Housing Benefit and

Council Tax Reduction

Legislation

Thirty second edition

2019/2020

Thirty second edition revised by
**Richard Poynter, Carolyn George, Stewart Wright,
Martin Williams, Susan Mitchell and Mark Brough**
Commentary by
Lorna Findlay, *LL.B (Hons) Barrister*
Employment Judge
Richard Poynter, *BCL, MA(Oxon)*
Judge of the Upper Tribunal
Carolyn George, *MA*
Freelance writer on welfare rights
Stewart Wright, *MA, Dip. Law, Barrister*
Judge of the Upper Tribunal
Martin Williams
Welfare rights worker, CPAG
Susan Mitchell
Freelance writer on welfare rights
Mark Brough
Freelance writer on welfare rights

Published by Child Poverty Action Group

Child Poverty Action Group works on behalf of the more than one in four children in the UK growing up in poverty. It does not have to be like this. We use our understanding of what causes poverty and the impact it has on children's lives to campaign for policies that will prevent and solve poverty – for good. We provide training, advice and information to make sure hard-up families get the financial support they need. We also carry out high-profile legal work to establish and protect families' rights. If you are not already supporting us, please consider making a donation, or ask for details of our membership schemes, training courses and publications.

Published by Child Poverty Action Group
30 Micawber Street, London N1 7TB
020 7837 7979
staff@cpag.org.uk
www.cpag.org.uk

Child Poverty Action Group is a charity registered in England and Wales (registration number 294841) and in Scotland (registration number SC039339), and is a company limited by guarantee, registered in England (registration number 1993854). VAT number: 690 808117

© Child Poverty Action Group 2019

A CIP record for this book is available from the British Library
ISBN: 978 1 910715 51 2

Content management system by Konnect Soft www.konnectsoft.com
Typeset by DLXML, a division of RefineCatch Limited, Bungay, Suffolk
Printed by CPI Group (UK) Ltd, Croydon CR0 4YY

Contents

Acknowledgements   vii
Table of cases   viii
Table of commissioners' decisions   xix
Table of Upper Tribunal decisions   xxiv
Housing Benefit Regulations: destination table   xxxii
Scotland: council tax reduction schemes comparative provisions   xxxvii
England: council tax reduction schemes comparative provisions   xl
Wales: council tax reduction schemes comparative provisions   xlii
Table of abbreviations   xlv

Part 1: **Main primary legislation – housing benefit**
Social Security Contributions and Benefits Act 1992 c4   3
Social Security Administration Act 1992 c5   21
Social Security (Consequential Provisions) Act 1992 c6   105
Social Security Act 1998 c14   106
Human Rights Act 1998 c42   111
Child Support, Pensions and Social Security Act 2000 c19   135
Constitutional Reform Act 2005 c4   160
Welfare Reform Act 2007 c5   162
Tribunals, Courts and Enforcement Act 2007 c15   167
Welfare Reform Act 2012 c5   207

Part 2: **Main secondary legislation – housing benefit**
The Housing Benefit Regulations 2006 No.213   219
The Housing Benefit (Persons who have attained the qualifying age for state pension   714
    credit) Regulations 2006 No.214
The Rent Officers (Housing Benefit Functions) Order 1997 No.1984   879
The Rent Officers (Housing Benefit Functions) (Scotland) Order 1997 No.1995 (S.144)   909
The Rent Officers (Housing Benefit Functions) (Local Housing Allowance) Amendment   929
    Order 2003 No.2398
The Rent Officers (Housing Benefit Functions) (Local Housing Allowance) Amendment   930
    Order 2005 No.236
The Rent Officers (Housing Benefit Functions) Amendment Order 2007 No.2871   931

Part 3: **Decision making and appeals – housing benefit**
The Housing Benefit and Council Tax Benefit (Decisions and Appeals) Regulations   937
    2001 No.1002
The Tribunal Procedure (First-tier Tribunal) (Social Entitlement Chamber) Rules 2008   983
    No.2685 (L.13
The Qualifications for Appointment of Members to the First-tier Tribunal and Upper   1027
    Tribunal Order 2008 No.2692
The Tribunal Procedure (Upper Tribunal) Rules 2008 No.2698   1029
The Transfer of Tribunal Functions Order 2008 No.2833   1057
The Appeals from the Upper Tribunal to the Court of Appeal Order 2008 No.2834   1060
The First-tier Tribunal and Upper Tribunal (Composition of Tribunal) Order 2008   1061
    No.2835
The Contracting Out (Administrative Work of Tribunals) Order 2009 No.121   1064
The First-tier Tribunal and Upper Tribunal (Chambers) Order 2010 No.2655   1065

Part 4: **Main primary legislation – council tax reduction schemes**
Local Government Finance Act 1992 c14   1071
Local Government Finance Act 2012 c17   1097

Contents

Part 5: Main secondary legislation – council tax reduction schemes
The Council Tax Reduction Schemes (Prescribed Requirements) (England)   **1103**
   Regulations 2012 No.2885
The Council Tax Reduction Schemes (Transitional Provision) (England) Regulations   **1185**
   2013 No.215
The Council Tax Reduction Schemes (Prescribed Requirements) (England)   **1187**
   (Amendment) Regulations 2015 No.2041
The Council Tax Reduction Schemes (Amendment) (England) Regulations 2017   **1188**
   No.1305
The Council Tax Reduction Schemes and Prescribed Requirements (Wales)   **1190**
   Regulations 2013 No.3029
The Council Tax Reduction Schemes (Default Scheme) (Wales) Regulations 2013   **1333**
   No.3035
The Council Tax Reduction Schemes (Transitional Provisions) (Wales) Regulations   **1450**
   2013 No.111 (W. 16)
The Council Tax Reduction (Scotland) Regulations 2012 No.303   **1452**
The Council Tax Reduction (State Pension Credit) (Scotland) Regulations 2012 No.319   **1574**
The Council Tax Reduction (Scotland) Amendment (No.2) Regulations 2013 No. 218   **1661**

Part 6: Valuation Tribunals and council tax reduction schemes – England and Wales
The Valuation Tribunal for England (Council Tax and Rating Appeals) (Procedure)   **1665**
   Regulations 2009 No.2269
The Valuation Tribunal for Wales Regulations 2010 No.713 (W.69)   **1684**

Part 7: Other primary legislation
Housing Act 1996 c52   **1699**
Welfare Reform and Pensions Act 1999 c30   **1700**
Immigration and Asylum Act 1999 c33   **1706**
Children (Leaving Care) Act 2000 c35   **1710**
Social Security Fraud Act 2001 c11   **1712**
Tax Credits Act 2002 c21   **1728**
Civil Partnership Act 2004 c33   **1729**

Part 8: Other secondary legislation – Common and transitional provisions
The Housing Benefit (Permitted Totals) Order 1996 No.677   **1735**
The Housing Benefit (Information from Landlords and Agents) Regulations 1997   **1741**
   No.2436
The Social Security (Penalty Notice) Regulations 1997 No.2813   **1745**
The Social Security (Immigration and Asylum) Consequential Amendments   **1747**
   Regulations 2000 No.636
The Discretionary Financial Assistance Regulations 2001 No.1167   **1751**
The Social Security (Notification of Change of Circumstances) Regulations 2001   **1759**
   No.3252
The Social Security (Loss of Benefit) Regulations 2001 No.4022   **1761**
The Contracting Out (Functions of Local Authorities: Income-Related Benefits) Order   **1769**
   2002 No.1888
The Social Security (Habitual Residence) Amendment Regulations 2004 No.1232   **1771**
The Civil Partnership Act 2004 (Relationships Arising Through Civil Partnership) Order   **1772**
   2005 No.3137
The Housing Benefit and Council Tax Benefit (Consequential Provisions) Regulations   **1773**
   2006 No.217
The Social Security (Persons from Abroad) Amendment Regulations 2006 No.1026   **1807**
The Housing Benefit and Council Tax Benefit (War Pension Disregards) Regulations   **1808**
   2007 No.1619
The Social Security (Claims and Information) Regulations 2007 No.2911   **1810**
The Housing Benefit (Local Housing Allowance and Information Sharing) Amendment   **1812**
   Regulations 2007 No.2868
The Housing Benefit (State Pension Credit) (Local Housing Allowance and Information   **1814**
   Sharing) Amendment Regulations 2007 No.2869
The Housing Benefit (Local Housing Allowance, Miscellaneous and Consequential)   **1816**
   Amendment Regulations 2007 No.2870

The Welfare Reform Act 2007 (Commencement No.4, and Savings and Transitional **1818**
  Provisions) Order 2007 No.2872
The Social Security (Local Authority Investigations and Prosecutions) Regulations 2008 **1821**
  No.463
The Welfare Reform Act 2007 (Commencement No.7, Transitional and Savings **1822**
  Provisions) Order 2008 No.2101
The Social Security (Use of Information for Housing Benefit and Welfare Services **1823**
  Purposes) Regulations 2008 No.2112
The Welfare Reform Act (Relevant Enactment) Order 2009 No.2162 **1825**
The Social Security (Information-sharing in relation to Welfare Services etc.) **1826**
  Regulations 2012 No.1483
The Welfare Reform Act 2012 (Commencement No.3, Savings Provision) Order 2012 **1838**
  No.1651
The Social Security (Civil Penalties) Regulations 2012 No.1990 **1839**
The Social Security (Overpayments and Recovery) Regulations 2013 No.384 **1840**
The Social Security (Information-sharing in relation to Welfare Services etc) **1848**
  Amendment and Prescribed Bodies Regulations 2013 No.454
The Welfare Reform Act 2012 (Commencement No.9 and Transitional and Transitory **1849**
  Provisions and Commencement No.8 and Savings and Transitional Provisions
  (Amendment)) Order 2013 No.983
The Social Security (Persons Required to Provide Information) Regulations 2013 **1854**
  No.1510
The Age-Related Payments Regulations 2013 No.2980 **1855**
The Social Security (Persons Required to Provide Information) Regulations 2013 **1856**
  No.1510
The Universal Credit (Transitional Provisions) Regulations 2014 No.1230 **1857**
The Welfare Reform Act 2012 (Commencement No.20 and Transitional and Transitory **1880**
  Provisions and Commencement No.9 and Transitional and Transitory Provisions
  (Amendment)) Order 2014 No.3094
The Welfare Reform Act 2012 (Commencement No.21 and Transitional and Transitory **1882**
  Provisions) Order 2015 No.33
The Welfare Reform Act 2012 (Commencement No.23 and Transitional and Transitory **1885**
  Provisions) Order 2015 No.634
The Welfare Reform Act 2012 (Commencement No.25 and Transitional and Transitory **1888**
  Provisions) Order 2015 No.1930
The Welfare Reform Act 2012 (Commencement No.26 and Transitional and Transitory **1889**
  Provisions and Commencement No.22, 23 and 24 and Transitional and Transitory
  Provisions (Modification)) Order 2016 No.33
The Welfare Reform Act 2012 (Commencement No.27 and Transitional and Transitory **1890**
  Provisions and Commencement No.22, 23 and 24 and Transitional and Transitory
  Provisions (Modification)) Order 2016 No.407
The Welfare Reform Act 2012 (Commencement No.13, 14, 16, 19, 22, 23 and 24 and **1891**
  Transitional and Transitory Provisions (Modification)) Order 2016 No.596
The Employment and Support Allowance and Universal Credit (Miscellaneous **1892**
  Amendments and Transitional and Savings Provisions) Regulations 2017 No.204
The Social Security (Restrictions on Amounts for Children and Qualifying Young **1894**
  Persons) Amendment Regulations 2017 No.376
The Welfare Reform Act 2012 (Commencement No.17, 19, 22, 23 and 24 and **1896**
  Transitional and Transitory Provisions (Modification) (No.2)) Order 2018 No.881
The Welfare Reform Act 2012 (Commencement No.31 and Savings and Transitional **1898**
  Provisions and Commencement No.21 and 23 and Transitional and Transitory
  Provisions (Amendment)) Order 2019 No.37 (C.1)

Index **1905**

Acknowledgements

We would like to thank all those who assisted with this publication, especially CPAG's Policy, Rights and Advocacy Team and staff at HM Courts and Tribunal Service and the Department for Work and Pensions, who all provide information on a regular basis.

We would like to acknowledge the previous authors, Paul Stagg, Martin Ward and Lorna Findlay.

Many thanks to Nicola Johnston who edited and managed the production of this book and Katherine Dawson for the index. Thanks also to Bryce Payton at Refinecatch.

We would like to thank all those who have taken the trouble to contact us with suggestions for improvements and notification of new developments since the last edition. We are always pleased to receive further such suggestions and information and can be contacted at the address below.

The legislation is up to date to 31 October 2019.

RICHARD POYNTER, CAROLYN GEORGE, STEWART WRIGHT, MARTIN WILLIAMS, SUSAN MITCHELL AND MARK BROUGH
c/o Publications Department
CPAG
30 Micawber Street
London
N1 7TB

Table of cases

Abdirahman and another v SSWP and another [2007] EWCA Civ 657; reported as *R(IS) 8/07*...
  328, 340, 338
Abdulaziz v UK (1985) 7 EHRR 471 at 501, para 78, ECtHR... **131**
Adan v Hounslow LBC [2004] EWCA Civ 101, CA... **557**
AF (Afghanistan) v Secretary of State for the Home Department [2019] EWCA Civ 208... **1054**
Ahmad v SSHD [2014] EWCA Civ 998... **331, 332**
Airey v Ireland (1979) 2 EHRR 305... **125**
AL (Serbia) v Home Secretary [2008] HL 42... **493**
Alarape and Tijani v SSHD (Case C-529/11)... **333**
Alcorn v SSWP , unreported, 12 April 2019... **1054**
AM (Somalia) v Entry Clearance Officer [2009] EWCA Civ 634... **395, 697**
Amos v SSHD [2011] EWCA Civ 552... **336**
Andersson v Sweden [1986] 46 DR 251, ECmHR... **127**
Andrew v City of Glasgow DC [1996] SLT 814 at 817H-L... **471**
Andronicou v Cyprus (1998) 25 EHRR 491, ECtHR... **125**
Appellant v Basingstoke and Deane BC (1705M219033/176C)... **1077**
Appellant v Folkestone and Hythe DC (Appeal No.2250M213194/084C)... **1078**
Appellants v Bury Council (Appeal No.4210M139633/254C)... **1079**
Attorney General's Reference No 4 of 2002 [2004] UKHL 43... **112**
Attorney Generals' Reference No2 of 2001 [2003] UKHL 68; [2004] 1 All ER 1041... **126**
B v SSWP [2005] EWCA Civ 929, [2005] 1 WLR 3796; reported as *R(IS) 9/06*... **38, 39, 593,**
  595, 968
Banks v Chief Adjudication Officer [2001] 1 WLR 1411, HL... **304**
Banger v SSHO (Case C-89/17) [2018] ECR **256**
Barrass v Reeve [1981] 1 WLR 408, DC... **53, 56**
Barry v LB Southwark [2008] EWCA Civ 1440... **306, 307**
Bate v Chief Adjudication Officer [1994] *The Times,*... **249**
Baumbast & R v SSHD (Case C-413/99) [2002] ECR I-07091... **337, 338, 341, 342, 343, 344**
Beattie v Secretary of State for Social Security [2001] 1 WLR 1404, CA... **458**
Begum v Tower Hamlets LBC [2003] 2 WLR 238, HL... **126**
Belgian State v Humbel (C-263/86) [1988] ECR 05365... **336**
Bellet v France (1995) unreported, case number A/333-B, ECtHR... **125**
Birmingham City Council v SSWP and Others [2016] EWCA Civ 1211; [2017] AACR 8... **1787,**
  1789
Blakiston v Cooper [1909] AC 104, HL... **440**
Bland v Chief Supplementary Benefit Officer [1983] 1 WLR 262, CA; reported as *R(SB) 12/83*...
  177, 178, 186
Botchett v Chief Adjudication Officer [1996] 2 CCLR 121, CA... **431**
BPP Holdings v HMRC [2017] UKSC 55... **1672**
Bradford MBC v Anderton [1991] RA 45, QBD... **1477**
Braintree DC v Thompson [2005] EWCA Civ 178, 7 March 2005, unreported... **186**
Bressol v Gouvernement de la Communauté Française (Case C-73/08) [2010] OJ C 148... **340**
Brewer v Mann [2012] EWCA Civ 246... **1019**
Brey Case C-140/12 [2013] ECR... **329, 330, 338**
Brown v Bullock [1961] 1 WLR 1095, CA... **442**
Bruton v London & Quadrant Housing Trust [1999] 3 WLR 150... **276**
Bull v Bull [1955] 1 QB 234... **393**
Burnip v Birmingham CC and Others [2012] EWCA Civ 629; [2013] AACR 7... **377, 378, 379,**
  380, 395, 396, 899, 1093
Burton v New Forest DC [2004] EWCA Civ 1510; reported as *R(H) 7/05*... **243**
Cameron v Cameron [1996] SLT 306 at 313F... **346**

Cameron v Henry [1992] SLT 586, IH… **1477**

Campbell and others v South Northamptonshire DC and SSWP [2004] EWCA Civ 409 CA; reported as *R(H) 8/04*… **93, 128, 283**

Campbell v Secretary of State for Social Services [1983] 4 FLR 138, QBD… **15**

Carpenter v SSWP [2003] EWCA Civ 33; reported as *R(IB) 6/03*… **140, 146, 177**

Carson and Reynolds (2005) UKHL 37 *The Times,*… **128, 129, 130**

Case of JD and A v the United Kingdom [2019] ECHR 753… **379**

Casewell v SSWP [2008] 11 March, WLR (D) 86, reported as *R(IS) 7/08*… **681**

Chief Adjudication Officer v Ahmed [1994] *The Times*… **347**

Chief Adjudication Officer v Bate [1996] 1 WLR 814… **157**

Chief Adjudication Officer v Carr [1994] 2 June, *The Times*… **273**

Chief Adjudication Officer v Combe [1998] SLT 15; reported as *R(IS) 8/98*… **947**

Chief Adjudication Officer v Ellis [1995] 15 February, CA… **254**

Chief Adjudication Officer v Leeves [1999] FLR 90, CA; reported as *R(IS) 5/99*… **418, 461, 462, 485**

Chief Adjudication Officer v McKiernon [1993] 3 July, CA… **955**

Chief Adjudication Officer v Palfrey [1995] *The Times,*… **476, 477**

Chief Adjudication Officer v Stafford [2000] 1 All ER 686 at 693g-694a, CA… **256**

Chief Adjudication Officer v Upton [1997] 2 CLY 4668, CA… **553**

Chief Adjudication Officer v Webber [1998] 1 WLR 625 at 633E, CA… **485**

Clayton's case [1861] 1 Mer 572… **61, 591, 600**

Clear v Smith [1981] 1 WLR 399 at 406, DC… **56**

Clift v United Kingdom (Application No 7205/07), 13 July 2010… **129**

Coates Brothers plc v General Accident Life Assurance Ltd [1991] 1 WLR 712 at 717… **441**

Codner v Wiltshire Valuation and Community Charge Tribunal [1994] 34 RVR 169, QBD… **1477**

Cooke v Glenrose Fish Company [2004] ICR 1188… **1020**

Cooke v Secretary of State for Social Security [2001] EWCA CIV 734; reported as *R(DLA) 6/01*… **186**

Cottingham v Chief Adjudication Officer [1992] appendix to *R(P) 1/93*… **11**

Coventry CC v Vassell [2011] EWHC 1542 (Admin)… **56**

Cox v London (South West) Valuation and Community Charge Tribunal [1994] 34 RVR 171, QBD… **1477**

Crabtree v Fern Spinning Co Ltd [1901] 85 LT 549 at 552, DC… **54**

Crake and Butterworth v Supplementary Benefit Commission [1982] 1 All ER 498… **14, 15**

Czop (Case C-147/11)… **343**

Dakneviciute (Case C-544/18) [2019] ECLI:EU:C:2019:261… **316**

Dano v Jobcentre Leipzig (Case C-333/13)… **340**

Davies v Child Support Commissioner and Child Support Agency [2008] EWHC 334 (Admin), QBD… **987**

De Brito v SSHD [2012] EWCA Civ 709… **311**

Denton v Chief Adjudication Officer [1999] ELR 86 at 87G-H… **485**

Denton v TH White [2014] EWCA Civ 906; [2014] 1 WLR 3927… **1683**

Deumeland v Germany (1986) 8 EHRR 448 at 468, para 74, ECtHR… **124**

DG v Liverpool City Council (Appeal No.43 10M140277/CTR) 1074

DH and others v Czech Republic (Appln No: 57325/00), (2008) 47 EHRR 3 (ECtHR)… **130**

Dias v SSWP (Case C-325/09) [2011] ECR I-06387; [2012] AACR 36… **333, 344**

Diatta v Land Berlin (Case C-267/83) [1985] ECR 00567… **318, 344**

DK v SSWP [2016] CSIH 84; [2017] AACR 10… **14**

DM v Lewisham LB and SSWP [2014] EWCA Civ 284; [2014] AACR 14… **268**

Doherty and others v Birmingham CC [2008] UKHL 57… **116**

Dombo Beheer BV v Netherlands (1993) 18 EHRR 213 at 226-8, ECtHR… **125**

Donaghue v Poplar Housing Association Ltd [2002] QB 58, CA… **116, 118**

Douglas v Phoenix Motors [1970] SLT 57, Sh Ct… **57**

DSS v Bavi [1996] COD 260 at 261, DC… **56**

DSS v Cooper [1994] 158 JPN 354, DC… **56**

Duggan v Chief Adjudication Officer [1988] *The Times*… **595**

E v SSHD [2004] EWCA Civ 49… **180**

Eba v Advocate General for Scotland [2010] CSIH 78... **169, 190**
Eba v Advocate General for Scotland [2011] UKSC 29; [2011] AACR 39... **169**
Eind (Case C-219/05) [2007] ECR I-10719... **304, 303**
Elmi v SSWP [2011] EWCA Civ 1403; [2012] AACR 22... **312**
Environmental Agency v Empress Cars (Abertillery) Ltd [1999] 2 AC 22, HL... **584**
Fairbank v Lambeth Magistrates' Court (2003) HLR 62... **56, 242**
Fedje v Sweden (1994) 17 EHRR 14, para 32, ECtHR... **126**
Feldbrugge v Netherlands (1986) 8 EHRR 425... **124**
Foster v Chief Adjudication Officer [1993] AC 754, HL... **179**
Foster v Chief Adjudication Officer [1992] QB 31 at 45... **10**
Francis v SSWP [2005] EWCA Civ 1303; reported as *R(IS) 6/06*... **129, 131**
Francois v LB Waltham Forest [2017] EWHC 2252 (Admin)... **689, 1181**
Franklin v Chief Adjudication Officer [1995] *The Times*... **595**
Frish Limited v Barclays Bank Limited [1955] 2 QB 541... **290**
Frost v Feltham [1981] 1 WLR 455... **1476, 1477**
Fryer-Kelsey v SSWP [2005] EWCA Civ 511; reported as *R(IB) 6/05*... **186**
Gargett, R (on the application of) v Lambeth LB [2008] EWCA Civ 1450... **1756**
Gaumont British Distributors Ltd v Henry [1939] 2 KB 711 at 719, 723, DC... **54**
Genc v Land Berlin (Case C-14/09) [2010] ECR... **307**
General Legal Council ex p Basil Whitter v Barrington Earl Frankson [2006] UKPC 42... **1007**
Ghaidan v Godin-Mendoza [2004] UKHL 30, 3 All ER 411... **113, 128, 131**
Gillies v SSWP [2006] UKHL 2; reported as *R(DLA) 5/06*... **123, 182**
Godwin v Rossendale BC [2002] *The Times*... **707**
Grant v Southwestern and County Properties Ltd [1975] Ch 185 at 197A-F, Ch D... **53**
Grice v Needs [1980] 1, WLR 45... **51**
Grzelcyzk (Case C-184/99) ECR I-06193... **330**
Gusa v Minister for Social Protection (C-422/16) [2017] ECR (ECLI:EC:C:2017:1004)... **313, 331**
Guygusuz v Austria (1997) 23 EHRR 364, ECtHR... **129, 130**
Hamblett v Godfrey [1987] 1 WLR 357, CA... **440**
Hammersmith and Fulham LBC v Monk [1991] UKHL 6... **393**
Haringey LBC v Awaritefe (1999) 32 HLR 517... **60, 183, 565, 600, 1745**
Haringey LBC v Cotter (1996) 29 HLR 682, CA... **127, 568**
Harrison v DSS [1997] COD 220 at 220-1, DC... **56**
Herbert v Byrne [1964] 1 WLR 519 at 527, 528, 529, CA... **265**
Hinchy v SSWP [2005] UKHL 16... **595**
Hobbs and others v UK (Application No.63684/00), 14 November 2006... **131**
Hochstrasser v Mayes [1959] Ch 22, CA... **440**
Hoekstra (Case C-75/73) [1964] ECR 00177... **305, 306**
Hooper v SSWP [2007] EWCA Civ 495; reported as *R(IB) 4/07*... **148**
Howker v SSWP [2003] ICR 405... **92**
Hrabkova v SSWP [2017] EWCA Civ 794... **343**
Humphreys v HMRC [2012] UKSC 18; [2012] AACR 46... **131, 408**
Industrial Properties (Barton Hill) Ltd v Associated Electrical Industries Ltd [1977] QB 580... **575**
Insurance Officer v McCaffrey [1985] 1 WLR 1353 at 1355H-1356C, HL... **26**
Jagoo v Bristol City Council [2017] EWHC 926 (Admin)... **1683**
James Miller & Partners Ltd v Whitworth Street Estates (Manchester) Ltd [1970] AC 572... **278**
Jany and Others v Staatssecretaris van Justitie (Case C-268/99) [2001] ECR I-08615... **308, 328**
JD and A v United Kingdom [2019] ECHR 753... **131**
Jeleniewicz v SSWP [2008] EWCA Civ 1163... **1181**
Jewish Blind Society Trustees v Henning [1961] 1 WLR 24 at 30, 34, CA... **431**
Jia v Migrationsverket (Case C-1/05) [2007] ECR I-00001... **319**
Jobcentre Berlin Newkolln v Alimanovic (Case C-67/14)... **315, 340**
John O'Flynn v CAO [1996] ECR I-02617, Case C-237/94... **269**
Jones v Chief Adjudication Officer [1994] 1 WLR 62 at 71H, 72F, CA... **595**
Jones v City of Glasgow DC HBRB [1997] unreported, 4 July, CSOH... **295**

Jones v Kernott [2011] UKSC 53… **461**
Jones v Waveney DC (1999) 33 HLR 3, CA… **568**
Jones v SSWP [2003] EWCA 964, unreported… **470**
JT v First-tier Tribunal [2018] EWCA Civ 1735… **188**
Kaczmarek v SSWP [2008] EWCA Civ 1310; reported as *R(IS) 5/09*… **338, 339**
Karanakaran v SSHD [2003] 3 All ER 449… **14**
Kazantzis v Chief Adjudication Officer [1999] *The Times*… **254**
Kerr v Department for Social Development [2004] UKHL 23; reported as *R 1/04 (SF)*… **139, 180, 318, 461, 586, 587, 589, 1181**
King v Kerrier DC [2006] EWHC 500 (Admin), unreported, 27 February (DC)… **56**
Kingston-upon-Thames BC v Prince (1998) 31 HLR 794, CA… **279**
Kits van Heijerungen v Staatssecretaris van Justitie (Case C-125/89) [1990] ECR I-01753… **306**
Kjeldsen Madsen v Denmark (1976) 1 EHRR 711, ECtHR… **129**
Kola and Another v SSWP [2007] 28 November, UKHL 54; reported as *R(IS) 1/08*… **1800**
Konodyba v Royal Borough of Kensington and Chelsea [2012] EWCA Civ 982… **311**
Lair v Universität Hannover (Case C-39/86) [1988] ECR 03161… **306**
Lambeth London BC v Kay [2006] 4 All ER 128… **276**
Langley v Bradford MDC and SSWP [2004] EWCA Civ 1343; reported as *R(H) 6/05*… **127, 288**
Lawrie-Blum v Land Baden-Wurtternberg (Case C-66/86) [1986] ECR 02121… **305**
LB Harrow v Ibrahim (Case C-310/08) [2010] ECR I-01065… **302, 337, 341, 342, 343, 344**
Leeds City Council v Price [2006] UKHL 10, [2006] 4 All ER 128… **112**
Levin v Staatssecretaris van Justitie (Case C-53/81) [1982] ECR 01035… **305**
Lillystone v Supplementary Benefits Commission [1982] 3 FLR 52, CA… **416**
Lloyd v Lewisham LB and SSWP [2013] EWCA Civ 923… **669**
LN v Styrelsen for Viderergaende Uddannelser of Uddannelsesstotte C-46/12 [2016] ECR… **309**
Locabail (UK) Ltd v Bayfield Properties Ltd [2000] QB 451 at 496F-497A, para 89, CA… **182**
Luisi & Carbone v Ministero del Tesoro (Cases C-286/82 & C-26/83) [1984] ECR 00377… **336**
Macastena v SSHD [2018] EWCA Civ 1558… **335**
Malcolm v Tweeddale District HBRB [1994] SLT 1212, CS(OH)… **1787, 1791, 1792, 1793**
Malekout v Secretary of State [2010] EWCA Civ 162; [2010] AACR 28… **669**
Manorlike Ltd v Le Vitas Travel Agency and Consultancy Services Ltd [1986] 1 All ER 573 at 575e-h, 576b-d, CA… **946**
Mansur v Turkey (1995) Series A No. 319–B… **1018**
Massachusetts Board of Retirement v Murgia [1976] 438 US 285… **130**
Mathieson v SSWP [2015] UKSC 47, [2015] 1 WLR 3250… **378**
McCarthy & Stone (Developments) Ltd v HMRC [2014] WLR 795… **1673**
McCarthy (Case C-434/09) [2011] ECR… **303, 304**
McLeod v HBRB for Banff and Buchan District HBRB [1988] SLT 753, CS(OH)… **1787, 1792**
McLoughlin and Jones [2002] QB 1312… **991**
Metock (Case C-127/08) [2008] ECR I-06241… **302, 319, 320**
Michalak v Wandsworth LBC [2003] 1 WLR 617… **128**
Miller v Secretary of State for Social Security [2002] GWD 25-861, CSIH… **181**
Minter v Kingston upon Hull City Council and Potter v SSWP [2011] EWCA Civ 1155; [2012] AACR 21… **418, 439, 440, 453**
Mirga and Samin v SSWP and Westminster City Council [2016] UKSC 1; [2016] AACR 26… **311, 332, 340**
Miskovic and Blazej v SSWP [2011] EWCA Civ 16; [2012] AACR 11… **324**
MM v Medway Council (Appeal No.2280M157095/084C)… **1080**
Mohammed and Parkes v DWP [2012] EWHC 4220 (Admin)… **67**
Mongan v Department for Social Development [2005] NICA 16; reported as *R3/05 (DLA)*… **145, 148**
Monteil v SSHD [1983] Imm AR 149 at 152, IAT… **307**
Mooney v SSWP [2004] SLT 1141; reported as *R(DLA) 5/04*… **148**
Moore v Branton [1974] 118 SJ 40, DC… **56**
Moore v Griffiths [1972] 1 WLR 1024, Ch D… **439**
Moorhouse v Dooland [1955] Ch 284, CA… **440**
Morgan v Warwick DC [2015] RVR 224… **1076**

Morrell v SSWP [2003] EWCA Civ 526; reported as *R(IS) 6/03*… **415**
Mullaney v Watford BC [1997] RA 225, QBD… **1477**
Müller v Austria (Commission) [1975] 3 D and R 25… **132**
Mulvey v Secretary of State for Social Security [1997] SLT 753 at 756, HL… **98**
Munro v UK [1986] 48 DR 154, ECmHR… **125**
NA (Pakistan) v SSHD [2014] EWCA Civ 995… **336**
Nessa v Chief Adjudication Officer [1998] 2 All ER 728… **345, 346**
Nimmo v Alexander Cowan & Sons Ltd [1968] AC 107, HL… **139**
Norwich and Peterborough Building Society v Steed [1991] 1 WLR 449… **1018**
Novitskaya v London Borough of Brent & Another [2009] EWCA Civ 1260; [2010] AACR 6…
    549
NS v SSHD (Case C-411/10) [2011] ECR I-13905… **340**
O v Minister voor Immigratie, Integratie en Asiel (Case C-456/12) [2014] ECR
    (ECLI:EU:C:2014:135)… **303**
Obrey and Others v SSWP [2013] EWCA Civ 1584… **272**
O'Connor v Chief Adjudication Officer [1999] ELR 209, CA… **493**
Ogieriakhi v Minister for Justice and Equality (Case C-244/13) [2014] ECR… **318**
Okafor and Others v SSHD [2011] EWCA Civ 499… **333**
Okun v London Borough of Lewisham [2016] EWHC 864 (Ch)… **1080**
Osinunga v DPP (1997) 30 HLR 853 at 856, DC… **41**
Osman v UK (1998) 29 EHRR 245, ECtHR… **157**
Owen v Chief Adjudication Officer [1999] *The Independent*… **10, 11**
Oxford City Council v Basey [2012] EWCA Civ 115; [2012] AACR 38… **625**
Page v Chief Adjudication Officer [1991] The Times 4 July, CA… **596**
Parry v Derbyshire Dales DC [2006] EWHC 988 (Admin), 5 May, unreported… **1477**
Patmalniece [2011] UKSC 11; [2011] AACR 34… **328, 340**
Patmalniece v SSWP [2009] EWCA Civ 621… **328, 340**
Pedro v SSWP [2009] EWCA Civ 1358; [2010] AACR 18… **319**
Perrot v Supplementary Benefit Commissioner [1980] 3 All ER 110 at 114j, 116a-e, 117b, CA…
    255
Petrovic v Austria [1998] 4 BHRC 232, ECtHR… **127, 131**
Plymouth CC v Gigg (1997) 30 HLR 284, CA… **600**
Poplar Housing Association Ltd v Donoghue [2002] QB 58, CA… **113, 115**
Porter v Magill [2002] 2 WLR 37… **182**
Prefeta v SSWP (Case C-618/16) [2018] ECR (ECLI:EU:C:2018:719)… **325**
Pretty v UK (2002) 35 EHRR 1, ECHR… **124**
Procurator Fiscal v Dyer and Watson [2002] UKPC D1… **125**
Punakova (Case 148/11)… **343**
R (A) v SSWP [2015] EWHC 159 (Admin)… **378**
*R (Alconbury Developments Ltd) v Secretary of State for the Environment, Transport and the
    Regions* [2003] 2 AC 295, HL… **112, 126**
R (Anufrijeva) v Southwark LBC [2003] EWCA Civ 1406, CA… **119, 127**
R (Anufrijeva) v SSHD [2003] 3 WLR 353, HL… **119, 1801**
R (Barber) v SSWP [2002] 2 FLR 1181… **130**
R (Beeson) v Dorset [2002] 6 CCLR 5, CA… **126**
R (Begum) v SSWP [2003] EWHC 3380 Admin; reported as *R(IS) 11/04*… **1708**
R (Ben-Abdelaziz) v SSHD [2001] 1 WLR 1485, CA… **123**
R (Bernard) v Enfield LBC [2002] 5 CCLR 589… **119**
R (Bierman) v SSWP [2004] EWHC 1024 (Admin)… **494**
R (Bono) v Harlow DC HBRB [2002] 1 WLR 2475… **115**
R (Buckley and others) v Sheffield City Council [2013] EWHC 512 (Admin)… **1092**
R (Carmichael and Rourke) v SSWP [2016] UKSC 58; [2017] AACR 9… **188, 377, 378**
R (Carson) v SSWP [2003] 3 All ER 577… **128, 130**
R (Cart and others) v Upper Tribunal and others [2009] EWHC 3052… **169**
R (Cart) v Upper Tribunal [2011] UKSC 28; [2011] AACR 38… **169**
R (Cotton and others) v SSWP and New Forest DC and Others [2014] EWHC 3437 (Admin)…
    373

R (CPAG) v SSWP [2011] EWHC 2616 (Admin)… **392, 394, 885**
R (Cumpsty) v Rent Officer [2002] EWHC 2526 (Admin)… **124, 125**
R (DA and others) v SSWP [2018] EWCA Civ 504… **523**
R (DA) and others v SSWP [2019] UKSC 21; [2019] 1 WLR 3289… **130, 131**
R (Douglas) v North Tyneside MBC and another [2004] 1 All ER 709… **133**
R (Fratila and Tanase) v SSWP (reference CO/3632/2019)… **328**
R (Greenfield) v SSHD [2005] UKHL 14, [2005] 2 All ER 240, HL… **119**
R (Gudanaviciene) v Director of Legal Aid Casework [2014] EWCA Civ 1622… **1009**
R (Hardy) v Sandwell MBC [2015] EWHC 890 (Admin)… **1077, 1753**
R (HC) v SSWP [2017] UKSC 73… **305, 328**
R (Heather) v The Leonard Cheshire Foundation [2001] 4 CCLR 211, Stanley Burton J… **116**
R (Hook) v The Social Security Commissioner [2007] EWHC 1705 (Admin), 3 July; reported as
    R(IS) 7/07… **471**
R (Hooper) v SSWP [2003] 1 WLR 2623, CA… **81**
R (Hurley, Jarrett and Palmer) v SSWP [2015] EWHC 3382 (Admin)… **523**
R (Iran) v SSHD [2005] EWCA Civ 982… **179**
R (Isle of Anglesey DC) v SSWP [2003] EWHC 2518 (Admin)… **90**
R (JL and AT Baird) v Environment Agency [2011] EWHC 939 (Admin)… **1092**
R (Knowles) v Valuation Agency, Lancashire CC and SSWP [2013] EWHC 19 (admin)… **628**
R (Laali) v Westminster CC HBRB (2002) HLR 179, QBD… **358**
R (Logan) v LB of Havering [2015] EWHC 3193 (Admin)… **1078, 1092**
R (MA and Others) v SSWP [2014] EWCA Civ 13… **377, 1751, 1753**
R (MA and Others) v SSWP and Birmingham City Council [2013] EWHC 2213 (QB)… **377, 396**
R (MA and Others) v SSWP and Birmingham City Council [2014] EWCA Civ 13… **373**
R (MA) v SSWP [2016] UKSC 58; [2016] 1 WLR 4550… **131**
R (Murphy) v Westminster CC (2002) HLR 447… **286, 288**
R (Naghshbandi) v Camden LBC [2001] EWHC Admin 813; (2003) HLR 280, CA… **266, 267,
    358, 486, 487, 1758**
R (on the application of DA and others) v SSWP [2017] EWHC 1446 (Admin)… **412, 522**
R (on the application of Heffernan) (FC) v The Rent Service [2008] UKHL 58… **893**
*R (on the application of Moseley (in substitution of Stirling Deceased)) v London Borough of
    Haringey* [2014] UKSC 56… **1091, 1092**
R (on the application of T) v Trafford MBC [2015] EWHC 369 (Admin)… **1091**
R (on the application of Tilianu) v SSWP [2010] EWCA Civ 1397… **313**
R (Painter) v Carmarthenshire CC HBRB (2002) HLR 447… **286, 288**
R (Reilly (No.2) and Hewstone) v SSWP [2014] EWHC 2182 (Admin)… **684**
R (Reilly and another) v SSWP [2013] EWCA Civ 66… **684**
R (Reilly and Wilson) v SSWP [2013] UKSC 68; [2014] AACR 9… **684**
R (Reynolds) v SSWP (2005) UKHL 37, *The Times*… **631**
R (Reynolds) v SSWP [2002] EWHC Admin 426… **127**
R (RJM) v SSWP [2008] UKHL 63… **112, 127, 129, 132, 493**
R (Rutherford and Others and 'A') v SSWP and New Forest DC and Others [2016] EWCA Civ
    29… **378**
R (S) v a Social Security Commissioner and Another [2009] EWHC 2221 (Admin)… **1780**
R (S) v Chief Constable of South Yorkshire Police (2004) 1 WLR 2196… **128, 129**
R (Saeedi) v Secretary of State for the Home Department [2010] EWHC 705 (Admin)… **340**
R (Sarabjeet Singh) v SSHD [2016] EWCA Civ 492… **182**
R (Sarah Stirling) v LB Haringey [2013] EWCA Civ 116… **1092**
R (SG and others (previously JS and others)) v SSWP [2015] UKSC 16 [2015] 1 WRL 1449…
    522
R (Sibley) v West Dorset DC [2001] EWHC Admin 365… **1758**
R (Sier) v Cambridge CC HBRB [2001] EWHC Admin 160, QBD; [2001] EWCA Civ 1523, CA…
    584, 585, 587, 588, 585, 594
R (Stott) v Secretary of State for Justice [2018] UKSC 59; [2018] 3 WLR 1831… **130**
R (T) v Richmond-upon-Thames LBC HBRB (2000) 33 HLR 65, QBD… **278**
R (Tucker) v Secretary of State for Social Security [2001] EWHC Admin 260; (2002) HLR 500,
    CA… **127, 289**

R (Waite) v Hammersmith and Fulham LB (2003) HLR 24… **272**

R (Wall) v Appeals Service [2003] EWHC 465 Admin… **126**

R (Winder and others) v Sandwell MBC [2014] EWHC 2617 (Admin)… **1075, 1078, 1082, 1091, 1090, 1117**

R (Zacchaeus 2000 Trust) v SSWP [2013] EWHC 233 (Admin)… **886**

R v A (No 2) [2001] 2 AC 91, HL… **113**

R v Allerdale DC HBRB ex p Doughty [2000] COD 462, QBD… **179, 621, 1790**

R v Armour [1997] 2 Cr App R(S) 240, CA… **41**

R v Aylesbury Vale DC ex p England (1996) 29 HLR 303… **553**

R v Barrow BC ex p Catnach [1997] unreported, 3 September, QBD… **297**

R v Beverley DC HBRB ex p Hare (1995) 27 HLR 637, QBD… **1787, 1789**

R v Birmingham CC HBRB ex p Ellery (1989) 21 HLR 398, QBD… **240**

R v Brent LBC ex p Gunning [1986] 84 LGR 168… **1091**

R v Brent LBC ex p Shah [1983] 2 AC 309 at 343H-344B, HL… **345, 346, 347**

R v Brent LBC HBRB ex p Connery (1989) 22 HLR 40 at 44, QBD… **39, 1788, 1789**

R v Bristol CC ex p Jacobs (1999) 32 HLR 841… **354**

R v Cambridge CC ex p Thomas [1995] unreported, 10 February, QBD… **275**

R v Camden LBC HBRB ex p W [1999] 21 May, unreported, QBD… **1790, 1791**

R v Canterbury CC ex p Woodhouse [1994] unreported, 2 August, QBD… **1790, 1791, 1792**

R v Chainey [1914] 1 KB 137 at 142, DC… **54**

R v Chesterfield BC ex p Fullwood (1993) 26 HLR 126 at 129, CA… **250, 520**

R v Coventry CC ex p Waite [1995] unreported, 7 July, QBD… **1787, 1789**

R v Coventry CC ex p Waite [1995] unreported, 7 October, QBD… **1788, 1791, 1793**

R v Deputy Industrial Injuries Commissioner ex p Moore [1965] 1 QB 456… **180**

R v Derby CC ex p Third Wave Housing (2000) 33 HLR 61, QBD… **277, 278**

R v Doncaster BC ex p Boulton (1992) 25 HLR 195, QBD… **668, 669**

R v Doncaster MBC ex p Nortrop [1998] unreported, 31 July, QBD… **465**

R v East Devon DC HBRB ex p Gibson (1993) 25 HLR, CA… **1787, 1788, 1791, 1793, 1792**

R v East Devon DC HBRB ex p Preston (1998) 31 HLR 936, QBD… **1793**

R v Ghosh [1982] QB 1053 at 1064D-G, CA… **53**

R v Gloucestershire CC ex p Barry [1997] AC 584, HL… **1753**

R v Gloucestershire CC ex p Dadds (1996) 29 HLR 700, QBD… **295, 297**

R v Greenwich LBC ex p Dhadly (1999) 32 HLR 829… **274, 295**

R v Greenwich LBC ex p Moult [1998] unreported, 19 June, CA… **285**

R v Haringey LBC ex p Ayub (1992) 25 HLR 566, QBD… **563, 575, 598, 600, 607**

R v Haringey LBC ex p Ayub (1990) 25 HLR 566, QBD… **572**

R v HMRC ex p Wilkinson [2005] UKHL 30… **131**

R v Ipswich BC ex p Flowers [1994] unreported, 1 March, QBD… **1793**

R v Islington LBC ex p Ewing [1992] unreported, 5 February, QBD… **565**

R v Kensington and Chelsea RBC ex p Abou-Jaoude [1996] unreported, 10 May, QBD… **1787, 1793**

R v Kensington and Chelsea RBC ex p Brandt (1995) 28 HLR 528, QBD… **354, 506, 598**

R v Kensington and Chelsea RBC ex p Carney [1997] COD 124 at 125, QBD… **1790, 1791**

R v Kensington and Chelsea RBC ex p Pirie [1997] unreported, 26 March, QBD… **1786, 1788, 1791**

R v Kensington and Chelsea RBC ex p Sheikh [1997] unreported, 14 January, QBD… **1790, 1792**

R v Kensington and Chelsea RBC HBRB ex p Robertson [1988] 28 RVR 84 at 85, QBD… **270**

R v Lambert [2002] 2 AC 545, para 80, HL… **113**

R v Lambeth LBC ex p Crookes (1995) 29 HLR 28 at 35, QBD… **564**

R v Lambeth LBC ex p Crookes (1998) 31 HLR 59, QBD… **567, 1007**

R v Lambeth LBC HBRB ex p Harrington [1996] unreported 22 November, QBD… **1791**

R v Liverpool CC ex p Griffiths (1990) 22 HLR 312, QBD… **572, 585, 590**

R v Liverpool CC ex p Johnson (No 1) [1994] unreported, 23 June, QBD… **564**

R v Macclesfield BC HBRB ex p Temsamani [1999] unreported, February 24, QBD… **361**

R v Manchester CC ex p Baragrove Properties Ltd (1991) 23 HLR 337, QBD… **296, 297, 576**

R v Manchester CC ex p Harcup (1993) 26 HLR 402 at 408, QBD… **1788**

R v Manchester City Council ex p Stennett [2002] UKHL 34… **687**

R v Middlesborough BC ex p Graville [1993] unreported, 26 March, QBD… **471**
R v Middlesborough BC ex p Holmes [1995] unreported, 15 February, QBD… **538, 1774**
R v Milton Keynes BC HBRB ex p Macklen [1996] unreported, 30 April, QBD… **295**
R v Milton Keynes CC HBRB ex p Saxby (2000) unreported, 11 August, QBD; [2001] 33 HLR 82, CA… **354**
R v National Insurance Commissioner ex p Stratton [1979] ICR 209… **418**
R v Newham LBC ex p Kaur (1997) 29 HLR 776 at 784, QBD… **565**
R v North and East Devon Health Authority ex p Coughlan [2001] QB 213… **1091**
R v Oadby and Wigston DC ex p Dickman (1995) 28 HLR 807… **1790, 1791, 1793**
R v Oldham MBC ex p G [1993] 1 FLR 645 at 662, CA… **279**
R v Oxford CC ex p Jack (1984) 17 HLR 419, QBD… **416, 417**
R v Passmore [2007] EWCA Crim 2053, 18 June, CA… **53**
R v Penwith DC ex p Burt (1990) 22 HLR 292 at 296, QBD… **264, 270**
R v Penwith DC ex p Menear (1991) 24 HLR 115, QBD… **14, 419, 490, 561**
R v Poole BC ex p Ross (1995) 28 HLR 351, QBD… **277, 283, 284, 296, 297**
R v Rugby BC HBRB ex p Harrison (1994) 28 HLR 36 at 48-9, QBD… **276, 283, 285**
R v Sandwell MBC ex p Wilkinson (1998) 31 HLR 22, QBD… **1788, 1793**
R v Secretary of State for Social Security ex p Grant [1997] unreported, 31 July, QBD… **1800**
R v Secretary of State for Social Services ex p CPAG [1990] 2 QB 540, CA… **564, 1010**
R v Secretary of State for Social Security ex p Association of Metropolitan Authoroties (1992) 25 HLR 131, QBD… **96**
R v Secretary of State for Social Security ex p Golding [1996] unreported, 1 July, CA… **61**
R v Secretary of State for Social Security ex p Sarwar [1997] 3 CMLR 647, CA… **6**
R v Secretary of State for Social Security ex p Smithson (Case C-243/90) [1992] ECR I-467, ECJ… **1775**
R v Secretary of State for the Environment ex p Hammersmith and Fulham LBC [1991] 1 AC 521 at 597E-H, HL… **89**
R v Secretary of State for the Home Department ex p Limbuela and others [2005] UKHL 66… **124**
R v Secretary of State for the Home Department ex p Pinochet (No 2) [2000] 1 AC 129, HL… **182**
R v Secretary of State for the Home Department, ex p Anderson [2002] UKHL 46… **112**
R v Sedgemoor DC HBRB ex p Weadon (1986) 18 HLR 355, QBD… **242**
R v Sefton MBC ex p Cunningham (1991) 23 HLR 534 at 538, QBD… **1787, 1790**
R v Sefton MBC HBRB ex p Brennan (1996) 29 HLR 735 at 741, QBD… **1792, 1793**
R v Sheffield CC HBRB ex p Smith (1994) 28 HLR 36 at 47-8, QBD… **242**
R v Slough BC ex p Green [1996] unreported, 15 November, QBD… **1791, 1793**
R v Solihull MBC HBRB ex p Simpson [1995] 1 FLR 140 at 148E-F, CA… **294, 295, 296**
R v South Hams DC ex p Ash (1999) 32 HLR 405, QBD… **81**
R v South Ribble DC HBRB ex p Hamilton (2000) 33 HLR 102, CA… **14, 136, 243, 419, 460, 490, 767**
R v South Tyneside MBC ex p Tooley [1996] COD 143 at 144, QBD… **295, 470**
R v SSHD ex p Brind [1991] 1 AC 696 at 747G-748F, 760D-762B, HL… **113**
R v SSHD ex p Jeyeanthan [2000] 1 WLR 354… **183**
R v SSWP ex p Hooper and others [2005] UKHL 29… **116, 129**
R v St Edmundsbury BC HBRB ex p Sandys (1997) 30 HLR 800; (1998) *The Times*… **108**
R v Stewart [1987] 2 All ER 363, CA… **41**
R v Stoke-on-Trent CC ex p Highgate Projects (1993) 26 HLR 551… **544**
R v Stoke-on-Trent CC ex p Highgate Projects (1996) 29 HLR 271 at 278, CA… **620**
R v Stratford-upon-Avon DC HBRB ex p White (1997) 30 HLR 178, QBD… **294, 295**
R v Stratford-upon-Avon DC HBRB ex p White (1998) 31 HLR 126… **276, 286, 296, 297, 576**
R v Supplementary Benefit Commission ex p Singer [1973] 1 WLR 713… **416, 417**
R v Sutton LBC HBRB ex p Keegan (1992) 27 HLR 92 at 99-100, QBD… **277, 296, 297**
R v Swale BC HBRB ex p Marchant [1999] 1 FLR 1087, QBD; [2000] 1 FLR 246, CA… **263, 269, 373, 881**
R v Thanet DC ex p Warren Court Hotels Ltd (2000) 33 HLR 339, CA… **565, 706**
R v Tilley [2009] EWCA Crim 1426… **54**
R v Tower Hamlets LBC HBRB ex p Kapur [2000] *The Times*… **694**
R v Waltham Forest LBC ex p Holder (1996) 29 HLR 71… **1791, 1792, 1793**

R v Warrington BC ex p Williams (1997) 29 HLR 872 at 876, QBD… **16, 275, 277**
R v West Dorset DC ex p Poupard [1988] 28 RVR 40, CA… **416, 417**
R v Westminster CC ex p Castelli and Tristan-Garcia [1995] 8 Admin LR 73 at 92E-F, QBD…
336
R v Westminster CC HBRB ex p Mehanne [1999] 2 All ER 319, CA… **286, 1789, 1790**
R v Westminster CC HBRB ex p Pallas [1997] unreported, 23 September, QBD… **1791, 1792**
R v Westminster CC HBRB ex p Sier (1999) 32 HLR 655 at 662-3, QBD… **275, 295**
R v Woking BC ex p Crawley [1996] unreported, 19 June, QBD… **276**
R v Wyre BC ex p Lord [1997] unreported, 24 October, QBD… **603**
R v SSHD ex p Anufrijeva [2003] UKHL 36 [2004] 1 AC 604… **420**
R (Beeson) v Dorset CC [2001] EWHC Admin 986, 30 November 2001… **469**
R v Liverpool City Council ex p Johnson (No 2) [1995] COD 200, QBD… **557**
R v Sutton LBC ex p Partridge (1994) 28 HLR 315 at 319-320… **283, 285, 286**
Rahman and others (Case C-83/11) [2012] ECR (ECLI:EU:C:2012:519)… **335**
Raulin (Case C-357/89) [1992] ECR I-01027… **307**
Re B (Minors) (Abduction) [1993] 1 FLR 993 at 995C-D, FD… **346**
Re C (Minors) (Adoption: Residence Order) [1994] Fam 1, CA… **288**
Re Collins [1990] Fam 56, FD… **288**
Re Forest of Dean Coal Mining Co [1879] 10 Ch D 451 at 453… **289**
Re J (A minor) (Abduction: Custody Rights) [1990] 2 AC 562… **345, 347**
Re Prince Blucher [1931] 2 Ch D 70… **1007**
Re S [2002] 2 AC 291, HL… **113**
Re Wyvern Developments Ltd [1974] 1 WLR 1097 at 1103D, Ch D… **275**
Ready-Mixed Concrete (South East) Ltd v Minister of Pensions and National Insurance [1968] 2
QB 497, CA… **289**
Reyes v Migrationsverket (Case C-423/12) [2014] ECR… **319**
Rider v Chief Adjudication Officer [1996] *Times*… **638**
Rinner-Kühn (Case C-171/88) … **306**
RR v SSWP [2019] UKSC 52 … **114, 115, 189, 380**
Robson v Secretary of State for Social Services [1982] 3 FLR 232, QBD… **15**
Ruiz-Mateos v Spain (1993) 16 EHRR 505… **125**
Rutherford and Others v SSWP [2014] EWHC 1613 (Admin)… **378**
Sabesan v LB Waltham Forest [2018] EWHC 2373 (Admin)… **1678, 1683**
Saint-Prix v SSWP (Case C-507/12) [2014] ECR; [2014] AACR 18… **315**
Saint-Prix v SSWP [2012] UKSC 49… **315**
Saker v Secretary of State for Social Security [1988] 16 January *The Times*… **588, 596, 947**
Salesi v Italy (1993) 26 EHRR 187 at 199, para 19, ECtHR… **124**
Samin v City of Westminster [2012] EWCA Civ 1468… **311**
Samuda v Secretary of SSWP [2014] EWCA Civ 1… **1054**
Saunders v Vautier [1841] 4 Bear 115… **472**
Saunderson v SSWP [2012] ScotCS CSIH 10… **255**
SC & Ors v SSWP & Ors [2018] EWHC 864 (Admin)… **412, 1127**
SC & Ors v SSWP & Ors [2019] EWCA Civ 615… **413, 1127**
SC v East Riding of Yorkshire Council [2014] EW Misc B46 (VT)… **1076, 1079, 1080, 1666**
Scott v SSWP [2011] EWCA Civ 103; [2011] AACR 23… **293**
Secretary of State for Social Security v Walter [2002] ICR 540… **492**
Secretary of State for Social Services v Solly [1974] 3 All ER 922… **594**
Sengupta v Holmes [2002] *The Times*… **126**
Shah v Secretary of State for Social Security [2002] EWCA Civ 285, CA; reported as *R(IS) 2/02*…
1708, 1750
Shepherd v Dundee CC [2002] SLT 1427, CS(IH)… **383**
Singh and Others v Minister for Justice and Equality (Case C-218/14) [2015] ECR not yet
reported… **331, 336**
Singh v Post Office [1973] ICR 437 at 440… **963**
Slezak v SSWP [2017] CSIH 4; [2017] AACR 21… **319**
SM (Order of the Court 14/03/2018 ECLI:EU:C:2018:191)… **318**
SM v Entry Clearance Officer [2018] UKSC 7… **318**

Smith v Chief Adjudication Officer [1994]; reported as *R(IS) 21/95*… **255**
Sodemare SA v Regione Lombardia (Case C-70/95) [1997] ECR I-03395… **336**
South Tyneside Council v Aitkin [2014] EWHC 4163 (Admin)… **1090**
Stec and others v United Kingdom (2006) 43 EHRR 47… **127, 131, 132**
SSHD v NA (Case C-115/15) … **336**
SSHD v Ojo [2015] EWCA Civ 1301… **334**
SSHD v Aibangbee [2019] EWCA Civ 339… **335**
SSWP v Carmichael and Sefton Council [2018] EWCA Civ 548… **114, 188, 379**
SSWP v Chiltern DC (2003) HLR 1019, CA; reported as *R(H) 2/03*… **557, 604**
SSWP v City of Glasgow Council and IB [2017] CSIH 35; [2017] AACR 29… **374, 376**
SSWP v Gubeladze [2017] EWCA Civ 1751… **320, 325**
SSWP v Gubeladze [2019] UKSC 31… **320, 325**
SSWP v Hockley and Nuneaton and Bedworth BC [2019] EWCA Civ 1080… **376**
SSWP v Miah; reported as *R(JSA) 9/03*… **16**
SSWP v Morina and Borrowdale [2007] EWCA Civ 749; reported as *R(IS) 6/07*… **177, 186**
SSWP v Payne and another [2011] UKSC 60; [2012] 2 All ER 46… **597**
SSWP v Roach [2006]; reported as *R(CS) 4/07*… **186**
SSWP v Selby DC and another [2006] EWCA Civ 271… **269**
SSWP v Slavin [2011] EWCA Civ 1515; [2012] AACR 30… **431**
SSWP v Wilson [2006] EWCA Civ 882; reported as *R(H) 7/06*… **24**
SSWP v Ahmed [2005] EWCA Civ 535; reported as *R(IS) 8/05*… **1708**
SSWP v Bhakta [2006] EWCA Civ 65; reported as *R(IS) 7/06*… **552**
SSWP v Chiltern DC [2003] EWCA Civ 508; reported as *R(H) 2/03*… **147**
SSWP v Gillies [2003] 2004 SLT 14; reported at 2006 SC (HL) 71… **123, 182**
SSWP v Hourigan [2003] 1 WLR 608… **477**
SSWP v Lassal (Case C-162/09) [2010] ECR; [2011] AACR 33… **332**
SSWP v M [2006] UKHL 11; reported as *R(CS) 4/06*… **127, 129**
SSWP v Robinson [2004], 11 February, CA; reported as *R(H) 4/04*… **534**
SSWP v Lassal [2009] EWCA Civ 157… **332**
Stach re application for Judicial Review [2018] NIQB 93… **326**
Steele v Steele [2001] CP Rep 106… **991**
Stevenson v Rogers [1992] SLT 558, IH… **1477**
Steymann v Staatssecretaris van Justitie (Case C-196/87) [1988] ECR 06159… **307, 336**
Street v Mountford [1995] AC 809, HL… **1476**
Swaddling v Chief Adjudication Officer (Case C-90/97) [1999] 2 CMLR 679, ECJ… **346**
Sweet v Parsley [1970] AC 132, 155A… **470**
Szeja v Land Berlin (Case C-424/10)… **333**
Szoma v SSWP [2005] UKHL 64, [2006] 1 All ER 1; reported as *R(IS) 2/06*… **1750**
Szpak v SSWP and SSHD [2013] EWCA Civ 46… **324**
Taylor's Central Garages (Exeter) Ltd v Roper [1951] 115 JP 445 at 449, 450, DC… **54, 56**
Teixeira v LB Lambeth and SSHD (Case C-480/08)… **337**
Teixeira v LB Lambeth (Case C-480/08) … **302, 341, 342, 343, 344**
Thamesdown BC v Goonery [1995] 1 CLY 2600, CA… **250**
The Belgian Linguistics Case (No.2) (1967) 1 EHRR 252 at 283-4, para 9, ECtHR… **129, 130**
The House of Lords [1999] 1 WLR 1937, [1999] 4 All ER 677… **345, 346**
The House of Lords [2001] 1 WLR 539… **1789**
Thlimmenos v Greece (2001) 31 EHRR 15… **697**
Thlimmenos v Greece (2001) 31 EHRR 411… **130, 395**
Thomas v Chief Adjudication Officer reported as an appendix to *R(SB) 17/87*… **461**
Thrasyvoulou v Secretary of State for the Environment [1990] 2 AC 273 at 289, HL… **152**
Tilling v Whiteman [1980] AC 1… **991**
Tkachuk v SSWP [2007] EWCA Civ 515; reported as *R(IS) 3/07*… **544**
Tolfree v Florence [1971] 1 WLR 141 at 144, DC… **56**
Toufik Lounes v SSHD (Case C-165/16);[2017] ECR (ECLI:EU:C:2017:862)… **304**
Trojani v Centre public d'aide sociale de Bruxelles (Case C-456/02) [2004] ECR I-07573… **337, 338**

Trustees of the Dennis Rye Pension Fund v Sheffield CC [1998] 1 WLR 840 at 849F-M, 850A, CA... **568**
Tsfayo v United Kingdom (2009) 48 EHRR 18... **126, 139, 969**
Turner v South Cambridgeshire DC [2016] EWHC 1017 (Admin)... **1683**
Tyrer v Smart [1979] 1 WLR 113, HL... **440**
Uratemp Ventures Ltd v Collins [2001] 3 WLR 806... **15, 16**
Van der Mussele v Belgium (1983) 6 EHRR 163, 179-180... **130**
W (China) & Another v Secretary of State for the Home Department [2006] EWCA Civ 1494... **331**
Walsh v Rother DC [1978] 1 All ER 510 at 514a-e, HC... **59**
Ward v Kingston upon Hull CC [1993] RA 71, QBD... **1477**
Warwick DC v Freeman (1994) 27 HLR 616, CA... **59, 60, 576, 587, 588, 600, 1745**
Watt v Ahsan [2007] UKHL 51; [2008] AC 696... **178**
Westminister CC v Clarke [1992] 2 AC 288 at 299, HL... **15**
Westminister CC v Croyalgrange Ltd [1986] 1 WLR 674 at 684E, HL... **54**
White v Chief Adjudication Officer [1986] 2 All ER 905, CA; reported as an appendix to *R(S) 8/85*... **177**
White v Chief Adjudication Officer [1993] *The Times*... **431**
Wilkinson v Chief Adjudication Officer; reported as *R(IS) 1/01*... **477**
Williams v Bayley [1866] LR 1 HL 200, HL... **60**
Williams v Horsham DC [2004] EWCA Civ 39... **1477**
Wilson v First County Trust Ltd (No 2) [2003] WLR 586... **123**
Wiltshire Council v Piggin [2014] EWHC 4386 (Admin)... **1080**
Wirral MBC v Salisbury Independent Living [2012] EWCA 84; [2012] AACR 37... **177, 942, 998**
Wirth v Landeshauptstadt Hannover (Case C-109/92) [1993] ECR I-06447... **336**
Wood v SSWP [2003] EWCA Civ 53; reported as *R(DLA) 1/03*... **140, 141, 146, 947, 954, 955, 972**
Wright v Howell [1947] 92 SJ 26, CA... **15**
X v Italy [1977] 11 DR 114... **133**
Yang v The Official Receiver and others [2013] EWHC 3577 (Ch)... **1080**
Yesiloz v LB Camden and SSWP [2009] EWCA Civ 145; reported as *R(H) 7/09*... **299, 1707**
YL (by her litigation friend the Official Solicitor) v Birmingham City Council and others [2007] UKHL 27, 20 June, HL... **116**
Zalewska v Department for Social Development [2008] UKHL 67... **324, 325**
Zambrano v Office national de l'emploi (ONEm) (Case C-34/09) [2011] ECR I-01177... **305, 328, 344, 1707, 1708**
Zhu and Chen (Case C-200/02) [2004] ECR I-09925... **344**
Ziolkowski v Land Berlin (Case C-425/10)... **333**

Table of commissioners' decisions

C 10/1995 (IS)... **309**
CCS 7967/1995... **458**
CCS 1535/1997... **151**
CCS 565/1999... **181**
CCS 557/2005... **182**
CDLA 7980/1995... **431**
CDLA 1347/1999... **123**
CDLA 5413/1999... **125**
CDLA 3432/2001... **126**
CDLA 4895/2001... **940**
CDLA 4977/2001... **566**
CDLA 1456/2002... **179, 180**
CDLA 2748/2002... **125, 181**
CDLA 2975/2002... **179, 180**
CDLA 4331/2002... **149**
CDLA 1685/2004... **1020**
CDLA 2014/2004... **1001**
CDLA 1589/2005... **559**
CF 6923/1999... **150**
CF 1863/2007... **318**
CFC 25/1989... **439**
CFC 1537/1995... **408**
CG 1479/1999... **948**
CG 2122/2001... **939**
CG 3844/2006... **549**
CH 3776/2001... **707**
CH 3853/2001... **151, 292**
CH 4065/2001... **584, 590**
CH 4838/2001... **590**
CH 4943/2001... **557, 565, 566, 603**
CH 5135/2001... **553**
CH 5147/2001... **283**
CH 5217/2001... **565**
CH 5221/2001... **180**
CH 393/2002... **265**
CH 396/2002... **282, 292**
CH 474/2002... **554**
CH 627/2002... **179**
CH 716/2002... **282, 287, 291**
CH 843/2002... **282**
CH 844/2002... **354, 355**
CH 999/2002... **557**
CH 1076/2002... **179, 284, 285**
CH 1085/2002... **181, 264**
CH 1129/2002... **145, 148**
CH 1171/2002... **145, 274, 276, 278**
CH 1172/2002... **589**
CH 1175/2002... **145, 149, 1754**
CH 1618/2002... **278**
CH 1992/2002... **1793**
CH 1993/2002... **1793**

CH 2191/2002... **554**
CH 2201/2002... **264, 265, 267, 584**
CH 2302/2002... **139, 182**
CH 2321/2002... **444, 447, 452, 463, 587, 674**
CH 2349/2002... **182, 604**
CH 2387/2002... **440**
CH 2443/2002... **595**
CH 2521/2002... **264, 265**
CH 2554/2002... **589, 591**
CH 2659/2002... **553**
CH 2888/2002... **589**
CH 3008/2002... **283, 293, 294**
CH 3009/2002... **145, 554, 941, 946, 955**
CH 3376/2002... **358**
CH 3594/2002... **181**
CH 3629/2002... **589**
CH 3679/2002... **585, 942, 180**
CH 4099/2002... **566**
CH 4465/2002... **589**
CH 4546/2002... **267**
CH 4922/2002... **277**
CH 4970/2002... **1789, 1793**
CH 4972/2002... **466**
CH 5125/2002... **93**
CH 5302/2002... **291**
CH 5553/2002... **603**
CH 69/2003... **587**
CH 216/2003... **566**
CH 296/2003... **243**
CH 329/2003... **434**
CH 393/2003... **553, 554**
CH 663/2003... **279, 283, 285**
CH 943/2003... **538, 586, 587**
CH 1176/2003... **590**
CH 1208/2003... **277, 400**
CH 1210/2003... **151**
CH 1278/2003... **242, 243**
CH 1325/2003... **286**
CH 1953/2003... **477**
CH 2214/2003... **1795**
CH 2329/2003... **283, 285, 353**
CH 2516/2003... **296**
CH 2743/2003... **241**
CH 3110/2003... **355**
CH 3197/2003... **477**
CH 3616/2003... **242, 290, 291**
CH 3743/2003... **283, 285**
CH 4354/2003... **582**
CH 4390/2003... **557**
CH 4574/2003... **127, 272**

CH 4733/2003... **289, 291**
CH 4854/2003... **284**
CH 4918/2003... **588, 589**
CH 296/2004... **284**
CH 609/2004... **589, 590**
CH 939/2004... **586**
CH 996/2004... **271, 553**
CH 1097/2004... **284**
CH 1237/2004... **270**
CH 1326/2004... **293**
CH 1586/2004... **282, 292**
CH 1762/2004... **508**
CH 1791/2004... **553**
CH 1854/2004... **269**
CH 2258/2004... **241**
CH 2517/2004... **671**
CH 2794/2004... **558, 560, 585, 586, 588**
CH 3439/2004... **584, 589**
CH 3656/2004... **286, 287**
CH 3817/2004... **39, 543, 553, 942**
CH 3857/2004... **268**
CH 3893/2004... **269, 270**
CH 257/2005... **277**
CH 318/2005... **248**
CH 704/2005... **152**
CH 1419/2005... **296**
CH 1450/2005... **435, 436**
CH 1561/2005... **415, 416, 538**
CH 1675/2005... **590**
CH 1786/2005... **264**
CH 2409/2005... **588**
CH 2484/2005... **338**
CH 2899/2005... **283, 285**
CH 2986/2005... **391, 392, 573**
CH 3083/2005... **585**
CH 3220/2005... **290, 291**
CH 3314/2005... **306, 311, 312**
CH 3497/2005... **976**
CH 3761/2005... **587, 585**
CH 3900/2005... **1779**
CH 4108 2005... **574, 575**
CH 48/2006... **520**
CH 180/2006... **574, 578**
CH 264/2006... **470**
CH 282/2006... **963**
CH 361/2006... **402**
CH 532/2006... **157, 563**
CH 533/2006... **157**
CH 542/2006... **287**
CH 687/2006... **587**
CH 858/2006... **585**
CH 1363/2006... **268**
CH 1400/2006... **336**
CH 1556/2006... **627**
CH 1578/2006... **355**
CH 1822 2006... **471**
CH 1911/2006... **266**

CH 2121/2006... **279**
CH 2638/2006... **270**
CH 2959/2006... **276**
CH 2995/2006... **965, 967, 968, 967, 969, 970**
CH 3282/2006... **283**
CH 3528/2006... **353, 1791, 1792**
CH 3622/2006... **39, 543**
CH 3736/2006... **532, 969, 970**
CH 3744/2006... **592**
CH 4371/2006... **452**
CH 4428/2006... **585, 586**
CH 4429/2006... **502**
CH 39/2007... **294**
CH 1289/2007... **1779, 1780**
CH 1672/2007... **418**
CH 2555/2007... **557**
CH 2805/2007... **1781**
CH 2943/2007... **589**
CH 3590/2007... **627**
CH 3631/2007... **978, 979**
CH 3729/2007... **461**
CH 3777/2007... **686**
CH 38/2008... **586**
CH 755/2008... **621**
CH 1096/2008... **284**
CH 1330/2008... **441**
CH 2198/2008... **553**
CH 2726/2008... **1779**
CH 3670/2008... **462**
CH 2194/2010... **270**
CH 567/2011... **264**
CH 2483/2012... **393**
CIB 5227/1999... **181**
CIB 3985/2001... **125**
CIB 4427/2002... **150**
CIB 4667/2002... **181**
CIB 2949/2005... **150**
CIS 124/1990... **469**
CIS 159/1990... **595**
CIS 93/1991... **460**
CIS 195/1991... **284**
CIS 222/1991... **595**
CIS 754/1991... **279**
CIS 93/1992... **950**
CIS 307/1992... **471**
CIS 395/1992... **595**
CIS 522/1992... **603**
CIS 671/1992... **17**
CIS 30/1993... **469**
CIS 77/1993... **441**
CIS 87/1993... **14, 15**
CIS 393/1993... **595**
CIS 590/1993... **418, 440**
CIS 166/1994... **6**
CIS 368/1994... **697**
CIS 372/1994... **595**

CIS 564/1994... **325**
CIS 683/1994... **38, 601**
CIS 1460/1995... **621, 625**
CIS 2326/1995... **345, 346, 347**
CIS 5136/1995... **347**
CIS 8111/1995... **345, 346, 347**
CIS 11304/1995... **17**
CIS 11481/1995... **345**
CIS 11293/1996... **1775**
CIS 12703/1996... **347**
CIS 13498/1996... **345, 346, 347**
CIS 13986/1996... **493**
CIS 14591/1996... **347**
CIS 14850/1996... **249**
CIS 15611/1996... **639**
CIS 15927/1996... **345**
CIS 16410/1996... **345**
CIS 85/1997... **254**
CIS 1137/1997... **1800**
CIS 1304/1997... **346**
CIS 1586/1997... **469**
CIS 2575/1997... **477**
CIS 3283/1997... **477, 476**
CIS 3287/1997... **11**
CIS 6002/1997... **181**
CIS 3418/1998... **1748**
CIS 4341/1998... **1800**
CIS 114/1999... **458**
CIS 217/1999... **948**
CIS 2428/1999... **149**
CIS 5825/1999... **602**
CIS 6249/1999... **946**
CIS 2943/2000... **461**
CIS 3508/2001... **1708**
CIS 47/2002... **1708**
CIS 521/2002... **678**
CIS 1277/2002... **961**
CIS 4901/2002... **974**
CIS 1870/2003... **130**
CIS 1972/2003... **346**
CIS 2505/2003... **142**
CIS 2532/2003... **250**
CIS 3228/2003... **582**
CIS 4348/2003... **595**
CIS 4474/2003... **345, 346**
CIS 1697/2004... **1707**
CIS 218/2005... **469**
CIS 2559/2005... **346**
CIS 3182/2005... **311, 316**
CIS 3573/2005... **338**
CIS 3875/2005... **336**
CIS 3890/2005... **310**
CIS 34/2006... **326**
CIS 1068/2006... **681**
CIS 1757 2006... **471**
CIS 1934/2006... **316**
CIS 2317/2006... **408**

CIS 2431/2006... **318**
CIS 2448/2006... **687**
CIS 3232/2006... **324**
CIS 4010/2006... **311**
CIS 4371/2006... **436**
CIS 647/2007... **436**
CIS 731/2007... **311, 316**
CIS 1793/2007... **307**
CIS 1813/2007... **436, 452**
CIS 1833/2007... **333**
CIS 1915/2007... **693**
CIS 2100/2007... **318**
CIS 2911/2007... **311**
CIS 3655/2007... **596, 947, 954, 955**
CIS 3799/2007... **312**
CIS 3960/2007... **342**
CIS 4144/2007... **306**
CIS 4237/2007... **311, 316**
CIS 4299/2007... **333**
CIS 4304/2007... **311, 316**
CIS 185/2008... **344**
CIS 612/2008... **335**
CIS 1042/2008... **309, 321**
CIS 1853/2008... **436**
CIS 2258/2008... **334**
CIS 2287/2008... **461, 475**
CIS 304/2009... **331**
CJSA 3979/1999... **559**
CJSA 2375/2000... **149**
CJSA 1332/2001... **559**
CJSA 5100/2001... **125, 180**
CJSA 549/2003... **453**
CJSA 825/2004... **492**
CJSA 1425/2004... **470**
CJSA 1223/2006... **346**
CJSA 3832/2006... **255**
CJSA 3960/2006... **974**
CJSA 1321/2007... **17**
CP 8001/1995... **15**
CP 5084/2001... **132**
CP 518/2003... **130, 131**
CPC 2920/2005... **338**
CPC 683/2007... **686**
CPC 2134/2007... **333**
CPC 3373/2007... **447, 449**
CPC 1433/2008... **319**
CPC 1446/2008... **250**
CPC 1935/2010... **343**
CS 249/1989... **431**
CS 130/1992... **595**
CS 12770/1996... **595**
CS 14430/1996... **149**
CS 2647/1997... **431**
CSB 150/1985... **15**
CSB 392/1985... **38**
CSB 1006/1985... **595**
CSB 64/1986... **595**

CSB 598/1987… **469**
CSB 950/1987… **534, 677**
CSDLA 855/1997… **182**
CSDLA 1019/1999… **123, 182**
CSDLA 336/2000… **180**
CSDLA 2/2002… **149**
CSDLA 606/2003… **182**
CSG 336/2003… **1042**
CSH 499/2006… **270**
CSHB 718/2002… **274, 278, 293, 587**
CSHB 405/2005… **269**
CSHB 606/2005… **275**
CSIB 848/1997… **181**
CSIB 588/1998… **180**
CSIS 62/1991… **603**
CSIS 100/1993… **250**
CSIS 185/1995… **250**
CSIS 754/2002… **142**
CSIS 652/2003… **250**
CSPC 677/2007… **293**
CTC 626/2001… **440**
CTC 3646/2007… **429**
CU 47/1993… **180**
DL and Redcar and Cleveland BC (CH 2658/
2015)… **380**
SSWP v RR and Sefton BC (CH 4674/2014)…
380
R(A) 1/72… **179**
R(CS) 5/96… **347**
R(CS) 3/04… **939**
R(DLA) 2/01… **149**
R(DLA) 3/01… **141, 149**
R(DLA) 4/02… **127**
R(DLA) 3/05… **940**
R(FC) 2/90… **254**
R(FC) 1/91… **448**
R(FC) 2/92… **687**
R(FC) 3/98… **157**
R(G) 1/79… **15**
R(H) 1/02… **180**
R(H) 1/03… **179, 283, 284**
R(H) 2/03… **981**
R(H) 3/03… **274, 582**
R(H) 1/04… **585, 587**
R(H) 2/04… **585, 587**
R(H) 3/04… **38, 39, 40, 60, 140, 143, 144,
145, 147, 151, 565, 566, 981**
R(H) 5/04… **557, 603**
R(H) 6/04… **140, 292**
R(H) 7/04… **38, 40, 147**
R(H) 8/04… **128, 130**
R(H) 9/04… **326**
R(H) 1/05… **603**
R(H) 2/05… **1791, 1792**
R(H) 3/05… **563**
R(H) 5/05… **275, 417, 669**
R(H) 6/05… **288**

R(H) 7/05… **243, 274, 295**
R(H) 9/05… **264, 267**
R(H) 10/05… **283, 294**
R(H) 1/06… **469**
R(H) 2/06… **559**
R(H) 4/06… **269**
R(H) 5/06… **287**
R(H) 6/06… **38, 39, 40, 147, 148, 592, 593,
594, 981**
R(H) 1/07… **947, 976, 1010**
R(H) 2/07… **1780, 1779, 1780**
R(H) 3/07… **242**
R(H) 4/07… **268**
R(H) 5/07… **448**
R(H) 6/07… **292**
R(H) 7/07… **1780**
R(H) 8/07… **242**
R(H) 9/07… **534, 552**
R(H) 10/07… **39**
R(H) 1/08… **575**
R(H) 2/08… **573, 581**
R(H) 3/08… **1476, 1478**
R(H) 4/08… **969, 981**
R(H) 5/08… **448**
R(H) 6/08… **1780, 1781**
R(H) 7/08… **688**
R(H) 8/08… **415**
R(H) 9/08… **355**
R(H) 10/08… **585, 587, 588**
R(H) 1/09… **969**
R(H) 2/09… **452**
R(H) 4/09… **1781**
R(H) 5/09… **6, 16**
R(H) 8/09… **372, 627, 881**
R(H) 9/09… **598**
R(I) 56/54… **955**
R(I) 7/62… **979**
R(I) 2/83… **979**
R(I) 2/88… **955**
R(I) 2/94… **955**
R(I) 5/02… **939**
R(I) 1/03… **157**
R(I) 2/06… **179**
R(IB) 4/02… **946**
R(IB) 3/03… **92**
R(IB) 2/04… **143, 145, 147, 148, 566, 575,
582, 946, 947, 954, 955, 969**
R(IB) 2/07… **93**
R(IS) 1/90… **461**
R(IS) 2/90… **465**
R(IS) 5/92… **603**
R(IS) 6/92… **440, 441**
R(IS) 12/92… **460**
R(IS) 1/93… **254**
R(IS) 3/93… **419**
R(IS) 14/93… **293, 471**
R(IS) 17/93… **273, 521**

R(IS) 21/93… **465**
R(IS) 17/94… **279**
R(IS) 5/95… **254**
R(IS) 7/95… **497**
R(IS) 8/95… **256**
R(IS) 16/95… **485, 497**
R(IS) 22/95… **254**
R(IS) 1/96… **492**
R(IS) 6/96… **249, 345, 346, 347**
R(IS) 8/96… **430**
R(IS) 12/96… **249**
R(IS) 3/97… **319**
R(IS) 11/98… **284**
R(IS) 12/98… **306, 311**
R(IS) 15/98… **485**
R(IS) 19/98… **484**
R(IS) 22/98… **417**
R(IS) 1/99… **17**
R(IS) 5/99… **485**
R(IS) 7/99… **493**
R(IS) 8/99… **10**
R(IS) 11/99… **179**
R(IS) 13/99… **254**
R(IS) 1/00… **485**
R(IS) 6/00… **309**
R(IS) 3/01… **815**
R(IS) 6/01… **979**
R(IS) 10/01… **458**
R(IS) 2/02… **1749**
R(IS) 4/03… **477**
R(IS) 5/03… **596**
R(IS) 6/03… **417**
R(IS) 1/04… **124, 125**
R(IS) 2/04… **125**
R(IS) 3/04… **978**
R(IS) 6/04… **123, 125, 126, 980**
R(IS) 12/04… **114**
R(IS) 15/04… **124, 946, 949**
R(IS) 16/04… **815, 974**
R(IS) 5/05… **686**
R(IS) 7/05… **595**
R(IS) 7/06… **346**
R(IS) 11/06… **130**
R(IS) 5/07… **477**
R(IS) 2/08… **143, 145, 148, 972, 973**
R(IS) 5/08… **688**
R(IS) 9/08… **419**
R(IS) 4/09… **339**

R(JSA) 1/02… **477**
R(JSA) 2/02… **493**
R(JSA) 3/02… **492**
R(JSA) 4/03… **256**
R(JSA) 2/04… **554**
R(JSA) 1/07… **255, 256**
R(P) 1/06… **133**
R(P) 2/06… **128**
R(PC) 3/08… **419, 433**
R(PC) 1/09… **1707**
R(S) 1/63… **549**
R(S) 2/63(T)… **553**
R(S) 4/84… **431**
R(S) 4/86… **947, 955**
R(SB) 10/81… **265, 688**
R(SB) 17/81… **15**
R(SB) 13/82… **17**
R(SB) 21/82… **595**
R(SB) 2/83… **180, 465**
R(SB) 4/83… **17**
R(SB) 20/83… **485**
R(SB) 30/83… **17**
R(SB) 41/83… **485**
R(SB) 54/83… **595**
R(SB) 13/84… **685**
R(SB) 25/84… **979**
R(SB) 27/84… **685**
R(SB) 40/84… **596**
R(SB) 1/85… **460**
R(SB) 4/85… **152**
R(SB) 8/85… **17**
R(SB) 9/85… **595**
R(SB) 18/85… **595**
R(SB) 35/85… **15**
R(SB) 38/85… **469**
R(SB) 40/85… **469**
R(SB) 21/86… **418, 440**
R(SB) 12/87… **646**
R(SB) 15/87… **595, 596**
R(SB) 22/87… **240, 287**
R(SB) 25/87… **484**
R(SB) 2/88… **564**
R(SB) 2/89… **458, 472**
R(SB) 9/91… **469**
R(SB) 12/91… **470**
R(TC) 2/03… **440**
R(TC) 1/05… **950**

Table of Upper Tribunal decisions

AA v Hounslow LB [2008] UKUT 13 (AAC)... **556, 967, 968**
AA v Leicester City Council [2009] UKUT 86 (AAC)... **967, 968**
AA v Cheshire and Wirral Partnership NHS Foundation Trust [2009] UKUT 195 (AAC); [2011]
AACR 37... **1023, 1024**
AA v Chesterfield BC [2011] UKUT 156 (AAC)... **361, 364, 393, 394, 395, 396**
AB v SSWP (JSA) [2013] UKUT 288 (AAC)... **114**
AD v Information Commissioner and Devon CC [2013] UKUT 550 (AAC)... **996**
AD v Information Commissioner [2016] UKUT 273 (AAC)... **1036**
AG v HMRC (TC) [2013] UKUT 530 (AAC)... **1009**
AG v Calderdale Council (HB) [2016] UKUT 396 (AAC)... **590**
AG v South Ayrshire Council (HB) [2017] UKUT 110 (AAC); [2018] AACR 18... **1780**
AH v Mendip DC [2008] UKUT 18 (AAC); R(H) 3/09... **592**
AH v London Borough of Hackney (HB) [2014] UKUT 47 (AAC)... **126**
AJ v SSWP (ESA) [2014] UKUT 208 (AAC)... **972**
AM v SSWP [2009] UKUT 224 (AAC)... **1024**
AM v Information Commissioner & FTT [2010] UKUT 438 (AAC)... **178**
AM v SSWP (IS) [2011] UKUT 387 (AAC)... **249**
AM v Chelmsford BC (HB) [2013] UKUT 245 (AAC)... **420**
AM v Information Commissioner [2014] UKUT 239 (AAC)... **995**
AMS v SSWP (PC) (second interim decision) [2017] UKUT 48 (AAC)... **330, 337**
AMS v SSWP (PC) (final decision) [2017] UKUT 381 (AAC)... **330, 341**
AP v SSWP (IS) [2018] UKUT 307 (AAC)... **327**
AP-H v SSWP [2010] UKUT 183 (AAC)... **148**
AR v Bradford MBC [2008] UKUT 30 (AAC); R(H) 6/09... **417, 447**
AS v SSWP (ESA) [2011] UKUT 159 (AAC)... **1019**
AS v SSWP (CA) [2015] UKUT 592 (AAC); [2016] AACR 22... **126**
AS v SSWP (UC) [2018] UKUT 260 (AAC)... **301**
AT v Broxstowe BC & JH (HB) [2015] UKUT 388 (AAC)... **575**
AW v SSWP (IB) [2012] UKUT 104 (AAC)... **1023**
AW v SSWP (ESA) [2013] UKUT 20 (AAC)... **552**
AW v Information Commissioner and Blackpool City Council [2013] UKUT 30 (AAC)... **996**
Aylesbury Vale DC v ER (HB) [2011] UKUT 160 (AAC)... **1792**
B v SSWP [2017] UKUT 472 (AAC)... **304**
BB v SSWP (ESA) [2014] UKUT 55 (AAC)... **999**
BM v Cheshire West and Chester Council [2009] UKUT 162 (AAC)... **1795**
BRG v SSWP (SPC) [2014] UKUT 246 (AAC)... **789**
BS v SSWP [2009] UKUT 16 (AAC)... **310, 322**
BV v SSWP (PIP) [2018] UKUT 444 (AAC); [2019] 1 WLR 3185... **990, 1015**
Babajanov (Continuity of residence – Immigration (EEA) Regulations) [2013] UKUT 513 (IAC)...
334
Babergh DC v GW (HB) [2017] UKUT 40 (AAC)... **275**
Basildon DC v AM [2009] UKUT 113 (AAC)... **283**
Bexley LB v LD (HB) [2010] UKUT 79 (AAC)... **382, 404, 879, 894**
Birmingham City Council v IB [2009] UKUT 116 (AAC)... **16, 265**
Blackburn with Darwen BC v DA (HB) [2014] UKUT 431 (AAC)... **245**
Bolton MBC v BF (HB) [2014] UKUT 48 (AAC)... **244, 374**
Bolton MBC v HY (HB) [2018] UKUT 103 (AAC); [2018] AACR 31... **343**
Bradford MDC v MR (HB) [2010] UKUT 315 (AAC)... **291**
Bristol CC v AW [2009] UKUT 109 (AAC)... **1781, 1782**
Bristol CC v FV (HB) [2011] UKUT 494 (AAC)... **308**
Bristol City Council v JKT [2016] UKUT 517 (AAC)... **240, 245, 282, 287**

Broxtowe BC v CS (HB) [2014] UKUT 186 (AAC)... **410**
Bury MBC v DC (HB) [2011] UKUT 43 (AAC)... **268**
C2/11-12(JSA) (MA v DSD (JSA) [2011] NICom 205)... **343**
Camden LB v FG (SEN) [2010] 249 (AAC)... **989**
CB v Suffolk CC [2010] UKUT 413 (AAC); [2011] AACR 22... **993**
CB v Liverpool City Council [2015] UKUT 359 (AAC)... **270**
CB v Manchester City Council and SSWP (HB) [2015] UKUT 556 (AAC)... **373**
CC v Braintree DC [2013] UKUT 104 (AAC)... **434**
CD v First-tier Tribunal (SEC) (CIC) [2010] UKUT 181 (AAC)... **989**
CG v SSWP (DLA) [2011] UKUT 453 (AAC)... **1019**
CH 4085/2007 [2008] UKUT 14 (AAC)... **25**
CH v Wakefield DC [2009] UKUT 20 (AAC)... **292**
CH v SSWP (DLA) [2012] UKUT 427 (AAC)... **1016**
CH v Plymouth City Council and DE (HB) [2018] UKUT 215 (AAC)... **146, 556, 969**
CIB 8/2008 [2009] UKUT 47 (AAC)... **125**
CJ v Stratford-on-Avon DC (HB) [2012] UKUT 357 (AAC)... **589**
CM v SSWP [2009] UKUT 43 (AAC), R(IS) 7/09... **492**
CM v HMRC (TC) [2014] UKUT 272 (AAC)... **998**
CO v LB Havering (CH) [2015] UKUT 28 (AAC)... **1007**
CP v M Technology School (SEN) [2010] UKUT 314 (AAC)... **181**
CP and Others v Aylesbury Vale DC v SSWP (HB) [2011] UKUT 22 (AAC)... **620**
CP v SSWP (IS) [2011] UKUT 157 (AAC)... **697**
CP v City of Brighton and Hove (HB) [2013] UKUT 543 (AAC)... **583**
CR v Wycombe DC [2009] UKUT 19 (AAC)... **241, 242**
CS v SSWP (DLA) 2011 UKUT 509 AAC... **1007**
CW v SSWP and another (CSM) [2014] UKUT 290 (AAC)... **997, 1018**
Camden LB v NW and SSWP (HB) [2011] UKUT 262 (AAC)... **408**
Cardiff CC v HM (HB) [2019] UKUT 271 (AAC)... **334**
Chorley BC v IT (HB) [2009] UKUT 107 (AAC); [2010] AACR 2... **1779, 1781**
DC v SSWP (ESA) [2015] UKUT 150 (AAC)... **1021, 1026**
DC v London Borough of Bromley (HB) [2018] UKUT 416 (AAC)... **393, 396**
DF v SSWP (ESA) [2015] UKUT 143 (AAC)... **1015**
DF v SSWP (ESA) [2015] UKUT 611 (AAC)... **461**
DF v LB Waltham Forest (HB) [2017] UKUT 306 (AAC)... **419, 420**
DH v Kirklees MBC and SSWP (HB) [2011] UKUT 301 (AAC); [2012] AACR 16... **93, 287**
DI v SSWP (PIP) [2018] UKUT 350 (AAC)... **999**
DJ v SSWP (JSA) [2013] UKUT 113 (AAC)... **342**
DL v Liverpool City Council [2009] UKUT 176 (AAC)... **39, 592, 594**
DL v LB Redbridge [2010] UKUT 293 (AAC)... **1023**
DLT v Eastleigh BC (HB) [2014] UKUT 242 (AAC)... **579**
DM v Lewisham LB and SSWP (HB) [2013] UKUT 26 (AAC)... **268**
DN v Leicester City Council (HB) [2010] UKUT 253 (AAC)... **144, 211, 956**
DP v Mid Suffolk DC (HB) [2013] UKUT 93 (AAC)... **972**
DTM v Kettering Borough Council (CTB) [2013] UKUT 625 (AAC)... **994, 995**
DV v HMRC (CHB) [2017] UKUT 155 (AAC)... **309**
DW v Oxford City Council (HB) [2012] UKUT 52 (AAC)... **1782**
Dorset Healthcare NHS Foundation Trust v MH [2009] UKUT 4 (AAC)... **178, 190**
E v Dacorum BC & M [2017] UKUT 93 (AAC)... **579**
E v Bristol City Council [2018] UKUT 287 (AAC)... **374**
EE v City of Cardiff (HB) [2018] UKUT 418 (AAC)... **1708**
EF v SSWP [2009] UKUT 92 (AAC); R(IB) 3/09... **190**
EG v SSWP (JSA) [2018] UKUT 285 (AAC)... **309**
EM v Waltham Forest LBC [2009] UKUT 245 (AAC)... **418, 538, 587, 588**
EM v SSWP (DLA) [2011] UKUT 320 (AAC)... **989**
ET v SSWP (II) [2014] UKUT 417 (AAC)... **1063**
ET v SSWP (PIP) [2017] UKUT 478 (AAC)... **148**
EW v Neath Port Talbot CBC [2009] UKUT 14 (AAC)... **603**

FC v Suffolk CC (SEN) [2010] UKUT 368 (AAC)... **997**
FI v HMRC (CHB) [2018] UKUT 226 (AAC)... **1009**
FK v Wandsworth BC (HB) [2016] UKUT 570 (AAC)... **275, 277**
FL v First-tier Tribunal and CICA [2010] UKUT 158 (AAC)... **145**
FR v Broadland DC [2012] UKUT 449 (AAC)... **554, 990**
FT v (1) Islington LB and (2) SSWP (HB) [2015] UKUT 121 (AAC)... **317**
FT v Perth and Kinross Council and SSWP (HB) [2019] UKUT 43 (AAC)... **368**
FW v SSWP (DLA) [2011] UKUT 88 (AAC)... **939**
FY v SSWP (ESA) [2017] UKUT 501 (AAC)... **1012**
FY v SSWP (RP) [2018] UKUT 146 (AAC)... **1012, 1017**
GA v Southwark LB (HB) [2013] UKUT 170 (AAC)... **1019, 1021**
GA v SSWP (ESA) [2014] UKUT 521 (AAC)... **150**
GA v SSWP [2018] UKUT 172 (AAC)... **336**
GB v Hillingdon LB [2010] UKUT 11 (AAC)... **419**
GB v Information Commissioner & FTT [2010] UKUT 432 (AAC)... **178**
GC v SSWP (ESA) [2012] UKUT 60 (AAC)... **1063**
GH v Scarborough BC (HB) [2015] UKUT 197 (AAC)... **586**
GJ v SSWP, JG and SW [2012] UKUT 447 (AAC)... **1016**
GK v SSWP (ESA) [2016] UKUT 465 (AAC)... **1014**
GM v SSWP (JSA) [2014] UKUT 57 (AAC)... **972, 973**
GN v Sevenoaks BC (HB) [2016] UKUT 271 (AAC)... **242, 290**
Gaskin v Information Commissioner and Norwich City Council [2016] UKUT 382 (AAC)... **1036**
Glasgow City Council v AL (HB) [2011] UKUT 354 (AAC); [2012] ACCR 20... **279**
Guildford BC v MW (HB) [2014] UKUT 49 (AAC)... **463, 466**
HC v Hull City Council (HB) [2013] UKUT 330 (AAC)... **585**
HD and GP v SSWP [2017] UKUT 11 (AAC)... **310, 316**
HG v SSWP (SPC) [2011] UKUT 382 (AAC)... **302, 305**
HK v South Hams DC (HB) [2017] UKUT 254 (AAC)... **270**
HK v SSWP [2017] UKUT 421 (AAC)... **311, 317**
HMRC v IT (CTC) [2016] UKUT 252 (AAC)... **308**
HMRC v HD (CHB) (Second Interim Decision) [2018] UKUT 148 (AAC)... **316**
HP v SSWP (ESA) [2014] UKUT 491 (AAC)... **1018, 1023**
Hackney LB v GA [2008] UKUT 26 (AAC); R(H) 5/09... **16, 265, 266, 285**
Hastings BC v PA and DA Hanlon (HB) [2013] UKUT 232 (AAC); [2014] AACR 4... **593**
IB v Barnsley MBC [2009] UKUT 279 (AAC)... **1476**
IB v Birmingham CC v SSWP v EHRC (HB) [2011] UKUT 23 (AAC)... **395**
IB v Information Commissioner [2011] UKUT 370 (AAC); [2012] AACR 26... **169, 979**
IB v Information Commissioner and Dorset Police [2013] UKUT 582 (AAC)... **1012**
IC v Glasgow City Council and SSWP (HB) [2016] UKUT 321 (AAC); [2017] AACR 1... **326**
ID v SSWP (IS) [2011] UKUT 401 (AAC); [2012] AACR 26... 319
IP v SSWP (IS) [2015] UKUT 691 (AAC)... **342**
Idezuna (EEA-permanent residence) Nigeria [2011] UKUT 474 (IAC)... **334**
Information Commissioner v PS [2011] UKUT 94 (AAC)... **178**
Islington LB v SJ [2008] UKUT 31 (AAC)... **573, 581**
Islington LB v JM (HB) [2014] UKUT 23 (AAC)... **973**
JA v SSWP (ESA) [2012] UKUT 122 (AAC); [2013] AACR 15... 307
JB v Oxford City Council and SSWP (HB) [2011] UKUT 136 (AAC)... **625**
JC v SSWP (DLA) [2013] UKUT 171 (AAC)... **1020**
JC v SSWP (PIP) [2018] UKUT 110 (AAC)... **988, 990**
JF v SSWP (IS) [2010] UKUT 267 (AAC)... **1015**
JH v SSWP [2009] UKUT 1 (AAC)... **685**
JK v SSWP [2017] UKUT 179 (AAC)... **325**
JM v SSWP [2009] UKUT 145 (AAC)... **470**
JM v Tower Hamlets LB [2015] UKUT 460 (AAC)... **603, 604**
JM v Eastleigh BC [2016] UKUT 464 (AAC)... **477**
JM v SSWP (PIP) [2018] UKUT 108 (AAC)... **1012**
JN v SSWP and Basingstoke and Deane BC (HB) [2014] UKUT 223 (AAC)... **408**

JP v SSWP (IB) [2011] UKUT 459 (AAC)... **1012**
JP v SSWP (IS) [2014] UKUT 17 (AAC)... **14**
JP v SSWP (ESA) [2016] UKUT 48 (AAC)... **989**
JP v Bournemouth BC (HB) [2018] UKUT 75 (AAC); [2018] AACR 30... **249**
JP v SSWP [2018] UKUT 161 (AAC)... **336**
JR v SSWP (IS); JR v Leeds CC and another (HB) [2014] UKUT 154 (AAC)... **305**
JRL v SSWP (JSA) [2011] UKUT 63 (AAC); [2011] AACR 30... **460, 465**
JS v Hull City Council [2012] UKUT 477 (AAC)... **589**
JS v SSWP (DLA) [2013] UKUT 100 (AAC); [2013] AACR 30... **1025**
JS v SSWP and Cheshire West and Chester BC (HB) [2014] UKUT 36 (AAC); [2014] AACR 26... **393**
JS v Kingston upon Hull City Council (HB) [2014] UKUT 43 (AAC)... **1024**
JS v SSWP (IS) [2019] UKUT 135 (AAC)... **316**
JS v South London and Maudsley NHS Foundation Trust and the Secretary of State for Justice [2019] UKUT 172 (AAC)... **1003**
JT v HMRC (TC) [2015] UKUT 81 (AAC)... **996**
KD v SSWP (DLA) [2013] UKUT 23 (AAC)... **947**
KH v CMEC (CSM) [2012] UKUT 329 (AAC)... **1016, 1019**
KKL v SSWP (PIP) [2018] UKUT 17 (AAC)... **148**
KM v South Somerset DC (HB) [2011] UKUT 148 (AAC)... **395**
KM v SSWP and DM (CSM) [2019] UKUT 48 (AAC)... **1015**
KO v SSWP (ESA) [2013] UKUT 544 (AAC)... **1012**
KP v Hertfordshire CC (SEN) [2010] UKUT 233 (AAC)... **1017**
KP v Royal Borough of Kensington and Chelsea [2014] UKUT 393 (AAC)... **38**
KQ v SSWP (IS) [2011] UKUT 102 (AAC); [2011] AACR 43... **689**
KR v City and County of Swansea (HB) [2015] UKUT 185 (AAC)... **590**
KS v SSWP (JSA) [2009] UKUT 122 (AAC); [2010] AACR 3... **462, 469**
KS v SSWP (PC) [2010] UKUT 156 (AAC)... **347**
KW v Lancaster CC (HB) [2011] UKUT 266 (AAC)... **416, 538**
KdeS v Camden LB (HB) [2011] UKUT 457 (AAC)... **270**
Kingston upon Hull CC v DLM (HB) [2010] UKUT 234 (AAC)... **418, 588**
Kirkham v Information Commissioner (Recusal and Costs) [2018] UKUT 65 (AAC)... **182**
Kirklees MBC v JM [2018] UKUT 219 (AAC)... **354**
LA v SSWP [2010] UKUT 109 (AAC)... **304**
LB Hillingdon v MJ [2009] UKUT 151 (AAC); [2010] AACR 4... **326**
LB v Lambeth LB & SSWP (HB) [2015] UKUT 237 (AAC)... **433**
LC v SSWP (DLA) [2015] UKUT 100 (AAC)... **1012**
LC v Bournemouth BC (HB) [2016] UKUT 175 (AAC)... **472**
LCC v SSWP [2009] UKUT 74 (AAC)... **25**
LG v SSWP (ESA) [2019] UKUT 153 (AAC)... **669**
LH v SSWP (IS) [2014] UKUT 60 (AAC)... **471**
LH v SSWP (PIP) [2018] UKUT 57 (AAC)... **1009**
LJT v SSWP (PIP) [2019] UKUT 21 (AAC)... **990, 1015, 1016**
LM v SSWP [2009] UKUT 185 (AAC)... **1024**
LM v Lewisham LB [2009] UKUT 204 (AAC); [2010] AACR 12... **178, 1002**
LM v LB Southwark (HB) [2015] UKUT 86 (AAC)... **1009**
LM v HMRC (CHB) [2016] UKUT 389 (AAC)... **311**
LO v SSWP (IS) [2017] UKUT 440 (AAC)... **341**
LP v SSWP (ESA) [2018] UKUT 389 (AAC)... **471**
LS v Lambeth LB (HB) [2010] UKUT 461 (AAC); [2011] AACR 27... **177, 178, 995**
Leicester CC v LG [2009] UKUT 155 (AAC)... **551, 553, 803, 816**
Liverpool City Council v (1) NM, (2) WD (HB) [2015] UKUT 532 (AAC); [2016] AACR 19... **357, 621, 625**
London Borough of Bexley v KM [2017] UKUT 354 (AAC)... **287**
M v SSWP [2017] UKUT 443 (AAC)... **375**
MA v SSWP [2009] UKUT 211 (AAC)... **986, 987, 990**
MAH (dual nationality – permanent residence) (Canada) [2010] UKUT 445 (IAC)... **320**

MB v Selby DC (HB) [2011] UKUT 5 (AAC)... **6, 505, 540**
MB v Wychavon DC (HB) [2013] UKUT 67 (AAC)... **1010**
MB and others v SSWP (ESA and DLA) [2013] UKUT 111 (AAC); [2014] AACR 1... **1063**
MB v Christchurch BC (HB) [2014] UKUT 201 (AAC); [2014] AACR 39... **586**
MB and Others v SSWP (JSA) [2016] UKUT 372 (AAC); [2017] AACR 6... **314**
MC v SSWP (IS) [2015] UKUT 600 (AAC)... **461**
MD v SSWP (Enforcement Reference) [2010] UKUT 202 (AAC); [2011] AACR 5... **993**
MD v SSWP (PC) [2016] UKUT 319 (AAC)... **344**
MG v Carmarthenshire CC and SSWP (HB) [2013] UKUT 363 (AAC)... **244**
MH v Wirral MBC [2009] UKUT 60 (AAC)... **290, 291**
MH v HMRC (TC) [2016] UKUT 79 (AAC)... **255**
MH v LB Waltham Forest (HB) [2016] UKUT 161 (AAC)... **419**
MH v SSWP and Rotherham MBC (HB) [2017] UKUT 401 (AAC)... **440**
MK v SSWP (ESA) [2018] UKUT 33 (AAC)... **1020**
MM v SSWP (ESA) [2011] UKUT 334 (AAC)... **1015**
MM v SSWP (IS) [2012] UKUT 358 (AAC)... **264**
MM v SSWP (IS) [2015] UKUT 128 (AAC)... **315**
MM v SSWP (ESA) [2017] UKUT 437 (AAC)... **341**
MMcF v Sefton BC (HB) [2016] UKUT 403 (AAC)... **1780**
MN v Bury Council and SSWP (HB) [2014] UKUT 187 (AAC)... **670**
MP v SSWP (DLA) [2010] UKUT 103 (AAC)... **999, 1013, 1019**
MQ v SSWP and SQ (CS) [2017] UKUT 392 (AAC)... **184, 1021**
MR v CMEC [2009] UKUT 284 (AAC), [2009] UKUT 285 (AAC), [2010] UKUT 38 (AAC)... **992**
MR v Bournmouth BC (HB) [2011] UKUT 284 (AAC)... **272**
MR v North Tyneside Council and SSWP [2015] UKUT 34 (AAC)... **373, 882**
MS v SSWP (JSA) [2011] UKUT 452 (AAC)... **325**
MS v SSWP (DLA) [2012] UKUT 463 (AAC)... **972**
MS v SSWP (IS) [2016] UKUT 348 (AAC)... **318, 319**
MT v SSWP (IS) [2010] UKUT 382 (AAC)... **992**
MW v SSWP (JSA) [2016] UKUT 469 (AAC); [2017] AACR 15... **460**
MW v Leeds CC (HB) [2018] UKUT 319 (AAC)... **151**
MW v SSWP (UC) [2019] UKUT 184 (AAC)... **300**
Martyres v Information Commissioner and Chief Constable of Cambridgeshire Police [2016] UKUT 471 (AAC)... **1036**
Middlesbrough BC v DS [2009] UKUT 80 (AAC)... **588**
N Warwickshire Travel Ltd and Michael James [2018] UKUT 11 (AAC)... **1016**
NC v Tonbridge & Malling BC [2010] UKUT 12 (AAC)... **433**
NG v SSWP (DLA) [2012] UKUT 291 (AAC)... **181**
NT v FtT (CIC) [2014] UKUT 210 (AAC)... **996**
Nuneaton and Bedworth BC v RH and SSWP [2017] UKUT 471 (AAC)... **376**
OB v SSHD [2010] UKUT 420 (IAC)... **304**
OB v SSWP (ESA) [2017] UKUT 255 (AAC)... **334**
ODS v SSWP (UC) [2019] UKUT 192 (AAC)... **305**
OFSTED v GM and WM [2009] UKUT 89 (AAC)... **145**
OFSTED v AF [2011] UKUT 72 (AAC); [2011] AACR 32... **178**
OR v SSWP and Isle of Anglesey CC [2013] UKUT 65 (AAC)... **16**
PA v CMEC [2009] UKUT 283 (AAC)... **992**
PC v SSWP (HB) [2014] UKUT 467 (AAC)... **373**
PJ v SSWP (ESA) [2011] UKUT 224 (AAC)... **1063**
PL v SSWP (JSA) [2016] UKUT 177 (AAC)... **114**
PM v SSWP [2009] UKUT 236 (AAC)... **324**
PM v SSWP (IS) [2014] UKUT 474 (AAC)... **148, 999**
PP v Basildon DC (HB) [2013] UKUT 505 (AAC)... **14**
PS v SSWP [2017] UKUT 55 (AAC)... **1020**
R (RB) v First-tier Tribunal (Review) [2010] UKUT 160 (AAC); [2010] AACR 41... **179, 1024**
R (LR by ER) v FtT (HESC) & Hertfordshire CC [2012] UKUT 213 (AAC)... **1016, 1019**

R (MP) v First-tier Tribunal and West London Mental Health NHS Trust [2012] UKUT 231 (AAC)... **179**

R (SB and others) v First-tier Tribunal and CICA [2014] UKUT 497 (AAC)... **991**

R(AM) v First-tier Tribunal (CIC) [2013] UKUT 333 (AAC)... **996**

RB v SSWP (ESA) [2016] UKUT 384 (AAC)... **471**

RC (Dec'd) v Maldon DC (HB) [2012] UKUT 333 (AAC)... **181**

RF v CMEC (CSM) [2010] UKUT 41 (AAC)... **987**

RF v LB Lambeth (HB) [2019] UKUT 52 (AAC)... **307**

RG v SSWP and North Wiltshire DC (HB) [2011] UKUT 198 (AAC)... **395**

RJ v SSWP (JSA) [2011] UKUT 447 (AAC); [2012] AACR 28... **313**

RK v SSWP [2008] UKUT 34 (AAC)... **250**

RM v SSWP [2009] UKUT 256 (AAC)... **1013**

RM v SSWP (IS) [2010] UKUT 238 (AAC)... **343**

RM v SSWP (IS) [2014] UKUT 401 (AAC); [2015] AACR 11... **343**

RM v Sefton Council (HB) [2016] UKUT 357 (AAC); [2017] AACR 5... **687**

RP v SSWP (ESA) [2016] UKUT 422 (AAC)... **325**

RR v SSWP (ESA) [2017] UKUT 403 (AAC)... **1021**

RS v Fife Council and SSP (HB) [2018] UKUT 322 (AAC)... **291**

RU v SSWP (ESA) [2014] UKUT 532 (AAC)... **1018**

Reigate and Banstead BC v SA (HB) [2014] UKUT 369 (AAC)... **433, 538**

Reigate and Banstead BC v GB [2018] UKUT 225 (AAC)... **477**

SA v Newham LB (HB) [2010] UKUT 191 (AAC)... **274**

SA v SSWP (PIP) [2017] UKUT 224 (AAC)... **1020**

SB v SSWP (ESA) [2012] UKUT 249 (AAC)... **1012**

SB v Oxford City Council (HB) [2014] UKUT 166 (AAC)... **497**

SC v SSWP (ESA) [2012] UKUT 98 (AAC) 11... **1019**

SD v Brent LB [2009] UKUT 7 (AAC)... **290**

SD v Newcastle City Council (HB) [2010] UKUT 306 (AAC)... **420**

SD v Eastleigh BC (HB) [2014] UKUT 325 (AAC)... **244**

SD v SSWP (ESA) [2015] UKUT 116 (AAC)... **184**

SD v SSWP (ESA) [2017] UKUT 278 (AAC)... **1018**

SE v SSWP [2009] UKUT 163 (AAC)... **1024, 1025**

SG v Tameside MBC (HB) [2010] UKUT 243 (AAC)... **331**

SH v SSWP (JSA) [2008] UKUT 21 (AAC)... **462**

SH v SSWP [2011] UKUT 428 (AAC)... **114**

SH v Tower Hamlets LB (HB) [2011] UKUT 500 (AAC)... **470**

SJ v SSWP (SPC) [2015] UKUT 505 (AAC); [2016] AACR 17... **1708**

SK v South Hams DC (HB) [2010] UKUT 129 (AAC); [2010] AACR 40... **263, 372, 382, 404, 627, 881**

SL v SSWP and KL-D [2014] UKUT 128 (AAC)... **995, 997**

SL v Renfrewshire Council (HB) [2014] UKUT 411 (AAC)... **533, 540**

SMcH v Perth and Kinross Council (HB) [2015] UKUT 126 (AAC)... **247**

SN v Hounslow LB [2010] UKUT 57 (AAC); [2010] AACR 27... **584, 585**

SOA v Ealing LB (HB) [2012] UKUT 437 (AAC)... **1021**

Southwark LB v JQ (HB) 2012 UKUT 232 AAC... **178**

SS v SSWP (ESA) [2011] UKUT 8 (AAC)... **335**

SS v Slough BC [2011] UKUT 128 (AAC)... **306**

SS v North East Lincolnshire Council (HB) [2011] UKUT 300 (AAC)... **139, 140, 968**

SS v Birmingham City and SSWP (HB) [2013] UKUT 418 (AAC)... **1787**

SSHD v FMB [2010] UKUT 447 (IAC)... **311**

SSHD v Lim [2013] UKUT 437 (IAC)... **319**

SSWP v AA [2009] UKUT 249 (AAC)... **305**

SSWP v AC [2017] UKUT 130 (AAC)... **341**

SSWP v AH (IS) [2010] UKUT 265 (AAC)... **339**

SSWP v AL (JSA) [2011] UKUT 451 (AAC)... **308, 310**

SSWP v AM and Northumberland CC (HB) [2015] UKUT 360 (AAC)... **373**

SSWP v CA [2009] UKUT 169 (AAC)... **339**

SSWP v Carmichael and Sefton BC (HB) [2017] UKUT 174 (AAC)... **114, 379**
SSWP v CO'N (ESA) [2018] UKUT 80 (AAC)... **1017**
SSWP v Czop (IS) [2013] UKUT 351 (AAC); [2013] AACR 6... **343**
SSWP v DL and RR (HB) [2018] UKUT 355 (AAC)... **188**
SSWP v EM [2009] UKUT 146 (AAC)... **311**
SSWP v FE [2009] UKUT 287 (AAC)... **312**
SSWP v GF (ESA) [2017] UKUT 333 (AAC)... **461**
SSWP v HH (SPC) [2015] UKUT 583 (AAC)... **331**
SSWP v IA [2009] UKUT 35 (AAC)... **317**
SSWP v IB (CSH) [2015] UKUT 282 (AAC)... **374**
SSWP v IG [2008] UKUT 5 (AAC)... **1708**
SSWP v IR [2009] UKUT 11 (AAC)... **316, 317**
SSWP v JP (JSA) [2010] UKUT 90 (AAC)... **418**
SSWP v JS (IS) [2010] UKUT 347 (AAC)... **342**
SSWP v JL (DLA) [2011] UKUT 293 (AAC)... **140**
SSWP v JS (IS) [2010] UKUT 240 (AAC)... **309, 313**
SSWP v LB Tower Hamlets and CT (IS and HB) [2018] UKUT 25 (AAC)... **461**
SSWP v LC (IS) [2011] UKUT 108 (AAC)... **343**
SSWP v LL (SPC) [2014] UKUT 136 (AAC)... **319**
SSWP v LS (IS) [2012] UKUT 207 (AAC)... **333**
SSWP v LZ (PC) [2014] UKUT 147 (AAC)... **335**
SSWP v MB and Others (JSA) [2016] UKUT 372 (AAC)... **319**
SSWP v MF (SPC) [2018] UKUT 179 (AAC)... **319**
SSWP v MK (IS) [2013] UKUT 163 (AAC)... **312, 317**
SSWP v MM and Northumberland CC [2015] UKUT 624 (AAC)... **373**
SSWP v MP (IS) [2011] UKUT 109 (AAC)... **343**
SSWP v Nelson and Nelson [2014] UKUT 525 (AAC); [2015] AACR 21... **373, 376**
SSWP v NZ (ESA) (third interim decision) [2017] UKUT 360 (AAC)... **325**
SSWP v NZ (ESA) (final decision) [2019] UKUT 250 (AAC)... **320**
SSWP v PE and Bolton MBC [2017] UKUT 393 (AAC)... **245, 377, 394**
SSWP v RK [2009] UKUT 209 (AAC)... **313**
SSWP v RR [2013] UKUT 21 (AAC)... **308**
SSWP v RR (HB) [2018] UKUT 180 (AAC)... **374**
SSWP v SFF and Others [2015] UKUT 502 (AAC); [2016] AACR 16... **315**
SSWP v Sister IS & Sister KM [2009] UKUT 200 (AAC)... **293**
SSWP v SS (DLA) [2010] UKUT 384 (AAC); [2011] AACR 24... **1017, 1063**
SSWP v SW (IS) [2011] UKUT 508 (AAC)... **331**
SSWP v ZA [2009] UKUT 294 (AAC)... **325**
SSWP v ZW [2009] UKUT 25 (AAC)... **312**
SSWP and Warwick DC v OB and JS and JS (CTB) [2012] UKUT 489 (AAC)... **272**
ST v SSWP [2009] UKUT 269 (AAC); [2010] AACR 23... **249**
ST v SSWP (ESA) [2012] UKUT 469 (AAC)... **1009**
ST v Sunderland City Council (CH) [2019] UKUT 33 (AAC)... **575**
SW v SSWP (IB) [2010] UKUT 73 (AAC)... **182**
Salford CC v PF [2009] UKUT 150 (AAC)... **246, 294, 1781**
Salisbury Independent Living v Wirral MBC (HB) [2011] UKUT 44 (AAC)... **998**
Sandwell MBC v NK (HB) [2016] UKUT 140 (AAC)... **585**
Secretary of State for Education v JN [2010] UKUT 248 (AAC)... **145**
Shabani v SSHD [2013] UKUT 315 (IAC)... **342**
Simpsons Malt & Ors v Jones & Ors (Valuation Officers) [2017] UKUT 460 (LC)... **1672**
Slough BC v PK [2019] UKUT 128 (AAC)... **270**
South Lanarkshire Council v DG [2018] UKUT 417 (AAC)... **288**
Stevenage BC v ML (HB) [2016] UKUT 164 (AAC)... **375**
Stroud DC v JG [2009] UKUT 67 (AAC); R(H) 8/09... **263, 269, 401, 627, 882**
Sunderland City Council v GH (HB) [2014] UKUT 3 (AAC)... **267**
T v SSWP (ESA) [2019] UKUT 59 (AAC)... **988**
TA v Islington LB (HB) [2014] UKUT 71 (AAC)... **589**

TA v SSWP (PIP) [2018] UKUT 26 (AAC)… **1012**
TD v SSWP and LB Richmond-upon-Thames (HB) [2013] UKUT 642 (AAC)… **408**
TG v SSWP [2009] UKUT 58 (AAC)… **309**
TG v SSWP (PC) [2015] UKUT 50 (AAC)… **320, 325**
TJ v SSWP (ESA) [2014] UKUT 445 (AAC)… **1016**
TM v HMRC (TC) [2013] UKUT 444 (AAC)… **1011**
TMcG v SSWP (ESA) [2013] UKUT 411 (AAC)… **1011**
Torbay BC v RF (HB) [2010] UKUT 7 (AAC); [2010] AACR 26… **272**
Torbay BC v BW (HB) [2011] UKUT 305 (AAC)… **979**
UH v Islington LB [2010] UKUT 64 (AAC)… **553**
VH v Suffolk CC [2010] UKUT 203 (AAC)… **1023**
VP v SSWP (JSA) [2014] UKUT 32 (AAC); [2014] AACR 25… **331**
VW v London Borough of Hackney (HB) [2014] UKUT 277 (AAC)… **946, 968, 969**
VW v SSWP (IS) [2015] UKUT 51 (AAC)… **470**
Walsall MBC v PL (HB) [2009] UKUT 27 (AAC)… **999**
Walsall BC v GP Ltd and others [2009] UKUT 247 (AAC); [2010] AACR 16… **39**
Walsall MBC v UM (HB) [2015] UKUT 99 (AAC)… **408**
Weldemichael and Another [2015] UKUT 540 (IAC)… **316**
West Somerset DC v JMA (HB) [2010] UKUT 190 (AAC)… **561, 586**
Westminster City Council v AT & SSWP (HB) [2013] UKUT 321 (AAC)… **25, 251**
Wirral MBC v AH and SSWP (HB) [2010] UKUT 208 (AAC); [2011] AACR 6… **395, 410**
Wirral MBC v AL (HB) [2010] UKUT 254 (AAC)… **579, 581**
Wirral MBC v Furlong, Perry and Salisbury Independent Living and SSWP (HB) [2013] UKUT 291 (AAC); [2014] AACR 12… **246, 1779**
Worcestershire CC v JJ (SEN) [2014] UKUT 406 (AAC)… **1019**
Wychavon DC v EM (HB) [2011] UKUT 144 (AAC)… **279**
Wychavon DC v EM (HB) [2012] UKUT 12 (AAC); [2012] AACR 41… **279**
ZB v SSWP (CSM) [2013] UKUT 367 (AAC)… **997, 1018**
ZN, BB, JHS V Redbridge LB (HB) [2013] UKUT 503 (AAC)… **1045**

Housing Benefit Regulations: destinations table

General

HB Regs 1987	HB Regs 2006		HB (SPC) Regs 2006	
Reg 1	1	p224	1	p718
Reg 2	2	p224	2	p718
Reg 2B	4	p251	4	p732
Reg 3	3	p248	3	p732
	New Reg 5	p252	New Reg 5	p733
Reg 4	6	p253	6	p733

Provisions affecting entitlement to housing benefit

HB Regs 1987	HB Regs 2006		HB (SPC) Regs 2006	
Reg 5	7	p256	7	p734
Reg 6	8	p273	8	p740
Reg 7	9	p280	9	p741
Reg 7A	10	p297	10	p742
Reg 7B	Sch 4 SI 2006 No 217	p1805	Sch 4 SI 2006 No 217	p1805
	New reg 10A	p347	New reg 10A	p744

Payments in respect of a dwelling

HB Regs 1987	HB Regs 2006		HB (SPC) Regs 2006	
Reg 8	11	p349	11	p744
Reg 10	12	p351	12	p745
	New reg 12B	p356	New reg 12B	p746
	New reg 12BA	p358		
	New reg 12C	p361	New reg 12C	p747
	New reg 12D	p362	New reg 12D	p748
	New regs	p707	New regs	p873
	12F–12K	p367	12F–12K	
	New reg A13			
	New reg B13	p369		
Reg 11	13	p380	13	p750
Old reg 12	Sch 3 paras 4 and	p1805	Sch 3 paras 4 and	p1774
	5 SI 2006 No 217		5 SI 2006 No 217	
	New reg 13ZA	p383	New reg 13ZA	p751
	New reg 13ZB	p385	New reg 13ZB	p752
	New reg 13C	p385	New reg 13C	p753
	New reg 13D	p388	New reg 13D	p754
	New reg 13E	p397	New reg 13E	p757
Reg 12A	14	p398	14	p757
Reg 12B	15	p402	15	p759
Reg 12C	17	p404	17	p760
Reg 12CA	16	p402	16	p760
Reg 12D	18	p404	18	p761
	New reg 18A	p405	New reg 18A	p761

Membership of a family

HB Regs 1987	HB Regs 2006		HB (SPC) Regs 2006	
Reg 13	19	p406	19	p762
Reg 14	20	p407	20	p762
Reg 15	21	p409	21	p762

Applicable amounts

HB Regs 1987	HB Regs 2006		HB&CTB (SPC) Regs 2003 substituted reg	HB (SPC) Regs 2006	
Reg 16	22	p411	Reg 16	22	p764
Reg 17	23	p413			
Reg 18	24 Now revoked	p415			

Income and capital

HB Regs 1987	HB Regs 2006		HB&CTB (SPC) Regs 2003 substituted reg	HB (SPC) Regs 2006	
Reg 19	25	p421	Reg 19	23	p765
Reg 20	26	p421		24	p765
Reg 21	27	p423	Reg 21	25	p766
Reg 21A	28	p424	Reg 22	26	p766
Reg 22	29	p431	Reg 23	27	p766
Reg 23	30	p434	Reg 24	28	p768
Reg 24	31	p434	Reg 25	29	p768
Reg 24A	32	p435	Reg 26	30	p772
Reg 25	33	p436	Reg 27	31	p773
Reg 28	35	p438	Reg 28	33	p777
Reg 29	36	p442	Reg 29	34	p780
	New reg 29A	p433			
Reg 30	37	p444	Reg 30	35	p780
Reg 31	38	p445	Reg 31	36	p781
Reg 32	39	p449	Reg 32	37	p782
Reg 33	40	p450	Reg 33	38	p783
Reg 34	41	p453	Reg 34	39	p784
Reg 35	42	p453	Reg 35	40	p786
Reg 37	43	p462	Reg 36	41	p787
Reg 38	44	p462	Reg 37	42	p789
Reg 39	45	p463	Reg 38	43	p790
Reg 40	46	p463	Reg 39	44	p790
Reg 41	47	p464	Reg 40	45	p790
Reg 42	48	p465	Reg 41	46	p791
Reg 43	49	p466	Reg 42	47	p791
Reg 43A	50	p472	Reg 43	48	p791
Reg 44	51	p476	Reg 44	49	p794
Reg 45	52	p478			

Students

HB Regs 1987	HB Regs 2006	
Reg 46	53	p480
Reg 47	54	p486
Reg 48	55	p487
Reg 48A	56	p487
Reg 50	57	p493
Reg 52	58	p495
Reg 53	59	p495
Reg 54	60	p498
Reg 55	61	p498
Reg 56	62	p499
Reg 57	63	p499
Reg 57A	64	p500
	New reg 64A	p502
	New reg 64B	p503
Reg 57B	65	p503
Reg 58	66	p503
Reg 58A	67	p504
Reg 59	68	p504
Reg 60	69	p504

Amount of benefit

HB Regs 1987	HB Regs 2006		HB&CTB (SPC) Regs 2003 inserted reg	HB (SPC) Regs 2006	
Reg 61	70	p505		50	p795
Reg 62	71	p506		51	p795
				New reg 52	p795
Reg 62A	72	p506			
	New reg 72A	p508			
	New reg 72B	p509			
	New reg 72C	p510			
	New reg 72D	p512			
	New reg 72E	p512			
Reg 62ZB	73	p512		53	p796
	New reg 73A	p513		New reg 53A	p796
	New reg 73B	p514		New reg 53B	p797
	New reg 73C	p515		New reg 53C	p798
	New reg 73D	p515		New reg 53D	p798
	New reg 73E	p516			
			Reg 62B	54	p799
Reg 63	74	p516		55	p800
Reg 64	75	p521		56	p802

Benefit cap

HB Regs 1987	HB Regs 2006	
	New reg 75A	p523
	New reg 75B	p524
	New reg 75C	p524
	New reg 75CA	p526
	New reg 75D	p527
	New reg 75E	p527
	New reg 75F	p528
	New reg 75G	p530
	New reg 75H	p531

Calculation of weekly amounts
and changes of circumstances

HB Regs 1987	HB Regs 2006		HB (SPC) Regs 2006	
Reg 65	76	p532	57	p803
Reg 65A	77	p534		
Reg 65B	78	p535	58	p803
Reg 66				
Reg 67				
Reg 68	79	p535	59	p804
Reg 68A				
Reg 68B			60	p806
Reg 69	80	p538	61	p809
Reg 70	81	p541	62	p810

Claims

HB Regs 1987	HB Regs 2006		HB (SPC) Regs 2006	
Reg 71	82	p542	63	p811
Reg 72	83	p544	64	p811
	New reg 83A	p554	New reg 64A	p816
Reg 72A	84	p554	65	p816
Reg 72B	85	p554	66	p817
Reg 72BA	No provision		64(1)	p811
Reg 73	86	p555	67	p817
Reg 74	87	p558	68	p818
Reg 75	88	p559	69	p819
	New reg 88ZA	p561	New reg 69ZA	p820
	New reg 88A	p562	New reg 69A	p821

Decisions on questions

HB Regs 1987	HB Regs 2006		HB (SPC) Regs 2006	
Reg 76	89	p563	70	p821
Reg 77	90	p564	71	p821

Payments

HB Regs 1987	HB Regs 2006		HB (SPC) Regs 2006	
Reg 88	91	p567	72	p822
	New reg 91A	p568	New reg 72A	p822
Reg 90	92	p569	73	p823
Reg 91	93	p571	74	p823
Reg 92	94	p572	75	p824
Reg 93	95	p573	76	p824
Reg 94	96	p577	77	p825
Reg 96	97	p580	78	p826
Reg 97	98	p581	79	p827

Overpayments

HB Regs 1987	HB Regs 2006		HB (SPC) Regs 2006	
Reg 98	99	p582	80	p827
Reg 99	100	p583	81	p827
Reg 100	101	p591	82	p828
Reg 101	102	p596	83	p829
Reg 102	103	p601	84	p830
Reg 103	104	p602	85	p830
	New reg 104A	p604	New reg 85A	p831
Reg 104	105	p605	86	p831
	New reg 106A	p607	New reg 87A	p831
1997/2435 106	106	p606	87	p832
1997/2435 107	107	p607	88	p833

Information

Source	IIB Regs 2006		HB (SPC) Regs 2006	
SI 2002 No 1132, reg 2	108	p608	89	p833
SI 2002 No 1132, reg 3	109	p608	90	p834
	New reg 109A	p609	New reg 90A	p834
SI 2002 No 1132, reg 4	110	p609	91	p834
SI 2002 No 1132, reg 5	111	p609	92	p834
SI 2002 No 1132, reg 6	112	p609	93	p835
SI 1997 No 2436, reg 1	113	p610	94	p835
HB Regs 1987, Reg 106	New reg 114A	p610	95A	p835
	114	p613	95	p838
SI 1988 No 662, reg 5	115	p613	96	p838
SI 1988 No 662, reg 6	116	p614	97	p839
SI 1997 No 2436, reg 2	117	p615	98	p840
SI 1997 No 2436, reg 3	118	p615	99	p840
SI 1997 No 2436, reg 4	119	p615	100	p840
SI 1997 No 2436, reg 5	120	p618	101	p842
SI 1997 No 2436, reg 6	121	p618	102	p842
	121A	p618	102A	p842
	New reg 122	p619	New reg 103	p842

Schedules

HB Regs 1987	HB Regs 2006		HB&CTB (SPC) Regs 2003	HB (SPC) Regs 2006	
Sch A1	Sch 4 SI 2006 No 217	p1805		Sch 4 SI 2006 No 217	p1805
Sch 1	Sch 1	p620		Sch 1	p843
Sch 1A	Sch 2	p625		Sch 2	p846
Sch 2	Sch 3	p630			
			Sch 2A	Sch 3	p848
Sch 3	Sch 4	p655			
			Sch 3A	Sch 4	p854
Sch 4	Sch 5	p664			
			Sch 4A	Sch 5	p857
Sch 5	Sch 6	p683			
			Sch 5ZA	Sch 6	p862
Sch 5A	Sch7	p701			
Sch 5B	Sch 8	p701		Sch 7	p870
Sch 6	Sch 9	p701		Sch 8	p870
	New Sch 10	p707		New Sch 9	p873
	New Sch 11	p712		New Sch 10	p877

Scotland: council tax reduction schemes comparative provisions

Scotland: working age	Scotland: pension credit age	HB Regulation	HB(SPC) Regulation
General			
2	2	2 (p239)	2 (p731)
3 (p1466)	3		
4	4	19 (p406)	
5 (p1471)	5	7 (p263)	7 (p740)
6	6	6 (p253)	
Families			
10	10	20 (p408)	
11 (p1473)	11	21 (p409)	
Application of the regulations			
12 (p1474)	12		
Entitlement to council tax reduction			
14 (p1475)	14		
15 (p1480)	15	7 (p263)	
16	16	10 (p297)	10 (p744)
19 (p1483)	19		
20 (p1485)		56 (p487)	
Applicable amount			
21		22 (p412)	
22		23 (p414)	
	20		22 (p765)
Income and capital			
24		25 (p421)	
25		26 (p422)	
27		27 (p424)	
28		28 (p429)	
29		29 (p432)	
30		30 (p434)	
31		31 (p434)	
32		32 (p435)	
33		33 (p437)	
34		35 (p439)	
35		36 (p443)	
36		37 (p445)	
37		38 (p447)	
38		39 (p450)	
39		40 (p452)	
40		41 (p453)	
41		42 (p457)	
42		43 (p462)	
43		44 (p463)	
44		45 (p463)	

Scotland: working age	Scotland: pension credit age	HB Regulation	HB(SPC) Regulation
45		46 (p464)	
46		47 (p465)	
47		48 (p466)	
48		49 (p468)	
49		50 (p475)	
50		51 (p476)	
51		52(1) and (6) (p479)	
	21	25 (p421)	
	22	26 (p422)	
	25		27 (p767)
	27		29 (p771)
	28	27 (p424)	
	29	28 (p429)	
	30	32 (p435)	
	31		33 (p779)
	32	35 (p439)	
	33	36 (p443)	
	34		37 (p783)
	35	37 (p445)	38 (p784)
	36	38 (p447)	
	37	39 (p450)	
	38		41 (p789)
	39		42 (p790)
	40	43 (p462)	43 (p790)
	41		44 (p790)
	42	47 (p465)	
	43	48 (p466)	
	44		47 (p791)
	45		48 (p794)
	46	51 (p476)	

Students

Scotland: working age	Scotland: pension credit age	HB Regulation	HB(SPC) Regulation
52 (p1516)		53 (p484)	
53		54 (p486)	
54		59 (p497)	
55		60 (p498)	
56		61 (p499)	
57		62 (p499)	
58		63 (p499)	
59		64 (p501)	
60		64A (p503)	
61		65 (p503)	
62		66 (p503)	
63		67 (p504)	
64		68 (p504)	
65		69 (p504)	

Amount of reduction

Scotland: working age	Scotland: pension credit age	HB Regulation	HB(SPC) Regulation
66 (p1522)	47		
67 (p1524)	48	74 (p516)	
68-72 (p1525)		72–72D (pp507-512)	
73	49	73 (p513)	
	55		54 (p799)
78 (p1529)	56		
79 (p1530)	57		

Scotland: working age	Scotland: pension credit age	HB Regulation	HB(SPC) Regulation
Effective date			
80		76 (p533)	
81		79 (p537)	
	58		57 (p803)
	59		59 (p806)
	60		60 (p808)
Applications			
82	61	82(1) (p543)	
	62		64 (1) and (1A) (p815)
83	63	83 (p549)	
84	64	83 (p549)	
85	65	83 (p549)	
86	66	86 (p555)	
87	67	87(1)–(3) (p559)	
88	68	87(4)–(6) (p559)	
Notifications of changes of circumstances			
89		88 (p560)	
	69		69 (p820)
90	70	88ZA (p562)	
Schedules			
Sch 1 Applicable amount (p1541)		Sch 3 (pp631–653)	
	Sch 1 applicable amount		Sch 3 (p848)
Sch 2 Amount of alternative maximum council tax reduction (p1551)	Sch 5		
Sch 3 Sums to be disregarded in the calculation of earnings	Sch 2	Sch 4 (pp655–663)	
Sch 4 Sums to be disregarded in the calculation of income other than earnings (p1556 and p1556)	Sch 3	Sch 5 (pp665–674)	
Sch 5 Capital to be disregarded (p1564)	Sch 4 [Commentary on para 30 only]	Sch 6 (pp684–699)	
Sch 6 Savings provisions (p1573)			

England: council tax reduction schemes comparative provisions

England: prescribed requirements	Scotland: workingage regulation	HB Regulation	HB(SPC) Regulations
General			
2		2 (p239)	2 (p731)
4			
6		19 (p406)	
7		20 (p408)	
8	11 (p1473)	21 (p410)	
9	3 (p1466)	3 (p249)	
10		6 (p253)	
Prescribed classes of persons			
11			43 (p790)
12		10 (p299)	10 (p744)
Schedules			
Sch 1: Pensioners: matters that must be included in an authority's scheme			
Sch 1 para 4	14 (p1475) and 79 (p1530)		
Sch 1 para 5	15 (p1480)	7(13), (16) and (17) (p263)	7 (p740)
Sch 1 para 6			22 (p765)
Sch 1 para 7	66 (p1522)		
Sch 1 para 8	67 (p1524)		
Sch 1 para 9	78 (p1529)		
Sch 1 para 11		25 (p421)	
Sch 1 para 12		26 (p422)	24 (p765)
Sch 1 para 14			27 (p767)
Sch 1 para 16			29 (p771)
Sch 1 para 17			33 (p779)
Sch 1 para 18		35 (p439)	
Sch 1 para 19		36 (p443)	
Sch 1 para 20			37 (p783)
Sch 1 para 21		37(1) (p445) and Sch 5 paras 26 and 27 (p673)	
Sch 1 para 22			41 (p789)
Sch 1 para 23			42 (p790)
Sch 1 para 24		27 (p424)	30 (p772)
Sch 1 paras 25		28 (p429)	
Sch 1 para 26		Sch 3 para 13 (p638)	
Sch 1 para 27		32 (p435)	
Sch 1 para 28		34 (p437)	
Sch 1 para 29		38 (p447)	
Sch 1 para 30		39 (p450)	
Sch 1 para 31			44 (p790)
		46 (p464)	
Sch 1 para 32		47 (p465)	

England: prescribed requirements	Scotland: working age regulation	HB Regulation	HB(SPC) Regulations
Sch 1 para 33		48 (p466)	
Sch 1 para 34		49(1), (5) and (7) (p468)	47 (p791)
Sch 1 para 35		50 (p475)	48 (p794)
		50 (p475)	
Sch 1 para 36		51 (p476)	
Sch 1 para 37			29(2) (p771)
Sch 1 para 38		73 (p513)	53 (p796)
Sch 1 para 39		73A (p513)	53A (p796)
Sch 1 para 43			54 (p799)
	71 (p1526)	72–72D (pp507–512)	
		73 (p513)	
Sch 1 para 45		76(1) and (2) (p533)	
Sch 1 para 47			60 (p808)
Sch 2: Applicable amounts	Sch 1 (p1541)	Sch 3 (pp631–653)	Sch 3 (p848)
Sch 3: Amount of alternative maximum CTR	Sch 2 (p1552)		
Sch 4: Sums disregarded from applicant's earnings			Sch 4 (p854)
Sch 5: Amounts to be disregarded in the calculation of income other than earnings			Sch 5 (p857)
Sch 6: Capital disregards			Sch 6 (p862)
Sch 8: All applicants: matters that must be included in an authority's scheme – other matters			
Sch 8 para 4		82 (p543)	
Sch 8 para 5		83 (p549)	64 (p815)
Sch 8 para 6			64 (p815)
Sch 8 para 7		86 (p556)	
Sch 8 para 8		87 (p559)	
Sch 8 para 9		88 (p560)	69 (p820)
Sch 8 para 11		89(2) (p563)	
Sch 8 para 12		90 (p564)	

Wales: council tax reduction schemes comparative provisions

Wales: Default Scheme	Wales: Prescribed Requirements	Scotland: Working Age Regulation	HB Regulation	HB(SPC) Regulation
Interpretation				
2	2		2 (p239)	2 (p731)
4	4		2 (p239)	
6			2 (p239)	
7	7		20 (p408)	
8	8	11 (p1473)	21 (p410)	
9	9	3 (p1466)	3 (p249)	
10	10		6 (p253)	
Classes entitled, etc	**Classes entitled etc**			
17	26	15 (p1480)	7(13), (16) and (17) (p263)	7 (p740)
Classes excluded etc	**Classes excluded etc**			
19	28		10 (p299)	10 (p744)
21	30			43 (p790)
Applicable amount				
23	Sch 1 para 1			22 (p765)
24	Sch 6 para 1		22 (p412)	
25	Sch 6 para 2		23 (p414)	
Maximum CTR				
27	Sch 1 para 2/Sch 6 para 4	66 (p1522)		
28	Sch 1 para 3/Sch 6 para 5	67 (p1524)		
Income and capital				
			25 (p421)	
31	Sch 1 para 6/Sch 6 para 8		26 (p422)	24 (p765)
33	Sch 1 para 8			27 (p767)
36	Sch 1 para 10			29 (p771)
37	Sch 1 para 11			33 (p779)
38	Sch 1 para 12		35 (p439)	
39	Sch 1 para 13		36 (p443)	
40	Sch 1 para 14			37 (p783)
41	Sch 1 para 15		37(1) (p445) and Sch 5 paras 26 and 27 (p673)	38 (p784)
42	Sch 1 para 16			41 (p789)
43	Sch 1 para 17			42 (p790)
44	Sch 6 para 10		29 (p432)	
45	Sch 6 para 11		30 (p434)	
46	Sch 6 para 12		31 (p434)	
47	Sch 6 para 13		33 (p437)	
48	Sch 6 para 14		35 (p439)	
49	Sch 6 para 15		36 (p443)	

Wales: Default Scheme	Wales: Prescribed Requirements	Scotland: Working Age Regulation	HB Regulation	HB(SPC) Regulation
50	Sch 6 para 16		37 (p445)	
51	Sch 6 para 17		40 (p452)	
52	Sch 6 para 18		41 (p453)	
53	Sch 6 para 19		42 (p457)	
54	Sch 1 para 18/Sch 6 para 20		27 (p424)	30 (p772)
55	Sch 1 para 19/Sch 6 para 21		28 (p429)	
56	Sch 1 para 21/Sch 6 para 22		32 (p435)	
57	Sch 1 para 22/Sch 6 para 23		34 (p437)	
58	Sch 1 para 23/Sch 6 para 24		38 (p447)	
59	Sch 1 para 24/Sch 6 para 25		39 (p450)	
60	Sch 1 para 25/Sch 6 para 26		44 (p463)	44 (p790)
61	Sch 6 para 27		46 (p464)	
62	Sch 1 para 26/Sch 6 para 28		47 (p465)	45 (p791)
63	Sch 1 para 27/Sch 6 para 29		48 (p466)	46 (p791)
64	Sch 1 para 28/Sch 6 para 30		49 (p468)	47 (p791)
65	Sch 1 para 29		50 (p475)	48 (p794)
66	Sch 6 para 31		50 (p475)	
67	Sch 1 para 30/Sch 6 para 32		51 (p476)	49 (p794)
68	Sch 1 para 31			29(2) (p771)
69	Sch 6 para 33		52(1) (p479)	
Students				
72	Sch 11 para 3			
73	Sch 11 para 4		59 (p497)	
74	Sch 11 para 5		60 (p498)	
75	Sch 11 para 6		61 (p499)	
76	Sch 11 para 7		62 (p499)	
77	Sch 11 para 8		63 (p499)	
78	Sch 11 para 9		64 (p501)	
79	Sch 11 para 10		64A (p503)	
80	Sch 11 para 11		65 (p503)	
81	Sch 11 para 12		66 (p503)	
82	Sch 11 para 13		67 (p504)	
83	Sch 11 para 14		68 (p504)	
84	Sch 11 para 15		69 (p504)	

Wales: Default Scheme	Wales: Prescribed Requirements	*Scotland:* *Working Age* *Regulation*	HB Regulation	*HB(SPC)* *Regulation*
Extended reductions				
91	Sch 1 para 37			54 (p799)
93	Sch 6 para 34		72 (p507)	
94	Sch 6 para 35		72A (p508)	
95	Sch 6 para 36		72B (p510)	
96	Sch 6 para 37		72C (p511)	
97	Sch 6 para 38		72D (p512)	
98	Sch 6 paras 39		73 (p513)	
Period of entitlement and change of circumstances				
106	Sch 1 para 41			60 (p808)
Applications				
107	Sch 13 para 1		82 (p543)	
109	Sch 13 para 3			64(1) and (1A) (p815)
111	Sch 13 para 5		86(1) and (2) to (5) (p556)	
112	Sch 13 para 6		87 (p559)	
&113	Sch 13 para 7		88 (p560)	69 (p820)
Decisions by authority				
114	Sch 13 para 8		89(2) (p563)	
115	Sch 13 para 9		90 (p564)	
Schedules				
Sch 2: Applicable amount: pensioners	Sch 2			Sch 3 (p848)
Sch 3: Applicable amount: other	Sch 7	Sch 1 Applicable amount (p1541)	Sch 3 (p631)	
Sch 4: Earnings disregards: pensioners	Sch 3			Sch 4 (p854)
Sch 5: Income disregards: pensioners	Sch 4		Sch 5 (p664)	
Sch 6: Earnings disregards: other	Sch 8		Sch 4 (p655)	
Sch 7: Income disregards: other	Sch 9	Sch 4 (p1556)	Sch 5 (p664)	
Sch 8: Capital disregards: pensioners	Sch 5			Sch 6 (p862)
Sch 9: Capital disregards: other	Sch 10	Sch 5 (p1564)	Sch 6 (p683)	
Sch 10: Notification	Sch 14		Sch 9 (p701)	

Table of abbreviations

Abbreviation	Meaning
AC	Appeal Cases Law Reports
AFIP	Armed forces independence payment
All ER	All England Reports
Art, Arts	Article, Articles
BC	Borough Council
BHRC	Butterworth's Human Rights Cases
CA	Carer's allowance
CA	Court of Appeal
CCLR	Community Care Law Reports
Ch	Chancery Division Law Reports
Ch D	Chancery Division
CIS, CH etc	Unreported Commissioner's decision
CMLR	Common Market Law Reports
CPA	Civil Partnership Act 2004
COD	Crown Office Digest
CSIH	Inner House of the Court of Session
CSOH	Outer House of the Court of Session
CSPSSA	Child Support, Pensions and Social Security Act 2000
CTB	Council tax benefit
CTC	Child tax credit
CTR	Council tax reduction
CTR(S) Regs	The Council Tax Reduction (Scotland) Regulations 2012 SI No.303
CTR(SPC)(S) Regs	The Council Tax Reduction (State Pensions Credit) (Scotland) Regulations 2012 SI No.319
CTRS(PR)(E) Regs	The Council Tax Reduction Schemes (Prescribed Requirements) (England) Regulations 2012 SI No.2885
CTRSPR(W) Regs 2012	The Council Tax Reduction Schemes and Prescribed Requirements (Wales) Regulations 2012 SI No.3144
CTRSPR(W) Regs	The Council Tax Reduction Schemes and Prescribed Requirements (Wales) Regulations 2013 SI No.3029
D&A Regs	Housing Benefit and Council Tax Benefit (Decisions and Appeals) Regulations 2001
DC	District Council
DFA Regs	The Discretionary Financial Assistance Regulations 2001 SI No.1167
DHP	Discretionary housing payment
DSS	Department of Social Security (predecessor to the DWP)
DWP	Department for Work and Pensions
EEA	European Economic Area
ECJ	European Court of Justice
ECR	European Court Reports
ECtHR	European Court of Human Rights
ECmHR	European Commission of Human Rights
EHRR	European Human Rights Reports

Abbreviation	Meaning
ESA	Employment and support allowance
EU	European Union
EWCA Civ	Court of Appeal Civil Division transcript
EWHC [number] (Admin), EWHC Admin	Administrative Court transcript
Ex p	Ex parte
FLR	Family Law Reports
First-tier Tribunal	First-tier Tribunal (Social Security and Child Support)
GM	*Housing Benefit and Council Tax Benefit Guidance Manual*
HB	Housing benefit
HB Regs	Housing Benefit Regulations 2006
HB(SPC) Regs	Housing Benefit (Persons who have attained the qualifying age for state pension credit) Regulations 2006
HB Regs 1987	Housing Benefit (General) Regulations 1987
H-B&CTB(CP) Regs	Housing Benefit and Council Tax Benefit (Consequential Provisions) Regulations 2006
HBRB	Housing Benefit Review Board
HHJ	His/Her Honour Judge
HL	House of Lords
HLR	Housing Law Reports
HMCTS	HM Courts and Tribunal Service
HMRC	HM Revenue and Customs
IAT	Immigration Appeal Tribunal
IB	Incapacity benefit
Imm AR	Immigration Appeal Reports
IS	Income support
J, JJ	Mr/Mrs Justice, Justices
JSA	Jobseeker's allowance
LBC	London Borough Council
LGFA 1992	Local Government Finance Act 1992
LGR	Local Government Reports
LHA	Local housing allowance
LJ, LJJ	Lord/Lady Justice, Lord/Lady Justices
MBC	Metropolitan Borough Council
PC	State pension credit
para, paras	Paragraph, Paragraphs
PIP	Personal independence payment
Prot	Protocol (to European Convention on Human Rights)
QB	Queen's Bench Law Reports
QBD	Queen's Bench Division of the High Court
r, rr	rule, rules
RBC	Royal Borough Council
reg, regs	Regulation, Regulations
R(IS), R(H) etc	Reported Commissioner's decision
RVR	Rating and Valuation Reporter
s, ss	Section, Sections

Abbreviation	Meaning
SC	Supreme Court
Sch, Schs	Schedule, Schedules
SDA	Severe disablement allowance
SDP	Severe disability premium
SI	Statutory Instrument
SLT	Scots Law Times
SPCA	State Pension Credit Act 2002
SSA	Social Security Act (of relevant year)
SSAA	Social Security Administration Act 1992
SSA(F)A	Social Security Administration (Fraud) Act 1997
SSCBA	Social Security Contributions and Benefits Act 1992
SSFA	Social Security Fraud Act 2001
SSHD	Secretary of State for the Home Department
SSWP	Secretary of State for Work and Pensions
TCA	Tax Credits Act 2007
TCEA 2007	Tribunals, Courts and Enforcement Act 2007
TFEU	Treaty on the Functioning of the European Union
TP(FTT) Rules	Tribunal Procedure (First-tier Tribunal) (Social Entitlement Chamber) Rules 2008

Abbreviation	Meaning
TP(UT) Rules	Tribunal Procedure (Upper Tribunal) Rules 2008
Tribunals Service	HM Courts and Tribunals Service
UC	Universal credit
UC Regs	Universal Credit Regulations 2013 SI No.376
UC(TP) Regs 2013	Universal Credit (Transitional Provisions) Regulations 2013 SI No.386
UC(TP) Regs 2014	Universal Credit (Transitional Provisions) Regulations 2013 SI No.1230
Upper Tribunal	Upper Tribunal (Administrative Appeals)
vol	Volume
VTE	Valuation Tribunal for England
VTE CPS 2017	Consolidated Practice Statement for the VTE, 2017 (as amended)
VTW	Valuation Tribunal for Wales
WLR	Weekly Law Reports
WRA 2007	Welfare Reform Act 2007
WRA 2009	Welfare Reform Act 2009
WRA 2012	Welfare Reform Act 2012
WRA 2016	Welfare Reform Act 2016
WRPA	Welfare Reform and Pensions Act 1999
WTC	Working tax credit

Part 1:

Main primary legislation – housing benefit

Social Security Contributions and Benefits Act 1992

(1992 c4)

PART VII
INCOME-RELATED BENEFITS

GENERAL
123.   Income-related benefits

HOUSING BENEFIT
130.   Housing benefit
130A.   Appropriate maximum housing benefit
130B.   Loss of housing benefit following eviction on certain grounds
130C.   Relevant orders for possession
130D.   Loss of housing benefit: supplementary
130E.   Couples
130F.   Information provision
130G.   Pilot schemes relating to loss of housing benefit
131.   Council tax benefit
132.   Couples
133.   Polygamous marriages

GENERAL
134.   Exclusions from benefit
135.   The applicable amount
136.   Income and capital
136A.   Effect of attaining qualifying age for state pension credit
137.   Interpretation of Part VII and supplementary provisions

PART XIII
GENERAL
INTERPRETATION
172.   Applications of Act in relation to territorial waters
173.   Age
174.   References to Acts

SUBORDINATE LEGISLATION
175.   Regulations, orders and schemes
176.   Parliamentary control

SHORT TITLE, COMMENCEMENT AND EXTENT
177.   Short title, commencement and extent

PART VII
Income-Related Benefits
General

Income-related benefits

123.–(1)   Prescribed schemes shall provide for the following benefits (in this Act referred to as "income-related benefits")–

(a)-(c) *[Omitted]*

(d)   housing benefit; and

[⁵ [¹(e)]]

(2)   *[Omitted]*

(3)   Every authority granting housing benefit–

(a)   shall take such steps as appear to them appropriate for the purpose of securing that persons who may be entitled to housing benefit from the authority become aware that they may be entitled to it; and

(b)   shall make copies of the housing benefit scheme, with any modifications adopted by them under the Administration Act, available for public inspection at their principal office at all reasonable hours without payment.

[⁵ [²(4)   [⁴]]]

Definitions
"Administration Act" – see s174.

Amendments
1.   Substituted by LGFA Sch 9 para 1(1) (1.4.93).
2.   Substituted by LGFA Sch 9 para 1(2).
3.   Substituted by Local Government etc. (Scotland) Act 1994 Sch 13 para 174(4) (1.4.96).
4.   Substituted by WRA 2007 s40 and Sch 5 para 1(2) (3.7.07).
5.   Repealed by WRA 2012 s147 and Sch 14 part 1 in so far as it relates to CTB (1.4.13).

General Note
This section provides the core basis in primary legislation for the HB scheme.

Subs (1) provides for the setting up of the HB scheme as one of the income-related benefits.

Subs (3) obliges the relevant authority to publicise the availability of assistance under the HB scheme. There are two separate obligations: to take steps to increase awareness of the availability of HB to those on low incomes; and to make copies of the scheme (this presumably being a reference to the relevant legislation) available for inspection free of charge. The duties are entirely general in nature and authorities adopt various methods of discharging them, from advertising to providing advice in courts where proceedings for possession of property are being heard.

It seems likely that the duties would be regarded as "target duties" in public law terms and hence not enforceable by a member of the general public, but it might be possible for a claimant to claim poor publicisation of HB entitlement in her/his locality as being a factor showing "good cause" for a late claim: see p552.

For the power to make modifications to the HB scheme, see s134(8) SSAA on p79.

Welfare Reform Act 2012
Universal credit (UC) began to be introduced in parts of Great Britain from April 2013 and was fully introduced throughout Great Britain by mid-December 2018. See the introductory commentary on the Universal Credit (Transitional Provisions) Regulations 2014 (the UC(TP) Regs) on p1857 for further information. Sections 123 to 137 SSCBA 1992 will ultimately be revoked, and consequently HB abolished, by s33 and Part 1 of Sch 14 of the Welfare Reform Act 2012. Although HB has not yet been abolished, the significance of the roll-out of UC for HB is that other than for those of at least the qualifying age for PC (but see below for "mixed-age couples") or for those of working-age in exceptional cases, new claims for, and entitlement to HB, are no longer allowed. For working-age claimants and for most mixed-age couples, HB is replaced by a housing element within UC. For single claimants and couples of at least the qualifying age for PC, HB will eventually be replaced by a housing credit within PC, though it is understood that the latter is unlikely to happen before October 2023.

The entitlement to HB of those with an existing award can continue, at least until there is a break in the claim or the claimant becomes a member of a mixed-age couple. But see below for when a new claim for HB may still be made. Note that the government intention is that those with an existing entitlement to HB will be transferred to UC under what is known as a "managed migration" process between January 2020 and June 2024. Up to 10,000 claimants will be transferred earlier (from July 2019) as the process is tested.

If the claimant is a UC claimant or entitled to UC

(1)   In most cases, new claims for HB are not allowed if the person is a "universal credit claimant": reg 6 UC(TP) Regs 2014. "UC claimant" is wider than the term suggests. It includes those entitled to UC, those who have claimed UC and those exempt from the requirement to claim UC. There are exceptions to the rule. A UC claimant *can* claim HB if this is in respect of "specified accommodation" or "temporary accommodation". A UC claimant can also complete an HB claim that pre-dates her/his claim for UC – eg, where s/he notified an intention to make an HB claim, or needs to correct an HB claim, made before that date.

(2)   A person cannot be entitled to HB in respect of any period when s/he is entitled to UC unless the HB is in respect of "specified accommodation" or "temporary accommodation", or is a "transitional housing payment" (a two-week run-on of entitlement to HB): regs 5, 8(2A), 46(1) and 47(2) UC(TP) Regs. Entitlement to HB can also be allowed for a short period if the claimant becomes entitled to UC when s/he becomes a member of a couple with a current UC claimant.

(3)   If someone is entitled to HB when s/he claims or becomes entitled to UC, transitional rules specify if and when entitlement to HB ends: regs 7, 8, 8A, 46 and 47 UC(TP) Regs 2014.

If the claimant is not a UC claimant or entitled to UC
While still preventing new claims for HB in most cases, the Welfare Reform Act 2012 (Commencement No.21 and Transitional and Transitory Provisions) Order 2015 (the No.21 Order on p1882) and the Welfare Reform Act 2012 (Commencement No.23 and Transitional and Transitory Provisions) Order 2015 (the No.23 Order on p1885) allow claims for HB in exceptional cases. These are as follows.

(1)   The claimant is a member of a "mixed-age couple" (ie, where one member is at least the qualifying age for PC, but not the other) who is allowed to claim HB by art 6 of the No.21 Order, art 7 of the No.23 Order and the Welfare Reform Act 2012 (Commencement No.31 and Savings and Transitional Provisions and Commencement No.21 and 23 and Transitional and Transitory Provisions (Amendment)) Order 2019 SI No.37 (the No.31 Order on p1898). Note: if the claimant is at least the qualifying age for PC, or if a member of a couple, s/he and her/his partner are both at least that age, the DWP intention is that s/he can claim and be entitled to HB under the HB(SPC) Regs, but the legislative basis making good such an intention is at best unclear.

(2)   The claimant's (or her/his partner's) entitlement to HB (or IS, income-based JSA or income-related ESA) in the last month included a severe disability premium and s/he is therefore prevented from claiming UC under reg 4A UC(TP) Regs.

(3)   If the Secretary of State has made a determination that UC claims cannot be made in an area or category of case and the claimant is therefore prevented from claiming UC under reg 4 UC(TP) Regs.

(4)   The claimant (or her/his partner) is a "frontier worker" (ie, s/he works in Great Britain or Northern Ireland but does not live there) and s/he is therefore prevented from claiming UC under art 4(11) Welfare Reform Act 2012 (Commencement No.32 and Savings and Transitional Provisions) Order 2019 SI No.167.

Housing benefit

Housing benefit
130.–(1)   A person is entitled to housing benefit if–
(a)   he is liable to make payments in respect of a dwelling in Great Britain which he occupies as his home;
(b)   there is an appropriate maximum housing benefit in his case; and
(c)   either–
  (i)   he has no income or his income does not exceed the applicable amount; or
  (ii)   his income exceeds that amount, but only by so much that there is an amount remaining if the deduction for which subsection (3)(b) below provides is made.

(2)   In subsection (1) above "payments in respect of a dwelling" means such payments as may be prescribed, but the power to prescribe payments does not include power to prescribe–
[¹[⁴ (a) payments to a billing authority or to a local authority in Scotland in respect of council tax;]
(b)   mortgage payments, or, in relation to Scotland, payments under heritable securities.]

(3)   Where a person is entitled to housing benefit, then–
(a)   if he has no income or his income does not exceed the applicable amount, the amount of the housing benefit shall be the amount which is the appropriate maximum housing benefit in his case; and
(b)   if his income exceeds the applicable amount, the amount of the housing benefit shall be what remains after the deduction from the appropriate maximum housing benefit of prescribed percentages of the excess of his income over the applicable amount.

(4)   [⁵]
(5)   [³]

Amendments
1.   Substituted by LGFA Sch 9 para 3 (1.4.93).
2.   Substituted by Local Government etc. (Scotland) Act 1994 Sch 13 para 174(4) (1.4.96).
3.   Deleted by Housing Act 1996 s227 and Sch 19 Pt IV (1.4.97).
4.   Substituted by WRA 2007 s40 and Sch 5 para 1(3) (3.7.07).
5.   Ceased to have effect by WRA 2007 s30(1) and Sch 8 (7.4.08).

Definitions

"dwelling" – see s137.
"Great Britain" – see s172(a).
"prescribed" – see s137.

Modifications

Subsection (4) ceased to have effect by s30(1) Welfare Reform Act 2007 from 7 April 2008, save for the transtitional and savings provisions in the Welfare Reform Act 2007 (Commencement No.4, and Savings and Transitional Provisions) Order 2007 No.2872 which could apply up to 6 April 2009 at the latest (see p1237 of the 23rd edition of this book).

General Note

Subs (1) and (2) set out the basic conditions of entitlement to HB. In case it were not obvious from the use of the word "and" after sub-paras (a) and (b), it was confirmed in *CIS 166/1994* that the conditions of entitlement in the comparable s124 in relation to IS are cumulative and must all be satisfied. The conditions, and the principal parts of the HB Regs specifying the detail, are as follows.

(1)   The claimant must be liable to make payments in respect of a dwelling in Great Britain which s/he occupies as her/his home: sub-section (1)(a). "Dwelling" is defined in s137 (on p12). Note that the dwelling which the claimant occupies as a home may comprise more than one property: *R(H) 5/09*. See p16 for a discussion.

The question of whether a claimant is liable to make payments is dealt with by regs 8, 9 and 10 of both the HB and the HB(SPC) Regs and reg 56 HB Regs. The question of occupation is dealt with by reg 7 and reg 21(3) of both the HB and the HB(SPC) Regs. "Great Britain" includes territorial waters by virtue of s172(a), a provision unlikely to be of relevance in this context, but excludes Northern Ireland which has its own benefit scheme. It is permissible to make regulations under s137(2)(i) to treat only a specified category of people as if they were not liable to make payments: *R v Secretary of State for Social Security ex p Sarwar* [1997] 3 CMLR 647, CA. Subs (2) prevents any regulations being made to allow council tax and mortgage payments or heritable securities to be met by the HB scheme. The "payments" for which liability can attract HB are set out in reg 12(1) of both the HB and the HB(SPC) Regs.

(2)   There must be an appropriate maximum HB in the claimant's case: sub-section (1)(b). See s130A below. Maximum HB is calculated under reg 70 HB Regs (see p505) and reg 50 HB(SPC) Regs (see p795).

(3)   The claimant's income must be sufficiently low: sub-section (1)(c). Income is calculated under Part 6 of both the HB and the HB(SPC) Regs. For the "applicable amount", see Part 5 and Sch 3 of those regs. Sub-section (c)(ii) is awkwardly worded. The second time the word "amount" is used, it does not refer to the applicable amount but refers to what is left of the claimant's appropriate maximum HB once the appropriate proportion of her/his income has been deducted as provided for by sub-section (3)(b). Before a claimant is entitled to be paid any HB, her/his "amount" must be at least the figure fixed by reg 75 HB Regs (reg 56 HB(SPC) Regs) (currently 50 pence).

Subs (3) provides for the amount of HB payable. Where the claimant's income is less than or equal to the applicable amount, the maximum HB is payable. Where the income exceeds the applicable amount, sub-section (b) provides for a "taper" under which entitlement declines gradually rather than instantly to nil. This is designed to minimise the impact of any poverty trap. The current percentage prescribed by reg 71 HB Regs (reg 51 HB(SPC) Regs) is 65 per cent. For example, if the applicable amount is £140 a week, the claimant has income to be taken into account of £90 a week and the appropriate maximum HB is £125 a week, the HB payable is the maximum HB minus 65 per cent of £50 (the difference between £140 and £90), namely £92.50 (£125 minus £32.50) a week.

In *MB v Selby DC (HB)* [2011] UKUT 5 (AAC), Judge Rowland considered a lacuna in the HB legislation and whether it could filled by judicial interpretation. The claimant was entitled to HB for two homes for four weeks under reg 7(6)(d) HB Regs because he had moved to a new home and could not reasonably have avoided liability in respect of both homes (see p256). The homes were in two different local authority areas (the "old" and the "new" authority). The claimant's income exceeded his applicable amount, so the new authority awarded HB calculated according to subs (3)(b). The old authority decided that the claimant's entitlement to HB continued for four weeks at the same rate as was paid prior to his moving – ie, also applying the taper. The claimant appealed as both the old and the new authority had taken his income into account, effectively meaning that the taper in his case was 130 percent and not 65 percent. It was common ground that that was an unfair result and could not have been intended by the legislature. Indeed, this would not have been the result had both his homes been in the same local authority area. Judge Rowland suggested that the draftsman had overlooked the need to make provision for cases where a person is treated as occupying two dwellings as a home in two different local authority areas, where there must be two separate claims for HB. He found it impossible to interpret the regulations in a way that would allow HB to be calculated in the same way that it would be calculated if the two homes had both been in the same local authority's area. However, he said:

"In my judgment, it is therefore section 130 that falls to be interpreted in this case and it is possible to construe it so that, where a person is treated as occupying two dwellings as his home and is required to make two claims for housing benefit because different local authorities are responsible for funding and administering housing benefit in respect of the two dwellings, his income is to be taken into account only once (although if part of the income is sufficient to extinguish entitlement on one claim, the balance may be taken into account on the other). That is how it should be construed, so as to give effect to the obvious intention of the draftsman."

Subs (4) allowed for regulations defining maximum HB. See now s130A(2). For transitional provisions, see the Welfare Reform Act 2007 (Commencement No.4 and Savings and Transitional Provisions) Order 2007 SI No.2872 on p1818.

[¹ Appropriate maximum housing benefit

130A.–(1)   For the purposes of section 130 above, the appropriate maximum housing benefit (in this section referred to as "the AMHB") is determined in accordance with this section.

(2)   Regulations must prescribe the manner in which the AMHB is to be determined.

(3)   [²The provision which may be made by the regulations includes provision] for the AMHB to be ascertained in the prescribed manner by reference to rent officer determinations.

(4)   The regulations may require an authority administering housing benefit in any prescribed case–

(a)   to apply for a rent officer determination, and

(b)   to do so within such time as may be specified in the regulations.

[² (5)   The regulations may, for the purpose of determining the AMHB, provide for the amount of the liability mentioned in section 130(1)(a) above to be taken to be an amount other than the actual amount of that liability (and, without prejudice to the generality of this subsection, may provide for it to be taken to be the amount of a rent officer determination).]

[² (6)   The regulations may, for that purpose, make provision for determining the amount of liability under section 130(1)(a) above which a person is treated as having by virtue of regulations under section 137(2)(j) below (and, without prejudice to the generality of this subsection, may provide for that amount to be the amount of a rent officer determination).]

(7)   A rent officer determination is a determination made by a rent officer in the exercise of functions under section 122 of the Housing Act 1996.]

Amendments

1.   Inserted by WRA 2007 s30(2) with effect from 1.10.07 (for making regulations) and 7.4.08.
2.   Amended by WRA 2012 s69 with effect from 27.11.12 (for making regulations) and 1.1.13.

General Note

This section was inserted to facilitate the local housing allowance rent restriction scheme, for which see regs 12C, 13C and 13D of both the HB and the HB(SPC) Regs. See p391 for a summary of the scheme.

Subs (2) and (3) set out what regulations must and may prescribe. Subs (2) replaced s130(4).

Subs (4) deals with regulations requiring local authorities to apply to rent officers for determinations.

Subss (5) and (6) deal with regulations allowing for the appropriate maximum HB to be an amount other than the claimant's (or her/his partner's) actual rent liability and allowing it to be the amount of a rent officer determination.

Welfare Reform Act 2012. s130A was amended by s69 of the WRA 2012 as from 27 November 2012 (for making regulations) and 1 April 2013. The explanatory notes to the Act say this is "to reflect the Secretary of State's intention to exercise the powers in that section to provide for [appropriate maximum housing benefit] to be determined by methods other than by reference to rent officer determinations". The powers were used to make regulations allowing eligible rent to be determined by reference to either rent officer determinations or the Consumer Prices Index (CPI) and to ensure the Secretary of State has powers to set local housing allowance rates by reference to either the bottom 30th percentile of private sector rents or (from April 2013) the CPI or (from January 2014) the previous year's local housing allowance rate increased by a set percentage or (from April 2016) the rate determined on 30 January 2015 or (from 26 January 2018) the rate last determined. For the current provisions see, for example, art 4B and Sch 3B of the Rent Officer (Housing Benefit Functions) Order 1997 (on p884 and p899). Also from April 2013, the powers were used to allow the HB of working age people in social sector housing (eg, local authority or housing association) to be restricted if they are underoccupying their homes (see regs 12BA, A13 and B13 HB Regs).

[¹Loss of housing benefit following eviction on certain grounds 130B.]

Amendment
1.   Inserted by WRA 2007 s31(1) from 1.11.07 until 31.12.10 (see s31(3) and (4) WRA 2007).

General Note
Section 31(1) of the Welfare Reform Act 2007 inserted ss130B–130G into the SSCBA 1992 from 1 November 2007, providing for the reduction, or non-payment, of a former occupier's HB following eviction for anti-social behaviour in specified circumstances. The rules were piloted in eight local authority areas in England from 1 November 2007 to 31 October 2009. The provisions have no effect after 31 December 2010. For commentary on s130B, and the detailed pilot rules, see the 22nd edition of this book.

[¹Relevant orders for possession 130C.]

Amendment
1.   Inserted by WRA 2007 s31(1) from 1.11.07 until 31.12.10 (see s31(3) and (4) WRA 2007).

[¹Loss of housing benefit: supplementary 130D.]

Amendment
1.   Inserted by WRA 2007 s31(1) from 1.11.07 until 31.12.10 (see s31(3) and (4) WRA 2007).

[¹Couples 130E.]

Amendment
1.   Inserted by WRA 2007 s31(1) from 1.11.07 until 31.12.10 (see s31(3) and (4) WRA 2007).

[¹Information provision 130F.]

Amendment
1.   Inserted by WRA 2007 s31(1) from 1.11.07 until 31.12.10 (see s31(3) and (4) WRA 2007).

[¹ Pilot schemes relating to loss of housing benefit 130G.]

Amendment
1.   Inserted by WRA 2007 s31(1) from 1.11.07 until 31.12.10 (see s31(3) and (4) WRA 2007).

[² [¹Council tax benefit 131.]

Amendments
1.   Substituted by LGFA Sch 9 para 4.
2.   Repealed by WRA 2012 s147 and Sch 14 part 1 (1.4.13).

Abolition of council tax benefit: savings and transitional provisions
Until CTB was abolished (from 1 April 2013) and help with payment of council tax was localised, s131 set out the basic conditions of entitlement to CTB. The following also made provision for CTB.

Sections 132 and 133 allowed regulations in respect of the entitlement and the amount of CTB of a claimant who was a member of a couple or who was married under a law which permits polygamy.

Sections 134 to 136A and 175 made the same provision for CTB as for HB.

Section 137 provided the definitions for CTB.

For savings and transitional provisions, see arts 9 and 10 Welfare Reform Act 2012 (Commencement No.8 and Savings and Transitional Provisions) Order 2013 SI No.358 on p1735 of the 26th edition. See Parts 4, 5 and 6 for the council tax reduction schemes which replaced CTB.

[⁷ Couples
132.]

Amendments
1.   Substituted by LGFA Sch 9 para 5(1) as from 1.4.93.
2.   Substituted by LGFA Sch 9 para 5(2) as from 1.4.93.
3.   Substituted by LGFA Sch 9 para 5(3) as from 1.4.93.
4.   Substituted by LGFA Sch 9 para 5(3) as from 1.4.93.
5.   Substituted by LGFA Sch 9 para 5(4) as from 1.4.93.
6.   Substituted by CPA 2004 Sch 24 para 45 as from 5.12.05.
7.   Repealed by WRA 2012 s147 and Sch 14 part 1 (1.4.13).

[² Polygamous marriages
133.]

Amendments
1.   Substitution made by LGFA Sch 9 para 6 (1.4.93).
2.   Repealed by WRA 2012 s147 and Sch 14 part 1 (1.4.13).

General

Exclusions from benefit
134.–(1)   No person shall be entitled to an income-related benefit if his capital or a prescribed part of it exceeds the prescribed amount.

(2)   Except in prescribed circumstances the entitlement of one member of a family to any one income-related benefit excludes entitlement to that benefit for any other member for the same period.

(3)   [¹ . . .]

(4)   Where the amount of any income-related benefit would be less than a prescribed amount, it shall not be payable except in prescribed circumstances.

Amendment
1.   Deleted by LGFA Sch 9 para 7.

Modification
Section 134 was repealed by WRA 2012 s147 and Sch 14 part 1 on 1.4.13 in so far as it related to CTB.

General Note
Subs (1) provides for a capital limit above which a claimant will not be entitled to HB. The prescribed figure is currently £16,000: see reg 43 of both the HB and the HB(SPC) Regs. Note that by reg 26 HB(SPC) Regs, where a claimant or her/his partner is in receipt of the guarantee credit of PC, the whole of her/his capital is ignored. This means that for those claimants, there is effectively no capital limit.

Subs (2) provides that generally if one member of a "family" receives an income-related benefit for a period, the other members may not receive the same benefit for that period (for the meaning of "family" see s137(1) and p17).

Subs (4) provides for the fixing of a minimum level below which HB is not payable. See reg 75 HB Regs (reg 56 HB(SPC) Regs) which provides a minimum level of fifty pence a week for HB.

The applicable amount
135.–(1)   The applicable amount, in relation to any income-related benefit, shall be such amount or the aggregate of such amounts as may be prescribed in relation to that benefit.

(2)   The power to prescribe applicable amounts conferred by subsection (1) above includes power to prescribe nil as an applicable amount.

(3)-(4)   [¹]

(5)   [²] the applicable amount for a severely disabled person shall include an amount in respect of his being a severely disabled person.

(6)   Regulations may specify circumstances in which persons are to be treated as being or as not being severely disabled.

Social Security Contributions and Benefits Act 1992

Amendments
1. Deleted by LGFA Sch 9 para 8 (1.4.93).
2. Amended by TCA Sch 6 (8.4.03).

Modification
Section 135 was repealed by WRA 2012 s147 and Sch 14 part 1 on 1.4.13 in so far as it related to CTB.

General Note
Subs (1) enables the making of regulations to quantify "applicable amounts", one of the necessary elements in the calculation of the amount of HB. See Part 5 and Sch 3 of both the HB and the HB(SPC) Regs. This subsection is supplemented by paras (2) under which nil can be a valid applicable amount and (5) and (6) under which an amount must be included for severely disabled people. See Sch 3 para 14 HB Regs and Sch 3 para 6 HB(SPC) Regs, which define "severely disabled" for these purposes.

Income and capital

136.–(1)   Where a person claiming an income-related benefit is a member of a family, the income and capital of any member of that family shall, except in prescribed circumstances, be treatcd as the income and capital of that person.

(2)   Regulations may provide that capital not exceeding the amount prescribed under section 134(1) above but exceeding a prescribed lower amount shall be treated, to a prescribed extent, as if it were income of a prescribed amount.

(3)   Income and capital shall be calculated or estimated in such manner as may be prescribed.

(4)   A person's income in respect of a week shall be calculated in accordance with prescribed rules; and the rules may provide for the calculation to be made by reference to an average over a period (which need not include the week concerned).

(5)   Circumstances may be prescribed in which–
(a)   a person is treated as possessing capital or income which he does not possess;
(b)   capital or income which a person does possess is to be disregarded;
(c)   income is to be treated as capital;
(d)   capital is to be treated as income.

Definitions
"family" – see s137.
"income-related benefits" – see s123.

Modification
Section 136 was repealed by WRA 2012 s147 and Sch 14 part 1 on 1.4.13 in so far as it related to CTB.

General Note
This section enables the making of regulations to quantify "income" and "capital" on the basis of which entitlement to, and the amounts of, HB are calculated.
Subs (1) deals with the aggregation of assets for members of a "family" – see reg 25 HB Regs (reg 23 HB(SPC) Regs).
Subs (2) enables the "tariff income rules" whereby capital between certain levels is deemed to produce income at a set level irrespective of the actual income received by the claimant. See reg 52 HB Regs and reg 29(2) HB(SPC) Regs for the tariff income rules.
Subs (3) to (5) introduce wide powers as to the treatment of resources, as to which generally see Part 6 of both the HB and HB(CTB) Regs. For examples of the uses of the powers specified by subs (5), see reg 49, Part 6 and Schs 4 to 6, reg 46, and reg 41 HB Regs.

Analysis
The scope of the very wide powers conferred by s136 has been the subject of judicial comment. In *Foster v Chief Adjudication Officer* [1992] QB 31 at 45, Sir John Donaldson MR noted in passing that s136 permits the Secretary of State "to prescribe that black is white and that nothing is something and vice versa in the context of income and capital".
The wide scope of the provisions was confirmed in *Owen v Chief Adjudication Officer* [1999] *The Independent* 13 April, CA (appendix to *R(IS) 8/99*). This case concerned an anomaly in the Income Support (General) Regulations 1987. The claimant became terminally ill and was signed off work by his doctor, receiving statutory and contractual sick pay. He was dismissed by his employer and was paid four weeks' sick pay in arrears on the last day of his employment. Notwithstanding the fact that the sick pay was paid in arrears, the regulations required

that the sick pay be taken into account as income for the first four weeks of the claim as it was not "earnings": see regs 29(1), 29(2), 31(1) and 35(2) IS Regs. It should be noted that the position under the HB Regs is different as statutory and contractual sick pay are treated as "earnings": see reg 35(1)(i) and (j) HB Regs; reg 35(1)(h) and (k) HB(SPC) Regs.

The argument in *Owen* was that the effect of the regulations was not authorised by s136 and that the closing words of reg 29(2) IS Regs were therefore *ultra vires*. It is plain that subs (4) envisages such regulations being made. However, as the Secretary of State conceded and the Court of Appeal accepted, that provision could not authorise the offending words in reg 29(2) IS Regs because s136(4) did not appear in s22 Social Security Act 1986 as originally enacted. It was inserted as s22(8A) with effect from 29 July 1988 by the Local Government Finance Act 1988. However, the IS Regs had come into force on 11 April 1988 and so the subsection could not retrospectively revive any regulations that had been *ultra vires* in the absence of s22(8A): *Cottingham v Chief Adjudication Officer* [1992] appendix to *R(P) 1/93*, CA. The same would apply to much of the HB Regs 1987, which came into force between 1 April 1988 and 4 April 1988. Thus any provision which appeared in the HB Regs 1987 as they stood on 28 July 1988 and which could only be justified by subs (4) would be *ultra vires*. Any provision that had been the subject of insertion or amendment since that date, however, could be validly made under subs (4).

It was, however, argued for the Chief Adjudication Officer that the scheme was justified by either subs (3) or (5)(a). As far as subs (5)(a) was concerned, it was submitted for the claimant that as he did possess the income in question (though most of it had been spent on the previous month's bills), subs (5)(a) could not be applicable. The Court rejected this submission:

"it is a deeming provision prescribing circumstances in which a person is treated as possessing income he does not possess. He may not in fact possess income in a relevant period for a number of reasons: he may never have possessed the income at all; he may have in fact possessed the income at an earlier period, but he does not possess it at a later period. In the latter case a person may be treated as possessing income in a later period, even though it was paid in respect of an earlier period and even though he has already spent all the income that he did in fact possess at the earlier period . . . These enabling terms are framed widely enough to authorise a provision spreading or apportioning income possessed by a claimant over a stated period by treating it as possessed by the claimant in which he did not in fact possess it."

The difficulty with this approach is that it does not deal with the case where the income is still possessed in the later period. If the income is all spent (and the evidence was that Mr Owen had spent most, but not all of it) then, because s136(5)(a) refers to income being deemed to be possessed "which he does not possess", the Court's approach is justified. However, if the income is still possessed, it cannot be said that on any normal reading of the language, s136(5)(a) can apply because the income is possessed during the relevant period. If a regulation would be *intra vires* when applied to some claimants, but *ultra vires* when applied to others, it must be struck down. Against this, it might be argued that once income is possessed beyond the period in which it is received, it becomes part of the claimant's capital and so s/he does not possess it as income.

The Court of Appeal did not deal with the argument concerning s136(3), which centred around whether, if no income was received during a period but the claimant was deemed to have such income, such a scheme could be said to involve a "calculation or estimation" of income. In *CIS 3287/1997* (Appendix paras 12–13), Commissioner Goodman stated that the outcome had to bear some resemblance to the reality.

The Court also vigorously rejected a second submission for the claimant that the regulations were *ultra vires* as irrational. Although it was accepted that the scheme operated unfairly, it could not be said to be irrational so as to justify the striking-down of the regulations.

[¹Effect of attaining qualifying age for state pension credit

136A.–(1)   Subsections (2) and (3) below apply in relation to housing benefit *[and council tax benefit]* in the case of any person who has attained the qualifying age for state pension credit.

(2)   Regulations may make provision for section 134(1) or any provision of section 136 above not to have effect in relation to those benefits in the case of any such person.

(3)   In relation to those benefits, regulations may make provision for the determination of the income and capital of any such person; and any such regulations may include provision applying (with such modifications as the Secretary of State thinks fit)–

(a)   section 5 of the State Pension Credit Act 2002 (provision for treating income of spouse as income of claimant, etc), and

(b)   section 15 of that Act (determination of income and capital for purposes of state pension credit).

(4)   Regulations under subsection (3) above may also include provision–

(a)   authorising or requiring the use of any calculation or estimate of a person's income or capital made by the Secretary of State for the purposes of the State Pension Credit Act 2002; or

    (b)   requiring that, if and so long as an assessed income period is in force under section 6 of that Act in respect of a person falling within subsection (1) above–

        (i)   the assessed amount of any element of his retirement provision shall be treated as the amount of that element for the purposes of housing benefit *[or council tax benefit]*; and

        (ii)   his income shall be taken for those purposes not to include any element of retirement provision which it is taken not to include for the purposes of state pension credit by virtue of a determination under subsection (5) of section 7 of that Act.

    (5)   In subsection (4) above "assessed amount", "element" and "retirement provision" have the same meaning as in the State Pension Credit Act 2002.

    (6)   The Secretary of State may by regulations make provision for the preceding provisions of this section to apply with modifications in cases to which section 12 of the State Pension Credit Act 2002 (polygamous marriages) applies.

    (7)   The provision that may be made by regulations under subsection (6) above includes any provision that may be made by regulations under section 133 above.]

Amendment
1.   Inserted by SPCA Sch 2 para 3 (27.01.03 (for making regulations) and 6.10.03).

Modification
Section 136A was repealed by WRA 2012 s147 and Sch 14 part 1 on 1.4.13 in so far as it related to CTB.

Definition
"qualifying age for state pension credit" – see s137.

General Note
s136A SSCBA gives extensive regulation-making powers in relation to the calculation of income and capital for HB purposes for those who have attained the qualifying age for PC (see the commentary to the definition on p17). The provisions for such claimants are in the HB(SPC) Regs.

Interpretation of Part VII and supplementary provisions
    137.–(1)   In this Part of this Act, unless the context otherwise requires–

[¹ "billing authority" has the same meaning as in Part I of the Local Government Finance Act 1992;]

"child" means a person under the age of 16;

[⁷ [¹¹, ¹² "couple" means–

    (a)   two people who are married to, or civil partners of, each other and are members of the same household; or

    (b)   two people who are not married to, or civil partners of, each other but are living together as a married couple otherwise than in prescribed circumstances;]]

"dwelling" means any residential accommodation, whether or not consisting of the whole or part of a building and whether or not comprising separate and self-contained premises;

"family" means–

    (a)   a [⁶ couple];

    (b)   a [⁶ couple] and a member of the same household for whom one of them is or both are responsible and who is a child or a person of a prescribed description;

    (c)   except in prescribed circumstances, a person who is not a member of a [⁶ couple] and a member of the same household for whom that person is responsible and who is a child or a person of a prescribed description;

"industrial injuries scheme" means a scheme made under Schedule 8 to this Act or section 159 of the 1975 Act or under the Old Cases Act;

[¹⁰ "local authority" in relation to Scotland means a council constituted under section 2 of the Local Government etc. (Scotland) Act 1994;]

[⁸ . . .]

[⁵ "pensionable age" has the meaning given by the rules in paragraph 1 of Schedule 4 to the Pensions Act 1995 (c. 26);]

"prescribed" means specified in or determined in accordance with regulations;
[⁵ "the qualifying age for state pension credit" is (in accordance with section 1(2)(b) and (6) of the State Pension Credit Act 2002)–

(a)   in the case of a woman, pensionable age; or

(b)   in the case of a man, the age which is pensionable age in the case of a woman born on the same day as the man;]

[⁵ "state pension credit" means state pension credit under the State Pension Credit Act 2002;]

[⁸ . . .]

"war pension scheme" means a scheme under which war pensions (as defined in section 25 of the Social Security Act 1989) are provided;

"week", in relation to [³ council tax benefit], means a period of 7 days beginning with a Monday.

[⁹ [¹¹, ¹² (1A)]]

(2)   Regulations may make provision for the purposes of this Part of this Act–

(a)   as to circumstances in which a person is to be treated as being or not being in Great Britain;

(b)   continuing a person's entitlement to benefit during periods of temporary absence from Great Britain;

(c)   as to what is or is not to be treated as remunerative work or as employment;

(d)   as to circumstances in which a person is or is not to be treated as

     (i)   engaged or normally engaged in remunerative work

     (ii)   [⁴ . . .]

(e)   as to what is or is not to be treated as relevant education;

(f)   as to circumstances in which a person is or is not to be treated as receiving relevant education;

(g)   specifying the descriptions of pension increases under war pension schemes or industrial injuries schemes that are analogous to the benefits mentioned in section 129(2)(b)(i) to (iii) above;

(h)   as to circumstances in which a person is or is not to be treated as occupying a dwelling as his home;

(i)   for treating any person who is liable to make payments in respect of a dwelling as if he were not so liable;

(j)   for treating any person who is not liable to make payments in respect of a dwelling as if he were so liable;

(k)   for treating as included in a dwelling any land used for the purposes of the dwelling;

(l)   as to circumstances in which persons are to be treated as being or not being members of the same household;

(m)   as to circumstances in which one person is to be treated as responsible or not responsible for another.

Amendments

1.   Substituted by LGFA Sch 9 para 9(a) (1.4.93).
2.   Definition of "levying authority" repealed by Local Government etc (Scotland) Act 1994 Sch 13 para 174(5) and Sch 14 (1.4.96).
3.   Substituted by LGFA Sch 9 para 9(d) (1.4.93).
4.   Deleted by Jobseekers Act 1995 Sch 2 para 35(2).
5.   Inserted by SPCA Sch 2 para 4 (2.7.02 (for making regulations) and 6.10.03).
6.   Substituted by CPA Sch 24 para 46(2) (5.12.05).
7.   Inserted by CPA Sch 24 para 46(3) (5.12.05).
8.   Omitted by CPA Sch 24 para 46(4) (5.12.05).
9.   Inserted by CPA Sch 24 para 46(5) (5.12.05).
10.   Inserted by WRA 2007 s40 and Sch 5 para 1(4) (3.7.07).
11.   Amended by art 2 and Sch 1 para 22(8) of SI 2014 No 560 as from 13.3.14 (in England and Wales).
12.   Amended by art 5(3) and Sch 4 para 2(13) of SI 2014 No 3229 as from 16.12.14 (in Scotland).

Modification

Section 137 was repealed by WRA 2012 s147 and Sch 14 part 1 on 1.4.13 in so far as it related to CTB.

General Note

Subs (1) defines certain terms for the purpose of this part of the Act. Subs (2) enables regulations to be made in order to implement the schemes set up under this Part of the Act.

Analysis

Subsection (1) : Definitions

"couple". Note that between 13 March 2014 and 16 December 2014, the definition of "couple" for HB purposes was different in Scotland than in England and Wales.

Two people are treated as a "couple" if they are married to or civil partners of each other and are members of the same household. Two people are also treated as a "couple" if they are not married to or civil partners of each other, but they are living together as a married couple otherwise than in prescribed circumstances.

On the question of when it is for the local authority to determine whether or not a claimant is a member of a couple (as opposed to the DWP), see the discussion on *R v Penwith DC ex p Menear* (1991) 24 HLR 115, QBD and *R v South Ribble DC HBRB ex p Hamilton* (2000) 33 HLR 102, CA in the General Note on p419.

Married couples and civil partners: para (a) of the definition. As to membership of the same household, see p17. A couple are civil partners if they have entered into a contract of civil partnership under the CPA 2004. Occasionally it may be necessary to consider the question of whether someone is actually married. If the marriage could be shown to be void, as distinct from voidable, under the relevant law of marriage in either England and Wales or in Scotland (which are markedly different), then it would be necessary to consider whether the two people in question are an unmarried couple: see below. The validity of foreign marriages can cause very difficult questions of law to arise. Note also the existence in Scotland of the doctrine of marriage by habit and repute. In cases where any of these issues arise, reference should be made to specialist textbooks on the subject. A useful short summary for advisers with references to caselaw can be found in the discussion of bereavement benefits (where these issues arise much more frequently) in CPAG's *Welfare Benefits and Tax Credits Handbook.*

Two people who are not married or civil partners of each other: para (b) of the definition. The main issue which arises is whether the people are "living together as a married couple". Prior to the amendments to the definitions of "couple", the main issue was the meaning of the phrase "living together as husband and wife". "Living together as a married couple" would seem to have the same effect as that phrase. "Living together as husband and wife", is a phrase that has been used widely in various means-tested and non-means-tested benefits schemes and is subject to a large body of caselaw.

Differences of interpretation led the predecessor of the DWP to issue guidance about indications as to whether the test of "living together as husband and wife" was satisfied. The first six of the principles below are the factors listed in the guidance, which is reproduced in the HB guidance: see GM C1 Annex A. They are "admirable signposts" (*Crake and Butterworth v Supplementary Benefit Commission* [1982] 1 All ER 498) and the starting point for deciding if two people who are not married or civil partners are a "couple". The "signposts" are also likely to be relevant to whether people are living together as a married couple. Note that *CIS 87/1993* emphasised the need to stand back once all the evidence has been considered and look at the overall quality of the relationship.

Note also that in *PP v Basildon DC (HB)* [2013] UKUT 505 (AAC), Judge Jacobs decided that although the "signposts" remain relevant, they are not exhaustive and an analysis of the evidence needs to recognise the importance of the emotional aspect of the relationship between the parties. The Court of Session in *DK v SSWP* [2016] CSIH 84; [2017] AACR 10 agreed with this approach – ie, that a tribunal must focus on the ultimate issue in the case without giving undue weight to any individual factor that may be relevant to that issue. It said that a tribunal:

"must address the applicable legal test on the basis of the whole of the evidence, but in doing so it is not necessary that it should provide a detailed analysis of the evidence divided into discrete components; nor is it necessary that the tribunal should explain what evidence it accepts or rejects in relation to each of those components and the relevance or otherwise of each component."

In the light of cases like *Karanakaran v SSHD* [2003] 3 All ER 449, the Court said that the facts found by a tribunal and the reasons it gives are treated as a totality, and that it is the inference drawn from that totality that is decisive.

If the result of this complex inquiry is that the couple are "living together as husband and wife" or (now) "living together as a married couple", only one of them may claim HB in respect of their dwelling and their needs and resources are aggregated.

Under previous versions of the definition, two people of the same sex were treated as a "couple" if they had not entered into a civil partnership contract, but were living together as if they were civil partners. Under subsection (1A) (now omitted), this last test was only satisfied if the same-sex couple would have been regarded as "living together as husband and wife" were they of the opposite sex. Similar considerations to those above were relevant in determining whether a same-sex couple was living together as if they were civil partners.

In *JP v SSWP (IS)* [2014] UKUT 17 (AAC), a claimant who owned her home jointly with a person of the same sex was deemed to be a member of a couple for IS purposes with her joint owner. The claimant had described her joint owner as a friend and carer. However, the First-tier Tribunal decided she was a member of a couple as she and her joint owner were living together as if they were civil partners. In granting leave to appeal, Judge Levenson suggested that if two people have not entered into a civil partnership and maintain that they are not living together as civil partners, a high degree of proof is required to establish that they are living together. In allowing the claimant's appeal he said (at para 33):

"It seems to me that in cases involving a suggestion that a couple are living together as if they were husband and wife or as though they were civil partners the current state of the law is that a committed emotional loving relationship must be established and publicly acknowledged. ... An unacknowledged relationship cannot be the equivalent of marriage or a registered civil partnership which are, in their very nature, public acknowledgement of an emotional relationship. In the case of same sex relationships ... some of the traditional signposts are of less assistance. It is for those alleging that two people are a couple within the meaning of section 137(1) to prove that there is a publicly acknowledged committed emotional loving relationship".

The "Signposts"

(1)   If the couple share a household, they will be more likely to be a "living together as husband and wife". For the meaning of "household", see p17. If they are not part of the same household, it is highly unlikely that they are "living together" in this sense. However, one of the most common pitfalls in these cases is to consider issues relating to the sharing of a household and stop the inquiry there. While the sharing of a household is consistent with a relationship akin to husband and wife, the caselaw is replete with examples where it has been held that the facts are equally consistent with other types of relationship such as simple friendship or brother and sister (*CP 8001/1995* para 10), patient and carer (*R(SB) 35/85* para 8), and landlord and lodger (*Campbell v Secretary of State for Social Services* [1983] 4 FLR 138, QBD, though rejected on the facts of that particular case).

(2)   The more stable the relationship, the more likely two people are to be "living together as husband and wife". However, again caution needs to be applied because some of the other relationships mentioned in the previous paragraph may last for a long time: *CP 8001/1995* para 12. A degree of permanency in a landlord and lodger relationship may take it over the line into cohabitation: see *Campbell* for an example. Note, however, point (7) below.

(3)   The closer the financial arrangements, the more likely that a finding of "living together as husband and wife" will be justified. However, in any case where this issue arises there will be some degree of financial connection between the parties and so it will only be a compelling factor if the financial arrangements are particularly close and involve, for example, joint bank accounts.

(4)   The presence of a sexual relationship is of importance: *R(SB) 17/81* (para 7). Claimants who are not involved in a sexual relationship may need to make this clear to the authorities at the outset. In *CIS 87/1993* (para 12) it was said that if there had never been a sexual relationship, strong alternative grounds will be required to permit a conclusion that the man and woman are a couple. In *CSB 150/1985* it was said that two Mormons engaged to each other and living in the same house could not be an unmarried couple. That decision probably goes too far in apparently excluding evidence of other factors, but it is an illustration of the significance of this factor. Its importance may vary according to the ages of the people in question and cultural factors, but authorities should be careful not to make assumptions.

(5)   If the couple have children "of their union", in the antiquated phrase that was used in the old supplementary benefit guidance, that will be a strong indication that they are "living together as husband and wife".

(6)   The degree of public acknowledgement of the relationship is a factor which is often underplayed and is often illuminating as to the true nature of the relationship and as to the intention of the parties (see below). If one partner uses the name of the other, that will be highly persuasive: *R(G) 1/79* (para 9).

(7)   The relevance of the intention of the parties is controversial. In *Crake and Butterworth,* Woolf J (at 504d-f) placed considerable emphasis on what the intention of the parties was, and Webster J thought that if the intention of the parties was capable of ascertainment, it was significant: see *Robson v Secretary of State for Social Services* [1982] 3 FLR 232, QBD. Subsequently, it was suggested that the intention of the parties could only be ascertained from their actions: see *R(SB) 17/81* (para 8). No doubt it is true that it would be wrong for an authority simply to accept a claimant's account of what her/his intention was without examining such a statement against the background of the objective evidence. However, it is suggested that if the objective evidence, perhaps coupled with credible evidence given by a claimant, clearly indicates an intention to adopt a different relationship, the two people will not be "living together as husband and wife": *CIS 87/1993* (para 14).

(8)   The nature of a relationship can change over time. Thus it is wrong for an authority to assume, just because it concludes that on a particular date that two people are an unmarried couple, that the relationship has always had that quality: *CP 8001/1995* (para 11).

"dwelling". See also reg 2(4) of both the HB Regs and the HB(SPC) Regs. The House of Lords decision in *Uratemp Ventures Ltd v Collins* [2001] 3 WLR 806 sheds light on the meaning of "dwelling". Previous authority had stated, in the context of statutory protection of residential tenants, that a room or rooms which a tenant was given a right to occupy could only be a "dwelling" if they provided for the three basic necessities of life: namely sleeping, cooking and eating. Of these, sleeping had been regarded as the most important factor: *Wright v Howell* [1947] 92 SJ 26, CA; *Westminister CC v Clarke* [1992] 2 AC 288 at 299, HL. In *Collins*, however, the House of Lords ruled that rooms were not excluded from the definition of "dwelling" simply by virtue of the fact that they did not contain cooking facilities. Lord Irvine stated (at 808D, para 3) that "dwelling ... connotes a place where one

lives, regarding and treating it as home". He said (at 808E, para 4) that it was not even necessary that the room or rooms should contain a bed if a person was sleeping there. Lord Bingham said (at 809G-H, para 12) that although premises would not normally be a "dwelling" unless the tenant sleeps there, there was no inflexible rule even as to this.

The House of Lords in *Collins* emphasised the importance of the statutory context in interpreting the word (at 808D, para 3, 809D–E, para 10, 810C, para 15, 822F–823A, para 57). The emphasis on the "residential" aspects in the definition given in s137 suggests that in the HB context it should be given a wide interpretation, because the essence of the HB scheme is to include all rent and allied payments for different types of accommodation. That this is the correct interpretation is further confirmed by the inclusive nature of the definition to include parts of a building and accommodation which is not self-contained. Some landlords of low-grade accommodation attempt to exclude it from the regime of statutory protection by, for example, providing that cooking facilities are not to be used. Even if these agreements are genuine, the absence of cooking facilities should not exclude the occupant from HB.

The dwelling which the claimant occupies as a home may comprise more than one property: *Hackney LB v GA* [2008] UKUT 26 (AAC); R(H) 5/09. The definition of "dwelling" in the HB context (for which see s130) is inseparable from occupation as the claimant's home. Judge Jacobs decided that the words "a dwelling in Great Britain which he occupies as his home" give rise to a single question of fact: what is the extent of the dwelling occupied by the claimant? In so deciding, the judge considered the decision of the Court of Appeal in *SSWP v Miah;* reported as *R(JSA) 9/03*. He accepted that although *Miah* is not a binding authority on the interpretation of the HB legislation, it is an authority that it is permissible, in appropriate circumstances, to take a functional approach to the definition of "dwelling". He did not read it as a restrictive definition, as it has to cover all sorts of residential accommodation. He said:

"The housing benefit legislation largely avoids terms of art from property law. For example: regulation 9 refers to payments in respect of a dwelling rather than rent and to agreement rather than tenancy. This reflects the breadth of the arrangements that are covered by the legislation. It is concerned with the economic substance of an arrangement rather than with the precise legal form. In that context, it is appropriate to take account of the reality of the claimant's living arrangements and not place too much emphasis on the legal structure."

Birmingham City Council v IB [2009] UKUT 116 (AAC) is consistent with the decision in *R(H) 5/09*. The claimant was a disabled student entitled to HB. To ensure full time attendance at university he needed a live-in carer and hence two-bedroom accommodation. The university did not have such accommodation available and therefore provided the claimant with two adjacent rooms, each with en-suite facilities, so that the carer could be on call 24 hours a day. The issue was whether two rooms which were physically separated from one another but had access onto the same corridor and required use of a common kitchen could constitute part of the same dwelling for HB purposes. Deputy Judge Mark decided that the claimant was entitled to HB on the basis that the dwelling occupied by him as a home included the room rented by him for his carer. Applying the tests set out in *Miah*, functionally and purposively, the judge decided that the claimant needed two rooms for living – one for himself and one for his carer. He said:

"Commonsense dictates that it should not matter whether there is a connecting door between the two, which the claimant might in any event be incapable of crossing, or whether the two rooms are in a larger flat as in this case or in a two room flat, or even a duplex with the carer's room on the first floor and inaccessible to the claimant. Nor should it matter if the landlord's internal billing system meant that the two rooms were separately billed."

OR v SSWP and Isle of Anglesey CC [2013] UKUT 65 (AAC) concerned a homeless claimant's entitlement to HB to cover the cost of staying overnight in a night shelter. Upper Tribunal Judge Wright summarised his decision by saying (at para 4) that "a person who is allowed to stay overnight (for a charge) at a night shelter but is not allowed to remain there during the day and so has to leave in the morning taking all his belongings with him, and has no right to stay in any part of the night shelter or indeed right generally to stay there (in the sense that if he turns up late and the shelter is full he will be turned away), is not occupying a dwelling as his home" and the decision has been widely misunderstood as holding that HB is never payable to those staying in night shelters. However, a reading of the decision as a whole contradicts that view. The issue on the appeal to the Upper Tribunal was whether (as the First-tier Tribunal had decided) the fact that a night shelter was a "hostel" for the purposes of HB meant that it was automatically a "dwelling". Judge Wright held that it did not: paras 22–26. That is the point of law decided in the *OR* case and therefore the point on which it is an authority. Having set the First-tier Tribunal decision aside, the judge then re-made the First-tier Tribunal's decision and decided that the individual claimant in *OR* did not occupy the particular night shelter in Anglesey *as his home*. That part of the *OR* decision was a decision on the facts of the case and is not a precedent that is binding on local authorities or the First-tier Tribunal: the judge stressed that at para 3, immediately before the summary quoted above. A number of factors were relevant but Judge Wright held that the decisive ones in that case were those identified in the summary namely "the very transient nature of his stays at the hostel, and ... the lack of any right of occupancy beyond the 12 hours he was allowed to be there overnight": para 47.

Besides the accommodation being residential in nature, it seems that the agreement under which the claimant occupies the home must reflect this fact. In *R v Warrington BC ex p Williams* (1997) 29 HLR 872 at 876, QBD, the claimant rented commercial premises and used them as a dwelling, in breach of the lease. He claimed that the landlord had orally agreed that he could stay overnight to act as a night watchman, and so was unable to assert the true character of the premises against the claimant. In view of that, it was contended that the premises had to be seen as having a joint residential and commercial use. This argument was rejected, as a waiver of a condition against use as a dwelling did not alter the commercial nature of the tenancy and so the premises were not a dwelling.

"family". This definition and its component parts determine the crucial question of who forms part of the assessment unit for HB purposes – eg, for the purposes of the "applicable amount". These are couples (para (a)), couples with children (para (b)) and lone parents (para (c)). Broadly speaking, a couple's resources are to be treated as the claimant's for the purposes of the assessment of those resources whereas those who do not form part of the family will only be taken into account as non-dependants, if at all.

For the critical issue of membership of a "household", see below. This is of equal importance to opposite-sex and same-sex couples. Section 137(2)(l) permits the making of regulations to define the situations in which people are not to be treated as being or not being members of the same household for these purposes. See reg 21 of both the HB and the HB(SPC) Regs. "Child" is defined in s137 as a person under the age of 16. A "person of a prescribed description" is a "young person", for which see reg 19 of both the HB and the HB(SPC) Regs. Reg 20 of both sets of regs sets out the circumstances in which someone is to be treated as responsible for a child or young person.

Meaning of "household" in the definitions of "couple" and "family". This word is of significance in three respects in determining the question of membership of a family. First, in order for a child or young person to form part of a claimant's family, s/he must live in the same household. Secondly, a "married couple" or "civil partnership couple" only comes within the definition of "couple" if the couple are members of the same household. Thirdly, the question of whether two people are "living together as husband and wife" or are "living together as a married couple" or whether a same-sex couple are living together as if they are civil partners involves consideration of, but is not determined by, the question of whether they share a household. Note that reg 21 of both the HB Regs and the HB(SPC) Regs provides circumstances in which a person is to be *treated as* a member of the household, but do not define the circumstances in which a person *is* a member of the household.

There is a considerable body of caselaw considering whether people are members of the same "household". As was observed in *R(SB) 4/83* (para 19), the word is an ordinary English word and the question is to be resolved by the use of common sense. More than one interpretation of the facts before the authority or the First-tier Tribunal may therefore be permissible. However, the following principles can be established from the caselaw.

(1)   A person cannot be a member of more than one household at once: *R(SB) 8/85* (para 12). However, it is possible for a person to follow a regular pattern of moving from one household to another: see *CIS 11304/ 1995* (para 10), where a claimant spent about six months in each year living with his wife and the other part of the year living with another partner.

(2)   The issue is not determined on a week-by-week basis but on the basis of the overall relationship between the parties: *R(SB) 30/83 (*para 5) concerning a university student moving in and out of the accommodation, who was held to be resident with her partner during the periods of absence during term-time. Note the special rules in reg 7(6)(b) HB Regs that can apply in these circumstances.

(3)   If the people are separately liable to pay for their accommodation, that is a good indication that they are not members of the same household: *R(SB) 13/82* (para 11).

(4)   If the people have completely separate living arrangements, then they cannot be members of the same household: *R(SB) 4/83* (para 19).

(5)   However, even if people share certain facilities, there must still be an element of domesticity about their arrangements. This is illustrated by *CIS 671/1992* (para 4) where the claimant and his wife had senile dementia and did not understand the fact that they were husband and wife. Accordingly, mere presence in the same room does not mean that the two people are sharing a household. The people must enjoy a reasonable level of independence and self-sufficiency: *R(IS) 1/99* (Appendix para 14). This will often be lacking where a person is living in communal accommodation and so it will be rare for the occupants to be sharing a single household: *CIS 671/1992*.

(6)   In considering whether the element of shared living is sufficiently strong to constitute a single household, a number of factors may be relevant. These may include: whether there are independent arrangements for the storage and cooking of food, whether there are independent financial arrangements (apart from the question of separate liabilities for the accommodation discussed above), whether the people eat separately, and the general evidence of family life within the accommodation: *CJSA 1321/2007*. Ultimately, however, it remains a question of fact and it will often not be easy to demonstrate an error of law in the approach taken by an authority or the First-tier Tribunal.

"The qualifying age for state pension credit". This age is relevant in determining whether the HB Regs or the HB(SPC) Regs apply to a claimant. The age at which someone qualifies for state pension credit (PC) is linked to the pensionable age for a woman. The qualifying age for PC for a woman is the minimum age she can receive state retirement pension. The qualifying age for PC for a man is the minimum age a woman born on the same day as him can receive state retirement pension. Note that from 6 December 2018, pensionable ages for men and women are equal and thus the qualifying age for PC is the person's pension age. For both men and women, the qualifying age for PC is therefore:

(1)   60, if s/he was born before 6 April 1950;
(2)   an age from 60 and one month to 64 and 11 months depending on her/his date of birth, if s/he was born on or after 6 April 1950 but before 6 December 1953;
(3)   65, if s/he was born on 6 November 1953;
(4)   an age from 65 and two months to 66 depending on her/his date of birth, if s/he was born on or after 6 December 1953 but before 5 October 1954;
(5)   66, if s/he was born on or after 6 October 1954 but before 6 April 1960;
(6)   67 if s/he was born on or after 6 March 1961 but before 6 April 1977.

Consequently, the rules in the HB(SPC) Regs will apply to individual claimants at different ages. For claimants born on or after 6 April 1950 but before 6 December 1953, there is a helpful table, setting out the relevant birth dates and pension ages, in an appendix to CPAG's *Welfare Benefits and Tax Credits Handbook*. Once pensionable age is 67, the age will rise to 68 between 2024 and 2046.

Subsection (2): Regulation-making powers
This sets out general regulation-making powers in relation to issues relating to entitlement to means-tested benefits. For regulation-making powers in relation to adjudication and administration, see ss5 and 6 SSAA. The principal regulations made under these powers are listed next to the letter of each paragraph below.

(a)   Reg 7(10) to (17) of both the HB and the HB(SPC) Regs.
(b)   Regs 7(13) to 17D) of both the HB and the HB(SPC) Regs.
(c)   Reg 6(1) to (4) HB and HB(SPC) Regs.
(d)   Reg 6(5) to (7) HB and HB(SPC) Regs.
(e)   Not relevant for HB. This concept has nothing to do with the HB rules about students but is used in the comparable IS and income-based JSA exclusions for students and others in full-time study.
(f)   See para (e).
(g)   Not relevant for HB.
(h)   See reg 7 of both the HB and HB(SPC) Regs.
(i)   See regs 8, 9, 10 and 56 HB Regs and regs 7, 9, and 10 HB(SPC) Regs.
(j)   See reg 8(1)(b) to (e) of both the HB and the HB(SPC) Regs.
(k)   See reg 2(4) of both the HB and the HB(SPC) Regs.
(l)   See reg 21 of both the HB and the HB(SPC) Regs.
(m)   See reg 20 of both the HB and the HB(SPC) Regs.

PART XIII
General
Interpretation

Applications of Act in relation to territorial waters
172.   In this Act–
(a)   any reference to Great Britain includes a reference to the territorial waters of the United Kingdom adjacent to Great Britain;
(b)   any reference to the United Kingdom includes a reference to the territorial waters of the United Kingdom.

Age
173.   For the purposes of this Act a person–
(a)   is over or under a particular age if he has or, as the case may be has not attained that age; and
(b)   is between two particular ages if he has attained the first but not the second;
and in Scotland (as in England and Wales) the time at which a person attains a particular age expressed in years is the commencement of the relevant anniversary of the date of his birth.

References to Acts
174.   In this Act–
"the 1975 Act" means the Social Security Act 1975;
"the 1986 Act" means the Social Security Act 1986;
"the Administration Act" means the Social Security Administration Act 1992;
"the Consequential Provisions Act" means the Social Security (Consequential Provisions) Act 1992;

"the Northern Ireland Contributions and Benefits Act" means the Social Security Contributions and Benefits (Northern Ireland) Act 1992;
"the Old Cases Act" means the Industrial Injuries and Diseases (Old Cases) Act 1975; and
"the Pensions Act" means the Social Security Pensions Act 1975.

Subordinate legislation

Regulations, orders and schemes

175.–(1)   Subject to section 145(5) above, regulations and orders under this Act shall be made by the Secretary of State.

[(1A)   *[Omitted]*]

(2)   Powers under this Act to make regulations, orders or schemes shall be exercisable by statutory instrument.

(3)   Except in the case of an order under section 145(3) above and in so far as this Act otherwise provides, any power under this Act to make regulations or an order may be exercised–

(a)   either in relation to all cases to which the power extends, or in relation to those cases subject to specified exceptions, or in relation to any specified cases or classes of case;

(b)   so as to make, as respects the cases in relation to which it is exercised–

(i)   the full provision to which the power extends or any less provision (whether by way of exception or otherwise),

(ii)   the same provision for all cases in relation to which the power is exercised, or different provision for different cases or different classes of case or different provision as respects the same case or class of case for different purposes of this Act,

(iii)   any such provision either unconditionally or subject to any specified condition;

and where such a power is expressed to be exercisable for alternative purposes it may be exercised in relation to the same case or any or all of those purposes; and powers to make regulations or an order for the purposes of any one provision of this Act are without prejudice to powers to make regulations or an order for the purposes of any other provision.

(4)   Without prejudice to any specific provision in this Act, any power conferred by this Act to make regulations or an order (other than the power conferred in section 145(3) above) includes power to make thereby such incidental, supplementary, consequential or transitional provision as appears to the Secretary of State to be expedient for the purposes of the regulations or order.

(5)   Without prejudice to any specific provisions in this Act, a power conferred by any provision of this Act except–

(a)   sections 30, 47(6), 57(9)(a) and 145(3) above and paragraph 3(9) of Schedule 7 to this Act;

(b)   section 122(1) above in relation to the definition of "payments by way of occupational or personal pension"; and

(c)   Part XI,

to make regulations or an order includes power to provide for a person to exercise a discretion in dealing with any matter.

(6)   Any power conferred by this Act to make orders or regulations relating to housing benefit or [¹ *council tax benefit*] shall include power to make different provisions for different areas.

(7)   Any power of the Secretary of State under any provision of this Act, except the provisions mentioned in subsection (5)(a) and (b) above and Part IX, to make any regulations or order, where the power is not expressed to be exercisable with the consent of the Treasury, shall if the Treasury so direct be exercisable only in conjunction with them.

(8)   Any power under any of sections 116 to 120 above to modify provisions of this Act or the Administration Act extends also to modifying so much of any other provision of this Act or that Act as re-enacts provisions of the 1975 Act which replaced provisions of the National Insurance (Industrial Injuries) Acts 1965 to 1974.

(9)   A power to make regulations under any of sections 116 to 120 above shall be exercisable in relation to any enactment passed after this Act which is directed to be construed as one with this Act; but this subsection applies only so far as a contrary intention is not expressed in the enactment so passed, and is without prejudice to the generality of any such direction.

(10)   Any reference in this section or section 176 below to an order or regulations under this Act includes a reference to an order or regulations made under any provision of an enactment passed after this Act and directed to be construed as one with this Act; but this subsection applies only so far as a contrary intention is not expressed in the enactment so passed, and without prejudice to the generality of any such direction.

Amendment

1.   Substituted by LGFA para 10 Sch 9 (1.4.93).

Modification

Section 175(5) was repealed by WRA 2012 s147 and Sch 14 part 1 on 1.4.13 in so far as it related to CTB.

Parliamentary control

176.–(1)-(2)   *[Omitted]*

(3)   A statutory instrument–

(a)   which contains (whether alone or with other provisions) any order, regulations or scheme made under this Act by the Secretary of State, other than an order under section 145(3) above; and

(b)   which is not subject to any requirement that a draft of the instrument shall be laid before and approved by a resolution of each House of Parliament,

shall be subject to annulment in pursuance of a resolution of either House of Parliament.

Short title, commencement and extent

Short title, commencement and extent

177.–(1)   This Act may be cited as the Social Security Contributions and Benefits Act 1992.

(2)   This Act is to be read, where appropriate, with the Administration Act and the Consequential Provisions Act.

(3)   The enactments consolidated by this Act are repealed, in consequence of the consolidation, by the Consequential Provisions Act.

(4)   Except as provided in Schedule 4 to the Consequential Provisions Act, this Act shall come into force on 1st July 1992.

(5)   The following provisions extend to Northern Ireland–

(a)   section 16 and Schedule 2;

(b)   section 116(2); and

(c)   this section.

(6)   Except as provided by this section, this Act does not extend to Northern Ireland.

Social Security Administration Act 1992
(1992 c5)

PART I
CLAIMS FOR AND PAYMENTS AND GENERAL ADMINISTRATION OF BENEFIT
Necessity of claim
1.   Entitlement to benefit dependent on claim
2.   Retrospective effect of provisions making entitlement to benefit dependent on claim

Work-focused interviews
2A.   Claim or full entitlement to certain benefits conditional on work-focused interview
2C.   Optional work-focused interviews

Claims and payments regulations
5.   Regulations about claims for and payments of benefit

Council tax benefits
6.   Regulations about council tax benefits administration
7.   Relationship between council tax benefit and other benefits
7A.   Sharing of functions as regards certain claims and information
7B.   Use of social security information

PART II
ADJUDICATION
Housing benefit and council tax benefit
63.   Adjudication

PART III
OVERPAYMENTS AND ADJUSTMENTS OF BENEFIT
Recovery of benefit payments
71ZC.   Deduction from benefit
71ZD.   Deduction from earnings
71ZE.   Court action etc

Housing benefit
75.   Overpayments of housing benefit

Council tax benefit
76.   Excess benefit
77.   Shortfall in benefit

PART VI
Enforcement
109A.   Authorisations for investigators
109B.   Power to require information
109C.   Powers of entry
110A.   Authorisations by local authorities
110AA. Power of local authority to require electronic access to information
111.   Delay, obstruction etc. of inspector
111A.   Dishonest representations for the purpose of obtaining benefit etc.
112.   False representations for obtaining benefit etc
113.   Breach of regulations
115.   Offences by bodies corporate
115A.   Penalty as alternative to prosecution
115B.   Penalty as alternative to prosecution: colluding employers etc

Civil penalties
115C.   Incorrect statements etc
115D.   Failure to disclose information

Legal proceedings
116.   Legal proceedings
116ZA.   Local authority powers to prosecute housing benefit and council tax benefit
         fraud
116A.   Local authority powers to prosecute benefit fraud
121DA.   Interpretation of Part VI

PART VII
PROVISION OF INFORMATION
Authorities administering housing benefit or council tax benefit
122C.   Supply of information to authorities administering benefit
122D.   Supply of information by authorities administering benefit
122E.   Supply of information between authorities administering benefit

Rent officers and housing benefit
122F.   Supply by rent officers of information relating to housing benefit
123.   Unauthorised disclosure of information relating to particular persons
126A.   Information from landlords and agents

EXPEDITED CLAIMS FOR HOUSING AND COUNCIL TAX BENEFIT
128A.   Disclosure of information by authorities

PART VIII
ARRANGEMENTS FOR HOUSING BENEFIT AND COUNCIL TAX BENEFITS AND RELATED
SUBSIDIES
Housing benefit
134.   Arrangements for housing benefit

Council tax benefit
138.   Nature of benefits
139.   Arrangements for council tax benefit

Reports
139A.   Persons to report on administration
139B.   Powers of investigation
139BA.   Interaction with Audit Commission
139C.   Reports

Directions by Secretary of State
139D.   Directions
139DA.   Directions: Variation and Revocation
139E.   Information about attainment of standards
139F.   Enforcement notices
139G.   Enforcement determinations
139H.   Enforcement determinations: supplementary

Subsidy
140A.   Subsidy
140B.   Calculation of amount of subsidy
140C.   Payment of subsidy
140D.   Rent rebate subsidy: accounting provisions

Supplementary provisions
140E.   Financing of joint arrangements
140F.   No requirement for annual orders
140G.   Interpretation: Part VIII

PART XIII
ADVISORY BODIES AND CONSULTATION
The Social Security Advisory Committee and the Industrial Injuries Advisory Council
170.   Consultation with representative organisations
172.   Functions of Committee and Council in relation to regulations
173.   Cases in which consultation is not required
174.   Committee's report on regulations and Secretary of State's duties

Housing benefit and council tax benefit
176.   Consultation with representative organisations

PART XV
MISCELLANEOUS
182A.   Return of social security post
182B.   Requirement to supply information about redirection of post
187.   Certain benefit to be inalienable

PART XVI
GENERAL
Subordinate legislation
189.   Regulations and orders – general
190.   Parliamentary control of orders and regulations

Supplementary
191.   Interpretation – general
192.   Short title, commencement and extent

SCHEDULES
4.   Persons Employed in Social Security Administration or Adjudication
10.   Supplementary Benefit etc

PART I
Claims for and Payments and General Administration of Benefit
Necessity of claim

Entitlement to benefit dependent on claim
    1.–(1)   Except in such cases as may be prescribed, and subject to the following provisions of this section and to section 3 below, no person shall be entitled to any benefit unless, in addition to any other conditions relating to that benefit being satisfied–
    (a)   he makes a claim for it in the manner, and within the time, prescribed in relation to that benefit by regulations under this Part of this Act; or
    (b)   he is treated by virtue of such regulations as making a claim for it.
    [²(1A)   No person whose entitlement to any benefit depends on his making a claim shall be entitled to the benefit unless subsection (1B) below is satisfied in relation both to the person making the claim and to any other person in respect of whom he is claiming benefit.
    (1B)   This subsection is satisfied in relation to a person if–
    (a)   the claim is accompanied by–
        (i)   a statement of the person's national insurance number and information or evidence establishing that that number has been allocated to the person; or

      (ii)   information or evidence enabling the national insurance number that has been allocated to the person to be ascertained; or

(b)   the person makes an application for a national insurance number to be allocated to him which is accompanied by information or evidence enabling such a number to be so allocated.

(1C)   Regulations may make provision disapplying subsection (1A) above in the case of–

(a)   prescribed benefits;

(b)   prescribed descriptions of persons making claims; or

(c)   prescribed descriptions of persons in respect of whom benefit is claimed, or in other prescribed circumstances.]

(2)   Where under subsection (1) above a person is required to make a claim or to be treated as making a claim for a benefit in order to be entitled to it–

(a)   if the benefit is a widow's payment, she shall not be entitled to it in respect of a death occurring more than 12 months before the date on which the claim is made or treated as made, and

(b)   if the benefit is any other benefit except disablement benefit or reduced earnings allowance, the person shall not be entitled to it in respect of any period more than 12 months before that date, except as provided by section 3 below.

(3)   *[Omitted]*

(4)   In this section and section 2 below "benefit" means–

(a)   benefit as defined in section 122 of the Contributions and Benefits Act; and

[[1](aa) a jobseeker's allowance;]

[[3](ab) state pension credit;]

[[4] (ac) an employment and support allowance;] and

[[5] (ad) personal independence payment.]

(b)   any income-related benefit.

(5)   This section (which corresponds to section 165A of the 1975 Act, as it had effect immediately before this Act came into force) applies to claims made on or after 1st October 1990 or treated by virtue of regulations under that section or this section as having been made on or after that date.

(6)   Schedule 1 to this Act shall have effect in relation to other claims.

Amendments

1.   Inserted by Jobseekers Act 1995 Sch 2 para 38 (22.4.96).
2.   Inserted by SSA(F) Act 1997, s19.
3.   Inserted by SCPA s11 and Sch 1 para 2 (2.7.02 for making regulations and 7.4.03).
4.   Inserted by WRA 2007 s28 and Sch 3 para 10(2) (18.3.08 for making regulations and 27.7.08).
5.   Inserted by WRA 2012 Sch 9 para 8 (8.4.13).

Definitions

"benefit" – see s1(4).
"claim" – see s191.
"income-related benefit" – see s191.
"prescribe" – see s191.

General Note

Subs (1) sets out the general condition of entitlement to any "benefit" (defined in s1(4) and including HB) that a person must make a claim for it in a prescribed manner and within a prescribed time, or must be treated as having made a claim. See Part 10 HB Regs and Part 9 HB(SPC) Regs. Note that there are now only limited situations in which a person may make a claim for HB. See the note on the Welfare Reform Act 2012 on p4 for further information.

Subs (1A) to (1C) provide a general requirement in relation to entitlement to any "benefit". By subs (1B), it is necessary that the claimant either supplies her/his national insurance number (NINO) or enough information to allow the number to be ascertained, or makes an application for a number. The phrase "any other person in respect of whom he is claiming benefit" in subsection (1A) includes the claimant's partner with whom s/he lives: *SSWP v Wilson* [2006] EWCA Civ 882, 29 June 2006; reported as *R(H) 7/06*. Reg 4 of each of the HB and HB(SPC) Regs sets out cases in which s1(1A) is disapplied. The requirement does not apply to the following:

(1) A person living in a hostel.
(2) A child or qualifying young person in respect of whom a person is claiming HB.
(3) A claimant's partner where the partner is a "person subject to immigration control" because s/he does not have leave to enter or remain in the UK, s/he is not "habitually resident" and s/he has not previously been allocated a NINO.

See, for example, reg 4 HB Regs on p251. See also the discussion of *Westminster City Council v AT & SSWP (HB)* [2013] UKUT 321 (AAC) on p251.

CH 4085/2007 [2008] UKUT 14 (AAC) considered the meaning in s1(1B)(b) of "accompanied by information or evidence enabling such a number" to be allocated. The tribunal had taken the view that the terms of s1(1B)(b) were not satisfied because the failure of the claimant's husband to attend an interview in respect of his application for a NINO, and the subsequent refusal of a NINO, showed that he had not provided sufficient information or evidence to enable a NINO to be allocated. Judge Rowland allowed the claimant's appeal. The requirement is merely to have applied for a NINO with the requisite information or evidence; the refusal of the NINO does not show conclusively that the requirement was not satisfied. What the Secretary of State actually requires in order to allocate a NINO is sufficient evidence to show that the applicant does not already have one, information that a claim for a benefit requiring an application for a NINO has been, or is to be, made and information as to identity so that the Secretary of State can be satisfied that the claimant is genuine. A person can only be expected to send what s/he has been told to send and the source of that information is likely to be those administering the benefit being claimed (here the local authority). The information and evidence mentioned in the legislation is only that information and evidence that the person concerned could reasonably have been expected to send when the application was made. The phrase "information or evidence enabling [a national insurance] number to be so allocated" cannot extend to information and evidence provided at an interview. In the judge's view, if Parliament had intended to include the information that is provided at interview, it would have made entitlement conditional on a NINO being allocated. The judge also pointed out that evidence of a failure to attend an interview is insufficient to show that an application was not, or has ceased to be, genuine. Regard must at least be had to the cause of the failure but even a lack of good cause may not indicate a lack of intention to pursue an application.

LCC v SSWP [2009] UKUT 74 (AAC) considered the NINO requirement in the context of a claimant's partner who had applied for, but was refused, a NINO. Judge Mesher confirmed that the NINO requirement applies not only on an initial claim but also where a decision making an indefinite award is being revised or superseded (*CH 4085/2007* approved in this respect). The judge also said that *CH 4085/2007* was right to hold that subsection (1B)(b) might be satisfied, even though the NINO was itself refused. However, he disagreed with the finding in that decision that the requirement can be satisfied simply by the submission of a form requesting a NINO interview. Rather, the information or evidence enabling a NINO to be allocated was to be regarded as encompassing all the information and evidence provided by the applicant during the process, down to and including the signing of the CA5400 form at the conclusion of the interview. He accepted that the essence of the interview was to obtain evidence of identity (and that immigration status, including not having the right to work, was irrelevant). As here such evidence had been provided (eg, a passport, student ID and utility bills in the applicant's name), the requirement was satisfied.

Retrospective effect of provisions making entitlement to benefit dependent on claim

2.–(1) This section applies where a claim for benefit is made or treated as made at any time on or after 2nd September 1985 (the date on which section 165A or the 1975 Act (general provision as to necessity of claim for entitlement to benefit), as originally enacted, came into force) in respect of a period the whole or any part of which falls on or after that date.

(2) Where this section applies, any question arising as to–

(a) whether the claimant is or was at any time (whether before, on or after 2nd September 1985) entitled to the benefit in question, or to any other benefit on which his entitlement to that benefit depends; or

(b) in a case where the claimant's entitlement to the benefit depends on the entitlement of another person to a benefit, whether that other person is or was so entitled,

shall be determined as if the relevant claim enactment and any regulations made under or referred to in that enactment had also been in force, with any necessary modifications, at all times relevant for the purpose of determining the entitlement of the claimant, and, where applicable, of the other person, to the benefit or benefits in question (including the entitlement of any person to any benefit on which that entitlement depends, and so on).

(3) In this section "the relevant claim enactment" means section 1 above as it has effect in relation to the claim referred to in subsection (1) above.

(4) In any case where–

(a)   a claim for benefit was made or treated as made (whether before, on or after 2nd September 1985, and whether by the same claimant as the claim referred to in subsection (1) above or not), and benefit was awarded on that claim, in respect of a period falling wholly or partly before that date; but

(b)   that award would not have been made had the current requirements applied in relation to claims for benefit, whenever made, in respect of periods before that date; and

(c)   entitlement to the benefit claimed as mentioned in subsection (1) above depends on whether the claimant or some other person was previously entitled or treated as entitled to that or some other benefit,

then, in determining whether the conditions of entitlement to the benefit so claimed are satisfied, the person to whom benefit was awarded as mentioned in paragraphs (a) and (b) above shall be taken to have been entitled to the benefit so awarded, notwithstanding anything in subsection (2) above.

(5)   In subsection (4) above "the current requirements" means–

(a)   the relevant claim enactment, and any regulations made or treated as made under that enactment, or referred to in it, as in force at the time of the claim referred to in subsection (1) above, with any necessary modifications; and

(b)   subsection (1) (with the omission of the words following "at any time") and subsections (2) and (3) above.

Definitions
"benefit" – see s1(4).
"claim" – see s191.
"current requirements" – see s2(5).
"relevant claim enactment" – see s2(1).

General Note
This section was introduced by the Social Security Act 1990 to confirm that the predecessor of s1 above had retrospective effect. It means that a claimant cannot claim HB from before September 1985 on the basis that before that date a claim was not a requirement of entitlement to benefit: *Insurance Officer v McCaffrey* [1985] 1 WLR 1353 at 1355H-1356C, HL.

Work-focused interviews

Claim or full entitlement to certain benefits conditional on work-focused interview
2A.–(1)   Regulations may make provision for or in connection with–

(a)   imposing, as a condition falling to be satisfied by a person who–
    (i)   makes a claim for a benefit to which this section applies, and
    [4 (ii) has not attained pensionable age at the time of making the claim (but see subsection (1A)),]
    a requirement to take part in [4 one or more work-focused interviews];

(b)   imposing, at a time when–
    (i)   a person [4 has not attained pensionable age and is] entitled to such a benefit, and
    (ii)   any prescribed circumstances exist,
    a requirement to take part in [4 one or more work-focused interviews] as a condition of that person continuing to be entitled to the full amount which is payable to him in respect of the benefit apart from the regulations.

[4 (1A)   For the purposes of subsection (1) a man born before [6 6 December 1953] is treated as attaining pensionable age when a woman born on the same day as the man would attain pensionable age.]

(2)   The benefits to which this section applies are–

(a)   income support;

(b)   housing benefit;

(c)   council tax benefit;

(d)   widow's and bereavement benefits falling within section 20(1)(e) and (ea) of the Contributions and Benefits Act (other than a bereavement payment);

(e)   incapacity benefit;

(f)   severe disablement allowance; and

(g)   [¹ carer's allowance].

[⁵ (2A)   No requirement may be imposed by virtue of this section on a person who–

(a)   is not a member of a couple, and

(b)   is responsible for, and a member of the same household as, a child under the age of one.

(2B)   For the purposes of subsection (2A)(b) regulations may make provision–

(a)   as to circumstances in which one person is to be treated as responsible or not responsible for another;

(b)   as to circumstances in which persons are to be treated as being or not being members of the same household.]

(3)   Regulations under this section may, in particular, make provision–

(a)   for securing, where a person would otherwise be required to take part in interviews relating to two or more benefits–

      (i)   that hc is only required to take part in one interview, and

      (ii)   that any such interview is capable of counting for the purposes of all those benefits;

(b)   for determining the persons by whom interviews are to be conducted;

(c)   conferring power on such persons or the designated authority to determine when and where interviews are to take place (including power in prescribed circumstances to determine that they are to take place in the homes of those being interviewed);

(d)   prescribing the circumstances in which persons attending interviews are to be regarded as having or not having taken part in them;

(e)   for securing that the appropriate consequences mentioned in subsection (4)(a) or (b) below ensue if a person who has been notified that he is required to take part in an interview–

      (i)   fails to take part in the interview, and

      (ii)   does not show, within the prescribed period, that he had good cause for that failure;

(f)   prescribing–

      (i)   matters which are or are not to be taken into account in determining whether a person does or does not have good cause for any failure to comply with the regulations, or

      (ii)   circumstances in which a person is or is not to be regarded as having or not having good cause for any such failure.

(4)   For the purposes of subsection (3)(e) above the appropriate consequences of a failure falling within that provision are–

(a)   where the requirement to take part in an interview applied by virtue of subsection (1)(a) above, that as regards any relevant benefit either–

      (i)   the person in question is to be regarded as not having made a claim for the benefit, or

      (ii)   if (in the case of an interview postponed in accordance with subsection (7)) that person has already been awarded the benefit, his entitlement to the benefit is to terminate immediately;

(b)   where the requirement to take part in an interview applied by virtue of subsection (1)(b) above, that the amount payable to the person in question in respect of any relevant benefit is to be reduced by the specified amount until the specified time.

(5)   Regulations under this section may, in relation to any such reduction, provide–

(a)   for the amount of the reduction to be calculated in the first instance by reference to such amount as may be prescribed;

(b)   for the amount as so calculated to be restricted, in prescribed circumstances, to the prescribed extent;

(c)   where the person in question is entitled to two or more relevant benefits, for determining the extent, and the order, in which those benefits are to be reduced in order to give effect to the reduction required in his case.

(6)   Regulations under this section may provide that any requirement to take part in an interview that would otherwise apply to a person by virtue of such regulations–

(a)   is, in any prescribed circumstances, either not to apply or not to apply until such time as is specified;

(b)   is not to apply if the designated authority determines that an interview–
  (i)   would not be of assistance to that person, or
  (ii)   would not be appropriate in the circumstances;

(c)   is not to apply until such time as the designated authority determines, if that authority determines that an interview–
  (i)   would not be of assistance to that person, or
  (ii)   would not be appropriate in the circumstances, until that time; and the regulations may make provision for treating a person in relation to whom any such requirement does not apply, or does not apply until a particular time, as having complied with that requirement to such extent and for such purposes as are specified.

(7)   Where–

(a)   a person is required to take part in an interview by virtue of subsection (1)(a), and

(b)   the interview is postponed by or under regulations made in pursuance of subsection (6)(a) or (c), the time to which it is so postponed may be a time falling after an award of the relevant benefit to that person.

[³ (7A)   Information supplied in pursuance of regulations under this section shall be taken for all purposes to be information relating to social security.]

(8)   In this section–

[⁵ "couple" has the meaning given by section 137(1) of the Contributions and Benefits Act;]

"the designated authority" means such of the following as may be specified, namely–

(a)   the Secretary of State,

(b)   a person providing services to the Secretary of State,

(c)   a local authority,

[² (ca) subject to subsection (9), a county council in England,]

(d)   [² subject to subsection (9),] a person providing services to, or authorised to exercise any function of, [² any authority mentioned in paragraph (c) or (ca)];

"interview" (in subsections (3) to (7)) means a work-focused interview;

"relevant benefit", in relation to any person required to take part in a work-focused interview, means any benefit in relation to which that requirement applied by virtue of subsection (1)(a) or (b) above;

"specified" means prescribed by or determined in accordance with regulations;

"work-focused interview", in relation to a person, means an interview conducted for such purposes connected with employment or training in the case of that person as may be specified; and the purposes which may be so specified include purposes connected with a person's existing or future employment or training prospects or needs, and (in particular) assisting or encouraging a person to enhance his employment prospects.

[² (9)   A county council in England or a person providing services to, or authorised to exercise any function of, such a council may be specified as the designated authority only in relation to interviews with persons to whom the council is required to make support services available under section 68(1) of the Education and Skills Act 2008 (support services: provision by local education authorities).]

Commencement

  11.11.99: see s89(4)(a) WRPA.

Amendments

  1.   Amended by art 2(2) and the Sch para 3 of SI 2002 No 1457 as from 1.4.03.
  2.   Amended by s169 and Sch 1 para 45 Education and Skills Act 2008 as from 26.1.09.
  3.   Amended by s34(1) WRA 2009 as from 12.1.10.
  4.   Amended by s35(2) and (4) WRA 2009 as from 10.2.10.

5.   Amended by s3(2) WRA 2009 as from 31.10.11 (6.10.11 for the purpose of making regulations under s2(2B)).
6.   Amended by s1 and Sch 1 para 2 Pensions Act 2011 as from 3.1.12.

Modification
Section 2A was repealed by WRA 2012 s147 and Sch 14 part 1 on 1.4.13 in so far as it related to CTB.

General Note
The principal innovation made by the WRPA in so far as the subject matter of this book is concerned was a greatly expanded role for local authorities as providers of benefit services. The Act sought to permit the implementation of the Single Work-Focused Gateway, or ONE as it was subsequently renamed.

    The aim of the scheme was to set up a number of offices to handle claims and inquiries relating to all benefits for which a person might be eligible. There are no longer any ONE offices. The provisions were included in this book because some ONE offices were run by local authorities: see subs (8)(c). The offices also provided "work-focused interviews" designed to assist claimants in finding employment. Note that subs (2) confirms that HB is among the benefits which, if claimed, may trigger a requirement to attend a work-focused interview, but there is not currently such a requirement. For an Analysis of the provisions, see pp30 and 31 of the 24th edition.

Optional work-focused interviews

2C.–(1)   Regulations may make provision for conferring on local authorities [² or, subject to subsection (3A), county councils in England] functions in connection with conducting work-focused interviews in cases where such interviews are requested or consented to by persons to whom this section applies.

(2)   This section applies to [¹
  (a)   persons making claims for or entitled to any of the benefits listed in section 2A(2) above or any prescribed benefit; and
  (b)   partners of persons entitled to any of the benefits listed in section 2AA(2) above or any prescribed benefit;]
      and it so applies regardless of whether such persons have, in accordance with regulations under section 2A [¹ or 2AA] above, already taken part in interviews conducted under such regulations.

(3)   The functions which may be conferred on a local authority [² or on a county council in England] by regulations under this section include functions relating to–
  (a)   the obtaining and receiving of information for the purposes of work-focused interviews conducted under the regulations;
  (b)   the recording and forwarding of information supplied at, or for the purposes of, such interviews;
  (c)   the taking of steps to identify potential employment or training opportunities for persons taking part in such interviews.

[² (3A)   Regulations under this section may confer functions on a county council in England only in relation to interviews with persons to whom the council is required to make support services available under section 68(1) of the Education and Skills Act 2008 (support services: provision by local education authorities).]

(4)   Regulations under this section may make different provision for different areas or different authorities.

(5)   In this section "work-focused interview", in relation to a person to whom this section applies, means an interview conducted for such purposes connected with employment or training in the case of such a person as may be prescribed; and the purposes which may be so prescribed include–
  (a)   purposes connected with the existing or future employment or training prospects or needs of such a person, and
  (b)   (in particular) assisting or encouraging such a person to enhance his employment prospects.

Commencement
11.11.99: see s89(4)(a) WRPA.

Amendments
1.   Amended by the Employment Act 2002 Sch 7 para 10 (5.7.03).
2.   Amended by s169 and Sch 1 para 47 Education and Skills Act 2008 as from 26.1.09.

Modification
Section 2C was repealed by WRA 2012 s147 and Sch 14 part 1 on 1.4.13 in so far as it related to CTB.

General Note
This authorised the pilot schemes for ONE that were run by local authorities. The Social Security (Claims and Information) Regulations 1999 SI No.3108 were made under this provision. The important point to note is the absence of any compulsion to attend an interview: see subs (1).

Claims and payments regulations

Regulations about claims for and payments of benefit

5.–(1) Regulations may provide–

(a)   for requiring a claim for a benefit to which this section applies to be made by such person, in such manner and within such time as may be prescribed;

(b)   for treating such a claim made in such circumstances as may be prescribed as having been made at such date earlier or later than that at which it is made as may be prescribed;

(c)   for permitting such a claim to be made, or treated as if made, for a period wholly or partly after the date on which it is made;

(d)   for permitting an award on such a claim to be made for such a period subject to the condition that the claimant satisfies the requirements for entitlement when benefit becomes payable under the award;

(e)   [⁴ for any such award to be revised under section 9 of the Social Security Act 1998, or superceded under section 10 of that Act, if any of those requirements are found not to have been satisfied;]

(f)   for the disallowance on any ground of a person's claim for a benefit to which this section applies to be treated as a disallowance of any further claim by that person for that benefit until the grounds of the original disallowance have ceased to exist;

(g)   for enabling one person to act for another in relation to a claim for a benefit to which this section applies and for enabling such a claim to be made and proceeded with in the name of a person who has died;

(h)   for requiring any information or evidence needed for the determination of such a claim or of any question arising in connection with such a claim to be furnished by such person as may be prescribed in accordance with the regulations;

[⁶(hh) for requiring such person as may be prescribed in accordance with the regulations to furnish any information or evidence needed for a determination whether a decision on an award of benefit to which this section applies–

   (i)   should be revised under section 9 of the Social Security Act 1998 [⁷ or, as the case may be, under paragraph 3 of Schedule 7 to the Child Support, Pensions and Social Security Act 2000]; or

   (ii)   should be superseded under section 10 of that Act [⁷ or, as the case may be, under paragraph 4 of that Schedule];]

(i)   for the person to whom, time when and manner in which a benefit to which this section applies is to be paid and for the information and evidence to be furnished in connection with the payment of such a benefit;

(j)   for notice to be given of any change of circumstances affecting the continuance of entitlement to such a benefit or payment of such a benefit;

(k)   for the day on which entitlement to such a benefit is to begin or end;

(l)   for calculating the amounts of such a benefit according to a prescribed scale or otherwise adjusting them so as to avoid fractional amounts or facilitate computations;

(m)   for extinguishing the right to payment of such a benefit if payment is not obtained within such period, not being less than 12 months, as may be prescribed from the date on which the right is treated under the regulations as having arisen;

[⁸. . .]

(p)   for the circumstances and manner in which payments of such a benefit may be made to another person on behalf of the beneficiary for any purpose, which may be to discharge, in whole or in part, an obligation of the beneficiary or any other person;

(q)   for the payment or distribution of such a benefit to or among persons claiming to be entitled on the death of any person and for dispensing with strict proof of their title;

(r)   for the making of a payment on account of such a benefit–

    (i)   where no claim has been made and it is impracticable for one to be made immediately;

    (ii)   where a claim has been made and it is impracticable for the claim or an appeal, reference, review or application relating to it to be immediately determined;

    (iii)   where an award has been made but it is impracticable to pay the whole immediately.

(2)   This section applies to the following benefits–

[15 (za) universal credit;]

(a)   benefits as defined in section 122 of the Contributions and Benefits Act;

[1(aa) a jobseeker's allowance;]

[12 (ab) state pension credit;]

[13 (ac) an employment and support allowance;]

[14 (ad) personal independence payment;]

(b)   income support;

[9]

[9]

(e)   housing benefit;

(f)   any social fund payments such as are mentioned in section 138(1)(a) or (2) of the Contributions and Benefits Act;

(g)   child benefit; and

(h)   Christmas bonus.

[10 (2A)   The regulations may also require such persons as are prescribed to provide a rent officer with information or evidence of such description as is prescribed.

(2B)   For the purposes of subsection (2A), the Secretary of State may prescribe any description of information or evidence which he thinks is necessary or expedient to enable rent officers to carry out their functions under section 122 of the Housing Act 1996.

(2C)   Information or evidence required to be provided by virtue of subsection (2A) may relate to an individual claim or award or to any description of claims or awards.]

[11 (3)]

[12 (3A)   *[Omitted]*]

[8]

(5)   *[Omitted]*

[2 (6)   As it has effect in relation to [15 universal credit or] housing benefit subsection (1)(p) above authorises provision requiring the making of payments of benefit to another person, on behalf of the beneficiary in such circumstances as may be prescribed.]

Definition

"prescribed" – see s191.

Amendments

1.   Inserted by Jobseekers Act 1996 Sch 2 para 39.

2.   Inserted by the Housing Act 1996, s120(1) and deemed always to have had effect by s120(2).

3.   Substituted by the Housing Act 1996 Sch 13 para 3(2).

4.   Substituted by SSA 1998 Sch 7 para 79(1)(a).

5.   Repealed by SSA 1998 Sch 7 para 79(1)(b) from 29.11.99. However, this repeal does not take effect in relation to HB and CTB: see Art 2(2)(a) and (b) of the Social Security Act 1998 (Commencement No 12 and Consequential and Transitional Provisions) Order 1999 SI No 3178.

6.   Inserted by SSA 1998 s74.

7.   Amended by CSPSSA Sch 7 para 21(1) (2.7.01).

8.   Repealed by SSA 1998 s86(2), Sch 8.

9.   Repealed by TCA Sch 6 (6.4.03).

10.   Inserted by WRA 2007 s35(2) (1.10.07 (for making regulations) and 7.4.08).
11.   Ceased to have effect by WRA 2007 s35(3) (7.4.08).
12.   Amended by SPCA s11 and Sch 1 para 3 (2.7.02 (for making regulations) and 7.4.03).
13.   Amended by WRA 2007 s28 and Sch 3 para 10(4) (27.10.08).
14.   Amended by WRA 2012 Sch 9 para 9 (8.4.13).
15.   Amended by WRA 2012 s31 and Sch 2 para 5 (25.1.13).

Modifications

Subsection (3) ceased to have effect by s35(3) Welfare Reform Act 2007 from 7 April 2008, save for the transitional and savings provisions in the Welfare Reform Act 2007 (Commencement No.4, and Savings and Transitional Provisions) Order 2007 No.2872 (see p1239 of the 23rd edition).

General Note

This enables the making of regulations in relation to the administration of claims and payments for HB and various other benefits.

For the authority's powers to treat claims not made in the required manner as valid, see reg 83 HB Regs and reg 64 HB(SPC) Regs.

Analysis

Paragraph (1)

By subs (2)(e), this subsection applies to HB. The list below refers to the lettered subparagraphs and which regulations, broadly speaking, are made under the powers given by the subparagraph.

(a)   See HB Regs regs 82 and 83 and HB(SPC) regs 63 and 64.
(b)   See HB Regs reg 83(12) and HB(SPC) Regs reg 64(1).
(c)   See HB Regs reg 83(10) and HB(SPC) Regs reg 64(11).
(d)   See HB Regs reg 83(10) and HB(SPC) Regs reg 64(11).
(e)   This power is not relevant to HB. See paras 3 and 4 of Sch 7 of the CSPSSA 2000 for the regulation-making powers for revisions and supersessions.
(f)   This power does not appear to have been exercised.
(g)   See HB Regs reg 82(2) to (6) and HB(SPC) Regs reg 63(2) to (6).
(h)   See HB Regs reg 86 and HB(SPC) Regs reg 67 and see paragraph (3) below.
(hh)   See HB Regs reg 86 and HB(SPC) Regs reg 67.
(i)   See HB Regs regs 91, 94 and 97 and HB(SPC) Regs reg 72, 75, 77 and 78.
(j)   See HB Regs regs 86 and 88 and HB(SPC) Regs 67 and 69.
(k)   See HB Regs reg 76 and HB(SPC) Regs 57.
(l)   See HB Regs reg 80(7) and HB(SPC) Regs reg 61(6).
(m)   This power does not appear to have been exercised.
(p)   See HB Regs regs 95 and 96 and HB(SPC) Regs reg 76 and 77. Note also subs (6).
(q)   See HB Regs reg 97 and HB(SPC) Regs reg 78.
(r)   See HB Regs reg 93 and HB(SPC) Regs reg 74.

Paragraphs (2A), (2B) and (2C)

These give power to make the provisions for a rent officer to require information: see the Rent Officers (Housing Benefit Functions) Order 1997 and the Rent Officers (Housing Benefit Functions) (Scotland) Order 1997 on p879 and p909. The power was formerly in para (3).

Paragraph (6)

The amendment made by the Housing Act 1996 removes any doubts about whether reg 93(1) HB Regs 1987 (now reg 95(1) HB Regs and reg 76(1) HB(SPC) Regs) was validly made under subs (1)(p), which only refers to circumstances in which payments of HB *may* be made, not circumstances when they *shall* be made to a third party. The amendment has retrospective effect.

Council tax benefits

[⁸ Regulations about council tax benefits administration 6.]

Amendments

1.   Substituted by LGFA Sch 9 para 12(1)(a) (1.4.93).
2.   Repealed by LGFA Sch 9 para 12(1)(b) and Sch 14 (1.4.93).
3.   Repealed by LGFA Sch 9 para 12(1)(c) and Sch 14 (1.4.93).
4.   Substituted by LGFA Sch 9 para 12(2) (1.4.93).
5.   Substituted by LGFA Sch 9 para 12(3) (1.4.93).
6.   Inserted by CSPSS Act 2000 Sch 7 para 21(2) (2.7.01).
7.   Repealed by SSA 1998 s86 (2), Sch 8 (2.7.01).
8.   Repealed by WRA 2012 s147 and Sch 14 part 1 (1.4.13).

Abolition of council tax benefit: savings and transitional provisions
Until CTB was abolished (from 1 April 2013) and help with payment of council tax was localised, s6 gave similar powers to make regulations in relation to CTB as are available under s5 in relation to the benefits listed in s5(2). For savings and transitional provisions, see arts 9 and 10 Welfare Reform Act 2012 (Commencement No.8 and Savings and Transitional Provisions) Order 2013 SI No.358. See Parts 4 and 5 of this book for the council tax reduction schemes.

Relationship between [⁴] benefits

7.–(1)   Regulations may provide for a claim for one relevant benefit to be treated, either in the alternative or in addition, as a claim for any other relevant benefit that may be prescribed.

(2)   Regulations may provide for treating a payment made or right conferred by virtue of regulations–
  (a)   under s5(1)(r) above; or
  [³ (b)]
as made or conferred on account of any relevant benefit that is subsequently awarded or paid.

(3)   For the purposes of [² subsection (1)] above relevant benefits are–
  (a)   any benefit to which section 5 above applies; [⁴]
  [⁴ (b)]]].

Definition
"prescribe" – see s191.

Amendment
  1.   Substitution made by LGFA Sch 9 para 13 (1.4.93).
  2.   Amended by WRA 2012 s33 and Sch 3 para 5 (1.4.13).
  3.   Repealed by WRA 2012 Sch 14 Part 11 (1.4.13).
  4.   Repealed by WRA 2012 s147 and Sch 14 part 1 (1.4.13).

Modification
Section 7(2) was repealed by WRA 2012 s147 and Sch 14 part 1 on 1.4.13 in so far as it related to CTB.

General Note
For an example of regulations made under subs (2), see reg 93 HB Regs (on p571). Under s1, there is no power to treat a claim for HB as a claim for any other benefit, or *vice versa*. However, the Secretary of State retains a power under reg 4(1) Social Security (Claims and Payments) Regulations 1987 to treat any written claim sent to her/him as being sufficient in the circumstances. So if a claimant mistakenly claims HB instead of help with housing costs with IS, income-based JSA, income-related ESA or PC and the HB claim was made through the DWP, it might be possible to ask the Secretary of State to exercise discretion to treat that as a claim for help with housing costs.

Sharing of functions as regards certain claims and information

7A.–(1)   Regulations may, for the purpose of supplementing the persons or bodies to whom claims for relevant benefits may be made, make provision–
  (a)   as regards housing benefit or council tax benefit, for claims for that benefit to be made to–
    (i)   a Minister of the Crown, or
    (ii)   a person providing services to a Minister of the Crown;
  (b)   as regards any other relevant benefit, for claims for that benefit to be made to–
    (i)   a local authority,
    (ii)   a person providing services to a local authority, or
    (iii)   a person authorised to exercise any function of a local authority relating to housing benefit or council tax benefit.
  [² (c)   as regards any relevant benefit, for claims for that benefit to be made to–
    (i)   a county council in England,
    (ii)   a person providing services to a county council in England, or
    (iii)   a person authorised to exercise any function a county council in England has under this section.]

(2) Regulations may make provision for or in connection with–

(a) the forwarding by a relevant authority of–

    (i) claims received by virtue of any provision authorised by subsection (1) above, and

    (ii) information or evidence supplied in connection with making such claims (whether supplied by persons making the claims or by other persons);

(b) the receiving and forwarding by a relevant authority of information or evidence relating to social security [¹ or work] matters supplied by, or the obtaining by a relevant authority of such information or evidence from–

    (i) persons making, or who have made, claims for a relevant benefit, or

    (ii) other persons in connection with such claims, including information or evidence not relating to the claims or benefit in question;

(c) the recording by a relevant authority of information or evidence relating to social security [¹ or work] matters supplied to, or obtained by, the authority and the holding by the authority of such information or evidence (whether as supplied or obtained or as recorded);

(d) the giving of information or advice with respect to social security [¹ or work] matters by a relevant authority to persons making, or who have made, claims for a relevant benefit.

[² (e) the verification by a relevant authority of information or evidence supplied to or obtained by the authority in connection with a claim for or an award of a relevant benefit.]

(3) In paragraphs (b) [², (d) and (e)] of subsection (2) above–

(a) references to claims for a relevant benefit are to such claims whether made as mentioned in subsection [² (1)(a), (b) or (c)] above or not; and

(b) references to persons who have made such claims include persons to whom awards of benefit have been made on the claims.

(4) Regulations under this section may make different provision for different areas.

(5) Regulations under any other enactment may make such different provision for different areas as appears to the Secretary of State expedient in connection with any exercise by regulations under this section of the power conferred by subsection (4) above.

(6) In this section–

(a) "benefit" includes child support or a war pension (any reference to a claim being read, in relation to child support, as a reference to an application under the Child Support Act 1991 for a maintenance assessment);

(b) "local authority" means an authority administering housing benefit or council tax benefit;

[² (c) "relevant authority" means–

    (i) a Minister of the Crown,

    (ii) a local authority;

    (iii) a county council in England;

    (iv) a person providing services to a person mentioned in sub-paragraphs (i) to (iii);

    (v) a person authorised to exercise any function of a local authority relating to housing benefit or council tax benefit;

    (vi) a person authorised to exercise any function a county council in England has under this section;]

(d) "relevant benefit" means housing benefit, council tax benefit or any other benefit prescribed for the purposes of this section;

[¹ (e) "social security or work matters" means matters relating to–

    (i) social security, child support or war pensions, or

    (ii) employment or training;]

Commencement

11.11.99: see s89(4)(a) WRPA.

Amendments

1.   Amended by the Employment Act 2002 Sch 7 para 12 (24.11.02).

2.   Amended by WRA 2007 s41(2) (3.7.07).

Modification
> Section 7A(1)-(5) was repealed by WRA 2012 s147 and Sch 14 part 1 on 1.4.13 in so far as it related to CTB.

General Note
> This is another provision that enabled the implementation of the ONE schemes (see p29) and their successors. It gave power to make regulations enabling such offices to receive claims for all benefits, to receive, forward and supply information to offices where claims were adjudicated. Note there are no longer any ONE offices.
>
> Since 3 July 2007, it has enabled claims for HB to be made to a county council: subs (1)(c). Note: this only applies in England and only if the local authority has arranged for claims to be received at the county council's offices: reg 83(4)(g) HB Regs and reg 64(5)(g) HB(SPC) Regs.

Use of social security information

7B.–(1)   A relevant authority may use for a relevant purpose any social security information which it holds.

(2)   Regulations may make provision as to the procedure to be followed by a relevant authority for the purposes of any function it has relating to the administration of a specified benefit if the authority holds social security information which–

(a)   is relevant for the purposes of anything which may or must be done by the authority in connection with a claim for or an award of the benefit, and

(b)   was used by another relevant authority in connection with a claim for or an award of a different specified benefit or was verified by that other authority in accordance with regulations under section 7A(2)(e) above.

(3)   A relevant purpose is anything which is done in relation to a claim which is made or which could be made for a specified benefit if it is done for the purpose of–

(a)   identifying persons who may be entitled to such a benefit;

(b)   encouraging or assisting a person to make such a claim;

(c)   advising a person in relation to such a claim.

(4)   Social security information means–

(a)   information relating to social security, child support or war pensions;

(b)   evidence obtained in connection with a claim for or an award of a specified benefit.

(5)   A specified benefit is a benefit which is specified in regulations for the purposes of this section.

(6)   Expressions used in this section and in section 7A have the same meaning in this section as in that section.

(7)   This section does not affect any power which exists apart from this section to use for one purpose social security information obtained in connection with another purpose.

Commencement
> 1.10.07: see s41(1) WRA 2007.

General Note
> Reg 5 of the Social Security (Claims and Information) Regulations 2007 SI No.2911 (for which see p1810) provides the definition of "specified benefit" for the purposes of s7B(5). The definition includes HB.

PART II
Adjudication
Housing benefit and council tax benefit

Adjudication

[¹**63.** ...]

Amendment
> 1.   Repealed by SSA 1998 s86(2) and Sch 8 (18.10.99).

General Note
> This was the enabling section for most of the regulations concerned with HB and CTB adjudication. See now s34 SSA 1998 on p106 and Sch 7 CSPSSA on p138.

PART III
Recovery of benefit payments

Deduction from benefit

71ZC.–(1)   An amount recoverable from a person under section 71ZB may be recovered by deducting the amount from payments of prescribed benefit.

Commencement

1.7.12 to insert s71ZC(1) for the purpose of prescribing the benefits from which deductions can be made in order to recover the penalties; 1.10.12 to insert s71ZC(1) for the purpose of enabling recovery of the penalities to take place by deduction from benefit (SI 2012 No.1246).

General Note

This section and ss71ZD and 71ZE are, in the main, concerned with recovery of overpayments of UC, JSA, ESA, and housing credit under the State Pension Credit Act 2002; and they allow for those overpayments to be recovered by deduction from prescribed benefits (s71ZC), deduction from earnings (s71ZD), and by civil action through the courts (s71ZE). However, by virtue of ss115B(4A), 115C(5) and (6) and 115D(5), those three methods of recovery also apply to local authorities recovering the "penalties" under ss115B, 115C and 115D of this Act.

Deduction from earnings

71ZD.–(1)   Regulations may provide for amounts recoverable under section 71ZB to be recovered by deductions from earnings.

(2)   In this section "earnings" has such meaning as may be prescribed.

(3)   Regulations under subsection (1) may include provision–

(a)   requiring the person from whom an amount is recoverable ("the beneficiary") to disclose details of their employer, and any change of employer, to the Secretary of State;

(b)   requiring the employer, on being served with a notice by the Secretary of State, to make deductions from the earnings of the beneficiary and to pay corresponding amounts to the Secretary of State;

(c)   as to the matters to be contained in such a notice and the period for which a notice is to have effect;

(d)   as to how payment is to be made to the Secretary of State;

(e)   as to a level of earnings below which earnings must not be reduced;

(f)   allowing the employer, where the employer makes deductions, to deduct a prescribed sum from the beneficiary's earnings in respect of the employer's administrative costs;

(g)   requiring the employer to keep records of deductions;

(h)   requiring the employer to notify the Secretary of State if the beneficiary is not, or ceases to be, employed by the employer;

(i)   creating a criminal offence for non-compliance with the regulations, punishable on summary conviction by a fine not exceeding level 3 on the standard scale;

(j)   with respect to the priority as between a requirement to deduct from earnings under this section and–

(i)   any other such requirement;

(ii)   an order under any other enactment relating to England and Wales which requires deduction from the beneficiary's earnings;

(iii)   any diligence against earnings.

Commencement

1.7.12 (SI 2012 No.1246).

Court action etc

71ZE.–(1)   Where an amount is recoverable under section 71ZB from a person residing in England and Wales, the amount is, if a county court so orders, recoverable–

(a)   under section 85 of the County Courts Act 1984, or

(b)   otherwise as if it were payable under an order of the court.

(2)   Where an amount is recoverable under section 71ZB from a person residing in Scotland, the amount recoverable may be enforced as if it were payable under an extract registered decree arbitral bearing a warrant for execution issued by the sheriff court of any sheriffdom in Scotland.

(3)   Any costs of the Secretary of State in recovering an amount of benefit under this section may be recovered by him as if they were amounts recoverable under section 71ZB.

(4)   In any period after the coming into force of this section and before the coming into force of section 62 of the Tribunals, Courts and Enforcement Act 2007, subsection (1)(a) has effect as if it read "by execution issued from the county court".

Commencement

1.10.12 to insert s71ZE for the purpose of enabling recovery of the penalities to take place by court action (SI 2012 No.1246).

Overpayments and Adjustments of Benefit
Housing benefit

Overpayments of housing benefit

75.–(1)   Except where regulations otherwise provide, any amount of housing benefit [¹ determined in accordance with regulations to have been] paid in excess of entitlement may be recovered [²] either by the Secretary of State or by the authority which paid the benefit.

(2)   Regulations may require such an authority to recover such an amount in such circumstances as may be prescribed.

[³ (3)   An amount recoverable under this section shall be recoverable–

(a)   except in such circumstances as may be prescribed, from the person to whom it was paid; and

(b)   where regulations so provide from such other person (as well as, or instead of, the person to whom it was paid) as may be prescribed.]

(4)   Any amount recoverable under this section may, without prejudice to any other method of recovery, be recovered by deduction from prescribed benefits.

[⁴ (5)   Where an amount paid to a person on behalf of another person is recoverable under this section, subsections (3) and (4) above authorise its recovery from the person to whom it was paid by deduction–

(a)   from prescribed benefits to which he is entitled;

(b)   from prescribed benefits paid to him to discharge (in whole or in part) an obligation owed to him by the person on whose behalf the recoverable amount was paid; or

(c)   from prescribed benefits paid to him to discharge (in whole or in part) an obligation owed to him by any other person.

(6)   Where an amount is recovered as mentioned in paragraph (b) of subsection (5) above, the obligation specified in that paragraph shall in prescribed circumstances be taken to be discharged by the amount of the deduction; and where an amount is recovered as mentioned in paragraph (c) of that subsection, the obligation specified in that paragraph shall in all cases be taken to be so discharged.

(7)   Where any amount recoverable under this section is to be recovered otherwise than by deduction from prescribed benefits–

(a)   if the person from whom it is recoverable resides in England and Wales and the county court so orders, it is recoverable by execution issued from the county court or otherwise as if it were payable under an order of that court; and

(b)   if he resides in Scotland, it may be enforced in the same manner as an extract registered decree arbitral bearing a warrant for execution issued by the sheriff court of any sheriffdom in Scotland.]

[⁵ (8)   Regulations may provide for amounts recoverable under this section to berecovered by deductions from earnings.

(9)   In subsection (8) above "earnings" has such meaning as may be prescribed.

(10)   Regulations under subsection (8) above may include provision–

(a)   requiring the person from whom an amount is recoverable ("the beneficiary") to disclose details of their employer, and any change of employer, to the Secretary of State or the authority which paid the benefit;

(b)   requiring the employer, on being served with a notice by the Secretary of State or the authority which paid the benefit, to make deductions from the earnings of the beneficiary and to pay corresponding amounts to the Secretary of State or that authority;

(c)   as to the matters to be contained in such a notice and the period for which a notice is to have effect;

(d)   as to how payment is to be made to the Secretary of State or the authority which paid the benefit;

(e)   as to a level of earnings below which earnings must not be reduced;

(f)   allowing the employer, where the employer makes deductions, to deduct a prescribed sum from the beneficiary's earnings in respect of the employer's administrative costs;

(g)   requiring the employer to keep records of deductions;

(h)   requiring the employer to notify the Secretary of State or the authority which paid the benefit if the beneficiary is not, or ceases to be, employed by the employer;

(i)   creating a criminal offence for non-compliance with the regulations, punishable on summary conviction by a fine not exceeding level 3 on the standard scale;

(j)   with respect to the priority as between a requirement to deduct from earnings under this section and–
   (i)   any other such requirement;
   (ii)   an order under any other enactment relating to England and Wales which requires deduction from the beneficiary's earnings;
   (iii) any diligence against earnings.]

Amendments

1.   Amended by SSA(F) Act, 1997 Sch 1 para (31.7.97).
2.   Repealed by SSA(F) Act 1997 Sch 2.
3.   Substituted by CSPSSA 2000 s71 (1.10.01).
4.   Amended by SSA(F) Act 1997 s16.
5.   Inserted by WRA 2012 s 106(3) (1.7.12).

Definition

"prescribe" – see s191.

General Note

This section provides for the scheme for recovery of overpaid HB to be provided for by Part 13 of the HB Regs and Part 12 of the HB(SPC) Regs.

As has been made clear by a tribunal of commissioners in *R(H) 3/04* and *R(H) 6/06* (the latter drawing on the Court of Appeal's decision in *B v SSWP* [2005] EWCA Civ 929, [2005] 1 WLR 3796; reported as *R(IS) 9/06*), recoupment of overpayments involves a two-stage process.

First, it is necessary for the local authority to decide that there has been an overpayment and that it is recoverable from someone. Secondly, there is the decision as to whether to enforce recovery and the method used to enforce recovery. Neither of the latter can be subject of challenge before the First-tier Tribunal: *R(H) 6/06* and *R(H) 7/04* respectively.

Note that HB paid under the pre-1988 scheme may be recovered by virtue of s75 and the regulations made thereunder: Sch 10 para 4(3). Note the effect of s68 Welfare Reform and Pensions Act 1999 on the recoverability of certain payments.

In refusing permission to appeal in *KP v Royal Borough of Kensington and Chelsea* [2014] UKUT 393 (AAC), Judge Wikeley ruled that a criminal court's imposition of a compensation order under the Powers of Criminal Courts (Sentencing) Act 2000 did not act to cap the maximum amount of HB that a local authority can recover under s75 SSAA 1992, and so nothing in the compensation order acted to prohibit the local authority from seeking to recover the balance of the overpayment under s75. In so doing, Judge Wikeley followed *CSB 392/1985* and *CIS 683/1994*.

Guidance has been issued to local authorities on overpayments in the form of the Housing Benefit Overpayments Guide (see www.gov.uk/government/publications/housing-benefit-overpayments-guide) and

Housing Benefit Overpayment Recovery Good Practice (see www.gov.uk/government/publications/housing-benefit-overpayment-recovery-good-practice).

Analysis

Subsection (1): The right to recover overpayments

This provides the basic power to prescribe the circumstances when an overpayment is recoverable in Part 13 of the HB Regs and Part 12 of the HB(SPC) Regs. There can be no recovery of HB by an authority unless a valid determination has been made that there is a recoverable overpayment. See the Analysis to reg 90 HB Regs on p565 regarding the validity of decisions. Note that subs (1) has not been amended by CSPSSA to refer to it being "decided" rather than "determined" that an overpayment is recoverable. This forms the basis of the decision of the tribunal of commissioners in *R(H) 3/04* that a right to appeal against an overpayment decision arises under Sch 7 para 6(6) CSPSSA rather than para 6(1). This, however, can cause its own difficulties: see the Analyses to Sch 7 paras 1 and 6 CSPSSA on p140 and p145.

Subsection (2): Required to recover

Where an interim payment on account proves to be excessive and the claimant continues to be entitled to HB, the authority must reduce the continuing payments to recover the overpayment: reg 93(3) HB Regs (reg 76(3) HB(SPC) Regs). Apart from that situation, as yet there are no circumstances where an authority is *required* by the Regulations to recover an overpayment.

Discretion to recover

In all other cases, the authority has a discretion as to whether to exercise its right of recovery, though the subsidy rules provide a strong incentive. Such a decision can encompass whether to recover all or part of the overpayment and the period over which it is to be recovered.

It is now clear from the tribunal of commissioners decision in *R(H) 6/06* and the Court of Appeal's decision in *B v SSWP* [2005] EWCA Civ 929, [2005] 1 WLR 3796; reported as *R(IS) 9/06* that, whatever may have been said in *R(H) 3/04*, a local authority has a general discretion as to whether to recover an overpayment of benefit which has been found to be recoverable; but that decision is not appealable. However, it must be remembered that all other overpayment decisions (ie, has there in fact been an overpayment, is it recoverable, and from whom is it recoverable) are all appealable: see further below and Part 13 of the HB Regs.

Like all discretionary powers, the authority must consider the circumstances of each individual case. If an authority fails to exercise its discretion in recovering overpayments, its decision to recover an overpayment may be vulnerable to judicial review.

It is impossible to compile a list of the matters that an authority may need to consider, but they will commonly include: the moral culpability of the person from whom recovery is sought, the effect of recovery on her/his life, the effect of recovery on her/his family, the likelihood of the claimant losing her/his accommodation and the possible resulting financial burden on the authority, and the cost-effectiveness of recovery. It is probably also legitimate for the authority to have regard to the financial implications of non-recovery of the overpayment: see eg, *R v Brent LBC HBRB ex p Connery* (1989) 22 HLR 40 at 44, QBD. However, this, like any other factor, cannot be treated as determinative. Financial or hardship grounds will be the usual factors which are taken into account, and terminal illness, senility or low intelligence and severe medical conditions might lead to non-recovery.

The authority may have a policy on recovery, but it must be sufficiently flexible to enable each case to be examined on its merits. If it is not, it will be vulnerable to challenge on judicial review. Policies that recovery will always be made or always be made from specified categories of claimants are unlawful.

Subsection (3): From whom recoverable?

See reg 101 HB Regs for the circumstances as to when an overpayment may be recoverable from persons other than those to whom benefit was paid. Section 75(3) is wide enough to fix recoverability on a landlord's agent if the overpaid benefit was paid to that agent, notwithstanding that, as an agent, s/he may have accounted to her/his principal (ie, the landlord) for all or part of the sum: *R(H) 10/07*. This analysis was taken further in *Walsall BC v GP Ltd and others* [2009] UKUT 247 (AAC); [2010] AACR 16, where it was held that the words "the person to whom" benefit was paid in s75(3)(a) did not require that only one person had had benefit paid to them and were wide enough to allow an overpayment to be legally recoverable from a landlord and their agent, as well as the claimant. By way of contrast, as there is no such thing as a joint claim for couples for HB (*CH 3817/2004*), where a couple is involved, an overpayment will only be recoverable from the claimant if it has been specifically decided that the overpayment is (also) recoverable from the claimants partner: reg 3(1)(d) D&A Regs and *CH 3622/2006*. Note also, in what the Upper Tribunal judge described as a provisional view, the perspective in *DL v Liverpool City Council* [2009] UKUT 176 (AAC) that, because s75(3)(a) refers to an amount of HB being recoverable "from the person to whom it was paid", the section does not extend to make recoverable payments of HB made to a claimant's rent account after her/his death.

The approach to s75(3) was given extensive consideration in *R(H) 6/06*. The tribunal of commissioners said that s75(3)(b):

> "requires that any regulation made under s75(3)(b) should specify whether a prescribed person is jointly liable with the person to whom the payment was made or is liable instead of that person. Under this construction the words in parentheses have a purpose. The construction is consistent with s75(3)(a) because, where the Secretary of State makes regulations providing that an overpayment is recoverable from a prescribed person

instead of the person to whom it was made, he is, in effect, providing for additional, but defined, circumstances in which the person to whom the payment was made is not liable to repay an overpayment. The circumstances are defined by the terms in which the prescribed person is defined or by the circumstances in respect of which he is prescribed (see s189(4)). This construction is also consistent with para 6(6) of Schedule 7, which provides a right of appeal to a tribunal in terms that do not limit it to points of law, because all issues arising under regulations made under s75(3) as to from whom an overpayment is recoverable are justiciable. If the Secretary of State makes regulations having the effect that an overpayment is recoverable from a prescribed person as well as the person to whom it is made, the non-justiciable choice as to from which of them the overpayment should actually be recovered falls to be made by the local authority at the stage of enforcing the right of recovery and so is not within the scope of the right of appeal".

It therefore concluded:

"under the legislation in force from 1 October 2001 to 9 April 2006, an overpayment of housing benefit is always recoverable from any person within the scope of regulation 101(2) as well as, if different, the person to whom the overpayment was made, except where regulation 101(1) applies in which case it is recoverable only from any person within the scope of regulation 101(2). No non-justiciable issues fall within the scope of the right of appeal and so there is no longer any need to apply *R(H) 3/04* and construe that right as being limited to points of law."

So the only appealable point (apart from whether there has in fact been an overpayment and whether it is recoverable) under s73(3) and reg 101 HB Regs 1987 is whether the person does in fact fall within reg 101. Once that point has been finally decided, *R(H) 6/06* makes it clear that no appeal right attaches to the enforcement decision of the local authority as against whom the recoverable overpayment should actually be recovered from.

Subsections (4) to (10): Methods of recovery

These provide for various methods of recovery of HB. Decisions as to what method of recovery to use are not appealable: *R(H) 7/04*. For recovery by deduction from other benefits, see regs 102 and 105 HB Regs and regs 83 and 86 HB(SPC) Regs. Subs (8) to (10) were introduced by s105 of the Welfare Reform Act 2012 and for the first time enable local authorities to effect recovery of overpayments of HB directly by way of deductions from earnings, without the need to apply to court for an attachment of earnings order. The detailed provision is set out in the Social Security (Overpayments and Recovery) Regulations 2013 (see p1840).

Subs (5), (6) and (7) were introduced by the 1997 Act. Subs (5) expands the scope for recovery by deduction from other benefits to include benefits paid on behalf of others to people from whom recovery is sought. The principal use of this power will be directed at recovery from landlords by deduction of HB paid direct in respect of other tenants. Subs (6) makes provision for the consequences of such recovery. See the Analysis to HB Regs regs 95 and 102 on p574 and p597.

Subs (7) allows authorities to use county court and sheriff court procedures for registration of the overpayment as a debt without having to bring an action against the person from whom recovery is sought. For convenience, further details are given in the Analysis to HB Regs reg 102 on p597.

Council tax benefit

Excess benefit

76.–(1)   Regulations may make provision as to any case where a [¹ billing authority] or a [⁵ local authority in Scotland] has allowed a [¹ council tax benefit] to a person and the amount allowed exceeds the amount to which he is entitled in respect of the benefit.

(2)   [² . . .] The regulations may provide that–

(a)   a sum equal to the excess shall be due from the person concerned to the authority (whatever the form the benefit takes);

(b)   any liability under any provision included under paragraph (a) above shall be met by such method mentioned in subsection (3) below as is prescribed as regards the case concerned, or by such combination or two or all three of the methods as is prescribed as regards the case concerned.

(3)   The methods are–

(a)   payment by the person concerned;

(b)   addition to any amount payable in respect of [³ council tax;]

(c)   deduction from prescribed benefits.

[⁴ (4)-(5) . . .]

(6)   In a case where the regulations provide that a sum or part of a sum is to be paid, and the sum or part is not paid on or before such day as may be prescribed, the regulations may provide that the sum or part shall be recoverable in a court of competent jurisdiction.

[⁴ (7)   . . .]

(8)   The regulations may provide that they are not to apply as regards any case falling within a prescribed category.

Definitions
"billing authority" – see s191.
"income-related benefit" – see s191.
"charge payer" – in subs (4), see Subs (7).

Amendments
1.   Substitutions by LGFA Sch 9 para 15(1) (1.4.93).
2.   Repealed by LGFA Sch 9 para 15(2) and Sch 14 (1.4.93).
3.   Substituted by LGFA Sch 9 para 15(3) (1.4.93).
4.   Repealed by LGFA Sch 9 para 15(4) and Sch 14 (1.4.93).
5.   Substituted by Local Government etc. (Scotland) Act 1994 Sch 13 para 175(3) (1.4.96).

General Note
This section deals with overpayments of CTB. An overpayment of CTB is termed an 'excess payment'. CTB was abolished on 1 April 2013 for commentary to this provision, see p45 of the 25th edition.

Shortfall in benefit

77.–(1)   Regulations may make provision as to any case where a [¹ billing authority] or a [² local authority in Scotland] has allowed [¹ council tax benefit] to a person and the amount allowed is less than the amount to which he is entitled in respect of the benefit.

Definition
"billing authority" – see s191.

Amendments
1.   Substituted by LGFA Sch 9 para 16(2) and Sch 14 (1.4.93).
2.   Substituted by Local Government etc (Scotland) Act 1994 Sch 13 para 175(3) (1.4.96).

General Note
See reg 79 CTB Regs and reg 64 CTB(SPC) Regs on p744 and p1006 of the 25th edition.

PART VI
Enforcement

General Note on Part VI
Part VI of the Act deals with specific criminal sanctions for abuse of the benefits system. The offences created apply to HB as well as benefits paid by the Secretary of State, and offences may be prosecuted by the local authority: see ss116, 116ZA and 116A.

Part VI has been subject to amendment since 1992 by no less than 15 different statutes. The result is a bloated, incoherent set of provisions. The description given by the former Law Lord, Lord Brightman, of Part VI as being a "drafting quagmire" (*Hansard* (HL) vol 623 col 338) may be thought to be flattering.

This repeated amending has been a direct product of the priority given by successive governments to investigating and combating social security fraud. There have been two Acts of Parliament specifically directed towards this issue: the Social Security Administration (Fraud) Act 1997 and the Social Security Fraud Act 2001. The 1997 Act was rushed through Parliament shortly before dissolution for the 1997 General Election amongst competition between the two major political parties as to which was "toughest" on benefit fraud. As a result, the measure had cross-party support. Besides widening the scope of the offences in s112 and introducing a new range of offences under s111A with higher penalties, the Act introduced a system of penalties which authorities may offer where prosecution is not thought economical. Part VII of the Act was also substantially recast.

For its part, the 2001 Act significantly expanded the information-seeking powers of local authorities and introduced a new scheme of penalising claimants convicted of more than one offence of benefit fraud. It also reformulated the criminal offences.

Despite the enacting of more serious offences under the Act, the practice has been to continue to prosecute such offences as general offences of dishonesty. In England and Wales, the relevant statute is the Theft Act 1968. A number of offences under that Act may be committed: theft under s1, obtaining property by deception under s15(1), and false accounting under s17(1). As to the last, it has been held that a HB claim form is a document created for accounting purposes: *Osinunga v DPP* (1997) 30 HLR 853 at 856, DC. In Scotland, a claimant could be prosecuted for the common law offences of theft or fraud.

For sentencing guidelines for the more serious offences under ss111A and 112, see *R v Stewart* [1987] 2 All ER 363, CA and *R v Armour* [1997] 2 Cr App R(S) 240, CA. There has been a noticeable toughening in sentencing for social security fraud in recent years.

[¹Authorisations for investigators

109A.–(1)   An individual who for the time being has the Secretary of State's authorisation for the purposes of this Part shall be entitled, for any one or more of the purposes mentioned in subsection (2) below, to exercise any of the powers which are conferred on an authorised officer by sections 109B and 109C below.

(2)   Those purposes are–

(a)   ascertaining in relation to any case whether a benefit is or was payable in that case in accordance with any provision of the relevant social security legislation;

(b)   investigating the circumstances in which any accident, injury or disease which has given rise, or may give rise, to a claim for–

(i)   industrial injuries benefit, or

(ii)   any benefit under any provision of the relevant social security legislation, occurred or may have occurred, or was or may have been received or contracted;

(c)   ascertaining whether provisions of the relevant social security legislation are being, have been or are likely to be contravened (whether by particular persons or more generally);

(d)   preventing, detecting and securing evidence of the commission (whether by particular persons or more generally) of benefit offences.

(3)   An individual has the Secretary of State's authorisation for the purposes of this Part if, and only if, the Secretary of State has granted him an authorisation for those purposes and he is–

(a)   an official of a Government department;

(b)   an individual employed by an authority administering housing benefit or council tax benefit;

(c)   an individual employed by an authority or joint committee that carries out functions relating to housing benefit or council tax benefit on behalf of the authority administering that benefit; or

(d)   an individual employed by a person authorised by or on behalf of any such authority or joint committee as is mentioned in paragraph (b) or (c) above to carry out functions relating to housing benefit or council tax benefit for that authority or committee.

(4)   An authorisation granted for the purposes of this Part to an individual of any of the descriptions mentioned in subsection (3) above–

(a)   must be contained in a certificate provided to that individual as evidence of his entitlement to exercise powers conferred by this Part;

(b)   may contain provision as to the period for which the authorisation is to have effect; and

(c)   may restrict the powers exercisable by virtue of the authorisation so as to prohibit their exercise except for particular purposes, in particular circumstances or in relation to particular benefits or particular provisions of the relevant social security legislation.

(5)   An authorisation granted under this section may be withdrawn at any time by the Secretary of State.

(6)   Where the Secretary of State grants an authorisation for the purposes of this Part to an individual employed by a local authority, or to an individual employed by a person who carries out functions relating to housing benefit or council tax benefit on behalf of a local authority–

(a)   the Secretary of State and the local authority shall enter into such arrangements (if any) as they consider appropriate with respect to the carrying out of functions conferred on that individual by or in connection with the authorisation granted to him; and

(b)   the Secretary of State may make to the local authority such payments (if any) as he thinks fit in respect of the carrying out by that individual of any such functions.

(7)   The matters on which a person may be authorised to consider and report to the Secretary of State under section 139A below shall be taken to include the carrying out by

any such individual as is mentioned in subsection (3)(b) to (d) above of any functions conferred on that individual by virtue of any grant by the Secretary of State of an authorisation for the purposes of this Part.

(8)   The powers conferred by sections 109B and 109C below shall be exercisable in relation to persons holding office under the Crown and persons in the service of the Crown, and in relation to premises owned or occupied by the Crown, as they are exercisable in relation to other persons and premises.

Commencement

1.11.00: see CSPSSA Sch 6 para 2 and 2001 SI No 1252.

Modification

Section 109A(3)(b-(d), (6) and (7) was repealed by WRA 2012 s147 and Sch 14 part 1 on 1.4.13 in so far as they related to CTB.

General Note

The powers introduced by CSPSSA extended the powers of fraud inspectors. Section 109A deals with authorisation of officers acting on behalf of the Secretary of State. It permits officers employed by the local authority to act both on behalf of the Secretary of State or the local authority employing her/him. Note, however, the important restrictions in subs (3) and (4). Subs (3) restricts the identity of people who can be granted a certificate to act as an inspector, and subs (4) gives power to restrict the scope of a certificate.

By subs (7) and (8), the Secretary of State may authorise inspectors to look into local authorities' administration of the HB scheme for the purposes of Pt VIII.

See reg 2 Social Security (Local Authority Investigations and Prosecutions) Regulations 2008 SI No.463 on p1821 for situations in which an authority can proceed for a purpose mentioned in subs (2)(a), (c) or (d); broadly the authorisation must relate to one or more of specified benefits and the authority must have commenced, in relation to a particular case, an investigation for a purpose mentioned in s110A(2).

Power to require information

109B.–(1)   An authorised officer who has reasonable grounds for suspecting that a person–

(a)   is a person falling within subsection (2) [¹ or (2A)] below, and

(b)   has or may have possession of or access to any information about any matter that is relevant for any one or more of the purposes mentioned in section 109A(2) above,

may, by written notice, require that person to provide all such information described in the notice as is information of which he has possession, or to which he has access, and which it is reasonable for the authorised officer to require for a purpose so mentioned.

(2)   The persons who fall within this subsection are–

(a)   any person who is or has been an employer or employee within the meaning of any provision made by or under the Contributions and Benefits Act;

(b)   any person who is or has been a self-employed earner within the meaning of any such provision;

(c)   any person who by virtue of any provision made by or under that Act falls, or has fallen, to be treated for the purposes of any such provision as a person within paragraph (a) or (b) above;

(d)   any person who is carrying on, or has carried on, any business involving the supply of goods for sale to the ultimate consumers by individuals not carrying on retail businesses from retail premises;

(e)   any person who is carrying on, or has carried on, any business involving the supply of goods or services by the use of work done or services performed by persons other than employees of his;

(f)   any person who is carrying on, or has carried on, an agency or other business for the introduction or supply, to persons requiring them, of persons available to do work or to perform services;

(g)   any local authority acting in their capacity as an authority responsible for the granting of any licence;

(h)   any person who is or has been a trustee or manager of a personal or occupational pension scheme;

(i)   any person who is or has been liable to make a compensation payment or a payment to the Secretary of State under section 6 of the Social Security (Recovery of Benefits) Act 1997 (payments in respect of recoverable benefits);

[¹³ (ia) a person of a prescribed description;] and

(j)   the servants and agents of any such person as is specified in any of paragraphs (a) to [¹³ (ia)] above.

[² (2A)   The persons who fall within this subsection are–

(a)   any bank;

[⁵ (aa) the Director of National Savings;]

(b)   any person carrying on a business the whole or a significant part of which consists in the provision of credit (whether secured or unsecured) to members of the public;

[⁶ (c) any insurer;]

(d)   any credit reference agency (within the meaning given by section 145(8) of the Consumer Credit Act 1974 (c. 39));

(e)   any body the principal activity of which is to facilitate the exchange of information for the purpose of preventing or detecting fraud;

(f)   any person carrying on a business the whole or a significant part of which consists in the provision to members of the public of a service for transferring money from place to place;

(g)   any water undertaker or sewerage undertaker, [¹⁰ Scottish Water or any local authority which is to collect charges by virtue of an order under section 37 of the Water Industry (Scotland) Act 2002 (asp 3);]

[⁶ (h) any person who;

    (i)   is the holder of a licence under section 7 of the Gas Act 1986 (c. 44) to convey gas through pipes, or

    (ii)   is the holder of a licence under section 7A(1) of that Act to supply gas through pipes;]

(i)   any person who (within the meaning of the Electricity Act 1989 (c. 29)) distributes or supplies electricity;]

(j)   any person who provides a telecommunications service;

(k)   any person conducting any educational establishment or institution;

(l)   any body the principal activity of which is to provide services in connection with admissions to educational establishments or institutions;

(m)   the Student Loans Company;

(n)   any servant or agent of any person mentioned in any of the preceding paragraphs.

(2B)   Subject to the following provisions of this section, the powers conferred by this section on an authorised officer to require information from any person by virtue of his falling within subsection (2A) above shall be exercisable for the purpose only of obtaining information relating to a particular person identified (by name or description) by the officer.

(2C)   An authorised officer shall not, in exercise of those powers, require any information from any person by virtue of his falling within subsection (2A) above unless it appears to that officer that there are reasonable grounds for believing that the identified person to whom it relates is–

(a)   a person who has committed, is committing or intends to commit a benefit offence; or

(b)   a person who (within the meaning of Part 7 of the Contributions and Benefits Act) is a member of the family of a person falling within paragraph (a) above.

(2D)   Nothing in subsection (2B) or (2C) above shall prevent an authorised officer who is an official of a Government department and whose authorisation states that his authorisation applies for the purposes of this subsection from exercising the powers conferred by this section for obtaining from–

(a)   a water undertaker or [¹⁰ Scottish Water,]

(b)   any person who (within the meaning the Gas Act 1986) supplies gas conveyed through pipes,

(c)   any person who (within the meaning of the Electricity Act 1989) supplies electricity conveyed by distribution systems, or

(d)   any servant or agent of a person mentioned in any of the preceding paragraphs,

any information which relates exclusively to whether and in what quantities water, gas or electricity are being or have been supplied to residential premises specified or described in the notice by which the information is required.

(2E)   The powers conferred by this section shall not be exercisable for obtaining from any person providing a telecommunications service any information other than information which (within the meaning of section 21 of the Regulation of Investigatory Powers Act 2000 (c. 23)) is communications data but not traffic data.

(2F)   Nothing in subsection (2B) or (2C) above shall prevent an authorised officer from exercising the powers conferred by this section for requiring information, from a person who provides a telecommunications service, about the identity and postal address of a person identified by the authorised officer solely by reference to a telephone number or electronic address used in connection with the provision of such a service.]

(3)   The obligation of a person to provide information in accordance with a notice under this section shall be discharged only by the provision of that information, at such reasonable time and in such form as may be specified in the notice, to the authorised officer who–

(a)   is identified by or in accordance with the terms of the notice; or

(b)   has been identified, since the giving of the notice, by a further written notice given by the authorised officer who imposed the original requirement or another authorised officer.

(4)   The power of an authorised officer under this section to require the provision of information shall include a power to require the production and delivery up and (if necessary) creation of, or of copies of or extracts from, any such documents containing the information as may be specified or described in the notice imposing the requirement.

[³ (5)   No one shall be required under this section to provide–

(a)   any information that tends to incriminate either himself or, in the case of a person who is [¹¹married or is a civil partner, his spouse or civil partner]; or

(b)   any information in respect of which a claim to legal professional privilege or, in Scotland, confidentiality as between client and professional legal adviser, would be successful in any proceedings;

and for the purposes of this subsection it is immaterial whether the information is in documentary form or not.]

[⁴ (6)   Provision may be made by order–

(a)   adding any person to the list of persons falling within subsection (2A) above;

(b)   removing any person from the list of persons falling within that subsection;

(c)   modifying that subsection for the purpose of taking account of any change to the name of any person for the time being falling within that subsection.

(7)   In this section–

[⁷ "bank" means–

(a)   a person who has permission under [¹² Part 4A] of the Financial Services and Markets Act 2000 to accept deposits;

(b)   an EEA firm of the kind mentioned in paragraph 5(b) of Schedule 3 to that Act which has permission under paragraph 15 of that Schedule (as a result of qualifying for authorisation under paragraph 12 of that Schedule) to accept deposits or other repayable funds from the public; or

(c)   a person who does not require permission under that Act to accept deposits, in the course of his business in the United Kingdom;]

"credit" includes a cash loan or any form of financial accommodation, including the cashing of a cheque;

[⁸ "insurer" means–

(a)   a person who has permission under [¹² Part 4A] of the Financial Services and Markets Act 2000 to effect or carry out contracts of insurance; or

(b)   an EEA firm of the kind mentioned in paragraph 5(d) of Schedule 3 to that Act, which has permission under paragraph 15 of that Schedule (as a result of

qualifying for authorisation under paragraph 12 of that Schedule) to effect or carry out contracts of insurance;]
"residential premises", in relation to a supply of water, gas or electricity, means any premises which–
(a) at the time of the supply were premises occupied wholly or partly for residential purposes, or
(b) are premises to which that supply was provided as if they were so occupied; and
"telecommunications service" has the same meaning as in the Regulation of Investigatory Powers Act 2000 (c. 23).]
[⁹ (7A) The definitions of "bank" and "insurer" in subsection (7) must be read with–
(a) section 22 of the Financial Services and Markets Act 2000;
(b) any relevant order under that section; and
(c) Schedule 2 to that Act.]

Commencement
1.11.00: see CSPSSA Sch 6 para 2 and 2001 SI No 1252.

Amendments
1. Amended by SSFA s1(2) SSFA (30.4.02).
2. Inserted by SSFA s1(2) (30.4.02).
3. Substituted by SSFA s1(3) (30.4.02).
4. Inserted by SSFA s1(4) (26.2.02).
5. Inserted by art 2(a) of SI 2002 No 817 as from 1.4.02.
6. Substituted by art 2(b) to (d) of SI 2002 No 817 as from 1.4.02.
7. Substituted by art 3(a)(i) of SI 2002 No 817 as from 1.4.02.
8. Inserted by art 3(a)(ii) of SI 2002 No 817 as from 1.4.02.
9. Inserted by art 3(b) of SI 2002 No 817 as from 1.4.02.
10. Amended by art 2 and the Sch of SI 2004 No 1822 as from 14.7.04.
11. Amended by CPA s254 and Sch 24 para 64 (5.12.05).
12. Amended by the Financial Services Act 2012 s114(1) and Sch 18 para 74 (1.4.13).
13. Amended by WRA 2012 s110 (17.6.13 for the purpose of making regulations; 1.10.13 for all other purposes).

General Note
The powers of an inspector to require information are expanded significantly by s109B. A written notice is required as a condition precedent to an obligation to provide information: subs (1). Subs (4) enables the information to be required in a form that suits the inspector. The only controls upon information requirements made under subs (2) are that they are limited to information to which a person has access, and that the requirement is reasonable. In the case of any dispute, the latter qualification is likely to prove vital. If, for example, an employee is required to breach some confidence by disclosing information about a colleague, it is unreasonable to require such steps since there are ample powers to require the employer to disgorge the same information. Similarly, if information can only be obtained following undue expense, it may be said to be unreasonable to require it to be furnished. The requirement of reasonableness qualifies the method of provision under subs (4) as well as the requirement to provide the information under subs (1). Thus, even if it would be reasonable to require a person to answer questions, it might be unreasonable to require a person to provide written answers, depending on the situation.

The breadth of the classes of people from whom information may be required under subs (2) is obvious. To take two examples, workers can be required to give information about colleagues, and charities may be required to reveal who is working for them. The Social Security (Persons Required to Provide Information) Regulations 2013 SI No.1510 (on p1856) prescribe the descriptions of people for the purpose of subsection (2)(ia).

Subs (2A) to (2F) vastly expand the range of bodies from which information may be sought. Subs (6) enables amendment of the bodies that may be required to supply information by statutory instrument, which requires an affirmative resolution under s190(1)(aza) SSAA.

There is some limitation in the powers under subs (2A). First, information may only be sought in relation to a specific person: subs (2B). Secondly, there must be "reasonable grounds" to suspect the commission of an offence by that person: subs (2C). Thirdly, the content of communications may not be disclosed to relevant officers but only the fact that communications are being made or the extent of the services provided: subs (2E).

Note that a breach of a duty to provide information under s109B does not of itself constitute an offence under this section. There may, however, be an offence committed under s111. Note also that subs (5) preserves the privilege against self-incrimination, and has now been expanded to cover information which is confidential or covered by legal professional privilege. It is likely that the courts would have implied such a limitation in any event.

Powers of entry

109C.–(1)   An authorised officer shall be entitled, at any reasonable time and either alone or accompanied by such other persons as he thinks fit, to enter any premises which–
(a)   are liable to inspection under this section; and
(b)   are premises to which it is reasonable for him to require entry in order to exercise the powers conferred by this section.

(2)   An authorised officer who has entered any premises liable to inspection under this section may–
(a)   make such an examination of those premises, and
(b)   conduct any such inquiry there, as appears to him appropriate for any one or more of the purposes mentioned in section 109A(2) above.

(3)   An authorised officer who has entered any premises liable to inspection under this section may–
(a)   question any person whom he finds there;
(b)   require any person whom he finds there to do any one or more of the following–
   (i)   to provide him with such information,
   (ii)   to produce and deliver up and (if necessary) create such documents or such copies of, or extracts from, documents, as he may reasonably require for any one or more of the purposes mentioned in section 109A(2) above; and
(c)   take possession of and either remove or make his own copies of any such documents as appear to him to contain information that is relevant for any of those purposes.

(4)   The premises liable to inspection under this section are any premises (including premises consisting in the whole or a part of a dwelling house) which an authorised officer has reasonable grounds for suspecting are–
(a)   premises which are a person's place of employment;
(b)   premises from which a trade or business is being carried on or where documents relating to a trade or business are kept by the person carrying it on or by another person on his behalf;
(c)   premises from which a personal or occupational pension scheme is being administered or where documents relating to the administration of such a scheme are kept by the person administering the scheme or by another person on his behalf;
(d)   premises where a person who is the compensator in relation to any such accident, injury or disease as is referred to in section 109A(2)(b) above is to be found;
(e)   premises where a person on whose behalf any such compensator has made, may have made or may make a compensation payment is to be found.

(5)   An authorised officer applying for admission to any premises in accordance with this section shall, if required to do so, produce the certificate containing his authorisation for the purposes of this Part.

(6)   Subsection (5) of section 109B applies for the purposes of this section as it applies for the purposes of that section.]

Amendment
1.   Substituted by CSPSSA Sch 6 para 2 (2.4.01).

General Note
The powers of authorised officers to enter premises are also extended under s109C. However, there is no power to enter a person's home without consent, unless there are reasonable grounds for suspecting that the home also falls into one of the categories in subs (4). Subs (3) gives powers in relation to making inquiries on premises.

[¹Authorisations by local authorities

110A.–(1)   An individual who for the time being has the authorisation for the purposes of this Part of an authority administering housing benefit or council tax benefit ("a local authority authorisation") shall be entitled, for [⁴ a relevant purpose], to exercise any of the powers which, subject to subsection (8) below, are conferred on an authorised officer by sections 109B and 109C above.

[⁴ (1A) Each of the following is a relevant purpose–
(a) a purpose mentioned in subsection (2) below;
(b) a purpose mentioned in section 109A(2)(a), (c) or (d).
(1B) If the Secretary of State prescribes conditions for the purposes of this section, an authority must not proceed under this section for a purpose mentioned in section 109A(2)(a), (c) or (d) unless any such condition is satisfied.
(1C) An authorisation made for a purpose mentioned in section 109A(2)(a), (c) or (d)–
(a) is subject to such restrictions as may be prescribed;
(b) is not valid in such circumstances as may be prescribed.]
(2) [⁴ The purposes in this subsection] are–
(a) ascertaining in relation to any case whether housing benefit or council tax benefit is or was payable in that case;
(b) ascertaining whether provisions of the relevant social security legislation that relate to housing benefit or council tax benefit are being, have been or are likely to be contravened (whether by particular persons or more generally);
(c) preventing, detecting and securing evidence of the commission (whether by particular persons or more generally) of benefit offences relating to housing benefit or council tax benefit.
(3) An individual has the authorisation for the purposes of this Part of an authority administering housing benefit or council tax benefit if, and only if, that authority have granted him an authorisation for those purposes and he is–
(a) an individual employed by that authority;
(b) an individual employed by another authority or joint committee that carries out functions relating to housing benefit or council tax benefit on behalf of that authority;
(c) an individual employed by a person authorised by or on behalf of–
  (i) the authority in question,
  (ii) any such authority or joint committee as is mentioned in paragraph (b) above,
  to carry out functions relating to housing benefit or council tax benefit for that authority or committee;
(d) an official of a Government department.
(4) Subsection (4) of section 109A above shall apply in relation to a local authority authorisation as it applies in relation to an authorisation under that section.
(5) A local authority authorisation may be withdrawn at any time by the authority that granted it or by the Secretary of State.
(6) The certificate or other instrument containing the grant or withdrawal by any local authority of any local authority authorisation must be issued under the hand of either–
(a) the officer designated under section 4 of the Local Government and Housing Act 1989 as the head of the authority's paid service; or
(b) the officer who is the authority's chief finance officer (within the meaning of section 5 of that Act).
(7) It shall be the duty of any authority with power to grant local authority authorisations to comply with any directions of the Secretary of State as to–
(a) whether or not such authorisations are to be granted by that authority;
(b) the period for which authorisations granted by that authority are to have effect;
(c) the number of persons who may be granted authorisations by that authority at any one time; and
(d) the restrictions to be contained by virtue of subsection (4) above in the authorisations granted by that authority for those purposes.
(8) The powers conferred by sections 109B and 109C above shall have effect in the case of an individual who is an authorised officer by virtue of this section as if those sections had effect–

(a)   with the substitution for every reference to the purposes mentioned in section 109A(2) above of a reference to the purposes mentioned in subsection (2) above; [² . . .]

(b)   with the substitution for every reference to the relevant social security legislation of a reference to so much of it as relates to housing benefit or council tax benefit [³ ; and

(c)   with the omission of section 109B(2D)].

[⁴ but paragraphs (a) and (b) above do not apply in any case where the relevant purpose is as mentioned in subsection (1A)(b) above.]

(9)   Nothing in this section conferring any power on an authorised officer in relation to housing benefit or council tax benefit shall require that power to be exercised only in relation to cases in which the authority administering the benefit is the authority by whom that officer's authorisation was granted.]

Amendments

1.   Substituted by CSPSSA 2000 Sch 6 para 3 (2.4.01).
2.   Amended by SSFA s19 (30.4.02).
3.   Inserted by SSFA s1(5) (30.4.02).
4.   Amended by WRA 2007 s46 (19.2.08 (for making regulations) and 7.4.08).

Modification

Section 110A was repealed by WRA 2012 s147 and Sch 14 part 1 on 1.4.13 in so far as it related to CTB.

General Note

Authorities are given the power to appoint inspectors under s110A. They have the same powers as those granted to the inspectors engaged by the Secretary of State. Note the certification requirements in subs (6). "Issued under the hand of" probably permits a junior officer directly under the supervision of the officers mentioned to sign the authorisation. Note also the power to issue directions in subs (7), a novel feature of the HB scheme. Local authority officers do not acquire any of the preserved powers under s109B(2D) by the back door.

[¹ Power of local authority to require electronic access to information

110AA.–(1)   Subject to subsection (2) below, where it appears to an authority administering housing benefit or council tax benefit–

(a)   that a person falling within section 109B(2A) keeps any electronic records,

(b)   that the records contain or are likely, from time to time, to contain information about any matter that is relevant for any one or more of the purposes mentioned in section 110A(2) above, and

(c)   that facilities exist under which electronic access to those records is being provided, or is capable of being provided, by that person to other persons,

that authority may require that person to enter into arrangements under which authorised officers are allowed such access to those records.

(2)   An authorised officer–

(a)   shall be entitled to obtain information in accordance with arrangements entered into under subsection (1) above only if his authorisation states that his authorisation applies for the purposes of that subsection; and

(b)   shall not seek to obtain any information in accordance with any such arrangements other than information which–

(i)   relates to a particular person; and

(ii)   could be the subject of any such requirement under section 109B above as may be imposed in exercise of the powers conferred by section 110A(8) above.

(3)   The matters that may be included in the arrangements that a person is required to enter into under subsection (1) above may include–

(a)   requirements as to the electronic access to records that is to be made available to authorised officers;

(b)   requirements as to the keeping of records of the use that is made of the arrangements;

(c)   requirements restricting the disclosure of information about the use that is made of the arrangements; and

(d)   such other incidental requirements as the authority in question considers appropriate in connection with allowing access to records to authorised officers.

(4)   An authorised officer who is allowed access in accordance with any arrangements entered into under subsection (1) above shall be entitled to make copies of, and to take extracts from, any records containing information which he is entitled to make the subject of a requirement such as is mentioned in subsection (2)(b) above.

(5)   An authority administering housing benefit or council tax benefit shall not–

(a)   require any person to enter into arrangements for allowing authorised officers to have electronic access to any records; or

(b)   otherwise than in pursuance of a requirement under this section, enter into any arrangements with a person specified in section 109B(2A) above for allowing anyone acting on behalf of the authority for purposes connected with any benefit to have electronic access to any private information contained in any records,

except with the consent of the Secretary of State and subject to any conditions imposed by the Secretary of State by the provisions of the consent.

(6)   A consent for the purposes of subsection (5) may be given in relation to a particular case, or in relation to any case that falls within a particular description of cases.

(7)   In this section "private information", in relation to an authority administering housing benefit or council tax benefit, means any information held by a person who is not entitled to disclose it to that authority except in compliance with a requirement imposed by the authority in exercise of their statutory powers.]

Amendment

1.   Inserted by SSFA s2(2) (30.4.02).

Commencement

1.4.02: SI 2002 No 1222.

Modification

Section 110AA was repealed by WRA 2012 s147 and Sch 14 part 1 on 1.4.13 in so far as it related to CTB.

General Note

Section 110AA enables a local authority to require access to electronic information. Subs (1) and (2) limit the scope of the powers to a similar extent to the powers in ss109B and 110A. By subs (3), there is power to impose requirements as to access, the keeping of records and the maintenance of confidentiality concerning the access arrangements. There is an important limitation in subs (5) to (7) which requires the Secretary of State to give consent for the use of the powers conferred by s110AA and also access agreed with those holding the information to "private information". The definition in subs (7) would cover "personal data" within the meaning of the Data Protection Act 1998 and information which was of a confidential nature so as to attract the protection of the law of breach of confidence.

A refusal to comply with a lawful request is an offence under s111(1)(ab).

Delay, obstruction etc of inspector

111.–(1)   If a person–

(a)   intentionally delays or obstructs an [² authorised officer] in the exercise of any power under this Act [¹ other than an Inland Revenue power];

[³ (ab) refuses or neglects to comply with any requirement under section 109BA or 110AA or with the requirements of any arrangements entered into in accordance with subsection (1) of that section, or]

(b)   refuses or neglects to answer any question or to furnish any information or to produce any document when required to do so under this Act [¹ otherwise than in the exercise of an Inland Revenue power],

he shall be guilty of an offence and liable on summary conviction to a fine not exceeding level 3 on the standard scale.

(2)   Where a person is convicted of an offence under [⁴ subsection (1)(ab) or (b)] above and the refusal or neglect is continued by him after his conviction, he shall be guilty of a further offence and liable on summary conviction to a fine not exceeding £40 for each day on which it is continued.

[¹ (3) and (4)   *[Omitted]*]

Amendments

1.　　Inserted by Transfer of Functions Act 1999 s5 and Sch 5 para 4 as from 1.4.99.
2.　　Amended by SSFA s1(6) (30.4.02).
3.　　Inserted by SSFA s2(3)(a) (30.4.02).
4.　　Amended by SSFA s2(3)(b) (30.4.02).

Modification

Section 111(1)(ab) and (3) amended by WRA 2012 s147 and Sch 14 part 1 on 1.4.13 in so far as they related to CTB.

General Note

Now that local authorities have power to appoint inspectors under s110A, this offence may be committed by anyone who obstructs an inspector or who fails to provide information when required to do so.

Analysis

Subs (1). The offence can only be committed when the inspector is acting within her/his powers. It is implicit in subs (1)(b) that the defendant either refused to answer a question or suppy information or failed to do so properly. A defendant who truthfully stated that s/he could not answer the question (whether because s/he did not know the answer or because there was some privilege in the information or documents) or did not have access to the information or documents does not commit the offence.

　　Subs (2). The fine is calculated on a daily rate between the date of conviction for the offence under subs (1) and the date of conviction under subs (2), not the date that the information is laid for the offence under subs (2): *Grice v Needs* [1980] 1, WLR 45 at 47F–G.

[¹Dishonest representations for the purpose of obtaining benefit etc

111A.–(1)　　If a person dishonestly–

(a)　　makes a false statement or representation; [⁴ or]

(b)　　produces or furnishes, or causes or allows to be produced or furnished, any document or information which is false in a material particular;

[⁵ . . .]

[⁵ . . .]

with a view to obtaining any benefit or other payment or advantage under the [² relevant] social security legislation (whether for himself or for some other person), he shall be guilty of an offence.

[⁶ (1A)　　A person shall be guilty of an offence if–

(a)　　there has been a change of circumstances affecting any entitlement of his to any benefit or other payment or advantage under any provision of the relevant social security legislation;

(b)　　the change is not a change that is excluded by regulations from the changes that are required to be notified;

(c)　　he knows that the change affects an entitlement of his to such a benefit or other payment or advantage; and

(d)　　he dishonestly fails to give a prompt notification of that change in the prescribed manner to the prescribed person.

(1B)　　A person shall be guilty of an offence if–

(a)　　there has been a change of circumstances affecting any entitlement of another person to any benefit or other payment or advantage under any provision of the relevant social security legislation;

(b)　　the change is not a change that is excluded by regulations from the changes that are required to be notified;

(c)　　he knows that the change affects an entitlement of that other person to such a benefit or other payment or advantage; and

(d)　　he dishonestly causes or allows that other person to fail to give a prompt notification of that change in the prescribed manner to the prescribed person.

(1C)　　This subsection applies where–

(a)　　there has been a change of circumstances affecting any entitlement of a person ('the claimant') to any benefit or other payment or advantage under any provision of the relevant social security legislation;

51

(b)   the benefit, payment or advantage is one in respect of which there is another person ('the recipient') who for the time being has a right to receive payments to which the claimant has, or (but for the arrangements under which they are payable to the recipient) would have, an entitlement; and

(c)   the change is not a change that is excluded by regulations from the changes that are required to be notified.

(1D)   In a case where subsection (1C) above applies, the recipient is guilty of an offence if–

(a)   he knows that the change affects an entitlement of the claimant to a benefit or other payment or advantage under a provision of the relevant social security legislation;

(b)   the entitlement is one in respect of which he has a right to receive payments to which the claimant has, or (but for the arrangements under which they are payable to the recipient) would have, an entitlement; and

(c)   he dishonestly fails to give a prompt notification of that change in the prescribed manner to the prescribed person.

(1E)   In a case where that subsection applies, a person other than the recipient is guilty of an offence if–

(a)   he knows that the change affects an entitlement of the claimant to a benefit or other payment or advantage under a provision of the relevant social security legislation;

(b)   the entitlement is one in respect of which the recipient has a right to receive payments to which the claimant has, or (but for the arrangements under which they are payable to the recipient) would have, an entitlement; and

(c)   he dishonestly causes or allows the recipient to fail to give a prompt notification of that change in the prescribed manner to the prescribed person.

(1F)   In any case where subsection (1C) above applies but the right of the recipient is confined to a right, by reason of his being a person to whom the claimant is required to make payments in respect of a dwelling, to receive payments of housing benefit–

(a)   a person shall not be guilty of an offence under subsection (1D) or (1E) above unless the change is one relating to one or both of the following–

    (i)   the claimant's occupation of that dwelling;

    (ii)   the claimant's liability to make payments in respect of that dwelling;

but

(b)   subsections (1D)(a) and (1E)(a) above shall each have effect as if after "knows" there were inserted "or could reasonably be expected to know".

(1G)   For the purposes of subsections (1A) to (1E) above a notification of a change is prompt if, and only if, it is given as soon as reasonably practicable after the change occurs.]

[³...]

(3)   A person guilty of an offence under this section shall be liable–

(a)   on summary conviction, to imprisonment for a term not exceeding six months, or to a fine not exceeding the statutory maximum, or to both; or

(b)   on conviction on indictment, to imprisonment for a term not exceeding seven years, or to a fine, or to both.

(4)   In the application of this section to Scotland, in [⁷ subsections (1) to (1E)] for "dishonestly" substitute "knowingly".]

Amendments

1.   Inserted by s11 of the SSA(F) Act 1997 as from 1.7.97.
2.   Inserted by CSPSSA 2000 s67 (2.4.01).
3.   Repealed by CSPSSA 2000 s85 (2.4.01).
4.   Amended by SSFA s16(1)(a) (18.10.01 and 30.4.02).
5.   Repealed by SSFA ss16(1)(a) and 19 and Sch (18.10.01 and 30.4.02).
6.   Inserted by SSFA s16(1)(b) and (2) (29.9.01 and 18.10.01).
7.   Amended by SSFA s16(1)(c) (18.10.01).

General Note

This section, inserted by s13 Social Security Administration (Fraud) Act 1997 and extensively amended by the Social Security Fraud Act 2001, creates an offence relating to fraudulent acts to complement the offence in s112. At first glance, the two offences appear quite similar in their ambit, but it is clear that this offence is intended to be used in prosecuting more serious offenders. Three factors lead to this conclusion. First, dishonesty must be shown. Secondly, there is a requirement that the act or omission in question must have been done with a view to obtaining benefit (contrast the position under s112). Finally, the offence is triable either way and the maximum penalties are substantially heavier.

No offence may be committed under this section by virtue of any act or omission committed before the section came into force on 1 July 1997: s25(5) of the 1997 Act. There is no equivalent provision in the 2001 Act, but the common law and Art 7 of the European Convention on Human Rights means that the new offences cannot apply to conduct committed before 18 October 2001, when the new provisions were brought into force by SI 2001 No.3551.

Analysis

These offences can all be committed by a "person". That wording will apply to legal as well as natural persons, and so companies and other bodies with legal personality may be charged with the offence: Sch 1 Interpretation Act 1978. Note also s115 SSAA, which provides that officers or members of a body corporate can be charged individually with the offence if the body corporate committed it "with the consent or connivance of" that officer.

Subsection (1)

"dishonestly". The meaning of "dishonesty" in English criminal law is well settled from its use in the Theft Act 1968. It must be shown that the defendant's actions would not have been seen as honest by ordinary people and that the defendant must have been aware of this: *R v Ghosh* [1982] QB 1053 at 1064D-G, CA. It is suggested that the requirement of dishonesty qualifies the whole of the subparagraph that follows. In other words, it is not just necessary for the prosecution to prove that the defendant was dishonest in relation to the act or omission alleged. It must also be shown that there was a dishonest intent to procure payment of benefit. This point is illustrated by the facts in *Barrass v Reeve* [1981] 1 WLR 408, DC. The claimant falsely claimed that he was incapable of work, but asserted that his objective in doing so was to deceive his employer. If he was believed, then that would require his acquittal on a charge under s111A, as he would have been dishonest in making a false statement, but not in relation to obtaining benefit. His dishonesty would not be "with a view" to obtaining benefit. Such a defendant can, however, be prosecuted under s112.

"(a) makes a false statement or representation". Proof of an actual statement is required, though the statement could presumably be oral or written.

"(b) produces or furnishes, or causes or allows to be produced or furnished ....". This is a very wide phrase. "Produces" means to personally hand something over. "Furnishes" has a slightly wider meaning and means that steps have been taken to ensure that the article in question has been handed over. It is questionable whether a defendant who has documents seized by an inspector "furnishes" them. A person "causes" documents or information to be given if s/he participates in the giving of the information. A person "allows" documents or information to be given if s/he passively stands by while the information is given. In the last case, care must be taken to ensure that the requisite dishonest intent is really present in relation to the omission. Mere carelessness or oversight will not suffice.

"any document". This tends to be given a flexible meaning by the courts to include any means by which information is stored: *Grant v Southwestern and County Properties Ltd* [1975] Ch 185 at 197A-F, Ch D. It, therefore, includes things like computer discs.

"with a view to obtaining any benefit". The complete offence is committed even though no benefit was actually paid as a result of the dishonesty, and so a defendant in such a case need not merely be charged with an attempt. All that is required is that the purpose (or one of the purposes) of the dishonesty was to procure payment.

"or other payment". This phrase prevents any argument as to whether any payment made is a payment of benefit. For example, if a landlord conspired with an individual in the HB office to send out two cheques for each claim, it might be arguable that the extra cheque was not "benefit". However, the second cheque would certainly fall within the scope of "other payment".

Subsection (1A)

This deals with dishonest failures to disclose by a claimant. There are four requirements.

(1)   There has been a change of circumstances which has affected entitlement to benefit: para (a). Note that it is necessary that entitlement to benefit *was* affected and not merely that the change might have affected entitlement: *R v Passmore* [2007] EWCA Crim 2053, 18 June, CA. Where this is disputed, it may be necessary to adjourn criminal proceedings pending resolution of the issue through the appeals process.

(2)   The change is not exempted from a disclosure requirement: para (b). See reg 88(3) HB Regs (reg 69(3) HB(SPC) Regs) for the types of information which need not be disclosed.

(3)   The defendant knows that the change affects entitlement: para (c). This requirement is narrowly drawn. It is not enough that the defendant *ought* to have known that the change was relevant. That is clear from the modification made by subs (1F)(b). It must be proven by the prosecution that there was knowledge

on the part of the defendant that there was a requirement to notify: *Gaumont British Distributors Ltd v Henry* [1939] 2 KB 711 at 719, 723, DC. It is suggested that there must have been knowledge at the time that the failure to notify occurred. This could lead to a number of difficult problems. First, it is suggested that where a defendant forgets about the obligation, having previously been aware of it, s/he does not have the requisite knowledge at that moment in time. If, of course, s/he subsequently remembers the duty and fails to notify, then s/he can be charged with the offence for that period of time. Secondly, it seems doubtful whether it can be said that a genuinely ignorant person who did not read the literature given to her/him and did not make any inquiries can be said to know what s/he is required to notify, unless it can be said that there was a deliberate attempt to refrain from seeking information: *Taylor's Central Garages (Exeter) Ltd v Roper* [1951] 115 JP 445 at 449, 450, DC; *Westminister CC v Croyalgrange Ltd* [1986] 1 WLR 674 at 684E, HL. Finally, if a person forms a false view that no disclosure is required, then provided that view is genuinely held, it cannot be said that he "knows" that such disclosure is necessary.

(4)   There is a dishonest failure to disclose promptly. See above on the meaning of "dishonesty". See reg 4 Social Security (Notification of Change of Circumstances) Regulations 2001 for the prescribed manner and person. The notification must be prompt, meaning as soon as reasonably practicable: subs (1G). In Scotland, the requirement "knowingly" is substituted: see subs (4).

Subsection (1B)

This deals with dishonestly allowing another person to omit disclosure. Again there are four requirements. The first three are identical to those in subs (1A)(a), (b) and (c) save that the change of circumstances and knowledge must relate to the effect on the other person's entitlement. "Causes or allows" requires that there must be some sort of implied permission given by the defendant to the person under the duty that s/he should not notify: *R v Chainey* [1914] 1 KB 137 at 142, DC. A person does not "allow" information to be given where s/he is unable to prevent it being given: *Crabtree v Fern Spinning Co Ltd* [1901] 85 LT 549 at 552, DC. So if a person knows that her/his partner is supplying false information or refraining from supplying information but s/he is threatened with violence, s/he does not "allow" that conduct. This issue was revisited by the Court of Appeal in *R v Tilley* [2009] EWCA Crim 1426, where the court said (paras 41–43) that "allowing" must mean something less than "causing" but for the prosecution to succeed it must be able to point to some action that the person could have taken that would have resulted in the other person making the relevant disclosure: simply doing nothing is not enough to establish the offence.

Subsections (1C) to (1F)

These create similar offences relating to those in receipt of benefit who are not claimants. They must be those having a right to receive payments in place of the claimant: see subs (1C)(b). These might be:

(1)   Landlords to whom rent allowance is paid directly: see regs 95 and 96 HB Regs (reg 76 and 77 HB(SPC) Regs).

(2)   Officials appointed to look after the affairs of those unable to act, and others so appointed: see regs 82(2), (3), (5) and 94(2) HB Regs (reg 63(2), (3), (5) and 75(2) HB(SPC) Regs).

(3)   Other people to whom the authority has agreed to pay benefit, notwithstanding that the claimant is capable of managing their affairs: see reg 94(3) HB Regs (reg 75(3) HB(SPC) Regs).

Subs (1D) creates an offence which may be committed by such an individual where the claimant's benefit entitlement is affected and the change is not excluded from notification. Knowledge of the effect of the change and dishonesty in failing to notify must normally be proved, but subs (1F) modifies their effect in relation to landlords in receipt of HB.

First, the relevant change must relate to the claimant's occupation of the dwelling or their liability to make payments. Given that this statute creates a criminal offence, it is suggested that these exceptions must be read narrowly. They cannot, therefore, relate to matters which affect the question of whether there is a legal liability at all or whether the liability falls within reg 9(1) of the HB and the HB(SPC) Regs. They can relate only to the question of whether the claimant is physically in occupation, or the amount of the liability for rent. Secondly, the requirement of knowledge is softened by requiring only proof that the landlord ought reasonably to have known, but given the requirement of dishonesty it seems unlikely that anything short of the landlord shutting his eyes to the obvious will suffice to constitute the criminal offence.

Subs (1E) creates a similar offence to that in subs (1B), and is similarly modified by subs (1F) in relation to landlords in receipt of HB.

False representations for obtaining benefit etc

112.–(1)   If a person for the purpose of obtaining any benefit or other payment under the [⁴ relevant] [³ social security legislation] whether for himself or some other person, or for any other purpose connected with that legislation–

(a)   makes a statement or representation which he knows to be false; or

(b)   produces or furnishes, or knowingly causes or knowingly allows to be produced or furnished, any document or information which he knows to be false in a material particular,

he shall be guilty of an offence.

[⁶(1A)   A person shall be guilty of an offence if–
(a)   there has been a change of circumstances affecting any entitlement of his to any benefit or other payment or advantage under any provision of the relevant social security legislation;
(b)   the change is not a change that is excluded by regulations from the changes that are required to be notified;
(c)   he knows that the change affects an entitlement of his to such a benefit or other payment or advantage; and
(d)   he fails to give a prompt notification of that change in the prescribed manner to the prescribed person.]–
(1B)   A person is guilty of an offence under this section if–
(a)   there has been a change of circumstances affecting any entitlement of another person to any benefit or other payment or advantage under any provision of the relevant social security legislation;
(b)   the change is not a change that is excluded by regulations from the changes that are required to be notified;
(c)   he knows that the change affects an entitlement of that other person to such a benefit or other payment or advantage; and
(d)   he causes or allows that other person to fail to give a prompt notification of that change in the prescribed manner to the prescribed person.
(1C)   In a case where subsection (1C) of section 111A above applies, the recipient is guilty of an offence if–
(a)   he knows that the change affects an entitlement of the claimant to a benefit or other payment or advantage under a provision of the relevant social security legislation;
(b)   the entitlement is one in respect of which he has a right to receive payments to which the claimant has, or (but for the arrangements under which they are payable to the recipient) would have, an entitlement; and
(c)   he fails to give a prompt notification of that change in the prescribed manner to the prescribed person.
(1D)   In a case where that subsection applies, a person other than the recipient is guilty of an offence if–
(a)   he knows that the change affects an entitlement of the claimant to a benefit or other payment or advantage under a provision of the relevant social security legislation;
(b)   the entitlement is one in respect of which the recipient has a right to receive payments to which the claimant has, or (but for the arrangements under which they are payable to the recipient) would have, an entitlement; and
(c)   he causes or allows the recipient to fail to give a prompt notification of that change in the prescribed manner to the prescribed person.
(1E)   Subsection (1F) of section 111A above applies in relation to subsections (1C) and (1D) above as it applies in relation to subsections (1D) and (1E) of that section.
(1F)   For the purposes of subsections (1A) to (1D) above a notification of a change is prompt if, and only if, it is given as soon as reasonably practicable after the change occurs.]
(2)   A person guilty of an offence under [⁴ this section] shall be liable on summary conviction to a fine not exceeding level 5 on the standard scale, or to imprisonment for a term not exceeding 3 months, or to both.
[⁵. . .]

Amendments
1.   Amended by SSA(F) Act 1997, s14(1A).
2.   Amended by SSA (F) Act 1997, s14(3).
3.   Substituted by SSA(F) Act 1997, Sch 1 para 4(2).
4.   Inserted by CSPSS Act, Sch 6 para 6 (2.4.01).
5.   Repealed by CSPSS Act 2000, s85 and Sch 9 (2.4.01).
6.   Substituted by SSFA s16(3) (29.9.01 and 18.10.01).

Social Security Administration Act 1992

General Note
This sets out the less serious offences that may be committed in relation to obligations of disclosure of information to an authority. Section 14 Social Security Administration (Fraud) Act 1997 considerably widened the scope of the offences to cover omissions as well as positive misstatements and again the offences have been reformulated by the Social Security Fraud Act 2001. Note the temporal effect of the provisions in subs (1A) to (1F): see the commentary to s111A. Note also the time limits for prosecutions imposed by s116.

Analysis
Subsection (1)
"If a person". See Analysis to s111A on p53.
"for the purpose of obtaining any benefit ... or for any other purpose connected with that legislation". The latter phrase means that it need not be shown that the defendant intended to obtain benefit. It suffices if the statement was made for purposes relating to benefit: *Clear v Smith* [1981] 1 WLR 399 at 406, DC (statement that no work was being done when claimant asserted that work was unremunerated); *Barrass v Reeve* [1981] 1 WLR 408, DC (statement that claimant was incapable of work allegedly only used to deceive employer); *DSS v Bavi* [1996] COD 260 at 261, DC (statement that claimant not working allegedly result of misunderstanding).
"(a) makes a statement or representation". An actual statement, whether written or oral, must be proved by the prosecution, though the place and date of the statement need not be proven: *DSS v Cooper* [1994] 158 JPN 354, DC.
In deciding whether a question on a claim form has been answered incorrectly, it is not necessary to analyse the question in a legalistic manner by reference to the meaning of a particular word in the HB Regs, but rather by taking a common-sense view. So where a claimant stated that he did not own property, but in fact was the registered owner of a house, it did not matter whether or not the claimant was an "owner" for the purposes of reg 2(1) HB and the HB(SPC) Regs. The fact that he had an interest in the property that made him the owner as a matter of common sense was sufficient: *Fairbank v Lambeth Magistrates' Court* (2003) HLR 62.
"which he knows to be false". The defendant must know of the falsity at the time the statement or representation is made: *Moore v Branton* [1974] 118 SJ 40, DC. It does not matter that a specific statement may have been true when made, if on a change of circumstances the claimant continues to sign forms stating that there has been no such change. The latter will be the requisite false statement: *Tolfree v Florence* [1971] 1 WLR 141 at 144, DC. Showing that a defendant was negligent or failed to make inquiries into facts does not establish knowledge of the falsity of those facts: *Taylor's Central Garages (Exeter) Ltd v Roper* [1951] 115 JP 445 at 449, 450, DC.
The prosecution must prove that the defendant knew that the statement was false, but as long as the defendant knows that the statement or representation is false, s/he need not know that the falsity was material to her/his entitlement to benefit, since there is no requirement of materiality in para (a), unlike para (b): *Harrison v DSS* [1997] COD 220 at 220-1, DC.
Para (b). See the requirement of knowledge discussed in the previous paragraph and see the Analysis of s111A(1)(b).
Subsections (1A) to (1F)
These subsections create similar criminal offences to those in s111A(1A) to (1G), except that there is no requirement of dishonesty. Each of the sub-paras (a) to (d) under subs (1A) must be established to the criminal standard of proof, and therefore it is for the prosecution to prove beyond a reasonable doubt that the defendant knew that the change *would* affect her/his benefit entitlement: simply showing that the change could affect entitlement will not be sufficient: *King v Kerrier DC* [2006] EWHC 500 (Admin), unreported, 27 February (DC). So where a claimant continued to receive HB and CTB after he thought he had reported a change of circumstances to the relevant office, and thus thought the change did not affect his entitlement, the element of the offence set out in s112(1A)(c) was not proved: *Coventry CC v Vassell* [2011] EWHC 1542 (Admin).
Subsection (2)
The offence is triable only summarily – ie, in the magistrates' court or sheriff court in Scotland.

[¹**Breach of regulations**
    113.–(1)   Regulations and schemes under any of the [² legislation to which this section applies] may provide that any person who contravenes, or fails to comply with, any provision contained in regulations made under [² that legislation]–
    (a)   in the case of a provision relating to contributions, shall be liable to a penalty;
    (b)   in any other case, shall be guilty of an offence under [² any enactment contained in the legislation in question].
[²(1A)   The legislation to which this section applies is–
    (a)   the relevant social security legislation; and
    (b)   the enactments specified in section 121DA(1) so far as relating to contributions [³].]
    (2)   *[Omitted]*

56

(3)   A person guilty of such an offence as is mentioned in subsection (1)(b) above shall be liable on summary conviction–
(a)   to a fine not exceeding level 3 on the standard scale;
(b)   in the case of an offence of continuing a contravention or failure after conviction, to a fine not exceeding £163.40 for each day on which it is so continued.
(4)   *[Omitted]*]

Amendments
1.   Substituted by SSA 1998 s60 (4.3.99/6.4.99).
2.   Amended by CSPSSA Sch 6 para 7 (1.11.00).
3.   Omitted by National Insurance Contributions and Statutory Payments Act 2004 s12 and Sch 2 (6.4.05).

General Note
The section allows regulations to provide that a failure to comply with requirements in such regulations amounts to a criminal offence under this section. Until 1997 there was no such provision in the HB or CTB schemes, but from 3 November 1997 the Social Security (Information from Landlords and Agents) Regulations 1997 made such a provision. This is now in regs 117–121 HB Regs (regs 98–102 HB(SPC) Regs). These regulations require landlords and their agents to furnish a wide range of information to an authority on request. A failure to comply with such a demand amounts to an offence under this section. See the commentary to those Regulations.
    As to the penalties, see the commentary to s111 on p50.

Offences by bodies corporate
115.–(1)   Where an offence under this Act [¹, or under the Jobseeker's Act 1995] which has been committed by a body corporate is proved to have been committed with the consent or connivance of, or to be attributable to any neglect on the part of, a director, manager, secretary or other similar officer of the body corporate, or any person who was purporting to act in any such capacity, he, as well as the body corporate, shall be guilty of that offence and be liable to be proceeded against accordingly.
(2)   Where the affairs of a body corporate are managed by its members, subsection (1) above applies in relation to the acts and defaults of a member in connection with his functions of management as if he were a director of the body corporate.

Amendment
1.   Amended by the Jobseekers Act 1995 Sch 2 para 116.

General Note
This section might apply in HB cases where a body corporate which is a landlord or an employer commits an offence under ss111A or 112 in relation to HB. It confirms that any officer or manager of such a body can be personally liable to prosecution if s/he has deliberately or negligently caused or contributed to the commission of the offence.
    It does not appear to be necessary for a prosecution under this section that the body corporate is also prosecuted, provided that it is guilty of the offence.
    A 'body corporate' is not defined in the Act. In England and Wales, it means a body which is incorporated under royal charter, Act of Parliament or the Companies Act 1985. In Scotland, however, it may include a partnership: *Douglas v Phoenix Motors* [1970] SLT 57, Sh Ct, where both English and Scottish law are discussed.

[¹Penalty as alternative to prosecution
115A.–(1)   This section applies where an overpayment is recoverable from a person by, or due from a person to, the Secretary of State or an authority under or by virtue of section 71, [⁶ 71ZB] 71A, 75 or 76 above and it appears to the Secretary of State or authority that–
(a)   the making of the overpayment was attributable to an act or omission on the part of that person; and
(b)   there are grounds for instituting against him proceedings for an offence (under this Act or any other enactment) relating to the overpayment.
[³ (1A)   This section also applies where–
(a)   it appears to the Secretary of State or an authority that there are grounds for instituting proceedings against a person for an offence (under this Act or any other enactment) relating to an act or omission on the part of that person in relation to any benefit, and

(b)   if an overpayment attributable to the act or omission had been made, the overpayment would have been recoverable from the person by, or due from the person to, the Secretary of State or an authority under or by virtue of section 71, 71ZB, 71A, 75 or 76 above.]

(2)   The Secretary of State or authority may give to the person a written notice–

(a)   stating that he may be invited to agree to pay a penalty and that, if he does so in the manner specified by the Secretary of State or authority, no [³ proceedings referred to in subsection (1) or (1A) above] will be instituted against him; and

(b)   containing such information relating to the operation of this section as may be prescribed.

[⁴ (3)   The amount of the penalty in a case falling within subsection (1) is 50% of the amount of the overpayment (rounded down to the nearest whole penny), subject to–

(a)   a minimum amount of £350, and

(b)   a maximum amount of [⁷ £5000].

(3A)   The amount of the penalty in a case falling within subsection (1A) is £350.

(3B)   The Secretary of State may by order amend–

(a)   the percentage for the time being specified in subsection (3);

(b)   any figure for the time being specified in subsection (3)(a) or (b) or (3A).]

(4)   If the person agrees in the specified manner to pay the penalty–

(a)   the amount of the penalty shall be recoverable by the same methods as those by which the overpayment is [³ or would have been] recoverable; and

(b)   no proceedings will be instituted against him for an offence (under this Act or any other enactment) relating to the overpayment [³ or to the act or omission referred to in subsection (1A)(a).].

(5)   The person may withdraw his agreement to pay the penalty by notifying the Secretary of State or authority, in the manner specified by the Secretary of State or authority, at any time during the period of [⁵ 14] days beginning with the day on which he agrees to pay it; and if he does so–

(a)   so much of the penalty as has already been recovered shall be repaid; and

(b)   subsection (4)(b) above shall not apply.

(6)   [³ In a case referred to in subsection (1)] Where, after the person has agreed to pay the penalty, it is decided on a review or appeal or in accordance with regulations that the overpayment is not recoverable or due, so much of the penalty as has already been recovered shall be repaid.

(7)   [³ In a case referred to in subsection (1)] Where, after the person has agreed to pay the penalty, the amount of the overpayment is revised on a review or appeal or in accordance with regulations–

(a)   so much of the penalty as has already been recovered shall be repaid; and

(b)   subsection (4)(b) above shall no longer apply by reason of the agreement;

but if a new agreement is made under this section in relation to the revised overpayment, the amount already recovered by way of penalty, to the extent that it does not exceed the amount of the new penalty, may be treated as recovered under the new agreement instead of being repaid.

[²(7A)   Subject to subsection (7B) below, the Secretary of State and an authority which administers housing benefit or council tax benefit may agree that, to the extent determined by the agreement, one may carry out on the other's behalf, or may join in the carrying out of, any of the other's functions under this section.

(7B)   Subsection (7A) above shall not authorise any delegation of–

(a)   the function of the person by whom any overpayment is [³ or would have been] recoverable, or to whom it is [³ or would have been] due, of determining whether or not a notice should be given under subsection (2) above in respect of that overpayment; or

(b)   the Secretary of State's power to make regulations for the purposes of paragraph (b) of that subsection.]

(8)   In this section "overpayment" means–

(a)   a payment which should not have been made;

(b)   a sum which the Secretary of State should have received;

(c)　　an amount of benefit paid in excess of entitlement; or

(d)　　an amount equal to an excess of benefit allowed;

and the reference in subsection (1)(a) [³ or (1A)(b)] above to the making of the overpayment is to the making of the payment, the failure to receive the sum, the payment of benefit in excess of entitlement or the allowing of an excess of benefit.]

Amendments

1.　　Inserted by SSA(F) Act 1997, s15.
2.　　Inserted by SSFA s14 (30.4.02).
3.　　Amended by WRA 2012 s113(2)-(7) (8.5.12).
4.　　Substituted by WRA 2012 s114(1) (8.5.12).
5.　　Substituted by WRA 2012 s115(2) (8.5.12).
6.　　Amended by WRA 2012 s105(3) (29.1.13).
7.　　Amended by art 2 of SI 2015 No 202 as from 1.4.15.

Modification

Section 115A(1), (1A), (2) and (5) was amended and s115A(7A) and (7B) were repealed by WRA 2012 s147 and Sch 14 part 1 on 1.4.13 in so far as it related to CTB.

General Note

One controversial innovation of the Social Security Administration (Fraud) Act 1997 was to enable an authority to offer a prospective defendant the option to pay a penalty rather than institute proceedings for the prosecution of that person. It may be argued that authorities might see this as a short-cut and a simple way of avoiding the expense of bringing criminal proceedings. In addition, there may be iniquity in the operation of the system if landlords are able to evade prosecution by accepting the penalty while claimants may be unable to do so.

A penalty may not be offered in relation to an offence alleged to have been committed before 18 December 1997, when the section came into force: s25(7) of the 1997 Act.

The scheme, in outline, is as follows. The authority may only offer a penalty when there are grounds for prosecuting for an offence either where an overpayment attributable to an act or omission has been made or where if such an overpayment had been made it would have been recoverable: subs (1) and (1A). A written notice offering the penalty must be given: subs (2). If the person in question agrees to pay, s/he receives immunity from prosecution and must pay a penalty on top of the overpayment: subs (3), (3A), (3B) and (4).

The person may withdraw from the agreement within 14 days: subs (5). Where there has been an overpayment and there is subsequently a decision that it is not recoverable, the penalty is not payable: subs (6). If the amount of the overpayment is revised, the agreement is void, but a new agreement may be made: subs (7).

Analysis

Subsection (1)

"where an overpayment is recoverable .... or due". An overpayment is not recoverable unless a valid determination has been issued by the local authority: *Warwick DC v Freeman* (1994) 27 HLR 616, CA. This is made clear beyond doubt, in relation to HB, by the amendment to Administration Act s75(1) made by Sch 1 para 3 of the 1997 Act.

It is difficult to see what "or due" adds to this. It cannot be said that it renders the penalty system operable before there has been a determination, because an overpayment cannot be "due" until it is recoverable, and until the amount has been calculated, it would not be possible to determine the level of the penalty. It might be thought that it is intended to cover situations where the overpayment arose before s115A came into force, but there is a specific provision against retrospectivity in relation to s115A in s25(7) of the 1997 Act. Finally, it was said in committee that "the definition of overpayment in [section 115A] does not go any wider than what is already covered by the 1992 Act": Oliver Heald MP, Standing Committee E, 21 January 1997, col. 319. There is no room for saying that it applies to overpayments that have yet to be determined to be recoverable.

It is suggested that the penalty system cannot come into operation until the local authority has made its initial determination under reg 89(1) HB Regs (reg 70(1) HB(SPC) Regs) as appropriate. However, there is no need to wait until the review or appeal procedure is exhausted: see subs (6).

"it appears to the Secretary of State or authority that". The prosecuting authority must satisfy itself that the two conditions set out in subsection (1) are met. If they do not carry out this thought process, the section has no application and so any notice served would be invalid.

"under or by virtue of section ... 75 or 76". Overpayments of HB and CTB are recoverable under ss75 and 76 respectively.

"the making of the overpayment was attributable to an act or omission". The word "attributable" requires some connection between the overpayment and the act or omission, but the latter need not be the sole cause of the former: *Walsh v Rother DC* [1978] 1 All ER 510 at 514a-e, HC.

59

"there are grounds for instituting ... proceedings for an offence". This must mean that there is at least enough evidence before the prosecuting authority to suggest that there is a *prima facie* case for the defendant to answer.

Subsection (1A)
This allows an authority to offer a penalty as an alternative to prosecution where an overpayment would have been recoverable had it been made. This would apply, for example, where a claim was found to be fraudulent before any HB was ever paid. For a discussion of terms, see the commentary to subs (1) above.

Subsection (2)
"may give". The power to offer a penalty is discretionary and there can be no question of the authority being under any duty to do so.

"if he does so in the manner specified". This phrase is a little vague. The notice words "the manner specified" apply to the invitation to make an agreement, rather than the payment of the penalty under that agreement. In other words, the notice is only required to state how the agreement is to be made. It does not have to set out how the penalty has to be paid.

It appears that there is no power for the Secretary of State to prescribe the means by which an agreement is reached and so this will be a matter for authorities. Needless to say, it ought to be in writing and authorities should take care that the chosen procedure leaves all parties clear as to whether the invitation has been accepted or not.

Paras (a) and (b). The notice must contain the specified information. If it does not, the notice will be invalid if the recipient has been disadvantaged thereby: *Freeman* (above), *Haringey LBC v Awaritefe* (1999) 32 HLR 517 and *R(H) 3/04*. It is suggested that in these circumstances, any agreement to pay a penalty may be unenforceable by reason of the invalidity of the notice, since the issue of a notice is the trigger for the making of the agreement. For the information that must be included in a penalty notice, see reg 2 Social Security (Penalty Notice) Regulations 1997 on p1745. Note the additional information required by reg 2(1A) of those regulations for offences for which notice is given under subsection (1A) that are committed wholly on or after 8 May 2012.

Subsection (3)
The amount of penalty for cases coming under subs (1) is 50 percent of the amount of the overpayment subject to a minimum of £350 and a maximum of £5,000. Note that the maximum was £2,000 before 1 April 2015. The amount of the overpayment is the amount as specified by the authority in its original determination that the overpayment is recoverable. Subs (6) deals with situations where the overpayment is later found not to be recoverable and subs (7) deals with the situation where the amount changes on review or appeal or in accordance with regulations. Prior to 8 May 2012, the penalty was 30 percent of the amount of the overpayment, with no fixed minimum or maximum.

Subsection (3A)
The amount of penalty for cases coming under subs (1A) is a fixed amount of £350.

Subsection (3B)
This subsection allows the Secretary of State to amend the percentage in subs (3) and any of the amounts in subs (3) or (3A).

Subsection (4)
"agrees in the specified manner to pay the penalty". The "specified manner" relates to the making of the agreement, not the payment: see subs (2). The significance of this is that if there is an agreement as to how the penalty is paid, but the person paying the penalty fails to adhere to that agreement, her/his failure does not render the agreement void and so the authority will not then be able to institute proceedings for a criminal offence.

Para (a). For the methods by which an overpayment is recoverable, see the Analysis to reg 102 HB Regs on p597.

Para (b). In return for paying the penalty, the person in question cannot be prosecuted under any of the offences set out above or under any other legislation, including in particular the Theft Act 1968. There could still be a prosecution under the common law, which may be relevant in Scotland, where there is no equivalent of the 1968 Act. Such a prosecution would probably be regarded as an abuse of process.

Subsection (5)
This gives a statutory 14-day 'cooling-off' period during which a person who has agreed to pay a penalty may withdraw from the agreement. Once that period has expired, it may still be possible to take civil proceedings to set the agreement aside if it was procured by undue influence on the part of the authority, namely the threat of prosecution: *Williams v Bayley* [1866] LR 1 HL 200, HL. It would have to be shown that the influence of the authority continued after the 14-day period (so that, for example, the paying person took no legal advice) and probably that there was some impropriety in the authority's actions. This latter requirement could be fulfilled by showing that the evidence would not have supported a criminal charge. The cooling-off period was 28 days prior to 8 May 2012.

"in the manner specified". By reg 2(1)(d) and (1A)(d) Social Security (Penalty Notice) Regulations 1997, a penalty notice served under subs (2) must contain a statement that the person in question may withdraw "in the manner specified by ... the authority". It is highly arguable that this requires the authority to specifically state in the notice how a person may withdraw from the agreement, rather than simply state "the manner specified" in the notice.

"so much of the penalty as has already been recovered shall be repaid". In many cases, the penalty and any overpayment will not be paid as a lump sum, but will be paid in instalments. If the payer withdraws from the agreement, do the instalments which s/he has already paid count towards the overpayment or to the penalty? Assuming the sums paid have not been specifically attributed to one or the other, the rule in *Clayton's case* [1861] 1 Mer 572 probably applies, so that payments are applied to the debt that first arose in time until it is extinguished.

The question then is which debt arose first in time. If there is no challenge to the recoverability of the overpayment, then that debt will have arisen before the penalty. However, it may be that review of the question of recoverability has been sought. It cannot be said that there is a debt in relation to the overpayment until it has been established that the overpayment is recoverable. In such a case, it may be that the penalty is the first debt in time and that the instalments will have been applied to reduce that debt. In that case, the instalments will have to be repaid.

Subsections (6) and (7)

These subsections only apply in cases coming under subs (1). If the overpayment is found not to be recoverable, then the penalty disappears: subs (6). Any payments made will have been attributable to the penalty, because there has never been any debt in relation to the overpayment. Note that the subsection does not provide that the claimant's immunity from prosecution disappears: compare subs (7)(b).

A change in the amount of the overpayment on review or appeal removes the effect of the agreement: subs (7). The reason for this is probably to allow an authority, where it is subsequently discovered that the amount of an overpayment is much higher, to take the decision to prosecute after all. Payments already made towards the penalty must be repaid, but if a new agreement is concluded, then those payments may be treated as being on account of the newly assessed penalty.

Subsection (8)

This subsection gives a wide definition to "overpayment" for the purposes of s115A. The following categories of payment are included in the definition.

(a) A payment which should not have been made. It might be thought that it was arguable that if there was an award of benefit pursuant to which the payments of benefit were made, it could not be said that the payment "should not have been made" because there was a legal obligation on the authority to pay that benefit until such time as the award was revised. However, a similar phrase also occurs in Sch 9A para 11 of the Social Security (Claims and Payments) Regulations 1987 which deals with recovery of overpaid mortgage interest paid as, for example, IS housing costs. In *R v Secretary of State for Social Security ex p Golding* [1996] unreported, 1 July, CA, the Court of Appeal held that a payment "ought not to have been made" if it was an overpayment, even though the payment was made pursuant to an award of an adjudication officer.

(b) This has no application to HB.

(c) An amount of benefit paid in excess of entitlement. This refers to payments not made pursuant to an award of benefit, such as double payments.

(d) An amount equal to an excess of benefit allowed. This refers to excess payments of CTB.

[¹ Penalty as alternative to prosecution: colluding employers etc

115B.–(1) This section applies where it appears to the Secretary of State or an authority that administers housing benefit or council tax benefit–

(a) that there are grounds for instituting proceedings against any person ('the responsible person') for an offence (whether or not under this Act) in respect of any conduct; and

(b) that the conduct in respect of which there are grounds for instituting the proceedings is conduct falling within subsection (2) below.

(2) Conduct in respect of which there appear to be grounds for instituting proceedings falls within this subsection if–

(a) those proceedings would be for an offence under this Act in connection with an inquiry relating to the employment of relevant employees or of any one or more particular relevant employees; or

(b) it is conduct which was such as to facilitate the commission of a benefit offence by a relevant employee (whether or not such an offence was in fact committed).

(3) The Secretary of State or authority may give to the responsible person a written notice–

(a) specifying or describing the conduct in question;

(b) stating that he may be invited to agree to pay a penalty in respect of that conduct;

(c) stating that, if he does so in the manner specified by the Secretary of State or authority, no criminal proceedings will be instituted against him in respect of that conduct; and

    (d)   containing such information relating to the operation of this section as may be prescribed.

    [⁴(4)   If the recipient of a notice under subsection (3) above agrees, in the specified manner, to pay the penalty–

    (a)   the amount of the penalty shall be recoverable from the recipient by the Secretary of State or authority; and

    (b)   no criminal proceedings shall be instituted against the recipient in respect of the conduct to which the notice relates.

    (4A)   Sections 71ZC, 71ZD and 71ZE above apply in relation to amounts recoverable under subsection (4)(a) above as to amounts recoverable by the Secretary of State under section 71ZB above (and, where the notice is given by an authority administering housing benefit or council tax benefit, those sections so apply as if references to the Secretary of State were to that authority).]

    (5)   The amount of the penalty shall be–

    (a)   in a case in which the conduct in question falls within paragraph (a) of subsection (2) above but not within paragraph (b) of that subsection, £1,000;

    (b)   in a case in which that conduct falls within paragraph (b) of that subsection and the number of relevant employees by reference to whom it falls within that subsection is five or more, £5,000; and

    (c)   in any other case, the amount obtained by multiplying £1,000 by the number of relevant employees by reference to whom that conduct falls within that subsection.

    (6)   The responsible person may withdraw his agreement to pay a penalty under this section by notifying the Secretary of State or authority, in the manner specified by the Secretary of State or authority, at any time during the period of [³ 14] days beginning with the day on which he agrees to pay it.

    (7)   Where the responsible person withdraws his agreement in accordance with subsection (6) above–

    (a)   so much of the penalty as has already been recovered shall be repaid; and

    (b)   subsection (4)(b) above shall not apply.

    (8)   For the purposes of this section an individual is a relevant employee in relation to any conduct of the responsible person if–

    (a)   that conduct was at or in relation to a time when that individual was an employee of the responsible person;

    (b)   that conduct was at or in relation to a time when that individual was an employee of a body corporate of which the responsible person is or has been a director; or

    (c)   the responsible person, in engaging in that conduct, was acting or purporting to act on behalf of, in the interests of or otherwise by reason of his connection with, any person by whom that individual is or has been employed.

    (9)   In this section–

"conduct" includes acts, omissions and statements;

"director"–

    (a)   in relation to a company (within the meaning of the Companies Act 1985), includes a shadow director;

    (b)   in relation to any such company that is a subsidiary of another, includes any director or shadow director of the other company; and

    (c)   in relation to a body corporate whose affairs are managed by its members, means a member of that body corporate;

"employee" means any person who–

    (a)   is employed under a contract of service or apprenticeship, or in an office (including an elective office), or

    (b)   carries out any work under any contract under which he has undertaken to provide his work,

and "employment" shall be construed accordingly;

[⁴]

"shadow director" means a shadow director as defined in [² section 251 of the Companies
Act 2006];
"subsidiary" means a subsidiary as defined in section 736 of the Companies Act 1985.]

Amendments
1.   Inserted by SSFA s15(1) (30.4.02).
2.   Amended by Art 10 and Sch 4 para 68 of SI 2007 No 2194 as from 1.10.07.
3.   Substituted by WRA 2012 s115(3) (8.5.12).
4.   Amended by WRA 2012 s105(4) (1.10.12).

Commencement
1.4.02: SI 2002 No 1222.

Modification
Section 115B(1), (3), (4), (4A), and (6) was amended by WRA 2012 s147 and Sch 14 part 1 on 1.4.13 in so far as
it related to CTB.

General Note
This makes special provision for penalties to be payable by employers who collude with employees to commit
benefit fraud. Penalties are to be paid into the Consolidated Fund: see subs (2). As with s115A, penalties are
payable only by way of agreement and give the person paying immunity from prosecution in relation to the
conduct giving rise to the giving of the notice.
    There is some doubt as to whether this provision may have effect in relation to conduct that took place prior
to the commencement date of this section. There was no provision in the SSFA equivalent to s25(7) SSA(F)A
which prevented penalties taking effect in relation to pre-commencement conduct. It is suggested that there is no
reason in principle why a penalty could not be offered, provided it could be shown that there was evidence of an
offence under the old law.

Analysis
Subsections (1) and (2): When a penalty may be offered
These subsections together impose two criteria which must be satisfied before a penalty may be offered. Any
notice served under subs (3) in circumstances where they are not made out would be invalid.
(1)   There must be "grounds for instituting proceedings" against a person. As in s115A(1)(b) SSAA, "grounds"
         would require that there should be at least sufficient evidence for there to be a case to answer. "Person"
         includes both natural and legal persons, such as companies and other corporations: Sch 1 to the
         Interpretation Act 1978. It does not, however, include a partnership since a partnership has no legal
         personality. It would have to be shown that there were grounds for proceedings against an individual
         partner and the notice would have to relate to that partner alone.
(2)   The person is guilty of relevant conduct within subs (2). This may relate to "an inquiry relating to" the
         employment of a relevant employee under para (a) or conduct facilitating an offence by such an employee
         under para (b). Para (a) relates to offences under s111 SSAA for refusing to supply information when
         required to do so. Local authority officers are entitled to demand information from employers under
         ss110A(1) and 109B(2)(a) SSAA. "Relating to" will probably include any information linked with the
         employment, even if the connection with the employment is indirect. Similarly under para (b), "facilitating"
         is a loose word and will probably cover conduct which makes it possible or even merely easier to commit
         a benefit offence as well as conduct which actively encourages or requires the commission of such
         offences. The employee need not have actually committed an offence; note, however, that the employer's
         conduct must itself be criminal or the first criterion above will not be satisfied.
Subsections (3) and (4): Making an agreement
Subs (3) and (4) are similar to s115A(2) and (4), with a few differences. First, the notice offering a penalty must
specify the conduct of which complaint is made in addition to explaining that a penalty is offered and that it offers
immunity from prosecution.
Subsection (5): The amount of the penalty
If the conduct falls within subs (2)(a) and relates to failure to respond to an inquiry, the penalty is £1,000. If it is
facilitating the commission of offences by employees, it is £1,000 multiplied by the number of employees affected,
up to a limit of £5,000.
Subsections (6) and (7): Withdrawing from an agreement
These are identical to s115A(5) and (6).
Subsections (8) and (9): Definitions
"Relevant employee" is given a very wide definition by subs (8). It relates not merely to employees in law by
para (a), but also employees of companies of which the responsible person is a director under para (b) (thus
confirming that directors may have a personal liability for a penalty) and employees of persons on behalf of whom

the responsible person was acting under para (c). The latter situation would cover a situation where an agent of the employer facilitates criminal offences.

"Director" is also given a wide definition. It may include the directors of sister companies, shadow directors or members of other bodies corporate. See the commentary to reg 9(1)(e) HB Regs on p289.

"Employee", by virtue of subs (9), includes independent contractors who provide labour under a contract. It also includes those who are apprentices or who are acting in an office.

Civil Penalties

Incorrect statements etc

115C.–(1)   This section applies where–
(a)   a person negligently makes an incorrect statement or representation, or negligently gives incorrect information or evidence–
    (i)   in or in connection with a claim for a relevant social security benefit, or
    (ii)   in connection with an award of a relevant social security benefit,
(b)   the person fails to take reasonable steps to correct the error,
(c)   the error results in the making of an overpayment, and
(d)   the person has not been charged with an offence or cautioned, or been given a notice under section 115A, in respect of the overpayment.
(2)   A penalty of a prescribed amount may be imposed by the appropriate authority–
(a)   in any case, on the person;
(b)   in a case where the person ("A") is making, or has made, a claim for the benefit for a period jointly with another ("B"), on B instead of A.
(3)   Subsection (2)(b) does not apply if B was not, and could not reasonably be expected to have been, aware that A had negligently made the incorrect statement or representation or given the incorrect information or evidence.
(4)   A penalty imposed under subsection (2) is recoverable by the appropriate authority from the person on whom it is imposed.
(5)   Sections 71ZC, 71ZD and 71ZE apply in relation to amounts recoverable by the appropriate authority under subsection (4) as to amounts recoverable by the Secretary of State under section 71ZB (and, where the appropriate authority is not the Secretary of State, those sections so apply as if references to the Secretary of State were to that authority).
(6)   In this section and section 115D–
"appropriate authority" means–
(a)   the Secretary of State, or
(b)   an authority which administers housing benefit or council tax benefit;
"overpayment" has the meaning given in section 115A(8), and the reference to the making of an overpayment is to be construed in accordance with that provision;
"relevant social security benefit" has the meaning given in section 121DA(7).

Commencement

10.5.12 for the purpose of prescribing amounts under s115C(2); 1.10.12 insofar as not already in force (SI 2012 No.1246).

General Note

Section 115C allows an "appropriate authority", defined in para (6), to impose a penalty in the circumstances set out in para (1). It can be imposed on the person who made the incorrect statement or representation or gave incorrect information or evidence, or if the person is a joint claimant – this can only be with the person's partner and is not relevant for HB – on that partner, unless para (3) applies. The prescribed amount of the penalty is £50: reg 2 Social Security (Civil Penalties) Regulations 2012 (see p1839).

Failure to disclose information

115D.–(1)   A penalty of a prescribed amount may be imposed on a person by the appropriate authority where–
(a)   the person, without reasonable excuse, fails to provide information or evidence in accordance with requirements imposed on the person by the appropriate authority in connection with a claim for, or an award of, a relevant social security benefit,

(b)   the failure results in the making of an overpayment, and
(c)   the person has not been charged with an offence or cautioned, or been given a notice under section 115A, in respect of the overpayment.
(2)   A penalty of a prescribed amount may be imposed on a person by the appropriate authority where–
(a)   the person, without reasonable excuse, fails to notify the appropriate authority of a relevant change of circumstances in accordance with requirements imposed on the person under relevant social security legislation,
(b)   the failure results in the making of an overpayment, and
(c)   the person has not been charged with an offence or cautioned, or been given a notice under section 115A, in respect of the overpayment.
(3)   Where a person is making, or has made, a claim for a benefit for a period jointly with another, and both of them fail as mentioned in subsection (1) or (2), only one penalty may be imposed in respect of the same overpayment.
(4)   A penalty imposed under subsection (1) or (2) is recoverable by the appropriate authority from the person on whom it is imposed.
(5)   Sections 71ZC, 71ZD and 71ZE apply in relation to amounts recoverable by the appropriate authority under subsection (4) as to amounts recoverable by the Secretary of State under section 71ZB (and, where the appropriate authority is not the Secretary of State, those sections so apply as if references to the Secretary of State were to that authority).
(6)   In this section "relevant change of circumstances", in relation to a person, means a change of circumstances which affects any entitlement of the person to any benefit or other payment or advantage under any provision of the relevant social security legislation.

Commencement

10.5.12 for the purpose of prescribing amounts under s115D(1) or (2); 1.10.12 insofar as not already in force (SI 2012 No.1246).

General Note

Section 115D allows an "appropriate authority", defined in s115C(6), to impose a penalty in the circumstances set out in either para (1) or para (2). The prescribed amount of the penalty in both cases is £50: regs 3 and 4 Social Security (Civil Penalties) Regulations 2012 (see p1839).

Legal proceedings

Legal proceedings

116.–(1)   Any person authorised by the Secretary of State in that behalf may conduct any proceedings [⁸ under any provision of this Act other than section 114 or under any provision of] [⁵ the Jobseekers Act 1995] before a magistrates' court although not a barrister or solicitor.
(2)   Notwithstanding anything in any Act–
(a)   proceedings for an offence under this Act [⁵, or the Jobseekers Act 1995] [¹¹ (other than proceedings to which paragraph (b) applies)] [⁵ , or for an offence under the Jobseekers Act 1995] may be begun at any time within the period of 3 months from the date on which evidence, sufficient in the opinion of the Secretary of State to justify a prosecution for the offence, comes to his knowledge or within a period of 12 months from the commission of the offence, whichever period last expires; and
(b)   proceedings [¹¹ brought by the appropriate authority] for an offence under this Act relating to housing benefit or [¹ council tax benefit] may be begun at any time within the period of 3 months from the date on which evidence, sufficient in the opinion of the appropriate authority to justify a prosecution for the offence, comes to the authority's knowledge or within a period of 12 months from the commission of the offence, whichever period last expires.
[⁴(2A)   Subsection (2) above shall not be taken to impose any restriction on the time when proceedings may begun for an offence under section 111A above.]
(3)   For the purposes of subsection (2) above–

(a)   a certificate purporting to be signed by or on behalf of the Secretary of State as to the date on which such evidence as is mentioned in paragraph (a) of the subsection came to his knowledge shall be conclusive evidence of that date; and

(b)   a certificate of the appropriate authority as to the date on which such evidence as is mentioned in paragraph (b) of that subsection came to the authority's knowledge shall be conclusive evidence of that date.

(4)   In subsections (2) and (3) above "the appropriate authority" means, in relation to an offence which relates to housing benefit and concerns any dwelling–

[⁶ (a) . . .]

(b)   if it relates to a rent rebate, the authority who are the appropriate housing authority by virtue of [⁷ section 134 below]; and

(c)   if it relates to rent allowance, the authority who are the appropriate local authority by virtue of [⁷ that section].

(5)   In subsections (2) and (3) above "the appropriate authority" means, in relation to an offence relating to [² council tax benefit], such authority as is prescribed in relation to the offence.

[⁸(5A)   *[Omitted]*]

(6)   [⁹ ...]

(7)   In the application of this section to Scotland, the following provisions shall have effect in substitution for subsections (1) [⁸ to (5A)] above–

(a)   proceedings for an offence under this Act [⁵, or the Jobseekers Act 1995] may, notwithstanding anything in [³ section 136 of the Criminal Procedure (Scotland) Act 1995], be commenced at any time within the period of 3 months from the date on which evidence, sufficient in the opinion of the Lord Advocate to justify proceedings, comes to his knowledge, or within the period of 12 months from the commission of the offence, whichever period last expires;

[¹⁰(aa) this subsection shall not be taken to impose any restriction on the time when proceedings may be commenced for an offence under section 111A above;]

(b)   for the purposes of this subsection–

(i)   a certificate purporting to be signed by or on behalf of the Lord Advocate as to the date on which such evidence as is mentioned above came to his knowledge shall be conclusive evidence of that date; and

(ii)   subsection (3) of section 331 of the said Act of 1975 (date of commencement of proceedings) shall have effect as it has effect for the purposes of that section.

Amendments

1.   Substituted by LGFA Sch 9 para 17(1) (1.4.93).
2.   Substituted by LGFA Sch 9 para 17(2) (1.4.93).
3.   Substituted by Criminal Procedure (Consequential Provisions) (Scotland) Act 1995 Sch 4 para 82 (1.4.96).
4.   Amended by SSA(F)A Sch 1 para 5.
5.   Amended by Jobseekers Act 1995 Sch 2 para 56.
6.   Deleted by Housing Act 1996 Sch 13 para 3(3).
7.   Substituted by Housing Act 1996 Sch 13 para 3(3).
8.   Amended by Social Security (Transfer of Functions etc) Act 1999 Sch 1 para 21.
9.   Repealed by SSA 1998 Sch 7 para 83.
10.   Inserted by SSFA s17 (30.4.02).
11.   Amended by WRA 2012 s111 (8.5.12).

Modification

Section 116(2)(a) was amended and s116(2)(b), (3(b), (4) and (5) was repealed by WRA 2012 s147 and Sch 14 part 1 on 1.4.13 in so far as they related to CTB.

General Note

This section deals with the prosecution of offences under the Act. It provides that officers of the authority may conduct proceedings in person if authorised by the Secretary of State and for time limits for certain prosecutions.

Analysis

Subsections (2)(a) and (2)(b)

Subs (2)(a) applies to proceedings other than those to which subs (2)(b) applies. According to the Explanatory Notes to the amendments made by the WRA 2012, this means that the Secretary of State can extend the period when proceedings for an HB offence may be commenced. Thus, proceedings may be commenced where the 12-month period after an offence was committed has expired but the date is within three months of the date on which evidence that is adequate to justify prosecution came to the Secretary of State's knowledge.

Subs (2)(b) places time limits upon prosecutions for HB offences brought by an authority in England and Wales. "Appropriate authority" is defined in subs (4). Subs (2)(b) only applies to offences "under this Act", so it does not apply to prosecutions under the Theft Act 1968 or any other statute, and nor does it apply to charges under s111A: subs (2A). It therefore applies to s112. A prosecution must be brought within two time periods, whichever ends later:

(1)   three months after the authority believes that it has sufficient evidence to justify a prosecution;

(2)   12 months after the commission of the offence.

Under the first of the two periods, a certificate by the authority stating when it believed that it had sufficient evidence is to be treated as conclusive evidence of that date: subs (3)(b). A defendant may question that date by way of judicial review.

See, generally, on the relationship between subsections (2)(a) and (2)(b), *Mohammed and Parkes v DWP* [2012] EWHC 4220 (Admin).

Subsection (7)

This makes equivalent provision to subs (2)(b) in relation to proceedings brought in Scotland.

Local authority powers to prosecute housing benefit and council tax benefit fraud

116ZA.–(1)   This section applies to an authority administering housing benefit or council tax benefit.

(2)   The authority may not bring proceedings against a person for a benefit offence relating to either of those benefits unless–

(a)   the authority has already started an investigation in relation to that person in respect of the offence,

(b)   in a case where the proceedings relate to housing benefit, the authority has already started an investigation in relation to the person in respect of a benefit offence relating to council tax benefit, or has already brought proceedings against the person in respect of such an offence,

(c)   in a case where the proceedings relate to council tax benefit, the authority has already started an investigation in relation to the person in respect of a benefit offence relating to housing benefit, or has already brought proceedings against the person in respect of such an offence,

(d)   the proceedings arise in prescribed circumstances or are of a prescribed description, or

(e)   the Secretary of State has directed that the authority may bring the proceedings.

(3)   The Secretary of State may direct that in prescribed circumstances, an authority may not bring proceedings by virtue of subsection (2)(a), (b) or (c) despite the requirements in those provisions being met.

(4)   A direction under subsection (2)(e) or (3) may relate to a particular authority or description of authority or to particular proceedings or any description of proceedings.

(5)   If the Secretary of State prescribes conditions for the purposes of this section, an authority may bring proceedings in accordance with this section only if any such condition is satisfied.

(6)   The Secretary of State may continue proceedings which have been brought by an authority in accordance with this section as if the proceedings had been brought in his name or he may discontinue the proceedings if–

(a)   the proceedings were brought by virtue of subsection (2)(a), (b) or (c),

(b)   he makes provision under subsection (2)(d) which has the effect that the authority would no longer be entitled to bring the proceedings in accordance with this section,

(c)   he withdraws a direction under subsection (2)(e) in relation to the proceedings, or

(d)   a condition prescribed under subsection (5) ceases to be satisfied in relation to the proceedings.

(7)   In exercising a power to bring proceedings in accordance with this section, a local authority must have regard to the Code for Crown Prosecutors issued by the Director of Public Prosecutions under section 10 of the Prosecution of Offences Act 1985–
(a)   in determining whether the proceedings should be instituted;
(b)   in determining what charges should be preferred;
(c)   in considering what representations to make to a magistrates'court about mode of trial;
(d)   in determining whether to discontinue proceedings.
(8)   Regulations shall define "an investigation in respect of a benefit offence" for the purposes of this section.
(9)   This section does not apply to Scotland."

Commencement
20.4.16 for the purposes of making regulations under section 116ZA(8) of the Social Security Administration Act 1992. 24.5.16 for all remaining purposes.

General Note
For the purposes of this section, "an investigation in respect of a benefit offence" is defined by reg 2 of the Social Security Administration Act 1992 (Local Authority Investigations) Regulations 2016 SI No.519 as an investigation which is being conducted with a view to determining whether there are grounds for instituting criminal proceedings in respect of a benefit offence against a person.

[¹Local authority powers to prosecute [² other] benefit fraud

116A–(1)   This section applies if an authority administering housing benefit or council tax benefit has power to bring proceedings for a benefit offence relating to that benefit.
(2)   The authority may bring proceedings for a benefit offence relating to any other relevant social security benefit [² only if]–
(a)   the proceedings relate to any benefit or circumstances or any description of benefit or circumstances which the Secretary of State prescribes for the purposes of this paragraph, or
(b)   the Secretary of State has directed that the authority [² may] bring the proceedings,
and a direction under paragraph (b) may relate to a particular authority or description of authority or to particular proceedings or any description of proceedings.
(3)   If the Secretary of State prescribes conditions for the purposes of this section, an authority must not bring proceedings under this section unless any such condition is satisfied.
(4)   The Secretary of State may continue proceedings which have been brought by an authority under this section as if the proceedings had been brought in his name or he may discontinue the proceedings if–
(a)   he makes provision under subsection (2)(a), such that the authority would no longer be entitled to bring the proceedings under this section,
(b)   he [² withdraws] a direction under subsection (2)(b) in relation to the proceedings, or
(c)   a condition prescribed under subsection (3) ceases to be satisfied in relation to the proceedings.
(5)   In the exercise of its power under subsection (2), a local authority must have regard to the Code for Crown Prosecutors issued by the Director of Public Prosecutions under section 10 of the Prosecution of Offences Act 1985–
(a)   in determining whether the proceedings should be instituted;
(b)   in determining what charges should be preferred;
(c)   in considering what representations to make to a magistrates' court about mode of trial;
(d)   in determining whether to discontinue proceedings.
(6)   An authority must not bring proceedings for a benefit offence which does not relate to housing benefit or council tax benefit otherwise than in accordance with this section.

(7)   In subsection (2), "relevant social security benefit" has the same meaning as in section 121DA below.

(8)   This section does not apply to Scotland.](1992 c5, s110A)

Amendments

1.   Inserted by WRA 2007 s47 (19.2.08 (for making regulations) and 7.4.08).
2.   Amended by WRA 2012 s112 (24.5.16).

Modification

Section 116A was repealed by WRA 2012 s147 and Sch 14 part 1 on 1.4.13 in so far as it related to CTB.

General Note

Reg 3 Social Security (Local Authority Investigations and Prosecutions) Regulations 2008 on p1821 prescribes the benefits for the purposes of subsection (2)(a). They are all relevant social security benefits except IS, JSA, IB, PC and ESA. "Relevant social security benefit" is defined in s121DA.

[¹Interpretation of Part VI

121DA.–(1)   In this Part "the relevant social security legislation" means the provisions of any of the following, except so far as relating to contributions, [⁴ . . .] statutory sick pay or statutory maternity pay, that is to say–

(a)   the Contributions and Benefits Act;
(b)   this Act;
(c)   the Pensions Act, except Part III;
(d)   section 4 of the Social Security (Incapacity for Work) Act 1994;
(e)   the Jobseekers Act 1995;
(f)   the Social Security (Recovery of Benefits) Act 1997;
(g)   Parts I and IV of the Social Security Act 1998;
(h)   Part V of the Welfare Reform and Pensions Act 1999;
[⁵ (hh) the State Pension Credit Act 2002;]
[⁶ (hi) Part 1 of the Welfare Reform Act 2007;]
[(hj)]
[⁷ (hk) Part 4 of that Act;]
(i)   the Social Security Pensions Act 1975;
(j)   the Social Security Act 1973;
(k)   any subordinate legislation made, or having effect as if made, under any enactment specified in paragraphs (a) to (j) above.]

[² (2)   In this Part "authorised officer" means a person acting in accordance with any authorisation for the purposes of this Part which is for the time being in force in relation to him.

(3)   For the purposes of this Part–
(a)   references to a document include references to anything in which information is recorded in electronic or any other form;
(b)   the requirement that a notice given by an authorised officer be in writing shall be taken to be satisfied in any case where the contents of the notice–
(i)   are transmitted to the recipient of the notice by electronic means; and
(ii)   are received by him in a form that is legible and capable of being recorded for future reference.

(4)   In this Part "premises" includes–
(a)   moveable structures and vehicles, vessels, aircraft and hovercraft;
(b)   installations that are offshore installations for the purposes of the Mineral Workings (Offshore Installations) Act 1971; and
(c)   places of all other descriptions whether or not occupied as land or otherwise;
and references in this Part to the occupier of any premises shall be construed, in relation to premises that are not occupied as land, as references to any person for the time being present at the place in question.

(5)   In this Part–
"benefit" includes any allowance, payment, credit or loan;
[² "benefit offence" means–

(a)   any criminal offence in connection with a claim for a relevant social security benefit;

(b)   any criminal offence in connection with the receipt or payment of any amount by way of such a benefit;

(c)   any criminal offence committed for the purpose of facilitating the commission (whether or not by the same person) of a benefit offence;

(d)   any attempt or conspiracy to commit a benefit offence;] and

"compensation payment" has the same meaning as in the Social Security (Recovery of Benefits) Act 1997.

(6)   In this Part–

(a)   any reference to a person authorised to carry out any function relating to housing benefit *[or council tax benefit]* shall include a reference to a person providing services relating to the benefit directly or indirectly to an authority administering it; and

(b)   any reference to the carrying out of a function relating to such a benefit shall include a reference to the provision of any services relating to it.]

[¹ (7)   In this section [³ "relevant social security benefit" means a benefit under any provision of the relevant social security legislation; and] "subordinate legislation" has the same meaning as in the Interpretation Act 1978.]

Amendments

1.   Inserted by CSPSS Act, Sch 6 para 8 (1.11.00 and 2.4.01).
2.   Amended by SSFA s1(7) (30.4.02).
3.   Amended by SSFA s1(8) (30.4.02).
4.   Amended by TCA Sch 6 (8.4.03).
5.   Amended by SPCA Sch 2 para 12 (October 2003).
6.   Amended by WRA 2007 s28 and Sch 3 para 10(12) (27.10.08).
7.   Amended by WRA 2012 Sch 9 para 12 (8.4.13).

Modification

Section 121DA(6) was repealed by WRA 2012 s147 and Sch 14 part 1 on 1.4.13 in so far as it related to CTB.

PART VII
Provision of Information

General Note on Part VII

The Social Security Administration (Fraud) Act 1997 significantly expanded the powers of the DWP and local authorities to share information with each other and with other government departments in an attempt to combat benefit fraud. Concern was expressed during the passage of the Act about the implications of giving such wide powers to share information and the consequences for the subjects of the information if it is inaccurate. One concern is the sharing of information with people providing services to social security authorities, who may well have other commercial interests which could benefit from the use of such information. It was said by the government during the committee stage of the Act that there were no current plans for wholesale privatisation of the social security authorities, but the wording of the Act leaves this possibility open: Alistair Burt MP, Standing Committee E, 14 January 1997, col.174.

If information is wrongfully disclosed, the law offers several possible avenues to prevent such abuse. First, there seems little doubt that information held by public bodies of this nature will be classified by the law as confidential information. It was said at the committee stage of the Act that all commercial organisations involved in work for social security authorities are generally required to sign agreements that information will be kept confidential: Oliver Heald MP, Standing Committee E, 12 December 1996, col.106. It would be possible to obtain an injunction to prevent the revealing of such information by a recipient.

Secondly, the Data Protection Act 2018 provides protections in respect of the processing of individuals' personal data.

Thirdly, there is a criminal sanction under s123 SSAA relating to unauthorised disclosure by officials. The Act extends the scope of this offence to local authority officials: see General Note to s123. Unauthorised access is covered by s1(1) Computer Misuse Act 1990. It was said in Committee that DWP officers were authorised to use computer records only for work purposes and any personal use would therefore be an offence under the 1990 Act: Oliver Heald MP, Standing Committee E, 17 December 1996, col.144.

Despite the concerns of many, the scope of Part VII and other similar provisions has been slowly expanded to provide for increased data-matching between different bodies holding information on claimants.

Authorities administering housing benefit or council tax benefit

[¹Supply of information to authorities administering benefit

122C.–(1)   This section applies to information relating to social security [², child support or war pensions, or employment or training,] which is held–
  (a)   by the Secretary of State or the Northern Ireland Department; or
  (b)   by a person providing services to the Secretary of State or the Northern Ireland Department in connection with the provision of those services.
  (2)   Information to which this section applies may be supplied to–
  (a)   an authority administering housing benefit or council tax benefit; or
  (b)   a person authorised to exercise any function of such an authority relating to such a benefit,
for use in the administration of such a benefit [⁴ or for the purposes of anything the authority is permitted to do in relation to any other benefit by virtue of section 110A or 116A above].
  (3)   But where information to which this section applies has been supplied to the Secretary of State, the Northern Ireland Department or the person providing services under section 122 or 122B above, it may only be supplied under subsection (2) above–
  (a)   for use in the prevention, detection, investigation or prosecution of [⁴ benefit offences (within the meaning of Part 6 above)]; or
  (b)   for use in checking the accuracy of information relating to housing benefit or to council tax benefit and (where appropriate) amending or supplementing such information.
  (4)   The Secretary of State or the Northern Ireland Department–
  (a)   may impose conditions on the use of information supplied under subsection (2) above; and
  (b)   may charge a reasonable fee in respect of the cost of supplying information under that subsection.
  (5)   Where information is supplied to an authority or other person under subsection (2) above, the authority or other person shall have regard to it in the exercise of any function relating to housing benefit or council tax benefit.
  (6)   Information supplied under subsection (2) above shall not be supplied by the recipient to any other person or body unless–
  (a)   it is supplied–
    (i)   by an authority to a person authorised to exercise any function of the authority relating to housing benefit or council tax benefit; or
    (ii)   by a person authorised to exercise any function of an authority relating to such a benefit to the authority;
  (b)   it is supplied for the purposes of any civil or criminal proceedings relating to the Contributions and Benefits Act, the Jobseekers Act 1995 [³, Part 1 of the Welfare Reform Act 2007] [⁵, Part 4 of the Welfare Reform Act 2012] or this Act or to any provision of Northern Ireland legislation corresponding to any of them; or
  (c)   it is supplied under section 122D or 122E below.
  (7)   This section does not limit the circumstances in which information may be supplied apart from this section (in particular by reason of section 122(4) or 122B(4) above).]
  [² (8)   In this section and section 122D below "war pension" has the same meaning as in section 25 of the Social Security Act 1989.]

Amendments
  1.   Inserted by SSA(F)A s3 (1.7.97).
  2.   Amended by the Employment Act 2002 s50 and Sch 6 para 22 (9.9.02).
  3.   Amended by WRA 2007 s28 and Sch 3 para 10(15) (27.10.08).
  4.   Amended by WRA 2007 s48(1) (2.7.09).
  5.   Amended by WRA 2012 Sch 9 para 14 (8.4.13).

Modification
  Section 122C was repealed by WRA 2012 s147 and Sch 14 part 1 on 1.4.13 in so far as it related to CTB.

General Note
> This allows any information held by the Secretary of State or someone providing the DWP with services to be passed to an authority for use in the administration of HB or for the purposes of anything the authority is permitted to do in relation to other benefits under s110A or 116A. Section 110A deals with the appointment of inspectors and s116A gives authorities the powers to prosecute fraud. Information may also be passed to a person carrying out functions on behalf of an authority. See also Sch 8 para 34 WRPA (on p1705). By subs (4), restrictions can be imposed on its use and a charge may be levied.
>
> A further restriction is imposed by subs (3) in relation to information which the DWP has itself only been supplied with under s122 or s122B. In such a case, the information may be disclosed for use in investigating fraud, or simply for comparison with information held by an authority. In relation to the latter, it appears at first sight that there must be some relevant information held by the local authority to be checked. However, it seems likely that "the accuracy of information" will be read as referring to the body of information held by an authority as a whole. So, where an authority has no information at all of the type which is supplied by the Secretary of State, it will be entitled to record that information under paragraph (b) as "supplementing" that body of information.
>
> Subs (6) restricts the right of the authority to pass the information to other bodies. It must be supplied for the purposes of court proceedings under the social security legislation or pursuant to s122D or s122E.

[¹Supply of information by authorities administering benefit

122D.–(1)   The Secretary of State or the Northern Ireland Department may require–
(a)   an authority administering housing benefit or council tax benefit; or
(b)   a person authorised to exercise any function of such an authority relating to such a benefit,
to supply [⁵ relevant benefit information] held by the authority or other person to, or to a person providing services to, the Secretary of State or the Northern Ireland Department for use for any purpose relating to social security [³, child support or war pensions, [⁴ employment or training, private pensions policy or retirement planning].

(2)   The Secretary of State or the Northern Ireland Department may require–
(a)   an authority administering housing benefit or council tax benefit; or
(b)   a person authorised to exercise any function of such an authority relating to such a benefit,
to supply benefit policy information held by the authority or other person to, or to a person providing services to, the Secretary of State or the Northern Ireland Department.

[⁴ (2A)   Information supplied under subsection (2) [⁵, in addition to any other purpose for which the information may be used,] may be used for any purpose relating to private pensions policy or retirement planning.]

(3)   Information shall be supplied under subsection (1) or (2) above in such manner and form, and in accordance with such requirements, as may be [² specified in directions given by the Secretary of State or, as the case may be, the Northern Ireland Department].

[⁵ (4)   In subsection (1) "relevant benefit information", in relation to an authority or other person, means any information which is relevant to the exercise of any function relating to a relevant social security benefit by the authority or other person.]

(5)   In subsection (2) above "benefit policy information" means any information which may be relevant to the Secretary of State or the Northern Ireland Department–
(a)   in preparing estimates of likely future expenditure on [⁵ any relevant social security benefit]; or
(b)   in developing policy relating to [⁵ any relevant social security benefit].]

[⁴ (6)   In this section–
"private pensions policy" means policy relating to occupational pension schemes or personal pension schemes (within the meaning given by section 1 of the Pension Schemes Act 1993);
"retirement planning" means promoting financial planning for retirement.]

[⁵ "relevant social security benefit" has the same meaning as in section 121DA above.]

Amendments
1.   Inserted by SSA(F)A s3 (1.7.97).
2.   Amended by SSFA s6 (30.4.02).
3.   Amended by the Employment Act 2002 s50 and Sch 6 para 22 (9.9.02).
4.   Amended by the Pensions Act 2004 s236 and Sch 10 para 3 (18.11.04).
5.   Amended by WRA 2007 s48(2) (2.7.09).

General Note
This section deals with information moving from local authority to DWP. See also Sch 8 para 34 WRPA (on p1705). The categories and uses of information are broader. "Relevant benefit information" is that relevant to any function relating to a relevant social security benefit (for the definition see s121DA) held by an authority, and it may be supplied for any purpose relating to social security. "Benefit policy information" is that helping the DWP forecast likely expenditure or to develop policy. There is little information relating to the benefits that could not be disclosed under these provisions.

[¹**Supply of information between authorities administering benefit**

122E.–(1) This section applies to [² relevant benefit information] which is held by–
   (a)   an authority administering housing benefit or council tax benefit; or
   (b)   a person authorised to exercise any function of such an authority relating to such a benefit.

(2)   Information to which this section applies may be supplied to another such authority or person–
   (a)   for use in the prevention, detection, investigation or prosecution of [² benefit offences (within the meaning of Part 6 above)]; or
   (b)   for use in checking the accuracy of information relating to housing benefit or to council tax benefit and (where appropriate) amending or supplementing such information.

(3)   The Secretary of State or the Northern Ireland Department may require information to which this section applies and which is of a prescribed description to be supplied in prescribed circumstances to another such authority or person for use in the administration of housing benefit or council tax benefit.

(4)   Information shall be supplied under subsection (3) above in such manner and form, and in accordance with such requirements, as may be prescribed.

(5)   Where information supplied under subsection (2) or (3) above has been used in amending or supplementing other information, it is lawful for it to be–
   (a)   supplied to any person or body to whom that other information could be supplied; or
   (b)   used for any purpose for which that other information could be used.

[² (6)   In this section "relevant benefit information", in relation to an authority or other person, means any information which is relevant to the exercise of any function relating to a relevant social security benefit (within the meaning of section 121DA above) by the authority or other person.]

(7)   This section does not limit the circumstances in which information may be supplied apart from this section.]

Amendments
1.   Inserted by SSA(F)A s3 (1.7.97).
2.   Amended by WRA 2007 s48(3) (2.7.09).

General Note
Benefit administration information may be shared voluntarily by local authorities or at the direction of the Secretary of State. In the former case, subs (2) requires the information to be used for the detection of fraud or the checking of information. Information transferred by order under subs (3) can be used more generally for administration. See also Sch 8 para 34 WRPA (on p1705).

The effect of subs (5) is that when information received is mixed with a body of information, it may be supplied to whoever is entitled to receive that body of information, even though the recipient would not be entitled to disclosure of the transferred information in the form in which it was received. This is to obviate the need for complex screening processes when mixed information is being passed on.

[¹ Rent officers and housing benefit

Supply by rent officers of information relating to housing benefit

122F.–(1)   The Secretary of State may require a rent officer to supply housing benefit information held by the rent officer to, or to a person providing services to, the Secretary of State for use for purposes relating to any of the following–

(a)   social security;

(b)   child support;

(c)   war pensions;

(d)   employment or training;

(e)   private pensions policy or retirement planning.

(2)   Information must be supplied under subsection (1) in such manner and form, and in accordance with such requirements, as may be specified in directions given by the Secretary of State.

(3)   A person who receives information by virtue of subsection (1) must not disclose the information to any person unless the disclosure is made–

(a)   for a purpose mentioned in that subsection (including disclosure to another rent officer in connection with any function he has under section 122 of the Housing Act 1996 relating to housing benefit),

(b)   in accordance with any other enactment, or

(c)   in accordance with the order of a court.

(4)   Housing benefit information is any information which relates to the exercise by the rent officer of any function he has under section 122 of the Housing Act 1996 relating to housing benefit.]

Amendment

1.   Inserted by WRA 2007 s36 (27.3.09).

Unauthorised disclosure of information relating to particular persons

123.–(1)   A person who is or has been employed in social security administration or adjudication is guilty of an offence if he discloses without lawful authority any information which he acquired in the course of his employment and which relates to a particular person.

(2)   A person who is or has been employed in the audit of expenditure or the investigation of complaints is guilty of an offence if he discloses without lawful authority any information

(a)   which he acquired in the course of his employment;

(b)   which is, or is derived from, information acquired or held by or for the purposes of any of the government departments or other bodies or persons referred to in Part I of Schedule 4 to this Act or Part I of Schedule 3 to the Northern Ireland Administration Act; and

(c)   which relates to a particular person.

(3)   It is not an offence under this section–

(a)   to disclose information in the form of a summary or collection of information so framed as not to enable information relating to any particular person to be ascertained from it; or

(b)   to disclose information which has previously been disclosed to the public with lawful authority.

(4)   It is a defence for a person charged with an offence under this section to prove that at the time of the alleged offence

(a)   he believed that he was making the disclosure in question with lawful authority and had no reasonable cause to believe otherwise; or

(b)   he believed that the information in question had previously been disclosed to the public with lawful authority and had no reasonable cause to believe otherwise.

(5)   A person guilty of an offence under this section shall be liable

(a)   on conviction on indictment, to imprisonment for a term not exceeding two years or a fine or both; or

(b)   on summary conviction, to imprisonment for a term not exceeding six months or a fine not exceeding the statutory maximum or both.

(6)   For the purposes of this section the persons who are "employed in social security administration or adjudication" are

(a)   any person specified in Part I of Schedule 4 to this Act or in any corresponding enactment having effect in Northern Ireland;

(b)   any other person who carries out the administrative work of any of the government departments or other bodies or persons referred to in that Part of that Schedule or that corresponding enactment; and

(c)   any persons who provides, or is employed in the provision of, services to any of those departments, persons or bodies;

and "employment", in relation to any such person, shall be construed accordingly.

[¹(6A)   Subsection (6) above shall have effect as if any [⁸ health care professional] who, for the purposes of [⁴ section 19 of the Social Security Act 1998], is provided by any person in pursuance of a contract entered into with the Secretary of State were specified in Part I of Schedule 4 to this Act.]

(7)   For the purposes of subsections (2) and (6) above, any reference in Part I of Schedule 4 to the Act or any corresponding enactment having effect in Northern Ireland to a government department shall be construed in accordance with Part II of that Schedule or any corresponding enactment having effect in Northern Ireland, and for this purpose "government department" shall be taken to include

(a)   the Commissioners of Inland Revenue; and

(b)   the Scottish Courts Administration.

(8)   For the purposes of this section, the persons who are "employed in the audit of expenditure or the investigation of complaints" are

(a)   the Comptroller and Auditor General;

(b)   the Comptroller and Auditor General for Northern Ireland;

(c)   the Parliamentary Commissioner for Administration;

(d)   the Northern Ireland Parliamentary Commissioner for Administration;

(e)   the Health Service Commissioner for England;

[⁶ (f)]

(g)   [⁵ the Scottish Public Services Ombudsman];

(h)   the Northern Ireland Commissioner for Complaints;

[² (ha) a member of the Local Commission for England;

[⁶ (hb)]

[⁵ (hc)]]

[⁶ (hd)]

[⁶ (he) the Public Services Ombudsman for Wales and any member of his staff;]

(i)   any member of the staff of the National Audit Office or the Northern Ireland Audit Office;

(j)   any other person who carries out the administrative work of either of those Offices, or who provides, or is employed in the provision of, services to either of them;

[²(ja) a member of the Audit Commission for Local Authorities and the National Health Service in England [⁷] and any auditor appointed by that Commission;

(jb)   a member of the Accounts Commission for Scotland and any auditor within the meaning of Part VII of the Local Government (Scotland) Act 1973;

(jc)   a Northern Ireland local government auditor; and]

(k)   any officer of any of the Commissioners [⁵, Ombudsman] [² or Commissions referred to in paragraphs (c) to [⁶ (ha)], (ja) and (jb) above and any person assisting an auditor referred to in paragraph (ja), (jb) or (jc) above;]

and "employment", in relation to any such person, shall be construed accordingly.

(9)   For the purposes of this section a disclosure is to be regarded as made with lawful authority, if, and only if, it is made

(a)   in accordance with his official duty

       (i)   by a civil servant; or

      (ii)   by a person employed in the audit of expenditure or the investing-action of complaints, who does not fall within subsection (8)(j) above;

(b)   by any other person either

       (i)   for the purposes of the function in the exercise of which he holds the information and without contravening any restriction duly imposes by the person responsible; or

      (ii)   to, or in accordance with an authorisation duly given by, the person responsible;

(c)   in accordance with any enactment or order or a court;

(d)   for the purpose of instituting, or otherwise for the purposes of, any proceedings before a court or before any tribunal or other body or person referred to in Part I of Schedule 4 to this Act or Part I of Schedule 3 to the Northern Ireland Administration Act; or

(e)   with the consent of the appropriate person;

and in this subsection "the person responsible" means the Secretary of State, the Lord Chancellor or any person authorised by the Secretary of State or the Lord Chancellor for the purposes of this subsection and includes a reference to "the person responsible" within the meaning of any corresponding enactment having effect in Northern Ireland.

   (10)   For the purposes of subsection (9)(e) above, "the appropriate person" means the person to whom the information in question relates, except that if the affairs of that person are being dealt with–

(a)   under a power or attorney;

(b)   by a receiver appointed under section 99 of the Mental Health Act 1983 or a controller appointed under Article 101 of the Mental Health (Northern Ireland) Order 1986;

(c)   by a Scottish mental health custodian, [³ that is to say a guardian or other person entitled to act on behalf of the person under the Adults with Incapacity (Scotland) Act 2000 (asp 4)]; or

(d)   by a mental health appointee, that is to say

       (i)   a person directed or authorised as mentioned in sub-paragraph (a) of rule 41(1) of the Court of Protection Rules 1984 or sub-paragraph (a) of rule 38(1) of Order 109 of the Rules of the Supreme Court (Northern Ireland) 1980; or

      (ii)   a receiver ad interim appointed under sub-paragraph (b) of the said rule 41(1) or a controller ad interim appointed under sub-paragraph (b) of the said rule 38(1),

the appropriate person is the attorney, receiver, controller, custodian or appointee, as the case may be, or, in a case falling within paragraph (a) above, the person to whom the information relates.

Amendments

1.   Inserted by Deregulation and Contracting Out Act 1994 (c.40) Sch 16 para 21 (3.1.95).
2.   Amended by SSA(F)A s4.
3.   Amended by art 3 of SI 2005 No 1790 as from 30.6.05.
4.   Amended by SSA 1998 Sch 7 para 88 (5.7.99).
5.   Amended by Art 12 of SI 2004 No 1823 as from 14.7.04.
6.   Amended by the Public Services Ombudsman (Wales) Act 2005 s39, Sch 6 para 26 and Sch 7 (1.4.06).
7.   Amended by the Local Government and Public Involvement in Health Act 2007 s146 and Sch 9 para 2(h) (1.4.07).
8.   Substituted by WRA 2007 s63 and Sch 7 para 3(3) (3.7.07).

General Note

This section makes it a criminal offence for officials involved in the administration or audit of benefits, or the investigation of complaints, to make an unauthorised disclosure of information which relates to particular people. It is applicable to local authority officers in relation to acts committed on or after 1 July 1997, when the amendments to Sch 4 naming officers as persons to whom s123 applies came into force.

[¹Information from landlords and agents

126A.–(1)   Regulations shall provide that where a claim for housing benefit in respect of a dwelling is made to an authority and the circumstances are such as are prescribed–

(a)   the authority; or

(b)   a person authorised to exercise any function of the authority relating to housing benefit,

may require any appropriate person to supply information of a prescribed description to the authority or other person.

(2)   Subject to subsection (4) below, for the purposes of subsection (1) above a person is an appropriate person in relation to a dwelling if he is–

(a)   a person to whom anyone is, or claims to be, liable to make relevant payments;

(b)   a person to whom, or at whose direction, a person within paragraph (a) above has agreed to make payments in consequence of being entitled to receive relevant payments; or

(c)   a person acting on behalf of a person within paragraph (a) or (b) above in connection with any aspect of the management of the dwelling.

(3)   In subsection (2) above "relevant payments", in relation to a dwelling, means payments in respect of the dwelling which are of a description in relation to which housing benefit may be paid.

(4)   Regulations may provide that any prescribed person, or any person of a prescribed description, is not an appropriate person for the purposes of subsection (1) above.

(5)   The descriptions of information which may be prescribed for the purposes of subsection (1) above include, in particular, any description of information relating to, or to any interest in or other connection with, dwellings and other property situated anywhere in the United Kingdom.

(6)   Information shall be supplied under subsection (1) above in such manner and form, and at such time and in accordance with such other requirements, as may be prescribed.

(7)   Information supplied to an authority or other person under subsection (1) above may be used by the authority or other person only in the exercise of any function relating to housing benefit or council tax benefit.

(8)   The provisions of sections 122D and 122E above apply in relation to any information supplied under subsection (1) above which is not [² relevant benefit information] (within the meaning of those provisions) as if it were.]

Amendments

1.   Inserted by SSA(F)A s11 (8.10.97).
2.   Amended by WRA 2007 s48(4) (2.7.09).

General Note

During the passage of the Social Security Administration (Fraud) Act 1997, one of the main concerns of the Labour members in Committee was the failure of the Bill to make specific provision for the problem of fraud by landlords. The creation of a landlord register was proposed with criminal sanctions for non-compliance, and a power to refuse to pay benefit where fraud was suspected.

The government's response was s11 of the Act, which inserted s126A. The section gives power to the authority to require information in circumstances to be prescribed by regulations. By subsection (5), it is made clear that the principal use of the provision will be to obtain lists of the landlord's property portfolio to enable cross-checks to be made. See also Sch 8 para 34 WRPA (on p1705).

For the information that may be required from landlords, see regs 117–121 HB Regs (reg 98–102 HB(SPC) Regs).

Analysis

Subsection (2)

This sets out the categories of people from whom information may be required under s126A.

(a)   Refers to the landlord or any person to whom the claimant is liable to make relevant payments. "Relevant payments" is defined in subs (3) as any payment (usually rent) which may lead to HB being paid. See reg 8 of both the HB and the HB(SPC) Regs for where a tenant may be so liable.

(b) This deals with situations where there is effectively a sub-letting arrangement. If A lets a flat to B, and B in turn takes in a lodger C after agreeing that A will receive a share of the rent in return for letting him take in C, A will be liable to provide information under s126A when C claims HB.

(c) This is a reference to agents.

Subsection (7)
The information supplied under s126A may only be used for purposes relating to benefits. See s123 for the consequences of a breach of this provision.

Subsection (8)
This subsection allows information collected under s126A to be passed to the Secretary of State or to other authorities under the powers conferred by ss122D and 122E.

Information for purposes of housing benefit
[¹**127.**]

Amendment
1. Repealed by the SSA(F) Act 1997.

Information for purposes of council tax benefit
[¹**128.**]

Amendment
1. Repealed by the SSA(F) Act 1997.

[¹ Expedited claims for housing [and council tax benefit]

Disclosure of information by authorities
128A.–(1)   Regulations may make provision requiring the disclosure by one authority ("the disclosing authority") to another authority ("the receiving authority"), in prescribed circumstances, of information of a prescribed description obtained by the disclosing authority in respect of persons who have been entitled to a jobseeker's allowance or to income support.

(2)   The regulations may in particular provide for–

(a)   information to be disclosed–
   (i)   at the request of the receiving authority;
   (ii)   at the request of any person who falls within a prescribed category; or
   (iii) otherwise than in response to such a request;

(b)   the period within which information is to be disclosed; and

(c)   information to be disclosed only if it has been obtained by the disclosing authority in the exercise of any of their functions in relation to housing benefit or council tax benefit.]

Amendments
1. Inserted by Jobseekers Act 1995, s28(2) (12.12.95 for regulation-making purposes, 1.4.96 for other purposes).
2. Whole section to be repealed by SSA(F)A, s22 Sch 2 when brought into force.

Modification
Section 128A was repealed by WRA 2012 s147 and Sch 14 part 1 on 1.4.13 in so far as it related to CTB.

General Note
This section was to be repealed by s22 Social Security Administration (Fraud) Act 1997, but the repealing provision has not yet been brought into force. It is not clear whether the reference to s128A in Sch 2 was a mistake. For regulations under this section, see reg 115 HB Regs (reg 96 HB(SPC) Regs).

PART VIII
Arrangements for Housing Benefit and Council Tax Benefits and Related Subsidies
Housing benefit

Arrangements for housing benefit

134.–[¹(1)   Housing benefit provided by virtue of a scheme under section 123 of the Social Security Contributions and Benefits Act 1992 (in this Part referred to as "the housing benefit scheme") shall be funded and administered by the appropriate housing authority or local authority.

(1A)   Housing benefit in respect of payments which the occupier of a dwelling is liable to make to a housing authority shall take the form of a rent rebate or, in prescribed cases, a rent allowance funded and administered by that authority.
The cases that may be so prescribed do not include any where the payment is in respect of property within the authority's Housing Revenue Account.

(1B)   In any other case housing benefit shall take the form of a rent allowance funded and administered by the local authority for the area in which the dwelling is situated or by such other local authority as is specified by an order made by the Secretary of State.]

(2)   The rebates and allowances referred to in [² subsections (1A) and (1B)] above may take any of the following forms, that is to say–

(a)   a payment or payments by the authority to the person entitled to the benefit;

(b)   a reduction in the amount of any payments which that person is liable to make to the authority by way of rent; or

(c)   such a payment or payments and such a reduction;

and in any enactment or instrument (whenever passed or made) "pay", in relation to housing benefit, includes discharge in any of those forms.

[¹ (3)]

[¹ (4)]

[¹ (5)   Authorities may–

(a)   agree that one shall discharge functions relating to housing benefit on another's behalf; or

(b)   discharge any such functions jointly or arrange for their discharge by a joint committee.

(5A)   Nothing in this section shall be read as excluding the general provisions of the Local Government Act 1972 or the Local Government (Scotland) Act 1973 from applying in relation to the housing benefit functions of a local authority.]

[¹ (6)]

[¹ (7)]

(8)   An authority may modify any part of the housing benefit scheme administered by the authority

(a)   so as to provide for disregarding, in determining a person's income (whether he is the occupier of a dwelling or any other person whose income falls to be aggregated with that of the occupier of a dwelling), the whole or part of any [⁴ prescribed] war disablement pension or [⁴ prescribed] war widow's [⁴] pension payable to that person;

(b)   to such extent in other respects as may be prescribed,

and any such modification may be adopted by resolution of an authority.

(9)   Modifications other than such modifications as are mentioned in subsection (8)(a) above shall be so framed as to secure that, in the estimate of the authority adopting them, the total of [¹ the housing benefit which will be paid by the authority in any year will not exceed the permitted total or any subsidiary limit specified by order of the Secretary of State.]

(10)   An authority who have adopted modifications may by resolution revoke or vary them.

(11)   If the housing benefit scheme includes power for an authority to exercise a discretion in awarding housing benefit, the authority shall not exercise that discretion so that the total of [¹ the housing benefit paid by them during the year exceeds the permitted total or any subsidiary limit specified by order of the Secretary of State.]

[¹ (12) The Secretary of State–
(a) shall by order specify the permitted total of housing benefit payable by any authority in any year; and
(b) may by order specify one or more subsidiary limits on the amount of housing benefit payable by any authority in any year in respect of any matter or matters specified in the order.

The power to specify the permitted total or a subsidiary limit may be exercised by fixing an amount or by providing rules for its calculation.]

(13) In this section "modifications" includes additions, omissions and amendments, and related expressions shall be construed accordingly.

[⁴ (14) In this section "war widow's pension" includes any corresponding pension payable to a widower or surviving civil partner.]

Definitions
"dwelling" – see s191.
"housing authority" – see s191.
"modifications" – see s134(13).
"war widow's pension" – see s134(14).

Amendments
1. Amended by the Housing Act 1996 Sch 12 para 1 and partially repealed by Sch 19, Part VI (1.4.97).
2. Amended by the LGA 2003 s127(1) and Sch 7 para 35 (deemed to come into force on 1.4.97).
3. Inserted by Art 7 of SI 2005 No 2053 as from 5.12.05.
4. Amended by WRA 2007 ss40 and 67 and Sch 5 para 3 and Sch 8 (3.7.07).

General Note
Subs (1A) and (1B) prescribe the two different forms that HB may take, depending on whether it is paid to a housing authority or to other types of landlord (eg, private or housing association). Note that under s191, "housing authority" means a local authority, a new town corporation or the Development Board for Rural Wales.

Subs (5) enables those administering the scheme to make arrangements whereby one will carry out the functions of the other (eg, where HB is payable in respect of two homes under reg 7(6)(d) of both the HB and the HB(SPC) Regs) the authority in the area the claimant has moved from may ask the authority in the new area to deal with HB in respect of both homes.

Subs (8)–(10) allow the authority to modify the basic HB scheme within limits. Subs (8) sets out the circumstances in which modifications may be made and how they may be adopted by the authority. Subs (10) permits the authority to revoke any modifications if its terms are complied with. Subs (9) sets a financial limit on the modifications which may be made.

Subs (11) puts a financial limit on the extent to which an authority may use its discretionary powers to award extra benefit. The financial limits in subs (9) and (11) are defined by subs (12).

Analysis
Subs (1) requires the HB scheme to be funded and administered by the appropriate "housing authority" or "local authority", both defined in s191.

Subs (1A) and (1B) specify the two types of HB: rent rebate which is generally paid to claimants who pay rent to the housing authority who administers the HB scheme, and rent allowance which is paid to those who pay rent to other landlords. This is not quite a rigid distinction, since certain prescribed occupiers who make payments to a housing authority may receive rent allowance instead: see reg 91A HB Regs and reg 72A HB (SPC) Regs. The proviso to subs (1A) limits the cases which by Secretary of State prescription may take the form of a rent allowance so as to exclude payments of HB in relation to properties within the authority's housing revenue account (HRA). Such properties are detailed in s74 Local Government and Housing Act 1989 (c.42) and include all mainstream council housing provided under Part II of the Housing Act 1985 and accommodation the authority has leased from the private sector of the same purpose where it has chosen to account for it within its HRA.

An important distinction in the treatment of claims in rent rebate and rent allowance cases is that the requirement to refer to the rent officer for determinations and then to apply certain of the rent restriction rules only applies to the latter, and not to the former: see regs 13, 13C and 14 of both the HB and the HB(SPC) Regs.

Subs (2) clarifies the forms of "payment" envisaged by the terms "rebate" and "allowance" and is also important in relation to overpayments of benefit. See note on the HB Regs reg 99 on p582.

Subs (8) allows an authority to modify the HB scheme by resolution. In the assessment of income for HB, £10 of certain war pensions must be disregarded. Subs 8(a) allows an authority to resolve to disregard more of (or all of) prescribed war pensions as income for the purposes of its HB scheme. The prescribed pensions are in the Schedule to the HB&CTB (War Pension Disregards) Regulations 2007 No.1619 (see p1808). Note that "war widow's pension" includes any corresponding pension payable to a widower or a surviving civil partner: subs (14).

The authority may change its mind by a further resolution: subs (10). For "occupier", see HB Regs reg 7 and for "income", see Section 1 of Part 6 of the HB Regs. No direct subsidy is paid in respect of extra benefit paid in accordance with this section.

Prior to the amendments made by SI 2007 No.1619 from 3 July 2007, reg 40(3) HB Regs (reg 33(13) HB(SPC) Regs) and reg 30(3) CTB Regs (reg 23(13) CTB(SPC) Regs), made under subs (8)(b), permitted a similar disregard in relation to a war widower's pension. A local authority would have to have found stringent justification for any disparity in treatment between widows and widowers if it was not to fall foul of Art 14 of the European Convention on Human Rights, and it would not be permitted a period of grace in order to carry out reforms: *R (Hooper) v SSWP* [2003] 1 WLR 2623, CA, affirmed on this point by the House of Lords in [2005] UKHL 29, *The Times,* 6 May.

A resolution usually only has effect from the date it is expressed to take effect. Thus where a claimant had been overpaid due to a late payment of an increase in his war pension, a resolution of the council to ignore war pension as income did not have retrospective effect: *R v South Hams DC ex p Ash* (1999) 32 HLR 405, QBD.

Subs (11) forbids authorities to exceed the permitted total of expenditure by allowing discretionary increases in benefit.

Housing benefit finance
[¹**135.**]

Amendment
1.   Repealed by the Housing Act 1996 Sch 19, Part VI (1.4.97).

Rent allowance subsidy and determinations of rent officers
[¹**136.**]

Amendment
1.   Repealed by the Housing Act 1996 Sch 19, Part VI (1.4.97).

[¹ Reports

Persons to report on administration
139A.–[²(1)   The Secretary of State may authorise persons to consider and report to him on the administration by authorities of housing benefit *[and council tax benefit]*.

(2)   The Secretary of State may ask persons authorised under subsection (1) to consider in particular–
(a)   authorities' performance in the prevention and detection of fraud relating to housing benefit *[and council tax benefit]*;
(b)   authorities' compliance with the requirements of Part I of the Local Government Act 1999 (best value).

(2A)   A person may be authorised under subsection (1)–
(a)   on such terms and for such period as the Secretary of State thinks fit;
(b)   to act generally or in relation to a specified authority or authorities;
(c)   to report on administration generally or on specified matters.]
(3)   In sections 139B and 139C below–
"benefit" means housing benefit *[or council tax benefit]*; and
"authority" means an authority which is administering either of those benefits.]

Amendments
1.   Inserted by the SSA(F)A 1997 s5.
2.   Substituted by the Local Government Act 1999 s14(1) (1.4.00).

Modification
Section 139A was repealed by WRA 2012 s147 and Sch 14 part 1 on 1.4.13 in so far as it related to CTB.

General Note
This section and those that follow it were introduced from 1 July 1997 by the Social Security Administration (Fraud) Act 1997 following concern at the apparent unwillingness of some authorities to tackle fraud. They give

the Secretary of State extensive powers over recalcitrant authorities and, ultimately, to require an authority's HB (and before 1 April 2013 its CTB) functions to be privatised.

This section gives the Secretary of State the power to appoint inspectors to examine the prevention of fraud and generally the administration of HB (and before 1 April 2013 CTB).

The section was amended by the Local Government Act 1999 to permit reports to consider whether the local authority is complying with the 'best value' provisions in Part I of the 1999 Act.

[¹Powers of investigation

139B.–(1)   A person authorised under section 139A(1) above–

(a)   has a right of access at all reasonable times to any document relating to the administration of benefit;

(b)   is entitled to require from any person holding or accountable for any such document such information and explanation as he thinks necessary; and

(c)   is entitled, if he thinks it necessary, to require any such person to produce any such document or to attend before him in person to give such information or explanation.

(2)   A person authorised under section 139A(1) above is entitled to require any officer or member of an authority or any person involved in the administration of benefit for an authority–

(a)   to give him such information and explanation relating to the administration of benefit as he thinks necessary; and

(b)   if he thinks it necessary, to require any such person to attend before him in person to give the information or explanation.

(3)   A person who without reasonable excuse fails to comply with a requirement under subsection (1) or (2) above is guilty of an offence and liable on summary conviction to a fine not exceeding level 3 on the standard scale.

(4)   A person authorised under section 139A(1) above may–

(a)   require any document or information which is to be given to him under subsection (1) or (2) above to be given in any form reasonably specified by him; and

(b)   take copies of any document produced to him.

(5)   In this section "document" means anything in which information of any description is recorded.]

Amendment

1.   Inserted by SSA(F)A s5.

Modification

Section 139B was repealed by WRA 2012 s147 and Sch 14 part 1 on 1.4.13 in so far as it related to CTB.

General Note

Extremely wide powers are given to the inspectors to look at documents, to require explanation of them under subs (1) and more generally to require information relating to benefit administration from local authority officials under subs (2). Such documents and information must be supplied in such form as the inspector requires and copies may be taken: subs (4). The definition of "document" in subs (5) covers items such as electronic data as well as paperwork.

[¹ [²139BA.]]

Amendments

1.   Inserted by of the Local Government and Public Involvement in Health Act 2007 s150 (1.4.08).

2.   Omitted by s45 and Sch 12 para 29 Local Audit and Accountability Act 2014 and art 3 SI 2015 No.841 (1.4.15).

Reports

[¹**139C.**–(1)   A report about an authority by a person authorised under section 139A(1) above may include recommendations about improvements which could be made by that authority in its administration of benefit and, [² in particular–

(a)   in the prevention and detection of fraud relating to benefit, or

(b)   for the purposes of complying with the requirements of Part I of the Local Government Act 1999 (best value).]

(2)   When the Secretary of State receives a report about an authority from a person authorised under section 139A(1) above, he shall send a copy to the authority.]

Amendments
1.   Inserted by SSA(F)A s5.
2.   Substituted by the Local Government Act 1999 s4(2) (1.4.00).

Modification
Section 139C was repealed by WRA 2012 s147 and Sch 14 part 1 on 1.4.13 in so far as it related to CTB.

General Note
By subs (2), the authority under investigation is entitled to receive a copy of any report made by the inspectors.

[¹ *Directions by Secretary of State*

[¹ **Directions**
139D.–(1)   This section applies where–
(a)   a copy of a report has been sent to an authority under section 139C(2) above;
(b)   a copy of a report has been sent to an authority under [² section 10(1) of the Audit Commission Act 1998] and to the Secretary of State under [² section 39 of that Act];
[³ (ba) a copy of a report has been sent to an authority under section 22(5) or (6) of the Public Audit (Wales) Act 2004 and to the Secretary of State under section 51(3) of that Act;]
[⁵ (bb) a copy of a report has been sent to a local authority under subsection (3) of section 13 of the Local Government Act 1999 and to the Secretary of State under subsection (4A) of that section;]
[⁴ (c) a copy of a report under section 102(1)(b) or (c) of the Local Government (Scotland) Act 1973 which to any extent relates to the administration of benefit has been sent to a local authority and the Secretary of State under section 102(2) of that Act;]
[⁴ (ca) a copy of a report which has been sent to a local authority under section 13A(3) of the Local Government Act 1999 and to the Secretary of State under section 13A(4A) of that Act;]
(d)   a copy of a report has been sent to an authority under [² section 38(7) of the Audit Commission Act 1998] or section 105A(7) of the Local Government (Scotland) Act 1973.

(2)   The Secretary of State may [⁴ require] the authority to consider the report and to submit proposals for–
(a)   improving its performance in relation to the prevention and detection of fraud relating to benefit or otherwise in relation to the administration of benefit; and
(b)   remedying any failings identified by the report.
[⁴ (2A)   A requirement under subsection (2) above may specify–
(a)   any information or description of information to be provided;
(b)   the form and manner in which the information is to be provided.
(2B)   The authority must respond to a requirement under subsection (2) above before the end of such period (not less than one month after the day on which the requirement is made) as the Secretary of State specifies in the requirement.
(2C)   The Secretary of State may extend the period specified under subsection (2B) above.]
[⁴ (3)   After considering–
(a)   the report,
(b)   any proposals made by the authority in response to it, and
(c)   any other information he thinks is relevant,
the Secretary of State may give directions to the authority under subsection (3A) or (3B) or both.
(3A)   Directions under this subsection are directions as to–

(a)   standards which the authority is to attain in the prevention and detection of fraud relating to benefit or otherwise in the administration of benefit;

(b)   the time within which the standards are to be attained.

(3B)   Directions under this subsection are directions to take such action as the Secretary of State thinks necessary or expedient for the purpose of improving the authority's exercise of its functions–

(a)   in relation to the prevention and detection of fraud relating to benefit;

(b)   otherwise in relation to the administration of benefit.

(3C)   A direction under subsection (3B) may specify the time within which anything is to be done.]

(4)   When giving directions to an authority under [⁴ subsection (3A)] above, the Secretary of State may make recommendations to the authority setting out any course of action which he thinks it might take to attain the standards which it is directed to attain.

[⁴ (4A)   If the Secretary of State proposes to give a direction under this section he must give the authority to which the direction is to be addressed an opportunity to make representations about the proposed direction.

(4B)   The Secretary of State may specify a period within which representations mentioned in subsection (4A) above must be made.

(4C)   The Secretary of State may extend a period specified under subsection (4B) above.

(4D)   Subsections (4A) to (4C) do not apply if the Secretary of State thinks that it is necessary for a direction to be given as a matter of urgency.

(4E)   If the Secretary of State acts under subsection (4D) he must give in writing to the authority to which the direction is addressed his reasons for doing so.]

(5)   In this section "benefit" means housing benefit or council tax benefit.

Amendments

1.   Inserted by SSA(F)A s8.
2.   Amended by the Audit Commission Act 1998 Sch 3 para 23.
3.   Amended by the Public Audit (Wales) Act 2004 s66 and Sch 2 para 15 (1.4.05).
4.   Amended by WRA 2007 s39 (1.4.08).
5.   Inserted by the Local Government and Public Involvement in Health Act 2007 s147(2) (1.4.08).

Modification

Section 139D was repealed by WRA 2012 s147 and Sch 14 part 1 on 1.4.13 in so far as it related to CTB.

General Note

Section 139D is the initial stage of the four-part enforcement process by which the Secretary of State can compel improvements in the detection of fraud and administration of HB generally, where the performance of a local authority is thought to be unsatisfactory. It will follow a report by an inspector under s139C(2) or by the appropriate local government auditor: subs (1). This section and the three following it were introduced at the last moment in Committee.

The starting point in the process is for the Secretary of State to invite the authority's response to the report and suggest how it thinks matters could be improved. If the minister is not happy with the response, s/he may issue directions under subs (3) requiring improvements.

Analysis

Before directions are given, it is an essential part of the process for the Secretary of State to seek the authority's views under subs (2). If this step is omitted, it would seem that directions under subs (3) would be *ultra vires* as these can only be given by the Secretary of State "after considering ... any proposals made by the authority".

The Secretary of State may require an authority to reach a certain standard within a certain period of time. In determining this standard, the Secretary of State must act reasonably but has the widest discretion and it would have to be shown that the standards set are wholly irrational before they can be subject to any challenge. However, the structure of subs (3) suggests that the Secretary of State may only have regard to the contents of the report and the authority's response in considering whether to make a direction, and if so what direction to make. If, for example, a direction was made following a petition, then it seems that such a direction could be challenged on grounds of procedural impropriety.

[¹ **Directions: variation and revocation**
139DA.–(1)   The Secretary of State may at any time in accordance with this section vary or revoke a direction under section 139D above.

(2)　A direction may be varied or revoked only if the Secretary of State thinks it is necessary to do so–
(a)　in consequence of representations made by the authority to which the direction is addressed,
(b)　to rectify an omission or error, or
(c)　in consequence of a material change in circumstances.
(3)　The Secretary of State must not vary a direction unless he first–
(a)　sends a copy of the proposed variation to the authority concerned,
(b)　gives the authority his reasons for making the variation, and
(c)　gives the authority an opportunity to make representations about the proposed variation.
(4)　The Secretary of State may specify a period of not less than one month within which representations mentioned in subsection (3)(c) above must be made.
(5)　The Secretary of State may extend a period specified under subsection (4) above.

Amendment
1.　Inserted by s39(9) WRA 2007 with effect from 1.04.08.

Modification
Section 139DA was repealed by WRA 2012 s147 and Sch 14 part 1 on 1.4.13 in so far as it related to CTB.

Information about attainment of standards
[¹**139E.**–(1)　Where directions have been given to an authority under [² section 139D(3A) or (3B)] above, the Secretary of State may require the authority to supply to him any information which he considers may assist him in deciding–
(a)　whether the authority has attained the standards which it has been directed to attain; or
[² (aa) whether the authority has taken the action which it has been directed to take;]
(b)　whether the authority is likely to attain those standards [² or take that action] within the time specified in the directions.
(2)　Information shall be supplied under subsection (1) above in such manner and form as the Secretary of State may require.]

Amendments
1.　Inserted by SSA(F)A s9.
2.　Amended by WRA 2007 s40 and Sch 5 para 5 (1.04.08).

Modification
Section 139E was repealed by WRA 2012 s147 and Sch 14 part 1 on 1.4.13 in so far as it related to CTB.

General Note
This is the second part of the enforcement process. It enables the Secretary of State to monitor the progress of the authority by requiring information to be supplied to her/him.

Enforcement notices
[¹**139F.**–(1)　Where directions have been given to an authority under [² section 139D(3A) or (3B)] above and the Secretary of State–
(a)　is not satisfied that the authority has attained the standards which it has been directed to attain; or
[² (aa) is not satisfied that the authority has taken the action which it has been directed to take;]
(b)　is not satisfied that the authority is likely to attain those standards [² or take that action] within the time specified in the directions,
he may serve on the authority a written notice under this section.
(2)　The notice shall–
(a)　identify the directions and state why the Secretary of State is not satisfied as mentioned in paragraph (a) [² , (aa)] or (b) of subsection (1) above; and

(b)   require the authority to submit a written response to the Secretary of State within a time specified in the notice.

(3)   If any person (other than the authority) carrying out work relating to the administration of benefit may be affected by any determination which may be made under section 139G below, the authority shall–

(a)   consult that person before submitting its response; and

(b)   include in its response any relevant observations made by that person.

(4)   [² If the notice identifies directions under section 139D(3A),] The authority's response shall either–

(a)   state that the authority has attained the standards, or is likely to attain them within the time specified in the directions, and justify that statement; or

(b)   state that the authority has not attained the standards, or is not likely to attain them within that time, and (if the authority wishes) give reasons why a determination under section 139G below should not be made or should not include any particular provision.

[² (4A)   If the notice identifies directions under section 139D(3B), the authority's response shall either–

(a)   state that the authority has taken the action, or is likely to take it within the time specified in the directions, and justify that statement; or

(b)   state that the authority has not taken the action, or is not likely to take it within that time, and (if the authority wishes) give reasons why a determination under section 139G below should not be made or should not include any particular provision.]

(5)   The notice may relate to any one or more matters covered by the directions.

(6)   The serving of a notice under this section relating to any directions or matter does not prevent the serving of further notices under this section relating to the same directions or matter.

(7)   In this section "benefit" means housing benefit *[or council tax benefit]*.]

Amendments
1.   Inserted by SSA(F)A s9.
2.   Amended by WRA 2007 s40 and Sch 5 para 6 (1.04.08).

Modification
Section 139F was repealed by WRA 2012 s147 and Sch 14 part 1 on 1.4.13 in so far as it related to CTB.

General Note
If it becomes clear to the Secretary of State that an authority has not taken action, or is unlikely to take action, it has been directed to take or has not attained, or is not likely to attain, the standards set by a direction under s139D(3A) or (3B), an enforcement notice may be served on the authority. A notice may be served before the expiry of any time limit specified in the direction: subs (1)(b). The notice must state, under subs (2)(a), the reasons for the Secretary of State's dissatisfaction.

The local authority is required to respond to the notice and state whether it has, or is going to be able to comply with the direction: subs (4) and (4A). Before it does so, it must consult those involved in the administration of benefit and incorporate their views in its response.

Subs (5) and (6) loosen possible restrictions on the Secretary of State's power to issue enforcement notices. Under subs (5), a notice may relate to particular matters identified in the direction, rather than the whole direction. More than one notice may be served in relation to a direction, and subs (6) confirms that subsequent notices may deal with the same matters as previous notices.

Analysis
"any person (other than the authority) carrying out work relating to the administration of benefit". On a wide reading, this might include the administrative staff employed by the local authority as well as people or business organisations outside the authority carrying out functions relating to the administration of HB.

Enforcement determinations
[¹**139G.**–(1)   Where, after the time specified in the notice under section 139F above has expired, the Secretary of State–

(a)   is not satisfied that the authority has attained the standards [² or taken the action] in question; or

(b)   is not satisfied that the authority is likely to attain those standards [² or take that action] within the time specified in the directions, he may make a determination under this section.

(2)   The determination may be made whether or not the authority has responded to the notice under section 139F above.

(3)   The determination shall be designed to secure the attainment of the standards [² or the taking of the action] in question and–

(a)   shall include provision such as is specified in subsection (4) below; and

(b)   may also include provision such as is specified in subsection (5) below.

(4)   The provision referred to in paragraph (a) of subsection (3) above is provision that the authority must comply with specified requirements as to inviting, preparing, considering and accepting bids to carry out any work which–

(a)   falls to be carried out in pursuance of the authority's functions relating to the administration of benefit; and

(b)   is of a description specified in the determination.

(5)   The provision referred to in paragraph (b) of that subsection is provision of any one or more of the following kinds relating to the work, or any specified category of the work, to which the determination relates–

(a)   provision that it may not be carried out by the authority;

(b)   provision that it may not be carried out by any person (other than the authority) who has been carrying it out; and

(c)   provision that any contract made by the authority with any person for carrying it out shall include terms requiring a level of performance which will secure, or contribute to securing, the attainment of the standards [² or the taking of the action] in question.

(6)   In this section "benefit" means housing benefit or council tax benefit.]

Amendments
1.   Inserted by SSA(F)A s9.
2.   Amended by WRA 2007 s40 and Sch 5 para 7 (1.04.08).

Modification
Section 139G was repealed by WRA 2012 s147 and Sch 14 part 1 on 1.4.13 in so far as it related to CTB.

General Note
The final step in the procedure is an enforcement determination. By this draconian step, the Secretary of State is able to require an authority to put its administration of HB, or any part thereof, out to tender: subs (4).

The Secretary of State may also impose further conditions under subs (5). The authority may be forbidden to carry out the work itself, a person who has been carrying out the work (see s139F) may be excluded, and the authority may be required to specify attainment of the standards, or the taking of action, as conditions of the contract awarded. See also s139H(3).

Enforcement determinations: supplementary

[¹**139H.**–(1)   The provisions included in a determination under section 139G above shall take effect from a date specified in the determination; and different dates may be specified in relation to different provisions.

(2)   The making of a determination under section 139G above in relation to any directions does not prevent the making of further determinations under that section in relation to the same directions.

(3)   The provision included in a determination by virtue of section 139G(3) above may include–

(a)   requirements that the Secretary of State be satisfied as to any specified matter; and

(b)   requirements that the Secretary of State authorise or consent to any specified matter.

(4)   The provision so included may also include provision as to the time at which any contract for the carrying out of work to which the determination relates (and which is not previously discharged) is to be taken to be frustrated by the determination.

(5)   A determination under section 139G above shall have effect in spite of any enactment under or by virtue of which an authority is required or authorised to carry out any work to which the determination relates.

(6)   A determination under section 139G above may make provision having effect, in relation to the work to which it relates, instead of any requirement which (apart from the determination) would have effect in relation to that work under or by virtue of the Local Government Act 1988.]

Amendment
1.   Inserted by SSA(F)A s9.

Modification
Section 139H was repealed by WRA 2012 s147 and Sch 14 part 1 on 1.4.13 in so far as it related to CTB.

General Note
This section makes a number of additional provisions in relation to enforcement determinations. By subs (1), time limits may be set for the determination to come into effect. More than one determination may be made in relation to a direction: subs (2). Subs (5) and (6) make it clear that the determination overrides any statutory provision requiring the authority to carry out the work in question and the requirements of the Local Government Act 1988 in relation to compulsory competitive tendering.

Finally, subs (3) allows the Secretary of State to control virtually any aspect of the tendering process or the work carried out pursuant to an enforcement direction.

[¹ Subsidy

Subsidy
140A.–(1)   For each year the Secretary of State shall pay a subsidy to each authority administering housing benefit *[or council tax benefit]*.

(2)   He shall pay–

(a)   rent rebate subsidy to each housing authority;

(b)   rent allowance subsidy to each local authority; and

[(c)   council tax benefit subsidy to each billing authority or levying authority.]

(3)   In the following provisions of this Part "subsidy", without more, refers to subsidy of any of those descriptions.]

Amendment
1.   Inserted by the Housing Act 1996 Sch 12 para 4.

Modification
Section 140A was repealed by WRA 2012 s147 and Sch 14 part 1 on 1.4.13 in so far as it related to CTB.

General Note
Sections 140A to 140G deal with the subsidy arrangements in respect of HB. Prior to 1 April 2013, they also dealt with the arrangements for CTB.

[¹Calculation of amount of subsidy
140B.–(1)   The amount of subsidy to be paid to an authority [⁴ determined in accordance with an] order made by the Secretary of State.

(2)   Subject as follows, the amount of subsidy shall be calculated by reference to the amount of relevant benefit paid by the authority during the year.
[³]

(3)   The order may provide that the amount of subsidy in respect of any matter shall be a fixed sum or shall be nil.

[² (4)   The Secretary of State may–

(a)   pay as part of subsidy an additional amount specified by, or calculated in a manner specified by, the order; or

(b)   deduct from the amount which would otherwise be payable by way of subsidy an amount specified by, or calculated in a manner specified by, the order.

(4A)   The additional amounts which may be paid by virtue of subsection (4)(a) above include amounts in respect of–

(a)   the costs of administering the relevant benefit; or

(b)   success in preventing or detecting fraud relating to the relevant benefit or action to be taken with a view to preventing or detecting such fraud.

(5)   The Secretary of State may–

(a)   where an application is made by an authority on his invitation, pay to the authority as part of the subsidy such additional amount as he considers appropriate in respect of–

(i)   success in preventing or detecting fraud relating to the relevant benefit; or

(ii)   action to be taken with a view to preventing or detecting such fraud; or

(b)   deduct from the subsidy which would otherwise be payable to an authority such amount as he considers it unreasonable to pay by way of subsidy.

(5A)   The amounts which may be deducted by virtue of subsection (4)(b) or (5)(b) above include amounts in respect of–

(a)   a failure to comply with directions under [⁵ section 139D(3A) or (3B)] above; and

(b)   other failures in preventing or detecting fraud relating to the relevant benefit.]

(6)   In this section "relevant benefit" means housing benefit *[or council tax benefit, as the case may be]*.

[³ (7)]

Amendments

1.   Inserted by the Housing Act 1996 Sch 12 para 4.
2.   Substituted by SSA(F)A s10.
3.   Omitted/repealed by the Local Government Act 2003, s127(1) and Sch 7 para 36 and s127(2) and Part 1 Sch 8 (18.11.03).
4.   Amended by SSA(F)A Sch 1 para 7 (1.7.97).
5.   Amended by WRA 2007 s40 and Sch 5 para 9 (1.04.08).

Modification

Section 140B was repealed by WRA 2012 s147 and Sch 14 part 1 on 1.4.13 in so far as it related to CTB.

General Note

Subsection (3) permits any element of a subsidy calculation to be made on a fixed basis or to be nil. The subsidy scheme gives greater powers to the Secretary of State to determine the amount of subsidy paid to relevant authorities, and in particular to reward success and punish failure regarding the prevention of fraud by giving extra subsidy or reducing it.

Analysis

Subs (5). The Secretary of State does not have to seek the approval of Parliament prior to making deductions from the amounts of subsidy under her/his powers. The analysis in *R v Secretary of State for the Environment ex p Hammersmith and Fulham LBC* [1991] 1 AC 521 at 597E-H, HL will not therefore apply and an order made by the Secretary of State can be subject to challenge on the grounds of unreasonableness. In particular, it is suggested that there can be no deduction from the subsidy unless the Secretary of State has some form of reliable evidence to justify such an approach, whether it be on the ground that the normal amount would be "unreasonable" under subs (4)(b) or that there have been failures in preventing fraud under subs (5A)(b).

Subs (5A). Note that the power to reduce subsidy is not limited to the two factors mentioned, they are merely "included" in the circumstances that can justify a reduction.

[¹Payment of subsidy

140C.–(1)   Subsidy shall be paid by the Secretary of State in such instalments, at such times, in such manner and subject to such conditions as to claims, records, certificates, audit or otherwise as may be provided by order of the Secretary of State.

[² (1A)   Conditions under subsection (1) above may (in particular) be imposed to obtain information for the purposes of the carrying-out by the Secretary of State of any of his functions relating to subsidy.]

(2)   The order may provide that if an authority has not, within such period as may be specified in the order, complied with the conditions so specified as to claims, records,

certificate, audit or otherwise, the Secretary of State may estimate the amount of subsidy payable to the authority and employ for that purpose such criteria as he considers relevant.

(3)   Where subsidy has been paid to an authority and it appears to the Secretary of State–

(a)   that subsidy has been overpaid; or

(b)   that there has been a breach of any condition specified in an order under this section, he may recover from the authority the whole or such part of the payment as he may determine.

Without prejudice to other methods of recovery, a sum recoverable under this subsection may be recovered by withholding or reducing subsidy.

(4)   An order made by the Secretary of State under this section may be made before, during or after the end of the year or years to which it relates.]

Amendments

1.   Inserted by the Housing Act 1996 Sch 12 para 4.

2.   Inserted by the Local Government Act 2003 s127(1) and Sch 7 para 37 (18.11.03).

Modification

Section 140C was repealed by WRA 2012 s147 and Sch 14 part 1 on 1.4.13 in so far as it related to CTB.

General Note

This deals with the calculation of subsidy and recovery of payments of subsidy which have either been overpaid or where there has been a breach of any condition.

Analysis

Subs (1) to (2). The Secretary of State may require the maintenance and production of records by the authority in order to calculate its subsidy and carry out estimates in default.

Subs (3)(a) expands the powers for rectifying errors in the payment of subsidy. Hitherto, the statutory powers were restricted to adjusting the following year's subsidy to rectify the error: s137(6), repealed by the Housing Act 1996 on 24 September 1996. Now the Secretary of State may require immediate repayment.

Subs (3)(b) appears to allow the Secretary of State a general discretion to recover part or the whole of a subsidy payment where an authority has failed to comply with requirements made under subs (1).

It is suggested, however, that this power cannot be exercised in a penal manner. Under subs (2), if it had been clear from the outset that the authority had failed to comply with the requirements, the Secretary of State would have had to estimate the amount of subsidy. Such method of estimation as was chosen would have to be rational and reasonable. It is not logical that the authority should be in a worse position if the failure only comes to light at a later stage. It is therefore suggested that subs (3)(b) does not allow the Secretary of State to recover so much of the subsidy that the authority has effectively received a lesser amount of subsidy than it would have received under an estimate carried out pursuant to subs (2).

This issue was to be considered in judicial review proceedings brought by Bridgnorth DC. That council had failed to implement a new version of reg 11 HB Regs 1987 properly, with the result that a large number of claims were determined without a proper reference from a rent officer. The Secretary of State decided to recover the full amount of subsidy paid in the relevant years, even though many of the claims must have been assessed correctly or even underpaid. This would have had dire consequences for the council. In its application for judicial review, the council argued that recovery of all the subsidy was disproportionate. The proceedings were settled with an agreed quashing of the decision to recover, the Secretary of State acknowledging flaws in the decision-making process and agreeing not to recover any of the subsidy.

Following a review of the Secretary of State's approach to this power, a new policy was set out in Circular S1/2002. The recovery of each overpayment of subsidy depends on all the circumstances, and criteria are set out which are to be taken into account. The implementation of the policy was challenged in *R (Isle of Anglesey DC) v SSWP* [2003] EWHC 2518 (Admin). The applicant local authority had made similar mistakes to Bridgnorth DC in its administration, and the Secretary of State proposed to recover 20 per cent of the subsidy paid to the council in respect of the claims that had not been properly administered. Lindsay J rejected the suggestion that Sch 4 para 6 Income-Related Benefits (Subsidy to Authorities) Order 1998, which awards nil subsidy where a claim has not been referred to the Rent Officer, was *ultra vires* (para 40) and also held that the decision of the Secretary of State on the particular facts of the case could not be castigated as penal, disproportionate or irrational.

[¹Rent rebate subsidy: accounting provisions

140D.–(1)   Rent rebate subsidy is payable–

(a)   in the case of a local authority in England and Wales, for the credit of a revenue account of theirs other than their Housing Revenue Account or Housing Repairs Account;

(b)   in the case of a local authority in Scotland, for the credit of their rent rebate account;

[² (c)]

(d)   in the case of a new town corporation in Scotland or Scottish Homes, for the credit of the account to which rent rebates granted by them, or it, are debited.

[² (2)]]

Amendments

1.   Inserted by Housing Act 1996 Sch 12 para 4.

2.   Omitted by the Local Government Act 2003, s127(1) and Sch 7 para 38 and s127(2) and Part 1 Sch 8 (18.11.03).

Modification

Section 140D was repealed by WRA 2012 s147 and Sch 14 part 1 on 1.4.13 in so far as it related to CTB.

[¹ Supplementary provisions

Financing of joint arrangements

140E.–(1)   Where two or more authorities make arrangements for the discharge of any of their functions relating to housing benefit or council tax benefit–

(a)   by one authority on behalf of itself and one or more other authorities; or

(b)   by a joint committee,

the Secretary of State may make such payments as he thinks fit to the authority or committee in respect of their expenses in carrying out those functions.

(2)   The provisions of sections 140B and 140C (subsidy: calculation and supplementary provisions) apply in relation to a payment under this section as in relation to a payment of subsidy.

(3)   The Secretary of State may (without prejudice to the generality of his powers in relation to the amount of subsidy) take into account the fact that an amount has been paid under this section in respect of expenses which would otherwise have been met in whole or in part by the participating authorities.]

Amendment

1.   Inserted by the Housing Act 1996 Sch 12 para 4.

Modification

Section 140E was repealed by WRA 2012 s147 and Sch 14 part 1 on 1.4.13 in so far as it related to CTB.

[¹No requirement for annual orders

140F.–(1)   Any power under this Part to make provision by order for or in relation to a year does not require the making of a new order each year.

(2)   Any order made under the power may be revoked or varied at any time, whether before, during or after the year to which it relates.]

Amendment

1.   Inserted by the Housing Act 1996 Sch 12 para 4.

Modification

Section 140F was repealed by WRA 2012 s147 and Sch 14 part 1 on 1.4.13 in so far as it related to CTB.

[¹Interpretation: Part VIII

140G.   In this Part, unless the context otherwise requires–

"Housing Repairs Account" means an account kept under section 77 of the Local Government and Housing Act 1989;

"Housing Revenue Account" means the account kept under section 74 of the Local Government and Housing Act 1989, and–

(a)   references to property within that account have the same meaning as in Part VI of that Act, [²]

[² (b)]

"rent rebate subsidy" and "rent allowance subsidy" shall be construed in accordance with section 134 above;

"year" means a financial year within the meaning of the Local Government Finance Act 1992.]

Amendments
1.   Inserted by the Housing Act 1996 s4.
2.   Omitted/repealed by the Local Government Act 2003, s127(1) and Sch 7 para 39 and s127(2) and Part 1 Sch 8 (18.11.03).

Modification
Section 140G was repealed by WRA 2012 s147 and Sch 14 part 1 on 1.4.13 in so far as it related to CTB.

PART X

Annual uprating of benefits
150.–(1)-(7)   *[Omitted]*
[² [¹ (7A)]]
(8)-(13)   *[Omitted]*

Amendments
1.   Inserted by s97(5) WRA 2012 as from 15.4.13.
2.   Omitted by s9(7) of the Welfare Reform and Work Act 2016 (16.3.16).

General Note
The power to review the benefit cap formerly found in s150(7A) is now in s96A of the Welfare Reform Act 2012 (on p209).

PART XIII

Advisory Bodies and Consultation

The Social Security Advisory Committee and the Industrial Injuries Advisory Council

General Note
The Social Security Advisory Committee (SSAC) is a body of experts, working on a voluntary basis, which advises the Secretary of State as to the implications of new legislation to be enacted. It serves a valuable function of bringing potential problems with proposals to the attention of officials of the DWP and in speaking with an authoritative voice in doing so. Historically, however, the SSAC has only rarely persuaded the Secretary of State to drop controversial proposals or modify them significantly, although there are exceptions such as the backdating restrictions which were due to replace the "good cause" test in reg 72(15) HB Regs 1987 and which were withdrawn mainly as a result of the SSAC's carefully reasoned opposition.

The process by which regulations are dealt with by the SSAC is that the Secretary of State first sends draft proposals to it. The Committee then decides whether or not the proposed regulations should be formally referred to it under s173(1)(b) and, if it concludes that they should be, consults the public if necessary and then produces a report under s174(1). When the regulations are laid, the Secretary of State is required to place a copy of the SSAC's report and the DWP's response before Parliament.

Certain categories of regulations are not required to be referred to the SSAC by virtue of s172(3). The categories are set out in Sch 7 SSAA, which is not reproduced in this book. In addition, s173(1) does not require the Secretary of State to refer regulations where "urgency" makes it "inexpedient" or the SSAC decides that it is unnecessary.

The SSAC seeks the views of the public on major regulations referred to it and details of current consultations can be found at www.gov.uk/government/organisations/social-security-advisory-committee.

The significance of the SSAC for the purposes of those advising claimants has increased as a result of the decision in *Howker v SSWP* [2003] ICR 405 (reported as *R(IB) 3/03*). In that decision, the Court of Appeal held that amendments to the regulations governing incapacity benefit were *ultra vires* because officials of the DWP had misled the SSAC as to the effect of the amending regulations, with the consequence that the SSAC did not ask for the amending regulations to be referred.

It need not be shown that the misleading advice was given deliberately: *Howker*, para 37. It is necessary to consider the significance of the advice (para 40) or to show that it was "seriously inaccurate" (*Howker*, para 54). The correct approach to determining whether the SSAC was misled is to look at all the material placed before the SSAC by the Secretary of State as the basis for the amendment (including answers given by DWP officials to the SSAC) and consider whether the overall effect was misleading; and, if it was, whether there is a real possibility that (a) the information might have misled the SSAC as to the effect of the proposed regulation, and (b) had the SSAC been aware of the regulations true effect it would have wished to have the proposed regulation formally referred to it: *R(IB) 2/07*.

In *CH 5125/2002*, a challenge was made to the 1998 amendments to reg 7 HB Regs 1987 on the basis that the SSAC had been misled. Commissioner Jacobs rejected the challenge (paras 68–69), holding that the adverse effect of the amendments had been made clear.

The Court of Appeal in *Campbell and others v South Northamptonshire DC and SSWP* [2004] EWCA Civ 409 CA; reported as *R(H) 8/04* – the appeal from *CH 5125/2002* – rejected the appeal and endorsed Commissioner Jacob's view that, as a whole, the adverse affects of the amendment regulations had been made clear to the SSAC and so it could not be said to have been misled.

In *DH v Kirklees MBC and SSWP (HB)* [2011] UKUT 301 (AAC); [2012] AACR 16, Judge Mesher noted that the documents put before the SSAC in *Campbell* did not make specific mention of what is now reg 9(1)(c) and that there had been some acceptance by the Court of a generally misleading effect of the amendments. He therefore considered all the SSAC-related documents that had been before the Court of Appeal in *Campbell*. He concluded that "the SSAC was not misled as to the specific effect of what became regulation 9(1)(c). There was generally misleading information provided to the SSAC, but since it decided not to require a reference after the expressions of concern it raised and the limited assurances it received, it would have made no difference to that conclusion if those general matters had been more accurately stated." He concluded that the amending regulation introducing what became reg 9(1)(c) was validly made.

The Social Security Advisory Committee

170.–(1)   The Social Security Advisory Committee (in this Act referred to as "the Committee") constituted under section 9 of the Social Security Act 1980 shall continue in being by that name–

(a)   to give (whether in pursuance of a reference under this Act or otherwise) advice and assistance to the Secretary of State in connection with the discharge of his functions under the relevant enactments;

(b)   to give (whether in pursuance of a reference under this Act or otherwise) advice and assistance to the Northern Ireland Department in connection with the discharge of its functions under the relevant Northern Ireland enactments; and

(c)   to perform such other duties as may be assigned to the Committee under any enactment.

(2)   Schedule 5 to this Act shall have effect with respect to the constitution of the Committee and the other matters there mentioned.

(3)   The Secretary of State may from time to time refer to the Committee for consideration and advice such questions relating to the operation of any of the relevant enactments as he thinks fit (including questions as to the advisability of amending any of them).

(4)   The Secretary of State shall furnish the Committee with such information as the Committee may reasonably require for the proper discharge of its functions.

(5)   In this Act–

"the relevant enactments" means–

(a)   the provisions of the Contributions and Benefits Act and this Act, except as they apply to industrial injuries benefit and Old Cases payments; and

(aa)-(ab) *[Omitted]*

[⁴ (ac) the provisions of the Social Security (Recovery of Benefits) Act 1997; and]

(ad)-(ae) *[Omitted]*

[¹ (af) section 42, [⁷] and [⁸ sections 69 and 70 of the Child Support, Pensions and Social Security Act 2000].]

[² (ag) [⁶ sections 6A to 11] of the Social Security Fraud Act 2001.]

[³ (ah) the provisions of the State Pension Credit Act 2002.]

(ai)-(aia) *[Omitted]*

[⁵ (aj) sections 32 and 33 of the Welfare Reform Act 2007;]

(ak)-(al) *[Omitted]*

[⁹ (ala) sections 96 to 97 of that Act *[the Welfare Reform Act 2012]*;]

(b)   *[Omitted]*

Amendments

1. Inserted by CSPSSA s73 (1.12.00).
2. Inserted by SSFA s12(3) (1.4.02).
3. Inserted by SPCA Sch 2 para 12 (6.10.03).
4. Inserted by the Social Security (Recovery of Benefits Act 1997) Sch 3 para 8 (6.10.97).
5. Inserted by WRA 2007 s33(7) (1.4.08 for making regulations and 6.10.08).
6. Amended by WRA 2009 s24 and Sch 4 para 9 (12.1.10 for making regulations and 1.4.10).
7. Amended by WRA 2009 s58 and Sch 7 (22.3.10).
8. Amended by WRA 2012 s31 and Sch 2 paras 3 and 26 (25.2.13).
9. Inserted by Welfare Reform and Work Act 2016 s10(1)(a) (9.6.16).

Functions of Committee and Council in relation to regulations

172.–(1) Subject–

(a) to subsection (3) below; and

(b) to section 173 below,

where the Secretary of State proposes to make regulations under any of the relevant enactments, he shall refer the proposals, in the form of draft regulations or otherwise, to the Committee.

(2) *[Omitted]*

(3) Subsection (1) above does not apply to the regulations specified in Part I of Schedule 7 to this Act.

(4)-(5) *[Omitted]*

Cases in which consultation is not required

173.–(1) Nothing in any enactment shall require any proposals in respect of regulations to be referred to the Committee or the Council if–

(a) it appears to the Secretary of State that by reason of the urgency of the matter it is inexpedient so to refer them; or

(b) the relevant advisory body have agreed that they shall not be referred.

(2) Where by virtue only of subsection (1)(a) above the Secretary of State makes regulations without proposals in respect of them having been referred, then, unless the relevant advisory body agrees that this subsection shall not apply, he shall refer the regulations to that body as soon as practicable after making them.

(3) Where the Secretary of State has referred proposals to the Committee or the Council, he may make the proposed regulations before the Committee have made their report or, as the case may be the Council have given their advice, only if after the reference it appears to him that by reason of the urgency of the matter it is expedient to do so.

(4) Where by virtue of this section regulations are made before a report of the Committee has been made, the Committee shall consider them and make a report to the Secretary of State containing such recommendations with regard to the regulations as the Committee thinks appropriate; and a copy of any report made to the Secretary of State on the regulations shall be laid by him before each House of Parliament together, if the report contains recommendations, with a statement–

(a) of the extent (if any) to which the Secretary of State proposes to give effect to the recommendations; and

(b) in so far as he does not propose to give effect to them, of his reasons why not.

(5) Except to the extent that this subsection is excluded by an enactment passed after 25th July 1986, nothing in any enactment shall require the reference to the Committee or the Council of any regulations contained in either–

(a) a statutory instrument made before the end of the period of 6 months beginning with the coming into force of the enactment under which those regulations are made; or

(b) a statutory instrument–

  (i) which states that it contains only regulations made by virtue of, or consequential upon, a specified enactment; and

  (ii) which is made before the end of the period of 6 months beginning with the coming into force of that specified enactment.

(6) In relation to regulations required or authorised to be made by the Secretary of State in conjunction with the Treasury, any reference in this section to the Secretary of State shall be construed as a reference to the Secretary of State and the Treasury.

(7) In this section "regulations" means regulations under any enactment, whenever passed.

Committee's report on regulations and Secretary of State's duties

174.–(1) The Committee shall consider any proposals referred to it by the Secretary of State under section 172 above and shall make to the Secretary of State a report containing such recommendations with regard to the subject-matter of the proposals as the Committee thinks appropriate.

(2) If after receiving a report of the Committee the Secretary of State lays before Parliament any regulations or draft regulations which comprise the whole or any part of the subject-matter of the proposals referred to the Committee, he shall lay with the regulations or draft regulations a copy of the Committee's report and a statement showing–

(a) the extent (if any) to which he has, in framing the regulations, given effect to the Committee's recommendations; and

(b) in so far as effect has not been given to them, his reasons why not.

(3) In the case of any regulations laid before Parliament at a time when Parliament is not sitting, the requirements of subsection (2) above shall be satisfied as respects either House of Parliament if a copy of the report and statement there referred to are laid before that House not later than the second day on which the House sits after the laying of the regulations.

(4) In relation to regulations required or authorised to be made by the Secretary of State in conjunction with the Treasury any reference in this section to the Secretary of State shall be construed as a reference to the Secretary of State and the Treasury.

Housing benefit and council tax benefit

Consultation with representative organisations

176.–(1) Subject to subsection (2) below, before making–

(a) regulations relating to housing benefit *[or [¹ council tax benefit]]* (other than regulations of which the effect is to increase any amount specified in regulations previously made);

[³(aa) regulations under section 69 of the Child Support, Pensions and Social Security Act 2000]

(b) an order under [² any provision of Part VIII above.]

the Secretary of State shall consult with organisations appearing to him to be representative of the authorities concerned.

(2) Nothing in subsection (1) above shall require the Secretary of State to undertake consultations if–

(a) it appears to him that by reason of the urgency of the matter it is inexpedient to do so; or

(b) the organisations have agreed that consultations should not be undertaken.

(3) Where the Secretary of State has undertaken such consultations, he may make any regulations or order to which the consultations relate without completing the consultations if it appears to him that by reason of the urgency of the matter it is expedient to do so.

Amendments

1. Substitution made by the Local Government Finance Act 1992 para 23 Sch 9 (1.4.93).
2. Amended by the Housing Act 1996 Sch 13 para 3(4) (1.4.97).
3. Inserted by CSPSSA s69(6) (2.7.01).

Modification

Section 176(1)(a) and (b) was repealed by WRA 2012 s147 and Sch 14 part 1 on 1.4.13 in so far as it related to CTB.

Analysis
The Secretary of State invoked the predecessor to subs (2)(a) as the reason for not consulting with the local authority associations when the Housing Benefit (General) Amendment Regulations 1992 SI No.201 were introduced. Those regulations followed the introduction by the London Borough of Hackney of a scheme whereby council tenants with rent arrears would be liable to a higher rent rise than those who were not. The amending regulations were aimed at ensuring that HB would not be paid with regard to the rent arrears supplement: see the Analysis of reg 11(3) HB Regs on p351.

R v Secretary of State for Social Security ex p Association of Metropolitan Authoroties (1992) 25 HLR 131, QBD found that, in relation to the making of the regulations, the Secretary of State could not invoke the exemption (then s61(8)(a) Social Security Act 1986) by leaving a decision until the last moment and thus creating the emergency her/himself.

PART XV
Miscellaneous

[¹**Return of social security post**

182A.–(1)   A social security authority may require–
(a)   the Post Office; or
(b)   any other person who conveys postal packets,
to return to the sender social security post sent by or on behalf of the authority which would otherwise be redirected.

(2)   A social security authority shall make payments of such amount as the Secretary of State considers reasonable in respect of the return of social security post in compliance with a requirement imposed by the authority under subsection (1) above.

(3)   In subsections (1) and (2) above "social security authority" means–
(a)   the Secretary of State;
(b)   the Northern Ireland Department; or
(c)   any local or other authority administering housing benefit *[or council tax benefit]* (including the Northern Ireland Housing Executive).

(4)   In subsections (1) and (2) above "social security post" means postal packets–
(a)   the contents of which relate to any benefit, contributions or national insurance number or to any other matter relating to social security; and
(b)   which are marked, in a manner approved by the Post Office or other person conveying them, with the name and address of the sender and with an indication that they are to be returned rather than redirected.

(5)   In this section–
(a)   "redirected", in relation to any postal packet, means delivered to an address other than that indicated by the sender on the packet; and
(b)   "postal packet" has the same meaning as in the Post Office Act 1953.

(6)   Any requirement imposed under subsection (1) above has effect subject to any order under–
(a)   section 371 of the Insolvency Act 1986 or Article 342 of the Insolvency (Northern Ireland) Order 1989 (redirection of bankrupt's letters to trustee in bankruptcy);
(b)   paragraph 10 of Schedule 1 to the Solicitors Act 1974 or paragraph 15 of Schedule 1 to the Solicitors (Northern Ireland) Order 1976 (redirection of letters following intervention by Law Society); or
(c)   paragraph 10 of Schedule 5 to the Administration of Justice Act 1985 (redirection of letters following intervention by Council for Licensed Conveyancers).]

Amendment
1.   Inserted by SSA(F)A s20 (27.3.99).

Modification
Section 182A(3)(c) was repealed by WRA 2012 s147 and Sch 14 part 1 on 1.4.13 in so far as it related to CTB.

General Note
Prior to the insertion of s182A, with the aim of preventing fraud, many local authorities had adopted the practice of marking envelopes containing HB cheques "Do Not Redirect", but the Post Office generally disregarded such

instructions, taking the view that without specific authority not to do so, it was obliged to obey directions from an addressee to redirect mail.

Subs (1) allows a "social security authority" to require return of mail which would be redirected. "Social security authority" includes a local authority: subs (3)(c). The requirement is imposed simply by indicating the requirement on the envelope: subs (4). The authority can be required by the Secretary of State to pay a fee for this service: subs (2).

Subs (6) makes the scheme subject to certain other statutory schemes requiring mail to be redirected.

[¹Requirement to supply information about redirection of post

182B.–(1)   The Secretary of State or the Northern Ireland Department may require the Post Office or any other person who conveys postal packets to supply information relating to arrangements for the redirection of postal packets to, or to a person supplying services to, the Secretary of State or the Department–

(a)   for use in the prevention, detection, investigation or prosecution of offences relating to social security; or

(b)   for use in checking the accuracy of information relating to benefits, contributions or national insurance numbers or to any other matter relating to social security and (where appropriate) amending or supplementing such information.

(2)   A local or other authority administering housing benefit *[or council tax benefit]* (including the Northern Ireland Housing Executive) may require the Post Office or any other person who conveys postal packets to supply information relating to arrangements for the redirection of postal packets to the authority or a person authorised to exercise any function of the authority relating to housing benefit *[or council tax benefit]*–

(a)   for use in the prevention, detection, investigation or prosecution of offences relating to such a benefit; or

(b)   for use in checking the accuracy of information relating to such a benefit and (where appropriate) amending or supplementing such information.

(3)   Information shall be supplied under subsection (1) or (2) above in such manner and form, and in accordance with such requirements, as may be prescribed.

(4)   Payments of such amount as the Secretary of State considers reasonable shall be made by a person or authority imposing a requirement under subsection (1) or (2) above in respect of the supply of information in compliance with the requirement.

(5)   Information supplied under subsection (1) or (2) above shall not be supplied by the recipient to any other person or body unless–

(a)   it could be supplied to that person or body under either of those subsections; or

(b)   it is supplied for the purposes of any civil or criminal proceedings relating to the Contributions and Benefits Act, the Jobseekers Act 1995 [², Part 1 of the Welfare Reform Act 2012] [³, Part 4 of that Act] or this Act or to any provision of Northern Ireland legislation corresponding to any of them.

(6)   But where information supplied under subsection (1) or (2) above has been used (in accordance with paragraph (b) of the subsection concerned) in amending or supplementing other information, it is lawful for it to be–

(a)   supplied to any person or body to whom that other information could be supplied; or

(b)   used for any purpose for which that other information could be used.

(7)   In subsections (1) and (2) above "arrangements for the redirection of postal packets" means arrangements made with the Post Office or other person conveying postal packets for the delivery of postal packets to addresses other than those indicated by senders on the packets.

(8)   In this section "postal packet" has the same meaning as in the Post Office Act 1953.]

Amendments
1.   Inserted by SSA(F)A s21 (27.3.99).
2.   Amended by WRA 2012 s31 and Sch 2 para 29 (29.4.13)
3.   Amended by WRA 2012 Sch 9 para 29 (8.4.13).

Modification
Section 182B(2) was repealed by WRA 2012 s147 and Sch 14 part 1 on 1.4.13 in so far as it related to CTB.

General Note

This requires the Post Office to gather information about the redirection of mail and supply it to local or other authorities administering HB at their request. It is similar in form to the provisions requiring and enabling the supply of information from one authority to another: see Part VII. A charge may be imposed: subs (4).

Subs (2) is in similar form to s122C(3), discussed in the General Note to s122C (on p72). Similarly, for discussion of the wording of subs (6), see the General Note to s122E as it relates to s122E(5) (on p73). Under subs (5) and (6), if the authority wishes to supply the information received to the Secretary of State or another authority, it must satisfy itself that the recipient would be entitled to receive the information under subs (1) or (2), or that it is being supplied for the purpose of civil or criminal proceedings under the social security legislation. Thus this provision could not, it appears, be used to justify the passing of information where a person is being prosecuted under the Theft Act 1968. See also Sch 8 para 34 WRPA (on p1705).

Certain benefit to be inalienable

187.–(1)   Subject to the provisions of this Act, every assignment of or charge on–
[⁴ (za) universal credit;]
  (a)   benefit as defined in section 122 of the Contributions and Benefits Act;
[¹ (ab) state pension credit;]
[² (ac) an employment and support allowance;]
[³ (ad) personal independence payment;]
  (b)   any income-related benefit; or
  (c)   child benefit,
and every agreement to assign or charge such benefit shall be void; and, on the bankruptcy of a beneficiary, such benefit shall not pass to any trustee or other person acting on behalf of his creditors.
  (2)   In the application of subsection (1) above to Scotland–
  (a)   the reference to assignment of benefit shall be read as a reference to assignation, "assign" being construed accordingly;
  (b)   the reference to a beneficiary's bankruptcy shall be read as a reference to the sequestration of his estate or the appointment on his estate of a judicial factor under section 41 of the Solicitors (Scotland) Act 1980.
  (3)   [. . .]

Amendments

1.   Inserted by SPCA Sch 2 para 23 (commenced October 2003).
2.   Inserted by WRA 2007 s28 and Sch 3 para 10(31) (27.10.08).
3.   Amended by WRA 2012 Sch 9 para 31 (8.4.13).
4.   Amended by WRA 2012 s31 and Sch 2 para 30 (29.4.13).

General Note

This provision prevents any assignment of a right to benefit by agreement or by operation of law. It does not prevent recovery of an overpayment by the Secretary of State (or a local authority) after the claimant has been made bankrupt: *Mulvey v Secretary of State for Social Security* [1997] SLT 753 at 756, HL. See further the Analysis to reg 102 HB Regs (p597).

PART XVI
General
Subordinate legislation

Regulations and orders – general

189.–(1)   Subject to [⁷] any [⁵ . . .] express provision of this Act, regulations and orders under this Act shall be made by the Secretary of State.
[⁷ (2)]
  (3)   Powers under this Act to make regulations or orders are exercisable by statutory instrument.
  (4)   Except in the case of regulations under section [⁷] [¹⁰] above and in so far as this Act otherwise provides, any power conferred by this Act to make an Order in Council, regulations or an order may be exercised
  (a)   either in relation to all cases to which the power extends, or in relation to those cases subject to specified exceptions, or in relation to any specified cases or classes of case;

(b) so as to make, as respects the cases in relation to which it is exercised–
   (i) the full provision to which the power extends or any less provision (whether by way of exception or otherwise);
   (ii) the same provision for all cases in relation to which the power is exercised, or different provision for different cases or different classes of case or different provision as respects the same case or class of case for different purposes of this Act;
   (iii) any such provision either unconditionally or subject to any specified condition;

and where such a power is expressed to be exercisable for alternative purposes it may be exercised in relation to the same case for any or all of those purposes; and powers to make an Order in Council, regulations or an order for the purposes of any one provision of this Act are without prejudice to powers to make regulations or an order for the purposes of any other provision.

(5) Without prejudice to any specific provision in this Act, a power conferred by this Act to make an Order in Council, regulations or an order [⁷] includes power to make thereby such incidental, supplementary, consequential or transitional provision as appears to Her Majesty, or the authority making the regulations or order, as the case may be, to be expedient for the purposes of the Order in Council, regulations or order.

(6) Without prejudice to any specific provisions in this Act, a power conferred by any provision of this Act, except [¹⁰ sections 14, 24 and 130], to make an Order in Council, regulations or an order includes power to provide for a person to exercise a discretion in dealing with any matter.

(7) Any power conferred by this Act to make orders or regulation relating to housing benefit *[or [¹ council tax benefit]]* shall include power to make different provision for different areas [² or different authorities].

[⁸ (7A) Without prejudice to the generality of any of the preceding provisions of this section, regulations under any of sections 2A to 2C and 7A above may provide for all or any of the provisions of the regulations to apply only in relation to any area or areas specified in the regulations.]

(8) An order under section [³ 140B, 140C,] 150, [⁹ 150A,] 152, 165(4) or 169 above [⁶] above shall not be made [⁴ by the Secretary of State] without the consent of the Treasury.

(9) Any power of the Secretary of State under any provision of this Act, except under [¹⁰ sections 80 and 154] and 178, to make any regulations or order, where the power is not expressed to be exercisable with the consent of the Treasury, shall if the Treasury so direct be exercisable only in conjunction with them.

[⁷ (10)]

(11) A power under any of sections 177 to 179 above to make provisions by regulations or Order in Council for modifications or adaptations of the Contributions and Benefits Actor this Act shall be exercisable in relation to any enactment passed after this Act which is directed to be construed as one with them, except in so far as any such enactment relates to a benefit in relation to which the power is not exercisable; but this subsection applies only so far as a contrary intention is not expressed in the enactment so passed, and is without prejudice to the generality of any such direction.

(12) Any reference in this section or section 190 below to an Order in Council, or an order or regulations, under this Act includes a reference to an Order in Council, an order or regulations made under any provision of an enactment passed after this Act and directed to be construed as one with this Act; but this subsection applies only so far as a contrary intention is not expressed in the enactment so passed, and without prejudice to the generality of any such direction.

Amendments
1. Substitution made by the Local Government Finance Act 1992 Sch 9 para 24 (1.4.93).
2. Amended by SSA(F)A Sch 1 para 10.
3. Amended by the Housing Act 1996 Sch 13 para 3(5) (1.4.97).
4. Amended by TCA Sch 4 para 3 (6.4.03).
5. Amended by TCA Sch 6 (8.4.03).

6.   Amended by the Social Security (Recovery of Benefits) Act 1997 Sch 3 para 11 (6.10.97).
7.   Amended by SSA 1998 Sch 7 para 109 (6.9.99).
8.   Inserted by WRPA Sch 12 para 83 (11.11.99).
9.   Amended by the Pensions Act 2007, Sch 1 para 29 (26.9.07).
10.   Amended by Art 4 and Sch of SI 2013 No 252 as from 7.2.13.

Modification

Section 189(7) and (7A) were repealed and section 189(8) amended by WRA 2012 s147 and Sch 14 part 1 on 1.4.13 in so far as they related to CTB.

Parliamentary control of orders and regulations

190.–(1)   Subject to the provisions of this section, a statutory instrument containing (whether alone or with other provisions)–

[¹⁰ (zza) an order under section 115A(3B);]

[¹¹ (zzb) regulations under section 115C(2) or 115D(1) or (2);]

[⁸ (za) regulations under section 132A(4);]

(a)   an order under section 141, 143, [¹ 143A,] 145, 150, [⁹ 150A,] 152 or 162(7) above; or

[⁶(aa) the first regulations to be made under section 2A;]

[⁷(ab) the first regulations to be made under section 2AA;]

[³(aza) any order containing provision adding any person to the list of persons falling within section 109B(2A) above;]

(b)   regulations under section [⁴] [⁵ 122B(1)(b) or] 154 above,

shall not be made unless a draft of the instrument has been laid before Parliament and been approved by a resolution of each House of Parliament.

(2)   Subsection (1) above does not apply to a statutory instrument by reason only that it contains regulations under section 154 above which are to be made for the purpose of consolidating regulations to be revoked in the instrument.

(3)   A statutory instrument–

(a)   which contains (whether alone or with other provisions) orders or regulations made under this Act by the Secretary of State; and

(b)   which is not subject to any requirement that a draft of the instrument be laid before and approved by a resolution of each House of Parliament,

shall be subject to annulment in pursuance of a resolution of either House of Parliament.

[² (4)   .....]

Amendments

1.   Inserted by SSA 1998 Sch 7 para 110 (8.10.98).
2.   Repealed by SSA 1998 Sch 7 para 110 (6.4.99).
3.   Inserted by SSFA s1(9) (26.2.02).
4.   Amended by the Social Security (Recovery of Benefits) Act 1997 Sch 3 para 11 (6.10.97).
5.   Amended by SSA(F)A Sch 1 para 11 (1.7.97).
6.   Inserted by WRPA Sch 12 para 83 (11.11.99).
7.   Inserted by the Employment Act 2002 Sch 7 para 15 (5.7.03).
8.   Amended by the National Insurance Contributions Act 2006 s7(3) (30.3.06).
9.   Amended by the Pensions Act 2007 Sch 1 para 30 (26.9.07).
10.   Inserted by WRA 2012 s114(2) (8.5.12).
11.   Inserted by WRA 2012 s116(2) (10.5.12).

Supplementary

Interpretation – general

191.   In this Act, unless the context otherwise requires–

"the 1975 Act" means the Social Security Act 1975;

"the 1986 Act" means the Social Security Act 1986;

"benefit" means benefit under the Contributions and Benefits Act [²⁶ and includes [²⁷ universal credit,] a jobseeker's allowance[¹⁶[²⁰[²⁴, state pension credit, an employment and support allowance and personal independence payment]]];

[²⁵ [¹]]

"the Consequential Provisions Act" means the Social Security (Consequential Provisions) Act 1992;

[⁵ "contribution-based jobseeker's allowance" has the same meaning as in the Jobseekers Act 1995;]

"the Contributions and Benefits Act" means the Social Security Contributions and Benefits Act 1992;

[²⁰ "contributory employment and support allowance" means a contributory allowance under Part 1 of the Welfare Reform Act 2007 (employment and support allowance);]

[²⁵ [¹⁴]]

"disablement benefit" is to be construed in accordance with section 94(2)(a) of the Contributions and Benefits Act;

"dwelling" means any residential accommodation, whether or not consisting of the whole or part of a building and whether or not comprising separate and self-contained premises;

[² "financial year" has the same meaning as in the Local Government Finance Act 1992;]

"5 year general qualification" is to be construed in accordance with section 71 of the Courts and Legal Services Act 1990;

"housing authority" means a local authority [¹⁷ or a new town corporation] or the Development Board for Rural Wales;

"housing benefit scheme" is to be construed in accordance with section 134(1) above;

[⁶ "income-based jobseeker's allowance" has the same meaning as in the Jobseekers Act 1995;]

"income-related benefit" means–

(a)   income support;

[¹⁵ . . .]

[¹⁵ . . .]

(d)   housing benefit; and

[³(e)   council tax benefit;]

[²⁰ "income-related employment and support allowance" means an income-related allowance under Part 1 of the Welfare Reform Act 2007 (employment and support allowance);]

"industrial injuries benefit" means benefit under Part V of the Contributions and Benefits Act, other than under Schedule 8;

"invalidity benefit" has the meaning assigned to it by section 20(1)(c) of that Act;

"local authority" means–

(a)   in relation to England [⁸ . . .], the council of a district or London borough, the Common Council of the City of London or the Council of the Isles of Scilly; and

[⁸(aa) in relation to Wales, the council of a county or county borough;] and

(b)   in relation to Scotland, [⁹ a council constituted under section 2 of the Local Government etc. (Scotland) Act 1994];

"medical examination" includes bacteriological and radiographical tests and similar investigations, and "medically examined" has a corresponding meaning;

"medical practitioner" means–

(a)   a registered medical practitioner; or

(b)   a person outside the United Kingdom who is not a registered medical practitioner, but has qualifications corresponding (in the Secretary of State's opinion) to those of a registered medical practitioner;

"medical treatment" means medical, surgical or rehabilitative treatment (including any course of diet or other regimen), and references to a person receiving or submitting himself to medical treatment are to be construed accordingly;

[²³ "money purchase contracted-out scheme" is to be construed in accordance with section 181A of the Pensions Act;]

"new town corporation" means–
    [²¹ (a) in relation to England–
        (i)   a development corporation established under the New Towns Act 1981; or
        (ii)   the Homes and Communities Agency so far as exercising functions in relation to anything transferred (or to be transferred) to it as mentioned in section 52(1)(a) to (d) of the Housing and Regeneration Act 2008; [²² or
        (iii) the Greater London Authority so far as exercising its new towns and urban development functions;]
    (ab) in relation to Wales–
        (i)   a development corporation established under the New Towns Act 1981; and
        (ii)   the Welsh Ministers so far as exercising functions in relation to anything transferred (or to be transferred) to them as mentioned in section 36(1)(a)(i) to (iii) of that Act;] and
    (b)   in relation to Scotland, a development corporation established under the New Towns (Scotland) Act 1968;
[¹⁸ "the Northern Ireland Department" means means the Department for Social Development but–
    (a)   in section 122 and sections 122B to 122E also includes the Department of Finance and Personnel; and
    (b)   in sections 121E, 121F, 122, 122ZA, 122C and 122D also includes the Department for Employment and Learning;]
"the Northern Ireland Administration Act" means the Social Security (Northern Ireland) Administration Act 1992;
"occupational pension scheme" has the same meaning as in section 66(1) of the Pensions Act;
"the Old Cases Act" means the Industrial Injuries and Diseases (Old Cases) Act 1975;
"Old Cases payments" means payments under Part I of Schedule 8 to the Contributions and Benefits Act;
[¹⁰ "pensionable age" has the meaning given by the rules in paragraph 1 of Schedule 4 to the Pensions Act 1995];
"the Pensions Act" means the[¹¹ Pension Schemes Act 1993];
"personal pension scheme" has the meaning assigned to it by [¹² section 1 of the Pensions Act] [¹² and "appropriate", in relation to such a scheme, shall be construed in accordance with [²³ section 181A(6)] of that Act];
"prescribe" means prescribe by regulations [¹⁹ and "prescribed" must be construed accordingly];
"rent rebate" and[¹³ …] "rent allowance" shall be construed in accordance with section 134 above;
[¹³ …] "tax year" means the 12 months beginning with 6th April in any year;
[¹⁶ "state pension credit" means state pension credit under the State Pension Credit Act 2002;]
"10 year general qualification" is to be construed in accordance with section 71 of the Courts and Legal Services Act 1990; and
"widow's benefit" has the meaning assigned to it by section 20(1)(e) of the Contributions and Benefits Act.

Amendments

1.   Substituted by LGFA Sch 9 para 25(a) (1.4.93).
2.   Inserted by LGFA Sch 9 para 25(b) (1.4.93).
3.   Substituted by LGFA Sch 9 para 25(c) (1.4.93).
4.   Substituted by LGFA Sch 9 para 25(d) (1.4.93).
5.   Inserted by the Jobseekers Act 1995 Sch 2 para 73(3) (22.4.96).
6.   Inserted by the Jobseekers Act 1995 Sch 2 para 73(4) (22.4.96).
7.   Definition of "levying authority" repealed by the Local Government etc. (Scotland) Act 1994 Sch 13 para 175(5)(a) and Sch 14 (1.4.96).
8.   Amended by the Local Government (Wales) Act 1994 Sch 1 para 94.

9.   Substituted bythe Local Government etc. (Scotland) Act 1994 Sch 13 para 175(5)(b) (1.4.96).
10. Substituted by the Pensions Act 1995 Sch 4 para 14 (19.7.95).
11. Substituted by the Pensions Schemes Act 1993 Sch 8 para 31(c) (7.2.94).
12. Amended by the Pensions Schemes Act 1993 Sch 8 para 31(d) (7.2.94).
13. Repealed by the Housing Act 1996 Sch 19 Part VI (1.4.97).
14. Inserted by the Housing Act 1996 Sch 13 para 6(a).
15. Amended by TCA Sch 6 (8.4.03).
16. Amended by SPCA Sch 2 para 24 (commenced October 2003).
17. Amended by the Housing (Scotland) Act 2001 Sch 10 para 17 (1.04.02).
18. Amended by the Employment Act 2002 Sch 7 para 16 (9.9.02).
19. Amended by WRA 2007 s40 and Sch 5 para 10 (3.7.07).
20. Amended by WRA 2007 s29 and Sch 3 para 10(32) (18.3.08 for making regulations and 27.7.08).
21. Amended by the Housing and Regeneration Act 2008 s56 and Sch 8 para 61 (1.12.08).
22. Amended by the Localism Act 2011 s195 and Sch 19 para 31 (1.4.12).
23. Amended by reg 2(3) of SI 2011 No 1724 as from 6.4.12.
24. Amended by WRA 2012 Sch 9 para 32 (8.4.13).
25. Repealed by WRA 2012 s147 and Sch 14 part 1 (1.4.13).
26. Amended by Jobseekers Act 1995 Sch 2 para 73(2) (22.4.96).
27. Amended by WRA 2012 Sch 2 para 31 (29.4.13).

Short title, commencement and extent

192.–(1)   This Act may be cited as the Social Security Administration Act 1992.

(2)   This Act is to be read, where appropriate, with the Contributions and Benefits Act and the Consequential Provisions Act.

(3)   The enactments consolidated by this Act are repealed, in consequence of the consolidation, by the Consequential Provisions Act.

(4)   Except as provided in Schedule 4 to the Consequential Provisions Act, this Act shall come into force on 1st July 1992.

(5)   The following provisions extend to Northern Ireland–

[² . . .]

[¹ . . .]

[³ section 132A (and sections 189 and 190, but only for the purposes of regulations under section 132A);]

section 170 (with Schedule 5);

section 177 (with Schedule 8); and

this section.

Except as provided by this section, this Act does not extend to Northern Ireland.

Amendments

1.   Amended by the Social Security (Recovery of Benefits) Act 1997 Sch 3 para 12 (6.10.97).
2.   Amended by the SSA 1998 Sch 7 para 112 (29.11.99).
3.   Inserted by the National Insurance Contributions Act 2006 s7(4) (3.3.06).

SCHEDULE 4

SECTION 123

PERSONS EMPLOYED IN SOCIAL SECURITY ADMINISTRATION OR ADJUDICATION

PART I

The Specified Persons

Government departments

A civil servant in

[² (a)   the Department for Work and Pensions;]

[² . . .]

(c)   the [⁴ Ministry of Justice].

Other public departments and offices

[Omitted]

[¹ Local authorities etc

A member, officer or employee of an authority administering housing benefit or council tax benefit.

A person authorised to exercise any function of such an authority relating to such a benefit or any employee of such a person.

A person authorised under section 139A(1) of this Act to consider and report to the Secretary of State on the administration of housing benefit *[or council tax benefit].*]

[³ A member, officer or employee of a county council in England who exercises–

(a)   any function conferred on the county council by regulations made under section 7A of this Act;

(b)   any function in connection with a relevant purpose within the meaning of section 7B(3) of this Act.

A person authorised to exercise any such function of such a county council or an employee of such a person.]

Modification

Paragraphs headed "Local authorities, etc" were repealed by WRA 2012 s147 and Sch 14 part 1 on 1.4.13 in so far as they related to CTB. For savings and transitional provisions, see Arts 9 and 10 of the Welfare Reform Act 2012 (Commencement No.8 and Savings and Transitional Provisions) Order 2013 SI No.358. See Part 4 for the council tax reduction schemes.

Adjudicating bodies

The clerk to, or other officer or member of staff of, any of the following bodies–

[⁴ (a)]

[Omitted]

Amendments

1.   Inserted by SSA(F)A s4.

2.   Amended by Sch para 8(4) of SI 2002 No 1397 as from 27.6.02.

3.   Inserted by WRA 2007 s41(3) (3.7.07).

4.   Amended by Art 9 and Sch 3 para 104 of SI 2008 No 2833 as from 3.11.08.

General Note

See also Sch 8 para 34 WRPA (on p1705).

SCHEDULE 10
Supplementary Benefit etc
Overpayments etc

4.–(1)-(2)   *[Omitted]*

(3)   The reference to housing benefit in section 75 above includes a reference to housing benefits under Part II of the Social Security and Housing Benefits Act 1982.

Social Security (Consequential Provisions) Act 1992
(1992 c6)

Meaning of "the consolidating Acts"
   1.   In this Act–
"the consolidating Acts" means the Social Security Contributions and Benefits Act 1992 ("the Contributions and Benefits Act"), the Social Security Administration Act 1992 ("the Administration Act") and, so far as it reproduces the effect of the repealed enactments, this Act; and
"the repealed enactments" means the enactments repealed by this Act.

Continuity of the law
   2.–(1)   The substitution of the consolidating Acts for the repealed enactments does not affect the continuity of the law.

   (2)   Anything done or having effect as if done under or for the purposes of a provision of the repealed enactments has effect, if it could have been done under or for the purposes of the corresponding provision of the consolidating Acts, as if done under or for the purposes of that provision.

   (3)   Any reference, whether express or implied, in the consolidating Acts or any other enactment, instrument or document to a provision of the consolidating Acts shall, so far as the context permits, be construed as including, in relation to the times, circumstances and purposes in relation to which the corresponding provision of the repealed enactments has effect, a reference to that corresponding provision.

   (4)   Any reference, whether express or implied, in any enactment, instrument or document to a provision of the repealed enactments shall be construed, so far as is required for continuing its effects, as including a reference to the corresponding provision of the consolidating Acts.

Social Security Act 1998
(1998 c14)

General Note
The Social Security Act (SSA) 1998 introduced a system for revision and supersession of decisions and a new structure for appeals. Its impact on HB, however, was modest but from 2 July 2001, new provision was made for HB decision making by CSPSSA s68 and Sch 7.

The principal provisions in the SSA 1998 relating to HB were ss34 and 35. The latter section was not brought into force. It related to the suspension of benefit pending resolution of questions or court decisions. For these now, see Sch 7 para 13 CSPSSA on p152.

Apart from s69, the balance of the Act as it relates to HB is concerned with regulation-making.

PART I

General

Appeals

Constitution of appeal tribunals
[²7.]

Amendments
1. Amended by the Tribunals, Courts and Enforcement Act 2007 s50 and Sch 10 para 29(3) and (4) (21.7.08).
2. Omitted by art 9 and Sch 3 para 147 of SI 2008 No 2833 (3.11.08).

General Note
Until 3 November 2008, this section provided for the constitution of appeal tribunals hearing benefit appeals under this act as well as HB (and CTB) appeals under Sch 7 para 6 CSPSSA. See now the Tribunals, Courts and Enforcement Act 2007 on p167.

For commentary on this former provision, see p109 of the 20th edition.

Social Security Decisions and Appeals

Housing benefit [and council tax benefit]

Determination of claims and reviews
34.–(1)   Regulations shall provide that, where a person claims–

(a)   housing benefit; or

[(b)   council tax benefit,]

the authority to whom the claim is made shall notify the person of its determination of the claim.

(2)   Any such notification shall be given in such form as may be prescribed.

(3)   Regulations may make provision requiring authorities to whom claims for housing benefit or council tax benefit are made by, or in respect of, persons who have been entitled to a jobseeker's allowance or to income support [² or state pension credit] to give priority, in prescribed circumstances, to those claims over other claims for any such benefit.

[¹ (4)]

[¹ (5)]

Amendments
1. Repealed by CSPSSA Sch 9 Pt VII (2.7.01).
2. Amended by SPCA Sch 2 para 41 (2.7.02 (for making regulations) and 6.10.03).

Commencement
18.10.99: Social Security Act 1998 (Commencement No 11, Savings and Consequential and Transitional Provisions) Order 1999 SI No.2860 Art 2(a).

Modification
Section 34 was repealed by WRA 2012 s147 and Sch 14 part 1 on 1.4.13 in so far as it related to CTB.

General Note

This replaced s63 SSAA as the basic piece of primary legislation upon which the decision-making structure for HB is (and until 1 April 2013 CTB was) based. So far as the mechanism for changing decisions is concerned, it has now in its turn been replaced by Sch 7 CSPSSA.

Analysis

Subs (1) to (3) are identical to the former subs (1), (2), (2A) and (3) SSAA s63. All regulations validly made under those provisions are treated by virtue of s17(2)(b) Interpretation Act 1978 as if they had been made under these provisions. The following list gives the principal regulations made under the powers granted by each numbered paragraph of this section.

(1)   See reg 90 HB Regs and reg 71 HB(SPC) Regs.

(2)   See Sch 9 HB Regs and Sch 8 HB(SPC) Regs.

(3)   See reg 89(3) HB Regs and reg 70(3) HB(SPC) Regs. Also note the different system for claiming HB for recipients of IS, JSA, ESA and PC (see reg 83(4) HB Regs and reg 64(5) HB(SPC) Regs).

Subs (4) and (5) formerly provided for regulations to make provision for reviews of determinations relating to HB (and CTB) (subs (4)) and matters arising out of the revision on review of such determinations (subs (5)). Both were repealed in July 2001, though preserved for certain purposes: to enable a Review Board to record its decision and send it out; to permit correction of accidental errors; to enable a Review Board to appear in judicial review proceedings; and to enable effect to be given to a Review Board's decision. The transitional provisions were in the Housing Benefit and Council Tax Benefit (Decisions and Appeals) (Transitional and Savings) Regulations 2001 SI No.1264. They governed what happened where the process for disputing an authority's determination commenced before 2 July 2001 but had not finished by that date.

See pp993–1000 of the 20th edition for the transitional rules and pp104–5 of the 18th edition for commentary on the repealed provisions.

PART III

Benefits

Validation of certain housing benefit determinations

69.–(1)   Subject to subsections (3) and (4) below, in so far as a housing benefit determination made before 18th August 1997 purported to determine that housing benefit was payable in respect of–

(a)   charges for medical care, nursing care or personal care; or

(b)   charges for general counselling or any other support services,

it shall be deemed to have been validly made if, on the assumption mentioned in subsection (2) below, it would have been so made.

(2)   The assumption is that, at all material times, such charges as are mentioned in subsection (1) above were eligible to be met by housing benefit where the claimant's right to occupy the dwelling was conditional on his payment of the charges.

(3)   Where the effect of a review carried out on or after 18th August 1997 was to revise the amount of housing benefit payable in respect of any validated charges–

(a)   the revision shall be deemed not to have been validly made in so far as it had the effect of increasing that amount; and

(b)   housing benefit shall cease to be payable in respect of those charges as from the beginning of the period for which the first payment of the revised amount of benefit was made.

(4)   Housing benefit shall not be payable in respect of any validated charges for any period falling after–

(a)   5th April 1998 where the rent is payable at intervals of a whole number of weeks; and

(b)   31st March 1998 in any other case.

(5)   In this section–

"the dwelling", in relation to a housing benefit determination, means the dwelling in respect of which the determination was made;

"housing benefit determination" means a determination under section 130 of the Contributions and Benefits Act or the corresponding provisions of the Social Security Act 1986, or a decision on a review of such a determination;

"medical care" includes treatment or counselling related to mental disorder, mental handicap, physical disablement or past or present alcohol or drug dependence;

"personal care" includes assistance at meal-times or with personal appearance or hygiene;
"validated charges" means charges in respect of which housing benefit is payable only
          by virtue of subsection (1) above.

General Note
This provision was made to alleviate accounting and subsidy difficulties experienced by local authorities following
the confusion over whether service charges for the types of services mentioned in subs (1) were properly payable
under the then HB Regs 1987 Sch 1 para 1(f)(i). It is now clear, following *R v St Edmundsbury BC HBRB ex p
Sandys* (1997) 30 HLR 800; (1998) *The Times* 9 September, CA that such services should not have been met
under that provision. Since the payments were unlawful, in the absence of a provision such as this some
authorities might have been faced with difficulties in justifying their expenditure on these items.
          Subs (1) and (2) retrospectively justify HB awards in respect of such service charges. The effect of the
retrospective validation is limited by subs (3) and (4). Subs (4) makes clear that the validation only lasted until the
end of the 1997 to 1998 financial year.
          For an analysis of these provisions, see pp117–18 of the 15th edition.

PART IV
Miscellaneous and Supplemental

Regulations and orders
79.–(1)   [³ Subject to subsection (2A) below,] regulations under this Act shall be
made by the Secretary of State.
    [³ (2)]
    [² (2A)   Subsection (1) has effect subject to any provision providing for regulations
to be made by the Treasury or the Commissioners of Inland Revenue.]
    (3)   Powers under this Act to make regulations or orders are exercisable by statutory
instrument.
    (4)   Any power conferred by this Act to make regulations or orders may be
exercised–
    (a)   either in relation to all cases to which the power extends, or in relation to those
           cases subject to specified exceptions, or in relation to any specified cases or
           classes of case;
    (b)   so as to make, as respects the cases in relation to which it is exercised–
           (i)   the full provision to which the power extends or any less provision
                  (whether by way of exception or otherwise);
           (ii)   the same provision for all cases in relation to which the power is exercised,
                  or different provision for different cases or different classes of case or
                  different provision as respects the same case or class of case for different
                  purposes of this Act;
           (iii) any such provision either unconditionally or subject to any specified
                  condition;
           and where such a power is expressed to be exercisable for alternative purposes
           it may be exercised in relation to the same case for any or all of those purposes.
    (5)   Powers to make regulations for the purposes of any one provision of this Act
are without prejudice to powers to make regulations for the purposes of any other
provision.
    (6)   Without prejudice to any specific provision in this Act, a power conferred by
this Act to make regulations includes power to make thereby such incidental,
supplementary, consequential or transitional provision as appears to the authority making
the regulations to be expedient for the purposes of those regulations.
    (7)   Without prejudice to any specific provisions in this Act, a power conferred by
any provision of this Act to make regulations includes power to provide for a person to
exercise a discretion in dealing with any matter.
    (8)   Any power conferred by this Act to make regulations relating to housing benefit
[or council tax benefit] shall include power to make different provision for different areas
or different authorities.
    [³ (9)]

Amendments
1.　　Amended by TCA Sch 4 para 13(2) (6.4.03).
2.　　Inserted by TCA Sch 4 para 13(3) (6.4.03).
3.　　Amended by art 9 and Sch 3 para 168 of SI 2008 No 2833 (3.11.08).

Modification
　　Section 79(8) was repealed by WRA 2012 s147 and Sch 14 part 1 on 1.4.13 in so far as it related to CTB.

Parliamentary control of regulations
　　80.–(1)　　Subject to the provisions of this section, a statutory instrument containing (whether alone or with other provisions) regulations under–
　　(a)　　section [³] 12(2) or 72 above; or
　　(b)　　[³] paragraph 9 of Schedule 2 [³] to this Act,
shall not be made unless a draft of the instrument has been laid before Parliament and been approved by a resolution of each House of Parliament.
　　(2)　　A statutory instrument–
　　(a)　　which contains (whether alone or with other provisions) regulations made under this Act by the Secretary of State[¹ , the Treasury or the Commissioners of Inland Revenue]; and
　　(b)　　which is not subject to any requirement that a draft of the instrument be laid before and approved by a resolution of each House of Parliament,
shall be subject to annulment in pursuance of a resolution of either House of Parliament.
　　[³ (3)]
　　[³ [² (4)]]

Amendments
1.　　Amended by TCA Sch 4 para 14 (6.4.03).
2.　　Amended by the Tribunals, Courts and Enforcement Act 2007 s50 and Sch 10 para 29(5) (21.7.08).
3.　　Amended by art 9 and Sch 3 para 169 of SI 2008 No 2833 (3.11.08).

Interpretation: general
　　84.　　In this Act–
"the Administration Act" means the Social Security Administration Act 1992;
"the Child Support Act" means the Child Support Act 1991;
"the Contributions and Benefits Act" means the Social Security Contributions and Benefits Act 1992;
"the Jobseekers Act" means the Jobseekers Act 1995;
"the Vaccine Damage Payments Act" means the Vaccine Damage Payments Act 1979;
"prescribe" means prescribe by regulations.

Short title, commencement and extent
　　87.–(1)　　This Act may be cited as the Social Security Act 1998.
　　(2)　　This Act, except–
　　(a)　　sections 66, 69, 72 and 77 to 85, this section and Schedule 6 to this Act; and
　　(b)　　subsection (1) of section 50 so far as relating to a sum which is chargeable to tax by virtue of section 313 of the Income and Corporation Taxes Act 1988, and subsections (2) to (4) of that section,
shall come into force on such day as may be appointed by order made by the Secretary of State; and different days may be appointed for different provisions and for different purposes.
　　(3)　　An order under subsection (2) above may make such savings, or such transitional or consequential provision, as the Secretary of State considers necessary or expedient–
　　(a)　　in preparation for or in connection with the coming into force of any provision of this Act; or
　　(b)　　in connection with the operation of any enactment repealed or amended by a provision of this Act during any period when the repeal or amendment is not wholly in force.

SCHEDULE 5

SECTION 16(1)

Regulations as to Procedure: Provision Which may be Made

General Note

These provisions authorise various regulations governing procedure. See p116 and p117 of the 20th edition for a list showing which regulations were made under which paragraphs.

1. Provision prescribing the procedure to be followed in connection with–
(a) the making of decisions or determinations by the Secretary of State [¹]; and
(b) the withdrawal of claims, applications, appeals or references falling to be decided or determined by the Secretary of State [¹].

Amendment

1. Amended by art 9 and Sch 3 para 173(a) of SI 2008 No 2833 (3.11.08).

[¹2.]

Amendment

1. Omitted by art 9 and Sch 3 para 173(b) of SI 2008 No 2833 (3.11.08).

3. Provision as to the form which is to be used for any document, the evidence which is to be required and the circumstances in which any official record or certificate is to be sufficient or conclusive evidence.
4. Provision as to the time within which, or the manner in which–
(a) any evidence is to be produced; or
(b) any application, reference or appeal is to be made.
[¹5.]

Amendment

1. Omitted by art 9 and Sch 3 para 173(b) of SI 2008 No 2833 (3.11.08).

[¹6.]

Amendment

1. Omitted by art 9 and Sch 3 para 173(b) of SI 2008 No 2833 (3.11.08).

[¹7.]

Amendment

1. Omitted by art 9 and Sch 3 para 173(b) of SI 2008 No 2833 (3.11.08).

[¹ 8.]

Amendment

1. Omitted by art 9 and Sch 3 para 173(b) of SI 2008 No 2833 (3.11.08).

9. Provision for the non-disclosure to a person of the particulars of any medical advice or medical evidence given or submitted for the purposes of a determination.

Human Rights Act 1998
(1998 c42)

General Note to the Act

The Human Rights Act 1998 was the result of the expressed intention of the Labour Government elected in 1997 to give domestic force to the European Convention on Human Rights and Fundamental Freedoms. Despite suggestions at the time it was passed that the British constitution and its traditions were under threat and that it would lead to judges, rather than Parliament, making the law, its actual impact has been modest in the social welfare field. Many challenges have been brought and few have succeeded. This is as true of challenges in the social security field as elsewhere. This is due to the fact that the Convention rights provide little by way of social rights, being directed principally to ensuring personal freedoms.

No attempt is made below to deal with the implications of the Convention in criminal proceedings, for which reference should be made to specialist works on criminal law.

Introduction
1. The Convention Rights
2. Interpretation of Convention rights

Legislation
3. Interpretation of legislation
4. Declaration of incompatibility
5. Right of Crown to intervene

Public authorities
6. Acts of public authorities
7. Proceedings
8. Judicial remedies
9. Judicial acts

Remedial action
10. Power to take remedial action

Other rights and proceedings
11. Safeguard for existing human rights
13. Freedom of thought, conscience and religion

Derogations and reservations (Omitted)
Judges of the European Court of Human Rights (Omitted)
Supplemental
20. Orders etc. under this Act
21. Interpretation, etc
22. Short title, commencement, application and extent

SCHEDULES
1. The Articles
2. Remedial Orders

Introduction

The Convention Rights

1.–(1) In this Act "the Convention rights" means the rights and fundamental freedoms set out in–

   (a)   Articles 2 to 12 and 14 of the Convention,

   (b)   Articles 1 to 3 of the First Protocol, and

   (c)   Articles 1 and 2 of the Sixth Protocol,

as read with Articles 16 to 18 of the Convention.

(2)   Those Articles are to have effect for the purposes of this Act subject to any designated derogation or reservation (as to which see sections 14 and 15).

(3)   The Articles are set out in Schedule 1.

(4)   The Secretary of State may by order make such amendments to this Act as he considers appropriate to reflect the effect, in relation to the United Kingdom, of a protocol.

(5)   In subsection (4) "protocol" means a protocol to the Convention–

(a)   which the United Kingdom has ratified; or

(b)   which the United Kingdom has signed with a view to ratification.

(6)   No amendment may be made by an order under subsection (4) so as to come into force before the protocol concerned is in force in relation to the United Kingdom.

Interpretation of Convention rights

2.–(1)   A court or tribunal determining a question which has arisen in connection with a Convention right must take into account any–

(a)   judgment, decision, declaration or advisory opinion of the European Court of Human Rights,

(b)   opinion of the Commission given in a report adopted under Article 31 of the Convention,

(c)   decision of the Commission in connection with Article 26 or 27(2) of the Convention, or

(d)   decision of the Committee of Ministers taken under Article 46 of the Convention, whenever made or given, so far as, in the opinion of the court or tribunal, it is relevant to the proceedings in which that question has arisen.

(2)   Evidence of any judgment, decision, declaration or opinion of which account may have to be taken under this section is to be given in proceedings before any court or tribunal in such manner as may be provided by rules.

(3)   In this section "rules" means rules of court or, in the case of proceedings before a tribunal, rules made for the purposes of this section–

(a)   by the Lord Chancellor or the Secretary of State, in relation to any proceedings outside Scotland;

(b)   by the Secretary of State, in relation to proceedings in Scotland; or

(c)   by a Northern Ireland department, in relation to proceedings before a tribunal in Northern Ireland–

(i)   which deals with transferred matters; and

(ii)   for which no rules made under paragraph (a) are in force.

General Note

This section deals with the effect of decisions of the European Court of Human Rights and the European Commission on Human Rights. The key words in s2 are "must take into account". Decisions are not therefore binding. However, great respect is accorded to Strasbourg decisions by the domestic courts, and it has been held that there should be a "special reason" for a departure from the learning of the Court or Commission: *R (Alconbury Developments Ltd) v Secretary of State for the Environment, Transport and the Regions* [2003] 2 AC 295, HL. This will especially be the case if the Strasbourg decision is recent and authoritative: see *Attorney General's Reference No 4 of 2002* [2004] UKHL 43 (para 33); and *R v Secretary of State for the Home Department, ex p Anderson* [2002] UKHL 46 (paras 17–18).

However, in almost all cases where there is a conflict between Strasbourg caselaw and a decision of a superior court in the UK, the inferior court or tribunal in the UK should follow the decision of the superior (UK) court: *Leeds City Council v Price* [2006] UKHL 10, [2006] 4 All ER 128 (paras 43–44). In *R (RJM) v SSWP* [2008] UKHL 63, the House of Lords confirmed that this is the correct approach where the Court of Appeal is faced with a conflict between a House of Lords decision and later Strasbourg caselaw. But the House of Lords went on to to to say in *RJM* that the same constraints do not necessarily apply where the Court of Appeal is faced with a conflict between an earlier Court of Appeal decision and a later decision of the European Court of Human Rights: "the Court of Appeal should be free (but not obliged) to depart from that decision" (*RJM* at para 66).

The most widely available, and most useful set of reports is the *European Human Rights Reports* (EHRR) published by Sweet and Maxwell. Butterworths' *Human Rights Cases* also publish some decisions which are not available in the EHRR. Reports of decisions are also available at http://hudoc.echr.coe.int/eng/.

Legislation

Interpretation of legislation

3.–(1)   So far as it is possible to do so, primary legislation and subordinate legislation must be read and given effect in a way which is compatible with the Convention rights.

(2)   This section–

(a)   applies to primary legislation and subordinate legislation whenever enacted;

(b)   does not affect the validity, continuing operation or enforcement of any incompatible primary legislation; and

(c)   does not affect the validity, continuing operation or enforcement of any incompatible subordinate legislation if (disregarding any possibility of revocation) primary legislation prevents removal of the incompatibility.

General Note

This is the first of the four sections that deal with the impact of the Convention on domestic law and administration. It is concerned with the technique for interpreting legislation that may be incompatible with a Convention right.

Analysis

Subs (1) states the general interpretative principle. It is a direction in strong terms: legislation must be read consistently with the Convention "so far as it is possible to do so". Before the 1998 Act came into force, resort could be had to the Convention as an aid to interpretation only to resolve an ambiguity in the meaning of a provision: see eg, *R v SSHD ex p Brind* [1991] 1 AC 696 at 747G-748F, 760D-762B, HL. It is clear that s3(1) requires a much more robust approach. The leading cases on the approach required by s3(1) are *R v A (No 2)* [2001] 2 AC 91, HL, *Re S* [2002] 2 AC 291, HL and *Ghaidan v Godin-Mendoza* [2004] UKHL 30, 3 All ER 411. In *R v A (No 2)*, a challenge was made to legislation excluding cross-examination of complainants in rape trials about previous sexual history, including any previous relationship with the accused. Lord Steyn set out the general approach required by s3(1):

"the interpretative obligation under section 3 of the 1998 Act is a strong one. It applies even if there is no ambiguity in the language in the sense of the language being capable of two different meanings. ... Section 3 places a duty on the court to strive to find a possible interpretation compatible with Convention rights. Under ordinary methods of interpretation a court may depart from the language of the statute to avoid absurd consequences: section 3 goes much further. Undoubtedly, a court must always look for a contextual and purposive interpretation: section 3 is more radical in its effect. It is a general principle of the interpretation of legal instruments that the text is the primary source of interpretation ... Section 3 qualifies this general principle because it requires a court to find an interpretation compatible with Convention rights if it is possible to do so. In the progress of the Bill through Parliament the Lord Chancellor observed that 'in 99% of the cases that will arise, there will be no need for judicial declarations of incompatibility' and the Home Secretary said 'We expect that, in almost all cases, the courts will be able to interpret the legislation compatibility with the Convention'. ... In accordance with the will of Parliament as reflected in section 3 it will sometimes be necessary to adopt an interpretation which linguistically may appear strained. The techniques to be used will not only involve the reading down of express language in a statute but also the implication of provisions. A declaration of incompatibility [under s4] is a measure of last resort. It must be avoided unless it is plainly impossible to do so." (at para 44)

Lord Hutton emphasised (at para 162) that s3(1) had to be utilised unless it was "impossible" to achieve the objective set out therein.

There are, however, limits to the exercise required by s3(1). It is limited to interpreting legislation, and does not allow judges "to act as legislators" and to override express or implied prohibitions in the legislation against adopting the proposed interpretation: *Re S* paras 37–41. The decision in *Re S* requires the court to be sure that the proposed modification is workable before it operates s3. Moreover, it is a precondition of carrying out the exercise under s3(1) that the ordinary interpretation of the legislation should conflict with a Convention right: *R v A (No 2)* at para 37; *Poplar Housing Association Ltd v Donoghue* [2002] QB 58, CA. The modification of the ordinary meaning of the legislation should be the minimum possible to achieve compatibility with the Convention: *Donoghue*, para 75(b). It should be possible to formulate, in words, the way in which the legislation has to be read in order for a compatible interpretation to be adopted: *R v Lambert* [2002] 2 AC 545, para 80, HL.

Ghaidan emphasises that use of the interpretive tool provided by s3(1) is not dependent on finding an ambiguity in the legislation, and s3 may require the tribunal or court to depart from the unambiguous meaning the legislation would otherwise bear. s3 may therefore require the decision-making body to depart from the intention of Parliament which enacted the legislation. However, the duty under s3 does not extend to allowing the courts to legislate, in the sense of reading in words which Parliament did not intend or otherwise adopting a meaning which is inconsistent with the underlying thrust of the legislation in question.

Subs (2) preserves the sovereignty of Parliament. The 1998 Act is no different to any other statute. It does not enable other statutes to be disregarded, and does not affect the continuing validity of such statutes. The same applies to secondary legislation such as regulations but *only* if "primary legislation prevents the removal of the incompatibility".

The view that secondary legislation which is made under powers in the primary legislation may be disapplied if it is incompatible with Convention rights has been firmly affirmed by the Supreme Court in *RR v SSWP* [2019] UKSC 52, which has found that the contary view taken by the majority of the Court of Appeal in *SSWP v Carmichael and Sefton Council* [2018] EWCA Civ 548 was wrong.

The three-judge panel of the Upper Tribunal in *SSWP v Carmichael and Sefton BC (HB)* [2017] UKUT 174 (AAC) which decided that where the secondary legislation in the case before it could not be read compatibly with a Convention right, but was not mandated by primary legislation, a tribunal could simply direct that benefit be awarded on a basis that was compatible with the Convention right.

As Lady Hale, President of the Supreme Court, pointed out in para 27 of *RR*:

"There is nothing unconstitutional about a public authority, court or tribunal disapplying a provision of subordinate legislation which would otherwise result in their acting incompatibly with a Convention right, where this is necessary in order to comply with the HRA. Subordinate legislation is subordinate to the requirements of an Act of Parliament. The HRA is an Act of Parliament and its requirements are clear."

Declaration of incompatibility

4.–(1)   Subsection (2) applies in any proceedings in which a court determines whether a provision of primary legislation is compatible with a Convention right.

(2)   If the court is satisfied that the provision is incompatible with a Convention right, it may make a declaration of that incompatibility.

(3)   Subsection (4) applies in any proceedings in which a court determines whether a provision of subordinate legislation, made in the exercise of a power conferred by primary legislation, is compatible with a Convention right.

(4)   If the court is satisfied–

(a)   that the provision is incompatible with a Convention right, and

(b)   that (disregarding any possibility of revocation) the primary legislation concerned prevents removal of the incompatibility,

it may make a declaration of that incompatibility.

(5)   In this section "court" means–

(a)   the House of Lords;

(b)   the Judicial Committee of the Privy Council;

(c)   the Courts-Martial Appeal Court;

(d)   in Scotland, the High Court of Justiciary sitting otherwise than as a trial court or the Court of Session;

(e)   in England and Wales or Northern Ireland, the High Court or the Court of Appeal.

(6)   A declaration under this section ("a declaration of incompatibility")–

(a)   does not affect the validity, continuing operation or enforcement of the provision in respect of which it is given; and

(b)   is not binding on the parties to the proceedings in which it is made.

General Note

The second means by which the Convention rights can impact on the law is through a declaration of incompatibility. But the effect of such a declaration is limited. It does not affect the validity of the legislation and is not binding upon the parties: see subs (6). Its sole purpose is to allow the Secretary of State to make a remedial order under s10 and Sch 2.

A declaration of incompatibility may only be made by a "court" as defined in subs (5). Thus authorities, the First-tier Tribunal and the Upper Tribunal have no power to grant such declarations. The usual mode of seeking a declaration of incompatibility will be by way of a claim for judicial review. It may be possible to do the same on appeal from the Upper Tribunal. On the other hand it may be difficult to show the Upper Tribunal erred law if the legislation in issue cannot admit of any different conclusion. For differing, though not inconsistent, perspectives on the role of the First-tier Tribunal and the Upper Tribunal in such cases see: *R(IS) 12/04*, *SH v SSWP* [2011] UKUT 428 (AAC), *AB v SSWP (JSA)* [2013] UKUT 288 (AAC) and *PL v SSWP (JSA)* [2016] UKUT 177 (AAC).

Right of Crown to intervene

5.–(1)   Where a court is considering whether to make a declaration of incompatibility, the Crown is entitled to notice in accordance with rules of court.

(2)   In any case to which subsection (1) applies–

(a)   a Minister of the Crown (or a person nominated by him),

(b)   a member of the Scottish Executive,
(c)   a Northern Ireland Minister,
(d)   a Northern Ireland department,
is entitled, on giving notice in accordance with rules of court, to be joined as a party to the proceedings.
(3)   Notice under subsection (2) may be given at any time during the proceedings.
(4)   A person who has been made a party to criminal proceedings (other than in Scotland) as the result of a notice under subsection (2) may, with leave, appeal to the House of Lords against any declaration of incompatibility made in the proceedings.
(5)   In subsection (4)–
"criminal proceedings" includes all proceedings before the Courts-Martial Appeal Court; and
"leave" means leave granted by the court making the declaration of incompatibility or by the House of Lords.

General Note
For guidance as to the procedure to adopt under s5, see *Poplar Housing Association Ltd v Donoghue* [2002] QB 58, CA.

Public authorities

Acts of public authorities

6.–(1)   It is unlawful for a public authority to act in a way which is incompatible with a Convention right.
(2)   Subsection (1) does not apply to an act if–
(a)   as the result of one or more provisions of primary legislation, the authority could not have acted differently; or
(b)   in the case of one or more provisions of, or made under, primary legislation which cannot be read or given effect in a way which is compatible with the Convention rights, the authority was acting so as to give effect to or enforce those provisions.
(3)   In this section "public authority" includes–
(a)   a court or tribunal, and
(b)   any person certain of whose functions are functions of a public nature,
but does not include either House of Parliament or a person exercising functions in connection with proceedings in Parliament.
(4)   In subsection (3) "Parliament" does not include the House of Lords in its judicial capacity.
(5)   In relation to a particular act, a person is not a public authority by virtue only of subsection (3)(b) if the nature of the act is private.
(6)   "An act" includes a failure to act but does not include a failure to–
(a)   introduce in, or lay before, Parliament a proposal for legislation; or
(b)   make any primary legislation or remedial order.

General Note
This forbids public authorities, with important exceptions, from infringing Convention rights by the way in which they act on a day-to-day basis.

Analysis
Subsections (1), (2) and (6): The basic prohibition
Subs (1) sets out the basic prohibition, which is then qualified by subs (2) and (6). For enforcement of this obligation, see s7.
Subs (2) follows the same aim of preserving Parliament as the supreme legislative authority. Under para (a), any public body which "could not have" acted in a different way as a result of obedience to primary legislation will not act unlawfully under subs (1). However, the words "could not have" emphasise that where the public body is given a discretion as to how it acts, it may breach s6(1) by acting unlawfully. Para (b) applies both to primary legislation and secondary legislation. It will only apply to secondary legislation if its existence in the incompatible form is made compulsory by primary legislation: see *R (Bono) v Harlow DC HBRB* [2002] 1 WLR 2475 at paras [34]–[35] and *RR v SSWP* [2019] UKSC 52 at para [29]. For further discussion on the reach of subsection (2),

see *R v SSWP ex p Hooper and others* [2005] UKHL 29 and *Doherty and others v Birmingham CC* [2008] UKHL 57.

Subs (6) makes it clear that "act" includes omissions. It then goes on to preserve Parliamentary sovereignty by excluding from the definition a failure by a minister or Parliament to legislate. A failure to make a remedial order may also not be impugned under s6, since this would have the effect of enforcing the court's declaration of incompatibility.

Subsections (3) to (5): "Public body"
The critical question is: what is a "public body" for the purposes of s6? The definition in subs (3) does not purport to be a complete guide. Clearly, a local authority or the Secretary of State for Work and Pensions is a "public body". However, in the context of HB, it may be important to know whether contractors performing functions on behalf of a local authority or social landlords assisting in verification work (see Circulars HB/CTB A21/2001 and A43/2001 for proposals about this) are "public bodies". For the purposes of possession proceedings, similarly, it will be necessary to know whether social landlords are constrained by the obligation in s6(1).

Subs (3)(a) and (4) confirm that courts, the First-tier Tribunal and the Upper Tribunal are public bodies and hence are bound by the prohibition in subs (1). Subs (4) confirms that the House of Lords, when acting in its judicial capacity, is obliged to comply with the Convention just as much as any other court.

Subs (3)(b) and (5) introduce the concept of a "functional" public authority; a body existing under private law but which is exercising functions of a public nature. The words "certain of whose" make it clear that the body may exercise private functions alongside its public functions without taking it outside the scope of "public body". Such a body will only be a "public body" in relation to its public acts, however, as subs (5) makes clear.

This distinction has been illuminated by caselaw. In *Donaghue v Poplar Housing Association Ltd* [2002] QB 58, CA, a tenant sought to impugn the decision of her landlord, a housing association, to seek possession of her home. She was an assured shorthold tenant under a tenancy conferred on her pursuant to an obligation of the local authority and her tenancy had been terminated under s21 Housing Act 1988, which gives a landlord an absolute right to possession. She contended that this was a breach of her right to respect for her home under Art 8 of the Convention. The Court of Appeal held that the meaning of "public body" should be given "a generous interpretation" (para 58). It went on to say (para 59):

"The purpose of s6(3)(b) is to deal with hybrid bodies which have both public and private functions. It is not to make a body, which does not have responsibilities to the public, a public body merely because it performs acts on behalf of a public body which would constitute public functions were such acts to be performed by the public body itself. An act can remain of a private nature even though it is performed because another body is under a public duty to ensure that that act is performed."

The court concluded (para 66) that the close links between the local authority and the housing association in that case meant that the association was a public body for the purposes of granting and terminating the claimant's tenancy. However, it went on to hold (paras 67-72) that there was no breach of Art 8.

The close links between the housing association and the local authority did not exist in *R (Heather) v The Leonard Cheshire Foundation* [2001] 4 CCLR 211, Stanley Burton J. In that case, the claimants challenged the closure of a care home on Art 8 grounds. The judge distinguished *Donaghue* on the ground that the special ties between the local authority and the landlord in *Donaghue* did not exist here. That decision was upheld by the Court of Appeal [2002] 2 All ER 936. That approach to the phrase "public authority" in the context of private care homes has been reaffirmed, albeit by a bare majority, by the House of Lords in *YL (by her litigation friend the Official Solicitor) v Birmingham City Council and others* [2007] UKHL 27, 20 June, HL.

It is suggested, however, that a private company carrying out HB functions on behalf of the local authority will be a "public body" in carrying out such functions. Furthermore, if a social landlord assists with verification work, it will be a "public body" for those purposes. However, a social landlord will not be a "public body" in acting as a landlord, without the special features present in *Donaghue v Poplar Housing Association Ltd* or something akin to them.

Proceedings

7.–(1)   A person who claims that a public authority has acted (or proposes to act) in a way which is made unlawful by section 6(1) may–

(a)   bring proceedings against the authority under this Act in the appropriate court or tribunal, or

(b)   rely on the Convention right or rights concerned in any legal proceedings,

but only if he is (or would be) a victim of the unlawful act.

(2)   In subsection (1)(a) "appropriate court or tribunal" means such court or tribunal as may be determined in accordance with rules; and proceedings against an authority include a counterclaim or similar proceeding.

(3)   If the proceedings are brought on an application for judicial review, the applicant is to be taken to have a sufficient interest in relation to the unlawful act only if he is, or would be, a victim of that act.

(4)   If the proceedings are made by way of a petition for judicial review in Scotland, the applicant shall be taken to have title and interest to sue in relation to the unlawful act only if he is, or would be, a victim of that act.

(5)   Proceedings under subsection (1)(a) must be brought before the end of–

(a)   the period of one year beginning with the date on which the act complained of took place; or

(b)   such longer period as the court or tribunal considers equitable having regard to all the circumstances,

but that is subject to any rule imposing a stricter time limit in relation to the procedure in question.

(6)   In subsection (1)(b) "legal proceedings" includes–

(a)   proceedings brought by or at the instigation of a public authority; and

(b)   an appeal against the decision of a court or tribunal.

(7)   For the purposes of this section, a person is a victim of an unlawful act only if he would be a victim for the purposes of Article 34 of the Convention if proceedings were brought in the European Court of Human Rights in respect of that act.

(8)   Nothing in this Act creates a criminal offence.

(9)   In this section "rules" means–

(a)   in relation to proceedings before a court or tribunal outside Scotland, rules made by the Lord Chancellor or the Secretary of State for the purposes of this section or rules of court,

(b)   in relation to proceedings before a court or tribunal in Scotland, rules made by the Secretary of State for those purposes,

(c)   in relation to proceedings before a tribunal in Northern Ireland–

(i)   which deals with transferred matters; and

(ii)   for which no rules made under paragraph (a) are in force,

rules made by a Northern Ireland department for those purposes,

and includes provision made by order under section 1 of the Courts and Legal Services Act 1990.

(10)   In making rules, regard must be had to section 9.

(11)   The Minister who has power to make rules in relation to a particular tribunal may, to the extent he considers it necessary to ensure that the tribunal can provide an appropriate remedy in relation to an act (or proposed act) of a public authority which is (or would be) unlawful as a result of section 6(1), by order add to–

(a)   the relief or remedies which the tribunal may grant; or

(b)   the grounds on which it may grant any of them.

(12)   An order made under subsection (11) may contain such incidental, supplemental, consequential or transitional provision as the Minister making it considers appropriate.

(13)   "The Minister" includes the Northern Ireland department concerned.

General Note

This deals with the procedure by which allegations of a breach of Convention rights can be raised for the consideration of the courts and tribunals.

Analysis

Subsections (1)(a), (2) to (5) and (7) to (13): Bringing proceedings for a breach of the Convention

Taken together, these subsections envisage the commencement of proceedings before a court or tribunal complaining of the breach of the Convention. By its terms, the right to commence proceedings under sub (1)(a) may apply even where the breach has not yet occurred, in which case an injunction (interdict in Scotland) may be sought to restrain the breach.

Sub (1)(a) and (2) restrict the right to bring proceedings to a court or tribunal that may be identified in accordance with rules as being the appropriate forum in which to proceed. By r7.11 of the Civil Procedure Rules 1998, in England and Wales proceedings may be issued in the High Court or the County Court, except where complaint is made about a judicial act in which case proceedings must be commenced in the High Court: see s9 below for complaints about judicial acts.

No rules have been made conferring a right to commence proceedings in the First-tier Tribunal or before the Upper Tribunal. However, Convention rights may be relied upon in an appeal under subs (1)(b).

Subs (1)(a), (3), (4) and (7) deal with the right to bring proceedings. A person must be a "victim" for the purposes of the Convention if s/he is to have the right to commence proceedings. That includes proceedings for judicial review, where the test of standing (England and Wales) or title and interest (Scotland) is different. Art 34 of the Convention, referred to in subs (7), does not define "victim". The following rules are a summary of the caselaw of the court and commissioner on the subject: see, for example, Starmer, *European Human Rights Law* (2000) paras 2.18–2.39.

(1)   The Convention applies to persons not in the country or acts taking place outside the country if they are done on behalf of the state.

(2)   A corporate body may be a victim. A governmental organisation, however, cannot bring proceedings.

(3)   Those potentially affected, as well as those who have already been affected, may bring proceedings as long as the risk of a breach of the Convention is not merely theoretical.

(4)   People indirectly affected, such as the family members of a claimant, or shareholders in a company that is a landlord, may be a "victim". Claims may also be brought by personal representatives on death or incapacity.

Subs (5) imposes a one-year limitation period in respect of the commencement of proceedings. That time limit is, however, subject to any stricter time limit provided for by relevant rules.

   Subs (9) to (13) deal with rule-making powers.

Subsections (1)(b) and (6): Relying on a breach of the Convention in proceedings

Breaches of Convention rights may be relied upon in any proceedings. These include appeals to the First-tier Tribunal or subsequent appeals to the Upper Tribunal or beyond. If proceedings are brought, for example for possession, it will be possible to allege that the court would act in breach of the Convention by granting possession as well as that the claimant is itself acting in breach of the Convention if it is a public body. For an example of this approach, see *Donaghue v Poplar Housing Association Ltd* [2002] QB 58, CA, where the tenant alleged that the court was in breach of Art 6 for proceeding in an unfair manner and the claimant landlord was in breach of Art 8 by seeking possession.

Judicial remedies

8.–(1)   In relation to any act (or proposed act) of a public authority which the court finds is (or would be) unlawful, it may grant such relief or remedy, or make such order, within its powers as it considers just and appropriate.

(2)   But damages may be awarded only by a court which has power to award damages, or to order the payment of compensation, in civil proceedings.

(3)   No award of damages is to be made unless, taking account of all the circumstances of the case, including–

(a)   any other relief or remedy granted, or order made, in relation to the act in question (by that or any other court), and

(b)   the consequences of any decision (of that or any other court) in respect of that act,

the court is satisfied that the award is necessary to afford just satisfaction to the person in whose favour it is made.

(4)   In determining–

(a)   whether to award damages, or

(b)   the amount of an award,

the court must take into account the principles applied by the European Court of Human Rights in relation to the award of compensation under Article 41 of the Convention.

(5)   A public authority against which damages are awarded is to be treated–

(a)   in Scotland, for the purposes of section 3 of the Law Reform (Miscellaneous Provisions) (Scotland) Act 1940 as if the award were made in an action of damages in which the authority has been found liable in respect of loss or damage to the person to whom the award is made;

(b)   for the purposes of the Civil Liability (Contribution) Act 1978 as liable in respect of damage suffered by the person to whom the award is made.

(6)   In this section–

"court" includes a tribunal;

"damages" means damages for an unlawful act of a public authority; and

"unlawful" means unlawful under section 6(1).

General Note

This section deals with the remedies that a court or tribunal may grant when proceedings are brought under s7 against a public body.

Analysis

Subs (1) and (2) allow a court (which includes, by virtue of subs (6), a tribunal) to grant remedies for acts which are unlawful under s6. However, the key phrase here is "within its powers". There is no additional power to grant remedies conferred by s8. It follows that tribunals and commissioners have no power to award damages or costs by virtue of the 1998 Act, as confirmed by subs (2).

Subs (3) to (5) deal with awards of damages. An award of damages is only to be made if it is necessary to give "just satisfaction" to the victim. This is a phrase which originates in Art 41, and indeed subs (4) requires a court to consider the caselaw under Art 41 in deciding whether to award damages and, if so, how much.

However, it is difficult to distil any clear principles from the Strasbourg caselaw. Domestic caselaw has now illuminated the situations in which damages will be awarded for breaches of Art 8 of the Convention. In *R (Anufrijeva) v Southwark LBC* [2003] EWCA Civ 1406, CA, the Court of Appeal gave guidance on this question. The court said (para 65) that a broad-brush approach should be adopted. Where there is pecuniary loss caused by the breach, that will ordinarily be calculated and awarded (para 59). However, non-pecuniary loss causes greater difficulty, as recognised by the Court at para 60:

"Infringements can involve a variety of treatment of an individual which is objectionable in itself. The treatment may give rise to distress, anxiety, and, in extreme cases, psychiatric trauma. The primary object of the proceedings will often be to bring the adverse treatment to an end. If this is achieved is this enough to constitute 'just satisfaction' or is it necessary to award damages to compensate for the adverse treatment that has occurred? More particularly, should damages be awarded for anxiety and distress that has been occasioned by the breach? It is in relation to these questions that Strasbourg fails to give a consistent or coherent answer."

In cases of maladministration such as those being considered by the Court, the "critical message is that the remedy has to be 'just and appropriate' and 'necessary' to afford 'just satisfaction'" (para 66). In deciding whether the breach of rights required an award of damages, the Court said that the scale and manner of the breach, and the conduct of the parties, would all be relevant (paras 66–68). As far as quantum was concerned, the amounts awarded should be modest but not minimal, and comparable awards by the Local Government Ombudsman are a useful comparator (paras 75 and 78). It appears that the £10,000 awarded to the claimants in *R (Bernard) v Enfield LBC* [2002] 5 CCLR 589 for leaving a severely disabled woman and her family in appalling and degrading living conditions for a considerable period of time is the very maximum award that should be made for a breach of Art 8.

The court also gave guidance as to the procedure that should be followed in relation to damages claims, having expressed its concern at the cost of the litigation before it (paras 81). Damages claims for maladministration should ordinarily proceed by way of judicial review and the claimant should be prepared to justify not using the Ombudsman or Adjudicator instead. Claims for damages should be determined on the papers by the appropriate level of judge, if necessary separately to any claim for other relief (such as an order to compel a local authority to determine a claim).

However, in *R (Greenfield) v SSHD* [2005] UKHL 14, [2005] 2 All ER 240, HL, the House of Lords, albeit in the context of a claim for damages for breach of Art 6, rejected the claimant's argument, which was predicated at least in part on the approach said to have been adopted in *R (Bernard) v Enfield* and *Anufrijeva*, that courts in England and Wales, when exercising their power to award damages under s8, should apply domestic scales of damages. In Lord Bingham's opinion, one of the broader reasons why this approach should not be followed was that the HRA is not a tort statute: its objects are different and broader. As such, even in a case where a finding of violation is not judged to afford the applicant just satisfaction (and in most Art 6 violation cases the finding of breach of Art 6 should, in Lord Bingham's view, of itself provide the just satisfaction or remedy), such a finding will be an important part of the claimant's remedy. Accordingly, in Art 6 cases at least awards of damages should be modestly low.

Overall, Lord Bingham's view in *Greenfield* was that courts in the UK, although not inflexibly bound by Strasbourg awards in what may be different cases, should not aim to be significantly more or less generous than the ECtHR might be expected to be, in a case where it was willing to make an award at all.

Judicial acts

9.–(1) Proceedings under section 7(1)(a) in respect of a judicial act may be brought only–

(a) by exercising a right of appeal;

(b) on an application (in Scotland a petition) for judicial review; or

(c) in such other forum as may be prescribed by rules.

(2) That does not affect any rule of law which prevents a court from being the subject of judicial review.

(3) In proceedings under this Act in respect of a judicial act done in good faith, damages may not be awarded otherwise than to compensate a person to the extent required by Article 5(5) of the Convention.

(4)   An award of damages permitted by subsection (3) is to be made against the Crown; but no award may be made unless the appropriate person, if not a party to the proceedings, is joined.

(5)   In this section–

"appropriate person" means the Minister responsible for the court concerned, or a person or government department nominated by him;

"court" includes a tribunal;

"judge" includes a member of a tribunal, a justice of the peace and a clerk or other officer entitled to exercise the jurisdiction of a court;

"judicial act" means a judicial act of a court and includes an act done on the instructions, or on behalf, of a judge; and

"rules" has the same meaning as in section 7(9).

Remedial action

Power to take remedial action

10.–(1)   This section applies if–

(a)   a provision of legislation has been declared under section 4 to be incompatible with a Convention right and, if an appeal lies–

(i)   all persons who may appeal have stated in writing that they do not intend to do so;

(ii)   the time for bringing an appeal has expired and no appeal has been brought within that time; or

(iii)   an appeal brought within that time has been determined or abandoned; or

(b)   it appears to a Minister of the Crown or Her Majesty in Council that, having regard to a finding of the European Court of Human Rights made after the coming into force of this section in proceedings against the United Kingdom, a provision of legislation is incompatible with an obligation of the United Kingdom arising from the Convention.

(2)   If a Minister of the Crown considers that there are compelling reasons for proceeding under this section, he may by order make such amendments to the legislation as he considers necessary to remove the incompatibility.

(3)   If, in the case of subordinate legislation, a Minister of the Crown considers–

(a)   that it is necessary to amend the primary legislation under which the subordinate legislation in question was made, in order to enable the incompatibility to be removed, and

(b)   that there are compelling reasons for proceeding under this section,

he may by order make such amendments to the primary legislation as he considers necessary.

(4)   This section also applies where the provision in question is in subordinate legislation and has been quashed, or declared invalid, by reason of incompatibility with a Convention right and the Minister proposes to proceed under paragraph 2(b) of Schedule 2.

(5)   If the legislation is an Order in Council, the power conferred by subsection (2) or (3) is exercisable by Her Majesty in Council.

(6)   In this section "legislation" does not include a Measure of the Church Assembly or of the General Synod of the Church of England.

(7)   Schedule 2 makes further provision about remedial orders.

Other rights and proceedings

Safeguard for existing human rights

11.   A person's reliance on a Convention right does not restrict–

(a)   any other right or freedom conferred on him by or under any law having effect in any part of the United Kingdom; or

(b)   his right to make any claim or bring any proceedings which he could make or bring apart from sections 7 to 9.

Freedom of thought, conscience and religion

13.–(1)   If a court's determination of any question arising under this Act might affect the exercise by a religious organisation (itself or its members collectively) of the Convention right to freedom of thought, conscience and religion, it must have particular regard to the importance of that right.

(2)   In this section "court" includes a tribunal.

Supplemental

Orders etc under this Act

20.–(1)   Any power of a Minister of the Crown to make an order under this Act is exercisable by statutory instrument.

(2)   The power of the Lord Chancellor or the Secretary of State to make rules (other than rules of court) under section 2(3) or 7(9) is exercisable by statutory instrument.

(3)   Any statutory instrument made under section 14, 15 or 16(7) must be laid before Parliament.

(4)   No order may be made by the Lord Chancellor or the Secretary of State under section 1(4), 7(11) or 16(2) unless a draft of the order has been laid before, and approved by, each House of Parliament.

(5)   Any statutory instrument made under section 18(7) or Schedule 4, or to which subsection (2) applies, shall be subject to annulment in pursuance of a resolution of either House of Parliament.

(6)   The power of a Northern Ireland department to make–

(a)   rules under section 2(3)(c) or 7(9)(c), or

(b)   an order under section 7(11),

is exercisable by statutory rule for the purposes of the Statutory Rules (Northern Ireland) Order 1979.

(7)   Any rules made under section 2(3)(c) or 7(9)(c) shall be subject to negative resolution; and section 41(6) of the Interpretation Act Northern Ireland) 1954 (meaning of "subject to negative resolution") shall apply as if the power to make the rules were conferred by an Act of the Northern Ireland Assembly.

(8)   No order may be made by a Northern Ireland department under section 7(11) unless a draft of the order has been laid before, and approved by, the Northern Ireland Assembly.

Interpretation etc

21.–(1)   In this Act–

"amend" includes repeal and apply (with or without modifications);

"the appropriate Minister" means the Minister of the Crown having charge of the appropriate authorised government department (within the meaning of the Crown Proceedings Act 1947);

"the Commission" means the European Commission of Human Rights;

"the Convention" means the Convention for the Protection of Human Rights and Fundamental Freedoms, agreed by the Council of Europe at Rome on 4th November 1950 as it has effect for the time being in relation to the United Kingdom;

"declaration of incompatibility" means a declaration under section 4;

"Minister of the Crown" has the same meaning as in the Ministers of the Crown Act 1975;

"Northern Ireland Minister" includes the First Minister and the deputy First Minister in Northern Ireland;

"primary legislation" means any–

(a)   public general Act;

(b)   local and personal Act;

(c)   private Act;

(d)   Measure of the Church Assembly;

(e)   Measure of the General Synod of the Church of England;

    (f)   Order in Council–
          (i)   made in exercise of Her Majesty's Royal Prerogative;
          (ii)   made under section 38(1)(a) of the Northern Ireland Constitution Act 1973 or the corresponding provision of the Northern Ireland Act 1998; or
          (iii)   amending an Act of a kind mentioned in paragraph (a), (b) or (c);

and includes an order or other instrument made under primary legislation (otherwise than by the National Assembly for Wales, a member of the Scottish Executive, a Northern Ireland Minister or a Northern Ireland department) to the extent to which it operates to bring one or more provisions of that legislation into force or amends any primary legislation;

"the First Protocol" means the protocol to the Convention agreed at Paris on 20th March 1952;

"the Sixth Protocol" means the protocol to the Convention agreed at Strasbourg on 28th April 1983;

"the Eleventh Protocol" means the protocol to the Convention (restructuring the control machinery established by the Convention) agreed at Strasbourg on 11th May 1994;

"remedial order" means an order under section 10;

"subordinate legislation" means any–

    (a)   Order in Council other than one–
          (i)   made in exercise of Her Majesty's Royal Prerogative;
          (ii)   made under section 38(1)(a) of the Northern Ireland Constitution Act 1973 or the corresponding provision of the Northern Ireland Act 1998; or
          (iii)   amending an Act of a kind mentioned in the definition of primary legislation;
    (b)   Act of the Scottish Parliament;
    (c)   Act of the Parliament of Northern Ireland;
    (d)   Measure of the Assembly established under section 1 of the Northern Ireland Assembly Act 1973;
    (e)   Act of the Northern Ireland Assembly;
    (f)   order, rules, regulations, scheme, warrant, byelaw or other instrument made under primary legislation (except to the extent to which it operates to bring one or more provisions of that legislation into force or amends any primary legislation);
    (g)   order, rules, regulations, scheme, warrant, byelaw or other instrument made under legislation mentioned in paragraph (b), (c), (d) or (e) or made under an Order in Council applying only to Northern Ireland;
    (h)   order, rules, regulations, scheme, warrant, byelaw or other instrument made by a member of the Scottish Executive, a Northern Ireland Minister or a Northern Ireland department in exercise of prerogative or other executive functions of Her Majesty which are exercisable by such a person on behalf of Her Majesty;

"transferred matters" has the same meaning as in the Northern Ireland Act 1998; and

"tribunal" means any tribunal in which legal proceedings may be brought.

    (2)   The references in paragraphs (b) and (c) of section 2(1) to Articles are to Articles of the Convention as they had effect immediately before the coming into force of the Eleventh Protocol.

    (3)   The reference in paragraph (d) of section 2(1) to Article 46 includes a reference to Articles 32 and 54 of the Convention as they had effect immediately before the coming into force of the Eleventh Protocol.

    (4)   The references in section 2(1) to a report or decision of the Commission or a decision of the Committee of Ministers include references to a report or decision made as provided by paragraphs 3, 4 and 6 of Article 5 of the Eleventh Protocol (transitional provisions).

    (5)   Any liability under the Army Act 1955, the Air Force Act 1955 or the Naval Discipline Act 1957 to suffer death for an offence is replaced by a liability to imprisonment for life or any less punishment authorised by those Acts; and those Acts shall accordingly have effect with the necessary modifications.

Short title, commencement, application and extent

22.–(1)   This Act may be cited as the Human Rights Act 1998.

(2)   Sections 18, 20 and 21(5) and this section come into force on the passing of this Act.

(3)   The other provisions of this Act come into force on such day as the Secretary of State may by order appoint; and different days may be appointed for different purposes.

(4)   Paragraph (b) of subsection (1) of section 7 applies to proceedings brought by or at the instigation of a public authority whenever the act in question took place; but otherwise that subsection does not apply to an act taking place before the coming into force of that section.

(5)   This Act binds the Crown.

(6)   This Act extends to Northern Ireland.

(7)   Section 21(5), so far as it relates to any provision contained in the Army Act 1955, the Air Force Act 1955 or the Naval Discipline Act 1957, extends to any place to which that provision extends.

Analysis

Subs (3) provides that the bulk of the 1998 Act was to come into force on the making of orders. The Human Rights Act (Commencement) Order 1998 SI No 2882 brought s19 (which allows ministers presenting legislation to Parliament to make statements about the compatibility of Bills with the Convention) into force from 24 November 1998. The remainder of the Act was brought into force by the Human Rights Act (Commencement No.2) Order 2000 No.1851 from 2 October 2000.

Subs (4) applies a limited retrospectivity to the Act. It is clear that where a public authority brings proceedings, a breach of Convention rights may be relied upon whenever the breach occurred. Thus a claimant who is prosecuted, or a person sued for recovery of an overpayment of HB, may rely on breaches of the Convention occurring prior to 2 October 2000 in those proceedings. 'Proceedings' means legal proceedings and so s22(4) does not apply to supersession (or revision) decisions instigated by a Secretary of State decision-maker as s/he only exercises administrative, and not legal, functions: *CDLA 1347/1999* para 29.

Judicial review proceedings are only technically brought in the name of the Crown. The reality is that they are instituted by the claimant, and accordingly damages cannot be claimed by a person whose Convention rights were breached prior to 2 October 2000 in judicial review proceedings: *R (Ben-Abdelaziz) v SSHD* [2001] 1 WLR 1485, CA.

The strict limits on the retrospectivity of the 1998 Act were confirmed by the House of Lords in *Wilson v First County Trust Ltd (No 2)* [2003] WLR 586. In *Wilson (No 2)*, it was confirmed that the 1998 Act has no application to events occurring prior to 2 October 2000 and so cannot give rise to any cause of action arising before that date save in the strictly limited circumstances set out in subs (4). Neither can the interpretative obligation in s3 apply to the law governing such a case (paras 10–23). The House of Lords did not find it necessary to decide whether the Court of Appeal's approach, in which it had decided that s6(1) obliged it to act compatibly with the Convention on an appeal, was incorrect in all cases. It could not, however, be correct in *Wilson (No 2)* because the court had purported to disapply primary legislation, which was prohibited by s6(2)(a) (paras 24–25).

The latter argument is, of course, of importance where a claimant asserts on an appeal heard after 2 October 2000 that a decision at a lower level in the appellate hierarchy breaches Convention Rights. In *CSDLA 1019/1999* (paras 70–89), the tribunal of commissioners ruled that an alleged breach of Art 6 in the constitution of a tribunal sitting prior to 2 October 2000 could not be relied upon on appeal. The tribunal's conclusion that the inclusion of a doctor who also carried out medical assessments for the Benefits Agency breached the common law rule against bias was overturned by the Court of Session in *SSWP v Gillies* [2003] 2004 SLT 14; reported at 2006 SC (HL) 71 (the decision of the Court of Session was upheld by the House of Lords in *Gillies v SSWP* [2006] UKHL 2; reported as *R(DLA) 5/06*. However, if a tribunal sitting after 2 October 2000 breaches a claimant's Convention rights, it does not matter whether the decision under appeal was made before or after that date: *Wilson (No 2)* para 21 and *R(IS) 6/04*; though if the decision under appeal was made before 2 October 2000, it cannot be challenged on the ground that it breached the claimant's Convention rights.

SCHEDULE 1

SECTION 1(3)

The Articles

General Note on Schedule 1

Only the Articles which might conceivably be relevant to HB entitlement are set out below and discussion is limited to that which is reasonably necessary to consider the arguments that might arise.

Article 3
Prohibition of torture

No one shall be subjected to torture or to inhuman or degrading treatment or punishment.

Analysis

A refusal of HB will not of itself give rise to any breach of Art 3. It is now established that while a state may have a positive obligation under Art 3 to prevent an individual suffering from "degrading treatment", the individual's condition must be of the requisite severity: *Pretty v UK* (2002) 35 EHRR 1, ECHR, para 52, where the ECHR said:

"As regards the types of "treatment" which fall within the scope of Article 3 of the Convention, the Court's case law refers to "ill-treatment" that attains a minimum level of severity and involves actual bodily injury or intense physical or mental suffering. Where treatment humiliates or debases an individual showing lack of respect for, or diminishing, his or her human dignity or arouses feelings of fear, anguish or inferiority capable of breaking an individual's moral and physical resistance, it may be characterised as degrading and also fall within the prohibition of Article 3. The suffering which flows from naturally occurring illness, physical or mental, may be treatment, where it is, or risks being, exacerbated by treatment, whether flowing from conditions of detention, expulsion or other measures, for which the authorities can be held responsible."

A claimant who is refused HB will ordinarily be able to avail her/himself of other forms of welfare support, whether by moving to a property where a claim for HB is unobjectionable or by other means. However, the threat of destitution may give rise to a breach of Art 3: *R v Secretary of State for the Home Department ex p Limbuela and others* [2005] UKHL 66. So, even homelessness or destitution may be sufficient.

Article 6
Right to a fair trial

1.   In the determination of his civil rights and obligations or of any criminal charge against him, everyone is entitled to a fair and public hearing within a reasonable time by an independent and impartial tribunal established by law. Judgment shall be pronounced publicly but the press and public may be excluded from all or part of the trial in the interest of morals, public order or national security in a democratic society, where the interests of juveniles or the protection of the private life of the parties so require, or to the extent strictly necessary in the opinion of the court in special circumstances where publicity would prejudice the interests of justice.

2.–3.   *[Omitted]*

Analysis

Paras 2 and 3 concern only criminal proceedings and accordingly are omitted here. A decision on recoverability of overpayments does not involve the determination of a "criminal charge": *R(IS) 1/04*. Art 6 is the cornerstone of the procedural protections envisaged by the Convention.

"the determination of his civil rights and obligations". Art 6 only has application if the matter in dispute is a "civil right" or "civil obligation". It now seems to be clear that the determination of entitlements to welfare benefits is the determination of a "civil right". Early cases established this principle in relation to contributory benefits, in which a right of property was recognised (see Prot 1 Art 1 below): see, for example, *Feldbrugge v Netherlands* (1986) 8 EHRR 425; *Deumeland v Germany* (1986) 8 EHRR 448 at 468, para 74, ECtHR. The objection taken by the states in those cases was that entitlement to benefits was a public law right and not "civil" in nature. The now generally accepted view is that where legislation confers an enforceable right to a benefit, Art 6 applies to proceedings in which entitlement to that benefit is considered. This is confirmed by *Salesi v Italy* (1993) 26 EHRR 187 at 199, para 19, ECtHR, which concerned a non-contributory pension. A similar perspective was adopted by the Tribunal of Commissioners in *R(IS) 15/04* in the context of a decision not to revise. The commissioners reasoned firstly that a claimant is entitled to apply for a revision on the grounds of official error and, if that ground is made out, is entitled to have the decision revised. Accordingly, there is a 'right' to the revision. Secondly, although the 'civil right' in question is the right to the social security benefit which was the subject of the decision on the claim, seeking a revision of that decision is part of the process whereby entitlement to the benefit is determined, and therefore falls within the scope of Art 6.

The issue of whether decisions relating to HB entitlement concern "civil rights and obligations" has been settled by the decision of Pitchford J in *R (Cumpsty) v Rent Officer* [2002] EWHC 2526 (Admin), paras 76–80.

The judge decided that even though the rent officer's determination did not itself decide the claimant's HB entitlement, it was such a vital and integral part of that decision that it was itself a determination of civil rights and obligations. See to similar effect the reasoning in *R(IS) 6/04*.

"a fair and public hearing". In many respects, the concept of a fair hearing mirrors the rules of natural justice in domestic law. The incorporation of Art 6, however, arguably broadens and emphasises these rules and, more importantly, gives them teeth where unfairness results from the application of a statutory rule.

The first aspect of a fair hearing is equality of arms. There must be equal opportunities on the two sides to a dispute to present their cases: *Dombo Beheer BV v Netherlands* (1993) 18 EHRR 213 at 226-8, ECtHR, paras 30–40. It is inherent in this that parties must ordinarily have sight of the evidence before the tribunal: *Ruiz-Mateos v Spain* (1993) 16 EHRR 505, para 63. In *CDLA 5413/1999* paras 49–51, it was suggested that the provisions for deemed notification of an oral hearing before a tribunal (and hence, presumably the similar provisions deeming receipt of a notification of a decision, a statement of reasons and so on) could offend against this principle if they caused injustice. In *CJSA 5100/2001*, the appeal to an appeal tribunal turned on a contested issue of fact, namely whether an investigating officer from the DWP had seen the claimant working, but the investigating officer failed to attend at the hearing and so could not be cross-examined by the claimant. Applying the 'equality of arms' principle, the commissioner ruled that while there was nothing the claimant could do to get the officer to attend, the Secretary of State could have secured his attendance, and the appeal tribunal then compounded this problem, and thereby erred in law, in failing to adjourn the case to enable the Secretary of State to seek the attendance of the investigating officer: see para 13. See also *CIB 3985/2001* where similar reasoning was applied to the Secretary of State's failure to make available to the tribunal relevant evidence in the form of a medical report which only he, and not the claimant, held. In *CDLA 2748/2002* (para 11), the commissioner held that if there were difficulties with interpretation that hampered the presentation of a claimant's case, Art 6 might be breached if the tribunal failed to take appropriate action to remedy the situation.

Secondly, the process of hearing a case must be reasonably accessible. If a party suffers the loss of her/his case through misleading rules of procedure, then there might be a violation of Art 6: *Bellet v France* (1995) unreported, case number A/333-B, FCtHR. This could apply if an appeal is inadvertently lodged out of time and not subsequently admitted.

The availability of legal aid is a controversial topic. In *Airey v Ireland* (1979) 2 EHRR 305, the Court found a violation in a family case where a woman was attempting to divorce a violent husband. The question posed was whether a claimant could effectively represent her/himself in the particular proceedings in question without legal representation. Since then, the court has qualified the effect of *Airey*. In *Munro v UK* [1986] 48 DR 154, ECmHR, which concerned defamation proceedings, the Commission contrasted the nature of those proceedings with the intimate nature of the family proceedings in *Airey* and the serious consequences for the family. Moreover, if there is some other means of assistance available, *Andronicou v Cyprus* (1998) 25 EHRR 491, ECtHR suggests that there will be no violation of Art 6. Since the consequences of the loss of HB entitlement are fairly intimate and serious, involving the potential loss of a home, it may be arguable that the absence of Community Legal Service funding for a sufficiently complex tribunal or commissioner hearing might infringe Art 6, particularly if an application for funding under the Access to Justice Act 1999 has been refused.

The concept of a fair hearing also involves the right to a reasoned decision and a public hearing, neither of which should present particular difficulties within the present adjudication system, save that tribunals should exercise caution in refusing an oral hearing if a claimant wants one.

One issue of particular concern within the HB system remains the rent officer system.

However, the question of whether the system of determinations by a rent officer was compliant with Art 6 was decided affirmatively in *Cumpsty*. There, the claimant had been given a re-determination, had been given reasons for the rent officer's conclusion as to the local reference rent level and had entered into extensive correspondence with the rent officer. Pitchford J held that the rent officer was "independent and impartial" (paras 81–82) and that there was sufficient involvement of the claimant in the process to give him a "fair hearing" (para 91). It remains open to question whether that would be so in a case where the rent officer refused to give reasons or gave insufficient reasons to enable a meaningful dialogue to take place, particularly in the light of *Tsfayo* (see below).

"within a reasonable time". *Feldbrugge*, *Denneland* and *Salesi* (cited above) are all examples of complaints of breach of the right to a determination within a reasonable time. In each case, the delay was several years. In the context of HB, however, since a home can be lost in as little as three to four months if HB is not put into payment, and a claim is supposed to be decided within 14 days, it may be that the tolerable period of delay is considerably less. However, in *R(IS) 1/04* and *R(IS) 2/04* delays of seven months and two years respectively in having initial decisions heard on an appeal were held to have met the reasonable time criterion and so did not breach Article 6.

In *CIB 8/2008* [2009] UKUT 47 (AAC), the DWP had delayed five years in preparing the claimant's appeal and forwarding it to the Tribunal Service, the delay being caused solely by administrative failure to progress the appeal. Judge Lane held that there had been a breach of Art 6. Citing *Procurator Fiscal v Dyer and Watson* [2002] UKPC D1, she said that where there is unreasonable delay, a breach of Art 6 is not dependant on proof of prejudice or detriment arising from the delay; prejudice is presumed if the delay is unreasonable. *Dyer* also confirmed that the manner in which administrative authorities deal with a dispute can be material to the issue of whether there has been unreasonable delay in providing a hearing.

Although Judge Lane's conclusion on remedy is consistent with the caselaw on Art 6, it has been decided in *AS v SSWP (CA)* [2015] UKUT 592 (AAC); [2016] AACR 22 that her view about Art 6 being breached in a case of unreasonable delay even where that delay has not prejudiced the right to a fair hearing is wrong. The decision in *AS* followed reason the decision of the House of Lords in the case of *Attorney Generals' Reference No2 of 2001* [2003] UKHL 68; [2004] 1 All ER 1041, which *AS* decides effectively overrules any contary authority such as *Dyer*. In *Attorney Generals' Reference No2 of 2001*, a nine-member House of Lords held (by a majority of 7 to 2), in the context of the remedy for criminal trial which had been the subject of unreasonable pre-trial delay but where no prejudice would have arisen to the defendant to proceed with the trial, that the hearing could only not proceed if a fair hearing was no longer possible. In other words, an unreasonable delay of itself is not enough and prejudice or lack of fairness has to be shown. The majority of the House of Lords held that the same considerations applied with equal (if not more) force to civil proceedings, and indicated that this analysis went not just to what remedy may be granted but whether Art 6 had been breached in the first place.

The decision in *AS* reiterates that it is not open to a First-tier Tribunal to remedy a breach of Art 6(1) by simply allowing the appeal. The tribunal's obligation is to decide the appeal on the evidence before it, making due allowance for any delay. Moreover, neither the First-tier Tribunal nor the Upper Tribunal has any statutory power to award the appellant compensation for the effects of any such delay: *AH v London Borough of Hackney (HB)* [2014] UKUT 47 (AAC).

"by an independent and impartial tribunal". At the time that the 1998 Act came into force, it was thought to be self-evident that the old Review Board system contravened Art 6 because a tribunal composed of members of the local authority could not be "independent and impartial". That has at long last been confirmed by the European Court of Human Rights in *Tsfayo v United Kingdom* (2009) 48 EHRR 18.

However, prior to *Tsfayo*, the courts in the UK had sought to limit this vital component of Art 6 as it is applied to decision-making by public authorities in social welfare matters. The reasoning of the UK courts rests on the decision of the House of Lords in *R (Alconbury Developments Ltd) v Secretary of State for the Environment, Transport and the Regions* [2003] 2 AC 295, HL, where it was held that although a planning inspector was not independent of the Secretary of State, Art 6 did not require a full appeal to an independent court on the facts as well as law and judicial review was a sufficient safeguard for those concerned with planning inquiries. A large part of the House of Lords' reasoning was that since planning matters raised matters of public interest as well as a dispute between individuals and the planning authority, it was right that the decisions on matters of fact should be taken by someone who was publicly accountable (such as the Secretary of State through her/his inspectors).

As a matter of principle, it is difficult to quarrel with such a conclusion. However, the same reasoning was then applied to situations where there is no general public interest in the outcome of the dispute between citizen and state beyond the question of expenditure of public funds. Thus in *Begum v Tower Hamlets LBC* [2003] 2 WLR 238, HL, it was held that no appeal on questions of fact was necessary in homelessness cases for compliance with Art 6, and in *R (Beeson) v Dorset* [2002] 6 CCLR 5, CA, a panel appointed by the local authority, controlled by judicial review, was held to be an adequate safeguard for a citizen aggrieved by a decision that he had deliberately disposed of capital in order to qualify for the provision of accommodation under s21 National Assistance Act 1948. The fears expressed by the courts of "over-judicialisation" of administrative procedures sit very uneasily with the existence of extensive rights of appeal on questions of fact in social security issues and the vital importance of the issues raised to the well-being of the individual. How much of *Alconbury* and *Begum* may read across to HB adjudication in a post-*Tsfayo* world – but one where there is a right of appeal to an independent appeal tribunal against most decisions – remains to be worked out.

In *R(IS) 6/04* (paras 36–49), the commissioner ruled that the exclusion of a right of appeal on questions relating to whether a valid claim had been made infringed Art 6. It is not a breach of Art 6 for a commissioner, who has previously decided that leave to appeal against a tribunal's decision, should be refused to decide whether or not to set aside the refusal of leave: see *CDLA 3432/2001* paras 2–3 and *Sengupta v Holmes* [2002] *The Times* 19 August, CA. The same will apply, therefore, to tribunal members sitting and determining whether to set aside their own decisions, unless perhaps there is some impropriety by the tribunal member alleged. Similarly, there can be no objection to a tribunal member hearing an appeal simply on the basis that the member has sat on a previous tribunal which dismissed an appeal by the same claimant: *R (Wall) v Appeals Service* [2003] EWHC 465 Admin, para 14. There must be some basis for satisfying the apparent bias test, as to which see the commentary to Sch 7 para 8 CSPSSA.

Application to appeals. While Art 6 does not require a state to provide a system of appeals from the court or tribunal which gives the initial independent determination required by Art 6, if such a system is provided then that system must also comply with the safeguards of the Article: *Fedje v Sweden* (1994) 17 EHRR 14, para 32, ECtHR.

Article 8
Right to respect for private and family life

1.   Everyone has the right to respect for his private and family life, his home and his correspondence.

2.   There shall be no interference by a public authority with the exercise of this right except such as is in accordance with the law and is necessary in a democratic society in the interests of national security, public safety or the economic well-being of the country, for the prevention of disorder or crime, for the protection of health or morals, or for the protection of the rights and freedoms of others.

Analysis

Art 8 is in far less absolute terms than Art 6. It confers a right only to "respect" for the matters set out therein. There is no absolute obligation on a state to provide welfare support of a particular kind: *Andersson v Sweden* [1986] 46 DR 251, ECmHR; *Petrovic v Austria* [1998] 4 BHRC 232, ECtHR (para 26); *R (Tucker) v Secretary of State for Social Security* [2001] EWHC Admin 260; (2002) HLR 500, CA (para 22).

Art 8, however, might be of relevance to a case in which a local authority had failed to adjudicate a claim for HB and a claimant lost her/his home as a result. No claim for damages for breach of statutory duty would lie in such circumstances: *Haringey LBC v Cotter* (1996) 29 HLR 682, CA. However, it is arguable that by failing to comply with obligations created by the state for the protection of a claimant's home, the local authority breached Art 8 in such a situation and would be liable in damages. There is a distinction between a complaint that the HB Regs exclude a claimant from entitlement (as in *Tucker*) and a complaint that the claimant is entitled to benefit but the relevant authority failed to decide so quickly enough.

Guidance as to the circumstances in which maladministration of a statutory scheme could give rise to a breach of Art 8 was given in *R (Anufrijeva) v Southwark LBC* [2003] EWCA Civ 1406, CA. Although there is no positive duty to provide particular forms of welfare support, nevertheless if in failing to adjudicate an HB claim the local authority failed to show respect for the home, then Art 8 might be breached: compare *Anufrijeva* para 43, where it was said that if withholding welfare support resulted in a lack of respect for family life, Art 8 could be breached. It is suggested that by analogy, since HB is a scheme designed to protect a person's home and thereby show "respect" for it, a failure to administer the HB scheme properly may give rise to a claim under Art 8 in principle. In para 45, the court said:

"In so far as Article 8 imposes positive obligations, these are not absolute. Before inaction can amount to a lack of respect for private and family life, there must be some ground for criticising the failure to act. There must be an element of culpability. At the very least there must be knowledge that the claimant's private and family life were at risk . . . Where the domestic law of a State imposes positive obligations in relation to the provision of welfare support, breach of those positive obligations of domestic law may suffice to provide the element of culpability necessary to establish a breach of Article 8, provided that the impact on private or family life is sufficiently serious and was foreseeable."

If the word "home" is transposed for "private and family" it seems, for example, that there is no reason why a local authority which ignores repeated pleas by a claimant and her/his representatives to adjudicate a HB claim for no good reason and which is aware that possession proceedings are pending would not be in breach of Art 8. Problems caused by lack of resources may, however, be taken into account when deciding whether Art 8 is breached: para 47. In para 48, the court said:

"Newman J suggested . . . that it is likely that the acts of a public authority will have to have so far departed from the performance of its duty as to amount to a denial or contradiction of that duty before Article 8 will be infringed. We think that this puts the position somewhat too high, for in considering whether the threshold of Article 8 has been reached it is necessary to have regard both to the extent of the culpability of the failure to act and to the severity of the consequence. Clearly, where one is considering whether there has been a lack of respect for Article 8 rights, the more glaring the deficiency in the behaviour of the public authority, the easier it will be to establish the necessary want of respect. Isolated acts of even significant carelessness are unlikely to suffice."

It is also possible that Art 8 might be invoked in relation to a failure to adjudicate a claim to a discretionary housing payment (DHP). Refusal of a DHP alone could not constitute a breach of Art 8, unless perhaps the authority was refusing to administer the scheme properly.

But Art 8 cannot be invoked to challenge the level of HB that is payable under the statutory schemes. In *R (Reynolds) v SSWP* [2002] EWHC Admin 426, it was stated that: "the broadly worded principle in Art 8 is [not] apt to a challenge to the level of a social security payment", and the Court of Appeal, agreeing, said the IS scheme did not *per se* come within the ambit of Art 8 (for the purposes of mounting an argument under Art 14). None of this reasoning was doubted by the House of Lords on a further appeal in *Reynolds*.

However, *CH 4574/2003* and Sedley LJ in *Langley v Bradford MDC and SSWP* [2004] EWCA Civ 1343; reported as *R(H) 6/05* both hold that the HB scheme does enage Art 8 as it is about respect for the home.

Although the judgment of the House of Lords in *SSWP v M* [2006] UKHL 11; reported as *R(CS) 4/06* may have laid down a narrower approach to the ambit of Art 8, given the decision in *Stec and others v United Kingdom* (2006) 43 EHRR 47 and the House of Lords in *R (RJM) v SSWP* [2008] UKHL 63, in relation to Art 1 Protocol 1 (see commentary on p132) it should no longer be a necessary step (in any Art 14 discrimination argument at least) to argue that HB (save for DHPs) comes within the scope of Art 8.

It is not a breach of respect for private life under Art 8 for an authority to film a claimant in public as part of an investigation of her/his entitlement to benefit, as long as the film is only used for that purpose: *R(DLA) 4/02* (para 21).

Article 9
Freedom of Thought, Conscience and Religion

1.   Everyone has the right to freedom of thought, conscience and religion; this right includes freedom to change his religion or belief and freedom, either alone or in community with others and in public or private, to manifest his religion or belief, in worship, teaching, practice and observance.

2.   Freedom to manifest one's religion or beliefs shall be subject only to such limitations as are prescribed by law and are necessary in a democratic society in the interests of public safety, for the protection of public order, health or morals, or for the protection of the rights and freedoms of others.

Analysis

While Art 9 does require some positive action on the part of a state to protect religious beliefs, it does not require the state to subsidise the manifestation of those beliefs. Any challenge, for example, to reg 9(1)(j) of either the HB Regs or the HB(SPC) Regs, or to reg 9(2) on the ground that it aims to exclude living arrangements such as those adopted by the Jesus Fellowship Church from entitlement to HB are unlikely to succeed on Art 9 grounds alone. However, they might form a basis for an Art 14 challenge, particularly in the light of the exhortation in s13. In *R(H) 8/04* (para 30), the commissioner indicated that the exclusion of church members from HB on the ground that they had adopted a communal lifestyle for religious reasons engaged Art 14 in conjunction with Art 9. This conclusion is to be challenged by the Secretary of State on the claimants' appeal to the Court of Appeal.

However, the question of whether Art 9 was 'engaged' on the facts was not given any clear or compelling answer by the Court of Appeal in *Campbell and others v South Northamptonshire DC and SSWP* [2004] EWCA Civ 409 CA; reported as *R(H) 8/04*. The only substantive judgment on this point was given by Jacobs LJ where he said that Art 14 was not engaged because there was no violation of Art 9 (or Arts 8 and 1 of Protocol 1). With respect this, however, is the wrong test: it is enough for Art 14 to come into play (or 'be engaged') if the facts of the case come within the ambit, or engage, one of the substantive articles of the Convention (see *The Belgian Linguistics* case), there is no need for that substantive article to itself have been breached. Moreover, in later parts of the judgment the judge considers (and rejects on the facts) arguments that reg 7(1)(a) HB Regs 1987 (now reg 9(1)(a) of both the HB and the HB(SPC) Regs) indirectly discriminated against members of the Jesus Fellowship in a disproportionate manner, all of which suggests that the Court of Appeal was proceeding on the footing that Art 14 could be in play. Perhaps the best explanation for this confusion lies in the Court's emphatic rejection of the claimants' argument that human rights considerations had any bearing on the factual assessment of whether the tenancy agreement was on a commercial basis (see the notes on p282 to reg 9(1) HB Regs), so that their comments on Arts 9, 8 and 14 are, strictly speaking, *obiter*.

Article 14
Prohibition of discrimination

The enjoyment of the rights and freedoms set forth in this Convention shall be secured without discrimination on any ground such as sex, race, colour, language, religion, political or other opinion, national or social origin, association with a national minority, property, birth or other status.

Analysis

Art 14 deals with discrimination in the enjoyment of Convention rights. The issues to be considered in ascertaining whether there is a breach of Art 14 in a particular case have been put in various ways. Perhaps the most straightforward formulation is the four questions posed by Brooke LJ in *Michalak v Wandsworth LBC* [2003] 1 WLR 617 (para 20):
"(i)   Do the facts fall within the ambit of one or more of the substantive Convention provisions . . .?
(ii)   If so, was there different treatment as respects that right between the complainant on the one hand and other persons put forward for comparison ("the chosen comparators") on the other?
(iii)   Were the chosen comparators in an analogous situation to the complainant's situation?
(iv)   If so, did the difference in treatment have an objective and reasonable justification: in other words, did it pursue a legitimate aim and did the differential treatment bear a reasonable relationship of proportionality to the aim sought to be achieved?"
In *R (Carson) v SSWP* [2003] 3 All ER 577, Laws LJ suggested that questions (iii) and (iv) should be conflated into a composite question: "are the circumstances of X and Y so similar as to call (in the mind of a rational and fair-minded person) for a positive justification for the less favourable treatment of Y in comparison with X?". However, a rigid adherence to these four tests has subsequently been deprecated by the House of Lords in cases such as *R (S) v Chief Constable of South Yorkshire Police* (2004) 1 WLR 2196 (para 24), *Ghaidan v Godin-Mendoza* [2004] UKHL 30, 3 All ER 411 (para 134) and *Carson and Reynolds* (2005) UKHL 37 *The Times*, 27 May (para 3). A Tribunal of Commissioner adopted Lord Nicholls approach in this last case, in *R(P) 2/06*, where they quoted as correct his view that the better approach in benefits cases was:
"to keep formulation of the relevant issues in these cases as simple and non-technical as possible. Article 14 does not apply unless the alleged discrimination is in connection with a Convention right and on a ground stated in article 14. If this prerequisite is satisfied, the essential question for the court is whether the alleged discrimination, that is, the difference in treatment of which complaint is made, can withstand scrutiny.

Sometimes the answer to this question will be plain. There may be such an obvious, relevant difference between the claimant and those with whom he seeks to compare himself that their situations cannot be regarded as analogous. Sometimes, where the position is not so clear, a different approach is called for. Then the court's scrutiny may best be directed at considering whether the differentiation has a legitimate aim and whether the means chosen to achieve the aim is appropriate and not disproportionate in its adverse impact".

Facts "within the ambit" of a Convention right. The major limitation on Art 14 is that it does not provide a free-standing right not to be discriminated against. On the other hand, it is not necessary to show that another Convention right has been breached, otherwise Art 14 would be devoid of meaning. It must be shown that the circumstances of the discrimination fall within the ambit of one of the other rights guaranteed by the Convention: *The Belgian Linguistics Case (No.2)* (1967) 1 EHRR 252 at 283-4, para 9, ECtHR; *Guygusuz v Austria* (1997) 23 EHRR 364, ECtHR.

In *Guygusuz*, the applicant complained that he had been denied entitlement to an emergency needs benefit on the basis of his nationality. Although the denial of benefit did not itself amount to a breach of Protocol 1 Art 1 (see below), his entitlement to benefit was a "pecuniary right" within the ambit of that article. It followed that while there was no entitlement to benefit under that article, as the state had chosen to provide that benefit it had to ensure it did so without discriminating against the claimant.

In *SSWP v M* [2006] UKHL 11; reported as *R(CS) 4/06*, the House of Lords rejected the view that even the most tenuous connection between the allegedly discriminatory rule or regulation under challenge and the rights protected by the other articles of the Convention will suffice to bring the rule or regulation within the ambit of the other article of the Convention. Lord Bingham stated (para 4):

"It is not difficult, when considering any provision of the Convention, including article 8 and article 1 of the First Protocol ("IFP"), to identify the core values which the provision is intended to protect. But the further a situation is removed from one infringing those core values, the weaker the connection becomes, until a point is reached when there is no meaningful connection at all. At the inner extremity a situation may properly be said to be within the ambit or scope of the right, nebulous though those expressions necessarily are. At the outer extremity, it may not. There is no sharp line of demarcation between the two. An exercise of judgment is called for ... I cannot accept that even a tenuous link is enough. That would be a recipe for artificiality and legalistic ingenuity of an unacceptable kind".

Even this approach is not necessarily free from difficulty where the ambit of Art 8 is concerned, because of its core focus being on *respect* for the home, family and private life: see Lord Walker in *M* at paras 83–84.

Differential treatment. Brooke LJ's questions (ii) and (iii) overlap to a considerable extent.

The grounds of discrimination which can be impugned under Art 14 are limited to discrimination relating to some personal characteristic of the claimant: *Kjeldsen Madsen v Denmark* (1976) 1 EHRR 711, ECtHR (para 56); *R (S) v Chief Constable of South Yorkshire Police* (2004) 1 WLR 2196; *R v SSWP ex p Hooper and others* [2005] UKHL 29 and *Carson and Reynolds*. However, this does not mean a personal attribute which is immutable or inherent to the claimant: see, eg, *Francis v SSWP* [2005] EWCA Civ 1303; reported as *R(IS) 6/06*. It can be a characterstic which has been acquired (eg, nationality in some circumstances, language, religion or property), and may be "more concerned with what people do, or with what happens to them, than who they are: but they may still come within article 14": per Lord Walker at para [5] of *R (RJM) v SSWP* [2008] UKHL 63. Moreover, a generous meaning should be given to the phrase "or other status" and it should not be too closely limited by the grounds which are specifically prohibited in Art 14 (para [43] of *RJM*), and the absence of one of the specifically prohibited grounds (eg, being homeless so *not* having 'property') may be enough to amount to a personal characteristic (para [44] of *RJM*). The fact that the status arises as a matter of choice is of little significance, and whether or not it is a legal status or has not been recognised by the ECtHR are of little weight (para [47] of *RJM*).

However, the decision of the ECtHR in *Clift v United Kingdom* (Application No 7205/07), 13 July 2010, may mark a step away from the "personal characteristic" thesis by the Strasbourg court. Having examined the derivation of the "personal characteristic" thesis in its own caselaw, but noted other such cases where they had not applied it, the ECtHR said that Art 14 prohibited differences in treatment "based on an identifiable, objective or personal characteristic, or "status" by which person or groups person are distinguishable from one another" (para [55]), and went on:

"[t]he Court therefore considers it clear that while it has consistently referred to a need for a distinction based on a "personal" characteristic in order to engage Article 14...the protection conferred by that Article is not limited to different treatment based on characteristics which are personal in the sense that they are innate or inherent...The question whether there is a difference of treatment based on a personal or identifiable characteristic in any given case is a matter to be assessed taking into consideration all the circumstances of the case and bearing in mind that the aim of the Convention is to guarantee not rights that are theoretical or illusory but rights that are practical and effective...the general purpose of Article 14 is to ensure that where a State provides for rights falling within the ambit of the Convention which go beyond the minimum guarantees set out therein, those supplementary rights are applied fairly and consistently to all those within its jurisdiction unless a difference of treatment is objectively justified" (paras [59] and [60]).

See further *R (Stott) v Secretary of State for Justice* [2018] UKSC 59; [2018] 3 WLR 1831. In *R (DA) and others v SSWP* [2019] UKSC 21; [2019] 1 WLR 3289, it was accepted that lone parents (and perhaps the children of lone parents) held a relevant status for Art 14 purposes.

Besides the need to bring the discrimination of which complaint is made within the scope of some other article, not all discrimination will result in a breach of Art 14. The state may escape censure if it is shown that the measure in question has a legitimate aim and the means adopted are proportionate to the aim: *The Belgian Linguistics Case (No.2)* (para 34).

Domestic discrimination law distinguishes between direct discrimination (discriminating against a woman because she is a woman) and indirect discrimination which, generally, involves the imposition of a requirement which fewer people of a particular group can comply with (discriminating against a woman by prohibiting pregnant people from participating in an activity). The Convention does not distinguish between direct and indirect discrimination and there has been some doubt as to whether Art 14 extends to the latter form of treatment. The Court in *Barber* doubted that it did but not all the relevant Strasbourg caselaw was cited and in *R(H) 8/04* (paras 39–52) the commissioner decided that the claimants, members of the Jesus Fellowship Church, could complain of the fact that it was impossible for them to follow their religion while complying with the requirement that their agreements should be made on a commercial basis. The view of the commissioner in *R(H) 8/04* has been followed by other commissioners in *CIS 1870/2003* and *CP 518/20033*. However, the Court of Appeal in *Esfandiari* (*R(IS) 11/06* – the appeal from *CIS 1870/2003*), stated that indirect discrimination claims under Art 14 should be treated with some care because the caselaw is limited. In its view, in so far as a uniform test can be distilled from the caselaw, the relevant test to be satisfied (in order to call for the discrimination to be justified) would seem to be whether the effects on the particular group are "disproportionately prejudicial". See also to similar effect para 175 of the Grand Chamber's decision in *DH and others v Czech Republic* (Appln No: 57325/00), (2008) 47 EHRR 3 (ECtHR).

Justification. In *Guygusuz*, the state did not attempt to justify the discrimination. Since the burden of proof in relation to justification rests firmly on the state, a breach of Art 14 was therefore established and the claimant recovered compensation for the loss of the benefit: at 380–1, paras 40–4. However, there are plenty of statements demonstrating the width of discretion accorded to governments in social welfare matters, for example the following statement of Laws LJ in *Carson* (para 73):

"In the field of what may be called macro-economic policy, certainly including the distribution of public funds upon retirement pensions, the decision-making power of the elected arms of government is all but at its greatest, and the constraining role of the courts, absent a florid violation by government of established legal principles, is correspondingly modest. I conceive this approach to be wholly in line with our responsibilities under the Human Rights Act 1998."

Upholding both *Carson and Reynolds* in the House of Lords, Lord Hoffmann stated what may now have to be viewed as the classic test for assessing justification in the social security field.

"14.   There is no doubt that Ms Carson is being treated differently from a pensioner who has the same contribution record but lives in the United Kingdom or a treaty country. But that is not enough to amount to discrimination. Discrimination means a failure to treat like cases alike. There is obviously no discrimination when the cases are relevantly different. Indeed, it may be a breach of article 14 not to recognise the difference: see *Thlimmenos v Greece* (2001) 31 EHRR 411. There is discrimination only if the cases are not sufficiently different to justify the difference in treatment. The Strasbourg court sometimes expresses this by saying that the two cases must be in an "analogous situation": see *Van der Mussele v Belgium* (1983) 6 EHRR 163, 179-180, para 46.

15.   Whether cases are sufficiently different is partly a matter of values and partly a question of rationality. Article 14 expresses the Enlightenment value that every human being is entitled to equal respect and to be treated as an end and not a means. Characteristics such as race, caste, noble birth, membership of a political party and (here a change in values since the Enlightenment) gender, are seldom, if ever, acceptable grounds for differences in treatment. In some constitutions, the prohibition on discrimination is confined to grounds of this kind and I rather suspect that article 14 was also intended to be so limited. But the Strasbourg court has given it a wide interpretation, approaching that of the 14th Amendment, and it is therefore necessary, as in the United States, to distinguish between those grounds of discrimination which prima facie appear to offend our notions of the respect due to the individual and those which merely require some rational justification: *Massachusetts Board of Retirement v Murgia* [1976] 438 US 285.

16.   There are two important consequences of making this distinction. First, discrimination in the first category cannot be justified merely on utilitarian grounds, eg that it is rational to prefer to employ men rather than women because more women than men give up employment to look after children. That offends the notion that everyone is entitled to be treated as an individual and not a statistical unit. On the other hand, differences in treatment in the second category (eg on grounds of ability, education, wealth, occupation) usually depend upon considerations of the general public interest. Secondly, while the courts, as guardians of the right of the individual to equal respect, will carefully examine the reasons offered for any discrimination in the first category, decisions about the general public interest

which underpin differences in treatment in the second category are very much a matter for the democratically elected branches of government.

17. There may be borderline cases in which it is not easy to allocate the ground of discrimination to one category or the other and, as I have observed, there are shifts in the values of society on these matters. *Ghaidan v Godin-Mendoza* [2004] UKHL 30, 3 All ER 411 recognised that discrimination on grounds of sexual orientation was now firmly in the first category. Discrimination on grounds of old age may be a contemporary example of a borderline case. But there is usually no difficulty about deciding whether one is dealing with a case in which the right to respect for the individuality of a human being is at stake or merely a question of general social policy. In the present case, the answer seems to me to be clear."

In social security cases, therefore, if the discrimination in question does not fall within Lord Hoffmann's specially prohibited first category, it may be relatively easy to justify on general public interest grounds (but note that *Francis* was successful).

In *Petrovic v Austria* [1998] 4 BHRC 232, ECtHR, the Court held that the disparity of provision by signatory states meant that a wide margin of appreciation was enjoyed in the field of social security, and that accordingly sex discrimination in relation to access to maternity allowances could not be impugned. Where the discrimination is on the ground of race or sex, the burden on the state to justify discrimination is usually particularly heavy: see, for example, *Abdulaziz v UK* (1985) 7 EHRR 471 at 501, para 78, ECtHR. However, the decision of the House of Lords in *Carson and Reynolds* left open whether a different test or less weighty reasons apply where the sex or race discrimination arises in respect of general measures of economic or social strategy. The commissioner in *CP 518/2003* said that if the claim for (indirect) sex discrimination in the allocation of pension entitlement could be made out then weighty reasons would be needed to justify it. But, in the final decision in *Stec* (12 April 2006), the Grand Chamber of the ECtHR set out what it described as the general approach to justification. This is that although in general weighty reasons are required to justify discrimination based on sex (or race), a wide margin of appreciation will usually be allowed to national governments when it comes to general measures of economic or social strategy. In such cases, *Stec* seems to suggest that the legislature's policy choice should generally be respected, unless it is manifestly without reasonable foundation. The Supreme Court in *Humphreys*, has now made it clear that it is the *Stec* "manifestly without reasonable foundation" test which applies when judging sex discrimination challenges in the context of state benefits: see *Humphreys* at para [19]. This has been confirmed twice since by the Supreme Court in *R (MA) v SSWP* [2016] UKSC 58; [2016] 1 WLR 4550 and *R (DA) and others v SSWP* [2019] UKSC 21; [2019] 1 WLR 3289. These authorities remain binding on decision makers, including tribunals and courts, notwithstanding the decision of the ECtHR in *JD and A v United Kingdom* [2019] ECHR 753, which on its face founded the test for justifying discrimination in the provision of state benefits on a need for "very weighty reasons" rather than the "manifestly without reasonable foundation" test.

Note, however, in terms of remedy, that just satisfaction may not require "levelling up" to award benefit to the discriminated party (if s/he has managed to show unjustified differential treatment) in all cases: *R v HMRC ex p Wilkinson* [2005] UKHL 30 at paras [26] to [28] and [47] to [53] and *Hobbs and others v UK* (Application No.63684/00), 14 November 2006.

Article 17
Prohibition of abuse of rights

Nothing in this Convention may be interpreted as implying for any State, group or person any right to engage in any activity or perform any act aimed at the destruction of any of the rights and freedoms set forth herein or at their limitation to a greater extent than is provided for in the Convention.

Article 18
Limitation on use of restrictions on rights

The restrictions permitted under this Convention to the said rights and freedoms shall not be applied for any purpose other than those for which they have been prescribed.

The First Protocol
Article 1
Protection of Property

Every natural or legal person is entitled to the peaceful enjoyment of his possessions. No one shall be deprived of his possessions except in the public interest and subject to the conditions provided for by law and by the general principles of international law.

The preceding provisions shall not, however, in any way impair the right of a State to enforce such laws as it deems necessary to control the use of property in accordance with the general interest or to secure the payment of taxes or other contributions or penalties.

Analysis

Art 1 of the First Protocol is breached if either (a) the State interferes with the peaceful enjoyment of the claimant's possessions; or (b) the claimant has been deprived of possessions by the State: or (c) the applicant's possessions have been subjected to control by the State.

By far the most important issue is whether benefits constitute 'possessions' under this article. All benefits which arise as a matter of right (such as HB) are now covered by Art 1 Prt 1: see *Stec and others v United Kingdom* (2006) 43 EHRR 47 and *R (RJM) v SSWP* [2008] UKHL 63.

Given its importance, it is worthwhile setting out the reasoning of the Grand Chamber of the ECtHR in *Stec* in full.

"It is in the interests of the coherence of the Convention as a whole that the autonomous concept of 'possessions' in Article 1 of Protocol No. 1 should be interpreted in a way which is consistent with the concept of pecuniary rights under Article 6. It is moreover important to adopt an interpretation of Article 1 of Protocol No.1 which avoids inequalities of treatment based on distinctions which, at the present day, appear illogical or unsustainable.

The Court's approach to Article 1 of Protocol No.1 should reflect the reality of the way in which welfare provision is currently organised within the Member States of the Council of Europe. It is clear that within those States, and within most individual States, there exists a wide range of social security benefits designed to confer entitlements which arise as of right. Benefits are funded in a large variety of ways: some are paid for by contributions to a specific fund; some depend on a claimant's contribution record; many are paid for out of general taxation on the basis of a statutorily defined status (see, with reference to the United Kingdom's system, Lord Hoffmann's comments in ex parte Carson). . . . Given the variety of funding methods, and the interlocking nature of benefits under most welfare systems, it appears increasingly artificial to hold that only benefits financed by contributions to a specific fund fall within the scope of Article 1 of Protocol No.1. Moreover, to exclude benefits paid for out of general taxation would be to disregard the fact that many claimants under this latter type of system also contribute to its financing, through the payment of tax.

In the modern, democratic State, many individuals are, for all or part of their lives, completely dependent for survival on social security and welfare benefits. Many domestic legal systems recognise that such individuals require a degree of certainty and security, and provide for benefits to be paid – subject to the fulfilment of the conditions of eligibility – as of right. Where an individual has an assertable right under domestic law to a welfare benefit, the importance of that interest should also be reflected by holding Article 1 of Protocol No.1 to be applicable.

Finally . . . the Court considers that to hold that a right to a non-contributory benefit falls within the scope of Article 1 of Protocol No. 1 no more renders otiose the provisions of the Social Charter than to reach the same conclusion in respect of a contributory benefit. Whilst the Convention sets forth what are essentially civil and political rights, many of them have implications of a social or economic nature. The mere fact that an interpretation of the Convention may extend into the sphere of social and economic rights should not be a decisive factor against such an interpretation; there is no water-tight division separating that sphere from the field covered by the Convention (see Airey v. Ireland)."

The ECtHR then concluded:

"therefore, if any distinction can still be said to exist in the caselaw between contributory and non-contributory benefits for the purposes of the applicability of Article 1 of Protocol No. 1, there is no ground to justify the continued drawing of such a distinction.

If . . . a Contracting State has in force legislation providing for the payment as of right of a welfare benefit – whether conditional or not on the prior payment of contributions – that legislation must be regarded as generating a proprietary interest falling within the ambit of Article 1 of Protocol No. 1 for persons satisfying its requirements.

In cases, such as the present, concerning a complaint under Article 14 in conjunction with Article 1 of Protocol No. 1 that the applicant has been denied all or part of a particular benefit on a discriminatory ground covered by Article 14, the relevant test is whether, but for the condition of entitlement about which the applicant complains, he or she would have had a right, enforceable under domestic law, to receive the benefit in question. Although Protocol No. 1 does not include the right to receive a social security payment of any kind, if a State does decide to create a benefits scheme, it must do so in a manner which is compatible with Article 14."

However, Art 1 Prt 1 does not confer a general right to be paid a benefit constituting a 'possession' at a particular rate (or, put another way, no right not to be deprived of a larger amount), *unless* the reduction is of such a substantial amount that it affects 'the very substance of the right': *Müller v Austria* (Commission) [1975] 3 D and R 25. *CP 5084/2001* lists the factors to help determine whether there was deprivation in this sense. These are: (a) does the provision in question reduce a benefit previously in payment; (b) was that provision in force throughout the time when the claimant was paying relevant contributions (or, presumably post *Stec*, claiming the benefit in question or, perhaps, being liable to pay tax); (c) the closeness of the link between the benefit and payment of contributions (arguably, post *Stec*, this factor is no longer relevant, or at least should carry less weight); and (d) the amount of the reduction in benefit.

Moreover, a claimant cannot be said to have been deprived of a possession if s/he had no entitlement to the possession at all under the rules of entitlement: *X v Italy* [1977] 11 DR 114, applied by the Court of Appeal in *Carson and Reynolds* (and not argued on the further appeals to the House of Lords). Therefore, the rules limiting backdating of the retirement pension to three months before the date of claim do not mean that a person has been 'deprived' of her/his pension for the period more than three months before the date s/he claim it: *R(P) 1/06*. However, these decisions, and the approach to this particular point which they exemplify, have now to be read subject to *Stec* if an Art 14 challenge is in play (it was not in *R(P) 1/06*). Accordingly, if the backdating rules for a pension (or, indeed, any benefit) had been changed or introduced in a discriminatory manner (eg, allowing more backdating for men than women), then *Stec*, in principle, may enable an Art 1 Prt 1 and Art 14 argument to be made. *X v Italy*, *Carson and Reynolds* and *R(P) 1/06* remain good law, however, if all that is being raised is an argument under Art 1 Prt 1.

As with Art 8, even if it can be shown that there has been deprivation of a posession in the sense described above, that can nonetheless be justified by the State if it can show that the deprivation was in accordance with the 'public interest'. A 'fair balance' test is applied in answering this question, in which compensation is a key factor. Compensation need not be full.

Article 2
Right to Education

No person shall be denied the right to education. In the exercise of any functions which it assumes in relation to education and to teaching, the State shall respect the right of parents to ensure such education and teaching in conformity with their own religious and philosophical convictions.

Analysis

This does not require a state to establish or facilitate a certain degree of education at its expense. All it requires is the right to enjoy such education that the state provides: *The Belgian Linguistics Case (No 2)* at 280–1, para 3. Thus it is difficult for students to argue that the severe restrictions on their entitlement to HB infringes Prt 1 Art 2: see *R (Douglas) v North Tyneside MBC and another* [2004] 1 All ER 709.

SCHEDULE 2

SECTION 10

Remedial Orders
Orders

1.–(1) A remedial order may–
(a) contain such incidental, supplemental, consequential or transitional provision as the person making it considers appropriate;
(b) be made so as to have effect from a date earlier than that on which it is made;
(c) make provision for the delegation of specific functions;
(d) make different provision for different cases.
(2) The power conferred by sub-paragraph (1)(a) includes–
(a) power to amend primary legislation (including primary legislation other than that which contains the incompatible provision); and
(b) power to amend or revoke subordinate legislation (including subordinate legislation other than that which contains the incompatible provision).
(3) A remedial order may be made so as to have the same extent as the legislation which it affects.
(4) No person is to be guilty of an offence solely as a result of the retrospective effect of a remedial order.

Procedure

2. No remedial order may be made unless–
(a) a draft of the order has been approved by a resolution of each House of Parliament made after the end of the period of 60 days beginning with the day on which the draft was laid; or
(b) it is declared in the order that it appears to the person making it that, because of the urgency of the matter, it is necessary to make the order without a draft being so approved.

Orders laid in draft

3.–(1) No draft may be laid under paragraph 2(a) unless–
(a) the person proposing to make the order has laid before Parliament a document which contains a draft of the proposed order and the required information; and
(b) the period of 60 days, beginning with the day on which the document required by this sub-paragraph was laid, has ended.

(2)   If representations have been made during that period, the draft laid under paragraph 2(a) must be accompanied by a statement containing–
(a)   a summary of the representations; and
(b)   if, as a result of the representations, the proposed order has been changed, details of the changes.

Urgent cases

4.–(1)   If a remedial order ("the original order") is made without being approved in draft, the person making it must lay it before Parliament, accompanied by the required information, after it is made.
(2)   If representations have been made during the period of 60 days beginning with the day on which the original order was made, the person making it must (after the end of that period) lay before Parliament a statement containing–
(a)   a summary of the representations; and
(b)   if, as a result of the representations, he considers it appropriate to make changes to the original order, details of the changes.
(3)   If sub-paragraph (2)(b) applies, the person making the statement must–
(a)   make a further remedial order replacing the original order; and
(b)   lay the replacement order before Parliament.
(4)   If, at the end of the period of 120 days beginning with the day on which the original order was made, a resolution has not been passed by each House approving the original or replacement order, the order ceases to have effect (but without that affecting anything previously done under either order or the power to make a fresh remedial order).

Definitions

5.   In this Schedule–
"representations" means representations about a remedial order (or proposed remedial order) made to the person making (or proposing to make) it and includes any relevant Parliamentary report or resolution; and
"required information" means–
(a)   an explanation of the incompatibility which the order (or proposed order) seeks to remove, including particulars of the relevant declaration, finding or order; and
(b)   a statement of the reasons for proceeding under section 10 and for making an order in those terms.

Calculating periods

6.   In calculating any period for the purposes of this Schedule, no account is to be taken of any time during which–
(a)   Parliament is dissolved or prorogued; or
(b)   both Houses are adjourned for more than four days.

Child Support, Pensions and Social Security Act 2000

(2000 c19)

PART III
SOCIAL SECURITY
Housing benefit and council tax benefit etc.

68. Housing benefit and council tax benefit: revisions and appeals
69. Discretionary financial assistance with housing
70. Grants towards cost of discretionary housing payments

Supplemental
84. Expenses
85. Repeals
86. Commencement and transitional provisions
87. Short title and extent

Schedules
7. Housing benefit and council tax benefit: revisions and appeals

General Note

This Act made a number of important reforms to social security, child support and pensions law. For HB purposes, the most significant changes are the introduction by s69 of a system of discretionary financial assistance which replaced exceptional hardship payments under the former HB Regs 1987 reg 61(3), and the introduction, by s68 and Sch 7, of a decision making and appeals system based on the Social Security Act 1998 (including the replacement of local authority Housing Benefit and Council Tax Benefit Review Boards by an independent appeal tribunal). The provisions governing appeals were further amended from 3 November 2008 by the establishment of the First-tier Tribunal and Upper Tribunal under the Tribunals Courts and Enforcement Act 2007.

PART III
Social Security
Housing benefit [and council tax benefit] etc

Housing benefit *[and council tax benefit]*: revisions and appeals

68. Schedule 7 (which makes provision for the revision of decisions made in connection with claims for housing benefit *[or council tax benefit]* and for appeals against such decisions) shall have effect.

Modification

Section 68 was repealed by WRA 2012 s147 and Sch 14 part 1 on 1.4.13 in so far as it related to CTB.

Discretionary financial assistance with housing

69.–(1)   The Secretary of State may by regulations make provision conferring a power on relevant authorities to make payments by way of financial assistance ("discretionary housing payments") to persons who–

(a)   are entitled to housing benefit or council tax benefit, or to both [1, universal credit]; and

(b)   appear to such an authority to require some further financial assistance (in addition to the benefit or benefits to which they are entitled) in order to meet housing costs.

(2)   Regulations under this section may include any of the following–

(a)   provision prescribing the circumstances in which discretionary housing payments may be made under the regulations;

(b)   provision conferring (subject to any provision made by virtue of paragraph (c) or (d) of this subsection or an order under section 70) a discretion on a relevant authority–

　　(i)   as to whether or not to make discretionary housing payments in a particular case; and

　　(ii)   as to the amount of the payments and the period for or in respect of which they are made;

(c)   provision imposing a limit on the amount of the discretionary housing payment that may be made in any particular case;

(d)   provision restricting the period for or in respect of which discretionary housing payments may be made;

(e)   provision about the form and manner in which claims for discretionary housing payments are to be made and about the procedure to be followed by relevant authorities in dealing with and disposing of such claims;

(f)   provision imposing conditions on persons claiming or receiving discretionary housing payments requiring them to provide a relevant authority with such information as may be prescribed;

(g)   provision entitling a relevant authority that are making or have made a discretionary housing payment, in such circumstances as may be prescribed, to cancel the making of further such payments or to recover a payment already made;

(h)   provision requiring or authorising a relevant authority to review decisions made by the authority with respect to the making, cancellation or recovery of discretionary housing payments.

(3)   Regulations under this section shall be made by statutory instrument, which shall be subject to annulment in pursuance of a resolution of either House of Parliament.

(4)   Subsections (4) to (6) of section 189 of the Social Security Administration Act 1992 (supplemental and incidental powers etc.) shall apply in relation to any power to make regulations under this section as they apply in relation to the powers to make regulations that are conferred by that Act.

(5)   Any power to make regulations under this section shall include power to make different provision for different areas or different relevant authorities.

(6)   *[Omitted]*

(7)   In this section–

"prescribed" means prescribed by or determined in accordance with regulations made by the Secretary of State; and

"relevant authority" means an authority administering housing benefit or council tax benefit.

Amendment

1.   Inserted by s31 and Sch 2 para 55 WRA 2012 (25.2.13).

General Note

This section gives power to set up the scheme for discretionary financial assistance with housing costs, which takes the form of discretionary housing payments (DHPs). DHPs replaced exceptional hardship payments which were formerly available under reg 61(3) HB Regs 1987. The detail of the scheme is found in the Discretionary Financial Assistance Regulations 2001 SI No.1167 (the DFA Regs) on p1751.

Analysis

Subs (1) introduces the scheme and sets out the two basic conditions for qualifying for a DHP, which are that a person is entitled to HB or UC and that s/he appears to require further assistance with housing costs. CTB was abolished from 1 April 2013 but the section was not amended to reflect the change. The subsection is implemented by reg 2 DFA Regs which, as amended from 1 April and 10 June 2013, provides that a person can only qualify for a DHP if, among other qualifying conditions, s/he is entitled to HB or a "relevant award of universal credit". "Entitled" in this context will almost certainly be construed as "lawfully entitled" and will hence exclude those who have obtained a decision awarding them benefit by deception: compare *R v South Ribble DC HBRB ex p Hamilton* (2000) 33 HLR 102, CA.

Subs (2) confers the usual very broad discretions as to the making of regulations upon the Secretary of State. The relevant provisions made under each paragraph are as follows:

(a)   Reg 3 DFA Regs.
(b)   Regs 2(2) and 5 DFA Regs.
(c)   Reg 4 DFA Regs.
(d)   Reg 2(3) DFA Regs.
(e)   Reg 6 DFA Regs.
(f)   Reg 7 DFA Regs.
(g)   Reg 8(2) DFA Regs.
(h)   Reg 8(1) DFA Regs.

Grants towards cost of discretionary housing payments

70.–(1)   The Secretary of State may, out of money provided by Parliament, make to a relevant authority such payments as he thinks fit in respect of–

(a)   the cost to that authority of the making of discretionary housing payments; and

(b)   the expenses involved in the administration by that authority of any scheme for the making of discretionary housing payments.

(2)   The following provisions, namely–

(a)   subsections (1), (3), (4), (5)(b) [¹] and (8) of section 140B of the Social Security Administration Act 1992 (calculation of amount of subsidy payable to authorities administering housing benefit or council tax benefit), and

(b)   section 140C of that Act (payment of subsidy),

shall apply in relation to payments under this section as they apply in relation to subsidy under section 140A of that Act.

(3)   The Secretary of State may by order make provision–

(a)   imposing a limit on the total amount of expenditure in any year that may be incurred by a relevant authority in making discretionary housing payments;

(b)   imposing subsidiary limits on the expenditure that may be incurred in any year by a relevant authority in making discretionary housing payments in the circumstances specified in the order.

(4)   An order imposing a limit by virtue of subsection (3)(a) or (b) may fix that limit either by specifying the amount of the limit or by providing for the means by which it is to be determined.

(5)   An order under this section shall be made by statutory instrument, which shall be subject to annulment in pursuance of a resolution of either House of Parliament.

(6)   Subsections (4) to (6) of section 189 of the Social Security Administration Act 1992 (supplemental and incidental powers etc.) shall apply in relation to any power to make an order under this section as they apply in relation to the powers to make an order that are conferred by that Act.

(7)   Any power to make an order under this section shall include power to make different provision for different areas or different relevant authorities.

(8)   In this section–

"discretionary housing payment" means any payment made by virtue of regulations under section 69;

"relevant authority" means an authority administering housing benefit or council tax benefit;

"subsidy" has the same meaning as in sections 140A to 140G of the Social Security Administration Act 1992;

"year" means a financial year within the meaning of the Local Government Finance Act 1992.

Amendment

1.   Repealed by the Local Government Act 2003 s127(2) and Part 1 Sch 8 (18.11.03).

General Note

This authorises a system of subsidy by the Secretary of State for DHPs made by local authorities. Note subs (2) which applies most of the provisions in SSAA ss140B and 140C to DHP subsidy. For regulations under this section, see the Discretionary Housing Payments (Grants) Order 2001 SI No.2340.

Supplemental

Expenses

84.   There shall be paid out of money provided by Parliament–

(a)   any expenditure incurred by the Secretary of State for or in connection with the carrying out of his functions under this Act; and

(b)   any increase attributable to this Act in the sums which are payable out of money so provided under any other Act.

Repeals

85.–(1)   The enactments mentioned in Schedule 9 (which include some spent provisions) are hereby repealed to the extent specified in the third column of that Schedule.

(2)   The repeals specified in that Schedule have effect subject to the commencement provisions and savings contained, or referred to, in the notes set out in that Schedule.

Commencement and transitional provisions

86.–(1)   This section applies to the following provisions of this Act–

(a)   Part I (other than section 24);

(b)   Part II (other than sections 38 and 39 and paragraphs 4 to 6, 8(1), (3) and (4) and 13 of Schedule 5);

(c)   Part III;

(d)   sections 82 and 83 and Schedule 8;

(e)   Parts I to VII and IX of Schedule 9.

(2)   The provisions of this Act to which this section applies shall come into force on such day as may be appointed by order made by statutory instrument; and different days may be appointed under this section for different purposes.

(3)   The power to make an order under subsection (2) shall be exercisable–

(a)   except in a case falling within paragraph (b), by the Secretary of State; and

(b)   in the case of an order bringing into force any of the provisions of sections 82 and 83, Schedule 8 or Part IX of Schedule 9, by the Lord Chancellor.

(4)   In the case of Part I (other than section 24) and of sections 62 to 66, the power under subsection (2) to appoint different days for different purposes includes power to appoint different days for different areas.

(5)   The Secretary of State may by regulations make such transitional provision as he considers necessary or expedient in connection with the bringing into force of any of the following provisions of this Act–

(a)   sections 43 to 46 and section (1) of Part III of Schedule 9;

(b)   sections 68 to 70 and Schedule 7 and Part VII of Schedule 9.

(6)   Regulations under subsection (5) shall be made by statutory instrument subject to annulment in pursuance of a resolution of either House of Parliament.

(7)   Section 174(2) to (4) of the Pensions Act 1995 (supplementary provision in relation to powers to make subordinate legislation under that Act) shall apply in relation to the power to make regulations under subsection (5) as it applies to any power to make regulations under that Act.

(8)   In this section "subordinate legislation" has the same meaning as in the Interpretation Act 1978.

Short title and extent

87.–(1)   This Act may be cited as the Child Support, Pensions and Social Security Act 2000.

(2)-(4)   *[Omitted]*

SCHEDULE 7

SECTION 68

Housing Benefit [And Council Tax Benefit]: Revisions And Appeals

Modification

Schedule 7 was repealed by WRA 2012 s147 and Sch 14 part 1 on 1.4.13 in so far as it related to CTB.

Abolition of council tax benefit: savings and transitional provisions

Until CTB was abolished (from 1 April 2013) and help with payment of council tax was localised, Sch 7 also applied to CTB. For savings and transitional provisions, see arts 9 and 10 Welfare Reform Act 2012 (Commencement No.8 and Savings and Transitional Provisions) Order 2013 SI No.358 on p1735 of the 26th edition.

General Note on Sch 7

Under reg 89 HB Regs and reg 70 HB(SPC) Regs, any matter that needs to be determined in order to decide a claim for HB falls to be determined by the relevant authority – ie, by a local government officer. Sch 7 and the D&A Regs (which are made under Sch 7 para 10) are concerned with the circumstances in which the initial decisions of local authorites can be changed.

There are only three such mechanisms, revision under para 3, supersession under para 4, and appeal, initially to the First-tier Tribunal. Unless a decision can be revised, superseded or changed on appeal, then it is final (see para 11). Contrary to what some local authorities – and the suppliers of their computer software – still seem to believe, there is no power for an authority simply to "cancel" or "withdraw" an award of HB: see, for example, *CH 2302/2002* and *SS v North East Lincolnshire Council (HB)* [2011] UKUT 300 (AAC) in which Upper Tribunal Judge Wikeley stated:

"5.   The benefits system, as Mr Commissioner Powell (as he then was) explained in Social Security Commissioner's decision CA/1020/2007 (at paragraph 12), is a "decision based" system:

"What is meant by this is that the system proceeds, or is based, on formal decisions being given. If a benefit is awarded it must be awarded by a formal and identifiable decision. If that decision is to be altered by, for example, increasing or decreasing the amount involved, it can only be done by another formal and identifiable decision. Likewise a decision is required if the period of the award is to be terminated, shortened or extended. If a payment of benefit is to be suspended, leaving the underlying entitlement in being, a formal decision is again required.""

Except where otherwise stated below, Sch 7 came into force on 2 July 2001 (art 2(2) Child Support, Pensions and Social Security Act 2000 (Commencement No.8) Order 2001 No.1252) and replaced the previous system of HB (and CTB) adjudication, under which the determinations of local authorities were subject to review by (usually) a more senior officer under reg 79 HB Regs 1987 (or reg 69 CTB Regs 1992), and then to a further review by a Review Board consisting of members (ie, councillors) of the authority concerned under regs 81–83 HB Regs 1987 (and regs 70–72 CTB Regs 1992). That system did not comply with Art 6 of the European Convention on Human Rights (see *Tsfayo v United Kingdom* (2009) 48 EHRR 18) and, therefore, could not remain in place after the Human Rights Act 1998 came into force.

Under Sch 7, those who are affected by a local authority decision on a claim for, or an award of, HB – and those from whom it is determined that an overpayment of HB is recoverable – have a right of appeal to the First-tier Tribunal and thereafter, on a point of law, to the Upper Tribunal and then (in England and Wales) the Court of Appeal or (in Scotland) the Inner House of the Court of Session. The effect is to align the appeal rights for HB (and CTB) with those for the social security benefits administered by the DWP and HMRC. The scheme of Sch 7 thus follows that set out in Part I, Ch II SSA 1998 very closely and decisions of the former social security commissioners, the Upper Tribunal and the courts on the comparable provisions will be of highly persuasive force in interpreting Sch 7. Care should be taken to note the differences between the two sets of legislation, however.

A system of revisions and supersessions is found in paras 3 and 4 which is identical to ss8 and 9 SSA 1998. Paras 6 and 7 govern appeals to the First-tier Tribunal in a similar fashion to ss12 and 13 (except that, in contrast to s12(3A)–(3C), para 6 does not provide for what is known colloquially as the "mandatory reconsideration" of a decision before a right of appeal arises), and paras 8 and 9 deal with further appeals to the Upper Tribunal and the courts in a similar fashion to ss14 and 15. There are also extensive powers to suspend benefit in paras 13 and 14 and an anti-test case rule in paras 16 to 18 which is not, however, being fully implemented.

The general approach to decision making in social security and, by implication, HB, was considered by the House of Lords in *Kerr v Department for Social Development* [2004] UKHL 23; reported as *R 1/04 (SF)*. The House of Lords set out five propositions of general application to the field of benefits adjudication. First, the determination of claims should be an inquisitorial process rather than adversarial. Second, facts which may reasonably be supposed to be within the claimant's own knowledge are for the claimant to supply at each stage in the assessment of the claim. However, s/he must be given a reasonable opportunity to supply them. Third, the knowledge as to the information that is needed to deal with a claim lies with the DWP (and/or the HB authority) and not with the claimant: so it is for the former to ask the relevant questions and the claimant is not to be faulted if the relevant questions to show whether or not the claim is excluded are not asked. Fourth, the general rule is that it is for the party who alleges an affirmative to make good her/his allegation. Fifth, it is also a general rule that a party who desires to take advantage of an exception must bring her/himself within the provisions of the exception. Exceptions (including grounds of disentitlement to benefit) are to be established by those who rely on them: *Nimmo v Alexander Cowan & Sons Ltd* [1968] AC 107, HL, so that in *Kerr* it was for the Department of Social Development in Northern Ireland to prove on the wording of the sub-regulation that was relevant in that case that the named close relatives of Mr Kerr were not in receipt of a relevant benefit, as proof of that condition acted as a ground of disentitlement to a social fund funeral payment.

Introductory

1.–(1)   In this Schedule "relevant authority" means an authority administering housing benefit *[or council tax benefit]*.

(2)   In this Schedule "relevant decision" means any of the following–

(a)   a decision of a relevant authority on a claim for housing benefit *[or council tax benefit]*;

(b)   any decision under paragraph 4 of this Schedule which supersedes a decision falling within paragraph (a), within this paragraph or within paragraph (b) of sub-paragraph (1) of that paragraph;

but references in this Schedule to a relevant decision do not include references to a decision under paragraph 3 to revise a relevant decision.

Analysis

"Relevant decision" is a decision of a local authority that either decides a claim for HB or that supersedes such a decision (or a decision of the First-tier Tribunal or Upper Tribunal) under para 4. The definition is important because it governs which decisions can be revised and superseded and which carry a right of appeal.

"Decision" in this context means what is sometimes described as an "outcome" decision – ie, that the claimant is not entitled to benefit or is so entitled at a specified weekly rate for a specified period. The decisions that an authority makes on the individual issues of fact and law that lead to a conclusion of entitlement or non-entitlement (eg, whether a claimant is liable to pay rent, the calculation of her/his applicable amount or the level of her/his income) are not outcome decisions but, rather, findings of fact or "determinations". Findings of fact and determinations cannot themselves be revised, superseded or (subject to what is said in the next paragraph) appealed: see *Carpenter v SSWP* [2003] EWCA Civ 33; reported as *R(IB) 6/03*. However, if there are grounds on which to change a finding of fact or determination, that may lead to a revision or supersession if the result is to change the outcome. Another way of putting the point is to say that what is revised, superseded or appealed against is the relevant decision itself and not the reason(s) for that decision.

For HB (but not for other social security benefits), there may be an exception to the principle that "determinations" cannot be appealed. As explained below, para 6(6) grants a right of appeal to "any person from whom it has been *determined* that [an amount of HB] is recoverable" (emphasis added). That formulation follows the wording of s75 SSAA, the primary legislation governing recover of HB overpayments. This is an unfortunate quirk of the drafting. A decision that there has been an overpayment of HB and that it is recoverable from one or more persons is plainly one that provides an outcome: it is not merely a finding of fact. Moreover, the equivalent decision in relation to a DWP benefit would be a "decision" (see s8(1)(c) and (4) SSA 1998) even though s71 SSAA uses the word "determine" in the same way as s75. It would have avoided confusion – and, in particular, would have avoided any argument about whether an overpayment "determination" can be revised or superseded by the local authority once it has been made – for the draftsman to have included overpayment "determinations" in the definition of "relevant decision" rather than to treat them as requiring a separate right of appeal. However, that course was not taken and it must therefore be remembered that, as it relates to HB overpayments, the nomenclature is inconsistent.

Decisions to revise an earlier decision under para 3 are not included in the definition of "relevant decision" because the effect of a revising decision is to alter or correct the terms of the original decision without replacing it. Any challenge (whether by way of an application for a further revision or an appeal) is therefore against the original decision as revised, rather than against the revising decision. This explains the words "whether as originally made or as revised under paragraph 3" in brackets in paras 4(1) and 6(1). By contrast, a superseding decision replaces the original decision, albeit (usually) with effect from a later date.

Some decisions suggest that revising decisions replace the earlier decision that is revised. So, for example, Upper Tribunal Judge Wikeley in *SS v North East Lincolnshire Council (HB)* [2011] UKUT 300 (AAC) at [6] states (in a passage that is repeated almost verbatim in relation to the social security system by a three-judge panel of the Upper Tribunal (Judges Mesher, Williams and Wikeley) in *SSWP v JL (DLA)* [2011] UKUT 293 (AAC) at [53]) that:

"a decision to award benefit may be altered later by a revision decision, *which typically replaces the original decision from the outset,* or a supersession decision, which usually replaces the original decision from some later date e.g. because of a subsequent change of circumstances" (added emphasis)

The point is a small one but it would be more technically correct to say that a revising decision typically changes the terms of the original decision from the outset. If it replaced the original decision any subsequent appeal would have to be against the revising decision, which is not the case.

Because para 1(2)(a) is not limited to decisions taken by the authority under Sch 7, decisions taken by local government officers before 2 July 2001 under regs 76 or 79 HB Regs 1987 (and regs 66 or 69 CTB Regs 1992) (which, at the time, were referred to as "determinations") are "relevant decisions" and can therefore be revised under para 3: *R(H) 6/04* (para 21). It follows that they can also be superseded under para 4. Decisions taken by review boards before 2 July 2001 under reg 83 HB Regs (or reg 72 CTB Regs 1992) (which, at the time, were referred to as "decisions") were treated (by reg 4(4) D&A Transitional Regs – see pp993–1000 of the 20th edition) as having been made by an appeal tribunal under para 6. An authority was therefore able to supersede them (at least until 3 November 2008: see the Analysis of para 4), but they could not be revised under para 3.

Note that a determination that an overpayment is recoverable is not a "relevant decision" within the definition in sub-para (2): *R(H) 3/04* (para 34). See the commentary to para 6 below and to s75 SSAA 1992 (see p39).

Refusals to revise and supersede. To supersede a decision is to alter it: see the decision of the majority of the Court of Appeal in *Wood v SSWP* [2003] EWCA Civ 53; reported as *R(DLA) 1/03* paras 42–43 and 78. By the same reasoning, to revise a decision is also to alter it. It follows that where an authority reconsiders an existing decision and does not change the outcome then it is not revising or superseding it (or even, as used to be said before *Wood*, superseding it "at the same rate") but *refusing* to revise or supersede it. That is so even if the reasoning or findings of fact that led to the original decision are changed, as long as the outcome remains the same.

Is a refusal to revise or supersede a "relevant decision" that gives rise to further rights of challenge?
For a refusal to revise, the answer is no. As revision changes the terms of the original decision without replacing it, a refusal to revise leaves the orginal decision unchanged. From 1 September 2009, where an application is made within one month of the original decision (or within that time limit as extended under reg 5 D&A Regs), the refusal has the effect of extending the time limit for an appeal against the original decision (Sch 1 TP(FT) Rules was amended by SI 2009 SI No.1975. See now r23(2)(iii) TP(FTT) Rules on p1006). That was also the position before 3 November 2008 under the former reg 18(3) D&A Regs. For the position between those two dates, see pp148–49 of the 21st edition.

For a refusal to supersede, the question is more difficult but it is suggested that the answer must be yes. In *Wood*, the Court of Appeal was considering ss10(1) and 12(1) and (9) SSA 1998. In order to avoid infringing art 6 of the European Convention on Human Rights, the majority adopted a strained construction of the phrase "decision superseding any such decision" in s12(9) as meaning "decision taken pursuant to the power to supersede". A refusal to supersede was therefore a "decision taken pursuant to the power to supersede". A refusal to supersede was therefore a "decision ... under section ... 10" for the purposes of the right of appeal in s12(1) even though no supersession had actually taken place (*Wood* paras 51 and 78). Paras 1, 4 and 6 of Sch 7 are not in the same terms as ss10 and 12 SSA 1998 and the analogy is therefore not exact. Nevertheless, it is suggested that the same approach should be applied to HB decisions. This would involve reading the words "any decision under paragraph 4 of this Schedule which supersedes a decision" in para 1(2)(b) as meaning "any decision *taken pursuant to the power* under paragraph 4 ...". Given the decision of the majority in *Wood* that to "supersede" an earlier decision, the superseding decision must change it, any other approach would inevitably infringe the Convention rights of the person affected. The approach is therefore required by s3(1) Human Rights Act 1998.

Decisions on claims for benefit

2.   Where at any time a claim for housing benefit *[or council tax benefit]* is decided by a relevant authority–
  (a)   the claim shall not be regarded as subsisting after that time; and
  (b)   accordingly, the claimant shall not (without making a further claim) be entitled to the benefit on the basis of circumstances not obtaining at that time.

Analysis

The effect of para 2 is that a decision refusing a claim for HB (sometimes called a "nil award") cannot be superseded on grounds of a change of circumstances that occurs after the *decision* was made. If someone is correctly refused benefit and her/his circumstances change, s/he must instead make a fresh claim for benefit. For the situation if someone's circumstances change after an appeal against a decision is made, see Sch 7 para 6(9).

Sub-para (a) confirms that the temporal effect of a claim ceases on the date that the authority makes its decision on the claim. The logical implication of the words "after that time" is that the claim does "subsist" prior to that time and so if a claimant is not entitled to benefit as at the date of claim but because of a change of circumstances becomes entitled on some later date before the authority makes its decision, the authority is obliged to award benefit from the later date. If this interpretation is correct, there may be some tension between sub-para (a) and reg 83(10) HB Regs (reg 64(11) HB(SPC) Regs), which appear to restrict the power to make such an award to a period of 13 weeks after the date of claim. Delays of more than that period in adjudicating claims are, unfortunately, endemic in some authorities. However, it may be argued that the regulations do no more than give a power to make an advance award *after* the date of claim.

To minimise any injustice caused by sub-para (a), it is suggested that benefit may be awarded from any date between the date of claim and the date on which the decision is made, even if the latter date is more than 13 weeks after the former. If, however, the decision is made quickly but it is apparent that the claimant would have become entitled to benefit within the 13-week period specified in reg 83(10) HB Regs (64(11) HB(SPC) Regs), such an award should be made.

Sub-para (b), if interpreted literally, leads to some bizarre results. What does "circumstances not obtaining at that time" mean? It appears to require the authority to consider only the circumstances as at the date of its decision. If that was so, then a claimant entitled to benefit on the date of claim but who subsequently loses entitlement as a result of a change of circumstances could not be awarded benefit at all. Again, this would give the severe delays occurring in many authorities even more serious consequences than the delays themselves.

The wording of sub-para (b) is similar to that used in para 6(9)(b) and the decisions of commissioners or the Upper Tribunal on the scope of s12(8)(b) SSA 1998 (the equivalent to para 6(9)(b) in relation to DWP benefits) will therefore assist. It is suggested that the position postulated in the previous paragraph would give rise to absurdities similar to those discussed in *R(DLA) 3/01* (see the commentary to para 6(9)(b) on p147). It is therefore appropriate to construe sub-para (b) as not excluding consideration of the position as at the date of claim and between the date of claim and date of the authority's initial decision. On that interpretation, it excludes consideration only of circumstances arising after the initial decision.

Two elements of the wording of sub-para (b) support that interpretation. First, the word "accordingly" links sub-para (b) to the rest of the paragraph and so focuses attention on the period after the decision is made. Secondly, "without making a further claim" again calls attention to the true focus of the sub-paragraph. The intention is that if a claim is rejected but a claimant subsequently becomes entitled, the claimant's means of securing benefit is a further claim and not an application to supersede the initial refusal.

"Closed period" supersessions. Para 2 has sometimes been misunderstood as preventing an authority from carrying out a "closed period" supersession. The problem occurs where:

(1)   the claimant is awarded benefit;

(2)   there is a change of circumstances which removes that entitlement; *and*

(3)   before the superseding decision is taken, there is a further change which re-establishes entitlement.

A common example may help: A, who is on HB as a person on low wages, works overtime during the month before Christmas with the result that he no longer satisfies the means test. By the time he receives his pay slip at the end of January, he has resumed his normal working pattern and is entitled to benefit again. In the past, some authorities have taken the view that when they make the superseding decision in February, the correct decision is that A has not been entitled to HB from the beginning of December because once his entitlement ended in December he could not become entitled to benefit again without a fresh claim (which has not been made).

That is not correct. As authorities have been reminded by Circular HB/CTB A6/2009, the award may be superseded for the period of non-entitlement and the supersession only replaces the original decision to that extent: see *CIS 2505/2003* and the authorities cited in that decision, particularly *CSIS 754/2002*. The reason – which is not explained adequately either in the Circular or the caselaw – is simply that any other outcome is unjust and that nothing in the Act or the D&A Regs requires the authority to reach such an outcome. In particular, para 2 does not have that effect: it is not concerned with revising or superseding decisions but with the initial decision on a claim. It says that if the initial decision is *refused* then the claimant cannot become entitled to benefit on the basis of circumstances not obtaining at the date of refusal because the claim has ceased to exist. It has no practical consequences where the initial decision is to *award* benefit because in such cases, although the claim still ceases to exist, the claimant does not have to rely upon the claim as the basis of his or her continuing entitlement: s/he can rely upon the decision awarding benefit. If, by the time that decision is superseded, there has been more than one change in circumstance then each such change is a ground for supersession and the authority is entitled – in fact, it will normally be obliged – to take each of those changes into account when making the superseding decision.

Revision of decisions

3.–(1)   Any relevant decision may be revised or further revised by the relevant authority which made the decision–

(a)   either within the prescribed period or in prescribed cases or circumstances; and

(b)   either on an application made for the purpose by a person affected by the decision or on their own initiative;

and regulations may prescribe the procedure by which a decision of a relevant authority may be so revised.

(2)   In making a decision under sub-paragraph (1), the relevant authority need not consider any issue that is not raised by the application or, as the case may be, did not cause them to act on their own initiative.

(3)   Subject to sub-paragraphs (4) and (5) and paragraph 18, a revision under this paragraph shall take effect as from the date on which the original decision took (or was to take) effect.

(4)   Regulations may provide that, in prescribed cases or circumstances, a revision under this paragraph shall take effect as from such other date as may be prescribed.

(5)   Where a decision is revised under this paragraph, for the purposes of any rule as to the time allowed for bringing an appeal, the decision shall be regarded as made on the date on which it is so revised.

(6)   Except in prescribed circumstances, an appeal against a decision of the relevant authority shall lapse if the decision is revised under this paragraph before the appeal is determined.

Definition

"relevant decision" – see Sch 7 para 1 CSPSSA 2000.

Analysis

Para 3 provides the statutory basis for a revision. The basic distinction between a revision and supersession is that the former corrects the original decision without replacing it and usually does not change the date from which that decision takes effect. A supersession replaces the original decision but usually only from some date subsequent to the date on which the decision was made.

Note that it is only a "relevant decision" as defined in para 1(2) that can be revised, or further revised, by the relevant authority that made the decision. This means that an authority cannot revise a decision of the First-tier Tribunal or the Upper Tribunal (or of the former appeal tribunals or social security commissioners). Such a decision may only be altered by a supersession under para 4 or on appeal.

The detailed procedure in relation to revisions is to be found in the commentary to regs 4, 5 and 6 D&A Regs. Only the bare outline is given here.

Note that following the decision of the tribunal of commissioners in *R(H) 3/04*, it may not be possible to revise a determination that an overpayment is recoverable. See the commentary to para 6 below.

Sub-para (1) introduces the power to revise. It includes a power to revise a decision more than once: "may be . . . further revised". A claimant may apply for a revision or it may be carried out by the authority of its own motion. For the mode of making an application, see regs 4(8) and (9) D&A Regs. For the "prescribed period", see reg 4(1) D&A Regs and note reg 5 giving power to extend time for an application by a claimant. For the "prescribed cases or circumstances", see reg 4(2), (3), (5), (7) and (7A)–(7H) on p942.

Sub-para (2) limits what the authority is required to consider in the course of a revision. The critical phrase here, however, is "need not" which confers a discretion: see *R(IB) 2/04*. Therefore, authorities should not shut their eyes where to do so would cause an injustice. However, claimants are best advised to raise all the points with which they disagree in their applications for revision and to provide relevant evidence and information to support the application. On an appeal against a revised decision (or against a refusal to revise) the First-tier Tribunal may exercise this discretion for itself. See commentary to Sch 7 para 6(9)(a) on p147.

Sub-paras (3) and (4) state the general rule that a revision takes effect from the same date as the original decision. Accordingly, where a claimant is seeking an increase in benefit, a revision is more advantageous than a supersession. For exceptions to the rule, see the anti-test case rule in para 18 on p156 and reg 6 D&A Regs on p951.

Sub-para (5) is necessary because there is no right of appeal against a revising decision: any appeal is against the original decision as revised. Without the extension of time established by sub-para (5), the appeal would be out-of-time whenever the process leading to the revising decision took more than a month.

Sub-para (6). If a decision is revised while there is an appeal pending against it, then the appeal lapses (ie, with the effect that the First-tier Tribunal or Upper Tribunal no longer has jurisdiction to hear it) if the revised decision is *more advantageous* to the person affected than the orginal decision: see reg 17 D&A Regs on p971. If the person affected remains dissatisfied with the revised decision (ie, because it remains less favourable than would have been the case had the appeal been completely successful), s/he must make a fresh appeal against the decision as revised. See, however, the discussion of *R(IS) 2/08* in the commentary to reg 17 D&A Regs.

Decisions superseding earlier decisions

4.–(1)   Subject to [¹ sub-paragraphs (4) and (4A)], the following, namely–

(a)   any relevant decision (whether as originally made or as revised under paragraph 3), [³]

[³ (aa)   any decision under this Schedule of an appeal tribunal or a Commissioner, and]

(b)   any decision under this Schedule [² of the First-tier Tribunal or any decision of the Upper Tribunal which relates to any such decision],

may be superseded by a decision made by the appropriate relevant authority, either on an application made for the purpose by a person affected by the decision or on their own initiative.

(2)   In this paragraph "the appropriate relevant authority" means the authority which made the decision being superseded, the decision appealed against to [³ the tribunal or] the [² First-tier Tribunal] or, as the case may be, the decision to which the decision being appealed against to [³ the Commissioner or] the [² Upper Tribunal] relates.

(3)   In making a decision under sub-paragraph (1), the relevant authority need not consider any issue that is not raised by the application or, as the case may be, did not cause them to act on their own initiative.

(4)   Regulations may prescribe the cases and circumstances in which, and the procedure by which, a decision may be made under this paragraph.

[¹ (4A)   Regulations may prescribe the cases and circumstances in which, and the procedure by which, a decision relating to housing benefit must be made by the appropriate relevant authority.]

(5)   Subject to sub-paragraph (6) and paragraph 18, a decision under this paragraph shall take effect as from the date on which it is made or, where applicable, the date on which the application was made.

(6)   Regulations may provide that, in prescribed cases or circumstances, a decision under this paragraph shall take effect as from such other date as may be prescribed.

[³ (7)   In this paragraph–

"appeal tribunal" means an appeal tribunal constituted under Chapter 1 of Part 1 of the Social Security Act 1998 (the functions of which have been transferred to the First-tier Tribunal);

"Commissioner" means a person appointed as a Social Security Commissioner under Schedule 4 to that Act (the functions of which have been transferred to the Upper Tribunal) and includes a tribunal of such persons.]

Amendments

1.   Amended by s30(3) of the WRA 2007 with effect from 1.10.07 (for making regulations) and 7.4.08.
2.   Amended by art 9 and Sch 3 para 190(2) of SI 2008 No 2833 (3.11.08).
3.   Amended by s103 and Sch 12 para 5 of the WRA 2012 (8.3.12).

Definitions

"relevant decision" – see Sch 7 para 1 CSPSSA 2000.

Analysis

>   *Sub-paras (1), (4) and (4A)* permit a supersession of a decision of an authority, as originally made or as revised or superseded, or of the First-tier Tribunal or the Upper Tribunal. Again, this may occur on the initiative of either the claimant or the authority. See reg 7 D&A Regs on p951 for the circumstances in which supersession is permitted, and note especially reg 7(6) which permits a notification of a change of circumstances to be treated as an application for a supersession. Note that, following the decision of the tribunal of commissioners in *R(H) 3/04*, it may not be possible to supersede a determination that an overpayment is recoverable. See the commentary to para 6 on p145. Inadequate drafting of Sch 3 para 190 Transfer of Tribunal Functions Order 2008 inadvertently removed the local authority's power to supersede a decision made by an appeal tribunal or a social security commissioner before 3 November 2008: see *DN v Leicester City Council (HB)* [2010] UKUT 253 (AAC). Amendments made by s103 and Sch 12 WRA 2012 (which apply as from 3 November 2008 by virtue of s103(2)) correct the error and confer a power to supersede the decisions of former appeal tribunals and the social security commissioners. See also the commentary to reg 7 D&A Regs on p954.

>   *Sub-para (3)* is similar in terms to para 3(2) (see p143).

>   *Sub-paras (5) and (6)* state the general rule as to the effective date of a supersession decision. It will normally take effect from the date it was made or from the date on which the application for it was made. For the extensive exceptions to this general rule, see regs 8 and 9 D&A Regs on p957 and p962.

Use of experts by relevant authorities

   5.   Where it appears to a relevant authority that a matter in relation to which a relevant decision falls to be made by them involves a question of fact requiring special expertise, they may direct that, in dealing with that matter, they shall have the assistance of one or more persons appearing to them to have knowledge or experience which would be relevant in determining that question.

Analysis

>   It is unclear why this provision was thought necessary. Perhaps it was designed to prevent any allegation that a decision was invalid because the part of the decision that required expertise had been effectively delegated to the expert. Little, if any, use has been made of this power.

Appeal to [¹ First-tier Tribunal]

   6.–(1)   Subject to sub-paragraph (2), this paragraph applies to any relevant decision (whether as originally made or as revised under paragraph 3) of a relevant authority which–

   (a)   is made on a claim for, or on an award of, housing benefit *[or council tax benefit]*; or

   (b)   does not fall within paragraph (a) but is of a prescribed description.

   (2)   This paragraph does not apply to–

   (a)   any decision terminating or reducing the amount of a person's housing benefit *[or council tax benefit]* that is made in consequence of any decision made under regulations under section 2A of the Administration Act (work-focused interviews);

   (b)   any decision of a relevant authority as to the application or operation of any modification of a housing benefit scheme *[or council tax benefit]* scheme under section 134(8)(a) or section 139(6)(a) of the Administration Act (disregard of war disablement and war widows' pensions);

   (c)   so much of any decision of a relevant authority as adopts a decision of a rent officer under any order made by virtue of section 122 of the Housing Act 1996 (decisions of rent officers for the purposes of housing benefit);

   (d)   any decision of a relevant authority as to the amount of benefit to which a person is entitled in a case in which the amount is determined by the rate of benefit provided for by law; or

   (e)   any such other decision as may be prescribed.

   (3)   In the case of a decision to which this paragraph applies, any person affected by the decision shall have a right to appeal to [¹ the First-tier Tribunal].

   (4)   Nothing in sub-paragraph (3) shall confer a right of appeal in relation to–

   (a)   a prescribed decision; or

   (b)   a prescribed determination embodied in or necessary to a decision.

   (5)   Regulations under sub-paragraph (4) shall not prescribe any decision or determination that relates to the conditions of entitlement to housing benefit *[or council tax benefit]* for which a claim has been validly made.

   (6)   Where any amount of housing benefit *[or council tax benefit]* is determined to be recoverable under or by virtue of section 75 or 76 of the Administration Act (overpayments and excess benefits), any person from whom it has been determined that it is so recoverable shall have a right of appeal to [¹ the First-tier Tribunal].

   (7)   A person with a right of appeal under this paragraph shall be given such notice of the decision in respect of which he has that right, and of that right, as may be prescribed.

   (8)   Regulations may make provision as to the manner in which, and the time within which, appeals are to be brought.

   (9)   In deciding an appeal under this paragraph, [¹ the First-tier Tribunal]–

   (a)   need not consider any issue that is not raised by the appeal; and

   (b)   shall not take into account any circumstances not obtaining at the time when the decision appealed against was made.

Amendment

1.   Amended by art 9 and Sch 3 para 190(3) of SI 2008 No 2833 (3.11.08).

Definitions

"relevant decision" – see para 1.
"relevant authority" – see para 1.

Analysis

The First-tier Tribunal

This paragraph sets out the scope of the right of appeal to the First-tier Tribunal. For the circumstances in which that tribunal was established and how it is constituted, see the commentary to the Tribunals, Courts and Enforcement Act 2007 on p167.

The approach to decision-making by the First-tier Tribunal

When it hears an appeal, the First-tier Tribunal (like the former appeal tribunals before it) is conducting a rehearing of the case: see *R(IB) 2/04* (paras 19–25), affirming *CH 1129/2002*, and the caselaw relating to other chambers of the First-tier Tribunal including *OFSTED v GM and WM* [2009] UKUT 89 (AAC) and *Secretary of State for Education v JN* [2010] UKUT 248 (AAC). Subject to the restrictions imposed by sub-para (9), it must decide whether it agrees the decision of the local authority was right, not (as the High Court used to do when considering judicial review challenges to the decisions of Review Boards) whether it thinks that the local authority was entitled to reach the decision that it did on the evidence before it: see *CH 1175/2002* (para 4). The First-tier Tribunal has power to remit issues to a local authority for consideration by it: *CH 3009/2002* (para 25).

A tribunal is entitled to, and must, ensure that it has jurisdiction to hear the case before it. That means that it must ensure that the challenge made by a claimant to the decision is one which the claimant is entitled to make: see the commentary to sub-para (1) below. However, the First-tier Tribunal should not decline jurisdiction simply because it considers the appeal is bound to fail: *FL v First-tier Tribunal and CICA* [2010] UKUT 158 (AAC).

Although a tribunal should consider every issue that is raised by the appeal, and that will include any issue that "has been raised by one of the parties at or before the...tribunal's decision" (see *R(IB) 2/04* at paras 32 and 192) or that is "clearly apparent from the evidence" (per *Mongan v Department for Social Development* [2005] NICA 16; reported as *R3/05 (DLA)*)), it does not follow that the tribunal must make a *decision* on *every* issue raised by the appeal if there is a more appropriate way of dealing with one or more issues: *R(IS) 2/08*. The tribunal of commissioners in that appeal went on to say:

"When an appeal against an outcome decision raises one issue on which the appeal is allowed but it is necessary to deal with a further issue before another outcome decision is substituted, a tribunal may set aside the original outcome decision without substituting another outcome decision, provided it deals with the original issue raised by the appeal and substitutes a decision on that issue."

It will then be for the Respondent authority to make a fresh decision on the new issue, against which new appeal rights will arise.

The tribunal of commissioners in *R(IS) 2/08* gave the following guidance:

–   in order to assist tribunals (now the First-tier Tribunal), the [Respondent's] submission to a tribunal should indicate whether it is considered that, if the appeal is allowed, there are any outstanding issues that need further consideration and whether the [Respondent] wishes the tribunal to deal with them;

–   where a tribunal, having dealt with the issues originally raised in an appeal, is not able immediately to give an outcome decision, it must decide whether to adjourn or whether to remit the question of entitlement to the [Respondent] if [it] would be in a better position to decide the issue and to seek further information from the claimant;

–   the tribunal's decision, as recorded on the decision notice issued at the conclusion of the hearing, should explicitly record what has and has not been decided and in particular, should make it absolutely clear whether the tribunal has made an outcome decision or has remitted the final decision on entitlement to the [Respondent authority].

For a more detailed discussion of the rules that must be followed by a tribunal, see the commentary to the TP(FTT) Rules.

Sub-para (1): Decisions that can be appealed

The first question that arises under para 6 is whether the decision of which complaint is made is one in respect of which the tribunal has jurisdiction. The tribunal has no jurisdiction beyond that conferred by legislation: *R(H) 3/04* (para 32). Sub-para (1) sets out the general rule, which is subject to sub-paras (2) and (3) discussed below.

"any relevant decision (whether as originally made or as revised ...)". See p140 for a discussion of a "relevant decision" and in particular for the question of whether a refusal to revise or to supersede is a relevant decision.

The tribunal must be careful, when determining an appeal against a decision which has been revised, to ensure that it is considering the decision as revised and not as it was originally made, otherwise it will err in law: *CH 1171/2002* (paras 3–8).

Sub-para (1) does not confer a right of appeal against a determination that an overpayment is recoverable: *R(H) 3/04* (para 33). The right of appeal arises under sub-para (6) instead: see below.

"made on a claim for, or on an award". An appeal may be brought against any decision (whether an original decision or a revised or superseded decision) "made on a claim for, or on an award of", HB. In *CH v Plymouth City Council and DE (HB)* [2018] UKUT 215 (AAC) at para 9, Judge Jacobs agreed that the words "on an award" in para 6(1)(a) "must mean a decision given on a claim or on supersession". No regulations have been made under sub-para (1)(b) and so every appeal must fall within the quoted words. They are wide enough to extend to issues arising under other legislation that must be determined for the purposes of an HB claim. Therefore, for example, an appeal may be validly made against a decision that a claimant is excluded from benefit under s115 Immigration and Asylum Act 1999.

There is an unfortunate tension between the definition of "relevant decision" in para 1(2) and these words in para 6(1). Para 1(2) defines a relevant decision only in terms of a decision on a claim or a supersession decision. The words "on an award" in para 6(1) must therefore be taken to refer to a decision superseding or refusing to supersede an earlier decision in order to avoid inconsistency between the two provisions.

For the question as to whether there is a right of appeal against a refusal to supersede, see p141.

In *Carpenter v SSWP* [2003] EWCA Civ 33; reported as *R(IB) 6/03*, the Court of Appeal had to consider whether a refusal by a tribunal to adjourn a hearing was of itself a "decision" which called for a statement of reasons under the former reg 53(4) SSCS D&A Regs. Laws LJ confirmed that a distinction had to be drawn between outcome decisions (which he described as "decisions upon the actual question whether an applicant is entitled to this or that benefit") on the one hand and "the many determinations which will fall to be made along the way to such a decision and which will inform it or indeed may determine it" and "procedural determinations": para 16. A refusal to adjourn fell within the latter category and was not appealable. Caution is required when applying the *Carpenter* decision to HB because of the anomaly whereby outcome decisions about the recovery of HB overpayments are not "relevant decisions" but are referred to using the verb "determine" (see p140). Even if such decisions are "determinations", they are not the type of determination to which Laws LJ was referring – ie, they are neither "findings of fact on particular issues" nor "procedural determinations".

The claimant's right to a fair hearing by an independent tribunal at common law and under art 6 must always inform any decision as to the scope of appeal rights: *Wood v SSWP* [2003] EWCA Civ 53; reported as *R(DLA) 1/03*. The tribunal's priority should at all times be to ensure that a person affected has a fair opportunity to challenge any aspect of a decision which affects her/him.

"of a prescribed description". No regulations have yet been made under para 6(1)(b), so if a decision is to be appealable it must fall within either para 6(1)(a) or para 6(6).

Sub-paras (2), (4) and (5): Decisions which cannot be appealed

Sub-paras (2) and (4) then set out a number of circumstances in which no appeal lies to the First-tier Tribunal against a decision.

(1) A decision terminating or reducing the amount of HB after a decision relating to a work-focused interview: head (a). However the decision relating to the interview attracted its own right of appeal: see reg 15 Social Security (Work-Focused Interviews) Regulations 2000 in the 2003/04 edition of this book. Note that work-focused interviews were only required in certain local authority areas operating within the ONE scheme, now largely replaced by Jobcentre Plus, which does not require work-focused interviews for HB.

(2) A decision as to whether war disablement and war widows' (or widowers') pensions should be disregarded for HB purposes: head (b). Such decisions are taken by resolution of the whole local authority. See the Analysis to s134(8) SSAA 1992 on p80.

(3) Any element of a decision relating to HB that follows inevitably from the conclusion reached by the rent officer: head (c). This prevents any indirect challenge to a rent officer's determinations. However, a danger can arise here if neither the appellant or the local authority in the appeal address the issue of whether the alternative version of reg 13 HB Regs (or of reg 13 HB(SPC) Regs) may apply (and hence that the rent officer's determination may not be determinative of the eligible rent). In such a situation, there is a danger that the appeal may be struck out by the tribunal under r8(2) TP(FT) Rules. It is therefore suggested that local authorities should set out in any response to an appeal raising issues under reg 13 that the alternative version of reg 13 does not apply and why that is the case. It is also suggested that, before striking out appeals for want of jurisdiction under para 6(2)(c), tribunal judges should ask for that information from local authorities if it has not already been provided. Note also the discussion on *Bexley LB v LD (HB)* [2010] UKUT 79 (AAC) and *SK v South Hams DC (HB)* [2010] UKUT 129 (AAC) on p404.

(4) Any element of a decision as to the rate of benefit: head (d). No one can therefore make an appeal on the ground that the benefit they are receiving is insufficient, or that a premium is insufficient to meet a need. This would include, it would seem, any argument relying on the Human Rights Act 1998. As any such appeal would be hopeless in any event, it seems that these are included so as to designate them as "out-of-jurisdiction" appeals and hence capable of being struck out under r8(2) TP(FT) Rules.

(5) Any prescribed decision or determination: head (e). See the Schedule to the D&A Regs and the commentary thereto. Sub-para (5) forbids the exclusion of any decision relating to whether the conditions of entitlement have been fulfilled. The exclusion of "a prescribed determination embodied in or necessary to a decision" from any right of appeal in para 6(4)(b) is puzzling because there is no right of appeal against such a determination in the first place: para 6(3) only gives a right of appeal against "decisions" and although para 6(6) may give a right of appeal against an overpayment "determination", that type of

"determination" is not "embodied in or necessary to a decision". However, the point is academic. No regulations have actually been made under para 6(6)(b).

Sub-paragraph (6): Appeals relating to recovery of overpayments

Sub-para (6) deals with the thorny subject of overpayment appeals. It was established by the decision of the tribunal of commissioners in *R(H) 3/04* (para 33) that the right to challenge decisions relating to recovery of overpayments arises under sub-para (6) and not under sub-para (1). The basis for that conclusion was that "determinations" that an overpayment is recoverable from a person does not fall within the definition of "relevant decision" in para 1. For the distinction between "decisions" and "determinations", see p140. That distinction would appear to lead to the conclusion that an overpayment "determination" cannot be altered once made by revision or supersession, other than on appeal. Two possible answers to this are as follows. First, it might be possible to argue that the former legislation was preserved. Secondly, since Sch 7 para 11 presumably does not apply (on the approach of the tribunal of commissioners) to overpayment determinations, reliance might be placed on the common law rule that a statutory power can be exercised repeatedly unless the legislation provides otherwise: s12 Interpretation Act 1978, though see Wade and Forsyth, *Administrative Law* (11th edition, 2014) pp191–93.

Most of the problems concerning the scope of the right of appeal under sub-para (6) have now been resolved by the tribunal of commissioners' decision in *R(H) 6/06*.

Challenging a decision that there has been an overpayment. Before a determination can be made that an overpayment is recoverable, it is normally a pre-condition that the decisions awarding benefit are altered: *R(H) 3/04* (para 34). Although the tribunal of commissioners referred only to the alteration being carried out by way of supersession, revision will be appropriate in the case of any award of benefit which is to be altered for the full period for which it was in effect.

There still seem to be some authorities who persist in asserting that a landlord has no right to challenge a decision that an overpayment has occurred but only that it is recoverable from her/him. That is plainly incorrect. The decision that an overpayment has occurred is made under ss75(1) or 76(1) SSAA and hence falls within the right of appeal conferred by sub-para (6). The tribunal of commissioners in *R(H) 3/04* (para 50) and *R(H) 6/06* have confirmed that a landlord may assert on an appeal that no overpayment has occurred, even if the claimant has not challenged the decision or decisions altering entitlement to benefit.

Challenging recovery of the overpayment. One of the most troublesome questions under the current adjudication regime has been the extent to which a decision to recover an overpayment (as distinct from a determination that it is recoverable) may be appealed.

Whatever the correctness of the Court of Appeal's decision in *SSWP v Chiltern DC* [2003] EWCA Civ 508; reported as *R(H) 2/03* and the tribunal of commissioners' decision in *R(H) 3/04* in respect of the regime in place prior to October 2001 (and the correctness of the Court of Appeal's decision is strongly doubted in *R(H) 6/06*), the tribunal of commissioners' decision in *R(H) 6/06* holds that rights of appeal only attach to decisions going to the recoverability of an overpayment and do not attach to decisions concerning the recovery (or enforcement) of such recoverable overpayment decisions. See further the commentary to s75 SSAA 1992 on p37.

Challenging the method of recovery. The First-tier Tribunal has no jurisdiction over *how* an overpayment is recovered. Methods of recovery are determined under s75(5) to (7) SSAA in a way that is outside the decision-making process as to recovery. Judicial review remains the only viable method of challenge.

This has been confirmed in *R(H) 7/04*, where the commissioner ruled that landlords had no right to challenge the decision to recover a recoverable overpayment by way of deduction from future payments of HB made to the landlords (per s75(4) SSAA 1992 and reg 102 HB Regs 1987 – now reg 102 HB Regs and reg 83 HB(SPC) Regs), where the decision that there had been an overpayment and that it was recoverable had been issued against the tenants. In the commissioner's view, a clear distinction needs to be made in such cases between the determination that there is a recoverable overpayment from a named person, and the means by which recovery is effected. The latter may have consequences on the amount of future HB received by the landlord but that does not constitute a decision that the overpayment is recoverable from the landlord.

Sub-paragraphs (3) and (7): Persons with a right of appeal

Sub-para (3) provides that any "person affected" will generally have the right of appeal. That phrase has the same meaning as in the D&A Regs: see para 23(2) on p159 and reg 3 D&A Regs on p941.

Sub-para (7) requires a person affected to be given notice of appeal rights. See Sch 9 HB Regs and Sch 8 HB(SPC) Regs for the consequences of non-compliance with those provisions, see the Analysis to reg 90 HB Regs on p565. See also reg 10 D&A Regs on p963.

Sub-paragraph (8): Making an appeal

See regs 19 and 20 D&A Regs (on p973 and p975) and r23 TP(FT) Rules (on p1006).

Sub-paragraph (9): Extent of a tribunal's jurisdiction

Head (a): Issues not raised "by the appeal". The First-tier Tribunal "need not" consider any issue not raised by the appeal. By implication, that rule has two consequences. First, the tribunal must consider all the issues which are "raised by the appeal". Second, it may consider issues which are not "raised by the appeal".

For these purposes, an issue is "raised by the appeal" if either:

– it has been raised by one of the parties at or before the appeal tribunal's decision (*R(IB) 2/04* paras 32 and 193); *or*

– if it is an issue which "obviously demands attention" (see *Mooney v SSWP* [2004] SLT 1141; reported as *R(DLA) 5/04*) or which is "clearly apparent from the evidence" (see *Mongan v Department for Social Development* [2005] NICA 16; reported as *R3/05 (DLA)*) and *Hooper v SSWP* [2007] EWCA Civ 495; reported as *R(IB) 4/07*).

That is so even if the appellant is represented and the representative does not raise the issue. As the Court in *Mongan* stated (at para 18):

"In carrying out their inquisitorial function, the tribunal should have regard to whether the party has the benefit of legal representation. It need hardly be said that close attention should be paid to the possibility that relevant issues might be overlooked where the appellant does not have legal representation. Where an appellant is legally represented the tribunal is entitled to look to the legal representatives for elucidation of the issues that arise. But this does not relieve them of the obligation to enquire into potentially relevant matters. A poorly represented party should not be placed at any greater disadvantage than an unrepresented party."

The inquisitorial role can extend to obtaining further evidence on issues that the first-tier agency has not investigated properly: eg, *PM v SSWP (IS)* [2014] UKUT 474 (AAC). Note, however, that although the tribunal may not refuse to deal with an issue that is "clearly apparent from the evidence", it is not always necessary for it to deal with such an issue by making a decision about it. In *R(IS) 2/08* (a decision concerning IS in which the decision maker was therefore the Secretary of State rather than a local authority) a tribunal of commissioners stated:

"47.   ...what a tribunal must not do is ignore an issue that is clearly apparent from the evidence. However, it does not follow that the tribunal must make a decision on every issue raised by the appeal if there is a more appropriate way of dealing with one or more issues.

48.   It is well established that a tribunal allowing an appeal because the decision under appeal was made without jurisdiction is entitled simply to set aside the decision without substituting another. So too may a tribunal when allowing an appeal on the ground that the original decision was not made against the correct parties and in such a case it is plainly open to the Sectretary of State to make another decision in place of the one that has been set aside (*R(H) 6/06*). In our judgment, the same approach can be applied where an issue first arises in the course of an appeal. When an appeal against an outcome decision raises one issue on which the appeal is allowed but it is necessary to deal with a further issue before another outcome decision is substituted, a tribunal may set aside the original outcome decision without substituting anotheroutcome decision, provided it deals with the original issue raised by the appeal and substitutes a decision on that issue. The Secretary of State must then consider the new issue and decide what outcome decision to give. In that outcome decision, he must give effect to the tribunal's decision on the original issue unless, at the time he makes the outcome decision, he is satisfied that there are grounds on which to supersede the tribunal's decision so as, for instance, to take account of any changes of circumstances that have occurred since he made the decision that was the subject of the appeal to the tribunal. Because his decision is an outcome decision, the claimant will have a right of appeal against it."

Although the First-tier Tribunal "need not" consider issues not raised by the appeal, it may do so. Para 6(9)(a) confers a discretion which must be exercised consciously and judicially, taking into account all relevant circumstances. If a statement of reasons is given, then reasons for the exercise of the discretion should be set out (whether the discretion is exercised to consider or not to consider the additional issue). In addition, the tribunal must be satisfied that there has been compliance with the requirements of Art 6 of the European Convention on Human Rights and of natural justice (*R(IB) 2/04* paras 88 to 97 and 194). Compliance with Art 6 requires that the parties should not be put at a disadvantage because they have been taken by surprise by a point which the tribunal takes of its own motion. (For example, in *CH 1129/2002*, the local authority refused benefit under reg 6 HB Regs 1987 (now reg 8 HB Regs) but the tribunal substituted a decision under reg 7 of those regs (now reg 9 HB Regs) without making it clear to the claimant's representative that it proposed to take that course. The commissioner held that to be a breach of natural justice: para 30.) This is particularly important if the effect of taking the new point may be to make a decision that is less favourable to the appellant than the decision appealed against. In such cases, fairness is likely to require an express warning and, at least where the appellant is unrepresented, an offer of an adjournment. For reasons to do with the structure of disability living allowance, the question whether to consider issues not raised by the appeal arises most often in appeals relating to that benefit. For a discussion of the issues raised by s12(8)(a) Social Security Act 1998 (equivalent to para 6(9)(a)) in that context, see *AP-H v SSWP* [2010] UKUT 183 (AAC) and the various decisions of the commissioners and the Upper Tribunal referred to in that case.

For a discussion of the approach to be taken by the First-tier Tribunal when it is not clear whether an issue is raised by the appeal, see the decision of Judge Wright in *ET v SSWP (PIP)* [2017] UKUT 478 (AAC).

Where the First-tier Tribunal accepts a concession from a party, the matter which forms the subject of the concession ceases to be an issue "raised by the appeal". However, the First-tier Tribunal still retains discretion to deal with it under para 6(9)(a). The First-tier Tribunal will normally be entitled to accept a concession that is offered by a competent representative without probing further. But that does not necessarily follow in the case of an unrepresented claimant. In such circumstances, the First-tier Tribunal should satisfy itself that the claimant has properly understood matters and is making an informed decision not to pursue a particular issue: see *KKL v SSWP (PIP)* [2018] UKUT 17 (AAC).

Head (b): Circumstances "not obtaining at the time when the decision ... was made". The purpose of this provision is to oust the "down to the date of hearing" rule under which a decision maker or tribunal was required by the decision in *CS 14430/1996* (Appendix para 3) to consider the claimant's entitlement not merely at the date of claim, but also in relation to each date up until the date of the hearing of the appeal. For example, if a claimant was refused benefit on the basis that s/he was not habitually resident in the UK, then a tribunal might have found that habitual residence had not been established as at the date of claim or of the decision maker's decision but was obtained by some later date. This was a rule which, although sounding impractical, when properly applied enabled tribunals to do practical justice and avoided the need for claimants to make repeated claims. Its application to HB (and CTB) was never, however, fully settled: see the Analysis to reg 83 HB Regs 1987 on p388 of the 13th edition.

Where an application has been made for a revision of the decision, which has been refused and the claimant has appealed against that refusal, the relevant date for the purposes of para 6(9)(b) is the date of the original decision, not the date of the refusal to revise: *CSDLA 2/2002* (para 22). The same is true of an appeal against an original decision that has been revised, but with which the appellant remains dissatisfied.

The equivalent provision relating to DWP benefits, s12(8)(b) SSA 1998, has had its scope substantially restricted by a number of commissioners' decisions. First, "circumstances" are the facts relevant to the decision and not the *evidence* of those facts. It is therefore perfectly permissible for the tribunal to have regard to evidence which is only made available, or even evidence that only comes into existence, after the decision was made: *R(DLA) 2/01* (para 9); *R(DLA) 3/01* (paras 58-60); *CH 1175/2002* (para 6). Furthermore, circumstances arising between the date of claim and the date that the decision was made must be considered: *R(DLA) 3/01* (paras 58–60); *CIS 2428/1999* (para 20). In *CJSA 2375/2000* (para 31), this principle was extended further to include circumstances which relate to the period prior to the decision, even if those circumstances did not come to light until after the decision was made. That case related to an appeal against a disqualification from JSA. After the decision was made, a previous disqualification was overturned on appeal and so the second disqualification fell to be reduced to two weeks, even if upheld. The commissioner held that it was necessary to interpret the provision so as to avoid absurdity and this convoluted interpretation was the only way in which this could be achieved. In *CDLA 4331/2002* (para 9), Commissioner Rowland said that s12(8)(b) SSA 1998 should not be read so as to prevent changes of circumstance to be taken into account which the decision maker is entitled to anticipate because they are almost certain to occur. See reg 7(2)(a)(ii) D&A Regs (on p955) which gives a local authority the power to supersede in such a situation.

The combined effect of this provision and that of Sch 7 para 2 above, along with the limits on backdating of benefit following a claim or a supersession (for these see reg 83(12) HB Regs; reg 64(1) and (1A) HB(SPC) Regs; and reg 8 D&A Regs) is that as a general rule, a claimant needs to consider making a fresh claim for benefit (or seeking a supersession) if circumstances change after the date of the decision being appealed. Once the appeal is determined, if the decision on the claim or supersession request (the new decision) would have been made differently by the decision maker had the result of the appeal been known, a revision of the new decision is possible. If the new decision has itself been appealed, see reg 4(1)(c) D&A Regs. If the new decision has not itself been appealed, see reg 4(7) D&A Regs on p947.

Redetermination etc of appeals by tribunal

7.–(1)   This paragraph applies where an application is made [¹ to the First-tier Tribunal for permission to appeal to the Upper Tribunal from any decision of the First-tier Tribunal under paragraph 6].

[¹ (2)]

(3)   If each of the principal parties to the case expresses the view that the decision was erroneous in point of law, [¹ the First-tier Tribunal] shall set aside the decision and refer the case for determination by a differently constituted [¹ First-tier Tribunal].

(4)   In this paragraph and paragraph 8 "principal parties" means–

(a)   where he is the applicant for leave to appeal or the circumstances are otherwise such as may be prescribed, the Secretary of State;

(b)   the relevant authority against whose decision the appeal to the appeal tribunal was brought; and

(c)   the person affected by the decision against which the appeal to the appeal tribunal was brought or by the tribunal's decision on that appeal.

Amendment

1.   Amended by art 9 and Sch 3 para 190(4) of SI 2008 No 2833 as from 3.11.08.

Analysis

Para 7 is equivalent, with the exception of sub-para (4), to s13 SSA 1998. As originally enacted, it contained two provisions. The first, in sub-para (2), permitted the person considering an application for leave to appeal against a decision of a former appeal tribunal to set that decision aside if it was "erroneous in point of law". The second, in sub-para (3), obliged that person to set aside the tribunal's decision if all the parties expressed the view that it was legally erroneous.

Sub-para (2) has now been replaced by the First-tier Tribunal's power of review in s9 TCEA (see p173).

Sub-para (3) is a provision that is capable of causing inconvenience: see (in the context of the equivalent rule in s13(3) Social Security Act 1998) *GA v SSWP (ESA)* [2014] UKUT 521 (AAC) at para 4. If *both* parties state that the decision contains an error of law, the First-tier Tribunal is *required* to set aside the decision. In such a case, the case *must* be remitted to a differently constituted tribunal. The reasonableness of the position taken by the parties is not, on the face of it, a factor; and the parties need not even agree that the same error of law has occurred.

Before 3 November 2008, the procedure by which appeal tribunals considered applications for leave to appeal meant that this provision was rarely used in practice. Although under reg 58 D&A Regs, an application for leave to appeal by the local authority had to be sent to every other party to the proceedings, there was no such requirement for applications made by the person affected by the decision. As such, the local authority was not usually in a position to comment on an application for leave by a claimant, preventing para 7(3) taking effect. Moreover, from 20 May 2002, reg 58(3) D&A Regs was revoked by SI 2002 No.1379 and a party who received a copy of an application for leave to appeal no longer had a right to make representations. However, under rr39(1) and 40(4) TP(FT) Rules, it may be that the First-tier Tribunal is faced with circumstances in which it must set aside the decision under sub-para (3) more frequently.

If one party makes an application for leave which is then refused, and the other party then makes an application, para 7(3) will not be applicable and the question as to whether leave should be granted must be determined in the normal way: *CF 6923/1999*. If, however, both parties to the appeal have expressed the view that the decision of the tribunal is erroneous before leave has been granted or refused to either party by the tribunal, then the mandatory terms of para 7(3) mean that the decision of the tribunal must be set aside and the Upper Tribunal can have no jurisdiction under para 8: *CIB 4427/2002* (paras 16–17). On the other hand, where one party is refused leave to appeal and renews the application for leave under para 8 of Sch 7, but at or about the same time the other party to the appeal applies for leave to appeal to the tribunal, whether para 7(3) or para 8 applies will depend upon the precise sequence of events: *CIB 2949/2005*. In that case, the commissioner took the view that as the renewed application for leave to appeal had been registered with the Commissioners' Office, the commissioner became seised of the matter under para 8 of Sch 7 and para 7(3) therefore could no longer apply.

Appeal from [¹ First-tier Tribunal to Upper Tribunal]

8.– [¹ (1)]

(2) An appeal [¹ to the Upper Tribunal under section 11 of the Tribunals, Courts and Enforcement Act 2007 from any decision of the First-tier Tribunal under paragraph 6 or 7 lies] at the instance of any of the following–

(a) the Secretary of State;

(b) the relevant authority against whose decision the appeal to the appeal tribunal was brought;

(c) any person affected by the decision against which the appeal to the [¹ First-tier Tribunal] was brought or by the tribunal's decision on that appeal.

[¹ (3)-(8)]

Amendment

1. Amended by art 9 and Sch 3 para 190(5) of SI 2008 No 2833 as from 3.11.08.

Analysis

For the Upper Tribunal, see the commentary to ss3 (p169), 5 (p170) and 11 (p176) TCEA.

Sub-para (2) supplements s11(2) TCEA. It is necessary because s11(2) confers a right of appeal to the Upper Tribunal on "[a]ny party to a case" without defining who is, or is not, a "party to a case": see the commentary on p176.

[¹ Applications for permission to appeal against a decision of the Upper Tribunal]

9.–[¹ (1)]

[¹ (2)]

(3) [¹ An application for permission to appeal from a decision of the Upper Tribunal in respect of a decision of the First-tier Tribunal under paragraph 6 or 7] may only be made by–

(a) a person who, before the proceedings before the [¹ Upper Tribunal] were begun, was entitled to appeal to the [¹ Upper Tribunal] from the decision to which the [¹ Upper Tribunal's] decision relates;

(b) any other person who was a party to the proceedings in which the decision to which the [¹ Upper Tribunal's] decision relates was given;

(c) any other person who is authorised by regulations to apply for [¹ permission];

[¹]

[¹ (4)]

[¹ (5)]

Amendment

1. Amended by art 9 and Sch 3 para 190(6) of SI 2008 No 2833 as from 3.11.08.

Analysis

Under s13 TCEA 2008 a further appeal lies from the Upper Tribunal, with permission, to either the Court of Appeal or to the Court of Session as appropriate.

Sub-paragraph (3): Who has the right to appeal?

Under sub-para (3), the people with a right of appeal are set out. First, there is any person who had a right of appeal to the Upper Tribunal: see para 8(2). Secondly, there is any other person who was a party to the tribunal proceedings. In fact, for HB purposes these are exactly the same parties as those with a right to appeal to the Upper Tribunal, since "party" means "principal party" under para 7(4): see reg 1(2) D&A Regs. No regulations have been made under sub-para (3)(c). Sub-para (2) overlaps with s13(2) TCEA 2008. It appears to have been retained because the reference in head (a) to a person who would have had an appeal to the Upper Tribunal, taken together with para 8(2), confers a right of appeal on the Secretary of State (who, in a HB case, may not have been a party to the appeal to the Upper Tribunal) which is not conferred by s13(2).

Procedure

10.–(1) Regulations may make for the purposes of this Schedule any such provision as is specified in Schedule 5 to the Social Security Act 1998, or as would be so specified if the references to the Secretary of State in paragraph 1 of that Schedule were references to a relevant authority.

[¹ (2)-(8)]

Amendment

1.   Omitted by art 9 and Sch 3 para 190(7) of SI 2008 No 2833 as from 3.11.08.

Analysis

From 3 November 2008, the power to make rules about tribunal procedure are contained in s22 and Sch 5 TCEA. This paragrapgh now contains residual regulation-making powers for those parts of the D&A Regs that do not concern tribunals and are not authorised by other provisions of Sch 7 – eg, para 3(4) and (6) and para 4(4) and (6).

Finality of decisions

11.   Subject to the provisions of this Schedule [¹ and to any provision made by or under Chapter 2 of Part 1 of the Tribunals, Courts and Enforcement Act 2007], any decision made in accordance with the preceding provisions of this Schedule shall be final.

Amendment

1.   Inserted by art 9 and Sch 3 para 190(8) of SI 2008 No 2833 as from 3.11.08.

Analysis

Para 11 covers the same ground as s17 SSA 1998, but is differently worded. It provides that a decision is final, except to the extent that it may be altered on revision, supersession or appeal. The scope of para 11 is restricted to what the previous decision maker actually decided – ie, the outcome decision. It does not extend to the findings of fact and law on which that outcome decision is based. Para 6(4), demonstrates that, for the purposes of the Schedule, there is a clear contrast between a "decision" and a "determination embodied in or necessary to a decision". Para 11 only applies to the former. Thus if claim A is rejected on the basis that the claimant has notional capital because s/he sold a capital asset at an undervalue so as to obtain HB, the decision is final as far as it affects claim A (subject to challenge). However, if the claimant makes claim B eight weeks later, the authority cannot simply rely on para 11 in rejecting claim B but must, at least in theory, reconsider the question of notional capital. Commissioner Jacobs confirmed this approach in *CH 1210/2003*. He said that a decision relates only to a claim. Although it may be taken into account when deciding a later claim, it is not conclusive on claims in respect of different periods. More recently, the same approach was taken by the Upper Tribunal (Judge Rowland) in *MW v Leeds CC (HB)* [2018] UKUT 319 (AAC).

It would also seem that, following the approach of the tribunal of commissioners in *R(H) 3/04*, para 11 has no application to a "determination" that an overpayment is recoverable.

The commissioners have consistently held that appeal tribunals were not bound by previous decisions of other appeal tribunals. Two decisions of Commissioner Jacobs deal with the point. It was held in *CH 3853/2001* (paras 18–19) that a Review Board decision on a question of fact does not bind an appeal tribunal deciding the same question in relation to a different claim. The commissioner said:

"Nor was the Tribunal bound by the Board's finding that the claimant was compelled to act as he did. That was so despite the fact that it was made in respect of the same claimant, the same premises, the same circumstances and the same arguments. The Board's finding was made on a different claim dealing with a different period."

The same must therefore be true of authorities determining subsequent claims, and of the First-tier Tribunal hearing an appeal where a previous tribunal has dismissed an appeal on the same facts: *CCS 1535/1997* (paras 24–27), where the commissioner suggested that the fact that tribunals exercised an inquisitorial jurisdiction meant that there could be no issue estoppel (under which a decision on a question between two parties is ordinarily binding on them in relation to future litigation) in tribunal proceedings.

This interpretation produces a desirable flexibility within the decision-making system. It is a common phenomenon for advisers to be consulted by claimants who have had an adverse decision on a question such as notional capital which cannot be challenged by the time that the adviser becomes involved. While any prospect of getting benefit on that claim may have been lost, it might cause serious injustice to such a claimant if s/he does not have the right to have the matter reconsidered on a fresh claim. The drawback of the interpretation is that it has the potential to cause administrative difficulties for authorities and the First-tier Tribunal where a claimant aggrieved by a decision adverse to her/him decides to make multiple claims at regular intervals. Authorities must adjudicate and decide each claim that is made in the correct time and manner and which satisfies the evidence requirements: reg 89 HB Regs and reg 70 HB(SPC) Regs. Authorities will probably simply rely on the reasoning of the first officer who determined the question under dispute and issue further decisions to identical effect. What authorities would have to be careful to avoid, in these circumstances, is ignoring any further information or evidence that may be presented on subsequent claims.

As far as repeated appeals are concerned, if there are several appeals outstanding at once, they can be listed for hearing and disposed of together: *R(SB) 4/85*. In cases where there is abuse of the appeals system, r8(3)(c) TP(FT) Rules permits the tribunal to strike out the appeal if it considers there is no reasonable prospect of the appellant's case, or part of it, succeeding.

However, paragraph 11 only applies to decisions made under Sch 7. It does not prevent the operation of the general rules about issue estoppel in public law decision making when the earlier decision was made, for example, by a court.

The principles underlying those rules were summarised by Lord Bridge in *Thrasyvoulou v Secretary of State for the Environment* [1990] 2 AC 273 at 289, HL as being the two maxims that there was a public interest in the finality of litigation and that no one should be vexed by litigation on the same question more than once. He said:

"In principle, they must apply equally to adjudications in the field of public law. In relation to adjudications subject to a comprehensive self-contained statutory code, the presumption, in my opinion, must be that where the statute has created a specific jurisdiction for the determination of any issue which establishes the existence of a legal right, the principle of res judicata applies to give finality to that determination unless an intention to exclude that principle can properly be inferred as a matter of construction of the relevant statutory powers."

CH 704/2005 decides that issue estoppel can apply in respect of an issue decided by the county court which is also an issue arising on a HB appeal. In that case, the issue was whether the claimant had a beneficial interest in a property and thus had capital in excess of £16,000. The commissioner said that issue estoppel could only apply if the parties to the appeal tribunal hearing were the same parties as in the county court and acting in the same capacity, but that was the case here as no valid distinction could be made between the local authority exercising its housing functions and its benefit functions. Nothing, in the commissioner's view, in the limited statutory estoppel created by para 11 of Sch 7, or the lack of any estoppel arising from findings of fact or determinations embodied in tribunal decisions created by s17(2) SSA 1998, meant that decisions made by courts in the exercise of their jurisdictions cannot create an issue estoppel for a later statutory appeal concerning the same parties.

CH 704/2005 also decides (para 14) that decisions of the statutory authorities (including tribunals) concerning HB and CTB (and all other benefits) cannot bind later decision makers within that statutory arena, save to the limited extent set out in Sch 7 para 11 (or s17(1) SSA 1998).

There is no direct authority as to whether decisions of other statutory tribunals (eg, of the Immigration and Asylum Chamber of the First-tier Tribunal) can give rise to an issue estoppel for the purposes of HB. The problem is unlikely to arise often as the parties to such appeals will usually be different from those in a HB appeal.

Matters arising as respects decisions
12. Regulations may make provision as respects matters arising–
(a) pending any decision under this Schedule of a relevant authority [¹ or the First-tier Tribunal, or any decision of the Upper Tribunal which relates to any decision under this Schedule of the First-Tier Tribunal,] which relates to–
    (i) any claim for housing benefit *[or council tax benefit]*;
    (ii) any person's entitlement to such a benefit or its receipt; or
(b) out of the revision under paragraph 3, or on appeal, of any such decision.

Amendment
1. Amended by art 9 and Sch 3 para 190(8) of SI 2008 No 2833 as from 3.11.08.

Suspension in prescribed circumstances
13.–(1) Regulations may provide for–
(a) suspending, in whole or in part, any payments of housing benefit *[or council tax benefit]*;
[(b) *suspending, in whole or in part, any reduction (by way of council tax benefit) in the amount that a person is or will become liable to pay in respect of council tax;]*

(c)   the subsequent making, or restoring, in prescribed circumstances of any or all of the payments, or reductions, so suspended.

(2)   Regulations made under sub-paragraph (1) may, in particular, make provision for any case where, in relation to a claim for housing benefit *[or council tax benefit]*–

(a)   it appears to the relevant authority that an issue arises whether the conditions for entitlement to such a benefit are or were fulfilled;

(b)   it appears to the relevant authority that an issue arises whether a decision as to an award of such a benefit should be revised (under paragraph 3) or superseded (under paragraph 4);

(c)   an appeal is pending against a decision of [¹ the First-tier Tribunal, the Upper Tribunal] or a court; or

(d)   it appears to the relevant authority, where an appeal is pending against the decision given by [¹ the Upper Tribunal] or a court in a different case, that if the appeal were to be determined in a particular way an issue would arise whether the award of housing benefit or council tax benefit in the case itself ought to be revised or superseded.

(3)   For the purposes of sub-paragraph (2), an appeal against a decision is pending if–

(a)   an appeal against the decision has been brought but not determined;

(b)   an application for [¹ permission] to appeal against the decision has been made but not determined; or

(c)   the time within which–

(i)   an application for [¹ permission] to appeal may be made, or

(ii)   an appeal against the decision may be brought,

has not expired and the circumstances are such as may be prescribed.

(4)   In sub-paragraph (2)(d) the reference to a different case–

(a)   includes a reference to a case involving a different relevant authority; but

(b)   does not include a reference to a case relating to a different benefit unless the different benefit is housing benefit *[or council tax benefit]*.

Amendment

1.   Amended by art 9 and Sch 3 para 190(10) of SI 2008 No 2833 as from 3.11.08.

Modification

Section 68, under which Sch 7 is given effect, was repealed by WRA 2012 s147 and Sch 14 part 1 on 1.4.13 in so far as it related to CTB.

Analysis

See regs 11 and 12 D&A Regs on p964 and p966. Note that the power in sub-para (3)(c) was only exercised with effect from 30 October 2008: reg 11(3) DA Regs inserted by SI 2008 No.2667. Until then, it appears that there was no power to suspend unless the authority had at least got to the stage of making an application for leave to appeal.

Note also the limited scope of the "different cases" which may trigger suspension under reg 11(2)(b)(ii) D&A Regs. Sub-para (4) provides that a case involving a different local authority may trigger a suspension, but cases involving other benefits may not give rise to suspension. Thus if the Upper Tribunal is due to give a ruling on the interpretation of a part of the IS legislation, it will not be open to the authority to impose a suspension on payment under HB claims which require consideration of an identical provision in the HB legislation.

Sub-para (4) does not, in terms, preclude suspension where a ruling is due in respect of legislation outside the area of social security. It would seem arguable that it would be legitimate for an authority to suspend payment where an authoritative ruling is due as to the meaning of a particular phrase replicated in the HB legislation. After all, the test is whether an issue would arise, not that the decision would make a difference for certain. Since "court" is not defined in the legislation, a pending appeal to the Court of Appeal from the High Court or some other statutory tribunal may well give a right to suspend payment.

Suspension for failure to furnish information etc

14.–(1)   The powers conferred by this paragraph are exercisable in relation to persons who fail to comply with information requirements.

(2)   Regulations may provide for–

(a)   suspending, in whole or in part, any payments of housing benefit *[or council tax benefit]*;

(b)   suspending, in whole or in part, any reduction (by way of *[council tax benefit]*) in the amount that a person is or will become liable to pay in respect of council tax;

(c)   the subsequent making, or restoring, in prescribed circumstances of any or all of the payments, or any right, so suspended.

(3)   In this paragraph and paragraph 15 "information requirement" means–

(a)   in the case of housing benefit, a requirement in pursuance of regulations made by virtue of section 5(1)(hh) of the Administration Act to furnish information or evidence needed for a determination whether a decision on an award of that benefit should be revised under paragraph 3 or superseded under paragraph 4 of this Schedule; and *[(b)   in the case of council tax benefit, a requirement made in pursuance of regulations under section 6(1)(hh) of the Administration Act to furnish information or evidence needed for a determination whether a decision on an award of that benefit should be so revised or superseded.]*

Modification

Section 68, under which Sch 7 is given effect, was repealed by WRA 2012 s147 and Sch 14 part 1 on 1.4.13 in so far as it related to CTB.

Analysis

See reg 13 D&A Regs on p966. Reg 86 HB Regs and reg 67 HB(SPC) Regs are partly made under ss5(1)(hh) and 6(1)(hh) SSAA.

Termination in cases of a failure to furnish information

15.   Regulations may provide that, except in prescribed cases or circumstances–

(a)   a person whose benefit has been suspended in accordance with regulations under paragraph 13 and who subsequently fails to comply with an information requirement, or

(b)   a person whose benefit has been suspended in accordance with regulations under paragraph 14 for failing to comply with such a requirement,

shall cease to be entitled to the benefit from a date not earlier than the date on which payments were suspended.

Analysis

See reg 14 D&A Regs on p968.

Decisions involving issues that arise on appeal in other cases

16.–(1)   This paragraph applies where–

(a)   a relevant decision, or a decision under paragraph 3 about the revision of an earlier decision, falls to be made in any particular case; and

(b)   an appeal is pending against the decision given in another case by [the Upper Tribunal] or a court.

(2)   A relevant authority need not make the decision while the appeal is pending if they consider it possible that the result of the appeal will be such that, if it were already determined, there would be no entitlement to benefit.

(3)   If a relevant authority consider it possible that the result of the appeal will be such that, if it were already determined, it would affect the decision in some other way–

(a)   they need not, except in such cases or circumstances as may be prescribed, make the decision while the appeal is pending;

(b)   they may, in such cases or circumstances as may be prescribed, make the decision on such basis as may be prescribed.

(4)   Where–

(a)   a relevant authority act in accordance with sub-paragraph (3)(b), and

(b)   following the making of the determination it is appropriate for their decision to be revised,

they shall then revise their decision (under paragraph 3) in accordance with that determination.

(5)   For the purposes of this paragraph, an appeal against a decision is pending if–

(a)   an appeal against the decision has been brought but not determined;

(b)   an application for leave to appeal against the decision has been made but not determined; or

(c)   the time within which–

(i)   an application for leave to appeal may be made, or

(ii)   an appeal against the decision may be brought,

has not expired and the circumstances are such as may be prescribed.

(6)   In paragraphs (a), (b) and (c) of sub-paragraph (5), any reference to an appeal against a decision, or to an application for leave to appeal against a decision, includes a reference to–

(a)   an application for judicial review of the decision under section 31 of the Supreme Court Act 1981 or for leave to apply for judicial review; or

(b)   an application to the supervisory jurisdiction of the Court of Session in respect of the decision.

(7)   In sub-paragraph (1)(b) the reference to another case–

(a)   includes a reference to a case involving a decision made, or falling to be made, by a different relevant authority; but

(b)   does not include a reference to a case relating to another benefit unless the other benefit is housing benefit *[or council tax benefit]*.

Amendment

1.   Amended by art 9 and Sch 3 para 190(11) of SI 2008 No 2833 as from 3.11.08.

Analysis

Para 16 is concerned with situations where an appeal in another case (known as a "test case") is pending and a decision falls to be made on a claim or through a revision (known as a "look-alike case"). It enables the local authority to postpone making the decision in the look-alike case until the decision is made in the test case. See para 18 where a decision has already been made on a test case.

Sub-para (2) temporarily absolves the authority from its duty to make the decision if it is *possible* that the result of the appeal would result in nil entitlement.

Sub-paras (3) and (4) deal with cases where there would be some other effect on the decision (such as a change in the rate of benefit). See reg 15 D&A Regs on p970 for the cases in which a decision may nonetheless be made. If the decision turns out to be wrong following the decision on the pending appeal, sub-para (4) requires the decision to be revised.

Sub-paras (5) to (7) deal with the type of appeals with which the court is concerned. Sub-paras (5) and (7) are identical to paras 13(3) and (4): see the Analysis to those provisions. Sub-para (6) confirms that "appeal" includes pending applications for judicial review in these circumstances.

Appeals involving issues that arise on appeal in other cases

17.–(1) This paragraph applies where–
(a) an appeal ("appeal A") in relation to a relevant decision (whether as originally made or as revised under paragraph 3) is made to [¹ the First-tier Tribunal, or from the First-tier Tribunal to the Upper Tribunal]; and
(b) an appeal ("appeal B") is pending against a decision given in a different case by [¹ the Upper Tribunal] or a court.

(2) If the relevant authority whose decision gave rise to appeal A consider it possible that the result of appeal B will be such that, if it were already determined, it would affect the determination of appeal A, they may serve notice requiring the [¹ First-tier Tribunal or Upper Tribunal]–
(a) not to determine appeal A but to refer it to them; or
(b) to deal with the appeal in accordance with sub-paragraph (4).

(3) Where appeal A is referred to the authority under sub-paragraph (2)(a), following the determination of appeal B and in accordance with that determination, they shall if appropriate–
(a) in a case where appeal A has not been determined by the [¹ First-tier Tribunal], revise (under paragraph 3) their decision which gave rise to that appeal; or
(b) in a case where appeal A has been determined by the [¹ First-tier Tribunal], make a decision (under paragraph 4) superseding the tribunal's decision.

(4) Where appeal A is to be dealt with in accordance with this sub-paragraph, the [¹ First-tier Tribunal or Upper Tribunal] shall either–
(a) stay appeal A until appeal B is determined; or
(b) if the [¹ First-tier Tribunal or Upper Tribunal] considers it to be in the interests of the appellant to do so, determine appeal A as if–
(i) appeal B had already been determined; and
(ii) the issues arising on appeal B had been decided in the way that was most unfavourable to the appellant.

(5) Where the [¹ First-tier Tribunal or Upper Tribunal] acts in accordance with sub-paragraph (4)(b), following the determination of appeal B the relevant authority whose decision gave rise to appeal A shall, if appropriate, make a decision (under paragraph 4) superseding the decision of the [¹ First-tier Tribunal or Upper Tribunal] in accordance with that determination.

(6) For the purposes of this paragraph, an appeal against a decision is pending if–
(a) an appeal against the decision has been brought but not determined;
(b) an application for leave to appeal against the decision has been made but not determined; or
(c) the time within which–
(i) an application for leave to appeal may be made, or
(ii) an appeal against the decision may be brought,
has not expired and the circumstances are such as may be prescribed.

(7) In this paragraph–
(a) the reference in sub-paragraph (1)(a) to an appeal to [¹ the Upper Tribunal] includes a reference to an application for leave to appeal to [¹ the Upper Tribunal];
(b) the reference in sub-paragraph (1)(b) to a different case–
(i) includes a reference to a case involving a different relevant authority; but
(ii) does not include a reference to a case relating to a different benefit unless the different benefit is housing benefit or council tax benefit; and
(c) any reference in paragraph (a), (b) or (c) of sub-paragraph (6) to an appeal, or to an application for leave to appeal, against a decision includes a reference to–
(i) an application for judicial review of the decision under section 31 of the Supreme Court Act 1981 or for leave to apply for judicial review; or
(ii) an application to the supervisory jurisdiction of the Court of Session in respect of the decision.

(8) In sub-paragraph (4) "the appellant" means the person who appealed or, as the case may be, first appealed against the decision mentioned in sub-paragraph (1)(a).

(9) Regulations may make provision supplementing the provision made by this paragraph.

Commencement

It is understood that the government does not intend to bring para 17 into force.

Amendment

1. Amended by art 9 and Sch 3 para 190(12) of SI 2008 No 2833 (3.11.08).

Restrictions on entitlement to benefit in certain cases of error

18.–(1) Subject to sub-paragraph (2), this paragraph applies where–

(a) the effect of the determination, whenever made, of an appeal [¹ to the Upper Tribunal] or the court ("the relevant determination") is that the relevant authority's decision out of which the appeal arose was erroneous in point of law; and

(b) after the date of the relevant determination a decision falls to be made by that relevant authority or another relevant authority in accordance with that determination (or would, apart from this paragraph, fall to be so made)–

 (i) in relation to a claim for housing benefit *[or council tax benefit]*;

 (ii) as to whether to revise, under paragraph 3, a decision as to a person's entitlement to such a benefit; or

 (iii) on an application made under paragraph 4 for a decision as to a person's entitlement to such a benefit to be superseded.

(2) This paragraph does not apply where the decision mentioned in sub-paragraph (1)(b)–

(a) is one which, but for paragraph 16(2) or (3)(a), would have been made before the date of the relevant determination; or

(b) is one made in pursuance of paragraph 17(3) or (5).

(3) In so far as the decision relates to a person's entitlement to benefit in respect of a period before the date of the relevant determination, it shall be made as if the relevant authority's decision had been found by [¹ the Upper Tribunal] or court not to have been erroneous in point of law.

(4) Sub-paragraph (1)(a) shall be read as including a case where–

(a) the effect of the relevant determination is that part or all of a purported regulation or order is invalid; and

(b) the error of law made by the relevant authority was to act on the basis that the purported regulation or order (or the part held to be invalid) was valid.

(5) It is immaterial for the purposes of sub-paragraph (1)–

(a) where such a decision as is mentioned in paragraph (b)(i) falls to be made, whether the claim was made before or after the date of the relevant determination;

(b) where such a decision as is mentioned in paragraph (b)(ii) or (iii) falls to be made on an application under paragraph 3 or (as the case may be) 4, whether the application was made before or after that date.

(6) In this paragraph "the court" means–

(a) the High Court;

(b) the Court of Appeal;

(c) the Court of Session;

(d) the House of Lords; or

(e) the Court of Justice of the European Community.

(7) For the purposes of this paragraph, any reference to entitlement to benefit includes a reference to entitlement–

(a) to any increase in the rate of a benefit; or

(b) to a benefit, or increase of benefit, at a particular rate.

(8) The date of the relevant determination shall, in prescribed cases, be determined for the purposes of this paragraph in accordance with any regulations made for that purpose.

(9) Regulations made under sub-paragraph (8) may include provision–

(a) for a determination of a higher court to be treated as if it had been made on the date of a determination by a lower court or by [¹ the Upper Tribunal]; or

(b) for a determination of a lower court or of [¹ the Upper Tribunal] to be treated as if it had been made on the date of a determination by a higher court.

Commencement

2.7.01, with the exception of para 18(2)(b) which has not been brought into force and it is understood that, as with para 17 to which it refers, it will not be brought into force.

Amendment

1. Amended by art 9 and Sch 3 para 190(13) of SI 2008 No 2833 as from 3.11.08.

Analysis

The aim of this para, known as the "anti-test case" rule, is to prevent large numbers of appellants taking advantage of a favourable ruling of the Upper Tribunal or of the court by deeming the law to have been as it had always previously been thought to be, except in relation to the successful appellant. It is an invidious and capricious concept and previous attempts by the then DSS to create a similar effect, principally in s69 SSAA (now repealed and replaced by s27 SSA 1998), caused a great deal of uncertainty and litigation.

It is suggested that para 18 may be vulnerable to challenge under Art 6 of the European Convention on Human Rights. In *Osman v UK* (1998) 29 EHRR 245, ECtHR, it was established that to create an exclusionary rule which prevented effective access to a court would infringe Art 6. As claimants caught by para 18 are effectively excluded from an effective remedy through the appeals system, it must be open to question whether para 18 complies with Art 6. Any challenge would, however, have to proceed by way of an application for a declaration of incompatibility since para 18 is primary legislation. The reasoning of the House of Lords in *Chief Adjudication Officer v Bate* [1996] 1 WLR 814 provides some support and justification for the existence of these rules.

See para 16 for the rules which allow a local authority to postpone making a decision pending a decision in a test case.

Sub-paragraphs (1), (2) and (4) to (6): Application of the rule

Sub-para (1) states the basic situation in which the rule takes effect. It deals with a decision ("decision B" – the "look-alike" case) that falls to be made after a decision of a court, as defined in sub-para (6), or the Upper Tribunal ("decision A" – the "test case"). This only applies where decision B is a decision on a claim, an application for a supersession under para 4 or as to whether to revise under para 3 (see sub-para (1)(b)). Where someone wants to challenge a decision on entitlement to HB as a result of a test case decision, the "anti-test case" rule can therefore be avoided by appealing against rather than seeking a revision or a supersession of the decision: see *CH 532/2006* and *CH 533/2006*.

First-tier Tribunal decisions are not, of course, binding and do not make the rule take effect. Decision A, termed "the relevant determination", must have been that the relevant authority's initial decision was erroneous in law. "Relevant authority" refers to the authority involved in the case before the court or commissioner, which may be different from the authority required to make decision B on which the rule bites.

The decision which was appealed to create decision A must have been "erroneous in point of law". In many cases, a point of principle is stated by a court or more often by a commissioner that was not considered by the authority at all. Thus it is entirely possible that an authority makes a decision which is overturned on the facts by the First-tier Tribunal. The authority then subsequently appeals to the Upper Tribunal, who in decision A upholds the First-tier Tribunal's decision on the facts and gives guidance as to the law. Unless it is clear that the commissioner finds some flaw in the *legal* approach of the council as opposed to its conclusions of fact, it would seem that the rule cannot bite in such a situation.

Another point of uncertainty concerns whether decision B is made "in accordance with that determination", that is in accordance with decision A. What happens if there is another binding decision, decision C, made prior to decision A but which the authority was bound to apply? In the past the former social security commissioners have given decisions, the implications of which are not realised until a further decision which achieves a greater degree of publicity. In these circumstances, it is the earliest authoritative decision which must be looked at for the purposes of deciding the relevant date: *R(FC) 3/98* (para 7) and *R(I) 1/03* (the latter is a decision of a tribunal of commissioners).

Sub-para (2) limits some of the most unfair effects of the rule by disapplying it in cases where a suspension was imposed under para 16 so as to avoid making a decision prior to decision A. However, there may be difficulties in ascertaining whether a decision "would have been made" prior to the date of decision A. It is suggested that it should be assumed that the authority is complying with the time limit imposed by reg 89(2) HB Regs and the HB(SPC) equivalent. There is no specific time limit for the carrying out of a revision or supersession but it is suggested that they ought to be carried out as soon as all relevant information is before the authority, which may be as soon as the application is made.

Sub-para (4) contains an extraordinary and profoundly undemocratic provision. Under this sub-paragraph, where the error of law that is identified in decision A is the application of a regulation which turns out to be *ultra vires*, the authority must assume the regulation to be valid for the purposes of applying this rule. Parliament appears to have effectively approved the making of any rules, even those clearly outside the scope of the enabling powers, as having what may be substantial effects on the entitlements of claimants. In this way, regulations may have effect prior to "the relevant determination" even if made in breach of consultation procedures designed to protect claimants or even, apparently, if made in bad faith or in breach of the European Convention on Human Rights. It is the sort of legislation designed to recreate the discredited approach of the first half of the twentieth century, namely that it is the Secretary of State (and hence the local authorities acting under her/his guidance) who determines the validity of regulations rather than the courts. It is not an exaggeration to say that provisions such as sub-para (4) undermine the rule of law.

Sub-para (5) confirms that the rule bites whenever the claim or application for revision or supersession was made.

Sub-paragraphs (3) and (7): The effect of the rule

Sub-para (3) states the effect of the rule. In relation to the period prior to decision A being made (and therefore not from the date of that decision), entitlement to benefit must be determined in decision B as if the authority's decision under attack in the proceedings giving rise to decision A was correct. Thus if decision A means that there was entitlement to benefit when decision A was on an appeal from an initial refusal of benefit, no benefit will be payable prior to the date of decision A. Similarly, where more benefit is payable as a result of decision A, the rule takes effect so as to deprive the claimant in decision B of that additional benefit in relation to the period prior to decision A: sub-para (7).

Sub-paragraphs (8) and (9): Regulations

No regulations have yet been made under sub-paras (8) and (9) and it is accordingly suggested that the normal rules will apply for ascertaining when a judgment takes effect.

In England and Wales, a court judgment normally takes effect from the day on which it is made or such later date as the court may specify: r40.7 Civil Procedure Rules 1998. In Scotland, a court decree is enforceable once the successful party has been issued with an extract decree. In the Sheriff Court, this is normally 14 days after the date of the decree. In the Court of Session, this is normally seven days after the date of the decree. In certain types of cases these periods can be shortened.

Correction of errors and setting aside of decisions

19.–(1)   Regulations may make provision with respect to–

(a)   the correction of accidental errors in any decision or record of a decision made [¹ by the relevant authority] under or by virtue of any relevant provision; [¹]

[¹ (b)]

(2)   Nothing in sub-paragraph (1) shall be construed as derogating from any power to correct errors [¹] which is exercisable apart from regulations made by virtue of that sub-paragraph.

(3)   In this paragraph "relevant provision" means–

(a)   any of the provisions of this Schedule;

(b)   any of the provisions of Part VII of the Social Security Contributions and Benefits Act 1992 so far as they relate to housing benefit or council tax benefit; or

(c)   any of the provisions of Part VIII of the Administration Act or of any regulations under section 2A of that Act, so far as the provisions or regulations relate to, or to arrangements for, housing benefit or council tax benefit.

Amendment

1.   Amended by art 9 and Sch 3 para 190(14) of SI 2008 No 2833 as from 3.11.08.

Analysis

This para permits local authorities to correct accidental errors in their decisions.

Until 3 November 2008, para 19 also governed the correction and setting aside of tribunal decisions: see now rr36 and 37 TP(FT) Rules on p1018.

Regulations

20.–(1)   The power to make regulations under this Schedule shall be [¹ exercisable by the Secretary of State]

(2)   Any power conferred by this Schedule to make regulations shall include power to make different provision for different areas or different relevant authorities.

(3)   Subsections (3) to (7) of section 79 of the Social Security Act 1998 (supplemental provision in connection with powers to make subordinate legislation under that Act) shall apply to any power to make regulations under this Schedule as they apply to any power to make regulations under that Act.

(4)   A statutory instrument containing (whether alone or with other provisions) regulations under paragraph 6(2)(e) or (4) shall not be made unless a draft of the instrument has been laid before Parliament and approved by a resolution of each House.

(5)   A statutory instrument–

(a)   which contains (whether alone or with other provisions) regulations made under this Schedule, and

(b)   which is not subject to any requirement that a draft of the instrument be laid before and approved by a resolution of each House of Parliament,

shall be subject to annulment in pursuance of a resolution of either House of Parliament.

[¹ (6)]

Amendment

1.   Amended by art 9 and Sch 3 para 190(15) of SI 2008 No 2833 as from 3.11.08.

Interpretation

23.–(1)   In this Schedule–

"the Administration Act" means the Social Security Administration Act 1992;

"affected" shall be construed subject to any regulations under sub-paragraph (2);

[¹]

[¹]

[¹]

"prescribed" means prescribed by regulations under this Schedule;

"relevant authority" has the meaning given by paragraph 1(1);

"relevant decision" has the meaning given by paragraph 1(2).

(2)   Regulations may make provision specifying the circumstances in which a person is or is not to be treated for the purposes of this Schedule as a person who is affected by any decision of a relevant authority.

(3)   For the purposes of this Schedule any decision that is made or falls to be made–

(a)   by a person authorised to carry out any function of a relevant authority relating to housing benefit or council tax benefit, or

(b)   by a person providing services relating to housing benefit or council tax benefit directly or indirectly to a relevant authority,

shall be treated as a decision of the relevant authority on whose behalf the function is carried out or, as the case may be, to whom those services are provided.

Amendment

1.   Amended by art 9 and Sch 3 para 190(16) of SI 2008 No 2833 as from 3.11.08.

Analysis

Sub-para (3) permits delegation of decision making functions in relation to HB either to officers authorised by local authorities to carry out their functions, or to contractors. The wording "directly or indirectly" covers cases of employees of contractors or, indeed, of sub-contractors.

PART 2
Arrangements to Modify the Office of Lord Chancellor
Continued judicial independence

Guarantee of continued judicial independence

3.–(1)   The Lord Chancellor, other Ministers of the Crown and all with responsibility for matters relating to the judiciary or otherwise to the administration of justice must uphold the continued independence of the judiciary.

(2)   Subsection (1) does not impose any duty which it would be within the legislative competence of the Scottish Parliament to impose.

(3)   *[Omitted]*

(4)   The following particular duties are imposed for the purpose of upholding that independence.

(5)   The Lord Chancellor and other Ministers of the Crown must not seek to influence particular judicial decisions through any special access to the judiciary.

(6)   The Lord Chancellor must have regard to–

(a)   the need to defend that independence;

(b)   the need for the judiciary to have the support necessary to enable them to exercise their functions;

(c)   the need for the public interest in regard to matters relating to the judiciary or otherwise to the administration of justice to be properly represented in decisions affecting those matters.

(7)   In this section "the judiciary" includes the judiciary of any of the following–

(a)   the Supreme Court;

(b)   any other court established under the law of any part of the United Kingdom;

(c)   any international court.

[¹ (7A)   In this section "the judiciary" also includes every person who–

(a)   holds an office listed in Schedule 14 or holds an office listed in subsection (7B), and

(b)   but for this subsection would not be a member of the judiciary for the purposes of this section.

(7B)   The offices are those of–

(a)   Senior President of Tribunals;

(b)-(e) *[Omitted]*

(8)   In subsection (7) "international court" means the International Court of Justice or any other court or tribunal which exercises jurisdiction, or performs functions of a judicial nature, in pursuance of–

(a)   an agreement to which the United Kingdom or Her Majesty's Government in the United Kingdom is a party, or

(b)   a resolution of the Security Council or General Assembly of the United Nations.

Amendment

1.   Amended by s1 Tribunals, Courts and Enforcement Act 2007 (19.9.2007)

SCHEDULE 14

SECTION 85

The Judicial Appointments Commission: Relevant Offices And Enactments

Part 1
Appointments by her Majesty

[¹ Judge of the Upper Tribunal by appointment under paragraph 1(1) of Schedule 3 to the Tribunals, Courts and Enforcement Act 2007

Paragraph 1(1) of Schedule 3 to the Tribunals, Courts and Enforcement Act 2007]

Part 3
Appointments by The Lord Chancellor: Offices to which Paragraph 2(2)(d) of Schedule 12 Applies

[¹ Chamber President of a chamber of the First-tier Tribunal, or of a chamber of the Upper Tribunal, by appointment under section 7(7) of the Tribunals, Courts and Enforcement Act 2007, but not where appointed in accordance with paragraph 2(2) to (5) of Schedule 4 to that Act

Section 7(7) of the Tribunals, Courts and Enforcement Act 2007

Judge of the First-tier Tribunal by appointment under paragraph 1(1) of Schedule 2 to the Tribunals, Courts and Enforcement Act 2007

Paragraph 1(1) of Schedule 2 to the Tribunals, Courts and Enforcement Act 2007

Other member of the First-tier Tribunal by appointment under paragraph 2(1) of Schedule 2 to the Tribunals, Courts and Enforcement Act 2007

Paragraph 2(1) of Schedule 2 to the Tribunals, Courts and Enforcement Act 2007

Other member of the Upper Tribunal by appointment under paragraph 2(1) of Schedule 3 to the Tribunals, Courts and Enforcement Act 2007

Paragraph 2(1) of Schedule 3 to the Tribunals, Courts and Enforcement Act 2007

Deputy judge of the Upper Tribunal by appointment under paragraph 7(1) of Schedule 3 to the Tribunals, Courts and Enforcement Act 2007

Paragraph 7(1) of Schedule 3 to the Tribunals, Courts and Enforcement Act 2007

Deputy Chamber President of a chamber of the First-tier Tribunal, or of a chamber of the Upper Tribunal, but not where appointed in accordance with paragraph 5(5) to (8) of Schedule 4 to the Tribunals, Courts and Enforcement Act 2007

Paragraph 5(1) of Schedule 4 to the Tribunals, Courts and Enforcement Act 2007]

Amendment

1. Amended by Sch 8 para 66 Tribunals, Courts and Enforcement Act 2007 (3.11. 2008).

Welfare Reform Act 2007
(2007 c5)

Loss of housing benefit following eviction for anti-social behaviour, etc.

31.–(1)-(2)   *[Omitted]*

(3)   The preceding provisions of this section have no effect after 31st December 2010.

(4)   The Secretary of State may by order made by statutory instrument make such provision as he thinks necessary or expedient in consequence of the operation of subsection (3) for the purpose of securing that, with effect from 1st January 2011, housing benefit to which a person who is a former occupier (within the meaning of section 130B of the Contributions and Benefits Act) is entitled is not subject to any restriction as mentioned in subsection (4) of that section.

Commencement

14.6.07 for the purpose only of the exercise of the power to make regulations; 1.11.07 for all other purposes.

General Note

Section 31(1) of the this Act inserted ss130B–130G into the SSCBA 1992 and s31(2) amended s176 of that Act. By s31(3), these provisions have no effect after 31 December 2010.

Housing benefit *[and council tax benefit]* for persons taking up employment

32.–(1)   Subsection (2) applies if a person is entitled to housing benefit *[or council tax benefit]* (by virtue of the general conditions of entitlement) and–

(a)   he is also entitled to a prescribed benefit or his partner is entitled to such a benefit,

(b)   he or his partner ceases to be entitled to the prescribed benefit in prescribed circumstances, and

(c)   the prescribed conditions are satisfied.

(2)   That person is entitled to housing benefit *[or council tax benefit]* in accordance with this section for a prescribed period.

(3)   Subsection (2) applies whether or not the person would be entitled to housing benefit *[or council tax benefit]* by virtue of the general conditions of entitlement for the whole or any part of the prescribed period.

(4)   A person who is entitled to housing benefit *[or council tax benefit]* by virtue of subsection (2) must be treated for all purposes–

(a)   as having made a claim for that benefit, and

(b)   as having complied with any requirement under or by virtue of any enactment in connection with the making of such a claim.

(5)   Housing benefit or council tax benefit to which a person is entitled by virtue of subsection (2) is to be funded and administered by the appropriate authority.

(6)   Subsection (5) applies whether or not, for the whole or any part of the prescribed period–

(a)   for the purposes of establishing an entitlement to housing benefit, the person occupies as his home a dwelling in the area of the authority;

[(b)   for the purposes of establishing an entitlement to council tax benefit, the person is a resident of a dwelling in the area of the authority.]

(7)   The amount of housing benefit or council tax benefit payable in respect of a person who is entitled to the benefit by virtue of subsection (2) is to be determined in accordance with regulations made for the purposes of this section.

(8)   If an amount of housing benefit *[or council tax benefit]* is, by virtue of subsection (2), payable in respect of a person by the appropriate authority for any period, no other amount of housing benefit *[or council tax benefit]* is (by virtue of the general conditions of entitlement) payable by that authority in respect of that person for the same period.

(9)   Regulations may make provision in connection with the effect of a person's entitlement to housing benefit or council tax benefit by virtue of subsection (2) on an

award of such benefit by virtue of the general conditions of entitlement in respect of that person or his partner.

(10)   Regulations may provide that where–

(a)   an amount of housing benefit *[or council tax benefit]* is, by virtue of subsection (2), payable in respect of a person by the appropriate authority for the whole or any part of a prescribed period, and

(b)   an amount of housing benefit *[or council tax benefit]* is (by virtue of the general conditions of entitlement) payable by a local authority which is not that appropriate authority in respect of that person for the whole or any part of that period,

the amount of the benefit payable by the local authority mentioned in paragraph (b) is to be reduced by an amount determined in such manner as is prescribed.

(11)   An amount determined for the purposes of subsection (10) may have the effect of reducing the amount mentioned in paragraph (b) of that subsection to nil.

(12)   Regulations may make provision as to circumstances in which–

(a)   subsection (8) does not apply;

(b)   entitlement to housing benefit *[or council tax benefit]* of a partner of the person mentioned in subsection (10) is to be treated as the entitlement of that person;

(c)   benefit is not to be reduced as mentioned in subsection (10).

(13)   For the purposes of subsection (1) a person must be treated as entitled to housing benefit or council tax benefit by virtue of the general conditions of entitlement if–

(a)   he is not so entitled to that benefit at the time he or his partner ceases to be entitled to the prescribed benefit as mentioned in subsection (1)(b), and

(b)   his entitlement to housing benefit *[or council tax benefit (as the case may be)]* ceased during the prescribed period before that time.

Commencement

6.10.08 (1.4.08. to make regulations).

Modification

Section 32 was repealed by WRA 2012 s147 and Sch 14 part 1 on 1.4.13 in so far as it related to CTB.

General Note

Sections 32 to 34 WRA 2007 establish a scheme for "extended payments" of HB to assist people who, having been on a specified benefit for a period, come off that benefit because they (or their partners) commence employment (or self-employment) or increase hours or earnings. The scheme provides financial assistance, in the form of continuing entitlement to HB, in the early weeks of that employment. Section 33 deals with administrative matters and s34 with interpretation. Note that prior to 1 April 2013, it also provided a scheme for extended payments of CTB and thus continuing entitlement to CTB. See previous editions of this book for details. From 1 April 2013, the localised council tax reduction schemes may provide such assistance (see Parts 4 and 5).

There are currently two schemes for extended payments of HB.

(1)   Extended payments of HB paid where the claimant or her/his partner was entitled to a "qualifying income-related benefit", defined as IS, income-based JSA (including joint-claim JSA) or income-related ESA: regs 2 and 72 to 72E HB Regs. Note that although there are no equivalent rules in the HB(SPC) Regs, claimants of at least the qualifying age for PC who were (or whose partners were) entitled to a qualifying income-related benefit and who satisfy the other rules of entitlement to extended payments would qualify for these under the HB Regs: see reg 5(1)(b) of the HB Regs. The amount of HB payable under the normal rules of entitlement can then be adjusted: reg 52 HB(SPC) Regs.

(2)   Extended payments of HB paid where the claimant or her/his partner was entitled to a "qualifying contributory benefit", defined as incapacity benefit, contributory ESA or severe disablement allowance: regs 2 and 73 to 73E HB Regs; regs 2 and 53 to 53D HB(SPC) Regs.

Note: under separate rules, there is a two week continuation of entitlement to HB (a transitional HB payment) for those who make a new claim for UC, whatever the reason for the claim. See regs 8 and 8A of the UC(TP) Regs on p1870 and p1871.

Analysis

Subss (1) to (3). Subs (1) sets out the general rules for entitlement to extended payments of HB. The prescribed benefits, circumstances and conditions are all to be found in regs 2, 72 and 73 HB Regs and regs 2 and 53 HB(SPC) Regs. The "general conditions of entitlement" are those in Part 7 of the SSCBA 1992: s34(2).

If the conditions for extended payments are met, HB entitlement continues for a prescribed period, even if it would otherwise cease (ie, if based on the claimant's new circumstances): subss (2) and (3). The prescribed period is one of up to four weeks: regs 72A and 73A HB Regs; reg 53A HB(SPC) Regs.

Subs (4) ensures that no claim for extended payments is required by deeming a person to have made such a claim and to have complied with any requirements for making a claim for HB.

Subss (5) and (6). Extended payments are funded and administered by the "appropriate authority", defined in s34(3) and (4) as the authority that funded and administered, as the case may be, the claimant's HB immediately before entitlement to the qualifying income-related or contributory benefit ceased. This is particularly relevant to "movers", that is, certain claimants who move from the area of one authority to another: regs 72C and 73C HB Regs; reg 53C HB(SPC) Regs.

Subss (7) and (8). The amount of extended payments is dealt with in regs 72B, 72C, 72E, 73B, 73C and 73E HB Regs and regs 53B and 53C HB (SPC) Regs.

Subss (9) to (12) prevent duplication of payments – eg, where a claimant receiving extended payments has a partner who claims HB in respect of the same period. See regs 72B(7), 72C(4), 73B(7) and 73C(4) HB Regs and regs 52, 53B(7) and 53C(4) HB(SPC) Regs.

Section 32: supplemental

33.–(1)   The administration provisions apply in relation to housing benefit *[or council tax benefit]* to which a person is entitled by virtue of subsection (2) of section 32 subject to–

(a)   subsections (4), (5) and (6) of that section;

(b)   any prescribed modifications of those provisions which the Secretary of State thinks are necessary or expedient in connection with such housing benefit or council tax benefit.

(2)   Modifications under subsection (1)(b) may, in particular, provide that housing benefit *[or council tax benefit]* to which a person is entitled by virtue of section 32(2) must or may take the form of a payment by the appropriate authority to another local authority in prescribed circumstances.

(3)   In this section the administration provisions are–

(a)   the Administration Act;

(b)   subordinate legislation (within the meaning of the Interpretation Act 1978 (c. 30)) made in pursuance of that Act.

(4)   The power to make regulations under this section or section 32 is exercisable by the Secretary of State by statutory instrument.

(5)   A statutory instrument containing regulations under this section or section 32 is subject to annulment in pursuance of a resolution of either House of Parliament.

(6)   Section 175(3) to (7) of the Contributions and Benefits Act (supplemental provision as to regulations) applies in relation to regulations under this section and section 32 above as it applies in relation to regulations under that Act.

(7)   *[Omitted]*

(8)   For the purposes of any enactment other than a relevant enactment–

(a)   entitlement to housing benefit by virtue of section 32(2) above is to be treated as entitlement under section 130 of the Contributions and Benefits Act;

[(b)   entitlement to council tax benefit by virtue of section 32(2) above is to be treated as entitlement under section 131 of that Act.]

(9)   In subsection (8), the relevant enactments are–

(a)   the administration provisions, and

(b)   Part 7 of the Contributions and Benefits Act, except sections 123 and 134(2) and (4).

Commencement

6.10.08 (1.4.08. to make regulations).

Modification

Section 33 was repealed by WRA 2012 s147 and Sch 14 Part 1 on 1.4.13 in so far as it related to CTB.

General Note

This deals with administrative matters in respect of the scheme for extended payments of HB (and until 1 April 2013 CTB). See the commentary to s32.

Sections 32 and 33: interpretation

34.–(1) This section has effect for the interpretation of sections 32 and 33.

(2) The general conditions of entitlement are the conditions governing entitlement to housing benefit *[or council tax benefit]* provided for by Part 7 of the Contributions and Benefits Act.

(3) The appropriate authority–

(a) in relation to housing benefit is the local authority or housing authority which, immediately before the person concerned ceased to be entitled to the prescribed benefit, funded and administered the housing benefit to which he was entitled;

[(b) in relation to council tax benefit is the billing authority or, in Scotland, local authority which, immediately before the person concerned ceased to be entitled to the rescribed benefit, funded and administered the council tax benefit to which he was entitled.]

(4) The following expressions have the same meaning as in the Administration Act–

(a) billing authority;

(b) housing authority;

(c) local authority.

(5) Partner, in relation to a person, is a person who is a member of the same couple (within the meaning of Part 7 of the Contributions and Benefits Act) as that person.

(6) Prescribed means prescribed by regulations.

Commencement
6.10.08 (1.4.08. to make regulations).

Modification
Section 34 was repealed by WRA 2012 s147 and Sch 14 part 1 on 1.4.13 in so far as it related to CTB.

General Note
This provides relevant definitions for the scheme for extended payments of HB (and until 1 April 2013 CTB). See the commentary to s32 on p163.

Information relating to certain benefits
[¹42.]

Commencement
5.8.08 for making orders or regulations; 1.9.08 for all other purposes.

Amendment
1.   Repealed by WRA 2012 s133(6) as from 2.7.12.

General Note
The Local Government Act 2000, by s93, introduced a system of grants to organisations providing welfare services such as counselling and support. This system replaced the provision made by Sch 1B of the HB Regs 1987.

Until 1 September 2008, ss94 and 95 of the 2000 Act contained provisions dealing with the disclosure of information. From 1 September 2008 to 2 July 2012, this was dealt with in ss42 and 43 WRA 2007. From 2 July 2012, disclosure of information is dealt with in ss130 to 133 WRA 2012. However, by art 3 of the Welfare Reform Act 2012 (Commencement No.3, Savings Provision) Order 2012 SI No.1651, s42 continues to have effect insofar as it permits the use, supply or provision by any person of information which came to that person before 2 July 2012 (see p1838).

Unlawful disclosure of certain information
[¹43.]

Commencement
5.8.08 (for making orders or regulations); 1.9.08 for all other purposes.

Amendment
1.   Repealed by WRA 2012 s133(6) as from 2.7.12.

General Note
See the General Note to s42. From 2 July 2012, disclosure of information is dealt with in ss130 to 133 WRA 2012. However, by art 3 of the Welfare Reform Act 2012 (Commencement No.3, Savings Provision) Order 2012 SI No.1651, s43 continues to have effect insofar as it relates to the disclosure by any person of information which came to that person before 2 July 2012 (see p1838).

Loss of benefit for commission of benefit offences

49.–(1)   In section 7 of the Social Security Fraud Act 2001 (c. 11) (loss of benefit for commission of benefit offences) in subsection (1)(b) (period within which later offence must be committed), for "three years" substitute "five years".

(2)   The amendment made by subsection (1) shall be disregarded insofar as the application of section 7(1)(b) of that Act involves considering whether an offence committed before the day on which this section comes into force was committed within the relevant period.

Commencement
1.4.08.

General Note
Section 7 SSFA 2001 sets up the so-called "two strikes" scheme for loss of benefit following commission of one or more benefit offences in two separate sets of proceedings. Prior to 1 April 2008, the later conviction must have been committed within three years of the earlier conviction. Para (1) increased this time period to five years. Para (2) makes transitional provisions.

Tribunals, Courts and Enforcement Act 2007
(2007 c15)

PART 1
TRIBUNALS AND INQUIRIES
CHAPTER 1: TRIBUNAL JUDICIARY: INDEPENDENCE AND SENIOR PRESIDENT
2.   Senior President of Tribunals

CHAPTER 2: FIRST-TIER TRIBUNAL AND UPPER TRIBUNAL
Establishment
3.   The First-tier Tribunal and the Upper Tribunal

Members and composition of tribunals
4.   Judges and other members of the First-tier Tribunal
5.   Judges and other members of the Upper Tribunal
6.   Certain judges who are also judges of First-tier Tribunal and Upper Tribunal
6A.   Certain judges who are also judges of the First-tier Tribunal
7.   Chambers: jurisdiction and Presidents
8.   Senior President of Tribunals: power to delegate

Review of decisions and appeals
9.   Review of decision of First-tier Tribunal
10.   Review of decision of Upper Tribunal
11.   Right to appeal to Upper Tribunal
12.   Proceedings on appeal to Upper Tribunal
13.   Right to appeal to Court of Appeal etc.
14.   Proceedings on appeal to Court of Appeal etc.
14A.   Appeal to Supreme Court: grant of certificate by Upper Tribunal
14B.   Appeal to Supreme Court: permission to appeal
14C.   Appeal to Supreme Court: exclusions

"Judicial review"
15.   Upper Tribunal's "judicial review" jurisdiction
16.   Application for relief under section 15(1)
17.   Quashing orders under section 15(1): supplementary provision
18.   Limits of jurisdiction under section 15(1)

Miscellaneous
22.   Tribunal Procedure Rules
23.   Practice directions
24.   Mediation
25.   Supplementary powers of Upper Tribunal
26.   First-tier Tribunal and Upper Tribunal: sitting places
27.   Enforcement
28.   Assessors
29.   Costs or expenses

CHAPTER 3: TRANSFER OF TRIBUNAL FUNCTIONS
30.   Transfer of functions of certain tribunals
31.   Transfers under section 30: supplementary powers
32.   Power to provide for appeal to Upper Tribunal from tribunals in Wales
33.   Power to provide for appeal to Upper Tribunal from tribunals in Scotland
34.   Power to provide for appeal to Upper Tribunal from tribunals in Northern Ireland
35.   Transfer of Ministerial responsibilities for certain tribunals

36.   Transfer of powers to make procedural rules for certain tribunals
37.   Power to amend lists of tribunals in Schedule 6
38.   Orders under sections 30 to 36: supplementary

CHAPTER 4: ADMINISTRATIVE MATTERS IN RESPECT OF CERTAIN TRIBUNALS
39.   The general duty
41.   Provision of accommodation
42.   Fees
43.   Report by Senior President of Tribunals

CHAPTER 5: OVERSIGHT OF ADMINISTRATIVE JUSTICE SYSTEM, TRIBUNALS AND
INQUIRIES
44.   The Administrative Justice and Tribunals Council
45.   Abolition of the Council on Tribunals

CHAPTER 6: SUPPLEMENTARY
49.   Orders and regulations under Part 1: supplemental and procedural provisions
Schedule 5: Procedure in First-tier Tribunal and Upper Tribunal
Schedule 6: Tribunals for the purposes of sections 30 to 36
Schedule 10: Amendments relating to judicial appointments

PART 1
Tribunals and Inquiries
Chapter 2
First-tier Tribunal and Upper Tribunal
Establishment

Senior President of Tribunals

2.–(1)   Her Majesty may, on the recommendation of the Lord Chancellor, appoint a person to the office of Senior President of Tribunals.

(2)   Schedule 1 makes further provision about the Senior President of Tribunals and about recommendations for appointment under subsection (1).

(3)   A holder of the office of Senior President of Tribunals must, in carrying out the functions of that office, have regard to–

(a)   the need for tribunals to be accessible,

(b)   the need for proceedings before tribunals–
          (i)   to be fair, and
          (ii)   to be handled quickly and efficiently,

(c)   the need for members of tribunals to be experts in the subject-matter of, or the law to be applied in, cases in which they decide matters, and

(d)   the need to develop innovative methods of resolving disputes that are of a type that may be brought before tribunals.

(4)   In subsection (3) "tribunals" means–

(a)   the First-tier Tribunal,

(b)   the Upper Tribunal,

(c)-(e) *[Omitted]*

Commencement
19.9.07.

General Note
The Senior President of Tribunals is the Rt Hon Lord Justice Ryder.

The First-tier Tribunal and the Upper Tribunal

3.–(1)   There is to be a tribunal, known as the First-tier Tribunal, for the purpose of exercising the functions conferred on it under or by virtue of this Act or any other Act.

(2)   There is to be a tribunal, known as the Upper Tribunal, for the purpose of exercising the functions conferred on it under or by virtue of this Act or any other Act.

(3)   Each of the First-tier Tribunal, and the Upper Tribunal, is to consist of its judges and other members.

(4)   The Senior President of Tribunals is to preside over both of the First-tier Tribunal and the Upper Tribunal.

(5)   The Upper Tribunal is to be a superior court of record.

Commencement
3.11.08.

General Note
The First-tier Tribunal and Upper Tribunal came into existence on 3 November 2008, as part of a programme of tribunal reform going far beyond social security appeals. On the same date:
(1)   Appeal tribunals and the social security commissioners were abolished (except for certain purposes in Scotland that have nothing to do with HB) (see art 4 of, and Sch 1 to, SI 2008 No.2833 on p1057).
(2)   The functions of appeal tribunals were transferred to the First-tier Tribunal and those of the commissioners to the Upper Tribunal (art 3 of, and Sch 1 to, SI 2008 No.2833 on p1057).
(3)   Sch 7 of CSPSSA was amended so that new appeals against local authority decisions about HB or CTB lie to the First-tier Tribunal rather than to an appeal tribunal.
(4)   Legally-qualified panel members of appeal tribunals became judges of the First-tier Tribunal and commissioners became judges of the Upper Tribunal.
(5)   Medically-, disability-, and financially-qualified members of appeal tribunals became members of the First-tier Tribunal.
(6)   New procedural rules came into force for both the First-tier Tribunal and the Upper Tribunal.
Administrative support for both the First-tier Tribunal and the Upper Tribunal is supplied by HM Courts and Tribunals Service (HMCTS), an executive agency of the Ministry of Justice. However, the two tribunals are not themselves part of HMCTS. HMCTS staff are civil servants responsible ultimately to the Lord Chancellor. The judges and members of the two tribunals are members of the judiciary with a guarantee of independence under s3 Constitutional Reform Act 2005.

Subs (5) provides that the Upper Tribunal is to be a "superior court of record". It is not clear what the practical consequences of this designation are or, indeed, whether it has any practical consequences. It was once suggested that the phrase had the effect that decisions of the Upper Tribunal were not subject to judicial review. However, that possibility has been rejected by both the Court of Appeal (in England and Wales) and the Inner House of the Court of Session (in Scotland) (see *R (Cart and others) v Upper Tribunal and others* [2009] EWHC 3052 at para 35 and [2010] EWCA Civ 859 at paras 16-17; *Eba v Advocate General for Scotland* [2010] CSIH 78 at para 48). It appears from these authorities that the expression is meaningless in Scotland and "a concept of uncertain import" in England and Wales.

Although the Upper Tribunal is not immune from judicial review by virtue of being a "superior court of record", the scope of judicial review in cases where a decision of the Upper Tribunal is challenged is restricted to circumstances in which the "second appeals criteria" are satisfied (see the decisions of the Supreme Court in *R (Cart) v Upper Tribunal* [2011] UKSC 28; [2011] AACR 38 and *Eba v Advocate General for Scotland* [2011] UKSC 29; [2011] AACR 39). The second appeals criteria are those specified in s13(6) TCEA. For the position as regards judicial review of decisions of the former social security commissioners, see p170 of the 23rd edition.

Both the Upper Tribunal and the First-tier Tribunal are "courts" for the purposes of vexatious litigant orders under s 42 Senior Courts Act 1981 (the former Supreme Court Act 1981). This means that if a person has been declared a vexatious litigant, s/he may not appeal to the First-tier Tribunal or the Upper Tribunal without first obtaining the permission of the High Court. The Upper Tribunal does not have power to grant such permission under s25(2)(c) TCEA: see *IB v Information Commissioner* [2011] UKUT 370 (AAC); [2012] AACR 26.

Members and composition of tribunals

Judges and other members of the First-tier Tribunal
    4.–(1)   A person is a judge of the First-tier Tribunal if the person–
(a)   is a judge of the First-tier Tribunal by virtue of appointment under paragraph 1(1) of Schedule 2,
(b)   is a transferred-in judge of the First-tier Tribunal (see section 31(2)),
(c)   is a judge of the Upper Tribunal,
[¹ (ca) is within section 6A,]
(d)-(e) *[Omitted]*
(2)   *[Omitted]*

(3)   A person is one of the other members of the First-tier Tribunal if the person–
(a)   is a member of the First-tier Tribunal by virtue of appointment under paragraph 2(1) of Schedule 2,
(b)   is a transferred-in other member of the First-tier Tribunal (see section 31(2)),
(c)   is one of the other members of the Upper Tribunal, or
(d)   is a member of a panel of members of employment tribunals that is not a panel of chairmen of employment tribunals.
(4)   Schedule 2–
contains provision for the appointment of persons to be judges or other members of the First-tier Tribunal, and
makes further provision in connection with judges and other members of the First-tier Tribunal.

Commencement
3.11.08.

Amendment
1.   Inserted by Sch 14 para 7 of the Crime and Courts Act 2013 as from 1.10.13 (art 3(g) of SI 2013 No.2200).

General Note
People who were chairmen of appeal tribunals on 2 November 2008 automatically became "transferred-in" judges of the First-tier Tribunal the following day. Part-time, fee-paid, judges of the First-tier Tribunal (ie, those who were previously referred to as "Deputy District Chairmen") are known by the informal title of "Tribunal Judge". Salaried judges are known informally as either "District Tribunal Judge" or "Regional Tribunal Judge" depending on the level of their administrative responsibilities.
     Judges and members of the Upper Tribunal are *ex officio* members of the First-tier Tribunal.
     Judges and other members should, strictly, be addressed as "sir" or "madam" when sitting on the First-tier Tribunal (even if their judicial rank would otherwise entitle them to some other title: see s6). However – except, perhaps, from counsel or solicitors – they are unlikely to object to any other respectful form of address.

Judges and other members of the Upper Tribunal

5.–(1)   A person is a judge of the Upper Tribunal if the person–
(a)   is the Senior President of Tribunals,
(b)   is a judge of the Upper Tribunal by virtue of appointment under paragraph 1(1) of Schedule 3,
(c)   is a transferred-in judge of the Upper Tribunal (see section 31(2)),
(d)   *[Omitted]*
(e)   is the Chief Social Security Commissioner, or any other Social Security Commissioner, appointed under section 50(1) of the Social Security Administration (Northern Ireland) Act 1992 (c. 8),
(f)   is a Social Security Commissioner appointed under section 50(2) of that Act (deputy Commissioners),
(g)   is within section 6(1),
(h)   is a deputy judge of the Upper Tribunal (whether under paragraph 7 of Schedule 3 or under section 31(2)), or
(i)   is a Chamber President or a Deputy Chamber President, whether of a chamber of the Upper Tribunal or of a chamber of the First-tier Tribunal, and does not fall within any of paragraphs (a) to (h).
(2)   A person is one of the other members of the Upper Tribunal if the person–
(a)   is a member of the Upper Tribunal by virtue of appointment under paragraph 2(1) of Schedule 3,
(b)   is a transferred-in other member of the Upper Tribunal (see section 31(2)),
(c)-(d) *[Omitted]*
(3)   Schedule 3–
contains provision for the appointment of persons to be judges (including deputy judges), or other members, of the Upper Tribunal, and
makes further provision in connection with judges and other members of the Upper Tribunal.

Commencement
    3.11.08.

General Note
    People who were social security commissioners or deputy social security commissioners on 2 November 2008 automatically became "transferred-in" judges and deputy judges of the Upper Tribunal the following day.

    Under s4(1)(c), judges (and other members) of the Upper Tribunal are *ex officio* members of the First-tier Tribunal. As ss4 and 5 contain no provision equivalent to s6(2), it would appear that this includes part-time judges.

    It is no longer the practice to distinguish informally between a (full-time) "Upper Tribunal Judge" and a (part-time) "Deputy Upper Tribunal Judge". This is because of s5(1)(h) which provides that a "deputy judge of the Upper Tribunal" is a "judge of the Upper Tribunal".

    Judges of the Upper Tribunal should be addressed as "sir" or "madam" when sitting (even if their judicial rank would otherwise entitle them to some other title – see s6).

    Social security commissioners used to sit either alone or as one of a tribunal of commissioners. Upper Tribunal judges may sit with "other members" who are not legally-qualified and subss(3) gives effect to Sch 3, which provides for the appointment of such members. In the Upper Tribunal the equivalent of a tribunal of commissioners is a "three-judge panel" of the Upper Tribunal.

Certain judges who are also judges of First-tier Tribunal and Upper Tribunal

    6.–(1)   A person is within this subsection (and so, by virtue of sections 4(1)(c) and 5(1)(g), is a judge of the First-tier Tribunal and of the Upper Tribunal) if the person–
[¹ (za) is the Lord Chief Justice of England and Wales,
(zb) is the Master of the Rolls,
(zc) is the President of the Queen's Bench Division of the High Court in England and Wales,
(zd) is the President of the Family Division of the High Court in England and Wales,
(ze) is the Chancellor of the High Court in England and Wales,]
(a)   is an ordinary judge of the Court of Appeal in England and Wales (including the vice-president, if any, of either division of that Court),
(b)   is a Lord Justice of Appeal in Northern Ireland,
(c)   is a judge of the Court of Session,
(d)   is a puisne judge of the High Court in England and Wales or Northern Ireland,
[¹ (da) is a deputy judge of the High Court in England and Wales,
(db) is the Judge Advocate General,]
(e)   is a circuit judge,
[² (ea) is a recorder,]
(f)   is a sheriff in Scotland,
(g)   is a county court judge in Northern Ireland,
(h)   is a district judge in England and Wales or Northern Ireland, [² or]
(i)   is a District Judge (Magistrates' Courts).
[² (j) is the President of Employment Tribunals (England and Wales),
(k)   is the President of Employment Tribunals (Scotland),
(l)   is the Vice President of Employment Tribunals (Scotland), or
(m) is a Regional Employment Judge.]
    (2)   References in subsection (1)(c) to (i) to office-holders do not include deputies or temporary office-holders.

Commencement
    3.11.08.

Amendments
    1.   Inserted by Sch 14 para 8 of the Crime and Courts Act 2013 as from 1.10.13 (art 3(g) of SI 2013 No 2200).
    2.   Amended by s1(2) of the Courts and Tribunals (Judiciary and Functions of Staff) Act 2018 as from 20.2.19 (s4(2) of the Act).

General Note
    Almost every salaried judge in the UK is *ex officio* a judge of the First-tier Tribunal and the Upper Tribunal. However, they will only sit as such if ticketed to do so by a Chamber President. It seems unlikely that the senior

members of the judiciary listed in heads (a) to (d) of para (1) will sit on social security appeals other than in exceptional circumstances.

The decision that district judges should automatically be judges of the Upper Tribunal is difficult to justify. District judges are of the same judicial rank (Group 7) as district tribunal judges and of lower rank than regional tribunal judges. District and regional tribunal judges, who are likely to have considerably more experience than district judges in the specialist law and procedures applied by the First-tier Tribunal, are judges of the First-tier Tribunal only, not the Upper Tribunal. Further, it is contrary to principle that a judge should hold a Group 6 office without having been appointed to it – or another equivalent or higher office – in an open competition by the Judicial Appointments Commission.

The judges listed in heads (a) to (d) of para (1) would normally be addressed as "my lord" or "my lady" in court and those in heads (e) to (g) as "your honour". However, when sitting as a judge of either the First-tier Tribunal or Upper Tribunal, they should be addressed as "sir" or "madam".

[¹ Certain judges who are also judges of the First-tier Tribunal

6A.   A person is within this section (and so, by virtue of section 4(1)(ca), is a judge of the First-tier Tribunal) if the person–

(a)   is a deputy Circuit judge,

[²]

(c)   is a person who holds an office listed–

    (i)   in the first column of the table in section 89(3C) of the Senior Courts Act 1981 (senior High Court Masters etc), or

    (ii)   in column 1 of Part 2 of Schedule 2 to that Act (High Court Masters etc),

(d)   is a deputy district judge appointed under section 102 of that Act or section 8 of the County Courts Act 1984,

(e)   is a Deputy District Judge (Magistrates' Court), or

(f)   is a person appointed under section 30(1)(a) or (b) of the Courts-Martial Apeals Act 1951 (assistants to the Judge Advocate General).]

Amendments

1.   Inserted by Sch 14 para 9 of the Crime and Courts Act 2013, with effect from 1.10.13 (art 3(g) of SI 2013 No 2200).

2.   Omitted by s1(3) of the Courts and Tribunals (Judiciary and Functions of Staff) Act 2018, as from 20.2.19 (s4(2) of the Act).

Chambers: jurisdiction and Presidents

7.–(1)   The Lord Chancellor may, with the concurrence of the Senior President of Tribunals, by order make provision for the organisation of each of the First-tier Tribunal and the Upper Tribunal into a number of chambers.

(2)   There is–

(a)   for each chamber of the First-tier Tribunal, and

(b)   for each chamber of the Upper Tribunal,

to be a person, or two persons, to preside over that chamber.

[¹ (3)   A person may at a particular time–

(a)   preside over more than one chamber of the First-tier Tribunal;

(b)   preside over more than one chamber of the Upper Tribunal;

(c)   preside over–

    (i)   one or more chambers of the First-tier Tribunal, and

    (ii)   one or more chambers of the Upper Tribunal.]

(4)   A person appointed under this section to preside over a chamber is to be known as a Chamber President.

(5)   Where two persons are appointed under this section to preside over the same chamber, any reference in an enactment to the Chamber President of the chamber is a reference to a person appointed under this section to preside over the chamber.

(6)   The Senior President of Tribunals may (consistently with [¹ subsection (2)]) appoint a person who is the Chamber President of a chamber to preside instead, or to preside also, over another chamber.

(7)   The Lord Chancellor may (consistently with [¹ subsection (2)]) appoint a person who is not a Chamber President to preside over a chamber.

(8)   Schedule 4 (eligibility for appointment under subsection (7), appointment of Deputy Chamber Presidents and Acting Chamber Presidents, assignment of judges and other members of the First-tier Tribunal and Upper Tribunal, and further provision about Chamber Presidents and chambers) has effect.

(9)   Each of the Lord Chancellor and the Senior President of Tribunals may, with the concurrence of the other, by order–

(a)   make provision for the allocation of the First-tier Tribunal's functions between its chambers;

(b)   make provision for the allocation of the Upper Tribunal's functions between its chambers;

(c)   amend or revoke any order made under this subsection.

Commencement

s7(1) and (9): 19.9.07; all other subsections: 3.11.08.

Amendment

1.   Amended by s1(4) of the Courts and Tribunals (Judiciary and Functions of Staff) Act 2018 as from 20.2.19 (s4(2) of the Act).

General Note

The power to organise the First-tier Tribunal and Upper Tribunal into chambers has been exercised by the First-tier Tribunal and Upper Tribunal (Chambers) Order 2008.

Since 1 July 2013, the First-tier Tribunal has been organised into the Social Entitlement Chamber, the War Pensions and Armed Forces Compensation Chamber, the Health Education and Social Care Chamber, the Immigration and Asylum Chamber, the Tax Chamber, the General Regulatory Chamber and the Property Chamber. Appeals against HB decisions (and other social security benefits and tax credits) are assigned to the Social Entitlement Chamber. From 15 February 2010, the Upper Tribunal has been organised into the Administrative Appeals Chamber, the Tax and Chancery Chamber, the Lands Chamber and the Immigration and Asylum Chamber. Appeals concerning HB (and other social security benefits and tax credits) are heard by the Administrative Appeals Chamber.

Under subs (2) each chamber of the First-tier Tribunal and Upper Tribunal must have at least one "Chamber President". The President of the Social Entitlement Chamber is Judge Aitken. The Acting President of the Administrative Appeals Chamber is Mrs Justice Farbey DBE.

Senior President of Tribunals: power to delegate

8.–(1)   The Senior President of Tribunals may delegate any function he has in his capacity as Senior President of Tribunals–

(a)   to any judge, or other member, of the Upper Tribunal or First-tier Tribunal;

(b)   to staff appointed under section 40(1).

(2)   Subsection (1) does not apply to functions of the Senior President of Tribunals under section 7(9).

(3)   A delegation under subsection (1) is not revoked by the delegator's becoming incapacitated.

(4)   Any delegation under subsection (1) that is in force immediately before a person ceases to be Senior President of Tribunals continues in force until varied or revoked by a subsequent holder of the office of Senior President of Tribunals.

(5)   The delegation under this section of a function shall not prevent the exercise of the function by the Senior President of Tribunals.

Commencement

3.11.08.

General Note

The Senior President of Tribunals may delegate the functions assigned to her/him by s2 as set out in this section.

Review of decisions and appeals

Review of decision of First-tier Tribunal

9.–(1)   The First-tier Tribunal may review a decision made by it on a matter in a case, other than a decision that is an excluded decision for the purposes of section 11(1) (but see subsection (9)).

(2)   The First-tier Tribunal's power under subsection (1) in relation to a decision is exercisable–

(a)   of its own initiative, or

(b)   on application by a person who for the purposes of section 11(2) has a right of appeal in respect of the decision.

(3)   Tribunal Procedure Rules may–

(a)   provide that the First-tier Tribunal may not under subsection (1) review (whether of its own initiative or on application under subsection (2)(b)) a decision of a description specified for the purposes of this paragraph in Tribunal Procedure Rules;

(b)   provide that the First-tier Tribunal's power under subsection (1) to review a decision of a description specified for the purposes of this paragraph in Tribunal Procedure Rules is exercisable only of the tribunal's own initiative;

(c)   provide that an application under subsection (2)(b) that is of a description specified for the purposes of this paragraph in Tribunal Procedure Rules may be made only on grounds specified for the purposes of this paragraph in Tribunal Procedure Rules;

(d)   provide, in relation to a decision of a description specified for the purposes of this paragraph in Tribunal Procedure Rules, that the First-tier Tribunal's power under subsection (1) to review the decision of its own initiative is exercisable only on grounds specified for the purposes of this paragraph in Tribunal Procedure Rules.

(4)   Where the First-tier Tribunal has under subsection (1) reviewed a decision, the First-tier Tribunal may in the light of the review do any of the following–

(a)   correct accidental errors in the decision or in a record of the decision;

(b)   amend reasons given for the decision;

(c)   set the decision aside.

(5)   Where under subsection (4)(c) the First-tier Tribunal sets a decision aside, the First-tier Tribunal must either–

(a)   re-decide the matter concerned, or

(b)   refer that matter to the Upper Tribunal.

(6)   Where a matter is referred to the Upper Tribunal under subsection (5)(b), the Upper Tribunal must re-decide the matter.

(7)   Where the Upper Tribunal is under subsection (6) re-deciding a matter, it may make any decision which the First-tier Tribunal could make if the First-tier Tribunal were re-deciding the matter.

(8)   Where a tribunal is acting under subsection (5)(a) or (6), it may make such findings of fact as it considers appropriate.

(9)   This section has effect as if a decision under subsection (4)(c) to set aside an earlier decision were not an excluded decision for the purposes of section 11(1), but the First-tier Tribunal's only power in the light of a review under subsection (1) of a decision under subsection (4)(c) is the power under subsection (4)(a).

(10)   A decision of the First-tier Tribunal may not be reviewed under subsection (1) more than once, and once the First-tier Tribunal has decided that an earlier decision should not be reviewed under subsection (1) it may not then decide to review that earlier decision under that subsection.

(11)   Where under this section a decision is set aside and the matter concerned is then re-decided, the decision set aside and the decision made in re-deciding the matter are for the purposes of subsection (10) to be taken to be different decisions.

Commencement

s9(3): 19.9.07; all other subsections: 3.11.08.

General Note

See the commentary to r40 TP(FT) Rules on p1023.

Review of decision of Upper Tribunal

10.–(1)   The Upper Tribunal may review a decision made by it on a matter in a case, other than a decision that is an excluded decision for the purposes of section 13(1) (but see subsection (7)).

(2)   The Upper Tribunal's power under subsection (1) in relation to a decision is exercisable–

(a)   of its own initiative, or

(b)   on application by a person who for the purposes of section 13(2) has a right of appeal in respect of the decision.

(3)   Tribunal Procedure Rules may–

(a)   provide that the Upper Tribunal may not under subsection (1) review (whether of its own initiative or on application under subsection (2)(b)) a decision of a description specified for the purposes of this paragraph in Tribunal Procedure Rules;

(b)   provide that the Upper Tribunal's power under subsection (1) to review a decision of a description specified for the purposes of this paragraph in Tribunal Procedure Rules is exercisable only of the tribunal's own initiative;

(c)   provide that an application under subsection (2)(b) that is of a description specified for the purposes of this paragraph in Tribunal Procedure Rules may be made only on grounds specified for the purposes of this paragraph in Tribunal Procedure Rules;

(d)   provide, in relation to a decision of a description specified for the purposes of this paragraph in Tribunal Procedure Rules, that the Upper Tribunal's power under subsection (1) to review the decision of its own initiative is exercisable only on grounds specified for the purposes of this paragraph in Tribunal Procedure Rules.

(4)   Where the Upper Tribunal has under subsection (1) reviewed a decision, the Upper Tribunal may in the light of the review do any of the following–

(a)   correct accidental errors in the decision or in a record of the decision;

(b)   amend reasons given for the decision;

(c)   set the decision aside.

(5)   Where under subsection (4)(c) the Upper Tribunal sets a decision aside, the Upper Tribunal must re-decide the matter concerned.

(6)   Where the Upper Tribunal is acting under subsection (5), it may make such findings of fact as it considers appropriate.

(7)   This section has effect as if a decision under subsection (4)(c) to set aside an earlier decision were not an excluded decision for the purposes of section 13(1), but the Upper Tribunal's only power in the light of a review under subsection (1) of a decision under subsection (4)(c) is the power under subsection (4)(a).

(8)   A decision of the Upper Tribunal may not be reviewed under subsection (1) more than once, and once the Upper Tribunal has decided that an earlier decision should not be reviewed under subsection (1) it may not then decide to review that earlier decision under that subsection.

(9)   Where under this section a decision is set aside and the matter concerned is then re-decided, the decision set aside and the decision made in re-deciding the matter are for the purposes of subsection (8) to be taken to be different decisions.

Commencement
s10(3): 19.9.07; all other subsections: 3.11.08.

General Note
See the commentary to r46 FT(UT) Rules on p1056.

Right to appeal to Upper Tribunal

11.–(1)   For the purposes of subsection (2), the reference to a right of appeal is to a right to appeal to the Upper Tribunal on any point of law arising from a decision made by the First-tier Tribunal other than an excluded decision.

(2)   Any party to a case has a right of appeal, subject to subsection (8).

(3)   That right may be exercised only with permission (or, in Northern Ireland, leave).

(4)   Permission (or leave) may be given by–

(a)   the First-tier Tribunal, or

(b)   the Upper Tribunal,

on an application by the party.

(5)   For the purposes of subsection (1), an "excluded decision" is–

(a)-(cb) [Omitted]

(d)   a decision of the First-tier Tribunal under section 9–

    (i)   to review, or not to review, an earlier decision of the tribunal,

    (ii)   to take no action, or not to take any particular action, in the light of a review of an earlier decision of the tribunal,

    (iii)   to set aside an earlier decision of the tribunal, or

    (iv)   to refer, or not to refer, a matter to the Upper Tribunal,

(e)   a decision of the First-tier Tribunal that is set aside under section 9 (including a decision set aside after proceedings on an appeal under this section have been begun), or

(f)   any decision of the First-tier Tribunal that is of a description specified in an order made by the Lord Chancellor.

(6)   A description may be specified under subsection (5)(f) only if–

(a)   in the case of a decision of that description, there is a right to appeal to a court, the Upper Tribunal or any other tribunal from the decision and that right is, or includes, something other than a right (however expressed) to appeal on any point of law arising from the decision, or

(b)   decisions of that description are made in carrying out a function transferred under section 30 and prior to the transfer of the function under section 30(1) there was no right to appeal from decisions of that description.

[[1] (6A)   Rules of court may make provision for permission not to be granted on an application under subsection (4) to the Court of Session that falls within subsection (7) unless the court considers–

(a)   that the proposed appeal would raise some important point of principle, or

(b)   that there is some other compelling reason for the court to hear the appeal.]

(7)   Where–

(a)   an order under subsection (5)(f) specifies a description of decisions, and

(b)   decisions of that description are made in carrying out a function transferred under section 30,

the order must be framed so as to come into force no later than the time when the transfer under section 30 of the function takes effect (but power to revoke the order continues to be exercisable after that time, and power to amend the order continues to be exercisable after that time for the purpose of narrowing the description for the time being specified).

(8)   The Lord Chancellor may by order make provision for a person to be treated as being, or to be treated as not being, a party to a case for the purposes of subsection (2).

Commencement

s11(5)(f) and (6) to (8): 19.9.07; all other subsections: 3.11.08.

Amendment

1.   Inserted by s23 of the Crime and Courts Act 2013 (15.7.13).

General Note

There is a right of appeal on a point of law to the Upper Tribunal against most decisions of the First-tier Tribunal. Permission to appeal (formerly called "leave to appeal") is required.

Analysis

Who may appeal?

Subs (2) confers a right of appeal on "any party to a case". The power conferred on the Lord Chancellor by subs (8) to provide for a person "to be treated as being ... or not being a party to the case" for the purposes of subs (2) has not been exercised and the phrase "any party to a case" is not defined in the Act. However, for HB purposes, CSPSSA Sch 7 para 8(2) confers a right of appeal on the Secretary of State, the relevant authority and any "person affected" by the decision against which the appeal to the First-tier Tribunal was brought or by the First-tier Tribunal's decision on the appeal. "Person affected" is defined for the purposes of Sch 7 in reg 3 D&A Regs. That definition is exhaustive (*Wirral MBC v Salisbury Independent Living* [2012] EWCA 84; [2012] AACR 37 at para 38): see further the commentary to reg 3 on p942.

Which decisions may be appealed against?

The scope of s11 was considered by a three-judge panel of the Upper Tribunal in *LS v Lambeth LB (HB)* [2010] UKUT 461 (AAC); [2011] AACR 27. In that case, a judge of the First-tier Tribunal had struck out an appeal which (as the Upper Tribunal confirmed) had been brought after the absolute 13-month time limit. The claimant challenged the decision by appealing against it and also by making an application for judicial review. However, she argued, in reliance on *SSWP v Morina and Borrowdale* [2007] EWCA Civ 749; reported as *R(IS) 6/07*, that the decision did not carry a right of appeal and that the correct way to challenge it was therefore by judicial review. The appeal and application were listed together before the Upper Tribunal, which held unanimously that *Morina* did not apply to decisions made under ss11 or 13 TCEA 2007. The consequence is that there is a right of appeal to the Upper Tribunal (and from the Upper Tribunal to the Court of Appeal) against any decision – ie, including interlocutory or case management decisions – except those that are excluded decisions under ss11(5) or 13(8). The Upper Tribunal stated:

"85.   In *Morina*, the Court of Appeal held that a decision of an appeal tribunal to refuse to admit an appeal on the ground of a lack of jurisdiction or to strike out an appeal would not constitute a "decision" within the meaning of that word for the purposes of section 14. In doing so, it referred to three other decisions of the Court of Appeal, all made in the context of social security cases. The first was *Bland v Chief Supplementary Benefit Officer* [1983] 1 WLR 262, CA; reported as *R(SB) 12/83*, in which the Court held that no appeal lay to it against a decision of a Commissioner refusing leave to appeal from a decision of an appeal tribunal under a predecessor of section 14. The second was *White v Chief Adjudication Officer* [1986] 2 All ER 905, CA; reported as an appendix to *R(S) 8/85*, in which it was said that a refusal of an extension of time in which to apply for leave to appeal was even less of a "decision" than a refusal of leave to appeal. The third was *Carpenter v SSWP* [2003] EWCA Civ 33; reported as *R(IB) 6/03*, where Laws LJ identified "a plain distinction between a decision (that is, a decision upon the actual question whether a claimant is entitled to a particular benefit or not) and what may conveniently be called a determination (that is, a determination of any matter along the way leading to a decision, including a determination of a procedural issue such as an application for an adjournment)".

86.   It is important, however, to note what Sir Anthony Clarke MR said in *Morina* at [50].

         "I add a few words only to emphasise the point made by Arden LJ that the question is entirely one of statutory construction of a particular statutory provision, namely section 14 of the Social Security Act 1998. In some contexts the word 'decision' might well include an interlocutory decision such as a refusal of an adjournment or an order to disclose documents. All depends on upon the particular circumstances. In the particular context of section 14 of the 1998 Act, I agree that neither of the decisions complained of was appealable."

87.   Section 11 of the 2007 Act is, of course, not confined to social security cases. Over the last two years there has been a number of cases in which the Upper Tribunal has drawn *Morina* to the attention of parties engaged in appeals against interlocutory decisions of the Health, Education and Social Care Chamber of the First-tier Tribunal. The parties' legal representatives have generally been bemused by the suggestion that the proceedings should have been brought by way of judicial review and no respondent has opposed the appeal on that ground. Consequently, the Upper Tribunal has accepted jurisdiction, albeit with varying degrees of certainty. In the Tax and Chancery Chamber of the Upper Tribunal it has similarly been assumed that there is jurisdiction to hear interlocutory appeals, without the point even being mentioned (see *Connect Global Ltd v HMRC* [2010] UKUT 372 (TCC) and *Capital Air Services Ltd v HMRC* [2010] UKUT 373 (TCC)).

88.   Moreover, s 11 of TCEA 2007 must be read with s 13, which concerns appeals from decisions of the Upper Tribunal...

89.   It would be very surprising indeed if the word "decision" in s 11(1) had a different meaning from its meaning in s 13(1), and even more surprising if it had a different meaning in cases concerning different subject-matter.

90.   We are satisfied that the word "decision" in both s 11(1) and s 13(1) must be read broadly. That is the natural reading of the word. This is particularly so where the structure of the section is to give a right of appeal generally, but then to carve out particular types of "excluded decision" in relation to which there is to be no right of appeal. It is not a question of granting a right of appeal in relation to particular types of pronouncement which are then classified as "decisions", but rather taking the general run of decisions, and identifying particular types of excluded decision so that the right of appeal applies to all that are not excluded.

91.   This must, as it seems to us, necessarily be the case when one examines what Parliament has said about excluded decisions in s 11 and s 13. In s 11(5)(d) and s 13(8)(d) all seven of the types of "decision"

mentioned are matters falling within Laws LJ's description of "determinations", matters "along the way leading to a decision [in a social security case, upon the actual question whether a claimant is entitled to a particular benefit or not]" Plainly Parliament did not intend to adopt the distinction drawn in *Carpenter*. And in each case the "decision" identified in paragraph (e) is something which has ceased to have effect: in so far as it exists at all it is far removed from "a decision upon the actual question whether a claimant is entitled to a particular benefit or not".

92.   A further and very powerful pointer to Parliament's intention is found in s 13. If it had been Parliament's intention that the word "decision" in s 13(1) should be interpreted in accordance with Bland, there would have been no need for s 13(8)(c). The words used by Parliament in s 13(8)(c) demonstrate a deliberate intention not to rely upon the courts to infer that the word "decision" has a limited meaning. Instead, in order to achieve a similar outcome to that achieved by *Bland* Parliament has expressly used the word "decision" in a broad sense, a sense which is broad enough to encompass decisions on permission or leave to appeal. As regards appeals from the Upper Tribunal, Parliament has deliberately categorised decisions on permission or leave to appeal as "excluded decisions".

93.   By parity of reasoning decisions by the First-tier Tribunal on permission or grant of leave to appeal fall within s 11(1). They have not been categorised as excluded decisions for the purposes of s 11, and the clear inference is that this is a deliberate decision by Parliament. As [counsel for the Secretary of State] points out, it was open to the Lord Chancellor under section 11(5)(f) and (6)(b) to make an order preserving the different approach in social security cases, but he did not do so. It seems to us that there were good reasons for him not making such an order, not the least of which is simplicity."

As with all rights of appeal to the Upper Tribunal and the Court of Appeal, the right of appeal against interlocutory and case management decisions, established by the decision in *LS v Lambeth LB (HB)* [2010] UKUT 461 (AAC); [2011] AACR 27, is subject to the requirement of permission in ss11(3) and 13(3).

A decision of the First-tier Tribunal refusing permission to appeal from the First-tier Tribunal to the Upper Tribunal is not an excluded decision within s11(5) TCEA. One consequence of the *LS* decision is therefore that such a decision is itself appealable (subject to permission being granted). In other words, *Bland v Chief Supplementary Benefit Officer* [1983] 1 WLR 262, CA; reported as *R(SB) 12/83* (see para 81 of *LS*) no longer applies to social security appeals. Presumably, a district tribunal judge faced with an application for permission to appeal against her/his decision refusing permission to appeal to the Upper Tribunal will forward it to the Upper Tribunal on the basis that it should be treated as a renewal of the original application under s11(4)(b). Note that a decision of the Upper Tribunal refusing permission to appeal from the First-tier Tribunal to the Upper Tribunal is an "excluded decision" under s13(8)(b) and therefore cannot be appealed to the Court of Appeal.

LS v Lambeth LB (HB) was concerned with an appeal that was made after the expiry of the absolute 13-month time limit. However, it is more common for late appeals to be made within 13 months so that the First-tier Tribunal has a discretion to extend time and admit them. Subsequent cases (*OFSTED v AF* [2011] UKUT 72 (AAC); [2011] AACR 32; *Information Commissioner v PS* [2011] UKUT 94 (AAC); *AM v Information Commissioner & FTT* [2010] UKUT 438 (AAC); and *GB v Information Commissioner & FTT* [2010] UKUT 432 (AAC)) suggest that the Upper Tribunal will be slow to interfere with the exercise of that discretion.

Moreover, the Upper Tribunal acknowledged (at para 94):

"it will be open to both the First-tier Tribunal and the Upper Tribunal to refuse permission to bring an interlocutory appeal on the ground that it is premature. The circumstances of the individual case must be considered. It is one thing to grant permission for an interlocutory appeal in a case where the final hearing may last for a fortnight. It is another to do so where the final hearing is likely to last about an hour, as is often the case in social security appeals. Moreover, as was suggested in *Dorset Healthcare NHS Foundation Trust v MH* [2009] UKUT 4 (AAC) at [19], where case-management decisions are being challenged, the First-tier Tribunal can treat an application for permission to appeal as an application for a new direction if it is satisfied that the challenged direction is not appropriate."

It therefore appears that, at least in cases where the decision under appeal does not finally dispose of all the issues, the question whether an appeal against the tribunal's final decision is an adequate remedy will remain relevant to the issue whether permission to appeal should be given even though it is no longer relevant to the issue whether a right of appeal exists (see *Dorset Healthcare* (above) and also *LM v Lewisham LB* [2009] UKUT 204 (AAC); [2010] AACR 12).

A further case in which it may not be premature to appeal an interlocutory decision before the tribunal has given its final decision is where a respondent objects to a decision to admit a late appeal. In *LS v Lambeth LB (HB)* itself, a tribunal judge had previously admitted the appeal for hearing but the District Tribunal Judge who eventually heard the case took the view that he was not bound by the earlier decision because there was no power to make a decision admitting an appeal that was more than 13 months late. The majority of the three-judge panel of the Upper Tribunal disagreed. The earlier decision was one that the judge had had power to make under former reg 18(4) of the D&A Regulations even though it was wrong and went to the appeal tribunal's jurisdiction to hear the appeal. It was established by *Watt v Ahsan* [2007] UKHL 51; [2008] AC 696 that an issue estoppel could arise from a decision by a tribunal as to whether it has jurisdiction. It was not necessary to decide whether an issue estoppel had arisen in the *LS* case because, even if it had not, the majority considered that it would not be appropriate to exercise any power to re-open the issue in all the circumstances of that case. In *Southwark LB v JQ (HB)* 2012 UKUT 232 AAC, the Upper Tribunal has suggested that a decision to extend time is a case management direction within r5(3)(a) TP(FTT) Rules and can therefore be challenged by applying for another direction setting the earlier direction aside under r5(2). In those circumstances, a respondent (and in the HB context, that does not just mean a local authority but would also include, for example, a claimant whose rights might be affected by an appeal by a landlord) who does not agree with a decision to admit a late appeal should make a prompt application for permission for that decision to be set aside under r5(2), and seek permission to appeal to the Upper Tribunal if that application is refused, rather than rely upon any residual power the First-tier Tribunal may have to reconsider the issue.

Although decisions taken under the power of review conferred by s9 are "excluded decisions" by virtue of s11(5)(d), and therefore cannot be appealed to the Upper Tribunal, such decisions can be challenged by judicial review: see, for example, *R (RB) v First-tier Tribunal (Review)* [2010] UKUT 160 (AAC); [2010] AACR 41 and *R (MP) v First-tier Tribunal and West London Mental Health NHS Trust* [2012] UKUT 231 (AAC). However, as was stated in the *RB* case (at para 30):

> "30.   The substantial element of judgment or discretion is no doubt a reason for review decisions not being appealable and it is also a reason for expecting that the Upper Tribunal will seldom interfere with review decisions when judicial review proceedings are brought. Moreover, the Upper Tribunal might in an appropriate case refuse permission to apply for judicial review on the ground that the applicant should wait for the case to be re-decided and then, if less successful than before, consider appealing on the ground that the review was unlawful."

In the *MP* case, Judge Wikeley commented (at para 19) that, in the light of those comments, "there will need to be a compelling case to give permission to apply for judicial review".

Grounds of appeal

Appeal lies to the Upper Tribunal "on any point of law arising from" the First-tier Tribunal decision. It cannot be over-emphasised that the First-tier Tribunal is the fact-finding forum and that, unless an error of law can be identified in a tribunal's decision, the Upper Tribunal will not be able to intervene, except possibly in the limited circumstances set out in category (10) below. A tribunal does not err in law simply because another tribunal or the Upper Tribunal would have assessed the combined significance of the facts differently or come to a different conclusion: *CDLA 1456/2002*; *CH 627/2002*; *CH 296/2004*.

In *CDLA 2975/2002* (para 15), the commissioner emphasised the importance of clearly identifying points of law:

> "Errors of law on the part of an experienced Tribunal . . . are not of course to be inferred, or imagined, simply because they reach a result on the questions of fact and degree they have to determine with which another Tribunal or professional person might possibly disagree; and appeals seeking to dispute the result on such grounds cannot of course succeed as all they are in effect doing is seeking to reargue the case again on the facts."

This illustrates the importance of claimants and authorities ensuring that they put all the points that they wish to put and call all the evidence they wish to call before the First-tier Tribunal, because unless an error of law is made by the First-tier Tribunal it will not be possible to remedy the situation at a later stage. See also the commentary to Sch 7 para 6(9)(a) CSPSSA on p147.

It is probably not possible to give an exhaustive summary of all the circumstances in which an error of law may arise. Nevertheless a number of different summaries exist, particularly in *R(A) 1/72*, *R(IS) 11/99* and the decision of the Court of Appeal in *R (Iran) v SSHD* [2005] EWCA Civ 982 (discussed by a tribunal of commissioners in *R(I) 2/06*). Those summaries are not inconsistent but may differ in emphasis and are inevitably influenced by the issues in the cases in which they are given. It is convenient to base this discussion on para 4 of *R(IS) 11/99*, which summaries the categories of error that can give rise to a right of appeal as follows.

(1)   A false proposition of law is evident from the tribunal's statement of reasons. This will include reliance on a provision in secondary legislation that is *ultra vires*: *Foster v Chief Adjudication Officer* [1993] AC 754, HL, though note CSPSSA Sch 7 para 18(4).

(2)   The tribunal has reached a decision that is supported by no evidence. Distinguishing between no evidence and little evidence is important in this context. A complaint in the latter category will only mean that there is an error of law if the conclusion reached is irrational: see below.

(3)   The tribunal has breached the relevancy principle, either by taking into account matters that should have been ignored, or ignoring matters that should have been taken into account. Where a tribunal is called upon to draw inferences from primary findings of fact, care must be taken to ensure that each of the factors relied upon in drawing the inference is relevant. A failure to do so will mean that the decision is erroneous in law, even if the tribunal has considered some of the relevant matters: *R v Allerdale DC HBRB ex p Doughty* [2000] COD 462, QBD. For that reason, the Upper Tribunal may feel more able to interfere with a tribunal's inferences rather than its findings of primary fact: see *CH 1076/2002* for an example.

(4)   The tribunal's decision is irrational, in that no tribunal properly instructed as to the law could have reached a conclusion of fact set out in the statement of reasons. There will be many types of case heard by tribunals in which different tribunals could quite legitimately come to different conclusions. There may be no "right" answer in law: see *R(H) 1/03* (paras 24–25); *CDLA 1456/2002* (paras 9–11); and the quotation

from *CDLA 2975/2002* above. It is rare for an appeal to succeed on this ground. Very often, appeals made on this ground are, on proper analysis, in fact complaining of some other error of law such as misconstruction of the relevant statutory provision. See *CDLA 1456/2002* (paras 9–13) for another particularly trenchant expression of this fundamental principle by Commissioner Howell.

(5) The tribunal has failed to exercise its inquisitorial jurisdiction (see below).

(6) There has been a breach of the rules of natural justice (see below).

(7) There has been a relevant breach of the procedural rules (see p183).

(8) The tribunal has acted in breach of the claimant's rights under the European Convention on Human Rights. Since a tribunal is a "public body" under s6(3)(a) Human Rights Act 1998, by virtue of s6(1) it is obliged to act in a way which is compatible with a party's Convention rights. Domestic public law often protects the same rights as those protected by the Convention, in particular Art 6 thereof. However, the commissioners were noticeably more enthusiastic than the courts about framing complaints of unfairness in terms of breach of Convention rights rather than trying to shoehorn them into the established grounds for complaint under domestic law set out above. See Commissioner Jacobs' decision in *CJSA 5100/2001* (paras 5–9) for a vivid example. Attention should therefore be paid to caselaw under the Convention as a possible additional source of complaint, while not neglecting the more mundane approach under domestic law. See also the commentary to Art 6 on p124.

(9) The tribunal has made a decision which it has no jurisdiction to make. This covers situations where a tribunal purports to hear appeals relating to matters over which it does not have jurisdiction under Sch 7 para 6 and the regulations made thereunder.

(10) Despite what has been said above about the distinction between errors of law and fact, it is possible that errors of fact may amount to errors of law in certain circumstances. In *E v SSHD* [2004] EWCA Civ 49 (paras 63–69), the Court of Appeal held that where on appeal a fact-finding tribunal could be shown to have made a clear and indisputable error of fact and injustice was caused to an appellant as a result, an appellate tribunal (in that case, the Immigration Appeal Tribunal) could intervene. "Injustice" would only be caused, however, in a case where the parties had a "common interest" in ensuring the correct result was reached. That test was satisfied in the context of *E* (claims for asylum) and it is highly arguable that it would also be satisfied in the context of social security appeals. The implications of this potentially ground-breaking decision for the social security appeals system will have to be fully worked out by the Upper Tribunal.

Scope of the right of appeal: failure to exercise inquisitorial jurisdiction. One of the fundamental distinctions between tribunals and courts is that the latter are generally concerned only with deciding disputes raised by the parties for their consideration. By contrast, tribunals are generally expected to be much more pro-active in identifying and resolving issues between the parties. They need not, therefore, come to a conclusion that is advocated by one of the parties to an appeal: *R v Deputy Industrial Injuries Commissioner ex p Moore* [1965] 1 QB 456 and *Kerr v Department for Social Development* [2004] UKHL 23; reported as *R 1/04 (SF)*. The question of when a tribunal's decision can be subject to appeal on this ground depends on all the circumstances of the case: *R(SB) 2/83* (paras 10–11). In deciding whether there has been a failure to exercise the inquisitorial function, it is helpful to consider whether it is an issue that is alleged to have been overlooked or whether it is relevant evidence that has not been considered. As far as issues are concerned, the tribunal has discretion by virtue of para 6(9)(a) to decline to consider issues which are not raised by the parties or at least by the appeal (see the Analysis on p147). Authorities on the scope of a tribunal's duty to consider new issues for itself must be read in the light of para 6(9)(a), though it is suggested that an unreasonable exercise of the discretion conferred by para 6(9)(a) may still constitute an error of law. The scope of the duty depends on the extent to which it appears that the parties have presented the relevant material to it. Where a representative appears to be competent, the omission will have to be obvious before the tribunal will err in law in failing to consider the issue: see *CSDLA 336/2000* (para 15). See also *R(H) 1/02* (paras 8–9). Where a representative specifically declines an opportunity to have a point addressed, the tribunal will not err in law by failing to do so itself: *CSIB 588/1998* (para 13).

The duty to consider or call for further evidence, on the other hand, may well be slightly wider. This is the case particularly where a claimant is unrepresented and may not be aware of the nature of the evidence that will be relevant to the determination of a question before the tribunal. It seems clear that if there is something to alert a tribunal that relevant evidence may exist that is not before it, it will err in law if it does not give the party the chance to produce that evidence: *CU 47/1993* (paras 4–11).

A tribunal does not generally err in law by failing to take documents not placed before it into account: *CH 5221/2001* (para 3.1). However, if it needs to examine a document to decide what impression it would have given to the reader, it will err in law if it does not call for a copy of the document rather than assuming the form that it took: *CH 5221/2001* (para 5).

Scope of the right of appeal: breach of natural justice. The rules of natural justice, which are now bolstered by the right to a fair hearing under Art 6 of the European Convention on Human Rights, comprise two basic principles: the first is the right to be heard and the second the rule against bias.

The right to be heard

The most obvious breach of the right to be heard is a case where a "person affected" is not notified of the proceedings. In *CH 3679/2002*, a claimant appealed against a decision that an overpayment was recoverable from a landlord. Commissioner Fellner held that the tribunal had erred in law because the landlord had not been made a party to the appeal and notified of the hearing: para 3. Provision for 14 days' notice of an oral hearing is made in r29 TP(FT) Rules. In *CH 3594/2002*, the commissioner said that to ensure a fair hearing, the equivalent rule in reg 49(2) Social Security and Child Support (Decisions and Appeals) Regulations 1999 had to be read as applying to provision of the submissions and evidence as well as the notice of the time and date of the hearing. He said that was so "unless the appeal tribunal is prepared to take the time during the oral hearing itself to redress the unfairness by ensuring that all the evidence and submissions are presented orally by both parties." In the absence of one of the parties, this could mean that the tribunal will find it necessary to adjourn the hearing. On the failure to give advance notice of documentary evidence, see also *RC (Dec'd) v Maldon DC (HB)* [2012] UKUT 333 (AAC).

If a party does not appear at a hearing through no fault of her/his own, then the tribunal's decision may be vitiated by an error of law even if no other person can be shown to be at fault: *CIB 5227/1999* (paras 9 and 10). If the claimant fails to attend a hearing due to a deliberate decision, there is no breach of the right: *CCS 565/1999* (para 12). Similarly, if a claimant fails to attend through carelessness, there is no error of law. However, before proceeding with a hearing in the absence of a party, the tribunal must be satisfied that (among other things) it is in the interests of justice to do so. Failure to consider that issue expressly is an error of law: see the commentary to r31 TP(FTT) Rules.

In *CIB 4667/2002*, the appellant's representative freely admitted that he had failed to attend a hearing because of a mistake about the date. The commissioner said that whether to adjourn a hearing in such circumstances is for the good sense, judgement and discretion of the tribunal. As tribunals are accustomed to dealing with unrepresented appellants and people who are not familiar with the legal process, the fact that a representative does not turn up to a hearing does not, in principle, make it wrong to proceed in her/ his absence. In order to give rise to an appeal on a point of law, "what has to be shown is that the tribunal's exercise of judgement was so unreasonable as to be perverse and to have deprived the claimant of a substantive opportunity for a fair hearing of the relevant issues in his or her case."

Experienced representatives who do not seek oral hearings on behalf of their clients might not then be able to argue that a tribunal should have nevertheless held one. In *Miller v Secretary of State for Social Security* [2002] GWD 25-861, CSIH, the appellant complained that she had not been allowed an oral hearing of her appeal to provide further evidence. However, the Court held that as the appellant's experienced representative had not sought an oral hearing and had stated that s/he was relying on specified paragraphs in the application for leave to appeal, the commissioner could not be said to have erred in law for not allowing an oral hearing.

Note the right to apply to set aside a tribunal decision under r37(1) and (2)(c) TP(FTT) Rules where a party to the proceedings or the party's representative was not present at a hearing (see p1019).

There is no obligation on a tribunal to adjourn a case to offer an unrepresented claimant a chance to obtain representation: *CSIB 848/1997* (para 9). However, if a claimant expresses the wish for an adjournment to be represented this ought ordinarily to be granted, particularly in a difficult case with serious consequences. Where a claimant suffers from difficulties such as illiteracy, this emphasises the need for a tribunal to decide whether it is appropriate to proceed in such circumstances: *CIS 6002/1997* (paras 9–11).

The right to be heard is not only relevant in cases where parties (or their representatives) do not attend the hearing. A fair procedure must be adopted in all cases and what fairness requires will differ according to the circumstances of the case. For example, local authorities all too frequently fail to explain their decision making processes with sufficient clarity in written submissions to a tribunal. If the process may have an impact on the outcome of the appeal, it is essential for a tribunal to explain it to an unrepresented claimant: *CH 1085/2002* (para 20).

Similarly, at a hearing, a party must be given a fair opportunity to present her/his case. The tribunal may exercise control over the presentation of the case to the extent of preventing disruption of its proceedings or the pursuit of irrelevant matters. It may also control undue length of presentation, though care must be taken to ensure that the case is not in reality more complex than it had first appeared. If insufficient time has been allocated for the hearing of the case and there is any danger that to restrict the amount of time available to a party to present its case would hamper its ability to place its full case before the tribunal, then the case should be adjourned and the clerk to the tribunal should be directed to list the case with a longer time estimate.

In order for a party to have a fair opportunity to present her/his case, s/he must have sufficient notice of the opposing party's case and, in particular, what is in dispute and what is not. The tribunal must therefore be vigilant not to allow one party to "ambush" another. But ambushes do not always come from the other party. The tribunal itself, in the exercise of its inquisitorial jurisdiction and the judicial discretion conferred by para 6(9)(a) of Sch 7 CSPSSA 2000, may take points that have not been raised by the parties and, if it does so, must ensure the parties have adequate notice of those points: see *CP v M Technology School (SEN)* [2010] UKUT 314 (AAC).

Where HM Courts and Tribunals Service appoints an interpreter to be used at a hearing, a claimant is entitled to expect the questions to her/him and her/his replies to be interpreted professionally. In *CDLA 2748/2002*, the commissioner did not accept that it was adequate to establish a fair hearing that the tribunal concluded it had "sufficient understanding". If the standard of interpretation appears inadequate, the tribunal should take appropriate action: see also *NG v SSWP (DLA)* [2012] UKUT 291 (AAC).

It is not part of the tribunal's judicial function to seek to bargain with an appellant or her/his representative as to which parts of the appeal the tribunal might accept if other parts are not pressed for at the hearing: *CSDLA 606/2003*. In this case, the appeal tribunal's record of proceedings noted that an offer had been put to the appellant by the chair of the tribunal just to reinstate her higher rate mobility component of DLA if she did not seek to argue for the care component, and the case was adjourned for 10 minutes for her to think about this. On reconvening the hearing the appellant, who at that point said she wished to proceed with her appeal, was then told that if she went ahead and sought to argue for the care component then she could risk losing everything, and she was told to think again about the matter. After a further short adjournment of five minutes the appellant "accepted the offer". Unsurprisingly, the commissioner concluded that this was not a fair and proper hearing. In her view, a "travesty of justice" had occurred in which the tribunal had pressurised the appellant into giving up her right to a hearing on the care component and had awarded the mobility component without any proper application of the relevant legal tests.

The rule against bias

The second aspect of the rules of natural justice is the rule against bias. Bias may be actual or apparent. Cases where it can be shown that a tribunal member has a direct interest in the outcome will be rare but even remote connections may be held to vitiate the fairness of proceedings: *R v Secretary of State for the Home Department ex p Pinochet (No 2)* [2000] 1 AC 129, HL. Members who are, for example, councillors of the relevant local authority or who are instructed by a party in private practice should disclose their interest or prior involvement. The same would be true of a member that had expressed strong views in an academic context that impinged upon the merits of one party's position: *Locabail (UK) Ltd v Bayfield Properties Ltd* [2000] QB 451 at 496F-497A, para 89, CA. If other parties are happy to proceed in knowledge of the full facts, any breach of this rule would be taken to be waived.

In cases of apparent bias, the question is "whether the fair-minded and informed observer, having considered the facts, would conclude that there was a real possibility that the tribunal was biased": *Porter v Magill* [2002] 2 WLR 37. For a detailed discussion of the application of the test in *Porter v Magill* [2002] 2 WLR 37, see the decision of the Upper Tribunal in *Kirkham v Information Commissioner (Recusal and Costs)* [2018] UKUT 65 (AAC) at paras 14–20. Note also *CSDLA 855/1997* (para 8), where the fact that a member of a tribunal was the partner of an examining medical practitioner whose report was being called into question was a breach of natural justice. The decision in *CSDLA 1019/1999* was overturned by the Court of Session in *SSWP v Gillies* [2003] 2004 SLT 14; reported at 2006 SC (HL) 71, in which the Court emphasised that the fair-minded observer is someone who is "neither complacent nor unduly sensitive or suspicious". The House of Lords upheld the decision of the Court of Session in *Gillies v SSWP* [2006] UKHL 2; reported as *R(DLA) 5/06*.

Examples of successful challenges for apparent bias can be found in *CCS 557/2005* and *SW v SSWP (IB)* [2010] UKUT 73 (AAC).

Representatives will need to exercise caution and restraint in making allegations of apparent bias based on the way in which hearings are conducted by tribunals. The commissioners have been critical about unparticularised complaints of bias which amount to nothing more than a complaint about the tribunal doing that which is its primary function, namely to closely test a party's case by questioning before accepting it in cases where the facts are in dispute: *CH 2302/2002* (para 10); *CH 2349/2002* (paras 12–13). In *R (Sarabjeet Singh) v SSHD* [2016] EWCA Civ 492, the Court of Appeal gave guidance as to the procedure to be followed in cases where an allegation of judicial bias is made as follows.

"52. It would not be appropriate, in my view, for this court to give, in the context of appeals to the Upper Tribunal, guidance of a kind replicating the detail of that found in the Practice Direction relating to Employment Appeal Tribunals. If this kind of appeal is to become more prevalent in this context then it would be much better for the Chamber Presidents, with their specialist expertise and their knowledge of the practicalities and in conjunction with the Senior President of Tribunals as appropriate, to decide whether or not to formulate any Practice Direction or Practice Statement or Guidance Note which may be considered necessary or desirable.

53. But that said, the problems that have been highlighted by the course of events in this particular case do for the present permit at least some observations to be made: and they are ones which, I think, should be made.

(1) An allegation of bias or misconduct can only too easily be raised by a disgruntled litigant. It is therefore important that any application for permission to appeal, if based (in whole or part) on such a ground, is closely scrutinised when consideration is given as to whether permission to appeal should be granted. Such an allegation, if to be sufficient to merit the grant of permission at all, should ordinarily be expected to be properly particularised and appropriately evidenced.

(2) If an allegation of bias or misconduct is raised which is adjudged sufficient to merit the grant of permission to appeal then it should be normal practice for the Upper Tribunal thereafter to obtain the written comments of the judge concerned: both in fairness to the judge and to provide the Upper Tribunal with a fuller picture.

(3) Such written comments of the judge, where obtained, should be provided to the parties for the purposes of the appeal hearing in the Upper Tribunal. In addition, such written comments should be

retained on the file pending any possible further appeal to the Court of Appeal (the present case indicates the potential awkwardness arising from that failure).

(4) Proceedings in the First-tier Tribunal are not ordinarily recorded (it is not a court of record) and no transcript of the hearing will be available. There may be some cases where it may also be necessary to obtain the Tribunal Judge's own note or record of the entire hearing.

(5) It will normally be likely in such as the present cases to be of assistance to the Upper Tribunal to know what the advocate for the respondent has to say as to what happened or what was said before the First-tier Tribunal. In the present case neither the Upper Tribunal nor this court had the assistance of any such observations. It should be borne in mind that to provide such observations is the more likely to help produce a fuller and more accurate picture of what actually happened or was said in the First-tier Tribunal. There may be cases where the advocate concerned has no precise note or recollection. In that case, the Upper Tribunal at least can be so told.

(6) Whether oral evidence is needed at the hearing of the appeal on the issue of what happened or was said below should be carefully considered by the parties.

(7) Reflecting all the foregoing, it is likely to be important, in appeals of this nature, for the file to be reviewed and any directions given by an Upper Tribunal Judge in good time before the substantive appeal hearing.

54. These suggestions which I make are borne out of this court's experience of what happened in this particular case. They are intended to be neither prescriptive nor exhaustive. The general position remains that it is for a party alleging bias (whether actual or apparent) to place before the appeal tribunal the evidence and materials necessary to make good – if he can – such an allegation; and the outcome for each such case will depend on its own facts and circumstances."

Scope of the right of appeal: breach of procedure. The courts have emphasised in recent years the need to consider the extent, nature and effect of non-compliance rather than whether the procedural provision is set out in the form of a duty or discretion: *Haringey LBC v Awaritefe* (1999) 32 HLR 517; *R v SSHD ex p Jeyeanthan* [2000] 1 WLR 354. A breach of the terms of a procedural requirement will not, therefore, of itself render a decision erroneous in law. As a rule of thumb, if the claimant is or might be prejudiced by the non-compliance then that will vitiate the decision. Further discussion as to when a breach of the procedural provisions in the TP(FTT) Rules is found in the commentary to those regulations. Note, however, that the First-tier Tribunal has power to waive any requirement of those Rules where it is just to do so: see r7(2)(a) on p992.

A common ground on which tribunal decisions are set aside is failure to give adequate reasons, which is a breach of procedure under r34(2) TP(FTT) Rules. However, if the shortcoming in the statement of reasons is immaterial because the case could only have been decided adversely to the claimant, the Upper Tribunal will either dismiss the appeal or will allow the appeal but substitute a decision to the same effect as that of the First-tier Tribunal.

Proceedings on appeal to Upper Tribunal

12.–(1) Subsection (2) applies if the Upper Tribunal, in deciding an appeal under section 11, finds that the making of the decision concerned involved the making of an error on a point of law.

(2) The Upper Tribunal–

(a) may (but need not) set aside the decision of the First-tier Tribunal, and

(b) if it does, must either–

    (i) remit the case to the First-tier Tribunal with directions for its reconsideration, or

    (ii) re-make the decision.

(3) In acting under subsection (2)(b)(i), the Upper Tribunal may also–

(a) direct that the members of the First-tier Tribunal who are chosen to reconsider the case are not to be the same as those who made the decision that has been set aside;

(b) give procedural directions in connection with the reconsideration of the case by the First-tier Tribunal.

(4) In acting under subsection (2)(b)(ii), the Upper Tribunal–

(a) may make any decision which the First-tier Tribunal could make if the First-tier Tribunal were re-making the decision, and

(b) may make such findings of fact as it considers appropriate.

Commencement
3.11.08.

General Note

This section sets out what the Upper Tribunal can do if it finds that the First-tier Tribunal's decision "involved the making of an error on a point of law". It is equivalent, and in similar terms, to the former Sch 7 paras 5 and 6 CSPSSA and s14(7) and (8) SSA 1998.

In those circumstances, the first decision for the Upper Tribunal is whether to set the First-tier Tribunal's decision aside: subs (2)(a). Although the Upper Tribunal has a discretion not to set the decision aside, justice to the party that is disadvantaged by the error will normally require that it do so, unless the error was not material – ie, it did not have any effect on the outcome of the appeal before the First-tier Tribunal. The discretion may also be a useful tool with which to do justice in other (rare) cases where it would be unjust to set aside the First-tier Tribunal's decision even though it was erroneous. For an example of circumstances in which the Upper Tribunal found a decision of the First-tier Tribunal to be wrong in law but declined to set it aside, see *MQ v SSWP and SQ (CS)* [2017] UKUT 392 (AAC).

Having decided to set the First-tier Tribunal's decision aside, the Upper Tribunal then has two possible courses of action: subs (2)(b).

The first is to remit the case to the First-tier Tribunal with directions for its reconsideration. In this case, it also has powers to direct that it is reconsidered by different members of the First-tier Tribunal from those who made the original decision and to give procedural directions: subs (3). The phrase "members of the First-tier Tribunal" in subs (3)(a) is presumably intended to include the judge who made the original decision, although elsewhere in the Act a sharp distinction is drawn between "judges" and "other members" of the First-tier Tribunal. In other words, the judge is a "member" of the First-tier Tribunal (using that word in its ordinary sense) even though s/he is not an "other member" as defined in s4(3). The First-tier Tribunal is required to comply with any directions given by the Upper Tribunal when remitting the case: see *SD v SSWP (ESA)* [2015] UKUT 116 (AAC) at para 9.

Alternatively, the Upper Tribunal may "re-make" the decision, in which case it may make any decision that the First-tier Tribunal could have made and make new or additional findings of fact: subs (4).

Right to appeal to Court of Appeal etc.

13.–(1)   For the purposes of subsection (2), the reference to a right of appeal is to a right to appeal to the relevant appellate court on any point of law arising from a decision made by the Upper Tribunal other than an excluded decision.

(2)   Any party to a case has a right of appeal, subject to subsection (14).

(3)   That right may be exercised only with permission (or, in Northern Ireland, leave).

(4)   Permission (or leave) may be given by–

(a)   the Upper Tribunal, or

(b)   the relevant appellate court,

on an application by the party.

(5)   An application may be made under subsection (4) to the relevant appellate court only if permission (or leave) has been refused by the Upper Tribunal.

(6)   The Lord Chancellor may, as respects an application under subsection (4) that falls within subsection (7) and for which the relevant appellate court is the Court of Appeal in England and Wales or the Court of Appeal in Northern Ireland, by order make provision for permission (or leave) not to be granted on the application unless the Upper Tribunal or (as the case may be) the relevant appellate court considers–

(a)   that the proposed appeal would raise some important point of principle [²or practice], or

(b)   that there is some other compelling reason for the relevant appellate court to hear the appeal.

[¹(6A)   Rules of court may make provision for permission not to be granted on an application under subsection (4) to the Court of Session that falls within subsection (7) unless the court considers–

(a)   that the proposed appeal would raise some important point of principle, or

(b)   that there is some other compelling reason for the court to hear the appeal.]

(7)   An application falls within this subsection if the application is for permission (or leave) to appeal from any decision of the Upper Tribunal on an appeal under section 11.

(8)   For the purposes of subsection (1), an "excluded decision" is–

(a)-(bb) *[Omitted]*

(c)   any decision of the Upper Tribunal on an application under section 11(4)(b) (application for permission or leave to appeal),

(d) a decision of the Upper Tribunal under section 10–
    (i) to review, or not to review, an earlier decision of the tribunal,
    (ii) to take no action, or not to take any particular action, in the light of a review of an earlier decision of the tribunal, or
    (iii) to set aside an earlier decision of the tribunal,
(e) a decision of the Upper Tribunal that is set aside under section 10 (including a decision set aside after proceedings on an appeal under this section have been begun), or
(f) any decision of the Upper Tribunal that is of a description specified in an order made by the Lord Chancellor.
(9) A description may be specified under subsection (8)(f) only if–
(a) in the case of a decision of that description, there is a right to appeal to a court from the decision and that right is, or includes, something other than a right (however expressed) to appeal on any point of law arising from the decision, or
(b) decisions of that description are made in carrying out a function transferred under section 30 and prior to the transfer of the function under section 30(1) there was no right to appeal from decisions of that description.
(10) Where–
(a) an order under subsection (8)(f) specifies a description of decisions, and
(b) decisions of that description are made in carrying out a function transferred under section 30,
the order must be framed so as to come into force no later than the time when the transfer under section 30 of the function takes effect (but power to revoke the order continues to be exercisable after that time, and power to amend the order continues to be exercisable after that time for the purpose of narrowing the description for the time being specified).
(11) Before the Upper Tribunal decides an application made to it under subsection (4), the Upper Tribunal must specify the court that is to be the relevant appellate court as respects the proposed appeal.
(12) The court to be specified under subsection (11) in relation to a proposed appeal is whichever of the following courts appears to the Upper Tribunal to be the most appropriate–
(a) the Court of Appeal in England and Wales;
(b) the Court of Session;
(c) the Court of Appeal in Northern Ireland.
(13) In this section except subsection (11), "the relevant appellate court", as respects an appeal, means the court specified as respects that appeal by the Upper Tribunal under subsection (11).
(14) The Lord Chancellor may by order make provision for a person to be treated as being, or to be treated as not being, a party to a case for the purposes of subsection (2).
(15) Rules of court may make provision as to the time within which an application under subsection (4) to the relevant appellate court must be made.

Commencement
    s13(6), (8)(f), (9), (10), (14) and (15): 19.9.07; all other subsections: 3.11.08.

Amendments
    1.   Inserted by s23 Crime and Courts Act 2013 by art 2 of SI 2013 No 1725 from 15.7.13.
    2.   Amended by s83(2) Criminal Justice and Courts Act 2015 from 13.4.15.

General Note
    A further appeal lies from the Upper Tribunal, with permission, to the "relevant appellate court".

Analysis
Who may appeal?
    The right of appeal is conferred on "any party to the case" subs (2). As with s11, that phrase is undefined. However, by subs (3) and (4), the right may only be exercised with permission to appeal and, under CSPSSA Sch 7 para 9(3), an application for permission to appeal may only be made by a person who was entitled to appeal to the Upper Tribunal (ie, under CSPSSA Sch 7 para 8(2)) or who was a party to the proceedings before the Upper Tribunal (ie, who was added or substituted as a party under r9 TP(UT) Rules) or who is authorised by

regulations to apply for permission. No such regulations have been made (SI 2005 No.2007 which was made under the previous version of para 9(3) was revoked by Sch 2 to SI 2008 No.2683 with effect from 3 November 2008).

The right of appeal conferred by subs (2) is subject to subs (14). However, no order has yet been made under that subsection.

Which decisions may be appealed against?

With two exceptions, subs (1) and (8) are in similar terms to s11(1) and (5): see the Analysis of s11 on p176. The exceptions are that:

– under subs (8)(c), a decision of the Upper Tribunal granting or refusing permission to appeal under s11(4)(b) (ie, permission to appeal from the First-tier Tribunal to the Upper Tribunal) is an "excluded decision". Any such decision can only be challenged by judicial review (if at all, see the discussion of *Cart* and *Eba* on p169). This codifies the law as it was before 3 November 2008: see *Bland v Chief Supplementary Benefit Officer* [1983] 1 WLR 262, CA; reported as *R(SB) 12/83* and *SSWP v Morina and Borrowdale* [2007] EWCA Civ 749; reported as *R(IS) 6/07* and the Analysis to s11; *and*

– no order has been made by the Lord Chancellor under subs (8)(f).

Grounds of appeal

Under subs (1), an appeal lies on "any point of law arising from a decision" of the Upper Tribunal: see the Analysis to s11(1) on p176. In addition, it will be an error of law for the Upper Tribunal to exceed its own jurisdiction by interfering with the decisions of the First-tier Tribunal where the Upper Tribunal disagrees with the decision on the facts but there has been no error of law. See, by analogy, *SSWP v Roach* [2006]; reported as *R(CS) 4/07* and *Braintree DC v Thompson* [2005] EWCA Civ 178, 7 March 2005, unreported.

The requirement for permission

Permission to appeal must first be sought from the Upper Tribunal: see subs (4) and r44 TP(UT) Rules (on p1055). Permission may only be sought from the relevant appellate court (see subs (12)) if the Upper Tribunal refuses permission.

In HB cases (and other cases on appeal from the Social Entitlement Chamber of the First-tier Tribunal), the time limit for applying for permission is three months after the date on which the Upper Tribunal sent the party written notice of its decision or (which will necessarily be later) notice of amended reasons, or correction of, the decision following a review under s10 and r46 or that an application to set aside the decision (ie, under r43) has been unsuccessful. That time limit may be extended or shortened: see rr5(3)(a) and 44(6) TP(UT) Rules.

In cases where the "relevant appellate court" is the Court of Appeal in England and Wales or the Court of Appeal in Northern Ireland, permission to appeal may only be granted if the Upper Tribunal or, where the Upper Tribunal refuses permission, the relevant appellate court, considers that the proposed appeal would raise some important point of principle or practice or there is some other compelling reason for the relevant appellate court to hear the appeal: see the Appeals from the Upper Tribunal to the Court of Appeal Order 2008 SI No.2834 made by the Lord Chancellor under the power conferred by subs (6). That order codifies the position that existed in practice before 3 November 2008: see *Cooke v Secretary of State for Social Security* [2001] EWCA CIV 734; reported as *R(DLA) 6/01, Fryer-Kelsey v SSWP* [2005] EWCA Civ 511; reported as *R(IB) 6/05* and the Analysis to Sch 7 para 9 CSPSSA on p167 of the 20th edition.

Which is the "relevant appellate court"?

Appeal under s13 lies to the "relevant appellate court" which may be the Court of Appeal in England and Wales, the Court of Session in Scotland or the Court of Appeal in Northern Ireland. Before the Upper Tribunal decides an application for permission to appeal, it must specify which of those courts is to be the "relevant appellate court" in that particular case: see subs (11) and (12). This will usually (but not necessarily) be the appellate court for the jurisdiction in which the claimant lives. Exceptions might be made where the claimant has moved or, possibly, where the parties were in the north of England and could more easily attend a hearing in Edinburgh rather than London.

What procedure must be followed on an appeal under s13?

For the requirements of an application to the Upper Tribunal for permission to appeal, see r44(7) TP(UT) Rules on p1055.

Procedure before the Court of Appeal or the Court of Session is beyond the scope of this book. Readers in England and Wales are referred to Part 52 of the Civil Procedure Rules 1998 SI No.3132 (as amended) and, in Scotland, to Chapter 41 of the Act of Sederunt (Rules of the Court of Session 1994) 1994 SI No.1443 (as amended).

Proceedings on appeal to Court of Appeal etc.

14.–(1)   Subsection (2) applies if the relevant appellate court, in deciding an appeal under section 13, finds that the making of the decision concerned involved the making of an error on a point of law.

(2)   The relevant appellate court–

(a)   may (but need not) set aside the decision of the Upper Tribunal, and

(b)   if it does, must either–

(i) remit the case to the Upper Tribunal or, where the decision of the Upper Tribunal was on an appeal or reference from another tribunal or some other person, to the Upper Tribunal or that other tribunal or person, with directions for its reconsideration, or

(ii) re-make the decision.

(3) In acting under subsection (2)(b)(i), the relevant appellate court may also–

(a) direct that the persons who are chosen to reconsider the case are not to be the same as those who–

(i) where the case is remitted to the Upper Tribunal, made the decision of the Upper Tribunal that has been set aside, or

(ii) where the case is remitted to another tribunal or person, made the decision in respect of which the appeal or reference to the Upper Tribunal was made;

(b) give procedural directions in connection with the reconsideration of the case by the Upper Tribunal or other tribunal or person.

(4) In acting under subsection (2)(b)(ii), the relevant appellate court–

(a) may make any decision which the Upper Tribunal could make if the Upper Tribunal were re-making the decision or (as the case may be) which the other tribunal or person could make if that other tribunal or person were re-making the decision, and

(b) may make such findings of fact as it considers appropriate.

(5) Where–

(a) under subsection (2)(b)(i) the relevant appellate court remits a case to the Upper Tribunal, and

(b) the decision set aside under subsection (2)(a) was made by the Upper Tribunal on an appeal or reference from another tribunal or some other person,

the Upper Tribunal may (instead of reconsidering the case itself) remit the case to that other tribunal or person, with the directions given by the relevant appellate court for its reconsideration.

(6) In acting under subsection (5), the Upper Tribunal may also–

(a) direct that the persons who are chosen to reconsider the case are not to be the same as those who made the decision in respect of which the appeal or reference to the Upper Tribunal was made;

(b) give procedural directions in connection with the reconsideration of the case by the other tribunal or person.

(7) In this section "the relevant appellate court", as respects an appeal under section 13, means the court specified as respects that appeal by the Upper Tribunal under section 13(11).

Commencement
3.11.08.

General Note
This section sets out the powers of the "relevant appellate Court" (eg, the Court of Appeal or Court of Session) when hearing an appeal against a decision of the Upper Tribunal under s13. Those powers are equivalent to those exercised by the Upper Tribunal under s12 when deciding an appeal against a decision of the First-tier Tribunal: see the Analysis to s12 on p184. The only exception is that the Court of Appeal or Court of Session may remit the case either to the Upper Tribunal or the First-tier Tribunal.

Under subs (5) and (6), where the Court of Appeal or Court of Session remits a case to the Upper Tribunal, the Upper Tribunal may in turn remit it to the First-tier Tribunal with the directions given by the Court and (if appropriate) further procedural directions.

Appeal to Supreme Court: grant of certificate by Upper Tribunal

14A.–(1) If the Upper Tribunal is satisfied that–

(a) the conditions in subsection (4) or (5) are fulfilled in relation to the Upper Tribunal's decision in any proceedings, and

(b) as regards that decision, a sufficient case for an appeal to the Supreme Court has been made out to justify an application under section 14B, the Upper Tribunal may grant a certificate to that effect.

(2)   The Upper Tribunal may grant a certificate under this section only on an application made by a party to the proceedings.

(3)   The Upper Tribunal may grant a certificate under this section only if the relevant appellate court as regards the proceedings is–

(a)   the Court of Appeal in England and Wales, or

(b)   the Court of Appeal in Northern Ireland.

(4)   The conditions in this subsection are that a point of law of general public importance is involved in the decision of the Upper Tribunal and that point of law is–

(a)   a point of law that–

    (i)   relates wholly or mainly to the construction of an enactment or statutory instrument, and

    (ii)   has been fully argued in the proceedings and fully considered in the judgement of the Upper Tribunal in the proceedings, or

(b)   a point of law–

    (i)   in respect of which the Uppper Tribunal is bound by a decision of the relevant appellate court or the Supreme Court in previous proceedings, and

    (ii)   that was fully considered in the judgements given by the relevant appellate court or, as the case may be, the Supreme Court in those previous proceedings.

(5)   The conditions in this subsection are that a point of law of general public importance is involved in the decision of the Upper Tribunal and that–

(a)   the proceedings entail a decision relating to a matter of national importance or consideration of such a matter,

(b)   the result of the proceedings is so significant (whether considered on its own or together with other proceedings or likely proceedings) that, in the opinion of the Upper Tribunal, a hearing by the Supreme Court is justified, or

(c)   the Upper Tribunal is satisfied that the benefits of earlier consideration by the Supreme Court outweigh the benefits of consideration by the Court of Appeal.

(6)   Before the Upper Tribunal decides an application made to it under this section, the Upper Tribunal must specify the court that would be the relevant appellate court if the application were an application for permission (or leave) under section 13.

(7)   In this section except subsection (6) and in sections 14B and 14C, "the relevant appellate court", as respects an application, means the court specified as respects that application by the Upper Tribunal under subsection (6).

(8)   No appeal lies against the grant or refusal of a certificate under subsection (1).

Commencement

8.8.16 (and applying only to decisions of the Upper Tribunal made on or after that date).

General Note

Sections 14A to 14C extend to the Upper Tribunal the "leapfrog" procedure that applies in the High Court under s12 of the Administration of Justice Act 1969. Where the conditions in s14A(4) or (5) apply, and the Upper Tribunal is satisfied that "a sufficient case for an appeal to the Supreme Court has been made out", the Upper Tribunal may grant a certificate that allows any application for permission to appeal to be made directly to the Supreme Court, rather than to the Court of Appeal.

In practice, this power is only likely to be used where a previous decision of the Court of Appeal would require that Court to decide the appeal in a particular way and one of the parties wishes to argue that the earlier decision of the Court of Appeal is wrong. At the time of writing, the only example of the Upper Tribunal issuing a "leapfrog" certificate followed the decision in *SSWP v DL and RR (HB)* [2018] UKUT 355 (AAC). Those appeals are *Carmichael* lookalikes: the claimants have had their HB reduced under the "bedroom tax" provisions of reg B13 HB Regus in circumstances which were held by the Supreme Court in *R (Carmichael and Rourke) v SSWP* [2016] UKSC 58; [2017] AACR 9 (*"Carmichael 1"*) to amount to unlawful discrimination (see p377). However, the Upper Tribunal is unable to give them an effective remedy because of the subsequent decision of the majority of the Court of Appeal in *SSWP v Carmichael and Sefton Council* [2018] EWCA Civ 548 (*"Carmichael 2"*). The decision in *Carmichael 2* has been widely doubted (including by the editors of this book: see p114) and a differently constituted panel of the Court of Appeal distinguished it in *JT v First-tier Tribunal* [2018] EWCA Civ 1735. There were therefore arguable grounds of appeal to the Supreme Court. However, if the claimants in *DL* and *RR* had appealed from the Upper Tribunal to the Court of Appeal, the Court would be bound to follow *Carmichael 2* and refuse the appeal. In those circumstances, Upper Tribunal Judge Lloyd-Davies has granted a certificate for the appeal to "leapfrog" to the Supreme Court. The appeal was allowed by the Supreme Court on 13 November 2019 (*RR v SSWP* [2019] UKSC 52).

Judge Lloyd-Davies also drew attention to a potential procedural trap for practitioners: the 14-day time limit for making an application for a "leapfrog" certificate are set out in The Supreme Court Practice Direction 3 at paragraph 3.6.2 and not in any tribunal procedure rules. The Upper Tribunal therefore does not have power to extend the time limit.

Appeal to Supreme Court: permission to appeal

14B.–(1)   If the Upper Tribunal grants a certificate under section 14A in relation to any proceedings, a party to those proceedings may apply to the Supreme Court for permission to appeal directly to the Supreme Court.

(2)   An application under subsection (1) must be made–

(a)   within one month from the date on which that certificate is granted, or

(b)   within such time as the Supreme Court may allow in a particular case.

(3)   If on such an application it appears to the Supreme Court to be expedient to do so, the Supreme Court may grant permission for such an appeal.

(4)   If permission is granted under this section–

(a)   no appeal from the decision to which the certificate relates lies to the relevant appellate court, but

(b)   an appeal lies from that decision to the Supreme Court.

(5)   An application under subsection (1) is to be determined without a hearing.

(6)   Subject to subsection (4), no appeal lies to the relevant appellate court from a decision of the Upper Tribunal in respect of which a certificate is granted under section 14A until–

(a)   the time within which an application can be made under subsection (1) has expired, and

(b)   where such an application is made, that application has been determined in accordance with this section.

Commencement
8.8.16 (and applying only to decisions of the Upper Tribunal made on or after that date).

Appeal to Supreme Court: exclusions

14C.–(1)   No certificate may be granted under section 14A in respect of a decision of the Upper Tribunal in any prooceedings where, by virtue of any enactment (other than sections 14A and 14B), no appeal would lie from that decision of the Upper Tribunal to the relevant appellate court, with or without the permission (or leave) of the Upper Tribunal or the relevant appellate court.

(2)   No certificate may be granted under section 14A in respect of a decision of the Upper Tribunal in any prooceedings where, by virtue of any enactment, no appeal would lie from a decision of the relevant appellate court on that decision of the Upper Tribunal to the Supreme Court, with or without the permission (or leave) of the relevant appellate court or the Supreme Court.

(3)   Where no appeal would lie to the relevant appellate court from the decision of the Upper Tribunal except with the permission (or leave) of the Upper Tribunal or the relevant appellate court, no certificate may be granted under section 14A in respect of a decision of the Upper Tribunal unless it appears to the Upper Tribunal that it would be a proper case for giving permission (or leave) to appeal to the relevant appellate court.

(4)   No certificate may be granted under section 14A in respect of a decision or order of the Upper Tribunal made by it in the exercise of its jurisdiction to punish for contempt.

Commencement
8.8.16 (and applying only to decisions of the Upper Tribunal made on or after that date).

General Note
Where the conditions in s14A(4) and (5) apply, and the Upper Tribunal is satisfied that "a sufficient case for an appeal to the Supreme Court has been made out", the Upper Tribunal may grant a certificate that allows any

appeal to "leapfrog" the Court of Appeal and be made directly to the Supreme Court. In practice, this power is only likely to be used where a previous decision of the Court of Appeal would require that Court to decide the appeal in a particular way and one of the parties wishes to argue that the earlier decision of the Court of Appeal is wrong.

"Judicial review"

General Note on ss15 to 21

One of the major changes introduced by the Act was the extension of the power of judicial review (which had previously only been exercisable by the High Court) to the Upper Tribunal. However, the power is limited. Under s15(2) the application must either satisfy s18 or have been transferred to the Upper Tribunal from the High Court under s31A of the Supreme Court Act 1981 (introduced by s19 TCEA, which is not reproduced in this book).

Section 18 sets out four conditions that must be satisfied if the Upper Tribunal is to have jurisdiction. If they are not satisfied then the application must be transferred to the High Court under s18(3). Conditions 1 and 2 (in s18(4) and (5)) are self-explanatory. By condition 3 (s18(6)) the Upper Tribunal only has jurisdiction where the application falls within a class specified in a Practice Direction given by the Lord Chief Justice of England and Wales or the Lord Chief Justice of Northern Ireland. The former has made the following Direction:

"It is ordered as follows:

1.   The following direction takes effect in relation to an application made to the High Court or Upper Tribunal on or after 3 November 2008 that seeks relief of a kind mentioned in section 15(1) of the Tribunals, Courts and Enforcement Act 2007 ("the 2007 Act")

2.   The Lord Chief Justice hereby directs that the following classes of case are specified for the purposes of section 18(6) of the 2007 Act–

a. *[Omitted as relating to criminal injuries compensation]*

b. Any decision of the First-tier Tribunal made under the Tribunal Procedure Rules or section 9 of the 2007 Act where there is no right of appeal to the Upper Tribunal and that decision is not an excluded decision under paragraph (b), (c) or (f) of section 11(5) of the 2007 Act.

3.   This Direction does not have effect where an application seeks (whether or not alone) a declaration of incompatibility under section 4 of the Human Rights Act 1998.

4.   This Direction is made by the Lord Chief Justice with the agreement of the Lord Chancellor. It is made in the exercise of powers conferred by section 18(6) of the 2007 Act and in accordance with Part 1 of Schedule 2 to the Constitutional Reform Act 2005."

Note that paragraphs (b), (c) and (f) of s11(5) have no application to HB or to social security appeals generally.

The terms of that Direction raise once again the vexed question of the extent of any right of appeal to the Upper Tribunal against interlocutory or procedural decisions made by the First-tier Tribunal: see the Analysis of s11 on p176. The effect of the Direction, however, is to resolve the difficulty. As pointed out by the three-judge panel of the Upper Tribunal in the *Dorset Healthcare* case (see p178), if there is no right of appeal against such a decision, the Upper Tribunal may treat the purported appeal as an application for permission to apply for judicial review.

Condition 4 is that the judge presiding at the hearing of the application is either a judge of the High Court, Court of Appeal or Court of Session, or a person agreed in accordance with s18(8)(b). The Chamber President of the Administrative Appeals Chamber is a High Court judge but judicial reviews are normally be heard by ordinary judges of the Upper Tribunal. The purpose of extending the judicial review jurisdiction to the Upper Tribunal was to relieve the pressure on the resources of the Administrative Court.

In cases where the Upper Tribunal has jurisdiction, it must apply the same principles as would be applied by the High Court in deciding an application for judicial review (s15(5) and any relief granted has the same effect as (and is enforceable as if it were) relief granted by the High Court on an application for judicial review (s15(4)).

For the procedure to be followed in applying to the Upper Tribunal for permission to apply for judicial review, see s16 (on p191) and Part 4 TP(UT) Rules (on p1048).

In Scotland, it is not possible for an application for judicial review to be made directly to the Upper Tribunal. Instead a petition must be presented to the Court of Session, which may then be transferred to the Upper Tribunal: see *EF v SSWP* [2009] UKUT 92 (AAC); *R(IB) 3/09* and *Eba* (at para 9).

Upper Tribunal's "judicial review" jurisdiction

15.–(1)   The Upper Tribunal has power, in cases arising under the law of England and Wales or under the law of Northern Ireland, to grant the following kinds of relief–

(a)   a mandatory order;

(b)   a prohibiting order;

(c)   a quashing order;

(d)   a declaration;

(e)   an injunction.

(2)   The power under subsection (1) may be exercised by the Upper Tribunal if–

(a) certain conditions are met (see section 18), or

(b) the tribunal is authorised to proceed even though not all of those conditions are met (see section 19(3) and (4)).

(3) Relief under subsection (1) granted by the Upper Tribunal–

(a) has the same effect as the corresponding relief granted by the High Court on an application for judicial review, and

(b) is enforceable as if it were relief granted by the High Court on an application for judicial review.

(4) In deciding whether to grant relief under subsection (1)(a), (b) or (c), the Upper Tribunal must apply the principles that the High Court would apply in deciding whether to grant that relief on an application for judicial review.

(5) In deciding whether to grant relief under subsection (1)(d) or (e), the Upper Tribunal must–

(a) in cases arising under the law of England and Wales apply the principles that the High Court would apply in deciding whether to grant that relief under section 31(2) of the Supreme Court Act 1981 (c. 54) on an application for judicial review, and

(b) in cases arising under the law of Northern Ireland apply the principles that the High Court would apply in deciding whether to grant that relief on an application for judicial review.

[¹ (5A) In cases arising under the law of England and Wales, subsections (2A) and (2B) of section 31 of the Senior Courts Act 1981 apply to the Upper Tribunal when deciding whether to grant relief under subsection (1) as they apply to the High Court when deciding whether to grant relief on an application for judicial review.

(5B) If the tribunal grants relief in reliance on section 31(2B) of the Senior Courts Act 1981 as applied by subsection (5A), the tribunal must certify that the condition in section 31(2B) as so applied is satisfied.]

(6) *[Omitted]*

Commencement

3.11.08.

Amendment

1. Inserted by Criminal Justice and Courts Act 2015 s84(4) (8.8.16, and applying only to applications for permission to apply for relief received by the Upper Tribunal on or after that date).

Application for relief under section 15(1)

16.–(1) This section applies in relation to an application to the Upper Tribunal for relief under section 15(1).

(2) The application may be made only if permission (or, in a case arising under the law of Northern Ireland, leave) to make it has been obtained from the tribunal.

(3) The tribunal may not grant permission (or leave) to make the application unless it considers that the applicant has a sufficient interest in the matter to which the application relates.

[¹ (3C) In cases arising under the law of England and Wales, in considering whether to grant permission to make the application, the tribunal–

(a) may of its own initiative consider whether the outcome for the applicant would have been substantially different if the conduct complained of had not occurred, and

(b) must consider that question if the respondent asks it to do so.

(3D) In subsection (3C) "the conduct complained of" means the conduct (or alleged conduct) of the respondent that the applicant claims justifies the tribunal in granting relief.

(3E) If, on considering the question mentioned in subsection (3C)(a) and (b), it appears to the tribunal to be highly likely that the outcome for the applicant would not have been substantially different, the tribunal must refuse to grant permission.

(3F) The tribunal may disregard the requirement in subsection (3E) if it considers that it is appropriate to do so for reasons of exceptional public interest.

(3G) If the tribunal grants permission in reliance on subsection (3F), the tribunal must certify that the condition in subsection (3F) is satisfied.]

(4) Subsection (5) applies where the tribunal considers–

(a) that there has been undue delay in making the application, and

(b) that granting the relief sought on the application would be likely to cause substantial hardship to, or substantially prejudice the rights of, any person or would be detrimental to good administration.

(5) The tribunal may–

(a) refuse to grant permission (or leave) for the making of the application;

(b) refuse to grant any relief sought on the application.

(6) The tribunal may award to the applicant damages, restitution or the recovery of a sum due if–

(a) the application includes a claim for such an award arising from any matter to which the application relates, and

(b) the tribunal is satisfied that such an award would have been made by the High Court if the claim had been made in an action begun in the High Court by the applicant at the time of making the application.

[¹ (6A) In cases arising under the law of England and Wales, subsections (2A) and (2B) of section 31 of the Senior Courts Act 1981 apply to the Upper Tribunal as regards the making of an award under subsection (6) as they apply to the High Court as regards the making of an award under section 31(4) of the Senior Courts Act 1981.

(6B) If the tribunal makes an award in reliance on section 31(2B) of the Senior Courts Act 1981 as applied by subsection (6A), the tribunal must certify that the condition in section 31(2B) as so applied is satisfied.]

(7) An award under subsection (6) may be enforced as if it were an award of the High Court.

(8) Where–

(a) the tribunal refuses to grant permission (or leave) to apply for relief under section 15(1),

(b) the applicant appeals against that refusal, and

(c) the Court of Appeal grants the permission (or leave),

the Court of Appeal may go on to decide the application for relief under section 15(1).

(9) Subsections (4) and (5) do not prevent Tribunal Procedure Rules from limiting the time within which applications may be made.

Commencement

3.11.08.

Amendment

1.   Inserted by Criminal Justice and Courts Act 2015 s84(5) and (6) (8.8.16, and applying only to applications for permission to apply for relief received by the Upper Tribunal on or after that date).

General Note

From 8 August 2016, in England and Wales, paras (3C) and (3D) of s16 *allow* the Upper Tribunal to consider "whether the outcome for the applicant would have been substantially different if the conduct complained of had not occurred" when deciding whether or not to grant permission to apply for judicial review. Where permission is granted, para (6A) *requires* the Upper Tribunal to refuse relief under para (6) unless either, that condition was met or the Upper Tribunal "considers that it is appropriate to do so for reasons of exceptional public interest": see s31(2A) and (2B) Senior Courts Act 1981. Where the Upper Tribunal relies on "reasons of exceptional public interest" condition when granting relief, para (6B) requires that it must certify that that condition applies.

Quashing orders under section 15(1): supplementary provision

17.–(1) If the Upper Tribunal makes a quashing order under section 15(1)(c) in respect of a decision, it may in addition–

(a) remit the matter concerned to the court, tribunal or authority that made the decision, with a direction to reconsider the matter and reach a decision in accordance with the findings of the Upper Tribunal, or

(b) substitute its own decision for the decision in question.

(2)　The power conferred by subsection (1)(b) is exercisable only if–
(a)　the decision in question was made by a court or tribunal,
(b)　the decision is quashed on the ground that there has been an error of law, and
(c)　without the error, there would have been only one decision that the court or tribunal could have reached.
(3)　Unless the Upper Tribunal otherwise directs, a decision substituted by it under subsection (1)(b) has effect as if it were a decision of the relevant court or tribunal.

Commencement
3.11.08.

Limits of jurisdiction under section 15(1)

18.–(1)　This section applies where an application made to the Upper Tribunal seeks (whether or not alone)–
(a)　relief under section 15(1), or
(b)　permission (or, in a case arising under the law of Northern Ireland, leave) to apply for relief under section 15(1).
(2)　If Conditions 1 to 4 are met, the tribunal has the function of deciding the application.
(3)　If the tribunal does not have the function of deciding the application, it must by order transfer the application to the High Court.
(4)　Condition 1 is that the application does not seek anything other than–
(a)　relief under section 15(1);
(b)　permission (or, in a case arising under the law of Northern Ireland, leave) to apply for relief under section 15(1);
(c)　an award under section 16(6);
(d)　interest;
(e)　costs.
(5)　Condition 2 is that the application does not call into question anything done by the Crown Court.
(6)　Condition 3 is that the application falls within a class specified for the purposes of this subsection in a direction given in accordance with Part 1 of Schedule 2 to the Constitutional Reform Act 2005 (c. 4).
(7)　The power to give directions under subsection (6) includes–
(a)　power to vary or revoke directions made in exercise of the power, and
(b)　power to make different provision for different purposes.
(8)　Condition 4 is that the judge presiding at the hearing of the application is either–
(a)　a judge of the High Court or the Court of Appeal in England and Wales or Northern Ireland, or a judge of the Court of Session, or
(b)　such other persons as may be agreed from time to time between the Lord Chief Justice, the Lord President, or the Lord Chief Justice of Northern Ireland, as the case may be, and the Senior President of Tribunals.
(9)　Where the application is transferred to the High Court under subsection (3)–
(a)　the application is to be treated for all purposes as if it–
(i)　had been made to the High Court, and
(ii)　sought things corresponding to those sought from the tribunal, and
(b)　any steps taken, permission (or leave) given or orders made by the tribunal in relation to the application are to be treated as taken, given or made by the High Court.
(10)　Rules of court may make provision for the purpose of supplementing subsection (9).
(11)　The provision that may be made by Tribunal Procedure Rules about amendment of an application for relief under section 15(1) includes, in particular, provision about amendments that would cause the application to become transferrable under subsection (3).
(12)　*[Omitted]*

Commencement
s18(10) and (11): 19.9.07; all other subsections: 3.11.08.

Miscellaneous

Tribunal Procedure Rules

22.–(1) There are to be rules, to be called "Tribunal Procedure Rules", governing–
(a) the practice and procedure to be followed in the First-tier Tribunal, and
(b) the practice and procedure to be followed in the Upper Tribunal.
(2) Tribunal Procedure Rules are to be made by the Tribunal Procedure Committee.
(3) In Schedule 5–
Part 1 makes further provision about the content of Tribunal Procedure Rules,
Part 2 makes provision about the membership of the Tribunal Procedure Committee,
Part 3 makes provision about the making of Tribunal Procedure Rules by the Committee, and
Part 4 confers power to amend legislation in connection with Tribunal Procedure Rules.
(4) Power to make Tribunal Procedure Rules is to be exercised with a view to securing–
(a) that, in proceedings before the First-tier Tribunal and Upper Tribunal, justice is done,
(b) that the tribunal system is accessible and fair,
(c) that proceedings before the First-tier Tribunal or Upper Tribunal are handled quickly and efficiently,
(d) that the rules are both simple and simply expressed, and
(e) that the rules where appropriate confer on members of the First-tier Tribunal, or Upper Tribunal, responsibility for ensuring that proceedings before the tribunal are handled quickly and efficiently.
(5) In subsection (4)(b) "the tribunal system" means the system for deciding matters within the jurisdiction of the First-tier Tribunal or the Upper Tribunal.

Commencement
19.9.07.

General Note
This section, together with Sch 5, establish the Tribunal Procedure Committee and empower it to make procedural rules for the First-tier Tribunal and the Upper Tribunal. Those powers have been exercised by the Committee to make the TP(FTT) Rules and the TP(UT) Rules. See further the commentary to those Rules on p983 and p1029.

Practice directions

23.–(1) The Senior President of Tribunals may give directions–
(a) as to the practice and procedure of the First-tier Tribunal;
(b) as to the practice and procedure of the Upper Tribunal.
(2) A Chamber President may give directions as to the practice and procedure of the chamber over which he presides.
(3) A power under this section to give directions includes–
(a) power to vary or revoke directions made in exercise of the power, and
(b) power to make different provision for different purposes (including different provision for different areas).
(4) Directions under subsection (1) may not be given without the approval of the Lord Chancellor.
(5) Directions under subsection (2) may not be given without the approval of–
(a) the Senior President of Tribunals, and
(b) the Lord Chancellor.
(6) Subsections (4) and (5)(b) do not apply to directions to the extent that they consist of guidance about any of the following–
(a) the application or interpretation of the law;
(b) the making of decisions by members of the First-tier Tribunal or Upper Tribunal.

(7)   Subsections (4) and (5)(b) do not apply to directions to the extent that they consist of criteria for determining which members of the First-tier Tribunal or Upper Tribunal may be chosen to decide particular categories of matter; but the directions may, to that extent, be given only after consulting the Lord Chancellor.

Commencement
3.11.08.

General Note
The Senior President of Tribunal has exercised the powers conferred by subs (1) to make two practice directions, *Child, Vulnerable Adult and Sensitive Witnesses* and *Use of the Welsh Language in Tribunals in Wales*. Both Directions apply to the First-tier Tribunal and the Upper Tribunal.
    In addition, there have been five 'Practice Statements': *Composition of Tribunals in Social Security and Child Support Cases in the Social Entitlement Chamber; Composition of Tribunals in Relation to Matters that Fall to be Decided by the Administrative Appeals Chamber of the Upper Tribunal; Delegation of Functions to Staff in Relation to the Social Entitlement Chamber of the First-tier Tribunal; Form of Decisions;* and *Neutral Citation First-tier Tribunal and Upper Tribunal and Record of Proceedings in Social Security and Child Support Cases in the Social Entitlement Chamber.* The first is made under powers conferred by art 2 First-tier Tribunal and Upper Tribunal (Composition of Tribunal) Order 2008 (see p1061). However, there is no specific power for the Senior President to make the last and it is open to question whether he has a general power to issue Practice Statements, as opposed to Practice Directions (which normally require the Lord Chancellor's consent under subs (4)).

Mediation
24.–(1)   A person exercising power to make Tribunal Procedure Rules or give practice directions must, when making provision in relation to mediation, have regard to the following principles–
(a)   mediation of matters in dispute between parties to proceedings is to take place only by agreement between those parties;
(b)   where parties to proceedings fail to mediate, or where mediation between parties to proceedings fails to resolve disputed matters, the failure is not to affect the outcome of the proceedings.
(2)   Practice directions may provide for members to act as mediators in relation to disputed matters in a case that is the subject of proceedings.
(3)   The provision that may be made by virtue of subsection (2) includes provision for a member to act as a mediator in relation to disputed matters in a case even though the member has been chosen to decide matters in the case.
(4)   Once a member has begun to act as a mediator in relation to a disputed matter in a case that is the subject of proceedings, the member may decide matters in the case only with the consent of the parties.
(5)   Staff appointed under section 40(1) may, subject to their terms of appointment, act as mediators in relation to disputed matters in a case that is the subject of proceedings.
(6)   In this section–
"member" means a judge or other member of the First-tier Tribunal or a judge or other member of the Upper Tribunal;
"practice direction" means a direction under section 23(1) or (2);
"proceedings" means proceedings before the First-tier Tribunal or proceedings before the Upper Tribunal.

Commencement
3.11.08.

Supplementary powers of Upper Tribunal
25.–(1)   In relation to the matters mentioned in subsection (2), the Upper Tribunal–
(a)   has, in England and Wales or in Northern Ireland, the same powers, rights, privileges and authority as the High Court, and
(b)   has, in Scotland, the same powers, rights, privileges and authority as the Court of Session.
(2)   The matters are–
(a)   the attendance and examination of witnesses,

    (b)   the production and inspection of documents, and

    (c)   all other matters incidental to the Upper Tribunal's functions.

    (3)   Subsection (1) shall not be taken–

    (a)   to limit any power to make Tribunal Procedure Rules;

    (b)   to be limited by anything in Tribunal Procedure Rules other than an express limitation.

    (4)   A power, right, privilege or authority conferred in a territory by subsection (1) is available for purposes of proceedings in the Upper Tribunal that take place outside that territory (as well as for purposes of proceedings in the tribunal that take place within that territory).

Commencement

3.11.08.

First-tier Tribunal and Upper Tribunal: sitting places

    26.   Each of the First-tier Tribunal and the Upper Tribunal may decide a case–

    (a)   in England and Wales,

    (b)   in Scotland, or

    (c)   in Northern Ireland,

even though the case arises under the law of a territory other than the one in which the case is decided.

Commencement

3.11.08.

Enforcement

    27.–(1)   A sum payable in pursuance of a decision of the First-tier Tribunal or Upper Tribunal made in England and Wales–

    (a)   shall be recoverable as if it were payable under an order of a county court in England and Wales;

    (b)   shall be recoverable as if it were payable under an order of the High Court in England and Wales.

    (2)   An order for the payment of a sum payable in pursuance of a decision of the First-tier Tribunal or Upper Tribunal made in Scotland (or a copy of such an order certified in accordance with Tribunal Procedure Rules) may be enforced as if it were an extract registered decree arbitral bearing a warrant for execution issued by the sheriff court of any sheriffdom in Scotland.

    (3)   A sum payable in pursuance of a decision of the First-tier Tribunal or Upper Tribunal made in Northern Ireland–

    (a)   shall be recoverable as if it were payable under an order of a county court in Northern Ireland;

    (b)   shall be recoverable as if it were payable under an order of the High Court in Northern Ireland.

    (4)   This section does not apply to a sum payable in pursuance of–

    (a)   an award under section 16(6), or

    (b)   an order by virtue of section 21(1).

    (5)   The Lord Chancellor may by order make provision for subsection (1) or (3) to apply in relation to a sum of a description specified in the order with the omission of one (but not both) of paragraphs (a) and (b).

    (6)   Tribunal Procedure Rules–

    (a)   may make provision as to where, for purposes of this section, a decision is to be taken to be made;

    (b)   may provide for all or any of subsections (1) to (3) to apply only, or not to apply except, in relation to sums of a description specified in Tribunal Procedure Rules.

Assessors

28.–(1)   If it appears to the First-tier Tribunal or the Upper Tribunal that a matter before it requires special expertise not otherwise available to it, it may direct that in dealing with that matter it shall have the assistance of a person or persons appearing to it to have relevant knowledge or experience.

(2)   The remuneration of a person who gives assistance to either tribunal as mentioned in subsection (1) shall be determined and paid by the Lord Chancellor.

(3)   The Lord Chancellor may–

(a)   establish panels of persons from which either tribunal may (but need not) select persons to give it assistance as mentioned in subsection (1);

(b)   under paragraph (a) establish different panels for different purposes;

(c)   after carrying out such consultation as he considers appropriate, appoint persons to a panel established under paragraph (a);

(d)   remove a person from such a panel.

Commencement

3.11.08.

Costs or expenses

29.–(1)   The costs of and incidental to–

(a)   all proceedings in the First-tier Tribunal, and

(b)   all proceedings in the Upper Tribunal,

shall be in the discretion of the Tribunal in which the proceedings take place.

(2)   The relevant Tribunal shall have full power to determine by whom and to what extent the costs are to be paid.

(3)   Subsections (1) and (2) have effect subject to Tribunal Procedure Rules.

(4)   In any proceedings mentioned in subsection (1), the relevant Tribunal may–

(a)   disallow, or

(b)   (as the case may be) order the legal or other representative concerned to meet,

the whole of any wasted costs or such part of them as may be determined in accordance with Tribunal Procedure Rules.

(5)   In subsection (4) "wasted costs" means any costs incurred by a party–

(a)   as a result of any improper, unreasonable or negligent act or omission on the part of any legal or other representative or any employee of such a representative, or

(b)   which, in the light of any such act or omission occurring after they were incurred, the relevant Tribunal considers it is unreasonable to expect that party to pay.

(6)   In this section "legal or other representative", in relation to a party to proceedings, means any person exercising a right of audience or right to conduct the proceedings on his behalf.

(7)   In the application of this section in relation to Scotland, any reference in this section to costs is to be read as a reference to expenses.

Commencement

3.11.08.

General Note

Rule 10 TP(FTT) Rules (made under subs (3)) provides that the Social Entitlement Chamber of the First-tier Tribunal has no power to award costs. Rule 10 TP(UT) Rules (also made under subs (3)) provides that the Upper Tribunal may only make an order in respect of costs when hearing an appeal from another tribunal if that other tribunal had power to order costs. The effect is that the Upper Tribunal has no power to make an order for costs on an appeal from a decision of the Social Entitlement Chamber.

Chapter 3
Transfer of tribunal functions

General Note to Chapter 3

Section 30 (together with the supplementary powers in ss31 and 36) permits the Lord Chancellor to make Orders transferring the functions of other tribunals to the First-tier Tribunal or Upper Tribunal, abolishing those other tribunals and making ancillary, transitional and savings provisions. Note, in particular, that under s38, such an order may amend repeal or revoke both primary and secondary legislation.

The power has been exercised to make the Transfer of Tribunal Functions Order 2008 (see p1057).

Transfer of functions of certain tribunals

30.–(1)   The Lord Chancellor may by order provide for a function of a scheduled tribunal to be transferred–

(a)   to the First-tier Tribunal,

(b)   to the Upper Tribunal,

(c)   to the First-tier Tribunal and the Upper Tribunal with the question as to which of them is to exercise the function in a particular case being determined by a person under provisions of the order,

(d)   to the First-tier Tribunal to the extent specified in the order and to the Upper Tribunal to the extent so specified,

(e)   to the First-tier Tribunal and the Upper Tribunal with the question as to which of them is to exercise the function in a particular case being determined by, or under, Tribunal Procedure Rules,

(f)-(i) *[Omitted]*

(2)   In subsection (1) "scheduled tribunal" means a tribunal in a list in Schedule 6 that has effect for the purposes of this section.

(3)   The Lord Chancellor may, as respects a function transferred under subsection (1) or this subsection, by order provide for the function to be further transferred as mentioned in any of paragraphs (a) to (i) of subsection (1).

(4)   An order under subsection (1) or (3) may include provision for the purposes of or in consequence of, or for giving full effect to, a transfer under that subsection.

(5)   A function of a tribunal may not be transferred under subsection (1) or (3) if, or to the extent that, the provision conferring the function–

(a)   would be within the legislative competence of the Scottish Parliament if it were included in an Act of that Parliament, or

(b)   *[Omitted]*

(6)-(7)   *[Omitted]*

(8)   A function of a tribunal may be transferred under subsection (1) or (3) only with the consent of the Welsh Ministers if any relevant function is exercisable in relation to the tribunal by the Welsh Ministers (whether by the Welsh Ministers alone, or by the Welsh Ministers jointly or concurrently with any other person).

(9)   In subsection (8) "relevant function", in relation to a tribunal, means a function which relates–

(a)   to the operation of the tribunal (including, in particular, its membership, administration, staff, accommodation and funding, and payments to its members or staff), or

(b)   to the provision of expenses and allowances to persons attending the tribunal or attending elsewhere in connection with proceedings before the tribunal.

Commencement

19.9.07.

Transfers under section 30: supplementary powers

31.–(1)   The Lord Chancellor may by order make provision for abolishing the tribunal by whom a function transferred under section 30(1) is exercisable immediately before its transfer.

(2)   The Lord Chancellor may by order make provision, where functions of a tribunal are transferred under section 30(1), for a person–

(a)   who is the tribunal (but is not the Secretary of State), or

(b)   who is a member of the tribunal, or

(c)   *[Omitted]*

to (instead or in addition) be the holder of an office specified in subsection (3).

(3)   Those offices are–

(a)   transferred-in judge of the First-tier Tribunal,

(b)   transferred-in other member of the First-tier Tribunal,

(c)   transferred-in judge of the Upper Tribunal,

(d)   transferred-in other member of the Upper Tribunal, and

(e)   deputy judge of the Upper Tribunal.

(4)   Where functions of a tribunal are transferred under section 30(1), the Lord Chancellor must exercise the power under subsection (2) so as to secure that each person who immediately before the end of the tribunal's life–

(a)   is the tribunal,

(b)   is a member of the tribunal, or

(c)   is an authorised decision-maker for the tribunal,

becomes the holder of an office specified in subsection (3) with effect from the end of the tribunal's life (if the person is not then already the holder of such an office).

(5)   Subsection (4) does not apply in relation to a person–

(a)   by virtue of the person's being the Secretary of State, or

(b)   by virtue of the person's being a Commissioner for the general purposes of the income tax;

and a reference in subsection (4) to the end of a tribunal's life is to when the tribunal is abolished or (without being abolished) comes to have no functions.

(6)   *[Omitted]*

(7)   Where a function of a tribunal is transferred under section 30(1), the Lord Chancellor may by order provide for procedural rules in force immediately before the transfer to have effect, or to have effect with appropriate modifications, after the transfer (and, accordingly, to be capable of being varied or revoked) as if they were–

(a)   Tribunal Procedure Rules, or

(b)   *[Omitted]*

(8)   In subsection (7)–

"procedural rules" means provision (whether called rules or not)–

(a)   regulating practice or procedure before the tribunal, and

(b)   applying for purposes connected with the exercise of the function;

"appropriate modifications" means modifications (including additions and omissions) that appear to the Lord Chancellor to be necessary to secure, or expedient in connection with securing, that the procedural rules apply in relation to the exercise of the function after the transfer.

(9)   The Lord Chancellor may, in connection with provision made by order under section 30 or the preceding provisions of this section, make by order such incidental, supplemental, transitional or consequential provision, or provision for savings, as the Lord Chancellor thinks fit, including provision applying only in relation to cases selected by a member–

(a)   of the First-tier Tribunal,

(b)   of the Upper Tribunal,

(c)-(d)   *[Omitted]*

(10)   Subsections (1), (2) and (7) are not to be taken as prejudicing the generality of subsection (9).

Commencement

19.9.07.

Power to provide for appeal to Upper Tribunal from tribunals in Wales

32.   *[Omitted]*

Commencement

19.9.07.

Power to provide for appeal to Upper Tribunal from tribunals in Scotland
    33. *[Omitted]*

Commencement
    19.9.07.

Power to provide for appeal to Upper Tribunal from tribunals in Northern Ireland
    34. *[Omitted]*

Commencement
    19.9.07.

Transfer of Ministerial responsibilities for certain tribunals
    35. *[Omitted]*

Commencement
    19.9.07.

Transfer of powers to make procedural rules for certain tribunals
    36. *[Omitted]*

Commencement
    19.9.07.

Power to amend lists of tribunals in Schedule 6
    37.–(1)   The Lord Chancellor may by order amend Schedule 6–
    (a)   for the purpose of adding a tribunal to a list in the Schedule;
    (b)   for the purpose of removing a tribunal from a list in the Schedule;
    (c)   for the purpose of removing a list from the Schedule;
    (d)   for the purpose of adding to the Schedule a list of tribunals that has effect for the purposes of any one or more of sections 30, 32(3), 35 and 36.
    (2)   The following rules apply to the exercise of power under subsection (1)–
    (a)   a tribunal may not be added to a list, or be in an added list, if the tribunal is established otherwise than by or under an enactment;
    (b)   a tribunal established by an enactment passed or made after the last day of the Session in which this Act is passed must not be added to a list, or be in an added list, that has effect for the purposes of section 30;
    (c)   if any relevant function is exercisable in relation to a tribunal by the Welsh Ministers (whether by the Welsh Ministers alone, or by the Welsh Ministers jointly or concurrently with any other person), the tribunal may be added to a list, or be in an added list, only with the consent of the Welsh Ministers;
    (d)   a tribunal may be in more than one list.
    (3)   In subsection (2)(c) "relevant function", in relation to a tribunal, means a function which relates–
    (a)   to the operation of the tribunal (including, in particular, its membership, administration, staff, accommodation and funding, and payments to its members or staff), or
    (b)   to the provision of expenses and allowances to persons attending the tribunal or attending elsewhere in connection with proceedings before the tribunal.
    (4)   In subsection (1) "tribunal" does not include an ordinary court of law.
    (5)   In this section "enactment" means any enactment whenever passed or made, including an enactment comprised in subordinate legislation (within the meaning of the Interpretation Act 1978 (c. 30)).

Commencement
    19.9.07.

Orders under sections 30 to 36: supplementary

38.–(1) Provision in an order under any of sections 30 to 36 may take the form of amendments, repeals or revocations of enactments.

(2) In this section "enactment" means any enactment whenever passed or made, including an enactment comprised in subordinate legislation (within the meaning of the Interpretation Act 1978).

(3) Any power to extend enactments to a territory outside the United Kingdom shall have effect as if it included–

(a) power to extend those enactments as they have effect with any amendments and repeals made in them by orders under any of sections 30 to 36, and

(b) power to extend those enactments as if any amendments and repeals made in them under those sections had not been made.

Commencement
19.9.07.

Chapter 4
Administrative matters in respect of certain tribunals

The general duty

39.–(1) The Lord Chancellor is under a duty to ensure that there is an efficient and effective system to support the carrying on of the business of–

(a) the First-tier Tribunal,

(b) the Upper Tribunal,

(c)-(e) *[Omitted]*

and that appropriate services are provided for those tribunals (referred to in this section and in sections 40 and 41 as "the tribunals").

(2) Any reference in this section, or in section 40 or 41, to the Lord Chancellor's general duty in relation to the tribunals is to his duty under subsection (1).

(3) The Lord Chancellor must annually prepare and lay before each House of Parliament a report as to the way in which he has discharged his general duty in relation to the tribunals.

Commencement
19.9.07.

Provision of accommodation

41.–(1) The Lord Chancellor may provide, equip, maintain and manage such tribunal buildings, offices and other accommodation as appear to him appropriate for the purpose of discharging his general duty in relation to the tribunals.

(2) The Lord Chancellor may enter into such arrangements for the provision, equipment, maintenance or management of tribunal buildings, offices or other accommodation as appear to him appropriate for the purpose of discharging his general duty in relation to the tribunals.

(3) The powers under–

(a) section 2 of the Commissioners of Works Act 1852 (c. 28) (acquisition by agreement), and

(b) section 228(1) of the Town and Country Planning Act 1990 (c. 8) (compulsory acquisition),

to acquire land necessary for the public service are to be treated as including power to acquire land for the purpose of its provision under arrangements entered into under subsection (2).

(4) In this section "tribunal building" means any place where any of the tribunals sits, including the precincts of any building in which it sits.

Fees

42.–(1) The Lord Chancellor may by order prescribe fees payable in respect of–

(a) anything dealt with by the First-tier Tribunal,

(b) anything dealt with by the Upper Tribunal,

(c) anything dealt with by the Asylum and Immigration Tribunal,

(d) anything dealt with by an added tribunal, and

(e) mediation conducted by staff appointed under section 40(1).

(2) An order under subsection (1) may, in particular, contain provision as to–

(a) scales or rates of fees;

(b) exemptions from or reductions in fees;

(c) remission of fees in whole or in part.

(3) In subsection (1)(d) "added tribunal" means a tribunal specified in an order made by the Lord Chancellor.

(4) A tribunal may be specified in an order under subsection (3) only if–

(a) it is established by or under an enactment, whenever passed or made, and

(b) is not an ordinary court of law.

(5) Before making an order under this section, the Lord Chancellor must consult–

(a) the Senior President of Tribunals, [¹]

[¹ (b)]

(6) The making of an order under subsection (1) requires the consent of the Treasury except where the order contains provision only for the purpose of altering amounts payable by way of fees already prescribed under that subsection.

(7) The Lord Chancellor must take such steps as are reasonably practicable to bring information about fees under subsection (1) to the attention of persons likely to have to pay them.

(8) Fees payable under subsection (1) are recoverable summarily as a civil debt.

(9) Subsection (8) does not apply to the recovery in Scotland of fees payable under this section.

[¹ (10)]

Commencement
19.9.07.

Amendment
1. Amended by Sch para 32 of SI 2013 No 2042 as from 19.8.13.

Report by Senior President of Tribunals

43.–(1) Each year the Senior President of Tribunals must give the Lord Chancellor a report covering, in relation to relevant tribunal cases–

(a) matters that the Senior President of Tribunals wishes to bring to the attention of the Lord Chancellor, and

(b) matters that the Lord Chancellor has asked the Senior President of Tribunals to cover in the report.

(2) The Lord Chancellor must publish each report given to him under subsection (1).

(3) In this section "relevant tribunal cases" means–

(a) cases coming before the First-tier Tribunal,

(b) cases coming before the Upper Tribunal,

(c)-(d) *[Omitted]*

Commencement
3.11.08.

Chapter 5
Oversight of administrative justice system, tribunals and inquiries

The Administrative Justice and Tribunals Council
[¹**44.**]

Amendment
1.   Omitted by Sch para 33 of SI 2013 No 2042 as from 19.8.13.

Abolition of the Council on Tribunals
[¹**45.**]

Amendment
1.   Omitted by Sch para 34 of SI 2013 No 2042 as from 19.8.13.

Chapter 6
Supplementary

Orders and regulations under Part 1: supplemental and procedural provisions
49.–(1)   Power–
(a)   of the Lord Chancellor to make an order, or regulations, under this Part,
(b)   of the Senior President of Tribunals to make an order under section 7(9), or
(c)   of the Scottish Ministers, or the Welsh Ministers, to make an order under paragraph 25(2) of Schedule 7,
is exercisable by statutory instrument.

(2)   The Statutory Instruments Act 1946 (c. 36) shall apply in relation to the power to make orders conferred on the Senior President of Tribunals by section 7(9) as if the Senior President of Tribunals were a Minister of the Crown.

(3)   Any power mentioned in subsection (1) includes power to make different provision for different purposes.

(4)   Without prejudice to the generality of subsection (3), power to make an order under section 30 or 31 includes power to make different provision in relation to England, Scotland, Wales and Northern Ireland respectively.

(5)   No order mentioned in subsection (6) is to be made unless a draft of the statutory instrument containing it (whether alone or with other provision) has been laid before, and approved by a resolution of, each House of Parliament.

(6)   Those orders are–
(a)   an order under section 11(8), 13(6) or (14), 30, 31(1), 32, 33, 34, 35, 36, 37 or 42(3);
(b)   an order under paragraph 15 of Schedule 4;
(c)   an order under section 42(1)(a) to (d) that provides for fees to be payable in respect of things for which fees have never been payable;
(d)   an order under section 31(2), (7) or (9), or paragraph 30(1) of Schedule 5, that contains provision taking the form of an amendment or repeal of an enactment comprised in an Act.

(7)   A statutory instrument that–
(a)   contains–
  (i)   an order mentioned in subsection (8), or
  (ii)   regulations under Part 3 of Schedule 9, and
(b)   is not subject to any requirement that a draft of the instrument be laid before, and approved by a resolution of, each House of Parliament,
is subject to annulment in pursuance of a resolution of either House of Parliament.

(8)   Those orders are–
(a)   an order made by the Lord Chancellor under this Part;
(b)   an order made by the Senior President of Tribunals under section 7(9).

(9)   A statutory instrument that contains an order made by the Scottish Ministers under paragraph 25(2) of Schedule 7 is subject to annulment in pursuance of a resolution of the Scottish Parliament.

(10)   A statutory instrument that contains an order made by the Welsh Ministers under paragraph 25(2) of Schedule 7 is subject to annulment in pursuance of a resolution of the National Assembly for Wales.

Commencement
19.9.07.

SCHEDULE 5

Commencement
19.9.07.

SECTION 22

Procedure in First-tier Tribunal and Upper Tribunal
Part 1
Tribunal Procedure Rules

Introductory

1.–(1) This Part of this Schedule makes further provision about the content of Tribunal Procedure Rules.

(2) The generality of section 22(1) is not to be taken to be prejudiced by–

(a) the following paragraphs of this Part of this Schedule, or

(b) any other provision (including future provision) authorising or requiring the making of provision by Tribunal Procedure Rules.

(3) In the following paragraphs of this Part of this Schedule "Rules" means Tribunal Procedure Rules.

Concurrent functions

2. Rules may make provision as to who is to decide, or as to how to decide, which of the First-tier Tribunal and Upper Tribunal is to exercise, in relation to any particular matter, a function that is exercisable by the two tribunals on the basis that the question as to which of them is to exercise the function is to be determined by, or under, Rules.

Delegation of functions to staff

3.–(1) Rules may provide for functions–

(a) of the First-tier Tribunal, or

(b) of the Upper Tribunal,

to be exercised by staff appointed under section 40(1).

(2) In making provision of the kind mentioned in sub-paragraph (1) in relation to a function, Rules may (in particular)–

(a) provide for the function to be exercisable by a member of staff only if the member of staff is, or is of a description, specified in exercise of a discretion conferred by Rules;

(b) provide for the function to be exercisable by a member of staff only if the member of staff is approved, or is of a description approved, for the purpose by a person specified in Rules.

Time limits

4. Rules may make provision for time limits as respects initiating, or taking any step in, proceedings before the First-tier Tribunal or the Upper Tribunal.

Repeat applications

5. Rules may make provision restricting the making of fresh applications where a previous application in relation to the same matter has been made.

Tribunal acting of its own initiative

6. Rules may make provision about the circumstances in which the First-tier Tribunal, or the Upper Tribunal, may exercise its powers of its own initiative.

Hearings

7. Rules may–

(a) make provision for dealing with matters without a hearing;

(b) make provision as respects allowing or requiring a hearing to be in private or as respects allowing or requiring a hearing to be in public.

Proceedings without notice

8. Rules may make provision for proceedings to take place, in circumstances described in Rules, at the request of one party even though the other, or another, party has had no notice.

Representation

9. Rules may make provision conferring additional rights of audience before the First-tier Tribunal or the Upper Tribunal.

Evidence, witnesses and attendance

10.–(1) Rules may make provision aboutevidence (including evidence on oath and administration of oaths).

(2)   Rules may modify any rules of evidence provided for elsewhere, so far as they would apply to proceedings before the First-tier Tribunal or Upper Tribunal.

(3)   Rules may make provision, where the First-tier Tribunal has required a person–

(a)   to attend at any place for the purpose of giving evidence,

(b)   otherwise to make himself available to give evidence,

(c)   to swear an oath in connection with the giving of evidence,

(d)   to give evidence as a witness,

(e)   to produce a document, or

(f)   to facilitate the inspection of a document or any other thing (including any premises),

for the Upper Tribunal to deal with non-compliance with the requirement as though the requirement had been imposed by the Upper Tribunal.

(4)   Rules may make provision for the payment of expenses and allowances to persons giving evidence, producing documents, attending proceedings or required to attend proceedings.

Use of information

11.–(1)   Rules may make provision for the disclosure or non-disclosure of information received during the course of proceedings before the First-tier Tribunal or Upper Tribunal.

(2)   Rules may make provision for imposing reporting restrictions in circumstances described in Rules.

Costs and expenses

12.–(1)   Rules may make provision for regulating matters relating to costs, or (in Scotland) expenses, of proceedings before the First-tier Tribunal or Upper Tribunal.

(2)   The provision mentioned in sub-paragraph (1) includes (in particular)–

(a)   provision prescribing scales of costs or expenses;

(b)   provision for enabling costs to undergo detailed assessment in England and Wales by a county court or the High Court;

(c)   provision for taxation in Scotland of accounts of expenses by an Auditor of Court;

(d)   provision for enabling costs to be taxed in Northern Ireland in a county court or the High Court;

(e)   provision for costs or expenses–

(i)   not to be allowed in respect of items of a description specified in Rules;

(ii)   not to be allowed in proceedings of a description so specified;

(f)   provision for other exceptions to either or both of subsections (1) and (2) of section 29.

Set-off and interest

13.–(1)   Rules may make provision for a party to proceedings to deduct, from amounts payable by him, amounts payable to him.

(2)   Rules may make provision for interest on sums awarded (including provision conferring a discretion or provision in accordance with which interest is to be calculated).

Arbitration

14.   Rules may provide for [¹ any of the provisions of sections 1 to 15 of and Schedule 1 to the Arbitration (Scotland) Act 2010 (which extends to Scotland) or] Part 1 of the Arbitration Act 1996 (c. 23) (which extends to England and Wales, and Northern Ireland, but not Scotland) not to apply, or not to apply except so far as is specified in Rules, where the First-tier Tribunal, or Upper Tribunal, acts as arbitrator.

Amendment

1.   Amended by art 2 and Sch para 8 of SI 2010 No 220 as from 5.6.10.

Correction of errors and setting-aside of decisions on procedural grounds

15.–(1)   Rules may make provision for the correction of accidental errors in a decision or record of a decision.

(2)   Rules may make provision for the setting aside of a decision in proceedings before the First-tier Tribunal or Upper Tribunal–

(a)   where a document relating to the proceedings was not sent to, or was not received at an appropriate time by, a party to the proceedings or a party's representative,

(b)   where a document relating to the proceedings was not sent to the First-tier Tribunal or Upper Tribunal at an appropriate time,

(c)   where a party to the proceedings, or a party's representative, was not present at a hearing related to the proceedings, or

(d)   where there has been any other procedural irregularity in the proceedings.

(3)   Sub-paragraphs (1) and (2) shall not be taken to prejudice, or to be prejudiced by, any power to correct errors or set aside decisions that is exercisable apart from rules made by virtue of those sub-paragraphs.

Ancillary powers

16.   Rules may confer on the First-tier Tribunal, or the Upper Tribunal, such ancillary powers as are necessary for the proper discharge of its functions.

Rules may refer to practice directions
    17.   Rules may, instead of providing for any matter, refer to provision made or to be made about that matter by directions under section 23.

Presumptions
    18.   Rules may make provision in the form of presumptions (including, in particular, presumptions as to service or notification).

Differential provision
    19.   Rules may make different provision for different purposes or different areas.

SCHEDULE 6

Commencement
    19.9.07.

SECTIONS 30 TO 37

Tribunals for the purposes of sections 30 to 36
Part 1
Tribunals for the purposes of sections 30, 35 and 36

Tribunal	*Enactment*
Appeal tribunal	Chapter 1 of Part 1 of the Social Security Act 1998 (c. 14)
Social Security Commissioner	Schedule 4 to the Social Security Act 1998 (c. 14)

SCHEDULE 10

SECTION 50

Amendments relating to judicial appointments
Part 1

Amendments
    29.–(1)   The Social Security Act 1998 (c. 14) is amended as follows.
    (2)-(7)   *[Omitted]*
    (8)   At any time before the coming into force of section 59(1) of the Constitutional Reform Act 2005 (c. 4) (renaming of Supreme Court), the reference to the Senior Courts in the section 7(2)(a) substituted by sub-paragraph (3) is to be read as a reference to the Supreme Court.

Commencement
    21.7.08.

Welfare Reform Act 2012
(2012 c5)

Universal credit and other benefits

Abolition of benefits

33.–(1) The following benefits are abolished–

(e) council tax benefit under section 131 of that Act;

Commencement

s33(1)(e): 1.4.13

General Note

CTB was abolished by s33(1)(e) of the Welfare Reform Act 2012 on 1 April 2013. Help with payment of council tax was localised from that date. See Parts 4 and 5 for details of the council tax reduction schemes. Note that s33 will also eventually abolish HB. However, as UC is being introduced, there are now only limited situations in which a person can make a claim for, and be entitled, to HB. See the note on p4 and the Universal Credit (Transitional Provisions) Regulations 2014 SI No.1230 on p1857 and the No.21, No.23 and 31 Orders on p1882, p1885 and p1898.

Benefit cap

Benefit cap

96.–(1) Regulations may provide for a benefit cap to be applied to the welfare benefits to which a single person or couple is entitled.

(2) For the purposes of this section, applying a benefit cap to welfare benefits means securing that, where a single person's or couple's total entitlement to welfare benefits in respect of the reference period exceeds the relevant amount, their entitlement to welfare benefits in respect of any period of the same duration as the reference period is reduced by an amount up to or equalling the excess.

(3) In subsection (2) the "reference period" means a period of a prescribed duration.

(4) Regulations under this section may in particular–

(a) make provision as to the manner in which total entitlement to welfare benefits for any period, or the amount of any reduction, is to be determined;

(b) make provision as to the welfare benefit or benefits from which a reduction is to be made;

(c) provide for exceptions to the application of the benefit cap;

(d) make provision as to the intervals at which the benefit cap is to be applied;

(e) make provision as to the relationship between application of the benefit cap and any other reduction in respect of a welfare benefit;

(f) provide that where in consequence of a change in the relevant amount, entitlement to a welfare benefit increases or decreases, that increase or decrease has effect without any further decision of the Secretary of State;

(g) make supplementary and consequential provision.

[¹ (5) Regulations under this section may make provision for determining the "relevant amount" for the reference period applicable in the case of a single person or couple by reference to the annual limit applicable in the case of that single person or couple.

(5A) For the purposes of this section the "annual limit" is–

(a) £23,000 or £15,410, for persons resident in Greater London;

(b) £20,000 or £13,400, for other persons.

(5B) Regulations under subsection (5) may–

(a) specify which annual limit applies in the case of–

(i) different prescribed descriptions of single person;

(ii) different prescribed descriptions of couple;

(b) define "resident" for the purposes of this section;

(c)   provide for the rounding up or down of an amount produced by dividing the amount of the annual limit by the number of periods of a duration equal to the reference period in a year.]

[¹ (6)]

[¹ (7)]

[¹ (8)]

(9)   Regulations under this section may not provide for any reduction to be made from a welfare benefit–

(a)   provision for which is within the legislative competence of the Scottish Parliament;

(b)   provision for which is within the legislative competence of the National Assembly for Wales;

(c)   provision for which is made by the Welsh Ministers, the First Minister for Wales or the Counsel General to the Welsh Assembly Government.

(10)   In this section–

"couple" means two persons of a prescribed description;

"prescribed" means prescribed in regulations;

"regulations" means regulations made by the Secretary of State;

"single person" means a person who is not a member of a couple;

"welfare benefit" [¹ means–

(a)   bereavement allowance (see section 39B of the Social Security Contributions and Benefits Act 1992),

(b)   child benefit (see section 141 of the Social Security Contributions and Benefits Act 1992),

(c)   child tax credit (see section 1(1)(a) of the Tax Credits Act 2002),

(d)   employment and support allowance (see section 1 of the Welfare Reform Act 2007), including income-related employment and support allowance (as defined in section 1(7) of the Welfare Reform Act 2007),

(e)   housing benefit (see section 130 of the Social Security Contributions and Benefits Act 1992),

(f)   incapacity benefit (see section 30A of the Social Security Contributions and Benefits Act 1992),

(g)   income support (see section 124 of the Social Security Contributions and Benefits Act 1992),

(h)   jobseeker's allowance (see section 1 of the Jobseekers Act 1995), including income-based jobseeker's allowance (as defined in section 1(4) of the Jobseekers Act 1995),

(i)   maternity allowance under section 35 or 35B of the Social Security Contributions and Benefits Act 1992,

(j)   severe disablement allowance (see section 68 of the Social Security Contributions and Benefits Act 1992),

(k)   universal credit,

(l)   widow's pension (see section 38 of the Social Security Contributions and Benefits Act 1992),

(m)   widowed mother's allowance (see section 37 of the Social Security Contributions and Benefits Act 1992), or

(n)   widowed parent's allowance (see section 39A of the Social Security Contributions and Benefits Act 1992).]

[¹ (11)]

Commencement

27.11.12 for making regulations; 15.4.13 for all other purposes.

Amendment

1.   Amended by s8(2)-(5) of the Welfare Reform and Work Act 2016 (16.3.16 for making regulations; 7.11.16 for all other purposes).

General Note

Sections 96 and 97 WRA 2012 make provision for limiting the amount of benefit certain working-age claimants can be paid if the total of their welfare benefits exceeds a "relevant amount". The "benefit cap" is applied by reducing the amount of the claimant's entitlement to universal credit (UC), or if the claimant is instead entitled to HB under the HB Regs, by reducing the amount of that entitlement. Note that if there is no entitlement to either UC or HB, no "benefit cap" can be applied.

Analysis

Subs (1) to (3) and (5) to (5B) set out the general framework for the "benefit cap". It is to be applied whether the claimant is single or a member of a couple. For HB purposes, "couple" is defined in reg 75G HB Regs by reference to the definition in reg 2(1) HB Regs, other than where the claimant is a member of a polygamous marriage. In this case, "couple" means the claimant and the member of the polygamous marriage to whom s/he was first married, and references to the claimant's partner are to that member.

Note that for HB purposes, the "benefit cap" can only apply to those entitled to HB under the HB Regs. It cannot apply to those entitled under the HB(SPC) Regs; no equivalent provisions have been made in the HB(SPC) Regs.

For HB purposes, unless any of the exceptions to the "benefit cap" apply (for which see regs 75E and 75F HB Regs), if the total welfare benefits of the claimant (and her/his partner) in respect of a "reference period" exceeds the "relevant amount", her/his entitlement to HB is reduced by an amount up to or equalling the excess. For HB, the "reference period" is a benefit week and the "relevant amount" is to be determined by reference to the applicable "annual limit" as set out in subs (5A) and as calculated under reg 75CA HB Regs. The method for calculating the total amount of welfare benefits is in reg 75C. A"welfare benefit" is defined in subs (10).

Subs (4). For the HB regulations made under this section, see regs 75A to 75H HB Regs. Note also regs 72E and 73E HB Regs for the calculation of extended payments of HB where the "benefit cap" applies.

Subs (5A) sets out what the "annual limit" is for people resident in Greater London and elsewhere. Reg 75CA is the regulation made under subs (5). The lower amounts in both cases apply to single claimants and the higher amounts to all other claimants: reg 75CA(2) HB Regs. Reg 2(1) HB Regs defines a "single claimant" as a claimant who neither has a partner nor is a lone parent. See reg 75CA(3) for when someone counts as resident in Greater London and reg 75CA(1) for how a weekly "relevant amount" is to be calculated. Note that both a requirement and a discretion to review the annual limits are found in s96A.

Subs (10). For HB purposes, the prescribed definition of "couple" is in regs 2(1) and 75G HB Regs.

From 7 November 2016, "welfare benefit" is defined in subs (10). Prior to this date, the definition was in reg 75G HB Regs. This list includes the only benefits that the local authority can use to calculate the total welfare benefits to which a claimant (and her/his partner) are entitled. No other benefits may be used. The definition includes child tax credit. It does not include carer's allowance, guardian's allowance, PC or retirement pension, or statutory payments (ie, statutory sick pay and statutory maternity, adoption, paternity and shared parental pay). For the manner of calculating the amount of a claimant's welfare benefits, see reg 75C HB Regs. Note that the definition includes UC, but a claimant is exempt from the HB benefit cap if s/he is receiving UC: reg 75F(1)(g) HB Regs.

[¹Benefit cap: review

96A.–(1)   The Secretary of State must at least once in each Parliament review the sums specified in section 96(5A) to determine whether it is appropriate to increase or decrease any one or more of those sums.

(2)   The Secretary of State may, at any other time the Secretary of State considers appropriate, review the sums specified in section 96(5A) to determine whether it is appropriate to increase or decrease any one or more of those sums.

(3)   In carrying out a review, the Secretary of State must take into account–

(a)   the national economic situation, and

(b)   any other matters that the Secretary of State considers relevant.

(4)   After carrying out a review, the Secretary of State may, if the Secretary of State considers it appropriate, by regulations amend section 96(5A) so as to increase or decrease any one or more of the sums specified in section 96(5A).

(5)   Regulations under subsection (4) may provide for amendments of section 96(5A) to come into force–

(a)   on different days for different areas;

(b)   on different days for different cases or purposes.

(6)   Regulations under subsection (4) may make such transitional or transitory provision or savings as the Secretary of State considers necessary or expedient in connection with the coming into force of any amendment made by regulations under subsection (4).

(7)   Regulations under subsection (6) may in particular–

(a)   provide for section 96(5A) to have effect as if the amendments made by regulations under subsection (4) had not been made, in relation to such persons or descriptions of persons as are specified in the regulations or generally, until a time or times specified in a notice issued by the Secretary of State;

(b)   provide for the Secretary of State to issue notices under paragraph (a) specifying different times for different persons or descriptions of person;

(c)   make provision about the issuing of notices under paragraph (a), including provision for the Secretary of State to issue notices to authorities administering housing benefit that have effect in relation to persons specified, or persons of a description specified, in the notices.

(8)   Section 176 of the Social Security Administration Act 1992 (consultation with representative organisations) does not apply in relation to regulations under subsection (4).

(9)   If an early parliamentary general election is to take place in accordance with section 2 of the Fixed-term Parliaments Act 2011, the duty in subsection (1) is to be disregarded.]

Amendment

1.   Inserted by s9(1) of the Welfare Reform and Work Act 2016 (16.3.16 for making regulations; 7.11.16 for all other purposes).

General Note

Section 96A(1) requires the Secretary of State to review the benefit cap "annual limits" found in s96(5A) at least once in each Parliament to determine if any of them should be increased or decreased. Note, however, that this duty is to be disregarded if an early general election is to take place in accordance with s2 of the Fixed-term Parliaments Act 2011: subs (9). Subs (2) gives the Secretary of State the discretion to review the annual limits at any other time. Note that the requirement to review the benefit cap was formerly in s150(7A) SSAA 1992.

Benefit cap: supplementary

97.–(1)   Regulations under section 96 [² or 96A] may make different provision for different purposes or cases.

(2)   Regulations under section 96 [² or 96A] must be made by statutory instrument.

[¹ (3)]

(4)   A statutory instrument containing [¹] regulations under section 96 is subject to annulment in pursuance of a resolution of either House of Parliament.

[² (4A)   A statutory instrument containing regulations under section 96A may not be made unless a draft of the instrument has been laid before, and approved by a resolution of, each House of Parliament.]

(5)-(6)   *[Omitted]*

Commencement

27.11.12

Amendments

1.   Amended by s8(6) of the Welfare Reform and Work Act 2016 (16.3.16 for making regulations; 7.11.16 for all other purposes).

2.   Amended by s9(2)-(5) of the Welfare Reform and Work Act 2016 (16.3.16 for making regulations; 7.11.16 for all other purposes).

Appeals

Supersession of decisions of former appellate bodies

103.–(1)   Schedule 12 contains amendments reinstating powers to make decisions superseding decisions made by appellate bodies before their functions were transferred to the First-tier Tribunal and Upper Tribunal.

(2)   The following have effect as if they had come into force on 3 November 2008–

(a)   the amendments made by Schedule 12, and

(b)   if regulations made in the exercise of the powers conferred by virtue of those amendments so provide, those regulations.

Commencement

8.3.12

General Note

Sch 12 amended para 4 of Sch 7 CSPSSA 2000 (on p143) retrospectively from 3 November 2008, to reverse the decision of the Upper Tribunal in *DN v Leicester City Council (HB)* [2010] UKUT 253 (AAC). See also regs 7 and 8 D&A Regs (on p951 and p957).

Information-sharing involving local authorities etc

Information-sharing in relation to provision of overnight care etc

130.–(1)   This section applies where a local authority holds information falling within subsection (2) in relation to a person who is receiving or is likely to receive a relevant service.

(2)   The information referred to in subsection (1) is–

(a)   information as to the fact of the provision or likely provision of the service;

(b)   information about when the provision of the service begins or ends or is likely to do so;

(c)   other prescribed information relating to the service provided and how it is funded (including the extent to which it is funded by the recipient).

(3)   In this section "relevant service" means–

(a)   a service consisting of overnight care in the individual's own home provided by or on behalf of a local authority;

(b)   a residential care service provided by or on behalf of a local authority;

(c)   a service consisting of overnight hospital accommodation.

(4)   In subsection (3)(c) "hospital accommodation" means–

(a)   in relation to England, hospital accommodation within the meaning of the National Health Service Act 2006 which is provided by [²] an NHS trust or an NHS foundation trust;

(b)   in relation to Wales, hospital accommodation within the meaning of the National Health Service (Wales) Act 2006 which is provided by a Local Health Board or an NHS trust;

(c)   in relation to Scotland, hospital accommodation within the meaning of the National Health Service (Scotland) Act 1978 which is provided by a Health Board or Special Health Board but excluding accommodation in an institution for providing dental treatment maintained in connection with a dental school.

(5)   The local authority may–

(a)   itself use the information for purposes relating to the payment of a relevant benefit to the individual, or

(b)   supply the information to a person specified in subsection (6) for those purposes.

(6)   The persons referred to in subsection (5) are–

(a)   the Secretary of State;

(b)   a person providing services to the Secretary of State;

(c)   a local authority;

(d)   a person authorised to exercise any function of a local authority relating to a relevant benefit;

(e)   a person providing services relating to a relevant benefit to a local authority.

(7)   In this section "relevant benefit" means–

(a)   universal credit;

(b)   housing benefit;

[¹ (c)]

(d)   any prescribed benefit.

(8)   Regulations under subsection (7)(d) may not prescribe a benefit provision for which is within the legislative competence of the Scottish Parliament.

Commencement
20.3.12 for the purpose of making regulations; 8.5.12 in so far as not already in force.

Amendments
1.   Repealed by WRA 2012 s147 and Sch 14 part 1 (1.4.13).
2.   Amended by art 7 of SI 2013 No 594 as from 1.4.13.

Information-sharing in relation to welfare services etc
131.–(1)   The Secretary of State, or a person providing services to the Secretary of State, may supply relevant information to a qualifying person for prescribed purposes relating to welfare services or council tax.

(2)   A qualifying person who holds relevant information for a prescribed purpose relating to welfare services may supply that information to–
(a)   the Secretary of State, or
(b)   a person providing services to the Secretary of State, for a prescribed purpose relating to a relevant social security benefit.

(3)   A qualifying person who holds relevant information for a prescribed purpose relating to welfare services, council tax or housing benefit may–
(a)   use the information for another prescribed purpose relating to welfare services, council tax or housing benefit;
(b)   supply it to another qualifying person for use in relation to the same or another prescribed purpose relating to welfare services, council tax or housing benefit.

(4)   Relevant information supplied under subsection (1) or (3) to a qualifying person may be supplied by that person to a person who provides qualifying welfare services for purposes connected with the provision of those services.

(5)   In subsection (4) services are qualifying welfare services if–
(a)   a local authority, or
(b)   a person who is a qualifying person by virtue of subsection (11)(g), contributes or will contribute to the expenditure incurred in their provision.

(6)   The Secretary of State may not exercise the power in subsection (3) to prescribe purposes for which information may be supplied by a qualifying person so as to prescribe an excepted purpose in relation to excepted information held by a Welsh body.

(7)   In subsection (6)–
(a)   excepted information is information held by the Welsh body that–
(i)   is not supplied by, or derived from information supplied to another person by, the Secretary of State or a person providing services to the Secretary of State or a person engaged in the administration of housing benefit, and
(ii)   is held only for an excepted purpose;
(b)   an excepted purpose is a purpose relating to a matter provision for which–
(i)   is within the legislative competence of the National Assembly for Wales, or
(ii)   is made by the Welsh Ministers, the First Minister for Wales or the Counsel General to the Welsh Assembly Government.

(8)   The Secretary of State may not exercise the power in subsection (3) to prescribe purposes for which information may be supplied by a qualifying person so as to prescribe an excepted purpose in relation to excepted information held by a Scottish body.

(9)   In subsection (8)–
(a)   excepted information is information held by the Scottish body that–
(i)   is not supplied by, or derived from information supplied to another person by, the Secretary of State or a person providing services to the Secretary of State or a person engaged in the administration of housing benefit, and
(ii)   is held only for an excepted purpose;
(b)   an excepted purpose is a purpose relating to a matter provision for which is within the legislative competence of the Scottish Parliament.

(10)   Subsections (1) to (4) do not apply in a case where the supply or use of information is authorised by section 130.

(11)   In this section "qualifying person" means–

(a) a local authority;
(b) a person authorised to exercise any function of such an authority relating to welfare services or council tax;
(c) a person providing services to a local authority relating to welfare services or council tax;
(d) an authority which administers housing benefit;
(e) a person authorised to exercise any function of such an authority relating to housing benefit;
(f) a person providing to such an authority services relating to housing benefit; or
(g) a person prescribed or of a description prescribed by the Secretary of State.
(12) In this section–
"council tax" includes any local tax to fund local authority expenditure;
"person engaged in the administration of housing benefit" means–
(a) an authority which administers housing benefit,
(b) a person authorised to exercise any function of such an authority relating to housing benefit, or
(c) a person providing to such an authority services relating to housing benefit;
"relevant information" means information relating to–
(a) any relevant social security benefit, or
(b) welfare services;
"relevant social security benefit" [¹ means–
(a) a relevant social security benefit as defined in section 121DA(7) of the Social Security Administration Act 1992, or
(b) a loan under section 18 of the Welfare Reform and Work Act 2016 (loans for mortgage interest etc);]
"Scottish body" means–
(a) a local authority in Scotland,
(b) a person authorised to exercise any function of such an authority relating to welfare services,
(c) a person providing to a local authority in Scotland services relating to welfare services, or
(d) a person prescribed or of a description prescribed by the Secretary of State;
"welfare services" includes services which provide accommodation, support, assistance, advice or counselling to individuals with particular needs, and for these purposes "assistance" includes assistance by means of a grant or loan or the provision of goods or services;
"Welsh body" means–
(a) a local authority in Wales,
(b) a person authorised to exercise any function of such an authority relating to welfare services,
(c) a person providing to a local authority in Wales services relating to welfare services, or
(d) a person prescribed or of a description prescribed by the Secretary of State.

Commencement
20.3.12 for the purpose of making regulations; 8.5.12 in so far as not already in force.

Amendment
1.   Amended by WRWA 2016 s20(10) (27.7.17)

General Note
The Scottish and Welsh bodies prescribed under s131(12) are in the Social Security (Information-sharing in relation to Welfare Services etc.) Amendment and Prescribed Bodies Regulations 2013 SI No.454 (on p1848).

Unlawful disclosure of information supplied under section 131
132.–(1)   A person to whom subsection (2) applies is guilty of an offence if the person discloses without lawful authority any information–
(a) which comes to the person by virtue of section 131(1), (3) or (4), and

(b)   which relates to a particular person.

(2)   This subsection applies to–

(a)   a person mentioned in section 131(11)(a) to (c);

(b)   a person who provides qualifying welfare services (within the meaning of section 131);

(c)   a person who is or has been a director, member of the committee of management, manager, secretary or other similar officer of a person mentioned in paragraph (a) or (b);

(d)   a person who is or has been an employee of a person mentioned in paragraph (a) or (b).

(3)   A person guilty of an offence under this section is liable–

(a)   on conviction on indictment, to imprisonment for a term not exceeding two years or a fine or both, or

(b)   on summary conviction, to imprisonment for a term not exceeding twelve months or a fine not exceeding the statutory maximum or both.

(4)   It is not an offence under this section–

(a)   to disclose information in the form of a summary or collection of information so framed as not to enable information relating to any particular person to be ascertained from it;

(b)   to disclose information which has previously been disclosed to the public with lawful authority.

(5)   It is a defence for a person ("D") charged with an offence under this section to prove that at the time of the alleged offence–

(a)   D believed that D was making the disclosure in question with lawful authority and had no reasonable cause to believe otherwise, or

(b)   D believed that the information in question had previously been disclosed to the public with lawful authority and had no reasonable cause to believe otherwise.

(6)   A disclosure is made with lawful authority if it is so made for the purposes of section 123 of the Social Security Administration Act 1992.

(7)   This section does not affect that section.

(8)   Regulations under section 131(11)(g) may include provision for applying the provisions of this section to–

(a)   a person who is a qualifying person within the meaning of section 131 by virtue of the regulations, or

(b)   a person associated with such a qualifying person by reason of the person's office or employment or otherwise.

(9)   In relation to an offence under this section committed in England and Wales before the commencement of section 154(1) of the Criminal Justice Act 2003 (increase in maximum term that may be imposed on summary conviction of offence triable either way) the reference in subsection (3)(b) to twelve months must be taken to be a reference to six months.

Commencement
20.3.12 s132(8); 8.5.12 in so far as not already in force

Sections 130 to 132: supplementary

133.–(1)   In sections 130 and 131–

"benefit" includes any allowance, payment, credit or loan;

"local authority" means–

(a)   a county or district council in England;

(b)   an eligible parish council (within the meaning of Chapter 1 of Part 1 of the Localism Act 2011);

(c)   a London borough council;

(d)   the Common Council of the City of London in its capacity as a local authority;

(e)   the Council of the Isles of Scilly;

(f)   a county or county borough council in Wales;

(g)   a council constituted under section 2 of the Local Government etc. (Scotland) Act 1994;

''prescribed'' means prescribed in regulations made by the Secretary of State.

(2)   Any power to make regulations under sections 130 and 131 includes power–

(a)   to make different provision for different purposes, cases and areas;

(b)   to make such incidental, supplemental, consequential, transitional or saving provision as the Secretary of State thinks necessary or expedient.

(3)   Regulations under sections 130 and 131 must be made by statutory instrument.

(4)   A statutory instrument containing regulations under section 130 or 131 is subject to annulment in pursuance of a resolution of either House of Parliament.

(6)   *[Omitted]*

Commencement

Paras (1) to (4): 20.3.12
Para (6): 2.7.12.

Part 2:

Main secondary legislation –
housing benefit

The Housing Benefit Regulations 2006
(SI 2006 No.213)

PART 1
General
1.   Citation and commencement
2.   Interpretation
3.   Definition of non-dependant
4.   Cases in which section 1(1A) of the Administration Act is disapplied
5.   Persons who have attained the qualifying age for state pension credit
6.   Remunerative work

PART 2
Provisions affecting entitlement to housing benefit
7.   Circumstances in which a person is or is not to be treated as occupying a dwelling as his home
8.   Circumstances in which a person is to be treated as liable to make payments in respect of a dwelling
9.   Circumstances in which a person is to be treated as not liable to make payments in respect of a dwelling
10.   Persons from abroad
10A.   Entitlement of a refugee to housing benefit

PART 3
Payments in respect of a dwelling
11.   Eligible housing costs
12.   Rent
12B.   Eligible rent
12BA.   Eligible rent and maximum rent (social sector)
12C.   Eligible rent and maximum rent
12D.   Eligible rent and maximum rent (LHA)
12L.   Transitional protection – larger properties
12M.   Transitional protection – reduction in LHA
A13.   When a maximum rent (social sector) is to be determined
B13.   Determination of a maximum rent (social sector)
13.   Maximum rent
13ZA.   Protection on death and 13 week protection
13ZB.   Change in reckonable rent
13C.   When maximum rent (LHA) is to be determined
13D.   Determination of a maximum rent (LHA)
13E.   Publication of local housing allowances
14.   Requirement to refer to rent officers
15.   Applications to the rent officer for redeterminations
16.   Application for a redetermination by a rent officer
17.   Substitute determinations or substitute redeterminations
18.   Application of provisions to substitute determinations or substitute redeterminations
18A.   Amended determinations

PART 4
Membership of a family
19.   Persons of prescribed description
20.   Circumstances in which a person is to be treated as responsible or not responsible for another
21.   Circumstances in which a person is to be treated as being or not being a member of the household

PART 5
Applicable amounts
22. Applicable amounts
23. Polygamous marriages
24. Patients

PART 6
Income and capital
SECTION 1
General
25. Calculation of income and capital of members of claimant's family and of a polygamous marriage
26. Circumstances in which income of non-dependant is to be treated as claimant's

SECTION 2
Income
27. Calculation of income on a weekly basis
28. Treatment of child care charges
29. Average weekly earnings of employed earners
29A. Date on which income consisting of earnings from employment as an employed earner are taken into account
30. Average weekly earnings of self-employed earners
31. Average weekly income other than earnings
32. Calculation of average weekly income from tax credits
33. Calculation of weekly income
34. Disregard of changes in tax, contributions etc

SECTION 3
Employed earners
35. Earnings of employed earners
36. Calculation of net earnings of employed earners

SECTION 4
Self-employed earners
37. Earnings of self-employed earners
38. Calculation of net profit of self-employed earners
39. Deduction of tax and contributions of self-employed earners

SECTION 5
Other income
40. Calculation of income other than earnings
41. Capital treated as income
42. Notional income

SECTION 6
Capital
43. Capital limit
44. Calculation of capital
45. Disregard of capital of child and young person
46. Income treated as capital
47. Calculation of capital in the United Kingdom
48. Calculation of capital outside the United Kingdom
49. Notional capital
50. Diminishing notional capital rule
51. Capital jointly held
52. Calculation of tariff income from capital

PART 7
Students
SECTION 1
General

53. Interpretation
54. Treatment of students

SECTION 2
Entitlement and payments in respect of a dwelling
55. Occupying a dwelling as a person's home
56. Full-time students to be treated as not liable to make payments in respect of a dwelling
57. Student's eligible housing costs
58. Student partners

SECTION 3
Income
59. Calculation of grant income
60. Calculation of covenant income where a contribution is assessed
61. Covenant income where no grant income or no contribution is assessed
62. Relationship with amounts to be disregarded under Schedule 5
63. Other amounts to be disregarded
64. Treatment of student loans
64A. Treatment of fee loans
64B. Treatment of special support loans
65. Treatment of payments from access funds
66. Disregard of contribution and rent
67. Further disregard of student's income
68. Amounts treated as capital
69. Disregard of changes occurring during summer vacation

PART 8
Amount of benefit
70. Maximum housing benefit
71. Housing benefit tapers
72. Extended payments
72A. Duration of extended payment period
72B. Amount of extended payment
72C. Extended payments – movers
72D. Relationship between extended payment and entitlement to housing benefit under the general conditions of entitlement
72E. Calculation of an extended payment where the benefit cap applies
73. Extended payments (qualifying contributory benefits)
73A. Duration of extended payment period (qualifying contributory benefits)
73B. Amount of extended payment (qualifying contributory benefits)
73C. Extended payments (qualifying contributory benefits) – movers
73D. Relationship between extended payment (qualifying contributory benefits) and entitlement to housing benefit under the general conditions of entitlement
73E. Calculation of an extended payment (qualifying contributory benefits) where the benefit cap applies
74. Non-dependant deductions
75. Minimum housing benefit

PART 8A
Benefit cap
75A.   Circumstances in which a benefit cap applies
75B.   Determinations
75C.   Manner of calculating the amount of welfare benefits
75CA.   Determinations of the relevant amount
75D.   Recuction of housing benefit
75E.   Exception to the benefit cap: current or recent work
75F.   Exception to the benefit cap: receipt of specified benefit
75G.   Interpretation
75H.   Specified accommodation

PART 9
Calculation of weekly amounts and changes of circumstances
76.   Date on which entitlement is to commence
77.   Date on which housing benefit is to end
78.   Date on which housing benefit is to end where entitlement to severe disablement allowance or incapacity benefit ceases
79.   Date on which change of circumstances is to take effect
80.   Calculation of weekly amounts
81.   Rent free periods

PART 10
Claims
82.   Who may claim
83.   Time and manner in which claims are to be made
83A.   Electronic claims for benefit
84.   Date of claim where claim sent or delivered to a gateway office
85.   Date of claim where claim sent or delivered to an office of a designated authority
86.   Evidence and information
87.   Amendment and withdrawal of claim
88.   Duty to notify changes of circumstances
88ZA.   Alternative means of notifying changes of circumstances
88A.   Notice of changes of circumstances given electronically

PART 11
Decisions on questions
89.   Decisions by a relevant authority
90.   Notification of decisions

PART 12
Payments
91.   Time and manner of payment
91A.   Cases in which payment to a housing authority are to take the form of a rent allowance
92.   Frequency of payment of a rent allowance
93.   Payment on account of a rent allowance
94.   Payment to be made to a person entitled
95.   Circumstances in which payment is to be made to a landlord
96.   Circumstances in which payment may be made to a landlord
97.   Payment on death of the person entitled
98.   Offsetting

PART 13
Overpayments
99.   Meaning of overpayment
100.   Recoverable overpayments
101.   Person from whom recovery may be sought
102.   Method of recovery
103.   Diminution of capital
104.   Sums to be deducted in calculating recoverable overpayments
104A. Sums to be deducted in calculating recoverable overpayments where the claimant has changed dwelling
105.   Recovery of overpayments from prescribed benefits
106.   Prescribed benefits
106A. Recovery by deduction from earnings
107.   Restrictions on recovery of rent and consequent notifications

PART 14
Information
SECTION 1
Claims and information
108.   Interpretation
109A. Verifying information
109.   Collection of information
110.   Recording and holding information
111.   Forwarding of information
112.   Request for information

SECTION 2
Information from landlords and agents and between authorities etc.
113.   Interpretation
114A. Information to be provided to rent officers
114.   Evidence and information required by rent officers
115.   Information to be supplied by an authority to another authority
116.   Supply of information: extended payments (qualifying contributory benefits)
117.   Requiring information from landlords and agents
118.   Circumstances for requiring information
119.   Relevant information
120.   Manner of supply of information
121.   Criminal offence
121A. Supply of benefit administration information between authorities

PART 15
Former pathfinder authorities
122.   Modifications in respect of former pathfinder areas

SCHEDULES
A1.   Treatment of claims for housing benefit by refugees
1.   Ineligible service charges
2.   Excluded tenancies
3.   Applicable amounts
4.   Sums to be disregarded in the calculation of earnings
5.   Sums to be disregarded in the calculation of income other than earnings
6.   Capital to be disregarded
7.   Extended payments of housing benefit
8.   Extended Payments (severe disablement allowance and incapacity benefit) of housing benefit
9.   Matters to be included in decision notice
10.   Former pathfinder authorities
11.   Electronic communication

General Note to the HB Regulations

These regulations, rather than the HB(SPC) Regs, apply where the neither the claimant nor her/his partner has attained the qualifying age for pension credit (PC), as defined in reg 2. The HB Regs also apply to any claimant who has attained that age who is on (or whose partner in on) IS, income-based JSA or income-related ESA (or UC): reg 5 (see p252).

Note that since 15 May 2019, where a claimant is a member of a "mixed-age couple" (ie, only one member of the couple is at least the qualifying age for PC), a new claim for, and entitlement to, HB is not generally allowed unless the claimant has been continuously entitled to PC or HB under the HB(SPC) Regs from before that date as part of the same mixed-age couple. For the rules for mixed-age couples on claims for, and termination of awards of, HB and the exceptions to the rules, see the Welfare Reform Act 2012 (Commencement No.31) Order 2019 SI No.37 (the No.31 Order) on p1898. Where a member of a mixed-age couple is excluded from entitlement to PC or HB and is also prevented from claiming UC because of the "SDP Gateway" in reg 4A of the UC(TP) Regs 2014 (see p1862), because s/he is a frontier worker or by virtue of reg 4 of the UC(TP) Regs 2014 (see p1861), the member of the couple who has reached the qualifying age for PC is treated as not having attained that age for the purposes of reg 5 and thus the HB Regs, instead of the HB(SPC) Regs, apply to such a claimant. See Art 8 of the No.31 Order on p1902.

Welfare Reform Act 2012

HB is to be abolished by the Welfare Reform Act 2012 (see p4). Note that, in many cases, new claims for, and entitlement to, HB are no longer allowed. Where they are allowed, these regulations continue to apply.

PART 1
General

General Note on Part I

This Part defines terms commonly used in the HB Regs. Reg 4 provides cases where the requirement to state a national insurance number when claiming HB does not apply.

Citation and commencement

1.–(1) These Regulations may be cited as the Housing Benefit Regulations 2006.

(2) These Regulations are to be read, where appropriate, with the Consequential Provisions Regulations and, in a case where regulation 5(2) applies, with the Housing Benefit (Persons who have attained the qualifying age for state pension credit) Regulations 2006.

(3) Except as provided in Schedule 4 to the Consequential Provisions Regulations, these Regulations shall come into force on 6th March 2006.

(4) The regulations consolidated by these Regulations are revoked, in consequence of the consolidation, by the Consequential Provisions Regulations.

Interpretation

2.–(1) In these Regulations–

"the Act" means the Social Security Contributions and Benefits Act 1992;

"the 1973 Act" means the Employment and Training Act 1973;

[1"the 2000 Act" means the Electronic Communications Act 2000;]

[50 "the 2012 Act" means the Welfare Reform Act 2012;]

"Abbeyfield Home" means an establishment run by the Abbeyfield Society including all bodies corporate or incorporate which are affiliated to that Society;

"adoption leave" means a period of absence from work on ordinary or additional adoption leave by virtue of section 75A or 75B of the Employment Rights Act 1996;

"the Administration Act" means the Social Security Administration Act 1992;

"appropriate DWP office" means an office of the Department for Work and Pensions dealing with state pension credit or an office which is normally open to the public for the receipt of claims for income support [17, a jobseeker's allowance or an employment and support allowance];

[9 "amended determination" means a determination made in accordance with article 7A of the Rent Officers Order;]

[75 "approved blood scheme" means a scheme established or approved by the Secretary of State, or trust established with funds provided by the Secretary of State, for the purpose of providing compensation in respect of a person having been infected from contaminated blood products;]

[51 "armed forces independence payment" means armed forces independence payment under the Armed Forces and Reserve Forces (Compensation Scheme) Order 2011;]

"assessment period" means such period as is prescribed in regulations 29 to 31 over which income falls to be calculated;

"attendance allowance" means–

(a)   an attendance allowance under Part 3 of the Act;

(b)   an increase of disablement pension under section 104 or 105 of the Act;

[56 (c)-d)]

(e)   a payment by virtue of article 14, 15, 16, 43 or 44 of the Personal Injuries (Civilians) Scheme 1983 or any analogous payment; or

(f)   any payment based on need for attendance which is paid as part of a war disablement pension;

[22 "basic rate", where it relates to the rate of tax, has the same meaning as in the Income Tax Act 2007 (see section 989 of that Act);]

"the benefit Acts" means the Act [17, the Jobseekers Act [50, Part 4 of the 2012 Act] [51, the Armed Forces and Reserve Forces (Compensation Scheme) Order 2011] [67, the Welfare Reform Act and the Pensions Act 2014];

"benefit week" means a period of 7 consecutive days commencing upon a Monday and ending on a Sunday;

[9 "broad rental market area" has the meaning specified in paragraph 4 of Schedule 3B to the Rent Officers Order;]

[9 "broad rental market area determination" means a determination made in accordance with article 4B(1A) of the Rent Officers Order;]

"care home" in England [77] has the meaning assigned to it by section 3 of the Care Standards Act 2000 [77 , in Wales means a care home service within the meaning of Part 1 of the Regulation and Inspection of Social Care (Wales) Act 2016 which is provided wholly or mainly to persons aged 18 or over] and in Scotland means a care home service within the meaning assigned to it by [42 paragraph 2 of schedule 12 to the Public Services Reform (Scotland) Act 2010];

[41 "the Caxton Foundation" means the charitable trust of that name established on 28th March 2011 out of funds provided by the Secretary of State for the benefit of certain persons suffering from hepatitis C and other persons eligible for payment in accordance with its provisions;]

[9 "change of dwelling" means, for the purposes of regulations 13C and 14, a change of dwelling occupied by a claimant as his home during the award where the dwelling to which the claimant has moved is one in respect of which the authority may make a rent allowance;]

"child" means a person under the age of 16;

"child tax credit" means a child tax credit under section 8 of the Tax Credits Act;

[58 "child who cannot share a bedroom" means a child–

(a)   who is entitled to the care component of disability living allowance at the highest or middle rate prescribed in accordance with section 72(3) of the Act; and

(b)   who the relevant authority is satisfied is, by virtue of his or her disability, not reasonably able to share a bedroom with another child;]

"the Children Order" means the Children (Northern Ireland) Order 1995;

"claim" means a claim for housing benefit;

"claimant" means a person claiming housing benefit;

"close relative" means a parent, parent-in-law, son, son-in-law, daughter, daughter-in-law, step-parent, step-son, step-daughter, brother, sister, or if any of the preceding persons is one member of a couple, the other member of that couple;

[19]

"concessionary payment" means a payment made under arrangements made by the Secretary of State with the consent of the Treasury which is charged either to the National Insurance Fund or to a Departmental Expenditure Vote to which payments of benefit [20 or tax credits under the benefit Acts or the Tax Credits Act] [12] are charged;

"the Consequential Provisions Regulations" means the Housing Benefit and Council Tax Benefit (Consequential Provisions) Regulations 2006;

[¹⁸ [⁵³ "contributory employment and support allowance" means an allowance under Part 1 of the Welfare Reform Act as amended by the provisions of Schedule 3, and Part 1 of Schedule 14, to the 2012 Act that remove references to an income-related allowance, and a contributory allowance under Part 1 of the Welfare Reform Act as that Part has effect apart from those provisions;]]

[³³ "converted employment and support allowance" means an employment and support allowance which is not income-related and to which a person is entitled as a result of a conversion decision within the meaning of the Employment and Support Allowance (Existing Awards) Regulations;]

"co-ownership scheme" means a scheme under which the dwelling is let by a housing association and the tenant, or his personal representative, will, under the terms of the tenancy agreement or of the agreement under which he became a member of the association, be entitled, on his ceasing to be a member and subject to any conditions stated in either agreement, to a sum calculated by reference directly or indirectly to the value of the dwelling;

[⁵⁹, ⁶² "couple" means–
  (a) two people who are married to, or civil partners of, each other and are members of the same household; or
  (b) two people who are not married to, or civil partners of, each other but are living together as a married couple;]

"Crown tenant" means a person who occupies a dwelling under a tenancy or licence where the interest of the landlord belongs to Her Majesty in right of the Crown or to a government department or is held in trust for Her Majesty for the purposes of a government department, except (in the case of an interest belonging to Her Majesty in right of the Crown) where the interest is under the management of the Crown Estate Commissioners [⁷² or a relevant person];

"date of claim" means the date on which the claim is made, or treated as made, for the purposes of regulation 83 (time and manner in which claims are to be made);

"the Decisions and Appeals Regulations" means the Housing Benefit and Council Tax Benefit (Decisions and Appeals) Regulations 2001;

"designated authority" means any of the following–
  (a) the Secretary of State;
  (b) a person providing services to the Secretary of State;
  (c) a local authority;
  (d) a person providing services to, or authorised to exercise any functions of, any such authority;

"designated office" means the office designated by the relevant authority for the receipt of claims to housing benefit–
  (a) by notice upon or with a form approved by it for the purpose of claiming housing benefit; or
  (b) by reference upon or with such a form to some other document available from it and sent by electronic means or otherwise on application and without charge; or
  (c) by any combination of the provisions set out in sub-paragraphs (a) and (b) above;

"disability living allowance" means a disability living allowance under section 71 of the Act;

"earnings" has the meaning prescribed in regulation 35 or, as the case may be, 37;

"the Eileen Trust" means the charitable trust of that name established on 29th March 1993 out of funds provided by the Secretary of State for the benefit of persons eligible for payment in accordance with its provisions;

[¹ "electronic communication" has the same meaning as in section 15(1) of the 2000 Act;]

[⁸ "eligible rent" means, as the case may require, an eligible rent determined in accordance with–

(a)   regulations 12B (eligible rent), [⁴⁷ 12BA (eligible rent and maximum rent (social sector)),] 12C (eligible rent and maximum rent) or 12D (eligible rent and maximum rent (LHA)); or

(b)   regulations 12 (rent) and 13 (restrictions on unreasonable payments) as set out in paragraph 5 of Schedule 3 to the Consequential Provisions Regulations in a case to which paragraph 4 of that Schedule applies;]

"employed earner" is to be construed in accordance with section 2(1)(a) of the Act and also includes a person who is in receipt of a payment which is payable under any enactment having effect in Northern Ireland and which corresponds to statutory sick pay or statutory maternity pay;

[⁵² "employment and support allowance" means an employment and support allowance under Part 1 of the Welfare Reform Act;]

[¹⁸ "Employment and Support Allowance Regulations" means the Employment and Support Allowance Regulations 2008;]

[³³ "Employment and Support Allowance (Existing Awards) Regulations" means the Employment and Support Allowance (Transitional Provisions, Housing Benefit and Council Tax Benefit) (Existing Awards) (No, 2) Regulations 2010;]

[³⁹]

"employment zone" means an area within Great Britain designated for the purposes of section 60 of the Welfare Reform and Pensions Act 1999 and an "employment zone programme" means a programme established for such an area or areas designed to assist claimants for a jobseeker's allowance to obtain sustainable employment;

"employment zone contractor" means a person who is undertaking the provision of facilities in respect of an employment zone programme on behalf of the Secretary of State for Work and Pensions;

[²⁶ "enactment" includes an enactment comprised in, or in an instrument made under, an Act of the Scottish Parliament [⁵⁶ or the National Assembly for Wales];]

[¹⁴ "extended payment" means a payment of housing benefit payable pursuant to regulation 72;]

[¹⁵ "extended payment period" means the period for which an extended payment is payable in accordance with regulation 72A or 73A;]

[¹⁴ "extended payment (qualifying contributory benefits)" means a payment of housing benefit payable pursuant to regulation 73;]

"family" has the meaning assigned to it by section 137(1) of the Act;

"the former Regulations" means the Housing Benefit (General) Regulations 1987;

"the Fund" means moneys made available from time to time by the Secretary of State for the benefit of persons eligible for payment in accordance with the provisions of a scheme established by him on 24th April 1992 or, in Scotland, on 10th April 1992;

[¹³]

"a guaranteed income payment" means a payment made under article 14(1)(b) or article 21(1)(a) of the Armed Forces and Reserve Forces (Compensation Scheme) Order 2005;

"hostel" means a building–

(a)   in which there is provided for persons generally or for a class of persons, domestic accommodation, otherwise than in separate and self-contained premises, and either board or facilities for the preparation of food adequate to the needs of those persons, or both; and

(b)   which is–

    (i)   managed or owned by a registered housing association; or

    (ii)   operated other than on a commercial basis and in respect of which funds are provided wholly or in part by a government department or agency or a local authority; or

    (iii)   managed by a voluntary organisation or charity and provides care, support or supervision with a view to assisting those persons to be rehabilitated or resettled within the community; and

(c)   which is not–
      (i)   a care home;
      (ii)   an independent hospital; or
      (iii) an Abbeyfield Home;

[36 "Housing Act functions" means functions under section 122 of the Housing Act 1996;]

[8 "housing association" has the meaning assigned to it by section 1(1) of the Housing Associations Act 1985;]

"Immigration and Asylum Act" means the Immigration and Asylum Act 1999;

"an income-based jobseeker's allowance" and "a joint-claim jobseeker's allowance" have the same meanings as they have in the Jobseekers Act by virtue of section 1(4) of that Act;

[18 "income-related employment and support allowance" means an income-related allowance under Part 1 of the Welfare Reform Act;]

"Income Support Regulations" means the Income Support (General) Regulations 1987;

[34 "independent hospital"–

(a)   in England, means a hospital as defined by section 275 of the National Health Service Act 2006 that is not a health service hospital as defined by that section;

(b)   in Wales, has the meaning assigned to it by section 2 of the Care Standards Act 2000; and

[42 (c) in Scotland, means an independent health care service as defined in section 10F(1)(a) and (b) of the National Health Service (Scotland) Act 1978;]]

[19]

[5 "the Independent Living Fund (2006)" means the Trust of that name established by a deed dated 10th April 2006 and made between the Secretary of State for Work and Pensions of the one part and Margaret Rosemary Cooper, Michael Beresford Boyall and Marie Theresa Martin of the other part;]

[19]
[19]
[19]
[11]

"invalid carriage or other vehicle" means a vehicle propelled by petrol engine or by electric power supplied for use on the road and to be controlled by the occupant;

"Jobseekers Act" means the Jobseekers Act 1995;

[52 "jobseeker's allowance" means a jobseeker's allowance within the meaning of Part 1 of the Jobseekers Act;]

"Jobseeker's Allowance Regulations" means the Jobseeker's Allowance Regulations 1996;]

[18 "limited capability for work" has the meaning given in section 1(4) of the Welfare Reform Act;

[18 "limited capability for work-related activity" has the meaning given in section 2(5) of the Welfare Reform Act;]

[9 "linked person" means–

(a)   any member of the claimant's family;

(b)   if the claimant is a member of a polygamous marriage, any partners of his and any child or young person for whom he or a partner is responsible and who is a member of the same household; or

(c)   any relative of the claimant or his partner who occupies the same dwelling as the claimant, whether or not they reside with him, except for a relative who has a separate right of occupation of the dwelling which would enable them to continue to occupy it even if the claimant ceased his occupation of it;]

[9 "local housing allowance" means an allowance determined in accordance with paragraph 2 of Schedule 3B to the Rent Officers Order;]

[49 "local welfare provision" means occasional financial or other assistance given by a local authority, the Scottish Ministers or the Welsh Ministers, or a person authorised to exercise any function of, or provide a service to, them, to or in respect of individuals for the purpose of–

(a) meeting, or helping to meet, an immediate short term need–
  (i) arising out of an exceptional event, or exceptional circumstances; and
  (ii) that requires to be met in order to avoid a risk to the well-being of an individual; or
(b) enabling individuals to establish or maintain a settled home, where those individuals have been or, without the assistance, might otherwise be–
  (i) in prison, hospital, a residential care establishment or other institution; or
  (ii) homeless or otherwise living an unsettled way of life;]

"the London Bombings Relief Charitable Fund" means the company limited by guarantee (number 5505072) and registered charity of that name established on 11th July 2005 for the purpose of (amongst other things) relieving sickness, disability or financial need of victims (including families or dependants of victims) of the terrorist attacks carried out in London on 7th July 2005;

[74 "the London Emergencies Trust" means the company of that name (number 09928465) incorporated on 23rd December 2015 and the registered charity of that name (number 1172307) established on 28th March 2017;]

"lone parent" means a person who has no partner and who is responsible for and a member of the same household as a child or young person;

"long tenancy" means a tenancy granted for a term of years certain exceeding twenty one years, whether or not the tenancy is, or may become, terminable before the end of that term by notice given by or to the tenant or by re-entry, forfeiture (or, in Scotland, irritancy) or otherwise and includes a lease for a term fixed by law under a grant with a covenant or obligation for perpetual renewal unless it is a lease by sub-demise from one which is not a long tenancy;

[7]

"the Macfarlane (Special Payments) Trust" means the trust of that name, established on 29th January 1990 partly out of funds provided by the Secretary of State, for the benefit of certain persons suffering from haemophilia;

"the Macfarlane (Special Payments) (No. 2) Trust" means the trust of that name, established on 3rd May 1991 partly out of funds provided by the Secretary of State, for the benefit of certain persons suffering from haemophilia and other beneficiaries;

"the Macfarlane Trust" means the charitable trust, established partly out of funds provided by the Secretary of State to the Haemophilia Society, for the relief of poverty or distress among those suffering from haemophilia;

[18 "main phase employment and support allowance" means an employment and support allowance where the calculation of the amount payable in respect of the claimant includes a component under section 2(1)(b) or 4(2)(b) of the Welfare Reform Act [73 or the claimant is a member of the work-related activity group] [23 except in Part 1 of Schedule 3];]

[38 "the Mandatory Work Activity Scheme" means a scheme within section 17A (schemes for assisting persons to obtain employment: "work for your benefit" schemes etc.) of the Jobseekers Act 1995 known by that name and provided pursuant to arrangements made by the Secretary of State that is designed to provide work or work-related activity for up to 30 hours per week over a period of four consecutive weeks with a view to assisting claimants to improve their prospects of obtaining employment;]

"maternity leave" means a period during which a woman is absent from work because she is pregnant or has given birth to a child, and at the end of which she has a right to return to work either under the terms of her contract of employment or under Part 8 of the Employment Rights Act 1996;

[8 "maximum rent" means the amount to which the eligible rent is restricted in a case where regulation 13 applies;]

[9 "maximum rent (LHA)" means the amount determined in accordance with regulation 13D;]

[70 "member of a couple who cannot share a bedroom" means a member of a couple–
- (a)   who is in receipt of–
    - (i)   attendance allowance at the higher rate in accordance with section 65(3) of the Act;
    - (ii)   the care component of disability living allowance at the highest or middle rate prescribed in accordance with section 72(3) of the Act;
    - (iii)   the daily living component of personal independence payment in accordance with section 78 of the 2012 Act; or
    - (iv)   armed forces independence payment; and
- (b)   whom the relevant authority is satisfied is, by virtue of his or her disability, not reasonably able to share a bedroom with the other member of the couple;]

[48 "member of the armed forces away on operations" means a member of the regular forces or the reserve forces (within the meaning of section 374 of the Armed Forces Act 2006) who is absent, while on operations, from the dwelling usually occupied as their home;]

[69 "member of the work-related activity group" means a [73 person] who has or is treated as having limited capability for work under either–
- (a)   Part 5 of the Employment and Support Allowance Regulations 2008 other than by virtue of regulation 30 of those Regulations; or
- (b)   Part 4 of the Employment and Support Allowance Regulations 2013 other than by virtue of regulation 26 of those Regulations;]

[27 "MFET Limited" means the company limited by guarantee (number 7121661) of that name, established for the purpose in particular of making payments in accordance with arrangements made with the Secretary of State to persons who have acquired HIV as a result of treatment by the NHS with blood or blood products;]

[14 "mover" means a claimant who changes the dwelling occupied as the claimant's home from a dwelling in the area of the appropriate authority to a dwelling in the area of a second authority;]

"net earnings" means such earnings as are calculated in accordance with regulation 36 (calculation of net earnings of employed earners);

"net profit" means such profit as is calculated in accordance with regulation 38 (calculation of net profit of self-employed earners);

"the New Deal options" means the employment programmes specified in regulation 75(1)(a)(ii) of the Jobseeker's Allowance Regulations and the training scheme specified in regulation 75(1)(b)(ii) of those Regulations;

[15 "new dwelling" means, for the purposes of the definition of "second authority" and regulations 72C, 73C, 115 and 116, the dwelling to which a claimant has moved, or is about to move, which is or will be occupied as the claimant's new home;]

"non-dependant" has the meaning prescribed in regulation 3;

[8 "non-dependant deduction" means a deduction that is to be made under regulation 74 (non-dependant deductions);]

"occupational pension" means any pension or other periodical payment under an occupational pension scheme but does not include any discretionary payment out of a fund established for relieving hardship in particular cases;

"ordinary clothing or footwear" means clothing or footwear for normal daily use but does not include school uniforms or clothing or footwear used solely for sporting activities;

"owner" means–
- (a)   in relation to a dwelling in England and Wales, the person who, otherwise than as a mortgagee in possession, is for the time being entitled to dispose of the fee simple, whether or not with the consent of other joint owners;
- (b)   in relation to a dwelling in Scotland, the proprietor under udal tenure or the proprietor of the dominion utile or the tenant's or the lessee's interest in a long tenancy, a kindly tenancy, a lease registered or registerable under the Registration of Leases (Scotland) Act 1857 or the Land Registration (Scotland) Act 1979 or a tenant-at-will as defined in section 20(8) of that Act of 1979;

"partner" means–
- (a) where a claimant is a member of a couple, the other member of that couple; or
- (b) where a claimant is polygamously married to two or more members of his household, any such member;

[[44] "paternity leave" means a period of absence from work on [[65]] paternity leave by virtue of section 80A or 80B of the Employment Rights Act 1996 [[65]];]"

"payment" includes part of a payment;

"pension fund holder" means with respect to a personal pension scheme or [[3] an occupational pension scheme], the trustees, managers or scheme administrators, as the case may be, of the scheme [[3]] concerned;

"person affected" shall be construed in accordance with regulation 3 of the Decisions and Appeals Regulations;

"person on income support" means a person in receipt of income support;

[[50] "personal independence payment" means personal independence payment under Part 4 of the 2012 Act;]

[[37] "person who requires overnight care" means a person ("P")–
- (a) who–
  - (i) is in receipt of attendance allowance;
  - (ii) is in receipt of the care component of disability living allowance at the highest or middle rate prescribed in accordance with section 72(3) of the Act; [[50]]
  - [[50] (iia) is in receipt of the daily living component of personal independence payment in accordance with section 78 of the 2012 Act;][[50]]
  - [[51] (iib) is in receipt of armed forces independence payment; or]
  - (iii) although not satisfying either paragraph (i) [[50][51,] (ii), (iia or (iib)]] above has provided [[70] or, where P is a child, the claimant has provided] the relevant authority with such certificates, documents, information or evidence as are sufficient to satisfy the authority that P requires overnight care; and
- (b) whom the relevant authority is satisfied reasonably requires, and has in fact arranged, that one or more people who do not occupy as their home the dwelling to which the claim or award for housing benefit relates should–
  - (i) be engaged in providing overnight care for P;
  - (ii) regularly stay overnight at the dwelling for that purpose; and
  - (iii) be provided with the use of a bedroom in that dwelling additional to those used by the persons who occupy the dwelling as their home,

but, in a case where P is treated as occupying a dwelling which P does not actually occupy, paragraph (b)(ii) and (iii) are to be treated as satisfied where the relevant authority is satisfied that the dwelling contains such an additional bedroom and that P did or will reasonably so require and so arrange at such time as P actually occupied or occupies the dwelling;]

[[12]]

[[3] "personal pension scheme" means–
- (a) a personal pension scheme as defined by section 1 of the Pension Schemes Act 1993;
- (b) an annuity contract or trust scheme approved under section 620 or 621 of the Income and Corporation Taxes Act 1988 or a substituted contract within the meaning of section 622(3) of that Act which is treated as having become a registered pension scheme by virtue of paragraph 1(1)(f) of Schedule 36 to the Finance Act 2004;
- (c) a personal pension scheme approved under Chapter 4 of Part 14 of the Income and Corporation Taxes Act 1988 which is treated as having become a registered pension scheme by virtue of paragraph 1(1)(g) of Schedule 36 to the Finance Act 2004;]

"policy of life insurance" means any instrument by which the payment of money is assured on death (except death by accident only) or the happening of any contingency dependent on human life, or any instrument evidencing a contract which is subject to payment of premiums for a term dependent on human life;

"polygamous marriage" means any marriage during the subsistence of which a party to it is married to more than one person and the ceremony of marriage took place under the law of a country which permits polygamy;

[²⁶ "public authority" includes any person certain of whose functions are functions of a public nature;]

"the qualifying age for state pension credit" means (in accordance with section 1(2)(b) and (6) of the State Pension Credit Act 2002)–
(a)   in the case of a woman, pensionable age; or
(b)   in the case of a man, the age which is pensionable age in the case of a woman born on the same day as the man;

[¹⁵ "qualifying contributory benefit" means–
(a)   severe disablement allowance;
(b)   incapacity benefit;]
[¹⁷ (c) contributory employment and support allowance;]

[¹⁵ "qualifying income-related benefit" means–
(a)   income support;
(b)   income-based jobseeker's allowance;]
[¹⁸ (c) income-related employment and support allowance;]

[⁴⁸ "qualifying parent or carer" means a person who has a bedroom in the dwelling they occupy as their home additional to those used by the persons who occupy the dwelling as their home and who–
(a)   has a child or qualifying young person placed with them as mentioned in regulation 21(3) who by virtue of that provision is not treated as occupying their dwelling; or
(b)   has been approved as a foster parent under regulation 27 of the Fostering Services (England) Regulations 2011 or regulation 28 of the Fostering Services (Wales) Regulations 2003 or as a kinship carer under regulation 10 or a foster carer under regulation 22 of the Looked After Children (Scotland) Regulations 2009 but does not have a child or qualifying young person placed with them and has not had a child or qualifying young person placed with them for a period which does not exceed 52 weeks;]

"qualifying person" means a person in respect of whom payment has been made from the Fund, the Eileen Trust[²⁸, MFET Limited], the Skipton Fund[⁴¹, the Caxton Foundation] [⁷¹, the Scottish Infected Blood Support Scheme] [⁷⁵, an approved blood scheme] [⁷⁴, the London Emergencies Trust, the We Love Manchester Emergency Fund] or the London Bombings Relief Charitable Fund;

[⁹ "reckonable rent" means payments which a person is liable to make in respect of the dwelling which he occupies as his home, and which are eligible, or would, but for regulation 13, be eligible for housing benefit;]]]

[⁹ [¹⁰ [³¹ "registered housing association" means–
(a)   a private registered provider of social housing;
(b)   a housing association which is registered in a register maintained by the Welsh Ministers under Chapter 1 of Part 1 of the Housing Act 1996 [⁴⁶ or a registered social landlord within the meaning of Part 1 of that Act]; or
(c)   a housing association which is registered by Scottish Ministers by virtue of section 57(3)(b) of the Housing (Scotland) Act 2001[⁴⁷ or a registered social landlord within the meaning of section 165 of that Act];]]]

"relative" means a close relative, grandparent, grandchild, uncle, aunt, nephew or niece;

"relevant authority" means an authority administering housing benefit;

[⁹ "relevant information" means information or evidence forwarded to the relevant authority by an appropriate DWP office regarding a claim on which rent allowance may be awarded, which completes the transfer of all information or evidence held by the appropriate DWP office relating to that claim;]

[^{72} "relevant person", in relation to any property, rights or interests to which section 90B(5) of the Scotland Act 1998 applies, means the person who manages that property or those rights or interests;]

"remunerative work" has the meaning prescribed in regulation 6 (remunerative work);

"rent" includes all those payments in respect of a dwelling specified in regulation 12(1);

[^{8} "Rent Officers Order" means the Rent Officers (Housing Benefit Functions) Order 1997 or, as the case may be, the Rent Officers (Housing Benefit Functions) (Scotland) Order 1997;]

[^{68} "Scottish basic rate" means the rate of income tax of that name calculated in accordance with section 6A of the Income Tax Act 2007;]

[^{71} "Scottish Infected Blood Support Scheme" means the scheme of that name administered by the Common Services Agency (constituted by section 10 of the National Health Service (Scotland) Act 1978;]

[^{68} "Scottish taxpayer" has the same meaning as in Chapter 2 of Part 4A of the Scotland Act 1998;]

[^{15} "second authority" means the authority to which a mover is liable to make payments for the new dwelling;]

[^{3}]

[^{16}]

"self-employed earner" is to be construed in accordance with section 2(1)(b) of the Act;

"self-employment route" means assistance in pursuing self-employed earner's employment whilst participating in–

(a)   an employment zone programme; [^{39}]

(b)   a programme provided or other arrangements made pursuant to section 2 of the 1973 Act (functions of the Secretary of State) or section 2 of the Enterprise and New Towns (Scotland) Act 1990 (functions in relation to training for employment, etc.); [^{39}][^{46} or]

[^{39} (c)]

[^{46} (c) a scheme prescribed in regulation 3 of the Jobseeker's Allowance (Schemes for Assisting Persons to Obtain Employment) Regulations 2013;]

[^{26} [^{61}]]

"shared ownership tenancy" means–

(a)   in relation to England and Wales, a [^{4} lease] granted on payment of a premium calculated by reference to a percentage of the value of the dwelling or the cost of providing it;

(b)   in relation to Scotland, an agreement by virtue of which the tenant of a dwelling of which he and the landlord are joint owners is the tenant in respect of the landlord's interest in the dwelling or by virtue of which the tenant has the right to purchase the dwelling or the whole or part of the landlord's interest therein;

[^{63} "shared parental leave" means leave under section 75E or 75G of the Employment Rights Act 1996;]

"single claimant" means a claimant who neither has a partner nor is a lone parent;

[^{9} "single room rent" means the rent determined by a rent officer under paragraph 5 of Schedule 1 to the Rent Officers Order;]

"the Skipton Fund" means the ex-gratia payment scheme administered by the Skipton Fund Limited, incorporated on 25th March 2004, for the benefit of certain persons suffering from hepatitis C and other persons eligible for payment in accordance with the scheme's provisions;

[^{27} "special account" means an account as defined for the purposes of Chapter 4A of Part 8 of the Jobseeker's Allowance Regulations or Chapter 5 of Part 10 of the Employment and Support Allowance Regulations;]

"sports award" means an award made by one of the Sports Councils named in section 23(2) of the National Lottery etc. Act 1993 out of sums allocated to it for distribution under that section;

[^{6} [^{24}]]

"student" has the meaning prescribed in regulation 53 (interpretation);

"subsistence allowance" means an allowance which an employment zone contractor has agreed to pay to a person who is participating in an employment zone programme;

"the Tax Credits Act" means the Tax Credits Act 2002;

"tax year" means a period beginning with 6th April in one year and ending with 5th April in the next;

"training allowance" means an allowance (whether by way of periodical grants or otherwise) payable–

(a) out of public funds by a Government department or by or on behalf of the Secretary of State, [²⁵ Skills Development Scotland,] Scottish Enterprise or Highlands and Islands Enterprise, [⁴³] [³⁵ [⁴⁵]] or the [²⁰ Welsh Ministers];

(b) to a person for his maintenance or in respect of a member of his family; and

(c) for the period, or part of the period, during which he is following a course of training or instruction provided by, or in pursuance of arrangements made with, that department or approved by that department in relation to him or so provided or approved by or on behalf of the Secretary of State, [²⁵ Skills Development Scotland,] Scottish Enterprise or Highlands and Islands Enterprise or the [²⁰ Welsh Ministers],

but it does not include an allowance paid by any Government department to or in respect of a person by reason of the fact that he is following a course of full-time education, other than under arrangements made under section 2 of the 1973 Act or is training as a teacher;

[⁵³ "universal credit" means universal credit under Part 1 of the 2012 Act;]

"voluntary organisation" means a body, other than a public or local authority, the activities of which are carried on otherwise than for profit;

[²]

[²¹ "war disablement pension" means any retired pay or pension or allowance payable in respect of disablement under an instrument specified in section 639(2) of the Income Tax (Earnings and Pensions) Act 2003;

"war pension" means a war disablement pension, a war widow's pension or a war widower's pension;

"war widow's pension" means any pension or allowance payable to a woman as a widow under an instrument specified in section 639(2) of the Income Tax (Earnings and Pensions) Act 2003 in respect of the death or disablement of any person;

"war widower's pension" means any pension or allowance payable to a man as a widower or to a surviving civil partner under an instrument specified in section 639(2) of the Income Tax (Earnings and Pensions) Act 2003 in respect of the death or disablement of any person;]

"water charges" means–

(a) as respects England and Wales, any water and sewerage charges under Chapter 1 of Part 5 of the Water Industry Act 1991,

(b) as respects Scotland, any water and sewerage charges established by Scottish Water under a charges scheme made under section 29A of the Water Industry (Scotland) Act 2002

in so far as such charges are in respect of the dwelling which a person occupies as his home;

[⁷⁴ "the We Love Manchester Emergency Fund" means the registered charity of that name (number 1173260) established on 30th May 2017;]

[¹⁸ "Welfare Reform Act" means the Welfare Reform Act 2007;]

"working tax credit" means a working tax credit under section 10 of the Tax Credits Act;

"Working Tax Credit Regulations" means the Working Tax Credit (Entitlement and Maximum Rate) Regulations 2002;

[⁸ "young individual" means a single claimant who has not attained the age of [⁴³ 35 years], but does not include such a claimant–

(a) whose landlord is a registered housing association;

(b) who has not attained the age of 22 years and has ceased to be the subject of a care order made pursuant to section 31(1)(a) of the Children Act 1989 which had previously been made in respect to him either–
(i) after he attained the age of 16 years; or
(ii) before he attained the age of 16 years, but had continued after he attained that age;

(c) who has not attained the age of 22 years and was formerly provided with accommodation under section 20 of the Children Act 1989 [⁷⁶ or section 76 of the Social Services and Well-being (Wales) Act 2014];

(d) who has not attained the age of 22 years and has ceased to be subject to a supervision requirement by a children's hearing under section 70 of the Children (Scotland) Act 1995 ("the 1995 Act") made in respect of him which had continued after he attained the age of 16 years, other than a case where–
(i) the ground of referral was based on the sole condition as to the need for compulsory measures of care specified in section 52(1)(i) of the 1995 Act (commission of offences by child); or
(ii) he was required by virtue of the supervision requirement to reside with a parent or guardian of his within the meaning of the 1995 Act, or with a friend or relative of his or of his parent or guardian;

(e) who has not attained the age of 22 years and has ceased to be a child in relation to whom the parental rights and responsibilities were transferred to a local authority under a parental responsibilities order made in accordance with section 86 of the 1995 Act or treated as so vested in accordance with paragraph 3 of Schedule 3 to that Act [⁴⁰ or has ceased to be a child in relation to whom a permanence order under section 80 of the Adoption and Children (Scotland) Act 2007 has been made, or treated as made], either–
(i) after he attained the age of 16 years; or
(ii) before he attained the age of 16 years, but had continued after he attained that age; or

(f) who has not attained the age of 22 years and has ceased to be provided with accommodation by a local authority under section 25 of the 1995 Act where he has previously been provided with accommodation by the authority under that provision either–
(i) after he attained the age of 16 years; or
(ii) before he attained the age of 16 years, but had continued to be in such accommodation after he attained that age;][³⁷ or

(g) who is a person who requires overnight care;][⁴³ [⁵⁸]

(h) who has attained the age of 25 years and to whom paragraph (1A), (1C) or both apply;][⁶⁰]

[⁵⁴ (i) who is a person who has not attained the age of 22 years and has ceased to be subject to a compulsory supervision order within the meaning of section 83 of the Children's Hearings (Scotland) Act 2011 ("the 2011 Act") which had continued after that person attained the age of 16 years, other than a case where–
(i) the section 67 ground (within the meaning of that Act) was based on the sole condition as to the need for compulsory measures of supervision specified in section 67(2)(j) (the child has committed an offence)of the 2011 Act; or
(ii) that person was required by virtue of the compulsory supervision order to reside with a parent or guardian of that person within the meaning of the 1995 Act, or with a friend or relative of that person or of that person's parent or guardian;]

[⁵⁸ [⁶⁰ (j)] who is a qualifying parent or carer;]

"young person" has the meaning prescribed in regulation 19(1) (persons of prescribed description).

[⁴³ (1A) This paragraph applies to a claimant ("C") if–
(a) C has, for a total of at least 3 months (whether or not continuously), occupied as his home one or more hostels for homeless people; and

(b)   whilst occupying such a hostel, C has been offered and has accepted support services with a view to assisting him to be rehabilitated or resettled within the community.

(1B)   For the purposes of determining whether C meets the condition in paragraph (1A)(a), "hostel for homeless people" means a hostel, as defined in paragraph (1), the main purpose of which is to provide accommodation together with care, support or supervision for homeless people with a view to assisting such persons to be rehabilitated or resettled within the community.

(1C)   This paragraph applies–

(a)   in England and Wales, to a claimant ("C") if C is the subject of active multi-agency management pursuant to arrangements established by a responsible authority under section 325(2) of the Criminal Justice Act 2003 (arrangements for assessing etc. risks posed by certain offenders); or

(b)   in Scotland, to a claimant ("C") if C is–

(i)   the subject of local inter-agency risk management or management by the multi-agency public protection panel pursuant to arrangements established by the responsible authorities under section 10(1) of the Management of Offenders etc. (Scotland) Act 2005 (arrangements for assessing and managing risks posed by certain offenders); or

(ii)   a person to whom section 10(1) of that Act does not apply by reason only of the fact that section 10(1)(b) or (d) has not been brought fully into force and C is considered by the relevant authority to be a person who may cause serious harm to the public at large; or

(iii)   a person to whom section 10(1) of that Act does not apply by reason only of the fact that section 10(1)(e) has not been brought fully into force and who has been convicted of an offence, if by reason of that conviction, C is considered by the relevant authority to be a person who may cause serious harm to the public at large.]

(2)   References in these Regulations to a person who is liable to make payments shall include references to a person who is treated as so liable under regulation 8 (circumstances in which a person is to be treated as liable to make payments in respect of a dwelling).

(3)   For the purposes of these Regulations, a person is on an income-based jobseeker's allowance on any day in respect of which an income-based jobseeker's allowance is payable to him and on any day–

(a)   in respect of which he satisfies the conditions for entitlement to an income-based jobseeker's allowance but where the allowance is not paid in accordance with [30 regulation 27A of the Jobseeker's Allowance Regulations or] section 19 or 20A [38 or regulations made under section 17A] of the Jobseekers Act (circumstances in which a jobseeker's allowance is not payable); or

(b)   which is a waiting day for the purposes of paragraph 4 of Schedule 1 to that Act and which falls immediately before a day in respect of which an income-based jobseeker's allowance is payable to him or would be payable to him but for [30 regulation 27A of the Jobseeker's Allowance Regulations or] section 19 or 20A [38 or regulations made under section 17A] of that Act; or

(c)   in respect of which he is a member of a joint-claim couple for the purposes of the Jobseekers Act and no joint-claim jobseeker's allowance is payable in respect of that couple as a consequence of either member of that couple being subject to sanctions for the purposes of section 20A of that Act; or

(d)   in respect of which an income-based jobseeker's allowance or a joint-claim jobseeker's allowance would be payable but for a restriction imposed pursuant to [29] [32 section 6B, 7, 8 or 9] of the Social Security Fraud Act 2001 (loss of benefit provisions).

[18 (3A)   For the purposes of these Regulations, a person is on an income-related employment and support allowance on any day in respect of which an income-related employment and support allowance is payable to him and on any day–

(a) in respect of which he satisfies the conditions for entitlement to an income-related employment and support allowance but where the allowance is not paid in accordance with section 18 of the Welfare Reform Act (disqualification); or

(b) which is a waiting day for the purposes of paragraph 2 of Schedule 2 to that Act and which falls immediately before a day in respect of which an income-related employment and support allowance is payable to him or would be payable to him but for section 18 of that Act.]

[[55] (3B) For the purposes of these Regulations, a person ("P") is on universal credit on any day in respect of which P is entitled to universal credit (whether it is in payment or not).]

(4) For the purposes of these Regulations, the following shall be treated as included in a dwelling–

(a) subject to sub-paragraphs (b) to (d) any land (whether or not occupied by a structure) which is used for the purposes of occupying a dwelling as a home where either–

    (i) the occupier of the dwelling acquired simultaneously the right to use the land and the right to occupy the dwelling, and, in the case of a person liable to pay rent for his dwelling, he could not have occupied that dwelling without also acquiring the right to use the land; or

    (ii) the occupier of the dwelling has made or is making all reasonable efforts to terminate his liability to make payments in respect of the land;

(b) where the dwelling is a caravan or mobile home, such of the land on which it stands as is used for the purposes of the dwelling;

(c) where the dwelling is a houseboat, the land used for the purposes of mooring it;

(d) where in Scotland, the dwelling is situated on or pertains to a croft within the meaning of section 3(1) of the Crofters (Scotland) Act 1993, the croft land on which it is situated or to which it pertains.

[[61] (5) References in these Regulations to a claimant participating as a service user are to–

(a) a person who is being consulted by or on behalf of–

    (i) a body which has a statutory duty to provide services in the field of health, social care or social housing; or

    (ii) a body which conducts research or undertakes monitoring for the purpose of planning or improving such services,

in their capacity as a user, potential user, carer of a user or person otherwise affected by the provision of those services; or

[[64] (ab) a person who is being consulted by or on behalf of–

    (i) the Secretary of State in relation to any of the Secretary of State's functions in the field of social security or child support or under section 2 of the Employment and Training Act 1973; or

    (ii) a body which conducts research or undertakes monitoring for the purpose of planning or improving such functions,

in their capacity as a person affected or potentially affected by the exercise of those functions or the carer of such a person;]

(b) the carer of a person consulted under [[64] sub-paragraph (a) or (ab)].]

[[70] (6) For the purpose of these Regulations, reference to a member of a couple who can share a bedroom is to a member of a couple where the other member of the couple is a member of a couple who cannot share a bedroom.]

Modifications

Definitions were substituted and inserted by reg 4(1) Housing Benefit (Local Housing Allowance and Information Sharing) Amendment Regulations 2007 SI No.2868, as amended by reg 4(3) of SI 2008 No.586, as from 7 April 2008, save that for a person to whom reg 1(5) of those regulations applied (see p1812), the amendments came into force on the day on or after 7 April 2008 when the first of the events specified in reg 1(6) applied to her/him, or on 6 April 2009 if none had before that date.

Definition of "eligible rent" modified and definition of "maximum rent (standard local rate)" inserted by Sch 10 para 2 (see p707). These apply only to former Pathfinder Authorities who administered the pilot local housing allowance scheme.

References to "step-parent", step-children and the various in-laws in the definition of "close relative" are modified by s246 Civil Partnership Act 2004 (see p1729) and Art 3 and Sch para 24 to SI 2005 No.3137 (see p1772).

Reg 2(1) was modified by reg 13 Jobseeker's Allowance (Work for Your Benefit Pilot Scheme) Regulations 2010 SI No.1222 from 22 November 2010 to 1 March 2012 in pilot areas only.

The amendments made by SI 2014 No.3255 which came into force on 5 April 2015 do not have effect in relation to ordinary statutory paternity pay which is paid, additional statutory paternity pay which is paid, a period in respect of which additional statutory paternity pay is payable which begins, or continues, ordinary paternity leave which is taken or additional paternity leave which is taken on or after 5 April 2015. See art 35 of SI 2014 No.3255.

Amendments

1. Inserted by art 2(2) of SI 2006 No 2968 as from 20.12.06.
2. Omitted by Reg 4(a) of SI 2007 No 1619 as from 3.7.07.
3. Amended by reg 4(2) of SI 2007 No 1749 as from 16.7.07.
4. Amended by reg 2(2) of SI 2007 No 1356 as from 1.10.07.
5. Amended by art 8(2) of SI 2007 No 2538 as from 1.10.07.
6. Inserted by reg 11(2) of SI 2007 No 2618 as from 1.10.07.
7. Revoked by reg 2 and the Sch of SI 2007 No 2618 as from 1.10.07.
8. Substituted by reg 4(1) of SI 2007 No 2868 as from 7.4.08 (or if reg 1(5) of that SI applies, on the day on or after 7.4.08 when the first of the events specified in reg 1(6) applies, or from 6.4.09 if none have before that date).
9. Inserted by reg 4(1) of SI 2007 No 2868, as amended by reg 4(3) of SI 2008 No 586, as from 7.4.08 (or if reg 1(5) of that SI applies, on the day on or after 7.4.08 when the first of the events specified in reg 1(6) applies, or from 6.4.09 if none have before that date).
10. Substituted by reg 4(3) of SI 2008 No 586 as from 7.4.08.
11. Omitted by reg 6(2) of SI 2008 No 698 as from 14.4.08.
12. Omitted by reg 3(2) of SI 2008 No 1042 as from 19.5.08.
13. Omitted by reg 2(2) of SI 2008 No 2299 as from 1.10.08.
14. Substituted by reg 4(2) of SI 2008 No 959 as from 6.10.08.
15. Inserted by reg 4(2) of SI 2008 No 959 as from 6.10.08.
16. Omitted by reg 4(2) of SI 2008 No 959 as from 6.10.08.
17. Amended by reg 5(2) of SI 2008 No 1082, as amended by reg 27 of SI 2008 No 2428, as from 27.10.08.
18. Inserted by reg 5(2) of SI 2008 No 1082, as amended by reg 27 of SI 2008 No 2428, as from 27.10.08.
19. Omitted by reg 6(2) of SI 2008 No 2767 as from 17.11.08.
20. Amended by reg 5(2) of SI 2008 No 3157 as from 5.1.09.
21. Inserted by reg 5(2) of SI 2008 No 3157 as from 5.1.09.
22. Inserted by reg 6(1)(a) of SI 2009 No 583 as from 6.4.09.
23. Amended by reg 6(2)(b) of SI 2009 No 583 as from 1.4.09 (6.4.09 where rent payable weekly or at intervals of a week).
24. Omitted by reg 6(2)(c) of SI 2009 No 583 as from 6.4.09.
25. Amended by reg 6(3)(a) of SI 2009 No 683 as from 6.4.09.
26. Inserted by reg 6(2) of SI 2009 No 2655 as from 2.11.09.
27. Inserted by reg 8(2) of SI 2010 No 641 as from 1.4.10 (5.4.10 where rent payable weekly or in multiples of a week).
28. Amended by reg 8(3) of SI 2010 No 641 as from 1.4.10 (5.4.10 where rent payable weekly or in multiples of a week).
29. Amended by reg 8 of SI 2010 No 424 as from 2.4.10 (the first day of the benefit week on or after 22.3.10 so far as it relates to a person who is subject to a restriction under section 62 or 63 of the Child Support, Pensions and Social Security Act 2000).
30. Amended by reg 4(1)(a) and (2) of SI 2010 No 509 as from 6.4.10.
31. Amended by art 4 and Sch 1 para 51 of SI 2010 No 671 as from 1.4.10.
32. Amended by reg 4 of SI 2010 No 1160 as from 1.4.10.
33. Inserted by reg 27 and Sch 5 para 1(2) of SI 2010 No 1907 as amended by reg 15 of SI 2010 No 2430 as from 1.10.10.
34. Substituted by arts 2 and 20 of SI 2010 No 1881 as from 1.10.10.
35. Amended by art 14(2) of SI 2010 No 1941 as from 1.9.10.
36. Substituted by reg 2(2) of SI 2010 No 2449 as from 1.11.10.
37. Inserted by reg 2(2) of SI 2010 No 2835 as from 1.4.11.
38. Inserted by regs 11 and 17 SI 2011 No 688 as from 25.4.11.
39. Amended by reg 11 of SI 2011 No 917 as from 20.5.11. SI 2011 No 917 was quashed by the Court of Appeal in *R (Reilly and another) v SSWP* [2013] EWCA Civ 66, 12 February 2013.
40. Amended by art 2 and Sch 1 para 39(2) of SI 2011 No 1740 as from 15.7.11.

41. Inserted by reg 19(2) of SI 2011 No 2425 as from 31.10.11.
42. Amended by art 2 and Sch 2 para 51 of SI 2011 No 2581 as from 28.10.11.
43. Amended by reg 2(2) and (3) of SI 2011 No 1736 as from 1.1.12.
44. Substituted by reg 7(2) of SI 2012 No 757 as from 1.4.12 (2.4.12 where rent payable weekly or in multiples of a week).
45. Amended by reg 11(2) of SI 2012 No 956 as from 1.5.12.
46. Inserted by reg 8 of SI 2013 No 276 as from 6.45 pm 17.2.13.
47. Amended by reg 5(2) of SI 2012 No 3040 as from 1.4.13.
48. Inserted by reg 2(2) of SI 2013 No 665 as from 1.4.13.
49. Inserted by reg 7(2) of SI 2013 No 443 as from 2.4.13.
50. Inserted or amended by reg 8 and Sch para 36(2) of SI 2013 No 388 as from 8.4.13.
51. Amended by art 7 and Sch para 34(2) of SI 2013 No 592 as from 8.4.13.
52. Inserted by reg 2(2) of SI 2013 No 2994 as from 15.4.13.
53. Amended by reg 35(2) of SI 2013 No 630 as from 29.4.13.
54. Amended by art 17 and Sch 1 para 23 of SI 2013 No 1465 as from 24.6.13.
55. Inserted by reg 7(2) of SI 2013 No 2070 as from 28.10.13.
56. Amended by reg 11(2) of SI 2013 No 2536 as from 29.10.13.
57. Inserted by Sch 2 para 93(2) of SI 2013 No 235 as from 1.4.13.
58. Amended by reg 2(2) of SI 2013 No 2828 as from 4.12.13.
59. Substituted (in England and Wales) by art 2 and Sch 1 para 40 of SI 2014 No 107 as from 13.3.14.
60. Amended by reg 3(2) of SI 2014 No 213 as from 1.4.14 (7.4.14 where rent payable weekly or in multiples of a week).
61. Amended by reg 8(2) of SI 2014 No 591 as from 28.4.14.
62. Substituted (in Scotland) by art 29 and Sch 6 para 27 of SI 2014 No 3229 as from 16.12.14.
63. Inserted by art 17(2)(c) of SI 2014 No 3255 as from 31.12.14.
64. Amended by reg 2 of SI 2015 No 67 as from 23.2.15.
65. Amended by reg 17(2)(a) and (b) of SI 2014 No 3255 as from 5.4.15.
66. Amended by art 2 and Sch 3 para 8(2) of SI 2015 No 971 as from 26.5.15.
67. Amended by art 28(2) of SI 2015 No 1985 as from 6.4.16.
68. Inserted by reg 4(2) of SI 2016 No 233 as from 6.4.16.
69. Inserted by Sch 1 para 6(2) of SI 2017 No 204 as from 3.4.17, subject to transitional and savings provisions in Sch 2 paras 1–7.
70. Amended by reg 4(2) of SI 2017 No 213 as from 1.3.17.
71. Inserted by reg 6(2) of SI 2017 No 329 as from 3.4.17.
72. Amended by Sch 5 para 102 of SI 2017 No 524 as from 31.3.17.
73. Amended by reg 5(2) of SI 2017 No 581 as from 23.6.17, subject to transitional and savings provision in reg 9.
74. Amended by reg 6(2) of SI 2017 No 689 as from 19.6.17.
75. Amended by reg 6(2) of SI 2017 No 870 as from 23.10.17.
76. Amended by art 11(2) of SI 2017 No 901 as from 3.11.17.
77. Amended by reg 9(2) of SI 2018 No 228 as from 2.4.18.

Definition

"dwelling" – see s137(1) SSCBA.

General Note

Reg 2 contains the bulk of the definitions of terms commonly used in the HB Regs. However, reg 3 defines "non-dependant", reg 5 "persons who have attained the qualifying age for pension credit", reg 6 "remunerative work" and reg 10 "person from abroad". Some regulations also give their own specialist meaning to terms used in them, and this will be pointed out where necessary in the relevant commentary. Note that some of the terms found in the regs are defined in s137 SSCBA 1992 (see p12) – an indication is also given where this applies.

Analysis

Paragraph (1): General definitions

"benefit week". In general, entitlement to HB accrues on a weekly basis, and by virtue of this definition, each week of entitlement runs from Monday to Sunday.

"change of dwelling" is a change of a dwelling occupied by a claimant, during an award of HB, to a dwelling in respect of which the authority may make a rent allowance – eg, to a housing association or private tenancy. The phrase is relevant for the local housing allowance scheme and the local reference rent scheme for rent restriction.

"child who cannot share a bedroom". The term is relevant for the size criteria for three of the rent restriction schemes. See regs B13 and 13D HB Regs, reg 13D HB(SPC) Regs and Sch 2 of both the Rent Officers (Housing Benefit Functions) Order 1997 and the Rent Officers (Housing Benefit Functions) (Scotland) Order 1997.

"close relative". The definition of "close relative" is relevant in a number of situations. See, for example, the definition of "linked person" that includes some relatives and thus the definition of "relative" that includes, among others, a close relative. See also reg 9(1)(b) and (e)(ii) under which a person is treated as not liable for rent payments if the liability is to a close relative in specified situations.

The term "couple" is defined later in this regulation. See also the modifications cited above.

In *Bristol City Council v JKT* [2016] UKUT 517 (AAC), Judge Ward decided that half-brothers and half-sisters come within the definition of "close relative", although not expressly included. He said:

"The inclusion of step-parent and step-son/daughter can be seen as an acknowledgement of the relationship between the child's actual parent and his/her new partner and the role of that in creating bonds of a degree of closeness. The importance of the role of the relationship between partners in the definition can be seen in the extension of the provisions to "the other member of a couple". The legislator did not see fit to include step-brothers and step-sisters, the degree of whose connection via the relationship between their respective parents is one degree more remote. The tribunal judge considered that step-siblings and half-siblings might be in "quite a similar position", but whilst I accept that family relationships are infinitely various, it is a question of drawing a line somewhere and a rationale for the inclusion of the "step" provisions so far as they go is in my view, for the reason above, apparent. "Step" relationships were considered by the legislator to require express inclusion, as were relationships by marriage. The argument that relationships of the half blood also do is not made out when, as noted by Mr Commissioner Rice at para 5 of *R(SB) 22/87*, as a use of language it is indeed possible to refer to a half-brother as a "brother", even if in contexts where specificity is demanded "half-brother" might be used."

"concessionary payment". These include, for example, extra statutory payments made during a strike.

"converted employment and support allowance". If a claimant is entitled to converted ESA, or in specified circumstances is appealing a conversion decision, s/he may be entitled to a protected amount of HB – a transitional addition. See regs 22(f) and 23(g) and Sch 3 Parts 7 and 8. By virtue of the definition here, income-related ESA can never be converted ESA.

"co-ownership scheme". The term "housing association" is defined later in the regulation; for land included with a "dwelling", see reg 2(4). The same wording was used in the 1985 HB Regs. A case based on those regs held that equity sharing schemes run by housing associations under the Housing Corporation's model rules, whereby on leaving the scheme after a minimum period of 12 months a participant would receive an equity share payment based on the increased value of the premises, were "co-ownership schemes": *R v Birmingham CC HBRB ex p Ellery* (1989) 21 HLR 398, QBD.

"couple". The definition is virtually the same as in s137 SSCBA. See p14 for commentary.

"crown tenant". See s137(1) SSCBA on p15 for "dwelling" and later in this regulation for "relevant person". HB is not payable in respect of payments by Crown tenants: reg 12(2). There is a separate scheme of relief for them, but Crown tenants entitled to IS, income-based JSA, income-related ESA or PC may be able to claim help with their "rent" under the housing costs rules for those benefits: see Sch 3 para 17(1)(e) Income Support (General) Regulations 1987, Sch 2 para 16(1)(e) Jobseeker's Allowance Regulations 1996, Sch 6 para 18(1)(e) Employment and Support Allowance Regulations 2008 and Sch 2 para 13(1)(e) State Pension Credit Regulations 2002.

"designated office". A claimant must generally give notice of changes in her/his circumstances to the local authority at its "designated office": reg 88(1) HB Regs and reg 4(1) Social Security (Notification of Change of Circumstances) Regulations 2001. This is the office designated for receipt of HB claims as set out in sub-paras (a) to (c) of the definition.

"employed earner". SSCBA s2(1)(a) defines this as "a person who is gainfully employed in Great Britain either under a contract of service, or in an office (including elective office) with earnings".

"the Fund" refers to money made available by the government from a trust set up by the relevant Secretary of State for persons infected (including infected partners and children) with HIV through NHS blood transfusions or tissue transfers.

"hostel". This definition serves several purposes. Hostels receive special treatment under the rent restrictions legislation: see regs 13(5)(d)(ii) and 14(2)(a). By reg 4, inhabitants of hostels are exempt from the "NINO requirement" imposed by s1(1A) SSAA. Certain single claimants aged 25 or over who have lived in a hostel for homeless people are excepted from the definition of "young individual" below: reg 2(1A) and (1B). Certain hostels come within the definition of "specified accommodation" defined in reg 75H. If the dwelling in respect of which HB is paid is "specified accommodation", the HB is disregarded in calculating the amount of the claimant's welfare benefits for the purpose of the "benefit cap": reg 75C(2)(a). Note also that a UC claimant is not precluded from entitlement to HB in respect of "specified accommodation", which for these purposes is defined in Sch 1 para 3A UC Regs: reg 5(2)(a) UC(TP) Regs 2014.

The following criteria must be fulfilled if a building is to qualify as a "hostel".

(1)   The accommodation must be for "persons generally or for a class of persons". In this context, in connection with the second criterion, this means that there must be a degree of multiple occupancy. However, there is no need for the people to have any particular need (eg, treatment for addiction) although this will be a feature of many of the dwellings that qualify.

(2)   It must provide "domestic accommodation, otherwise than in separate and self-contained premises". This appears to require that the facilities required for the basic functions of life must be shared to some degree. At minimum, it is suggested, to be "separate and self-contained" units would have to have facilities for eating, sleeping, cooking and washing.

(3)   There must either be board provided or facilities for the preparation of food adequate to the needs of the people accommodated, or both.

(4)   The condition in sub-para (b) of the definition as to ownership or management must be fulfilled in one of three ways. First, under head (i), a building qualifies if it is owned *or* managed (but not necessarily both) by a "registered housing association" (also defined in reg 2(1)).

Alternatively, under head (ii) a building qualifies if it is operated other than on a commercial basis. The caselaw set out in the Analysis to reg 9(1)(a) (see p282) may assist, although the running of the accommodation as a whole must be examined rather than just the agreement with the individual tenant in question. It must also be funded in whole or in part by one of the relevant public bodies listed. It would appear that anything more than minimal funding would suffice, so a modest local authority grant would allow the dwelling to qualify.

Finally, under head (iii), a building qualifies if it is managed by a "voluntary organisation" (defined later in this regulation) or a charity, by which is presumably meant a registered charity. It must also provide suitable "care, support or supervision" to allow inhabitants to be "rehabilitated or resettled" into the community. These are general words that should be given a wide meaning. They carry no pejorative implication and so the newly disabled, for example, require rehabilitation or resettlement just as do those with addictions.

(5)   The building cannot be a "care home", "independent hospital" or an "Abbeyfield Home" (all defined elsewhere in this regulation).

"housing association"*.* By s1(1) Housing Associations Act 1985, this means a "society, body of trustees or a company (a) which is established for the purposes of, or amongst whose objects and powers are included, those of providing, constructing, improving or managing, or facilitating or encouraging the construction or improvement of, housing accommodation, and (b) which does not trade for profit or whose constitution or rules prohibit the issue of capital with interest or dividend exceeding such rate as may be prescribed by the treasury, whether with or without differentiation between share and loan capital". It does not include Scottish Homes. See also the definition of "registered housing association" below.

"an income-based jobseeker's allowance" is defined by reference to s1(4) Jobseeker's Act 1995. Thus where income-based JSA is referred to in these regulations it means a JSA entitlement which is based on the claimant satisfying the income-based JSA conditions in s3 of that Act, or a joint-claim JSA.

"linked person"*.* The definition is relevant for determining whether rent restrictions can be delayed under reg 12BA(3) or (6), reg 12D(3) or (5) or reg 13ZA. "Partner" and "relative" are defined later in this regulation. See also reg 3(4) for when a person resides with another.

"local housing allowance"*.* Where reg 12D applies, HB is calculated by reference to the appropriate local housing allowance, here defined as an allowance determined in accordance with para 2 Sch 3B Rent Officers Order. "Rent Officers Order" is defined later in this regulation.

"local welfare provision" is the DWP term for the replacement of social fund community care grants and crisis loans by local provision. The definition is self-explanatory. For HB purposes, the term is relevant for income other than earnings and capital that can be disregarded: Sch 5 para 31A and Sch 6 para 20A.

"lone parent"*.* "Child and "partner" are defined in this regulation. See also Part 4 of the HB Regs: "young person" is defined in reg 19; reg 20, deals with circumstances in which an adult is treated as "responsible" for a child or young person; reg 21 deals with those in which people are to be treated as sharing a household. See also p17 for more on the meaning of household.

"long tenancy"*.* HB is not payable in respect of payments made under a long tenancy, other than where this is a shared ownership tenancy: reg 12(2)(a). Note that reg 12(2)(a) does not exclude payments by someone entitled to dispose of the leasehold interest under a long lease – a formulation similar to that for excepting payment by an owner under reg 12(2)(c). If rent is payable by the claimant under, for example, an assured shorthold tenancy and not under the long leasehold interest, HB might be payable in respect of the rent: *CR v Wycombe DC* [2009] UKUT 19 (AAC). However, consideration needs to be given to whether the claimant is to be treated as not liable to pay rent under reg 9 (see p280) and to whether any of the rental income belongs to the claimant and is to be taken into account. A "term of years certain" means that the length of the lease may be ascertained and that it is intended to last for more than 21 years, subject to the potential terminating factors here set out. The term will be set out in the lease. "Re-entry" is a landlord's remedy for the breach of a condition in a lease which can no longer be exercised without a court order while someone is lawfully residing in the dwelling concerned: see Protection from Eviction Act 1977. "Forfeiture" is a similarly restricted remedy for non-payment of rent. A tenancy for life takes effect as a tenancy for 90 years in England and Wales by virtue of s149(6) Law of Property Act 1925, and so is a "long tenancy" for HB purposes: *CH 2743/2003* para 8 and *CH 2258/2004* para 16.

An oral agreement cannot create a long tenancy. Moreover, an agreement in writing (but not by deed) is not enough to create a long tenancy, as the effect of ss52, 53 and 54(2) of the Law of Property Act 1925 is to require leases in excess of three years to be made by deed. Accordingly, a written agreement purporting to create a long tenancy but which was not made by deed (ie, under seal), is not a "tenancy granted" for a term in excess of 21 years and is not, therefore, a long tenancy: *R(H) 3/07*.

"Lease for a term fixed by law . . . perpetual renewal" refers to the provisions of s145 and Sch 15 Law of Property Act 1922 which convert perpetually renewable leases into leases lasting for a term of 2,000 years but such leases will not count as long tenancies if they are sub-leases and the person sub-letting does not have a long tenancy her/himself. The term "irritancy", used in the definition, is a Scots law remedy – the landlord's right to end the lease and repossess the property if certain terms of the lease are broken.

"main phase employment and support allowance". The components referred to in the definition are the support component and the work-related activity component. Note that, from 3 April 2017, the work-related activity component was abolished for new ESA claims. This definition was amended from 23 June 2017 to include ESA where the claimant is a "member of the work-related activity group" defined later in this regulation.

"maximum rent" is the amount to which the eligible rent is restricted under regs 12C, 13 and 14 (referred to as the "local reference rent" rules).

"maximum rent (LHA)" is the amount to which eligible rent is restricted under regs 12D, 13C and 13D (referred to as the "local housing allowance" rules).

"member of a couple who cannot share a bedroom". The definition is relevant for the size criteria in the local housing allowance, social sector and local reference rent schemes for rent restriction. The member of the couple must be in receipt of one of the benefits or payments listed and the local authority must be satisfied that, because of her/his disability, s/he cannot reasonably share a bedroom with the other member of the couple.

"member of the work-related activity group". A person comes within the definition if s/he has, or is treated as having, limited capability for work under the regulations cited, other than if s/he is treated as such while awaiting a decision on ESA eligibility – eg, pending assessment.

"mover", *"new dwelling"*, *"qualifying contributory benefit"*, *"qualifying income-related benefit"* and *"second authority"* are relevant to the rules for extended payments of HB in regs 72 to 73E.

"non-dependant" and *"non-dependant deduction"*. Reg 74 provides that the maximum amount of HB payable to a claimant shall be reduced by fixed amounts if certain "non-dependants" live with her/him, defined in reg 3.

"owner". Reg 12(2)(c) renders any payments by an "owner" ineligible for HB. The definition of "owner" in reg 2(1) also applies to cognate expressions such as "own", "owned" and "ownership" elsewhere in the HB Regs – eg, in reg 9(1)(h): *CH 1278/2003* para 13; *CH 3616/2003* para 7.

In England and Wales, an owner is "the person who, otherwise than as a mortgagee in possession, is for the time being entitled to dispose of the fee simple, whether or not with the consent of joint owners". In *GN v Sevenoaks BC (HB)* [2016] UKUT 271 (AAC), Judge Levenson decided that a claimant had not owned his dwelling from the date of a restraint order under the terms of which he was prohibited from disposing of his assets himself or in any other way, because he was *not* entitled to dispose of the fee simple. The mortgagee is the lending institution which lends the person money on mortgage to buy the home. The other persons who have the right to sell or otherwise dispose of the dwelling should be listed on the title deeds or on the office copies relating to the title in the property which are held at the Land Registry. The inclusion in this definition of persons who cannot sell without consent is designed to overturn the decision in *R v Sedgemoor DC HBRB ex p Weadon* (1986) 18 HLR 355, QBD. That decision had held that a co-owner was able to get HB for rent paid to the other owners in respect of her occupation of the dwelling.

In *R(H) 8/07*, the claimant was the registered proprietor of the freehold of a property. He occupied a flat in it, and paid rent to the person to whom he had granted a long lease of it. He claimed HB in respect of his liability for that rent. Commissioner Turnbull said that although, for most practical purposes, the long leaseholder, rather than the claimant, would be regarded as the "owner" of the flat, "owner" for HB purposes is defined by reference to the ability to dispose of the fee simple, and not by reference to the ability to dispose of any long leasehold interest in it which may have been granted. The claimant here had the right to dispose of the fee simple. Although the definition applies "unless the context otherwise requires", it was not possible to conclude that the context of what is now reg 12(2)(c) HB Regs requires that, where a long leasehold interest has been granted at a low rent, the person with the ability to dispose of that leasehold interest, rather than the person who is entitled to dispose of the freehold, is the owner.

In *R v Sheffield CC HBRB ex p Smith* (1994) 28 HLR 36 at 47-8, QBD, Blackburne J suggested that if a person has a joint beneficial interest giving her/him a right to a share in the proceeds of sale, it does not follow that s/he is a person "for the time being, entitled to dispose of the fee simple". If this is right, it appears from his rejection of the argument for the respondents (at 46–7) that it will probably be necessary to show that the individual claimant has a specific power to dispose of the legal title to the property. Following on from *ex p Smith*, in *CR v Wycombe DC* [2009] UKUT 19 (AAC) it was suggested, though not decided, that a person who has a beneficial interest will not be caught by this definition of "owner" if s/he is not the owner, or one of the owners, of the legal estate: in other words, if the person only has a beneficial interest.

In *Fairbank v Lambeth Magistrates' Court* (2003) HLR 62, the claimant asserted that he held a property as trustee for his father. The court ruled that it was not necessary for him to come within the definition of "owner" to be guilty of the offence with which he was charged but went on to hold that a claimant who merely needs to consult beneficiaries under a trust of land is an "owner" for the purposes of reg 2(1). That finding was technically *obiter* but is fully reasoned and was followed by Commissioner Fellner in *R(H) 7/05* paras 35–41 and Commissioner Mesher in *CH 1278/2003* para 16.

The claimant in *R(H) 7/05* appealed against the decision of the commissioner but his appeal was rejected by the Court of Appeal in *Burton v New Forest DC* [2004] EWCA Civ 1510; reported as *R(H) 7/05*. The commissioner had decided that the claimant came within the definition of "owner" – and was thus disqualified from receiving HB by virtue of reg 10(2)(c) HB regs 1987 (now reg 12(2)(c) HB Regs) – because the claimant was the registered proprietor of the property (on the Land Charges Register) and so, by virtue of s20(1) Land Registration Act 1925 (LRA), was "entitled to dispose of the fee simple" without the consent of other joint owners, regardless of whether so selling the property would give rise to a breach of trust.

In rejecting the further appeal, the Court of Appeal held that there is no true distinction between the words "entitled to dispose of the fee simple" in reg 2(1)(a) and being "able" to dispose of the fee simple under s20(1) LRA 1925. Given this, it was quite impossible to construe the term "owner" in reg 2(1) as meaning exclusively a beneficial owner. Because his name remained on the title at the Land Registry as sole owner with title absolute, he was, as a matter of law, entitled to dispose of the fee simple at any point up until the Land Registry was rectified. But until any such rectification, the claimant was the "owner" and not entitled to any HB. Moreover, in the Court of Appeal's view, nothing in the terms of reg 7 HB Regs 1987 (now reg 9 HB Regs) acted to alter this conclusion.

In *CH 1278/2003*, the commissioner commented that administrators of estates may also fall within the definition since they have a right to dispose of the fee simple: paras 18–19.

It appears that local authorities are having to deal with unorthodox arrangements for the holding of property with increasing frequency. Rather than grapple with the complexities as to whether the claimant is an "owner", some are simply finding that the arrangements fall foul of the provisions in reg 9(1) (circumstances in which a person is to be treated as not liable to make payments). However, it is important that authorities do not make an assumption of non-commerciality or contrivance simply on the basis of the unusual nature of an arrangement. Such arrangements for the holding of property are often the reflection of the values of religious or ethnic groups, and caution will be required to ensure that the relevant tests are met. See the Analysis to reg 9 on p282 for more details.

It is important to bear in mind that the definition of "owner" cannot apply to a person who is a leaseholder, as opposed to a freeholder, in England and Wales: *CH 296/2003* para 29. Long tenancy holders (defined above) are excluded from HB by virtue of reg 12(2)(a).

"Udal tenure" is a form of land holding only found in the Orkney and Shetland Islands. The "proprietor of the dominium utile" is the person with the right to use and occupy the land; again, this should be apparent from the title deeds. "Long tenancy" is defined above. "Registered" leases are registered in the Land Register of Scotland or the Register of Sasines in Register House, Edinburgh. "Registrable" leases in Scotland are those: (1) executed in probative writing; and (2) lasting for a period of more than 20 years, or for a shorter period if there is an obligation to renew the lease so that it will actually endure for a period exceeding that number of years.

"partner". "Couple" is defined above and by s137(1) SSCBA (see p14). "Polygamous marriage" is defined below.

"person on income support". *R v South Ribble DC HBRB ex p Hamilton* (2000) 33 HLR 102, CA confirmed that the definition of "person on income support" must be read as a person lawfully in receipt of IS. See also the discussion of *SD v Newcastle City Council (HB)* [2010] UKUT 306 (AAC) on p420.

"person who requires overnight care". This definition is relevant for the local housing allowance, the social sector and the local reference rent schemes for rent restriction. Since 1 April 2011, there has been a requirement to take account of an additional bedroom for a non-resident carer where the claimant or her/his partner is a "person who requires overnight care" (see regs B13, 13 and 13D HB Regs and Sch 2 para 1A of both the Rent Officers (Housing Benefit Functions) Order 1997 and the Rent Officers (Housing Benefit Functions) (Scotland) Order 1997). Until 1 April 2017, it could only apply to a claimant and her/his partner, and another person who was jointly liable with the claimant or her/his partner (or both) along with that person's partner. From that date, it can apply to a claimant's child, qualifying young person or non-dependant, including a child or qualifying young person for whom the claimant or her/his partner is a "qualifying parent or carer" defined later in this regulation. In the case of the social sector scheme, it can also include a child or young person in respect of whom other specified people occupying the claimant's dwelling are qualifying parents or carers.

Someone is a "person who requires overnight care" if s/he:

(1)   is in receipt of AA, the highest or middle rate of DLA care component, either rate of the daily living component of PIP or armed forces independence payment: sub-para (a)(i)-(iib). AA, DLA, PIP and armed forces independence payment are all defined in this regulation; *or*

(2)   is not in receipt of any of the benefits or payments listed in (1) above, but has provided (or where the person is a child, the claimant has provided) the local authority with sufficient certificates, documents, information or evidence to satisfy it that s/he requires overnight care: sub-para (a)(iii).

In addition, the local authority must be satisfied that the person "reasonably requires", and has arranged for, at least one person who does not occupy the dwelling to which the HB claim or award relates to provide overnight care, to stay overnight regularly for this purpose and to be provided with the use of a bedroom additional to those used by the occupiers of the dwelling: sub-para (b).

"Regularly" is not defined and thus should be given its ordinary meaning. *SD v Eastleigh BC (HB)* [2014] UKUT 325 (AAC) concerned the meaning of the word "regularly" in the definition. The First-tier Tribunal, although unhappy with it, had decided that it meant "something which happens at intervals which, if not precisely fixed, are at least reasonably even". Judge Rowland, pointed out that regularly can also be a synonym for "habitually", "customarily" or "commonly" and that this was a more sensible understanding of the meaning in the context of the definition. The issue is whether the claimant's need for care arises often and steadily enough so that a bedroom has to be available for that purpose. He said:

"A bedroom cannot be switched on and off and, if the object of the legislation is to encourage claimants to move to smaller accommodation or take lodgers into their spare rooms, it is to be presumed that whether overnight care is regular or not has to be considered over a fairly long period. Moreover, there is nothing in the word "regularly" that requires that the carer must be required to stay overnight on the majority of nights for the claimant to meet the criterion. That may be why that word was chosen. It does not mean the same as "normally" or "ordinarily". A bedroom may be required even if the help is required only on a minority of nights. Whether a carer must "regularly" stay overnight must be considered in that context."

The local authority had initially decided that because the claimant was getting middle rate DLA care component for her care needs during the day, and not the night, she did not have a regular need for a bedroom for a non-resident carer. In view of this approach, Judge Rowland said that the basis for an award of DLA care component (ie, whether it is for day or night needs) may be relevant evidence, but cannot be determinative of the question whether a claimant is a "person who requires overnight care".

In *MG v Carmarthenshire CC and SSWP (HB)* [2013] UKUT 363 (AAC), the claimants had night carers who worked on a "wakeful" system – ie, a carer was awake at night to see to their care needs as required. An additional room was provided for the use of the carers, but this was an office which did not contain a bed or facilities for sleeping. The local authority only allowed the single room rate of HB on the basis that the carers had not been provided with the use of a bedroom additional to those used by the people who occupied the dwelling as a home. The claimants' representatives argued the word "bedroom" should be read as extending to any room occupied by a carer providing night-time care, whether or not the room contains a bed or is used for sleeping in. The appeal was dismissed on the basis that the room used by an overnight carer had to be in fact a bedroom.

Bolton MBC v BF (HB) [2014] UKUT 48 (AAC) concerned the meaning of "bedroom" in para (b) of the definition. The claimant occupied a two-bedroom dwelling with his wife. The local authority accepted that the claimant required someone to provide him with overnight care, that he had arranged for and received such care and that his home had an extra bedroom. However, it decided that he was only entitled to one bedroom under the relevant size criteria (in his case those in reg 13D) because for health reasons, he slept in the second bedroom, not his overnight carer, and his carer (his daughter) slept on a portable bed in the lounge. The First-tier Tribunal decided that the claimant did come within the definition of "person who requires overnight care" and that his HB should be calculated based on the two-bedroom local housing allowance rate. The local authority appealed. Upper Tribunal Judge West dismissed the appeal. Considering the ordinary meaning of "bedroom", he concluded that the claimant's carer had been provided with the use of a bedroom additional to those used by the people who occupied the dwelling as a home (ie, the claimant and his wife). The fact that the room his daughter used was also the lounge did not preclude it from being a bedroom. He distinguished the case from *MG v Carmarthenshire CC and SSWP (HB)*. He said:

"The legislation does not require that the 'bedroom' must be a room primarily intended for sleeping in, such that a lounge or other living room is necessarily precluded from being a bedroom because it can be used for another purpose when it is not being used to be slept in. ... [T]he fact that the bed may have been folded up or put away in the course of the day when the room was being used as a lounge or living room does not mean that it was not a bedroom within the meaning of the regulations when [the carer] slept in it at night. It is sufficient if the room in question, of which the overnight carer has use, is furnished with a bed or is used for sleeping in. It would therefore make no difference if the claimant's daughter had, for example, slept on the sofa, or in a sleeping bag on cushions on the floor, as opposed to sleeping on a portable bed."

By the closing words of para (b), someone can come within the definition even if s/he does not occupy the dwelling if s/he can be treated as doing so, for which see reg 7. In this case, the local authority must be satisfied that the dwelling contains an extra bedroom and that the person did reasonably require and arrange overnight care when s/he occupied the dwelling or will do so when s/he occupies it.

Note that s130 WRA 2012 (on p211) makes provision for information sharing in relation to the provision of overnight care. This, for example, enables local authority HB departments to use information provided by the authority's social services department in determining whether someone is a person who requires overnight care.

"polygamous marriage". This only covers marriages that are lawful where and when they occur. An authority faced with a problem as to the validity of a polygamous marriage should seek expert advice from a specialist lawyer.

"the qualifying age for state pension credit". This age is relevant in determining whether the HB Regs or the HB(SPC) Regs apply to a claimant: reg 5. The age at which someone qualifies for state pension credit (PC) is linked to pensionable age for a woman.

The process of equalising men's and women's pension ages began on 6 April 2010. From that date, women's pension age began to rise, as did the qualifying age for pension credit (PC). Note that pension ages for men and women are equal from 6 December 2018.

Under the definition, the qualifying age for PC for a woman is the minimum age she can receive state retirement pension. The qualifying age for PC for a man is the minimum age a woman born on the same day as him can receive state retirement pension. So for both men and women, the qualifying age for PC is:

(1)   60, if s/he was born before 6 April 1950;

(2)   an age from 60 and one month to 64 and 11 months depending on her/his date of birth, if s/he was born on or after 6 April 1950 but before 6 December 1953;

(3)   65, if s/he was born on 6 November 1953;

(4)   an age from 65 to 66 depending on her/his date of birth, if s/he was born on or after 6 December 1953 but before 5 October 1954;

(5)   66, if s/he was born on or after 6 October 1954 but before 6 April 1960;

(6)   67, if s/he was born on or after 6 March 1961 but before 6 April 1977.

Consequently, the rules in the Housing Benefit (Persons who have attained the qualifying age for state pension credit) Regulations 2006 No.214 can apply to individual claimants at different ages. For claimants born on or after 6 April 1950 but before 6 December 1953, there is a helpful table, setting out the relevant birth dates and pension ages, in an Appendix to CPAG's *Welfare Benefits and Tax Credits Handbook*.

Pensionable age for both men and women will rise to 68 between 2024 and 2046.

"qualifying parent or carer". A "qualifying parent or carer" is someone who is an approved foster parent or carer or a kinship carer who has a child or qualifying young person placed with her/him or has had one placed with her/him within the previous 52 weeks. If s/he has only recently been approved and has not had a child or qualifying young person placed with her/him, s/he counts as a qualifying parent or carer for up to 52 weeks. The definition is relevant for determining the number of bedrooms allowed under the size criteria within the the local housing allowance, the social sector and the local reference rent schemes for rent restriction: see regs B13, 13 and 13D HB Regs. Broadly, it allows foster parents and carers and kinship carers one additional bedroom. To come within the definition, the person must not only satisfy either para (a) or (b), but must also actually have a bedroom in the dwelling s/he occupies as her/his home that is additional to those used by others who occupy it. Note that if the child or qualifying young person is a "person who requires overnight care" (defined above), a further additional bedroom can be allowed. The definition does not include people who provide care to an adult placed with them. It only includes those who provide relevant care to children and young people. However, see *SSWP v PE and Bolton MBC* [2017] UKUT 393 (AAC), discussed on p377.

"qualifying person". "The Fund", "the Eileen Trust", "MFET Ltd", "the Skipton Fund", "the Caxton Foundation", "Scottish Infected Blood Support Scheme", " approved blood scheme", "the London Emergencies Trust", "the We Love Manchester Emergency Fund" and the "London Bombings Relief Charitable Fund" are all defined elsewhere in this regulation. The significance of the term is in respect of certain income and capital disregards.

"registered housing association". The definition is relevant when determining whether a claimant's eligible rent for HB purposes is to be restricted under any of the rent restriction schemes, for which see the General Note on Part 3 on p348 and regs 12BA, 12C and 12D and para 4 of Sch 3 of the HB&CTB(CP) Regs. The definition was substituted from 1 April 2010 as a consequence of changes to the registration process for providers of social housing in England. Such providers are covered by para (a). Sections 68–71 Housing and Regeneration Act 2008 define social housing as low cost rental accommodation (ie, accommodation that is available to rent at below the market rate) and low cost ownership accommodation (ie, accommodation occupied or made available to occupy in accordance with shared ownership or equity percentage arrangements or shared ownership trusts). Rental and ownership accommodation are only social housing if the accommodation is available to people whose needs are not adequately served by the commercial housing market. A "registered provider of social housing" is a person or body registered by the Homes and Communities Agency. A current list of registered providers is at www.gov.uk/government/publications/current-registered-providers-of-social-housing.

Private registered providers can be either non-profit or profit-making.

In Wales and Scotland, a registered housing association is one registered in a register maintained by the Welsh Ministers or the Scottish Ministers respectively.

"relative". "Close relative" is defined earlier in this regulation. Note that neither definition expressly covers half-sisters and brothers, but see the discussion of *Bristol City Council v JKT* [2016] UKUT 517 (AAC) on p240.

"self-employed earner". SSCBA s2(1)(b) defines this as "a person who is gainfully employed in Great Britain otherwise than in employed earner's employment (whether or not he is also employed in such employment)". For "employed earner", see above.

"shared ownership tenancy". For "dwelling", see SSCBA s137(1) (p15) and reg 2(4). For "owner", see above.

Judge Mesher considered whether the definition of shared ownership tenancy could apply to a claimant who had acquired the long tenancy of a dwelling under the right to buy legislation: *Blackburn with Darwen BC v DA (HB)* [2014] UKUT 431 (AAC). He concluded that para (a) of the definition had to be qualified by reading in some element of shared ownership, with "ownership" here given its everyday meaning. He said:

"A shared ownership tenancy is one in which the tenant, in the case of a flat, takes a long-term leasehold interest in only part of the dwelling concerned (typically, 25%, 50% or 75%), while paying rent as a short-term tenant would on the remainder. The tenant then has the right to buy additional percentages on the long-term basis, when amount of the short-term rent will reduce proportionately. The essence is that there is a sharing of what would in ordinary language be regarded as the ownership of the dwelling, between the tenant in the case of the long-term tenancy element and the landlord in the case of the short-term tenancy aspect. The claimant here did not share the ownership of his flat in that sense, and neither would anyone else who acquired a long tenancy of the dwelling as a whole under the right to buy legislation. His ownership under the 125 year lease was not shared with the landlord in that sense, even though there was still a split between the freehold interest of the landlord and his leasehold interest. Therefore, the ordinary application of regulation 12(2)(a) of the 2006 Regulations to long tenancies was not excluded in the claimant's case. That conclusion is in my view confirmed by the terms of head (b) of the definition of "shared ownership tenancy" applying to Scotland. There would be no rational reason for applying a different practical policy to the scope of the application of regulation 12(2)(a) as between Scotland and England and Wales."

A *"single claimant"* is a claimant who has neither a partner nor is a lone parent. "Partner and "lone parent" are also defined in reg 2(1).

"special account". The definition is relevant for an income disregard under Sch 5 para 58.

"voluntary organisation". In determining whether activities are "carried on otherwise than for profit" it is relevant to look not simply at the constitution of the body but at its actual activities: *Salford CC v PF* [2009] UKUT 150 (AAC). See also the discussion of *Wirral MBC v Furlong, Perry and Salisbury Independent Living and SSWP (HB)* [2013] UKUT 291 (AAC); [2014] AACR 12 on p1779.

"young individual". Reg 13(5) requires that where the claimant is a "young individual" (ie, a "single claimant" under 35 who does not come within any of the exceptions set out) and the rent officer has supplied the authority with a single room rent, the maximum rent under the local reference rent rules is based on that figure. "Single claimant" is also defined in reg 2(1). Reg 13D(2)(a) specifies the category of dwelling normally applicable to a "young individual" which in turn sets the maximum rent (LHA) for such a claimant under the "local housing allowance" rules. Note that prior to 1 January 2012, the age limit was 25.

There are a number of exceptions set out in sub-paras (a) to (j). A claimant is *not* a "young individual", if any of the following apply.

(1)   Her/his landlord is a "registered housing association": sub-para (a). For the definition, see above.

(2)   S/he is under 22 and was formerly in the care of, or supervised by or provided with accommodation by, a local authority under specified provisions: sub-paras (b)–(f).

         In England and Wales, a single claimant under 22 is not a "young individual" if s/he was the subject of a care order made under s31(I)(a) Children Act 1989 which was made after s/he turned 16 or made before age 16 but continued after that age. For this exemption to apply, the court must have made an order putting the child in the care of a designated authority. A single claimant is also not a "young individual" if s/he is under 22 years and was formerly provided with accommodation under s20 Children Act 1989 or s76 Social Services and Well-being (Wales) Act 2014. These require social services departments to provide accommodation to children (anyone aged under 18 years) in need. It also permits social services to provide accommodation to any child within its area – eg, if it considers that doing so would safeguard or promote the child's welfare.

         In Scotland, a single claimant under 22 is not a "young individual" if parental rights were assumed by a local authority under s86 Children (Scotland) Act 1995 or s/he was provided with accommodation by a local authority under s25 of that Act or if s/he has ceased to be a child in relation to whom a permanence order has been made or treated a made, in all cases after s/he turned 16 or before age 16 but continuing after that age. A single claimant under 22 is also not a "young individual" if s/he was subject to a supervision requirement under s70 Children (Scotland) Act 1995 ("provided that the supervision requirement was not made as a result of the child having committed an offence"). For this exemption to apply, the authority should be satisfied that the child was living away from her/his normal place of residence but not with friends or relatives.

(3)   S/he is under 22 and, unless any of the listed exceptions in sub-para (i)(i) or (ii) apply, s/he has ceased to be subject to a compulsory supervision order which had continued after s/he was 16: sub-para (i). Under s83 of the Children's Hearings (Scotland) Act 2011, a compulsory supervision order is an order including any of specified measures. These include, among other measures, a requirement that a child resides at a specified place (in England, Wales or Scotland) and a direction authorising the person in charge of the specified place to restrict the child's liberty.

(4)   S/he is a "person who requires overnight care": sub-para (g). For the definition, see above.

(5)   S/he is aged at least 25 and has occupied one or more hostels for homeless people (as defined), for a total of at least three months (this does not have to be continuous), if while in occupation, s/he has been offered and accepted support services with a view to being assisted to be "rehabilitated or resettled within the community": sub-para (h) and reg 2(1A) and (1B).

(6)   S/he is aged at least 25 and is the subject of active multi-agency risk management under s325(2) Criminal Justice Act 2000 (in England or Wales) or s10(1) Management of Offenders etc (Scotland) Act 2005 (a

person who may cause serious harm to the public): sub-para (h) and reg 2(1C). Also exempt are claimants in Scotland not covered by the duty under s10 for specified reasons but who the local authority considers may cause serious harm to the public at large. Multi-Agency Public Protection Arrangements (MAPPA) Guidance at www.justice.gov.uk/downloads/offenders/mappa/mappa-guidance-2012-part1.pdf says that this applies to level 2 and level 3 MAPPA offenders.

(7)   S/he is a "qualifying parent or carer": sub-para (j). "qualifying parent or carer" is also defined in reg 2(1).

Paragraph (2)

This confirms that persons liable to make payments include those deemed to be so liable under reg 8.

Paragraph (3)

For the meaning of "payable", see the discussion of *SMcH v Perth and Kinross Council (HB)* in the Analysis of para (3A) below.

Someone is considered to be on income-based JSA (defined in para (1) above) on any day in respect of which it is payable to her/him, and also on the following.

(1)   Days on which the claimant is entitled to income-based (or joint-claim) JSA but is disqualified from payment under reg 27A Jobseeker's Allowance Regulations 1996 SI No.207 (JSA Regs), ss19 or 20A Jobseekers Act 1995 (JSA 1995) or regulations made under s17A of that Act – ie, because s/he failed to participate in an interview as required or has been "sanctioned", for example, for failing to apply for a job or for losing a job through misconduct. See the commentary in the latest edition of *Social Security Legislation* Vol II for further details. Note that from 22 October 2012, s19 JSA 1995 was substituted under s46 WRA 2012 and reg 27A JSA Regs was revoked by SI 2012 No.2568, but at the time this book was written, no consequential amendments had been made to this provision. Note also that no amendments have yet been made to reflect the different JSA sanction provisions for JSA claimants to whom ss6J and 6K JSA 1995 apply (for which see s49 WRA 2012) – ie, for those entitled to contribution-based JSA who come under the UC system. This may be because the concept under the new provisions is that where a JSA claimant has been "sanctioned", JSA is paid at a reduced rate – ie, it technically continues to be payable (even if this is at a "nil" rate) during the sanction period.

(2)   So-called "waiting days". Under Sch 1 para 4 JSA 1995, a claimant is generally not entitled to JSA for the first seven days (it was three days before 27 October 2014) of any jobseeking period ("waiting days"). If the waiting days immediately precede a day for which income-based JSA is payable (or would be payable were it not for a sanction under reg 27A JSA Regs, ss19 or 20A JSA 1995 or regulations made under s17A of that Act, for which see above), the claimant is entitled to maximum HB for the waiting days.

(3)   Where income-based (or joint-claim) JSA would be payable but for the loss of JSA due to the operation of the provisions for loss of benefit on repeat convictions for benefit fraud.

Paragraph (3A)

Someone is considered to be on income-related ESA on any day in respect of which it is payable to her/him. In *SMcH v Perth and Kinross Council (HB)* [2015] UKUT 126 (AAC), Judge Mesher decided that "payable" here does not mean "actually paid" or "actually paid under an award whether right or wrong". It means "properly or lawfully paid" or something akin to that. A consequence is that the disregard of income in Sch 5 para 4 HB Regs cannot be triggered by payments of income-related ESA subsequently found to have been made in error – eg, if there was no entitlement to income-related ESA.

Someone is also considered to be on income-related ESA on the following.

(1)   Days on which the claimant is entitled to income-related ESA but is disqualified from payment under s18 WRA 2007 – eg, because s/he has limited capability for work through misconduct or for failing without good cause to follow medical advice or where s/he has failed without good cause to observe "prescribed rules of behaviour".

(2)   So called "waiting days". Under Sch 2 para 2 WRA 2007 and reg 144 Employment and Support Allowance Regulations 2008 SI No.794, a claimant is generally not entitled to ESA for the first seven days (it was three days before 27 October 2014) of any "period of limited capability for work".

Paragraph (3B)

Someone is considered to be on UC on any day s/he is entitled to it, even if it is not in payment. Although a person is generally precluded from entitlement to HB if s/he is entitled to UC, UC claimants may be entitled to HB for "specified accommodation" or "temporary accommodation" (as defined in Sch 1 paras 3A and 3B UC Regs) and in other limited cases, including where the claimant is entitled to a two-week run on of HB (a transitional HB payment): see the Universal Credit (Transitional Provisions) Regulations 2014 SI No.1230 on p1857. The definition in para (3B) is relevant for regs 5, 7, 56 and 83. The earnings, other income and capital of a claimant on UC are disregarded in full under Sch 4 para 12, Sch 5 para 4 and Sch 6 para 5 respectively.

Paragraph (4)

This does not define the term "dwelling" exclusively: the full definition is in s137 SSCBA (see p15). This paragraph merely lists certain areas of land which are to be treated as part of a dwelling. The main application will be to include the land in capital disregarded under Sch 6 para 1. The basic aim is to avoid the payment of HB in respect of commercially used land.

Sub-para (a) requires that land must be used "for the purposes of occupying the dwelling as a home" as opposed to occupation for business or other purposes. Additionally, if the occupier obtained the use of the land

and the dwelling at the same time, it must not have been possible for her/him to obtain the use of the one without the other. Otherwise, if the use of the land and the dwelling were obtained at different times, or the dwelling could have been occupied without the land, s/he must have made or be making "all reasonable efforts" to get rid of the liability for the land before it can be treated as part of the dwelling for HB purposes.

Sub-paras (b) and (c) include land under a caravan or mobile home or where a houseboat is moored in the definition of "dwelling". Note *CH 318/2005* which, although not relying on this provision, decided that a narrowboat can constitute a "dwelling" for the purposes of the HB scheme.

Sub-para (d). The Crofters (Scotland) Act 1993 s3(1), as amended by s21 of the Crofters Reform etc Act 2007 and s22 of the Crofting Reform (Scotland) Act 2010, sets out the conditions which must be complied with before land will count as a "croft". It must be situated in one of the former "crofting counties". A croft is a small landholding, usually in the Highlands, Western Isles or Northern Isles of Scotland.

Paragraph (5)

"Claimant participating as a service user" is relevant for certain disregards of expenses and notional expenses as income. Note that prior to 28 April 2014, there were similar disregards for those in a "service user group". See p226 of the 26th edition.

Paragraph (6)

This paragraph is needed to define "member of a couple who can share a bedroom" references to which are found in the size criteria in regs B13(5) and 13D(3) HB Regs, and Sch 2 para 1 of both the Rent Officers (Housing Benefit Functions) Order 1997 and the Rent Officers (Housing Benefit Functions) (Scotland) Order 1997.

Definition of non-dependant

3.–(1)   In these Regulations, "non-dependant" means any person, except someone to whom paragraph (2) applies, who normally resides with a claimant or with whom a claimant normally resides.

(2)   This paragraph applies to–

(a)   any member of the claimant's family;

(b)   if the claimant is polygamously married, any partner of his and any child or young person who is a member of his household and for whom he or one of his partners is responsible;

(c)   a child or young person who is living with the claimant but who is not a member of his household by virtue of regulation 21 (circumstances in which a person is to be treated as being or not being a member of the same household);

(d)   subject to paragraph (3), a person who jointly occupies the claimant's dwelling and is either a co-owner of that dwelling with the claimant or his partner (whether or not there are other co-owners) or is liable with the claimant or his partner to make payments in respect of his occupation of the dwelling;

(e)   subject to paragraph (3)–

  (i)   any person who is liable to make payments on a commercial basis to the claimant or the claimant's partner in respect of the occupation of the dwelling;

  (ii)   any person to whom or to whose partner the claimant or the claimant's partner is liable to make payments on a commercial basis in respect of the occupation of the dwelling; or

  (iii)   any other member of the household of the person to whom or to whose partner the claimant or the claimant's partner is liable to make payments on a commercial basis in respect of the occupation of the dwelling;

(f)   a person who lives with the claimant in order to care for him or a partner of his and who is engaged by a charitable or voluntary organisation which makes a charge to the claimant or his partner for the services provided by that person.

(3)   Sub-paragraphs (d) and (e) of paragraph (2) shall not apply to any person who is treated as if he were not liable to make payments in respect of a dwelling under paragraph (1) of regulation 9 (circumstances in which a person is to be treated as not liable to make payments in respect of a dwelling).

(4)   For the purposes of this regulation [¹, regulations 9 and 13(6)(c) and the definition of "linked person" in regulation 2] a person resides with another only if they share any accommodation except a bathroom, a lavatory or a communal area within the meaning prescribed in paragraph 8 of Schedule 1 but not if each person is separately liable to make payments in respect of his occupation of the dwelling to the landlord.

Modifications

Amendments were made to para (4) by reg 4(2) Housing Benefit (Local Housing Allowance and Information Sharing) Amendment Regulations 2007 No.2868 as from 7 April 2008, save that for a person to whom reg 1(5) of those regulations applied (see p1812), the amendments came into force on the day on or after 7 April 2008 when the first of the events specified in reg 1(6) applied to her/him, or on 6 April 2009 if none had before that date.

Amendment

1.   Amended by reg 4(2) of SI 2007 No 2868 as from 7.4.08 (or if reg 1(5) of that SI applies, on the day on or after 7.4.08 when the first of the events specified in reg 1(6) applies, or from 6.4.09 if none have before that date).

Definitions

"child" – see s137(1) SSCBA and reg 2(1).
"claimant" – see reg 2(1).
"communal area" – see para 8 of Sch 1.
"dwelling" – see s137(1) SSCBA and reg 2(4).
"linked person" – see reg 2(1).
"partner" – see reg 2(1).
"young person" – see regs 2(1) and 19.

General Note

This defines which of the people who "reside" with the claimant or with whom the claimant resides are to be treated as "non-dependants" and therefore in respect of whom a claimant's maximum HB may be reduced under reg 74 by a "non-dependant deduction". Note that all payments made to a claimant by a non-dependant are disregarded under Sch 5 para 21. The definition is also relevant for the qualifying conditions for a severe disability premium: Sch 3 para 14.

Para (1) provides the general rule, subject to the exceptions listed in para (2). In particular, para (2)(e), provides that those residing with the claimant or her/his partner (or with whom the claimant or the partner resides) on a commercial basis are not to be treated as non-dependants.

Para (4) qualifies the term "resides with another" for these purposes, and also for the purposes of reg 9 (circumstances in which a person is to be treated as not liable to make payments in respect of a dwelling), reg 13(6)(c) (a situation when, in the case of a "young individual", maximum rent is not restricted to the single room rent) and the definition of "linked person" in reg 2.

Analysis

Paragraphs (1) and (4): Persons normally residing with the claimant

The basic rule is that a "non-dependant" is anyone who normally resides with the claimant or with whom the claimant normally resides, subject to the exceptions in para (2). The addition of the latter category excludes any possibility of arguing that the claimant resides with the supposed non-dependent rather than the other way round – an argument accepted by the Court of Appeal in *Bate v Chief Adjudication Officer* [1994] *The Times,* 12 December, but rejected by the House of Lords when overturning the decision of the Court of Appeal (*R(IS) 12/ 96*). If the person does not come within the definition, the person is *not* a non-dependant and maximum HB cannot be reduced under reg 74.

AM v SSWP (IS) [2011] UKUT 387 (AAC) pointed out that for a person to count as a non-dependant, three questions must be answered. First, does the person "reside" in the same dwelling as the claimant? Second, does the person "normally reside" in in the same dwelling as the claimant? Finally, does the person "reside with" the claimant?

Does the person "reside" in the same dwelling? In *AM*, Judge Parker decided that in determining whether someone "resides" in the same dwelling as the claimant, there are analogies to habitual residence cases and, citing *R(IS) 6/96*, that to count as resident in a dwelling, a person must be seen to be making a home there, even if it is not the only or permanent home. The judge accepted that it was possible for a person to be resident in more than one place at the same time and also to have no residence at all. She said:

"It is a question of fact whether the quality of a person's stay in a particular dwelling constitutes it as a home for the person concerned; or alternatively is only a place where that person transiently or temporarily lives."

Does the person "normally reside" in the same dwelling? Whether someone "normally resides" with the claimant is a purely factual question. It involves no element of judgment on the quality of the residence: *ST v SSWP* [2009] UKUT 269 (AAC); [2010] AACR 23. Note, however, that where a person stays in other places besides the claimant's home, it is a matter of fact and degree as to whether s/he is *normally* resident with the claimant. A person must have lived there for long enough to regard it as her/his usual home: *CIS 14850/1996* para 7. Relevant factors for deciding whether a person is normally resident may include: the relationship between the parties, how much time s/he spends at the claimant's address, where her/his post is sent, where s/he keeps clothes and other belongings, whether the stay or absence is temporary, and whether there is another permanent base that s/he could regard as home. In *JP v Bournemouth BC (HB)* [2018] UKUT 75 (AAC); [2018] AACR 30, the First-tier Tribunal decided that someone could be resident in more than one place at the same time and that s/he could be normally resident in both places. Judge Wikeley agreed with the former conclusion, but not the latter. Thus he decided that it is not possible for someone to have a normal residence in one place (eg, for the purpose of reg 3), but to have a normal home elsewhere (eg, for the purpose of reg 74(7)(a), a situation when no non-dependant deduction can be made). Where a person has connections with more than one home, it is possible that s/he may not be normally residing in any of them: *CSIS 100/1993*.

Does the person "reside with" the claimant? Para (4) restricts the circumstances in which a person "resides with another". There must be some shared accommodation other than a bathroom, lavatory or communal area (defined in Sch 1 para 8 as an area of common access including a hall or passageway and rooms of common use in sheltered accommodation).

It is plain from the wording of para (4) that a person does not "reside with" another person unless there is relevant shared accommodation. However, the existence of such sharing is not determinative of the issue, and all that need be shown is that the two people "reside with" each other in normal use of that phrase.

In *CPC 1446/2008*, the claimant lived in a "granny annexe" built on to the back of her son's house. She had her own lounge and bathroom but used the kitchen of her son's house to heat up food in a microwave. A kitchen clearly counts as "any accommodation except a bathroom, a lavatory or a communal area". The question was whether the claimant was sharing the kitchen with a non-dependant. Approving *CIS 2532/2003* and *CSIS 652/2003*, Deputy Commissioner Wikeley decided that if a claimant makes use of a kitchen, s/he shares it, even if s/he does not actually visit it. The contrary view taken in the earlier *CSIS 185/1995* was disapproved. The Deputy Commissioner said that this is in accord with the plain meaning of the expression "normally resides with". He thought that if the claimant's son were asked "Where does your mother live?" or "Where does your mother reside?" his answer most probably would be "She can't manage by herself any more; she lives [or resides] with me – we have had a granny annex built out the back of our house".

A person shares a kitchen with another even though s/he is never there at the same time as the other person and even though s/he pays for the use of the kitchen: *Thamesdown BC v Goonery* [1995] 1 CLY 2600, CA.

RK v SSWP [2008] UKUT 34 (AAC) decided that people are only to be regarded as residing with each other if they are sharing accommodation in a way that is consistent with living in the same household. Judge Rowland said that "share" does not mean "use with another person", but means "have the use of with another person" in the sense of "have a shared right to use". Actual use of accommodation is evidence of a right to use it but is neither necessary nor conclusive. The members of a household have shared use of the accommodation the household has the right to occupy. Where members of a family (in the non-technical sense of that word) are living in the same household on a non-commercial basis, they can usually be regarded as sharing the whole of the dwelling. The way accommodation is actually used may also be relevant when considering whether people are residing together. In particular, the fact that one member of a family frequently cooks for another member may be powerful evidence that they live in the same household. The fact that adults and older children respect each other's privacy and do not in fact make use of each other's bedrooms is immaterial. However, it is not invariably the case that members of the same family living in the same building are living in the same household. They may deliberately constitute themselves into different households – eg, because they are estranged or wish to establish their independence. In those circumstances, a person resides only with the members of the family who are members of the same household and the fact that the household may share accommodation with other family members living in a different household does not mean that they also reside with those other family members. But where a claimant in receipt of attendance allowance (AA) lives in the same building as other members of her/his family, it is unlikely that they are living in separate households because the purpose of living in the same building will usually have been precisely so that the claimant can receive the attention or supervision that entitlement to AA implies is needed from those other members of the family, at least to some extent.

Paragraphs (2) and (3): The exceptions
The following categories of people are *not* non-dependants even if they fall within the definition set out above. For the meaning of "household", see p17.

(1)   A member of the claimant's family: para (2)(a). "Family" means the claimant's partner (if s/he has one) and any dependent children and qualifying young people who are members of the same household and for whom s/he or her/his partner is responsible: s137(1) SSCBA and regs 19–21. Reg 20 deals with the situations in which an adult is to be treated as responsible for a child or young person, and reg 21, with those in which s/he may be treated as sharing a household with such a person.

(2)   Where a claimant is in a polygamous marriage, any partner and any dependent children (and qualifying young people) who are members of the same household and for whom either s/he or a partner is responsible: para (2)(b). See regs 19-21 on p405.

(3)   A child or young person living with the claimant, but excluded from counting as a member of the household under reg 21 – eg, a foster child: para (2)(c).

(4)   A joint occupier who is also either a co-owner with the claimant or her/his partner or is liable with the claimant or her/his partner to make payments in respect of her/his occupation of the dwelling: para (2)(d). A "joint occupier" is someone who has a joint legal right to occupy the property, rather than merely someone who occupies the property along with the claimant or her/his partner: *R v Chesterfield BC ex p Fullwood* (1993) 26 HLR 126 at 129, CA. Thus it covers joint tenants and people who have signed a

single license agreement. It has been argued in previous editions that it may be possible to argue that "payments in respect of his occupation of the dwelling" does not mean the same as "payments in respect of a dwelling" in reg 8(1) and could cover situations such as utility bills which are in joint names. In view of the fact that para (3) envisages that reg 9 may apply to the liability under this paragraph so as to render the person a non-dependent after all, this seems to be incorrect, and the payments must be payments of rent or similar.

(5)   Those residing with the claimant who are liable to make payments on a commercial basis to her/him or her/his partner: para (2)(e)(i). For liability to make payments, see reg 9 on p280. For whether such payments are "on a commercial basis", see the Analysis to reg 9(1)(a) on p282. Where the person is not a non-dependant, some (or all) of the payments made to the claimant can be disregarded. See in particular Sch 5 paras 22 and 42 on p669 and p677.

(6)   The person to whom the claimant or her/his partner are liable to make payments on a commercial basis (or that person's partner) – eg, a resident landlord: para (2)(e)(ii).

(7)   Any member of the household of a person excluded by (6): para (2)(e)(iii).

(8)   A person who lives with the claimant in order to care for her/him or her/his partner and who is employed by a charity or voluntary organisation, where a charge is made for her/his services: para (2)(f). This applies whether or not there is assistance with the charges from a public or local authority.

By para (3), anyone in categories (4) to (7) above may be a non-dependent if her/his liability to pay rent falls foul of any of the exclusions from HB in reg 9(1) – eg, where the liability was created to take advantage of the HB scheme or the claimant is a close relative.

Cases in which section 1(1A) of the Administration Act is disapplied

4.   Section 1(1A) of the Administration Act (requirement to state national insurance number) shall not apply–

(a)   to a claim for housing benefit where the person making the claim, or in respect of whom the claim is made, is liable to make payments in respect of a dwelling which is a hostel;

(b)   to any child or young person in respect of whom housing benefit is claimed.

[¹ (c)   to a person who–

(i)   is a person in respect of whom a claim for housing benefit is made;

(ii)   is subject to immigration control within the meaning of section 115(9)(a) of the Immigration and Asylum Act;

(iii)   is a person from abroad for the purposes of these Regulations as defined in regulation 10(2); and

(iv)   has not previously been allocated a national insurance number.]

Amendment

1.   Amended by reg 9 of SI 2009 No 471 as from 6.4.09.

Definitions

"child" – see reg 2(1).
"hostel" – see reg 2(1).
"young person" – see regs 2(1) and 19.

General Note

The National Insurance number (NINO) requirement imposed by s1(1A) SSAA (see p23) is removed by para (a) in respect of inhabitants of hostels. See the discussion on the complex definition of "hostel", on p240.

Para (b) clarifies that the NINO requirement does not apply to a child or young person in respect of whom HB is claimed.

Para (c) disapplies the NINO requirement for anyone in respect of whom a claim for HB is made (eg, a partner) where s/he has not previously been allocated a NINO and the following conditions are satisfied:

(1)   s/he is "subject to immigration control" because s/he requires leave to enter or remain in the UK but does not have it: s115(9)(a) Immigration and Asylum Act 1999 (see p1706); *and*

(2)   s/he is not "habitually resident" in the UK, the Channel Islands, the Isle of Man or the Republic of Ireland: reg 10(2) (see p297). However, note that given that none of those who are subject to immigration control because they require leave to enter or remain and do not have it can count as "habitually resident" it appears that para (c)(iii) is *otiose*.

Para (c) ensures that in such a case, the claim for HB can still be allowed. However, it is important to note that where a claim for HB is made in respect of someone "subject to immigration control" there might be consequences for that person's immigration status. Immigration advice is essential in such a situation.

Both paras (b) and (c) apply to those in respect of whom HB is claimed. The judge in *Westminster City Council v AT & SSWP (HB)* [2013] UKUT 321 (AAC) said that reg 4 has to be read consistently with s1(1A) SSAA which draws a distinction between "the person making the claim" and "any other person in respect of whom he is claiming benefit". In other words, the HB claimant cannot also be a person in respect of whom the claim is made. Thus, in this appeal, a claimant who was a child was not exempt from the NINO requirement under reg 4(b), and could not satisfy it because she did not have a NINO, nor had she applied for one.

Persons who have attained the qualifying age for state pension credit

5.–(1)   These Regulations apply to a person who–
(a)   has not attained the qualifying age for state pension credit; or
(b)   has attained the qualifying age for state pension credit if he, or if he has a partner, his partner, is a person [³ on universal credit,] on income support [², on an income-based jobseeker's allowance or on an income-related employment and support allowance].
[¹ (2)]
(3)   Except as provided in [¹ paragraph (1)], these Regulations shall not apply in relation to any person if he, or if he has a partner, his partner, has attained the qualifying age for state pension credit.

Amendments

1.   Amended by reg 4(3) of SI 2008 No 959 as from 6.10.08.
2.   Amended by reg 6 of SI 2008 No 1082 as from 27.10.08.
3.   Amended by reg 7(3) of SI 2013 No 2070 as from 28.10.13.

Definitions

"an income-based jobseeker's allowance – see reg 2(1).
"partner" – see reg 2(1).
"person on an income-based jobseeker's allowance" – see reg 2(3).
"person on an income-related employment and support allowance" – see reg 2(3A).
"person on income support" – see reg 2(1).
"person on universal credit" – see reg 2(3B).
"qualifying age for state pension credit" – see reg 2(1).

General Note

The HB Regs apply in two situations.
(1)   If neither the claimant nor her/his partner have reached the qualifying age for PC: paras (1)(a) and (3).
(2)   If the claimant or her/his partner has reached the qualifying age for PC, but s/he or her/his partner is on IS, income-based JSA, income-related ESA or UC: paras (1)(b) and (3).
Before 15 May 2019, a claimant who was a member of a "mixed-age couple" (ie, where only one member of the couple was at least the qualifying age for PC) could claim and be entitled to HB under these regulations if para (1)(b) applied, or under the HB(SPC) Regs if para (1)(b) did not apply: reg 5 HB(SPC) Regs. New claims for HB by members of a mixed-age couple on or after 15 May 2019 are generally no longer allowed under either the HB Regs or the HB(SPC) Regs unless the claimant has been continuously entitled to PC or HB under the HB(SPC) Regs from before that date as part of the same mixed-age couple. If a claimant who has been entitled to HB under the HB Regs becomes a member of a mixed-age couple on or after that date, her/his entitlement to HB generally ends. For the rules for mixed-age couples on claims for, and termination of awards of, HB and the exceptions to the rules, see the Welfare Reform Act 2012 (Commencement No.31) Order 2019 SI No.37 (the No.31 Order) on p1898.
    Note that where a person is excluded from entitlement to PC or HB because s/he is a member of a mixed-age couple and is also prevented from claiming UC because of the "SDP Gateway" in reg 4A of the UC(TP) Regs 2014 (see p1862) or because s/he is a frontier worker or by virtue of reg 4 of the UC(TP) Regs 2014 (see p1861), the member of the couple who has reached the qualifying age for PC is treated as not having attained that age for the purposes of reg 5 and thus the HB Regs *do* apply to such a claimant. S/he is also treated as meeting the age conditions for IS, JSA and ESA so can potentially claim those benefits. See Art 8 of the No.31 Order on p1902.
    Note that a person on UC can only claim and be entitled to HB in limited circumstances, including if the HB is in respect of "specified accommodation" or "temporary accommodation" (defined in Sch 1 Paras 3A and 3B UC Regs). See the Universal Credit (Transitional Provisions) Regulations 2014 SI No.1230 on p1857.
    Because those born on or after 6 April 1950 may reach the qualifying age for PC on different dates, reg 5 may be relevant to claimants at different ages. See the note on the definition of "qualifying age for state pension credit" on p244.

Remunerative work

6.–(1)   Subject to the following provisions of this regulation, a person shall be treated for the purposes of these Regulations as engaged in remunerative work if he is engaged, or, where his hours of work fluctuate, he is engaged on average, for not less than 16 hours a week, in work for which payment is made or which is done in expectation of payment.

(2)   Subject to paragraph (3), in determining the number of hours for which a person is engaged in work where his hours of work fluctuate, regard shall be had to the average of hours worked over–

(a)   if there is a recognisable cycle of work, the period of one complete cycle (including, where the cycle involves periods in which the person does no work, those periods but disregarding any other absences);

(b)   in any other case, the period of 5 weeks immediately prior to the date of claim, or such other length of time as may, in the particular case, enable the person's weekly average hours of work to be determined more accurately.

(3)   Where, for the purposes of paragraph (2)(a), a person's recognisable cycle of work at a school, other educational establishment or other place of employment is one year and includes periods of school holidays or similar vacations during which he does not work, those periods and any other periods not forming part of such holidays or vacations during which he is not required to work shall be disregarded in establishing the average hours for which he is engaged in work.

(4)   Where no recognisable cycle has been established in respect of a person's work, regard shall be had to the number of hours or, where those hours will fluctuate, the average of the hours, which he is expected to work in a week.

(5)   A person shall be treated as engaged in remunerative work during any period for which he is absent from work referred to in paragraph (1) if the absence is either without good cause or by reason of a recognised, customary or other holiday.

(6)   A person on income support [¹, an income-based jobseeker's allowance or an income-related employment and support allowance] for more than 3 days in any benefit week shall be treated as not being in remunerative work in that week.

(7)   A person shall not be treated as engaged in remunerative work on any day on which the person is on maternity leave, paternity leave [², shared parental leave] or adoption leave, or is absent from work because he is ill.

(8)   A person shall not be treated as engaged in remunerative work on any day on which he is engaged in an activity in respect of which–

(a)   a sports award has been made, or is to be made, to him; and

(b)   no other payment is made or is expected to be made to him.

Amendments

1.   Amended by reg 7 of SI 2008 No 1082 as from 27.10.08.
2.   Amended by art 17(3) of SI 2014 No 3255 as from 31.12.14.

Definitions

"benefit week" – see reg 2(1).
"claim" – see reg 2(1).
"an income-based jobseeker's allowance" – see reg 2(1).
"maternity leave", "paternity leave", "shared parental leave" and "adoption leave" – see reg 2(1).
"payment" – see reg 2(1).
"person on an income-based jobseeker's allowance" – see reg 2(3).
"person on an income-related employment and support allowance" – see reg 2(3A).
"person on income support" – see reg 2(1).
"sports award" – see reg 2(1).

General Note

This defines the term "remunerative work" for the purposes of these regulations. The test is of much greater significance in the context of working tax credit and other means-tested benefits (ie, IS, income-based JSA, income-related ESA), because it is a condition of entitlement to (or an exclusion of entitlement from) those benefits. Its significance for HB arises in relation to the treatment of earned income (Sch 4 para 1), additional earnings disregards and childcare costs disregards (Sch 4 para 17 and regs 27(1)(c) and 28) and, where a non-dependant is in remunerative work, to the appropriate non-dependant deduction (reg 74).

Note that the exception to the "benefit cap" in reg 75E if the claimant or her/his partner is in work, or has worked recently, does not refer to, or rely on, the definition in reg 6.

Analysis
Paragraphs (1) and (5) to (8): Definition of remunerative work
By para (1), a person is in "remunerative work" if s/he is engaged for at least 16 hours a week (or where hours flucuate for an average of at least 16 hours a week) in paid work or work done in the expectation of payment. This is qualified as follows.

(1)   If someone is absent from work "without good cause" or on a "recognised, customary or other holiday", s/he is treated as being at work for the period of absence: para (5). "Good cause" is not defined for these purposes. It is suggested that whether or not the employer has authorised the absence is not conclusive, but if the absence is authorised the claimant is likely to have good cause.

(2)   A person on IS, income-based JSA or income-related ESA for more than three days in a benefit week (see the definitions in reg 2(1), (3) and (3A)) is not in remunerative work for that week: para (6). Note that if this applies to a non-dependant, a lower (or no) non-dependant deduction is applicable: reg 74.

(3)   A person on maternity, adoption, paternity or shared parental leave or sick leave is not treated as being in remunerative work for the days that s/he is absent from work: para (7). But see reg 28(2) to (4), (14) and (15) on p424 for situations when such a person *can* be treated as in remunerative work for the purpose of the childcare charge deduction from earnings. See also the commentary to reg 35(1)(i) and (j) on "paternity leave" on p441. Note also that the scheme of shared parental leave only affects those whose baby is (or was) due on or after 5 April 2015.

(4)   A person is not treated as being in remunerative work on any day where her/his sole remuneration is, or is expected to be, in the form of a "sports award" (defined in reg 2(1) on p233): para (8). The definition requires that the claimant "is engaged in an activity in respect of which" the sports award is payable. A broad reading should be taken of this wording. If, for example, a person is receiving treatment for injury or is engaged in promotional activities relating to her/his sport, then it should be found to be satisfied. It is also a requirement that no other payment is made to her/him (or is expected to be made) in respect of the sporting activities in respect of that day.

To determine if a person is in "remunerative work" three questions must be answered.
(1)   Is the person engaged in work?
(2)   Is the work done in expectation of payment?
(3)   Does the person work at least 16 hours a week on average?

"Engaged". The person must be "engaged" in remunerative work. Thus if s/he is engaged in other activities awaiting an opportunity to work, it is arguable that s/he is in a different situation from being engaged in work. In *CIS 85/1997* para 7, the commissioner distinguished between a claimant who waited in her flat above her shop until a customer called and the claimant in the case before him, who was a self-employed taxi-driver who would wait in the cab company's office for customers. The former claimant was not engaged in work, the latter was. This is not a particularly easy distinction to draw, but if the claimant pursues other activities at her/his own home while awaiting a call from a client, it is hard to see how s/he can be said to be "engaged" in work. The commissioner's decision was upheld by the Court of Appeal in *Kazantzis v Chief Adjudication Officer* [1999] *The Times* 30 June (*R(IS) 13/99*). It was not possible to draw a dividing line between the waiting time and the time spent driving when determining entitlement to IS. The same will be true of the operation of reg 6.

See the commentary to paras (2) and (4) for a discussion of the issues for seasonal workers and the commentary to para (3) for a discussion of the issues for "term-time only" workers.

"Work done in the expectation of payment". Even if the person is not receiving any payment for the work, it may be necessary to decide whether s/he is expecting payment for work, whether immediately or at some future time. There are a number of useful decisions on IS which must be seen as highly persuasive.

The work must be done in the *expectation*, not merely the hope, of payment. So there must be a realistic expectation of payment within the foreseeable future: *R(IS) 1/93* para 11. Usually, where the person in question is employed this will not present much difficulty, though two points should be noted. First, it is not necessary that the payment comes from the employer: *R(FC) 2/90* concerning receipt of religious covenants. Secondly, the payment must be received for the current work. It is not sufficient for someone to be doing voluntary work in the hope of being offered a paid job: *R(IS) 5/95* para 8.

The most difficult problems arise with self-employed people. Millett LJ gave useful guidance for such cases in *Chief Adjudication Officer v Ellis* [1995] 15 February, CA (appendix to *R(IS) 22/95*). The guidance can be summarised as follows.

(1)   The question whether the work is paid for, or done in the expectation of, payment must be judged on a week by week basis at the time the work is done.

(2)   The type of work is not important. The issue to be determined is whether the work was paid for or expected to be paid for.

(3)   If the person in question was actually paid for the work done, s/he is in remunerative work. Only when it is not paid for does the question of whether the business can be expected to be profitable come in for

consideration. However, insignificant sums received may be ignored, such as the £200 received in a year by the would-be music agent in *Smith v Chief Adjudication Officer* [1994]; reported as *R(IS) 21/95.*

(4)   Remuneration may take many forms. Just because a person's expenses in running a business are greater than her/his income from it does not prevent the income from being remuneration: *Perrot v Supplementary Benefit Commissioner* [1980] 3 All ER 110 at 114j, 116a-e, 117b, CA. However, in the case of retail and similar businesses, remuneration comes from the profit made from the store and not from the sale of the goods therein. Receipt of an Enterprise Allowance or similar payment does not amount to "payment" for the work: *Smith.*

(5)   Where the person in question is in a partnership, monies received by the partnership do not amount to remuneration until there is a distribution of profits. However, where the person is in business with her/his partner, the authority will be justified in viewing the partnership as a single economic unit.

(6)   If such a person draws on the funds of the business, this may be by way of wage, advance on profit or consumption of the capital of the business. Only if the nature of the drawings can be seen to represent the last of these can it be found that the person is not in remunerative work.

(7)   If the partners are not making drawings, they are in remunerative work if they expect to receive a share of the profits. This does not depend on the state of the annual accounts but on whether they have a realistic expectation that they will receive a share. But they must hope to be paid for the work they are currently doing, not that they will put themselves in a situation to be able to earn money from future work. Lord Bingham MR added (transcript at 16B) that the expectation of profit had to come from that financial year, when the accounts were finalised.

In *MH v HMRC (TC)* [2016] UKUT 79 (AAC), Judge Rowland considered whether a self-employed tax credits claimant was working in expectation of payment. The claimant was the managing director of a company he owned with his wife. HMRC had decided that although he had worked, because he had been resigned to the fact that the company would not make enough to pay him a salary, he had not worked in expectation of payment and thus was not in remunerative work. Judge Rowland said that for work to be "remunerative work", it must be done with the expectation that the claimant will be paid personally and that an expectation that the company for whom the work is done will be paid is not enough. However, he also decided that work can be done in expectation of payment even if a company makes no profit, or if it is known that it will not make a profit for some time but is expected to become profitable in the future.

Paragraphs (2), (3) and (4): Determination of hours worked

"regard shall be had". Paras (2) and (4) appear to offer some discretion to authorities in the way they determine the hours of work where these flucuate in that an authority need only pay "regard" to the hours (or average of hours) mentioned in those paras. The primary question is whether the person is working for at least 16 hours a week "on average": para (1). It is suggested that if the authority thinks that the provisions under paras (2) and (4) give an unfair or unrealistic result, it is open to it to adopt a different approach. Caution is therefore required in applying the extensive IS caselaw, for which reference should be made to the corresponding IS provisions in *Social Security Legislation Vol II.*

Paras (2) and (4). The first thing the authority must decide is whether the person has a recognisable cycle of work, despite the fact that the weekly hours fluctuate. If so, under para (2)(a), the average number of hours worked is obtained by dividing the total number of hours in the cycle by the number of weeks it lasts, ignoring weeks in which no work is done unless this is part of the cycle. For example, if someone works 30 hours one week, 20 the next and then has the next week off (on a regular basis), the total hours worked over the cycle would be divided by three. If the person has a four-week cycle but is off during the last week due to sickness, the hours worked in that particular cycle would be divided by three only, not four.

If the person works casually or intermittently (eg, as a seasonal worker who works in the summer but is unemployed the rest of the year), the "work cycle" is that part of the year in which s/he is working and does not include the period of unemployment. Commissioner Howell dealt with the similar provision for JSA in *R(JSA) 1/ 07* and two other appeals. The claimants worked from March to October in summer employment. During the out-of-season months they had no earnings or work at all. The decision maker said that as they had had their summer employment for more than one year in a row, they had a cycle of work of a year and as the average hours of work over this period was greater than 16 hours a week they were in "remunerative work". Commissioner Howell disagreed. He said that the recurrence of an inability to get work at all during the winter months could not turn the whole calendar year into one continuous period of the claimants being "engaged in work" so as to be able to call the whole year a "recognisable cycle of work". The real question is whether the person is "in" work at the material time. That means that there must be some sort of continuing relationship between the employee and the employer and, where a contract of employment has been terminated, a committment to resume the relationship: *CJSA 3832/2006.*

In *Saunderson v SSWP* [2012] ScotCS CSIH 10, the claimant was a self-employed golf caddy whose necessary authorisation to work as a caddy had been withdrawn because of reduced demand in the winter months. On claiming JSA, the DWP decided he was a self-employed "seasonal worker" who was in remunerative work. The Court of Session confirmed that the notion of a "recognisable cycle of work", for averaging hours of work, only comes into play once it has been decided that the person concerned is "in work". It was "not legitimate to seek to identify some 'recognisable cycle of work' as being the test for that primary criterion whether the person concerned is 'in work'." The Court also decided that no distinction should be drawn between previously employed or self-employed claimants. It said (at para 20):

> "Plainly there may be many self-employed trading or professional activities in which it is not difficult to say that the professional or trading activity continues notwithstanding an idle period. An example might be the arable farmer who, having ploughed and sowed the winter wheat in the autumn, has relatively little to do until the arrival of the spring. In some respects, one might draw an analogy with a schoolteacher whom one would readily say was in work albeit that his teaching duties are punctuated by school holidays in which he has little by way of professional activity to perform. But conversely, there will be seasonally pursued activities which, while treated in their exercise for contractual or fiscal reasons as a "self-employed" activity, are in their substance little different from employment. Typically (but not exclusively), such quasi employed activities might be those in which the individual has no significant commercial capital invested and the temporal limit on his exercise of that technically self-employed activity is dictated by seasonal factors affecting demand for the person's services. In that context, any distinction between self-employment and employment may be of little or no materiality when addressing the question whether the claimant is in work. Thus the categorisation of a claimant's limited seasonal activity as being 'self-employed' does not in itself detract from the need to reach a proper answer on the primary question whether, the seasonal activity having come to an end, the claimant may yet properly be said to be 'in work'."

Paras (2)(b) and (4), at first sight, appear to contradict each other. The best way to resolve the difficulty is probably to follow the approach taken by the commissioner in *R(IS) 8/95* Appendix paras 10 to 12. A claimant who normally worked a full week was on a period of working one week on and one week off, although he might be called in on non-working days. The commissioner holds that para (4) addresses the situation where there is insufficient evidence of recent working hours to resolve the question of the average working hours. It is forward-looking, with reference to the number of hours (or average of hours) a person is *expected* to work. Para (2) applies where such evidence exists and shows a fluctuation. If a recognisable cycle of work has been "established", then para (2)(a) applies. If not, para (2)(b) requires consideration of the average hours worked in the period of five weeks immediately before the date of claim, unless a different period (shorter or longer) provides a more accurate average. It is therefore backward-looking. The commissioner states that the point at which the calculation moves from being made under para (4) to that under para (2)(b) depends on the circumstances.

Para (3): "Term-time only" workers. Para (3) provides a particular method by which the average weekly number of hours worked is calculated where a person's recognisable cycle of work at a school, other educational establishment or any other place of employment, is one year and includes school holidays or similar vacations during which s/he does not work. In such cases, school holidays and any other periods during which s/he is not required to work must be disregarded in calculating the average weekly hours worked – ie, average weekly hours should generally be calculated by reference only to average weekly hours worked during term time.

It is not open to evade the effect of para (3) by treating the vacations as being excluded from the cycle of work on the basis that no work is being done at those times: *Chief Adjudication Officer v Stafford* [2000] 1 All ER 686 at 693g-694a, CA, upheld by a majority of three to two in *Banks v Chief Adjudication Officer* [2001] 1 WLR 1411, HL. That would mean that the "cycle" was effectively being ignored. Nevertheless, in the HB context it is suggested that the authority may adopt a different approach if it feels that the result of the calculation in para (3) is unfair. Although it is in mandatory terms, para (3) applies "for the purposes of paragraph (2)(a)" and so the authority is only required to have regard to the calculation and is not bound by it. Reference should be made to the very powerful dissenting speech of Lord Scott in the House of Lords in *Stafford* for the unfair results of reliance on the "cycle" and the differing (and fairer) result reached by a tribunal of commissioners in the context of JSA in *R(JSA) 4/03* in such cases. See also the commentary on *R(JSA) 1/07* and *Saunderson v SSWP* above.

PART 2
Provisions affecting entitlement to housing benefit

General Note on Part 2

By virtue of s130 SSCBA 1992, a person is entitled to HB in respect of certain payments that s/he is liable to make in relation to the dwelling s/he occupies as her/his home. Reg 7 deals with the meaning of the phrase "occupies as his home". Regs 8 and 9 respectively deal with the situations in which a person is or is not to be treated as "liable" for payments on that home. Reg 10 provides that certain "persons from abroad" are to be treated as not being liable for payments. See also reg 56 for full-time students who are treated as not being liable for payments.

Circumstances in which a person is or is not to be treated as occupying a dwelling as his home

7.–(1) Subject to the following provisions of this regulation, a person shall be treated as occupying as his home the dwelling normally occupied as his home–

(a) by himself or, if he is a member of a family, by himself and his family; or

(b)   if he is polygamously married, by himself, his partners and any child or young person for whom he or any partner of his is responsible and who is a member of that same household,

and shall not be treated as occupying any other dwelling as his home.

(2)   In determining whether a dwelling is the dwelling normally occupied as a person's home for the purpose of paragraph (1) regard shall be had to any other dwelling occupied by that person or any other person referred to in paragraph (1) whether or not that dwelling is in Great Britain.

(3)   Where a single claimant or a lone parent is a student, other than one to whom regulation 56(1) applies (circumstances in which certain students are treated as not liable to make payments in respect of a dwelling), or is on a training course and is liable to make payments (including payments of mortgage interest or, in Scotland, payments under heritable securities or, in either case, analogous payments) in respect of either (but not both) the dwelling which he occupies for the purpose of attending his course of study or, his training course, or as the case may be, the dwelling which he occupies when not attending his course, he shall be treated as occupying as his home the dwelling in respect of which he is liable to make such payments.

(4)   Where a claimant has been required to move into temporary accommodation by reason of essential repairs being carried out to the dwelling normally occupied as his home, and is liable to make payments (including payments of mortgage interest or, in Scotland, payments under heritable securities or, in either case, analogous payments) in respect of either (but not both) the dwelling which he normally occupied as his home or the temporary accommodation, he shall be treated as occupying as his home the dwelling in respect of which he is liable to make payments.

(5)   Where a person is required to reside in a dwelling which is a bail hostel or probation hostel approved by the Secretary of State under [⁵ section 13 of the Offender Management Act 2007], he shall not be treated as occupying that dwelling as his home.

(6)   Where a person is liable to make payments in respect of two (but not more than two) dwellings, he shall be treated as occupying both dwellings as his home only–

(a)   for a period not exceeding 52 weeks in the case where he has left and remains absent from the former dwelling occupied as his home through fear of violence in that dwelling or by a former member of his family and–

    (i)   it is reasonable that [⁸ payments should be made (whether by way of housing benefit or universal credit)] in respect of both his former dwelling and his present dwelling occupied as the home; and

    (ii)   he intends to return to occupy the former dwelling as his home; or

(b)   in the case of a couple or a member of a polygamous marriage, where he or one partner is a student, other than one to whom regulation 56(1) applies (circumstances in which certain students are treated as not liable to make payments in respect of a dwelling), or is on a training course and it is unavoidable that the partners should occupy two separate dwellings and reasonable that housing benefit should be paid in respect of both dwellings; or

(c)   in the case where, because of the number of persons referred to in paragraph (1), they have been housed by a housing authority in two separate dwellings; or

(d)   in the case where a person has moved into a new dwelling occupied as the home, except where paragraph (4) applies, for a period not exceeding 4 benefit weeks [¹ from the date on which he moved] if he could not reasonably have avoided liability in respect of two dwellings; or

(e)   in the case where a person–

    (i)   is treated by virtue of paragraph (8) as occupying a dwelling as his home ("the new dwelling") and sub-paragraph (c)(i) of that paragraph applies; and

    (ii)   he has occupied another dwelling as his home on any day within the period of 4 weeks immediately preceding the date he moved to the new dwelling,

for a period not exceeding 4 benefit weeks immediately preceding the date on which he moved.

(7)   Where–
(a)   a person has moved into a dwelling for which he is not liable to make payments ("the new dwelling"); and
(b)   immediately before that move, he was liable to make payments for the dwelling he previously occupied as his home ("the former dwelling"); and
(c)   that liability continues after he has moved into the new dwelling,
he shall be treated as occupying the former dwelling as his home for a period not exceeding 4 benefit weeks if he could not reasonably have avoided liability in respect of that former dwelling.
(8)   [² Where]–
(a)   [² a person] has moved into a dwelling and was liable to make payments in respect of that dwelling before moving in; and
[² (b)   either–
    (i)   that person had claimed housing benefit before moving in and either no decision has yet been made on that claim or it has been refused but a further claim has been made or treated as made within 4 weeks of the date on which the claimant moved into the new dwelling occupied as the home; or
    (ii)   that person notified the move to the new dwelling as a change of circumstances under regulation 88 (duty to notify changes of circumstances) before the move, or the move to the new dwelling was otherwise notified before the move under that regulation; and]
(c)   the delay in moving into the dwelling in respect of which there was liability to make payments before moving in was reasonable and–
    (i)   that delay was necessary in order to adapt the dwelling to meet the disablement needs of that person or any member of his family; or
    (ii)   the move was delayed pending [⁷ local welfare provision or] the outcome of an application under [³ Part 8] of the Act for a social fund payment to meet a need arising out of the move or in connection with setting up the home in the dwelling and either a member of the claimant's family is aged 5 or under or the claimant's applicable amount includes a premium under paragraph [³] 12, 14 or 16 of Schedule 3 [⁴ or a component under paragraph [¹⁰] 24 of that Schedule [¹⁰ or the claimant or the claimant's partner is a member of the work-related activity group]]; or
    (iii)   the claimant became liable to make payments in respect of the dwelling while he was a patient or in residential accommodation,
[² the person shall be treated] as occupying the dwelling as his home for any period not exceeding 4 weeks immediately prior to the date on which he moved into the dwelling and in respect of which he was liable to make payments.
(9)   Where a person is treated by virtue of paragraph (8) as occupying a dwelling as his home in respect of the period before moving in, his claim for housing benefit in respect of that dwelling shall be treated as having been made on either–
(a)   in the case of a claim in respect of which a decision has not yet been made the date that claim was or was treated as made in accordance with regulation 83 (time and manner in which claims are to be made); or
(b)   in the case of a claim for housing benefit in respect of that dwelling which has been refused and a further claim was or was treated as made in accordance with Part 10 (claims) within 4 weeks of the date on which he moved into the dwelling, the date on which the claim was refused or was treated as made; or
(c)   the date from which he is treated by virtue of paragraph (8) as occupying the dwelling as his home,
whichever of those dates is the later.
(10)   Where a person to whom neither paragraph (6)(a) nor (16)(c)(x) applies–
(a)   formerly occupied a dwelling but has left and remains absent from it through fear of violence–
    (i)   in the dwelling; or

(ii)　by a person who was formerly a member of the family of the person first mentioned; and

(b)　has a liability to make payments in respect of that dwelling which is unavoidable, he shall be treated as occupying the dwelling as his home for a period not exceeding 4 benefit weeks.

(11)　This paragraph shall apply to a person who enters residential accommodation [⁹ in Great Britain]–

(a)　for the purpose of ascertaining whether the accommodation suits his needs; and

(b)　with the intention of returning to the dwelling which is normally occupied by him as his home should, in the event, the residential accommodation prove not to suit his needs; and

(c)　while the part of the dwelling which is normally occupied by him as his home is not let, or as the case may be, sublet.

(12)　A person to whom paragraph (11) applies shall be treated as if he is occupying the dwelling he normally occupies as his home for a period not exceeding, subject to an overall limit of 52 weeks on the absence from that home, 13 weeks beginning from the first day he enters [⁹ the residential accommodation].

[⁹ (13)　Subject to paragraphs (13B) and (17), where a person is temporarily absent within Great Britain from his main dwelling, he shall be treated as occupying that dwelling as his home whilst he is so absent, subject to an overall limit of a period of 13 weeks beginning with the first day of the absence from the main dwelling, provided that–

(a)　the person intends to return to occupy the main dwelling as his home;

(b)　the part of the main dwelling normally occupied by the person has not been let or, as the case may be, sub-let; and

(c)　the period of the absence within Great Britain is unlikely to extend beyond the overall limit.]

[⁹ (13A)　The period of 13 weeks referred to in paragraph (13) shall run or continue to run during any period of absence from Great Britain.

(13B)　Where–

(a)　a person returns to Great Britain after a period of absence from Great Britain;

(b)　he has been absent from the main dwelling for less than 13 weeks beginning with the first day of absence from that dwelling; and

(c)　at the outset of, or during, the period of absence from Great Britain, he ceased to be treated as occupying the main dwelling as his home,

then, for any day that follows the period of absence from Great Britain and precedes his return to the main dwelling, he shall not be treated as occupying the main dwelling as his home under paragraph (13).

(13C)　This paragraph applies to a person who is temporarily absent from Great Britain and who occupied the main dwelling as his home, or was treated as occupying that dwelling as his home, immediately before the period of absence from Great Britain.

(13D)　Subject to paragraphs (13E), (13G), (17C) and (17D) a person to whom paragraph (13C) applies shall be treated as occupying the main dwelling as his home whilst he is absent from Great Britain, for a period not exceeding 4 weeks beginning with the first day of that absence from Great Britain, provided that–

(a)　the person intends to return to occupy the main dwelling as his home;

(b)　the part of the main dwelling normally occupied by the person has not been let or, as the case may be, sub-let; and

(c)　the period of absence outside Great Britain is unlikely to exceed 4 weeks.

(13E)　If the temporary absence from the main dwelling is in connection with the death of–

(a)　the person's partner or a child or young person for whom the person or the person's partner is responsible;

(b)　the person's close relative;

(c)　the close relative of the person's partner; or

(d)　the close relative of a child or young person for whom the person or the person's partner is responsible, then the period of 4 weeks in the opening words of paragraph (13D) may be extended by up to 4 further weeks if the relevant authority considers it unreasonable to expect the person to return to Great Britain within the first 4 weeks (and so that the reference in sub-paragraph (c) of that paragraph to a period of 4 weeks shall, where the period is extended, be taken as referring to the period as so extended).

(13F)   This paragraph applies to a person who is temporarily absent from Great Britain as a member of Her Majesty's forces posted overseas, a mariner or a continental shelf worker, and who occupied the main dwelling as his home, or was treated as occupying that dwelling as his home, immediately before the period of absence from Great Britain.

(13G)   A person to whom paragraph (13F) applies shall be treated as occupying the main dwelling as his home whilst he is absent from Great Britain, for a period not exceeding 26 weeks beginning with the first day of that absence from Great Britain, provided that–

(a)   the person intends to return to occupy the main dwelling as his home;

(b)   the part of the main dwelling normally occupied by the person has not been let or, as the case may be, sub-let; and

(c)   the period of absence outside Great Britain is unlikely to exceed 26 weeks.]

(14)   This paragraph applies to a person who is–

(a)   detained in custody pending sentence upon conviction or under a sentence imposed by a court, other than a person who is detained in hospital under the provisions of the Mental Health Act 1983, or, in Scotland, under the provisions of the Mental Health (Care and Treatment) (Scotland) Act 2003 or the Criminal Procedure (Scotland) Act 1995; and

(b)   on temporary release from such detention in accordance with Rules made under the provisions of the Prison Act 1952 or the Prisons (Scotland) Act 1989.

(15)   Where paragraph (14) applies to a person, then, for any day when he is on temporary release–

(a)   if such temporary release was immediately preceded by a period of temporary absence under paragraph (13) or (16), he shall be treated as if he continues to be absent from the dwelling, despite any occupation of the dwelling;

(b)   for the purposes of paragraph (16)(c)(i), he shall be treated as if he remains in detention; and

(c)   if he does not fall within sub-paragraph (a), he shall be treated as if he does not occupy his dwelling as his home despite any such occupation of the dwelling.

(16)   This paragraph shall apply to a person who is temporarily absent from the [⁹ main dwelling], if–

(a)   he intends to return to occupy the [⁹ main dwelling] as his home; and

(b)   while the part of the [⁹ main dwelling] which is normally occupied by him has not been let, or as the case may be, sublet; and

(c)   he is–

[⁷ (i)   a person to whom paragraph (16A) applies;]

(ii)   resident in a hospital or similar institution as a patient; or

(iii)   undergoing, or as the case may be, his partner or his dependant child is undergoing [⁹] medical treatment, or medically approved convalescence, in accommodation other than residential accommodation; or

(iv)   following [⁹] a training course; or

(v)   undertaking medically approved care of a person [⁹]; or

(vi)   undertaking the care of a child whose parent or guardian is temporarily absent from the dwelling normally occupied by that parent or guardian for the purpose of receiving medically approved care or medical treatment; or

(vii)   a person who is [⁹] receiving medically approved care provided in accommodation other than residential accommodation; or

(viii) a student to whom paragraph (3) or (6)(b) does not apply;

(ix)   a person who is receiving care provided in residential accommodation other than a person to whom paragraph (11) applies; or

(x)   a person who has left the dwelling he occupies as his home through fear of violence, in that dwelling, or by a person who was formerly a member of the family of the person first mentioned, and to whom paragraph (6)(a) does not apply; and

[⁹ (d) in the case of–

(i)   absence within Great Britain, any period of absence from the dwelling is unlikely to extend beyond or, in exceptional circumstances is unlikely substantially to extend beyond, an overall limit of 52 weeks beginning with the first day of the absence from the dwelling;

(ii)   absence from Great Britain by a person to whom any of sub-paragraphs (c)(ii), (iii), (vii) or (x) apply, any period of absence from Great Britain is unlikely to exceed or, in exceptional circumstances is unlikely substantially to exceed, 26 weeks beginning with the first day of the absence from Great Britain; or

(iii)   absence from Great Britain by a person to whom paragraph (ii) of this sub-paragraph does not apply, any period of absence from Great Britain is unlikely to exceed or, in exceptional circumstances is unlikely substantially to exceed, 4 weeks beginning with the first day of absence from Great Britain.]

[⁷ (16A)   This paragraph applies to a person ("P") who is–

(a)   detained in custody on remand pending trial;

(b)   detained pending sentence upon conviction; or

(c)   as a condition of bail required to reside–

(i)   in a dwelling, other than a dwelling P occupies as P's home; or

(ii)   in premises approved under section 13 of the Offender Management Act 2007,

and who is not also detained in custody following sentence upon conviction.]

[⁹ (17)   Subject to paragraph (17B), a person to whom paragraph (16) applies who is absent within Great Britain, shall be treated as occupying the main dwelling as his home whilst he is so absent, subject to an overall limit of a period of 52 weeks beginning with the first day of the absence from the dwelling.]

[⁹ (17A)   The period of 52 weeks referred to in paragraph (17) shall run or continue to run during any period of absence from Great Britain.

(17B)   Where–

(a)   a person returns to Great Britain after a period of absence from Great Britain;

(b)   he has been absent from the main dwelling for less than 52 weeks beginning with the first day of absence from that dwelling; and

(c)   at the outset of, or during, the period of absence from Great Britain, he ceased to be treated as occupying the main dwelling as his home,

then, for any day that follows the period of absence from Great Britain and precedes his return to the main dwelling, he shall not be treated as occupying the main dwelling as his home under paragraph (17).

(17C)   A person to whom paragraph (16) applies who–

(a)   is a person described in any of sub-paragraphs (c)(ii), (iii), (vii) or (x) of that paragraph;

(b)   is temporarily absent from Great Britain; and

(c)   immediately before that period of temporary absence, occupied the main dwelling as his home or was treated as so occupying that dwelling,

shall be treated as occupying that dwelling as his home whilst he is absent from Great Britain, for a period not exceeding 26 weeks beginning with the first day of the absence from Great Britain.

(17D)   A person to whom paragraph (16) applies who–

(a)   is a person described in any of sub-paragraphs (c)(i), (iv), (v), (vi), (viii) or (ix) of that paragraph;

(b)   is temporarily absent from Great Britain; and

(c)   immediately before that period of temporary absence, occupied the main dwelling as his home or was treated as so occupying that dwelling, shall be treated as occupying that dwelling as his home whilst he is absent from Great Britain, for a period not exceeding 4 weeks beginning with the first day of the absence from Great Britain.]

(18) In this regulation–

[⁹ "continental shelf worker" means a person who is employed, whether under a contract of service or not, in a designated area or a prescribed area in connection with any activity mentioned in section 11(2) of the Petroleum Act 1998;

"designated area" means any area which may from time to time be designated by Order in Council under the Continental Shelf Act 1964 as an area within which the rights of the United Kingdom with respect to the seabed and subsoil and their natural resources may be exercised;

"main dwelling" means the dwelling that a person normally occupies as his home;

"mariner" means a person who is employed under a contract of service either as a master or member of the crew of any ship or vessel, or in any other capacity on board any ship or vessel, where–

(a) the employment in that capacity is for the purposes of that ship or vessel or its crew or any passengers or cargo or mails carried by the ship or vessel; and

(b) the contract is entered into in the United Kingdom with a view to its performance (in whole or in part) while the ship or vessel is on its voyage;]

"medically approved" means certified by a medical practitioner;

[⁹ "member of Her Majesty's forces posted overseas" means a person who is a member of the regular forces or the reserve forces (within the meaning of section 374 of the Armed Forces Act 2006), who is absent from the main dwelling because the person has been posted outside of Great Britain to perform the duties of a member of Her Majesty's regular forces or reserve forces;]

"patient" means a person who is undergoing medical or other treatment as an in-patient in any hospital or similar institution;

[⁹ "prescribed area" means any area over which Norway or any member State (other than the United Kingdom) exercises sovereign rights for the purpose of exploring the seabed and subsoil and exploiting their natural resources, being an area outside the territorial seas of Norway or such member State, or any other area which is from time to time specified under section 10(8) of the Petroleum Act 1998;]

"residential accommodation" means accommodation which is provided in–

(a) a care home;

(b) an independent hospital;

(c) an Abbeyfield Home; or

(d) an establishment managed or provided by a body incorporated by Royal Charter or constituted by Act of Parliament other than a local social services authority;

"training course" means a course of training or instruction provided wholly or partly by or on behalf of or in pursuance of arrangements made with, or approved by or on behalf of, [⁶ Skills Development Scotland,] Scottish Enterprise, Highlands and Islands Enterprise, a government department or the Secretary of State.

Amendments

1. Amended by reg 5 of SI 2006 No 3274 as from 8.1.07.
2. Amended by reg 11(3) of SI 2007 No 2618 as from 1.10.07.
3. Amended by reg 3(3) of SI 2008 No 1042 as from 19.5.08.
4. Amended by reg 7A of SI 2008 No 1082, as inserted by reg 28 of SI 2008 No 2428, as from 27.10.08.
5. Amended by reg 6(3) of SI 2008 No 2767 as from 17.11.08.
6. Amended by reg 6(3)(b) of SI 2009 No 583 as from 6.4.09.
7. Amended by reg 7(3) of SI 2013 No 443 as from 2.4.13.
8. Amended by reg 7(4) of SI 2013 No 2070 as from 28.10.13.
9. Amended by reg 2(2) of SI 2016 No 624 as from 28.7.16, subject to transitional provision in reg 5 of SI 2016 No 624.
10. Amended by reg 5(3) of SI 2017 No 581 as from 23.6.17, subject to transitional and savings provision in reg 9.

Definitions

"benefit week" – see reg 2(1).
"child" – see s137 SSCBA and reg 2(1).
"claim" – see reg 2(1).
"claimant" – see reg 2(1).
"close relative" – see reg 2(1).
"course of study" – see reg 53.
"dwelling" – see s137 SSCBA and reg 2(4).
"family" – see s137 SSCBA.
"housing authority" – see s191 SSAA.
"liable to make payments" – see regs 2(2) and 8.
"local welfare provision" – see reg 2(1).
"lone parent" – see reg 2(1).
"member of the work-related activity group" – see reg 2(1).
"partner" – see reg 2(1).
"polygamous marriage" – see reg 2(1).
"single claimant" – see reg 2(1).
"student" – see regs 2(1) and 53.
"young person" – see reg 2(1).

General Note

To be entitled to HB, a claimant must be liable to make payments in respect of a dwelling which s/he occupies as her/his home: s130 SSCBA (see p16). Paras (1) and (2) set out the general rule that a claimant is only usually treated as occupying one dwelling as a home, namely that normally occupied by her/him (and her/his family if s/he is a member of one). The remainder of the regulation provides for various exceptions to this rule.

(1)   Paras (3) and (4) provide situations where if a claimant has two homes but only pays for one of them, s/he will be treated as occupying the one that is paid for. Broadly, para (3) applies to students and people on training courses who occupy one home during their courses and one during vacations, and para (4) applies to claimants who have had to move into temporary accommodation due to essential repairs.

(2)   Residence in an approved bail or probation hostel is to be ignored in considering where a person's normal home is: para (5).

(3)   Para (6) sets out a number of cases in which a claimant can be treated as occupying two homes and therefore receive HB for both.

(4)   Paras (7) to (10) deal with situations where a claimant can be treated as occupying a property which s/he has moved from or is about to move (or has moved) into.

(5)   Paras (11) to (17D) deal with when someone can be treated as occupying a dwelling during a temporary absence within or outside Great Britain. Note that prior to 28 July 2016, under the rules on temporary absence from home, it did not in general matter if a person was absent from Great Britain. For details of the rules prior to that date, and commentary, see pp248–60 of the 28th edition of this book. For details of the transitional provisions, see the Analysis below.

Two provisions deal with claimants who are "students" who are not excluded from eligibility to HB under reg 56(1), or who are on "training courses": paras (3) and (6)(b). See also reg 55 that deals with accommodation occupied by a full-time student to enable her/him to attend the course and absence outside the period of study.

The application of reg 7 is not restricted to the question of whether or not the claimant is entitled to HB. As the headnote suggests, the regulation determines the issue of whether or not a person is occupying the home. Thus where a claimant's children spent most of their time with their mother and she received child benefit in respect of them, each child was resident in the property where her/his "family" (as defined in s137 SSCBA) lived and so could not be treated as occupying the father's home for the purposes of the rent officer's assessment: *R v Swale BC HBRB ex p Marchant* [1999] 1 FLR 1087, QBD; [2000] 1 FLR 246, CA. See also reg 21(3) on p410 under which, from 1 November 2010, specified children and young people placed with the claimant under child protection legislation are not to be treated as occupying the claimant's dwelling.

Reg 7 is also relevant in determining whether someone is an occupier of a dwelling with the claimant for the purposes of determining the number of bedrooms allowed under the size criteria within the rent restriction schemes (for which see Part 3 of the HB Regs), and for determining if there has been a change in the number of occupiers for the purposes of a reference to the rent officer under reg 14(1)(c): *Stroud DC v JG* [2009] UKUT 67 (AAC); R(H) 8/09; *SK v South Hams DC (HB)* [2010] UKUT 129 (AAC); [2010] AACR 40.

In *R(H) 8/09*, the claimant's son was a student who lived away from home during term time. Judge Williams concluded that he was to be treated as occupying the claimant's dwelling as his home under reg 7(16)(c)(viii) and (17) (student who is temporarily absent from home). As such, there was not a change in the number of occupiers in the claimant's home and a reference under reg 14 therefore could not be made. Note that where it is determined that someone occupies a dwelling with the claimant, it will also be necessary to determine whether a non-dependant deduction is to be made under reg 74.

Analysis

Paragraphs (1) and (2): The general rule

The home in question is that "normally occupied" by the people listed in paras (1)(a) or (b), as appropriate. There is no definition of "normally occupied". In *CH 1085/2002* para 13, the commissioner pointed out that "normally occupied" was a lower standard to "permanently occupied". He also suggested that the views of officers administering JSA or the social fund were relevant: para 14. It is suggested that this could only be the case if the issue has been specifically considered by such officers, and tribunals must not, of course, treat their views as binding.

Note that specified children and young people living with the claimant (eg, foster children) are not to be treated as occupying the claimant's dwelling: reg 21(3). However, if the claimant or her/his partner is a "qualifying parent or carer" for the purposes of the size criteria within the rent restriction schemes (in Part 3 of the HB Regs and the Rent Officer Orders), an additional bedroom may be allowed even if specified children and young people are excluded by reg 21(3) from being treated as occupying the claimant's dwelling: regs B13(6)(b) and 13D(3A)(b) HB Regs and Sch 2 para 1A(b) of both the Rent Officer Orders. A further additional bedroom can be allowed if a child or young person in respect of whom the claimant or partner is a qualifying parent or carer is a "person who requries overnight care" (defined in reg 2(1)). In the case of the social sector scheme (for which see reg B13), an additional bedroom can also be allowed for a child or young person who requires overnight care in respect of whom other people occupying the claimant's dwelling are qualifying parents or carers.

In *MM v SSWP (IS)* [2012] UKUT 358 (AAC), Judge Wikeley pointed out that a tribunal acts at its peril if it defines the relevant legal test in terms of "living at" or "permanently residing at" a property; the proper test is whether or not the claimant "normally occupies" a property as her/his home.

In *R(H) 9/05*, the commissioner said that occupation does not require the personal presence of the tenant if the property is under her/his control and is being used by her/him to store her/his belongings and for no other purpose. The claimant took out a tenancy of a new flat from February 2004 but she could not move in immediately as the property needed to be adapted to met her needs as a disabled person. On 15 March 2004, the disabled adaptations had been completed and so she terminated her former tenancy and her family moved all her furniture and possessions into the new flat. However, the claimant herself was unable to move in on this date – and did not in fact move in until 9 August 2004 – because she became ill and had to be admitted to hospital. On these facts, the deputy commissioner decided that the claimant had normally occupied the flat as her home within reg 5(1) HB Regs 1987 (now reg 7(1) HB Regs) from the date her furniture and possessions had been moved into it, notwithstanding that the claimant herself had not begun living in the flat until five months later. The use of the word "normally" did not speak to the length of time present in the property but was rather in place to help resolve cases where the claimant might be regarded as living in more than one property. Moreover, the claimant could be said to have "moved in" to the flat on 15 March, and so could be treated as occupying it for the four weeks beforehand: reg 7(8)(c)(i) HB Regs. Further, the claimant's temporary absence from the property (to August 2004) did not affect these conclusions because it is possible for the claimant to intend to return to occupy the flat as her home even though she had never physically lived there.

The decision in *R(H) 9/05*, although no doubt welcome on the facts, places a strained interpretation on the word "return" as used in sub-paras (13) to (17D) of reg 7. *CH 2521/2002* rules that the comparable sub-paras in reg 5(1) HB Regs 1987 (now reg 7(1) HB Regs) could be used as an aid to construe the test. However, given that *R(H) 9/05* is a reported decision it must be preferred over any conflicting unreported decisions (such as, at least implicitly, *CH 2201/2002* and *CH 2521/2002*).

Some factors which are relevant to the question of which home is "normally occupied" if more than one property is involved are the following:

(1)   The amount of time that the person spends at the property, compared with other properties with which a comparison is being made under para (2): *R v Penwith DC ex p Burt* (1990) 22 HLR 292 at 296, QBD.

(2)   The reason for any absence from the property, though note the possible application of paras (10) to (16A).

(3)   Where the person's personal belongings are kept and if the premises are under her/his control: see *R(H) 9/05* above.

(4)   The reason why the person is not living in the premises full-time and whether s/he intends to live there permanently: *CH 567/2011*.

(4)   Where the person is registered to vote, registers with GPs and dentists, is liable for council tax and utilities bills, etc.

(5)   Whether the person has any local ties such as memberships of clubs and associations.

Previous versions of this book have suggested another relevant factor as being where the claimant regards the centre of her/his existence and where s/he intends it should be in the future. However, *CH 1786/2005* (rightly) points out that a "centre of interests" test is not a substitute for making an overall assessment of the circumstances and evidence in each case in deciding which home is "normally occupied" by the claimant (per *CH 2521/2002*); and warns against chopping up what is essentially a single factual issue into series of individual tests for particular factors.

The "dwelling" which the claimant occupies as a home may comprise more than one property or more than one room in a property: *Hackney LB v GA* [2008] UKUT 26 (AAC); R(H) 5/09; *Birmingham City Council v IB* [2009] UKUT 116 (AAC). See p16 for a discussion.

Under para (2), the authority must pay regard to any other "dwelling" occupied by the claimant or by any of the other people listed in para (1) in order to decide which is the "normal" home. This includes dwellings outside Great Britain, but GM A3.356 warns authorities that this provision is not intended to exclude from entitlement someone who has set up home in this country but whose family is no longer part of her/his household and remains abroad. The GM says that the purpose of taking account of homes outside Great Britain is to avoid simultaneous payment of HB under both the Northern Irish and British schemes.

Evidence of a claimant having made a claim for HB and JSA in the area of another authority will be adequate evidence that a claimant is residing elsewhere, at least in the absence of contradictory evidence: *CH 2201/2002* para 10.

In *CH 2521/2002* para 10, Commissioner Fellner cautioned against over-heavy reliance on *Herbert v Byrne* [1964] 1 WLR 519 at 527, 528, 529, CA, noting that it was a case under a different statutory provision. She went on to question (paras 11–12) whether a person may have two dwellings and still qualify for benefit on their usual residence under reg 5(1) HB regs 1987 (now reg 7(1) HB Regs). It is suggested that it is plain from para (2) that this is possible.

Paragraph (3): Absence due to study or training
This provides for the situation in which an eligible student (ie, one who is *not* treated as not liable to pay rent under reg 56(1)) or a person on a training course (defined in para (18)) who is a single claimant (ie, someone without a partner – see the definition of "single claimant" in reg 2(1)) or a lone parent, occupies two dwellings, one to enable her/him to attend the course, and one which s/he uses at other times, but is only *liable* for payments in respect of one of them. Note also that the payments in question can be mortgage and similar payments as well as payments of the nature that could attract HB. So if a claimant pays rent for two homes, or rent for one and mortgage payments for the other, s/he does not come within the scope of this provision.

When the paragraph applies, the claimant is treated for HB purposes, as occupying the dwelling for which s/he is liable to pay. This is of benefit, for example, to a student who pays for term-time accommodation but stays at her/his parents' home, at no cost to her/himself, during the vacations (but see Part 7 of these Regulations and in particular reg 55). Note para (6)(b) for couples who are liable to make payments for two homes, where one member of the couple is an eligible student and paras (16)(c)(viii) and (17D) for students to whom neither para (3) nor para (6)(b) applies.

Paragraph (4): Absence due to essential repairs
This ensures that a claimant required to leave the home s/he normally occupies due to essential repair work can qualify for HB provided that s/he is liable to make such payments as are referred to in respect of either the normal home or the temporary accommodation. If s/he is liable to make relevant payments on *both*, the payments are not covered by this paragraph, but see para (6). As with para (3), the payments in question can be mortgage and similar payments as well as payments of the nature that could attract HB. So if a claimant pays rent for both the normal and the temporary home, or rent for one and mortgage payments for the other, s/he does not come within the scope of this provision.

There is no guidance on the meaning of "essential", but when this term was used in relation to the old supplementary benefit scheme in respect of grants for redecoration, a commissioner interpreted the term as covering work which was "necessary" rather than a luxury, but not necessarily "indispensable if life was to be maintained": *R(SB) 10/81*.

Commissioner Williams approved the relevance of the test propounded in *R(SB) 10/81* in *CH 393/2002*. He also held that it was not necessary for all the repairs to be completed in order for the deeming provision in para (4) to cease to have effect, as long as the essential repairs had been completed and the property was habitable: paras 15–16. However, consideration of the claimant's illness would be relevant in determining whether the property was habitable.

Paragraph (5): Approved bail and probation hostels
This provision effectively requires a local authority to ignore enforced residence in an approved bail or probation hostel when deciding where someone's "normal home" is. Residence in the hostel must be "required" which will normally mean that it will be a condition of the person's bail or licence on release from prison. In England and Wales, documentary evidence of this may be obtained from the relevant magistrates' or Crown Court. See paras (16)(c)(i), (16A)(c)(ii) and (17D) for the provision that allows HB to be paid in respect of the home the claimant normally occupies during a temporary absence in approved premises.

Paragraph (6): HB on two homes
Para (6) allows the claimant to be treated as occupying two dwellings as her/his home, and hence to qualify for HB in respect of both of them in the circumstances there set out (or if a UC claimant has left her/his former home through fear of violence in specified circumstances, HB in respect of one home and UC in respect of the other). Note that para (6) is only relevant if the claimant is occupying two or more dwellings. If the claimant occupies a single "dwelling" it is not relevant even if the dwelling is comprised of more than one property: *Hackney LB v GA* [2008] UKUT 26 (AAC); R(H) 5/09; *Birmingham City Council v IB* [2009] UKUT 116 (AAC). See p16 for a

discussion. Note also that in order to qualify for HB for a home, it must be in Great Britain (ie, England, Scotland or Wales): s130(1)(a) SSCBA 1992.

Fear of violence: sub-para (a). Sub-para (a) enables people forced to leave home through fear of actual or threatened violence to receive benefit in respect of both the former and the new home where it is considered reasonable that payments (of either HB or UC) should be made for both. The claimant is treated as occupying both homes for up to 52 weeks in such circumstances. A claimant can thus be paid HB for both homes. A person is generally precluded from entitlement to HB if entitled to UC: the Universal Credit (Transitional Provisions) Regulations 2014 SI No.1230 – the UC(TP) Regs 2014 (see p1857). However, if the new home comes within the definition (in reg 2 of those regulations) of "specified accommodation" (specified types of supported accommodation and of temporary accommodation for those who have left home as a result of domestic violence) or "temporary accommodation" (specified types of homeless accommodation), a claimant can be paid HB for the new home while entitled to UC, but not for the former home (unless it also comes within either definition). However, s/he may continue to qualify for UC for the former home. Also see the commentary on paras (10) and (16)(c)(x).

No violence need yet have occurred – the mere fear of violence is sufficient. GM A3.411 states that this fear of violence must be reasonably held and suggests that corroborative evidence may be obtained from the police or a supportive organisation to whom reports of violence may have been made. It is suggested that provided there is an honest fear of violence which has some basis, this would suffice. Furthermore, authorities should not fall into the trap of rejecting a claimant's assertions of fear of violence if no report is made to the police. Many victims of domestic violence find it very difficult to seek official help.

The fear of violence can come from either of two sources.

(1) Fear of violence in the dwelling formerly occupied as a home. A "dwelling" can include some land – eg, that used for the purpose of occupying a dwelling or land on which a caravan or mobile home stands: s137 SSCBA and reg 2(4). So fear of violence in, for example, the garden of the former home should suffice. Fear of attacks in the street will not suffice. However, it is suggested that abuse in the street towards a claimant living in her/his home which gives rise to a fear of being attacked in the home should be enough to qualify. Note that a fear of violence in the former home need not come from a former member of the claimant's family; attacks on the home by neighbours, racial violence or hate crimes can come within this heading.

(2) Fear of violence by a former member of the claimant's family. For the meaning of family, see p17. This does not have to be a fear of violence in the former home.

Students and training courses: sub-para (b). Sub-para (b) deals with claims from people who are members of a couple or a polygamous relationship where one of the partners is a student who is not excluded from HB by reg 56(1) (see p487) or is on a training course (defined in para (18)). In this situation, HB can be paid in respect of both the term-time residence and the dwelling in which the other partner(s) live indefinitely, but the need for two homes must be "unavoidable" and payment of HB in respect of both homes must be reasonable in the circumstances of the particular claim. See also reg 55. Note that although a person entitled to UC may qualify for HB in respect of "specified accommodation" or "temporary accommodation" (both defined in reg 2 of the UC(TP) Regs 2014), and that a student entitled to UC is not excluded from HB by reg 56(1) unless the UC includes an amount in respect of the accommodation s/he occupies as a home, it appears that sub-para (b) cannot apply to a couple entitled to UC if only one of the homes is "specified accommodation" or "temporary accommodation".

See para (3) for single claimants or lone parents who occupy two dwellings and paras 16(c)(viii) and (17D) for students to whom neither para (3) nor para (6)(b) applies.

The decision of the Court of Appeal in *R (Naghshbandi) v Camden LBC* [2001] EWHC Admin 813; (2003) HLR 280, CA may produce a potential anomaly in the operation of sub-para (b). See the commentary to regs 12B(4) and 54 for a discussion of the decision. Since, following *Naghshbandi*, reg 56(1) only applies in relation to a student who is a claimant, it arguably cannot apply in any case where the claimant is the student's partner. Thus if the claimant becomes liable for the rent on the student partner's accommodation, provided that the other conditions in sub-para (b) are met it may be possible for the claimant to claim HB on both properties even though if the student made a claim her/himself in respect of the student accommodation, it would be rejected because s/he does not fall into any of the categories in reg 56(2).

Large families: sub-para (c). Sub-para (c) caters for very large families. The dwellings need not be adjacent: GM A3.660. However, the housing must be provided by the local authority. But note the reference to *Hackney LB v GA* [2008] UKUT 26 (AAC); R(H) 5/09 above where the dwelling a claimant occupies as a home may comprise of more than one property.

Moving home: sub-para (d). Sub-para (d) makes provision for HB claimants who move home and who could not reasonably avoid liability for payments in respect of both the old and the new home – eg, where a claimant had to move quickly to take advantage of better accommodation and so had to leave a former home without being able to give notice to her/his landlord. HB can be paid in respect of both dwellings for up to four weeks from the date on which the claimant moved. See para (7) where there is no liability in respect of the new home and paras (8) and (9) where there is a delay in moving.

CH 1911/2006 emphasises that the "person" to which reg 5(5)(d) HB Regs 1987 (now reg 7(6)(d)) refers must be the HB claimant. Accordingly, sub-para (d) cannot cover a situation where the partner of the claimant moves into the new dwelling to get it ready for the rest of the family to move in.

Note that although a person entitled to UC cannot normally qualify for HB, s/he may qualify for HB in respect of "specified accommodation" or "temporary accommodation" (both defined in reg 2 UC(TP) Regs 2014). S/he can be treated as occupying two homes under sub-para (d), but can only qualify for HB for a home if it comes within either definition. It would appear that the claimant cannot qualify for a UC housing costs element for a former home in this situation.

In previous editions it has been suggested that before a claimant can get HB on both the old and new homes, s/he must have actually moved – ie, HB can be paid to cover payments on the old home after a move but not on a new home before the claimant moves in. This approach was adopted in *CH 2201/2002*. The commissioner was considering a case where a claimant's move into a new housing association property from his council flat was delayed for just over three weeks from the start of the new tenancy due to his disability and a delay in obtaining a grant to cover removal expenses. The claimant sought HB on both properties for that period. The commissioner stated (para 6) that reg 5(5) HB Regs 1987 (now reg 7(6)) had no application. But note now the decision in *R(H) 9/05* and its view – albeit in a slightly different context – that a person can be said to have moved in once her/his furniture and personal possessions have been placed in the property.

In *CH 4546/2002*, the claimant's partner and carer took a tenancy of a property and sub-let a part of the property to the claimant, who then moved in with them. The commissioner held that on the facts, the dual liability could have been avoided (para 29) but more importantly for general purposes, decided that sub-para (d) could operate even where the new liability fell foul of reg 7(1) HB Regs 1987 (now reg 9(1)), as the deeming of non-liability under reg 7(1) had no impact on whether there is a liability in fact in respect of the new dwelling for the purposes of sub-para (d). It is not clear whether the commissioner considered *Naghshbandi* (see above). It is not mentioned in the decision and it is arguably inconsistent with the Court of Appeal's reasoning in that case.

Adaptations to meet disablement needs: sub-para (e). Under this provision, where a person is treated as occupying a new home under para (8)(c)(i) (ie, because a move was delayed while adaptations were made to meet her/his disablement needs or those of any member of her/his family) and occupied another dwelling within the four weeks immediately preceding the move, HB can be paid for both dwellings for up to four weeks.

Paragraph (7): Moving to a new home in respect of which there is no liability for payments
Para (7) deals with situations where a claimant has moved from a home for which s/he was liable to make payments, to a new dwelling for which there is no such liability. The latter could include, for example, prison or hospital (see GM A3.430–432) or staying with friends or relatives. It allows HB to be paid for the former home for up to four weeks where liability continues after the move, so long as the claimant could not reasonably have avoided the liability – eg, where s/he had to leave a former home without being able to give notice to her/his landlord. See para (6)(d) and (e) where there *is* liability for payments for both homes and paras (11) to (17D) for when a claimant can qualify for HB while temporarily absent from home.

Paragraphs (8) and (9): Delays in moving into new home
Like paragraph (6)(d), these paragraphs deal with the situation where a claimant has moved house, but this provision does not authorise the treatment of more than one dwelling as the claimant's home: only para (6) lists the situation in which this is possible. In *CH 2201/2002,* the judge decided that if an award of HB in respect of the former home had not been superseded, there was no power for the local authority to award HB for the new home under para (8) for an overlapping period. Thus, unless para (6) applied, para (8) could only apply to a claimant who was not receiving HB in respect of her/his former home. However, in *Sunderland City Council v GH (HB)* [2014] UKUT 3 (AAC), Judge Mark declined to follow *CH 2201/2002*. The claimant had claimed HB for a new home, but then delayed moving in while awaiting a payment from the social fund. She continued to receive HB for the refuge in which she resided while waiting. It was accepted that in respect of the new home, para (8)(c)(ii) applied to her, but she was not a person who could be entitled to HB for more than one home so the local authority did not award HB for the new home until she moved in. The judge decided that the claimant was entitled to HB for her new home for the four weeks prior to her move on the basis that the new home was the dwelling she occupied as her home for HB purposes, rather than the refuge. He said that if *CH 2201/2002* was correct in finding that a local authority has no power to make an HB award if it has failed to terminate an earlier one, it would follow that even if a claimant moved home, but the local authority in error failed to supersede the HB award in respect of the former home, so long as that error continued there would be no power to make an award in respect of the new home. Note that as a consequence, HB was overpaid in respect of the claimant's former home. In such situations, as the judge pointed out, the local authority can suspend payment of HB pending a decision on which of the two dwellings the claimant occupies as her/his home, and for which of these HB should therefore be awarded.

Where this provision does apply, it permits payment of HB in respect of rent due up to four weeks before the claimant actually moved into the new home (where s/he was liable to pay in respect of that period). This is done by deeming the claimant to occupy the accommodation during that period, even though s/he had not in fact moved in. In addition, the following conditions must be satisfied.

(1) The provision may only take effect after the claimant moves in: para (8)(a). But note here the decision in *R(H) 9/05*, which holds, in effect, that this does not require personal presence by the claimant, but can be met by the claimant's furniture and possessions being "moved in".

(2) The claimant must either have claimed HB or have notified the authority of the move to the new dwelling before the move: para (8)(b)(i) and (ii). In the former case, the claim must either have been refused or not

yet have been determined. If the claim has been refused, the claimant must make a fresh claim within four weeks of moving to the new home. At first sight, para (9) appears to relax the second condition, by allowing a claim made within four weeks of the move to be treated as if made prior to it. But on a careful reading the paragraph does not have this effect, because it only applies if the conditions in para (8)(a) to (c) are satisfied. Para (9) therefore simply governs the date on which a claim which was made prior to moving is treated as being effective.

(3)   If (1) and (2) are satisfied, the delay between taking on liability for the home and moving in must have been "reasonable": para (8)(c).

(4)   One or more of the conditions in para (8)(c)(i)–(iii) must be fulfilled.

Under para (8)(c)(i), the delay in moving must be necessary in order to adapt the dwelling to meet specified disablement needs. See para (6)(e) where someone is treated as occupying a dwelling under para (8)(c)(i) and is also liable to make payments in respect of her/his former home.

CH 3857/2004 confirms the, perhaps obvious, point that the adaptations have to meet the needs of the claimant or family member which arise from or are particular to her/his disabilities (eg, handrails), rather than being works which would be necessary regardless of disability. This was emphasised in *R(H) 4/07*, where the commissioner followed an earlier decision of his (*CH 1363/2006*) in holding that the word "adapt" entails a change to the fabric or structure of the dwelling and so did not encompass furnishing (eg, carpeting) or decorating the dwelling.

In *Bury MBC v DC (HB)* [2011] UKUT 43 (AAC) the claimant, due to his obsessive compulsive disorder, could not move into his new home until it had been redecorated and carpeted. Judge Jacobs decided that "disablement" included mental as well as physical disablement. He considered whether "necessary" meant "essential" or "reasonably required" and decided it meant the latter. However, following *R(H) 4/07*, he concluded that the works required in this case did not amount to adaptations of the dwelling. He considered whether the condition could be satisfied if the works that are needed have to be done in a way that takes account of the claimant's disability but concluded that this was not sufficient to bring a case within the provision. He said: "It is the adapting of the dwelling that has to be necessary, not the manner in which it may have to be carried out."

Judge Mesher, in *DM v Lewisham LB and SSWP (HB)* [2013] UKUT 26 (AAC), rejected arguments that *R(H) 4/07* was wrongly decided and said that, subject to human rights arguments, the meaning of regulation 7(8)(c)(i) was to be regarded as settled at the level of the Upper Tribunal. He then went on to consider whether the interpretation of "adapt the dwelling" adopted in *R(H) 4/07*, and other decisions, discriminated against disabled people contrary to article 14 of the European Convention on Human Rights (the ECHR) in conjunction with article 8 (right to respect for private and family life) and/or article 1 of Protocol 1 (protection of property). Judge Mesher decided that there was a not a difference of treatment on the ground of a personal characteristic under article 14 of the ECHR, but in any event, even on the assumption that the claimant's case under that article did not fail, the difference of treatment of the claimant was objectively and reasonably justified, so that there was no contravention of article 14. The claimant appealed to the Court of Appeal in *DM v Lewisham LB and SSWP* [2014] EWCA Civ 284; [2014] AACR 14. The Court considered the meaning of "adapt the dwelling" and concluded that reg 7(8)(c) cannot have been intended to exclude a disabled person who is unable to move into her/his home while it is being decorated to meet her/his disablement needs but to include one who is, for example, unable to move in while the bathroom and kitchen are being refitted to meet her/his disablement needs. It agreed with the approach the First-tier Tribunal suggested it would have followed had it not been constrained by *R(H) 4/07*, that adapt "can mean to make fit, to change or modify to suit a purpose. What in any individual case will amount to adapting a dwelling to meet the disablement needs of a person will depend very much on the nature of those needs. Adapting a dwelling need not … involve works of any particular type and specifically need not involve any physical interference with the structure of the dwelling or any physical addition to it. Provided the result of the process which the dwelling has undergone is that it has been changed to make it more suitable for the needs of the disabled person, it can fairly be said to have been adapted."

In respect of para (8)(c)(ii), the relevant paragraphs refer to people entitled to have a disability, severe disability or disabled child premium included in their applicable amounts and the component is the support component – see Sch 3 (on p630). "Member of the work-related activity group" is defined in reg 2(1).

For the definitions of "patient" and "residential accommodation" in para (8)(c)(iii), see para (18) and for "local welfare provision" see reg 2(1). Local welfare provision is the DWP term for the replacement of social fund community care grants and crisis loans from April 2013 by local provision.

Para (9) governs the date on which payment of HB for a period prior to that on which the claimant actually occupied the dwelling may be authorised subject to the four-week maximum provided in para (8). That period commences on the later of the appropriate dates ascertained under (a) to (c). For "made or treated as made", see regs 76 and 83. Note also that reg 79(10) sets the effective date for a change of circumstances as the first day on which the person is treated as occupying the new dwelling as a home under reg 7(8).

Paragraph (10): Absence due to domestic violence

Where neither para (6)(a) nor (16)(c)(x) applies, if the claimant has left a former home through fear of relevant violence and has an unavoidable liability to make payments in respect of that former home, this provision requires the authority to treat the claimant as occupying the dwelling as a home (and therefore as potentially entitled to HB) for up to four weeks. So where the claimant cannot be treated as occupying both the former and the new home (eg, because s/he is only liable for payments on the former home) or s/he is not temporarily absent from the former home (eg, because s/he does not intend to return to it), HB can be paid on the former home for the period specified. For the types of violence to which this provision applies, see the Analysis to para (6)(a). Unlike the circumstances covered by para (6)(a) this provision applies even where there is no liability to make payments in respect of the new dwelling and regardless of whether or not the claimant intends to return to the former home.

Paragraph (11) and (12): Absence for a trial period in residential accommodation

If a claimant enters residential accommodation, as defined in para (18), on a permanent basis s/he is no longer entitled to HB on her/his former home.

Where a claimant enters such accommodation with the intention of returning home s/he is entitled to benefit for her/his normal home for up to 52 weeks: paras 16(c)(ix) and (17D). Some people, however, go into residential accommodation on a trial basis to see if it suits them. In these circumstances, so long as the residential accommodation is in Great Britain (ie, England, Scotland or Wales), paras (11) and (12) may allow them to continue to receive HB for up to 13 weeks, subject to an overall limit of 52 weeks on the absence from home. This would, for example, allow for further trial periods in other residential accommodation, or for absences from home allowed under paras (13) to (17D), before or after the trial period.

The Court of Appeal's decision in *SSWP v Selby DC and another* [2006] EWCA Civ 271, reported as *R(H) 4/ 06* (overturning *CH 1854/2004*) holds that the language used in sub-para (7B)(b) HB Regs 1987 (now para (11)(b)) requires that the intention of returning to the dwelling which is normally occupied as the home must be present at the moment the person enters the residential accommodation; no more, no less. In other words, the intention to return home is to be gauged and fixed as at the date the person enters the residential accommodation.

On the other hand, the terms of sub-para (11)(c) are not confined to the present and have a temporal span which covers the whole of a person's time in residential accommodation. Accordingly, if at any time during the "trial" stay in residential accommodation the dwelling normally occupied is let, then the claimant will fall outside the parameters of para (11) and lose her/his entitlement to HB. But that will not arise if all that has happened is that the claimant has given in her/his notice to quit the dwelling.

What reg 5(7C) HB Regs 1987 provided for (now reg 7(12)), in the Court of Appeal's view, was to *treat* the claimant as if s/he was occupying the dwelling s/he normally occupied for 13 weeks, even though s/he had manifested the intention of not returning to it (or more accurately not returning to it after her/his right to exclusive possession has ended by operation of her/his notice to quit). The Court of Appeal noted that its construction of reg 5(7B) and (7C) HB Regs 1987 was supported by the *different* language used in reg 5(8B) and (8C) HB Regs 1987 (now reg 7(16) and (17)), which, in the court's view, by inference, shows that the intention there has to be present throughout the whole of the period of temporary absence (therefore endorsing, though not expressly, the views in *CH 3893/2004*).

In *CSHB 405/2005*, the commissioner stated (para 30) that "desire" is not equivalent to "intention" in this statutory context, the former being a less certain or fixed state of mind than the latter. More controversially, perhaps, the commissioner said that in the context of reg 5 HB Regs 1987 (now reg 7) an intention to return to occupy the dwelling as the home must involve not only a subjective purpose to do so but also the objective fact that such a return is a realistic possibility. It is arguable that adding this gloss to the statutory words is both unnecessary and unhelpful. What has to be ascertained under reg 7 is the "intention" of the person, albeit to do a particular thing. As a matter of evidence the ability of the claimant to return and occupy the dwelling as her/his home may go to the cogency of her/his intention, and may reduce an intention to a desire to return, but this is all a matter of weight to be attached to the evidence when deciding whether the claimant has the relevant intention. If the commissioner is saying that, even if it is determined that a person has the relevant intention, the claim under reg 7 can still be defeated if it is decided that such a return is not a realistic possibility, it is suggested that the decision is wrong.

Paragraph (13) to (13G) and (16) to (17D): Temporary absence

A claimant who is absent from her/his "main dwelling" (defined in para (18) as the dwelling the person normally occupies as her/his home) for a specified temporary period can be treated as occupying the home for that period, and thus can qualify for HB for her/his main dwelling while away from home. The period is up to:

(1)   13 weeks if the person is absent from home, whatever the reason: para (13);

(2)   26 weeks if the person is absent from Great Britain (ie, England, Scotland and Wales) as a member of the armed forces posted overseas, a mariner or a continental shelf worker: paras (13F) and (13G);

(3)   52 weeks if the person is absent from home in the particular circumstances set out in paras (16) and (16A).

In all cases, the period runs from the first day of absence. Under the rules allowing 13 or 52 weeks absence from home, the period can be shorter if the person is not only absent from her/his main dwelling, but is also absent from Great Britain: paras (13A)–(13E) and (17A)–(17D). A non-British EEA national is more likely to be affected by the rules that limit the amount of time a claimant can be absent from Great Britain. The differential treatment of absences in and outside of Great Britain may be unlawful in the specific case of EU nationals with a right to reside. See, in particular, *John O'Flynn v CAO* [1996] ECR I-02617, Case C-237/94.

Paras (13) to (13G) and (16) to (17D) may also be relevant in determining whether someone occupies a dwelling with the claimant. See the discussion of *Swale* and *Stroud DC v JG* [2009] UKUT 67 (AAC); R(H) 8/09 in the General Note on p263.

Note: the amendments made by the Housing Benefit and State Pension Credit (Temporary Absence) (Amendment) Regulations 2016 SI No.624 did not apply in respect of a person who was temporarily absent from Great Britain on 28 July 2016 until s/he returned to Great Britain: reg 5(1) of SI 2016 No.624.

General rules

In *HK v South Hams DC (HB)* [2017] UKUT 254 (AAC), the judge considered how a claimant's absence from a dwelling under reg 7(1), (13) and (17) should be approached. A determination must first be made as to whether the claimant normally occupies the dwelling as her/his home under para (1). If s/he does not, there can be no entitlement to HB for it. If s/he does, it is necessary to then consider whether the claimant's absence from the dwelling is temporary – ie, whether the conditions in paras (13) to (13G) or (16) to (17D) are satisfied. It is possible to continue to qualify for HB during a temporary absence from home even if the home is uninhabitable during that absence: *CH 2194/2010*.

CSH 499/2006 considered the phrase **"the first day of that absence from home"**. The claimant had been treated as occupying his home during an absence while in prison on remand under reg 5(8B)(c)(i) HB Regs 1987 (becoming reg 7(16)(c)(i), and now reg 7(16A)(a)). The issue was whether he could then be treated as occupying his home for 13 weeks from the date he was sentenced to a term of imprisonment under reg 5(8) HB Regs 1987 (now reg 7(13)). Commissioner May refused the claimant's appeal. He said that the calculation of temporary absence was dependent upon the application of reg 5(8) HB Regs 1987. For the purposes of that paragraph, "the first day of that absence from the home" was, as a matter of fact, the date the claimant had first been detained in prison.

In *R v Penwith DC ex p Burt* (1990) 22 HLR 292 at 296, QBD, it was held that the absence must be for a continuous unbroken period – ie, without any returns. In cases where a claimant is moving backwards and forwards between two properties, authorities must consider reg 7(1) in order to decide what is the "normal" home in respect of which HB should be paid. It follows that authorities cannot "aggregate" periods of absence so as to make up the period allowed. Consequently if the claimant, with the exception of prisoners on temporary leave under paras (14) and (15), returns to and occupies the dwelling as a home, even for a short time, the allowable period of temporary absence starts again. The DWP suggests that a stay at home lasting, for example, only a few hours may not be acceptable but one that lasts for at least 24 hours may be acceptable: GM A3.460.

To be treated as occupying the main dwelling during a period of absence from home within Great Britain (or of absence from Great Britain) *all* of the following are required.

(1) **Intention to return to the home**. The person must intend to return to live in the main dwelling: paras (13)(a), (13D)(a), (13G)(a) and (16)(a). Often, a good indicator of an intention to return is personal belongings and furniture being left in the home: *R v Kensington and Chelsea RBC HBRB ex p Robertson* [1988] 28 RVR 84 at 85, QBD. Other factors might be where the claimant pays council tax, where s/he is registered to vote and other local connections. However, once a notice to quit has been given by a tenant in respect of the dwelling then s/he can no longer have a continuing intention to return to occupy the dwelling as her/his home: *CH 3893/2004* para 6. In such a situation the giving of the notice to quit cannot be treated simply as an expression of a future intention not to return to the dwelling upon the expiry of the tenancy, as the wording of the relevant paragraphs requires the continuance in the current benefit week of a positive intention to return to the dwelling: *CH 3893/2004* para 8. See also *CH 1237/2004* below which is to similar effect.

(2) **Home not let or sub-let.** The part of the main dwelling normally occupied by the person must not have been let or sublet: paras (13)(b), (13D)(b), (13G)(b) and (16)(b).

(3) **Period of absence unlikely to exceed specified period.** The period of absence from home (or from Great Britain) must be unlikely to exceed the period allowed, or for those who may be absent from home for up to 52 weeks (and absent from Great Britain for four or 26 weeks within those 52 weeks), unlikely to substantially exceed the period: para (13)(c), (13D)(c), (13G)(c) and (16)(d).

GM A3.532 suggests that the term "unlikely to substantially exceed" in respect of the 52-week period relates to periods of absence of up to 15 months but it is for the individual authority to determine this, subject to appeal.

The issue is not whether the person has been absent for more than the period allowed, but whether her/his absence is likely to be for more than that period. In working out whether the period of absence is unlikely to exceed 4/13/26/52 weeks, the day the claimant leaves her/his home is to be included, but the day s/he is likely to return home is not: *KdeS v Camden LB (HB)* [2011] UKUT 457 (AAC). In *Slough BC v PK* [2019] UKUT 128 (AAC), the judge said that that decision, and *CH 2638/2006* and *CB v Liverpool City Council* [2015] UKUT 359 (AAC), are directly applicable to the question of when the period of a claimant's temporary absence from Great Britain starts. The judge said: "In any event, the language used in Regulation 7(13D) is "beginning with" not "beginning from" and it is clear that such language results in the first day of the relevant period being the date on which the specified event occurs." Once it becomes clear that a claimant is going to be away for more than the period allowed, HB entitlement ends, even if the claimant has not yet been away for the maximum number of weeks allowed. What is crucial is not whether the period does, in the event, exceed 4/13/26/ 52 weeks, but whether it is likely to do so on each successive day of the absence. *CH 1237/2004* confirmed that a claimant remains entitled to HB until it is no longer likely that s/he will return within the number of weeks allowed. The main point of that decision is that the point from which the period of absence is to be calculated – for the purpose of determining whether the absence is likely to exceed 4/13/26/52 weeks – is the date the claimant left the house (para 12 of the decision), or left Great Britain, and not the date of claim. However, the decision goes on to say that continued entitlement has to be judged on a week by week basis, so that if at any date in the period of absence it becomes likely that the absence will exceed the number of weeks allowed, that is a change of circumstances allowing for a supersession of the entitlement decision from that date. The decision also emphasises that the test of likely period of absence is an objective one, to which the claimant's belief or opinion about the likely period of absence is relevant evidence but is not determinative.

Example: a claimant leaves home to look for work in another town within Great Britain intending to return within 13 weeks. He has a train ticket for return within that period. He is treated as occupying his home and is entitled to HB. After he has been away from home for 10 weeks, he notifies the local authority that he is unable to return to his home for the foreseeable future. As his period of absence is no longer unlikely to exceed 13 weeks, he is no longer treated as occupying his home and his entitlement to HB for that home ends.

There is no requirement that the intention to be temporarily absent from the dwelling needs to be notified in writing to the authority prior to departure: *CH 996/2004* para 17.

Paras (13) to (13B): absence from the main dwelling for up to 13 weeks. If the person is absent from her/his main dwelling within Great Britain, s/he is treated as occupying that dwelling as her/his home for up to 13 weeks, whatever the reason for her/his absence: para (13). Within that 13-week period, a person can continue to qualify for HB for up to four weeks while absent from Great Britain under paras (13C) to (13E).

The 13-week period under para (13) runs, or continues to run while the person is absent from Great Britain: para (13A). When the person returns to Great Britain, s/he can continue to be treated as occupying her/his main dwelling while absent from it, for the remainder (if any) of the 13-week period allowed. However, this does not apply if at the start of the period of absence from Great Britain or during that period, s/he ceased to be treated as occupying her/his main dwelling as a home. In this case, s/he is treated as *not* occupying the main dwelling on any day following the period of absence from Great Britain until s/he returns to the main dwelling: para (13B).

Paras (13C) to (13E): absence from Great Britain for up to four weeks. A person is treated as occupying her/his main dwelling as a home for up to four weeks while absent from Great Britain, so long as s/he occupied that dwelling as her/his home, or was treated as doing so, immediately before the period of absence from Great Britain: paras (13C) and (13D). This is subject to paras (13E), (13G), (17C) and (17D) which provide additional situations in which a person can continue to be treated as occupying her/his main dwelling while absent from Great Britain. The four-week period can be extended by up to four weeks if the absence is in connection with the death of any of the people listed in para (13E) and the local authority considers it unreasonable to expect the person to return to Great Britain within the first four weeks.

Examples
- A claimant notifies the local authority that he is going to stay with his sister in Great Britain prior to a two-week holiday abroad and that, after his holiday, he intends to stay with her for a further week before returning home. He is treated as occupying his main dwelling for 2 + 2 + 1 = 5 weeks and thus continues to qualify for HB for his main dwelling for that period.
- A claimant goes abroad to visit relatives with the intention of returning within four weeks. After an absence of two weeks, she notifies the local authority that she is extending her visit by three weeks. She then returns to Great Britain, but does not return home for a further two weeks. She ceases to be treated as occupying her main dwelling after two weeks absence from Great Britain because she no longer intends to return within the four-week period allowed. Her entitlement to HB therefore ends. She cannot be treated as occupying her main dwelling again until she returns home (see para (13B) above).

Paras (13F) and (13G): absence from Great Britain for up to 26 weeks. If the person is absent from Great Britain as a "member of Her Majesty's forces posted overseas", or as a "mariner" or a "continental shelf worker" (all defined in para (18)), s/he is treated as occupying her/his main dwelling as a home for up to 26 weeks. S/he must have occupied that dwelling as a home, or have been treated as doing so, immediately before the period of absence from Great Britain.

Paras (16) to (17D): absence from the main dwelling for up to 52 weeks. In the particular circumstances specified in paras (16) and (16A), if the person is absent from her/his main dwelling within Great Britain, s/he is treated as occupying that dwelling as her/his home for up to 52 weeks: para (17). Also in the circumstances specified, and within that 52-week period, a person is treated as occupying her/his main dwelling as a home for up to four or 26 weeks while absent from Great Britain, so long as s/he occupied that dwelling as her/his home, or was treated as doing so, immediately before the period of absence from Great Britain: paras (17C) and (17D). See also the situations in paras (13D) and (13G) that allow for periods of absence from Great Britain.

The 52-week period runs, or continues to run, while the person is absent from Great Britain: para (17A). When the person returns to Great Britain, s/he can continue to be treated as occupying her/his main dwelling while absent from it, for the remainder (if any) of the 52-week period allowed. However, this does not apply if at the start of the period of absence from Great Britain or during that period, s/he ceased to be treated as occupying her/his main dwelling as a home. In this case, s/he is treated as *not* occupying the main dwelling on any day following the period of absence from Great Britain until s/he returns to the main dwelling: para (17B).

Examples
- The claimant leaves home to stay in London to be near her child who is receiving medical treatment in a hospital. Prior to leaving home she notifies the local authority that she intends to return home within 52

weeks. After 18 weeks, she takes her child to Spain for further medical treatment in a hospital there. She returns home from Spain after 10 weeks. She is treated as occupying her main dwelling for 18 + 10 = 28 weeks (see paras (16)(c)(iii) and (d)(ii) and (17C)) and thus continues to be entitled to HB for her main home during that period.

– The claimant goes to Italy for a two-week training course and following that a two-week holiday there. He notifes the local authority of this before his departure. He is treated as occupying his main dwelling for two weeks under para (17D) and for a further two weeks under paras (13C) and (13D). He is treated as occupying his main dwelling for four weeks. After four weeks, he cannot be treated as occupying his main dwelling until he returns home.

Categories of people who may be absent from home for up to 52 weeks. The categories of claimant who may be temporarily absent for up to 52 weeks and retain their HB entitlement are set out in paras (16)(c) and (16A). There must be some causal link between the reason for the absence from home and being within one of the categories: *Torbay BC v RF (HB)* [2010] UKUT 7 (AAC); [2010] AACR 26. They are:

(i)   A person on remand pending trial or detained pending sentence, as well as a person required to live in approved premises (eg, a bail hostel) or at an address away from her/his normal home as a condition of bail: para (16A). S/he can be temporarily absent from Great Britain for up to four weeks: paras (16)(d)(iii) and (17D). The words at the end of para (16A) making it a requirement that the person is not also detained in custody following a sentence upon conviction, were added from 2 April 2013 to reverse the effect of *MR v Bournmouth BC (HB)* [2011] UKUT 284 (AAC). In that decision, the judge decided that "detained in custody on remand pending trial" and "detained pending sentence upon conviction" could apply to a person while s/he was simultaneously serving another sentence. The category of those required to live in an address away from their normal home removes the prior restriction in reg 5(8B)(c)(i) HB Regs 1987 to persons in bail hostels only. That rule had been challenged – by a claimant who was required to live away from her home as a condition of her bail – in *CH 4574/2003*. The commissioner held, however, that the restriction of the rule to bail hostel cases only, did not discriminate in a way which infringed the claimant's Art 14 Convention rights, as the difference in treatment between the two categories of person was within the margin of judgement that is allowed to the legislature when enacting social legislation: paras 63–66 applying *R (Waite) v Hammersmith and Fulham LB* (2003) HLR 24. See paras (14) and (15) for additional rules where a detained or sentenced prisoner is given temporary release.

(ii)   A person resident in a hospital or similar institution as a patient as defined in para (18). S/he can be temporarily absent from Great Britain for up to 26 weeks: paras (16)(d)(ii) and (17C). Note that, unlike in the definition of "patient" in reg 28(11)(e), the medical or other treatment need not be provided free. In *SSWP and Warwick DC v OB and JS and JS (CTB)* [2012] UKUT 489 (AAC), the claimants were seriously mentally ill and as they had been hospital in-patients for in excess of 52 weeks, their entitlement had ended under reg 7(16)(c)(ii) and (17). One of the claimants argued that the rule interfered with his rights under Art 8 ECHR (right to respect for the home) and the interference was not proportionate. All of the claimants argued that the rule had a disproportionate impact on the mentally ill and that the discrimination was not justified. Judge Lloyd-Davies did not accept that the provision touched upon the right to respect for the home. However, he was prepared to assume that the provision indirectly discriminated against the mentally ill as it adversely affects a significantly greater proportion of mental health patients than other hospital patients because they represent a significantly greater proportion of the patients staying in hospital for over 52 weeks and because patients who are mentally ill are more likely to be in receipt of HB than are other patients. However, he concluded that the discrimination was justified.

The claimants' appeal against the decision of the Upper Tribunal was unsuccessful: *Obrey and Others v SSWP* [2013] EWCA Civ 1584.

(iii)   A person undergoing, or whose partner or dependant child is undergoing, medical treatment or "medically approved" convalescence, but not in "residential accommodation". S/he can be temporarily absent from Great Britain for up to 26 weeks: paras (16)(d)(ii) and (17C).

(iv)   A person undertaking a training course. S/he can be temporarily absent from Great Britain for up to four weeks: paras (16)(d)(iii) and (17D).

(v)   A person providing "medically approved" care. S/he can be temporarily absent from Great Britain for up to four weeks: paras (16)(d)(iii) and (17D).

(vi)   A person providing care for a child (defined in reg 2(1) as a person under the age of 16), whose parent or guardian is temporarily away from home receiving medical treatment or "medically approved" care. S/he can be temporarily absent from Great Britain for up to four weeks: paras (16)(d)(iii) and (17D).

(vii)   A person receiving "medically approved" care but not in "residential accommodation". S/he can be temporarily absent from Great Britain for up to 26 weeks: paras (16)(d)(ii) and (17C).

(viii)   A student to whom paras (3) or (6)(b) do not apply. S/he can be temporarily absent from Great Britain for up to four weeks: paras (16)(d)(iii) and (17D).

(ix)   A person receiving temporary care in "residential accommodation" but not if residing there on a trial basis. S/he can be temporarily absent from Great Britain for up to four weeks: paras (16)(d)(iii) and (17D). For those residing in such accommodation on a trial basis, see paras (11) and (12).

(x)   A person in fear of violence to whom para (6)(a) does not apply because, for example, s/he is staying with close relatives and is not liable to pay rent on two homes but intends to return to occupy her/his original home. S/he can be temporarily absent from Great Britain for up to 26 weeks: paras (16)(d)(iii) and (17C). Where there is no intention to return home, see para (10).

"Medically approved", "residential accommodation" and "training course" are defined in para (18).

Paragraphs (14) and (15): Temporary release from imprisonment

The purpose of this provision is to ensure that most people detained in custody who are temporarily released cannot claim HB for the home they are temporarily occupying. A similar provision in the HB Regs 1987 was inserted following the decision in *Chief Adjudication Officer v Carr* [1994] 2 June, *The Times*, CA which held that a prisoner on home release could claim IS.

    Where para (14) applies:

(1)   If the person's temporary release was immediately preceded by a period of temporary absence under paras (13) or (16), 13 or 52 weeks as the case may be, s/he is treated as still absent. If not, s/he is treated as not occupying the dwelling as a home: sub-paras (a) and (c).

(2)   For the purposes of para (16)(c)(i) (temporary absence of up to 52 weeks), the person is treated as if still detained.

The provision only applies to a person "detained in custody" pending sentence or under a sentence. It does not therefore apply to someone required to reside in approved premises or some other address away from home pending sentence: *R(IS) 17/93*. In addition, it does not apply to somebody detained under the mental health legislation listed in para (14)(a). Note also that someone serving a very short sentence might still qualify under the temporary absence provision in para (13).

Circumstances in which a person is to be treated as liable to make payments in respect of a dwelling

8.–(1)   Subject to regulation 9 (circumstances in which a person is to be treated as not liable to make payments in respect of a dwelling), the following persons shall be treated as if they were liable to make payments in respect of a dwelling–

(a)   the person who is liable to make those payments;

(b)   a person who is a partner of the person to whom sub-paragraph (a) applies;

(c)   a person who has to make the payments if he is to continue to live in the home because the person liable to make them is not doing so and either–

    (i)   he was formerly a partner of the person who is so liable; or

    (ii)   he is some other person whom it is reasonable to treat as liable to make the payments;

(d)   a person whose liability to make such payments is waived by his landlord as reasonable compensation in return for works actually carried out by the tenant in carrying out reasonable repairs or redecoration which the landlord would otherwise have carried out or be required to carry out but this sub-paragraph shall apply only for a maximum of 8 benefit weeks in respect of any one waiver of liability;

(e)   a person who is a partner of a student to whom regulation 56(1) (circumstances in which certain students are treated as not liable to make payments in respect of a dwelling) applies.

(2)   A person shall be treated as liable to make a payment in respect of a dwelling for the whole of the period in, or in respect of, which the payment is to be made notwithstanding that the liability is discharged in whole or in part either before or during that period and, where the amount which a person is liable to pay in respect of a period is varied either during or after that period, he shall, subject to regulations 79 to 81 (dates of relevant changes of circumstances, weekly amounts and housing benefit for rent free periods), be treated as liable to pay the amount as so varied during the whole of that period.

Definitions

"benefit week" – see reg 2(1).
"claimant" – see reg 2(1).
"dwelling" – see reg 2(4) and s137(1) SSCBA.
"partner" – see reg 2(1).
"payment" – see reg 2(1).

General Note

One of the basic conditions of entitlement to HB is that the claimant must be liable to make payments in respect of a dwelling: s130(1)(a) SSCBA. Reg 8 deals with the circumstances in which a person is treated as liable to make such payments. References in the HB Regs to a person who is liable to make payments includes references to a person who is treated as liable under reg 8: reg 2(2). Note that a claimant need not be liable personally. Particular issues for young claimants and claimants with a degree of mental incapacity are discussed below.

The question of whether there is a genuine liability to make payments is dealt with under reg 8 (see p278 for a discussion on genuine liability and so-called "sham" agreements). However, reg 8 must be read subject to reg 9. Reg 9 treats certain classes of people who are (or may be) under a legal liability to make payments as not being liable, thereby disqualifying them from HB.

Cases often raise issues under both reg 8 and reg 9. In *SA v Newham LB(HB)* [2010] UKUT 191 (AAC), Judge Lane pointed out that the question of genuine liability needs to be considered first under reg 8 and the question of whether the claimant is to be treated as not having a liability to make payments then considered under reg 9. She said:

"As a matter of practicality, a tribunal may bypass regulation 8 if it sees an obvious ground under regulation 9 upon which it can decide the appeal, but there are dangers in doing so. Bypassing regulation 8 may not amount to a material error of law if the tribunal gives a satisfactory explanation for disallowing the appeal under regulation 9, but if the tribunal turns out to be wrong under regulation 9, the Upper Tribunal may have no alternative but to set aside and remit the appeal."

Where a case raises issues under both regs 8 and 9, because the issues overlap sufficiently, the First-tier Tribunal should determine all issues at once. In *CSHB 718/2002* para 21, the commissioner said that it would be "sensible" to deal with all issues in one hearing and this course was also approved in *R(H) 7/05* para 3.

Issues under reg 9(1)(a) to (l) may be linked with the issue as to whether there is a genuine liability under reg 8. However, the issues are different, and it is important to consider the legal requirements separately so as to avoid confusion: *CH 1171/2002* para 12.

Note that if the First-tier Tribunal decides to overturn an authority's decision that there is no liability (ie, the tribunal accepts that there is a genuine liability), it is under a duty to warn the parties if it is going on to consider whether reg 9 applies: *R(H) 3/03*. The following approach is suggested.

(1)   First, the question of whether a claimant is liable, or is to be treated as liable, to make payments in respect of a dwelling must be decided under reg 8. There must be evidence of liability, though this need not be in writing, and the liability must be genuine.

(2)   If there is a genuine liability, but there is a question whether the claimant is to be treated as not liable to make payments in respect of a dwelling, consideration should be given to whether any of the circumstances in reg 9(1) apply. This includes whether the agreement is on a commercial basis or the liability was created to take advantage of the HB scheme. See the General Note and Analysis to reg 9 from p281 for a discussion.

The need to draw a careful distinction between issues arising under reg 8 and reg 9 was vividly illustrated by *R v Greenwich LBC ex p Dhadly* (1999) 32 HLR 829. The claimant occupied a three-bedroom property owned by his son, who lived in America. The local authority initially refused HB on the basis that there was no true liability to pay rent (though referring to SSCBA s130 rather than reg 6 HB Regs 1987 – now reg 8) and also on the basis that if there was a liability to pay rent, it fell foul of the former reg 7(1)(b) HB Regs 1987, now reg 9(1)(l). On review, the refusal of HB was based solely on the absence of a liability. The Review Board stated that it was "not satisfied that Mr Dhadly was genuinely liable to pay rent".

Mr Dhadly applied in person for judicial review of the Board's decision. His application was refused at first instance by Collins J [1998] 31 HLR 446. The judge held that the Board was wrong to rely on reg 7 HB Regs 1987 but as it was possible to justify its decision on the basis that there was no genuine liability for rent (ie, by reliance on reg 6 HB Regs 1987 – now reg 8), permission to seek judicial review would be refused. However, that decision was overturned by the Court of Appeal, which granted permission and remitted the case to a High Court judge for hearing.

The substantive application was heard by Richards J [1999] 32 HLR 829. Counsel for the local authority argued that even if the Board's findings on reg 7 HB Regs 1987 could not be supported, judicial review should nevertheless be refused on the ground that the Board's findings clearly supported a conclusion that there was no liability to pay rent. Richards J rejected that submission in these terms:

"I am not persuaded that the matter can be dealt with as easily as that. The Board's decision fails to show that the Board has properly understood the legal issues and the precise legal test that it was applying at each stage of the analysis. If it was applying section 130, it has conspicuously failed to say so and has, on the contrary, purported to be applying regulation 7(1)(b). .... in circumstances where there is no mention of section 130, and the decision is expressed to be on a different basis, the court should be slow to hold that the Board did approach section 130 in the right way and that the decision can be upheld as a proper application of that provision."

Analysis

Paragraph (1)

Para (1) sets out the categories of people who are to be treated as liable to make payments in respect of a dwelling, subject to reg 9.

If reg 9 applies to exclude the people listed here, they cannot be treated as liable.

The people that are to be treated as liable to make payments are as follows.

(1)   The person who is liable – ie, under an agreement – and the partner of that person: sub-paras (a) and (b). Note that only one partner in a couple can claim HB: see reg 82.

(2)   A person who has to make the payments if s/he is to continue to live in the home because the person who is actually liable is not doing so: sub-para (c). This only applies if the person who has to make the payments is either the former partner of the liable person, or is not the former partner but is someone it is reasonable to treat as liable. Where consideration is being given to whether reg 8(1)(c)(ii) applies, the liable "person" can include a limited company and is not restricted to a natural person: *R(H) 5/05* para 33. It is not possible to deem a co-tenant to be liable for a co-tenant's share of the rent in addition to his own under this provision: *CH 3376/2002* para 37. In *CSHB 606/2005*, the commissioner accepted (para 15) that it was not reasonable to treat a child of 15 as liable to make payments in place of her mother who was the tenant, where the mother was ineligible for HB under the terms of (what is now) reg 9(1)(d). On the facts, the claim by the child was simply a device to circumvent reg 9(1)(d) and to hold otherwise would negate the effect of reg 9(1)(d). The use of the term "reasonable" within regulation 8(1)(c)(ii) means reasonable in all the circumstances and in light of the overall purpose of the HB scheme: *FK v Wandsworth BC (HB)* [2016] UKUT 570 (AAC); *Babergh DC v GW (HB)* [2017] UKUT 40 (AAC).

(3)   A person given a rent-free period as "reasonable compensation" in return for carrying out repairs or decoration: sub-para (d). This only applies for up to eight weeks in any one rent-free period. The work done must be reasonable and that which the landlord would have carried out or be required to carry out if the claimant had not.

There is no prohibition on claiming for a subsequent eight-week period, so works that will take longer can be split up into periods of eight weeks or less, separated by at least one complete benefit week where payment of rent is resumed. In *R v Westminster CC HBRB ex p Sier* (1999) 32 HLR 655 at 662-3, QBD (Latham J), it was pointed out that where the eight-week period pre-dated any payment for rent, the authority would have to satisfy itself that there was actually an obligation to pay rent (in the absence of the waiver) prior to the payments of rent starting. In that case there was no evidence to support the existence of any such pre-existing liability. The judge also ruled that the eight-week period had to run from the beginning of any rent-free period. Thus it is not possible to select a convenient eight-week period – eg, in order to preserve transitional protection.

(4)   A person who is the partner of a student treated as not liable to pay rent (and hence excluded from entitlement to HB) by reg 56(1): sub-para (e).

The liability to make payments must be in respect of a dwelling. In *R v Cambridge CC ex p Thomas* [1995] unreported, 10 February, QBD, a mother assisted one of her sons in raising funds to purchase a house. A declaration of trust was made in respect of the property, which included an obligation on the son to pay any rent received from lodgers to his mother. The property was registered solely in the son's name. The son lived there but the mother did not. Another son, the claimant, moved in and started to pay rent to the mother. It was held that since the mother had no legal title, she could not grant the claimant any right to reside in the property, and so the payments that he had agreed to make to her were not "payments in respect of a dwelling".

This conclusion seems rather dubious. It was not apparently in issue that the son was happy for his brother to move in, and it seems wrong to say that the claimant had no rights against the son. It is basic contract law that payments (or "consideration") made in return for goods or services need not be made to the person providing those goods or services. Payment to a third party is sufficient: see, for example, *re Wyvern Developments Ltd* [1974] 1 WLR 1097 at 1103D, Ch D. Therefore it is suggested that the claimant's payments in *Thomas* were indeed made in return for his occupation of the dwelling, the son having given the claimant a right to occupy in exchange for payments to the mother. The case would have been better dealt with as a "contrived tenancy" case under reg 7(1) HB Regs 1987 (now reg 9(1)).

The fact that payments must be made in respect of a "dwelling" confirms that if the payments are made under a business tenancy, they do not qualify. However, there may be difficulties where the tenancy is a mixed one or where there has been a change of use during the tenancy. With mixed tenancies, an apportionment must be made as to the rent payable for the business premises and for the residential premises and only the latter payments can be eligible rent under reg 12: see, for example, reg 12B(3).

A change of use during a tenancy could result in premises becoming eligible for HB. It would depend on the actual use to which the premises were now put and some evidence of conversion to living accommodation would be required. However, there must also be some change in the nature of the payments made. In *R v Warrington BC ex p Williams* (1997) 29 HLR 872 at 876, QBD, the claimant took garage premises under a commercial lease containing a covenant forbidding use of the premises as a dwelling. The claimant claimed that he had started to sleep on the premises as a night watchman, and therefore could claim HB in respect of the premises. The landlord's agents denied that the agreement was anything other than commercial. Hidden J held (at 875–6) that the agreement remained as a commercial one, even if the landlord was aware of the fact that the claimant was living on the premises. Accordingly, the claimant was not entitled to HB.

Paragraph (2)

This ensures that a claimant may receive HB in respect of all of the rent due for a particular period, even when payment is made wholly or partly in advance. Benefit is to be calculated on the basis of the period to which a payment *relates*, irrespective of when payment is actually *made*. Likewise, where rent is varied, HB is calculated on the basis of the period the variation affects, irrespective of when the variation is announced to, or paid by, the claimant. So, subject to regs 79 to 81, if rent is due on the first day of every month and the claimant's landlord informs her/him on the 15th that s/he is putting the rent up as of that month, for HB purposes the increase is treated as taking effect on the first day of the month.

Liability

"Liable" is not itself defined. The Oxford English Dictionary defines it as "legally bound, answerable for .... under obligation to do ....". The need for the obligation to be legal as opposed to moral was confirmed by Blackburne J in *R v Rugby BC HBRB ex p Harrison* (1994) 28 HLR 36 at 48-9, QBD. In that case, the claimants were members of a religious commune who signed a detailed agreement headed "Statement of Conditions of Residence". It was held that there was a question of law as to whether the agreement was intended to create legal relations between the claimants and the commune, and Blackburne J decided that there was such an intention (at 51). He also decided that it was not necessary to demonstrate that the landlord would probably take proceedings to recover unpaid payments, in order to demonstrate that the obligation was a legal one (at 51). The Court of Appeal approved this analysis in *R v Stratford-upon-Avon DC HBRB ex p White* (1998) 31 HLR 126 a case concerning the same commune (the Jesus Fellowship Church). The court stated that there was no reason why a relationship with a spiritual basis should not have legally enforceable aspects to it, and on a proper analysis of the commune's documents the obligation to make regular payments was a legal one.

In *R v Woking BC ex p Crawley* [1996] unreported, 19 June, QBD, Sedley J confirmed that the distinction that has to be drawn is between arrangements for living which will usually be made between friends and family (and, one might add, religious communities such as those in *Harrison* and *White*) and legally enforceable arrangements. If payment were made in the former cases, it would be "no more than subsidising a family arrangement which would in any event have resulted in the claimant sharing someone else's accommodation" (transcript at 7H–8B). The claimant had stayed with a friend who held an assured shorthold tenancy on condition that he paid half the rent. There was a clause in the tenancy prohibiting sub-letting.

There is a conflict in the approaches of Blackburne J and Sedley J as to whether the issue of whether an agreement gives rise to a legal liability is a question of law or fact. *CH 1171/2002* para 11 held that it was a question of fact whether or not a legal liability is created by an agreement.

What is required for there to be a legal liability? The three basic elements of a binding contract must be shown.

(1)   There must be a "consideration" (broadly, that both parties are giving up something in return for something). This will not be an issue in HB cases.

(2)   There must be a settled agreement between the parties. Again, this will not usually present a problem. There is no need for the parties to reach a detailed written agreement (see under "Evidence of liability" below). If A orally agrees to rent a room to B for £50 a week, that is all that is required to establish a settled agreement for HB purposes. If there is no specific agreement about what facilities B can use and about house rules, that does not prevent there being a binding agreement.

(3)   There must be an intention to create legal relations. Did the parties intend their agreement to be legally enforceable? It is on this third element that cases such as *Harrison* and *Crawley* turned. In deciding whether there is such an intention, local authorities should be careful to separate their consideration of this question from the question as to whether any of the grounds in reg 9(1) applies.

Those who do not have an interest in land can nevertheless enter into a tenancy agreement with another party, with a consequent liability for rent. In *CH 2959/2006*, the claimant had said that his brother (MI), to whom he paid rent, was acting as agent for the landlord. His claim for HB was refused on the basis that he was not liable to pay rent to the registered owner of the property (A) and that MI had no right to grant occupation. The tribunal upheld the decision. It said that in the absence of clear evidence that MI was the agent of A, he had no legal ability to enter into any contract with the claimant for the renting out of the property and consequently there could be no legal liability to make payments in respect of it. Deputy Commissioner Whybrow QC had sympathy with the difficult task faced by the tribunal but said that it erred in law by misdirecting itself that there could be no valid agreement creating a liability to make payments where the grantor had no power to let the property. He said (at para 22) that *Bruton v London & Quadrant Housing Trust* [1999] 3 WLR 150 and *Lambeth London BC v Kay* [2006] 4 All ER 128 (both House of Lords decisions):

"establish that a party who does not have an interest in land such as to enable him to grant a leasehold estate or tenancy in favour of another party can nevertheless enter into a tenancy agreement with another party which is valid and effective between the parties to the agreement, albeit that the agreement will not be effective to create an interest or estate in land binding on third parties, including the registered owner of the relevant land. While *Bruton and Kay were* concerned with cases where the landlord could not create an estate because he was only a licensee of the owner of the legal interest, in my judgement the principle in those cases apply equally to circumstances, as found by the tribunal in this case, where MI had no authority from the registered owner to let the premises. Thus, assuming that there was an otherwise valid agreement between MI and the claimants, such an agreement would be as binding and effective as between these parties, notwithstanding it could not confer on the claimants an interest or estate binding A. The tribunal in holding otherwise erred in law."

In *FK v Wandsworth BC (HB)* [2016] UKUT 570 (AAC), the claimant lived in a property that was the sole tenancy of her sister, without the agreement of the landlord. Her sister had not intended to live in, and had never lived in, the property, renting it only to enable the claimant to obtain accommodation. The First-tier Tribunal decided that the arrangement between the claimant and her sister did not create a legal liability – ie, that the claimant was not entitled to HB because she was not liable to make payments in respect of the dwelling to the landlord or her sister. Judge Hemingway decided that the tribunal had not erred in this regard, but it had, in failing to go on to consider whether the claimant could be treated as liable under reg 8(1)(c)(ii), ie if she had to make the payments to continue to live in the dwelling because the liable person (her sister) was not doing so and it was reasonable to treat her as liable. The judge pointed out that there is an argument that where there is dishonesty, it will not necessarily be appropriate to conclude that it is reasonable to treat a claimant as liable under reg 8(1)(c). He said:

"... the use of the term "reasonable" within regulation 8(1)(c)(ii) is to be regarded as meaning reasonable in all the circumstances and in light of the overall purpose of the housing benefit scheme. That was the way in which I think Commissioner Mesher (as he then was) had approached the matter in CH/3013/2003 (see in particular paragraph 34 of that decision). Looked at in that way, although I was concerned about the point when I granted permission, it does not seem to me it can properly be said that any dishonesty either on the part of a claimant or on the part of someone intimately involved with the process of claiming (perhaps in this case *[the claimant's sister]*) should necessarily lead to a conclusion that it would not be reasonable to treat a claimant as being liable. Rather, such might be regarded as one of many factors which may have relevance to that question."

Identifying the source of the liability may be of difficulty in cases where claimants have been placed by local authorities in accommodation pursuant to their duties. In *CH 1208/2003*, the claimant argued that his HB was not subject to restriction because he had been placed in accommodation by a local authority and his obligation to pay rent was to the authority rather than the owner of the accommodation. The commissioner, reversing the decision of the tribunal, stated that the mere fact that the local authority owed a statutory duty to house the claimant did not mean that his liability for rent was to the local authority: para 17. It was necessary to analyse how the local authority had actually discharged its duty.

The mere fact that payments are made to a person does not mean that the payments are made pursuant to a legal liability to that person. It is possible that the claimant is making payments of rent to a third party for the convenience of the landlord and her/his creditor. Thus in *CH 4922/2002* paras 16–17, the mere fact that the claimant was making payments to the landlord's mortgagee did not mean that they had taken on a legal liability for those payments which was excluded from HB under s130(2)(b).

Note also the, arguably *obiter*, view in *CH 257/2005* which holds that a failure of the landlord to supply an address for service contrary to s48(1) Landlord and Tenant Act 1987 only postpones when the rent is in fact to be paid (until the address is in fact provided) but does not mean that the claimant is not liable for the rent. Regrettably, the decision gives no real guidance as to what a HB authority should in fact do where there is a continuing failure by the landlord to comply with s48(1) Landlord and Tenant Act 1987 at the time of its decision on the claim. It is not immediately obvious that payment of the HB in this situation could lawfully be suspended under either regs 11 or 13 of the D&A Regs.

The fact that the liability must be legal can produce problems with young claimants and claimants with a degree of mental incapacity. These matters are discussed under separate headings below.

Evidence of liability. An agreement to pay rent can be enforceable even if it is not in writing so authorities should be prepared to take a broad view of the evidence required to establish liability for rent. HB is paid not only in respect of payments under a lease but also in respect of payments referable to licence agreements and other types of arrangement: see reg 12(1). Evidence of liability for rent may take various forms – eg, letter from a landlord, receipts for payment, bank withdrawal slips. Where the agreement is oral and the evidence is sparse, the authority should give due weight to the claimant's declaration on a claim form that s/he is liable to pay rent: *R v Sutton LBC HBRB ex p Keegan* (1992) 27 HLR 92 at 99-100, QBD. This cannot be carried too far, however; in *R v Derby CC ex p Third Wave Housing* (2000) 33 HLR 61, QBD, it was pointed out that although a party's stated understanding may be genuine, such a statement cannot be determinative of the legal status of an agreement.

There should be no need to produce a rent book, since a tenancy can exist without one: *R v Warrington BC ex p Williams* (1997) 29 HLR 872 at 876, QBD. In *R v Poole BC ex p Ross* (1995) 28 HLR 351, QBD, the Review Board decided that the claimant was not "liable" to pay rent because "there was no tenancy agreement and no steps had been taken to recover rent". Sedley J held (at 357–8) that neither of these findings could form a basis for the conclusion reached. As to the absence of a written agreement, it was clear from reg 10 HB Regs 1987 (now reg 12) that any kind of legal obligation sufficed to show that the claimant was obliged to make a relevant payment. As to the fact that the claimant's landlady had not sought to take proceedings, the short delay before the Board hearing and the fact that the landlady was aware of the HB dispute and could expect to be paid backdated benefit negated this factor.

In *Third Wave Housing*, Gibbs J provided guidance as to the requirements of a valid Review Board decision in a case where liability was in dispute. The applicant landlord (no point having been taken about the landlord's right to bring proceedings) was a voluntary organisation that arranged for foreign nationals to come to the UK to do voluntary work. They stayed in a hostel and claimed HB to pay their rent. Gibbs J stated that in considering whether the Board's decision that there was no liability for rent could be upheld, three matters had to be considered.

(1)   Was there material on which the finding could be made, whether individually or cumulatively?

(2)   Had the Board failed to take into account any evidence that was relevant to the question of liability?

(3)   Had the Board given adequate reasons or were they invalid as being sufficiently inadequate "so as not properly to indicate the basis of its findings"?

In that case, the judge concluded that the Review Board did have material before it in the form of evidence from the claimant to the effect that she had understood that she would not be pursued for rent arrears, her documentation had promised free accommodation, and she had made arrangements with a sister company to meet any shortfall in HB.

A further illustration of the range of factors that may be relevant to a determination as to whether a true liability exists may be found in *R (T) v Richmond-upon-Thames LBC HBRB* (2000) 33 HLR 65, QBD. In that case, a claimant with Alzheimer's disease lived with his landlady, who acted as his carer. The Board gave three findings as reasons for its conclusion that there was no liability for rent: that the carer acted as appointee for benefit purposes, that there was a close friendship between them, and that it was unclear how much rent had been paid prior to the HB claim. The judge rejected submissions that these factors were irrelevant and that it was irrational to use them as a basis for its finding (paras 25 and 26).

In *CH 1618/2002* para 12, the commissioner suggested that it was not permissible to consider evidence as to how the parties actually implement an agreement in determining the question as to whether a legal liability was created. The decision of the House of Lords in *James Miller & Partners Ltd v Whitworth Street Estates (Manchester) Ltd* [1970] AC 572 was cited for that proposition, but *Chitty* paras 12–124 points out that the decision only supports a proposition that subsequent conduct cannot be used as an aid to interpretation of the *terms* of the contract. Such conduct can be considered in determining whether in fact a legal liability was created at all. Such restrictions upon the evidence that may be considered seem to be inappropriate in the context of informal proceedings before a tribunal.

Is the liability genuine?: "sham" agreements. Particular difficulties may be created by cases in which a written agreement exists, but the local authority takes the view that it does not reflect the true intention of the parties. This was the issue in *CH 1171/2002*, where the commissioner referred to cases on general contract law as to the meaning of "sham": paras 10 and 11. *CH 1618/2002* was another such case. The commissioner stated that the first question was whether the document, on a proper interpretation and on the assumption that it was a genuine agreement, imposed a duty to pay rent: para 13. If that question was answered positively, then the issue of whether the obligation to pay rent was a sham needs to be considered:

"If as interpreted the document produced by the claimant does impose a duty to pay rent, the tribunal must consider whether the obligation to pay rent is a genuine part of the arrangement between the parties. If it is not, the term is a mere sham that was never intended to be implemented, but which was brought into existence to misrepresent the true arrangement between the parties and to conceal the truth from those dealing with them." (para 14)

The commissioner went on to give some useful guidelines as to the principles to be applied in answering this basic question.

(1)   It need not be shown that the whole document is a sham. "The sham may extend to the whole of the document or be confined to one or more of its terms": para 13. It is the term creating the liability for rent which is of importance, although the fact that other terms are intended to be genuine is probably at least some evidence that the whole document is genuine.

(2)   It is for the person alleging that a document is a sham to prove it. The local authority must therefore prove that the document is a sham: paras 15–16.

(3)   Whether a term is a sham is a question of fact: para 17.

(4)   The term is only a sham if neither party regards it as a genuine term: para 17.

(5)   If a term is genuine, the motivation behind the term is irrelevant to the question of whether there is a legal liability: para 17. So if an obligation to pay rent was only inserted to bring the claimant within the scope of the HB scheme, that does not mean that there is no liability for rent, although that may call into question whether the agreement falls foul of reg 9(1)(l).

(6)   The tribunal may take account of the way in which the contract has been implemented by the parties: para 18. However, a careful distinction must be drawn between a term which will never be implemented and one which might be implemented but has not in fact been enforced. Only the former terms are shams: para 19. Thus where a landlord does not enforce an obligation to pay rent while an appeal against a refusal of HB under reg 8 is outstanding, it does not necessarily follow that the obligation as to payment is a sham: paras 20–22.

CSHB 718/2002 considered the Scottish law on the subject of the creation of leases. Some of the points made in this decision are, however, of general application. The commissioner held (para 26) that where there is more than one agreement, each must be considered separately in deciding whether they are shams. She also said that non-payment of rent was evidence that the agreement was a sham (para 28). However, any explanation for non-payment (eg, lack of resources) would need to be taken into account.

Liability of the young. There is currently no lower age limit for claiming HB so claims by those under the age of 18 are possible. The law in England and Wales and that in Scotland require separate explanation.

In England and Wales, the age of capacity is 18: s1 Family Law Reform Act 1969. It is not possible for a minor to hold any legal estate in land: s1(6) Law of Property Act 1925. So if a person under the age of 18 signs a tenancy agreement, the agreement is treated as an undertaking by the landlord to hold the property in trust for the tenant: Sch 1 para 1(1) Trusts of Land and Appointment of Trustees Act 1996. However, that would not mean that the minor was not liable to make payments of rent, since the minor would still be obliged to meet the consideration for the creation of the statutory trust: namely the payments set out in the agreement. This issue does not arise in the case of other types of contract for the occupation of property such as a contractual license, in which no estate in land passes. Note also that a minor may succeed to certain statutory tenancies: see, for example, *Kingston-upon-Thames BC v Prince* (1998) 31 HLR 794, CA.

A minor is bound by a contract for "necessities" and it is therefore likely that accommodation would be regarded as a necessity. However, in deciding whether a minor can make a contract for the provision of accommodation, bear in mind the following statement of Scott LJ in *R v Oldham MBC ex p G* [1993] 1 FLR 645 at 662, CA:

> "If a minor is to enter into a contract with the limited efficacy that the law allows, the minor must at least be old enough to understand the nature of the transaction and, if the transaction involves obligations of a continuing nature, the nature of those obligations."

In Scotland, the position is governed by the Age of Legal Capacity (Scotland) Act 1991. Unless an exception applies (for which see s2 of the 1991 Act), any contract entered into by a person under the age of 16 is void: s1(1)(a). A contract entered into by a person aged between 16 and 18 may be voidable in certain circumstances: ss1(1)(b) and 3. In the latter case it is suggested that the analysis above applies. Even if the contract is void, *R(IS) 17/94* points out that the claimant might be liable under the law of reparation. Reference should be made to that decision for a detailed analysis.

Liability of the mentally incapacitated. This is now governed exclusively by the Mental Capacity Act 2005. It is not appropriate for this commentary to seek to summarise the terms of that Act. Where issues of mental capacity arise, readers should refer to one of the standard works on this Act.

Caselaw prior to the Mental Capacity Act 2005 held as follows. Firstly, where the claimant is contracting for accommodation, it is unlikely that a high degree of comprehension is required: see, for example, *CIS 754/1991* (an IS claimant with Down's syndrome had sufficient contractual capacity). In any event, in *CH 663/2003* paras 8–10, the commissioner held that a claimant incapable of making a contract could be entitled to HB, since the contract was only voidable and the claimant could not take the benefit of the contract for the provision of accommodation without accepting the burden of paying rent. Following on from *CH 663/2003*, *CH 2121/2006* emphasises that there is no minimum level of understanding of a party to a transaction that can act to render the contract void from the outset.

The judge in *Wychavon DC v EM (HB)* [2011] UKUT 144 (AAC) pointed out that decisions in *CH 663/2003* and *CH 2121/2006* must have proceeded on the basis that there was a contract. In *Whychavon DC v EM (HB)*, the tenancy agreement was expressed to be between the claimant's father and the claimant, signed by the father as landlord, but in the space for the claimant's signature it stated that the claimant was "profoundly disabled and cannot communicate at all." There was no one with the power to contract on the claimant's behalf. Hence, the judge decided that the claimant was not a party to any agreement and therefore had no liability to pay rent or any of the other types of payment in reg 12 HB Regs in respect of the dwelling she occupied as her home. Note that subsequent to the decision under appeal, an order was made in the Court of Protection giving the claimant's mother power to act on behalf of the claimant in some respects and so it was then possible that she could enter into a tenancy agreement on the claimant's behalf, allowing entitlement to HB. The claimant sought permission to appeal to the Court of Appeal on two grounds, first that Judge Mark was wrong to decide that there was no contract and second that he had failed to consider the claimant's liability to pay a sum for the occupation of her home under s7 Mental Capacity Act 2005. Judge Mark reviewed his decision and redecided the appeal in *Wychavon DC v EM (HB)* [2012] UKUT 12 (AAC); [2012] AACR 41. Although he decided that the first ground had no merit, he accepted that the claimant was liable to make payments in respect of her home, despite the absence of a contractual obligation. Because the accommodation was a "necessary" for her, the obligation arose either at common law or under s7 Mental Capacity Act 2005.

In Scotland, an agreement entered into by a person incapable of understanding the nature of her/his obligations is void and not merely voidable: *The Laws of Scotland* (1990) vol 15 para 661. The analysis in *R(IS) 17/94* would also apply in this situation however: see above. *Glasgow City Council v AL (HB)* [2011] UKUT 354 (AAC); [2012] ACCR 20 concerned the correct test to be applied to the issue of a claimant's legal capacity to enter contracts. The three-judge panel decided that a "transaction by transaction approach" to deciding legal capacity to contract represents the current common law of Scotland. It said:

"10.   We consider that the law is correctly stated by Professor W McBryde in Contract (Third Edition) paragraph 3–46 where he puts matters thus:

"The issue is primarily one of fact. There must have been a mental (or physical) defect which rendered the contracting party incapable of understanding what was being done so that there was no consent to that contract. (Our italics). A person's ability to understand or consent to other types of acts, or other contracts, is not the test, although evidence of surrounding circumstances is always relevant. The question of capacity will be decided on medical evidence and evidence of behaviour."

The above statement of the law is consistent with the legislative approach taken in The Adults with Incapacity (Scotland) Act 2000 relating to the appointment of guardians. The transaction by transaction approach described above by Professor McBryde should be followed by decision makers and tribunals faced with an issue of a claimant's legal capacity to contract. Paragraph 23 of the Appendix to R(IS) 17/94 and paragraph 6 of CSH 5/2009, insofar as it follows the contents of paragraph 23, no longer represent good law and should not be followed. The tribunal's application of a test of the claimant's general incapability of managing his own affairs was an error of law on their part.

11.   For the sake of completeness, we also specifically accept the submission of Mr Collins that it is not at all appropriate to base a conclusion of incapacity to contract (following the transaction by transaction approach) on a concession made by parties, especially by parties with an interest. In that regard also paragraph 23 of the Common Appendix to R(IS) 17/94 should not be followed. We also accept his submission that there is a presumption in favour of capacity and that that presumption can only be overcome by independent and informed evidence. In addition, we agree with Mr Collins that the appointment of an appointee for benefit purposes is by no means conclusive on an issue of incapacity to contract and is only an adminicle of evidence on that question."

Circumstances in which a person is to be treated as not liable to make payments in respect of a dwelling

9.–(1)   A person who is liable to make payments in respect of a dwelling shall be treated as if he were not so liable where–

(a)   the tenancy or other agreement pursuant to which he occupies the dwelling is not on a commercial basis;

(b)   his liability under the agreement is to a person who also resides in the dwelling and who is a close relative of his or of his partner;

(c)   his liability under the agreement is–

    (i)   to his former partner and is in respect of a dwelling which he and his former partner occupied before they ceased to be partners; or

    (ii)   to his partner's former partner and is in respect of a dwelling which his partner and his partner's former partner occupied before they ceased to be partners;

(d)   he is responsible, or his partner is responsible, for a child of the person to whom he is liable under the agreement;

(e)   subject to paragraph (3), his liability under the agreement is to a company or a trustee of a trust of which–

    (i)   he or his partner;

    (ii)   his or his partner's close relative who resides with him; or

    (iii)   his or his partner's former partner;

is, in the case of a company, a director or an employee, or, in the case of a trust, a trustee or a beneficiary;

(f)   his liability under the agreement is to a trustee of a trust of which his or his partner's child is a beneficiary;

(g)   subject to paragraph (3), before the liability was created, he was a non-dependant of someone who resided, and continues to reside, in the dwelling;

(h)   he previously owned, or his partner previously owned, the dwelling in respect of which the liability arises and less than five years have elapsed since he or, as the case may be, his partner, ceased to own the property, save that this sub-paragraph shall not apply where he satisfies the appropriate authority that he or his partner could not have continued to occupy that dwelling without relinquishing ownership;

[¹ (ha) he or his partner–

    (i)   was a tenant under a long tenancy in respect of the dwelling; and

(ii) less than five years have elapsed since that tenancy ceased,
except where he satisfies the appropriate authority that he or his partner could
not have continued to occupy that dwelling without relinquishing the tenancy;]

(i) his occupation, or his partner's occupation, of the dwelling is a condition of his
or his partner's employment by the landlord;

(j) he is a member of, and is wholly maintained (disregarding any liability he may
have to make payments in respect of the dwelling he occupies as his home) by,
a religious order;

(k) he is in residential accommodation;

(l) in a case to which the preceding sub-paragraphs do not apply, the appropriate
authority is satisfied that the liability was created to take advantage of the
housing benefit scheme established under Part 7 of the Act.

(2) In determining whether a tenancy or other agreement pursuant to which a person
occupies a dwelling is not on a commercial basis regard shall be had inter alia to whether
the terms upon which the person occupies the dwelling include terms which are not
enforceable at law.

(3) Sub-paragraphs (e) and (g) of paragraph (1) shall not apply in a case where the
person satisfies the appropriate authority that the liability was not intended to be a means
of taking advantage of the housing benefit scheme.

(4) In this regulation "residential accommodation" means accommodation which is
provided in–

(a) a care home; or

(b) an independent hospital.

Modifications

Reg 9 applies as modified by Sch 3 para 9(3)(a) HB&CTB(CP) Regs (see p1803) to a claimant who on 3 October 2005 was someone to whom reg 7(2) HB Regs 1987 as then in force applied.

Reg 9 applies as modified by Sch 3 para 9(5)(a) HB&CTB(CP) Regs (see p1803) to a claimant who on 3 October 2005 was someone to whom reg 7(5) HB Regs 1987 as then in force applied.

Reg 9 applies as modified by Sch 3 para 9(7)(a) HB&CTB(CP) Regs (see p1803) to a claimant who on 3 October 2005 was someone to whom reg 7(7) HB Regs 1987 as then in force applied.

Amendment

1. Inserted by reg 2(3) of SI 2007 No 1356 as from 1.10.07.

Definitions

"care home" – see reg 2(1).
"close relative" – reg 2(1).
"dwelling" – see reg 2(4) and s137(1) SSCBA.
"independent hospital" – see reg 2(1).
"long tenancy" – see reg 2(1).
"partner" – reg 2(1).
"payment" – see reg 2(1).
"resides with" – see reg 3(4).

General Note

The question of whether there is a genuine liability to make payments is dealt with under reg 8. However, reg 9 (made under powers conferred by s137(2)(i) SSCBA 1992) treats certain classes of people who are (or may be treated as) under a genuine liability to make payments as not being liable, thereby disqualifying them from HB. Cases often raise issues under both reg 8 and reg 9. See the General Note on reg 8 on p274 for how such cases should be dealt with.

The predecessor to reg 9(1) – reg 7(1) HB (General) Regs 1987 – was intended to identify cases deemed unacceptable to attract entitlement to HB – ie, where there was a risk of abuse of the HB scheme. Reg 9(1) lists the classes of people who are treated as not liable to make payments – eg, because of the category of agreement or the relationship between the landlord and the tenant. It requires careful treatment by authorities to determine the question of whether an agreement falls foul of its provisions. Local authorities and the First-tier Tribunal may find the following systematic approach helpful.

(1) Consider which of the sub-paras in para (1) may be applicable to the case under consideration. Examine carefully the various issues that arise under each and what must be proven and by whom.

(2) Ensure that the parties have had a fair opportunity to prepare cases on any new sub-paras identified by the First-tier Tribunal as being potentially relevant and which have not been dealt with in the submissions

of the parties. Note the discretion in Sch 7 para 6(9)(b) CSPSSA to decline to consider fresh issues, and the fact that a failure to give an opportunity to consider the evidence will render a tribunal decision erroneous in law: see below.

(3)   Consider all the evidence and make full findings of fact on all evidence, particularly where the evidence is in conflict.

(4)   Examine any of sub-paras (a) to (k) that may be applicable. Decide whether, on the findings of fact, the claimant's case falls within any of them. Give full reasons why this is found to be so, ensuring that all relevant factors have been explicitly considered.

(5)   If the case is found to fall within either of sub-paras (e) or (g), consider the question of whether the claimant has proved that the liability was not intended to take advantage of the HB scheme: para (3).

(6)   If none of the preceding sub-paras are found to be applicable, consider whether sub-para (l) applies (and see *CH 1586/2004* referred to below). Note the difference in language between sub-para (1)(l) and para (3) discussed below. Give full reasons for the conclusion on this issue. It may be prudent to consider sub-para (l) even if a case is found to fall within one of the other sub-paras.

In the discussion below, the words "landlord", "tenant", and "tenancy" are used as convenient shorthand for the person to whom payment is made, the person making payment for the home, and the agreement under which the home is occupied, even where the use of these words is not strictly correct as a matter of law.

Analysis
Paragraph (1): Introduction
The interpretation of the various sub-paras of para (1) must be informed by the fact that reg 9(1) has the potential to work "rough justice" and that "it is appropriate to give them [*the sub-paras*] the narrowest interpretation that is consistent with the policy of protecting the scheme": *CH 716/2002* para 11. But note that the judge in *Bristol City Council v JKT* [2016] UKUT 517 (AAC) was of the view that to rely on the fact that reg 9 is a deeming provision without taking into account the important part the regulation plays in protecting the HB scheme, in order to justify giving the claimant the benefit of the doubt and applying a narrow interpretation, is not the correct approach.

When considering sub-paras (a) to (l), it must be borne in mind that these offer 13 entirely separate grounds on which the authority may refuse HB on the basis that someone must be treated as if not liable for rent. As will appear from the Analysis below, certain issues will be of relevance to more than one of the grounds. However, it is important to consider the possible application of each of the sub-paras separately, to avoid confusion.

If the facts of a particular case bring it within the meaning of more than one of the sub-paras in reg 9(1), some general principles emerge.

(1)   If the First-tier Tribunal forms the view that a sub-para other than that relied upon by the authority in reaching its decision may be applicable, it is under a duty to warn the parties of that possibility and give them a fair opportunity to deal with the point, otherwise there will be a breach of natural justice and its decision will be set aside on appeal: *CH 396/2002* para 7. It makes no difference that there is evidence to support the tribunal's alternative ground for its decision: *CH 843/2002* para 7.

(2)   There is nothing in the language of reg 9(1) which compels the decision maker to consider para (1)(l) (whether a liability was created to take advantage of the HB scheme) in every case. If it were otherwise, and the opening words in 9(1)(l) "in a case to which the preceding sub-paragraphs do not apply" were said to create the duty, then in order for the local authority or the tribunal to be able to rely on reg 9(1)(l) it would first have to show that it had considered and rejected all of sub-paras (a) to (k). Moreover, it is suggested that on a reg 9(1) case the "issue" (eg, per Sch 7 para 6(9)(a) CSPSSA 2000) is not whether reg 9(1) in general is satisfied, but whether the claimant is not be be treated as liable to pay rent *because* s/he comes within one or more of the sub-paras in reg 9(1). Note, however, the view of Commissioner Levenson in *CH 1586/2004* that where a local authority or a tribunal has decided that none of the provisions in para (1)(a) to (1)(k) applies, the authority or tribunal is under a duty to consider para (1)(l). In his view, this duty arose because of the structure of reg 7(1) HB Regs 1987 (now reg 9(1)) and because "the very fact that regulation 7(1) was raised at all put 7(1)(l) into issue". With respect, it is suggested that the commissioner is wrong on both of these points and the conclusion he then draws from them for the reasons set out above.

(3)   Correct terminology should be used to avoid confusion: *CH 396/2002*. In that decision, the commissioner pointed out that speaking of any of the sub-paragraphs in terms of contrivance led to a danger of superimposing the test in sub-para (l) on the considerations appropriate to the other sub-paragraphs under consideration: para 11.

Paragraphs (1)(a) and (2): Non-commercial agreements
Para (1)(a) treats a person as not liable to make payments in respect of a dwelling if the agreement under which s/he occupies the dwelling is not on a commercial basis. It is to be noted that it is the agreement between the parties, and not just the payment made pursuant to that agreement, that must be assessed to ascertain whether it is made other than "on a commercial basis". In determining whether an agreement is not on a commercial basis, para (2) requires the authority to consider whether any of the terms upon which the person occupies the dwelling are not enforceable at law. See p286 for a discussion.

The agreement, and the relationship between the parties, must be looked at as a whole: *R v Sutton LBC ex p Partridge* (1994) 28 HLR 315 at 319-320; *R v Rugby BC HBRB ex p Harrison* (1994) 28 HLR 36 at 48-9, QBD. See also *R(H) 1/03* para 16.4. In paras 21–22 of that decision, the commissioner described a finding as to commerciality as a "compound fact" which depended on the primary facts found by the tribunal. In *CH 5147/2001* para 9, the commissioner stated that "the regulation is in the most general terms, allowing decision makers to take a variety of circumstances into account." All the relevant circumstances must be taken into account, but the weight given to them is a matter for the tribunal and a challenge to the weight given to the factors will only succeed if no reasonable tribunal could have approached the case in the way that the tribunal did: *R(H) 8/04* paras 23 and 29. On a further appeal, the Court of Appeal in *Campbell and others v South Northamptonshire DC and SSWP* [2004] EWCA Civ 409 CA; reported as *R(H) 8/04* ruled that the weighing of the relevant circumstances is not analogous to the exercise of a discretion (as to which factors to take into account or not); everything in the evaluation is purely factual. Accordingly, there can be no scope for ruling certain relevant facts out of consideration because to take them into account would be to infringe a claimant's rights under the European Convention on Human Rights (here, Art 9, concerning freedom of religion). See also the decision of Judge Wikeley in *Basildon DC v AM* [2009] UKUT 113 (AAC).

In *CH 3008/2002*, the commissioner pointed out that the first step under sub-para (a) is to identify the agreement which is alleged not to have a commercial basis. Unlike sub-para (l), it may be possible for an agreement to pass in and out of the scope of sub para (a). In that case, the reversionary interest of the landlord under an assured tenancy agreement had been transferred to the claimant's sister during the contractual term. At the end of the contractual term, a statutory tenancy came into existence by the operation of the Housing Act 1988. The commissioner remarked that he could not "understand how a tenancy that is created by law cannot be on a commercial basis" (para 11). This, at best, misleading sentence has been held to be wrong in *R(H) 10/05*, which should be preferred to *CH 3008/2002* on this point. As Commissioner Turnbull puts it in *R(H) 10/05*:

"the . . . words [in *CH 3008/2002*] would appear to mean that a statutory tenancy cannot, at the point when it arises, be non-commercial, and that it can only become so by virtue of factors subsequently occurring (eg the sorts of events which the commissioner went on to mention). That is in my view plainly not correct. The statutory periodic tenancy arising under the 1988 Act has essentially the same terms as those of the preceding fixed term tenancy (section 5(3)(e) of the 1988 Act). Further, it arises simply by reason of the termination of the previous contractual tenancy. If that contractual tenancy was not on a commercial basis, then it is likely that the statutory one will also not be so. For example, if, by reason of the relationship between the parties, the terms of the contractual tenancy are very unusual, those terms will be carried over into the statutory tenancy. It is true that either the landlord or the tenant can under section 6 of the 1988 Act serve a notice proposing different terms, in which case in the event of dispute a rent assessment committee is to fix such terms "as might reasonably be expected to be found in an assured tenancy". A failure to use those provisions might be an additional factor pointing to non-commerciality, but the mere fact that the tenancy had arisen by force of the statute would not mean that it would be necessary to point to such a failure, or to some other matter arising subsequent to the arising of the statutory tenancy, in order to demonstrate non-commerciality."

However, if the agreement under which a claimant occupies a dwelling is *genuinely* on commercial terms then it follows that the agreement is necessarily on a commercial basis: *CH 3282/2006* para 15.

It is for the authority to produce evidence to satisfy itself or the First-tier Tribunal that the agreement is not on a commercial basis. In dealing with a reg 9(1)(a) case, the tribunal should "ask themselves whether the evidence has satisfied them on the balance of probability that the principal basis on which the agreement was made was a non-commercial one. If the test is not met the liability is not excluded.": *R v Poole BC ex p Ross* (1995) 28 HLR 351, QBD at 358 (see below).

The word "commercial" is not susceptible of further elaboration and it is probably not possible to definitively state when an agreement is commercial and when it is not. An attempted formulation in *CH 2329/2003* para 7 that "the arrangement ... will be other than commercial only if it confers no benefit on the owner which is proportionate to the benefit conferred on the occupier" was rejected in *CH 3743/2003* paras 32–35. Commissioner Jacobs said in the latter case (para 34) that "rigid rules are inappropriate" when assessing whether or not an agreement was made on a commercial basis. However, in *CH 663/2003* the commissioner suggested that the term "on a commercial basis" connotes a financially justifiable relationship and also some generality as to who may take up the tenancy, which would shut out (as being "commercial") an arrangement set up exclusively for the benefit of a particular claimant. This test would also seem to fall foul of the broader approach advocated in *CH 3743/2003*, as it seeks to elevate one relevant factor to being a decisive factor. The approach in *CH 663/2003* conflicts directly with *CH 296/2004,* where Commissioner Jacobs again emphasised that no factor is decisive in deciding commerciality and, rightly it is suggested, pointed out that accepting less than the contractual rent rather than evicting the tenant may simply be bowing to reality and does not necessarily mean that the arrangment is non-commercial. *CH 296/2004* also makes the rather pithy point that "[Rachman] is not the only model of a commercial landlord". What this division in the caselaw seems to reflect is the truth of the statement made above that it is not possible to definitively state when an agreement is or is not "commercial". It is suggested that the approach advocated in *CH 3743/2003* and *CH 296/2004* should be preferred. This suggestion is given added force by *CH 2899/2005*, which holds that in so far as *CH 2329/2003* and *CH 663/2003* put forward what may be described as the *only* relevant factors for determining commerciality they are inconsistent with *R(H) 1/03* and should not be followed.

In *CH 1096/2008*, the claimant was a disabled person who was the beneficiary of a trust created for him by his mother and another of her sons. In *CH 663/2003* it had been held that the tenancy he had in accommodation rented to him by the trust was not on a commercial basis, in particular because the arrangement was essentially and strictly personal to him. Subsequently, the property was sold and another purchased, with the claimant's mother and the trust owners in the form of joint tenants in common. Accommodation was rented to the claimant, with his mother as landlord. Judge Mesher decided that the claimant's tenancy was not on a commercial basis. The existence of the family trust was an essential background. As tenants in common, the trust had a right to possession of the whole property and in practical terms the claimant was either living in the trustees' half of the property or in property in which the trustees were entitled to a half-share of the income. Secondly, the claimant's mother had testified to the tribunal that she would never evict the claimant. Thirdly, the claimant's mother had signed the agreement for the claimant as tenant and as landlord, and she had control (as trustee) of the account into which the claimant's DLA was paid, and so in effect she controlled how much rent was paid to her as landlord. Taken altogether, all these factors strongly indicated that there was something other than a commercial arrangement. However, the judge accepted that a motive other than profit and concern that the claimant had accommodation where he could receive the necessary care and attention did not make the arrangement non-commercial, nor did the mere fact that the claimant's landlord was his mother. Judge Mesher commented that the legislation "seems very ill-suited to providing humane outcomes in these cases."

The factors which may be relevant in assessing whether the agreement is on a commercial basis include the following.

The relationship between the parties. Even if the parties are not "close relatives" so as to bring them within the scope of sub-para (b), the authority may take into account the relationship between them: *R v Poole BC ex p Ross* (1995) 28 HLR 351, QBD. However, as Sedley J in *Ross* makes clear, there is nothing inherently non-commercial about letting to a close friend or relative, though the closer the relationship, the more critically the agreement may be examined. This point was emphasised by Commissioner Howell in *CH 4854/2003* where, following *Ross*, he stressed (para 11) that what is important is the nature of the arrangement: "the fact that the parties are friendly or related to one another cannot by itself turn a commercial arrangement or agreement into a non-commercial one". It is also relevant to have regard to factors such as the desire to have a reliable and trustworthy tenant and someone companionable, particularly in cases involving single elderly people such as *Ross*: see Sedley J at 359. Such factors may explain why friends have decided not to live on their own. In *CH 1076/2002*, the claimant's adult son was the half-brother of the landlord. The commissioner stated, at para 19.1, that such a fact was of very little significance in view of the time that had elapsed since the relationship between the claimant and the landlord's father. The mere fact that the parties knew each other and could trust each other "proves nothing".

The 1997 GM A3.66iv made the point that fostering children is a commercial arrangement and so former foster children who remain in the family home when they are no longer dependent should be treated as paying rent on a commercial basis.

The fact that a claimant is residing with her/his landlord should not, of itself, be a factor suggesting that the agreement is non-commercial. Anyone who has shared a property with a resident landlord will be aware how intensely commercial the relationship can sometimes be. It will be much more instructive to have regard to the personal ties, if any, between landlord and tenant. Not all cases where there is a close relationship between landlord and tenant will fall foul of sub-para (a). It depends on all the facts of the case.

In *CH 296/2004*, the commissioner considered what difference, if any, the fact that the claimant's father was his landlord made to whether the tenancy was on a commercial basis. He concluded that there is nothing necessarily incompatible in a commercial arrangement being made between a parent and adult child, though the close family element in the relationship may make such a finding less likely: see *R(IS) 11/98* para 8 and *CIS 195/ 1991*. Moreover, care and support being provided to a disabled adult son by a parent under the tenancy, although different in quality from that which a stranger would provide, is not necessarily incompatible with the arrangement being commercial. If it were otherwise – and the provision of care and counselling by the landlord to the tenant would render such a tenancy arrangement automatically non-commercial – then there would have been no need to make such service charges ineligible under Sch 1 para 1(f) HB Regs. Thirdly, the commissioner noted that the motivation for such arrangements will be different. However, even if the sole motivation for the arrangement is to ensure that the adult son or daughter is properly housed and supported, this does not necessarily mitigate against it being a commercial arrangement. Indeed, arrangements for supported independent living are a recognised part of the commercial rented sector. Fourthly, the commissioner emphasised that when considering the issue of eviction a realistic view should be taken about whether a landlord who is not a family member would have taken steps towards eviction, particularly where (as on the facts of this case) the claimant is able to pay a significant part of her/his rent even without HB.

In *CH 1097/2004*, the deputy commissioner confirmed (para 15), following *CH 296/2004*, that there is nothing inherently non-commercial in a tenancy agreement between members of the same family or between a provider and recipient of personal care. Neither did the fact that the landlords would not have let a room to anyone other than the claimant (a friend of theirs) mean that the tenancy was not on a commercial basis, considering all the facts of the case (paras 18–20). The friends wanted a commercial return for the room and without that return they would ultimately want the room back. Although they only considered letting the room to the claimant to assist her in difficult times (and would not have let it to anyone else), the letting was on a commercial basis even though the motivation for it was largely non-commercial.

However, in *CH 663/2003*, the commissioner – following *R v Rugby BC HBRB ex p Harrison* (1994) 28 HLR 36 at 48-9, QBD, and what he characterised as the peculiar and personal rights of occupation in play in that case – agreed that the agreement was not on a commercial basis because, although the rent may have been a commercial rent in that it had been assessed as a "fair rent", on the facts of the case the arrangement looked at as a whole was one which was strictly personal to, and set up for the benefit of the claimant and the claimant alone. It was not, therefore, an arrangement which would have been offered on the open market to anyone other than the claimant. "On a commercial basis" connotes a financially justifiable relationship and also some general class of person who may take the benefit of the arrangement, rather than one person for whom the arrangement is exclusively conceived. But see *CH 3743/2003* and *CH 2899/2005* above.

The living arrangements. If the living arrangements are of an unusual character, this may suggest that the agreement is not commercial. In *R v Greenwich LBC ex p Moult* [1998] unreported, 19 June, CA, the claimant's agreement gave him occupation of the sole bedroom, but the rest of the accommodation was stated to be shared with the landlady. On a renewed application for leave to move for judicial review, it was observed that the fact that the owner jointly occupied the common parts but kept no part of the property for her sole use was "not something which one would expect to find in a commercial letting". In such a case, however, the authority should give due weight to any explanation given by the claimant for an unusual arrangement.

The amount payable. In *R v Sutton LBC ex p Partridge* (1994) 28 HLR 315 at 319-320 319-320, Laws J rejected a submission that "commercial" simply meant that some payment which was more than minimal was made for the accommodation. The same point was made in *R v Rugby BC HBRB ex p Harrison* (1994) 28 HLR 36 at 48-9, QBD at 55, where it was said that even if the rent was broadly a market rent, the rest of the agreement might still lead to the conclusion that it was non-commercial. Profit is not necessary, provided the recompense is reasonable. GM A3.262 correctly emphasises the need not to place too much importance on this factor:

"Charging a low rent does not on its own make an agreement non-commercial. Many charities, voluntary bodies, and some individuals, choose to let properties at below market rents or do not want to make a profit from letting, but their tenancies may still be commercial arrangements if that is what the parties to the agreement intended."

Evidence of the making and amount of payments under the agreement. If there is no such evidence, that will be a factor the authority may take into account in deciding that the agreement is not a commercial one: *Moult* (see above). Such evidence may, of course, call into question the existence of any legal liability at all as well as the commerciality of the agreement. See the commentary to reg 8.

A careful distinction needs, however, to be drawn between a case where there is no evidence that *any* payments have been made and cases where the landlord has been accepting less than the contractual rent. In *CH 1076/2002*, the contractual rent was £400 and had been subject to a restriction of about 25 percent by the rent officer. The landlord accepted the amount payable by way of HB. The only reason given by the tribunal for finding that the agreement in question was on a non-commercial basis was the fact that the landlord had declined to sue for the balance. The landlord adduced independent evidence from a letting agent who stated that it was not unusual for private landlords to accept the amount of HB payable and not enforce entitlement to the rest. The commissioner held that in the light of that evidence and his own experience to the same effect, the landlord's decision not to enforce the balance could not be castigated as a non-commercial decision: paras 18 and 19.3. It was not irrelevant to the commerciality issue, but neither was it conclusive as the tribunal had found. Furthermore, the fact that the parties had not formally varied the agreement so as to provide for the new lower agreed rent was of little significance, since "lay people do not always attach the same significance to legal form as lawyers do": para 19.2.

A very common issue arising in these cases concerns the significance of a landlord deciding not to take immediate possession proceedings but deciding to await the outcome of an appeal against a refusal of HB. Considerable caution needs to be exercised before heavy reliance is placed on this factor. HB claimants are generally impecunious, having little or no disposable income and few or no assets against which a judgment can be enforced. Local authorities argue that no commercial landlord would wait long for rent; but the contrary argument in these circumstances is that if evicted, a tenant will have little incentive to pursue an appeal against a refusal of HB and there will be no chance, as against at least some chance, that a landlord will ever receive her/his money. A decision to await the outcome of a hearing by the First-tier Tribunal, even if that takes a few months, will rarely demonstrate non-commerciality. A decision to wait considerably longer, perhaps a year or more if the case gets to the Upper Tribunal, would have to be examined with more care. Legal advice received or the landlord's perceptions as to the prospects of success of the appeal would be of importance in such a case. Independent evidence from letting agents as to common practice in such a situation, similar to that adduced in *CH 1076/2002*, would also be of assistance.

If payments are made to a third party instead of the landlord, it does not necessarily follow that the agreement is uncommercial (or that the true liability is to the payee: see the commentary to reg 8). In *CH 2329/2003*, the claimant and his wife moved into their daughter's house while she was abroad and paid all the outgoings on it themselves. The commissioner upheld the tribunal's conclusion that the agreement was a commercial one, saying (para 7):

> "the arrangement between the owner of a property and the occupier will be other than commercial only if it confers no benefit on the owner which is proportionate to the benefit conferred on the occupier. In this case, the owner clearly benefits from the arrangement because it enables her to retain the house while she is abroad and have it occupied by somebody whom she can trust to look after it and its contents."

The parties' views. How the parties view the agreement may be relevant, but their views as to the nature of the agreement cannot be conclusive: *Partridge* at 318 (see p282).

Bad faith. As with sub-para (I), if there is evidence of bad faith on the part of the parties, it may lead the First-tier Tribunal to view their evidence with suspicion. However, the conclusion that the agreement is non-commercial would not automatically follow. In *CH 1325/2003*, the parties had created a tenancy agreement which had been backdated to 1998 to attempt to justify a claim for backdating. The commissioner held that despite that conduct, the tribunal had been entitled to decide that there was a binding commercial agreement from 2001, the year in which the agreement was created (paras 12–14).

Para (2): Non-enforceable terms. Para (2) explicitly requires the authority to consider whether the agreement includes terms that are not enforceable at law. However, it must be emphasised that it is not determinative of the question of non-commerciality, but is merely a factor to be placed in the equation. On the other hand, the fact that the Secretary of State has identified this as a factor of relevance means that it should be given considerable weight in the scales: compare *R v Westminster CC HBRB ex p Mehanne* [1999] 2 All ER 319, CA.

The presence of this factor requires careful disentanglement of the consideration of reg 8 and of reg 9(1)(a). Under reg 8, the question is whether there is a legal liability to make a payment. Provided that the landlord could sue for rent under the agreement, reg 8 is satisfied, whether or not there are extraneous, non-legal terms: see *R v Stratford-upon-Avon DC HBRB ex p White* (1998) 31 HLR 126. Under reg 9(2) the issue is whether *any* of the terms are incapable of enforcement in the courts, not merely those relating to the payment of the rent.

A number of points need to be made about the effect of para (2). First, only "terms upon which the person occupies the dwelling" are relevant. It might be, for example, that one agreement contained the terms of the claimant's tenancy and also provided for details of her/his employment. Provided that the agreement did not make the occupation of the accommodation conditional of the employment (as to which see sub-para (i) below) the terms of the employment cannot be considered under para (2).

The question of whether a term agreed between the parties is enforceable at law should be considered broadly. This is only one factor in determining commerciality and so authorities should not overly concern themselves with technical issues of whether a landlord or tenant could sue for breach of a particular term. It must also be borne in mind that contractual terms can be "enforceable" in a number of ways. Thus a term cannot be said to be unenforceable simply because a party would not suffer any financial loss as a result of a breach and so could not sue the other party for damages. It may well be that an injunction (interdict in Scotland) could be obtained to prevent the other party breaking the agreement.

Once non-enforceable terms have been identified, the issue arises as to how much weight they should be given. It is suggested that the more fundamental they are to the whole agreement between the parties, the stronger their presence suggests that the agreement is non-commercial. The clear thrust of para (2) is to deal with cases like *White* where the legal liability is merely incidental to the spiritual relationship between landlord and tenant.

Paragraph (1)(b): Payments to resident landlords who are close relatives

Para (1)(b) treats a person as not liable to make payments in respect of a dwelling if the liability under the agreement is to someone who is also resident in the dwelling and who is a "close relative". As the categories of unacceptable relationships between landlord and tenant have been more exhaustively defined than under an older version of the rule, it is suggested that it is questionable whether this provision is compatible with Art 8 of the European Convention on Human Rights.

"Who also resides in the dwelling". A subtle change in the wording of the provision may substantially change its effect. An older version of reg 7(1)(a)(i) HB Regs 1987 spoke of a claimant "who resides with" the landlord. That imported the definition in reg 3(4). Now, however, the reference is to a landlord "who also resides in the dwelling". This would appear to oust the definition in reg 3(4), though this may not have been intended.

The critical factor is what is meant by "the dwelling" for these purposes. Must the landlord share *all* the tenant's accommodation, or is it sufficient if common parts are shared? By SSCBA s137(1), "dwelling" is defined as:

> "any residential accommodation, whether or not consisting of the whole or part of a building and whether or not comprising separate and self-contained premises."

The effect of *R (Painter) v Carmarthenshire CC HBRB* (2002) HLR 447 and *R (Murphy) v Westminster CC* (2002) HLR 447 is that careful attention must be paid to the agreement between the parties and its legal effect and it is likely that most house-sharing arrangements will be construed as being an agreement to share a single dwelling, rather than an agreement to create two separate dwellings within the same building: see paras 11 and 12 of the judgment. The view stated in previous editions of this book – that if the claimant has a tenancy, rather than a licence, in the property, it is impossible to conclude that the landlord "resides in the dwelling" because that would be inconsistent with the exclusive possession that is the hallmark of a tenancy – was found in *CH 3656/2004* to constrain para (1)(b) too narrowly. Commissioner Fellner accepted that this view might apply where the claimant rented a bed-sit and shared only the common parts. It is not the case that the only circumstances which could come within para (1)(b) is where the claimant and landlord share a room; everything will depend on the facts. *CH 3656/2004* was followed in *R(H) 5/06*, where the claimant and her sister shared the living room, kitchen and common parts, and the commissioner said that the claimant and her sister were residing in the same dwelling: the test for the commissioner was whether the landlord and the claimant were sharing the majority of the accommodation in the residential unit. (The commissioner also rejected an argument that the terms of reg 7(1)(b) HB Regs 1987 (now reg 9(1)(b)) were discriminatory and breached Art 14 of the European Convention on Human Rights.) The same commissioner put the issue somewhat differently in *CH 542/2006* where he said (para 13) that where "a person is entitled to and does share essential living accommodation such as living rooms and a kitchen, it is not in my judgment right to regard the "dwelling" in respect of which he pays rent as being only the rooms of which he has exclusive occupation". On that basis the claimant in *CH 542/2006* was caught by para 1(b) because his son, who was his landlord, also resided in the dwelling. Following *CH 3656/2004*, it was not necessary that the landlord son was entitled to occupy all the accommodation comprised in that dwelling.

However, even where there is no tenancy, there may be sufficient physical separation between the parts occupied by the "landlord" and the parts occupied by the tenant to lead to the conclusion that sub-para (b) does not bite. An example of this might be a self-contained "granny flat" where there is insufficient evidence of a tenancy but where the elderly relative is left to live her/his own life.

"Close relative". This is defined in reg 2(1) on p225. GM A3.240 suggests, on the authority of *R(SB) 22/87*, that "brother" and "sister" includes half-brother and half-sister. That decision also establishes that a child, when adopted, no longer has any relation with her/his natural parents and other relatives. See also the discussion of *Bristol City Council v JKT* [2016] UKUT 517 (AAC) on p240. Note that step-brothers and step-sisters (unlike step-parents and children) do not fall within the definition. GM A3.243-245 gives useful examples of how divorce and death can affect who a person's "close relatives" are. Broadly, divorce and death sever the links with the family by marriage – eg, so that a parent-in-law is no longer to be treated as such.

Paragraph (1)(c): Liability to former partners

Para (1)(c) treats a person as not liable to make payments in respect of a dwelling if the liability under the agreement is to her/his former partner or her/his partner's former partner. The liability must be in respect of the dwelling formerly occupied by the claimant/partner and the former partner before they ceased to be partners.

It is regrettable that the exception in para (3) does not apply to these agreements. One of the most common forms of financial settlement on divorce consists of partner A, formerly the main breadwinner, taking on responsibility for the mortgage, and partner B living in the property until their children become independent (the so-called *Mesher* order). The agreement will often include some kind of contribution made by B towards the mortgage payments. Such arrangements are excluded from HB, and it is likely to cause substantial difficulties for those in the position of such claimants.

The definition of "partner" is in reg 2(1). There is no explicit requirement that the two relationships be consecutive and not separated in time, or that the occupation of the accommodation is continuous, provided that the accommodation remains the same. The phrase used in sub-para (c)(i) is "his former partner". Previous editions have suggested that in this context, "former" means "last", because if a relationship is in the distant past, the case for regarding such a liability as necessarily unacceptable is much reduced and this could justify a narrow interpretation of the sub-para under the principle identified in *CH 716/2002* para 11. This suggestion was rejected in *DH v Kirklees MBC and SSWP (HB)* [2011] UKUT 301 (AAC); [2012] AACR 16. Judge Mesher decided that "former partner" meant any former partner. He said (at para 23):

"I find nothing in [the claimant's] submissions to divert me from applying what in my view is the plain and ordinary meaning of the words of regulation 9(1)(c), that they apply where the liability is to anyone who at any time has been a partner of the claimant (or the claimant's partner), providing that the liability is in respect of a dwelling that they occupied together while they were a couple. To adopt any narrower meaning would involve an artificially strained construction that cannot be justified on the ordinary principles of statutory interpretation."

Judge Mesher considered whether the amending regulation (in the Housing Benefit (General) (Amendment) (No 2) Regulations 1998) which became reg 9(1)(c) was validly made and decided that it was. He also considered whether para (1)(c) should be given a narrow construction by virtue of s3 HRA 1998 if more women than men were disadvantaged by the provision. He decided that any difference of treatment did not amount to discrimination contrary to Art 14 of the Convention because it was justified as a proportionate response to a legitimate aim.

It appears that the liability must be to the former partner alone. If, for example, the former partner jointly owned the property with a third party, it would appear that sub-para (c) does not apply. It would, however, apply if the liability was to joint landlords who were *both* former cohabitees of the claimant and/or her/his partner, there being nothing to exclude the usual principle that the singular includes the plural: see s6(c) Interpretation Act 1978. However, in *London Borough of Bexley v KM* [2017] UKUT 354 (AAC), where the claimant's liability was not to her former partner alone, but to the former partner and another owner of the dwelling, Judge Jacobs said that the First-tier Tribunal should have considered the issue as discussed here. The judge had not had argument on the issue and thus did not decide on the issue, but commented that it was possible that, in an anti-avoidance measure, it would be sufficient if the liability were to the former partner along with others.

The argument that the "dwelling" occupied by the claimant must be the same as the "dwelling" occupied when the claimant and her/his landlord were a couple and that if the claimant occupies a bedroom plus the common parts in a property while being excluded from the landlord's bedroom, sub-para (c) does not bite, was rejected in *R (Painter) v Carmarthenshire CC HBRB (*2002) HLR 447 and *R (Murphy) v Westminster CC* (2002) HLR 447 by Lightman J. Mr Painter and Mr Murphy had lived as lodgers in properties owned by their landladies before forming relationships with them and sharing their bedrooms. When the relationships broke down, they reverted to their status as lodgers. In Mr Painter's case, a deed of separation between the parties declared that he had a right to live in the property on paying rent but that the parties would respect each others' privacy. Lightman J held, as a matter of construction, that the agreement gave Mr Painter a right to occupy the whole property and so he was occupying the same dwelling as he formerly occupied (para 11). The agreement to respect each other's privacy, while it effectively amounted to an agreement not to go into each other's bedrooms, did not define rights of occupation.

The judge went on to hold (para 12) that a similar agreement would be inferred in Mr Murphy's case in the absence of any evidence as to the precise terms that had been agreed between the parties. The judge then went on to decide that even if the "dwelling" presently occupied by the two claimants was only part of the "dwelling" formerly occupied by each of them, that would suffice to trigger the exclusion because "it is only necessary that it was in fact occupied by the claimant and his former partner during the period of their relationship" (para 13).

It was further argued that sub-para (c) discriminated against the claimants as being people who had formerly been in a relationship with their landlady, whereas a lodger who had never been involved in such a relationship would not be excluded from HB. The sub-para therefore infringed the claimants' rights under Art 14 of the European Convention on Human Rights, taken in conjunction with Art 8. Lightman J rejected that argument (paras 15–21 of his judgment).

A further human rights challenge to sub-para (c) was raised in *R(H) 6/05*. It was argued that since claimants with a liability for rent to their former same-sex partners were not caught by the sub-paragraph (because their former partners would not have been a "partner" as then defined in reg 2(1)), the regulation discriminated against heterosexual claimants. The challenge failed and a further appeal to the Court of Appeal was also unsuccessful: *Langley v Bradford MDC and SSWP* [2004] EWCA Civ 1343; reported as *R(H) 6/05*. Note that same-sex partners *do* now come within the definition of "partner".

Paragraph (1)(d): Responsible for landlord's child

Para (1)(d) treats a person as not liable to make payments in respect of a dwelling if s/he or her/his partner is "responsible" for a child of the person to whom s/he is liable. A person is only **"responsible"** for a child if s/he falls to be treated as part of the responsible person's family for benefit purposes. See the commentary on Part 4 of the HB Regs and in particular reg 20 (see p408). It follows that it is not sufficient that the claimant or her/his partner spends a lot of time caring for the child.

One issue of interpretation under this sub-para is the meaning of **"child of"** the landlord. It must be broader than a child for whom the landlord is "responsible", because under reg 20 only one person can be "responsible" for a child. Logically, it would mean any child of which the landlord was the genetic parent. It will also apply to a child who is adopted, who will not be regarded as being the child of her/his genetic parents: s39(2) Adoption Act 1976 and *Re Collins* [1990] Fam 56, FD. The genetic parents will also cease to be regarded as parents of the child when a freeing order is made under the 1976 Act prior to adoption: *Re C (Minors) (Adoption: Residence Order)* [1994] Fam 1, CA. Likewise, any child in respect of whom a parental order has been made pursuant to s54 of the Human Fertilisation and Embryology Act 2008 (the 2008 Act) is regarded as being the child of those in favour of whom the parental order is made. However, a man who provided sperm for "licensed" treatment under s28(6)(a) of the 2008 Act is not to be regarded as a father of the child. In a case where the Human Fertilisation And Embryology Act 1990 applies, if the woman receiving treatment has a partner, s/he is regarded as her/his child: s28(3). Where the 2008 Act applies, the person who is treated as the father or other parent of the child will depend upon whether the woman receiving treatment was married at the time of treatment (s35), whether agreed fatherhood conditions apply in relation to a man who was not the sperm donor (ss36 and 37), or whether the woman was in a civil partnership at the time of treatment (s42).

Those are the statutory presumptions that can be stated with confidence. Other situations are not so clear. It is not clear whether step-children are properly to be regarded as a "child of" the step-parent. It is suggested that unless the step-parent has parental responsibility for the child, the definition does not apply. Any person in whose favour a child responsibility order is made acquires parental responsibility for a child: s12(2) Children Act 1989. Guardians acquire parental responsibility for a child: s5(6) of the 1989 Act. In any of these cases, the child is probably to be regarded as a "child of" the guardian: s5(6) Children Act 1989.

The above concerns the legislation in England and Wales. Scottish family law is to be found in different statutes.

Para (1)(d) excludes a claimant from entitlement to HB if s/he (or her/his partner) is responsible for a child of **"the person"** to whom s/he is liable under the agreement. In *South Lanarkshire Council v DG* [2018] UKUT 417 (AAC), Judge Poole decided that the words "the person" may include "a person" – ie, the provision can apply if "the person" is only one of the claimant's landlords. The judge said:

"If, just by adding another person as landlord in a tenancy agreement, the effect of this provision could be avoided, it would lose much of its effectiveness. If housing benefit was payable, the landlord parent of the child would still benefit, resulting in a state subsidy, even if only one of multiple landlords. The general policy aim of Regulation 9(1)(d) would be subverted."

The validity of sub-para (d) was subjected to an attack in *R (Tucker) v Secretary of State for Social Security* [2001] EWHC Admin 260; (2002) HLR 500, CA. Maurice Kay J rejected arguments of invalidity in domestic law on the basis of conflict with the primary legislation governing child support (paras 5–9), that it offended against the principle of legality (paras 10–14), and that it was irrational (paras 15–20). He went on to hold that sub-para (d) did not infringe Art 8 European Convention on Human Rights on its own or in conjunction with Art 14 (paras 21–29, discussed on p128). The Court of Appeal rejected the claimant's appeal, essentially adopting the same approach as the judge.

Paragraph (1)(e): Liability to connected company or trustee

Para (1)(e) treats a person as not liable to make payments in respect of a dwelling if the liability is to a company or a trustee of a trust, but only if the person, or any of the other people listed in sub-para (e)(i) to (iii), is a director or employee (if the liability is to a company) or a trustee or beneficiary (if the liability is to a trust). This seeks to exclude a number of devices that in the DWP's view have been adopted in the past to circumvent the definition of "owner" in reg 2(1) and an older version of reg 7(1)(a)(i) and (ii) HB Regs 1987. These schemes have typically used the separate legal personality of a company or a trust as a vehicle to hold the freehold or leasehold interest in the home. The sub-para excludes agreements with a landlord that is a trust or a company where there is some connection between the landlord and the claimant or someone close to her/him. For convenience, in the following discussion the landlord is referred to as a "connected" company or trust, A is the claimant and B is the claimant's partner.

Who must have the connection? There are three categories of people that can have a relationship with the connected company or trust that brings the claim within the scope of sub-para (e) (collectively referred to below as "a relevant person"):

(1)   A (the claimant) or B (the claimant's partner);

(2)   C, who is a "close relative" of A or B who "resides with" A. See reg 2(1) for the definition of "close relative", and reg 3(4) for the issue of whether C "resides with" A. Note that the use of that phrase excludes the argument discussed under sub-para (1)(b) above;

(3)   D, who is A or B's former partner. See the Analysis to sub-para (c) above, though note that there is no requirement here that the home be the same as the one that D formerly occupied.

Connection with a company. The legal and everyday uses of the word "company" are different. Many people use the word loosely to denote any arrangement under which people trade in company with other people. In this context, a "company" is a company registered under the Companies Act 2006.

The agreement falls within sub-para (e) if a relevant person (see above) is a director or an employee of the company. A company is required by ss9(4)(c) of the 2006 Act to register the names of the officers, including directors, of the company Details of a company's directors may be obtained by carrying out a company search. These are held at the relevant Companies House for England and Wales or for Scotland. Company searches are also carried out by many independent organisations providing business services. The registration requirements, however, are frequently flouted and a person may still be treated as being a director of a company even when s/he is not registered as such. A director "includes any person occupying the position of director, by whatever name called": s250 of the 2006 Act. This may not extend to include a "shadow director". A shadow director is "a person in accordance with whose directions or instructions the directors of a company are accustomed to act": s251. However, in *CH 4733/2003*, Commissioner Howell said that it was "for consideration whether the term "director" in reg 7(1)(e) HB Regs 1987 (now reg 9(1)(e)) may need extending to include the concept of "shadow director" which it does not ordinarily do": para 37. Apart from those provisions, the term is not defined and the closest that caselaw has come to a definition is probably the following definition in *Re Forest of Dean Coal Mining Co* [1879] 10 Ch D 451 at 453: "commercial men managing a trading concern for the benefit of themselves and all the other shareholders in it".

A person is not necessarily an "employee" of a company simply because s/he does work for it. It may be that s/he is correctly to be seen as an independent contractor. The principal indicia of a contract of employment are an undertaking to provide work *personally* in exchange for remuneration and a sufficient degree of control by the employer over the employee: *Ready-Mixed Concrete (South East) Ltd v Minister of Pensions and National Insurance* [1968] 2 QB 497, CA. Authorities may find examination of the treatment of the claimant by the tax authorities helpful, but must be careful to reach their own conclusions. In *CH 4733/2003*, the commissioner said that the term "employee" has to be understood in the absence of any more extended definition as a person with some form of contract of service or an office holder: para 37.

Connection with a trust. This is likely to be a much more troublesome concept for authorities to apply, and so a short summary of the nature of trusts is attempted here. A trust may be defined as a relationship in which property is held by a person or persons (the trustees) for the benefit of a person or persons (known as beneficiaries). The law imposes strict obligations on trustees as to their dealings with the property that is the subject-matter of the trust and requires them to act absolutely in the interest of the beneficiaries. One person may be both a trustee and a beneficiary.

The trust is a flexible concept and trusts range from small trusts of family property right up to huge corporate trusts such as pension funds and charities. Under reg 9(1), it will be mainly the former category of trust with which authorities will be concerned. In England and Wales, where there is a trust of real property, there must be at least two trustees unless the trustee is a trust company.

Trusts may be express or implied. In the case of an express trust, there will be a document setting out the terms of the trust and usually spelling out who the trustees and beneficiaries are, though informal documents may suffice to create an express trust if sufficiently certain. In certain circumstances, the courts may substitute trustees or alter the terms of a trust, including who is to benefit thereunder. Placing property in a trust constitutes a "disposition" of property, and the express trust is therefore only valid if evidenced in writing: see s53(1) Law of Property Act 1925 and s2(1) Law of Property (Miscellaneous Provisions) Act 1989 in relation to trusts created before and after 1989. If there is no document complying with the statutory requirements, then an implied trust may exist. There is nothing in sub-para (e) to prevent it applying to implied trusts. Broadly speaking, implied trusts are of two types. A resulting trust is imposed by the law when Z purchases property, or contributes towards the purchase of property, and it is agreed or understood between the trustees and Z that Z will be entitled to the property or, in the latter case, a proportional interest in it. A constructive trust arises in the absence of an agreement wherever it is unconscionable for the trustees to ignore Z's interests in the property.

This is only the briefest sketch of the law in England and Wales and reference should be made to standard works on equity for a full treatment of the law of trusts. Scottish trusts law has many similarities but also many fundamental differences: see *The Laws of Scotland* (1992) vol 14 para 1 and the full discussion in that volume.

Under sub-para (e), a relevant person (see above) must be "a trustee" or a "beneficiary". As regards liability to a trustee, the normal rule in s6(c) of the Interpretation Act 1978 will apply here, so liability to more than one trustee will fall within the scope of the provision. However, it is suggested that the liability must be to a trustee *as such*, otherwise the landlord is not properly described as a "trustee". Where the home is not trust property, the provision does not apply. This is best illustrated with an example. A, X and Y are the joint trustees of a charity assisting the blind. X makes his living by buying, selling and renting property and rents one of his properties to A. Although A's liability to X is to a trustee of a trust of which he is also a trustee, X is not acting as a trustee when he rents the property to A and the agreement does not fall foul of sub-para (e).

As regards liability to a beneficiary, in *SD v Brent LB* [2009] UKUT 7 (AAC), Judge Bano rejected the claimant's contention that the term "beneficiary" does not extend to objects of a discretionary trust in whose favour no power of appointment has been exercised, but decided that for the purposes of reg 9(1)(e), a person is only a "beneficiary" of a trust if under the terms of the trust s/he can be permitted to occupy the dwelling which is the subject of the HB claim. He went on to consider and apply *Frish Limited v Barclays Bank Limited* [1955] 2 QB 541 and decided that reg 9(1)(e) is limited to cases where there is power under the trust (other than by the grant of a lease) to provide the claimant with the accommodation in respect of which the claim for HB has been made.

The exception. Para (3) applies to cases falling within sub-para (e). See p297 for a discussion.

Paragraph (1)(f): Liability to child's trustee

Para (1)(f) treats a person as not liable to make payments in respect of a dwelling if the liability is to a trustee of a trust, of which her/his or her/his partner's child is a beneficiary. For an explanation of the trust concept see the Analysis to sub-para (e) above. Again it is suggested that the provision only applies where the liability is to a trustee as such.

"His or his partner's child" is not to be equated with a child for whom either is responsible under Pt 4. It is wider than that. It would appear that it should be interpreted in the same way as the phrase "a child of the person" in sub-para (d): see the Analysis to that sub-paragraph.

Paragraph (1)(g): Liability of former non-dependant

Para (1)(g) treats a person as not liable to make payments in respect of a dwelling if, before the liability was created, s/he was a non-dependant of someone (B) who lived and continues to live in the dwelling. For the definition of "non-dependant", see reg 3 and the commentary thereto. It appears that someone could fall within this provision even if B has never claimed HB. B must, however, have resided, and must continue to reside in "the dwelling": see the Analysis to sub-paras (b) and (c) for the suggested significance of this phrase.

The exception. Para (3) applies to sub-para (g). See p297 for a discussion.

Paragraph (1)(h): Former owners

Para (1)(h) treats a person as not liable to make payments in respect of a dwelling in any case in which the claimant or her/his partner previously owned the dwelling if less than five years have elapsed since ownership ceased. A person ceases to own property, in England and Wales in any event, when a sale is completed and not when a contract of sale is entered into. Again the phrase "the dwelling" is used: see the Analysis to sub-paras (b) and (c), although the distinction discussed there is less likely to be of significance in this context. This para applies regardless of whether there has been a continutiy of residence – ie, even if the claimant lived elsewhere before returning to the property in question: *CH 3616/2003*; *CH 3220/2005*; *MH v Wirral MBC* [2009] UKUT 60 (AAC). Continuity is only necessary to come within the exception to para (1)(h), for which see below.

Sub-para (h) may apply even if a property has been divided into two separate properties or extended since the claimant owned it: *CH 3616/2003* paras 14–16. So if a claimant continues to occupy only part of the dwelling that was sold, s/he still falls within the scope of this provision because the new dwelling was part of the old dwelling.

Unless the claimant or partner fell within the definition of "owner" in reg 2(1), s/he cannot fall within the provision. See, for example, *GN v Sevenoaks BC (HB)* [2016] UKUT 271 (AAC).

Note: there is no requirement that the ownership of the claimant or partner immediately preceded that of the landlord, though it might be possible to make a similar argument as was adopted by the commissioner in *CH 716/2002* para 11 to support a conclusion that an intervening owner or owners would make sub-para (h) inapplicable.

As originally enacted in the HB Regs 1987, sub-para (h) had no application where the claimant had lived elsewhere before returning to the property in question: *CH 716/2002* para 11; *CH 5302/2002* para 14. From 21 May 2001, the harsh effect of the provision was mitigated by applying it only to cases where less than five years have elapsed since the relevant person ceased to own the property. The provision did not have retrospective effect in relation to claims made prior to 21 May 2001, but the five years could start to run prior to that date. In *CH 3616/2003* para 12, the commissioner decided that there was no longer any reason to hold that the provision should be limited in its effect. This conclusion sits uneasily with the commissioner's view in the earlier decisions that the word "continued" supported a view that the occupation of the property had to be continuous in order for the provision to apply: *CH 716/2002* paras 8–9. Since the regulation had not been amended save as to impose the five-year limit of its operation, it does not seem logical or in accordance with the normal rule of interpretation (that phrases used in previous versions of legislation and retained for present versions should be given the same interpretation as was adopted under the previous version) to give a more restricted meaning to "continued" under the new form. However, in *CH 4733/2003* Commissioner Howell was of the view, albeit *obiter*, that the interpretation placed on the wording of the amended form of reg 7(1)(h) HB Regs 1987 (now reg 9(1)(h)) in *CH 3616/2003* was the correct interpretation of the wording both of the amended and the unamended form of reg 7(1)(h). Commissioner Angus agreed with this interpretation in *CH 3220/2005*. He said that there is no ambiguity in the wording of either the old or the new version of sub-para (h) which would warrant reading into them a proviso or a precondition of continual occupation: para 10. In *MH v Wirral MBC* [2009] UKUT 60 (AAC), Judge Jacobs confirmed his interpretation in *CH 3616/2003* for the reasons given in that decision. The judge said that he gave a different interpretation to the previous version of the legislation in *CH 716/2002*, because it was open-ended in its operation. This is what led him to interpret the provision differently from the natural meaning of its language. That consideration no longer applies, as the provision is limited to five years.

The exception. There is an exception for anyone "who satisfies the appropriate authority that he or his partner could not have continued to occupy that dwelling without relinquishing ownership". Continuity of residence is needed to come within the exception (ie, the claimant must show that s/he was in occupation of the dwelling both before and after the sale); *CH 3616/2003; Bradford MDC v MR (HB)* [2010] UKUT 315 (AAC). The judge in *Bradford MDC v MR*, although he did not decide the issues, pointed out that para (1)(h) does not state that the occupation of the dwelling must be as a home (as is necessary for entitlement to HB under s130 SSCBA 1992) and that if all that is required is occupation of the dwelling by the claimant, and not occupation of it as a home, there would be a question whether gaining possession of a dwelling, while leaving it empty, could amount to occupying it for the purpose of the exception to para (1)(h).

GM A3.282 suggests that this exception is principally aimed at those who sell their home when a mortgage lender is "on the point of seeking possession". It is arguable that this is too strict an interpretation of the wording. A claimant who is in substantial mortgage arrears which are mounting and who has no realistic prospect of stopping the increase in the arrears could be said to fall within the provision, even if the mortgage lender has not yet taken proceedings. It would not be sound policy to require a claimant to run up a large amount of debt where s/he has a ready solution to the problem. Judge Poole in *RS v Fife Council and SSP (HB)* [2018] UKUT 322 (AAC) rejected the SSWP's submission that the exception could only be met if there was an immediate threat to continued occupation. It is not necessary to decide how far off threat of losing occupation is for the claimant to fall within the exception. She said:

> "No doubt the more distant the compulsion, the harder it may be to satisfy the exception, if that is the only operative factor. After all, the further off something is, the more time there is for other alternatives to crop up. But that is not to say it is impossible in all cases. In my view, it is not the law that people have to wait until there is an emergency or immediate threat before it can be found that there is practical compulsion *[the test adopted in CH 3853/2001]*. People should not be penalised for sensible planning when, put colloquially, the writing is on the wall, if they are not involved in avoidance. In *Simms v Registrar of Probates* [1900] AC 323 at 335, Lord Hobhouse stated "Where there are two meanings, each adequately satisfying the meaning (of a statute), and great harshness is produced by one of them, that has a legitimate influence in inclining the mind to the other....it is more probable that the legislature should have used the word in that interpretation which least offends our sense of justice". It seems to me that great hardship could potentially be caused by adopting the narrow interpretation suggested by the SSWP, if people facing genuine problems with continued ownership were excluded from HB. But it is not necessary to adopt such a restrictive interpretation as suggested by the SSWP to give effect to the wording in Regulation 9(1)(h). Practical compulsion leading to a person being unable to continue to occupy without relinquishing ownership is sufficient. In difficult cases, tribunals may be assisted by bearing in mind the mischief that Regulation 9(1)(h) aims to prevent, *[...]*. Where there is a genuine and serious problem with continued occupation without a sale and no real alternatives, then the circumstances may disclose practical compulsion."

GM A3.282 also suggests that the rule applies in cases of shared-ownership, where a tenant cannot afford the payments on the percentage owned and the housing organisation agrees to take back a part of the ownership and enable the tenant to rent a larger share. However, as sub-para (h) treats the claimant as not liable only where s/he or her/his partner previously owned "the dwelling" and has ceased to own "the property", it is arguable that as the claimant (or partner) has not given up ownership of the whole dwelling sub-para (h) cannot apply at all in such cases.

In *CH 3853/2001*, the claimant had inherited a house from his mother. He felt under a moral obligation to share the property with his sisters. He sold it and divided the proceeds of sale between them, and then agreed with the purchaser that he could continue to live in the property. The commissioner adopted a test (para 16) of whether the claimant was under a "practical compulsion" to sell the property. He held that the claimant was not, since it would have been possible for the claimant to take out a mortgage in order to meet the moral obligation. This will include consideration of both the reasonableness of the sale as well surrounding matters which could have acted to remove the need to relinquish ownership (eg, finding a new or alternative employment or sub-letting part of the property): *CH 1586/2004* para 12.

CH v Wakefield DC [2009] UKUT 20 (AAC) considered the relevance of whether the claimant has made enquiries as to alternatives, or has taken advice. Judge Ward thought that here, the tribunal may have applied the wrong test, concerning itself with the adequacy of enquiry of itself, rather than as a route to establishing what alternative options were open to the claimant. Although it is true that sub-para (h) is not applying a test based on a claimant's conduct of itself, showing what steps have been taken to explore alternatives, whether by direct action taken by a claimant or by the claimant obtaining suitable advice, may well be an integral part of establishing whether or not it was possible for the claimant and partner to remain in occupation without relinquishing ownership. Judge Ward pointed out that as it is for a claimant to make out her/his case on this aspect, a claimant who does not address what steps have been taken to explore alternatives does so at her/his peril. As indicated in *R(H) 6/07*, there may be exceptional cases where a claimant's circumstances mean that investigation of options may not be required, but it follows that in cases which are not exceptional, it is likely to be a material factor.

The motive of the claimant in disposing of the property is irrelevant in determining the applicability of sub-para (h): *CH 396/2002* para 7. It is also important to note that the "practical compulsion" in *CH 3853/2001* does not require some *legal* compulsion to dispose of the property: *CH 396/2002* para 15. However, although the claimant's perceptions may be relevant as evidence of what is actually possible – so that in an exceptional case a claimant may be under so much stress that it is the interests of her/his own mental health to dispose of ownership as quickly as possible without investigating other possibilities short of sale – it has to be borne in mind that the statutory test to be applied is "could not" and not "believes s/he could not": *R(H) 6/07*.

A further important limitation of sub-para (h) is demonstrated by *R(H) 6/04*, in which the former owner was the claimant's husband who had left the country at the time that the property was let by the new owner to the claimant. The commissioner held that in order for sub-para (h) to bite, the former owner had to be the claimant's *current* partner: para 31. There was evidence in the case that the husband might no longer be living in the same household as the claimant, which would mean that he was no longer her partner.

Paragraph (1)(ha): Former tenants of long tenancies

Para (1)(ha) treats a person as not liable to make payments in respect of a dwelling if s/he or her/his partner was previously a tenant of a long tenancy of the dwelling, if less than five years have elapsed since the long tenancy ceased. This is a similar provision to that in sub-para (h). "Long tenancy" is defined in reg 2(1) and must be for a term of more than 21 years (see p229).

The exception. There is an exception for anyone who satisfies the appropriate authority that s/he or her/his partner could not have continued to occupy that dwelling without relinquishing the tenancy. See above for commentary on the similar exception in sub-para (h).

Paragraph (1)(i): Tied accommodation

Para (1)(i) treats a person as not liable to make payments in respect of a dwelling if s/he or or her/his partner is employed by the landlord, and it is a condition of the employment that the dwelling be occupied. There must be a relationship of employment: see the Analysis to sub-para (e) above. Furthermore the occupancy must be a *condition* of the employment. That means that it must be compulsory and not merely a "perk of the job" or provided by the employer to assist resettlement. Where the claimant or partner has a written contract of employment, it will normally be apparent from the terms and conditions therein whether occupying the property is truly a "condition". Otherwise the best indicator will come from considering the nature of the job: is there something about it which makes residence on a premises necessary? The classic example is a pub landlord.

Sub-para (i) only applies during the period of employment. Once the employment ends, a liability to the former employer for rent may attract HB.

Paragraph (1)(j): Members of religious orders

Para (1)(j) treats a person as not liable to make payments in respect of a dwelling if s/he is a member of, and wholly maintained by, a religious order. The words in brackets "disregarding any liability he may have to makes payments in respect of the dwelling he occupies as his home", preclude any argument that the liability for rent prevents the claimant from being "wholly" maintained by the order. However, the maintenance must be whole and not partial.

"Religious order" is not defined. GM A3.256 suggests that a religious order "consists of a group of people who have given up all material belongings and have offered their services free for the benefit of the order". GM A3.257 draws a contrast with religious communities, which "may do paid work or keep their own possessions" and may therefore qualify for HB.

The principal question in *CSPC 677/2007* was whether the claimant was a member of a religious order who was "fully" maintained by the order for the purposes of pension credit (PC). Commissioner May decided that she was. The claimant was a member of a religious order of Carmelite Nuns in which each sister paid all her own income into the monastery's account. Although only certain people could withdraw the money from the bank, each sister retained the right to her share of the money and if anything was needed, she could request cash, or payment for what was needed out of the account. If any of the sisters could not contribute to the funds, her expenses were covered by others' contributions. Commissioner May said that once funds are held in common for their application for the accommodation and maintenance of the members, it was difficult to advance the proposition that the members who benefit from this are not fully maintained, albeit that they themselves have, in some instances, made a contribution towards the funds of the order. He decided that for the purposes of whether a sister is maintained fully, her income, and the contribution of that income to the order, must be ignored. The government had (eg, through letters from the Minister at the time) given the impression that there was a distinction to be made between self-maintaining and other religious orders. However, the statutory language did not permit such a distinction. The commissioner considered whether, but did not accept that, the provisions were contrary to the European Convention on Human Rights, Art 1 Protocol 1 and Arts 8 and 14.

The meaning of "religious order" and the issue of being "fully" maintained by an order for PC purposes were considered by a three-judge panel in *SSWP v Sister IS & Sister KM* [2009] UKUT 200 (AAC). The claimants argued that they were not members of a religious order because their orders were without centralised authority. This was not accepted by the Upper Tribunal who said that the term was used in a broad sense. Both claimants were "fully" maintained by their orders even though they were themselves the source of funds for the order, via their work and state benefits. The focus is on who it is that maintains a claimant, not where the money comes from. Both claimants were bound by vows of poverty and had no personal benefit from income they generated or received. The income therefore did not maintain the claimants; they were wholly reliant on the religious order for maintenance. The Upper Tribunal also decided that the provision barring entitlement to PC was not unlawful discrimination under the Human Rights Act 1998 because the discriminatory effect of the provision could be removed without conferring any advantage on the claimants. As the claimants would still be caught by the provision if it referred to "members of orders" rather than "members of religious orders", they were not victims for the purpose of the Act. An appeal to the Court of Appeal against the decision in *SSWP v Sister IS* was dismissed: *Scott v SSWP* [2011] EWCA Civ 103; [2011] AACR 23.

Paragraphs (1)(k) and (4): People in residential accommodation
Para (1)(k) treats a person as not liable to make payments in respect of a dwelling if s/he is in residential accommodation. "Residential accommodation" is defined in para (4). Note also the modifications made by para 9 Sch 3 HB&CTB(CP) Regs (see p1803).

In *CH 1326/2004* (which was dealing with the pre-October 2005 form of paras (1)(k) and (3) of reg 7 HB Regs 1987, but the reasoning may remain applicable), it was accepted that where a person is living in a home run by a person registered to run a care home but is not in fact receiving the care which is contemplated in the registration then para (1)(k) will not apply to that person, as it is the care provided to the person in such a home (and not just residence in such a home) which is key to whether they fall within the meaning of "residential accommodation".

Paragraph (1)(l): Liability created to take advantage of the HB scheme – "contrived" agreements
Para (1)(l) treats a person as not liable to make payments in respect of a dwelling if the liability was created to take advantage of the HB scheme. It only applies where none of the preceding sub-paragraphs apply. There is a reference to the HB scheme established under Part 7 of the SSCBA 1992. This would suggest that if the liability was created when one of the predecessor schemes was in force, the provision cannot apply: compare *R(IS) 14/93* para 15.

Authorities need to consider all the evidence and relevant factors in determining whether an agreement was created to take advantage of the HB scheme. The usual trap into which decision makers fall is to identify one factor which they find particularly persuasive and rely solely on that matter without considering the entire background to the agreement and its contents.

1. General principles.
Before setting out the factors which will usually fall to be taken into account in para (1)(l) cases, it is useful to set out some points of general application.

"The liability was created". What must be examined is whether the liability to make payments was created to take advantage of the HB scheme. It would follow that the importance of the relevant factors (see below) must be judged as at that time and not in the light of events which only became known to the parties subsequently: *CSHB 718/2002* para 33. However, that decision also notes (para 34) that an intention to abuse the HB scheme in the future would suffice to bring sub-para (l) into play. In *CH 3008/2002,* the claimant took a tenancy from a landlord with whom she had no relationship. During the contractual term, the landlord transferred the property to the claimant's sister. The contractual term subsequently expired and a statutory tenancy came into force by virtue of the Housing Act 1988. The commissioner confirmed (para 14) that since the claimant was unrelated to her landlord at the time that the tenancy was created, sub-para (l) could not apply to the creation of the contractual agreement. However, as to whether the liability could be "created to take advantage" of the HB scheme thereafter, he said (para 14):

"But what about the statutory protected [this should probably be 'periodic'] tenancy? The claimant's liability for rent has arisen under that tenancy since 16th July 1995. That tenancy was created by operation of law. How can a tenancy that exists by operation of law have been created with the necessary purpose? One answer may be this. If the sisters allowed the tenancy to come into existence when it could have been prevented, then it may be possible to find that the liability arising under the tenancy was created to take advantage of the scheme."

It is suggested that this is contrary to the wording of sub-para (l). When a statutory periodic tenancy is created at the point that the contractual period elapses, it is created by the Housing Act 1988 and not by the parties. It is hard to see how the parties "create" anything when a statutory periodic tenancy is allowed to come into force; rather, they allow the legislation to extend the tenancy. Moreover, nothing which is said in *R(H) 10/05* about the correctness of parts of *CH 3008/2002* detracts from this argument.

Even if the commissioner is right, extreme caution is required before it will be legitimate to make a finding along the lines that he indicates. If the tenancy is not an assured shorthold tenancy giving an absolute right to terminate it under s21 of the 1988 Act, the landlord may be powerless to act. As to the tenant, it will be a rare case in which they can be blamed for choosing to stay in existing accommodation rather than face a move into new accommodation.

It should be borne in mind in similar cases that it may be necessary to examine the motivation of the original agreement. Thus, if the relative agreed with the original landlord that the property would be purchased shortly after the original tenancy, it might be possible to find that the original agreement fell foul of sub-para (l) if all the other circumstances justified such a finding.

"To take advantage of the HB scheme".The meaning of "to take advantage" in this context means "to abuse" and not, as in some other parts of social security legislation such as SSCBA s73(1)(d), to benefit from or to avail oneself of the scheme. If that were the case, no one could qualify for HB.

Commissioner Jacobs dealt with the meaning of "to take advantage of the scheme" in *CH 39/2007*. He said that it means something akin to abuse of the scheme or taking improper advantage of it. It did not mean merely using the scheme, nor did it mean "make the most of the opportunities that it presents". If it did, there would be no market for tenants requiring financial support for their rent. He said at para 19: "Many landlords use the housing benefit scheme as a way of financing the purchase of property as an investment or of financing a business, but it is not the function of regulation 9(1)(l) to impede the proper operation of the private rented housing sector." The provision has to be interpreted in the context of other control mechanisms provided for in the legislation – eg, the various rules for restricting "eligible rent", now in regs 12C to 14 of both the HB and the HB(SPC) Regs and in Sch 3 paras 4 and 5 HB&CTB(CP) Regs.

In general, the mere fact of letting only to tenants who have a genuine need for support, and to whom the landlord will provide support, with a view to obtaining a higher rent eligible for HB, is not an abuse: *Salford CC v PF* [2009] UKUT 150 (AAC). However, there will be an abuse if the rent is unfairly or improperly high, having regard in particular to the cost of providing the accommodation.

In *R vSolihull MBC HBRB ex p Simpson* [1995] 1 FLR 140 at 148E-F, CA, Kennedy LJ in the Court of Appeal cited Sedley J at first instance (1993) 26 HLR 370 at 378 as describing the purpose of the former reg 7(1)(a), (b) and (c) HB Regs 1987 as being "to shut out certain arrangements which, in the Secretary of State's view, would amount to an abuse of the system" and added:

"I believe that to be a correct approach, provided that abuse is not equated with bad faith on the part of the applicant. Bad faith would, of course, be persuasive evidence of abuse, but the appropriate Authority might in some cases properly conclude that there was a breach of regulation 7[(1)(l)] without it. In other words, the use of the words "take advantage" shows that at least in the eye of the beholder there has to be conduct which appears to some extent improper."

In *R v Stratford-upon-Avon DC HBRB ex p White* (1997) 30 HLR 178, QBD, Dyson J criticised this test on a number of grounds. He asked who was to judge whether there was impropriety, by what criteria, and what the policy of reg 7 HB Regs 1987 (now reg 9 HB Regs) was. The decision was reversed on appeal (1998) 31 HLR 126, CA. Mr White was a member of a religious commune, the Jesus Fellowship Church, that required certain categories of members to live in a commune, maximise their income and pool it. The Review Board found that there was a legal liability between Mr White and the Trust set up by the commune for the purposes of reg 6 HB Regs 1987 (now reg 8) but found that the obligation to make payments was "inextricably bound up" with the obligation to pool income. The Court of Appeal, holding that Mr White did not fall foul of subpara (1)(l), endorsed the interpretation of the subparagraph in *Simpson*:

"In my judgement the precise language of subpara [(l)] indicates that there must have been some purposive conduct on the part of those seeking benefit, the liability must appear "to have been created to take advantage". This connotes that something has been contrived or devised for the purpose of taking advantage of or exploiting the scheme. There is no evidence to suggest that Mr White (and, I would add, the landlord) has behaved in such a manner or been motivated by dubious ingenuity to create the liability." (Otton LJ at 137)

"For my part I share the judge's unhappiness at attempts to graft onto the express language of regulation 7(1)[(l)] an additional requirement .... having said that, I have little difficulty in finding in the language of paragraph [(l)] the connotation of an abuse of the housing benefit scheme." (Peter Gibson LJ at 141)

The mere fact that the arrangements between landlord and tenant are unusual and involve the creation of a "device of some sort" does not necessarily lead to the conclusion that the agreement is contrived: *R(H) 7/05* paras 46–47, though obviously the use of such means will call for some sort of innocent explanation.

No presumption against the claimant. Finally, there is no presumption against the claimant that s/he is guilty of abusing the scheme: see Sedley J in *Simpson* at 378. Once it is established that the claimant is under a liability to make the payments, the burden of proof is on the authority to show some grounds for believing that abuse exists. The words "the appropriate authority is satisfied" allow the authority to reach its own conclusion on the point but, as elsewhere in administrative law, it cannot make a decision for which there is insufficient evidence or which is not properly reasoned. In *White*, Dyson J suggested that the concept of the onus of proof was unhelpful. However, it may well be useful in cases where evidence is sparse, since if there is not enough information before an authority or the First-tier Tribunal to give rise to an inference of impropriety, reg 9(1)(l) cannot be applied. If there is enough evidence to allow the inference to be drawn, however, it may then be legitimate to examine whether the claimant has any explanation for the circumstances which do not relate to the obtaining of HB: see Kennedy LJ in *Simpson* at 148F.

A failure by a Review Board to apply the burden of proof under sub-para (1)(l) properly was Richards J's primary reason for the quashing of the Board's decision in *R v Greenwich LBC ex p Dhadly* (1999) 32 HLR 829. It is worthy of note that this step was taken even though the Board specifically reminded itself at the start of its statement of reasons that the burden of proof to show the applicability of para (1)(l) rested on the local authority. Richards J examined the whole of the decision and considered that it showed that the Board might well not have applied the principle it stated at the outset.

2. Obligations of the First-tier Tribunal.

In *R v South Tyneside MBC ex p Tooley* [1996] COD 143 at 144, QBD, Ognall J stated that a Review Board's decision letter relating to a decision that a claimant falls foul of reg 7(1)(l) HB regs 1987 (now reg 9(1)(l)) must include the following matters. It is suggested that the same approach is applicable to the First-tier Tribunal.

(1) A summary of the claimant's case as to why s/he does not come within para (1)(l) (though note there is no presumption against the claimant).

(2) An account of the evidence, if any, given by the claimant in support of her/his case.

(3) The conclusion.

(4) A reasoned statement as to why it was concluded that the tenancy was created to take advantage of the HB scheme. The facts will often be open to a number of possible interpretations and if a tribunal concludes that a tenancy is "contrived" its decision must contain a statement of reasons which is sufficiently detailed for the claimant to be able to understand why an adverse interpretation has been preferred to a favourable one: see Sedley J in *Simpson* at 378 and *Sier* (Latham J). In *ex p Dhadly*, Richards J also emphasised failures by the Board to deal with aspects of the evidence called and submissions made by the claimant as a reason for quashing its decision. The message is clear: a decision must show that all relevant evidence and factors have been considered or it will be vulnerable to challenge.

It is not essential that the First-tier Tribunal should consider the intentions of landlord, tenant and any other relevant party separately in every case. What is necessary depends on the facts: *Jones v City of Glasgow DC HBRB* [1997] unreported, 4 July, CSOH.

3. The relevant factors.

It must be emphasised that the whole of the circumstances of the case must be considered and that none of the following can be determinative in any one case.

The means, circumstances and intention of the tenant. A tenant will often have a number of motives or purposes in entering into an agreement to pay rent. The relevant question for the purposes of reg 9(1)(l) is which of these purposes was the tenant's dominant purpose. In *Simpson*, Kennedy LJ observed, at 149A-C:

"Of course [attracting HB] was one of the aims. That is why the applicant properly made inquiries to try to establish if Housing Benefit would be payable before he made the agreement, but it is at least arguable that his dominant purpose when he entered into the tenancy agreement was not to obtain Housing Benefit but to provide accommodation for his family .... In my judgment, the Board had to reject that conclusion if it was to find that the applicant created his liability to make payments to take advantage of the Housing Benefit Scheme ...."

It follows that, subject to what is said below about the circumstances and intentions of the landlord, reg 9(1)(l) cannot apply where the claimant's dominant purpose is to provide a home for her/himself and her/his family. In cases where it is accepted that the claimant and her/his family are actually living in the accommodation, it will often be difficult for the authority to show that this was not the dominant purpose of the tenancy, even when the circumstances surrounding the creation of the tenancy seem to be unusual. Tenants who are reliant on income-related benefits do not have much bargaining power in the housing market and often have to take whatever is available. This will often be the explanation for cases where relatives have purchased a house and rented it to the claimant. *Simpson* was one such case, where the applicant and his partner had a severely disabled daughter and lived in unsatisfactory council accommodation. The council was unable to move the family, and the partner's father purchased the home so as to facilitate proximity to schools and the hospital. Other cases of this type are *R v Milton Keynes BC HBRB ex p Macklen* [1996] unreported, 30 April, QBD and *R v Gloucestershire CC ex p Dadds* (1996) 29 HLR 700, QBD.

In particular, it is not sufficient to establish abuse for the authority to show that one or both of the parties knew at the time the agreement was made that the claimant would be unable to pay the rent without recourse to HB. This may be taken into account: Sedley J in *Simpson* at 376; *R v Sutton LBC HBRB ex p Keegan* (1992) 27 HLR 92 at 99-100, QBD; *R v Poole BC ex p Ross* (1995) 28 HLR 351, QBD; *CH 2516/2003* para 4. However, it will rarely be a factor of great weight. Many recipients of HB will be in this position and, as Sedley J stated in *Simpson* at 379:

"To use this fact to deny an applicant benefit is to undermine the whole purpose of the Scheme by making the claimant's need count against instead of for him."

This point was re-emphasised by Peter Gibson LJ in *White* at 142.

However, the converse to this, namely that the claimant did not anticipate having to claim HB when s/he took on the rent liability or has met the liability her/himself from time to time, may often be a very good indication that there was no attempt to take advantage of the HB scheme: Kennedy LJ in *Simpson* at 149E and Otton LJ in *White* at 137.

Whether or not the claimant has sought other accommodation on the open housing market before entering into the tenancy may be relevant in some circumstances but equally it may be entirely reasonable for someone who is offered a tenancy on beneficial terms by a friend or relative to take up that offer without bothering to search elsewhere. The absence of a prior search for accommodation elsewhere does not necessarily mean that the tenant's dominant purpose in entering into the agreement was other than to provide her/himself and any family with a roof over their heads.

In some cases, it may be appropriate to consider the conduct of someone other than the tenant: *CH 1419/2005* para 15. In that case, the claimant was a young man who was severely mentally impaired and had severe learning difficulties. His mother worked in the HB section of the local authority and helped her son enter into a joint tenancy agreement with herself and her husband in respect of a flat the claimant had previously lived in with his grandmother. On these facts, Commissioner Jacobs accepted that the mother's conduct could in principle be relevant to the question of whether the tenancy had been created to take advantage of the HB scheme. In his view, in a case where a tenant is unable to act wholly independently it is relevant to take account of the motives and purposes of those who help in setting up the tenancy.

The means, circumstances and intention of the landlord. In many cases the best pointers as to whether an agreement falls foul of reg 9(1)(l) will be found in analysing the landlord's motives. As Peter Gibson LJ said in *White*:

"A liability cannot be created unilaterally, but the reality, as Sir Christopher Slade pointed out in the course of argument, is that the purpose of the landlord is likely to be more significant than that of the tenant who will usually be incurring the liability for the proper purpose of providing himself with accommodation."

The fact that the landlord will make a profit from the rent charged is not conclusive evidence of abuse, as profit is the usual purpose and effect of any commercial letting. However, it is clear from *White* and the decision in *R v Manchester CC ex p Baragrove Properties Ltd* (1991) 23 HLR 337, QBD, that the landlord's intentions and circumstances can give rise to a finding of abuse even in the absence of any complicity or impropriety on the part of the tenant.

In *Baragrove Properties*, the applicant was a property management company managing about 340 houses on behalf of 140 landlords. They applied for judicial review of a policy adopted by the council on October 22 1990 to the effect that where the rent payable exceeded the "market rent" fixed by the rent officer by 50 per cent plus £20, it would treat tenancies granted to persons covered by an older version of reg 11(3) HB Regs 1987 as having been "created to take advantage of the housing benefit scheme" pursuant to reg 7(1)(l) HB Regs 1987 (now reg 9(1)(l) HB Regs) and therefore no HB would be payable. Where such claimants renegotiated their rents after such a refusal, the council would continue to refuse benefit under reg 7(1)(l) HB Regs 1987 where the new rent exceeded the "market rent" by 50 per cent plus £20 "save in the most exceptional of circumstances".

It was not disputed by the applicants that they were deliberately "targeting" people in so-called "exempt groups" (ie, exempt from certain rent restrictions) in terms of offering tenancies by advertising for such tenants and that they were not willing to let the properties concerned to HB claimants outside these groups. Nor would they have been able to levy the sort of rents involved, between twice and five times the "market rent", from non-HB tenants. Further, it was again not disputed that the sole and specific purpose of letting these properties at these rents to "exempt groups" was in order to "charge very high rents which they could not otherwise command". The case must be viewed against these rather remarkable circumstances.

The applicants argued that restrictions on excessive rents were governed by regs 11 and 12 HB Regs 1987 (provisions now found in Sch 3 para 5 of the HB&CTB(CP) Regs – see p1776) and could not therefore be used as the foundation for a refusal under reg 7(1)(l) HB Regs 1987 (now reg 9(1)(l) HB Regs). The respondents argued that these tenancies at these rents simply would not have been created but for the so-called "exemption" provisions of reg 11(3) HB Regs 1987 and that they therefore came within reg 7(1)(l). It was part of the applicant's case that the rent officer set the market rent too low. This was rejected. Stuart-Smith LJ held (at 345-6) that "given that the applicants have been deliberately targeting the exempt groups .... for the purpose of charging very high rents" the creation of such tenancies could fall within reg 7(1)(l).

The tenancies in *Baragrove Properties* were found to be "contrived" even though the tenants did not benefit from the abuse and were unlikely to have been motivated to enter into the agreements by the prospect of extra profits which would accrue to their landlord. It seems to follow that an abusive intention on the part of the landlord can, in an appropriate case, bring the tenancy within reg 9(1)(l) even though the tenant's dominant purpose in entering the tenancy was to provide a home for her/himself and her/his family. In the more conventional case where the focus is on the tenant, it is important for the authority to investigate what the consequences will be for the landlord if HB is not payable. If the landlord will be forced, or will wish, to evict the claimant if rent is not paid and is unable to maintain the property without the receipt of rent, those factors will be suggestive of the agreement not being contrived: *R v Sutton LBC HBRB ex p Keegan* (1992) 27 HLR 92 at 99-100, QBD. However, if the evidence is that the landlord will take a commercial view and will not chase a tenant for rent where it would be uneconomical to do so, that will not justify a finding of contrivance: *R v Stratford-upon-Avon DC HBRB ex p White* (1998) 31 HLR 126.

Prior relationship of landlord and tenant. The fact that the landlord and tenant knew each other or were friends before the tenancy was created, while it may be relevant, is far from being conclusive evidence of abuse. It may be a reasonable and commercial decision for a landlord to let to someone s/he knows, as s/he will be more certain of having a good tenant. Likewise, a tenant may feel more secure with a landlord who is known to her/ him. If friends can reach a mutually acceptable agreement, then nothing in reg 9 compels them to go into the market, as long as the tenant's dominant purpose is to provide her/himself and her/his family with a home and the landlord's dominant purpose is to provide accommodation for a reasonable return: see *R v Poole BC ex p Ross* (1995) 28 HLR 351, QBD. Similarly, it is of little relevance that the parties are related, unless they reside together in which case see para (1)(b). Contrary to what seems to be popular belief, there is no legal rule which prevents members of the same family entering into binding legal agreements with each other, as long as all the parties intend to create legal relations. Again the question is what the dominant purpose of the agreement was at the time it was entered into.

The rent charged. If the rent payable under the agreement is high in comparison with the market rates prevailing in the area or if the accommodation is larger than is needed by the claimant and any family, then that may be evidence (taken together with other relevant factors) that the liability was created to take advantage of the scheme: see *Dadds* at 705 and *R v Barrow BC ex p Catnach* [1997] unreported, 3 September, QBD. If these are the only factors which suggest abuse, the authority does not need to rely on reg 9 and can restrict the claimant's eligible rent under a rent restriction scheme (if relevant): regs 12C to 14. These schemes make it difficult to "take advantage" of the scheme by charging an excessive rent.

Where the rent officer has made a valuation which is not much lower than the contractual rent, it will be irrational for the authority to conclude that the agreement is contrived without other factors being present: *Dadds* at 705, where the contractual rent was £95 and the rent officer's assessment was £78.

Paragraph (3): The exception

This sets out an important escape route from paras (1)(e): liability to connected company or trustee and (g): liability of former non-dependant (but not the others). It applies where the person satisfies the local authority that the liability "was not intended to be a means of taking advantage" of the HB scheme. The burden of proof is therefore on the person, not the local authority. However, where there is adequate evidence relating to the issues, this is unlikely to be of great significance: see the discussion on para (1)(l). A bold assertion by the claimant or landlord that there was no intention to abuse the scheme need not be accepted if their actions give the lie to that assertion. Clearly, however, in such a case careful findings of fact and reasons will have to be given by authorities and the First-tier Tribunal.

The critical concept of a liability taking advantage of the HB scheme is also present in para (1)(l). However, there are critical differences between para (1)(l) and this provision. In para (3), the question for consideration is whether or not the liability was intended to be a means of taking advantage of the HB scheme. In considering this question, particularly close attention must be had to the knowledge of the claimant and the landlord of the HB scheme and its operation. The paradigm case of an intention to abuse the HB scheme is *Baragrove Properties*, discussed above. It does not appear that it is necessary for *both* landlord and tenant to have the requisite intention. It will be sufficient if one of them does. But it is entirely possible that an agreement could take advantage of the HB scheme, without landlord or tenant necessarily having intended to produce that result.

Persons from abroad

10.–(1)   A person from abroad who is liable to make payments in respect of a dwelling shall be treated as if he were not so liable but this paragraph shall not have effect in respect of a person to whom and for a period to which regulation 10A (entitlement of a refugee to housing benefit) and Schedule A1 (treatment of claims for housing benefit by refugees) apply.

[¹ (2)   In paragraph (1), "person from abroad" means, subject to the following provisions of this regulation, a person who is not habitually resident in the United Kingdom, the Channel Islands, the Isle of Man or the Republic of Ireland.

(3)   No person shall be treated as habitually resident in the United Kingdom, the Channel Islands, the Isle of Man or the Republic of Ireland unless he has a right to reside in (as the case may be) the United Kingdom, the Channel Islands, the Isle of Man or the

Republic of Ireland other than a right to reside which falls within paragraph (3A) [¹⁶ or (3AA)].

(3A)   A right to reside falls within this paragraph if it is one which exists by virtue of, or in accordance with, one or more of the following–

(a)   regulation 13 of the [¹⁶ Immigration (European Economic Area) Regulations 2016];

(b)   regulation 14 of those Regulations, but only in a case where the right exists under that regulation because the person is–

(i)   a jobseeker for the purpose of the definition of "qualified person" in regulation 6(1) of those Regulations, or

(ii)   a family member (within the meaning of regulation 7 of those Regulations) of such a jobseeker;

[¹⁶ (bb) regulation 16 of those Regulations, but only in a case where the right exists under that regulation because the person satisfies the criteria in paragraph (5) of that regulation;]

(c)   Article 6 of Council Directive No. 2004/38/EC; [⁹]

(d)   Article 39 of the Treaty establishing the European Community (in a case where the person is seeking work in the United Kingdom, the Channel Islands, the Isle of Man or the Republic of Ireland) [⁹; or

(e)   Article 20 of the Treaty on the Functioning of the European Union (in a case where the right to reside arises because a British citizen would otherwise be deprived of the genuine enjoyment of the substance of their rights as a European Union citizen).]

[¹⁶ (3AA)   A right to reside falls within this paragraph if it exists by vrtue of a person having been granted limited leave to enter, or remain in, the United Kingdom under the Immigration Act 1971 by virtue of–

(a)   Appendix EU to the immigration rules made under section 3(2) of that Act; or

(b)   being a person with a Zambrano right to reside as defined in Annex 1 of Appendix EU to the immigration rules made under section 3(2) of that Act.]

(3B)   A person is not a person from abroad if he is–

[¹⁵ (za) a qualified person for the purposes of regulation 6 of the [¹⁶ Immigration (European Economic Area) Regulations 2016] as a worker or a self-employed person;]

[¹⁵ (zb) a family member of a person referred to in sub-paragraph (za) within the meaning of regulation 7(1)(a), (b) or (c) of those Regulations;]

[¹⁵ (zc) a person who has a right to reside permanently in the United Kingdom by virtue of regulation 15(1)(c), (d) or (e) of those Regulations;]

[¹⁵ (a)]

[¹⁵ (b)]

[¹⁵ (c)]

[¹⁵ (d)]

[¹⁵ (e)]

[¹⁵ [⁵ [¹⁰ (f)]]]

(g)   refugee;

[⁴ [¹¹ (h) a person who has been granted leave or who is deemed to have been granted leave outside the rules made under section 3(2) of the Immigration Act 1971 where that leave is

(i)   discretionary leave to enter or remain in the United Kingdom;

(ii)   leave to remain under the Destitution Domestic Violence concession; or

(iii)   leave deemed to have been granted by virtue of regulation 3 of the Displaced Persons (Temporary Protection) Regulations 2005;]

(hh)   a person who has humanitarian protection granted under those rules;]

(i)   a person who is not a person subject to immigration control within the meaning of section 115(9) of the Immigration and Asylum Act and who is in the United Kingdom as a result of his deportation, expulsion or other removal by compulsion of law from another country to the United Kingdom; [¹¹ [¹²]]

[¹¹ (j)]

[⁷ [¹¹ (jj)]
(k)   in receipt of income support [⁶, [¹³] or on an income-related employment and support allowance][¹⁴;or
(l)   in receipt of an income-based jobseeker's allowance and has a right to reside other than a right to reside falling within paragraph (3A).]]
[¹¹ (4)]
[²]
(6)   In this regulation–
[²]
"refugee" means a person recorded by the Secretary of State as a refugee within the definition in Article 1 of the Convention relating to the Status of Refugees.

Modifications

The amendments made by SI 2006 No.1026 do not affect the continued operation of the transitional and savings provided for in reg 12 Social Security (Persons From Abroad) Miscellaneous Amendments Regulations 1996 (see p1633 of the 26th edition), reg 6 Social Security (Habitual Residence) Amendment Regulations 2004 (see p1771) or Sch 3 para 6 HB&CIB(CP) Regs (see p1795). See reg 11 of SI 2006 No.1026 (p1807).

From 25 July 2006 until 31 January 2007, a para (3B)(jj) was inserted by the Social Security (Lebanon) Amendment Regulations 2006 SI No.1981. See p241 of the 20th edition for the text of the insertion.

The amendment made to para (3B) by the Housing Benefit (Habitual Residence) Amendment Regulations 2014 SI No.513 does not apply to a person who, on or after 31 March 2014, is entitled to HB and income-based JSA, but only until the person ceases to be entitled to income-based JSA, or makes a new claim for HB (whichever event occurs first): the savings are provided by reg 3 of those regulations.

Amendments

1.   Substituted by reg 4(2)(a) of SI 2006 No 1026 as from 30.4.06.
2.   Omitted by reg 4(2)(b) and (c) of SI 2006 No 1026 as from 30.4.06.
3.   Amended by reg 5 of SI 2006 No 1981 from 25.7.06 until 31.1.07 only.
4.   Amended by reg 5 of SI 2006 No 2528 as from 9.10.06.
5.   Substituted by reg 5 of SI 2006 No 3341 as from 1.1.07.
6.   Amended by reg 8 of SI 2008 No 1082 as from 27.10.08.
7.   Amended by reg 5 of SI 2009 No 362 as from 18.3.09.
8.   Omitted by reg 19(3) of SI 2011 No 2425 as from 31.10.11.
9.   Amended by reg 5 of SI 2012 No 2587 as from 8.11.12.
10.   Substituted by reg 5 of SI 2013 No 1474 as from 1.7.13.
11.   Amended by reg 11(3) of SI 2013 No 2536 as from 29.10.13.
12.   Omitted by reg 2(1)(a) of SI 2014 No 539 as from 1.4.14.
13.   Omitted by reg 2(1)(b) of SI 2014 No 539 as from 1.4.14.
14.   Inserted by reg 2(1)(c) of SI 2013 No 539 as from 1.4.14
15.   Substituted by reg 5 of SI 2014 No 902 as from 31.5.14.
16.   Amended by reg 5 of SI 2019 No 872 as from 7.5.19.

General Note

The scheme of the regulation

This regulation has the effect of excluding certain categories of "persons from abroad" from entitlement to HB by deeming them not to be liable to make payments in respect of their home.

Before dealing with this question, however, a prior question may need to be addressed, namely whether the claimant is excluded from benefit altogether under s115 Immigration and Asylum Act 1999 and the Social Security (Immigration and Asylum) Consequential Provisions Regulations 2000 (see p1706 and p1747) as a "person subject to immigration control". A person falling within s115 of the 1999 Act is barred from HB unless s/he can take advantage of the provisions in reg 2 of the 2000 Regs.

It is only if the person is not excluded under s115 that it may become necessary to address whether s/he is caught by reg 10.

Note that even if a person who is subject to immigration control can avoid the exclusion under s115 of the 1999 Act due to coming within the 2000 Regulations, s/he will still need not to be a "person from abroad" under reg 10 – see *Yesiloz v LB Camden and SSWP* [2009] EWCA Civ 145; reported as *R(H) 7/09*.

The label of "person from abroad" should thus be confined to those falling foul of reg 10. The regulation is a classic example of obscure social security drafting, but once unpicked its meaning is relatively plain.

The starting point is para (1), which sets out that a "person from abroad" shall be treated as not liable to make payments in respect of a dwelling, and so is not entitled to HB. Who then is a "person from abroad"? The short answer is given in para (2), namely a person who is not habitually resident in the UK, the Channel Islands, the Isle of Man or the Republic of Ireland (referred to collectively as the Common Travel Area or CTA); unless that person falls within para (3B), in which case s/he is simply not a person from abroad. Para (3) then provides that a person cannot be treated as habitually resident unless s/he has a "right to reside" in the CTA, other than one of the rights to reside which falls within para (3A) or (3AA). This requires some elucidation.

Firstly, the test in para (3) is a separate test from that in (3B), notwithstanding the fact that nearly all of the heads under the latter concern categories of person who will have a right of residence in the UK in any event (see *MW v SSWP (UC)* [2019] UKUT 184 (AAC) at para 5 which gives a clear explanation of the analogous regulation for universal credit).

Secondly, if the only right to reside a person has is one which falls within para (3A)–(3AA) then, in effect, it does not amount to a sufficient right to reside, and that person will be a "person from abroad" (because s/he is not habitually resident in the UK) and not entitled to HB. Paras (3A)–(3AA) exclude as a sufficient right of residence those non-UK EEA nationals, whose only right of residence is due to their being within their first three months of residence in the CTA (para (3A)(a) and (c)), non-UK EEA nationals (or their family members – (3A)(b)(ii)) who have never previously worked in the CTA and are here looking for work (para (3A)(b)(i) and (d)), those whose right of residence arises because they are responsible for a British child who would have to leave the UK if they were not allowed to remain whether that right is in the form of recognition under the I(EEA) Regs (para (3A)(bb)) or from 7 May 2019, under the Immigration Act 1971. Also, from 7 May 2019, para (3AA)(a) *purports to exlcuse* from entitlement those whose only right of residence is limited leave to remain issued under Appendix EU to the Immigration Rules (on this point see below in the Analysis).

Thirdly, for those not coming within (3B), having a right to reside in the CTA is a necessary but not a sufficent condition for being habitually resident in the CTA; to meet the latter s/he will also have to show that s/he is habitually resident in the UK as a matter of fact (see below). This may most obviously apply to UK nationals returning to the UK from abroad. If, however, the person falls within para (3B), s/he cannot be a "person from abroad" and is exempted for the habitual residence test altogether. Para 3B covers:

(1) Some of those who have a right of residence under the Immigration (European Economic Area) Regulations 2016 (SI No.1052) (see the note in "Modifications" above regarding references to the now revoked Immigration (European Economic Area) Regulations 2006): para (3B)(za)–(zc).

(2) Those who have been recorded by the Secretary of State as refugees (defined in para (6)) under asylum law: para (3B)(g). Note that, perhaps confusingly and unnecessarily, such people are *also* said not to be "persons from abroad" at all under para (1) (see reg 10A and Sch A1 in Sch 4 HB&CTB(CP) Regs – on p1805 – and the special rules for retrospectively dealing with HB claims by refugees).

(3) Those granted certain forms of leave within the Immigration Rules or similar leave outside the rules: para (3B)(h) and (hh).

(4) Those who have been deported or removed *to* the UK from another country: para (3B)(i).

(5) Those in receipt of IS or on income-related ESA: para (3B)(k).

(6) Those in receipt of income-based JSA who have a right to reside other than that as a jobseeker: para (3B)(l).

So, in summary, the claimant will not be a "person from abroad" (and so will be treated as not liable for rent) if either:

(a) s/he falls within para (3B) – eg, because s/he is in receipt of IS or is a person who has retained the status of a worker in EU law; *or*

(b) s/he has a right to reside in the CTA (eg, as a British or Irish citizen, under the Immigration Act 1971, or under some provision of the Immigration (EEA) Regulations 2016 or of EU law that is not specifically provided for in (3B) – eg, someone who is the primary carer of the child of former worker where that child is receiving education) *and* s/he is habitually resident in the CTA as a matter of fact.

Given that receipt of IS or income-related ESA in effect allows a person to bypass the habitual residence/right to reside tests for HB purposes (see para (3B)(k)), in reality right to reside or habitual residence disputes for HB purposes are often bypassed on the basis of the outcome of a claim for one of those benefits. As a reflection of this, the commentary below is not as comprehensive as it is to the corresponding commentary in Volume II of Sweet and Maxwell's *Social Security Legislation* (which contains annotations to the I(EEA) Regs 2016) and Volume III of that work (which contains annotations to EU Directive 2004/38). It is suggested that reference should be made to those sources, as well as to the commentary here, in cases where the right to reside or habitual residence tests are genuinely determinative of the HB claim.

Brexit

At the time of writing, the UK is set to leave the European Union at 11pm on 31 January 2020. At the time of writing, it is not known with any certainty what, if any, transitional arrangements will be put in place. However, at minimum, the Immigration (European Economic Area) Regulations 2016 will continue as part of the domestic law (see s7 of the European Union (Withdrawal) Act 2018). It may be the case that nationals of other EEA states will then be required to apply for leave to remain within a certain period. Close attention will, therefore, need to be paid to developments in this area after the publication of the present work.

The "EU Settled Status Scheme" is the vehicle under which the status of EEA nationals and their family members, resident in the UK, will be turned into leave to remain under the Immigration Act 1971. Appendix EU to the Immigration Rules provides for leave to remain under the Act to be granted to EEA citizens and their family members on receipt of an application under the Scheme. Those resident in he UK for five years or more are granted indefinite leave to remain ("settled status"). Those resident for less than five years are granted a limited leave to remain for a five-year period which is not subject to any conditions ("pre-settled status").

At present, people with either of these statuses may also have an EU law right of residence.

As mentioned above, the amendments to regulation 10 from 7 May 2019, are designed to prevent a person whose only right to reside is limited leave to remain issued under the Scheme. Those who are granted settled status can rely on that to pass the right to reside test. See futher below in the Analysis to para (3AA) for consideration of the validity of the rule excluding pre-settled status from being a sufficient right of residence.

Analysis

The length of this analysis of a single regulation reflects the complexity of the subject matter with which it deal: EU residence law and its interactions with benefit entitlements. *AS v SSWP (UC)* [2018] UKUT 260 (AAC) contains a useful warning about how decision makers should approach such cases:

"19.   The law about the right to reside is not straightforward and the claimant was entitled to expect the First-tier Tribunal to exercise its inquisitorial jurisdiction by asking all the questions that needed to be asked so as to enable the claimant's father to put the claimant's case in the best possible way.

20.   The fact that the First-tier Tribunal has such an enabling and inquisitorial jurisdiction is routinely used as a reason for not extending legal aid to tribunal proceedings. The system does not work properly if the First-tier Tribunal confines itself to the facts highlighted by the [decision maker] – or by unrepresented claimants who cannot be expected to know what facts are potentially relevant – and rubber-stamps the [decision maker's] decision without investigating the other issues that are apparent from the evidence."

As discussed in the General Note, anyone who comes within one of the heads of para (3B) cannot be a "person from abroad". Virtually all of the people whose circumstances bring them within one of the heads of para (3B) have a right of residence by virtue of those circumstances in any event. However, it is only those who do not come within para (3B) who are formally required to have a right to reside in order to count as habitually resident and therefore not be persons from abroad.

This analysis is therefore structured as follows.

[1]   Paragraph (3B): Groups who cannot be "persons from abroad"

[2]   Paragraph (3): Who has a right to reside in the CTA (other than those covered by para (3B) and not excluded by para (3A))

[3]   Paragraph (2): "habitually resident in fact"

For commentary on reg 10(4), see p1795.

As this is a long note, for ease of reference, these broad headings have been further broken down with sub-headings as follows.

[1] Paragragh (3B): Groups who cannot be persons from abroad (p302)

    [1.1] Para (3B)(za): Workers (p305)

    [1.2] Para (3B)(za): Self-employed (p308)

    [1.3] Para (3B)(za): Those who retain worker/self-employed status (p310)

        [1.3.1] "temporarily unable to work as a result of an illness or accident" (p310)

        [1.3.2] Involuntary unemployment (p311)

            [1.3.2.1] "voluntary" and "involuntary" unemployment (p311)

            [1.3.2.2] "registered as a jobseeker with the relevant employment office" (p312)

            [1.3.2.3] Self-employed and involuntary unemployment (p313)

            [1.3.2.4] The limitations in reg 6(2) I(EEA) Regs (see p313)

        [1.3.3] Pregnancy (p315)

        [1.3.4] Gaps and switching between ways of retaining status (p316)

    [1.4] Para (3B)(zb): Family members of workers or the self-employed (p317)

    [1.5] Para (3B)(zc): Former workers/self-employed (p319)

    [1.6] Para (3B): A2, Croatian and A8 workers (p320)

        [1.6.1] Modifications of the rights of residence of A2 and Croatian nationals during their accession periods (p321)

        [1.6.2] Which A2 or Croatian nationals are subject to worker authorisation (p322)

        [1.6.3] What counts as authorised work (p322)

        [1.6.4] The rights of residence of A8 nationals during their accession period and its potential effect on HB/CTB entitlement after 1 May 2011 (p323)

        [1.6.5] The lawfulness of the A8 scheme during the time it was in force (p324)

    [1.7] Para (3B)(g): Refugees (p325)

    [1.8] Para (3B)(h) and (hh): Persons granted certain forms of leave to remain or enter/humanitarian protection (p326)

    [1.9] Para (3B)(k): Claimants in receipt of IS or on income-related ESA (p326)

    [1.10] Para (3B)(l): Those in receipt of income-based JSA who have a right to reside other than as a jobseeker (p327)

[2] Paragraph (3)– (3AA): Who has a right to reside in the Common Travel Area sufficient to claim HB (p327)
    [2.1] Para (3A)–(3AA): Non qualifying rights of residence (p327)
        [2.1.1] The *Zambrano* right (p328)
        [2.1.2] Lawfulness of the pre-settled status exclusion (p328)
    [2.2] Initial right to reside (p328)
    [2.3] Extended right to reside (p328)
        [2.3.1] Self-sufficient (p329)
            [2.3.1.1] sufficient resources (p329)
            [2.3.1.2] comprehensive sickness insurance (p331)
        [2.3.2] Students (p332)
        [2.3.3] Family members of anyone with an extended right of residence (p332)
    [2.4] Permanent right to reside (p332)
        [2.4.1] Legal residence/residence in "accordance with these Regulations" (p332)
        [2.4.2] Continuity of residence (p334)
    [2.5] The rights of extended family members (p335)
    [2.6] Retention of a right of residence: death, divorce and departure (p335)
    [2.7] EU Rights of residence other than those in the Directive (p336)
        [2.7.1] Service recipients (p336)
        [2.7.2] Article 21 TFEU (p337)
        [2.7.3] Rights of carer's of the children in education of former workers and the formerly self-employed
(p341)
        [2.7.4] Rights of carer's of children who themselves have a right to reside (p344)
    [2.8] Residence documentation (p344)
[3] Paragraph (2): "habitually resident in fact" (p344)
    [3.1] Basic principles (p345)
    [3.2] Acquisition of habitual residence (p345)
        [3.2.1] An "appreciable period of time" (p345)
        [3.2.2] A "settled intention" (p346)
    [3.3] Loss of habitual residence (p347)

[1] Paragraph (3B): Groups who cannot be persons from abroad
If a person is covered by one of the heads within para (3B), s/he is not a person from abroad. Accordingly, s/he does not need to have a right to reside or to be habitually resident in fact.

Until 31 May 2014, the first five heads, (a) to (e), all made reference to EU Directive 2004/38 (sometimes called the "Residence Directive" or even the "Citizenship Directive"). However, from that date, para (3B) was amended so that those were replaced with references to those with certain positions under the Immigration (European Economic Area) Regulations 2006 No.1003 (I(EEA) Regs 2006). From 1 February 2017, the I(EEA) Regs 2006 were revoked and replaced by the Immigration (European Economic Area) Regulations 2016 No.1052 ("I(EEA) Regs" hereafter). By reg 45 and Sch 7 para 1 of the I(EEA) Regs, references in other legislation (such as reg 10 HB Regs considered here) to the I(EEA) Regs 2006 are to be read as references to the corresponding provisions in the 2016 set (Sch 7 of which also provides a table of correspondences). This note therefore now refers to the I(EEA) Regs.

An understanding of both the Residence Directive and the I(EEA) Regs, and their relationship to each other, is necessary to determine whether an EEA national, or her/his family member, is defined as a "person from abroad" under reg 10.

–   *Directive:* this came into effect on 30 April 2006. It is a codifying measure which seeks to bring together the many previously disparate provisions of EU law concerning residence rights within the EU. It repeals and replaces many previous Directives (eg, Directive 68/360/EEC) and amends EC Regulation 1612/68. Although a codifying measure, it is important to realise that another purpose of the Directive is to strengthen residence rights and the ECJ approaches its interpretation in this light (see *Metock* (Case C-127/08) [2008] ECR I-06241 at para 59). The Directive does not, however, codify all rights of residence for EU nationals. For example, it is now clear from the decisions in *LB Harrow v Ibrahim* (Case C-310/08) [2010] ECR I-01065 and *Teixeira v LB Lambeth* (Case C-480/08) [2010] ECR I-01107 that rights of residence for the children of former workers who are in education (and their primary carers) arise outside the Directive: the ECJ explicitly rejected the arguments of the UK and others that this was not the case (see *Teixeira*, paras 55 to 60).

–   *I(EEA) Regs:* these regulations are supposed to implement the Directive within domestic law.
Although it is sometimes easier to satisfy a decision maker of a right of residence by reference to the I(EEA) Regs, it should be noted that the Directive can be relied upon directly by EU nationals in the UK. In some cases, the domestic regulations may provide for a right of residence which the Directive does not – ie, be more generous: see, for example, *HG v SSWP (SPC)* [2011] UKUT 382 (AAC) (although that is a historical example as the I(EEA) Regs were subsequently amended). However, given the tightening of the I(EEA) Regs it is more common to find

situations where one can argue a right arises under the Directive but not the I(EEA) Regs. The relationship between the two instruments, and with the structure of reg 10, results in two possibilities.

(1)   A claimant with a right of residence under the I(EEA) Regs referred to in para (3B)(za) to (zc) (or indeed any of the other sub-paras) means the claimant cannot be a person from abroad.

(2)   A claimant with a right that arises under the Directive which is not mirrored in the I(EEA) Regs or someone who has a right of residence under the I(EEA) Regs which is not one of those referred to specifically in para (3B)(za) to (zc) of reg 10, provided that right is not excluded under para (3A), will have a right of residence sufficient to come within para (3): provided s/he is also habitually resident in fact s/he will not be a person from abroad.

A note on EEA nationals. The EEA is a larger grouping than the EU as it also includes Iceland, Norway and Liechtenstein. The I(EEA) Regs apply to all EEA nationals (except the British – see below) and also treat Swiss nationals as EEA nationals. On a European law level, the EEA Treaty (the "Oporto Agreement") provides for the same residence rights for EEA citizens as for EU citizens and the "Luxembourg Agreement" (*Agreement between the European Community and its Member States, or the one part, and the Swiss Confederation, of the other, on the Free Movement of Persons*, Luxembourg, June 21, 1999, Cm.5369) provides the same rights for the Swiss from 1 June 2002. Reg 10(c) Social Security (Persons from Abroad) Amendment Regulations 2006 No.1026 provides that nationals of these states are to be treated as if they were EU nationals for the purposes of the now replaced para (3B)(a) to (e) (see p1807). That treatment is no longer needed as now para (3B)(za) to (zc) refers only to persons with rights under the I(EEA) Regs.

A note on British Citizens and the Directive. The UK is a member state of the EU and of the EEA. However, British citizens do not usually need to invoke EU law residence rights as they have rights of residence in the UK under British law. The issue of whether a British citizen may also have such rights under EU law becomes relevant when a family member of a British citizen seeks to derive a right of residence from the British citizen – eg, where a British person is married to an economically inactive EU national and that person's dependent parent seeks to claim HB.

At the outset it must be noted that the Directive does not apply to British citizens resident in the UK who have not moved within the EU: see Art 3(1) on who is a "beneficiary" of the Directive. This is now confirmed by the European Court of Justice in *McCarthy* (Case C-434/09) [2011] ECR, 103375 (see "Group 2" below for a further discussion). However, note that there are three groups of British citizens who may, nonetheless, have an EU law right of residence from which a non-British family member may derive a right to reside despite the fact no leave to remain has been granted to them by the Home Office. Of these three groups, it is really only Group 1 who properly comes within para (3B) but it is convenient to discuss all three groups to some degree at this point.

Group 1: British citizens who have been migrants in another EEA state. The family members of British citizens have rights of residence in EU law if the British citizen has her/himself exercised EU rights of freedom of movement in another EU state and then returned to the UK: *Eind* (Case C-219/05) [2007] ECR I-10719. This is in part reflected in the I(EEA) Regs: although they generally adopt the device as treating British citizens as if they were not EEA nationals (to give effect to Art 3(1) of the Directive excluding them from being beneficiaries), reg 9 provides that the family members of a British citizen who has resided in another EEA state as a "qualified person" (see [2.3]) will have the regulations applied to her/him as if that British citizen was a non-British EEA national. Thus, if the British citizen would count as a worker/self-employed person etc in the UK were s/he a non-British EEA national, her/his family members have a right of residence. However, in *Eind* it was held that there was no need for a Union citizen who had been a worker in another EU country to carry out an economic activity on return to the home state, in order for his family members to have an EU law right of residence on the national's return, with them, to the home state.

The ECJ returned to this issue in *O v Minister voor Immigratie, Integratie en Asiel* (Case C-456/12) [2014] ECR (ECLI:EU:C:2014:135). It considered the cases of two families, each comprised of a Netherlands citizen married to a non-EEA national. The non-EEA nationals sought residence in the Netherlands. In the case of the O family, he had resided in Belgium while his wife, the Netherlands citizen, resided in the Netherlands and she visited him at weekends. In the case of the other family, B, prior to marriage they had lived together in Spain. However, they had only married once Ms B, again the Netherlands citizen, had returned to the Netherlands. The Court was asked questions which aimed to establish what quality of residence the EEA citizen must have in another member state to trigger rights for their non-EEA family members to reside with them in their home state. The Court's formulation was that:

"where a Union citizen has created or strengthened a family life with a third-country national during genuine residence, pursuant to and in conformity with the conditions set out in Article 7(1) and (2) and Articles 16(1) and (2) of [the Directive] [...] in a Member State other than that of which he is a national, the provisions of the directive apply by analogy where that Union citizen returns, with the family member in question, to his Member State of origin."

That made clear that the UK regulations at the time were not wide enough in that they limited the rights to those who have worked or been self-employed in another EEA state (as those who, for example, had resided in another member state as a self-sufficient person would also acquire rights for their non EEA family members – an error now fixed in the I(EEA) Regs) but does seem to contradict what was said in *Eind* where, as stated, there was no requirement for the returning resident to meet any conditions as to working in her/his home state in order for the non-EEA family member to acquire EU law rights.

In *LA v SSWP* [2010] UKUT 109 (AAC), the claimant was the Greek mother-in-law of a British citizen who had worked on a self-employed basis in Greece and then returned to the UK with his Greek wife and the claimant. Judge Lane remitted the case to the First-tier Tribunal to make findings about both the issue of dependency and whether the British citizen had been a worker in the UK at the date of the refusal of his mother-in-law's pension credit claim on the basis that she did not have a right of residence. The need to make such a finding as to whether the British citizen was a worker on his return to the UK is inconsistent with the judgment in *Eind* (although possibly correct given what was said in *O* as discussed above). The judge in *LA v SSWP* does not mention the decision in *Eind*.

In *B v SSWP* [2017] UKUT 472 (AAC), the claimant was a French national who had lived with her British partner in France from 1998 to 2002. While living in France, her partner was a self-employed art dealer. The couple moved to the UK at the end of 2002 and married shortly after. Her husband was self-sufficient in the UK until his death in 2008. Reg 9(2)(b) (in that case of the I(EEA) Regulations 2006 – similar provision is made in reg 9(2)(d) of the current I(EEA) Regs) required the British citizen to have been married to the partner while living in the other EEA state. The Upper Tribunal held that the claimant could not benefit from reg 9 as she was not a family member of her late husband while he was exercising his EU law right of residence in France. The subsequent case of *Banger v SSHD* (Case C 89/17) [2018] ECR (ECLI:EU:C:2018:570) held that where the unmarried partner of a UK citizen had lived with that citizen in another member state and enjoyed a right of residence there granted as an "extended family member" (see [2.5] below at p335), then s/he had returned to the UK, the UK was required to facilitate the entry and residence of that unmarried partner in a similar way as for extended family members.

In *OB v SSHD* [2010] UKUT 420 (IAC), a three-judge panel of the Immigration and Asylum Chamber of the Upper Tribunal considered a case where there had been a 13-month gap between the appellant's wife (a British national who had been working in Ireland) ceasing work and returning to the UK. The First-tier Tribunal had dismissed the case on the basis, it seems, that it had determined the exercise of free movement rights in another state had to have taken place immediately or very shortly prior to the return to the UK. The Upper Tribunal held this was not the case. The appellant had argued that either there was no need for any temporal connection between the exercise of treaty rights in another member state and the right to family reunification on return to the UK or, in the alternative, that the facts of this case were sufficient for the appellant's wife to still have the right to install the appellant in the UK. The Upper Tribunal assumed but did not decide that there did need to be "some link" between the exercise of free movement rights in another state and return to the UK for the right to install family members to exist. The link in the case before it was sufficiently clear. Given this decision, it would be wise for advisers to argue, where possible, that a link between the free movement rights and the return to the UK does exist (see para 15 of the decision for a list of the factors taken into account in that case). It is worth noting though that in the *O* case, a similar question was asked of the ECJ (ie, did it matter that a period of residing togther in another member state had been two years prior to the period for which the non-EEA national sought a right of residence in the home member state of his partner?). The ECJ did not need to answer this question as, on the facts, the couple had not been married while living in the other member state and so had not been family members of one another at that time.

Group 2: dual nationals. The ECJ has now made clear in *McCarthy* that a British citizen who is also a citizen of another EU state, but who has never exercised a right of freedom of movement within the EU, cannot in general rely upon EU citizenship to assert a right of residence here. It is not clear that *McCarthy* would have been decided in the same way had Mrs McCarthy worked in the UK (or indeed had there been any cross border movement). Thus at paras 25 and 26 of the judgment it seems the Court is clear about the context of the case it is being asked to decide:

"25.   There is no indication in the order for reference, in the case-file or in the observations submitted to the Court that Mrs McCarthy has ever exercised her right of free movement within the territory of the Member States, either individually or as a family member of a Union citizen who has exercised such a right. Likewise, Mrs McCarthy is applying for a right of residence under European Union law even though she does not argue that she is or has been a worker, self-employed person or self-sufficient person."

The Court says that this means it has to understand the question it is being asked in that particular light:

"26.   Thus, the first question from the national court must be understood as asking, in essence, whether Article 3(1) of Directive 2004/38 or Article 21 TFEU is applicable to the situation of a Union citizen who has never exercised his right of free movement, who has always resided in a Member State of which he is a national and who is also a national of another Member State."

Two caveats need to be born in mind when considering the rule in *McCarthy*.

(1)   On 14 November 2017, the ECJ gave judgment in *Toufik Lounes v SSHD* (Case C-165/16);[2017] ECR (ECLI:EU:C:2017:862). That case considered the case of an EU national who, unlike in *McCarthy*, had exercised his freedom of movement to come to the UK and then acquired British nationality (becoming a dual national). The dual national then married a third-country national several years later and the issue arose whether she could obtain an EU law right of residence via her dual national partner. Although the

ECJ is clear that a dual national in this situation no longer has a right of residence under the Directive, it held nonetheless that:

"The third-country national is however eligible for a derived right of residence under Article 21(1) TFEU, on conditions which must not be stricter than those provided for by Directive 2004/38 for the grant of such a right to a third-country national who is a family member of a Union citizen who has exercised his right of freedom of movement by settling in a Member State other than the Member State of which he is a national."

ODS v SSWP (UC) [2019] UKUT 192 (AAC) confirms that *Lounes* will also benefit an EEA national who is the family member of a British citizen who had, before becoming a British citizen, been an EEA national exercising a right of residence in he UK – ie, it does not onl apply to third-country national relatives of dual British/EEA citizens.

(2)　In *SSWP v AA* [2009] UKUT 249 (AAC), given prior to the ECJ's judgment in *McCarthy*, Judge Rowland considered a case concerning the right of residence of the Spanish dependent father of a dual Spanish/ British national. The dual national had lived in the UK all his life and was working but had never moved from another EU state or exercised a right of freedom of movement to go and work in another EU state. The judge held that such a dual national did have a right of residence under the I(EEA) Regs 2006. He also held that s/he had such a right under the Directive and, although that part of the ruling may be regarded as incorrect following *McCarthy*, the principle that a right of residence under the I(EEA) Regs 2006 can exist for a person who is a dual national of Britain and another EEA state, even if it does not under the Directive, was confirmed in *HG v SSWP (SPC)* [2011] UKUT 382 (AAC). However, from 16 October 2012, the I(EEA) Regs 2006 have been amended (by SI 2012 No.1547) so that such a right cannot arise under those regulations. This means that the family member of a dual British/other EEA national cannot, from that date, have a right of residence under the UK Regs. The amending regulations contain limited saving provisions (at Sch 3 para 3) for family members of such dual nationals who, as at 16 July 2012, had already acquired permanent residence or for those who had either applied for, been issued with residence documentation or were in the process of appealing against a refusal to issue such documentation. In practice, few EEA nationals apply for such residence documentation themselves (such applications only being made where a non-EEA family member requires a right of residence) and so it seems these savings are unlikely to benefit many people who may have had a right of residence prior to 16 October 2012. Challenges may arise, in a benefit context, concerning the limited scope of the savings, particularly perhaps for those for whom the changes mean a loss of an existing benefit entitlement with the loss of the qualifying right of residence as the family member of a dual British/other EEA national.

Group 3: parents of British children. In *Zambrano v Office national de l'emploi* (ONEm) (Case C-34/09) [2011] ECR I-01177, the ECJ held that where a child who is an EU national resides in the EU state of which s/he is a national and is dependent on a "third country" (ie, non-EU state) national, that third-country national must be granted a right of residence in the member state of residence and nationality of the child. From 8 November 2012, however, reg 10(3A) has been amended (with the insertion of sub-paragraphs (bb) and (e)) to provide that such a right of residence is not a sufficient right of residence to satisfy the test for entitlement to HB. In *R (HC) v SSWP* [2017] UKSC 73 it was held that these amendments were lawful. Further consideration of *Zambrano*, is given at [2.1] alongside the other provisions of paragraph (3A).

[1.1] Para (3B)(za): Workers

The I(EEA) Regs define a "worker" as someone who is a worker for the purposes of Art 45 TFEU (formerly Art 39 EC): see reg 4(1)(a) I(EEA) Regs. Freedom of movement for workers and their families is one of the fundamental principles of EU law. As such, a liberal interpretation must be given to the phrase: *Levin v Staatssecretaris van Justitie* (Case C-53/81) [1982] ECR 01035.

The term is to be construed in accordance with EU law rather than domestic law: *Hoekstra* (Case C-75/73) [1964] ECR 00177; *Levin* paras 11–12. The ECJ has held that a worker is someone in an employment relationship and that this concept must be defined by objective criteria which distinguish it by reference to the rights and duties of the persons concerned. The essential features of an employment relationship are that for a certain period of time a person:

–　　provides services;

–　　in return for remuneration;

–　　under the direction of another person (*Lawrie-Blum v Land Baden-Wurtternberg* (Case C-66/86) [1986] ECR 02121).

In *JR v SSWP (IS); JR v Leeds CC and another (HB)* [2014] UKUT 154 (AAC) it was held that a person in receipt of carer's allowance (a condition of entitlement for which is that the person is regularly and substantially caring for another for at least 35 hours a week) could not thereby argue that s/he is a worker. The case provides a useful review of the elements that comprise an employment relationship in EU law.

Further questions then arise concerning how much remuneration must be received and how many services must be provided in order for a person to gain the privileged status of worker. In addition, there is the question of when someone ceases to be a worker. The issue of loss of status is better dealt with in section [1.3] on p310.

In terms of what makes someone a worker and how that status is acquired, then the work must be "genuine and effective" rather than "marginal or ancillary": *Levin* para 17. This will be a question of fact in each case. GM

C4 Annex B (para 6) suggests five factors which need to be weighed in deciding whether the work is "genuine and effective". To the extent indicated below, the first four of these provide a useful guide, but it must be stressed that *all* the relevant factors must be taken into account (the fifth more properly relates to loss of status and is not considered here). None will be decisive of itself.

(1)   **The period of employment.** The shorter the period of employment, the less likely it is that the status of "worker" is acquired, but it will not require a long period of employment to acquire the status. In *Lair v Universität Hannover* (Case C-39/86) [1988] ECR 03161, the ECJ explicitly held that member states may not impose a fixed minimum period before worker status is obtained. In *Barry v LB Southwark* [2008] EWCA Civ 1440, the Court of Appeal held that Mr Barry's two weeks' of work at the Wimbledon Tennis Championships were sufficient to have made him a worker.

(2)   **The number of hours worked.** A person may be a "worker" even if s/he only works part-time but there will be a point at which the length of time spent working is so short that the work can be described as "marginal". In *Rinner-Kühn* (Case C-171/88) [1989] ECR 02743, a claimant working 10 hours a week was a worker and in *Kits van Heijerungen v Staatssecretaris van Justitie* (Case C-125/89) [1990] ECR I-01753, a man working four hours a week was not. In *R(IS) 12/98* (para 15), an au pair who had worked for 13 hours a week for a modest wage plus board and lodging was held to be a worker. See also the discussion of *Genc* below.

(3)   **The level of earnings.** When assessing whether or not work is "genuine and effective" as opposed to "marginal and ancillary", there has been some controversy in domestic caselaw over whether one can have regard to the fact the work was remunerated at such a level that means tested benefits were payable. In *CH 3314/2005*, Commissioner Rowland considered the question of whether the work for which a claimant was looking was sufficient to make her/him a workseeker: the issue was whether the claimant would have counted as in genuine and effective work had s/he obtained the work s/he was looking for. The commissioner separated out the question of whether the search was "genuine" from whether it was "effective" and in respect of the latter held that reference could be had to whether a person will continue to need to have recourse to social assistance even if s/he finds the work s/he is looking for in order to decide if the work is "effective". The commissioner suggested a formula whereby one compared the potential earnings with the person's potential entitlement to benefits. However, on that test, he held that the work sought in the specific case before him would have counted (just) as effective had it been obtained. Commissioner Jacobs declined to follow Commissioner Rowland's approach in *CIS 4144/2007* (para 24).

Undeterred, Mr Rowland (now Judge Rowland) returned to the issue in *SS v Slough BC* [2011] UKUT 128 (AAC). While he acknowledges (at para 6) that it is probably wrong to seek to separate out whether work is "effective" from whether it is "genuine", and (at para 25) that a formulaic approach comparing wages with benefit rates is probably not correct, he still maintains that it is permissible to have regard to whether the level of earnings means that social assistance can be claimed as a top-up by the worker in deciding whether s/he is in fact a worker. The judge finds that the proper approach is to consider what is proportionate. He suggests that in doing this one could also consider the fact that if one does not recognise the person is a worker s/he may still (if looking for work) have a right of residence as a workseeker and that this is a factor which could mean it was not disproportionate to find s/he is a worker. The judge found, applying the "proportionality" approach, that the claimant in the case before him was a worker.

With respect to the judge, it is suggested that this approach cannot be correct. The approach appears to allow a decision maker to take into account, in determining whether someone is in genuine and effective employment (and hence a worker), what the consequences of that decision will be in terms of the package of social advantages s/he will then have access to. This appears strangely circular: one judges whether someone is a worker and hence has access to equal treatment and social advantages by reference to her/his potential need to get those social advantages. In other words, for Judge Rowland, the extent of the burden on social assistance which will arise if someone is recognised as a worker is an allowable consideration in deciding whether s/he is a worker or not. If that is correct, it is surprising that the Directive did not caveat the rights of residence of workers by reference to whether or not they would be a burden on social assistance (as it did for the self-sufficient). It is also difficult to see how on Judge Rowland's analysis "worker" can be a "community concept": as held consistently by the ECJ since at least 1964 in *Hoekstra* (Case C-75/73) [1964] ECR 00177. In that case, the ECJ commented that: "If the definition of this term were a matter within the competence of national law, it would therefore be possible for each member state to modify the meaning of the concept of "migrant worker" and to eliminate at will the protection afforded by the treaty to certain categories of person."

If the levels of UK benefits and whether a claimant will have recourse to them are a factor in determining whether a person is a worker or not, then presumably a person doing the same job in a different EU state which had lower levels of benefit could still be a worker: where then is the supra-national community wide meaning of worker? Given the above, it is suggested that decision makers will follow a safer course if they hold with the approach suggested in *CIS 4144/2007* and apply the language of the decisions of the ECJ in approaching the factual question of whether work is genuine and effective: a language which is throughout free of reference to the need for a proportionality type approach in coming to a decision on such issues.

Remuneration may also be in kind: *Steymann v Staatssecretaris van Justitie* (Case C-196/87) [1988] ECR 06159.

(4)   **Whether the work is regular or erratic.** Periods of work and unemployment will not prevent the acquisition of worker status: *Monteil v SSHD* [1983] Imm AR 149 at 152, IAT. However, some types of job where the worker is only given work at the whim of the employer may be too ancillary. For example, in *Raulin* (Case C-357/89) [1992] ECR I-01027, the claimant was a waitress who made herself available, and was to be paid only when her employer required her services. In *CIS 1793/2007*, the judge distinguishes between a situation where "work is undertaken for what is expected from the outset to be for a very short period and indefinite employment that has curtailed prematurely" (in such a case the claimant is obliged to keep looking for work and often should be regarded as not being a worker) and that of an agency worker where "short periods of temporary work are not separated by longer periods of no work" in which case the person could be a worker throughout. It is clear that work which is not declared to the DWP can still make a claimant a worker: *Barry v LB Southwark* [2008] EWCA Civ 1440 – here the appellant had not declared to the DWP his two weeks' work at the Wimbledon Tennis Championships. Further, "cash in hand" work in which proper payment of tax and national insurance does not take place can still make a person a worker. Thus, in *JA v SSWP (ESA)* [2012] UKUT 122 (AAC); [2013] AACR 15 it was held that "the Court had defined worker as an economic status, not a legal one".

The ECJ considered again the concept of "worker" in *Genc v Land Berlin* (Case C-14/09) [2010] ECR. The Court refused to be drawn by a plea from the referring national court that it lay down a minimum threshold in terms of hours and pay below which work would be considered marginal and ancillary. However, the Court was prepared to declare that the very limited amount of work which Ms Genc had done was potentially capable of making her a worker. It is worth, therefore, looking at the facts of her case, which concerned the refusal to renew her residence permit in 2007:

"Since 18 June 2004, Ms Genc has been working as a cleaner...According to the contract of employment, which was put down in writing on 9 November 2007, the working time per week is 5.5 hours at an hourly rate of EUR 7.87. That contract provides for entitlement to 28 days of paid leave and continued payment of wages in the event of sickness. The contract is, moreover, subject to the relevant collective agreement. For this employment, Ms Genc receives monthly wages of approximately EUR 175."

The Court referred again to its caselaw establishing that the fact that wages were so low that the worker was still dependent on benefits (para 20) was irrelevant and went on to say:

"26.   Although the fact that a person works for only a very limited number of hours in the context of an employment relationship may be an indication that the activities performed are marginal and ancillary (*Raulin* (Case C-357/89) [1992] ECR I-01027, paragraph 14), the fact remains that, independently of the limited amount of the remuneration for and the number of hours of the activity in question, the possibility cannot be ruled out that, following an overall assessment of the employment relationship in question, that activity may be considered by the national authorities to be real and genuine, thereby allowing its holder to be granted the status of 'worker' within the meaning of Article 39 EC.

27.   The overall assessment of Ms Genc's employment relationship makes it necessary to take into account factors relating not only to the number of working hours and the level of remuneration but also to the right to 28 days of paid leave, to the continued payment of wages in the event of sickness, and to a contract of employment which is subject to the relevant collective agreement, in conjunction with the fact that her contractual relationship with the same undertaking has lasted for almost four years.

28.   Those factors are capable of constituting an indication that the professional activity in question is real and genuine."

Once someone has attained the status of worker, if s/he ceases to be a worker, s/he may retain that status in certain situations (see [1.3]). However, prior to the question of whether worker status can be retained under the provisions discussed at [1.3] is the question of whether worker status ceases immediately on the employment relationship ending – also dealt with in that section.

Minimum earnings threshold

HB Circular A3/2014 contains guidance on how to determine whether someone is a worker. The guidance envisages a two-stage test. In the first stage, the decision maker should consider whether the claimant has earned 16x the national minimum wage for at least three months (the "minimum earnings threshold" – "MET"). If s/he has, the enquiry can stop at that point as it must be accepted the person has achieved worker status. Importantly, however, the guidance then provides that for those who have done less than this amount of work either in terms of earnings, hours or duration, decision makers should have regard to the concept of worker under Art 45 TFEU as discussed above.

The risk is that decision makers will have regard only to the first stage of the analysis the guidance requests they undertake. That runs the possibility of wrongly excluding from entitlement those who are workers under Art 45 even though they do not satisfy the MET. Given the MET is set to require much more work than might make someone a worker under EU law, such cases arise frequently. *RF v LB Lambeth (HB)* [2019] UKUT 52 (AAC) was just such a case. Judge Jacobs draws attention to the importance of always considering the second stage required by the guidance – ie, the EU law test for whether someone is a worker.

Offers of employment. In *SSWP v RR* [2013] UKUT 21 (AAC), a three-judge panel of the Upper Tribunal dealt with a case where, on the facts, the claimant, a German citizen, had entered the UK in 2006 with an offer of employment. Taking up the offer of employment was delayed initially because the job involved working from home and a lack of suitable conditions at home precluded this. Then the claimant was diagnosed with breast cancer and this caused further delays. She claimed income support at a time when the job offer still remained open to her and the claim was refused.

The three-judge panel, highlighted that Art 39 EC (now Art 45 TFEU) in addition to granting residence rights to those who are in work (as discussed thus far in this section), to seek work (an excluded right of residence for HB purposes due to para (3A)(b) and (d) of this regulation as discussed at [2.1]) and to remain in residence if certain conditions are met once work ceases (as discussed at [1.3]), also contains a distinct free movement right to move to, and reside in, a member state for the purpose of accepting an offer of employment actually made (Art 39(3)(a) and (b)).

The Upper Tribunal commented as follows:

"41.   In very many cases, a person moving to another Member State holding an offer of employment will take up that offer within a matter of days or weeks. It will often be the case, however, that a short period before actually beginning the employment will be needed while the person holding the offer sorts out the practical matters which are inherent in any relocation connected with work. It will only be in very unusual cases that a person holding a job offer will not have taken up an immediate offer of employment within three months. We choose that period for two reasons. Firstly, the Citizenship Directive gives all Union citizens an unconditional right of residence for up to three months. Secondly, the period of derogation provided by Article 24(2) of the Citizenship Directive within which there is no obligation on a host Member State to provide social assistance is also three months.

42.   The case before us is one which we consider to be exceptional. Circumstances conspired to prevent the claimant from being able to take up the offer of employment actually made for a considerable period, but the offer had not been withdrawn. The possibility of taking it up was becoming more problematic when the accommodation problems were compounded by the serious health condition of the claimant. But, and we regard this as significant, the putative employer had confirmed in emails before the First-tier tribunal that the offer remained open at all material times."

It goes on to find that a person with a right of residence which exists in such a scenario does count as a worker under Directive 2004/38. As such, a person in this situation comes within para (3B)(a) of reg 10 and cannot be a person from abroad (see paras 53 to 56 of the judgment which holds that is the position for the income support provision which is equivalent to para (3B)(za) of reg 10 for HB).

Although the facts of *SSWP v RR* are clearly exceptional, the case may be of wider importance for those claiming HB in the usual period of days or weeks when they have an offer of employment which they have not yet taken up – such persons cannot be persons from abroad and thus do not need to demonstrate they are "habitually resident in fact" (see [3] at p344).

[1.2] Para (3B)(za): Self-employed

Reg 4(1)(b) I(EEA) Regs defines a "self employed person" as someone "who establishes himself in order to perform activities as a self employed person in accordance with Article 49 [TFEU]". Reg 6(1)(c) I(EEA) Regs defines such a person as a "qualified person". Art 49 TFEU (previously Art 43) on freedom of establishment, includes the right to take up and pursue activities as a self-employed person in an EU state.

The ECJ has taken the approach of defining as self-employed all those who are providing services in return for remuneration *but not under the direction of another person* – in other words, the distinction between a worker and a self-employed person turns on whether or not the services are provided outside a relationship of subordination: where they are (ie, there is no subordination of the service provider to another) then that activity must be regarded as self-employment (*Jany*, para 33). Cases such as *SSWP v AL (JSA)* [2011] UKUT 451 (AAC) highlight that the fact someone is taxed on a self-employed basis is not determinative of whether that is the case and emphasises the need to take particular care as to whether a relationship of subordination does exist in construction worker cases (where the "Construction Industry Scheme" may hide the fact that someone is really a worker and not self-employed in an EU law sense).

Furthermore, the ECJ in *Jany* is clear that the same considerations as to the activities being genuine and effective, as opposed to marginal and ancillary, apply to self-employment (see the discussion at [1.1] in relation to workers). The Upper Tribunal has frequently considered whether self-employment on the part of *Big Issue* sellers meets the genuine and effective threshold.

In *Bristol CC v FV (HB)* [2011] UKUT 494 (AAC), the Upper Tribunal considered whether a tribunal had been entitled to conclude that a seller of the *Big Issue* was self-employed and decided, on the evidence, that it was. The case serves as a reminder that the question of whether (1) the elements of self-employment (providing services, for remuneration, not under the direction of another) and (2) whether it is genuine and effective, are ones of fact. *HMRC v IT (CTC)* [2016] UKUT 252 (AAC) also concerned a *Big Issue* seller. There the judge found the work was not sufficient to count as genuine and effective. The facts were that the claimant had a profit of £2.36 per hour worked for a four and a half month period (working 16 hours a week). The judge also notes "this was the sole work during this period and was being done to support the claimant, his wife and their seven children". If that is meant to form part of the reasoning as to why the self-employment was not genuine and effective, then it is suggested that this is not a relevant factor in determining the issue (where the caselaw of the Court of Justice makes clear one takes account only of the factors concerned with the economic activity itself – see, for example, para 43 of *LN v Styrelsen for Viderergaende Uddannelser of UddannelsesstotteC-46/12* [2016] ECR). *DV v HMRC (CHB)* [2017] UKUT 155 (AAC) remarks that the *Bristol CC* case is not authority that all *Big Issue* sellers are in genuine and effective self-employment and finds, in the particular case it considers, that the claimant's activity did not meet the required threshold.

Someone who is merely seeking opportunities to become self-employed will not count: see the Northern Ireland Commissioner's decision in *C 10/1995 (IS)*. However, what of those who have taken some positive steps towards becoming self-employed but are not yet trading? In *R(IS) 6/00*, Commissioner Mesher considered the case of a French national who returned to the UK while she was pregnant. She placed an advert in a newspaper advertising French tuition. It was argued that she had a right of residence under Directive 73/148 (now repealed but with similar rights existing in Directive 2004/38). The commissioner held that the conclusions and reasoning in *C 10/1995 (IS)* could not be accepted in their entirety. He stated (paras 29–31) that there had to be a right of residence before a self-employed person actually began to trade in order to give effect to the Community objective of freedom of movement. Thus a person taking preparatory steps to setting up a business would acquire a right of residence under Directive 73/148. He then considered whether a claimant with an intention to trade, but who had not yet taken any steps towards doing so, could qualify.

"The difficult question is whether the right extends not merely to those who are taking steps towards offering their services to the public (or whatever final step is appropriate to the nature of the business) in a Member State, but also to those who wish to do that, but have not yet taken any steps beyond arriving in the Member State concerned. In my judgment, it does not. It would be going further than justified by the purposes of the Directive to extend a right of residence, rather than the mere right of entry to the Member State under Article 3, to such persons. It also seems to me that the crucial factor is not so much whether the person's intentions are for the present or for the future or are conditional in some way, but whether the person is taking steps towards offering services to the public, or otherwise setting up as a self-employed person." (para 31)

In *TG v SSWP* [2009] UKUT 58 (AAC), at the date of decision under consideration (in July 2006), the claimant had been working for about two months as a self-employed interpreter. Most of his work had been marketing and preparation and he had only been doing three or four hours of work a week and had made no profit (his first payment came after the date of the decision and for work done after that date). He had not registered with HMRC as a self-employed person. The judge held that the failure to register with HMRC was not fatal to the claimant being counted as self-employed (although it "may in some circumstances be evidence from which it may be inferred that a person is not self-employed"). He held on these facts that the claimant was self-employed.

In *EG v SSWP (JSA)* [2018] UKUT 285 (AAC), the Upper Tribunal considered a case of someone who had been on the New Enterprise Allowance Scheme (a Jobcentre Plus scheme to help jobseekers start or develop a self-employed business). Unfortunately, the judge in that case considered the issue as whether participation in the scheme should have paused the running of the 91 days during which the claimant could be accepted as a jobseeker without needing to show compelling evidence of a genuine prospect of work, rather than considering the sort of issues raised in *TG* and *R(IS) 6/00*. Nonetheless, there is certainly nothing in *EG* which undermines the authority of those decisions.

It is therefore clear that someone who is taking steps to become self-employed, but has not yet had any income as a result of those steps, may count as self-employed. Having said that, those cases all turned on consideration of the EU law. It might be said that they make clear EU law allows for a right of residence of those taking steps to establish themselves as well as those in fact established (see, for example, *R(IS) 6/00* at paras 31 to 32 – at that time it seems the relevant domestic legislation implementing EU rights also applied to those "seeking" to establish themselves). However, the I(EEA) Regs define a self-employed person as someone who is established. It may be the case, therefore, that those seeking to establish themselves would struggle to argue they came within para (3B) of reg 10 given that it now refers to the I(EEA) Regs (but could still say they had a right sufficient for para (3)).

How though does one determine whether someone has ceased to be self-employed?

CIS 1042/2008 held that a woman who takes a period of leave from her self-employment for reasons of maternity but intends to return, continues to count as self-employed (so the issue of whether she is a person who retains the status of a self-employed person and so comes within para (3B)(c) does not arise). That decision is argued to be incorrect by the DWP and a reference has been made (see the discussion of pregnancy at [1.3.3] on p315).

In *SSWP v JS (IS)* [2010] UKUT 240 (AAC), Judge Jacobs considered the situation of a Polish claimant who had been working on a self-employed basis providing language support in schools. At the date of decision on her claim for IS, she appeared not to have had any ongoing work (or very little such ongoing work). The judge held:

"5.   I do not accept that a claimant who is for the moment doing no work is necessarily no longer self-employed. There will commonly be periods in a person's self-employment when no work is done. Weekends and holiday periods are obvious examples. There may also be periods when there is no work to do. The concept of self-employment necessarily encompasses periods of both feast and famine. During the latter, the person may be engaged in a variety of tasks that are properly seen as part of continuing self-employment: administrative work, such as maintaining the accounts; in marketing to generate more work; or developing the business in new directions. Self-employment is not confined to periods of actual work. It includes natural periods of rest and the vicissitudes of business life. This does not mean that self-employment survives no matter how little work arrives. It does mean that the issue can only be decided in the context of the facts at any particular time. The amount of work is one factor. Whether the claimant is taking any other steps in the course of self-employment is also relevant. The claimant's motives and intentions must all be taken into account, although they will not necessarily be decisive."

Therefore, it seems that there are circumstances in which a claimant experiencing a period with no ongoing business can continue to count as self-employed, although, as the judge notes, "So much depends on the circumstances, and, therefore, on the evidence."

SSWP v AL (JSA) (above) was one case where the tribunal had been entitled to conclude that the facts did support continued self-employment. *HD and GP v SSWP* [2017] UKUT 11 (AAC) provides an example of where such a conclusion was not supported on the facts but emphasises the need for careful fact finding in this area (both of the claimants in this joined decision had stopped self-employment due to pregnancy and a final decision is stayed behind resolution of whether a right of residence exists in such a situation: see [1.3.4] below).

[1.3] Para (3B)(za): Those who retain worker/self-employed status

A person who is no longer a worker or self-employed may, if certain conditions are met, continue to be treated as having the status of worker or self employed person.

In all cases, before considering whether a person retains the status of worker/self-employed person, it is first necessary to consider whether s/he is in fact still a worker or self-employed. Part of the answer to this seems to be that someone remains a worker while on a period of leave from work, even if that leave is unpaid: see *BS v SSWP* [2009] UKUT 16 (AAC). The other issue is whether the person has left the labour market, and the position seems to be that this does not happen automatically once a contract of employment ends (see [1.3.3] on p316).

It is to be noted that sub-para (za) refers to those who are workers or self-employed people under reg 6 I(EEA) Regs. Reg 6(2) and (4) set out situations in which a person who has ceased to be a worker or self-employed person for EU law purposes nonetheless continues to be treated as a worker or self-employed person. The conditions for falling within the reg 6(2) situations are further set out in reg 6(3) to (10). Art 7(3) of Directive 2004/38 also provides for situations where a person may retain her/his right as a worker/self-employed person. It is fair to say that the rules set out in the Directive make considerably easier reading and understanding than those provided in the I(EEA) Regs. More seriously, it may be the case that the limitations in reg 6(3) to (10) are more restrictive than the Directive rights which they are supposed to transpose. Given that the complexities of the I(EEA) Regs mainly relate to the position of those who may retain worker status while involuntarily unemployed, this issue is discussed at [1.3.2]. For the present, it is enough to refer to the situations in which status may be retained by reference to Art 7(3) of the Directive, which provides that a person who is no longer a worker/self-employed person continues to have that status if s/he is:

(a) temporarily unable to work as a result of an illness or accident (see [1.3.1]);

(b) in duly recorded involuntary unemployment after having been employed for more than one year and has registered as a jobseeker with the relevant employment office;

(c) in duly recorded involuntary unemployment after having worked for less than a year and has registered as a jobseeker with the relevant employment office. The Directive states that in such circumstances "the status of worker shall be retained for no less than six months";

(d) embarked upon vocational training. Unless involuntarily unemployed, the retention of the status of worker requires that the training be related to the previous employment (see [1.3.2] for a discussion of Art 7(3)(b) to (d) as compared to the provisions of the I(EEA) Regs).

The removal of the reference to income-based JSA in reg 10(3B)(k) (see [1.9]) means that authorities will now need to determine whether claimants receiving income-based JSA are in fact retaining worker status under Art 7(3)(b) or (c) (or have some other right of residence better than that of a jobseeker). The commentary at [1.9] explores the relationship between a DWP decision to award income-based JSA and HB decision-making: where income-based JSA is awarded on the basis that the claimant has a right of residence as a jobseeker, the procedure is that the DWP will notify the authority that its view is that the claimant only has a right of residence as a jobseeker (see HB Circular A6/2014).

Art 7(3) of the Directive is now known not to be an exhaustive list of the situations in which a person may retain her/his status as a worker. This is discussed at [1.3.3 below] with particular reference to women who are not working due to pregnancy or having recently had a child.

[1.3.1] "temporarily unable to work as a result of an illness of accident"

The meaning of this provision was considered in *CIS 3890/2005*. In that case, the tribunal directed itself that an incapacity was only temporary if there was a certainty of recovery. In the view of the tribunal, this was not the case with the claimant's back problems. The commissioner allowed the claimant's appeal and held that while the tribunal was permitted to conclude that the back problems could be a permanent illness, the test was whether or not the inability to work produced by the illness was temporary.

A useful summary of the cases that concern the distinction between temporary and permanent incapacity for work is contained in the Court of Appeal's decision in *Samin v City of Westminster* [2012] EWCA Civ 1468 at paras 17 to 19. The cases show that:

(1)   Temporary is to be contrasted with permanent: there is no middle ground between these two terms – an incapacity is either one or the other (*SSHD v FMB* [2010] UKUT 447 (IAC)), approved in *De Brito v SSHD* [2012] EWCA Civ 709). So a claimant unable to work due to illness or accident, whose incapacity is not temporary will have a permanent incapacity and may be able to benefit from Article 17 of Directive 2004/38 and come within reg 10(3B)(e) – discussed at [1.5].

(2)   *Samin, De Brito* and a further Court of Appeal case (*Konodyba v Royal Borough of Kensington and Chelsea* [2012] EWCA Civ 982) hold that the question of whether someone is permanently incapable is an objective one (although the claimant's views may be relevant to assessing this). The question to be asked is whether there is a realistic prospect of the person returning to work in the foreseeable future. They also highlight that the question is always whether it is the health problems of the person which must be preventing the return to work rather than some other factor.

An appeal against the decision in *Samin* was dismissed by the Supreme Court in *Mirga and Samin v SSWP and Westminster City Council* [2016] UKSC 1; [2016] AACR 26, although the issue as to the distinction between permanent and temporary incapacity did not figure in the appeal. *LM v HMRC (CHB)* [2016] UKUT 389 (AAC) also confirms incapacity for work is either temporary or it is permanent – there is no grey area in between.

In *CIS 4304/2007*, the commissioner held that the test of whether a claimant was "unable to work" was not the same as the UK test for whether a person could receive benefits on the basis of incapacity for work, but was an autonomous EU concept:

"in order to ensure uniformity in that legislation between Member States, it must be interpreted in the same way throughout the EU. It cannot, therefore, depend upon the particular domestic legislation governing incapacity benefits. The language of the legislation has to be interpreted and applied as it stands. The context provides some guidance. It ensures continuity of worker status for someone who would otherwise be employed or looking for work. That employment or search for employment provides the touchstone against which the claimant's disabilities must be judged. The question is: can she fairly be described as unable to do the work she was doing or the sort of work that she was seeking?"

In *HK v SSWP* [2017] UKUT 421 (AAC), *CIS 4304/2007* was followed. The judge also makes the further point that there is no need for any claim to benefit to have been made for periods where a claimant asserts s/he retains worker/self-employed status when temporarily unable to work due to illness. Finally, while the test of inability to work is not the ESA test, evidence of how the claimant is assessed under the ESA test may help evidence if the claimant meets the EU law test.

It has been held that pregnancy per se is not an illness and therefore a pregnant woman who gives up work during pregnancy does not necessarily retain her status as a worker on the basis of being temporarily unable to work as a result of an illness. Although in *CIS 4010/2006*, it was held that pregnancy is not an illness and, therefore, a pregnant woman does not retain her status on this basis, *Saint Prix* (discussed at [1.3.3], which confirms that point) holds that such women may still count as workers in any event. If there is pregnancy-related ill health which prevents work, status will be retained: *CIS 731/2007*. Note also that a woman on maternity leave remains a worker and so the question of retaining status does not arise: *CIS 4237/2007*.

Arguments that the worker/self-employed person was temporarily unable to work as a result of an illness experienced by someone else for whom s/he had to care have failed: *CIS 3182/2005, CIS 2911/2007* (although again given it is now clear that the situations in which worker status is retained are not exhaustively set out in Art 7(3) of the Directive (or reg 6(2) I(EEA) Regs) the correctness of those decisions may be reconsidered).

[1.3.2] Involuntary unemployment

It is necessary to consider:

(1)   The meaning of "involuntary unemployment" in Art 7(3)(b)–(d) of the Directive and of "voluntary unemployment" in Art 7(3)(d) – see [1.3.2.1].

(2)   The circumstances in which someone is to be regarded as having "registered as a jobseeker with the relevant employment office" – see [1.3.2.2].

(3)   The issue of whether a self-employed person whose business folds can retain status under Art 7(3)(b)–(d) – see [1.3.2.3].

(4)   The precise terms of reg 6(2)–(10) I(EEA) Regs and the extent to which they are consistent with the rights set forth in Art 7(3)(b)–(d) of the Directive – see [1.3.2.4].

[1.3.2.1] "voluntary" and "involuntary unemployment".

For reg 6(2) I(EEA) Regs and Art 7(3)(b) and (c), in terms of retaining status as a worker/self-employed person while involuntarily unemployed, it is clear that "involuntarily" relates not to the circumstances of leaving work but to the ongoing relationship to the labour market: *CH 3314/2005* (para 11) and *R(IS) 12/98*.

In *SSWP v EM* [2009] UKUT 146 (AAC), the Upper Tribunal considered the distinction between being "voluntarily" and "involuntarily" unemployed for the purposes of Art 7(3)(d) of the Directive (equivalent to reg 6(2)(e) of the I(EEA) Regs). That provision provides for worker status to be retained when the worker has entered vocational education. Importantly, if the unemployment is voluntary, then worker status can only be retained where the vocational education is related to the previous employment. It is only where the person is involuntarily unemployed that worker status can be retained regardless of any connection between the content of the vocational education and the content of previous employment. EM needed to show that she was involuntarily unemployed because she could not argue that her former employment in a chicken processing factory was related to her vocational education training to be a teaching assistant. It was argued for her that in this provision one must look at how the person became unemployed in order to determine whether she was involuntarily unemployed. However, the judge disagreed and held that someone is involuntarily unemployed for the purposes of this provision:

"Only where a person has to retrain in order to find work reasonably equivalent to his or her former employment. [......] it does not look back at the circumstances in which the person has become unemployed, although that may be part of the background; it is concerned with the situation where a person cannot reasonably be expected to be in the labour market because there is no appropriate market."

The Secretary of State's attempt to argue, again, that this approach was incorrect, was defeated in *SSWP v MK (IS)* [2013] UKUT 163 (AAC): in that case the claimant had left work voluntarily. The Upper Tribunal on this occasion again confirmed that the test was whether the claimant remained in the labour market – the circumstances of leaving work may be evidence useful in deciding that question but that is all (see paras 41 to 47).

It should also be noted with regard to Art 7(3)(d) that there is no requirement for the claimant to have registered her/his unemployment with the relevant employment office.

[1.3.2.2] "registered as a jobseeker with the relevant employment office". The requirement to have "registered as a jobseeker with the relevant employment office", necessary to retain status when involuntarily unemployed, can certainly be met by claiming JSA at a Jobcentre Plus and signing on thereafter.

What is less clear is what happens in situations where the claimant has not done this. Prior to 30 April 2006, the Secretary of State had conceded in *CH 3314/2005* that a requirement that a claimant be "duly recorded by the relevant employment office" was met by an IS claimant who declared that she was seeking work on her "Right to Reside Stencil" – ie, in the claim process. That concession was not made again in other cases, and in *CIS 3799/2007* it was held the test could only be met where a claimant had claimed JSA. In *SSWP v ZW* [2009] UKUT 25 (AAC), the Upper Tribunal held that participation in a work-focused interview by an IS claimant did not constitute registration with a relevant employment office. The first of two of those decisions is now shown to have clearly been wrong and the second is arguably so.

In *SSWP v FE* [2009] UKUT 287 (AAC), a three-judge panel of the Upper Tribunal considered the situation of someone who had worked for six months and who had, on being made redundant, claimed IS as a lone parent, stating on the HRT2(R) form issued to her by the Jobcentre that she was looking for work. The Upper Tribunal concluded by a 2:1 majority as follows:

"29.   We conclude that the Secretary of State has not shown that the UK has defined specific mechanisms as being the only ways in which an individual can, for the purposes of Article 7(3)(c) "register as a job-seeker with the relevant employment office". That being so, the tribunal was entitled to hold that the Secretary of State's factual concessions meant that the claimant succeeded in her appeal. In summary:

a.   What the Directive contemplates is that a claimant has done what is needed in order to have his or her name recorded as looking for work by the relevant employment office

b.   Whether or not this has been done is a question of fact

c.   There is no rule of law that such registration can be effected only by way of registering for jobseeker's allowance or national insurance credits, less still only by successfully claiming one or other of those benefits

d.   Nor was there at the material time an administrative practice to that effect (even assuming – without deciding – that to be a lawful way of implementing the Directive)

e.   Successfully claiming jobseeker's allowance or national insurance credits will no doubt provide sufficient evidence to satisfy Article 7(3)(c); but

f.   Those who are able to show not merely that they were seeking work, but that they had done what is needed in order to have their name recorded as looking for work by the relevant employment office – will meet the registration requirement of Article 7(3)(c);

g.   It being conceded that the claimant had stated on the Habitual Residence Test documents that she was seeking work and that the extent of the work being sought was sufficient, it follows that she met the relevant test."

The Secretary of State's appeal against the decision was unanimously dismissed by the Court of Appeal on 18 October 2011: *Elmi v SSWP* [2011] EWCA Civ 1403; [2012] AACR 22.

As the Secretary of State may well fail to consider whether a claimant has an *Elmi*-type case and refuse IS, despite the fact the claimant has declared s/he is looking for work, following a period of employment there are situations where decision makers in HB matters will need to consider the issue for themselves. It cannot be over-emphasised that a claim for JSA will almost always be in the best interests of a claimant who is involuntarily unemployed (having been a worker) given the ease with which it can then be argued that such a claimant retains worker status compared to *Elmi*-type cases.

[1.3.2.3] Self-employed and involuntary unemployment. The I(EEA) Regs did not, until 24 July 2018, provide for a self-employed person who stops working to be able to retain her/his status through looking for work and registering with the relevant employment office. *Gusa v Minister for Social Protection* (C-422/16) [2017] ECR (ECLI:EC:C:2017:1004) established that this was wrong. The ECJ held:

> "Article 7(3)(b) of Directive 2004/38/EC [...] must be interpreted as meaning that a national of a Member State retains the status of self-employed person for the purposes of Article 7(1)(a) of that directive where, after having lawfully resided in and worked as a self-employed person in another Member State for approximately four years, that national has ceased that activity, because of a duly recorded absence of work owing to reasons beyond his control, and has registered as a jobseeker with the relevant employment office of the latter Member State."

This means that *SSWP v RK* [2009] UKUT 209 (AAC) and *R (on the application of Tilianu) v SSWP* [2010] EWCA Civ 1397 were wrongly decided.

SB v SSWP (UC) [2019] UKUT 219 (AAC) confirms that a self-employed person who has worked for less than one year can retain status for six months (ie, that Art 7(3)(c) also applies to the self-employed – the facts of *Gusa* came within Art 7(3)(b) but there is no reason why the principle would not also extend to sub-para (c)).

From 24 July 2018, the I(EEA) Regs are amended to make clear that a person who was self-employed can retain status under any of the heads of article 7(3): see reg 6(4).

In some cases, one can avoid needing to consider the issue of *retaining* self employed status by asking the logically prior question which is whether the person has in fact *stopped* being a self-employed person (in which case no question of retaining that status need arise). Because a person who is merely taking steps to establish self-employment may count as a self-employed person (see [1.2] above), it must be the case that someone who has in fact established her/himself in that capacity and worked on that basis for some time and who is then in a period where no work is coming in, but who is actively taking steps to obtain more work, will still be considered self-employed: that has been confirmed in *SSWP v JS (IS)* [2010] UKUT 240 (AAC). One might think that such considerations are irrelevant now a claimant can rely on *Gusa,* but factual situations could arise where it mattered – eg, if the self-employment proper (as opposed to merely retaining that status) continued until a later date then the six-month period might start to run from a later date.

RJ v SSWP (JSA) [2011] UKUT 447 (AAC); [2012] AACR 28 agrees with *SSWP v JS (IS)* [2010] UKUT 240 (AAC) to the effect that a person may be self-employed despite the fact no work is coming in at present.

[1.3.2.4] The limitations in reg 6(2) I(EEA) Regs. Reg 6 I(EEA) Regs 2006 was amended three times between December 2013 and November 2014. The main effect sought by the amendments was to limit the situations in which status as a worker can be maintained. Those amendments are carried over into the current I(EEA) Regs. Given that reg 10(3B)(za) HB Regs refers only to people who are workers or self-employed under the I(EEA) Regs, it is necessary to pay careful attention to the wording.

The current version now reads as follows, so far as is relevant to looking at how Art 7(3)(b) and (c) of the Directive are now transposed in UK law (the specific provisions relevant to jobseekers – that is those who do not retain status as a worker but merely have a right of residence as a jobseeker are discussed at [1.9] below):

"Qualified person"

6.–(1)   In these Regulations–

"jobseeker" means an EEA national who satisfies conditions A, B and, where relevant, C;

"qualified person" means a person who is an EEA national and in the United Kingdom as–

(a)   a jobseeker;

(b)   a worker;

(c)   a self-employed person;

(d)   a self-sufficient person; or

(e)   a student;

"relevant period" means–

(a)   in the case of a person retaining worker status under paragraph (2)(b) or self-employed person status under paragraph (4)(b), a continuous period of six months;

(b)   in the case of a jobseeker, 91 days, minus the cumulative total of any days during which the person concerned previously enjoyed a right to reside as a jobseeker, not including any days prior to a continuous absence from the United Kingdom of at least 12 months.

(2)   A person who is no longer working must continue to be treated as a worker provided that the person–

(a)   is temporarily unable to work as the result of an illness or accident;

(b)   is in duly recorded involuntary unemployment after having been employed in the United Kingdom for at least one year, provided the person–

   (i)   has registered as a jobseeker with the relevant employment office; and

   (ii)   satisfies conditions A and B;

(c)   is in duly recorded involuntary unemployment after having been employed in the United Kingdom for less than one year, provided the person–

   (i)   has registered as a jobseeker with the relevant employment office; and

   (ii)   satisfies conditions A and B;

(d)   is involuntarily unemployed and has embarked on vocational training; or

(e) has voluntarily ceased working and has embarked on vocational training that is related to the person's previous employment.

(3) A person to whom paragraph (2)(c) applies may only retain worker status for a maximum of six months.

(4) A person who is no longer in self-employment must continue to be treated as a self-employed person provided that the person–

(a) is temporarily unable to engage in activities as a self-employed person as the result of an illness or accident;

(b) is in duly recorded involuntary unemployment after having worked as a self-employed person in the United Kingdom for at least one year provided the person–

 (i) has registered as a jobseeker with the relevant employment office; and

 (ii) satisfies conditions D and E;

(c) is in duly recorded involuntary unemployment after having worked as a self-employed person in the United Kingdom for less than one year, provided the person–

 (i) has registered as a jobseeker with the relevant employment office; and

 (ii) satisfies conditions D and E;

(d) is involuntarily no longer in self-employment and has embarked on vocational training; or

(e) has voluntarily ceased self-employment and has embarked on vocational training that is related to the person's previous occupation.

(4A) A person to whom paragraph (4)(c) applies may only retain self-employed person status for a maximum of six months.

(4B) Condition D is that the person–

(a) entered the United Kingdom as a self-employed person or in order to seek employment as a self-employed person; or

(b) is present in the United Kingdom seeking employment or self-employment, immediately after enjoying a right to reside under sub-paragraphs (c) to (e) of the definition of qualified person in paragraph (1) (disregarding any period during which self-employed status was retained pursuant to paragraph (4)(b) or (c)).

(4C) Condition E is that the person provides evidence of seeking employment or self-employment and having a genuine chance of being engaged.

(5) Condition A is that the person–

(a) entered the United Kingdom in order to seek employment; or

(b) is present in the United Kingdom seeking employment, immediately after enjoying a right to reside under sub-paragraphs (b), (d) or (e) of the definition of qualified person in paragraph (1) (disregarding any period during which worker status was retained pursuant to paragraph (2)(b) or (c)).

(6) Condition B is that the person provides evidence of seeking employment and having a genuine chance of being engaged.

(7) A person may not retain the status of–

(a) a worker under paragraph (2)(b);

(b) a jobseeker; or

(c) a self-employed person under paragraph (4)(b)

for longer than the relevant period without providing compelling evidence of continuing to seek employment and having a genuine chance of being engaged.

(8) Condition C applies where the person concerned has, previously, enjoyed a right to reside under this regulation as a result of satisfying conditions A and B or, as the case may be, conditions D and E–

(a) in the case of a person to whom paragraph (2)(b) or (c) or (4)(b) or (c) applied, for at least six months; or

(b) in the case of a jobseeker, for at least 91 days in total,

unless the person concerned has, since enjoying the above right to reside, been continuously absent from the United Kingdom for at least 12 months.

(9) Condition C is that the person has had a period of absence from the United Kingdom.

(10) Where condition C applies–

(a) paragraph (7) does not apply; and

(b) condition B or, as the case may be, condition E has effect as if "compelling" were inserted before "evidence".

The effect of this regulation on when worker status can be retained in periods of unemployment are as follows.

(1) A person who has worked (employed or self-employed) in excess of a year and is then involuntarily unemployed (ie, someone within para (2)(b) or (4)(b)) will retain status if s/he registers as a jobseeker (para (2)(b)(i)) and also meets conditions A and B (para (2)(b)(ii)/(4)(b)(ii) – where condition A and B map to condition D and E). Condition A is defined in para (5). Condition B is simply that evidence of seeking employment is being provided and the claimant has a genuine chance of being engaged. However, by para (7) such a person will only retain status beyond a relevant period (defined in para (1) as a continuous period of six months) where s/he can provide *compelling* evidence that s/he is seeking employment and has a genuine chance of being engaged. The compelling evidence requirement also applies to the jobseeker's right of residence and its meaning was considered in *MB and Others v SSWP (JSA)* [2016] UKUT 372 (AAC); [2017] AACR 6. Effectively, the phrase adds nothing to the EU law test of whether

someone has a genuine chance of being engaged which means a chance of obtaining employment that is "real" as opposed to fanciful as shown by the objective facts of the case.

(2) For those who have been employed/self-employed for less than a year, the UK provision now means worker status can be retained for no more than six months.

The contrast between the wording of the Directive at Art 7(3)(b) and (c) and the I(EEA) Regs are stark.

(1) For those who have worked for more than a year, Art 7(3)(b) does not place any limit on how long worker status may be retained for, or require demonstration of a search for work or reasonable prospects of being engaged (compelling or otherwise), but simply requires that the person has "registered as a jobseeker with the relevant employment office": presumably the fact that a person has been employed for a year is sufficient evidence of her/his employability and being registered with the jobcentre of her/his search for work. The Upper Tribunal in *MM v SSWP (IS)* [2015] UKUT 128 (AAC) took the view that Art 7(3)(b) allowed worker status to be retained for a period that was "open-ended though not for evermore". Further, there the judge found it to be "eminently reasonable" to conclude someone retained status under that provision for a year "in the absence of some intervening event which indicates that the person has withdrawn from the labour market entirely". Although the judge was not considering there the provisions of the I(EEA) Regs, the decision was given after their coming into force and the judgment gives a binding interpretation of Art 7(3)(b) to decision makers which is at odds with what is said in the I(EEA) Regs. The Upper Tribunal is considering whether the I(EEA) Regs are more limiting than the Directive in file reference CH/2389/2016.

(2) For those who have been employed for less than a year, Art 7(3)(c) requires registration as a jobseeker with the relevant employment office and states that "the status of worker shall be retained for **no less than** six months". However, the UK provision means worker status could be retained for **no more than** six months. Under the I(EEA) Regs 2006, prior to the 2014 amendments, the then reg 6(2)(b)(iii) allowed for worker status to be retained for a longer period where the claimant could provide evidence that s/he was looking for work and had a genuine chance of being engaged. That could be seen as having been more consistent with the wording of the Directive. However, in *Jobcentre Berlin Newkolln v Alimanovic* (Case C-67/14), the Court of Justice accepted, without comment, the German transposition of the Directive which provided worker status in such a case could only be retained for a maximum of six months as being all that Art 7(3)(c) requires. Again, however, it should be noted that the Directive does not require demonstration of the effectiveness of the search for work at any point.

(3) The approach of the UK Regulations to periods of self-employment to the effect that the person must now show evidence of a genuine chance of becoming self-employed is also perhaps wrong – a person who is no longer self-employed following *Gusa* presumably needs to show s/he is actively seeking employment – which is after all what JSA requires.

Given that the amendment of reg 10(3B)(k) (see [1.9]) to remove receipt of income-based JSA as a passport through the person from abroad test means that those whose only right to reside is as a jobseeker are now excluded from HB entitlement, whether Art 7(3)(b) and (c) do confer more rights, as suggested above, than reg 6 I(EEA) Regs is an issue which arises in HB disputes. If it is held that a person has a right of residence under Art 7(3)(b) or (c) but not under the I(EEA) Regs then that would be a sufficient right of residence for reg 10(3) even if it not one referred to in reg 10(3B)(za).

[1.3.3] Pregnancy

The Supreme Court in *Saint-Prix v SSWP* [2012] UKSC 49 referred the following questions to the Court of Justice:
"1. Is the right of residence conferred upon a 'worker' in Article 7 of the Citizenship Directive to be interpreted as applying only to those (i) in an existing employment relationship, (ii) (at least in some cicumstances) seeking work, or (iii) covered by the extensions in article 7(3), or is the Article to be interpreted as not precluding the recognition of further persons who remain 'workers' for this purpose?
2. (i) If the latter, does it extend to a woman who reasonably gives up work, or seeking work, because of the physical constraints of the late stages of pregnancy (and the aftermath of childbirth)?
   (ii) If so, is she entitled to the benefit of the national law's definition of when it is reasonable for her to do so?"

In *Saint-Prix v SSWP* (Case C-507/12) [2014] ECR; [2014] AACR 18, the ECJ answered the questions as follows:
"Article 45 TFEU must be interpreted as meaning that a woman who gives up work, or seeking work, because of the physical constraints of the late stages of pregnancy and the aftermath of childbirth retains the status of 'worker', within the meaning of that article, provided she returns to work or finds another job within a reasonable period after the birth or her child."

At para 42, the Court gave guidance on how to determine what a "reasonable period" is:
"In order to determine whether the period that has elapsed between childbirth and starting work again may be regarded as reasonable, the national court concerned should take account of all the specific circumstances of the case in the main proceedings and the applicable national rules on the duration of maternity leave, in accordance with Article 8 of Council Directive 92/85/EEC [the "pregnancy directive"]"

The Upper Tribunal has now clarified the scope of *Saint-Prix*. In *SSWP v SFF and Others* [2015] UKUT 502 (AAC); [2016] AACR 16 it was held that:

(1)   There is no requirement that there be, at the outset of a *Saint-Prix*-period, an intention to return to work (or seeking work). However, if a firm intention not to return to work is formed at some stage, the right of residence would come to an end at that point. This is contrary to what is said in DMG Memo 25/14 which suggests that a woman must declare at the outset of a claim for IS that she intends to return to work.

(2)   A woman may start to have a *Saint-Prix* right either after having been employed immediately beforehand or in a situation where immediatley before the *Saint-Prix* period she was retaining her worker status under Art 7(3) of the Directive (disagreeing with the Memo).

(3)   Typically a *Saint-Prix* right would commence 11 weeks before the expected week of birth but it could be different depending on the nature of the work that the woman had been doing. Note, though, that a three-judge panel of the Upper Tribunal's Immigration and Asylum Chamber decided in *Weldemichael and Another* [2015] UKUT 540 (IAC) that an earlier start date could arise in a case of multiple births or where the work was particularly onerous but cogent evidence would be needed.

(4)   Applying para 42 of the judgment in *Saint-Prix* a "reasonable period" would normally be 52 weeks (again contrary to the DWP Memo).

(5)   It is sufficient for the woman to return to seeking work at the expiry of this reasonable period; there is no requirement the woman actually gets a job.

(6)   A *Saint-Prix* right can count towards a permanent right of residence.

In *HMRC v HD (CHB) (Second Interim Decision)* [2018] UKUT 148 (AAC), Judge Ward referred questions to the Court of Justice effectively asking if the *Saint-Prix* right also extends to those who have to stop self-employment due to late stage pregnancy. Judgment was given on 19 September 2019 in *Dakneviciute* (Case C-544/18) [2019] ECLI:EU:C:2019:261 where the Court delcared that the *Saint-Prix* right did so extend.

In a first interim decision involving the same claimant heard with a linked case in which a final decision is given (*HD and GP v SSWP* [2017] UKUT 11 (AAC)), emphasis is given to the need for careful fact finding in cases involving self-employed women and pregnancy: one possibility is that the woman is actually still engaged in genuine and effective self-employment (as was the case in *GP*) – see further the discussion at [1.2].

Taking a step back from the rights of pregnant women, the *Saint-Prix* judgment is also significant in that the Court explicitly holds that the heads in Art 7(3) of Directive 2004/38 (and, therefore, also the heads of reg 6(2) I(EEA) Regs) are not an exhaustive list of the circumstances in which someone who is no longer working nonetheless should still be treated as a worker (para 38). There may be other circumstances where one has to regard a person as still a worker after the employment relationship has ended: although what these circumstances are remains to be determined – it could be suggested that a person who stops work to care for a child who is temporarily ill (eg, that *CIS 3182/2005* was wrongly decided) or for other compelling reasons that are nonetheless clearly temporary will retain her/his status. That line of argument did not find success at the Upper Tribunal in *JS v SSWP (IS)* [2019] UKUT 135 (AAC). The judge held that the Court of Justice in *Saint-Prix* did not open the door to other categories by analogy (para 33).

The *Saint-Prix* case arose against the background that it had been held that pregnancy per se is not an illness and therefore a pregnant woman who gives up work during pregnancy does not necessarily retain her status as a worker on the basis of being temporarily unable to work as a result of an illness. However, if there is pregnancy-related ill health which prevents work, status will be retained (*CIS 731/2007*) and it will not be necessary to consider whether the *Saint-Prix* conditions are met. Note also that a woman on maternity leave remains a worker and so the question of retaining status does not arise: *CIS 4237/2007*.

[1.3.4] Gaps and switching between ways of retaining status

In *CIS 4304/2007* and *SSWP v IR* [2009] UKUT 11 (AAC), it has been decided that a person may move from retaining status as a worker in one way to retaining it under another – ie, a person who had been a worker, then had a period of retaining status while claiming JSA and then became temporarily unable to work due to illness would count as a person who retained the status of worker.

What, though, of situations where there is a gap between the person ceasing to be a worker/self-employed person and coming within one of Art 7(3)(a)–(d), or one of the provisions in reg 6(2) of the I(EEA) Regs? In *CIS 1934/2006,* the commissioner commented that "it may well be that some gap between employment and a person starting to seek work again will not be fatal"; however on the facts of the case before him – where the gap was two years, which is longer than the time abroad allowed for a person who wishes not to lose her/his permanent right of residence (see below) – this had not occurred. Interestingly, the commissioner commented that gaps where the "person had taken time away from the labour market for a short holiday or while giving birth" could possibly count. A more concrete example arose in *SSWP v IR*. In that case, there had been a gap of just over two months between the claimant finishing work and claiming JSA. The judge remitted the case to a fresh tribunal to determine whether this gap was fatal and held as follows:

"A gap between becoming involuntarily unemployed and claiming jobseeker's allowance is not necessarily fatal. Whether it is significant or not will depend on the length of the gap and the reasons for it. Put into the legal terms of the EC analysis, the question is whether the gap shows that the claimant has withdrawn from the labour market. A claimant may take a few days to think about the future or to rest after a stressful period leading to redundancy. That may be consistent with remaining in the labour market. In contrast, a claimant who decides to spend six months backpacking in the Australian outback before looking for work has clearly left the labour market for the time being."

So the position following *SSWP v IR*, for people having a gap between stopping work and signing on, depends upon the specific facts of their case and whether those facts show that they remained in the labour market. However, the issue has been re-examined in *SSWP v MK (IS)* [2013] UKUT 163 (AAC) and a slightly different conclusion has been reached, following extensive consideration of the caselaw. The judge found that the earlier cases were decided prior to the introduction of the specific wording in Directive 2004/38 which now requires, for retaining status when involuntarily unemployed, "registration" with the employment office as well as being "duly recorded" as in involuntary unemployment. The judge holds that the requirement for registration may be a new tightening of the rules that did not previously exist (para 53). The issue in that case was whether a gap of slightly over three months between stopping work and claiming JSA allowed worker status to be retained. The judge concluded that "where there is delay of more than a very few days between the end of employment and the completion of the formalities required to take the benefit of Article 7(3)(b) [...] the proper approach is to ask whether, having regard to all the circumstances of the case, there has been undue delay". The judge holds that the test of "undue delay" involves "a full enquiry into the reasons for and circumstances of any delay" that entails "full and careful findings of fact about what a claimant did between the ending of employment and [registration]" in the light of which decision makers need to "exercise a judgment as to whether there are reasonable grounds for the delay such that it is not right to regard it as an undue delay" (paras 70–72). A longer delay will require more compelling reasons to count as not "undue".

In an interim decision in *FT v (1) Islington LB and (2) SSWP (HB)* [2015] UKUT 121 (AAC) given on 6 March 2015, the Upper Tribunal found that a gap of six weeks between the claimant ceasing employment and claiming JSA was not sufficient to break the retention of worker status. The judge observes the case may be useful from "a practitioner's point of view" as an aide to understanding how the principle in *SSWP v MK (IS)* should be applied. The SSWP (and local authority) conceded in that case that they would not argue that a gap of six weeks was down to undue delay. The reasons given by the SSWP were:

(a) the appellant's history of looking for, and speedily obtaining, jobs previously;

(b) the availability of existing savings to tide her over; *and*

(c) the evidence provided by the backdating claim form, containing very specific details of the steps which this appellant had taken at the time to look for work and confirmation of the SSWP's view at the time that what she had said was reliable.

The judge (para 15) stated that a key bit of evidence in the case before him (about a HB matter) had to be obtained from the DWP – he does this to draw attention to local authority submission writers, claimant representatives, and tribunals that this may be source of evidence in similar cases.

The position for people who have a short gap between stopping work and becoming temporarily incapable of work is less clear. In *SSWP v IA* [2009] UKUT 35 (AAC), the judge comments that:

"There is nothing in either the Directive or the Regulations that confers a right to reside on someone who becomes unable to work unless immediately before that the person was either a worker or retained worker status. Worker status can be gained and retained. There is no power for it to be revived after it has been lost other than by working."

This is somewhat odd as it seems to assume that worker status must have been lost. Take, as an example, the case of a person who stops work and takes a short rest after a stressful period leading up to a redundancy but intends to sign on after that (which the same judge accepted was permissible in *SSWP v IR*). Why should that claimant not retain status if, for example, she breaks a leg during that period of rest and is then unable to sign on? It is suggested that the same considerations as apply to people who can retain status through involuntary unemployment should apply to those who become temporarily incapable of work – particularly where the incapacity was unforeseen.

HK v SSWP [2017] UKUT 421 (AAC) states that the caselaw on gaps will apply equally to situations where the gap is not immediately after working, but is instead between retaining status under one head of Art 7(3) and retaining it under another head (that would apply in a case where, for example, a claimant ceased work and a couple of weeks later became temporarily unable to work due to illness and claimed ESA; although if the claimant was unwell at the point s/he stopped work then, of course, s/he meet the condition in art 7(3)(a) from that point in any event).

Reg 6(5)(b) of the I(EEA) Regs requires, for retention of worker status on the grounds of involuntary unemployment, that the period of unemployment is "immediately after" enjoying some other right of residence. Making that rule fit with the decided cases referred to above can be achieved by noting that in the gap period the person is regarded as continuing to be a worker.

[1.4] Para (3B)(zb): Family members of workers or the self-employed

Para (3B)(zb) provides that the family member within the meaning of reg 7(1)(a) to (c) I(EEA) Regs of a worker/ self-employed person cannot be a "person from abroad" (the family member of a person who retains status as a worker etc will similarly be within this provision as such persons are treated as workers for the purposes of reg 6(1) I(EEA) Regs).

Regulation 7(1) defines a family member as:

(1) a spouse or civil partner;

(2) a direct descendant of the worker/self-employed person, or of her/his spouse or civil partner, who is *either* under 21 *or* is dependant;

(3)   direct relatives in the ascendant line (parents, grandparents etc) of the worker/self-employed person, or their spouse or civil partner, who are dependent.

Art 2(2) of the Directive makes the same provision. "Extended family members" (those not falling within the above definition who are nonetheless treated by reg 7(3) I(EEA) Regs as family members) are dealt with below at [2.5] as it is only family members under reg 7(1)(a)–(c) who come within sub-paragraph (zb) and do not have to be habitually resident in fact as well as showing a right of residence.

Direct descendant. In *MS v SSWP (IS)* [2016] UKUT 348 (AAC), it was held that legal guardianship did not create a parental relationship so as to make a child under such guardianship a direct descentdant of their guardian (in that case the child's brother). However, in *SM v Entry Clearance Officer* [2018] UKSC 7, the Supreme Court referred to the Court of Justice (case C-129/18) the following questions:

"(1)   Is a child who is in the permanent legal guardianship of a Union citizen or citizens, under "kefalah" or some equivalent arrangement provided for in the law of his or her country of origin, a "direct descendant" within the meaning of article 2.2(c) of Directive 2004/38?

(2)   Can other provisions in the Directive, in particular articles 27 and 35, be interpreted so as to deny entry to such children if they are the victims of exploitation, abuse or trafficking or are at risk of such?

(3)   Is a member state entitled to inquire, before recognising a child who is not the consanguineous descendant of the EEA national as a direct descendant under article 2.2(c), into whether the procedures for placing the child in the guardianship or custody of that EEA national was such as to give sufficient consideration to the best interests of that child?"

The Supreme Court refers to guidance from the Commission as follows:

"24.   Firstly, there is the Communication from the Commission to the European Parliament and the Council on guidance for better transposition and application of Directive 2004/38/EC (Com (2009) 313 final). Paragraph 2.1.2 is headed "Family members in direct line" and thus apparently refers to article 2.2(c). It says this:

> "Without prejudice to issues related to recognition of decisions of national authorities, the notion of **direct relatives in the descending and ascending lines** extends to adoptive relationships or minors in custody of a permanent legal guardian. Foster children and foster parents who have temporary custody may have rights under the Directive, depending upon the strength of the ties in the particular case. There is no restriction as to the degree of relatedness. National authorities may request evidence of the claimed family relationship." (Original emphasis)

That guidance does not appear to have been before the judge in *MS.* More importantly, given the Supreme Court has held the point is not *acte clair* and therefore referred the issue, *MS* which decided the point, should not currently be regarded as binding. In cases where the claimants right of residence depends on being a family member of their legal guardian, then decisions ought perhaps to be stayed. Unfortunately, the Court of Justice has refused to adopt an expedited procedure in dealing with the reference from *SM* (Order of the Court 14/03/2018 ECLI:EU:C:2018:191).

Spouse/civil partner. It is important to note that a person remains a spouse/civil partner even if separated from the worker/self-employed person. A spouse/civil partner will only cease to count as a family member on divorce/termination of the civil partnership: *Diatta v Land Berlin* (Case C-267/83) [1985] ECR 00567 and *CIS 2431/2006*. Similarly, a child aged under 21 is not required to live with the qualifying worker/self-employed person and there may be complete alienation: *CF 1863/2007. Ogieriakhi v Minister for Justice and Equality* (Case C-244/13) [2014] ECR confirms this is the correct position: in that case even where the spouses had separated and found new partners and the home occupied by the family member was no longer provided or made available by the EU national with the primary right of residence. In cases of separated spouses relying on the residence rights of their husband or wife, it can be difficult for the claimant to obtain information about whether that person is working/self-employed or retaining that status – eg, a woman who has fled her husband due to domestic violence cannot easily obtain his most recent wage-slip. It is suggested that in such cases the DWP or HMRC be asked to provide what information they can by the local authority. Where the status of the spouse cannot be established, it may be the case that the local authority cannot show the claimant is a person from abroad. Given that being a person from abroad is an exception to the general principle that if one is liable for rent then it can be met by way of HB, it may be arguable that the correct decision in such cases would be to allow the claim – see *Kerr v Department for Social Development* [2004] UKHL 23; reported as *R 1/04 (SF)*. That will certainly be the case if the local authority has not made any efforts to establish itself whether the separated spouse is working through contacting the DWP and asking it to check its systems of national insurance contributions and benefit payments from which an answer to that question may be derived.

Dependant. In *CIS 2100/2007*, the commissioner considered a number of ECJ decisions on the meaning of dependence and concluded they stand for the following principles.

(1)   A person is only dependent who actually receives support from another.

(2)   There need be no right to that support and it is irrelevant that there are alternative sources of support available.

(3)   That support must be material, although not necessarily financial, and must provide for, or contribute towards, the basic necessities of life.

SSWP v MB and Others (JSA) [2016] UKUT 372 (AAC) accepts that a person may still be dependent on another when in receipt of a subsistence benefit. However, receipt of such benefits might made it difficult to show a situation of "real" dependence. The issue is one of evidence.

SSWP v MF (SPC) [2018] UKUT 179 (AAC) held that emotional support and support in translating was not "material support" and so could not found a claim of dependancy.

In *Pedro v SSWP* [2009] EWCA Civ 1358; [2010] AACR 18, the Court of Appeal considered an appeal from *CPC 1433/2008*, in which the deputy commissioner had held that *Jia v Migrationsverket* (Case C-1/05) [2007] ECR I-00001 was authority that the relationship of dependence must have existed in the country of origin. The Court held that, following the introduction of the Directive, *Jia* did not have this effect. Further, it reasoned, following *Metock*, that the Directive strengthened previous rights of residence. The Court also explains the purposive construction that must be given to the Directive:

"if a particular interpretation of the Directive would mean that a national of a Member State might realistically be discouraged from leaving that state and going to another Member State to work or if, when working or having worked, in another Member State, he might be encouraged to leave, that would not be consistent with the purpose of the Directive, or give effect to it."

The Court held that a Union citizen who wished to work in another member state may be deterred from doing so if he knows that his elderly, but not then dependent mother, will not be regarded as his dependent for the purposes of Art 2(2) if she joins him and later becomes dependent upon him: that would not be consistent with the purpose of the Directive. Accordingly, the Court held that a person would still be dependent on another (and hence her/his family member) even if the relationship of dependency existed for the first time in the UK.

In *SSHD v Lim* [2013] UKUT 437 (IAC), the Upper Tribunal held that dependency can still exist where the dependent person would have adequate resources for her/himself but chooses to rely on assistance from the EEA citizen, provided that this is not done for the sole purpose of creating an EU law right. The case also makes the point that it is not necessary for a person to be wholly or even mainly dependent (receiving a contribution to material needs is sufficient). A similar ruling by the ECJ was given in *Reyes v Migrationsverket* (Case C-423/12) [2014] ECR (not yet reported). In that case, it was held that a child aged over 21 of an EU national with a primary right of residence, who was themselves able to work but had not done so, could still count as a dependent family member (again dependency through choice was acceptable).

Note that for "extended family members" (see [2.4]) the requirement for the dependence to have existed in the country of origin will still exist.

SSWP v LL (SPC) [2014] UKUT 136 (AAC) makes the point that the family member of someone is themselves a mere jobseeker – ie, who does not retain worker status through jobseeking, does not have a right of residence sufficient to avoid being a person from abroad. Note though the different position if the jobseeker has left the UK: *Slezak v SSWP* [2017] CSIH 4; [2017] AACR 21.

MS v SSWP (IS) [2016] UKUT 348 (AAC) rejected the proposition that the claimant could argue she was the family member of her brother who had obtained legal guardianship of the claimant in Poland and who was a worker in the UK.

[1.5] Para (3B)(zc): Former workers/self-employed

Sub-para (zc) refers to those who have a permanent right of residence under reg 15(1)(c), (d) or (e) I(EEA) Regs.

Regulation 15(1)(c) refers to a "worker or self-employed person who has ceased activity" – that is defined in reg 5(1) which transposes Art 17 of Directive 2004/38/EC. This gives certain former workers/self-employed persons the right to remain permanently in the territory of the host state. The following people are covered.

(1)   A former worker/self-employed person who, at the time s/he stops working, has reached pensionable age (or has taken early retirement) and who has been employed in that state for the last 12 months and has resided there continuously for more than three years: see reg 5(2). Only work in the host state counts: *R(IS) 3/97* para 16.

(2)   A former worker/self-employed person who ceases to work as a result of permanent (as opposed to merely temporary – see [1.3.1] above at p311) incapacity: see reg 5(3). In addition, s/he must have *either* resided continuously for two years in the host state *or* if the incapacity is the result of an accident at work or occupational disease entitling her/him to a benefit payable in full or in part by the UK state.

(3)   A former worker/self-employed person who has worked and resided for three years in the host state before working in another member state, while retaining her/his residence in the host state and returning there at least once a week: see reg 5(4) and (5).

Periods of involuntary unemployment, recorded by the relevant employment office and periods not worked for reasons not of the person's own making, or cessation of work due to illness or accident, must be regarded as periods of employment for the purposes of the rules as to the time for which a person must work to come within the above groups.

In *ID v SSWP (IS)* [2011] UKUT 401 (AAC); [2012] AACR 26, the judge held that where Art 17 requires a certain period of residence before the acquisition of a permanent right of residence then residence only counts if it is legal residence within the meaning of the Directive. The principle reason for so holding is that Art 17 must be considered as a derogation from the general rule on acquisition of a permanent right of residence after five year's legal residence set out in Art 16 (see [2.3]) and there is "nothing to indicate that it changes the nature or quality of the residence that is [...] required" (ie, only the quantity of residence is changed for those coming within Art 17).

The judge went on to hold that the same is true of the provisions which mimic Art 17 in the I(EEA) Regs 2006 (reg 5). It is important to note that the judge in this case, before providing this analysis of how to correctly construe the legal provisions in Art 17, had held that the evidence in this case failed to show that the claimant had ever been a worker or self-employed and also that in any event it appeared he was not permanently incapable of work. Given those findings, it is difficult to see how the pronouncement as to what quality of residence would be required *had the claimant been a permanently incapable former worker or self-employed person* is anything other than dicta. Furthermore, it is to be noted that Art 17 has its origin in Regulation (EEC) 1251/70: that regulation was silent on the question of the quality of residence required. If it was not a requirement under this predecessor regulation that residence during the periods required be legal residence then it is difficult to see how Directive 2004/38 (which is intended to *strengthen* residence rights – see *Metock*) can have introduced that requirement.

The correctness of the decision in *ID v SSWP (IS)* doubted in the above paragraph, was considered by the Upper Tribunal in *TG v SSWP (PC)* [2015] UKUT 50 (AAC) under "ISSUE A" of that decision, characterized by the judge as follows:

"Does the requirement in Article 17(1)(a) of the Directive for a person to "have resided [in another Member State] continuously for more than three years" at the material time refer to actual residence or to residence that is in accordance with specific legal instruments (the point equally apples to the IEEA Regulations)?"

The Upper Tribunal reviewed the history of Art 17 in previous instruments – eg, Regulation (EEC) 1251/70 referred to above. The tribunal also considered *MAH (dual nationality – permanent residence) (Canada)* [2010] UKUT 445 (IAC), para 26 of which stated that there was no requirement that residence be in accordance with the regulations in order to come within the definition of reg 5(1) of the I(EEA) Regs 2006. *MAH* was a three-judge panel of the Upper Tribunal's Immigration and Asylum Chamber. The tribunal notes that *MAH* was not cited to the judge in *ID v SSWP*. The Upper Tribunal holds that it should follow *MAH* (either as he is bound to follow the decision of a three-judge panel from another Chamber or as a matter of comity and in recognition of the seniority of the judges who dealt with that case – which included the Chamber President). For that and other reasons which are expounded in detail, the Upper Tribunal in *TG v SSWP (PC)* found that the residence needed to come within reg 5(1) or Art 17 does not have to be residence that is in accordance with the I(EEA) Regs or the Directive. In *SSWP v Gubeladze* [2017] EWCA Civ 1751, the Court of Appeal reversed that aspect of the decision but the Supreme Court in *SSWP v Gubeladze* [2019] UKSC 31 restored it (with the result that the required residence periods in Art 17 do not have to be residence in accordance with the Directive/I(EEA) Regs).

The *Gubeladze* litigation concerned that actual residence was sufficient for Art 17(1)(a) (retired workers): *SSWP v NZ (ESA) (final decision)* [2019] UKUT 250 (AAC) confirms that this is also the case for Art 17(1)(b) (permanently incapacitated workers).

The conditions as to length of residence and employment in (1) and (2) above are waived where the former worker/self-employed person's spouse is a British citizen (or was but lost that nationality by marriage to the worker/self-employed person): Art 17(2) and reg 5(6).

Once acquired, a permanent right to reside under Art 17 can only be lost by absence from the UK in excess of two years (reg 15(2) and Art 16(4), discussed at [2.3]).

Reg 15(1)(d): provides that the family members of the worker or self-employed person, residing with them in the host member state also acquire a permanent right of residence provided they were residing with the worker as a family member at the point they ceased activity.

Reg 15(1)(e): provides that, if a worker or self-employed person dies having resided continuously for at least two years (or for any period if the death was the result of an accident at work or occupational disease), then the family members who were residing with the worker will also acquire a permanent right of residence.

See [2.4] below regarding the more general route to obtaining a permanent right of residence by residing in accordance with Art 7 of the Directive or as a qualified person or her/his family member for a five-year period under the I(EEA) Regs. Such a right does not come within sub-para (zc) but these persons will have a sufficient right of residence to satisfy para (3) and so, subject to being habitually residenct in fact, will not be persons from abroad.

[1.6] The former para (3B)(f): Croatian, A2 and A8 workers
Until 31 May 2014, para (3B)(f) provided for Bulgarian, Romanian or Croatian workers who are "subject to worker authorisation". Note that no Bulgarian or Romanian worker ("A2 national") can be so defined from 1 January 2014 (from which point those countries are no longer in the seven year "accession period" as new EU members). As indicated in the 26th edition, this paragraph was not strictly speaking necessary (as such persons would count come (3B)(a) if it were not present). That is the approach now taken by reg 10 HB Regs – Croatian workers who met the conditions discussed for being authorised to work came within sub-para (za) for the period to 30 June 2018.

From 31 October 2011, the former sub-para (f) was amended so that it no longer refers to A8 nationals (see below at [1.6.4] for the countries whose nationals are "A8 nationals"). However, from 1 May 2011 (in fact, following *Gubeladze* discussed below at [1.6.5], from 1 May 2009), it has not been possible to treat A8 nationals differently to other EU nationals and that is the important date rather than the October one, which is of no significance.

That was provided for in domestic law by the changes brought about by the Accession (Immigration and Worker Registration (Revocation, Savings and Consequential Provisions) Regulations 2011 No.544. However, whether an A8 national had a right of residence in the period 1 May 2004 to 1 May 2011 will often be crucial to whether s/he or her/his family members have a right of residence after the latter date.

Similarly for A2 nationals, up until 1 January 2013, whether they met the authorisation requirements during their period of access can have a bearing on whether they, or their family members, now have a right to reside.

Finally, from 1 July 2013 to 30 June 2018, Croatian nationals also had to meet authorisation requirements in order to count as workers.

Given that the rules of those schemes and a person's position under them during the applicable accession period can make a difference to present entitlement to HB, it is still important to understand how the schemes worked. The analysis in this part is therefore organised as follows.

(1)   The modifications to the rights of residence of A2 and Croatian nationals during the "accession period" are discussed generally [1.6.1].
(2)   An explanation is given of which A2 and Croatian nationals were "subject to worker authorisation" during the accession period which applied to them [1.6.2].
(3)   An explanation is given of what counted as "authorised employment" for A2 or Croatian nationals [1.6.3].
(4)   The position of A8, A2 or Croatian nationals during their accession period and how that can affect current entitlement to HB is discussed [1.6.4].
(5)   Consideration is given to the lawfulness of the A8 provisions that were in force [1.6.5].

[1.6.1] Modifications of the rights of residence of A2 and Croatian nationals during their accession period
On 1 January 2007, Bulgaria and Romania joined the EU; their citizens are referred to here as "A2 nationals". Croatia joined the EU on 1 July 2013.

The treaties under which these states joined allowed existing member states to limit access to their labour markets by nationals of the new states, subject to certain conditions being met, for a maximum period of seven years from the date of accession (for Croation nationals, the UK decided the conditions to extend the restrictions for the final two of the seven years was not met and so they ended on 30 June 2018). Thus the treaties allowed derogations from Art 39 EC (now Art 45 TFEU), which provides freedom of movement for workers.

A2 Nationals. The UK took advantage of the ability to derogate and the modifications to the usual EU rights for A2 nationals are set out in the Accession (Immigration and Worker Authorisation) Regulations 2006 No.3317. These regulations can be found in Volume II of Sweet and Maxwell's *Social Security Legislation.* They derogated from the rights of residence for A2 nationals *as workers and work seekers* provided for in Art 45 TFEU (ex-Art 39 EC Treaty) during their accession period (1 January 2007 to 31 December 2013). They also modified the rights of residence set forth in the I(EEA) Regs 2006 for nationals of these states.

It is important to understand that these special rules did not effect any rights of residence which A2 nationals may have had under other provisions of EU law (ie, as self-employed or retaining that status, self-sufficient people or students) – as shown by *CIS 1042/2008* in relation to the scheme that was applied to A8 nationals.

Croatian Nationals. The position of Croatian nationals is broadly speaking similar to the position of A2 nationals during their accession period (1 July 2013 to 30 June 2018). The rules setting out the derogations and modifications to free movement rights as workers for Croatian nationals are contained in the Accession of Croatia (Immigration and Worker Authorisation) Regulations 2013 No.1460 (which again can be found in Volume II of *Social Security Legislation*).

As with A2 nationals there are no negative effects to the rights of Croatian citizens other than to those they may have as EEA workers (or work seekers).

The rules for A2 and Croatian nationals, although in different sets of regulations set up a broadly similar scheme – the differences relate to who exactly is a person required to be authorised in order to work (see [1.6.2] below).

The special rules provided that most Croatian and A2 nationals during their accession period were "accession state national[s] subject to worker authorisation" (discussed further at [1.6.3]). Where a Croatian or A2 national during their accession period was subject to worker authorisation, her/his rights under Art 45 TFEU (and the I(EEA) Regs) were modified in the following ways.

(1)   There was no right to reside as a jobseeker.
(2)   The status of worker could not be retained when out of work.
(3)   S/he did not count as a worker (and therefore did not have a right to reside through working) while in work *unless* s/he had complied with the conditions for authorisation.

In order to determine whether a claimant qualified as a worker, it was therefore necessary to examine which Croatian or A2 nationals were subject to worker authorisation (see [1.6.2]) and what counted as being in registered/authorised employment (see [1.6.3]): it is only if a person is subject to worker authorisation and is authorised to do the work s/he is doing that s/he will count as a worker.

It can be seen that a Croatian or A2 nationals fell within one of the following groups during their accession period:

(1)   S/he was not a Croatian or A2 national subject to worker authorisation – if this is the case, her/his right to reside in that period should be considered in the same way as with any other EU national.
(2)   S/he was a Croatian or A2 national subject to worker authorisation – if this is the case, whether s/he had a right to reside during the accession period depended on:
(a)   if s/he was working in authorised work then s/he counted as a worker;

(b)   if s/he was not working or was working but had not complied with the requirement to obtain authorisation, s/he did not have a right of residence as a worker or (if the job ended) as someone retaining her/his status as a worker (or as a jobseeker) but s/he may have had a right to reside on some other basis – eg, as a self-employed person or as someone with five years' legal residence (see below).

[1.6.2] Which Croatian and A2 nationals were subject to worker authorisation?

An A2 national was not subject to worker authorisation if s/he fell within reg 2(2)–(11) of the 2006 Accession Regs. A Croatian national was not subject to worker authorisation if s/he falls within reg 2(2)–(19) of the 2013 Accession of Croatia Regs. As mentioned, the two sets of rules are somewhat different. The differences, where they exist, are explained below.

An A2 or Croatian national was not subject to worker authorisation where s/he:

–   had on 31 December 2006 (for A2 nationals) or 30 June 2013 (for Croats) leave to enter/remain which has no restriction on right to employment, or is given such leave after that date;

–   was legally working in the UK for an uninterrupted period of 12 months, up to and including 31 December 2006 (for A2 nationals) or 30 June 2013 (for Croats);

–   has legally worked for an uninterrupted period of 12 months for a period falling partly or wholly after 31 December 2006 (for A2 nationals) or 1 July 2013 (for Croats);

–   (A2 nationals only) has dual nationality with the UK or another (non-A2) EEA state;

–   (Croatian nationals only) has dual nationality with the UK or another EEA state (unless under that dual nationality s/he would count as an A2 national subject to worker authorisation and s/he is not working with such authorisation);

–   is the spouse/civil partner of UK a national or of a person settled in the UK (in addition for Croatian nationals it will suffice to be the unmarried or same sex partner of such a person);

–   is the spouse/civil partner/child under 18 of a person with leave to enter/remain in the UK that allows employment (in addition for Croatian nationals it will suffice to be the unmarried or same sex partner of such a person);

–   has a permanent right of residence under the I(EEA) Regs 2006 (see [2.4] at p332);

–   is the member of a diplomatic mission, or the family member of such a person, or a person otherwise entitled to diplomatic immunity;

–   is a student with a registration certificate, which includes a statement that s/he shall not work more than 20 hours a week (unless it is part of vocational training or during vacations) and s/he complies with this. If the certificate confirms the student can work during the four months after the course ends, the exemption continues for this period;

–   is a family member of an EEA national who has a right to reside unless the EEA national is an accession state national subject to worker authorisation (or the only reason that person is not an accession state national subject to worker authorisation is because s/he is a family member of a self-employed person, a self-sufficient person or a student);

–   is the spouse, civil partner or descendant (and if a descendant aged 21 or over is dependent on) of an accession state national subject to worker authorisation who has a right to reside as a worker;

–   is a highly skilled person with a registration certificate stating s/he has unconditional access to the UK's labour market (issued under reg 4 of the 2006 Accession Regs for an A2 national or reg 7 of the 2013 Accession of Croatia Regs for a Croatian);

–   is a posted worker – ie, is working in the UK providing services on behalf of an EEA employer who is not established in the UK.

Croatian nationals and A2 nationals were legally working for an uninterrupted period of 12 months if they were working legally at the start and end of that period and the total of any days during the period when they were not so working is 30 or less. Work is legal for periods prior to accession if it was in accordance with any condition of their leave under the Immigration Act 1971 or no such leave was required because a right of residence existed under the I(EEA) Regs 2006. For periods after that, work is legal if it is in accordance with the requirement to be authorised (see below), or if it is work done while the claimant is not a Croatian or A2 national who is subject to worker authorisation (see above). The latter would apply, for example, in the case of a Bulgarian national who was married to a British citizen. That Bulgarian national would not be an A2 national subject to worker authorisation while married to the British citizen. If the couple then divorce, the Bulgarian national would become an A2 national subject to worker authorisation unless s/he had done 12 months' work while married (which would have counted as legal work: see reg 2(12)(b)(i) 2006 Accession Regs). In *BS v SSWP* [2009] UKUT 16 (AAC), the judge held that a claimant was "legally working" for the purposes of the 2006 Accession Regulations when she was on unpaid sick leave (and in Bulgaria).

[1.6.3] What counted as authorised work?

A Croatian, or A2 national during her/his accession period, who was subject to worker authorisation had to be authorised to work, and where working but not in authorised work, was treated as if s/he were not a worker: see regs 5 and 6 of the 2006 Accession Regs (for A2 natioanls) and regs 4 and 5 of the 2013 Accession of Croatia Regs (for Croatian nationals). A Croatian, or A2 national during her/his respective accession periods, who was subject to worker authorisation was only authorised to work if s/he held an accession worker authorisation document and was working in accordance with the rules set out in that document. These documents were either passports (stamped with visas showing limited leave to enter under the Immigration Act 1971 which gave some (restricted) rights to work in a particular category) or, for particular employers, seasonal agricultural worker cards (A2 nationals only) or "accession worker cards" which were issued under the relevant Accesssion Regs. To obtain the latter, an A2 national had to meet the conditions for work in a category of employment set out in Schedule 1 to the 2006 Accession Regulations (such as au pair, domestic worker, work permit employment etc), whereas a Croatian national had to have a certificate of sponsorship from an employer under Tier 2 or Tier 5 of the points-based system operated under Part 6A of the Immigration Rules.

[1.6.4] The rights of residence of A8 nationals during their accession period and its potential effect on HB entitlement after 1 May 2011

As stated above, from 1 May 2011 (and following *Gubeladze* discussed below at [1.6.5] in fact from 1 May 2009), A8 nationals could not be treated any differently from other EEA nationals. However, many cases will continue to arise where the claimant's right to reside, and therefore entitlement to HB, depend in full or in part on whether or not s/he, or an A8 national of whom s/he is a family member, had a right of residence during the A8 accession period (1 May 2004 to 30 April 2011). Before the reasons for this can be explained, it is necessary to understand how the system worked in that period.

On 1 May 2004, 10 new countries joined the EU: Malta, Cyprus, Czech Republic, Poland, Hungary, Estonia, Latvia, Lithuania, Slovakia and Slovenia. Citizens of all but the first two are referred to here as "A8 nationals".

Similar to the accession of the A2 states (and to previous accessions to the EU), the treaties under which these states joined allowed existing member states to limit access to their labour markets by nationals of the new states, subject to certain conditions being met, for a period of seven years from the date of accession.

The UK did not derogate in respect of Cyprus an Malta but did in respect of A8 states. The scheme worked differently than that for A2 nationals. However, its fundamentals were not dissimilar and were set out in the Accession (Immigration and Worker Registration) Regulations 2004 No.1219 (reproduced in Vol II of Sweet and Maxwell's *Social Security Legislation*).

(1)   There was a definition of "A8 national requiring registration".

(2)   For persons falling within that definition then: (a) if they were working but not for an "authorised employer" they did not have a right of residence as a worker, (b) they could not have a right of residence as a jobseeker and (c) worker status could not be retained.

(3)   Those persons who were A8 nationals requiring registration and were working for an authorised employer came within para (3B)(f) but more importantly for present purposes had a right of residence as EU workers.

An A8 national was not required to register if s/he fell within reg 2(2) to (6) of the 2004 Accession Regs. That is if:

–   on 30 April 2004 s/he had leave to enter or remain in the UK under the Immigration Act 1971 which was not subject to any condition restricting her/his employment;

–   s/he was working legally (ie, in accordance with any conditions as to employment attached to her/his leave to enter or remain (if there were any): reg 2(7)(a)) on 30 April 2004 and who had been so working without interruption for the previous 12 months;

–   s/he has worked legally (ie, for periods prior to accession as above and for periods after accession in accordance with the conditions of the scheme) without interruption for a continuous period of 12 months – in essence this means that once an A8 national has worked in accordance with the scheme for 12 months, s/he is treated as any other EU national;

–   s/he is the spouse/civil partner/child under 18 of a person with leave to enter/remain in the UK that allows employment;

–   s/he has dual nationality with the UK or another (non-A8/A2) EEA state or Switzerland;

–   s/he is a family member of another EEA or Swiss national who has a right to reside under the I(EEA) Regs 2006 (other than an A8/A2 national subject to registration/authorisation if her/his only right to reside is for the first three months in the UK);

–   s/he is the member of a diplomatic mission, or the family member of such a person, or the person otherwise entitled to diplomatic immunity;

–   s/he is a posted worker – ie, is working in the UK providing services on behalf of an employer who is not established in the UK.

A8 nationals who were required to register (ie, fell outside the circumstances set out in the above list) could only work for "authorised employers". They only counted as workers for the purposes of reg 6(1) I(EEA) Regs or Art 39 EC (now Art 45 TFEU) when so doing (regs 4 and 5 of the 2004 Accession Regs). In other words, an A8 national who was required to register and was working but not for an authorised employer, as stated above, did not have a right of residence as a worker.

An employer was an authorised employer in relation to a worker in the circumstances set out in reg 7(2) of the 2004 Accession Regs if:

–   the worker was legally working for that employer on 30 April 2004 and has not ceased working for it;

–   the worker was within the first month of employment with that employer;

–   the worker was outside the first month of employment but during that month applied for a registration certificate and had not received it;

–   the worker had received a valid registration certificate in respect of that employer;

– where, during the period 1 May to 31 December 2004 only, the worker began working as a seasonal worker at an agricultural camp after 1 May 2004 but had been issued, prior to 1 May 2004, with leave to enter under the Immigration Act 1971 as a seasonal worker at such a camp, then the employer at such a camp is an authorised employer (this may seem archaic but could have some relevance to determining whether this person had a permanent right of residence several years later).

"Legally working" was similarly defined as for A2 workers: after accession a person was only legally working if working for an authorised employer or during a period when s/he was working and not an A8 national required to register. Working for a "continuous period without interruption" had the same meaning as for A2 nationals.

The regulations which revoked the 2004 Accession Regs (SI 2011 No.544) did so with certain savings. Those savings preserve the effect of the 2004 Accession Regs in respect of periods within the Accession period (see regs 7A and 7B I(EEA) Regs 2006 which they inserted and reg 45 and Sch 4(2) of the I(EEA) Regs which, in turn, saves that provision). The effect of this can be seen if we consider a claim for HB made by a 19-year-old, whose A8 national parent worked from January 2009 to February 2011, before being unable to work due to illness for three months and then claiming JSA. If that parent had not registered her/his work and completed the 12 months' of uninterrupted work discussed below, it would seem that s/he is a mere jobseeker and not someone who retained worker status. If that is correct, it will not assist the 19-year-old, as being a family member of a jobseeker is not a sufficient right to reside to obtain HB. Therefore, it is likely that advisers and those concerned with the determination of HB claims will need to have regard to the A8 restrictions for some time after the ending of the accession period. Similarly, a case may arise where someone worked but did not register their employment properly for a period 2005 to 2010 and wishes to assert a permanent right of residence on the basis of having been a worker for a five-year period. Thus one can see that the special rules that did apply to A8 nationals during their accession period are likely to continue to have relevance to HB cases for some time – hence the reason for setting them out in some detail here.

[1.6.5] The lawfulness of the A8 scheme

In *Zalewska v Department for Social Development* [2008] UKHL 67, the House of Lords rejected an argument that an A8 national who had claimed IS after she had ceased working in registered employment for less than 12 months was protected by Art 7(2) of EC Regulation 1612/68. The court ruled, unanimously on this point, that the effect of the Annexes to the Accession Treaty was to modify the impact of the rights of migrant workers under Art 39 of the EC Treaty and Arts 1–6 of Regulation 1612/68 so as to enable national rules to be applied to regulate A8 nationals' access to the state's employment markets. Of their very nature, these differential rules were intended to be, and were allowed to be, discriminatory. Once an A8 national had been admitted to the labour market in the UK (by taking up registered employment), s/he would be a "worker" and fall under the protection of Art 7(2) of Regulation 1612/68 (now a worker covered by para (3B)(a)). However, the central question in the appeal was whether Ms Zalewska remained as a "worker" and so was protected when she made her claim for IS. It was clear that the status of A8 nationals was intended to be different from that of other EU nationals and it was clearly not the intention of the Act of Accession to tie the hands of national authorities as to how they regulated their national labour markets. As the relevant Annexes to the Accession Treaty made plain, an A8 national properly admitted to the UK's labour market for 12 months would acquire full EU "worker" rights. But as the UK had been left to determine the conditions in which an A8 national has been properly admitted to the labour market for 12 months, whether Ms Zaleskwa had or had not had to be determined by considering UK law. That law showed that in order to be properly admitted to the labour market, Ms Zaleskwa would need to have been in registered employment for 12 months before her claim for IS, which she had not. By a bare majority of three to two, the House of Lords ruled that the registration scheme was a reasonable and proportionate concomitant of the permitted derogation. In so doing, the majority of the House of Lords followed and adopted Commissioner Rowland's reasoning in *CIS 3232/2006*.

That, however, has not been the end of arguments about the rules for A8 workers.

– In *PM v SSWP* [2009] UKUT 236 (AAC), an A8 national had temporary admission as an asylum seeker prior to accession. He had obtained permission to work as an asylum seeker and worked from June 2003 to April 2005. He had not registered this work after accession. The issue in the case before the Upper Tribunal was whether the claimant was an A8 national required to register. Reg 2(7)(a)(i) of the 2004 Accession Regs provides that a person is legally working before accession if s/he had leave to enter (note temporary admission is not leave to enter) under the Immigration Act 1971 and was working in accordance with the conditions of that leave. The claimant sought to argue that this was not an exhaustive description of when a person was legally working. If the claimant was legally working at the date of accession, then he would not have been required to register that work at accession for it to be legal (see first bullet above and reg 7(2)(a)). The claimant's argument was to the effect that legally working (as it was a phrase which appeared in the Accession Treaty) must have a Community meaning. The judge dismissed this argument. The claimant's appeal was dismissed by the Court of Appeal as *Miskovic and Blazej v SSWP* [2011] EWCA Civ 16; [2012] AACR 11.

– On 13 February 2013, the Court of Appeal gave judgment in *Szpak v SSWP and SSHD* [2013] EWCA Civ 46. The issue was whether a registration certificate applied for after the first month of employment, operated, once issued, retrospectively, such that the period of work between the end of the first month of employment and the issuance of the registration certificate was then to be regarded as for an authorised employer. The Court of Appeal unanimously held that a registration certificate, issued in these circumstances, had no such retrospective effect. The decision endorses the decision of the Upper Tribunal in *SSWP v ZA* [2009] UKUT 294 (AAC) (*Szpak* was an appeal against, *MS v SSWP (JSA)* [2011] UKUT 452 (AAC), a decision following *SSWP v ZA* by the same Upper Tribunal judge who had decided that case). *SSWP v ZA* also contains an interesting observation on the burden of proof in such cases. The certificate itself does not include details of the date on which it was applied for and a claimant could not generally be expected to have kept a record. However, the DWP can readily obtain that information. Therefore, in general, it would be for the DWP (or local authority in a HB case) to obtain evidence about when the certificate was applied for, so it could be determined whether the whole of a claimant's work was for an authorised employer (where the application was made after the first month) or whether the work only had that character for the first month and then from when the certificate was issued (where the application was made outside the initial month). The judge commented (at para 73) that where the DWP (or presumably the authority) has failed to make the relevant enquiries and the relevant facts cannot be otherwise established, the matter may be determined in favour of the worker (see *Kerr v Department for Social Development* [2004] UKHL 23; reported as *R 1/04 (SF)*).

– The Upper Tribunal held in *TG v SSWP (PC)* [2015] UKUT 50 (AAC) that there was no legal power for the goverment to extend the A8 restrictions beyond 30 April 2009. That decision was upheld by both the Court of Appeal (*SSWP v Gubeladze* [2017] EWCA Civ 1751) and the Supreme Court (*SSWP v Gubeladze* [2019] UKSC 31).

– The Upper Tribunal in *RP v SSWP (ESA)* [2016] UKUT 422 (AAC), referred to the Court of Justice questions concerning whether the Act of Accession allowed the UK to prevent a person who was in registered work, but whose employment ceased before they completed 12 months' employment from (effectively) retaining status as a worker. The tribunal distinguished this issue from that considered in *Zalewska*. The following questions were put to the ECJ:

"(1) Did Annex XII of the Treaty of Accession permit Member States to exclude Polish nationals from the benefits of Article 7(2) of the Workers Regulation1 and Article 7(3) of the Citizenship Directive2 where the worker, though he had belatedly complied with the national requirement that his employment be registered, had not yet worked for an uninterrupted registered twelve month period?

(2) If the answer to the first question is "no," may a Polish national worker in the circumstances in question 1 rely on Article 7(3) of the Citizenship Directive which concerns retention of worker status?"

The Court answered those questions in *Prefeta v SSWP* (Case C-618/16) [2018] ECR (ECLI:EU:C:2018:719) by holding the the Treaty of Accession:

"must be interpreted as permitting, during the transitional period provided for by that act, the United Kingdom of Great Britain and Northern Ireland to exclude a Polish national, such as Mr Rafal Prefeta, from the benefits of Article 7(3) of Directive 2004/38/EC [...] when that person has not satisfied the requirement imposed by national law of having completed an uninterrupted 12-month period of registered work in the United Kingdom."

– In *JK v SSWP* [2017] UKUT 179 (AAC), the claimant was the family member of a Polish worker who had not registered any of his various jobs from 2004 to 2011 as required. The Upper Tribunal accepted a concession from the SSWP that given the claimant had worked legally before accession, had striven not to work illegally when his visa expired and had lived in the UK for 10 years at the time of decision, it would be disproportionate to insist on the fulfillment of the conditions in the worker registration scheme. Importantly, the judgment holds that in such cases the assessment of proportionality relates to whether it is proportionate to apply the worker registration scheme rules – *Zalewska* was confined to its facts and did not prevent this approach.

– *SSWP v NZ (ESA) (third interim decision)* [2017] UKUT 360 (AAC) deals with an A8 national who had been in registered employment for less than the 12 months when she became permanently incapable of work. She had been resident in the UK for more than two years. The judge holds that, assuming the Upper Tribunal was correct to find that residence for the purpose of Art 17 is simply factual (and not legal) residence (which the Court of Appeal rejected in *Gubeladze* but on which the Supreme Court may come to a different view – see [1.5]), then she would have acquired a permanent right of residence. The reason for that conclusion is that the permissible restrictions on A8 residence rights during the accession period under the Teaty of Accession did not extend to derogating from Art 17 of the Directive (which replaces EC Regulation 1251/70) on permanent right of residence for former workers.

[1.7] Paragraph (3B)(g): Refugees

Prior to 15 October 1996, a "refugee" was defined as being a person who came within the meaning of that term under the Convention Relating to the Status of Refugees. In *CIS 564/1994* (paras 23–24), it was confirmed that a person who fulfilled the criteria under the Convention for being a refugee was a refugee even if the immigration authorities had yet to decide so. The suggestion to the contrary was described as "callous, unprincipled nonsense". Had that definition remained in place, it would therefore have been necessary for authorities and tribunals to decide for themselves whether a claimant was a refugee.

But from 15 October 1996, the definition in para (6) took effect, so that a person is only a "refugee" when the Secretary of State has recorded her/him as such. There was special provision for the often lengthy period while refugees had their claims for asylum determined: see reg 10A and Sch A1 in Sch 4 HB&CTB(CP) Regs on p1805. However, this provision no longer exists for those claimants not recorded as refugees by 14 June 2007.

[1.8] Paragraph (3B)(h) and (hh): Persons granted certain forms of leave to remain or enter/humanitarian protection

Sub-para (h) is amended such that it now covers those granted leave (or deemed to have been granted leave outside the rules) which is (1) discretionary leave, (2) leave under the Destitution Domestic Violence Concession or (3) leave under reg 3 Displaced Persons (Temporary Protection) Regs 2005. Sub-para (hh) covers those granted humanitarian protection usually granted by the Secretary of State to those who could show compelling humanitarian reasons why they should not be deported.

[1.9] Paragraph (3B)(k): Claimants in receipt of IS or on income-related ESA

Until 1 April 2014, when the reference to income-based JSA was removed, this was a most important category. That was not just because there is no need for an authority to enquire into the residence rights or ordinary habitual residence of a person in receipt of one of these benefits, but because the right to reside requirement, as it applies to entitlement to income-based JSA (reg 85A Jobseekers Allowance Regulations 1996), does not exclude from entitlement someone whose only right to reside is as an EEA jobseeker. In effect that meant that any EEA national (other than a Croatian national subject to worker authorisation) whose only right to reside stemmed from the fact that s/he was looking for work and met the means test requirement for income-based JSA could, by obtaining that benefit, get entitlement to HB. Reg 3 of the amending regulations (SI 2014 No.539), as explained in the Modifications note to this regulation, does not apply to a person who, on or after 31 March 2014, is entitled to HB and income-based JSA but this protection ceases as soon as the person ceases to be entitled to income-based JSA or makes a new claim for HB. For those with this transitional protection, it is important to note that moving home such that a new authority becomes responsible for HB will lead to a new claim (although moving within the same authority should not do so).

The policy of removing HB entitlement for those on income-based JSA was announced on 13 December 2013. SI 2014 No.539 was made on 5 March 2014 and laid on 11 March 2014. The Secretary of State declared in the introductory text to the regulations that he was not going to consult with the representative organisations of authorities (see s176 SSAA at p95) or the Social Security Advisory Committee (see ss170–174 at p93 and onwards) as "it appear[ed] to him that by reason of the urgency of the matter it is inexpedient to do so". A three-judge panel of the Upper Tribunal considered whether the failure to consult rendered the removal of "passporting" through the habitual residence test for income-based JSA claimants unlawful in *IC v Glasgow City Council and SSWP (HB)* [2016] UKUT 321 (AAC); [2017] AACR 1 and decided that it did not. The Northern Ireland High Court confirmed in *Stachre application for Judicial Review* [2018] NIQB 93 that the denial of HB to an EU jobseeker did not constitute a human rights breach.

A person "on income support" [or "on income-based jobseeker's allowance" before the amendment] includes those who are entitled but not being paid it due to a sanction, "waiting days" or because of the "loss of benefit" provisions, and a person "on an income-related ESA" includes those on "waiting days" as well as certain claimants disqualified from payment of ESA: reg 2(3) and (3A).

In *R(H) 9/04*, the deputy commissioner commented, *obiter*, that an award of one of those benefits to a claimant did not bind the local authority in making a decision on HB/CTB: para 24. However, the terms of reg 10(2) and (3B) when read together, show that if a person is in receipt of IS, and so falls within para (3B), s/he cannot by the terms of para (2) fall within para (2), and so s/he cannot be a person from abroad. Fortunately, the same deputy commissioner has now accepted the criticisms put in previous volumes of this work in *CIS 34/2006 and others* (para 47), and has recanted from what he said in *R(H) 9/04* (para 39). He went on to rule in *CIS 34/2006* that a person is not "in receipt" of IS for a period where it has later been established that s/he was not entitled to that benefit. In *LB Hillingdon v MJ* [2009] UKUT 151 (AAC); [2010] AACR 4, the exact relationship between DWP decision making on right to reside and that of authrorities administering HB is further clarified. At para 23, Judge Humphreys held that where both DWP and a local authority needed to make a decision on right to reside, then the *obiter* remarks at paras 38 and 39 of *R(H) 9/04* are an accurate reflection of the position. She also held that where reg 10(3B)(k) applied, the local authority was bound by that. The para 38 remarks criticises, correctly, a mistake in an earlier edition of this work. The parts of the para 39 remarks that are relevant would, therefore, seem to be only those which relate to situations where the DWP has decided a claimant is not entitled to a means-tested benefit. In those cases, the authority should be slow to reach a different conclusion in the absence of other evidence:

"39.   [...] I do not consider that the local authority is precluded from disagreeing with such a decision. On the other hand, I do not consider that the local authority is obliged to decide the issue from scratch as though the Jobcentre Plus decision did not exist. Where the local authority is satisfied that a considered decision on the issue has been made by Jobcentre Plus, the local authority is entitled, in the absence of anything to compel a contrary conclusion, to regard the existence of that decision as satisfactory evidence that the claimant is not a person from abroad."

[1.10] Paragraph (3B)(l): Claimants in receipt of income-based JSA with a non-excluded right of residence
This applies to those who are in receipt of income-based JSA and who have a right of residence other than (practically it would be a right "in addition to") as a jobseeker. The effect is that such persons, therefore, cannot be excluded from entitlement to HB on the basis that they are not "habitually resident in fact" (see [3] on p344).

Given that an award of income-based JSA is no longer a passport through the residence test, authorities will have to make many decisions where the DWP has awarded income-based JSA and informs them that the claimant's only right of residence is as a jobseeker. It is suggested that in such cases, the threshold for when an authority may depart from that view is much lower than is set out in *LB Hillingdon v MJ* discussed in [1.9] above: from the DWP decision maker's point of view in awarding income-based JSA, it will not have mattered that the only right of residence is as a jobseeker. Thus all the decision really represents is that the claimant is at least someone with that right of residence. The DWP decision maker has no interest in going on to determine whether a claimant may have some other right of residence (as the HB decision maker must do) and thus her/his opinion on that matter, it is suggested, should carry little weight: this is a different situation from that referred to in the decided cases as in those a negative DWP decision would, if correct, have also meant HB should be refused. It is therefore suggested that the guidance issued to local authorities, HB Circular A6/2014, which at Q.7 of Annex B indicates authorities should follow the DWP decision, rather overstates the case: the decision makers are not applying the same test and crucially the DWP decision maker's view on what other rights of residence exist is not a necessary part of their decision.

[2] Paragraphs (3) and (3A)–(3AA): Who has a right to reside in the Common Travel Area sufficient to claim HB
As detailed above, for those not coming within para (3B) then para (3) provides that they will not be habitually resident under para (2), unless they have a right to reside in the CTA. Para (3) also provides that a person whose right of residence is only one of those set out in para (3A)-(3AA) does not have a sufficient right of residence to satisfy that requirement – para (3A)–(3AA) are discussed at [2.1].

Advisers should note the transitional protection which may allow some claimants to count as habitually resident without needing to have a right of residence (see p1783 and p1795): *AP v SSWP (IS)* [2018] UKUT 307 (AAC). A claimant who can take advantage of this protection does not need to have a right to reside (but will be subject to the requirement of habitual residence in fact, unless exempt under para (3B)).

British citizens, Irish citizens and citizens of the other states in the CTA clearly all have a right to reside in the CTA. So too do those who have valid leave to remain under the Immigration Act 1971 other than, following the insertion of para (3AA) from 7 May 2019, those who have limited leave granted under Appendix EU to the Immigraion Rules (pre-settled status) – although see below on the challenge to that exclusion. Persons with leave to remain under the Immigration Act 1971 may well be excluded on the separate basis that they are "persons subject to immigration control". In reality, therefore, it is largely only non-British or Irish EEA nationals (or their family members) who may be found not to have a right to reside in the CTA: all other persons clearly have a right of residence or are excluded at an earlier stage because they are subject to immigration control.

As discussed above for EU nationals, the starting point for determining whether a right to reside exists is Directive 2004/38. As noted, the EEA is a larger grouping than the EU. It includes Norway, Iceland and Liechtenstein. EEA nationals enjoy the same rights of residence as EU nationals under the EEA Treaty (the "Oporto Agreement"). The I(EEA) Regs 2006 treat nationals from any EEA state (save Britain – see above) and Swiss nationals in the same manner.

The Directive, and the I(EEA) Regulations, set out three main types of residence right.
(1)   An initial right to reside for all EEA nationals (see [2.2] on p328).
(2)   An extended right to reside for EEA nationals and their family members who are workers, self-employed, self-sufficient or students (see [2.3] on p328).
(3)   A permanent right of residence for those who have resided legally for five years (or less if they come within Art 17 discussed above) (see [2.4] on p332).
It is helpful to consider each of these in turn before looking at:
–   the rights of extended family members (see [2.5] on p335);
–   certain other situations where a right of residence may be retained (see [2.6] on p335);
–   the difficult question of when someone may have a right to reside not provided for in the Directive or the I(EEA) Regs 2006 (see [2.7] on p336);
–   whether possession of an EU residence document issued by the Home Office can be relied upon to establish a right of residence (see [2.8] on p344).

[2.1] Paragraph (3A): Non-qualifying rights of residence
If a claimant's only right of residence is one which falls within para (3A) or (3AA) that is expressed, in para (3), not to be a sufficient right of residence to meet the test for HB entitlement. Para (3A) and (3AA) deal with:
(1)   At (3A)(b) and (d), those whose only right of residence was as a jobseeker or family member of a jobseeker. See [1.10] in this note for those who are in receipt of income-based JSA and have a right of residence other than that of a jobseeker. See also the modification on p299 for those continually entitled to HB and income-based JSA since 31 March 2014, and p326 concerning the lawfulness of the change

which prevents simple receipt of income-based JSA from passporting a claimant through the "person from abroad" test in all circumstances.

(2)   At (3A)(a) and (c), those whose only right of residence is the initial right of residence that all EEA nationals and their family members may have during their initial three months in the UK. See [2.2].

(3)   Fom 8 November 2012, the excluded categories of claimant have been expanded to include (at (3A)(bb) and (e)) those who have what is referred to in this note as a "*Zambrano* right" (discussed further below at [2.1.1]).

(4)   At (3AA), from 7 May 2019, under sub-para (a), those whose only right to reside is "pre-settled status" – ie, limited leave to remain granted under Appendix EU to the Immigration Rules and under sub-para (b) *Zambrano* carers recognised under the EU Settled Status Scheme.

[2.1.1] The Zambrano right

In *Zambrano v Office national de l'emploi* (ONEm) (Case C-34/09) [2011] ECR I-01177, the claimant and his wife were Colombian nationals. They applied for asylum in Belgium. That was refused, but while they were in Belgium they had two children who acquired Belgian nationality – ie, under the relevant Belgian law. They applied to take up residence as ascendants of a Belgian national; Mr Zambrano also applied for unemployment benefit. Both applications were rejected. The latter rejection involved the application of a rule regarding foreigners' residence and employment of foreign workers. That decision was the subject of a further appeal, and was referred to the ECJ. The ECJ allowed the claimant's appeal. Article 20 of the Treaty on the Functioning of the European Union precluded national measures which have the effect of depriving citizens of the EU of the genuine enjoyment of the substance of the rights conferred by virtue of their status as EU citizens. Regarding the facts of this case, the Court said "a refusal to grant a right of residence to a third-country national with dependent minor children in the Member State where those children are nationals and reside…has such an effect" (para 43). The Court said that was because:

"it must be assumed that such a refusal would lead to a situation where those children, citizens of the Union, would have to leave the territory of the Union in order to accompany their parents… In those circumstances, those citizens of the Union would, as a result, be unable to exercise the substance of the rights conferred on them by virtue of their status as citizens of the Union" (para 44).

At issue in the *Zambrano* case was also Mr Zambrano's entitlement to unemployment benefit. It seems that a requirement for receipt of this was that he had a work permit. The Court ruled specifically that:

"Similarly, if a work permit were not granted to such a person, he would risk not having sufficient resources to provide for himself and his family, which would also result in the children, citizens of the Union, having to leave the territory of the Union."

The I(EEA) Regs 2006 were amended to recognise such a right to reside (and to a work permit) with effect from 8 November 2012 (reg 15A(4A) as inserted by SI 2012 No.2560) (now reflected in reg 16(5) of the I(EEA) Regs). However, the amendments from the same date to para (3A) of reg 10 HB Regs seeks to ensure that such a right of residence does not give rise to a HB entitlement. Now that *Zambrano* carers can also be granted leave to remain under the EU Settled Status Scheme, para (3AA)(b) also excludes that form of leave from being a sufficient right to reside.

The Supreme Court considered a challenge to the exclusion of *Zambrano* carer's from accessing benefits in *R (HC) v SSWP* [2017] UKSC 73 and decided this was lawful in terms of EU and ECHR law.

[2.1.2] Lawfulness of the pre-settled status exclusion

Reg 10(3AA)(a) from 7 May 2019 exlcudes from entitlement those with pre-settled status (limited leave to remain issued under Appendix EU to the Immigration Rules). Permission for a judicial review against the exclusion of EU nationals with pre-settled status has been granted in the ongoing case of *R (Fratila and Tanase) v SSWP* (reference CO/3632/2019). The case is listed to be heard on 18 and 19 February 2020. The argument in the case is essentially that in *Jany and Others v Staatssecretaris van Justitie* (Case C-268/99) [2001] ECR I-08615 it was held that Art 18 TFEU prevents the refusal of such benefits to EU nationals who are resident under domestic law. The UK Courts have consistently stated that this is the principle which *Trojani* stands for (*Abdirahman and another v SSWP and another* [2007] EWCA Civ 657; reported as *R(IS) 8/07* at para 32(iv); *Patmalniece* [2011] UKSC 11; [2011] AACR 34 at paras 105–106 and most importantly as part of the ratio of *Patmalniece v SSWP* [2009] EWCA Civ 621) at para 56.

[2.2] Initial right to reside

All EEA nationals have an initial right of residence for up to three months (Art 6 of the Directive and reg 13 I(EEA) Regs). Art 24 of the Directive provides in general that those with a right of residence under the Directive are entitled to equal treatment. However, Art 24(2) allows member states to derogate from this requirement of equal treatment by stating that "the host Member State shall not be obliged to confer entitlement to social assistance during the first three months of residence". Thus, para (3A)(a) and (c) of this regulation provides that the initial right of residence is not a sufficient right to reside to satisfy para (3). The effect is that, where a claimant's *only* right to reside is because s/he is an EEA national within her/his first three months of residence in the UK, that right will not entitle her/him to HB.

[2.3] Extended right to reside

The Directive provides (Art 7(1)) that those who are workers, self-employed, self-sufficient, students or their family members shall have a right to reside for longer than the first three months. Similar provision is made by regs 6 and 14 I(EEA) Regs (although whether it is entirely similar and the results under reg 10 if it is not, is discussed at [1.3.2.4]). The I(EEA) Regs also give this right to jobseekers and their family members: however, para (3A)(b) and (d) again provide that this is not a sufficient right to reside to satisfy para (3).

What then of the other groups with an extended right to reside? Workers, the self-employed and those who retain one of those statuses are specifically provided for under para (3B) (although that is subject to the qualification about whether reg 6(2) is now as generous as Art 7(3)(b) and (c) of the Directive referred to above).

[2.3.1] Self-sufficient

Self-sufficient persons have an extended right of residence. The Directive and the I(EEA) Regs require that to be self-sufficient the person must have "sufficient resources for themselves and their family members not to become a burden on the social assistance system of the host Member State and have comprehensive sickness insurance cover in the host Member State" (Art 7(1)(b)). It is helpful to consider the two requirements separately. However, it should be emphasised that they both serve a similar purpose: limiting the degree of financial solidarity member states are required to show to economically inactive migrants in cases where it is proportionate to do so. Those wishing to argue they are self-sufficient should also see the analysis concerning Art 21 TFEU at [2.7.2] on p337.

[2.3.1.1] Sufficient resources. Art 8(4) provides that member states may not lay down a fixed amount which they regard as "sufficient resources" and cannot in any event require a person to have more resources than the threshold below which nationals of the host state become eligible for social assistance. Reg 4(4) I(EEA) Regs 2006, until 1 June 2011, was slightly different in that resources were "to be regarded as sufficient if they exceed the maximum level of resources which a UK national and his family members may possess if he is to become eligible for social assistance under the United Kingdom benefit system". That said nothing about whether resources below this level *might* be regarded (as opposed to *must* be regarded) as sufficient. However, from 2 June 2011, SI 2011 No.1247 amends the definition so that if it appears appropriate a lower level of resources might be regarded as sufficient "taking into account the personal situation of the person concerned" (and any family members). As HB does count as social assistance, any person who would qualify for some HB cannot automatically be regarded as having sufficient resources.

The approach to addressing the question of whether or not a person who claims a social assistance benefit counts as having "sufficient resources" to not become a burden on the social assistance system of the host member state was addressed by the ECJ in *Brey* Case C-140/12 [2013] ECR.

The Court explains that the aim of the Directive is to facilitate and strengthen the exercise of the primary and individual right to move and reside freely within the EU, and to set the conditions governing the exercise of that right. These conditions include the condition in Art 7(1)(b) that economically inactive migrants must, after the first three months' residence, have sufficient resources (para 53).

The Court held explicitly, by reference to recital 10, that the purpose of Art 7(1)(b) is to prevent such persons from becoming an unreasonable burden on the social assistance system.

The Court goes on to hold that the fact that an economically inactive migrant may be entitled to a means-tested benefit could be an indication s/he does not have sufficient resources to avoid becoming such an unreasonable burden (para 63).

However, that conclusion cannot be arrived at automatically. The Court holds that there must be an individual examination of the specific burden which granting that benefit to that particular claimant would place on the social assistance system as a whole, which takes account of the personal circumstances of the claimant:

"64.   However, the competent national authorities cannot draw such conclusions [eg that the claimant does not have sufficient resources] without first carrying out an overall assessment of the specific burden which granting that benefit would place on the national social assistance system as a whole, by reference to the personal circumstances characterising the individual situation of the person concerned."

The Court of Justice goes on to comment (at para 70) that the requirement for sufficient resources, as a restriction on a fundamental right, should be construed narrowly.

At para 77 the Court is clear that an automatic decision that a claimant who meets the means test for a benefit such as the compensatory supplement at issue in that case (a benefit similar to the UK's pension credit) does not have a right to reside is unlawful as it precludes the necessary inquiry into the individual circumstances of the claimant:

"77.   Such a mechanism, whereby nationals of other Member States who are not economically active are automatically barred by the host Member State from receiving a particular social security benefit, […], does not enable the competent authorities of the host Member State, where the resources of the person concerned fall short of the reference amount for the grant of that benefit, to carry out – in accordance with the requirements under, inter alia, Articles 7(1)(b) and 8(4) of that directive and the principle of proportionality – an overall assessment of the specific burden which granting that benefit would place on the social assistance system as a whole by reference to the personal circumstances characterising the individual situation of the person concerned."

In para 78 the Court lists the factors that must be taken into account in this individual enquiry:

"[….] the amount and the regularity of the income which he receives; the fact that those factors have led those authorities to issue him with a certificate of residence; and the period during which the benefit applied for is likely to be granted to him."

The Court goes on to suggest that it may be relevant in undertaking the assessment of whether awarding benefit would constitute a burden on the social assistance system, to consider the proportion of claimants of a particular benefit who would be economically inactive EU migrants.

The further cases of *Dano* and *Alimanovic* in which the ECJ dealt with other factual matrices where it held there was no need for an assessment of proportionality are fully cited and discussed at [2.7.2] below. Those cases did cast some doubt on when, if ever, an individualised assessment as called for in *Brey* should be carried out. The answer to this is now given in *AMS v SSWP (PC) (second interim decision)* [2017] UKUT 48 (AAC). There, it is held that such an individual assessment of proportionality is necessary in any case where the claimant has for a time satisfied the conditions as to having sufficient resources and comprehensive sickness insurance but no longer does so.

The final decision for AMS (*AMS v SSWP (PC) (final decision)* [2017] UKUT 381 (AAC)) gives an example of how the *Brey* test should be considered. The key points emerging from the judgment are:

–   one should look at the actual amounts of means-tested benefits the claimant would receive were they to be regarded as having a right to reside. In doing this, the fact that some of the income possessed by the claimant would not count as income under the relevant benefit rules and would not therefore reduce the amount of benefit s/he received is relevant. Furthermore, the assessment is not just of the value of the benefit at issue in an appeal but all the other benefits the claimant could then receive;

–   in looking at the duration of the likely recourse to social assistance by the claimant, one cannot limit matters to the position at the point the claimant would have achieved five-years residence (in that case, the judge looked at how long the pensioner in question was likely to go on living); *and*

–   that in looking at the collective impact of allowing claimants in the category of a particular case to receive benefit it will be for the decision maker to bring evidence as to this.

In the case before the tribunal, those principles were applied and led to findings that the claimant would have received in excess of £13,000 for a period of at least four years. It was concluded that it was not disproportionate to insist on sufficient resources.

SG v Tameside MBC, was until the judgment in *Brey,* the main UK authority on what constituted sufficient resources. The claimant was a Swedish national in receipt of a Swedish invalidity pension of £121.68 a week. The claimant had lived in the UK since December 2007 and had initially stayed with her sister, before moving to stay with friends in February 2008. In May 2008, the claimant was given a tenancy of a housing association flat but HB was refused on the basis that she had no right to reside. Judge Ward considered both whether the test of sufficient resources was met and also whether the claimant had comprehensive sickness insurance (see [2.3.1.2]).

With regard to the issue of sufficient resources, the Upper Tribunal noted *Grzelcyzk* (Case C-184/99) ECR I-06193. The Upper Tribunal concluded (albeit tentatively) that, following that case, it is arguable that a claimant who can demonstrate that s/he was self-sufficient for a time but then ceased to be self-sufficient, might only lawfully be denied benefit if s/he has become an unreasonable burden on the social assistance system. That then left the judge to decide the sub-issues arising.

(1)   Whether the claimant had ever been self-sufficient? That involves asking how much resources she needed to count as self-sufficient.

(2)   Whether at the time of claim for HB she was likely to be an unreasonable burden on the social assistance system?

In looking at whether the claimant had ever been self-sufficient, the judge noted that the requirement under Art 7(1)(b) of the Directive is to have sufficient resources not to become a burden *during her/his period of residence.* He then looked at how much resources a claimant would need to avoid being a burden on the social assistance scheme in that period. Judge Ward noted that the claimant had a higher income than the personal allowance for IS purposes. However, HB counts as social assistance and, to be self-sufficient, a person needs a roof over her/his head. Therefore, the judge rules that one can take into account whether the claimant has housing (or sufficient income to obtain housing) in determining sufficiency of resources (at para 50). That said, it is possible that where a claimant has accommodation provided by a third party for free, it will count as part of the claimant's resouces. However, the judge then ruled that in this case the arrangements the claimant had for the provision of accommodation from her sister, which had fallen through when her violent ex-husband discovered her location, and her later residence with friends in Manchester were not sufficiently secure to be able to say the claimant had sufficient accommodation. The judge also considered that if the level of resources required was thought to be the level above which the claimant would become eligible for some HB (arguably taking into account premiums that she would have included in her applicable amount to calculate this) then the claimant always had inadequate resources. Thus the judge found that the claimant did not have sufficient resources at any point. In the light of *Brey*, the ruling that someone whose resources were not sufficient to mean they would be excluded from HB entitlement on income grounds must be incorrect. That is precisely the kind of automatic conclusion the Court warned against. As stated above, it is also likely that the emphasis on whether the claimant was self-sufficient in the past is incorrect given the approach of the ECJ.

The Upper Tribunal judge went on to consider whether the claimant would be, were he wrong on the need to demonstrate self-sufficiency in a past period, an unreasonable burden at the date of decision. He concluded that she would be. It is worth noting that the main factors the judge took into account in considering this were the fact that the claimant would in all likelihood be indefinitely in need of benefits and that these would be for a significant portion of her housing costs. That approach seems to have included at least some of the factors which the ECJ subsequently found were relevant in *Brey.*

The same judge considered the scope of *Brey* in *VP v SSWP (JSA)* [2014] UKUT 32 (AAC); [2014] AACR 25 and that decision was endorsed by the Court of Appeal in *Ahmad v SSHD* [2014] EWCA Civ 998.

The Court of Justice ruled in *Singh and Others v Minister for Justice and Equality* (Case C-218/14) [2015] ECR not yet reported, that an EU citizen could rely upon the income from work in the host member state of her/his third country national spouse in order to satisfy the sufficient resources test. This means that *W (China) & Another v Secretary of State for the Home Department* [2006] EWCA Civ 1494 is incorrect in holding the contrary.

All of the above carefully worked out positions may change when the ECJ gives judgment in *Gusa v Minister for Social Protection* (C-422/16) [2017] ECR (ECLI:EC:C:2017:1004). In that case, the Advocate General suggests that, in his opinio, a person who has in fact lived in a country without recourse to the social assistance system must be presumed to have had sufficient resources: "[t]hey cannot be retrospectively regarded as having been insufficient for the purposes of Directive 2004/38, given that the Union Citizen was not [...] a 'burden on the social assistance system of the host Member State'" (para 34, AG opinion). It is to be noted though that the ECJ could simply ignore that part of the opinion as it does not go to any of the specific questions asked.

[2.3.1.2] Comprehensive sickness insurance. The requirement for comprehensive sickness insurance was considered by the Court of Appeal in *W (China) & Another v Secretary of State for the Home Department* [2006] EWCA Civ 1494. The Court held that the fact the appellant could rely on NHS treatment was not sufficient as the NHS is largely tax funded and not insurance-based. Furthermore, as the purpose of the requirement that comprehensive health insurance was in place was precisely to prevent a burden on the host state, then the fact that free NHS services were obtainable in fact precisely created that burden. The European Commission takes the opposite view and has said that "in practice that this condition will always be met if the host country has a residence based health care system and a non-active person moves his or her... residence there" (see the European Commission's *Explanatory Notes on Modernised Social Security*, January 2011). Unfortunately for claimants, the view of the Commission is not binding whereas the judgment of the Court of Appeal is. Nonetheless, given it is plain that the Commission takes a different view on the issue that might open the way for a referral to the ECJ in an appropriate case.

An alternative approach might be to argue that, given at para 10 of *W (China),* Buxton LJ held that the purpose of the requirement for health insurance was to prevent the presence of the EU migrant placing a burden on the public finances of the host state. That may open the way to say that the requirement for health insurance should be approached in the same way as in *Brey*: by reference to whether the recourse to the NHS is an unreasonable burden given the personal circumstances of the claimant (that was also the approach of the ECJ in *Baumbast* (see [2.7.2] at p337).

However, it is also important to note that *W (China)* did not consider whether a claimant who came within the personal scope of EC Regulation 1408/71 or 883/2004 and had a right to access NHS treatment under the equal treatment provision of that legislation (as a sickness benefit in kind) could meet the requirement of comprehensive sickness insurance.

In *SG v Tameside MBC (HB)* Judge Ward summarised the issue on comprehensive sickness insurance for him to decide as follows:

"Do the provisions of Regulation (EEC) No.1408/71 applicable to the receipt by an EU citizen of National Health Service care mean that she has "comprehensive sickness insurance cover in the host member State"

The Upper Tribunal held, accepting a concession from the Secretary of State (who was joined as a party to the case), that as the claimant was in receipt of a Swedish invalidity benefit, the UK would be able, under Art 28a of EC Regulation 1408/71 and Art 95 of EC Regulations 574/72, to claim from the Swedish state. Accordingly, the purpose of the requirement that comprehensive sickness insurance, identified by the Court of Appeal in *W (China),* was not frustrated by receipt of free NHS treatment as the UK would be reimbursed for that treatment.

Thus, provided that under these EC Regulations (or their replacements: EC Regulations 883/04 and 987/2009) the UK would be able to claim any NHS costs for treating someone from another member state, that will satisfy the requirement of comprehensive medical insurance. Note that this right to reclaim costs appears only to arise in limited circumstances – ie, where that other member state was the one whose legislation was applicable to the claimant (see Title II of EC Regulation 883/04 for when that is the case) and typically where that state is paying a benefit to the claimant. An example is provided by *SSWP v HH (SPC)* [2015] UKUT 583 (AAC). Here the claimant was initially found to have comprehensive sickness insurance on the basis that he had a Dutch pension and hence the UK could recoup the costs of NHS treatment from the Netherlands. However, this ceased to be the case as soon as he also started to receive a UK pension due to the effect of Art 23 Regulation 883/2004.

Until the decision of the Upper Tribunal in *VP,* now endorsed by the Court of Appeal in *Ahmad v SSHD,* it remained arguable at First-tier Tribunal that anyone who is within the personal scope of those EC Regulations should count as having the required sickness insurance. This was argued before the Upper Tribunal in file reference *CIS 304/2009* but the SSWP conceded in that case that the claimant had had private health insurance. More pertinently, Judge Rowland commented in *SSWP v SW (IS)* [2011] UKUT 508 (AAC), when remitting the case before him to a fresh First-tier Tribunal, that time during which a Swiss national was reliant on the income of her British partner, during which she had access to NHS treatment under domestic law, would be time spent as a self-sufficient person. That is also the view of the European Commission, which on 26 April 2012 announced it had sent a reasoned opinion to the UK government stating it may take infringement proceedings against the UK on the basis that, amongst other issues:

"Under the Free Movement Directive, EU citizens who settle in another EU country but do not work there may be required to have sufficient resources and sickness insurance. The United Kingdom, however, does not consider entitlement to treatment by the UK public healthcare scheme (NHS) as sufficient. This breaches EU law."

However, the Court of Appeal in *Ahmad* agreed with Judge Ward in *VP* that the commission's view was incompatible with EU law.

The decision of the Supreme Court in *Mirga and Samin v SSWP and Westminster City Council* [2016] UKSC 1; [2016] AACR 26 does not mention the decision in *Ahmad* but it appears from the judgment that, in appropriate cases, the application of a strict requirement for comprehensive medical insurance will be disproportionate.

[2.3.2] Students

Students also have an extended right of residence. Note, however, that they must have made a declaration to the Home Secretary to the effect that they have sufficient resources to avoid becoming a burden on the social assistance system (see above in [2.3.1] for what this means). They must also have comprehensive sickness insurance.

Note also that for a student's family members, it is only the spouse and dependent children who can derive a right of residence from the student (dependent direct relatives in the ascending line are treated as extended family members): see Art 7(4) and reg 7(2).

[2.3.3] Family members of anyone with extended right of residence

Art 7 provides that the family members of anyone with an extended right of residence also has a right of residence. The meaning of family members within the directive has been considered at [1.4] above. Reg 14(2) I(EEA) Regs makes similar provision. Note that the I(EEA) Regs provide that someone who is an "extended family member" (see [2.4]) and has the required residence documentation counts as a family member and may therefore have a right to reside if the person of whom s/he is a family member has such a right.

[2.4] Permanent right to reside

Art 16 of the Directive provides that those who "have resided legally for a continuous period of five years in the host Member State shall have the right of permanent residence there". Reg 15(1)(a) and (b) of the I(EEA) Regs makes similar provision for those who have "resided in accordance with these Regulations". Once acquired, this right is not subject to the claimant meeting other conditions (eg, being a worker, self-employed person etc) and the right can only be lost by absence from the host state of more than two consecutive years (reg 15(3)/Art 16(4)). It helps to firstly consider what "legal residence" or residence "in accordance with these Regulations" means ([2.4.1]) and, secondly, the need for continuity of residence ([2.4.2]).

[2.4.1] Legal residence/residence in "accordance with these Regulations"

One issue arose because reg 15 I(EEA) Regs 2006 sought to implement Art 16 in domestic law but failed to do so adequately. A person acquires a permanent right of residence when s/he has resided for five years "in accordance with these regulations". The Regulations treat residence before their coming into force (30 April 2006) as residence "in accordance with these regulations" if it was residence in accordance with the Immigration (European Economic Area) Regulations 2000 No.2326 (I(EEA) Regs 2000) (see Sch 4 para 6 I(EEA) Regs 2006). The 2000 Regulations were in force from 2 October 2000. That, it was argued, meant periods of residence prior to the 2000 date could not be counted towards the acquisition of the permanent right. Another argument put forward was that given the Directive only created a permanent right of residence from 30 April 2006 and given preamble 17 to the Directive referred to the need to create a right of permanent residence for those who have resided for a five-year period "in compliance with the conditions laid down in this Directive" then no one could obtain a permanent right of residence under the Directive until 30 April 2011.

In *SSWP v Lassal* [2009] EWCA Civ 157, the Court of Appeal referred to the ECJ the following question:

"Is Article 16(1) of Directive 2004/38 of the European Parliament and the Council of 29 April 2004 to be interpreted as entitling that EU citizen to a right of permanent residence by virtue of the fact that she had been legally resident, in accordance with earlier community law instruments conferring rights of residence on workers, for a continuous period of five years which ended prior to 30 April 2006 (the date by which member States had to transpose the Directive)?"

Ms Lassal had, after completing her five years' residence in accordance with earlier provisions, left the UK for a 10-month period before 30 April 2006 and the Court of Appeal also asked whether that could affect her permanent right of residence.

The ECJ gave its judgment on 7 March 2010 in *SSWP v Lassal* (Case C-162/09) [2010] ECR; [2011] AACR 33. The Court held in clear terms that:

"– continuous periods of five years' residence completed before the date of transposition of Directive 2004/38, namely 30 April 2006, in accordance with earlier European Union law instruments, must be taken into account for the purposes of the acquisition of the right of permanent residence pursuant to Article 16(1) thereof, and

– absences from the host Member State of less than two consecutive years, which occurred before 30 April 2006 but following a continuous period of five years' legal residence completed before that date do not affect the acquisition of the right of permanent residence pursuant to Article 16(1) thereof."

Lassal cleared up, to some extent, whether periods of residence before the coming into force of the Directive could count towards the acquisition of a permanent right of residence. However, a separate issue arose in *Dias v SSWP* (Case C-325/09) [2011] ECR I-06387; [2012] AACR 36. *Lassal* was, in part, concerned with what happens when someone has done five years' legal residence before 30 April 2006 but then left the UK for a period before that date: as we have seen the answer is that provided the absence was less than two consecutive years, a permanent right of residence arises on 30 April 2006. In *Dias,* the issue was what happens when someone has done five years' or more of legal residence before 30 April 2006 but has had a further period after doing so when s/he remained in the UK but without a basis in EU law for residence in that further period? The ECJ ruled effectively that provided the period of residence prior to 30 April 2006 in which the person had no EU law right to reside was less than two years then, by analogy with the rules about continuous absence, the right to reside would still exist on 30 April 2006.

While *Lassal* and *Dias* address the time periods that can potentially be taken into account, they do not particularly address the issue of what is meant by "resided legally" in Art 16. The following would appear to be the current position – the position under the Directive is considered separately from that under the I(EEA) Regs as this is an area where the two instruments contain differences.

Under the Directive

(1) Following *Ziolkowski* and *Szeja v Land Berlin* (joined cases C-424/10 and C-425/10) [2011] ECR I-14035, then periods of residence where a person has a right of residence under Art 7(1) of the Directive count as legally residing for the purposes of obtaining the permanent right of residence under Art 16: ie, periods where the person was a worker, self-employed person (or retained either of those statuses), self-sufficient, a student, or the family member of a person in the preceding categories. This appears to exclude from qualifying rights of residence under EU law, the right of residence as a jobseeker (as opposed to someone who retains the status of worker while unemployed) and also persons with rights as primary carers of the children in education of former workers (discussed at [2.6.3]). In *Okafor and Others v SSHD* [2011] EWCA Civ 499 (a decision given prior to *Ziolkowski*), the Court of Appeal explicitly held that time spent where the only right of residence was as a primary carer of this sort did not count. In *Alarape and Tijani v SSHD* (Case C-529/11), the Court also explicitly held that to be the case:

"Periods of residence in a host Member State which are completed by family members of a Union citizen who are not nationals of a Member State solely on the basis of Article 12 of Regulation No 1612/68, as amended by Directive 2004/38, where the conditions laid down for entitlement to a right of residence under that directive are not satisfied, may not be taken into consideration for the purposes of acquisition by those family members of a right of permanent residence under that directive."

(2) For periods before the coming into force of the Directive, then certainly any right of residence under a provision that is now replaced and codified in Art 7(1) of the Directive will count (*Ziolkowski* and *Dias*). It is arguable that *CIS 4299/2007* still binds UK decision makers at First-tier Tribunal and below to hold that where a person had a right of residence under a different provision of EU law (ie, not just those provisions which were replaced by the rights now contained in Art 7 as set out above), prior to 30 April 2006, that can count towards the acquisition of a permanent right. *Ziolkowski* suggests that the EU may ultimately decide that in periods prior to the coming into force of the Directive then only time spent in exercise of a right that is now codified in Art 7 of the Directive can count.

(3) Following, *Ziolkowski*, then time a person spends in the UK prior to becoming an EU citizen can, contrary to *R(IS) 3/08, CIS 1833/2007, CIS 4299/2007* and *CPC 2134/2007*, count towards the acquisition of a permanent right to reside, provided the person would have had a right under Art 7(1) had it been in force at the time and had that person been an EU citizen at the time. DMG Memo 18/12 indicates that the DWP believes that a further requirement is that the person had leave to remain under UK law and, if working, then that any work was done in accordance with any visa conditions imposed as a condition of leave. Further the Memo explicitly excludes time spent with temporary admission – eg, as an asylum seeker etc. The litigants in *Ziolkowski* did have residence in the EU state in which they had lived (Germany). However, it is difficult to discern from the text that this fact was viewed by the ECJ as a separate requirement which the claimants had to meet and the Memo does not provide any other authority for the position. However, the Upper Tribunal appears to have concurred with the Memo in *SSWP v LS (IS)* [2012] UKUT 207 (AAC).

Sch 4 para 6(3)(a) I(EEA) Regs 2006, as amended from 16 July 2012, also provided that leave to remain during a period prior to accession is an essential requirement for being able to use that period towards qualifying for a permanent right of residence. That rule is now in Sch 6 para 8(3)(b) of the I(EEA) Regs.

Under the I(EEA) Regs

(1) The acquisition of a permanent right of residence under the I(EEA) Regs is in some ways more generous than under the Directive.

(2)   Residence which was in compliance with any provision of the I(EEA) Regs, except a derivative right of residence under reg 16 (see reg 15(2)), can count (reg 15). Those who had a right under the I(EEA) Regs 2000 or I(EEA) Regs 2006 are treated as having had a right under the 2016 Regs: see Sch 6 para 8. That has two important effects:

(a)   Importantly, as jobseekers have an explicit right of residence under the I(EEA) Regs (reg 6(1)(a)) then periods where the claimant is a mere jobseeker from 30 April 2006 can count (jobseekers did not have a right of residence under the 2000 Regs).

(b)   Similarly, it appears that time spent as a "family member who has retained the right of residence" (under reg 10) can count.

(3)   The *Ziolkowski* point discussed above in relation to periods of residence prior to accession, is dealt with domestically at Sch 6 para 8(3): para 8(3)(b) makes leave to remain during a period prior to accession an essential requirement for being able to use that period towards qualifying for a permanent right of residence.

[2.4.2] Continuity of residence

Art 16(1) and reg 15(1) I(EEA) Regs are at least the same in referring to those who have resided *continuously* for a five-year period. Art 16(3) and reg 3(2) both also provide that continuity of residence shall not be affected by absences, for any reason, of up to six months in total in any year, one absence of up to 12 months for reason of pregnancy, childbirth, serious illness, study or vocational training or overseas posting (or similar), or for an undefined period for compulsory military service. In *CIS 2258/2008*, the commissioner held that, although this means that such absences allow periods of residence to be linked up, they do not themselves count as periods spent legally residing. However, in *Idezuna (EEA-permanent residence) Nigeria* [2011] UKUT 474 (IAC), a three-judge panel of the Upper Tribunal's Immigration and Asylum Chamber, concluded that the appellant did have a permanent right of residence and in calculating the period by which this would have occurred included allowable periods of absence from the UK: it held at paragraph 3 that the appellant acquired his permanent right of residence exactly five years after coming to the UK (throughout the time in the UK he was residing with his spouse who was an EU national with a right of residence) despite the fact that at paragraph 5 the tribunal explained that there had been two periods of absence in one of those years: "one in October when he travelled to the Netherlands and the other between 29 October and 17 December when he went back to Nigeria on the death of his father". The judgment in *Idezuna*, did not contain an reasoning for why that should be the case. However, the Upper Tribunal (Immigration and Asylum Chamber) returned to the issue in *Babajanov (Continuity of residence – Immigration (EEA) Regulations)* [2013] UKUT 513 (IAC). In that case, it held that the allowable absences did count towards calculation of the five-year period – indeed it was even possible that the permanent right of residence could crystallize, as in that case, at a point when the individual concerned was not in the UK. *CIS 2258/2008* should therefore no longer be followed.

     In *Babajanov*, the Upper Tribunal also commented that, in determining whether an absence of up to a year was of a sort which was "similar" to the listed situations (pregnancy, serious illness etc), regard should be had to the quality of integration in the UK prior to the absence and the way in which that integration is affected by the absence (para 19).

     There is nothing in the Directive or the 2006 Regs which touches on what is to be made, for the purposes of continuity of residence to acquire a permanent right, of time spent in the UK where there is no right to reside. This work previously suggested that such gaps should be treated in the same way as absences abroad. If that was right then a person who worked for three years and then remained in the UK but ceased being economically active for five months before returning to work for a further two years, would not, because of that gap, lose continuity of residence just as s/he would not had s/he returned to her/his country of origin for that five-month period. However, in *OB v SSWP (ESA)* [2017] UKUT 255 (AAC), the Upper Tribunal considered a similar case. Rather than applying the analysis suggested here, the tribunal considers the three previous cases and determined that:

(1)   continuity of residence does not need to be continuity of residence with a right of residence; but

(2)   the aggregate time of the periods with a right of residence needed to exceed five years.

That appears to mean that the position is now as follows:

–   *Absences from the UK:* such absences, following *Babajanov* and *Idezuna*, if allowable under Art 16(3) (or reg 3(2)), count towards the five-year period.

–   *Periods in the UK with no right of residence:* such periods, if they would be allowable under Art 16(3) (or reg 3(2)) were the claimant to have left the UK, do not break continuity of residence but do not count towards the five-year period (applying *OB v SSWP*).

Unfortunately, *OB v SSWP* was decided without the decision of the Court of Appeal in *SSDH v Ojo* [2015] EWCA Civ 1301. The Court in that case held that there was no scope to aggregate periods of residence separated by a break not covered by Art 16(3) – ie, where the claimant remained in the UK without a right of residence. The Upper Tribunal noted this in *Cardiff CC v HM (HB)* [2019] UKUT 271 (AAC) and held that *OB was per incuriam* on this point and should not be followed.

[2.5] The rights of extended family members
Art 3(2) of the Directive provides that member states shall, in accordance with national legislation, facilitate the entry and residence of those not coming within the narrow definition of family member set out in Art 2(2) (see [1.4]) for the following:
- any other family members who, in the country from which they have come, are dependants or members of the household of the Union citizen;
- other such family members who strictly require personal care due to serious health grounds;
- partners with whom the Union citizen has a durable relationship, duly attested.

The I(EEA) Regs provide that persons in such circumstances are "extended family members" (reg 8), and reg 7(3) provides that if they have obtained a residence certificate/card, they will count as family members. As family members they can derive a right of residence from the Union citizen of whom they are a family member who has such a right. Such persons will still have to satisfy the test of being "habitually resident in fact" (see [3] below) as they do not come under reg 10(3B)(zc) of the HB Regs.

In *CIS 612/2008*, the commissioner comments, *obiter,* at para 53, that in the absence of the required residence documentation an extended family member cannot have a right of residence. This is because, although the ECJ has held that generally a residence document is not necessary to have the right of residence which it describes, the right of residence for an extended family member does not arise directly under Art 3(2) but is merely one which the UK is required to facilitate. Thus, unless the Home Secretary has granted such a right of residence (as shown by the issue of the residence document), it does not exist. In *SS v SSWP (ESA)* [2011] UKUT 8 (AAC), the Upper Tribunal has confirmed that this is the situation. In that case, the facts were particularly clear that the claimant was an extended family member. The judge held that such a person will "only [have] a right of residence if that is conferred by the immigration authorities" (para 14). In *Rahman and others* (Case C-83/11) [2012] ECR (ECLI:EU:C:2012:519), the ECJ confirmed that a person could not rely directly on Art 3(2) of the Directive to establish a right of residence. That appears consistent with the above mentioned social security cases which require the domestic procedure for obtaining the right to have been gone through in order for it to exist and in *SSWP v LZ (PC)* [2014] UKUT 147 (AAC) this was the view taken of the effect of *Rahman.* The Court of Appeal has confirmed in *Macastena v SSHD* [2018] EWCA Civ 1558 that for these rights to exist the Home Secretary must grant them and also held that they could not be retrospectively attested to (see also *SSHD v Aibangbee* [2019] EWCA Civ 339).

As it is only the claimant of HB who is required not to be a person from abroad, in many cases of unmarried/civil-partnered couples then the failure of the Directive to confer a right on such partners by virtue of their relationship will not be problematic, provided it is the partner who has the right of residence who has claimed benefit. It may be relevant if, for example, the claimant is the child of an extended family member (who has not obtained a residence document) of a worker, but is not the child of the worker.

[2.6] Retention of a right of residence: death, divorce and departure
There are rules in Arts 12 and 13 of the Directive and reg 10 of the I(EEA) Regs which provide for the retention of the right of residence by a family member where the person who had a right of residence as a worker, self-employed person, self-sufficient person or student has died, divorced her/him or departed from the UK. For many years, this work expressed the view that this was an area where EU law and domestic law appeared to diverge and thus dealt separately with the provisions to highlight the differences. That view was wrong for the reasons discussed below.

Reg 14(3) of the I(EEA) Regs gives a "family member who has retained the right of residence" a right to reside. A family member who has retained the right of residence is defined in reg 10.

Where the person was the family member of an EEA national with a right of residence who died, the rules mean:
(1)   If the person is a non-EEA national who resided for at least a year with a right of residence under the regulations before the death and would now if an EEA national count as a worker, self-employed person or self-sufficient person (or the family member of any such person), s/he will have a right of residence (reg 10(2) and (6) – the equivalent rights within the Directive are at Art 12(2)).
(2)   Regardless of whether the person is an EEA national or not, if s/he was the descendant family member of the EEA national who died and was attending an educational course, which s/he continue to attend, when the EEA national died, s/he will have a right of residence (reg 10(3) / Art 12(3)).
(3)   The parent with actual custody of a child (again regardless of nationality) who satisfies the rule in 2 above will also have a right of residence (reg 10(4) / Art 12(3)).

The latter two rules also apply where the EEA national has not died but has departed from the UK.

The rule on divorce only applies where the person is a non-EEA national (reg 10(5) and (6) / Art 13(2)). Such a person will be a "family member who has retained the right of residence" if:
(1)   the person had ceased to be a family member on termination of the marriage or civil partnership;
(2)   was residing in the UK in accordance with the Regulations at that date; *and*
(a)   the marriage or civil partnership had lasted for at least three years and the parties to the marriage had resided for at least one year during the marriage in the UK;
(b)   the former spouse has custody of the child of the EEA national or a right of access to that child or EEA national; *or*

(c)   the continued residence is warranted by particularly difficult circumstances such as there having been domestic violence in the marriage or civil partnership.

The mistake made in previous editions came from an incorrect consideration of Arts 12(1) and 13(1). Those provide that the death or departure of the EU citizen (art 12), or their divorce (art 13), "shall not affect the right of residence of his/her family members who are EU citizens". The only qualification to this is that such persons cannot themselves acquire a right of permanent residence until they themselves are a worker, self-employed or self-sufficient person or a student. However, *JP v SSWP* [2018] UKUT 161 (AAC) and *GA v SSWP* [2018] UKUT 172 (AAC) hold that the first paragraph of each of these articles does not in itself confer any separate right of residence, but simply makes clear that in such circumstances the EU citizens affected can continue to have a right of residence in their own rights under Art 7 or whichever provision may apply to them. The UK Regulations thus do not give a more restrictive right that what is provided in the Directive.

In *Singh and Others v Minister for Justice and Equality* (Case C-218/14) [2015] ECR not yet reported, the ECJ was asked by an Irish Court to consider the following questions (the other questions referred relate to a different issue).

"(1)   Where marriage involving EU and non-EU citizens ends in divorce obtained following departure of the EU citizen from a host member state where EU rights were exercised by the EU citizen, and where Arts 7 and 13(2)(a) of Council Directive 2004/38/EC apply, does the non-EU citizen retain a right of residence in the host member state thereafter? If the answer is in the negative: does the non- EU citizen have a right of residence in the host Member State during the period before divorce following departure of the EU citizen from the host Member State?"

The Court answered:

"Article 13(2) of Directive 2004/38 [....] must be interpreted as meaning that a third-country national, divorced from a Union citizen, whose marriage lasted for at least three years before the commencement of divorce proceedings, including at least one year in the host Member State, cannot retain a right of residence in that Member State on the basis of that provision where the commencement of the divorce proceedings is preceded by the departure from that Member State of the spouse who is a Union Citizen."

In *NA (Pakistan) v SSHD* [2014] EWCA Civ 995, the Court of Appeal referred to the ECJ the question of whether a third-country national ex-spouse must be able to show that her/his former spouse was exercising Treaty rights at the time of the divorce in order to come within Art 13(2) of the Directive. In doing so, the Court observed (para 21) that the earlier decision of *Amos v SSHD* [2011] EWCA Civ 552, was not authority for viewing the I(EEA) Regs as correctly transposing Art 13 on the issue of the question they were asking. The Court of Justice decided the case as *SSHD v NA (Case C-115/15)*. It held that Art 13(2)(c) of the Directive could not be relied upon in a case where the divorce proceedings post-dated the exit from the host member state of the EU national to whom NA had been married.

[2.7] EU Rights of residence other than those in the Directive

The subject of what rights of residence a person not coming within the Directive may have has proved a troubled one.

[2.7.1] Service recipients

EU nationals wishing to be recipients of services in other member states were previously covered by Art 1(1)(b) of Directive 73/148, but Directive 2004/38/EC is silent about recipients as is reg 10 HB Regs. This probably does not matter as recipients of services have a right to reside under EC Treaty Arts 49 and 50. "Services" are normally provided for remuneration: EC Treaty Art 60; *R v Westminster CC ex p Castelli and Tristan-Garcia* [1995] 8 Admin LR 73 at 92E-F, QBD (R Henderson QC) (EU national cannot seek to be recipient of NHS services to show right of residence). Examples of services which may be sought are tourism, business, education and medical treatment: *Luisi & Carbone v Ministero del Tesoro* (Cases C-286/82 & C-26/83) [1984] ECR 00377. Note that the services received must be being provided for the purpose of making a profit: see *CH 1400/2006* in which the commissioner held, following cases *Belgian State v Humbel* (C-263/86) [1988] ECR 05365 and *Wirth v Landeshauptstadt Hannover* (Case C-109/92) [1993] ECR I-06447, that a claimant attending a postgraduate course at the University of London for which she had paid the foreign student fee rate was not a recipient of services.

The limitations of the derivative residence rights under Arts 49 and 50 for those seeking to claim benefits were revealed in *CIS 3875/2005*. The commissioner accepted that the provision of accommodation, social services and medical services are all capable of falling within the scope of Art 50. However, two important limiting factors then have to be considered. Firstly, the services must normally be provided for remuneration. Secondly, Art 50 does not apply where a national of a member state goes to the territory of another member state and establishes her/his principal residence there in order to provide or receive services there for an *indefinite* period: *Steymann v Staatssecretaris van Justitie* (Case C-196/87) [1988] ECR 06159 and *Sodemare SA v Regione Lombardia* (Case C-70/95) [1997] ECR I-03395. The residence right only arises if the services are being sought for a temporary period. However, from a practical perspective, establishing that fact would itself undermine any claim (for the habitual residence test) that the claimant had a settled intention to remain in the UK. In addition, the right to reside for recipients of services can only arise if the claimant came to the UK in order to receive services here, and not simply whether the claimant travelled to the UK in circumstances where it was likely that s/he would receive services, even if that was not the purpose of the journey.

[2.7.2] Article 21 TFEU

All nationals of EU member states are citizens of the EU (Art 20 TFEU, formerly Art 17 EC Treaty). By Art 20(2)(a) and Art 21(1) (formerly Art 18), EU citizens have the right to move and reside freely within the EU. However, for both articles these rights are expressed to be subject to the "limitations and conditions defined by the Treaties and by the measures adopted to give them effect".

In addition, Art 18 TFEU (formerly Art 12 EC Treaty) provides that it is unlawful to discriminate on the basis of nationality within the scope of application of the Treaty.

The question of whether an EU national who does not meet the conditions set out in Directive 2004/38 for a right of residence should nonetheless, at least in some cases, be regarded as possessing such a right directly under Art 21 has proved a difficult one. In many cases it may be closely related to the question of whether a person should be regarded as having a right of residence under Art 7(1)(b) of the Directive as a self-sufficient person (see the discussion at [2.3.1] on p329 for consideration of when someone who may be entitled to means-tested benefits may nonetheless not thereby become a burden on the social assistance system of the UK). However, *AMS v SSWP (PC) (second interim decision)* [2017] UKUT 48 (AAC) now demonstrates the difference between self-sufficiency cases and more general Art 21 cases: the former deal with a test of proportionality within a rule in the Directive (ie, whether the claimant has sufficient resources not to be an unreasonable burden on the host state) and the latter deal with whether the Directive is proportionate given the specific facts of the case.

Related to both questions, is the further issue of whether denial of benefits to someone who does not have a right of residence (even directly under Art 21) is consistent with the anti-discrimination provision in Art 18 TFEU.

Baumbast has had more attention of late for being the first in the line of cases which has culminated in *Teixeira* and *Ibrahim*. However, the ECJ in that case also considered the residence rights of Mr Baumbast. Mr Baumbast, a German national, had been a worker in the UK for several years but was, at the relevant time, employed by a German company to work in China. He thus had sufficient resources to avoid being a burden on the social assistance system of the UK. However, he did not meet the condition for a right of residence as a self-sufficient person in the then applicable Directive because his comprehensive medical insurance did not cover emergency treatment in the UK (in other words he did not satisfy the "limitations and conditions" in the measures adopted under the then Art 18 (now Art 21). Nonetheless, the ECJ held that:

"90.   In any event, the limitations and conditions which are referred to in Article 18 EC and laid down by Directive 90/364 are based on the idea that the exercise of the right of residence of citizens of the Union can be subordinated to the legitimate interests of the Member States. In that regard, according to the fourth recital in the preamble to Directive 90/364 beneficiaries of the right of residence must not become an 'unreasonable' burden on the public finances of the host Member State.

91.   However, those limitations and conditions must be applied in compliance with the limits imposed by Community law and in accordance with the general principles of that law, in particular the principle of proportionality. That means that national measures adopted on that subject must be necessary and appropriate to attain the objective pursued (see, to that effect, Joined Cases C-259/91, C-331/91 and C-332/91 *Alluè and Others* [1993] ECR I-4309, paragraph 15).

92.   In respect of the application of the principle of proportionality to the facts of the Baumbast case, it must be recalled, first, that it has not been denied that Mr Baumbast has sufficient resources within the meaning of Directive 90/364; second, that he worked and therefore lawfully resided in the host Member State for several years, initially as an employed person and subsequently as a self-employed person; third, that during that period his family also resided in the host Member State and remained there even after his activities as an employed and self-employed person in that State came to an end; fourth, that neither Mr Baumbast nor the members of his family have become burdens on the public finances of the host Member State and, fifth, that both Mr Baumbast and his family have comprehensive sickness insurance in another Member State of the Union.

93.   Under those circumstances, to refuse to allow Mr Baumbast to exercise the right of residence which is conferred on him by Article 18(1) EC by virtue of the application of the provisions of Directive 90/364 on the ground that his sickness insurance does not cover the emergency treatment given in the host Member State would amount to a disproportionate interference with the exercise of that right."

Mr Baumbast thus received his residence permit. The *Baumbast* judgment is therefore authority for the principle that a right of residence can arise directly under Art 21 where it is not proportionate to insist on satisfaction of the precise terms of Directive 2004/38. The UK courts, in the cases discussed below, have generally determined that the situations in which it would not be proportionate to deny a residence right to a person, due to a need to pursue the legitimate aim of protecting the public finances of the UK from an "unreasonable" burden, are extremely rare.

In *Trojani v Centre public d'aide sociale de Bruxelles* (Case C-456/02) [2004] ECR I-07573, the ECJ gives an example of where it is proportionate to insist on fulfilment of the conditions in the Directives. Mr Trojani was a French national living in a Salvation Army hostel in Belgium. He was not a worker. He claimed and was refused the minimex. The Court (at para 36) held clearly that, in those circumstances, it was not disproportionate to hold that he did not have a right of residence under then Art 18 (now Art 21). However, Mr Trojani had been given a residence permit by the local municipal authority. The Court went on to hold that an EU national who "has been lawfully resident in the host Member State for a certain time or possesses a residence permit" could rely on the anti-discrimination rule in Art 12 (now Art 18). As benefits were within the scope of the Treaty (see para 42), then it was unlawful discrimination to deny him the minimex.

The first two main domestic cases which grappled with the principles in *Baumbast* and *Trojani* discussed above were *Abdirahman and another v SSWP and another* [2007] EWCA Civ 657; reported as *R(IS) 8/07* and *Kaczmarek v SSWP* [2008] EWCA Civ 1310; reported as *R(IS) 5/09*. In *Abdirahman*, the Court of Appeal rejected appeals by two claimants whose appeals had been dismissed by a tribunal of commissioners in *CIS 3573/2005*, *CH 2484/2005* and *CPC 2920/2005*. The claimants were born in Somalia and were nationals of Sweden and Norway respectively and had entered the UK lawfully as EEA nationals. Neither claimant was at the relevant time a worker or economically self-sufficient. One claimed IS, HB and CTB, the other claimed PC. All claims were refused on the basis that the claimants did not have a right to reside in the UK.

The Court of Appeal held, firstly, that being lawfully present in the UK (as the claimants were) was not to be equated with a "right to reside", as UK law made a distinction between a right to reside and any lesser status (including, and here particularly, an EEA national who was in this country having entered lawfully and had committed no breach of immigration law, but who was not a "qualified person" under I(EEA) Regs 2000). The claimants in this case, although lawfully present, did not have a right to reside, under UK law, at the time relevant to the appeals, because they were not qualified persons. Having considered Art 18 (now Art 21) of the Treaty, Directive 90/364/EEC and ECJ caselaw thereunder (especially *Trojani* – the Court of Appeal noting with approval the view of the Advocate General in that case that "the basic principle of Community law is that persons who depend on social assistance will be taken care of in their own Member State"), the Court of Appeal concluded that Art 18 (now Art 21) does not create a right of residence for an EU citizen in another member state, in a case in which the limitations imposed under Directive 90/364 (note these are now the same limitations as those requiring self-sufficiency for those who are not workers or self-employed found in Directive 2004/38) are not satisfied, and where those limitations are proportionate to the legitimate objective in protecting the public finances of the host member state. Following *Brey*, (discussed at [2.3.1] on p329) this approach must perhaps be modified to recognise that there can be no automatic conclusion that any amount of social assistance entitlement generates a prohibited burden on the social assistance system.

This then left the claimants' second argument, based on Art 12 of the EC Treaty (now Art 18 TFEU) and that article's prohibition on discrimination. The tribunal of commissioners had found that the claimants' cases fell within Art 12 and thus called for the discrimination in not awarding them benefit on the grounds of nationality to be justified, but had found such justification. However, in the Court of Appeal's view, the appeals did not even get that far as the claims did not come within "the scope of application of this Treaty", which are the opening words of Art 12. Surprisingly, they held (at para 43) that the benefits themselves were not within the scope of the Treaty (although this was said to be a "misreport" in *Kaczmarek* – see below). Nonetheless, they held that if they were wrong on this, then the discrimination was justified as a proportionate way to achieve the legitimate aim articulated by the SSWP to protect the UK finances from EU nationals coming to the UK in order to live off the benefit system.

In *Kaczmarek*, the Court of Appeal considered the case of a claimant who had lived in the UK since 2002, initially as a student and then as a worker for the period June 2003 to February 2005. She applied for IS in May 2005. It was argued for the claimant that she had been lawfully resident in the UK for a three-year period at the date of her claim, mostly as a worker, and had therefore demonstrated the sort of social integration that the ECJ had in mind in *Trojani* when it held that a person who had been "lawfully resident in the host Member State for a certain time" could rely upon the anti-discrimination measure in Art 12 (now Art 18). The Court of Appeal dismissed the appeal and held that the reference in *Trojani* to residence "for a certain time" did not "open the door to eligibility based on residence of unspecified but significant duration and of a type which evidences a degree of social integration in the host Member State" (para 16). The Court held that the reference to residence "for a certain time" was a reference to a specific qualifying period which gives rise to an express right of residence – "it would be wholly undesirable if Article 12 were to give rise to an open-textured temporal qualification of the kind suggested on behalf of the appellant. Eligibility is primarily and more appropriately a matter for normative regulation rather than discretion or subjective evaluation on a case by case basis". With respect to the Court, given that at the time the ECJ decided in *Trojani* that there was no general rule about specific qualifying periods in EU law which gave rise to an express right of residence (Art 16 of Directive 2004/38 being a development which postdated that decision), it is difficult to see how this can be said to be what the ECJ actually had in mind.

The Court in *Kaczmarek* then revisited the issue of the proportionality of the denial of a right of residence to this claimant. The Court referred to those passages from *Baumbast* set out above. However, it agreed with the commissioner below who had held that the approach to the proportionality in such cases should be informed by the concept of whether there was a "lacuna" in the Directive. It is necessary to explain this in some detail.

–   At para 120 of the Advocate General's opinion in *Baumbast* it was observed that the rules on freedom of movement "had not kept up with the pace of developments". In particular, the Advocate General noted that when the legislation at issue in that case had been created (1968), no account was taken of a case where a person might live in one member state while working outside that state for a firm established in a different state.

–   In such a case, there was an unintended lacuna (hole) in the rules which it would be proportionate to fill.

–   The Court of Appeal was of the view that the ECJ had been informed by that analysis.

–   Residence rules were brought up to date by Directive 2004/38 (which was not in force at the time of the decision under consideration in *Kaczmarek*).

–   That Directive now provides an "authoritative insight into the parameters of proportionality when applied to the economically inactive migrant".

–   Where it appears, therefore, that the Directive has deliberately excluded a class of persons from the rights of residence it provides, it will not be proportionate to set those limitations aside on the grounds of proportionality. Or, in the words of the Court, "it would be inappropriate and presumptuous for us to characterize something as a lacuna when it was not identified by the Council when it most recently moved to enlarge eligibility".

An example of a case where there was a lacuna which ought to be filled is provided in *R(IS)4/09*: decided by the same commissioner whose lacuna-filling approach was subsequently endorsed by the Court of Appeal in *Kaczmarek*. There the claimant was a French national who had given up work to care for her husband, a national of Cameroon who had been working but had had to stop due to illness. The French national did not retain her status as a worker, and because her husband was a non-EEA national, he had no independent right of residence as a worker who was temporarily incapable of work on which she could rely as his family member. In these circumstances, the commissioner was satisfied that the claimant had a right of residence pursuant to Art 18 (now Art 21) notwithstanding the fact that she was not self-sufficient etc. For the commissioner, the questions to be asked in such cases are as follows:

"whether there is a lacuna in that directive, whether recognising a right of residence under Article 18(1) of the Treaty would be inconsistent with the directive and whether the principle of proportionality requires a right of residence to be recognised..."

He went on to set out the factors taken into account:

"54.   In my judgment, having regard to all these considerations, the claimant's wife's right of free movement for the purpose of working, guaranteed to her by Article 39 of the Treaty, would be infringed if she and the claimant were not recognised as having the right to reside in the United Kingdom in the circumstances of this case. There was a lacuna in the directives in force at the time of the claimant's claim for income support and there is now a lacuna in Directive 2004/38/EC but I am satisfied that the claimant and his wife retained rights of residence by virtue of Article 18(1) of the Treaty. Where a worker exercising rights under Article 39 of the Treaty in the United Kingdom is obliged to cease work and cannot be available for alternative work due to a need to care for his or her spouse who is a not a citizen of the Union but who is temporarily seriously disabled, they both retain rights of residence in the United Kingdom in the circumstances that arise in this case. Among those circumstances are the facts that:

(a)   the disabled person had been exercising his Community law right to work in the United Kingdom and had become temporarily incapable of work;

(b)   the disability had first manifested itself some considerable time after the disabled person had arrived in the United Kingdom, after he had married and after he had started work;

(c)   the disabled person had qualified for free National Health Service treatment by virtue of his period of residence in the United Kingdom, which was at least in part by virtue of his right of residence under Community law, and was continuing to undergo such treatment while being cared for by his wife;

(d)   the recognition of the claimant's right of residence under Community law when he married had led to him losing the opportunity of establishing a right of residence in his own right as a refugee.

        Whether any of those circumstances is determinative can be decided when the need arises. (If point (a) is not determinative, it may follow that a person retains a right of residence while temporarily unable to be available for work due to the need to care for a dependant child, although, I would suggest, only where the child's need for care is temporary and is wholly due to the seriousness of the disability rather than the child's age.)"

In *SSWP v CA* [2009] UKUT 169 (AAC), the judge holds that this type of "lacuna-filling" approach is the only correct approach to the question of proportionality in right to reside cases. However, the judge in *SSWP v AH (IS)* [2010] UKUT 265 (AAC) takes a different view. The judge in that case comments that, although the lacuna-filling approach is one way in which proportionality operates (although he would not have read the *Baumbast* judgment in that way), the other approach is that proportionality overrides conditions that normally apply:

"Freedom of movement for EU citizens is a fundamental right. Any exceptions or conditions must be narrowly interpreted and applied. They must not be given an effect out of proportion with the policy objective that they seek to fulfil."

It is suggested that, following the decision in *Brey,* this is the correct approach and is now binding in the UK; attempts to restrict proportionality reviews to a (usually fruitless) search for a lacuna as described above are incorrect.

        The exact parameters of who may have a right of residence directly under Art 21 TFEU, or failing that, who may rely on Art 18 TFEU, remain to be worked out in further cases. At present it is suggested that the case of *R(IS) 4/09* provides one benchmark as to when an Art 21 TFEU right may arise. In other cases, it is apparent that, if there would need to be reliance on benefits for a considerable period of time were an Art 21 right recognised, that will present a significant barrier.

Finally, it is also worth noting that since the coming into force of the TFEU, the Charter of Fundamental Rights of the European Union now has the same legal value as the EU Treaties (see Art 6 TFEU). It is likely that the provisions of Title IV of the Charter, entitled "Solidarity", will increasingly be relied upon in cases where no clear right of residence exists and a claim for HB is made. In particular, a question to be asked is whether Article 34 of the Charter which states that the EU "recognises and respects the right to social and housing assistance so as to ensure a decent existence for all who lack sufficient resources" actually adds anything to existing law. It may be that the incorporation of the Charter shifts the tenor of judgments on these issues further towards the importance of recognising the solidarity that EU states have to display towards nationals of other EU states within their boundaries.

Note that although the UK has, with Poland, attempted to opt out of that rule under Protocol 30 to TFEU, this provision does not change the enforceability of the Charter before UK Courts: in *R (Saeedi) v Secretary of State for the Home Department* [2010] EWHC 705 (Admin), Cranston J had held that the Charter could not be "directly relied on as against the United Kingdom" by virtue of the Protocol (para 155). However, on appeal to the Court of Appeal, the Master of the Rolls recorded that the Home Secretary no longer supported that finding. She conceded that "the fundamental rights set out in the Charter can be relied on as against the United Kingdom and ... that [Cranston J] erred in holding otherwise". The Court of Justice confirmed that the Charter has to be applied and enforced by UK Courts in a question referred from the proceedings: *NS v SSHD* (Case C-411/10) [2011] ECR I-13905.

In *Patmalniece v SSWP* [2009] EWCA Civ 621, the Court of Appeal held that the justification accepted for any discrimination that did exist in *Abdirahman* was also sufficient to justify the discrimination that did arise for the purposes of Art 3 EC Regulation 1408/71. That article is the anti-discrimination provision within EC Regulation 1408/71 and can be relied upon by all those within the personal scope of the regulation as defined in Art 2. The Court of Appeal held (at para 24) that, although the right to reside test was indirectly discriminatory against non-UK EU nationals, that discrimination was not overt (ie, direct) because some EU nationals would pass the test. The Court went on to hold that as PC (the benefit at issue in that case) was a special non-contributory benefit, then the justification advanced in *Abdirahman* sufficed here in as much as PC still had characteristics of social assistance. Where that leaves those benefits to which the right to reside test applies that are not special-contributory benefits or social assistance for the purposes of the Regulation (eg, child benefit) is not a subject for this volume as it is accepted that HB is not covered by EC Regulation 1408/71.

The Supreme Court gave judgment in *Patmalniece* [2011] UKSC 11; [2011] AACR 34 on 16 March 2011. The Court proceeded on the basis that if the habitual residence test was directly discriminatory against EU nationals then it would be unlawful. However, the Court confirmed that the habitual residence test was not directly discriminatory against EU nationals as compared with UK and Irish nationals. In doing so, the Court followed the ECJ in *Bressol v Gouvernement de la Communauté Française* (Case C-73/08) [2010] OJ C 148 which held that a similar composite test to the habitual resident test, one bit of which (ie, in the UK situation the right to reside requirement in the habitual residence test) would automatically be satisfied by UK citizens but the other bit of which (ie, the "habitually resident in fact" part of the test) might be failed by some was not directly discriminatory. Although the judgment is concerned with the anti-discrimination provision in Art 3 of EC Regulation 1408/71 (which does not apply to HB as that is not within the material scope of that Regulation), it must also apply to potential challenges to the habitual residence test brought under other anti-discrimination provisions in EU law (eg, Art 24 of the Directive or Art 21 TFEU).

The ECJ has analysed the issue differently but come to effectively the same conclusion in a series of recent cases:

(1)   In *Dano v Jobcentre Leipzig* (Case C-333/13), the Court ruled that "social assistance" for the purposes of Directive 2004/38 included benefits that would be referred to a special non-contributory benefits under EC Regulation 1408/71 (now 883/2004) and that EU nationals without a right of residence under Directive 2004/38 could legitimately be excluded from accessing those benefits.

(2)   In *Jobcentre Berlin Newkolln v Alimanovic* (Case C-67/14), the Court decided that those whose only right of residence was as a jobseeker could legitimately be excluded from accessing any benefits that were not benefits of a financial nature intended to faciliate access to the labour market of the host state. The Court went further and stated that in such cases there was no need of an individual assessment of proportionality (paras 59–62). That aspect of the decision is most troubling as it is by no means clear from what the Court has said when a *Brey*-style assessment would be needed and when it can be dispensed with.

The Supreme Court gave judgment in *Mirga and Samin v SSWP and Westminster City Council* [2016] UKSC 1; [2016] AACR 26 on 27 January 2016. The facts for Ms Mirga were that she was born in Poland in 1988. She was in the UK from 1998 to 2002 before returning to Poland and re-entering the UK in 2004 when Poland acceded to the EU. She finished her education in 2005 and worked from April to November of that year in registered work. She became pregnant in February 2006 and did some unregistered work. The SSWP refused her claim to IS on the grounds of pregnancy from August 2006 holding that she did not have a right to reside. Two arguments were put to the Supreme Court:

"38.   The first argument [...] is that, in the light of her right to respect for her private and family life, under article 8 of the European Convention on Human Rights, she cannot be removed from the UK, and therefore her right of residence in the UK, as accorded by article 21.1 of TFEU, cannot be limited or cut back in the way that the Income Support Regulations seek to do, namely by restricting her rights to income support because she has not achieved a continuous 12 month period in registered employment. His alternative argument is that, even if it would be permissible to refuse Ms Mirga income support on that ground, it is only possible in practice if it would be proportionate to do so, and in particular if the grant of income support to her would place an unreasonable burden on the social assistance system of the UK, and there has been no inquiry into that question."

The Supreme Court rejected both arguments. In respect of the first it held that the art 21(1) right was explicitly subject to the "limitations and condition" in the Directive that required sufficient resources which were not present (paras 43–46). In respect of the second, the Court held at 69 and 70:

"Where a national of another member state is not a worker, self-employed or a student, and has no, or very limited, means of support and no medical insurance ...it would severely undermine the whole thrust and purpose of the 2004 Directive if proportionality could be invoked to entitle that person to have the right of residence and social assistance in another member state, save perhaps in extreme circumstances. It would also place a substantial burden on a host member state if it had to carry out a proportionality exercise in every case where the right of residence (or indeed the right against discrimination) was invoked.

Even if there is a category of exceptional cases where proportionality could come into play, I do not consider that [Ms Mirga] could possibly satisfy it.'"

What is to be noted about this ruling is that:

(1)   The Court seems to accept that where a claimant has more than just "very limited" means of subsistence then proportionality may come into play.

(2)   The Court also does not rule out the possibility of a category of exceptional cases.

Since *Mirga,* the caselaw could be summarised as a largely fruitless search for circumstances that may fall into this category of exceptional cases. *MM v SSWP (ESA)* [2017] UKUT 437 (AAC) at para 44 and *LO v SSWP (IS)* [2017] UKUT 440 (AAC) at para 51 both confirm that such a category exists and is not confined to someone entirely on all fours with the *Baumbast* facts. Cases which have been held not to fall into the category include:

–   *LO v SSWP:* the claimant, a Spanish national, had two children under school age who were British nationals. She claimed income support when she separated from their British father, her unmarried partner. She was prevented by order of the Family Court from taking the children out of the UK and thus from returning to her Spain where she could have potentially accessed social assistance.

–   *MM v SSWP:* the claimant was Swedish and came to the UK in 2004 with her parents. Due to learning difficulties she needed full time care and support and had been awarded disability living allowance. Her (step)father had worked in the UK but subsequently left the country and it was accepted that the claimant could not derive a right to reside from his residence. Her mother had claimed income support for a number of years as a lone parent, although no immigration checks had been undertaken when she made her claims and she had no right to reside that could assist the claimant. The claimant was refused income related ESA. Judge Ward holds:

"It is clear from Mirga that for a proportionality argument to stand any chance of success, the case must involve 'extreme circumstances' and will be 'an exceptional case' (Mirga [69] and [70]). I term these, together, the 'exceptionality requirement'. I am mindful that in those paragraphs Lord Neuberger was guarded as to whether a window of opportunity to rely on proportionality exists at all, even when the exceptionality requirement is fulfilled. In the remainder of this decision I proceed on the basis that it may do so. In assessing what might fulfil the exceptionality requirement, one has to bear in mind the purposes of the Directive as expounded in Dano, Alimanovic and Mirga itself and the clear preference of the Supreme Court for a rule based system over one based on the examination of individual circumstances. It is clear from the Supreme Court's review of the authorities that reliance on Brey can get the appellant no further than this."

The claimant's reliance on others in order to live in the community at all were not regarded as the sort of extreme factors needed.

–   *AMS v SSWP (PC) (final decision)* [2017] UKUT 381 (AAC): the claimant was a pensioner whose case was really about disapplying the rules for sufficient resources (see that section).

–   *SSWP v AC* [2017] UKUT 130 (AAC): the claimant was Greek and had been in the UK 30 years. This was held to be the type of case the limitations on residence rights in Art 21 were designed to catch – although the claimant could potentially have a domestic law basis for obtaining leave to remain.

[2.7.3] Rights of carer's of the children in education of former workers and the formerly self-employed

On 23 February 2010, in *Teixeira v LB Lambeth* (Case C-480/08) [2010] ECR I-01107 and *LB Harrow v Ibrahim* (Case C-310/08) [2010] ECR I-01065, the ECJ confirmed its decision in *Baumbast & R v SSHD* (Case C-413/99) [2002] ECR I-07091 and held that the children of EU workers or former workers and their primary carers have a right of residence by virtue of Art 12 of EEC Regulation 1612/68 (replaced by Art 10 of Regulation (EU) 492/2011 from 16 June 2011 to the same effect) and are thereby entitled to access social assistance in the UK. Art 12 provides that the children of a national of a member state who is, or has been, employed in the territory of another member state shall be admitted to that state's education system under the same conditions as the nationals of that State.

The principal issue in both cases was the same: namely, whether the appellants had a right of residence deriving directly from Art 12 of Regulation 1612/68, it being accepted by all parties that they could not derive such a right from EC Directive 2004/38.

The ECJ dismisses the UK's arguments (that such a right was dependent on self-sufficiency or that the Directive had limited the scope of *Baumbast*) in both judgments, holding that a national of a member state who was employed in the UK can claim a right of residence as the primary carer of a child in education solely on the basis of Art 12 of Regulation of 1612/68, without being required to satisfy the conditions laid down in Directive 2004/38. Paragraphs 53 and 54 of *Teixeira* state that Art 12 must be applied independently of other rights of residence in EU law and para 58 notes that this interpretation is confirmed by the *travaux preparatoires* to Directive 2004/38, which show that the Directive was designed to be consistent with the judgment in *Baumbast*.

With regard to the requirement of self-sufficiency, the ECJ again refers to its judgment in *Baumbast* and notes that the right of residence accorded to the children and their mother in that case was not based on their self-sufficiency but on the purpose of Regulation 1612/68 to promote and facilitate freedom of movement for workers which necessitated the best possible conditions for the integration of the worker's family in the host state. The ECJ, therefore, holds that the right of residence deriving from Art 12 "is not conditional on that parent having sufficient resources not to become a burden on the social assistance system of that Member State during the period of residence and having comprehensive sickness cover there."

The Court also clarified in *Teixeira* that there was no requirement that the child first entered education when the EU citizen was a worker in order to have a right to reside under Art 12 of Regulation 1612/68. There was nothing in the wording of the Article that required that, and it was "enough that the child who is in education in the host Member State became installed there when one of his or her parents was exercising rights of residence there as a migrant worker" (para 74). In terms of the duration of the Art 12 right of residence, the Court notes that in terms of access to, and the completion of, education, the right extends to higher education. Consequently, the date a child completes her/his education may be after reaching the age of majority and also after ceasing to be dependent on a parent. In terms of the primary carer, the Court held (at para 86) that her right to reside may extend beyond the age of majority of the child "if the child continues to need the presence and the care of that parent in order to be able to pursue and complete his or her education."

Finally, it should be noted that there is no requirement that the primary carer is or was a worker, or continues to reside with the parent who was the worker (see *Ibrahim*). This means that a woman (of whatever nationality) who has separated from her partner who is an EEA national who has worked in the UK can establish a right to reside on the basis of being a lone parent of their child in education.

The judgments mean that claimants covered by the *Baumbast* principle are entitled to HB (providing they are also habitually resident in the ordinary sense), including new claimants, and those whose appeals are yet to be determined or have been stayed pending the ECJ judgments. In practical terms, the claimant will need to establish the following:

(1)   a parent has worked in the UK and attained the status of worker for the purposes of EU law; *and*
(2)   a child of that worker has resided in the UK at the same time as the worker; *and*
(3)   the child has entered and remains in the UK education system; *and*
(4)   the claimant is the child's primary carer.

Note that in *CIS 3960/2007,* it was held that enrolling in nursery education does not count as a child having entered education for the purposes of Art 12 of EC Reg 1612/68. The same view was arrived at in *SSWP v IM (IS)* [2011] UKUT 231 (AAC). Reg 15A I(EEA) Regs 2006 sought to express that rule in domestic law. However, in *Shabani v SSHD* [2013] UKUT 315 (IAC), a three-judge panel of the Immigration and Asylum Chamber of the Upper Tribunal determined that the primary carer of a child who had entered reception class had acquired Art 12 rights and that "nursery education" for the purposes of reg 15A did not encompass reception class. The three-judge panel distinguish the two social security cases holding the opposite position on the basis that the Education Act 2006 had changed the position since those cases were decided (para 78).

In *SSWP v JS (IS)* [2010] UKUT 347 (AAC), the Upper Tribunal held that the child in education of an A8 worker who has done some authorised work, but less than the 12 months (and was therefore still an A8 worker requiring registration or would have been if s/he got a job), still had a right of residence under Art 12 of Regulation 1612/68, and therefore that the primary carer of that child also enjoyed a right of residence. It is worth noting that the first month of employment by an A8 national was always regarded as for an authorised employer and so it seems that all A8 nationals who did some work during the accession period and had children in the UK at that time who are now in education will benefit from this decision.

DJ v SSWP (JSA) [2013] UKUT 113 (AAC) confirms that this is the correct approach. In that case the claimant had never registered her work, but was able to rely on the fact that the first month was legal work in any event, to found a *Baumbast* right.

In *IP v SSWP (IS)* [2015] UKUT 691 (AAC), the Upper Tribunal holds that where the child in education is the child of the unmarried partner of an EU worker but not the child of the worker themselves, the primary carer will not have a right of residence. In *SSWP v JS (ESA)* [2016] UKUT 314 (AAC), the tribunal holds that although a grandparent can be a primary carer, it is a requirement that a *parent* has worked in the UK. It is not sufficient that the grandparent has done so.

In C-115/15 *SSHD v NA*, the Court of Justice expressly holds that a residence right for a child and her/his primary carer will arise in a case where the worker parent had left the host Member State prior to the child commencing education. *Bolton MBC v HY (HB)* [2018] UKUT 103; [2018] AACR 31 confirmed at para 40 that there does need to be a common period where the worker parent is in the UK and the child is installed here as their family member.

Another issue, is whether the family member of the primary carer with a right of residence following the *Teixeira* and *Ibrahim* cases can have a right of residence. The judge in *RM v SSWP (IS)* [2010] UKUT 238 (AAC) suggests, *obiter*, at para 9 that they do. However, in the same paragraph the judge decides (without any reasoning) that an A8 worker who has done some work (the first month of which must be regarded as for an authorised employer) and is then the primary carer of children in education does not have a right of residence – ie, decides differently to the Upper Tribunal in the case of *JS* referred to above. The claimant, RM, has sought permission to appeal to the Court of Appeal on this and other grounds. The point about whether family members of the primary carer with a *Teixeira* right of residence themselves have a right to reside also arises in another case awaiting determination by the Upper Tribunal – file *CPC 1935/2010*). In a Northern Ireland case, C2/11-12(JSA) (*MA v DSD (JSA)* [2011] NICom 205)), the Department conceded, and the concession was accepted with reasons as to why, that the partner of a primary carer with *Teixeira* rights (ie, the father of the child in education where the mother was the primary carer on the facts) also had a right of residence. That seems consistent with Art 24.3 of the Charter of Fundamental Rights discussed above at [1]. In *CPC 1935/2010* (neutral citation unavailable at the time of writing) the Upper Tribunal decided:

(1)   That, the answer to the question posed at the start of this paragraph (ie, whether the family member of a primary carer with a *Teixeira* right can derive a right of residence through that relationship?) is no.

(2)   That there may be some cases where a person other than a parent can be a primary carer, but that would require examination of the facts.

The judge also regards the Northern Irish decision in *MA v DSD (JSA)* referred to above as correct: "it is no doubt realistic to accept that parents jointly share the care or their children" and that the SSWP consistently makes the same concession in other cases.

In *SSWP v LC (IS)* [2011] UKUT 108 (AAC) and *SSWP v MP(IS)* [2011] UKUT 109 (AAC) (*Punakova* (Case 148/11) and *Czop* (Case C-147/11) respectively before the ECJ), the Upper Tribunal referred to the ECJ questions concerning whether the child in education of someone who is or has been self-employed (and therefore that child's primary carer) enjoys a similar right of residence to that of the child of someone who is or has been a worker. Specifically, the judge asks whether a right of residence will exist because:

"(a)   Regulation 1612/68 applies, together with the reasoning of the European Court of Justice in *Baumbast & R v SSHD* (Case C-413/99) [2002] ECR I-07091, *LB Harrow v Ibrahim* (Case C-310/08) [2010] ECR I-01065 and *Teixeira v LB Lambeth* (Case C-480/08) [2010] ECR I-01107;

(b)   there is a general principle of EU law that equates the position of workers and the self-employed;

(c)   it would impede or deter the freedom of establishment if the claimant did not have a right to reside; *or*

(d)   some other basis."

The ECJ ultimately only answered the first of those questions (negatively) as the SSWP conceded in both of the referred cases that a right of residence existed on another basis. The final decision of the Upper Tribunal made clear that this is the position at para 7 of *SSWP v Czop (IS)* [2013] UKUT 351 (AAC); [2013] AACR 6.

In disposing of the *Punakova* and *Czop* cases on their return from the ECJ, Judge Jacobs also expresses the view that the ECJ had only dealt with the first question and that the other questions will still need to be decided.

However, in *RM v SSWP (IS)* [2014] UKUT 401 (AAC); [2015] AACR 11 Judge Jacobs returned to the issue. He held that although *Czop* had not decided the answer to the other questions, it had decided that there was no right to education for the children of the formerly self-employed. That was sufficient to mean that a right of residence for the primary carer of such a child did not arise. Although the claimant in *RM* did not appeal, Judge Jacobs granted permission to appeal to the Court of Appeal on the question of whether the children of a formerly self-employed person have a right to reside in order to pursue education in another case. The Court of Appeal in *Hrabkova v SSWP* [2017] EWCA Civ 794 dismissed that appeal and Ms Hrabkova is seeking permission to appeal to the Supreme Court.

The UK amended the I(EEA) Regs 2006 from 16 July 2012, in order to, among other reasons, attempt to put the judgment in *Teixeira* on a domestic law footing. SI 2012 No.1547 inserts a new reg 15A into the I(EEA) Regs 2006. Paragraphs (3), (4) and (5) of that regulation deal with issues relating to *Teixeira.*

Reg 16 of the I(EEA) Regs now attempts to codify the *Baumbast/Teixeira* rights in domestic law:

–   Paragraph (3) provides for the child in education's right of residence where one of her/his parents is, or has previously been, a worker at a point where the child resided in the UK.

–   Paragraph (4) provides for the right of residence of any primary carer of a child coming within paragraph (3) provided only that the child would not be able to continue to be educated in the UK if the primary carer were required to permanently leave.

–   Paragraph (6) also provides for the other children aged under 18 (for whom the primary carer is responsible) to have a right of residence if the primary carer would have to leave the UK were such other children required to leave.

It is worth also noting paragraphs (7) and (8):

– Paragraph (7), consistent with *SSWP v IM (IS)*, provides that nursery education is excluded but not education received prior to compulsory school age that is equivalent to education that would be received at or after compulsory school age – ie, reception class. However it also provides that a person only counts as a worker for the purposes of their children resident in the state acquiring a right to enter education and therefore gain a right of residence if they are actually in work at the same time a child is in the UK. If the parent is merely retaining worker status at this point, that will not do. It is not clear that this latter condition is correct. Finally, paragraph (7) now also prevents a derivative right of residence arising for any person unless they would have no other right of residence.

– Paragraph (8) defines "primary carer" as someone who is a direct relative or legal guardian of the child in education and who either has primary responsibility for caring or shares that responsibility equally with one other person who has no other right to reside in the UK (that is arguably inconsistent with *MA v DSD (JSA)* referred to above).

[2.7.4] Rights of carer's of children who themselves have a right of residence

A further issue that may arise following *Teixeira* and *Ibrahim* (see above) concerns the situations of primary carers of children where the child has a right of residence as the family member of someone who has either an Art 7 extended right of residence or an Art 16 or Art 17 permanent right of residence but where **either** that child is not in education **and/or** the non-primary carer parent's right of residence is not as a worker or someone retaining that status.

In *Teixeira* and *Ibrahim,* the children had no right of residence as the family member of a worker, as their parents were not at the relevant time in work or retaining that status. However, as they were the children of people who had been workers and as they were in education, then they had a right of residence directly under Art 12 of EC Regulation 1612/68.

However, in many cases of separated unmarried partners, it may be that while the parent looking after the children has no right of residence in her/his own right, the other parent will have a right of residence as a worker or self-employed person. That is sufficient to give the child a right of residence as a family member (see the case of *Diatta*). However, it will not provide a right of residence to the ex-partner of that worker (as they are not married, they do not count as family members of each other under Art 2 of the Directive).

In such situations, the case of *Zhu and Chen* (Case C-200/02) [2004] ECR I-09925 suggests that the primary carer of the child will still have a right of residence. While in the cases of *Baumbast*, *Teixeira* and *Ibrahim*, the ECJ had to locate the right of residence for the child in the fact that they were the children of those who had been workers and were in education, in *Chen*, the ECJ had found the child had a right of residence as a self-sufficient person. However, in all four cases the ECJ went on to find that the fact that the child had a right of residence meant that her/his primary carer too had to have such a right (to facilitate that of the child). Similarly, in *Zambrano* once the Court had decided that the child had a right of residence, it went on to find that the primary carer on whom the child was dependent also had such a right. It can, therefore, be argued that whenever a child has a right of residence (whether that arises because s/he is a child in education of a former worker or on some other basis, such as because s/he is the family member of a person who is in fact a worker albeit not living with that worker or s/he is the child of a self-employed person etc), then the primary carer of that child must have a right of residence.

The Upper Tribunal is to consider this argument in file *CJSA 1637/2017* and two other linked appeals by the same claimant.

[2.8] Residence documentation

It is now clear that the possession of residence documentation issued to certify a right of residence under EU law does not in and of itself confer a right of residence: *Dias v SSWP* (Case C-325/09) [2011] ECR I-06387; [2012] AACR 36 . Thus, *CIS 185/2008* (ie, Ms Dias' case at commissioner level), in which the commissioner held that a valid residence permit, issued under the provisions in force before Directive 2004/38, must be accepted as proof that the bearer had a right of residence, despite the fact that the claimant was no longer pursuing the economic activity which had entitled her to the issue of the permit in the first place, should no longer be followed. *MD v SSWP (PC)* [2016] UKUT 319 (AAC) establishes that a residence card certifying permanent residence is not conclusive evidence that the underlying right exists.

This means that, save for extended family members (for whom possession of residence card or certificate is essential to acquire the right to be treated as a family member and therefore have a right of residence under domestic law), residence documentation is of little or no value to an EEA national.

[3] Paragraph (2): "habitually resident in fact"

To repeat, for emphasis, the points made in the General Note, habitual residence in fact will only arise as an issue for those people who have a right to reside and who do not fall within para (3B).

The phrase "habitual residence" has been frequently used in international conventions, many of which have been incorporated into English law by statute. As "habitual residence" does not have a special meaning for HB purposes (see below), caselaw on the meaning of the phrase in other contexts may be examined to determine the meaning in this context. In particular, there is a large amount of caselaw on the phrase as used in the Hague Convention on the Civil Aspects of Child Abduction 1980 Art 3 and the Child Abduction and Custody Act 1985. In addition, an identical test was introduced for IS claimants along with the amendments adding the HB/CTB test. There are now many decisions in relation to IS which must be regarded as highly persuasive authority.

[3.1] Basic principles

The basic principles established by this large body of caselaw are now enumerated below. For a helpful review of the law on habitual residence, see *CIS 4474/2003*. The quotations constituting the first two principles are taken from the speech of Lord Brandon in In *Re J (A minor) (Abduction: Custody Rights)* [1990] 2 AC 562.

(1) "the expression "habitually resident", as used in Art 3 of the Convention, is nowhere defined. It follows, I think, that the expression is not to be treated as a term of art with special meaning, but is rather to be understood according to the ordinary and natural meaning of the two words which it contains." This statement was approved and followed in *R(IS) 6/96* (paras 17, 20) and *CIS 2326/1995* (para 17).

(2) "the question whether a person is or is not habitually resident in a specified country is a question of fact to be decided by reference to all the circumstances of any particular case". So it has been held that it is not possible to draw up a comprehensive list of factors to be considered: *R(IS) 6/96* (paras 17, 20); *CIS 13498/1996* (para 9). All the facts of the case must be considered.

(3) It is possible for a claimant to be habitually resident in more than one state at once: *CIS 2326/1995* (para 27).

(4) In deciding whether a claimant is habitually resident, authorities and tribunals must examine the whole period down to the date that the decision is made, because the time period between the claim and the decision being made may be sufficient to allow the "appreciable period of time" to have accrued: *CIS 2326/1995* (para 29); *CIS 11481/1995* (paras 10–12).

(5) It is for the authority to justify a decision that the claimant is not habitually resident. It follows that if no evidence is available to support such a decision, the authority must accept the claimant as habitually resident: *R(IS) 6/96* (para 15).

(6) A person cannot be habitually resident unless s/he is resident. If s/he is not resident, there is no need to consider the quality of the claimant's existence here. A future intention to reside here is insufficient: *CIS 15927/1996* (paras 6, 9). Residence may be in the CTA (see p299). The residence must be lawful: *R v Brent LBC ex p Shah* [1983] 2 AC 309 at 343H–344B, HL. Residence is not the same as physical presence. One may be resident without being present: see the discussion of loss of habitual residence below. It is possible for a claimant to be resident in more than one country: *CIS 16410/1996* (para 10). Likewise, one may be present without being resident. In *R(IS) 6/96* (para 19) the following was said:

> "Residence to my mind involves a more settled state than mere physical presence in a country, so that a person who is a short stay visitor, or has come here for an operation or to receive medical treatment other than long-term care, is neither resident nor habitually resident. To count as resident, a person must be seen to be making a home here; even though it need not be his or her home, nor need it be intended to be a permanent one, provided that it is genuinely home for the time being."

In many cases, the claimant will not previously have spent any substantial period of time in the CTA. The sole question will then be whether the claimant has acquired habitual residence status. However, there will also be cases in which the claimant was present in the CTA for a substantial period or periods of time before going away to another country. In such cases, the claimant may have been habitually resident in the CTA before s/he left and before considering the present period of residence, it will be necessary to decide whether the status of habitual residence was ever lost: *R(IS) 6/96* (paras 31–32); *CIS 8111/1995* (para 11). If it was not lost, it will not be necessary for the claimant to show that s/he has acquired the status during the present period of residence. It is therefore necessary to consider both [3.2] how the status is acquired and [3.3] how it is lost.

[3.2] Acquisition of habitual residence

The starting point is the third point made by Lord Brandon in *Re J (A minor) (Abduction: Custody Rights)* [1990] 2 AC 562 at 578G–H:

> "there is a significant difference between a person ceasing to be habitually resident in country A, and his subsequently becoming resident in country B instead. A person may cease to be habitually resident in country A in a single day if he or she leaves it with a settled intention not to return to it but to take up long-term residence in country B instead. Such a person cannot, however, become habitually resident in country B in a single day. An appreciable period of time and a settled intention will be necessary to enable him or her to become so. During that appreciable period of time the person will have ceased to be habitually resident in country A but not yet have become resident in country B."

In essence, therefore, two basic requirements need to be fulfilled: [3.2.1] an appreciable period of time must elapse and the claimant must have [3.2.2] a settled intention to reside in the UK.

[3.2.1] "An appreciable period of time" The need for an "appreciable period of time" to elapse before a person can become habitually resident has been a reasonably constant feature of the caselaw: see *R(IS) 6/96* (para 21) and *CIS 2326/1995* (paras 20–21), despite strenuous argument in the latter case that Lord Brandon's statement was *obiter* and of no assistance in the benefits context. This was confirmed by the majority in *Nessa v Chief Adjudication Officer* [1998] 2 All ER 728, which was an appeal from the latter decision, despite a powerful dissent from Thorpe LJ. *The House of Lords* [1999] 1 WLR 1937, [1999] 4 All ER 677 subsequently upheld the commissioner's decision unanimously. However, it is arguably noteworthy that Lord Slynn, in giving the only substantial judgment of the House of Lords in *Nessa* did not use the word "appreciable". Instead, he stated that it was "plain as a matter of ordinary language [that] a person is not habitually resident in any country unless he has taken up residence and lived there for a period". Although there would be some types of legislation which could not work if there could be a gap between leaving country A and establishing habitual residence in country B, the IS legislation (and hence the HB legislation) did not fall into that category. He then went on to give some general guidance:

"I do not consider that, when he spoke of residence for an appreciable period, Lord Brandon meant more than this. It is a question of fact to be determined on the date where the determination has to be made on the circumstances of each case whether and when that habitual residence had been established. Bringing possessions, doing everything necessary to establish residence before coming, having a right of abode, seeking to bring family, 'durable ties' with the country of residence or intended residence, and many other factors have to be taken into account.

The requisite period is not a fixed period. It may be longer where there are doubts. It may be short ... There may indeed be special cases where the person concerned is not coming here from the first time, but is resuming an habitual residence previously had ... On such facts, the adjudication officer may or of course may not be satisfied that the previous habitual residence has been resumed. This position is quite different from that of someone coming to the United Kingdom for the first time." (see *The House of Lords* [1999] 1 WLR 1937, [1999] 4 All ER 677 at 682f–683d)

The decision in *Nessa* therefore settles a number of points. First, unless, for benefits within its material scope (not HB), the claimant falls within the scope of Regulation 1408/71 and can take advantage of the ruling in *Swaddling v Chief Adjudication Officer* (Case C-90/97) [1999] 2 CMLR 679, ECJ, or in some cases is a returning resident (see below), the claimant must demonstrate that s/he has resided in the CTA for some period of time.

Secondly, it confirmed that the period of time may vary and depends on the facts of the individual case.

In *R(IS) 6/96* (para 28), the commissioner gave examples of periods of time which would normally be necessary for residence to have been for an appreciable period. This approach has been rejected in *CIS 2326/1995* (para 24) and *CIS 8111/1995* (para 17) as likely to lead to the suggested periods being treated as rules of thumb. In *Cameron v Cameron* [1996] SLT 306 at 313F CS(IH), it was said that there was no minimum period of residence that could be described as "habitual". This approach was followed in *CIS 2326/1995* (para 24). In paras 25–27, the commissioner pointed out that Lord Brandon's statement that habitual residence could not be acquired in a single day had to be seen in the child abduction context, where a child was removed and where intention or preparation for her/him taking up residence in the country where s/he was taken by the abductor has to be ignored. If there is a "sharp-edged" change of residence, where the claimant unequivocally abandons the former state of residence and commits to the CTA, the period may be quite short. In *CIS 4474/2003*, the commissioner confirms that what constitutes the required period will depend on the circumstances of the particular case. However, he added that in the general run of cases the period will lie between one and three months and that cogent reasons would need to be given by a tribunal supporting a decision that required a significantly longer period. This approach was subsequently doubted by the tribunal of commissioners in *CIS 2559/2005* (para 17), a view echoed in *CIS 1972/2003* as reducing the relevant period of residence to a fixed tariff. In *R(IS) 7/06* (an appeal against which was dismissed by the Court of Appeal), the commissioner had supported the comments in *CIS 4474/2003* to the effect that cases outside the one- to three-month range were exceptional. The same commissioner who decided *CIS 4474/2003* has replied, in *CJSA 1223/2006*, by stating that his decision should not be regarded as setting a tariff, but that he remained of the view that for most cases an appreciable period is likely to be between one and three months. It is suggested that the fact that in most cases such a period will be appropriate that is not the same as setting a tariff but merely recognises what is decided in most cases. Thus a case outside this range is a strange one and will require a cogent explanation.

Note that in *CIS 1304/1997*, the commissioner held that a person who had previously been habitually resident in the UK and had stopped being habitually resident during a period of absence (see [3.3]) could nonetheless be habitually resident immediately on return to the UK – ie, without the need for the new period of residence to have been for an appreciable period of time. This might be the case if the claimant is returning to take up a way of life previously settled. This was said to depend on factors such as (1) the circumstances of loss of habitual residence, (2) any links maintained while the claimant was away, and (3) the circumstances of the return to the UK.

The "length, continuity and nature" of the residence will be relevant to whether it has been for a sufficient period: *R(IS) 6/96* (para 21). However, in *CIS 2326/1995* (para 26), the commissioner suggested that the period need not be continuous and preparatory acts in other states or preparatory visits to the CTA may be relevant if they are evidence of the claimant's settled intention (see below). It seems to follow from this that a strongly settled intention will tend to reduce the necessary period: *Re B (Minors) (Abduction)* [1993] 1 FLR 993 at 995C-D, FD (Waite J).

The provisions of the United Nations Convention on the Rights of the Child have no direct application here as it does not form part of domestic UK law. However, it can be taken into account in deciding what on the facts of a particular case may amount to a sufficient period: *CIS 1972/2003* para 17.

[3.2.2] A "settled intention" The claimant must also have a "settled intention" to reside in the CTA. The intention need not be to reside permanently in the CTA: *Shah* at 344C-D, *Cameron* at 313G-I, *CIS 13498/1996* (para 12). Evidence of settled intention usually comes from the claimant's actions before entering the CTA and between that time and claiming benefit. However, the actions between the claim and a tribunal hearing may be relied on to show that the intention was always there: *CIS 2326/1995* para 28. In addition, the claimant's behaviour during a previous period of residence in the CTA may assist: *CIS 8111/1995* para 15.

Factors which may be relevant in assessing "settled intention" include:

(1) The claimant's employment or prospects of employment. Her/his education and qualifications may be highly significant: *CIS 5136/1995* para 4. A higher proportion of time spent working and a stable job are good evidence. The work done by the claimant's partner may also be relevant and an imminent offer of work will also be good evidence.

(2) The claimant's reasons for coming to the CTA. A clear reason for presence is more likely to demonstrate a settled intention. 1997 GM C13 Annex 3 para 18 gave retirement, studying, medical treatment, visiting relatives or domestic political unrest as examples.

(3) The claimant's intentions as to where her/his future lies, which can be shown by an intention to move family and property here.

(4) Where the claimant's "centre of interest" lies: *CIS 2326/1995* (para 22). This means the strength of ties to this country. Is her/his immediate family in this country? What about extended family? Has s/he joined clubs or associations? Where does s/he hold real or personal property? Has s/he registered with a doctor? Is s/he seeking work? Has money been spent in this country with a view to establishing residence?

(5) The viability of continued residence in the CTA. Note that this is a relevant factor and not a separate requirement. *R(IS) 6/96* (paras 28–29) suggested it was an additional requirement for the claimant to be able to demonstrate that s/he can maintain her/himself during the appreciable period without reliance on state benefits. The supposed requirement of viability has been heavily criticised. As was pointed out in *CIS 5136/1995* (para 4), it produces an "absurd circularity". A claimant cannot attain an appreciable period and hence be entitled to benefit unless s/he has had a viable existence, but many claimants cannot have a viable existence unless they receive benefit. This supposed requirement could result in the sick or retired never being habitually resident. It is now reasonably clear that the viability of residence without benefits is not a separate requirement, but is merely another factor giving evidence of settled intention: *CIS 2326/1995* (para 28); *CIS 12703/1996* (para 10); *CIS 2326/1995* (para 20 – where it was said to be of "considerable relevance"): see below.

(6) In *CIS 2326/1995* (para 17) and *R(CS) 5/96* (para 9), it was stated that while habitual residence has a common meaning in all the statutory contexts in which it occurs, different factors may have different weight in different contexts. In the case of HB, it is suggested that the agreement pursuant to which HB is claimed will be of particular significance. Thus lodgers who can leave at will are less likely to have a settled intention to remain than tenants with statutory protection. The length of any lease or licence may also be relevant.

[3.3] Loss of habitual residence

In *Re J*, Lord Brandon stated that habitual residence may be lost in a day, but this will only happen where there is clear, unequivocal evidence of complete abandonment of the state by the claimant: see the comments in *CIS 2326/1995* referred to above. A "temporary absence" from the CTA will not prevent a claimant remaining habitually resident in the CTA: *R(IS) 6/96* (para 21); *Shah* at 342D-E. This is so whether the absence is short or long, provided that the absence can be described as "temporary". Holidays are usually regarded as "temporary": *CIS 5136/1995* para 5 (three weeks); 1997 GM C13 Annex 3 para 29(i) (three months). *CIS 12703/1996* (para 7) suggests that an absence was not "temporary" where the return date was uncertain and habitual residence was lost, though this suggestion may be in conflict with *Chief Adjudication Officer v Ahmed* [1994] *The Times* 6 April, CA. A five-year absence lost the claimant her habitual residence status in *CIS 13498/1996* (para 16). On the other side of the dividing line was *CIS 14591/1996* in which the claimant and his wife were resident in the UK for 15 months before leaving in October 1994 to be with their daughter-in-law pending her entry clearance. That process took 13 months. The family then returned and the claimant's IS claim was refused. It was held that as the absence abroad had always been intended to be temporary, the claimant had not lost his habitual residence status. Similarly, in *KS v SSWP (PC)* [2010] UKUT 156 (AAC), Judge Levenson held that a person who had left the UK on a two-year Voluntary Service Overseas assignment had not lost her/his habitual residence during the temporary absence.

Entitlement of a refugee to Housing Benefit
[¹ 10A]

Modification

Reg 10A was inserted by Sch 4 para 2(1) of the HB&CTB(CP) Regs. It only applied to claims for HB by some refugees. Sch A1 was also inserted by Sch 4 para 2(2) of the HB&CTB(CP) Regs.

Amendment

1. Lapsed by s12(2)(e) of the Asylum and Immigration (Treatment of Claimants etc) Act 2004 (for those recorded as refugees after 14.6.07).

General Note

Reg 10A and Sch A1 as inserted by Sch 4 HB&CTB(CP) Regs dealt with a refugee's retrospective entitlement to HB. See pp1126–27 of the 20th edition for the full text of reg 10A and Sch A1 and commentary on these, and p322 of the 26th edition for a note on the commencement of s12 Asylum and Immigration (Treatment of Claimants etc) Act 2004.

PART 3
Payments in respect of a dwelling

General Note on Part 3

This Part of the Regulations deals with the type of payments in respect of which HB may be paid (and the amount of these). The power to make such regulations is granted by s130(2) SSCBA 1992. It is important to note the transitional protection and modifications that exist in relation to these regulations.

The starting point in deciding whether a particular payment will attract HB is reg 11(1), which confirms that HB is to be paid in respect of all those payments set out in reg 12(1). Categories of payments which HB will not meet are set out in regs 11(2) and (3) and 12(2). Note also s130(2) SSCBA which confirms that there is no power to make regulations extending HB coverage to council tax payments (which, until April 2013, were met by CTB), or payments under mortgages or heritable securities in Scotland (which could, until 6 April 2018, be met as housing costs under the IS, income-based JSA, income-related ESA, PC or UC schemes). From 6 April 2018, claimants of those benefits may be able to take out a loan from the DWP to help pay such housing costs, referred to as a "support for mortage interest loan" (see the Loans for Mortgage Interest Regulations 2017 SI No.725). Note that a charge on the claimant's property is made in favour of the DWP (a standard security in Scotland) and that interest on the loan is generally payable.

The amount of HB payable depends on, among other factors, the claimant's "maximum housing benefit" defined in reg 70 as the weekly "eligible rent" minus any deductions for non-dependants under reg 74.

Regs 12B, 12BA, 12C and 12D HB Regs and reg 12 as provided in Sch 3 para 5 HB&CTB(CP) Regs set out what "eligible rent" is for HB purposes. Which of these regulations is to be used to determine eligible rent depends on whether HB is payable as a rent rebate or a rent allowance, and whether any of the rent restriction schemes are applicable.

There are four potential schemes that can restrict eligible rent.

(1) **The "pre-January 1996" scheme** provides transitional protection for people living in "exempt accommodation" and for certain "exempt claimants": Sch 3 paras 4 and 5 HB&CTB(CP) Regs (from p1776). Under this scheme, the form of the HB rules prior to 2 January 1996 applies and the authority can restrict eligible rent by an amount it considers appropriate.

(2) **The "social sector" scheme**, often referred to as the "bedroom tax", or by the DWP as the "removal of the spare room subsidy" or the "under-occupation charge", can only apply to social sector tenancies: regs 12BA, A13 and B13. Under this scheme, eligible rent is determined by reference to the "maximum rent (social sector)."

(3) **The "local housing allowance" (LHA) scheme** can only apply if HB is paid as a rent allowance: regs 12D and 13C to 13E HB Regs. Under this scheme, eligible rent is determined by reference to the "maximum rent (LHA)".

(4) **The "local reference rent" scheme** can only apply if HB is paid as a rent allowance: regs 12C, 13, 13ZA, 13ZB and 14 HB Regs. Under this scheme, eligible rent is determined by reference to the "maximum rent".

Even where none of the rent restriction rules apply, there may be a general discretion to decrease eligible rent under reg 12B(6).

In cases of hardship, where extra financial assistance is needed to meet housing costs, authorities can pay discretionary housing payments under the Discretionary Financial Assistance Regulations 2001 (see p1751).

Which rent restriction rules apply

The type of tenancy determines which of the four schemes may potentially apply.

If the claimant is a private tenant, the local housing allowance, local reference rent or pre-January 1996 scheme may apply.

If the claimant is a housing association tenant, the local reference rent scheme, or in exceptional cases the pre-January 1996 or local housing allowance schemes may apply. If none of these apply, the social sector scheme may apply.

If the claimant is a local authority tenant, in exceptional cases, the pre-January 1996 scheme may apply. If this does not apply, the social sector scheme may apply.

If **HB is paid as a rent allowance** (eg, to a private or housing association tenant), to work out which of the rent restriction rules (if any) apply, the following steps are suggested. "Rent allowance" is defined in s134(1B) SSAA.

(1) Work out if the claimant has an "excluded tenancy".

The "LHA" rules, the "local reference rent" rules and the "pre-January 1996" rules do not apply if the tenancy is excluded under Sch 2 paras 3 to 12: regs 13C(5)(a) and (c) and 14(2)(b). Excluded tenancies include, for example, regulated and protected tenancies (ie, tenancies entered into before 15 January 1989 or, in Scotland, 2 January 1989) and many lettings by registered housing associations (see reg 2(1) for the definition).

Unless the claimant's landlord is a registered housing association, the "social sector" rules do not apply if the tenancy is excluded under Sch 2 paras 4 to 11: reg A13(2)(a).

(2) If the claimant does not have an "excluded tenancy", work out which, if any, of the four rent restriction schemes apply.

(3) Where a claim for HB is made on or after 7 April 2008 (or where there is a change of dwelling during an award of HB on or after that date):

– the "pre-January 1996" rules apply if the claimant lives in "exempt accommodation" or is what is referred to as an "exempt claimant": reg 13C(5)(b) HB Regs and Sch 3 para 4(1) and (2) to (7) HB&CTB(CP) Regs. Note that although entitlement to HB is generally precluded if the claimant is entitled to UC, UC claimants in "exempt accommodation" may qualify for HB for this accommodation: see the Universal Credit (Transitional Provisions) Regulations 2014 SI No.1230 in Part 8. Exempt claimants are certain claimants who have been entitled to HB since 1 January 1996 and who have not moved home, and certain claimants who inherit this protection;

– the "local reference rent" rules apply if the claimant lives in a hostel, houseboat, mobile home or caravan or her/his rent includes board and attendance. In some cases, the rules can also apply if the landlord is a registered housing association (see reg 2(1) for the definition) or the tenancy is a former local authority or new town letting which has been transferred to a new owner: regs 13(1), 13C(5)(a) to (e) and (6) and 14 and Sch 2 HB Regs;

– in all other cases, the "LHA" rules may apply: reg 13C HB Regs.

(4) If the claimant is the tenant of a social landlord (eg, a housing association), and the "pre-January 1996", "local reference rent" and "LHA" rules do not apply, the "social sector" rules may apply if the claimant's accommodation is larger than allowed under the relevant size criteria. The rules are the same as for local authority tenants (see below).

If **HB is paid as a rent rebate** (ie, to a local authority tenant), in exceptional cases, the "pre-January 1996" rules may apply. If they do not apply, the "social sector" rules may apply if the claimant's accommodation is larger than allowed under the size criteria. "Rent rebate" is defined in s134(1A) SSAA. The social sector rules do *not* apply:

– if the claimant or her/his partner is at least the qualifying age for PC: regs 2(1) and A13(2)(d);

– in respect of a shared ownership tenancy, mooring charges for houseboats or caravan or mobile home site fees: reg A13(2)(b) and (c);

– if the dwelling is a specified type of temporary accommodation: reg A13(2)(e) and (3).

Rules before 7 April 2008

The "LHA" rules were piloted in 18 Pathfinder areas from late 2003. The "LHA" rules as now in force apply to those living in a former Pathfinder area to whom the pilot rules applied before 7 April 2008. The pilot rules were more generous in some respects. Some transitional protection was provided: regs 12E to 12K as inserted by Sch 10 para 6 HB Regs.

Other than where the pilot rules applied, if a claimant's eligible rent was being restricted under any of the rules that applied before 7 April 2008, it continues to be restricted under the same rules, until there is a break in the claim or the claimant moves to a new home while entitled to HB. From that point, eligible rent is restricted (if relevant) under whichever rules then apply. It is important for a claimant to assess any financial impact before a new claim or a change of dwelling occurs.

If a claimant would be entitled to more HB under the "LHA" scheme than under the "local reference rent" scheme, s/he may be able to surrender her/his HB claim and make a fresh claim to be assessed by reference to the "LHA" rules. DWP Guidance (HB/CTB G10/2008) reminded authorities that although there is no statutory mechanism expressly permitting a claim to be withdrawn once a decision has been made on it, a claimant should not be prevented from surrendering an award of benefit if s/he indicates that s/he no longer wishes to claim HB. Note that because of amendments made to the "LHA" scheme, there are very few, if any, cases where a claimant would now be entitled to more HB under that scheme than under the "local reference rent" scheme. However, see p302 of the 24th edition for a discussion of the issues to bear in mind.

Eligible housing costs

11.–[¹ (1) Subject to the following provisions of this regulation, housing benefit shall be payable in respect of the payments specified in regulation 12(1) (rent) and a claimant's maximum housing benefit shall be calculated under Part 8 (amount of benefit) by reference to the amount of his eligible rent determined in accordance with–

(a) regulation 12B (eligible rent);

[⁴ (ab) regulations 12BA (eligible rent and maximum rent (social sector)), A13 (when a maximum rent (social sector) is to be determined) and B13 (determination of a maximum rent (social sector));]

(b)   regulations 12C (eligible rent and maximum rent), 13 (maximum rent), 13ZA (protection on death and 13 week protection) and 13ZB (change in reckonable rent);

(c)   regulations 12D (eligible rent and maximum rent (LHA)), 13C (when a maximum rent (LHA) is to be determined) and 13D (determination of a maximum rent (LHA)); or

(d)   regulations 12 (rent) and 13 (restrictions on unreasonable payments) as set out in paragraph 5 of Schedule 3 to the Consequential Provisions Regulations,

whichever is applicable in his case.]

(2)   Subject to paragraph (4), housing benefit shall not be payable in respect of payments made by a person on income support [³, an income-based jobseeker's allowance or an income-related employment and support allowance] whose applicable amount for that benefit includes an amount in respect of those payments.

(3)   Where any payment for which a person is liable in respect of a dwelling and which is specified in regulation 12(1) (payments of rent for which housing benefit is payable), is increased on account of–

(a)   outstanding arrears of any payment or charge; or

(b)   any other unpaid payment or charge,

to which [² paragraphs (1) or (2) of that regulation or paragraph (2) of regulation 12B] or Schedule 1 (ineligible service charges) refer and which is or was formerly owed by him in respect of that or another dwelling, a rent rebate or, as the case may be, a rent allowance shall not be payable in respect of that increase.

(4)   Where a person who has been awarded housing benefit in respect of a dwelling becomes entitled to income support [³, an income-based jobseeker's allowance or an income-related employment and support allowance] and his applicable amount for the purpose of calculating his entitlement to that benefit includes an amount in respect of a payment made by him in respect of that dwelling, the payments made by him in respect of that dwelling shall continue to be eligible for housing benefit for a period of 4 benefit weeks beginning with the benefit week after the date on which he becomes entitled to income support [³, an income-based jobseeker's allowance or an income-related employment and support allowance].

Modifications

Para (1) was substituted and para (3) amended by reg 4(3) Housing Benefit (Local Housing Allowance and Information Sharing) Amendment Regulations 2007 SI No.2868 as from 7 April 2008, save that for a person to whom reg 1(5) of those regulations applied (see p1812), the amendments came into force on the day on or after 7 April 2008 when the first of the events specified in reg 1(6) applied to her/him, or on 6 April 2009 if none had before that date.

Para (1) is modified by Sch 10 para 3 (see p707). This applies only to former Pathfinder Authorities who administered the pilot local housing allowance scheme.

Amendments

1.   Substituted by reg 4(3)(a) of SI 2007 No 2868 as from 7.4.08 (or if reg 1(5) of that SI applies, on the day on or after 7.4.08 when the first of the events specified in reg 1(6) applies, or from 6.4.09 if none have before that date).

2.   Amended by reg 4(3)(b) of SI 2007 No 2868 as from 7.4.08 (or if reg 1(5) of that SI applies, on the day on or after 7.4.08 when the first of the events specified in reg 1(6) applies, or from 6.4.09 if none have before that date).

3.   Amended by reg 9 of SI 2008 No 1082 as from 27.10.08.

4.   Inserted by reg 5(3) of SI 2012 No 3040 as from 1.4.13.

Definitions

"applicable amount" – see s135 SSCBA.
"benefit week" – see reg 2(1).
"dwelling" – see reg 2(4) and s137(1) SSCBA.
"an income-based jobseeker's allowance" – see reg 2(1).
"maximum housing benefit" – see reg 70.
"rent allowance" – see s134(1A) SSAA.
"rent rebate" – see s134(1B) SSAA.
"payment" – see reg 2(1).

"person on an income-based jobseeker's allowance" – see reg 2(3).
"person on an income-related employment and support allowance" – see reg 2(3A).
"person on income support" – see reg 2(1).

General Note
Even if a payment is covered by para (1), no HB may be paid in respect of it if paras (2) or (3) apply.

Analysis
Paragraph (1): The general rule
The general rule is that HB is payable in respect of all those categories of payment set out in reg 12(1). As can be seen from the commentary on that regulation, a wide variety of payments can be met by HB. Maximum HB is calculated under Part 8 HB Regs by reference to "eligible rent" which is determined by the regulations listed in sub-paras (a) to (d).

Reg 12B is the general rule where none of the rent restriction schemes apply: sub-para (a).

Regs 12BA, A13 and B13 are the "social sector" scheme: sub-para (ab).

Regs 12C, 13, 13ZA and 13ZB are the "local reference rent" scheme: sub-para (b).

Regs 12D, 13C and 13D are the "LHA" scheme: sub-para (c).

Regs 12 and 13 as set out in Sch 3 para 5 HB&CTB(CP) Regs are the "pre-January 1996" scheme: sub-para (d).

Paragraphs (2) and (4): Exclusion for payments met by IS, income-based JSA or income-related ESA
Para (2) excludes payment of HB in respect of payments which are already covered by IS, income-based JSA or income-related ESA. Para (4) provides an exception to this rule for people already receiving HB for a dwelling who become entitled to IS, income-based JSA or income-related ESA with an applicable amount that includes amounts in respect of payments made for that dwelling – eg, where they buy a home that they formerly rented. In that situation, HB may continue to be paid for an overlap period of four benefit weeks. Note that from 6 April 2018, IS, income-based JSA and income-related ESA can no longer include amounts for mortgage interest or interest on other other home loans, and can only include amounts for other housing costs such as ground rent and service charges.

Paragraph (3): Exclusion for increased rent to cover arrears
Para (3) provides that where a claimant's liability in respect of a dwelling is increased on account of outstanding arrears or unpaid sums which are owed or formerly owed by the claimant in respect of the current or former dwelling, then HB is not payable in respect of that increase. Nevertheless as a result of the rules relating to the housing authority's housing revenue account contained in Part VI of and the Schedule to the Local Government and Housing Act 1989, an authority has to increase the general level of rents for all tenants as the result of its need to provide for, or write off, bad debts and rent arrears. The general increase in rents due to such provision remains eligible for HB.

Rent
12.–(1) Subject to the following provisions of this regulation, the payments in respect of which housing benefit is payable in the form of a rent rebate or allowance are the following periodical payments which a person is liable to make in respect of the dwelling which he occupies as his home–

(a) payments of, or by way of, rent;

(b) payments in respect of a licence or permission to occupy the dwelling;

(c) payments by way of mesne profits or, in Scotland, violent profits;

(d) payments in respect of, or in consequence of, use and occupation of the dwelling;

(e) payments of, or by way of, service charges payment of which is a condition on which the right to occupy the dwelling depends;

(f) mooring charges payable for a houseboat;

(g) where the home is a caravan or a mobile home, payments in respect of the site on which it stands;

(h) any contribution payable by a person resident in an almshouse provided by a housing association which is either a charity of which particulars are entered in the register of charities established under section 3 of the Charities Act 1993 (register of charities) or an exempt charity within the meaning of that Act, which is a contribution towards the cost of maintaining that association's almshouses and essential services in them;

(i) payments under a rental purchase agreement, that is to say an agreement for the purchase of a dwelling which is a building or part of one under which the whole or part of the purchase price is to be paid in more than one instalment and the completion of the purchase is deferred until the whole or a specified part of the purchase price has been paid; and

(j) where, in Scotland, the dwelling is situated on or pertains to a croft within the meaning of section 3(1) of the Crofters (Scotland) Act 1993, the payment in respect of the croft land.

(2) A rent rebate or, as the case may be, a rent allowance shall not be payable in respect of the following periodical payments–

(a) payments under a long tenancy except a shared ownership tenancy [¹];

(b) payments under a co-ownership scheme;

(c) payments by an owner;

(d) payments under a hire purchase, credit sale or conditional sale agreement except to the extent the conditional sale agreement is in respect of land; and

(e) payments by a Crown tenant.

[¹ (f) payments by a person in respect of a dwelling where his partner is an owner of that dwelling.]

[⁴ (2A) Where a reduction in any of the payments listed in paragraph (1) for which a person would otherwise be liable is applied by a provider of social housing under an approved tenant incentive scheme, for the purposes of paragraph (1) the amount of the payment is to be treated as if no such reduction had been applied.

(2B) For the purposes of paragraph (2A)–

"approved tenant incentive scheme" means a scheme which is–

(a) operated by a provider of social housing and designed to avoid rent arrears by allowing reductions in the payments listed in paragraph (1) or other advantages in return for meeting specified conditions; and

(b) approved by the Secretary of State;

"provider of social housing" means–

(a) a local authority;

(b) a non-profit registered provider of social housing;

(c) in relation to accommodation which is social housing, a profit-making registered provider of social housing;

(d) a registered social landlord;

"registered social landlord" means–

(a) a body which is registered in the register maintained by the Welsh Ministers under Chapter 1 of Part 1 of the Housing Act 1996;

(b) a body which is registered in the register maintained by the Scottish Housing Regulator under the Housing (Scotland) Act 2010;

"social housing" has the meaning given in section 68 of the Housing and Regeneration Act 2008.]

[² (3)-(7)]

(8) In this regulation [³, regulation 12B (eligible rent)] and Schedule 1 (ineligible service charges)–

"service charges" means periodical payments for services, whether or not under the same agreement as that under which the dwelling is occupied, or whether or not such a charge is specified as separate from or separately identified within other payments made by the occupier in respect of the dwelling; and

"services" means services performed or facilities (including the use of furniture) provided for, or rights made available to, the occupier of a dwelling.

Modifications

Paras (3) to (7) were omitted and para (8) amended by reg 4(4) Housing Benefit (Local Housing Allowance and Information Sharing) Amendment Regulations 2007 SI No.2868 as from 7 April 2008, save that for a person to whom reg 1(5) of those regulations applied (see p1812), the amendments came into force on the day on or after 7 April 2008 when the first of the events specified in reg 1(6) applied to her/him, or on 6 April 2009 if none had before that date.

A different version of reg 12 is substituted and used to determine eligible rent for some claimants entitled to HB on 1 January 1996. See Sch 3 paras 4 and 5(1) HB&CTB(CP) Regs (p1776).

Amendments

1. Amended by reg 2(4) of SI 2007 No 1356 as from 1.10.07.
2. Omitted by reg 4(4)(a) of SI 2007 No 2868 as from 7.4.08 (or if reg 1(5) of that SI applies, on the day on or after 7.4.08 when the first of the events specified in reg 1(6) applies, or from 6.4.09 if none have before that date).
3. Amended by reg 4(4)(b) of SI 2007 No 2868 as from 7.4.08 (or if reg 1(5) of that SI applies, on the day on or after 7.4.08 when the first of the events specified in reg 1(6) applies, or from 6.4.09 if none have before that date).
4. Inserted by reg 20 of SI 2017 No 995 as from 7.11.17.

Definitions

"co-ownership scheme" – see reg 2(1).
"dwelling" – see reg 2(4) and s137(1) SSCBA.
"housing association" – see reg 2(1).
"croft" – see "owner", reg 2.
"long tenancy" – see reg 2(1).
"owner" – see reg 2(1).
"payment" – see reg 2(1).
"rent rebate", "rent allowance" – see s134(1A) and (1B) SSAA 1992.
"shared ownership tenancy" – see reg 2(1).

General Note

This deals with the types of payments that may be met by HB. For what is then "eligible rent" for HB purposes, see regs 12B, 12BA, 12C and 12D. Note: for the rules on eligible payments under the "pre-January 1996" scheme, see reg 12 as set out in Sch 3 para 5 HB&CTB(CP) Regs (on p1783).

Para (1) (qualified by paras (2A) and (2B)) defines payments which qualify as rent, and therefore in respect of which HB, by way of rent rebate or rent allowance, may be paid. Para (2) sets out payments in respect of which HB is not payable. Para (8) defines the terms "services" and "service charges" for the purposes of this regulation, reg 12B and Sch 1.

Analysis

Paragraph (1), (2A) and (2B): Payments that qualify for HB

In the same way that many people use "rent" as a portmanteau term for most types of payments that they are liable to make in return for occupying their home, the HB Regs use it as a convenient shorthand for various categories of payments. Some claimants may make payments falling into more than one of these categories, all of which are eligible.

Note that where a provider of social housing applies a reduction to any of the payments listed in para (1) under an "approved tenant incentive scheme", the reduction must be ignored in calculating rent for HB purposes, so long as the person would otherwise be liable for the full payment: para (2A). "Provider of social housing" and "approved tenant incentive scheme" are defined in para (2B).

In order to attract HB, the payments must be "periodical": para (1). In *CH 2329/2003*, the claimant and his wife were paying all the outgoings on their daughter's property while she was abroad. It was held that there was a commercial agreement: see the commentary to reg 9(1)(a) on p282. The payments made to the mortgagees on behalf of the daughter, therefore, could be met by HB, but the commissioner held that one-off payments for repairs fell outside the scope of the scheme (para 9). Discussing reg 10 HB Regs 1987 the commissioner said:

"For the occupier's payments to or on behalf of the landlord to come within the scope of regulation 10 they must, therefore, be made at regular intervals and be of an ascertainable amount so that the weekly rental figure can be calculated in accordance with regulation 69 of the regulations."

(Regs 10 and 69 HB regs 1987 are now regs 12 and 80 HB Regs.)

For the issue of whether payments are those a person is "liable to make", see reg 8. For the question of whether a dwelling is occupied as the home, see reg 7.

Sub-para (a): rent. "Rent" in this sub-para, of course, refers to rent properly so-called and not merely some payment that the claimant refers to as rent and which does not fall into one of the other categories. It refers, therefore, to payments made to a landlord under a tenancy. It includes all payments described as or deemed to be rent in the tenancy agreement. It can include charges for voids and long term maintenance: *CH 3528/2006*. Commissioner Jacobs said that the first question is whether a payment is a "service charge" (defined in reg 12(8)). If it is not, the charge *may* be taken into account as part of the rent under sub-para (a), if it relates to a matter that is properly considered in setting the rent.

Sub-para (b): licence or permission to occupy. The main indicators of a tenancy are that exclusive occupation is granted to the tenant or tenants for a certain period in return for periodic payments of rent. However, many claimants do not have tenancies because they have not been granted exclusive occupation of the premises. This is most obviously the case with lodgers, but may occur in cases where the landlord is not obviously resident. Although this can create headaches in other areas of law, such claimants occupy under a licence and so qualify for HB under sub-para (b). The use of the word "permission" is probably aimed at cases of tolerated trespassers, where no formal licence is granted but the landlord agrees to refrain from seeking possession for a period.

Reg 10 HB Regs 1987 (now reg 12) was the battleground between authorities and the Jesus Fellowship Church, following the leading cases on liability for rent and contrived tenancies (see the commentary to regs 8 and 9 on p275 and p282). In *R v Milton Keynes CC HBRB ex p Saxby* (2000) unreported, 11 August, QBD; [2001] 33 HLR 82, CA, the courts were concerned with a claim by an Elder of the church. In broad terms, condition 4 required both "style 3" members (who are the rank and file members of the communities) and Elders (who are the heads of the communities and licensees of the trust property) to pay £55 to the common purse. Condition 6 required Elders to ensure that the payment due to the church's central trust fund from the common purse of £30 a resident, including themselves, was made.

The Review Board held that the Elder's liability for rent was that payable under condition 4 and not that under condition 6. Hidden J held that to be a wrong approach; the payments under condition 6 were sufficiently connected with the licence held by the Elders to enable it to be a payment "in respect of" that licence. The Court of Appeal upheld his decision. Hale LJ said:

"15.   The argument is therefore about whether "payments in respect of a dwelling which he occupies as his home" means "payments in respect of his own (or his own and his family's) occupation of a dwelling as his home". This would be to rewrite both section 123(1) of the Act and regulation 10(1). The non-dependant deduction provisions make it quite clear that the payments may relate to a dwelling in which other people also live. It would be strange indeed, and most unfair, if an Elder could only make a claim based upon his own contribution to the common purse, but then suffer fixed non-dependant deductions for all the adult residents (indeed that was what the local authority had earlier decided in this case).

16.   It is also quite clear that the clause 6 payments made by the Elders are the rent paid by them, as licensees, in respect of their licence to occupy the house. They have to make those payments irrespective of whether or not the residents make their clause 4 payments: it is not therefore the simple transmission of payments made by others."

It should, however, be noted that it would appear that the full amount of each condition 6 payment has to be made by the Elder. If that is so, the amount of HB payable may fall to be restricted under the rent restrictions provisions.

Sub-paras (c) and (d): mesne profits, violent profits and payments for use and occupation of the dwelling. "Mesne profits" in England and Wales are the damages for which a former tenant whose lease is forfeit may be liable to pay as compensation for depriving the landlord of the use or occupation of her/his land. They are usually assessed according to the ordinary letting value of the land. These categories of payment cannot include any interest which a claimant has been ordered to pay a landlord by a court: *R v Kensington and Chelsea RBC ex p Brandt* (1995) 28 HLR 528, QBD.

In Scotland, "violent profits" are damages which a possessor of land in bad faith is liable to pay to the true occupier. They are assessed according to the profit the latter could have made from letting the land during the period s/he was dispossessed, plus compensation for any damage caused.

Payments for "use and occupation" is another phrase borrowed from the law of real property. Such payments are assessed by a court in the same way as mesne profits except that they are paid by a trespasser for use of the land rather than a former tenant. Sub-para (d) is to be interpreted as referring to payments for use and occupation in that sense rather than according to the normal meaning of those words which might include payments that must be made as an incidence of the occupation. In *R v Bristol CC ex p Jacobs* (1999) 32 HLR 841 (Owen J), the claimant was liable to pay water rates as a consequence of her tenancy and argued that the rates fell within sub-para (d). The argument was rejected. Although leave to appeal was granted, it is understood that *ex parte Jacobs* never went to the Court of Appeal.

In *CH 844/2002*, for which see the notes to sub-para (f) below, the commissioner thought that a boat licence fee giving permission to use the boat on waterways fell within sub-para (d) as a "payment in respect of, or in consequence of, use and occupation of the" boat: at para 13. That decision did not refer to the analysis in *ex parte Jacobs*. In *Kirklees MBC v JM* [2018] UKUT 219 (AAC), the claimant lived on a narrow boat. The local authority refused his claim for HB in respect of a continuous cruiser licence, which allowed him to cruise and to moor overnight on specified terms. The First-tier Tribunal decided that the licence fee came within sub-para (d). The Upper Tribunal judge, having considered both *ex parte Jacobs* and *CH 844/2002*, decided that the First-tier Tribunal was wrong and confirmed the local authority's decision. Deciding that the First-tier Tribunal should have followed *ex parte Jacobs* he said:

"The starting point is that the Commissioner [in *CH 844/2002*] did not address the question whether 'use and occupation' was limited to its established, specialist meaning that Owen J [in *ex parte Jacobs*] accepted. As far as his decision shows, this was not put to the Commissioner, and Owen J's decision seems not to have been cited. As always, it is necessary to consider the statutory context. Regulation 12(1) prescribes the periodical payments in respect of which housing benefit is payable. The first five are in summary: (a) rent; (b) licence payments; (c) mesne profits; (d) payments for use and occupation; and (e) service charges. Sub-paragraph (d) is surrounded by expressions that have an established meaning in property law. I would expect in that context that it would bear that meaning. The remaining five, again in summary, are: (f) mooring charges; (g) site payments for caravans and mobile homes; (h) contribution by the resident of an almshouse; (i) rental purchase payments; and (j) payments for croft land in Scotland. These share the characteristic of being narrow in their scope and specific to particular contexts. If a charge for being on a waterway were included as an eligible payment, I would expect to find it among this miscellaneous collection, not nestling between mesne profits and service charges. In other words, there appears to be a logical structure and sequence to the structure of regulation 12 and the Commissioner's interpretation subverts it."

Sub-para (e): service charges. "Service charges" are defined by para (8). The payments must be made in return for "services", also defined in para (8). Under this sub-para only those charges paid as a condition of occupying the premises are treated as rent. Thus if it is something the landlord provides at the tenant's request, it is not a service charge. The payments must be periodical, which means that they must relate to a specified period. The periods need not be even and they need not correlate to the periods over which rent is paid.

Sch 1 para 4 requires a local authority to make a reduction from a service charge to which para (1)(e) applies if it considers the amount of the charge to be excessive in relation to the service provided for the claimant or her/his family. See also reg 12B(2) which restricts the category of charges that can be included in a claimant's "eligible rent" under that regulation and under reg 12BA (see reg B13(2)(a)). For a claimant's "eligible rent" under regs 12C and 12D, the adjustments on account of ineligible charges are generally made when the rent officer sets the local housing allowances (for the "LHA" scheme) and makes determinations (for the "local reference rent" scheme).

Sub-para (f): houseboat mooring charges. "Houseboat" is not defined in the HB legislation. In *R(H) 9/08*, Commissioner Levenson pointed out that the legislation could have defined the term but did not. He said (at para 19) that for HB purposes "houseboat" is an ordinary English word without a technical meaning and that it is a matter of fact in any particular case whether a boat is a "houseboat" in this sense. He found it difficult to imagine a case in which a reasonable tribunal would conclude that a boat which is fitted out as a dwelling suitable for permanent residence is not a houseboat. Definitions in other legislation or regulations for different purposes (eg, tax liability) are not relevant. These might reflect or inform common usage but cannot define "houseboat" for HB purposes. Neither can the classification for the purposes of licensing, or the operation of other schemes, such as the definition of a houseboat used in paragraph 38 of the British Waterways Boat Licence and Permit Conditions.

This provision was considered by Commissioner Williams in *CH 844/2002*, which concerned the question of whether the claimant could claim HB in respect of the cost of a mooring permit. The commissioner held (para 8) that a houseboat did not necessarily have no engine and could be capable of movement. The commissioner also held (para 13) that "mooring charges" could cover both a houseboat certificate granted by the British Waterways Board as well as a mooring fee. Note that the Commissioner also considered whether a claimant could claim HB in respect of a boat licence fee payable to British Waterways. But see the Analysis to sub-para (d) above.

Sub-para (g): caravan and mobile home site fees. Again, "caravan" and "mobile home" are not defined. This sub-para covers all payments "in respect of the site on which it stands", not just those for the space occupied by the caravan or mobile home. It covers things like charges for electricity supply, toilet and shower facilities etc. Payments by mobile home owners are regulated by the Mobile Homes Act 1983. *CH 3110/2003* makes the valuable point that if the claimant's home does not count as a caravan or a mobile home (in this case it was a prefabricated chalet type structure resting on the land), s/he should nevertheless be entitled under reg 12(1)(a) to HB to meet the rent paid in respect of the land on which the home stands because it counts as "rent" for which s/he is "liable to make [periodical payments] in respect of the dwelling which he occupies as his home": per reg 12(1). The fact that the rent was called "ground rent" was irrelevant, since the tenancy of the land was not a "long tenancy" falling within reg 12(2)(a) (the rent under such a tenancy ordinarily being called "ground rent").

Sub-para (h): contributions in almshouses. The "register of charities" is kept by the Charity Commission. "Exempt" charities are those listed in Sch 2 to the Charities Act 1993. This includes certain universities and colleges, the Church Commissioners, societies registered under the Industrial and Provident Societies Act 1893, and the Friendly Societies Act 1896. A registrar maintains a list of those bodies registered under each of those Acts.

Sub-para (i): rental purchase agreements is self-explanatory.

Sub-para (j): croft land relates to agricultural land in Scotland.

Paragraph (2): Payments that do not qualify

This sets out categories of payments ineligible for HB. "Long tenancy", "co-ownership scheme" and "owner" are all defined in reg 2 and reference should be made to the commentary to that regulation, particularly in relation to ownership. Note that since 1 October 2007, the exception for long tenancies which are shared ownership tenancies (also defined in reg 2) applies to all such tenancies – ie, private sector shared ownership leases as well as shared ownership tenancies granted by a housing association or a housing authority.

CH 1578/2006 dealt with issues of general principle about the liability of one co-owner to another and the treatment of any such liability for the purposes of HB. The legal position is governed by the Trusts of Land and Appointment of Trustees Act 1996. s13(6)(a) of that Act provides that where the entitlement of any beneficiary to occupy land under section 12 has been excluded or restricted, the conditions which may be imposed on any other beneficiary in relation to his occupation of the land include conditions requiring him to make payments by way of compensation to the beneficiary whose entitlement has been excluded or restricted. The HB scheme is intended to cover payments made to secure occupation, not payments made to compensate another person for not exercising a right to occupy. Here, the payments which were made to the claimant's son were repayments of the mortgage loan and were not rent within the meaning of the HB Regs. The claimant's liability to make such payments arose as a result of acquiring a beneficial interest in the property, not in consequence of her use and occupation of the dwelling.

Crown tenants (sub-para (e)), defined in reg 2(1), have their own scheme to assist with rent: see p240.

[¹ **Eligible rent**

12B.–[² (1)   The amount of a person's eligible rent shall be determined in accordance with the provisions of this regulation except where any of the following provisions applies–

(a)   regulation 12BA (eligible rent and maximum rent (social sector));

(b)   regulation 12C (eligible rent and maximum rent);

(c)   regulation 12D (eligible rent and maximum rent (LHA));

(d)   paragraph 4 of Schedule 3 to the Consequential Provisions Regulations.]

(2)   Subject to paragraphs (3), (4) and (6), the amount of a person's eligible rent shall be the aggregate of such payments specified in regulation 12(1) as that person is liable to pay less–

(a)   except where he is separately liable for charges for water, sewerage or allied environmental services, an amount determined in accordance with paragraph (5);

(b)   where payments include service charges which are wholly or partly ineligible, an amount in respect of the ineligible charges determined in accordance with Schedule 1; and

(c)   where he is liable to make payments in respect of any service charges to which regulation 12(1)(e) does not apply, but to which paragraph 3(2) of Part 1 of Schedule 1 (unreasonably low service charges) applies in the particular circumstances, an amount in respect of such charges determined in accordance with paragraph 3(2) of Part 1 of Schedule 1.

(3)   Where the payments specified in regulation 12(1) are payable in respect of accommodation which consists partly of residential accommodation and partly of other accommodation, only such proportion of those payments as is referable to the residential accommodation shall count as eligible rent for the purposes of these Regulations.

(4)   Where more than one person is liable to make payments in respect of a dwelling, the payments specified in regulation 12(1) shall be apportioned for the purpose of calculating the eligible rent for each such person having regard to all the circumstances, in particular, the number of such persons and the proportion of rent paid by each such person.

(5)   The amount of the deduction referred to in paragraph (2) shall be–

(a)   if the dwelling occupied by the claimant is a self-contained unit, except in a case to which sub-paragraph (c) applies, the amount of the charges;

(b)   in any other case, except one to which sub-paragraph (c) applies, the proportion of those charges in respect of the self-contained unit which is obtained by dividing the area of the dwelling occupied by the claimant by the area of the self-contained unit of which it forms part;

(c)   where the charges vary in accordance with the amount of water actually used, the amount which the appropriate authority considers to be fairly attributable to water, and sewerage services, having regard to the actual or estimated consumption of the claimant.

(6)   In any case where it appears to the relevant authority that in the particular circumstances of that case the eligible rent as determined in accordance with the preceding paragraphs of this regulation is greater than it is reasonable to meet by way of housing benefit, the eligible rent shall be such lesser sum as seems to that authority to be an appropriate rent in that particular case.]

Modifications

Reg 12B is modified by Sch 10 para 4 (see p707). This applies only to former Pathfinder Authorities who administered the pilot local housing allowance scheme.

Amendments

1. Inserted by reg 5 of SI 2007 No 2868 as from 7.4.08 (or if reg 1(5) of that SI applies, on the day on or after 7.4.08 when the first of the events specified in reg 1(6) applies, or from 6.4.09 if none had before that date).
2. Subsituted by reg 5(4) of SI 2012 No 3040 as from 1.4.13.

Definitions

"claimant" – see reg 2(1).
"dwelling" – see reg 2(4) and s137(1) SSCBA.
"eligible rent" – see reg 2(1).
"payment" – see reg 2(1).
"service charges" – see reg 12(8).

General Note

"Eligible rent" for HB purposes is determined under reg 12B, together with Sch 1, unless regs 12BA, 12C or 12D HB Regs (respectively, the "social sector", the "local reference rent" and "local housing allowance" schemes) or Sch 3 para 4 HB&CTB(CP) Regs (the "pre-January 1996" scheme) apply. It can apply both where HB is paid as a rent rebate and where it is paid as a rent allowance, where the tenancy is excluded from the application of all of the rent restriction schemes.

Analysis

Paragraphs (2) to (5): Calculation of eligible rent

If reg 12B applies, these paragraphs set out the system of determining the claimant's "eligible rent". An apportionment under paras (3) and (4) may be relevant. Finally, there is a general discretion to restrict "eligible rent" under para (6).

The following stages need to be followed in making the calculation. "Eligible rent" is the aggregate of the payments under reg 12(1) that a person is liable to pay, less the deductions set out in para (2)(a) to (c) of reg 12B – ie, it is the contractual rent, minus ineligible services.

(1)   The first deduction is for water, sewerage and allied environmental services, which is only made if a claimant is not liable for such services separately from her/his tenancy: para (2)(a). Para (5) then sets out the rules for the calculation of the deduction. In *Liverpool City Council v (1) NM, (2) WD (HB)* [2015] UKUT 532 (AAC); [2016] AACR 19, Judge Knowles decided that para (5) only applies to water charges for personal use by the claimant, and not therefore to charges in respect of communal areas – eg, in sheltered accommodation. She also decided that water charges in respect of the commmunal areas in sheltered and supported accommodation are eligible services. See the discussion on Sch 1 para 1(g) on p621.

If the claimant lives in a self-contained unit, the whole of the charges are deducted under para (5)(a). If the dwelling is not self-contained, a share of the charges is deducted. This is calculated by dividing the total area of the unit in which the dwelling is contained (such as a block of flats) by the area of the dwelling: para (5)(b). If in either case the amount of the charges varies, the authority may deduct a sum that is fairly attributable to charges: para (5)(c).

(2)   The second deduction is for ineligible service charges: para (2)(b). This is determined under Sch 1 para 1: see the commentary on p620. Note that "service charges" for these purposes are defined in reg 12(8).

(3)   Finally, a higher deduction must be made in respect of certain service charges: para (2)(c). They must be charges not falling within reg 12(1)(e) – ie, because occupation of the property is not conditional on payment. They must also be ineligible charges in respect of which the local authority has decided that the amounts levied are unreasonably low. See the commentary to Sch 1 para 3(2) on p623.

Note that Sch 1 para 4 requires a local authority to make a reduction from an eligible service charge to which reg 12(1)(e) applies if it considers the amount of the charge to be excessive in relation to the service provided for the claimant or her/his family. The amount of the deduction is then ineligible for HB.

Paragraph (3): Apportionment where accommodation only partly residential

Where the accommodation occupied by the claimant is not solely residential accommodation, only that portion of the payments specified in reg 12(1) referable to the residential element can form part of the "eligible rent". This will typically arise in the case of accommodation that has both residential and commercial parts.

Paragraph (4): Apportionment of joint liabilities

An apportionment of the payments specified in reg 12(1) must be carried out if there is a joint liability – eg, where three tenants in a property have all signed the tenancy agreement. If each of the tenants has a separate tenancy agreement with the landlord, no apportionment is appropriate. The local authority has a discretion to decide the proportions to be attributed to each person, "having regard to" all the circumstances. It may not be appropriate to divide the amounts equally. This will be the case, for example, where one person occupies a much larger room than another. Particular regard must be paid to the number of such persons and to the amounts paid by each, but the weight given to the latter could be reduced, for example, where it was clear that the division of the amounts had been arranged deliberately to maximise benefit entitlement.

A problem that has arisen is whether a person who is deemed not to be liable for rent by virtue of regs 9, 10 or 56 must be excluded from the apportionment exercise under reg 12B(4) HB Regs. In *R (Naghshbandi) v Camden LBC* [2001] EWHC Admin 813; (2003) HLR 280, CA, Rafferty J decided that the apportionment must be between the people who are actually liable to pay the rent and any deemed non-liability should be ignored for these purposes. Rafferty J's decision was upheld by the Court of Appeal.

In *CH 3376/2002*, the elderly claimant was a joint tenant of a property with his son, who had moved out some considerable time previously. He was no longer in contact with the son. He was in poor health. The local authority assessed his HB on the basis that he was liable for half the rent and he appealed.

Commissioner Jacobs first dealt with an argument for the claimant that he could be treated as liable for the son's share of the rent under reg 6(1)(c) HB Regs 1987 (now reg 8(1)(c)) as well as his own share under reg 6(1)(a) (now reg 8(1)(a)) and that no apportionment could therefore be made. He held that reg 10(5) HB Regs 1987 (a provision now in reg 12B(4)) required apportionment only of actual liabilities rather than liabilities which were deemed to exist under reg 6(1) HB Regs 1987: para 37.

He then went on to consider the discretion as to apportionment and concluded that the whole of the rent should be apportioned to the claimant: para 60. He gave useful general guidance on the exercise of the discretion.

(1)   The proportion of the rent that had been paid by each joint tenant might be an important factor, but was not an overriding or even the predominant factor in every case: para 45.

(2)   The right to respect for the home under Art 8 European Convention on Human Rights was a relevant consideration: para 53. It was not determinative. Unless a failure to pay full HB would be a breach of Art 8.1, it is hard to see what the relevance of the Convention would be.

(3)   Para (4) specifies the number of tenants and the total rent paid as relevant: para 54.

(4)   The ability of the tenants to pay was relevant, but did not of itself justify placing a disproportionate responsibility on the claimant for HB: para 55.

(5)   The views of the landlord as to who is expected to pay in practice are relevant, but the fact that a landlord has foreborn to enforce the full rent pending the outcome of a dispute about HB should not be held against the claimant: para 56.

(6)   Whether the claimant could be expected to move might be relevant. This would involve consideration of issues such as the claimant's age, state of health, connections with the local area and the availability of property in the locality: para 58.

The commissioner pointed out that it was possible for the local authority to make a different apportionment for a limited period only, to give the claimant a fair chance to move or to find another co-tenant: para 57. However, caution needs to be exercised over the latter course because most tenancies strictly control the right of the tenant to get another person into the property. He also stated that it was possible for an apportionment to be changed if a change of circumstances occurred: para 63.

Paragraph (6): Discretion to restrict eligible rent

Para (6) contains a general discretion to reduce the eligible rent still further. The power to reduce the eligible rent under para (6) is additional to the foregoing provisions of this regulation, but only where the "eligible rent" as determined under the provisions above is greater than it is reasonable to meet by way of HB. The generality of the power enables authorities to ensure that where reg 12B applies, HB should not be paid on any rent above a level which the authority considers to be appropriate in any particular case. Note, however, that para (6) is not to be applied in determining a maximum rent (social sector), for which see reg B13(2)(a).

Note: regs 12C and 12D(3)(a)(ii) and the definition of "cap rent" in reg 13D(12) are said to be subject to reg 12B(6). See the commentary to regs 12C and 13D on p361 and p392 for a discussion.

Para (6) raises a number of questions of judgment that must be considered rationally. If the authority or the First-tier Tribunal reaches a decision that no sensible decision maker could reach then it may be held to be vulnerable to attack on appeal. There is no restriction in the paragraph as to which factors may be taken into account and so all facts relevant to the making of a restriction may be considered. No fixed rules or policies may be adopted. It is clear from the wording of the provision that each case must be considered individually. Decision makers should be prepared to give coherent reasons for imposing a restriction.

It was confirmed in *R (Laali) v Westminster CC HBRB* (2002) HLR 179, QBD that when deciding whether or not to make a reduction under reg 10(6B) HB Regs 1987 (now reg 12B(6)), the claimant's personal circumstances were relevant. The Review Board had therefore been in error to disregard the claimant's need to live in St John's Wood because his daughter lived nearby, because of the length of time he had lived in the area, because the accommodation was all on one floor and hence more suitable for him (he was disabled) and that he was unable to pay a deposit or rent in advance on another property. The authority's contention that those matters fell to be considered on an application for an exceptional hardship payment pursuant to a former version of reg 61 HB Regs 1987 (later substituted) was rejected, though permission to appeal was granted.

[¹ **Eligible rent and maximum rent (social sector)**

12BA.–(1)   This regulation applies where a maximum rent (social sector) has been, or is to be, determined in accordance with regulation A13 (when a maximum rent (social sector) is to be determined).

(2)　Except where paragraph (3) or (6) applies, the amount of a person's eligible rent is the maximum rent (social sector).

(3)　Where the claimant occupies a dwelling which is the same as that occupied by the claimant at the date of death of a linked person, the eligible rent is–

(a)　the eligible rent which applied on the day before the death occurred; or

(b)　in a case where no eligible rent applied on that day, an eligible rent determined in accordance with regulation 12B(2),

where that eligible rent is more than the eligible rent determined in accordance with paragraph (2).

[²(4)　For the purpose of paragraph (3), a claimant is treated as occupying the dwelling if–

(a)　any of paragraphs (13), (13D) (with (13E) where applicable) or (13G) of regulation 7 (circumstances in which a person is or is not to be treated as occupying a dwelling as his home) is satisfied and for that purpose those paragraphs shall have effect as if sub-paragraph (b) of those paragraphs were omitted; or

(b)　any of paragraphs (17), (17C) or (17D) of regulation 7 is satisfied and for that purpose those paragraphs shall have effect as if sub-paragraph (b) of paragraph (16) of that regulation were omitted.]

(5)　Where a person's eligible rent has been determined in accordance with paragraph (3) (protection on death), it shall apply until the first of the following events occurs–

(a)　the period of 12 months from the date of death has expired;

(b)　the determination of an eligible rent in accordance with paragraph (3) (protection on death) in relation to a subsequent death;

(c)　there is a change of circumstances and the relevant authority determines a new eligible rent in accordance with paragraph (2) which is equal to or more than the eligible rent determined in accordance with paragraph (3);

(d)　there is a change of dwelling; or

(e)　the determination of an eligible rent under regulation 12B.

(6)　Where the relevant authority is satisfied that the claimant or a linked person was able to meet the financial commitments for the dwelling when they were entered into, the eligible rent is an eligible rent determined in accordance with regulation 12B(2) where that eligible rent is more than the eligible rent determined in accordance with paragraph (2).

(7)　Paragraph (6) shall not apply where the claimant or the claimant's partner was previously entitled to benefit in respect of an award of housing benefit which fell wholly or partly less than 52 weeks before the commencement of the claimant's current award of housing benefit.

(8)　Where a person's eligible rent has been determined in accordance with paragraph (6) (13 week protection), it shall apply until the first of the following events occurs–

(a)　the first 13 weeks of the claimant's award of housing benefit have expired;

(b)　the determination of an eligible rent in accordance with paragraph (3) (protection on death);

(c)　there is a change of circumstances and the relevant authority determines a new eligible rent in accordance with paragraph (2) which is equal to or more than the eligible rent determined in accordance with paragraph (6);

(d)　there is a change of dwelling; or

(e)　the determination of an eligible rent under regulation 12B.]

Amendments

1.　Inserted by reg 5(5) of SI 2012 No 3040 as from 1.4.13.

2.　Substituted by reg 2(3) of SI 2016 No 624 as from 28.7.16, subject to transitional provision in reg 5 of SI 2016 No 624.

Definitions

"claimant" – see reg 2(1).

"eligible rent" – see reg 2(1).

"linked person" – see reg 2(1).

"partner" – see reg 2(1).

General Note

"Eligible rent" for HB purposes is only determined under reg 12BA if "maximum rent (social sector)" is (or is to be) determined under reg A13 (the "social sector" scheme rules). See p371 for a summary of the "social sector" scheme. It is often referred to as the "bedroom tax" or by the DWP as the "removal of the spare room subsidy" or the "under-occupation charge". Note: restriction of eligible rent can be delayed in specified circumstances: paras (3) to (8).

Analysis

Reg 12BA applies if a "maximum rent (social sector)" has been, or is to be, determined under reg A13: para (1). Unless there is protection on death or 13-week protection under paras (3) or (6), the claimant's eligible rent is the "maximum rent (social sector)": para (2). So in simple terms, eligible rent under the "social sector" scheme is the contractual rent, minus any ineligible charges, reduced by a set percentage if the claimant's dwelling has more bedrooms than are allowed under the size criteria and then apportioned (if there is a joint liability).

Paras (3) to (5): Protection on death

Para (3) provides a degree of protection for the recently bereaved if a claimant is continuing to occupy a home which s/he occupied at the time a "linked person" died.

A "linked person" for these purposes is a member of the claimant's family (defined in s137(1) SSCBA), a partner in a polygamous marriage or a child or young person for whom the claimant or a partner is responsible and who lives in the same household, or a relative of the claimant or her/his partner who occupies the same dwelling without a separate right to do so: reg 2(1). As to the last of these categories, "relative" is also defined in reg 2(1). The deceased person need not have been residing with the claimant, provided only that s/he occupied the same dwelling. Oddly, reg 3(4) specifies when a person "resides with" another for the purposes of the definition of "linked person", but the term used in the definition is "occupies the same dwelling ... whether or not they reside with him". In this context, "occupies the same dwelling" arguably means someone living within the same building, provided that the living units of the claimant and the deceased are not completely self-contained. It might cover those who were sharing only a toilet, or some similar part of the accommodation. The relative should not have had a separate right of occupation. If the relative had her/his own tenancy from a landlord, the claimant cannot therefore take advantage of this provision. However, if the claimant and the relative were joint tenants, it could be argued that the relative's right of occupation was not "separate" because it was held jointly with the claimant.

By para (4), "occupation" of a home for the purposes of para (3) can include deemed occupation under reg 7(13), (13D) (including any extension allowed under (13E)), (13G), (17), (17C) or (17D) that is, where someone is treated as occupying a dwelling while temporarily absent from it. The claimant need not, however, comply with sub-para (b) of those paragraphs, so it does not matter if the home was let or sublet.

Unless the eligible rent as determined under para (2), ie the maximum rent (social sector), is the same or higher, eligible rent is either:

(1) the eligible rent that applied on the day before the date of death; *or*

(2) in a case where no eligible rent applied on the date of death (eg, where there was no current award of HB at the time of death), the eligible rent as determined under reg 12B(2) (the normal rules). See the commentary to reg 12B on p357.

This protected eligible rent continues to apply until the first of the events in para (5) occurs, ie:

(1) It is more than 12 months since the date of death.

(2) The authority determines another protected eligible rent under para (3) because another "linked person" has died.

(3) There has been a change of circumstances and the local authority determines an eligible rent that is the same or higher than the protected eligible rent.

(4) The claimant moves.

(5) An eligible rent is determined under reg 12B (the normal rules), that is, none of the rent restriction rules (including the "social sector" rules) now apply.

Paras (6) to (8): 13-week protection

Para (6) can postpone the application of a restricted eligible rent determined under para (2) if the claimant or a "linked person" (see above) was able to meet the financial commitments for the dwelling (which includes things like bills as well as the rent) at the time they were taken on. By para (7), the protection does not apply where the claimant or her/his partner has been entitled to HB at some time within the 52 weeks prior to the commencement of the claimant's current HB award.

Unless eligible rent as determined under para (2) (ie, the maximum rent (social sector)) is the same or higher, eligible rent is to be determined under reg 12B(2) (the normal rules). See the commentary to reg 12B on p357.

This protected eligible rent continues to apply until the first of the events in para (8) occurs, ie:

(1) It is more than 13 weeks since HB was awarded.

(2) The authority determines another protected eligible rent because a "linked person" has died: see para (3).

(3) There has been a change of circumstances and the local authority determines an eligible rent that is the same or higher than the protected eligible rent.

(4)   The claimant moves.

(5)   An eligible rent is determined under reg 12B (the normal rules), that is, none of the rent restriction rules (including the "social sector" rules) now apply.

[¹ Eligible rent and maximum rent

12C.–(1)   This regulation applies where a maximum rent has been, or is to be, determined in accordance with regulation 13 (maximum rent).

(2)   Where this regulation applies, except where paragraph (3) applies, the amount of a person's eligible rent shall be the maximum rent, subject to paragraphs (3), (4) and (6) of regulation 12B.

(3)   In a case where the maximum rent is derived from a single room rent determined by a rent officer under paragraph 5 of Schedule 1 to the Rent Officers Order the eligible rent shall be the maximum rent subject to paragraphs (3) and (6) of regulation 12B.]

Amendment

1.   Inserted by reg 5 of SI 2007 No 2868 as from 7.4.08 (or if reg 1(5) of that SI applies, on the day on or after 7.4.08 when the first of the events specified in reg 1(6) applies, or from 6.4.09 if none have before that date).

Definitions

"eligible rent" – see reg 2(1).
"maximum rent" – see reg 2(1).
"Rent Officers Order"– see reg 2(1).
"single room rent" – see reg 2(1).

General Note

"Eligible rent" for HB purposes is only determined under reg 12C if "maximum rent" is (or is to be) determined under reg 13 (the "local reference rent" rules). "Maximum rent" is determined under reg 13 where reg 14 is relevant. See p382 for a summary of the "maximum rent" calculation under the "local reference rent" scheme. Note that the use of the maximum rent in calculating HB may be delayed under reg 13ZA (protection on death and 13-week protection).

Analysis

Reg 12C applies if "maximum rent" has been, or is to be, determined under reg 13. In this case, "eligible rent" is the "maximum rent". Where the claimant is a "young individual", broadly most single claimants under 35 (but see the full definition in reg 2(1), the exceptions and the commentary on p246), "eligible rent" is the maximum rent derived from the "single room rent": see the commentary to reg 13(5). Prior to 1 January 2012, the "young individual" age limit was 25.

So, in simple terms, eligible rent under the "local reference rent" scheme is the contractual rent, minus any amount above the level to which maximum rent is restricted. Note that, except in the circumstances set out in reg 13(5) and (7), the authority does not make deductions under reg 12C for ineligible charges; these have generally been dealt with in the determinations made by the rent officer.

In all cases, where the accommodation occupied by the claimant is not solely residential accommodation, only that portion of the payments referable to the residential element can form part of the eligible rent: see paras (2) and (3) and reg 12(B)(3).

Where the claimant is jointly liable to make the payments set out in reg 12(1), an apportionment must be made: see para (2) and reg 12B(4). This of course does not apply where the maximum rent is derived from the single room rent.

Both paras (2) and (3) are said to be subject to reg 12B(6) which purports to give the authority a general discretion to reduce the eligible rent calculated under reg 12C. The wording of reg 12B(6) states it only applies where eligible rent has been determined in accordance with the preceding paragraphs of that regulation, so the judge in *AA v Chesterfield BC* [2011] UKUT 156 (AAC), an appeal concerning the "LHA scheme" rules, thought that it was arguable that the discretion to restrict eligible rent under reg 12B(6) had no or little relevance. However, see the discussion on *DC v London Borough of Bromley (HB)* [2018] UKUT 416 (AAC) on p396.

If reg 12C(2) and (3) *is* subject to reg 12B(6), caution is required where a rent officer's determinations have already restricted the claimant's eligible rent under reg 13: see p382. After all, that process should mean that the claimant's rent has been reduced to a reasonable level already. However, in *R v Macclesfield BC HBRB ex p Temsamani* [1999] unreported, February 24, QBD, the High Court confirmed that, under the provisions as they applied before 7 April 2008, an authority could properly reduce the eligible rent even where the rent officer had not given a significantly high rent determination provided that it had sufficient evidential basis to do so.

[¹ **Eligible rent and maximum rent (LHA)**

12D.–(1) [² Except where regulation 12M (transitional protection – reduction in LHA) applies,] This regulation applies where, by virtue of paragraphs (2) or (3) of regulation 13C (when a maximum rent (LHA) is to be determined), a maximum rent (LHA) has been, or is to be, determined in accordance with regulation 13D (determination of a maximum rent (LHA)).

(2) Where this regulation applies, except where paragraphs (3)(a) (protection on death) or (5)(a) (13 week protection) apply–

(a) the amount of a person's eligible rent shall be the maximum rent (LHA); and

(b) it shall apply until the earlier of–

(i) the determination of a maximum rent (LHA) by virtue of regulation 13C(2)(d) (change of category of dwelling, death or change of dwelling for an LHA case);

(ii) the determination of a maximum rent (LHA) by virtue of regulation 13C(3) (anniversary of LHA date); or

(iii) the determination of a maximum rent by virtue of regulation 13 or an eligible rent under regulation 12B.

(3) Subject to paragraph (7), where the relevant authority is required to determine a maximum rent (LHA) by virtue of regulation 13C(2)(a), (b) (new claim on or after 7th April 2008) or (d)(i) or (ii) (change of category of dwelling or death relating to an LHA case) and the claimant occupies a dwelling which is the same as that occupied by him at the date of death of any linked person, the eligible rent shall be–

(a) either–

(i) the eligible rent which applied on the day before the death occurred; or

(ii) in a case where there was no eligible rent, subject to regulation 12B(3) (mixed use accommodation), (4) (more than one person liable to make payments) and (6) (discretion in relation to eligible rent), the reckonable rent due on that day; or

(b) the eligible rent determined in accordance with paragraph (2), where it is equal to or more than the eligible rent determined in accordance with sub-paragraph (a).

[⁴ (4) For the purpose of paragraph (3), a claimant is treated as occupying the dwelling if–

(a) any of paragraphs (13), (13D) (with (13E) where applicable) or (13G) of regulation 7 (circumstances in which a person is or is not to be treated as occupying a dwelling as his home) is satisfied and for that purpose those paragraphs shall have effect as if sub-paragraph (b) of those paragraphs were omitted; or

(b) any of paragraphs (17), (17C) or (17D) of regulation 7 is satisfied and for that purpose those paragraphs shall have effect as if sub-paragraph (b) of paragraph (16) of that regulation were omitted.]

(5) Subject to paragraphs (6) and (7), where a relevant authority is required to determine a maximum rent (LHA) by virtue of regulation 13C(2)(a) or (b) (new claim on or after 7th April 2008) and the relevant authority is satisfied that the claimant or a linked person was able to meet the financial commitments for his dwelling when they were entered into, the eligible rent shall be–

(a) an eligible rent determined in accordance with regulation 12B(2); or

(b) the eligible rent determined in accordance with paragraph (2), where it is equal to or more than the eligible rent referred to in sub-paragraph (a).

(6) Paragraph (5) shall not apply where a claimant or the claimant's partner, was previously entitled to benefit in respect of an award of housing benefit which fell wholly or partly less than 52 weeks before the commencement of the claimant's current award of housing benefit.

(7) Where a person's eligible rent has been determined in accordance with–

(a) paragraph (3)(a) (protection on death), it shall apply until the first of the following events occurs–

(i) the period of 12 months from the date of death has expired;

(ii) the relevant authority determines an eligible rent in accordance with paragraph (2) which is equal to or exceeds it or is based on a maximum rent (LHA) determined by virtue of regulation 13C(2)(d)(iii) (change of dwelling);

(iii) the determination of an eligible rent in accordance with paragraph (3)(a) (protection on death) in relation to a subsequent death; or

(iv) the determination of a maximum rent by virtue of regulation 13[³, a maximum rent (social sector) by virtue of regulation A13] or an eligible rent under regulation 12B.

(b) paragraph (5)(a) (13 week protection), it shall apply until the first of the following events occurs–

(i) the first 13 weeks of the claimant's award of housing benefit have expired;

(ii) the relevant authority determines an eligible rent in accordance with paragraph (2) which is equal to or exceeds it or is based on a maximum rent (LHA) determined by virtue of regulation 13C(2)(d)(iii) (change of dwelling);

(iii) the determination of an eligible rent in accordance with paragraph (3)(a) (protection on death); or

(iv) the determination of a maximum rent by virtue of regulation 13[³, a maximum rent (social sector) by virtue of regulation A13] or an eligible rent under regulation 12B.

(8) Where an eligible rent ceases to apply by virtue of paragraph (7)(a)(i) (expiry of protection on death) or (7)(b)(i) (expiry of 13 week protection), the eligible rent that shall apply instead shall be the one which would have applied but for paragraphs (3)(a) and (5)(a).]

Modifications

Reg 12D is modified by Sch 10 para 5 (see p707). This applies only to former Pathfinder Authorities who administered the pilot local housing allowance scheme.

Amendments

1. Inserted by reg 5 of SI 2007 No 2868 as from 7.4.08 (or if reg 1(5) of that SI applies, on the day on or after 7.4.08 when the first of the events specified in reg 1(6) applies, or from 6.4.09 if none have before that date).
2. Amended by reg 2(3) of SI 2010 No 2835 as from 1.4.11.
3. Amended by reg 5(6) of SI 2012 No 3040 as from 1.4.13.
4. Substituted by reg 2(3) of SI 2016 No 624 as from 28.7.16, subject to transitional provision in reg 5 of SI 2016 No 624.

Definitions

"claimant" – see reg 2(1).
"dwelling" – see reg 2(4) and s137(1) SSCBA.
"eligible rent" – reg 2(1).
"linked person" – see reg 2(1).
"maximum rent (social sector)" – see regs A13 and B13.
"partner" – see reg 2(1).
"reckonable rent" – see reg 2(1).

General Note

"Eligible rent" for HB purposes is only determined under reg 12D if "maximum rent (LHA)" is (or is to be) determined under reg 13D (the "LHA" scheme rules), unless the claimant is entitled to transitional protection under reg 12M (against rules reducing local housing allowance rates from 1 April 2011). See p391 for a summary of the "LHA" scheme. Note:

(1) The period over which the eligible rent applies is set out in para (2)(b). Note that local authorities can generally only re-assess a claimant's eligible rent annually (on 1 April) – eg, even if the rate of the appropriate local housing allowance changes.

(2) Restriction of eligible rent can be delayed in specified circumstances: paras (3) to (8).

Transitional protection was provided to those living in former Pathfinder areas whose HB was calculated on the basis of the "maximum rent (standard local rate)": reg 122 and Sch 10.

Analysis

Reg 12D applies if "maximum rent (LHA)" has been, or is to be, determined under reg 13D: para (2)(a). In this case, "eligible rent" is generally the maximum rent (LHA). So in simple terms, eligible rent under the "LHA" scheme is the contractual rent, minus any amount above the level to which maximum rent (LHA) is restricted. The authority does not make deductions under reg 12D for ineligible charges; these are generally dealt with in the local housing allowances set by the rent officer upon which maximum rent (LHA) is based.

Unlike the "local reference rent" scheme, eligible rent is not apportioned where the accommodation occupied by the claimant is not solely residential or where the claimant is jointly liable to make the payments set out in reg 12(1). However, an apportionment of the claimant's "cap rent" (an element in the calculation of maximum rent (LHA)) *is* made, which has the same effect: see reg 13D(12).

Para (2). Under para (2), eligible rent is the maximum rent (LHA) unless the claimant has protection on death under para (3)(a) or 13-week protection under para (5)(a). This applies until the earliest of the three circumstances in para (2)(b), that is until:

(1)   A new maximum rent (LHA) has been determined following a specified change: para 2(b)(i). The specified changes are a change in the category of dwelling that applies to the claimant (ie, s/he is allowed more or fewer bedrooms), the death of a member of the claimant's family (or a relative of the claimant or her/his partner living with the claimant), the claimant moving to a new home or a change affecting the amount of the claimant's "cap rent" (ie, her/his rent has increased or decreased). For full details see reg 13C(2)(d).

(2)   A new maximum rent (LHA) has been determined under reg 13C – ie, on 1 April in any year: para (2)(b)(ii).

(3)   A "maximum rent" has been determined under reg 13 (the "local reference rent" rules) or an eligible rent has been determined under reg 12B (the normal rules), that is, where the "LHA" rules no longer apply to the claimant (eg, because her/his landlord is now a registered provider of social housing or s/he has moved to a rented mobile home): para (2)(b)(iii).

Paras (3), (4), (7) and (8): Protection on death

Para (3) provides a degree of protection for the recently bereaved if a claimant is continuing to occupy a home which s/he occupied at the time a "linked person" died. Para (3) only applies where the authority is required to determine a new maximum rent (LHA) under any of reg 13C(2)(a), (b) or (d)(i) or (ii) – eg, where because of the death of the "linked person", a new claim for HB is necessary or there is a change in the category of dwelling that applies to the claimant.

A "linked person" for these purposes is a member of the claimant's family (defined in s137(1) SSCBA), a partner in a polygamous marriage or a child or young person for whom the claimant or a partner is responsible and who lives in the same household, or a relative of the claimant or her/his partner who occupies the same dwelling without a separate right to do so: reg 2(1). As to the last of these categories, "relative" is also defined in reg 2(1). The deceased person need not have been residing with the claimant, provided only that s/he occupied the same dwelling. Oddly, reg 3(4) specifies when a person "resides with" another for the purposes of the definition of "linked person", but the term used in the definition is "occupies the same dwelling ... whether or not they reside with him". In this context, "occupies the same dwelling" arguably means someone living within the same building, provided that the living units of the claimant and the deceased are not completely self-contained. It might cover those who were sharing only a toilet, or some similar part of the accommodation. The relative should not have had a separate right of occupation. If the relative had her/his own tenancy from a landlord, the claimant cannot therefore take advantage of this provision. However, if the claimant and the relative were joint tenants, it could be argued that the relative's right of occupation was not "separate" because it was held jointly with the claimant.

By para (4), "occupation" of a home for the purposes of para (3) can include deemed occupation under reg 7(13), (13D) (including any extension under (13E)), (13G), (17), (17C) or (17D) that is, where someone is treated as occupying a dwelling while temporarily absent from it. The claimant need not, however, comply with sub-para (b) of those paragraphs, so it does not matter if the home was let or sublet.

Unless eligible rent determined on the basis of the new circumstances is the same or higher, eligible rent is either the eligible rent that applied on the day before the date of death, or in a case where there was no eligible rent in force (eg, where there was no current award of HB at the time of death), the "reckonable rent" on the date of death. "Reckonable rent" means the payments a person is liable to make in respect of the dwelling s/he occupies as her/his home and which are eligible (or but for reg 13 would be eligible) for HB. Note that where the eligible rent is the reckonable rent, this is subject to reg 12B(3), (4) and (6). See reg 12B for a discussion of these provisions. Note, however, the wording of reg 12B(6), which states it only applies where eligible rent has been determined in accordance with the preceding paragraphs of that regulation, so the judge in *AA v Chesterfield BC* [2011] UKUT 156 (AAC), thought that it was arguable that the discretion to restrict eligible rent under reg 12B(6) had no or little relevance. However, see the discussion on *DC v London Borough of Bromley (HB)* [2018] UKUT 416 (AAC) on p396.

The protected eligible rent continues to apply until the first of the the events in para (7)(a) occurs – ie:

(1)   It is more than 12 months since the date of death. Where the protection ceases for this reason, the eligible rent that applies is that which would have applied but for the protection provided by para (3)(a): para (8).

Note that if there was protection on death before 1 April 2011 and this ceased on or after that date, the claimant may then have become entitled to transitional protection under reg 12M (see below).

(2) The authority determines an eligible rent that is the same or higher than the protected eligible rent, or is based on a different maximum rent (LHA) because the claimant has moved.

(3) The authority determines another eligible rent under para (3)(a) because another "linked person" has died.

(4) A "maximum rent" has been determined under reg 13 (the "local reference rent" rules), a "maximum rent (social sector)" has been determined under reg A13 (the "social sector" rules) or an eligible rent has been determined under reg 12B (the normal rules), that is, the "LHA" rules no longer apply.

Paras (5) to (7) and (8): 13-week protection

Para (5) can postpone the application of the restricted eligible rent during the first 13 weeks of an HB award if the claimant or a "linked person" (see above) was able to meet the financial commitments for the dwelling (which includes things like bills as well as the rent) at the time they were taken on. Para (5) only applies on a new claim for HB on or after 7 April 2008. By para (6), the protection in para (5) does not apply where the claimant or her/his partner has been entitled to HB at some time within the 52 weeeks prior to the commencement of the claimant's current HB award.

Unless eligible rent as determined under para (2) is the same or higher, eligible rent is to be determined under reg 12B(2) (the normal rules). See the commentary to reg 12B on p357.

The protected eligible rent continues to apply until the first of the the events in para (7)(b) occurs – ie:

(1) It is more than 13 weeks since HB was awarded. Where the protection ceases for this reason, the eligible rent that applies is that which would have applied but for the protection provided by para (5)(a): para (8). Note that if there was 13-week protection before 1 April 2011 and this ceased on or after that date, the claimant may then have become entitled to transitional protection under reg 12M (see below).

(2) The authority determines an eligible rent that is the same or higher than the protected eligible rent, or is based on a different maximum rent (LHA) because the claimant has moved.

(3) The authority determines another eligible rent under para (3)(a) because a "linked person" has died: see para (3)(a).

(4) A "maximum rent" has been determined under reg 13 (the "local reference rent" rules), a "maximum rent (social sector)" has been determined under reg A13 (the "social sector" rules) or an eligible rent has been determined under reg 12B (the normal rules), that is, the "LHA" rules no longer apply.

Transitional protection for pathfinder cases
12E.–12K.

General Note

Regs 12E to 12K are inserted by Sch 10 para 6 (see p707). They only apply to former Pathfinder Authorities which administered the pilot local housing allowance scheme.

[¹ [² Transitional protection – larger properties
12L.]]

Amendments

1. Inserted by reg 2(2) of SI 2009 No 614 as from 6.4.09.
2. Omitted by reg 2(4) of SI 2010 No 2835 as from 1.4.11.

[¹ Transitional protection – reduction in LHA

12M.–(1) This regulation applies where–

(a) reference was made to a maximum rent (LHA) in determining the amount of the eligible rent which applied immediately before 1st April 2011;

(b) on or after 1st April 2011 the relevant authority is required to determine a maximum rent (LHA) by virtue of–

   (i) regulation 13C(2)(d)(i) (change of category of dwelling) because the claimant has become entitled to a larger category of dwelling; or

   (ii) regulation 13C(3) (anniversary of LHA date); and

(c) the determination referred to in sub-paragraph (b) is the first determination of a maximum rent (LHA) the relevant authority is required to make on or after 1st April 2011.

(2) Where this regulation applies, the claimant's eligible rent is–

(a) the maximum rent (LHA) where that is equal to or higher than the eligible rent which applied immediately before 1st April 2011; or

(b)   in any other case, the lower of–
    (i)   the amount of the eligible rent which applied immediately before 1st April 2011; or
    (ii)   the amount of the cap rent by reference to which the maximum rent (LHA) referred to in paragraph (1)(b) was determined.

(3)   Where the claimant's eligible rent is determined in accordance with paragraph (2)(b) it will continue to apply until, on or after 1st April 2011, the first of the following events occurs–

(a)   the period 9 months after the determination of the maximum rent (LHA) referred to in paragraph (1)(b) has expired;

(b)   the relevant authority is required to determine a new maximum rent (LHA) by virtue of regulation 13C(2)(d)(i) (change of category of dwelling) because the claimant has become entitled to a larger category of dwelling and the maximum rent (LHA) is equal to or higher
than the eligible rent referred to in paragraph (2)(b);

(c)   the relevant authority is required to determine a new maximum rent (LHA) by virtue of regulation 13C(2)(d)(i) (change of category of dwelling) because the claimant has become entitled to a smaller category of dwelling;

(d)   the relevant authority is required to determine an eligible rent following a change of dwelling; or

(e)   the relevant authority is required to determine an eligible rent in accordance with regulation 12D(3) (protection on death).

(4)   [² Subject to paragraph (4A), where] the eligible rent ceases to apply because of paragraph (3)(a), the eligible rent will be the maximum rent (LHA) which would have applied but for the transitional protection in paragraph (2)(b).

[² (4A)   Where on the date when the eligible rent ceases to apply because of paragraph (3)(a), the claimant is a young individual who has attained the age of 25 years–

(a)   the eligible rent will be the maximum rent (LHA) which would apply if the relevant authority were to determine one by reference to that date, but

(b)   the LHA date for the purposes of regulation 13C will remain the date by reference to which the local housing allowance used in the determination referred to in paragraph (1)(b) was identified.]

(5)   Where the eligible rent is the maximum rent (LHA), it shall be treated as if it had been determined in accordance with regulation 12D(2)(a) (eligible rent is maximum rent (LHA)) and shall apply according to the provisions of regulation 12D.]

Amendments

1.   Inserted by reg 2(5) of SI 2010 No 2835 as from 1.4.11.
2.   Amended by reg 2(4) and (5) of SI 2011 No 1736 as from 1.1.12.

Definitions

"cap rent" – see reg 13D(12).
"claimant" – see reg 2(1).
"eligible rent" – see reg 2(1).
"maximum rent (LHA)" – see regs 2(1) and 13D.
"young individual" – see reg 2(1).

General Note

Changes to the "local housing allowance" scheme rules from 1 April 2011 potentially reduced the amount of a claimant's eligible rent, and hence the amount of her/his HB, when entitlement was reassessed on or after that date. The changes were:

(1)   A reduction in the maximum number of bedrooms allowed under the size criteria in reg 13D, to four bedrooms.

(2)   A change in the way local housing allowance rates were determined under Sch 3B of the Rent Officers Orders, reducing these from the median of rents in each broad rental market area to the 30th percentile.

(3)   A cap on the local housing allowance rates allowed under Sch 3B of the Rent Officer Orders for each category of property.

(4)   A potential reduction in the "maximum rent (LHA)" to the lower of the appropriate local housing allowance or the claimant's "cap rent", rather than the "cap rent" plus £15.

Reg 12M provided transitional protection against a reduction in HB for some claimants. See pp325–26 of the 25th edition of this work for details and commentary.

A claimant could be entitled to protection on the death of a "linked person" under reg 12D(3) before or after entitlement to transitional protection under reg 12M. A claimant could be entitled to 13-week protection under reg 12D(5) before s/he was entitled to transitional protection under reg 12M. For some examples, see pp317–18 of the 24th edition.

[¹ When a maximum rent (social sector) is to be determined

A13.–(1)   Subject to paragraph (2), the relevant authority must determine a maximum rent (social sector) in accordance with regulation B13 (determination of a maximum rent (social sector)) where the relevant authority has not determined, and is not required to determine–

(a)   a maximum rent in accordance with regulation 13 (maximum rent); [²]

(b)   a maximum rent (LHA) by virtue of regulation 13C (when a maximum rent (LHA) is to be determined).[² or]

[² (c)   an eligible rent in a case where paragraph 4 of Schedule 3 (transitional and savings provisions) to the Consequential Provisions Regulations applies.]

(2)   This regulation does not apply–

(a)   in a rent allowance case where the tenancy is an excluded tenancy of a type mentioned in any of paragraphs 4 to 11 of Schedule 2 (excluded tenancies) and the landlord is not a registered housing association;

(b)   in respect of shared ownership tenancies;

(c)   in respect of mooring charges for houseboats and payments in respect of the site on which a caravan or mobile home stands;

(d)   where the claimant or the claimant's partner has attained the qualifying age for state pension credit, or where both have attained that age; or

(e)   where the dwelling is temporary accommodation.

(3)   In this regulation "temporary accommodation" means accommodation of a kind listed in paragraph (4) which the relevant authority makes available to the claimant, or which a registered housing association makes available to the claimant in pursuance of arrangements made with it by the authority–

(a)   to discharge any of the authority's functions under Part 3 of the Housing Act 1985, Part 7 of the Housing Act 1996 or (in Scotland) Part 2 of the Housing (Scotland) Act 1987; or

(b)   to prevent the claimant being or becoming homeless within the meaning of Part 7 of the Housing Act 1996 or (in Scotland) Part 2 of the Housing (Scotland) Act 1987.

(4)   The accommodation referred to in paragraph (3) is–

(a)   accommodation–

    (i)   provided for a charge, where that charge includes the provision of that accommodation and some cooked or prepared meals which are also cooked or prepared, and consumed, in that accommodation or associated premises; or

    (ii)   provided in a hotel, guest house, lodging house or similar establishment,

but does not include accommodation which is provided in a care home, an independent hospital or a hostel;

(b)   accommodation which the authority or registered housing association holds on a lease and, in the case of an authority in England, is held outside the Housing Revenue Account on a lease granted for a term not exceeding 10 years;

(c)   accommodation which the authority or registered housing association has a right to use under an agreement other than a lease with a third party.

Amendments

1.   Inserted by reg 5(7) of SI 2012 No 3040 as from 1.4.13.
2.   Amended by reg 3 of SI 2014 No 212 as from 3.3.14.

Definitions

"care home" – see reg 2(1).
"Consequential Provisions Regulations" – see reg 2(1).

"hostel" – see reg 2(1).
"independent hospital" – see reg 2(1).
"qualifying age for state pension credit" – see reg 2(1).
"registered housing association" – see reg 2(1).
"relevant authority" – see reg 2(1).
"rent allowance" – see s134(1A) and (1B) SSAA 1992.
"shared ownership tenancy" – see reg 2(1).

General Note

The starting point for deciding whether maximum rent (social sector) is to be calculated under reg B13 (the "social sector" rules), and hence eligible rent under reg 12BA, is reg A13. Reg A13 prescribes the circumstances in which this must be done, and the situations in which the "social sector" rules do not apply. It provides a definition of "temporary accommodation" for these purposes.

The rules do not specifically set out to whom the "social sector" rules apply. However, as paras (1) and (2) set out when the rules do *not* apply, broadly reg A13 can apply if the claimant is the tenant of a local authority or a registered housing association (defined in reg 2(1) to include a registered social landlord). This means that the rules can apply both where HB is paid in the form of a rent allowance and in the form of a rent rebate.

Note that in *FT v Perth and Kinross Council and SSWP (HB)* [2019] UKUT 43 (AAC) Judge Poole decided that the application of regs A13 and B13 in the case of a traveller did not violate the claimant's Convention rights under articles 8 and 14 ECHR because DHPs were available to mitigate the adverse effect.

Analysis

Para (1). Unless any of the exceptions in para (2) apply, the local authority must determine a maximum rent (social sector) under reg B13 if it has not determined, and is not required to determine, a maximum rent under the "local reference rent" rules, a maximum rent (LHA) under the "local housing allowance" rules or an eligible rent under the "pre-January 1996" rules (ie, where Sch 3 para 4 HB&CTB(CP) Regs applies). Thus the local authority must first decide whether any of the other rent restriction schemes apply, and then, if none of these apply, whether any of the exceptions in para (2) apply. If a maximum rent (social sector) is determined, eligible rent is determined under reg 12BA.

Para (2): exceptions. A maximum rent (social sector) does not have to be determined if any of the exceptions in para (2) apply – ie:

(1)   Where HB is paid in the form of a rent allowance and the claimant has an "excluded tenancy" of a type in any of paras 4 to 11 of Sch 2 (for which see pp629–629), but only if the landlord is *not* a registered housing association: sub-para (a). This ensures that, unless the landlord is a registered housing association, those excluded by regs 13C(5)(c) and 14(2)(a) and those paras of Sch 2 from the application of the "local housing allowance" or the "local reference rent" scheme rules are also excluded from the "social sector" scheme rules.

(2)   The payments for which HB is claimed are in respect of a shared ownership tenancy (for which see reg 2(1) and p245): sub-para (b). This is the case whether or not the landlord is a registered housing association.

(3)   The payments for which HB is claimed are in respect of mooring charges for a houseboat or the site on which a caravan or mobile home stands: sub-para (c). For the latter to apply, there must be an identifiable payment in respect of the site: *FT v Perth and Kinross Council and SSWP (HB)* [2019] UKUT 43 (AAC). Note that cases where HB would be paid as a rent allowance and rent is paid in relation to a houseboat, a mobile home or a caravan are generally dealt with under the "local reference rent" scheme: see reg 13C(5)(d) and the General Note to reg 14.

(4)   The claimant or her/his partner is at least the qualifying age for PC (for which see reg 2(1) and p244): sub-para (d). By reg 5, the HB regs can apply to a claimant of at least that age (or who has a partner of at least that age) if one of them is on IS, income-based JSA or income-related ESA (or UC). Thus the "social sector" rules apply to single claimants who are under the qualifying age for PC or couples where both members are under that age.

The position may be different if the claimant is a member of a mixed-age couple – ie, if only one member is at least the qualifying age for PC. If a person is excluded from entitlement to PC or HB because s/he is a member of a mixed age couple and is also prevented from claiming UC because of the "SDP Gateway" in reg 4A of the UC(TP) Regs 2014 (see p1862) or because s/he is a frontier worker or by virtue of reg 4 of the UC(TP) Regs 2014 (see p1861), the member of the couple who has reached the qualifying age for PC is treated as not having attained that age for the purposes of reg 5 and thus the HB Regs apply to such a claimant. See Art 8 of the Welfare Reform Act 2012 (Commencement No.31 and Savings and Transitional Provisions and Commencement No.21 and 23 and Transitional and Transitory Provisions (Amendment) Order 2019 SI No.37 (the No.31 Order) on p1902. While it appears that sub-para (d) excludes such claimants from the application of the "social sector" rules, the effect of art 8(2)(b) of the No.31 Order may be to treat the older member of the couple as not having attained the qualifying age for PC because it allows the HB regs to apply "to the assessment of the award". DWP guidance to local authorities, A9/2019 *Mixed age couples: further guidance (revised)*, 10 July 2019, suggests that this is the intention and that the HB regs apply in full to the assessment of the award. However, it may be arguable that art 8(2)(b) has the more limited effect of simply allowing for claims to be made under the HB Regs and that the provision here in para (d) continues to apply.

(5)   The claimant's dwelling is "temporary accommodation", defined for these purposes in paras (3) and (4): sub-para (e).

Paras (3) and (4): temporary accommodation. The "social sector" rules do not apply if the claimant lives in "temporary accommodation" as defined in paras (3) and (4), broadly temporary accommodation provided for homeless people or to prevent homelessness. The accommodation must be of a type described in para (4). The accommodation must have been made available by the local authority (see the definition of "relevant authority" in reg 2(1)), or by a registered housing association in pursuance of arrangements made with the local authority under the provisions specified in para (3)(a) or (b). Note that for the purposes of determining whether a UC claimant may claim HB for her/his temporary accommodation (for which see the UC(TP) Regs 2014 on p1857), this definition is similar to that provided in Sch 1 para 3B UC Regs for those regulations. Thus, such claimants may fall within the exception in para (2)(e).

[¹ **Determination of a maximum rent (social sector)**

B13.–(1)   The maximum rent (social sector) is determined in accordance with paragraphs (2) to (4).

(2)   The relevant authority must determine a limited rent by–

(a)   determining the amount that the claimant's eligible rent would be in accordance with regulation 12B(2) without applying regulation 12B(4) and (6);

(b)   where the number of bedrooms in the dwelling exceeds the number of bedrooms to which the claimant is entitled in accordance with [² paragraphs (5) to (7)], reducing that amount by the appropriate percentage set out in paragraph (3); and

(c)   where more than one person is liable to make payments in respect of the dwelling, apportioning the amount determined in accordance with sub-paragraphs (a) and (b) between each such person having regard to all the circumstances, in particular, the number of such persons and the proportion of rent paid by each person.

(3)   The appropriate percentage is–

(a)   [⁶ 14%] where the number of bedrooms in the dwelling exceeds by one the number of bedrooms to which the claimant is entitled; and

(b)   [⁶ 25%] where the number of bedrooms in the dwelling exceeds by two or more the number of bedrooms to which the claimant is entitled.

(4)   Where it appears to the relevant authority that in the particular circumstances of any case the limited rent is greater than it is reasonable to meet by way of housing benefit, the maximum rent (social sector) shall be such lesser sum as appears to that authority to be an appropriate rent in that particular case.

(5)   The claimant is entitled to one bedroom for each of the following categories of person whom the relevant authority is satisfied occupies the claimant's dwelling as their home (and each person shall come within the first category only which is applicable)–

[⁷ (za) a member of a couple who cannot share a bedroom;

(zb)   a member of a couple who can share a bedroom;]

(a)   a couple [⁷];

(b)   a person who is not a child;

[³ (ba) a child who cannot share a bedroom;]

(c)   two children of the same sex;

(d)   two children who are less than 10 years old;

(e)   a child,

[²]]

[² (6)   The claimant is entitled to one additional bedroom in any case where–

[⁷ (a) one or more relevant persons in paragraph (9)(a), (b) or [⁸ (e)] is a person who requires overnight care;

(ab)   one or more relevant persons in paragraph (9)(c) or (d) is a person who requires overnight care; or]

(b)   [³ a relevant person is] a qualifying parent or carer.]

[²[³ (7)   Where
(a)   more than one sub-paragraph of paragraph (6) applies the claimant is entitled to an additional bedroom for each sub-paragraph that applies;
(b)   more than one person falls within [⁷ paragraph (6)(b)] the claimant is entitled to an additional bedroom for each person falling within that sub-paragraph, except that where a person and that person's partner both fall within the same subparagraph the claimant is entitled to only one additional bedroom in respect of that person and that person's partner.]]

[² (8)   For the purposes of determining the number of occupiers of the dwelling under paragraph (5), the relevant authority must include any member of the armed forces away on operations who–
(a)   is the son, daughter, step-son or step-daughter of the claimant or the claimant's partner;
(b)   was the claimant's non-dependant before they became a member of the armed forces away on operations; and
(c)   intends to resume occupying the dwelling as their home when they cease to be a member of the armed forces away on operations.]

[³ (9)   In this regulation "relevant person" means–
(a)   the claimant;
(b)   the claimant's partner;
(c)   a person ("P") other than the claimant or the claimant's partner who is jointly liable with the claimant or the claimant's partner (or both) to make payments in respect of the dwelling occupied as the claimant's home;
(d)   P's partner.]
[⁷ (e)   for the purposes of paragraph (6)(a)–
(i)   a person (other than the claimant, the claimant's partner, P or P's partner) who occupies the claimant's dwelling as their home;
(ii)   a child or young person in respect of whom a relevant person under sub-paragraphs (a) to (e)(i) is a qualifying parent or carer.]

Amendments

1.   Inserted by reg 5(7) of SI 2012 No 3040 as from 1.4.13.
2.   Amended by reg 2(3) of SI 2013 No 665 as from 1.4.13.
3.   Amended by reg 2(3) of SI 2013 No 2828 as from 4.12.13.
4.   Confirmed by art 17(2) of SI 2014 No 516 as from 1.4.14 (7.4.14 where rent payable weekly or in multiples of a week).
5.   Confirmed by art 17(2) of SI 2015 No 547 as from 1.4.15 (6.4.15 where rent payable weekly or in multiples of a week).
6.   Confirmed by art 22(2) of SI 2017 No 260 as from 1.4.17 (3.4.17 where rent payable weekly or in multiples of a week).
7.   Amended by reg 4(3) of SI 2017 No 213 as from 1.4.17.
8.   Amended by correction slip to SI 2017 No 213 dated 15.3.17.

Definitions

"child" – see reg 2(1).
"child who cannot share a bedroom" – see reg 2(1).
"couple" – see reg 2(1).
"member of a couple who can share a bedroom" – see reg 2(6).
"member of a couple who cannot share a bedroom" – see reg 2(1).
"member of the armed forces away on operations" – see reg 2(1).
"partner" – see reg 2(1).
"person who requires overnight care" – see reg 2(1).
"qualifying parent or carer" – see reg 2(1).

General Note

From 1 April 2013, rules were introduced that may restrict the HB of claimants in social sector rented housing if they are under-occupying their homes. Reg B13 deals with the calculation of the claimant's "maximum rent (social sector)" for HB purposes under the "social sector" scheme. The scheme is often referred to as the "bedroom tax" or, by the DWP, as the "removal of the spare room subsidy" or the "under-occupation charge". The significance of the maximum rent (social sector) is that the claimant's eligible rent cannot normally exceed it: reg 12BA. Reg B13 applies in the circumstances set out in reg A13.

Summary of the scheme

(1)   If the "social sector" scheme rules apply, the local authority must determine a "limited rent" as follows: reg B13(2) and (3).

Step one. The number of bedrooms a claimant is allowed under the size criteria is determined – ie, the number of bedrooms allowed for all of the people occupying the claimant's dwelling as a home: reg B13(5)–(9). Unlike under the "local housing allowance" rules, there is no maximum number of bedrooms allowed.

Step two. The number of bedrooms in the claimant's dwelling is determined. See p373 for a discussion on the meaning of "bedroom" for these purposes.

Step three. Eligible rent is calculated, broadly as if the normal rules apply (in accordance with reg 12B(2)). If the number of bedrooms in step two is the same as, or lower than, the number allowed in step one, unless step five applies, this is the "limited rent".

Step four. If the number of bedrooms in step two exceeds the number allowed in step one, the amount in step three is reduced. Unless step five applies, the resulting amount is the "limited rent". The reduction is 14 per cent of the amount in step three if the number of bedrooms exceeds the number allowed by one, or 25 per cent if the number of bedrooms exceeds the number allowed by two or more.

Step five. If more than one person is liable to make payments in respect of the dwelling – ie, the claimant is a joint tenant, the "limited rent" determined under either step three or step four is apportioned between the liable people. The amount apportioned to the claimant is the "limited rent" for her/him.

(2)   The "limited rent" is normally the maximum rent (social sector). However, if it appears to the local authority that it is greater than it would be reasonable to meet by way of HB, the maximum rent (social sector) can be a lower amount: reg B13(4).

(3)   A restriction can be delayed for a period – ie, a claimant's eligible rent can be higher than her/his maximum rent (social sector) for a period. This can apply for up to 12 months when there has been a death of a "linked person" (defined in reg 2(1)), or for up to 13 weeks where the claimant or a "linked person" could meet the financial commitments for the dwelling at the time they were taken on: reg 12BA(3) to (8).

(4)   There are no rules specifying when the maximum rent (social sector) may or must be reassessed, or requiring a reassessment at any particular time. However, an "outcome" decision on a claim for HB can be revised or superseded under Sch 7 para 3 or 4 CSPSSA 2000 when it is no longer correct – eg, if the number of bedrooms a claimant is allowed under the size criteria changes and hence the maximum rent (social sector) should be lower or higher.

Future changes

The government intended to introduce rules from 1 April 2019 that would cap the amount of HB payable to social sector tenants at the local housing allowance (LHA) rate that would apply to them under the LHA rules (for which see reg 13D), if this was lower than the amount as calculated under reg B13. It said this would apply to a claimant who took on a new, or renewed a, social sector tenancy agreement on or after 1 April 2016 (or 1 April 2017 if s/he lived in supported accommodation). Examples given of supported accommodation included refuges for those fleeing domestic abuse, homeless provision, housing for ex-offenders, as well as supported housing for older and disabled people. However, on 25 October 2017 at Prime Minister's question time, the Prime Minister said "as part of our response to the review [*of supported housing*], we will not be applying the local housing allowance cap to supported housing; indeed, we will not be implementing it in the wider social rented sector. The full details will be made available when we publish our response to the consultation." The response, *Funding Sheltered Housing*, was published on 31 October 2017. The government's intention was, from April 2020, to continue to fund sheltered and extra care housing, as well as long-term supported accommodation, via the benefit system with a "sheltered rent" introduced from April 2020. In England, short-term supported housing was to be funded via a ring-fenced grant to local authorities. However, in a further response published in August 2018, *Funding for Supported Housing, Government Response to Two Consultations*, the government said that it would be maintaining HB for all supported housing, including short-term. It also said that it would not be pursuing the "sheltered rent" model.

Analysis

Paragraphs (1) to (4): The calculation of a maximum rent (social sector)

If a local authority is required by reg A13 to determine a maximum rent (social sector) under reg B13, the basis for doing so is set out in paras (2) to (4).

Para (2) sets out the steps for calculating what is referred to as a "limited rent", which, unless the discretion in para (4) to reduce this figure is applied, is the claimant's maximum rent (social sector).

(1)   The amount a claimant's eligible rent would be – ie, but for these provisions – is determined under reg 12B(2): sub-para (a). Note that reg 12B(4) (apportionment of joint liabilities) and (6) (discretion to restrict eligible rent) must not be applied. Thus the figure arrived at is the contractual rent for the whole dwelling

occupied by the claimant (even if there is a joint liability with someone other than a member of the claimant's family), minus any ineligible service charges.

(2)   The number of bedrooms allowed under the size criteria is determined, for which see paras (5) to (9). If the number of bedrooms in the dwelling exceeds the number of bedrooms allowed, the amount arrived at under sub-para (a) is reduced by the appropriate percentage in para (3): sub-para (b).

(3)   If more than one person is liable to make payments in respect of the dwelling, the amount determined under sub-para (a) or (b) is apportioned between the liable people having regard to the matters set out: sub-para (c).

Para (3) fixes the appropriate percentages as 14 percent if the claimant's dwelling has one bedroom too many and 25 percent if the dwelling has two or more bedrooms too many.

Examples

(1)   The claimant rents a three-bedroom council house. She is the lone parent of two boys, aged 10 and 12. The eligible rent as calculated under reg 12B(2) is £180 a week. Under the size criteria she is allowed two bedrooms – one for her and one for her two boys. She therefore has one bedroom too many. 14 per cent of £180 = £25.20. The claimant's maximum rent (social sector) and therefore her eligible rent is £154.80 (£180 – £25.20): reg 12BA(1). As the claimant does not have non-dependants residing with her, it is also the "maximum housing benefit" (reg 70). HB is then calculated using this figure.

(2)   The claimant and his partner rent a four bedroom housing association house. They have two girls aged 15 and 17. The claimant's father lives with them but is not a joint tenant of the claimant and his partner. The eligible rent as calculated under reg 12B(2) is £225 a week. Under the size criteria, the claimant is allowed four bedrooms – one for him and his partner, one for his father and one for each of their daughters. No reduction is therefore applicable. The claimant's maximum rent (social sector) and therefore his eligible rent is £225: reg 12BA(1). The claimant has a non-dependant residing with him. Thus, the "maximum housing benefit" (reg 70) is £225 minus the appropriate non-dependant deduction (reg 74) and HB is calculated using this figure.

Para (4) contains a general discretion to reduce the "limited rent" calculated under para (2), but only where it is greater than it is reasonable to meet by way of HB. In this case, the maximum rent (social sector) is the amount which the authority considers to be an appropriate rent in any particular case. As with the similar power in reg 12B(6), para (4) raises a number of questions of judgment that must be considered rationally. See the commentary to reg 12B(6) on p358 for a discussion.

Paragraphs (5) to (9): The size criteria

The number of bedrooms a claimant is allowed under the size criteria is the number of bedrooms s/he is entitled to under para (5) and, if appropriate, additional bedrooms under para (6).

Paras (5) and (8). Under para (5), the claimant is allowed one bedroom for each of the categories of people listed in sub-paras (za) to (e) who the local authority is satisfied occupy the dwelling as a home, each coming only into the first category for which s/he is eligible.

A "member of a couple who cannot share a bedroom" is defined in reg 2(1) and is member of a couple receiving higher rate AA, highest or middle rate DLA care component, either rate of the daily living component of PIP or armed forces independence payment and who the local authority is satisfied is not reasonably able to share a bedroom with the other member of the couple by virtue of her/his disability. A "member of a couple who can share a bedroom" is defined in reg 2(6) and is a member of a couple whose partner is a "member of a couple who cannot share a bedroom". Note that, until 1 April 2017, the rules did not specifically allow a bedroom for a member of a couple who could not share a bedroom. See below for a discussion of the legal challenges made to the rules.

A person who is not a child is someone aged 16 or over (see the definition of "child" in reg 2(1)). A "child who cannot share a bedroom" is defined in reg 2(1) and is a child under 16 entitled to highest or middle rate DLA care component and who the local authority is satisfied is not reasonably able to share a bedroom with another child under 16 by virtue of her/his disability.

Para (8) includes as someone occupying the claimant's dwelling as a home: a son, daughter, step-son or step-daughter of the claimant or of her/his partner who was the claimant's non-dependant before becoming a "member of the armed forces away on operations" – ie, who is away from the dwelling usually occupied as her/his home (see the definition in reg 2(1) on p230). This only applies if s/he intends to resume occupation of the dwelling as a home when s/he ceases to be a "member of the armed forces away on operations". Note, however, that no non-dependant deduction can be made for her/him: reg 74(7)(g).

Occupation of the dwelling. For a discussion of when a person might count as occupying a dwelling as a home, see reg 7 on p256.

The people occupying the claimant's dwelling as a home include not only those who count as members of the claimant's family for benefit purposes (for which see s137(1) SSCBA), but also those who are not part of the family – eg, non-dependants or live-in carers, or joint tenants whether or not they are members of the claimant's household. It is suggested that it can also include people who normally live with the claimant but who are temporarily absent from the dwelling: *R(H) 8/09*; *SK v South Hams DC (HB)* [2010] UKUT 129 (AAC); [2010] AACR 40. It does not, however, include children or young people placed with the claimant under specified child protection legislation (eg, foster children): reg 21(3). However, some foster carers and kinship carers may be allowed one or more additional bedrooms under para (6).

Note that a child is considered to be occupying the home of only one parent – the parent with whom the child normally lives: *R v Swale BC HBRB ex p Marchant* [1999] 1 FLR 1087, QBD; [2000] 1 FLR 246, CA. In a claim for judicial review on behalf of a number of separated parents with shared care of their children, a ruling was sought that reg B13 was incompatible with the claimants' and their and their children's rights under Art 8 and/or Art 14 of the European Convention and was therefore unlawful under s6 Human Rights Act 1998. The claim was unsuccessful: *R (Cotton and others) v SSWP and New Forest DC and Others* [2014] EWHC 3437 (Admin). A judge in the Upper Tribunal decided in a similar case, *PC v SSWP (HB)* [2014] UKUT 467 (AAC), that although Art 8 was engaged, any relevant interference did not have consequences of sufficient gravity to require the DWP to show justification. Following *R (MA and Others) v SSWP and Birmingham City Council* [2014] EWCA Civ 13, he took into account the availability of discretionary housing payments (DHPs). He decided it was not seriously arguable that the decision to apply a reduction under reg B13 to the claimant involved a breach of Art 8.

MR v North Tyneside Council and SSWP [2015] UKUT 34 (AAC) was a lead case that considered an approach some First-tier Tribunals had adopted to assist claimants faced with a reduction in HB under reg B13. The claimant's son was the subject of a shared residence order and spent time in both parent's houses. The claimant was not receiving child benefit for him, but his other parent was. The local authority decided that as the claimant's son could not be treated as occupying her dwelling, she therefore could not be allowed a bedroom for him under the size criteria and it reduced her HB accordingly. The First-tier Tribunal, treating the words "dwelling" and "home" in reg B13(5) as undefined ordinary words, decided that the claimant's son occupied her dwelling on a continuing basis with temporary weekly absences and that he occupied his other parent's home on the same basis – ie, the son had more than one home, lived in more than one household and occupied more than one property on a normal basis. Judge Jacobs allowed the local authority's appeal. The meanings of the words used in para (5) are not freestanding but have to be read in the context of other HB provisions, in particular reg 7(1)(a) that treats a claimant who is a member of a "family" as occupying as her/his home, the dwelling s/he normally occupies as a home with her/his "family" (defined in s137(1) SSCBA 1992) and reg 20(2), which deals with situations where a child spends equal amounts of time in different households. Judge Jacobs confirmed this view in *SSWP v AM and Northumberland CC (HB)* [2015] UKUT 360 (AAC) in which he said that he could "see nothing in the structure of the Regulations as a whole or in the content of individual regulations to justify interpreting regulation B13 on its own and in isolation from the basic concepts that apply to all other provisions."

In *SSWP v MM and Northumberland CC* [2015] UKUT 624 (AAC), the same First-tier Tribunal judge had not decided that there had been a breach of Art 8 of the European Convention on Human Rights (right to respect for private and family life), but he had used Art 8 as part of his analysis of the interpretation of reg B13, in accordance with s3(1) of the Human Rights Act 1998. Judge Jacobs confirmed the view he held in his earlier decisions. He said:

"I do not see any way in which the interpretative duty under section 3 of the Human Rights Act 1998 can produce a different outcome. The judge's argument is premised on regulation B13 being freestanding. Once that premise is shown to be invalid, as the language of the regulation itself does, there is no scope for any other interpretation than the one I have given, which is the inexorable result of the chain of relevant provisions."

Bedroom. "Bedroom" is not defined in the regulations, so it is the ordinary meaning of the word that is relevant. It is for the local authority to determine whether or not a room in a particular dwelling is a bedroom before going on to determine how many bedrooms that dwelling contains and whether the number of bedrooms exceeds the number allowed: paras (2)(b) and (5) to (7). It is suggested that it is not sufficient for a local authority simply to consider the designation of a house (eg, as a two- or three-bedroom dwelling as the case may be (as the dwelling was designated when built)), but must take at least some account of factors such as the size of a room and the personal use of a room by the claimant and her/his family – eg, if a designated bedroom is not used as a bedroom but is instead used to store equipment required because of a severe disability (but see the discussion below). However, *CB v Manchester City Council and SSWP (HB)* [2015] UKUT 556 (AAC) decided that the basis on which the claimant's rent is calculated is not relevant – eg, if although a flat has two bedrooms, the landlord only charges the rent for a one-bedroom flat.

DWP guidance in HB U6/2013 suggested that when local authorities apply the size criteria, the only consideration should be the composition of the household and the number of bedrooms as designated by the landlord, not by measuring rooms. However, it said that in "determining whether or not a room is a bedroom the landlord may consider a number of factors, but one of these must be whether or not a room is large enough to accommodate at least a single bed." It also suggested that landlords should classify a room as a bedroom notwithstanding that the tenant has habitually used it for something else, such as storage.

In *SSWP v Nelson and Nelson* [2014] UKUT 525 (AAC); [2015] AACR 21, the First-tier Tribunal had decided that a room that had been classified as a bedroom was not a bedroom because the floor area was too small. A three-judge panel considered the approach that should be taken in determining what a bedroom is for the purposes of reg B13 (what the judges referred to as the "bedroom criteria").

The Upper Tribunal said that when an ordinary or familiar word is used in a statutory test and is not defined, the well established approach is that the test should not be re-written or paraphrased, and the word should be construed and applied in its context having regard to the underlying purposes of the legislation. Applying this approach to reg B13, in considering whether an HB claimant is under-occupying her/his home, it decided:

(1)   The use or potential use of a room can be by any of the people listed in paras (5) and (6).

(2)   Consideration must be given to whether the room could be used by any of the people listed in paras (5) or (6). This is because the test is focused on the availability of rooms that could be used as bedrooms by any of those people. However, the Upper Tribunal did not agree that a bedroom must generally be reasonably fit for full-time occupation as a bedroom, as opposed to short-term or irregular occupation by a visitor or overnight guest.

(3)   The occupier's designation or choice as to which person (or people) should occupy which rooms as bedrooms or how rooms should be used is unlikely to have an impact on the application of reg B13, but note that the judges did not consider that it would be appropriate to say that such a designation or choice would never be relevant.

(4)   Although the starting point in deciding how many bedrooms a home contains is the description of the property by the person renting it out, the Upper Tribunal said (at para 31) that "when an issue arises as to whether a particular room falls to be treated as a bedroom that could be used by any of the persons listed in Regulation B13(5) and (6) a number of case sensitive factors will need to be considered including (a) size, configuration and overall dimensions, (b) access, (c) natural and electric lighting, (d) ventilation, and (c) privacy."

The room must also be safe to sleep in – eg, it must not be contaminated with asbestos: *E v Bristol City Council* [2018] UKUT 287 (AAC).

Note that in the First-tier Tribunal's reasons for its decision in *Nelson*, it had suggested that under-occupancy was the flip side of overcrowding and that if Parliament had intended that the long-standing statutory minimum standards on overcrowding should be disregarded by the tribunal, it would have been clearly stated in the HB legislation. The Upper Tribunal did not agree.

In a later decision, the Upper Tribunal, considering *SSWP v Nelson and Nelson*, said that the decision went "no further than saying that normally the family designation and choice is not a relevant factor, but leaves open the question of whether or not there might be exceptional circumstances where re-designation might be appropriate": *SSWP v IB (CSH)* [2015] UKUT 282 (AAC). Judge Sir Crispin Agnew went on to decide that it was a relevant factor in the appeal, in considering whether or not a room was available for use as a bedroom, that a room had been designated on professional advice for a particular use by a claimant with a mental health condition. The DWP appealed to the Court of Session in *SSWP v City of Glasgow Council and IB* [2017] CSIH 35; [2017] AACR 29. It argued that in deciding if a room is a bedroom, even if actual use by the claimant is relevant, only physical alteration of the room would be sufficient for a room to be redesignated. The main issue in the appeal was whether the established use of a room and its designation are relevant factors to be taken into account in determining whether a room is a bedroom. The Court thought that there was merit in the Upper Tribunal's approach in so far as it recognised that the assessment of whether a room is a bedroom should focus on the property when vacant rather than how it is actually being used. However, it did not agree with the Upper Tribunal's view that the designation of a room, or the choices made by a claimant on the use of a room or the person who should occupy it, had relevance. It said (at paragraph 20):

"In our opinion the classification and description of a property used as a dwelling is a matter of fact to be determined objectively according to relevant factors such as size, layout and specification of the particular property in its vacant state. That classification cannot be changed except by structural alterations made with the landlord's approval which have the result of changing the classification of the property having regard objectively to its potential use in a vacant state. Thus the classification of a property as having one or more bedrooms does not change depending on the actual needs of the occupants or how they use the rooms for whatever reason from time to time. This may work both in favour of and against the applicant for housing benefit. For example, if the property considered objectively is classified as three bedrooms, the fact that the tenant always uses the livingroom as a bedroom should not result in reclassification of the property for the purposes of the 2006 Regulations as a four bedroom property. In contrast, if a tenant chooses or requires to use one of the three bedrooms as a storeroom for essential medical equipment, that should not result in a reclassification of the property from a three bedroom property to a two bedroom property."

In *SSWP v RR (HB)* [2018] UKUT 180 (AAC), the claimant lived in a property that had two bedrooms on the upper floor and two rooms and a bathroom and kitchen on the ground floor. The landlord classified the property as a three-bedroom house – ie, saying that one of the ground floor rooms was a bedroom. However, the claimant did not use either of the ground floor rooms as a bedroom. He had a team of carers. The overnight carers used one of the upstairs bedrooms.The two ground floor rooms were shared as living rooms, the claimant and carers each using one of these to give the other space. On his claim for HB, the local authority allowed two bedrooms under the relevant size criteria and applied a 14 per cent reduction on finding that the claimant's dwelling had three bedrooms – ie one bedroom too many. The First-tier Tribunal, following *Bolton MBC v BF (HB)* [2014] UKUT 48 (AAC) (discussed on p244), decided that the claimants dwelling was a two bedroom property, and thus that no deduction should be made. In the appeal to the Upper Tribunal, Judge Rowland said that *Bolton* was not relevant. However, he considered that *Nelson* and *SSWP v City of Glasgow Council and IB* were both relevant. He said that those decisions both make it clear that reg B13 requires an objective approach to be taken, despite there being many contexts in which a room is described by the way it is used by the occupier of the property. The judge went on to say:

"23.   To describe a landlord's designation, as expressed in a tenancy agreement, as a starting point seems to me to be partly an acceptance of the practical point that a landlord's view is likely to be the only evidence before a housing benefit decision-maker that is at least largely independent of the claimant, but it may also reflect an unexpressed view that a social sector landlord is likely to have a realistic view of the potential value of the property in terms of occupancy and an interest in using the property efficiently and therefore in a way consistent with the underlying purpose behind regulation B13. The *Glasgow* case makes it absolutely clear that the landlord's designation is not definitive but it does not assist with the question whether or not it is to be given any weight in an otherwise borderline case.

24.   A further point worth emphasising is that it was accepted in *Nelson* that, when considering whether a room can reasonably be used in a way consistent with the landlord's designation, one material consideration is how similar rooms are used in other properties in the area (see paragraph [32] which is among the paragraphs with which the Court of Session expressed broad approval in the *Glasgow* case). This, it seems to me, is important. The 2006 Regulations do not provide that all rooms in a house bar one must be regarded as bedrooms if they could be used as such. They require a distinction to be drawn between bedrooms and other types of room. Therefore, insofar as the Secretary of State argued that the only question was whether the room could reasonably be used as a bedroom, I do not agree. Nonetheless, the test is objective and, if a type of room is conventionally used in more than one way, the fact that it is more often used in one particular way rather than an another is unlikely by itself to be determinative."

However, applying the caselaw, the judge decided that the claimant's actual use of the downstairs room was immaterial as were his personal characteristics and his and his parents' reasons for renting the property. He decided that looking at the property objectively as it would be in its vacant state, it could be be used as either a two-bedroom or a three-bedroom house. Thus, he regarded the landlord's designation as determinative and decided that the claimant's dwelling should be classified as three-bedroom.

In *M v SSWP* [2017] UKUT 443 (AAC), the Upper Tribunal considered whether, to be a bedroom for the purposes of the HB and UC under-occupancy provisions, a room had to have space for a bedside table in addition to furniture for clothes storage. Judge Mitchell decided that this was not, as a general rule, required. He said (at paragraphs 65 and 66):

"In my judgment, paragraph 33 of *Nelson* recognises that, taking into account the normal and ordinary understanding of 'bedroom', a bedroom's function extends beyond merely a place to sleep. For a room to function as a bedroom properly so-called, *[it]* must also provide for clothes storage, a flat surface of some sort on which to place necessary items and avoid obvious safety risks as well as sufficient free space for dressing and un-dressing. Clearly, there are a range of different ways in which those requirements may be met.

In this context, a chest of drawers of appropriate height and placement can serve a dual function. It supplies a flat surface alongside a bed as well as space in the drawers underneath for storing clothes. In such circumstances, that single piece of furniture allows a room to satisfy two of the minimum functional requirements of a bedroom identified in *Nelson.*"

In *Stevenage BC v ML (HB)* [2016] UKUT 164 (AAC), the claimant argued that *Nelson* did not take the provisions of the Housing Act 2004, the Housing Health and Safety Rating System established under that Act or the guidance given by Local Authorities Coordinators of Regulatory Services (LACORS) dealing with space and overcrowding into account, and so should not be followed. Judge Lloyd-Davies did not agree. His analysis was as follows:

(1)   In *Nelson*, the Upper Tribunal decided that legislation relating to space and overcrowding is not to be read across into HB legislation relating to under occupation.

(2)   The Housing Act 2004 and the operating guidance and enforcement guidance given under s9 of that Act in relation to space and overcrowding do not mention specific room sizes.

(3)   Under the guidance and reg 6(7)(e) of the Housing Health and Safety Rating System (England) Regulations 2005, questions arising on space and overcrowding can only be decided by reference to actual occupiers and thus can only be taken into account where there are actual space issues or overcrowding. Those applying the HB Regs (eg, local authorities and the First-tier Tribunal) cannot therefore be expected to apply standards which those charged with applying those standards cannot themselves apply.

(4)   The LACORS guidance is simply guidance relating to best practice in connection with space and overcrowding and cannot be prayed in aid in construing reg B13 HB Regs.

The judge also pointed out that provisions relating to houses in multiple occupation can have no effect where the dwelling concerned is not a house in multiple occupation

The judge in *M v SSWP* [2017] UKUT 443 (AAC) also considered the relevance of the Housing Act 2004 housing safety scheme and the LACORS guidance. He pointed out that the 2004 Act scheme is designed to be operated by professional environmental health officers who are required to exercise professional judgment. He agreed with the judge in *Stevenage BC v ML (HB)* that the First-tier Tribunal "cannot properly carry out its own assessment of whether a dwelling presents a category 1 or 2 hazard nor can it properly try and predict if a local authority inspector would be likely to decide that such a hazard exists."

In some cases, it may be possible for a landlord to re-designate a property as having a lower number of bedrooms than as originally built – eg, if a property has been adapted for a disabled person, or two small bedrooms have been converted into one bedroom. However, local authorities need to be aware that although the DWP does not object in principle to this practice, Lord Freud, the Minister for Welfare Reform, said in a letter to local authority chief executives, 20 June 2013, that the DWP expects the designation of a property to be consistent for HB and rent purposes. He said: "Where it is found that a local authority has re-designated properties without reasonable grounds and without reducing rents, [the DWP] would consider either restricting or not paying their Housing Benefit subsidy".

In *Nuneaton and Bedworth BC v RH and SSWP* [2017] UKUT 471 (AAC), the claimant, her husband and two sons aged nine and seven lived in a three-bedroom property. Two of the bedrooms were too small to share and the tenancy agreement specified that the maximum number of residents was four. On the basis of the size criteria, the local authority decided that the sons could share a bedroom and that the claimant was entitled to only one bedroom for them (presumably under para (5)(c)). Thus, because it concluded the claimant's dwelling had one too many bedrooms, it applied a 14 per cent reduction under para (3)(a). The First-tier Tribunal found in the claimant's favour on the basis that neither of the two small bedrooms could be shared and the local authority appealed. A three-judge panel considered the size criteria in para (5) in terms of what it referred to as the "connection issue", that is whether a room must be one that can be used by the actual occupants or class of occupants of the dwelling as a bedroom, as opposed to in terms of what it referred to as the "classification issue", that is whether a room can be used as a bedroom at all. Para (5) states that a claimant is entitled to one bedroom "for each of the ... categories of person" who occupy the dwelling as their home. Thus, the local authority must first identify the individuals who occupy the dwelling as their home and then place them into the categories listed in sub-paras (a) to (e). The DWP and local authority argued that next, the local authority had to identify the number of bedrooms in the dwelling without reference to the categories of person who would occupy them. The Upper Tribunal disagreed. It said that as para (5) provides that the claimant is entitled to a bedroom "for" each category, the "natural expectation of that language is that the room would be a bedroom for the persons bearing the characteristics of that category, not a room that ignored those characteristics." The opening words of para (5) state that a person comes within the first category only that is applicable. Applying this to this claimant's case, because two of the bedrooms were too small to accommodate two children, the categories in para (5)(c) and (d) could not be applicable. Alternatively, reading para (5) as a whole, if there is no room that can accommodate two children of the same sex, neither head (c) nor head (d) is an applicable category within the meaning of the paragraph. Para (5)(e) thus has to be applied twice to ensure that the claimant is entitled to one room for each of the children. The Upper Tribunal declined to follow *SSWP v City of Glasgow Council and IB* [2017] CSIH 35; [2017] AACR 29 and *SSWP v Nelson and Nelson* [2014] UKUT 525 (AAC); [2015] AACR 21. One of the reasons for this was because those decisions were concerned with the classification issue and not the connection issue. The DWP's appeal to the Court of Appeal succeeded: *SSWP v Hockley and Nuneaton and Bedworth BC* [2019] EWCA Civ 1080. The Court decided that in the phrase "one bedroom for each of the following categories of person" in para (5), the word "bedroom" means a room capable of being used as a "bedroom" by any of the listed categories in that paragraph and that it did *not* mean a room capable of being used as a "bedroom" by a particular claimant. This was because the word "bedroom" has to be construed and applied in its context having regard to the underlying purposes of the legislation, that being to limit the entitlement to HB of those in social housing. The local authority's assessment of the number of bedrooms a claimant is allowed is objective in nature. The local authourity is not required to take account of how a property and the bedrooms in the property would be used by a particular family unit. The Court said that this is consistent with *Nelson* and with *SSWP v City of Glasgow Council and IB*. The Upper Tribunal in this case had introduced a subjective element into the assessment, which the Court said was not supported by the words of the regulation or the intention of the legislation.

Paras (6), (7) and (9). Under para (6), one additional bedroom is allowed under each of the sub-paras (6)(a), (ab) and (b) that apply: para (7)(a). A "person who requires overnight care" is defined in reg 2(1) (see p243 for a discussion on the meaning), as is a "qualifying parent or carer" (certain foster carers and kinship carers – see p245). To come within either of the definitions, the person must actually have a bedroom in the dwelling s/he occupies as her/his home that is additional to those used by the others who occupy it. "Relevant person" is defined in para (9). Thus additional bedrooms are allowed as follows.

(1)   One additional bedroom is allowed if the claimant, the claimant's partner, a person (other than the claimant, her/his partner or a person coming under para (9)(c) or (d)) who occupies the claimant's dwelling as a home (eg, a child or non-dependant) or a child or young person in respect of whom any "relevant person" (as defined in para 9) is a qualifying parent or carer is a "person who requires an overnight care"; paras (6)(a) and 9(a), (b) and (e). Even if more than one person requires an overnight carer, only one additional bedroom is allowed under this sub-para.

(2)   One additional bedroom is allowed if a person who is jointly liable to make payments with the claimant or the claimant's partner for the dwelling occupied as the claimant's home, or that person's partner, is a "person who requires overnight care": paras (6)(ab) and (9)(c) and (d). Even if more than one person requires overnight carer, only one additional bedroom is allowed under this sub-para.

(3)   One or more additional bedrooms are allowed if any "relevant person" (as defined in para (9) is a "qualifying parent or carer": para (6)(b). If this applies to more than one "relevant person", the claimant is

allowed an additional bedroom for each of them: para (7)(b). However, if a person and her/his partner are each a "qualifying parent or carer", only one additonal bedroom is allowed for them. See also the discussion of *SSWP v PE and Bolton MBC* [2017] UKUT 393 (AAC) below.

Note that prior to 1 April 2017, "relevant person", in all cases, only included the claimant, her/his partner, any person who was jointly liable to make payments with the claimant or her/his partner, and that person's partner.

Examples

1.   The claimant and her partner live in a four-bedroom council house with their two girls aged seven and 11. The seven-year-old is severely disabled, gets the highest rate of DLA care component and is a "person who requires overnight care". The claimant's partner is also severely disabled, receives the daily living component of PIP and cannot share a bedroom with the claimant because of his disability. The claimant is allowed four bedrooms: one for her partner under para (5)(za), one for her under para (5)(zb), one for her two girls under para (5)(c) and one additional bedroom under para (6)(a) and (9)(e) for the child who cannot share a bedroom.

2.   The claimant has a joint tenancy of a three-bedroom flat with a couple who are his friends. Both members of the couple are foster parents to two boys aged six and eight. The claimant is allowed three bedrooms: one for him under para (5)(b), one for his joint tenants under para (5)(a) and one additional bedroom under para (6)(b), (7)(b) and (9).

For the purposes of para (6)(b), the definition of "qualifying parent or carer" does not include people who provide care to an adult placed with them. It only includes those who provide relevant care to children and young people. In *SSWP v PE and Bolton MBC* [2017] UKUT 393 (AAC), the claimant was approved under an adult placement scheme to provide accommodation and one-to-one support to adults placed with her because of their disabilities. The adults lived with her on a short- or long-term basis. She had a three-bedroom home in which she lived with her son. Because the third bedroom was empty, a 14 per cent reduction was made when calculating her HB as the local authority decided that she had one bedroom too many. She appealed and the First-tier Tribunal found in her favour, deciding that the HB Regs were manifestly without reasonable foundation in so far as they required people in the claimant's position to be subject to a reduction on account of a spare bedroom. The Upper Tribunal decided that the First-tier Tribunal had not made an error of law. The DWP argued that the claimant's appeal could not succeed, because she was not herself disabled. Judge Jacobs said that this was irrelevant; the First-tier Tribunal's analysis of the discrimination involved was based on a comparison with the position of foster carers. The DWP argued that that there was no analogy between foster carers and people taking adults under an adult placement scheme. Judge Jacobs disagreed. The DWP argued that there could not be discrimination in situations like the claimant's because the adults placed with her may be entitled to HB personally. Thus, the local authority would be liable to pay HB in respect of the same room to both the claimant and to the adult placed with her. Judge Jacobs rejected this argument on the facts. In addition, he said:

"Moreover, the Upper Tribunal has no power on an appeal to quash a regulation for violating the Human Rights Act 1998. All that this tribunal can do is to disapply it: *Chief Adjudication Officer v Foster* [1993] AC 754. That power only applies to someone who is a victim: section 7(1) and *Langley v Bolton Metropolitan Borough Council* reported as *R(H) 6/05*. The claimant would be a victim when the room was standing empty, but not when it was occupied. Accordingly, the regulation would not be disapplied when an adult was placed with her and receiving housing benefit. It would only be disapplied at other times. That is why the Secretary of State's argument does not work."

An argument that the case was analogous to claims that were dismissed by the Supreme Court in *R (Carmichael and Rourke) v SSWP* [2016] UKSC 58; [2017] AACR 9 was also rejected.

The size criteria do not expressly include an additional bedroom where this is needed for any other reason. Note, however, that even before the amendments made on 4 December 2013, the government accepted, following the Court of Appeal decision in *Burnip v Birmingham CC and Others* [2012] EWCA Civ 629; [2013] AACR 7 (*Burnip, Trengove* and *Gorry*), that local authorities should allow an extra bedroom for children who are unable to share because of severe disabilities. See the discussion on p395. For the position prior to the amendments made on 1 April 2017, see the discussion on the legal challenges to the rules discussed below.

Challenges to the legal validity of the rules

The "social sector" rules were unsuccessfuly challenged in *R (MA and Others) v SSWP and Birmingham City Council* [2013] EWHC 2213 (QB) on the basis that the regulations discriminated against disabled people. The Court declined to strike out the regulations. However, in the proceedings, the DWP assured the Court that it would amend the HB Regs to conform with the *Gorry* judgment, which it did with effect from 4 December 2013.

In the claimants' appeal to the Court of Appeal in *R (MA and Others) v SSWP* [2014] EWCA Civ 13, the Court considered two grounds.

(1)   *Whether the reduction in eligible rent under reg B13 discriminates against disabled people under Art 14 of the ECHR when read with Art 1 of the First Protocol and, if so, was this justified.* The Court said that reg B13, if read in isolation, clearly discriminates against disabled people. However, it said (at para 40) that it was not realistic to confine the enquiry to reg B13 because the regulation is part of a package dealing with the problem of under-occupation. The Court decided that the discrimination was justified. The test (ie, whether the measure was "manifestly without reasonable foundation") was a stringent one. In addition, it said (at para 81) that "the need for the court to be cautious about finding unlawful

discrimination of a statutory instrument passed by affirmative resolution of Parliament is heightened by the fact that some of the principal complaints that are made by the claimants were expressly raised and discussed during the Parliamentary debates and rejected".

(2) *Whether the measures were introduced in breach of the Secretary of State's public sector equality duty under s149 Equality Act 2010 to have "due regard" to the need to eliminate discrimination and advance equality of opportunity for disabled people.* The Court decided that the process leading to the introduction of the measures did not breach this duty.

The claimants appeal to the Supreme Court was heard with *R (Rutherford and Others and 'A') v SSWP and New Forest DC and Others* (for which see the discussion on *R (Carmichael and Rourke)* below).

Rutherford and Others v SSWP [2014] EWHC 1613 (Admin) was an application for judicial review made on the basis that the "social sector" rules discriminate unlawfully against disabled children who need overnight care contrary to Art 14 of the European Convention on Human Rights, and that there is no rational justification for this. The claimants, who were unable to look after their severely disabled grandson themselves, lived with him in a specially adapted home which contained an extra bedroom for the grandson's overnight carers. Although DHPs were not initially awarded by the claimants' local authority, by the time the application for judicial review came to be heard by the Court, DHPs had been awarded to cover the HB shortfall for the period up to 6 April 2015. Refusing the application, the Court considered both *R (MA and Others)* and *Burnip*, noting that in *Burnip* DHPs did not cover the HB shortfall, but that in *R (MA and Others)* the budget for DHPs had been increased, and DHPs were accepted as part of the overall scheme considered and approved by Parliament. Stuart-Smith J said (at para 48): "The effect of *Burnip* and *MA* taken together is that, while a scheme including the use of DHPs as the conduit for payment may be justifiable, it will not be justified if it fails to provide suitable assurance of present and future payment in appropriate circumstances. For my part, I see no conflict of principle between *Burnip* and *MA* on this point; and it is apparent that the Court of Appeal in *MA* also saw none."

An attempt by a claimant housed under a Sanctuary Scheme to challenge the "social sector" rules was unsuccessful: *R (A) v SSWP* [2015] EWHC 159 (Admin). The claimant's HB had been reduced because she was deemed to be underoccupying her home under reg B13. The problem for the claimant was not that she required an additional bedroom, but that she would have to move from her home, specially adapted for her under a Sanctuary Scheme, because she could not afford the HB shortfall. Sanctuary Schemes provide for properties to be adapted (eg, by provision of a secured room) to provide security for people threatened with violence. Under the schemes, a quick police response is ensured, and specialist support is provided.

The claimant made an application for judicial review of the SSWP's failure to provide an appropriate exception for HB recipients who are victims of domestic violence living in accommodation adapted under the provisions of a Sanctuary Scheme. The application was made on the grounds that (1) the HB Regs discriminate against women contrary to Art 14 of the ECHR taken together with Arts 3 and/or 8 and/or Art 1 Protocol 1, (2) the SSWP had failed to comply with his public sector equality duty under s149 of the Equality Act 2010 and (3) the system (that is the combination of the HB Regs and DHPs) is unlawful because it carries, inherent within it, an unacceptable risk of breaches of Art 8 ECHR.

The Court accepted that the rules were discriminatory, but, following *R (MA)* and later decisions, decided that the discrimination was justified – ie, that the SSWP had established that it is not irrational or manifestly without reasonable foundation to have adopted a locally administered scheme of discretionary payments (DHPs) to deal with the issues for HB which arise for those helped under Sanctuary Schemes. The court also decided that the SSWP did enough to satisfy his public sector equality duty.

The appeals in *Rutherford and Others* and *R (A)* were heard together by the Court of Appeal: *R (Rutherford and Others and 'A') v SSWP and New Forest DC and Others* [2016] EWCA Civ 29. In both appeals, the Court decided that there was discrimination in reg B13 HB Regs, in breach of Art 14 of the ECHR, and that, despite the potential provision of DHPs, the discrimination was not objectively and reasonably justified. In 'A', the Court said that it was bound by the decision in *Burnip, Trengove and Gorry* and thus that the Secretary of State was not entitled to decide that the better way of providing for 'A' and other HB claimants in a similar position was by way of DHPs. The claimants in *Rutherford and Others* succeeded on the same basis. In addition, having considered the decision in *Mathieson v SSWP* [2015] UKSC 47, [2015] 1 WLR 3250, the Court said that the Secretary of State should have had specific regard to the best interests of disabled children who needed an overnight carer as a primary consideration when devising the regulations. The Secretary of State was given permission to appeal to the Supreme Court in both cases. Appeals to the Supreme Court in both cases were heard with the appeal in *R (MA)*: *R (Carmichael and Rourke) v SSWP* [2016] UKSC 58; [2017] AACR 9. In its judgment on 9 November 2016, the Supreme Court accepted that there was a reasonable foundation not to create a blanket exception from the provisions in reg B13 for anyone with a disability and to regard the DHP scheme as an appropriate remedy. However, this was not the end of the matter. Lord Toulson said (at para 42):

"... there are some people who suffer from disabilities such that they have a transparent medical need for an additional bedroom. *Burnip* and *Gorry* were in that category. Even before the decision in those cases there had been an amendment of the Regulations to '... include one additional bedroom in any case where the claimant or the claimant's partner is a person who requires overnight care (or in any case where both of them are)'. *Burnip* was such a case. *Gorry* was a case where children required separate bedrooms for disability reasons. In those cases, which were rightly identified by the Court of Appeal as ones where the individuals' medical condition was easy to recognise and gave rise to the need for a separate bedroom, there was no reasonable cause to apply the same cap on HB as if the bedrooms were truly under-occupied."

Going on to consider the case of Mrs Carmichael, who because of her disabilities could not share a bedroom with her husband, the Court decided that her position could not be distinguished from that of the *Gorry* children, who could not share a bedroom because of their disabilities. Going on to consider the Rutherfords' case, the Court said that their position could not be distinguished from that of *Burnip* – ie, the situaton between adults and children in need of an overnight carer was comparable. Applying the "manifestly without reasonable foundation" test, it therefore dismissed the SSWP's appeal in *Rutherford* and allowed the claimant's appeal in *Carmichael*. Note that reg B13 was then amended from 1 March 2017.

The Court found against all the other claimants, including, in a majority decision, in the case of *R (A)*. The claimant in *R (A)* took her case to the European Court of Human Rights. Her case was decided along with that of a claimant whose home had been specifically designed to accommodate her severely disabled daughter: *Case of JD and A v the United Kingdom* [2019] ECHR 753. 'A' made a complaint of sex discrimination as the victim of gender-based violence. 'JD' made an unsuccessful complaint of disability discrimination on the basis of her daughter's disability. In a majority decision, the court held that in A's case, there had been a violation of art 14 of the Convention in conjunction with art 1, Protocol 1. It said:

"103.   In the case of the second applicant *[A]* the Court notes that the legitimate aim of the present scheme – to incentivise those with 'extra' bedrooms to leave their homes for smaller ones – was in conflict with the aim of Sanctuary Schemes, which was to enable those at serious risk of domestic violence to remain in their own homes safely, should they wish to do so ... .

104.   Given those two legitimate but conflicting aims the Court considers that the impact of treating the second applicant, or others housed in Sanctuary Schemes, in the same way as any other Housing Benefit recipient affected by the impugned measure, was disproportionate in the sense of not corresponding to the legitimate aim of the measure. The Government have not provided any weighty reasons to justify the prioritisation of the aim of the present scheme over that of enabling victims of domestic violence who benefitted from protection in Sanctuary Schemes to remain in their own homes safely. In that context, the provision of DHP *[discretionary housing payments]* could not render proportionate the relationship between the means employed and the aim sought to be realised where it formed part of the scheme aimed at incentivising residents to leave their homes, as demonstrated by its identified disadvantages ...

105.   Accordingly, the imposition of Regulation B13 on this small and easily identifiable group has not been justified and is discriminatory. In coming to that conclusion, the Court also recalls that in the context of domestic violence it has found that States have a duty to protect the physical and psychological integrity of an individual from threats by other persons, including in situations where an individual's right to the enjoyment of his or home free of violent disturbance is at stake (see Kalucza v. Hungary, no. 57693/10, § 53, 24 April 2012)."

It is not yet known if the government intends to amend the rules in the light of the Court's decision. However, the Supreme Court's contrary decision in *R (A)* remains binding on decision makers and tribunals in Great Britain.

As well as seeking a judicial review, Mr Carmichael had appealed to the First-tier Tribunal against the local authority's decision to calculate his HB with a reduction of 14 per cent under para (3)(a). A three-judge panel dealt with the Secretary of State's appeal to the Upper Tribunal in *SSWP v Carmichael and Sefton BC (HB)* [2017] UKUT 174 (AAC). A lead case in more than 200 appeals, it considered the powers of the First-tier Tribunal where the ordinary application of the words of secondary legislation results in an undisputed breach of a claimant's Convention rights under the Human Rights Act 1998. The First-tier Tribunal had found in Mr Carmichael's favour. To avoid a breach of Convention rights, it had read words into reg B13(5)(a) (the "size criteria") to the effect that no 14 per cent reduction applied in Mr Carmichael's case. The Upper Tribunal decided that it should not have done so, but should have instead directed the local authority to calculate his HB without making a deduction of 14 per cent, giving the same outcome. It said:

"We conclude that in such cases, and in the light of *Mathieson* [*Mathieson v Secretary of State for Work and Pensions* [2015] UKSC 47] and similar authorities discussed below, courts and tribunals ultimately have the power to determine and so order or direct that to the extent that subordinate legislation is incompatible with a person's Convention rights it should not be given effect to in determining the person's lawful entitlement, or should be otherwise applied or disapplied in a way that does not breach the person's Convention rights. In our judgment that is a "relief or remedy" which a court or tribunal may make "within its powers as it considers just and appropriate" under section 8(1) of the 1998 Act. Indeed, an analogous power exists at common law, predating the 1998 Act (see *R v Lord Chancellor ex parte Witham* [1998] 2 WLR 849). For a court, especially one exercising the discretionary judicial review jurisdiction, it may be sufficient to make a declaration to the effect that the individual's rights have been breached. Statutory tribunals, however, are charged with making an actual decision on a person's lawful benefit entitlement."

Thus the Secretary of State's appeal was allowed but the Upper Tribunal made a decision to the same effect as the First-tier Tribunal.

The Secretary of State appealed to the Court of Appeal: *SSWP v Carmichael and Sefton Council* [2018] EWCA Civ 548. In the leading judgment, allowing the appeal, Flaux LJ said that the Upper Tribunal had exceeded what was permissible and should have limited itself to determining that reg B13 was incompatible with Convention rights. As regards to any loss Mr Carmichael had suffered as a consequence, the remedy was to bring a claim for damages in the civil courts under s8(2) HRA 1998. He said:

"The answer to the conclusion of the Upper Tribunal that this would render any remedy for violation of Convention rights ineffective or illusory is the twofold one which Mr Eadie QC gave: (i) that is clearly what Parliament intended by providing that the remedy of damages under section 8(2) could only be awarded by a court and the executive has not chosen to expand the powers of tribunals under section 7(11) to enable them to award damages; and (ii) in the present case, because the first respondent had received DHPs to make up the shortfall in housing benefit, he would not appear to have suffered any loss as a consequence of the violation which would sound in damages under section 8(2). Whilst as the Supreme Court held in Carmichael, that is not an answer to whether or not there was a violation, it seems to me that it is an answer to whether or not the first respondent requires a remedy beyond a declaration that Regulation B13 as originally enacted was incompatible with his Convention rights. He does not, in marked contrast to Mr Mathieson [in *Mathieson v SSWP* [2015] UKSC 47; [2015] 1 WLR 3250]."

The dissenting judge, Leggatt LJ did not agree. He held that the First-tier Tribunal and the Upper Tribunal had the power, and the duty, to disapply and treat as having no effect, provisions of the HB Regs in so far as those provisions, when applied in calculating Mr Carmichael's HB, violated a Convention right and are therefore overridden by the HRA 1998. Here the local authority was applying provisions of subordinate legislation of a kind which a court or tribunal is entitled and obliged by s6(1) HRA 1998 not to enforce or apply in so far as they are incompatible with a Convention right. He said:

"Not giving effect to provisions of subordinate legislation in an individual case where to do so would violate a Convention right does not involve "re-writing" the legislation. It shows a proper respect for constitutional boundaries by leaving it to Parliament or to the Secretary of State with delegated legislative authority to decide what changes to make to avoid further violations of Convention rights."

Note that although Mr Carmichael did not appeal, two further claimants were granted "leap frog" certificates by the Upper Tribunal under s14A TCEA 2007 to apply directly to the Supreme Court for permission to appeal, to challenge the correctness of the Court of Appeal's decision in *SSWP v Carmichael and Sefton BC*: *SSWP v RR and Sefton BC* (*CH 4674/2014*) and *SSWP v (1) DL, (2) Redcar and Cleveland BC (HB)* [2018] UKUT 355 (AAC). The appellant in *SSWP v RR* was granted permission to appeal and the appeal was heard on 3 July 2019. Judgement was given on 13 November 2019: *RR v SSWP* [2019] UKSC 52. In a unanimous decision, the Supreme Court held that secondary legislation which is made under powers in the primary legislation may be disapplied or disregarded if it is incompatible with Convention rights. Thus the Court allowed the claimant's appeal decided that RR's HB was to be recalculated without a 14 per cent reduction.

While appeals in the Upper Tribunal and the Courts are pending, claimants who have been affected by the "social sector" rules who consider that they have not been allowed enough rooms under the size criteria should pursue appeals to the First-tier Tribunal and Upper Tribunal, citing *Burnip, Trengove and Gorry, Carmichael* and *Rutherford*. In relevant cases, it may also be possible to argue that the local authority has wrongly identified a room as a "bedroom".

[¹ Maximum rent

13.–(1) The maximum rent shall be determined in accordance with paragraphs (2) to (8) where–

(a) a local authority has applied for a determination in accordance with regulation 14 (requirement to refer to rent officers), a redetermination in accordance with regulation 15 or 16, or a substitute determination or substitute redetermination in accordance with regulation 17 and a rent officer has made a determination, redetermination, substitute determination or substitute redetermination in exercise of the Housing Act functions; or

(b) an authority is not required to apply to the rent officer for a determination because–

(i) regulation 14(2)(a) applies; or

(ii) regulation 14(2)(b) applies because paragraph 2(2) of Schedule 2 applies.

(2) In a case where the rent officer has determined a claim-related rent, but is not required to notify the relevant authority of a local reference rent or a single room rent, the maximum rent shall be that claim-related rent.

(3) Subject to the limit specified in paragraph (4), in a case where the rent officer has determined both a local reference rent of which he is required to notify the relevant authority and a claim-related rent, the maximum rent shall be the local reference rent.

(4) In a case to which paragraph 8 of Schedule 3 to the Consequential Provisions Regulations applies, where the rent officer has determined and is required to notify the relevant authority of a local reference rent the maximum rent shall not exceed twice that local reference rent.

(5)   Subject to paragraph (6), in the case of a young individual–

(a)   except where sub-paragraph (b) applies, where the rent officer has determined a single room rent and is required to notify the relevant authority of it, the maximum rent shall not exceed that single room rent;

(b)   where–

    (i)   the rent officer has determined a single room rent and a claim-related rent and is required to notify the authority of them;

    (ii)   the claim-related rent includes payment in respect of meals; and

    (iii)   the single room rent is greater than the claim-related rent less an amount in respect of meals determined in accordance with paragraph 2 of Part 1 of Schedule 1 (ineligible service charges),

the maximum rent shall not exceed the claim-related rent less that amount in respect of meals.

(6)   Paragraph (5) shall not apply in the case of a claimant–

(a)   to whom paragraph 4 of Schedule 3 to the Consequential Provisions Regulations (saving provision) applies;

(b)   to whom paragraph 14 of Schedule 3 (severe disability premium) applies; or

(c)   where a non-dependant resides with him.

(7)   Where the maximum rent is derived from–

(a)   a claim-related rent and the notification under paragraph 9(1)(c) of Schedule 1 to the Rent Officers Order states that an ineligible amount in respect of meals has been included in that claim-related rent; or

(b)   a local reference rent and the notification under paragraph 9(1)(da) of Schedule 1 to the Rent Officers Order states that an ineligible amount in respect of meals has been included in that local reference rent,

in determining the maximum rent the relevant authority shall deduct an amount determined in accordance with paragraph 2 of Schedule 1 to these Regulations in respect of meals.

(8)   This regulation is subject to regulations 13ZA (protection on death and 13 week protection) and 13ZB (change in reckonable rent).

(9)

In this regulation–

"claim-related rent" means the rent notified by the rent officer under paragraph 9(1) of Schedule 1 to the Rent Officers Order;

"local reference rent" means the rent determined by a rent officer under paragraph 4 of Schedule 1 to the Rent Officers Order.]

Modifications

Reg 13 was substituted by reg 6 Housing Benefit (Local Housing Allowance and Information Sharing) Amendment Regulations 2007 SI No.2868 as from 7 April 2008, save that for a person to whom reg 1(5) of those regulations applied (see p1812), the amendments came into force on the day on or after 7 April 2008 when the first of the events specified in reg 1(6) applied to her/him, or on 6 April 2009 if none had before that date.

A different version of reg 13 is substituted for some claimants entitled to HB on 1 January 1996. See Sch 3 paras 4 and 5(2) HB&CTB(CP) Regs on p1776.

Reg 13 applies as modified by Sch 3 para 8 HB&CTB(CP) Regs (see p1785) for some claimants entitled to HB on or before 5 October 1997.

Amendment

1.   Substituted by reg 6 of SI 2007 No 2868 as from 7.4.08 (or if reg 1(5) of that SI applies, on the day on or after 7.4.08 when the first of the events specified in reg 1(6) applies, or from 6.4.09 if none have before that date).

Definitions

"non-dependant" – see reg 3.

"Rent Officers Order" – see reg 2(1).

"single room rent" – see reg 2(1).

"young individual" – see reg 2(1).

General Note

Reg 13 deals with the calculation of the claimant's "maximum rent" for HB purposes under the "local reference rent" scheme. The significance of the maximum rent is that the claimant's "eligible rent" cannot exceed it: reg

12C. The application of the maximum rent can be delayed in the circumstances set out in reg 13ZA (protection on death and 13 week protection). Note that there are now only a limited number of situations in which HB is calculated by reference to the local reference rent scheme. These include if the claimant lives in a hostel, houseboat, mobile home or caravan, or the claimant's rent includes board and attendance, or where the claim was made before 7 April 2008: see regs 13(1), 13C(5)(a)–(e) and 14(1) HB Regs.

The maximum rent is derived from rent officer's determinations. The rent officer's determinations are extremely difficult to attack in judicial review proceedings and cannot, by virtue of Sch 7 para 6(2)(c) CSPSSA 2000, be appealed to the First-tier Tribunal. For further discussion of challenges to rent officers' decisions and of the possible human rights issues involved, see reg 16 for redeterminations by a rent officer and the Rent Officers (Housing Benefit Functions) Order 1997 on p879. Although there is no right of appeal to the First-tier Tribunal against a decision of the rent officer, the claimant can appeal the local authority's decision on HB entitlement (the "outcome" decision) and, as such, can challenge the factual basis upon which the rent officer decision was made – eg, the number of occupiers given to the rent officer by the local authority: *Bexley LB v LD (HB)* [2010] UKUT 79 (AAC) and *SK v South Hams DC (HB)* [2010] UKUT 129 (AAC); [2010] AACR 40.

Summary of the maximum rent calculation

One of the difficult aspects of reg 13 is the terminology applied to the various figures used to calculate maximum rent. The terms are summarised here, with cross-reference to other commentary. Not all the various terms will be relevant in every case.

Maximum rent is calculated as follows:

(1)   The authority applies for a rent officer determination under reg 14 (unless not required to do so in the circumstances specified in para (1)(b) – broadly where there are existing determinations it can use): reg 13(1).

(2)   The following rent determinations are made by the rent officer:

(a)   A significantly high rent (SHR) determination is made if the claimant's rent is significantly higher than a reasonable rent: Sch 1 para 1 of the Rent Officer (Housing Benefit Functions) Order 1997 or its Scottish equivalent, which are referred to collectively as the RO Orders in this commentary.

(b)   A size-related rent determination is made (SizeRR) under Sch 1 para 2 of the RO Orders if it is decided that the property exceeds the size criteria set out in Sch 2 of the RO Orders. Note that no size-related rent determination can be made if the determination relates to mooring charges for houseboat or payments in respect of the site on which a caravan or a mobile home stands: Sch 4 of the RO Orders.

(c)   An exceptionally high rent determination is made (EHR) if the rent officer decides under Sch 1 para 3 of the RO Orders that it needs to be given.

(d)   The local reference rent (LRR) is calculated under Sch 1 para 4 of the RO Orders. The LRR is broadly the mid-point of reasonable market rents for comparable assured tenancies in the same area (called the "broad rental market area (local reference rent)").

(e)   The single room rent (SRR) is calculated under Sch 1 para 5 of the RO Orders. It is used in the calculation of the maximum rent of a "young individual" (broadly, most single claimants under 35 but see the full definition in reg 2(1) for exceptions). It is assessed on the basis of the mid-point of reasonable rents for comparable assured tenancies in the same area (called the "broad rental market area (local reference rent)") comprising a single room occupied exclusively, with a shared, toilet, bathroom, kitchen and living room and which does not include payments for board and attendance. Note: the "young individual" age limit was 25 prior to 1 January 2012.

(3)   The claim-related rent (CRR) is the lowest of the determinations in (2)(a)–(c) above, or if none of them are determined, the rent payable under the tenancy: Sch 1 para 6 of the RO Orders. The rent officer notifies the authority of the CRR (and if an ineligible amount in respect of meals has been included) and, if lower, the LRR or SRR.

(4)   Unless Sch 3 paras 4 and 5 HB&CTB(CP) Regs apply (the "pre-January 1996" scheme), maximum rent is calculated by the authority using the determinations notified in (3) above: reg 13(2)–(7). Maximum rent is the lowest of the CRR, the LRR, or if relevant the SRR unless the claimant has transitional protection, for which, see Sch 3 para 8 HB&CTB(CP) Regs (on p1802) and the commentary to paras (2) to (4).

(5)   The authority decides whether the use of the maximum rent in calculating HB entitlement can be delayed: reg 13ZA.

The eligible rent is then calculated by the authority in accordance with reg 12C.

Analysis

Paragraph (1): The general rule

Reg 13 applies where an authority has applied for a rent officer determination under reg 14. It also applies where it is not required to do so because an application was made in respect of a claim within the previous 52 weeks (sub-para (b)(ii)) or where the dwelling is a hostel and a determination has been made within the previous 12 months in respect of a similar dwelling in that hostel and there has been no change of circumstances in relation to the similar dwelling (sub-para (b)(i)). In both of these situations, there will already be rent officer determinations the authority can use. See the commentary to reg 14 on p400 for when an authority must apply to the rent officer. The maximum rent is then to be determined as set out in the paras that follow.

Once maximum rent is set, HB is calculated using this figure until the next time the authority is required to apply to the rent officer for a determination. This is usually annually: reg 14(1)(f) and (g). Note, however, that where a claimant's rent liability is reduced to an amount lower than the maximum rent, maximum rent can be reduced: reg 13ZB.

Paragraphs (2) to (8): Calculation of maximum rent
These set out the bases on which the maximum rent is calculated. Generally, the maximum rent is the lowest of the CRR, the LRR or, in the case of a "young individual", the SRR (see the General Note above). Note that a restriction can be delayed in some circumstances under reg 13ZA and that some changes in rent can be taken into account under reg 13ZB: para (8).

Paras (2) to (4). The effect of paras (2) and (3) is that unless para (5) applies, maximum rent is the lower of the CRR and the LRR. There is transitional protection for some claimants. A 50 per cent taper is preserved in relation to certain categories of claimants (broadly, those continuously entitled to, and in receipt of, HB for the same property since 5 October 1997): see para 8 Sch 3 HB&CTB(CP) Regs on p1802. For protected claimants, para (3) as modified provides that the maximum rent is the LRR plus half the difference between the CRR and the LRR. In this case, the maximum rent cannot be more than twice the LRR: para (4).

For example, if the rent officer's CRR for the dwelling is £100 and the rent officer's LRR figure is £40, the maximum rent is £70 if the claimant has the transitional protection but only £40 if s/he does not have it.

Paras (5) and (6). Para (5) applies where the claimant is a "young individual" as defined in reg 2(1) (broadly most single claimants aged under 35 but see the full definition and exceptions in reg 2(1) and the commentary on p246) and the rent officer has notified a SRR. The maximum rent is restricted to the SRR, or the CRR minus any payments included for meals if this is lower. Note that someone does not count as a young individual if her/his landlord is a registered housing association, or if s/he is a "person who requires overnight care" or a "qualifying parent or carer" (also defined in reg 2(1)), or if s/he is under 22 and was in the care of, or under the supervision of, a local authority under specified provisions after aged 16, or was provided with accommodation by a local authority under s20 Children Act 1989, or if s/he is under 25 and living in a homeless hostel in specified circumstances or is an offender subject to specific multi-agency risk management arrangements: see sub-paras (a) to (j) of the definition.

The effect of this provision is softened by para (6), which provides that para (5) is not applicable where the "pre-January 1996" scheme rules apply or where the claimant qualifies for a severe disability premium or has a non-dependent residing with her/him, for which see reg 3. It is not clear why the exception for those to whom the "pre-January 1996" scheme rules apply was felt necessary as a different version of reg 13 is substituted for these claimants: Sch 3 paras 4 and 5(2) HB&CTB(CP) Regs.

From 1 January 2012, the definition of "young individual" was amended and the age limit was increased from 25 to 35. Prior to that date, if a claimant was aged at least 25, para (5) did not apply and her/his maximum rent could not be restricted to the SRR. However, para (5) *will* apply the next time the local authority is required to apply to the rent officer for determinations under reg 14 if the claimant has not yet reached aged 35 and comes within the definition of "young individual".

Paragraph (7): Deductions
This sets out the rules for deducting amounts for meals from the maximum rent, where an ineligible amount in respect of these has been included in the CRR or LRR. In a decision concerning the old form of the rules, in *Shepherd v Dundee CC* [2002] SLT 1427, CS(IH), the claimant asserted that where eligible rent had already been restricted to a sum less than the contractual rent, it was not open to the local authority to make a further deduction in respect of the cost of board. Unsurprisingly, the court rejected that submission (paras 14–15).

[¹ Protection on death and 13 week protection

13ZA–(1) In a case where the claimant occupies a dwelling which is the same as that occupied by him at the date of death of a linked person, the maximum rent shall be either–

 (a) the maximum rent which applied before the death occurred; or

 (b) in a case where there was no maximum rent, the reckonable rent due before the death occurred,

 (c) for a period of 12 months from the date of such a death.

[² (2) For the purpose of paragraph (1), a claimant is treated as occupying the dwelling if–

 (a) any of paragraphs (13), (13D) (with (13E) where applicable) or (13G) of regulation 7 (circumstances in which a person is or is not to be treated as occupying a dwelling as his home) is satisfied and for that purpose those paragraphs shall have effect as if sub-paragraph (b) of those paragraphs were omitted; or

    (b)   any of paragraphs (17), (17C) or (17D) of regulation 7 is satisfied and for that purpose those paragraphs shall have effect as if sub-paragraph (b) of paragraph (16) of that regulation were omitted.]

(3)   Subject to paragraph (4), where the relevant authority is satisfied that the claimant or a linked person was able to meet the financial commitments for his dwelling when they were entered into, there shall be no maximum rent during the first 13 weeks of the claimant's award of housing benefit.

(4)   Paragraph (3) shall not apply where a claimant or the claimant's partner was previously entitled to benefit in respect of an award of housing benefit which fell wholly or partly less than 52 weeks before the commencement of the claimant's current award of housing benefit.]

Modifications

A different version of reg 13ZA is substituted for some claimants living in exempt accommodation or entitled to HB on 1 January 1996. It concerns restrictions on rent increases, not protection on death or 13 week protection. See Sch 3 paras 4 and 5(3) HB&CTB(CP) Regs on p1776.

Amendments

1.   Inserted by reg 6 of SI 2007 No 2868 as from 7.4.08 (or if reg 1(5) of that SI applies, on the day on or after 7.4.08 when the first of the events specified in reg 1(6) applies, or from 6.4.09 if none have before that date).

2.   Substituted by reg 2(4) of SI 2016 No 624 as from 28.7.16, subject to transitional provision in reg 5 of SI 2016 No 624.

Definitions

"child" – see reg 2(1).
"claimant" – see reg 2(1).
"dwelling" – see reg 2(4) and s137(1) SSCBA.
"linked person" – see reg 2(1).
"maximum rent" – see reg 13.
"partner" – see reg 2(1).
"reckonable rent" – see reg 2(1).
"young person" – see reg 2(1).

Analysis

Delay in application of the maximum rent

Reg 13ZA provides for limited protection for two classes of claimants whose eligible rent is to be calculated under the "local reference rent" scheme.

    Paras (1) and (2): Protection on death. Para (1) provides a degree of protection for the recently bereaved. If a claimant continues to occupy a home which s/he occupied at the time a "linked person" died, the maximum rent under reg 13 that applied at the date of death continues to apply for 12 months from the date of death. In cases where there was no maximum rent in force (eg, if a new claim for HB was made following the death), the maximum rent is the "reckonable rent". Again, this protection lasts for 12 months from the date of death. "Reckonable rent" means the payments a person is liable to make in respect of the dwelling s/he occupies as her/his home and which are eligible (or but for reg 13 would be eligible) for HB: reg 2(1).

    A "linked person" for these purposes is a member of the claimant's family (defined in s137(1) SSCBA – see p17), a partner in a polygamous marriage or a child or young person for whom s/he or a partner is responsible and who lives in the same household, or a relative of the claimant or her/his partner who occupies the same dwelling without a separate right to do so: reg 2(1). As to the last of these categories, "relative" is also defined in reg 2(1). The deceased person need not have been residing with the claimant, provided only that s/he occupied the same dwelling. Oddly, reg 3(4) specifies when a person "resides with" another for the purposes of the definition of "linked person", but the term used in the definition is "occupies the same dwelling ... whether or not they reside with him". In this context, "occupies the same dwelling" arguably means someone living within the same building, provided that the living units of the claimant and the deceased are not completely self-contained. It might cover those who were sharing only a toilet, or some similar part of the accommodation. The relative should not have had a separate right of occupation. If the relative had her/his own tenancy from a landlord, the claimant cannot therefore take advantage of this provision. However, if the claimant and the relative were joint tenants, it could be argued that the relative's right of occupation was not "separate" because it was held jointly with the claimant. By para (2), "occupation" of a home for the purposes of para (1) can include deemed occupation under reg 7(13), (13D) (including any extension under (13E)), (13G), (17), (17C) or (17D), that is, where someone is treated as occupying a dwelling while temporarily absent from it. The claimant need not, however, comply with sub-para (b) of those paragraphs, so it does not matter if the home was let or sublet.

Paras (3) and (4): 13-week protection. Para (3) postpones the application of the maximum rent during the first 13 weeks of an HB award if the claimant or a "linked person" (see above) was able to meet the financial commitments for the dwelling (which will include things like bills as well as the rent) at the time they were taken on. By para (4), the protection in para (3) does not apply where the claimant or her/his partner has been entitled to HB at some time within the 52 weeks prior to the commencement of the claimant's current HB award.

[¹ Change in reckonable rent

13ZB.–(1)   In a case where–

(a)   the authority has determined a maximum rent under regulation 13 or 13ZA; and

(b)   during the period for which that maximum rent applies the reckonable rent in respect of the dwelling by reference to which that maximum rent was determined is reduced to a sum which is less than that maximum rent,

the maximum rent shall be reduced to an amount equal to the reduced reckonable rent.

(2)   This paragraph applies in a case where–

(a)   a rent officer has made a determination in exercise of the Housing Act functions pursuant to an application by an authority under regulation 14(1)(e) (pre-tenancy determination);

(b)   subsequent to that determination the reckonable rent for that dwelling is changed; and

(c)   a maximum rent is to be determined in relation to a claim for housing benefit by a claimant.

(3)   In a case to which paragraph (2) applies, where the reckonable rent is reduced to a figure below the figure that would have been the maximum rent if the reckonable rent had not changed, the maximum rent shall be the reckonable rent as so reduced.

(4)   In any other case to which paragraph (2) applies, the authority shall treat the reckonable rent to be that applicable to the determination by the rent officer referred to in paragraph (2)(a).]

Amendment

1.   Inserted by reg 6 of SI 2007 No 2868 as from 7.4.08 (or if reg 1(5) of that SI applies, on the day on or after 7.4.08 when the first of the events specified in reg 1(6) applies, or from 6.4.09 if none have before that date).

Definitions

"claimant" – see reg 2(1).

"dwelling" – see reg 2(4) and s137(1) SSCBA.

"maximum rent" – see reg 13.

"reckonable rent" – see reg 2(1).

Analysis

Reg 13ZB deals with the effect on the maximum rent of changes in the claimant's "reckonable rent" during an award of HB. "Reckonable rent" means the payments a person is liable to make in respect of the dwelling s/he occupies as her/his home and which are eligible (or but for reg 13 would be eligible) for HB: reg 2(1). Generally the maximum rent is only changed when the local authority is required to apply to the rent officer for a determination under reg 14, usually annually, but under para (1), where the claimant's reckonable rent reduces during the award to a figure below the maximum rent figure determined by the authority under either reg 13 or reg 13ZA, the maximum rent is set to an amount equal to the new lower reckonable rent figure.

Para (2) deals with the situation where a maximum rent is to be determined after a claimant has obtained a pre-tenancy determination under reg 14(1)(e) and the reckonable rent is subsequently changed. If the reckonable rent is lower than the maximum rent would have been had the reckonable rent not changed, the maximum rent is the reckonable rent: para (3). In any other case (ie, where the reckonable rent is now higher than the maximum rent would have been), the authority must treat the reckonable rent to be that determined by the rent officer in the application for the pre-tenancy determination.

[¹ When a maximum rent (LHA) is to be determined

13C.–(1)   A relevant authority shall determine a maximum rent (LHA) in accordance with regulation 13D (determination of a maximum rent (LHA)) in any case where paragraphs (2) or (3) apply.

(2)   This paragraph applies where a relevant authority has received–

(a)   a claim on which a rent allowance may be awarded, where the date of claim falls on or after 7th April 2008;

(b)   relevant information regarding a claim on which a rent allowance may be awarded, where the date of claim falls on or after 7th April 2008;

(c)   in relation to an award of housing benefit where the eligible rent was determined without reference to regulation 13A or 13D, a notification of a change of dwelling (as defined in regulation 2) where the change occurs on or after 7th April 2008; or

(d)   in relation to an award of housing benefit where a maximum rent (LHA) was determined in accordance with regulation 13D–

    (i)   notification of a change of a kind which affects the category of dwelling applicable to the claim;

    (ii)   notification of the death of a linked person, where the notification does not fall within head (i); [⁵]

    (iii)   notification of a change of dwelling.[⁵ or

    (iv)   notification of a change of a kind which affects the amount of the claimant's cap rent as determined in accordance with regulation 13D (determination of a maximum rent (LHA)).]

[⁴ (3)   This paragraph applies on 1st April in any year.]

[⁴ (4)]

(5)   This regulation does not apply in a case where–

[³ (a)   the landlord is–

    (i)   a registered social landlord,

    (ii)   a non-profit registered provider of social housing, or

    (iii)   in relation to a dwelling which is social housing (within the meaning of sections 68 to 77 of the Housing and Regeneration Act 2008), a profit-making registered provider of social housing;]

(b)   paragraph 4(1)(b) of Schedule 3 to the Consequential Provisions Regulations (savings provision) applies;

(c)   the tenancy is an excluded tenancy of a type [² mentioned in any of paragraphs 4 to 11] of Schedule 2;

(d)   the claim or award relates to–

    (i)   periodical payments of kind falling within regulation 12(1) (rent) which a person is liable to make in relation to a houseboat, caravan or mobile home which he occupies as his home; or

    (ii)   rent payable in relation to a hostel; or

(e)   rent under the tenancy is attributable to board and attendance, and–

    (i)   the relevant authority has made an application to the rent officer in accordance with regulation 13D(10) (board and attendance determination), regulation 15 (applications to the rent officer for determinations) or regulation 17 (substitute determinations or substitute redeterminations); and

    (ii)   the rent officer has determined that a substantial part of the rent under the tenancy is fairly attributable to board and attendance and has notified the relevant authority of this in accordance with article 4C, 4D or 4E of the Rent Officers Order.

(6)   In this regulation–

[⁴]

"registered social landlord" has the same meaning as in Part 1 of the Housing Act 1996 or, in Scotland, sections 57 and 59 of the Housing (Scotland) Act 2001.]

Modifications

Reg 13C is modified by Sch 10 para 7 (see p707). This applies only to former Pathfinder Authorities who administered the pilot local housing allowance scheme.

Amendments
1.   Inserted by reg 7 of SI 2007 No 2868 as from 7.4.08 (or if reg 1(5) of that SI applies, on the day on or after 7.4.08 when the first of the events specified in reg 1(6) applies, or from 6.4.09 if none have before that date).
2.   Amended by reg 4(4)(a) of SI 2008 No 586 as from 7.4.08.
3.   Substituted by art 4 and Sch 1 para 52 of SI 2010 No 671 as from 1.4.10.
4.   Amended by reg 3(2)(b)–(d) of SI 2012 No 3040 as from 1.1.13.
5.   Amended by reg 3(2)(a) of SI 2012 No 3040 as from 1.4.13.

Definitions
"change of dwelling" – see reg 2(1).
"hostel" – see reg 2(1).
"linked person" – see reg 2(1).
"relevant information" – see reg 2(1).
"rent allowance" – see s134(1B) SSAA 1992.

General Note
The starting point for deciding whether maximum rent (LHA) is to be calculated under reg 13D (the "LHA" rules), and hence eligible rent under reg 12D, is reg 13C. Reg 13C prescribes the circumstances in which this must be done, and those where the "LHA" rules do not apply.
Unless any of the circumstances in para (5) apply, broadly reg 13C will apply if, on or after 7 April 2008, a claim for HB is made or a claimant with an award of HB moves to a new home, and in both cases, HB would be paid as a rent allowance. Thus, reg 13C can apply if the claimant lives in private rented accommodation. It does not apply if the landlord is a registered social landlord or a non-profit registered provider of social housing (see reg 13C(5)(a)(i) and (ii)), and does not apply to the social housing of a profit-making registered provider of social housing: reg 13C(5)(a).
Claimants whose HB was assessed under the "local reference rent" rules before 7 April 2008, are effectively provided with transitional protection until there is a new claim (ie, following a break in claim) or the claimant moves. See p400 for a discussion of the issues.

Analysis
Paragraphs (1), (2) and (3): When maximum rent (LHA) is to be determined under reg 13D
Paras (2) and (3) set out the circumstances in which a maximum rent (LHA) must be determined under reg 13D, unless excepted by para (5).
Para (2)(a) and (b): Claims. These sub-paras apply where a claim for HB is received or an authority has received "relevant information" about a claim on which a rent allowance may be awarded. In both cases, the date of claim must fall on or after 7 April 2008. Relevant information is defined in reg 2(1) as "information or evidence forwarded to the authority by an appropriate DWP office regarding a claim on which rent allowance may be awarded, which completes the transfer of all information or evidence held by the appropriate DWP office relating to that claim" – eg, where the claim for HB has been made with a claim to the DWP for IS, JSA, ESA or PC.
Para (2)(c): Change of dwelling to one where the "local housing allowance" rules apply. Sub-para (c) applies where the authority has received notification of a change of dwelling during an award of HB where eligible rent was determined otherwise than by reference to reg 13D or the local housing allowance pilot rules that applied in former Pathfinder areas. By the definition of "change of dwelling" in reg 2(1), the change must be to a dwelling in respect of which the authority may make a rent allowance. See sub-para (d)(iii) where there is a change of dwelling and eligible rent was already determined by reference to reg 13D. Note that the reference to reg 13A in para (2)(c) is to the regulation under which maximum rent was determined under the pilot local housing allowance rules in Pathfinder areas between late 2003 and 7 April 2008. See p514 of the 20th edition of this work for details.
Para (2)(d): Other changes. Sub-para (d) only applies where there is an award of HB made on the basis of a maximum rent (LHA) and one of the circumstances in sub-paras (d)(i) to (iv) occurs. In these circumstances, the local authority is required to determine a new maximum rent (LHA). Those in sub-paras (d)(i) to (iii) are self-explanatory. The "cap rent" referred to in sub-para (d)(iv) is broadly the amount of rent the claimant is liable, or treated as liable, to pay (including service charges): reg 13D(12).
Para (3). Para (3) ensures that even if none of the circumstances in para (2) have occurred, maximum rent (LHA) is reassessed annually, on 1 April in any year, based on the local housing allowance (see the summary on p391) that is then appropriate. Note that prior to 1 January 2013, the reassessment in any particular claimant's case took place on the anniversary of the "LHA date" relevant in her/his case – ie, the date by reference to which the local housing allowance used to determine the maximum rent (LHA) for her/him was identified.
Paragraph (5): The exceptions
Para (5) sets out a number of exceptions. Note that some of these are also excluded from other rent restriction schemes.
(1)   The landlord is a registered social landlord (since 1 April 2010, this applies in Wales and Scotland only) or a non-profit or a profit making registered provider of social housing (in England only): sub-para (a).

Lettings by profit-making registered providers of social housing are only excepted if the claimant's dwelling is "social housing" within the meaning of ss68 to 77 Housing and Regeneration Act 2008 (H&RA 2008), that is, low cost rental accommodation (ie, accommodation that is available to rent at below the market rate) and low cost ownership accommodation (ie, accommodation occupied or made available to occupy in accordance with shared ownership or equity percentage arrangements or shared ownership trusts) that is available to people whose needs are not adequately served by the commercial housing market. A "registered provider of social housing" is a person or body registered by the Homes and Communities Agency (the Regulator of Social Housing): s80 and Chapter 3 H&RA 2008. See www.gov.uk/government/publications/current-registered-providers-of-social-housing for the list of the current registered providers. "Registered social landlord" is defined in para (6). Note that lettings by the landlords listed in sub-para (a) may also be excluded from the "local reference rent" scheme if they come within the definition of a registered housing association (in reg 2(1): reg 14(2)(b) and Sch 2 para 3(1)(a) and (1A).

(2) The claimant occupies "exempt accommodation" as defined in Sch 3 para 4(10) HB&CTB(CP) Regs: sub-para (b) and Sch 3 para 4(1)(b) HB&CTB(CP) Regs. Broadly, this is supported accommodation. Note that such lettings are also excluded from the "local reference rent" scheme, but may be affected by the "pre-January 1996" rules found in Sch 3 paras 4 and 5 HB&CTB(CP) Regs.

This exception does not cover the "exempt claimants" set out in Sch 3 para 4(1)(a) HB&CTB(CP) Regs. Such claimants lose their transitional protection under the "pre-January 1996" rules in any of the circumstances of reg 13C(2)(a) to (c). See the commentary to Sch 3 para 4 HB&CTB(CP) Regs on p1778.

(3) The tenancy is an "excluded tenacy" under Sch 2 paras 4 to 11 HB Regs: sub-para (c). See the commentary to those provisions for details. Tenancies excluded under Sch 2 para 3 are not covered, but may come within the exception for registered social landlords and providers of social housing above. Tenancies excluded under Sch 2 para 12 (shared ownership tenancies) are not covered, but may come within other exceptions in reg 13C(5) – eg, where the landlord is a registered social landlord or provider of social housing. Note that tenancies excluded under Sch 2 paras 4 to 10 and 12 are also excluded from the "local reference rent" scheme, and that those excluded under Sch 2 para 11 generally are. Tenancies under Sch 2 paras 4 to 11 where the landlord is not a registered housing association, as well as shared ownership tenancies, are also excluded from the "social sector" scheme.

(4) Periodical payments are made in relation to a houseboat, caravan or mobile home which is occupied as a home, or rent is payable in relation to a hostel: sub-para (d). For a discussion of the meaning of "periodical payments", see the commentary to reg 12(1).

(5) Rent is attributable to board and attendance: sub-para (e). The authority must have made an application to the rent officer for a board and attendance determination under the provisions cited and the rent officer must have determined that a substantial part of the rent is "fairly attributable" to board and attendance. If so, the claimant's eligible rent may still be restricted under regs 12C and 13. See reg 14(1).

[¹ **Determination of a maximum rent (LHA)**

13D.–(1)   Subject to paragraph (3) to (11), the maximum rent (LHA) shall be the local housing allowance determined by the rent officer by virtue of article 4B(2A) or (4) of the Rent Officers Order which is applicable to–

(a)   the broad rental market area in which the dwelling to which the claim or award of housing benefit relates is situated at the relevant date; and

(b)   the category of dwelling which applies at the relevant date in accordance with paragraph (2).

(2)   The category of dwelling which applies is–

(a)   the category specified in paragraph 1(1)(a) of Schedule 3B to the Rent Officers Order (one bedroom shared accommodation) where–

(i)   the claimant is a young individual who has no non-dependant residing with him and to whom paragraph 14 of Schedule 3 (severe disability premium) does not apply; or

(ii)   paragraph (b) does not apply because neither sub-paragraph (b)(i) nor (ii) are satisfied in the claimant's case and neither the claimant nor his partner (where he has one) is a person to whom paragraph 14 of Schedule 3 (severe disability premium) applies, or to whom the circumstances in any of paragraphs (b) to (f) [⁶ or (i)] of the definition of young individual applies (certain care leavers);

(b)   except where paragraph (a)(i) applies, the category specified in paragraph 1(1)(b) of Schedule 3B to the Rent Officers Order (one bedroom self-contained accommodation) where that applies in the claimant's case at the relevant date in accordance with the size criteria [² as set out in paragraph (3)] and–

     (i)   the claimant (together with his partner where he has one) has the exclusive use of two or more rooms; or

     (ii)   the claimant (together with his partner where he has one) has the exclusive use of one room, a bathroom and toilet and a kitchen or facilities for cooking,

and in this sub-paragraph "room" means a bedroom or room suitable for living in except for a room which the claimant shares with any person other than a member of his household, a non-dependant of his, or a person who pays rent to him or his partner;

  (c)   in any other case, the category which corresponds with the number of bedrooms to which the claimant is entitled in accordance with [⁵ paragraphs (3) to (3B)] [³ [⁴ up to a maximum of four bedrooms]].

  (3)   The claimant shall be entitled to one bedroom for each of the following categories of occupier (and each occupier shall come within the first category only which applies to him)–

  [⁸ (za) a member of a couple who cannot share a bedroom;

  (zb) a member of a couple who can share a bedroom;]

  (a)   a couple [⁸];

  (b)   a person who is not a child;

  [⁷ (ba) a child who cannot share a bedroom;]

  (c)   two children of the same sex;

  (d)   two children who are less than 10 years old;

  (e)   a child.

[⁷ but the claimant is only entitled to a bedroom in respect of a child who cannot share a bedroom [⁸ or a member of a couple who cannot share a bedroom] if there is a bedroom in the dwelling occupied as the home that is additional to those to which the claimant would be entitled if the child [⁸ or the member of the couple] were able to share a bedroom.]

  [⁴ [⁵]]

  [⁵ (3A)   The claimant is entitled to one additional bedroom in any case where–

  [⁸ (a) one or more of the following persons is a person who requires overnight care–

     (i)   the claimant;

     (ii)   the claimant's partner;

     (iii) a person (other than the claimant or the claimant's partner) who occupies the claimant's dwelling as their home;

     (iv) a child or young person in respect of whom the claimant or the claimant's partner is a qualifying parent or carer; or]

  (b)   the claimant or the claimant's partner is (or each of them is) a qualifying parent or carer.]

  [⁵ (3B)   The claimant is entitled to two additional bedrooms where paragraph (3A)(a) and (b) both apply.]

  (4)   The relevant authority shall determine–

  (a)   the cap rent (in accordance with the definition in paragraph (12)); and

  (b)   whether the cap rent exceeds the applicable local housing allowance.

  [⁴ (5)   Where the applicable local housing allowance exceeds the cap rent, the maximum rent (LHA) shall be the cap rent.]

  [⁴ (6)]

  [³ (7)]

  [⁴ (8)]

  [⁴ (9)]

  (10)   The relevant authority shall apply to the rent officer for a board and attendance determination to be made in accordance with article 4C of the Rent Officers Order where–

  (a)   the relevant authority is required to determine a maximum rent (LHA) by virtue of regulation 13C; and

  (b)   part of the rent under the tenancy appears to the relevant authority to be likely to be attributable to board and attendance.

(11)   Where an application to a rent officer is required in accordance with paragraph (10) it shall be made within the same period following the day on which the relevant authority becomes obliged to determine a maximum rent (LHA) by virtue of regulation 13C as would be required if the application were to be made under regulation 14(1).

(12)   In this regulation–

"cap rent" means the aggregate of such payments specified in regulation 12(1) (rent) which the claimant is liable to pay, or is treated as liable to pay by virtue of regulation 8 (circumstances in which a person is treated as liable to make payments in respect of a dwelling), subject to regulation 12B(3) (mixed use accommodation), (4) (more than one person liable to make payments) and (6) (discretion in relation to eligible rent);

[⁵ "occupiers" means–

(a)   the persons whom the relevant authority is satisfied occupy as their home the dwelling to which the claim or award relates except for any joint tenant who is not a member of the claimant's household; and

(b)   any member of the armed forces away on operations who–
   (i)   is the son, daughter, step-son or step-daughter of the claimant or the claimant's partner;
   (ii)   was the claimant's non-dependant before they became a member of the armed forces away on operations; and
   (iii)   intends to resume occupying the dwelling as their home when they cease to be a member of the armed forces away on operations;]

"relevant date" means, as the case may require–

(a)   the date of the claim to which the claim or relevant information referred to in regulation 13C(2)(a) or (b) relates;

(b)   the date of the change of dwelling, change which affects the category of dwelling, or date of death, to which a notification referred to in regulation 13C(2)(c) or (d) relates; or

(c)   the date on which the anniversary of the LHA date referred to in regulation 13C(3) falls.

"tenancy" includes

(a)   in Scotland, any other right of occupancy; and

(b)   in any other case, a licence to occupy premises,

and reference to a tenant, landlord or any other expression appropriate to a tenancy shall be construed accordingly.]

Modifications

Reg 13D is modified by Sch 10 para 8 (see p707). This applies only to former Pathfinder Authorities who administered the pilot local housing allowance scheme.

Amendments

1.   Inserted by reg 7 of SI 2007 No 2868 as from 7.4.08 (or if reg 1(5) of that SI applies, on the day on or after 7.4.08 when the first of the events specified in reg 1(6) applies, or from 6.4.09 if none have before that date).
2.   Amended by reg 4(4)(b) of SI 2008 No 586 as from 7.4.08.
3.   Amended by reg 2(3) of SI 2009 No 614 as from 6.4.09.
4.   Amended by reg 2(6) of SI 2010 No 2835 as from 1.4.11.
5.   Amended by reg 2(4) of SI 2013 No 665 as from 1.4.13.
6.   Amended by art 17 and Sch 1 para 23 of SI 2013 No 1465 as from 24.6.13.
7.   Amended by reg 2(4) of SI 2013 No 2828 as from 4.12.13.
8.   Amended by reg 4(4) of SI 2017 No 213 as from 1.4.17.

Definitions

"board and attendance determination" – see eg art 2(1) of the relevant Rent Officer Order.
"broad rental market area" – see reg 2(1).
"child" – see reg 2(1).
"child who cannot share a bedroom" – see reg 2(1).
"claimant" – see reg 2(1).
"local housing allowance" – see reg 2(1).

"member of a couple who can share a bedroom" – see reg 2(6).
"member of a couple who cannot share a bedroom" – see reg 2(1).
"member of the armed forces away on operations" – see reg 2(1).
"non-dependant" – see reg 3.
"partner" – see reg 2(1).
"person who requires overnight care" – see reg 2(1).
"qualifying parent or carer" – see reg 2(1).
"rent allowance" – see s134(1B) SSAA 1992.
"young individual" – see reg 2(1).

General Note

Reg 13D deals with the calculation of the claimant's "maximum rent (LHA)" for HB purposes under the "LHA" scheme. The significance of the maximum rent (LHA) is that the claimant's "eligible rent" generally cannot exceed it: reg 12D. Reg 13D applies in the circumstances set out in reg 13C.

The DWP guidance to local authorities, the *Local Housing Allowance Guidance Manual* and *Local Housing Allowance Good Practice Guide* are available at www.gov.uk/government/publications/local-housing-allowance-guidance-and-good-practice-for-local-authorities.

Summary of the scheme

It is important to remember that the "LHA" is not a different form of HB. Strictly speaking, it is a determination made by the rent officer upon which the calculation of HB for a relevant claimant is based. As Commissioner Williams pointed out in *CH 2986/2005*, the HB Regs apply in full, and the administrative provisions applying to decision making and appeals are the same as those applying to HB generally. Although the decision dealt with the pilot scheme rules in Pathfinder areas, the same would apply under the national scheme rules.

The scheme includes the following:

(1)   The "maximum rent (LHA)" is the local housing allowance that is appropriate for the claimant, or if lower, her/his "cap rent": reg 13D(1), (5) and (6). Note: prior to 1 April 2011, the "maximum rent (LHA)" was the appropriate local housing allowance, or if lower, the "cap rent" plus £15.

(2)   The "LHA" that is appropriate for a particular claimant depends on the category of dwelling that applies to her/him – ie, the number of bedrooms allowed under the size criteria (up to a maximum of four) and whether the claimant lives in shared accommodation: reg 13D(2) and (3). Note: prior to 6 April 2009, there was no maximum number of bedrooms allowed under the size criteria. The number of bedrooms allowed was restricted to a maximum of five from 6 April 2009 to 1 April 2011. Claimants who were allowed five bedrooms prior to 1 April 2011 may have been entitled to transitional protection under reg 12M (see p365).

(3)   For those only allowed one bedroom under the size criteria who live in shared accommodation and for a "young individual" (defined in reg 2(1) – broadly single claimants under 35, but there are a number of exceptions), the local housing allowance is based on accommodation in which the tenant has exclusive use of one bedroom only and all or some of the other facilities are shared. This does not apply if the claimant (or her/his partner) qualifies for a severe disability premium or has a non-dependant living with her/him. See also the exceptions in the definition of "young individual" in reg 2(1), including a claimant who is "a person who requires overnight care" or who is a "qualifying parent or carer", and the commentary on p246. The "young individual" age limit was 25 prior to 1 January 2012.

(4)   Local housing allowances for each size category of properties up to four bedrooms are set by the rent officer annually. This must be done on the last working day of January of each year: reg 13D(1) HB Regs and art 4B(2A) and (2B) of the RO Orders. The local housing allowances take effect the following 1 April: art 4B(3A) of the RO Orders. The LHA rates are capped at the lower of the amount of rent at the 30th percentile point of local market rents for assured tenancies in a "broad rental market area" or the latest rate determined by the rent officer (or in some local authority areas only, that rate plus 3 per cent): Sch 3B paras 2 and 5A of the RO Orders. They can be lower than those rates, but never higher. Note that from 1 April 2015, LHA rates were effectively capped at the rates determined on 30 January 2015 (or from 23 January 2017, in some local authority areas only, that rate plus 3 per cent).

(5)   Local housing allowances are made public: reg 13E. These are available at http://lha-direct.voa.gov.uk/search.aspx.

(6)   Maximum rent (LHA) is based on the local housing allowance that is appropriate when the claim is assessed. The local authority reassesses claims annually on 1 April in any year, using the allowance that is then appropriate for the property. However, claims can be reassessed earlier if there are certain changes in circumstances and this means a different allowance is appropriate – eg, a change in the amount of the "cap rent", a change in the size of the household or a change in the category of dwelling that applies such as where a single claimant turns 35: regs 12D(2) and 13C(2) and (3). Note: those whose eligible rent was higher prior to 1 April 2011 than it was when the claim was reassessed may have been entitled to transitional protection under reg 12M (see p365).

(7)   If the appropriate local housing allowance for a claimant should be reduced, because of the death of a member of the claimant's family or a relative of the claimant or her/his partner who occupies the same dwelling, the decrease in "eligible rent" can be delayed for 12 months: reg 12D(3), (4), (7) and (8).

(8)   A restriction of a claimant's "eligible rent" can be delayed for 13 weeks if the claimant or a member of her/his family or a relative of the claimant or her/his partner who occupies the same dwelling could meet the costs of the dwelling when these were taken on: reg 12D(5) to (8).

(9)   In most cases, HB is paid to the claimant, not to the landlord (or agent). However, direct payments to landlords are still possible in some situations: regs 95 and 96. In order to transfer payment of HB to a tenant from a landlord, a supersession decision is needed. The landlord has a right of appeal against the decision and the tenant is a party to any such appeal as a "person affected": *CH 2986/2005*.

In *R (CPAG) v SSWP* [2011] EWHC 2616 (Admin), the High Court considered a challenge to two changes to the LHA scheme for rent restriction made with effect from 1 April 2011.

(1)   The introduction of maximum weekly caps on the LHA rates. These had the effect of making it more difficult for HB to meet the rental costs in high rent areas (such as London). The challenge here was on the basis that the introduction of caps went beyond the powers given by Parliament to the Secretary of State in setting up the HB scheme because the effect of the caps was to stop HB from being a national scheme. It was also argued that the Secretary of State had failed to comply with his general equality duty under the Race Relations Act 1976.

(2)   The reduction in the maximum size of dwelling upon which HB can be based from five bedrooms to four. This challenge was on the basis that the Secretary of State failed to fulfil properly his general equality duties under the Race Relations Act 1976 and the Sex Discrimination Act 1975.

The High Court dismissed the claim. It agreed with the Secretary of State that the purpose of the HB scheme is not to prevent homelessness but to help claimants with their rent, while also protecting the public purse. In that context, there was nothing in the statutory scheme to prevent the government from setting an overall cap in the way it did. Further, by preparing an Equality Impact Assessment on the amending provisions, the government had "due regard" to the need to eliminate unlawful discrimination and that was sufficient for it to show that it had acted lawfully.

Analysis

Paragraph (1): The general rule

Where reg 13C applies, maximum rent (LHA) is to be determined as set out in reg 13D. Maximum rent (LHA) is the local housing allowance determined by the rent officer that, at the "relevant date", is applicable to the "broad rental market area" in which the dwelling the claimant occupies is situated, and the category of dwelling that applies to the claimant. However, the maximum rent (LHA) is the claimant's "cap rent" (defined in para (12)) if this is lower; para (5). The "relevant date" is either the date of claim or the date of any of the changes specified in reg 13C(2)(c) or (d) (change of dwelling, etc): para (12). Note that the reference to the anniversary of "the LHA date" in the definition was not amended when reg 13C(3) was substituted by SI 2012 No.3040. Reg 13C(3) now refers to the 1st April in any year.

A broad rental market area is defined as an area within which a person could reasonably be expected to live having regard to facilities and services for the purposes of health, education, recreation, personal banking and shopping and the travel distance by public and private transport. It must contain a variety of types of residential accommodation and types of lettings, and have sufficient private rented housing to ensure that the local housing allowance for the category of dwelling in the area is representative of the rents that a landlord might reasonably be expected to obtain in that area: Sch 3B para 4 of the RO Orders.

Once maximum rent (LHA) is set, HB is calculated on the basis of this until the next time the authority is required to determine maximum rent (LHA). This is usually annually on 1 April in any year: reg 12D(2)(b)(ii) and reg 13C(3).

Paragraph (2): The category of dwelling

Para (2) sets out the category of dwelling that applies in any particular case. There are three possibilities.

Para (2)(a): One-bedroom shared accommodation. This category applies if the claimant is a "young individual" (broadly a single claimant under 35, but there are a number of exceptions) who does not qualify for a severe disability premium and does not have any non-dependants residing with her/him (for which see reg 3), whether or not the claimant lives in shared accommodation: para (2)(a)(i). It does not apply if the claimant is a lone parent – see the definition of "single claimant" in reg 2(1). It appears that this category would apply to a "young individual" who has a boarder.

This category also applies if the claimant (and her/his partner if any) is only allowed one bedroom under the size criteria and neither sub-paras (b)(i) or (ii) are satisfied – ie, s/he lives in shared accommodation: para (2)(a)(ii). For the size criteria, see paras (3) to (3B). It does not apply if the claimant (or her/his partner) qualifies for a severe disability premium (for which see Sch 3 para 14). It also does not apply if any of the exceptions in paras (b) to (f) or (i) of the definition of "young individual" apply to the claimant or her/his partner (it is not known why the exception in para (h) was not included). Broadly, those paragraphs exclude a person from the definition if s/he is under 22 and was in the care of, or under the supervision of, a local authority under specified provisions, or ceased to be subject to a compulsory supervision order, after aged 16, or was provided with accommodation by a local authority under s20 Children Act 1989. In these cases, the category in para (2)(b) instead applies (one bedroom self-contained accommodation), even if the claimant lives in shared accommodation. Note that the category in para (2)(c) (two bedroom accommodation) applies if the claimant or her/his partner is a "person who requires overnight care" or a "qualifying parent or carer": exceptions in paras (g) and (j) of the definition of "young individual".

Note that someone is not a "young individual" if her/his landlord is a registered housing association (defined in reg 2(1)), but such claimants are generally excepted from the "LHA" rules in any event: reg 13C(5)(a).

From 1 January 2012, the definition of "young individual" was amended and the age limit was increased from 25 to 35. If a claimant was aged at least 25, the category that applied was that for one bedroom self-contained accommodation, unless s/he was living in shared accommodation. However, the category that applied was that for one bedroom shared accommodation the next time the claim was reassessed if the claimant had not yet reached age 35 and came within the definition of "young individual". See also reg 12M for those entitled to HB prior to 1 April 2011.

Para (2)(b): One-bedroom self-contained accommodation. Unless para (2)(a)(i) applies, this category applies if the claimant is only allowed one bedroom under the size criteria – eg, s/he is a single claimant or a member of a couple without children, neither s/he nor her/his partner is a "member of a couple who cannot share a bedroom", a "person who requires overnight care" or a "qualifying parent or carer" and s/he has no non-dependants residing with her/him. In addition, the claimant must not be living in shared accommodation – ie, s/he (and her/his partner) must have the exclusive use of at least two rooms or the exclusive use of one room, a bathroom and toilet and a kitchen or facilities for cooking. "Room" here means a bedroom or room suitable for living in, other than one the claimant shares with a member of her/his household, a non-dependant or someone who pays rent to the claimant or her/his partner. "Exclusive use" is not defined. Though the point was *obiter*, the judge in *AA v Chesterfield BC* [2011] UKUT 156 (AAC) commented on the interpretation of the phrase. He said that a claimant has exclusive use of a room if s/he has a legal right under the tenancy to exclude all others. Citing *Bull v Bull* [1955] 1 QB 234 and *Hammersmith and Fulham LBC v Monk* [1991] UKHL 6, he pointed out that joint tenants have joint and several right to possession of the whole property and thus one joint tenant cannot exclude the other joint tenant from any part of the property concerned.

In *DC v London Borough of Bromley (HB)* [2018] UKUT 416 (AAC), the claimants were a married couple, claiming HB separately. Although they had a joint tenancy of the dwelling that was their home, it was accepted that they were not members of the same household and thus, for HB purposes, they were not considered to be a "couple" as defined in s137 SSCBA 1992 and reg 2(1) HB Regs. They each had separate accommodation within the dwelling and a legal agreement between them was in place that set out that each claimant had the exclusive use of a bedroom and a living room. Nevertheless, the local authority decided that in both claimant's cases, because the dwelling was let as a joint tenancy on a shared basis, the LHA for one-bedroom shared accommodation applied. Judge Rowland disagreed and decided that the appropriate LHA for both claimants was that for one-bedroom self-contained accommodation. The issue of exclusive use of a room and of sharing a room concern a person's rights rather than her/his actual use. However, this did not necessarily mean that a claimant's tenancy agreement is the only relevant source for the purpose for determining the rights. He said:

"... I do not see why an agreement between joint tenants should not be taken into account in determining their rights to use rooms within a dwelling, provided that it has some legal force. Once it is accepted that they live in different households, it seems to me that each occupies a separate dwelling as a home within the premises that was originally let. If regulation 12B were to apply, the payments due in respect of that dwelling could be ascertained by apportioning the rent due in respect of the whole premises. If regulation 13D applies and each household consists of a single person, it is necessary to determine whether all or part of the dwelling is shared. It is true that neither person can unilaterally exclude the other from any part of the property and that, as against the landlord, they remain jointly and severally liable for the whole rent, but it does not follow that they are not at liberty to agree between themselves the way in which each will occupy the premises and the proportion of the rent that each will pay in consequence and to do so by way of a binding contract."

JS v SSWP and Cheshire West and Chester BC (HB) [2014] UKUT 36 (AAC); [2014] AACR 26 concerned the meaning of the phrase "has the exclusive use of" in reg 13D(2) HB(SPC) Regs (which is identical to reg 13D(2) HB Regs). Judge Wright considered whether it meant rooms a person practically has control over and sole use of (a "practical control test") or, as found by the First-tier Tribunal, a legal right to exclude others from the rooms. He said that the correct starting point was ascertaining the meaning of the phrase in the context of the statutory scheme within which it appears, and that the context must include reading reg 13D(2) together with the relevant terms of the Rent Officers (Housing Benefit Functions) Order 1997. He rejected the claimant's argument that as a matter of law or a matter of approach the starting point is that the phrase "exclusive use" has to be given a non-technical and ordinary meaning. Agreeing with Judge Wikeley's opinion in *AA v Chesterfield BC*, which was followed by the judge in *CH 2483/2012*, he concluded that "exclusive use" means the legal right to exclude others from the rooms and not, as the claimant contended, as a matter of fact or practice has the sole use of the rooms.

This category does not apply if the single claimant or couple are allowed more than one bedroom under the size criteria, for which see paras (2)(c) and (3) to (3B) below.

Para (2)(c): Other cases. In any other case, the category that applies is that which corresponds with the number of bedrooms the claimant is entitled to under the size criteria in paras (3) to (3B), up to a maximum of four bedrooms. This category therefore applies, for example, if the claimant is a lone parent or a couple with children, a "member of a couple who cannot share a bedroom", a "person who requires overnight care" or a "qualifying parent or carer", or if the claimant has any non-dependants living with her/him. It can also apply if the claimant is a joint tenant with someone who is a member of her/his household: *AA v Chesterfield BC*.

Note: the four-bedroom limit has only existed since 1 April 2011. Between 6 April 2009 and 1 April 2011, there was a five-bedroom limit. The amended rules apply to new claims from 1 April 2011. Those with an award of HB based on a category of dwelling of five bedrooms prior to 1 April 2011 may have been entitled to transitional protection under reg 12M (see p365). Prior to 6 April 2009 there was no limit. See the commentary to regs 12L (for transitional protection) and 13D in earlier editions of this work. See also the discussion of *R (CPAG) v SSWP* [2011] EWHC 2616 (Admin) on p392.

Paragraphs (3) to (3B): The size criteria

Under the size criteria, firstly, the claimant is allowed one bedroom for each of the categories of occupier specified in para (3)(za) to (e), each only coming into the first of these that applies.

(1)   A "member of a couple who cannot share a bedroom", defined in reg 2(1) as a member of a couple receiving higher rate AA, highest or middle rate DLA care component, either rate of the daily living component of PIP or armed forces independence payment and who the local authority is satisfied is not reasonably able to share a bedroom with the other member of the couple by virtue of her/his disability: sub-para (za). This category has only applied since 1 April 2017.

(2)   A "member of a couple who can share a bedroom", defined in reg 2(6) as a member of a couple whose partner is a "member of a couple who cannot share a bedroom": sub-para (zb).

(3)   A couple, defined in reg 2(1): sub-para (a).

(4)   A person who is not a child – ie, someone aged 16 or over: sub-para (b). See the definition of "child" in reg 2(1).

(5)   A "child who cannot share a bedroom": sub-para (ba). This category has only applied since 4 December 2013. "Child who cannot share a bedroom" is defined in reg 2(1) as a child under 16 who is entitled to DLA care component at the middle or highest rate and who the local authority is satisfied is not reasonably able to share a bedroom with another child because of her/his disability.

(6)   Two children of the same sex: sub-para (c).

(7)   Two children who are less than 10 years old: sub-para (d)

(8)   A child – ie, someone aged under 16: sub-para (e). See the definition in reg 2(1).

Note that by the closing words of para (3), a bedroom is only allowed for the child or member of the couple who cannot share a bedroom if there is a bedroom in the home additional to those to which the claimant would be entitled if the child or member of the couple could share a bedroom.

Paras (3A) and (3B): additional bedrooms. Under para (3A)(a), one additional bedroom is allowed for a non-resident carer if one or more of the people listed in para (3A)(a) is a **"person who requires overnight care"** (for which see reg 2(1) and the discussion on p243). Note that those listed in sub-para (a)(iii) can include a child or young person and a non-dependant. It may be arguable that it can also include a claimant's joint tenant as there is no requirement for the person to be an "occupier" as defined in para (12); the requirement here is that the person must occupy the claimant's dwelling as a home. Sub-para (a)(iv) is needed as the children and young people referred to do not count as occupying the claimant's dwelling as a home: see reg 21(3).

Under para (3A)(b), one additional bedroom is allowed if the claimant or her/his partner is a **"qualifying parent or carer"** (for which see reg 2(1) and the discussion on p245).

A "qualifying parent or carer" is someone who is an approved foster carer or a kinship carer who has a child placed with her/him or has had a child placed with her/him within the previous 52 weeks. If s/he has only recently been approved and has not had a child placed with her/him, s/he counts as a qualifying parent or carer for up to 52 weeks. The definition does not include people who provide care to an adult placed with them. However, see the discussion of *SSWP v PE and Bolton MBC* [2017] UKUT 393 (AAC) on p377.

Two additional bedrooms are allowed if both paras (3A)(a) and (b) apply: para (3B). Note that to come within either definition, the person must actually have a bedroom in the dwelling s/he occupies as her/his home that is additional to those used by the others who occupy it.

"Bedroom" is not here defined. See p373 for a discussion of what may be considered a bedroom.

Example: the claimant and her partner live in a four-bedroom private rented house. They have two boys aged four and seven. The seven-year-old is entitled to DLA care component at the highest rate and needs his own bedroom because of the effects of his disability. The claimant and her partner are the foster parents of two girls aged 10 and 12. The claimant is entitled to three bedrooms under para (3): one for a couple, one for a "child who cannot share a bedroom", and one for a child. She is also entitled to an additional bedroom under para (3A)(b), because she and her partner are both a "qualifying parent or carer". The claimant is therefore entitled to four bedrooms under the size criteria.

"Occupiers" is defined in para (12) to include two categories of people. For when a person might count as occupying a dwelling as a home, see reg 7 on p256. See also the discussion on occupation of the dwelling on p372.

The first category is people who the authority is satisfied occupy the dwelling to which the claim or award relates as a home, other than a joint tenant who is not a member of the claimant's household. This therefore includes not only those who count as members of the claimant's family for benefit purposes (for which see s137(1) SSCBA), but also those who are not part of the family – eg, non-dependants, boarders or live-in carers, or joint tenants who *are* members of the claimant's household: *AA v Chesterfield BC*.

The second category is any "member of the armed forces away on operations" – ie, who is away from the dwelling usually occupied as her/his home: see the definition in reg 2(1). The person must be a son, daughter, step-son or step-daughter of the claimant or her/his partner, who was the claimant's non-dependant before going away on operations and the person must intend to resume occupation of the dwelling as a home when s/he ceases to be away on operations.

Prior to 1 November 2010, "occupiers" could also include foster children: *Wirral MBC v AH and SSWP (HB)* [2010] UKUT 208 (AAC); [2011] AACR 6. This was because, although reg 21(3) prevented such children from counting as a member of claimant's household (and hence as a member of her/his family), it did not prevent the foster children from counting as occupying the claimant's dwelling. However, reg 21(3) was amended with effect from 1 November 2010 (see p409).

Challenges to the legality of the rules

Additional bedrooms. Prior to 1 April 2011, the size criteria did not include an additional bedroom for a non-resident carer if the claimant or her/his partner required overnight care. The claimant in *IB v Birmingham CC v SSWP v EHRC (HB)* [2011] UKUT 23 (AAC) was a severely disabled student who needed accommodation that included an extra bedroom for a team of non-resident carers. The local authority calculated his HB on the basis of the local housing allowance for one bedroom self-contained accommodation (under reg 13D(2)(b)) not that for two bedroom accommodation (under reg 13D(2)(c)). The First-tier Tribunal decided that the local authority had been correct to do so because the claimant's carers could not be regarded as occupying his dwelling as their home. As such, the claimant was the only "occupier" and so was only entitled to one bedroom under the size criteria in reg 13D(3). On appeal to the Upper Tribunal, the claimant contended that this amounted to unlawful discrimination against him contrary to s6 Human Rights Act 1998 and Article 14 of the Convention (prohibition of discrimination) read in conjunction with either Art 8 (right to respect for private and family life and home) or Art 1 of Protocol 1 (peaceful enjoyment of possessions), or both. Thus, he argued that the First-tier Tribunal should have held that he was entitled to have his HB calculated on the basis of the local housing allowance for a two bedroom property as if his carers together constituted an additional single adult also residing with him in his home. The discrimination was said to arise in two ways.

(1) The operation of the LHA limits imposed an adverse differential effect on the claimant as compared with non-disabled claimants.

(2) There was discrimination contrary to Art 14 in a failure to take positive measures to treat the claimant differently than non-disabled claimants (the requirement of positive differential treatment established by the ECHR in *Thlimmenos v Greece* (2001) 31 EHRR 411, acknowledged and approved by the Court of Appeal in *AM (Somalia) v Entry Clearance Officer* [2009] EWCA Civ 634).

Judge Howell considered the issues against the background of the additional help that disabled people get from benefits, namely that disabled full-time students are not barred from claiming HB, the calculation of HB includes adjustments for disability (including higher income disregards and applicable amounts) and entitlement to HB when renting privately and under 25 is based on one bedroom self-contained accommodation as opposed to one bedroom shared accommodation. He also pointed out that if the carers were to be treated as residing with the claimant, the claimant could lose more than he would gain as he would potentially lose his entitlement to a severe disability premium. Judge Howell refused the claimant's appeal. He said that because the objective limitation of the room rates to "occupiers" was unrelated to disability or any other personal characteristic of the claimant and applied to all alike, there was not a breach of Art 14 based on direct or indirect adverse differential treatment of the claimant as a severely disabled person. He also dismissed the argument that there was a violation of Article 14 in the failure to provide the claimant with extra HB outside the rules, at the two-bedroom rate.

Judge Mark said that similar considerations as in *IB v Birmingham CC* applied in *KM v South Somerset DC (HB)* [2011] UKUT 148 (AAC). Here, the claimant and her husband needed separate bedrooms because of her disability, but because they were a couple (as defined in s137 SSCBA 1992) HB was calculated on the basis that the appropriate LHA was that for one bedroom accommodation. The judge said: "It does not appear to me that the provisions that have been made, giving 'couple' its normal meaning under Part 7 of the 1992 Act, and the failure to make special provision for this type of case beyond the provision of the limited funds available by way of a discretionary housing payment involve any breach of Article 8 or Article 14."

In *RG v SSWP and North Wiltshire DC (HB)* [2011] UKUT 198 (AAC), the claimant needed an extra bedroom because his disabled daughters needed separate bedrooms. His representative argued that there was a difference between this case and *IB v Birmingham CC* in that in the latter the claimant wanted to be treated as entitled to an extra bedroom for someone who was not an occupier, whereas here the extra bedroom was for an occupier. Judge Turnbull decided that the differences were not such as to enable him to say that the reasoning in *IB v Birmingham CC* did not apply. The discrimination in the failure to treat the claimant's case differently was objectively justified.

The claimants in *IB v Birmingham*, another similar case and *RG v SSWP and North Wiltshire DC (HB)* appealed to the Court of Appeal: *Burnip v Birmingham CC and Others* [2012] EWCA Civ 629; [2013] AACR 7 (*Burnip, Trengove* and *Gorry*). All three appeals were allowed. In *Gorry*, the Court held that the size criteria in reg

13D(3) discriminated unlawfully against a family with two disabled children under 10 who could not share a room because of the nature of their disabilities, contrary to Art1 Protocol 1 and Art 14 ECHR. In the joined cases of *Burnip* and *Trengove*, the Court held that the size criteria similarly discriminated against claimants who needed 24 hour care provided by "rolling carers". The fact that the case involved the allocation of additional resources by the state did not preclude the application of Art 14. The claimants were not asking for preferential treatment, but were asking to be put in the same position as other claimants who were not affected by disability. The payment of other benefits for subsistence and of discretionary housing payments (DHPs), which did not cover the full amount or the full period of the shortfall in HB did not justify the discrimination either. The SSWP applied to the Supreme Court for permission to appeal, but later dropped the appeal.

The current position. The regulations were amended, with effect from 1 April 2011, to cover the circumstances of the claimants in *Burnip* and *Trengove*. The size criteria now allow an additional bedroom if the claimant or her/his partner is a "person who requires overnight care": para (3A)(a). The carer(s) are not "occupiers", so entitlement to the severe disability premium (if applicable) should not be affected. The regulations were not, until 4 December 2013, amended to cover the circumstances of the claimant in *Gorry*.

Prior to the December 2013 amendments, in the wake of the judgment in *Burnip, Trengove* and *Gorry*, the DWP issued guidance in the form of circular HB/CTB U2/2013 which stated that from 15 May 2012, local authorities "should allow an extra bedroom for children who are unable to share because of their severe disabilities". However, the circular suggested that the judgment should not be applied in other circumstances – eg, where members of a couple are unable to share a bedroom due to a disability, or where an extra room is needed to store equipment needed in connection with a disability. In *R (MA and Others) v SSWP and Birmingham City Council*, the "social sector" rules in regs A13 and B13 (in which the size criteria are broadly the same as here) were unsuccessfully challenged on the basis that they discriminated against disabled people. The Court declined to strike out the regulations and an appeal to the Court of Appeal was unsuccessful. See p377 for a discussion of *R (MA) and Others)* and a later case, *Rutherford and Others v SSWP*. In the latter case, the claimants, who were unable to look after their severely disabled grandson themselves, lived with him in a specially adapted home which contained an extra bedroom for the grandson's overnight carers. Note that the claimants in *R (MA and others)* were given permission to appeal to the Supreme Court. The appeal was heard from 29 February to 2 March 2016. The claimants in *Rutherford* were successful in an appeal to the Court of Appeal. An appeal by the SSWP to the Supreme Court was heard with *R (MA)* and was unsuccessful. One of the appellants in *R (MA and others)* (Mrs Carmichael) was successful in her appeal. Subsequently, from 1 April 2017, reg 13D was amended.

Claimants who have been affected by the "local housing allowance" rules who consider that they have not been allowed enough rooms under the size criteria (eg, they have not been allowed an extra bedroom for a partner who is unable to share a bedroom because of severe disabilities, or for an overnight carer for a child) should pursue appeals to the First-tier Tribunal and Upper Tribunal, citing *Burnip, Trengove and Gorry, Rutherford* and *Carmichael*. In relevant cases, it may also be possible to argue that the local authority has wrongly identified a room as a "bedroom". See p373 for a discussion of what may be considered a bedroom.

Paragraphs (1), (4) and (5): Calculation of maximum rent (LHA)
Under para (4), the authority is required to determine a "cap rent" and also whether this exceeds the local housing allowance that applies to the claimant. Maximum rent (LHA) is then the local housing allowance that applies or, if lower, the cap rent: paras (1) and (5).

"Cap rent" is defined in para (12). It is the payments in reg 12(1) that the claimant is liable to pay (or treated as liable to pay – see reg 8). Where the accommodation occupied by the claimant is not solely residential accommodation, only that portion of the payments referable to the residential element can form part of the cap rent: reg 12(B)(3). Where the claimant is jointly liable to make the payments, an apportionment must be made: reg 12B(4).

The definition is also said to be subject to reg 12B(6) which purports to give the authority a general discretion to reduce the cap rent. Note, however, the wording of reg 12B(6), which states it only applies in cases where eligible rent, as determined in accordance with the preceding paragraphs of reg 12B, is greater than it is reasonable to meet by way of HB. Under the LHA scheme, eligible rent is set by reg 12D, so the judge in *AA v Chesterfield BC* thought that it was arguable that the discretion to restrict eligible rent under reg 12B(6) had no or little relevance. However, in *DC v London Borough of Bromley (HB)* [2018] UKUT 416 (AAC), Judge Rowland said:

"The reference to an amount based on "the aggregate of such payments specified in regulation 12(1) (rent)" is common to both regulation 12B(2) and the beginning of the definition of "cap rent" in regulation 13D(12) and it seems obvious that the draftsman intended that paragraphs (3), (4) and (6) of regulation 12B should apply to reduce such payments for the purposes of the definition of "cap rent" as they would apply to reduce them in regulation 12B itself. Given that there is nothing else material in regulation 12B, because paragraph (1) is merely introductory and paragraph (5) merely supplements paragraph (2), the reference to "the preceding paragraphs" in paragraph (6) does not cause any difficulty (although it is true that the deduction of ineligible charges has been omitted and it is not obvious to me why that should be so). The need for provision such as is made by regulation 12B(3), (4) and (6) in the definition is clear if the most obvious purpose of the "cap rent" – i.e., preventing a local housing allowance from being greater than the housing benefit that would have been allowed under regulation 12B – was to be achieved. However, the "cap rent" assumes a greater role than it might otherwise have as a result of the lack of any other provision for apportionment within regulation 13D."

If the amount of the cap rent *is* subject to reg 12B(6), an authority will need to be cautious in using its discretion to decrease it. If the cap rent is relevant in the formula for calculating maximum rent (LHA) under reg 13D, this is because it is lower than the appropriate LHA rate.

Examples

(1)   The claimant is a joint tenant of a private flat with two friends. The rent for the flat is £300 a week. The local housing allowance that applies is that for one-bedroom shared accommodation, determined to be £125 by the rent officer. The cap rent is £100 (£300 divided by 3). Maximum rent (LHA) is therefore the cap rent (£100) as this figure is lower than the local housing allowance. This is also the "eligible rent": reg 12D(2)(a) and as the claimant does not have non-dependants residing with her/him, it is also the "maximum housing benefit" (reg 70). HB is then calculated using this figure: £100.

(2)   The claimant and her partner are joint tenants of a three-bedroom house. They live there with their daughter, aged 10. The rent for the house is £400 a week. The local housing allowance that applies is that for a two-bedroom dwelling, determined to be £300 by the rent officer. The cap rent is £400. Maximum rent (LHA) is therefore £300, the local housing allowance, because this is lower than the cap rent. This is also the "eligible rent": reg 12D(2)(a) and as the claimant does not have non-dependants residing with her, it is also the "maximum housing benefit" (reg 70). HB is then calculated using this figure: £300.

(3)   The claimant, aged 40, cares for his mother who is a member of the same household. They are joint tenants. The rent for the flat is £250 a week. The local housing allowance that applies is that for two-bedroom accommodation, determined to be £200 by the rent officer. The cap rent is £125 (half of the contractual rent). Maximum rent (LHA) is therefore £125 as this figure is lower than the local housing allowance. This is also the "eligible rent": reg 12D(2)(a) and as the claimant does not have non-dependants residing with him, it is also the maximum housing benefit" (reg 70). HB is then calculated using this figure: £125.

Paragraphs (10) and (11): Board and attendance determinations

Paras (10) and (11) require the authority to apply to the rent officer for a board and attendance determination, that is, a determination on whether or not a substantial part of the rent under the tenancy is fairly attributable to board and attendance. If this is the case, the "local housing allowance" rules do not apply: reg 13C(5)(e). Instead, the "local reference rent" rules may apply (see regs 13 and 14). Note that where the rent officer decides that a substantial part of the rent under the tenancy is fairly attributable to board and attendance, s/he must treat the application for a determination as one made under reg 14(1): see, for example, art 4C Rent Officers (Housing Benefit Functions) Order 1997 on p886.

Transitional protection

Changes to the "local housing allowance" scheme rules from 1 April 2011 could potentially reduce the amount of a claimant's eligible rent, and hence the amount of her/his HB, when entitlement was re-assessed on or after that date. Reg 12M (on p365) provided transitional protection against a reduction in HB in some cases. This could apply if the claimant's HB was affected by:

(1)   a reduction in the maximum number of bedrooms allowed under the size criteria, to four bedrooms: reg 13D(2)(c);

(2)   a change in the way local housing allowance rates are determined by the rent officer, reducing these from the median of rents in each broad rental market area to the 30th percentile;

(3)   a cap on the local housing allowance rates allowed for each category of property: Sch 3B para 1(12) of both the Rent Officers (Housing Benefit Functions) Order 1997 and the Rent Officers (Housing Benefit Functions) (Scotland) Order 1997.

[¹ Publication of local housing allowances

13E.–(1)   A relevant authority shall take such steps as appear to it to be appropriate for the purpose of securing that information in relation to broad rental market areas falling in whole or in part within its area, and local housing allowances applicable to such broad rental market areas, is brought to the attention of persons who may be entitled to housing benefit from the authority.

Amendment

1.   Inserted by reg 7 of SI 2007 No 2868 as from 7.4.08 (or if reg 1(5) of that SI applies, on the day on or after 7.4.08 when the first of the events specified in reg 1(6) applies, or from 6.4.09 if none have before that date).

General Note

Local housing allowance rates are available at http://lha-direct.voa.gov.uk/search.aspx.

[¹ **Requirement to refer to rent officers**

14.–(1)   Subject to the following provisions of this regulation, a relevant authority shall apply to a rent officer for a determination to be made in pursuance of the Housing Act functions where–

(a)   it has received a claim on which rent allowance may be awarded and any of the circumstances specified in regulation 13C(5)(a) to (e) (rent allowance cases for which a maximum rent (standard local rent) is not to be determined) apply;

(b)   it has received relevant information regarding a claim on which rent allowance may be awarded and any of the circumstances specified in regulation 13C(5)(a) to (e) apply;

(c)   it has received a notification of a change relating to a rent allowance and a maximum rent (LHA) does not fall to be determined under regulation 13C (determination of a maximum rent (LHA));

(d)   it has received a notification of a change of dwelling and any of the circumstances specified in regulation 13C(5)(a) to (e) apply;

(e)   it has received, except in the case where any liability to make payments in respect of a dwelling would be to a housing authority, a request from a person ("the prospective occupier"), on a properly completed form approved for the purpose by the relevant authority, which includes the specified matters and any of the circumstances specified in regulation 13C(5)(a) to (d) apply;

(f)   52 weeks have expired since it last made an application under sub-paragraph (a), (b), (c), (d) [², (e) or (h)] in relation to the claim or award in question and–

   (i)   a maximum rent (LHA) determined under regulation 13D does not apply; and

   (ii)   a maximum rent (LHA) is not to be determined under regulation 13D; [²]

(g)   52 weeks have expired since an application was made under sub-paragraph (f) or a previous application was made under this sub-paragraph, whichever last occurred, and–

   (i)   a maximum rent (LHA) determined under regulation 13D does not apply; and

   (ii)   a maximum rent (LHA) is not to be determined under regulation 13D. [² or

(h)   has received notification that any of the circumstances in regulation 13C(5) apply.]

(2)   An application shall not be required under paragraph (1) where a claim, relevant information regarding a claim, notification or request relates to either–

(a)   a dwelling in a hostel if, during the period of 12 months ending on the day on which that claim, relevant information regarding a claim, notification or request is received by the relevant authority–

   (i)   a rent officer has already made a determination in the exercise of the Housing Act functions in respect of a dwelling in that hostel which is a similar dwelling to the dwelling to which the claim, relevant information regarding a claim, notification or request relates; and

   (ii)   there has been no change relating to a rent allowance that has affected the dwelling in respect of which that determination was made; or

(b)   an "excluded tenancy" within the meaning of Schedule 2 (excluded tenancies).

(3)   The provision of information to the rent officer in accordance with regulation 114A(5) shall be treated as an application to the rent officer under paragraph (1).

(4)   Where a relevant authority receives a request pursuant to paragraph (1)(e) (request from prospective occupier) and it is a case where, by reason of paragraph (2) (hostels or excluded tenancies), an application to a rent officer is not required, the authority shall–

(a)   return it to the prospective occupier, indicating why no such application is required; and

(b)   where it is not required by reason of either paragraph (2)(a) (hostels) of this regulation or paragraph 2 of Schedule 2 (cases where the rent officer has already made a determination), shall also send him a copy of that determination within 4 days of the receipt of that request by the authority.

(5)　Where an application to a rent officer is required by paragraph (1) it shall be made within 3 days, or as soon as practicable after that date, of–

(a)　the relevant authority receiving a claim on which rent allowance may be awarded;

(b)　the relevant authority receiving relevant information regarding a claim on which rent allowance may be awarded;

(c)　the relevant authority receiving a notification of a change relating to a rent allowance;

(d)　the relevant authority receiving a notification of a change of dwelling; or

(e)　the day on which the period mentioned in paragraph (1)(f) or (g) expired,

except that, in the case of a request to which paragraph (1)(e) (request from prospective occupier) applies, the application shall be made within 2 days of the receipt of that request by the authority.

(6)　In calculating any period of days mentioned in paragraphs (4) or (5), no regard shall be had to a day on which the offices of the relevant authority are closed for the purposes of receiving or determining claims.

(7)　For the purpose of this regulation a dwelling in a hostel shall be regarded as similar to another dwelling in that hostel if each dwelling provides sleeping accommodation for the same number of persons.

(8)　In this regulation–

"change relating to a rent allowance" means a change or increase to which paragraph 2(3)(a), (b), (c) [³, (d) [⁴ (f) [⁵, (g) or (h)]]] of Schedule 2 applies;

"prospective occupier" shall include a person currently in receipt of housing benefit in respect of a dwelling which he occupies as his home and who is contemplating entering into a new agreement to occupy that dwelling, but only where his current agreement commenced 11 months or more before the request under paragraph (1)(e);

"specified matters" means–

(a)　the signature of the prospective occupier;

(b)　the signature of the person to whom the prospective occupier would incur liability to make such payments;

(c)　a statement that the person in paragraph (b) agrees to the application being made for that determination; and

(d)　an indication that the prospective occupier is contemplating occupying the dwelling as his home and that if he does so, he is likely to claim housing benefit;

"tenancy" includes–

(a)　in Scotland, any other right of occupancy; and

(b)　in any other case, a licence to occupy premises,

and reference to a tenant, landlord or any other expression appropriate to a tenancy shall be construed accordingly;

[²]]

Modifications

Reg 14 was substituted by reg 8 Housing Benefit (Local Housing Allowance and Information Sharing) Amendment Regulations 2007 SI No.2868 as from 7 April 2008, save that for a person to whom reg 1(5) of those regulations applied (see p1812), the amendments came into force on the day on or after 7 April 2008 when the first of the events specified in reg 1(6) applied to her/him, or on 6 April 2009 if none had before that date.

Amendments

1.　Substituted by reg 8 of SI 2007 No 2868 as from 7.4.08 (or if reg 1(5) of that SI applies, on the day on or after 7.4.08 when the first of the events specified in reg 1(6) applies, or from 6.4.09 if none have before that date).

2.　Amended by reg 4(5) of SI 2008 No 586 as from 4.7.08.

3.　Amended by reg 2(7) of SI 2010 No 2835 as from 1.4.11.

4.　Amended by reg 2(5) of SI 2013 No 665 as from 1.4.13.

5.　Amended by reg 2(5) of SI 2013 No 2828 as from 4.12.13.

Definitions

"change of dwelling" – see reg 2(1).
"hostel" – see reg 2(1).
"maximum rent (LHA)" – see reg 2(1).
"relevant information" – see reg 2(1).
"rent allowance" – see s134(1B) SSAA 1992.
"Housing Act functions" – see reg 2(1).

General Note

The starting point for deciding whether maximum rent is to be calculated under reg 13 (the "local reference rent" rules) is to consider whether the authority is required to apply to the rent officer for a determination under reg 14. Reg 14, together with Sch 2, prescribes the circumstances in which the authority must ask the rent officer for a determination to be made and the time limits which must be observed. For the rent officer's functions under the Housing Act see the Rent Officers (Housing Benefit Functions) Order 1997 and the Rent Officers (Housing Benefit Functions) (Scotland) Order 1997. Reg 114A deals with the information which must be given to the rent officer. Although there is no right of appeal against rent officer determinations, authorities may ask for redeterminations on a claimant's behalf under reg 16. Other provisions for redeterminations and substitute determinations are found in regs 15, 17 and 18. Note also that where an application for a board and attendance determination is made under reg 13D(10) and the rent officer decides that a substantial part of the rent under the tenancy is fairly attributable to board and attendance, s/he must treat the application for a determination as one made under reg 14(1): see, for example, art 4C Rent Officers (Housing Benefit Functions) Order 1997 on p886.

Unless the claimant has an "excluded tenancy", broadly, reg 14 applies if, on or after 7 April 2008, a claim for HB is made or a claimant with an award of HB moves to a new home, HB would be paid as a rent allowance and one of the following applies: regs 13C(5)(a)–(e) and 14(1) and (2)(b).

(1)   Rent is paid in relation to a hostel, a houseboat, a mobile home or a caravan: reg 13C(5)(d).
(2)   A substantial part of the rent is attributable to board and attendance: reg 13C(5)(e).
(3)   The landlord is a registered social landlord or a non-profit or profit-making registered provider of social housing (in the case of profit-making providers, the claimant's dwelling must be "social housing", that is, low cost rental or ownership accommodation that is available to people whose needs are not adequately served by the commercial housing market): reg 13C(5)(a). See the commentary on p387 for further information.
        If the landlord is a "registered housing association" (as defined in reg 2(1)), this only applies if the authority considers the rent unreasonably high. Otherwise, such a registered housing association tenancy is an "excluded tenancy" under Sch 2 para 3. Note that prior to 1 April 2013, this also applied if the authority considered the accommodation to be unreasonably large. Now such cases are "excluded tenancies" for the purpose of reg 14, but the "social sector" scheme may apply: regs A13 and B13.
(4)   The tenancy was a local authority or new town letting, that was transferred to a new owner.
        This only applies if there has been a rent increase since the transfer and the authority considers the rent to be unreasonably high or, if the transfer took place before 7 October 2002, the authority considers the accommodation to be unreasonably large: reg 13C(5)(c). Otherwise, the tenacy is an "excluded tenancy" under Sch 2 para 11.
(5)   The claimant lives in "exempt accommodation" under Sch 3 para 4(b) HB&CTB(CP) Regs (p1776): reg 13C(5)(b) HB Regs. However, in such cases, eligible rent must be determined under regs 12 and 13 as set out in Sch 3 para 5 HB&CTB(CP) Regs.

Claimants entitled to HB before 7 April 2008

Reg 14 (in either its previous or substituted form) can also apply to other rent allowance cases not covered in the list above – ie, those who live in a private rented property. If the claimant was entitled to HB immediately before 7 April 2008 under the "local reference rent" rules that then applied, these continue to apply until a new claim for HB is made (eg, after a break in entitlement) or the claimant moves to a new home: reg 13C(2)(a)–(c).

The "local reference rent" rules continue to apply, even following any of the changes of circumstance listed in Sch 2 para 2(3)(a)–(d) (and Sch 2 para 2(3)(a)–(d) HB Regs as substituted by reg 18 HB(LHA&IS)A Regs), and then when the local authority has to apply to the rent officer for determinations every 52 weeks thereafter: regs 13(1) and 14(1)(c), (f) and (g) and (8) HB Regs.

Analysis

Paragraph (1): When referrals are to be made

Pursuant to para (1), there are eight circumstances in which a local authority is obliged to apply to a rent officer for a determination. These are subject to para (2), which provides for circumstances in which no application is required. In all of the circumstances, an application is only required where the "LHA" rules (for which see regs 13C and 13D) do not apply.

An application to the rent officer must only be made in cases where HB would be paid as a rent allowance and not as a rent rebate. This may cause difficulties in cases where claimants have been placed in accommodation by local housing authorities: for an example, see *CH 1208/2003* referred to in the commentary to reg 8. The situations when HB takes the form of rent allowance and rent rebate are in s134(1A) and (1B) SSAA 1992. Generally speaking, HB takes the form of a rent allowance in cases other than where rent is paid to the authority administering the HB scheme – eg, where a claimant is a private or housing association tenant.

Note that oddly, an application to the rent officer is required where Sch 3 para 4(1)(b) HB&CTB(CP) Regs applies, that is, where the claimant lives in "exempt accommodation": see paras (a), (b) and (d) to (h) below and reg 13C(5)(b). However, Sch 3 para 4(1)(b) HB&CTB(CP) Regs requires the authority to determine the eligible rent in such cases under the versions of reg 12 and 13 HB Regs set out in Sch 3 para 5 HB&CTB(CP) Regs.

Sub-paras (a) and (b): Claims. These sub-paras apply where a claim for HB is received or an authority has received "relevant information" regarding a claim on which a rent allowance may be awarded. Relevant information is defined in reg 2(1) as "information or evidence forwarded to the authority by an appropriate DWP office regarding a claim on which rent allowance may be awarded, which completes the transfer of all information or evidence held by the appropriate DWP office relating to that claim" – eg, where the claim for HB has been made with a claim to the DWP for IS, JSA, ESA or PC. In both cases, one of the circumstances in reg 13C(5)(a) to (e) must apply, in other words, the claimant must be exempt from the application of the "LHA" rules. See the commentary to reg 13C(5) for details of the circumstances.

Sub-para (c): Change relating to a rent allowance. This applies where the authority has received a notification of a change relating to a rent allowance. A "change relating to a rent allowance" is defined in para (8) by reference to various parts of Sch 2 and covers changes in the number of occupiers, someone becoming or ceasing to be a "person who requires overnight care" or a "qualifying parent or carer" (a specified foster or kinship carer) or an occupier ceasing to be a "child who cannot share a bedroom" or a "member of a couple who cannot share a bedroom" and affecting the applicable size criteria, changes in the condition of the dwelling, certain rent increases and changes in the composition of the household or a child becoming 10 or 16. See the commentary to those provisions for full details and note in particular the discussion of *Stroud DC v JG* [2009] UKUT 67 (AAC); R(H) 8/09. The words from "and a maximum rent (LHA)" to the end of the sub-para are needed to ensure that where a "maximum rent (LHA)" is to be determined under reg 13C, an application is not to be made under reg 14 which would lead to a "maximum rent" under reg 13 also being determined for the same claimant.

Sub-para (d): Change of dwelling. This sub-para applies where the authority has received a notification of a change of dwelling. "Change of dwelling" is defined in reg 2(1) as a change of dwelling during an award of HB, to a dwelling in respect of which the authority may make a rent allowance. As with sub-paras (a) and (b) above, one of the circumstances in reg 13C(5)(a)–(e) must apply.

Sub-para (e): Pre-tenancy determinations. This establishes a scheme of pre-tenancy determinations for prospective occupiers to whom one of the circumstances in reg 13C(5)(a)–(d) applies. The policy aim is to prevent a tenant taking on a tenancy and then finding that her/his eligible rent is restricted. The determinations inform prospective tenants, current tenants and landlords of the likely amount of rent that HB will meet.

Pre-tenancy determinations are available to "prospective occupiers". By para (8), this term does not just include those considering taking on a tenancy but also includes HB claimants who are already occupying accommodation and who are considering entering into a new agreement. In the latter case, however, any existing agreement must have started not less than 11 months prior to the request being made.

No claim for HB is required, but one must be likely: see sub-para (d) in the the definition of "specified matters" in para (8).

The prospective occupier must submit her/his request to the authority on a "properly completed form approved ... by the relevant authority" which includes "specified matters", defined in para (8) as including the signature of the prospective occupier and the landlord or letting agent.

The pre-tenancy determinations are rent officer determinations for the purpose of reg 13 and are binding on the authority in the event of an HB claim in respect of that accommodation, either from the prospective tenant who made the original application or another tenant. However, in the latter case, the conditions under which the pre-tenancy determination was given by the rent officer must remain the same. For example, the size criteria should accord with the composition of the household.

Sub-paras (f) and (g): 52 weeks since previous application. These sub-paras apply where 52 weeks have elapsed since a previous application to the rent officer was made in relation to the claim or award in question under any of the other sub-paras in reg 14(1). This effectively provides for an annual re-assessment of maximum rent under reg 13. The qualification made by sub-sub-paras (i) and (ii) in both cases is needed to ensure that where a "maximum rent (LHA)" is to be (or has been) determined under reg 13D, an application is not to be made under reg 14 which would lead to a "maximum rent" also being determined for the same claimant.

Sub-para (h): Maximum rent (LHA) no longer applies. Sub-para (h) applies where HB has been determined by reference to the "LHA" rules under reg 13D, but these no longer apply – eg, where a claimant lives in private rented accommodation which has passed into the ownership of a registered housing association.

Paragraphs (2), (4) and (7): The exceptions

Para (2) sets out the two exceptions to the requirement to apply to a rent officer. Under para (a), no dwelling within a hostel need be referred if a determination has been made within the previous 12 months in respect of a similar dwelling in that hostel and there has been no change of circumstances in relation to the similar dwelling. "Similar dwelling" means one sleeping the same number of people: para (7). Under para (b), no "excluded tenancy" as set out in Sch 2 need be referred. Note that a number of the excluded tenancies are therefore excluded from the rent restriction schemes altogether. See the commentary to that Schedule on p625.

Under para (4), where a request for a pre-tenancy determination would relate to a case where application to the rent officer is not required by reason of para (2), the local authority must return the request indicating why a referral is not necessary and, where the reason is that a determination has already been made, enclose a copy of that determination.

Paragraphs (3), (5) and (6): Making the referral

Para (3) treats the provision of information to the rent officer under reg 114A(5) as an application for a determination under para (1). This applies in cases where a substantial part of rent is attributable to board and attendance.

Paras (5) and (6) set out the time limits with which the authority must comply. Applications for pre-tenancy determinations must be referred to the rent officer within two working days. In other cases, the referral to the rent officer must be made within three working days from the authority receiving the claim, relevant information or notification or "as soon as practicable after". Note that the two working day limit for pre-tenancy determinations is absolute and not subject to the "as soon as is practicable after" qualification.

By para (6), days on which the local authority's offices are closed do not count.

In *CH 361/2006,* the deputy commissioner pointed out that the intention is that the application to the rent officer should be one of the very first stages of the processing of a claim for HB and not something that need only be dealt with once it is established that all the other conditions of entitlement are satisfied. Although there may be cases and situations where it is not "practicable" for the authority to satisfy the time limit, what is not permissible is for an authority to take a conscious decision not to make a reference to a rent officer because it is believes that the claim will eventually fail on other grounds. Note that a failure to apply to the rent officer in respect of a claim may amount to an official error for the purposes of reg 100 (recoverable overpayments): para 34.

[¹ Application to the rent officer for redeterminations

15.–(1) Subject to paragraph (2) and regulation 16 (application for redetermination by rent officer), where a relevant authority has obtained from a rent officer either or both of the following–

(a) a determination on a reference made under regulation 13D(10) (board and attendance determination) or regulation 14 (requirement to refer to rent officers);

(b) a redetermination on a reference made under regulation 16(2) (application for redetermination by rent officer),

the authority may apply to the rent officer for a redetermination of any determination or redetermination he has made which has effect at the date of the application.

(2) No application shall be made for a further redetermination of a redetermination made in response to an application under paragraph (1).]

Modifications

Reg 15 was substituted by reg 9 Housing Benefit (Local Housing Allowance and Information Sharing) Amendment Regulations 2007 SI No.2868 as from 7 April 2008, save that for a person to whom reg 1(5) of those regulations applied (see p1812), the amendments came into force on the day on or after 7 April 2008 when the first of the events specified in reg 1(6) applied to her/him, or on 6 April 2009 if none had before that date.

Amendment

1. Substituted by reg 9 of SI 2007 No 2868 as from 7.4.08 (or if reg 1(5) that SI applies, on the day on or after 7.4.08 when the first of the events specified in reg 1(6) applies, or from 6.4.09 if none have before that date).

General Note

Regs 15, 16, 17 and 18 allow for applications for redeterminations and substitute determinations by a rent officer. Under reg 15, an authority may apply for a redetermination of a rent officer determination, or for a second redetermination following one made at the person affected's request under reg 16(2). It may apply only once: see reg 15(2).

[¹ Application for a redetermination by a rent officer

16.–(1) This paragraph applies where–

(a) a person affected makes written representations which are signed by him, to a relevant authority concerning a decision which it makes in relation to him;

(b) those representations relate, in whole or in part, to a rent officer's determination or redetermination in exercise of the Housing Act functions except for functions relating to broad rental market area determinations and local housing allowance determinations or amended determinations; and

(c)   those representations are made no later than one month after the day on which the person affected was notified of the decision by the relevant authority.

(2)   Subject to paragraphs (3) and (4), where paragraph (1) applies, the relevant authority shall, within 7 days of receiving the representations, apply to the rent officer for a redetermination or, as the case may be, a further redetermination in exercise of the Housing Act functions and a copy of those representations shall accompany the local authority's application.

(3)   Except where paragraph (4) applies, a relevant authority, in relation to any determination by a rent officer of an application under regulation 13D(10) (board and attendance determination) or 14(1) (requirement to refer to rent officers), shall not apply for a redetermination under paragraph (2) more than once in respect of an individual claimant's dwelling to which that determination relates.

(4)   Paragraph (2) shall operate so as to require a relevant authority to make a second application where the following conditions are met in addition to those imposed by that paragraph–

(a)   the written representations made under paragraph (1) relate to a redetermination by a rent officer made in response to an application by the relevant authority under regulation 15 (application to the rent officer for redetermination);

(b)   by the time of that application, the rent officer has already provided a redetermination under this regulation of a determination made in response to an application under regulation 13D(10) or 14(1); and

(c)   both the application under this regulation referred to in sub-paragraph (b) and the second application for which this paragraph provides relate to the same claimant.

(5)   Where a decision has been revised in consequence of a redetermination, substitute determination or substitute redetermination by a rent officer in exercise of the Housing Act functions (except for those relating to broad rental market area determinations and local housing allowance determinations or amended determinations) and that redetermination, substitute determination or substitute redetermination has led to–

(a)   a reduction in the maximum rent, the redetermination, substitute determination or substitute redetermination shall be a change of circumstances;

(b)   an increase in the maximum rent, the redetermination, substitute determination or substitute redetermination shall have effect in place of the original determination.]

Modifications

Reg 16 was substituted by reg 9 Housing Benefit (Local Housing Allowance and Information Sharing) Amendment Regulations 2007 SI No.2868 as from 7 April 2008, save that for a person to whom reg 1(5) of those regulations applied (see p1812), the amendments came into force on the day on or after 7 April 2008 when the first of the events specified in reg 1(6) applied to her/him, or on 6 April 2009 if none had before that date.

Amendment

1.   Substituted by reg 9 of SI 2007 No 2868 as from 7.4.08 (or if reg 1(5) of that SI applies, on the day on or after 7.4.08 when the first of the events specified in reg 1(6) applies, or from 6.4.09 if none have before that date).

General Note

Under para 6(2)(c) CSPSSA, "so much of any decision of a relevant authority as adopts a decision of a rent officer under any order made by virtue of section 122 of the Housing Act 1996" does not carry a right of appeal to the First-tier Tribunal. Reg 16 provides a limited opportunity for a "person affected" to apply for a redetermination of a rent officer determination. "Person affected" is defined in reg 2(1) by reference to reg 3 D&A Regs and so can include, as well as a claimant, a landlord or her/his agent.

The procedure is for the "person affected" to make signed written representations to the authority about a decision, which relates to the rent officer's determination. These must be made no later than one month after the day on which s/he was notified of the authority's HB decision. The authority must then apply within seven days to the rent officer for a redetermination.

Claimants and advisers should note that such representations may lead to a *decrease* in the maximum rent as well as to an increase. If a decrease occurs, it is treated by para (5)(a) as a change of circumstances and will lead to the supersession of the earlier award. By contrast an increase in the maximum rent takes effect as a revision of the original award: para (5)(b). It therefore leads to a payment of back-dated benefit: see also regs 4(3), 7(2)(c) and 8(6) D&A Regs. Paras (3) and (4) make it clear that only one redetermination can be required for each original rent officer determination except where, in relation to the same claimant, there has been a first redetermination at the claimant's request, then a further redetermination at the authority's request, and the claimant then makes further representations about the second redetermination.

Note that although there is no right of appeal to the First-tier Tribunal against a decision of the rent officer, the claimant can appeal the local authority's "outcome" decision on HB entitlement and, as such, can challenge the factual basis upon which the rent officer decision was made – eg, the number of occupiers given to the rent officer by the local authority: *Bexley LB v LD (HB)* [2010] UKUT 79 (AAC) and *SK v South Hams DC (HB)* [2010] UKUT 129 (AAC); [2010] AACR 40.

[¹ Substitute determinations or substitute redeterminations

17.–(1)   In a case where either–
(a)   the appropriate authority discovers that an application it has made to the rent officer contained an error in respect of any of the following–
  (i)   the size of the dwelling;
  (ii)   the number of occupiers;
  (iii)   the composition of the household;
  (iv)   the terms of the tenancy; or
(b)   the rent officer has, in accordance with article 7A(1) or (2) of the Rent Officers Order, notified an appropriate authority of an error he has made (other than in the application of his professional judgement),
the authority shall apply to the rent officer for a substitute determination, substitute redetermination, board and attendance redetermination, substitute board and attendance determination or substitute board and attendance redetermination, as the case may be.

(2)   In its application to the rent officer the relevant authority shall state the nature of the error and withdraw any previous application relating to the same case for a redetermination or substitute determination or substitute redetermination, which it has made but to which the rent officer has not yet responded.]

Modifications

Reg 17 was substituted by reg 9 of the Housing Benefit (Local Housing Allowance and Information Sharing) Amendment Regulations 2007 SI No.2868 as from 7 April 2008, save that for a person to whom reg 1(5) of those regulations applied (see p1812), the amendments came into force on the day on or after 7 April 2008 when the first of the events specified in reg 1(6) applied to her/him, or on 6 April 2009 if none had before that date.

Amendment

1.   Substituted by reg 9 of SI 2007 No 2868 as from 7.4.08 (or if reg 1(5) of that SI applies, on the day on or after 7.4.08 when the first of the events specified in reg 1(6) applies, or from 6.4.09 if none have before that date).

General Note

Reg 17 requires an authority to apply for a substitute determination where any of the errors listed in para (1) comes to light. It appears that the error may be one of law as well as fact, but it would seem that if the local authority reaches a conclusion from primary facts, for example as to the composition of a household, it cannot describe that conclusion as an "error" merely because another officer later takes a different view.

There is no mechanism for a claimant to apply for a substitute determination, but an authority could be invited to exercise its duty under reg 17 and could be vulnerable to judicial review if it refuses to do so.

The references to "the appropriate authority" in paras (1)(a) and (b) appear to have been overlooked by the draftsman of SI 2001 No.1605 which amended reg 12C HB Regs 1987 (now reg 17 HB Regs). s34 WRA 2007 now provides a definition, but only for the purposes of the interpretation of ss32 and 33 WRA 2007 (the scheme for extended payments of HB, and previously CTB, on a person taking up employment or increasing earnings).

[¹ Application of provisions to substitute determinations or substitute redeterminations

18.   Regulations 15, 16 and 17 apply to a substitute determination or substitute redetermination as they apply to the determination or redetermination it replaces.]

Modifications

Reg 18 was substituted by reg 9 of the Housing Benefit (Local Housing Allowance and Information Sharing) Amendment Regulations 2007 SI No.2868 as from 7 April 2008, save that for a person to whom reg 1(5) of those regulations applied (see p1812), the amendments came into force on the day on or after 7 April 2008 when the first of the events specified in reg 1(6) applied to her/him, or on 6 April 2009 if none had before that date.

Amendment

1.   Substituted by reg 9 of SI 2007 No 2868 as from 7.4.08 (or if reg 1(5) of that SI applies, on the day on or after 7.4.08 when the first of the events specified in reg 1(6) applies, or from 6.4.09 if none have before that date).

General Note

Reg 18 confirms that substitute determinations may themselves be the subject of applications for redeterminations.

[¹ Amended determinations

18A.–(1)   This regulation applies where a decision has been revised in consequence of an amended broad rental market area determination or amended local housing allowance determination by a rent officer.

(2)   Where that amended determination has led to a reduction in the maximum rent (LHA) applicable to a claimant, the amended determination shall be a change of circumstances in relation to that claimant.

(3)   Where that amended determination has led to an increase in the maximum rent (LHA) applicable to a claimant, the amended determination shall have effect in place of the original determination.]

Amendment

1.   Inserted by reg 10 of SI 2007 No 2868 as from 7.4.08 (or if reg 1(5) of that SI applies, on the day on or after 7.4.08 when the first of the events specified in reg 1(6) applies, or from 6.4.09 if none have before that date).

Definitions

"amended determination" – see reg 2(1).
"claimant" – see reg 2(1).
"broad rental market area determination" – see reg 2(1).

General Note

The regulations do not provide a right of appeal or internal review against the broad rental market area determinations or the local housing allowance determinations made by the rent officer. However, where a rent officer is of the opinion that s/he has made an error (other than in the application of her/his professional judgement) in relation to either of these, s/he is required to notify the authority under art 7A(4) of the Rent Officer Orders. S/he must also provide an amended determination, as soon as practicable.

Reg 18A then sets out when the amended determination applies. A decrease in the maximum rent (LHA) is treated by para (2) as a change of circumstances and will lead to the supersession of the earlier award. By contrast an increase in the maximum rent (LHA) takes effect as a revision of the original award: para (3). It therefore leads to a payment of backdated benefit: see also regs 4(3), 7(2)(c) and 8(6) D&A Regs.

PART 4
Membership of a family

General Note on Part 4

"Family" is defined in s137(1) SSCBA. Note that it has a specific meaning for HB purposes – ie, a "family" is a couple or lone parent and any child or "person of a prescribed description" who is a member of the same household and for whom the claimant (or partner or both of them) is responsible. "Couple" and "child" are also defined in s137(1) SSCBA as well as in reg 2 HB Regs. Reg 19 sets out who is a person of a prescribed description for these purposes (a "qualifying young person"). Reg 20 provides circumstances in which the claimant and her/his partner are to be treated as responsible (or not responsible) for a child or young person. Reg 21 provides circumstances in which people (ie, the claimant, any partner and any child or young person) are to be treated as being (or not being) a member of the same household.

Note that the definition of "couple" for HB purposes has been amended, with effect from 13 March 2014 in England and Wales and from 16 December 2014 in Scotland, as a result of the introduction of same-sex marriage.

Among other things, being a member of the claimant's "family" is relevant for the following.

(1) Working out the claimant's applicable amount: see Part 5.

(2) Assessing the claimant's income and capital: see Part 6. Note: only the income and capital of a partner of the claimant is treated as the claimant's.

(3) For some of the rules for assessing the number of bedrooms allowed under the size criteria for the rent restriction schemes.

Note that if someone is a member of the "family", s/he cannot be a non-dependant and hence no non-dependant deduction can be made for her/him: see regs 3(2)(a) and 74.

Note also that reg 21(3), as well as preventing certain children or young people placed with a claimant or her/his partner under child protection legislation from being treated as members of the claimant's family, prevents them from being treated as occupying the claimant's home, and hence from being taken into account as occupiers for the purposes of the size criteria under the "social sector" scheme, the "local housing allowance" scheme and the "local reference rent" scheme rules. However, a "qualifying parent or carer" (a specified foster and kinship carer) is entitled to one additional bedroom under those criteria: regs B13(6)(b) and 13D(3A)(b) HB Regs and Sch 2 para 1A(b) of the RO Orders.

Persons of prescribed description

19.–(1) Subject to paragraph (2), a person of a prescribed description for the purposes of section 137(1) of the Act as it applies to housing benefit (definition of family) is a person [¹ who falls within the definition of qualifying young person in section 142 of the Act (child and qualifying young person)], and in these Regulations such a person is referred to as a "young person".

(2) Paragraph (1) shall not apply to a person who is–

(a) on income support [³, an income-based jobseeker's allowance or an income-related employment and support allowance]; [¹ [⁴]]

[² (b)]

(c) a person to whom section 6 of the Children (Leaving Care) Act 2000 (exclusion from benefits) applies. [⁴; or]

[⁴ (d) entitled to an award of universal credit]

(3) A person of a prescribed description for the purposes of section 137(1) of the Act as it applies to housing benefit (definition of the family) includes a child or young person in respect of whom section 145A of that Act applies for the purposes of entitlement to child benefit but only for the period prescribed under section 145A(1) of that Act.

Amendments

1. Amended by reg 4(2)(a) and (b) of SI 2006 No 718 as from 10.4.06.
2. Omitted by reg 4(2)(c) of SI 2006 No 718 as from 10.4.06.
3. Amended by reg 10 of SI 2008 No 1082 as from 27.10.08.
4. Amended by reg 35(3) of SI 2013 No 630 as from 29.4.13.

Definitions

"an income-based jobseeker's allowance" – see reg 2(1).
"person on income support" – see reg 2(1).
"person on an income-based jobseeker's allowance" – see reg 2(3).
"person on an income-related employment and support allowance" – see reg 2(3A).

General Note

s137(1) SSCBA 1992 refers to "child" and "person of a prescribed description" in the definition of "family" for HB purposes (see p12). That section and reg 2(1) define "child" and this reg deals with those covered by the latter term, and provides that they shall be referred to as a "young person" elsewhere in these regulations.

Analysis

Para (1). "Young person" is defined by reference to the definition of a "qualifying young person" for child benefit purposes. s142 SSCBA 1992 and the Child Benefit (General) Regulations 2006 SI No.223 (the CB Regs) prescribe who may be treated as a "qualifying young person" for these purposes.

First, the young person must be 16 or over and under 20 and on a course of "full-time non-advanced education", in "approved training" or, in England only, in "appropriate full-time education" under s4 Education and Skills Act 2008 (ie, a "16–19 study programme"), or having undertaken such a course or training, have been accepted or be enrolled to undertake a further such course or training: reg 3(2) CB Regs. S/he must have started the course or the training, or have been enrolled or accepted on the course or the training, before reaching age 19: reg 3(2) and (4) CB Regs.

The course of full-time non-advanced education must be at a school, college or similar institution: reg 3(2)(a)(i) CB Regs. Education received elsewhere (eg, at home) also qualifies if approved by the Commissioners for Her Majesty's Revenue and Customs (HMRC) and the young person was receiving the education before reaching age 16: reg 3(2)(a)(ii) and (3) CB Regs. If the student is not at a recognised educational establishment, it is the nature of the course that matters, not where s/he is studying, provided the Commissioners for the HMRC have approved the studies.

For the purposes of "full-time non-advanced education", "full-time" means over 12 hours a week excluding meal breaks and unsupervised study: reg 1(3) CB Regs. "Non-advanced" for these purposes (and for the purposes of "appropriate full-time education" under s4 Education and Skills Act 2008) means not above A level or Higher/Advanced Higher standard: regs 1(3) and 3(2)(ab)(i) CB Regs.

"Approved training" means arrangements made by the government. At the time of writing, these were known in Wales as "Foundation Modern Apprenticeships", and in Scotland as "Employability Fund activity": reg 1(3) CB Regs. The training cannot be provided under a contract of employment: reg 3(2)(c) CB Regs.

If a young person leaves education or approved training before reaching age 20, s/he is still treated as a qualifying young person in any of the following circumstances.

(1)   If s/he is 16, up to and including 31 August following her/his 16th birthday or if her/his 16th birthday is on 31 August, up to and including the day after: reg 4 CB Regs.

(2)   If s/he is 16 or 17, has left education or training, is registered for work, education or training and is not in remunerative work (here defined as 24 hours or more a week), until the end of her/his "extension period" – ie, from the Monday after the education/training ends and ending 20 weeks later: reg 1(3) and 5 CB Regs.

(3)   If s/he is at least 16 but under 20, and has not yet passed the end of the week that includes her/his "terminal date", up to and including the week (Monday to Sunday) that includes her/his "terminal date" or, if s/he reaches 20 before that date, the week including the last Monday before her/his 20th birthday: reg 7 CB Regs. The "terminal date" is whichever of the following dates first follows the date s/he leaves the education or training: the last day in February, May, August or November: reg 7 CB Regs. A young person who is to return to take an external exam in connection with the education is treated as still being in the education until the date of the last exam. In Scotland, a young person who has taken the Higher or Advanced Higher Certificate can be treated as still being in education until the date a comparable course in England would end if this is later.

Some interruptions in satisfying the conditions for being a "qualifying young person" can be ignored: reg 6 CB Regs.

Para (2). A young person is not part of the claimant's family if s/he is her/himself on IS, income-based JSA or income-related ESA (see reg 2(1) for the definitions) or is entitled to an award of UC. Neither is a person who is excluded from entitlement to benefits under s6 Children (Leaving Care) Act 2000 (see p1710).

Para (3). s145A SSCBA, inserted by s55 TCA 2002, provides for entitlement to child benefit to continue for a prescribed period after the death of a child or qualifying young person. The prescribed period is eight weeks for a child under 16. For a "qualifying young person" it is also eight weeks unless s/he would have attained the age of 20 during that period. In this case, if it is shorter, it is the period commencing the week in which the death occurred and finishing on the Monday in the week following the week in which the qualifying young person would have attained the age of 20: reg 20 CB Regs. The effect of reg 19(3) is that the deceased child continues to be treated as part of the claimant's family for HB purposes during that prescribed period.

Circumstances in which a person is to be treated as responsible or not responsible for another

20.–(1)   Subject to the following provisions of this regulation a person shall be treated as responsible for a child or young person who is normally living with him and this includes a child or young person to whom paragraph (3) of regulation 19 applies.

(2)   Where a child or young person spends equal amounts of time in different households, or where there is a question as to which household he is living in, the child or young person shall be treated for the purposes of paragraph (1) as normally living with–

(a)   the person who is receiving child benefit in respect of him; or

(b)   if there is no such person–

    (i)   where only one claim for child benefit has been made in respect of him, the person who made that claim, or

    (ii)   in any other case the person who has the primary responsibility for him.

(3)   For the purposes of these Regulations a child or young person shall be the responsibility of only one person in any benefit week and any person other than the one treated as responsible for the child or young person under this regulation shall be treated as not so responsible.

Definitions

"benefit week" – see reg 2(1).
"child" – see s137(1) SSCBA and reg 2(1).
"household" – see note on s137 SSCBA.
"young person" – see reg 19.

General Note

For a child or young person to count as a member of a claimant's family for HB purposes, s/he must be a member of the claimant's household (see reg 21) and the claimant or her/his partner must be "responsible" for her/him: s137(1) SSCBA 1992. A child or young person being a member of a claimant's family is important for a number of reasons, the main one being that the claimant's applicable amount includes allowances and premiums for her/him and hence the claimant's rate of HB is potentially higher.

Reg 20 sets out the situations in which a person is treated as responsible. By para (3) only one person can be treated as responsible for a particular child or young person in any benefit week. Para (1) sets out the general rule that a person is responsible for a child or young person "normally living with" her/him. That includes a deceased child or young person falling within reg 19(3). Para (2) sets out the rules for deciding who the responsible person is, if the child or young person spends equal time in different households or if there is doubt or dispute as to which household the child or young person lives in.

Analysis

Para (1). The primary rule is that a person is responsible for a child or young person who is "normally living with" her/him. This means that the child or young person is spending more time with that person than with anyone else: *CFC 1537/1995*.

Para (2) contains deeming provisions to resolve cases in two sets of circumstances.

(1)   It applies where the amount of time spent in different households is equal. It need not be exactly equal in order to trigger the operation of para (2): *CFC 1537/1995*. Authorities should therefore consider the position in the round rather than carrying out an exact calculation.

(2)   It applies "where there is a question" as to which household a child or young person is living in. It is suggested that there must be a "question" of some difficulty, otherwise para (1) would be deprived of all effect. In granting permission to appeal in *Walsall MBC v UM (HB)* [2015] UKUT 99 (AAC), Judge Jacobs raised the issue of when a question arose. He said: "This is a difficult expression to understand. Paragraph (2) has to be interpreted in the context of the regulation as a whole. It must not be interpreted in a way that renders other paragraphs redundant. It is not an excuse for a local authority to avoid the need to investigate. It clearly applies if, having investigated, there is no evidence on the matter or if the evidence is insufficient for the local authority or tribunal to make a soundly based finding."

Where para (2) applies, the test is determined in three stages. The child is treated as "normally living with":

(1)   The person who is in receipt of child benefit in respect of the child: sub-para (a). A person is not "receiving child benefit" where it is being paid to her/him, or, for example, paid into her/his bank account, by the person entitled to the child benefit: *CIS 2317/2006*.

(2)   If no one is receiving child benefit, the person who has claimed it in respect of the child: sub-para (b)(i).

(3)   In any other case (including where more than one person has claimed child benefit for the child), the person who has "primary responsibility" for the child: sub-para (b)(ii). This will require consideration of all the circumstances, financial and pastoral.

In *Camden LB v NW and SSWP(HB)* [2011] UKUT 262 (AAC), the claimant's attempt to challenge the use of the receipt of child benefit as a deciding factor in cases where a child spends exactly equal time in different households failed. The appeal was decided before the Supreme Court made its decision in *Humphreys v HMRC* [2012] UKSC 18; [2012] AACR 46. The Supreme Court rejected Human Rights Act arguments in the context of CTC, albeit in an appeal concerning a different rule than for HB, and not about exactly equal shared care.

TD v SSWP and LB Richmond-upon-Thames (HB) [2013] UKUT 642 (AAC) was an appeal by a father who had exactly equal shared care of his child but did not receive child benefit for him. He argued that the rule in reg 20(2)(a) HB Regs indirectly discriminated against men as fewer men than women in his situation received child benefit. Judge Wright, having considered statistical evidence, agreed, but decided that the discrimination was justified; it could not be said that per *Humphreys* the discrimination was manifestly without reasonable foundation. The claimant's argument that the discrimination was not justified on the facts of his case because he was not seeking HB to be paid twice or for it to be apportioned (his child's mother was not an HB claimant) was rejected because what has to be justified is the indirectly discriminatory effects of the rule and not its effect in any particular case, though the latter may inform the former. The same result was reached in respect of "substantial minority carers" in *JN v SSWP and Basingstoke and Deane BC (HB)* [2014] UKUT 223 (AAC), though in the alternative to the parent being an exactly equal shared carer.

Circumstances in which a person is to be treated as being or not being a member of the household

21.–(1)   Subject to paragraphs (2) to (4), the claimant and any partner and, where the claimant or his partner is treated as responsible by virtue of regulation 20 (circumstances in which a person is to be treated as responsible or not responsible for another) for a child or young person, that child or young person and any child of that child or young person, shall be treated as members of the same household notwithstanding that any of them is temporarily living away from the other members of his family.

(2)   Paragraph (1) shall not apply to a person who is living away from the other members of his family where–

(a)   that person does not intend to resume living with the other members of his family; or

(b)   his absence from the other members of his family is likely to exceed 52 weeks, unless there are exceptional circumstances (for example where the person is in hospital or otherwise has no control over the length of his absence) and the absence is unlikely to be substantially more than 52 weeks.

(3)   A child or young person shall not be treated as a member of the claimant's household [¹, nor as occupying the claimant's dwelling,] where he is–

(a)   placed with the claimant or his partner by a local authority under [⁴ section 22C(2)] of the Children Act 1989 [⁴ or section 81(2) of the Social Services and Well-being (Wales) Act 2014] or by a voluntary organisation under section 59(1)(a) of that Act, or in Scotland boarded out [³ or placed] with the claimant or his partner under a relevant enactment; or

(b)   placed, or in Scotland boarded out, with the claimant or his partner prior to adoption; or

(c)   placed for adoption with the claimant or his partner in accordance with the Adoption and Children Act 2002 or [² the Adoption Agencies (Scotland) Regulations 2009].

(4)   Subject to paragraph (5), paragraph (1) shall not apply to a child or young person who is not living with the claimant and he–

(a)   is being looked after by, or in Scotland is in the care of, a local authority under a relevant enactment; or

(b)   has been placed, or in Scotland boarded out, with a person other than the claimant prior to adoption; or

(c)   has been placed for adoption in accordance with the Adoption and Children Act 2002 or [² the Adoption Agencies (Scotland) Regulations 2009].

(5)   An authority shall treat a child or young person to whom paragraph (4)(a) applies as being a member of the claimants' household in any benefit week where–

(a)   that child or young person lives with the claimant for part or all of that benefit week; and

(b)   the authority considers that it is reasonable to do so taking into account the nature and frequency of that child's or young person's visits.

(6)   In this regulation "relevant enactment" means the Army Act 1955, the Air Force Act 1955, the Naval Discipline Act 1957, the Matrimonial Proceedings Children Act 1958, the Social Work (Scotland) Act 1968, the Family Law Reform Act 1969, the Children and Young Persons Act 1969, the Matrimonial Causes Act 1973, the Children Act 1975, the Domestic Proceedings and Magistrates' Courts Act 1978, [² the Adoption and Children (Scotland) Act 2007], the Child Care Act 1980, the Family Law Act 1986, the Children Act 1989 [³] the Children (Scotland) Act 1995 [³ and the Children's Hearings (Scotland) Act 2011].

Amendments

1.   Amended by reg 2(3) of SI 2010 No 2449 as from 1.11.10.
2.   Amended by art 2 and Sch 1 para 39(3) of SI 2011 No 1740 as from 15.7.11.
3.   Amended by art 17 and Sch 1 para 23 of SI 2013 No 1465 as from 24.6.13.
4.   Amended by arts 11(3) and 25(2) of SI 2017 No 901 as from 3.11.17.

Definitions

"benefit week" – see reg 2(1).
"child" – see reg 2(1) and s137(1) SSCBA.
"claimant" – see reg 2(1).
"family" – see reg 2(1) and s137(1) SSCBA.
"household" – see note to s137 SSCBA.
"partner" – see reg 2(1).
"relevant enactment" – see para (6).
"young person" – see reg 19.

General Note

Reg 21 deals with the situations in which a claimant's family for HB purposes (that is her/his partner and children or qualifying young people) are treated as being members of the same household and when they are not so treated, and when certain children and young people (specified in para (3)) are not to be treated as members of the household or as occupying the claimant's dwelling. Note that for a child or young person to count as a member of a claimant's family at all, s/he *must* be a member of the claimant's household and the claimant or her/his partner must be "responsible" for her/him (for which see reg 20): s137(1) SSCBA. The first thing to notice is that this regulation does not define "household". See the discussion of the meaning in the Analysis to s137 SSCBA on p17. It does, however, set out the situations in which a person is to continue to be treated as a member of a household despite physical absence from it.

Analysis

Para (1). The general rule is that claimants, their partner(s), any child or young person for whom they are responsible, and any child of such a child or young person shall be treated as members of the same household even where one of them is temporarily living away from the other members of the family. Exceptions to the rules are found in paras (2) to (5).

For a claimant to have a "partner" as defined in reg 2(1), s/he must be a member of a couple (also defined in reg 2(1)) or be polygamously married.

It is only then that the claimant can be treated as a member of the same household with a partner under para (1). As the judge in *Broxtowe BC v CS (HB)* [2014] UKUT 186 (AAC) said (at para 25):

"[I]f people are in different households, they cannot be a couple, and regulation 21 cannot turn them into a couple. Regulation 21 is about how long the status of being in the same household lasts, but only once it has been established that people are in fact in the same household. If two people are not a couple, regulation 21 is irrelevant."

Para (2) treats a person who is living away from the other members of the family (eg, a partner working abroad, or in another part of the country) as not being a member of the household if s/he does not intend to resume living with the family or s/he is likely to be absent for more than 52 weeks (unless there are exceptional circumstances). Examples of exceptional circumstances are given in sub-para (b). If such a person is the claimant's partner, her/his income will no longer fall to be treated as the claimant's under reg 25 and any money actually received from her/him should be treated as maintenance under Section 5 of Part 6.

Para (3) provides that certain children or young people placed with (or in Scotland boarded out or placed with) a claimant (or her/his partner) under the specified child protection legislation are not to be treated as members of the claimant's household, and hence out of her/his benefit family. Para (3) was amended from 1 November 2010 and now also provides that these children and young people are not to be treated as occupying the claimant's dwelling. This reverses the decision in *Wirral MBC v AH and SSWP (HB)* [2010] UKUT 208 (AAC); [2011] AACR 6 and now prevents the children and young people being taken into account as occupiers for the purposes of the size criteria under the social sector scheme rules, the local housing allowance scheme rules or the local reference rent scheme rules: see regs B13, 13 and 13D(3) HB Regs and Sch 2 para 1 of the RO Orders. Note, however, that a "qualifying parent or carer" (a specified foster or kinship carer – see the definition in reg 2(1)) is entitled to one additional bedroom under those criteria: regs B13(6)(b) and 13D(3A)(b) HB Regs and Sch 2 para 1A(b) of the RO Orders.

Under sub-para (a), s23(1)(a) Children Act 1989 placed a duty upon the local authority to provide accommodation for a child when s/he is in care. By s23(2)(a) of the Act, the authority was to provide that accommodation by placing the child with a family, a relative of hers/his, or any other suitable person. Sub-para (a) has now been amended to reflect the fact that these duties are now to be found in s22C of the Act and in s81(2) of the Social Services and Well-being (Wales) Act 2014. Where a voluntary organisation provides accommodation for a child under s59(1)(a) Children Act 1989 it must do so by placing the child with the same persons identified above. For the definition of "relevant enactment", see para (6).

Under sub-paras (b) and (c), a child placed with the claimant (boarded out in Scotland) as part of the adoption process is not to be treated as being a member of the claimant's family or as occupying the claimant's dwelling.

Paras (4) and (5). Para (4) treats a child or young person who is being "looked after" (in care in Scotland) or is being prepared for adoption, as not being a member of the household (and hence part of the claimant's benefit family). However, if the child or young person is being "looked after" (or is in care) but lives with the claimant for part or all of any benefit week, then para (5) allows them to be treated as a member of the claimant's household, in that week. Para (5), however, only applies if the authority considers this reasonable taking into account the nature and frequency of the visits. The "nature" of the visits might refer to length of stay, and whether the child is treated as a member of the family during the stay, etc. Reading paras (4) and (5) together, the phrase "living with" seems to have the narrow meaning of physical presence, because if a child or young person is physically present in any particular week, if para (5) applies it may be used to override the effect of para (4).

PART 5
Applicable amounts

General Note on Part 5
This Part is made under s135 SSCBA 1992 and, together with Sch 3, prescribes the rules for ascertaining a claimant's applicable amount. The "applicable amount" is an essential component in the calculation of HB: see s135 SSCBA (p9) and Part 8 (p504).

Sch 3 sets out the different elements that can make up an applicable amount. The "allowances" depend on whether a claimant is single, a lone parent, part of a couple or polygamously married, and whether s/he is responsible for a child or qualifying young person. In addition to these basic amounts, the claimant may qualify to have one or more of the premiums set out in Parts 3 and 4 of Sch 3 included in her/his applicable amount (see p634 and p646) and the support component, as set out in Parts 5 and 6 of Sch 3 (see p647 and p650). If the claimant has been transferred (the conversion) from IS "on the grounds of disability", IB or SDA to ESA which is not income-related, or is appealing a conversion decision, s/he may also qualify for a transitional addition under Parts 7 and 8 of Sch 3.

Applicable amounts

22.–(1) Subject to regulations 23, 24, 80 and 81 and Schedule A1 (polygamous marriages, patients, calculation of weekly amounts, rent free periods and treatment of claims for housing benefit by refugees), a claimant's weekly applicable amount shall be the aggregate of such of the following amounts as may apply in his case–

(a)   an amount in respect of himself or, if he is a member of a couple, an amount in respect of both of them, determined in accordance with paragraph 1(1), (2) or (3), as the case may be, of Schedule 3;

[⁵ (b) an amount determined in accordance with paragraph 2 of Schedule 3 in respect of up to two individuals who are either children or young persons and who are members of his family;]

[³ (c)]

(d)   the amount of any premiums which may be applicable to him, determined in accordance with Parts 3 and 4 of Schedule 3 (premiums).

[¹, ⁴ (e) the amount of the support component which may be applicable to him in accordance with Part 5 of Schedule 3 (the component);]

[² (f) the amount of any transitional addition which may be applicable to him in accordance with Parts 7 and 8 of Schedule 3 (transitional addition).]

[⁵ (2)   For the purposes of paragraph (1)(b), as it applies apart from paragraph (4), where the family includes more than two individuals who are either children or young persons, and, under paragraph 2 of Schedule 3, a different amount applies to different individuals, the two amounts to be included in the applicable amount shall be those that result in the greatest possible total amount.

(3)   Paragraph (4) applies where–

(a)   (whether or not as part of a tax credit couple) the claimant has an award of child tax credit in respect of a child or young person who is a member of his family, and whether or not any amount is payable by way of such credit; and

(b)   the total amount to be included in the applicable amount under paragraph (1)(b) as substituted by paragraph (4) would be higher than the total amount that would be included under paragraph (1)(b) apart from paragraph (4).

(4)   Where this paragraph applies, for paragraph (1)(b) substitute–

"(b) an amount determined in accordance with paragraph 2 of Schedule 3 in respect of any child or young person who is a member of his family and in respect of whom the individual element of child tax credit has been included in the determination of the maximum rate of that credit;".

(5)   In this regulation, "tax credit couple" means a couple as defined in section 3(5A) of the Tax Credits Act 2002.]

Amendments
1.   Inserted by reg 11 of SI 2008 No 1082, as amended by reg 29 of SI 2008 No 2428, as from 27.10.08.
2.   Inserted by reg 27 and Sch 5 para 1(3) of SI 2010 No 1907 as amended by reg 15 of SI 2010 No 2430 as from 1.10.10.
3.   Omitted by reg 2(1)(a) of SI 2015 No 1857 as from 1.5.16, subject to transitional provisions in reg 4.
4.   Substituted by Sch 1 para 6(3) of SI 2017 No 204 as from 3.4.17, subject to transitional and savings provisions in Sch 2 paras 1–7.
5.   Amended by reg 7(2) of SI 2017 No 376 as from 6.4.17, subject to transitional provision in reg 9.

Definitions
"applicable amount" – see s135 SSCBA.
"child" – reg 2(1).
"claimant" – see reg 2(1).
"couple" – see reg 2(1).
"family" – see s137(1) SSCBA.
"polygamous marriage" – see reg 2(1).
"young person" – regs 2(1) and 19(1).

General Note
This regulation sets out the basic rules for ascertaining the applicable amount (notional financial needs) for the purpose of working out HB entitlement, for any claimant who is not polygamously married. The basic rules are subject to regs 23, 24, 80 and 81 and Sch A1. A claimant's weekly applicable amount is the total of the amounts applicable to her/him under sub-paras (a) to (f) of para (1). Note that reg 24 was revoked in April 2006 and that Sch A1 can only be relevant to those recorded as refugees on or before 14 June 2007. Reg 23 sets out the applicable amount for a claimant who is polygamously married.

Analysis
Para (1)(a). The amount applicable under sub-para (a) is the "personal allowance" which varies according to the claimant's age and to whether the claimant is a single person, a lone parent or a member of a couple.
        Para (1)(b). Sch 3 para 2 provides allowances for children and qualifying young people (for which see reg 19). Note that, from 6 April 2017, this is generally restricted to allowances for two children or young people. Paras (2) to (5) prescribe that the local authority will use a child tax credit (CTC) decision, where relevant, as the basis for its decision on whether to include a third or subsequent child in the applicable amount. The restriction to two allowances is subject to transitional protection (set out in reg 9 of the Social Security (Restrictions on Amounts for Children and Qualifying Young Persons) Amendment Regulations 2017 SI No.376 – see p1894) for those who were entitled to HB on 5 April 2017 and responsible for more than two children or young people. Transitional protection continues until a new claim for HB is made or the claimant becomes responsible for a new child or young person. Note that the fact that allowances for some children or young people may not be included in the applicable amount does not prevent those children or young people from being treated as occupying the claimant's home, and hence from being taken into account as occupiers for the purposes of the size criteria under the "social sector" scheme, the "local housing allowance" scheme and the "local reference rent" scheme rules. For membership of a "family", see p17 and Part 4 of these regulations.
        In a judicial review case, *SC & Ors v SSWP & Ors* [2018] EWHC 864 (Admin), the High Court held that the two-child provision as a whole is compatible with the ECHR. The Court rejected the reasoning set out by Mr Justice Collins in *R (on the application of DA and others) v SSWP* (see p522) that the effect of welfare cuts amounts to unlawful discrimination contrary to Art 14. It found no support for a conclusion that the two-child limit leads to non-justifiable discrimination.
        However, one of the parties to the action was a family who looked after a child under a child arrangement, taking the child in as the family's second child before the couple went on to have a further child of their own. The family would have been excepted from the two-child limit if the looked-after child had counted as their third child. The Court found that the operation of the exception in respect of non-parental caring arrangements (provided for in the Child Tax Credit (Amendment) Regulations 2017 and the Social Security (Restriction on Amounts for Children and Qualifying Young Persons) Amendment Regulations 2017) was unlawful to the extent that it depended on whether the looked-after child joined the family before or after the second child was born to the family. Mr Justice Ouseley found (at paras 216 and 217) that:
        "The purpose of the exception is to encourage, or at least to avoid discouraging, a family from looking after a child who would otherwise be in local authority care…The choice which the family is being asked to make…is not rationally connected to the purposes of the legislation, and indeed it is in conflict with them...It is not the exception itself which is unlawful, but the sequencing or ordering part of it."

The Court held that it would hear counsel on the appropriate form of relief for that unlawful provision. The government subsequently announced that it would extend the exception for children who would otherwise be likely to be in local authority care, including children who are adopted or looked after by non-parental carers, so that it applies regardless of the order in which they joined the household. Amendments to the Child Tax Credit Regulations 2002 were made from 28 November 2018 (as a result of the Child Tax Credit (Amendments) Regulations 2018 SI No.1130). The effect is that a child element will be payable for a third or subsequent child or qualifying young person where all, or all but one, of the other children or young people for whom the claimant is responsible are adopted or cared for under a non-parental caring arrangement. Parents who have adopted children or who are kinship carers can, therefore, receive child elements for two further children for whom no exception applies. The amendments also ensure that, where a person adopts a child and subsequently dies, the exception from the two-child rule will continue to apply to that person's surviving partner.

In *SC & Ors v SSWP & Ors* [2019] EWCA Civ 615, the Court of Appeal upheld the High Court's decision on the two-child provision as a whole. The Court concluded that:

"(a)   the admittedly greater impact of the measure on women and (b) the difference in treatment between families according to whether there are more than two, or no more than two, children in the family are both differences in treatment which fall within the ambit of article 14...However, the aims of the measure are undoubtedly legitimate and, given the wide area of judgment afforded to the legislature in matters of social and economic policy, it cannot be said that either difference in treatment is manifestly not a proportionate means of pursuing legitimate aims."

Para (1)(c). Prior to 1 May 2016, sub-para (c) provided a family premium under Sch 3 para 3. The family premium was abolished from that date subject to transitional rules. See the commentary on p634.

Para (1)(d). See the notes to Sch 3 for the details of the premiums. They are designed to meet the additional specific needs of some claimants. Note Sch 3 para 13(9) limits the award of the disability premium if the claimant has, or is treated as having, limited capabilty for work. In this case, s/he may instead be entitled to the component in sub-para (e) below.

Para (1)(e). See the notes to Sch 3 for details of the component. A component can be included if the claimant or her/his partner has, or is treated as having, limited capability for work. Note that, prior to 3 April 2017, such a claimant or her/his partner could have one of two components included. The work-related activity component is no longer available for claims made on or after 3 April 2017. Transitional provision made under Sch 2 paras 1–7 of the Employment and Support Allowance and Universal Credit (Miscellaneous Amendments and Transitional and Savings Provisions) Regulations 2017 SI No.204 (see p1892) for claims made before 3 April 2017 means that those who continue to have, or to be treated as having, limited capability for work are entitled to continue to receive that component. Sch 3 paras 21 and 21A prevent the award of more than one component. Para 22 limits the award of a component if the claimant is entitled to a disability premium.

Para (1)(f). This amount is applicable where a claimant or her/his partner has been transferred to ESA which is not income-related (the conversion) from IS "on the grounds of disability", IB or SDA , or in specified circumstances is appealing a conversion decision. The transitional addition (calculated under Sch 3 para 30) is meant to provide protection against a reduction in HB as a consequence of the conversion.

Polygamous marriages

23.–(1)   Subject to regulations 24, 80 and 81 and Schedule A1 (patients, calculation of weekly amounts, rent free periods and treatment of claims for housing benefit by refugees), where a claimant is a member of a polygamous marriage, his weekly applicable amount shall be the aggregate of such of the following amounts as may apply in his case–

(a)   the highest amount applicable to him and one of his partners determined in accordance with paragraph 1(3) of Schedule 3 as if he and that partner were a couple;

(b)   an amount equal to the difference between the amounts specified in sub-paragraphs (3)(b) and (1)(b) of paragraph 1 of Schedule 3 in respect of each of his other partners;

[⁵ (c)   an amount determined in accordance with paragraph 2 of Schedule 3 in respect of up to two individuals who are either children or young persons and for whom he or a partner of his is responsible and who are members of the same household;]

[³ (d)]

(e)   the amount of any premiums which may be applicable to him determined in accordance with Parts 3 and 4 of Schedule 3 (premiums).

[¹,⁴ (f)   the amount of the support component which may be applicable to him in accordance with Part 5 of Schedule 3 (the component);]

[² (g)   the amount of any transitional addition which may be applicable to him in accordance with Parts 7 and 8 of Schedule 3 (transtional addition).]

[⁵ (2)   For the purposes of paragraph (1)(c), as it applies apart from paragraph (4), where the claimant and his partners are between them responsible for more than two individuals who are either children or young persons and who are members of the same household, and, under paragraph 2 of Schedule 3, a different amount applies to different individuals, the two amounts to be included in the applicable amount shall be those that result in the greatest possible total amount.

(3)   Paragraph (4) applies where–

(a)   (as part of a polygamous unit) the claimant has an award of child tax credit in respect of any child or young person for whom he or a partner of his is responsible and who is a member of the same household, and whether or not any amount is payable by way of such credit; and

(b)   the total amount to be included in the applicable amount under paragraph (1)(c) as substituted by paragraph (4) would be higher than the total amount that would be included under paragraph (1)(c) apart from paragraph (4).

(4)   Where this paragraph applies, for paragraph (1)(c) substitute–

"(c)   an amount determined in accordance with paragraph 2 of Schedule 3 in respect of any child or young person for whom he or a partner of his is responsible and who is a member of the same household and in respect of whom the individual element of child tax credit has been included in the determination of the maximum rate of that credit;".

(5)   In this regulation, "polygamous unit" has the same meaning as in regulation 2 of the Tax Credits (Polygamous Marriages) Regulations 2003.]

Amendments

1.   Inserted by reg 12 of SI 2008 No 1082, as amended by reg 30 of SI 2008 No 2428, as from 27.10.08.
2.   Inserted by Reg 27 and Sch 5 para 1(4) of SI 2010 No 1907 as amended by reg 15 of SI 2010 No 2430 as from 1.10.10.
3.   Omitted by reg 2(1)(b) of SI 2015 No 1857 as from 1.5.16, subject to transitional provisions in reg 4.
4.   Substituted by Sch 1 para 6(4) of SI 2017 No 204 as from 3.4.17, subject to transitional and savings provisions in Sch 2 paras 1–7.
5.   Amended by reg 7(3) of SI 2017 No 376 as from 6.4.17, subject to transitional provision in reg 9.

Definitions

"applicable amount" – see s135 SSCBA.
"child" – see reg 2(1).
"claimant" – see reg 2(1).
"partner" – see reg 2(1).
"polygamous marriage" – see reg 2(1).
"young person" – see reg 19.

General Note

These rules apply solely to claimants who are polygamously married: defined in reg 2(1). Because of the definition of "partner" in reg 2(1), an increased applicable amount can only be obtained under this regulation in respect of partners to a polygamous marriage who share the same household. The rules are subject to regs 24, 80 and 81 and Sch A1. Note that reg 24 was revoked in April 2006 and that Sch A1 can only be relevant to those recorded as refugees on or before 14 June 2007.

Sub-paras (c) to (g) of para (1) of this regulation have the same effect as sub-paras (b) to (f) of reg 22(1): see notes on that regulation. The applicable amount is the total due under sub-paras (a) to (g).

Prior to 1 May 2016, sub-para (d) provided a family premium under Sch 3 para 3. The family premium was abolished from that date subject to transitional rules. See the commentary on p634.

Analysis

Para (1)(a) and (b). The basic personal allowance awarded in respect of polygamously married couples is calculated by taking the highest amount awarded under Sch 3 para 1(3) in respect of any of the couples (depending on age and whether the claimant is entitled to ESA which includes a work-related activity component or a support component). An additional personal allowance is then awarded for the other partner(s): the amount is the difference between the allowance for a single claimant aged not less than 25 and a couple aged not less than 18. So, for example, if a male claimant, A, aged 45 has two wives, B aged 37 and C aged 17, the couple allowance is calculated as between A and B and is for couples where at least one member is more than 18. A further amount is then awarded for C as stated above.

Para (1)(c) and (e). The allowances and premiums awarded are identical to those awarded under reg 22(1)(b) and (d), save that in relation to child premiums the claimant is entitled if any of her/his partners is responsible for the children. The restriction from 6 April 2017 to payment of allowances for two children or young people, and the transitional provision for those entitled to HB before that date, operates in the same way as described for reg 22(1)(b).

Para (1)(f). The removal of the work-related activity component from 3 April 2017, and the transitional provision for claims made before that date, operates in the same way as described for reg 22(1)(e).

Patients
[¹24.]

Amendment

1.   Omitted by reg 2(4) of SI 2005 No 2502 as amended by Sch 2 para 27 of SI 2006 No 217 as from 1.4.06 (3.4.06 where rent payable weekly or at intervals of a week).

General Note

Until omitted, reg 24 varied the applicable amounts due under regs 22 or 23 as appropriate, in relation to claimants who had been patients for more than 52 weeks. Whether someone is a patient is still of relevance in the treatment of childcare costs (under reg 28) and to entitlement to the disability and enhanced disability premiums (Sch 3 paras 13 and 15). The definition of "patient" for these purposes is in reg 28(11)(e) (see p430).

Long-term hospital patients may still be caught by the requirement in reg 7 that they must be occupying the home, but see reg 7(16)(c)(ii). The definition of "patient" for these purposes is in reg 7(18) (see p262). The definition there also applies in determining whether a non-dependant deduction is applicable under reg 74(7)(f).

PART 6
Income and capital

General Note on Part 6

The claimant's income and capital and that of her/his partner, together with her/his applicable amount (see Part 5) and her/his "eligible rent" (see Part 3) are the basic components of the HB calculation: see s130(1)(c) SSCBA 1992 (p5).

The income rules are very detailed and are largely in line with the rules for IS, income-based JSA and income-related ESA. Caselaw in relation to those benefits and that decided under the old supplementary benefit scheme will often be highly persuasive. Only the most significant court judgments and commissioners' and Upper Tribunal decisions are examined in the commentary to Part 6. See the current volume of *Social Security Legislation Vol II* for a more comprehensive treatment.

There is provision for assessment of capital, and a capital limit on entitlement of £16,000.

Income and capital: the distinction

No attempt has been made in the rules at any sort of definition of the difference between income and capital. What is very clear is that a resource must be either one or the other; there is nothing inbetween. However, although a resource at any one time must be income or capital, it does not follow that such status is immutable as a sum of money can alter in status, particularly over time: *CH 1561/2005* paras 17 and 18. See also regs 41 and 46 on p453 and p463 for the situations in which capital is to be treated as income and income is to be treated as capital, as well as the analysis to reg 32 on p435 for when payments of tax credits might not count as income.

In *R(H) 8/08*, the claimant's accountant had paid his rent, on a number of occasions, direct to his landlord, as a loan on a temporary basis while his HB application was being considered. The local authority took the rent payments into account as the claimant's income. Deputy Commissioner Mark reviewed the caselaw on the meaning of "income" and decided that, as stated by the Court of Appeal in *Morrell v SSWP* [2003] EWCA Civ 526; reported as *R(IS) 6/03*, the word must be given its ordinary and natural meaning, subject only to specific provisions of the regulations giving it a different meaning. Loans can be income, but it is necessary to examine all the facts before coming to a conclusion. He said that while loans, in particular recurrent loans, may well be income if there is no immediate repayment obligation, all the facts and circumstances need to be examined to decide if this is the case. He made some useful points on the factors that need to be considered (at para 31).

(1)   If a claimant receives regular loans from family or friends to cover rent or other outgoings before applying for benefit, and is not expected to repay them until some time in the indefinite future, this suggests that the loans are "income".

(2)   If a claimant and another person (eg, her/his accountant) agree that s/he should lend the claimant money for her/his rent for a month or two, while a claim for HB is being processed, then this suggests the loans are not "income", particularly if the person would expect repayment as soon as the claim was processed and arrears of benefit paid.

(3)   If a person was lending money regularly in ignorance of an application for HB, or would have gone on lending it regardless of its outcome, then this may suggest the loans are "income".

(4)   The fact that loans are not made every month is a factor to be taken into account with all the other circumstances, both in considering whether all or some of the loans are income, and in considering what the claimant's income was at any particular time.

The deputy commissioner pointed out that it would not appear to be the intention of the legislation to penalise somebody in need who made a legitimate application for benefit, because, through no fault of her/his own, the application took time to process and s/he needed to borrow temporarily to cover her/his needs while the application was being considered.

In order to decide whether a particular resource is income or capital, careful note should be taken of the provisions for treatment of income as capital and *vice versa*: see regs 41 and 46 respectively. Further indications as to the nature of a resource may be found in Schs 5 and 6, which set out the categories of income and capital that are to be disregarded in the assessment process. If a resource is required to be partially disregarded as income or as capital, that is a good indication that the resource (or those of a similar nature) is intended by the regulations to be treated as such. For example, Sch 6 para 10(a) requires insurance payments relating to damage to the home to be ignored as capital for up to 26 weeks. It follows that such payments will be treated as capital, and it can be deduced from that that most insurance pay-outs will fall to be treated as capital rather than income.

However, *CH 1561/2005* warns against assuming that the provisions of the legislation can determine the classification of whether a sum of money is income or capital. Indeed the decision goes further than this and holds that the regulations do not provide any definition of income or capital (either expressly – which is true – or by implication) but instead are predicated on the classification already having been made. Even if this approach is correct, it is suggested that the provisions of the regulations may provide helpful guidance as to whether an initial classification of a sum of money into income or capital is correct (which the commissioner in *CH 1561/2005* himself would seem to have done when deciding in that case that arrears of working families' tax credit were to be treated as income).

Where the legislation does not specifically or implicitly define how a payment should be treated, resort must be had to the caselaw. A useful starting point is the decision of Bridge J in *R v Supplementary Benefit Commission ex p Singer* [1973] 1 WLR 713. He stated that the "essential feature of receipts by way of income is that they display an element of periodic recurrence. Income cannot include ad hoc receipts." So for example, *KW v Lancaster CC (HB)* [2011] UKUT 266 (AAC) decided that arrears of child support maintenance, calculated with reference to weekly liabilities but paid as a lump sum, were income. This is a useful rule of thumb but it does not provide a complete answer, because periodic payments may constitute capital in certain circumstances. It is also necessary to consider the nature of the obligation under which the payments are made. In *Lillystone v Supplementary Benefits Commission* [1982] 3 FLR 52, CA, the claimant was receiving £70 a month for 10 years towards the purchase price of his house. Because the payments went towards the sale price of a capital asset, it was held that they constituted capital.

Two cases decided under a former version of the HB Regs 1987 may also be of assistance. In *R v Oxford CC ex p Jack* (1984) 17 HLR 419, QBD, the High Court considered the meaning of "income other than earnings" and quashed a decision of a review board to base its assessment of the claimant's income on withdrawals from his current account. This was because "the Board failed to enquire where the various sums paid into the account had come from". It might have been reasonable to base the claimant's income on his current account if no other evidence was available, but there was in this case. The judge referred to the definition of income in the Shorter Oxford English Dictionary. The current definition of income is:

"that which comes in as the periodical produce of one's work, business, lands or investment (commonly expressed in terms of money) annual or periodical receipts; revenue.".

On the basis of the definition of "income", the judge made the following general remarks about the nature of income:

"income, in my view, is what would in the colloquial sense, be regarded as a person's income, including not merely periodical payments received as of legal right, but periodical payments received, not necessarily at regular intervals, as a result of parental or family feeling or as a result of an agreement not enforceable by law.".

"[if] regular payments are made . . . it is much more likely that it will appear to be income than if it is an irregular amount which is paid at less regular intervals [although] the precise period for which payment is made is not critical".

Therefore, a lump sum paid at the start of a year with the expectation that it should gradually be drawn on for living expenses "would properly fall to be considered as income".

In *R v West Dorset DC ex p Poupard* [1988] 28 RVR 40, CA, Balcombe LJ considered the point and stated (at p43):

"if and insofar as what Glidewell J was saying was that it was a question of fact in any case, within the discretion of the review board, whether withdrawals from a bank account could be taken into account in estimating income, I respectfully agree [but] if he was intending to accept the concession 'prima facie that a withdrawal is not income', then in my judgment . . . his remarks were obiter and I do not accept them as laying down any general principle . . ."

In *Poupard,* the claimant's business was shown to have made a loss, but the claimant had made drawings both from the business receipts and from a bank overdraft facility in order to pay for living expenses, and those drawings were treated as income. Balcombe LJ's conclusions were as follows (at p43):

"(1)   Income is that which comes in to the applicant;

(2)   It may, depending on the facts of the case, be appropriate to take into account cash withdrawals from the gross receipts of an applicant's business, or withdrawals from an applicant's business, or withdrawals from an applicant's bank account or other moneys received by way of loan, notwithstanding that these may not be classified as income on accounting principles and notwithstanding that the loan may eventually be repaid out of capital.

(3)   Capital which is in no way utilised cannot be deemed to constitute or create income.

(4)   However, again depending on the facts of the particular case, the utilisation of capital, whether directly so as to pay for living expenses, or indirectly as security for a loan which is used to pay for living expenses, may thereby 'convert' the capital so used into 'income'."

Some care is required in using these cases, however, for two reasons. First, specific provision is now made to meet some of the points made. see, for example, reg 52(1) which *does* deem capital to create income. Secondly, the old HB scheme did not contain any capital limit. In *ex p Jack,* Glidewell J had referred extensively to Bridge J's views as to the nature of "income" in *Singer* (see above). In *Poupard,* Balcombe LJ found this case "of no help" because the supplementary benefit legislation had separate provision for the assessment of income and capital in the same way that the current HB Regs do. Consequently the comments in *Singer* are more relevant now than when they were considered in *Poupard.* Despite the fact that *Poupard* is a decision of the Court of Appeal, it is submitted that this case is of little assistance given the current HB scheme's distinction between capital and income.

Because income and capital are treated separately under these regulations, as they were in *Singer,* the relevance of *Poupard* to the current regulations must be debatable where, say, only sporadic withdrawals of differing amounts are made. The Court of Appeal held in *Poupard* that borrowings by way of a bank overdraft secured by capital and used for day-to-day living expenses constitute "income" for HB purposes. This decision is not necessarily inconsistent with *ex p Jack* as the Court did have regard to the source of the money and the fact that the loan was secured by capital. Certainly, the more general comments in *ex p Jack* regarding the nature of income payments have not been interfered with.

In *AR v Bradford MBC* [2008] UKUT 30 (AAC); R(H) 6/09, Judge Mesher went further. He said that the factors of the absence of any provision in the statute and regulations for taking capital into account and of any real definition of income that no doubt stood behind the impetus in *Poupard* to regard loans or the utilisation of a person's own capital for living expenses as income, are entirely absent from the current scheme. Nor is there room in that context for the adoption of a simplistic starting point like "income is that which comes in". The starting point must be the particular highly detailed statutory context. There is nothing in the statutory context here to point against the conclusion that drawings from a business are not to be taken into account as either income from self-employment or other income. *Poupard* never stood for any rigid rule that loans always have to count as income, but in Judge Mesher's judgment the decision should no longer be considered as of any relevance to the current HB scheme (and the then current CTB scheme) and should now be consigned to a historical footnote at most.

In *R(H) 5/05,* Commissioner Mesher held that "the resources provided by the use of the overdraft facility do not amount to income" (para 47); though it would appear that the contrary was not argued before him nor was *Poupard* cited to him. His reasoning, in paras 44 to 47, was as follows:

"It is just possible that it could have been argued that the claimant's use of the overdraft facility with his bank produced income in his hands. Nowhere in his comprehensive written and oral submissions did Mr Stagg make that specific argument, and it does not specifically appear anywhere else in the papers. In those circumstances I have not sought any further submissions and explain only briefly why I conclude that that argument would not work."

"The argument could have run as follows. On the statements before me, the first cheque paid by the bank without funds in the account to cover it was paid on 28 March 2001. By 18 April 2001 the overdraft stood at £2,799.55. The overdraft seems initially not to have been agreed, although it probably was by 18 April 2001. But it is established that the drawing of a cheque in excess of the amount standing to a customer's credit is a request for a loan and if the cheque is honoured the customer has borrowed money (see paragraph 11 of *R(IS) 22/98*). Money drawn down under an agreed limit is also borrowing, as is the honouring of cheques taking an overdraft over an agreed limit. The first two payments from Ms LB reduced the amount by which the claimant was overdrawn. The payments on 17 July 2001 and 7 November 2001 took him into credit, but the effect did not last for more than a few weeks in either case. The payment on 14 January 2002 did enable the claimant to stay in credit until 2 April 2002. It might have been argued that the approach endorsed by the Court of Appeal in *Morrell, R(IS) 6/03,* applied to the loans made to the claimant by his bank by way of overdraft. That would have been on the basis that a purpose must have been to allow the claimant to meet the recurrent expenses ordinarily met out of his current account. Chief among these was the monthly rent of £1,785.33, and there were other regular payments for items like home and contents insurance and water rates, as well as payments for cable services and credit card bills. It could have been argued that the provision of resources for such regularly recurring items resulted in the receipt of income."

"That on its face is a powerful argument. But it seems to me that it is undermined by the principles laid down in *Chief Adjudication Officer v Leeves* [1999] FLR 90, CA; reported as *R(IS) 5/99*, as followed in *Morrell*. In that case, a student abandoned his course on 27 April 1995 having received the summer term's instalment of grant from his local education authority on 24 April 1995 (and spent it all on paying off mortgage arrears and debts). He had undertaken, in accordance with the legislation then in force on student grants, to repay such sum as might be determined by the authority if he ceased to attend the course before its normal termination date. On 24 May 1995 the authority wrote to the student terminating his grant with effect from 27 April 1995 and requiring repayment of a particular amount. Under the income support rules the payment of grant on 24 April 1995 would be attributed as income to the whole of the summer term. The Court of Appeal held that as from 24 May 1995 the grant monies were not income. The court agreed with counsel for the student that "income" should be given its natural and ordinary meaning and that moneys accruing or to be treated as accruing "under a certain obligation of immediate payment (ie, an equivalent debt) do not amount to income". From 27 April 1995 to 23 May 1995, although there was no reason to think that the discretion to call for repayment would not be exercised, it was not clear when the student would be required to repay or what the precise sum would be. So there was no "crystallised" obligation. But there was from 24 May 1995."

"Although I have no evidence in the present case of the precise terms on which the overdraft was granted to the claimant, I can take judicial notice of the fact that the standard terms are that bank overdrafts are repayable on demand, although the demand may not be made while the amount stays within an agreed limit. Those terms bring the claimant's repayment obligation within the *Leeves* principles. The obligation is certain, as the amount overdrawn can be identified day by day, and is immediate, even though the bank chooses not to enforce the immediate obligation. Accordingly, the resources provided by the use of the overdraft facility do not amount to income. In my judgment, that result is also in accord with the ordinary and natural meaning of "income". One would not naturally speak of a person having an income from incurring expenditure and running up an overdraft."

In *CH 1672/2007*, there was a decree absolute of judicial separation in effect between the claimant and his wife. As part of the arrangements associated with the issue of the decree, he was ordered by the High Court to pay a monthly sum to his wife that was one half of his monthly occupational pension. The order was enforceable against him. However, the local authority decided that his income was his full pension income and that no account could be taken of the sums he paid to his wife. The claimant argued that his weekly income should be calculated after deducting the sum he had to pay to his wife. Commissioner Williams said that a review of the cases showed the difficulty that courts, tribunals and the Secretary of State have had in drawing a line between receipts by a claimant that are properly regarded as income as against those that are not income (and are termed by default of any alternative as capital). Within the category of payments that on receipt are regarded as income there was a further difficulty in deciding in what circumstances those receipts should be reduced fully or partly by reference to payments made by the recipient from those receipts, whether to the original payer or to some third party. The cases also all showed the importance of noting the immediate statutory context of the questions to be asked, and the terms to be applied, and in those contexts, the precise financial transactions taking place and the importance of distinguishing between informal arrangements and formal liabilities. The commissioner accepted that a literal interpretation of the rules would mean here that the income transferred by the claimant to his wife would be regarded both as his income and as her income at the same time. In his view it militated against introducing an "ordinary" meaning of income that allowed the same income to be counted twice in the hands of different recipients as equally income of both of them. He therefore decided that the proper interpretation of the relevant statutory test of income, in its ordinary sense, but also in the context of the arrangements in this appeal, was that the claimant's income should be regarded as the amount he had left from his occupational pension after he had passed on the sums he was required to pay to his wife from that pension under the High Court pension-splitting order.

There have been a number of decisions on the treatment of payments made by local authority employers as arrears or compensation payments made in respect of equal pay, equal treatment, sex discrimination claims or similar, when the employee in question has also been in receipt of means-tested benefits during the period of the payment. *EM v Waltham Forest LBC* [2009] UKUT 245 (AAC) concerned treatment of bonus payments which were held to be capital payments. *SSWP v JP (JSA)* [2010] UKUT 90 (AAC) concerned treatment of a payment made in offer of settlement under the Equal Pay Act 1970, which was held to be income (specifically "earnings"). *Kingston upon Hull CC v DLM (HB)* [2010] UKUT 234 (AAC) concerned an equal pay "final settlement" compensation offer made by reference to the claimant's past income. In that decision, Judge Howell held that the payment was "earnings". He said that the First-tier Tribunal was right to apply the principle of *R(SB) 21/86* which was followed in *CIS 590/1993* and in *SSWP v JP*.

The claimants in *Kingston upon Hull v DLM* and *SSWP v JP* appealed to the Court of Appeal: *Minter v Kingston upon Hull City Council and Potter v SSWP* [2011] EWCA Civ 1155; [2012] AACR 21, 13 October 2011. Citing *R v National Insurance Commissioner ex p Stratton* [1979] ICR 209, the Court of Appeal said that first the true characteristics of payments made in the hands of the recipients must be determined, taking into consideration the reason why the payment was made. The label that the parties attach to a payment is irrelevant as is the method of settlement – ie, the manner of payment, and the size of the payment, for example, in comparison to a claimants' weekly or monthly wages. The Court decided that the payments to both claimants were income. In

Minter, the claimant was paid compensation for lower wages. In *Potter*, the claimant was paid an on account payment for lost wages. In both cases, the payments were due to breaches of the Equal Pay Act 1970, the equality clause applied by that Act and other legislation relating to unequal pay. Thus, for HB purposes, for example, the payment to the claimant in *Minter* fell within reg 35 as "any remuneration". If not, it was "payment in lieu of remuneration" under reg 35(1)(b). If the payment was not income under reg 35, it was earnings to be treated as income under reg 41(3).

When income converts to capital

Another important point is the effect of retention of income. The most common example of a capital asset is, perhaps, a bank account which contains the accumulated earnings of the account-holder, minus outgoings. Thus there comes a point at which income metamorphoses into capital. The general rule is that a payment is treated as income for a period equal to that to which it is attributable, whereon it becomes part of the claimant's capital: see *R(IS) 3/93*; *R(IS) 9/08*; *R(PC) 3/08*.

Decision-making on income and capital issues

The rules in this Part only apply, effectively, to claimants who are not in receipt of IS, income-based JSA or income-related ESA (or UC). There is no need for an authority to work out income and capital for recipients of those benefits under this Part. Indeed an authority is generally bound by the DWP decision awarding IS, income-based JSA or income-related ESA (or UC): see *R v Penwith DC ex p Menear* (1991) 24 HLR 115, QBD. Whatever income or capital such recipients *do* possess is disregarded under Sch 4 para 12, Sch 5 para 4 and Sch 6 para 5. If they satisfy the other conditions of entitlement, they are therefore entitled to HB under s130(1)(c)(i) SSCBA. By definition, IS, income-based JSA and income-related ESA (and UC) claimants have capital worth less than £16,000 and income less than their applicable amounts. Note that there are only limited situations in which someone can claim and be entitled to HB and UC at the same time. See the Universal Credit (Transitional Provisions) Regulations 2014 on p1857.

There are two exceptions to this cardinal rule.

(1)   Where an authority has evidence which has not already been considered by the DWP and which raises a reasonable doubt as to whether the DWP decision on the means test was correct, the authority may notify the DWP of its views under the information-sharing powers in Part VII SSAA and may suspend payment of HB pending consideration by the DWP as to whether the award of benefit should be revised or superseded: see reg 11 D&A Regs.

(2)   The second exception is a product of the decision of the Court of Appeal in *R v South Ribble DC HBRB ex p Hamilton* (2000) 33 HLR 102, CA. In that case, the Review Board upheld the council's determinations that HB should be refused to the claimant on the basis that he was fraudulently concealing income and capital from the then DSS and the local authority. There was, indeed, strong evidence before the Board to this effect, but the authority did not refer the matter to the DSS for investigation. The Court of Appeal approved the decision in *ex p Menear*, but said that the decision did not require a council to pay HB (or even to award it and then withhold benefit pending examination of the issue). If the authority can conclude that the claimant is fraudulently concealing resources from the DWP, it may lawfully refuse to award benefit.

On its facts, the decision is justifiable as a matter of public policy. However, caution is required in its application. In *Hamilton*, there was apparently no evidence that the then DSS had ever considered whether it shared the local authority's view that the claimant was acting fraudulently. However, there may be cases where the DWP has examined a claim and has concluded that there is no basis for taking away the claimant's IS, JSA or ESA, or where a decision by a decision maker that a claimant has been acting fraudulently is reversed on appeal to the First-tier Tribunal. In that event, *Hamilton* should not be read as giving the local authority an entitlement to take a different view. The judge in *GB v Hillingdon LB* [2010] UKUT 11 (AAC) said that although this comment was helpful, it may not be the end of the matter. The structure of the legislation, as emphasised in *Menear*, is that in such cases it is for the DWP (and subsequently the First-tier Tribunal) to make decisions on income and capital. Where there is an award of eg IS, an authority is bound by the DWP (or tribunal) decision and the claimant is deemed to have no income and capital for HB purposes for the period of that IS award. However, an authority can make its own decision on income and capital if it can show, on the balance of probabilities, that the IS award underpinning the HB award was obtained by fraud or dishonesty: *ex p Hamilton*; *GB v LB Hillingdon*. This may apply if the DWP has not had an adequate opportunity to decide whether the claimant is concealing resources, ie where the DWP has been unaware of any basis for questioning the decision to award benefit, and also to cases where the DWP (or tribunal) has decided that benefit should not be withdrawn but the authority has fresh evidence at its disposal. In *DF v LB Waltham Forest (HB)* [2017] UKUT 306 (AAC), Judge Wikeley emphasised that an authority can depart from a DWP decision on benefit entitlement or income and capital matters only if the authority has strong and clear evidence of fraud – suspicion is not sufficent.

Note, however, *MH v LB Waltham Forest (HB)* [2016] UKUT 161 (AAC) where Judge Turnbull dealt with a HB/CTB appeal heard at the same time as an appeal that had decided that IS was payable. The appellant's IS was stopped on supersession, on the basis that her capital from a beneficial interest in property was in excess of the prescribed limit. The local authority subsequently made a decision revising and removing the awards of HB and CTB. The First-tier Tribunal found that the appellant had capital that exceeded £16,000 at all material times. Despite this finding, it allowed the IS appeal and found her entitled to IS for the periods that benefit had been awarded and paid, but dismissed her appeals against the decisions made by the local authority. The appellant appealed the HB/CTB decision to the Upper Tribunal but the Secretary of State chose not to appeal the IS decision.

Judge Turnbull decided that he could ignore the outcome of the IS appeal and decide the HB/CTB appeal as if the First-tier Tribunal had (as it ought to have done) applied its finding that the claimant throughout had capital worth more than £16,000 to the IS appeal as well. His reasoning included:

(1)   The provision that a claimant on IS is in effect deemed to have no income or capital for HB/CTB purposes is to allow the assumption that the claimant's means have been examined for IS, and that it would be wrong to require that exercise to be carried out again. But that rationale does not apply when, in concurrent appeals, the claimant's means have been examined by a First-tier Tribunal and s/he has been found to have had assets.

(2)   What causes the difficulty for the local authority is the provision in Sch 6 para 5 HB Regs that the whole of the capital of a claimant on IS is disregarded. At the time of the local authority's revising decisions, the claimant had not been 'on IS' in respect of any of the material period in that her awards of IS had been removed by supersession and revision decisions made by the DWP. The later decision of the First-tier Tribunal should in the exceptional circumstances of this case be ignored for this purpose.

It should also be noted that if the DWP *refuses* IS, income-based JSA or income-related ESA on the basis of excess income or capital, there is nothing in the legislation that requires or entitles the authority to follow suit – ie, the authority is *not* bound by a decision that a person is *not* entitled to one of those benefits, other than in not being permitted to disregard all of the person's income and capital under Schs 4, 5 and 6: *AM v Chelmsford BC (HB)* [2013] UKUT 245 (AAC). The authority must carry out its own assessment of income and capital and is entitled to come to a different conclusion, though it is entitled to inquire of the DWP under Pt VII of the SSAA as to the basis for its refusal of benefit.

What if the DWP fails to notify a claimant of a decision that her/his entitlement to, for example, IS has ended? In *SD v Newcastle City Council (HB)* [2010] UKUT 306 (AAC), Judge Mesher decided, applying *R v SSHD ex p Anufrijeva* [2003] UKHL 36 [2004] 1 AC 604, that such a decision could only have legal effect once notified and thus the claimant here was to continue to be considered as "on IS" until such time as she was notified. Judge Mesher appreciated the difficulty for local authorities when receiving information from the DWP that an award of IS or another passporting benefit has been terminated. He said (at para 15):

"A local authority cannot reasonably be expected to go behind such information at that stage and start making enquiries about whether the claimant has been notified of the income support decision. It seems to me that an authority would, unless there was some positive indication to the contrary, be entitled to take the information at face value and make the necessary housing benefit and CTB decisions in consequence. But once the issue of notification of the income support decision by the DWP is raised by or on behalf of the claimant or by some other evidence that comes before the local authority, things are different. Local authorities must then deal with the issue consistently with the approach of law set out above either in its own decisions or before tribunals on appeal."

Note, however, that once a claimant is notified by the DWP of a decision to end entitlement to a passporting benefit, the decision is effective. The local authority can then supersede the relevant HB decision.

In *DF v LB Waltham Forest (HB)*, the authority stopped the claimant's entitlement to HB on the basis that she no longer had passported entitlement after it became aware that her entitlement to IS had stopped. IS had apparently been paid in error for a number of weeks after entitlement ended and the authority sought to recover a sum it regarded as overpaid HB for those weeks. The claimant was subsequently awarded JSA and requested backdating. Judge Wikeley concluded that the evidence indicated that JSA was backdated to the date entitlement to IS had stopped, but arrears of JSA were not paid as they were offset by IS paid in error for the same period. The claimant had, therefore, been entitled to a passporting benefit throughout. Judge Wikeley stated that a conclusion that HB entitlement should cease as soon as the qualifying criteria for a passporting benefit are no longer met is far too sweeping an approach.

Structure of the Part

Section 1 contains general rules about when another person's income/capital may be treated as belonging to the claimant, and when the HB calculation may be based on a non-dependant's income and capital rather than the claimant's own. The provisions of Sections 2 to 5 apply to the claimant's income as defined by Section 1 (thus including that of her/his partner or partners falling within reg 25).

Section 2 contains general rules about the calculation of income on a weekly basis and what counts as "income" for these purposes. Regs 27 to 31 provide a definition of the different categories of income which are subject to the specific rules in Sections 3 to 5. Reg 33 applies generally to convert payments of assessable income into weekly amounts where they are paid for periods other than a week, as HB is calculated on a weekly basis. Reg 34 deals with the effect of changes in certain statutory deductions from income and is really a provision to help authorities administer the scheme more efficiently. The total amount of weekly income to be taken into account under this Part is the claimant's weekly income assessed under regs 29 to 32, plus any "tariff income" and capital treated as income.

Section 3 contains specific rules about the assessment of earnings from "employed earners" employment.

Section 4 contains specific rules about earnings from employment as a "self-employed" earner.

Section 5 sets out specific rules about the assessment of income which is not earnings.

Section 6 contains the rules about the assessment of capital.

SECTION 1
General

General Note on Section 1
This Section deals with two matters pursuant to s136 SSCBA 1992 (see p10) in relation to the calculation of a claimant's income and capital.
(1)   Reg 25, by authority of s136(1) SSCBA, prescribes the circumstances in which the income and capital of members of the claimant's family is or is not to be treated as the claimant's own. It also sets out the circumstances in which a claimant who is polygamously married is to be treated as possessing the income and capital of her/his partners.
(2)   Reg 26, in pursuance of s136(5)(a) and (b) SSCBA, enables the authority assessing HB to treat the claimant as possessing the income and capital of a non-dependant rather than her/his own resources, which are then disregarded. This is an anti-abuse provision.

Calculation of income and capital of members of claimant's family and of a polygamous marriage

25.–(1)   The income and capital of a claimant's partner which by virtue of section 136(1) of the Act is to be treated as income and capital of the claimant, shall be calculated or estimated in accordance with the following provisions of this Part in like manner as for the claimant; and any reference to the "claimant" shall, except where the context otherwise requires, be construed for the purposes of this Part as if it were a reference to his partner.

(2)   Where a claimant or the partner of a claimant is married polygamously to two or more members of his household–
(a)   the claimant shall be treated as possessing capital and income belonging to each such member; and
(b)   the income and capital of that member shall be calculated in accordance with the following provisions of this Part in like manner as for the claimant.

(3)   The income and capital of a child or young person shall not be treated as the income and capital of the claimant.

Definitions
"capital" – see General Note on Section 6.
"child" – see reg 2(1).
"claimant" – see reg 2(1).
"family" – see s137(1) SSCBA.
"household" – see "family".
"income" – see General Note on Part 6.
"married polygamously" – see reg 2(1).
"partner" – see reg 2(1).
"young person" – see reg 19.

General Note
According to s136(1) SSCBA 1992, a claimant is to be treated as possessing the income and capital of members of her/his "family" "except in prescribed circumstances". Under s136(5)(a) SSCBA, regulations may prescribe circumstances in which a claimant may be treated as possessing income which s/he does not in fact possess. This effectively only applies to the income and capital of any partner of the claimant as this regulation, together with the other provisions of this Part, prescribes that a child or young person's income and capital are *not* to be treated as the claimant's. Using the powers in s136(5)(a), reg 25 provides that claimants who are polygamously married are to be treated as possessing the income/capital of their partners who share their household.

Analysis
Para (1). The effect of para (1) is that whenever a reference to the claimant's capital or income is made it is to be treated as including the income and capital of her/his partner.
Para (2) provides that where the claimant is polygamously married s/he is to be treated as possessing the income and capital of all partners to the marriage with whom s/he shares a household (see p17).
Para (3) states that the income and capital of a child or young person is not treated as that of the claimant.

Circumstances in which income of non-dependant is to be treated as claimant's

26.–(1)   Where it appears to the relevant authority that a non-dependant and the claimant have entered into arrangements in order to take advantage of the housing benefit scheme and the non-dependant has more capital and income than the claimant, that authority shall, except where the claimant is on income support [¹, an income-based jobseeker's allowance or an income-related employment and support allowance], treat the claimant as possessing capital and income belonging to that non-dependant and, in such a case, shall disregard any capital and income which the claimant does possess.

(2)   Where a claimant is treated as possessing capital and income belonging to a non-dependant under paragraph (1) the capital and income of that non-dependant shall be calculated in accordance with the following provisions of this Part in like manner as for the claimant and any reference to the "claimant" shall, except where the context otherwise requires, be construed for the purposes of this Part as if it were a reference to that non-dependant.

Amendment

1.   Amended by reg 13 of SI 2008 No 1082 as from 27.10.08.

Definitions

"capital" – see General Note on Part 6.
"claimant" – see reg 2(1).
"income" – see General Note on Part 6.
"an income-based jobseeker's allowance" – see reg 2(1).
"non-dependant" – see reg 3.
"person on income support" – see reg 2(1).
"person on an income-based jobseeker's allowance" – see reg 2(3).
"person on an income-related employment and support allowance" – see reg 2(3A).
"relevant authority" – see reg 2(1).

General Note

Made under s136(5)(a) and (b) SSCBA, this regulation gives an authority the power to assess entitlement to HB on the basis of a non-dependant's capital and income, rather than on the basis of the claimant's own, where the circumstances suggest to the authority that the claimant and non-dependant have made arrangements so as to take advantage of the HB scheme and the non-dependant has more income and capital than the claimant.

Analysis

Para (1). The language used in para (1), in particular the phrase "take advantage of the housing benefit scheme", is similar to that used in reg 9(1)(l) and so it is suggested that similar considerations arise and the caselaw will assist in resolving disputes on the application of this provision. Reference should be made to the Analysis on p293, but some modification will be necessary.

The first step is to identify some "arrangements" that the claimant and non-dependant have entered into. Some evidence of collusion will usually be required. Thus where A is a tenant whose uncle B lives with him and A becomes unemployed and claims HB to meet his rent liability, there is no basis for fixing him with B's resources. It is clear that the power cannot be used just because the non-dependant is wealthier than the claimant, and it is suggested that it should be used only where good reason exists.

If challenged, the onus is on the authority to show grounds for its belief that arrangements have been made so as to take advantage of the HB scheme. The words "appears to the relevant authority" do not absolve the authority from determining the question on proper principles and if it fails to do so, its decision will be vulnerable to challenge.

Note that this power may be used only where the non-dependant's income and capital *both* exceed that of the claimant and that it cannot be used where the claimant is on IS, income-based JSA (as defined in reg 2(1) this includes joint-claim JSA) or income-related ESA. For when a person counts as on IS, income-based JSA or income-related ESA, see reg 2(1), (3) and (3A) and note that for income-based JSA and income-related ESA, it can include, for example, days when those benefits are not payable to the person.

Para (2). If the authority does decide to use this power, it must base the HB calculation on the non-dependant's income and capital. Previous editions have suggested that this includes resources belonging to the non-dependant's family, but it is suggested that is incorrect. Para (2) requires the non-dependant's resources to be calculated under the "following provisions of this Part" and it would appear that phrase excludes consideration of reg 25 which deals with the treatment of the resources of family members and of reg 26 itself.

If the power is exercised, the claimant's income and capital is to be disregarded under para (1).

Every reference to "claimant" in the remainder of this part should be read as referring to the "non-dependant" unless the context of the regulation in question makes it clear that this is not intended. See particularly the note to Sch 4 para 3 on p658.

SECTION 2
Income

Calculation of income on a weekly basis

27.–(1)   Subject to regulations 34 (disregard of changes in tax, contributions etc), and 80 and 81 (calculation of weekly amounts and rent free periods) for the purposes of section 130(1)(c) of the Act (conditions of entitlement to housing benefit) the income of a claimant shall be calculated on a weekly basis–

(a)   by estimating the amount which is likely to be his average weekly income in accordance with this Section and Sections 3 to 5 of this Part and Sections 1 and 3 of Part 7;

(b)   by adding to that amount the weekly income calculated under regulation 52 (calculation of tariff income from capital); and

(c)   by then deducting any relevant child care charges to which regulation 28 (treatment of child care charges) applies from any earnings which form part of the average weekly income or, in a case where the conditions in paragraph (2) are met, from those earnings plus whichever credit specified in sub-paragraph (b) of that paragraph is appropriate, up to a maximum deduction in respect of the claimant's family of whichever of the sums specified in paragraph (3) applies in his case.

(2)   The conditions of this paragraph are that–

(a)   the claimant's earnings which form part of his average weekly income are less than the lower of either his relevant child care charges or whichever of the deductions specified in paragraph (3) otherwise applies in his case; and

(b)   that claimant or, if he is a member of a couple either the claimant or his partner, is in receipt of either working tax credit or child tax credit.

(3)   The maximum deduction to which paragraph (1)(c) above refers shall be–

(a)   where the claimant's family includes only one child in respect of whom relevant child care charges are paid, [[13] £175.00] per week;

(b)   where the claimant's family includes more than one child in respect of whom relevant child care charges are paid, [[13] £300] per week.

(4)   For the purposes of paragraph (1) "income" includes capital treated as income under regulation 41 (capital treated as income) and income which a claimant is treated as possessing under regulation 42 (notional income).

Amendments

1.   Confirmed by art 19(2) of SI 2006 No 645 and reg 8 of SI 2006 No 217 as from 1.4.06 (3.4.06 where rent payable weekly or at intervals of a week).

2.   Confirmed by art 19(2) of SI 2007 No 688 as from 1.4.07 (2.4.07 where rent payable weekly or at intervals of a week).

3.   Confirmed by art 19(3) of SI 2008 No 632 as from 1.4.08 (7.4.08 where rent payable weekly or in multiples of a week).

4.   Confirmed by art 19(3) of SI 2009 No 497 as from 1.4.09 (6.4.09 where rent payable weekly or in multiples of a week).

5.   Confirmed by art 19(2) of SI 2010 No 793 as from 1.4.10 (5.4.10 where rent payable weekly or in multiples of a week).

6.   Confirmed by art 20(2) of SI 2011 No 821 as from 1.4.11 (4.4.11 where rent payable weekly or in multiples of a week).

7.   Confirmed by art 20(2) of SI 2012 No 780 as from 1.4.12 (2.4.12 where rent payable weekly or in multiples of a week).

8.   Confirmed by art 19(2) of SI 2013 No 574 as from 1.4.13.

9.   Confirmed by art 17(3) of SI 2014 No 516 as from 1.4.14 (7.4.14 where rent payable weekly or in multiples of a week).

10.   Confirmed by art 17(3) of SI 2015 No 547 as from 1.4.15 (6.4.15 where rent payable weekly or in multiples of a week).

11.   Confirmed by art 22(3) of SI 2017 No 260 as from 1.4.17 (3.4.17 where rent payable weekly or in multiples of a week).

12.   Confirmed by art 23(2) of SI 2018 No 281 as from 1.4.18 (2.4.18 where rent payable weekly or in multiples of a week).

13.   Confirmed by art 23(2) of SI 2019 No 480 as from 1.4.19.

Definition
> "capital" – see General Note on Part 6.
> "child" – see reg 2(1).
> "claimant" – see reg 2(1).
> "couple" – see reg 2(1).
> "family" – see s137(1) SSCBA.
> "income" – see General Note on Part 6.
> "relevant child care charges" – see reg 28(5).

General Note
> Reg 27 sets out the basic formula for the calculation of income. It is the total income assessed under Sections 2 to 5 of this Part (and the special provisions for students in Part 7) plus any tariff income deemed to be generated by capital under reg 52, minus deductible child care charges up to the maximum figures stated in para (3). "Income" in this context includes notional income and capital deemed to be income as well as actual income: see para (4).

Analysis
> *Para (1)* sets out how income is to be calculated on a weekly basis, subject to regs 34 (disregard of changes in tax, contributions, etc), 80 (calculation of weekly amounts) and 81 (rent-free periods). Under sub-para (b), the income calculated under reg 52 is income a claimant is treated as receiving from her/his capital if the latter is worth more than £6,000 (£10,000 if living in residential accommodation) but less than £16,000 as assessed under Section 6 of this Part and Sch 6. Any actual income from capital is generally treated as capital under reg 46(4).
>
> *Paras (1)(c), (2) and (3)* provide for relevant childcare charges (as defined by reg 28) to be deducted from earnings subject to weekly maxima of a set amount where those charges are incurred in respect of one child and a higher amount where they are incurred in respect of more than one child. Where the claimant's earnings are lower than the childcare charges or the amounts specified in para (3), any working tax credit or child tax credit to which s/he is entitled is added to the earnings for the purpose of calculating the deduction.
>
> *Para (4)* confirms that capital treated as income (reg 41) and notional income (reg 42) should be included in the calculation of income on a weekly basis.

Treatment of child care charges

28.–(1)   This regulation applies where a claimant is incurring relevant child care charges and–

   (a)   is a lone parent and is engaged in remunerative work;

   (b)   is a member of a couple both of whom are engaged in remunerative work; or

   (c)   is a member of a couple where one member is engaged in remunerative work and the other–

      (i)   is incapacitated;

      (ii)   is an in-patient in hospital; or

      (iii)   is in prison (whether serving a custodial sentence or remanded in custody awaiting trial or sentence).

   (2)   For the purposes of paragraph (1) and subject to paragraph (4), a person to whom paragraph (3) applies shall be treated as engaged in remunerative work for a period not exceeding 28 weeks during which he–

   (a)   is paid statutory sick pay;

   (b)   is paid short-term incapacity benefit at the lower rate under sections 30A to 30E of the Act;

   [⁴ (ba) is paid an employment and support allowance;]

   (c)   is paid income support on the grounds of incapacity for work under regulation 4ZA of, and paragraph 7 or 14 of Schedule 1B to, the Income Support Regulations; or

   (d)   is credited with earnings on the grounds of incapacity for work [⁴ or limited capability for work] under regulation 8B of the Social Security (Credits) Regulations 1975.

   (3)   This paragraph applies to a person who was engaged in remunerative work immediately before–

   (a)   the first day of the period in respect of which he was first paid statutory sick pay, short-term incapacity benefit [⁴, an employment and support allowance] or income support on the grounds of incapacity for work; or

(b) the first day of the period in respect of which earnings are credited, as the case may be.

(4) In a case to which paragraph (2)(c) or (d) applies, the period of 28 weeks begins on the day on which the person is first paid income support or on the first day of the period in respect of which earnings are credited, as the case may be.

(5) Relevant child care charges are those charges for care to which paragraphs (6) and (7) apply, and shall be calculated on a weekly basis in accordance with paragraph (10).

(6) The charges are paid by the claimant for care which is provided–

(a) in the case of any child of the claimant's family who is not disabled, in respect of the period beginning on that child's date of birth and ending on the day preceding the first Monday in September following that child's fifteenth birthday; or

(b) in the case of any child of the claimant's family who is disabled, in respect of the period beginning on that person's date of birth and ending on the day preceding the first Monday in September following that person's sixteenth birthday.

(7) The charges are paid for care which is provided by one or more of the care providers listed in paragraph (8) and are not paid–

(a) in respect of the child's compulsory education;

(b) by a claimant to a partner or by a partner to a claimant in respect of any child for whom either or any of them is responsible in accordance with regulation 20 (circumstances in which a person is treated as responsible or not responsible for another); or

(c) in respect of care provided by a relative of a child wholly or mainly in the child's home.

(8) The care to which paragraph (7) refers may be provided–

(a) out of school hours, by a school on school premises or by a local authority–

(i) for children who are not disabled in respect of the period beginning on their eighth birthday and ending on the day preceding the first Monday in September following their fifteenth birthday; or

(ii) for children who are disabled in respect of the period beginning on their eighth birthday and ending on the day preceding the first Monday in September following their sixteenth birthday;

(b) by a child care provider approved in accordance with the Tax Credit (New Category of Child Care Provider) Regulations 1999;

(c) by persons registered under Part 10A of the Children Act 1989; or

[⁸ (d) by a person who is excepted from registration under Part 2 of the Children and Families (Wales) Measure 2010 because the child care that person provides is in a school or establishment referred to in article 11, 12 or 14 of the Child Minding and Day Care Exceptions (Wales) Order 2010;]; or

[⁹ (e) by–

(i) persons registered under section 59(1) of the Public Services Reform (Scotland) Act 2010; or

(ii) local authorities registered under section 83(1) of that Act,

where the care provided is child minding or daycare of children within the meaning of that Act; or]

(f) by a person prescribed in regulations made pursuant to section 12(4) of the Tax Credits Act. [⁶ or

(g) by a person who is registered under Chapter 2 or 3 of Part 3 of the Childcare Act 2006; or

(h) by any of the schools mentioned in section 34(2) of the Childcare Act 2006 in circumstances where the requirement to register under Chapter 2 of Part 3 of that Act does not apply by virtue of section 34(2) of that Act; or

(i) by any of the schools mentioned in section 53(2) of the Childcare Act 2006 in circumstances where the requirement to register under Chapter 3 of Part 3 of that Act does not apply by virtue of section 53(2) of that Act; or

(j)   by any of the establishments mentioned in section 18(5) of the Childcare Act 2006 in circumstances where the care is not included in the meaning of "childcare" for the purposes of Part 1 and Part 3 of that Act by virtue of that subsection; or

(k)   by a foster parent [7 or kinship carer] under the Fostering Services Regulations 2002, the Fostering Services (Wales) Regulations 2003 or the [7 Looked After Children (Scotland) Regulations 2009] in relation to a child other than one whom the foster parent is fostering [7 or kinship carer is looking after]; or

(l)   by a domiciliary care worker under the Domiciliary Care Agencies Regulations 2002 or [19 by a person who is employed, or engaged under a contract for services, to provide care and support by the provider of a domiciliary support service within the meaning of Part 1 of the Regulation and Inspection of Social Care (Wales) Act 2016]; or

(m)   by a person who is not a relative of the child wholly or mainly in the child's home.]

(9)   In paragraphs (6) and (8)(a), "the first Monday in September" means the Monday which first occurs in the month of September in any year.

(10)   Relevant child care charges shall be estimated over such period, not exceeding a year, as is appropriate in order that the average weekly charge may be estimated accurately having regard to information as to the amount of that charge provided by the child minder or person providing the care.

(11)   For the purposes of paragraph (1)(c) the other member of a couple is incapacitated where–

[3 (a)   the claimant's applicable amount includes a disability premium on account of the other member's incapacity [4 or the support component or [18 the other member is a member of the work-related activity group] on account of the other member having limited capability for work];]

(b)   the claimant's applicable amount would include a disability premium [3] on account of the other member's incapacity but for that other member being treated as capable of work by virtue of a determination made in accordance with regulations made under section 171E of the Act;

[4 (ba)   the claimant's applicable amount would include the support component or [18 the other member would be a member of the work-related activity group] on account of the other member having limited capability for work but for that other member being treated as not having limited capability for work by virtue of a determination made in accordance with the Employment and Support Allowance Regulations [13 or the Employment and Support Allowance Regulations 2013];]

(c)   the claimant (within the meaning of regulation 2) is, or is treated as, incapable of work and has been so incapable, or has been so treated as incapable, of work in accordance with the provisions of, and regulations made under, Part 12A of the Act (incapacity for work) for a continuous period of not less than 196 days; and for this purpose any two or more separate periods separated by a break of not more than 56 days shall be treated as one continuous period;

[4 (ca)   the claimant (within the meaning of regulation 2(1)) has, or is treated as having, limited capability for work and has had, or been treated as having, limited capability for work in accordance with the Employment and Support Allowance Regulations [13 or the Employment and Support Allowance Regulations 2013] for a continuous period of not less than 196 days and for this purpose any two or more separate periods separated by a break of not more than 84 days must be treated as one continuous period;]

(d)   there is payable in respect of him one or more of the following pensions or allowances–

(i)   long-term incapacity benefit or short-term incapacity benefit at the higher rate under Schedule 4 to the Act;

(ii)   attendance allowance under section 64 of the Act;

(iii)   severe disablement allowance under section 68 of the Act;

(iv)   disability living allowance under section 71 of the Act;

(v)   increase of disablement pension under section 104 of the Act;

(vi)   a pension increase [⁵ paid as part of a war disablement pension or under] an industrial injuries scheme which is analogous to an allowance or increase of disablement pension under head (ii), (iv) or (v) above;

[⁴ (vii) main phase employment and support allowance;]

[¹¹ (viii) personal independence payment;]

[¹² (ix) armed forces independence payment;]

(e)   a pension [¹⁴, allowance or payment to which head (ii), (iv), (v), (vi) or (viii)] of sub-paragraph (d) above refers was payable on account of his incapacity but has ceased to be payable in consequence of his becoming a patient [¹, which in this regulation shall mean a person (other than a person who is serving a sentence of imprisonment or detention in a youth custody institution) who is regarded as receiving free in-patient treatment within the meaning of [² regulation 2(4) and (5) of the Social Security (Hospital In-Patients) Regulations 2005].];

(f)   sub-paragraph (d) or (e) would apply to him if the legislative provisions referred to in those sub-paragraphs were provisions under any corresponding enactment having effect in Northern Ireland; or

(g)   he has an invalid carriage or other vehicle provided to him by the Secretary of State under section 5(2)(a) of and Schedule 2 to the National Health Service Act 1977 or by Scottish Ministers under section 46 of the National Health Service (Scotland) Act 1978 or provided by the [³ Department of Health, Social Services and Public Safety in Northern Ireland] under Article 30(1) of the Health and Personal Social Services (Northern Ireland) Order 1972.

(12)   For the purposes of paragraph (11), once paragraph (11)(c) applies to the claimant, if he then ceases, for a period of 56 days or less, to be incapable, or to be treated as incapable, of work, that paragraph shall, on his again becoming so incapable, or so treated as incapable, of work at the end of that period, immediately thereafter apply to him for so long as he remains incapable, or is treated as remaining incapable, of work.

[⁴ (12A)   For the purposes of paragraph (11), once paragraph (11)(ca) applies to the claimant, if he then ceases, for a period of 84 days or less, to have, or to be treated as having, limited capability for work, that paragraph is, on his again having, or being treated as having, limited capability for work at the end of that period, immediately thereafter to apply to him for so long as he has, or is treated as having, limited capability for work.]

(13)   For the purposes of paragraphs (6) and (8)(a), a person is disabled if he is a person–

(a)   in respect of whom disability living allowance is payable, or has ceased to be payable solely because he is a patient;

[¹⁵ (b) who is certified as severely sight impaired or blind by a consultant ophthalmologist;] [¹¹]

(c)   who ceased to be [¹⁵ certified as severely sight impaired or blind] within the period beginning 28 weeks before the first Monday in September following that person's fifteenth birthday and ending on the day preceding the first Monday in September following that person's sixteenth birthday. [¹¹ [¹²]]

[¹¹ (d) in respect of whom personal independence payment is payable, or [¹⁴ has ceased to be payable solely by virtue of] regulations made under section 86(1) (hospital in-patients) of the 2012 Act][¹² or]

[¹² (e) in respect of whom armed forces independence payment is payable.]

(14)   For the purposes of–

(a)   paragraph (1) a person on maternity leave, paternity leave [¹⁶, shared parental leave] or adoption leave shall be treated as if she is engaged in remunerative work for the period specified in sub-paragraph (b) ("the relevant period") provided that–

(i)   in the week before the period of maternity leave, paternity leave [¹⁶, shared parental leave] or adoption leave began she was in remunerative work;

(ii)   the claimant is incurring relevant child care charges within the meaning of paragraph (5); and

(iii)   she is entitled to statutory maternity pay under section 164 of the Act, [¹⁰ [¹⁷] statutory paternity pay by virtue of section 171ZA or 171ZB of the Act, [¹⁷]], statutory adoption pay by virtue of section 171ZL of the Act, maternity allowance under section 35 of the Act [¹⁶, statutory shared parental pay by virtue of section 171ZU or 171ZV of the Act] or qualifying support;

(b)   sub-paragraph (a) the relevant period shall begin on the day on which the person's maternity leave, paternity leave or adoption leave commences and shall end on–

(i)   the date that leave ends;

(ii)   if no child care element of working tax credit is in payment on the date that entitlement to maternity allowance, qualifying support, statutory maternity pay, [¹⁰ [¹⁷ statutory paternity pay]] or statutory adoption pay [¹⁶ or statutory shared parental pay] ends, the date that entitlement ends; or

(iii)   if a child care element of working tax credit is in payment on the date that entitlement to maternity allowance, qualifying support, statutory maternity pay, [¹⁰ [¹⁷ statutory paternity pay]] or statutory adoption pay [¹⁶ or statutory shared parental pay] ends, the date that entitlement to that award of the child care element of working tax credit ends,

whichever shall occur first.

(15) In paragraph (14)–

(a)   "qualifying support" means income support to which that person is entitled by virtue of paragraph 14B of Schedule 1B to the Income Support Regulations; and

(b)   "child care element" of working tax credit means the element of working tax credit prescribed under section 12 of the Tax Credits Act (child care element).

Modifications

The amendments made by SI 2014 No.3255 which came into force on 5 April 2015 do not have effect in relation to ordinary statutory paternity pay which is paid, additional statutory paternity pay which is paid, a period in respect of which additional statutory paternity pay is payable which begins, or continues, ordinary paternity leave which is taken or additional paternity leave which is taken, on or after 5 April 2015. See art 35 of SI 2014 No.3255. See also s126 Children and Families Act 2014.

Amendments

1.   Amended by reg 2(5) of SI 2005 No 2502 as amended by Sch 2 para 27 of SI 2006 No 217 as from 1.4.06 (3.4.06 where rent payable weekly or at intervals of a week).
2.   Amended by reg 5(2) of SI 2005 No 3360 as subsituted by Sch 2 para 30 of SI 2006 No 217 as from 10.4.06.
3.   Amended by reg 3(4) of SI 2008 No 1042 as from 19.5.08.
4.   Amended by reg 14 of SI 2008 No 1082 as from 27.10.08.
5.   Amended by reg 5(3) of SI 2008 No 3157 as from 5.1.09.
6.   Amended by reg 2 of SI 2009 No 1848 as from 5.8.09.
7.   Amended by reg 7(2) of SI 2010 No 2429 as from 1.11.10.
8.   Substituted by art 5 and Sch 4 para 10 of SI 2010 No.2582 (W.216)(C.123) as inserted by Art 2 of SI 2011 No.577 (W.82)(C.20) as from 1.4.11.
9.   Substituted by art 2 and Sch 2 para 51 of SI 2011 No 2581 as from 28.10.11.
10.   Amended by reg 7(3) of SI 2012 No 757 as from 1.4.12 (2.4.12 where rent payable weekly or in multiples of a week).
11.   Amended by reg 8 and Sch para 36(3) of SI 2013 No 388 as from 8.4.13.
12.   Amended by art 7 and Sch para 34(3) of SI 2013 No 591 as from 8.4.13.
13.   Inserted by reg 35(4) of SI 2013 No 630 as from 29.4.13.
14.   Amended by reg 3(3) of SI 2014 No 213 as from 1.4.14 (7.4.14 where rent payable weekly or in multiples of a week).
15.   Amended by reg 3(5)(a) of SI 2014 No 2888 as from 26.11.14.
16.   Amended by art 17(4)(a), (b), (c)(iii), (d)(ii) and (e)(ii) of SI 2014 No 3255 as from 31.12.14.
17.   Amended by art 17(4)(c)(iii), (d)(i) and (e)(i) of SI 2014 No 3255 as from 5.4.15.
18.   Amended by Sch 1 para 6(5) of SI 2017 No 204 as from 3.4.17, subject to transitional and savings provisions in Sch 2 paras 1–7.
19.   Amended by reg 9(3) of SI 2018 No 228 as from 2.4.18.

Definitions

"the Act" – see reg 2(1).
"armed forces independence payment" – see reg 2(1).
"claimant" – see reg 2(1).
"couple" – see reg 2(1).
"disability living allowance" – see reg 2(1).
"an employment and support allowance" – see reg 2(1).
"family" – see s137(1) SSCBA.
"lone parent" – see reg 2(1).
"main phase employment and support allowance" – see reg 2(1).
"maternity leave", "paternity leave", "shared parental leave" and "adoption leave" – see reg 2(1).
"partner" – see reg 2(1).
"personal independence payment" – see reg 2(1).
"remunerative work" – see reg 6.

General Note

This defines the circumstances in which child care charges may be deducted (subject to the weekly maxima in reg 27(3)) from a claimant's earnings (and in some cases, WTC or CTC) under reg 27(1)(c).

Analysis

Para (1) lists the categories of people who are entitled to have child care charges deducted from their earnings (and in some cases from WTC or CTC). The relevant categories are lone parents who are in "remunerative work" (for which see reg 6 and paras (2) to (4), (14) and (15)), and couples with children where either both partners are in remunerative work or one partner is and the other is "incapacitated" as defined by paras (11), (12) and (12A), an in-patient in hospital as defined in para (11)(e) or in prison (on remand or serving a sentence).

Paras (2) to (4). A person who is absent from work because s/he is ill cannot be treated as in remunerative work under reg 6. However, for the purposes of the child care charges disregard, paras (2) to (4) *can* treat someone as in remunerative work for the first 28 weeks of a period of sickness, so long as s/he was in such work immediately before getting one of the benefits specified in para (2)(a) to (c) or national insurance credits for incapacity or limited capability for work (para (2)(d)). Note that after the 28-week period, lone parents are no longer entitled to have a deduction made for child care charges. However, couples are, if one of the couple is in remunerative work and the other is "incapacitated" as defined in paras (11), (12) and (12A).

Paras (5) to (9) define the type of child care charges ("relevant child care charges") which are eligible to be deducted. There are four basic rules.

(1)   The charges must be paid by the claimant, or by the claimant's partner: see below.
(2)   The child must be a member of the claimant's family: see s137 SSCBA (p17) and Part 4.
(3)   The care must be provided by one of the care providers listed in para (8) – eg, by a registered child minder or through certain types of official scheme. There is no requirement for the claimant (or partner) to be at work when the child care is being provided.
(4)   The charges must relate to a period before the first Monday in September following the child's 15th birthday or, if the child is disabled within the definition in para (13), following her/his 16th birthday.

The charges cannot be made by the claimant to her/his partner (or vice versa) or made in respect of care provided by a relative of the child wholly or mainly in the child's home: para (7). Para (7) also says that payments made to the claimant by her/his partner are also ineligible but, given that the earlier part of the regulation suggests that payments can only be eligible in the first place if they are made "by the claimant" the effect of this part of the para is unclear. It seems to imply that payments made by a claimant's partner to, say, a registered child minder would be eligible and that the reference to "the claimant" rather than to "the claimant or the claimant's partner" is an oversight.

The charges cannot be payments in respect of the child's "compulsory education": para (7)(a). In *CTC 3646/ 2007*, a decision on the very similarly worded rule for WTC, the child attended a fee paying school that provided, at no additional cost, "classes" (called waiting classes) that pupils could attend before the start and at the end of the school day. The commissioner accepted that the "classes" were childcare and were not compulsory education. However, the "classes" could only qualify as relevant child care charges if a separate charge was made for them. He said (at para 12):

"... [I]n circumstances where the charge covered compulsory education and was the same whether or not a particular child attended the waiting class, I do not consider that it is possible to say some proportion of the charge is not paid in respect of compulsory education, on the basis that the overall charge is set so as to cover the cost of the waiting class in addition to the cost of the education proper."

This was because, although the attendance amounted to child care, the claimant was not incurring any cost in respect of that attendance that was not equally being incurred by the parents of a child who did not attend the "classes". Note, however, that the commissioner did accept that if the school had adopted a different charging policy under which there was a separate fee for the waiting class, this would not have been excluded from the definition.

Para (10) tells the authority to estimate the child care charges over an appropriate period of no more than one year so as to reduce them accurately to a weekly amount for inclusion in the means test calculation.

Paras (11) to (12A) define who is incapacitated and a patient for the purposes of para (1)(c). For a discussion on the definition of "patient", see below.

The situations in which a member of a couple is "incapacitated" are largely self-explanatory. However, note the following.

Sub-para (11)(b) applies if the claimant's applicable amount would include a disability premium but for her/his partner being treated as capable of work under the provision cited – ie, because the partner became incapable of work through misconduct or failed without good cause to attend for, or submit to, medical or other treatment or to observe prescribed rules of behaviour. It is unlikely to have much application as most of those claiming benefits for incapacity for work have been transferred to ESA.

Sub-paras (c) and (ca) only apply if the *claimant* is the member of the couple who is incapable of work or has limited capability for work. Note that under paras (12) and (12A), breaks in the period of incapacity or limited capability of 56 days or 84 days respectively are ignored.

The WTC rules now allow a couple to qualify for an increase in their WTC for child care costs (a child care costs element) where one is in remunerative work and the other is not, but is entitled to carers allowance. However, reg 28 was not amended to enable such a couple to qualify for a deduction for child care costs under reg 27(1)(c). Thus, the amount of the WTC child care costs element will be taken into account in full for HB purposes. It is understood that this was not an omission; the government was aware of this consequence.

Para (13) defines who is disabled for the purposes of paras (6) and (8)(a).

Paras (14) and (15). People who are absent from work on maternity, adoption, shared parental or paternity leave cannot be treated as in remunerative work under reg 6. However, for the purposes of the child care charge deduction, paras (14) and (15) *can* treat someone who is on such leave as in remunerative work. The person must have been in remunerative work immediately before the leave began, must be paying relevant child care charges and must be entitled to statutory maternity, adoption, paternity or shared parental pay or maternity allowance, or "qualifying support" (defined in para (15) as IS because of being on paternity leave (or if the baby was due before 5 April 2015, ordinary paternity leave)). Para 14(b) provides that this special treatment ends when the leave ends (in which case it is no longer necessary) or, if earlier, when the claimant ceases to be entitled to statutory maternity, adoption, shared parental or paternity pay or maternity allowance or "qualifying support" unless s/he was being paid a childcare element of WTC at that date. In the latter case, the special treatment continues until the end of entitlement to the child care element of WTC. Note:

(1)   Until 1 April 2012, there was a difference in treatment between those on paternity leave and SPP, and those on maternity leave and SMP. Paternity leave, as defined in reg 2(1), only included ordinary paternity leave – ie, not additional paternity leave. Further, s11(2) Work and Families Act 2006 states that references to SPP in any instrument or document made before the date of commencement of specified provisions (ie, 6 April 2010) are to be read after that date as references to ordinary SPP – ie, not as references to additional SPP. It is understood that this was an omission and not the intention.

(2)   The scheme of shared parental leave and statutory shared parental pay affects those whose baby is (or was) due on or after 5 April 2015. For those whose baby was due before that date, "paternity leave" included both ordinary and additional paternity leave and statutory paternity pay included both ordinary and additional statutory paternity pay.

Who is a patient?

Para (11)(e) defines "patient" for the purposes of this regulation. Note that a person does not come within the definition of patient for these purposes if s/he is a serving a sentence of imprisonment or detention in youth custody.

Reg 2(4) and (5) Social Security (Hospital In-Patients) Regulations 2005 provide as follows:

"(4)   For the purposes of this regulation, a person shall be regarded as receiving or having received free in-patient treatment for any period for which he is or has been maintained free of charge while undergoing medical or other treatment as an in-patient–

(a)   in a hospital or similar institution under the National Health Service Act 1977, the National Health Service (Scotland) Act 1978 or the National Health Service and Community Care Act 1990, or

(b)   in a hospital or similar institution maintained or administered by the Defence Council,

and such a person shall for the purposes of sub-paragraph (a) be regarded as being maintained free of charge in a hospital or similar institution unless his accommodation and services are provided under s65 National Health Service Act 1977, s57 National Health Service (Scotland) Act 1978 or para 14 Sch 2 National Health Service and Community Care Act 1990.

(5)   For the purposes of paragraph (4), a period during which a person is regarded as receiving or having received free in-patient treatment shall be deemed to begin on the day after the day on which he enters a hospital or similar institution referred to in that paragraph and to end on the day on which he leaves such a hospital or similar institution."

Four questions need to be posed.

Is the person an "in-patient"? A period of in-patient treatment begins on the day after the day of admission and ends on the day on which the person leaves. This affirms the commissioner's reasoning in *R(IS) 8/96*. There is an area of doubt in respect of the "day" on which a person enters hospital. The commissioner proceeded on the basis that a "day" for these purposes was the 24 hours between midnight and midnight. This interpretation does have the benefit of certainty, but is not necessarily inherent in the use of the word "day": *Halsbury's Laws of England* (1984 4th edn) vol 45 para 1113. The powerful arguments in favour of requiring a 24 hour stay in *R(S) 4/ 84* do not appear to be explicitly overridden by para (5).

Is the person receiving relevant treatment? The scope of the regulation is not confined to medical treatment but includes other treatment. Medical or other treatment is treatment by a doctor, dentist or professionally qualified or trained nurse or by someone under the supervision of such a person: *SSWP v Slavin* [2011] EWCA Civ 1515; [2012] AACR 30. In *Botchett v Chief Adjudication Officer* [1996] 2 CCLR 121, CA the claimant had severe learning difficulties, although not a patient within the meaning of the Mental Health Act 1983, and required a high degree of care and supervision. She lived in a nursing home administered by a trust, which would take any amount of IS to which she was entitled over and above the standard nursing home rates. It was argued that the claimant was receiving care and not treatment in the home. However, the Court of Appeal ruled that the attention she received constituted "medical or other treatment".

Is the person in a "hospital or similar institution"? *White v Chief Adjudication Officer* [1993] *The Times* 2 August, CA decided that the definitions in s128 National Health Service Act 1977 must be applied. The definition of "Hospital" (now in s275 National Health Service Act 2006) is "(a) any institution for the reception and treatment of persons suffering from illness; (b) any maternity home; and (c) any institution for the reception and treatment of persons during convalescence or persons requiring medical rehabilitation." "Illness" includes "mental disorder within the meaning of the Mental Health Act 1983 and any injury or disability requiring medical or dental treatment or nursing". It does not appear to cover those with disabilities if such disabilities do not of themselves require medical treatment – eg, blindness: *Jewish Blind Society Trustees v Henning* [1961] 1 WLR 24 at 30, 34, CA. In *Botchett*, it was held that the definition of "mental disorder" in the 1983 Act was wide enough to cover the claimant in that case. The home was therefore a "similar institution". In order to be an "institution", however, it would have to be a "building used by .... a society or organisation": see the *Shorter Oxford English Dictionary*. It might be possible to argue that very small, privately-run nursing homes are not therefore within the scope of the definition.

This suggestion is supported by *CDLA 7980/1995*, a decision on reg 8 Social Security (Disability Living Allowance) Regulations 1991, which is in similar terms to reg 2(4). In that case, the claimant had a learning disability and was epileptic. She lived in a privately rented house along with six people in a similar position. 24-hour care was provided by specialist carers from the local authority. Medication was provided by the claimant's GP. The tribunal decided that the house was not a "similar institution" and the commissioner upheld its ruling. He said (para 9):

"In my judgement, when those words are used in connection with the word 'hospital', they connote some sort of formal body or structure which controls all aspects of the treatment or care that is provided including the premises in which that treatment or care is carried out. They mean more than just a building in which care or treatment takes place. In this appeal, the treatment or care takes place in a private house which is let to the six occupants. They are the persons responsible for the payment of rent and other outgoings and for the purchase of their food. The appeal tribunal so found as they were bound to find on the evidence presented to them. .... On the appeal tribunal's findings there is simply no institution in the sense in which I consider the words must be construed. Further, no-one would suggest that the arrangements at No 167 could be described as 'a hospital' in any popular sense even though treatment and care is carried out there."

The authority of the decision is undermined slightly by the fact that *Botchett* was not apparently cited. However, it is suggested that it is correct. Note also that the treatment must be provided under one of the Acts mentioned in sub-para (a) or by the institutions mentioned in sub-para (b). If it is provided under the National Assistance Act 1948 or otherwise, the claimant will not be a "patient". Another authority supporting this interpretation of reg 2(4) is *CS 2647/1997* in which a resident at a hostel was held to fall outside its scope.

Is the person maintained free of charge? The effect of the closing words of para (4) is that a person is deemed to satisfy this condition unless s/he is a privately paying patient under the legislation mentioned there. Thus in *CS 249/1989* where the claimant's wife brought him meals every day because the hospital could not satisfy his dietary requirements, it was held that as he was not a private patient; he was deemed to be maintained free of charge even though it was costing his family money to feed him: para 11.

Average weekly earnings of employed earners

29.–(1)   Where a claimant's income consists of earnings from employment as an employed earner his average weekly earnings shall be estimated by reference to his earnings from that employment–

(a)   over a period immediately preceding the benefit week in which the claim is made or treated as made and being a period of–

(i)   5 weeks, if he is paid weekly; or

(ii)   2 months, if he is paid monthly; or

(b)   whether or not sub-paragraph (a)(i) or (ii) applies, where a claimant's earnings fluctuate, over such other period preceding the benefit week in which the claim is made or treated as made as may, in any particular case, enable his average weekly earnings to be estimated more accurately.

(2)   Where the claimant has been in his employment for less than the period specified in paragraph (1)(a)(i) or (ii)–

(a)   if he has received any earnings [¹ or expects to receive an amount of earnings] for the period that he has been in that employment and those earnings are likely to represent his average weekly earnings from that employment his average weekly earnings shall be estimated by reference to those earnings;

(b)   in any other case, the relevant authority shall require the claimant's employer to furnish an estimate of the claimant's likely weekly earnings over such period as the relevant authority may require and the claimant's average weekly earnings shall be estimated by reference to that estimate.

(3)   Where the amount of a claimant's earnings changes during an award the relevant authority shall estimate his average weekly earnings by reference to his likely earnings from the employment over such period as is appropriate in order that his average weekly earnings may be estimated accurately but the length of the period shall not in any case exceed 52 weeks.

(4)   For the purposes of this regulation the claimant's earnings shall be calculated in accordance with Section 3 of this Part.

Amendment

1.   Amended by reg 2(2) of SI 2015 No 6 as from 9.2.15.

Definitions

"benefit week" – see reg 2(1).
"claimant" – see reg 2(1).
"earnings" – see regs 2(1) and 35(1).
"employment as an employed earner" – see reg 2(1).
"income" – see General Note on Part 6.
"relevant authority" – reg 2(1).

General Note

This regulation deals with the earnings of an employed, as opposed to a self-employed, claimant. Para (4) refers to Section 3 for the assessment of earnings in this respect. Para (1) specifies the period over which a claimant's weekly earnings are to be averaged and reg 33 provides a mechanism for calculating weekly amounts of earnings where payment has been made for a period other than a week. For the date on which earnings from employment are to be taken into account, see reg 29A.

Remember that the earnings of a partner or partners of a claimant are included.

GM BW2.248 points out that earnings are usually verified from pay slips or a certificate of earnings. It reminds authorities that because of the government's overall policy of reducing the burden on business, they should avoid asking employers about a claimant's earnings unless no other source of information is available or there is doubt about the authenticity of the evidence provided by the claimant.

Para (2) modifies the rules in para (1) for people who have recently started work and para (3) deals with the situation where a claimant's earnings change during an award.

Analysis

Para (1). The wording of this regulation is unfortunate. The use of the word "consists" suggests that it only applies to claimants whose sole income is earnings from employment, although this cannot be the intention. For "benefit week in which the claim is made or treated as made", see reg 83 on p544.

If the claimant's weekly earnings fluctuate, the authority must use sub-para (b) to calculate her/his weekly average rather than sub-para (a). The wording suggests that where sub-para (b) applies, the periods mentioned in sub-para (a) cannot be used even if they do accurately reflect the claimant's weekly average. Note that the period chosen under sub-para (a) or sub-para (b) must precede the week in which the claim is made or treated as made, rather than be based on estimated future earnings.

See reg 33 if the claimant is paid in respect of a period other than a week, in order to work out the weekly amount due.

Para (2) deals with the situation where the claimant has not yet been in employment for the appropriate period under para (1)(a)(i) or (ii).

Sub-para (a) deals with claimants who have already been paid earnings, or expect to receive an amount of earnings, that reflect their likely average earnings; for "earnings", see para (4). See also reg 33 where the amount paid relates to a period other than a week.

Sub-para (b) deals with all other cases – ie, claimants who have not yet been paid any earnings, or who have been paid, but the amount expected or received is not representative of what they will receive in the future. Note that it is the local authority that must require the employer to provide an estimate of the claimant's likely earnings, not the claimant. An award of HB can then be made on the basis of the estimate. The local authority may then instruct the claimant to notify it if s/he actually earns more than the estimate and adjust the original estimate accordingly under para (3): *NC v Tonbridge & Malling BC* [2010] UKUT 12 (AAC).

For the treatment of advance earnings, see reg 46(5).

Para (3) deals with changes in a claimant's earnings during an award – ie, relevant changes of circumstance. Claimants are under a duty to report such changes: see reg 88. Reg 79 specifies the date on which the changes will take effect. This paragraph obliges the authority to amend the claimant's entitlement to HB when such a change becomes effective. The averaging process is not bound by para (1), which applies only to the determination of entitlement on a claim, but the authority must choose an appropriate period in order to estimate earnings accurately. While the authority has wide discretion, it must actively consider whether the chosen period accurately identifies future average weekly earnings. It is not sufficient simply to take payslips submitted by a claimant, average them and, if this produces a different figure from that used previously, reassess benefit from the start of the period covered by the first payslip. *LB v Lambeth LB & SSWP (HB)* [2015] UKUT 237 (AAC). The length of the period can in no case exceed 52 weeks. Reg 33 applies to help ascertain the weekly value of earnings for these purposes.

Para (4). See section 3 of this part and Sch 4, for the assessment of earnings.

[¹ Date on which income consisting of earnings from employment as an employed earner are taken into account

29A.–(1)   A claimant's average weekly earnings from employment estimated pursuant to regulation 29 (Average weekly earnings of employed earners) and Section 3 (Employed earners) of this Part shall be taken into account–

(a)   in the case of a claim, on the date that the claim was made or treated as made and the first day of each benefit week thereafter, regardless of whether those earnings were actually received in that benefit week;

(b)   in the case of a claim or award where the claimant commences employment, the first day of the benefit week following the date the claimant commences that employment, and the first day of each benefit week thereafter, regardless of whether those earnings were actually received in that benefit week; or

(c)   in the case of a claim or award where the claimant's average weekly earnings from employment change, the first day of the benefit week following the date of the change, and the beginning of each benefit week thereafter, regardless of whether those earnings were actually received in that benefit week.]

Amendment

1.   Inserted by reg 2(3) of SI 2015 No 6 as from 9.2.15.

Definitions

"benefit week" – see reg 2(1).
"claimant" – see reg 2(1).
"earnings" – see regs 2(1) and 35(1).

General Note

From 9 February 2015, reg 29A provides the date on which earnings from employment estimated under reg 29 and Section 3 of this Part, which have been paid or are expected to be paid, are to be taken into account. The relevant dates are as follows.

Sub-para (a) provides the date if a claimant is in employment when her/his claim is made. In this case, actual or expected earnings are taken into account from the date the claim is made or treated as made and thereafter on the first day of each benefit week.

Sub-para (b) applies if the claimant commences employment after her/his claim or an award of HB is made. In this case, actual or expected earnings are taken into account on the first day of the benefit week that follows the date the employment started and thereafter on the first day of each benefit week.

Sub-para (c) applies if the claimant's average weekly earnings change after her/his claim or an award of HB is made. In this case, actual or expected earnings are taken into account from the first day of the benefit week after the change and thereafter on the first day of each benefit week.

Until 9 February 2015, like for PC, there was no rule for HB specifying that earnings were to be treated as paid on any particular date or were to be taken into account for any particular period. In *Reigate and Banstead BC v SA (HB)* [2014] UKUT 369 (AAC), Judge West, having considered *R(PC) 3/08* in which Judge Mesher said that the PC legislation must operate on "an assumed notion of a period of attribution of income", decided that the HB scheme must also operate on that basis. The claimant had started work part-way through a month and was paid wages at the end of that part-month. She was then paid a full month's wages at the end of the next month. The local authority, following what was then the current practice, attributed the earnings backwards over the period in which they were earned. The First-tier Tribunal, however, decided that the earnings should be attributed forwards from the date they were received – ie, that the claimant's earnings were to be averaged under reg 29 over the period from when they were paid. Judge West agreed with the First-tier Tribunal. Note that HB Bulletin G8/2014 reminded local authorities that Judge West's decision was binding on all attribution decisions until the rules were amended.

Average weekly earnings of self-employed earners

30.–(1)   Where a claimant's income consists of earnings from employment as a self-employed earner his average weekly earnings shall be estimated by reference to his earnings from that employment over such period as is appropriate in order that his average weekly earnings may be estimated accurately but the length of the period shall not in any case exceed a year.

(2)   For the purposes of this regulation the claimant's earnings shall be calculated in accordance with Section 4 of this Part.

Definitions
"claimant" – see reg 2(1).
"earnings" – see regs 2(1) and 37(1).
"income" – see General Note on Part 6.
"self-employed earner" – see reg 2(1).

General Note
This deals with the earnings from self-employment of claimants and their partners. Reg 33 applies to ascertain the weekly amounts of such earnings if payment is made for a period other than a week. Para (2) provides that earnings are to be assessed for these purposes under Section 4 of this Part.

Analysis
Unlike the provisions in respect of *employed* earners, there is no mechanism for dealing with unforeseen changes in the claimant's income over the period of an award. Also there is no prescribed period over which income should be averaged. The authority must simply choose a period it thinks appropriate that will enable it to estimate the claimant's income from this source accurately. The averaging period must not exceed a year.

It was emphasised in *CH 329/2003* that it may not always be appropriate to use the last year's accounts.

In *CC v Braintree DC* [2013] UKUT 104 (AAC), Judge Mark concluded that, where there has been a significant change in weekly earnings from the previous year, to simply use the previous year's earnings taking into account any downturn or upturn "is the antithesis of estimating the earnings accurately". As this is so both in the year in question and in any subsequent year, this does not lead to the same period being used twice. Judge Mark also pointed out that a period shorter than a year can be used where appropriate.

Average weekly income other than earnings

31.–(1)   A claimant's income which does not consist of earnings shall, except where paragraph (2) applies, be estimated over such period as is appropriate in order that his average weekly income may be estimated accurately but the length of the period shall not in any case exceed 52 weeks; and nothing in this paragraph shall authorise an authority to disregard any such income other than that specified in Schedule 5.

(2)   The period over which any benefit under the benefit Acts is to be taken into account shall be the period in respect of which that benefit is payable.

(3)   For the purposes of this regulation income other than earnings shall be calculated in accordance with Section 5 of this Part.

Definitions
"benefit Acts" – see reg 2(1) and s123 SSCBA.
"claimant" – see reg 2(1).
"earnings" – see regs 2(1), 35(1) and 37(1).
"income" – see General Note on Part 6.

General Note
This deals with income which is not "earnings" under regs 29 and 30. Para (3) provides that such income is to be taken into account as specified by Section 5 of this Part. Under reg 27(1)(a), this "other income" is to be assessed

on the basis of what a claimant is likely to receive on an average weekly basis. See reg 33 on p436 for the conversion of payments made in respect of periods other than a week into weekly amounts.

Analysis

As with regs 29 and 30, the authority must estimate such income over an appropriate period in order to estimate earnings accurately. Here the length of the period can in no case exceed 52 weeks. The authority can only disregard such amounts as are authorised by Sch 5.

The effect of para (2) is that benefits paid under the benefit Acts (as defined in reg 2(1)) should only be taken into account during the period in respect of which they are payable (eg, the two weeks before actual payment if made two-weekly in arrears); and if not paid for every week, they should only be taken into account in respect of the number of weeks for which they actually are paid.

Calculation of average weekly income from tax credits

32.–(1)   This regulation applies where a claimant receives a tax credit.

(2)   Where this regulation applies, the period over which a tax credit is to be taken into account shall be the period set out in paragraph (3).

(3)   Where the instalment in respect of which payment of a tax credit is made is–

(a)   a daily instalment, the period is 1 day, being the day in respect of which the instalment is paid;

(b)   a weekly instalment, the period is 7 days, ending on the day on which the instalment is due to be paid;

(c)   a two weekly instalment, the period is 14 days, commencing 6 days before the day on which the instalment is due to be paid;

(d)   a four weekly instalment, the period is 28 days, ending on the day on which the instalment is due to be paid.

(4)   For the purposes of this regulation "tax credit" means child tax credit or working tax credit.

Definitions

"child tax credit" and "working tax credit" – see reg 2(1).
"claimant" – see reg 2(1).

Analysis

This provides the mechanism for determining the period over which tax credits income is to be taken into account. "Tax credits" are child tax credit (CTC) and working tax credit (WTC): para (4). For the calculation of the weekly amount to be taken into account, see reg 33 for the conversion of payments made in respect of periods other than a week. Note that reg 34(e) allows a local authority to ignore legislative changes in the maximum rate of tax credits (ie, the annual uprating) for up to 30 weeks.

The regulation applies where the claimant "receives a tax credit".

Para (2) then sets out how the instalments are to be calculated for HB purposes. The instalments should be set out in the claimant's tax credit award notice. There are some important issues and implications.

(1)   It is the amount of tax credits the claimant is actually receiving that is relevant, whether HMRC calculated the amount correctly or not. Where an overpayment that occurred during the current year's award of tax credits is being recovered by HMRC, it is the reduced amount of tax credits (the "instalment") that should be taken into account for HB purposes. Note that where an overpayment of tax credits from a previous year is being recovered from the current year's award, the amount of tax credits that is taken into account is, similarly, the amount actually being paid: reg 40(6). But see below if tax credits are currently in payment, but are being overpaid.

(2)   Where the amount of an award of tax credits changes during the year, the local authority takes this into account when the instalment reflecting this is "due to be paid", not when the change occurs.

(3)   Where a payment is not a regular instalment, but a payment of arrears of tax credits (eg, at the beginning of an award or after a change in circumstances has been taken into account), it should not be treated as income, but as capital and disregarded for up to 52 weeks: reg 46(9) and Sch 6 para 9(1)(e).

(4)   Tax credit "additional payments" or "top-up payments" (discretionary payments made by HMRC where a reduced tax credits award causes hardship) are effected by increasing the tax credit award for the relevant year and hence the instalments due to be paid for the remainder of that year.

Are all payments of tax credits income?

Where tax credits are being overpaid to a claimant, issues arise as to how the payments should be treated for HB purposes. The question is whether the payments are to be taken into account as income.

In *CH 1450/2005*, the claimant continued to be paid tax credits, having informed HMRC that she was no longer entitled. She informed the local authority of the change in her circumstances. The commissioner rejected an argument that as the claimant was putting the overpaid sums of tax credits aside pending recovery, she was holding the sums on trust for HMRC, had no beneficial interest in the sums, and so they should have been ignored as income in the year in which they were actually paid. The sums were clearly received by the claimant and were her income, and any different result would mean that the overpaid sums stood to be disregarded both in the year in which they were received and the following year (see now reg 40(6)), which would amount to a double disregard. However, in *CIS 1813/2007*, the claimant also informed HMRC immediately when she stopped working because she knew that she ceased to be eligible for WTC. Despite her best efforts to stop being paid, WTC continued to be paid for nearly two months. HMRC then sought to recover the overpayment. When she had claimed IS on ceasing work, the WTC payments were taken into account as income in calculating her entitlement. Deputy Commissioner Mark decided that the payments of WTC were not income or, if that was wrong, that they were "voluntary payments" to be disregarded. Although normally WTC does count as part of a claimant's income for IS purposes, it appeared to the deputy commissioner to be an abuse of language to treat payments as income, if they are payments the claimant has asked that s/he should not receive, having correctly explained why s/he should not be receiving them. As regards voluntary payments, he said (at para 12):

"The position would be different at a time before disclosure is made of facts which give [HMRC] grounds to vary the award, and may be different if there is an element of uncertainty whether a variation can or should be made. But once there has been proper disclosure by the claimant which allows for only one decision, and even more so where the claimant has asked not to be paid, or for that decision to be made, it is entirely a matter for [HMRC] whether the payments continue to be made or whether it varies the award and ceases the payments."

He distinguished the case from *CIS 647/2007* where it had been held that an overpayment of WTC did count as income for IS purposes. In that case, the claimant had *not* informed HMRC of the change in her circumstances. Hence, HMRC continued to be under an obligation to make the payments of WTC that had been awarded and had no basis on which to consider amending the WTC award. No question of the payment being a voluntary one, and no question of its stopping being her income, could therefore arise.

In *CIS 4371/2006*, Deputy Commissioner Mark considered *CH 1450/2005* and in *obiter* comments stood by his reasoning in *CIS 1813/2007*. In *CIS 1853/2008*, Judge Jacobs made a decision without reasons on the basis that the Secretary of State had conceded that the tax credits the claimant had received were not income on the reasoning applied in *CIS 1813/2007*. It is therefore suggested that *CIS 1813/2007* should now be followed in preference to *CH 1450/2005*.

Applying the caselaw to HB, if a claimant is continuing to receive payments of tax credits to which s/he is not entitled and has reported relevant changes in her/his circumstances to HMRC and/or asked that payments cease, an authority should not treat the payments as income and should not take them into account in calculating HB: *CIS 1813/2007*. This is despite the provision in reg 40(6) (see p450) under which, where an overpayment is being recovered from a tax credits award, it is the amount of tax credits in payment that is taken into account: *CH 4371/2006* para 12. However, where a claimant does not report a change in circumstances to HMRC or ask for tax credits payments to stop, applying *CIS 647/2007*, the payments would be income. Likewise, where a claimant retains some entitlement to tax credits under an award, the amount of that entitlement would be income. It is therefore vital for a claimant to notify HMRC of relevant changes of circumstance timeously and to ask that payment of tax credits cease, and at the same time to notify the local authority of the change and to ask for her/his award of HB to be recalculated.

Calculation of weekly income

33.–(1) For the purposes of regulations 29 (average weekly earnings of employed earners), 31 (average weekly income other than earnings) and 32 (calculation of average weekly income from tax credits), where the period in respect of which a payment is made–

(a) does not exceed a week, the weekly amount shall be the amount of that payment;

(b) exceeds a week, the weekly amount shall be determined–

(i) in a case where that period is a month, by multiplying the amount of the payment by 12 and dividing the product by 52;

(ii) in any other case, by dividing the amount of the payment by the number equal to the number of days in the period to which it relates and multiplying the quotient by 7.

(2) For the purposes of regulation 30 (average weekly earnings of self-employed earners) the weekly amount of earnings of a claimant shall be determined by dividing his earnings over the assessment period by the number equal to the number of days in that period and multiplying the quotient by 7.

Definitions

"assessment period" – see reg 2(1).

"claimant" – see reg 2(1).

"earnings" – see regs 2(1) and 35(1).

General Note

This provides the means for converting the sums to be taken into account under regs 29, 30, 31 and 32 into weekly amounts.

Analysis

Para (1) deals with the earnings of an employed earner under reg 29, income other than earnings under reg 31 and income from tax credits under reg 32. Where a payment is made for a period of up to a week, the weekly amount is the amount of the payment: sub-para (a).

Para (1)(b) deals with payments made in respect of a period exceeding a week. Under sub-para (b)(i), payments in respect of a month are to be converted by multiplying by 12 to give the annual figure then dividing by 52 to produce a weekly figure. Sub-para (b)(ii) converts payments in respect of periods not covered by sub-para (b)(i) by dividing by the number of days in the period to which the payment relates and multiplying by seven. Note that days during weekends must also be counted as days for this purpose.

Para (2) deals with the earnings of a self-employed earner. These are based on the estimated average of earnings received over the assessment period (up to one year – see reg 30). The average weekly amount of earnings is obtained by dividing those earnings by the number of days in the assessment period and multiplying the result by seven.

Disregard of changes in tax, contributions etc

34. In calculating the claimant's income the appropriate authority may disregard any legislative change–

(a) in the basic or other rates of income tax;

[⁴ (aa) in the Scottish basic or other rates of income tax;]

(b) in the amount of any personal tax [⁴ reliefs under Chapters 2, 3 and 3A of Part 3 of the Income Tax Act 2007];

(c) in the rates of [¹ national insurance contributions] payable under the Act or in the lower earnings limit or upper earnings limit for Class 1 contributions under the Act, the lower or upper limits applicable to Class 4 contributions under the Act or the amount specified in section 11(4) of the Act ([² small profits threshold] exception in relation to Class 2 contributions);

(d) in the amount of tax payable as a result of an increase in the weekly rate of Category A, B, C or D retirement pension or any addition thereto or any graduated pension payable under the Act [³ or a state pension under Part 1 of the Pensions Act 2014];

(e) in the maximum rate of child tax credit or working tax credit,

for a period not exceeding 30 benefit weeks beginning with the benefit week immediately following the date from which the change is effective.

Amendments

1. Amended by reg 3(4)(a) of SI 2014 No 213 as from 1.4.14 (7.4.14 where rent payable weekly or in multiples of a week).

2. Amended by reg 33(2) of SI 2015 No 478 as from 6.4.15.

3. Amended by art 28(3) of SI 2015 No 1985 as from 6.4.16.

4. Amended by reg 4(3) of SI 2016 No 233 as from 6.4.16.

Definitions

"child tax credit" and "working tax credit" – see reg 2(1).

"claimant" – see reg 2(1).

"benefit week" – see reg 2(1).

"income" – see General Note on Part 6.

"Scottish basic rate" – see reg 2(1).

General Note

This regulation is intended to assist the authority in administering the HB scheme by modifying the other provisions of this Part and reg 79 so that the effect of certain changes in the claimant's income is ignored for up to 30 benefit weeks after they take effect, giving an authority time to gather information and recalculate an affected claimant's HB. The changes listed could reduce or increase a claimant's entitlement to HB. If an authority exercises its discretion under this paragraph it does not mean that the claimant has been over- or under-paid, so when the authority does take the change into account there is no adjustment to be made to HB paid in the intervening period. This is because during that period entitlement has been correctly assessed according to the treatment of income rules.

See also reg 42(8), about changes in the rate of certain benefits.

Analysis

Note that the "changes" which may be ignored as set out in sub-paras (a) to (e) are only those arising from changes in the legislation, not extra-statutory concessions.

Para (b) covers changes in personal tax relief by which is meant the tax thresholds.

Para (d). Pensioners will only pay tax on these amounts if their total income is sufficient to use up their tax allowances. Therefore the change in the amount of tax payable may not change some pensioners' HB entitlement in any case. Note that most pensioner claimants have their HB assessed under the HB(SPC) Regs (see reg 5 HB Regs) so this provision only has limited application.

SECTION 3
Employed earners

General Note on Section 3

See also regs 27 and 29 and the General Note to Section 2.

Reg 29(4) provides that for the purposes of that reg (ie, quantification of the employee's weekly earnings together with the earnings of any partner), this Section is to govern the amounts which are to be taken into account as earnings, and how they are to be assessed.

Reg 35 defines earnings.

Reg 36 provides that for the purposes of reg 29 it is net earnings that are to be taken into account, minus the amounts which may be disregarded under Sch 4, and sets out how "net" earnings are to be ascertained.

Earnings of employed earners

35.–(1)   Subject to paragraph (2), "earnings" means in the case of employment as an employed earner, any remuneration or profit derived from that employment and includes–

(a)   any bonus or commission;

(b)   any payment in lieu of remuneration except any periodic sum paid to a claimant on account of the termination of his employment by reason of redundancy;

(c)   any payment in lieu of notice or any lump sum payment intended as compensation for the loss of employment but only in so far as it represents loss of income;

(d)   any holiday pay except any payable more than 4 weeks after termination or interruption of the employment;

(e)   any payment by way of a retainer;

(f)   any payment made by the claimant's employer in respect of expenses not wholly, exclusively and necessarily incurred in the performance of the duties of the employment, including any payment made by the claimant's employer in respect of–

(i)   travelling expenses incurred by the claimant between his home and place of employment;

(ii)   expenses incurred by the claimant under arrangements made for the care of a member of his family owing to the claimant's absence from home;

(g)   any award of compensation made under section 112(4) or 117(3)(a) of the Employment Rights Act 1996 (remedies and compensation for unfair dismissal);

[¹ (gg) any payment or remuneration made under section 28, 34, 64, 68 or 70 of the Employment Rights Act 1996 (right to guarantee payments, remuneration on suspension on medical or maternity grounds, complaints to employment tribunals);]

(h)   any such sum as is referred to in section 112 of the Act (certain sums to be earnings for social security purposes);

(i)   any statutory sick pay, statutory maternity pay, [³ [⁶ statutory paternity pay]] or statutory adoption pay, [⁵ statutory shared parental pay] or a corresponding payment under any enactment having effect in Northern Ireland;

(j)   any remuneration paid by or on behalf of an employer to the claimant who for the time being is on maternity leave, paternity leave or adoption leave [⁵ or shared parental leave] or is absent from work because he is ill;

(k)   the amount of any payment by way of a non-cash voucher which has been taken into account in the computation of a person's earnings in accordance with Part 5 of Schedule 3 to the Social Security (Contributions) Regulations 2001.

(2)   Earnings shall not include–

(a)   subject to paragraph (3), any payment in kind;

(b)   any payment in respect of expenses wholly, exclusively and necessarily incurred in the performance of the duties of the employment;

(c)   any occupational pension.

[² (d) any payment in respect of expenses arising out of the [⁴ the claimant participating as a service user].]

(3)   Paragraph (2)(a) shall not apply in respect of any non-cash voucher referred to in paragraph (1)(k).

Modifications

The amendments made by SI 2014 No.3255 which came into force on 5 April 2015 do not have effect in relation to ordinary statutory paternity pay which is paid, additional statutory paternity pay which is paid, a period in respect of which additional statutory paternity pay is payable which begins, or continues, ordinary paternity leave which is taken or additional paternity leave which is taken on or after 5 April 2015. See art 35 of SI 2014 No.3255. See also s126 Children and Families Act 2014.

Amendments

1.   Inserted by reg 11(4) of SI 2007 No 2618 as from 1.10.07.
2.   Inserted by reg 6(3) of SI 2009 No 2655 as from 2.11.09.
3.   Amended by reg 7(4) of SI 2012 No 757 as from 1.4.12 (2.4.12 where rent payable weekly or in multiples of a week).
4.   Amended by reg 8(3) of SI 2014 No 591 as from 28.4.14.
5.   Amended by art 17(5)(a)(ii) and (b) of SI 2014 No 3255 as from 31.12.14.
6.   Amended by art 17(5)(a)(i) of SI 2014 No 3255 as from 5.4.15.

Definitions

"employed earner" – see reg 2(1).
"maternity leave", "paternity leave", "shared parental leave" and "adoption leave" – see reg 2(1).
"occupational pension" – see reg 2(1).
"participating as a service user" – see reg 2(5).

General Note

This regulation defines "earnings" for the purposes of this Part. It includes all those payments listed in para (1) but excludes those listed in para (2).

Analysis

Paragraph (1): General

"Remuneration or profit derived from ... employment". Sub-paras (a) to (k) of this paragraph do not exclusively define earnings; they are simply a list of items which are deemed to be earnings for these purposes. The true test of which other payments are "earnings" is the phrase "remuneration or profit derived from . . . employment". See also the discussion on *Minter v Kingston upon Hull City Council and Potter v SSWP* [2011] EWCA Civ 1155; [2012] AACR 21 on p418.

The phrase is well known to tax lawyers as defining the payments which may become liable to tax as employment income. In *CFC 25/1989*, the commissioner held that the similarity of wording under tax and social security legislation "cannot be accidental" and that income tax cases were "a useful guide". "Remuneration or profit" would seem to exclude payments of expenses, but see paras (1)(f) and (2)(b) for a detailed look at the treatment of expenses. The issue of whether a payment is "derived from" employment is constantly before the courts regarding the question of liability to tax. A number of tests have evolved to decide whether a payment is so derived.

Generally, the phrase has been widely interpreted in relation to tax so that it is unusual for a payment passing between employer and employee not to be treated as "derived from" employment. A payment made to an employee by a third party is less likely to be so regarded. See, for example, *Moore v Griffiths* [1972] 1 WLR 1024, Ch D, where a payment made to Bobby Moore after the 1966 World Cup by a company seeking publicity from the prize-giving was not "derived from" employment despite the "work" relationship.

Where the payment has been made by an employer, the case of *Hochstrasser v Mayes* [1959] Ch 22, CA, is often quoted. In that case, the test of derivation was held to be whether the payment was made in return for services "past, present or future". This case also established that, in relation to tax at least, the employment relationship need only be one reason for the payment before it will be treated as "derived from" employment. Other important factors in deciding whether a payment is "derived from" employment have been held to be:

(1)   Whether the employee has a contractual right to payment: *Moorhouse v Dooland* [1955] Ch 284, CA.

(2)   Whether the employer's purpose in making the payment was to provide an incentive to the employee to work harder: *Tyrer v Smart* [1979] 1 WLR 113, HL.

(3)   The fact that the payment relates to terms and conditions of employment: *Hamblett v Godfrey* [1987] 1 WLR 357, CA. In that case, payments of £1,000 made to GCHQ employees to give up trade union rights were held to be derived from employment on this basis.

(4)   Whether the payment was of a recurrent nature; if so, it is more likely to be treated as derived from employment: *Blakiston v Cooper* [1909] AC 104, HL.

In *CH 2387/2002*, Commissioner Fellner considered a case in which a company director had put forward accounts showing payment of directors' emoluments of £6,400. In fact, the claimant had only drawn just under £3,000 and the balance had been added to a loan account showing monies owed by the company to the claimant. This approach had been suggested by the company's accountants as a means of saving tax. The commissioner held (para 11) that it was not permissible to put forward one set of earnings figures for tax purposes and another set for benefits purposes. In *CTC 626/2001*, Commissioner Williams upheld a refusal of tax credit to a husband and wife who had adopted an artificial means of payment to themselves from their partnership to save tax, and then argued that for tax credits purposes the true position had to be taken into account. Commissioner Fellner applied that decision and held that the claimant's income for CTB purposes had to be calculated in accordance with the figure given in the accounts. The same will apply for HB purposes.

Payments made in respect of offices. "Employed earner" is defined in s2(1)(a) SSCBA: see reg 2(1) on p227. The definition provides as follows:

"a person who is gainfully employed in Great Britain either under a contract of service, or in an office (including elective office) with general earnings".

Thus it can be seen that the definition of "employed earner" does not solely relate to employment but also to office-holders, provided that they have "general earnings". "General earnings" are defined in s7(3) Income Tax (Earnings and Pensions) Act 2003: s122 SSCBA 1992. The reference to elective office means that councillors' allowances will be treated as "earnings" for the purposes of Part 6: see *R(IS) 6/92* para 5. There is important caselaw on the treatment of councillors' allowances: see the commentary to para (1)(f) below. Note that an office holder who comes within the definition of employed earner may count as in remunerative work for HB purposes: see reg 6 on p253. See the General Note to reg 6 for the significance for HB.

Paragraph (1): Categories of earnings

"Earnings" includes the payments listed in paragraphs (a) to (k) of para (1).

Sub-para (a) is self-explanatory.

Sub-para (b). Payments "in lieu of remuneration" include awards made by employment tribunals and courts to compensate for loss of earnings. It does not, however, apply to redundancy payments. In *MH v SSWP and Rotherham MBC (HB)* [2017] UKUT 401 (AAC), the claimant, having received a redundancy payment, was offered his old job back on condition that he repaid that sum over the same tax year by monthly deduction from his wages. The deduction amounts were treated as part of his earnings in the calculation of HB. Judge Wikeley decided that the amounts did not amount to income and earnings, finding that the claimant had agreed a contractual variation to allow repayment such that the money in question did not amount to income in the first place. This is quite different from the other types of deductions commonly made from wages that are not allowable in calculating a person's income for benefit purposes. *R(TC) 2/03* considered and applied.

A compensatory award made by an employment tribunal falls under this sub-para, in so far as it consists of compensation for loss of earnings: *R(SB) 21/86* para 12. Similarly, where an applicant is awarded any compensation in a claim for discrimination which relates to lost earnings, it falls under sub-para (b): *CIS 590/1993* para 7. It was also decided in that case, however, that awards covering injury to feelings and the loss of a tax rebate did not fall within sub-para (b). See also the discussion on *Minter v Kingston upon Hull City Council and Potter v SSWP* [2011] EWCA Civ 1155; [2012] AACR 21 on p418.

Sub-para (c) applies, for example, to basic awards for unfair dismissal, payments explicitly made in lieu of notice, or payments made by the Secretary of State under s167 Employment Rights Act 1996 to employees whose employer goes into liquidation before they can work their notice.

Sub-para (d). Note that holiday pay payable more than four weeks after employment terminates is treated as capital under reg 46(3).

Sub-para (e). "Retainer" is not defined, but GM BW2.70 says this is "a payment made for a period when no actual work is carried out, such as payment made to employees of the school meals service during school holidays". Payments made during a period of "garden leave" would probably also fall under this provision.

Sub-para (f). The wording "wholly exclusively and necessarily" is the same test as is applied to ascertain deductible expenditure from earnings in relation to income tax. For a discussion of the meaning of the phrase, see the note on para (2)(b) below, which provides that expenses which are so incurred are not to count as earnings for these purposes. That means that under this paragraph, all expenses not so incurred are to be seen as "earnings".

Heads (i) and (ii) deem that the items there specified are *not* to be treated as "wholly exclusively and necessarily" incurred for the purposes of the employment. So travelling expenses to work (but not those incurred while *at* work) are to be treated as earnings, and so are childminding and other care expenses necessitated when the carer goes to work. For the treatment of such expenses, see reg 28.

In *CH 1330/2008*, the claimant was a careworker whose contract of employment showed that her "place of work" was "at any location within [a specified London Borough]". The local authority decided that her place of employment for the purposes of reg 35 was the first place she went to work on any particular day. Expenses for that journey therefore counted as earnings under reg 35(1)(f). Commissioner Jacobs disagreed. He said that reg 35(1) only applies if the claimant *has* a place of employment. If there is no place of employment, which he accepted was the case here, the provision does not apply. Referring to the approach taken by Millett J in *Coates Brothers plc v General Accident Life Assurance Ltd* [1991] 1 WLR 712 at 717 he said that as a matter of interpretation, it is permissible to imply the words "if any" into reg 35(1)(f)(i) so that it reads: "travelling expenses incurred by the claimant between his home and place of employment *if any*". The commissioner accepted that everyone who works must work somewhere. However, that is not the sense of reg 35, which is referring to a fixed place at which work is done or a base from which work is undertaken. The distinction is between travelling done in order to get to work and travelling done while working. Put into the context of this case, the issue was whether, when the claimant left her home, she was travelling (i) in order to take up her duties or (ii) as part of her duties.

There is important caselaw on the treatment of councillors' allowances, concerning arguments that the allowances are supposed to cover expenses of councillors. The allowances are paid, in England and Wales, under s18 Local Government and Housing Act 1989 and the Local Authorities (Members' Allowances) (England) Regulations 2003 and the Local Authorities (Allowances for Members) (Wales) Regulations 2007, and under equivalent legislation in Scotland. None of that legislation gives a clue as to how the allowances are to be treated. In *R(IS) 6/92* para 8, the commissioner concluded that the attendance allowance payable to councillors was "not a payment to meet expenses, but a payment to recompense a councillor for his attendance at authorised meetings". In *CIS 77/1993* para 8, however, the same commissioner pointed out that Department of the Environment Circular 2/91, which was issued following the introduction of the system of allowances, suggested that the purpose of the basic allowance was *both* to recompense a councillor for her/his efforts and for her/his expenses. He therefore concluded that if the councillor could show that s/he had incurred expenses which satisfied the stringent test (for HB set out in para (2)(b)), it was only the amount (if any) to recompense a councillor for her/his efforts that could be regarded as falling within the provision.

It is therefore suggested that what is important is not the purpose for which any allowance is paid but rather whether the evidence shows that the councillor has incurred expenses "wholly, exclusively and necessarily" as a consequence of her/his work as a councillor. Councillors claiming HB but not IS, JSA or income-related ESA are therefore advised to keep full records of their expenses. It should also be noted that they have the right to have income tax deducted from an attendance allowance at the basic rate and then to ask HMRC to direct the council to deduct expenses from the tax.

Sub-para (g) covers compensation awards made under ss112(4) and 117(3)(a) Employment Rights Act 1996. The former provision refers to compensatory awards made by industrial tribunals where the complainant has established unfair dismissal but the tribunal does not recommend reinstatement or re-engagement. The latter provision refers to the higher rate awards made where reinstatement or re-engagement has been recommended but the employer has failed to comply.

Sub-para (gg) covers the payments or remuneration made under the sections of the Employment Rights Act 1996 listed. They are guarantee payments (ss28 and 34), remuneration to an employee who is suspended from work by her/his employer on medical grounds (ss64 and 70) or on maternity grounds (ss68 and 70).

Sub-para (h). The payments covered are:

(1) Amounts representing arrears of pay paid in pursuance of an order for reinstatement or re-engagement under the Employment Rights Act 1996.

(2) Amounts payable by way of pay in pursuance of an order for continuation of a contract of employment under the Employment Rights Act 1996 or the Trade Union and Labour Relations (Consolidation) Act 1992.

(3) "Protective awards" made to employees where the employer has failed to comply with the consultation procedure for redundancies under the Trade Union and Labour Relations (Consolidation) Act 1992.

Sub-paras (i) and (j) confirm that sick pay and maternity, paternity, shared parental and adoption pay, whether made under statute or as additional payments under contract, count as earnings.

Sub-para (k). The principle is that if a "non-cash voucher" counts as earnings when calculating liability to pay national insurance contributions under the regulations cited, it also counts as earnings for HB. Note that the contributions legislation is changed very frequently, so in any case of doubt reference should be made to the current version of the regulations or current tax handbooks. Current versions of social security regulations are available at www.legislation.gov.uk.

Paragraphs (2) and (3): Exclusions from the definition of earnings

Sub-paras (a) to (d) of para (2) exclude certain types of payment from the definition of "earnings" in para (1). Such payments therefore count as "income other than earnings" to be assessed under Section 5, but note that under Sch 5 payments in kind, expenses "wholly, exclusively and necessarily incurred" for the purposes set out and expenses for a claimant's participating as a service user are to be disregarded completely: see Sch 5 paras 23, 3 and 2A respectively.

Sub-para (a) excludes any payment in kind, with the exception of vouchers that fall to be taken into account under para (1)(k) above: see para (3).

Sub-para (b). The phrase "wholly, exclusively and necessarily incurred in performing the duties of the employment" has been rigidly interpreted in relation to tax law. Before a payment may fall into this category it must display all three attributes referred to.

(1)   "Wholly" means that all of the payment in question must be dedicated to this purpose, not just part. However, if a lump sum is paid in respect of some expenses which qualify and others which do not, there would seem to be no reason why an apportionment cannot be made: see the authorities on councillors' allowances referred to under para (1)(f).

(2)   "Exclusively" means that the payment must be for no other purpose than the duties of the employment – eg, expenditure on an item which is to be used partly for domestic use would not qualify.

(3)   Finally, before expenditure may be excluded from the definition of earnings on this basis, it must be "necessary" for the performance of the duties of employment. In relation to tax, the case of *Brown v Bullock* [1961] 1 WLR 1095, CA, decided that only expenditure necessitated by the duties themselves, and not simply the employer's policies, would qualify. For example, if the job is such that protective clothing is necessary, expenditure on that clothing which is reimbursed will not be "earnings", but if an employer insists that employees wear suits, when the job could be done adequately without the wearing of a suit, expenses in that respect will not be "necessarily" incurred for the purpose of performing the duties and so *will* count as earnings.

There is a vast amount of caselaw concerned with the phrase in relation to tax and reference should be made to textbooks on tax law in any case of doubt.

Note that expenses deemed not to be earnings by sub-para (b) are disregarded as "income other than earnings" by Sch 5 para 3.

Sub-para (c). See reg 2(1) (p230) for the definition of "occupational pension".

Sub-para (d). See reg 2(5) (p237) for the definition of "participating as a service user".

Calculation of net earnings of employed earners

36.–(1)   For the purposes of regulation 29 (average weekly earnings of employed earners), the earnings of a claimant derived or likely to be derived from employment as an employed earner to be taken into account shall, subject to paragraph (2), be his net earnings.

(2)   There shall be disregarded from a claimant's net earnings, any sum, where applicable, specified in paragraphs 1 to 14 of Schedule 4.

(3)   For the purposes of paragraph (1) net earnings shall, except where paragraph (6) applies, be calculated by taking into account the gross earnings of the claimant from that employment over the assessment period, less–

(a)   any amount deducted from those earnings by way of–
(i)   income tax;
(ii)   primary Class 1 contributions under the Act;

(b)   one-half of any sum paid by the claimant by way of a contribution towards an occupational pension scheme;

(c)   one-half of the amount calculated in accordance with paragraph (5) in respect of any qualifying contribution payable by the claimant; and

(d)   where those earnings include a payment which is payable under any enactment having effect in Northern Ireland and which corresponds to statutory sick pay, statutory maternity pay, [³ [⁵] statutory paternity pay]] or statutory adoption pay [⁴ or statutory shared parental pay], any amount deducted from those earnings by way of any contributions which are payable under any enactment having effect in Northern Ireland and which correspond to primary Class 1 contributions under the Act.

(4)   In this regulation "qualifying contribution" means any sum which is payable periodically as a contribution towards a personal pension scheme.

(5)   The amount in respect of any qualifying contribution shall be calculated by multiplying the daily amount of the qualifying contribution by the number equal to the

number of days in the assessment period; and for the purposes of this regulation the daily amount of the qualifying contribution shall be determined–

(a) where the qualifying contribution is payable monthly, by multiplying the amount of the qualifying contribution by 12 and dividing the product by 365;

(b) in any other case, by dividing the amount of the qualifying contribution by the number equal to the number of days in the period to which the qualifying contribution relates.

(6) Where the earnings of a claimant are estimated under sub-paragraph (b) of paragraph (2) of regulation 29 (average weekly earnings of employed earners), his net earnings shall be calculated by taking into account those earnings over the assessment period, less–

(a) an amount in respect of income tax equivalent to an amount calculated by applying to those earnings [²] the basic rate [⁶, or in the case of a Scottish taxpayer, the Scottish basic rate,] of tax applicable to the assessment period less only the [⁶ personal reliefs to which the claimant is entitled under Chapters 2, 3 and 3A of Part 3 of the Income Tax Act 2007 as are] appropriate to his circumstances but, if the assessment period is less than a year, the earnings to which the [¹ [² basic] rate] [⁶, or the Scottish basic rate,] of tax is to be applied and the amount of the personal [⁶ reliefs] deductible under this sub-paragraph shall be calculated on a pro rata basis;

(b) an amount equivalent to the amount of the primary Class 1 contributions that would be payable by him under the Act in respect of those earnings if such contributions were payable; and

(c) one-half of any sum which would be payable by the claimant by way of a contribution towards an occupational or personal pension scheme, if the earnings so estimated were actual earnings.

Modifications

The amendments made by SI 2014 No.3255 which came into force on 5 April 2015 do not have effect in relation to ordinary statutory paternity pay which is paid, additional statutory paternity pay which is paid, a period in respect of which additional statutory paternity pay is payable which begins, or continues, ordinary paternity leave which is taken or additional paternity leave which is taken on or after 5 April 2015. See art 35 of SI 2014 No.3255. See also s126 Children and Families Act 2014.

Amendments

1. Amended by reg 11(5) of SI 2007 No 2618 as from 1.10.07.
2. Amended by reg 6(4) of SI 2009 No 583 as from 6.4.09.
3. Amended by reg 7(5) of SI 2012 No 757 as from 1.4.12 (2.4.12 where rent payable weekly or in multiples of a week).
4. Amended by art 17(6)(b) of SI 2014 No 3255 as from 31.12.14.
5. Amended by art 17(6)(a) of SI 2014 No 3255 as from 5.4.15.
6. Amended by reg 4(4) of SI 2016 No 233 as from 6.4.16.

Definitions

"claimant" – see reg 2(1).
"earnings" – see reg 35.
"employed earner" – see reg 2(1).
"occupational pension" – see reg 2(1).
"personal pension scheme" – see reg 2(1).
"Scottish basic rate" – see reg 2(1).
"Scottish taxpayer" – see reg 2(1).

General Note

Paras (1) and (2) set out the general rule that "earnings" to be taken into account under reg 29 are "net" earnings minus sums disregarded under Sch 4.

Paras (3) and (6) define "net" for these purposes. Para (3) relates to claimants whose earnings are to be averaged under reg 29(1). Their net earnings are to be ascertained by deducting income tax, national insurance (NI) contributions and half of occupational/personal pension contributions made by the employee from the gross figure. Para (6) deals with those whose earnings are estimated under reg 29(2)(b).

Analysis

Para (2). In considering the scope of any disregard, decisions on similarly-worded disregards in other means-tested benefit schemes must be taken into account: *CH 2321/2002* para 8.

Paras (3) to (5) set out amounts which are to be deducted to generate a net earnings figure. See also reg 34 where the amounts of statutory deductions change during an award. The deductions are:

(1)   Amounts deducted by way of income tax and Class 1 NI contributions: para (3)(a).

(2)   Half of any contributions made by a claimant towards an occupational pension scheme: para (3)(b).

(3)   Half of any "qualifying contributions": para (3)(c). These are those made to a personal pension scheme: see para (4). Para (5) sets out the method of calculation.

(4)   Sums deducted from statutory sick pay and statutory maternity, adoption, shared parental and paternity pay in Northern Ireland which correspond to Class 1 contributions: para (3)(d).

Para (6)(a). The wording of para (6)(a) is odd, but the effect is that the appropriate personal allowance for tax purposes is deducted from gross earnings and the basic rate applied to what remains. Details of tax rates and NI contributions are available at www.hmrc.gov.uk/rates. Note that, from tax year 2018/19, Scottish rates and bands of income tax have been different from those elsewhere in the UK. (Note also that the definition of "Scottish basic rate" in reg 2(1) is by reference to s6A Income Tax Act 2007. That section was repealed on 30 November 2016 by virtue of s14(5) Scotland Act 2016.)

"on a pro-rata basis" requires, for example, that if the assessment period is six months, one half of the appropriate personal reliefs should be deducted. Notice that if the HB is being assessed outside the year of assessment in which the claim was made, the basic rate of tax due in that year is used, but the personal relief applying in the current tax year is to be applied.

SECTION 4
Self-employed earners

General Note on Section 4

This section deals with the assessment of earnings from self-employment for the purposes of regs 27 and 30.

Reg 37 defines "earnings" so far as self-employed earners are concerned.

Reg 38 provides the rules under which such a person's "net profit" is to be calculated and reg 39 provides the details necessary in relation to reg 38 to enable deductions in respect of tax and NI contributions to be made.

The main disputes in relation to this Section are likely to be about the quantification of "profit". In particular it may be difficult for the claimant or those whose income is aggregated with the claimant's to provide adequate evidence of net profit.

Earnings of self-employed earners

37.–(1)   Subject to [5 paragraphs (2) and (2A)], "earnings", in the case of employment as a self-employed earner, means the gross income of the employment [3].

(2)   "Earnings" shall not include any payment to which paragraph [4 26, 27 or 27A] of Schedule 5 refers (payments in respect of a person accommodated with the claimant under arrangements made by a local authority or voluntary organisation [4, payments] made to the claimant by a health authority, local authority or voluntary organisation in respect of persons temporarily in the claimant's care [4 and any payments made to a claimant under section 73(1)(b) of the Children and Young People (Scotland) Act 2014 (kinship care assistance)]) nor shall it include any sports award.

[5 (2A)   Earnings shall also not include any payment made in accordance with section 26A of the Children (Scotland) Act 1995 (duty to provide continuing care)–

(a)   to a claimant; or

(b)   where paragraph (2B) applies, to another person ("A") which A passes on to the claimant.

(2B)   This paragraph applies only where A–

(a)   was formerly in the claimant's care;

(b)   is aged 16 or over; and

(c)   continues to live with the claimant.]

[1 [2 (3)   This paragraph applies to–

(a)   royalties or other sums paid as a consideration for the use of, or the right to use, any copyright, design, patent or trade mark; or

(b)   any payment in respect of any–

(i)   book registered under the Public Lending Right Scheme 1982; or

(ii)   work made under any international public lending right scheme that is analogous to the Public Lending Right Scheme 1982, where the claimant is the first owner of the copyright, design, patent or trade mark, or an original contributor to the book or work concerned.]

(4)   Where the claimant's earnings consist of any items to which paragraph (3) applies, those earnings shall be taken into account over a period equal to such number of weeks as is equal to the number obtained (and any fraction shall be treated as a corresponding fraction of a week) by dividing the earnings by the amount of housing benefit which would be payable had the payment not been made plus an amount equal to the total of the sums which would fall to be disregarded from the payment under Schedule 4 (sums to be disregarded in the calculation of earnings) as appropriate in the claimant's case.]

Amendments
1.   Inserted by reg 6(3) of SI 2008 No 698 as from, as it relates to a particular beneficiary, the first day of the benefit week on or after 7.4. 08.
2.   Substituted by reg 6(5) of SI 2009 No 583 as from the first day of the first benefit week to commence for the claimant on or after 6.4.09.
3.   Omitted by reg 19(4) of SI 2011 No 2425 as from 31.10.11.
4.   Amended by reg 5(2) of SI 2017 No 995 as from 7.11.17.
5.   Amended by reg 12 of SI 2017 No 995 as from 7.11.17.

Definitions
"claimant" – reg 2(1).
"self-employed earner" – see reg 2(1).

General Note
This regulation provides a general definition of the term "earnings" in relation to self-employed earners. Para (2) clarifies that local authority payments to foster parents (and certain payments to kinship carers) should not be treated as self-employed earnings. Such payments in fact are considered to be income other than earnings and are disregarded under Sch 5 paras 26 and 27A, as are certain payments made to those providing respite care (Sch 5 para 27). Paras (2A) and (2B) clarify that certain payments made by a local authority in Scotland to persons who are providing "continuing care" to children over 16 who were previously looked after by the authority should also not be treated as self-employed earnings. Paras (3) and (4) deal with the period over which royalties, copyright, design, patent, trade mark and Public Lending Right Scheme payments are to be taken into account.
The reference is to *gross* earnings and the other regulations in this Section provide for deductions from earnings to arrive at "net profit" for the purposes of reg 30.

Analysis
Para (1). The "earnings" of a self-employed earner are the gross income of the employment.
Paras (3) and (4). Under para (4), any of the payments listed in para (3) are taken into account over a period of weeks obtained by dividing the amount of the payments by the amount of HB which would be payable had the claimant not received the payments, plus the amount that would have been disregarded from the earnings under Sch 4.

Calculation of net profit of self-employed earners

38.–(1)   For the purposes of regulation 30 (average weekly earnings of self-employed earners) the earnings of a claimant to be taken into account shall be–
(a)   in the case of a self-employed earner who is engaged in employment on his own account, the net profit derived from that employment;
(b)   in the case of a self-employed earner whose employment is carried on in partnership or is that of a share fisherman within the meaning of the Social Security (Mariners' Benefits) Regulations 1975, his share of the net profit derived from that employment, less–
(i)   an amount in respect of income tax and of [² national insurance contributions] payable under the Act calculated in accordance with regulation 39 (deduction of tax and contributions for self-employed earners); and
(ii)   one-half of the amount calculated in accordance with paragraph (11) in respect of any qualifying premium.
(2)   There shall be disregarded from a claimant's net profit, any sum, where applicable, specified in paragraphs 1 to 14 of Schedule 4.

(3)   For the purposes of paragraph (1)(a) the net profit of the employment shall, except where paragraph (9) applies, be calculated by taking into account the earnings of the employment over the assessment period less–

(a)   subject to paragraphs (5) to (7), any expenses wholly and exclusively incurred in that period for the purposes of that employment;

(b)   an amount in respect of–

(i)   income tax; and

(ii)   [² national insurance contributions] payable under the Act, calculated in accordance with regulation 39 (deduction of tax and contributions for self-employed earners); and

(c)   one-half of the amount calculated in accordance with paragraph (11) in respect of any qualifying premium.

(4)   For the purposes of paragraph (1)(b) the net profit of the employment shall be calculated by taking into account the earnings of the employment over the assessment period less, subject to paragraphs (5) to (7), any expenses wholly and exclusively incurred in that period for the purposes of the employment.

(5)   Subject to paragraph (6), no deduction shall be made under paragraph (3)(a) or (4), in respect of–

(a)   any capital expenditure;

(b)   the depreciation of any capital asset;

(c)   any sum employed or intended to be employed in the setting up or expansion of the employment;

(d)   any loss incurred before the beginning of the assessment period;

(e)   the repayment of capital on any loan taken out for the purposes of the employment;

(f)   any expenses incurred in providing business entertainment; and

(g)   any debts, except bad debts proved to be such, but this sub-paragraph shall not apply to any expenses incurred in the recovery of a debt.

(6)   A deduction shall be made under paragraph (3)(a) or (4) in respect of the repayment of capital on any loan used for–

(a)   the replacement in the course of business of equipment or machinery; and

(b)   the repair of an existing business asset except to the extent that any sum is payable under an insurance policy for its repair.

(7)   The relevant authority shall refuse to make a deduction in respect of any expenses under paragraph (3)(a) or (4) where it is not satisfied given the nature and the amount of the expense that it has been reasonably incurred.

(8)   For the avoidance of doubt–

(a)   a deduction shall not be made under paragraph (3)(a) or (4) in respect of any sum unless it has been expended for the purposes of the business;

(b)   a deduction shall be made thereunder in respect of–

(i)   the excess of any value added tax paid over value added tax received in the assessment period;

(ii)   any income expended in the repair of an existing business asset except to the extent that any sum is payable under an insurance policy for its repair;

(iii)   any payment of interest on a loan taken out for the purposes of the employment.

(9)   Where a claimant is engaged in employment as a child minder the net profit of the employment shall be one-third of the earnings of that employment, less–

(a)   an amount in respect of–

(i)   income tax; and

(ii)   [² national insurance contributions] payable under the Act, calculated in accordance with regulation 39 (deduction of tax and contributions for self-employed earners); and

(b)   one-half of the amount calculated in accordance with paragraph (11) in respect of any qualifying premium.

(10)   For the avoidance of doubt where a claimant is engaged in employment as a self-employed earner and he is also engaged in one or more other employments as a self-

employed or employed earner any loss incurred in any one of his employments shall not be offset against his earnings in any other of his employments.

(11) The amount in respect of any qualifying premium shall be calculated by multiplying the daily amount of the qualifying premium by the number equal to the number of days in the assessment period; and for the purposes of this regulation the daily amount of the qualifying premium shall be determined–

(a) where the qualifying premium is payable monthly, by multiplying the amount of the qualifying premium by 12 and dividing the product by 365;

(b) in any other case, by dividing the amount of the qualifying premium by the number equal to the number of days in the period to which the qualifying premium relates.

(12) In this regulation, "qualifying premium" means any premium which is payable periodically in respect of [¹] a personal pension scheme and is so payable on or after the date of claim.

Amendments

1. Omitted by reg 4(3) of SI 2007 No 1749 as from 16.7.07.
2. Amended by reg 3(4)(b) of SI 2014 No 213 as from 1.4.14 (7.4.14 where rent payable weekly or in multiples of a week).

Definitions

"assessment period" – see reg 2(1).
"capital" – see General Note on Section 6.
"claimant" – see reg 2(1).
"date of claim" – reg 2(1).
"earnings" – see reg 37.
"employed earner" – see reg 2(1).
"partner" – reg 2(1).
"qualifying premium" – see para (12).
"relevant authority" – see reg 2(1).
"self-employed earner" – reg 2(1).

General Note

This deals with the assessment of "net profit" for the purposes of reg 30. It produces detailed rules as to what expenditure may be deducted from the gross "earnings" of a self-employed earner (see reg 37 on p444) to arrive at the net figure. The wording follows the income tax law quite closely in relation to allowable deductions from chargeable income.

Analysis

Paragraphs (1) and (2): The basic calculation

Para (1) sets out the basic rule for what is to be taken into account as earnings for the self-employed under reg 30. See p439 for the meaning of "derived from". Earnings to be taken into account are "net profit" minus sums disregarded under Sch 4. Whether or not the business is in profit, any drawings cannot be regarded as earnings, nor can they be taken into account as other income. To do so would involve taking into account both the claimant's share of the profits (independent of whether any profits were withdrawn) and the actual drawings from that share of profits: *AR v Bradford MBC* [2008] UKUT 30 (AAC); R(H) 6/09. See also the General Note to Part 6 on p415.

There are two categories of self-employed persons.

(1) Those who are in self-employment in their own account: para (1)(a). Their net profit is calculated under para (3).
(2) Those who are in partnerships or are share fishermen: para (1)(b). Their net profit is calculated under para (4).

Note that childminders are dealt with separately. Their net profit is calculated under para (9).

Para (2) requires the deduction of the disregarded amounts set out in paras 1 to 14 of Sch 4. In considering the scope of any disregard, decisions on similarly-worded disregards in other means-tested benefit schemes must be taken into account: *CH 2321/2002* para 8.

Note that the deputy commissioner in *CPC 3373/2007*, dealing with the equivalent provision for PC purposes, pointed out that when the difference between receipts and expenditure is a positive figure the regulations refer to it as a "profit" and where it is a negative figure, they refer to it as a "loss". He said that it followed that when a loss is made the net "profit" of the employment for these purposes is nil and not a negative figure.

Paragraph (3): Those who are self-employed on their own account

Note that this does not apply to childminders, who are dealt with under para (9). The total of the amounts available under sub-paras (a) to (c) must be deducted to arrive at the net profit.

Sub-para (a) must be read together with paras (5) to (8) to ascertain exactly which expenses are deductible. The expenses set out in para (5) cannot be deducted, whereas those in para (6) must be deducted. There is a general requirement under para (7) that the expenses must be "reasonably incurred". Para (8) then sets out further deeming provisions. See the discussion of the terms "wholly" and "exclusively" in the commentary to reg 35(2)(b). Note that here there is no requirement that the expenses be necessary. Instead, the test of reasonableness is used.

In *R(H) 5/07*, the commissioner followed *R(FC) 1/91* in holding that the part of the interest on a car loan apportionable to business use could be allowed as an expense "wholly and exclusively incurred . . . for the purposes of [the] employment".

Only expenses incurred during the period over which the profit is averaged out under reg 30 may be considered.

Sub-para (b) requires deduction of income tax and NI contributions. See reg 39, which supplements this.

Sub-para (c) requires the deduction of half of a "qualifying premium" paid in respect of a personal pension scheme (defined in paras (11) and (12)).

Paragraph (4): Partners and share fishermen

Where someone is a partner or a share fisherman, this paragraph, with para (1)(b), is used to calculate earnings. Under para (1)(b)(i) and (ii), from the claimant's share of the net profit, deductions are made corresponding to para (3)(b) and (c). Para (4) enables business expenses to be deducted on a similar basis to that provided by para (3)(a) in relation to all other self-employed people except child minders.

See also the note to para (10) below.

Paragraph (5): Items which are not expenses

This lists items which are deemed not to satisfy para (3)(a) or para (4), except to the extent that para (6) provides otherwise.

Sub-para (a) capital expenditure. Note that where para (6) applies, the expenditure to which it relates is deductible under para (3)(a) or para (4), despite this provision.

Sub-para (b) depreciation. There can be no deduction in this respect as tax relief and other allowances are already available.

Sub-para (d) losses incurred before the assessment period. Although losses incurred during the assessment period may be deducted as allowable expenses this can only ever take the net "profit" (per para (1)(a)) to a figure of nil; it cannot reduce the profit to a negative figure to be set off against any other income which the claimant may have: *R(H) 5/08* (paras 26–28).

Sub-para (e) excludes repayments of capital on loans taken out for the purposes of the employment. However, para (8)(b)(iii) states that interest on such a loan may be an allowable expense. See also para (6).

Sub-para (g) prevents debts owed to the business being taken into account when calculating net profit. "Bad debts", however, may be taken into account. Bad debts are irrecoverable in accounting terms – eg, because the debtor is insolvent. The requirement that bad debts be "proven to be such" indicates that the claimant must prove that a debt is a bad debt. Expenses incurred in recovering a business debt are deductible in assessing "net profit" if para (3)(a), or paras (4) and (7) are satisfied.

Paragraph (6): Items deemed to be expenses

This qualifies para (5) by providing that capital used to repay loans for the items listed shall be deducted under para (3)(a) or para (4) when calculating net profit.

Sub-para (a). Note that the replacement must be in the "course of business" and not for personal use.

However, in *R(H) 5/07* the commissioner held that capital repayments in respect of a replacement car are deductible as a car is perfectly capable of amounting to "business equipment or machinery", regardless of how good accounting practice may view it.

Sub-para (b). If a sum is "payable" (whether or not actually paid) under an insurance policy for the repair in question, para (5)(e) operates to prevent deduction of capital repayments in this respect, to the extent that the insurance payment would cover them. See also para (8)(b)(iii).

Paragraph (7): Reasonableness of expenses

In deciding whether a business expense has been "reasonably" incurred, the authority has to take account of the nature as well as the amount of the expense, given the character of the claimant's business. The question is whether expenditure of this kind is reasonable. If para (6) or para (8)(b) deems expenses to be deductible, they need to also satisfy the "reasonableness" test under para (7).

Paragraph (8): Deeming provisions

Para (8) contains a number of deeming provisions confirming the effect of paras (3) to (6). Any amounts referred to here which are deductible must still be subjected to the reasonableness test in para (7).

Sub-para (a) simply reinforces the use of the word "wholly" in para (3)(a), confirming that any expenditure of which any part is not for business purposes is not deductible.

Sub-para (b) confirms that net payments of VAT, repair expenditure (except sums paid under insurance policies) and interest payments on loan may be deducted when calculating net profit.

Paragraph (9): Childminders

Para (9) provides special rules for the assessment of the net profit of childminders. "Childminder" is not defined but as "child" is defined as any person under the age of 16, it is suggested that any person looking after a "child" at any period of the day by way of a business will fall within that provision. Paras (3) to (7) do not apply. Instead, childminders are deemed to have net profit of one-third of their earnings. Para (2) still applies and so the sums listed in Sch 4 paras 1 to 14 are deductible from a childminder's net profit for the purposes of reg 30.

As to deductions under sub-para (a), see reg 39. "Qualifying premiums" in sub-para (b) are defined in para (12) and the amount is to be calculated in accordance with para (11). Half a qualifying premium may be deducted.

Paragraph (10): Offsetting

This paragraph provides that if a claimant has more than one employment, losses made in one during the averaging period cannot be offset against gains made in respect of another. It is, however, not possible to imply a general rule, that losses may be offset: *CPC 3373/2007*. Para (10) states expressly that it has been made "for the avoidance of doubt" and it is intended merely to clarify the law as it would exist even if the regulation had not been made.

Paragraphs (11) and (12): "Qualifying premiums"

Para (11) deals with calculation of qualifying premiums. Para (12) defines the term and clarifies that the amount initially to be deducted should be based on the amounts payable on or after the date of claim.

Deduction of tax and contributions of self-employed earners

39.–(1) The amount to be deducted in respect of income tax under regulation 38(1)(b)(i), (3)(b)(i) or (9)(a)(i) (calculation of net profit of self-employed earners) shall be calculated on the basis of the amount of chargeable income and as if that income were assessable to income tax at [²...] the basic rate [⁶, or in the case of a Scottish taxpayer, the Scottish basic rate,] of tax applicable to the assessment period less only the [⁶ personal reliefs to which the claimant is entitled under Chapters 2, 3 and 3A of Part 3 of the Income Tax Act 2007 as are] appropriate to his circumstances; but, if the assessment period is less than a year, the earnings to which the [¹ [³ basic] rate] [⁶, or the Scottish basic rate,] of tax is to be applied and the amount of the personal [⁶ reliefs] deductible under this paragraph shall be calculated on a pro rata basis.

(2) The amount to be deducted in respect of [⁴ national insurance contributions] under regulation 38(1)(b)(i), (3)(b)(ii) or (9)(a)(ii) shall be the total of–

(a) the amount of Class 2 contributions payable under section [⁵ 11(2)] or, as the case may be, [⁵ 11(8)] of the Act at the rate applicable to the assessment period except where the claimant's chargeable income is less than the amount specified in section 11(4) of the Act ([⁵ small profits threshold]) for the tax year applicable to the assessment period; but if the assessment period is less than a year, the amount specified for that tax year shall be reduced pro rata; and

(b) the amount of Class 4 contributions (if any) which would be payable under section 15 of the Act (Class 4 contributions recoverable under the Income Tax Acts) at the percentage rate applicable to the assessment period on so much of the chargeable income as exceeds the lower limit but does not exceed the upper limit of profits and gains applicable for the tax year applicable to the assessment period; but if the assessment period is less than a year, those limits shall be reduced pro rata.

(3) In this regulation "chargeable income" means–

(a) except where sub-paragraph (b) applies, the earnings derived from the employment less any expenses deducted under paragraph (3)(a) or, as the case may be, (4) of regulation 38;

(b) in the case of employment as a child minder, one third of the earnings of that employment.

Amendments

1. Amended by reg 11(6) of SI 2007 No 2618 as from 1.10.07.
2. Omitted by reg 6(4)(a) of SI 2009 No 583 as from 6.4.09.
3. Amended by reg 6(4)(b) of SI 2009 No 583 as from 6.4.09.
4. Amended by reg 3(4)(c) of SI 2014 No 213 as from 1.4.14 (7.4.14 where rent payable weekly or in multiples of a week).
5. Amended by reg 33(3) of SI 2015 No 478 as from 6.4.15.
6. Amended by reg 4(4) of SI 2016 No 233 as from 6.4.16.

Definitions

"basic rate" – see reg 2(1).
"self-employed earner" – see reg 2(1).
"Scottish basic rate" – see reg 2(1).
"Scottish taxpayer" – see reg 2(1).

General Note

This relates to the calculation of "net profit" under reg 38 and in particular to deductions for income tax and national insurance (NI) made under paras (1)(b), (3)(b) and (9)(a) of that regulation. Para (1) deals with the quantification of income tax to be deducted from "earnings" as defined in reg 37 under paras (1)(b)(i), (3)(b)(i) or (9)(a)(i) as appropriate.

Para (2) deals with the amount of NI contributions to be deducted from earnings; and para (3) defines the term "chargeable income" as used in this regulation.

Analysis

Para (2). A self-employed person may be liable to both class 2 and class 4 contributions depending on the level of her/his profits. The amount due is calculated on the basis of "chargeable income": see para (3) for the definition. Deductions for NI should be based on the rates applicable to the assessment period (for which see reg 2(1)).

Para (3) defines "chargeable income" as the amount remaining after the deductions in paras (3)(a) and (4) of reg 38, as appropriate, have been made from gross earnings. In the case of a child minder, it is one-third of her/his earnings. See the Analysis to reg 38(9) on p448.

SECTION 5
Other income

General Note on Section 5

This Section provides the rules under which income which is not "earnings" under Sections 3 or 4 is to be assessed. Note, however, that student income is dealt with in Part 7.

Calculation of income other than earnings

40.–(1) For the purposes of regulation 31 (average weekly income other than earnings), the income of a claimant which does not consist of earnings to be taken into account shall, subject to paragraphs (2) to (7) be his gross income and any capital treated as income under regulation 41 (capital treated as income).

(2) There shall be disregarded from the calculation of a claimant's gross income under paragraph (1), any sum, where applicable, specified in Schedule 5.

[² (3)]

[² (4)]

[¹, ² (4A)]

(5) Where the payment of any benefit under the benefit Acts is subject to any deduction by way of recovery the amount to be taken into account under paragraph (1) shall be the gross amount payable.

[⁴ (5A) Where the claimant or, where the claimant is a member of a couple, his partner is receiving a contributory employment and support allowance and that benefit has been reduced under regulation 63 of the Employment and Support Allowance Regulations [⁵ or section 11J of the Welfare Reform Act] the amount of that benefit to be taken into account is the amount as if it had not been reduced.]

(6) Where an award of any working tax credit or child tax credit under the Tax Credits Act is subject to a deduction by way of recovery of an overpayment of working tax credit or child tax credit which arose in a previous tax year the amount to be taken into account under paragraph (1) shall be the amount of working tax credit or child tax credit awarded less the amount of that deduction.

(7) [³ Paragraphs (8) and (8A) apply] where–

(a) a relevant payment has been made to a person in an academic year; and

(b) that person abandons, or is dismissed from, his course of study before the payment to him of the final instalment of the relevant payment.

(8) [³ Where a relevant payment is made quarterly, the] amount of a relevant payment to be taken into account for the assessment period for the purposes of paragraph (1) in respect of a person to whom paragraph (7) applies, shall be calculated by applying the formula–

$$\frac{A - (B \text{ X } C)}{D}$$

where–

A= the total amount of the relevant payment which that person would have received had he remained a student until the last day of the academic term in which he abandoned, or was dismissed from, his course, less any deduction under regulation 64(5);

B= the number of benefit weeks from the benefit week immediately following that which includes the first day of that academic year to the benefit week which includes the day on which the person abandoned, or was dismissed from, his course;

C= the weekly amount of the relevant payment, before the application of the £10 disregard, which would have been taken into account as income under regulation 64(2) had the person not abandoned or been dismissed from, his course and, in the case of a person who was not entitled to housing benefit immediately before he abandoned or was dismissed from his course, had that person, at that time, been entitled to housing benefit;

D= the number of benefit weeks in the assessment period.

[³ (8A)   Where a relevant payment is made by two or more instalments in a quarter, the amount of a relevant payment to be taken into account for the assessment period for the purposes of paragraph (1) in respect of a person to whom paragraph (7) applies, shall be calculated by applying the formula in paragraph (8) but as if–

A = the total amount of relevant payments which that person received, or would have received, from the first day of the academic year to the day the person abandoned the course, or was dismissed from it, less any deduction under regulation 64(5).]

(9)   [³ In this regulation]–

"academic year" and "student loan" shall have the same meanings as for the purposes of Part 7;

[³ "assessment period" means–

(a)   in a case where a relevant payment is made quarterly, the period beginning with the benefit week which includes the day on which the person abandoned, or was dismissed from, his course and ending with the benefit week which includes the last day of the last quarter for which an instalment of the relevant payment was payable to that person;

(b)   in a case where the relevant payment is made by two or more instalments in a quarter, the period beginning with the benefit week which includes the day on which the person abandoned, or was dismissed from, his course and ending with the benefit week which includes–

(i)   the day immediately before the day on which the next instalment of the relevant payment would have been due had the payments continued; or

(ii)   the last day of the last quarter for which an instalment of the relevant payment was payable to that person,

whichever of those dates is earlier;]

"relevant payment" means either a student loan or an amount intended for the maintenance of dependants referred to in regulation 59(7) or both.

[³ "quarter" in relation to an assessment period means a period in that year beginning on–

(a)   1st January and ending on 31st March;

(b   1st April and ending on 30th June;

(c)   1st July and ending on 31st August; or

(d)   1st September and ending on 31st December;]

(10)   For the avoidance of doubt there shall be included as income to be taken into account under paragraph (1)–

(a)   any payment to which regulation 35(2) (payments not earnings) applies; or

(b)   in the case of a claimant who is receiving support under section 95 or 98 of the Immigration and Asylum Act including support provided by virtue of regulations made under Schedule 9 to that Act, the amount of such support provided in respect of essential living needs of the claimant and his dependants (if any) as is specified in regulations made under paragraph 3 of Schedule 8 to the Immigration and Asylum Act.

Amendments

1. Inserted by reg 2 of SI 2006 No 2813 as from 20.11.06.
2. Omitted by reg 4(b) of SI 2007 No 1619 as from 3.7.07.
3. Amended by reg 5(2) of SI 2008 No 1599 as from, for students whose period of study begins on or after 1.8.08 but before 1.9.08, on the day the period of study begins; in any other case 1.9.08.
4. Inserted by reg 15 of SI 2008 No 1082 as from 27.10.08.
5. Amended by reg 35(5) of SI 2013 No 630 as from 29.4.13.

Definitions

"benefit Acts" – see reg 2(1).
"benefit week" – see reg 2(1).
"capital" – see General Note on Section 6.
"child tax credit" and "working tax credit" – see reg 2(1).
"claimant" – see reg 2(1).
"contributory employment and support allowance" – see reg 2(1).
"couple" – see reg 2(1).
"earnings" – see regs 2(1), 35 and 37.
"Employment and Support Allowance Regulations" – see reg 2(1).
"Immigration and Asylum Act" – see reg 2(1).
"income" – see General Note on Part 6.
"partner" – see reg 2(1).
"student" – see regs 2(1) and 53.
"Tax Credit Act" – see reg 2(1).
"tax year" – see reg 2(1).
"Welfare Reform Act" – see reg 2(1).

General Note

Unlike in sections 3 and 4 of this Part, the general rule is that gross, rather than net, income is to be taken into account together with any capital treated as income under reg 41. Amounts specified in Sch 5 are disregarded; this includes tax paid on the income.

Analysis

Para (1) confirms that, subject to paras (2) to (7), gross income is taken into account. Note, however, that tax paid on the income is to be disregarded under Sch 5 para 1. For general comments about the nature of income, see the General Note to this Part.

Para (2) permits the disregards in Sch 5. In considering the scope of any disregard, decisions on similarly-worded disregards in other means-tested benefit schemes must be taken into account: *CH 2321/2002* para 8.

Para (5) refers only to the situation where a "deduction by way of recovery" is made from gross benefit paid under the benefit Acts (defined in reg 2(1)) – eg, to recoup an overpayment – not to the situation where there is a *reduction* in benefit for some other reason such as a trade dispute or for a JSA sanction, or where ESA is reduced where occupational pension is in payment: *R(H) 2/09*. Tax credits are not dealt with under this paragraph, but under para (6) instead.

Para (5A) means that where a claimant or her/his partner is receiving a reduced rate of contributory ESA under reg 63 ESA Regs 2008 or under s11J WRA 2012, the amount of ESA as if *not* reduced is to be taken into account. Reg 63 ESA Regs 2008 (applying to "old style" ESA claimants) provides for a reduction in ESA where the ESA claimant is required to take part in work-related activity or a work-focused interview, but has failed to do so without good cause. Section 11J WRA 2012 (applying to "new style" ESA claimants) provides for a reduction in ESA for "sanctionable failures" such as a failure to comply with work-related requirements.

Para (6) makes it plain that where an award of WTC or CTC for the current year is subject of a deduction in order to recover an overpayment of tax credits from the previous year (pursuant to s28(1) Tax Credits Act 2002), the amount of CTC or WTC to be taken into account in calculating the weekly level of income for HB purposes is the current year award of tax credits less the deduction for the overpayment: generally, the amount being paid.

However, note that where tax credits continue to be paid incorrectly after a claimant has asked that they cease, the continuing payments can be disregarded while the overpayment continues: see the commentary to reg 32 and in particular the discussion of *CIS 1813/2007* on p435. This means that, although there could in effect be a double deduction (ie, where incorrect payments of tax credits were disregarded as income for a past period), for a current period, an authority must make a deduction for the recovery of the overpayment if the conditions of para (6) are met, and only take into account the amount of tax credits being paid. In *CH 4371/2006*, the deputy commissioner said that for HB, he did not consider his construction of the provisions in *CIS 1813/2007* to be affected by the introduction of reg 33(3AA) HB Regs 1987 (now reg 40(6) HB Regs). It is therefore vital for a claimant to ensure that s/he notifies HMRC of relevant changes of circumstance timeously and to ask that payment of tax credits cease, and at the same time to notify the local authority of the change and to ask for her/his award of HB to be recalculated.

Paras (7) to (9) deal with students who leave their courses prematurely. Where the student has received a "relevant payment" (as defined in para (9)), that payment is apportioned according to the formula in para (8). The effect is that the former student is treated as having the same weekly income from the relevant payment as if s/he had completed the course but only for the period during which s/he was actually on the course. Para (8A) modifies the formula in para (8) where the student has received the relevant payment in two or more instalments in a quarter.

In *CJSA 549/2003* para 6, the commissioner confirmed that the formula in para (8) has to be applied even in a case where the student had repaid a student loan that she had taken out in full. He was critical of the unfairness of this rule.

Para (10)(a) makes it clear that payments which are disregarded under reg 35(2) in the calculation of earnings are to be taken into account as "other income" under para (1). See, however, Sch 5 paras 3 and 23 for when these can be disregarded.

Capital treated as income

41.–(1) Any capital payable by instalments which are outstanding at the date on which the claim is made or treated as made, or, at the date of any subsequent revision or supersession, shall, if the aggregate of the instalments outstanding and the amount of the claimant's capital otherwise calculated in accordance with Section 6 exceeds £16,000, be treated as income.

(2) Any payment received under an annuity shall be treated as income.

(3) Any earnings to the extent that they are not a payment of income shall be treated as income.

(4) Any Career Development Loan paid pursuant to section 2 of the 1973 Act shall be treated as income.

(5) Where an agreement or court order provides that payments shall be made to the claimant in consequence of any personal injury to the claimant and that such payments are to be made, wholly or partly, by way of periodic payments, any such periodic payments received by the claimant (but not a payment which is treated as capital by virtue of this Part), shall be treated as income.

Definitions
"1973 Act" – see reg 2(1).
"capital" – see General Note on Section 6.
"claim" – see reg 2(1).
"claimant" – see reg 2(1).
"earnings" – see regs 35 and 37.
"income" – see General Note on Part 6.

General Note
Reg 41 provides for the treatment as income of some payments which would normally be regarded as capital. They are disregarded as capital under Sch 6 para 22.

Analysis
Para (1) aims to give a benevolent treatment of outstanding instalments of capital owed to a claimant. If the sum of the claimant's capital and the instalments outstanding is worth more than £16,000 (the capital limit) and hence would normally disqualify the claimant from benefit, the value of the right to receive the instalments is disregarded as a capital asset under Sch 6 para 18 and the outstanding instalments are treated as income. This question is decided both on the date of claim (see reg 83) and on any subsequent revision or supersession.

Para (3) requires that earnings be treated as income in all cases. See also the discussion on *Minter v Kingston upon Hull City Council and Potter v SSWP* [2011] EWCA Civ 1155; [2012] AACR 21 on p418.

Para (5) deals with periodic payments made under an agreement or court order in consequence of personal injury. Note that such payments can be disregarded under Sch 5 para 14.

Notional income

42.–(1) A claimant shall be treated as possessing income of which he has deprived himself for the purpose of securing entitlement to housing benefit or increasing the amount of that benefit.

(2)　Except in the case of–

(a)　a discretionary trust;

(b)　a trust derived from a payment made in consequence of a personal injury;

(c)　a personal pension scheme [¹, occupational pension scheme] [² [⁵] or a payment made by the Board of the Pension Protection Fund] where the claimant [¹⁴ has not attained the qualifying age for state pension credit];

[⁴ (d) any sum to which paragraph 45(2)(a) of Schedule 6 (capital to be disregarded) applies which is administered in the way referred to in paragraph 45(1)(a);

(da)　any sum to which paragraph 46(a) of Schedule 6 refers;]

(e)　rehabilitation allowance made under section 2 of the 1973 Act;

(f)　child tax credit; or

(g)　working tax credit,

[¹² (h) any sum to which paragraph (12A) applies;]

any income which would become available to the claimant upon application being made, but which has not been acquired by him, shall be treated as possessed by the claimant but only from the date on which it could be expected to be acquired were an application made.

[⁸ (3)]

[⁸ [⁵ (3A)]]

[⁸ (4)]

[⁸ (5)]

(6)　Any payment of income, other than a payment of income specified in paragraph (7), made–

(a)　to a third party in respect of a single claimant or a member of the family (but not a member of the third party's family) shall, where that payment is a payment of an occupational pension [², a pension or other periodical payment made under a personal pension scheme or a payment made by the Board of the Pension Protection Fund], be treated as possessed by that single claimant or, as the case may be, by that member;

(b)　to a third party in respect of a single claimant or in respect of a member of the family (but not a member of the third party's family) shall, where it is not a payment referred to in sub-paragraph (a), be treated as possessed by that single claimant or by that member to the extent that it is used for the food, household fuel or, subject to paragraph (13), rent or ordinary clothing or footwear, of that single claimant or, as the case may be, of any member of that family or is used for any council tax or water charges for which that claimant or member is liable;

(c)　to a single claimant or a member of the family in respect of a third party (but not in respect of another member of that family) shall be treated as possessed by that single claimant or, as the case may be, that member of the family to the extent that it is kept or used by him or used by or on behalf of any member of the family.

(7)　Paragraph (6) shall not apply in respect of a payment of income made–

(a)　under [¹³ or by] the Macfarlane Trust, the Macfarlane (Special Payments) Trust, the Macfarlane (Special Payments) (No. 2) Trust, the Fund, the Eileen Trust [¹³, MFET Limited] [¹⁷, the Skipton Fund, the Caxton Foundation] [²³, the Scottish Infected Blood Support Scheme] [²⁵, an approved blood scheme] [²⁴, the London Emergencies Trust, the We Love Manchester Emergency Fund] or the Independent Living [⁹ Fund (2006)];

(b)　pursuant to section 19(1)(a) of the Coal Industry Act 1994 (concessionary coal);

(c)　pursuant to section 2 of the 1973 Act in respect of a person's participation–

(i)　in an employment programme specified in regulation 75(1)(a)(ii) of the Jobseeker's Allowance Regulations;

(ii)　in a training scheme specified in regulation 75(1)(b)(ii) of those Regulations;

(iii)　in the Intensive Activity Period specified in regulation 75(1)(a)(iv) of those Regulations [⁷]; [¹¹]

(iv)   in a qualifying course within the meaning specified in regulation 17A(7) of those Regulations; [¹¹ or]

[¹¹ (v) in the Flexible New Deal specified in regulation 75(1)(a)(v) of those Regulations;]

[*(ca)*]

[¹⁵ (cb) in respect of a person's participation in the Mandatory Work Activity Scheme;]

[¹⁶ (cc)]

[¹⁸ (cc) in respect of a claimant's participation in a scheme prescribed in regulation 3 of the Jobseeker's Allowance (Schemes for Assisting Persons to Obtain Employment) Regulations 2013;]

[²⁰ (cd)]

[²¹ (ce)]

(d)   under an occupational pension scheme [², in respect of a pension or other periodical payment made under a personal pension scheme or a payment made by the Board of the Pension Protection Fund] where–

(i)   a bankruptcy order has been made in respect of the person in respect of whom the payment has been made or, in Scotland, the estate of that person is subject to sequestration or a judicial factor has been appointed on that person's estate under section 41 of the Solicitors (Scotland) Act 1980;

(ii)   the payment is made to the trustee in bankruptcy or any other person acting on behalf of the creditors; and

(iii)   the person referred to in (i) and any member of his family does not possess, or is not treated as possessing, any other income apart from that payment.

(8)   Where a claimant is in receipt of any benefit (other than housing benefit) under the benefit Acts and the rate of that benefit is altered with effect from a date on or after 1st April in any year but not more than 14 days thereafter, the relevant authority shall treat the claimant as possessing such benefit at the altered rate–

(a)   in a case in which the claimant's weekly amount of eligible rent falls to be calculated in accordance with regulation 80(2)(b) [³ or (c)] (calculation of weekly amounts), from 1st April in that year;

(b)   in any other case, from the first Monday in April in that year,

to the date on which the altered rate is to take effect.

(9)   Subject to paragraph (10), where–

(a)   a claimant performs a service for another person; and

(b)   that person makes no payment of earnings or pays less than that paid for a comparable employment in the area,

the relevant authority shall treat the claimant as possessing such earnings (if any) as is reasonable for that employment unless the claimant satisfies the authority that the means of that person are insufficient for him to pay or to pay more for the service.

(10)   Paragraph (9) shall not apply–

(a)   to a claimant who is engaged by a charitable or voluntary organisation or who is a volunteer if the relevant authority is satisfied in any of those cases that it is reasonable for him to provide those services free of charge; or

(b)   in a case where the service is performed in connection with–

(i)   the claimant's participation in an employment or training programme in accordance with regulation 19(1)(q) of the Jobseeker's Allowance Regulations, other than where the service is performed in connection with the claimant's participation in the Intense Activity Period specified in regulation 75(1)(a)(iv) of those Regulations [⁷]; or

(ii)   the claimant's or the claimant's partner's participation in an employment or training programme as defined in regulation 19(3) of those Regulations for which a training allowance is not payable or, where such an allowance is payable, it is payable for the sole purpose of reimbursement of travelling or meal expenses to the person participating in that programme. [⁶; or

(c)   to a claimant who is participating in a work placement approved by the Secretary of State (or a person providing services to the Secretary of State) before the placement starts.

(10A)   In paragraph (10)(c) "work placement" means practical work experience which is not undertaken in expectation of payment.]

(11)   Where a claimant is treated as possessing any income under any of paragraphs (1) to (8), the foregoing provisions of this Part shall apply for the purposes of calculating the amount of that income as if a payment had actually been made and as if it were actual income which he does possess.

(12)   Where a claimant is treated as possessing any earnings under paragraph (9) the foregoing provisions of this Part shall apply for the purposes of calculating the amount of those earnings as if a payment had actually been made and as if they were actual earnings which he does possess except that paragraph (3) of regulation 36 (calculation of net earnings of employed earners) shall not apply and his net earnings shall be calculated by taking into account those earnings which he is treated as possessing, less–

(a)   an amount in respect of income tax equivalent to an amount calculated by applying to those earnings the [¹⁰] the basic rate [²², or in the case of a Scottish taxpayer, the Scottish basic rate,] of tax applicable to the assessment period less only the [²² personal reliefs to which the claimant is entitled under Chapters 2, 3 and 3A of the Income Tax Act 2007 as are] appropriate to his circumstances; but, if the assessment period is less than a year, the earnings to which the [⁶ [¹⁰ basic] rate] [²², or the Scottish basic rate,] of tax is to be applied and the amount of the personal [²² reliefs] deductible under this sub-paragraph shall be calculated on a pro rata basis;

(b)   an amount equivalent to the amount of the primary Class 1 contributions that would be payable by him under the Act in respect of those earnings if such contributions were payable; and

(c)   one-half of any sum payable by the claimant by way of a contribution towards an occupational or personal pension scheme.

[¹² (12A)   Paragraphs (1), (2), (6) and (9) shall not apply in respect of any amount of income other than earnings, or earnings of an employed earner, arising out of the [¹⁹ claimant participating as a service user].]

(13)   In paragraph (6) "rent" means eligible rent less any deductions in respect of non-dependants which fall to be made under regulation 74 (non-dependant deductions).

Modifications

Reg 42(7) was modified by reg 14 Jobseeker's Allowance (Work for Your Benefit Pilot Scheme) Regulations 2010 SI No.1222 and sub-para (ca) inserted from 22 November 2010 to 1 March 2012 in pilot areas only.

Reg 42(7) was modified by reg 11 of the Jobseeker's Allowance (Supervised Job Search Pilot Scheme) Regulations 2014 SI No.1913 and sub-para (cd) inserted from 18 July 2014 to 30 April 2015 for those selected to participate in the pilot scheme only.

Reg 42(7) was modified by reg 15 of the Jobseeker's Allowance (18–21 Work Skills Pilot Scheme) Regulations 2014 SI No.3117 and sub-para (ce) inserted from 25 November 2014 to 24 November 2016 for those selected to participate in the pilot scheme in pilot areas only.

Amendments

1.   Amended by reg 5A(2) of SI 2005 No 2465 as inserted by Sch 2 para 28(5) of SI 2006 No 217 as from 6.4.06.
2.   Amended by reg 8(2)(a)–(c) of SI 2006 No 588 as from 6.4.06.
3.   Amended by reg 8(2)(d) of SI 2006 No 588 as from 1.4.06.
4.   Substituted by reg 6(2) of SI 2007 No 719 as from 2.4.07.
5.   Amended by reg 4(4) of SI 2007 No 1749 as from 16.7.07.
6.   Amended by reg 11(7) of SI 2007 No 2618 as from 1.10.07.
7.   Omitted by reg 6(4) of SI 2008 No 698 as from 14.4.08.
8.   Omitted by reg 3(5) of SI 2008 No 1042 as from 19.5.08.
9.   Amended by reg 6(4)(a) of SI 2008 No 2767 as from 17.11.08.
10.   Amended by reg 6(4) of SI 2009 No 583 as from 6.4.09.
11.   Amended by reg 3 of SI 2009 No 480 as from 5.10.09.
12.   Inserted by reg 6(4) of SI 2009 No 2655 as from 2.11.09.

13. Amended by reg 8(3) and (5) of SI 2010 No 641 as from 1.4.10 (5.4.10 where rent payable weekly or in multiples of a week).
14. Amended by reg 8(4) of SI 2010 No 641 as from 6.4.10.
15. Inserted by reg 12 of SI 2011 No 688 as from 25.4.11.
16. Inserted by reg 12 of SI 2011 No 917 as from 20.5.11. SI 2011 No 917 was quashed by the Court of Appeal in *R (Reilly and another) v SSWP* [2013] EWCA Civ 66, 12 February 2013.
17. Inserted by reg 19(5) of SI 2011 No 2425 as from 31.10.11.
18. Inserted by reg 9 of SI 2013 No 276 as from 6.45 pm 12.2.13.
19. Amended by reg 8(4) of SI 2014 No 591 as from 28.4.14.
20. Inserted by reg 11 of SI 2014 No 1913 as from 18.7.14. The amendment ceases to have effect on 30.4.15.
21. Inserted by reg 15 of SI 2014 No 3117 as from 25.11.14. The amendment ceases to have effect at the end of 24 months beginning with that date.
22. Amended by reg 4(4) of SI 2016 No 233 as from 6.4.16.
23. Amended by reg 6(3)(a) of SI 2017 No 329 as from 3.4.17.
24. Amended by reg 6(3)(a) of SI 2017 No 689 as from 19.6.17.
25. Amended by reg 6(3)(a) of SI 2017 No 870 as from 23.10.17.

Definitions

"1973 Act" – see reg 2(1).
"benefit Acts" – see SSCBA.
"benefit week" – see reg 2(1).
"child tax credit" and "working tax credit" – see reg 2(1).
"claimant" – see reg 2(1).
"earnings" – see regs 35 and 37.
"eligible rent" – see reg 2(1).
"family" – see s137(1) SSCBA.
"income" – see General Note on Part 6.
"Jobseeker's Allowance Regulations" – see reg 2(1).
"Mandatory Work Activity Scheme" – see reg 2(1).
"occupational pension/personal pension scheme" – see reg 2(1).
"participating as a service user" – see reg 2(5).
"relevant authority" – see reg 2(1).
"Scottish basic rate" – see reg 2(1).
"Scottish taxpayer" – see reg 2(1).
"the Macfarlane Trust" and other schemes listed in para (7)(a) – see reg 2(1).
"voluntary organisation" – see reg 2(1).

General Note

This highly complex regulation deals with the situations in which a claimant may be treated as possessing income that s/he does not in fact possess. It covers a variety of situations.

Para (1) deals with income of which a claimant has deprived her/himself.

Para (2) deals with income which is available to a claimant on application.

Paras (6) and (7) deal with payments involving third parties. Para (6)(b) requires an equivalent amount of payments made to third parties on behalf of a claimant to cover basic living expenses to be taken into account as income. Para (6)(c) requires income paid to a claimant or a member of the family in respect of someone else who is not a member of the family to be taken into account if it is retained or used by the claimant or the member of the family.

Para (8) deals with the effect of changes in benefit rates.

Para (9) requires a claimant to be treated as possessing any earnings which would be reasonable if s/he is not paid or is paid too little; para (12) deals with how the earnings are to be calculated.

Para (10) provides exceptions to para (9).

Para (12A) disapplies paras (1), (2), (6) and (9) for income other than earnings and earnings of employees arising out of a claimant "participating as a service user".

Analysis

Paragraph (1): Income of which the claimant has deprived himself

The wording of this provision dates back to the old supplementary benefits scheme, though there is no discretion as there then was as to whether the consequences of the provision should apply. Caselaw decided by the commissioners and the Upper Tribunal will be highly relevant to deciding whether or not the terms of para (1) are met. That caselaw is summarised in the Analysis to reg 49(1) on p468.

The effect of the provision is that the claimant is deemed to possess income which s/he has got rid of in order to qualify for, or increase entitlement to, HB. That apparently simple question involves a fairly complex analysis and so careful reference needs to be made to the caselaw. Note that para (1) does not apply in respect of any amount of income other than earnings, or earnings from employment, arising out of a claimant participating as a service user (see para (12A)).

A child support commissioner has decided, in relation to the equivalent child support provision, that a refusal to take up an offer of employment does not amount to deprivation of income: *CCS 7967/1995*. In relation to claimants who do carry out work for which they are not paid or are paid too little, see para (9).

Paragraph (2): Income available on application

This makes it clear that, unless excepted by sub-paras (a) to (h), income a claimant could obtain on application being made is treated as possessed by the claimant, even if it is has not actually been acquired by her/him. Note that para (2) does not apply in respect of any amount of income other than earnings, or earnings from employment, arising out of a claimant participating as a service user (see para (12A)).

Certain payments from trusts falling within the sub-paras are excluded. In relation to potential payments from other types of trust, s31 Trustee Act 1925 must be borne in mind. In most cases trustees are under a duty to pay the income produced by property held in trust for a beneficiary who is aged 18 or over to that beneficiary, unless the terms of the trust itself exclude such payments. Accordingly, in such a case, a beneficiary *would* be entitled to the income on application and therefore it must be taken into account under this paragraph. *Actual* payments of this kind should be assessed under reg 40 instead. The section only gives trustees a *power* to pay income where the potential beneficiary is aged under 18 so there is no guarantee that a beneficiary *would* be entitled to income on application in such a case, and therefore the potential income will not be assessable under this paragraph.

Para (2) may apply to entitlement to social security benefits, but the authority would have to be certain not merely that application for the benefit would result in entitlement, but also as to the amount of any entitlement. Where benefits are concerned, entitlement decisions are for decision makers within the social security system. If there is any uncertainty, it is suggested that the wording of para (2) is not met because it is necessary for the authority to satisfy itself that income *would* be available on application.

Another point that needs to be borne in mind is that payments of benefits are often ignored in whole or in part as income for the purposes of assessing HB. If a benefit is disregarded under Sch 5, it cannot be taken into account as notional income under para (2).

With income from some sources, the problem will be in deciding what the claimant really could be paid if s/he applied. But if the authority decides that money would become available on application it must treat the claimant as possessing it, unless the source of the funds is set out in sub-paras (a) to (h).

Sub-para (a): Exclusion of discretionary trusts. This is because, by definition, a potential beneficiary has no right to payment. A discretionary trust is one in relation to which the trustees have a choice as to the beneficiary they should pay, or how much they pay. But if a claimant actually receives such a payment it is assessable under reg 40.

Sub-para (b): "Trust derived from a payment made in consequence of personal injury". This would include a trust of funds from a vaccine damage payment, as well as an out-of-court settlement or actual damages under court order which are placed in a trust following a court order. The regulation does not apply to potential payments from such a source but reg 40 might apply to any actual payments of income: see *CIS 114/1999* para 21, upheld in *Beattie v Secretary of State for Social Security* [2001] 1 WLR 1404, CA, and both reported as *R(IS) 10/01*. Note, however, that some payments from trusts set up out of money paid because of personal injury to the claimant can be ignored under Sch 5 para 14 and that any payments from certain trusts (eg, the McFarlane Trust or the Eileen Trust) are ignored under Sch 5 para 35. In *R(SB) 2/89* para 15, it was held that "personal injury" included injury suffered as a result of a disease (as well as accidental injury).

Sub-para (c) requires income to which a claimant would be entitled from a personal pension scheme or occupational pension scheme or a payment by the Board of the Pension Protection Fund if it was applied for not to be taken into account, so long as s/he is under the qualifying age for PC. However, see reg 41(4) to (6) HB(SPC) Regs where the claimant is at least that age and neither s/he nor her/his partner is on IS, income-based JSA or income-related ESA (or UC).

Sub-paras (d) and (da) refer to funds derived from awards of damages for personal injury, administered either by a relevant court or by the Court of Protection. See the Analysis to Sch 6 para 45 on p697.

Sub-para (e). Rehabilitation allowance is paid to those on full-time rehabilitation courses. They are designed to help those who have been incapable of work for long periods to return to work.

Sub-paras (f) and (g). A claimant cannot be treated as in possession of CTC or WTC if s/he does not claim them.

Sub-para (h) refers to payments of income other than earnings, and earnings of an employee arising out of a claimant participating as a service user (see reg 2(5)).

Paragraphs (6), (7) and (13): Payments involving third parties

Para (6) deals with a number of different circumstances in which third parties are involved in relevant funds. The authority here is obliged to treat the claimant or family member as possessing income if one of the sub-paras applies. There is no discretion. However, if a payment to a third party is a voluntary payment (ie, one where the payer does not receive anything in return) this income or part of it may be disregarded under Sch 5 para 14. If the payment is made from one of the sources specified in para (7), it is ignored. Note also that para (6) does not apply in respect of any amount of income other than earnings, or earnings from employment, arising out of participation in a service user group (see para (12A)).

Para (6)(a) prevents a person depriving her/himself of income to which s/he is entitled from the pension schemes listed by assigning it to a third party. The amounts of any payments to third parties will be taken into account as the income of that person, but see para (7)(d).

Para (6)(b) deals with when income for the benefit of a single claimant or a member of the family is paid direct to a third party. Payments are taken into account as income to the extent that they are used for specified items. The aim is to prevent third parties paying for basic items which are usually covered by means-tested benefits. But if the payment is used for a purpose other than those listed (eg, for a leisure item or educational purposes), the payment should be disregarded. The relevant items are:

(1)   Food.

(2)   Household fuel. This will cover coal (though note the effect of para (7)(b) in relation to concessionary coal), gas and electricity but will not cover, for example, petrol for a car purchased by someone outside the claimant's family.

(3)   Rent. This is defined in para (13) as being eligible rent less deductions made for non-dependants. For the determination of eligible rent see regs 12B, 12BA, 12C and 12D HB Regs as well as reg 12 as set out in Sch 3 para 5 HB&CTB(CP) Regs. The consequence of the wording of para (13) is that if the claimant's HB is reduced because certain payments of rent are not eligible or is restricted under the rent restriction provisions in Part 3 or the HB&CTB(CP) Regs, the shortfall may be paid by a third party direct to the landlord without it being taken into account as the income of the claimant or other person liable for the rent.

(4)   Ordinary clothing or footwear. This is defined in reg 2(1) as clothing or footwear "for normal daily use" but does not include school uniforms or clothing or footwear used solely for sporting activities. What "normal daily use" means will be a question of fact. Whether, for example, a suit would fall under this sub-para might depend on the person's circumstances. For example, if s/he is in low paid work and wears the suit every day, it is probably an item for "normal daily use". If a suit is purchased for a single event such as a wedding or a funeral, that is arguably not "normal daily use". The provision therefore has the perverse effect that the price of luxuries will often not be taken into account as income but the cost of basic items bought for someone will be.

Para (6)(c) is more restrictive in its terms than sub-para (b). It applies to payments made to a claimant or a member of her/his family in respect of a third party – eg, which actually belong to someone else, or are to be used for someone else's benefit. If the payee keeps the money or uses it for the benefit of her/himself or the member of the family, or any other member of her/his family so uses it, s/he will be treated as possessing it to the extent that it was so kept or used. This is the case no matter the purpose to which the money is put.

Para (7) states that any payments made from the trusts and funds listed in sub-para (a) are exempt from the treatment in para (6) as are payments in lieu of concessionary coal (on which see also the Analysis to Sch 5 para 14) and certain payments under s2 Employment and Training Act 1973 (sub-para (c)) and payments in respect of specified schemes (sub-paras (cb), (cc), (cd) and (ce)). Note that the schemes in sub-para (c)(i)–(iii) and (v) are no longer available: reg 75(1) JSA Regs was substituted by SI 2012 No.2568 from 22 October 2012. Note also that the regulations inserting sub-paras (cd) and (ce) no longer have effect.

For the purposes of sub-para (cc), the Schemes prescribed in reg 3 Jobseeker's Allowance (Schemes for Assisting Persons to Obtain Employment) Regulations 2013 from 12 February 2013, at the time of writing, are the Work Programme, Skills Conditionality, the sector-based work academy, New Enterprise Allowance, Full-time Training Flexibility and the Work and Health Programme.

Para (7)(d) constitutes an exception to the treatment of assigned pension entitlements under para (6)(a) above. If the person entitled to the payments has been made bankrupt or sequestrated and the payments are being made to her/his trustee in bankruptcy or other person administering her/his affairs, and no member of the family has any other income, the payments will not be taken into account.

Paragraph (8): Treatment of benefits

Para (8) provides that where a claimant receives a benefit other than HB and it is due to be altered between April 1 and 15 in any given year, the authority is obliged to treat the claimant as receiving the altered amount up to two benefit weeks before that week in which the different amount is actually paid. This rule is for the authority's administrative convenience to enable it to alter amounts so as to coincide with changes in rent, rather than cope with changes of circumstances later on.

Paragraphs (9), (10) and (10A): Notional earnings

Para (9) is sometimes known as the "notional earnings" rule. The effect is to treat the claimant as having an income from unpaid or low paid work which s/he does, with the limited exceptions in para (10). Note also that para (9) does not apply in respect of any amount of income other than earnings, or earnings from employment, arising out of a claimant participating as a service user (see para (12A)).

The exceptions are work for charitable or voluntary bodies or other voluntary work (para (10)(a)), services performed in connection with certain employment or training schemes for which a training allowance is not payable or where the allowance is only for travel or meal expenses (para (10)(b)) and certain approved work placements (para (10)(c)). "Work placement" is defined in para (10A). See also Sch 5 para 2 on p665. Note that the Intensive Activity Period in para (10)(b) is a scheme no longer in existence: reg 75(1)(a) of the JSA Regs was substituted by SI 2012 No.2568 as from 22 October 2012.

The provision is directed at employers who pay too little and aims to prevent low-paid work being subsidised by the public purse. It is not directed at claimants who declare less than they earn, yet the effect is to penalise the claimant.

In applying the paragraph, however, the authority has many value judgments to make.

(1)   If the claimant is working for a charitable or voluntary organisation or is a volunteer, the authority must decide if it is "reasonable" for her/him to work free of charge. A "volunteer" is a person who without any obligation performs a service for someone else without expecting payment: *R(IS) 12/92* para 6. It might be reasonable for such work to be done where the worker is trying to obtain work experience. Other relevant factors are the closeness of the relationship between the volunteer and the beneficiary of the service, the expectations of family members if there is a family relationship, the housing arrangements of the parties and why, if s/he did, the volunteer gave up paid employment: see *CIS 93/1991* para 4.

(2)   Does the person for whom the work is performed pay less than the amount paid for "comparable employment" in the area? If there is no "comparable employment" and something is paid, it is arguable that the paragraph cannot apply. A particular difficulty that has arisen concerns employees who are paid less than the national minimum wage. Some authorities have proceeded on the basis that since it is generally unlawful to pay less than the minimum wage, employees working for less than the minimum wage have to be treated as being in receipt of notional earnings. This seems particularly harsh and wholly out of touch with the reality of work in tight labour markets in areas of high unemployment, where workers may have little option but to accept low-paid work to keep themselves in the job market. Thus unless the authority has evidence of comparable jobs paying higher wages, authorities ought readily to find that it is not reasonable to treat the relevant person as receiving more money.

(3)   What is a "reasonable" amount to treat the claimant as possessing from the employment? In certain circumstances it may be "reasonable" to treat the claimant as possessing *no* income from this source.

Even if the authority considers the terms of para (9)(a) and (b) to be satisfied, the claimant can still avoid the effect of the paragraph by satisfying the authority that the person for whom the work is done cannot afford to pay, or to pay more. It may be difficult to provide evidence of the other person's means.

Paragraphs (11) and (12): Quantification of notional income

Para (11) deals with the quantification of income which a claimant is treated as possessing under paras (1) to (8). Basically, the notional income is quantified as if it were real.

Para (12) quantifies notional earnings which a claimant is deemed to receive under para (9). The deductions made under sub-paras (a) to (c) are the same as those in reg 36(6). See the Analysis on p444.

Paragraph (12A): Payments to "service user groups"

Para (12A) disapplies paras (1), (2), (6) and (9) for the payments set out to a claimant who is participating as a service user, for which see reg 2(5) on p237.

SECTION 6
Capital

General Note on Section 6

This Section deals with the quantification of a claimant's "capital" for HB purposes. The term "capital" itself is not defined by the regulations. For the capital/income distinction, see p415.

There is a bar on entitlement for anyone with capital exceeding £16,000 as assessed under this Section: see reg 43. If a claimant has capital worth between £6,000 (£10,000 if living in residential accommodation) and £16,000, s/he is treated as receiving "tariff income" from that capital: see reg 52. *Actual* income produced by capital which is taken into account is itself treated as capital and disregarded as income: see reg 46(4) and Sch 5 para 17. Income produced by some *disregarded* capital is taken into account under Section 5: Sch 5 para 17. See regs 44, 47 and 48 for the calculation of capital and the discussion of *JRL v SSWP (JSA)* [2011] UKUT 63 (AAC); [2011] AACR 30 on p465.

There is a total disregard of capital belonging to IS, income-based JSA and income-related ESA (and UC) claimants as their capital has already been taken into account in the assessment of that benefit, though note the potential effect of the decision in *R v South Ribble DC HBRB ex p Hamilton* (2000) 33 HLR 102, CA: see the discussion on p419.

It is important to remember that a capital resource which appears to belong to the claimant (eg, property in her/his name) may in fact legally belong to someone else because it is held subject to a trust or pursuant to some other form of equity. For example, a house in the claimant's name but purchased with someone else's money, not as a gift for the claimant, was held not to belong to the claimant, but to be held on "resulting trust" for the person advancing the money: *R(SB) 1/85* para 9. In *MW v SSWP (JSA)* [2016] UKUT 469 (AAC); [2017] AACR 15, similar questions arose in respect of entitlement to income-based JSA for a claimant who had been lent £20,000 by his mother for the purpose of buying his home. Given the obligation to repay the funds if not used for that specific purpose, the claimant's situation in Scots Private Law was held to be analogous to holding the sum on trust and it did not fall to be considered as the claimant's capital. Likewise, if a claimant is paid money for a particular purpose in circumstances which make her/him a trustee for the carrying out of that purpose, and for some reason that purpose is not, or cannot, be carried out, s/he would normally not own the money but would hold it on trust for the person it originally belonged to. In *R(IS) 1/90*, the claimant tried to argue that he had transferred over £6,000 from a redundancy payment to his son, to pay for his education. It was held in a high interest account in the claimant's name as he feared his son might misuse the money. It was held that although the money was clearly earmarked for his son's education, he had done nothing to renounce ownership and control. A person should not be treated as voluntarily giving up an interest in property unless there is a very clear indication that this is his/her intention. There was no express or implied declaration of trust in this case. See the discussion in the commentary to reg 46 Income Support (General) Regulations 1987 in the current edition of vol II of *Social Security Legislation* for a more extensive analysis of the caselaw on beneficial ownership of capital. There can be a "legal owner" of an asset, with all the formal rights of ownership but no right to benefit from it, who holds the asset on trust for the "beneficial owner". It is the beneficial ownership that is relevant to entitlement to HB. In *SSWP v LB Tower Hamlets and CT (IS and HB)* [2018] UKUT 25 (AAC), the claimant was the legal owner of a property but only held a small share of it as a beneficial owner. Another person held the vast majority of the beneficial ownership, having contributed 99.6 per cent of the non-mortgage purchase price. The Upper Tribunal held (considering *Jones v Kernott* [2011] UKSC 53) that, in the absence of evidence of express agreement to that effect, it would be unfair to calculate the claimant's HB as if she had received a gift from the beneficial owner of a substantial share in the property that she had not in fact received.

In *SSWP v GF (ESA)* [2017] UKUT 333 (AAC), the claimant had capital of over £50,000 in a fixed-rate bond. He did not disclose the funds because he had earmarked them to cover costs in a civil litigation in which he was unsuccessful. When liability to pay over £48,000 in costs was issued, the claimant's brother-in-law settled it, effectively by way of an informal loan, due to the claimant's capital being tied up in the bond. Judge Wikeley found that the existence of outstanding liabilities, even if they are due, does not affect the calculation of capital for benefit purposes. The claimant had the sole legal and beneficial ownership of the capital in the bond. In this case, there was no court order restricting the use of the funds, and no question of the claimant being deemed to hold the funds in an implied trust for his brother-in-law.

A claimant who acts as appointee for the purposes of administering another person's entitlement to benefit can be regarded as effectively acting as that person's trustee. If benefit, when received, is then saved and converted into capital it should not be deemed to be the claimant's capital. In *MC v SSWP (IS)* [2015] UKUT 600 (AAC), a mother who saved her two daughters' DLA for them, but at one point used a substantial amount of the funds to pay off the rent arrears on the home she shared with them, was refused IS for six years because the capital was deemed to belong to her and exceeded the prescribed limit. Judge Wikeley rejected the argument that the claimant's use of the capital for this purpose effectively meant that in some way the capital belonged to her. The claimant, as appointee, acted perfectly reasonably in paying off rent arrears to help keep a roof over her daughters' heads. This was consistent with the purpose of what was, in effect, an informal trust to benefit them.

In *Thomas v Chief Adjudication Officer* reported as an appendix to *R(SB) 17/87*, CA, it was held that money held by a solicitor for a client was an actual, not a notional resource, and that the solicitor should be looked at in the same way as a bank. See also the discussion of *LC v Bournemouth BC (HB)* [2016] UKUT 175 (AAC) on p472.

In *DF v SSWP (ESA)* [2015] UKUT 611 (AAC), the claimant held an individual savings account (ISA) in his name, but stated that all of the funds (which exceeded the capital limit for benefit) belonged to his daughter. The Secretary of State argued that an ISA by definition belongs only to the account holder and the funds must be beneficially owned by that person. Judge Mitchell decided that, despite the particular legal framework for ISAs (and, as outlined in para 17 of the decision, the legal risks to a claimant of doing so), a claimant may argue that the beneficial interest in the amount lies elsewhere. In giving guidance on how to deal with an issue of beneficial interest, he highlighted that if a claimant account-holder argues the beneficial interest lies elsewhere, certain evidence relevant to that issue can only be supplied by the claimant. The claimant is expected to supply it once asked, so that, if s/he does not, a decision maker or tribunal is entitled to draw an adverse factual inference (*Kerr v Department for Social Development* [2004] UKHL 23; reported as *R 1/04 (SF)*). Given that the Individual Savings Account Regulations 1998 require that the original agreement must include a 'no beneficial interests' term and a declaration that all the cash deposited in the ISA belongs to the account-holder, he suggested that the DWP should seek such evidence as a matter of course where a claimant argues the beneficial interest in the ISA deposits lies elsewhere. The claimant, he observed, "may well have an evidential mountain to climb".

CIS 2287/2008 concerned, among other issues, the classification of an asset as capital. Agreeing with *CIS 2943/2000* and disagreeing with *CH 3729/2007*, Commissioner Jacobs decided that the decision in *Chief Adjudication Officer v Leeves* [1999] FLR 90, CA; reported as *R(IS) 5/99*, although a decision in respect of income, applied to capital, that is, that capital that should in law be immediately repaid is not capital, the focus being on the moment of receipt or notional attribution. However, he pointed out that as with income, it is relevant only to the classification of money or an asset as capital and only applies if the capital never became a resource in the claimant's hands from the moment of receipt or attribution. He said (at paras 27 and 28):

"A claimant may receive capital in circumstances that render it immediately subject to a bare trust for the transferor. If so, the capital never comes into the beneficial ownership of the claimant. But if the circumstances do not create a trust, it is possible that the claimant is under a certain and immediate obligation to return the asset transferred. If so, *Leeves* applies. ... However, it only applies at the moment of receipt or attribution and for the purpose of classification. It does not apply thereafter. In particular, it does not apply to reduce the amount on account of liability that has arisen after the payment (or attribution) but in respect of, or otherwise connected with, it."

Commissioner Jacobs said that a demand for repayment after something has become capital in the claimant's hands is outside the scope of *Leeves*. In this appeal, the claimant had been overpaid benefit and the overpayment decisions had created liabilities. However, Commissioner Jacobs said that they did not affect the character of the assets held by the claimant. What the overpayment decisions did was to create new liabilities that reduced the net worth of the claimant's assets. That is outside the scope of *Leeves*, because they did not prevent the assets becoming capital.

In *KS v SSWP (JSA)* [2009] UKUT 122 (AAC); [2010] AACR 3, the claimant had been adjudged bankrupt and a trustee in bankruptcy had been appointed prior to his claim for JSA. He was refused JSA because he was said to have capital in excess of the limit. Under s284(1) to (3) Insolvency Act 1986, where a person is adjudged bankrupt, any disposition of property made by that person from the date of presentation of the petition to the vesting of her/his estate in a trustee, is void unless made with the consent of the court or subsequently ratified by the court. That includes payments in cash or otherwise by the bankrupt, so that where a payment is void by virtue of that section, the person paid holds the sum paid for the bankrupt as part of her/his estate. Prior to the making of a bankruptcy order, a claimant may deprive her/himself of her/his capital as explained by Judge Jacobs in *CH 3670/2008*. However, s/he cannot deprive her/himself of anything of value following the making of the order. Agreeing with the decision in *SH v SSWP (JSA)* [2008] UKUT 21 (AAC) (a case concerning a restraint order), Judge Mark said that in the context of bankruptcy proceedings, where the provisions of the Insolvency Act 1986 are designed to transfer property automatically to the trustee as soon as the necessary formalities have been gone through to appoint a trustee, the claimant has been stripped of her/his beneficial interest in the property once the bankruptcy order has been made, and the provisions invalidating subsequent transactions by her/him are designed to protect the interests of the trustee and the creditors. It was unnecessary for Judge Mark to come to any firm conclusion on the question whether it remains capital with a nil value or ceases to be capital at all, as the effect on the claimant's entitlement to benefit will be the same in either case. That conclusion also was a reasonable one, as a bankrupt ought not to be at a disadvantage because there is a delay in appointing a trustee. The purpose of the provisions as to capital is to ensure that the state does not provide benefit to somebody with capital assets over a certain amount out of which s/he can legally provide for her/himself. It ought not to be able to say that the claimant cannot legally spend the money and at the same time that s/he is not entitled to benefit because s/he can spend it unlawfully. However, Judge Mark went on to say that a claimant may fall foul of the notional capital rule (for which see reg 49). If s/he presents a petition (or possibly, fails to resist a petition presented by a creditor) and is declared bankrupt as a result, s/he may be found to have deprived her/himself of capital for the purpose of the notional capital rule if s/he has taken this step, or held back from opposing the petition for the purpose of securing entitlement to benefit. He said that this may also be the case if the claimant fails to take reasonable steps either to ensure that the debts are paid off and the bankruptcy annulled, or if the claimant fails to co-operate with the trustee in bankruptcy to ensure that the bankruptcy proceeds smoothly, that all liabilities are discharged and that any surplus is paid to her/him.

Sch 6 provides a long list of disregards for a claimant's capital. Reg 41 provides that certain capital is treated as income.

Capital limit

43. For the purposes of section 134(1) of the Act as it applies to housing benefit (no entitlement to benefit if capital exceeds prescribed amount), the prescribed amount is £16,000.

General Note

The "prescribed amount" has been £16,000 since April 1990.

Calculation of capital

44.–(1) For the purposes of Part 7 of the Act (income-related benefits) as it applies to housing benefit, the capital of a claimant to be taken into account shall, subject to paragraph (2), be the whole of his capital calculated in accordance with this Part and any income treated as capital under regulation 46 (income treated as capital).

(2) There shall be disregarded from the calculation of a claimant's capital under paragraph (1), any capital, where applicable, specified in Schedule 6.

Definitions

"capital" – see General Note on Section 6.

"claimant" – see reg 2(1).

General Note
This regulation provides the general authority for assessing capital according to the rules set out in the rest of this Part, not just this Section, so income treated as capital under reg 46 is specifically included. See regs 47 and 48 for the calculation of capital in and outside of the UK.

Para (2), together with Sch 6, provides for the disregard of certain items of capital. In considering the scope of any disregard, decisions on similarly-worded disregards in other means-tested benefit schemes must be taken into account: *CH 2321/2002* para 8. A disregard of certain payments made to qualifying Equitable Life annuitants must also be made: reg 5 Age-Related Payments Regulations 2013 SI No.2980 (on p1855). Note also the effect of reg 25 which treats the capital of the claimant's partner(s) as the claimant's.

The proper approach is to disregard (or consider disregarding) capital under Sch 6 without determining its value, rather than determining the value and then only considering whether the capital can be disregarded if it is above a relevant limit: *Guildford BC v MW (HB)* [2014] UKUT 49 (AAC).

Disregard of capital of child and young person
45. The capital of a child or young person who is a member of the claimant's family shall not be treated as capital of the claimant.

Definitions
"capital" – see General Note on Section 6.
"child" – see reg 2(1).
"family" – see s137(1) SSCBA.
"membership of a family" – see Part 4.
"young person" – see reg 19.

General Note
The effect of this regulation is that the capital of a child or young person for whom the claimant or her/his partner is "responsible" (for which, see reg 20), and who lives in the same household, is *not* to be treated as the claimant's.

Income treated as capital
46.–(1) Any bounty derived from employment to which paragraph 8 of Schedule 4 applies and paid at intervals of at least one year shall be treated as capital.

(2) Any amount by way of a refund of income tax deducted from profits or emoluments chargeable to income tax under Schedule D or E shall be treated as capital.

(3) Any holiday pay which is not earnings under regulation 35(1)(d) (earnings of employed earners) shall be treated as capital.

(4) Except any income derived from capital disregarded under paragraphs 1, 2, 4, 8, 14 [¹, 25 to 28, 45 or 46] of Schedule 6, any income derived from capital shall be treated as capital but only from the date it is normally due to be credited to the claimant's account.

(5) In the case of employment as an employed earner, any advance of earnings or any loan made by the claimant's employer shall be treated as capital.

(6) Any charitable or voluntary payment which is not made or due to be made at regular intervals, other than a payment which is made under [³ or by] the Macfarlane Trust, the Macfarlane (Special Payments) Trust, the Macfarlane (Special Payments) (No. 2) Trust, the Fund, the Eileen Trust [³, MFET Limited] [⁴, the Skipton Fund, the Caxton Foundation] [⁵, the Scottish Infected Blood Support Scheme] [⁷, an approved blood scheme] [⁶, the London Emergencies Trust, the We Love Manchester Emergency Fund] or the Independent Living [² Fund (2006)], shall be treated as capital.

(7) There shall be treated as capital the gross receipts of any commercial activity carried on by a person in respect of which assistance is received under the self-employment route, but only in so far as those receipts were payable into a special account [³] during the period in which that person was receiving such assistance.

(8) Any arrears of subsistence allowance which are paid to a claimant as a lump sum shall be treated as capital.

(9) Any arrears of working tax credit or child tax credit shall be treated as capital.

Amendments
1. Amended by reg 15(2) of SI 2006 No 2378 from the first day of the first benefit week to commence on or after 2.10.06.
2. Amended by reg 6(4)(b) of SI 2008 No 2767 as from 17.11.08.

3. Amended by reg 8(3), (5) and (6) of SI 2010 No 641 as from 1.4.10 (5.4.10 where rent payable weekly or in multiples of a week).
4. Inserted by reg 19(5) of SI 2011 No 2425 as from 31.10.11.
5. Amended by reg 6(3)(b) of SI 2017 No 329 as from 3.4.17.
6. Amended by reg 6(3)(b) of SI 2017 No 689 as from 19.6.17.
7. Amended by reg 6(3)(b) of SI 2017 No 870 as from 23.10.17.

Definitions

"capital" – see General Note on Section 6.
"child tax credit" and "working tax credit" – see reg 2(1).
"claimant" – see reg 2(1).
"derived from" – see Analysis of reg 35.
"earnings" – see regs 35 and 36.
"employed earner" – see reg 2(1).
"the Macfarlane Trust" and other schemes listed in para (6) – see reg 2(1).
"self-employment route" – see reg 2(1).
"special account" – see reg 2(1).
"subsistence allowance" – see reg 2(1).

General Note

This regulation sets out certain types of income that are to be treated as capital and Sch 5 para 30 provides that these are to be *ignored* for the purposes of assessing a claimant's income, to avoid double counting.

Analysis

Para (1). The relevant employments are part-time firefighters, auxiliary coastguards, those involved in launching lifeboats part-time, and reservists. Note that para (1) only applies where the bounty is paid at intervals of at least one year.

Para (2) deals with income tax refunded on earnings from employed earners or self-employment.

Para (3). Under regulation 35(1)(d), holiday pay payable more than four weeks after termination or interruption of employment is not treated as earnings. However, it is treated as capital under para (3).

Para (4). Most income from capital is treated as capital. Instead, capital is treated as producing "tariff income". Only income from disregarded capital as specified is treated as income. See the General Note to reg 52 on p479. The word "normally" is used so that occasional deviations from this date may be ignored. See also Sch 5 para 17 on p670 and Sch 6 para 15 on p690.

Para (5) is self-explanatory.

Para (6). For "charitable or voluntary payment", see the Analysis of Sch 5 para 14 on p668. Regular charitable or voluntary payments are income and may be disregarded in whole or in part under that paragraph.

Para (6) treats *irregular* charitable or voluntary payments (other than those specified) as capital. They do not affect entitlement to benefit at all if the claimant's total capital after receipt is less than £6,000. If total capital after receipt is between £6,000 (or £10,000 if living in residential accommodation) and £16,000, the tariff income rule in reg 52 applies. Note that payments (even if they are irregular) from the Macfarlane Trusts etc are disregarded as capital by Sch 6 para 24. See also Sch 5 para 35(1) for provision for such payments (even if they are regular) also to be disregarded as income.

Para (7). "Self-employment route" is defined in reg 2(1). The definition of the special account referred to is in reg 102A Jobseeker's Allowance Regulations 1996 and reg 100 Employment and Support Allowance Regulations 2008. See also Sch 5 para 58 for payments to those following this route that can be disregarded as income.

Para (8). "Subsistence allowance" means that which an employment zone contractor has agreed to pay someone who is participating in an employment zone programme. "Employment zone" and "employment zone contractor" are defined in reg 2(1). It is understood that it is unlikely that anyone would now be participating in an employment zone programme.

Para (9) provides that "any arrears" of WTC and CTC are to be treated as capital. Note also that Sch 6 para 9(1)(e) provides for such arrears to be disregarded as capital for a period of 52 weeks from the date of receipt.

HMRC pays tax credits by direct credit transfer either one week or four-weekly in arrears. It is clear that this provision is not intended to apply to such four-weekly payments (payments "in arrears") as distinct from payments made in respect of a period prior to the current period (payments "of arrears"). However, it may be open to argument that payments in arrears, at least in so far as they relate to the three weeks previous to the week in which the payments are made, are "arrears" and should be treated as capital rather than income.

Calculation of capital in the United Kingdom

[¹**47.** Capital which a claimant possesses in the United Kingdom shall be calculated at its current market or surrender value less–

(a)   where there would be expenses attributable to the sale, 10 per cent; and

(b)   the amount of any encumbrance secured on it.]

Amendment

1.   Substituted by reg 11(8) of SI 2007 No 2618 as from 1.10.07.

Definitions

"capital" – see General Note on this Section.
"claimant" – see reg 2(1).

General Note

This deals with the quantification of capital which is taken into account for HB purposes and which is situated in the UK (a term which includes Northern Ireland).

Analysis

The authority has to decide what the current market or surrender value is. Authorities should avoid asking for evidence which would cause the claimant inordinate expenditure – eg, surveyor's reports.

From the current market/surrender value should be deducted the amounts referred to in sub-paras (a) and (b). In sub-para (b), the words "encumbrance secured on it" would include any debts secured on the capital – eg, a mortgage on a house. In *R(IS) 21/93* para 19(7)(a), the commissioner concluded that a mere unsecured loan could not be an "incumbrance". The word should therefore be read as it applies in the law of real property.

In *JRL v SSWP (JSA)* [2011] UKUT 63 (AAC); [2011] AACR 30, the claimant had three accounts with the same bank: the first had a nil balance, the second had a credit balance of £7,700.09 and the third was overdrawn by £1,994.90. The DWP decided that he had capital in excess of the £6,000 lower limit and hence that tariff income was to be taken into account in calculating his JSA. The claimant argued that the capital to be taken into account was the net amount produced by deducting the overdraft in the third account from the credit balance in the second. However, the First-tier Tribunal said it was bound by *R(SB) 2/83* (a decision of a Tribunal of Commissioners) to decide that the capital to be taken into account was the gross value of the claimant's capital, without any deduction for the overdraft. A three-judge panel decided that the tribunal had erred in law. It said that the tribunal had overlooked the crucial fact that, unlike the situation in *R(SB) 2/83*, the claimant's capital consisted of bank accounts with the same bank – ie, he was both a creditor and a debtor of the same body. The tribunal should have sought, and have taken into account the meaning and effect of, the terms and conditions of the claimant's bank accounts in calculating "the current market ... value" of his capital. Having itself examined the terms and conditions, the Upper Tribunal decided that the market value of the claimant's capital was the net value of the account in credit – ie, the amount after deduction of the overdraft in the account in debit.

Valuation

Where there is a conflict of valuation evidence, the First-tier Tribunal is not obliged to give more weight to a lower valuation so as to grant rather than deny benefit. Valuation is "an art rather than a science" and, in an appropriate case, a tribunal is entitled to resolve the conflict by taking an average of the competing figures. The tribunal does not err by accepting valuation assumptions which were reasonable at the time the value of the capital has to be assessed, even if subsequent evidence has shown those assumptions to be incorrect: see *R v Doncaster MBC ex p Nortrop* [1998] unreported, 31 July, QBD.

Property. GM BW1.470 suggests that as regards valuation of property (eg, a second home or business premises), authorities should obtain a current market valuation unless one is already available.

Stocks and shares. GM BW1.513 suggests that where capital consists of stocks and shares "valuation should relate to the value on the date the claim for benefit is made, or treated as made, and be based on relevant information, such as Stock Market pages in a national newspaper". *R(IS) 2/90* concerned the valuation of shares in a private company. The articles of association of the private company provided that the shares must be offered first to the other shareholders at a "fair" value, determined by the company's auditors. Commissioner Rice held that the DWP could not just come to its own, higher valuation and the value of the shares could not be more than that set by the auditor. The value could have been lower as IS presupposed a quick sale.

Calculation of capital outside the United Kingdom

48.   Capital which a claimant possesses in a country outside the United Kingdom shall be calculated–

(a)   in a case where there is no prohibition in that country against the transfer to the United Kingdom of an amount equal to its current market or surrender value in that country, at that value;

(b)   in a case where there is such a prohibition, at the price which it would realise if sold in the United Kingdom to a willing buyer,

less, where there would be expenses attributable to sale, 10 per cent. and the amount of any encumbrances secured on it.

Definitions

"capital" – see General Note on this Section.
"claimant" – see reg 2(1).

General Note

This provides for the quantification of capital which is taken into account for HB purposes and which is situated outside the UK, with different rules depending on whether or not an amount equivalent to the value of that asset in the country in which it is situated may be transferred to the UK. There will undoubtedly be problems in quantifying the market value of such assets overseas and in converting the amount in question to sterling. GM BW1.400-407 gives some guidance.

If there is no prohibition on the transfer of the value of the asset to the UK from the country, para (a) applies and the claimant is treated as possessing an amount equal to the market or surrender value in that country, minus the same deductions as available under reg 47 above. It is the "current market or surrender value *in that country*" which is relevant. Thus in *CH 4972/2002* (para 9) the commissioner stated that the market value of a property in France had to be assessed for a sale in France rather than the UK.

An argument that the "willing buyer" test in para (b) does not apply in cases of valuing property outside the United Kingdom was rejected in *Guildford BC v MW (HB)* [2014] UKUT 49 (AAC). The local authority's argument was that it does not apply because the words "willing buyer" appear in reg 48(b) HB Regs but not reg 48(a). However, the words have to be implied into the "current market value" test. The judge said that the words willing buyer are used explicitly in para (b) "to make good the fictional ability to sell in the UK and to avoid the argument that there would be no willing buyer in the UK if there was such a prohibition."

If there *is* a prohibition on the transfer of the value of the asset to the UK from the country in which it is situated, para (b) applies. The claimant is treated as possessing the amount, if any, which a "willing buyer" in the UK would pay to purchase the asset from the claimant, bearing in mind that such a buyer would not her/himself be able to liquidate the assets and transfer them here either. As with para (a), the same deductions as available under reg 47 must be made. The amounts a claimant can be treated as possessing on this basis will usually be much smaller than the actual value of the asset if sold in the country in which it is situated.

Notional capital

49.–(1)   A claimant shall be treated as possessing capital of which he has deprived himself for the purpose of securing entitlement to housing benefit or increasing the amount of that benefit except to the extent that that capital is reduced in accordance with regulation 50 (diminishing notional capital rule).

(2)   Except in the case of–

(a)   a discretionary trust; or

(b)   a trust derived from a payment made in consequence of a personal injury; or

(c)   any loan which would be obtained only if secured against capital disregarded under Schedule 6; or

(d)   a personal pension scheme [¹, occupational pension scheme] [² [⁴] or a payment made by the Board of the Pension Protection Fund]; or

[³ (e)   any sum to which paragraph 45(2)(a) of Schedule 6 (capital to be disregarded) applies which is administered in the way referred to in paragraph 45(1)(a); or

(ea)   any sum to which paragraph 46(a) of Schedule 6 refers; or]

(f)   child tax credit; or

(g)   working tax credit,

any capital which would become available to the claimant upon application being made, but which has not been acquired by him, shall be treated as possessed by him but only from the date on which it could be expected to be acquired were an application made.

(3)   Any payment of capital, other than a payment of capital specified in paragraph (4), made–

(a)   to a third party in respect of a single claimant or a member of the family (but not a member of the third party's family) shall, where that payment is a payment of an occupational pension [², a pension or other periodical payment made under a personal pension scheme or a payment made by the Board of the Pension Protection Fund], be treated as possessed by that single claimant or, as the case may be, by that member;

(b)   to a third party in respect of a single claimant or in respect of a member of the family (but not a member of the third party's family) shall, where it is not a payment referred to in sub-paragraph (a), be treated as possessed by that single claimant or by that member to the extent that it is used for the food, household fuel or, subject to paragraph (8), rent or ordinary clothing or footwear, of that single claimant or, as the case may be, of any member of that family or is used for any council tax or water charges for which that claimant or member is liable;

(c) to a single claimant or a member of the family in respect of a third party (but not in respect of another member of the family) shall be treated as possessed by that single claimant or, as the case may be, that member of the family to the extent that it is kept or used by him or used by or on behalf of any member of the family.

(4) Paragraph (3) shall not apply in respect of a payment of capital made–

(a) under [⁸ or by] the Macfarlane Trust, the Macfarlane (Special Payments) Trust, the Macfarlane (Special Payments) (No. 2) Trust, the Fund, the Eileen Trust [⁸, MFET Limited], the Independent Living [⁶ Fund (2006)], the Skipton Fund [¹¹, the Caxton Foundation] [¹⁵, the Scottish Infected Blood Support Scheme] [¹⁷, an approved blood scheme] [¹⁶, the London Emergencies Trust, the We Love Manchester Emergency Fund] or the London Bombings Relief Charitable Fund;

(b) pursuant to section 2 of the 1973 Act in respect of a person's participation–
  (i) in an employment programme specified in regulation 75(1)(a)(ii) of the Jobseeker's Allowance Regulations;
  (ii) in a training scheme specified in regulation 75(1)(b)(ii) of those Regulations;
  (iii) in the Intense Activity Period specified in regulation 75(1)(a)(iv) of those Regulations [⁵]; [⁷]
  (iv) in a qualifying course within the meaning specified in regulation 17A(7) of those Regulations; [⁷ or]
  [⁷ (v) in the Flexible New Deal specified in regulation 75(1)(a)(v) of those Regulations;]

[(ba)]

[⁹ (bb) in respect of a person's participation in the Mandatory Work Activity Scheme;]
[¹⁰ (bc)]
[¹² (bc) in respect of a claimant's participation in a scheme prescribed in regulation 3 of the Jobseeker's Allowance (Schemes for Assisting Persons to Obtain Employment) Regulations 2013;]
[¹³ (bd)]
[¹⁴ (be)]

(c) under an occupational pension scheme [², in respect of a pension or other periodical payment made under a personal pension scheme or a payment made by the Board of the Pension Protection Fund] where–
  (i) a bankruptcy order has been made in respect of the person in respect of whom the payment has been made or, in Scotland, the estate of that person is subject to sequestration or a judicial factor has been appointed on that person's estate under section 41 of the Solicitors (Scotland) Act 1980;
  (ii) the payment is made to the trustee in bankruptcy or any other person acting on behalf of the creditors; and
  (iii) the person referred to in (i) and any member of his family does not possess, or is not treated as possessing, any other income apart from that payment.

(5) Where a claimant stands in relation to a company in a position analogous to that of a sole owner or partner in the business of that company, he may be treated as if he were such sole owner or partner and in such a case–

(a) the value of his holding in that company shall, notwithstanding regulation 44 (calculation of capital) be disregarded; and

(b) he shall, subject to paragraph (6), be treated as possessing an amount of capital equal to the value to him or, as the case may be, his share of the value of the capital of that company and the foregoing provisions of this Section shall apply for the purposes of calculating that amount as if it were actual capital which he does possess.

(6) For so long as the claimant undertakes activities in the course of the business of the company, the amount which he is treated as possessing under paragraph (5) shall be disregarded.

(7)   Where a claimant is treated as possessing capital under any of paragraphs (1) to (3) the foregoing provisions of this Section shall apply for the purposes of calculating its amount as if it were actual capital which he does possess.

(8)   In paragraph (3) "rent" means eligible rent less any deductions in respect of non-dependants which fall to be made under regulation 74 (non-dependant deductions).

Modifications

Reg 49(4) was modified by reg 15 Jobseeker's Allowance (Work for Your Benefit Pilot Scheme) Regulations 2010 SI No.1222 and sub-para (ba) inserted from 22 November 2010 to 1 March 2012 in pilot areas only.

Reg 49(4) was modified by reg 13 of the Jobseeker's Allowance (Supervised Job Search Pilot Scheme) Regulations 2014 SI No.1913 and sub-para (bd) inserted from 18 July 2014 to 30 April 2015 for those selected to participate in the pilot scheme only.

Reg 49(4) was modified by reg 16 of the Jobseeker's Allowance (18–21 Work Skills Pilot Scheme) Regulations 2014 SI No.3117 and sub-para (be) inserted from 25 November 2014 to 24 November 2016 for those selected to participate in the pilot scheme in pilot areas only.

Amendments

1.   Amended by reg 5A(3) of SI 2005 No 2465 as inserted by Sch 2 para 28(5) of SI 2006 No 217 as from 6.4.06.
2.   Amended by reg 8(3) of SI 2006 No 588 as from 6.4.06.
3.   Substituted by reg 6(3) of SI 2007 No 719 as from 2.4.07.
4.   Amended by reg 4(5) of SI 2007 No 1749 as from 16.7.07.
5.   Omitted by reg 6(4) of SI 2008 No 698 as from 14.4.08.
6.   Amended by reg 6(4)(c) of SI 2008 No 2767 as from 17.11.08.
7.   Amended by reg 3 of SI 2009 No 480 as from 5.10.09.
8.   Amended by reg 8(3) and (5) of SI 2010 No 641 as from 1.4.10 (5.4.10 where rent payable weekly or in multiples of a week).
9.   Inserted by reg 13 of SI 2011 No 688 as from 25.4.11.
10.   Inserted by reg 13 of SI 2011 No 917 as from 20.5.11. SI 2011 No 917 was quashed by the Court of Appeal in *R (Reilly and another) v SSWP* [2013] EWCA Civ 66, 12 February 2013.
11.   Inserted by reg 19(6)(b) of SI 2011 No 2425 as from 31.10.11.
12.   Inserted by reg 10 of SI 2013 No 276 as from 6.45 pm 12.2.13.
13.   Inserted by reg 12 of SI 2014 No 1913 as from 18.7.14. The amendment ceases to have effect on 30.4.15.
14.   Inserted by reg 16 of SI 2014 No 3117 as from 25.11.14. The amendment ceases to have effect at the end of 24 months beginning on that date.
15.   Amended by reg 6(3)(c) of SI 2017 No 329 as from 3.4.17.
16.   Amended by reg 6(3)(c) of SI 2017 No 689 as from 19.6.17.
17.   Amended by reg 6(3)(c) of SI 2017 No 870 as from 23.10.17.

Definitions

"capital" – see General Note on this section.
"child tax credit" and "working tax credit" – see reg 2(1).
"claimant" – see reg 2(1).
"family" – see s137(1) SSCBA.
"Jobseeker's Allowance Regulations" – see reg 2(1).
"the Macfarlane Trust" and the other schemes listed in para (4)(a) – see reg 2(1).
"Mandatory Work Activity Scheme" – see reg 2(1).
"membership of family" – see Part 4.
"occupational pension/personal pension scheme" – see reg 2(1).
"ordinary clothing or footware" – see reg 2(1).

General Note

This regulation sets out the situations in which a claimant must or may be treated as possessing capital even when s/he does not actually possess it. This regulation corresponds to reg 42 in respect of income.

Paras (1) to (5) set out these situations, para (6) qualifies para (5), and para (7) provides how capital that a claimant is deemed to possess under this regulation is to be quantified. Para (8) defines the term "rent" as it is used in para (3).

Analysis

Paragraph (1): Capital of which a claimant has deprived her/himself

Para (1) is similar to reg 42(1) in its effect. The notes below on the wording of this paragraph will be equally applicable to reg 42(1).

It is important to note that para (1) only applies if there has been a deprivation of capital, and if the deprivation was for the purpose of securing or increasing entitlement to HB. The reference to reg 50 ensures that the claimant is only treated as possessing the notional capital remaining after any reduction provided by that regulation.

The key factors in reaching a decision that a claimant is to be treated as possessing capital of which s/he has deprived her/himself are:

(1)   that the resource had actually belonged to the claimant; *and*
(2)   that the dates and period over which disposal occurred indicate at least a partial motive for the deprivation. The capital of which the claimant is said to have deprived her/himself must be capital which would normally fall to be taken into account. Thus if the capital does not belong to the claimant in the first case (perhaps because it is subject to a trust: see the General Note on this Section) or if it falls to be disregarded under Sch 6, para (1) can have no application.

"of which he has deprived himself". The word "deprived" is an ordinary English word and does not have any special meaning: *R(SB) 38/85* para 21. It is sufficient if a claimant ceases to possess the relevant asset, even if s/he receives something in exchange for the asset: *R(SB) 40/85* para 8.

It appears that a person can have "deprived himself" of an asset of which s/he was never in possession. So a deliberate failure to cash a cheque may amount to a "deprivation" (*CSB 598/1987*) as may a release of a debtor (*CIS 1586/1997*). A person may also have deprived her/himself of an asset if s/he presents a petition (or possibly fails to resist a petition by a creditor) and is declared bankrupt as a result: *KS v SSWP (JSA)* [2009] UKUT 122 (AAC); [2010] AACR 3.

Much of the relevant DWP guidance is useful but care must be taken to give precedence to the wording of the regulation and the caselaw.

GM BW1.714, lists certain circumstances where the DWP suggests deprivation may have occurred:

(1)   A lump sum payment made to someone else – eg, as a gift or to repay a debt.
(2)   Substantial expenditure incurred on a non-essential item – eg, on an expensive holiday.
(3)   Title deeds of property which is not, or will soon cease to be, the claimant's home transferred into someone else's name.
(4)   Money put into an irrevocable trust.
(5)   Money converted into a form (eg, personal possessions) which would fall to be disregarded.
(6)   Money reduced by extravagant living.

However, while the guidance provides a useful indication of the types of situation in which a claimant is likely to be subject to an inquiry as to the circumstances of the deprivation, the wording of the legislation and the relevant caselaw must always be followed. Note, therefore, some of the criticisms of the guidance set out below.

"for the purpose of securing entitlement to housing benefit or increasing the amount of that benefit". Two different issues arise from this part of the paragraph.

The first issue: "purpose". The relevant "purpose" must be established. In deciding whether a person has deprived her/himself of capital to obtain or increase HB, the authority must consider whether the obtaining of benefit was a "significant operative purpose" behind the decision to divest her/himself of the asset: *R(SB) 40/85* para 10. It is insufficient that the claimant knows that the obtaining of benefit is a natural consequence of the transaction: *R(SB) 9/91*. There must be a positive finding that the claimant actually knew of the capital limit in the light of all the facts, and it will not necessarily be sufficient for the authority to show that the information was available to the claimant in literature supplied by it: *CIS 124/1990* para 11; *CIS 30/1993*. These principles have been restated with force in *R(H) 1/06*, a case concerning a claimant with a severe and enduring mental illness. Commissioner Howell in considering reg 43 HB Regs 1987 (now reg 49 HB Regs) at para 13 stated:

> "there is no doubt that the test of whether a claimant is shown to have deprived himself of capital "for the purpose of" securing entitlement to housing benefit so as to fall within the notional capital provisions of regulation 43 Housing Benefit (General) Regulations 1987 SI No 1971 is a subjective one, depending on the evidence about the particular claimant in question. It does not in my view adequately address or answer the point to say as the chairman did that because a person is not completely incapable of managing his affairs or of realising he was spending his money imprudently, it follows as a matter of course and without further analysis that all such spending is done for the purpose of securing entitlement to benefit. Such a jump is impermissible as it omits any real consideration of the actual purpose of the particular person involved".

This decision was endorsed and followed by Commissioner Bano in *CIS 218/2005* (para 7), where he said that "the issue requires a determination of the actual, or subjective, intention of the claimant".

Commissioner Howell returned to this point later in *R(H) 1/06*, where he said (para 22):

> "Whether the securing of entitlement to benefit was, in this sense, among the purposes which led any particular claimant to act as he did is a question that must be determined by the tribunal of fact in the circumstances of each individual case, the test as already noted being one of subjective purpose: see in the housing benefit context *R (Beeson) v Dorset CC* [2001] EWHC Admin 986, 30 November 2001, *per* Richards J at paragraphs 9, 37 (not challenged on this point in the Court of Appeal). In the great majority of cases this must be a matter of drawing such inferences as the tribunal of fact thinks fit from the surrounding circumstances, such as the claimant's state of knowledge of the rules, the nature and timing of the disposals he makes and the timing and manner of his claims for benefit; since direct evidence to show such a purpose is in the nature of things unlikely. Such a task is however a perfectly normal one for a tribunal of fact to have

to undertake, and this is of course by no means the only instance in the law when the purpose for which a thing is done may not be express, and has to be ascertained "as a matter of substance and of fact": *re South African Supply and Cold Storage Company* [1904] 2 Ch 268, per Buckley J at p282. In using the word "significant" Mr Monroe may perhaps have had in mind what was said by Lord Morris of Borth-y-Gest in *Sweet v Parsley* [1970] AC 132, 155A:

"In my opinion, the words 'premises ... used for the purposes of ...' denote a purpose which is other than quite incidental or casual or fortuitous: they denote a purpose which is or has become either a significant one or a recognised one though certainly not necessarily an only one."

The mere fact that an asset has been disposed of at a substantial undervalue is insufficient, of itself, for an authority to conclude that a claimant should be treated as having notional capital. The claimant's explanation for the disposition needs to be properly considered: *R v South Tyneside MBC ex p Tooley* [1996] COD 143 at 144, QBD.

The caselaw on the correct approach to be taken to "purpose" where the deprivation is constituted in paying off a commercial debt (in this case credit cards) was reviewed in *CJSA 1425/2004*. Commissioner Rowland stressed that the approach of the Court of Appeal in *Jones v SSWP* [2003] EWCA 964, unreported, does not undermine the point in *R(SB) 12/91* that, if the debtor has no practical choice but to pay her/his debt, the repayment of the debt cannot reasonably be regarded as having been for the purpose of obtaining benefit and that, normally, if a debt is immediately repayable, the debtor has no practical choice. Moreover, *Jones* is not authority for the proposition that if the debtor thought that the debt would not be called in for some time, payment of the debt would be for the purpose of obtaining benefit. Commissioner Rowland commented (at para 38) that he found it:

"difficult to envisage a case where it would be unreasonable for a claimant to pay a debt that had become due, merely because the creditor had decided not to enforce it for the time being, unless, perhaps, the decision not to enforce the debt was entirely unconnected to the claimant's lack of means and amounted, in effect, to a variation of the terms upon which the debt became repayable."

He went on (para 40) to conclude:

"The effect of all these decisions is therefore that, if a claimant realised that one consequence of depriving himself of capital was that he might become entitled to jobseeker's allowance or income support and he nonetheless deprived himself of that capital, there arises the question whether obtaining benefit was a significant operative purpose of the deprivation. Because there will almost always be some other purpose as well, that question is determined by deciding whether, given his knowledge, it was reasonable in all the circumstances for him to act as he did, bearing in mind not only his obligation to tax payers to support himself, but also his obligations to other people. Moreover, insofar as his obligation to support himself is concerned, it is necessary to have regard to the long term as well as the short term."

In approaching the facts of the case before him, Commissioner Rowland made a number of useful observations.

(1)   If a claimant has mixed motives, the question whether the purpose of obtaining benefits is a significant operative purpose is to be determined by deciding whether it was reasonable for the claimant to act in the way that s/he did: *CJSA 1425/2004* para 46. Note, however, that in *CH 264/2006*, Commissioner Jacobs disapproved of this approach saying it "erroneously converts an evidentiary factor of reasonableness into a legal test and a subjective test of purpose into an objective test of reasonableness." In a later decision, *JM v SSWP* [2009] UKUT 145 (AAC), Judge Rowlands disagreed. However, the judge in *SH v Tower Hamlets LB (HB)* [2011] UKUT 500 (AAC), while noting the comments in *JM v SSWP*, agreed with *CH 264/2006*.

(2)   The true significance of the timing of the deprivation is that the closer the deprivation was to the date of claim, the stronger the inference will be that the deprivation was made in the expectation that there would be a claim and with the knowledge that the deprivation would affect the claimant's entitlement to benefit: para 48.

(3)   Even if the appellant's forthcoming application for "review" of his benefit claim may have prompted him into paying his credit card debts when he did, that merely suggested that obtaining benefit was one purpose behind the payments; leaving the question whether it was a significant operative purpose still to be answered (and that was to be determined by considering whether making the payments was reasonable). In other words, although a claimant's desire to obtain benefit may explain the timing of the payments, it is not necessarily to be taken to have been a significant operative purpose behind the making of the payments: para 49.

(4)   The threat of having to make high interest payments is just as capable of making it reasonable to pay a debt as the threat of enforcement of a liability to repay: para 50.

In *VW v SSWP (IS)* [2015] UKUT 51 (AAC), Judge Rowland pointed out that in determining whether repayment of a debt to a friend or relative amounts to a deprivation of capital for the purpose of securing or increasing entitlement to benefit, decision makers and tribunals may need to investigate the facts thoroughly and obtain relevant evidence. He said, for example, that evidence may be required on whether there was a loan giving rise to a legally-enforceable debt, as well as evidence of the transfer to the claimant of the money that was lent and of the transfer of money to the alleged lender. A claimant's word can be accepted without corroboration. However, the judge said that "it may be reasonable to expect a friend or relative to provide written and documentary evidence in support of a claimant who claims they were both parties to a legitimate transaction involving a substantial amount of money."

It is for the Secretary of State to prove on the balance of probabilities that deprivation has been for the purpose of claiming benefit. The relevant authority must make a sufficiently clear positive finding that the claimant knew of the capital limit and its effect on entitlement: *LP v SSWP (ESA)* [2018] UKUT 389 (AAC). However, in *RB v SSWP (ESA)* [2016] UKUT 384 (AAC), the appellant received a lump-sum divorce settlement and subsequently made two payments to repay loans to his parents and a payment of a year's rent in advance, bringing his capital below the threshold. In dismissing the appellant's appeal against a decision that he had deprived himself of capital for the purpose of claiming benefit, Judge Markus said that the tribunal was entitled to expect the appellant to provide evidence to support his explanation for the payments. The credibility of the appellant's claim that he had repaid loans turned significantly on whether there had been such loans in the first place. The advance payment of rent was not a condition of the tenancy. In the absence of any other explanation, the tribunal was entitled to decide that the payment was made for the purpose of claiming benefit.

In *LH v SSWP (IS)* [2014] UKUT 60 (AAC), it appeared that the claimant had told a DWP visiting officer that she had used capital from an endowment policy to pay off existing debts. The visiting officer advised that using capital in this manner was acceptable and she then acted on this advice when making further disposals of her capital before reclaiming benefit. The question was whether, if in acting on the (alleged) advice that if she disposed of capital to pay off debts she would again secure entitlement to IS, that on then disposing of the capital in that manner, the claimant was depriving herself of capital for the "significant operative purpose" of securing entitlement to IS. In the end, the appeal was decided on a different basis. However, in *obiter* remarks, Judge Wright said that whether the significant operative purpose of such a disposal of capital is securing entitlement to benefit depends on the nature of the advice sought and given. He disagreed with *CIS 307/1992*, which found that advice that a disposal of capital would not affect benefit entitlement would act to nullify any finding of adverse intention under reg 51(1) IS Regs (the equivalent to reg 49(1) HB Regs) and thus would insulate the person provided with the advice from being caught by reg 51(1). He said that if the claimant in *CIS 307/1992* had sought advice from the DWP about whether the disposal of her capital would affect her ability to remain on IS or to reclaim it, and the advice was that it would not, it was difficult to see why her intention in then paying out the money was not for the purpose of securing entitlement to IS, as that was precisely what she sought the advice about.

The second issue: securing, or increasing the amount of, HB. The purpose must be to secure, or increase the amount of, "housing benefit". The regulation does not operate where the claimant has deprived her/himself of capital in order to get other means-tested benefits. If, for example, it could be shown that a claimant had deprived her/himself of capital but that her/his purpose in doing so was to secure entitlement to IS, income-based JSA or income-related ESA rather than HB then s/he might be entitled to continue to receive HB even though the other benefit was stopped or reduced.

In practice, this would probably be difficult to establish but it might be possible to show in some cases that the claimant had no knowledge of the existence of HB (perhaps because s/he had never previously rented property). This principle also applies when one benefit is abolished and replaced by another: in *R(IS) 14/93* paras 16–17 it was held that a claimant who had deprived himself of substantial amounts of capital in 1987 in order to secure entitlement to supplementary benefit was nevertheless entitled to IS because, at the date of the deprivation, that benefit did not exist and therefore the deprivation could not have had the purpose of securing entitlement to it. It is not unknown for similar cases to emerge even now and it is suggested that the reference to "housing benefit" in reg 49(1) must be read as a reference to "housing benefit" under the HB Regs and not under the previous schemes: compare *R v Middlesborough BC ex p Graville* [1993] unreported, 26 March, QBD and *Andrew v City of Glasgow DC* [1996] SLT 814 at 817H-L. Note also that this may have application when HB is replaced by universal credit.

Already getting the maximum entitlement to HB may, in effect, mean that a claimant cannot be said to be able to secure, or increase the amount of, HB by failing to disclose, or disposing of, capital. However, in *LP v SSWP (ESA)* [2018] UKUT 389 (AAC), Judge Mesher rejected the argument, advanced by the Secretary of State, that such a situation meant that the notional capital rules did not apply. He said that to take that approach would undermine the duty to report relevant changes of circumstances that a claimant might reasonably be expected to know might affect entitlement.

In some circumstances, a claimant may be fixed with notional capital even though the deprivation was by her/his partner *before* they became a couple: *CH 1822 2006*, a decision refusing leave to appeal to a commissioner (decided with *CIS 1757 2006*). This is because the focus of reg 49 is at the time when entitlement is in issue but in respect of a past disposal of capital. In this situation, the notional capital rule will only apply to a future partner when there has been conduct that is related to future entitlement to benefit either for the person alone or as a member of a family, and then only when there has been a deprivation of capital with the necessary intention. Note that the claimant failed in his application for a judicial review of the commissioner's decision: *R (Hook) v The Social Security Commissioner* [2007] EWHC 1705 (Admin), 3 July; reported as *R(IS) 7/07*.

Paragraph (2): Capital available on application

This is similar to reg 42(2): see the commentary on p458. The authority is obliged to treat the claimant as possessing any capital which would become available to her/him on application, unless it comes within the exceptions in sub-paras (a) to (g). If a claimant is a potential beneficiary under a discretionary trust or a trust derived from a payment made in consequence of personal injury (see reg 42), or could raise money on a loan, but only if the loan was secured by capital disregarded under Sch 6, s/he is not to be treated as possessing capital under this regulation. See also Sch 6 para 14 in respect of entitlement under a trust of funds paid in consequence of personal injury.

Actual payments made to the claimant under a discretionary or other type of trust will be dealt with under the rest of this Section and not this regulation.

If the trust or other source from which a claimant could obtain capital is not excluded from this regulation, it must still be established by the authority that s/he actually could get payment if s/he asked. This will cause problems. In relation to trusts, under s32 Trustee Act 1925 (as amended by s9 of the Inheritance and Trustees' Powers Act 2014), trustees have a restricted power to advance the whole of a claimant's potential share of capital under a trust, whether or not the claimant's right to such capital is vested or subject to her/him satisfying a contingency. But the trustees cannot be *obliged* to exercise this power, so it is by no means certain that if a claimant is a potential beneficiary under a trust s/he *would* be paid on application. Further information will be necessary.

If the claimant is absolutely entitled to trust funds under the rule in *Saunders v Vautier* [1841] 4 Bear 115, s/he is treated as the legal owner of the funds so that it is arguable that the trust funds will be treated as *actual* capital and not be subject to this regulation. However, in *R(SB) 2/89*, which concerned a trust of personal injury compensation, the beneficiary of the trust was the sole beneficiary and therefore, under the law, absolutely entitled to the money in the trust fund, but this did not stop it being disregarded under the analogous provision. This makes sense, because otherwise sub-para (e) would be deprived of any effect.

Disputed matrimonial assets may require careful consideration. In *LC v Bournemouth BC (HB)* [2016] UKUT 175 (AAC), the claimant's partner had an interest in a former matrimonial home. The proceeds, totalling over £400,000, were held in a solicitor's account pending agreement as to how the money would be split between him and his ex-wife. The local authority decided the proceeds should be treated as notional capital as soon as they reached the solicitor's account, and that (under reg 51) the claimant's partner should be regarded as entitled to an equal share of the total amount. These arguments were rejected. The disbursement of the proceeds of sale of a matrimonial home held in this way requires the agreement of both parties or an order or the court, and a valuation of the capital will be minimal until agreement is reached. Regulation 49(2) places an obligation on a local authority to allow time for a claimant to apply for capital in dispute before it is held to be notional capital. The authority must consider the practicalities of gaining access to disputed matrimonial assets. Before making an entitlement decision based on the possession of notional capital, it needs to make a judgment as to the likely distribution of the proceeds of sale and, where agreement cannot be reached between the parties to the failed relationship, to decide how long it is reasonable to allow before application for the court to determine the distribution is required, and how long to allow between application for the capital and its notional acquisition.

Paragraphs (3), (4) and (8): Payments involving third parties

This is identical in effect to paras (6) and (7) of reg 42. See the Analysis on p458.

Paragraph (5) and (6): Business assets

The application of para (5) by an authority is discretionary. Sub-paras (a) and (b) and para (6) quantify how much capital a claimant is to be treated as possessing in this respect, if the authority decides to exercise its discretion.

If this paragraph applies while the claimant is actually working for the company, the capital value of her/his share of it is to be totally ignored in assessing the claimant's assets; if para (6) does *not* apply, under para (5)(a) and (b) s/he is treated as possessing the capital value of the company or her/his share of that value, rather than the actual value of her/his *holding* which is ignored.

The valuation is made according to the rules in the rest of this Section – ie, at market value, minus allowable deductions: see reg 47. If the claimant is the sole owner, see Sch 6 para 8, which allows its value to be ignored for a "reasonable" period after s/he stops work to allow the company to be sold.

Paragraph (7): Valuation

If a claimant is treated as possessing capital under paras (1) to (5), it is to be quantified according to the rules which pertain to *actual* capital assets under this Section.

Diminishing notional capital rule

50.–(1) Where a claimant is treated as possessing capital under regulation 49(1) (notional capital), the amount which he is treated as possessing–

(a) in the case of a week that is subsequent to–

   (i) the relevant week in respect of which the conditions set out in paragraph (2) are satisfied; or

   (ii) a week which follows that relevant week and which satisfies those conditions,

   shall be reduced by an amount determined under paragraph (3);

(b) in the case of a week in respect of which paragraph (1)(a) does not apply but where–

     (i)   that week is a week subsequent to the relevant week; and

     (ii)   that relevant week is a week in which the condition in paragraph (4) is satisfied,

shall be reduced by the amount determined under paragraph (4).

(2)   This paragraph applies to a benefit week where the claimant satisfies the conditions that–

(a)   he is in receipt of housing benefit; and

(b)   but for regulation 49(1), he would have received an additional amount of housing benefit in that week.

(3)   In a case to which paragraph (2) applies, the amount of the reduction for the purposes of paragraph (1)(a) shall be equal to the aggregate of–

(a)   the additional amount to which sub-paragraph (2)(b) refers;

(b)   where the claimant has also claimed council tax benefit, the amount of any council tax benefit or any additional amount of council tax benefit to which he would have been entitled in respect of the benefit week to which paragraph (2) refers but for the application of regulation 39(1) of the Council Tax Benefit Regulations 2006 (notional capital);

(c)   where the claimant has also claimed income support, the amount of income support to which he would have been entitled in respect of the benefit week to which paragraph (2) refers but for the application of regulation 51(1) of the Income Support Regulations (notional capital); [²]

(d)   where the claimant has also claimed a jobseeker's allowance, the amount of an income-based jobseeker's allowance to which he would have been entitled in respect of the benefit week to which paragraph (2) refers but for the application of regulation 113 of the Jobseeker's Allowance Regulations (notional capital).

[² (e)   where the claimant has also claimed an employment and support allowance, the amount of an income-related employment and support allowance to which he would have been entitled in respect of the benefit week to which paragraph (2) refers but for the application of regulation 115 of the Employment and Support Allowance Regulations (notional capital).]

(4)   Subject to paragraph (5), for the purposes of paragraph (1)(b) the condition is that the claimant would have been entitled to housing benefit in the relevant week but for regulation 49(1), and in such a case the amount of the reduction shall be equal to the aggregate of–

(a)   the amount of housing benefit to which the claimant would have been entitled in the relevant week but for regulation 49(1) and, for the purposes of this sub-paragraph, if the relevant week is a week to which [¹ regulation 80(3)(a)] refers (calculation of weekly amounts), that amount shall be determined by dividing the amount of housing benefit to which he would have been so entitled by the number of days in that week for which he was liable to make payments in respect of the dwelling he occupies as his home and multiplying the quotient so obtained by 7;

(b)   if the claimant would, but for regulation 39(1) of the Council Tax Benefit Regulations 2006, have been entitled to council tax benefit or to an additional amount of council tax benefit in respect of the benefit week which includes the last day of the relevant week, the amount which is equal to–

     (i)   in a case where no council tax benefit is payable, the amount to which he would have been entitled; or

     (ii)   in any other case, the amount equal to the additional amount of council tax benefit to which he would have been entitled;

and, for the purposes of this sub-paragraph, if the amount is in respect of a part-week, that amount shall be determined by dividing the amount of the council tax benefit to which he would have been so entitled by the number equal to the number of days in the part-week and multiplying the quotient so obtained by 7;

(c)   if the claimant would, but for regulation 51(1) of the Income Support Regulations, have been entitled to income support in respect of the benefit week, within the meaning of regulation 2(1) of those Regulations (interpretation), which includes the last day of the relevant week, the amount to which he would have been entitled and, for the purposes of this sub-paragraph, if the amount is in respect of a part-week, that amount shall be determined by dividing the amount of the income support to which he would have been so entitled by the number equal to the number of days in the part-week and multiplying the quotient so obtained by 7;

(d)   if the claimant would, but for regulation 113 of the Jobseeker's Allowance Regulations, have been entitled to an income-based jobseeker's allowance in respect of the benefit week, within the meaning of regulation 1(3) of those Regulations (interpretation), which includes the last day of the relevant week, the amount to which he would have been entitled and, for the purposes of this sub-paragraph, if the amount is in respect of a part-week, that amount shall be determined by dividing the amount of the income-based jobseeker's allowance to which he would have been so entitled by the number equal to the number of days in the part-week and multiplying the quotient so obtained by 7.

[² (e) if the claimant would, but for regulation 115 of the Employment and Support Allowance Regulations, have been entitled to an income-related employment and support allowance in respect of the benefit week, within the meaning of regulation 2(1) of those Regulations (interpretation), which includes the last day of the relevant week, the amount to which he would have been entitled and, for the purposes of this sub-paragraph, if the amount is in respect of a part-week, that amount must be determined by dividing the amount of the income-related employment and support allowance to which he would have been so entitled by the number equal to the number of days in that part-week and multiplying the quotient so obtained by 7.]

(5)   The amount determined under paragraph (4) shall be re-determined under that paragraph if the claimant makes a further claim for housing benefit and the conditions in paragraph (6) are satisfied, and in such a case–

(a)   sub-paragraphs (a) to (d) of paragraph (4) shall apply as if for the words "relevant week" there were substituted the words "relevant subsequent week"; and

(b)   subject to paragraph (7), the amount as re-determined shall have effect from the first week following the relevant subsequent week in question.

(6)   The conditions are that–

(a)   a further claim is made 26 or more weeks after–

(i)   the date on which the claimant made a claim for housing benefit in respect of which he was first treated as possessing the capital in question under regulation 49(1);

(ii)   in a case where there has been at least one redetermination in accordance with paragraph (5), the date on which he last made a claim for housing benefit which resulted in the weekly amount being re-determined; or

(iii)   the date on which he last ceased to be entitled to housing benefit, whichever last occurred; and

(b)   the claimant would have been entitled to housing benefit but for regulation 49(1).

(7)   The amount as re-determined pursuant to paragraph (5) shall not have effect if it is less than the amount which applied in that case immediately before the redetermination and in such a case the higher amount shall continue to have effect.

(8)   For the purposes of this regulation–

(a)   "part-week" in paragraph (4)(b) means a period of less than a week for which council tax benefit is allowed;

(b)   "part-week" in paragraph (4)(c) [², (d) and (e)] means–

(i)   a period of less than a week which is the whole period for which income support [² an income-related employment and support allowance], or, as the case may be, an income-based jobseeker's allowance, is payable; and

(ii)   any other period of less than a week for which it is payable;

(c)   "relevant week" means the benefit week in which the capital in question of which the claimant has deprived himself within the meaning of regulation 49(1)–

(i)   was first taken into account for the purpose of determining his entitlement to housing benefit; or

(ii)   was taken into account on a subsequent occasion for the purpose of determining or re-determining his entitlement to housing benefit on that subsequent occasion and that determination or redetermination resulted in his beginning to receive, or ceasing to receive, housing benefit;

and where more than one benefit week is identified by reference to heads (i) and (ii) of this sub-paragraph the later or latest such benefit week;

(d)   "relevant subsequent week" means the benefit week which includes the day on which the further claim or, if more than one further claim has been made, the last such claim was made.

Modifications

Para (4)(a) was amended by reg 11 Housing Benefit (Local Housing Allowance and Information Sharing) Amendment Regulations 2007 SI No.2868 as from 7 April 2008 save that, for a person to whom reg 1(5) of those regulations applied (see p1812), the amendments came into force on the day on or after 7 April 2008 when the first of the events specified in reg 1(6) applied to her/him, or on 6 April 2009 if none had before that date.

Amendments

1.   Amended by reg 11 of SI 2007 No 2868 as from 7.4.08 (or if reg 1(5) of that SI applies, on the day on or after 7.4.08 when the first of the events specified in reg 1(6) applies, or from 6.4.09 if none have before that date).

2.   Amended by reg 16 of SI 2008 No 1082 as from 27.10.08.

Definitions

"benefit week" – see reg 2(1).
"capital" – see General Note on this Section.
"claimant" – see reg 2(1).
"employment and support allowance" and "income-related employment and support allowance" – see reg 2(1).
"Income Suppport Regulations" – see reg 2(1).
"jobseeker's allowance" and "an income-based jobseeker's allowance" – see reg 2(1).
"Jobseeker's Allowance Regulations" – see reg 2(1).

General Note

Although this regulation is lengthy, the principle is simple enough. Reg 49(1), if applied, could result in unfairness. Without a mechanism for reducing "notional capital", a claimant's HB entitlement could be affected permanently. In other words, had the claimant not disposed of capital, s/he would be able to use her/his capital resources and would eventually regain entitlement to (or gain an increased rate of) HB. Reg 50 therefore provides the mechanism whereby the amount of notional capital which the claimant has as a result of the operation of reg 49(1) is reduced by the weekly amount of benefits lost as a result of the application of the rule.

Reg 50 does not apply to *actual* capital: *CIS 2287/2008*. However, Commissioner Jacobs said that although there is no formal "diminishing" rule for actual capital, a similar result can be attained using inferences in the fact finding process.

Analysis

Paragraphs (1) to (4): The basic calculation

Para (1) provides the source of the reductions to notional capital. The calculation starts at the "relevant week" which is defined in para (8)(c) and hence can apply retrospectively. The "relevant week" is ordinarily the first week in which the notional capital was taken into account for the purposes of determining entitlement to HB. If, however, there are one or more subsequent determinations and benefit is actually awarded under that determination, the "relevant week" is the week of the most recent determination.

First, under sub-para (a), in relation to any subsequent week where the conditions in para (2) are met, a reduction is made according to the calculation in para (3). In relation to any other week in which the condition in para (4) is met, a reduction is made under that paragraph.

Paras (2) and (3): claimant is in receipt of HB. Para (2) applies where a claimant is in receipt of HB and the effect of reg 49(1) has been to reduce her/his entitlement in that week. This would apply where the claimant's capital (notional and actual) is below the upper, but above the lower, capital limit and hence tariff income calculated under reg 52 reduces the amount to which s/he is entitled.

If para (2) applies, para (3) requires the amount of the notional capital in that week to be reduced by the additional amount of HB to which the claimant would have been entitled in the absence of reg 49(1) plus any IS, income-based JSA (defined in reg 2(1) to include joint-claim JSA) and income-related ESA to which s/he would have been entitled in the absence of the operation of the equivalent provisions for those benefits.

The claimant will need to show that a valid claim had been made, subject to the rules for deeming claims. See the current volume II of *Social Security Legislation* for the rules relating to claims for those benefits. Note that CTB is also mentioned: para (3)(a). CTB was abolished from 1 April 2013 but may be relevant for calculating a reduction in notional capital before that date.

Para (4): claimant not entitled to HB. Para (4) imposes the condition for para (1)(b), which is that there would have been entitlement to HB but for the operation of reg 49(1). This applies where there is no current entitlement to HB – ie, because the claimant's capital (notional and actual) is above the capital limit, or is below the upper, but above the lower, capital limit and hence tariff income calculated under reg 52 reduces the amount of HB to which s/he is entitled to nil. The amount of notional capital is reduced in a similar way to para (3). Part-weeks are dealt with on a pro rata basis.

Paragraphs (5) to (7): Redeterminations

Under para (5), if the claimant then reclaims HB 26 or more weeks after the latest date set out in para (6), and is still not entitled due to the "notional capital" rule in reg 49(1), the rate of diminution is recalculated at that point. Any changes which would reduce the rate of diminution are ignored under para (7), although factors which would increase that rate (eg, annual uprating) are taken into account.

It follows that claimants excluded from benefit by this rule should reclaim at 26-week intervals to ensure that the "notional capital" reduces at the maximum rate. If the "diminishing capital" rule results in a claimant becoming entitled again at some later date any remaining "notional capital" reduces according to the rules in paras (1)(a), (2), (3) and (8)(b)(ii).

Capital jointly held

51. Except where a claimant possesses capital which is disregarded under regulation 49(5) (notional capital) where a claimant and one or more persons are beneficially entitled in possession to any capital asset they shall be treated as if each of them were entitled in possession to the whole beneficial interest therein in an equal share and the foregoing provisions of this Section shall apply for the purposes of calculating the amount of capital which the claimant is treated as possessing as if it were actual capital which the claimant does possess.

Definitions

"capital" – see General Note on this Section.

"claimant" – see reg 2(1).

General Note

The legal owner of an asset may be, but is not always, the same as the beneficial owner – eg, if one person buys a house in her/his name, but part of the purchase price is paid by someone else, and that person does not intend to make the nominal purchaser an outright gift, or only intends to lend the nominal purchaser the money, that other person has a "beneficial interest" in the house, despite the fact that the legal ownership is in the person whose name is on the title deeds. The term "in possession" means that ownership can be enjoyed at present and is not postponed to some other legal interest (eg, a life interest) or dependent on the satisfaction of some contingency. As the law on quantification of beneficial interests is complex, this regulation simply deems each of those who have such an interest in a particular capital asset to have an equal share in it. See also Sch 5 para 17 in respect of income produced by such an asset.

Analysis

Reg 51 has what is probably the most chequered legislative history of any regulation in this book. Before 2 October 1995, the wording of reg 44 HB Regs 1987 (now reg 51) was exactly the same as it is now. Then, as part of a series of changes to the rules for all the income-related benefits, it was amended. Those amendments were designed to reverse the decision of the Court of Appeal in *Chief Adjudication Officer v Palfrey* [1995] *The Times*, 8 February; reported as *R(IS) 5/98*, CA. Then, in May 1998 the equivalent amendment to the IS Regs was held to be *ultra vires* in *CIS 3283/1997*. The then DSS did not appeal that decision and accepted the commissioner's reasoning by returning the regulation to its original wording.

The regulation deals with the common situation where property is owned by more than one person. Rather than become embroiled in difficult disputes as to the relative shares actually owned by each co-owner, the policy of the DWP has long been to calculate benefit entitlement as if the asset were owned in equal shares. However, whether or not reg 51 successfully carries that policy into effect is open to question. Two problems arise. The first is whether the wording of the regulation is apt to include all forms of co-ownership and the second is the basis on which the claimant's deemed equal share is to be valued.

Forms of co-ownership. Under English law, there are two forms of co-ownership, namely joint tenancy and tenancy in common. The word "tenancy" might seem to suggest leasehold ownership or entitlement under a tenancy agreement but in this context applies to freehold ownership as well. Under a joint tenancy, all co-owners own the whole property (and hence if one dies, her/his interest is simply subsumed in the interest(s) of the other(s) by a process known as "survivorship" rather than passing under the will of the deceased owner). By contrast each owner under a tenancy in common owns an undivided share in the property. There was disagreement between commissioners as to whether reg 44 HB Regs 1987 (now reg 51) applied to both forms of co-ownership or merely to joint tenancies. It was confirmed by the Court of Appeal in *SSWP v Hourigan* [2003] 1 WLR 608 (reported as *R(IS) 4/03*), paras 17–21, 30 and 32 that reg 51 has no application to tenants in common.

In *CIS 2575/1997*, the commissioner held that the regulation also applied to foreign property and covered all forms of co-ownership whether existing under English law or not. Whether or not the latter finding can stand with *Hourigan* remains to be seen. Logically, if a form of foreign co-holding is akin to tenancy in common, the regulation should be inapplicable. If that is correct, evidence from a local lawyer in the country where the property was held would be required to ascertain the nature of the co-ownership.

Valuation of the deemed share. If the regulation does apply, there are two possible approaches to the valuation of the deemed share. These may be illustrated by the example of a house which is owned jointly by two people. The first approach values the house as a whole and then, after deductions for the costs of sale and any mortgages or other charges, divides that figure by two and values each co-owner's deemed share at an amount equal to the dividend. The second approach looks at the value which would be obtained on the open market if, rather than sell the house as a whole, the claimant's deemed equal share was sold but the deemed equal share of the co-owner was not. In other words the second approach values the claimant's share on the basis that any purchaser would have to continue to share the property with the co-owner. The difference between the approaches can be summed up as being between "half the value" and the "value of half".

The Court of Appeal in *Palfrey* favoured the "value of half" approach, the 1995 amendments purported to replace it with the "half the value" rule and, as a result of *CIS 3283/1997* and amendments in October 1998, the "value of half" rule has now regained supremacy.

The "value of half" approach has, for the claimant, the advantage of consistently returning a lower valuation. In the case of a jointly-owned house, common sense suggests that the value of half (or a third or any other part-share) will quite often be nil simply because there will be no evidence of an actual market in part shares of houses and because it would not be possible for the buyer of a part-share to take out a mortgage on it. The correctness of this view is reinforced by the decision in *CH 1953/2003* which concerned the former matrimonial home occupied by the claimant's wife. The tribunal had simply found that the claimant had to be treated as entitled to half the property which would take him over the capital limit. Following *Hourigan*, that approach was incorrect as the form of co-ownership had to be investigated (para 11). The tribunal was not entitled to assume that the claimant's wife would buy him out of the property on his request (para 14). In valuing the property, account had to be taken of the potential difficulties with sale in the light of the rights of the claimant's wife (para 15). The commissioner observed that "I would need evidence of the existence of a real market for the claimant's interest in his former home" (para 16).

In *JM v Eastleigh BC* [2016] UKUT 464 (AAC), Judge Jacobs stated that this is perhaps too pessimistic a view of the possibilities of realising the value of a part share in a property. He cited the decision of the Court of Appeal in *Wilkinson v Chief Adjudication Officer;* reported as *R(IS) 1/01*, which was decided on the equivalent provisions in income support legislation. The value of the claimant's share depends simply on whether it can be realised, and not on the difficulties those who held the other shares in the property may have in buying the claimant's share. Whether it can be realised depends on the circumstances of each case, but Judge Jacobs noted that there is increased awareness of markets that exist for investors in such shares. In deciding *Reigate and Banstead BC v GB* [2018] UKUT 225 (AAC), Judge Jacobs stated that evidence used to value a share in jointly owned property must be read fairly and as a whole in assessing its reliability. He confirmed that, while it may not be easy to produce evidence of a market for investment in interests that do not allow immediate exclusive possession, it is now well-established by Upper Tribunal decisions that such a market exists.

In *R(IS) 5/07*, Commissioner Williams sets out the approach to be taken in assessing the capital value of a claimant's share in a former joint home. The question of the value of a former joint home is only to be considered if none of the relevant capital disregards apply on the facts of the case (for which see Sch 6). If none of the disregards apply, next one has to consider whether the claimant's interest in the former home is as a tenant in common or a joint tenant. A joint tenancy should not be assumed (because nowadays it is far more common, for tax planning reasons for example, for couples to be advised to buy as tenants in common). However, this factual issue can be resolved easily by payment of a small fee and searching the land registry (at www.landregistry.gov.uk). If the interest is as a joint tenant, it is the current market value of the claimant's half of the house that is relevant (ie, with the former partner still living in it and perhaps unwilling or unable to move out or buy out the claimant's half share), not half the value of the sale of proceeds of the whole house: *R(IS) 4/03*, *CH 3197/2003* and *R(JSA) 1/02* considered.

It is advisable for claimants involved in disputes to obtain their own valuation evidence. Although District Valuers can usually claim special expertise because details of every property purchase need to be produced to HMRC as part of the conveyancing process, it is doubtful whether any such claim can be made in relation to sales of part shares. This is because there are unlikely to be many such sales. It is therefore always worth asking for the number of real-life examples on which the official valuation is based.

Calculation of tariff income from capital

52.–(1)   Except where the circumstances prescribed in paragraph [¹] (4) apply to the claimant, where the claimant's capital calculated in accordance with this Part exceeds [¹ £6,000] it shall be treated as equivalent to a weekly tariff income of £1 for each complete £250 in excess of [¹ £6,000] but not exceeding £16,000.

[¹ (2)]

(3)   Where the circumstances prescribed in paragraph (4) apply to a claimant and that claimant's capital calculated in accordance with this Part exceeds £10,000, it shall be treated as equivalent to a weekly tariff income of £1 for each complete £250 in excess of £10,000 but not exceeding £16,000.

(4)   For the purposes of paragraph (3), the prescribed circumstances are that the claimant–

(a)   occupies residential accommodation as his home; or

(b)   is a person–

    (i)   to whom on 3rd October 2005 paragraph (2) of regulation 7 of the former regulations as in force on that date applied; or

    (ii)   to whom on 3rd October 2005, paragraph (5) or paragraph (7) of regulation 7 of those Regulations as in force on that date applied and continues to apply;

(5)   For the purposes of paragraph (4), the claimant shall be treated as–

(a)   occupying residential accommodation as his home; or

(b)   a person to whom regulation 9(1A) as inserted by paragraph 9(3)(a) of Schedule 3 to the Consequential Provisions Regulations, applies; or

(c)   a person to whom regulation 9(6) as inserted by paragraph 9(5)(a) of Schedule 3 to the Consequential Provisions Regulations, applies; or

(d)   a person to whom regulation 9(6) as inserted by paragraph 9(7)(a) of Schedule 3 to the Consequential Provisions Regulations, applies,

in any period during which he is treated as occupying the accommodation as his home pursuant to regulation 7(12), (13) or (17).

(6)   Notwithstanding paragraphs (1) [¹] and (3) where any part of the excess is not a complete £250 that part shall be treated as equivalent to a weekly tariff income of £1.

(7)   For the purposes of paragraphs (1) [¹] and (3), capital includes any income treated as capital under regulation 46 (income treated as capital).

(8)   For the purposes of this regulation and subject to paragraph (9), "residential accommodation" means accommodation which is provided by an establishment–

(a)   under sections 21 to 24 of the National Assistance Act 1948 (provision of accommodation) [² or under Part 1 of the Care Act 2014 (care and support)] or under section 59 of the Social Work (Scotland) Act 1968 (provision of residential and other establishments) [³ or under section 35 or 36 of the Social Services and Well-being (Wales) Act 2014 (duty and power to meet care and support needs of an adult)] where board is not available to the claimant and the home in which the accommodation is provided is either owned or managed or owned and managed by a local authority;

(b)   which is managed or provided by a body incorporated by Royal Charter or constituted by Act of Parliament (other than a social services authority) and provides both board and personal care for the claimant; and in this sub-paragraph, "personal care" means care which includes assistance with bodily functions where such assistance is required;

(c)   which is an Abbeyfield Home,

and in this definition, "board" refers to the availability to the claimant in the home in which his accommodation is provided of cooked or prepared food, where the food is made available to him in consequence solely of his paying the charge for the accommodation or any other charge which he is required to pay as a condition of occupying the accommodation, or both those charges and is made available for his consumption without any further charge to him.

(9)   Paragraph (8) shall not apply to residential accommodation of the type referred to in sub-paragraphs (a) to (c) of paragraph (8) where such accommodation is residential

accommodation for the purpose of regulation 9 unless the claimant is a person to whom paragraphs 10, 11 or 12 of Schedule 3 to the Social Security (Care Homes and Independent Hospitals) Regulations 2005 apply.

Modifications

Reg 52 applies as modified by Sch 3 para 9(3)(b) HB&CTB(CP) Regs (see p1803) to a claimant who on 3 October 2005 was someone to whom reg 7(2) of the HB Regs 1987 as then in force applied.

Reg 52 applies as modified by Sch 3 para 9(5)(b) HB&CTB(CP) Regs (see p1803) to a claimant who on 3 October 2005 was someone to whom reg 7(5) of the HB Regs 1987 as then in force applied.

Reg 52 applies as modified by Sch 3 para 9(7)(b) HB&CTB(CP) Regs (see p1804) to a claimant who on 3 October 2005 was someone to whom reg 7(7) of the HB Regs 1987 as then in force applied.

Amendments

1.   Amended by reg 5A(4) of SI 2005 No 2465 as inserted by Sch 2 para 28(5) of SI 2006 No 217 as from 1.4.06.
2.   Amended by art 2 and Sch para 24(2) of SI 2015 No 643 as from 1.4.15.
3.   Amended by art 11(4) of SI 2017 No 901 as from 3.11.17.

Definitions

"capital" – see General Note on this Section.
"claimant" – see reg 2(1).

General Note

This regulation applies to create "tariff income" which is deemed to be generated by capital held by a claimant which is between the upper and lower limits set out in paras (1) and (3) – ie, where s/he has capital insufficient to take her/him over the capital limit. Actual income from assessable capital is usually treated as capital itself under reg 46. For income from disregarded capital, see Sch 5 para 17 and reg 46(4).

Analysis

Paras (1), (6) and (7) set out the normal rule. Where para (4) does not apply to a claimant, and the total capital falling to be assessed under this Section is between £6,000 and £16,000, the claimant is treated as having income of £1 a week from each £250 or part of £250 in excess of £6,000. For example, a claimant has £7,765 assessed under this Part. S/he is treated as receiving £1,750 divided by 250 = 7. £15 left over gives rise to another £1 and so s/he is deemed to have £8 a week income from that capital.

Paras (3) to (9) set out a special rule for certain claimants in "residential accommodation" as defined in paras (8) and (9). By para (5), those who are deemed to be in occupation by relevant provisions in reg 7 also qualify. For these claimants the lower capital limit is increased from £6,000 to £10,000, and they are treated as having weekly tariff income of £1 for each £250, or part thereof, of capital in excess of £10,000.

PART 7
Students

General Note on Part 7

Since 1 September 1990, government policy has been to exclude most, but not all, full-time students from entitlement to HB. This is done by treating them (under reg 56) as not liable to make payments in respect of their dwelling; a person can only be entitled to HB if, among other conditions, s/he *is* liable (or treated as liable) to make such payments: s130 SSCBA. These changes were part of a more general change in the structure of student finance, the aim of which was to provide for students' financial needs wholly through the system of grants and student loans. Educational establishments have further "access funds" to assist students experiencing financial hardship. Full-time students are not generally eligible for IS, ESA or JSA or for UC (except for limited categories).

For further information about other types of financial support available to students, see CPAG's *Student Support and Benefits Handbook: England, Wales and Northern Ireland* and *Benefits for Students in Scotland Handbook*.

Part 7 deals with the following.

(1)   The definitions relevant to the rules for students and student income: reg 53.
(2)   Students entitled to and excluded from entitlement to HB: regs 55 to 58.
(3)   The treatment of student income: regs 59 to 69.

Note that the provisions in Parts 2 to 4 also apply to students subject to the provisions in Part 7: reg 54.

There are no comparable rules for students in the HB(SPC) Regs so claimants covered by those regulations are *not* excluded from entitlement to HB for being students. In addition, student loan and grant income is ignored under those regulations; it does not come within the definition of "income" in reg 29 HB(SPC) Regs.

The excluded students

Reg 56(1) excludes anyone who is a "full-time student" (defined in reg 53) from entitlement to HB subject to certain exceptions listed in reg 56(2). See also reg 55. It must be borne in mind that a claimant may fall within the definition of "full-time student" from the date on which her/his course starts until the day it ends or that s/he abandons it or is dismissed from it: reg 53(2) to (4). This means that the special rules for full-time students can apply even if the claimant is not studying at the material time – eg, during the summer vacation or absences from a course due to illness or pregnancy. For the difficult questions arising for students who have taken time off in the middle of their courses, see the Analysis to reg 56.

The treatment of student claims

Even if a student is not excluded from entitlement to HB by reg 56, s/he must still satisfy the other rules in this Part before qualifying. The general rule is that claims by students will, subject to the special rules in this Part, be decided in the same way as claims by non-students. The special rules can be summarised as follows.

(1) If a full-time student is absent from her/his home where s/he lives to study outside a period of study, then s/he is deemed not to occupy the dwelling, unless the absence is due to hospitalisation: reg 55.

(2) Unless a full-time student is entitled to HB by virtue of the exceptions in reg 56(2), HB is not payable during a period of study in respect of payments made to the student's educational establishment, except in limited circumstances: reg 57.

(3) There are detailed rules for the treatment of the sources of income for students – eg, grants, covenant income, student loans and access funds: regs 59 to 69. Note that education maintenance allowances and 16 to 19 bursaries (and similar payments) paid to young people on certain non-advanced courses are dealt with separately. They are disregarded as income under para 11 of Sch 5 and as capital under para 51 of Sch 6. Career development loans paid under s2 Employment and Training Act 1973 are taken into account as income (reg 41(4)) with provision for some or all of it to be disregarded (Sch 5 para 13).

Claimants with a student partner

The general exclusion of full-time students from HB does not prevent a claimant whose partner is a student from claiming HB. However, the provisions of reg 57 concerning claimants who pay rent to educational establishments apply to such claimants: reg 58.

SECTION 1
General

Interpretation

53.–(1)   In this Part–

"academic year" means the period of twelve months beginning on 1st January, 1st April, 1st July or 1st September according to whether the course in question begins in the winter, the spring, the summer or the autumn respectively but if students are required to begin attending the course during August or September and to continue attending through the autumn, the academic year of the course shall be considered to begin in the autumn rather than the summer;

"access funds" means–

(a) grants made under section 68 of the Further and Higher Education Act 1992 for the purpose of providing funds on a discretionary basis to be paid to students;

(b) grants made under sections 73(a) and (c) and 74(1) of the Education (Scotland) Act 1980; or

(c) grants made under Article 30 of the Education and Libraries (Northern Ireland) Order 1993 or grants, loans or other payments made under Article 5 of the Further Education (Northern Ireland) Order 1997 in each case being grants, or grants, loans or other payments as the case may be, for the purpose of assisting students in financial difficulties;

(d) discretionary payments, known as "learner support funds", which are made available to students in further education by institutions out of funds provided by the [7 [8 Secretary of State under section 14 of the Education Act 2002] [9] under sections 100 and 101 of [8 the Apprenticeships, Skills, Children and Learning Act 2009]]; or

(e) Financial Contingency Funds made available by the [4 Welsh Ministers];

"college of further education" means a college of further education within the meaning of Part I of the Further and Higher Education (Scotland) Act 1992;

[5 "contribution" means–

(a)   any contribution in respect of the income of a student or any person which the Secretary of State, the Scottish Ministers or an education authority takes into account in ascertaining the amount of a student's grant or student loan; or

(b)   any sums, which in determining the amount of a student's allowance or bursary in Scotland under the Education (Scotland) Act 1980, the Scottish Ministers or education authority takes into account being sums which the Scottish Ministers or education authority consider that it is reasonable for the following persons to contribute towards the holder's expenses–

    (i)   the holder of the allowance or bursary;

    (ii)   the holder's parents;

    (iii)   the holder's parent's spouse, civil partner or a person ordinarily living with the holder's parent as if he or she were the spouse or civil partner of that parent; or

    (iv)   the holder's spouse or civil partner;]

"course of study" means any course of study, whether or not it is a sandwich course and whether or not a grant is made for undertaking or attending it;

"covenant income" means the gross income payable to a full-time student under a Deed of Covenant by his parent;

"education authority" means a government department, [⁶ a local authority as defined in section 579 of the Education Act 1996 (interpretation)], a local education authority as defined in section 123 of the Local Government (Scotland) Act 1973, an education and library board established under Article 3 of the Education and Libraries (Northern Ireland) Order 1986, any body which is a research council for the purposes of the Science and Technology Act 1965 or any analogous government department, authority, board or body, of the Channel Islands, Isle of Man or any other country outside Great Britain;

"full-time course of study" means a full-time course of study which–

(a)   is not funded in whole or in part by the [⁷ [⁸ Secretary of State under section 14 of the Education Act 2002] [⁹ or under section 100 of the Apprenticeships, Children, Skills and Learning Act 2009]] or by the [¹ [⁴ Welsh Ministers]] or a full-time course of study which is not funded in whole or in part by the Scottish Ministers at a college of further education or a full-time course of study which is a course of higher education and is funded in whole or in part by the Scottish Ministers;

(b)   is funded in whole or in part by the [⁷ [⁸Secretary of State under section 14 of the Education Act 2002] [⁹ or under section 100 of the Apprenticeships, Children, Skills and Learning Act 2009]] or by the [¹ [⁴ Welsh Ministers]] if it involves more than 16 guided learning hours per week for the student in question, according to the number of guided learning hours per week for that student set out–

    [⁷ (i)   in the case of a course funded by the [⁸ Secretary of State [⁹] in the student's learning agreement signed on behalf of the establishment which is funded by [⁹ the Secretary of State] for the delivery of that course; or]

    (ii)   in the case of a course funded by the [¹ [⁴ Welsh Ministers]], in a document signed on behalf of the establishment which is funded by that Council for the delivery of that course; or

(c)   is not higher education and is funded in whole or in part by the Scottish Ministers at a college of further education and involves–

    (i)   more than 16 hours per week of classroom-based or workshop-based programmed learning under the direct guidance of teaching staff according to the number of hours set out in a document signed on behalf of the college; or

    (ii)   16 hours or less per week of classroom-based or workshop-based programmed learning under the direct guidance of teaching staff and it involves additional hours using structured learning packages supported by the teaching staff where the combined total of hours exceeds 21 hours per week, according to the number of hours set out in a document signed on behalf of the college;

"full-time student" means a person attending or undertaking a full-time course of study and includes a student on a sandwich course;

"grant" (except in the definition of "access funds") means any kind of educational grant or award and includes any scholarship, studentship, exhibition, allowance or bursary but does not include a payment from access funds or any payment to which paragraph 11 of Schedule 5 or [² paragraph 51] of Schedule 6 applies;

"grant income" means–
   (a)   any income by way of a grant;
   (b)   any contribution whether or not it is paid;

"higher education" means higher education within the meaning of Part 2 of the Further and Higher Education (Scotland) Act 1992;

"last day of the course" means–
   (a)   in the case of a qualifying course, the date on which the last day of that course falls or the date on which the final examination relating to that course is completed, whichever is the later;
   (b)   in any other case, the date on which the last day of the final academic term falls in respect of the course in which the student is enrolled;

"period of study" means–
   (a)   in the case of a course of study for one year or less, the period beginning with the start of the course and ending with the last day of the course;
   (b)   in the case of a course of study for more than one year, in the first or, as the case may be, any subsequent year of the course, other than the final year of the course, the period beginning with the start of the course or, as the case may be, that year's start and ending with either–
      [⁵ (i)   the day before the start of the next year of the course in a case where the student's grant or loan is assessed at a rate appropriate to his studying throughout the year or, if he does not have a grant or loan, where a loan would have been assessed at such a rate had he had one; or]
      (ii)   in any other case, the day before the start of the [⁵ normal] summer vacation appropriate to his course;
   (c)   in the final year of a course of study of more than one year, the period beginning with that year's start and ending with the last day of the course;

"periods of experience" means periods of work experience which form part of a sandwich course;

[¹⁰ "postgraduate master's degree loan" means a loan which a student is eligible to receive under the Education (Postgraduate Master's Degree Loans) Regulations 2016;]

"qualifying course" means a qualifying course as defined for the purposes of Parts 2 and 4 of the Jobseeker's Allowance Regulations;

[² "sandwich course" has the meaning prescribed in regulation 2(9) of the Education (Student Support) Regulations 2008, regulation 4(2) of the Education (Student Loans) (Scotland) Regulations 2007 or regulation 2(8) of the Education (Student Support) Regulations (Northern Ireland) 2007, as the case may be;]

"standard maintenance grant" means–
   (a)   except where paragraph (b) or (c) applies, in the case of a student attending or undertaking a course of study at the University of London or an establishment within the area comprising the City of London and the Metropolitan Police District, the amount specified for the time being in paragraph 2(2)(a) of Schedule 2 to the Education (Mandatory Awards) Regulations 2003 ("the 2003 Regulations") for such a student;
   (b)   except where paragraph (c) applies, in the case of a student residing at his parent's home, the amount specified in paragraph 3 thereof;
   (c)   in the case of a student receiving an allowance or bursary under the Education (Scotland) Act 1980, the amount of money specified as "standard maintenance allowance" for the relevant year appropriate for the student set out in the Student Support in Scotland Guide issued by the Student Awards Agency for Scotland,

or its nearest equivalent in the case of a bursary provided by a college of further education or a local education authority [³];

(d)   in any other case, the amount specified in paragraph 2(2) of Schedule 2 to the 2000 Regulations other than in sub-paragraph (a) or (b) thereof;

"student" means a person, other than a person in receipt of a training allowance, who is attending or undertaking–

(a)   a course of study at an educational establishment; or

(b)   a qualifying course;

"student loan" means a loan towards a student's maintenance pursuant to any regulations made under section 22 of the Teaching and Higher Education Act 1998, section 73 of the Education (Scotland) Act 1980 or Article 3 of the Education (Student Support) (Northern Ireland) Order 1998 and shall include, in Scotland, a young student's bursary paid under regulation 4(1)(c) of the [² Students' Allowances (Scotland) Regulations 2007].

(2)   For the purposes of the definition of "full-time student" in paragraph (1), a person shall be regarded as attending or, as the case may be, undertaking a full-time course of study or as being on a sandwich course–

(a)   subject to paragraph (3), in the case of a person attending or undertaking a part of a modular course which would be a full-time course of study for the purposes of this Part, for the period beginning on the day on which that part of the course starts and ending–

(i)   on the last day on which he is registered with the educational establishment as attending or undertaking that part as a full-time course of study; or

(ii)   on such earlier date (if any) as he finally abandons the course or is dismissed from it;

(b)   in any other case, throughout the period beginning on the date on which he starts attending or undertaking the course and ending on the last day of the course or on such earlier date (if any) as he finally abandons it or is dismissed from it.

(3)   For the purposes of sub-paragraph (a) of paragraph (2), the period referred to in that sub-paragraph shall include–

(a)   where a person has failed examinations or has failed to successfully complete a module relating to a period when he was attending or undertaking a part of the course as a full-time course of study, any period in respect of which he attends or undertakes the course for the purpose of retaking those examinations or that module;

(b)   any period of vacation within the period specified in that paragraph or immediately following that period except where the person has registered with the educational establishment to attend or undertake the final module in the course and the vacation immediately follows the last day on which he is required to attend or undertake the course.

(4)   In paragraph (2), "modular course" means a course of study which consists of two or more modules, the successful completion of a specified number of which is required before a person is considered by the educational establishment to have completed the course.

Amendments

1.   Amended by reg 2 of SI 2005 No 3238 as amended by Sch 2 para 31 of SI 2006 No 217 as from 1.4.06.
2.   Amended by reg 3(6) of SI 2008 No 1042 as from 19.5.08.
3.   Amended by reg 6(5) of SI 2008 No 2767 as from 17.11.08.
4.   Amended by reg 5(4) of SI 2008 No 3156 as from 5.1.09.
5.   Substituted by reg 6(6) of SI 2009 No 583 as from 6.4.09.
6.   Amended by art 4 and Sch 3 para 64 of SI 2010 No 1172 as from 5.5.10.
7.   Amended by art 14(3) of SI 2010 No 1941 as from 1.9.10.
8.   Amended by reg 11(3) of SI 2012 No 956 as from 1.5.12.
9.   Amended by art 2 and Sch 3 para 8(3) of SI 2015 No 971 as from 26.5.15.
10.   Inserted by reg 4(2) of SI 2016 No 743 as from 4.8.16.

Analysis

"academic year". This definition is relevant to the treatment of student loans and postgraduate master's degree loans. See reg 64(2) on p500.

"access funds". See reg 65 for the treatment of certain access funds.

"contribution". The definition includes any contribution in respect of the income of the student or any other person taken into account in the assessment of a student's grant or loan or in Scotland, allowance or bursary, including amounts which the student, her/his spouse, civil partner or parents (or in some cases in Scotland, parent's partners) could reasonably be expected to contribute. Note that this allows the reduction in the student's grant or loan on the basis of her/his own income to be treated as a "contribution". Note also that a contribution counts as "grant income" (para (b) of the definition also in reg 53(1)) or loan income (for which see reg 64(4)(a)(ii)) whether or not it is paid. See regs 66 and 67 where the claimant or her/his partner is assessed as liable to make a contribution. See Sch 5 paras 19 and 20 for income disregards where a claimant is making a parental contribution in respect of a student.

"course of study". A course counts as a course of study whether or not it is a sandwich course and whether or not a grant is made for it. For the meaning of a "sandwich course", see below. It must be a course of study, and purely vocational work may not qualify: see, for example, *R(SB) 25/87* which decides that a pupil barrister is not studying; s/he is attending a barrister to assimilate vocational skills. However, where there is active tuition, the fact that the skills are vocational does not prevent the course being a course of study. Many such "courses" may be excluded by the requirement that no training allowance is being received (see the definition of "student" below). So in *R(IS) 19/98* para 11 it was held that a nurse on the Project 2000 scheme who was paid a bursary by the Department of Health during her training was on a course of study. For when a full-time student is treated as attending a full-time course of study, see para (2).

"covenant income". Notice that this covers only income covenanted by a parent, not grandparent, etc and that the beneficiary must be a "full-time student" (defined below). This definition refers to the gross amount of the payment. See regs 60 and 61 for the calculation of covenant income.

"full-time course of study". See the Analysis of "full-time student" below.

"full-time student". Under the definition, a full-time student "means a person attending or undertaking a full-time course of study and includes a student on a sandwich course". "Student", "course of study", "full-time course of study" and "sandwich course" are all defined in reg 53(1). Note that a claimant cannot be a "student" if s/he is receiving a training allowance. If the claimant is not on a "course of study", s/he cannot be affected by the general exclusion of students from HB under reg 56(1).

The phrase "full-time course of study" is defined as comprising three categories of course.

(1) Sub-para (b) covers students whose courses at colleges of further education (CFEs) are funded in whole or in part by the Secretary of State under s14 Education Act 2002 or s100 of the Apprenticeships, Children, Skills and Learning Act 2009 or by the Welsh Ministers as appropriate. For such students, the categorisation of the course depends on the number of guided learning hours a week. A course of more than 16 guided learning hours a week is full-time. The number of guided learning hours a student does is set out in her/his learning agreement which is signed by the student and the college.

Broadly, guided learning hours are the times when a member of staff is present to give specific guidance towards the learning aim being studied on a programme, including lectures, tutorials and supervised study in eg, open learning centres or learning workshops and time spent by staff assessing a learner's achievements where the learner is present – eg, in the assessment of competence for National Vocational Qualifications. CFEs provide a document, called a learning agreement in England, which makes it clear how many guided learning hours a course entails.

(2) Sub-para (c) covers Scottish students on courses at a college of further education that are not higher education and are funded in whole or in part by the Scottish Ministers. For such students, the categorisation of a course depends on the number of hours of classroom-based or workshop-based "programmed learning" under the direct guidance of a teacher. A course of more than 16 hours a week is full-time. Also full-time is a course of more than 21 hours a week, 16 or less of which involve classroom-based or workshop-based "programmed learning" and the rest of which involve structured learning supported by a teacher. As in England and Wales, the CFE provides a document stating the number of hours of "learning" per week.

(3) Sub-para (a) covers students on full-time courses of study *not* funded in whole or in part by the Secretary of State under s14 Education Act 2002 or s100 Apprenticeships, Children, Skills and Learning Act 2009 or by the Welsh Ministers as appropriate. It also covers Scottish students on full-time courses of study at CFEs that are not higher education and *not* funded in whole or in part by the Scottish Ministers or which are courses of higher education funded in whole or in part by the Scottish Ministers.

In the first two categories, whether someone counts as a full- or part-time student depends on her/his personal pattern of attendance on the course. In the third category, this depends on the course as a whole.

The question as to how an authority is to judge whether a further or higher education course is full- or part-time arises frequently in courses coming under the third category (sub-para (a)). In the absence of any definition, local authorities should seek the advice of the establishment where the student is studying. It is suggested that the view of the establishment as to whether the course is full-time or part-time is not conclusive, but it may require weighty evidence to rebut it. The assessment is based on the amount of time that is normally expected of a student on the course, not the time that the individual claimant devotes to her/his studies: *R(SB) 41/83* paras 11–12. A good indicator of whether a course is full-time, in relation to further or higher education courses, is whether or not the student is in receipt of a loan, since these are generally only available to full-time students. All the points in this paragraph were confirmed by the Court of Appeal in dismissing an application for leave to appeal in *Denton v Chief Adjudication Officer* [1999] ELR 86 at 87G-H.

Flexible (modular) courses. August 2000 reforms aimed to cope with the problems with modular courses posed by *Chief Adjudication Officer v Webber* [1998] 1 WLR 625 at 633E, CA (reported as *R(IS) 15/98*), and *R(IS) 1/00* paras 14–17. Paras (2) to (4) of reg 53 deal with full-time students on modular courses. "Modular course" is defined in para (4) as a course of study of two or more modules, a specified number of which the student must complete successfully before the educational establishment considers her/him to have completed the course.

If the part of the modular course the student is attending "would be a full-time course of study" (see above), para (2)(a) deems her/him to be a full-time student from the day on which that part of the course began until the last day s/he is registered with the educational establishment as attending or undertaking that part as a full-time course or until s/he abandons the course or is dismissed from it. Included are periods of attendance to retake examinations or the module: para (3)(a). Also included are periods of vacation within the module as well as vacation that immediately follows it, unless this is the last day on which the student is required to attend or undertake the course: para (3)(b).

The effect of the rules is that a claimant should not come within the definition of "full-time student" while studying part-time on a modular course or where s/he has changed from full-time to part-time or has taken time out from the course.

"grant" means any kind of educational grant or award other than a payment from "access funds" or an education maintenance allowance or a 16 to 19 bursary or other allowance which can be disregarded as income under Sch 5 para 11 or as capital under Sch 6 para 51 HB Regs. GM Annex A C2.11 advises local authorities not to include payments derived from funds made available by the Secretary of State to assist students in financial difficulties under s100 Education Act 1944, s65 Further and Higher Education Act 1992, s73 Education (Scotland) Act 1980 or s40 Further and Higher Education (Scotland) Act 1992.

There are conflicting decisions of the commissioners in relation to whether "award" can include loans made to students by educational authorities. In *R(SB) 20/83* para 10(3), it was held that it could, but in *R(IS) 16/95* para 10 it was pointed out that the word usually connoted an absolute gift when used in an educational context. It is suggested that this is plainly right in view of the examples of sources of income such as scholarships, which are almost invariably in the nature of gifts rather than loans. Likewise, it cannot apply to bank loans or overdrafts obtained by students. Note the special provisions for assessing income from student loans in reg 64.

"grant income". A contribution (see above) is deemed to have been received by the student whether paid or not. Note that when a student abandons a course, s/he falls under an obligation to repay any grant made by the education authority. The amount of the grant which is repayable cannot be treated as income from that date: *R(IS) 5/99* para 12. Changes were made to the IS scheme to provide for such treatment, but no corresponding amendments were made to the HB regulations. The commissioner's decision was upheld on a different basis by the Court of Appeal in *Chief Adjudication Officer v Leeves* [1999] FLR 90, CA; reported as *R(IS) 5/99*. Potter LJ held that once the education authority demanded repayment of an ascertained sum, the amount of the grant could not be treated as income from that date.

"last day of the course". This clarifies the treatment of those cases where, for example, the student is able to leave the course a few weeks early after having taken final exams. For "qualifying courses" (see below), since these are not organised along the lines of terms, the last day of the course is the later of the date of the final exam or the last day of the course. In other cases "the last day of the course" always means the date on which the last day of the final academic term is scheduled to fall and not the earlier date on which the student actually left.

Note that GM C2.352-354 says that full-time postgraduate students cease to be treated as full-time students when their course is completed. The guidance goes on to say that whether such a student who is doing further research or writing a thesis after this should be regarded as a full-time student depends on the amount of work being undertaken, not on the fact that the course was full-time.

"period of study". In a "course of study" (see above) of more than one year, the date on which a "period of study" ends depends on whether grants or loans for that course are assessed on the basis of a full year's study, or whether no grant or loan is assessed for the summer vacation. In the latter case, which will be the norm, it ends at the beginning of that vacation and starts again when the vacation ends. This is the case whether or not the student in question receives a grant or loan. During the final year of a course, the "period of study" always ends on "the last day of the course" (see above). See further the Analysis to regs 55, 56 and 57.

"periods of experience". "Periods of work experience", the definition of which is, for England for example, found in reg 2 Education (Student Support) Regulations 2011 SI No.1986, means–

"(a)   periods of industrial, professional or commercial experience associated with full-time study at an institution but at a place outside the institution,

(b)   periods during which a student is employed and residing in a country whose language is one that he is studying for his course (provided that the period of residence in that country is a requirement of his course and the study of one or more modern languages accounts for not less than one half of the total time spent studying on the course)."

"qualifying course". These courses form part of the elaborate package aimed at assisting the long-term unemployed. The definition of such a course is to be found in reg 17A(7) Jobseeker's Allowance Regulations 1996 (JSA Regs). Note that the regulations only apply to those claiming old-style JSA – ie, those who do not come under the UC system. Certain claimants on such courses may continue to receive JSA throughout the period of study. Three conditions must be fulfilled.

(1)   It must be an "employment-related course". By reg 1(3) JSA Regs, this is defined as "a course the purpose of which is to assist persons to acquire or enhance skills required for employment, for seeking employment or for a particular occupation".

(2)   It must last for no more than 12 consecutive months.

(3)   It must be a course of an appropriate level. The definition of what is an appropriate level is different in England and Wales on one hand and Scotland on the other. In England and Wales, Sch 2 Further and Higher Education Act 1992 provides the definition, but note that Sch 2 was repealed by the Learnings and Skills Act 2000. Sch 2 lists vocational courses approved by the Secretary of State, GCSE and A-Level courses, preparation for further education, preparatory courses for the foregoing, English and Welsh classes, basic mathematics courses, and courses teaching independent living and communication skills. In Scotland, s6 Further and Higher Education (Scotland) Act 1992 lists courses that: prepare people for vocational qualifications, prepare for a qualification awarded by the Scottish Qualifications Authority or, for GCE exams, assist those with learning difficulties, assist access to higher education, assist with English for those for whom it is not their first language, and preparatory courses covering the above. Note that there are wide powers to add categories of course. Not all such courses are capable of fulfilling the first condition above. Note also that by reg 17A(8) JSA Regs, any courses of a higher standard may nonetheless be determined to be qualifying courses even if they do not fall within the scope of the definition above.

"sandwich course". Note that the current regulations for England are the Education (Student Support) Regulations 2011 SI No.1986. The definition in the 2008 regulations cited, says that a course is a sandwich course if it is not a course for the initial training of teachers, it consists of alternate periods of full-time study in an institution and periods of work experience, and taking the course as a whole, the student attends the periods of full-time study for an average of not less than 18 weeks in each year. For the purposes of calculating attendance, the course is treated as beginning with the first period of full-time study and ending with the last such period.

"student". A person in receipt of a training allowance does not come within the definition of student. For "training allowance", see reg 2(1). The definition of student includes those on a "course of study" or a "qualifying course": see above.

Paras (2) to (4). By para (2), a full-time student is treated as attending the course throughout all vacations as well as during the term, or until s/he abandons or is dismissed from the course if earlier. The effect of this is partly offset by the use of the phrase "period of study" in various regulations: see above. See also the analysis of "course of study" and the discussion on flexible (modular) courses above.

Treatment of students

54.   The provisions of Parts 2, 3 and 4 (entitlement to housing benefit, payments in respect of a dwelling, membership of a family) shall have effect in relation to students subject to the following provisions of this Part.

General Note

See General Note to Part 7 on p479. These regulations also affect Part 6.

Analysis

In *R (Naghshbandi) v Camden LBC* [2001] EWHC Admin 813; (2003) HLR 280, CA, the court was considering the inter-relationship between Pts II and VII of the HB Regs 1987 (now Pts 2 and 7 HB Regs). The claimant had an adult son living in his household who was a student. There were a total of five members of the family who shared the rent liability and the issue was whether reg 48A(1) HB Regs 1987 (now reg 56(1) HB Regs) operated to deem the son not to be liable for rent and so to exclude him from the apportionment of the rent between those liable under reg 10(5) HB Regs 1987 (now reg 12B(4) HB Regs). The council and Rafferty J decided that the deemed non-liability did not apply to reg 10(5).

On appeal, the Secretary of State intervened to support the council's position. Counsel for the Secretary of State argued that the rule had to be read as if it said "shall have effect in relation to students who are claimants for housing benefit". The court accepted that argument and dismissed the claimant's appeal. But reading reg 54 in this way produces some potentially odd results. See the commentary to regs 7(6)(b) and 55.

SECTION 2
Entitlement and payments in respect of a dwelling

General Note on Section 2
See the General Note on this Part on p479. The rules in Parts 2, 3 and 4 apply to students, but they are modified as set out below.
This should be read together with reg 7(3) and (6)(b) (see p257), which also makes provision for students.

Occupying a dwelling as a person's home
55.–(1)   Subject to paragraph (2), a full-time student shall not be treated as occupying a dwelling as his home during any benefit week outside the period of study if he is absent from it for the whole of that week and if the main purpose of his occupation during the period of study would be to facilitate attendance on his course.

(2)   The provisions of paragraph (1) shall not apply to any absence occasioned by the need to enter hospital for treatment.

Definitions
"benefit week" – see reg 2(1).
"dwelling" – see reg 2(4).
"full-time student" – see reg 53.
"period of study" – see reg 53.
"student" – see reg 53.

General Note
To qualify for HB, a claimant must be liable to make payments in respect of a dwelling which s/he occupies as her/his home: s130 SSCBA. Thus, even if a full-time student is able to claim HB, this regulation prevents her/him claiming in respect of accommodation occupied to enable her/him to attend the course, for any whole week s/he is absent from it outside her/his period of study (defined in reg 53).
This regulation does not apply where the student is in hospital for treatment: para (2).
It is suggested that where the student is not the claimant, reg 55 has no application because the application of this Part is limited to cases where the student is the claimant: *R (Naghshbandi) v Camden LBC* [2001] EWHC Admin 813; (2003) HLR 280, CA. Accordingly where a student's partner claims HB both in respect of the normal home and the student accommodation under reg 7(6)(b), HB remains payable during the vacations.

Analysis
Para (1). For the meaning of "occupying a dwelling as his home", see reg 7 and particularly reg 7(3) and (6)(b) for special rules relating to students.
The student is only deemed *not* to be occupying the accommodation if the "main purpose" of her/his occupation during the "period of study" is to facilitate her/his attendance on the course – eg, if s/he would not normally be living there were it not for the course. So the provision cannot apply to a student who would stay in her/his term-time residence even if not attending a course, or who has other, equally important, reasons for staying at that place. Examples include where the claimant is fully independent of, does not have, or is estranged from her/his parents, or where s/he was already settled in the accommodation prior to study. GM C2.73 states that authorities may "readily accept" that the claimant's main purpose of residence is not study where the student's dependent children are living with her/him or where the student has no other accommodation which could be regarded as her/his home. Where the student is under 25, whether or not the student has parents is also relevant. Authorities should "look carefully" at other categories of case: GM C2.74.
Para (2). "Hospital" is not defined. It is suggested that it can cover a wider range of residential treatment than that offered by the NHS. It may cover private treatment and clinics where alternative medicine is practised, provided that there is a respectable medical basis for the treatment being given.

Full-time students to be treated as not liable to make payments in respect of a dwelling
56.–(1)   A full-time student shall be treated as if he were not liable to make payments in respect of a dwelling.

(2)   Paragraph (1) shall not apply to a full-time student–

(a)   who is a person on income support[³, an income-based jobseeker's allowance or an income-related employment and support allowance];

[⁸ (aa) who is a person on universal credit, except where the award of universal credit to that person includes an amount in respect of a liability to make payments in respect of the accommodation they occupy as their home, in accordance with section 11 of the Welfare Reform Act 2012 (housing costs);]

(b) who is a lone parent;

(c) whose applicable amount would, but for paragraph (1), include the [²] disability premium or severe disability premium;

(d) whose applicable amount would include the disability premium but for his being treated as capable of work by virtue of a determination made in accordance with regulations made under section 171E of the Act;

(e) who is, or is treated as, incapable of work and has been so incapable, or has been so treated as incapable, of work in accordance with the provisions of, and regulations made under, Part 12A of the Act (incapacity for work) for a continuous period of not less than 196 days; and for this purpose any two or more separate periods separated by a break of not more than 56 days shall be treated as one continuous period;

[³ (ea) who has, or is treated as having, limited capability for work and has had, or been treated as having, limited capability for work in accordance with the Employment and Support Allowance Regulations [⁷ or the Employment and Support Allowance Regulations 2013] for a continuous period of not less than 196 days and for this purpose any two or more separate periods separated by a break of not more than 84 days must be treated as one continuous period;]

(f) who has a partner who is also a full-time student, if he or that partner is treated as responsible for a child or young person;

(g) who is a single claimant with whom a child is–

    (i) placed by a local authority or voluntary organisation under [⁹ section 22C(2)] or section 59(1)(a) of the Children Act 1989 (provision of accommodation and maintenance); [⁹

    (ia) in Wales, placed by a local authority under section 81(2) of the Social Services and Well-being (Wales) Act 2014; or]

    (ii) in Scotland, boarded out by a local authority or voluntary organisation within the meaning of the Social Work (Scotland) Act 1968;

[¹ [⁶ (h) who is–

    (i) aged under 21 and whose course of study is not a course of higher education;

    (ii) aged 21 and attained that age during a course of study which is not a course of higher education; or

    (iii) a qualifying young person or child within the meaning of section 142 of the Act (child and qualifying young person);]] or

(i) in respect of whom–

    (i) a supplementary requirement has been determined under paragraph 9 of Part 2 of Schedule 2 to the Education (Mandatory Awards) Regulations 2003; or

    [² (ii) an allowance or, as the case may be, bursary has been granted which includes a sum under paragraph (1)(d) of regulation 4 of the Students' Allowances (Scotland) Regulations 2007 or, as the case may be, under paragraph (1)(d) of regulation 4 of the Education Authority Bursaries (Scotland) Regulations 2007, in respect of expenses incurred; or]

    (iii) a payment has been made under section 2 of the Education Act 1962 or under, or by virtue of regulations made under, the Teaching and Higher Education Act 1998; or

    (iv) a grant has been made under [² regulation 37 of the Education (Student Support) Regulations 2008] or under [² regulation 39 of the Education (Student Support) Regulations (Northern Ireland) 2007]; or

    (v) a supplementary requirement has been determined under paragraph 9 of Schedule 6 to the [² Students Awards Regulations (Northern Ireland) 2003] or a payment has been made under Article 50(3) of the Education and Libraries (Northern Ireland) Order 1986,

on account of his disability by reason of deafness; or

(j)   who–
    (i)   immediately before 1st September 1990 was in receipt of income support by virtue of paragraph 7 of Schedule 1 to the Income Support (General) Regulations 1987 as then in force; or
    (ii) on or after that date makes a claim for income support or housing benefit (or both) and at any time during the period of 18 months immediately preceding the date of that claim was in receipt of income support either by virtue of that paragraph or regulation 13(2)(b) of those Regulations,
but this sub-paragraph shall cease to apply where the person has ceased to be in receipt of income support for a continuous period of 18 months or more.

[⁴ [⁶ (2A)   Paragraph (2)(h)(ii) only applies to a claimant until the end of the course during which the claimant attained the age of 21.]]

(3)   For the purposes of paragraph (2), once paragraph (2)(e) applies to a full-time student, if he then ceases, for a period of 56 days or less, to be incapable, or to be treated as incapable, of work, that paragraph shall, on his again becoming so incapable, or so treated as incapable, of work at the end of that period, immediately thereafter apply to him for so long as he remains incapable, or is treated as remaining incapable, of work.

(4)   In paragraph (2)(h) reference to a course of higher education is a reference to a course of any description mentioned in Schedule 6 to the Education Reform Act 1988 [²].

(5)   A full-time student to whom sub-paragraph (i) of paragraph (2) applies shall be treated as satisfying that sub-paragraph from the date on which he made a request for the supplementary requirement, allowance, bursary or payment, as the case may be.

(6)   Paragraph (1) shall not apply to a full-time student for the period specified in paragraph (7) if–
(a)   at any time during an academic year, with the consent of the relevant education establishment, he ceases to attend or undertake a course because he is–
    (i)   engaged in caring for another person; or
    (ii) ill;
(b)   he has subsequently ceased to be engaged in caring for that person or, as the case may be, he has subsequently recovered from that illness; and
(c)   he is not eligible for a grant or a student loan in respect of the period specified in paragraph (7).

(7)   The period specified for the purposes of paragraph (6) is the period not exceeding one year beginning on the day on which he ceased to be engaged in caring for that other person or, as the case may be, the day on which he recovered from that illness and ending on the day before–
(a)   the day on which he resumes attending or undertaking the course; or
(b)   the day from which the relevant educational establishment has agreed that he may resume attending or undertaking the course,
whichever shall first occur.

Amendments

1.   Inserted by reg 4(3) of SI 2006 No 718 as from 10.4.06.
2.   Amended by reg 3(7) of SI 2008 No 1042 as from 19.5.08.
3.   Amended by reg 17 of SI 2008 No 1082 as from 27.10.08.
4.   Amended by reg 6(7) of SI 2009 No 583 as from 6.4.09.
5.   Amended by reg 8(7) of SI 2010 No 641 as from 1.4.10 (5.4.10 where rent payable weekly or in multiples of a week).
6.   Amended by reg 12 of SI 2012 No 757 as from 1.4.12 (2.4.12 where rent payable weekly or in multiples of a week).
7.   Amended by reg 35(6) of SI 2013 No 630 as from 29.4.13.
8.   Inserted by reg 7(5) of SI 2013 No 2070 as from 28.10.13.
9.   Amended by arts 11(5) and 25(3) of SI 2017 No 901 as from 3.11.17.

Definitions

"disability premium" – see para 12 Sch 3.
"full-time student" – see reg 53.
"an income-based jobseeker's allowance" – see reg 2(1).
"lone parent" – see reg 2(1).

"partner" – see reg 2(1).
"person on income support" – see reg 2(1).
"person on an income-based jobseeker's allowance" – see reg 2(3).
"person on an income-related employment and support allowance" – see reg 2(3A).
"person on universal credit" – see reg 2(3B).
"responsible for a child or young person" – see reg 20.
"severe disability premium" – see para 14 Sch 3.
"single claimant" – see reg 2(1).
"student" – see reg 53.

General Note

To qualify for HB, a claimant must be liable or treated as liable to make payments in respect of her/his dwelling (see s130(1)(a) SSCBA 1992 and reg 8 on p8 and p273). Para (1) seeks to exclude most full-time students from entitlement to HB by treating them as not liable to make payments in respect of their dwelling. See the Analysis on p484 for the difficult question of what a full-time student is. Paras (2) to (7) define the exceptions.

If someone comes within the definition of full-time student, s/he is then treated as attending or undertaking a full-time course of study for the duration of the course or until s/he abandons the course or is dismissed from it: reg 53(2). In limited circumstances, claims for HB can be made during breaks from study: paras (6) and (7).

Analysis

Para (1): The general exclusion

A "full-time student" is treated as not liable to make payments in respect of a dwelling by para (1). Note that even if the student falls within the exclusion, her/his partner can be treated as liable to make payments in respect of the dwelling (and can therefore qualify for HB) unless s/he is also an excluded student: see reg 8(1)(e) on p273. The definition of "full-time student" is in reg 53(1). See p484 for a discussion. If the claimant does not come withing the definition, s/he cannot be affected by the general exclusion.

Note that unlike with IS and JSA, there are no special rules for those in "relevant education" (essentially full-time non-advanced education for those under 20 – eg, see s124(1)(d) SSCBA 1992 and reg 12 Income Support (General) Regulations 1987 SI No.1967). For this reason, a young person might be able to claim HB while in "relevant education" even if s/he cannot claim IS or JSA.

Paras (2) to (7): The exceptions

Para (2) exempts the following categories of "full-time student" from the general exclusion from HB provided for by para (1).

(1)   Those **on IS, income-based JSA or income-related ESA**: sub-para (a). Once the claimant shows that s/he is on IS, income-based JSA or income-related ESA, the authority is not entitled to treat the claimant as a full-time student not liable to make payments in respect of a dwelling. It is not entitled to look into the position for itself: compare the income and capital case of *R v Penwith DC ex p Menear* (1991) 24 HLR 115, QBD. However, in *R v South Ribble DC HBRB ex p Hamilton* (2000) 33 HLR 102, CA, the Court of Appeal confirmed that the definition of "person on income support" must be read as a person lawfully in receipt of IS. See also the discussion of *SD v Newcastle City Council (HB)* [2010] UKUT 306 (AAC) on p420. If the authority suspects that the claimant should not be receiving IS, income-based JSA or income-related ESA, it ought to award HB, but could then suspend payment under reg 11 D&A Regs pending a query with the DWP. For a full discussion of *Menear* and *Hamilton*, see the General Note to Part 6 on p419. See also the discussion on the definitions of "person on income-based JSA" and "person on income-related ESA" on p247.

(2)   Those **on UC**, other than where the UC includes a housing costs element for the accommodation occupied as a home: sub-para (aa). A person is generally precluded from entitlement to HB if entitled to UC: the Universal Credit (Transitional Provisions) Regulations 2014 SI No.1230 (the UC(TP) Regs 2014 – see p1857). However, a person entitled to UC living in "specified accommodation" (specified types of supported accommodation, or specified types of temporary accommodation for those who have left home as a result of domestic violence) or "temporary accommodation" (specified types of homeless accommodation) may qualify for HB in respect of that accommodation: regs 5(2)(a) and 6(8) UC(TP) Regs 2014. Sub-para (aa), allows a student on UC who is living in "specified accommodation" or "temporary accommodation" to qualify for HB for that accommodation. "Specified accommodation" is defined in reg 2 of the UC(TP) Regs 2014 by reference to the definition in Sch 1 para 3A of the UC Regs which is broadly the same as that in reg 75H HB Regs. "Temporary accommodation" is defined in reg 2 UC(TP) Regs 2014 by reference to Sch 1 para 3B of the UC Regs. See reg 7 if the student is a member of a couple who are living separately.

(3)   **Lone parents** (defined in reg 2(1)) **and lone foster parents** where the child has been formally placed or boarded out with them by a local authority or voluntary organisation (also defined in reg 2(1)): sub-paras (b) and (g).

(4)   Full-time students whose **applicable amount would include the disability or severe disability premium**: sub-para (c). Note that on the wording of sub-para (c), this exception would appear to apply to

a full-time student whose applicable amount would include one of the premiums listed on the basis of her/his partner's circumstances, even if it would not include one of these based on the student's.

Now, a student cannot usually fall within this exception unless s/he qualifies for a severe disability premium, or s/he qualifies for a disability premium for a reason other than incapacity for work – eg, receipt of a qualifying benefit such as DLA or PIP. From 27 October 2008, new claims for IS "on the grounds of disability", IB and SDA (benefits based on incapacity for work) were only possible in limited cases and existing claimants of those benefits have almost all been transferred to ESA (a benefit based on limited capability for work). Any remaining claimants were to be transferred by April 2018. Thus few, if any, claimants will now qualify for the disability premium on grounds of incapacity for work. Note that those who did qualify on the grounds of incapacity, who were not terminally ill did not normally qualify for disability premium on this basis until they had been incapable of work for 364 days: see Sch 3 para 13(1)(b)(ii). For a discussion on who may have qualified for a disability premium on the basis of incapacity for work after 27 October 2008, see the analysis to Sch 3 para 13 on p638.

A claimant who has (or is treated as having) limited capability for work (eg, s/he is claiming ESA or NI credits for limited capability for work) cannot ever qualify for a disability premium, even if s/he is in receipt of DLA or PIP (see Sch 3 para 13(9) on p637) so cannot fall within this exception unless s/he qualifies for the severe disability premium. The student may instead qualify under sub-paras (e) or (ea). However, note that a student cannot qualify under those sub-paragraphs until s/he has been incapable of work, or has had limited capability for work (or has been treated as either), for 196 days. Thus, if a claimant is receiving DLA and would only be exempt from the general exclusion from HB because s/he qualifies for a disability premium, it may be advisable not to claim ESA – eg, if s/he would not be eligible for income-related ESA while studying (and therefore would not come within sub-para (a)), s/he would not come within para (ea) for 196 days.

(5)   Full-time students who **would be entitled to a disability premium but for being treated as capable of work** under specified provisions: sub-para (d). See above for the position on claims on grounds of incapacity for work from 27 October 2008. In situations where a DWP decision maker had made a determination under reg 18 Social Security (Incapacity for Work) Regulations 1995 (ie, where the claimant was disqualified from receiving benefit due to misconduct or failure to accept treatment), if the student was *actually* incapable of work, the determination was to be ignored. See also the discussion of sub-para (c) above.

(6)   Full-time students who who **have (or have been treated as having) limited capability for work, or who have been (or have been treated as) incapable of work for a period of not less than 196 days**: sub-paras (e) and (ea). See above for the position on claims on grounds of incapacity for work from 27 October 2008. In determining whether there has been limited capability or incapacity for work for 196 days, a number of periods may be added together if there are not more than 84 days (in the case of limited capability for work) or 56 days (in the case of incapacity for work) between them.

Para (3) simply put it beyond doubt that once the 196-day period had been attained, if the claimant became capable of work and then became incapable again within 56 days, s/he fell within sub-para (e) without having to build up a further period of 196 days first. It is suggested that on the wording of para (e), para (3) was not necessary. See also the discussion of sub-para (c) above.

The starting date for calculating the period will generally be the date shown on the first medical certificate furnished by the claimant. Such certificates can be granted retrospectively. The decision as to whether a claimant has or is treated as having limited capability for work, or is incapable or is treated as incapable of work, is one for the DWP. Until a decision is made as to whether a claimant has limited capability for work, s/he can be treated as having it under reg 30 ESA Regs 2008 or reg 26 ESA Regs 2013 pending the decision if s/he supplies medical certificates. Although it is now only of historic relevance, under reg 28 Social Security (Incapacity for Work) Regulations 1995, until the decision maker applied the "personal capability assessment" to the claimant, it could be deemed to be satisfied by virtue of the fact that medical certificates were being supplied: see the discussion of sub-para (c) above and the analysis to Sch 3 para 13 on p638. Note also the transitional protection in Sch 3 paras 2 and 3 HB&CTB(CP) Regs (see p1774).

(7)   A **full-time student claimant with a full-time student partner if either is "treated as responsible for a child or young person"**, as to which see regs 19 and 20: sub-para (f).

(8)   Claimants **under the age of 21, or** who are aged 21 and **attained that age during a course of study**, who are not on a course of higher education or claimants who are **qualifying young people or children within the meaning of s142 SSCBA 1992**: sub-para (h). In the case of a claimant aged 21 not on a course of higher education, this only applies until the end of the course during which s/he attained that age: para (2A).

"Higher education" is defined in para (4) by reference to Sch 6 Education Reform Act 1988. This includes the following types of course: teacher and youth worker training, first and postgraduate degree courses, HND and HNC courses as well as courses at a higher level in preparation for a professional qualification. See GM C2 Annex A C2.12–14 for a list of the types of courses regarded as providing higher education.

"Qualifying young person" is defined by regs 2 to 7 Child Benefit (General) Regulations 2006 SI No 223. It includes certain young people aged at least 16 but under 20 on full-time courses of non-advanced education or in approved training and some who have left courses or training. They must have begun their course or training (or be enrolled or accepted on it) before reaching the age of 19. For further information, see CPAG's *Welfare Benefits and Tax Credits Handbook*.

(9)   Certain categories of students **entitled to disabled students allowance or a payment under the discretionary awards scheme** on the same basis **orand the equivalents available in Scotland and Northern Ireland, because they are deaf**: sub-para (i). This includes cases where the underlying conditions for the disabled students allowance are satisfied but no actual payment is made as a result of means-testing parental income, since what is required is that an additional requirement has been determined by the education authority, not that it has been paid. Note that this exception takes effect from the date of application for the payment: para (5).

(10)   Certain disabled students who **fulfill either of two criteria in relation to receipt of IS**: sub-para (j). This exception ensured that disabled students who were entitled to IS under the rules as they were prior to 1 September 1990 continued to qualify for HB. It is therefore unlikely that there are any students to whom this exception would still apply. For details, see p374 of the 13th edition.

Paras (6) and (7): Breaks from study

A question which has caused acute controversy was whether students who take time out in the middle of their courses, for whatever reason, are deemed to retain the status of a full-time student for the period until they return to their courses. August 2000 reforms softened the harshest aspects of the treatment of such students, which had generated particularly sharp judicial criticism. See pp277–79 of the 12th edition for the caselaw in relation to the old provisions.

For the current rules, the starting point is to reproduce the definition of "full-time student" from reg 53. "Full-time student" means a person attending or undertaking a full-time course of study and includes a student on a sandwich course. For the purposes of the definition, someone continues to be treated as a undertaking a full-time course of study (or as being on a sandwich course) until the last day of the course or on such earlier date as s/he abandons or is dismissed from the course: reg 53(2) to (4).

This differs from the situation where someone completes a course and is to start another. In *R(IS) 1/96*, the claimant was studying to be an architect. He had completed his university degree course, but then was to undertake a work placement prior to a further period of postgraduate study. Commissioner Howell said that as a matter of ordinary language "a course" is "a unified sequence of study, tuition and/or practical training, undertaken at or by arrangement with the education or training establishment, and intended to lead to one or more qualifications obtained on its completion," including modular courses leading to a single degree. He said that "a person who aspires to practice in a profession that requires more than one separately obtained qualification for which educational establishments do not provide a single sequence of tuition and/or experience, starts and completes one "course" and then moves on to another, rather than being engaged on one continuous "course" gaining intermediate qualifications and experience along the way": para 17. Thus if such a claimant has completed one course, s/he is not a full-time student in the period until s/he starts the next course. Note, however, the special rules for "sandwich courses".

Paras (6) and (7) of reg 56 provide welcome relief for full-time students who have to temporarily leave their courses with the consent of the educational establishment, due to illness or through having to care for another person. Such students cannot generally claim HB while caring or ill (however note the exceptions under paras (2)(c) to (ea)), but can when the illness or caring responsibilities come to an end. The relief is available for a period of up to one year, so long as the student is not eligible for a grant or loan in respect of the period. The period starts on the day the illness or caring ceased and ends on the earlier of the day the student resumes the course or the day from which the educational establishment has agreed s/he could do so: para (7). "Caring for another person" in sub-para (6)(a)(i) is not further defined. It is suggested that it is not necessary, for example, for the carer to fulfil the conditions of entitlement to carer's allowance or to be caring for a person in any specific circumstances. Nor does the sub-para set out the number of hours a person would have to be caring for another.

What, however, of other breaks from study?

Pregnancy. If someone is taking time-out from study because of pregnancy, the rules do not provide relief. The JSA rules were challenged on the grounds that they directly discriminated against women. However, the Court of Appeal in *Secretary of State for Social Security v Walter* [2002] ICR 540 (reported as *R(JSA) 3/02*) rejected the arguments for the claimant. The Court did not, however, consider or decide on whether the rules were *indirectly* discriminatory (ie, whether they had a disproportionate impact on women) nor if such discrimination was proved, whether it could be objectively justified. It also did not consider whether the rules were incompatible with the Human Rights Act.

CJSA 825/2004 did consider the question of indirect discrimination in relation to a pregnant student who had taken leave of absence from her course but only EU law was raised. The commissioner held that the relevant pools for comparison were (1) male students who had taken leave of absence and (2) female students who had taken such leave, but that there was no statistical evidence to demonstrate that the latter class were disproportionately affected by the legislation.

Human Rights Act arguments *were* considered by the Upper Tribunal in *CM v SSWP* [2009] UKUT 43 (AAC), R(IS) 7/09. The claimant argued that the provision preventing a pregnant student claiming IS while taking a leave of absence from her course was indirectly discriminatory against women, alternatively pregnant women, because only women could become pregnant. Judge Lloyd Davies refused the claimant's appeal. He held as follows.

(1)   The right to claim a non-contributory social security benefit was within the scope or ambit of Art 1 of Protocol 1 to the European Convention on Human Rights so as to enable Art 14 to be engaged: *R (RJM) v SSWP* [2008] UKHL 63.

(2)   The denial of the claimant's claim was not within the ambit of Art 2 of Protocol 1 (right to education). The claimant had argued that the denial of IS to pregnant intercalating students meant that such students would be more likely to be forced to abandon their course (rather than take a leave of absence) so as to have means of subsistence. However, the claimant did not in fact abandon her course, but chose to intercalate. The judge therefore decided that there had been no denial of the right of education to the claimant (whose personal circumstances caused her to interrupt her course).

(3)   Statistics are not a necessary pre-condition for indirect discrimination to be adduced for the purposes of Art 14, taken with Art 1 of Protocol 1. Pregnancy is an "other status" for the purposes of Art 14. Rather than seeking to establish comparators, it is better to concentrate on the reasons for the difference in treatment and whether they amount to an objective and reasonable justification: *AL (Serbia) v Home Secretary* [2008] HL 42.

(4)   Having considered whether there was an objective and reasonable justification for the policy of disentitling pregnant intercalating students from IS (thereby distinguishing them from students who intercalate for other reasons), the judge held that there was. He said that, notwithstanding the lack of mention of pregnancy, "the policy behind the regulatory structure is that students who intercalate for essentially transient reasons (even through no fault of their own) should not receive benefit, but should rely on such support as might be available from the education authorities concerned. The later period of pregnancy cannot, given this policy, be distinguished from the periods (such as of illness or caring responsibilities) for which other students, who might also be regarded as hard cases, are denied benefit: once the policy of non-recognition of transient reasons for non-entitlement to benefit is accepted (and there was no general challenge to that policy before me), then I consider that there is objective and reasonable justification for the inclusion of intercalating students during the later term of their pregnancy within that policy."

Note that once the baby is born, the claimant may qualify for HB on the grounds of one of the exceptions in para (2) – eg, because s/he qualifies for IS or because s/he is a lone parent.

    Breaks to re-take exams. If a student fails exams, or hits financial trouble and is forced to take a year out, it does not appear possible to revive the analysis of Commissioner Howell in *CIS 13986/1996* paras 10–14, which was disapproved by *O'Connor v Chief Adjudication Officer* [1999] ELR 209, CA (*R(IS) 7/99*). The reasoning of the majority in that case proceeded on the basis that a student taking time out would return to the same "course".

    O'Connor does, however, leave open the position of students who have failed exams or otherwise broken off their studies and who know that they will be invited back (if at all) to follow what is undoubtedly a different course from the one they originally commenced (eg, because it is in a different subject or leads to a pass degree rather than an honours degree). It is suggested that such students must be treated as following a different course when they return and hence as not being full-time students when they are away from their studies.

    R(JSA) 2/02 dealt with a claimant who had been attending a course at an educational establishment that provided training and education to enable her/him to take examinations that were set and marked by another, unconnected body. He failed the examinations and intended to re-sit them. Commissioner Williams said that it was possible to abandon, or be dismissed from, a course of training without abandoning or being dismissed from a course of examinations: para 11. This means that someone could cease to be a full-time student when a course is abandoned, even if s/he intends to re-sit the examinations at a later date.

Student's eligible housing costs

57.–(1)   Subject to paragraphs (2) and (4), housing benefit shall not be payable during the period of study in respect of payments made by a student to an educational establishment which the student is attending.

(2)   Subject to paragraph (4), where the educational establishment itself pays rent for the dwelling occupied by the student as his home to a third party (other than to another educational establishment) the provisions of paragraph (1) shall only apply if rent is payable under the terms of a long tenancy or to an education authority which has provided the dwelling in exercise of its functions as an education authority.

(3)   Where it appears to the relevant authority that an educational establishment has arranged for accommodation to be provided by a person or body other than itself in order to take advantage of the housing benefit scheme, housing benefit shall not be payable during the period of study in respect of payments made to that person or body by a student.

(4)   Housing benefit shall be payable during the period of study in respect of payments made by a student to an educational establishment which the student is attending where the student–

(a)   is one who falls within a category specified in regulation 56(2); or

(b)   would fall within a category specified in regulation 56(2)(b) to (j) if he were a full-time student.

Definitions

"education authority" – see reg 53.

"dwelling" – see reg 2(4) and s137(1) SSCBA.

"long tenancy" – see reg 2(1).

"payments" – see reg 2(1).

"period of study" – see reg 53.

"rent" – see Part 3.

"student" – see reg 53.

General Note

The object of this regulation is to prevent students who pay rent to the educational establishment which they are attending, other than those to whom para (4) applies, from being paid HB, at least during their "period of study" (for which see reg 53(1)), whether they are full-time students or not (see the definition of "student" in reg 53). The rule also applies if a claimant's *partner* is a student but the claimant is not: see reg 58. In this case, the claimant is treated as if s/he is a student.

Para (2) provides an exception where the educational establishment itself pays rent for the dwelling to a third party.

Para (3) is an "anti-avoidance" device designed to stop bogus arrangements where the student pays a third party but the money ends up with the educational establishment.

Analysis

Para (1). The provision only has effect during the period of study, so students who rent from their institution during the summer vacation do not fall within its scope if the vacation is not part of their "period of study". Moreover, the institution from which the claimant rents must be the same one that the claimant is attending. However, such students may fall foul of para (3). An argument that para (1) is *ultra vires* was rejected by the High Court in *R (Bierman) v SSWP* [2004] EWHC 1024 (Admin). Mr Justice Davis rejected the argument that ss130 and 137(2) SSCBA 1992 only empower the making of regulations which state that a person is not liable to pay rent and do not allow for regulations which speak of HB not being "payable". In the Court's view, the precise form of language used in reg 50(1) HB Regs 1987 (now reg 57(1) HB Regs) was not important; the intent was clearly to exclude entitlement for students who pay rent to the educational establishment which they are attending, and that intent is within the broad powers conferred by s130(2) SSCBA 1992. Moreover, the power to prescribe in s130(2) is not limited by the terms of s137(2) to regulations which speak about treating persons as not being "liable" to make payments in respect of a dwelling.

Para (2) provides an exception where the educational establishment is effectively acting as a letting agency for a third party, provided that third party is not another educational establishment, and that the establishment which is being paid does not have the property in question on a long tenancy from the third party. For the meaning of "dwelling occupied by the student as his home", see reg 7(3) and (6)(b) and reg 55. If the other establishment is not providing the accommodation "in the exercise of its functions", as where the institution has purchased property as an investment, the student should be able to claim HB if the rest of this paragraph is satisfied.

Para (3). It is suggested that the question of whether the institution has sought to "take advantage" of the HB scheme must be determined in the same way as a question as to whether a tenancy has been created for that purpose. See the Analysis to reg 9(1)(l) on p293. A student refused HB under this provision has the normal rights to challenge a decision. GM C2.94 states that the exclusion will not apply when rent is paid to a housing association. There is no statutory basis for this statement, but it is unlikely that an arrangement at arms' length will fall foul of this paragraph.

Para (4). Living away from campus can prevent some students (in particular disabled students and lone parents) from having easy access to all the facilities that an educational establishment provides and to mix easily with other students. Those who need to live in accommodation provided by the educational establishment in order to attend a course, who cannot afford such accommodation, might be prevented from taking up places on courses. Para (4) enables certain students to be paid HB in respect of accommodation which they rent from their educational establishment. There are two categories.

(1)   Full-time students who are exempt from the general exclusion from HB by reg 56(2): sub-para (a).

(2)   Part-time students who would be exempt from the general exclusion from HB by reg 56(2) if they were full-time students, unless they would only be exempt under reg 56(2)(a) or (aa) – ie, because they are on IS, income-based JSA or income-related ESA (or UC): sub-para (b).

Note that students who are only exempt from the general exclusion from HB under reg 56(6) (ie, while waiting to return to a course following a period of incapacity or caring) do not come within either category. Presumably few of these students would be living in accommodation rented from the educational establishment during a "period of study" in any case, in which case reg 57 would not apply: see para (1).

Student partners

58. Where a claimant is not, but his partner is, a student, the provisions of regulation 57 (student's eligible housing costs) shall apply as if the claimant were a student.

General Note
See commentary to reg 57 on p494.

SECTION 3
Income

General Note on Section 3
See the General Note on this Part on p479. This Section sets out the special rules for treatment of student income, namely grant, loan, fee loan and special support loan income (regs 59, 64, 64A and 64B) as well as covenant income (regs 60 and 61) and payments from access funds (reg 65). It supplements, and to some extent modifies, the provisions of Part 6 of these regulations. Regs 63, 66 and 67 provide for additional disregards from a student's income which is other than grants, loans or covenant income. Reg 68 sets out situations when certain student income is to be treated as capital.

Other types of income received by students are dealt with under the ordinary income and capital rules found in Part 6. Note:

(1)   All of the income of a student on IS, income-based JSA or income-related ESA (or UC) is disregarded: Sch 5 para 4.
(2)   Education maintenance allowances and 16 to 19 bursaries (and similar payments) paid to young people on certain non-advanced courses are excluded from the definition of "grant" and are dealt with separately. They are disregarded as income under Sch 5 para 11 and as capital under Sch 6 para 51.
(3)   Career development loans paid under s2 Employment and Training Act 1973 are taken into account as income (reg 41(4)) with provision for some or all of such loans to be disregarded (Sch 5 para 13).

The effect of the apportionment rules on entitlement to HB
Grant income is in general spread over the weeks in a student's "period of study": see reg 53(1). A period of study can be a period of less than a calendar year – eg, it can exclude the summer vacation. Loan income is generally spread over the weeks in a student's "academic year": see reg 53(1). An academic year is a period of up to 12 months. Covenant income is spread over both the period of study and the academic year. For this reason, grant, loan and covenant income can be taken into account over different periods. This means that a student may be entitled to HB (or have increased entitlement to HB) outside her/his period of study. A fresh claim or a supersession request is required in these circumstances.

Calculation of grant income

59.–(1)   The amount of a student's grant income to be taken into account shall, subject to paragraphs (2) and (3), be the whole of his grant income.

(2)   There shall be excluded from a student's grant income any payment–
(a)   intended to meet tuition fees or examination fees;
(b)   in respect of the student's disability;
(c)   intended to meet additional expenditure connected with term time residential study away from the student's educational establishment;
(d)   on account of the student maintaining a home at a place other than that at which he resides during his course;
(e)   on account of any other person but only if that person is residing outside of the United Kingdom and there is no applicable amount in respect of him;
(f)   intended to meet the cost of books and equipment;
(g)   intended to meet travel expenses incurred as a result of his attendance on the course;
(h)   intended for the child care costs of a child dependant.
[⁴ (i) of higher education bursary for care leavers made under Part III of the Children Act 1989 [⁸ or Part 6 of the Social Services and Well-being (Wales) Act 2014].]

(3) Where a student does not have a student loan [⁷ or a postgraduate master's degree loan] and is not treated as possessing [⁷ a student loan or a postgraduate master's degree loan], there shall be excluded from the student's grant income–
(a) the sum of [⁵ £303] in respect of travel costs; and
(b) the sum of [⁵ £390] towards the costs of books and equipment,
whether or not any such costs are incurred.

[¹ (4) There shall also be excluded from a student's grant income the grant for dependants known as the parents' learning allowance paid pursuant to regulations made under Article 3 of the Education (Student Support) (Northern Ireland) Order 1998 or section 22 of the Teaching and Higher Education Act 1998 [⁶ or paid under section 63(6) of the Health Services and Public Health Act 1968].]

(5) Subject to paragraphs (6) and (7), a student's grant income shall be apportioned–
(a) subject to paragraph (8), in a case where it is attributable to the period of study, equally between the weeks in the period beginning with the benefit week, the first day of which coincides with, or immediately follows, the first day of the period of study and ending with the benefit week, the last day of which coincides with, or immediately precedes, the last day of the period of study;
(b) in any other case, equally between the weeks in the period beginning with the benefit week, the first day of which coincides with, or immediately follows, the first day of the period for which it is payable and ending with the benefit week, the last day of which coincides with, or immediately precedes, the last day of the period for which it is payable.

(6) Any grant in respect of dependants paid under section 63(6) of the Health Services and Public Health Act 1968 (grants in respect of the provision of instruction to officers of hospital authorities) and any amount intended for the maintenance of dependants under Part 3 of Schedule 2 to the Education (Mandatory Awards) Regulations 2003 shall be apportioned equally over the period of 52 weeks or, if there are 53 benefit weeks (including part-weeks) in the year, 53.

(7) In a case where a student is in receipt of a student loan or where he could have acquired a student loan by taking reasonable steps but had not done so, any amount intended for the maintenance of dependants to which neither paragraph (6) nor regulation 63(2) (other amounts to be disregarded) apply, shall be apportioned over the same period as the student's loan is apportioned or, as the case may be, would have been apportioned.

(8) In the case of a student on a sandwich course, any periods of experience within the period of study shall be excluded and the student's grant income shall be apportioned equally between the weeks in the period beginning with the benefit week, the first day of which immediately follows the last day of the period of experience and ending with the benefit week, the last day of which coincides with, or immediately precedes, the last day of the period of study.

Amendments
1. Substituted by reg 3(2) and (3) of SI 2006 No 1752 as from, for students whose period of study begins on or after 1.8.06 but before 1.9.06, on the day the period of study begins; in any other case 1.9.06.
2. Substituted by reg 4(2) of SI 2007 No 1632 as from, in the case of a person whose period of study begins on or after 1.8.07 but before 1.9.07, on the day the period of study begins; in any other case, 1.9.07.
3. Amended by reg 5(3) of SI 2008 No 1599 as from, for students whose period of study begins on or after 1.8.08 but before 1.9.08, on the day the period of study begins; in any other case 1.9.08.
4. Inserted by reg 6(8) of SI 2009 No 583 as from 6.4.09.
5. Amended by reg 2 of SI 2009 No 1575 as from, for students whose period of study begins on or after 1.8.09 but before 1.9.09, on the day the period of study begins; in any other case 1.9.09.
6. Amended by reg 6 of SI 2015 No 67 as from 23.2.15.
7. Amended by reg 4(3) of SI 2016 No 743 as from 4.8.16.
8. Amended by art 11(6) of SI 2017 No 901 as from 3.11.17.

Definitions
"applicable amount" – see Part 5.
"benefit week" – see reg 2(1).
"child" – see reg 2(1).
"full-time student" – see reg 53.

"grant" and "grant income" – see reg 53.
"periods of experience" – see reg 53.
"period of study" – see reg 53.
"postgraduate master's degree loan" – see reg 53.
"sandwich course" – see reg 53.
"student" – see reg 53.
"student loan" – see reg 53.
"UK" – includes Northern Ireland.

General Note

Para (1) provides the general rule that a student's grant income is to be taken into account in full, whether or not s/he is studying full-time (see the definition of "student" in reg 53). Paras (2) to (4) list parts of the student's grant income which must be ignored. Note that grant income cannot be disregarded under Sch 5 para 14 – eg, as a charitable or voluntary payment: reg 62.

Paras (5) to (7) set out the period over which grant income as calculated in paras (1) to (4) is to be taken into account, and how weekly amounts are to be calculated.

Regs 66 and 67 provide for a disregard if a student (or her/his partner) has been assessed for a contribution to the student's grant.

Reg 69 (on p504) provides for treatment of changes in the amount of standard maintenance grant that occur in the recognised summer vacation. If that summer vacation does not form part of the student's period of study, the change is ignored from the date it occurs to the end of the vacation.

Note that if a student is eligible for a student loan or a postgraduate master's degree loan in addition to a grant, the amounts disregarded for travel, books and equipment under para (3) are applied to the loan income rather than the grant income under reg 64(5).

Analysis

Para (1). For the meaning of "grant income", see the Analysis to reg 53 on p484.

Paras (2) and (4). The total of any amounts listed under these paragraphs which apply to a claimant are to be disregarded. The categories are in general self-explanatory.

Note that the payments disregarded under para (2) are those "intended" for or paid "on account of" the types of expenditure mentioned or in respect of a student's disability. It is the intention of the body paying the grant that is relevant: *R(IS) 7/95*; *R(IS) 16/95*; *SB v Oxford City Council (HB)* [2014] UKUT 166 (AAC). However, there is no requirement that the student uses the payments for the items listed. See also regs 62, 63 and 67.

Under para (2)(a), payments intended to meet tuition or examination fees are to be disregarded. *SB v Oxford City Council (HB)* concerned how much of a bursary was to be taken into account as grant income. The local authority had only disregarded the element of the bursary that was intended for the "start-up costs" of going to university. The claimant had argued, referring to DWP guidance, that although she had obtained a loan to pay her tuition fees, the remainder of the bursary should be disregarded under para (2)(a) as intended to meet those fees. Judge Rowland was not satisfied that the First-tier Tribunal had erred in law in finding that the claimant's university did not in fact intend any part of the bursary to be used to meet tuition fees. However, he said that although it was not necessary for him to decide the point, he would have been minded to accept that, in principle, a claimant's bursary could have been intended to meet tuition fees, even if s/he had received a loan for that purpose.

Under para (2)(b), payments in respect of the student's disability are to be disregarded. For example GM C2.322 tells local authorities to disregard Disabled Students Allowances as they are paid to provide help towards the costs of a non-medical helper, major items of equipment, travel costs and other items.

Under para (2)(e), payments "on account of any other person" outside the UK who is not residing with the claimant could include, for example, payments on account of a partner or child, but only if there is no HB applicable amount in respect of her/him.

Under para (2)(h), payments intended for the childcare costs of a child dependant may only be disregarded if they are for a child under the age of 16: see the definition of "child" in reg 2(1).

Para (3) permits the deductions from grant income listed, but only where a student does not have a student loan or a postgraduate master's degree loan and cannot be treated as having one – eg, under reg 64(3). These are flat-rate deductions in respect of books, equipment and travel, whether or not the costs are incurred. In the past they were uprated annually, but they have not been uprated since 2009. If the student has a loan, see reg 64(5).

Apportionment of grant income

Para (5)(a). Except in the case of a sandwich course (see para (8)) where a grant is said to be in respect of the "period of study" (see reg 53) it is divided equally between the weeks which that period covers.

Para (5)(b). In any other case (ie, where a grant is not said to be in respect of the "period of study"), grant income is divided equally between the weeks in the period for which it is payable.

Para (6) deals with apportionment of grants for dependants paid under specific provisions. These are divided equally over 52 (or 53) benefit weeks.

Para (7) deals with grants for dependants not covered by para (6), paid to students in receipt of student loans or students who could receive a loan by taking reasonable steps. Note that reg 63(2) referred to was omitted by SI 2009 No.583 from 6 April 2009.

The grant for dependants is apportioned over the same period as the loan (see reg 64). Note that where a claimant could have obtained a student loan but did not in fact do so, s/he is treated as being in receipt of one: reg 64(3)(b). If a student abandons or is dismissed from a course, the rules in reg 40(7), (8) and (9) specify how payments referred to in para (7) must be treated.

Para (8). If the student is on a "sandwich course" and the grant is said to be in respect of the "period of study", it should be divided equally over the weeks in that period during which the student is not on a "period of experience".

Calculation of covenant income where a contribution is assessed

60.–(1)   Where a student is in receipt of income by way of a grant during a period of study and a contribution has been assessed, the amount of his covenant income to be taken into account for that period and any summer vacation immediately following shall be the whole amount of the covenant income less, subject to paragraph (3), the amount of the contribution.

(2)   The weekly amount of the student's covenant income shall be determined–

(a)   by dividing the amount of income which falls to be taken into account under paragraph (1) by 52 or 53, whichever is reasonable in the circumstances; and

(b)   by disregarding from the resulting amount, £5.

(3)   For the purposes of paragraph (1), the contribution shall be treated as increased by the amount (if any) by which the amount excluded under regulation 59(2)(g) (calculation of grant income) falls short of the amount specified in paragraph 7(2) of Schedule 2 to the Education (Mandatory Awards) Regulations 2003 (travel expenditure).

Definitions
"contribution" – see reg 53.
"covenant income" – see reg 53.
"grant" – see reg 53.
"income" – see Part 6 also.
"period of study" – see reg 53.
"student" – see reg 53.

General Note
Prior to 1988, there was a provision for students to be paid under a deed of covenant whereby the payer could deduct the appropriate rate of tax from the gross amount of the payment and pay the student the net amount. The student could then claim a refund of the tax deducted, the refund being treated as capital under reg 68(1). Such tax relief has not been available since April 1988.

It is unlikely that there are any students still receiving covenant income. For an analysis of the rules for covenant income, see earlier editions of this work.

Covenant income where no grant income or no contribution is assessed

61.–(1)   Where a student is not in receipt of income by way of a grant the amount of his covenant income shall be calculated as follows–

(a)   any sums intended for any expenditure specified in regulation 59(2)(a) to (e) (calculation of grant income) necessary as a result of his attendance on the course shall be disregarded;

(b)   any covenant income, up to the amount of the standard maintenance grant, which is not so disregarded, shall be apportioned equally between the weeks of the period of study;

(c)   there shall be disregarded from the amount so apportioned the amount which would have been disregarded under regulation 59(2)(f) and (3) (calculation of grant income) had the student been in receipt of the standard maintenance grant; and

(d)   the balance, if any, shall be divided by 52 or 53 whichever is reasonable in the circumstances and treated as weekly income of which £5 shall be disregarded.

(2)   Where a student is in receipt of income by way of a grant and no contribution has been assessed, the amount of his covenanted income shall be calculated in accordance with sub-paragraphs (a) to (d) of paragraph (1), except that–

(a)   the value of the standard maintenance grant shall be abated by the amount of such grant income less an amount equal to the amount of any sums disregarded under regulation 59(2)(a) to (e); and

(b)   the amount to be disregarded under paragraph (1)(c) shall be abated by an amount equal to the amount of any sums disregarded under regulation 59(2)(f) and (g) and (3).

General Note
See General Note to reg 60 above.

Relationship with amounts to be disregarded under Schedule 5

62.   No part of a student's covenant income or grant income shall be disregarded under [¹ paragraph 14] of Schedule 5 [²].

Amendments
1.   Substituted by reg 3(4) of SI 2006 No 1752 as from, for students whose period of study begins on or after 1.8.06 but before 1.9.06, on the day the period of study begins; in any other case 1.9.06.
2.   Amended by reg 15(3) of SI 2006 No 2378 from the 1st day of the 1st benefit week to commence on or after 2.10.06.

General Note
This provides that the disregard of, for example, charitable or voluntary payments under Sch 5 para 14 cannot apply to a claimant's covenant or grant income at all.

Other amounts to be disregarded

63.–(1)   For the purposes of ascertaining income other than grant income, covenant income and loans treated as income in accordance with regulation 64 (treatment of student loans), any amounts intended for any expenditure specified in regulation 59(2) (calculation of grant income), necessary as a result of his attendance on the course shall be disregarded but only if, and to the extent that, the necessary expenditure exceeds or is likely to exceed the amount of the sums disregarded under regulation 59(2) or (3), 60(3), 61 (1)(a) or (c) or 64(5) (calculation of grant income, covenant income and treatment of student loans) on like expenditure.

[² (2)]

Amendments
1.   Amended by reg 3(8) of SI 2008 No 1042 as from 19.5.08.
2.   Omitted by reg 6(9) of SI 2009 No 583 as from 6.4.09.

Definitions
"covenant income" – see reg 53.
"grant income" – see reg 53.

General Note
This deals with income other than grant income, covenant income and student loans treated as income under reg 64 – eg, gifts, etc. Any amounts intended for some or all of the items listed in reg 59(2) which are necessary for attendance on the student's course are disregarded, but only to the extent that the total necessary expenditure on these items exceeds (or is likely to exceed) the amounts actually disregarded (from grant, covenant and loan income) by the regulations listed: para (1).

It is unclear whether sums covered by this regulation, and which are not to be disregarded, are to be taken into account over a full year or just over the "period of study". It is submitted that how the money is intended to be used is relevant – eg, if a grandparent makes a gift for the student's maintenance during the period of study it should only be taken into account over that period.

Treatment of student loans [⁵ and postgraduate master's degree loans]

64.–(1)   A student loan [⁵ and a postgraduate master's degree loan] shall be treated as income.

(2)   In calculating the weekly amount of the loan to be taken into account as income–

(a)   in respect of a course that is of a single academic year's duration or less, a loan which is payable in respect of that period shall be apportioned equally between the weeks in the period beginning with–

(i)   except in a case where head (ii) applies, the benefit week, the first day of which coincides with, or immediately follows, the first day of the single academic year;

(ii)   where the student is required to start attending the course in August or where the course is less than an academic year's duration, the benefit week, the first day of which coincides with, or immediately follows, the first day of the course,

and ending with the benefit week, the last day of which coincides with, or immediately precedes, the last day of the course;

(b)   in respect of an academic year of a course which starts other than on 1st September, a loan which is payable in respect of that academic year shall be apportioned equally between the weeks in the period beginning with the benefit week the first day of which coincides with or immediately follows, the first day of that academic year and ending with the benefit week, the last day of which coincides with or immediately precedes, the last day of that academic year but excluding any benefit weeks falling entirely within the quarter during which, in the opinion of the Secretary of State, the longest of any vacation is taken and for the purposes of this sub-paragraph, "quarter" shall have the same meaning as for the purposes of the Education (Student Support) Regulations 2005;

(c)   in respect of the final academic year of a course (not being a course of a single year's duration), a loan which is payable in respect of that final academic year shall be apportioned equally between the weeks in the period beginning with–

(i)   except in a case where head (ii) applies, the benefit week, the first day of which coincides with, or immediately follows, the first day of that academic year;

(ii)   where the final academic year starts on 1st September, the benefit week, the first day of which coincides with, or immediately follows, the earlier of 1st September or the first day of the autumn term,

and ending with the benefit week, the last day of which coincides with, or immediately precedes, the last day of the course;

(d)   in any other case, the loan shall be apportioned equally between the weeks in the period beginning with the earlier of–

(i)   the first day of the first benefit week in September; or

(ii)   the benefit week, the first day of which coincides with, or immediately follows the first day of the autumn term,

and ending with the benefit week, the last day of which coincides with, or immediately precedes, the last day of June,

and, in all cases, from the weekly amount so apportioned there shall be disregarded £10.

(3)   A student shall be treated as possessing a student loan [⁵ or a postgraduate master's degree loan] in respect of an academic year where–

(a)   a student loan [⁵ or a postgraduate master's degree loan] has been made to him in respect of that year; or

(b)   he could acquire [⁵ a student loan or a postgraduate master's degree loan] in respect of that year by taking reasonable steps to do so.

(4)   Where a student is treated as possessing a student loan under paragraph (3), the amount of the student loan to be taken into account as income shall be, subject to paragraph (5)–

(a)   in the case of a student to whom a student loan is made in respect of an academic year, a sum equal to–

(i)   the maximum student loan he is able to acquire in respect of that year by taking reasonable steps to do so; and

(ii)   any contribution whether or not it has been paid;

(b)   in the case of a student to whom a student loan is not made in respect of an academic year, the maximum student loan that would be made to the student if–

(i)   he took all reasonable steps to obtain the maximum student loan he is able to acquire in respect of that year; and

(ii)   no deduction in that loan was made by virtue of the application of a means test.

[[5] (4A)   Where a student is treated as possessing a postgraduate master's degree loan under paragraph (3) in respect of an academic year, the amount of that loan to be taken into account as income shall be, subect to paragraph (5), a sum equal to 30 per cent. of the maximum postgraduate master's degree loan the student is able to acquire in respect of that academic year by taking reasonable steps to do so.]

(5)   There shall be deducted from the amount of a student's loan income–

(a)   the sum of [[4] £303] in respect of travel costs; and

(b)   the sum of [[4] £390] towards the cost of books and equipment,

whether or not any such costs are incurred.

Amendments

1.   Substituted by reg 3(2) of SI 2006 No 1752 as from, for students whose period of study begins on or after 1.8.06 but before 1.9.06, on the day the period of study begins; in any other case 1.9.06.

2.   Substituted by reg 4(3) of SI 2007 No 1632 as from, in the case of a person whose period of study begins on or after 1.8.07 but before 1.9.07, on the day the period of study begins; in any other case, 1.9.07.

3.   Amended by reg 5(4) of SI 2008 No 1599 as from, for students whose period of study begins on or after 1.8.08 but before 1.9.08, on the day the period of study begins; in any other case 1.9.08.

4.   Amended by reg 2 of SI 2009 No 1575 as from, for students whose period of study begins on or after 1.8.09 but before 1.9.09, on the day the period of study begins; in any other case 1.9.09.

5.   Amended by reg 4(4) of SI 2016 No 743 as from 4.8.16.

Definitions

"academic year" – see reg 53.

"benefit week" – see reg 2(1).

"contribution" – see reg 2(1).

"last day of course" – see reg 53.

"postgraduate master's degree loan" – see reg 53.

"student loan" – see reg 53.

General Note

Under para (1), a "student loan" and a "postgraduate master's degree loan" are treated as income. They are disregarded as capital under para 22 of Sch 6. Special support loans are dealt with under reg 64B and are disregarded as income. Career development loans paid pursuant to s2 Employment and Training Act 1973 are dealt with under reg 41(4) and Sch 5 para 13.

Under para (2), the loan is apportioned on a weekly basis over the length of the course or the academic year. Note that the definition of "academic year" (reg 53(1)) specifies that where a course begins during August or September, the academic year of the course is considered to start on 1 September.

Under para (3), a student is treated as having a student loan or a postgraduate master's degree loan even where s/he has not applied for one, provided that s/he could obtain one.

Under para (4), if the student is treated as having a student loan, s/he is deemed to have the maximum student loan available.

Under para (4A), if the student is treated as having a postgraduate master's degree loan, the amount to be taken into account is 30 per cent of the maximum loan available.

Under para (5), set deductions are made from loan income in respect of travel, books and equipment, whether or not the costs are incurred.

The special support element of a student loan is ignored under reg 64B. Regs 66 and 67 provide for a disregard if a student (or her/his partner) has been assessed for a contribution to the student's loan.

Note that if a student abandons or is dismissed from a course, the rules in reg 40(7) to (9) specify how a loan must be treated.

Loans paid to part-time students towards books and travel are dealt with under this regulation. So if they are paid at a lower rate than the combination of disregards available for books and equipment and travel costs they are disregarded in full.

Analysis

Para (2). How a student loan or a postgraduate master's degree loan is to be apportioned, in general depends on whether the course lasts for one year or for a longer period. There are four possibilities.

(1)   Courses that last for a single academic year or less: sub-para (a). The loan is divided equally between the weeks in the period beginning with the start of the academic year (or for courses starting in August or lasting less than a year, the first day of the course) and ending on the last day of the course.

(2)   Courses that start other than on 1 September: sub-para (b). If the academic year of a course starts other than on 1 September, the loan is divided equally between the weeks in the period from the first to the last days of the academic year. Any benefit weeks falling entirely within the quarter during which, in the opinion of the DWP, the longest vacation is taken, must be disregarded. "Quarter" in relation to an academic year, means a period in that year from 1 January to 31 March, 1 April to 30 June, 1 July to 31 August, or 1 September to 31 December. If it is the final academic year of the course, see (3) below.

(3)   The final academic year of a course: sub-para (c). Unless the course is for a single year (for which see (1) above), the loan payable in respect of the final academic year of a student's course is apportioned as follows. If the academic year starts on 1 September, the loan is to be divided equally between the weeks in the period beginning with the earliest of 1 September or the first day of the autumn term and ending with the benefit week the last day of which coincides with or immediately precedes the last day of the course. In other cases, the loan is divided equally between the weeks in the period from the first day of the academic year to the benefit week the last day of which coincides with or immediately precedes the last day of the course.

(4)   Any other case: sub-para (d). Unless it is the final year of the course (for which see (3) above), sub-para (d) applies to courses of more than an academic year's duration where the academic year starts on 1 September. The loan is divided equally between the weeks in the period beginning with the earlier of the first benefit week in September or in the autumn term and ending on the benefit week the last day of which coincides with or immediately precedes the last day of June.

In all four cases, a £10 weekly disregard must be applied. Note, however, that this disregard can overlap with disregards from covenant income and access funds as well as disregards from certain types of war pension income. A combined maximum of £20 is allowed: Sch 5 para 34.

Paras (3), (4) and (4A). A student is treated as possessing a student loan or a postgraduate master's degree loan where one has been made to her/him, as well as where s/he could acquire a loan by taking reasonable steps to do so: para (3).

The meaning of the phrase "he could acquire such a loan ... by taking reasonable steps to do so" was considered in *CH 4429/2006.* The claimant's partner had not taken out a student loan because strongly held religious beliefs prohibited him from doing so. The claimant argued that it was therefore not reasonable for her partner to apply for a student loan. However, the commissioner said that the regulation refers to "reasonable steps", that is, it qualifies the steps which must be taken to acquire a loan. It is not concerned with other matters such as the motives and religious beliefs of the claimant. It is the mechanics of obtaining a loan that must be considered. The commissioner also decided that there was no breach of Art 14 of the European Convention on Human Rights. This reasoning should apply equally to postgraduate master's degree loans.

The amount of student loan then taken into account is the maximum amount of loan the student would be able to acquire if s/he took reasonable steps to do so, even if less than this amount (or no loan) is actually borrowed: para (4). In the case of a student who has taken out a student loan, any contribution assessed is also taken into account, even if it has not been paid: para (4)(a)(ii). In the case of a student who has not taken out such a loan, no account is taken of any deduction in that loan that could have been made as a result of the means-test.

The amount of a postgraduate master's degree loan then taken into account is 30 per cent of the maximum amount of loan the student would be able to acquire if s/he took reasonable steps to do so, even if less than this amount (or no loan) is actually borrowed: para (4A).

Para (5). Flat rate deductions must be made for travel costs, books and equipment, whether or not costs are incurred. In the past, they were uprated annually, but they have not been uprated since 2009.

[¹ Treatment of fee loans

64A.   A loan for fees, known as a fee loan or a fee contribution loan, made pursuant to regulations made under Article 3 of the Education (Student Support) (Northern Ireland) Order 1998, section 22 of the Teaching and Higher Education Act 1998 or section 73(f) of the Education (Scotland) Act 1980, shall be disregarded as income.]

Amendment

1.   Inserted by reg 3(5) of SI 2006 No 1752 as from, for students whose period of study begins on or after 1.8.06 but before 1.9.06, on the day the period of study begins; in any other case 1.9.06.

General Note
Eligible full-time higher education students can take out student loans to pay their fee contribution to the college or university – known as "fee loans" or "fee contribution loans". Reg 64A allows for these loans to be disregarded in full. Note that any amount of a student's grant income intended to meet tuition fees is disregarded under reg 59(2)(a) (see p495).

[¹Treatment of special support loans

64B. A special support loan within the meaning of regulation 68 of the Education (Student Support) Regulations 2011 is to be disregarded as income.]

Amendment
1. Inserted by reg 4(5) of SI 2016 No 743 as from 4.8.16.

Treatment of payments from access funds

65.–(1) This regulation applies to payments from access funds that are not payments to which regulation 68(2) or (3) (income treated as capital) applies.

(2) A payment from access funds, other than a payment to which paragraph (3) applies, shall be disregarded as income.

(3) Subject to paragraph (5) of this regulation and paragraph 34 of Schedule 5, any payments from access funds which are intended and used for food, household fuel or rent or ordinary clothing or footwear, of a single claimant or any other member of his family, and any payments from access funds which are used for any council tax or water charges for which that claimant or member is liable shall be disregarded as income to the extent of £20 per week.

(4) For the purposes of paragraph (3), "rent" means eligible rent less any deductions in respect of non-dependants which fall to be made under regulation 74 (non-dependant deductions).

(5) Where a payment from access funds is made–

(a) on or after 1st September or the first day of the course, whichever first occurs, but before receipt of any student loan in respect of that year and that payment is intended for the purpose of bridging the period until receipt of the student loan; or

(b) before the first day of the course to a person in anticipation of that person becoming a student,

that payment shall be disregarded as income.

General Note
Access funds (defined in reg 53) are discretionary funds administered by colleges and universities who may call these funds by other names – eg, access bursaries, mature students' bursaries, childcare support, the Financial Contigency Fund in Wales, hardship funds or discretionary learner support funds. They should be distinguished from payments from other sources.

Most payments from access funds which do not fall to be treated as capital under reg 68 (ie, which are not single lump sums) are disregarded: para (2). However, those intended for and used for specified basic necessities will be taken into account with a £20 a week disregard: para (3). Note, however, that this disregard can overlap with disregards from covenant income and student loan income as well as disregards from certain types of war pension income. A combined maximum of £20 is allowed: Sch 5 para 34. "Rent" is defined in para (4) and "ordinary clothing or footwear" in reg 2(1). Note that "eligible rent", referred to in para (4), is also defined in reg 2(1). Under para (5), an access fund payment used to bridge the period until a loan can be obtained is ignored, as is a payment made before the student commences study.

Disregard of contribution and rent

66. Where the claimant or his partner is a student and, for the purposes of assessing a contribution to the student's grant or student loan, the other partner's income has been taken into account, an amount equal to that contribution shall be disregarded for the purposes of assessing that other partner's income.

General Note
This provides for an income disregard where a student's partner has been assessed for a contribution to her/his grant or loan. That contribution is taken into account as income and so, to avoid double counting, an equal amount of the contributing partner's income is disregarded. Note that the words "and rent" were apparently not omitted from the title of reg 58 HB Regs 1987 (now reg 66) when para (2) of that regulation was omitted in 2002.

Further disregard of student's income

67. Where any part of a student's income has already been taken into account for the purposes of assessing his entitlement to a grant [¹, student loan or postgraduate master's degree loan], the amount taken into account shall be disregarded in assessing that student's income.

Amendment

1.   Amended by reg 4(6) of SI 2016 No 743 as from 4.8.16.

General Note

Reg 67 applies where a student has been assessed as liable to make a contribution towards his/her *own* grant or loan by the education authority. In this case, the amount of income taken into account is disregarded under this regulation.

Amounts treated as capital

68.–(1)   Any amount by way of a refund of tax deducted from a student's covenant income shall be treated as capital.

(2)   An amount paid from access funds as a single lump sum shall be treated as capital.

(3)   An amount paid from access funds as a single lump sum which is intended and used for an item other than food, household fuel, rent, ordinary clothing or footwear of a single claimant or, as the case may be, of the claimant or any other member of his family, or which is used for any council tax or water charges for which that claimant or member is liable, shall be disregarded as capital but only for a period of 52 weeks from the date of the payment.

(4)   In paragraph (3), "rent" means eligible rent less any deductions in respect of non-dependants which fall to be made under regulation 74 (non-dependant deductions).

General Note

Single lump sum access fund payments are treated as capital as are refunds of income tax deducted from a student's covenant income. See p498 on covenant income. However, a lump sum payment from access funds intended for and used for items other than specified basic necessities must be disregarded for 52 weeks from payment. "Rent" is defined in para (4), "access funds" in reg 53 and "ordinary clothing and footwear" in reg 2(1). "Eligible rent" referred to in para (4) is also defined in reg 2(1).

Disregard of changes occurring during summer vacation

69.   In calculating a student's income the relevant authority shall disregard any change in the standard maintenance grant, occurring in the recognised summer vacation appropriate to the student's course, if that vacation does not form part of his period of study from the date on which the change occurred to the end of that vacation.

General Note

See the General Note to reg 59 on p497.

PART 8
Amount of benefit

General Note on Part 8

This Part provides the rules under which the amount of HB to which a person is entitled is calculated, as well as the two schemes for extended payments of HB.

Reg 70 sets out the rules for ascertaining the appropriate maximum HB to which a particular claimant may be entitled. Reg 71 prescribes the taper – the percentage of the claimant's excess income which is to be deducted from maximum HB to arrive at the amount of HB payable.

Regs 72 to 73E make provisions for extended payments of HB, where HB was payable, in the circumstances prescribed – ie, where entitlement to IS, income-based JSA, ESA, IB or SDA ceases on account of the commencement of employment or self-employment or an increase in the hours or earnings from such.

Reg 74 is ancillary to reg 70 in that a person's maximum HB is arrived at by deducting certain amounts in respect of "non-dependants" (defined in reg 3) from the "eligible rent" figure calculated under regs 12B, 12BA, 12C or 12D, or under regs 12 and 13 as set out in Sch 3 para 5 HB&CTB(CP) Regs (see p1783). Reg 74 sets out the appropriate amounts to be deducted in respect of different categories of non-dependant as well as the situations when no deduction can be made.

Reg 75 is made under s134(4) SSCBA and prescribes the minimum weekly amount of HB to which a claimant may be entitled and actually paid.

A lower amount of HB than as calculated in this Part might be payable in the following circumstances.

(1)   A reduction can be applied for a specified period (four, 13 or 26 weeks or three years) where the claimant or a member of her/his family is convicted of one or more benefit offences or agrees to pay a penalty or accepts a formal caution instead of being prosecuted (the "one strike" rule) or if convicted of two or more offences within five years (the "two strikes" rule). The reduction is 20 or 40 per cent of the appropriate personal allowance for a single person of the claimant's age: ss6A, 6B, 7 and 9 SSFA 2001 (see p1712) and the Social Security (Loss of Benefit) Regulations 2001 (see p1761).

(2)   From 15 April 2013, a "benefit cap" can be applied, limiting the amount of HB of certain working-age claimants if their total entitlement to specified welfare benefits exceeds the "relevant amount": see s96 WRA 2012 and regs 75A to 75H in Part 8A.

[¹ Maximum housing benefit

70.   The amount of a person's appropriate maximum housing benefit in any week shall be 100 per cent. of his eligible rent calculated on a weekly basis in accordance with regulation 80 and 81 (calculation of weekly amounts and rent free periods) less any deductions in respect of non-dependants which fall to be made under regulation 74 (non-dependant deductions).]

Modifications

Reg 70 was substituted by reg 12 Housing Benefit (Local Housing Allowance and Information Sharing) Amendment Regulations 2007 SI No.2868 as from 7 April 2008, save that for a person to whom reg 1(5) of those regulations applied (see p1812), the amendments came into force on the day on or after 7 April 2008 when the first of the events specified in reg 1(6) applied to her/him, or on 6 April 2009 if none had before that date.

Amendment

1.   Substituted by reg 12 of SI 2007 No 2868 as from 7.4.08 (or if reg 1(5) of that SI applies, on the day on or after 7.4.08 when the first of the events specified in reg 1(6) applies, or from 6.4.09 if none have before that date).

Definitions

"eligible rent" – see reg 2(1).
"non-dependants" – see reg 3.

General Note

Where a claimant is entitled to HB under s130(1)(c)(i) SSCBA 1992 (ie, where s/he has no income or her/his income does not exceed her/his applicable amount), unless the "benefit cap" is applied (for which see regs 75A to 75H), the maximum HB is what s/he will actually receive. Where s/he is entitled under s130(1)(c)(ii) SSCBA (ie, where her/his income exceeds her/his applicable amount) the HB due is to be calculated by deducting the percentage of the claimant's "excess income" prescribed by reg 71 from the maximum HB to which s/he is potentially entitled and, if relevant, then applying the "benefit cap", and a reduction for "benefit offences" if relevant (for which see the SSFA 2001 on p1712 and the Social Security (Loss of Benefit) Regulations 2001 on p1761). "Excess income" is the amount by which a claimant's income assessed under Part 6 (and Part 7 if relevant) exceeds her/his "applicable amount" under Part 5.

Note that authorities have powers to top up HB with discretionary housing payments under the Discretionary Financial Assistance Regulations 2001 (see p1751).

Analysis

This regulation (together with reg 74) sets out the maximum HB which can be paid in any week (though note the situation where there is entitlement to "extended payments" of HB under reg 72 or 73).

A person's maximum HB is calculated by reference to her/his weekly eligible rent. "Eligible rent" is calculated under regs 12B, 12BA, 12C or 12D HB Regs, or under regs 12 and 13 as set out in Sch 3 para 5 HB&CTB(CP) Regs (see p1783). Note the three rent restriction schemes that can reduce eligible rent where HB is paid as a rent allowance and the "social sector" scheme which can reduce eligible rent where HB is paid to a social sector tenant: regs A13, B13, 13, 13C and 13D HB Regs, and reg 13 as set out in Sch 3 para 5 HB&CTB(CP) Regs (see p1784).

Where the claimant is entitled to HB for two homes under reg 7(6), maximum housing benefit is the aggregate of the eligible rents for the two homes, less any deductions in respect of non-dependents: *MB v Selby DC (HB)* [2011] UKUT 5 (AAC).

Regs 80 and 81 set out how eligible rent is to be calculated on a weekly basis. Any of the non-dependant deductions listed in reg 74 which apply must be deducted from the eligible rent to produce the appropriate maximum HB in any case. Note that any actual payments made to the claimant by the non-dependant are disregarded under Sch 5 para 21.

Where the claimant has for any reason to pay interest on the eligible rent, that interest cannot form part of the HB: *R v Kensington and Chelsea RBC ex p Brandt* (1995) 28 HLR 528, QBD.

Housing benefit tapers

71. The prescribed percentages for the purpose of sub-section (3)(b) of section 130 of the Act (percentage of excess of income over applicable amount which is deducted from maximum housing benefit) shall be 65 per cent.

Analysis

Reg 71 provides the percentage of excess income to deduct from maximum HB when calculating HB entitlement where s130(1)(c)(ii) SSCBA applies. HB in such a case is calculated as follows.

(1)   Work out weekly "eligible rent" under the relevant provision (see Part 3 HB Regs and regs 80 and 81).

(2)   Work out weekly maximum HB under reg 70 by deducting non-dependant deductions under reg 74 (if applicable) from "eligible rent".

(3)   Work out by how much the claimant's income exceeds her/his applicable amount (for which see Parts 5 and 6 (and 7 if relevant) and Sch 3).

(4)   To calculate HB due, deduct 65 per cent of the excess income so calculated from maximum HB.

(5)   If the "benefit cap" applies, the amount of HB entitlement is reduced, if the claimant's total entitlement to specified welfare benefits exceeds the "relevant amount": s96 WRA 2012 and regs 75A to 75H. The amount of HB may also be reduced for "benefit offences". See the SSFA 2001 on p1712 and the Social Security (Loss of Benefit) Regulations 2001 on p1761.

Example: The claimant, aged 45, is the sole tenant of a private rented, one-bedroom self-contained flat where she lives alone. She works part-time and has net earnings of £174.50 a week. The contractual rent is £150 a week. The appropriate local housing allowance is £128.

Eligible rent is £128: reg 12D.

Maximum HB is £128: reg 70 (the claimant has no non-dependants).

Applicable amount is £73.10: Sch 3 para 1.

Income to be taken into account is £169.50: £5 of her earnings are disregarded under Sch 4 para 10.

The difference between income and applicable amount is £96.40 (£169.50 – £73.10). 65 per cent of £96.40 is £62.66.

The claimant is entitled to HB of £65.34 (£128 – £62.66).

As HB is the only benefit to which the claimant is entitled, the "benefit cap" does not apply as her/his benefit income does not exceed the "relevant amount" for her in reg 75CA (£257.69).

[²Extended payments

72.–(1)   A claimant who is entitled to housing benefit (by virtue of the general conditions of entitlement) shall be entitled to an extended payment where–

(a)   the claimant or the claimant's partner was entitled to a qualifying income-related benefit;

(b)   entitlement to a qualifying income-related benefit ceased because the claimant or the claimant's partner–

(i)   commenced employment as an employed or self-employed earner;

(ii)   increased their earnings from such employment; or

(iii)   increased the number of hours worked in such employment,

and that employment is or, as the case may be, increased earnings or increased number of hours are expected to last five weeks or more; and

(c)   the claimant or the claimant's partner had been entitled to and in receipt of a qualifying income-related benefit, jobseeker's allowance or a combination of those benefits for a continuous period of at least 26 weeks before the day on which the entitlement to a qualifying income-related benefit ceased.

(2)   For the purpose of paragraph (1)(c), a claimant or a claimant's partner is to be treated as having been entitled to and in receipt of a qualifying income-related benefit or jobseeker's allowance during any period of less than five weeks in respect of which the claimant or the claimant's partner was not entitled to any of those benefits because the claimant or the claimant's partner was engaged in remunerative work as a consequence of their participation in an employment zone programme.

(3)   For the purpose of this regulation, where a claimant or a claimant's partner is entitled to and in receipt of joint-claim jobseeker's allowance they shall be treated as being entitled to and in receipt of jobseeker's allowance.

(4)   A claimant must be treated as entitled to housing benefit by virtue of the general conditions of entitlement where–

(a)   the claimant ceased to be entitled to housing benefit because the claimant vacated the dwelling occupied as the claimant's home;

(b)   the day on which the claimant vacated the dwelling was either in the week in which entitlement to a qualifying income-related benefit ceased, or in the preceding week; and

(c)   entitlement to the qualifying income-related benefit ceased in any of the circumstances listed in paragraph (1)(b).

(5)   This regulation shall not apply where, on the day before a claimant's entitlement to income support ceased, regulation 6(5) of the Income Support Regulations (remunerative work: housing costs) applied to that claimant.]

Amendments

1.   Amended by reg 13 of SI 2007 No 2868 as from 7.4.08 (or if reg 1(5) of that SI applies, on the day on or after 7.4.08 when the first of the events specified in reg 1(6) applies, or from 6.4.09 if none have before that date).

2.   Substituted by reg 2(2) of SI 2008 No 959 as from 6.10.08.

Definitions

"claimant" – see reg 2(1).
"dwelling" – see reg 2(4) and s137(1) SSCBA.
"employed earner" – see reg 2(1).
"employment zone programme" – see reg 2(1).
"general conditions of entitlement" – see s34(2) WRA 2007.
"jobseeker's allowance" – see reg 2(1).
"partner" – see reg 2(1).
"qualifying income-related benefit" – see reg 2(1).
"remunerative work" – see regs 2(1) and 6.
"self-employed earner" – see reg 2(1).

General Note

Sections 32 to 34 WRA 2007 and regs 72 to 72E provide a scheme for "extended payments" of HB to be made to certain people who have been (or whose partners have been) on IS, income-based JSA or income-related ESA for at least 26 weeks, who come off that benefit because they or their partners start employment as an employed or self-employed earner or increase hours or earnings. Extended payments can be made for up to four weeks: reg 72B. It is important to note that entitlement to HB does not end when the entitlement to the qualifying income-related benefit ends but continues until at least the end of the extended payment period: reg 72D(1). Entitlement can continue beyond the end of the extended payment period under the normal rules of entitlement to HB.

Reg 72 sets out the general rules of entitlement to extended payments. Reg 72B, qualified by reg 72E if the "benefit cap" has been applied, deals with the amount of the extended payments. Reg 72C provides special rules for "movers" (defined in reg 2(1) on p230), also qualified by reg 72E if the "benefit cap" has been applied. Reg 72D deals with the relationship between extended payments and HB entitlement under the normal rules of entitlement.

No separate claim for extended payments of HB is necessary: s32(4) WRA 2007 (see p162).

See regs 73 to 73E for a similar scheme where entitlement to contributory ESA, incapacity benefit or severe disablement allowance ceases for employment reasons.

See reg 52 HB(SPC) Regs (on p795) if a claimant claims (and is awarded) HB under the HB(SPC) Regs for the same period in which s/he is entitled to an extended payment under reg 72.

Rules prior to 6 October 2008

Prior to 6 October 2008, the scheme for extended payments of HB was found in the former version of reg 72 and Sch 7. The scheme was broadly similar to the current scheme, but with an important difference; HB entitlement under the normal rules of entitlement ended in the same circumstances in which a claimant qualified for extended payments: reg 77, omitted by the Housing Benefit and Council Tax Benefit (Extended Payments) Amendment Regulations 2008 SI No.959. For entitlement to continue under the former version after the extended payment period, a fresh claim was therefore required. Such claims were given priority under reg 89(3) (also omitted by SI 2008 No.959). See the 20th edition for commentary on the former version of the rules.

Analysis

Paras (1) to (3). Para (1) sets out the basic conditions of entitlement to extended payments:

(1) the claimant was entitled to HB under the general conditions of entitlement while either s/he or her/his partner was entitled to a "qualifying income-related benefit", defined in reg 2(1) as IS, income-based JSA and income-related ESA: s32(1) and (3) WRA 2007 and para (1)(a). "Income-based JSA" includes "joint-claim JSA" (see reg 2(1)). The "general conditions of entitlement" are those in Part 7 of the SSCBA 1992: s34(2) WRA 2007. Note that certain claimants who move home are deemed to satisfy the general conditions of entitlement under para (4);

(2) entitlement to the "qualifying income-related benefit" ceased because of the commencement of employment or self-employment, or an increase in earnings from, or hours in, the employment. This must be expected to last at least five weeks: para (1)(b); *and*

(3) the claimant or her/his partner had been entitled to and receiving IS, JSA (income-based, joint-claim or contribution-based) or income-related ESA or a combination of those benefits for a continuous period of 26 weeks. This includes periods of less than five weeks when the claimant or partner counted as in remunerative work because of being on an "employment zone programme": paras (1)(c), (2) and (3). It is understood that there are no longer any employment zone programmes.

Para (4). The claimant is to be treated as entitled to HB under the general conditions of entitlement where s/he ceased to be entitled because s/he moved home either in the week entitlement to a "qualifying income-related benefit" ceased, or the week before that, and s/he ceased to be entitled to the qualifying income-related benefit in any of the circumstances set out in para (1)(b). See also the additional rules for "movers" in reg 72C.

For the importance of meeting the precise timing in the former (similar) version of reg 72(1)(b), see *CH 1762/ 2004*, where the claimant failed to qualify for an extended payment because, although he had moved from his previous accommodation to take up employment, he did not do so either in the week in which he started his new job or in the previous week.

Para (5). This regulation does not apply to a person who, on the day before IS ceased, was being treated as not in remunerative work under reg 6(5) IS Regs. That regulation provides a similar scheme for extended payments of IS for home ownership costs (known as "housing costs run-on"). Note that this no longer covers mortgage interest.

General issues

The circumstances set out in para (1)(b) are changes that must be reported to both the DWP and the local authority under, respectively, reg 32 Social Security (Claims and Payments) Regulations 1987 and reg 88(1) HB Regs. A failure to report such a change would not affect entitlement to extended payments, but could result in an overpayment of HB from the end of the extended payment period.

[¹ Duration of extended payment period

72A.–(1)   Where a claimant is entitled to an extended payment, the extended payment period starts on the first day of the benefit week immediately following the benefit week in which the claimant, or the claimant's partner, ceased to be entitled to a qualifying income-related benefit.

(2)   For the purpose of paragraph (1), a claimant or a claimant's partner ceases to be entitled to a qualifying income-related benefit on the day immediately following the last day of entitlement to that benefit.

(3)   The extended payment period ends–

(a)   at the end of a period of four weeks; or

(b)   on the date on which the claimant to whom the extended payment is payable has no liability for rent, if that occurs first.]

Amendment

1.   Inserted by reg 2(2) of SI 2008 No 959 as from 6.10.08.

Definitions

"benefit week" – see reg 2(1).
"claimant" – see reg 2(1).
"extended payment period" – see reg 2(1).
"partner" – see reg 2(1).
"qualifying income-related benefit" – see reg 2(1).
"rent" – see reg 2(1).

Analysis

Under reg 72A, extended payments are made for four weeks, or until liability for rent ends if this is sooner: para (3). The period starts on the Monday following the benefit week in which entitlement to a qualifying income-related benefit ceased: paras (1) and (2). Note that even where the claimant moves, extended payments can in some cases continue to be paid until the end of the extended payment period: reg 72C.

[¹ Amount of extended payment

72B.–(1)   For any week during the extended payment period the amount of the extended payment payable to a claimant shall be the higher of–

(a)   the amount of housing benefit to which the claimant was entitled under the general conditions of entitlement in the last benefit week before the claimant or the claimant's partner ceased to be entitled to a qualifying income-related benefit;

(b)   the amount of housing benefit to which the claimant would be entitled under the general conditions of entitlement for any benefit week during the extended payment period, if regulation 72 (extended payments) did not apply to the claimant; or

(c)   the amount of housing benefit to which the claimant's partner would be entitled under the general conditions of entitlement, if regulation 72 did not apply to the claimant.

(2)   Paragraph (1) is subject to paragraphs (3) to (6) and does not apply in the case of a mover.

(3)   Where the last benefit week referred to in paragraph (1)(a) fell, in whole or in part, within a rent free period, the last benefit week for the purposes of that paragraph is the last benefit week that did not fall within the rent free period.

(4)   Where–

(a)   a claimant is entitled to an extended payment by virtue of regulation 72(4) (early vacation of dwelling); and

(b)   the last benefit week before the claimant ceased to be entitled to a qualifying income-related benefit was a week in which the claimant's eligible rent was calculated in accordance with regulation 80(3)(c) (calculation of rent for a partial week),

the last benefit week for the purpose of calculating the amount of the extended payment under paragraph (1)(a) shall be the benefit week before the partial week.

(5)   Where–

(a)   a claimant was treated as occupying two dwellings as the claimant's home under regulation 7(6) (liability to make payments in respect of two homes) at the time when the claimant's entitlement to a qualifying income-related benefit ceased; and

(b)   the claimant's liability to pay rent for either of those dwellings ceases during the extended payment period,

the amount of the extended payment for any week shall be reduced by a sum equivalent to the housing benefit which was payable in respect of that dwelling.

(6)   No extended payment is payable for any rent free period as defined in regulation 81(1) (rent free periods).

(7)   Where a claimant is in receipt of an extended payment under this regulation and the claimant's partner makes a claim for housing benefit, no amount of housing benefit shall be payable by the appropriate authority during the extended payment period.]

Amendment

1.   Inserted by reg 2(2) of SI 2008 No 959 as from 6.10.08.

Definitions

"appropriate authority" – see s34(3) WRA 2007.

"benefit week" – see reg 2(1).

"claimant" – see reg 2(1).

"dwelling" – see reg 2(4) and s137(1) SSCBA.

"extended payment period" – see reg 2(1).

"the general conditions of entitlement" – see s34(2) WRA 2007.

"mover" – see reg 2(1).

"partner" – see reg 2(1).

"qualifying income-related benefit" – see reg 2(1).

"rent" – see reg 2(1).

Analysis

Paras (1) to (4). Other than for a "mover" (for which see reg 72C), para (1) sets out the amount of extended payments of HB that are payable during the "extended payment period" (defined in reg 2(1) as the period for which an extended payment is payable in accordance with either reg 72A or 73A). For any week during the period, the amount payable is the highest of the following:

(1)   the HB to which the claimant was entitled in the last (non-rent-free) benefit week before entitlement to a qualifying income-related benefit ceased: paras (1)(a) and (3). Note that where a claimant is entitled to an extended payment by virtue of reg 72(4) and the last benefit week is one in which HB was calculated on a partial week, the amount of the extended payment is the HB in the week before the partial week: para (4). A change in the claimant's circumstances during the extended payment period will not affect the amount that applies under this sub-para: reg 72D(2) disapplies Part 9 HB Regs where extended payments are paid in accordance with reg 72B(1)(a); *or*

(2)   the weekly rate of HB to which the claimant would be entitled, as if the extended payment rules did not apply – ie, the amount of HB to which the claimant would be entitled on the basis of her/his new circumstances: para (1)(b); *or*

(3)   the weekly rate of HB to which the claimant's partner would be entitled, as if the extended payment rules did not apply – ie, the amount of HB to which the claimant's partner would be entitled if s/he claimed on the basis of her/his circumstances: para (1)(c).

At the end of the extended payment period, HB entitlement (if any) continues, but at the weekly rate of HB based on the new circumstances. Note that although the amount set by para (1)(a) cannot change, a change in the claimant's circumstances during the extended payment period can affect the weekly amount of the extended payments if, as a result of the change, the amount in either para (1)(b) or (c) is then higher or lower than that in (1)(a). The extended payment will then be whichever amount is now highest.

See also reg 72C where a claimant moves from the area of one authority to another during the extended payment period.

If the "benefit cap" has been applied. Although not specifically stated, reg 72B is subject to reg 72E if the "benefit cap" has been applied and hence HB entitlement is reduced under reg 75D. If the "benefit cap" has been applied, in all three cases above, the extended payments must be calculated using the amount of HB entitlement before the reduction was made.

Example: The claimant is a local authority tenant with a non-dependant. The "benefit cap" has not been applied. She was entitled to HB of £100 (which took into account a non-dependant deduction of £49.20) in the week before her entitlement to IS ceased. Her weekly entitlement based on her new circumstances in work is £69.21. Her extended payments are therefore £100 a week. In the second week of the extended payment period the non-dependant moves out. Her weekly entitlement based on her new circumstances is now £118.41 (£69.21 + £49.20) and as this is higher than the weekly rate of HB in the week before entitlement to IS ceased, this is now her weekly extended payment for the remainder of the period.

Para (5). A claimant may be treated as occupying two homes under reg 7(6) and can be entitled to HB (and therefore extended payments of HB) for both. Para (5) ensures that where liability to pay rent for either of the two dwelling ceases during the extended payment period, the extended payments are reduced by the amount of HB payable for that dwelling.

Para (6) prevents payment of extended payments during a rent-free period.

Para (7) prevents duplication of payments where the partner of the person being paid extended payments claims HB – ie, on the basis of the couple's new circumstances. See also reg 52 HB(SPC) Regs on p795 where the claimant claims HB under those rules while entitled to extended payments under reg 72 or reg 73.

[¹ Extended payments – movers

72C.–(1) This regulation applies–

(a)   to a mover; and

(b)   from the Monday following the day of the move.

(2)   The amount of the extended payment payable from the Monday from which this regulation applies until the end of the extended payment period shall be the amount of housing benefit which was payable to the mover for the last benefit week before the mover, or the mover's partner, ceased to be entitled to a qualifying income-related benefit.

(3)   Where a mover's liability to make payments for the new dwelling is to the second authority, the extended payment may take the form of a payment from the appropriate authority to–

(a)   the second authority; or

(b)   the mover directly.

(4)   Where–

(a)   a mover, or the mover's partner, makes a claim for housing benefit to the second authority after the mover, or the mover's partner, ceased to be entitled to a qualifying income-related benefit; and

(b)   the mover, or the mover's partner, is in receipt of an extended payment from the appropriate authority,

the second authority shall reduce the weekly amount of housing benefit that the mover, or the mover's partner, is entitled to by a sum equal to the amount of the extended payment until the end of the extended payment period.

(5)   The reduction of housing benefit made by the second authority under paragraph (4) is subject to any entitlement the claimant may have pursuant to regulation 7(6) (liability to make payments in respect of two homes).

(6)   Where the last benefit week referred to in paragraph (2) fell, in whole or in part, within a rent free period, the last benefit week for the purposes of that paragraph is the last benefit week that did not fall within the rent free period.

(7)   No extended payment is payable for any rent free period as defined in regulation 81(1) (rent free periods).]

Amendment

1.   Inserted by reg 2(2) of SI 2008 No 959 as from 6.10.08.

Definitions

"appropriate authority" – see s34(3) WRA 2007.
"benefit week" – see reg 2(1).
"dwelling" – see reg 2(4) and s137(1) SSCBA.
"extended payment period" – see reg 2(1).
"person liable to make payments" – see reg 2(2).
"mover" – see reg 2(1).
"partner" – see reg 2(1).
"qualifying income-related benefit" – see reg 2(1).
"second authority" – see reg 2(1).

Analysis

Reg 72C deals with the amount of extended payments paid to "movers".

Movers, as defined by reg 2(1), are claimants who move home from the area of the "appropriate authority" (ie, the authority that was administering the HB claim immediately before entitlement to a qualifying income-related benefit ceased) to a home in the area of a "second authority". As a "second authority" (defined in reg 2(1)) is the authority "to which" (as opposed to *in* which) a mover is liable to make payments for the new dwelling (which in this context would appear to be a reference to payments of rent), reg 72C can only apply where the claimant pays rent to the second authority and therefore does not apply where the claimant pays rent to, for example, a private landlord or housing association. In such cases, there does not appear to be a provision as in paras (4) and (5) to reduce HB where a claim for HB is made to the second authority.

Paras (1), (2) and (6). The weekly amount of a mover's extended payments is the amount of HB which was payable in the last (non-rent free) benefit week before entitlement to a qualifying income-related benefit ceased: paras (2) and (6). Although not specifically stated, reg 72C is subject to reg 72E if the "benefit cap" has been applied and hence HB entitlement reduced under reg 75D. If the "benefit cap" has been applied, the extended payments must be calculated using the amount of HB entitlement before the reduction was made.

This amount of HB applies from the Monday following the move until the end of the extended payment period (for which see reg 72A): paras (1) and (2). Note that a change in the claimant's circumstances during the extended payment period will not affect the weekly amount of the extended payments: reg 72D(2) disapplies Part 9 HB Regs where extended payments are paid in accordance with reg 72C(2). However, a change might affect the amount by which the second authority can "top up" the extended payments under paras (4) and (5) below.

Para (3). Where the rent liability is to the second authority, the extended payments can be made either to the mover or to the second authority: para (3). But note that given the definition of "second authority" in reg 2(1), the mover will always be so liable.

Paras (4) and (5) require the second authority to reduce the amount of HB paid to the mover or her/his partner by the amount of the extended payments in the circumstances described in para (4)(a) and (b). This applies where the mover or her/his partner makes a claim for HB to the second authority while either of them is being paid extended payments by the appropriate authority after entitlement to a qualifying income-related benefit ceased. The effect of this is that if HB at the new home is higher than HB was at the former home, the extended payments are effectively "topped up" by any additional entitlement to HB based on the new circumstances. This is subject to any entitlement the claimant may have to HB for two homes under reg 7(6).

Para (7) prevents payment of extended payments during a rent-free period.

[¹Relationship between extended payment and entitlement to housing benefit under the general conditions of entitlement

72D.–(1) Where a claimant's housing benefit award would have ended when the claimant ceased to be entitled to a qualifying income-related benefit in the circumstances listed in regulation 72(1)(b), that award will not cease until the end of the extended payment period.

(2) Part 9 (calculation of weekly amounts and changes of circumstances) shall not apply to any extended payment payable in accordance with regulation 72B(1)(a) or 72C(2) (amount of extended payment – movers).]

Amendment

1. Inserted by reg 2(2) of SI 2008 No 959 as from 6.10.08.

Definitions

"claimant" – see reg 2(1).
"extended payment period" – see reg 2(1).
"qualifying income-related benefit" – see reg 2(1).

Analysis

Reg 72D confirms that entitlement to HB does not end until the end of the extended payment period, even if entitlement would have ended if based only on the claimant's new circumstances: para (1). It also confirms that the general rules for calculating weekly amounts and for changes of circumstances do not apply to extended payments payable in accordance with reg 72B(1)(a) or 72C(2): para (2).

[¹ Calculation of an extended payment where the benefit cap applies

72E. Where a claimant's housing benefit in the benefit week with respect to which the extended payment is to be calculated is reduced in accordance with regulation 75D, the extended payment must be calculated using the amount of housing benefit before any such reduction is made.]

Amendment

1. Inserted by reg 2(3) of SI 2012 No 2994 as from 15.4.13.

Definitions

"claimant" – see reg 2(1).
"extended payment period" – see reg 2(1).
"qualifying income-related benefit" – see reg 2(1).

Analysis

The amount of HB entitlement of certain working-age claimants can be reduced (ie, a "benefit cap" is applied) if their total entitlement to specified welfare benefits exceeds the "relevant amount": regs 75A to 75H. However, under reg 72E, extended payments of HB must be calculated using the amount of HB before any such reduction where the claimant's HB is reduced "in the benefit week with respect to which the extended payment is to be calculated". So reg 72E would apply to the calculation of the amounts in reg 72B(1)(a), (b) and (c) and in reg 72C(2).

[²Extended payments (qualifying contributory benefits)

73.–(1) A claimant who is entitled to housing benefit (by virtue of the general conditions of entitlement) shall be entitled to an extended payment (qualifying contributory benefits) where–

(a) the claimant or the claimant's partner was entitled to a qualifying contributory benefit;

(b) entitlement to a qualifying contributory benefit ceased because the claimant or the claimant's partner–

  (i) commenced employment as an employed or self-employed earner;

  (ii) increased their earnings from such employment; or

  (iii) increased the number of hours worked in such employment,

  and that employment is or, as the case may be, increased earnings or increased number of hours are expected to last five weeks or more;

(c)   the claimant or the claimant's partner had been entitled to and in receipt of a qualifying contributory benefit or a combination of qualifying contributory benefits for a continuous period of at least 26 weeks before the day on which the entitlement to a qualifying contributory benefit ceased; and

(d)   the claimant or the claimant's partner was not entitled to and not in receipt of a qualifying income-related benefit in the last benefit week in which the claimant, or the claimant's partner, was entitled to a qualifying contributory benefit.

(2)   A claimant must be treated as entitled to housing benefit by virtue of the general conditions of entitlement where–

(a)   the claimant ceased to be entitled to housing benefit because the claimant vacated the dwelling occupied as the claimant's home;

(b)   the day on which the claimant vacated the dwelling was either in the week in which entitlement to a qualifying contributory benefit ceased, or in the preceding week; and

(c)   entitlement to the qualifying contributory benefit ceased in any of the circumstances listed in paragraph (1)(b).]

Amendments

1.   Amended by reg 13 of SI 2007 No 2868 as from 7.4.08 (or if reg 1(5) of that SI applies, on the day on or after 7.4.08 when the first of the events specified in reg 1(6) applies, or from 6.4.09 if none have before that date).

2.   Substituted by reg 3(2) of SI 2008 No 959 as from 6.10.08.

Definitions

"benefit week" – see reg 2(1).
"claimant" – see reg 2(1).
"dwelling" – see reg 2(4) and s137(1) SSCBA.
"employed earner" – see reg 2(1).
"the general conditions of entitlement" – see s34(2) WRA 2007.
"partner" – see reg 2(1).
"qualifying contributory benefit" – see reg 2(1).
"qualifying income-related benefit" – see reg 2(1).
"self-employed earner" – see reg 2(1).

General Note

Extended payments of HB are available to those whose entitlement (or whose partner's entitlement) to a "qualifying contributory benefit" (defined in reg 2 as IB, contributory ESA and SDA) ended because they started employment as an employed or self-employed earner, or increased earnings from, or hours of, the employment. The claimant (or her/his partner) must not have been entitled to, or in receipt of, a "qualifying income-related benefit" (defined in reg 2 as IS, income-based JSA (including joint-claim JSA) and income-related ESA). See also regs 73A to 73E.

The qualifying rules are broadly the same as the extended payment rules for those coming off a "qualifying income-related benefit" (see the commentary on regs 72 to 72E).

See reg 52 HB(SPC) Regs (on p795) if a claimant claims (and is awarded) HB under the HB(SPC) Regs for the same period in which s/he is entitled to an extended payment under reg 73.

[¹ Duration of extended payment period (qualifying contributory benefits)

73A.–(1)   Where a claimant is entitled to an extended payment (qualifying contributory benefits), the extended payment period starts on the first day of the benefit week immediately following the benefit week in which the claimant, or the claimant's partner, ceased to be entitled to a qualifying contributory benefit.

(2)   For the purpose of paragraph (1), a claimant or a claimant's partner ceases to be entitled to a qualifying contributory benefit on the day immediately following the last day of entitlement to that benefit.

(3)   The extended payment period ends–

(a)   at the end of a period of four weeks; or

(b)   on the date on which the claimant to whom the extended payment (qualifying contributory benefits) is payable has no liability for rent, if that occurs first.]

Amendment

1.   Inserted by reg 3(2) of SI 2008 No 959 as from 6.10.08.

[¹ Amount of extended payment (qualifying contributory benefits)

73B.–(1)   For any week during the extended payment period the amount of the extended payment (qualifying contributory benefits) payable to a claimant shall be the higher of–

(a)   the amount of housing benefit to which the claimant was entitled under the general conditions of entitlement in the last benefit wcck before the claimant or the claimant's partner ceased to be entitled to a qualifying contributory benefit;

(b)   the amount of housing benefit to which the claimant would be entitled under the general conditions of entitlement for any benefit week during the extended payment period, if regulation 73 (extended payments (qualifying contributory benefits)) did not apply to the claimant; or

(c)   the amount of housing benefit to which the claimant's partner would be entitled under the general conditions of entitlement, if regulation 73 did not apply to the claimant.

(2)   Paragraph (1) is subject to the paragraphs (3) to (6) and does not apply in the case of a mover.

(3)   Where the last benefit week referred to in paragraph (1)(a) fell, in whole or in part, within a rent free period, the last benefit week for the purposes of that paragraph is the last benefit week that did not fall within the rent free period.

(4)   Where–

(a)   a claimant is entitled to an extended payment (qualifying contributory benefits) by virtue of regulation 73(2) (early vacation of dwelling); and

(b)   the last benefit week before the claimant ceased to be entitled to a qualifying contributory benefit was a week in which the claimant's eligible rent was calculated in accordance with regulation 80(3)(c) (calculation of rent for a partial week),

the last benefit week for the purpose of calculating the amount of the extended payment (qualifying contributory benefits) under paragraph (1)(a) shall be the benefit week before the partial week.

(5)   Where–

(a)   a claimant was treated as occupying two dwellings as the claimant's home under regulation 7(6) (liability to make payments in respect of two homes) at the time when the claimant's entitlement to a qualifying contributory benefit ceased; and

(b)   the claimant's liability to pay rent for either of those dwellings ceases during the extended payment period,

the amount of the extended payment (qualifying contributory benefits) for any week shall be reduced by a sum equivalent to the housing benefit which was payable in respect of that dwelling.

(6)   No extended payment (qualifying contributory benefits) is payable for any rent free period as defined in regulation 81(1) (rent free periods).

(7)   Where a claimant is in receipt of an extended payment (qualifying contributory benefits) under this regulation and the claimant's partner makes a claim for housing benefit, no amount of housing benefit shall be payable by the appropriate authority during the extended payment period.]

Amendment
1.   Inserted by reg 3(2) of SI 2008 No 959 as from 6.10.08.

"claimant" – see reg 2(1).
"dwelling" – see reg 2(4) and s137(1) SSCBA.
"the general conditions of entitlement" – see s34(2) WRA 2007.
"mover" – see reg 2(1).
"partner" – see reg 2(1).
"qualifying contributory benefit" – see reg 2(1).

[¹ Extended payments (qualifying contributory benefits) – movers

73C.–(1) This regulation applies–

(a) to a mover; and

(b) from the Monday following the day of the move.

(2) The amount of the extended payment (qualifying contributory benefits) payable from the Monday from which this regulation applies until the end of the extended payment period shall be the amount of housing benefit which was payable to the mover for the last benefit week before the mover, or the mover's partner, ceased to be entitled to a qualifying contributory benefit.

(3) Where a mover's liability to make payments for the new dwelling is to the second authority, the extended payment (qualifying contributory benefits) may take the form of a payment from the appropriate authority to–

(a) the second authority; or

(b) the mover directly.

(4) Where–

(a) a mover, or the mover's partner, makes a claim for housing benefit to the second authority after the mover, or the mover's partner, ceased to be entitled to a qualifying contributory benefit; and

(b) the mover, or the mover's partner, is in receipt of an extended payment (qualifying contributory benefits) from the appropriate authority,

the second authority shall reduce the weekly amount of housing benefit that the mover, or the mover's partner, is entitled to by a sum equal to the amount of the extended payment (qualifying contributory benefits) until the end of the extended payment period.

(5) The reduction of housing benefit made by the second authority under paragraph (4) is subject to any entitlement the claimant may have pursuant to regulation 7(6) (liability to make payments in respect of two homes).

(6) Where the last benefit week referred to in paragraph (2) fell, in whole or in part, within a rent free period, the last benefit week for the purposes of that paragraph is the last benefit week that did not fall within the rent free period.

(7) No extended payment (qualifying contributory benefits) is payable for any rent free period as defined in regulation 81(1) (rent free periods).]

Amendment

1. Inserted by reg 3(2) of SI 2008 No 959 as from 6.10.08.

Definitions

"appropriate authority" – see s34(3) WRA 2007.
"benefit week" – see reg 2(1).
"dwelling" – see reg 2(4) and s137(1) SSCBA.
"extended payment period" – see reg 2(1).
"mover" – see reg 2(1).
"partner" – see reg 2(1).
"person liable to make payments" – see reg 2(2).
"qualifying contributory benefit" – see reg 2(1).
"second authority" – see reg 2(1).

[¹ Relationship between extended payment (qualifying contributory benefits) and entitlement to housing benefit under the general conditions of entitlement

73D.–(1) Where a claimant's housing benefit award would have ended when the claimant ceased to be entitled to a qualifying contributory benefit in the circumstances listed in regulation 73(1)(b), that award will not cease until the end of the extended payment period.

(2)   Part 9 (calculation of weekly amounts and changes of circumstances) shall not apply to any extended payment (qualifying contributory benefits) payable in accordance with regulation 73B(1)(a) or 73C(2) (amount of extended payment – movers).]

Amendment

1.   Inserted by reg 3(2) of SI 2008 No 959 as from 6.10.08.

Definitions

"claimant" – see reg 2(1).
"extended payment period" – see reg 2(1).
"qualifying contributory benefit" – see reg 2(1).

[¹ Calculation of an extended payment (qualifying contributory benefits) where the benefit cap applies

73E.   Where a claimant's housing benefit in the benefit week with respect to which the extended payment (qualifying contributory benefits) is to be calculated is reduced in accordance with regulation 75D, the extended payment (qualifying contributory benefits) must be calculated using the amount of housing benefit before any such reduction is made.]

Amendment

1.   Inserted by reg 2(4) of SI 2012 No 2994 as from 15.4.13.

Definitions

"benefit week" – see reg 2(1).
"claimant" – see reg 2(1).

[¹ Non-dependant deductions

74.–(1) Subject to the following provisions of this regulation, the deductions referred to in regulation 70 (maximum housing benefit) shall be–
  (a)   in respect of a non-dependant aged 18 or over in remunerative work, [³¹ £100.65] per week;
  (b)   in respect of a non-dependant aged 18 or over to whom sub-paragraph (a) does not apply, [³¹ £15.60] per week.
    (2)   In the case of a non-dependant aged 18 or over to whom paragraph (1)(a) applies because he is in remunerative work, where it is shown to the appropriate authority that his normal weekly gross income is–
  (a)   less than [³¹ £143.00], the deduction to be made under this regulation shall be that specified in paragraph 1(b);
  (b)   not less than [³¹ £143.00] but less than [³¹ £209.00], the deduction to be made under this regulation shall be [³¹ £35.85];
  (c)   not less than [³¹ £209.00] but less than [³¹ £272.00], the deduction to be made under this regulation shall be [³¹ £49.20];
  (d)   not less than [³¹ £272.00] but less than [³¹ £363.00], the deduction to be made under this regulation shall be [³¹² £80.55];
  (e)   not less than [³¹ £363.00] but less than [³¹ £451.00], the deduction to be made under this regulation shall be [³¹ £91.70].
    (3)   Only one deduction shall be made under this regulation in respect of a couple or, as the case may be, members of a polygamous marriage and, where, but for this paragraph, the amount that would fall to be deducted in respect of one member of a couple or polygamous marriage is higher than the amount (if any) that would fall to be deducted in respect of the other, or any other, member, the higher amount shall be deducted.
    (4)   In applying the provisions of paragraph (2) in the case of a couple or, as the case may be, a polygamous marriage, regard shall be had, for the purpose of paragraph (2) to the couple's or, as the case may be, all members of the polygamous marriage's joint weekly gross income.
    (5)   Where a person is a non-dependant in respect of more than one joint occupier of a dwelling (except where the joint occupiers are a couple or members of a polygamous

marriage), the deduction in respect of that non-dependant shall be apportioned between the joint occupiers (the amount so apportioned being rounded to the nearest penny) having regard to the number of joint occupiers and the proportion of the payments in respect of the dwelling payable by each of them.

(6)   No deduction shall be made in respect of any non-dependants occupying a claimant's dwelling if the claimant or his partner is–

(a)   [²⁰ severely sight impaired or blind or treated as severely sight impaired or blind] by virtue of paragraph 13 of Schedule 3 (additional condition [⁹ for the disability premium]); or

(b)   receiving in respect of himself either–
     (i)   attendance allowance; [¹⁶]
     (ii)   the care component of the disability living allowance. [¹⁶ [¹⁷]]
     [¹⁶ (iii) the daily living component of personal independence payment;][¹⁷ or]
     [¹⁷ (iv) armed forces independence payment.]

(7)   No deduction shall be made in respect of a non-dependant if–

(a)   although he resides with the claimant, it appears to the appropriate authority that his normal home is elsewhere; or

(b)   he is in receipt of a training allowance paid in connection with [⁶ youth training] established under section 2 of the 1973 Act or section 2 of the Enterprise and New Towns (Scotland) Act 1990; or

(c)   he is a full-time student during a period of study within the meaning of Part 7 (Students); or

(d)   he is a full time student and during a recognised summer vacation appropriate to his course he is not in remunerative work; or

(e)   he is a full-time student and the claimant or his partner has attained [³⁰ pensionable age]; or

(f)   he is not residing with the claimant because he has been a patient for a period in excess of 52 weeks, or a prisoner, and for these purposes–
     (i)   "patient" has the meaning given in paragraph (18) of regulation 7 (circumstances in which a person is or is not to be treated as occupying a dwelling as his home);
     (ii)   where a person has been a patient for two or more distinct periods separated by one or more intervals each not exceeding 28 days, he shall be treated as having been a patient continuously for a period equal in duration to the total of those distinct periods; and
     (iii)   "prisoner" means a person who is detained in custody pending trial or sentence upon conviction or under a sentence imposed by a court other than a person who is detained in hospital under the provisions of the Mental Health Act 1983, or, in Scotland, under the provisions of the Mental Health (Care and Treatment) (Scotland) Act 2003 or the Criminal Procedure (Scotland) Act 1995.

[¹⁵ (g) he is not residing with the claimant because he is a member of the armed forces away on operations.]

[¹⁸ (8)   No deduction shall be made in calculating the amount of a rent rebate or allowance in respect of a non-dependant aged less than 25 who is–

(a)   on income support, an income-based jobseeker's allowance or an income-related employment and support allowance which does not include an amount under section 4(2)(b) of the Welfare Reform Act (the support component [²³]) [²³, ²⁶ and where the non-dependant is not a member of the work-related activity group]; or

(b)   entitled to an award of universal credit where the award is calculated on the basis that the non-dependant does not have any earned income.]

(9)   In the case of a non-dependant to whom paragraph (2) applies because he is in remunerative work, there shall be disregarded from his weekly gross income–

(a)   any attendance allowance[¹⁶, disability living allowance[¹⁷, armed forces independence payment] or personal independence payment] received by him;

(b)   any payment made under [⁹ or by] the Macfarlane Trust, the Macfarlane (Special Payments) Trust, the Macfarlane (Special Payments) (No. 2) Trust, the Fund, the Eileen Trust[⁹, MFET Limited] [¹², the Skipton Fund, the Caxton Foundation] [²⁵, the Scottish Infected Blood Support Scheme] [²⁸, an approved blood scheme] [²⁷, the London Emergencies Trust, the We Love Manchester Emergency Fund] or the Independent Living [⁵ Fund (2006)] which had his income fallen to be calculated under regulation 40 (calculation of income other than earnings) would have been disregarded under paragraph 23 of Schedule 5 (income in kind); and

(c)   any payment which had his income fallen to be calculated under regulation 40 would have been disregarded under paragraph 35 of Schedule 5 (payments made under certain trusts and certain other payments);

[²⁸ (d) any payment made under or by a trust, established for the purpose of giving relief and assistance to disabled persons whose disabilities were caused by the fact that during their mother's pregnancy she had taken a preparation containing the drug known as Thalidomide, and which is approved by the Secretary of State.]

(10)   No deduction shall be made in respect of a non-dependant who is on state pension credit.]

[¹⁸ (11)   For the purposes of paragraph (8), "earned income" has the meaning given in regulation 52 of the Universal Credit Regulations 2013.]

Modifications

Reg 74 was substituted by reg 14 Housing Benefit (Local Housing Allowance and Information Sharing) Amendment Regulations 2007 SI No.2868 as from 7 April 2008, save that for a person to whom reg 1(5) of those regulations applied (see p1812), the amendments came into force on the day on or after 7 April 2008 when the first of the events specified in reg 1(6) applied to her/him, or on 6 April 2009 if none had before that date.

Amendments

1.   Substituted by reg 14 of SI 2007 No 2868 as from 7.4.08 (or if reg 1(5) of that SI applies, on the day on or after 7.4.08 when the first of the events specified in reg 1(6) applies, or from 6.4.09 if none have before that date).

2.   Confirmed by art 19(4) of SI 2008 No 632 as from 1.4.08 (7.4.08 where rent payable weekly or in multiples of a week).

3.   Amended by art 19(4) of SI 2008 No 632 as from 1.4.08 (7.4.08 where rent payable weekly or in multiples of a week).

4.   Amended by reg 18 of SI 2008 No 1082 as from 27.10.08.

5.   Amended by reg 6(4)(d) of SI 2008 No 2767 as from 17.11.08.

6.   Amended by reg 6(6) of SI 2008 No 2767 as from 17.11.08.

7.   Confirmed by art 19(4) of SI 2009 No 497 as from 1.4.09 (6.4.09 where rent payable weekly or in multiples of a week).

8.   Amended by art 19(4) of SI 2009 No 497 as from 1.4.09 (6.4.09 where rent payable weekly or in multiples of a week).

9.   Amended by reg 8(3), (5) and (8) of SI 2010 No 641 as from 1.4.10 (5.4.10 where rent payable weekly or in multiples of a week).

10.   Confirmed by art 19(3) of SI 2010 No 793 as from 1.4.10 (5.4.10 where rent payable weekly or in multiples of a week).

11.   Amended by art 20(3) of SI 2011 No 821 as from 1.4.11 (4.4.11 where rent payable weekly or in multiples of a week).

12.   Inserted by reg 19(5) of SI 2011 No 2425 as from 31.10.11.

13.   Amended by art 20(3) of SI 2012 No 780 as from 1.4.12 (2.4.12 where rent payable weekly or in multiples of a week).

14.   Amended by art 19(3) of SI 2013 No 574 as from 1.4.13.

15.   Amended by reg 2(6) of SI 2013 No 655 as from 1.4.13.

16.   Amended by reg 8 and Sch para 36(4) of SI 2013 No 388 as from 8.4.13.

17.   Amended by art 7 and Sch para 344) of SI 2013 No 591 as from 8.4.13.

18.   Amended by reg 35(7) of SI 2013 No 630 as from 29.4.13.

19.   Amended by art 19(4) of SI 2014 No 516 as from 1.4.14 (7.4.14 where rent payable weekly or in multiples of a week).

20.   Amended by reg 3(5)(b) of SI 2014 No 2888 as from 26.11.14.

21.   Amended by art 17(4) of SI 2015 No 547 as from 1.4.15 (6.4.15 where rent payable weekly or in multiples of a week).

22. Amended by reg 5 of SI 2016 No 242 as from 1.4.16 (4.4.16 where rent payable weekly or in multiples of a week).
23. Amended by Sch 1 para 6(6) of SI 2017 No 204 as from 3.4.17, subject to transitional and savings provisions in Sch 2 paras 1-7 of SI 2017 No 204.
24. Amended by art 22(4) of SI 2017 No 260 as from 1.4.17 (3.4.17 where rent payable weekly or in multiples of a week).
25. Amended by reg 6(3)(d) of SI 2017 No 329 as from 3.4.17.
26. Amended by reg 5(4) of SI 2017 No 581 as from 23.6.17, subject to transitional and savings provision in reg 9.
27. Amended by reg 6(3)(d) of SI 2017 No 689 as from 19.6.17.
28. Amended by reg 6(3)(d) and (4) of SI 2017 No 870 as from 23.10.17.
29. Amended by art 23(3) of SI 2018 No 281 as from 1.4.18 (2.4.18 where rent payable weekly or in multiples of a week).
30. Amended by reg 6 of SI 2017 No 1187 as from 6.12.18.
31. Amended by art 23(3) of SI 2019 No 480 as from 1.4.19.

Definitions

"appropriate authority" – see s34(3) WRA 2007.
"armed forces independence payment" – see reg 2(1).
"attendance allowance" – see reg 2(1).
"claimant" – see reg 2(1).
"couple" – see reg 2(1).
"disability living allowance" – see reg 2(1).
"dwelling" – see s137(1) of SSCBA and reg 2(4).
"an income-based jobseeker's allowance" – see reg 2(1).
"the Macfarlane Trust" and other schemes listed in para (9)(b) – see reg 2(1).
"member of the armed forces away on operations" – see reg 2(1).
"member of the work-related activity group" – see reg 2(1).
"non-dependant" – see reg 3.
"partner" – see reg 2(1).
"period of study" – see reg 53.
"person on an income-based jobseeker's allowance" – see reg 2(3).
"person on income support" – see reg 2(1).
"person on an income-related employment and support allowance" – see reg 2(3A).
"personal independence payment" – see reg 2(1).
"polygamous marriage" – see reg 2(1).
"rent rebate/allowance" – see ss134(1A) and (1B) and 191 SSAA.
"remunerative work" – see reg 6.
"student" – see reg 53.
"universal credit" – see reg 2(1).
"Welfare Reform Act" – see reg 2(1).

General Note

This regulation sets out the situations in which non-dependant deductions must be made from a claimant's "eligible rent" to arrive at maximum HB under reg 70, and the amounts of the relevant deductions. It is suggested that the appropriate procedure for determining whether a non-dependant deduction is to be made, and if so the amount of the deduction, is as follows.

(1) The authority should first determine whether the claimant has any "non-dependants" normally residing with her/him. Reg 3 sets out who counts as a non-dependant and who does not. No deduction is applicable at *all* in respect of a person who does not come within the definition of "non-dependant".

(2) If someone *is* a non-dependant, her/his age is relevant; it is only if a non-dependant is aged 18 or over that a deduction can be applied: paras (1) and (2).

(3) Even if the claimant has non-dependants aged 18 or over, para (6) sets out the situations in which no deduction may be made for any of the non-dependants and paras (7), (8) and (10) set out the situations in which no deductions are to be made in respect of a particular non-dependant.

(4) If the claimant has non-dependants aged 18 or over and paras (6) to (8) or (10) do *not* apply, paras (1) and (2) set out the relevant amounts of the deductions for different categories of non-dependants. These depend on whether or not the non-dependant is in "remunerative work" (for which see reg 6). If not in remunerative work, the lowest rate deduction is made, whatever the source of, and amount of, the non-dependant's income: para (1)(b). If the non-dependant is in remunerative work, the amount of the deduction depends on the gross income of the non-dependant, disregarding the amounts set out in para (9): paras (1)(a) and (2).

Paras (3) and (4) deal with non-dependants who are couples or partners to a polygamous marriage. Para (5) deals with the apportionment of non-dependant deductions where more than one person is liable for the rent on the dwelling in which the non-dependant is living.

Any actual payments made to the claimant by the non-dependant are disregarded as income under Sch 5 para 21.

The non-dependant deduction rates did not increase between April 2001 and April 2011. Since April 2011, they have been uprated annually on the basis of prices.

Analysis

Paragraphs (1) to (4) and (9): Amounts of deductions

Para (1) sets out the general rule. The deductions provided by this paragraph shall only be made if the non-dependant is 18 or over, and if none of paras (6) to (8) and (10) apply. The lowest rate deduction is made where the non-dependant is not in remunerative work, whatever her/his income: para (1)(b). The highest rate deduction is made where the non-dependant is in remunerative work: (1)(a). This is qualified by para (2) where the non-dependant has income below set levels. Both sub-paras (a) and (b) are qualified by paras (3) to (5).

Higher rates of non-dependant deductions are specified in respect of people who are in "remunerative work" as defined in reg 6: see p253. It is suggested that it is for the authority to prove that a person is a non-dependant, and also that such a non-dependant is (or is to be treated as) in remunerative work.

Under reg 6(5)–(8), a person is treated as not in remunerative work in various circumstances. These include where s/he has good cause for her/his absence from it, and where s/he is on, for example, sick leave or maternity, adoption, shared parental or paternity leave. It would be wrong to assume that only "extended" absences should qualify as "good cause", although of course the absence will have to last at least one benefit week (Monday to Sunday) to be of significance. Likewise, a person on IS, income-based JSA or income-related ESA for more than three days in a benefit week is treated as not in remunerative work in that week. In such circumstances, paras (1)(a) and (2) do not apply.

Para (2) requires lower rate deductions than those provided by para (1)(a) to be made where the non-dependant is aged 18 or over and is in remunerative work with normal weekly gross income below the levels shown in sub-paras (a) to (e). It is suggested that the burden of proof is on the claimant to show that the non-dependant has a low income. This follows from the words "where it is shown to". However, authorities should bear in mind that non-dependants will often be reluctant to disclose personal financial details and should not just sit back and expect the claimant to obtain the information unassisted.

In *CH 48/2006,* the local authority assumed, in the absence of any actual evidence as to what the non-dependant was earning, that the highest rate of non-dependent deduction was to be made from the claimant's maximum council tax benefit (CTB). Both the local authority and the tribunal had proceeded on the basis that because no positive evidence from the non-dependant or the claimant had been produced, the very worst had to be assumed. The commissioner recognised that a local authority was entitled to require evidence from claimants under reg 63 CTB Regs 1992 (from 6 March 2006, reg 72 CTB Regs 2006; the equivalent for HB is reg 86 HB Regs) and that, in the absence of such evidence, it may make adverse inferences. However, any such adverse inferences have to be based in some sense of reality. Authorities have the duty to assess what the likely level of a non-dependant's earnings are, on the evidence available and on the balance of probabilities, and estimate a non-dependant's income, with reasonable adverse assumptions being made where inferences have to be drawn because no evidence is available.

All the non-dependant's income under Part 6 and not just her/his wages must be taken into account.

It is income before the various deductions allowable for tax and other factors under Part 6 have been made, but para (9) provides for certain payments to be disregarded in calculating a non-dependant's gross weekly income.

Para (3) provides that there can only be one non-dependant deduction made per couple or polygamous marriage. The deduction to be made is the highest amount that would apply to any of the individual partners under reg 74(1) or (2).

Para (4) must be read together with para (3). In deciding whether para (2) applies, the gross income of both/all partners is to be taken into account.

Para (9) provides that in calculating the gross weekly income of a non-dependant in remunerative work income from any of the sources listed is disregarded.

Paragraph (5): Apportionment

The authority must first decide on the appropriate non-dependant deduction, then apportion it, not simply according to the number of joint occupiers, but also according to the share of the rent each of them pays. Note that this para does not apply where joint occupiers are members of a couple or polygamous marriage as only one of them will be eligible for HB in any case. This para does not apply in respect of boarders who are not non-dependants: see reg 3(2)(e) on p248.

"Joint occupier" refers to a person with a joint legal right to occupy the property rather than a person who merely happens to live in the same building: see *R v Chesterfield BC ex p Fullwood* (1993) 26 HLR 126 at 129, CA cited in the Analysis to reg 3(2)(d) on p250.

Paragraphs (6) to (8) and (10): When no non-dependant deduction is to be made

Para (6) sets out circumstances in which no non-dependant deduction is to be made for *any* of the claimant's non-dependants.

(1) The claimant or her/his partner is severely sight impaired or blind, or is treated as severely sight impaired or blind: para (6)(a). See Sch 3 para 13 for the circumstances in which a person may be treated as severely sight impaired or blind.

(2) The claimant or her/his partner is receiving AA, DLA care component or PIP daily living component (any level of these will suffice) or armed forces independence payment: para (6)(b).

Paras (7), (8), (10) and (11). If para (6) does not apply, paras (7), (8) and (10) set out circumstances in which a deduction is not to be made in respect of a particular non-dependant. These are as follows.

(1) The non-dependant's normal home is not with the claimant: para (7)(a). See p264 for a discussion of "normal home".

(2) The non-dependant is in receipt of a training allowance in connection with youth training under the provisions listed, irrespective of her/his age: para (7)(b).

(3) The non-dependant is a "full-time student" during a "period of study" or where the claimant or her/his partner is 65 or over only, the non-dependant is a "full-time student", whether or not during a period of study: paras (7)(c) and (e). Sub-para (e) can only apply where the claimant or partner is on IS, income-based JSA or income-related ESA (or UC) as otherwise the HB(SPC) Regs apply: reg 5. See reg 53 for the definition of the terms.

(4) The non-dependant is a "full-time student", it is the summer vacation and s/he is not in remunerative work: para (7)(d).

(5) The non-dependant has been a patient as defined in reg 7(18) for more than 52 weeks: para (7)(f). Note the linking rule in sub-para (f)(ii). This allows those who are continuously in and out of hospital to be treated as "patients" in due course. The effect of this is that separate periods spent as a patient which are not more than 28 days apart are added together when calculating the 52 weeks.

(6) The non-dependant is a prisoner: para 7(f). A "prisoner" includes those who are remanded in custody pending trial or sentence as well as those actually serving sentences. It does not, however, include those detained under the mental health legislation listed, nor those resident in bail hostels: para (7)(f)(iii) and *R(IS) 17/93* para 6.

(7) The non-dependant is not residing with the claimant because s/he is a "member of the armed forces away on operations", defined in reg 2(1) as "a member of the regular or reserve forces (within the meaning of the Armed Forces Act 2006) who is absent, while on operations, from the dwelling usually occupied as their home": para 7(g). This exception is needed as, for the purposes of determining the number of bedrooms the claimant is allowed under the various size criteria (see, for example, reg B13), a son, daughter, step-son or step-daughter of the claimant or her/his partner who was the claimant's non-dependant before becoming a "member of the armed forces away on operations" continues to count as occupying the clamant's home if s/he intends to resume living there.

(8) The non-dependant is aged under 25 and is on IS, income-based JSA or income-related ESA which does not include a support component and is not a member of the work-related activity group, defined in reg 2(1): para (8)(a). If the non-dependant is on income-related ESA, this para can only apply until a component is awarded by the DWP or s/he becomes a member of the work-related activity group. For the situations when a person is deemed to be "on" IS, income-based JSA or income-related ESA, see reg 2(1), (3) and (3A) respectively. Note that someone is considered to be "on" income-based JSA not only on days when it is payable to her/him, but also on other days (eg, when sanctioned for losing a job through misconduct) and "on" income-related ESA eg, when it is not payable to a claimant who is disqualified in certain circumstances. See the note on reg 2(3) and (3A) on p247.

(9) The non-dependant is aged under 25 and is entitled to an award of UC, provided the non-dependant does not have earned income: para 8(b) and (11). Reg 52 of the UC Regs 2013 SI No.376 defines "earned income" as (1) the remuneration or profits derived from employment under a contract of service or in an office, including elective office, a trade, profession or vocation or any other paid work; or (2) any income treated as earned income under Chapter 2 of Part 6 of those regulations. On the wording of para 8(b), it is sufficient that the non-dependant is entitled to UC; UC does not have to be in payment – eg, if the claimant has been sanctioned and the amount of the UC award has been reduced to nil.

(10) The non-dependant is on PC: para (10).

Minimum housing benefit

75. Where housing benefit is payable in the form of a rent rebate or allowance, it shall not be payable where the amount to which a person would otherwise be entitled is less than 50 pence per benefit week.

Definitions

"benefit week" – see reg 2(1).

"rent rebate/allowance" – see ss134(1A) and (1B) and 191 SSAA.

General Note

This prescribes the minimum weekly amount that may be paid to a claimant in respect of both forms of HB: rent rebate and rent allowance. If the claimant is entitled to less than 50p, that rebate or allowance shall not be paid.

From April 2013, total benefit payments to working age claimants can be capped. Until UC is fully introduced, local authorities apply the "benefit cap" by reducing the claimant's HB. However, HB cannot be reduced below the minimum amount found in reg 75: reg 75D.

PART 8A
Benefit cap

General Note on Part 8A

Sections 96, 96A and 97 WRA 2012 make provision for limiting the amount of HB entitlement of certain working-age claimants if their total entitlement to welfare benefits exceeds a specified amount – the "relevant amount". Note that for HB purposes, the "benefit cap" can only apply to those entitled to HB under the HB Regs. It does not apply if either the claimant or her/his partner is at least the qualifying age for PC so long as neither is on IS, income-based JSA, income-related ESA or UC – ie, if the claimant is entitled to HB under the HB(SPC) Regs. Note: new claims for HB by members of a mixed-age couple (ie, where only one member of the couple is at least the qualifying age for PC) are generally no longer allowed on or after 15 May 2019. See the General Note to reg 5 HB(SPC) Regs on p733 for a discussion.

For HB purposes, this "benefit cap" applies in the circumstances set out in reg 75A. The "relevant amount" is determined by reference to the applicable "annual limit" as set out in s96(5A) WRA 2012 and as calculated under reg 75CA.

See reg 75B for when a local authority is to make a determination whether a benefit cap applies and reg 75C for the manner of calculating the amount of welfare benefits. "Welfare benefit" is defined in s96(10) WRA 2012; not all social security benefits and tax credits are included (see p208). Note that if the claimant lives in "specified accommodation" (defined in reg 75H, broadly, as specified types of supported accommodation and of temporary accommodation for those who have left home as a result of domestic violence), HB for that dwelling is disregarded.

Exceptions are provided, and the benefit cap does not apply in the following circumstances.

(1)   The claimant or her/his partner is currently, or has recently been, in work in specified circumstances: reg 75E.

(2)   The claimant or her/his partner or a dependent child or qualifying young person is receiving a specified benefit: reg 75F.

Unless any of the exceptions to the benefit cap apply, if the claimant's total entitlement to welfare benefits in respect of the "reference period" (for HB a benefit week) exceeds the relevant amount, the local authority must reduce her/his entitlement to HB under reg 75D by the amount of the excess (or a lower sum so as to leave the claimant with a minimum amount of HB). Note also the special rules for calculating extended payments of HB in regs 72E and 73E.

Challenging a benefit cap

For UC purposes, a decision to apply the benefit cap is not an appealable decision; s97(6) WRA 2012 adds a new paragraph 8A to the list of unappealable decisions in Sch 2 SSA 1998. However, for HB purposes, no comparable amendments were made to para 6 Sch 7 CSPSSA, nor has a benefit cap decision been prescribed by the HB&CTB(DA) Regs as a decision against which there is no right of appeal. There *is* therefore a right of appeal against an HB benefit cap decision – eg, the decision whether any of the exceptions to the benefit cap apply or the amount of a claimant's welfare benefits that were taken into account. In any event, a decision on an award of HB (the "outcome" decision – ie, the amount of HB entitlement eventually arrived at) is appealable.

A challenge to the way the benefit cap operates failed in *R (on the application of SG and others) v SSWP* [2014] EWCA Civ 156. The claimants (single mothers and their children) argued that the cap had been implemented in a way that discriminated against women and large families contrary to Art 14 of the Convention, breached their right to private and family life and was irrational under common law. The claimants had all experienced extreme domestic violence and abuse and were in danger of becoming homeless as a result of the benefit cap. The claimants appealed to the Supreme Court: *R (SG and others (previously JS and others)) v SSWP* [2015] UKSC 16 [2015] 1 WRL 1449. Although the Supreme Court found that in introducing the benefit cap the government had failed to comply with the UN Convention on the Rights of the Child, in a 3:2 split decision, it decided that the benefit cap did not breach Art 14 of the Convention, and that it is, therefore, lawful.

The application of the benefit cap to lone parents of children under two was, however, subsequently found by the High Court to be unlawful because of its discriminatory impact: *R (on the application of DA and others) v SSWP* [2017] EWHC 1446 (Admin). Four lone parents argued that, because of their caring responsibilities for young children, they were unable to work the required 16 hours to meet one of the exemptions from the cap. The High Court found that the aim pursued by the benefit cap was legitimate and that, given the detailed parliamentary consideration that it had been subject to, the Court should be circumspect in interfering with it. However, Mr Justice Collins considered the powerful evidence of the damaging effect of the cap on the claimants and the lack of specific assessment of the ability of lone parents of children under two to enter work. He concluded that the different effect of the cap on such families is manifestly without reasonable foundation and so amounts to unlawful discrimination contrary to Art 14. In doing so, he also found that the children's rights to respect for private and family life under Art 8 were likely to be affected by cuts to benefits specifically intended to provide for their support, differentiating his conclusion on this point from that of the Supreme Court in *R (SG and others)* above.

The Court of Appeal subsequently allowed an appeal by the DWP, overturning the decision: *R (DA and others) v SSWP* [2018] EWCA Civ 504. Leave to appeal to the Supreme Court was granted. The case was heard – together with a related case, *R (on the application of DS and others) v SSWP,* which had been granted permission by the High Court to 'leapfrog' to the Supreme Court so as to be heard jointly – in July 2018. In these cases, the Supreme Court ([2019] UKSC 21) decided by a majority that discrimination faced by lone parents of young children subject to the benefit cap is not "manifestly without reasonable foundation" and that the government and Parliament both gave proper consideration to the interests of the children affected to objectively justify the impact of the cap upon them. The court acknowledged that the benefit cap has had a major impact on lone parent households with a child aged under five and, in particular, under two. It noted "striking evidence" about the effect on children of an early life of poverty and accepted evidence that a substantial reduction in benefit awards due to the benefit cap pulls incomes of lone parents below poverty levels. However, the court stated that the government "did evaluate the likely impact of the revised cap on lone parents with young children; and that it did assess their best interests at a primary level of its overall consideration. This court must impose on itself the discipline not, from its limited perspective, to address whether the government's evaluation of its impact was questionable". It concluded by "a narrow margin" that "the government's decision to treat the appellant cohorts similarly to all others subjected to the revised cap was not manifestly without reasonable foundation".

In *R (Hurley, Jarrett and Palmer) v SSWP* [2015] EWHC 3382 (Admin), the claimants argued that not to exempt those who receive carer's allowance (CA) from the benefit cap was unlawful because this was irrational or disproportionate. Alternatively, CA should not have been included in the definition of "welfare benefit" – ie, the list of benefits that must be used to calculate whether the total welfare benefits to which the claimant (and her/his partner) are entitled exceeds the cap. The claimants also argued that the benefit cap unlawfully discriminates against carers and those for whom they care contrary to Art 14 of the ECHR. Mr Justice Collins found in favour of the claimants. He concluded that the failure to exempt at least individual family carers from the benefit cap was unlawful because this amounted to indirect discrimination which was not objectively justifiable. He added (at paragraph 75):

" ... whether or not the defendant accepts my decision reconsideration will I hope be given to whether the present regulatory regime is appropriate having regard to the hardship it can and does produce and the lack of real benefit to the State in terms of the objectives of the benefit cap. As I have said, a bright line approach is available by simply exempting those single recipients of CA who provide family care."

Note that from 7 November 2016, CA is no longer included in the definition of "welfare benefit": s96(10) WRA 2012. Also from that date, the benefit cap does not apply if the claimant, her/his partner or a qualifying young person for whom the claimant or partner is responsible is entitled to CA: reg 75F(h).

[¹Circumstances in which a benefit cap will apply

75A. Unless regulation 75E or 75F applies, a benefit cap applies where the relevant authority makes a determination that during the reference period the total amount of welfare benefits to which–

(a)   where the claimant is a member of a couple, each member of the couple is or jointly are entitled; or

(b)   in any other case, the claimant is entitled,

exceeds the relevant amount.]

Amendment

1.   Inserted by reg 2(5) of SI 2012 No 2994 as from 15.4.13.

Definitions

"claimant" – see reg 2(1).
"couple" – see reg 75G.
"reference period" – see reg 75G.
"relevant amount" – see regs 75CA and 75G.
"relevant authority" – see reg 2(1).
"welfare benefit" – see s96(10) WRA 2012.

Analysis

For HB purposes, unless any of the exceptions in regs 75E or 75F apply, the "benefit cap" applies in the circumstance set out in reg 75A – ie, where the local authority makes a determination that during a benefit week (the "reference period" as defined in reg 75G) the total amount of welfare benefits (defined in s96(10) WRA 2012) to which the claimant and, if s/he is a member of a couple, her/his partner, are entitled exceeds the "relevant amount" (for which see reg 75CA). Note that "couple" is defined in reg 75G HB Regs by reference to the definition in reg 2(1) HB Regs, other than where the claimant is a member of a polygamous marriage. In this case, "couple" means the claimant and the member of the polygamous marriage to whom s/he was first married, references to the claimant's partner are to that member, and it is the total amount of welfare benefits of the claimant and that member only that are relevant.

If the benefit cap applies, the local authority must reduce the claimant's HB under reg 75D. See reg 75B for when a local authority is to make a determination whether a benefit cap applies and reg 75C for the manner of calculating the amount of welfare benefits.

[¹ [² Determinations

75B.–(1)   A relevant authority may make a determination as to whether the benefit cap applies or whether to change the amount of any reduction made in accordance with regulation 75D (reduction of housing benefit) but a relevant authority is not required to do so unless paragraph (2) applies.

(2)   This paragraph applies where a relevant authority receives notification from the Secretary of State that–

(a)   the benefit cap may apply;

(b)   there has been a change in the amount of a welfare benefit to which a claimant is entitled; or

(c)   there has been a change to the relevant amount which may affect the amount of housing benefit to which a claimant is entitled.]]

Amendments

1.   Inserted by reg 2(5) of SI 2012 No 2994 as from 15.4.13.
2.   Substituted by reg 2(2) of SI 2016 No.909 as from 7.11.16.

Definitions

"claimant" – see reg 2(1).
"relevant amount" – see regs 75G and 75CA.
"relevant authority" – see reg 2(1).
"welfare benefit" – see s96(10) WRA 2012.

Analysis

Under para (1), the local authority can, at any time, determine whether the benefit cap applies, or whether to change the amount of any reduction to a claimant's HB made because it does apply (either upwards or downwards). It is suggested that this includes determining whether, following a change of circumstances (eg, an award of an exempting benefit specified in reg 75F), the benefit cap no longer applies. The use of the words "may" and "not required" makes this discretionary, but this discretion must be exercised fairly. In any case, the decision as to the amount of a claimant's HB entitlement (the local authority's outcome decision) can be revised under reg 4 D&A Regs or superseded under reg 7 of those regulations.

Under para (2), the local authority is required to determine whether the benefit cap applies or whether to change the amount of any reduction to a claimant's HB made because it does apply if it is notified by the DWP of any of the following:

(1)   The benefit cap may apply.

(2)   The amount of a "welfare benefit" to which the claimant is entitled has changed. Note that welfare benefit is defined in s96(10) WRA 2012.

(3)   There has been a change to the "relevant amount" which may affect the amount of a claimant's entitlement to HB. For the relevant amount, see reg 75CA.

[¹ Manner of calculating the amount of welfare benefits

75C.–(1)   When calculating the total amount of welfare benefits, the relevant authority must use the amount of a welfare benefit to which a person is entitled unless paragraph (2), (3) or (4) applies.

(2)   Where the welfare benefit is housing benefit, the relevant authority–

(a)   where the dwelling is [² accommodation specified in regulation 75H (specified accommodation)], must use the amount of nil; and

(b)   in any other case, must not take account of any reduction under regulation 75D and must use the amount to which the claimant would be entitled by virtue of section 130 of the Act.

(3)   Where the welfare benefit is an employment and support allowance, the relevant authority must disregard that benefit where a person is disqualified for receiving it by virtue of section 18 of the Welfare Reform Act.

(4)   Where an amount of a welfare benefit other than jobseeker's allowance or employment and support allowance is taken into account as income in accordance with Part 6 (income and capital), or would be so taken into account if the relevant authority were required to calculate the claimant's income, the relevant authority must use that amount.

(5)   The amount of a welfare benefit for the purpose of paragraph (4) includes any amount of that benefit which would have been payable but for any loss of benefit under, or by virtue of, section 6B, 7 or 9 of the Social Security Fraud Act 2001.]

Amendments

1.   Inserted by reg 2(5) of SI 2012 No 2994, as amended by reg 2(2) of SI 2013 No 546, as from 15.4.13.
2.   Amended by reg 3(2) of SI 2014 No 771 as from 10.4.14.

Definitions

"claimant" – see reg 2(1).
"dwelling" – see reg 2(4) and s137(1) SSCBA.
"employment and support allowance" – see reg 2(1).
"income" – see General Note on Part 6.
"jobseeker's allowance" – see reg 2(1).
"partner" – see reg 2(1), but also the definition of "couple" in reg 75G.
"relevant authority" – see reg 2(1).
"specified accommodation" – see reg 75H.
"welfare benefit" – see s96(10) WRA 2012.
"Welfare Reform Act" – see reg 2(1).

Analysis

Reg 75C sets out the amount of a welfare benefit the local authority must use when calculating a claimant's (and her/his partner's) total welfare benefits. Note that it is only the welfare benefits listed in s96(10) WRA 2012 (on p208) that are to be included in the total, and only those of the claimant (and partner) – ie, not those of any children or qualifying young people. If the claimant is a member of a polygamous marriage, see the definition of "couple" in reg 75G for who counts as her/his "partner" for these purposes.

Para (1): the general rule. Para (1) is the general rule. If para (1) applies, the amount of the welfare benefit used is the amount to which the claimant or partner is entitled – ie, not the amount of the benefit that is in payment. The amount being paid may be lower than the amount of entitlement, for example, if an overpayment is being recovered or deductions are being made for direct payments (eg, for fuel arrears) or if the benefit is JSA or ESA and the claimant has been sanctioned. The general rule in para (1) applies unless any of paras (2) to (4) apply. Thus, para (1) applies to the following.

(1)   A welfare benefit (other than HB) that is not taken into account as income for HB (or would not be taken into account were the local authority required to calculate the claimant's income) – ie, child benefit, IS, income-based JSA, income-related ESA and UC. Note that a claimant is exempt from the benefit cap if s/he is receiving UC, or if s/he or her/his partner is receiving ESA that includes a support component. Note also that prior to 7 November 2016, guardian's allowance came within the definition of "welfare benefit" and para (1) applied, and that UC did *not* come within the definition of "welfare benefit".

(2)   Contribution-based JSA and contributory ESA (but see para (3) if the person is disqualified from receiving ESA).

Para (2): HB. Para (2) sets out the amount that a local authority must use if the welfare benefit is HB.

(1)   If the dwelling in respect of which the HB is paid is "specified accommodation" (defined in reg 75H), broadly specified types of supported accommodation and of temporary accommodation for those who have left home as a result of domestic violence, the HB is disregarded: sub-para (a).

(2)   In all other cases, the amount of HB used is the amount to which the person is entitled before any reduction is made for the benefit cap under reg 75D: sub-para (b).

Para (3): ESA where the person is disqualified from receiving it. Para (3) applies if the benefit is ESA and the person has been disqualified from receiving it under s18 WRA 2007. In this case, ESA is disregarded. Under s18 WRA 2007, and regulations made under it, a person can be disqualified from receiving ESA for up to six weeks if s/he has limited capability for work through her/his own misconduct or through failing without good cause to follow medical advice which would be likely to overcome her/his limited capability for work, s/he failed without good cause to cease behaviour that retards her/his recovery or s/he is absent from home without advising the DWP where s/he can be found without good cause. A person can also be disqualified from receiving ESA if s/he is absent abroad or is imprisoned or detained in legal custody.

Paras (4) and (5): benefits taken into account as income for HB. Para (4) applies to the welfare benefits in s96(10) WRA 2012 (other than JSA or ESA) that are taken into account as income, or would be taken into account were the local authority required to calculate the claimant's income. The latter would apply, for example, if the claimant is on IS, income-based JSA or income-related ESA. Thus, para (4) applies to bereavement allowance, child tax credit, incapacity benefit, maternity allowance, severe disablement allowance, widowed mother's allowance, widowed parent's allowance and widow's pension. Note that prior to 7 November 2016, carer's allowance came within the definition of "welfare benefit" and paras (4) and (5) applied.

The amount of the welfare benefit used is the amount as calculated in accordance with Part 6, including any amount that would have been payable but for any of the loss of benefit for benefit offences provisions cited in para (5). Generally this will be the amount to which the claimant or partner is entitled – ie, not the amount of the benefit that is in payment. However, there are exceptions.

(1)   If the welfare benefit is widowed mother's allowance or widowed parent's allowance, the amount used is the amount of the benefit minus a £15 disregard: Sch 5 para 16.

(2)   If the welfare benefit is CTC which is subject to deduction by way of recovery of an overpayment which arose in the previous tax year, the amount used is the amount of the award of CTC minus the deduction: see reg 40(6).

[¹Determination of relevant amount

75CA.–(1)   The relevant amount is determined by dividing the applicable annual limit by 52 and rounding that amount by disregarding any amount of less than half a penny and treating any amount of half a penny or more as a whole penny.

(2)   The applicable annual limit is–

(a)   £15,410 in the case of single claimants resident in Greater London;

(b)   £23,000 in the case of all other claimants resident in Greater London;

(c)   £13,400 in the case of single claimants not resident in Greater London;

(d)   £20,000 in the case of all other claimants not resident in Greater London.

(3)   For the purposes of section 96 of the 2012 Act (benefit cap) and this regulation a claimant is resident in Greater London if–

(a)   the dwelling that the claimant normally occupies as the claimant's home is in Greater London; or

(b)   where the claimant is treated as occupying more than one dwelling as the claimant's home pursuant to regulation 7(6) (circumstances in which a person is or is not to be treated as occupying a dwelling as his home), one of those dwellings is in Greater London.]

Amendment

1.   Inserted by reg 2(3) of SI 2016 No.909 as from 7.11.16.

Definitions

"claimant" – see reg 2(1).
"dwelling" – see reg 2(4) and s137(1) SSCBA.
"relevant amount" – see reg 75G.
"single claimant" – see reg 2(1).

Analysis

Under s96 WRA 2012, where a single person's or a couple's total entitlement to welfare benefits in respect of a "reference period" exceeds the "relevant amount", the claimant's entitlement to HB is reduced by an amount up to or equalling the excess. Reg 75CA provides the means for determining the relevant amount for the reference period by reference to the applicable annual limit.

Paras (1) and (2). For HB, the reference period is a benefit week – ie, a period of seven days starting on a Monday and ending on a Sunday: regs 2(1) and 75G. Thus a weekly relevant amount is needed and the formula for determining this is in para (1). Para (2) provides the annual limits. The weekly amounts are therefore as follows.

(1)   The weekly relevant amount for a single claimant, defined in reg 2(1) as a claimant who neither has a partner nor is a lone parent, is £296.35 if s/he is resident in Greater London, or £257.69 if s/he is resident elsewhere.

(2)   The weekly relevant amount for a claimant who is *not* a single claimant (ie, who is lone parent or a member of a couple) is £442.31 if s/he is resident in Greater London, or £384.62 if s/he is resident elsewhere.

Note that the weekly relevant amounts were higher prior to 7 November 2016. See reg 75G HB Regs on p492 of the 28th edition of this book.

Para (3) defines when a person is "resident in Greater London". For when a person is, or is not, to be treated as normally occupying a home, see reg 7 (on p256). If the claimant is treated as occupying more than one dwelling as a home, only one of the homes needs to be in Greater London.

[¹ Reduction of housing benefit

75D.–(1) Subject to paragraph (2), where the benefit cap applies, the relevant authority must reduce the amount of housing benefit to which the claimant is entitled by virtue of section 130 of the Act by the amount by which the total amount of welfare benefits exceeds the relevant amount.

(2) Where the reduction would reduce the claimant's housing benefit to less than the minimum amount of housing benefit provided for in regulation 75 (minimum housing benefit), the relevant authority must reduce the claimant's housing benefit by such amount as will leave the claimant entitled to that minimum amount.]

Amendment

1.   Inserted by reg 2(5) of SI 2012 No 2994 as from 15.4.13.

Definitions

"claimant" – see reg 2(1).
"relevant amount" – see regs 75CA and 75G.
"relevant authority" – see reg 2(1).
"total amount of welfare benefits" – see reg 75C.
"welfare benefit" – see s96(10) WRA 2012.

Analysis

Reg 75D provides the method for applying the benefit cap. Simply put, if the benefit cap applies, the local authority works out the amount by which the total welfare benefits (calculated under reg 75C) exceeds the claimant's "relevant amount" (determined under reg 75CA) and must reduce her/his HB entitlement by this amount. The claimant must be left with the minimum HB entitlement in reg 75 – currently 50 pence a week. If the "relevant amount" exceeds the total amount of welfare benefits, no reduction is made.

Examples

(1)   A claimant and his partner, who have four children, get income-based JSA (£114.85), child benefit (£61.80) and CTC (£223.23). They live in a private rented house in Newcastle upon Tyne. Their HB is £240 a week.
The total amount of welfare benefits is: £639.88. JSA, child benefit, CTC and HB are all taken into account.
The relevant amount is: £384.62.
The excess is: £255.26 (£639.88 – £384.62).
The excess is higher than the HB to which the claimant is entitled. HB entitlement is therefore the minimum HB entitlement: £0.50.

(2)   The claimant is living in a women's refuge in Greater London having left home because of domestic violence. She is entitled to HB for two homes. She gets income support (£73.10). Her HB for the refuge is £200 a week. HB for her normal home is £180 a week.
The total amount of welfare benefits is £253.10. IS is taken into account. Only the HB for the claimant's normal home is taken into account.
The relevant amount is £296.35.
There is no excess (the relevant amount is higher than the total amount of welfare benefits).
HB entitlement is therefore: £380 (£200 + £180).

[¹ Exception to the benefit cap: current or recent work

75E.–(1) The benefit cap does not apply where paragraph (2) applies or during the period specified in paragraph (3).

(2) This paragraph applies where the claimant is, or the claimant and the claimant's partner are jointly, entitled to working tax credit.

(3) The specified period is, where paragraph (4) applies, the consecutive period of 39 consecutive weeks starting on the day specified in paragraph (5).

(4) This paragraph applies where the relevant authority is satisfied that, for at least 50 weeks out of the 52 weeks immediately preceding their last day of work, the claimant or the claimant's partner ("P")–

  (a)   was employed or engaged in work for payment, or in the expectation of payment; and

  (b)   was not entitled to income support, a jobseeker's allowance or an employment and support allowance, and, for the purposes of sub-paragraph (a), P is employed or engaged in work for any day on which P is on maternity leave, paternity leave [², adoption leave or shared parental leave] or is in receipt of statutory sick pay.

(5)   The specified day is the day after the last day on which P was employed or engaged in the work referred to in paragraph (4).]

Modifications

The amendments made by SI 2014 No.3255 which came into force on 5 April 2015 do not have effect in relation to ordinary statutory paternity pay which is paid, additional statutory paternity pay which is paid, a period in respect of which additional statutory paternity pay is payable which begins, or continues, ordinary paternity leave which is taken or additional paternity leave which is taken on or after 5 April 2015. See art 35 of SI 2014 No.3255.

Amendments

1.   Inserted by reg 2(5) of SI 2012 No 2994 as from 15.4.13.
2.   Amended by art 17(7) of SI 2014 No 3255 as from 31.12.14.

Definitions

"adoption leave", "maternity leave", "shared parental leave" and "paternity leave" – see reg 2(1).
"claimant" – see reg 2(1).
"employment and support allowance" – see reg 2(1).
"jobseeker's allowance" – see reg 2(1).
"partner" – see reg 2(1), but also the definition of "couple" in reg 75G.
"working tax credit" – see reg 2(1).

General Note

Reg 75E provides an exemption from the benefit cap if the claimant or her/his partner is in work and entitled to WTC, or has recently worked. See also reg 75F for exemption for receipt of a specified benefit.

Analysis

The benefit cap does not apply if para (2) applies, or during the "grace period" provided by paras (3) to (5).

Para (2): entitlement to WTC. Under para (2), the benefit cap does not apply if the claimant is entitled to WTC, on her/his own or jointly with her/his partner. Note that the rule does not exempt a claimant if there is no entitlement to WTC – eg, if neither the claimant nor her/his partner works sufficient hours to qualify. However, if a person (or her/his partner) is in qualifying remunerative work (ie, working sufficient hours) and satisfies the other rules of entitlement to WTC, including making a claim, s/he (or they) can be awarded WTC at a nil rate under s14(3) of the Tax Credits Act 2002 – ie, if income is above the relevant threshold. In these circumstances, it is suggested s/he should be considered to be entitled to WTC and therefore exempt from the benefit cap. Claimants may need to be advised to make a protective WTC claim in this situation.

Paras (3) to (5): the "grace period". Under para (3), the benefit cap does not apply during a 39-week grace period, if the claimant (or her/his partner) has worked recently. There are two criteria.

(1)   The claimant (or partner) must have been employed or engaged in work for payment, or in expectation of payment, for at least 50 of the 52 weeks immediately before the last day of employment or work: para (4)(a). Note that there is no minimum number of hours, so part-time work will suffice. Note also that a person is to be considered as employed or engaged in work while on maternity leave, paternity leave, shared parental leave or adoption leave, or when receiving SSP.

(2)   The claimant (or partner) must not have been entitled to IS, JSA or ESA in at least 50 of the 52 weeks immediately before the last day of employment or work – ie, if s/he (or her/his partner) was entitled to any of those benefits in three or more weeks in the 52 weeks, the claimant will not be exempt from the benefit cap under reg 75E. To be entitled to IS, JSA or ESA, the claimant (or partner) must have made a claim for the benefit.

The 39-week grace period starts on the day after the last day on which the claimant (or partner) was employed or engaged in work: para (5).

[¹ Exception to the benefit cap: receipt of specified benefit

75F.–(1)   The benefit cap does not apply where–

(a)   the claimant or the claimant's partner is receiving an employment and support allowance under Part 1 of the Welfare Reform Act which includes a support component;

(b)   the claimant or the claimant's partner is receiving an industrial injuries benefit by virtue of Part 5 of the Act;

(c)   the claimant or the claimant's partner is receiving an attendance allowance;

(d)   the claimant or the claimant's partner is receiving a war pension;

(e)   the claimant, the claimant's partner or a child or young person for whom the claimant or the claimant's partner is responsible, is receiving a disability living allowance;

(ea)   the claimant, the claimant's partner or a young person for whom the claimant or the claimant's partner is responsible, is receiving a personal independence payment or an armed forces independence payment under the Armed Forces and Reserve Forces (Compensation) Scheme Order 2011;

(f)   the claimant, the claimant's partner or a child or young person for whom the claimant or the claimant's partner is responsible is entitled to a payment listed in sub-paragraph (b), (c), (d), (e) or (ea) but–

    (i)   that person is not receiving it under regulation 6 (hospitalisation) or regulation 7 (persons in care homes) of the Social Security (Attendance Allowance) Regulations 1991;

    (ii)   it is withheld under article 53 of the Naval, Military and Air Forces Etc (Disablement and Death) Service Pensions Order 2006 (maintenance in hospital or an institution);

    (iii)   that person is not receiving it under regulation 8 (hospitalisation) or regulation 9 (persons in care homes) of the Social Security (Disability Living Allowance) Regulations 1991;

    (iv)   that payment is not payable in accordance with regulations made under section 85 (care home residents) or section 86(1) (hospital in-patients) of the Welfare Reform Act 2012;

(g)   the claimant is receiving universal credit.

[² (h)   the claimant, the claimant's partner, or a young person for whom the claimant or the claimant's partner is responsible, is entitled to a carer's allowance under section 70 of the Act;]

[² (i)   the claimant, the claimant's partner or a young person for whom the claimant or the claimant's partner is responsible, is entitled to a guardian's allowance under section 77 of the Act.]

(2)   In this regulation "war pension" has the meaning in regulation 2 (interpretation) and includes–

(a)   a guaranteed income payment;

(b)   a pension payable to a person as a widow, widower or surviving civil partner under any power of Her Majesty otherwise than under an enactment to make provision about pensions for or in respect of persons who have been disabled or have died in consequence of service as members of the armed forces of the Crown;

(c)   a payment which is made under any of–

    (i)   the Order in Council of 19th December 1881;

    (ii)   the Royal Warrant of 27th October 1884;

    (iii)   the Order by His Majesty of 14th January 1922, to a widow, widower or surviving civil partner of a person whose death was attributable to service in a capacity analogous to service as a member of the armed forces of the Crown and whose service in such capacity terminated before 31st March 1973 (d) a pension paid by the government of a country outside Great Britain which is analogous to a war pension or any of the pensions or payments mentioned in subparagraphs (a) to (c).]

Amendments

1.   Inserted by reg 2(5) of SI 2012 No 2994, as amended by reg 8 and Sch para 51 of SI 2013 No 388, reg 2(3) of SI 2013 No 546 and Art 7 and Sch para 48 of SI 2013 No 591, as from 15.4.13.

2.   Inserted by reg 2(4) of SI 2016 No.909 as from 7.11.16.

Definitions

"armed forces independence payment", "attendance allowance", "disability living allowance" and "personal independence payment" – see reg 2(1).

"child" – see reg 2(1).

"claimant" – see reg 2(1).
"employment and support allowance" – see reg 2(1).
"partner" – see reg 2(1), but also the definition of "couple" in reg 75G.
"responsible for a child or young person" – see reg 20.
"support component" – see Sch 3 para 24.
"universal credit" – see reg 2(1).
"war pension" – see reg 2(1).
"Welfare Reform Act" – see reg 2(1).
"young person" – see regs 2(1) and 19.

General Note

Reg 75F provides an exemption from the benefit cap if the claimant or her/his partner, or a child or young person who is a member of her/his "family" for HB purposes, is in receipt of a specified benefit. Note that receipt of a specified benefit by any other person (eg, a non-dependant) does not exempt the claimant from the benefit cap.

See also reg 75E for exemption if the claimant or her/his partner is in work and entitled to WTC, or has worked recently.

Analysis

The benefit cap does not apply if the claimant, her/his partner or child or qualifying young person is receiving one of the specified benefits, or in some cases would be receiving it but for being in hospital or a care home.

Claimant. The claimant is exempt from the benefit cap if s/he is receiving universal credit (UC): para (1)(g). This will generally only apply if the UC claimant's HB is for "specified accommodation" (defined in reg 75H): see regs 5 and 6 Universal Credit (Transitional Provisions) Regulations 2014 SI No.1230 on p1862 and p1864. Note that in any event, HB for "specified accommodation" is disregarded in calculating the total welfare benefits under reg 75C(2)(a).

Claimant or partner. The claimant is exempt from the benefit cap if s/he or her/his partner is receiving any of the following.

(1)   ESA that includes a support component (for which see ss2(2) and 4(4) WRA 2007): para (1)(a). Note that if the person is disqualified from receiving ESA under s18 WRA 2007, the claimant would not be exempt from the benefit cap. However, the ESA must be disregarded when the local authority calculates the claimant's total welfare benefits: reg 75C(3).

(2)   An industrial injuries benefit: para (1)(b). These are industrial injuries disablement benefit, reduced earnings allowance, retirement allowance and industrial death benefit. Note that the latter is now only payable in respect of deaths before 11 April 1988.

(3)   Attendance allowance (AA), disability living allowance (DLA), personal independence payment (PIP), armed forces independence payment (AFIP), carer's allowance (CA) or guardian's allowance: para (1)(c), (e), (ea), (h) and (i).

(4)   A war pension. For the definition, see para (2).

Child or qualifying young person. The claimant is exempt from the benefit cap if a child or qualifying young person for whom the claimant or her/his partner is responsible is receiving DLA: para (1)(e). The claimant is also exempt if a qualifying young person is receiving PIP, AFIP, CA or guardian's allowance: paras (1)(ea), (h) and (i). For when someone counts as responsible for a child or qualifying young person, see reg 20 on p407.

The effect of hospitalisation or residence in a care home. The claimant is also exempt if s/he, her/his partner or a child or qualifying young person is entitled to one of the relevant benefits in para (1)(b) to (ea), but is not receiving it after being a hospital patient or resident in a care home for a specified period: para (1)(f).

[¹ Interpretation

75G.   For the purposes of section 96 of the Welfare Reform Act 2012 and this Part–
"couple" has the meaning in regulation 2 unless the claimant is a member of a polygamous
            marriage, in which case it means the claimant and the member of the polygamous
            marriage to whom the claimant was first married and references to the claimant's
            partner are to that member of that marriage;
"reference period" means a benefit week;
"relevant amount" [² means the amount determined in accordance with regulation 75CA];
[²]

Amendments

1.   Inserted by reg 2(5) of SI 2012 No 2994 as from 15.4.13.
2.   Amended by reg 2(5) of SI 2016 No.909 as from 7.11.16.

General Note

Reg 75G contains some definitions relevant to the benefit cap.

"Couple" is defined by reference to the definition in reg 2(1) HB Regs, other than where the claimant is a member of a polygamous marriage. In this case, "couple" means the claimant and the member of the polygamous marriage to whom s/he was first married, and references to the claimant's partner are to that member. Thus, it is the total amount of welfare benefits of the claimant and that member only that are relevant. Likewise, the claimant can only be exempt from the benefit cap under reg 75F if s/he or that member (or a child or qualifying young person of either of them) is receiving a specified benefit (or would be receiving it but for hospitalisation or residence in a care home).

"Reference period". "Benefit week" is defined in reg 2(1) as a period of seven days starting on a Monday and ending on a Sunday.

"Relevant amount" is defined by reference to reg 75CA.

Prior to 7 November 2016, "welfare benefit" was defined in reg 75G. Now see s96(10) WRA 2012.

[¹Specified accommodation

75H.–(1)   The accommodation referred to in regulation 75C(2)(a) is accommodation to which one or more of the following paragraphs applies.

(2)   This paragraph applies to accommodation which is exempt accommodation within the meaning of paragraph 4(10) of Schedule 3 to the Consequential Provisions Regulations.

(3)   This paragraph applies to accommodation–

(a)   which is provided by a relevant body;

(b)   into which the claimant has been admitted in order to meet a need for care, support or supervision; and

(c)   where the claimant receives care, support or supervision.

(4)   This paragraph applies to accommodation which–

(a)   is provided by a relevant authority or a relevant body to the claimant because the claimant has left the home as a result of domestic violence; and

(b)   consists of a building, or part of a building, which is used wholly or mainly for the non-permanent accommodation of persons who have left their homes as a result of domestic violence.

(5)   This paragraph applies to accommodation–

(a)   which would be a hostel within the meaning of regulation 2(1) (interpretation) but for it being owned or managed by a relevant authority; and

(b)   where the claimant receives care, support or supervision.

(6)   In this regulation–

"coercive behaviour" means an act of assault, humiliation or intimidation or other abuse that is used to harm, punish or frighten the victim;

"controlling behaviour" means an act designed to make a person subordinate or dependent by isolating them from sources of support, exploiting their resources and capacities for personal gain, depriving them of the means needed for independence, resistance or escape or regulating their everyday behaviour;

"domestic violence" means any incident, or pattern of incidents, of controlling behaviour, coercive behaviour, violence or abuse, including but not limited to–

(a)   psychological abuse;

(b)   physical abuse;

(c)   sexual abuse;

(d)   emotional abuse;

(e)   financial abuse,

regardless of the gender or sexuality of the victim;

"relevant body" means a–

(a)   council for a county in England for each part of whose area there is a district council;

(b)   housing association;

(c)   registered charity; or

(d)   voluntary organisation.]

Amendment

1.   Inserted by reg 3(3) of SI 2014 No 771 as from 10.4.14.

Definitions
"claimant" – see reg 2(1).
"the Consequential Provisions Regulations" – see reg 2(1).
"hostel" – see reg 2(1).
"housing association" – see reg 2(1).
"relevant authority" – see reg 2(1).
"voluntary organisation" – see reg 2(1).

General Note
Under reg 75C(2)(a), in calculating the total amount of a claimant's welfare benefits, the local authority must disregard HB if the dwelling is accommodation specified in reg 75H. Note that prior to 10 April 2014, HB was only disregarded if the dwelling was "exempt accommodation".

There are four categories of "specified accommodation".

"Exempt accommodation" as defined in Sch 3 para 4(10) HB&CTB(CP) Regs (on p1777): para (2). This is accommodation which is a "resettlement place", or accommodation provided by specified bodies where care, support or supervision is provided to the claimant by that body or a person acting on its behalf. See the commentary from p1779.

Accommodation where the claimant receives care, support or supervision provided by a "relevant body" (defined in para (6)): para (3). The claimant must have been admitted into the accommodation to meet a need for care, support or supervision. Note that here, the care, support or supervision does not have to be provided by the relevant body or on its behalf.

Temporary accommodation for people who have left home because of domestic violence. The accommodation must be provided by a "relevant authority" or a "relevant body" (defined in para (6)) – eg, a women's refuge: para (4). The claimant must have left home as a result of the domestic violence. Note the wide definition of "domestic violence" in para (6).

Hostel accommodation owned or managed by a "relevant authority" where the claimant receives care, support or supervision. The care, support or supervision does not have to be provided by the relevant authority.

PART 9
Calculation of weekly amounts and changes of circumstances

General Note on Part 9
Reg 76 provides the rules for deciding in which benefit week the claimant first becomes entitled to HB. Reg 79 sets out the dates on which changes of circumstance are to take effect for the purposes of calculating HB entitlement. Reg 80 deals with how eligible rent is to be worked out on a weekly basis. Reg 81 deals with the effect of "rent-free periods" on the calculation of weekly amounts of HB.

It is important to note that if IS, income-based JSA or income-related ESA entitlement ends, for whatever reason, HB entitlement does *not* end automatically, although there could be grounds for revision or supersession of the HB award – eg, where income has changed. This was confirmed in *CH 3736/2006*, a decision that pre-dated the introduction of income-related ESA. The deputy commissioner reminded authorities that after the abolition of "benefit periods" in October 2003 (for claimants 60 or over) and in April 2004 (for other claimants), except in the circumstances contemplated by the then reg 77 (see the General Note on p534), the cessation of IS or income-based JSA is an ordinary change of circumstances that must be assessed like any other and it does not have the effect of automatically ending entitlement to HB. It cannot even be assumed that the cessation of IS, income-based JSA or income-related ESA will reduce entitlement to HB. Until the authority knows why entitlement has ended, it cannot conclude that it ended in circumstances that provide grounds upon which to supersede the claimant's entitlement to HB. In cases where it is unclear why benefit has stopped, the correct approach is for the authority to suspend payment of benefit and make further enquiries to establish whether there are grounds for superseding the HB award.

Date on which entitlement is to commence
76.–(1) Subject to [¹ paragraphs (2) and (3)], a person who makes a claim and is otherwise entitled to housing benefit shall be entitled to that benefit from the benefit week following the date on which his claim is or is treated as made.

(2) Where a claimant is otherwise entitled to housing benefit and becomes liable, for the first time, to make payments in respect of the dwelling which he occupies as his home in the benefit week in which his claim is or is treated as made, he shall be so entitled from that benefit week.

[¹ (3) A claimant shall become entitled to housing benefit from the benefit week in which the first day in respect of which his claim is made falls, where–
(a) he is otherwise entitled to housing benefit;

(b)   paragraph (2) does not apply to him; and

[² (c) he becomes liable in that benefit week to make payments, which fall due on a daily basis, in respect of the accommodation listed in paragraph (4) which he occupies as his home.]]

[³ (4) The accommodation referred to in paragraph (3)(c) is–

(a)   a hostel;

(b)   board and lodging accommodation where the payments are to an authority under section 206(2) of the Housing Act 1996 or section 35(2)(b) of the Housing (Scotland) Act 1987;

(c)   accommodation which the authority holds on a licence agreement where the payments are to an authority under section 206(2) of the Housing Act 1996 or section 35(2)(b) of the Housing (Scotland) Act 1987; or

(d)   accommodation outside that authority's Housing Revenue Account which the authority holds on a lease granted for a term not exceeding 10 years.

(5)   In this regulation–

"board and lodging accommodation" means–

(a)   accommodation provided to a person or, if he is a member of a family, to him or any other member of his family, for a charge which is inclusive of the provision of that accommodation and at least some cooked or prepared meals which both are cooked or prepared (by a person other than a person to whom the accommodation is provided or by a member of his family) and are consumed in that accommodation or associated premises; or

(b)   accommodation provided to a person in a hotel, guest house, lodging house or some similar establishment,

but it does not include accommodation in a care home, an Abbeyfield Home, an independent hospital or a hostel; and

"Housing Revenue Account" has the same meaning as for the purposes of Part VIII of the Social Security Administration Act 1992.]

Amendments

1.   Amended by reg 8(4) of SI 2006 No 588 as from 1.4.06.
2.   Substituted by reg 2(2)(a) of SI 2007 No 294 as from 1.4.07.
3.   Inserted by reg 2(2)(b) of SI 2007 No 294 as from 1.4.07.

Definitions

"Abbeyfield Home", "care home", "hostel" and "independent hospital" – see reg 2(1).
"benefit week" – see reg 2(1).
"dwelling" – see s137(1) SSCBA and reg 2(4).
"liable to make payments" – see regs 2(2), 8 and 9.

General Note

Reg 76 deals with when entitlement to HB commences and therefore from when it can be paid. Para (1) sets out the general rule and paras (2) and (3) provide exceptions where people who become liable for rent on their home claim (or are treated as claiming) HB during the same benefit week.

Analysis

Para (1). The general rule is that unless paras (2) or (3) apply, a claimant's entitlement to HB usually begins from the "benefit week" (running from Monday to Sunday) following the week in which the claim is made (or is treated as made) – ie, the Monday after the date of claim. Reg 83 determines the date of claim (the date on which a claim is, or is to be treated as, made). This can be a date earlier (or later) than the date the claim is actually received by the authority.

Para (2). There are two conditions which must be satisfied before a claimant's entitlement to HB commences in the benefit week in which s/he claims rather than the one which follows.

(1)   S/he must become liable for rent on the dwelling she occupies as her/his home (see reg 7) for the *first time* during that benefit week (eg, s/he moves into a new home).

(2)   S/he must make her/his claim or be treated as doing so under reg 83 during that week.

The practical effect of this is that if para (2) applies, entitlement to HB starts from the same day the liability for rent began: see reg 80(2), (3)(a), (4) and (8). Note that the claimant must both occupy the dwelling as a home *and* be liable to make payments in respect of it: *SL v Renfrewshire Council (HB)* [2014] UKUT 411 (AAC).

In *SSWP v Robinson* [2004], 11 February, CA; reported as *R(H) 4/04*, the Court of Appeal allowed the Secretary of State's appeal in a case where a claim had been made on 11 March, the same day on which the claimant became liable for rent, but had not moved into the property until 20 March. The commissioner had awarded benefit under para (2) from the benefit week in which 11 March fell. However, the Court of Appeal held that para (2) could not apply on the facts of Ms Robinson's case as, although in the week in which 11 March fell the claimant was liable for the rent on the new dwelling, she was not occupying it as her home, and reg 65(2) HB Regs 1987 (now reg 76(2) HB Regs) – by its use of the phrase "becomes liable for the first time" – only applies where the liability to make payments in respect of the property for the first time coincides with the benefit week in which the claimant meets the other conditions of entitlement to HB. In Ms Robinson's case that did not arise as her liability arose for the first time in the week before she met the other conditions of entitlement for HB (ie, occupying the dwelling as her home) and so the general rule in reg 65(1) HB Regs 1987 applied. However, see reg 7 which allows for some claimants who are moving (or have moved) home to be treated as occupying the new home although they are not actually doing so.

In *R(H) 9/07*, the claimant had made a claim for HB in advance of satisfying the rules of entitlement. A few weeks later he moved into his new home. This was in the benefit week following the week his liability for rent began. Applying *Robinson,* the local authority awarded HB from the Monday following the date the claimant had moved into his new home. Commissioner Williams agreed this was the date on which this claimant's entitlement commenced. He gave detailed consideration to the interaction between an authority's discretion to treat a claim in advance of entitlement as made in the benefit week preceding the first week of entitlement under reg 76(11) HB Regs 1987 (now reg 83(10)), and the rules on commencement of entitlement to HB in reg 65(1) and (2) HB Regs 1987 (now reg 76(1) and (2)). The rules in reg 76(1) and (2) apply both to the actual date of claim and to the date treated as the date of claim. He therefore concluded that where a claim in advance is made, and reg 83(10) has been found to be relevant, it must be applied to both. The commissioner set out a helpful step-by-step approach authorities should take in reaching decisions in such cases. An authority should:
(1)   Identify the actual date of claim.
(2)   If the claim is made in the same week as that in which the claimant first becomes liable to make payments for her/his home, apply reg 76(2).
(3)   If on the facts reg 76(2) does not apply, apply reg 76(1).
(4)   Consider if reg 83(10) applies on the facts.
(5)   If reg 83(10) does not apply, the answer is that at step (3).
(6)   If reg 83(10) does apply, apply the date on which the claim is to be treated as made by reg 83(10) to reg 76(2).
(7)   If on the assumption in step (6), reg 76(2) is relevant to the claim, consider, as a matter of discretion, if reg 83(10) is to be applied.
(8)   If reg 76(2) is not relevant on the assumption in step (6), apply the assumption to reg 76(1). If the answer is different to that given at step (3) consider if that answer should, as a matter of discretion, be applied instead of the answer at step (3).
Note that para (3) was inserted into reg 76 in April 2006. Reg 76(1) is now subject to reg 76(2) *and* (3).

Para (3) provides assistance to those living in the types of accommodation listed in para (4), who become liable for daily payments in respect of that accommodation which they occupy as a home. Unless para (2) applies, entitlement to HB commences in the benefit week in which the first day in respect of which the claim is made falls, which could include where a claim is made for a past period: reg 83.

"Board and lodging accommodation" is defined as accommodation in which cooked or prepared meals are provided and consumed. This element of the definition is identical to that found in reg 2(1) Income Support (General) Regulations 1987. Preparation, in the context of this definition, requires something more than merely leaving the ingredients out for the lodger: *CSB 950/1987.*

[¹Date on which housing benefit is to end
77.]

Amendment
1.   Omitted by reg 4(4)(a) of SI 2008 No 959 as from 6.10.08.

General Note
Until 6 October 2008, reg 77 provided a change of circumstances which terminated entitlement to HB, even where there would otherwise have been continued entitlement. This was that entitlement to IS or income-based (or joint-claim) JSA had ceased because of the commencement of employment (or self-employment) or because of increased earnings from, or hours worked in, such employment – the same circumstances that led to entitlement to extended payments of HB under the former version of reg 72. This meant that in such circumstances, a fresh claim for HB was necessary for entitlement to continue. For commentary, see pp367–86 of the 20th edition. See also the General Note to this Part on p532.

[¹Date on which housing benefit is to end where entitlement to severe disablement allowance or incapacity benefit ceases
78.]

Amendment

1.   Omitted by reg 4(4)(b) of SI 2008 No 959 as from 6.10.08.

General Note

Until 6 October 2008, entitlement to HB ended, even where there would otherwise be continued entitlement, where entitlement to severe disablement allowance or incapacity benefit ceased because of employment or increased earnings. The rules were broadly the same as those in reg 77 – see in particular the General Note above and the General Note to this Part on p532.

Date on which change of circumstances is to take effect

79.–(1)   Except in cases where [⁵ regulation 34 (disregard of changes in tax, contributions, etc) applies, and subject to regulation 8(3) of the Decisions and Appeals Regulations and] the following provisions of this regulation, and to [⁷ regulation 80(5)], a change of circumstances which affects entitlement to, or the amount of, housing benefit ("change of circumstances") shall take effect from the first day of the benefit week following the date on which the change of circumstances actually occurs, and where that change is cessation of entitlement to any benefit under the benefit Acts, the date on which the change actually occurs shall be the day immediately following the last day of entitlement to that benefit.

[¹(2)   Subject to paragraph (8) [⁵ and regulation 8(3) of the Decisions and Appeals Regulations] where the change of circumstances is a change in the amount of rent payable in respect of a dwelling, that change shall take effect from the day on which it actually occurs.]

[²(2A)   Subject to paragraphs (8) [⁶ to (10)], except in a case where regulation 8(3) of the Decisions and Appeals Regulations applies, where the change of circumstances is–

(a)   that a person moves into a new dwelling occupied as the home, or

(b)   any other event which–

    (i)   entitles a person to be treated as occupying two dwellings as his home under regulation 7(6), or

    (ii)   brings to an end a person's right to be treated as occupying two dwellings as his home under that regulation, in a case where he has, immediately prior to the event, been treated as occupying two dwellings as his home,

    that change of circumstances shall take effect on the day on which it actually occurs.

(2B)   Subject to paragraph (8), where the change of circumstances is the expiry of a maximum period of time, referred to in regulation 7(6), for which a person can be treated as occupying two dwellings as his home, that change shall take effect on the day after the last day of that period]

(3)   Subject to paragraphs (8) [³], where the change of circumstances is an amendment to these Regulations that change, subject to [⁷ regulation 80(5)], shall take effect as follows–

(a)   where the amendment is made by an order under section 150 of the Administration Act (annual up-rating of benefits)–

    (i)   in a case in which the claimant's weekly amount of eligible rent falls to be calculated in accordance with regulation 80(2)(b) [³ or (c)] (calculation of weekly amounts), from 1st April;

    (ii)   in any other case, from the first Monday in April,

    in the year in which that order comes into force;

(b)   in respect of any other amendment, from the date on which the amendment of these Regulations comes into force in the particular case.

[¹(4)   Subject to paragraph (8), if two or more changes of circumstances occurring in the same benefit week would, but for this paragraph, take effect in different benefit weeks in accordance with this regulation, they shall all take effect on the first day of the benefit week in which they occur, unless a change taking effect under paragraphs (2), (2A) or

(2B) takes effect in that week, in which case the changes shall all take effect on the day on which that change takes effect.]

(5)   Where, during a benefit week commencing on the first Monday in April–

(a)   a change of circumstances takes effect in accordance with paragraph (3)(a)(ii);

(b)   one or more changes of circumstances occur to which paragraph (1) applies; and

(c)   no other change of circumstances occurs to which this regulation applies,

any change of circumstances to which paragraph (1) applies and which occurs in that benefit week shall take effect from the first day of that benefit week.

(6)   Where the change of circumstances is that income, or an increase in the amount of income, other than a benefit or an increase in the amount of a benefit under [¹⁰ the Act,] [⁹ [¹⁰] or part 4 of the 2012 Act] [¹⁰ or article 24A of the Armed Forces and Reserve Forces (Compensation Scheme) Order 2011], is paid in respect of a past period and there was no entitlement to income of that amount during that period, the change of circumstances shall take effect from the first day on which such income, had it been paid in that period at intervals appropriate to that income, would have fallen to be taken into account for the purposes of these Regulations.

(7)   Without prejudice to paragraph (6), where the change of circumstances is the payment of income, or arrears of income, in respect of a past period, the change of circumstances shall take effect from the first day on which such income, had it been timeously paid in that period at intervals appropriate to that income, would have fallen to be taken into account for the purposes of these Regulations.

[¹(8) Subject to paragraph (9), where a change of circumstances occurs which has the effect of bringing entitlement to an end it shall take effect on the first day of the benefit week following the benefit week in which that change actually occurs except in a case where a person is liable to make payments, which fall due on a daily basis, [⁴] in which case that change shall take effect on the day on which it actually occurs.

(9)   Where the change of circumstances is that a person moves to a new dwelling and immediately after the move he is treated as occupying his former dwelling as his home in accordance with regulation 7(7) or (10) then that change of circumstances shall take effect on the day after the last day for which he is treated as [⁸ occupying] the former dwelling in accordance with whichever of those regulations applies in his case.]

[⁶(10)   Where the change of circumstances is that the person moves to a new dwelling and immediately before the move that person is treated as occupying the new dwelling in accordance with regulation 7(8) then that change of circumstances shall take effect on the first day on which the person is treated as occupying the new dwelling as the home under that regulation.]

Modifications

Paras (1) and (3) were amended by reg 15 Housing Benefit (Local Housing Allowance and Information Sharing) Amendment Regulations 2007 SI No.2868 as from 7 April 2008, save that for a person to whom reg 1(5) of those regulations applied (see p1812), the amendments came into force on the day on or after 7 April 2008 when the first of the events specified in reg 1(6) applied to her/him, or on 6 April 2009 if none had before that date.

Reg 79 applies as if para (7) was omitted where a change of circumstances occurs as a result of the payment of arrears of any income which affects a determination or decision in respect of entitlement to, or the amount of, HB or CTB before 6 March 1995. See Sch 3 para 1 HB&CTB(CP) Regs on p1774.

Amendments

1.   Substituted by reg 2(10)(b), (e) and (f) of SI 2005 No 2502 as amended by Sch 2 para 27 of SI 2006 No 217 as from 1.4.06 (3.4.06 where rent payable weekly or at intervals of a week).

2.   Inserted by reg 2(10)(c) of SI 2005 No 2502 as amended by Sch 2 para 27 of SI 2006 No 217 as from 1.4.06 (3.4.06 where rent payable weekly or at intervals of a week).

3.   Amended by reg 2(10)(d) of SI 2005 No 2502 as amended by Sch 2 para 27 of SI 2006 No 217 as from 1.4.06 (3.4.06 where rent payable weekly or at intervals of a week).

4.   Amended by reg 2(3) of SI 2007 No 294 as from 1.4.07.

5.   Substituted by reg 4 of SI 2007 No 2470 as from 24.9.07.

6.   Amended by reg 11(9) of SI 2007 No 2618 as from 1.10.07.

7. Substituted by reg 15 of SI 2007 No 2868 as from 7.4.08 (or if reg 1(5) of that SI applies, on the day on or after 7.4.08 when the first of the events specified in reg 1(6) applies, or from 6.4.09 if none have before that date).
8. Substituted by reg 5 of SI 2008 No 2667 as from 30.10.08.
9. Amended by reg 8 and Sch para 36(5) of SI 2013 No 388 as from 8.4.13.
10. Amended by Art 7 and Sch para 34(5) of SI 2013 No 591 as from 8.4.13.

Definitions

"the Act" – see reg 2(1).
"the 2012 Act" – see reg 2(1).
"the Administration Act" – see reg 2(1).
"benefit Acts" – see reg 2(1).
"benefit week" – see reg 2(1).
"the Decisions and Appeals Regulations" – see reg 2(1).
"dwelling" – see reg 2(4) and s137(1) SSCBA.
"eligible rent" – see reg 2(1).
"income" – see General Note on Part 6.
"rent" – see Part 3.

General Note

Para (1) lays down the general rule as to the date on which changes take effect. Paras (2) to (5) and (8) to (10) set out some exceptional circumstances in which the change affects benefit from the benefit week in which the change actually occurs. But see also regs 34 and 42(8) HB Regs, and regs 7 and 8 UC(TP) Regs 2014 on p1868 and p1870. Reg 79 is not made subject to regs 7 and 8 UC(TP) Regs 2014. However, the government intention is that if reg 7 or 8 UC(TP) Regs 2014 applies, if an HB award would terminate under this provision later than it would under reg 7 or 8 UC(TP) Regs 2014, this provision does not apply: regs 7(6) and 8(5) UC(TP) Regs 2014.

This regulation is to be read together with regs 80 and 81 (see p538 and p541).

Analysis

Para (1) contains the general rule that changes in the claimant's circumstances, or those of anyone else whose circumstances affect the claimant's entitlement to HB or how much benefit s/he is due, are to take effect on the first day of the benefit week following the week in which the change takes place – ie, the Monday following the change. The changes referred to in this paragraph need not only be in the claimant's own circumstances. It is the effect of such a change on the claimant's entitlement to HB which is important, rather than who suffers the change.

The general rule does not apply where reg 34 applies. Reg 34 enables certain changes in a claimant's income to be ignored for up to 30 benefit weeks after the week in which they actually take effect.

Para (1) is subject to two provisions.

(1) By reg 8(3) D&A Regs, where a change is one that is required to be notified and it is advantageous to the claimant, it must be notified within one month of the change (or a longer period in limited circumstances). If the change is notified outside this period, the date of notification is treated as if it is the date the change occurred.

(2) Reg 80(5) sets the effective date for changes in applicable amounts, income or non-dependant deductions which occur in the same benefit week that a claimant has moved or her/his eligible rent has altered (in specified circumstances).

Paras (2) to (5) and (8) to (10) set out the exceptions to the general rule specified in para (1).

(1) Changes in rent payable usually take effect from the day the change occurs: para (2). As with para (1), this is subject to reg 8(3) D&A Regs.

(2) If the change is that the claimant has moved to a new home, or can be (or can no longer be) treated as occupying more than one home under reg 7(6), the change usually takes effect from the day the change occurs: para (2A). As with para (1), this is subject to reg 8(3) D&A Regs.

(3) If the change is that the maximum period of time for which the claimant can be treated as occupying two homes under reg 7(6) has ended, the change usually takes effect on the day after the last day of the period: para (2B).

(4) Changes consequent on benefit uprating usually take effect from the first Monday in April. However, where rent is payable monthly or daily, the change usually takes effect from 1 April: para (3)(a). Any other amendments to the regulations usually take effect on the date they come into force: para (3)(b).

(5) Where more than one change of circumstances occurs in the same benefit week but would take effect in different weeks, they all take effect on the first day of the benefit week in which they occur: para (4). However, where a change referred to in para (2), (2A) or (2B) takes effect that week, all the changes take effect on the day that change takes effect.

(6) Where a change consequent on benefit uprating takes effect from the first Monday in April under para (3)(a) and there are changes falling under para (1) in the same week, all changes take effect on the same

537

date if there are no others: para (5). The purpose of these complex rules is to minimise the need to issue multiple notices of determination each covering just a few days.

(7)   Where a change ends entitlement to HB, it usually takes effect from the first day of the benefit week following the benefit week in which the change occurred: para (8). However, where the claimant is liable for daily payments, the change takes effect on the day it occurs.

(8)   If the change is that the claimant has moved to a new home and immediately after this is treated as occupying a former home under reg 7(7) or (10) (ie, where liability for rent there continues and could not be avoided or where there was a fear of violence), the change takes effect on the day after the last day for which s/he is treated as occupying the former home: para (9).

(9)   If the change is that the claimant has moved to a new home and immediately before the move is treated as occupying the new home under reg 7(8) (ie, where there was a delay in moving for specified reasons), the change takes effect on the day on which s/he is treated as occupying the new home.

Para (6) provides that income or an increase in income paid for a past period, other than the benefit income specified, should be taken into account over the period that it would have been taken into account if entitlement had existed and it had been paid on time. PIP, armed forces independence payment and benefits paid under the SSCBA are excluded. Thus it would seem that para (6) can apply to ESA and JSA.

Para (6) only applies if there was no entitlement to the income (or the increase) during that period. For example, if the claimant has a pay award finalised at the end of August which takes effect from the previous May, the arrears should be treated as if received at the end of May. Note that where there *was* entitlement to the income during the past period, para (7) may instead apply. Para (7) will also apply to benefit income.

Para (7) applies to payments of income or arrears of income (including benefit income) for a past period which were due earlier but paid late (ie, where entitlement to the income existed all along): *EM v Waltham Forest LBC* [2009] UKUT 245 (AAC) paras 63–69; *KW v Lancaster CC (HB)* [2011] UKUT 266 (AAC). It does not, however, apply to earnings paid in arrears, but on the contractually stipulated date: *Reigate and Banstead BC v SA (HB)* [2014] UKUT 369 (AAC). The change in circumstances takes effect from the first day the income would have been taken into account had it been paid in time at appropriate intervals.

Para (7) deals with difficulties posed by payment of benefit in arrears. Reg 31(2) provides that: "The period over which any benefit . . . is to be taken into account shall be the period in respect of which that benefit is payable." Where claimants have received awards of a benefit for past periods, authorities may be able to retrospectively alter benefit entitlement under the above rule and reg 4(2)(b) of the D&A Regs (and see also *CH 1561/2005*), thus creating potentially recoverable overpayments. But note the possible official error arguments which may arise in these situations: see *CH 943/2003* and commentary to reg 100(2) on p583. Note also that arrears of some benefits as well as tax credits and discretionary housing payments count as capital not income and can be disregarded for a period after receipt (see Sch 6 para 9).

Reg 79 is modified by Sch 3 para 1 HB&CTB(CP) Regs on p1774 and the regulation applies as if para (7) was omitted where a change of circumstances occurs as a result of the payment of arrears of any income which affects a determination or decision about entitlement to, or the amount of, HB before 6 March 1995. This is a transitional provision, following amendments made by the Housing Benefit and Council Tax Benefit (Amendment) Regulations 1995 SI N0.511 following the decision in *R v Middlesborough BC ex p Holmes* [1995] unreported, 15 February, QBD. It may be of continuing relevance in overpayment cases involving a failure to disclose receipt of income. See p407 of the 17th edition.

[¹ Calculation of weekly amounts

80.–(1)   A person's entitlement to housing benefit in any benefit week shall be calculated in accordance with the following provisions of this regulation.

(2)   The weekly amount of a claimant's eligible rent shall be–

(a)   subject to paragraph (3), where rent is payable at intervals of one week or a multiple thereof, the amount of eligible rent payable weekly or, where it is payable at intervals of a multiple of a week, the amount determined by dividing the amount of eligible rent payable by the number equal to the number of weeks in respect of which it is payable; or

(b)   subject to paragraph (3), where the rent is payable at intervals of a calendar month or multiples thereof, the amount determined by dividing the amount payable by the number equal to the number of calendar months in respect of which it is payable, multiplying by 12 and dividing by 52;

(c)   subject to paragraph (3), where the rent is payable at intervals of a day or multiples thereof, the amount determined by dividing the amount payable by the number equal to the number of days in respect of which it is payable and multiplying by 7.

(3)   In a case–

(a)   to which regulation 76(2) or (3) (date on which entitlement is to commence) applies, his eligible rent for the benefit week in which he becomes liable to make payments in respect of a dwelling which he occupies as his home shall be calculated by multiplying his daily rent by the number equal to the number of days in that benefit week for which he is liable to make such payments;

(b)   where a change of circumstances takes effect in a benefit week under regulation 79(2A), (but is not a change described in sub-paragraph (c)(ii) of this regulation), (2B), (8) or (9) other than on the Monday of a benefit week then the claimant's eligible rent for that benefit week shall be calculated by multiplying his daily rent by the appropriate number of days in that benefit week;

(c)   where–

    (i)   the amount of eligible rent which the claimant is liable to pay in respect of a dwelling is altered and that change of circumstances takes effect under regulation 79(2); or

    (ii)   the claimant–

        (aa)   moves to a new dwelling occupied as the home,

        (bb)   he is not entitled to be treated, immediately after that move, as occupying two dwellings as his home or as occupying his former dwelling as his home, and

        (cc)   that change of circumstances takes effect under regulation 79(2A),

other than on the Monday of a benefit week, then the claimant's eligible rent for that benefit week shall be calculated by multiplying his old and new daily rent by the number equal to the number of days in that week which relate respectively to the old and new amounts which he is liable to pay.

(4)   In the case of a claimant whose weekly eligible rent falls to be calculated in accordance with paragraph (3)(a) or (b) by reference to the daily rent in his case, his weekly applicable amount, weekly income, the weekly amount of any non-dependant deductions and the minimum amount payable in his case shall be calculated in the same manner as his weekly eligible rent by reference to the amounts determined in his case in accordance with Parts 5 to 8 (applicable amounts, income and capital, students and amount of benefit).

(5)   Where a change in the amount of a claimant's applicable amount, income or non-dependant deductions falls to be taken into account in the same benefit week as a change in his eligible rent to which paragraph (3)(c) applies, it shall be taken into account in that week on a daily basis in the same manner and as if it had occurred on the same day as that change in his eligible rent.

[² (6)]

(7)   Any amount determined under these Regulations may, if it is appropriate, be rounded to the nearest whole penny by disregarding any amount less than half a penny and treating any amount of half a penny or more as a whole penny.

(8)   In this regulation "daily rent" shall mean the amount determined by dividing by 7 the amount determined under whichever sub-paragraph of paragraph (2) is appropriate in each case.

(9)   Where a claimant is entitled to benefit in respect of two (but not more than two) dwellings in accordance with regulation 7(6) his eligible rent shall be calculated in respect of each dwelling in accordance with this regulation.]

Modifications

Reg 80 was substituted by reg 16 Housing Benefit (Local Housing Allowance and Information Sharing) Amendment Regulations 2007 SI No.2868 as from 7 April 2008, save that for a person to whom reg 1(5) of those regulations applied (see p1812), the amendments came into force on the day on or after 7 April 2008 when the first of the events specified in reg 1(6) applied to her/him, or on 6 April 2009 if none had before that date.

Amendments

1.   Substituted by reg 16 of SI 2007 No 2868 as from 7.4.08 (or if reg 1(5) of that SI applies, on the day on or after 7.4.08 when the first of the events specified in reg 1(6) applies, or from 6.4.09 if none have before that date).

2.   Omitted by reg 4(4)(c) of SI 2008 No 959 as from 6.10.08.

Definitions

"applicable amount" – see Part 5 and s135 SSCBA.

"benefit week" – see reg 2(1).

"claimant" – see reg 2(1).

"dwelling" – see reg 2(4) and s137(1) SSCBA.

"eligible rent" – see reg 2(1).

"income" – see General Note on Part 6.

"liable to make payments" – see regs 2(2), 8 and 9.

"non-dependant deductions" – see regs 3 and 74.

General Note

The calculation of HB is based on weekly amounts. This regulation deals with how a claimant's "eligible rent" (for which see regs 12B, 12BA, 12C and 12D and regs 12 and 13 as set out in Sch 3 para 5 HB&CTB(CP) Regs – see p1783) is to be calculated on a weekly basis for the purpose of the HB calculation. Note also reg 81 where a claimant has a "rent free period".

The other components in the calculation, namely applicable amounts (Part 5), income (Part 6), student income (Part 7) and amount of benefit (Part 8), are converted into weekly figures by the Parts which specifically deal with them, and are only affected by this regulation so far as paras (4) and (5) allow.

The interaction between reg 79 and reg 80(3) to (5) is that reg 79 operates to fix the benefit week in which changes of circumstances are to take effect, and paras (3) to (5) of reg 80 provide how such a change is to affect the weekly amount of benefit due for the benefit week in question.

Para (1) gives effect to the rest of this regulation.

Para (2) is the general rule. A distinction is drawn between claimants who pay rent on a weekly basis or for a period equivalent to a number of weeks (para (2)(a)) and those who pay rent at intervals of a month or a day or multiples of these (paras (2)(b) and (c)).

Para (3) deals with situations where eligible rent must be calculated for part-weeks (ie, where a claimant is not liable for rent for a full week), certain changes of circumstance affect rent due in a week or the amount of rent changes during a week.

Paras (4) and (5) are consequential on para (3) and refer to the quantification of the other components in the HB calculation where a change covered by para (3) has occurred.

Para (7) allows for the rounding of figures determined under the regulations.

Para (8) defines "daily rent" for the purpose of para (3).

Para (9) makes it clear that, where a claimant is entitled to HB for two homes, the eligible rent for each dwelling is calculated separately under this regulation. Maximum HB calculated under reg 70 will then be the aggregate of the eligible rents for the two homes, less any deductions in respect of non-dependents: *MB v Selby DC (HB)* [2011] UKUT 5 (AAC).

Analysis

Para (2) sets out the general rules for determining weekly amounts of eligible rent in circumstances where para (3) is not applicable.

Para (2)(a) provides that where rent is payable weekly, the weekly eligible rent is the amount payable weekly. Where rent is paid for a multiple of weeks, weekly eligible rent is the total payable for that period divided by the number of weeks in it – eg, where rent is paid fortnightly, the rent payable is divided by 2.

Para (2)(b) provides that where rent is payable at intervals of (or in multiples of) a calendar month, weekly eligible rent is the total payable for the period divided by the number of months in that period, then multiplied by 12 and divided by 52.

Para (2)(c) provides that where rent is payable at intervals of (or in multiples of) a day, weekly eligible rent is the amount payable divided by the number of days in the period, then multiplied by 7.

Para (3) sets out the circumstances in which the normal rules in para (2) do not apply. The effect of para (3) combined with paras (4) and (5) is that, for the week affected, eligible rent is calculated for a part-week on a daily basis. There are three situations.

(1)   Where a claimant's entitlement to HB commences in her/his week of claim (rather than the week after) – ie, s/he both claims (or is treated as claiming) HB and first becomes liable to pay rent on her/his dwelling in the same week or becomes liable for daily payments in specified types of accommodation which s/he occupies as a home (see reg 76(2) and (3)): sub-para (a). In such cases, eligible rent for the week in which s/he becomes liable (ie, the first week of claim) is calculated by multiplying "daily rent" by the number of days in the week for which the claimant is both liable to make payments in respect of the dwelling and occupies it: *SL v Renfrewshire Council (HB)* [2014] UKUT 411 (AAC).

(2)   Where a change of circumstances takes effect other than on a Monday under reg 79(2A) (other than where para (c)(ii) of this regulation applies, for which see below), (2B), (8) or (9) (all situations where the change takes effect during the week the change occurred rather than from the start of the next benefit week): sub-para (b). In such cases, eligible rent for the week in which the change takes effect is calculated by multiplying "daily rent" by the appropriate number of days in the benefit week.

(3)   Where a change in the rent payable takes effect on the day it occurs under reg 79(2) or a claimant moves, cannot be treated as occupying the former home for HB purposes and the change takes effect on the day it occurs under reg 79(2A) and, in both cases, this is other than on the Monday of a benefit week: sub-para (c). In such cases, eligible rent for the week in which the change takes effect is calculated by multiplying the old and the new "daily rent" by the number of days in the week for which the claimant is liable to pay each of these.

"Daily rent" for all three purposes is defined in para (8).

Para (4). Where either para (3)(a) or (b) applies, HB entitlement is calculated for the part-week only. The applicable amount, income, non-dependant deductions and the minimum amount of HB payable are adjusted in the same manner as her/his eligible rent so that they, too, only relate to the number of days for which the claimant is liable for rent.

Para (5). Where para (3)(c) applies and, in the same benefit week as a claimant's eligible rent alters, a change in the applicable amount, income or non-dependant deductions takes effect, the weekly amount of any of these is calculated in the same way as the eligible rent, that is by apportioning the old and new amounts according to the number of days to which they relate.

Example: A claimant moves into a new home and claims HB in the same week (on a Friday). Her rent is £325 a calendar month. Applying reg 80(2)(b), her normal weekly eligible rent is £325 times 12 divided by 52 = £75. Applying reg 80(3)(a), her eligible rent for the first benefit week of entitlement is £75 divided by 7 times three days = £32.14. The other components determining the amount of HB are also apportioned for that week, applying reg 80(5).

[¹ Rent free periods

81.–(1)   This regulation applies to a claimant for any period (referred to in this regulation as a rent free period) in, or in respect of, which he is not liable to pay rent except for any period to which regulation 8(1)(d) (waiver of rent by landlord in return for work done) applies.

(2)   In the case of the beginning or ending of a claimant's rent-free period, his eligible rent for the benefit week in which the rent free period begins and ends shall be calculated on a daily basis as if those benefit weeks were weeks to which regulation 80(3) applies.

(3)   For the purpose of determining the weekly applicable amount and income of a claimant to whom this regulation applies, the weekly amount of any non-dependant deductions and the minimum amount payable in his case–

(a)   in a case to which regulation 80(2)(a) applies, the amounts determined in his case in accordance with Parts 5 to 8 (applicable amounts, income and capital, students and amount of benefit) shall be multiplied by 52 or 53, whichever is appropriate, and divided by the number equal to the number of weeks in that 52 or 53 week period in respect of which he is liable to pay rent;

(b)   subject to paragraph (4), in a case to which regulation 80(2)(b) or (c) applies, the amounts determined in his case in accordance with Parts 5 to 8 shall be multiplied by 365 or 366, whichever is appropriate and divided by the number of days in that 365 or 366 day period in respect of which he is liable to pay rent.

(4)   In a case to which paragraph (3)(b) applies, where either regulation 80(4) or (5) also applies or it is the beginning or end of a rent-free period, the weekly amounts referred to in paragraph (3) shall first be calculated in accordance with sub-paragraph (b) of that paragraph and then determined on a daily basis in the same manner as the claimant's eligible rent.]

Modifications

Reg 81 was substituted by reg 16 Housing Benefit (Local Housing Allowance and Information Sharing) Amendment Regulations 2007 SI No.2868 as from 7 April 2008, save that for a person to whom reg 1(5) of those regulations applied (see p1812), the amendments came into force on the day on or after 7 April 2008 when the first of the events specified in reg 1(6) applied to her/him, or on 6 April 2009 if none had before that date.

Amendment

1.   Substituted by reg 16 of SI 2007 No 2868 as from 7.4.08 (or if reg 1(5) of that SI applies, on the day on or after 7.4.08 when the first of the events specified in reg 1(6) applies, or from 6.4.09 if none have before that date).

Definitions
"applicable amount" – see reg 22 and s135 SSCBA.
"benefit week" – see reg 2(1).
"claimant" – see reg 2(1).
"eligible rent" – see reg 2(1).
"income" – see General Note on Part 6.
"liable to make payments" – see regs 2(2), 8 and 9.
"non-dependant deductions" – see regs 3 and 74.
"rent" – see Part 3.

General Note
Para (1) applies this regulation to a claimant in a "rent-free period". Those are periods in which (or in respect of which) a claimant who is normally liable to pay rent is not liable – eg, where a tenant pays rent over 48 weeks and has a rent-free period for the Christmas holidays. Reg 81 does not apply where the claimant is treated as liable for rent under reg 8(1)(d) – ie, where her/his rent has been waived temporarily to compensate for work done.

Para (2) deals with eligible rent for the weeks in which the rent free period begins and ends.

Paras (3) and (4) deal with adjustments to the applicable amount, income, non-dependant deductions and minimum amount of HB payable. Because the claimant will not be entitled to HB during a rent-free period because s/he is not then *liable* for rent as required by s130(1)(a) SSCBA or treated as liable by reg 8, this regulation provides that these other components in the calculation of HB are adjusted to ensure that the claimant does not receive more HB than s/he otherwise would during a year on account of having rent-free weeks. It works by ensuring that *all* of her/his assessable income for that year including that paid in respect of rent-free weeks, is taken into account during the weeks in which s/he actually pays rent, and correspondingly that the non-dependant deductions and applicable amounts which would normally be taken into account over a whole year are taken into account during those same weeks.

Analysis
Para (2). In all cases, eligible rent in the benefit weeks in which the rent free period begins and ends is calculated on a daily basis as if reg 80(3) applies. See the note on that provision. Sch 1 para 7(2) also affects the calculation of weekly fixed rate ineligible service charges where there are rent free periods.

Para (3). A distinction is drawn between situations where rent is payable weekly (sub-para (a)) or monthly or daily (sub-para (b)) or in multiples of those periods. Where rent is payable weekly, weekly income, applicable amounts and non-dependant deductions are multiplied by 52 (or 53 as appropriate) to give annual amounts. These are then divided by the number of weeks in that 52 (or 53) week period in respect of which there is a liability to pay rent. Where rent is payable monthly or daily, the figures are multiplied by 365 (or 366 as appropriate) and the result then divided by the number of days in that 365 (or 366) day period in respect of which there is a liability to pay rent. So for example, where rent is payable monthly other than in December (31 days), all the figures are multiplied by 365 and divided by 334 (365 – 31).

Para (4) qualifies the process under para (3)(b) where reg 80(4) or (5) applies or it is the beginning or end of the rent free period. Amounts produced under para (3)(b) are calculated first, then the daily rate is worked out in the same way as eligible rent under reg 80.

PART 10
Claims

General Note on Part 10
This Part regulates how, and by whom, claims for HB are to be made, the fixing of the date on which the claim is treated as having been made, the authority's rights to require supporting evidence and the duty of the claimant (and certain other people) to notify the authority of changes in circumstances.

Who may claim
82.–(1) In the case of a couple or members of a polygamous marriage a claim shall be made by whichever one of them they agree should so claim or, in default of agreement, by such one of them as the relevant authority shall determine.

(2) Where a person who is liable to make payments in respect of a dwelling is unable for the time being to act, and–

(a) a [¹ deputy] has been appointed by the Court of Protection with power to claim, or as the case may be, receive benefit on his behalf; or

(b) in Scotland, his estate is being administered by a judicial factor or any guardian acting or appointed under the Adults with Incapacity (Scotland) Act 2000 who has power to claim or, as the case may be, receive benefit on his behalf; or

(c)   an attorney with a general power or a power to claim or as the case may be, receive benefit, has been appointed by that person under [¹ the Powers of Attorney Act 1971, the Enduring Powers of Attorney Act 1985 or the Mental Capacity Act 2005 or otherwise],

that [¹ deputy], judicial factor, guardian or attorney, as the case may be, may make a claim on behalf of that person.

(3)   Where a person who is liable to make payments in respect of a dwelling is unable for the time being to act and paragraph (2) does not apply to him, the relevant authority may, upon written application made to them by a person who, if a natural person, is over the age of 18, appoint that person to exercise on behalf of the person who is unable to act, any right to which that person might be entitled under the Act and to receive and deal on his behalf with any sums payable to him.

(4)   Where the relevant authority has made an appointment under paragraph (3) or treated a person as an appointee under paragraph (5)–

(a)   it may at any time revoke the appointment;

(b)   the person appointed may resign his office after having given 4 weeks notice in writing to the relevant authority of his intention to do so;

(c)   any such appointment shall terminate when the relevant authority is notified that a receiver or other person to whom paragraph (2)(b) or (c) applies has been appointed.

(5)   Where a person who is liable to make payments in respect of a dwelling is for the time being unable to act and the Secretary of State has appointed a person to act on his behalf for the purposes of the Act the relevant authority may, if that person agrees, treat him as if he had been appointed by them under paragraph (3).

(6)   Anything required by these Regulations to be done by or to any person who is for the time being unable to act may be done by or to the [¹ deputy], judicial factor, guardian or attorney, if any, or by or to the person appointed or treated as appointed under this regulation and the receipt of any such person so appointed shall be a good discharge to the relevant authority for any sum paid.

[² (7)]

Amendments
1.   Substituted by reg 11(10) of SI 2007 No 2618 as from 1.10.07.
2.   Omitted by reg 2(3) of SI 2008 No 2299 as from 1.10.08.

Definitions
"the Act" – see reg 2(1).
"claim" – see reg 2(1).
"couple" – see reg 2(1).
"dwelling" – see reg 2(4) and s137(1) SSCBA.
"liable to make payments" – see regs 2(2), 8 and 9.
"polygamous marriage" – see reg 2(1).
"relevant authority" – see reg 2(1).

General Note
The general rule (which is not expressly spelt out in the regulations) is that it is the person who "is liable to make payments in respect of a dwelling . . . which he occupies as his home" (see s130 SSCBA 1992) who must make the claim for benefit required by s1 SSAA 1992. Problems can arise, however, if that person is unable to manage her/his own affairs, or if more than one member of the household is potentially eligible to claim by virtue of reg 8(1). This regulation makes provision for such cases.

Analysis
Paragraph (1): The general rule
The effect of this paragraph is that only one partner in a couple or a polygamous marriage may claim HB in respect of the same dwelling. There is, therefore, no such thing as a joint claim for HB: *CH 3817/2004* para 8; *CH 3622/2006*. If the parties to the relationship cannot agree who is to claim, the authority must decide.
Paragraphs (2) to (5): Claims on behalf of claimants
Paras (2) to (5) are made under powers given to the Secretary of State by s5(1)(g) and (2)(e) SSAA and cover the situation where the person who is liable to pay the rent is "unable for the time being to act". This will usually be because o/he is mentally or physically incapable of managing her/his affairs permanently, but it would also

cover a temporary incapacity – eg, following an accident. The quoted phrase is apt to cover inability to act, however caused, and the regulation is not restricted either to medical incapacities or to mental illness or disability. It could, for example, apply to those with language difficulties.

Para (2) states that the representative of a person unable to act will be an attorney with powers to claim and receive benefit; or a deputy appointed by the Court of Protection in England and Wales with such powers; or a judicial factor or guardian in Scotland. The attorney, deputy, or judicial factor etc may claim and receive HB on the liable person's behalf. Note that if the conditions of para (2) are satisfied, the authority has no choice but to accept a claim from a person who comes within sub-paras (a) to (c).

Paras (3) to (5) permit the authority to appoint someone to act on the claimant's behalf if s/he is unable to act. An appointee must, if s/he is a natural person as opposed to a corporate body, be aged over 18 and must apply for the appointment in writing: para (3). The authority may revoke the appointment under para (4)(a) or the appointee may resign on four weeks' notice under para (4)(b). This is so even if there is no other person who is prepared to claim on behalf of the liable person. If a person falling within para (2) is appointed, any appointment made under para (3) ceases: para (4)(c). If an appointment has been made by the DWP, the appointee may also act in relation to HB: para (5). A person unable to act but otherwise eligible for HB will probably also be entitled to other benefits under SSCBA. This will usually be the most convenient course, but the authority is not under an absolute duty to accede to the request. Again, the only legal obligation is to exercise the discretion reasonably, having regard to all the relevant circumstances of each individual case and directing itself properly as to the applicable law.

In most cases, the identity of the most suitable appointee will be readily apparent. If, however, there are competing candidates, or if the most obvious person is thought to be unsuitable (eg, because s/he is felt to be taking advantage of the liable person's vulnerability or has criminal convictions for benefit offences), the authority must exercise the discretion to appoint in accordance with the general principles of administrative law, having regard to all the relevant circumstances of each individual case. Although the paragraph is silent on this point, it is doubted that an authority could lawfully stop a person who is unable to act from claiming HB by refusing everyone who applies to be appointed. If it is felt desirable to do so in order to protect the interests of the person who is unable to act, the authority could, in an appropriate case, appoint one of its own officers or an officer of the local social services authority to claim and receive HB (which would then usually be paid direct to the landlord). Any local government officer so appointed should always bear in mind her/his personal obligations under para (6) and possible liability to repay any benefit which may be overpaid.

Claims by agents. It may be that a liable person who is mentally competent is able to appoint an agent to claim benefit on her/his behalf whether or not s/he is "unable for the time being to act" and without formally granting the agent a power of attorney. It is a general principle of the common law that a person who may lawfully do an act her/himself may appoint another to do it for her/him as agent and in *R v Stoke-on-Trent CC ex p Highgate Projects* (1993) 26 HLR 551 it was said in the context of an application for review that, as the claimants were legally competent, they could authorise their landlords to act for them as agent. In *Tkachuk v SSWP* [2007] EWCA Civ 515; reported as *R(IS) 3/07*, it was held that the common law of agency did apply in the context of claims for benefit.

As a matter of the law of agency, there is no reason why the appointment of an agent should even be in writing but, in practical terms, an authority is unlikely to accept on a balance of probabilities that an agency has been created unless the agent can produce some written evidence of her/his authority.

Para (6) empowers anyone appointed under paras (2) or (3) (or treated as appointed under para (5)) to do anything the regulations require a claimant to do and allows the authority to act towards the appointee as if s/he were a claimant. A receipt for HB received by the appointee discharges the authority from any obligation under the regulations to pay that HB to the claimant.

Time and manner in which claims are to be made

83.–(1) [¹ Subject to [⁴ paragraphs (4A) to (4AE)],] Every claim shall be in writing and made on a properly completed form approved for the purpose by the relevant authority or in such written form as the relevant authority may accept as sufficient in the circumstances of any particular case or class of cases having regard to the sufficiency of the written information and evidence.

(2) The forms approved for the purpose of claiming shall be provided free of charge by the relevant authority or such persons as they may authorise or appoint for the purpose.

(3) Each relevant authority shall notify the Secretary of State of the address to which claims delivered or sent to the appropriate DWP office are to be forwarded.

(4) A claim [¹ in writing]–

(a) may be sent or delivered to the appropriate DWP office where the claimant or his partner is also claiming income support, incapacity benefit, state pension credit [⁶, a jobseeker's allowance or an employment and support allowance];

(b)   where it has not been sent or delivered to the appropriate DWP office, shall be sent or delivered to the designated office;

(c)   sent or delivered to the appropriate DWP office, other than one sent on the same form as a claim being made to income support, incapacity benefit [⁶, a jobseeker's allowance or an employment and support allowance] and as approved by the Secretary of State for the purpose of the benefits being claimed, shall be forwarded to the relevant authority within two working days of the date of the receipt of the claim at the appropriate DWP office, or as soon as practicable thereafter;

[⁴ (d)]

[⁴ (e)]

(f)   where the claimant has attained the qualifying age for state pension credit, may be sent or delivered to an authorised office.

[³ (g) may be sent or delivered to the offices of a county council in England if the council has arranged with the relevant authority for claims to be received at their offices ("county offices").]

[¹ (4A)   Where the relevant authority has published a telephone number for the purpose of receiving claims for housing benefit, a claim may be made by telephone to that telephone number.

[⁴ (4AA)   If the Secretary of State agrees, where–

(a)   a person makes a claim for a benefit referred to in paragraph (4)(a); and

(b)   the Secretary of State has made provision in the Social Security (Claims and Payments) Regulations 1987 for that benefit to be claimed by telephone,

that person may claim housing benefit by telephone to the telephone number specified by the Secretary of State.

(4AB)   A claim for housing benefit may be made in accordance with paragraph (4AA) at any time before a decision has been made on the claim for the benefit referred to in paragraph (4)(a).

(4AC)   If the Secretary of State agrees, where a person, in accordance with regulation 32 of the Social Security (Claims and Payments) Regulations 1987 (information to be given and changes to be notified)–

(a)   furnishes the Secretary of State with such information or evidence as he may require; or

(b)   notifies the Secretary of State of any change of circumstances,

that person may claim housing benefit in the same manner in which the information or evidence was furnished or the notification was given.

(4AD)   If the Secretary of State agrees, where a person, in accordance with regulation 24 of the Jobseeker's Allowance Regulations (provision of information and evidence)(7)–

(a)   furnishes the Secretary of State with such certificates, documents and other evidence as he may require; or

(b)   notifies the Secretary of State of any change of circumstances,

that person may claim housing benefit in the same manner as the certificate, document and other evidence was furnished or the notification was given.

(4AE)   A claim for housing benefit may be made in accordance with paragraphs (4AC) or (4AD) at any time before a decision has been made on the award of benefit to which the information, evidence, certificates, documents or notification relates.]

(4B)   The relevant authority may determine, in any particular case, that a claim made by telephone [⁴ in accordance with paragraph (4A)] is not a valid claim unless the person making the claim approves a written statement of his circumstances, provided for the purpose by the relevant authority.

[⁴ (4BA)   The relevant authority or the Secretary of State may determine that a claim made by telephone in accordance with paragraphs (4AA) to (4AE) is not a valid claim unless the person making the claim approves a written statement of his circumstances, provided for the purpose by the Secretary of State.]

[⁴ (4C)   A claim made by telephone in accordance with paragraphs (4A) to (4AE) is defective unless the relevant authority or the Secretary of State is provided with all the information requested during that telephone call.]

(4D)   Where a claim made by telephone in accordance with paragraph (4A) is defective, the relevant authority [⁴ must] provide the person making it with an opportunity to correct the defect.

[⁴ (4DA)   Where a claim made by telephone in accordance with paragraphs (4AA) to (4AE) is defective–
   (a)   the Secretary of State may provide the person making it with an opportunity to correct the defect;
   (b)   the relevant authority must provide the person making it with an opportunity to correct the defect if the Secretary of State has not already done so, unless it considers that it has sufficient information to determine the claim.]

(4E)   If the person corrects the defect within one month, or such longer period as the relevant authority considers reasonable, [⁴ of the date the relevant authority or the Secretary of State] last drew attention to it, the relevant authority shall treat the claim as if it had been duly made in the first instance.]

[⁴ (4F)   If the person does not correct the defect within one month, or such longer period as the relevant authority considers reasonable, of the date the relevant authority or the Secretary of State last drew attention to it, the relevant authority may treat the claim as if it had been duly made in the first instance where it considers that it has sufficient information to determine the claim.]

(5)   Subject to paragraph (10), [⁴] the date on which a claim is made shall be–
   (a)   in a case where an award of income support [⁶, an income-based jobseeker's allowance or an income-related employment and support allowance] has been made to the claimant or his partner and the claim for housing benefit is made within one month of the date on which the claim for that income support [⁶, jobseeker's allowance or employment and support allowance] was received at the appropriate DWP office, the first day of entitlement to income support [⁶, an income-based jobseeker's allowance or an income-related employment and support allowance] arising from that claim; [⁶]

[¹⁰ (aa) in a case where an award of universal credit has been made to the claimant and the claim for housing benefit is made–
   (i)   within one month of the date on which the claim for universal credit was made in accordance with regulation 8 of the Universal Credit, Personal Independence Payment, Jobseeker's Allowance and Employment and Support Allowance (Claims and Payments) Regulations 2013 ("the Claims and Payments Regulations"); or
   (ii)   in a case where the award of universal credit was made without a claim in accordance with regulation 6 (claims not required for entitlement to universal credit in certain cases) or 9(6), (7) or (10) (claims for universal credit by members of a couple) of the Claims and Payments Regulations, or the claimant was treated as making a claim for universal credit under regulation 9(8) of those Regulations, within one month of the date on which the Secretary of State sent notification of the award to the claimant, the first day of entitlement to universal credit arising from the award;]

   (b)   in a case where the claimant or his partner is a person on [¹⁰ universal credit] income support [⁶, an income-based jobseeker's allowance or an income-related employment and support allowance] and he becomes liable for the first time to make payments in respect of the dwelling which he occupies as his home, where the claim is received at the designated office or appropriate DWP office within one month of the claimant first becoming liable for such payments, the date he became liable for those payments;

   (c)   in a case where the claimant is the former partner of a person who was, at the date of his death or their separation, entitled to housing benefit and the claimant makes a claim within one month of the date of the death or the separation, that date;

[⁴ (d)   except where [¹⁰ sub-paragraph (a), (aa), (b) or (c)] is satisfied, in a case where a properly completed claim is received in a designated office, an authorised office, county offices or an appropriate DWP office within one month, or such longer period as the relevant authority considers reasonable, of the date on which–

    (i)   a claim form was issued to the claimant following the claimant first notifying, by whatever means, a designated office, an authorised office or an appropriate DWP office of an intention to make a claim; or

    (ii)   a claimant notifies, by whatever means, a designated office, an authorised office or an appropriate DWP office of an intention to make a claim by telephone in accordance with paragraphs (4A) to (4AE),

the date of first notification; and]

(e)   in any other case, the date on which the claim is received at the designated office, authorised office [³, county offices] or appropriate DWP office.

[⁶ (5A)   For the purposes only of sub-paragraph (5)(a) a person who has been awarded an income-based jobseeker's allowance or an income-related employment and support allowance is to be treated as entitled to that allowance for any days which immediately precede the first day in that award and on which he would have been entitled to that allowance but for regulations made under–

(a)   in the case of income-based jobseeker's allowance, paragraph 4 of Schedule 1 to the Jobseekers Act (waiting days); or

(b)   in the case of income-related employment and support allowance, paragraph 2 of Schedule 2 to the Welfare Reform Act (waiting days).]

(6)   Where a claim received at the designated office [⁷ or appropriate DWP office] has not been made in the manner prescribed in paragraph (1), that claim is for the purposes of these Regulations defective.

(7)   Where a claim [⁷, which is received by a relevant authority,] is defective because–

(a)   it was made on the form approved for the purpose but that form is not accepted by the relevant authority as being properly completed; or

(b)   it was made in writing but not on the form approved for the purpose and the relevant authority does not accept the claim as being in a written form which is sufficient in the circumstances of the case having regard to the sufficiency of the written information and evidence,

the relevant authority may, in a case to which sub-paragraph (a) applies, request the claimant to complete the defective claim or, in the case to which sub-paragraph (b) applies, supply the claimant with the approved form or request further information or evidence.

[⁷ (7A)   Where a claim is received at an appropriate DWP office and it appears to the Secretary of State that the form has not been properly completed, the Secretary of State may request that the claimant provides the relevant authority with the information required to complete the form.]

[⁷ (8)   The relevant authority shall treat a defective claim as if it had been validly made in the first instance if, in any particular case, the conditions specified in sub-paragraph (a), (b) or (c) of paragraph (8A) are satisfied.

(8A)   The conditions are that–

(a)   where paragraph (7)(a) (incomplete form) applies, the authority receives at the designated office the properly completed claim or the information requested to complete it or the evidence within one month of the request, or such longer period as the relevant authority may consider reasonable; or

(b)   where paragraph (7)(b) (claim not on approved form or further information requested by relevant authority) applies–

    (i)   the approved form sent to the claimant is received at the designated office properly completed within one month of it having been sent to him; or, as the case may be,

    (ii)   the claimant supplies whatever information or evidence was requested under paragraph (7) within one month of the request,

or, in either case, within such longer period as the relevant authority may consider reasonable; or

(c)   where paragraph (7A) (further information requested by Secretary of State) applies, the relevant authority receives at the designated office the properly completed claim or the information requested to complete it within one month of the request by the Secretary of State or within such longer period as the relevant authority considers reasonable.]

(9)   A claim which is made on an approved form for the time being is, for the purposes of this regulation, properly completed if completed in accordance with the instructions on the form, including any instructions to provide information and evidence in connection with the claim.

[² (10)   Except in the case of a claim made by a person from abroad, where the claimant is not entitled to housing benefit in the benefit week immediately following the date of his claim but the relevant authority is of the opinion that unless there is a change of circumstances he will be entitled to housing benefit for a period beginning not later than the thirteenth benefit week following the date on which the claim is made, the relevant authority may treat the claim as made on a date in the benefit week immediately preceding the first benefit week of that period of entitlement and award benefit accordingly.]

(11)   In the case of a person who has attained, or whose partner has attained, [⁸ the age which is 17 weeks younger than the qualifying age for state pension credit], paragraph (10) shall apply as if for the reference to the thirteenth benefit week, there was substituted a reference to the seventeenth benefit week.

[⁹ (12)   Where a claimant ("C")–
(a)   makes a claim which includes (or which C subsequently requests should include) a period before the claim is made; and
(b)   from a day in that period, up to the date when C made the claim (or subsequently requested that the claim should include a past period), C had continuous good cause for failing to make a claim (or request that the claim should include that period),
the claim is to be treated as made on the date determined in accordance with paragraph (12A).
(12A)   That date is the latest of–
(a)   the first day from which C had continuous good cause;
(b)   the day [¹¹ one month] before the date the claim was made;
(c)   the day [¹¹ one month] before the date when C requested that the claim should include a past period.]

(13)   In this regulation "authorised office" means an office which is nominated by the Secretary of State and authorised by the relevant authority for receiving claims for decision by the relevant authority.

Amendments

1.   Inserted by reg 2(2) of SI 2006 No 2967 as from 20.12.06.
2.   Substituted by reg 3 of SI 2007 No 1331 as from 23.5.07.
3.   Amended by reg 7(2) of SI 2007 No 2911 as from 31.10.07.
4.   Amended by reg 2(4) of SI 2008 No 2299 as from 1.10.08.
5.   Substituted by reg 4 of SI 2008 No 2424 as from 6.10.08.
6.   Amended by reg 19 of SI 2008 No 1082 as from 27.10.08.
7.   Amended by reg 2(2) of SI 2008 No 2987 as from 22.12.08.
8.   Amended by reg 25 of SI 2009 No 1488 as from 6.4.10.
9.   Substituted by reg 2(4) of SI 2010 No 2449 as from 1.11.10.
10.   Amended by reg 7(6) of SI 2013 No 2070 as from 28.10.13.
11.   Amended by reg 3 of SI 2015 No 1857 as from 1.04.16.

Definitions

"appropriate DWP office" – see reg 2(1).
"benefit week" – see reg 2(1).
"claimant" – see reg 2(1).
"claim" – see reg 2(1).
"an employment and support allowance" and "an income-related employment and support allowance" – see reg 2(1).

"Jobseeker's Act" – see reg 2(1).
"a jobseeker's allowance" and "an income-based jobseeker's allowance" – see reg 2(1).
"Jobseeker's Allowance Regulations" – see reg 2(1).
"partner" – see reg 2(1).
"person from abroad" – see reg 10.
"relevant authority" – see reg 2(1).
"remunerative work" – see reg 6.
"universal credit" – see reg 2(1).
"Welfare Reform Act" – see reg 2(1).

General Note

Paras (1) to (4AE) and (9) deal with how claims are to be made. Para (5) determines the date to be taken as the date of claim. Paras (4E), (4F), (8), (8A), (10), (12) and (12A) effectively qualify para (5) as they affect the date of claim.

Paras (4B) to (4D) deal with when a telephone claim is defective and paras (4D) to (4F) with how such claims can be rectified. Paras (6) to (8A) deal with rectification of written claims not made in the proper manner. Para (10) deals with claims made in advance of entitlement and paras (12) and (12A) with backdating.

See also reg 86 for the evidence and information that can be required by an authority to support a claim and reg 87 for when a claim may be amended or withdrawn.

Finally, note reg 7(9) which operates to set the date from which a claim is treated as made for those treated under reg 7(8) as occupying a dwelling before they have moved in.

Analysis

Paragraphs (1) to (3): General requirements in relation to claims

Para (1) deals with the form a claim must take. Unless a telephone claim can be made, for which see paras (4A) and (4AA), claims must be in writing, and normally made on a form, approved by the local authority for this purpose, which has been "properly completed": see para (9). However, the authority has a discretion to accept a claim in some other written form if it considers the written information and evidence to be "sufficient in the circumstances". Note also that a claim can be made by means of an electronic communication if the conditions in Sch 11 are satisfied: reg 83A.

In *Novitskaya v London Borough of Brent & Another* [2009] EWCA Civ 1260; [2010] AACR 6, the Court of Appeal decided that a document may constitute a claim even where it does not use explicit wording or expressly name the benefit being claimed: the correct approach is that the meaning of a document (ie, whether it constitutes a claim) should be construed in the light of the relevant surrounding facts, including other documents. Distinguishing the decision in *R(S) 1/63* on the meaning of "claim", the Court said that excessive reliance should not be placed on the statement there that the intention to claim must appear on the face of the document. Distinguishing comments made in *CG 3844/2006*, the Court held that most situations would call for a "generous approach to the interpretation of such documents".

Local authorities may have their own approved forms.

A "rapid reclaim" form (HBRR1) can be accepted where a claimant is reclaiming IS, JSA or incapacity benefit (IB) at the same time as HB and this is within 26 weeks of a previous entitlement ending. This only applies if s/he is also reclaiming IS, JSA or IB, is entitled to IS, income-based JSA or IB and her/his circumstances have not changed since s/he was last claiming HB: GM A2.560-565. A rapid reclaim form can also be accepted where a claimant is reclaiming ESA at the same time as HB within 12 weeks of a previous entitlement ending. The form is issued by Jobcentre Plus offices to claimants who may be eligible. Note that from December 2018, new claims for IS, income-based JSA and income-related ESA are only possible in limited circumstances.

Para (2) enables the authority to provide the approved forms referred to in para (1) itself, or to authorise or appoint someone else to provide them. Either way, the forms must be provided free of charge to claimants. Note paras (7) and (7A) where the claim is not made on an approved form or the form is not properly completed.

Para (3) is linked with para (4) and deals with the situation in which an HB claim is sent by an IS, JSA, ESA, IB or PC claimant to a DWP office. The authority must tell the Secretary of State where it wishes the DWP to forward such claims.

Paragraph (4): Place of claim

Para (4) deals with the place to which a written HB claim may be sent or delivered. There are a number of possibilities according to the circumstances of the claimant.

(1)   If the claimant (or her/his partner) is also claiming IS, JSA, ESA, IB or PC, the HB claim can be sent or delivered to either the "appropriate DWP office" or the authority's "designated office" (both defined in reg 2(1)): sub-paras (a) and (b). The standard practice where IS or income-based JSA are claimed on a written claim form is to issue the claimant with a standard HB claim form. If claims for IS, income-based

JSA, ESA or IB are made via a Jobcentre Plus contact centre, or a PC claim is made by telephone, the HB claim is usually completed at the same time (and is referred to as an "input document").

In these circumstances, an authority may then send a claimant its own form to fill in, but the date of claim remains that determined by para (5). See also Paras (4AA) to (4AE) for when a claim for HB made in connection with a claim for one of the benefits referred to in para (4)(a) can be made by telephone.

Sub-para (c) then provides that where a claim has been sent or delivered to the "appropriate DWP office", that office should send the claim to the authority within two working days of the date on which the HB claim is actually received. If this is not achieved, the claim must be sent on "as soon as practicable" after that. This requirement does not apply if the HB claim is made on the same form as that for IS, JSA, ESA or IB. The regulation does not set a time limit in such a situation.

Note that sub-paras (a) and (b) make reference to those claiming PC. The time and manner in which HB claims are to be made by those of at least the qualifying age for PC, not on IS, income-based JSA or income-related ESA are now dealt with by reg 64 HB(SPC) Regs. However, where someone is making an advance claim for PC prior to reaching the qualifying age, and an advance claim for HB under para (10), her/his claim would be dealt with under the HB Regs initially.

(2)   Other HB claimants *must* send or deliver their claims to the authority's "designated office" (defined in reg 2(1): sub-para (b).

(3)   Sub-paras (f) and (g) allow claims to be sent or delivered to an "authorised office" or the offices of a county council in the circumstances set out.

Paragraphs (4A) and (4B): Telephone claims to the local authority
Under para (4A), a claim for HB can be made by telephone where the local authority has published a telephone number for this purpose and the claim is made to that number. The local authority can decide in a particular case to provide a written statement of the claimant's circumstances for her/him to approve. The telephone claim might not be accepted as valid if the statement is not then approved: para (4B).

Note that even where a telephone claim is not permitted, a claimant can notify her/his intention to claim by telephone (or other means). If a written claim is then submitted within one month, the date of claim is the date of the notification of intention to claim: see para (5)(d).

Paragraphs (4AA) to (4AE) and (4BA): Telephone claims to the DWP
Under para (4AA), if the Secretary of State agrees, where a claim for IS, JSA, ESA, IB or PC is made by telephone under the provisions set out, a claim for HB can also be made by telephone to the number specified by the Secretary of State. This can be done at any time before a decision is made on the claim for the DWP benefit: para (4AB). See the commentary to para (4) above for a discussion on the position where there is a claim for PC.

A claim for HB can also be made, if the Secretary of State agrees, when a claimant is furnishing information or evidence as required or notifies a change of circumstances in accordance with either reg 32 Social Security (Claims and Payments) Regulations 1987 or reg 24 Jobseeker's Allowance Regulations 1996: paras (4AC) and (4AD). This can be done at any time before a decision is made on the award of the DWP benefit to which the evidence, information or change of circumstances relates: para (4AE). Although there is no express reference here, it is understood the intention is for this provision to allow for a telephone claim for HB in this situation: explanatory memorandum to SI 2008 No.2299.

Where the HB claim is made by telephone, the DWP can decide to provide a written statement of the claimant's circumstances for her/him to approve. The telephone claim might not be accepted as valid if the statement is not then approved: para (4BA).

Note: because of the provisions cited, these paragraphs can only apply to claims for "old-style" JSA and ESA – ie, those for whom the provisions in the Welfare Reform Act 2012 have not yet been commenced. Note also that from December 2018, new claims for IS, income-based JSA and income-related ESA are possible only in limited circumstances.

Paragraphs (4C) to (4F): Validity of telephone claims
These mirror the rules in paras (6) to (9) which allow a claimant to remedy a defective written claim. A claim made by telephone is defective unless the claimant provides the local authority (or the DWP where the claim is made to the DWP) with all the information it requires during the telephone call: para (4C). Where a telephone claim is made in accordance with para (4A) and it is defective, the local authority must provide the claimant with an opportunity to correct the defect: para (4D). If the claim is made in accordance with paras (4AA) to (4AE) and it is defective, the DWP may provide the claimant with an opportunity to correct the defect. However, if it does not, the local authority must do so, unless it considers it has sufficient information to determine the HB claim: para (4DA).

If the defect is corrected within one month of the last time it was drawn to the claimant's attention, or within a longer period considered "reasonable" by the authority, the claim *must* be treated as if it was properly made in the first instance: para (4E). If the defect is not corrected within the month (or longer period), although the local authority is not compelled to treat the claim as properly made in the first instance, it has the discretion to do so if it considers it has sufficient information to determine the claim: para (4F).

Paragraphs (5), (5A), (10) and (11): The date of claim
The date on which a claim is (or is treated as) made is important because, subject to paras (12) and (12A), it is used to determine the date on which entitlement to HB commences under reg 76. Para (5) expressly provides

what the date of claim shall be (be it in writing, by telephone or by electronic communication), other than where the claim is made in advance. Paras (10) and (11) provide the date a claim in advance is treated as made.

Para (5). It is important to note that the date of claim is not necessarily the date the claim is actually received by the authority – eg, the date the claimant submits a claim form or makes the telephone call which is the claim for HB. Para (5) is subject to para (10). It should also be read together with paras (4E), (4F), (8) and (8A). So, for example, if a claimant claims and is awarded IS from 1 October, makes a defective written claim for HB on 15 October, but then submits a properly completed claim form on 12 November, it can be argued that the date of claim for HB purposes is 1 October. This is because the HB claim is treated as if validly made on 15 October by para (8), and then as made on the first date of entitlement to IS under para 5(a). It is suggested that this is consistent with *Leicester CC v LG* [2009] UKUT 155 (AAC). For a discussion of that decision, see p815.

Note also that a claim can be backdated under paras (12) and (12A).

Para (5)(d) and (e): The general rules. The date to be taken as the date on which a claim is made is usually the earliest of the following.

(1)   The date the claimant first notified a "designated office", an "authorised office" (see para (13)), or an "appropriate DWP office", by whatever means, of her/his intention to claim. This applies if a "properly completed claim" (only defined in para (9) if the claim is made on an approved form) is received in one of those offices (or a "county office", for which see para (4)(g)) within one month of the form being issued or the claimant notifying her/his intention to make a claim by telephone in accordance with paras (4A) to (4AE) (or a longer period if the authority considers this reasonable): sub-para (d).

"By whatever means" could include by telephone or in person, or where someone notifies the claimant's intention on her/his behalf.

However, claimants and advisers should note that in the event of a subsequent dispute, the absence of a written notification may cause evidential difficulties. Claimants should keep careful contemporaneous notes of any oral notification.

Note that where a claim form is issued for completion after a claimant notifies her/his intention to claim, the one month (or longer) time limit for returning the claim form runs from the date it was issued: sub-para (d)(i). If that time limit is met then the claim can be fixed as having been made on an earlier date than this even if there is a gap between the claimant contacting one of the offices saying s/he wants to claim HB and the claim form then being issued to her/him, thus insulating the claimant from any administrative delays on the part of the authority in issuing the claim form. Where the claimant notifies her/his intention to claim by telephone in accordance with paras (4A) to (4AE), the time limit for receipt of the "properly completed claim" runs from the date of notification: sub-para (d)(ii). It is presumed that a "properly completed claim" would be one that is not deemed defective, for example, by para (4C).

(2)   The date the claim is received at the "designated office", "authorised office", "county offices" or "appropriate DWP office": sub-para (e).

Para (5)(a) to (c): The exceptions. There are three exceptions to the general rule in this regulation (and one in another set of provisions as explained below).

(1)   If a claimant (or her/his partner) has been awarded IS, income-based JSA (defined in reg 2(1) to include joint-claim JSA) or income-related ESA, and the HB claim is made within one month of the date on which the claim for IS, JSA or ESA was received at the "appropriate DWP", the date of claim for HB is the first day of entitlement to IS/income-based JSA/income-related ESA – ie, the effective date of the award of IS/income-based JSA/income-related ESA: sub-para (a); *Leicester CC v LG* [2009] UKUT 155 (AAC). For example, where the claim for IS is backdated, the date of claim for HB would be the date to which the IS claim was backdated. Note that from December 2018, new claims for IS, income-based JSA and income-related ESA are only possible in limited circumstances.

On new claims for income-based JSA or income-related ESA, the claimant normally has to serve seven waiting days before being entitled to that benefit. However, for the purposes of para (5)(a) claimants are to be treated as if they are entitled to income-based JSA or income-related ESA for any waiting days (which can be seven or fewer if the claimant has interrupted the claim), if the waiting days immediately precede the first day in the award of income-based JSA or income-related ESA: para (5A). This means that they will be entitled to maximum HB from the outset. Liaison between the DWP and authorities in this respect could give rise to problems: both will have to be careful about recording the relevant dates.

(2)   From 28 October 2013, sub-para (aa) provides for a similar rule to that above in the case of a person who has been awarded universal credit (UC). If such a person claims HB within a month of the claim for that benefit being made (sub-sub-para (i)) or within a month of the notification of the UC award in a case where no claim for UC is required in order for an entitlement to arise (sub-sub-para (ii)) then the date of claim for HB purposes is the first day of entitlement to UC.

Given that UC is supposed to replace HB as the means through which housing costs for tenants are met there will not be many people covered by this rule: people who have an award of UC can only be entitled to HB in the limited exceptional cases set out in regs 5 and 6 UC(TP) Regs 2014 (at p1862 and p1864) – ie, generally only those living in "specified accommodation" (specified types of supported accommodation and of temporary accommodation for those who have left home as a result of domestic violence) or "temporary accommodation" ie, where a local authority has housed a person in temporary accommodation under its duties to people who are homeless. Claimants covered by the transitional provision in reg 8A UC(TP) Regs 2014 may also receive HB for a period where a claim for UC has been made.

A larger problem has been people who mistakenly claimed UC, only to find they did not meet the tightly drawn conditions for who could claim that benefit during its protracted "roll out" (see reg 6 UC(TP) Regs 2014 – p1864). Such persons may have had their date of claim for HB determined by Art 3A Welfare Reform Act 2012 (Commencement No.9 and Transitional and Transitory Provisions and Commencement No.8 and Savings and Transitional Provisions (Amendment)) Order 2013 as explained at p1850.

(3)   If a claimant (or her/his partner) is on UC, IS, income-based JSA or income-related ESA when s/he becomes liable for rent in a dwelling occupied as a home for the first time (eg, where s/he moves), her/his date of claim for HB is the date s/he first became liable, if the HB claim is received at a "designated office" or "appropriate DWP office" within one month of becoming liable: sub-para (b).

(4)   Sub-para (c) gives some relief from immediately having to claim when a couple relationship comes to an end either due to separation or the death of one of the couple. Where the claimant's former partner was entitled to HB at the time of her/his death or separation from the claimant, then if the claim is made within one month of the death or separation, the date of claim for HB is the date of the death or separation.

Paragraphs (10) and (11): Advance claims

Other than where the claimant is a "person from abroad" (see reg 10), this paragraph gives an authority the discretion to treat an advance claim as made in the benefit week before the first week of entitlement to HB. This applies where a claimant is not entitled to HB in the benefit week after the actual date of claim, but the authority considers s/he will become entitled in the next 13 weeks unless there is a change in circumstances. Note that it is 17 weeks if the claimant or her/his partner is 17 weeks younger than the qualifying age for PC (para 11). See reg 76(1) and (2) for the effect of para (10) and, in particular, the note on *R(H) 9/07*. Excluding people from abroad from this advance claim rule reverses the effect of the Court of Appeal's decision in *SSWP v Bhakta* [2006] EWCA Civ 65; reported as *R(IS) 7/06*. See also reg 7(8) for claimants becoming entitled for the first time when they move to a new home.

AW v SSWP (ESA) [2013] UKUT 20 (AAC) finds that the weight of authority is that a claim is "made" on each day between the date of claim and the date of decision. Accordingly, if a claim is submitted more than 13 weeks prior to any potential entitlement arising but is not decided until 13 or less prior to that entitlement arising then an advance award can still be made. Thus when looking to see whether an advance award should have been made, it is appropriate to look at whether entitlement could have arisen at any point in the 13 weeks after the decision was given.

The judge in *AW v SSWP* also comments on the discretionary nature of the power to make an advance award: he concludes that there would in general be no reason not to exercise this discretion in a claimant's favour where the conditions are met.

Paragraphs (6) to (9): Validity of written claims

Paras (6) and (9). Under para (6), written claims which do not comply with para (1) are to be termed "defective" for the purposes of these regulations, but see paras (8) and (8A). Para (9) defines when a claim made on an approved form amounts to a "properly completed claim" – ie, when the claimant has followed the instructions as to its completion, including those as to provision of information and evidence. So s/he will not be penalised if the instructions are inadequate. See also reg 86 for situations when additional evidence and information must be provided when requested.

Para (7) goes on to say that if a claim received by the local authority is defective, for either of the reasons listed in sub-paras (a) (approved form but not properly completed) or (b) (not on approved form and not sufficient), the authority may give the claimant a chance to remedy things. It can return the form for completion if sub-para (a) applies, or supply her/him with an approved form or request further information and evidence if sub-para (b) applies. However, see also para (9).

Para (7A) allows the DWP, where the HB claim is received at an appropriate DWP office and appears not to have been completed properly, to request a claimant to provide information to the local authority needed to complete the form.

Paras (8) and (8A). A defective claim must be treated as if it had been validly made if any of the conditions in para (8A) are satisfied: para (8). So as regards the date to be taken as the date of claim, para (5) will apply, for example, to the date on which the claim was first sent or delivered, rather than the date on which a remedied form (or information or evidence) is returned or provided. The conditions are:

(1)   Where the authority gives the claimant a chance to remedy a defective claim under para (7)(a) or (b), the properly completed form (or information or evidence) is returned within one month: para (8A)(a) and (b).

(2)   Where the DWP has requested the claimant to provide information to the local authority under para (7A), the properly completed form (or information or evidence) is provided to the local authority within one month: para (8A)(c).

In all cases, the one-month period can be such longer period as the local authority considers "reasonable".

Paragraph (12) and (12A): Backdating

A claim made on or after 1 April 2016 can only be backdated for up to one month, rather than the six months that was possible before that date. This is intended to match the one-month backdating possible for universal credit. Prior to 6 October 2008 a claim could be backdated for up to 52 weeks.

For para (12) to apply, the claimant must have requested HB in respect of a past period (previously the rules required a "claim for backdating"); secondly, from a date in that past period up to the date on which the claimant requested HB for a past period, the claimant must have had continuous "good cause" for her/his failure to make a claim for HB (or failure to request that the claim should include the past period). If these two conditions are met, the claim for the past period is treated as made on the latest of the days listed in para (12A): either the first day from which the claimant had continuous good cause, the day one month before HB was claimed or the day one month before HB in respect of a past period was requested.

Thus the regulations now deal with what is to be taken as the date of the "claim for backdating" under the old terminology. Prior to amendment that was important as it determined the date from which HB could be paid retrospectively. Was it the date the claim for backdating was actually made (ie, the date a claimant requests backdating, in writing or by telephone) or was the date to be determined by para (5) above? As the claim for backdating was a claim for HB, it was arguable that the date should have been determined by para (5). If this was right, it would have produced the same result as In *Leicester CC v LG* [2009] UKUT 155 (AAC), such that the claimant could have the backdated payment commence from, for example, the date of a claim for IS, income-based JSA or income-related ESA where a HB claim was then submitted within a month of that claim, or some other earlier date determined by para (5).

Now, however, it is clear that, where a claimant has made a claim for benefit and asks for HB in respect of a period of backdating before that claim was made, the earliest commencement of entitlement will be one month before that request was made (unless the date from which the continuous good cause is established is later). This provision sits somewhat uneasily alongside reg 87, which allows an amendment of an undecided claim to be treated as if it was made when the claim was made. It may be that this will mean that where a claim is amended to include a request for a backdated period before the claim is decided, the request for a past period will be treated as made on the same date the claim is made. That would seem to mitigate this rule to some extent.

Unless a person has been appointed under reg 82(3) to act on behalf of the claimant, the test of "good cause" applies to the claimant her/himself and not her/his landlord, even where the claimant is in supported housing and the landlord may, in fact, have been assisting the claimant with her/his claims for benefit: *CH 1791/2004* para 25. However, this decision emphasises that in the latter situation the actions or errors of the landlord will not be irrelevant, but have to be viewed from the perspective of whether the claimant acted reasonably in all the circumstances, in particular in allowing his or her landlord to act for her/him.

In the case of a couple (see reg 82(1)), it is for the member of the couple who makes the claim for backdating to show that s/he has "good cause" and it is irrelevant whether the other member of the couple can show good cause or not: *CH 3817/2004* para 8.

The Court of Appeal held in *R v Aylesbury Vale DC ex p England* (1996) 29 HLR 303 that ordinarily a claim for HB is to be treated as prospective only, so an express request must be included if backdating is required. For the position where a request for backdating was made before 1 April 1996, see p236 of the 9th edition and p7 of the supplement to that edition.

CH 996/2004 states that the issue of backdating does not arise (and so need not be considered) if the other conditions of entitlement are not satisfied in any event. Although perhaps this will be an issue of little practical importance, it is respectfully suggested that *CH 996/2004* is wrong on this point and is putting the proverbial horse before the cart. Axiomatically, the other conditions of entitlement cannot arise unless and until a claim has been made (including for a backdated period), and so establishing if a claim has been made for a backdated period must be logically prior to deciding whether the other conditions of entitlement are met.

The phrase "good cause" has frequently been considered by social security commissioners and in *R(S) 2/63(T)* was defined by a tribunal of commissioners as:

"... some fact which, having regard to all the circumstances (including the claimant's state of health and the information which he had received and that which he might have obtained) would probably have caused a reasonable person of his age and experience to act (or fail to act) as the claimant did."

CH 2198/2008 makes the point that the test is not how a reasonable person would have acted, but is rather whether *the claimant has good cause* for not claiming earlier. While whether, given a claimant's circumstances, it can be said s/he acted reasonably is a factor in whether s/he had good cause that is not necessarily determinative. In *UH v Islington LB* [2010] UKUT 64 (AAC), the Upper Tribunal agrees with that, but notes that the more reasonable a person's behaviour in not claiming earlier, given her/his age, experience and the information available to her/him, the more likely s/he will have good cause.

However, it is clear from *Chief Adjudication Officer v Upton* [1997] 2 CLY 4668, CA that, as long as the authority has regard to this legal test, the question of whether "good cause" exists is one of fact. The commissioner approved this view of *Upton* in *CH 2659/2002* para 24.

The burden of proof to establish "good cause" rests on the claimant: *CH 5135/2001* para 1.4. That case involved a claimant who relied on an illness from which he was suffering during the relevant period. The tribunal decided that an illness must be severe for a claimant to succeed in asserting "good cause", but the commissioner decided that was incorrect: para 6. The question was "whether the nature of the illness is sufficient to constitute or lead to good cause".

Where a claimant has a mental illness, the reasonableness of her/his actions must be judged by her/his mental age or capacity rather than chronological age, though medical evidence would be required: *CH 393/2003* paras 5–6; *CH 474/2002* para 9. An illness is not rendered irrelevant just because a claimant does not have an appointee: *CH 393/2003* para 7.

In *FR v Broadland DC* [2012] UKUT 449 (AAC) the judge commented:

"If a claimant simply chooses not to make a claim and then changes his mind, he does not show that he had good cause for not making it. It is for him to show in some detail why he did not make it at the start of the period for which backdating is claimed and why he continued not to make it. It is possible, as in the examples of old cases that I have given, that a tribunal could properly regard a claimant as having good cause not to claim benefit for a limited period, when he is devoting his time to making real efforts to obtain work and avoid what the claimant here has referred to as the benefits trap and in the process to avoid becoming a burden on the state or the local authority. Indeed he may be applauded for his efforts in that respect. On the other hand a person who decides not to claim benefit ought not generally to expect to be able to change his mind and have his claim backdated. Also, the greater the delay in claiming benefit, the harder it may be to show good cause. It is a matter for the tribunal to determine as a question of fact whether all the facts in the particular case amount to continuing good cause for failing to make the claim."

In *CH 2191/2002*, the claimant failed to disclose to the DWP that her husband had started work. When the change of circumstances was discovered, her JSA was terminated retrospectively which led to a disallowance of HB during the same period. The commissioner held that the only conclusion that the tribunal could come to was that backdating should be refused, because she had failed to disclose the change of circumstances. This is to ask entirely the wrong question. The question is why the claimant did not make a claim earlier, not why she did not disclose a change of circumstances earlier. In any event, it is hard to see why she was not entitled to have her notional entitlement to HB offset under reg 104(1) HB Regs 1987 (now reg 104(1)).

A tribunal may, when hearing an appeal against refusal to backdate a claim to the date when a previous entitlement ended, treat that claim as an application for revision or appeal against the decision which brought the previous entitlement to HB to an end: *R(JSA) 2/04*; *CH 3009/2002*. In such a case, the tribunal needs to consider not just whether a claim can be backdated but also whether the decision to stop the benefit in the first place was correct.

For a discussion of the caselaw on the position for renewal claims prior to the abolition of benefit periods in April 2004, see pp460–61 of the 21st edition.

[1Electronic claims for benefit

83A. A claim for housing benefit may be made by means of an electronic communication in accordance with Schedule 11.]

Amendment

1.   Inserted by art 2(3) of SI 2006 No 2968 as from 20.12.06.

Definition

"electronic communication" – see reg 2(1).

General Note

If authorisation is given by means of a direction of the Chief Executive of the authority, a claim for HB can be made by electronic communication and such a claim is effectively dealt with as a written claim. The authorisation requirements and conditions for claims by electronic communication are found in Sch 11. By Sch 11 para 4, any claim, certificate, notice, information or evidence which is delivered by means of an electronic communication must generally be treated as having been delivered in the manner or form required by any provision of the HB Regs, on the day the conditions imposed are satisfied.

The DWP reminds authorities (in *HB/CTB General Information Bulletin G11/2007*) that claims made electronically where an authority has *not* obtained a Chief Executive's direction are not valid claims and that any benefit paid or credited as a result will not attract any subsidy.

[1Date of claim where claim sent or delivered to a gateway office 84.]

Amendment

1.   Omitted by reg 2(5) of SI 2008 No 2299 as from 1.10.08.

[1Date of claim where claim sent or delivered to an office of a designated authority 85.]

Amendment

1.   Omitted by reg 2(6) of SI 2008 No 2299 as from 1.10.08.

Evidence and information

86.–(1)   Subject to [³ paragraphs (1A) and (2)] and to paragraph 5 of Schedule A1 (treatment of claims for housing benefit by refugees), a person who makes a claim, or a person to whom housing benefit has been awarded, shall furnish such certificates, documents, information and evidence in connection with the claim or the award, or any question arising out of the claim or the award, as may reasonably be required by the relevant authority in order to determine that person's entitlement to, or continuing entitlement to, housing benefit and shall do so within one month of [³ the relevant authority requiring him, or the Secretary of State requesting him, to do so] or such longer period as the relevant authority may consider reasonable.

[³ (1A)   Where a person notifies a change of circumstances to the appropriate DWP office under regulation 88(6), the Secretary of State may request that the claimant provides to the relevant authority the information or evidence that the Secretary of State considers the relevant authority may require to determine the claimant's continuing entitlement to housing benefit.]

(2)   Nothing in this regulation shall require a person to furnish any certificates, documents, information or evidence relating to a payment to which paragraph (4) applies.

(3)   Where a request is made under paragraph (1), the relevant authority shall–

(a)   inform the claimant or the person to whom housing benefit has been awarded of his duty under regulation 88 (duty to notify change of circumstances) to notify the designated office of any change of circumstances; and

(b)   without prejudice to the extent of the duty owed under regulation 88, indicate to him either orally or by notice or by reference to some other document available to him on application and without charge, the kind of change or circumstances which is to be notified.

(4)   This paragraph applies to any of the following payments–

(a)   a payment which is–

   (i)   disregarded under paragraph 23 of Schedule 5 (income in kind) or paragraph 34 of Schedule 6 (certain payments in kind); and

   (ii)   made under [⁴ or by] the Macfarlane Trust, the Macfarlane (Special Payments) Trust, the Macfarlane (Special Payments) (No 2) Trust, the Fund, the Eileen Trust [⁴, MFET Limited], the Skipton Fund [⁶, the Caxton Foundation] [⁷, ⁹] [⁸, the London Emergencies Trust, the We Love Manchester Emergency Fund] or the London Bombings Relief Charitable Fund;

(b)   a payment which is disregarded under paragraph 35 of Schedule 5 or paragraph 24 of Schedule 6 (payments made under certain trusts and certain other payments), other than a payment made under the Independent Living [² Fund (2006)];

(c)   a payment which is disregarded under regulation 74(9)(b) or (c) (income of non-dependant) other than a payment made under the Independent Living [² Fund 2006].

(5)   Where a claimant or a person to whom housing benefit has been awarded or any partner [⁵ has attained the qualifying age for state pension credit] and is a member of, or a person deriving entitlement to a pension under, a personal pension scheme, [¹] he shall where the relevant authority so requires furnish the following information–

(a)   the name and address of the pension fund holder;

(b)   such other information including any reference or policy number as is needed to enable the personal pension scheme [¹] to be identified.

(6)   Where the pension fund holder receives from a relevant authority a request for details concerning a personal pension scheme [¹] relating to a person or any partner to whom paragraph (5) refers, the pension fund holder shall provide the relevant authority with any information to which paragraph (7) refers.

(7)   The information to which this paragraph refers is–

(a)   where the purchase of an annuity under a personal pension scheme has been deferred, the amount of any income which is being withdrawn from the personal pension scheme;

(b)　in the case of–
　　(i)　a personal pension scheme where income withdrawal is available, the [10 rate of the annuity which may have been purchased with the funds held under the scheme]; or
　　(ii)　a personal pension scheme where income withdrawal is not available, [1] the [10 rate of the annuity which might have been purchased with the fund] if the fund were held under a personal pension scheme where income withdrawal was available,

calculated by or on behalf of the pension fund holder by means of tables prepared from time to time by the Government Actuary which are appropriate for this purpose.

Amendments

1.　　Amended by reg 4(6) of SI 2007 No 1749 as from 16.7.07.
2.　　Amended by reg 6(4)(e) of SI 2008 No 2767 as from 17.11.08.
3.　　Amended by reg 2(3) of SI 2008 No 2987 as from 22.12.08.
4.　　Amended by reg 8(3) and (5) of SI 2010 No 641 as from 1.4.10 (5.4.10 where rent payable weekly or in multiples of a week).
5.　　Amended by reg 8(9) of SI 2010 No 641 as from 6.4.10.
6.　　Inserted by reg 19(6)(b) of SI 2011 No 2425 as from 31.10.11.
7.　　Amended by reg 6(3)(e) of SI 2017 No 329 as from 3.4.17.
8.　　Amended by reg 6(3)(e) of SI 2017 No 689 as from 19.6.17.
9.　　Amended by reg 6(5) of SI 2017 No 870 as from 23.10.17.
10.　　Amended by reg 11 of SI 2017 No 1015 as from 16.11.17.

Definitions

"appropriate DWP office" – see reg 2(1).
"claim" – see reg 2(1).
"claimant" – see reg 2(1).
"designated office" – see reg 2(1).
"the Macfarlane Trust" and other schemes listed in para (4)(a)(ii) – see reg 2(1).
"partner" – see reg 2(1).
"pension fund holder" – see reg 2(1).
"personal pension scheme" – see reg 2(1).
"qualifying age for state pension credit" – see reg 2(1).
"relevant authority" – see reg 2(1).

General Note

This obliges the claimant to provide evidence to support her/his claim, if required to do so by the authority (either on the claim form or subsequently) or requested to do so by the DWP. S/he must do so within one month of the request, or such longer period as the authority considers reasonable.

The authority must inform the claimant of her/his obligation (under reg 88) to report certain changes of circumstance. See also reg 83 for the information and evidence requirements for valid claims.

Analysis

Paragraphs (1), (1A), (2) and (4): Power to require information

The time at which information may be demanded is the whole period during which HB is being claimed. The claimant or person to whom HB is awarded must provide "certificates, documents, information and evidence" (not further defined) as may be reasonably required. This will depend upon the personal circumstances of each individual claimant and on whether the authority has reasonable cause to doubt any previous statements made, or information given, by her/him. However, the information must be required for the purpose of determining entitlement to HB and not for any other purpose. The requirement to supply information under reg 86 must actually have been communicated to the person in question; proof of posting to the last known address is not sufficient: *AA v Hounslow LB* [2008] UKUT 13 (AAC).

Where there is a failure to comply with the requirements in reg 86(1), note the possibility of payment of HB being suspended under regs 11 or 13 D&A Regs (see p964 and p966). Entitlement to HB might then be terminated under reg 14 of those regulations (see p968). Note, however, that suspension and termination of an award under those regulations are only possible where the information and evidence relates to a question that has arisen about *entitlement* to HB. In *CH v Plymouth City Council and DE (HB)* [2018] UKUT 215 (AAC), the Upper Tribunal held that a local authority has no power to terminate an award on account of failure to provide information that the authority has asked for in order to make *payment* of HB (in this case, a claimant's failure to provide bank details to allow payment to be made by the authority's preferred method, BACS). While Judge

Jacobs confirmed that there is no appeal against a decision of a local authority under reg 86, the tribunal has jurisdiction where the decision is on a claim or an award.

Under para (1A), if a change of circumstances is notified to the DWP under reg 88(6), the DWP can request that a claimant provides information or evidence to the local authority if it is needed to determine the claimant's continuing entitlement to HB.

There is no duty to disclose details of certain specific payments which are wholly disregarded: para (2). These are listed in para (4), namely:

(1)   Income or payments in kind disregarded under Sch 5 para 23 or Sch 6 para 34.

(2)   Payments from any of the Macfarlane Trusts (which were established by the Secretary of State for Social Security for the benefit of haemophiliacs), the Fund, the Eileen Trust, MFET Limited, the Skipton Fund, the Caxton Foundation, the London Emergencies Trust, the We Love Manchester Emergency Fund or the London Bombings Relief Charitable Fund.

(3)   Payments which are disregarded under Sch 5 para 35 or Sch 6 para 24 (except for payments from the Independent Living Funds). These are payments from the Macfarlane Trusts or any of the other trusts and funds mentioned in (2) above, plus the Scottish Infected Blood Support Scheme and an approved blood scheme.

(4)   Payments to a non-dependant which are disregarded under reg 74(9)(b) or (c) (other than payments from the Independent Living Fund (2006)). Again these are payments under the Macfarlane Trusts or any of the other trusts, funds and schemes mentioned in (3) above.

The power is to require information from "a person who makes a claim or a person to whom housing benefit has been awarded". This includes anyone claiming on behalf of a claimant as appointee under reg 82 or as a duly appointed agent. The fact that specific mention is made of such payments indicates that claimants are potentially under an obligation to disclose all other income and capital (even where it falls to be disregarded in its entirety), at least when requested to do so. It might be argued that the existence of the disregard means that the authority does not need to know the amount of such income or capital to determine the claim but the reality is otherwise: the authority needs to know the amount and nature of all such payments in order to be satisfied that the disregard applies in the first place. It is perfectly reasonable for a local authority to require information or evidence not only at the time the claim form is completed but also "from time to time in the form of a signed statement given in response to direct questions from a council officer at a home visit": *CH 4390/2003* para 11. Moreover, a local authority is entitled (and, indeed, required) to demand information under reg 86(1) notwithstanding the fact that entitlement had ceased in order to correctly calculate the amount of an overpayment: *CH 4943/2001* paras 65–70. The decision in *SSWP v Chiltern DC* (2003) HLR 1019, CA; reported as *R(H) 2/03*, which reversed Commissioner Jacobs' decision on two points, does not affect this conclusion. The Court of Appeal did not endorse the submission for the local authority before the commissioner to the effect that the only way in which it could obtain information in order to operate reg 104 HB Regs 1987 (now reg 104 HB Regs) was by inviting a fresh claim and that it could only operate reg 104 if backdating for "good cause" is granted. The Court of Appeal says "can use that fresh claim" and does not say "can only use that fresh claim" or that the local authority is precluded from obtaining information by other means. Moreover, such an approach would be inconsistent with the Court of Appeal's decision in *Adan* (*R(H) 5/04*): see the commentary to reg 104 on p603.

In *R v Liverpool City Council ex p Johnson (No 2)* [1995] COD 200, QBD, it was held that reg 73(1) HB Regs 1987 (now reg 86(1)) did not empower an authority to insist that a claimant attend for an interview or to decline to determine the claim if s/he did not do so. However, in the absence of such an interview, the authority may decide that it is not satisfied that the claimant has established her/his entitlement to HB, in which case the claim will be refused and the claimant left to her/his remedies of revision or appeal.

The authority may extend the one-month time limit within which the claimant must supply the evidence required or requested for as long as it considers reasonable. An authority's practice of never extending the time limit, however reasonable the request, would be liable to be overturned on judicial review as imposing a fetter on the authority's discretion. An individual refusal could also be challenged if it could be shown that the authority had failed to have regard to a relevant factor – eg, the claimant's state of health or the difficulty of obtaining the information.

The requirement in para (1) that information must be "*reasonably* required", and the prohibition in para (2) of requiring information of the types set out in para (4), override any general guidance given to local authorities by the DWP on the types of evidence they should require of claimants when a claim is made. *CH 999/2002* paras 13–15 upheld the reasonableness of a requirement to provide utility bills as proof of residence. However, the commissioner made it clear that the reasonableness of any requirement would depend on the circumstances of the individual case: para 14. In short, it is reg 86(1) with which the claimant must comply, not any requirements of government verification guidance.

The decision to seek certain information or seek it in certain ways (eg, a home visit) is not itself appealable. However, *CH 2555/2007* reminds the First-tier Tribunal that when an appeal has been made against a decision altering or stopping an award of benefit on the grounds of an alleged failure to provide information, the tribunal has to satisfy itself of the reasonableness of the request for information (or a home visit) in the individual case before it as part of its deciding whether the failure to provide the information gave sufficient grounds to alter or stop the benefit award. Accordingly, in cases where the need for a particular piece of information or a home visit is challenged on an appeal, the tribunal must decide for itself on the facts whether the information or home visit was reasonably required, rather than limiting itself to deciding (on judicial review type grounds) whether the request under reg 86(1) was one which a reasonable local authority could make.

Paragraph (3): The authority's obligations

This obliges the authority to inform the claimant of her/his duty to report changes of circumstances to the authority (sub-para (a)), and also tell her/him what *kind* of change s/he should report (sub-para (b)). The latter duty may be discharged by word of mouth but it is good practice to provide a written guide in every case and to get the claimant to sign to say that s/he has received and read it. A document is of more use to the claimant because s/he can refer to it in the future and if the duty is discharged by telling the claimant orally of the kinds of changes which should be reported, disputes may arise subsequently as to what was said and indeed whether such a conversation ever took place at all. Needless to say, the authority should be as explicit as possible so that the claimant is not misled in any way.

The duty under this para is stated to arise "where a request is made under paragraph (1)" but taken on its own this is apt to cause confusion. In practice, a request under para (1) is made in every case because information, documents and evidence, etc are always requested by the questions in the authority's printed claim form and there is no power other than reg 86(1) to require such information. It follows that the para (3) information should be given to the claimant at the time of the claim in every case and *again* if a supplementary request for further information or evidence is made.

The wording of para (3)(a) does not mean that a claimant is under a duty to provide information to an authority only where a prior request for information has been made by the authority: *CH 2794/2004* para 18. While the duty to provide evidence or information will only arise under reg 86(1) where that evidence or information has been requested, nothing in para (3) qualifies the claimant focused duty in reg 88(1).

Paragraphs (5) to (7): Pension funds

Para (5) entitles the authority to require a claimant or person to whom HB has been awarded (or any partner) who is at least the qualifying age for PC to supply information about pension fund holders and suppliers of pension schemes. Paras (6) and (7) require the provision of information by those administering the schemes. It is not clear what purpose these paras now serve, given the amendments to reg 42(2)(c) and omission of reg 42(3) (see p453).

Prior to 16 July 2007, reference was also made to "retirement annuity contracts". These were a method of saving for retirement. However, from April 2007 they were subsumed into "personal pension schemes" so it was no longer necessary to draw a distinction between retirement annuity contracts and personal pension schemes.

[²Amendment and withdrawal of claim

[³ **87.**–[⁴ (1)   A person who has made a claim for benefit may amend it at any time before a [⁵ decision] has been made on the claim by notice in writing received at the designated office, by telephone call to a telephone number specified by the relevant authority under regulation 83(4A) (time and manner in which claims are to be made) or by the Secretary of State under regulation 83(4AA) or in such other manner as the relevant authority or the Secretary of State may decide or accept.]

[⁴ (2)]

(3)   Any claim amended in accordance with paragraph (1) [⁴] shall be treated as if it had been amended in the first instance.

(4)   A person who has made a claim may withdraw it at any time before a decision has been made on it by notice to the designated office.

(5)   Where the claim was made by telephone in accordance with paragraphs (4AA) to (4AE) of regulation 83, the withdrawal may also be made by telephone to the telephone number specified by the Secretary of State.

(6)   Any notice of withdrawal given in accordance with paragraph (4) or (5) shall have effect when it is received.]]

Amendments

1.   Inserted by reg 2(3) of SI 2006 No 2967 as from 20.12.06.
2.   Substituted by reg 6(4) of SI 2007 No 719 as from 2.4.07.
3.   Substituted by reg 2(7) of SI 2008 No 2299 as from 1.10.08.
4.   Amended by reg 11(4) of SI 2013 No 2536 as from 29.10.13.
5.   Amended by reg 3(5) of SI 2014 No 213 as from 1.4.14 (7.4.14 where rent payable weekly or in multiples of a week).

Definitions

"claim" – see reg 2(1).
"designated office" – see reg 2(1).
"relevant authority" – see reg 2(1).

Analysis

Paras (1) to (3). Before a decision has been made the claimant needs no permission to amend her/his claim. The claim is then treated as if made as amended.

Para (4) to (6). A claim can be withdrawn by notice to the "designated office" at any time before a decision is made on it. There is no requirement as to the form of "notice" required to withdraw a claim; according to para (4) it need not even be in writing. Where the claim was made by telephone to the DWP in accordance with reg 83(4AA) to (4AE), it can be withdrawn by telephone to the number specified by the Secretary of State.

Once properly withdrawn, the claim ceases to exist and no decision or award can be made on it, nor can the claim then be reinstated: *R(H) 2/06* para 9. It may be possible to show that the decision to withdraw was not freely made – thus depriving the withdrawal of legal effect – but this will only arise in an exceptional case where, for example, the claimant was acting under duress (*CJSA 3979/1999* para 26). However, even in a case of alleged duress, where a claimant is ordinarily able to understand the consequences of her/his actions, what will need to be shown is threatening or overbearing behaviour, or deception, leading to the claim being withdrawn: the fact that withdrawing the claim was not, with the benefit of hindsight, in the claimant's best interests will not be enough (*R(H) 2/06* para 11).

Although there is no statutory mechanism expressly permitting withdrawal from an award once a decision has been made on a claim, DWP Guidance (HB/CTB G10/2008) reminds authorities that a claimant should not be prevented from surrendering an award of benefit if s/he indicates that s/he no longer wishes to claim HB. See also: *CJSA 1332/2001*, *CDLA 1589/2005* and *CJSA 3979/1999* cited therein.

Duty to notify changes of circumstances

88.–(1)   Subject to [³ [⁵ paragraphs (3) and (6)]], if at any time between the making of a claim and a decision being made on it, or during the award of housing benefit, there is a change of circumstances which the claimant, or any person by whom or on whose behalf sums payable by way of housing benefit are receivable, might reasonably be expected to know might affect the claimant's right to, the amount of or the receipt of housing benefit, that person shall be under a duty to notify that change of circumstances by giving notice [¹] to the designated office

[¹[⁶ (a)   in writing; or

(b)   by telephone–

    (i)   where the relevant authority has published a telephone number for that purpose or for the purposes of regulation 83 (time and manner in which claims are to be made) unless the authority determines that in any particular case or class of case notification may not be given by telephone; or

    (ii)   in any case or class of case where the relevant authority determines that notice may be given by telephone; or

(c)   by any other means which the relevant authority agrees to accept in any particular case.]]

[³ (2)]

(3)   The duty imposed on a person by paragraph (1) does not extend to changes in–

(a)   the amount of rent payable to a housing authority;

(b)   the age of the claimant or that of any member of his family or of any non-dependants;

(c)   these Regulations;

(d)   in the case of a claimant on income support [² [⁴, an income-based jobseeker's allowance or an income-related employment and support allowance]], any circumstances which affect the amount of income support [⁴, an income-based jobseeker's allowance or an income-related employment and support allowance] but not the amount of housing benefit to which he is entitled, other than the cessation of that entitlement to income support [⁴, an income-based jobseeker's allowance or an income-related employment and support allowance].

(4)   Notwithstanding paragraph (3)(b) or (d) a claimant shall be required by paragraph (1) to notify the designated office of any change in the composition of his family arising from the fact that a person who was a member of his family is now no longer such a person because he ceases to be a child or young person.

[³ (5)]

[⁵ (6)   Where–

(a)   the claimant or the claimant's partner is in receipt of income support or jobseeker's allowance;

(b)   the change of circumstance is that the claimant or the claimant's partner starts employment; and

(c)   as a result of that change of circumstance, either entitlement to that benefit will end or, where the claimant or claimant's partner is in receipt of a contribution-based jobseeker's allowance, the amount of that benefit will be reduced,

the claimant may discharge the duty in paragraph (1) by notifying the change of circumstance by telephoning the appropriate DWP office if a telephone number has been provided for that purpose.]

Amendments

1.   Amended by reg 2(4) of SI 2006 No 2967 as from 20.12.06.
2.   Inserted by reg 3(9) of SI 2008 No 1042 as from 19.5.08.
3.   Amended by reg 2(8) of SI 2008 No 2299 as from 1.10.08.
4.   Amended by reg 20 of SI 2008 No 1082 as from 27.10.08.
5.   Amended by reg 2(4) of SI 2008 No 2987 as from 22.12.08.
6.   Amended by reg 2(5) of SI 2010 No 2449 as from 1.11.10.

Definitions

"appropriate DWP office" – see reg 2(1).
"claim" – see reg 2(1).
"claimant" – see reg 2(1).
"designated office" – see reg 2(1).
"designated authority" – see reg 2(1).
"family" – see s137(1) SSCBA and Part 4.
"housing authority" – see s191 SSAA.
"person on an income-based jobseeker's allowance" – see reg 2(3).
"person on an income-related employment and support allowance" – see reg 2(3A).
"person on income support) – see reg 2(1).
"non-dependant" – see reg 3.
"rent" – see Part 3.

General Note

This regulation imposes a general duty on the claimant (and anyone by whom, or on whose behalf, HB may be receivable) to report to the authority any change of circumstances which might affect the claimant's right to, the amount of, or the payment of, benefit.

The regulation links to the rules on overpayments: see Part 13. Local authorities should act promptly when notified of changes in circumstance as any subsequent overpayment may be irrecoverable as having been caused by official error.

Note also the possible offences where someone dishonestly fails to give a prompt notification of a change of circumstances: ss111A and 112 SSAA (on p51 and p54). For these purposes, the acceptable form of notification is provided for in reg 4 Social Security (Notification of Change of Circumstances) Regulations 2001 (on p1759). In addition to possible criminal offences, from 1 October 2012, ss115C and 115D SSAA also provide for the imposition of civil penalties (in the sum of £50) for negligently making an incorrect statement, and certain failures to disclose (in both cases if this leads to an overpayment) (see p64).

Analysis

Paragraph (1): The duty to report changes

The duty to report changes in circumstances is placed not merely on the claimant but on appointees and landlords who are in receipt of direct payment of HB: see regs 95 and 96. It is not contingent on a prior request being made by the local authority: *CH 2794/2004* para 18.

Notification must usually be given to the local authority (but see para (6) for an exception) and must be:
–   in writing;
–   by telephone where the relevant authority has published a telephone number for the purposes of telephone claims or notification of changes of circumstances or in other cases specified; *or*
–   in a form other than in writing or by telephone.

Note that notice may also be given by means of an electronic communication in accordance with Sch 11 (if authorised) (reg 88A) and that there are alternative means for notice (reg 88ZA). Notice may be given to the DWP in specified circumstances under reg 88(6).

Telephoning the local authority with the information would, in many cases, be bad practice as it does not provide a permanent record. It is always best to ensure receipt of notifications by the authority by sending letters by recorded delivery post. Some authorities adopt a helpful practice of giving a receipt for documents handed over in person, and such receipts should always be kept in a safe place.

The changes which must be reported are those which might effect the claimant's right to HB (eg, if s/he moves address or her/his capital increases above the capital limit), the amount of HB s/he is entitled to (eg, if her/his income increases, or s/he inherits capital which will increase her/his "tariff income" under reg 52); and her/his right to receive HB (eg, rent arrears which might justify payment to a landlord).

In *West Somerset DC v JMA (HB)* [2010] UKUT 190 (AAC), the local authority was found by the First-tier Tribunal not to have informed the claimant that changes of circumstances were required to be reported in writing (at a time before the amendments allowed reporting of changes via other methods in certain circumstances). The claimant was found to have visited the designated office to make disclosure. On appeal to the Upper Tribunal, the authority argued that the cause of the overpayment was the failure to report the change in writing as, at that time, required by para (1). The judge held that the failure to inform the claimant of her duty under para (1) to report the change in writing was in part the cause of the overpayment (the other element being the failure of the officer to whom disclosure was made to pass the information on). The case shows that although the duty is to report changes in the prescribed manner, where the claimant has not been put on notice of that requirement, then in at least some cases, breach of the duty will not rebound to the loss of the claimant.

There are back up arrangements between local authorities and DWP local offices where the claimant is also in receipt of IS, income-related ESA or income-based JSA. The DWP should notify the authority of any changes which are reported to them and if the claimant ceases to be entitled to IS or income-based JSA. There is often delay in this happening so claimants should *not* rely on it. The primary duty is imposed on the claimant (and/or appointee or landlord as the case may be) to report all relevant changes to the correct office irrespective of whether the DWP also does so. A breakdown in the back-up procedure will not mean that a resulting overpayment is unrecoverable as being the result of an official error: see the Analysis to reg 100.

Paragraphs (3), (4) and (6): Exceptions to the general rule

Para (3) lists four types of change of circumstance which do not have to be reported to the local authority by someone under the general duty in para (1).

(1) Changes in the rent charged by the authority to its own tenants: sub-para (a).

(2) Changes in the ages of the claimant and her/his family or of any non-dependants: sub-para (b). This is subject to the qualification in para (4).

(3) Changes in the regulations themselves: sub-para (c).

(4) Changes which affect the amount of IS, income-based JSA or income-related ESA but not HB, other than the cessation of entitlement to one of those benefits: sub-para (d). This is subject to the qualification in para (4).

The changes in sub-paras (a), (b) and (c) are included because, although they do potentially affect entitlement, the authority will already be aware of them from other sources, as with those changes in sub-paras (a) and (c) or from the dates of birth supplied at the time of the claim.

The change set out in sub-para (d) would include, for example, a change in income or capital that reduces (but does not end) entitlement to IS, income-based JSA or income-related ESA. HB claimants who are also entitled to IS, income-based JSA or income-related ESA receive maximum HB whatever the amount of their IS, income-based JSA or income-related ESA (see s130(3)(a) of SSCBA, HB Regs Sch 4 para 12, Sch 5 para 4 and Sch 6 para 5 and the discussion on *R v Penwith DC ex p Menear* (1991) 24 HLR 115, QBD in the General Note to Part 6). Apart from the change set out in para (4) (to which this sub-paragraph is subject), changes in the amount of IS/income-based JSA/income-related ESA payable to the claimant have no effect on her/his entitlement to, nor the amount of, HB.

Para (4). Although the general rule in para (2)(b) is that changes in the age of members of the family do not need to be reported, this paragraph requires disclosure when someone ceases to be a "child" or a "young person" for HB purposes (see commentary to reg 19 on p406). This is because the effect of such a change could be that the person concerned ceases to be a member of the "family" and instead becomes a non-dependant: see reg 3 and s137(1) SSCBA.

The change from family member to non-dependant affects the level of HB payable even if the claimant continues to receive IS, income-based JSA or income-related ESA, because maximum HB is defined as eligible rent less non-dependant deductions: see reg 70. It must therefore be reported notwithstanding sub-para (3)(d).

Para (6). There is one situation in which a claimant, instead of notifying the local authority, can report a change in circumstances by telephoning the DWP, if a telephone number has been provided for this purpose. This only applies where the change of circumstances is that the claimant or her/his partner has started employment, the claimant or her/his partner is in receipt of IS or JSA, and as a result of the change, entitlement to IS or JSA will end, or if the benefit is *contribution-based* JSA, the amount will be reduced.

[¹ Alternative means of notifying changes of circumstances

88ZA.–(1)   In such cases and subject to such conditions as the Secretary of State may specify, the duty in regulation 88(1) to notify a change of circumstances may be discharged by notifying the Secretary of State–

(a)   where the change of circumstances is a birth or death, through a relevant authority, or a county council in England, by personal attendance at an office specified by that authority or county council, provided the Secretary of State has agreed with that authority or county council for it to facilitate such notification; or

(b)   where the change of circumstances is a death, by telephone to a telephone number specified for that purpose by the Secretary of State.

(2)   Paragraph (1) only applies if the authority administering the claimant's housing benefit agrees with the Secretary of State that notifications may be made in accordance with that paragraph.

(3)   The Secretary of State must forward information received in accordance with paragraph (1) to the authority administering the claimant's housing benefit.]

Amendment

1.   Inserted by reg 5 of SI 2010 No 444 as from 5.4.10.

Definitions

"claimant" – see reg 2(1).
"relevant authority" – see reg 2(1).

General Note

If the condition in para (2) is met, reg 88ZA provides an alternative means of notifying a change of circusmtances where the change is a birth or a death. Such a change can be reported in person at a local authority office (or in England a county council office), if such an office has been specified for reporting these changes: para (1)(a). If the change is a death, this can also be notified to the DWP by telephone to a number specified for this purpose: para (1)(b). This provision is sometimes referred to as "Tell Us Once". Notification of a death may also be made by electroinc communication in the circumstances set out in reg 88A.

[¹Notice of changes of circumstances given electronically

[²88A.–(1)]   A person may give notice of a change of circumstances required to be notified under regulation 88 by means of an electronic communication in accordance with Schedule 11.

[² (2)   Where–
(a)   the change of circumstances required to be notified is a death; and
(b)   the authority administering the claimant's housing benefit agrees with the Secretary of State that notifications may be made in accordance with regulation 88ZA(1) (alternative means of notifying changes of circumstances),
a person may give notice of the change to the Secretary of State by means of an electronic communication in accordance with the provisions set out in Schedule 9ZC to the Social Security (Claims and Payments) Regulations 1987 (electronic communication).

(3)   The provisions set out in that Schedule shall apply for the purposes of paragraph (2) as they apply for the purposes of regulation 32ZA of the Social Security (Claims and Payments) Regulations 1987 (information given electronically).

(4)   The Secretary of State must forward information received in accordance with paragraph (2) to the authority administering the claimant's housing benefit.]

Amendments

1.   Inserted by Art 2(4) of SI 2006 No 2968 as from 20.12.06.
2.   Amended by Art 6 of SI 2011 No 2943 as from 23.1.12.

Definition

"claimant" – see reg 2(1).

General Note

If a local authority authorises it, notifications can be made by electronic communication. The authorisation requirements are found in Sch 11. By Sch 11 para 4, any claim, certificate, notice, information or evidence which is delivered by means of an electronic communication must generally be treated as having been delivered in the manner or form required by any provision of the HB Regs, on the day the conditions imposed are satisfied.

Since 21 January 2012, if the change of circumstances is a death, this may be reported by electronic communication to the DWP if the conditions in para (2) are satisfied. This provision is sometimes referred to as "Tell Us Once". See also reg 88ZA.

PART 11
Decisions on questions

General Note on Part 11
This Part deals with decisions and their notification to those affected by them. Reg 89 provides that initial decisions are generally to be taken by the "relevant authority" and provides a flexible time limit for reaching decisions. Reg 90 prescribes how and when authorities are to notify any person affected by a decision (this is not just claimants) of their decisions and requires every notification to include a statement as to the matters set out in Sch 9.

Decisions by a relevant authority
89.–(1) Unless provided otherwise by these Regulations, any matter required to be determined under these Regulations shall be determined in the first instance by the relevant authority.

(2)   The relevant authority shall make a decision on each claim within 14 days of the provisions of regulations 83 and 86 being satisfied or as soon as reasonably practicable thereafter.

[¹ (3)]

Amendment
1.   Omitted by reg 4(4)(d) of SI 2008 No 959 as from 6.10.08.

Definitions
"claim" – see reg 2(1).
"relevant authority" – see reg 2(1).

General Note
This reinforces s34 SSA 1998 by providing that the relevant authority is to have primary responsibility for taking decisions under these regulations: para (1). Para (2) sets out a flexible time limit for taking decisions.

Analysis
Paragraph (1)
Decisions must be made by the "relevant authority", defined as the authority administering HB: reg 2(1). This rule is subject to other bodies being given decision-making powers by individual regulations: the rent officer's involvement in determining the claimant's maximum rent under reg 13 is an example. See also s134(5) SSAA 1992.

Paragraph (2)
The relevant authority must make a decision on each claim. This includes where a claim is defective. The previous version of this paragraph in the HB Regs 1987 – which stated that an authority was under no duty to make a decision on a claim which had not been properly made or where the claimant had failed to provide evidence or information in connection with the claim – was ruled *ultra vires* and of no effect by a tribunal of commissioners in *R(H) 3/05*. The essence of the commissioners' decision was that there was no power given by primary legislation to local authorities to decide not to determine a claim. See *CH 532/2006* for the retrospective application of this decision.

The effect of the decision and the subsequent amendments to reg 76 HB Regs 1987 (now consolidated in reg 89 HB Regs) is that a local authority *must* decide a defective claim at the point in time when the alleged defect will not or cannot reasonably be remedied, and when such a decision is made the claimant has a right of appeal to the First-tier Tribunal against the entitlement decision then arrived at. The decisions made by local authorities in these situations are simply decisions on claims, made on the evidence available, which in most cases will be negative decisions given the likely lack of evidence.

If any support for this is needed it can be gained from what was said in Committee by the Parliamentary Under-Secretary of State (Maria Eagle) when reg 4(3) of (the then draft) SI 2004 No.3368 (which amended reg 76 HB Regs 1987) was being considered. She made it plain that the intent of the amendment was to implement in full *R(H) 3/05* and that the terms of reg 76(1) HB Regs 1987 required an authority to make a decision on every claim, defective or otherwise.

The time limit for making a decision. Where the authority is under a duty to make a decision on the claim, the general rule is that it must be done within 14 days. However, the time limit is qualified by the phrase "or as soon as reasonably practicable thereafter".

If the authority has made a decision on a claim but is delaying actual payment, see the Analysis to reg 91(3) on p568. Note also the obligation to make a payment on account in certain circumstances under reg 93 if the claim is not decided within 14 days. This does not require the claimant to make a further application for such payment: *R v Haringey LBC ex p Ayub* (1992) 25 HLR 566, QBD. See the Analysis to reg 93 on p571.

Delays in making a decision can cause severe difficulties for private tenants. A threat to apply for judicial review may have a salutary effect on an authority failing to make a decision on a claim. In *R v Liverpool CC ex p Johnson (No 1)* [1994] unreported, 23 June, QBD, it was said that it was "of the essence" that claims for HB should be determined speedily and an order of *mandamus* was granted to compel the authority to determine the claims. Of the corresponding provision for the adjudication of general benefits in s21(1) SSAA, Commissioner Goodman stated that the word "imposes a fairly strict requirement ... and every effort should be made to secure compliance with the statutory provision ...": *R(SB) 2/88* (para 14).

Many authorities have sought to justify delays by staffing and financial constraints. In *R v Secretary of State for Social Services ex p CPAG* [1990] 2 QB 540, CA, a submission that the Secretary of State was under a duty to appoint enough adjudication officers (the term then used for decision makers) to enable every claim to be determined within 14 days was rejected. It was said, however, that s/he could not simply ignore the requirement and would be obliged to take it into account when determining how many officers to appoint. That discretion had to be exercised reasonably· at 555B‑D. This suggests that a complete failure to have regard to the statutory duty under reg 89(2) will result in grounds for judicial review.

An alternative method of dealing with delays in assessment is to complain to the local government ombudsman. If s/he considers the delay constitutes maladministration s/he may order compensation to be paid. As to when judicial review proceedings will be appropriate, note the suggestion in *R v Lambeth LBC ex p Crookes* (1995) 29 HLR 28 at 35, QBD that the ombudsman should normally be the first port of call in cases of delay. However, if the allegation is one of complete failure to make a decision rather than delay, the same analysis ought not to apply.

Paragraph (3)
Until 6 October 2008, a claimant's entitlement to HB ceased under reg 77 when her/his entitlement to IS or income-based JSA ceased on account of work or an increase in hours or earnings. A new claim for HB was given priority under para (3) in specified circumstances: see pp393–94 of the 20th edition for details. Under the current versions of regs 72 to 72E, entitlement to HB continues at least until the end of the extended payment period so no new claim is needed.

Notification of decisions

90.–(1)   An authority shall notify in writing any person affected by a decision made by it under these Regulations–

(a)   in the case of a decision on a claim, forthwith or as soon as reasonably practicable thereafter;

(b)   in any other case, within 14 days of that decision or as soon as reasonably practicable thereafter,

and every notification shall include a statement as to the matters set out in Schedule 9.

(2)   A person affected to whom an authority sends or delivers a notification of decision may, by notice in writing signed by him [¹ within one month of the date of the notification of that decision (or, if the decision was notified before 1st November 2010, before 1st December 2010)], request the authority to provide a written statement setting out the reasons for its decision on any matter set out in the notice.

(3)   For the purposes of paragraph (2), where a person affected who requests a written statement is not a natural person, the notice in writing referred to in that paragraph shall be signed by a person over the age of 18 who is authorised to act on that person's behalf.

(4)   The written statement referred to in paragraph (2) shall be sent to the person requesting it within 14 days or as soon as is reasonably practical thereafter.

Amendment
1.   Amended by reg 2(6) of SI 2010 No 2449 as from 1.11.10.

Definitions
"claim" – see reg 2(1).
"person affected" – see reg 2(1).

General Note
Once an authority has made a decision, reg 90 makes it mandatory for the authority to notify any person affected by the decision and sets out the rules which it must observe when notifying such a person (see also reg 93 in respect of payments on account of rent allowance).

Every notification must include a statement as to the matters set out in Sch 9. While Sch 9 obliges an authority to provide information in its notification in specified circumstances, paras (2) and (4) enable a person affected to ask for a statement of the *reasons* for a decision on any matter set out in the notice. Note also the additonal requirements for a notice of a decision against which there is a right of appeal in reg 10 D&A Regs (see p963).

There are no specifications as to the form or content of the decision but authorities are encouraged to give full details rather than just quoting regulation numbers.

Analysis

Paragraph (1): General

"Person affected" is defined in reg 2(1) by reference to reg 3 D&A regs and is not just the claimant: see p942 for a discussion of its meaning. See also the General Note to reg 95 on p574.

By reg 82(6) a notification to a deputy, judicial factor, guardian, attorney or appointee for a claimant who is unable to act is validly given even if (as will be usual) it is not also given to the claimant. A written notification can be validly given to a claimant who cannot read English, at least where such a claimant has assistance from friends, relatives or advisers available: *R v Newham LBC ex p Kaur* (1997) 29 HLR 776 at 784, QBD.

Sub-paras (a) and (b) give the time limits for making notifications in respect of decisions on claims and decisions on other matters.

Although the time limit for deciding on a claim is given by reg 89(2), once it is made the decision must be sent out "forthwith": sub-para (a). In any other case, the decision must be sent out within 14 days: sub-para (b). However, where this is not possible, both sub-paragraphs qualify the time periods. In this case, an authority must provide the notice "as soon as reasonably practicable thereafter". In respect of delays, see the Analysis to reg 89(2).

Paragraph (1): Validity of notifications

The duty in para (1) to provide a notification and the duty to ensure that the notification contains the matters prescribed by Sch 9 is mandatory. The question of whether a notification is valid has particular significance in the context of overpayments, but may also arise in other contexts. For example, a claimant may have missed the time limit for appealing and it may be necessary to decide upon the validity of a document purporting to be a decision, since if the decision has not been validly notified to the claimant, the authority can be compelled by judicial review proceedings to issue a proper notification which then attracts rights of appeal.

It must be borne in mind that a local authority is not precluded from issuing a valid decision by a tribunal's ruling that a previous purported decision is invalid and of no effect: *CH 5217/2001* para 12.

The form of the decision. The general approach of the High Court has been to look at the substance rather than the form of a communication to the claimant. Even if a communication to a claimant is not described as a "decision", the High Court has indicated that the communication will be examined to see whether it does in fact amount to a decision: *R v Islington LBC ex p Ewing* [1992] unreported, 5 February, QBD. In that case, letters from the authority refusing increases of benefit under what was reg 61(2) HB Regs 1987 (now revoked) were held arguably to be "decisions".

The Court of Appeal held that if a defect in a notice does not cause prejudice to a person affected, its validity should be upheld: *Haringey LBC v Awaritefe* (1999) 32 HLR 517. In that case the notice failed to refer to the defendant's right to seek a statement of reasons under reg 77(4) HB regs 1987 (now reg 90(2)), referred to the right to seek a review as a right of "appeal" and did not refer to a right to seek a further hearing before a Review Board. The Court held that as there was no evidence that these failures had prevented the defendant from challenging the decision that an overpayment was recoverable, she had not suffered any prejudice and so the non-compliance with the requirements of Sch 6 HB Regs 1987 (now Sch 9) did not invalidate the determination and the overpayment was recoverable.

However, *Awaritefe* and another Court of Appeal decision, *R v Thanet DC ex p Warren Court Hotels Ltd* (2000) 33 HLR 339, CA, may now need to be treated with a little caution as they were decided when the ultimate challenge to a decision was by way of judicial review, where the substantive factual basis of the overpayment decision could not be considered, whereas on an appeal, the First-tier Tribunal can consider the factual basis of the decision and, if necessary, adjourn the hearing of the appeal so as to give the appellant sufficient opportunity to address points which may not have been addressed in the initial decision notice. Accordingly, the better starting point for considering alleged deficiencies in the decision notice may be the commissioners' decisions referred to below, in particular *R(H) 3/04*.

Awaritefe was applied in *R(H) 1/02* para 10. Since there was no prejudice to the claimant in not having detailed calculations of an overpayment, if there had been a duty to state those details (which the commissioner held there was not) then the omission would not have rendered the overpayment irrecoverable: para 10.

Commissioner Jacobs applied *Awaritefe* in *CH 4943/2001* and held that, although the constituent parts of the decision had emerged in dribs and drabs leading up to the appeal hearing, the landlord had sufficient information to be able to appeal and then argue its case before the tribunal (para 21). Accordingly the decision was not invalidated by the failure to provide all the required information at the outset. The same commissioner reached a consistent conclusion in *CH 5217/2001*, where the claimant complained that she had never been provided with a calculation of excess CTB alleged to have been paid to her. The commissioner held that the deprivation of a possible ground of appeal amounted to significant prejudice: paras 7, 9. Had the claimant been provided with a calculation before the tribunal, it would have been possible for her to address the point, with an adjournment if necessary, and the decision would not have been invalid. But it was too late to provide a calculation before the commissioner: para 13.

The terms of a decision may be proved by extraneous evidence even if the actual decision cannot be provided: *CH 4099/2002* paras 9–11; *CH 4943/2001* paras 10–11; *CH 216/2003* paras 12–16, though note para 20 where the commissioner is critical of the shortcomings of authorities' computer systems.

What impact deficiences in the decision notice may have on any subsequent appeal was considered by a tribunal of commissioners in *R(H) 3/04*. They concluded in respect of reg 77 HB Regs 1987 (now reg 90 HB Regs), at paras 74–76, as follows:

"74.   . . .the question of the effect of any procedural defect in the steps taken by the authority will only fall to be considered by an appeal tribunal on a properly constituted appeal, by a particular appellant against a recoverable overpayment determination for a particular amount made against him pursuant to section 75. Here the introduction of a full statutory right of appeal to a judicial tribunal having full jurisdiction to rehear and redetermine for itself the factual basis of the determination as to recoverability as well as its legality, coupled with the requirement to give a full statement of reasons for its decision if requested, means that many of the arguments which formerly occupied the courts on judicial review applications concerning procedural defects on the part of an authority will cease to have so much practical effect.

75.   Failures for example by a local authority to provide particulars of the facts, grounds, amount and period of the overpayment as required by regulation 77, or to notify the appellant of the existence of his rights of appeal, will for practical purposes in the normal case have ceased to cause any significant injustice to an appellant by the time a properly constituted appeal does get before the tribunal. This is because the appeal process affords him the opportunity to adduce evidence and have a full rehearing before a judicial body able to go into the factual basis of the claim that the money is legally recoverable from him, as well as any maintainable challenge to the lawfulness of the whole process. It may still be necessary, in an extreme case where the Council's attempt at operation of the procedure has been so far defective or non-existent that the tribunal is satisfied there has never been a valid basis for a determination against the appellant at all, for the whole process to be held abortive and the appeal summarily allowed on that ground; but such cases of total rejection where the authority will have to abandon its attempt at recovery or start again will now be rarer than in the days when the only judicial control was by way of review.

76.   Thus if the tribunal is satisfied on the facts before it that the case for a recoverable overpayment determination against the appellant is made out, incidental procedural defects in the local authority's determination that no longer have any continuing practical effect and have not caused any injustice still unremedied by the tribunal itself will not in our judgment prevent it confirming the authority's determination, or if necessary making its own findings and substituting its own decision as to the amount legally recoverable. Consequently we accept the arguments of the authorities and the Secretary of State summarised in paragraph 31 above, with the test of "significant prejudice" or "substantial compliance" explained in *Haringey LBC v Awaritefe* [1999] 32 HLR 517 applied as indicated above to take into account what happens in the tribunal appeal process itself. By the same token we reject the arguments for the landlords that any past failure of procedure must be fatal to recovery, or that past administrative cost and delay is a sufficient prejudice in this context to deprive a tribunal of the ability to confirm a determination or substitute its own, even where the original failures of notification, etc., have ceased to be of any practical effect."

Defective attempt at revision or supersession. The decision of the tribunal of commissioners in *R(IB) 2/04* has settled the law on defective attempts to make a decision to revise or supersede. It is suggested that these parts of the tribunal's decision will apply to the HB scheme. After detailed consideration of the statutory scheme under the SSA 1998, the tribunal concluded (para 55) that it was open to an appeal tribunal to substitute a revising decision for a superseding decision. It was also decided that defects in a revising or superseding decision would not generally render the decision invalid (para 72). It was said that:

". . . a decision should generally be regarded as having been made under Section 10, regardless of the form in which it may be expressed, if it has the effect of terminating an existing entitlement from the date of the decision (or from some later date than the effective date of the original decision). That is simply because there is no other general power which enables an existing entitlement to be terminated in that manner." (para 76)

The tribunal of commissioners' decision is not particularly helpful about the circumstances in which a revising or superseding decision would be invalid. It stated that:

"there may be some decisions made by the Secretary of State which have so little coherence or connection to legal powers that they do not amount to decisions under Section 10 at all. In the absence of specific facts, we do not consider it would be helpful here to seek to identify the characteristics which might lead to that conclusion in a particular case, but deal with the general principles below." (para 72)

Some assistance may be found in *CDLA 4977/2001* para 28, in which Commissioner Jacobs suggested cases where the officer took a decision without authority, where a similar decision had already been made by another officer, and where there had not been some step taken that was necessary to give the officer authority: para 28.

Paragraphs (2) to (4): Written statement of reasons

Para (2). The request for reasons must be made in writing, within one month of the date of the notification of the decision. Prior to 1 November 2010, no time limit was specified. Note: if the decision was notified before that date, the request for reasons must have been made before 1 December 2010.

The right to reasons extends to "any matter set out in the notice". Sch 9 deals with what should be included in the notice. Note that the requirement that the request is "signed by him" may mean that the person affected must sign it personally and it will be insufficient for it to be signed by a duly authorised agent such as a solicitor: *R v Lambeth LBC ex p Crookes* (1998) 31 HLR 59, QBD. But see the commentary to r23 of the TP(FTT) Rules on p1006 for a possible alternative argument.

Note that if a written statement is requested under reg 10 D&A Regs (where one has not already been provided): days between the date the authority receives the request and the date on which it is provided are ignored when calculating the time limit for seeking a revision (reg 4(4) D&A Regs); the time limit for appealing runs for 14 days after the later of the normal one-month time limit for appealing or after the written statement of reasons is provided (r23 TP(FTT) Rules).

Para (3) requires that where a person affected is not a "natural person" (eg, a corporate body, such as a landlord that is a company), the notice seeking a written statement of reasons must be signed by an authorised person who is over age 18.

Para (4). The authority must provide a written statement within 14 days of the request, or as soon as "reasonably practicable" after. See notes on reg 89(2) in respect of delays.

PART 12
Payments

General Note on Part 12

This Part governs when (reg 91(3)), how (regs 91(1) and 91A), how frequently (regs 91 and 92) and to whom (regs 94 to 96) HB shall be paid, and makes provision for payment on account of rent allowance if an authority is slow in calculating actual entitlement (reg 93).

Reg 97 deals with payment where the person entitled has died. Reg 98 provides for the offsetting of benefit already paid when the amount to which the claimant is entitled is revised.

Time and manner of payment

91.–(1) Subject to paragraphs (2) and (3) and regulations 92 to 98 (frequency of payment of a rent allowance, and payment on account of a rent allowance, payment provisions, offsetting) the relevant authority shall pay housing benefit to which a person is entitled under these Regulations at such time and in such manner as is appropriate, having regard to–

(a) the times at which and the frequency with which a person's liability to make payment of rent arises; and

(b) the reasonable needs and convenience of the person entitled thereto.

(2) Where a person's entitlement to housing benefit is less than £1 weekly the relevant authority may pay that benefit at 6 monthly intervals.

(3) Subject to regulations 92 to 97 (frequency of payment of and payment on account of a rent allowance, payment provisions), every authority shall make the first payment of any housing benefit awarded by it within 14 days of the receipt of the claim at the designated office or, if that is not reasonably practical, as soon as possible thereafter.

Modifications

Reg 91(3) has effect as modified by Sch 3 para 7 of the HB&CTB(CP) Regs (see p1801) for some claimants entitled to and in receipt of HB in respect of their current home on 6 October 1996 and continuously since then.

Definitions

"liable to make payments" – see regs 2(2), 8 and 9.
"payment" – see reg 2(1).
"relevant authority" – see reg 2(1).
"rent" – see Part 3.

General Note

Although the language in which this regulation is expressed is mandatory, it merely sets out the boundaries within which the authority's discretion may be exercised.

Para (1) lists certain factors which the authority must consider in deciding how and when to pay HB. Para (2) provides a discretion to pay at six monthly intervals where only a small amount of benefit is involved. Para (3) gives the time limit within which payment should be made after a successful claim.

Analysis

Para (1) is expressly subject to regs 92 to 98. The implication is that, if the authority's choice of time and method of payment is not "appropriate", it may be challenged. The factors in sub-paras (a) and (b) must be considered in deciding what is appropriate. Authorities who delay in paying rent rebates or allowances yet expect claimants to continue paying full rent in the meantime cannot be said to be taking account of a claimant's reasonable needs and convenience. In the case of private tenants, there will be no option but to pay in full despite outstanding HB entitlement. Such practices should be avoided.

Para (2) merely gives the authority discretion to pay at six monthly intervals when the claimant is entitled to less than £1 a week.

Para (3). The 14-day time limit for payment following a successful claim is qualified by the phrase "or if this is not reasonably practical, as soon as possible thereafter", and also by regs 92 to 97. For "reasonably practical" see the Analysis of reg 89(2) but note that payment must in any event be made "as soon as possible" after the 14-day limit expires, which may be an even more stringent test than that in reg 89(2). If it is impracticable for the authority to make a decision on a claim within 14 days, see reg 93 for when payments on account ("interim payments") must be made.

If a particular authority is persistently late in paying, legal action may be possible. See the Analysis of reg 89(2) in respect of dealing with delays. In an individual case, once entitlement to HB has been notified, that entitlement may be classed as a debt owed to the claimant, and if the authority delays unreasonably in paying thereafter, some success has been achieved in the past by suing in the county court for the HB owed.

It is clear from two decisions of the Court of Appeal that if an authority determines that a claimant is entitled to HB (or a landlord is entitled to direct payments) but then fails to make payment, the person entitled to receive the payment may bring an action in the county court in England and Wales or the sheriff court in Scotland. First, the Court of Appeal has stated that where a public body has decided that sums should be payable to an individual pursuant to statute but then fails to do so, it may be sued in debt: *Trustees of the Dennis Rye Pension Fund v Sheffield CC* [1998] 1 WLR 840 at 849F-M, 850A, CA. This principle was applied in the HB context in *Jones v Waveney DC* (1999) 33 HLR 3, CA. The claimant, Mr Jones, was a landlord of a number of properties with tenants in receipt of HB from the defendant council. He was paid by regular cheques for the HB due to him from his tenants. The council took the view that one of his tenants was overpaid just over £1,000. No determination to that effect was issued and the sum was deducted from one of the regular cheques. Mr Jones brought proceedings in the county court for the balance of the HB due to him. The county court judge found in Mr Jones' favour and the council appealed. Pill LJ, dismissing the appeal, set out the position as follows:

"A claimant who seeks to obtain relief must normally follow the procedures set out in the Regulations, as this Court held in *Haringey LBC v Cotter* (1996) 29 HLR 682, CA. Where, however, as in this case, the Council have not themselves followed the procedures which they are obliged to follow under the regulations, and have thereby deprived the claimant of the protection and opportunities offered him by the regulations, he is entitled to bring a County Court action. In substance, by their defence the Council were seeking to "recover", under the regulations, what they had determined to be an overpayment under the regulations.

It is conceded that if a Council purported to make a payment by cheque of housing benefit they had determined to be due, but declined to sign the cheque, the sum determined to be due would be recoverable in the County Court. That would be a mere debt collecting exercise for which an ordinary action is appropriate."

The position can therefore be summarised as follows. Proceedings in the county court or sheriff court may be brought by a claimant if benefit has been awarded to her/him but not paid. Proceedings may also be brought by a landlord where the benefit has been awarded and the council has also decided that direct payments should be made to her/him. Proceedings may be brought if a cheque has been issued but has been lost or, as Pill LJ suggested, not properly filled out with the result that it cannot be cashed by the intended recipient. However, proceedings may *never* be brought unless the council has actually awarded HB. If there is any dispute as to whether HB should have been awarded, the appeal process must be used to determine that issue.

[¹Cases in which payments to a housing authority are to take the form of a rent allowance

91A.–(1) Where the occupier of a dwelling is liable to make payments in respect of that dwelling to a housing authority as a result of the making of an order specified in paragraph (2), housing benefit in respect of those payments shall take the form of a rent allowance.

(2) The orders specified for the purposes of paragraph (1) are–

(a) a management control order made in accordance with section 74 of the Antisocial Behaviour etc. (Scotland) Act 2004;

(b) an interim management order made in accordance with section 102 of the Housing Act 2004;

(c) a final management order made in accordance with section 113 of that Act;

(d) an interim empty dwelling management order made in accordance with section 133 of that Act; and

(e) a final empty dwelling management order made in accordance with section 136 of that Act.]

[² (3) Where–

(a) the occupier of a caravan, mobile home or houseboat is liable to make payments in respect of that caravan, mobile home or houseboat and housing benefit in relation to those payments takes the form of a rent allowance; and

(b) the occupier is also liable to make payments to a housing authority in respect of the site on which that caravan or mobile home stands, or in respect of the mooring to which the houseboat is attached,

housing benefit in respect of payments to the housing authority shall take the form of a rent allowance.]

Amendments
1. Inserted by reg 2 of SI 2006 No 644 as from 3.4.06.
2. Inserted by reg 2(2) of SI 2008 No 2824 as from 6.4.09.

Definitions
"dwelling" – see reg 2(4) and s137(1) SSCBA.
"liable to make payments" – see regs 2(2), 8 and 9.
"rent allowance" – see s134(1A) and (1B) SSAA.

General Note
HB takes the form of a rent rebate where rent is paid to the authority paying the HB and otherwise takes the form of a rent allowance: s134(1A) and (1B) SSAA 1992. Various provisions within the HB Regs apply only where a rent allowance is payable – eg, three of the rent restriction schemes, for which see the General Note to Part 3.

Paras (1) and (2). Where an occupier becomes liable to pay rent to an authority as a result of any of the orders specified in para (2) being made, rather than to her/his landlord, a rent rebate would ordinarily become payable. Reg 91A was inserted into the HB Regs to ensure that rent allowances continue to be paid so that claimants in this situation do not unfairly gain (eg, because their rent is not referred to the rent officer under reg 14 or the LHA rules no longer apply) or lose out.

Para (3) similarly deems HB paid in respect of payments made to the authority to be rent allowance in the situations set out. Note that such a tenancy may be an "excluded tenancy" for the purposes of the local reference rent scheme for rent restriction under Sch 2 para 3(1)(c) (see p628). Such a tenancy may also be excluded from the local housing allowance scheme – eg, if the landlord is a registered social landlord or provider of social housing.

Frequency of payment of a rent allowance

92.–(1) Subject to the following provisions of this regulation any rent allowance other than a payment made in accordance with regulation 91(2) or (3) or 93 (time and manner of payment, payment on account of rent allowance) shall be paid at intervals of 2 or 4 weeks or one month or, with the consent of the person entitled, at intervals greater than one month.

(2) Except in a case to which paragraph (3) applies, any payment of a rent allowance shall be made, in so far as it is practicable to do so, at the end of the period in respect of which it is made.

(3) Except in a case to which regulation 96(2) applies and subject to paragraph (4), this paragraph applies where payment of a rent allowance is being made to a landlord (which for these purposes has the same meaning as in regulations 95 and 96 (payments to a landlord)), when that payment shall be made–

(a) at intervals of 4 weeks; and

(b) at the end of the period in respect of which it is made.

(4) Where paragraph (3) applies–

(a) in a case where the liability in respect of which the rent allowance is paid is monthly, the authority may make payment at intervals of 1 month;

(b) in a case where the authority is paying a rent allowance to a landlord in respect of more than one claimant, then the first such payment in respect of any claimant may be made to that landlord at such lesser interval as that authority considers is in the best interest of the efficient administration of housing benefit.

(5) Except in a case to which paragraph (3) applies, where a person's weekly entitlement to a rent allowance is more than £2 he may require payment at two weekly intervals and the relevant authority shall pay at two weekly intervals in such a case.

(6) Except in a case to which paragraph (3) applies, the relevant authority may pay a rent allowance at weekly intervals where either–

(a) it considers that unless the rent allowance is paid at weekly intervals an overpayment is likely to occur; or

(b) the person entitled is liable to pay his rent weekly and it considers that it is in his interest that his allowance be paid weekly.

(7) Subject to paragraphs (2), (3) and (5), the relevant authority may pay a rent allowance to a student once a term.

Modifications

Reg 92 has effect as modified by Sch 3 para 7 HB&CTB(CP) Regs (see p1801) for some claimants entitled to and in receipt of HB in respect of their current home on 6 October 1996 and continuously since then.

Definitions

"claimant" – see reg 2(1).
"payment" – see reg 2(1).
"overpayment" – see reg 99.
"rent" – see Part 3.
"rent allowance" – see s134(1A) and (1B) SSAA.
"student" – see Part 7.
"weekly entitlement" – see regs 80 and 81 and Part 8.

General Note

This applies solely to rent allowances – eg, HB paid to private and housing association tenants. It effectively limits the authority's choice in deciding how frequently to pay this form of HB. The regulation only applies where a claim is made or treated as made on or after 7 October 1996 and the claimant is not exempt from these payment rules. See Sch 3 para 7 HB&CTB(CP) Regs (p1801) for the saving provision.

Where the authority has a choice about how frequently to pay HB, it must take into account the factors in reg 91(1).

Analysis

Paragraphs (1) and (2): Payments to claimants

Para (1). Under para (1), except where the claimant is entitled to less than £1 a week and the authority has used its powers in reg 91(2) or where an initial payment is made following a claim under reg 91(3), or where payment on account is made under reg 93, the authority may choose between the following periods of payment frequency: every two weeks, four weeks or monthly. This para is specifically qualified by paras (2) to (7). Payment may only be made at longer intervals if the claimant agrees. If para (6) is satisfied, the authority can choose to pay weekly instead. Where the "person entitled" is unable to consent, see reg 82(3) and (6).

Para (2). The authority should make any payment of a rent allowance at the end of the period to which it relates ("in so far as it is practicable") – ie, in arrears.

Paragraphs (3) and (4): Payments to landlords

Para (3). Where HB takes the form of a rent allowance and payment is made to a landlord (excluding those cases where the authority is only making a first payment of benefit to the landlord) payment must be made at intervals of four weeks under sub-para (a); and at the end of the period in respect of which it is made under sub-para (b) – ie, in arrears.

Para (4) sets out two exceptions to the rule set out in para (3). First, where there is a calendar monthly rent liability, the authority has the discretion to make payment at calendar monthly intervals: sub-para (a). Second, where the authority is paying a rent allowance to a landlord in respect of more than one claimant, the first payment for any claimant may be made to that landlord at such shorter interval as the authority considers is in the best interest of the efficient administration of HB: sub-para (b). The latter might be appropriate where the authority has adopted a fixed cycle for a landlord with a number of properties – eg, agreeing to pay all monies due in respect of the tenants of that particular landlord on, say, every fourth Monday. The first direct payment in respect of any individual claimant could then be made in respect of a period of less than four weeks to bring it into cycle. Thereafter, payments should be made four-weekly in arrears on the pay-day agreed with the landlord.

Paragraphs (5) to (7): Special cases

Para (5). If this para applies, the authority must pay a rent allowance at two-weekly intervals if requested to do so. For "weekly entitlement", see regs 80 and 81 and Part 8.

Para (6). The authority has a discretion to pay a rent allowance weekly if either of the sub-paras apply. Sub-para (a) might apply where an authority is uncertain about a claimant's circumstances. Payment under sub-para (b) would be in a claimant's interest, for example, if rent is due weekly, to help her/him avoid getting into arrears.

Para (7) applies to payments to a "student" (defined in reg 2(1) by reference to reg 53(1)) and is expressly subject to paras (2), (3) and (5) above: eg, if this para is used, payment should be made on the date ascertained under para (2), and the claimant's right to request fortnightly payment under para (5) is protected. Even if para (5) does not apply, the authority is not obliged to use its powers under para (7) and may choose to pay a student at one of the intervals listed in para (1), or, impliedly, weekly under para (6).

Payment on account of a rent allowance

93.–(1)   Where it is impracticable for the relevant authority to make a decision on a claim for a rent allowance within 14 days of the claim for it having been made and that impracticability does not arise out of the failure of the claimant, without good cause, to furnish such information, certificates, documents or evidence as the authority reasonably requires and has requested or which has been requested by the Secretary of State, the authority shall make a payment on account of any entitlement to a rent allowance of such amount as it considers reasonable having regard to–

(a)   such information which may at the time be available to it concerning the claimant's circumstances; and

(b)   any relevant determination made by a rent officer in exercise of the Housing Act functions.

(2)   The notice of award of any payment on account of a rent allowance made under paragraph (1) shall contain a notice to the effect that if on the subsequent decision of the claim the person is not entitled to a rent allowance, or is entitled to an amount of rent allowance less than the amount of the payment on account, the whole of the amount paid on account or the excess of that amount over the entitlement to an allowance, as the case may be, will be recoverable from the person to whom the payment on account was made.

(3)   Where on the basis of the subsequent decision the amount of rent allowance payable differs from the amount paid on account under paragraph (1), future payments of rent allowance shall be increased or reduced to take account of any underpayment or, as the case may be, overpayment.

Definitions

"claim" – see reg 2(1).
"claimant" – see reg 2(1).
"Housing Act functions" – see reg 2(1).
"overpayment" – see Part 13.
"payment" – see reg 2(1).
"relevant authority" – see reg 2(1).
"rent allowance" – see s134(1A) and (1B) SSAA.

General Note

This regulation only applies to claimants entitled to rent allowance – eg, HB paid to private and housing association tenants. Under it, the authority is obliged to make payments on account of HB to the claimant (interim payments) where it has been unable to make a formal decision on the claim under reg 89 and where the reason for the delay is not the claimant's failure to provide information or evidence, or, if it is, the claimant can show good cause for failing to do so.

The provision aims to ensure that private tenants do not lose accommodation due to delays in benefit administration.

Subject only to the claimant not having failed to produce information or evidence without good cause when s/he has been required to do so, there is no exception of "reasonable practicability" in relation to this provision (see notes on regs 89 and 91). Payments are mandatory.

Under paras (2) and (3), if a claimant is paid more or less than s/he is entitled to under this provision, future payments of rent allowance are altered accordingly.

Analysis

Para (1). Where it is impracticable for an authority to make a decision on a claim before the fourteenth day after a claim is made (ie, it has not been able to assess the claim within the required period), the authority has a duty to make payment on account, so long as it is not impracticable because of the claimant's failure to provide information etc without good cause. However, the amount of the payment is, to a certain extent, at the authority's discretion. In *R v Haringey LBC ex p Ayub* (1990) 25 HLR 566, QBD it was held that there is no need for a separate claim for a payment on account.

Reg 95(1)(b) can require an authority to pay HB to a landlord where the tenant is eight weeks or more in arrears of rent. Schiemann J went on to find that if the tenant is eight weeks or more in arrears of rent and the conditions in reg 91 HB regs 1987 (now reg 93) are satisfied, then the authority is under a duty to make payment on account to the *claimant's landlord.* But that duty only arises if the landlord or someone else informs the authority that there are eight weeks or more arrears – ie, it is not up to the authority to find this out for itself. He stated that if the tenant disputes that there are eight weeks arrears, the landlord can ask the council to make a determination on the issue. If it goes against the landlord the council's duty to pay the landlord direct would not arise unless and until the dispute was resolved in her/his favour.

The judge confirmed that there was no duty to pay rent allowance under reg 88 HB Regs 1987 (now reg 91), as opposed to making a payment on account, until a decision is made (but the claimant might be entitled to an order of *mandamus* requiring the council to make a decision if prejudiced by the amount or frequency of payments on account).

For the date on which a claim is treated as made, see reg 83. For the authority's powers to request information, see reg 86. Examples of "good cause" might be illness or difficulty in contacting someone who can supply the relevant information.

The amount of a payment depends on what the authority considers "reasonable" having regard to:

(1)   Such information which may at the time be available to it concerning the claimant's circumstances.

(2)   Any relevant determination made by a rent officer in exercise of the Housing Act functions – eg, the determination the authority must apply for under reg 14 (see that reg and the relevant Rent Officers (Housing Benefit Functions) Order).

Para (2) supplements reg 90 and Sch 9 by providing that the notice issued is to warn the claimant that if any excess payment to which s/he is not entitled is made under para (1), it can be recovered from the person to whom it was paid.

Para (3) supplements para (2) by providing that where a claimant is underpaid or overpaid under para (1), the overpayment shall be recovered or the underpayment made good by increasing or decreasing future payments of HB. There is no time limit specified in the regulation during which this must be done so that if a claimant is not actually entitled to HB when the para (1) payment is made, it may be recovered if s/he becomes entitled in the future.

If, on the "subsequent decision" referred to, it does transpire that the claimant is not entitled at all, however, the mere fact that s/he has been notified under para (2) that the payment made is a payment on account which may or may not be accurate does not of itself entitle the authority to recover the overpayment under reg 100: see *R v Liverpool CC ex p Griffiths* (1990) 22 HLR 312, QBD, and the note on reg 100.

Payment to be made to a person entitled

94.–(1)   Subject to regulations 95 to 97 (payment to landlords, payment on death) and the following provisions of this regulation, payment of any rent allowance to which a person is entitled shall be made to that person.

(2)   Where a person other than a person who is entitled to a rent allowance made the claim and that first person is a person referred to in regulation 82(2), (3) or (5) (persons appointed to act for a person unable to act), payment may be made to that person.

(3)   A person entitled to a rent allowance, although able to act on his own behalf, may request in writing that the appropriate authority make payments to a person, who if a natural person must be aged 18 or more, nominated by him, and the authority may make payments to that person.

Definitions

"claim" – see reg 2(1).
"payment" – see reg 2(1).
"rent allowance" – see s134(1A) and (1B) SSAA.

General Note

A rent allowance must be paid to a person entitled to it under para (1) or, if s/he is unable to act, may be paid to the person who claimed on her/his behalf under para (2). This is qualified by regs 95 and 96 (which set out when payments can or must be made to a landlord) and reg 97 (which deals with payment where the person entitled has died). A further exception is provided by para (3): an authority may agree to pay the rent allowance to someone else, aged 18 or over, nominated by the person entitled.

Analysis

Para (1). Under para (1) payment is to be made to the person entitled (ie, the claimant) unless payment is to be made to the landlord or the person entitled has died. Once a payment of HB has in fact been lawfully made to a claimant under this provision, then a second payment may not be made to a landlord covering the same period, even though had the local authority been made aware of the true state of affairs at the time of the payment to the claimant (more than eight weeks' arrears of rent) it would have made the payment instead to the landlord under reg 95(1)(b): *R(H) 2/08* para 39, relying on reg 98. However, in most cases this problem should be avoided if local authorities properly notify both parties (ie, landlord and claimant) of the decision changing who is to be paid: see *CH 2986/2005.*

In *Islington LB v SJ* [2008] UKUT 31 (AAC), an award of HB was made with payment to be made to the claimant. The local authority later decided to backdate the award and pay the arrears of HB direct to the claimant's landlord. Nevertheless, the arrears of HB were paid to the claimant who did not use them to satisfy his liability for arrears of rent. When the landlord asked for payment of the arrears of HB, the local authority said that it could not pay these to the landlord because they had already been paid to the claimant and that it could not lawfully make payment of the same benefit twice. The First-tier Tribunal, allowing the landlord's appeal, decided that the arrears of HB were to be paid to the landlord on the basis that, although the principle stated in *R(H) 2/08* was accepted, namely that no second payment of HB can be made to a landlord once the claimant has been lawfully paid for the period in question, the local authority here did not lawfully pay arrears of HB to the claimant. Judge Turnbull upheld the tribunal's decision. The reasoning behind *R(H) 2/08* was that if HB has been paid in accordance with a decision (eg, to the claimant) and then that decision is revised so as to make the HB payable to another (eg, the landlord), the amount which has been paid to the claimant cannot be paid to the landlord, because that amount is required by reg 98 to be offset against the arrears which would otherwise be payable to the landlord under the revised decision. However, reg 98 can only apply where the first payment is made under and in accordance with a decision, that decision is then revised and payment is made in accordance with the revised decision. Here the decision was to pay HB to the landlord but this was incorrectly paid to the claimant. Further, the decision to pay to the landlord was never revised. The problem was simply that owing to an administrative error, payment had not been made in accordance with its terms. Note that the judge suggests (at para 16) that the payment made to the claimant was an "overpayment" within the definition in reg 99 and that it may be recoverable under reg 100. It is respectfully suggested that this is incorrect; "overpayment" means an amount paid to which there was no entitlement. The claimant here *was* entitled to the HB paid, it was simply paid to the wrong person.

Para (2). Payment to the appointee is discretionary so payment could still be made to the person entitled although this would be at the authority's risk as that person may not have mental capacity to give a valid receipt.

Para (3). For this to apply, the person entitled must be able to act for her/himself at the time the request is made. The reference to a "natural person" is to make a distinction between human beings and legal personalities such as companies. The authority has discretion whether or not to pay the nominee but the general principles of administrative law which govern the exercise of such discretions means that the authority must have a valid reason if it decides to depart from the claimant's wishes.

GM A6.181 refers to this procedure as nominating an "agent" and also misleadingly says that this power is to be used where the claimant is unable to collect money for her/himself – eg, when s/he is away from home. There is nothing in the regulation to restrict it in this way.

Circumstances in which payment is to be made to a landlord

95.–(1)   Subject to paragraph (2) and paragraph 8(4) of Schedule A1 (treatment of claims for housing benefit by refugees), a payment of rent allowance shall be made to a landlord (and in this regulation the "landlord" includes a person to whom rent is payable by the person entitled to that allowance)–

(a)   where under Regulations made under the Administration Act an amount of income support [², a jobseeker's allowance or an employment and support allowance] payable to the claimant or his partner is being paid direct to the landlord; or

(b)   where sub-paragraph (a) does not apply and the person is in arrears of an amount equivalent to 8 weeks or more of the amount he is liable to pay his landlord as rent, except where it is in the overriding interest of the claimant not to make direct payments to the landlord.

(2)   Any payment of rent allowance made to a landlord pursuant to this regulation or to regulation 96 (circumstances in which payment may be made to a landlord) shall be to discharge, in whole or in part, the liability of the claimant to pay rent to that landlord in respect of the dwelling concerned, except in so far as–

(a)   the claimant had no entitlement to the whole or part of that rent allowance so paid to his landlord; and

(b)   the overpayment of rent allowance resulting was recovered in whole or in part from that landlord.

[¹ (2A)   In a case where–

(a)   a relevant authority has determined a maximum rent (LHA) in accordance with regulation 13D; and

(b)   the rent allowance exceeds the amount which the claimant is liable to pay his landlord by way of rent,

any payment of rent allowance made to a landlord pursuant to this regulation or to regulation 96 may include all or part of any amount by which the rent allowance exceeds the amount which the claimant is liable to pay his landlord as rent but shall not include any amount by which the rent allowance exceeds the amount which the claimant is liable to pay his landlord as rent and arrears of rent.]

(3)   Where the relevant authority is not satisfied that the landlord is a fit and proper person to be the recipient of a payment of rent allowance no such payment shall be made direct to him under paragraph (1).

Amendments

1.   Amended by reg 17 of SI 2007 No 2868 as from 7.4.08 (or if reg 1(5) of that SI applies, on the day on or after 7.4.08 when the first of the events specified in reg 1(6) applies, or from 6.4.09 if none have before that date).

2.   Amended by reg 21 of SI 2008 No 1082 as from 27.10.08.

Definitions

"Administration Act" – see reg 2(1).

"claimant" – see reg 2(1).

"dwelling" – see reg 2(4) and s137(1) SSCBA.

"an employment and support allowance" – see reg 2(1).

"income support" – see reg 2(1).

"a jobseeker's allowance" – see reg 2(1).

"partner" – see reg 2(1).

"relevant authority" – see reg 2(1).

"rent" – see Part 3.

"rent allowance" – see s134(1A) and (1B) SSAA.

General Note

Reg 95 is an exception to reg 94(1) which requires payment to be made to the "person entitled".

Under this regulation payment *must* be made to the landlord (as defined by the regulation itself) rather than the person entitled. By contrast, reg 96 provides instances in which payment *may* be made to the landlord. See reg 97(5) if the person entitled to HB has died.

Once an authority has made a decision, reg 90(1) requires it to notify any "person affected" by the decision. A landlord is a "person affected" where a decision is made under reg 95 whether or not to pay HB direct to her/ him: *CH 180/2006.*

Decisions made under reg 95 may be appealed to the First-tier Tribunal by either the claimant or the landlord, and it will be an error of law not to invite the claimant or landlord to the hearing of the other party's appeal as both are person's affected by such a decision: *CH 4108 2005.*

Like regs 92 to 94, this regulation only applies to payment of rent allowances.

Following a decision under reg 89(2), there is no duty to pay the landlord direct under reg 95 unless the DWP is paying part of the claimant's or her/his partner's IS, JSA or ESA direct to the landlord for rent arrears (para (1)(a)) or until the authority is told that eight or more weeks' arrears exist (para (1)(b)). Even then the duty does not arise until any dispute as to the amount of arrears has been resolved if necessary.

Major changes were made in the rules on the payment of HB, introduced with effect from 3 November 1997, in the context of a number of other regulations implementing the SSA(F)A. These were described in guidance as measures to combat fraud. The regulations were, however, made under provisions of SSAA, principally ss5 and 6, which existed before the Fraud Act was passed.

The principal provisions are:

(1)   Authorities have discretion not to pay rent allowance to a landlord or agent who is not a "fit and proper person" to receive it: regs 95(3) and 96(3).

(2)   Landlords to whom direct payments are made are notified of their duty to report changes in the tenant's circumstances: Sch 9 Part 4.

Analysis

Paragraph (1): The duty to pay to the landlord

There are two circumstances in which the authority is obliged to make direct payments to the landlord (this includes a person to whom rent is payable), provided there has been no finding that the landlord is not a "fit and proper" person under para (3).

(1)   Where direct payments of IS, JSA or ESA are being made to the claimant's landlord by the DWP: sub-para (a). There is a power in Sch 9 Social Security (Claims and Payments) Regulations 1987 to make deductions from a claimant's IS, JSA or ESA to pay small amounts towards arrears of rent. Note that sub-para (a) does not apply if direct payments of UC are being made to the claimant's landlord – ie, where the claimant is getting HB for "specified accommodation" or "temporary accommodation". However, sub-para (b) could apply.

(2)   Where sub-para (a) does not apply (eg, if no IS, JSA or ESA is paid direct to the landlord), payment must be made to the landlord where the person entitled to HB is in arrears equivalent to eight weeks' rent or more: sub-para (b). In *AT v Broxstowe BC & JH (HB)* [2015] UKUT 388 (AAC), the claimant's tenancy began before the date on which a previous tenancy on the property expired. Judge Mark dismissed the claimant's query as to whether he was liable for rent (and therefore in arrears not having paid that rent) for the period before the previous tenancy ended. As long as a tenant remains in possession undisturbed by any adverse claim, then s/he cannot dispute the landlord's title to grant the tenancy: *Industrial Properties (Barton Hill) Ltd v Associated Electrical Industries Ltd* [1977] QB 580. Rent payable in advance can be immediate arrears for the purposes of reg 95. In the case of *ST v Sunderland City Council (CH)* [2019] UKUT 33 (AAC), the tenants were required to pay two months' rent in advance. They were unable to pay this by the time they took possession, meaning that they were already more than eight weeks in arrears. The Upper Tribunal decided that HB should be paid to the landlord.

Even where a tenant is in arrears equivalent to eight weeks' rent or more, the authority can still decide *not* to make payment to the landlord where this would not be in the claimant's "overriding interest". In *ST v Sunderland City Council*, the housing authority argued that, once the arrears dropped below the level of eight weeks' rent, direct payment should cease. Judge Gray rejected this argument, determining that the regulation envisages direct payment continuing until the arrears are cleared. Otherwise, direct payment would stop every time a nominal payment reduced arrears below eight weeks' rent, leading to a proliferation of decision-making where circumstances had not necessarily altered.

Note that what reg 95(1)(b) is concerned with is the tenant being eight weeks or more in arrears of liability for rent; it is not concerned with any set-off from that figure: *CH 4108 2005*. However, the view is that decision – that the decision of a local authority as to whether it is in the overriding interest of the claimant not to make direct payments to a landlord may only be interfered with on appeal on judicial review error of law grounds (ie, that it is not for the First-tier Tribunal to decide for itself whether payment direct is not in the overriding interest of the claimant) – has, rightly it is suggested, not been followed in *R(H) 1/08*. That later decision makes it plain that on an appeal it is for the First-tier Tribunal to exercise its normal decision making powers (per *R(IB) 2/04* para 25) on the evidence available and form its own judgment as to whether direct payment is not in the overriding interest of the claimant. Judge Gray stated in *ST v Sunderland City Council* that this decision involves an exercise of judgement on issues of fact, but it is not a discretionary decision. Generic reasons why it may be in a tenant's interests to receive rent direct (eg, a desire to pursue a policy of financial inclusion) cannot resolve the question. Individual circumstances must be considered in each case. *R(H) 1/08* also decides that it is permissible to suspend payment of HB (under reg 11(2)(a)(ii) of the D&A Regs) while enquiries are made as to which person the benefit should be paid to, as a change in payee requires the award to be revised or superseded.

Paragraph (2): Effect of recovery of an overpayment on rent liability

This purports to reverse the effect of *R v Haringey LBC ex p Ayub* (1992) 25 HLR 566, QBD by providing that where an overpayment is recovered from the landlord, rent arrears of the amount of the overpayment are created. It therefore purports to affect the substantive obligations and rights, under the general law of landlord and tenant, of the claimant and landlord *inter se*. It is strongly arguable that, in doing so, the paragraph is *ultra vires*. The regulation was made under s5(1)(p) SSAA which empowers the Secretary of State to make regulations which provide "for the circumstances and manner in which payments of such a benefit may be made to another person on behalf of the beneficiary for any purpose, which may be to discharge in whole or in part, an obligation of the beneficiary or any other person."

The enabling power therefore only provides for "the circumstances and manner" of payments to persons other than the claimant. Discharging an obligation is only a *purpose* for which payments can be made. Section 5(1)(p) does not give any power to prescribe *whether* an obligation is in fact discharged by the payment or, *a fortiori*, that an obligation which would under the general law be regarded as discharged should in the future revive upon the recovery of an overpayment from the landlord. See p597 for the changes brought in by the SSA(F)A.

Paragraph (2A): Where a maximum rent (LHA) has been determined

This limits the amount that can be paid to a landlord where the "local housing allowance" rules apply and a maximum rent (LHA) has been determined in accordance with reg 13D. If HB exceeds the claimant's rent liability, the maximum that can be paid to her/his landlord is the amount which the claimant is liable to pay the landlord as rent and arrears of rent. The remainder must be paid to the claimant. This is now only of historic relevance as from 1 April 2011 HB cannot exceed a claimant's rent liability, even under the transitional rules in reg 12M.

Paragraph (3): Landlord not a "fit and proper person"

Para (3) prevents authorities from making direct payments to landlords under this regulation where they are not satisfied that the landlord is "a fit and proper person to be the recipient of a payment of rent allowance". This applies even if direct payments would otherwise be compulsory – eg, where the rent is more than eight weeks in arrears. A similar para is also in reg 96 where its effect is to allow authorities not to make direct payments to landlords who are not "fit and proper" even when the criteria for a discretionary direct payment would otherwise be met. Guidance as to the meaning of the words "fit and proper person" in the context of HB is given in GM A6.196-207 which identifies four basic principles.

(1)   The test only applies where the landlord's honesty in connection with HB is in doubt. It should not be applied in every case where a request for direct payments has been made.

(2)   The test must be applied on an individual basis. So, for example, an authority could not decide that all landlords of a particular class (eg, those who let houses in multiple occupation) are *ipso facto* not fit and proper persons.

(3)   Each case has to be decided on its own individual facts. The circumstances in which a landlord is not a fit and proper person cannot be listed exhaustively in advance and the examples in the guidance are illustrative only.

(4)   Before a landlord can be said not to be a fit and proper person s/he must have engaged in undesirable activity in relation to HB. It is suggested that an authority cannot take non-HB-related behaviour into account (even, it would seem, where the behaviour is housing-related – eg, failure to comply with a Housing Act notice).

The guidance's insistence that the undesirable activity should be HB-related is probably over-cautious. It is suggested that any serious dishonesty or criminality should suffice to make a landlord not "fit and proper" at least where such criminality or dishonesty is social security related. If a landlord has, for example, been convicted of a multiple-claim IS fraud, it is difficult to see an authority's decision that s/he is not a fit and proper person being overturned merely because benefits other than HB were involved.

On the other hand, some convictions may not suffice even when they are HB-related. The offences introduced by the Fraud Act have the effect, in some cases, of criminalising what would in other contexts amount to no more than a negligent omission. It is difficult to see how a single failure, by oversight, to report a change in a tenant's circumstances, which is now *prima facie* criminal under s112(1A) SSAA 1992 calls a landlord's honesty into sufficient question to make her/him not "fit and proper" (although the position would be different if there were habitual failures).

It is suggested that a failure or refusal to comply with a notice requiring information under s126A of the Administration Act would also be a factor which would legitimately be taken into account in reaching a decision. Such a failure or refusal is a criminal offence: see reg 121 and s113 SSAA 1992.

It is unclear whether an agreement to pay an administrative penalty under s115A SSAA 1992 is a matter which can be taken into account in deciding whether or not a landlord is a fit and proper person. Such an agreement is not the same as accepting a caution for a criminal offence as it does not amount to an admission of guilt, and the local authority only needs grounds for commencing criminal proceedings before serving a penalty notice rather than proof beyond a reasonable doubt. In some cases, a landlord might agree to pay a penalty on the strictly commercial basis that to do so would be cheaper than to pay for legal representation against a criminal prosecution. On the other hand, the regulations clearly do not regard an agreement to pay a penalty as morally neutral. For example, reg 107 prevents a landlord who has agreed to pay an administrative penalty in respect of an overpayment from suing the tenant for any money which the authority has recovered under s75(5)(b) SSAA 1992. It is therefore suggested that an agreement to pay a penalty is a factor which the authority can take into account but that it does not carry as much weight as a criminal conviction. One administrative penalty would probably not usually (depending on the precise circumstances) be sufficient on its own to prevent a landlord from being "fit and proper", but payment of a series of administrative penalties would almost certainly justify such a decision against a landlord.

Some behaviour which falls short of criminality may also justify a decision that a landlord is not a fit and proper person. The Guidance suggests that a habitual failure to repay an overpayment which the authority has decided is recoverable from her/him would be sufficient. However, before a decision is based on this ground, the authority should ensure that the notifications relating to the overpayments comply fully with the requirements of Sch 9 as otherwise the landlord would be within her/his rights not to have paid: see the decision of the Court of Appeal in *Warwick DC v Freeman* (1994) 27 HLR 616, CA.

It seems likely that there is an overlap between the "fit and proper test" and other anti-abuse provisions, in particular the contrived tenancy rules in reg 9(1)(l) HB Regs. The Court of Appeal has held in *R v Stratford-upon-Avon DC HBRB ex p White* (1998) 31 HLR 126 that the words "take advantage" in reg 7 HB Regs 1987 (now reg 9 HB Regs) bear their "common meaning of avail oneself unfairly or improperly". In the circumstances, it would seem to be open to an authority to decide that a landlord who habitually created or was a party to contrived tenancies was not a fit and proper person. For example, although it would not today be possible to repeat the scheme devised by the landlords in *R v Manchester CC ex p Baragrove Properties Ltd* (1991) 23 HLR 337, QBD, a landlord who habitually targeted a particular class of claimant for no reason other than to exploit the favourable treatment afforded to that class by the HB scheme might be acting in a way which would justify a conclusion that s/he was not a fit and proper person.

Circumstances in which a landlord has otherwise acted to obtain HB to which it is or was not entitled may mean the landlord is not a "fit and proper person". One possible example of this would be the use of limited companies to avoid repayment of overpayments. Where one company had been closed down owing money to the authority and another set up with similar directors and/or shareholders, it might be possible for the authority to conclude that the second company was not a fit and proper person to receive direct payments even though it was the first company, which is a separate person from a legal point of view, which was responsible for the impropriety.

Whether or not a landlord is a fit and proper person to receive payments of rent allowance is a decision which can be made at the beginning of the claim and also during the period of an award if there are grounds for revision or supersession – eg, if there has been a change of circumstances or if the original decision was based on a mistake of fact or law.

Paradoxically, it does not follow automatically from a finding that a landlord is not a fit and proper person to receive payments of rent allowance, that rent allowance will not be paid to her/him. There is, of course, no question of payment to the landlord being mandatory in such circumstances but there is still a discretion to pay the landlord direct under reg 96. An authority might decide that the claimant's overriding interests require that direct payments be made to the landlord, but that the landlord is not "fit and proper" to receive them. In this unusual situation the authority would need to balance the risks and could decide to make direct payments. An authority could instead find alternative methods of payment. If direct payments are made, regular and frequent checks should be made on the claim.

Circumstances in which payment may be made to a landlord

96.–(1)   Subject to paragraph 8(4) of Schedule A1 (treatment of claims for housing benefit by refugees), where regulation 95 (circumstances in which payment is to be made to a landlord) does not apply but subject to [¹ paragraphs (3) and (3A)] of this regulation, a payment of a rent allowance may nevertheless be made to a person's landlord where–

(a)   the person has requested or consented to such payment;

(b)   payment to the landlord is in the interest of the claimant and his family;

(c)   the person has ceased to reside in the dwelling in respect of which the allowance was payable and there are outstanding payments of rent but any payment under this sub-paragraph shall be limited to an amount equal to the amount of rent outstanding.

(2)   Without prejudice to the power in paragraph (1), in any case where in the opinion of the authority–

(a)   the claimant has not already discharged his liability to pay his landlord for the period in respect of which any payment is to be made; and

(b)   it would be in the interests of the efficient administration of housing benefit,

a first payment of a rent allowance following the making of a decision on a claim or a supersession under paragraph 4 of Schedule 7 to the Child Support, Pensions and Social Security Act 2000 may be made, in whole or in part, [³] to that landlord.

(3)   In a case where the relevant authority is not satisfied that the landlord is a fit and proper person to be the recipient of a claimant's rent allowance, the authority may either–

(a)   not make direct payments to the landlord in accordance with paragraph (1) [¹, (3A) or (3B)]; or

(b)   make such payments to the landlord where the authority is satisfied that it is nonetheless in the best interests of the claimant and his family that the payments be made.

[² (3A)   In a case where a relevant authority has determined a maximum rent in accordance with regulation 13D–

(a)   sub-paragraphs (a) and (b) of paragraph (1) shall not apply; and

(b)   payment of a rent allowance to a person's landlord may be made where–

(i)   the relevant authority considers that the claimant is likely to have difficulty in relation to the management of his financial affairs;

(ii)   the relevant authority considers that it is improbable that the claimant will pay his rent; or

(iii)   a direct payment has previously been made by the relevant authority to the landlord in accordance with regulation 95 in respect of the current award of housing benefit.[⁴ or

(iv)   the relevant authority considers that it will assist the claimant in securing or retaining a tenancy.]

(3B)   Where the relevant authority suspects that the grounds in paragraph (3A)(b)(i) or (ii) apply and is considering whether to make payments on one of those grounds, it may make a payment of a rent allowance to the person's landlord for a period not exceeding 8 weeks.]

[⁴ (4)   In this regulation–

"landlord" has the same meaning as in regulation 95 and paragraph (2) of that regulation shall have effect for the purposes of this regulation; and

"tenancy" includes–

(a)   in Scotland, any other right of occupancy; and

(b)   in England and Wales, a licence to occupy premises.]

Modifications

Paras (1) and (3) were amended and paras (3A) and (3B) inserted by reg 17 Housing Benefit (Local Housing Allowance and Information Sharing) Amendment Regulations 2007 SI No.2868 as from 7 April 2008, save that for a person to whom reg 1(5) of those regulations applied (see p1812), the amendments came into force on the day on or after 7 April 2008 when the first of the events specified in reg 1(6) applied to her/him, or on 6 April 2009 if none had before that date.

Amendments

1.   Amended by reg 17(2) of SI 2007 No 2868 as from 7.4.08 (or if reg 1(5) of that SI applies, on the day on or after 7.4.08 when the first of the events specified in reg 1(6) applies, or from 6.4.09 if none have before that date).

2.   Inserted by reg 17(2) of SI 2007 No 2868 as from 7.4.08 (or if reg 1(5) of that SI applies, on the day on or after 7.4.08 when the first of the events specified in reg 1(6) applies, or from 6.4.09 if none have before that date).

3.   Amended by reg 2(7) of SI 2010 No 2449 as from 1.11.10.

4.   Amended by reg 3(8) of SI 2010 No 2835 as from 1.4.11.

Definitions

"claimant" – see reg 2(1).

"dwelling" – see reg 2(4) and s137(1) SSCBA.

"family" – see reg 2(1) and s137(1) SSCBA.

"landlord" – see para (4) and reg 95.

"payment" – see reg 2(1).

"relevant authority" – see reg 2(1).

"rent" – see Part 3.

"rent allowance" – see s134(1A) and (1B) SSAA.

General Note

Para (1) sets out three situations in which the authority has the discretion to pay rent allowance direct to the landlord, even though not obliged to do so under reg 95, or until it is obliged to do so under that regulation – eg, when eight weeks rent arrears have accrued.

Para (2) enables the authority to make the first payment of a rent allowance (in whole or in part) to the "landlord".

Para (3) sets out the options available to an authority which would otherwise be prepared to make discretionary direct payments but which is not satisfied that a landlord is a "fit and proper person to be the recipient of a claimant's rent allowance".

Paras (3A) and (3B) set out the situations in which the authority may not, and additional situations in which it may, pay rent allowance direct to the landlord, where the "local housing allowance" rules apply and a maximum rent (LHA) has been determined in accordance with reg 13D.

Para (4) defines "landlord" by reference to reg 95 and purports to apply the rule in reg 95(2) to cases where discretionary direct payments have been made and then recovered as overpayments. It also defines "tenancy".

See also the General Note to reg 95. Note that once an authority has made a decision, reg 90(1) requires it to notify any "person affected" by the decision. A landlord is a "person affected" where a decision is made under reg 96 whether or not to pay HB direct to her/him: *CH 180/2006*. See reg 97(5) if the person entitled to HB has died.

Analysis

Para (1) gives a discretion to the authority to make direct payments to the landlord (this includes a person to whom rent is payable) in three instances.

(1)   Where the claimant requests or consents to such payments: sub-para (a). Even if such a request is made, payment to the landlord is at the authority's discretion.

(2)   Where the authority considers it to be in the interest of the claimant and her/his family (as defined in s137(1) SSCBA, if any: sub-para (b). It is not necessary for the claimant to have a "family" living with her/

him for payment to be to a landlord under this provision; *DLT v Eastleigh BC (HB)* [2014] UKUT 242 (AAC). Payment can be made under this sub-para without the consent of the claimant.

(3)   Sub-para (c) covers the situation where the claimant has moved, leaving arrears of rent. The authority can only pay HB due in respect of the *former* home to the landlord and then only to the extent necessary to clear outstanding rent. Payment can be made under this sub-para without the consent of the claimant.

Note that sub-paras (a) and (b) do *not* apply where a maximum rent (LHA) has been determined in accordance with reg 13D – ie, where the "local housing allowance" rules apply: para (3A)(a).

In *E v Dacorum BC & M* [2017] UKUT 93 (AAC), Judge Mitchell considered the circumstances in which sub-para (c) applies. In that case, a tenant had been evicted for non-payment of rent. The payment of subsequent arrears of HB to the landlord to clear outstanding rent arrears was disputed by the tenant. Judge Mitchell emphasised that sub-para (c) does not give an unrestricted power to authorities to pay arrears of HB to a landlord in such circumstances. The authority must be satisfied that there are outstanding payments of rent, and payment to a landlord is limited to the amount of those arrears. The amount may be reduced by factors such as whether a deposit was retained, depending on the terms of the lease in regard to the purpose of the deposit. In the absence of specific contractual terms, other costs, such as those incurred by the landlord to secure eviction, cannot be added to the outstanding rent. Outstanding rent may be reduced by any costs incurred by the tenant that s/he would be likely to succeed in having taken into account had s/he faced an action for recovery of rent arrears.

Para (2) enables the authority to make the first payment of a rent allowance following the determination of a claim or a supersession of an award, in whole or in part, to the landlord. This rule only applies, however, if, in the authority's opinion, both the following conditions are met.

(1)   The claimant has not already discharged her/his liability to pay the landlord for the period in respect of which any payment is to be made.

(2)   It would be in the interests of the "efficient administration" of HB.

The DWP described this power as tackling "an existing abuse when tenants abscond with the benefit without paying their rent", (*Social Security Departmental Report: The Government's Expenditure Plans, 1996–97 to 1998–99*, HMSO, March 1996, p40).

The authority's "opinion" should be based on information held at the time the claim (or supersession) is dealt with. The authority is not required to make special enquiries, for example, to establish from the landlord or specifically of the claimant whether the rental liability for the period in question has been discharged.

GM A6.163-166 advises authorities that they have a duty to safeguard the public purse by minimising the opportunities for fraud or abuse and that this duty would meet the criterion of the "efficient administration" of the benefit scheme. It suggests that an authority may wish to consider the amount of benefit payable and, if there is evidence that the claimant has paid some or all of the rent for the period in question, the rent outstanding. If either the benefit due or the rent debt is small it may be inappropriate to invoke this power. Equally, it would be inappropriate to pay to the landlord more than the outstanding eligible rent. The guidance suggests that the authority should consider paying the first payment to the landlord where, for example: the amount due is £100 or more, or the authority has reason to think that the claimant might default (perhaps because a previous landlord has reported non-payment), or there is a rent debt but the case is not appropriate for longer-term direct payment arrangements. The authority does not need to invoke this power where the claimant's circumstances warrant a permanent direct payment from the outset.

Para (3) applies the "fit and proper person" test to reg 96. See Analysis to reg 95(3) on p575.

Paras (3A) and (3B) are only relevant where the "local housing allowance" rules apply and a maximum rent (LHA) has been determined in accordance with reg 13D. In this case, the authority has the discretion to pay HB direct to a landlord under para (1)(c) (ie, where the claimant has moved leaving arrears of rent) but not (1)(a) or (b): para (3A)(a). In addition, it can do so in four further situations.

(1)   Where the authority considers that the claimant is likely to have difficulty managing her/his financial affairs: para (3A)(b)(i).

(2)   Where the authority considers that it is improbable that the claimant will pay her/his rent: para (3A)(b)(ii).

(3)   Where a direct payment has previously been made under reg 95 in respect of the current HB award: para (3A)(b)(iii).

(4)   Where the authority considers it will assist the claimant in securing or retaining a tenancy: para (3A)(b)(iv). This situation was added from 1 April 2011. It is understood that the government's intention was that it should only apply if the rent is at a level that the claimant can afford, but the provision makes no reference to this.

If the authority suspects that paras (3A)(b)(i) or (ii) apply, it can pay rent allowance direct to the claimant's landlord while it considers whether to make payments on one of those grounds (for a maximum of eight weeks): para (3B).

In *Wirral MBC v AL (HB)* [2010] UKUT 254 (AAC), the questions arose whether a decision of the local authority not to exercise its discretion under para (3A) was appealable by the landlord under Sch 7 para 6 CSPSSA 2000 and, if it was, what the scope of the appeal was – ie, whether the appeal was a complete re-exercise by the First-tier Tribunal of an administrative discretion given to the local authority, or something narrower. Judge Howell refrained from giving an actual decision on the questions, accepting that there was a right of appeal and that the nature of the appeal was a complete re-hearing. However, he said (at para 19):

"At some point the principles involved may need to be reconsidered, perhaps at a higher level, because it does seem odd and unusual if the discretionary and administrative matters housing benefit authorities are charged with considering for themselves under regulation 96, which must include non-justiciable questions, are to be reconsidered at large by a tribunal consisting of a lawyer without any of the responsibilities and constraints of such an authority, who is then supposed to substitute his or her own subjective view on the merits retrospectively: a far cry from the more normal judicial control of such matters by way of review to ensure administrative authorities invested with discretionary powers stay within them and act properly and legally."

Note that reg 95(2A) also applies to payments of rent allowance made to landlords under reg 96 – ie, where a maximum rent (LHA) has been determined in accordance with reg 13D and HB exceeds the claimant's rent liability. This is now only of historic relevance. See discussion on p575.

Para (4). If, as is argued above, reg 95(2) is *ultra vires*, it will be equally ineffective in the context of reg 96.

Payment on death of the person entitled

97.–(1)   Subject to paragraphs (3) and (5) where the person entitled to an allowance has died the relevant authority shall make payment either to his personal representative or, where there is none, his next of kin if aged 16 or over.

(2)   For the purposes of paragraph (1) "next of kin" means in England and Wales the persons who would take beneficially on an intestacy and in Scotland the persons entitled to the moveable estate on intestacy.

(3)   A payment under paragraph (1) or (5) shall not be made unless the landlord, the personal representative or the next of kin, as the case may be, makes written application for the payment of any sum of benefit to which the deceased was entitled, and such written application is sent to or delivered to the relevant authority at its designated office within 12 months of the deceased's death or such longer period as the authority may allow in any particular case.

(4)   The authority may dispense with strict proof of title of any person claiming under paragraph (3) and the receipt of such a person shall be a good discharge to the authority for any sum so paid.

(5)   Subject to paragraph (3), where the relevant authority determines, before the death of the person first mentioned in paragraph (1), that a rent allowance was payable to his landlord in accordance with regulation 95 or 96, that authority shall pay to that landlord so much of that allowance as does not exceed the amount of rent outstanding at the date of the person's death.

Definition

"designated office" – see reg 2(1).
"relevant authority" – see reg 2(1).
"rent allowance" – see s134(1A) and (1B) SSAA.

General Note

This deals with the situation where a claimant has died before receiving HB to which s/he was entitled. Para (1) sets out to whom such benefit should be paid, para (3) how someone may apply for payment and paras (2) and (4) define those people and enable such a payee to give the authority a good receipt for payments made under this regulation. Para (5) deals with situations where HB was payable direct to a landlord before the claimant's death.

Analysis

Para (1) just talks about "an allowance" (presumably "rent allowance"). Subject to paras (3) and (5), payment to the personal representative (or next of kin) is mandatory.

Para (2) defines "next of kin". In England and Wales, the "persons who would take beneficially on an intestacy" are set out in the Administration of Estates Act 1925, the Intestates Act 1952, the Family Provision Act 1966 and the Family Law Reform Act 1969. In Scotland, the Succession (Scotland) Act 1964 provides the rules. A "personal representative" is someone appointed by a will (eg, an executor) to carry out the provisions of that will. Under para (4) the authority is not required to demand strict proof of whether the payee is a personal representative or next-of-kin.

Para (3). Before payment can be made to a landlord, personal representative or next-of-kin, s/he must apply in writing to the authority at its designated office, within 12 months of the deceased's death, or a longer period if the authority agrees.

Para (4). See also para (2) and the "General Note".

Para (5) makes clear that where the authority has decided to make HB payments direct to the landlord under regs 95 or 96 before the time of the claimant's death, any outstanding benefit, limited to the amount of rent outstanding at the time of the claimant's death, must be paid to the landlord if the landlord has made a written application for it: para (3).

Offsetting

98.–(1)   Where a person has been paid a sum of housing benefit under a decision which is subsequently revised or [¹ superseded or further revised or superseded], any sum paid in respect of a period covered by a subsequent decision shall be offset against arrears of entitlement under the subsequent decision except to the extent that the sum exceeds the arrears and shall be treated as properly paid on account of them.

(2)   Where an amount has been deducted under regulation 104(1) (sums to be deducted in calculating recoverable overpayments) an equivalent sum shall be offset against any arrears of entitlement under the subsequent decision except to the extent that the sum exceeds the arrears and shall be treated as properly paid on account of them.

(3)   No amount may be offset under paragraph (1) which has been determined to be an overpayment within the meaning of regulation 99 (meaning of overpayment).

Amendment

1.   Amended by reg 5(2)(a) of SI 2012 No 824 as from 17.4.12.

General Note

This is an extremely tortuous piece of legislation designed, it seems, to cover the situation where a claimant has been underpaid for a period.

Analysis

Paras (1) and (2). If someone has been paid a sum of HB under a decision which is later revised or superseded (or further revised or superseded), and it is decided to pay her/him more for a particular period, what s/he will get under para (1) is the difference between what s/he has already been paid and what s/he was actually entitled to. "Revised" includes a decision being revised by a tribunal altering it on appeal: *Wirral MBC v AL (HB)* [2010] UKUT 254 (AAC).

Note that payment of HB in respect of the same period of entitlement cannot be made to both the claimant and the landlord because the amount which has been paid to the claimant is required by reg 98 to be offset against the arrears which would otherwise be payable to the landlord: *R(H) 1/08*; *R(H) 2/08*. However, this only applies where the first payment is made under and in accordance with a decision, that decision is then revised and payment is made in accordance with the revised decision. See also the commentary on *Islington LB v SJ* [2008] UKUT 31 (AAC) on p572.

Where, in calculating the amount of a recoverable overpayment, a sum of HB has been deducted under reg 104(1) which should have been determined to be payable, the same sum is offset against the arrears of entitlement under the revised decision under para (2).

The phrase "except to the extent … arrears" means that this regulation cannot be used with the result that the claimant owes the authority money. HB can only be recovered from a claimant under reg 100. For example, if the claimant has been paid £100 for a period and on revision s/he should have got £95, s/he will not owe the authority anything. £95 of what s/he has been paid is offset against revised entitlement, but the extra £5 will be ignored unless reg 100 makes it recoverable.

Para (3). But under para (3), in computing what s/he has already been paid, anything which has been determined to be an overpayment (see reg 99) paid during the same period is to be left out of account. Under reg 102, however, such a recoverable overpayment may be deducted from arrears of HB paid so that in the end the claimant is no better off.

PART 13
Overpayments

General Note on 13

This part of the regulations deals with the calculation and recovery of overpayments of HB. Note: if reg 10 UC(TP) Regs 2014 (p1872) applies to the overpayment, Part 13 of these regulations cannot apply to the overpayment. Incentives to detect fraud, recover overpayments and avoid official errors are given by the percentages of subsidy which are payable in respect of different categories of overpayment.

Disputes about alleged overpayments (most often, whether an overpayment is recoverable) make up a large part, if not the majority, of HB appeals. A systematic approach is required by advisers, authorities and the First-tier Tribunal. The following stepped approach is suggested.

(1)   Has there been an overpayment? The definition is set out in reg 99.

(2)   What is the amount of the overpayment? This involves a complex process of calculation which is set out in the commentary to reg 103. Regs 103 and 104 set out deductions to be made from the gross amount of HB paid.

(3)   Is the overpayment recoverable? The test is different from that applicable to DWP benefits. The criteria for recoverability are set out in reg 100.

(4)   If there is a recoverable overpayment, from whom is it recoverable? The persons from whom it is recoverable are set out in reg 101.

[Note: disputes as to decisions given by a local authority on each of the above four questions may be appealed to a First-tier Tribunal. However, disputes arising under points (5) and (6) below cannot be appealed.]

(5)   Should the overpayment be recovered, and if so from whom? SSAA s75(2) and (3) give the local authority the power to recover.

(6)   How should the overpayment be recovered? SSAA s75(4)–(5) and regs 101(4), 102 and 105 provide for various means of recovery. A full guide is in the Analysis to reg 102.

Meaning of overpayment

99.   In this Part, "overpayment" means any amount which has been paid by way of housing benefit and to which there was no entitlement under these Regulations (whether on the initial decision [¹ or as subsequently revised or superseded or further revised or superseded]) and includes any amount paid on account under regulation 93 (payment on account of a rent allowance) which is in excess of the entitlement to housing benefit as subsequently decided.

Amendment

1.   Amended by reg 2 of SI 2005 No 2904 as amended by Sch 2 para 29 of SI 2006 No 217 as from 10.4.06.

General Note

This defines an "overpayment" for the purposes of Part 13. It must be borne in mind that just because an amount comes within the above definition it does not follow that it can be recovered. That question is dealt with by reg 100.

Analysis

"any amount which has been paid by way of housing benefit". The provisions apply equally to rent allowance and rent rebate, though there are differences in the rules as to recoverability.

"and to which there was no entitlement ... whether on the initial decision or as subsequently revised or superseded or further revised or superseded". It is fundamental to the social security benefits system, and HB is no exception to this, that a decision awarding benefit remains valid unless and until changed, and those changes can only be effected under the decision-making rules specifically provided for this purpose. Accordingly, an overpayment of HB can only arise if the decision awarding HB is first revised or superseded by the local authority. Hence, the compendious nature of the phrase above.

Following the decision of the tribunal of commissioners in *R(IB) 2/04*, where the commissioners concluded (para 55) that it was open to an appeal tribunal to substitute a revising decision for a superseding decision and also decided that defects in a revising or superseding decision would not generally render the decision invalid (para 72), and *CH 4354/2003*, a defective attempt by the local authority, to revise or supersede the awarding decision can and should be corrected by a tribunal on any appeal against the resultant overpayment decision. Accordingly, the absence of a proper revision or supersession decision by the local authority is not to be equated with there being no revision or supersession decision at all, and so will not render void the overpayment decision. The only exceptions to this are where the revision or supersession decision of the local authority is so incoherent or lacking any legal basis that it does not amount to a decision at all: *R(IB) 2/04* para 72; or the evidence is not available to the tribunal to enable it to identify the details of the past awarding decision(s), without which the tribunal may not be able to identify any appropriate revision or supersession ground: *CIS 3228/2003*. But if there is no local authority revision or supersession decision at all, or no evidence of such a decision having been made (though this may not be too high a hurdle for the authority to pass – see para 76 of *R(IB) 2/04*), there is nothing for the tribunal to correct and there will be no overpayment.

In overpayment cases, it is also important to determine any question of whether the claimant was actually entitled to benefit according to the legislation as it stood at the time: *R(H) 3/03* para 8. Account must also be taken of any transitional protection conferred by subsequent amending legislation.

It must be borne in mind that when determining whether a claimant has been overpaid, it is the legislation in force at the date of the payment that determines her/his eligibility and not the version effective at the time that the authority comes to consider whether s/he has been overpaid. The only exception to this is where amending legislation is expressed to have retrospective effect.

CP v City of Brighton and Hove (HB) [2013] UKUT 543 (AAC) makes the valuable, but much missed, point that there cannot be two or more separate overpayments covering the same period. If a local authority has made a decision that a claimant has been overpaid HB for a period due to, for example, failure to disclose an increase in her/his earnings, and the authority then identifies that the claimant's partner's earnings had also increased during the same period, the correct legal approach is not for it to make a separate overpayment decision arising from the partner's earnings but for it to revise the first overpayment decision so as to take account of this second basis for the overpayment over the period.

"any amount paid on account ... in excess of the entitlement ... as subsequently decided". The third broad category is excessive estimated payments. So if the local authority estimates the claimant's entitlement at £100 a week and it is subsequently found to be £80, the £20 a week excess constitutes an overpayment.

Recoverable overpayments

100.–(1)   Any overpayment, except one to which paragraph (2) applies, shall be recoverable.

(2)   Subject to paragraph (4) this paragraph applies to an overpayment [¹ which arose in consequence of] an official error where the claimant or a person acting on his behalf or any other person to whom the payment is made could not, at the time of receipt of the payment or of any notice relating to that payment, reasonably have been expected to realise that it was an overpayment.

(3)   In paragraph (2), "overpayment which arose [¹ in consequence of an official error]" means an overpayment caused by a mistake made whether in the form of an act or omission by–

(a)   the relevant authority;

(b)   an officer or person acting for that authority;

(c)   an officer of–

   (i)   the Department for Work and Pensions; or

   (ii)   Revenue and Customs,

   acting as such; or

(d)   a person providing services to the Department for Work and Pensions or to the Commissioners for Her Majesty's Revenue and Customs,

where the claimant, a person acting on his behalf or any other person to whom the payment is made, did not cause or materially contribute to that mistake, act or omission.

(4)   Where in consequence of an official error, a person has been awarded rent rebate to which he was not entitled or which exceeded the benefit to which he was entitled, upon the award being revised [¹ or superseded] any overpayment of benefit, which remains credited to him by the relevant authority in respect of a period after the date on which the revision [¹ or supersession] took place, shall be recoverable.

Amendment

1.   Amended by reg 4 of SI 2005 No 2904 as amended by Sch 2 para 29 of SI 2006 No 217 as from 10.4.06.

Definitions

"claimant" – see reg 2(1).
"overpayment" – see reg 99.

General Note

The rules governing the recoverability of HB overpayments are arguably more stringent than the rules set out in s71 Administration Act for recovery of benefits paid by the DWP. Disputes about HB overpayments make up a significant number, if not the majority, of appeals to First-tier Tribunals against HB decisions.

For HB overpayments the starting point is that all overpayments are recoverable. The only exception to this general rule is if:

(1)   the overpayment was caused by an official error which no relevant person caused or contributed to; *and*

(2)   no relevant person could reasonably have been expected to realise that there was an overpayment either at the time it was made or when they were notified of the payment.

Analysis

Paragraph (1)

This states the general rule that, unless the criteria in para (2) apply, the overpayment is recoverable. Note that s68 Welfare Reform and Pensions Act 1999 renders certain overpayments irrecoverable even where the criteria specified in para (2) do not apply.

It is for the local authority to show that the overpayment is recoverable including, arguably, that it was not caused by official error: see *CH 4065/2001* para 1.3. However, it is for the claimant (or other relevant person) to prove that s/he could not reasonably have been expected to realise that s/he was being overpaid: *CH 3439/2004*.

Paragraphs (2) and (3)

These paragraphs together set out the criteria which have to be shown for the overpayment to be irrecoverable. Note that overpayments falling within para (4) will always be recoverable, regardless of whether the criteria are fulfilled.

Whether the criteria are met must be considered during the whole period of the overpayment not merely at the beginning. A recoverable overpayment may therefore need to be split between differing causes of the overpayment: *SN v Hounslow LB* [2010] UKUT 57 (AAC); [2010] AACR 27 at paras 16–18.

First criterion: Official error which no relevant person caused or contributed to

The overpayment must be caused by an error or mistake made by the authority or a relevant person acting as such. Unless the person from whom recovery is sought can show such an error, the overpayment will always be recoverable regardless of the merits of the case: see, for example, *CH 2201/2002* para 9, where it was confirmed that an overpayment was recoverable where a claimant moved out without informing either the landlord or the local authority. (The only official error which might arise on these type of facts is if the local authority did not act timeously after it had been made aware that the claimant had moved out.) Equally, even if there is an error or mistake by a relevant official, it will not amount to an "official error" if the claimant or another relevant person caused or contributed to it, and so such an overpayment will also always be recoverable. But the caselaw has eschewed an overly refined approach to causation in this context. The result is that the key question to be asked in a case where an overpayment has arisen after a mistake by an official is not whether the claimant (or other relevant person) caused or contributed to that mistake, but rather whether s/he caused or contributed to the overpayment. The starting point in this caselaw is the case of *Sier.*

In *R (Sier) v Cambridge CC HBRB* [2001] EWHC Admin 160, QBD; [2001] EWCA Civ 1523, CA (dealing with reg 99 HB Regs 1987 – now reg 100), the claimant lived in Cambridge and claimed HB for a long period while he was recovering from a long illness. On his recovery, he decided to seek accommodation in London and live there during the week to assist his search for work. He gave evidence to the Review Board that he had sought advice from two London authorities where he was proposing to live as to whether he would be entitled to claim HB on two homes and that he received (erroneous) advice that he would be able to do so. The Board accepted that evidence. As a result of the advice he received, he did not inform Cambridge City Council when he took a tenancy in London and it became his normal home. The council did not ask any questions directed to the location of the claimant's normal home on its claim form. The claimant also moved his IS claim to a London Employment Service office, but no form NHB 8 was sent to Cambridge City Council in accordance with the normal procedure. An overpayment resulted. On the facts, Mr Sier had not contributed to the "mistake" (the failure of the DSS – as it then was – to send the form NHB 8 to Cambridge City Council), and had that omission not occurred then Cambridge City Council would in all likelihood have stopped his HB. (Equally, on the facts it seemed that if there was an official error then the overpayment would not have been recoverable because of the erroneous advice which Mr Sier had been given upon which – per sub-para (3) – he could not reasonaby have been expected to realise that he was not entitled to get HB on his Cambridge and London homes and so could not have realised he was being overpaid.) But it was also true on the facts that Mr Sier had failed in his own duty to inform Cambdrige City Council that he had moved to London. On a literal reading of what is now reg 100(2) and (3), Mr Sier argued that the overpayment of HB on his Cambridge home was irrecoverable because he had not caused or contributed to the failure of the DSS to send the form NH8 to Cambridge City Council.

The High Court rejected this argument. It accepted that the failure to send the NHB 8 form was a relevant mistake, but it held that the mistake did not cause the overpayment. Accordingly, it was not an "official error" overpayment as defined in what is now reg 100(3) and was therefore recoverable from Mr Sier under what is now reg 100(1). The High Court accepted that an overpayment could have more than one cause but, as a matter of common sense, the cause of the overpayment was the claimant's failure to notify Cambridge City Council. The common sense approach was required by *Environmental Agency v Empress Cars (Abertillery) Ltd* [1999] 2 AC 22, HL. The Court of Appeal upheld the judge's approach.

"In the present case, one has to have regard to the general legislative purpose, which seems to me to be clear. Parliament has laid down in the Regulations that a person is to be relieved of the obligation to repay an overpayment when that has been occasioned by an administrative mistake and not by any fault on the part of the recipient. That seems to me to be the basic thrust of the Regulation and one should approach the meaning of the word 'cause' and its application to the facts on that basis." (Latham LJ, para 25)

"Such a result … seems to me so entirely surprising and unsatisfactory that it requires one to approach regulation 99(3) rather differently. In my judgment a single composite question falls to be asked under regulation 99(3). One must ask: 'was the overpayment the result of a wholly uninduced official error, or was it rather the result of the claimant's own failings, here his failure in breach of duty to report a change of circumstance?' The answer to that question on the facts of this case is, of course, self-evident … It would be remarkable indeed if the claimant was liable to make repayment in a case where he merely contributed to what might be a fundamental error on the part of the department, and yet wholly escapes such liability even when himself primarily responsible for the overpayment." (Simon Brown LJ, paras 30–31)

Sier has been followed and applied in a number of subsequent commissioner's decisions. In *R(H) 1/04*, the claimant had informed the local authority that he was in receipt of occupational pensions, but had failed to disclose that information on his claim forms for IS. IS was duly awarded and CTB was awarded as a result of the award of IS. The commissioner decided that even had there been an official error (as to which see the discussion below), the substantial cause of the overpayment was the claimant's failure to notify the DWP of the award of IS: para 26. No attempt was made by the claimant to argue that there was an error on the part of the DWP, and the commissioner held that the fact that he had not challenged the decision disallowing IS was some evidence that there was no such error: para 24.

A similar conclusion was reached in *R(H) 2/04* para 14. The true cause was the claimant's failure to disclose her new working families' tax credit (WFTC) award rather than the council's failure to await the level of the award before adjudicating her renewal claim for HB.

The paraphrasing of one paragraph in *CH 2794/2004* in previous editions of this book has been criticised (rightly) in *SN v Hounslow LB* [2010] UKUT 57 (AAC); [2010] AACR 27 (at para 24) as oversimplifying, and thus potentially misleading, the approach on official error and causation following *Sier*. As the Upper Tribunal puts it in *SN v LB Hounslow*, "the test is the simple common sense one explained in *Sier* of what was the substantial (ie, not just a contributory) cause of the overpayment". What the previous commentary on *CH 2794/2004* was seeking to make clear was that even if a claimant did not cause or contribute to the official error that will not avail her/him if her/his act or omission was still the (substantial) cause of the overpayment occurring. Similar views to *SN v LB Hounslow* had previously been expressed in *CH 3083/2005* (para 38) and *CH 3761/2005*. In the latter case, at least for part of the period, the commissioner found that the substantial cause of the overpayment was the Jobcentre's mistakes in (i) telling the claimant that it would notify the local authority of his JSA stopping and he therefore did not need to do so, and (ii) its failure to then notify the local authority of that information. In *R(H) 10/08*, the deputy commissioner said that a tribunal must consider and determine whether the overpayment was caused by a wholly uninduced official error or was rather the result of the claimant's own failings – ie, her/his failure to inform the "designated office" of a change in circumstances under reg 88 (or reg 69 HB(SPC) Regs).

"a mistake made, whether in the form of an act or omission". No fault is required for the act or omission to amount to a "mistake". All that is necessary is that, with the benefit of hindsight, something is done which should not have been done or something is not done which should have been. An example of this point, although it did not arise for decision in the case, is *R v Liverpool CC ex p Griffiths* (1990) 22 HLR 312, QBD, in which the authority's HB department was unable to implement changes to the HB scheme which had been brought in at very short notice. Estimated awards were made on review and reviewed again when the authority was able to work out claimants' exact entitlement. Some of the estimated awards were too high and the authority sought to recover the difference. Even though the authority could not have avoided making the error, it still amounted to a relevant mistake.

Delay can amount to an official error: *CH 858/2006* (para 20) and *HC v Hull City Council (HB)* [2013] UKUT 330 (AAC) (para 26). The latter decision emphasises that how long the period of delay needs to be before amounting to an official error will depend on the facts of each individual case. A relevant consideration may be official guidance the authority may be expected to act under in terms of processing and acting on information, though in *HC v Hull City Council (HB)* it was pointed out that the guidance did not act to provide a complete code for official error in delay cases. The decision in *Sandwell MBC v NK (HB)* [2016] UKUT 140 (AAC) discusses a potential difference between *CH 858/2006* and *HC v Hull City Council (HB)* and suggests the latter decision might have the "effect that claimants living in the areas of less efficient, or more overstretched, local authorities are treated less favourably than claimants in other areas". Judge Rowland continued:

"Moreover, it seems odd that recoverability should be determined by factors such as the impact of staff sickness that are not only beyond a claimant's control but also upon which it is difficult for the First-tier Tribunal to make an independent judgement without disproportionate cost to both the local authority and the tribunal."

However, this point did not need to be decided by Judge Rowland as the claimant in that case could not in any event show that she could not reasonably have been expected to realise that she was being overpaid.

In *Sier*, the claim form failed to ask any questions designed to elicit information about where the claimant's normal home was. It was argued that as this was a basic issue under the HB scheme, it was a relevant mistake not to ask the relevant question. Richards J rejected the submission, holding that the very complexity of reg 5 HB Regs 1987 (now reg 7) and the rarity of claimants with two homes meant that it could not be said to be unreasonable not to ask any questions directed towards that point. That argument was not pursued before the Court of Appeal. However, note *CH 3679/2002*, where an overpayment occurred when a claimant continued to claim HB in respect of a liability to his ex-wife. The local authority's claim forms were not changed after January 1999 to seek information relevant to the then new form of reg 7 HB Regs 1987 (now reg 9). The commissioner held, accepting a concession by the local authority, that there was an "official error" in not changing the forms: paras 2, 7. The value of this holding was doubted in *CH 4428/2006* because it was based on a concession and was not decided by the commissioner, but in an inquisitorial jurisdiction it is a little difficult to see why this should wholly undermine the decision. Indeed, the commissioner in *CH 4428/2006* seemingly accepted (despite his stated rejection of *CH 3679/2002*) that "a failure to amend forms to accord with amending legislation may, in certain circumstances, amount to an official error but will not do so in every case" (para 33). However, for reasons which, with respect, are not particularly clear or convincing, he did not accept in the case before him that the failure to amend the claim forms promptly after the new form of reg 7(1)(d) HB Regs 1987 had come into effect amounted to an official error. The commissioner focused narowly on whether it had been an error on the part of the local authority not to have changed its forms so as to seek information relevant to the reg 7(1)(d) issues (ie, whether the landlord is a parent of the claimant's child). However, with respect, it is surely arguable that the focus should have been on whether it had been an error not to have made any changes to its claims forms to capture all the information required after the wholesale changes to reg 7(1) HB Regs 1987, rather than just looking at whether the form should have been changed to elicit the reg 7(1)(d) information. It is suggested that, in the context of the complete reshaping of reg 7(1) HB Regs 1987 with effect from 25 January 1999, it is a false exercise to seek to ask whether the local authority erred in not changing its forms to obtain just one of the pieces of information required for the new reg 7(1): not rewriting all claim forms may be quite justified for some period of time if the change required is quite a minor one or one which impacts on only a small minority of claimants; but not rewriting claim forms for a period of time may well not be justified where the changes are extensive.

The Upper Tribunal has since reviewed the law on whether errors or omissions in official claim forms can amount to an 'official error' in *MB v Christchurch BC* (HB) [2014] UKUT 201 (AAC); [2014] AACR 39. Judge Wikeley extracted from *CH 4428/2006*, and endorsed, the general legal principle that "a failure to amend the forms to accord with amending legislation may, in certain circumstances, amount to official error but will not do so in every case". He went on to emphasise that whether a failure to ask a particular question on a standard claim form amounts to an 'official error' is very much a question of fact and degree, and the number of cases likely to be affected by the 'missing question' would be a very important consideration. It was also relevant, in Judge Wikeley's view, to take account of wider considerations when applying a test of reasonableness in this context. First, reg 86(1) HB Regs requires claimants to furnish evidence "as may reasonably be required by the relevant authority in order to determine that person's entitlement". The local authority, therefore, has to ask the right questions on the claim for benefit, and claimants "cannot be assumed to have either an encyclopaedic knowledge of the rules of entitlement to housing benefit or a paranormal ability to read the minds of council staff". Second, the decision of the House of Lords in *Kerr v Department for Social Development* [2004] UKHL 23; reported as *R 1/04 (SF)*, showed that decision making in the field of benefits was a co-operative process that depended on the department or local authority asking the right questions and claimants answering them as best they can. In Judge Wikeley's view, any decision on whether a failure to ask a specific question on a claim form amounts to an official error must bear all of these considerations in mind.

On the facts, in *MB* there was an official error. It was a case where the parent's shared care of their son. At the time in question, the child spent more time each week with his father than with his mother (who was the claimant), and so the mother ought not to have received any HB for her son but had done so and so had been overpaid. This was because on the local authority's claim form she answered "yes" to a question "Are there any children in your household?" The official error lay in the claim form not going on to ask whether the child normally lived with the mother and/or whether he also lived at any other address, nor had any guidance notes sought to explain this important aspect of the statutory test. The DWP's model claim form HCTB1 contained such additional questions. In that context the local authority's claim form was, in Judge Wikeley's view, not "fit for purpose in terms of the fundamental principles of eligibility for housing benefit".

Where a tribunal on an appeal finds a decision on benefits or tax credits entitlement to have been wrongly made by the DWP or HMRC, this, in effect, is binding authority that the benefits or tax credits decision was made in "error" or was a "mistake" for the purposes of reg 100(3), and it is not open to the HB authority to go behind the tribunal's decision to try and identify the exact basis on which it set aside the DWP's or HMRC's decision: *CH 943/2003*. The commissioner did, however, point out that the claimant might have contributed to the error if s/he failed to put evidence before the HMRC decision maker which led the tribunal to allow her/his appeal, or might be taken to be aware that s/he was being overpaid if the decision maker's decision was clearly wrong: para 39. *CH 943/2003* was followed and applied, and a contrary decision in *CH 38/2008* expressly disapproved of, in *GH v Scarborough BC* (HB) [2015] UKUT 197 (AAC).

If an officer of the DWP undertakes to forward information to the local authority and fails to do so, s/he will be guilty of an official error even if the undertaking is given outside normal procedures: *CH 939/2004* para 11. Equally, a failure to operate the verification framework properly or at all is capable of amounting to a "mistake or omission": *CH 2794/2004* para 22; but this does not override the claimant's responsibility to answer the questions on claim forms accurately and completely. Further, a failure by a local authority to inform a claimant that changes of circumstances were required to be reported in writing (at a time before the regulations allowed for reporting of changes other than by writing – see p560) has been held to constitute an official error: *West Somerset DC v JMA (HB)* [2010] UKUT 190 (AAC). In that case, the claimant had visited the designated office and told it verbally about a change in her circumstances, namely that her IS was about stop, but the local authority took no action on this information and an overpayment arose. On appeal to the Upper Tribunal, the local authority argued that the cause of the overpayment was the failure of the claimant to report the change in writing, as was the required method of notifying changes in circumstances at that time. Rejecting this argument, the Upper Tribunal held that the failure of the local authority to inform the claimant of her duty to report the change in writing and the failure of the officer to whom disclosure was made to pass the information on were both official errors, and as these were substantial causes of the overpayment it was not recoverable from the claimant.

When will there be an official error in a local authority failing to identify and query an apparent discrepancy in information before it? It is suggested that the problem will have to be clear and obvious before an official error will be made. In *R(H) 1/04* (see above), it was contended that the local authority should have queried the award of IS and it was an official error for it not to do so. Commissioner Turnbull rejected that contention (para 22), since the claimant might have been getting mortgage interest payments which would have entitled him to IS and "the information before the Council did not demonstrate that the income support award had been wrongly made".

This analysis will not, of course, be capable of application to a case involving an HB overpayment because the claimant ought not to be getting mortgage interest as part of an IS or JSA claim as well as HB. It is suggested that a failure to follow up a glaring discrepancy may involve an official error. See, however, the discussion on causation above.

To similar effect is the decision in *R(H) 2/04*, where a claimant was awarded HB on a renewal claim when her award of WFTC was about to expire. It was argued that the local authority should have realised that the new award of WFTC might be different and that benefit should not have been paid until the new award was made. Commissioner Howell rejected that submission, holding that it was the claimant's fault that the local authority had not been made aware of the new award: para 12. There had to be a "clear and obvious" error of fact as to the facts disclosed: para 13. A further illustration of the difficulty in demonstrating official error in cases of this nature is *CH 69/2003*, where the local authority was held to be under no duty to analyse the payments going into a bank account from statements before it (para 9). Nor can it be argued that there was an official error in not suspending payment on the basis of a suspicion: *CSHB 718/2002* para 42. *CH 687/2006* holds that nothing said by the House of Lords in *Kerr* [2004] 1 WLR 1374 cuts down on the "clear and obvious discrepancy" analysis in *R(H) 1/04* and *R(H) 2/04*.

Before 1 April 1997, this phrase was worded "a mistake made or something done or omitted to be done". It is arguable that this wording did not require a "mistake" at all and rendered it unnecessary for this criterion to be met, because there was always "something done" which caused the overpayment, namely the act of authorising the payment. There was nothing in the amending regulations (SI 1997 No.65) to suggest that the phrase applied to payments made before April 1997 and so this argument can still be used in relation to periods prior to that date.

Who must make the mistake? The overpayment must have been caused by a mistake made by the authority or a relevant official. The relevant official could be any of the following.

(1) The relevant authority. "Relevant authority" is defined in reg 2 as an authority administering HB.

(2) An officer or person acting for the "relevant authority". This includes employees of bodies carrying out HB functions which have been privatised or put out to tender under an enforcement determination issued by the Secretary of State (see s139G SSAA on p86). The officer need not be an officer working in the HB section: *CH 2321/2002* para 37. For example, if a claimant is visited by an officer from the social services department, who then promises to notify the HB department of a change in the claimant's circumstances and fails to do so, that will be a relevant mistake. In *R(H) 10/08*, the deputy commissioner agreed. He could see no justification for construing the term "relevant authority" in a way which confines it to one department within the authority. It would have been easy to limit the term expressly. He noted the contrast between the absence of a restrictive definition of the term "relevant authority" with the deliberately restrictive way in which the separate duty imposed on claimants to report change of circumstances was drafted. There, the claimant is required to report changes to the "designated office" as defined in reg 2, not to the authority generally. However, it would be insufficient to base a conclusion that a mistake had been made on the mere fact that information was given to a department, or an officer in a department, other than the HB department. A tribunal would need to be satisfied that either the claimant had a reasonably based expectation that the information would be passed on, for example, because s/he was told, or could reasonably infer, that this would happen, or because there were internal arrangements or practices within the authority for dealing with information potentially relevant to entitlement to HB and that those arrangements or practices had not been followed.

(3) An officer of the DWP. The typical situation here will be where there has been a failure to follow the standard procedures for passing information between the departments and the authority in relation to claimants claiming IS or income-based JSA. In *Freeman* [1994] 27 HLR 616 at 621, Hale J said that it was "quite plain" that there was an official error, and the only possible mistake was the omission by the DSS to inform the authority of the cessation of the claimant's IS, and this was confirmed in *Sier* (in the High Court). Note *CH 943/2003*, which holds that an error here will include where the DWP (or HMRC – see para (4)) officer's decision is overturned by an appeal tribunal. But note also the comment of the commissioner in *CH 3761/2005* that the failure of an automatic computer notification system, without more, may not amount to an error on the part of an official of the DWP. As the Rent Service is an executive agency of the DWP, rent officers are also officers of the DWP and so a mistake made by a rent officer which leads to an overpayment may amount to an "official error".

(4) An officer of HMRC.

(5) A person providing services to any of the above Departments. Again, this covers the possibility of privatisation of functions of the DWP and HMRC.

"acting as such". These words only qualify sub-paragraphs (c)(i) and (ii), and thus refer to DWP and HMRC officers acting as such. They would add nothing to sub-para (h) as it already has that qualification. *EM v Waltham*

Forest LBC [2009] UKUT 245 (AAC) was thus correct to point out (at para 82) that the commentary in previous editions of this book was wrong in referring to a "neighbour working for the council" when commenting on the phrase "acting as such". That commentary would have been perfectly apposite had it been referring to sub-para (b). However, in the context of sub-para (c) the phrase "acting as such" means that the DWP or HMRC official must be acting in her/his official capacity. Thus the claimant whose neighbour works for the DWP (or HMRC) and gives her/him wrong advice as to entitlement to HB cannot rely on his advice as the relevant mistake. This is for two reasons. Arguably these reasons depend on the same underpinning logic and so some of the criticisms of the previous commentary in *EM v Waltham Forest LBC* may, it is suggested, be misplaced. The first reason is because the neighbour was not acting in his official capacity as a DWP (or HMRC) officer when he gave the advice. Secondly, and perhaps alternatively, as *EM v Waltham Forest LBC* suggests (in para 82), because following *R(H) 10/08*, the claimant in the above example would not have a reasonable expectation that the neighbour's advice was advice that he could formally rely on. But, put this way, it is suggested this latter characterisation of the neighbour's advice collapses into the former; because it is only if the claimant can show that the neighbour was acting officially that he would have a reasonable expectation that the advice was correct and could be relied upon.

Does any mistake count? Despite the breadth of the wording in para (3), not every mistake made by a local authority will count. For example, errors in the calculation of employee pensions administered on behalf of the local authority in respect of its employees, or an error in a local authority's employee's wages, will not, without more, amount to an error by a relevant authority or a person acting for such an authority within the terms of reg 100(3): *Middlesbrough BC v DS* [2009] UKUT 80 (AAC) para 13, *EM v Waltham Forest LBC* paras 83–84 and *Kingston upon Hull CC v DLM (HB)* [2010] UKUT 234 (AAC) paras 38–41.

No contribution to the mistake. By para (3), the person from whom recovery is sought cannot rely on the mistake if a relevant person has contributed to it. Who is a relevant person? Para (3) provides that contribution to the mistake may be made by three categories of person.

(1)   The claimant.

(2)   A person acting on her/his behalf. People appointed under reg 82 to look after an incapacitated claimant's interests fall under this heading but it probably also includes those who are dealing with the authority on her/his behalf on an informal basis.

(3)   Any other person to whom the payment is made. This includes appointees who made the original claim paid under reg 94(2), landlords paid under regs 95 and 96, or personal representatives or next of kin of deceased claimants paid under reg 97. Where the person is the landlord and that landlord is a company or a housing association, the tests in reg 100(2) focus on, say, what the housing association as a whole could reasonably have been expected to realise and not what any particular employee of the association may reasonably have been expected top realise: *CH 4918/2003* (para 18).

The view expressed in previous editions of this book that, contrary to *Freeman*, the overpayment may only be recoverable from the person who caused or materially contibuted to the mistake was, it is suggested, wrong, and in any event arguably cannot sit with para 19 of *CH 4918/2003* (see below). This is for a number of reasons. Firstly, reg 100 is concerned with whether an overpayment is recoverable and not from whom it is recoverable (which falls to be determined under reg 101), and so it is arguably legally impermissible for the terms of reg 100 to constrain or calibrate the categories of person from whom an overpayment is recoverable, save where the wording of reg 100 clearly compels such a result. Secondly, the closing words of para (3) do not, without more, carry the import that it is only the person who causes or materially contributes to the mistake that the overpayment may be recoverable from. Suppose it is the claimant who has contributed to the mistake and the landlord has not. It is suggested that this, of itself, cannot render the overpayment irrecoverable from the landlord where the overpayment was paid to the landlord because, assuming the landlord cannot rely on the regulation 101(1) "defence", that would render the terms of reg 101(2) below *otiose*. Thirdly, the parallel wording in para (2) has been held not to be met if any one of the claimant, person acting on her/his behalf, or the person to whom the payment was made, could reasonably have been expected to realise that it was an overpayment, and, moreover, determination of that question is separate from the question of from whom the overpayment is recoverable (*CH 4918/2003*, paras 19 and 20 respectively).

"did not cause or materially contribute". The relevant person need not be solely to blame. For the contribution to be "material", it must be shown that if the relevant person had acted differently s/he might have prevented the overpayment: *Saker v Secretary of State for Social Security* [1988] 16 January *The Times*, CA (reported as *R(I) 2/88)*). A claimant will not automatically have caused or materially contributed to the mistake if s/he notifies the authority of information other than in writing as required by reg 88(1): *CH 2409/2005* (para 22). In that case, the claimant had not caused or materially contributed to the mistake, despite his breach of regulation 88(1), because he had given the authority the information by telephone, which it accepted, and had never been told by the authority that information had to be provided in writing. However, bear in mind the the view of the Court of Appeal in *Sier* (as explained in *CH 2794/2004* para 13), that the broad question to be asked is whether the claimant's act or omission caused or contributed to the overpayment being made; and so a more focused enquiry on whether the claimant contributed to the 'official error' is unlikely, in most cases, to lead to any different conclusion.

Second criterion: Knowledge of the overpayment
It must be shown that a relevant person could not reasonably have known that there was an overpayment. It is for the person seeking to rely on reg 100(2) to prove that s/he could not reasonably have been expected to realise that an overpayment was being made and not for the authority to prove that s/he could reasonably have been expected to realise that an overpayment was being made: *CH 4918/2003* (para 16) and *CH 3439/2004* (para 22 – applying ratio of *Kerr v Department for Social Development* [2004] UKHL 23; reported as *R 1/04 (SF)*. The "defence" under para (2) is not made out if any one of the claimant, person acting on her/his behalf, or the person to whom the payment was made, could reasonably have been expected to realise that it was an overpayment: *CH 4918/2003* para 19.

"could not ... reasonably have been expected to realise". The test here is subjective – ie, whether the particular person with her/his experience, abilities and education could reasonably have been expected to realise: *JS v Hull City Council* [2012] UKUT 477 (AAC) at para 16 and *TA v Islington LB (HB)* [2014] UKUT 71 (AAC) at para 14.

This had been partially confirmed by Commissioner Jacobs in *CH 2554/2002*, in which he was critical of a statement by a tribunal that it did not impute "any more knowledge about the HB scheme than an ordinary reasonable person might have". He said (para 13):

"The question of imputation of knowledge to the claimant did not arise. The issue for the Tribunal was what could reasonably be expected of *the claimant*. There may be exceptional cases in which it is reasonable to expect a claimant to find out more about the housing benefit scheme, probably from the local authority or (possibly) elsewhere. If those cases exist in reality rather than theory, they will involve claimants with a special knowledge of the scheme, such as former housing benefit officers. They will, in any event, be rare. This case is not one of them. In the overwhelming majority of cases, there is no scope for imputing any knowledge to the claimant. The issue will be what could reasonably be deduced from the information available to the claimant. What a claimant could reasonably have been expected to realise is a question of fact. It depends on the information available to the person and on an analysis of what that information could have revealed." (para 13). See also *CH 609/2004* at para 8.

This statement of principle is a useful rebuttal to the arguments put forward by some local authorities in overpayment cases as to what can be reasonably expected of claimants. Some authorities appear to believe that any HB claimant should know the legislation inside out and should know instinctively when s/he is being overpaid. Plainly, such an approach is preposterous. As the commissioner goes on to state, in most cases the claimant's only sources of knowledge are past experience with the scheme and the documents provided by the local authority: para 15.

On the facts of the case, which concerned a failure to report income, the commissioner did not regard as conclusive the warnings given in the HB award letter to report changes of income: paras 20–22. However, he decided that since it was clear from the award letter that tax credits reduced the HB entitlement, the claimant ought to have realised that her income from employment should also do so: para 23.

A number of decisions now illustrate how critical close attention to the facts of an individual case will be. In *CH 2888/2002* para 15, the commissioner held that where a claimant had disclosed an increase in income and his wife had repeatedly enquired as to when his HB was to be reduced, the only permissible conclusion was that he should have known that he was being overpaid. This conclusion requires caution, since it is possible for such a claimant eventually to form the view, reasonably, that the local authority does not regard the increased income as relevant to her/his HB entitlement.

In *CH 2943/2007*, the claimant had correctly stated her earnings in her HB and CTB claims and in later enquiries, but the local authority had calculated her benefit on incorrect (lower) earnings and these were shown on its decision notices. The commissioner pointed out that a claimant cannot reasonably be expected to seek advice about a local authority's decision notice because s/he does not understand all the figures unless s/he has some reason to believe that the figures are wrong. A claimant who has given clear and correct information is entitled to start from the basis that the local authority has such information when stating her/his weekly earnings.

CH 2493/2007 was approved and followed in *CJ v Stratford-on-Avon DC (HB)* [2012] UKUT 357 (AAC), where the Upper Tribunal observed: "Claimants are not to be expected to be particularly numerate or familiar with either accounting practice or benefit law ... they cannot reasonably be expected to realise that they are being overpaid if that would involve them realising that a trained benefit officer using the correct information was not calculating their earnings properly" (paragraph 15), and "In judging what a claimant can reasonably have been expected to realise, it is very important to look at the case from his or her perspective."

Where a landlord was clearly informed that she should report the departure of a tenant from a property, her belief that she was entitled to receive HB during the claimant's notice period did not preclude a finding that she could reasonably be expected to know that she was being overpaid: *CH 1172/2002* para 8. Rather more obviously, in *CH 4465/2002* para 9, a landlord's argument that it could not reasonably be expected to know that it was being overpaid when it was aware of the claimant's departure from the premises and had indeed placed another tenant therein was rejected.

A less rigorous view was taken in *CH 3629/2002* where the claimant started low-paid work. She knew that her HB would decrease, but did not know when or by how much. The commissioner held that for a few weeks at least she could not reasonably have been expected to know that she was being overpaid.

If a claimant receives clear advice from a local authority that a certain income source is disregarded, then s/he cannot reasonably be expected to know that he is being overpaid: *CH 4838/2001* para 8. However, the effect of any contradictory advice in the documentation made available to a claimant should be taken into account in determining what is reasonable.

In *CH 4065/2001*, a claimant had been overpaid because the local authority had incorrectly calculated her income from IB. The authority alleged that she ought to have known that she was being overpaid and her response was that she had telephoned the local authority to query the award and had been told that it was correct. The authority's retort that there was no record of the call (as should have been the case on the office system) was held not to be a complete answer by Commissioner Jacobs. He said that "it is not my experience of life that administrative systems work perfectly in every case" (para 13). See also similar comments by the same commissioner in *CH 609/2004* para 24. It is implicit from the directions given to the tribunal in *CH 4065/2001*, that the commissioner took the view that if the claimant's evidence was accepted, the claimant could not reasonably have been expected to know that she was being overpaid. The directions (para 21) are a very useful summary of the correct approach to this very common type of case.

"at the time of receipt of the payment or of any notice relating to that payment". It seems that the person whom it is alleged ought to have known should be the person receiving the payment or the notice. For example, a person should probably realise at the time of receipt of a duplicate payment that they s/he has overpaid: *R v Liverpool CC ex p Griffiths* (1990) 22 HLR 312, QBD (Nolan J).

The purpose of this part of reg 99(2) HB Regs 1987 (now reg 100(2)), and the basis for its interpretation, was explained clearly by Commissioner Jacobs in *CH 1176/2003* para 8:

"The context in which regulation 99(2) will operate is relevant. It only applies to cases in which the claimant was on low income at the time of the payment. And the payment involved will have been made to help the claimant pay rent on a dwelling. In those circumstances, it is likely that the money will be spent fairly quickly. That, I believe, accounts for the emphasis on the time of payment or notice relating to payment. If the claimant could not reasonably have been expected to realise that an overpayment had been made, it is likely that the money will have been spent and spent in reliance on the claimant being properly entitled to it. In other words, regulation 99(2) contains an element of protection for a claimant who has relied on being entitled to the payment. The provision is not worded in those terms or limited to cases where there has been reliance. But that rationale provides a context in which the terms of the legislation must be interpreted."

The phrase relating to notices causes difficulty. The amendment was apparently made to deal with rent rebate cases where the claimant never actually receives any rent: Circular HB/CTB 90/23, and see *CH 1675/2005*. The wording is not restricted to such cases: *CH 1176/2003* para 9. In the same case, the commissioner suggested that if notice of an erroneous payment is sent out but promptly corrected by a telephone call to the claimant, it might be possible to see the whole process as one transaction: paras 32–33. This seems to be an unwarranted gloss on the legislation and adds an additional complication to a tribunal's task.

In *R(H) 1/02*, the commissioner was concerned with a case where a claimant had omitted to inform the local authority of an increase in her wages until she signed a review form some six weeks later. However, the authority recalculated her benefit on the basis of an incorrect figure being entered into its computer for the benefit calculations. That recalculation was carried out at a later stage, with a result that a lump sum was payable to the claimant. The claimant was sent notifications which set out the calculation with the incorrect figure used for the amount of her wages.

The commissioner held, at para 6(2)(a) of the decision, that where a claimant both receives a notice relating to a payment and receives it, knowledge or presumed knowledge on the date of either event will suffice to make the overpayment recoverable. He also held that "notice relating to that payment" requires that the notice in question be sufficiently closely related to the payment: para 6(2)(b).

This point was also addressed in *CH 1176/2003*, where the commissioner held (para 31) that, although the notice need not be the notice *of* payment, and so is wider than the actual decision notice, it must relate to the *payment* and not the overpayment, otherwise para (2) would provide no protection as, by definition, at the time of the overpayment notice the claimant must have been able to realise that it was an overpayment (see also *CH 1675/2005*). In *CH 1176/2003*, a cheque for HB was mistakenly issued to the claimant's bank on 18 February and credited to her account on the following day. The claimant made a series of withdrawals from her bank account before being informed by the local authority on 26 February of the mistake. Commissioner Jacobs held that a payment made by cheque is only received when it is credited to the claimant's bank account and not when the cheque is received by the claimant or presented at the bank: paras 20–23. He also held, remitting the case to the tribunal for reconsideration, that the "time" of receipt should not be judged according to the split-second at which the cheque was credited: para 26. It was a question of fact for the tribunal but one possible approach was to examine the claimant's knowledge over the day of receipt: para 27.

KR v City and County of Swansea (HB) [2015] UKUT 185 (AAC) emphasises that if a decision notice is the sole basis of it being argued or concluded that a person could reasonably have been expected to realise they were being overpaid, that expectation could not arise before the person had received the decision notice and read it.

Care may need to be taken, however, in not reading *KR* too widely as its concern was only with when a claimant might be fixed with knowledge of the information provided in a notice. However, as *AG v Calderdale*

Council (HB) [2016] UKUT 396 (AAC) points out, a notice (once received and read) might still be effective for the purposes of reg 100(2) for a period prior to its receipt if it relates sufficiently closely to a payment made for that period.

"that it was an overpayment". It must be shown that the relevant person should have known that there was an overpayment, not that there might have been an overpayment. In *Griffiths* (above), the authority had sent out letters warning claimants that they might receive the wrong amount of benefit under the estimated award. It was argued that it was sufficient that Mrs Griffiths knew that she might be being overpaid. Nolan J held (at 317) that this was not enough. It was not reasonable to expect her to work out her entitlement herself to decide whether she was getting too much HB. This approach was confirmed in *CH 2554/2002* para 9. The corollary of this, as pointed out by Commissioner Jacobs in that case, is that the claimant need not be aware of the amount by which s/he is being overpaid. All that is necessary is that that the claimant "could reasonably have been expected to realise that the amount she was receiving definitely contained some element of overpayment".

Paragraph (4)
This provides that certain overpayments of rent rebate are always recoverable. There are four conditions for its operation.

(1)   There has been a revision of the award. It does not appear to apply if the award is correct but, for example, the claimant is credited twice on her/his account due to a clerical error.

(2)   It also appears that the claimant's rent account must be in credit for the paragraph to come into effect. So, if a claimant is wrongly awarded £100 rather than £50 rent rebate for four weeks, but incurs an annual service charge on the rent account of £500, the account will be £300 in the red and so the paragraph does not apply.

(3)   The credit is in respect of a period after the date of the revision. In respect of past periods, the exception does not apply and the three criteria can be considered.

(4)   Even if there is a credit after the date of the revision, that credit must be the overpayment and not subsequent payments of rent rebate or made by the claimant. If the latter is the case, then the surplus ought to be presumed to relate to the latest of the payments made into the rent account: *Clayton's case* [1861] 1 Mer 572. For example, a claimant wrongly awarded £100 rather than £80 for four weeks then has her/his rent rebate suspended for two weeks. After one week, the £80 credit has gone; after two, the claimant is £80 in the red. However, at the end of the two weeks, before a revision is carried out, the claimant pays £160 into the rent account. There is an £80 credit on the account when the review is carried out, but that represents the claimant's voluntary payment rather than the overpayment.

Person from whom recovery may be sought

101.–(1)   For the purposes of section 75(3)(a) of the Administration Act (prescribed circumstances in which an amount recoverable shall not be recovered from the person to whom it was paid), the prescribed circumstance is–

(a)   housing benefit has been paid in accordance with regulation 95 (circumstances in which payment is to be made to the landlord) or regulation 96 (circumstances in which payment may be made to a landlord);

(b)   the landlord has notified the relevant authority or the Secretary of State in writing that he suspects that there has been an overpayment;

[¹ (bb) the relevant authority is satisfied that the overpayment did not occur as a result of any change of dwelling occupied by the claimant as his home;]

(c)   it appears to the relevant authority that, on the assumption that there has been an overpayment–

(i)   there are grounds for instituting proceedings against any person for an offence under section 111A or 112(1) of the Administration Act (dishonest or false representations for obtaining benefit); or

(ii)   there has been a deliberate failure to report a relevant change of circumstances contrary to the requirement of regulation 88 (duty to notify a change of circumstances) and the overpayment occurred as a result of that deliberate failure; and

(d)   the relevant authority is satisfied that the landlord–

(i)   has not colluded with the claimant so as to cause the overpayment;

(ii)   has not acted, or neglected to act, in such a way so as to contribute to the period, or the amount, of the overpayment.

[² [⁴ (2)   For the purposes of section 75(3)(b) of the Administration Act (recovery from such other person, as well as or instead of the person to whom the overpayment was made), where recovery of an overpayment is sought by a relevant authority–

(a)　subject to paragraph (1) and where sub-paragraph (b) or (c) does not apply, the overpayment is recoverable from the claimant as well as the person to whom the payment was made, if different;

(b)　in a case where an overpayment arose in consequence of a misrepresentation of or a failure to disclose a material fact (in either case, whether fraudulently or otherwise) by or on behalf of the claimant, or by or on behalf of any person to whom the payment was made, the overpayment is only recoverable from any person who misrepresented or failed to disclose that material fact instead of, if different, the person to whom the payment was made; or

(c)　in a case where an overpayment arose in consequence of an official error where the claimant, or a person acting on the claimant's behalf, or any person to whom the payment was paid, or any person acting on their behalf, could reasonably have been expected, at the time of receipt of the payment or of any notice relating to that payment, to realise that it was an overpayment, the overpayment is only recoverable from any such person instead of, if different, the person to whom the payment was made.]

[³ (2A)　Where an overpayment is made in a case where a relevant authority has determined a maximum rent (LHA) in accordance with regulation 13D (determination of a maximum rent (LHA)), and the housing benefit payable exceeds the amount which the claimant is liable to pay his landlord by way of rent, the relevant authority must not recover from the landlord more than the landlord has received.]

(3)　For the purposes of [³ paragraphs (1) and (2A)], "landlord" shall have the same meaning as it has for the purposes of regulation 95.

[¹ (3A)　For the purposes of [⁴ paragraph (2)(c)], "overpayment arose in consequence of an official error" shall have the same meaning as in regulation 100(3) above.]

[⁴ (4)]

Amendments

1.　Inserted by reg 6(2) and (4) of SI 2005 No 2904 as amended by Sch 2 para 29 of SI 2006 No 217 as from 10.4.06.
2.　Substituted by reg 6(3) of SI 2005 No 2904 as amended by Sch 2 para 29 of SI 2006 No 217 as from 10.4.06.
3.　Amended by reg 2 of SI 2008 No 586 as from 7.4.08.
4.　Amended by reg 4(2) of SI 2008 No 2824 as from 6.4.09.

Definitions

"claimant" – see reg 2(1).
"membership of household" – see Part 4 and note on s20(11).
"partner" – see reg 2(1).
"overpayment" – see reg 99.
"recoverable" – see reg 100.

General Note

SSAA s75(3) provides that a recoverable overpayment is recoverable from the person to whom it was paid unless regulations provide otherwise, and also gives a power to make regulations allowing recovery to be made from other persons in certain circumstances. This regulation exercises those powers. See commentary to s75 SSAA on p39 and the tribunal of commissioners' decision in *R(H) 6/06*. Note also the view in *DL v Liverpool City Council* [2009] UKUT 176 (AAC) that payments of HB made to a claimant's rent account after her/his death are not recoverable from the claimant under reg 101.

Despite the title of reg 101, it is clear that it is dealing with the recoverability stage rather than (the later) enforcement of recovery: *R(H) 6/06*.

Note also the commissioners' recommendation in para 60 of *R(H) 6/06* that in every case where reg 101 provides for joint liability, the local authority should make a single decision referring to all of those from whom the overpayment is recoverable, rather than separate decisions addressed to each of them. Moreover, where a local authority decides that an overpayment is not recoverable from the person to whom it was made, a proper decision to that effect should be made and included in the decision about the person from whom the overpayment is recoverable, and that decision issued to both parties. Unless and until this is done any alleged overpayment will not be recoverable from any person: *CH 3744/2006* para 33.

R(H) 3/09 decided that it was not unfair for the immediately prior form of reg 101 to have retrospective effect, in the sense that if the reg 101 decision was made on or after 10 April 2006 then it would be the reg 101 in place at that time that would act to fix from whom the overpayment may be recoverable notwithstanding that the overpayment may be for a period arising wholly or partly before 10 April 2006 (when the result under the then version of reg 101 may have been different). Reg 101 (and para 2 in particular) has been amended again since the version of reg 101 that *R(H) 3/09* ruled on. However, as it would seem that the 6 April 2009 changes to reg 101(2) were intended merely to tidy up the wording of para (2), and as the scope of para (2) arguably remains the same, it is likely that *R(H) 3/09* remains good law.

One contentious issue which may still arise in respect of the post-9 April 2006 version of reg 101, however, is when a landlord may be said to have breached a legal duty to disclose so that s/he can be said to have failed to disclose (following *B v SSWP* [2005] EWCA Civ 929, [2005] 1 WLR 3796; reported as *R(IS) 9/06*). This is because regs 86(1) and 88(1) (and the equivalent regulations in the HB(SPC) Regs – regs 67(1) and 69(1)) would seem to only impose a legal duty on a landlord to disclose if there is a subsequent change in circumstances after the claim has been awarded, and then only if s/he knows about the change and "might reasonably be expected to know" that it "might affect" the claimant's HB. This issue was addressed in *Hastings BC v PA and DA Hanlon (HB)* [2013] UKUT 232 (AAC); [2014] AACR 4, in the context of whether a landlord knew or ought to have known that his tenant had left the dwelling for which housing benefit continued to be paid. Judge Rowland said (paras 27–29):

> "Regulation 69(1) clearly imposes on a landlord a duty to inform a local authority if he or she knows that a claimant has ceased to occupy the relevant dwelling as his home, since that is obviously relevant to the claimant's entitlement to housing benefit. It equally clearly imposes on a landlord a duty to inform a local authority if he or she is aware of any other change of circumstances that he or she "might reasonably be expected to know" might affect the claimant's entitlement to housing benefit. The words "might reasonably be expected to know" refer not to whether the landlord might reasonably be expected to know of the change of circumstances but to whether he or she might reasonably be expected to know its materiality. It imposes an objective test but in applying it regard would need to be had to what the landlord had been told in the notice issued under paragraph 11 of Schedule 8. What, however, regulation 69(1) does not do is impose on a landlord any duty positively to seek out information relevant to claimants' entitlement to housing benefit. There may be good reasons for that, given tenants' rights to quiet enjoyment and privacy. It is one thing to encourage landlords to report information they acquire in the normal course of events, perhaps because a landlord lives in the same building as a tenant, but it is another to encourage them to snoop on their tenants. A person may occupy a dwelling and be liable for rent even though he or she does not live there and is therefore not entitled to housing benefit and it may not always be immediately obvious when a person has ceased to occupy, or has even ceased to live at, an address.
>
> It may well be that a person can be under a legal duty to disclose facts to a local authority notwithstanding that the duty is not imposed by any statutory provision. It is noteworthy that, since it refers only to a change of circumstances, regulation 69 does not impose on a landlord a duty to disclose a fact that he or she knows made a claim for housing benefit fraudulent from the start but a duty to disclose such a fact might possibly be implied from the circumstances surrounding the acceptance of the payments. However, I see no warrant in regulation 69 or under the general law for implying a duty to disclose facts of which one is unaware or to take active steps to discover facts so that they may be disclosed. One has only to raise the questions of what those steps might be and how far such a duty might extend to appreciate that there might be difficulties with implying such an approach and, indeed, with the application of a provision such as regulation 82(1)(d)(ii)".

Para (1) deals with the case where a person receiving HB will not be liable to repay benefit, namely a blameless landlord in certain limited cases.

All reg 101 is concerned with is fixing who, as a matter of law, is legally liable to repay the overpayment, and disputes as to whether a person falls within reg 101 are appealable. However, once those reg 101 issues have been finally decided there then arises one final decision to be made, namely who out of those people who are legally liable to repay the overpayment the local authority will actually seek to enforce recovery against as a matter of fact. That is a discretionary decision of the local authority and, as *R(H) 6/06* makes plain, it is *not* appealable.

Analysis

Paragraph (1): Cases where an overpayment is not recoverable from a landlord

As *R(H) 6/06* explains, para (1) provides a limited exception to the entitlement to recover from landlords. Para (1) sets out five conditions that must all be satisfied if the landlord is to escape liability.

If the five conditions in para (1) are satisfied, the overpayment is *irrecoverable* from the landlord even if the HB was paid to her/him. However, the five conditions must all be satisfied and, hence, if the landlord fails to meet just one of them it will lose the protection of para (1), and the question of whether the overpayment is recoverable from it will have to be determined under para (2). *Hastings BC v PA and DA Hanlon (HB)* [2013] UKUT 232 (AAC); [2014] AACR 4 points out that the insertion of sub-paragraph (bb) with effect from 10 April 2006, with no concomitant restriction on the reach of paragraph (2)(b), significantly limits the protection afforded to landlords in the situation where the cause of the overpayment is the claimant moving out of the rental property. This is because in such a situation the landlord cannot rely on para (1) and may be caught by para (2)(b). However, it is suggested that the significance of this change may be more apparent than real given the very real difficulty a landlord would have in meeting all of the conditions in para (1) (even before sub-para (bb)) and the failure to disclose limb at least of para (2)(b) not having any application to a landlord if the landlord did not know the claimant had moved out (as per *Hasting BC*).

Sub-para (a): Direct payments made to landlord. A landlord cannot take advantage of para (1) unless direct payments were made under reg 95 or 96.

Note, however, that the HB that has been paid direct arguably must be the same as the HB of which recovery is sought, given the scope of the enabling power in s75(3) (and see further the like reasoning in *DL v Liverpool City Council* above). So if the landlord received direct payments prior to the overpayment period but not during that period, the overpayment will not be recoverable (though not because the landlord has met the five conditions in reg 101(1) but because the overpayment does not fall within reg 101 in the first place).

Direct payments to a landlord's agent will satisfy this condition, since reg 101(3) imports the definition in reg 95: "a person to whom rent is payable". If a landlord appoints an agent to receive the rent, then for the purposes of reg 101, the agent will be treated as if s/he is the landlord.

Sub-para (b): Notification of overpayment. There must be a written notification. "Writing" should extend to communication by fax and also ought to extend to correspondence by email. It is also suggested that it will be sufficient if a landlord makes an oral statement to an officer which is recorded by that officer, as long as if it is then signed by the landlord.

A notice given by an agent or company director should be sufficient for the purposes of sub-para (b), certainly if it is explicitly made on behalf of the landlord.

Sub-para (bb): Not due to change of dwelling. If the authority, or on appeal the tribunal, is satisfied that the overpayment arose because of the claimant moving out of the dwelling for which s/he was getting HB, the landlord cannot rely on reg 101(1). The wording of sub-para (bb) would still seem to allow reg 101(1) to apply, however, to those parts of the overpayment that did not occur as a result of a change of dwelling.

Sub-para (c): Offence committed or deliberate failure to disclose. On appeal, the First-tier Tribunal must decide for itself whether it appears that the condition is satisfied.

The two limbs of sub-para (c) are alternatives. Under head (i), it is not necessary to prove that the relevant person is guilty of the offence, merely that there is a case for her/him to answer. See ss111A and 112(1) for the question of whether an offence is committed.

Under head (ii), there must have been a failure to report a change of circumstances by a claimant, a recipient of HB or an agent of a recipient. The breach must be deliberate. The *Shorter Oxford English Dictionary* defines "deliberate" as "carefully thought out, studied; intentional, done on purpose". A breach that is inadvertent or even negligent will not suffice. The breach must also have caused the overpayment. It need not be the sole cause. It will suffice if it is one of joint causes: *R (Sier) v Cambridge CC HBRB* [2001] EWHC Admin 160, QBD; [2001] EWCA Civ 1523, CA, Richards J, discussed on p584.

Sub-para (d): No fault of landlord. It appears that both limbs under sub-para (d) must be satisfied. Again the wording "the relevant authority is satisfied" does not confine the First-tier Tribunal to a review of the authority's decision; it must decide the question for itself afresh.

In head (i), "colluded" is not defined. The *Shorter Oxford English Dictionary* gives "conspire, plot, connive, act in secret concert …. stir up or bring about by collusion". Effectively, there must be an agreement to act in such a way that an overpayment occurs, but it may be that a specific intention to commit fraud is not required.

Under head (ii), it must be shown that the landlord "has not acted, or neglected to act" in a way that caused the claimant to be overpaid. One of two things must be shown: a positive action of the landlord (or, it would seem, the landlord's agent) or some degree of inaction. The latter must involve "neglect". So if the landlord did not know of the relevant facts or if a reasonable person in the landlord's position would not have informed the local authority of the position, then the overpayment does not become recoverable.

Paragraph (2): Targets for recovery

In most cases para (1) will not be satisfied. Therefore, for the vast majority of cases from whom the overpayment is recoverable will be governed by reg 101(2). The wording of para (2) was amended in April 2009. This rewriting of para (2) was not intended to alter its scope but to make clearer who para (2) was aimed at after criticism of the wording of prior versions of reg 101(2) by the Tribunal of Commissioners in *R(H) 6/06*.

Para (2) seeks to define the circumstances under s75(3)(b) SSAA in which an overpayment shall be recoverable from such other person as well as, or instead of, the person to whom it was paid. Thus the regulation making power in s75(3)(b) expressly contemplates that an overpayment may be recoverable from a person in addition to the person to whom the HB was paid or a person instead of the payee, and reg 101(2) then, in its now clearer terms, sets out how that is effected.

General rule: claimant and payee. The general rule is set out in para (2)(a). This provides that that an overpayment is recoverable from the claimant and the person, if different, to whom the overpayment was made.

However this general rule will not apply if reg 101(1) (above) applies, nor will it apply if either sub-paras (b) or (c) apply.

Note further, however, in respect of the claimant, what Judge Mesher called his "provisional view" in *DL v Liverpool City Council* that, although following *Secretary of State for Social Services v Solly* [1974] 3 All ER 922 an HB overpayment could in principle be recoverable from the claimant's estate after her/his death, this could only be where the overpayment was in respect of periods before the claimant's death, as only in that circumstance could the overpayment be said to be a liability of the claimant's estate.

First exception to general rule: claimant or payee fails to disclose or misrepresents. The first exception to the general rule is set out in sub-para (b) of para (2). The net effect of this exception is that where the overpayment has arisen in consequence of a misrepresentation of, or a failure to disclose, a material fact then (a) the general rule above does not apply, and (b) the overpayment is *only* recoverable from the person who made the misrepresentation or failed to disclose. The misrepresentation or failure to disclose may be made by or in behalf of the claimant or by or on behalf of the person the benefit was paid to (eg, the landlord). However, it must be noted that for reg 101(2)(b) to apply to a landlord (or agent) then either the overpayment in question must have been paid to the landlord (or agent) or, if it was paid to the claimant, the misrepresentation or failure to disclose was made by the landlord (or agent) acting on behalf of the claimant. Absent these considerations, however, where the overpayment was paid to the claimant then a landlord cannot be caught by reg 101(2) and the overpayment will *only* be recoverable from the claimant.

Second exception to the general rule: claimant or payee should realise official error overpayment being made. The second exception to the general rule is set out in sub-para (c) of para (2). Here the overpayment in question must have arisen in consequence of an "official error" under regulation 100(3) HB Regs. The net effect of the second exception is that where the overpayment has arisen in consequence of an official error then the overpayment is only recoverable from those out of the claimant, the payee, or those acting on either's behalf, who, under the regulation 100(2) test, could reasonably have been expected to realise that an overpayment was being made. Note again, however, that this will only apply to a landlord (or agent) where either the official error overpayment was made to it or where it was acting on behalf of the claimant.

"in consequence of". There must be a clear link between the misrepresentation or failure to disclose and the making of the overpayment. However, the misleading of the authority need not be the sole cause of the overpayment. It is sufficient if it is a significant contributing factor. So, where there has been a failure to disclose by a relevant person, it is not an answer that the authority could have discovered the true situation by contacting the DWP or some other person: *Duggan v Chief Adjudication Officer* [1988] *The Times* 18 December, CA; *CSB 64/1986* para 11.

On the other hand, where the authority knows of the true situation, the misleading may not be sufficiently significant. The "clear link" will not be established where it can be shown that the authority has actually been informed of the true situation by the DWP or some other third person: *CIS 159/1990* para 4; *CS 12770/1996* para 9. When the relevant person has previously informed the authority of the true facts but later inadvertently misleads the authority, provided it is reasonable for them to assume the previous information has been acted on, the later misrepresentation may not be an effective cause of the overpayment: *CS 130/1992* paras 15–16. Furthermore, where the information before the authority clearly makes it clear that there is a need for further inquiries, and those inquiries are not made, then the sole cause of the overpayment may be the authority's error: *CIS 222/1991* paras 4–5.

Where there has been criminal activity by a third person, such as the theft of a cheque, that activity may be found to be the true cause of a resulting overpayment: *CIS 395/1992* para 10.

"a misrepresentation". A misrepresentation is an actual statement which is untrue or misleading: *CSB 1006/1985* para 5. It may be made in writing, orally or even by conduct if sufficiently unambiguous: *R(SB) 18/85* para 10.

Claim forms provided by authorities often require a person claiming on behalf of the claimant to sign a declaration at the end of the form. If the declaration is false then that may amount to a misrepresentation even if none of the details given on the form are untrue of themselves. However, the courts have tended to give a narrow reading to such declarations: see *Jones v Chief Adjudication Officer* [1994] 1 WLR 62 at 71H, 72F, CA; *Franklin v Chief Adjudication Officer* [1995] *The Times* 29 December, CA; *CIS 393/1993* para 7; *CIS 372/1994* para 6.

"or failure to disclose". Following the case of *B* (see below for details) the authority must now establish only two matters; the additional test of whether disclosure was "reasonably to be expected" having been held to be unnecessary in *B*.

(1)   That the relevant person was under a duty to disclose. See reg 86 for the duty to provide information to the authority and reg 88 for the statutory duty to notify a change of circumstances. In *CH 2443/2002* para 14, the commissioner held that an employer could not be under a duty to disclose because reg 75 HB Regs 1987 (now reg 88) had no application to an employer. The Court of Appeal in *B v SSWP* [2005] EWCA Civ 929, [2005] 1 WLR 3796; reported as *R(IS) 9/06* – affirming the decision of the tribunal of commissioners in *CIS 4348/2003* – has held that a failure to disclose can only arise if the person was under a legal duty which s/he has breached *R(SB) 21/82*. However, there can be no duty to disclose information which is not known: *Franklin*; *R(SB) 54/83* para 13(2); *R(SB) 9/85* para 7.

(2)   That the relevant person did not disclose the relevant information. Disclosure means informing the authority in such a way that the information can be expected to come to the attention of a person with responsibility for handling the claim: *R(SB) 15/87* paras 25, 28 and *Hinchy v SSWP* [2005] UKHL 16 (*R(IS) 7/05*). Although reg 88 HB Regs require changes of circumstances to be notified "in writing to the designated office" oral disclosure has always been treated as sufficient in relation to DWP benefits, even before reg 32 Social Security (Claims and Payments) Regulations 1987 was amended to permit oral

disclosure to be accepted: see *R(SB) 40/84* para 5; *R(SB) 15/87* para 13. Once disclosure has been made, there is no duty to disclose the same information again: *R(SB) 15/87* para 28.

"a material fact". The better view may now arguably be that a 'material fact' is one that itself would justify a different outcome decision (per *CIS 3655/2007*) rather than the lesser test of a fact that might well have affected the decision (per *Saker v Secretary of State for Social Security* [1988] 16 January *The Times*, CA (reported as *R(I) 2/88*))).

"in either case whether fraudulently or otherwise". No moral culpability need be shown on the part of the relevant person. The misleading of authority may have been entirely innocent: *Page v Chief Adjudication Officer* [1991] The Times 4 July, CA.

"the person who misrepresented or failed to disclose that material fact". In all cases, this includes the individual responsible who misled the authority. It probably also includes corporate entities for whom the individual works: see Interpretation Act 1978 Sch 1.

Recovery from appointees. The mechanism in reg 82(3) for appointment of a person to act on behalf of another is similar to the procedure for appointment by the DWP under reg 33 Social Security (Claims and Payments) Regulations 1987. The question of whether appointees can be personally liable to repay an overpayment has caused controversy in relation to DWP benefits. This has been settled by the decision of a tribunal of commissioners in *R(IS) 5/03*, which held that such personal liability would ordinarily exist: para 57. Recovery will normally be available against both claimant and appointee: para 58. However, it was said that if the benefit was not paid over to the claimant, recovery could only be made from the appointee: para 59. It was also said that the appointee would have a right under general principles of agency law to be indemnified by her/his principal except in cases where s/he was guilty of negligence or a breach of duty: para 61. The principal is the local authority, because the local authority appoints the appointee to act. Accordingly, in cases where it is alleged that there is strict liability for a misrepresentation made by an appointee but the appointee acted with due diligence, the appointee will be able to counterclaim to proceedings brought by the local authority for an indemnity, and the claim for the amount of the overpayment and the counterclaim for the indemnity will cancel each other out.

Method of recovery

102.–(1) Without prejudice to any other method of recovery, [² a relevant authority] may recover a recoverable overpayment from any person referred to in regulation 101 (persons from whom recovery may be sought) by deduction from any housing benefit to which that person is entitled (including arrears of entitlement after offsetting under regulation 98 (offsetting)) or, where it is unable to do so, may request the Secretary of State to recover any recoverable overpayment from the benefits prescribed in [³ regulation 105(1)] (recovery of overpayments from prescribed benefits).

[³ (1ZA) Where an overpayment is recoverable from a claimant who has one or more partners, a relevant authority may recover the overpayment by deduction from any housing benefit payable to the claimant's partner, or where it is unable to do so, may request the Secretary of State to recover any recoverable overpayment from the benefits prescribed in regulation 105(1B) (recovery of overpayments from prescribed benefits), provided that the claimant and that partner were a couple both at the time of the overpayment and when the deduction is made.]

[² [⁴]]

(2) Subject to paragraphs [² [⁴]] (4) and (5), where [¹ a relevant authority] makes deductions permitted by paragraph (1) [³ or (1ZA)] from the housing benefit it is paying to a claimant [³ or a claimant's partner] (other than deductions from arrears of entitlement), the deduction in respect of a benefit week shall be–

(a) in a case to which paragraph (3) applies, not more than the amount there specified; and

(b) in any other case, not more than three times five per cent. of the personal allowance for a single claimant aged not less than 25, that five per cent. being, where it is not a multiple of five pence, rounded to the next higher such multiple.

(3) Where [¹ a relevant authority] makes deductions from housing benefit it is paying to a claimant [³ or a claimant's partner, where the claimant has] , in respect of the whole or part of the recoverable overpayment–

(a) been found guilty of an offence whether under a statute or otherwise;

(b) made an admission after caution of deception or fraud for the purpose of obtaining relevant benefit; or

(c) agreed to pay a penalty under section 115A of the Administration Act (penalty as an alternative to prosecution) and the agreement has not been withdrawn, the amount deducted under paragraph (2) shall be not more than [⁵ five times] five per cent. of the personal allowance for a single claimant aged not less than 25, [⁵ that five per cent. being, where it is not a multiple of 5 pence, rounded to the next higher such multiple].

(4)   Where, in the calculation of housing benefit, the amount of earnings or other income falling to be taken into account is reduced by reason of paragraphs 3 to 10 of Schedule 4 (sums to be disregarded in the calculation of earnings) [⁴ , or paragraph 10A of that Schedule in a case where the amount of earnings to be disregarded under that paragraph is the amount referred to in regulation 45(2) of the Employment and Support Allowance Regulations [⁶ regulation 39(1)(a) of the Employment and Support Allowance Regulations 2013] or regulation 17(2) of the Social Security (Incapacity for Work) (General) Regulations 1995,] or paragraph 14 or 15 of Schedule 5 (sums to be disregarded in the calculation of income other than earnings), the deduction under paragraph (2) may be increased by not more than half the amount of the reduction.

(5)   No deduction made under this regulation [² [⁴]] shall be applied so as to reduce the housing benefit in respect of a benefit week to less than 50 pence.

(6)   In this regulation–
"admission after caution" means–
(i)   in England and Wales, an admission after a caution has been administered in accordance with a Code issued under the Police and Criminal Evidence Act 1984;
(ii)   in Scotland, admission after a caution has been administered, such admission being duly witnessed by two persons; and
"personal allowance for a single claimant aged not less than 25" means the amount specified in paragraph 1(1)(b) of column 2 of Schedule 3 (applicable amounts).

(7)   This regulation shall not apply in respect of an offence committed or an admission after caution or an agreement to pay a penalty made before 2nd October 2000.

Amendments

1.   Substituted by reg 7(2) of SI 2005 No 2904 as amended by Sch 2 para 29 of SI 2006 No 217 as from 10.4.06.
2.   Inserted by reg 7(3)-(5) of SI 2005 No 2904 as amended by Sch 2 para 29 of SI 2006 No 217 as from 10.4.06.
3.   Amended by reg 4(3) of SI 2008 No 2824 as from 6.4.09.
4.   Amended by reg 2(2) of SI 2009 No 2608 as from 1.4.10 (5.4.10 where rent payable weekly or in multiples of a week).
5.   Amended by reg 3(2) of SI 2012 No 645 as from 1.4.12.
6.   Amended by reg 35(8) of SI 2013 No 630 as from 29.4.13.

Definitions

"authority" – see reg 2(2) and s134(4) SSAA.
"overpayment" – see reg 99.
"recoverable" – see reg 100.

Analysis

In the detailed consideration of the various methods of recovery available that follows, the person from whom recovery is sought will be referred to as "D". Recovery can also be from the claimant's partner (or partners) (per para (1ZA)), provided the following conditions are met.

(1)   D is the claimant. The power cannot be used to recover, for example, from the partner of D who is an executor of the claimant's will and who has received benefit after the claimant's death.
(2)   D was receiving the HB. It does not apply where payment was made to the landlord under regs 93 or 94 or to any other payee.
(3)   D and her/his partner(s) were living in the same household *both* at the time of the overpayment *and* at the time the deduction is made. It is suggested that the authority cannot make recovery of a proportion of the overpayment where her/his partner was only in the same household for some of the weeks of the period of the overpayment. The "overpayment" is the full amount found to be recoverable. The partner must have been living in the same household for the full period before the provision can be used.

Bankruptcy and debt relief orders

The decision of the Supreme Court in *SSWP v Payne and another* [2011] UKSC 60; [2012] 2 All ER 46, recasts substantially (at least as far as England and Wales is concerned) the law relating to the application of bankruptcy orders and debt relief orders (DROs) to the recovery of overpayments of HB. Giving the leading judgment for the Supreme Court, dismissing the Secretary of State's appeal, Lady Hale said (at paras 21–26):

"This Court is in the fortunate position of being able to adopt a coherent approach which it would have been difficult for the courts below to achieve. In my view, there is no such thing as the so-called "net entitlement principle". The claimant to any kind of social security benefit has a statutory entitlement to the amount of benefit which she is awarded by the Secretary of State or a tribunal. ... Some claimants may have a prior liability to repay previously overpaid benefits, whether of the same or an entirely different kind, or they may have taken out a Social Fund loan which they are liable to repay. By no stretch of the imagination does a Social Fund loan to buy a cooker amount to an advance payment of retirement pension to which the claimant later becomes entitled. It could more plausibly be regarded as an advance payment of future income support. But at the point when the loan is made and the liability to repay arises it cannot be known whether the claimant will continue to be reliant on income support. She may get a job, marry a rich man, or win the lottery. The liability to repay arises independently of her entitlement to any benefit from which the Secretary of State may later decide to recoup it.

"In any ordinary use of language, the power to recover the debt by deduction from benefit is a "remedy in respect of the debt".

"Furthermore, I do not see any reason to distinguish between the DRO scheme and bankruptcy in this respect….It is just as much a remedy against the property of the bankrupt as it is a remedy in respect of a debt listed in a DRO. For my part, therefore, I would hold that *Taylor and Chapman* [1997] BPIR 505 was wrongly decided. The Secretary of State loses the power to recoup overpayments and Social Fund loans on the making of a bankruptcy order just as he does on the making of a DRO.

"This result is inconsistent with the result reached in Mulvey 1997 SC (HL) 105. But Mulvey depended on the Scottish common law of bankruptcy together with the Bankruptcy (Scotland) Act 1985, which has no exact equivalent of the English provisions with which we are concerned. In those circumstances, it cannot be for this Court in an English case to over-turn the decision of the House of Lords in a Scottish case. We can merely place a question mark against that element in the reasoning which has been referred to as the "net entitlement principle".

"Finally, it is clear that *Balding* [2007] EWCA Civ 1327 was rightly decided and that the principle applies equally to the DRO scheme. It is worth noting, therefore, that the impact of this decision is not as great as might have been thought. All those liabilities to repay overpaid benefits, tax credits and Social Fund loans listed in DROs …. will in any event be wiped out at the end of the moratorium period. We are talking about the power to continue to deduct during that period. The sums involved, though not insignificant, will be much less than the total of the liabilities involved. It would, of course, be open to the Government to promote delegated legislation to exclude these liabilities from the definition of "qualifying debts" in the DRO scheme altogether (and, indeed, to seek corresponding amendment to section 382 with regard to "bankruptcy debt"), but that would raise policy issues which are not for this Court."

The effect of the Supreme Court's decision is as follows. If the overpayment decision is made before a bankruptcy order is made in respect of D, then the local authority will not be able to recover the overpayment from D from the date of the bankruptcy order, and the liability to repay the overpayment will in any event be discharged once D is discharged from bankruptcy. Likewise, if, instead, D has been granted a DRO under section 251G of the Insolvency Act 1986 and the overpayment of HB is specified as a debt under the DRO, then the local authority is precluded from recovering the overpayment both during the one-year moratorium period that arises after the DRO has been made and at the end of that moratorium period. The only exception to these rules would seem to be where the overpayment decision is made after D is adjudged bankrupt. In this circumstance, following *R(H) 9/ 09*, the Insolvency Act 1986 has no application and the overpayment will remain a debt D is liable to repay.

The authority may not add interest to the overpayment: *R v Kensington and Chelsea RBC ex p Brandt* (1995) 28 HLR 528, QBD (Dyson J).

Recovery from HB payable to D

Under reg 102, there may be recovery from any HB owing to D to which D is entitled. This can be arrears owed to D (even if the arrears are referable to dates outside the period of the overpayment) or future payments. The effect of reg 102 is duplicated by SSAA s75(5)(a) and reg 106(2).

Where D is a claimant in receipt of rent allowance, this should not cause any difficulties. When determining the appropriate rate of recovery, the authority will wish to balance the need for enforcement against the need to avoid making the tenant homeless and possibly liable to be housed by the authority. The authority may deduct from payments made to D's landlord. Since the landlord has never been paid, this will create rent arrears as between landlord and claimant.

Reg 102 only authorises deduction from HB where D is not a claimant, if it is HB paid to D in her/his role as claimant. In particular, where D is a landlord, reg 102 does not authorise recovery from HB paid to D in respect of tenants other than the overpaid claimant. The recovery is only from HB "to which that person [ie, the person from whom recovery is sought] is entitled". D is not entitled to HB; her/his tenants are.

In *R v Haringey LBC ex p Ayub* (1992) 25 HLR 566, QBD, the applicant was a landlord owning a large stock of housing in the authority's area. Many of his tenants received HB. When overpayments were made, the authority sought to withhold payment of HB payable in respect of other tenants. On judicial review, the authority admitted that this course of action was not sanctioned by reg 102. Instead, it was said that this was a convenient method of recovery. Furthermore, as the other tenants were debtors of the landlord, the authority could "garnish" their debts (that is, seize payments made to a debtor by his debtors). Schiemann J held that there was no right to garnish a debt until a court order was obtained, and then stated:

"When a council is making a payment to a landlord under regulations 93 or 94 *[now regs 95 and 96 HB Regs]* of rent allowance to which tenants B-Z are entitled it is in effect acting as the agent of those tenants and paying their rent for them. Upon such a payment being made the tenant's liability to the landlord is *pro tanto* extinguished and the latter cannot thereafter sue the former for more payment of that rent or repossess the property on the basis of non-payment of that rent. The authority is not allowed to use a tenant's rent allowance in order to extinguish any liability of the landlord to the authority. That is not a purpose for which Parliament has authorised the payment of rent allowance. The general right of set-off for which the authority contends would leave it totally unclear as to which unfortunate tenant's rent allowance is to be used for this purpose and indeed whether the choice of the unlucky tenant is to be in the hands of the landlord or in those of the authority."

However, s75(5)(b) and (c) SSAA (inserted by s16 Social Security (Administration) Fraud Act 1997) gives the authority the right to recover from "prescribed benefits" paid to D in respect of an obligation owed to him by another person. See reg 106(3) and note the effect of reg 107 on tenants' liabilities.

Paras (2) and (3) impose maximum weekly amounts that may be recovered from ongoing HB. This applies only to ongoing entitlement and not to arrears, as is clear from the words in parentheses in para (2). The maximum amount is subject to a needlessly complicated calculation. First, one takes the personal allowance for a single claimant aged over 25, then takes 5 per cent of that. That figure is then multiplied by three to give the maximum deduction.

A higher maximum applies wherever the claimant is convicted of an offence, admits the offence under caution or agrees to pay a penalty. However, that only applies where the offence, admission or agreement occurs after 2 October 2000: see para (7). An admission under caution must comply with Code C issued under the Police and Criminal Evidence Act 1984 in England and Wales. Some guidance is given on this in para 19 of Circular HB/CTB A42/2000, but careful reference should be made to the Code.

In either case, where the claimant (or her/his partner) has earnings which are being partially disregarded, a further amount of half of the disregard may be added to the amount being recovered.

It is to be noted, however, that these amounts remain the maxima and so authorities should give careful consideration to any hardship that may result in deciding whether to deduct the full amount: see para 20 of the Circular.

Recovery from other benefits

The procedure for recovery from other benefits is specified by reg 105. It applies to benefits payable by the DWP and recovery is carried out by the Secretary of State on the authority's behalf.

Conditions for recovery from other benefits. The authority may only make a request to the Secretary of State to recover from other benefits payable to D when it is "unable" to recover by deduction from D's HB. It is suggested that this requires that there is no HB in payment which the authority can withhold, not merely that the authority consider that the amount is insufficient.

The Secretary of State may not recover the overpayment unless requested to by the authority, and must be satisfied of three conditions before making recovery. However, once the three conditions are present, the minister has no discretion to decline to recover.

(1)   That there is a recoverable overpayment of HB. The Secretary of State will invariably follow the authority's final determination, but ought to refuse recovery where D is still exercising statutory rights of review or is seeking judicial review. Where an application is made by the authority under reg 102 in this situation, D is well advised to inform the local office in writing of the fact that recoverability is in dispute.

(2)   The overpayment is due to the misleading of the authority. For the meaning of the wording in the phrase in para (3)(a), see the Analysis of reg 101. It appears that it is for the Secretary of State to decide whether this condition is met, even if the authority has already concluded that it has been misled.

(3)   D is receiving a "sufficient" amount of a relevant benefit to enable recovery. What is a "sufficient" amount depends on the facts of individual cases.

The relevant benefits. The categories of benefits that are prescribed by reg 105 as being candidates for recovery differ depending on whether recovery is from benefits payable to the claimant or the claimant's partner.

For the claimant the following categories of benefit are prescribed by reg 105(1) as being candidates for recovery.

(1)   Any benefit except guardian's allowance: reg 105(1)(a). These include maternity allowance, widow's benefits, retirement pension, carer's allowance, industrial injuries benefits, disability living allowance and attendance allowance. It would also include arrears of defunct benefits such as sickness, invalidity and unemployment benefit.

(2)   Income support: reg 105(1)(b).

(3)   Benefits payable to the claimant from other EU member states under Regulation (EEC)1408/71: reg 105(1)(c).

(4)   Jobseeker's allowance, whether contribution-based or income-based: reg 105(1)(d).

(5)   State pension credit: reg 105(1)(e).

(6)   Employment and support allowance, whether contributory or income-related: reg 105(1)(f).

(7)   Personal independence payment: reg 105(1)(g).

(8)   Universal credit: reg 105(1)(h).

For the claimant's partner the categories of benefit are more limited. They are prescribed by reg 105(1B) and are: IS, income-based JSA, PC, income-related ESA, PIP and UC.

Debit from D's rent account

Where D is in receipt of rent rebate, the authority may add the overpayment as a debit to the rent account. Caution is required, however. The debit must be carefully distinguished from any rent arrears that exist at the point of the debit and any that subsequently arise: 1997 GM A7.37.

The reason for this is that recovery of an overpayment of benefit from a landlord did not allow the landlord to recover the overpayment from the tenant as rent arrears. Once HB was paid to the landlord, the claimant's liability for rent is discharged to the extent of that HB payment: see the quotation from *Ayub* above. At most, the claimant owes the landlord a debt once there is recovery from the latter. But the debt is not rent arrears and the landlord cannot use the debt as the basis of a claim for possession for non-payment of rent.

This rule *may* have been abrogated in relation to rent allowance from April 1997 (see the Analysis to reg 95(2)), but the same principle applies to debits from the claimant's rent account. SSAA s134(2)(b) makes it clear that the effect of rent rebate is to reduce the claimant's liability to pay rent by the amount of the rebate. If the claimant fails to pay any balance, that will create rent arrears. However, once the rebate is credited to the rent account, the claimant's liability to pay the amount of the rebate is discharged, and it is not resurrected by a decision that the rebate should not have been paid. If an authority fails to distinguish between the overpayment and the rent arrears, it will be difficult to tell whether there is a valid claim for possession.

A further complication is the treatment of payments by the claimant after the overpayment is debited from the rent account. The general rule is that a debtor owing more than one debt to a creditor may elect to attribute a payment to any of the debts and in such proportions as s/he chooses. If, as will usually be the case, D does not indicate whether s/he is seeking to pay off the rent arrears or the overpayment, and the authority does not indicate to which debt it wishes to apply the payment, the debt is applied to the debt that first arose in time: *Clayton's case* [1861] 1 Mer 572. Two examples help clarify how this rule works.

(1)   In week 1, D is in rent arrears of £100. In week 2, a £500 overpayment is debited from the rent account, putting D £600 in the red. In week 3, D pays £200 into the rent account. Even though the account is in arrears to the sum of £400, the authority cannot seek possession on the basis of non-payment of rent, since the whole of that sum is attributable to the debited overpayment.

(2)   D's rent is £100 a week. In week 1, D's account is £200 in credit. In week 2, the day before the rent becomes due, a £500 overpayment is debited, making arrears of £300. D does not pay rent in either week 2 or week 3, but then pays £200 into the account in week 4. The account is £300 in the red. If D specifically states that s/he is paying off the rent arrears, then the £300 would represent part of the overpayment. If s/he does not, then the £200 s/he paid is treated as paying off the overpayment, since that preceded the rent arrears in time. Claimants in such situations are therefore advised to specifically state that they are paying off their rent arrears rather than the overpayment.

Court proceedings

Once a determination has been made that an overpayment is recoverable, a debt is created between the authority and D for which the authority may sue in the County Court. The claim must be brought within the relevant time limit, which is six years in England and Wales: s2 Limitation Act 1980. In Scotland, it is five years: s6, Sch 1 para 1 Prescription and Limitation (Scotland) Act 1973.

A number of recent cases have considered the extent to which D can raise a defence or counterclaim to such proceedings.

Defence alleging invalid determination. It is an essential pre-condition of recovery that a valid determination be issued by the authority complying with the requirements of Sch 9 para 15. If no such determination is issued, no debt is created and the authority may not sue for the amount: *Warwick DC v Freeman* (1994) 27 HLR 616, CA. In *Plymouth CC v Gigg* (1997) 30 HLR 284, CA, *Freeman* was distinguished and it is submitted that it remains good law on this point. The Court of Appeal so confirmed in *Haringey LBC v Awaritefe* (1999) 32 HLR 517.

Registration as a recoverable debt at court

SSAA s75(7) will permit the authority to avoid the need to bring proceedings by registering the overpayment at the relevant local court. Once registration is carried out, the authority may utilise the court's powers of enforcement such as the use of bailiffs and attachment of earnings orders.

In England and Wales, the relevant procedure is prescribed by Order 25 rule 12 of the County Court Rules 1981, now found in Sch 2 of the Civil Procedure Rules 1998. The authority must complete Form N322 certifying the amount due and attach a "copy of the award" which presumably means a copy of the final determination that the overpayment is recoverable and is to be recovered. This must be done within six years of the final determination: s7 Limitation Act 1980. The court order will be made by a court officer. If D wishes to challenge the validity of the determination, an application should be made to the District Judge to set aside the officer's order as one given in the absence of D.

There are equivalent procedures available in relation to the "extract registered decree arbitral" in the Sheriff Court in Scotland.

Compensation order

Where D is convicted of an offence in relation to the overpayment, the authority can ask the court to make a compensation order under s35 Powers of Criminal Courts Act 1973. This option is rarely used. Any authority with a compensation order in its favour must deduct the amount of the order from the amount it seeks to recover, otherwise there will be double recovery: *CIS 683/1994* para 5.

Diminution of capital

103.–(1)   Where in the case of a recoverable overpayment, in consequence of a misrepresentation or failure to disclose a material fact (in either case whether fraudulent or otherwise) as to a person's capital, or an error, other than one to which regulation 100(2) (effect of official error) refers, as to the amount of a person's capital, the overpayment was in respect of a period ("the overpayment period") of more than 13 benefit weeks, the relevant authority shall, for the purpose only of calculating the amount of that overpayment–

   (a)   at the end of the first 13 benefit weeks of the overpayment period, treat the amount of that capital as having been reduced by the amount of housing benefit overpaid during those 13 weeks;

   (b)   at the end of each subsequent period of 13 benefit weeks, if any, of the overpayment period, treat the amount of that capital as having been further reduced by the amount of housing benefit overpaid during the immediately preceding 13 benefit weeks.

   (2)   Capital shall not be treated as reduced over any period other than 13 benefit weeks or in any circumstances other than those for which paragraph (1) provides.

Definitions

"capital" – see Part 6, Section 6.
"overpayment" – see reg 99.

General Note

Regs 103 and 104 deal with three categories of deduction that may be made in calculating the amount of the recoverable overpayment. Calculation of amounts can be a complex process and a systematic approach is required. The following method should ensure that mistakes are minimised.

(1)   Determine the dates between which the claimant has been paid too much benefit.

(2)   Check that the criteria for recovery are met for the whole of that period. This will often not be the case. For example, A is overpaid for 10 weeks due to the authority failing to adjust her/his benefit after s/he told them about an award of contributory ESA. On the facts of the case, it was not reasonable for A to realise that s/he was being overpaid until the fourth week. The first three weeks of benefit will not be recoverable and should be disregarded for the purposes of calculating the amount. The period that is left is the relevant period.

(3)   Calculate the full amount of benefit paid during the relevant period.

(4)   Determine whether the claimant, or her/his partner, should have been receiving any lesser amount during the relevant period. If so, this should be deducted from the amount of benefit obtained under step (3): reg 104(1).

(5)   In a rent rebate case, determine whether the claimant has paid too much rent for the period. If so, deduct the excess: reg 104(2).

(6)   Where the claimant has had too much capital, consider the application of the diminishing capital rule under reg 103.

The claimant is not entitled to have other amounts deducted, such as housing costs which ought to have been met under IS or income-based JSA where the claimant mistakenly claimed HB instead. However, the authority can be asked to consider exercising its discretion not to recover an appropriate portion of the overpayment in such circumstances.

Analysis

The injustice that reg 103 seeks to address concerns cases where overpayments arise through excess capital. Had HB been refused or reduced because of excess capital, the claimant would presumably have spent part of the capital on rent and eventually the level of capital would have reduced below the statutory limits. Without this provision, a claimant who would have fallen below one of the limits through such expenditure had the capital been properly taken into account would never qualify for the correct level of HB, since s/he did not in fact spend any of the capital.

Paragraph (1)

When the regulation applies. The rule comes into operation only where the relevant period is at least 13 weeks and then only in the following two cases.

(1)   Where the authority is misled as to an amount of the capital. For the meaning of "misrepresentation" and the other words and phrases in the first part of reg 103(1), see the Analysis to reg 101. It does not have to be the claimant who misled the authority about the amount of capital. Moreover, it does not have to be the claimant's capital.

(2)   Where there is an error as to the amount of the claimant's capital. It does not matter who makes the error. The reference to reg 100(2) means that if the error is an official error and the overpayment is irrecoverable because the other two criteria are met (see the Analysis to reg 100), the regulation has no application. If, however, there is more than one official error and the three criteria are met in relation to only one of them, then reg 103 will apply to such overpayment as has been made in consequence of the other error.

"for the purpose only of calculating the amount of that overpayment". This makes it clear that reg 100 has no application in other cases. It cannot, for example, assist a claimant seeking to backdate a claim who had capital of just over one of the relevant limits. More importantly, it does not apply in respect of the claimant's future entitlement to HB after the end of the overpayment period. Until the actual capital goes below the relevant limit, the claimant's actual capital will affect her/his entitlement.

The operation of the rule. At the end of each successive period of 13 weeks, the claimant's capital is treated as if reduced by the amount of the overpayment during that 13 weeks. However, in calculating the correct amount of HB which should have been payable (so as to calculate the amount actually overpaid), note the possible effect of the 65 per cent taper under s130(3)(b) SSCBA 1992 and reg 71 of these regulations if the tariff income from the capital gave the claimant an income figure in excess of her/his applicable amount.

It is not clear whether expenditure by the claimant during the same period should be taken into account, assuming that such expenditure is not caught by the diminishing capital rule. Para (2) probably does not mean that such expenditure should be ignored. It is suggested that it should be taken into account, since the regulation refers to "that capital" which is the capital that was not disclosed. As the claimant's capital, which was not disclosed, varied from time to time, logic would suggest that the reference to "that capital" must be read as being the capital (notional and actual) which the claimant actually had at the beginning of each 13-week period. If that is right, at the beginning of each 13-week period, any capital spent should be deducted and any capital acquired should be added. If this is not done, the diminishing capital rule would not work in such cases, because a claimant who reasonably purchased a car and reduced her/his capital from £7,000 to £3,500 would not get the benefit of the rule, whereas a claimant who received a legacy of £10,000 during the overpayment period could effectively insist that it was ignored. This interpretation is in accordance with the decision of the commissioner in *CIS 5825/ 1999* para 15.

Paragraph (2)

This makes it clear that no reduction can be applied where the overpayment period is less than 13 weeks or for any residue of less than that length of time. There is therefore no room to argue that the principle should be applied weekly.

Sums to be deducted in calculating recoverable overpayments

104.–(1)   Subject to paragraph (2), in calculating the amount of a recoverable overpayment, the relevant authority shall deduct any amount of housing benefit which should have been determined to be payable [² to the person from whom the overpayment is recoverable or their partner] in respect of the whole or part of the overpayment period–

(a)   on the basis of the claim as presented to the authority;

(b)   on the basis of the claim as it would have appeared had any misrepresentation or non-disclosure been remedied before the decision; or

(c)   on the basis of the claim as it would have appeared if any change of circumstances [¹, except a change of the dwelling which the claimant occupies as his home,] had been notified at the time that change occurred.

(2)   In the case of rent rebate only, in calculating the amount of a recoverable overpayment the relevant authority may deduct so much of any payment by way of rent in respect of the overpayment period which exceeds the amount, if any, which the claimant was liable to pay for that period under the original erroneous decision.

Amendments

1.   Amended by reg 8 of SI 2005 No 2904 as amended by Sch 2 para 29 of SI 2006 No 217 as from 10.4.06.

2.   Amended by reg 2(2) of SI 2012 No 645 as from 1.4.12.

Definitions
"payment" – see reg 2(1).
"rent" – see Part 3.
"rent rebate" – see ss134(1) and (2) and 191 SSAA.

General Note
This deals with two other deductions from the amount of an overpayment. See the General Note to reg 103. The rule was amended from 2 October 2000 to reverse the effect of the decision in *R v Wyre BC ex p Lord* [1997] unreported, 24 October, QBD (which itself was later overruled by the Court of Appeal in *R(H) 5/04*). The broad purpose of the new provisions is to ensure that an overpayment is "calculated with regard to the claimant's correct circumstances and any underlying entitlement deducted" (Circular HB/CTB A42/2000). In any case of doubt, regard should be had to that policy intent. This now covers the claimant's partner's entitlement to HB as well (and see the commentary to *JM v Tower Hamlets LB* [2015] UKUT 460 (AAC), in the Analysis below). However, *R(H) 1/05* holds (para 16) that it is for the claimant to prove the correct amount that s/he is entitled to for the overpayment period.

EW v Neath Port Talbot CBC [2009] UKUT 14 (AAC) pointed out that although the First-tier Tribunal need not consider any issue not raised by an appeal, in a challenge to recoverability of an overpayment, it is always wise for the tribunal to satisfy itself as to the calculation of that overpayment, and in particular, that the local authority has taken steps to calculate any amounts which it might be appropriate to offset. However, claimants should beware: where the local authority seeks further information from the claimant to enable it to make an appropriate offset, and the information is not provided, the local authority and the tribunal are unable to apply the relevant offsetting provisions and it will be difficult for the claimant to argue that they have not complied with reg 104.

Analysis
Para (1) deals with the basic entitlement to an offset. The wording "which should have been determined to be payable" emphasises that the exercise is looking into the past with the benefit of hindsight to see what the true circumstances are and to award benefit on that basis. Para (1) bears some resemblance to reg 13(b) Social Security (Payments on Account, Overpayments and Recovery) Regulations 1988 and so the commissioners' decisions on that provision may provide some assistance. There are important differences, however. There is no equivalent of sub-para (c) in reg 13(b) of the 1988 Regulations. Moreover, an amount may only be deducted if it was payable "in respect of the whole or any part of the overpayment period", which words do not appear in reg 13(b). The ruling in *R(IS) 5/92* (para 6), that it was permissible to offset an amount which should have been payable in a period before the overpayment period, cannot therefore be applied here.

Bearing in mind those differences in the provisions and having regard to the policy intention, the three considerations set out in sub-paras (a) to (c) need to be examined as follows.
(1)   Any additional amount that should have been awarded "on the basis of the claim as presented to the authority" must be deducted. This may include additional amounts that have nothing to do with the overpayment. If, for example, a claimant can show that an additional premium should have been awarded on the basis of assertions in the initial claim, it is open to her/him to present further evidence to support those assertions: *CIS 522/1992* para 10. Furthermore, "the claim as presented" includes any information that would have been elicited on a reasonable enquiry by the local authority: *R(IS) 5/92* para 8. However, since there is no appeal against the Secretary of State's decision as to whether to issue a certificate under Sch 7 para 1, it will not be possible to offset an alleged entitlement to extended payments against an overpayment: *CH 5553/2002* paras 15–18.
(2)   Any additional amount that should have been awarded if any misrepresentation or non-disclosure had been remedied before determination. This obviously means, for example, that if a claimant has been claiming as a single person while living together as husband and wife with a partner, any entitlement on the basis of a claim as a couple should be awarded: *CSIS 62/1991* para 10. However, sub-para (b) potentially has a wider application. The word "any" is of importance. If there are other erroneous statements or omissions on the form besides the statement or statements that led to the overpayment, they can also be corrected. It might be arguable that if a claimant failed to state matters that might have led to a higher award of benefit, that could be said to be a non-disclosure which should allow the true facts to be brought into account.
(3)   Sub-para (c), as already noted, is not to be found in reg 13 of the 1988 Regulations and is at first sight worded a little strangely. When "change of circumstances" is being talked about, it is usually in the context of a change that occurs in the benefit period after the claim is made and so it seems odd to talk of how a claim would have appeared had a change been notified. The point, however, is that sub-para (c) applies both to the claim that was extant at the beginning of the overpayment period and to any renewal claims within the overpayment period.
The local authority is not entitled to absolve itself from applying reg 104 by the non-return of a fresh claim form sent to the claimant after IIB had ceased. It was entitled to demand information under reg 86(1) notwithstanding the fact that the claim had ceased: *CH 4943/2001* paras 65–70. It is suggested that there is nothing in the Court

of Appeal's reasoning in *SSWP v Chiltern DC* (2003) HLR 1019, CA; reported as *R(H) 2/03* which allowed an appeal from some aspects of the commissioner's decision, which detracts from his reasoning on this point.

This issue was revisited by the Upper Tribunal in *JM v Tower Hamlets LB* [2015] UKUT 460 (AAC). In this case, the claimant's entitlement to HB had ceased when he went abroad for too long. His wife and four children remained in the rental properly but the wife did not make a claim for HB. The local authority argued that as the husband and wife could not make a joint claim for HB, the wife's entitlement was contingent on her making her own claim for HB. This argument found favour with the First-tier Tribunal but was rejected by the Upper Tribunal. Judge Knowles ruled (at paras 30–35):

"The Respondent acknowledges that regulation 104(1) was amended in 2002 to offset any entitlement attributable to a claimant's partner from the calculation of a recoverable overpayment. Its submission that a partner's entitlement cannot be considered to be part of the claim in which the overpayment occurred conflates two entirely separate matters.

The underlying entitlement of a partner as provided for in regulation 104(1) only affects the amount of the recoverable overpayment. It does not entitle the partner to the payment of benefit – the only way that could happen in these circumstances would be for the partner to make their own claim for benefit.

In this case there was no dispute that the original claim included details of the Appellant's wife and four children on the basis that she was dependent on the Appellant. There was no dispute that she and the children had occupied the property throughout the Appellant's absence and it was also accepted that she had made no claim for benefit during the Appellant's absence.....

The wording of regulation 104(1) is plain. Housing benefit to which either the claimant or his partner would have been entitled in respect of the whole or part of the overpayment period shall be deducted from the amount of the recoverable overpayment. Application of regulation 104(1) requires a two stage process: first of all to look into the past to see what the true circumstances of a claim were had the claimant submitted a valid claim for benefit and to calculate benefit due to either the claimant or his partner on that basis. Having calculated the amount of benefit due, regulation 104(1) then requires the local authority to deduct that amount from the overpayment recoverable from the claimant. This two stage process is consistent with the comments made by the Court of Appeal in R(H) 5/04....

The tribunal found that the Appellant's claim ended when his entitlement ended in accordance with regulations 7 and 8 of the HB Regulations and the relevant council tax regulations. He had no underlying entitlement and thus the amount of the recoverable overpayment had been correctly calculated. The tribunal said it had no jurisdiction over any matters pertaining to the "separate claim and entitlement" of the Appellant's wife to either housing or council tax benefit.

What the tribunal failed to exercise was its jurisdiction to determine the amount of the recoverable overpayment from the Appellant by applying regulation 104(1) correctly. The exercise of that jurisdiction required it to go through the steps I have outlined....above...."

It appears from *CH 2349/2002* (para 11) that in considering non-disclosed income and the effect of it on the claimant's notional HB entitlement under reg 104, the claimant's income may be assessed on a week-by-week basis and need not be averaged out under reg 27(1)(a) HB Regs.

Para (2) will principally deal with errors in handling local authority rent accounts. If the overpayment has been wholly or partly caused by the claimant being asked to pay too much rent, as a result of which too much HB is credited to the rent account, then the extra rent is deductible from the amount. The authority will already have received the excess rent.

[¹Sums to be deducted in calculating recoverable overpayments where the claimant has changed dwelling

104A.–(1)   This regulation applies where an overpayment has occurred in the following circumstances–

(a)   a claimant has moved from the dwelling previously occupied as his home ("dwelling A") to another dwelling which he occupies as his home ("dwelling B");

(b)   the claimant has been awarded housing benefit in the form of a rent allowance in respect of dwelling A to which he is not entitled because he is no longer occupying or treated as occupying dwelling A as his home;

(c)   housing benefit is paid to the same person in respect of the claimant's occupation of dwelling B as it was paid to in respect of dwelling A; and

(d)   the same relevant authority is responsible for paying the housing benefit in respect of dwelling A and dwelling B.

(2)   Where this regulation applies, in calculating the amount of the overpayment which is recoverable the relevant authority may at its discretion deduct an amount equal to the claimant's weekly entitlement to housing benefit in respect of dwelling B for the

number of benefit weeks equal to the number of weeks during which the claimant was overpaid housing benefit in respect of dwelling A.

(3) Where a sum has been deducted under paragraph (2), an equivalent sum shall be treated as having been paid in respect of the claimant's entitlement to housing benefit in respect of dwelling B for the number of benefit weeks equal to the number of weeks during which the claimant was overpaid housing benefit in respect of dwelling A.]

Amendment

1. Inserted by reg 2(3) of SI 2009 No 2608 as from 1.4.10 (5.4.10 where rent payable weekly or in multiples of a week).

Recovery of overpayments from prescribed benefits

105.–(1) [³ Subject to paragraph (1B),] For the purposes of section 75(4) of the Administration Act (recovery of overpaid housing benefit by deduction from other benefits), the benefits prescribed by this regulation are–

(a) any benefit except guardian's allowance;

(b) income support under Part 7 of the Act;

(c) any benefit payable under the legislation of any member State other than the United Kingdom concerning the branches of social security mentioned in Article 4(1) of Regulation (EEC) No 1408/71 [⁶, as amended from time to time,] on the application of social security schemes to employed persons, to self-employed persons and to members of teir families moving within the Community, [⁶ or in Article 3(1) of Regulation (EC) No 883/2004 of the European Parliament and of the Council of 29 April 2004, as amended from time to time, on the coordination of social security systems,] whether or not the benefit has been acquired by virtue of the provisions of [⁶ either Regulation, as amended from time to time];

(d) a jobseeker's allowance;

(e) state pension credit.

[² (f) an employment and support allowance.]

[⁴ (g) personal independence payment.]

[⁵ (h) universal credit.

[¹ (1A) For the purposes of paragraph (1)(c) the term "member State" shall be understood to include Switzerland in accordance with and subject to the provisions of Annex II of the Agreement between the European Community and its Member States and the Swiss Confederation on the free movement of persons, signed at Brussels on 21st June 1999 [⁶ ,as amended from time to time].]

[³ (1B) For the purposes of section 75(4) of the Administration Act, where recovery is sought from the claimant's partner under regulation 102(1ZA), the benefits prescribed by this regulation are–

(a) income support under Part 7 of the Act;

(b) income-based jobseeker's allowance;

(c) state pension credit; and

(d) income-related employment and support allowance.]

[⁴ (e) personal independence payment.]

[⁵ (f) universal credit.]

[³ (2) The Secretary of State shall, if requested to do so by an authority under regulation 102 (method of recovery), recover a recoverable overpayment by deduction from any of the benefits prescribed in paragraph (1) or (in the case of the claimant's partner) any of the benefits prescribed in paragraph (1B) provided that the Secretary of State is satisfied that–

(a) a recoverable overpayment has been made in consequence of a misrepresentation of or a failure to disclose a material fact (in either case whether fraudulently or otherwise), by a claimant or any other person to whom a payment of housing benefit has been made; and

(b) the person from whom it is sought to recover the overpayment is receiving sufficient amounts of any of the benefits prescribed in paragraph (1) or (1B) (as the case may be) to enable deductions to be made for the recovery of the overpayment.]

(3)   In paragraph (1)(a), "benefit" has the meaning it has in section 122(1) of the Act.

Amendments

1.   Inserted by reg 9 of SI 2005 No 2904 as amended by Sch 2 para 29 of SI 2006 No 217 as from 10.4.06.
2.   Amended by reg 22 of SI 2008 No 1082 as from 27.10.08.
3.   Amended by reg 4(4) of SI 2008 No 2824 as from 6.4.09.
4.   Amended by reg 33(2) of SI 2013 No 384 as from 8.4.13.
5.   Amended by reg 33(2) of SI 2013 No 384 as from 29.4.13.
6.   Amended by reg 4 and Sch para 10 of SI 2018 No 1084 as from 15.11.18.

Definitions

"claimant" – see reg 2(1).
"member State" of the EEC – see para (1)(c) and (1A).
"recoverable overpayment" – see reg 100.

General Note

This specifies the categories of benefit from which the Secretary of State may make reductions to recover an overpayment of HB. See the Analysis to reg 102 for full details. See also reg 106.

Prescribed benefits

106.–(1)   The benefits prescribed for the purposes of section 75(5) and (7) of the Administration Act (recovery of overpayments) are those set out in the following paragraphs.

(2)   Prescribed benefits within section 75(5) of the Administration Act (benefits to which a landlord or agent is entitled) are–

(a)   housing benefit; and

(b)   those benefits prescribed from time to time in regulation 105(1) (recovery of overpayments from prescribed benefits), but only in cases where–

(i)   an authority has, pursuant to regulation 102 (method of recovery), requested the Secretary of State to recover an overpayment of housing benefit from such benefits; and

(ii)   the Secretary of State is satisfied as to the matters prescribed in paragraph (3)(a) and (b) of regulation 105.

(3)   Housing benefit is prescribed for the purposes of section 75(5)(b) or (c) of the Administration Act (benefits paid to a landlord or agent to discharge an obligation owed by another person).

(4)   Prescribed benefits within section 75(7) of the Administration Act (benefits recoverable from the county court or the sheriff court) are housing benefit and those benefits prescribed from time to time in regulation 105(1).

General Note

This specifies the benefits from which recovery may be made under SSAA s75(5). There is a certain amount of duplication of the powers which already exist under other regulations in Part 13.

Analysis

Para (2). SSAA s75(5)(a) authorises recovery from benefits to which the landlord or agent is entitled personally. HB is prescribed, along with benefits falling within reg 105(1), provided the normal procedure prescribed by regs 102 and 105 is followed. This provision does not appear to add to the powers that authorities already had.

Para (3). SSAA s75(5)(b) authorises recovery from benefits which the landlord or agent is paid on behalf of claimant A, when claimant A was overpaid. SSAA s75(5)(c) authorises recovery from benefits paid on behalf of claimant A, when claimant B was overpaid. For the effect on rent obligations in the former case, see reg 107, and in the latter case see s75(6) which provides that B's obligation is discharged. Note also Sch 9 para 15(2) that requires both landlord and claimant B to be informed of this fact.

Para (4). SSAA s75(7) provides that prescribed benefits may be recovered simply by registering the debt as recoverable under the respective procedures in the County Court and Sheriff Court. Para (4) provides that these powers apply to recovery of HB.

[¹ Recovery by deduction from earnings

106A.–(1)   Any overpayment which is recoverable by virtue of regulation 100 may be recovered by a relevant authority by deduction from the earnings of the person from whom it is recoverable.

(2)   Part 6 of the Social Security (Overpayments and Recovery) Regulations 2013 applies in relation to the recovery of overpayments by deduction from the earnings of a person specified in paragraph (1) by a relevant authority as it applies to the recovery of recoverable amounts by deduction from the earnings of persons under that Part of those Regulations by an appropriate authority]

Amendment

1.   Inserted by reg 33(3) of SI 2013 No 384 as from 8.4.13.

Restrictions on recovery of rent and consequent notifications

107.–(1)   Where, pursuant to section 75(5)(b) of the Administration Act, an amount has been recovered by deduction from housing benefit paid to a person (referred to as "the landlord" in this regulation) to discharge (in whole or in part) an obligation owed to him by the person on whose behalf the recoverable amount was paid (referred to as "the tenant" in this regulation) that obligation shall, in a case to which paragraph (2) applies, be taken to be discharged by the amount of the deduction.

(2)   This paragraph applies in a case where the amount recoverable from the landlord relates to an overpayment of housing benefit in relation to which the landlord has–

(a)   agreed to pay a penalty pursuant to section 115A of the Administration Act (penalty as an alternative to prosecution); or

(b)   been convicted of an offence arising under the Act or any other enactment.

(3)   In any case to which paragraph (2) applies or will apply when recovery is made the authority that has determined that there is an overpayment and that it is recoverable from the landlord shall notify both the landlord and the tenant that–

(a)   the overpayment that it has recovered or that it has determined to recover ("that sum") is or will be one to which paragraph (2) applies; and

(b)   the landlord has no right in relation to that sum against the tenant, and that his obligation to the landlord shall be taken to be discharged by the amount so recovered.

General Note

This provides for the effects of recovery from a landlord by deductions from future payments of HB in respect of a claimant, where the same claimant was the one overpaid. By s75(6), where recovery is made from a different claimant's HB, her/his obligation to pay rent is always discharged.

Analysis

The effect of recovery of an overpayment from a landlord on the extent of the overpaid tenant's rent arrears has always been a cause of controversy. See the Analysis to regs 95(2) and 105. Reg 95(2) is in conflict with the provisions in reg 107. Even if reg 95(2) is validly made (as to which see p575) it is suggested that reg 107, made as it is under a specific rather than a general enabling power, must take precedence in relation to overpayments made after 3 November 1997.

Para (1) confirms the effect of the regulation. If the case falls within para (2), then the tenant's obligation is to be treated as discharged by the amount of the deduction. Presumably, the time of deemed payment of rent is the time when the deduction is made. This may be significant in possession proceedings – eg, where the landlord is seeking a compulsory order under Ground 2 in Sch 2 Housing Act 1988.

Curiously, the regulation does not state what happens in cases that do not fall within para (2). If reg 95(2) is valid, then the tenant is in rent arrears. If it is not, then the analysis in *R v Haringey LBC ex p Ayub* (1992) 25 HLR 566, QBD suggests that the tenant's obligation will be discharged. If reg 95(2) is invalid, the question is whether s75(6) and reg 107 change the position by implication. Certainly it can be argued that by saying that the obligation is discharged in prescribed cases, s75(6) is saying that it is not discharged in other cases. However, s75(6) does not say that the obligation is discharged *only* in prescribed cases and so there would be a powerful contrary argument that Parliament cannot be deemed to have changed the existing law as between landlord and tenant without explicitly saying so.

Para (2). The requirement is that the landlord has been required to pay a penalty under SSAA s115A or convicted of an offence "in relation to" that overpayment. It is suggested that this would cover, for example, a conviction under SSAA s113 for failing to supply information under the Housing Benefit (Information from

Landlords and Agents) Regulations 1997 that is connected with the making of the overpayment. It would appear that the landlord itself must be convicted of the offence. So if a company officer is convicted of an offence, that is insufficient to bring para (2) into effect because the company has a separate legal existence. On the other hand, as the singular must include the plural, conviction of one of joint landlords will bring para (2) into force, as will conviction of one of the partners in a partnership that holds property.

Para (3) provides that both landlord and tenant must be informed of the applicability of para (2) and that the landlord has no right to recover it from the tenant. It should logically have been an amendment to Sch 9.

PART 14
Information

SECTION 1
Claims and information

General Note on Section 1

The regulations in this Section, made principally under s7A SSAA, confirm the powers of local authorities in relation to the obtaining, retention and transmission of information in relation to claims for HB. This will prevent any allegation of a breach of the Data Protection Act 2018 where any dealing with information in the ways specified below takes place.

For powers to compel the provision of information, see Part 7 of the SSAA as amended by the SSFA (see p70). Reg 112 enables the Secretary of State or parties acting under her/his direction to demand information from a local authority.

Interpretation
108. In this Section–
[¹ "county council" means a county council in England, but only if the council has made an arrangement in accordance with regulation 83(4)(g) or 109(3);]
"local authority" means an authority administering housing benefit;
"relevant authority" means–
  (a)   the Secretary of State; or
  (b)   a person providing services to the Secretary of State; [¹ or
  (c)   a county council;]
"relevant information" means information or evidence relating to the administration of claims to or awards of housing benefit.

Amendment

1.   Amended by reg 7(3) of SI 2007 No 2911 as from 31.10.07.

[¹Collection of information
109.–(1)   The Secretary of State, or a person providing services to him, may receive or obtain relevant information from–
  (a)   persons making, or who have made, claims for housing benefit; or
  (b)   other persons in connection with such claims.
  (2)   In paragraph (1) references to persons who have made claims for housing benefit include persons to whom awards of benefit have been made on those claims.
  (3)   Where a county council has made an arrangement with a local authority, or a person authorised to exercise any function of a local authority relating to housing benefit [²], to receive and obtain information or evidence relating to claims for housing benefit, the council may receive or obtain the information or evidence from–
  (a)   persons making claims for housing benefit; or
  (b)   other persons in connection with such claims.
  (4)   A county council may receive information or evidence relating to an award of housing benefit which is supplied by–
  (a)   the person to whom the award has been made; or
  (b)   other persons in connection with the award.]

Amendments

1.   Substituted by reg 7(4) of SI 2007 No 2911 as from 31.10.07.
2.   Amended by reg 3 and Sch 1 of SI 2013 No 458 as from 1.4.13.

[¹Verifying information

109A. A relevant authority may verify relevant information supplied to, or obtained by, the authority in accordance with regulation 109.]

Amendment

1. Inserted by reg 7(5) of SI 2007 No 2911 as from 31.10.07.

[¹Recording and holding information

110. A relevant authority which obtains relevant information or to whom such information is supplied–

(a) shall make a record of such information; and

(b) may hold that information, whether as supplied or obtained or recorded, for the purpose of forwarding it to the person or authority for the time being administering housing benefit.]

Amendment

1. Substituted by reg 7(6) of SI 2007 No 2911 as from 31.10.07.

Forwarding of information

111. A relevant authority which holds relevant information–

(a) shall forward it to the person or authority for the time being administering claims to or awards of housing benefit to which the relevant information relates, being–

(i) a local authority;

(ii) a person providing services to a local authority; or

(iii) a person authorised to exercise any function of a local authority relating to housing benefit; and

[¹ (b) may, if the relevant authority is the Secretary of State or a person providing services to the Secretary of State, continue to hold a record of such information, whether as supplied or obtained or recorded, for such period as he considers appropriate.]

Amendment

1. Substituted by reg 7(7) of SI 2007 No 2911 as from 31.10.07.

Request for information

112. A relevant authority which holds information or evidence relating to social security matters shall forward such information or evidence as may be requested to the person or authority making that request, provided that–

(a) the request is made by–

(i) a local authority;

(ii) a person providing services to a local authority; or

(iii) a person authorised to exercise any function of a local authority relating to housing benefit; and

(b) the information or evidence requested includes relevant information;

(c) the relevant authority is able to provide the information or evidence requested in the form in which it was originally supplied or obtained; and

(d) provision of the information or evidence requested is considered necessary by the relevant authority to the proper performance by a local authority of its functions relating to housing benefit.

SECTION 2

Information from landlords and agents and between authorities etc.

General Note on Section 2

The Housing Benefit (Information from Landlords and Agents) Regulations 1997 SI No.2436 implemented s126A SSAA. These provisions are now in reg 113 (in part) and regs 117 to 121 HB Regs and reg 94 (in part) and regs 98 to 102 HB(SPC) Regs. These set out the circumstances in which local authorities may require information from landlords and agents, the information which must be supplied, the time limit for supplying it and the manner in which the information must be provided. Failure to comply with a notice requiring information under s126A is a criminal offence and is a factor which a local authority could take into account when considering whether a landlord is a "fit and proper person" to receive payments of HB under regs 95 and 96 HB Regs (or regs 76 and 77 HB(SPC) Regs).

Interpretation

113. In this Section–

"the notice" means the notice prescribed in regulation 118(1)(b) (circumstances for requiring information);

"relevant information" means such information as is prescribed in regulation 119 (relevant information);

"the requirer" means a person within regulation 117 (requiring information from landlords and agents), who requires information pursuant to that regulation;

"the supplier" means an appropriate person who is required, pursuant to regulations 117 and 118, to supply relevant information and any person who is not so required is not, for the purpose of supplying information pursuant to section 126A of the Administration Act and these Regulations, an appropriate person.

[¹ Information to be provided to rent officers

114A.–(1) This paragraph applies to every claim for or award of housing benefit in the form of a rent allowance where the eligible rent has been, or is to be determined, in accordance with–

(a) regulation 12(3)(a) (rent) or 12C (eligible rent and maximum rent), as the case may require;

(b) [² regulation 12D] (eligible rent and the maximum rent (LHA)) or any of regulations 12E to 12K (transitional protection for pathfinder cases), as the case may require; or

(c) regulations 12 (rent) and 13 (maximum rent) as set out in paragraph 5 of Schedule 3 to the Consequential Provisions Regulations.

(2) No earlier than the first, and no later than the fifth, working day of every month a relevant authority shall provide the following information to the rent officer in relation to every claim for or award of housing benefit to which paragraph (1) applied in the preceding month–

(a) the address, including any room or unit number, house or flat number or name, and the postcode of the dwelling to which the claim or award relates;

(b) where the claim or award relates to mooring charges for a houseboat, or payments in respect of the site on which a caravan or mobile home stands, the mooring or plot number and the address of the mooring or site, including the postcode;

(c) the date on which the tenancy began;

(d) the amount of rent and the rental period, whether calendar monthly, four weekly, weekly or some other period;

(e) where the claimant has the use of two or more bedrooms, the number of bedrooms and rooms suitable for living in that there are in the dwelling, and in this sub-paragraph "bedroom" does not include a bedroom which the claimant shares with any person other than a member of his household, a non-dependant of his, or a person who pays rent to him or his partner;

(f) whether the tenant (together with his partner where he has one) has exclusive use of only one bedroom, and if so, whether they have exclusive use of a kitchen, bathroom, toilet and a room suitable for living in;

(g) whether the tenant has exclusive use of only one bedroom, and if so, which, if any, of the following the tenancy provides for him to share–

(i) a kitchen;

(ii) a bathroom;

(iii) a toilet; or

(iv) a room suitable for living in;

(h) the date on which entitlement to housing benefit began; and

(i)   where applicable, the date on which entitlement to housing benefit ended.

(3)   Where the relevant authority is required to apply to the rent officer for a board and attendance determination by virtue of regulation 13D(10) (determination of a maximum rent (LHA)), it shall provide the following information in the application to the Rent Officer–

(a)   the address, including any room or unit number, house or flat number or name and the postcode of the dwelling to which the claim or award relates;

(b)   the date on which the tenancy began;

(c)   the length of the tenancy;

(d)   the total amount of those payments referred to in regulation 12(1) (rent) which the claimant is liable to make in respect of the dwelling which he occupies as his home;

(e)   whether those payments include any charges for water, sewerage or allied environmental services or charges in respect of meals or fuel which are ineligible for housing benefit; and

(f)   where those payments include any charges that are ineligible for housing benefit by reason of paragraph 1(a)(iv) and (c) to (f) of Schedule 1 (ineligible service charges), that such charges are included, and the value of those charges as determined by that authority pursuant to regulation 12B(2) and that Schedule.

(4)   Where the relevant authority has identified charges to which paragraph (3)(f) applies, it shall–

(a)   deduct those charges from the total amount of those payments which, in accordance with paragraph (3)(d), it has stated that the claimant is liable to make in respect of the dwelling which he occupies as his home; and

(b)   notify that total so reduced to the rent officer in its application.

(5)   Where a relevant authority has received notification from the rent officer that a substantial part of the rent is attributable to board and attendance, it shall provide the information referred to in paragraphs (7) and (8), except for such information as it has already provided in accordance with paragraphs (3) and (4).

(6)   Where the relevant authority is required to apply to the rent officer for a determination by virtue of regulation 14(1) (requirement to refer to rent officers), it shall provide the information referred to in paragraphs (7) to (9) in the application to the rent officer.

(7)   In relation to the dwelling to which the claim or award relates, the relevant authority shall provide the following information–

(a)   the address, including any room or unit number, house or flat number or name and the postcode of the dwelling;

(b)   where the claim or award relates to mooring charges for a houseboat, or payments in respect of the site on which a caravan or mobile home stands, the mooring or plot number and the address of the mooring or site, including the postcode;

(c)   whether the dwelling is–

    (i)   a detached house;

    (ii)   a semi-detached house;

    (iii)   a terraced house;

    (iv)   a maisonette;

    (v)   a detached bungalow;

    (vi)   a semi-detached bungalow;

    (vii)   a flat in a house;

    (viii)   a flat in a block;

    (ix)   a flat over a shop;

    (x)   a bedsit or rooms or a studio flat;

    (xi)   a hostel;

    (xii)   a caravan, mobile home or houseboat;

    (xiii)   board and lodgings;

    (xiv)   a hotel;

    (xv)   a care home;

       (xvi) an independent hospital; or

       (xvii) some other description of dwelling, and if so what;

  (d)   whether the dwelling has central heating, a garden, a garage or a parking space;

  (e)   how many rooms suitable for living in there are–

      (i)   in the dwelling;

      (ii)   in the dwelling which the claimant shares with any person other than a member of his household, a non-dependant of his, or a person who pays rent to him or his partner;

  (f)   how many bedsitting rooms there are in the categories (e)(i) and (ii);

  (g)   how many bedrooms there are in the categories (e)(i) and (ii);

  (h)   how many bathrooms or toilets there are in the categories (e)(i) and (ii); and

  (i)   such other information as the rent officer may reasonably require to make a determination.

(8)   In relation to the tenancy to which the claim or award relates, the relevant authority shall provide the following information–

  (a)   the information referred to in paragraphs (3)(d) to (f) and (4);

  (b)   if the tenancy is furnished, and if so, to what extent;

  (c)   the rental period, whether calendar monthly, four weekly, weekly or some other period;

  (d)   the length of the tenancy;

  (e)   when the tenancy began and, if appropriate, when it ended;

  (h)   the landlord's or letting agent's name;

  (i)   the landlord's or letting agent's business address;

  (j)   whether the landlord is a housing association [3, private registered provider of social housing] or registered social landlord; and

  (k)   such other information as the rent officer may reasonably require to make a determination.

(9)   In relation to the claimant and the other occupiers of the dwelling to which the claim or award relates, the relevant authority shall provide the following information–

  (a)   such information regarding the relationship of the claimant to the occupiers and the occupiers to each other, as is necessary for the rent officer to make the determination;

  (b)   the age and sex of each occupier under 18;

  (c)   whether the claimant is or may be a young individual;

[4 (ca) whether [5 any person mentioned in regulation 13D(3A)(a)] is a person who requires overnight care;] and

  (d)   any other information that is relevant to the rent officer in making the determination, including visits to the dwelling.

(10)   Where a rent officer serves a notice under article 5 (insufficient information) of the Rent Officers Order the relevant authority shall supply the further information required under this regulation, or confirm whether information already supplied is correct and, if it is not, supply the correct information.

(11)   Where the relevant authority refers a case to the rent officer in accordance with regulation 14 as in force before the coming into force of regulation 8 of the Housing Benefit (Local Housing Allowance and Information Sharing) Amendment Regulations 2007, it shall notify the rent officer that the referral is made in accordance with regulation 14 as in force before the coming into force of regulation 8 of those Regulations.

(12)   In this regulation–

"tenancy" includes–

  (a)   in Scotland, any other right of occupancy; and

  (b)   in any other case, a licence to occupy premises,

and reference to a tenant, landlord or any other expression appropriate to a tenancy shall be construed accordingly;

"working day" means any day other than a Saturday, a Sunday, Christmas Day, Good Friday or a day which is a bank holiday under the Banking and Financial Dealings Act 1971 in the jurisdiction in which the area of the relevant authority is situated.]

Amendments

1.   Inserted by reg 3(2) of SI 2007 No 2868, as amended by reg 4(2)(b) of SI 2008 No 586, as from 7.4.08.
2.   Amended by reg 4(2)(b) of SI 2008 No 586 as from 7.4.08.
3.   Amended by art 4 and Sch 1 para 53 of SI 2010 No 671 as from 1.4.10.
4.   Inserted by reg 2(9) of SI 2010 No 2835 as from 1.4.11.
5.   Amended by reg 4(5) of SI 2017 No 213 as from 1.4.17.

General Note

The information required by para (3)(e) and (f) relates to applications for board and attendance determinations and whether the rent paid includes payments in respect of certain items that are ineligible to be met by HB. The authority must state the total amounts eligible to be met by HB under reg 12(1) and then set out information about ineligible charges relating to the following.

(1)   Water, sewerage and allied environmental services: sub-para (e).
(2)   Ineligible charges for meals and fuel: sub-para (e).
(3)   The cleaning of rooms and windows except the exterior of windows which cannot be cleaned by anyone in the household or communal areas: sub-para (f).
(4)   The provision of an emergency alarm system: sub-para (f).
(5)   Medical expenses: sub-para (f).
(6)   Nursing or personal care: sub-para (f).
(7)   General counselling or support services: sub-para (f).

Paras (6) to (9) set out the information which the local authority must give to the rent officer when it applies for a determination under reg 14(1) HB Regs. Note that under para (9), if the authority believes the claimant is or may be a "young individual" or a person is a "person who requires overnight care" (see reg 2(1) for the definitions), the authority must say so.

[¹ Evidence and information required by rent officers 114.]

Amendment

1.   Omitted by reg 3(3) of SI 2007 No 2868 as from 7.4.08.

[¹Information to be supplied by an authority to another authority

115.–(1)   This regulation applies for the purposes of section 128A of the Administration Act (duty of an authority to disclose information to another authority).

(2)   Information is to be disclosed by one authority to another where–

(a)   there is a mover who is or was in receipt of housing benefit from Authority "A";

(b)   either the mover's new dwelling is within the area of another Authority "B" or the mover is liable or treated as liable to make payments in respect of the new dwelling to housing authority B; and

(c)   the mover is entitled to an extended payment in accordance with regulation 72.

(3)   Authority A shall disclose to Authority B–

(a)   the amount of the extended payment calculated in accordance with regulation 72C(2) (amount of extended payment – movers);

(b)   the date that entitlement to the extended payment will commence or has commenced;

(c)   the date that entitlement to the extended payment ceased or will cease;

(d)   the date of the move from Authority A to Authority B;

(e)   where the extended payment will be paid by Authority A to Authority B in accordance with regulation 72C(3)(a) (payment of extended payment to the second authority)–

    (i)   the amount that Authority A will pay to Authority B in accordance with that paragraph; and

    (ii)   any other information required by Authority B to enable Authority A to make the payment in accordance with that paragraph; and

(f)   if any deduction was being made in respect of a recoverable overpayment.

(4)   Authority B shall disclose to Authority A–

(a)   if a mover's liability to make payments for the new dwelling is to Authority B; and

(b)   where the extended payment will be paid by Authority A to Authority B in accordance with regulation 72C(3)(a)–

    (i)   any information required by Authority A to enable Authority A to make the payment in accordance with that paragraph; and

    (ii)   the date on which Authority B receives any such payment.]

Amendment

1.   Substituted by reg 2(3) of SI 2008 No 959 as from 6.10.08.

General Note

This facilitates the passing of information between authorities where there is entitlement to extended payments under regs 72 to 72E and the claimant moves from the area of the authority where s/he had previously been in receipt of HB to another. Reg 72C deals with these so-called "movers". See also s128A SSAA on p78. See reg 116 where there is entitlement to an extended payment under regs 73 to 73E.

[¹Supply of information – extended payments (qualifying contributory benefits)

116.–(1) This regulation applies for the purposes of section 122E(3) of the Administration Act (duty of an authority to supply information to another authority).

(2)   Information is to be disclosed by one authority to another where–

(a)   there is a mover who is or was in receipt of housing benefit from Authority "A";

(b)   either the mover's new dwelling is within the area of another Authority "B" or the mover is liable or treated as liable to make payments in respect of the new dwelling to housing authority B; and

(c)   the mover is entitled to an extended payment (qualifying contributory benefits) in accordance with regulation 73.

(3)   Authority A shall disclose to Authority B–

(a)   the amount of the extended payment (qualifying contributory benefits) calculated in accordance with regulation 73C(2) (amount of extended payment – movers);

(b)   the date that entitlement to the extended payment will commence or has commenced;

(c)   the date that entitlement to the extended payment ceased or will cease;

(d)   the date of the move from Authority A to Authority B;

(e)   where the extended payment will be paid by Authority A to Authority B in accordance with regulation 73C(3)(a) (payment of the extended payment to the second authority)–

    (i)   the amount that Authority A will pay to Authority B in accordance with that paragraph; and

    (ii)   any other information required by Authority B to enable Authority A to make the payment in accordance with that paragraph; and

(f)   if any deduction was being made in respect of a recoverable overpayment.

(4)   Authority B shall disclose to Authority A–

(a)   if a mover's liability to make payments for the new dwelling is to Authority B; and

(b)   where the extended payment will be paid by Authority A to Authority B in accordance with regulation 73C(3)(a)–

    (i)   any information required by Authority A to enable Authority A to make the payment in accordance with that paragraph; and

    (ii)   the date on which Authority B receives any such payment.]

Amendment

1.   Substituted by reg 3(3) of SI 2008 No 959 as from 6.10.08.

General Note

This facilitates the passing of information between authorities where there is entitlement to extended payments under regs 73 to 73E and the claimant moves from the area of the authority where s/he had previously been in receipt of HB to another. See reg 115 where there is entitlement to extended payments under reg 72 to 72E.

Requiring information from landlords and agents

117. Pursuant to section 126A of the Administration Act (information from landlords and agents), where a claim is made to an authority, on which a rent allowance may be awarded, then, in the circumstances prescribed in regulation 118 (circumstances for requiring information), that authority, or any person authorised to exercise any functions of the authority relating to housing benefit, may require an appropriate person to supply to that authority or person relevant information, in the manner prescribed in regulation 120 (manner of supply of information).

General Note

This confirms that the circumstances in which information may be sought are set out in reg 118 and the manner of the supply of information is set out in reg 120. Note that information may also be demanded by any body administering HB on behalf of an authority. Note also that it is not necessary that rent allowance has been awarded before the information may be required. The authority is probably entitled to delay determination of a claim pending the supply of the information by the landlord, but the delay must be reasonable in all the circumstances.

Circumstances for requiring information

118.–(1) A person is required to supply information in the following circumstances–

(a) he is an appropriate person in relation to any dwelling in respect of which–

    (i) housing benefit is being paid to an appropriate person pursuant to regulation 95 or 96 (circumstances in which payment is to be or may be made to a landlord); or

    (ii) a request has been made by an appropriate person or by the claimant for housing benefit to be so paid; and

(b) the requirer serves upon that appropriate person, whether by post or otherwise, a written notice stating that the requirer–

    (i) suspects that there is or may be an impropriety in relation to a claim in respect of any dwelling wherever situate in relation to which he is an appropriate person; or

    (ii) is already investigating an allegation of impropriety in relation to that person.

(2) In formation required to be supplied under paragraph (1) shall be supplied to the requirer at the address specified in the notice.

General Note

This sets out the circumstances in which information must be supplied by an "appropriate person".

Analysis

Para (1). A number of conditions must be fulfilled before the "appropriate person" comes under an obligation to supply the information requested.

(1) S/he must be an "appropriate person" in relation to a relevant dwelling. "Appropriate person" is defined in SSAA s126A(2) (see p77). It includes landlords and their agents.

(2) HB is being paid direct to the "appropriate person" under reg 95 or reg 96, or a request has been made for such payment by her/him or a claimant.

(3) A written notice is served in relation to the authority's grounds for making the request. This must be either that an impropriety in relation to a claim is suspected in respect of a dwelling where the "appropriate person" is involved, or that there is an investigation of impropriety in relation to the "appropriate person": sub-para (b). Under sub-para (b)(i), the impropriety need not relate to the same property, it need not be the same claimant and s/he need not be the "appropriate person" in respect of the same capacity. The authority is not obliged to inform the person of the reasons for its suspicion, nor is it restricted in seeking information that relates only to that suspicion. However, it is clear that the authority must have formed a suspicion, which provided it is held in good faith is probably immune from challenge. The only basis for a challenge would be judicial review.

Para (2). The notice must specify an address and the information must be supplied at that address.

Relevant information

119.–(1) The information the supplier is to supply to the requirer is that prescribed in paragraphs (2) and (3) (referred to in this Part as "the relevant information").

(2)   For a supplier who falls within paragraph (4) or section 126A(2)(b) of the Administration Act ("the landlord"), the information is–

(a)   where the landlord is a natural person–

    (i)   his appropriate details;

    (ii)   the relevant particulars of any residential property in which he has an interest; and

    (iii)   the appropriate details of any body corporate, in which he is a major shareholder or of which he is a director and which has an interest in residential property;

(b)   where the landlord is a trustee, except a trustee of a charity, in addition to any information that he is required to supply in accordance with sub-paragraph (a) or (c), as the case may be, the relevant particulars of any residential property held by the trust of which he is a trustee and the name and address of any beneficiary under the trust or the objects of that trust, as the case may be;

(c)   where the landlord is a body corporate or otherwise not a natural person, other than a charity–

    (i)   its appropriate details;

    (ii)   the relevant particulars of any residential property in which it has an interest;

    (iii)   the names and addresses of any directors of it;

    (iv)   the appropriate details of any person–

        (aa)   who owns 20 per cent. or more of it; or

        (bb)   of whom it owns 20 per cent. or more; and

    (v)   the names and addresses of its major shareholders;

(d)   where the landlord is a charity or is a recognised body, the appropriate details relating to the landlord and particulars of the landlord's registration as a charity.

(3)   For a supplier who falls within section 126A(2)(c) of the Administration Act or paragraph (5)("the agent"), the information is–

(a)   the name and address of any person ("his principal")–

    (i)   to whom the agent has agreed to make payments in consequence of being entitled to receive relevant payments: or

    (ii)   for whom the agent is acting on behalf of or in connection with any aspect of the management of a dwelling,

    as the case may be;

(b)   the relevant particulars of any residential property in respect of which the agent–

    (i)   has agreed to make payments in consequence of being entitled to receive relevant payments; or

    (ii)   is acting on behalf of his principal in connection with any aspect of its management;

(c)   where the agent is a natural person–

    (i)   the relevant particulars of any residential property in which he has an interest;

    (ii)   the appropriate details of any body corporate or any person not a natural person, in which he is a major shareholder or of which he is a director and which has any interest in residential property; or

(d)   where the agent is a body corporate or other than a natural person–

    (i)   the relevant particulars of any residential property in which it has an interest;

    (ii)   the names and addresses of any directors of or major shareholders in the agent; and

    (iii)   the appropriate details of any person–

        (aa)   who owns 20 per cent. or more of the agent; or

        (bb)   of whom the agent owns 20 per cent. or more.

(4)   A supplier falls within this paragraph (landlord receiving rent), if he falls within section 126A(2)(a) of the Administration Act, but does not fall within paragraph (5).

(5)   A supplier falls within this paragraph (agent receiving the rent), if he falls within subsection (2)(a) of section 126A of the Administration Act and has agreed to make

payments, in consequence of being entitled to receive relevant payments, to a person falling within subsection (2)(b) of that section.

(6) For the purposes of this regulation–

"appropriate details" means the name of the person and (in the case of a company) its registered office and, in any case, the full postal address, including post code, of the principal place of business of that person and the telephone and facsimile number (if any) of that place;

"charity" means a charity which is registered under section 3 of the Charities Act 1993 and is not an exempt charity within the meaning of that Act;

"major shareholder" means, where a body corporate is a company limited by shares, any person holding one tenth or more of the issued shares in that company and, in any other case, all the owners of that body;

"recognised body" has the same meaning as in section 1(7) of the Law Reform (Miscellaneous Provisions) (Scotland) Act 1990;

"relevant particulars" means the full postal address, including post code, and number of current lettings of or within that residential property and, if that property includes two or more dwellings, that address and the number of such lettings for each such dwelling;

"residential property" includes any premises, situate within the United Kingdom–

(a) used or which has, within the last six months, been used; or

(b) which may be used or is adapted for use,

as residential accommodation,

and other expressions used in this regulation and also in the Companies Act 1985 shall have the same meaning in this regulation as they have in that Act.

General Note

This sets out the type of information that is to be supplied. It is worthy of note that all the information is to be supplied and there is no obligation on the authority to make a specific request for any of the information. However, it could presumably request only certain categories of information and if the rest was not supplied, a criminal prosecution might be regarded as an abuse of process. It would be useful for authorities to draw up questionnaires for different categories of suppliers of information to use.

A large amount of information may be supplied under this regulation about parties who will not be mixed up in the authority's investigation. It may be arguable that the low threshold in reg 118 for the requiring of the information is insufficient justification for the invasion of privacy that the supply of the information involves. There may well be grounds for challenge under the Human Rights Act 1998.

Analysis

Paragraph (2)

This sets out the information to be supplied by landlords. That expression is defined as covering both landlords directly receiving the rent and tenants that sublet. The former are under the obligation provided that they do not fulfil para (5) as being agents: see para (4). The latter fall within SSAA s126A(2)(b).

The information to be provided depends on the status of the landlord. Four cases are dealt with.

(1) A "natural person" must supply her/his "appropriate details". S/he must also supply the "relevant particulars" of any residential property in which s/he has an interest. Those expressions are defined in para (6). The property must be residential, but it is suggested that information in relation to properties with both business and residential elements must be supplied. The word "interest" must relate to a property interest, but could be legal or equitable (ie, as a beneficiary under a trust). The "appropriate details" of any body corporate must be supplied provided that s/he is a "major shareholder" or a director, and the body corporate holds an interest in residential property. See para (6) for the meaning of "major shareholder".

(2) Trustees must supply further information *in addition* to any other information supplied under one of the other heads. Details of residential property held by the trust, its beneficiaries and the objects of the trust must be supplied. The latter can be satisfied by supplying the requirer with a copy of the trust deed.

(3) Bodies corporate (including partnerships in Scotland but not in England and Wales) must give their appropriate details, particulars of residential property, names and addresses of directors, the details of any person (which could be a natural or legal person) that owns 20 per cent or more of the body corporate or of which the body corporate owns 20 per cent or more, and the details of its major shareholders.

(4) Charities must give their appropriate details and matters relating to their registration.

Paragraph (3)

This deals with the agent falling within s126A(2)(c) SSAA. Under sub-para (a), details of the principal must be given (ie, the person on whose behalf the agent is acting), along with particulars of any property in respect of which the agent is receiving HB or is acting on behalf of his principal: sub-para (b). This must be the same principal as the one whose name and address is disclosed under sub-para (a).

Where the agent is a natural person, details of any residential property in which he has an interest must be given. Again, "interest" can only refer to a legal or equitable interest in land and not merely a property that the agent is dealing with in the course of her/his business. S/he must also give details of interests in body corporate or "any person otherwise not a natural person" in which a major shareholding or directorship is held and which holds an interest in residential property. The latter expression would cover a partnership.

An agent that is a body corporate must give details of all residential property in which it is interested, the names and addresses of major shareholders and directors, and details of major ownership (see the Analysis to para (2) relating to bodies corporate).

Manner of supply of information

120.–(1)   Subject to paragraph (2), the relevant information shall be supplied–
(a)   in typewritten or printed form; or
(b)   with the written agreement of the requirer, in electronic or handwritten form,
within a period of 4 weeks commencing on the date on which the notice was sent or given.
(2)   Where–
(a)   within a period of 4 weeks commencing on the date on which the notice was sent or given, the supplier requests that the time for the supply of the relevant information be extended; and
(b)   the requirer provides written agreement to that request,
the time for the supply of the relevant information shall be extended to a period of 8 weeks commencing on the date on which the notice was sent or given.

General Note
The time limit for supplying the "relevant information" (for which see reg 119) is four weeks, which may be extended to eight weeks with the written agreement of the authority. It must normally be delivered in typewritten or printed form but may, with the written agreement of the authority, be delivered in handwritten or electronic form.

Criminal offence

[¹**121.**   Any supplier who fails to supply relevant information to the requirer as, when and how required under regulations 117 to 120 shall be guilty of an offence under section 113 of the Administration Act.]

Amendment
1.   Substituted by reg 2(9) of SI 2008 No 2299 as from 1.10.08.

General Note
See the commentary to s113 SSAA on p56.

[¹ Supply of benefit administration information between authorities

121A.–(1)   For the purpose of section 122E(3) of the Administration Act (supply of information between authorities administering benefit) the circumstances in which information is to be supplied and the information to be supplied are set out in paragraph (2).

(2)   Where the functions of an authority ("Authority A") relating to housing benefit are being exercised, wholly or in part, by another authority ("Authority B")–
(a)   Authority A must supply to Authority B any benefit administration information it holds which is relevant to, and necessary for, Authority B to exercise those functions; and
(b)   Authority B must supply to Authority A any benefit administration information it holds which is relevant to, and necessary for, Authority A to exercise those functions.

(3)   The circumstances in which paragraph (2) applies include cases where the authorities have agreed to discharge functions jointly.

(4)   In paragraph (2) "Authority A" and "Authority B" include any person authorised to exercise functions relating to housing benefit on behalf of the authority in question.

(5)   This regulation shall not apply if the person or authority to whom the information is to be supplied agrees that the information need not be supplied.]

Amendment

1.   Inserted by reg 2(10) of SI 2008 No 2299 as from 1.10.08.

[¹ PART 15
Former pathfinder authorities

Modifications in respect of former pathfinder authorities

122.–(1)   In this regulation and in Schedule 10, "former pathfinder authority" means a relevant authority specified in Part 1 of that Schedule.

(2)   The provisions of Part 2 of Schedule 10 apply in relation to the area of a former pathfinder authority.]

Amendment

1.   Substituted by reg 20(1) of SI 2007 No 2868 as from 7.4.08.

General Note

The "local housing allowance" scheme for rent restriction, found in regs 12D, 13C and 13D, was piloted in 18 Pathfinder areas from late 2007 until 7 April 2008. The pilot rules were more generous in a number of respects than the current "local housing allowance" rules. Sch 10 provides transitional rules for determining eligible rent for those living in former Pathfinder areas where, prior to 7 April 2008, eligible rent was determined by reference to the maximum rent (standard local rate).

Prior to 7 April 2008, the HB Regs were modified by Sch 10 for those in Pathfinder areas as follows.

(1)   Regs 11, 12, 14-17, 95 and 96 HB Regs were amended.

(2)   Regs 11A, 12A, 13A and 13B, 18A HB Regs were inserted.

See pp510–18 of the 20th edition for the full text of the provisions and a summary of the Pathfinder scheme.

[¹ SCHEDULE A1]
TREATMENT OF CLAIMS FOR HOUSING BENEFIT BY REFUGEES

Modification

Sch A1 was inserted by Sch 4 para 2(2) HB&CTB(CP) Regs in respect of claims for HB by some refugees. Sch A1 was further modifed by Sch 4 para 4(2) for some HB claimants who were refugees who claimed asylum on or before 2 April 2000.

Amendment

1.   Lapsed by s12(2)(e) of the Asylum and Immigration (Treatment of Claimants, etc.) Act 2004 (for those recorded as refugees after 14.6.07).

General Note

Reg 10A and Sch A1 as inserted by Sch 4 HB&CTB(CP) Regs dealt with a refugee's retrospective entitlement to HB.

Section 12 Asylum and Immigration (Treatment of Claimants, etc.) Act 2004 came into force on 14 June 2007 by the Asylum and Immigration (Treatment of Claimants, etc.) Act 2004 (Commencement No.7 and Transitional Provisions) Order 2007 SI No.1602. However, the commencement does not apply to those recorded as refugees on or before 14 June 2007. For these purposes, a person is "recorded as a refugee" on the day the Secretary of State notifies her/him that s/he has been recognised as a refugee and granted asylum in the UK.

See the 20th edition pp1127–29 for the full text of Sch A1 and pp1126–27 for commentary on it.

Note that reg 10A and Sch A1 paras 3 and 7 of both the HB Regs and the HB(SPC) Regs, as inserted by para 2, were substituted by reg 6 Housing Benefit (Local Housing Allowance, Miscellaneous and Consequential) Amendment Regulations 2007 SI No.2870 as from 7 April 2008, save that for a person to whom reg 1(3) of those regulations applied, the amendments came into force on the day on or after 7 April 2008 when the first of the events specified in reg 1(4) applied to her/him, or on 6 April 2009 if none had before that date. Sch 4 para 3(4) HB&CTB(CP) Regs was amended by reg 7(5) Social Security (Miscellaneous Amendments) (No.2) Regulations 2008 SI No.1042 as from 19 May 2008.

SCHEDULE 1

REGULATION 11

Ineligible service charges

General Note

The general rule in reg 12(1)(e) is that services charges are "rent" for HB purposes and hence eligible to be met by HB under reg 11(1). This Schedule lists the exceptions to that rule. If a service charge is listed in the Schedule (and hence is ineligible) a deduction must be made under reg 12B(2) or if the "pre-January 1996" scheme of rent restriction applies, under reg 12(3) as set out in Sch 3 para 5(1) HB&CTB(CP) Regs. Note that the amount calculated in accordance with reg 12B(2) is also relevant for determining eligible rent under reg 12BA and "maximum rent (social sector)" under reg B13. See also Sch 1 paras 4(3)(b) and (7) and Sch 3B para 2(7(b) Rent Officers (Housing Benefit Functions) Order 1997 and the Scotland equivalent.

PART 1
Service charges other than for fuel

Ineligible service charges

1.   The following service charges shall not be eligible to be met by housing benefit–
(a)   charges in respect of day-to-day living expenses including, in particular, all provision of–
   (i)   subject to paragraph 2 meals (including the preparation of meals or provision of unprepared food);
   (ii)   laundry (other than the provision of premises or equipment to enable a person to do his own laundry);
   [¹ (iii)   leisure items such as either sports facilities (except a children's play area), or television rental, licence and subscription fees (except radio relay charges and charges made in respect of the conveyance and installation and maintenance of equipment for the conveyance of a television broadcasting service);]
   (iv)   cleaning of rooms and windows except cleaning of–
      (aa)   communal areas; or
      (bb)   the exterior of any windows where neither the claimant nor any member of his household is able to clean them himself,
   where a payment is not made in respect of such cleaning by a local authority (including, in relation to England, a county council) or the [² Welsh Ministers] to the claimant or his partner, or to another person on their behalf; and
   (v)   transport;
(b)   charges in respect of–
   (i)   the acquisition of furniture or household equipment; and
   (ii)   the use of such furniture or equipment where that furniture or household equipment will become the property of the claimant by virtue of an agreement with the landlord;
(c)   charges in respect of the provision of an emergency alarm system;
(d)   charges in respect of medical expenses (including the cost of treatment or counselling related to mental disorder, mental handicap, physical disablement or past or present alcohol or drug dependence);
(e)   charges in respect of the provision of nursing care or personal care (including assistance at meal-times or with personal appearance or hygiene);
(f)   charges in respect of general counselling or of any other support services, whoever provides those services;
(g)   charges in respect of any services not specified in sub-paragraphs (a) to (f) which are not connected with the provision of adequate accommodation.

Amendments

1.   Substituted by reg 6(5) of SI 2007 No 719 as from 2.4.07.
2.   Amended by reg 5(5) of SI 2008 No 3157 as from 5.1.09.

Analysis

This lists the ineligible services, including a catch-all para 1(g) which refers to charges in respect of services "which are not connected with the provision of adequate accommodation". Note the definition of "communal areas" in para 8. GM A4.730 provides a non-exhaustive list of the items which are *not* covered here and are therefore still "eligible": wardens and caretakers (in so far as they provide eligible accommodation-related services); removal of refuse; lifts; radio and TV relay; portering; communal telephone charges; entry-phones; cleaning of communal areas; children's play areas.

It is for the claimant to satisfy the authority that a service charge is not ineligible: *R v Stoke-on-Trent CC ex p Highgate Projects* (1996) 29 HLR 271 at 278, CA.

CP and Others v Aylesbury Vale DC v SSWP (HB) [2011] UKUT 22 (AAC) considered whether service charges attributable to the maintenance of a communal garden were eligible for HB. Judge Turnbull, distinguishing

CH 755/2008, concluded that they could be eligible where a tenant only has a right to use a communal garden, as opposed to exclusive possession of it (alone or with other tenants). Gardening charges are not excluded by para 1(a) ("day-to-day living expenses") nor by para 1(g). He pointed out that the "distinction drawn in para 1(a)(iv) of Schedule 1, between (i) cleaning of rooms and windows in communal areas and external windows which cannot be reached by the tenant and (ii) cleaning of other rooms and windows, shows that the question whether the tenant is able (whether legally or in practice) to carry out the activity himself is potentially important, in determining whether a charge by the landlord for that service is eligible."

In *Liverpool City Council v (1) NM, (2) WD (HB)* [2015] UKUT 532 (AAC); [2016] AACR 19, Judge Knowles, decided that water charges for the communal areas of supported or sheltered accommodation were eligible service charges. Such charges are not specifically listed in Sch 1 para 1. Communal water charges are services connected to the provision of adequate accommodation and thus are not excluded by Sch 1 para 1(g).

Sub-paragraphs (e), (f) and (g)
Most of the categories of ineligible charge are self-explanatory, but the scope of sub-paras (e), (f) and (g) has caused considerable difficulty.

Sub-para (e): charges in respect of the provision of nursing care or personal care. It is suggested that a service only falls under sub-para (e) if it involves a degree of physical proximity in the assistance that is given, and consists of doing something for the claimant rather than reminding or persuading the claimant to do it for her/himself. The distinction is perhaps easier to recognise than to state. A valid analogy might be the difference between "attention" and "supervision" in the context of awards of disability living allowance. Some assistance in drawing this distinction may also be obtained from the decision in *R v Allerdale DC HBRB ex p Doughty* [2000] COD 462, QBD. In that case, the applicant lived in a religious home. An application for registration of the home as a small residential home was rejected by the Registered Homes Tribunal. The Housing Benefit Review Board found that because the home was not registered under the Registered Homes Act 1984, it could not therefore be said to be providing "personal care" under the scope of the previous definition and so the home was not "supported accommodation".

The judge held this approach to be wrong. The effect of the rejection of registration was that the landlord could not provide "personal care" as defined in s20(1) of the 1984 Act: "care which includes assistance with bodily functions where such assistance is required".

"[Counsel for the applicant] accepts that the concept will also embrace other forms of care, such as psychiatric and certain physical care, but submits that it clearly does not extend to general counselling and support services such as fall within the scope of para 1(f)(iii). This is, in my view, plainly correct, and, as I have already indicated, in the schedule itself the concept of personal care is found in para (e) and the concept of 'general counselling' or 'any other support services' are found in para (f). In my view, the concept of 'personal care' in para (e) is the same as that found in the Registered Homes Act, but in any event, even if that were not so, it would be, in substance, a similar concept."

Sub-para (f): charges in respect of general counselling or support services. The scope of para 1(f) has been considered by the courts on a number of occasions and it was usually amended in consequence. Following the introduction of the Supporting People scheme, the complex former provisions were repealed and the question is now much simpler. For the old law, see pp397–8 of the 12th edition.

Under para 1(f), charges in respect of general counselling or any other support services are ineligible. It does not matter who provides the services.

Sub-para (g): charges not connected with the provision of adequate accommodation. *CIS 1460/1995* provides valuable guidance on the scope of para 1(g). Although it excludes services which relate purely to meeting the personal needs of residents, this does not mean that in deciding whether a service is related to the provision of adequate accommodation the question of suitability for the personal needs of the residents is not relevant (as the cleaning of the outside of windows – per para 1(a)(iv) – is connected both with adequate accommodation and the personal needs of the claimant), and therefore the Schedule itself contemplates that some personal needs may be relevant to assessing what are eligible service charges. What constitutes "adequate accommodation" is a question of fact in each case. The terms of GM A4.730 set out above would suggest that the approach in *CIS 1460/1995* is accepted by the DWP as being correct.

Amount ineligible for meals
2.–(1)   Where a charge for meals is ineligible to be met by housing benefit under paragraph 1, the amount ineligible in respect of each week shall be the amount specified in the following provisions of this paragraph.

(2)   Subject to sub-paragraph (4), where the charge includes provision for at least three meals a day, the amount shall be–
(a)   for a single claimant, [¹³ £28.55];
(b)   if the claimant is a member of a family–
(i)   for the claimant and for each member of his family aged 16 or over, [¹³ £28.55];
(ii)   for each member of his family under age 16, [¹³ £14.50].

(3)   Except where sub-paragraph (5) applies and subject to sub-paragraph (4), where the charge includes provision for less than three meals a day, the amount shall be–
(a)   for a single claimant, [¹³ £19.05];

(b)　　if the claimant is a member of a family–
　　　　(i)　　for the claimant and for each member of his family aged 16 or over, [¹³ £19.05];
　　　　(ii)　　for each member of his family under age 16, [¹³ £9.55].
　　(4)　　For the purposes of sub-paragraphs (2)(b) and (3)(b), a person attains the age of 16 on the first Monday in September following his 16th birthday.
　　(5)　　Where the charge for meals includes the provision of breakfast only, the amount for the claimant and, if he is a member of a family, for the claimant and for each member of his family, shall be [¹³ £3.55].
　　(6)　　Where a charge for meals includes provision for meals for a person who is not a member of the claimant's family sub-paragraphs (2) to (5) shall apply as if that person were a member of the claimant's family.
　　(7)　　For the avoidance of doubt where the charge does not include provision for meals for a claimant or, as the case may be, a member of his family, sub-paragraphs (2) to (5) shall not apply in respect of that person.

Amendments

1.　　Amended by art 19(4) of SI 2006 No 645 and reg 8 of SI 2006 No 217 as from 1.4.06 (3.4.06 where rent payable weekly or at intervals of a week).
2.　　Amended by art 19(4) of SI 2007 No 688 as from 1.4.07 (2.4.07 where rent payable weekly or at intervals of a week).
3.　　Amended by art 19(5) of SI 2008 No 632 as from 1.4.08 (7.4.08 where rent payable weekly or in multiples of a week).
4.　　Amended by art 19(5) of SI 2009 No 497 as from 1.4.09 (6.4.09 where rent payable weekly or at intervals of a week).
5.　　Amended by art 19(4) of SI 2010 No 793 as from 1.4.10 (5.4.10 where rent payable weekly or in multiples of a week).
6.　　Amended by art 20(4) of SI 2011 No 821 as from 1.4.11 (4.4.11 where rent payable weekly or in multiples of a week).
7.　　Amended by art 20(4) of SI 2012 No 780 as from 1.4.12 (2.4.12 where rent payable weekly or in multiples of a week).
8.　　Amended by art 19(4) of SI 2013 No 574 as from 1.4.13.
9.　　Amended by art 17(5) of SI 2014 No 16 as from 1.4.14 (7.4.14 where rent payable weekly or in multiples of a week).
10.　　Amended by art 17(5) of SI 2015 No 547 as from 1.4.15 (6.4.15 where rent payable weekly or in multiples of a week).
11.　　Amended by art 22(5) of SI 2017 No 260 as from 1.4.17 (3.4.17 where rent payable weekly or in multiples of a week).
12.　　Amended by art 23(4) of SI 2018 No 281 as from 1.4.18 (2.4.18 where rent payable weekly or in multiples of a week).
13.　　Amended by art 23(4) of SI 2019 No 480 as from 1.4.19.

Analysis

Para 2 makes it clear that when a service charge is paid for meals, only the appropriate amounts shown in the paragraph are to be treated as ineligible, whatever the actual charge for meals. The leeway afforded by paras 3 and 4 in relation to other types of service charge does not apply here. The amount ineligible varies according to the number of meals per day included in the charge and the age of the members of the claimant's "family", defined in s137(1) SSCBA (see p17). However, where the charge does not include meals for the claimant or a member of her/his family, no deduction is made for that person: sub-para (7). "Single claimant" is defined in reg 2(1) and is a claimant who neither has a partner nor is a lone parent.

Where the charge for meals included in the claimant's charge includes meals not only for members of a claimant's family but for someone else (eg, a non-dependant), the appropriate deduction is to be made in respect of that person as though s/he was a member of the claimant's family: sub-para (6).

Amount of ineligible charges

3.–(1)　　Subject to paragraph 2 where an ineligible service charge is not separated from or separately identified within other payments made by the occupier in respect of the dwelling, the appropriate authority shall apportion such charge as is fairly attributable to the provision of that service, having regard to the cost of comparable services and such portion of those payments shall be ineligible to be met by housing benefit.
　　(2)　　Subject to paragraph 2, where the relevant authority considers that the amount of any ineligible service charge which is separately identified within other payments made by the occupier in respect of the dwelling is unreasonably low having regard to the service provided, it shall substitute a sum for the charge in question which it considers represents the value of the services concerned and the amount so substituted shall be ineligible to be met by housing benefit.
　　(3)　　In sub-paragraph (2) the expression "ineligible service charge" includes any service charge which does not qualify as a periodical payment under regulation 12(1)(e) (rent).
　　(4)　　In any other case, the whole amount of the ineligible service charge shall be ineligible to be met by housing benefit.

Analysis
The general rule subject to para 2 above, as set out in para 3(4), is that the whole amount of an ineligible charge is ineligible for HB. However, this is subject to two qualifications. Firstly, in many cases, the amount of such a charge will not be identifiable and in such a case para 3(1) gives the authority power to make an amount "fairly attributable" to it ineligible for HB, having regard to the actual cost of comparable services.

Secondly, para 3(2) gives authorities the power to substitute their own valuation for ineligible service charges in a case where the amounts are considered to be unreasonably low for the services provided. See para 4 where *eligible* charges are thought to be excessive.

Excessive service costs
4. Subject to paragraph 2, where the relevant authority considers that the amount of a service charge to which regulation 12(1)(e) (rent) applies is excessive in relation to the service provided for the claimant or his family, having regard to the cost of comparable services, it shall make a deduction from that charge of the excess and the amount so deducted shall be ineligible to be met by housing benefit.

PART 2
Payments in respect of fuel charges

5. A service charge for fuel except a charge in respect of services for communal areas shall be ineligible to be met by housing benefit.

General Note
The term "communal areas" is defined in para 8.

6.–(1) Where a charge is ineligible to be met by housing benefit under paragraph 5–
(a) in the calculation of entitlement to a rent rebate; or
(b) in the calculation of entitlement to a rent allowance if the amount of the charge is specified or is otherwise readily identifiable (except where the amount of the charge is unrealistically low in relation to the fuel provided or the charge cannot readily be distinguished from a charge for a communal area),
the amount ineligible to be met by housing benefit shall be the full amount of the service charge.

(2) In any other case, subject to sub-paragraphs (3) and (4) and paragraph 7, the amount ineligible to be met by housing benefit shall be the following amounts in respect of each week–
(a) for heating (other than hot water) [¹⁴ £32.70];
(b) for hot water [¹⁴ £3.80];
(c) for lighting [¹⁴ £2.60];
(d) for cooking [¹⁴ £3.80].

(3) Where the accommodation occupied by the claimant or, if he is a member of a family, by the claimant and the members of his family, consists of one room only, the amount ineligible to be met by housing benefit in respect of each week where heating only is, or heating and either hot water or lighting (or both) are, provided, shall be one-half of the aggregate of the amounts specified in sub-paragraphs (2)(a), (b) and (c).

(4) In a case to which sub-paragraph (2) or (3) applies, if a claimant provides evidence on which the actual or approximate amount of the service charge for fuel may be estimated, the amount ineligible to be met by housing benefit under this paragraph shall be that estimated amount.

Amendments
1. Amended by art 19(5) of SI 2006 No 645 and reg 8 of SI 2006 No 217 as from 1.4.06 (3.4.06 where rent payable weekly or at intervals of a week).
2. Amended by art 19(5) of SI 2007 No 688 as from 1.4.07 (2.4.07 where rent payable weekly or at intervals of a week).
3. Confirmed by art 19(6) of SI 2008 No 632 as from 1.4.08 (7.4.08 where rent payable weekly or in multiples of a week).
4. Amended by art 19(6) of SI 2009 No 497 as from 1.4.09 (6.4.09 where rent payable weekly or at intervals of a week).
5. Confirmed by art 19(5) of SI 2010 No 793 as from 1.4.10 (5.4.10 where rent payable weekly or in multiples of a week).
6. Confirmed by art 20(5) of SI 2011 No 821 as from 1.4.11 (4.4.11 where rent payable weekly or in multiples of a week).
7. Amended by art 20(5) of SI 2012 No 780 as from 1.4.12 (2.4.12 where rent payable weekly or in multiples of a week).
8. Amended by art 19(5)(a) of SI 2013 No 574 as from 1.4.13.
9. Confirmed by art 19(5)(b) and (c) of SI 2013 No 574 as from 1.4.13.
10. Amended by art 17(6) of SI 2014 No 16 as from 1.4.14 (7.4.14 where rent payable weekly or in multiples of a week).

11.   Amended by art 17(6) of SI 2015 No 547 as from 1.4.15 (6.4.15 where rent payable weekly or in multiples of a week).
12.   Confirmed by art 22(6) of SI 2017 No 260 as from 1.4.17 (3.4.17 where rent payable weekly or in multiples of a week).
13.   Amended by art 23(5) of SI 2018 No 281 as from 1.4.18 (2.4.18 where rent payable weekly or in multiples of a week).
14.   Amended by art 23(5) of SI 2019 No 480 as from 1.4.19.

Analysis
Under para 6(1), the full amount of the service charge for fuel is ineligible in all cases where the claimant has a rent rebate, and in rent allowance cases where the charge is specified or can otherwise be readily identified. In the latter case, this does not apply if the charge is unrealistically low or if the charge cannot be distinguished from a portion relating to "communal areas" (defined in para 8). "Rent allowance" and "rent rebate" are defined in s134 SSAA.

If para 6(1) does not apply, regard must be had to sub-paras (2), (3) and (4) to work out the the amount ineligible. Specified amounts are in sub-para (2). If, however, the claimant provides evidence to allow the actual amounts to be estimated, those amounts are to be taken instead: sub-para (4).

Under sub-para (3), where the claimant and her/his family (if applicable) occupy a single room, lower deductions apply. GM A4.912-913 suggests that this applies where the claimant occupies one room only, including cases where the room or other communal areas are shared and that the reference to "one room only" is not a reference to the number of rooms occupied solely by the claimant, that is that if a claimant has her/his own room and shared occupation of other rooms the higher amount is ineligible. However, the guidance also suggests that bathrooms, toilets and shared kitchens should not count as rooms occupied by the claimant and family.

The scope of sub-para (3) is uncertain in two respects. Firstly, this calculation only applies where "heating only is, or heating and either hot water or lighting (or both) are, provided", that is where there is a charge for heating, or heating and hot water, or heating and lighting, or heating, hot water and lighting.

Secondly, there are difficulties in determining how much is to be ineligible. Sub-para (3) provides that the ineligible amount is to be half the aggregate of the amounts set out in sub-para (2) for heating, hot water and lighting. What about, however, the case where a charge is only made for heating, or only for heating and one of the latter two categories of charge? On a literal reading of sub-para (3), it would appear that all the amounts are to be aggregated, yet this seems illogical in view of the fact that charges for hot water, lighting or both are not actually being made.

7.–(1)   Where rent is payable other than weekly, any amount ineligible to be met by housing benefit which is specified in this Schedule as a weekly amount shall–
(a)   where rent is payable in multiples of a week, be multiplied by the number equal to the number of weeks in respect of which it is payable; or
(b)   in any other case, be divided by 7 and multiplied by the number of days in the period to be used by the relevant authority for the purpose of calculating the claimant's weekly eligible rent under regulation 80 (calculation of weekly amounts).
(2)   In a case to which regulation 81 applies (rent free periods), any amount ineligible to be met by housing benefit which is specified in this Schedule as a weekly amount shall, where appropriate, be converted in accordance with sub-paragraph (1) and shall–
(a)   where rent is payable weekly, or in multiples of a week, be multiplied by 52 or 53, whichever is appropriate, and divided by the number equal to the number of weeks in that 52 or 53 week period in respect of which he is liable to pay rent; or
(b)   in any other case, be multiplied by 365 or 366, whichever is appropriate, and divided by the number of days in that 365 or 366 day period in respect of which he is liable to pay rent.

Analysis
Para 7 deals with the arithmetic of calculating ineligible charges where rent is paid other than weekly or where there are rent-free periods. Under para 7(1), the charges are converted to weekly amounts. Under para 7(2), where there are rent-free periods (see reg 81) the amount of ineligible charges is adjusted. Suppose, for example, the claimant has eligible rent of £150 a week and ineligible charges of £10 a week. She has a rent-free period of four weeks during a 52 week year. The £10 is multiplied by 52 and divided by 48, giving £10.84 as the ineligible amount during each week.

---

8.   In this Schedule–
"communal areas" mean areas (other than rooms) of common access (including halls and passageways) and rooms of common use in sheltered accommodation;
"fuel" includes gas and electricity and a reference to a charge for fuel includes a charge for fuel which includes an amount in respect of the facility of providing it other than a specified amount for the provision of a heating system.

Analysis

"Communal areas". The definition of "communal areas" is relevant for whether some charges for cleaning of rooms and windows (under para 1(a)(iv)) or fuel (under para 5) are eligible for HB. It is also relevant for the deduction to make from eligible rent for water charges in respect of communal areas in sheltered and supported accommodation under reg 12B(2)(a).

"Sheltered accommodation" is not defined. The meaning of the phrase was considered in *JB v Oxford City Council and SSWP (HB)* [2011] UKUT 136 (AAC). The claimant, a man with severe learning disabilities, was a housing association tenant. He had his own bedroom, but shared other rooms. 24-hour care, support and supervision were provided. The local authority decided that this was not "sheltered accommodation" and so certain charges for cleaning and fuel could not be included in his HB. Judge Levenson agreed with the claimant that, in the context of the HB scheme, "sheltered accommodation" must be given a meaning consistent with the underlying purpose of the legislation and that because the term was not defined it should not be given a narrow or technical meaning. He said:

"32.   "Sheltered accommodation" clearly means something more than ordinary accommodation or shelter, otherwise the distinction would not be made in paragraph 8 of Schedule 1 to the regulations. This can only really mean that it is accommodation provided for people who are in some way (and probably for some defined reason) more vulnerable than most people are, or are vulnerable in a particular kind of way.

33.   If, for reasons relating to the nature of claimant's vulnerability, there are resident or other staff on hand, then I see no reason why, as part of the definition, there has to be a warden/[manager] and/or an alarm system. Subject to that, I agree with the comments of Judge Mesher [in *CIS 1460/1995*] referred to in paragraph 10 above.

34.   The First-tier Tribunal went wrong in unduly emphasising the presence of a warden/manager and an alarm system. More significantly, the First-tier Tribunal and the respondents have gone wrong in emphasising a need for the accommodation to be self-contained. By definition we cannot be talking about totally self-contained accommodation, because the relevant provisions of Schedule 1 only come into play if there are common rooms that have to be lit, heated and cleaned. I see absolutely nothing in the regulations that prevents housing benefit being available for these costs because a claimant could happily chose not to ever use any of these common rooms. Indeed, that would be perverse – to say that the less need there is to use such rooms, the more likely it is that housing benefit should cover their cost.

35.   There are some types of accommodation that are clearly not "sheltered accommodation" – such as (and these are only examples) (a) accommodation of the type that most people probably occupy which is not designed for any kind of vulnerable person or where there is absolutely no special provision, (b) residential or nursing care homes, (c) standard student accommodation and (d) other types dealt with by other provisions of the housing benefit scheme. However, unless accommodation is excluded by virtue of being in one of those categories, a broad view should be taken of the meaning of "sheltered accommodation" for these purposes and, in my opinion, it certainly includes the type of accommodation occupied by the claimant."

The Court of Appeal refused the local authority's appeal in *Oxford City Council v Basey* [2012] EWCA Civ 115; [2012] AACR 38. Deciding that the Upper Tribunal had been correct to conclude that the claimant occupied sheltered accommodation, it said that, as Parliament did not choose to define sheltered accommodation, "the Court should not impose a prescriptive definition upon an inherently flexible concept which can take many different forms, and which now includes very sheltered or extra care sheltered accommodation". See also *Liverpool City Council v (1) NM, (2) WD (HB)* [2015] UKUT 532 (AAC); [2016] AACR 19 on sheltered and supported accommodation.

[¹ SCHEDULE 2

Excluded tenancies

REGULATION 14

Modifications

Schedule 2 was substituted by reg 18 Housing Benefit (Local Housing Allowance and Information Sharing) Amendment Regulations 2007 No.2868 as from 7 April 2008, save that for a person to whom reg 1(5) of those regulations applied (see p1812), the amendments came into force on the day on or after 7 April 2008 when the first of the events specified in reg 1(6) applied to her/him, or on 6 April 2009 if none had before that date.

Amendment

1.   Substituted by reg 18 of SI 2007 No 2868 as from 7.4.08 (or if reg 1(5) of that SI applies, on the day on or after 7.4.08 when the first of the events specified in reg 1(6) applies, or from 6.4.09 if none have before that date).

General Note

This Schedule lists circumstances in which the general obligation in reg 14 (see p398) – requiring local authorities in claims for a rent allowance to seek determinations from the rent officer – does not apply. Although under para

1, these are referred to as "excluded tenancies", this is a misleading term because not all the agreements referred to in the Schedule relate to tenancies as distinct from licences and so on, and also because many of the exclusions relate not so much to the tenancy but to the person claiming. A tenancy may gain and lose its status as an "excluded tenancy" during its existence.

In a number of cases, the "excluded tenancies" are not only excluded from the requirement to apply to the rent officer, but are excluded from the application of the "local reference rent", the "local housing allowance" and the "social sector" schemes of rent restriction altogether.

(1)   A claimant is excluded from the application of the "local reference rent" scheme where any of paras 4 to 9 or 12 apply. Where paras 3 or 11 apply, a claimant *may* be excluded from the application of that scheme: regs 12C and 13.

(2)   A claimant is excluded from the application of the "local housing allowance" scheme where the tenancy is of a type mentioned in any of paras 4 to 11. Tenancies excluded under paras 3 and 12 are not covered, but may come within other exceptions in reg 13C(5): regs 12D, 13C and 13D.

(3)   So long as the landlord is not a registered housing association, a claimant is excluded from the application of the "social sector" scheme where the tenancy is of a type mentioned in any of paras 4 to 11: reg A13(2)(a). A claimant is also excluded if her/his tenancy is a shared ownership tenancy, whether or not the landlord is a registered housing association: reg A13(2)(b).

Note that although an application to the rent officer is required where Sch 3 para 4(1)(b) HB&CTB(CP) Regs applies (ie, where the claimant lives in "exempt accommodation"), that provision requires the authority to determine the eligible rent in such cases under the versions of reg 12 and 13 HB Regs set out in Sch 3 para 5 HB&CTB(CP) Regs.

These rules are quite complex and careful analysis will often be required to ascertain whether a decision to apply to the rent officer can be challenged. Even where that has been done, it may be to the claimant's advantage to allow an application to the rent officer in certain circumstances, particularly if rents have increased since a previous determination was made. The outcome of the application may well be a higher eligible rent and therefore entitlement to increased HB.

---

1.   An excluded tenancy is any tenancy to which any of the following paragraphs applies.

2.–(1)   Subject to the following sub-paragraphs, where a rent officer has made a determination, which relates to the tenancy in question or any other tenancy of the same dwelling this paragraph applies to–

(a)   the tenancy in respect of which that determination was made; and

(b)   any other tenancy of the same dwelling on terms which are substantially the same, other than the term relating to the amount of rent, as those terms were at the time of that determination or, if earlier, at the end of the tenancy.

(2)   For the purposes of any claim, notification, request or application under regulation 14(1) ("the later application"), a tenancy shall not be an excluded tenancy by virtue of sub-paragraph (1) by reference to a rent officer's determination made in consequence of an earlier claim, notification, request or application ("the earlier application") where–

(a)   the earlier and later applications were made in respect of the same claimant or different claimants; and

(b)   the earlier application was made more than 52 weeks before the later application was made.

(3)   Sub-paragraph (1) shall not apply where subsequent to the making of the determination mentioned in that sub-paragraph–

(a)   the number of occupiers of the dwelling has changed and that dwelling is not in a hostel;

(b)   there has been a substantial change in the condition of the dwelling (including the making of improvements) or the terms of the tenancy other than a term relating to rent;

(c)   there has been a rent increase under a term of the tenancy and the term under which that increase was made was either included in the tenancy at the time when the application for that determination was made (or was a term substantially the same as such a term) and that determination was not made under paragraph 1(2), 2(2) or 3(3) of Schedule 1 to the Rent Officers Order;

(d)   in a case where the rent officer has made a determination under paragraph 2(2) of Schedule 1 to the Rent Officers Order (size and rent determinations), but since the date of the application for that determination–

(i)   a child, who is a member of the household occupying the dwelling, has attained the age of 10 years; or

(ii)   a young person, who is a member of the household occupying that dwelling, has attained the age of 16 years; or

(iii)   there is a change in the composition of the household occupying the dwelling;

(e)   the claimant is a young individual, except in a case where the determination mentioned in sub-paragraph (1) was, or was made in conjunction with, a determination of a single room rent pursuant to paragraph 5 of Schedule 1 to the Rent Officers Order on or after 2nd July 2001.

[1, 4 (f)   any person mentioned in paragraph 1A(a) of Schedule 2 to the Rent Officers Order becomes or ceases to be a person who requires overnight care where that affects the size criteria, as set out in that Schedule to that Order, applicable in the claimant's case;]

[² (g) the claimant or the claimant's partner becomes, or ceases to be, a qualifying parent or carer where that affects the size criteria, as set out in Schedule 2 to the Rent Officers Order, applicable in the claimant's case.]

[³ (h) an occupier becomes or ceases to be a child who cannot share a bedroom [⁴ or a member of a couple who cannot share a bedroom] where that affects the size criteria, as set out in Schedule 2 to the Rent Officers Order, applicable in the claimant's case.]

[² (4) For the purposes of sub-paragraph (3)(d)(iii) it does not amount to a change in the composition of the household where a son, daughter, step-son or step-daughter of the claimant or the claimant's partner who is the claimant's non-dependant ceases to occupy the dwelling as their home because they become a member of the armed forces away on operations, or subsequently resumes occupying the dwelling as their home on ceasing to be a member of the armed forces away on operations.]

Amendments

1.   Inserted by reg 2(10) of SI 2010 No 2835 as from 1.4.11.
2.   Inserted by reg 2(7) of SI 2013 No 665 as from 1.4.13.
3.   Amended by reg 2(6) of SI 2013 No 2828 as from 4.12.13.
4.   Amended by reg 4(6) of SI 2017 No 213 as from 1.4.17.

Analysis

This is by far the most common type of "excluded tenancy" and is designed to avoid the need for constant applications to be made for properties where there are continual changes of tenant.

The general rule, as set out in sub-para (1), is that once a rent officer has made a determination in relation to accommodation, it remains valid during the term of the existing tenancy (which, it is suggested, will include any period during which the claimant becomes a statutory tenant by virtue of the operation of the Housing Act 1988 or similar legislation). It also remains valid in relation to subsequent tenancies, provided that they are on substantially the same terms as the tenancy in existence when the application was made, except in relation to the amount of rent payable. It is to be noted that it does not matter if the claimant changes.

However, the effect of this exclusion is limited. It only applies for 52 weeks: sub-para (2). Furthermore, sub-para (3) disapplies it in a case where any of the following changes of circumstance occur subsequent to the making of the determination:

(1)   Where the **number of occupiers of the dwelling changes**, whether or not they are members of the claimant's family: sub-para (3)(a). This does not apply to hostel accommodation. There is no definition of "occupier" for these purposes. However, reg 7 determines the issue of whether a person is, or is not, to be treated as occupying a dwelling as a home: *Stroud DC v JG* [2009] UKUT 67 (AAC); R(H) 8/09; *SK v South Hams DC (HB)* [2010] UKUT 129 (AAC); [2010] AACR 40. In *R(H) 8/09*, the claimant's son was a student who lived away from home during term time. Judge Williams concluded that he was to be treated as occupying the claimant's dwelling as his home under reg 7(16)(c)(viii) and (17) (student who is temporarily absent from home). As such, there was not a change in the number of occupiers in the claimant's home and a reference under reg 14 could therefore not be made on this ground.
Note: sub-para (3)(a) was not amended when the government introduced rules from 1 April 2013 to protect the position of a claimant whose (or whose partner's) son, daughter, step-son or step-daughter is a "member of the armed forces away on operations (defined in reg 2(1)), but see instead sub-paras (3)(d)(iii) and (4).

(2)   Where there is a **substantial change in the condition of the dwelling or the terms of the tenancy** except in so far as they relate to rent: sub-para (3)(b).

(3)   Where there has been a **rent increase under a term of the tenancy**: sub-para (3)(c). This only applies where the term, or one like it, was in the tenancy when the previous application for a determination was made. It also only applies where the rent officer did not made a significantly high rent determination, an exceptionally high rent determination, or a size-related rent determination following the previous application. That should be clear from the terms of the rent officer's determination. It is important for the First-tier Tribunal to establish the correct legal basis for an increase in rent before going on to consider whether the authority is under a duty to apply to the rent officer under reg 14: *CH 1556/2006*.
In *CH 3590/2007*, the claimant's rent was increased and he sought an increase in his HB. However, the authority decided it was unable to refer the increased rent to the rent officer until 52 weeks had expired since the previous referral and so his HB remained unchanged. The tribunal decided that, as the claimant had a monthly periodic assured shorthold tenancy that had arisen after a fixed term had ended, under a process set out in s13 Housing Act 1988 the rent could be increased once a year and that this was an implied term of the claimant's tenancy. Hence it decided that the 52 week rule could be displaced as sub-para (3)(c) applied. The deputy commissioner agreed that the "term" referred to in sub-para (3)(c) can be express or implied. However, he did not agree that s13 Housing Act 1988 operates by implying such a term. He said (para 11): "Rather it operates by establishing a free-standing statutory procedure under which a landlord may increase the rent payable under the tenancy even though it does not contain a term that would allow her to do so on a contractual basis. The tribunal was not correct to say that the rent could not be increased unless the process set out in section 13 was a term of the appellant's tenancy. The legal

basis for the increased rent is section 13(4). Where it applies, that subsection imposes the increase in the rent as a matter of statute law and does not require contractual authority, whether express or implied, to do so." He concluded that the rent increase notified to the authority was not one to which sub-paras (3)(a)–(d) applied and was therefore not notification of a "change relating to a rent allowance" within reg 14(1)(c).

(4) Where the **previous determination contained a size-related rent determination and there has been a specified change in circumstances**: sub-para (3)(d). These are a change in the composition of the household occupying the dwelling, or a child (or young person) becoming 10 (or 16). This changes the number of bedrooms required: see Sch 2 para 1 Rent Officers (Housing Benefit Functions) Order 1997 on p897 and its Scottish equivalent on p923. Sub-para (3)(d)(iii) is qualified by sub-para (4). It therefore does not amount to a change in the composition of the household if a non-dependant ceases to occupy the claimant's dwelling because s/he is a "member of the armed forces away on operations" (defined in reg 2(1)), or s/he resumes occupation having ceased to be such a member. The non-dependant must be the claimant's (or her/his partner's) son, daughter, step-son or step-daughter.

(5) Where the **claimant is a "young individual"** (defined in reg 2(1) as most single claimants under the age of 35 – there are a number of exceptions) and the **previous determination did not include a single room rent**: sub-para (3)(e). This would be the case if the previous tenant was not a young individual. Note: the age was 25 prior 1 January 2012.

(6) Where an **occupier becomes or ceases to be a "child who cannot share a bedroom"** or a **"member of a couple who cannot share a bedroom"** or a **relevant person** (as mentioned in the provision cited) **becomes or ceases to be a "person who requires overnight care"** or **the claimant or her/his partner ceases to be a "qualifying parent or carer"** (all defined in reg 2(1)) if this affects the applicable size criteria: sub-para (3)(f), (g) and (h). This would be the case if the claimant is now entitled to, or ceases to be entitled to, an additional bedroom.

[¹**3.**–(1) Subject to [² sub-paragraphs (1A) and (2)], this paragraph applies where the landlord is–
(a) a registered housing association;
(b) a county council, with regard to gypsies' and travellers' caravan or mobile home sites and caravans or mobile homes provided on those sites; or
(c) a housing authority, with regard to caravan or mobile home sites or houseboat moorings, payments in respect of which are to take the form of a rent allowance in accordance with regulation 91A(3).
[² (1A) In relation to a profit-making registered provider of social housing, sub-paragraph (1)(a) only applies to its social housing (within the meaning of sections 68 to 77 of the Housing and Regeneration Act 2008).]
(2) Sub-paragraph (1) does not apply where the local authority considers that–
[³ (a)]
(b) the rent payable for that dwelling is unreasonably high.
(3) Where the circumstances set out in head [³] (b) of sub-paragraph (2) exist, the authority must state this in their application for a determination.
(4) In this Schedule "gypsies and travellers" means–
(a) persons with a cultural tradition of nomadism or of living in a caravan; and
(b) all other persons of a nomadic habit of life, whatever their race or origin, including–
    (i) such persons who, on grounds only of their own or their family's or dependant's educational or health needs or old age, have ceased to travel temporarily or permanently; and
    (ii) members of an organised group of travelling show people or circus people (whether or not travelling together as such).]

Amendments
1. Substituted by reg 2(3) of SI 2008 No 2824 as from 6.4.09.
2. Amended by art 4 and Sch 1 paras 54 and 55 of SI 2010 No 671 as from 1.4.10.
3. Amended by reg 5(8) of SI 2012 No 3040 as from 1.4.13.

Analysis
"Housing association" and "registered housing association" are defined in reg 2(1). Note that if the registered housing association is a profit-making registered provider of social housing, the exclusion only applies to the association's social housing: sub-para (1A).

The tenancies listed in sub-para (1) are excluded unless the authority considers the claimant's rent to be unreasonably high: sub-para (2). No specific comparison with suitable alternative accommodation is called for. However, it would be hard for a local authority to reach a conclusion that the home was unreasonably expensive without carrying out such a comparison. See p1784 for the extensive caselaw relating to these concepts. Note that prior to 1 April 2013, the exclusion also applied if the authority considered the accommodation to be unreasonably large. Now such cases may be affected by the "social sector" scheme in regs A13 and B13.

Tenancies on gypsies and travellers sites are only excluded tenancies if the landlord is a county council or a housing authority (a local authority): para (1)(b) and (c). An argument that the rules as they apply to tenancies on private sector sites were unlawful under Human Rights law was unsuccessful: *R (Knowles) v Valuation Agency, Lancashire CC and SSWP* [2013] EWHC 19 (admin).

4.   This paragraph applies to a tenancy entered into before–
(a)   in Scotland, 2nd January 1989; and
(b)   in any other case, 15th January 1989.
5.   This paragraph applies to a regulated tenancy within the meaning of–
(a)   in Scotland, the Rent (Scotland) Act 1984; and
(b)   in any other case, the Rent Act 1977.
6.   This paragraph applies to a housing association tenancy which–
(a)   in Scotland, is a tenancy to which Part 6 of the Rent (Scotland) Act 1984 applies; and
(b)   in any other case, is a housing association tenancy to which Part 6 of the Rent Act 1977 applies.
7.   This paragraph applies to a protected occupancy or statutory tenancy within the meaning of the Rent (Agriculture) Act 1976.
8.   This paragraph applies to a tenancy at a low rent within the meaning of Part 1 of the Landlord and Tenant Act 1954 or Schedule 10 to the Local Government and Housing Act 1989.

Analysis of paragraphs 4 to 8 and 10
Paras 4 to 8 and 10 exclude a number of tenancies, which arose under old legislation. The common theme with tenancies under the old legislation is that the rent will usually be very low in any event. Reference should be made to the legislation mentioned in the paragraphs in any case of doubt.

9.   This paragraph applies to a tenancy of any dwelling which is a bail hostel or probation hostel approved by the Secretary of State under [[1] section 13 of the Offender Management Act 2007].

Amendment
1.   Amended by reg 6(7) of SI 2008 No 2767 as from 17.11.08.

Analysis
Para 9 excludes a tenancy of a dwelling which is an approved bail hostel or probation hostel but note that those required to live in such accommodation are treated as not occupying the dwelling as a home and so cannot qualify for HB in respect of that accommodation: reg 7(5).

10.   This paragraph applies to a tenancy of a housing action trust established under Part 3 of the Housing Act 1988.
11.–(1)   Subject to sub-paragraphs (2) and (3) this paragraph applies to a tenancy–
(a)   in respect of a dwelling comprised in land which has been disposed of under section 32 of the Housing Act 1985 or section 12 of the Housing (Scotland) Act 1987;
(b)   in respect of a dwelling comprised in land which has been disposed of with the consent required by section 43 of the Housing Act 1985 or section 12 of the Housing (Scotland) Act 1987;
(c)   in respect of which the fee simple estate has been acquired, under the right conferred by Chapter 2 of Part 1 of the Housing Act 1996, otherwise than from a housing action trust within the meaning of Part 3 of the Housing Act 1988, or in respect of which the house has been acquired under the right conferred by Part 3 of the Housing (Scotland) Act 1988; or
(d)   in respect of a dwelling disposed of under the New Towns (Transfer of Housing Stock) Regulations 1990 to a person who is an approved person for the purposes of disposal under those Regulations or in respect of a dwelling disposed of pursuant to powers contained in the New Towns (Scotland) Act 1968 to a housing association.
(2)   This paragraph shall not apply to a tenancy to which sub-paragraph (1) refers if–
(a)   there has been an increase in rent since the disposal or acquisition, as the case may be, occurred; and
(b)   the local authority stated in the application for determination that–
    (i)   the claimant occupies a dwelling larger than is reasonably required by him and any others who occupy that dwelling (including any non-dependant of his and any person paying rent to him); or
    (ii)   the rent payable for that dwelling is unreasonably high.
(3)   Where the disposal or acquisition, as the case may be, took place on or after 7th October 2002, sub-paragraph (2)(b) shall apply to a tenancy to which sub-paragraph (1) refers as if head (i) were omitted.

Analysis
Para 11 excludes former local authority or new town lettings which have been transferred to a new owner (eg, a housing association) under the powers cited. It also excludes properties the authority has a duty to sell to "approved landlords" under the "Tenants' Choice" provisions of the Housing Act 1988. The exclusion does not apply, however, if there has been an increase in rent since the transfer and the authority thinks that the rent is unreasonably high, or if the transfer took place before 7 October 2002, the accommodation is unreasonably large: para 11(3). See the commentary to para 3 and to the version of reg 13 mentioned there.

12.   This paragraph applies to a shared ownership tenancy.

Analysis

Para 12 excludes shared ownership tenancies (defined in reg 2(1)). Note, however, that the "local housing allowance" scheme may instead apply – eg, if the ownership is shared with a private landlord.

---

13. In this Schedule, "rent" shall be construed in accordance with paragraph (8) of regulation 14 (interpretation of "tenancy" and other expressions appropriate to a tenancy) and, subject to that paragraph, has the same meaning–

(a) in Scotland, as in section 25 of the Housing (Scotland) Act 1988, except that the reference to the house in subsection (3) shall be construed as a reference to the dwelling;

(b) in any other case, as in section 14 of the Housing Act 1988, except that the reference to the dwelling-house in subsection (4) shall be construed as a reference to the dwelling,

and–

    (i) other expressions have the same meanings as in regulation 14(8);

    (ii) in the case of a determination by a rent officer pursuant to a request for such a determination under regulation 14(1)(e), any reference to a "tenancy" shall be taken as a reference to a prospective tenancy and any reference to an "occupier" or any person "occupying" a dwelling shall, in the case of such a determination, be taken to be a reference to a potential occupier or potential occupation of that dwelling.]

SCHEDULE 3

REGULATION 22

Applicable amounts

Definitions

"the 2012 Act" – see reg 2(1).
"armed forces independence payment" – see reg 2(1).
"attendance allowance" – see reg 2(1).
"child" – see reg 2(1).
"claimant" – see reg 2(1).
"concessionary payment" – see reg 2(1).
"disability living allowance" – see reg 2(1).
"an employment and support allowance", "converted employment and support allowance" and "main phase employment and support allowance" – see reg 2(1).
"Employment and Support Allowance Regulations" – see reg 2(1).
"Employment and Support Allowance (Existing Awards) Regulations" – see reg 2(1).
"family" – see s137(1) SSCBA and Part 4.
"limited capability for work" – see reg 2(1).
"limited capability for work-related activity" – see reg 2(1).
"lone parent" – see reg 2(1).
"member of household" – see s137(1) SSCBA and reg 21.
"member of the work-related activity group" – see reg 2(1).
"non-dependant" – see reg 3.
"partner" – see reg 2(1).
"personal independence payment" – see reg 2(1).
"person in receipt of benefit" – see para 19.
"polygamous marriage" – see reg 2(1).
"qualifying age for state pension credit" – see reg 2(1).
"responsibility for a child" – see Part 4.
"single claimant" – see reg 2(1).
"training allowance" – see reg 2(1).
"Welfare Reform Act" – see reg 2(1).
"Working Tax Credit Regulations" – see reg 2(1).
"young person" – see regs 2(1) and 19(1).

General Note on Schedule 3

This Schedule sets out the amounts of the various elements to be added together under regs 22 and 23 to arrive at a claimant's "applicable amount" on which the calculation of HB is based. For the calculation of HB, see regs 70 to 75.

    Part 1 sets out the personal allowances and allowances for children.

    Part 2 set out the conditions for the family premium. The family premium was abolished from 1 May 2016, subject to transitional rules. See the commentary on p634.

    Parts 3 and 4 set out the rules under which a claimant may qualify for one or more "premiums" and the amounts of the premiums.

Parts 5 and 6 set out the rules under which a claimant may qualify for a "support component" and the amounts of the component. A second component (the "work-related activity component") was abolished from 3 April 2017, subject to transitional rules. See the General Note to Part 5 on p647.

Parts 7 and 8 set out the rules under which a claimant may qualify for a "transitional addition" when transferred to ESA from IS, IB or SDA, or appealing a decision not to transfer the claimant from one of those benefits to ESA, and the rules for calculating the transitional addition.

PART 1

General Note

This Part sets out the amounts of the personal allowances and allowances for children and qualifying young people which form the primary part of the applicable amount. The highest rate personal allowance (for a single person, lone parent or couple, as the case may be) is applicable where the claimant is entitled to main phase ESA, defined in para 1A. See the Analysis to para 1A below.

Otherwise, whether the highest rate personal allowance is applicable depends on: for single people, whether the claimant is aged at least 25; and for lone parents and members of couples, whether the claimant or her/his partner is at least 18.

The different personal allowances for single people under and over the age of 25 do not infringe Arts 8, 14 or Prot 1 Art 1 of the European Convention on Human Rights: *R (Reynolds) v SSWP (*2005) UKHL 37, *TheTimes*, 27 May.

Personal allowances

1. The amounts specified in column (2) below in respect of each person or couple specified in column (1) shall be the amounts specified for the purposes of regulations 22[¹² (1)](a) and 23[¹² (1)](a) and (b)–

Column (1) Person or couple	Column (2) Amount
[⁴ (1) Single claimant who–	(1)
(a) is entitled to main phase employment and support allowance;	(a) [¹¹ £73.10];
(b) is aged not less than 25;	(b) [¹¹ £73.10];
(c) is aged less than 25	(c) [¹¹ £57.90].
(2) Lone parent who–	(2)
(a) is entitled to main phase employment and support allowance;	(a) [¹¹ £73.10];
(b) is aged not less than 18;	(b) [¹¹ £73.10];
(c) is aged less than 18	(c) [¹¹ £57.90].
(3) Couple where–	(3)
(a) the claimant is entitled to main phase employment and support allowance;	(a) [¹¹ £114.85];
(b) at least one member is aged not less than 18;	(b) [¹¹ £114.85];
(b) both members are aged less than 18.	(c) [¹¹ £87.50.]

Amendments

1. Amended by art 19(6) and Sch 6 para 1 of SI 2006 No 645 and reg 8 of SI 2006 No 217 as from 1.4.06 (3.4.06 where rent payable weekly or at intervals of a week).
2. Amended by art 19(6) and Sch 6 para 1 of SI 2007 No 688 as from 1.4.07 (2.4.07 where rent payable weekly or at intervals of a week).
3. Amended by art 19(7) and Sch 6 para 1 of SI 2008 No 632 as from 1.4.08 (7.4.08 where rent payable weekly or in multiples of a week).
4. Substituted by reg 23(a) of SI 2008 No 1082 as from 27.10.08.
5. Amended by art 19(7) and Sch 5 para 1 of SI 2009 No 497 as from 1.4.09 (6.4.09 where rent payable weekly or in multiples of a week).
6. Amended by art 19(6) and Sch 5 para 1 of SI 2010 No 793 as from 1.4.10 (5.4.10 where rent payable weekly or in multiples of a week).
7. Amended by art 20(6) and Sch 5 of SI 2011 No 821 as from 1.4.11 (4.4.11 where rent payable weekly or in multiples of a week).
8. Amended by art 20(6) and Sch 5 of SI 2012 No 780 as from 1.4.12 (2.4.12 where rent payable weekly or in multiples of a week).
9. Amended by art 19(6) and Sch 5 para 1 of SI 2013 No 574 as from 1.4.13.
10. Amended by art 7 and Sch 2 of SI 2014 No 147 as from 1.4.14 (7.4.14 where rent payable weekly or in multiples of a week).
11. Amended by art 7 and Sch 2 of SI 2015 No 30 as from 1.4.15 (6.4.15 where rent payable weekly or in multiples of a week).
12. Amended by reg 7(4) of SI 2017 No 376 as from 6.4.17, subject to transitional provision in reg 9.

[¹ [²**1A.** For the purposes of paragraph 1 a claimant is entitled to main phase employment and support allowance if–

(a) each of the conditions in paragraph 21 is satisfied in relation to the claimant personally [⁴ or the claimant is personally a member of the work-related activity group]; or

(b) the claimant personally is entitled to a converted employment and support allowance [³, or would be entitled but for the application of section 1A of the Welfare Reform Act (duration of contributory allowance)].]]

Amendments

1. Inserted by reg 6(10(a) of SI 2009 No 583 as from 1.4.09 (6.4.09 where rent payable weekly or at intervals of a week).
2. Substituted by reg 27 and Sch 5 para 1(5)(a) of SI 2010 No 1907 as amended by reg 15 of SI 2010 No 2430 as from 1.10.10.
3. Amended by reg 7 of SI 2012 No.913 as from 1.5.12.
4. Amended by reg 5(5) of SI 2017 No 581 as from 23.6.17, subject to transitional and savings provision in reg 9.

Analysis

For the purposes of determining if the highest rate personal allowance is applicable, a claimant is treated as entitled to main phase ESA if s/he personally satisfies all of the conditions in para 21 or is personally a member of the work-related activity group (see reg 2(1)). See p648 for a discussion. A claimant is also treated as entitled to main phase ESA in the following situations.

(1) S/he is personally entitled to a converted ESA.

(2) S/he would be personally entitled to a converted ESA but for the application of s1A WRA 2007. Under s1A WRA 2007 (inserted by s51 WRA 2012) entitlement to contributory ESA ends once the claimant has been entitled for 365 days (disregarding any days spent in the so-called "support group"). A claimant whose entitlement has ended for this reason alone is still treated as entitled to main phase ESA under para 1A.

Converted ESA (defined in reg 2(1)) is ESA which is not income-related to which the claimant is entitled on being transferred from IS "on the grounds of disability", IB or SDA. See Parts 7 and 8 for situations when there may be entitlement to a transitional addition.

2.–(1) The amount specified in column (2) below in respect of each person specified in column (1) shall, for the relevant period specified in column (1), be the amounts specified for the purposes of regulations 22[¹³ (1)](b) and 23[¹³ (1)](c)–

Column (1) Child or young person Persons in respect of the period–	Column (2) Amount
(a) beginning on that person's date of birth and ending on the day preceding the first Monday in September following that person's sixteenth birthday;	(a) [¹⁵ £66.90];
(b) beginning on the first Monday in September following that person's sixteenth birthday and ending on the day preceding that person's [² twentieth] birthday.	(b) [¹⁵ £66.90].

(2) In column (1) of the table in paragraph (1), "the first Monday in September" means the Monday which first occurs in the month of September in any year.

Amendments

1. Amended by art 19(6) and Sch 6 para 2 of SI 2006 No 645 and reg 8 of SI 2006 No 217 as from 1.4.06 (3.4.06 where rent payable weekly or at intervals of a week).
2. Amended by reg 4(4) of SI 2006 No 718 as from 10.4.06.
3. Amended by art 19(6) and Sch 6 para 2 of SI 2007 No 688 as from 1.4.07 (2.4.07 where rent payable weekly or at intervals of a week).
4. Amended by art 19(7) and Sch 6 para 2 of SI 2008 No 632 as from 1.4.08 (7.4.08 where rent payable weekly or in multiples of a week).
5. Amended by art 19(7) and Sch 5 para 2 of SI 2009 No 497 as from 1.4.09 (6.4.09 where rent payable weekly or in multiples of a week).
6. Amended by art 19(6) and Sch 5 para 2 of SI 2010 No 793 as from 1.4.10 (5.4.10 where rent payable weekly or in multiples of a week).
7. Amended by art 20(6) and Sch 5 of SI 2011 No 821 as from 1.4.11 (4.4.11 where rent payable weekly or in multiples of a week).
8. Amended by art 20(6) and Sch 5 of SI 2012 No 780 as from 1.4.12 (2.4.12 where rent payable weekly or in multiples of a week).

9.   Amended by art 19(6) and Sch 5 para 2 of SI 2013 No 574 as from 1.4.13.
10. Amended by art 17(7) and Sch 5 of SI 2014 No 16 as from 1.4.14 (7.4.14 where rent payable weekly or in multiples of a week).
11. Amended by art 17(7) and Sch 5 of SI 2015 No.547 as from 1.4.15 (6.4.15 where rent payable weekly or in multiples of a week).
12. Confirmed by art 22(7) and Sch 5 of SI 2017 No 260 as from 1.4.17 (3.4.17 where rent payable weekly or in multiples of a week).
13. Amended by reg 7(4) of SI 2017 No 376 as from 6.4.17, subject to transitional provision in reg 9.
14. Confirmed by art 23(6) and Sch 4 of SI 2018 No 281 as from 1.4.18 (2.4.18 where rent payable weekly or in multiples of a week).
15. Confirmed by art 23(6) of SI 2019 No 480 as from 1.4.19.

Analysis

An amount is applicable under para 2 in respect of any child or qualifying young person who is a member of the claimant's family (see reg 22(b)), or if the claimant is a member of a polygamous marriage, in respect of any child or qualifying young person for whom the claimant or a partner is responsible and who is a member of the same household (see reg 23(c)). Although there are two bands depending on the age of the child or young person, the amounts for both age bands are currently the same. From 6 April 2017, payment is restricted to allowances for two children or young people, subject to exceptions and transitional rules – see the commentary to reg 22 on p412.

[²¹ PART 2]

Amendments

1.   Confirmed by art 19(7) of SI 2006 No 645 and reg 8 of SI 2006 No 217 as from 1.4.06 (3.4.06 where rent payable weekly or at intervals of a week).
2.   Amended by art 19(7) of SI 2006 No 645 and reg 8 of SI 2006 No 217 as from 1.4.06 (3.4.06 where rent payable weekly or at intervals of a week).
3.   Confirmed by art 19(7) of SI 2007 No 688 as from 1.4.07 (2.4.07 where rent payable weekly or at intervals of a week).
4.   Amended by art 19(7) of SI 2007 No 688 as from 1.4.07 (2.4.07 where rent payable weekly or at intervals of a week).
5.   Confirmed by art 19(8) of SI 2008 No 632 as from 1.4.08 (7.4.08 where rent payable weekly or in multiples of a week).
6.   Amended by art 19(8) of SI 2008 No 632 as from 1.4.08 (7.4.08 where rent payable weekly or in multiples of a week).
7.   Amended by reg 3(10)(a) and (b) of SI 2008 No 1042 as from 19.5.08.
8.   Confirmed by art 19(8) of SI 2009 No 497 as from 1.4.09 (6.4.09 where rent payable weekly or in multiples of a week).
9.   Amended by art 19(8) of SI 2009 No 497 as from 1.4.09 (6.4.09 where rent payable weekly or in multiples of a week).
10. Amended by reg 6(10)(b) of SI 2009 No 583 as from 1.4.09 (6.4.09 where rent payable weekly or at intervals of a week).
11. Confirmed by art 19(7)(a) and (c) of SI 2010 No 793 as from 1.4.10 (5.4.10 where rent payable weekly or in multiples of a week).
12. Amended by art 19(7)(b) of SI 2010 No 793 as from 1.4.10 (5.4.10 where rent payable weekly or in multiples of a week).
13. Substituted by reg 2(8)(a) of SI 2010 No 2449 as from 1.4.11 (4.4.11 where rent payable weekly or in multiples of a week).
14. Confirmed by art 20(7) of SI 2011 No 821 as from 1.4.11 (4.4.11 where rent payable weekly or in multiples of a week).
15. Amended by reg 19(7)(a) of SI 2011 No 2425 as from 31.10.11.
16. Confirmed by art 20(7) of SI 2012 No 780 as from 1.4.12 (2.4.12 where rent payable weekly or in multiples of a week).
17. Confirmed by art 19(7) of SI 2013 No 574 as from 1.4.13.
18. Confirmed by art 17(8) of SI 2014 No 16 as from 1.4.14 (7.4.14 where rent payable weekly or in multiples of a week).
19. Amended by art 17(8) of SI 2014 No 16 as from 1.4.14 (7.4.14 where rent payable weekly or in multiples of a week).
20. Confirmed by art 17(8) of SI 2015 No 547 as from 1.4.15 (6.4.15 where rent payable weekly or in multiples of a week).
21. Omitted by reg 2(1)(c) of SI 2015 No 1857 as from 1.05.16, subject to transitional provisions in reg 4.

General Note

Until 1 May 2016, Part 2 (ie, para 3) provided the rules for entitlement to a family premium if at least one member of a claimant's family was a child or qualifying young person. The premium was abolished from that date subject to transitional rules. See pp592–94 of the 28th edition of this book for details of the entitlement rules and commentary. Note also that a higher rate family premium for lone parents was abolished for most claimants in April 1998. Para 3(3) to (5) gave transitional protection to certain claimants.

Under reg 4 of the Housing Benefit (Abolition of the Family Premium and date of claim) (Amendment) Regulations 2015 SI No.1857, a claimant can still qualify for a family premium if s/he was entitled to HB on 30 April 2016 and on that date either of the following applied.

(1)   The claimant was a member of a family that included a child or qualifying young person.

(2)   The claimant was a partner in a polygamous marriage where s/he or another partner was responsible for a child or qualifying young person who was a member of her/his household.

See the definition of family in s137 SSCBA 1992 and of "child" and "young person" in reg 2(1) HB Regs. See also regs 19 to 21 HB Regs. This transitional protection continues until the relevant condition in (1) or (2) above ceases to apply, or the claimant makes a new claim for HB.

PART 3
Premiums

General Note to Part 3

This Part sets out the rules under which a claimant may qualify to have one or more "premiums" (in addition to the family premium under Part 2 if still entitled – see above) included in her/his applicable amount: see regs 22(d) and 23(e). The aim is to allow those claimants that have particular financial burdens or responsibilities arising out of their circumstances to qualify for higher rates of benefit. For a discussion of some issues to consider in respect of maximising entitlement to HB, see the commentary to para 13 on p638.

Paras 4 to 7, 18 and 19 set out some general rules governing entitlement to premiums, including the rules when a claimant qualifies for more than one premium: see paras 5 and 6. Paras 12 to 17 set out the specific rules relating to entitlement to individual premiums. The premiums that are currently available are:

(1)   Disability premium: paras 12 and 13.

(2)   Severe disability premium: para 14.

(3)   Enhanced disability premium: para 15.

(4)   Disabled child premium: para 16.

(5)   Carer premium: para 17.

The rules of entitlement for some of the premiums are made more complicated by inconsistencies in the terminology used, specifically where a premium is affected by entitlement to, and/or receipt of, and/or payment of, or an award of, another benefit – a "qualifying benefit". As a result, a number of issues arise, including the following.

(1)   A carer needs to consider how her/his claim for carer's allowance (CA) or universal credit (UC) that includes the carer element will affect the severe disability premium entitlement of the person s/he cares for, or of that person's partner (under para 14), particularly where the only financial advantage for the carer is the value of the carer premium (under para 17). For example, a single claimant will lose the severe disability premium if her/his carer is entitled to *and* receiving CA, or has an award of UC that includes the carer element, in respect of caring for her/him. However, a carer can qualify for the carer premium, and a severely disabled person can at the same time qualify for the severe disability premium, if the carer is entitled to, but *not* receiving, CA – eg, where CA overlaps with contributory ESA.

(2)   Severely disabled couples may qualify for two carer premiums, and at the same time the severe disability premium at the couple rate (under paras 14 and 17). This could be the case, for example, where both members of the couple are receiving attendance allowance or the highest or middle rate of disability living allowance care component or the daily living component of PIP and both members are entitled to (but not receiving) CA – eg, because it overlaps with contributory ESA.

Note that contributory ESA is only paid for 365 days, although any time when the ESA claimant has limited capability for work-related activity (when s/he qualifies for a support component) is ignored. If payment of contributory ESA ends, it will no longer overlap with CA, and the carer's receipt of CA would then affect the severe disability premium of the person s/he cares for. If the carer then gives up her/his claim for CA, the notional income rules in reg 42 may be relevant to her/his HB claim. DWP guidance (albeit for IS and JSA) suggests that if a claimant ends her/his claim for CA solely to enable a person other than a member of her/his family for benefit purposes to secure or increase entitlement to benefit, s/he should not be treated as possessing the CA: paras 28608-16 Decision Makers Guide. However, consideration may then be given as to whether the CA is then available on application: reg 42(2).

Note that where there is an award of HB and a "qualifying benefit" is later awarded (or reinstated), regs 4(7B) and (7C), 7(2)(i) and 8(14) D&A Regs effectively allow for backdating of entitlement to premiums which depend on entitlement to (or receipt of) that qualifying benefit, for the period for which arrears of that benefit are paid. See the commentary to those provisions.

4.   Except as provided in paragraph 5, the premiums specified in Part 4 of this Schedule shall, for the purposes of regulations 22[¹ (1)](d) and 23[¹ (1)](e), be applicable to a claimant who satisfies the condition specified in paragraphs 8 to 17 in respect of that premium.

Amendment
1.   Amended by reg 7(4) of SI 2017 No 376 as from 6.4.17, subject to transitional provision in reg 9.

Analysis
Para 4 gives effect to the rates of the various premiums which are set out in Part 4 of the Schedule.

---

5.   Subject to paragraph 6, where a claimant satisfies the conditions in respect of more than one premium in this Part of this Schedule, only one premium shall be applicable to him and, if they are different amounts, the higher or highest amount shall apply.

Analysis
Para 5 states a general rule that where a claimant is entitled to more than one of the premiums in Part 3, only the highest is included in her/his applicable amount. This is subect to the exceptions in para 6. Therefore, since the omission of the bereavement premium (para 8) and pensioner premiums (paras 9–11) from Part 3, the overall effect is as follows.
(1)   The severe disability premium, the enhanced disability premium, the disabled child premium and the carer premium may all be included in addition to each other, and in addition to the disability premium – the only "other premium which may apply": para 6. They can also be paid in addition to the family premium (if the claimant is still entitled – see p634).
(2)   The transitional protection leading to the higher rate family premium for lone parents is lost if the disability premium is applicable (see pp592–94 of the 28th edition of this book).
Note also that a disability premium cannot be included if the claimant has, or is treated as having, "limited capability for work": para 13(9). However, the claimant may instead qualify for a support component under Part 5 of the Schedule. For a discussion of some issues to consider in respect of maximising entitlement to HB, see the commentary to para 13 on p638.

[¹**6.**   The following premiums, namely–
(a)   a severe disability premium to which paragraph 14 applies;
(b)   an enhanced disability premium to which paragraph 15 applies;
(c)   a disabled child premium to which paragraph 16 applies; and
(d)   a carer premium to which paragraph 17 applies,
may be applicable in addition to any other premium which may apply under this Schedule.]

Amendment
1.   Amended by reg 3(10)(c) of SI 2008 No 1042 as from 19.5.08.

7.–(1)   Subject to sub-paragraph (2), for the purposes of this Part of this Schedule, once a premium is applicable to a claimant under this Part, a person shall be treated as being in receipt of any benefit for–
(a)   in the case of a benefit to which the Social Security (Overlapping Benefits) Regulations 1979 applies, any period during which, apart from the provisions of those Regulations, he would be in receipt of that benefit; and
(b)   any period spent by a person in undertaking a course of training or instruction provided or approved by the Secretary of State under section 2 of the 1973 Act, or by [¹ Skills Development Scotland,] Scottish Enterprise or Highlands and Islands Enterprise under section 2 of the Enterprise and New Towns (Scotland) Act 1990 or for any period during which he is in receipt of a training allowance.
(2)   For the purposes of the carer premium under paragraph 17, a person shall be treated as being in receipt of carer's allowance by virtue of sub-paragraph (1)(a) only if and for so long as the person in respect of whose care the allowance has been claimed remains in receipt of attendance allowance, [² the care component of disability living allowance at the highest or middle rate prescribed in accordance with section 72(3) of the Act [³ ,] the daily living component of personal independence payment at the standard or enhanced rate in accordance with section 78(3) of the 2012 Act][³ or armed forces independence payment].

Amendments
1.   Amended by reg 6(3)(c) of SI 2009 No 583 as from 6.4.09.
2.   Amended by reg 8 and Sch para 36(6)(a) of SI 2013 No 388 as from 8.4.13.
3.   Amended by art 7 and Sch para 34(6)(a) of SI 2013 No 591 as from 8.4.13.

Analysis
Para 7 deals with the situation where entitlement to one of the premiums depends on the claimant being in receipt of some other benefit. The effect of para 7(1)(a) is that where a claimant is not receiving a benefit because the

Social Security (Overlapping Benefits) Regulations 1979 apply, s/he will nevertheless be treated as being in receipt of that benefit for the purposes of Part 3. Under para 7(1)(b), if a claimant moves off benefit because s/he is participating in specified training, s/he is treated as being in receipt of benefit for the purposes of Part 3.

Para 7(2) was effectively made irrelevant by amendments to the carer premium rules (in April 2000 and October 2003). The issue for a carer premium under para 17 is whether the claimant or her/his partner is *entitled* to CA. The claimant or the partner are not required to be "in receipt" of that benefit. See the commentary to para 17. Note, however, that entitlement to CA will in any event end when the person being cared for is no longer in receipt of AA, the highest or middle rate of the care component of DLA, the daily living component of PIP or armed forces independence payment.

See also paras 18 and 19 on p645.

[¹ Bereavement premium]
[¹ **8.**]

Amendment
1.　　Revoked by reg 2 and the Sch of SI 2007 No 2618 as from 1.10.07.

[¹ Pensioner Premium for persons under 75
9.]

Amendment
1.　　Omitted by reg 3(10)(d) of SI 2008 No 1042 as from 19.5.08.

[¹ Pensioner Premium for persons 75 and over
10.]

Amendment
1.　　Omitted by reg 3(10)(d) of SI 2008 No 1042 as from 19.5.08.

[² Higher Pensioner Premium
11.]

Amendments
1.　　Amended by reg 15(5) of SI 2006 No 2378 as from 9.10.06.
2.　　Omitted by reg 3(10)(d) of SI 2008 No 1042 as from 19.5.08.

Disability Premium
12.　　The condition is that–

(a)　　where the claimant is a single claimant or a lone parent, he [¹ has not attained the qualifying age for state pension credit] and the additional condition specified in paragraph 13 is satisfied; or

(b)　　where the claimant has a partner, either–

　　(i)　　the claimant [¹ has not attained the qualifying age for state pension credit] and the additional condition specified in paragraph 13(1)(a) or (b) is satisfied by him; or

　　(ii)　　his partner [¹ has not attained the qualifying age for state pension credit] and the additional condition specified in paragraph 13(1)(a) is satisfied by his partner.

Amendment
1.　　Amended by reg 26(2) of SI 2009 No 1488 as from 6.4.10.

General Note
There are two conditions for entitlement to a disability premium. If the claimant is single or a lone parent, s/he must be under the qualifying age for PC (defined in reg 2(1) and discussed on p731) and satisfy the condition in para 13. If s/he has a partner, there are two ways to qualify. Either the claimant must be under the qualifying age for PC and satisfy a condition in para 13(1)(a) or (b), or the partner must be under that age and satisfy the condition in para 13(1)(a). Satisfying para 13(1)(b) will not suffice in the case of a partner.

Additional Condition for the [³ Disability Premium]
13.–(1)　　Subject to sub-paragraph (2) and paragraph 7, the additional condition referred to in paragraphs 11 and 12 is that either–

(a)　　the claimant or, as the case may be, his partner–

　　(i)　　is in receipt of one or more of the following benefits: attendance allowance, disability living allowance, [⁶ personal independence payment,] [⁷ , armed forces independence payment] the disability element or the severe disability element of working tax credit as specified in regulation 20(1)(b) and (f) of the Working Tax Credit Regulations, mobility supplement, long-term incapacity benefit under Part 2 of the Act or severe disablement allowance under Part 3 of the Act but, in the case of long-term incapacity benefit or severe disablement allowance only where it is paid in respect of him; or

(ii)   was in receipt of long-term incapacity benefit under Part 2 of the Act when entitlement to that benefit ceased on account of the payment of a retirement pension under that Act [¹⁰ or a state pension under Part 1 of the Pensions Act 2014] and the claimant has since remained continuously entitled to housing benefit and, if the long-term incapacity benefit was payable to his partner, the partner is still a member of the family; or

(iii)   [¹] was in receipt of attendance allowance or disability living allowance but payment of benefit has been suspended in accordance with regulations made under section 113(2) of the Act or otherwise abated as a consequence of the claimant or his partner becoming a patient within the meaning of [¹ regulation 28(11)(e) (treatment of child care charges)]; or

[⁶ [⁸ (iiia) was in receipt of personal independence payment that is no longer payable by virtue of regulations made under section 86(1) (hospital in-patients) of the 2012 Act.]]

(iv)   is provided by the Secretary of State with an invalid carriage or other vehicle under section 5(2) of the National Health Service Act 1977 (other services) or, in Scotland by the Scottish Ministers, under section 46 of the National Health Service (Scotland) Act 1978 (provision of services) or receives payments by way of grant from the Secretary of State under paragraph 2 of Schedule 2 to the Act of 1977 (additional provisions as to vehicles) or, in Scotland by the Scottish Ministers, under section 46 of the Act of 1978; or

[⁹ (v)   is certified as severely sight impaired or blind by a consultant ophthalmologist; or]

(b)   the claimant–

(i)   is, or is treated as, incapable of work in accordance with the provisions of, and regulations made under, Part 12A of the Act (incapacity for work); and

(ii)   has been incapable, or has been treated as incapable, of work for a continuous period of not less than–

(aa)   in the case of a claimant who is terminally ill within the meaning of section 30B(4) of the Act, 196 days;

(bb)   in any other case, 364 days.

[⁹ (2)   For the purposes of sub-paragraph (1)(a)(v), a person who has ceased to be certified as severely sight impaired or blind on regaining his eyesight shall nevertheless be treated as severely sight impaired or blind, as the case may be, and as satisfying the additional condition set out in that sub-paragraph for a period of 28 weeks following the date on which he ceased to be so certified].

(3)   For the purposes of sub-paragraph (1)(b), once [³] the disability premium is applicable to a claimant by virtue of his satisfying the additional condition specified in that provision, if he then ceases, for a period of 8 weeks or less, to be treated as incapable of work or to be incapable of work he shall, on again becoming so incapable of work, immediately thereafter be treated as satisfying the condition in sub-paragraph (1)(b).

[³ (4)]

(5)   For the purposes of sub-paragraph (1)(b), once the disability premium is applicable to a claimant by virtue of his satisfying the additional condition specified in that provision, he shall continue to be treated as satisfying that condition for any period spent by him in undertaking a course of training provided under section 2 of the 1973 Act or for any period during which he is in receipt of a training allowance.

(6)   For the purposes of sub-paragraph (1)(b), where any two or more periods of incapacity are separated by a break of not more than 56 days, those periods shall be treated as one continuous period.

(7)   For the purposes of this paragraph, a reference to a person who is or was in receipt of long-term incapacity benefit includes a person who is or was in receipt of short-term incapacity benefit at a rate equal to the long-term rate by virtue of section 30B(4)(a) of the Act (short-term incapacity benefit for a person who is terminally ill), or who would be or would have been in receipt of short-term incapacity benefit at such a rate but for the fact that the rate of short-term incapacity benefit already payable to him is or was equal to or greater than the long-term rate.

(8)   In the case of a claimant who is a welfare to work beneficiary [³ (a person to whom regulation 13A(1) of the Social Security (Incapacity for Work) (General) Regulations 1995 applies, and who again becomes incapable of work for the purposes of Part 12A of the Act)]–

(a)   the reference to a period of 8 weeks in sub-paragraph (3); and

(b)   the reference to a period of 56 days in sub-paragraph (6),

shall in each case be treated as a reference to a period of [² 104 weeks].

[⁴ (9)   The claimant is not entitled to the disability premium if the claimant has, or is treated as having, limited capability for work [⁵].]

Amendments

1.   Amended by reg 2(15)(b) of SI 2005 No 2502 as amended by Sch 2 para 27 of SI 2006 No 217 as from 1.4.06 (3.4.06 where rent payable weekly or at intervals of a week).

2.   Amended by reg 15(5) of SI 2006 No 2378 as from 9.10.06.

3.   Amended by reg 3(10)(e)-(h) of SI 2008 No 1042 as from 19.5.08.

4.   Inserted by reg 23(b) of SI 2008 No 1082 as from 27.10.08.

5.   Amended by reg 31(a) of SI 2008 No 2428 as from 27.10.08.

6.   Amended by reg 8 and Sch para 36(6)(b) of SI 2013 No 388 as from 8.4.13.
7.   Amended by art 7 and Sch para 34(6)(b) of SI 2013 No 591 as from 8.4.13.
8.   Amended by reg 3(6)(a) of SI 2014 No 213 as from 1.4.14 (7.4.14 where rent payable weekly or in multiples of a week).
9.   Amended by reg 3(5)(c) of SI 2014 No 2888 as from 26.11.14.
10.   Amended by art 28(4) of SI 2015 No 1985 as from 6.4.16.

Analysis

This highly complex piece of legislation sets out the additional conditions for a disability premium specified in para 12. Only one of the conditions in sub-para (1)(a) or (b) need be satisfied. To satisfy sub-para (1)(a), either the claimant or her/his partner must fulfil any one of the six heads. To satisfy sub-para (1)(b), the claimant must fulfill all the criteria set out there. Note the deeming provisions in paras 7, 18 and 19 relating to receipt and payment of benefit.

Additional condition for a claimant or a partner

Sub-para (1)(a)(i). The claimant or her/his partner must be **receiving one of the benefits or elements of WTC listed**. Note that the relevant person must be receiving incapacity benefit (IB) or severe disablement allowance (SDA) for themselves and not on behalf of some other person. This prevents arguments such as those raised in *Rider v Chief Adjudication Officer* [1996] *Times* 30 January, CA. See also para 19.

In the case of IB, only long-term IB normally suffices but if a claimant is getting short-term IB as a terminally ill person or would qualify as such were s/he not already getting a higher rate than that applicable to the terminally ill, s/he is deemed to be getting long-term IB for this purpose: sub-para (7). This is very unlikely now to apply because new claims for IB are now only possible if the claimant is entitled to IS: see reg 2 Employment and Support Allowance (Transitional Provisions) Regulations 2008 SI No.795 as amended by SI 2008 No.2783 and SI 2010 No.1907. If, after the claim for IB, the claimant is still on IS, the disability premium is not needed as the amount of HB entitlement is assessed without reference to an applicable amount.

Sub-para (1)(a)(ii). The claimant or her/his partner must have been **receiving long-term IB and subsequently retirement pension or state pension**. If the IB was payable to the claimant's partner, the partner must still be a member of the family.

Only long-term IB normally suffices but if a claimant or her/his partner is getting short-term IB as a terminally ill person or would qualify as such were s/he not already getting a higher rate than that applicable to the terminally ill, s/he is deemed to be getting long-term IB for this purpose: sub-para (7). However, see the discussion of sub-para (1)(a)(i) above.

Note that this sub-para will generally not be relevant because if the claimant or her/his partner is of at least the qualifying age for PC (defined in reg 2(1)) and neither is on IS, income-based JSA or income-related ESA, her/his claim is assessed under the HB(SPC) Regs: reg 5. If the claimant or her/his partner is on one of those benefits, the amount of HB entitlement is assessed without reference to an applicable amount. Note also that, from 15 May 2019 a "mixed-age couple" is generally not able to make a new claim for HB under either the HB Regs or the HB(SPC) Regs – see the General Note to reg 5 on p252.

Sub-para (1)(a)(iii) and (iiia) applies where the claimant or her/his partner is a **"patient" and payment of AA, DLA or PIP has been suspended**. See reg 28(11)(e) on p430 for the meaning of patient in sub-para (1)(a)(iii). Either the claimant or her/his partner must have been in receipt of AA, DLA or PIP. For AA and DLA, payment must then have been suspended under the Social Security (Attendance Allowance) Regulations 1991 or the Social Security (Disability Living Allowance) Regulations 1991 due to her/him being a "patient". Both sets of regulations do not speak in terms of suspension of benefit but rather of it being a "condition of receipt" of AA or DLA that the relevant person does not become a patient. Loss of benefit under the relevant provisions should be seen as a suspension of benefit for the purposes of this sub-paragraph. For PIP, the relevant regulations are the Social Security (Personal Independence Payment) Regulations 2013. See specifically regs 29 and 30 of those regulations.

Sub-para (1)(a)(iv) applies where the claimant or her/his partner is **provided with one of the vehicles or payments listed**. The reference to s5(2) NHS Act 1977 (which has been repealed) should now be read as a reference to Sch 1 para 9 NHS Act 2006 under which a clinical commissioning group "may make arrangements for the provision of vehicles (including wheelchairs) for persons for whom the group has responsibility and who appear to it to who have a physical impairment which has a substantial and long-term adverse effect on their ability to carry out normal day-to-day activities".

Sub-para (1)(a)(v) applies to those who are **certified as severely sight impaired or blind** by a consultant ophthalmologist. Under sub-para (2) (note that SI 2014 No.2888 said to substitute the para as now shown above, but with the paragraph number (ii) which it is presumed was an error), a person who has ceased to be certified is treated as fulfilling this condition for 28 weeks after ceasing to be so certified.

Additional condition for a claimant

Sub-para (1)(b) requires that the claimant is **incapable of work** for the purposes of the IB legislation. Pursuant to Part 12A SSCBA, the question as to whether a claimant is, or is treated as, incapable for work is conclusively determined by the DWP decision maker. Therefore, if there is any dispute as to whether a claimant is incapable of work, it must be referred to the DWP even if the claimant is not claiming DWP benefits. A claimant who does not receive (and does not need to claim) DWP benefits (eg, IB or ESA) may qualify for incapacity credits, in which case there will be a determination that s/he is incapable of work which the local authority must then act upon. There does not appear to be anything in the HB regulations requiring an application for incapacity credits, which has implications for the question of entitlement to a disability premium under sub-para (1)(b) for a period starting on or after 27 October 2008. See below for a discussion. If the claimant does not want to claim ESA, and would not be better-off were s/he to qualify for the support component under Part 5 (see p648 for a discussion), s/he should write to the DWP stating s/he wants the Secretary of State to assess her/his capacity for work under Part 12A SSCBA for the purposes of HB disability premium.

The claimant must be incapable or so treated for at least 364 days. The period is reduced to 196 days in the case of a claimant who is terminally ill. It seems that the question of whether someone is terminally ill must be resolved by the local authority and not by the DWP decision maker. By SSCBA s30B(4), "a person is terminally ill if he suffers from a progressive disease and his death in consequence of that disease can reasonably be expected within 6 months."

A prisoner may remain incapable of work. Serving as a prisoner prevents receipt of IB but does not deem her/him to be capable of work: *CIS 15611/1996.*

From 27 October 2008 IS awarded "on the grounds of disability", IB and SDA were replaced with employment and support allowance (ESA). Under the Employment and Support Allowance (Transitional Provisions) Regulations 2008 SI No.795 (as amended by SI 2008 No.2428, SI 2008 No.2783 and SI 2010 No.1907) and the Income Support (Prescribed Categories of Person) Regulations 2009 No 3152, people can retain entitlement to IS "on the grounds of disability", IB and SDA after 27 October 2008 until transferred to ESA. However, if a claim is made for a period starting on or after 27 October 2008, the claim is generally treated as a claim for ESA. Since 31 January 2011, there have only been two exceptions: where a claim for IS "on the grounds of disability" is made by a claimant entitled to IB or SDA, or where a claim for IB is made by a claimant entitled to IS "on the grounds of disability".

For HB, if a claimant qualifies for the disability premium on the basis of incapacity for work before 27 October 2008, s/he will continue to do so at least until s/he is entitled to ESA or NI credits on the basis of limited capability for work (see sub-para (9) and the discussion on maximising entitlement). However, to enable the transitional provisions for IS, IB and SDA to continue, s67 and Sch 8 WRA 2007, which repeal ss171A to 171G SSCBA (ie, Part 12A SSCBA) have not yet been brought into force. This suggests that for HB, a claimant could still be, or could still be treated as, incapable of work, even where the issue arises for the first time on or after 27 October 2008 – ie, where s/he does not make a claim for ESA.

Note that most of those entitled to IS "on the grounds of disability", IB and SDA have been assessed and, if they qualify, transferred to ESA. HB claimants who (or whose partners) are entitled to "converted employment and support allowance" (defined in reg 2(1) as ESA which is not income-related and to which there is entitlement as a result of a "conversion decision", broadly ESA paid to those transferred from IS "on the grounds of disability", IB or SDA) will have qualified for a component instead of a disability premium. As discussed below, in some cases, the HB entitlement of those who qualify for a disability premium is more generous than the HB entitlement of those who qualify for a component. To ensure a claimant is no worse off if s/he (or her/his partner) is entitled to converted ESA, or in specified circumstances is appealing a conversion decision, s/he may also be entitled to a protected amount of HB – a transitional addition: Sch 3 Parts 7 and 8.

Those transferred to income-related ESA will eventually be transferred to UC.

Sub-paragraphs (3) to (6), (8) and (9)

Sub-paras (3) to (6) are deeming provisions meant to protect entitlement to the disability premium once a claimant has qualified for one under sub-para (1)(b).

(1)   A period where the claimant is capable of work for eight weeks or less does not prevent the claimant satisfying the condition in sub-para (1)(b): sub-para (3). In the case of a "welfare to work beneficiary" (see below), this period is extended to 104 weeks: sub-para (8)(a).

(2)   A claimant is treated as satisfying the condition in para (1)(b) during a period spent undertaking training under the Employment and Training Act 1973 or in receipt of a training allowance (see reg 2(1) for a definition): sub-para (5).

(3)   A break in a period of incapacity of not more than 56 days is ignored: sub-para (6). In the case of a "welfare to work beneficiary" (see below), this period is extended to 104 weeks: sub-para (8)(b).

Note the transitional protection in Sch 3 para 2 HB&CTB(CP) Regs (see p1774).

However, where there has been a break in entitlement to a benefit claimed on the basis of incapacity for work (ie, IS "on the grounds of disability", IB or SDA) and the claimant becomes incapable of work again, s/he will only be able to claim one of those benefits in limited circumstances. If s/he instead claims ESA, and is treated as having limited capability for work, s/he will not qualify for a disability premium: see para (9). Thus the linking periods as set out, and as extended by para (8), will have limited application – eg, they can only potentially apply where the claimant has not made a claim for ESA. See the discussion above about the rules from 27 October 2008.

A "welfare to work beneficiary" is someone falling within the scope of reg 13A(1) Social Security (Incapacity for Work) (General) Regulations 1995, which prescribes the conditions. First, the claimant must have been incapable of work for more than 196 days. Second, s/he must have stopped receiving the benefit s/he was receiving as a result of the incapacity (eg, IB or IS) on or after 5 October 1998. Third, s/he must have commenced remunerative work or a training course for which training allowance is received within a month of benefit ceasing. S/he is a welfare to work beneficiary for a fixed period of 104 weeks for the purposes of this Schedule. In cases of doubt, seek clarification from the DWP as to whether a claimant has acquired this status. However, it appears that it is for the local authority and not the DWP to decide whether this condition is met for HB purposes (although the decision as to whether a claimant is incapable of work is made by the DWP: see above).

Sub-para (9). Under sub-para (9), a claimant is not entitled to a disability premium if s/he has, or is treated as having, limited capability for work (defined in reg 2(1) as having the meaning given in s1(4) of the WRA 2007). This is one of the basic conditions of entitlement to ESA, and to NI credits where the claimant is not fit for work. A claimant who has (or is treated as having) limited capability for work-related activity may instead be entitled to a support component: see paras 21 to 26. (Note that the work-related activity component is no longer available for claims made on or after 3 April 2017, subject to transitional rules. See the General Note to Part 5 on p647 and the transitional rules on p1892.)

Note that sub-para (9) does *not* disentitle a claimant to the disability premium if it is only her/his *partner* who has, or is treated as having, limited capability for work. See below for a discussion of the potential effect of this.

Sub-para (9) applies even if a claimant would otherwise qualify for the disability premium on a ground not related to fitness for work – eg, under para 13(1)(a)(ii) on the basis of her/his (or her/his partner's) entitlement to DLA or PIP or under para 13(1)(a)(v) because s/he (or her/his partner) is certified as severely sight-impaired or blind.

For the position of those claiming IS "on grounds of disability", IB or SDA from 27 October 2008, see the discussion above. See also the commentary to sub-para (1)(b).

Maximising entitlement

On the face of it, the situation appears to be straightforward: if an HB claimant is incapable of work for the purposes of incapacity benefit legislation, s/he qualifies for a disability premium under para 13(1)(b); if s/he has limited capability for work-related activity for the purposes of ESA legislation, s/he qualifies for a support component under para 24. Those claiming before 3 April 2017 who continue to have, or be treated as having, limited capability for work are entitled to continue to receive the work-related activity component (see p1892).

Because (currently) the disability premium for a single claimant is higher in value than the work-related activity component, but lower in value than the support component, and because there is a higher rate of disability premium where the claimant is a member of a couple, but there is no couple rate of the work-related activity component or support component, there are some important issues to bear in mind, in particular for those HB claimants still entitled to the work-related activity component.

Unless a claimant is entitled to maximum HB because s/he or her/his partner is on IS, income-based JSA or income-related ESA (or UC), there are situations where consideration needs to be given to how the claimant can qualify for the highest rate of HB for her/him. If a single claimant has limited capability for work, it may be beneficial not to claim ESA (or not to apply for NI credits on the basis of limited capability for work), to avoid a determination that may result in her/him failing to qualify for, or losing entitlement to, a disability premium – ie, if s/he would only qualify for the work-related activity component and not the support component. In the case of couples, it is only if the *claimant* has (or is treated as having) limited capability for work that there is no entitlement to the disability premium. It does not matter if the claimant's *partner* has (or is treated as having) limited capability for work. It may therefore be beneficial for a couple to consider which member should be the HB claimant if this would mean they would qualify for a disability premium (instead of a support component) – eg, if only one member of the couple (person A) has (or is treated as having) limited capability for work and receives DLA. In this case, if the other member of the couple (person B) claims HB, s/he qualifies for a disability premium at the rate for a couple under paras 13(1)(a)(i) and 20(5)(b). Note that most of those on IS "on grounds of disability", IB or SDA, have been assessed and, if qualifying, transferred to ESA by the end of March 2014. In this situation, if the person transferred to ESA was an HB claimant, s/he no longer qualified for a disability premium, but instead qualified for a component and possibly a transitional addition: Sch 3 Parts 5 to 8.

It is important to take the following into account.

(1)   The personal allowance of a single claimant under 25, a lone parent under 18 or a member of a couple both under 18 increases when the claimant is "entitled to main phase ESA": see paras 1 and 1A. Note, however, that a claimant will in some cases only count as entitled to main phase ESA after what is known as the "assessment phase" (the first 13 weeks after a claim for ESA or NI credits).

(2)   Based on the 2019/20 benefit rates, the amount of the disability premium for a single claimant is higher than the work-related activity component, but lower than the support component. However, the amount of the disability premium for a couple is higher than both components.

(3)   If a claimant qualifies for a support component, s/he also qualifies for an enhanced disability premium under para 15. Otherwise, to qualify for that premium for her/himself or her/his partner, the claimant or the partner must be aged less than the qualifying age for PC and qualify for the highest rate DLA care component, the enhanced rate of the PIP daily living component or armed forces independence payment.

(4)   A claimant cannot qualify for a disability premium if s/he has, or is treated as having, limited capability for work – ie, if s/he has qualified for ESA or NI credits on the basis of limited capability for work: para 13(9). This applies even if the claimant might qualify for a disability premium on grounds other than limited

capability for work – eg, where s/he or her/his partner is receiving DLA or PIP. However, s/he also cannot qualify for either the work-related activity component or the support component until one of the conditions in para 21(c) is met, that is, when the "assessment phase" has ended or would have ended, unless the claimant (or her his partner) is someone who can qualify for a component before it has ended. So potentially, there is a period during which HB will be calculated with neither the disability premium, nor one of the components.

(5) Where both the claimant and her/his partner satisfy the conditions for a component, the component to be included is that to which the *claimant* is entitled, even if the partner qualifies for a higher rate component: para 22(2).

(6) It may be important for the claimant to apply for NI credits. These help claimants satisfy the contribution conditions for certain contributory benefits, including state pension. See CPAG's *Welfare Benefits and Tax Credits Handbook* for details.

Note: the claimant and her/his partner may need to consider swapping the claimant role to ensure entitlement to the highest possible rate of HB. It will be important to bear in mind not just issues in respect of maximising entitlement, but also whether any of the various forms of transitional protection will be lost. Note also possible application of the notional income rule in reg 42(2) if a person elects not to claim ESA, but see the commentary on p458.

Severe Disability Premium

14.–(1) The condition is that the claimant is a severely disabled person.

(2) For the purposes of sub-paragraph (1), a claimant shall be treated as being a severely disabled person if, and only if–

(a) in the case of a single claimant, a lone parent or a claimant who is treated as having no partner in consequence of sub-paragraph (3)–

    (i) he is in receipt of attendance allowance, [⁴ the care component of disability living allowance at the highest or middle rate prescribed in accordance with section 72(3) of the Act or the daily living component of personal independence payment at the standard or enhanced rate in accordance with section 78(3) of the 2012 Act][⁵ or armed forces independence payment]; and

    (ii) subject to sub-paragraph (4), he has no non-dependants aged 18 or over normally residing with him or with whom he is normally residing; and

    (iii) no person is entitled to, and in receipt of, a carer's allowance under section 70 of the Act [⁸ or has an award of universal credit which includes the carer element under regulation 29 of the Universal Credit Regulations 2013] in respect of caring for him;

(b) in the case of a claimant who has a partner–

    (i) the claimant is in receipt of attendance allowance, [⁴ the care component of disability living allowance at the highest or middle rate prescribed in accordance with section 72(3) of the Act or the daily living component of personal independence payment at the standard or enhanced rate in accordance with section 78(3) of the 2012 Act][⁵ or armed forces independence payment]; and

    (ii) his partner is also in receipt of such an allowance [⁴ or payment] or, if he is a member of a polygamous marriage, all the partners of that marriage are in receipt of such an allowance [⁴ or payment]; and

    (iii) subject to sub-paragraph (4), the claimant has no non-dependants aged 18 or over normally residing with him or with whom he is normally residing,

and either a person is [² entitled to and in receipt of a carer's allowance] [⁸ or has an award of universal credit which includes the carer element] in respect of caring for only one of a couple or, in the case of a polygamous marriage, for one or more but not all the partners of the marriage, or as the case may be, no person is entitled to and in receipt of such an allowance [⁸ or has such an award of universal credit] in respect of caring for either member of a couple or any partner of a polygamous marriage.

(3) Where a claimant has a partner who does not satisfy the condition in sub-paragraph (2)(b)(ii), and that partner is [⁷ severely sight impaired or blind or treated as severely sight impaired or blind] within the meaning of paragraph 13(1)(a)(v) and (2), that partner shall be treated for the purposes of sub-paragraph (2) as if he were not a partner of the claimant.

(4) For the purposes of sub-paragraph (2)(a)(ii) and (2)(b)(iii) no account shall be taken of–

(a) a person receiving attendance allowance, [⁴ the care component of disability living allowance at the highest or middle rate prescribed in accordance with section 72(3) of the Act or the daily living component of personal independence payment at the standard or enhanced rate in accordance with section 78(3) of the 2012 Act][⁵ or armed forces independence payment]; or

(b) a person who is [⁷ severely sight impaired or blind or treated as severely sight impaired or blind] within the meaning of paragraph 13(1)(a)(v) and (2).

(5) For the purposes of sub-paragraph (2)(b) a person shall be treated–

(a) as being in receipt of attendance allowance, or the care component of disability living allowance at the highest or middle rate prescribed in accordance with section 72(3) of the Act, if he would, but for his being a patient for a period exceeding 28 days, be so in receipt;

(b)   as being entitled to and in receipt of a carer's allowance [⁸ or having an award of universal credit which includes the carer element] if he would, but for the person for whom he was caring being a patient in hospital for a period exceeding 28 days, be so entitled and in receipt [⁸ or have such an award of universal credit].

[⁴ (c)   as being in receipt of the daily living component of personal independence payment at the standard or enhanced rate in accordance with section 78 of the 2012 Act, if he would, but for [⁶ payment ceasing by virtue of] regulations made under section 86(1) (hospital inpatients) of the 2012 Act, be so in receipt.]

(6)   For the purposes of sub-paragraph (2)(a)(iii) and (2)(b), no account shall be taken of an award of carer's allowance [⁸ or universal credit which includes the carer element] to the extent that payment of such an award is backdated for a period before [¹ the date on which the award is first paid].

(7)   In sub-paragraph (2)(a)(iii) and (b), references to a person being in receipt of a carer's allowance [⁸ or as having an award of universal credit which includes the carer element] shall include references to a person who would have been in receipt of that allowance [⁸ or had such an award of universal credit] but for the application of a restriction under section [³ 6B or] 7 of the Social Security Fraud Act 2001 (loss of benefit provisions).

Amendments

1.   Amended by reg 6(6) of SI 2007 No 719 as from 2.4.07.
2.   Amended by reg 6(10(c) of SI 2009 No 583 as from 6.4.09.
3.   Amended by reg 4 of SI 2010 No 1160 as from 1.4.10.
4.   Amended by reg 8 and Sch para 36(6)(c) of SI 2013 no 388 as from 8.4.13.
5.   Amended by art 7 and Sch para 34(6)(c) of SI 2013 No 591 as from 8.4.13.
6.   Amended by reg 3(6)(b) of SI 2014 No 213 as from 1.4.14 (7.4.14 where rent payable weekly or in multiples of a week).
7.   Amended by reg 3(5)(c)(ii) of SI 2014 No 2888 as from 26.11.14.
8.   Inserted by reg 17(2) of SI 2015 No 1754 as from 4.11.15.

Analysis

To qualify for the severe disability premium, the claimant must be a "severely disabled person": sub-para (1). The claimant may be treated as such only in accordance with the terms of sub-para (2). See also the General Note to Part 3 of this Schedule (on p634).

Sub-para (2)(a): single claimants and lone parents, and those treated as having no partner under sub-para (3).

There are three criteria, all of which must be fulfilled.

(1)   The claimant must be in receipt of attendance allowance (AA), disability living allowance (DLA) highest or middle rate care component, either rate of PIP daily living component or armed forces independence payment (AFIP). Note the deeming provisions in paras 18 and 19 relating to receipt and payment of benefit.

(2)   There are no non-dependants normally residing with her/him. For the meaning of "non-dependant" and "normally resides", see reg 3. Note that if such people are themselves receiving AA, highest or middle rate DLA care component, either rate of PIP daily living component or AFIP, or are severely sight-impaired or blind or treated as such for the purposes of para 13(1)(a)(v) and (2) then they are ignored: sub-para (4).

(3)   No one is entitled to and in receipt of carer's allowance (CA), or has an award of universal credit (UC) that includes the carer element, in respect of caring for him/her. Backdated CA or UC that includes the carer element will not count: sub-para (6).

Sub-para (2)(b): claimants with partners. Note that a person can be treated as if s/he were not a claimant's partner under sub-para (3).

There are four criteria which must be fulfilled. The claimant must satisfy the first two of the criteria listed under sub-para (2)(a) above: sub-paras (2)(b)(i) and (iii). In addition:

(1)   The partner, or all the parties to a polygamous marriage, must also be in receipt of AA, highest or middle rate DLA care component, either rate of PIP daily living component or AFIP. Again, note the deeming provisions in paras 18 and 19 relating to receipt and payment of benefit.

(2)   Either someone is entitled to and in receipt of CA, or has an award of UC that includes the carer element, in respect of caring for only one member of the couple (or one but not all the members of a polygamous marriage) or no one is entitled to and in receipt of CA, or an award of UC that includes the carer element, for either (or any) partner.

For the purposes of sub-para (2)(b) (ie, for a claimant with a partner), suspension of payment of AA, DLA or PIP due to the disabled person becoming a "patient" is ignored: sub-para (5). Likewise, any carer is treated as receiving CA, or as having an award of UC that includes the carer element, if s/he would have been entitled to and receiving CA, or would have such an award of UC, but for the fact that the disabled person has been a patient for longer than 28 days. This means that if someone is in receipt of CA or UC that includes the carer element for only one member of a couple (or polygamous marriage) or a claimant satisfies the conditions in sub-para (2)(b) only because of sub-para (5), a severe disability premium is included in the claimant's applicable amount at the single person's rate: para 20(6)(b)(i). Note that a comparable rule is not needed for AFIP as it continues in payment while the claimant is a patient. Again, backdated CA or UC that includes the carer element is ignored: sub-para (6).

For the purposes of both sub-para (a) and (b), someone is treated as in receipt of CA (or as having an award of UC that includes the carer element) if s/he would have been in receipt of CA (or have such an award of UC) but for the "loss of benefit" provisions cited: sub-para (7).

Note that a claimant's entitlement to the severe disability premium is only affected if a person is both entitled to *and* in receipt of CA. So where the person is *not* receiving CA because s/he receives another "overlapping benefit" (sometimes known as an "underlying entitlement"), the claimant's entitlement to the severe disability premium is not affected. For the overlapping benefit rules, see the Social Security (Overlapping Benefits) Regulations 1979 SI No.597 (as amended). The benefits which overlap with CA are contribution-based JSA, contributory ESA, maternity allowance, incapacity benefit, retirement pension, state pension, widow's or bereavement benefits, severe disablement allowance and training allowances.

Sub-para (3). Under sub-para (3), where a claimant's partner is not in receipt of AA, highest or middle rate DLA care component, either rate of PIP daily living component or AFIP, but is severely sight impaired or blind for the purposes of para 13(1)(a)(v) and (2), s/he is treated as not the claimant's partner for the purpose of sub-para (2). Note that, in practical terms, to qualify for a severe disability premium where one member of a couple is in receipt of a relevant benefit or payment and the other is severely sight-impaired or blind, the one who is in receipt of the benefit or payment should be the HB claimant.

Enhanced disability premium

15.–[² (1)   Subject to sub-paragraph (2), the condition is that–

[³ (a)   the Secretary of State has decided that the claimant has, or is to be treated as having, limited capability for work-related activity; or]

(b)   the care component of disability living allowance is, or would, but for a suspension of benefit in accordance with regulations made under section 113(2) of the Act or but for an abatement as a consequence of hospitalisation be payable at the highest rate prescribed under section 72(3) of the Act in respect of–
   (i)   the claimant; or
   (ii)   a member of the claimant's family,
   who [⁵ has not attained the qualifying age for state pension credit].][⁸ or]

[⁸ (c)   the enhanced rate of the daily living component of personal independence payment is [¹⁰ payable, or has ceased to be payable by virtue of regulations made under section 86(1) (hospital in-patients) of the 2012 Act,] in respect of–
   (i)   the claimant; or
   (ii)   a member of the claimant's family,
   who has not attained the qualifying age for state pension credit][⁹; or]

[(d)   armed forces independence payment is payable in respect of (i) the claimant, or (ii) a member of the claimant's family, who has not attained the qualifying age for state pension credit,]

[⁶ (1A)   Where the condition in sub-paragraph (1) ceases to be satisfied because of the death of a child or young person, the condition is that the claimant [⁷ or partner] is entitled to child benefit in respect of that person under section 145A of the Act (entitlement to child benefit after death of child or qualifying young person).]

(2)   [⁶ The condition is not satisfied if the person to whom sub-paragraph (1) refers is]–

(a)   a claimant who–
   (i)   is not a member of a couple or a polygamous marriage; and
   (ii)   is a patient within the meaning of [¹ regulation 28(11)(e)] and has been for a period of more than 52 weeks; or

(b)   a member of a couple or a polygamous marriage where each member is a patient within the meaning of [⁴ regulation 28(11)(e)] and has been for a period of more than 52 weeks.

Amendments

1.   Amended by reg 2(15)(c) of SI 2005 No 2502 as amended by Sch 2 para 27 of SI 2006 No 217 as from 1.4.06 (3.4.06 where rent payable weekly or at intervals of a week).
2.   Substituted by reg 23(c) of SI 2008 No 1082 as from 27.10.08.
3.   Substituted by reg 31(b) of SI 2008 No 2428 as from 27.10.08.
4.   Amended by reg 6(8) of SI 2008 No 2767 as from 17.11.08.
5.   Amended by reg 26(3) of SI 2009 No 1488 as from 6.4.10.
6.   Amended by reg 12(2) of SI 2011 No 674 as from 1.4.11 (4.4.11 where rent payable weekly or in any multiple of whole weeks).
7.   Amended by reg 19(7)(b) of SI 2011 No 2425 as from 31.10.11.
8.   Amended by reg 8 and Sch para 36(6)(d) of SI 2013 No 388 as from 8.4.13.
9.   Amended by art 7 and Sch para 34(6)(d) of SI 2013 No 591 as from 8.4.13.
10.   Amended by reg 3(6)(c) of SI 2014 No 213 as from 1.4.14 (7.4.14 where rent payable weekly or in multiples of a week).

Analysis

Para (1). The enhanced disability premium is included where either the Secretary of State has decided that the claimant has, or is to be treated as having, limited capability for work-related activity (defined in reg 2 as having the meaning given in s2(5) WRA 2007) or the highest rate of the care component of DLA, the enhanced rate of the daily living component of PIP or armed forces independence payment (AFIP) is "payable" to the claimant or a member of her/his family who is under the qualifying age for PC (defined in reg 2(1)) – ie, a partner or child, or if the specified rates of DLA or PIP have ceased to be payable under specified provisions because of a stay in hospital. A comparable rule is not needed for AFIP as it continues in payment while a claimant is in hospital. Note that a person under 18 will now also still be paid DLA or PIP while a patient. It is suggested that "payable" here must mean entitled to (or entitled to be paid) DLA, PIP or AFIP, but does not necessarily mean that it is actually in payment. Note also the deeming provisions in paras 18 and 19 relating to receipt and payment of benefit. The premium is included for each child who satisfies the conditions – ie, more than one can be included: para 20(9)(a). Where an adult satisfies the conditions (ie, the claimant or her/his partner or both of them), there is a single or couple rate as relevant: para 20(9)(b) and (c).

Para (1A) ensures that where a child or young person dies, entitlement to the enhanced disability premium continues for eight weeks if the claimant or her/his partner is entitled to child benefit under the provision specified.

Para (2). If the claimant is single, the enhanced disability premium is not applicable where s/he is a hospital in-patient, and has been for more than 52 weeks. See p430 for a discussion on the meaning of "patient". If the claimant is a member of a couple or of a polygamous marriage, the enhanced disability premium remains applicable unless both members of the couple, or every member of the polygamous marriage, are patients and have been so for more than 52 weeks. Note, however, that the claimant and partner may no longer count as a couple for HB purposes where one of them has been absent from the home for more than 52 weeks (see reg 21).

For a discussion on maximising entitlement to HB, see p640.

Disabled child premium

16. The condition is that a child or young person for whom the claimant or a partner of his is responsible and who is a member of the claimant's household–
(a) is in receipt of disability living allowance or is no longer in receipt of such allowance because he is a patient, provided that the child or young person continues to be a member of the family; or
(b) is [5 severely sight impaired or blind or treated as severely sight impaired or blind] within the meaning of paragraph 13; or
[1 (c) is a child or young person in respect of whom section 145A of the Act (entitlement to child benefit after death of child or qualifying young person) applies for the purposes of entitlement to child benefit but only for the period prescribed under that section, and in respect of whom a disabled child premium was included in the claimant's applicable amount immediately before the death of that child or young person, or ceased to be included in the claimant's applicable amount because of that child or young person's death.] [2 or]
[2 (d) is a young person who is in receipt of personal independence payment or who would, but for [4 payment ceasing by virtue of] regulations made under section 86(1) (hospital in-patients) of the 2012 Act be so in receipt, provided that the young person continues to be a member of the family] [3; or]
[3 (e) is a young person who is in receipt of armed forces independence payment.]

Amendments
1. Substituted by reg 12(3) of SI 2011 No 674 as from 1.4.11 (4.4.11 where rent payable weekly or in any multiple of whole weeks).
2. Amended by reg 8 and Sch para 36(6)(e) of SI 2013 No 388 as from 8.4.13.
3. Amended by art 7 and Sch para 34(6)(e) of SI 2013 No 591 as from 8.4.13.
4. Amended by reg 3(6)(d) of SI 2014 No 213 as from 1.4.14 (7.4.14 where rent payable weekly or in multiples of a week).
5. Amended by reg 3(5)(c)(iii) of SI 2014 No 2888 as from 26.11.14.

Analysis
To get disabled child premium, the claimant or her/his partner must be responsible for a child or qualifying young person who is a member of the claimant's household (see Part 4 from p405). One of three critera must then be satisfied.
(1) The child or young person is in receipt of DLA, PIP or armed forces independence payment (AFIP), or is no longer being paid DLA or PIP because s/he is a patient so long as s/he continues to count as a member of the family (see p17). A comparable rule is not needed for AFIP as it continues in payment while a claimant is a patient. Note that a person under 18 will now also still be paid DLA or PIP while a patient.
(2) The child or young person is severely sight impaired or blind (or treated as severely sight impaired or blind) within the meaning in para 13.

(3)   The child or young person has died, the disabled child premium was included in the claimant's applicable amount for the child or young person immediately before the death, or ceased to be included because of the death, and child benefit is paid for the child or young person following the death. This only applies for a period of eight weeks.

The premium is included for each child who satisfies the conditions – ie, more than one can be included: para 20(7).

Carer premium
17.–(1)   The condition is that the claimant or his partner is, or both of them are, entitled to a carer's allowance under section 70 of the Act.

(2)   Where a carer premium is awarded but–

(a)   the person in respect of whose care the carer's allowance has been awarded dies; or

(b)   in any other case the person in respect of whom a carer premium has been awarded ceases to be entitled to a carer's allowance,

the condition for the award of the premium shall be treated as satisfied for a period of eight weeks from the relevant date specified in sub-paragraph (3).

(3)   The relevant date for the purposes of sub-paragraph (2) shall be–

(a)   where sub-paragraph (2)(a) applies, the Sunday following the death of the person in respect of whose care a carer's allowance has been awarded or the date of death if the death occurred on a Sunday;

(b)   in any other case, the date on which the person who has been entitled to a carer's allowance ceases to be entitled to that allowance.

(4)   Where a person who has been entitled to a carer's allowance ceases to be entitled to that allowance and makes a claim for housing benefit, the condition for the award of the carer premium shall be treated as satisfied for a period of eight weeks from the date on which–

(a)   the person in respect of whose care the carer's allowance has been awarded dies;

(b)   in any other case, the person who has been entitled to a carer's allowance ceased to be entitled to that allowance.

Analysis
To qualify for the carer premium the claimant or her/his partner must be entitled to carer's allowance (CA). See also the General Note to Part 3 of this Schedule (on p634) and the Analysis of para 7(2) (on p635).

A carer premium is applicable even if the claimant or her/his partner is not actually receiving CA – ie, s/he already receives another "overlapping benefit". This is sometimes referred to as "underlying entitlement" to CA. For the overlapping benefit rules, see the Social Security (Overlapping Benefits) Regulations 1979 SI No.597 (as amended). The benefits which overlap with CA are contribution-based JSA, contributory ESA, maternity allowance, incapacity benefit, retirement pension, state pension, widow's or bereavement benefits, severe disablement allowance and training allowances. It is important to note that for someone to be entitled to CA, a claim must be made: s1 SSAA. GM BW3.271 points out that claimants with an underlying entitlement to CA are notified by the DWP's CA Unit of that fact.

The premium is payable for each person who satisfies the condition, so if both the claimant and her/his partner qualify, two are payable: para 20(8).

Where a carer is paid CA (or has an award of UC that includes the carer element), the person being cared for might not be able to qualify for a severe disability premium. Careful benefit advice is therefore needed before a claim for CA (or UC) is made.

Sub-paras (2), (3) and (4) allow entitlement to the premium to continue for eight weeks after caring or entitlement to CA ceases. This also applies where the person being cared for has died. The eight weeks runs from the same day if the death occurs on a Sunday and from the following Sunday if occurring on another day.

Persons in receipt of concessionary payments
18.   For the purpose of determining whether a premium is applicable to a person under paragraphs 13 to 17, any concessionary payment made to compensate that person for the non-payment of any benefit mentioned in those paragraphs shall be treated as if it were a payment of that benefit.

Analysis
Under para 18, a concessionary payment to compensate for non-payment of a benefit must be treated as a payment of that benefit. It has been suggested in previous editions that payment from non-governmental sources would suffice but that is not correct: see the definition of "concessionary payment" in reg 2(1) on p225.

Where a concessionary payment is "treated as if it were a payment of that benefit" under para 18, the benefit would be "payable" for the purpose of para 15 and a person would be "in receipt" of the benefit for the purposes of paras 13, 14 and 16. However, in para 17 the issue is whether someone is "entitled to" a benefit. It is suggested that where a payment is made in the circumstances set out in para 18, there has been a concession that there was an entitlement to the benefit concerned.

Person in receipt of benefit

19. For the purposes of this Part of this Schedule, a person shall be regarded as being in receipt of any benefit if, and only if, it is paid in respect of him and shall be so regarded only for any period in respect of which that benefit is paid.

Analysis

This clarifies what it means to be "in receipt of" benefit, a concept that occurs in several places in Part 3 – eg, paras 13 to 16. It was added to reverse *R(SB) 12/87*. Under para 19, a person is "in receipt" of benefit only if it is actually paid in respect of her/him. The words "in respect of" mean that it does not have to be paid *to* her/him: it might be paid to an appointee. However, the person "in receipt" is the one who is entitled to the benefit. So, for example, where a claimant is entitled to AA but it is being paid to another person on her/his behalf, it is the claimant who is "in receipt" of the AA, not the other person.

PART 4
Amounts of premiums specified in Part 3

Premium	Amount
20.–[⁴ (1)]	[⁴ (1)]
[⁶ (2)]	[⁶ (2)]
[⁶ (3)]	[⁶ (3)]
[⁶ (4)]	[⁶ (4)]
(5) Disability Premium–	(5)
(a) where the claimant satisfies the condition in paragraph 12(a);	(a) [¹⁸ £34.35];
(b) where the claimant satisfies the condition in paragraph 12(b).	(b) [¹⁸ £48.95].
(6) Severe Disability Premium–	(6)
(a) where the claimant satisfies the condition in paragraph 14(2)(a);	(a) [¹⁸ £65.85];
(b) where the claimant satisfies the condition in paragraph 14(2)(b)–	
(i) in a case where there is someone in receipt of carer's allowance [¹⁵ or who has an award of universal credit which includes the carer element under regulation 29 of the Universal Credit Regulations 2013] or if he or any partner satisfies that condition only by virtue of paragraph 14(5);	(b)(i) [¹⁸ £65.85];
(ii) in a case where there is no one in receipt of such an allowance [¹⁵ or such an award of universal credit].	(b)(ii) [¹⁸ £131.70].
(7) Disabled Child Premium.	(7) [¹⁸ £64.19] in respect of each child or young person in respect of whom the condition specified in paragraph 16 of Part 3 of this Schedule is satisfied.
(8) Carer Premium.	(8) [¹⁸ £36.85] in respect of each person who satisfies the condition specified in paragraph 17.
(9) Enhanced Disability Premium [⁹].	(9)(a) [¹⁸ £26.04] in respect of each child or young person in respect of whom the conditions specified in paragraph 15 are satisfied;
	(b) [¹⁸ £16.80] in respect of each person who is neither–
	(i) a child or young person;
	nor
	(ii) a member of a couple or a polygamous marriage, in respect of whom the conditions specified in paragraph 15 are satisfied;
	(c) [¹⁸ £24.10] where the claimant is a member of a couple or a polygamous marriage and the conditions specified in paragraph 15 are satisfied in respect of a member of that couple or polygamous marriage.

Amendments

1. Amended by art 19(8) and Sch 7 of SI 2006 No 645 and reg 8 of SI 2006 No 217 as from 1.4.06 (3.4.06 where rent payable weekly or at intervals of a week).

2.　Confirmed by art 19(8) and Sch 7 of SI 2007 No 688 as from 1.4.07 (2.4.07 where rent payable weekly or at intervals of a week).

3.　Amended by art 19(8) and Sch 7 of SI 2007 No 688 as from 1.4.07 (2.4.07 where rent payable weekly or at intervals of a week).

4.　Revoked by reg 2 and the Sch of SI 2007 No 2618 as from 1.10.07.

5.　Amended by art 19(9) and Sch 7 of SI 2008 No 632 as from 1.4.08 (7.4.08 where rent payable weekly or in multiples of a week).

6.　Omitted by reg 3(10)(i) of SI 2008 No 1042 as from 19.5.08.

7.　Amended by art 19(9) and Sch 6 of SI 2009 No 497 as from 1.4.09 (6.4.09 where rent payable weekly or in multiples of a week).

8.　Amended by art 19(8) and Sch 6 of SI 2010 No 793 as from 1.4.10 (5.4.10 where rent payable weekly or in multiples of a week).

9.　Amended by reg 2(8)(b) of SI 2010 No 2449 as from 1.11.10.

10.　Amended by art 20(8) and Sch 6 of SI 2011 No 821 as from 1.4.11 (4.4.11 where rent payable weekly or in multiples of a week).

11.　Amended by art 20(8) and Sch 6 of SI 2012 No 780 as from 1.4.12 (2.4.12 where rent payable weekly or in multiples of a week).

12.　Amended by art 19(8) and Sch 6 of SI 2013 No 574 as from 1.4.13.

13.　Amended by art 17(9) and Sch 6 of SI 2014 No 16 as from 1.4.14 (7.4.14 where rent payable weekly or in multiples of a week).

14.　Amended by art 17(9) and Sch 6 of SI 2015 No 547 as from 1.4.15 (6.4.15 where rent payable weekly or in multiples of a week).

15.　Inserted by reg 17(3) of SI 2015 No 1754 as from 4.11.15.

16.　Amended by art 22(9) and Sch 6 of SI 2017 No 260 as from 1.4.17 (3.4.17 where rent payable weekly or in multiples of a week).

17.　Amended by art 23(8) and Sch 5 of SI 2018 No 281 as from 1.4.18 (2.4.18 where rent payable weekly or in multiples of a week).

18.　Amended by art 23(8) and Sch 3 of SI 2019 No 480 as from 1.4.19.

General Note

This simply quantifies the appropriate amounts for the premiums set out in Part 3.

[¹ PART 5

Amendment

1.　Inserted by reg 23(d) of SI 2008 No 1082, as substituted by reg 31(c) of SI 2008 No 2428, as from 27.10.08.

General Note to Part 5

This Part sets out the rules under which a claimant may qualify to have the "support component" included in her/his applicable amount: see regs 22(1)(e) and 23(1)(f). This component is only relevant where the claimant or her/his partner has, or is treated as having, limited capability for work-related activity under the ESA legislation. A second component, the "work-related activity component" was available for claims made before 3 April 2017. It is no longer available for claims made on or after that date. Transitional provision is made under Sch 2 paras 1–7 of the Employment and Support Allowance and Universal Credit (Miscellaneous Amendments and Transitional and Savings Provisions) Regulations 2017 SI No.204 (see p1892) so that those claiming before that date who continue to have, or be treated as having, limited capability for work are entitled to continue to receive it. Paras 21, 21A and 22 set out some general rules governing entitlement to a component; there can only be entitlement to one of the components and not both. Para 24 sets out the specific rules relating to entitlement to the support component. For full details of the rules relating to the work-related activity component, see the 29th edition of this volume.

　　Note that where there is an award of HB and a "qualifying benefit" (eg, ESA) is later awarded or reinstated, regs 4(7B) and (7C), 7(2)(i) and 8(14) D&A Regs effectively allow for backdating of entitlement to components which depend on entitlement to (or receipt of) that qualifying benefit for the period for which arrears of that benefit are paid – see the commentary to those provisions. Note also regs 7(2)(o), (p) and (q) and 8(14D) and (14E) D&A Regs where subsequent to the first day of entitlement to HB, the Secretary of State decides that the claimant or her/his partner has, or is to be treated as having, limited capability for work or the claimant or her/his partner has an award of benefit (IS, IB or SDA) converted to ESA or is appealing a decision not to convert an award to ESA, or where following an award of converted ESA, the claimant or her/his partner is awarded a different component.

　　There may also be entitlement to a transitional addition if the claimant is on ESA which is not income-related following being transferred from IS "on grounds of disability", IB or SDA: Sch 3 Parts 7 and 8.

The[³component]

[¹ **21**–(1)   Subject to paragraph 22, the claimant is entitled to [³ the component in paragraph] 24 if–
(a)   the claimant or the claimant's partner has made a claim for employment and support allowance;
[³ (b)   the Secretary of State has determined that the claimant or the claimant's partner has or is treated as having limited capability for work-related activity; and]
(c)   one of the following applies–
   (i)   the assessment phase as defined in section 24(2) of the Welfare Reform Act (interpretation) has ended;
   (ii)   regulation 7 of the Employment and Support Allowance Regulations [² or regulation 7 of the Employment and Support Allowance Regulations 2013](circumstances where the condition that the assessment phase has ended before entitlement to the support component [³] arises does not apply) applies; or
   (iii)   the conditions in sub-paragraph (2) apply.
(2)   The conditions referred to in sub-paragraph (1)(c)(iii) are–
(a)   neither the claimant nor the claimant's partner is entitled to an employment and support allowance;
(b)   either is or both are entitled to be credited with earnings equal to the lower earnings limit then in force under regulation 8B(2)(a)(iv) of the Social Security (Credits) Regulations 1975 (credits for incapacity for work or limited capability for work); and
(c)   paragraph (1)(c)(i) or (ii) would have applied to the claimant or the claimant's partner (or both) had they been entitled to an employment and support allowance.]

Amendments
1.   Substituted by reg 7(4)(a) of SI 2013 No 443 as from 2.4.13.
2.   Amended by reg 35(9)(a) of SI 2013 No 630 as from 29.4.13.
3.   Amended by Sch 1 para 6(7) of SI 2017 No 204 as from 3.4.17, subject to transitional and savings provisions in Sch 2 paras 1–7.

[¹**21A.**   Subject to paragraph 22, the claimant is entitled to one, but not both, of the components in paragraphs 23 or 24 if the claimant or the claimant's partner is entitled to a converted employment and support allowance [², or would be entitled but for the application of section 1A of the Welfare Reform Act (duration of contributory allowance)].]

Amendments
1.   Inserted by reg 27 and Sch 5 para 1(5)(b) of SI 2010 No 1907 as amended by reg 15 of SI 2010 No 2430 as from 1.10.10.
2.   Amended by reg 7 of SI 2012 No.913 as from 1.5.12.

22.–(1)   The claimant has no entitlement under paragraph 23 or 24 if the claimant is entitled to the disability premium under paragraphs 12 and 13.
(2)   Where the claimant and the claimant's partner each satisfies paragraph [¹] 24, the component to be included in the claimant's applicable amount is that which relates to the claimant.

Amendment
1.   Amended by Sch 1 para 6(7)(a)(iii) of SI 2017 No 204 as from 3.4.17, subject to transitional and savings provisions in Sch 2 paras 1–7.

Analysis of paras 21, 21A and 22
The general rules of entitlement to the support component are found in paras 21, 21A and 22. Note that the work-related activity component is no longer available for claims made on or after 3 April 2017, subject to transitional rules (see the General Note to this Part on p647 and the transitional rules on p1892). Under paras 21 and 21A, in the circumstances where the transitional rules apply, the claimant is entitled to one of the components but never both, if s/he or her/his partner satisfies the conditions.

Para 21. Under para 21, a claimant is entitled to a support component if the general conditions are met. First, the claimant or her/his partner must have made a claim for ESA: sub-para (1)(a). Second, the Secretary of State must have decided that s/he or the partner has limited capability for work-related activity (defined in reg 2 by reference to the WRA 2007), or is to be treated as having limited capability for work-related activity: sub-para (1)(b). Finally, one of the following conditions must be met.
(1)   The "assessment phase" has ended: sub-para (1)(c)(i). The assessment phase is normally the first 13 weeks of entitlement to ESA, during which the claimant is paid ESA at a lower rate. During this phase, the DWP gathers further information relevant to the ESA claim (including assessing whether the claimant has "limited capability for work-related activity"). See CPAG's *Welfare Benefits and Tax Credits Handbook* for further details.

(2)   The claimant is someone to whom reg 7 of either the ESA Regs 2008 or the ESA Regs 2013 apply: sub-para (1)(c)(ii). Those regulations set out situations when a claimant can qualify for an ESA support component before the end of the assessment phase – eg, if s/he is terminally ill, or where a period of limited capability for work is linked to an earlier one for which the assessment phase had ended.

(3)   Neither the claimant nor her/his partner is entitled to ESA, but either or both of them are entitled to NI credits and the condition in sub-para (1(c)(i) or (ii) would have applied had the claimant or partner been entitled to ESA: sub-paras (1)(c)(iii) and (2).

Where none of the three conditions are yet met, there is no entitlement to a component, nor can there be entitlement to a disability premium – ie, where the claimant has claimed ESA (or applied for NI credits) and has, or is treated as having, limited capability for work: para 13(9). See p640 for a discussion.

Para 21A. Under this para, a claimant is entitled to a component if s/he or her/his partner is entitled to a "converted employment and support allowance", or would be entitled but for the application of s1A WRA 2007. Under s1A WRA 2007 (inserted by s51 WRA 2012) entitlement to contributory ESA ends once the claimant has been entitled for 365 days (disregarding any days spent in the "support group"). A claimant whose entitlement has ended for this reason alone is still entitled to a component. "Converted employment and support allowance" is defined in reg 2(1) as ESA which is not income-related and to which there is entitlement as a result of a "conversion decision", broadly ESA paid to those transferred from IS "on the grounds of disability", IB or SDA. See Parts 7 and 8 of this Schedule for when such a claimant may be entitled to a protected amount of HB – a transitional addition.

Para 22. Both paras 21 and 21A are subject to para 22. Under para 22(1), there can be no entitlement to a component if the claimant is entitled to a disability premium (for which see paras 12 and 13 on p636 and p636 and the commentary). For example, where a claimant who is capable of work is receiving DLA and is therefore entitled to the disability premium, there would be no entitlement to a component, even if her/his partner has limited capability for work-related activity.

Where both the claimant and her/his partner satisfy the conditions for a component, the component to be included is that to which the claimant is entitled: para 22(2). This may mean that because the support component is of a higher value, the member of the couple who qualifies for that component should be the HB claimant. If a claimant and her/his partner are considering swapping the claiming role, bear in mind not just issues in respect of maximising entitlement, but also whether any of the various forms of transitional protection would be lost.

See p640 for a discussion of other issues to consider in maximising entitlement to HB.

The transitional protection leading to the higher rate family premium for lone parents is lost if a component under either para 23 or 24 applies. See pp592–94 of the 28th edition of this book for details.

[¹ **The work-related activity component**
23.]

Amendment

1.   Omitted by Sch 1 para 6(7)(a)(iv) of SI 2017 No 204 as from 3.4.17, subject to transitional and savings provisions in Sch 2 paras 1–7.

The support component
24.   The claimant is entitled to the support component if the Secretary of State has decided that the claimant or the claimant's partner has, or is to be treated as having, limited capability for work-related activity.]

Analysis to paras 23 and 24

For claims made prior to 3 April 2017, a claimant is entitled to a work-related activity component if the DWP has decided that either s/he or her/his partner has, or is to be treated as having, "limited capability for work" (defined in reg 2 by reference to s1(4) WRA 2007): para 23. (Note that, for claims made on or after 3 April 2017, the work-related activity component is no longer available. See the General Note to Part 5 on p647. For the transitional rules, see p1892.) This is one of the basic conditions of entitlement to ESA and to NI credits on new claims on or after 27 October 2008. However, entitlement to the component is generally initially precluded: see para 21(1)(b) and (c) and (2). Limited capability for work is determined by the DWP by reference to reg 19 and Sch 2 Employment and Support Allowance Regulations 2008 SI No.794 (the ESA Regs 2008) and reg 15 and Sch 2 Employment and Support Allowance Regulations 2013 SI No.379 (the ESA Regs 2013). Claimants can be treated as having limited capability for work under regs 20 and 30 of the ESA Regs 2008 and regs 16 and 26 ESA Regs 2013.

A higher rate of ESA is payable where the ESA claimant not only has limited capability for work, but has limited capability for work-related activity which makes it unreasonable to require her/him to undertake such activity. This is determined by the DWP under reg 34 and Sch 3 ESA Regs 2008 and reg 30 and Sch 3 ESA Regs 2014. For HB purposes, this higher rate of ESA is offest by entitlement to the support component under para 24. A claimant is entitled to the support component if the DWP has decided that either s/he or her/his partner has limited capability for work-related activity.

Effectively all claimants who meet the conditions for the support component will also meet the conditions for the work-related activity component. However, a claimant is entitled to one, but not both, of the components: see para 21. The rules do not set out which component is applicable in this situation. For single claimants or lone parents, or couples where only one member satisfies paras 23 and 24, it is suggested that it is the support component. For couples, note para 22(2) if both of them satisfy para 23 or 24.

Note that where the claimant's partner has limited capability for work but the claimant does not, the claimant may instead qualify for a disability premium under paras 12 and 13 – eg, if the claimant is receiving DLA or is incapable of work under the incapacity benefit legislation. See the commentary to para 13 on p640 for a discussion of some financial implications.

[¹ PART 6
Amount of[⁹component]

[⁹**25.**]

26. The amount of the support component is [¹² £38.55].]

Amendments

1.   Inserted by reg 23(d) of SI 2008 No 1082, as substituted by reg 31(c) of SI 2008 No2428, as from 27.10.08.
2.   Amended by art 19(10) of SI 2009 No 497 as from 1.4.09 (6.4.09 where rent payable weekly or in multiples of a week).
3.   Amended by art 19(9) of SI 2010 No 793 as from 1.4.10 (5.4.10 where rent payable weekly or in multiples of a week).
4.   Amended by art 20(9) of SI 2011 No 821 as from 1.4.11 (4.4.11 where rent payable weekly or in multiples of a week).
5.   Amended by art 20(9) of SI 2012 No 780 as from 1.4.12 (2.4.12 where rent payable weekly or in multiples of a week).
6.   Amended by art 19(9) of SI 2013 No 574 as from 1.4.13.
7.   Amended by art 17(10) of SI 2014 No 16 as from 1.4.14 (7.4.14 where rent payable weekly or in multiples of a week).
8.   Amended by art 17(10) of SI 2015 No 547 as from 1.4.15 (6.4.15 where rent payable weekly or in multiples of a week).
9.   Omitted by Sch 1 para 6(7)(b) of SI 2017 No 204 as from 3.4.17, subject to transitional and savings provisions in Sch 2 paras 1–7.
10.   Amended by art 22(10) of SI 2017 No 260 as from 1.4.17 (3.4.17 where rent payable weekly or in multiples of a week).
11.   Amended by art 23(9) of SI 2018 No 281 as from 1.4.18 (2.4.18 where rent payable weekly or in multiples of a week).
12.   Amended by art 23(9) of SI 2019 No 480 as from 1.4.19.

General Note

Paras 25 and 26 simply quantify the appropriate amounts for the components set out in Part 5. Para 25: note that the work-related activity component is no longer available for claims made on or after 3 April 2017. See the General Note to Part 5 on p647. For the transitional rules relating to previous claims, see p1892.

[¹ PART 7

Amendment

1.   Inserted by reg 27 and Sch 5 para 1(5)(c) of SI 2010 No 1907 as amended by reg 15 of SI 2010 No 2430 as from 1.10.10.

General Note to Part 7

IS awarded "on the grounds of disability", IB and SDA were replaced with ESA on new claims from 27 October 2008. If a claim is made for one of those benefits for a period starting on or after 27 October 2008, the claim is generally treated as a claim for ESA. Since 31 January 2011, there have only been two exceptions: where a claim for IS "on the grounds of disability" is made by a claimant entitled to IB or SDA, or where a claim for IB is made by a claimant entitled to IS "on the grounds of disability". Under the Employment and Support Allowance (Transitional Provisions) Regulations 2008 SI No.795 (as amended by SI 2008 No.2428, SI 2008 No.2783 and SI 2010 No.1907) and the Income Support (Prescribed Categories of Person) Regulations 2009 No.3152, people can retain entitlement to IS "on the grounds of disability", IB and SDA after 27 October 2008 until transferred to ESA.

Most of those claiming IS "on the grounds of disability", IB and SDA were assessed for and, if they qualifed, transferred to ESA by the end of March 2014. The transfer process for the remainder has now been completed. HB claimants who (or whose partners) are entitled to "converted employment and support allowance" may qualify for a component (under Part 5) instead of a disability premium (under Part 3 para 12). HB entitlement for those who qualify for a disability premium can in some cases be more generous than HB entitlement for those who qualify for a component. See p640 for a discussion of the issues. To ensure that a claimant continues to qualify for the same rate of HB as before the transfer to ESA, or in specified circumstances while s/he or her/his partner is appealing a conversion decision, s/he may be entitled to a protected amount of HB – a transitional addition under Part 7 is included in her/his applicable amount: regs 22(1)(f) and 23(1)(g). The amount of the transitional addition is calculated under Part 8.

Para 27 sets out the rules of entitlement to a transitional addition and when the entitlement ends.

Para 28 provides a linking rule where there is a break in entitlement to HB.

Para 29 provides a linking rule where there is a break in entitlement to ESA.

Note that in all cases, entitlement to a transitional addition will end on 5 April 2020 if it has not already ended before that date. But note that in any event, existing HB claimants will be transferred to UC (from 2019 to 2023).

Transitional addition

27.–(1) The claimant is entitled to the transitional addition calculated in accordance with paragraph 30 where the claimant or the claimant's partner ("the relevant person")–

(a) is entitled to a converted employment and support allowance [¹, or would be entitled but for the application of section 1A of the Welfare Reform Act (duration of contributory allowance)]; or

(b) is appealing a conversion decision as described in regulation 5(2)(b) of the Employment and Support Allowance (Existing Awards) Regulations and–

   (i) is treated as having limited capability for work by virtue of regulation 30 of the Employment and Support Allowance Regulations [² or regulation 26 of the Employment and Support Allowance Regulations 2013, in either case] as modified by the Employment and Support Allowance (Existing Awards) Regulations; and

   (ii) is not in receipt of an income-related employment and support allowance,

unless the amount of the transitional addition calculated in accordance with paragraph 30 would be nil.

(2) The claimant's entitlement to a transitional addition by virtue of this paragraph ends on any of the following–

(a) the reduction of the transitional addition to nil in accordance with paragraph 31;

(b) the termination of the claimant's award of housing benefit;

(c) the relevant person ceasing to meet the requirements of sub-paragraph (1)(a) or (b), as the case may be;

(d) the claimant or the claimant's partner becoming entitled to an income-related employment and support allowance, an income-based jobseeker's allowance or income support;

(e) 5th April 2020.

Amendments

1. Amended by reg 7 of SI 2012 No.913 as from 1.5.12.
2. Amended by reg 35(9)(b)(i) of SI 2013 No 630 as from 29.4.13.

Analysis

Sub-para (1). An HB claimant can qualify for a transitional addition in two circumstances.

(1) S/he or her/his partner is entitled to a "converted employment and support allowance" (or would be entitled but for the application of s1A WRA 2007): sub-para (1)(a). Converted ESA is defined in reg 2(1) as ESA to which there is entitlement as a result of a "conversion decision" (broadly ESA that is not income-related, paid to those transferred from IS "on the grounds of disability", IB or SDA). Under s1A WRA 2007 (inserted by s51 WRA 2012) entitlement to contributory ESA ends once the claimant has been entitled for 365 days (disregarding any days spent in the so-called "support group"). A claimant whose entitlement has ended for this reason alone can still qualify for a transitional addition.

(2) S/he or her/his partner is appealing a conversion decision: sub-para (1)(b). In this case, the claimant or partner must be treated as having limited capability for work pending the appeal under the regulations cited – ie, by providing medical evidence of limited capability for work. In addition, s/he must not be receiving income-related ESA. Where someone is appealing a conversion decision, if entitled to ESA, it is paid at the assessment phase rate – ie, without a work-related activity component or a support component. Note that, from 3 April 2017, the work-related activity component was withdrawn for new claims (see the General Note to Part 5 on p647).

There is no entitlement to a transitional addition if the claimant (or her/his partner) is entitled to converted *income-related* ESA, or is receiving income-related ESA while appealing a conversion decision. In such cases a transitional addition is not needed as someone entitled to income-related ESA has passported entitlement to maximum HB under reg 70 without reference to an applicable amount.

Sub-para (2). Entitlement to the transitional addition ends if any of the circumstances listed in sub-para (2)(a) to (d) occur, or on 5 April 2020 if none have occurred before that date. See also the General Note to Part 7 on p650. There are linking rules in paras 28 and 29 that may revive entitlement to a transitional addition where there is a break in entitlement to HB or to ESA.

28.–(1)   This paragraph applies where–
(a)   the claimant's entitlement to a transitional addition ends, by virtue of the termination of the claimant's award of housing benefit, under–
  (i)   paragraph 27(2)(b);
  (ii)   sub-paragraph (3)(b) of this paragraph; or
  (iii)   paragraph 29(3)(b);
(b)   within [¹ 12] weeks of that termination but before 5th April 2020 the claimant again becomes entitled to housing benefit;
(c)   in the benefit week in which the claimant again becomes entitled to housing benefit the relevant person [² satisfies the requirements of paragraph 27(1) or] is entitled to an employment and support allowance which is not income-related; [¹ and]
[¹ (d)]
(e)   at the date on which the claimant again becomes entitled to housing benefit, neither the claimant nor the claimant's partner is entitled to an income-related employment and support allowance, an income-based jobseeker's allowance or income support.
(2)   Where this paragraph applies, the claimant is entitled, with effect from the day on which the claimant again becomes entitled to housing benefit, to a transitional addition of the amount of the transitional addition that would have applied had the claimant's entitlement to a transitional addition not ended (but taking account of the effect which any intervening change of circumstances would have had by virtue of paragraph 31), unless the amount of the transitional addition would be nil.
(3)   The claimant's entitlement to a transitional addition by virtue of this paragraph ends on any of the following–
(a)   the reduction of the transitional addition to nil in accordance with paragraph 31;
(b)   the termination of the claimant's award of housing benefit;
(c)   the relevant person [² no longer satisfying the requirements of paragraph 27(1) or] no longer being entitled to the employment and support allowance referred to in sub-paragraph (1)(c);
(d)   the claimant or the claimant's partner becoming entitled to an income-related employment and support allowance, an income-based jobseeker's allowance or income support;
(e)   5th April 2020.

Amendments
1.   Amended by reg 3 of SI 2012 No.919 as from 1.5.12.
2.   Amended by reg 7(4)(b) of SI 2013 No 443 as from 2.4.13.

Analysis
Sub-para (1). Para 28 provides a linking rule where a claimant's entitlement to a transitional addition ends under para 27(2)(b), para 28(3)(b) or para 29(3)(b) – ie, because her/his award of HB is terminated. S/he is entitled to a transitional addition again if the conditions in sub-para (1)(b) to (e) are satisfied. The effect of these is as follows.
(1)   The original claimant must become entitled to HB again before 5 April 2020 and within 12 weeks of the termination of her/his award of HB: sub-para (1)(a) and (b). The linking rule, therefore, does not apply if the claimant is unable to make a new claim for HB because s/he is someone who must instead claim UC.
(2)   The "relevant person" must satisfy the requirements of para 27(1) or be entitled to ESA which is not income-related in the benefit week in which entitlement to HB begins again: sub-para (1)(c). The "relevant person" is the person who is entitled to converted ESA or is appealing a conversion decision – ie, the claimant or her/his partner as the case may be: para 27(1).
(3)   Neither the claimant nor her/his partner can be entitled to IS, income-based JSA or income-related ESA on the date entitlement to HB begins again: sub-para (1)(e).
Note that this linking rule can only apply if the person claiming HB when entitlement begins again is the person who was claiming HB before the award terminated: see the wording of sub-para (1)(b). For this reason, careful consideration needs to be given to the financial implications before the claimant and her/his partner swap the claimant role.
Sub-para (2). The amount of the transitional addition that applies is the amount that would have applied had entitlement to the addition not ended, taking into account any changes that would have decreased that transitional addition under para 31.
Sub-para (3). Entitlement to the transitional addition ends if any of the circumstances listed in sub-para (3)(a) to (d) occur, or on 5 April 2020 if none have occurred before that date. Note that where there is a break in entitlement to ESA or the HB award is terminated again, the linking rules both in this para and in para 29 may still apply. See also the General Note to Part 7 on p650.

29.–(1)   This paragraph applies where–
(a)   the claimant's entitlement to a transitional addition ends, by virtue of the relevant person ceasing to be entitled to an employment and support allowance, under–
  (i)   paragraph 27(2)(c);
  (ii)   paragraph 28(3)(c); or
  (iii)   sub-paragraph (3)(c) of this paragraph;

(b)   before 5th April 2020 the relevant person again becomes entitled to an employment and support allowance which is not income-related;

[¹ (c) at the date on which the relevant person again becomes entitled to an employment and support allowance which is not income-related, regulation 145(1) of the Employment and Support Allowance Regulations [² or regulation 86 of the Employment and Support Allowance Regulations 2013] applies to the relevant person; and]

(d)   at the date on which the relevant person again becomes entitled to an employment support allowance which is not income-related, neither the claimant nor the claimant's partner is entitled to an income-related employment and support allowance, an income-based jobseeker's allowance or income support.

(2)   Where this paragraph applies, the claimant is entitled, with effect from the day that the relevant person's entitlement to employment and support allowance takes effect for housing benefit purposes, to a transitional addition of the amount of the transitional addition that would have applied had the claimant's entitlement to a transitional addition not ended (but taking account of the effect which any intervening change of circumstances would have had by virtue of paragraph 31), unless the amount of the transitional addition would be nil.

(3)   The claimant's entitlement to a transitional addition by virtue of this paragraph ends on any of the following–

(a)   the reduction of the transitional addition to nil in accordance with paragraph 31;

(b)   the termination of the claimant's award of housing benefit;

(c)   the relevant person no longer being entitled to the employment and support allowance referred to in sub-paragraph (1)(b);

(d)   the claimant or the claimant's partner becoming entitled to an income-related employment and support allowance, an income-based jobseeker's allowance or income support;

(e)   5th April 2020.]

Amendments

1.   Substituted by reg 3 of SI 2012 No 919 as from 1.5.12.
2.   Amended by reg 35(9)(b)(ii) of SI 2013 No 630 as from 29.4.13.

Analysis

Sub-para (1). Para 29 provides a linking rule where entitlement to HB continues, but entitlement to a transitional addition ends under paras 27(2)(c), 28(3)(c) or 29(3)(c) – ie, because the relevant person's entitlement to ESA ends, including where this is because s/he is no longer appealing a conversion decision. The "relevant person" is the person who is entitled to converted ESA or is appealing a conversion decision – ie, the claimant or her/his partner as the case may be: para 27(1). The HB claimant is entitled to a transitional addition again if the conditions in sub-para (2)(b) to (d) are satisfied. The effect of these is as follows.

(1)   The "relevant person" must become entitled to ESA (which is not income-related ESA) again before 5 April 2020 and within 12 weeks of entitlement ceasing: sub-para (1)(a) to (c) and reg 145(1) ESA Regs 2008 and reg 86 ESA Regs 2013.

(2)   The claimant and her/his partner must not be entitled to IS, income-based JSA or income-related ESA on the date the "relevant person" becomes entitled to ESA again: sub-para (1)(d).

Note that where entitlement to HB ends (eg, as a consequence of entitlement to ESA ending), it appears that it is the linking rule in para 28 that is relevant, not the linking rule in para 29.

Sub-para (2). The amount of the transitional addition that applies is the amount that would have applied had entitlement to the addition not ended, taking into account any changes that would have decreased that transitional addition under para 31.

Sub-para (3). Entitlement to the transitional addition ends if any of the circumstances listed in sub-para (3)(a) to (d) occur, or on 5 April 2020 if none have occurred before that date. Note that where there is a further break in entitlement to ESA or the HB award is terminated, the linking rules both in this para and in para 28 may still apply. See also the General Note to Part 7 on p650.

[¹ PART 8

Amendment

1.   Inserted by reg 27 and Sch 5 para 1(5)(c) of SI 2010 No 1907 as amended by reg 15 of SI 2010 No 2430 as from 1.10.10.

General Note to Part 8

If an HB claimant is entitled to a transitional addition under Part 7, the amount of the addition is calculated under para 30. This is subject to para 31 which sets out how the amount of the transitional addition is to be reduced where there are specified changes in circumstance. Once a claimant's transitional addition is reduced to nil, s/he cannot regain entitlement: paras 27(2)(a), 28(3)(a) and 29(3)(a).

Amount of transitional addition

30.–(1)   Subject to paragraph 31, the amount of the transitional addition is the amount by which Amount A exceeds Amount B.

(2)   Where a conversion decision as described in regulation 5(2)(a) of the Employment and Support Allowance (Existing Awards) Regulations is made in respect of the relevant person–

(a)   Amount A is the basic amount that would have applied on the day that decision took effect had that decision not been made; and

(b)   Amount B is the basic amount that applied on that day as a result of that decision.

(3)   Where the relevant person is appealing a conversion decision as described in regulation 5(2)(b) of the Employment and Support Allowance (Existing Awards) Regulations and is treated as having limited capability for work by virtue of regulation 30 of the Employment and Support Allowance Regulations as modified by the Employment and Support Allowance (Existing Awards) Regulations–

(a)   Amount A is the basic amount that would have applied on the day the relevant person was first treated as having limited capability for work if the relevant person had not been so treated; and

(b)   Amount B is the basic amount that applied on that day as a result of the relevant person being so treated.

(4)   In this paragraph and paragraph 31, "basic amount" means the aggregate of such amounts as may apply in the claimant's case in accordance with regulation 22[¹ (1)](a) to (e) or regulation 23[¹ (1)](a) to (f).

Amendment

1.   Amended by reg 7(4) of SI 2017 No 376 as from 6.4.17, subject to transitional provision in reg 9.

Analysis

Simply put, the amount of the transitional addition is the difference between Amount A and Amount B, where Amount A is higher than Amount B: sub-para (1). This is subject to reduction under para 31. The effect is that the claimant's HB applicable amount after conversion (or an appeal against a refusal to award converted ESA) is equal to her/his applicable amount before the conversion (or appeal).

Sub-para (2) defines Amount A and Amount B if the claimant or her/his partner was awarded converted ESA (see reg 2(1) for the definition). In this case, Amount A is the applicable amount under reg 22 or 23 that would have applied on the day the decision to award ESA took effect had that decision not been made – ie, the claimant's applicable amount immediately before entitlement to ESA began. Amount B is the applicable amount under reg 22 or 23 that applied on the day the decision to award ESA took effect.

Example. In May 2013, a single HB claimant aged 50 was entitled to long-term rate IB and was then awarded converted ESA which included a work-related activity component. Amount A is £71.70 (personal allowance) *plus* £31 (disability premium) = £102.70. Amount B is £71.70 (personal allowance) *plus* £28.45 (work-related activity component) = £100.15. The transitional addition is £2.55 (Amount A *minus* Amount B). Thus the claimant's applicable amount is £71.70 (personal allowance) *plus* £28.45 (work-related activity component) *plus* £2.55 (transitional addition) = £102.70.

Sub-para (3) defines Amount A and Amount B if the claimant or her/his partner is treated as having limited capability for work while appealing a decision not to award converted ESA. In this case, Amount A is the applicable amount under reg 22 or 23 that would have applied on the day the claimant or partner was first treated as having limited capability for work had s/he not been so treated – ie, the claimant's applicable amount immediately before appealing. Amount B is the applicable amount under reg 22 or 23 that applied on the day the claimant or partner was treated as having limited capability for work.

Example. In July 2013, a claimant who is a member of a couple is appealing a decision that he is not entitled to converted ESA. Prior to the decision, he was entitled to long-term rate IB and DLA. Amount A is £112.55 (personal allowance) *plus* £44.20 (disability premium couple rate) = £156.75. Amount B is £112.55 (personal allowance). The transitional addition is £44.20 (Amount A *minus* Amount B). Thus the claimant's applicable amount is £112.55 (personal allowance) *plus* £44.20 (transitional addition) = £156.75.

Para (4) defines "basic amount" for the purposes of both paras 30 and 31.

31.–(1)   Subject to sub-paragraph (2), where there is a change of circumstances which leads to an increase in the claimant's basic amount, the transitional addition that applies immediately before the change of circumstances shall be reduced by the amount by which Amount C exceeds Amount D.

(2)   If Amount C exceeds Amount D by more than the amount of the transitional addition that applies immediately before the change of circumstances, that transitional addition shall be reduced to nil.

(3)   Amount C is the basic amount that applies as a result of the increase.

(4)   Amount D is the basic amount that applied immediately before the increase.]

Analysis

The transitional addition as calculated under para 30 is subject to reduction if there is a change of circumstances which leads to an increase in the claimant's applicable amount under reg 22 or 23, until the addition is reduced to nil, when it is lost altogether: paras (1) and (2). The reduction is the difference between the applicable amount as so increased (Amount C) and the applicable amount prior to the increase (Amount D). Note that "basic amount" is defined in para 30(4).

Example. A claimant who is a member of a couple was entitled to long-term rate IB. In May 2013, she was awarded converted ESA which included a work-related activity component. Amount A is £112.55 (personal allowance) *plus* £44.20 (disability premium) = £156.75. Amount B is £112.55 (personal allowance) *plus* £28.45 (work-related activity component) = £141.00. The transitional addition is £15.75 (Amount A *minus* Amount B). In April 2014, when benefit rates increase, Amount C is £113.70 (personal allowance) *plus* £28.75 (work-related activity component) = £142.45. Amount D is the same as Amount B = £141.00. The transitional addition is reduced by £1.45 (Amount C *minus* Amount D) and is therefore £14.30. Thus the claimant's applicable amount is £113.70 (personal allowance) *plus* £28.75 (work-related activity component) *plus* £14.30 (transitional addition) = £156.75 – ie, the same amount as it was in May 2013.

In September 2014, the claimant's partner is awarded CA and so her applicable amount should be increased by £34.20 to include a carer premium. Amount C is £113.70 (personal allowance) *plus* £28.75 (work-related activity component) *plus* £34.20 (carer premium) = £176.65. Amount D is £113.70 (personal allowance) *plus* £28.75 (work-related activity component) = £142.45. Amount C exceeds Amount D by more than £14.30 so the transitional addition is reduced to nil. Thus the claimant's applicable amount is £113.70 (personal allowance) *plus* £28.75 (work-related activity component) *plus* £34.20 (carer premium) = £176.65.

SCHEDULE 4

REGULATIONS 36(2) AND 38(2)

Sums to be disregarded in the calculation of earnings

Definitions

"applicable amount" – see Part 5.

"child" – see reg 2(1).

"claimant" – see reg 2(1).

"couple" – see s137(1) SSCBA.

"earnings" – see regs 35 and 37.

"employed earner" – see reg 2(1).

"family" – see s137(1) SSCBA.

"Great Britain" – excludes Northern Ireland.

"lone parent" – see reg 2(1).

"member of the work-related activity group" – see reg 2(1)

"partner" – see reg 2(1).

"part-time employment" – see para 16.

"person on an income-based jobseeker's allowance" – see reg 2(3).

"person on an income-related employment and support allowance" – see reg 2(3A).

"person on income support" – see reg 2(1).

"person on universal credit" – see reg 2(3B).

"polygamous marriage" – see reg 2(1).

"remunerative work" – see reg 6.

"self-employed earner" – see reg 2(1).

"service user group" – see reg 2(1).

"support component" – see Sch 3 para 24.

"United Kingdom" – includes Northern Ireland.

"Working Tax Credit Regulations" – see reg 2(1).

"young person" – see reg 19.

---

1.   In the case of a claimant who has been engaged in remunerative work as an employed earner or, had the employment been in Great Britain, would have been so engaged–

(a)   where–

(i)   the employment has been terminated because of retirement; and

(ii)   on retirement he is entitled to a retirement pension under the Act, or is not so entitled solely because of his failure to satisfy the contribution conditions,

any earnings [¹ paid or due to be paid] in respect of that employment, but only for a period commencing on the day immediately after the date on which the employment was terminated;

[³ (aa)   where–

(i)   the employment has been terminated because of retirement; and

(ii)   on retirement he is entitled to a state pension under Part 1 of the Pensions Act 2014, or is not so entitled solely because he does not have the minimum number of qualifying years,

any earnings paid or due to be paid in respect of that employment, but only for a period commencing on the day immediately after the date the employment was terminated;]

[¹ (b)   where before the first day of entitlement to housing benefit the employment has been terminated otherwise than because of retirement, any earnings paid or due to be paid in respect of that employment except–

[² (i)   any payment of the nature described in–

(aa)   regulation 35(1)(e), or

(bb)   section 28, 64 or 68 of the Employment Rights Act 1996 (guarantee payments, suspension from work on medical or maternity grounds); and]

(ii)   any award, sum or payment of the nature described in–

(aa)   regulation 35(1)(g) or (h), or

(bb)   section 34 or 70 of the Employment Rights Act 1996 (guarantee payments and suspension from work: complaints to employment tribunals),

including any payment made following the settlement of a complaint to an employment tribunal or of court proceedings;

(c)   where before the first day of entitlement to housing benefit–

(i)   the employment has not been terminated, but

(ii)   the claimant is not engaged in remunerative work,

any earnings paid or due to be paid in respect of that employment except any payment or remuneration of the nature described in [² paragraph 1(b)(i) or (ii)(bb) or regulation 35(1)(i)] or (j).]

Amendments

1.   Amended by reg 11(11)(a) of SI 2007 No 2618 as from 1.10.07.
2.   Amended by reg 6(5) of SI 2009 No 2655 as from 2.11.09.
3.   Inserted by art 28(5) of SI 2015 No 1985 as from 6.4.16.

Analysis

This paragraph applies only to claimants who have been in "remunerative work" as employed earners (see regs 2(1) and 6 for definitions), or who would have been had their employment been in Great Britain. Sub-paras (a), (aa) and (b) deal with situations where the employment has been terminated. Para (c) deals with situations where employment has *not* been terminated, but the person is no longer in "remunerative work" – eg, where s/he is no longer doing sufficient hours or is on sick leave. By reg 25, para 1 also applies to claimants' partners. It provides a complete disregard of earnings paid on retirement and a more restricted disregard for earnings received where employment has ceased or has been interrupted as at the first day of entitlement to HB. If a claimant receives wages or is due to receive wages on the termination or interruption of part-time work, see para 2. If s/he has been a self-employed earner, see para 2A.

Sub-para (a) deals with the treatment of earnings on termination of employment because of retirement. In this case, if the claimant is entitled to retirement pension when s/he retires (or would be but for failing to satisfy the contribution conditions), earnings (paid or due to be paid) from that employment are disregarded, but only for the period starting on the day after the day the employment ended. It is the date on which the employment terminated which is important, not the date on which the claimant last worked, which may be earlier. So where HB entitlement commences *after* the employment has terminated, all earnings from that employment should be disregarded.

Sub-para (aa) makes similar provision in respect of a claimant who is (or would be but for the contribution conditions) entitled to state pension. Note that by reg 5, these paras are effectively redundant as the HB Regs do not apply to a single claimant if s/he has, or a claimant who is a member of a couple and her/his partner have both, reached the qualifying age for PC unless either is on IS, income-based JSA or income-related ESA (or UC). Claims by such claimants are instead dealt with under the HB(SPC) Regs. New claims for HB by members of a mixed-age couple (ie, where only one member of the couple is at least the qualifying age for PC) are generally no longer allowed on or after 15 May 2019 – see the General Note to reg 5 HB(SPC) Regs on p733 for a discussion). Note that if a claimant *is* on IS, income-based JSA or income-related ESA (or UC), earnings are disregarded under para 12.

Sub-para (b) deals with the treatment of earnings on termination of employment before the first day of entitlement to HB, otherwise than on retirement. In this case, any earnings (paid or due to be paid) in respect of that employment should be disregarded, except those earnings shown in reg 35(1)(e), (g) and (h) (ie, retainers, compensation for unfair dismissal and payments deemed to be earnings by regulations made under s112 SSCBA 1992) and guarantee payments and remuneration on suspension from work on medical or maternity grounds following a complaint to an employment tribunal under ss28, 34, 64, 68 or 70 Employment Rights Act 1996. So where the employment terminates *after* the first day of entitlement to HB, earnings from that employment should be taken into account, subject only to the appropriate earnings disregard below.

Sub-para (c) deals with earnings that are disregarded on "remunerative work" ending but where the person's employment has not been terminated – eg, where working hours have decreased to less than 16, or the person is ill, or is on maternity leave. Where that person was not engaged in remunerative work at the first day of entitlement to HB, any earnings (paid or due to be paid) in respect of that employment are disregarded except those earnings shown in para 1(b)(i) and (ii)(bb) and reg 35(1)(i) and (j) – ie, retainers, any statutory sick pay, statutory maternity, adoption, paternity or shared parental pay and any employer's sick pay or maternity, adoption, paternity or shared parental pay. So where the remunerative work ceases *after* the first day of entitlement to HB, earnings from that employment should be taken into account, subject only to the appropriate earnings disregard below.

---

2. In the case of a claimant who, before the [¹ first day of entitlement to housing benefit]–

(a) has been engaged in part-time employment as an employed earner or, where the employment has been outside Great Britain, would have been so engaged had the employment been in Great Britain; and

(b) has ceased to be engaged in that employment, whether or not that employment has been terminated, any earnings [¹ paid or due to be paid] in respect of that employment except–

    (i) where that employment has been terminated, [¹ any payment of the nature described in [² paragraph 1(b)(i) or (ii)(bb)]];

    (ii) where that employment has not been terminated, [¹ any payment or remuneration of the nature described in [² paragraph 1(b)(i) or (ii)(bb) or regulation 35(1)(i)] or (j)].

Amendments
1.   Amended by reg 11(11)(b) of SI 2007 No 2618 as from 1.10.07.
2.   Amended by reg 6(5) of SI 2009 No 2655 as from 2.11.09.

Analysis
Para 2 deals with earnings disregarded on termination or interruption of part-time employment (defined as less than 16 hours a week in para 16). It clarifies that where a person has been in such employment (or would have been had her/his employment been in Great Britain) but this ceased before the first day of entitlement to HB (irrespective of whether or not that employment has terminated), then any earnings (paid or due to be paid) from that employment should be disregarded, except for:

(1)   where the employment terminated, any payments of the nature of those in para 1(b)(i) or (ii)(bb);

(2)   where, although that employment has not been terminated, that person has ceased to be engaged in that employment (eg, because s/he is ill), payments of the nature of those in para 1(b)(i) and (ii)(bb) and in reg 35(1)(i) and (j) of the HB Regs (ie, statutory sick pay, statutory maternity, adoption, paternity or shared parental pay and any employer's sick pay or maternity, adoption, paternity or shared parental pay).

So where the employment was terminated or interrupted *after* the first day of entitlement to HB, earnings from that employment should be taken into account, subject only to the appropriate earnings disregard below.

[¹**2A.** In the case of a claimant who has been engaged in remunerative work or part-time employment as a self-employed earner or, had the employment been in Great Britain would have been so engaged and who has ceased to be so employed, from the date of the cessation of his employment any earnings derived from that employment except earnings to which regulation 37(3) and (4) (earnings of self-employed earners) apply.]

Amendment
1.   Inserted by reg 6(11) of SI 2009 No 583 as from 6.4.09.

Analysis
This deals with earnings disregarded when employment as a self-employed earner ends, whether this was remunerative work (for which see reg 6) or part-time employment (defined as less than 16 hours a week in para 16). In this case, all earnings derived from that employment are disregarded from the date it ended, other than royalties, sums paid for the use of, or the right to use, any copyright, design, patent or trade mark, or Public Lending Right Scheme payments.

3.–(1) In a case to which this paragraph applies and paragraph 4 does not apply, £20; but notwithstanding regulation 25 (calculation of income and capital of members of a claimant's family and of a polygamous marriage) if this paragraph applies to a claimant it shall not apply to his partner except where, and to the extent that, the earnings of the claimant which are to be disregarded under this paragraph are less than £20.

(2) This paragraph applies where the claimant's applicable amount includes an amount by way of the disability premium [² , severe disability premium[⁴] or support component] under Schedule 3 (applicable amounts) [⁴ or where the claimant or the claimant's partner is a member of the work-related activity group].

(3) This paragraph applies where–

[¹ (a) the claimant is a member of a couple and his applicable amount includes an amount by way of the disability premium under Schedule 3; and]

(b) he or his partner [³ has not attained the qualifying age for state pension credit] and at least one is engaged in employment.

[¹ (4)]

[¹ (5)]

Amendments
1.   Amended by reg 3(11)(a) and (b) of SI 2008 No 1042 as from 19.5.08.
2.   Amended by reg 24(a) of SI 2008 No 1082 as from 27.10.08.
3.   Amended by reg 27 of SI 2009 No 1488 as from 6.4.10.
4.   Amended by Sch 1 para 6(8)(a) of SI 2017 No 204 as from 3.4.17, subject to transitional and savings provisions in Sch 2 paras 1–7.

Analysis

Para 3 provides a **£20 earnings disregard**. It applies if either of the conditions in sub-paras (2) or (3) is satisfied. The condition in sub-para (2) is that the claimant's applicable amount includes the disability or severe disability premium or the support component (see paras 12, 13, 14 and 24 of Sch 3). Transitional provision is made under Sch 2 paras 1–7 of the Employment and Support Allowance and Universal Credit (Miscellaneous Amendments and Transitional and Savings Provisions) Regulations 2017 SI No.204 for claims made before 3 April 2017 that include the work-related activity component (previously provided for in para 23 of Sch 3). Receipt of that component is also a qualifying condition for the £20 disregard. Even if a non-dependant's earnings are used (see reg 26), it is still the *claimant* who must satisfy these conditions as they relate to applicable amount, not resources. Note that para 3(3) was amended oddly when pensioner premiums were omitted on 19 May 2008. Where a claimant qualifies for a disability premium, s/he will qualify for a £20 earnings disregard under para 3(2) whether or not para 3(3) is satisfied. Note the following.
(1)   This disregard does not apply if the claimant qualifies for a lone parent disregard under para 4 or for an "exempt work" disregard under para 10A.
(2)   The claimant may also qualify for an additional earnings disregard under para 17.
(3)   In the case of couples, there is a maximum £20 deduction, not a disregard of £20 of the earnings of each partner who has earnings. The disregard is first applied to the earnings of the claimant, then anything left over may be applied to the earnings, if any, of the partner(s). For example, if the claimant earns £10 a week and her/his partner earns £23, the claimant's earnings are totally disregarded, but only £10 (balance of the disregard) of her/his partner's.

---

4.   In a case where the claimant is a lone parent, £25.

Analysis

Para 4 provides a **£25 earnings disregard** where the claimant is a lone parent (defined in reg 2(1)). Note that the claimant may also qualify for an additional earnings disregard under para 17. Para 4 can only apply where the claimant is not on IS, income-based JSA or income-related ESA (or UC). If s/he is on one of those benefits, all of her/his earnings are disregarded under para 12. See para 10A if the claimant is doing "exempt work" while receiving IB, ESA, SDA or NI credits for incapacity for work or limited capability for work.

5.–(1)   In a case to which neither paragraph 3 nor paragraph 4 applies to the claimant, and subject to sub-paragraph (2), where the claimant's applicable amount includes an amount by way of the carer premium under Schedule 3 (applicable amounts), £20 of the earnings of the person who is, or at any time in the preceding eight weeks was, in receipt of carer's allowance or treated in accordance with paragraph 17(2) of that Schedule as being in receipt of carer's allowance.

(2)   Where the carer premium is awarded in respect of the claimant and of any partner of his, their earnings shall for the purposes of this paragraph be aggregated, but the amount to be disregarded in accordance with sub-paragraph (1) shall not exceed £20 of the aggregated amount.

Analysis

Para 5 provides a **£20 earnings disregard** for claimants whose applicable amount includes the carer premium: see Sch 3 para 17. It does not apply if the claimant qualifies for a lone parent disregard under para 4 or for an "exempt work" disregard under para 10A. Para 5 applies to the earnings of the carer: sub-para (1). Where both the claimant and her/his partner qualifiy for the carer premium, £20 is disregarded from their combined earnings: sub-para (2). See para 6 where the claimant is a carer and her/his partner is engaged in employment. Note that the claimant may also qualify for an additional earnings disregard under para 17.

---

6.   Where the carer premium is awarded in respect of a claimant who is a member of a couple and whose earnings are less than £20, but is not awarded in respect of the other member of the couple, and that other member is engaged in an employment–
(a)   specified in paragraph 8(1), so much of the other member's earnings as would not when aggregated with the amount disregarded under paragraph 5 exceed £20;
(b)   other than one specified in paragraph 8(1), so much of the other member's earnings from such other employment up to £10 as would not when aggregated with the amount disregarded under paragraph 5 exceed £20.

Analysis

Where the claimant is the carer, has earnings less than £20 and is a member of a couple whose partner is engaged in any of the employments specified in para 8(1) (eg, auxiliary coastguard), the remainder of the £20 disregard under para 5 can be applied to the partner's earnings: sub-para (a). If the partner is engaged in any other employment, up to £10 of her/his earnings can be disregarded: sub-para (b). The total can never exceed £20.

---

7.   In a case where paragraphs 3, 5, 6 and 8 do not apply to the claimant and he is one of a couple and a member of that couple is in employment, £10; but, notwithstanding regulation 25 (calculation of income and capital of members of claimant's family and of a polygamous marriage), if this paragraph applies to a claimant it shall not apply to his partner except where, and to the extent that, the earnings of the claimant which are to be disregarded under this paragraph are less than £10.

Analysis

Para 7 provides a **£10 earnings disregard** for claimants who are members of a couple and who do not satisfy the provisions of paras 3, 5, 6 or 8. It does not apply if the claimant qualifies for a disregard under para 10A. Note that the claimant may also qualify for an additional earnings disregard under para 17.

It is not clear how this provision affects partners to polygamous marriages; presumably the claimant and one other partner would count as a "couple" for these purposes.

A flat-rate disregard of £10 is available, irrespective of whether the earnings are from full-time or part-time work. Despite reg 25, the context requires that "partner" should not be substituted for "claimant" where the partner has earnings, as specific provision is made for the earnings of partners by the regulation. The effect is that there is only one disregard per couple, rather than a disregard of £10 of *each* of their earnings if each earn. See para 3 for an example of how this works. If reg 26 has been used, the rules apply to the earnings of the non-dependant and her/his partner as only the assessment of resources is involved. See para 8 if the claimant or her/his partner is engaged in any of the employments specified in para 8(1) (eg, part-time fire fighter). See para 9 if a claimant her/himself has earnings which would normally be covered by this paragraph as well as by para 8. See para 10A if the claimant or her/his partner is doing "exempt work" while receiving IB, ESA, SDA or NI credits for incapacity for work or limited capability for work.

8.–(1)   In a case where paragraphs 3, 4, 5 and 6 do not apply to the claimant, £20 of earnings derived from one or more employments as–

[¹ (a)   a part-time fire-fighter employed by a fire and rescue authority under the Fire and Rescue Services Act 2004 or by the Scottish Fire and Rescue Service established under section 1A of the Fire (Scotland) Act 2005;]

[¹ (b)]

(c)   an auxiliary coastguard in respect of coast rescue activities;

(d)   a person engaged part-time in the manning or launching of a life boat;

(e)   a member of any territorial or reserve force prescribed in Part 1 of Schedule 6 to the Social Security (Contributions) Regulations 2001;

but, notwithstanding regulation 25 (calculation of income and capital of members of claimant's family and of a polygamous marriage), if this paragraph applies to a claimant it shall not apply to his partner except to the extent specified in sub-paragraph (2).

(2)   If the claimant's partner is engaged in employment–

(a)   specified in sub-paragraph (1), so much of his earnings as would not in aggregate with the amount of the claimant's earnings disregarded under this paragraph exceed £20;

(b)   other than one specified in sub-paragraph (1), so much of his earnings from that employment up to £10 as would not in aggregate with the claimant's earnings disregarded under this paragraph exceed £20.

Amendment

1.   Substituted by reg 11(5) of SI 2013 No 2536 as from 29.10.13.

Analysis

Para 8 provides a **£20 earnings disregard** in respect of the employments listed in para (1) if the claimant is not covered by paras 3, 4, 5 or 6 above. It does not apply if the claimant qualifies for a disregard under para 10A. Note that the claimant may also qualify for an additional earnings disregard under para 17. If the claimant has a partner and s/he or her/his partner has earnings from any other source of employment, see sub-para (2) if it is the partner who has such earnings, and para 9 if the claimant has earnings from other work. Because of para 9 it does not seem to be the intent that the claimant should be able to use the disregards in both paras 7 and 8, as paras 8 and 9 together provide a complete code where the claimant or her/his partner has earnings which would normally be covered by para 7 as well as by para 8(1) employment.

Sub-para (1) sets out the employments covered. Under sub-para (1)(e), the forces listed are: retired and emergency lists of officers of the Royal Navy; Royal Naval reserves; Royal Marines reserves; Army reserves;

Territorial Army and Volunteer reserves; RAF reserves; Royal Auxiliary Air Force; Royal Irish Regiment. Note under that reg 46(1), payments of annual bounty in relation to these employments paid at intervals of at least one year are to be treated as capital.

Sub-para (2) deals with the situation where the claimant is in any of the employments specified in sub-para (1) and a partner of the claimant also has earnings from a listed employment (sub-para (2)(a)), or from other work (sub-para (2)(b)).

The partner's earnings are only disregarded if the claimant's sub-para (1) earnings do not exhaust the disregard available under that sub-paragraph, and even then only up to the maximum amount specified.

Sub-para (2)(a). If the claimant's earnings from an employment listed in sub-para (1) are less than £20, the unused part of the disregard may be set against her/his partner's earnings from a listed employment.

Sub-para (2)(b). If the claimant's earnings from listed employment do not exhaust the £20 disregard under sub-para (1), up to £10 of what remains of the disregard may be set against her/his partner's earnings from other work.

9.   Where the claimant is engaged in [¹ one or more employments] specified in paragraph 8(1), but his earnings derived from such employments are less than £20 in any week and he is also engaged in any other employment so much of his earnings from that other employment, up to £5 if he is a single claimant, or up to £10 if he has a partner, as would not in aggregate with the amount of his earnings disregarded under [¹ paragraph 8] exceed £20.

Amendment

1.   Amended by reg 3(11)(c) of SI 2008 No 1042 as from 19.5.08.

Analysis

This appears to substitute for para 7 where the claimant has employment covered by para 8(1) and also does other work. Where such a claimant has not exhausted her/his £20 disregard under para 8(1) if s/he is single, s/he can offset up to £5 of what is left against earnings covered by this paragraph, or if s/he has a partner s/he can offset up to £10 against such earnings, subject to a total disregard of £20 of the claimant's earnings as assessed under this paragraph and para 8. The relationship between this paragraph and para 8(2) is not clear. It could be argued that this provision is in addition to, rather than in substitution for, para 8(2) on the basis that the claimant's earnings here cannot be intended also to refer to her/his partner's earnings as specific provision has been made for the partner's earnings under para 8(2) so that, if both have earnings, the claimant's earnings covered by this para and those of her/his partner under para 8(2), disregards under both para 8(2) and this para may be available. However, the "aggregate disregard" of the claimant's earnings covered by this paragraph and para 8 must not exceed £20, which implies that sums due to a partner and covered by para 8(2) are to be treated as the "claimant's" for these purposes, so no duplication occurs.

10.   In a case to which none of the paragraphs 3 to 9 applies, £5.

Analysis

Para 10 provides a **£5 earnings disregard** where none of paras 3 to 9 apply, that is, where a claimant is single, is not a lone parent and does not qualify for a £20 earnings disregard. See para 9 where the claimant also has earnings from any of the employments specified in para 8(1). This para does not apply if the claimant qualifes for a disregard under para 10A. The claimant may also qualify for an additional earnings disregard under para 17.

[¹**10A.**–(1)   Where–
(a)   the claimant (or if the claimant is a member of a couple, at least one member of that couple) is a person to whom sub-paragraph (5) applies;
(b)   the Secretary of State is satisfied that that person is undertaking exempt work as defined in sub-paragraph (6); and
(c)   paragraph 12 does not apply,
the amount specified in sub-paragraph (7) ("the specified amount").

(2)   Where this paragraph applies, paragraphs 3 to 10 do not apply; but in any case where the claimant is a lone parent, and the specified amount would be less than the amount specified in paragraph 4, then paragraph 4 applies instead of this paragraph.

(3)   Notwithstanding regulation 25 (calculation of income and capital of members of claimant's family and of a polygamous marriage), if sub-paragraph (1) applies to one member of a couple ("A") it shall not apply to the other member of that couple ("B") except to the extent provided in sub-paragraph (4).

(4)   Where A's earnings are less than the specified amount, there shall also be disregarded so much of B's earnings as would not when aggregated with A's earnings exceed the specified amount; but the amount of B's earnings which may be disregarded under this sub-paragraph is limited to a maximum of £20 unless the Secretary of State is satisfied that B is also undertaking exempt work.

(5)   This sub-paragraph applies to a person who is–
(a)   in receipt of a contributory employment and support allowance;

(b)   in receipt of incapacity benefit;

(c)   in receipt of severe disablement allowance; or

(d)   being credited with earnings on the grounds of incapacity for work or limited capability for work under regulation 8B of the Social Security (Credits) Regulations 1975.

(6)   "Exempt work" means work of the kind described in–

(a)   regulation 45(2), (3) or (4) of the Employment and Support Allowance Regulations [² or regulation 39(1)(a), (b) or (c) of the Employment and Support Allowance Regulations 2013]; or (as the case may be)

(b)   regulation 17(2), (3) or (4) of the Social Security (Incapacity for Work) (General) Regulations 1995, and, in determining for the purposes of this paragraph whether a claimant or a member of a couple is undertaking any type of exempt work, it is immaterial whether that person or their partner is also undertaking other work.

(7)   The specified amount is the amount of money from time to time mentioned in any provision referred to in sub-paragraph (6) by virtue of which the work referred to in sub-paragraph (1) is exempt (or, where more than one such provision is relevant and those provisions mention different amounts of money, the highest of those amounts).]

Amendments

1.   Inserted by reg 2(4)(a) of SI 2009 No 2608 as from 1.4.10 (5.4.10 where rent payable weekly or in multiples of a week).

2.   Amended by reg 35(10) of SI 2013 No 630 as from 29.4.13.

Analysis

Para 10A provides an **earnings disregard where the claimant or her/his partner is undertaking "exempt work"** (defined in sub-para (6)) while receiving contributory ESA, IB, SDA or NI credits for incapacity for work or limited capability for work, often referred to as "permitted work". This is to ensure that claimants (and partners) are not disadvantaged financially by attempting such work. Para 10A applies instead of paras 3 to 10, unless the claimant is a lone parent and the amount to be disregarded under para 4 would be higher than the disregard under this paragraph: sub-para (2). The claimant may also qualify for an additional earnings disregard under para 17.

Para 10A does not apply if the claimant is on IS, income-based JSA or income-related ESA (or UC), in which case all of the claimant's (and partner's) earnings are disregarded under para 12.

"Exempt work" (see para (6)) is any of the following.

(1)   Work as part of a treatment programme under medical supervision in a hospital or while regularly attending hospital as an outpatient for which earnings are no more than a set amount a week. The amount is 16 times the national living wage for a person aged 25 or over, rounded up to the nearest 50p where the amount includes an amount less than 50p, or rounded up to the nearest £1 where the amount includes an amount less than £1 but more than 50p. The national living wage was established on 1 April 2016, and was increased to a rate of £8.21 per hour from 1 April 2019. The set amount from 1 April 2019 is therefore £8.21 x 16 = £131.36, which is rounded up to £131.50.

(2)   Work for which earnings are no more than a set amount a week (calculated as in (1) above) which is supervised by a public or local authority or by a voluntary organisation or community interest company engaged in the provision or procurement of work for people with disabilities – often referred to as "supported permitted work".

(3)   For up to 52 weeks (indefinitely in limited cases, for which see the regulations specified in para (6)), work done for less than 16 hours a week and for which earnings are no more than a set amount a week (calculated as in (1) above) (often referred to as "permitted work higher limit").

(4)   Work for which earnings do not exceed £20 a week (often referred to as "permitted work lower limit").

The DWP must be satisfied that the person is undertaking exempt work as defined: para 10A(1)(b). It is understood that information on whether work falls into one of the categories and whether a time limit is appropriate is provided to local authorities by Jobcentre Plus.

The disregard that applies is the amount of weekly earnings allowed for the type of exempt work being undertaken (from 1 April 2019 £20 or £131.50 as the case may be), or where more than one type of exempt work is being undertaken, the highest of the amounts: sub-para (7). The disregard is not only applied to the earnings from the exempt work; it can be applied to any earnings from other work (see the wording of sub-para (1)). However, for a single claimant, the other work can only be other work s/he is permitted to do without affecting her/his entitlement to the benefits or NI credits specified – eg, work as a local councillor or disability member of the First-tier Tribunal. Where the claimant is a member of a couple and the earnings of the member doing exempt work are lower than the relevant disregard, the remainder can be used up on the earnings of the other member of the couple. This is limited to a maximum disregard of £20 unless the other member is also undertaking exempt work: sub-para (4).

11.   Any amount or the balance of any amount which would fall to be disregarded under paragraph 19 or 20 of Schedule 5 had the claimant's income which does not consist of earnings been sufficient to entitle him to the full disregarded thereunder.

Analysis
This applies where the claimant has insufficient income to use up the disregards under Sch 5 paras 19 and 20. Those paras deal with situations where the claimant is making a parental contribution to a student's grant or loan or contributes to a student's maintenance. In such a case, the unused part of the disregards may be applied to the claimant's earnings. This provision is available in addition to any other disregard available under this Schedule.

---

12. Where a claimant is on [² universal credit,] income support [, an income-based jobseeker's allowance or an income-related employment and support allowance], his earnings.

Amendments
1. Amended by reg 24(b) of SI 2008 No 1082 as from 27.10.08.
2. Amended by reg 7(7) of SI 2013 No 2070 as from 28.10.13.

Analysis
This paragraph is necessary as claimants on IS, income-based JSA or income-related ESA (or UC) have already had their income taken into account for those purposes. "Person on income support" is defined by reg 2(1), "person on an income-based jobseeker's allowance" by reg 2(3), "person on an income-related employment and support allowance" by reg 2(3A) and "person on universal credit" by reg 2(3B). Note that a person is generally precluded from claiming and entitlement to HB if entitled to UC: the Universal Credit (Transitional Provisions) Regulations 2014 SI No.1230 – the UC(TP) Regs 2014 (see p1857). However, a person entitled to UC living in "specified accommodation" or "temporary accommodation" may qualify for HB in respect of the specified accommodation: reg 5 UC(TP) Regs 2014. "Specified accommodation" and "temporary accommodation" are defined in reg 2 UC(TP) Regs by reference to the definitions in, respectively, Sch 1 para 3A Universal Credit Regulations 2013 SI No.376 (which is broadly the same as that in reg 75H HB Regs) and Sch 1 para 3B of those 2013 Regulations (which relates to certain types of accommodation provided for homeless persons).

---

13. Any earnings derived from employment which are payable in a country outside the United Kingdom for such period during which there is a prohibition against the transfer to the United Kingdom of those earnings.
14. Where a payment of earnings is made in a currency other than Sterling, any banking charge or commission payable in converting that payment into Sterling.
15. Any earnings of a child or young person.
16. In this Schedule "part-time employment" means employment in which the person is engaged on average for less than 16 hours a week.
17.–(1) In a case where the claimant is a person who satisfies at least one of the conditions set out in sub-paragraph (2), and his net earnings equal or exceed the total of the amounts set out in sub-paragraph (3), the amount of his earnings that falls to be disregarded under [⁷ paragraphs 3 to 10A] of this Schedule shall be increased by [²¹ £17.10].
(2) The conditions of this sub-paragraph are that–
(a) the claimant, or if he is a member of a couple, either the claimant or his partner, is a person to whom regulation 20(1)(c) of the Working Tax Credit Regulations applies; or
(b) the claimant–
  (i) is, or if he is a member of a couple, at least one member of that couple is aged at least 25 and is engaged in remunerative work for on average not less than 30 hours per week; or
  (ii) is a member of a couple and–
    (aa) at least one member of that couple, is engaged in remunerative work for on average not less than 16 hours per week; and
    [¹⁵ (bb) his family includes at least one child or young person;] or
  (iii) is a lone parent who is engaged in remunerative work for on average not less than 16 hours per week; or
  [¹⁹ (iv) not being a member of a couple, is engaged in remunerative work for on average not less than 16 hours per week and–
    [⁵ (aa) the claimant's applicable amount includes a disability premium under paragraph 12, or [¹⁶] the support component under paragraph 24, of Schedule 3 [¹⁶] ;] or
    (bb) the claimant is a member of the work-related activity group [⁴] [⁵ [¹⁶]] [¹⁶] [¹⁸]; or
  (v) is a member of a couple and at least one member of that couple is engaged in remunerative work for on average not less than 16 hours per week and that member of the couple–
    (aa) satisfies the qualifying conditions for the disability premium under paragraph 12 or the support component under paragraph 24 of Schedule 3; or
    (bb) is a member of the work-related activity group; or]
(c) the claimant is, or, if he has a partner, one of them is, a person to whom regulation 18(3) of the Working Tax Credit Regulations (eligibility for 50 plus element) applies, or would apply if an application for working tax credit were to be made in his case.
(3) The following are the amounts referred to in sub-paragraph (1)–
(a) the amount to be disregarded from the claimant's earnings under [⁹ paragraphs 3 to 10A] of this Schedule;

(b)   the amount of child care charges calculated as deductible under [⁴ regulation 27(1)(c)]; and
(c)   [²¹ £17.10].
(4)   The provisions of regulation 6 shall apply in determining whether or not a person works for on average not less than 30 hours per week, but as if the reference to 16 hours in paragraph (1) of that regulation were a reference to 30 hours.

Amendments

1.   Amended by art 19(9) of SI 2006 No 645 and reg 8 of SI 2006 No 217 as from 1.4.06 (3.4.06 where rent payable weekly or at intervals of a week).
2.   Amended by art 19(9) of SI 2007 No 688 as from 1.4.07 (2.4.07 where rent payable weekly or at intervals of a week).
3.   Amended by art 19(10) of SI 2008 No 632 as from 1.4.08 (7.4.08 where rent payable weekly or in multiples of a week).
4.   Amended by reg 3(11)(d)-(f) of SI 2008 No 1042 as from 19.5.08.
5.   Amended by reg 24(c) of SI 2008 No 1082, as amended by reg 32 of SI 2008 No 2428, as from 27.10.08.
6.   Amended by art 19(11) of SI 2009 No 497 as from 1.4.09 (6.4.09 where rent payable weekly or at intervals of a week).
7.   Amended by reg 2(4)(b) of SI 2009 No 2608 as from 1.4.10 (5.4.10 where rent payable weekly or in multiples of a week)
8.   Amended by art 19(10) of SI 2010 No 793 as from 1.4.10 (5.4.10 where rent payable weekly or in multiples of a week).
9.   Amended by reg 2(9) of SI 2010 No 2449 as from 1.11.10.
10.   Confirmed by art 20(10) of SI 2011 No 821 as from 1.4.11 (4.4.11 where rent payable weekly or in multiples of a week).
11.   Confirmed by art 20(10) of SI 2012 No 780 as from 1.4.12 (2.4.12 where rent payable weekly or in multiples of a week).
12.   Confirmed by art 19(10) of SI 2013 No 574 as from 1.4.13.
13.   Confirmed by art 17(11) of SI 2014 No 16 as from 1.4.14 (7.4.14 where rent payable weekly or in multiples of a week).
14.   Confirmed by art 17(11) of SI 2015 No 547 as from 1.4.15 (6.4.15 where rent payable weekly or in multiples of a week).
15.   Substituted by reg 2(1)(d) of SI 2015 No 1857 as from 1.05.16, subject to transitional provisions in reg 4.
16.   Amended by Sch 1 para 6(8)(b) of SI 2017 No 204 as from 3.4.17, subject to transitional and savings provisions in Sch 2 paras 1–7.
17.   Confirmed by art 22(11) of SI 2017 No 260 as from 1.4.17 (3.4.17 where rent payable weekly or in multiples of a week).
18.   Amended by reg 5(6) of SI 2017 No 581 as from 23.6.17, subject to transitional and savings provision in reg 9.
19.   Substituted by art 25(4) of SI 2017 No 901 as from 3.11.17.
20.   Confirmed by art 23(10) of SI 2018 No 281 as from 1.4.18 (2.4.18 where rent payable weekly or in multiples of a week).
21.   Confirmed by art 23(10) of SI 2019 No 480 as from 1.4.19.

Analysis

Para 17 provides an **additional earnings disregard** for some working claimants, broadly, those who qualify for a 30-hour element in the calculation of their working tax credit (WTC), or those working sufficient hours as set out in sub-para (2)(b). It lessens the impact of earnings on HB entitlement for those in low paid work. The categories of claimant who qualify are set out below.

If the claimant's (and partner's) net earnings are equal to or exceed the sum of the amounts set out in sub-para (3), the relevant disregard in paras 3 to 10A is to be increased by the amount of the additional disregard set out in sub-para (1). The amount in sub-para (1) has not been uprated since April 2010. See Sch 5 para 56 if net earnings are less than the sum of the amounts in sub-para (3). In this case, the equivalent of the additional earnings disregard is deducted from any WTC awarded.

Five categories of claimant qualify for an additional disregard.

(1)   A claimant to whom (or to whose partner) reg 20(1)(c) Working Tax Credit (Entitlement and Maximum Rate) Regulations 2002 applies: sub-para (2)(a). These are those who qualify for a 30-hour element with WTC, that is those who work 30 hours or more a week, or in the case of a couple with children, those who between them work 30 hours or more a week. The latter only applies if at least one of the couple is working 16 hours or more a week.
(2)   A claimant who is aged at least 25 and who works for at least 30 hours a week, or who has a partner who fulfils that description: sub-para (2)(b)(i).
(3)   A claimant who is a member of a couple, one of whom is working 16 hours or more a week, and whose family includes at least one child or young person. Transitional provision is made for those entitled to HB

on 30 April 2016, by reg 4 Housing Benefit (Abolition of the Family Premium and date of claim) (Amendment) Regulations 2015 SI No.1857: sub-para (2)(b)(ii).

(4)   A claimant who is a lone parent working 16 hours or more a week: sub-para (2)(b)(iii).

(5)   A single claimant who works 16 hours or more a week and whose applicable amount includes a disability premium or a support component, or who is a member of the work-related activity group (defined in reg 2(1)): sub-para (2)(b)(iv). In the case of couples, the one of them who satisfies the conditions for a disability premium or a support component, or who is a member of the work-related activity group, must be working at least 16 hours a week: sub-para (2)(b)(v). It is important to note that a person who works in any week is treated as not having limited capability for work under regs 40 and 44 ESA Regs 2008 or regs 37 and 38 ESA Regs 2013, unless it is work s/he may do while claiming: reg 40(2) ESA Regs 2008 and reg 37(2) ESA Regs 2013. To qualify for the support component under Sch 3 para 24, the claimant or her/his partner must have limited capability for work-related activity. So where there is entitlement to a component, this sub-para can only apply if the claimant (or partner) is doing work that is permitted by reg 40(2) ESA Regs 2008 or reg 37(2) ESA Regs 2013. Transitional provision is made under Sch 2 paras 1–7 of the Employment and Support Allowance and Universal Credit (Miscellaneous Amendments and Transitional and Savings Provisions) Regulations 2017 SI No.204 for claims made before 3 April 2017 that include the work-related activity component (see p1892). Where a claimant (or partner) works 16 or more hours a week and qualifies for that component, the additional earnings disregard will apply.

On the face of it, sub-para (2)(c), provides a further situation in which a claimant could qualify for an additional disregard – ie, if s/he or her/his partner qualifies (or would qualify) for a 50 plus element with WTC. However, reg 18 WTC Regs was omitted with effect from 6 April 2012 and the WTC 50-plus element has not been available since that date.

In deciding how many hours a week are worked, the averaging rules in reg 6 apply: sub-para (4).

SCHEDULE 5

REGULATION 40

Sums to be disregarded in the calculation of income other than earnings

Modifications

Para 51 was substituted by Sch 4 para 2(4) and paras 55A and 55B inserted by Sch 4 para 2(5) HB&CTB(CP) Regs in respect of claims for HB by some refugees.

A different version of para 55B was substituted for para 56 by Sch 4 para 4(2)(b) HB&CTB(CP) Regs for some HB claimants who were refugees who claimed asylum on or before 2 April 2000.

See also reg 10A and Sch A1 inserted by Sch 4 para 2 HB&CTB(CP) Regs.

Note that paras 55A and 55B lapsed by s12(2)(e) Asylum and Immigration (Treatment of Claimants, etc.) Act 2004 (for those recorded as refugees after 14 June 2007) and were deleted by reg 5(6)(k) of SI 2008 No.3157 as from 5 January 2009. For the full text of para 51 as substituted and paras 55A and 55B as inserted, see p1129 of the 20th edition.

A para A1 was inserted by reg 16 Jobseeker's Allowance (Work for Your Benefit Pilot Scheme) Regulations 2010 SI No.1222 from 22 November 2010 to 1 March 2012 in pilot areas only.

A para A4 was inserted by reg 13 Jobseeker's Allowance (Supervised Job Search Pilot Scheme) Regulations 2014 SI No.1913 from 18 July 2014 to 30 April 2015 for those selected to participate in the pilot scheme only.

A para A5 was inserted by reg 17 Jobseeker's Allowance (18–21 Work Skills Pilot Scheme) Regulations 2014 SI No.3117 from 25 November 2014 to 24 November 2016 for those selected to participate in the pilot scheme in pilot areas only.

Definitions

"armed forces independence payment" – see reg 2(1).

"attendance allowance" – see reg 2(1).

"benefit week" – see reg 2(1).

"boarder" – see reg 2(1).

"capital" – see reg 2(1).

"child" – see reg 2(1).

"claimant" – see reg 2(1).

"claimant participating as a service user" – see reg 2(5).

"disability living allowance" – see reg 2(1).

"dwelling" – see s137(1) SSCBA.

"earnings" – see regs 35 and 37.

"eligible rent" – see reg 2(1).

"employment zone contractor" – see reg 2(1).

"employment zone programme" – see reg 2(1).

"family" – see reg 2(1).

"a guaranteed income payment" – see reg 2(1).

"income" – see Part 6.
"Jobseekers Act" – see reg 2(1).
"local authority" – see s191 SSAA.
"local welfare provision" – see reg 2(1).
"the Mandatory Work Activity Scheme" – see reg 2(1).
"Macfarlane Trust" and other schemes listed in para 35(1) and (7) – see reg 2(1).
"non-dependant" – reg 3.
"partner" – see reg 2(1).
"participating as a service user" – see reg 2(5).
"payment" – see reg 2(1).
"personal independence payment" – see reg 2(1).
"person on an income-based jobseeker's allowance" – see reg 2(3).
"person on an income-related employment and support allowance" – see reg 2(3A).
"person on income support" – see reg 2(1).
"person on universal credit" – see reg 2(3B).
"occupies as a home" – see reg 7.
"ordinary clothing or footwear – see reg 2(1).
"self-employment route" – see reg 2(1).
"special account" – see reg 2(1).
"sports award" – see reg 2(1).
"student" – see reg 2(1) and Part 7.
"student contribution" – see Part 7.
"student loans" – see reg 53.
"subsistence allowance" – see reg 2(1).
"voluntary organisation" – see reg 2(1).
"young person" – see reg 19.

[A1.]
[¹**A2.** Any payment made to the claimant in respect of any travel or other expenses incurred, or to be incurred, by him in respect of his participation in the Mandatory Work Activity Scheme.]

Amendment

1.   Inserted by reg 14 of SI 2011 No 688 as from 25.4.11.

*[¹**A3.**]*

Amendment

1.   Inserted by reg 14 of SI 2011 No 917 as from 20.5.11. SI 2011 No 917 was quashed by the Court of Appeal in *R (Reilly and another) v SSWP* [2013] EWCA Civ 66, 12 February 2013.

[²**A3.** Any payment made to the claimant in respect of any travel or other expenses incurred, or to be incurred, by him in respect of his participation in a scheme prescribed in regulation 3 of the Jobseeker's Allowance (Schemes for Assisting Persons to Obtain Employment) Regulations 2013.]

Amendment

1.   Inserted by reg 11 of SI 2013 No 276 as from 6.45 pm 12.2.13.

General Note

The Schemes currently prescribed in the regulations cited are the Work Programme, Skills Conditionality, the sector-based work academy, New Enterprise Allowance, Full-time Training Flexibility and Work and Health Programme.

[A4.]
[A5.]
1.   Any amount paid by way of tax on income which is to be taken into account under regulation 40 (calculation of income other than earnings).

Analysis

This requires the deduction of any income tax *actually* paid on income other than earnings covered by reg 40.

2.   Any payment in respect of any expenses incurred or to be incurred by a claimant who is–
(a)   engaged by a charitable or voluntary organisation; or

(b)   a volunteer,

if he otherwise derives no remuneration or profit from the employment and is not to be treated as possessing any earnings under regulation 42(9) (notional income).

Analysis

Notice that the types of expenses to be disregarded are unrestricted, unlike under regs 35(2)(b) or 38, but that the requirement that no "remuneration or profit" be made excludes any element of *gain* from the disregard. See reg 42(9) for where someone can be treated as having "notional" earnings.

[¹**2A.**   Any payment in respect of expenses arising out of the [² claimant participating as a service user].]

Amendments

1.   Inserted by reg 6(6)(a) of SI 2009 No 2655 as from 2.11.09.
2.   Amended by reg 8(5) of SI 2014 No 591 as from 28.4.14.

3.   In the case of employment as an employed earner, any payment in respect of expenses wholly, exclusively and necessarily incurred in the performance of the duties of the employment.

Analysis

The purpose is to avoid expenses which are deemed not to be "earnings" by reg 35(2)(b) being taken into account under any other regulation.

4.   Where a claimant is on [² universal credit,] income support [¹, an income-based jobseeker's allowance or an income-related employment and support allowance] the whole of his income.

Amendments

1.   Amended by reg 25(a) of SI 2008 No 1082 as from 27.10.08.
2.   Amended by reg 7(8) of SI 2013 No 2070 as from 28.10.13.

Analysis

This para and para 5 are necessary as IS, income-based JSA and income-related ESA (and UC) claimants have already had their income fully considered in relation to that benefit – see General Note on Part 6 on p415. "Person on income support" is defined by reg 2(1), "person on an income-based jobseeker's allowance" by reg 2(3), "person on an income-related employment and support allowance" by reg 2(3A) and "person on universal credit" by reg 2(3B). Note that a person is generally precluded from entitlement to HB if entitled to UC: the Universal Credit (Transitional Provisions) Regulations 2014 SI No.1230 – the UC(TP) Regs 2014 (see p1857). However, a person entitled to UC living in "specified accommodation" or "temporary accommodation" may qualify for HB in respect of that accommodation: reg 15 UC(TP) Regs 2014. "Specified accommodation" and "temporary accommodation" are defined in reg 2 UC(TP) Regs by reference to the definitions in, respectively, Sch 1 para 3A Universal Credit Regulations 2013 SI No.376 (which is broadly the same as that in reg 75H HB Regs) and Sch 1 para 3B of those 2013 Regulations.

5.   Where the claimant is a member of a joint-claim couple for the purposes of the Jobseekers Act and his partner is on an income-based jobseeker's allowance, the whole of the claimant's income.

6.   Any disability living allowance [², armed forces independence payment][¹ or personal independence payment].

Amendments

1.   Amended by reg 8 and Sch para 36(7) of SI 2013 No 388 as from 8.4.13.
2.   Amended by art 7 and Sch para 34(7) of Si 2013 No 591 as from 8.4.13.

Analysis

See para 7 for the treatment of concessionary payments of DLA, armed forces independence payment or PIP. See also Sch 6 para 9 (on p687) where the concessionary payments are capital payments for arrears, or to compensate for arrears due. See para 9 for attendance allowance.

7.   Any concessionary payment made to compensate for the non-payment of–
(a)   any payment specified in paragraph 6 or 9;
(b)   income support;
(c)   an income-based jobseeker's allowance.
[¹ (d)   an income-related employment and support allowance.]
[² (e)   universal credit]

Amendments
1. Inserted by reg 25(a) of SI 2008 No 1082 as from 27.10.08.
2. Inserted by reg 35(11) of SI 2013 No 630 as from 29.4.13.

Analysis
See also Sch 6 para 9 where the concessionary payments are capital payments for arrears, or to compensate for arrears due.

8. Any mobility supplement under [¹ article 20 of the Naval, Military and Air Forces Etc. (Disablement and Death) Service Pensions Order 2006] (including such a supplement by virtue of any other scheme or order) or under article 25A of the Personal Injuries (Civilians) Scheme 1983 or any payment intended to compensate for the non-payment of such a supplement.

Amendment
1. Amended by reg 5(6)(a) of SI 2008 No 3157 as from 5.1.09.

Analysis
Art 20 of the Order referred to relates to mobility supplement paid to members of the armed forces who are in receipt of retired pay or a pension due to a specified injury. Art 25A refers to similar payments made to civilians and former civil defence volunteers due to "war/war service injuries sustained during the period September 3, 1939 to March 19, 1946". Notice that the paragraph also covers sums paid as compensation for non-payment of the benefits referred to.

9. Any attendance allowance.

Analysis
See para 7 for the treatment of concessionary payments of attendance allowance. See also Sch 6 para 9 (on p687) where the concessionary payments are capital payments for arrears, or to compensate for arrears due. See para 6 for DLA, PIP and armed forces independence payment.

10. Any payment to the claimant as holder of the Victoria Cross or of the George Cross or any analogous payment.
11.–(1) Any payment–
(a) by way of an education maintenance allowance made pursuant to–
    (i) regulations made under section 518 of the Education Act 1996 (payment of school expenses; grant of scholarships etc.);
    (ii) regulations made under section 49 or 73(f) of the Education (Scotland) Act 1980 (power to assist persons to take advantage of educational facilities);
    [¹ (iii) directions made under section 73ZA of the Education (Scotland) Act 1980 and paid under section 12(2)(c) of the Further and Higher Education (Scotland) Act 1992; [²]
(b) corresponding to such an education maintenance allowance, made pursuant to–
    (i) section 14 or section 181 of the Education Act 2002 (power of Secretary of State and National Assembly for Wales to give financial assistance for purposes related to education or childcare, and allowances in respect of education or training); or
    (ii) regulations made under section 181 of that Act [² ;or
(c) in England, by way of financial assistance made pursuant to section 14 of the Education Act 2002.]
(2) Any payment, other than a payment to which sub-paragraph (1) applies, made pursuant to–
(a) regulations made under section 518 of the Education Act 1996;
(b) regulations made under section 49 of the Education (Scotland) Act 1980; or
[¹ (c) directions made under section 73ZA of the Education (Scotland) Act 1980 and paid under section 12(2)(c) of the Further and Higher Education (Scotland) Act 1992,]
in respect of a course of study attended by a child or a young person or a person who is in receipt of an education maintenance allowance [² or other payment] made pursuant to any provision specified in sub-paragraph (1).

Amendments
1. Substituted by reg 5(6)(b) of SI 2008 No 3157 as from 5.1.09.
2. Amended by reg 19(8) of SI 2011 No 2425 as from 31.10.11.

Analysis
This provides for a disregard of education maintenance allowance (in Wales payments corresponding to such an allowance) and payments made to people aged above compulsory school leaving age, whether or not that education is in, or equivalent to, secondary education. Also disregarded are payments paid to children below school leaving age to enable them to take part in activities at state schools, or, where appropriate, help pay fees

for fee-paying schools, to avoid hardship to children or their parents. Education maintenance allowances have been abolished in England, but from 31 October 2011, financial assistance provided under s14 Education Act 2002 is disregarded – eg, 16 to 19 bursaries. Note that the payments listed are also disregarded as capital under para 51 of Sch 6.

12. Any payment made to the claimant by way of a repayment under regulation 11(2) of the Education (Teacher Student Loans) (Repayment etc) Regulations 2002.

13.–(1) Any payment made pursuant to section 2 of the 1973 Act or section 2 of the Enterprise and New Towns (Scotland) Act 1990 except–

(a) a payment made as a substitute for income support, a jobseeker's allowance, incapacity benefit [¹ , severe disablement allowance or an employment and support allowance];

(b) a payment of an allowance referred to in section 2(3) of the 1973 Act or section 2(5) of the Enterprise and New Towns (Scotland) Act 1990;

(c) a payment intended to meet the cost of living expenses which relate to any one or more of the items specified in sub-paragraph (2) whilst a claimant is participating in an education, training or other scheme to help him enhance his employment prospects unless the payment is a Career Development Loan paid pursuant to section 2 of the 1973 Act and the period of education or training or the scheme, which is supported by that loan, has been completed; or

(d) for the purpose only of assessing entitlement to housing benefit in respect of a dwelling other than the one which the claimant normally occupies as his home, a payment made to a person to whom regulation 7(5)(b) (circumstances in which a person is or is not to be treated as occupying a dwelling as his home) applies to the extent that the payment is made in respect of the cost of living away from home.

(2) The items specified in this sub-paragraph for the purposes of sub-paragraph (1)(c) are food, ordinary clothing or footwear, household fuel or rent of the claimant or, where the claimant is a member of a family, any other member of his family, or any council tax or water charges for which that claimant or member is liable.

(3) For the purposes of this paragraph, "rent" means eligible rent less any deductions in respect of non-dependants which fall to be made under regulation 74 (non-dependant deductions).

Amendment

1. Amended by reg 8(10)(a) of SI 2010 No 641 as from 1.4.10 (5.4.10 where rent payable weekly or in multiples of a week).

Analysis

This relates to any arrangements for training made under s2 of the Acts referred to. Only the payments referred to in sub-paras (a) to (d) are to be taken into account.

14.–(1) Subject to sub-paragraph (2), any of the following payments–

(a) a charitable payment;

(b) a voluntary payment;

(c) a payment (not falling within sub-paragraph (a) or (b) above) from a trust whose funds are derived from a payment made in consequence of any personal injury to the claimant;

(d) a payment under an annuity purchased–
   (i) pursuant to any agreement or court order to make payments to the claimant; or
   (ii) from funds derived from a payment made,
   in consequence of any personal injury to the claimant; or

(e) a payment (not falling within sub-paragraphs (a) to (d)) received by virtue of any agreement or court order to make payments to the claimant in consequence of any personal injury to the claimant.

(2) Sub-paragraph (1) shall not apply to a payment which is made or due to be made by–

(a) a former partner of the claimant, or a former partner of any member of the claimant's family; or

(b) the parent of a child or young person where that child or young person is a member of the claimant's family.

Analysis

Note, firstly that para 35 provides a complete disregard of certain charitable payments. Note, secondly, that unlike previous versions of this paragraph, if the income payment falls within para (1) – this includes payments made in consequence of personal injury suffered by a claimant – and is not caught by para (2), all of the payment is ignored. There is no £20 limit under this para as there was under previous versions of this paragraph, nor does para 34 apply to limit the total amount of income that may be ignored.

Sub-paras (a) and (b). The nature of charitable and voluntary payments was examined in detail in *R v Doncaster BC ex p Boulton* (1992) 25 HLR 195, QBD. Laws J held that:

"The effect of specifying both charitable and voluntary payments is to enable payments which are not made for the payer's own benefit to be brought within the scope of the disregard without the need to engage with fine distinctions between charitable and non-charitable payments."

In addition it was found that the reference to charitable payments "must be to payments made under a charitable trust" – eg, those made by a registered charity. As with charitable payments, the Court decided that a payment is voluntary if it is made without anything being obtained by the payer in return.

The case itself dealt with the question of whether or not payments of cash in lieu of concessionary coal made to the widow of a miner by British Coal were voluntary payments which qualified for the disregard. This was found not to be the case on the basis that the agreement between British Coal and the Unions under which they are paid was entered into in the interests of good labour relations and for the efficient running of the coal industry. Laws J concluded that:

"This legitimate and proper purpose is, however, far away from the purpose and benevolence behind voluntary payments in the regulations . . . and that as a matter of the law the payments made to the applicant were not voluntary within the meaning of the relevant regulations."

Consequently authorities should take payments of cash in lieu of concessionary coal made by British Coal to ex-miners and their widows into account as "remuneration or profit derived from that employment" and should treat them as earnings. See also reg 42(6) and (7).

In *R(H) 5/05*, Commissioner Mesher concluded that the phrase "voluntary payment" should have the same meaning here as it did in reg 40(6) HB Regs 1987 (now reg 46(6) HB Regs), even though the contexts are somewhat different, and that *Boulton* was correctly decided and applied as much to reg 40(6) HB regs 1987 as it did to this para. However, on the facts of the case before him, where an "informal loan" had been made to the claimant, the commissioner concluded that there had been no intention to create legal relations and therefore no legally enforceable rights or obligations were created by the payments to the claimant. This was a crucial point which distinguished the case from *Boulton*, because here the person making the "loan" payments to the claimant got nothing in return, tangible or otherwise, whereas in *Boulton* the Coal Board did at least benefit from the payments of cash in lieu of concessionary coal in the sense of fostering good labour relations. The maintenance of a relationship of personal affection or of familial duty on the part of the payer, in Commissioner Mesher's view, did not constitute an intangible benefit for the payer sufficient to disqualify the payments as voluntary payments: para 42.

Payments from a trust can be voluntary. The specific terms of the trust deed must be considered. In *LG v SSWP (ESA)* [2019] UKUT 153 (AAC) (a case decided on the provisions in the ESA Regulations 2008 equivalent to reg 46(6) HB Regs and para 14 above), Judge Poole considered a trust that was a liferent trust with the power to advance capital. The liferenter was entitled to payment of the income of the trust, and so these payments were not 'voluntary'. For payments to be voluntary, there must be discretion about whether or not to make payments, not simply about matters such as the timing and manner of making them. Any decision to advance capital from the trust would have been voluntary.

Sub-para (c) covers payments from trusts whose funds are derived from payments made in consequence of personal injury to the claimant. The value of the trust itself is disregarded under para 14 of Sch 6, as is the value of the right to receive payments under it. See also para 14A Sch 6 for capital payments made from such a trust and paras 45 and 46 Sch 6 where damages paid to children or young people are administered by the Court.

Sub-para (e) *Lloyd v Lewisham LB and SSWP* [2013] EWCA Civ 923 concerned whether an income loss award paid following an injury at work could be disregarded for HB purposes under sub-para (e). The right to claim the award formed part of the claimant's terms of employment and was therefore "pre-injury" compensation, rather than compensation paid under an agreement made after she suffered an injury. The Upper Tribunal had decided that the income could not be disregarded, applying *Malekout v Secretary of State* [2010] EWCA Civ 162; [2010] AACR 28 which had decided in respect of the similarly worded IS provision that an employee's early ill-health pension from his employer, paid in consequence of an injury to him, was not "received by virtue of any agreement" because the "agreement" had to be made after the injury for it to be an agreement "in consequence of any personal injury". In the Court of Appeal, the claimant argued for a wide meaning, that sub-para (e) included payments made after the injury but pursuant to agreements or orders made at any time – ie, including payments under occupational pension schemes. The Secretary of State argued for a narrow meaning, that the agreement or order must have been made after the injury. The Court of Appeal decided that, although not bound by *Malekout*, its reasoning was persuasive and that sub-para (e) only excludes sums paid under agreements which are made after an injury occurs.

---

15.   Subject to paragraph 34, £10 of any of the following, namely–

(a)   a war disablement pension (except insofar as such a pension falls to be disregarded under paragraph 8 or 9);

[¹ (b)   a war widow's pension or [³ war widower's pension] ;]

(c)   a pension payable to a person as a widow, widower or surviving civil partner under [²] any power of Her Majesty otherwise than under an enactment to make provision about pensions for or in respect of persons who have been disabled or have died in consequence of service as members of the armed forces of the Crown;

(d)   a guaranteed income payment [² and, if the amount of that payment has been abated to less than £10 by a [³ pension or payment falling within article 31(1)(a) or (b) of the Armed Forces and Reserve Forces (Compensation Scheme) Order 2005], so much of [³ that pension or payment] as would not, in aggregate with the amount of [³ any] guaranteed income payment disregarded, exceed £10];

(e)   a payment made to compensate for the non-payment of such a pension or payment as is mentioned in any of the preceding sub-paragraphs;

(f)   a pension paid by the government of a country outside Great Britain which is analogous to any of the pensions or payments mentioned in sub-paragraphs (a) to (d) above;

[⁴ (g) a pension paid by a government to victims of National Socialist persecution .]

Amendments
1.   Substituted by reg 3(12)(a) of SI 2008 No 1042 as from 19.5.08.
2.   Amended by reg 5(6)(c of SI 2008 No 3157 as from 5.1.09.
3.   Amended by reg 6(6)(b) of SI 2009 No 2655 as from 2.11.09.
4.   Substituted by reg 5 of SI 2017 No 174 as from 20.3.17.

Analysis
A guaranteed income payment (defined in reg 2(1)) can be abated in part or in full by a payment under the schemes set out in sub-para (d). The amendment made by SI 2008 No.3157 ensures that the claimant can benefit from the full £10 disregard in this situation. Great Britain does *not* include Northern Ireland. Para 15(f) extends the £10 statutory disregard to analogous payments made by the governments of other countries. This disregard can overlap with disregards from student covenant income and access funds as well as the disregard in para 16. A combined maximum of £20 is allowed: Sch 5 para 34.

In *MN v Bury Council and SSWP (HB)* [2014] UKUT 187 (AAC), Judge Williams decided (on the version of sub-para (g) in force prior to its substitution on 20 March 2017) that sums received by the appellant from the Netherlands WUV scheme, for compensation for victims of national socialist persecution, were to be treated as if they were received from one of the funds identified in para 15(g). He concluded that the failure to include the Netherlands scheme within the same provisions as the German and Austrian schemes for social security purposes was a form of discrimination based on eligibility for one scheme rather than another, which itself was based on nationality. The claimant was to be viewed as a victim of discrimination under Article 14 read with Article 1 of Protocol 1 to the ECHR and the discrimination was manifestly without reasonable justification. The version of sub-para (g) in force from 20 March 2017 ensures that the same disregard applies in all cases.

Note: s134(8) SSAA (on p79) allows an authority to resolve to disregard more than £10 of (or all of) prescribed war pensions.

---

16.   Subject to paragraph 34, £15 of any–
(a)   widowed mother's allowance paid pursuant to section 37 of the Act;
(b)   widowed parent's allowance paid pursuant to section 39A of the Act.

Analysis
This disregard can overlap with disregards from student covenant income and access funds as well as the disregard in para 15. A combined maximum of £20 is allowed: Sch 5 para 34.

17.–(1)   Any income derived from capital to which the claimant is or is treated under regulation 51 (capital jointly held) as beneficially entitled but, subject to sub-paragraph (2), not income derived from capital disregarded under paragraphs 1, 2, 4, 8, 14 or 25 to 28 of Schedule 6.

(2)   Income derived from capital disregarded under paragraphs 2, 4 or 25 to 28 of Schedule 6 but only to the extent of–
(a)   any mortgage repayments made in respect of the dwelling or premises in the period during which that income accrued; or
(b)   any council tax or water charges which the claimant is liable to pay in respect of the dwelling or premises and which are paid in the period during which that income accrued.

(3)   The definition of "water charges" in regulation 2(1) shall apply to sub-paragraph (2) of this paragraph with the omission of the words "in so far as such charges are in respect of the dwelling which a person occupies as his home".

Analysis
The effect of this para is that unless the *capital* to which the person is entitled is disregarded under the provisions listed, the income produced by capital is to be disregarded. Income from capital disregarded under the provisions listed is to be taken into account, however, except so far as sub-para (2) provides otherwise. See also reg 51 (on p476). Note that reg 52 (on p478) provides a formula for calculating "tariff" (deemed) income from capital that is not disregarded.

Sub-para (2). Where income is produced from capital disregarded under paras 2, 4, or 25 to 28 of Sch 6, it can be disregarded to the extent that mortgage repayments (of capital as well as interest) were made in respect of the premises in question during the period to which the income relates. Deductions can also be made for any payments of council tax or water charges for which the claimant is liable during the period to which the income relates.

[¹**18.**]

Amendment

1.   Omitted by reg 3(12)(b) of SI 2008 No 1042 as from 19.5.08.

---

19.   Where the claimant makes a parental contribution in respect of a student attending a course at an establishment in the United Kingdom or undergoing education in the United Kingdom, which contribution has been assessed for the purposes of calculating–

(a)   under, or pursuant to regulations made under powers conferred by, sections 1 or 2 of the Education Act 1962 or section 22 of the Teaching and Higher Education Act 1998, that student's award;

(b)   under regulations made in exercise of the powers conferred by section 49 of the Education (Scotland) Act 1980, that student's bursary, scholarship, or other allowance under that section or under regulations made in exercise of the powers conferred by section 73 of that Act of 1980, any payment to that student under that section; or

(c)   the student's student loan,

an amount equal to the weekly amount of that parental contribution, but only in respect of the period for which that contribution is assessed as being payable.

Analysis

Under this para, a parental contribution taken into account in computing a student's grant or loan under the provisions listed is disregarded in computing the payer's "other" income during the period for which the contribution is payable. If "other" income is insufficient to use up the disregard, the unused part can be disregarded from earnings: see Sch 4 para 11. See also para 20 below.

Sub-para (a). Section 1 of the 1962 Act deals with full time courses designated as first degree courses or comparable to these, at universities, colleges or other institutions in the UK.

Sub-para (b). Under s73 of the 1980 Act, the Secretary of State may award grants to assist the carrying out of educational research (Subs (1)(e)) or payments of allowances to persons attending "courses of education" (Subs (1)(f)).

Sub-para (c) refers to student loans. See reg 53 for the definition.

20.–(1)   Where the claimant is the parent of a student aged under 25 in advanced education who either–

(a)   is not in receipt of any award, grant or student loan in respect of that education; or

(b)   is in receipt of an award under section 2 of the Education Act 1962 or an award bestowed by virtue of the Teaching and Higher Education Act 1998, or regulations made thereunder, or a bursary, scholarship or other allowance under section 49(1) of the Education (Scotland) Act 1980, or a payment under section 73 of that Act of 1980,

and the claimant makes payments by way of a contribution towards the student's maintenance, other than a parental contribution falling within paragraph 19, an amount specified in sub-paragraph (2) in respect of each week during the student's term.

(2)   For the purposes of sub-paragraph (1), the amount shall be equal to–

(a)   the weekly amount of the payments; or

(b)   the amount by way of a personal allowance for a single claimant under 25 less the weekly amount of any award, bursary, scholarship, allowance or payment referred to in sub-paragraph (1)(b),

whichever is less.

Analysis

This provides a partial disregard in computing the payer's "other income" for payments made by a parent to a student in advanced education who is aged under 25 and is not receiving a grant or loan (or who gets one of the awards listed). If "other" income is insufficient to use up the disregard, the unused part can be disregarded from earnings: see Sch 4 para 11. See also para 19 above.

Note the, albeit very *obiter*, view in *CH 2517/2004* that the word "parent" in Sch 4 para 18 HB Regs 1987 (now Sch 5 para 20) should arguably not be restricted to a natural or adoptive parent.

Sub-para (2) quantifies how much of the parent's income may be disregarded in this respect.

---

21.   Any payment made to the claimant by a child or young person or a non-dependant.

Analysis

This provides a disregard of payments received by the claimant from a child, young person or non-dependant – but see reg 74 (on p516) for the deductions that can be made from "eligible rent" in respect of non-dependants. See also paras 22 and 42 if payments are being made by someone residing in the claimant's home who is other than a child, young person or non-dependant.

---

22.   Where the claimant occupies a dwelling as his home and the dwelling is also occupied by a person other than one to whom paragraph 21 or 42 refers and there is a contractual liability to make payments to the claimant in respect of the occupation of the dwelling by that person or a member of his family–

[³ (a) where the aggregate of any payments made in respect of any one week in respect of the occupation of the dwelling by that person or a member of his family, or by that person and a member of his family, is less than £20, the whole of that amount; or

(b) where the aggregate of any such payments is £20 or more per week, £20.]

Amendments

1. Amended by art 19(10)(a) of SI 2006 No 645 and reg 8 of SI 2006 No 217 as from 1.4.06 (3.4.06 where rent payable weekly or at intervals of a week).
2. Amended by art 19(10)(a) of SI 2007 No 688 as from 1.4.07 (2.4.07 where rent payable weekly or at intervals of a week).
3. Substituted by reg 11(12) of SI 2007 No 2618 as from 1.4.08 (7.4.08 where rent payable weekly or at intervals of a week).

Analysis

This deals with payments from people other than a child, a young person or a non-dependant (for which see para 21) or someone to whom the claimant is providing "board and lodging accommodation" (for which see para 42). There must be a contractual liability (ie, as a licensee or tenant) to pay the claimant in return for living in her/his home. Such income is *not* treated as "earnings" and the only disregards are those set out here.

23.–(1) Any income in kind, except where regulation 40(10)(b) (provision of support under section 95 or 98 of the Immigration and Asylum Act in the calculation of income other than earnings) applies.

(2) The reference in sub-paragraph (1) to "income in kind" does not include a payment to a third party made in respect of the claimant which is used by the third party to provide benefits in kind to the claimant.

Analysis

Income in kind is excluded from the calculation of HB, as long as it is not caught by sub-para (2) and is not income to be taken into account under reg 40(10)(b).

---

24. Any income which is payable in a country outside the United Kingdom for such period during which there is a prohibition against the transfer to the United Kingdom of that income.

25.–(1) Any payment made to the claimant in respect of a person who is a member of his family–

(a) pursuant to regulations under section 2(6)(b), 3 or 4 of the Adoption and Children Act 2002 or [¹ in accordance] with a scheme approved by the Scottish Ministers under [² section 51A] of the Adoption (Scotland) Act 1978 (schemes for payments of allowances to adopters) [⁵ or in accordance with a scheme made under section 71 of the Adoption and Children (Scotland) Act 2007];

[² (b)]

[³ (ba) which is a payment made by a local authority in pursuance of section 15(1) of, and paragraph 15 of Schedule 1 to, the Children Act 1989 (local authority contribution to a child's maintenance where the child is living with a person as a result of a [⁶child arrangements] order) or in Scotland section 50 of the Children Act 1975 (payments towards maintenance of children);]

(c) which is a payment made by an authority, as defined in Article 2 of the Children Order, in pursuance of Article 15 of, and paragraph 17 of Schedule 1 to, that Order (contribution by an authority to child's maintenance);

(d) in accordance with regulations made pursuant to section 14F of the Children Act 1989 (special guardianship support services);

[⁴]

(2) Any payment, other than a payment to which sub-paragraph (1)(a) applies, made pursuant to regulations under section 2(6)(b), 3 or 4 of the Adoption and Children Act 2002.

[⁴ (3)]

Amendments

1. Amended by reg 3(12)(c) of SI 2008 No 1042 as from 19.5.08.
2. Amended by reg 5(6)(d) of SI 2008 No 3157 as from 5.1.09.
3. Inserted by reg 6(6)(c) of SI 2009 No 2655 as from 2.11.09.
4. Amended by reg 2(10) of SI 2010 No 2449 as from 1.4.11 (4.4.11 where rent payable weekly or in multiples of a week).
5. Amended by art 2 and Sch 1 para 39(4) of SI 2011 No 1740 as from 15.7.11.
6. Amended by art 13 of SI 2014 No 852 as from 22.4.14.

Analysis

Note that where a payment is made in respect of a child or young person who does not count as a member of the claimant's "family" for HB purposes (eg, where the child or young person has not yet been placed with the claimant but is staying with her/him), the payment is fully disregarded in England: para (2). In Scotland and

Wales, see reg 42(6)(c) under which any amount of the payment used by or spent on the child or young person is not to be treated as the claimant's income.

Until 5 January 2009, sub-para (1)(b) allowed for a disregard of contributions towards the cost of accommodation and maintenance of a child made by a local authority under s15(1) and para 15 Sch 1 Children Act 1989 where a child lived, or was to live, with someone as a result of a residence order. It also allowed a disregard (in Scotland) of certain payments made under s50 Children Act 1975 – eg, to "kinship carers". See also para 27A. Sub-para (1)(b) was omitted in error and so the provision has now been re-inserted as sub-para (1)(ba).

[²**26.** Any payment made to the claimant with whom a person is accommodated by virtue of arrangements made–
(a) by a local authority under–
[³ (i) section 22C(2) of the Children Act 1989 (ways in which looked after children are to be accommodated and maintained),
(ia) section 81(2) of the Social Services and Well-being (Wales) Act 2014 (ways in which looked after children are to be accommodated and maintained),]
(ii) section 26 of the Children (Scotland) Act 1995 (manner of provision of accommodation to child looked after by local authority), or
(iii) regulations 33 or 51 of the Looked After Children (Scotland) Regulations 2009 (fostering and kinship care allowances and fostering allowances); or
(b) by a voluntary organisation under section 59(1)(a) of the Children Act 1989 (provision of accommodation by voluntary organisations).]

Amendments
1. Amended by reg 15(6) of SI 2006 No 2378 as from 2.10.06.
2. Substituted by reg 7(3) of SI 2010 No 2429 as from 1.11.10.
3. Amended by arts 11(7)(a) and 25(5) of SI 2017 No 901 as from 3.11.17.

Analysis
This provides a total disregard of the payments referred to.

Sections 23(2)(a) (as referred to in the previous version of para (a)(i)) and 59(1)(a) Children Act 1989 refer to the local authority powers to provide accommodation and maintenance for a child they are looking after and for the provision of accommodation to voluntary organisations. The powers previously in s23 are now to be found in ss22A–C of the Act. Section 81(2) of the Welsh Act gives authorities duties to make arrangements for children under 18 they are looking after to live with certain persons or to be given appropriate placements. Section 26 of the 1995 Act gives authorities wide powers to make provision for children and young people aged less than 21 where such arrangements would safeguard or promote the welfare of the child or young person.

The regulations provide the same in respect of children already in care.

---

27. Any payment made to the claimant or his partner for a person ("the person concerned"), who is not normally a member of the claimant's household but is temporarily in his care, by–
(a) a health authority;
(b) a local authority but excluding payments of housing benefit made in respect of the person concerned;
(c) a voluntary organisation;
(d) the person concerned pursuant to section 26(3A) of the National Assistance Act 1948; [¹]
[³ (dza) the person concerned where the payment is for the provision of accommodation in respect of the meeting of that person's needs under section 18 or 19 of the Care Act 2014 (duty and power to meet needs for care and support);]
[⁴ (dzb) the person concerned where the payment is for the provision of accommodation to meet the person's needs for care and support under section 35 or 36 of the Social Services and Well-being (Wales) Act 2014 (duty and power to meet care and support needs of an adult);]
[² (da) a clinical commissioning group established under section 14D of the National Health Service Act 2006;]
[² (db) the National Health Service Commissioning Board; or]
[² (e)]
[¹ (f) a Local Health Board established under section 16BA of the National Health Service Act 1977 or established by an order made under section 11 of the National Health Service (Wales) Act 2006.]

Amendments
1. Amended by reg 5(6)(e) of SI 2008 No 3157 as from 5.1.09.
2. Amended by Sch 2 para 93(3) of SI 2013 No 235 as from 1.4.1.3.
3. Inserted by art 2 and Sch para 24(3)(a) of SI 2015 No 643 as from 1.4.15.
4. Inserted by art 11(7)(b) of SI 2017 No 901 as from 3.11.17.

Analysis

For "membership of the claimant's household", see p17 and Part 4 of these regulations.

This paragraph covers expenses plus any inducement element paid to enable a claimant to provide temporary respite care for someone (eg, an elderly or disabled person) so that, for example, a principal family carer can go on holiday. There is a total disregard of such payments.

Sch 4 para 25 HB Regs 1987 (now Sch 5 para 27) was considered by Commissioner Williams in *CH 2321/ 2002*. He decided it was part of a set of disregards designed to enable landlords to receive income in return for caring for vulnerable people without their benefit being affected (para 21). The provisions were, between them, designed to apply to all such payments (para 23). Guidance was also given on the meaning of "temporarily in his care" (para 32).

[¹**27A.** Any payment made to a claimant under section 73(1)(b) of the Children and Young People (Scotland) Act 2014 (kinship care assistance).]

Amendment

1. Inserted by reg 5(3) of SI 2017 No 995 as from 7.11.17.

Analysis

Under section 73(1)(b) of the 2014 Act and the Kinship Care Assistance (Scotland) Order 2016 (SSI 2016 No 153), payments can be made to a person who is, or is considering, applying for a kinship care order for a child who is at risk of going into care and who was previously looked after by a local authority. Payment is in the form of an allowance paid to the carer until the child is aged 16, at which point the child may be entitled to an allowance in her/his own right. The payments are not intended to cover the accommodation and maintenance of the child, but are intended to meet extra costs which would normally be provided to children living at home, such as extra-curricular activities. All such payments made to a claimant are disregarded as income. They are also disregarded as capital (see Sch 6 para 64 on p700).

28. Any payment made by a local authority in accordance with section 17, [¹ 23B, 23C or 24A] of the Children Act 1989 or, as the case may be, section 12 of the Social Work (Scotland) Act 1968 or section [² 22,] [³ 26A, 29 or 30 of the Children (Scotland) Act 1995 (provision of services to children and their families and provision of advice and assistance for certain young persons)] [⁴ or section 37 or 38 of the Social Services and Well-being (Wales) Act 2014, but excluding any direct payment made in accordance with regulations made under section 51 of that Act, or section 109, 110, 114 or 115 of that Act.]

Amendments

1. Amended by reg 6(9)(a) of SI 2008 No 2767 as from 17.11.08.
2. Inserted by reg 7(4) of SI 2010 No 2429 as from 1.11.10.
3. Amended by art 6(2)(a) of SI 2016 No 732 as from 5.8.16.
4. Amended by art 11(7)(c) of SI 2017 No 901 as from 3.11.17.

Analysis

See Analysis of Sch 6 para 19 on p690.

[¹**28A.**–(1) Subject to sub-paragraph (2), any payment (or part of a payment) made by a local authority in accordance with section 23C of the Children Act 1989 [² or section 26A or 29 of the Children (Scotland) Act 1995 (local authorities' duty to promote welfare of children, duty to provide continuing care and provision of advice and assistance for certain young persons)] [³ or section 110 of the Social Services and Well-being (Wales) Act 2014 (support for category 3 young people)] to a person ("A") which A passes on to the claimant.

(2) Sub-paragraph (1) applies only where A–

(a) was formerly in the claimant's care, and

[² (b) is aged 18 or over or, in the case of a payment or part of a payment made in accordance with section 26A of the Children (Scotland) Act 1995, aged 16 or over, and]

(c) continues to live with the claimant.]

Amendments

1. Inserted by reg 6(5)(a) of SI 2008 No 698 as from, as it relates to a particular beneficiary, the first day of the benefit week on or after 7.4.08.
2. Amended by art 6(2)(b) of SI 2016 No 732 as from 5.8.16.
3. Amended by art 11(7)(d) of SI 2017 No 901 as from 3.11.17.

Analysis

This provides a disregard of payments made by a local authority in accordance with the provisions listed. This only applies where the payment is made to someone formerly in the claimant's care as a child or young person, who is now aged 18 or over (or, in Scotland, 16 or over in certain circumstances) but continues to live with her/ him, and who has passed the payment on to the claimant.

29.–(1)   Subject to sub-paragraph (2), any payment received under an insurance policy taken out to insure against the risk of being unable to maintain repayments–
  (a)   on a loan which is secured on the dwelling which the claimant occupies as his home; or
  (b)   under a regulated agreement as defined for the purposes of the Consumer Credit Act 1974 or under a hire-purchase agreement or a conditional sale agreement as defined for the purposes of Part 3 of the Hire-Purchase Act 1964.
  (2)   A payment referred to in sub-paragraph (1) shall only be disregarded to the extent that the payment received under that policy does not exceed the amounts, calculated on a weekly basis, which are used to–
  (a)   maintain the repayments referred to in sub-paragraph (1)(a) or, as the case may be, (b); and
  (b)   meet any amount due by way of premiums on–
    (i)   that policy; or
    (ii)   in a case to which sub-paragraph (1)(a) applies, an insurance policy taken out to insure against loss or damage to any building or part of a building which is occupied by the claimant as his home and which is required as a condition of the loan referred to in sub-paragraph (1)(a).

Analysis

Payments received under an insurance policy taken out to insure against the risk of being unable to maintain certain loan repayments are disregarded. The loan insured must be secured on the home or an agreement of the types specified in sub-para (1)(b). The maximum disregarded is the total of the amounts in sub-para (2)(a) and (b).

30.   Any payment of income which by virtue of regulation 46 (income treated as capital) is to be treated as capital.

Analysis

This paragraph is necessary to aviod double counting.

31.   Any social fund payment made pursuant to Part 8 of the Act (the Social Fund).

Analysis

With effect from 16 September 2019, applicants in Scotland can no longer apply for a funeral payment under the social fund. They may instead qualify for "funeral expense assistance" paid in accordance with regulations made under s34 Social Security (Scotland) Act 2018. Such assistance is also disregarded in full for the purposes of HB (see para 70 of this Schedule on p683).

[¹**31A.**   Any local welfare provision.]

Amendment
  1.   Inserted by reg 7(5)(a) of SI 2013 No 443 as from 2.4.13.

General Note

"Local welfare provision" is defined in reg 2(1) (see p228). It is the DWP term for the replacement of social fund community care grants and crisis loans by local provision. Capital payments can also be disregarded: Sch 6 para 20A.

32.   Any payment under Part 10 of the Act (Christmas bonus for pensioners).
33.   Where a payment of income is made in a currency other than sterling, any banking charge or commission payable in converting that payment into sterling.
34.   The total of a claimant's income or, if he is a member of a family, the family's income and the income of any person which he is treated as possessing under regulation 25(2) (calculation of income and capital of members of claimant's family and of a polygamous marriage) to be disregarded under regulation 60(2)(b) and regulation 61(1)(d) (calculation of covenant income where a contribution assessed), covenant income where no grant income or no contribution is assessed regulation 64(2) (treatment of student loans), regulation 65(3) (treatment of payments from access funds) and paragraphs 15 and 16 shall in no case exceed £20 per week.

Analysis

Under this paragraph, the combined maximum disregard for the types of income listed is £20.

35.–(1)   Any payment made under [³ or by] the Macfarlane Trust, the Macfarlane (Special Payments) Trust, the Macfarlane (Special Payments) (No. 2) Trust ("the Trusts"), the Fund, the Eileen Trust [³, MFET Limited] [⁴, the Skipton Fund, the Caxton Foundation] [⁵, the Scottish Infected Blood Support Scheme] [⁷, an approved blood scheme] [⁶, the London Emergencies Trust, the We Love Manchester Emergency Fund] or the Independent Living [¹ Fund (2006)].

(2)   Any payment by or on behalf of a person who is suffering or who suffered from haemophilia or who is or was a qualifying person, which derives from a payment made under [³ or by] any of the Trusts to which sub-paragraph (1) refers and which is made to or for the benefit of–

(a)   that person's partner or former partner from whom he is not, or where that person has died was not, estranged or divorced or with whom he has formed a civil partnership that has not been dissolved or, where that person has died, had not been dissolved at the time of that person's death;

(b)   any child who is a member of that person's family or who was such a member and who is a member of the claimant's family; or

(c)   any young person who is a member of that person's family or who was such a member and who is a member of the claimant's family.

(3)   Any payment by or on behalf of the partner or former partner of a person who is suffering or who suffered from haemophilia or who is or was a qualifying person provided that the partner or former partner and that person are not, or if either of them has died were not, estranged or divorced or, where the partner or former partner and that person have formed a civil partnership, the civil partnership has not been dissolved or, if either of them has died, had not been dissolved at the time of the death, which derives from a payment made under [³ or by] any of the Trusts to which sub-paragraph (1) refers and which is made to or for the benefit of–

(a)   the person who is suffering from haemophilia or who is a qualifying person;

(b)   any child who is a member of that person's family or who was such a member and who is a member of the claimant's family; or

(c)   any young person who is a member of that person's family or who was such a member and who is a member of the claimant's family.

(4)   Any payment by a person who is suffering from haemophilia or who is a qualifying person, which derives from a payment under [³ or by] any of the Trusts to which sub-paragraph (1) refers, where–

(a)   that person has no partner or former partner from whom he is not estranged or divorced or with whom he has formed a civil partnership that has not been dissolved, nor any child or young person who is or had been a member of that person's family; and

(b)   the payment is made either–

(i)   to that person's parent or step-parent; or

(ii)   where that person at the date of the payment is a child, a young person or a student who has not completed his full-time education and has no parent or step-parent, to his guardian,

but only for a period from the date of the payment until the end of two years from that person's death.

(5)   Any payment out of the estate of a person who suffered from haemophilia or who was a qualifying person, which derives from a payment under [³ or by] any of the Trusts to which sub-paragraph (1) refers, where–

(a)   that person at the date of his death (the relevant date) had no partner or former partner from whom he was not estranged or divorced or with whom he had formed a civil partnership that had not been dissolved, nor any child or young person who was or had been a member of his family; and

(b)   the payment is made either–

(i)   to that person's parent or step-parent; or

(ii)   where that person at the relevant date was a child, a young person or a student who had not completed his full-time education and had no parent or step-parent, to his guardian,

but only for a period of two years from the relevant date.

(6)   In the case of a person to whom or for whose benefit a payment referred to in this paragraph is made, any income which derives from any payment of income or capital made under or deriving from any of the Trusts.

(7)   For the purposes of sub-paragraphs (2) to (6), any reference to the Trusts shall be construed as including a reference to the Fund, the Eileen Trust [³, MFET Limited], the Skipton Fund [⁴, the Caxton Foundation] [⁵, the Scottish Infected Blood Support Scheme] [⁷, an approved blood scheme] [⁶, the London Emergencies Trust, the We Love Manchester Emergency Fund] or the London [² Bombings] Relief Charitable Fund.

Modifications

References to "step-parent" in sub-paras (4)(b)(i) and (ii) and (5)(b)(i) and (ii) are modified by s246 Civil Partnership Act 2004 (see p1729) and art 3 and para 25 Sch to SI 2005 No.3137 (see p1772).

Amendments

1.   Amended by reg 6(4)(f) of SI 2008 No 2767 as from 17.11.08.
2.   Amended by reg 5(6)(f) of SI 2008 No 3157 as from 5.1.09.
3.   Amended by reg 8(3) and (5) of SI 2010 No 641 as from 1.4.10 (5.4.10 where rent payable weekly or in multiples of a week).
4.   Inserted by reg 19(5) and (6)(b) of SI 2011 No 2425 as from 31.10.11.
5.   Amended by reg 6(3)(f) of SI 2017 No 329 as from 3.4.17.
6.   Amended by reg 6(3)(f) of SI 2017 No 689 as from 19.6.17.
7.   Amended by reg 6(3)(e) of SI 2017 No 870 as from 23.10.17.

Analysis

Sub-para (1) provides an absolute disregard of payments from the various trusts, funds and schemes listed.

Sub-paras (2)–(6) extend this disregard to certain situations where a payment made to someone who has (or had) haemophilia or who is (or was) a "qualifying person" (defined in reg 2(1)) from the trusts, funds and schemes referred to in sub-para (1) or included by sub-para (7), is passed on to someone else by the person who originally received it. The sub-paragraphs are relevant where the claimant or her/his partner is the person to whom the money has been passed.

36.   Any payment made by the Secretary of State to compensate for the loss (in whole or in part) of entitlement to housing benefit.

[¹37.]

Amendment
1.   Omitted by reg 6(5)(b) of SI 2008 No 698 as from 14.4.08.

[¹38.]

Amendment
1.   Omitted by reg 5(6)(g) of SI 2008 No 3157 as from 5.1.09.

39.   Any payment to a juror or witness in respect of attendance at a court other than compensation for loss of earnings or for the loss of a benefit payable under the benefit Acts.

Analysis

This would cover, for example, payments for travel, subsistence or accommodation.

[¹ 40.]

Amendment
1.   Omitted by reg 6(9)(b) of SI 2008 No 2767 as from 17.11.08.

41.   Any payment in consequence of a reduction of council tax under section 13 [², section 13A] or [¹] section 80 of the Local Government Finance Act 1992 (reduction of liability for council tax).

Amendments
1.   Omitted by reg 6(5)(c) of SI 2008 No 698 as from 14.4.08.
2.   Amended by reg 7(5)(b) of SI 2013 No 443 as from 2.4.13.

General Note

Among other things, para 41 allows payments in consequence of a local authority's council tax reduction scheme (the replacement for council tax benefit from 1 April 2013) to be disregarded.

42.–(1)   Where the claimant occupies a dwelling as his home and he provides in that dwelling board and lodging accommodation, an amount, in respect of each person for whom such accommodation is provided for the whole or any part of a week, equal to–
(a)   where the aggregate of any payments made in respect of any one week in respect of such accommodation provided to such person does not exceed £20.00, 100 per cent. of such payments; or
(b)   where the aggregate of any such payments exceeds £20.00, £20.00 and 50 per cent. of the excess over £20.00.
(2)   In this paragraph "board and lodging accommodation" means accommodation provided to a person or, if he is a member of a family, to him or any other member of his family, for a charge which is inclusive of the provision of that accommodation and at least some cooked or prepared meals which both are cooked or prepared (by a person other than the person to whom the accommodation is provided or a member of his family) and are consumed in that accommodation or associated premises.

Analysis

This provides a disregard of a portion of the payments made to a claimant by people to whom s/he provides "board and lodging accommodation" (as defined in sub-para (2)) in the dwelling s/he occupies as her/his home. "Board and lodging accommodation" is accommodation in which cooked or prepared meals are provided and consumed. Preparation, in the context of this definition, requires something more than merely leaving the ingredients out for the lodger: *CSB 950/1987*.

The first £20 of each boarder's payment is ignored plus half of the amount in excess of £20. Where the claimant has a business partner, the paragraph does not say to apportion the disregard, even if the claimant's income includes just her/his share of the weekly charge to the boarders. The full disregard for each boarder as set out in this para should be made: *CIS 521/2002*.

There is no requirement that the board and lodgings be provided on a commercial basis, and no bar on this paragraph applying if, for example, the lodger is a close relative of the claimant. However, if the arrangement is not commercial, the lodger could come within the definition of a "non-dependant" in reg 3. If so, the payments made by her/him would instead be disregarded in full under para 21 above, but a non-dependant deduction would be made under reg 74 (see p516).

[¹**43.**]

Amendment

1.   Omitted by reg 5(6)(g) of SI 2008 No 3157 as from 5.1.09.

[²**44.**–(1)   Any payment or repayment made–
(a)   as respects England, under regulation 5, 6 or 12 of the National Health Service (Travel Expenses and Remission of Charges) Regulations 2003 (travelling expenses and health service supplies);
(b)   as respects Wales, under regulation 5, 6 or 11 of the National Health Service (Travelling Expenses and Remission of Charges) (Wales) Regulations 2007 (travelling expenses and health service supplies);
(c)   as respects Scotland, under regulation 3, 5 or 11 of the National Health Service (Travelling Expenses and Remission of Charges) (Scotland) (No. 2) Regulations 2003 (travelling expenses and health service supplies).

(2)   Any payment or repayment made by the Secretary of State for Health [³ and Social Care], the Scottish Ministers or the Welsh Ministers which is analogous to a payment or repayment mentioned in sub-paragraph (1).]

Amendments

1.   Amended by reg 3(12)(d)-(f) of SI 2008 No 1042 as from 19.5.08.
2.   Substituted by reg 5(6)(h) of SI 2008 No 3157 as from 5.1.09.
3.   Amended by the Sch para 21(m) of SI 2018 No 378 as from 11.4.18.

Analysis

Para 44 provides a disregard of payments made in respect of certain NHS charges – eg, hospital travel costs.

[²**45.**   Any payment made to such persons entitled to receive benefits as may be determined by or under a scheme made pursuant to section 13 of the Social Security Act 1988 in lieu of vouchers or similar arrangements in connection with the provision of those benefits (including payments made in place of healthy start vouchers, milk tokens or the supply of vitamins).]

Amendments

1.   Amended by reg 3(12)(g) of SI 2008 No 1042 as from 19.5.08.
2.   Substituted by reg 5(6)(h) of SI 2008 No 3157 as from 5.1.09.

Analysis

Para 45 provides a disregard of payments made in lieu of vouchers for Healthy Start food and vitamins or for milk tokens. Healthy Start food is milk, and fresh or frozen fruit and vegetables. Information is at www.healthystart.nhs.uk. The disregard will also apply to the value of the payment card issued under the "Best Start" foods scheme which replaces the Healthy Start food scheme in Scotland from 12 August 2019 (under the Welfare Foods (Best Start Foods) (Scotland) Regulations 2019 SSI No.193, which are also made under authority of s13 of the 1988 Act). See also Sch 6 para 41 on p696 for the extent to which such payments are disregarded as capital.

46.   Any payment made by either the Secretary of State for [¹ Justice] or by Scottish Ministers under a scheme established to assist relatives and other persons to visit persons in custody.

Amendment

1.   Amended by Art 8 and the Sch para 23 of SI 2007 No 2128 as from 22.8.07.

[¹**47.**–(1)   Where a claimant's [² family includes at least one child or young person,] £15 of any payment of maintenance, other than child maintenance, whether under a court order or not, which is made or due to be made by the claimant's former partner, or the claimant's partner's former partner.

(2)   For the purpose of sub-paragraph (1) where more than one maintenance payment falls to be taken into account in any week, all such payments shall be aggregated and treated as if they were a single payment.

(3)   A payment made by the Secretary of State in lieu of maintenance shall, for the purposes of sub-paragraph (1), be treated as a payment of maintenance made by a person specified in sub-paragraph (1).]

Amendments

1.   Substituted by reg 3(12)(h) of SI 2008 No 1042 as from 27.10.08.
2.   Amended by reg 2(1)(e) of SI 2015 No 1857 as from 1.05.16, subject to transitional provisions in reg 4.

Analysis

This provides a £15 disregard of maintenance payments other than child maintenance (for which see para 47A) where the claimant's family includes at least one child or young person. Prior to 1 May 2016, the condition was that the claimant's applicable amount included a family premium. Transitional provision is made for those entitled to HB on 30 April 2016, by reg 4 Housing Benefit (Abolition of the Family Premium and date of claim) (Amendment) Regulations 2015 SI No.1857.

[¹[²**47A.**–(1)   Any payment of child maintenance made or derived from a liable relative where the child or young person in respect of whom the payment is made is a member of the claimant's family, except where the person making the payment is the claimant or the claimant's partner.

(2)   In paragraph (1)–
"child maintenance" means any payment towards the maintenance of a child or young person, including any payment made voluntarily and payments made under–
(a)   the Child Support Act 1991;
(b)   the Child Support (Northern Ireland) Order 1991;
(c)   a court order;
(d)   a consent order;
(e)   a maintenance agreement registered for execution in the Books of Council and Session or the sheriff court books;
"liable relative" means a person listed in regulation 54 (interpretation) of the Income Support (General) Regulations 1987, other than a person falling within sub-paragraph (d) of that definition.]]

Amendments

1.   Inserted by reg 3(12)(h) of SI 2008 No 1042 as from 27.10.08.
2.   Substituted by reg 6(6)(d) of SI 2009 No 2655 as from 1.4.10 (5.4.10 where rent payable weekly or in multiples of a week).

Analysis

This provides a complete disregard of "child maintenance" payments, defined in sub-para (2) which are made by a "liable relative" (also defined in sub-para (2)), except where the person making the payments is the claimant or her/his partner. Liable relatives as defined in reg 54 of the IS Regs include spouses, former spouses, civil partners and former civil partners of the claimant or of a member of her/his family. It also includes parents of a child or young person who is a member of the claimant's family and certain people who are contributing to the maintenance of a child or young person and who may reasonably be treated as the father of that child or young person.

[¹**48.**]

Amendment

1.   Omitted by reg 6(5)(b) of SI 2008 No 698 as from 14.4.08.

49.   Any payment (other than a training allowance) made, whether by the Secretary of State or any other person, under the Disabled Persons (Employment) Act 1944 to assist disabled persons to obtain or retain employment despite their disability.
50.   Any guardian's allowance.
[² [¹**51.**]]

Amendments

1.   Substituted by reg 5(6)(i) of SI 2008 No 3157 as from 5.1.09.
2.   Deleted by reg 3 and Sch 1 of SI 2013 No 458 as from 1.4.13.

General Note

Para 51 provided a complete disregard of council tax benefit until it was abolished on 1 April 2013. For a disregard of payments under a council tax reduction scheme, see para 41.

[¹**52.**–(1)   If the claimant is in receipt of any benefit under Part 2, 3 or 5 of the Act, any increase in the rate of that benefit arising under Part 4 (increases for dependants) or section 106(a) (unemployability supplement) of the Act, where the dependant in respect of whom the increase is paid is not a member of the claimant's family.

(2)   If the claimant is in receipt of any pension or allowance under Part 2 or 3 of the Naval, Military and Air Forces Etc. (Disablement and Death) Service Pensions Order 2006, any increase in the rate of that pension

or allowance under that Order, where the dependant in respect of whom the increase is paid is not a member of the claimant's family.]

Amendment

1. Substituted by reg 5(6)(i) of SI 2008 No 3157 as from 5.1.09.

[¹**53.** Any supplementary pension under article 23(2) of the Naval, Military and Air Forces Etc. (Disablement and Death) Service Pensions Order 2006 (pensions to surviving spouses and surviving civil partners) and any analogous payment made by the Secretary of State for Defence to any person who is not a person entitled under that Order.]

Amendment

1. Substituted by reg 5(6)(i) of SI 2008 No 3157 as from 5.1.09.

---

54.   In the case of a pension awarded at the supplementary rate under article 27(3) of the Personal Injuries (Civilians) Scheme 1983 (pensions to widows, widowers or surviving civil partners), the sum specified in paragraph 1(c) of Schedule 4 to that Scheme.

55.–(1)   Any payment which is–
(a)   made under any of the Dispensing Instruments to a widow, widower or surviving civil partner of a person–
    (i)   whose death was attributable to service in a capacity analogous to service as a member of the armed forces of the Crown; and
    (ii)   whose service in such capacity terminated before 31st March 1973; and
[¹ (b)   equal to the amount specified in article 23(2) of the Naval, Military and Air Forces Etc. (Disablement and Death) Service Pensions Order 2006.]
(2)   In this paragraph "the Dispensing Instruments" means the Order in Council of 19th December 1881, the Royal Warrant of 27th October 1884 and the Order by His Majesty of 14th January 1922 (exceptional grants of pay, non-effective pay and allowances).

Amendment

1. Substituted by reg 5(6)(j) of SI 2008 No 3157 as from 5.1.09.

---

56.   Except in a case which falls under sub-paragraph (1) of paragraph 17 of Schedule 4, where the claimant is a person who satisfies any of the conditions of sub-paragraph (2) of that paragraph, any amount of working tax credit up to [¹³ £17.10].

Amendments

1. Amended by art 19(10)(b) of SI 2006 No 645 and reg 8 of SI 2006 No 217 as from 1.4.06 (3.4.06 where rent payable weekly or at intervals of a week).
2. Amended by art 19(10)(b) of SI 2007 No 688 as from 1.4.07 (2.4.07 where rent payable weekly or at intervals of a week).
3. Amended by art 19(11) of SI 2008 No 632 as from 1.4.08 (7.4.08 where rent payable weekly or in multiples of a week).
4. Amended by art 19(12) of SI 2009 No 497 as from 1.4.09 (6.4.09 where rent payable weekly or at intervals of a week).
5. Amended by art 19(11) of SI 2010 No 793 as from 1.4.10 (5.4.10 where rent payable weekly or in multiples of a week).
6. Confirmed by art 20(11) of SI 2011 No 821 as from 1.4.11 (4.4.11 where rent payable weekly or in multiples of a week).
7. Confirmed by art 20(11) of SI 2012 No 780 as from 1.4.12 (2.4.12 where rent payable weekly or in multiples of a week).
8. Confirmed by art 19(11) of SI 2013 No 574 as from 1.4.13.
9. Confirmed by art 17(12) of SI 2014 No 16 as from 1.4.14 (7.4.14 where rent payable weekly or in multiples of a week).
10. Confirmed by art 17(12) of SI 2015 No 547 as from 1.4.15 (6.4.15 where rent payable weekly or in multiples of a week).
11. Confirmed by art 22(12) of SI 2017 No 260 as from 1.4.17 (3.4.17 where rent payable weekly or in multiples of a week).
12. Confirmed by art 23(11) of SI 2018 No 281 as from 1.4.18 (2.4.18 where rent payable weekly or in multiples of a week).
13. Confirmed by art 23(11) of SI 2019 No 480 as from 1.4.19.

Analysis

This allows for a disregard of working tax credit up to the amount specified where earnings are too low to use the whole of the disregard allowed by Sch 4 para 17.

57.   Any payment made [¹] [³ as a direct payment as defined in section 4(2) of the Social Care (Self-directed Support) (Scotland) Act 2013] [², or under sections 12A to 12D of the National Health Service Act 2006 (direct payments for health care)] [⁴ or under sections 31 to 33 of the Care Act 2014 (direct payments)] or under regulations made under section 57 of the Health and Social Care Act 2001 (direct payments) [⁵ or in accordance with regulations made under section 50 or 52 of the Social Services and Well-being (Wales) Act 2014 (direct payments)].

Amendments
1.   Amended by reg 6(12) of SI 2009 No 583 as from 6.4.09.
2.   Amended by reg 8(11) of SI 2010 No 641 as from 1.4.10 (5.4.10 where rent payable weekly or in multiples of a week).
3.   Amended by art 2 and Sch para 10(a) of SI 2014 No 513 as from 1.4.14.
4.   Amended by art 2 and Sch para 24(3)(b) of SI 2015 No 643 as from 1.4.15.
5.   Amended by art 11(7)(e) of SI 2017 No 901 as from 3.11.17.

Analysis
Rather than provide services to disabled people directly, local authorities can make "direct payments" to them to buy their own services. Payments can also be made under the National Health Service Act directly to patients in lieu of their health care ("Direct Payments for Health Care"). Under this paragraph, direct payments are disregarded. They are also disregarded as capital under Sch 6 para 58.

   Note that "direct payments" could count as "earnings" if the person who is paid them is a member of a couple and "employs" her/his partner as her/his carer. In *CIS 1068/2006*, the claimant was caring for his severely disabled wife, and claiming IS. Direct payments were made by the local authority to the claimant's wife. She used these to employ the claimant as her carer. The issue was whether the direct payments should be fully disregarded under Sch 9 para 58 Income Support (General) Regulations 1987 (the equivalent of this paragraph) or taken into account as the claimant's earnings (making an appropriate earnings disregard). Allowing the Secretary of State's appeal, Commissioner Turnbull held that it was not open to the tribunal to hold on the evidence before it that the claimant was not in receipt of earnings from his wife in the form of the payment made to him. In determining the claimant's wife's income the "direct payments" to her had to be disregarded under Sch 9 para 58. However, the claimant's wife then used those payments to "employ" him as her carer. It did not matter whether she formally employed him or he was engaged as a self-employed earner to provide services for her: in either case the sums paid to the claimant were earnings and fell to be taken into account in calculating his IS. Nothing in s136(1) SSCBA 1992 altered this conclusion, or meant that the claimant had to be treated as receiving the payments as "direct payments" rather than earnings. The Court of Appeal upheld the decision in *Casewell v SSWP* [2008] 11 March, WLR (D) 86, reported as *R(IS) 7/08*.

58.–(1)   Subject to sub-paragraph (2), in respect of a person who is receiving, or who has received, assistance under the self-employment route, any payment to that person–
   (a)   to meet expenses wholly and necessarily incurred whilst carrying on the commercial activity;
   (b)   which is used or intended to be used to maintain repayments on a loan taken out by that person for the purpose of establishing or carrying on the commercial activity,
in respect of which such assistance is or was received.
   (2)   Sub-paragraph (1) shall apply only in respect of payments which are paid to that person from the special account [¹].

Amendment
1.   Amended by reg 8(10)(b) of SI 2010 No 641 as from 1.4.10 (5.4.10 where rent payable weekly or in multiples of a week).

Analysis
The payments set out in sub-para (1) to those following the "self-employment route" (defined in reg 2(1)) to meet expenses or to service loans are ignored, but only where paid into a special account referred to in sub-para (2) and also defined in reg 2(1). See also reg 46(7) for receipts paid to those following this route which are treated as capital.

59.–(1)   Any payment of a sports award except to the extent that it has been made in respect of any one or more of the items specified in sub-paragraph (2).
   (2)   The items specified for the purposes of sub-paragraph (1) are food, ordinary clothing or footwear, household fuel or rent of the claimant or where the claimant is a member of a family, any other member of his family, or any council tax or water charges for which that claimant or member is liable.
   (3)   For the purposes of sub-paragraph (2)–
"food" does not include vitamins, minerals or other special dietary supplements intended to enhance the performance of the person in the sport in respect of which the award was made;
"rent" means eligible rent less any deductions in respect of non-dependants which fall to be made under regulation 74 (non-dependant deductions).

Analysis

Sports awards (defined in reg 2(1)) are ignored as income except in so far as they provide for basic needs. On the wording of para (2), see the analysis to reg 42(6) on p459.

60. Where the amount of subsistence allowance paid to a person in a benefit week exceeds the amount of income-based jobseeker's allowance that person would have received in that benefit week had it been payable to him, less 50p, that excess amount.

61. In the case of a claimant participating in an employment zone programme, any discretionary payment made by an employment zone contractor to the claimant, being a fee, grant, loan or otherwise.

62. Any discretionary housing payment paid pursuant to regulation 2(1) of the Discretionary Financial Assistance Regulations 2001.

63.–(1) Any payment made by a local authority or by the [¹ Welsh Ministers], to or on behalf of the claimant or his partner relating to a service which is provided to develop or sustain the capacity of the claimant or his partner to live independently in his accommodation.

(2) For the purposes of sub-paragraph (1) "local authority" includes, in England, a county council.

Amendment

1. Amended by reg 5(6)(l) of SI 2008 No 3157 as from 5.1.09.

Analysis

Under this para, payments made by a local authority or the Welsh Ministers for support services to help the claimant or her/his partner live independantly are ignored as the claimant's income. This disregard does not apply to landlords receiving such payments for providing the services, although other paragraphs in this Schedule might apply.

[¹ [²**64.**]

Amendments

1. Inserted by reg 4 of SI 2008 No 3140 as from 5.1.09.
2. Revoked by reg 1(3) and (4) of SI 2008 No 3140 as from 6.4.09 (1.4.09 in relation to a claimant whose eligible rent falls to be calculated in accordance with reg 80(2)(b) or (c) HB Regs.

[¹**65.** Any payment of child benefit.]

Amendment

1. Inserted by reg 3 of SI 2009 No 2848 as from 2.11.09.

[¹**66.** Any payments to a claimant made under section 49 of the Children and Families Act 2014 (personal budgets and direct payments)]

Amendment

1. Inserted by reg 20(2) of SI 2014 No.2103 as from 1.9.14.

Analysis

Under section 49 of the 2014 Act, a local authority in England can make a 'personal budget' for a child or young person who has a plan to ensure that special educational provision is made to cover her/his education, health care and social care needs (an EHC plan). All or part of the personal budget can be in the form of direct payments to a parent of the child or to a young person to allow them to make direct provision to secure any services required under the EHC plan. All such payments made to a claimant are disregarded as income. They are also disregarded as capital (see Sch 6 para 61 on p700).

[¹**67.** Any bereavement support payment under section 30 of the Pensions Act 2014 (bereavement support payment) except any such payment which is disregarded as capital under paragraph 9(1)(h) or 62 of Schedule 6.]

Amendment

1. Inserted by art 25(2) of SI 2017 No 422 as from 6.4.17, subject to transitional provisions in arts 2 and 3.

[¹**68.** Any payment of carer's allowance supplement made under section 81 of the Social Security (Scotland) Act 2018.]

Amendment

1. Inserted by art 5 of SI 2018 No 872 as from 3.9.18.

Analysis

Para 68 provides a complete disregard of payments of the carer's allowance supplement. This supplement is paid under section 81 Social Security (Scotland) Act 2018 to any person resident in Scotland who is in receipt of carer's allowance (CA). The supplement is paid twice-yearly, with the first payment of £221 covering the period 1 April to 30 September 2018 being made in September/October 2018 to those who were in receipt of CA on 16 April 2018. The supplement is intended to bring income from CA up to the same level as the rate of JSA for a single person aged not less that 25. Part of the agreement for devolution of certain social security powers to the Scottish Parliament was that any new benefits or discretionary payments introduced should produce additional income for claimants and should not, therefore, result in an automatic offsetting reduction in other benefits. Note that no provision has been made in Schedule 6 to disregard payments of the supplement as capital.

[¹**69.** Any early years assistance given in accordance with section 32 of the Social Security (Scotland) Act 2018.]

Amendment

1.   Inserted by reg 8(2) of SI 2018 No 1138 as from 10.12.18.

Analysis

See Sch 6 para 65.

[¹**70.** Any funeral expense assistance given in accordance with section 34 of the Social Security (Scotland) Act 2018.]

Amendment

1.   Inserted by reg 13(2) of SI 2019 No 1060 as from 16.9.19.

Analysis

See Sch 6 para 66.

SCHEDULE 6

REGULATION 44

Capital to be disregarded

Modifications

Paras 48A and 48B were inserted by para 2(6) HB&CTB(CP) Regs in respect of claims for HB by some refugees.
     A different version of para 48B was substituted for para 55B by Sch 4 para 4(2)(c) of the HB&CTB(CP) Regs for some HB claimants who are refugees who claimed asylum on or before 2 April 2000. See also reg 10A and Sch A1 inserted by Sch 4 para 2 HB&CTB(CP) Regs.
     Note that paras 48A and 48B lapsed by s12(2)(e) of the Asylum and Immigration (Treatment of Claimants, etc.) Act 2004 (for those recorded as refugees after 14 June 2007) and were omitted by reg 5(7)(b) of SI 2008 No.3157 as from 5 January 2009. For the full text of paras 48A and 48B, see p1129 and p1133 of the 20th edition.
     A para A1 was inserted by reg 17 Jobseeker's Allowance (Work for Your Benefit Pilot Scheme) Regulations 2010 SI No.1222 from 22 November 2010 to 1 March 2012 in pilot areas only.
     A para A4 was inserted by reg 13 Jobseeker's Allowance (Supervised Job Search Pilot Scheme) Regulations 2014 SI No.1913 from 18 July 2014 to 30 April 2015 for those selected to participate in the pilot scheme only.
     A para A5 was inserted by reg 18 Jobseeker's Allowance (18–21 Work Skills Pilot Scheme) Regulations 2014 SI No.3117 from 25 November 2014 to 24 November 2016 for those selected to participate in the pilot scheme in pilot areas only.

Definitions

"capital" – see General Note on Part 6 Section 6.
"child tax credit" and "working tax credit" – see reg 2(1).
"claimant" – see reg 2(1).
"concessionary payment" – see reg 2(1).
"croft land" – see note on reg 2(4).
"Decisions and Appeals Regulations" – see reg 2(1).
"dwelling" – see reg 2(4) and s137(1) SSCBA.
"eligible rent" – see reg 2(1).
"family" – see s137(1) SSCBA.
"income" – see General Note on Part 6.
"income related benefit" – see s123(1) SSCBA.
"local authority" – see s191 SSAA.
"local welfare provision" – see reg 2(1).
"lone parent" – see reg 2(1).

"Macfarlane Trust" and other schemes listed in paras 24(1) and (7) and 34 – see reg 2(1).
"the Mandatory Work Activity Scheme" – see reg 2(1).
"non-dependant" – see reg 3.
"occupational pension" and "personal pension scheme" – see reg 2(1).
"partner" – see reg 2(1).
"person on an income-based jobseeker's allowance" – see reg 2(3).
"person on an income-related employment and support allowance" – see reg 2(3A).
"person on income support" – see reg 2(1).
"person on universal credit" – see reg 2(3B).
"polygamous marriage" – see reg 2(1).
"qualifying age for state pension credit" – see reg 2(1).
"relative" – see reg 2(1).
"rent" – see Part 3.
"self-employed earner" – see reg 2(1).
"self-employment route" – see reg 2(1).
"sports award" – see reg 2(1).
"subsistence allowance" – see reg 2(1).
"young person" – see reg 19.

General Note on Schedule 6

This sets out the items of a claimant's and her/his partner's capital which must be ignored for the purposes of calculating HB. See reg 44(2) and, generally, Section 6 of Part 6. The disregards under the following paragraphs are cumulative unless specified otherwise. The effect is a mandatory disregard, but sometimes the *period* of the disregard is at the authority's discretion.

Note: payments made to qualifying Equitable Life annuitants under the Age Related Payments Regulations 2013 SI No.2980 are disregarded under reg 5 of those regulations (see p1855).

[A1.]

[¹**A2.** Any payment made to the claimant in respect of any travel or other expenses incurred, or to be incurred, by him in respect of his participation in the Mandatory Work Activity Scheme but only for 52 weeks beginning with the date of receipt of the payment.]

Amendment

1. Inserted by reg 15 of SI 2011 No 688 as from 25.4.11.

[¹A3.]

Amendment

1. Inserted by reg 15 of SI 2011 No 917 as from 20.5.11. SI 2011 No 917 was quashed by the Court of Appeal in *R (Reilly and another) v SSWP* [2013] EWCA Civ 66, 12 February 2013.

[²**A3.** Any payment made to the claimant in respect of any travel or other expenses incurred, or to be incurred, by him in respect of his participation in a scheme prescribed in regulation 3 of the Jobseeker's Allowance (Schemes for Assisting Persons to Obtain Employment) Regulations 2013 but only for 52 weeks beginning with the date of receipt of the payment.]

Amendment

1. Inserted by reg 12 of SI 2013 No 276 as from 6.45 pm 12.2.13.

General Note

The Schemes now prescribed in the regulations cited are the Work Programme, Skills Conditionality, the sector-based work academy, New Enterprise Allowance, Full-time Training Flexibility and the Work and Health Programme. Note that SI 2011 No.917, which inserted an earlier version of para A3, was quashed on 12 February 2013 by the Court of Appeal in *R (Reilly and another) v SSWP* [2013] EWCA Civ 66. The Secretary of State's appeal to the Supreme Court was unsuccessful: *R (Reilly and Wilson) v SSWP* [2013] UKSC 68; [2014] AACR 9.

That version of para A3 allowed payments made in respect of travel or other expenses in respect of a claimant's participation in the Employment, Skills and Enterprise Scheme (which included a number of the schemes listed above) to be disregarded. The government legislated to retrospectively validate SI 2011 No.917 under s1 Jobseekers (Back to Work Schemes) Act 2013 up to 12 February 2013. However, in *R (Reilly (No.2) and Hewstone) v SSWP* [2014] EWHC 2182 (Admin) the Court decided that the Act was incompatible with the claimants rights under Art 6(1) ECHR and granted a declaration of incompatibility to that effect, as the claimants had made appeals before the 2013 Act came into effect.

[A4.]
[A5.]
1.　　　The dwelling together with any garage, garden and outbuildings, normally occupied by the claimant as his home including any premises not so occupied which it is impracticable or unreasonable to sell separately, in particular, in Scotland, any croft land on which the dwelling is situated; but, notwithstanding regulation 25 (calculation of income and capital of members of claimant's family and of a polygamous marriage), only one dwelling shall be disregarded under this paragraph.

Analysis

For the dwelling "normally occupied" by the claimant as her/his home, see reg 7. To be included as the home, provided they are part of the same "dwelling", are any premises it is "impractical or unreasonable" to sell separately.

This disregard is in addition to land already treated as a dwelling under reg 2(4). This wording was used in respect of the meaning of the word "home" in reg 2(1) of the Supplementary Benefit (Resources) Regs 1987. In *R(SB) 13/84* and *R(SB) 27/84*, it was said that whether it is "impractical or unreasonable" to sell is a subjective question – ie, to be looked at from the claimant's point of view and circumstances. A dwelling could include an extension built to accommodate a relative, but not where this is separately rated or self-contained. Only one "dwelling" may be ignored under this paragraph. But note that the dwelling a claimant occupies as a home may comprise more than one property: *Hackney LB v GA* [2008] UKUT 26 (AAC); R(H) 5/09.

Note that para 1 would cease to apply if the claimant no longer occupies a dwelling as a home (eg, s/he moves home) but other paras below might apply to the now former home so that its value can continue to be disregarded (see, for example, paras 4, 25, 26 and 28) or the proceeds of sale might be disregarded (see para 3).

2.　　　Any premises acquired for occupation by the claimant which he intends to occupy as his home within 26 weeks of the date of acquisition or such longer period as is reasonable in the circumstances to enable the claimant to obtain possession and commence occupation of the premises.

Analysis

Under this para, a claimant may have premises acquired for occupation as a home ignored for the purpose of calculating her/his entitlement to HB. The claimant must intend to occupy the premises as her/his home within 26 weeks of acquiring it (longer if reasonable). This is a week-by-week test and the disregard could cease to apply immediately if the claimant no longer intends to occupy the premises at all or within the 26-week (or longer) period: *JH v SSWP* [2009] UKUT 1 (AAC).

The words "as his home" show that only potential residential premises are covered. Once the claimant moves into the premises, para 2 would no longer apply, but para 1 would if they are "normally occupied" by the claimant.

3.　　　Any sum directly attributable to the proceeds of sale of any premises formerly occupied by the claimant as his home which is to be used for the purchase of other premises intended for such occupation within 26 weeks of the date of sale or such longer period as is reasonable in the circumstances to enable the claimant to complete the purchase.

Analysis

This covers the situation where the claimant has sold her/his former home, but has not yet purchased a new one. It applies where the proceeds of the sale are to be used to purchase premises which the claimant intends to occupy as a home, within 26 weeks of the date of sale. A longer period can be allowed if this is "reasonable", and is necessary to allow the claimant to complete the purchase. Once the new home is actually purchased, paras 1 or 2 could apply to the acquired premises, depending on whether the claimant moves in immediately or not. For the meaning of "occupied as home", see reg 7.

4.　　　Any premises occupied in whole or in part–
(a)　　　by a partner or relative of a single claimant or any member of the family as his home [¹ where that person has attained the qualifying age for state pension credit or is incapacitated];
(b)　　　by the former partner of the claimant as his home; but this provision shall not apply where the former partner is a person from whom the claimant is estranged or divorced or with whom he had formed a civil partnership that has been dissolved.

Amendment

1.　　　Amended by reg 28 of SI 2009 No 1488 as from 6.4.10.

Analysis

This allows the disregard of any dwelling owned by the claimant occupied by the people set out in sub-paras (a) or (b). This para is not restricted to the disregard of *one* dwelling only. It allows the whole premises to be ignored whether the partner/former partner/relative/member of the family occupies all or part of them.

Sub-para (a). The partner, relative or family member in question must either be at least the qualifying age for PC (defined in reg 2(1)) or "incapacitated". "Incapacitated" is not defined here but would appear to have a broader meaning than those who would qualify for disability premium or for a component (see Sch 3).

Sub-para (b) provides a disregard where the claimant's former partner occupies the premises as a home, so long as s/he and the claimant are not estranged or divorced nor their civil partnership dissolved. This would include situations where a couple continue to see themselves as a couple, but for HB purposes, are not treated as such – eg, because they are no longer members of the same household: regs 2(1) (definitions of "partner" and "couple") and 21.

The meaning of "estranged" is not supplied by the paragraph. In *R(IS) 5/05*, Commissioner Rowland said that it has a connotation of emotional disharmony. The question will be whether the parties have ceased to consider themselves to be a couple and not whether, despite that, they continue to maintain friendly relations. In *CPC 683/ 2007*, there was no emotional disharmony between the claimant and the former partner as adults, but there was emotional disharmony between them as partners. Commissioner Jacobs said that was a key distinction because the language used in the legislation is attempting to identify those cases in which the relationship between the parties is such that it is appropriate for their finances to be treated separately for the purposes of benefit entitlement. In *CH 3777/2007*, Commissioner Howell did not accept that "estranged" required an element of disharmony. He said: "the word "estranged" in this context implies no more than that the reason for the two people concerned no longer living together as a couple in the same household is that the relationship between them has broken down. It is not a necessary, or for that matter a sufficient, requirement to come within the term that dealings and communications between the two of them should be acrimonious."

See para 25 when the claimant *is* "estranged" or divorced from the former partner or where a civil partnership has been dissolved.

5. Where a claimant is on [² universal credit,] income support [¹, an income-based jobseeker's allowance or an income-related employment and support allowance], the whole of his capital.

Amendments

1.   Amended by reg 26(a) of SI 2008 No 1082 as from 27.10.08.
2.   Amended by reg 7(9) of SI 2013 No 2070 as from 28.10.13.

Analysis

This paragraph and para 6 are necessary to avoid double counting – see General Notes on Part 6 and Sch 4 para 12 and Sch 5 paras 4 and 5.

6. Where the claimant is a member of a joint-claim couple for the purposes of the Jobseekers Act and his partner is on income-based jobseeker's allowance, the whole of the claimant's capital.

7. Any future interest in property of any kind, other than land or premises in respect of which the claimant has granted a subsisting lease or tenancy, including sub-leases or sub-tenancies.

Analysis

A "future interest", or "reversionary interest", covers the situation where the claimant or her/his partner (see reg 25) will become entitled to possession of the asset at some future date, but someone else has that right at present – eg, where property has been left to another person for life, then to the claimant on that other person's death. The value of any such interest must be totally disregarded.

8.–(1)   The assets of any business owned in whole or in part by the claimant and for the purposes of which he is engaged as a self-employed earner, or if he has ceased to be so engaged, for such period as may be reasonable in the circumstances to allow for disposal of any such asset.

(2)   The assets of any business owned in whole or in part by the claimant where–

(a)   he is not engaged as a self-employed earner in that business by reason of some disease or bodily or mental disablement; but

(b)   he intends to become engaged or, as the case may be, re-engaged as a self-employed earner in that business as soon as he recovers or is able to become engaged or re-engaged in that business,

for a period of 26 weeks from the date on which the claim for housing benefit is made, or is treated as made, or, if it is unreasonable to expect him to become engaged or re-engaged in that business within that period, for such longer period as is reasonable in the circumstances to enable him to become so engaged or re-engaged.

(3)   In the case of a person who is receiving assistance under the self-employment route, the assets acquired by that person for the purpose of establishing or carrying on the commercial activity in respect of which such assistance is being received.

(4)   In the case of a person who has ceased carrying on the commercial activity in respect of which assistance was received as specified in sub-paragraph (3), the assets relating to that activity for such period as may be reasonable in the circumstances to allow for disposal of any such asset.

Analysis

This allows the disregard of business assets owned by the claimant while s/he is working for the business and also for a "reasonable" period after s/he ceases working for the business to allow time to sell or otherwise dispose of the assets: sub-para (1). What is a "reasonable" period will depend on the type of business as well as the current economic situation. See also reg 49(5). Sub-para (2) ensures the disregard is also applicable during any period a self-employed claimant is temporarily unable to work due to an illness or injury for a period of up to 26 weeks from the date the HB claim is, or is treated as, made. The initial 26 week period should be extended where it is considered unreasonable to expect the claimant to become (re-)engaged in that period.

In *RM v Sefton Council (HB)* [2016] UKUT 357 (AAC); [2017] AACR 5, Judge Jacobs held (reviewing *R(FC) 2/92* and other relevant caselaw) that receiving rent and carrying out landlord's duties in respect of a single dwelling did not constitute carrying out a business as a self-employed person and so the value of the property could not be disregarded as a business asset.

9.–(1)   Subject to sub-paragraph (2), any arrears of, or any concessionary payment made to compensate for arrears due to the non-payment of–

(a)   any payment specified in paragraphs 6, 8 or 9 of Schedule 5;

[² (b)   an income-related benefit under Part 7 of the Act;]

(c)   an income-based jobseeker's allowance;

(d)   any discretionary housing payment paid pursuant to regulation 2(1) of the Discretionary Financial Assistance Regulations 2001;

(e)   working tax credit and child tax credit [¹],

[³ (f)   an income-related employment and support allowance,]

[⁴ (g)   universal credit,]

[⁵ (h)   bereavement support payment under section 30 of the Pensions Act 2014,]

[⁷ (i)   maternity allowance under section 35 of the Act (state maternity allowance for employed or self-employed earner),]

but only for a period of 52 weeks from the date of the receipt of arrears or of the concessionary payment.

(2)   In a case where the total of any arrears and, if appropriate, any concessionary payment referred to in sub-paragraph (1) relating to one of the specified payments, benefits or allowances amounts to £5,000 or more (referred to in this sub-paragraph and in sub-paragraph (3) as "the relevant sum") and is–

[⁶ (a)   paid in order to rectify, or to compensate for–

(i)   an official error as defined in regulation 1(2) of the Decisions and Appeals Regulations, or

(ii)   an error on a point of law; and]

(b)   received by the claimant in full on or after 14th October 2001,

sub-paragraph (1) shall have effect in relation to such arrears or concessionary payment either for a period of 52 weeks from the date of receipt, or, if the relevant sum is received in its entirety during the award of housing benefit, for the remainder of that award if that is a longer period.

(3)   For the purposes of sub-paragraph (2), "the award of housing benefit" means–

(a)   the award in which the relevant sum is first received (or the first part thereof where it is paid in more than one instalment); and

(b)   where that award is followed by one or more further awards which, or each of which, begins immediately after the end of the previous award, such further award provided that for that further award the claimant–

(i)   is the person who received the relevant sum; or

(ii)   is the partner of the person who received the relevant sum, or was that person's partner at the date of his death.

Amendments

1.   Amended by reg 2(16) of SI 2005 No 2502 as amended by Sch 2 para 27 of SI 2006 No 217 as from 1.4.06 (3.4.06 where rent payable weekly or at intervals of a week).

2.   Substituted by reg 6(6)(a) of SI 2008 No 698 as from 14.4.08.

3.   Inserted by reg 26(b) of SI 2008 No 1082 as from 27.10.08.

4.   Inserted by reg 35(12) of SI 2013 No 630 as from 29.4.13.

5.   Inserted by art 25(3)(a) of SI 2017 No 422 as from 6.4.17, subject to transitional provisions in arts 2 and 3.

6.   Substituted by reg 5 of SI 2018 No 932 as from 11.9.18.

7.   Inserted by reg 5 of SI 2019 No 1314 as from 31.10.19.

Analysis

This allows payments of arrears of, or compensation in respect of, the benefits listed to be ignored for a period of up to 52 weeks after they are received. If anything is left of such a payment after the 52 weeks, the payment is taken into account as normal. WTC and CTC and discretionary housing payments also receive the same treatment. Where a payment is £5,000 or over and is made to compensate for an official error or error on a point of law having been made in a case, the amount is disregarded for 52 weeks or for the duration of the HB award, whichever is the longer.

In *CIS 2448/2006*, the local authority had paid the claimant compensation because it had wrongly charged him for aftercare services pursuant to s117 Mental Health Act 1983: per *R v Manchester City Council ex p Stennett* [2002] UKHL 34. The claimant argued that the payment should be treated as arrears of compensation for non-payment of IS and so should be disregarded under Sch 10 para 7(1) IS Regs 1987 (the equivalent to para 9(1)) because, had the local authority not in fact charged him under the MHA for the costs of his residential accommodation, he would have received the full amount for IS and not just the sum for "personal expenses". The argument was rejected on the facts of the case. As the claimant had been paid full IS at all relevant times and then paid the residential fees element onto the care home, no arrears of IS were due. Even assuming that some of the IS was paid direct to the care home by the DWP, the argument was still ill-founded because whatever may have later been held in *Stennett*, at the time the IS would properly have been paid to the care home and so there could be no question of the claimant establishing that any sum of IS had been wrongfully withheld from him. Even if that was wrong, the payment here was not a payment of "arrears" of IS as that refers to a sum paid by the Secretary of State in satisfaction of an award of IS. The decision was approved by *R(IS) 5/08*.

See also Sch 5 para 7 where the concessionary payments are income payments.

---

10.   Any sum–

(a)   paid to the claimant in consequence of damage to, or loss of the home or any personal possession and intended for its repair or replacement; or

(b)   acquired by the claimant (whether as a loan or otherwise) on the express condition that it is to be used for effecting essential repairs or improvement to the home,

which is to be used for the intended purpose, for a period of 26 weeks from the date on which it was so paid or acquired or such longer period as is reasonable in the circumstances to effect the repairs, replacement or improvement.

Analysis

This provides that certain sums for repairs to, or replacement of, personal possessions, or repairs or improvements to the home are to be ignored for a limited period. The initial 26-week period may be extended where this is considered reasonable where the claimant needs the extra time to get the repairs, etc done.

Sub-para (a) covers sums paid as a result of damage to, or the loss of, the claimant's home or personal possessions, intended for their repair or replacement. "Personal possession" is not defined but would cover, for example, a car. See the analysis to para 12 below.

Sub-para (b). This might even cover a payment from a relative – it is the terms of the payment which are important, not the source. "Essential" work was distinguished in *R(SB) 10/81* from that which is a luxury, but it need not be so vital as to be indispensable for life to be maintained (that case was about a single payment for "essential redecoration").

An "improvement" may be distinguished from a repair in that it connotes the adding of something new other than remedying a damaged, pre-existing feature.

---

11.   Any sum–

(a)   deposited with a housing association as defined in section 1(1) of the Housing Associations Act 1985 or section 338(1) of the Housing (Scotland) Act 1987 as a condition of occupying the home;

(b)   which was so deposited and which is to be used for the purchase of another home, for the period of 26 weeks or such longer period as may be reasonable in the circumstances to enable the claimant to complete the purchase.

Analysis

Sub-para (a) provides a disregard for deposits held by a housing association, sub-para (b) for deposits which *were* so held until the claimant decided to purchase a home.

Sub-para (a). s1 Housing Act 1985 refers to s5 of that Act. The definition in s338(1) of the 1987 Act is precisely the same. The payment of the deposit must be a condition of occupying the home for the paragraph to apply.

Sub-para (b). Here the disregard is a limited one. The initial 26-week period may be extended where this is considered reasonable in view of the fact that the claimant needs the extra time to complete purchase.

---

12.   Any personal possessions except those which have been acquired by the claimant with the intention of reducing his capital in order to secure entitlement to housing benefit or to increase the amount of that benefit.

Analysis

"Personal possessions" is not defined but could cover everything from clothing to paintings, furniture, cars or even a caravan based at a non-residential site. In *R(H) 7/08*, Commissioner Jacobs concluded that "personal possessions" means any physical assets other than land and assets used for business purposes. The only such items which cannot be ignored are those bought for the purposes of securing or increasing HB entitlement. See the analysis of reg 49(1) on p468. See also para 10 where a sum has been paid to the claimant for damage to, or loss of, personal possessions.

---

13.   The value of the right to receive any income under an annuity or the surrender value (if any) of such an annuity.

Analysis

This provides a total disregard of the surrender value of annuities or the right to receive income under them. For the treatment of income *actually* received under an annuity, see reg 41(2) and Sch 5 para 18.

---

14. Where the funds of a trust are derived from a payment made in consequence of any personal injury to the claimant [¹ or the claimant's partner], the value of the trust fund and the value of the right to receive any payment under that trust.

Amendment

1. Amended by reg 15(7)(a) of SI 2006 No 2378 from the first day of the first benefit week to commence on or after 2.10.06.

Analysis

The paragraph provides a disregard of the value of a trust fund derived from payments made in consequence of personal injury, and the right to receive payments, for an indefinite period in all cases. See reg 42(2) in respect of income from such trusts. Payments of income are disregarded under Sch 5 para 14. See para 14A of this Schedule for capital payments and paras 45 and 46 where damages paid to children or young people are administered by the Court.

Payments made "in consequence of any personal injury" covers out of court settlements and insurance payments as well as damages under a court order. It can also include payments made in respect of a claim for professional negligence. In *KQ v SSWP (IS)* [2011] UKUT 102 (AAC); [2011] AACR 43, an appeal concerning IS provisions identical to this para and para 14A, the claimant had instructed solicitors to seek compensation for personal injury. The solicitors failed to make the claim in time. The claimant then instructed a second firm of solicitors to seek compensation from the first firm for professional negligence. The claim was settled and an amount of compensation was paid. The First-tier Tribunal decided that the payment was not made in consequence of personal injury and therefore could not be disregarded. As Judge Levenson pointed out, the compensatory element of damages for professional negligence is generally intended to put a claimant in the same position as had the negligence not occurred. The First-tier Tribunal had failed to give due weight to the meaning of the words "in consequence of". The whole of the payment made to the claimant was what would have been claimed for personal injury. The judge could not see how in these circumstances the payment could be said not to be in consequence of the personal injury. However, he pointed out that the chain of causation does not go on for ever and that, for example, amounts paid in respect of stress caused by professional negligence or punitive damages might not be covered by the disregards.

In *Francois v LB Waltham Forest* [2017] EWHC 2252 (Admin), the High Court determined in a council tax reduction case that a claimant had not satisfied the onus of proof about capital held in a personal injury trust when she supplied a solicitor's letter in general terms about the trust but failed to comply with subsequent requests by the authority to supply bank statements. The Court found that, while the fact that there was a personal injury trust was established, the authority (and subsequently the Valuation Tribunal for England) were entitled to conclude that this was not enough in itself and the onus of proof remained with the claimant to provide the further information requested.

[¹**14A.**–(1) Any payment made to the claimant or the claimant's partner in consequence of any personal injury to the claimant or, as the case may be, the claimant's partner.

(2) But sub-paragraph (1)–

(a) applies only for the period of 52 weeks beginning with the day on which the claimant first receives any payment in consequence of that personal injury;

(b) does not apply to any subsequent payment made to him in consequence of that injury (whether it is made by the same person or another);

(c) ceases to apply to the payment or any part of the payment from the day on which the claimant no longer possesses it;

(d) does not apply to any payment from a trust where the funds of the trust are derived from a payment made in consequence of any personal injury to the claimant.

(3) For the purposes of sub-paragraph (2)(c), the circumstances in which a claimant no longer possesses a payment or a part of it include where the claimant has used a payment or part of it to purchase an asset.

(4) References in sub-paragraphs (2) and (3) to the claimant are to be construed as including references to his partner (where applicable).]

Amendment

1. Inserted by reg 15(7)(b) of SI 2006 No 2378 from the first day of the first benefit week to commence on or after 2.10.06.

Analysis

A payment made in consequence of a personal injury to the claimant or her/his partner is disregarded for 52 weeks from the day the claimant first receives any payment in consequence of that injury, though the amount of the disregard decreases as the payment is disposed of (eg, as the claimant spends it): sub-paras (1), (2)(a) and

(c) and (3). This gives the claimant time to spend all or part of the payment, or to put it into a trust which can itself be disregarded under para 14. For the meaning of payments "in consequence of any personal injury", see the analysis of para 14.

However, para 14A does not apply to:

(1)   Subsequent payments made in consequence of the same injury: sub-para (2)(b). However, it is suggested that the amount could be disregarded if put into a trust (see reg 49(2)(b) and para 14).

(2)   Payments of capital made from a trust derived from payments made in consequence of a personal injury to the claimant or her/his partner: sub-para (2)(d). Note that payments of income from such a trust are disregarded under Sch 5 para 14.

Sub-para (4) confirms that in sub-paras (2) and (3) the references to "claimant" should also be read as "partner" where relevant.

15.   The value of the right to receive any income under a life interest or from a life rent.

Analysis

The terms "life interest" or "life rent" (in Scots law) cover the situation where a beneficiary under a trust gets the right to enjoy an asset during her/his lifetime, but that asset will pass on her/his death to someone else. Such a right can be bought and sold and is therefore given a capital value, but that value is to be ignored for the purpose of assessing HB. If, however, a claimant receives actual payments (eg, of income, under such a life interest or life rent) that income is assessable under Section 5 of Part 6.

16.   The value of the right to receive any income which is disregarded under [¹ paragraph 13 of Schedule 4] or paragraph 24 of Schedule 5.

Amendment

1.   Amended by reg 3(13)(a) of SI 2008 No 1042 as from 19.5.08.

Analysis

The right to receive income can be bought and sold and so has a capital value. However, where the right is to receive income disregarded under the paragraphs cited, that value is ignored for HB purposes. Para 13 Sch 4 and para 24 Sch 5 refer to earnings and income payable in a country outside the UK for a period during which there is a prohibition against the transfer of the earnings to the UK.

17.   The surrender value of any policy of life insurance.

18.   Where any payment of capital falls to be made by instalments, the value of the right to receive any outstanding instalments.

Analysis

Reg 41 deems capital payable by instalments which are outstanding as at the date of claim to be treated as income in certain circumstances. Under this paragraph, the value of the right to receive the outstanding instalments is ignored in the assessment of capital.

19.   Any payment made by a local authority in accordance with section 17, [¹ 23B,] 23C or 24A of the Children Act 1989 or, as the case may be, section 12 of the Social Work (Scotland) Act 1968 or [³ section 22, 26A, 29 or 30 of the Children (Scotland) Act 1995 (provision of services to children and their families and advice and provision of assistance for certain young persons) [⁴ or section 37 or 38 of the Social Services and Well-being (Wales) Act 2014, but excluding any direct payment made in accordance with regulations made under section 51 of that Act, or section 109, 110, 114 or 115 of that Act].]

Amendments

1.   Amended by reg 6(10)(a) of SI 2008 No 2767 as from 17.11.08.
2.   Inserted by reg 7(4) of SI 2010 No 2429 as from 1.11.10.
3.   Amended by art 6(3)(a) of SI 2016 No 732 as from 5.8.16.
4.   Amended by art 11(8)(a) of SI 2017 No 901 as from 3.11.17.

Analysis

Section 17 Children Act 1989 enables the local authority to give children in need, their families and others cash payments "in exceptional circumstances". Section 12 of the 1968 Act is to the same effect for Scotland. Sections 23B, 23C and 24A enable the local authority to give individuals under 21 who at any time after reaching the age of 16 but while still a child had been looked after, accommodated or fostered by the local authority, cash payments "in exceptional circumstances". Sections 22, 26A, 29 and 30 of the 1995 Act are to the same effect for Scotland. Section 37 of the Welsh Act requires authorities to meet the needs of a child for care and support, to the extent that those needs are not met by the child's family or a carer. For income payments, see Sch 5 para 28. For the circumstances in which payments made under s23C Children Act 1989, s29 Children (Scotland) Act 1995 or s110 Social Services and Well-being (Wales) Act 2014 which are passed on to a former carer can be disregarded, see para 19A and Sch 5 para 28A.

[¹**19A.**–(1)   Subject to sub-paragraph (2), any payment (or part of a payment) made by a local authority in accordance with section 23C of the Children Act 1989 [² or section 26A or 29 of the Children (Scotland) Act 1995 (local authorities' duty to promote welfare of children, duty to provide continuing care and provision of advice and assistance for certain young persons)] [³ or section 110 of the Social Services and Well-being (Wales) Act 2014 (support for category 3 young people)] to a person ("A") which A passes on to the claimant.

(2)   Sub-paragraph (1) applies only where A–

(a)   was formerly in the claimant's care, and

[² (b)   is aged 18 or over or, in the case of a payment or part of a payment made in accordance with section 26A of the Children (Scotland) Act 1995, aged 16 or over, and]

(c)   continues to live with the claimant.]

Amendments

1.   Inserted by reg 6(6)(b) of SI 2008 No 698 as from, as it relates to a particular beneficiary, the first day of the benefit week on or after 7.4.08.

2.   Amended by art 6(3)(b) of SI 2016 No 732 as from 5.8.16.

3.   Amended by art 11(8)(b) of SI 2017 No 901 as from 3.11.17.

Analysis

This provides a disregard of payments made by a local authority in accordance with the provisions listed. This only applies where the payment is made to someone formerly in the claimant's care as a child or young person, who is now aged 18 or over (or, in Scotland, aged 16 or over in certain circumstances) but continues to live with her/him, and who has passed the payment on to the claimant.

20.   Any social fund payment made pursuant to Part 8 of the Act.

General Note

With effect from 16 September 2019, applicants in Scotland can no longer apply for a funeral payment under the social fund. They may instead qualify for "funeral expense assistance" paid in accordance with regulations made under s34 Social Security (Scotland) Act 2018. Such assistance is also disregarded in full for the purposes of HB (see para 66 of this Schedule on p701).

[¹**20A.**   Any local welfare provision.]

Amendment

1.   Inserted by reg 7(6)(a) of SI 2013 No 443 as from 2.4.13.

Analysis

"Local welfare provision" is defined in reg 2(1) (on p228). It is the DWP term for the replacement of social fund community care grants and crisis loans by local provision. Income payments can also be disregarded: Sch 5 para 31A.

21.   Any refund of tax which falls to be deducted under section 369 of the Income and Corporation Taxes Act 1988 (deduction of tax from certain loan interest) on a payment of relevant loan interest for the purpose of acquiring an interest in the home or carrying out repairs or improvements to the home.

22.   Any capital which by virtue of regulation 41 or 64 (capital treated as income and treatment of student loans) is to be treated as income.

Analysis

As capital under reg 41 and student loans under reg 64 are to be treated as part of the claimant's income, this paragraph is necessary to avoid double counting. See also para 18, above.

23.   Where any payment of capital is made in a currency other than Sterling, any banking charge or commission payable in converting that payment into Sterling.

24.–(1)   Any payment made under [² or by] the Macfarlane Trust, the Macfarlane (Special Payments) Trust, the Macfarlane (Special Payments) (No. 2) Trust ("the Trusts"), the Fund, the Eileen Trust [², MFET Limited], the Independent Living [¹ Fund (2006)], [³ the Skipton Fund, the Caxton Foundation] [⁴, the Scottish Infected Blood Support Scheme] [⁶, an approved blood scheme] [⁵, the London Emergencies Trust, the We Love Manchester Emergency Fund] or the London Bombings Relief Charitable Fund.

(2)   Any payment by or on behalf of a person who is suffering or who suffered from haemophilia or who is or was a qualifying person, which derives from a payment made under [² or by] any of the Trusts to which sub-paragraph (1) refers and which is made to or for the benefit of–

    (a)   that person's partner or former partner from whom he is not, or where that person has died was not, estranged or divorced or with whom he has formed a civil partnership that has not been dissolved or, where that person has died, had not been dissolved at the time of that person's death;

    (b)   any child who is a member of that person's family or who was such a member and who is a member of the claimant's family; or

    (c)   any young person who is a member of that person's family or who was such a member and who is a member of the claimant's family.

    (3)   Any payment by or on behalf of the partner or former partner of a person who is suffering or who suffered from haemophilia or who is or was a qualifying person provided that the partner or former partner and that person are not, or if either of them has died were not, estranged or divorced or, where the partner or former partner and that person have formed a civil partnership, the civil partnership has not been dissolved or, if either of them has died, had not been dissolved at the time of the death, which derives from a payment made under [² or by] any of the Trusts to which sub-paragraph (1) refers and which is made to or for the benefit of–

    (a)   the person who is suffering from haemophilia or who is a qualifying person;

    (b)   any child who is a member of that person's family or who was such a member and who is a member of the claimant's family; or

    (c)   any young person who is a member of that person's family or who was such a member and who is a member of the claimant's family.

    (4)   Any payment by a person who is suffering from haemophilia or who is a qualifying person, which derives from a payment under [² or by] any of the Trusts to which sub-paragraph (1) refers, where–

    (a)   that person has no partner or former partner from whom he is not estranged or divorced or with whom he has formed a civil partnership that has not been dissolved, nor any child or young person who is or had been a member of that person's family; and

    (b)   the payment is made either–

        (i)   to that person's parent or step-parent; or

        (ii)   where that person at the date of the payment is a child, a young person or a student who has not completed his full-time education and has no parent or step-parent, to his guardian,

but only for a period from the date of the payment until the end of two years from that person's death.

    (5)   Any payment out of the estate of a person who suffered from haemophilia or who was a qualifying person, which derives from a payment under [² or by] any of the Trusts to which sub-paragraph (1) refers, where–

    (a)   that person at the date of his death (the relevant date) had no partner or former partner from whom he was not estranged or divorced or with whom he had formed a civil partnership that had not been dissolved, nor any child or young person who was or had been a member of his family; and

    (b)   the payment is made either–

        (i)   to that person's parent or step-parent; or

        (ii)   where that person at the relevant date was a child, a young person or a student who had not completed his full-time education and had no parent or step-parent, to his guardian,

but only for a period of two years from the relevant date.

    (6)   In the case of a person to whom or for whose benefit a payment referred to in this paragraph is made, any capital resource which derives from any payment of income or capital made under or deriving from any of the Trusts.

    (7)   For the purposes of sub-paragraphs (2) to (6), any reference to the Trusts shall be construed as including a reference to the Fund, the Eileen Trust[², MFET Limited], the Skipton Fund[³, the Caxton Foundation] [⁴, the Scottish Infected Blood Support Scheme] [⁶, an approved blood scheme] [⁵, the London Emergencies Trust, the We Love Manchester Emergency Fund] or the London Bombings Relief Charitable Fund.

Modifications

References to "step-parent" in sub-paras (4)(b)(i) and (ii) and (5)(b)(i) and (ii) are modified by s246 Civil Partnership Act 2004 (see p1729) and art 3 and para 26 of the Schedule to SI 2005 No.3137 (see p1772).

Amendments

1.   Amended by reg 6(4)(g) of SI 2008 No 2767 as from 17.11.08.
2.   Amended by reg 8(3) and (5) of SI 2010 No 641 as from 1.4.10 (5.4.10 where rent payable weekly or in multiples of a week).
3.   Amended by reg 19(6) of SI 2011 No 2425 as from 31.10.11.
4.   Amended by reg 6(3)(g) of SI 2017 No 329 as from 3.4.17.
5.   Amended by reg 6(3)(g) of SI 2017 No 689 as from 19.6.17.
6.   Amended by reg 6(3)(f) of SI 2017 No 870 as from 23.10.17.

Analysis

See analysis of Sch 5 para 35.

    25.–(1)   Where a claimant has ceased to occupy what was formerly the dwelling occupied as the home following his estrangement or divorce from, or dissolution of his civil partnership with, his former partner, that dwelling for a period of 26 weeks from the date on which he ceased to occupy that dwelling or, where the dwelling is occupied as the home by the former partner who is a lone parent, for so long as it is so occupied.

(2)   In this paragraph "dwelling" includes any garage, garden and outbuildings, which were formerly occupied by the claimant as his home and any premises not so occupied which it is impracticable or unreasonable to sell separately, in particular, in Scotland, any croft land on which the dwelling is situated.

Analysis

Sub-para (1) allows the disregard of a claimant's former home s/he left following estrangement or divorce from her/his partner or where her/his civil partnership with the partner has been dissolved. The home must be occupied by the former partner. For "occupied as the home", see the note to reg 7. See para 4 above for a discussion of the term "estranged" and where the claimant and the former partner are not estranged or divorced from the former partner or where a civil partnership has not been dissolved.

(1)   If the former partner is a lone parent, the dwelling can be disregarded indefinitely, so long as s/he continues to occupy it as a home. "Lone parent" is defined in reg 2(1).

(2)   In all other cases, the dwelling can be disregarded for 26 weeks from the date the claimant ceased to occupy it. There is no discretion to extend (although a claimant subject to this paragraph may also be covered by other paras below – eg, paras 26 or 27). It may be difficult to ascertain on which date the claimant finally ceased to occupy the dwelling for these purposes.

This provision is likely to give rise to a number of practical difficulties where there are no children or the former partner leaves the home (eg, for it to be sold) not least because the short time during which the disregard is available will frequently be inadequate to enable a couple's financial affairs to be sorted out in the case of a divorce. At the end of the 26-week period, even if financial arrangements have been made following the breakdown of a relationship, matters may not be clear-cut as the divorce courts sometimes make what are known as "Mesher" orders which order that the former matrimonial home be held on trust for the former partners in their respective shares, but that it should not be sold until the occurrence of a particular event – eg, the death or remarriage of the partner who remains in residence. In such a case, the partner who has left will continue to have an interest in the home which, after the initial 26-week period, will not be disregarded unless the other partner is a lone parent and continues to live in the home, or one of the other paragraphs of Sch 6 applies. A practical solution lies in the method of valuation of such capital – see regs 47 and 51. The asset (here the claimant's share) is to be valued at its current market value less 10 per cent and the value of any encumbrance secured on it. If what a claimant possesses is an interest in a house which s/he is unable to sell because her/his partner is still living in it and/or because a court order forbids the sale, the market value of that asset is likely to be very low. Authorities should be careful to take a realistic and humane approach to this problem.

Sub-para (2) is the same definition of a "dwelling" as appears in para 1.

---

26.   Any premises where the claimant is taking reasonable steps to dispose of those premises, for a period of 26 weeks from the date on which he first took such steps, or such longer period as is reasonable in the circumstances to enable him to dispose of those premises.

Analysis

The question of what are "reasonable steps" to dispose of premises initially rests with the authority. Here the 26-week disregard runs from the date on which reasonable steps are first taken and may be extended where it appears "reasonable" to do so in the circumstances. In *CIS 1915/2007*, the claimant had fled domestic violence and an arranged marriage and began divorce proceedings. However, under family pressure these were temporarily suspended. The DWP decided that the value of her interest in the former matrimonial home could no longer be disregarded as she was no longer taking reasonable steps to dispose of it. Deputy Commissioner Mark allowed the claimant's appeal. He said that in considering the reasonableness of the period taken by the claimant to secure a divorce (and the resulting disposal of the premises), including any temporary suspension of such action, it was necessary to look at all the facts, including the pressures that were brought on her. The steps she took to temporarily suspend her divorce proceedings until she had moved to a new address and changed her name to secure her safety did not mean that she was no longer taking reasonable steps to dispose of the premises through divorce proceedings.

Once the property has been disposed of, para 3 above may apply to the proceeds.

---

27.   Any premises which the claimant intends to occupy as his home, and in respect of which he is taking steps to obtain possession and has sought legal advice, or has commenced legal proceedings, with a view to obtaining possession, for a period of 26 weeks from the date on which he first sought such advice or first commenced such proceedings whichever is the earlier, or such longer period as is reasonable in the circumstances to enable him to obtain possession and commence occupation of those premises.

Analysis

The starting date for the period of disregard under this para is the date on which the claimant first sought legal advice if this is earlier (as it usually will be by several weeks if not months) than the date on which s/he commenced legal proceedings. There could be overlap between this para and para 25 above, in which case this para may operate to extend any period of disregard available under para 25: eg, if a claimant leaves the matrimonial home and 10 weeks later seeks advice on commencing divorce proceedings in which there is an application for the other partner, who is childless, to leave the premises and for the claimant to be permitted to re-enter, para 25 applies initially and then the full period in para 27 applies after advice is sought. In many cases, for reasons beyond the claimant's control, it is possible that possession proceedings will not be completed within six months of their commencement, and this should be reflected by the use of the discretion to extend the period of the disregard where necessary.

28. Any premises which the claimant intends to occupy as his home to which essential repairs or alterations are required in order to render them fit for such occupation, for a period of 26 weeks from the date on which the claimant first takes steps to effect those repairs or alterations, or such longer period as is necessary to enable those repairs or alterations to be carried out.

Analysis

"Essential" repairs or alterations are not defined but they must be such as are necessary to make the premises fit for the claimant's occupation. It is possible that cases will arise where this paragraph overlaps with Sch 6 para 2, and the scheme should be operated with the claimant's interests in mind.

The scope of this paragraph was considered in *R v Tower Hamlets LBC HBRB ex p Kapur* [2000] *The Times* 28 June, QBD. The applicant owned a derelict house valued at £240,000 which was unfit for habitation. He wished to renovate the property and move back into it and made extensive efforts to obtain funding for the necessary works from lenders, relatives and public authorities in the form of various types of renovation grant. It took a great deal of time to assemble the funds. The Housing Benefit Review Board held that "the date on which the claimant first takes steps to effect those repairs" could not be earlier than the date on which works actually commenced. Scott Baker J quashed the Board's decision, holding that to be a wrong approach. The judge had regard to the *Adjudication Officer's Guide*, which stated, in relation to the similar Sch 10 para 28 Income Support (General) Regulations 1987, that the relevant "steps" could include getting a grant or loan to pay for repairs or alterations, employing an architect, getting planning permission or finding someone to do the work, and that the relevant "date" could be the first date on which inquiries about those matters were made. It was a question of fact for the authority as to when the first steps were taken, but the Board's approach was clearly too restrictive and its decision was therefore quashed.

[[1]**29.**]

Amendment

1. Omitted by reg 6(6)(c) of SI 2008 No 698 as from, as they relate to a particular beneficiary, the first day of the benefit week on or after 7.4.08.

30. Any payment made by the Secretary of State to compensate for the loss (in whole or in part) of entitlement to housing benefit.
31. The value of the right to receive an occupational or personal pension.
32. The value of any funds held under a personal pension scheme [[1]].

Amendment

1. Amended by reg 4(7) of SI 2007 No 1749 as from 16.7.07.

33. The value of the right to receive any rent except where the claimant has a reversionary interest in the property in respect of which rent is due.
34. Any payment in kind made by a charity or under [[3] or by] the Macfarlane (Special Payments) Trust, the Macfarlane (Special Payments) (No. 2) Trust, [[1] the Fund [[4], MFET Limited] [[5], the Skipton Fund, the Caxton Foundation], [[2]] [[6], the Scottish Infected Blood Support Scheme] or the Independent Living Fund (2006)].

Amendments

1. Amended by art 8(3) of SI 2007 No 2538 as from 1.10.07.
2. Amended by reg 6(9)(b) of SI 2008 No 2767 as from 17.11.08.
3. Amended by reg 8 (5) of SI 2010 No 641 as from 1.4.10 (5.4.10 where rent payable weekly or in multiples of a week).
4. Amended by reg 8(11) of SI 2010 No 641 as from 1.4.10 (5.4.10 where rent payable weekly or in multiples of a week).
5. Inserted by reg 19(5) of SI 2011 No 2425 as from 31.10.11.
6. Amended by reg 6(3)(g) of SI 2017 No 329 as from 3.4.17.

Analysis

The implication of this para is that (except where the claimant is on IS, an income-based JSA or an income-related ESA (or UC) – see Sch 4 para 12, Sch 5 paras 4 and 5 and Sch 6 paras 5 and 6) other, non-charitable capital payments in kind are to be taken into account. The regulations provide no mechanism for quantifying the value of other payments in kind.

35. Any payment made pursuant to section 2 of the 1973 Act or section 2 of the Enterprise and New Towns (Scotland) Act 1990, but only for the period of 52 weeks beginning on the date of receipt of the payment.

[¹**36.**]

Amendment

1. Omitted by reg 6(9)(c) of SI 2008 No 2767 as from 17.11.08.

37. Any payment in consequence of a reduction of council tax under section 13 [¹ , section 13A or] section 80 of the Local Government Finance Act 1992 (reduction of liability for council tax), but only for a period of 52 weeks from the date of the receipt of the payment.

Amendment

1. Amended by reg 7(6)(b) of SI 2013 No 443 as from 2.4.13.

Analysis

Among other things, para 37 allows payments in consequence of a local authority's council tax reduction scheme (the replacement for council tax benefit from 1 April 2013) to be disregarded.

38. Any grant made to the claimant in accordance with a scheme made under section 129 of the Housing Act 1988 or section 66 of the Housing (Scotland) Act 1988 (schemes for payments to assist local housing authority and local authority tenants to obtain other accommodation) which is to be used–
(a)   to purchase premises intended for occupation as his home; or
(b)   to carry out repairs or alterations which are required to render premises fit for occupation as his home,
for a period of 26 weeks from the date on which he received such a grant or such longer period as is reasonable in the circumstances to enable the purchase, repairs or alterations to be completed and the claimant to commence occupation of those premises as his home.

[¹**39.** Any arrears of supplementary pension which is disregarded under paragraph 53 of Schedule 5 (sums to be disregarded in the calculation of income other than earnings) or of any amount which is disregarded under paragraph 54 or 55 of that Schedule, but only for a period of 52 weeks from the date of receipt of the arrears.]

Amendment

1. Substituted by reg 5(7)(a) of SI 2008 No 3157 as from 5.1.09.

[²**40.**–(1) Any payment or repayment made–
(a)   as respects England, under regulation 5, 6 or 12 of the National Health Service (Travel Expenses and Remission of Charges) Regulations 2003 (travelling expenses and health service supplies);
(b)   as respects Wales, under regulation 5, 6 or 11 of the National Health Service (Travelling Expenses and Remission of Charges) (Wales) Regulations 2007 (travelling expenses and health service supplies);
(c)   as respects Scotland, under regulation 3, 5 or 11 of the National Health Service (Travelling Expenses and Remission of Charges) (Scotland) (No. 2) Regulations 2003 (travelling expenses and health service supplies),
but only for a period of 52 weeks from the date of receipt of the payment or repayment.
(2)   Any payment or repayment made by the Secretary of State for Health [³ and Social Care], the Scottish Ministers or the Welsh Ministers which is analogous to a payment or repayment mentioned in sub-paragraph (1), but only for a period of 52 weeks from the date of receipt of the payment or repayment.]

Amendments

1. Amended by reg 3(13)(b)-(d) of SI 2008 No 1042 as from 19.5.08.
2. Substituted by reg 5(7)(a) of SI 2008 No 3157 as from 5.1.09.
3. Amended by the Sch para 21(m) of SI 2018 No 378 as from 11.4.18.

Analysis

Paras 40, 41 and 42 provide a disregard of payments made in respect of certain NHS charges (eg, hospital travel costs), payments in lieu of healthy start food vouchers (for which see Sch 5 para 45), milk tokens or the supply of vitamins, and for assisted prison visits. In all cases the disregard is only for 52 weeks.

[²**41.** Any payment made to such persons entitled to receive benefits as may be determined by or under a scheme made pursuant to section 13 of the Social Security Act 1988 in lieu of vouchers or similar arrangements in connection with the provision of those benefits (including payments made in place of healthy start vouchers, milk tokens or the supply of vitamins), but only for a period of 52 weeks from the date of receipt of the payment.]

Amendments
1.   Amended by reg 3(13)(e) of SI 2008 No 1042 as from 19.5.08.
2.   Substituted by reg 5(7)(a) of SI 2008 No 3157 as from 5.1.09.

Analysis
Para 41 provides a disregard for 52 weeks of payments made in lieu of vouchers for Healthy Start food and vitamins or for milk tokens. Healthy Start food is milk, and fresh or frozen fruit and vegetables. Information is at www.healthystart.nhs.uk. The disregard will also apply to the value of the payment card issued under the "Best Start" foods scheme which replaces the Healthy Start food scheme in Scotland from 12 August 2019 (under the Welfare Foods (Best Start Foods) (Scotland) Regulations 2019 SSI No.193, which are also made under authority of s13 of the 1988 Act). See also Sch 5 para 45 on p678 for the disregard of such payments as income.

[¹**41A.** Any payment made under Part 8A of the Act (entitlement to health in pregnancy grant).]

Amendment
1.   Inserted by reg 6(13)(a) of SI 2009 No 583 as from the first day of the first benefit week for the claimant on or after 6.4.09.

Analysis
Para 41A provided a complete and indefinite disregard of the health in pregnancy grant, a non-means-tested grant (£190) paid to pregnant women to help them prepare for the birth of the baby. Note: health in pregnancy grants have now been abolished. From 1 January 2011, a woman could only qualify for a health in pregnancy grant if she had reached the 25th week of her pregnancy before that date.

42. Any payment made either by the Secretary of State for [¹ Justice] or Scottish Ministers under a scheme established to assist relatives and other persons to visit persons in custody, but only for a period of 52 weeks from the date of the receipt of the payment.

Amendment
1.   Amended by Art 8 and the Sch para 23 of SI 2007 No 2128 as from 22.8.07.

43. Any payment (other than a training allowance) made, whether by the Secretary of State or any other person, under the Disabled Persons (Employment) Act 1944 [¹] to assist disabled persons to obtain or retain employment despite their disability.

Amendment
1.   Amended by reg 3(13)(f) of SI 2008 No 1042 as from 19.5.08.

44. Any payment made by a local authority under section 3 of the Disabled Persons (Employment) Act 1958 [¹ or under Part 4 of the Social Services and Well-being (Wales) Act 2014] to homeworkers assisted under the Blind Homeworkers' Scheme.

Amendment
1.   Amended by art 11(8)(c) of SI 2017 No 901 as from 3.11.17.

[¹ **45.**–(1)   Any sum of capital to which sub-paragraph (2) applies and–
(a)   which is administered on behalf of a person by the High Court or the County Court under Rule 21.11(1) of the Civil Procedure Rules 1998 or by the Court of Protection;
(b)   which can only be disposed of by order or direction of any such court; or
(c)   where the person concerned is under the age of 18, which can only be disposed of by order or direction prior to that person attaining age 18.
(2)   This sub-paragraph applies to a sum of capital which is derived from–
(a)   an award of damages for a personal injury to that person; or
(b)   compensation for the death of one or both parents where the person concerned is under the age of 18.]

Amendment

1.   Substituted by reg 15(7)(c) of SI 2006 No 2378 from the 1st day of the 1st benefit week to commence on or after 2.10.06.

Analysis

An adult who receives compensation for personal injuries can prevent it from reducing her/his entitlement to HB by putting it in a trust (see para 14). However, where children and young people under 18 are awarded such compensation that is not possible as the money is not paid to them but retained in court until their 18th birthday. Paras 45 and 46 make it clear that compensation paid to children and young people for personal injury or the death of a parent is also disregarded while it is held by the court. At least as far as personal injury compensation is concerned they are probably unnecessary given the unreported decision of a commissioner in *CIS 368/1994*. Note that compensation paid for the death of a parent can only be disregarded until the claimant is 18 – ie, sub-para (2)(b) is not concerned with the claimant's age when the compensation was paid or when the death of the parent occurred: *CP v SSWP (IS)* [2011] UKUT 157 (AAC). In *CP v SSWP*, the claimant, who was severely disabled, had been paid compensation on the death of her mother to pay for her care needs. Her representative argued that the material difference between her position and that of non-disabled people was such that the failure to provide some form of differential treatment amounted to unlawful discrimination within the principle of *Thlimmenos v Greece* (2001) 31 EHRR 15, as acknowledged and approved by the Court of Appeal in *AM (Somalia) v Entry Clearance Officer* [2009] EWCA Civ 634. Judge Wikeley did not agree.

---

46.   Any sum of capital administered on behalf of a person in accordance with an order made under section 13 of the Children (Scotland) Act 1995 or under Rule 36.14 of the Ordinary Cause Rules 1993 or under Rule 128 of those Rules, where such sum derives from–

(a)   award of damages for a personal injury to that person; or

(b)   compensation for the death of one or both parents where the person concerned is under the age of 18.

47.   Any payment to the claimant as holder of the Victoria Cross or George Cross.

[¹**48.**]

Amendment

1.   Omitted by reg 12(4) of SI 2011 No 674 as from 1.4.11 (4.4.11 where rent payable weekly or in any multiple of whole weeks).

---

49.   In the case of a person who is receiving, or who has received, assistance under the self-employment route, any sum of capital which is acquired by that person for the purpose of establishing or carrying on the commercial activity in respect of which such assistance is or was received but only for a period of 52 weeks from the date on which that sum was acquired.

50.–(1)   Any payment of a sports award for a period of 26 weeks from the date of receipt of that payment except to the extent that it has been made in respect of any one or more of the items specified in sub-paragraph (2).

(2)   The items specified for the purposes of sub-paragraph (1) are food, ordinary clothing or footwear, household fuel or rent of the claimant or, where the claimant is a member of a family, any other member of his family, or any council tax or water charges for which that claimant or member is liable.

(3)   For the purposes of sub-paragraph (2)–

"food" does not include vitamins, minerals or other special dietary supplements intended to enhance the performance of the person in the sport in respect of which the award was made;

"rent" means eligible rent less any deductions in respect of non-dependants which fall to be made under regulation 74 (non-dependant deductions).

Analysis

See Sch 5 para 59.

51.–(1)   Any payment–

(a)   by way of an education maintenance allowance made pursuant to–

(i)   regulations made under section 518 of the Education Act 1996 (payment of school expenses; grant of scholarships etc);

(ii)   regulations made under section 49 or 73(f) of the Education (Scotland) Act 1980 (power to assist persons to take advantage of educational facilities);

[¹ (iii)   directions made under section 73ZA of the Education (Scotland) Act 1980 and paid under section 12(2)(c) of the Further and Higher Education (Scotland) Act 1992; [²]

(b)   corresponding to such an education maintenance allowance, made pursuant to–

(i)   section 14 or section 181 of the Education Act 2002 (power of Secretary of State and National Assembly for Wales to give financial assistance for purposes related to education or childcare, and allowances in respect of education or training); or

(ii)   regulations made under section 181 of that Act [² or

(c) in England, by way of financial assistance made pursuant to section 14 of the Education Act 2002.]

(2) Any payment, other than a payment to which sub-paragraph (1) applies, made pursuant to–

(a) regulations made under section 518 of the Education Act 1996;

(b) regulations made under section 49 of the Education (Scotland) Act 1980; or

[¹ (c) directions made under section 73ZA of the Education (Scotland) Act 1980 and paid under section 12(2)(c) of the Further and Higher Education (Scotland) Act 1992,]

in respect of a course of study attended by a child or a young person or a person who is in receipt of an education maintenance allowance [² or other payment] made pursuant to any provision specified in sub-paragraph (1).

Amendments

1. Amended by reg 5(7)(c) of SI 2008 No 3157 as from 5.1.09.
2. Amended by reg 19(8) of SI 2011 No 2425 as from 31.10.11.

Analysis

See Sch 5 para 11.

---

52. In the case of a claimant participating in an employment zone programme, any discretionary payment made by an employment zone contractor to the claimant, being a fee, grant, loan or otherwise, but only for the period of 52 weeks from the date of receipt of the payment.

53. Any arrears of subsistence allowance paid as a lump sum but only for the period of 52 weeks from the date of receipt of the payment.

54. Where an ex-gratia payment of £10,000 has been made by the Secretary of State on or after 1st February 2001 in consequence of the imprisonment or interment of–

(a) the claimant;

(b) the claimant's partner;

(c) the claimant's deceased spouse or deceased civil partner; or

(d) the claimant's partner's deceased spouse or deceased civil partner,

by the Japanese during the Second World War, £10,000.

55.–(1) Subject to sub-paragraph (2), the amount of any trust payment made to a claimant or a member of a claimant's family who is–

(a) a diagnosed person;

(b) the diagnosed person's partner or the person who was the diagnosed person's partner at the [² date] of the diagnosed person's death;

(c) a parent of a diagnosed person, a person acting in place of the diagnosed person's parents or a person who was so acting at the date of the diagnosed person's death; or

(d) a member of the diagnosed person's family (other than his partner) or a person who was a member of the diagnosed person's family (other than his partner) at the date of the diagnosed person's death.

(2) Where a trust payment is made to–

(a) a person referred to in sub-paragraph (1)(a) or (b), that sub-paragraph shall apply for the period beginning on the date on which the trust payment is made and ending on the date on which that person dies;

(b) a person referred to in sub-paragraph (1)(c), that sub-paragraph shall apply for the period beginning on the date on which the trust payment is made and ending two years after that date;

(c) a person referred to in sub-paragraph (1)(d), that sub-paragraph shall apply for the period beginning on the date on which the trust payment is made and ending–

(i) two years after that date; or

(ii) on the day before the day on which that person–

(aa) ceases receiving full-time education; or

(bb) attains the age of [¹ 20],

whichever is the latest.

(3) Subject to sub-paragraph (4), the amount of any payment by a person to whom a trust payment has been made or of any payment out of the estate of a person to whom a trust payment has been made, which is made to a claimant or a member of a claimant's family who is–

(a) the diagnosed person's partner or the person who was the diagnosed person's partner at the date of the diagnosed person's death;

(b) a parent of a diagnosed person, a person acting in place of the diagnosed person's parents or a person who was so acting at the date of the diagnosed person's death; or

(c) a member of the diagnosed person's family (other than his partner) or a person who was a member of the diagnosed person's family (other than his partner) at the date of the diagnosed person's death,

but only to the extent that such payments do not exceed the total amount of any trust payments made to that person.

(4) Where a payment as referred to in sub-paragraph (3) is made to–

(a) a person referred to in sub-paragraph (3)(a), that sub-paragraph shall apply for the period beginning on the date on which that payment is made and ending on the date on which that person dies;

(b) a person referred to in sub-paragraph (3)(b), that sub-paragraph shall apply for the period beginning on the date on which that payment is made and ending two years after that date; or

(c)   a person referred to in sub-paragraph (3)(c), that sub-paragraph shall apply for the period beginning on the date on which that payment is made and ending–

     (i)   two years after that date; or

     (ii)   on the day before the day on which that person–

          (aa)   ceases receiving full-time education; or

          (bb)   attains the age of [¹ 20],

whichever is the latest.

(5)   In this paragraph, a reference to a person–

(a)   being the diagnosed person's partner;

(b)   being a member of a diagnosed person's family;

(c)   acting in place of the diagnosed person's parents,

at the date of the diagnosed person's death shall include a person who would have been such a person or a person who would have been so acting, but for the diagnosed person residing in a care home, an Abbeyfield Home or an independent hospital on that date.

(6)   In this paragraph–

"diagnosed person" means a person who has been diagnosed as suffering from, or who, after his death, has been diagnosed as having suffered from, variant Creutzfeld-Jakob disease;

"relevant trust" means a trust established out of funds provided by the Secretary of State in respect of persons who suffered, or who are suffering, from variant Creutzfeld-Jakob disease for the benefit of persons eligible for payments in accordance with its provisions;

"trust payment" means a payment under a relevant trust.

Amendments

1.   Amended by reg 4(5) of SI 2006 No 718 as from 10.4.06.

2.   Amended by reg 3(13)(g) of SI 2008 No 1042 as from 19.5.08.

Analysis

Para 55 provides a complex disregard covering payments from trusts (referred to as "relevant trusts") set up by the Secretary of State to compensate those with variant Creutzfeldt-Jakob disease. Part of the reason for the complexity is that some people may only be diagnosed as having that disease after they have died and payments from such trusts may therefore need to be made to other family members.

Where a payment is made to someone who has the disease her/himself ("the diagnosed person") or to that person's partner or to a person who was the partner of a diagnosed person when the latter died, the disregard lasts for the life of the payee. In other cases, the disregard lasts for two years unless the payee is a child or young person for whom the diagnosed person is (or was at the date of her/his death) responsible: in the latter case, the period of the disregard ends on the day before the child or young person's 20th birthday, or the day before s/he leaves full-time education or two years from the date of payment, whichever is the latest. See sub-para (5) for an extension of the definitions of "partner", member of the "family" and person acting in place of parents for these purposes.

Sub-para (3) establishes a similar disregard for payments made *by* a diagnosed person who has received money from a relevant trust to any of the people listed in heads (a) to (c). This includes payments made from the diagnosed person's estate after her/his death. The maximum amount which can be disregarded under sub-para (3) is the total sum received by the diagnosed person from any relevant trust.

---

56.   The amount of any payment, other than a war pension [¹], to compensate for the fact that the claimant, the claimant's partner, the claimant's deceased spouse or deceased civil partner or the claimant's partner's deceased spouse or deceased civil partner–

(a)   was a slave labourer or a forced labourer;

(b)   had suffered property loss or had suffered personal injury; or

(c)   was a parent of a child who had died,

during the Second World War.

Amendment

1.   Amended by reg 5(7)(d) of SI 2008 No 3157 as from 5.1.09.

Analysis

This paragraph provides a capital disregard of the amount of payments made to people who were slaves or forced labourers, suffered property loss or personal injury, or who were parents of a child who died during the Second World War. The disregard lasts for an unlimited time and even if there is a break in the claimant's benefit entitlement. It is additional to any other disregard, including the disregard for pensions for victims of persecution under Sch 5 para 15(g).

57.–(1)   Any payment made by a local authority, or by the [¹ Welsh Ministers], to or on behalf of the claimant or his partner relating to a service which is provided to develop or sustain the capacity of the claimant or his partner to live independently in his accommodation.

(2)   For the purposes of sub-paragraph (1) "local authority" includes in England a county council.

Amendment

1.   Amended by reg 5(7)(e) of SI 2008 No 3157 as from 5.1.09.

Analysis

See Sch 5 para 63.

58.   Any payment made under [¹] regulations made under section 57 of the Health and Social Care Act 2001 or [³ as a direct payment as defined in section 4(2) of the Social Care (Self-directed Support) (Scotland) Act 2013] [², or under sections 12A to 12D of the National Health Service Act 2006 (direct payments for health care)] [⁴ or under sections 31 to 33 of the Care Act 2014 (direct payments)] [⁵, or in accordance with regulations made under section 50 or 52 of the Social Services and Well-being (Wales) Act 2014]

.
Amendments

1.   Amended by reg 6(13b) of SI 2009 No 583 as from 6.4.09.
2.   Amended by reg 8(11) of SI 2010 No 641 as from 1.4.10 (5.4.10 where rent payable weekly or in multiples of a week).
3.   Amended by art 2 and Sch para 10(b) of SI 2014 No 513 as from 1.4.14.
4.   Amendedby art 2 and Sch para 24(4) of SI 2015 No.643 as from 1.4.15.
5.   Amended by art 11(8)(d) of SI 2017 No 901 as from 3.11.17.

Analysis

See Sch 5 para 57.

59.   Any payment made to the claimant pursuant to regulations under section 2(6)(b), 3 or 4 of the Adoption and Children Act 2002.
60.   Any payment made to the claimant in accordance with regulations made pursuant to section 14F of the Children Act 1989 (special guardianship support services).
[¹**61.**   Any payments to a claimant made under section 49 of the Children and Families Act 2014 (personal budgets and direct payments)]

Amendment

1.   Inserted by reg 20(3) of SI 2014 No.2103 as from 1.9.14.

Analysis

See the analysis of Sch 5 para 66 on p682.

[¹**62.**   Any bereavement support payment in respect of the rate set out in regulations 3(2) or (5) of the Bereavement Support Payment Regulations 2017 (rate of bereavement support payment), but only for a period of 52 weeks from the date of receipt of the payment.

Amendment

1.   Inserted by art 25(3)(b) of SI 2017 No 422 as from 6.4.17, subject to transitional provisions in arts 2 and 3.

[¹**63.**   Any payment made under or by a trust, established for the purpose of giving relief and assistance to disabled persons whose disabililties were caused by the fact that during their mother's pregnancy she had taken a preparation containing the drug known as Thalidomide, and which is approved by the Secretary of State.]

Amendment

1.   Inserted by reg 6(6) of SI 2017 No 870 as from 23.10.17.

[¹ **64.**   Any payment made to a claimant under section 73(1)(b) of the Children and Young People (Scotland) Act 2014 (kinship care assistance).]

Amendment

1.   Inserted by reg 5(4) of SI 2017 No 995 as from 7.11.17.

Analysis

See the analysis of Sch 5 para 27A on p674.

[¹**65.**   Any early years assistance given in accordance with section 32 of the Social Security (Scotland) Act 2018.]

Amendment

1.   Inserted by reg 8(3) of SI 2018 No 1138 as from 10.12.18.

Analysis

With effect from 10 December 2018, applicants in Scotland may qualify for "early years assistance" in the form of a lump-sum pregnancy and baby grant payable to people who have, or expect to have, a new baby in the family. Two further lump-sum early years assistance payments has since been introduced: with effect from 29 April 2019, an early learning grant payable in respect of a young child (defined as from her/his second birthday until the end of the day s/he reaches 3 1/2 years); and, with effect from 3 June 2019, a school age grant payable in respect of a child who has reached, or will reach within the year, the age at which children in Scotland normally start primary school (which is age 4 or 5, depending on when the child's birthday falls). See the Early Years Assistance (Best Start Grants) (Scotland) Regulations 2018 SSI No.370, made under s32 Social Security (Scotland) Act 2018. Such assistance is disregarded in full. It is also disregarded as income – see Sch 5 para 69 on p683.

[¹**66.**   Any funeral expense assistance given in accordance with section 34 of the Social Security (Scotland) Act 2018.]

Amendment

1.   Inserted by reg 13(3) of SI 2019 No 1060 as from 16.9.19.

Analysis

With effect from 16 September 2019, applicants in Scotland can no longer apply for a funeral payment under the social fund – see para 20 of this Schedule on p691 for the disregard of social fund payments. They may instead qualify for "funeral expense assistance" paid in accordance with regulations made under s34 Social Security (Scotland) Act 2018 – the Funeral Expense Assistance (Scotland) Regulations 2019 SSI No.292. Such assistance is disregarded in full. It is also disregarded as income – see Sch 5 para 70 on p683.

[² SCHEDULE 7]

Amendments

1.   Amended by reg 19 of SI 2007 No 2868, as amended by reg 4(6) of SI 2008 No 586, as from 7.4.08 (or if reg 1(5) of that SI applies, on the day on or after 7.4.08 when the first of the events specified in reg 1(6) applies, or from 6.4.09 if none have before that date).
2.   Omitted by reg 4(4)(e) of SI 2008 No 959 as from 6.10.08.

[² SCHEDULE 8]

Amendments

1.   Amended by reg 19 of SI 2007 No 2868 as from 7.4.08 (or if reg 1(5) of that SI applies, on the day on or after 7.4.08 when the first of the events specified in reg 1(6) applies, or from 6.4.09 if none have before that date).
2.   Omitted by reg 4(4)(f) of SI 2008 No 959 as from 6.10.08.

SCHEDULE 9

REGULATION 90

Matters to be included in decision notice

Definitions

"applicable amount" – see Part 5.
"benefit week" – see reg 2(1).
"claimant" – see reg 2(1).
"Decisions and Appeals Regulations" – see reg 2(1).
"earnings" – see regs 35 and 37.
"eligible rent" – see Part 3.
"income" – see General Note on Section 2 of Part 6.
"non-dependant" – see reg 3.
"person affected" – see reg 2(1).
"person on an income-based jobseeker's allowance" – see reg 2(3).
"person on an income-related employment and support allowance" – see reg 2(3A).
"person on income support" – see reg 2(1).

"relevant authority" – see reg 2(1).
"rent allowance", "rent rebate" – see s134(1A) and (1B) SSAA.

General Note on Schedule 9

This lists matters to be included in written notices of decisions issued to "persons affected" by a relevant authority: see reg 90. See the Analysis to reg 90 for the effects of a failure to provide the necessary information. Note that reg 10(1) D&A Regs may require the inclusion of additional information where a decision carries a right of appeal.

There are seven parts specifying information to be included in a notice in different circumstances.

(1)   Part 1 lists general matters which *always* need to appear within the terms of a notice of decision.

(2)   Part 2 applies only to notifications of a successful claim made by an IS, income-based JSA or income-related ESA recipient or where "extended payments" of HB are payable. See Part 6 where no HB award is made.

(3)   Part 3 applies only to notifications on a successful claim, this time when IS, income-based JSA and income-related ESA are *not* payable. See Part 6 where no HB award is made.

(4)   Part 4 applies where the authority has used its powers under regs 95 and 96 to pay HB direct to a landlord, whether or not on the decision of a claim.

(5)   Part 5 applies when the authority uses its powers to treat a non-dependant's income as if it was the claimant's under reg 26, whether or not on the decision of a claim.

(6)   Part 6 only applies to notices informing a claimant that a claim for HB has been unsuccessful.

(7)   Part 7 applies to notifications informing a person affected that s/he has been overpaid where the overpayment is recoverable under reg 100.

PART 1
General

1.   The statement of matters to be included in any decision notice issued by a relevant authority to a person, and referred to in regulation 90 (notification of decisions) and in regulation 10 of the Decisions and Appeals Regulations are those matters set out in the following provisions of this Schedule.

Analysis

Para 1 makes it clear that the requirements of the Schedule are mandatory. They are not optional and they are not to be seen by authorities as a piece of unnecessary bureaucracy. Clear notices assist claimants in understanding how a decision has been reached and reduce confusion and dispute. On the question of validity of notifications, see the Analysis to reg 90(1).

The requirements apply to decision notices issued under reg 90 and also under reg 10 D&A Regs. They apply both to initial decisions and decisions following revision or supersession, except as otherwise stated.

2.   Every decision notice shall include a statement as to the right of any person affected by that decision to request a written statement under regulation 90(2) (requests for statement of reasons) and the manner and time in which to do so.

Analysis

Para 2 requires every notice to state that persons affected have the right to request a statement of reasons under reg 90(2), and the time limit within, and manner in which, this must be done. This applies to initial decisions and decisions following a revision or supersession.

3.   Every decision notice shall include a statement as to the right of any person affected by that decision to make an application for a revision in accordance with regulation 4(1)(a) of the Decisions and Appeals Regulations and, where appropriate, to appeal against that decision and the manner and time in which to do so.

Analysis

Para 3 requires every notice to set out the right to seek a revision under reg 4 D&A Regs. Note also reg 10 D&A Regs which specifies when a "person affected" must be notified of her/his right of appeal.

4.   Every decision notice following an application for a revision in accordance with regulation 4(1)(a) of the Decisions and Appeals Regulations shall include a statement as to whether the original decision in respect of which the person made his representations has been confirmed or revised and where the relevant authority has not revised the decision the reasons why not.

Analysis

If a claimant has requested a revision of an authority's decision under reg 4(1)(a) D&A Regs (an "any grounds" revision), this paragraph specifies the matters which must be included in the notice informing the person affected of the authority's decision on revision. Reasons need to be given only where the authority decides not to revise its original decision, but note the separate right to request reasons for a decision under reg 10 D&A Regs where there is a right of appeal against a decision.

5. Every decision notice following an application for a revision in accordance with regulation 4(1)(a) of the Decisions and Appeals Regulations shall, if the original decision has been revised, include a statement as to the right of any person affected by that decision to apply for a revision in accordance with regulation 4(1)(a) of those Regulations and the manner and time in which to do so.

Analysis

Para 5 specifies that the notice sent out following an application for a revision must mention the right of any other person affected to apply for a further revision.

6. An authority may include in the decision notice any other matters not prescribed by this Schedule which it sees fit, whether expressly or by reference to some other document available without charge to the person.

Analysis

The authority is not restricted to giving the information set out in the Schedule and there will be cases in which further information is appropriate.

7. Parts 2, 3 and 6 of this Schedule shall apply only to the decision notice given on a claim.
8. Where a decision notice is given following a revision of an earlier decision–
(a) made of the authority's own motion which results in a revision of that earlier decision; or
(b) made following an application for a revision in accordance with regulation 4(1)(a) of the Decisions and Appeals Regulations, whether or not resulting in a revision of that earlier decision,
that notice shall, subject to paragraph 6, contain a statement only as to all the matters revised.

Analysis

Para 8 refers to the notices covered by paras 4 and 5, whether or not the authority's decision is to revise. It also covers, by sub-para (a), notices which are issued following an authority's own decision to revise a decision. The interaction of this paragraph with paras 4 and 5 is not totally clear, but the net effect seems to be that, apart from the factors listed in these paragraphs, the authority should not put information about matters which were not involved in the revision in the notice. The exception is those matters that it sees fit to include under para 6, to which para 8 is expressly subject. Para 6 is sufficiently wide, however, to completely negate para 8.

PART 2
Awards where income support [², an income-based jobseeker's allowance, an income-related employment and support allowance] [¹, an extended payment or an extended payment (qualifying contributory benefits)] is payable

9. Where a person on income support [², an income-based jobseeker's allowance or an income-related employment and support allowance] is awarded housing benefit [¹ or a claimant is entitled to an extended payment in accordance with regulation 72 or an extended payment (qualifying contributory benefits) in accordance with regulation 73], the decision notice shall include a statement as to–
(a) his weekly eligible rent, if any; and
(b) the amount and an explanation of any deduction made under paragraph 6(2) or (3) of Schedule 1 (fuel deductions), if any, and that the deduction may be varied if he provides to the authority evidence on which it may estimate the actual or approximate amount of that service charge; and
(c) the amount of and the category of non-dependant deductions made under regulation 74, if any; and
(d) the normal weekly amount of rent allowance, or rent rebate as the case may be, to which he is entitled; and
(e) in the case of a rent allowance or a rent rebate paid as if it were a rent allowance, the day of payment, and the period in respect of which payment of that allowance is to be made; and
(f) the first day of entitlement to an allowance or rebate; and
(g) his duty to notify any change of circumstances which might affect his entitlement to, or the amount of, housing benefit and (without prejudice to the extent of the duty owed under regulation 88 (duty to notify changes of circumstances)) the kind of change of circumstances which is to be notified, either upon the notice or by reference to some other document available to him on application and without charge.

Amendments
1. Amended by reg 4(5) of SI 2008 No 959 as from 6.10.08.
2. Amended by reg 27(a) of SI 2008 No 1082 as from 27.10.08.

Analysis

Where IS, income-based JSA or income-related ESA is claimed, much of the authority's decision-making is simplified because it has no need to consider the question of the claimant's resources. However, the relevant authority is still responsible for taking all decisions on the HB claim (except those expressly reserved to someone else under these regulations or the primary legislation) and, by virtue of reg 90 and the D&A Regs, for issuing notices of those decisions.

The requirements of Part 2 only apply to initial decisions following a claim: see para 7. Moreover, they only apply to notices sent when the claimant is on IS, income-based JSA, income-related ESA and *successfully* claims HB or where the claimant is entitled to extended payments of HB under either reg 72 or reg 73. If HB is refused, see Part 6. Paras 2, 3 and 6 of Part 1 of this Schedule also apply. Note that Part 2 does not apply in the albeit limited cases where the claimant is on UC. It is not known if this is an omission or the intention.

The following sub-paras specify the necessary information.

(a) The weekly eligible rent: see Part 3 HB Regs.

(b) The amount of any deductions made under Sch 1 para 6 in respect of fuel charges and the fact that the deductions may be varied if material is provided to allow the authority to estimate the service charge.

(c) The amount and type of non-dependant deductions under reg 74. See reg 3 for who is a non-dependant.

(d) The weekly amount of rent allowance or rent rebate: see Part 8 HB regs.

(e) In the case of rent allowance, or a rent rebate that is paid to the claimant as if it were, the day of payment and period in respect of which payment is made: see Part 12 HB Regs.

(f) The first day of entitlement: see reg 76.

(g) Notification of the duty to notify changes of circumstances: see reg 88. The authority is obliged to give examples of the kinds of changes that must be notified. It would appear that it is also obliged to make it clear that the obligation under reg 88 is a general one and that the examples are just that. A failure to make such a statement could well constitute an "official error" for the purposes of overpayment recoverability: see reg 100. It may also affect the question of whether the claimant could reasonably be expected to know that s/he was being overpaid.

PART 3

Awards where no income support [¹, an income-based jobseeker's allowance or an income-related employment and support allowance] is payable

10. Where a person is not on income support [¹, an income-based jobseeker's allowance or on an income-related employment and support allowance] but is awarded housing benefit, the decision notice shall include a statement as to–

(a) the matters set out in paragraph 9; and

(b) his applicable amount and how it is calculated; and

(c) his weekly earnings; and

(d) his weekly income other than earnings.

Amendment

1. Amended by reg 27(b) of SI 2008 No 1082 as from 27.10.08.

Analysis

The requirements of Part 3 only apply to initial decisions following a claim: see para 7. In addition to the information set out in para 9, additional information must be given where the claimant is awarded HB but is not on IS, income-based JSA or income-related ESA (see reg 2 for the definitions), since the authority is required to carry out its own assessment of the claimant's resources. Note that as Part 2 has not been amended to apply to a claimant on UC, Part 3 would appear to apply to such claimants.

The following information is required, in addition to the matters in paras 2, 3, 6 and 9.

(1) The applicable amount and "how it is calculated": sub-para (a). This means that the applicable amount itself must be stated, but a full breakdown should also be given of the personal allowances, premiums and components to which the claimant is entitled.

(2) The claimant's weekly earnings: see regs 29, 30, 35 and 37.

(3) The claimant's weekly income other than earnings: see regs 31 and 40.

It is curious that there is no requirement to state the amount of the capital that the claimant has. If there is capital between the lower limit and £16,000 and tariff income is calculated, without showing the source of the income, the claimant may well be left mystified.

PART 4

Awards where direct payments made to landlords

11. Where a decision has been made under regulation 95 or 96 (circumstances in which payment is to be made, or may be made, direct to a landlord), the decision notice shall include a statement–

(a)   as to the amount of housing benefit which is to be paid direct to the landlord and the date from which it is to be paid; and

(b)   informing the landlord of the duty imposed upon him to notify the local authority of–

    (i)   any change in circumstances which might affect the claimant's entitlement to housing benefit, or the amount of housing benefit payable in his case; and

    (ii)   the kind of change of circumstances which is to be notified;

(c)   informing both landlords and claimants that where a payment of housing benefit is recoverable from a landlord and the recovery is made from housing benefit payable to the landlord to discharge (in whole or in part) an obligation owed to him by a claimant, then, in a case where that claimant is not the person on whose behalf the recoverable amount was paid, that obligation shall nonetheless be taken to be discharged by the amount so recovered,

and the notice shall be sent both to the claimant and to the landlord.

Analysis

The requirements of Part 4 apply on the initial decision following a claim and on subsequent decisions – eg, following a revision or a supersession. The requirements as to content were substantially increased following the changes made by the Social Security Administration (Fraud) Act 1997 and the secondary legislation made thereunder.

"Landlord" in this paragraph has the same meaning as in reg 95: see para 12. The notice must be sent to both the landlord and the claimant and must contain the following information, in addition to the matters in paras 2, 3 and 6.

(1)   The amount of HB to be paid direct and the date from which it is to be paid: para 11(a).

(2)   A notification of the landlord's duty to notify changes of circumstances and the kind of changes that are to be notified: para 11(b). See the Analysis to para 9(g) above for commentary on this provision.

(3)   A warning to both landlord and tenant A that if payments in respect of tenant A's HB are withheld to recover an overpayment made to tenant B and recovered from the landlord, then tenant A's obligation is taken to be discharged: para 11(c). This is a consequence of SSAA s75(6). Note also the obligation in reg 107(3) when there is a decision that an overpayment is recoverable from the landlord.

Note that as a decision under regs 95 or 96 attracts a right of appeal (see para 1 Sch to the D&A Regs on p980), notice of this right and the right to a written statement of reasons for the decision where not already provided) are also required under reg 10 D&A Regs.

---

12.   In this Schedule, "landlord" has the same meaning as in regulation 95.

PART 5
Notice where income of non-dependant is treated as claimant's

13.   Where an authority makes a decision under regulation 26 (circumstances in which income and capital of a non-dependant is to be treated as claimant's) the decision notice shall contain a statement as to–

(a)   the fact that a decision has been made by reference to the income and capital of the claimant's non-dependant; and

(b)   the relevant authority's reasons for making that decision.

Analysis

The requirements of Part 5 apply on the initial decision following a claim and on subsequent decisions – eg, following a revision or a supersession. Reg 26(1) permits an authority to treat a claimant as having her/his non-dependant's income and capital where it appears that they have entered into an arrangement to take advantage of the HB scheme. See the Analysis to reg 26 on p421.

Where such a decision is made, in addition to the matters in paras 2, 3 and 6, the decision notice must state the fact that reg 26(1) has been utilised and the reasons for making that decision, an unhelpfully vague phrase. It is suggested that authorities should give the following information.

(1)   The fact that it appears that the claimant and the non-dependant (who should be identified) have entered into an arrangement falling within reg 26 and a summary of the reasons why that view is taken. See the Analysis to reg 9(1)(l) on p293 for the meaning of "take advantage" in this context.

(2)   The assessment made by the authority of the income and capital of both the claimant and the non-dependant and details of the calculation made under the non-dependant's resources (which is probably required anyway by virtue of para 10).

It would appear that since a non-dependant is not a "person affected" within the meaning of reg 2(1), s/he is not entitled to receive notification of the decision or to challenge it.

PART 6
Notice where no award is made

14.   Where a person is not awarded housing benefit–

(a) either on grounds of income or because the amount of any housing benefit is less than the minimum housing benefit prescribed by regulation 75, the decision notice shall include a statement as to–
  (i) the matters set out in paragraphs 9(a) to (c), and in a case where the amount of entitlement is less than the minimum amount of housing benefit prescribed, paragraph 9(d) also; and
  (ii) the matters set out in paragraphs 10(b) to (d) where the person is not on income support [¹, an income-based jobseeker's allowance or an income-related employment and support allowance]; and
  (iii) where the amount of entitlement is less than the minimum amount of housing benefit prescribed, that fact and that such entitlement is not payable;
(b) for any reason other than one mentioned in sub-paragraph (a), the decision notice shall include a statement as to the reason why no award has been made.

Amendment
1. Amended reg 27(c) of SI 2008 No 1082 as from 27.10.08.

Analysis
The requirements of Part 6 only apply to initial decisions following a claim: see para 7. Para 14 applies where HB is refused. Two categories of notices are set out. If the refusal is on income grounds, the information prescribed by paras 9(a) to (c) must be given, and where the claimant is not on IS, income-based JSA or income-related ESA (defined in reg 2), the information in paras 10(b) to (d). If HB is refused because the entitlement is less than the minimum HB payable under reg 75, the fact must be stated and the information in para 9(d) given.

If refusal is not for a reason specified in para (a), only the reason for the refusal need be given. It would be good practice for more information to be given under para 6, particularly where there has been a finding of no liability or of a contrived tenancy.

Paras 2, 3 and 6 apply to notices under para 14.

PART 7
Notice where recoverable overpayment

15.–(1) Where the appropriate authority makes a decision that there is a recoverable overpayment within the meaning of regulation 100 (recoverable overpayments), the decision notice shall include a statement as to–
(a) the fact that there is a recoverable overpayment; and
(b) the reason why there is a recoverable overpayment; and
(c) the amount of the recoverable overpayment; and
(d) how the amount of the recoverable overpayment was calculated; and
(e) the benefit weeks to which the recoverable overpayment relates; and
(f) where recovery of the recoverable overpayment is to be made by deduction from a rent allowance or rebate, as the case may be, that fact and the amount of the deduction.
(2) In a case where it is–
(a) determined that there is a recoverable overpayment;
(b) determined that that overpayment is recoverable from a landlord; and
(c) decided that recovery of that overpayment is to be made by deduction from a rent allowance paid to that landlord to discharge (in whole or in part) an obligation owed to him by a claimant ("claimant A"), not being the claimant on whose behalf the recoverable amount was paid,
the decision notice sent to that landlord shall identify both–
  (i) the person on whose behalf the recoverable amount was paid to that landlord; and
  (ii) claimant A.

Analysis
Paras 2, 3 and 6 also apply to notices under para 15. The requirements of the notices were expanded following changes made by the Social Security Administration (Fraud) Act 1997 and the secondary legislation made thereunder. The following content is required.
(1) The fact that there is a recoverable overpayment and the reason why there is one: sub-paras (1)(a) and (b). It is suggested that authorities should go systematically through each of the issues in reg 100 to determine the answer to this question. In *R v Thanet DC ex p Warren Court Hotels Ltd* (2000) 33 HLR 339, CA, the notifications of overpayment contained a statement that there had been a change in the claimant's circumstances, as a result of which an overpayment had occurred because the local authority was unaware of the change in circumstances. The council argued that for the purposes of Sch 6 para 14(1)(b) HB Regs 1987 (now Sch 9 para 15(1)(b) HB Regs), "the reason why there is a recoverable overpayment", it was sufficient to state that there had been a change in circumstances. Jackson J disagreed, holding that it was necessary to spell out what the change of circumstances was (see the Analyses to s75(2) SSAA on p39 and reg 90 on p565 for the effect of this defect and the other issues in the case).
"The phrase 'change of circumstances' in that letter could cover a multitude of events. To take one example, it could mean that Mr H was in paid employment from 12 October onwards. To take another

example, it could mean that although Mr H was unemployed, there was a three-week break in his entitlement to housing benefit." (para 36).

The requirement to identify how an overpayment has occurred does not require detailed calculations of the revised amounts of benefit: *CH 3776/2001* para 10. All that is required is the old and new figures and the difference.

(2)   The amount of the overpayment and how it is calculated: sub-paras (1)(c) and (d). Enough detail should be given to enable the claimant to follow the calculation through. That should include a complete breakdown of how much benefit is recoverable in each week it was paid, and details of a diminishing capital calculation if necessary. See regs 103 and 104 on p601 and p602.

(3)   The benefit weeks to which the overpayment relates: sub-para (1)(e). "Benefit week" is defined in reg 2(1).

(4)   Where recovery is to be made by deduction from ongoing payments of rent allowance or rent rebate, that fact and the amount of the deduction: sub-para (1)(f).

(5)   Where the overpayment is recoverable from the landlord and recovery is to be made from claimant A's benefit where claimant B was overpaid, the landlord must be told the identities of claimants A and B: sub-para (2). Under SSAA s75(6), claimant A's obligation is deemed to be discharged by the amount of the deduction.

In *Godwin v Rossendale BC* [2002] *The Times* 24 May, [2002] EWCA Civ 726, para 51, the court stated that a notice under Sch 6 para 14(2) HB Regs 1987 (now Sch 9 para 15(2) HB Regs) should be given before recovery is made. However, the court rejected the suggestion that a failure to do so rendered the recovery unlawful, since there was no prejudice to the landlord by the omission.

Note the additional information that has to be provided under reg 107(3) in certain cases.

[¹ SCHEDULE 10

REGULATION 122

Former pathfinder authorities

Amendment

1.   Substituted by reg 20(2) of SI 2007 No 2868 as from 7.4.08.

General Note

Until 7 April 2008, Sch 10 contained the modified rules for determining the maximum rent (standard local rate), and hence the maximum HB, for tenants in the deregulated private sector in Pathfinder areas – the pilot "local housing allowance" scheme for rent restriction. From that date, the "local housing allowance" scheme was introduced nationwide (see Part 3). As the national scheme is less generous in a number of respects than the pilot scheme, Sch 10 contains modifications which provided transitional protection for claimants in former Pathfinder areas.

Para 6 inserts a number of regulations. A claimant could have transitional protection if, before 7 April 2008:

(1)   Her/his HB was calculated on the basis of the maximum rent (standard local rate): regs 12E and 12I.

(2)   A rent restriction was delayed because of the death of a member of the family or a relative: regs 12F and 12J.

(3)   A rent restriction was delayed for 13 weeks because the claimant or a member of the family or a relative could meet the costs of the dwelling: reg 12G.

Where a claimant has transitional protection and a member of the family or a relative of the claimant or her/his partner who lives in the same accommodation without a separate right to do so died before 7 April 2009, a consequent rent restriction could be delayed: regs 12H and 12K.

PART 1
Former pathfinder authorities

Argyll and Bute
Blackpool
Brighton and Hove
Conwy
Coventry
East Riding of Yorkshire
Edinburgh
Guildford
Leeds
Lewisham
North East Lincolnshire
Norwich
Pembrokeshire
St Helens

Salford
South Norfolk
Teignbridge
Wandsworth

PART 2
Application of the Regulations
1.   These Regulations shall apply to former pathfinder authorities subject to the provisions of this Part of this Schedule.

Amendment of regulation 2
2.   In regulation 2(1) (interpretation)–
(a)   in the definition of "eligible rent", in sub-paragraph (a) for "or 12D (eligible rent and maximum rent (LHA))" substitute ", 12D (eligible rent and maximum rent (LHA)) or any of regulations 12E to 12K (transitional protection for pathfinder cases)";
(b)   after the definition of "maximum rent (LHA)" insert–

""maximum rent (standard local rent)" means a maximum rent (standard local rate) determined in accordance with regulation 13A;".

Amendment of regulation 11
3.   In regulation 11(1) (eligible housing costs)–
(a)   in paragraph (c) omit "or"; and
(b)   after sub-paragraph (d) insert–

"; or
(e)   any of regulations 12E to 12K (transitional protection for pathfinder cases) and regulations 13C (when a maximum rent (LHA) is to be determined) and 13D (determination of a maximum rent (LHA)),".

Amendment of regulation 12B
[¹**4.**   In regulation 12B(1) (eligible rent) after sub-paragraph (c) insert–

"(ca)   any of regulations 12E to 12K (transitional protection for pathfinder cases);".]

Amendment
1.   Substituted by reg 5(9) of SI 2012 No 3040 as from 1.4.13.

Amendment of regulation 12D
5.   In regulation 12D (eligible rent and maximum rent (LHA)) before paragraph (1) insert–

"(A1)   This regulation shall not apply where any of regulations 12E to 12K (transitional protection for pathfinder cases) apply."

Insertion of regulations 12E to 12K
6.   After regulation 12D (eligible rent and maximum rent (LHA)) insert–

"Basic transitional protection for pathfinder cases
12E.–(1)   This regulation applies where–
(a)   reference was made to a maximum rent (standard local rate) in determining the amount of the eligible rent which applied immediately before 7th April 2008;
(b)   on 7th April 2008 the local authority determines a maximum rent (LHA) by virtue of regulation 13C(4A)(a); and
(c)   regulations 12F (cases where the claimant enjoyed protection on death before 7th April 2008) and 12G (cases where the claimant enjoyed 13 week protection before 7th April 2008) do not apply.
(2)   Where this regulation applies, the claimant's eligible rent is–
(a)   the maximum rent (LHA) where that is higher than the eligible rent which applied immediately before 7th April 2008; or
(b)   the amount of the eligible rent which applied immediately before 7th April 2008.
(3)   Where the eligible rent is the amount of the eligible rent which applied immediately before 7th April 2008, it will continue to apply until, on or after 7th April 2008, the first of the following events occurs–
(a)   the relevant authority is required to determine a maximum rent (LHA) by virtue of regulation 13C(2)(d)(i) (change of category of dwelling) because the claimant has become entitled to a larger category of dwelling and the maximum rent (LHA) is higher than that eligible rent;

(b) the relevant authority is required to determine a maximum rent (LHA) by virtue of regulation 13C(2)(d)(i) (change of category of dwelling) because the claimant has become entitled to a smaller category of dwelling;

(c) the relevant authority is required to determine an eligible rent following a change of dwelling;

(d) the relevant authority is required to determine an eligible rent in accordance with regulation 12H (cases where a death occurs in the first year on or after 7th April 2008) following the death of a linked person;

(e) the relevant authority determines a maximum rent (LHA) on 7th April 2009 by virtue of regulation 13C(4A)(b).

(4) Where the eligible rent is the maximum rent (LHA), it shall be treated as if it had been determined in accordance with regulation 12D(2)(a) (eligible rent is maximum rent (LHA)) and shall apply according to the provisions of regulation 12D (eligible rent and maximum rent (LHA)).

Cases where the claimant enjoyed protection on death before 7th April 2008
12F.–(1) This regulation applies where–

(a) immediately before 7th April 2008 the claimant enjoyed protection on death in accordance with regulation 12A(4)(a)(ii) (pathfinder protection on death based on reckonable rent); and

(b) on 7th April 2008 the local authority determines a maximum rent (LHA) by virtue of regulation 13C(4A)(a).

(2) Where this regulation applies, the claimant's eligible rent is–

(a) the maximum rent (LHA) where that is higher than the eligible rent which applied immediately before 7th April 2008; or

(b) the amount of the eligible rent which applied immediately before 7th April 2008.

(3) Where the eligible rent is the amount of the eligible rent which applied immediately before 7th April 2008, it will continue to apply until, on or after 7th April 2008, the first of the following events occurs–

(a) the end of 12 months after the death to which the protection relates;

(b) the relevant authority is required to determine a maximum rent (LHA) by virtue of regulation 13C(2)(d)(i) (change of category of dwelling) and it is higher than that eligible rent;

(c) the relevant authority is required to determine an eligible rent following a change of dwelling;

(d) the relevant authority is required to determine an eligible rent in accordance with regulation 12H (cases where a death occurs in the first year on or after 7th April 2008) following the death of a linked person;

(4) Where the eligible rent ceases to apply because of paragraph (3)(a), the eligible rent will be the maximum rent (LHA) which would have applied but for the transitional protection.

(5) Where the eligible rent is the maximum rent (LHA), it shall be treated as if it had been determined in accordance with regulation 12D(2)(a) (eligible rent is maximum rent (LHA)) and shall apply according to the provisions of regulation 12D (eligible rent and maximum rent (LHA)).

Cases where the claimant enjoyed 13 week protection before 7th April 2008
12G.–(1) This regulation applies where–

(a) immediately before 7th April 2008 the claimant enjoyed 13 week protection in accordance with regulation 12A(6)(a) (local housing allowance pathfinder 13 week protection); and

(b) on 7th April 2008 the local authority determines a maximum rent (LHA) by virtue of regulation 13C(4A)(a).

(2) Where this regulation applies, the claimant's eligible rent is–

(a) the maximum rent (LHA) where that is higher than the eligible rent which applied immediately before 7th April 2008; or

(b) the amount of the eligible rent which applied immediately before 7th April 2008.

(3) Where the eligible rent is the amount of the eligible rent which applied immediately before 7th April 2008, it will continue to apply until, on or after 7th April 2008, the first of the following events occurs–

(a) the end of the day when the protection expires, namely 13 weeks after the date of the claim;

(b) the relevant authority is required to determine a maximum rent (LHA) by virtue of regulation 13C(2)(d)(i) (change of category of dwelling) and it is higher than that eligible rent;

(c) the relevant authority is required to determine an eligible rent following a change of dwelling;

(d) the relevant authority is required to determine an eligible rent in accordance with regulation 12H (cases where a death occurs in the first year on or after 7th April 2008) following the death of a linked person.

(4) Where the eligible rent ceases to apply because of paragraph (3)(a), the eligible rent will be the maximum rent (LHA) which would have applied but for the transitional protection.

(5) Where the eligible rent is the maximum rent (LHA), it shall be treated as if it had been determined in accordance with regulation 12D(2)(a) (eligible rent is maximum rent (LHA)) and shall apply according to the provisions of regulation 12D (eligible rent and maximum rent (LHA)).

Cases where a death occurs in the first year on or after 7th April 2008
12H.–(1) This regulation applies where–

(a) the eligible rent is that specified in regulation 12E(2)(b) (basic transitional protection for pathfinder cases), 12F(2)(b) (transitional protection where the claimant enjoyed protection on death before 7th

April 2008), 12G(2)(b) (transitional protection where the claimant enjoyed 13 week protection before 7th April 2008) or paragraph (2)(b) of this regulation;
(b) a linked person dies on or after 7th April 2008 and before 7th April 2009;
(c) the claimant occupies the same dwelling as the linked person at the date of death; and
(d) the relevant authority determines a maximum rent (LHA) by virtue of regulation 13C(2)(d)(i) or (ii) (change of category of dwelling or death of a linked person).
(2) Where this regulation applies, the claimant's eligible rent is–
(a) the maximum rent (LHA) where that is higher than the eligible rent which applied immediately before the date of the death; or
(b) the amount of the eligible rent which applied immediately before the date of the death.
(3) Where the eligible rent is the amount of the eligible rent which applied immediately before the date of death, it will continue to apply until, on or after the date of the death, the first of the following events occurs–
(a) the end of 12 months from the date of the death;
(b) the relevant authority is required to determine a maximum rent (LHA) by virtue of regulation 13C(2)(d)(i) (change of category of dwelling) and it is higher than that eligible rent;
(c) the relevant authority is required to determine an eligible rent following a change of dwelling;
(d) the relevant authority is required to determine an eligible rent in accordance with this regulation following the death of another linked person.
(4) Where the eligible rent is the maximum rent (LHA), it shall be treated as if it had been determined in accordance with regulation 12D(2)(a) (eligible rent is maximum rent (LHA)) and shall apply according to the provisions of regulation 12D (eligible rent and maximum rent (LHA)).
(5) For the purposes of paragraph (1)(c), a claimant shall be treated as occupying the dwelling if regulation 7(13) is satisfied and for that purpose paragraph (13) of regulation 7 shall have effect as if sub-paragraph (b) were omitted.

Basic transitional protection in the second year and subsequent years after 7th April 2008
12I.–(1) This regulation applies where–
(a) immediately before 7th April 2009 the claimant was enjoying basic transitional protection under regulation 12E; and
(b) the local authority determines a maximum rent (LHA) by virtue of 13C(4A)(b) on 7th April 2009.
(2) Where this regulation applies, the claimant's eligible rent is–
(a) the maximum rent (LHA) where it is higher than the eligible rent applying immediately before 7th April 2008; or
(b) in any other case, the lower of–
(i) the amount of the eligible rent applying immediately before 7th April 2008; or
(ii) the amount of the cap rent by reference to which the maximum rent (LHA) was determined [¹].
(3) Where the claimant's eligible rent is determined in accordance with paragraph (2)(b), it continues to apply until, on or after 7th April 2009, the first of the following events occurs–
(a) the relevant authority is required to determine a maximum rent (LHA) by virtue of regulation 13C(2)(d)(i) (change of category of dwelling) because the claimant has become entitled to a larger category of dwelling or 13C(3) (anniversary of the LHA date) and the maximum rent (LHA) is higher than that eligible rent;
(b) the relevant authority is required to determine a maximum rent (LHA) by virtue of regulation 13C(2)(d)(i) (change of category of dwelling) because the claimant has become entitled to a smaller category of dwelling;
(c) the relevant authority is required to determine an eligible rent following a change of dwelling;
(d) the relevant authority is required to determine an eligible rent in accordance with regulation 12K (protection on death in the second and subsequent years after 7th April 2008) following the death of a linked person.
(4) Where the eligible rent is the maximum rent (LHA), it shall be treated as if it had been determined in accordance with regulation 12D(2)(a) (eligible rent is maximum rent (LHA)) and shall apply according to the provisions of regulation 12D (eligible rent and maximum rent (LHA)).

Amendment
1.   Amended by reg 2(11) of SI 2010 No 2835 as from 1.4.11.

Transitional protection in the second year after 7th April 2008 where the claimant is already enjoying protection on death
12J.–(1) This regulation applies where–
(a) immediately before 7th April 2009 the claimant was enjoying transitional protection on death under regulation 12H (cases where a death occurs in the first year on or after 7th April 2008); and
(b) the local authority determines a maximum rent (LHA) by virtue of regulation 13C(4A)(b) on 7th April 2009.
(2) Where this regulation applies, the claimant's eligible rent is–
(a) the maximum rent (LHA) where that is higher than the eligible rent which applied immediately before the date of the death to which the protection relates; or

(b)   the amount of the eligible rent which applied immediately before the date of the death.

(3)   Where the eligible rent which applies is the one that applied immediately before the date of the death, it continues to apply until, on or after the date of the death, the first of the following events occurs–

(a)   the end of 12 months after the date of the death to which the protection relates;

(b)   the relevant authority is required to determine a maximum rent (LHA) by virtue of regulation 13C(2)(d)(i) (change of category of dwelling) and it is higher than that eligible rent;

(c)   the relevant authority is required to determine an eligible rent following a change of dwelling;

(d)   the relevant authority is required to determine an eligible rent in accordance with regulation 12K (protection on death in the second and subsequent years after 7th April 2008) following the death of a linked person.

(4)   Where the eligible rent ceases to apply because of paragraph (3)(a) the eligible rent is the one that would have applied if the relevant authority not determined an eligible rent in accordance with regulation 12H(2)(b) (transitional protection where a death occurs in the first year on or after 7th April 2008).

(5)   Where the eligible rent is the maximum rent (LHA), it shall be treated as if it had been determined in accordance with regulation 12D(2)(a) (eligible rent is maximum rent (LHA)) and shall apply according to the provisions of regulation 12D (eligible rent and maximum rent (LHA)).

Protection on death in the second and subsequent years after 7th April 2008

12K.–(1)   This regulation applies where–

(a)   the claimant's eligible rent is that specified in regulation 12I(2)(b) (basic transitional protection in the second and subsequent years after 7th April 2008), 12J(2)(b) (transitional protection in the second year after 7th April 2008 where the claimant is already enjoying protection on death) or paragraph (2)(b) of this regulation;

(b)   a linked person dies on or after 7th April 2009;

(c)   the claimant occupies the same dwelling as the linked person at the date of death; and

(d)   the relevant authority determines a maximum rent (LHA) by virtue of regulation 13C(2)(d)(i) or (ii) (change of category of dwelling or death of a linked person).

(2)   Where this regulation applies, the claimant's eligible rent is–

(a)   the maximum rent (LHA) where that is higher than the eligible rent which applied immediately before the date of the death; or

(b)   the amount of eligible rent which applied immediately before the death.

(3)   Where the eligible rent which applies is the one that applied immediately before the date of the death, it will continue to apply until, on or after the date of the death, the first of the following events occurs–

(a)   the end of 12 months from the date of the death;

(b)   the relevant authority is required to determine a maximum rent (LHA) by virtue of regulation 13C(2)(d)(i) or (3) (change of category of dwelling or anniversary of the LHA date) and it is higher than that eligible rent;

(c)   the relevant authority is required to determine an eligible rent following a change of dwelling;

(d)   the relevant authority is required to determine an eligible rent in accordance with this regulation following the death of another linked person.

(4)   Where the eligible rent ceases to apply because of paragraph (3)(a) the eligible rent is the one that would have applied but had the relevant authority not determined an eligible rent in accordance with this regulation.

(5)   Where the eligible rent is the maximum rent (LHA), it shall be treated as if it had been determined in accordance with regulation 12D(2)(a) (eligible rent is maximum rent (LHA)) and shall apply according to the provisions of regulation 12D (eligible rent and maximum rent (LHA)).

(6)   For the purposes of paragraph (1)(c), a claimant shall be treated as occupying the dwelling if regulation 7(13) is satisfied and for that purpose paragraph (13) of regulation 7 shall have effect as if sub-paragraph (b) were omitted.".

Amendment of regulation 13C

7.   In regulation 13C (when a maximum rent (LHA) is to be determined)–

(a)   in paragraph (1) for "paragraphs (2) or (3)" substitute "paragraphs (2), (3) or (4A)";

(b)   in paragraph (3) after "LHA date" insert "except where paragraph (4A)(b) applies";

(c)   after paragraph (4) insert–

"(4A)   This paragraph applies where it is–

(a)   7th April 2008 and reference was made to a maximum rent (standard local rate) in determining the amount of the eligible rent which applied immediately before 7th April 2008; or

(b)   7th April 2009 and the eligible rent which applies on that date was determined in accordance with regulation 12E(2)(b) (basic transitional protection for pathfinder cases) or 12H(2)(b) (transitional protection where a death occurs in the first year on or after 7th April 2008).".

Amendment of regulation 13D

8.   In regulation 13D(12) (determination of a maximum rent (LHA)) in the definition of "relevant date" after sub-paragraph (c) insert–

"(d)   7th April 2008;

(e)   7th April 2009."]

[¹SCHEDULE 11
Electronic Communication

Amendment
1.   Inserted by art 2(5) of SI 2006 No 2968 as from 20.12.06.

General Note to Schedule 11
Reg 83A allows claims for HB to be made by electronic communication. The authorisation requirements and conditions for such claims are found in Sch 11. See the General Note to reg 83A on p554.

PART 1
Introduction

Interpretation
1.   In this Schedule "official computer system" means a computer system maintained by or on behalf of the relevant authority or of the Secretary of State for sending, receiving, processing or storing of any claim, certificate, notice, information or evidence.

PART 2
Electronic Communication – General Provisions

Conditions for the use of electronic communication
2.–(1)   The relevant authority may use an electronic communication in connection with claims for, and awards of, benefit under these Regulations.

(2)   A person other than the relevant authority may use an electronic communication in connection with the matters referred to in sub-paragraph (1) if the conditions specified in sub-paragraphs (3) to (6) are satisfied.

(3)   The first condition is that the person is for the time being permitted to use an electronic communication by an authorisation given by means of a direction of the Chief Executive of the relevant authority.

(4)   The second condition is that the person uses an approved method of–

(a)   authenticating the identity of the sender of the communication;

(b)   electronic communication;

(c)   authenticating any claim or notice delivered by means of an electronic communication; and

(d)   subject to sub-paragraph (7), submitting to the relevant authority any claim, certificate, notice, information or evidence.

(5)   The third condition is that any claim, certificate, notice, information or evidence sent by means of an electronic communication is in a form approved for the purposes of this Schedule.

(6)   The fourth condition is that the person maintains such records in written or electronic form as may be specified in a direction given by the Chief Executive of the relevant authority.

(7)   Where the person uses any method other than the method approved of submitting any claim, certificate, notice, information or evidence, that claim, certificate, notice, information or evidence shall be treated as not having been submitted.

(8)   In this paragraph "approved" means approved by means of a direction given by the Chief Executive of the relevant authority for the purposes of this Schedule.

Use of intermediaries
3.   The relevant authority may use intermediaries in connection with–

(a)   the delivery of any claim, certificate, notice, information or evidence by means of an electronic communication; and

(b)   the authentication or security of anything transmitted by such means,

and may require other persons to use intermediaries in connection with those matters.

PART 3
Electronic Communication – Evidential Provisions

Effect of delivering information by means of electronic communication
4.–(1)   Any claim, certificate, notice, information or evidence which is delivered by means of an electronic communication shall be treated as having been delivered in the manner or form required by any provision of these Regulations, on the day the conditions imposed–

(a)   by this Schedule; and

(b)   by or under an enactment,

are satisfied.

(2)   The relevant authority may, by a direction, determine that any claim, certificate, notice, information or evidence is to be treated as delivered on a different day (whether earlier or later) from the day provided for in sub-paragraph (1).

(3)   Information shall not be taken to have been delivered to an official computer system by means of an electronic communication unless it is accepted by the system to which it is delivered.

Proof of identity of sender or recipient of information

5.   If it is necessary to prove, for the purpose of any legal proceedings, the identity of–

(a)   the sender of any claim, certificate, notice, information or evidence delivered by means of an electronic communication to an official computer system; or

(b)   the recipient of any such claim, certificate, notice, information or evidence delivered by means of an electronic communication from an official computer system,

the sender or recipient, as the case may be, shall be presumed to be the person whose name is recorded as such on that official computer system.

Proof of delivery of information

6.–(1)   If it is necessary to prove, for the purpose of any legal proceedings, that the use of an electronic communication has resulted in the delivery of any claim, certificate, notice, information or evidence this shall be presumed to have been the case where–

(a)   any such claim, certificate, notice, information or evidence has been delivered to the relevant authority, if the delivery of that claim, certificate, notice, information or evidence has been recorded on an official computer system; or

(b)   any such claim, certificate, notice, information or evidence has been delivered by the relevant authority, if the delivery of that certificate, notice, information or evidence has been recorded on an official computer system.

(2)   If it is necessary to prove, for the purpose of any legal proceedings, that the use of an electronic communication has resulted in the delivery of any such claim, certificate, notice, information or evidence, this shall be presumed not to be the case, if that claim, certificate, notice, information or evidence delivered to the relevant authority has not been recorded on an official computer system.

(3)   If it is necessary to prove, for the purpose of any legal proceedings, when any such claim, certificate, notice, information or evidence sent by means of an electronic communication has been received, the time and date of receipt shall be presumed to be that recorded on an official computer system.

Proof of content of information

7.   If it is necessary to prove, for the purpose of any legal proceedings, the content of any claim, certificate, notice, information or evidence sent by means of an electronic communication, the content shall be presumed to be that recorded on an official computer system.]

The Housing Benefit (Persons who have attained the qualifying age for state pension credit) Regulations 2006

(SI 2006 No.214)

PART 1
GENERAL

1.   Citation and commencement
2.   Interpretation
3.   Definition of non-dependant
4.   Cases in which section 1(1A) of the Administration Act is disapplied
5.   Persons who have attained the qualifying age for state pension credit
6.   Remunerative work

PART 2
PROVISIONS AFFECTING ENTITLEMENT TO HOUSING BENEFIT

7.   Circumstances in which a person is or is not to be treated as occupying a dwelling as his home
8.   Circumstances in which a person is to be treated as liable to make payments in respect of a dwelling
9.   Circumstances in which a person is to be treated as not liable to make payments in respect of a dwelling
10.   Persons from abroad
10A.   Entitlement of a refugee to Housing Benefit

PART 3
PAYMENTS IN RESPECT OF A DWELLING

11.   Eligible housing costs
12.   Rent
12B.   Eligible rent
12C.   Eligible rent and maximum rent
12D.   Eligible rent and maximum rent (LHA)
12L.   Transitional prorection – larger properties
12M.   Transitional protection – reduction in LHA
13.   Maximum rent
13ZA.   Protection on death and 13 week protection
13ZB.   Change in reckonable rent
13C.   When a maximum rent (LHA) is to be determined
13D.   Determination of a maximum rent (LHA)
13E.   Publication of local housing allowances
14.   Requirement to refer to rent officers
15.   Application to the rent officer for redeterminations
16.   Application for redeterrmination by a rent officer
17.   Substitute determinations or substitute redeterminations
18.   Application of provisions to substitute determinations or substitute redeterminations
18A.   Amended determinations

PART 4
MEMBERSHIP OF A FAMILY

19.   Persons of prescribed description
20.   Circumstances in which a person is to be treated as responsible or not responsible for another
21.   Circumstances in which a person is to be treated as being or not being a member of the household

PART 5
APPLICABLE AMOUNTS

22.   Applicable amounts

PART 6
ASSESSMENT OF INCOME AND CAPITAL
SECTION 1
General

23.   Calculation of income and capital of members of claimant's family and of a polygamous marriage
24.   Circumstances in which income of non-dependant is to be treated as claimant's

SECTION 2
Income

25.   Calculation of income and capital
26.   Claimant in receipt of guarantee credit
27.   Calculation of claimant's income and capital in savings credit only cases
28.   Calculation of income and capital where state pension credit is not payable
29.   Meaning of "income"
30.   Calculation of income on a weekly basis
31.   Treatment of child care charges
32.   Calculation of average weekly income from tax credits
33.   Calculation of weekly income
34.   Disregard of changes in tax, contributions etc

SECTION 3
Employed earners

35.   Earnings of employed earners
36.   Calculation of net earnings of employed earners

SECTION 4
Self-employed earners

37.   Calculation of earnings of self-employed earners
38.   Earnings of self-employed earners
39.   Calculation of net profit of self-employed earners
40.   Deduction of tax and contributions of self-employed earners

SECTION 5
Other income

41.   Notional income
42.   Income paid to third parties

SECTION 6
Capital

43.   Capital limit
44.   Calculation of capital
45.   Calculation of capital in the United Kingdom
46.   Calculation of capital outside the United Kingdom
47.   Notional capital
48.   Diminishing notional capital rule
49.   Capital jointly held

PART 7
Amount of benefit

50.   Maximum housing benefit
51.   Housing benefit tapers

52.   Amount payable during extended payment period when an extended payment is payable pursuant to regulation 72 or 73 of the Housing Benefit Regulations
53.   Extended payments (qualifying contributory benefits)
53A.   Duration of extended payment period (qualifying contributory benefits)
53B.   Amount of extended payment (qualifying contributory benefits)
53C.   Extended payments (qualifying contributory benefits) – movers
53D.   Relationship between extended payment (qualifying contributory benefits) and entitlement to housing benefit under the general conditions of entitlement
54.   Continuing payments where state pension credit claimed
55.   Non-dependant deductions
56.   Minimum housing benefit

PART 8
Calculation of weekly amounts and changes of circumstances
57.   Date on which entitlement is to commence
58.   Date on which housing benefit is to end where entitlement to severe disablement allowance or incapacity benefit ceases
59.   Date on which change of circumstances is to take effect
60.   Change of circumstances where state pension credit payable
61.   Calculation of weekly amounts
62.   Rent free periods

PART 9
Claims
63.   Who may claim
64.   Time and manner in which claims are to be made
64A.   Electronic claims for benefit
65.   Date of claim where claim sent or delivered to a gateway office
66.   Date of claim where claim sent or delivered to an office of a designated authority
67.   Evidence and information
68.   Amendment and withdrawal of claim
69.   Duty to notify changes of circumstances
69ZA.   Alternative means of notifying changes of circumstances
69A.   Notice of changes of circumstances given electronically

PART 10
Decisions on questions
70.   Decisions by a relevant authority
71.   Notification of decision

PART 11
Payments
72.   Time and manner of payment
72A.   Cases in which payments to a housing authority are to take the form of a rent allowance
73.   Frequency of payment of a rent allowance
74.   Payment on account of a rent allowance
75.   Payment to be made to a person entitled
76.   Circumstances in which payment is to be made to a landlord
77.   Circumstances in which payment may be made to a landlord
78.   Payment on death of the person entitled
79.   Offsetting

PART 12
Overpayments

80. Meaning of overpayment
81. Recoverable overpayments
82. Person from whom recovery may be sought
83. Method of recovery
84. Diminution of capital
85. Sums to be deducted in calculating recoverable overpayments
85A. Sums to be deducted in calculating overpayments where the claimant has changed dwelling
86. Recovery of overpayments from prescribed benefits
87. Prescribed benefits
87A. Recovery by deduction from earnings
88. Restrictions on recovery of rent and consequent notifications

PART 13
Information
SECTION 1
Claims and information

89. Interpretation
90. Collection of information
90A. Verifying information
91. Recording and holding information
92. Forwarding of information
93. Request for information

SECTION 2
Evidence and Information

94. Interpretation
95A. Information to be provided to rent officers
95. Evidence and information required by rent officers
96. Information to be supplied by an authority to another authority
97. Supply of information – extended payments (qualifying contributory benefits)
98. Requiring information from landlords and agents
99. Circumstances for requiring information
100. Relevant information
101. Manner of supply of information
102. Criminal offence
102A. Supply of benefit administration information between authorities

PART 14
Former Pathfinder authorities

103. Modifications in respect of former pathfinder authorities

SCHEDULES

A1. Treatment of claims for housing benefit by refugees
1. Ineligible service charges
2. Excluded Tenancies
3. Applicable amounts
4. Sums disregarded from claimant's earnings
5. Amounts to be disregarded in the calculation of income other than earnings
6. Capital to be disregarded
7. Extended payments (severe disablement allowance and incapacity benefit) of housing benefit
8. Matters to be included in decision notice
9. Former pathfinder authorities
10. Electronic communication

General Note to the HB(SPC) Regulations

These regulations, rather than the HB Regs, apply where the claimant has attained the qualifying age for pension credit (PC), as defined in reg 2. However, they do not apply in relation to any claimant who remains (or whose partner remains) on IS, income-based JSA or income-related ESA (or UC): reg 5 (see p733). It is vital to note that receipt of PC by an HB claimant is not a requirement for these regulations to apply to her/him.

Note that since 15 May 2019, where a claimant is a member of a "mixed-age couple" (ie, only one member of the couple is at least the qualifying age for PC), a new claim for, and entitlement to, HB is not generally allowed unless the claimant has been continuously entitled to PC or HB under the HB(SPC) Regs from before that date as part of the same mixed-age couple. For the rules for mixed-age couples on claims for, and termination of awards of, HB and the exceptions to the rules, see the Welfare Reform Act 2012 (Commencment No.31) Order 2019 SI No.37 (the No.31 Order) on p1898. Where a member of a mixed-age couple is excluded from entitlement to PC or HB and is also prevented from claiming UC because of the "SDP Gateway" in reg 4A of the UC(TP) Regs 2014 (see p1862) or because s/he is a frontier worker or by virtue of reg 4 of the UC(TP) Regs 2014 (see p1861), the member of the couple who has reached the qualifying age for PC is treated as not having attained that age for the purposes of reg 5 and thus the HB Regs, instead of the HB(SPC) Regs, apply to such a claimant. See Art 8 of the No.31 Order on p1902.

Many of the regulations are the same as, or similar to, the Housing Benefit Regulations 2006 (SI 2006 No.213), referred to in this book as "the HB Regs". Where a regulation is substantially the same as a corresponding regulation in the HB Regs, no commentary appears below and reference should be made to the comparison HB Regulation, for which see the Destinations table on pxxxi.

Note: there is no equivalent in the HB(SPC) Regs to the **social sector scheme for rent restriction**, sometimes referred to as the **"bedroom tax"** or the "removal of the spare room subsidy". Also, there is no **"benefit cap"** for those entitled to HB under the HB(SPC) Regs.

Welfare Reform Act 2012

HB is to be abolished by the Welfare Reform Act 2012 (see p4). For claimants of at least the qualifying age for PC, the government intends to replace HB with a housing credit within PC from October 2023. Until then, these claimants will continue to qualify for HB.

PART 1
General

Citation and commencement

1.–(1)　These Regulations may be cited as the Housing Benefit (Persons who have attained the qualifying age for state pension credit) Regulations 2006.

(2)　These Regulations are to be read, where appropriate, with the Consequential Provisions Regulations.

(3)　Except as provided in Schedule 4 to the Consequential Provisions Regulations, these Regulations shall come into force on 6th March 2006.

(4)　The regulations consolidated by these Regulations are revoked, in consequence of the consolidation, by the Consequential Provisions Regulations.

Interpretation

2.–(1)　In these Regulations–

"the Act" means the Social Security Contributions and Benefits Act 1992;

"the 1973 Act" means the Employment and Training Act 1973;

[² "the 2000 Act" means the Electronic Communications Act 2000;]

[⁴⁵ "the 2012 Act" means the Welfare Reform Act 2012;]

"Abbeyfield Home" means an establishment run by the Abbeyfield Society including all bodies corporate or incorporate which are affiliated to that Society;

"adoption leave" means a period of absence from work on ordinary or additional adoption leave by virtue of section 75A or 75B of the Employment Rights Act 1996;

"the Administration Act" means the Social Security Administration Act 1992;

[¹⁰ "amended determination" means a determination made in accordance with article 7A of the Rent Officers Order;]

"appropriate DWP office" means an office of the Department for Work and Pensions dealing with state pension credit or an office which is normally open to the public for the receipt of claims for income support [¹⁶, a jobseeker's allowance or an employment and support allowance];

[⁶⁶ "approved blood scheme" means a scheme established or approved by the Secretary of State, or trust established with funds provided by the Secretary of State, for the purpose of providing compensation in respect of a person having been infected from contaminated blood products;]

[⁴⁶ "armed forces independence payment" means armed forces independence payment under the Armed Forces and Reserve Forces (Compensation Scheme) Order 2011;]

"assessment period" means the period determined–

(a)   in relation to the earnings of a self-employed earner, in accordance with regulation 37 (calculation of earnings of self-employed earners) for the purpose of calculating the weekly earnings of the claimant; or

(b)   in relation to any other income, in accordance with regulation 33 (calculation of weekly income) for the purpose of calculating the weekly income of the claimant;

"attendance allowance" means–

(a)   an attendance allowance under Part 3 of the Act;

(b)   an increase of disablement pension under section 104 or 105 of the Act;

[⁴⁸ (c)]

[⁴⁸ (d)]

(e)   a payment by virtue of article 14, 15, 16, 43 or 44 of the Personal Injuries (Civilians) Scheme 1983 or any analogous payment; or

(f)   any payment based on need for attendance which is paid as part of a war disablement pension;

[²¹ "basic rate", where it relates to the rate of tax, has the same meaning as in the Income Tax Act 2007 (see section 989 of that Act);]

"the benefit Acts" means the Act, the Jobseekers Act [¹⁶, the Welfare Reform Act] [⁴⁵, Part 4 of the 2012 Act], [⁵⁸ the Pensions Act 2014] [⁴⁶, the Armed Forces and Reserve Forces (Compensation Scheme) Order 2011] and the State Pension Credit Act;

"benefit week" means a period of 7 consecutive days commencing upon a Monday and ending on a Sunday;

"board and lodging accommodation" means accommodation provided to a person or, if he is a member of a family, to him or any other member of his family, for a charge which is inclusive of the provision of that accommodation and at least some cooked or prepared meals which both are cooked or prepared (by a person other than the person to whom the accommodation is provided or a member of his family) and are consumed in that accommodation or associated premises;

[¹⁰ "broad rental market area" has the meaning specified in paragraph 4 of Schedule 3B to the Rent Officers Order;]

[¹⁰ "broad rental market area determination" means a determination made in accordance with article 4B(1A) of the Rent Officers Order;]

"care home" in England [⁶⁷] has the meaning assigned to it by section 3 of the Care Standards Act 2000 [⁶⁷, in Wales means a care home service within the meaning of Part 1 of the Regulation and Inspection of Social Care (Wales) Act 2016 which is provided wholly or mainly to persons aged 18 or over] and in Scotland means a care home service within the meaning assigned to it by [³⁸ paragraph 2 of schedule 12 to the Public Services Reform (Scotland) Act 2010];

[³⁷ "the Caxton Foundation" means the charitable trust of that name established on 28th March 2011 out of funds provided by the Secretary of State for the benefit of certain persons suffering from hepatitis C and other persons eligible for payment in accordance with its provisions;]

[¹⁰ "change of dwelling" means, for the purposes of regulations 13C and 14, a change of dwelling occupied by a claimant as his home during the award where the dwelling to which the claimant has moved is one in respect of which the authority may make a rent allowance;]

"child" means a person under the age of 16;

"child tax credit" means a child tax credit under section 8 of the Tax Credits Act;

[⁵⁰ "child who cannot share a bedroom means a child–
  (a)   who is entitled to the care component of disability living allowance at the highest or middle rate prescribed in accordance with section 72(3) of the Act; and
  (b)   who the relevant authority is satisfied is, by virtue of his or her disability, not reasonably able to share a bedroom with another child;]
"the Children Order" means the Children (Northern Ireland) Order 1995;
"claim" means a claim for housing benefit;
"claimant" means a person claiming housing benefit;
"close relative" means a parent, parent-in-law, son, son-in-law, daughter, daughter-in-law, step-parent, step-son, step-daughter, brother, sister, or if any of the preceding persons is one member of a couple, the other member of that couple;
[¹⁹ "concessionary payment" means a payment made under arrangements made by the Secretary of State with the consent of the Treasury which is charged to a Departmental Expenditure Vote to which payments of benefit or tax credits under the benefit Acts or the Tax Credits Act are charged;]
"the Consequential Provisions Regulations" means the Housing Benefit and Council Tax Benefit (Consequential Provisions) Regulations 2006;
[¹⁷ [⁴⁷ "contributory employment and support allowance" means an allowance under Part 1 of the Welfare Reform Act as amended by the provisions of Schedule 3, and Part 1 of Schedule 14, to the 2012 Act that remove references to an income-related allowance, and a contributory allowance under Part 1 of the Welfare Reform Act as that Part has effect apart from those provisions;]]
"co-ownership scheme" means a scheme under which the dwelling is let by a housing association and the tenant, or his personal representative, will, under the terms of the tenancy agreement or of the agreement under which he became a member of the association, be entitled, on his ceasing to be a member and subject to any conditions stated in either agreement, to a sum calculated by reference directly or indirectly to the value of the dwelling;
[⁵³ "couple" means–
  (a)   two people who are married to, or civil partners of, each other and are members of the same household; or
  (b)   two people who are not married to, or civil partners of, each other but are living together as a married couple;]
[⁵¹ "couple" means–
  (a)   two people who are married to, or civil partners of, each other and are members of the same household; or
  (b)   two people who are not married to, or civil partners of, each other but are living together as a married couple;]
"course of study" means any course of study, whether or not it is a sandwich course and whether or not a grant is made for undertaking or attending it;
"Crown tenant" means a person who occupies a dwelling under a tenancy or licence where the interest of the landlord belongs to Her Majesty in right of the Crown or to a government department or is held in trust for Her Majesty for the purposes of a government department, except (in the case of an interest belonging to Her Majesty in right of the Crown) where the interest is under the management of the Crown Estate Commissioners [⁶³ or a relevant person];
"date of claim" means the date on which the claim is made, or treated as made, for the purposes of regulation 64 (time and manner in which claims are to be made);
"the Decisions and Appeals Regulations" means the Housing Benefit and Council Tax Benefit (Decisions and Appeals) Regulations 2001;
"the designated authority" means any of the following–
  (a)   the Secretary of State;
  (b)   a person providing services to the Secretary of State;
  (c)   a local authority;
  (d)   a person providing services to, or authorised to exercise any function of, any such local authority;

"designated office" means the office designated by the relevant authority for the receipt of claims to housing benefit–
- (a) by notice upon or with a form approved by it for the purpose of claiming housing benefit; or
- (b) by reference upon or with such a form to some other document available from it and sent by electronic means or otherwise on application and without charge; or
- (c) by any combination of the provisions set out in sub-paragraphs (a) and (b) above;

"disability living allowance" means a disability living allowance under section 71 of the Act;

"dwelling occupied as the home" means the dwelling, together with any garage, garden and outbuildings, normally occupied by the claimant as his home, including any premises not so occupied which it is impracticable or unreasonable to sell separately, in particular, in Scotland, any croft land on which the dwelling is situated;

"earnings" has the meaning prescribed in regulation 35 (earnings of employed earners) or, as the case may be, 38 (earnings of self-employed earners);

"the Eileen Trust" means the charitable trust of that name established on 29th March 1993 out of funds provided by the Secretary of State for the benefit of persons eligible for payment in accordance with its provisions;

[² "electronic communication" has the same meaning as in section 15(1) of the 2000 Act;]

[⁹ "eligible rent" means as the case may require, an eligible rent determined in accordance with–
- (a) regulations 12B (eligible rent), 12C (eligible rent and maximum rent) or 12D (eligible rent and maximum rent (LHA)); or
- (b) regulations 12 (rent) and 13 (restrictions on unreasonable payments) as set out in paragraph 5 of Schedule 3 to the Consequential Provisions Regulations in a case to which paragraph 4 of that Schedule applies;]

"employed earner" is to be construed in accordance with section 2(1)(a) of the Act and also includes a person who is in receipt of a payment which is payable under any enactment having effect in Northern Ireland and which corresponds to statutory sick pay or statutory maternity pay;

[¹⁷ "Employment and Support Allowance Regulations" means the Employment and Support Allowance Regulations 2008;]

[²⁴ "enactment" includes an enactment comprised in, or in an instrument made under, an Act of the Scottish Parliament [⁴⁸ or the National Assembly of Wales];]

[¹³ "extended payment (qualifying contributory benefits)" means a payment of housing benefit payable pursuant to regulation 53 of these Regulations or regulation 73 of the Housing Benefit Regulations 2006;]

[¹⁴ "extended payment period" means the period for which an extended payment is payable in accordance with regulation 53A of these Regulations or regulation 72A or 73A of the Housing Benefit Regulations 2006;]

"family" has the meaning assigned to it by section 137(1) of the Act;

[¹²]

"the Fund" means moneys made available from time to time by the Secretary of State for the benefit of persons eligible for payment in accordance with the provisions of a scheme established by him on 24th April 1992 or, in Scotland, on 10th April 1992;

[¹⁵]

[¹ "the Graduated Retirement Benefit Regulations" means the Social Security (Graduated Retirement Benefit) Regulations 2005;]

"guarantee credit" is to be construed in accordance with sections 1 and 2 of the State Pension Credit Act;

"a guaranteed income payment" means a payment made under article 14(1)(b) or article 21(1)(a) of the Armed Forces and Reserve Forces (Compensation Scheme) Order 2005;

"hostel" means a building–
(a) in which there is provided for persons generally or for a class of persons, domestic accommodation, otherwise than in separate and self-contained premises, and either board or facilities for the preparation of food adequate to the needs of those persons, or both; and
(b) which is–
(i) managed or owned by a registered housing association; or
(ii) operated other than on a commercial basis and in respect of which funds are provided wholly or in part by a government department or agency or a local authority; or
(iii) managed by a voluntary organisation or charity and provides care, support or supervision with a view to assisting those persons to be rehabilitated or resettled within the community; and
(c) which is not–
(i) a care home;
(ii) an independent hospital; or
(iii) an Abbeyfield Home;
[³³ "Housing Act functions" means functions under section 122 of the Housing Act 1996;]
[⁹ "housing association" has the meaning assigned to it by section 1(1) of the Housing Associations Act 1985;]
"an income-based jobseeker's allowance" and "a joint-claim jobseeker's allowance" have the same meaning as they have in the Jobseekers Act by virtue of section 1(4) of that Act;
[¹⁷ "income-related employment and support allowance" means an income-related allowance under Part 1 of the Welfare Reform Act;]
"Income Support Regulations" means the Income Support (General) Regulations 1987;
[³¹ "independent hospital"–
(a) in England, means a hospital as defined by section 275 of the National Health Service Act 2006 that is not a health service hospital as defined by that section;
(b) in Wales, has the meaning assigned to it by section 2 of the Care Standards Act 2000; and
[³⁸ (c) in Scotland, means an independent healthcare service as defined in section 10F(1)(a) and (b) of the National Health Service (Scotland) Act 1978];]
[¹⁸]
[⁶ "the Independent Living Fund (2006)" means the Trust of that name established by a deed dated 10th April 2006 and made between the Secretary of State for Work and Pensions of the one part and Margaret Rosemary Cooper, Michael Beresford Boyall and Marie Theresa Martin of the other part;]
[¹⁸]
[¹⁸]
[¹⁸]
"invalid carriage or other vehicle" means a vehicle propelled by petrol engine or by electric power supplied for use on the road and to be controlled by the occupant;
"Jobseekers Act" means the Jobseekers Act 1995;
"Jobseeker's Allowance Regulations" means the Jobseeker's Allowance Regulations 1996;
[¹⁰ "linked person" means–
(a) any member of the claimant's family;
(b) if the claimant is a member of a polygamous marriage, any partners of his and any child or young person for whom he or a partner is responsible and who is a member of the same household; or
(c) any relative of the claimant or his partner who occupies the same dwelling as the claimant, whether or not they reside with him, except for a relative who has a separate right of occupation of the dwelling which would enable them to continue to occupy it even if the claimant ceased his occupation of it;]

[¹⁰ "local housing allowance" means an allowance determined in accordance with paragraph 2 of Schedule 3B to the Rent Officers Order;]

[⁴⁴ "local welfare provision" means occasional financial or other assistance given by a local authority, the Scottish Ministers or the Welsh Ministers, or a person authorised to exercise any function of, or provide a service to, them, to or in respect of individuals for the purpose of–

  (a) meeting, or helping to meet, an immediate short term need–

      (i)   arising out of an exceptional event, or exceptional circumstances; and

      (ii)   that requires to be met in order to avoid a risk to the well-being of an individual; or

  (b) enabling individuals to establish or maintain a settled home, where those individuals have been or, without the assistance, might otherwise be–

      (i)   in prison, hospital, a residential care establishment or other institution; or

      (ii)   homeless or otherwise living an unsettled way of life;]

"the London Bombings Relief Charitable fund" means the company limited by guarantee (number 5505072) and registered charity of that name established on 11th July 2005 for the purpose of (amongst other things) relieving sickness, disability or financial need of victims (including families or dependants of victims) of the terrorist attacks carried out in London on 7th July 2005;

[⁶⁵ "the London Emergencies Trust" means the company of that name (number 09928465) incorporated on 23rd December 2015 and the registered charity of that name (number 1172307) established on 28th March 2017;]

"lone parent" means a person who has no partner and who is responsible for and a member of the same household as a child or young person;

"long tenancy" means a tenancy granted for a term of years certain exceeding twenty one years, whether or not the tenancy is, or may become, terminable before the end of that term by notice given by or to the tenant or by re-entry, forfeiture (or, in Scotland, irritancy) or otherwise and includes a lease for a term fixed by law under a grant with a covenant or obligation for perpetual renewal unless it is a lease by sub-demise from one which is not a long tenancy;

[⁸]

"the Macfarlane (Special Payments) Trust" means the trust of that name, established on 29th January 1990 partly out of funds provided by the Secretary of State, for the benefit of certain persons suffering from haemophilia;

"the Macfarlane (Special Payments) (No.2) Trust" means the trust of that name, established on 3rd May 1991 partly out of funds provided by the Secretary of State, for the benefit of certain persons suffering from haemophilia and other beneficiaries;

"the Macfarlane Trust" means the charitable trust, established partly out of funds provided by the Secretary of State to the Haemophilia Society, for the relief of poverty or distress among those suffering from haemophilia;

[¹⁷ "main phase employment and support allowance" means an employment and support allowance where the calculation of the amount payable in respect of the claimant includes a component under section 2(1)(b) or 4(2)(b) of the Welfare Reform Act [⁶⁴ or the claimant is a member of the work-related activity group];]

"maternity leave" means a period during which a woman is absent from work because she is pregnant or has given birth to a child, and at the end of which she has a right to return to work either under the terms of her contract of employment or under Part 8 of the Employment Rights Act 1996;

[⁹ "maximum rent" means the amount to which the eligible rent is restricted in a case where regulation 13 applies;]

[¹⁰ "maximum rent (LHA)" means the amount determined in accordance with regulation 13D;]

[⁶¹ "member of a couple who cannot share a bedroom" means a member of a couple–

  (a) who is in receipt of–

      (i)   attendance allowance at the higher rate in accordance with section 65(3) of the Act;

      (ii)   the care component of disability living allowance at the highest or middle rate prescribed in accordance with section 72(3) of the Act;

      (iii)   the daily living component of personal independence payment in accordance with section 78 of the 2012 Act; or

      (iv)   armed forces independence payment; and

  (b)   whom the relevant authority is satisfied is, by virtue of his or her disability, not reasonably able to share a bedroom with the other member of the couple;]

[⁴³ "member of the armed forces away on operations" means a member of the regular forces or the reserve forces (within the meaning of section 374 of the Armed Forces Act 2006) who is absent, while on operations, from the dwelling usually occupied as their home;]

[⁶⁰ "member of the work-related activity group" means a [⁶⁴ person] who has or is treated as having limited capability for work under either–

  (a)   Part 5 of the Employment and Support Allowance Regulations 2008 other than by virtue of regulation 30 of those Regulations; or

  (b)   Part 4 of the Employment and Support Allowance Regulations 2013 other than by virtue of regulation 26 of those Regulations;]

[²⁵ "MFET Limited" means the company limited by guarantee (number 7121661) of that name, established for the purpose in particular of making payments in accordance with arrangements made with the Secretary of State to persons who have acquired HIV as a result of treatment by the NHS with blood or blood products;]

[¹⁴ "mover" means a claimant who changes the dwelling occupied as the claimant's home from a dwelling in the area of the appropriate authority to a dwelling in the area of a second authority;]

"net earnings" means such earnings as are calculated in accordance with regulation 36 (calculation of net earnings of employed earners);

"net profit" means such profit as is calculated in accordance with regulation 39 (calculation of net profit of self-employed earners);

[¹⁴ "new dwelling" means, for the purposes of the definition of "second authority" and regulations 53C, 96 and 97, the dwelling to which a claimant has moved, or is about to move, which is or will be occupied as the claimant's new home;]

"non-dependant" has the meaning prescribed in regulation 3;

[⁹ "non-dependant deduction" means a deduction that is to be made under regulation 55 (non-dependant deductions);]

"occupational pension" means any pension or other periodical payment under an occupational pension scheme but does not include any discretionary payment out of a fund established for relieving hardship in particular cases;

"owner" means–

  (a)   in relation to a dwelling in England and Wales, the person who, otherwise than as a mortgagee in possession, is for the time being entitled to dispose of the fee simple, whether or not with the consent of other joint owners;

  (b)   in relation to a dwelling in Scotland, the proprietor under udal tenure or the proprietor of the dominion utile or the tenant's or the lessee's interest in a long tenancy, a kindly tenancy, a lease registered or registerable under the Registration of Leases (Scotland) Act 1857 or the Land Registration (Scotland) Act 1979 or a tenant-at-will as defined in section 20(8) of that Act of 1979;

"partner" means–

  (a)   where a claimant is a member of a couple, the other member of that couple; or

  (b)   where a claimant is polygamously married to two or more members of his household, any such member;

[⁴⁰ "paternity leave" means a period of absence from work on [⁵⁶] paternity leave by virtue of section 80A or 80B of the Employment Rights Act 1996 [⁵⁶];]

"payment" includes part of a payment;

"pension fund holder" means with respect to a personal pension scheme or [⁴ an occupational pension scheme], the trustees, managers or scheme administrators, as the case may be, of the scheme [⁴] concerned;

"person affected" shall be construed in accordance with regulation 3 of the Decisions and
      Appeals Regulations;

"person on income support" means a person in receipt of income support;

"person on state pension credit" means a person in receipt of state pension credit;

[²⁴ "person who requires overnight care" means a person ("P")–
- (a) who–
  - (i) is in receipt of attendance allowance;
  - (ii) is in receipt of the care component of disability living allowance at the highest or middle rate prescribed in accordance with section 72(3) of the Act; [⁴⁵]
  - [⁴⁵ (iia) is in receipt of the daily living component of personal independence payment in accordance with section 78 of the 2012 Act; [⁴⁶]]
  - [⁴⁶ (iib) is in receipt of armed forces independence payment; or]
  - (iii) although not satisfying either paragraph (i) [⁴⁵ [⁴⁶ , (ii), (iia) or (iib)]] above has provided [⁶¹ or, where P is a child, the claimant has provided] the relevant authority with such certificates, documents, information or evidence as are sufficient to satisfy the authority that P requires overnight care; and
- (b) whom the relevant authority is satisfied reasonably requires, and has in fact arranged, that one or more people who do not occupy as their home the dwelling to which the claim or award for housing benefit relates should–
  - (i) be engaged in providing overnight care for P;
  - (ii) regularly stay overnight at the dwelling for that purpose; and
  - (iii) be provided with the use of a bedroom in that dwelling additional to those used by the persons who occupy the dwelling as their home,

[³⁷ but, in a case where P is treated as occupying a dwelling which P does not actually occupy, sub-paragraphs (b)(ii) and (iii) are to be treated as satisfied where the relevant authority is satisfied that the dwelling contains such an additional bedroom and that P did or will reasonably so require and so arrange at such time as P actually occupied or occupies the dwelling;]

[⁴⁵ "personal independence payment" means personal independence payment under Part 4 of the 2012 Act;]

[⁴ "personal pension scheme" means–
- (a) a personal pension scheme as defined by section 1 of the Pension Schemes Act 1993;
- (b) an annuity contract or trust scheme approved under section 620 or 621 of the Income and Corporation Taxes Act 1988 or a substituted contract within the meaning of section 622(3) of that Act which is treated as having become a registered pension scheme by virtue of paragraph 1(1)(f) of Schedule 36 to the Finance Act 2004;
- (c) a personal pension scheme approved under Chapter 4 of Part 14 of the Income and Corporation Taxes Act 1988 which is treated as having become a registered pension scheme by virtue of paragraph 1(1)(g) of Schedule 36 to the Finance Act 2004;]

"policy of life insurance" means any instrument by which the payment of money is assured on death (except death by accident only) or the happening of any contingency dependent on human life, or any instrument evidencing a contract which is subject to payment of premiums for a term dependent on human life;

"polygamous marriage" means any marriage during the subsistence of which a party to it is married to more than one person and the ceremony of marriage took place under the law of a country which permits polygamy;

[²⁴ "public authority" includes any person certain of whose functions are functions of a public nature;]

"qualifying age for state pension credit" means (in accordance with section 1(2)(b) and (6) of the State Pension Credit Act)–
- (a) in the case of a woman, pensionable age; or

    (b)   in the case of a man, the age which is pensionable age in the case of a woman born on the same day as the man;

[¹⁴ "qualifying contributory benefit" means–
    (a)   severe disablement allowance;
    (b)   incapacity benefit;]
    [¹⁵ (c) contributory employment and support allowance;]

"qualifying course" means a qualifying course as defined for the purposes of Parts 2 and 4 of the Jobseeker's Allowance Regulations;

[¹⁴ "qualifying income-related benefit" means–
    (a)   income support;
    (b)   income-based jobseeker's allowance;]
    [¹⁵ (c) income-related employment and support allowance;]

[⁴⁵ "qualifying parent or carer" means a person who has a bedroom in the dwelling they occupy as their home additional to those used by the persons who occupy the dwelling as their home and who–
    (a)   has a child or qualifying young person placed with them as mentioned in regulation 21(3) who by virtue of that provision is not treated as occupying their dwelling; or
    (b)   has been approved as a foster parent under regulation 27 of the Fostering Services (England) Regulations 2011 or regulation 28 of the Fostering Services (Wales) Regulations 2003 or as a kinship carer under regulation 10 or a foster carer under regulation 22 of the Looked After Children (Scotland) Regulations 2009 but does not have a child or qualifying young person placed with them and has not had a child or qualifying young person placed with them for a period which does not exceed 52 weeks;]

"qualifying person" means a person in respect of whom payment has been made from the Fund, the Eileen Trust[²⁶, MFET Limited], the Skipton Fund[³⁷, the Caxton Foundation] [⁶², the Scottish Infected Blood Support Scheme] [⁶⁶, an approved blood scheme] [⁶⁵, the London Emergencies Trust, the We Love Manchester Emergency Fund] or the London Bombings Relief Charitable Fund;

[¹⁰ "reckonable rent" means payments which a person is liable to make in respect of the dwelling which he occupies as his home, and which are eligible, or would, but for regulation 13, be eligible for housing benefit;]

[¹⁰ [¹¹[²⁹ "registered housing association" means–
    (a)   a private registered provider of social housing;
    (b)   a housing association which is registered in a register maintained by the Welsh Ministers under Chapter 1 of Part 1 of the Housing Act 1996 [⁴² or a registered social landlord within the meaning of Part 1 of that Act]; or
    (c)   a housing association which is registered by Scottish Ministers by virtue of section 57(3)(b) of the Housing (Scotland) Act 2001 [⁴² or a registered social landlord within the meaning of section 165 of that Act];]]]

"relative" means a close relative, grandparent, grandchild, uncle, aunt, nephew or niece;

"relevant authority" means an authority administering housing benefit;

[¹⁰ "relevant information" means information or evidence forwarded to the relevant authority by an appropriate DWP office regarding a claim on which rent allowance may be awarded, which completes the transfer of all information or evidence held by the appropriate DWP office relating to that claim;]

[⁶³ "relevant person", in relation to any property, rights or interests to which section 90B(5) of the Scotland Act 1998 applies, means the person who manages that property or those rights or interests;]

"remunerative work" has the meaning prescribed in regulation 6 (remunerative work);

"rent" includes all those payments in respect of a dwelling specified in regulation 12(1);

[⁹ "Rent Officers Order" means the Rent Officers (Housing Benefit Functions) Order 1997 or, as the case may be, the Rent Officers (Housing Benefit Functions) (Scotland) Order 1997;]

[⁴]

[¹² "sandwich course" has the meaning prescribed in regulation 2(9) of the Education (Student Support) Regulations 2008, regulation 4(2) of the Education (Student Loans) (Scotland) Regulations 2007 or regulation 2(8) of the Education (Student Support) Regulations (Northern Ireland) 2007, as the case may be;]

"savings credit" shall be construed in accordance with sections 1 and 3 of the State Pension Credit Act;

[⁵⁹ "Scottish basic rate" means the rate of income tax of that name calculated in accordance with section 6A of the Income Tax Act 2007;]

[⁶² "Scottish Infected Blood Support Scheme" means the scheme of that name administered by the Common Services Agency (constituted by section 10 of the National Health Service (Scotland) Act 1978;]

[⁵⁹ "Scottish taxpayer" has the same meaning as in Chapter 2 of Part 4A of the Scotland Act 1998;]

[¹⁴ "second authority" means the authority to which a mover is liable to make payments for the new dwelling;]

"self-employed earner" is to be construed in accordance with section 2(1)(b) of the Act;

[²⁴ [⁵²]]

"shared ownership tenancy" means–

(a) in relation to England and Wales, a [⁵ lease] granted on payment of a premium calculated by reference to a percentage of the value of the dwelling or the cost of providing it;

(b) in relation to Scotland, an agreement by virtue of which the tenant of a dwelling of which he and the landlord are joint owners is the tenant in respect of the landlord's interest in the dwelling or by virtue of which the tenant has the right to purchase the dwelling or the whole or part of the landlord's interest therein;

[⁵⁴ "shared parental leave" means leave under section 75E or 75G of the Employment Rights Act 1996;]

"single claimant" means a claimant who neither has a partner nor is a lone parent;

"the Skipton Fund" means the ex-gratia payment scheme administered by the Skipton Fund Limited, incorporated on 25th March 2004, for the benefit of certain persons suffering from hepatitis C and other persons eligible for payment in accordance with the scheme's provisions;

"sports award" means an award made by one of the Sports Councils named in section 23(2) of the National Lottery etc Act 1993 out of sums allocated to it for distribution under that section;

[⁷ [²²]]

"State Pension Credit Act" means the State Pension Credit Act 2002;

"student" means a person, other than a person in receipt of a training allowance, who is attending or undertaking–

(a) a course of study at an educational establishment; or

(b) a qualifying course;

"the Tax Credits Act" means the Tax Credits Act 2002;

"tax year" means a period beginning with 6th April in one year and ending with 5th April in the next;

"training allowance" means an allowance (whether by way of periodical grants or otherwise) payable–

(a) out of public funds by a Government department or by or on behalf of the Secretary of State, [²³ Skills Development Scotland,] Scottish Enterprise or Highlands and Islands Enterprise, [⁴¹][³² [⁴¹] [⁵⁷]] or the [¹⁹ Welsh Ministers];

(b) to a person for his maintenance or in respect of a member of his family; and

(c) for the period, or part of the period, during which he is following a course of training or instruction provided by, or in pursuance of arrangements made with, that department or approved by that department in relation to him or so provided or approved by or on behalf of the Secretary of State, [²³ Skills Development Scotland,] Scottish Enterprise or Highlands and Islands Enterprise or the [¹⁹ Welsh Ministers], but it does not include an allowance paid by any Government department to or in respect of a person by reason of the fact that he is following a course of full-time education, other than under arrangements made under section 2 of the 1973 Act or is training as a teacher;

[⁴⁷ "universal credit" means universal credit under Part I of the 2012 Act;]

"voluntary organisation" means a body, other than a public or local authority, the activities of which are carried on otherwise than for profit;

[³]

[²⁰ "war disablement pension" means any retired pay or pension or allowance payable in respect of disablement under an instrument specified in section 639(2) of the Income Tax (Earnings and Pensions) Act 2003;

"war pension" means a war disablement pension, a war widow's pension or a war widower's pension;

"war widow's pension" means any pension or allowance payable to a woman as a widow under an instrument specified in section 639(2) of the Income Tax (Earnings and Pensions) Act 2003 in respect of the death or disablement of any person;

"war widower's pension" means any pension or allowance payable to a man as a widower or to a surviving civil partner under an instrument specified in section 639(2) of the Income Tax (Earnings and Pensions) Act 2003 in respect of the death or disablement of any person;]

"water charges" means–

(a) as respects England and Wales, any water and sewerage charges under Chapter 1 of Part 5 of the Water Industry Act 1991;

(b) as respects Scotland, any water and sewerage charges established by Scottish Water under a charges scheme made under section 29A of the Water Industry (Scotland) Act 2002,

in so far as such charges are in respect of the dwelling which a person occupies as his home;

[⁶⁵ "the We Love Manchester Emergency Fund" means the registered charity of that name (number 1173260) established on 30th May 2017;]

[¹⁷ "Welfare Reform Act" means the Welfare Reform Act 2007;]

"working tax credit" means a working tax credit under section 10 of the Tax Credits Act;

"Working Tax Credit Regulations" means the Working Tax Credit (Entitlement and Maximum Rate) Regulations 2002;

[³⁹]

"young person" has the meaning prescribed in regulation 19(1).

(2)   References in these Regulations to a person who is liable to make payments shall include references to a person who is treated as so liable under regulation 8 (circumstances in which a person is to be treated as liable to make payments in respect of a dwelling).

(3)   For the purposes of these Regulations, a person is on an income-based jobseeker's allowance on any day in respect of which an income-based jobseeker's allowance is payable to him and on any day–

(a) in respect of which he satisfies the conditions for entitlement to an income-based jobseeker's allowance but where the allowance is not paid in accordance with [²⁸ regulation 27A of the Jobseeker's Allowance Regulations or] section 19 or 20A [³⁵ or regulations made under section 17A] of the Jobseekers Act (circumstances in which a jobseeker's allowance is not payable); or

(b) which is a waiting day for the purposes of paragraph 4 of Schedule 1 to that Act and which falls immediately before a day in respect of which an income-based jobseeker's allowance is payable to him or would be payable to him but for [²⁸ regulation 27A of the Jobseeker's Allowance Regulations or] section 19 or 20A [³⁵ or regulations made under section 17A] of that Act; or

(c) in respect of which he is a member of a joint-claim couple for the purposes of the Jobseekers Act and no joint-claim jobseeker's allowance is payable in respect of that couple as a consequence of either member of that couple being subject to sanctions for the purpose of section 20A of that Act; or

(d)   in respect of which an income-based jobseeker's allowance or a joint-claim jobseeker's allowance would be payable but for a restriction imposed pursuant to [²⁷] section [³⁰ 6B,] 7, 8 or 9 of the Social Security Fraud Act 2001 (loss of benefit provisions).

[¹⁷ (3A)   For the purposes of these Regulations, a person is on an income-related employment and support allowance on any day in respect of which an income-related employment and support allowance is payable to him and on any day–

(a)   in respect of which he satisfies the conditions for entitlement to an income-related employment and support allowance but where the allowance is not paid in accordance with section 18 of the Welfare Reform Act (disqualification); or

(b)   which is a waiting day for the purposes of paragraph 2 of Schedule 2 to that Act and which falls immediately before a day in respect of which an income-related employment and support allowance is payable to him or would be payable to him but for section 18 of that Act.]

(4)   For the purposes of these Regulations, the following shall be treated as included in a dwelling–

(a)   subject to sub-paragraphs (b) to (d) any land (whether or not occupied by a structure) which is used for the purposes of occupying a dwelling as a home where either–

(i)   the occupier of the dwelling acquired simultaneously the right to use the land and the right to occupy the dwelling, and, in the case of a person liable to pay rent for his dwelling, he could not have occupied that dwelling without also acquiring the right to use the land; or

(ii)   the occupier of the dwelling has made or is making all reasonable efforts to terminate his liability to make payments in respect of the land;

(b)   where the dwelling is a caravan or mobile home, such of the land on which it stands as is used for the purposes of the dwelling;

(c)   where the dwelling is a houseboat, the land used for the purposes of mooring it;

(d)   where in Scotland, the dwelling is situated on or pertains to a croft within the meaning of section 3(1) of the Crofters (Scotland) Act 1993, the croft land on which it is situated or to which it pertains.

(5)   In these Regulations references to any person in receipt of a guarantee credit, a savings credit or state pension credit includes a reference to a person who would be in receipt thereof but for regulation 13 of the State Pension Credit Regulations 2002 (small amounts of state pension credit).

[⁵² (6)   References in these Regulations to a claimant participating as a service user are to–

(a)   a person who is being consulted by or on behalf of–

(i)   a body which has a statutory duty to provide services in the field of health, social care or social housing; or

(ii)   a body which conducts research or undertakes monitoring for the purpose of planning or improving such services,

in their capacity as a user, potential user, carer of a user or person otherwise affected by the provision of those services; or

[⁵⁵ (ab) a person who is being consulted by or on behalf of–

(i)   the Secretary of State in relation to any of the Secretary of State's functions in the field of social security or child support or under section 2 of the Employment and Training Act 1973; or

(ii)   a body which conducts research or undertakes monitoring for the purpose of planning or improving such functions,

in their capacity as a person affected or potentially affected by the exercise of those functions or the carer of such a person;]

(b)   the carer of a person consulted under [⁵⁵ sub-paragraph (a) or (ab)].]

[⁶¹ (7)   For the purpose of these Regulations, reference to a member of a couple who can share a bedroom is to a member of a couple where the other member of the couple is a member of a couple who cannot share a bedroom.]

Modifications

Definitions substituted and inserted by reg 4(1) Housing Benefit (State Pension Credit) (Local Housing Allowance and Information Sharing) Amendment Regulations 2007 SI No.2869, as amended by reg 5(3) of SI 2008 No.586, as from 7 April 2008, save that for a person to whom reg 1(5) of those regulations applied (see p1814), the amendments came into force on the day on or after 7 April 2008 when the first of the events specified in reg 1(6) applies to her/him, or on 6 April 2009 if none had before that date.

Definition of "eligible rent" modified and definition of "maximum rent (standard local rate)" inserted by Sch 9 para 2 (see p873). These apply only to former Pathfinder Authorities who administered the pilot local housing allowance scheme.

References to "step-parent", step-children and the various in-laws in the definition of "close relative" are modified by s246 Civil Partnership Act 2004 (see p1729) and art 3 and Sch para 24 to SI 2005 No.3137 (see p1772).

From 1 December 2008, in England and Wales, in the definition of "registered housing association", the reference to the Housing Corporation is to be treated as if it were a reference to the Regulator of Social Housing: art 3 and Sch para 7 Transfer of Housing Corporation Functions (Modifications and Transitional Provisions) Order 2008 SI No.2839.

The amendments made by SI 2014 No.3255 which came into force on 5 April 2015 do not have effect in relation to ordinary statutory paternity pay which is paid, additional statutory paternity pay which is paid, a period in respect of which additional statutory paternity pay is payable which begins, or continues, ordinary paternity leave which is taken or additional paternity leave which is taken on or after 5 April 2015. See art 35 of SI 2014 No.3255.

Amendments

1. Inserted by reg 11(2) of SI 2005 No 2677 and reg 2 of SI 2006 No 217 as from 6.4.06.
2. Inserted by art 3(2) of SI 2006 No 2968 as from 20.12.06.
3. Omitted by reg 6(a) of SI 2007 No 1619 as from 3.7.07.
4. Amended by reg 5(2) of SI 2007 No 1749 as from 16.7.07.
5. Amended by reg 3(2) of SI 2007 No 1356 as from 1.10.07.
6. Amended by art 9 of SI 2007 No 2538 as from 1.10.07.
7. Inserted by reg 12(2) of SI 2007 No 2618 as from 1.10.07.
8. Revoked by reg 2 and the Sch of SI 2007 No 2618 as from 1.10.07.
9. Substituted by reg 4(1) of SI 2007 No 2869 as from 7.4.08 (or if reg 1(5) of that SI applies, on the day on or after 7.4.08 when the first of the events specified in reg 1(6) applies, or from 6.4.09 if none have before that date).
10. Inserted by reg 4(1) of SI 2007 No 2869 as from 7.4.08 (or if reg 1(5) of that SI applies, on the day on or after 7.4.08 when the first of the events specified in reg 1(6) applies, or from 6.4.09 if none have before that date).
11. Substituted by reg 5(3) of SI 2008 No 586 as from 7.4.08.
12. Amended by reg 4(2) of SI 2008 No 1042 as from 19.5.08.
13. Substituted by reg 6(2) of SI 2008 No 959 as from 6.10.08.
14. Inserted by reg 6(2) of SI 2008 No 959 as from 6.10.08.
15. Omitted by reg 3(2) of SI 2008 No 2299 as from 1.10.08.
16. Amended by reg 29(2) of SI 2008 No 1082 as from 27.10.08.
17. Inserted by reg 29(2) of SI 2008 No 1082, as amended by reg 33 of SI 2008 No 2428, as from 27.10.08.
18. Amended by reg 7(2) of SI 2008 No 2767 as from 17.11.08.
19. Amended by reg 6(2) of SI 2008 No 3157 as from 5.1.09.
20. Inserted by reg 6(2) of SI 2008 No 3157 as from 5.1.09.
21. Inserted by reg 7(2)(a) of SI 2009 No 583 as from 6.4.09.
22. Omitted by reg 7(2)(b) of SI 2009 No 583 as from 6.4.09.
23. Amended by reg 7(3)(a) of SI 2009 No 583 as from 6.4.09.
24. Inserted by reg 7(2) of SI 2009 No 2655 as from 2.11.09.
25. Inserted by reg 9(2) of SI 2010 No 641 as from 1.4.10 (5.4.10 where rent payable weekly or in multiples of a week).
26. Inserted by reg 9(3) of SI 2010 No 641 as from 1.4.10 (5.4.10 where rent payable weekly or in multiples of a week).
27. Amended by reg 8 of SI 2010 No 424 as from 2.4.10.
28. Amended by reg 4(1)(b) and (2) of SI 2010 No 509 as from 6.4.10.
29. Amended by art 4 and Sch 1 para 57 of SI 2010 No 671 as from 1.4.10.
30. Amended by reg 5 of SI 2010 No 1160 as from 1.4.10.
31. Substituted by arts 2 and 21 of SI 2010 No 1881 as from 1.10.10.
32. Amended by art 15 of SI 2010 No 1941 as from 1.9.10.
33. Amended by reg 3(2) of SI 2010 No 2449 as from 1.11.10.
34. Inserted by reg 3(2) of SI 2010 No 2835 as from 1.4.11.

35.   Inserted by reg 17 of SI 2011 No 688 as from 25.4.11.
36.   Amended by art 2 and Sch 1 para 40(2) of SI 2011 No 1740 as from 15.7.11.
37.   Amended by reg 20(2) of SI 2011 No 2425 as from 31.10.11.
38.   Amended by art 2 and Sch 2 para 52 of SI 2011 No 2581 as from 28.10.11.
39.   Omitted by reg 3 of SI 2011 No 1736 as from 1.1.12.
40.   Substituted by reg 8(2) of SI 2012 No 757 as from 1.4.12 (2.4.12 where rent payable weekly or in multiples of a week).
41.   Amended by reg 12 of SI 2012 No 956 as from 1.5.12.
42.   Amended by reg 6 of SI 2012 No 3040 as from 1.4.13.
43.   Inserted by reg 3(2) of SI 2013 No 665 as from 1.12.13.
44.   Inserted by reg 8(2) of SI 2013 No 443 as from 2.4.13.
45.   Amended by reg 8 and Sch para 37(2) of SI 2013 No 388 as from 8.4.13.
46.   Amended by art 7 and Sch para 35(2) of SI 2013 No 591 as from 8.4.13.
47.   Amended by reg 36(2) of SI 2013 No 630 as from 29.4.13.
48.   Amended by reg 12(2) of SI 2013 No 2536 as from 29.10.13.
49.   Inserted by Sch 2 para 94(2) of SI 2013 No 235 as from 1.4.13.
50.   Amended by reg 3(2) of SI 2013 No 2828 as from 4.12.13.
51.   Substituted (in England and Wales only) by art 2 and Sch 1 para 41 of SI 2014 No107 as from 13.3.14.
52.   Amended by reg 9(2) of SI 2014 No 591 as from 28.4.14.
53.   Substituted (in Scotland only) by art 29 and Sch 6 para 28 as from 16.12.14.
54.   Amended by art 18(2)(b) of SI 2014 No 3255 as from 31.12.14.
55.   Amended by reg 2 of SI 2015 No 67 as from 23.2.15.
56.   Amended by reg 18(2)(a) of SI 2014 No 3255 as from 5.4.15.
57.   Amended by art 2 and Sch 3 para 9 of SI 2015 No 971 as from 26.5.15.
58.   Amended by art 29(2) of SI 2015 No 1985 as from 6.4.16.
59.   Inserted by reg 5(2) of SI 2016 No 233 as from 6.4.16.
60.   Inserted by Sch 1 para 7(2) of SI 2017 No 204 as from 3.4.17, subject to transitional and savings provisions in Sch 2 paras 1–7.
61.   Amended by reg 5(2) of SI 2017 No 213 as from 1.4.17.
62.   Inserted by reg 7(2) of SI 2017 No 329 as from 3.4.17.
63.   Amended, as reg 2 applies in relation to Scotland, by Sch 5 para 103 of SI 2017 No 524 as from 31.3.17.
64.   Amended by reg 6(2) of SI 2017 No 581 as from 23.6.17, subject to transitional and savings provision in reg 9.
65.   Amended by reg 7(2) of SI 2017 No 689 as from 19.6.17.
66.   Amended by reg 7(2) of SI 2017 No 870 as from 23.10.17.
67.   Amended by reg 10(2) of SI 2018 No 228 as from 2.4.18.

Analysis
"board and lodging accommodation" is defined as accommodation in which cooked or prepared meals are provided and consumed. This definition is identical to that found in Sch 5 para 42(2) HB Regs (on p677). It is relevant for reg 38(2)(a) and the income disregard found in Sch 5 para 9 of the HB(SPC) Regs.

"qualifying age for state pension credit" is relevant in determining whether these regs or the HB Regs apply to a claimant: reg 5. The age at which someone qualifies for state pension credit (PC) is linked to pensionable age for a woman.

The process of equalising men's and women's pension ages began on 6 April 2010. From that date, women's pension age began to rise, as did the qualifying age for PC. Note that pension ages for men and women are equal from 6 December 2018.

Under the definition, the qualifying age for PC for a woman is the minimum age she can receive state retirement pension. The qualifying age for PC for a man is the minimum age a woman born on the same day as him can receive state retirement pension. So for both men and women, the qualifying age for PC is:
(1)   60, if s/he was born before 6 April 1950;
(2)   an age from 60 and one month to 64 and 11 months depending on her/his date of birth, if s/he was born on or after 6 April 1950 but before 6 December 1953;
(3)   65, if s/he was born on 6 November 1953;
(4)   an age from 65 and two months to 66 depending on her/his date of birth, if s/he was born on or after 6 December 1953 but before 5 October 1954;
(5)   66, if s/he was born on or after 6 October 1954.
Consequently, the rules in the HB(SPC) Regs can apply to individual claimants at different ages. For claimants born on or after 6 April 1950 but before 6 December 1953, there is a helpful table, setting out the relevant birth dates and pension ages, in an Appendix to CPAG's *Welfare Benefits and Tax Credits Handbook*. Note: pensionable age for both men and women will rise to 68 between 2024 and 2046.

Definition of non-dependant

3.–(1)   In these Regulations, "non-dependant" means any person, except someone to whom paragraph (2) applies, who normally resides with a claimant or with whom a claimant normally resides.

(2)   This paragraph applies to–

(a)   any member of the claimant's family;

(b)   if the claimant is polygamously married, any partner of his and any child or young person who is a member of his household and for whom he or one of his partners is responsible;

(c)   a child or young person who is living with the claimant but who is not a member of his household by virtue of regulation 21 (circumstances in which a person is to be treated as being or not being a member of the same household);

(d)   subject to paragraph (3), a person who jointly occupies the claimant's dwelling and is either a co-owner of that dwelling with the claimant or his partner (whether or not there are other co-owners) or is liable with the claimant or his partner to make payments in respect of his occupation of the dwelling;

(e)   subject to paragraph (3)–

    (i)   any person who is liable to make payments on a commercial basis to the claimant or the claimant's partner in respect of the occupation of the dwelling;

    (ii)   any person to whom or to whose partner the claimant or the claimant's partner is liable to make payments on a commercial basis in respect of the occupation of the dwelling; or

    (iii)   any other member of the household of the person to whom or to whose partner the claimant or the claimant's partner is liable to make payments on a commercial basis in respect of the occupation of the dwelling;

(f)   a person who lives with the claimant in order to care for him or a partner of his and who is engaged by a charitable or voluntary organisation which makes a charge to the claimant or his partner for the services provided by that person.

(3)   Sub-paragraphs (d) and (e) of paragraph (2) shall not apply to any person who is treated as if he were not liable to make payments in respect of a dwelling under paragraph (1) of regulation 9 (circumstances in which a person is to be treated as not liable to make payments in respect of a dwelling).

(4)   For the purposes of this regulation and regulation 9 [¹ and the definition of "linked person" in regulation 2] a person resides with another only if they share any accommodation except a bathroom, a lavatory or a communal area within the meaning prescribed in paragraph 8 of Schedule 1 but not if each person is separately liable to make payments in respect of his occupation of the dwelling to the landlord.

Modifications

Amendments made to para (4) by reg 4(2) Housing Benefit (State Pension Credit) (Local Housing Allowance and Information Sharing) Amendment Regulations 2007 SI No.2869 as from 7 April 2008, save that for a person to whom reg 1(5) of those regulations applied (see p1814), the amendments came into force on the day on or after 7 April 2008 when the first of the events specified in reg 1(6) applied to her/him, or on 6 April 2009 if none had before that date.

Amendment

1.   Amended by reg 4(2) of SI 2007 No 2869 as from 7.4.08 (or if reg 1(5) of that SI applies, on the day on or after 7.4.08 when the first of the events specified in reg 1(6) applies, or from 6.4.09 if none have before that date).

Cases in which section 1(1A) of the Administration Act is disapplied

4.   Section 1(1A) of the Administration Act (requirement to state national insurance number) shall not apply–

(a)   to a claim for housing benefit where the person making the claim, or in respect of whom the claim is made, is liable to make payments in respect of a dwelling which is a hostel;

(b)   to any child or young person in respect of whom housing benefit is claimed.

[¹ (c) to a person who–
    (i)   is a person in respect of whom a claim for housing benefit is made;
    (ii)   is subject to immigration control within the meaning of section 115(9)(a) of the Immigration and Asylum Act 1999;
    (iii) is a person from abroad for the purposes of these Regulations as defined in regulation 10(2); and
    (iv) has not previously been allocated a national insurance number.]

Amendment
1.   Amended by reg 10 of SI 2009 No 471 as from 6.4.09.

Persons who have attained the qualifying age for state pension credit

5.–(1)   Except as provided in paragraph (2), these Regulations apply to a person who has attained the qualifying age for state pension credit.

(2)   These Regulations shall not apply in relation to any person if he, or if he has a partner, his partner, is a person [³ on universal credit,] on income support [¹, [² on] an income-based jobseeker's allowance or on an income-related employment and support allowance].

Amendments
1.   Amended by reg 30 of SI 2008 No 1082 as from 27.10.08.
2.   Amended by reg 34 of SI 2008 No 2428 as from 27.10.08.
3.   Amended by reg 8 of SI 2013 No 2070 as from 28.10.13.

Definitions
"person on an income-based jobseeker's allowance" – see reg 2(3).
"person on an income-related employment and support allowance" – see reg 2(3A).
"person on income support" – see reg 2(1).
"qualifying age for state pension credit" – see reg 2(1).

General Note
The HB(SPC) Regs apply where a person has reached the qualifying age for PC (see p731). However, they do not apply if either the claimant or her/his partner is on UC, IS, income-based JSA or income-related ESA. In this case, the HB Regs instead apply. Note that, unlike with the HB Regs, "person on universal credit" is not defined.

Before 15 May 2019, a claimant who was a member of a "mixed-age couple" (ie, only one member of the couple was at least the qualifying age for PC) could claim and be entitled to HB under these regulations unless para (2) applied. If para (2) applied, claims and entitlement were allowed under the HB Regs: reg 5 HB Regs. New claims for HB by members of a mixed-age couple on or after 15 May 2019 are generally no longer allowed. However, claims are allowed under the HB(SPC) Regs if the claimant has been continuously entitled to PC or HB under the HB(SPC) Regs from before 15 May 2019 as part of the same mixed-age couple. If a claimant who has been entitled to HB under the HB Regs becomes a member of a mixed-age couple on or after that date, her/his entitlement to HB generally ends. For the rules for mixed-age couples on claims for, and termination of awards of, HB and the exceptions to the rules, see the Welfare Reform Act 2012 (Commencement No.31) Order 2019 SI No.37 (the No.31 Order) on p1898.

Note that where a person is excluded from entitlement to PC or HB because s/he is a member of a mixed-age couple and is also prevented from claiming UC because of the "SDP Gateway" in reg 4A of the UC(TP) Regs 2014 (see p1862) or because s/he is a frontier worker or by virtue of reg 4 of the UC(TP) Regs 2014 (see p1861), the member of the couple who has reached the qualifying age for PC is treated as not having attained that age for the purposes of reg 5 of the HB Regs, thus those regulations, instead of the HB(SPC) Regs, apply to such a claimant. S/he is also treated as meeting the age conditions for IS, JSA and ESA so can potentially claim those benefits. See art 8 of the No.31 Order on p1902.

Remunerative work

6.–(1)   Subject to the following provisions of this regulation, a person shall be treated for the purposes of these Regulations as engaged in remunerative work if he is engaged, or, where his hours of work fluctuate, he is engaged on average, for not less than 16 hours a week, in work for which payment is made or which is done in expectation of payment.

(2)   Subject to paragraph (3), in determining the number of hours for which a person is engaged in work where his hours of work fluctuate, regard shall be had to the average of hours worked over–

(a) if there is a recognisable cycle of work, the period of one complete cycle (including, where the cycle involves periods in which the person does no work, those periods but disregarding any other absences);

(b) in any other case, the period of 5 weeks immediately prior to the date of claim, or such other length of time as may, in the particular case, enable the person's weekly average hours of work to be determined more accurately.

(3) Where, for the purposes of paragraph (2)(a), a person's recognisable cycle of work at a school, other educational establishment or other place of employment is one year and includes periods of school holidays or similar vacations during which he does not work, those periods and any other periods not forming part of such holidays or vacations during which he is not required to work shall be disregarded in establishing the average hours for which he is engaged in work.

(4) Where no recognisable cycle has been established in respect of a person's work, regard shall be had to the number of hours or, where those hours will fluctuate, the average of the hours, which he is expected to work in a week.

(5) A person shall be treated as engaged in remunerative work during any period for which he is absent from work referred to in paragraph (1) if the absence is either without good cause or by reason of a recognised, customary or other holiday.

(6) A person on income support[1, income-based jobseeker's allowance or an income-related employment and support allowance] for more than 3 days in any benefit week shall be treated as not being in remunerative work in that week.

(7) A person shall not be treated as engaged in remunerative work on any day on which the person is on maternity leave, paternity leave [2, adoption leave or shared parental leave], or is absent from work because he is ill.

(8) A person shall not be treated as engaged in remunerative work on any day on which he is engaged in an activity in respect of which–

(a) a sports award has been made, or is to be made, to him; and

(b) no other payment is made or is expected to be made to him.

Amendments

1. Amended by reg 31 of SI 2008 No 1082 as from 27.10.08.
2. Amended by art 18(3) of SI 2014 No 3255 as from 31.12.14.

PART 2

Provisions affecting entitlement to housing benefit

Circumstances in which a person is or is not to be treated as occupying a dwelling as his home

7.–(1) Subject to the following provisions of this regulation, a person shall be treated as occupying as his home the dwelling normally occupied as his home–

(a) by himself or, if he is a member of a family, by himself and his family; or

(b) if he is polygamously married, by himself, his partners and any child or young person for whom he or any partner of his is responsible and who is a member of that same household,

and shall not be treated as occupying any other dwelling as his home.

(2) In determining whether a dwelling is the dwelling normally occupied as a person's home for the purpose of paragraph (1) regard shall be had to any other dwelling occupied by that person or any other person referred to in paragraph (1) whether or not that dwelling is in Great Britain.

(3) Where a single claimant or a lone parent is a student, other than one to whom regulation 56(1) of the Housing Benefit Regulations 2006 applies (circumstances in which certain students are treated as not liable to make payments in respect of a dwelling), or is on a training course and is liable to make payments (including payments of mortgage interest or, in Scotland, payments under heritable securities or, in either case, analogous payments) in respect of either (but not both) the dwelling which he occupies for the purpose of attending his course of study or, his training course, or as the case may be, the dwelling which he occupies when not attending his course, he shall be treated as

occupying as his home the dwelling in respect of which he is liable to make such payments.

(4)   Where a claimant has been required to move into temporary accommodation by reason of essential repairs being carried out to the dwelling normally occupied as his home, and is liable to make payments (including payments of mortgage interest or, in Scotland, payments under heritable securities or, in either case, analogous payments) in respect of either (but not both) the dwelling which he normally occupied as his home or the temporary accommodation, he shall be treated as occupying as his home the dwelling in respect of which he is liable to make payments.

(5)   Where a person is required to reside in a dwelling which is a bail hostel or probation hostel approved by the Secretary of State under [⁴section 13 of the Offender Management Act 2007], he shall not be treated as occupying that dwelling as his home.

(6)   Where a person is liable to make payments in respect of two (but not more than two) dwellings, he shall be treated as occupying both dwellings as his home only–

(a)   for a period not exceeding 52 weeks in the case where he has left and remains absent from the former dwelling occupied as his home through fear of violence in that dwelling or by a former member of his family and–

(i)   it is reasonable that housing benefit should be paid in respect of both his former dwelling and his present dwelling occupied as the home; and

(ii)   he intends to return to occupy the former dwelling as his home; or

(b)   in the case of a couple or a member of a polygamous marriage, where he or one partner is a student, other than one to whom regulation 56(1) of the Housing Benefit Regulations 2006 applies (circumstances in which certain students are treated as not liable to make payments in respect of a dwelling), or is on a training course and it is unavoidable that the partners should occupy two separate dwellings and reasonable that housing benefit should be paid in respect of both dwellings; or

(c)   in the case where, because of the number of persons referred to in paragraph (1), they have been housed by a housing authority in two separate dwellings; or

(d)   in the case where a person has moved into a new dwelling occupied as the home, except where paragraph (4) applies, for a period not exceeding four benefit weeks [¹ from the date on which he moved] if he could not reasonably have avoided liability in respect of two dwellings; or

(e)   in the case where a person–

(i)   is treated by virtue of paragraph (8) as occupying a dwelling as his home ("the new dwelling") and sub-paragraph (c)(i) of that paragraph applies; and

(ii)   he has occupied another dwelling as his home on any day within the period of 4 weeks immediately preceding the date he moved to the new dwelling, for a period not exceeding 4 benefit weeks immediately preceding the date on which he moved.

(7)   Where–

(a)   a person has moved into a dwelling for which he is not liable to make payments ("the new dwelling"); and

(b)   immediately before that move, he was liable to make payments for the dwelling he previously occupied as his home ("the former dwelling"); and

(c)   that liability continues after he has moved into the new dwelling,

he shall be treated as occupying the former dwelling as his home for a period not exceeding four benefit weeks if he could not reasonably have avoided liability in respect of that former dwelling.

(8)   [² Where]–

(a)   [² a person] has moved into a dwelling and was liable to make payments in respect of that dwelling before moving in; and

[² (b) either–

(i)   that person had claimed housing benefit before moving in and either no decision has yet been made on that claim or it has been refused but a further claim has been made or treated as made within 4 weeks of the date on which the claimant moved into the new dwelling occupied as the home; or

(ii) that person notified the move to the new dwelling as a change of circumstances under regulation 69 (duty to notify changes of circumstances) before the move, or the move to the new dwelling was otherwise notified before the move under that regulation; and]

(c) the delay in moving into the dwelling in respect of which there was liability to make payments before moving in was reasonable and–

(i) that delay was necessary in order to adapt the dwelling to meet the disablement needs of that person or any member of his family; or

(ii) the move was delayed pending [⁶ local welfare provision or] the outcome of an application under [³ Part 8] of the Act for a social fund payment to meet a need arising out of the move or in connection with setting up the home in the dwelling and either a member of the claimant's family is aged 5 or under or the claimant is a person who has attained or whose partner has attained the qualifying age for state pension credit; or

(iii) the claimant became liable to make payments in respect of the dwelling while he was a patient or in residential accommodation,

[² the person shall be treated] as occupying the dwelling as his home for any period not exceeding 4 weeks immediately prior to the date on which he moved into the dwelling and in respect of which he was liable to make payments.

(9) Where a person is treated by virtue of paragraph (8) as occupying a dwelling as his home in respect of the period before moving in, his claim for housing benefit in respect of that dwelling shall be treated as having been made on–

(a) in the case of a claim in respect of which a decision has not yet been made the date that claim was or was treated as made in accordance with regulation 64 (time and manner in which claims are to be made); or

(b) in the case of a claim for housing benefit in respect of that dwelling which has been refused and a further claim was or was treated as made in accordance with Part 9 (claims) within 4 weeks of the date on which he moved into the dwelling, the date on which the claim was refused or was treated as made; or

(c) the date from which he is treated by virtue of paragraph (8) as occupying the dwelling as his home,

whichever of those dates is the later.

(10) Where a person to whom neither paragraph (6)(a) nor (16)(c)(x) applies–

(a) formerly occupied a dwelling but has left and remains absent from it through fear of violence–

(i) in the dwelling; or

(ii) by a person who was formerly a member of the family of the person first mentioned; and

(b) has a liability to make payments in respect of that dwelling which is unavoidable,

he shall be treated as occupying the dwelling as his home for a period not exceeding 4 benefit weeks.

(11) This paragraph shall apply to a person who enters residential accommodation [⁷ in Great Britain]–

(a) for the purpose of ascertaining whether the accommodation suits his needs; and

(b) with the intention of returning to the dwelling which is normally occupied by him as his home should, in the event, the residential accommodation prove not to suit his needs; and

(c) while the part of the dwelling which is normally occupied by him as his home is not let, or as the case may be, sublet.

(12) A person to whom paragraph (11) applies shall be treated as if he is occupying the dwelling he normally occupies as his home for a period not exceeding, subject to an overall limit of 52 weeks on the absence from that home, 13 weeks beginning from the first day he enters [⁷ the residential accommodation].

[⁷ (13) Subject to paragraphs (13B) and (17), where a person is temporarily absent within Great Britain from his main dwelling, he shall be treated as occupying that dwelling as his home whilst he is so absent, subject to an overall limit of a period of 13 weeks beginning with the first day of the absence from the main dwelling, provided that–

(a) the person intends to return to occupy the main dwelling as his home;

(b) the part of the main dwelling normally occupied by the person has not been let or, as the case may be, sub-let; and

(c) the period of the absence within Great Britain is unlikely to extend beyond the overall limit.]

[[7](13A)] The period of 13 weeks referred to in paragraph (13) shall run or continue to run during any period of absence from Great Britain.

(13B) Where–

(a) a person returns to Great Britain after a period of absence from Great Britain;

(b) he has been absent from the main dwelling for less than 13 weeks beginning with the first day of absence from that dwelling; and

(c) at the outset of, or during, the period of absence from Great Britain, he ceased to be treated as occupying the main dwelling as his home,

then, for any day that follows the period of absence from Great Britain and precedes his return to the main dwelling, he shall not be treated as occupying the main dwelling as his home under paragraph (13).

(13C) This paragraph applies to a person who is temporarily absent from Great Britain and who occupied the main dwelling as his home, or was treated as occupying that dwelling as his home, immediately before the period of absence from Great Britain.

(13D) Subject to paragraphs (13E), (13G), (17C) and (17D) a person to whom paragraph (13C) applies shall be treated as occupying the main dwelling as his home whilst he is absent from Great Britain, for a period not exceeding 4 weeks beginning with the first day of that absence from Great Britain, provided that–

(a) the person intends to return to occupy the main dwelling as his home;

(b) the part of the main dwelling normally occupied by the person has not been let or, as the case may be, sub-let; and

(c) the period of absence outside Great Britain is unlikely to exceed 4 weeks.

(13E) If the temporary absence from the main dwelling is in connection with the death of–

(a) the person's partner or a child or young person for whom the person or the person's partner is responsible;

(b) the person's close relative;

(c) the close relative of the person's partner; or

(d) the close relative of a child or young person for whom the person or the person's partner is responsible,

then the period of 4 weeks in the opening words of paragraph (13D) may be extended by up to 4 further weeks if the relevant authority considers it unreasonable to expect the person to return to Great Britain within the first 4 weeks (and so that the reference in sub-paragraph (c) of that paragraph to a period of 4 weeks shall, where the period is extended, be taken as referring to the period as so extended).

(13F) This paragraph applies to a person who is temporarily absent from Great Britain as a member of Her Majesty's forces posted overseas, a mariner or a continental shelf worker, and who occupied the main dwelling as his home, or was treated as occupying that dwelling as his home, immediately before the period of absence from Great Britain.

(13G) A person to whom paragraph (13F) applies shall be treated as occupying the main dwelling as his home whilst he is absent from Great Britain, for a period not exceeding 26 weeks beginning with the first day of that absence from Great Britain, provided that–

(a) the person intends to return to occupy the main dwelling as his home;

(b) the part of the main dwelling normally occupied by the person has not been let or, as the case may be, sub-let; and

(c) the period of absence outside Great Britain is unlikely to exceed 26 weeks.]

(14) This paragraph applies to a person who is–

    (a)   detained in custody pending sentence upon conviction or under a sentence imposed by a court (other than a person who is detained in hospital under the provisions of the Mental Health Act 1983, or, in Scotland, under the provisions of the Mental Health (Care and Treatment) (Scotland) Act 2003 or the Criminal Procedure (Scotland) Act 1995); and

    (b)   on temporary release from detention in accordance with Rules made under the provisions of the Prison Act 1952 or the Prisons (Scotland) Act 1989.

(15)   Where paragraph (14) applies to a person, then, for any day when he is on temporary release–

    (a)   if such temporary release was immediately preceded by a period of temporary absence under paragraph (13) or (16), he shall be treated as if he continues to be absent from the dwelling, despite any occupation of the dwelling;

    (b)   for the purposes of paragraph (16)(c)(i), he shall be treated as if he remains in detention; and

    (c)   if he does not fall within sub-paragraph (a), he shall be treated as if he does not occupy his dwelling as his home despite any such occupation of the dwelling.

(16)   This paragraph shall apply to a person who is temporarily absent from the [⁷ main dwelling], if–

    (a)   he intends to return to occupy the [⁷ main dwelling] as his home; and

    (b)   while the part of the [⁷ main dwelling] which is normally occupied by him has not been let, or as the case may be, sublet; and

    (c)   he is–

        [⁶ (i)   a person to whom paragraph (16A) applies;]

        (ii)   resident in a hospital or similar institution as a patient; or

        (iii) undergoing, or as the case may be, his partner or his dependant child is undergoing [⁷] medical treatment, or medically approved convalescence, in accommodation other than residential accommodation; or

        (iv) following [⁷] a training course; or

        (v)   undertaking medically approved care of a person residing [⁷]; or

        (vi) undertaking the care of a child whose parent or guardian is temporarily absent from the dwelling normally occupied by that parent or guardian for the purpose of receiving medically approved care or medical treatment; or

        (vii) a person who is [⁷] receiving medically approved care provided in accommodation other than residential accommodation; or

        (viii) a student to whom paragraph (3) or (6)(b) does not apply; or

        (ix) a person who is receiving care provided in residential accommodation other than a person to whom paragraph (11) applies; or

        (x)   a person who has left the dwelling he occupies as his home through fear of violence, in that dwelling, or by a person who was formerly a member of the family of the person first mentioned, and to whom paragraph (6)(a) does not apply; and

[⁷ (d) in the case of–

        (i)   absence within Great Britain, any period of absence from the dwelling is unlikely to extend beyond or, in exceptional circumstances is unlikely substantially to extend beyond, an overall limit of 52 weeks beginning with the first day of the absence from the dwelling;

        (ii)   absence from Great Britain by a person to whom any of sub-paragraphs (c)(ii), (iii), (vii) or (x) apply, any period of absence from Great Britain is unlikely to exceed or, in exceptional circumstances is unlikely substantially to exceed, 26 weeks beginning with the first day of the absence from Great Britain; or

        (iii) absence from Great Britain by a person to whom paragraph (ii) of this sub-paragraph does not apply, any period of absence from Great Britain is unlikely to exceed or, in exceptional circumstances is unlikely substantially to exceed, 4 weeks beginning with the first day of absence from Great Britain.]

[⁶ (16A)   This paragraph applies to a person ("P") who is–

(a)   detained in custody on remand pending trial;
(b)   detained pending sentence upon conviction; or
(c)   as a condition of bail required to reside–
   (i)   in a dwelling, other than a dwelling P occupies as P's home; or
   (ii)   in premises approved under section 13 of the Offender Management Act 2007,
and who is not also detained in custody following sentence upon conviction.]

[⁷ (17)   Subject to paragraph (17B), a person to whom paragraph (16) applies who is absent within Great Britain, shall be treated as occupying the main as his home whilst he is so absent, subject to an overall limit of a period of 52 weeks beginning with the first day of the absence from the dwelling.]

[⁷ (17A)   The period of 52 weeks referred to in paragraph (17) shall run or continue to run during any period of absence from Great Britain.

(17B)   Where–
(a)   a person returns to Great Britain after a period of absence from Great Britain;
(b)   he has been absent from the main dwelling for less than 52 weeks beginning with the first day of absence from that dwelling; and
(c)   at the outset of, or during, the period of absence from Great Britain, he ceased to be treated as occupying the main dwelling as his home,
then, for any day that follows the period of absence from Great Britain and precedes his return to the main dwelling, he shall not be treated as occupying the main dwelling as his home under paragraph (17).

(17C)   A person to whom paragraph (16) applies who–
(a)   is a person described in any of sub-paragraphs (c)(ii), (iii), (vii) or (x) of that paragraph;
(b)   is temporarily absent from Great Britain; and
(c)   immediately before that period of temporary absence, occupied the main dwelling as his home or was treated as so occupying that dwelling,
shall be treated as occupying that dwelling as his home whilst he is absent from Great Britain, for a period not exceeding 26 weeks beginning with the first day of the absence from Great Britain.

(17D)   A person to whom paragraph (16) applies who–
(a)   is a person described in any of sub-paragraphs (c)(i), (iv), (v), (vi), (viii) or (ix) of that paragraph;
(b)   is temporarily absent from Great Britain; and
(c)   immediately before that period of temporary absence, occupied the main dwelling as his home or was treated as so occupying that dwelling,
shall be treated as occupying that dwelling as his home whilst he is absent from Great Britain, for a period not exceeding 4 weeks beginning with the first day of the absence from Great Britain.]

(18)   In this regulation–
[⁷ "continental shelf worker" means a person who is employed, whether under a contract of service or not, in a designated area or a prescribed area in connection with any activity mentioned in section 11(2) of the Petroleum Act 1998;
"designated area" means any area which may from time to time be designated by Order in Council under the Continental Shelf Act 1964 as an area within which the rights of the United Kingdom with respect to the seabed and subsoil and their natural resources may be exercised;
"main dwelling" means the dwelling that a person normally occupies as his home;
"mariner" means a person who is employed under a contract of service either as a master or member of the crew of any ship or vessel, or in any other capacity on board any ship or vessel, where–
(a)   the employment in that capacity is for the purposes of that ship or vessel or its crew or any passengers or cargo or mails carried by the ship or vessel; and
(b)   the contract is entered into in the United Kingdom with a view to its performance (in whole or in part) while the ship or vessel is on its voyage;]
"medically approved" means certified by a medical practitioner;

[⁷ "member of Her Majesty's forces posted overseas" means a person who is a member of the regular forces or the reserve forces (within the meaning of section 374 of the Armed Forces Act 2006), who is absent from the main dwelling because the person has been posted outside of Great Britain to perform the duties of a member of Her Majesty's regular forces or reserve forces;]

"patient" means a person who is undergoing medical or other treatment as an in-patient in any hospital or similar institution;

[⁷ "prescribed area" means any area over which Norway or any member State (other than the United Kingdom) exercises sovereign rights for the purpose of exploring the seabed and subsoil and exploiting their natural resources, being an area outside the territorial seas of Norway or such member State, or any other area which is from time to time specified under section 10(8) of the Petroleum Act 1998;]

"residential accommodation" means accommodation which is provided in–

    (a)   a care home;

    (b)   an independent hospital;

    (c)   an Abbeyfield Home; or

    (d)   an establishment managed or provided by a body incorporated by Royal Charter or constituted by Act of Parliament other than a local social services authority;

"training course" means a course of training or instruction provided wholly or partly by or on behalf of or in pursuance of arrangements made with, or approved by or on behalf of, [⁵ Skills Development Scotland,] Scottish Enterprise, Highlands and Islands Enterprise, a government department or the Secretary of State.

Amendments

1.   Amended by reg 6 of SI 2006 No 3274 as from 8.1.07.
2.   Amended by reg 12(3) of SI 2007 No 2618 as from 1.10.07.
3.   Amended by reg 4(3) of SI 2008 No 1042 as from 19.5.08.
4.   Amended by reg 7(3) of SI 2008 No 2767 as from 17.11.08.
5.   Amended by reg 7(3)(b) of SI 2009 No 583 as from 6.4.09.
6.   Amended by reg 8(3) of SI 2013 No 443 as from 2.4.13.
7.   Amended by reg 3(2) of SI 2016 No 624 as from 28.7.16, subject to transitional provision in reg 5 of SI 2016 No 624.

General Note

Reg 7 is nearly identical to reg 7 HB Regs (see p264). The only difference is in para (8)(c)(ii). Here, among the other conditions, rather than requiring that the claimant's applicable amount includes one of specific premiums or components, the claimant or her/his partner need only have reached the qualifying age for PC (defined in reg 2(1)).

Circumstances in which a person is to be treated as liable to make payments in respect of a dwelling

8.–(1)   Subject to regulation 9 (circumstances in which a person is to be treated as not liable to make payments in respect of a dwelling), the following persons shall be treated as if they were liable to make payments in respect of a dwelling–

    (a)   the person who is liable to make those payments;

    (b)   a person who is a partner of the person to whom sub-paragraph (a) applies;

    (c)   a person who has to make the payments if he is to continue to live in the home because the person liable to make them is not doing so and either–

        (i)   he was formerly a partner of the person who is so liable; or

        (ii)   he is some other person whom it is reasonable to treat as liable to make the payments;

    (d)   a person whose liability to make such payments is waived by his landlord as reasonable compensation in return for works actually carried out by the tenant in carrying out reasonable repairs or redecoration which the landlord would otherwise have carried out or be required to carry out but this sub-paragraph shall apply only for a maximum of 8 benefit weeks in respect of any one waiver of liability;

(e)   a person who is a partner of a student to whom regulation 56(1) of the Housing Benefit Regulations 2006 (circumstances in which certain students are treated as not liable to make payments in respect of a dwelling) applies.

(2)   A person shall be treated as liable to make a payment in respect of a dwelling for the whole of the period in, or in respect of, which the payment is to be made notwithstanding that the liability is discharged in whole or in part either before or during that period and, where the amount which a person is liable to pay in respect of a period is varied either during or after that period, he shall, subject to regulations 59 to 62 (dates of relevant changes of circumstances, weekly amounts and housing benefit for rent free periods), be treated as liable to pay the amount as so varied during the whole of that period.

Circumstances in which a person is to be treated as not liable to make payments in respect of a dwelling

9.–(1)   A person who is liable to make payments in respect of a dwelling shall be treated as if he were not so liable where–

(a)   the tenancy or other agreement pursuant to which he occupies the dwelling is not on a commercial basis;

(b)   his liability under the agreement is to a person who also resides in the dwelling and who is a close relative of his or of his partner;

(c)   his liability under the agreement is–

    (i)   to his former partner and is in respect of a dwelling which he and his former partner occupied before they ceased to be partners; or

    (ii)   to his partner's former partner and is in respect of a dwelling which his partner and his partner's former partner occupied before they ceased to be partners;

(d)   he is responsible, or his partner is responsible, for a child of the person to whom he is liable under the agreement;

(e)   subject to paragraph (3), his liability under the agreement is to a company or a trustee of a trust of which–

    (i)   he or his partner;

    (ii)   his or his partner's close relative who resides with him; or

    (iii)   his or his partner's former partner,

    is, in the case of a company, a director or an employee, or, in the case of a trust, a trustee or a beneficiary;

(f)   is liability under the agreement is to a trustee of a trust of which his or his partner's child is a beneficiary;

(g)   subject to paragraph (3), before the liability was created, he was a non-dependant of someone who resided, and continues to reside, in the dwelling;

(h)   he previously owned, or his partner previously owned, the dwelling in respect of which the liability arises and less than five years have elapsed since he or, as the case may be, his partner, ceased to own the property, save that this sub-paragraph shall not apply where he satisfies the appropriate authority that he or his partner could not have continued to occupy that dwelling without relinquishing ownership;

[¹ (ha) he or his partner–

    (i)   was a tenant under a long tenancy in respect of the dwelling; and

    (ii)   less than five years have elapsed since that tenancy ceased,

    except where he satisfies the appropriate authority that he or his partner could not have continued to occupy that dwelling without relinquishing the tenancy;]

(i)   his occupation, or his partner's occupation, of the dwelling is a condition of his or his partner's employment by the landlord;

(j)   he is a member of, and is wholly maintained (disregarding any liability he may have to make payments in respect of the dwelling he occupies as his home) by, a religious order;

(k)   he is in residential accommodation;

(1) in a case to which the preceding sub-paragraphs do not apply, the appropriate authority is satisfied that the liability was created to take advantage of the housing benefit scheme established under Part 7 of the Act.

(2) In determining whether a tenancy or other agreement pursuant to which a person occupies a dwelling is not on a commercial basis regard shall be had inter alia to whether the terms upon which the person occupies the dwelling include terms which are not enforceable at law.

(3) Sub-paragraphs (e) and (g) of paragraph (1) shall not apply in a case where the person satisfies the appropriate authority that the liability was not intended to be a means of taking advantage of the housing benefit scheme.

(4) In this regulation "residential accommodation" means accommodation which is provided in–

(a) a care home; or

(b) an independent hospital.

Modifications

Reg 9 applies as modified by Sch 3 para 9(3)(a) HB&CTB(CP) Regs (see p1803) to a claimant who on 3 October 2005 was someone to whom reg 7(2) of the HB Regs 1987 as then in force applied.

Reg 9 applies as modified by Sch 3 para 9(5)(a) HB&CTB(CP) Regs (see p1803) to a claimant who on 3 October 2005 was someone to whom reg 7(5) of the HB Regs 1987 as then in force applied.

Reg 9 applies as modified by Sch 3 para 9(7)(a) HB&CTB(CP) Regs (see p1803) to a claimant who on 3 October 2005 was someone to whom reg 7(7) of the HB Regs 1987 as then in force applied.

Amendment

1. Inserted by reg 3(3) of SI 2007 No 1356 as from 1.10.07.

Persons from abroad

10.–(1) A person from abroad who is liable to make payments in respect of a dwelling shall be treated as if he were not so liable but this paragraph shall not have effect in respect of a person to whom and for a period to which regulation 10A (entitlement of a refugee to housing benefit) and Schedule A1 (treatment of claims for housing benefit by refugees) apply.

[¹ (2) In paragraph (1), "person from abroad" means, subject to the following provisions of this regulation, a person who is not habitually resident in the United Kingdom, the Channel Islands, the Isle of Man or the Republic of Ireland.

(3) No person shall be treated as habitually resident in the United Kingdom, the Channel Islands, the Isle of Man or the Republic of Ireland unless he has a right to reside in (as the case may be) the United Kingdom, the Channel Islands, the Isle of Man or the Republic of Ireland other than a right to reside which falls within paragraph (4) [¹² or (4ZA)].

(4) A right to reside falls within this paragraph if it is one which exists by virtue of, or in accordance with, one or more of the following–

(a) regulation 13 of the [¹² Immigration (European Economic Area) Regulations 2016];

(b) regulation 14 of those Regulations, but only in a case where the right exists under that regulation because the person is–

(i) a jobseeker for the purpose of the definition of "qualified person" in regulation 6(1) of those Regulations, or

(ii) a family member (within the meaning of regulation 7 of those Regulations) of such a jobseeker;

[¹² (bb) regulation 16 of those Regulations, but only in a case where the right exists under that regulation because the person satisfies the criteria in paragraph (5) of that regulation;]

(c) Article 6 of Council Directive No. 2004/38/EC; [⁸]

(d) Article 39 of the Treaty establishing the European Community (in a case where the person is seeking work in the United Kingdom, the Channel Islands, the Isle of Man or the Republic of Ireland).[⁸; or

(e) Article 20 of the Treaty on the Functioning of the European Union (in a case where the right to reside arises because a British citizen would otherwise be deprived of the genuine enjoyment of the substance of their rights as a European Union citizen).]

[¹² (4ZA) A right to reside falls within this paragraph if it exists by vrtue of a person having been granted limited leave to enter, or remain in, the United Kingdom under the Immigration Act 1971 by virtue of–

(a) Appendix EU to the immigration rules made under section 3(2) of that Act; or

(b) being a person with a Zambrano right to reside as defined in Annex 1 of Appendix EU to the immigration rules made under section 3(2) of that Act.]

(4A) A person is not a person from abroad if he is–

[¹¹ (za) a qualified person for the purposes of regulation 6 of the [¹² Immigration (European Economic Area) Regulations 2016] as a worker or a self-employed person;]

[¹¹ (zb) a family member of a person referred to in sub-paragraph (za) within the meaning of regulation 7(1)(a), (b) or (c) of those Regulations;]

[¹¹ (zc) a person who has a right to reside permanently in the United Kingdom by virtue of regulation 15(1)(c), (d) or (e) of those Regulations;]

[¹¹ (a)–(e)]

[¹¹ [⁵ [⁹ (f)]]]

(g) a refugee;

[⁴ [¹⁰ (h) a person who has been granted leave or who is deemed to have been granted leave outside the rules made under section 3(2) of the Immigration Act 1971 where that leave is–

(i) discretionary leave to enter or remain in the United Kingdom;

(ii) leave to remain under the Destitution Domestic Violence concession; or

(iii) leave deemed to have been granted by virtue of regulation 3 of the Displaced Persons (Temporary Protection) Regulations 2005;]

(hh) a person who has humanitarian protection granted under those rules;]

(i) a person who is not a person subject to immigration control within the meaning of section 115(9) of the Immigration and Asylum Act 1999 and who is in the United Kingdom as a result of his deportation, expulsion or other removal by compulsion of law from another country to the United Kingdom; [¹⁰ or]

[¹⁰ (j)] [⁶]

[¹⁰ [⁶ (jj)]

(k) on state pension credit.]

[¹⁰ (5)]

(6) In this regulation–

[²]

"refugee" in this regulation means a person recorded by the Secretary of State as a refugee within the definition in Article 1 of the Convention relating to the Status of Refugees.

Modifications

Reg 10(4A)(a) to (e) applies in relation to a national of Norway, Iceland, Liechtenstein or Switzerland or a member of her/his family (within the meaning of Art 2 of Council Directive No.2004/38/EC) as if such a national were a national of a member state. See reg 10 of SI 2006 No.1026 on p1807.

The amendments made by SI 2006 No.1026 do not affect the continued operation of the transitional and savings provided for in reg 12 Social Security (Persons From Abroad) Miscellaneous Amendments Regulations 1996 (see p1633 of the 26th edition), reg 6 Social Security (Habitual Residence) Amendment Regulations 2004 (see p1771) or Sch 3 para 6 HB&CTB(CP) Regs (see p1795). See reg 11 of SI 2006 No.1026 on p1807.

From 25 July 2006 until 31 January 2007, a para (4A)(jj) was inserted by the Social Security (Lebanon) Amendment Regulations 2006 SI No.1981. See p701 of the 20th edition for the text of the insertion.

Amendments

1. Substituted by reg 5(2)(a) of SI 2006 No 1026 as from 30.4.06.
2. Omitted by reg 5(2)(b) of SI 2006 No 1026 as from 30.4.06.
3. Amended by reg 6 of SI 2006 No 1981 from 25.7.06 until 31.1.07 only.
4. Amended by reg 6 of SI 2006 No 2528 as from 9.10.06.

5.	Substituted by reg 6 of SI 2006 No 3341 as from 1.1.07.
6.	Amended by reg 6 of SI 2009 No 362 as from 18.3.09.
7.	Omitted by reg 20(3) of SI 2011 No 2425 as from 31.10.11.
8.	Amended by reg 6 of SI 2012 No 2587 as from 8.11.12.
9.	Substituted by reg 6 of SI 2013 No 1474 as from 1.7.13.
10.	Amended by reg 12(3) of SI 2013 No 2536 as from 28.10.13.
11.	Substituted by reg 6 of SI 2014 No 902 as from 31.5.14.
12.	Amended by reg 6 of SI 2019 No 872 as from 7.5.19.

Definition

"person on state pension credit" – see reg 2(1).

General Note

This regulation is substantially the same as reg 10 of the HB Regs. See the commentary to that provision at p297. The key difference is that claimants on PC (as defined in reg 2(1) this means in receipt of PC) are exempt from having the habitual residence test applied to them for HB purposes: para (4A)(k). That is similar to the rule about claimants on IS, income-based JSA and income-related ESA in reg 10(3B)(k) of the HB Regs – see the analysis at p326.

Note that it is not possible for a person over state retirement age whose only right of residence is as a jobseeker to employ the device of claiming income-based JSA in order to then get HB. When pension ages for men and women differ, that raises potential discrimination issues for a woman who can claim SPC but not income-based JSA as compared to a man of the same age who can claim income-based JSA and therefore obtain HB. Such a case may arise under EC Directive 79/7 (outside the scope of this work but discussed in Volume III of Sweet and Maxwell's *Social Security Legislation*).

Entitlement of a refugee to Housing Benefit
[¹ **10A.**]

Modification

Reg 10A was inserted by Sch 4 para 2(1) HB&CTB(CP) Regs. It only applied to claims for HB by some refugees.

Amendment

1.   Lapsed by s12(2)(e) of the Asylum and Immigration (Treatment of Claimants, etc.) Act 2004 (for those recorded as refugees after 14.6.07).

PART 3
Payments in respect of a dwelling

Eligible housing costs

[¹**11.**–(1)   Subject to the following provisions of this regulation, housing benefit shall be payable in respect of the payments specified in regulation 12(1) (rent) and a claimant's maximum housing benefit shall be calculated under Part 7 (amount of benefit) by reference to the amount of his eligible rent determined in accordance with–

(a)   regulation 12B (eligible rent);

(b)   regulations 12C (eligible rent and maximum rent), 13 (maximum rent), 13ZA (protection on death and 13 week protection) and 13ZB (change in reckonable rent);

(c)   regulations 12D (eligible rent and maximum rent (LHA)), 13C (when a maximum rent (LHA) is to be determined) and 13D (determination of a maximum rent (LHA)); or

(d)   regulations 12 (rent) and 13 (restrictions on unreasonable payments) as set out in paragraph 5 of Schedule 3 to the Consequential Provisions Regulations,

whichever is applicable in his case.]

(2)   Where any payment for which a person is liable in respect of a dwelling and which is specified in regulation 12(1) (payments of rent for which housing benefit is payable), is increased on account of–

(a)   outstanding arrears of any payment or charge; or

(b)   any other unpaid payment or charge,

to which [¹ paragraphs (1) or (2) of that regulation or paragraph (2) of regulation 12B] or Schedule 1 (ineligible service charges) refer and which is or was formerly owed by him in respect of that or another dwelling, a rent rebate or, as the case may be, a rent allowance shall not be payable in respect of that increase.

Modifications

Para (1) substituted by reg 4(3)(a) Housing Benefit (State Pension Credit) (Local Housing Allowance and Information Sharing) Amendment Regulations 2007 SI No.2869 as from 7 April 2008, save that for a person to whom reg 1(5) of those regulations applied (see p1814), the amendments came into force on the day on or after 7 April 2008 when the first of the events specified in reg 1(6) applied to her/him, or on 6 April 2009 if none had before that date.

Reg 11 is modified by Sch 9 para 3 (see p873). This applies only to former Pathfinder Authorities who administered the pilot local housing allowance scheme.

Amendment

1.   Substituted by reg 4(3) of SI 2007 No 2869 as from 7.4.08 (or if reg 1(5) of that SI applies, on the day on or after 7.4.08 when the first of the events specified in reg 1(6) applies, or from 6.4.09 if none have before that date).

General Note

Reg 4(3)(b) Housing Benefit (State Pension Credit) (Local Housing Allowance and Information Sharing) Amendment Regulations 2007 SI No.2869 says in respect of reg 11 HB(SPC) Regs: in paragraph (3) for "paragraphs (1) to (3) of that regulation" substitute "paragraphs (1) or (2) of that regulation or paragraph (2) of regulation 12B"". It is clear that this is meant to be an amendment to sub-paragraph (2).

Rent

12.–(1)   Subject to the following provisions of this regulation, the payments in respect of which housing benefit is payable in the form of a rent rebate or allowance are the following periodical payments which a person is liable to make in respect of the dwelling which he occupies as his home–

(a)   payments of, or by way of, rent;

(b)   payments in respect of a licence or permission to occupy the dwelling;

(c)   payments by way of mesne profits or, in Scotland, violent profits;

(d)   payments in respect of, or in consequence of, use and occupation of the dwelling;

(e)   payments of, or by way of, service charges payment of which is a condition on which the right to occupy the dwelling depends;

(f)   mooring charges payable for a houseboat;

(g)   where the home is a caravan or a mobile home, payments in respect of the site on which it stands;

(h)   any contribution payable by a person resident in an almshouse provided by a housing association which is either a charity of which particulars are entered in the register of charities established under section 3 of the Charities Act 1993 (register of charities) or an exempt charity within the meaning of that Act, which is a contribution towards the cost of maintaining that association's almshouses and essential services in them;

(i)   payments under a rental purchase agreement, that is to say an agreement for the purchase of a dwelling which is a building or part of one under which the whole or part of the purchase price is to be paid in more than one instalment and the completion of the purchase is deferred until the whole or a specified part of the purchase price has been paid; and

(j)   where, in Scotland, the dwelling is situated on or pertains to a croft within the meaning of section 3(1) of the Crofters (Scotland) Act 1993, the payment in respect of the croft land.

(2)   A rent rebate or, as the case may be, a rent allowance shall not be payable in respect of the following periodical payments–

(a)   payments under a long tenancy except a shared ownership tenancy [¹];

(b)   payments under a co-ownership scheme;

(c)   payments by an owner;

(d)   payments under a hire purchase, credit sale or conditional sale agreement except to the extent the conditional sale agreement is in respect of land; and

(e)   payments by a Crown tenant.

[¹ (f) payments by a person in respect of a dwelling where his partner is an owner of that dwelling.]

[⁴ (2A) Where a reduction in any of the payments listed in paragraph (1) for which a person would otherwise be liable is applied by a provider of social housing under an approved tenant incentive scheme, for the purposes of paragraph (1) the amount of the payment is to be treated as if no such reduction had been applied.

(2B) For the purposes of paragraph (2A)–

"approved tenant incentive scheme" means a scheme which is–

(a) operated by a provider of social housing and designed to avoid rent arrears by allowing reductions in the payments listed in paragraph (1) or other advantages in return for meeting specified conditions; and

(b) approved by the Secretary of State;

"provider of social housing" means–

(a) a local authority;

(b) a non-profit registered provider of social housing;

(c) in relation to accommodation which is social housing, a profit-making registered provider of social housing;

(d) a registered social landlord;

"registered social landlord" means–

(a) a body which is registered in the register maintained by the Welsh Ministers under Chapter 1 of Part 1 of the Housing Act 1996;

(b) a body which is registered in the register maintained by the Scottish Housing Regulator under the Housing (Scotland) Act 2010;

"social housing" has the meaning given in section 68 of the Housing and Regeneration Act 2008.]

[² (3)–(7)]

(8) In this regulation [³, regulation 12B (eligible rent)] and Schedule 1 (ineligible service charges)–

"service charges" means periodical payments for services, whether or not under the same agreement as that under which the dwelling is occupied, or whether or not such a charge is specified as separate from or separately identified within other payments made by the occupier in respect of the dwelling; and

"services" means services performed or facilities (including the use of furniture) provided for, or rights made available to, the occupier of a dwelling.

Modifications

Paras (3) to (7) omitted and para (8) amended by reg 4(4) Housing Benefit (State Pension Credit) (Local Housing Allowance and Information Sharing) Amendment Regulations 2007 SI No.2869 as from 7 April 2008, save that for a person to whom reg 1(5) of those regulations applied (see p1814), the amendments came into force on the day on or after 7 April 2008 when the first of the events specified in reg 1(6) applied to her/him, or on 6 April 2009 if none had before that date.

A different version of reg 12 is substituted and used to determine eligible rent for some claimants entitled to HB on 1 January 1996. See Sch 3 paras 4 and 5 (1) HB&CTB(CP) Regs on p1776.

Amendments

1. Inserted by reg 3(4) of SI 2007 No 1356 as from 1.10.07.
2. Omitted by reg 4(4)(a) of SI 2007 No 2869 as from 7.4.08 (or if reg 1(5) of that SI applies, on the day on or after 7.4.08 when the first of the events specified in reg 1(6) applies, or from 6.4.09 if none have before that date).
3. Amended by reg 4(4)(b) of SI 2007 No 2869 as from 7.4.08 (or if reg 1(5) of that SI applies, on the day on or after 7.4.08 when the first of the events specified in reg 1(6) applies, or from 6.4.09 if none have before that date).
4. Inserted by reg 21 of SI 2017 No 995 as from 7.11.17.

[¹ **Eligible rent**

12B.–(1) The amount of a person's eligible rent shall be determined in accordance with the provisions of this regulation except where regulations 12C (eligible rent and maximum rent) or 12D (eligible rent and maximum rent (LHA)) apply, or paragraph 4 of Schedule 3 to the Consequential Provisions Regulations applies.

(2)   Subject to paragraphs (3), (4) and (6), the amount of a person's eligible rent shall be the aggregate of such payments specified in regulation 12(1) as that person is liable to pay less–

(a)   except where he is separately liable for charges for water, sewerage or allied environmental services, an amount determined in accordance with paragraph (5);

(b)   where payments include service charges which are wholly or partly ineligible, an amount in respect of the ineligible charges determined in accordance with Schedule 1; and

(c)   where he is liable to make payments in respect of any service charges to which regulation 12(1)(e) does not apply, but to which paragraph 3(2) of Part 1 of Schedule 1 (unreasonably low service charges) applies in the particular circumstances, an amount in respect of such charges determined in accordance with paragraph 3(2) of Part 1 of Schedule 1.

(3)   Where the payments specified in regulation 12(1) are payable in respect of accommodation which consists partly of residential accommodation and partly of other accommodation, only such proportion of those payments as is referable to the residential accommodation shall count as eligible rent for the purposes of these Regulations.

(4)   Where more than one person is liable to make payments in respect of a dwelling, the payments specified in regulation 12(1) shall be apportioned for the purpose of calculating the eligible rent for each such person having regard to all the circumstances, in particular, the number of such persons and the proportion of rent paid by each such person.

(5)   The amount of the deduction referred to in paragraph (2) shall be–

(a)   if the dwelling occupied by the claimant is a self-contained unit, except in a case to which sub-paragraph (c) applies, the amount of the charges;

(b)   in any other case, except one to which sub-paragraph (c) applies, the proportion of those charges in respect of the self-contained unit which is obtained by dividing the area of the dwelling occupied by the claimant by the area of the self-contained unit of which it forms part;

(c)   where the charges vary in accordance with the amount of water actually used, the amount which the appropriate authority considers to be fairly attributable to water, and sewerage services, having regard to the actual or estimated consumption of the claimant.

(6)   In any case where it appears to the relevant authority that in the particular circumstances of that case the eligible rent as determined in accordance with the preceding paragraphs of this regulation is greater than it is reasonable to meet by way of housing benefit, the eligible rent shall be such lesser sum as seems to that authority to be an appropriate rent in that particular case.]

Modifications

Reg 12B is modified by Sch 9 para 4 (see p873). This applies only to former Pathfinder Authorities who administered the pilot local housing allowance scheme.

Amendment

1.   Inserted by reg 5 of SI 2007 No 2869 as from 7.4.08 (or if reg 1(5) of that SI applies, on the day on or after 7.4.08 when the first of the events specified in reg 1(6) applies, or from 6.4.09 if none have before that date).

General Note

This regulation is broadly the same as reg 12B HB Regs. However, here, there is no reference in para (1) to eligible rent and maximum rent (social sector) as there is no equivalent to the "social sector" scheme for rent restriction in the HB(SPC) Regs. Thus, "eligible rent" for HB purposes under the HB(SPC) Regs is determined under reg 12B, together with Sch 1, unless regs 12C or 12D (respectively the "local reference rent" and "local housing allowance" schemes) or Sch 3 para 4 HB&CTB(CP) Regs (the "pre-January 1996" scheme) apply.

[¹ Eligible rent and maximum rent

12C.–(1)   This regulation applies where a maximum rent has been, or is to be, determined in accordance with regulation 13 (maximum rent).

(2)   Where this regulation applies the amount of a person's eligible rent shall be the maximum rent, subject to paragraphs (3), (4) and (6) of regulation 12B.]

Amendment

1.   Inserted by reg 5 of SI 2007 No 2869 as from 7.4.08 (or if reg 1(5) of that SI applies, on the day on or after 7.4.08 when the first of the events specified in reg 1(6) applies, or from 6.4.09 if none have before that date).

[¹ Eligible rent and maximum rent (LHA)

12D.–(1)   [² Except where regulation 12M (transitional protection – reduction in LHA) applies,] this regulation applies where, by virtue of paragraphs (2) or (3) of regulation 13C (when a maximum rent (LHA) is to be determined), a maximum rent (LHA) has been, or is to be, determined in accordance with regulation 13D (determination of a maximum rent (LHA)).

(2)   Where this regulation applies, except where paragraphs (3)(a) (protection on death) or (5)(a) (13 week protection) apply–

(a)   the amount of a person's eligible rent shall be the maximum rent (LHA); and

(b)   it shall apply until the earlier of–

(i)   the determination of a maximum rent (LHA) by virtue of regulation 13C(2)(d) (change of category of dwelling, death or change of dwelling for an LHA case);

(ii)   the determination of a maximum rent (LHA) by virtue of regulation 13C(3) (anniversary of LHA date); or

(iii)   the determination of a maximum rent by virtue of regulation 13 or an eligible rent under regulation 12B.

(3)   Subject to paragraph (7), where the relevant authority is required to determine a maximum rent (LHA) by virtue of regulation 13C(2)(a), (b) (new claim on or after 7th April 2008) or (d)(i) or (ii) (change of category of dwelling or death relating to an LHA case) and the claimant occupies a dwelling which is the same as that occupied by him at the date of death of any linked person, the eligible rent shall be–

(a)   either–

(i)   the eligible rent which applied on the day before the death occurred; or

(ii)   in a case where there was no eligible rent, subject to regulation 12B(3) (mixed use accommodation), (4) (more than one person liable to make payments) and (6) (discretion in relation to eligible rent), the reckonable rent due on that day; or

(b)   the eligible rent determined in accordance with paragraph (2), where it is equal to or more than the eligible rent determined in accordance with sub-paragraph (a).

[³ (4)   For the purpose of paragraph (3), a claimant is treated as occupying the dwelling if–

(a)   any of paragraphs (13), (13D) (with (13E) where applicable) or (13G) of regulation 7 (circumstances in which a person is or is not to be treated as occupying a dwelling as his home) is satisfied and for that purpose those paragraphs shall have effect as if sub-paragraph (b) of those paragraphs were omitted; or

(b)   any of paragraphs (17), (17C) or (17D) of regulation 7 is satisfied and for that purpose those paragraphs shall have effect as if sub-paragraph (b) of paragraph (16) of that regulation were omitted.]

(5)   Subject to paragraphs (6) and (7), where a relevant authority is required to determine a maximum rent (LHA) by virtue of regulation 13C(2)(a) or (b) (new claim on or after 7th April 2008) and the relevant authority is satisfied that the claimant or a linked person was able to meet the financial commitments for his dwelling when they were entered into, the eligible rent shall be–

(a)   an eligible rent determined in accordance with regulation 12B(2); or

(b)   the eligible rent determined in accordance with paragraph (2), where it is equal to or more than the eligible rent referred to in sub-paragraph (a).

(6)   Paragraph (5) shall not apply where a claimant or the claimant's partner, was previously entitled to benefit in respect of an award of housing benefit which fell wholly or partly less than 52 weeks before the commencement of the claimant's current award of housing benefit.

(7)   Where a person's eligible rent has been determined in accordance with–

(a)   paragraph (3)(a) (protection on death), it shall apply until the first of the following events occurs–

    (i)   the period of 12 months from the date of death has expired;

    (ii)   the relevant authority determines an eligible rent in accordance with paragraph (2) which is equal to or exceeds it or is based on a maximum rent (LHA) determined by virtue of regulation 13C(2)(d)(iii) (change of dwelling);

    (iii)   the determination of an eligible rent in accordance with paragraph (3)(a) (protection on death) in relation to a subsequent death; or

    (iv)   the determination of a maximum rent by virtue of regulation 13 or an eligible rent under regulation 12B.

(b)   paragraph (5)(a) (13 week protection), it shall apply until the first of the following events occurs–

    (i)   the first 13 weeks of the claimant's award of housing benefit have expired;

    (ii)   the relevant authority determines an eligible rent in accordance with paragraph (2) which is equal to or exceeds it or is based on a maximum rent (LHA) determined by virtue of regulation 13C(2)(d)(iii) (change of dwelling);

    (iii)   the determination of an eligible rent in accordance with paragraph (3)(a) (protection on death); or

    (iv)   the determination of a maximum rent by virtue of regulation 13 or an eligible rent under regulation 12B.

(8)   Where an eligible rent ceases to apply by virtue of paragraph (7)(a)(i) (expiry of protection on death) or (7)(b)(i) (expiry of 13 week protection), the eligible rent that shall apply instead shall be the one which would have applied but for paragraphs (3)(a) and (5)(a).]

Modifications

Reg 12D is modified by Sch 9 para 5 (see p873). This applies only to former Pathfinder Authorities who administered the pilot local housing allowance scheme.

Amendments

1.   Inserted by reg 5 of SI 2007 No 2869 as from 7.4.08 (or if reg 1(5) of that SI applies, on the day on or after 7.4.08 when the first of the events specified in reg 1(6) applies, or from 6.4.09 if none have before that date).

2.   Amended by reg 3(3) of SI 2010 No 2835 as from 1.4.11.

3.   Substituted by reg 3(3) of SI 2016 No 624 as from 28.7.16, subject to transitional provision in reg 5 of SI 2016 No 624.

Transitional protection for pathfinder cases
12E.–12K.

General Note

Regs 12E to 12K are inserted by Sch 9 para 6 (see p873). They only apply to former Pathfinder Authorities who administered the pilot local housing allowance scheme.

[² [¹ Transitional protection – larger properties
12L.]

Amendments

1.   Inserted by reg 3(2) of SI 2009 No 614 as from 6.4.09.

2.   Omitted by reg 3(4) of SI 2010 No 2835 as from 1.4.11.

[¹ Transitional protection – reduction in LHA

12M.–(1)   This regulation applies where–
(a)   reference was made to a maximum rent (LHA) in determining the amount of the eligible rent which applied immediately before 1st April 2011;
(b)   on or after 1st April 2011 the relevant authority is required to determine a maximum rent (LHA) by virtue of–
    (i)   regulation 13C(2)(d)(i) (change of category of dwelling) because the claimant has become entitled to a larger category of dwelling; or
    (ii)   regulation 13C(3) (anniversary of LHA date); and
(c)   the determination referred to in sub-paragraph (b) is the first determination of a maximum rent (LHA) the relevant authority is required to make on or after 1st April 2011.
(2)   Where this regulation applies, the claimant's eligible rent is–
(a)   the maximum rent (LHA) where that is equal to or higher than the eligible rent which applied immediately before 1st April 2011; or
(b)   in any other case, the lower of–
    (i)   the amount of the eligible rent which applied immediately before 1st April 2011; or
    (ii)   the amount of the cap rent by reference to which the maximum rent (LHA) referred to in paragraph (1)(b) was determined.
(3)   Where the claimant's eligible rent is determined in accordance with paragraph (2)(b) it will continue to apply until, on or after 1st April 2011, the first of the following events occurs–
(a)   the period 9 months after the determination of the maximum rent (LHA) referred to in paragraph (1)(b) has expired;
(b)   the relevant authority is required to determine a new maximum rent (LHA) by virtue of regulation 13C(2)(d)(i) (change of category of dwelling) because the claimant has become entitled to a larger category of dwelling and the maximum rent (LHA) is equal to or higher than the eligible rent referred to in paragraph (2)(b);
(c)   the relevant authority is required to determine a new maximum rent (LHA) by virtue of regulation 13C(2)(d)(i) (change of category of dwelling) because the claimant has become entitled to a smaller category of dwelling;
(d)   the relevant authority is required to determine an eligible rent following a change of dwelling; or
(e)   the relevant authority is required to determine an eligible rent in accordance with regulation 12D(3) (protection on death).
(4)   Where the eligible rent ceases to apply because of paragraph (3)(a), the eligible rent will be the maximum rent (LHA) which would have applied but for the transitional protection in paragraph (2)(b).
(5)   Where the eligible rent is the maximum rent (LHA), it shall be treated as if it had been determined in accordance with regulation 12D(2)(a) (eligible rent is maximum rent (LHA)) and shall apply according to the provisions of regulation 12D.]

Amendment
1.   Inserted by reg 3(5) of SI 2010 No 2835 as from 1.4.11.

Maximum rent

[¹ **13.**–(1)   The maximum rent shall be determined in accordance with paragraphs (2) to (6) where–
(a)   a local authority has applied for a determination in accordance with regulation 14 (requirement to refer to rent officers), a redetermination in accordance with regulation 15 or 16, or a substitute determination or substitute redetermination in accordance with regulation 17 and a rent officer has made a determination, redetermination, substitute determination or substitute redetermination in exercise of the Housing Act functions; or

(b)　　an authority is not required to apply to the rent officer for a determination because–
　　(i)　　regulation 14(2)(a) applies; or
　　(ii)　　regulation 14(2)(b) applies because paragraph 2(2) of Schedule 2 applies.

(2)　　In a case where the rent officer has determined a claim-related rent, but is not required to notify the relevant authority of a local reference rent, the maximum rent shall be that claim-related rent.

(3)　　Subject to the limit specified in paragraph (4), in a case where the rent officer has determined both a local reference rent of which he is required to notify the relevant authority and a claim-related rent, the maximum rent shall be the local reference rent.

(4)　　In a case to which paragraph 8 of Schedule 3 to the Consequential Provisions Regulations applies, where the rent officer has determined and is required to notify the relevant authority of a local reference rent the maximum rent shall not exceed twice that local reference rent.

(5)　　Where the maximum rent is derived from–
(a)　　a claim-related rent and the notification under paragraph 9(1)(c) of Schedule 1 to the Rent Officers Order states that an ineligible amount in respect of meals has been included in that claim-related rent; or
(b)　　a local reference rent and the notification under paragraph 9(1)(da) of Schedule 1 to the Rent Officers Order states that an ineligible amount in respect of meals has been included in that local reference rent,

in determining the maximum rent the relevant authority shall deduct an amount determined in accordance with paragraph 2 of Schedule 1 to these Regulations in respect of meals.

(6)　　This regulation is subject to regulations 13ZA (protection on death and 13 week protection) and 13ZB (change in reckonable rent).

(7)　　In this regulation–

"claim-related rent" means the rent notified by the rent officer under paragraph 9(1) of Schedule 1 to the Rent Officers Order;

"local reference rent" means the rent determined by a rent officer under paragraph 4 of Schedule 1 to the Rent Officers Order.]

Modifications

Reg 13 substituted by reg 6 Housing Benefit (State Pension Credit) (Local Housing Allowance and Information Sharing) Amendment Regulations 2007 No.2869 as from 7 April 2008, save that for a person to whom reg 1(5) of those regulations applied (see p1814), the amendments came into force on the day on or after 7 April 2008 when the first of the events specified in reg 1(6) applied to her/him, or on 6 April 2009 if none had before that date.

A different version of reg 13 is substituted for some claimants entitled to HB on 1 January 1996. See Sch 3 paras 4 and 5(2) HB&CTB(CP) Regs on p1776.

Reg 13 applies as modified by Sch 3 para 8 HB&CTB(CP) Regs (see p1785) for some claimants entitled to HB on or before 5 October 1997.

Amendment

1.　　Inserted by reg 6 of SI 2007 No 2869 as from 7.4.08 (or if reg 1(5) that SI applies, on the day on or after 7.4.08 when the first of the events specified in reg 1(6) applies, or from 6.4.09 if none have before that date).

General Note

Reg 13 is nearly identical to reg 13 HB Regs (see p380). In the HB(SPC) Regs, there are naturally no rules in respect of a "young individual".

[¹ **Protection on death and 13 week protection**

13ZA.–(1)　　In a case where the claimant occupies a dwelling which is the same as that occupied by him at the date of death of a linked person, the maximum rent shall be either–
(a)　　the maximum rent which applied before the death occurred; or
(b)　　in a case where there was no maximum rent, the reckonable rent due before the death occurred,

for a period of 12 months from the date of such a death.

[² (2)   For the purposes of paragraph (1), a claimant is treated as occupying the dwelling if–

(a)   any of paragraphs (13), (13D) (with (13E) where applicable) or (13G) of regulation 7 (circumstances in which a person is or is not to be treated as occupying a dwelling as his home) is satisfied and for that purpose those paragraphs shall have effect as if sub-paragraph (b) of those paragraphs were omitted; or

(b)   any of paragraphs (17), (17C) or (17D) of regulation 7 is satisfied and for that purpose those paragraphs shall have effect as if sub-paragraph (b) of paragraph (16) of that regulation were omitted.]

(3)   Subject to paragraph (4), where the relevant authority is satisfied that the claimant or a linked person was able to meet the financial commitments for his dwelling when they were entered into, there shall be no maximum rent during the first 13 weeks of the claimant's award of housing benefit.

(4)   Paragraph (3) shall not apply where a claimant or the claimant's partner was previously entitled to benefit in respect of an award of housing benefit which fell wholly or partly less than 52 weeks before the commencement of the claimant's current award of housing benefit.]

Modifications

A different version of reg 13ZA is substituted for some claimants entitled to HB on 1 January 1996. See Sch 3 paras 4 and 5(3) HB&CTB(CP) Regs on p1776.

Amendments

1.   Inserted by reg 6 of SI 2007 No 2869 as from 7.4.08 (or if reg 1(5) that SI applies, on the day on or after 7.4.08 when the first of the events specified in reg 1(6) applies, or from 6.4.09 if none have before that date).

2.   Substituted by reg 3(4) of SI 2016 No 624 as from 28.7.16, subject to transitional provision in reg 5 of SI 2016 No 624.

[¹ Change in reckonable rent

13ZB.–(1)   In a case where–

(a)   the authority has determined a maximum rent under regulation 13 or 13ZA; and

(b)   during the period for which that maximum rent applies the reckonable rent in respect of the dwelling by reference to which that maximum rent was determined is reduced to a sum which is less than that maximum rent,

the maximum rent shall be reduced to an amount equal to the reduced reckonable rent.

(2)   This paragraph applies in a case where–

(a)   a rent officer has made a determination in exercise of the Housing Act functions pursuant to an application by an authority under regulation 14(1)(e) (pre-tenancy determination);

(b)   subsequent to that determination the reckonable rent for that dwelling is changed; and

(c)   a maximum rent is to be determined in relation to a claim for housing benefit by a claimant.

(3)   In a case to which paragraph (2) applies, where the reckonable rent is reduced to a figure below the figure that would have been the maximum rent if the reckonable rent had not changed, the maximum rent shall be the reckonable rent as so reduced.

(4)   In any other case to which paragraph (2) applies, the authority shall treat the reckonable rent to be that applicable to the determination by the rent officer referred to in paragraph (2)(a).]

Amendment

1.   Inserted by reg 6 of SI 2007 No 2869 as from 7.4.08 (or if reg 1(5) that SI applies, on the day on or after 7.4.08 when the first of the events specified in reg 1(6) applies, or from 6.4.09 if none have before that date).

[¹ When a maximum rent (LHA) is to be determined
13C.–(1)   A relevant authority shall determine a maximum rent (LHA) in accordance with regulation 13D (determination of a maximum rent (LHA)) in any case where paragraphs (2) or (3) apply.
(2)   This paragraph applies where a relevant authority has received–
(a)   a claim on which a rent allowance may be awarded, where the date of claim falls on or after 7th April 2008;
(b)   relevant information regarding a claim on which a rent allowance may be awarded, where the date of claim falls on or after 7th April 2008;
(c)   in relation to an award of housing benefit where the eligible rent was determined without reference to regulation 13A or 13D, a notification of a change of dwelling (as defined in regulation 2) where the change occurs on or after 7th April 2008; or
(d)   in relation to an award of housing benefit where a maximum rent (LHA) was determined in accordance with regulation 13D–
(i)   notification of a change of a kind which affects the category of dwelling applicable to the claim;
(ii)   notification of the death of a linked person, where the notification does not fall within head (i); [⁵]
(iii)   notification of a change of dwelling.[⁵ or
(iv)   notification of a change of a kind which affects the amount of the claimant's cap rent as determined in accordance with regulation 13D (determination of a maximum rent (LHA)).]
[⁴ (3)   This paragraph applies on 1st April in any year.]
[⁴ (4)]
(5)   This regulation does not apply in a case where–
[³ (a)   the landlord is–
(i)   a registered social landlord,
(ii)   a non-profit registered provider of social housing, or
(iii)   in relation to a dwelling which is social housing (within the meaning of sections 68 to 77 of the Housing and Regeneration Act 2008), a profit-making registered provider of social housing;]
(b)   paragraph 4(1)(b) of Schedule 3 to the Consequential Provisions Regulations (savings provision) applies;
(c)   the tenancy is an excluded tenancy of a type [² mentioned in any of paragraphs 4 to 11] of Schedule 2;
(d)   the claim or award relates to–
(i)   periodical payments of kind falling within regulation 12(1) (rent) which a person is liable to make in relation to a houseboat, caravan or mobile home which he occupies as his home; or
(ii)   rent payable in relation to a hostel; or
(e)   rent under the tenancy is attributable to board and attendance, and–
(i)   the relevant authority has made an application to the rent officer in accordance with regulation 13D(10) (board and attendance determination), regulation 15 (applications to the rent officer for determinations) or regulation 17 (substitute determinations or substitute redeterminations); and
(ii)   the rent officer has determined that a substantial part of the rent under the tenancy is fairly attributable to board and attendance and has notified the relevant authority of this in accordance with article 4C, 4D or 4E of the Rent Officers Order.
(6)   In this regulation–
[⁴]
"registered social landlord" has the same meaning as in Part 1 of the Housing Act 1996 or, in Scotland, sections 57 and 59 of the Housing (Scotland) Act 2001.]

Modifications

Reg 13C is modified by Sch 9 para 7 (see p873). This applies only to former Pathfinder Authorities who administered the pilot local housing allowance scheme.

Amendments

1. Inserted by reg 7 of SI 2007 No 2869 as from 7.4.08 (or if reg 1(5) that SI applies, on the day on or after 7.4.08 when the first of the events specified in reg 1(6) applies, or from 6.4.09 if none have before that date).
2. Amended by reg 5(4)(a) of SI 2008 No 586 as from 7.4.08.
3. Substituted by art 4 and Sch 1 para 58 of SI 2010 No 671 as from 1.4.10.
4. Amended by reg 4(2)(b)-(d) of SI 2012 No 3040 as from 1.1.13.
5. Amended by reg 4(2)(a) of SI 2012 No 3040 as from 1.4.13.

[¹ **Determination of a maximum rent (LHA)**

13D.–(1)   Subject to paragraph (3) to (11), the maximum rent (LHA) shall be the local housing allowance determined by the rent officer by virtue of article 4B(2A) or (4) of the Rent Officers Order which is applicable to–

(a)   the broad rental market area in which the dwelling to which the claim or award of housing benefit relates is situated at the relevant date; and

(b)   the category of dwelling which applies at the relevant date in accordance with paragraph (2).

(2)   The category of dwelling which applies is–

(a)   the category specified in paragraph 1(1)(a) of Schedule 3B to the Rent Officers Order (one bedroom shared accommodation) where paragraph (b) does not apply because neither sub-paragraph (b)(i) nor (ii) are satisfied in the claimant's case and–

    (i)   neither the claimant nor his partner (where he has one) is a person to whom paragraph 6 of Schedule 3 (severe disability premium) applies; or

    [² (ii) the claimant's partner is not a care leaver;]

(b)   the category specified in paragraph 1(1)(b) of Schedule 3B to the Rent Officers Order (one bedroom self contained accommodation) where that applies in the claimant's case at the relevant date in accordance with the size criteria [² as set out in paragraph (3)] and–

    (i)   the claimant (together with his partner where he has one) has the exclusive use of two or more rooms; or

    (ii)   the claimant (together with his partner where he has one) has the exclusive use of one room, a bathroom and toilet and a kitchen or facilities for cooking,

    and in this sub-paragraph "room" means a bedroom or room suitable for living in except for a room which the claimant shares with any person other than a member of his household, a non-dependant of his, or a person who pays rent to him or his partner; or

(c)   in any other case, the category which corresponds with the number of bedrooms to which the claimant is entitled in accordance with [⁵ paragraphs (3) to (3B)] [³ [⁴ up to a maximum of four bedrooms]].

(3)   The claimant shall be entitled to one bedroom for each of the following categories of occupier (and each occupier shall come within the first category only which applies to him)–

[⁹ (za) a member of a couple who cannot share a bedroom;

(zb)   a member of a couple who can share a bedroom;]

(a)   a couple [⁹];

(b)   a person who is not a child;

[⁸ (ba) a child who cannot share a bedroom;]

(c)   two children of the same sex;

(d)   two children who are less than 10 years old;

(e)   a child.

[⁸ but the claimant is only entitled to a bedroom in respect of a child who cannot share a bedroom [⁹ or a member of a couple who cannot share a bedroom] if there is a bedroom in the dwelling occupied as the home that is additional to those to which the claimant would be entitled if the child [⁹ or the member of the couple] were able to share a bedroom.]

[⁴ [⁵]]

[⁶ (3A)   The claimant is entitled to one additional bedroom in any case where–

[⁹ (a)   one or more of the following persons is a person who requires overnight care–

    (i)   the claimant;

    (ii)   the claimant's partner;

    (iii) a person (other than the claimant or the claimant's partner) who occupies the claimant's dwelling as their home;

    (iv) a child or young person in respect of whom the claimant or the claimant's partner is a qualifying parent or carer; or]

(b)   the claimant or the claimant's partner is (or each of them is) a qualifying parent or carer.]

[⁶ (3B)   The claimant is entitled to two additional bedrooms where paragraphs (3A)(a) and (b) both apply.]

(4)   The relevant authority shall determine–

(a)   the cap rent (in accordance with the definition in paragraph (12)); and

(b)   whether the cap rent exceeds the applicable local housing allowance.

[⁴ (5)   Where the applicable local housing allowance exceeds the cap rent, the maximum rent (LHA) shall be the cap rent.]

[⁴ (6)]

[³ (7)]

[⁴ (8)]

[⁴ (9)]

(10)   The relevant authority shall apply to the rent officer for a board and attendance determination to be made in accordance with article 4C of the Rent Officers Order where–

(a)   the relevant authority is required to determine a maximum rent (LHA) by virtue of regulation 13C; and

(b)   part of the rent under the tenancy appears to the relevant authority to be likely to be attributable to board and attendance.

(11)   Where an application to a rent officer is required in accordance with paragraph (10) it shall be made within the same period following the day on which the relevant authority becomes obliged to determine a maximum rent (LHA) by virtue of regulation 13C as would be required if the application were to be made under regulation 14(1).

(12)   In this regulation–

"cap rent" means the aggregate of such payments specified in regulation 12(1) (rent) which the claimant is liable to pay, or is treated as liable to pay by virtue of regulation 8 (circumstances in which a person is treated as liable to make payments in respect of a dwelling) subject to regulation 12B(3) (mixed use accommodation), (4) (more than one person liable to make payments) and (6) (discretion in relation to eligible rent);

"care leaver" means a person who has not attained the age of 22 and–

(a)   has ceased to be the subject of a care order made pursuant to section 31(1)(a) of the Children Act 1989 which had previously been made in respect to him either–

    (i)   after he attained the age of 16 years; or

    (ii) before he attained the age of 16 years, but had continued after he attained that age;

(b)   was formerly provided with accommodation under section 20 of the Children Act 1989 [¹⁰ or section 76 of the Social Services and Well-being (Wales) Act 2014];

(c)   has ceased to be subject to a supervision requirement by a children's hearing under section 70 of the Children (Scotland) Act 1995 ("the 1995 Act") made in respect of him which had continued after he attained the age of 16 years, other than a case where–

      (i)   the ground of referral was based on the sole condition as to the need for compulsory measures of care specified in section 52(1)(i) of the 1995 Act (commission of offences by child); or

      (ii)   he was required by virtue of the supervision requirement to reside with a parent or guardian of his within the meaning of the 1995 Act, or with a friend or relative of his or of his parent or guardian;

[⁷(ca) that person has ceased to be subject to a compulsory supervision order within the meaning of section 83 of the Children's Hearings (Scotland) Act 2011 ("the 2011 Act") which had continued after that person attained the age of 16 years, other than a case where–

      (i)   the section 67 ground (within the meaning of that Act) was based on the sole condition as to the need for compulsory measures of supervision specified in section 67(2)(j) of the 2011 Act (the child has committed an offence); or

      (ii)   that person was required by virtue of the compulsory supervision order to reside with a parent or guardian of that person within the meaning of the 1995 Act, or with a friend or relative of that person or of that person's parent or guardian;]

(d)   has ceased to be a child in relation to whom the parental rights and responsibilities were transferred to a local authority under a parental responsibilities order made in accordance with section 86 of the 1995 Act or treated as so vested in accordance with paragraph 3 of Schedule 3 to that Act [⁵ or has ceased to be a child in relation to whom a permanence order under section 80 of the Adoption and Children (Scotland) Act 2007 has been made, or treated as made], either–

      (i)   after he attained the age of 16 years; or

      (ii)   before he attained the age of 16 years, but had continued after he attained that age; or

(e)   has ceased to be provided with accommodation by a local authority under section 25 of the 1995 Act where he has previously been provided with accommodation by the authority under that provision either–

      (i)   after he attained the age of 16 years; or

      (ii)   before he attained the age of 16 years, but had continued to be in such accommodation after he attained that age;

[⁶ "occupiers" means–

(a)   the persons whom the relevant authority is satisfied occupy as their home the dwelling to which the claim or award relates except for any joint tenant who is not a member of the claimant's household; and

(b)   any member of the armed forces away on operations who–

      (i)   is the son, daughter, step-son or step-daughter of the claimant or the claimant's partner;

      (ii)   was the claimant's non-dependant before they became a member of the armed forces away on operations; and

      (iii) intends to resume occupying the dwelling as their home when they cease to be a member of the armed forces away on operations;]

"relevant date" means, as the case may require–

(a)   the date of the claim to which the claim or relevant information referred to in regulation 13C (2) (a) or (b) relates;

(b)   the date of the change of dwelling, change which affects the category of dwelling, or date of death, to which a notification referred to in regulation 13C(2)(c) or (d) relates; or

(c)   the date on which the anniversary of the LHA date referred to in regulation 13C(3) falls.

"tenancy" includes

(a)   in Scotland, any other right of occupancy; and

(b)   in any other case, a licence to occupy premises,

and reference to a tenant, landlord or any other expression appropriate to a tenancy shall be construed accordingly.]

Modifications

Reg 13D is modified by Sch 9 para 8 (see p873). This applies only to former Pathfinder Authorities who administered the pilot local housing allowance scheme.

Amendments

1.   Inserted by reg 7 of SI 2007 No 2869 as from 7.4.08 (or if reg 1(5) that SI applies, on the day on or after 7.4.08 when the first of the events specified in reg 1(6) applies, or from 6.4.09 if none have before that date).
2.   Amended by reg 5(4)(b) of SI 2008 No 586 as from 7.4.08.
3.   Amended by reg 3(3) of SI 2009 No 614 as from 6.4.09.
4.   Amended by reg 3(6) of SI 2010 No 2835 as from 1.4.11.
5.   Inserted by art 2 and Sch 1 para 40(3) of SI 2011 No 1740 as from 15.7.11.
6.   Amended by reg 3(3) of SI 2013 No 665 as from 1.4.13.
7.   Amended by art 17 and Sch 1 para 24 of SI 2013 No 1465 as from 24.6.13.
8.   Amended by reg 3(3) of SI 2013 No 2828 as from 4.12.13.
9.   Amended by reg 5(3) of SI 2017 No 213 as from 1.4.17.
10.   Amended by art 12(2) of SI 2017 No 901 as from 3.11.17.

General Note

Reg 13D is nearly identical to reg 13D HB Regs (see p388). In the HB(SPC) Regs, there are naturally no rules in respect of a "young individual". However, here if the claimant (and any partner) live in shared accommodation, the LHA for one-bedroom shared accommodation only applies if neither the claimant nor her/his partner qualifies for a severe disability premium or the partner is not a "care leaver" (defined in para (12): para (2)(a)).

[¹Publication of local housing allowances

13E.–(1)   A relevant authority shall take such steps as appear to it to be appropriate for the purpose of securing that information in relation to broad rental market areas falling in whole or in part within its area, and local housing allowances applicable to such broad rental market areas, is brought to the attention of persons who may be entitled to housing benefit from the authority.]

Amendment

1.   Inserted by reg 7 of SI 2007 No 2869 as from 7.4.08 (or if reg 1(5) that SI applies, on the day on or after 7.4.08 when the first of the events specified in reg 1(6) applies, or from 6.4.09 if none have before that date).

[¹ Requirement to refer to rent officers

14.–(1)   Subject to the following provisions of this regulation, a relevant authority shall apply to a rent officer for a determination to be made in pursuance of the Housing Act functions where–
(a)   it has received a claim on which rent allowance may be awarded and any of the circumstances specified in regulation 13C(5)(a) to (e) (rent allowance cases for which a maximum rent (standard local rent) is not to be determined) apply;
(b)   it has received relevant information regarding a claim on which rent allowance may be awarded and any of the circumstances specified in regulation 13C(5)(a) to (e) apply;
(c)   it has received a notification of a change relating to a rent allowance and a maximum rent (LHA) does not fall to be determined under regulation 13C (determination of a maximum rent (LHA));
(d)   it has received a notification of a change of dwelling and any of the circumstances specified in regulation 13C(5)(a) to (e) apply;
(e)   it has received, except in the case where any liability to make payments in respect of a dwelling would be to a housing authority, a request from a person ("the prospective occupier"), on a properly completed form approved for the purpose by the relevant authority, which includes the specified matters and any of the circumstances specified in regulation 13C(5)(a) to (d) apply;
(f)   52 weeks have expired since it last made an application under sub-paragraph (a), (b), (c), (d) [², (e) or (h)] in relation to the claim or award in question and–
    (i)   a maximum rent (LHA) determined under regulation 13D does not apply; and

(ii) a maximum rent (LHA) is not to be determined under regulation 13D; [²]

(g) 52 weeks have expired since an application was made under sub-paragraph (f) or a previous application was made under this sub-paragraph, whichever last occurred, and–

(i) a maximum rent (LHA) determined under regulation 13D does not apply; and

(ii) a maximum rent (LHA) is not to be determined under regulation 13D. [²

or

(h) has received notification that any of the circumstances in regulation 13C(5) apply.]

(2) An application shall not be required under paragraph (1) where a claim, relevant information regarding a claim, notification or request relates to either–

(a) a dwelling in a hostel if, during the period of 12 months ending on the day on which that claim, relevant information regarding a claim, notification or request is received by the relevant authority–

(i) a rent officer has already made a determination in the exercise of the Housing Act functions in respect of a dwelling in that hostel which is a similar dwelling to the dwelling to which the claim, relevant information regarding a claim, notification or request relates; and

(ii) there has been no change relating to a rent allowance that has affected the dwelling in respect of which that determination was made; or

(b) an "excluded tenancy" within the meaning of Schedule 2 (excluded tenancies).

(3) The provision of information to the rent officer in accordance with regulation 95A(5) shall be treated as an application to the rent officer under paragraph (1).

(4) Where a relevant authority receives a request pursuant to paragraph (1)(e) (request from prospective occupier) and it is a case where, by reason of paragraph (2) (hostels or excluded tenancies), an application to a rent officer is not required, the authority shall–

(a) return it to the prospective occupier, indicating why no such application is required; and

(b) where it is not required by reason of either paragraph (2)(a) (hostels) of this regulation or paragraph 2 of Schedule 2 (cases where the rent officer has already made a determination), shall also send him a copy of that determination within 4 days of the receipt of that request by the authority.

(5) Where an application to a rent officer is required by paragraph (1) it shall be made within 3 days, or as soon as practicable after that date, of–

(a) the relevant authority receiving a claim on which rent allowance may be awarded;

(b) the relevant authority receiving relevant information regarding a claim on which rent allowance may be awarded;

(c) the relevant authority receiving a notification of a change relating to a rent allowance;

(d) the relevant authority receiving a notification of a change of dwelling; or

(e) the day on which the period mentioned in paragraph (1)(f) or (g) expired,

except that, in the case of a request to which paragraph (1)(e) (request from prospective occupier) applies, the application shall be made within 2 days of the receipt of that request by the authority.

(6) In calculating any period of days mentioned in paragraphs (4) or (5), no regard shall be had to a day on which the offices of the relevant authority are closed for the purposes of receiving or determining claims.

(7) For the purpose of this regulation a dwelling in a hostel shall be regarded as similar to another dwelling in that hostel if each dwelling provides sleeping accommodation for the same number of persons.

(8) In this regulation–

"change relating to a rent allowance" means a change or increase to which paragraph 2(3)(a), (b), (c) [³, (d) [⁴ (e) [⁵, (f) or (g)]]] of Schedule 2 applies;

"prospective occupier" shall include a person currently in receipt of housing benefit in respect of a dwelling which he occupies as his home and who is contemplating entering into a new agreement to occupy that dwelling, but only where his current agreement commenced 11 months or more before the request under paragraph (1)(e);

"specified matters" means–

    (a)   the signature of the prospective occupier;

    (b)   the signature of the person to whom the prospective occupier would incur liability to make such payments;

    (c)   a statement that the person in paragraph (b) agrees to the application being made for that determination; and

    (d)   an indication that the prospective occupier is contemplating occupying the dwelling as his home and that if he does so, he is likely to claim housing benefit;

"tenancy" includes–

    (a)   in Scotland, any other right of occupancy; and

    (b)   in any other case, a licence to occupy premises,

and reference to a tenant, landlord or any other expression appropriate to a tenancy shall be construed accordingly;

[²]]

Modifications

Reg 14 substituted by reg 8 Housing Benefit (State Pension Credit) (Local Housing Allowance and Information Sharing) Amendment Regulations 2007 SI No.2869, as amended by reg 5(5) of SI 2008 No.586, as from 7 April 2008, save that for a person to whom reg 1(5) of those regulations applied (see p1814), the amendments came into force on the day on or after 7 April 2008 when the first of the events specified in reg 1(6) applied to her/him, or on 6 April 2009 if none had before that date.

Amendments

    1.   Substituted by reg 8 of SI 2007 No 2869 as from 7.4.08 (or if reg 1(5) of that SI applies, on the day on or after 7.4.08 when the first of the events specified in reg 1(6) applies, or from 6.4.09 if none have before that date).

    2.   Amended by reg 5(5) of SI 2008 No 586 as from 7.4.08.

    3.   Amended by reg 3(7) of SI 2010 No 2835 as from 1.4.11.

    4.   Amended by reg 3(4) of SI 2013 No 665 as from 1.4.13.

    5.   Amended by reg 3(4) of SI 2013 No 2828 as from 4.12.13.

[¹ Application to the rent officer for redeterminations

15.–(1)   Subject to paragraph (2) and regulation 16 (application for redetermination by rent officer), where a relevant authority has obtained from a rent officer either or both of the following–

    (a)   a determination on a reference made under regulation 13D(10) (board and attendance determination) or regulation 14 (requirement to refer to rent officers);

    (b)   a redetermination on a reference made under regulation 16(2) (application for redetermination by rent officer),

the authority may apply to the rent officer for a redetermination of any determination or redetermination he has made which has effect at the date of the application.

    (2)   No application shall be made for a further redetermination of a redetermination made in response to an application under paragraph (1).]

Modifications

Reg 15 substituted by reg 9 Housing Benefit (State Pension Credit) (Local Housing Allowance and Information Sharing) Amendment Regulations 2007 No.2869 as from 7 April 2008, save that for a person to whom reg 1(5) of those regulations applied (see p1814), the amendments came into force on the day on or after 7 April 2008 when the first of the events specified in reg 1(6) applied to her/him, or on 6 April 2009 if none had before that date.

Amendment

    1.   Substituted by reg 9 of SI 2007 No 2869 as from 7.4.08 (or if reg 1(5) of that SI applies, on the day on or after 7.4.08 when the first of the events specified in reg 1(6) applies, or from 6.4.09 if none have before that date).

[¹ Application for a redetermination by a rent officer

16.–(1)   This paragraph applies where–
(a)   a person affected makes written representations which are signed by him, to a relevant authority concerning a decision which it makes in relation to him;
(b)   those representations relate, in whole or in part, to a rent officer's determination or redetermination in exercise of the Housing Act functions except for functions relating to broad rental market area determinations and local housing allowance determinations or amended determinations; and
(c)   those representations are made no later than one month after the day on which the person affected was notified of the decision by the relevant authority.

(2)   Subject to paragraphs (3) and (4), where paragraph (1) applies, the relevant authority shall, within 7 days of receiving the representations, apply to the rent officer for a redetermination or, as the case may be, a further redetermination in exercise of the Housing Act functions and a copy of those representations shall accompany the local authority's application.

(3)   Except where paragraph (4) applies, a relevant authority, in relation to any determination by a rent officer of an application under regulation 13D(10) (board and attendance determination) or 14(1) (requirement to refer to rent officers), shall not apply for a redetermination under paragraph (2) more than once in respect of an individual claimant's dwelling to which that determination relates.

(4)   Paragraph (2) shall operate so as to require a relevant authority to make a second application where the following conditions are met in addition to those imposed by that paragraph–
(a)   the written representations made under paragraph (1) relate to a redetermination by a rent officer made in response to an application by the relevant authority under regulation 15 (application to the rent officer for redetermination);
(b)   by the time of that application, the rent officer has already provided a redetermination under this regulation of a determination made in response to an application under regulation 13D(10) or 14(1); and
(c)   both the application under this regulation referred to in sub-paragraph (b) and the second application for which this paragraph provides relate to the same claimant.

(5)   here a decision has been revised in consequence of a redetermination, substitute determination or substitute redetermination by a rent officer in exercise of the Housing Act functions (except for those relating to broad rental market area determinations and local housing allowance determinations or amended determinations) and that redetermination, substitute determination or substitute redetermination has led to–
(a)   a reduction in the maximum rent, the redetermination, substitute determination or substitute redetermination shall be a change of circumstances;
(b)   an increase in the maximum rent, the redetermination, substitute determination or substitute redetermination shall have effect in place of the original determination.]

Modifications

Reg 16 substituted by reg 9 Housing Benefit (State Pension Credit) (Local Housing Allowance and Information Sharing) Amendment Regulations 2007 No.2869 as from 7 April 2008, save that for a person to whom reg 1(5) of those regulations applied (see p1814), the amendments came into force on the day on or after 7 April 2008 when the first of the events specified in reg 1(6) applied to her/him, or on 6 April 2009 if none had before that date.

Amendment

1.   Substituted by reg 9 of SI 2007 No 2869 as from 7.4.08 (or if reg 1(5) of that SI applies, on the day on or after 7.4.08 when the first of the events specified in reg 1(6) applies, or from 6.4.09 if none have before that date).

[¹ Substitute determinations or substitute redeterminations

17.–(1)   In a case where either–
(a)   the appropriate authority discovers that an application it has made to the rent officer contained an error in respect of any of the following–

      (i)   the size of the dwelling;
      (ii)   the number of occupiers;
      (iii) the composition of the household;
      (iv) the terms of the tenancy; or

  (b)   the rent officer has, in accordance with article 7A(1) or (2) of the Rent Officers Order, notified an appropriate authority of an error he has made (other than in the application of his professional judgement),

the authority shall apply to the rent officer for a substitute determination, substitute redetermination, board and attendance redetermination, substitute board and attendance determination or substitute board and attendance redetermination, as the case may be.

  (2)   In its application to the rent officer the relevant authority shall state the nature of the error and withdraw any previous application relating to the same case for a redetermination or substitute determination or substitute redetermination, which it has made but to which the rent officer has not yet responded.]

Modifications

Reg 17 substituted by reg 9 Housing Benefit (State Pension Credit) (Local Housing Allowance and Information Sharing) Amendment Regulations 2007 No.2869 as from 7 April 2008, save that for a person to whom reg 1(5) of those regulations applied (see p1814), the amendments came into force on the day on or after 7 April 2008 when the first of the events specified in reg 1(6) applied to her/him, or on 6 April 2009 if none had before that date.

Amendment

1.   Substituted by reg 9 of SI 2007 No 2869 as from 7.4.08 (or if reg 1(5) of that SI applies, on the day on or after 7.4.08 when the first of the events specified in reg 1(6) applies, or from 6.4.09 if none have before that date).

[¹ Application of provisions to substitute determinations or substitute redeterminations

  18.   Regulations 15, 16 and 17 apply to a substitute determination or substitute redetermination as they apply to the determination or redetermination it replaces.]

Modifications

Reg 18 substituted by reg 9 Housing Benefit (State Pension Credit) (Local Housing Allowance and Information Sharing) Amendment Regulations 2007 No.2869 as from 7 April 2008, save that for a person to whom reg 1(5) of those regulations applied (see p1814), the amendments came into force on the day on or after 7 April 2008 when the first of the events specified in reg 1(6) applied to her/him, or on 6 April 2009 if none had before that date.

Amendment

1.   Substituted by reg 9 of SI 2007 No 2869 as from 7.4.08 (or if reg 1(5) of that SI applies, on the day on or after 7.4.08 when the first of the events specified in reg 1(6) applies, or from 6.4.09 if none have before that date).

[¹ Amended determinations

  18A.–(1)   This regulation applies where a decision has been revised in consequence of an amended broad rental market area determination or amended local housing allowance determination by a rent officer.

  (2)   Where that amended determination has led to a reduction in the maximum rent (LHA) applicable to a claimant, the amended determination shall be a change of circumstances in relation to that claimant.

  (3)   Where that amended determination has led to an increase in the maximum rent (LHA) applicable to a claimant, the amended determination shall have effect in place of the original determination.]

Amendment

1.   Inserted by reg 10 of SI 2007 No 2869 as from 7.4.08 (or if reg 1(5) of that SI applies, on the day on or after 7.4.08 when the first of the events specified in reg 1(6) applies, or from 6.4.09 if none have before that date).

PART 4

Membership of a family

Persons of prescribed description

19.–(1) Subject to paragraph (2), a person of a prescribed description for the purposes of section 137(1) of the Act as it applies to housing benefit (definition of family) is a person [¹ who falls within the definition of qualifying young person in section 142 of the Act (child and qualifying young person)], and in these Regulations such a person is referred to as a "young person".

(2) Paragraph (1) shall not apply to a person who is–

(a) on income support [⁴, an income-based jobseeker's allowance or an income-related employment and support allowance]; [² [⁵]]

[³ (b)]

(c) a person to whom section 6 of the Children (Leaving Care) Act 2000 (exclusion from benefits) applies [⁵; or]

[⁵ (d) entitled to an award of universal credit]

(3) A person of a prescribed description for the purposes of section 137(1) of the Act as it applies to housing benefit (definition of the family) includes a child or young person in respect of whom section 145A of that Act applies for the purposes of entitlement to child benefit but only for the period prescribed under section 145A(1) of that Act.

Amendments

1. Substituted by reg 4(2)(a) of SI 2006 No 718 as from 10.4.06.
2. Inserted by reg 4(2)(b) of SI 2006 No 718 as from 10.4.06.
3. Omitted by reg 4(2)(c) of SI 2006 No 718 as from 10.4.06.
4. Amended by reg 32 of SI 2008 No 1082 as from 27.10.08.
5. Amended by reg 36(3) of SI 2013 No 630 as from 29.4.13.

General Note

This regulation is identical to reg 19 HB Regs (see p406).

Circumstances in which a person is to be treated as responsible or not responsible for another

20.–(1) Subject to the following provisions of this regulation a person shall be treated as responsible for a child or young person who is normally living with him and this includes a child or young person to whom paragraph (3) of regulation 19 applies.

(2) Where a child or young person spends equal amounts of time in different households, or where there is a question as to which household he is living in, the child or young person shall be treated for the purposes of paragraph (1) as normally living with–

(a) the person who is receiving child benefit in respect of him; or

(b) if there is no such person–

(i) where only one claim for child benefit has been made in respect of him, the person who made that claim; or

(ii) in any other case the person who has the primary responsibility for him.

(3) For the purposes of these Regulations a child or young person shall be the responsibility of only one person in any benefit week and any person other than the one treated as responsible for the child or young person under this regulation shall be treated as not so responsible.

General Note

This regulation is identical to reg 20 HB Regs (see p407).

Circumstances in which a person is to be treated as being or not being a member of the household

21.–(1) Subject to paragraphs (2) to (4), the claimant and any partner and, where the claimant or his partner is treated as responsible by virtue of regulation 20 (circumstances in which a person is to be treated as responsible or not responsible for another) for a child or young person, that child or young person and any child of that child or young person, shall be treated as members of the same household notwithstanding that any of them is temporarily living away from the other members of his family.

(2)   Paragraph (1) shall not apply to a person who is living away from the other members of his family where–

(a)   that person does not intend to resume living with the other members of his family; or

(b)   his absence from the other members of his family is likely to exceed 52 weeks, unless there are exceptional circumstances (for example where the person is in hospital or otherwise has no control over the length of his absence) and the absence is unlikely to be substantially more than 52 weeks.

(3)   A child or young person shall not be treated as a member of the claimant's household[1, nor as occupying the claimant's dwelling,] where he is–

(a)   placed with the claimant or his partner by a local authority under [4 section 22C(2)] of the Children Act 1989 [4 or section 81(2) of the Social Services and Well-being (Wales) Act 2014] or by a voluntary organisation under section 59(1)(a) of that Act, or in Scotland boarded out [3 or placed] with the claimant or his partner under a relevant enactment; or

(b)   placed, or in Scotland boarded out, with the claimant or his partner prior to adoption; or

(c)   placed for adoption with the claimant or his partner in accordance with the Adoption and Children Act 2002 or [2 the Adoption Agencies (Scotland) Regulations 2009].

(4)   Subject to paragraph (5), paragraph (1) shall not apply to a child or young person who is not living with the claimant and he–

(a)   is being looked after by, or in Scotland is in the care of, a local authority under a relevant enactment; or

(b)   has been placed, or in Scotland boarded out, with a person other than the claimant prior to adoption; or

(c)   has been placed for adoption in accordance with the Adoption and Children Act 2002 or [2 the Adoption Agencies (Scotland) Regulations 2009].

(5)   An authority shall treat a child or young person to whom paragraph (4)(a) applies as being a member of the claimants' household in any benefit week where–

(a)   that child or young person lives with the claimant for part or all of that benefit week; and

(b)   the authority considers that it is reasonable to do so taking into account the nature and frequency of that child's or young person's visits.

(6)   In this regulation "relevant enactment" means the Army Act 1955, the Air Force Act 1955, the Naval Discipline Act 1957, the Matrimonial Proceedings Children Act 1958, the Social Work (Scotland) Act 1968, the Family Law Reform Act 1969, the Children and Young Persons Act 1969, the Matrimonial Causes Act 1973, the Children Act 1975, the Domestic Proceedings and Magistrates' Courts Act 1978, [2 the Adoption and Children (Scotland) Act 2007], the Child Care Act 1980, the Family Law Act 1986, the Children Act 1989 [3] the Children (Scotland) Act 1995 [3 and the Children's Hearings (Scotland) Act 2011.].

Amendments

1.   Amended by reg 3(3) of SI 2010 No 2449 as from 1.11.10.

2.   Amended by art 2 and Sch 1 para 40(4) of SI 2011 No 1740 as from 15.7.11.

3.   Amended by art 17 and Sch 1 para 24 of SI 2013 No 1465 as from 24.6.13.

4.   Amended by arts 12(3) and 26(2) of SI 2017 No 901 as from 3.11.17.

General Note

This regulation is identical to reg 21 HB Regs (see p409).

PART 5
Applicable amounts

Applicable amounts

22.–(1)   Subject to regulations 61 and 62 and Schedule A1 (calculation of weekly amounts, rent free periods and treatment of claims for housing benefit by refugees), the applicable amount of a claimant shall be the aggregate of such of the following amounts as apply in his case–

(a)   an amount in respect of his personal allowance, determined in accordance with paragraph 1 of Schedule 3;

[⁷ (b)   an amount determined in accordance with paragraph 2 of that Schedule in respect of up to two individuals who are either children or young persons and who are members of his family;]

[⁶ (c)]

[⁵ (d)]

(e)   the amount of any premiums which may be applicable to him, determined in accordance with Parts 3 and 4 of that Schedule (premiums).

[¹ (2)]

[¹ (3)]

[¹ (4)]

[² (5)   In [⁴ Schedule 3]–

"additional spouse" means a spouse of either party to the marriage who is additional to the other party to the marriage;

"patient" means a person (other than a person who is serving a sentence of imprisonment or detention in a youth custody institution) who is regarded as receiving free in-patient treatment within the meaning of [³ regulation 2(4) and (5) of the Social Security (Hospital In-Patients) Regulations 2005].]

[⁷ (5A)   For the purposes of paragraph (1)(b), as it applies apart from paragraph (5C), where the family includes more than two individuals who are either children or young persons, and, under paragraph 2 of that Schedule, a different amount applies to different individuals, the two amounts to be included in the applicable amount shall be those that result in the greatest possible total amount.

(5B)   Paragraph (5C) applies where–

(a)   (whether or not as part of a tax credit couple) the claimant has an award of child tax credit in respect of a child or young person who is a member of his family, whether or not any amount is payable by way of such credit; and

(b)   the total amount to be included in the applicable amount under paragraph (1)(b) as substituted by paragraph (5C) would be higher than the total amount that would be included under paragraph (1)(b) apart from paragraph (45C.

(5C)   Where this paragraph applies, for paragraph (1)(b) substitute–

"(b)   an amount determined in accordance with paragraph 2 of that Schedule in respect of any child or young person who is a member of his family and in respect of whom the individual element of child tax credit has been included in the determination of the maximum rate of that credit;".

(5D)   In this regulation, "tax credit couple" means a couple as defined in section 3(5A) of the Tax Credits Act 2002.]

[¹ (6)]

[¹ (7)]

Amendments

1.   Omitted by reg 2(3)(a) of SI 2005 No 2502 as amended by Sch 2 para 27 of SI 2006 No 217 as from 1.4.06 (3.4.06 where rent payable weekly or at intervals of a week).

2.   Substituted by reg 2(3)(b) of SI 2005 No 2502 as amended by Sch 2 para 27 of SI 2006 No 217 as from 1.4.06 (3.4.06 where rent payable weekly or at intervals of a week).

3.   Amended by reg 5(1) of SI 2005 No 3360 as amended by Sch 2 para 30 of SI 2006 No 217 as from 10.4.06.

4.   Amended by reg 4(5) of SI 2008 No 1042 as from 19.5.08.

5.   Omitted by reg 20(4) of SI 2011 No 2425 as from 31.10.11.

6.   Omitted by reg 2(2)(a) of SI 2015 No 1857 as from 1.05.16, subject to transitional provision in reg 4 of SI 2015 No 1857.

7.   Amended by reg 8(2) of SI 2017 No 376 as from 6.4.17, subject to transitional provision in reg 9.

Analysis

Para (1). The same technique for calculating applicable amounts is used as under regs 22 and 23 HB Regs. Note, however, that there is no entitlement to a component under the HB(SPC) Regs, nor is there entitlement to a "transitional amount" if the claimant or her/his partner is transferred from IS "on the grounds of disability", IB or SDA to ESA (see Parts 7 and 8 of Sch 3 HB Regs). The amounts and conditions of the premiums are as stated in Sch 3. Note: the family premium (under para (1)(c)) was abolished from 1 May 2016 subject to transitional rules. See the commentary on p634. Note also that, from 6 April 2017, para (1)(b) restricts payment of allowances for children or young people to two per claim, subject to exceptions and transitional rules. See the commentary on p412. The transitional rules in both cases are the same as for those entitled to HB under the HB Regs.

Para (5). The definition of "patient" is relevant in the treatment of childcare costs (under reg 29). See p430 for a discussion of the meaning of "patient".

Note that long-term hospital patients may be caught by the requirement that they be occupying the home in reg 7, but see reg 7(16)(c)(ii). The definition of patient for these purposes is in reg 7(18). The definition there also applies in determining whether a non-dependant deduction is applicable under reg 55(7)(f).

PART 6
Assessment of income and capital
SECTION 1
General

Calculation of income and capital of members of claimant's family and of a polygamous marriage

23.–(1)   The income and capital of a claimant's partner which by virtue of section 136(1) of the Act is to be treated as income and capital of the claimant, shall be calculated or estimated in accordance with the following provisions of this Part in like manner as for the claimant; and any reference to the "claimant" shall, except where the context otherwise requires, be construed for the purposes of this Part as if it were a reference to his partner.

(2)   Where a claimant or the partner of a claimant is married polygamously to two or more members of his household–

(a)   the claimant shall be treated as possessing capital and income belonging to each such member; and

(b)   the income and capital of that member shall be calculated in accordance with the following provisions of this Part in like manner as for the claimant.

(3)   The income and capital of a child or young person shall not be treated as the income and capital of the claimant.

General Note

This regulation is identical to reg 25 HB Regs (see p421).

Circumstances in which income of non-dependant is to be treated as claimant's

24.–(1)   Where it appears to the relevant authority that a non-dependant and the claimant have entered into arrangements in order to take advantage of the housing benefit scheme and the non-dependant has more capital and income than the claimant, that authority shall, except where the claimant is on [¹ a guarantee credit], treat the claimant as possessing capital and income belonging to that non-dependant and, in such a case, shall disregard any capital and income which the claimant does possess.

(2)   Where a claimant is treated as possessing capital and income belonging to a non-dependant under paragraph (1) the capital and income of that non-dependant shall be calculated in accordance with the following provisions of this Part in like manner as for the claimant and any reference to the "claimant" shall, except where the context otherwise requires, be construed for the purposes of this Part as if it were a reference to that non-dependant.

Amendment

1.   Amended by reg 6(3) of SI 2008 No 3157 as from 5.1.09.

SECTION 2
Income

General Note to Section 2
Although the heading for Section 2 is "Income", the capital of some claimants is also dealt with in this section. Section 2 requires the treatment of resources in three ways.

(1)   If a claimant (or her/his partner) is in receipt of the guarantee credit of PC, all her/his income and capital are disregarded: reg 26. There is effectively no capital limit for such claimants. See p419 for the question of how far the decisions of the DWP are binding on the local authority.

(2)   If a claimant (or her/his partner) is in receipt of the savings credit of PC but not the guarantee credit, the special rules in reg 27 apply. There is a £16,000 capital limit in such cases.

(3)   If a claimant (or her/his partner) is not receiving either the guarantee credit or savings credit of PC, the rules in regs 29 to 49 apply: reg 28. There is a £16,000 capital limit in such cases.

Calculation of income and capital
25.   The income and capital of–
(a)   the claimant; and
(b)   any partner of the claimant,
shall be calculated in accordance with the rules set out in this Part; and any reference in this Part to the claimant shall apply equally to any partner of the claimant.

Claimant in receipt of guarantee credit
26.   In the case of a claimant who is in receipt, or whose partner is in receipt, of a guarantee credit, the whole of his capital and income shall be disregarded.

Calculation of claimant's income and capital in savings credit only cases
27.–(1)   In determining the income and capital of a claimant who has, or whose partner has, an award of state pension credit comprising only the savings credit, the relevant authority shall, subject to the following provisions of this regulation, use the calculation or estimate of the claimant's or, as the case may be, the claimant's partner's income and capital made by the Secretary of State for the purpose of determining that award.

(2)   The Secretary of State shall provide the relevant authority with details of the calculation or estimate–
(a)   if the claimant is on housing benefit or has claimed housing benefit, within the two working days following the day the calculation or estimate was determined, or as soon as reasonably practicable thereafter; or
(b)   if sub-paragraph (a) does not apply, within the two working days following the day he receives information from the relevant authority that the claimant or his partner has claimed housing benefit, or as soon as reasonably practicable thereafter.

(3)   The details provided by the Secretary of State shall include the amount taken into account in that determination in respect of the net income of the person claiming state pension credit.

(4)   The relevant authority shall modify the amount of the net income provided by the Secretary of State only in so far as necessary to take into account–
(a)   the amount of the savings credit payable;
(b)   in respect of any dependent children of the claimant, childcare charges taken into account under regulation 30(1)(c) (calculation of income on a weekly basis);
(c)   the higher amount disregarded under these Regulations in respect of–
(i)   lone parent's earnings;
(ii)   payments of maintenance, whether under a court order or not, which is made or due to be made by–

      (aa)   the claimant's former partner, or the claimant's partner's former partner; or

      (bb)   the parent of a child or young person where that child or young person is a member of the claimant's family except where that parent is the claimant or the claimant's partner;

(d)   any amount to be disregarded by virtue of [¹ paragraph 5A or 9(1)] of Schedule 4;

(e)   the income and capital of any partner of the claimant who is treated as a member of the claimant's household under regulation 21 (circumstances in which a person is to be treated as being or not being a member of the household) to the extent that it is not taken into account in determining the net income of the person claiming state pension credit;

(f)   regulation 24 (circumstances in which income of a non-dependent is to be treated as claimant's), if the relevant authority determines that this provision applies in the claimant's case;

(g)   any modification under section 134(8) of the Administration Act (modifications by resolution of an authority) which is applicable in the claimant's case.

(5)   Regulations 29 to 49 shall not apply to the amount of the net income to be taken into account by the local authority under paragraph (1), but shall apply (so far as relevant) for the purpose of determining any modifications which fall to be made to that amount under paragraph (4).

(6)   The relevant authority shall for the purpose of determining the claimant's entitlement of housing benefit use, except where paragraphs (7) and (8) apply, the calculation of the claimant's capital made by the Secretary of State, and shall in particular apply the provisions of regulation 43 if the claimant's capital is calculated as being in excess of £16,000.

(7)   If paragraph (8) applies, the relevant authority shall calculate the claimant's capital in accordance with regulations 43 to 49 below.

(8)   This paragraph applies if–

(a)   the Secretary of State notifies the relevant authority that the claimant's capital has been determined as being £16,000 or less;

(b)   subsequent to that determination the claimant's capital rises to more than £16,000; and

(c)   the increase occurs whilst there is in force an assessed income period within the meaning of sections 6 and 9 of the State Pension Credit Act.

Amendment

1.   Amended by reg 3(2) of SI 2009 No 2608 as from 1.4.10 (5.4.10 where rent payable weekly or in multiples of a week).

General Note

Reg 27 sets out the capital and income rules if the claimant or her/his partner has been awarded the savings credit of PC, but not the guarantee credit. In these cases, income and capital for HB purposes are the income and capital figure used by the DWP to work out PC, as modified by paras (4) to (8). The DWP figure is sometimes referred to as the "assessed income figure" or AIF.

Analysis

Paras (1) to (3). The general rule is that, for the purpose of working out HB entitlement, authorities must use the calculation or estimate of income and capital made by the DWP in determining entitlement to the savings credit of PC. It is suggested that the mandatory wording of para (1) means that the reasoning of the Court of Appeal in *R v South Ribble DC HBRB ex p Hamilton* (2000) 33 HLR 102, CA cannot apply to such claimants. See p419 for a full discussion of the *Hamilton* decision, but it is suggested that the local authority is not entitled to disregard the DWP's assessment merely because it believes that there has been a failure by the claimant to disclose resources to the DWP. It must refer its evidence to the DWP with a view to revision or supersession of the award of savings credit, suspending HB entitlement if necessary.

    See also reg 41(10) (where a claimant is in receipt of a benefit other than HB and the rate of that other benefit alters on or after 1 April in any year) and reg 60(6) (where there is a change in the DWP assessment of income and capital).

    Para (2) imposes strict time limits for the provision of the information to the authority by the DWP on behalf of the Secretary of State.

Modifications to the income figure

Paras (4) and (5) deal with modifications an authority must make to the income figure provided by the DWP. By para (5), the rules in the remainder of Section 2 are used to determine the modifications (eg, reg 31 forms the basis for the calculation of childcare charges under para (4)(b)) but are not to be used to determine the amount of net income to be taken into account.

The following modifications must be made (if relevant).

(1) The authority must add the savings credit that is payable: para (4)(a).

(2) Childcare charges must be deducted from earnings under reg 30(1)(c): para (4)(b).

(3) The more generous HB disregards for lone parents' earnings and maintenance must be applied: para (4)(c). Lone parents have only £20 of earnings disregarded for PC purposes but £25 is ignored for HB purposes (see Sch 4 para 1(a) on p854), so such claimants will have an additional £5 disregard applied to the assessment of income for HB purposes. If a family premium is included in the claimant's applicable amount, £15 of any maintenance paid for her/him or her/his partner made by her/his or the partner's spouse, civil partner, former spouse or former civil partner is disregarded: Sch 5 para 20. None of this type of maintenance is disregarded for PC purposes.

(4) The additional earnings disregard under Sch 4 paras 5A (where the claimant or partner is undertaking "exempt work") and 9(1) (additional earnings disregard for some claimants in work) must be applied: para (4)(d).

(5) The income and capital of the claimant's partner (if s/he is treated as a member of the claimant's household) must be added, if it was not taken into account for PC purposes (eg, where the claimant is treated as a single claimant for PC purposes but under reg 21 is treated as having a partner): para (4)(e).

(6) The income of a non-dependant must be added, but only if the authority decides the income of that non-dependant is to be treated as the claimant's under reg 24: para (4)(f). Note that in this case, the income and the capital of the claimant are disregarded under reg 24(1).

(7) Any disregard of war pensions adopted by the authority must be applied: para (4)(g).

Modifications to the capital figure

Paras (6) to (8) deal with the calculation of capital. The DWP's assessment must be used and the capital limit of £16,000 applies. The only time when the authority does its own capital assessment is where capital rises above £16,000 after entitlement to PC has been assessed and during an "assessed income period" – broadly, a set period during which the PC claimant is not required to report changes in retirement provision to the DWP, including the amount of her/his capital. Note that unless the increase in capital has the effect of disqualifying the claimant from HB, there can be no departure from the DWP's figure. For example, where there is an increase in capital but the amount is still less than the £16,000 limit, the authority is not permitted to add (or increase) deemed income from capital under reg 29(2); see para (5) above.

Calculation of income and capital where state pension credit is not payable

28. The income and capital of a person to whom neither regulation 26 nor regulation 27 applies shall be calculated or estimated by the relevant authority in accordance with regulations 29 to 49.

Meaning of "income"

29.–(1) For the purposes of these Regulations, "income" means income of any of the following descriptions–

(a) earnings;

(b) working tax credit;

(c) retirement pension income within the meaning of the State Pension Credit Act;

(d) income from annuity contracts (other than retirement pension income);

(e) a war disablement pension or war widow's or widower's pension;

(f) a foreign war disablement pension or war widow's or widower's pension;

(g) a guaranteed income payment;

[4 (h) a payment made under article 21(1)(c) of the Armed Forces and Reserve Forces (Compensation Scheme) Order 2005, in any case where article 23(2)(c) applies;]

(i) income from capital, other than capital disregarded under Part 1 of Schedule 6;

(j) social security benefits, other than retirement pension income or any of the following benefits–

(i) disability living allowance;

[9 (ia) personal independence payment;]

[10 (ib) armed forces independence payment;]

(ii) attendance allowance payable under section 64 of the Act;

(iii) an increase of disablement pension under section 104 or 105 of the Act;

    (iv)   a payment under regulations made in exercise of the power conferred by paragraph 7(2)(b) of Part 2 of Schedule 8 to the Act;

    (v)   an increase of an allowance payable in respect of constant attendance under paragraph 4 of Part 1 of Schedule 8 to the Act;

    (vi)   child benefit;

    (vii)   any guardian's allowance payable under section 77 of the Act;

    (viii)   any increase for a dependant, other than the claimant's partner, payable in accordance with Part 4 of the Act;

    (ix)   any social fund payment made under Part 8 of the Act;

    (x)   Christmas bonus payable under Part 10 of the Act;

    (xi)   housing benefit;

    [8 (xii)]

    [14 (xiii) bereavement support payment under section 30 of the Pensions Act 2014;]

    (xiv)   statutory sick pay;

    (xv)   statutory maternity pay;

    [7 (xvi) [12] statutory paternity pay payable under Part 12ZA of the Act;]

    [12 [7 (xvia)]]

    (xvii) statutory adoption pay payable under Part 12ZB of the Act;

    [11 (xviia) statutory shared parental pay payable under Part 12ZC of the Act;]

    [16 (xviib) carer's allowance supplement payable under section 81 of the Social Security (Scotland) Act 2018;]

    [17 (xviic) early years assistance given in accordance with section 32 of the Social Security (Scotland) Act 2018;]

    [18 (xviid) funeral expense assistance given in accordance with section 34 of the Social Security (Scotland) Act 2018.]

    (xviii) any benefit similar to those mentioned in the preceding provisions of this paragraph payable under legislation having effect in Northern Ireland;

(k)   all foreign social security benefits which are similar to the social security benefits prescribed above;

[4 (l)   a payment made–

    (i)   under article 30 of the Naval, Military and Air Forces Etc. (Disablement and Death) Service Pensions Order 2006, in any case where article 30(1)(b) applies; or

    (ii)   under article 12(8) of that Order, in any case where sub-paragraph (b) of that article applies;]

[13 (m) a pension paid by a government to victims of National Socialist persecution;]

(n)   payments under a scheme made under the Pneumoconiosis etc. (Worker's Compensation) Act 1979;

(o)   payments made towards the maintenance of the claimant by his spouse, civil partner, former spouse or former civil partner or towards the maintenance of the claimant's partner by his spouse, civil partner, former spouse or former civil partner, including payments made–

    (i)   under a court order;

    (ii)   under an agreement for maintenance; or

    (iii)   voluntarily;

(p)   payments due from any person in respect of board and lodging accommodation provided by the claimant;

[5 (q) royalties or other sums paid as a consideration for the use of, or the right to use, any copyright, design, patent or trade mark;]

[5 (r)   any payment in respect of any–

    (i)   book registered under the Public Lending Right Scheme 1982; or

    (ii)   work made under any international public lending right scheme that is analogous to the Public Lending Right Scheme 1982;]

(s)   any payment, other than a payment ordered by a court or made in settlement of a claim, made by or on behalf of a former employer of a person on account of the early retirement of that person on grounds of ill-health or disability;

(t)   any sum payable by way of pension out of money provided under the Civil List Act 1837, the Civil List Act 1937, the Civil List Act 1952, the Civil List Act 1972 or the Civil List Act 1975;

(u)   any income in lieu of that specified in sub-paragraphs (a) to (r);

(v)   any payment of rent made to a claimant who–
  (i)   owns the freehold or leasehold interest in any property or is a tenant of any property;
  (ii)   occupies part of the property; and
  (iii)   has an agreement with another person allowing that person to occupy that property on payment of rent; [¹]

(w)   any payment made at regular intervals under an equity release scheme.

[² (x) PPF periodic payments within the meaning of section 17(1) of the State Pension Credit Act.]

[⁶ (2)   For the purposes of these Regulations and subject to regulation 44(2) (capital to be disregarded), a claimant's capital shall be treated as if it were a weekly income of–

(a)   £1 for each £500 in excess of £10,000; and

(b)   £1 for any excess which is not a complete £500.]

(3)   Where the payment of any social security benefit prescribed under paragraph (1) [¹⁵, or retirement pension income to which section 16(1)(za) to (e) of the State Pension Credit Act applies,] is subject to any deduction (other than an adjustment specified in paragraph (4)) the amount to be taken into account under paragraph (1) shall be the amount before the deduction is made.

(4)   The adjustments specified in this paragraph are those made in accordance with–

(a)   the Social Security (Overlapping Benefits) Regulations 1979;

(b)   the Social Security (Hospital In-Patients) Regulations 1975;

(c)   section 30DD or section 30E of the Act (reductions in incapacity benefit in respect of pensions and councillor's allowances).

[³ (d) section 3 of the Welfare Reform Act (deductions from contributory employment and support allowance in respect of pensions and councillor's allowances).]

[¹⁵ (e) section 14 of the Pensions Act 2014 (pension sharing: reduction in the sharer's section 4 pension);

(f)   section 45B or 55B of the Social Security Contributions and Benefits Act 1992 (reduction of additional pension in Category A retirement pension and shared additional pension: pension sharing).]

(5)   Where an award of any working tax credit or child tax credit under the Tax Credits Act 2002 is subject to a deduction by way of recovery of an overpayment of working tax credit or child tax credit which arose in a previous tax year the amount to be taken into account under paragraph (1) shall be the amount of working tax credit or child tax credit awarded less the amount of that deduction.

[⁶ (6)]

[⁶ (7)]

(8)   In paragraph (1)(w), "equity release scheme" means a loan–

(a)   made between a person ("the lender") and the claimant;

(b)   by means of which a sum of money is advanced by the lender to the claimant by way of payments at regular intervals; and

(c)   which is secured on a dwelling in which the claimant owns an estate or interest and which he occupies as his home.

Modifications

The amendments made by SI 2014 No.3255 which came into force on 5 April 2015 do not have effect in relation to ordinary statutory paternity pay which is paid, additional statutory paternity pay which is paid, a period in respect of which additional statutory paternity pay is payable which begins, or continues, ordinary paternity leave which is taken or additional paternity leave which is taken on or after 5 April 2015. See art 35 of SI 2014 No.3255.

Amendments

1.   Amended by reg 10(2)(a) of SI 2006 No 588 as from 6.4.06.
2.   Inserted by reg 10(2)(b) of SI 2006 No 588 as from 6.4.06.
3.   Amended by reg 33 of SI 2008 No 1082 as from 27.10.08.

4. Substituted by reg 6(4) of SI 2008 No 3157 as from 5.1.09.
5. Substituted by reg 7(4) of SI 2009 No 583 as from the first day of the first benefit week for a claimant on or after 6.4.09.
6. Amended by reg 5 of SI 2009 No 1676 as from 2.11.09.
7. Substituted by reg 8(3) of SI 2012 No 757 as from 1.4.12 (2.4.12 where rent payable weekly or in multiples of a week).
8. Amended by reg 3 and Sch 1 of SI 2013 No 458 as from 1.4.13.
9. Inserted by reg 8 and Sch para 37(3) of SI 2013 No 388 as from 8.4.13.
10. Amended by art 7 and Sch para 35(3) of SI 2013 No 591 as from 8.4.13.
11. Inserted by art 18(4)(c) of SI 2014 No 3255 as from 31.12.14.
12. Amended by art 18(4)(a) and (b) of SI 2014 No 3255 as from 5.4.15.
13. Substituted by reg 6(2) of SI 2017 No 174 as from 20.3.17.
14. Substituted by art 26(2) of SI 2017 No 422 as from 6.4.17, subject to transitional provisions in arts 2 and 3.
15. Amended by reg 12(2) of SI 2017 No 1015 as from 16.11.17.
16. Inserted by art 6 of SI 2018 No 872 as from 3.9.18.
17. Inserted by reg 9(2) of SI 2018 No 1138 as from 10.12.18.
18. Inserted by reg 15(2) of SI 2019 No 1060 as from 16.9.19.

Analysis
Paragraph (1): The definition of "income"
Unlike under the HB Regs, "income" is defined by reg 29(1). Therefore, any category of income that does not fall within any of the categories listed does not count as income and is not taken into account at all. Note that there are earnings disregards in Sch 4 (see p854) and amounts to be disregarded from income other than earnings in Sch 5 (see p857).

Most of the categories are self-explanatory but some require explanation.

Sub-para (c): "retirement pension income". Retirement pension income is defined in s16 SPCA. It includes Category A, B, C and D state retirement pension, occupational and personal pension schemes and other private arrangements.

Sub-para (i): "income from capital". This counts as income, unless it is from capital disregarded under Sch 6 Part 1. See also reg 33(11)(a) which confirms this. The combined effect of sub-para (1)(i) and Sch 5 paras 22 and 24 is that it is only actual income from the types of capital specified in Sch 6 Part 2 that is taken into account, and then only if the total value of the capital exceeds £10,000. Note that capital, other than capital disregarded under *either* Part 1 or 2 of Sch 6, is deemed to produce a weekly income under para (2).

Sub-para (j): social security benefits. Social security benefits, other than retirement pension (which instead counts as income under sub-para (c)) and the benefits listed in sub-paras (j)(i) to (xviii), count as income. Note that statutory sick, maternity, paternity, shared parental and adoption pay are disregarded under sub-para (j), but count as earnings under reg 35(1)(h)-(j), and hence are taken into account under sub-para (a) above. Note also that, while carer's allowance counts as income, carer's allowance supplement (sub-para (j)(xviib)) paid in Scotland does not. Lump sum payments available to applicants in Scotland for early years assistance and funeral expense assistance (sub-para (j)(xviic) and (xviid)) also do not count. (See HB Regs Sch 5 para 68 on p682 for an explanation of the carer's allowance supplement and Sch 6 paras 65 and 66 on p700 for an explanation of the lump sum payments.)

Sub-para (o): maintenance. The specified payments towards the maintenance of the claimant count as income, but note the possible disregard in Sch 5 para 20.

Sub-para (p): board and lodging payments. Payments due to the claimant in respect of board and lodging accommodation (defined in reg 2(1)) provided by her/him count as income, but note the possible disregard in Sch 5 para 9.

Sub-para (s) seems to be directed at income from private health insurance schemes provided by an employer.

Sub-para (w). Note that "equity release scheme" is defined in para (8).

Paragraph (2): Deemed income from capital
Para (2) deals with deemed income from capital, sometimes referred to as "tariff income". The tariff is lower than under the HB Regs: under the HB(SPC) Regs, a claimant is to be treated as having £1 weekly income for every £500 of capital over the lower capital limit (£10,000 since 2 November 2009). Because para (2) is subject to reg 44(2) and because of reg 33(11), it is only capital other than capital disregarded under Sch 6 that is treated as producing a deemed weekly income as set out.

Paragraphs (3) to (5): Miscellaneous rules about income
Under paras (3) and (4), where there are adjustments in the amount of a social security benefit other than under the overlapping benefits provisions or the other circumstances listed in para (4), the unadjusted amount of income is taken into account.

Para (5) makes it plain that where an award of WTC or CTC for the current tax year is subject to a deduction in order to recover an overpayment of tax credit(s) from the previous year (pursuant to s28(1) Tax Credits Act

2002), the amount of WTC or CTC to be taken into account in calculating the weekly level of income for HB purposes is the current year award of tax credit(s) less the deduction for the overpayment.

Calculation of income on a weekly basis

30.–(1) Subject to regulation 34 (disregard of changes in tax, contributions etc.) and 61 and 62 (calculation of weekly amounts and rent free periods), for the purposes of section 130(1)(c) of the Act (conditions for entitlement to housing benefit) the income of a claimant who has reached the qualifying age for state pension credit shall be calculated on a weekly basis–

(a) by calculating or estimating the amount which is likely to be his average weekly income in accordance with this Part;

(b) by adding to that amount the weekly income calculated under regulation 29(2);

(c) by then deducting any relevant child care charges to which regulation 31 (treatment of child care charges) applies from any earnings which form part of the average weekly income or, in a case where the conditions in paragraph (2) are met, from those earnings plus whichever credit specified in sub-paragraph (b) of that paragraph is appropriate, up to a maximum deduction in respect of the claimant's family of whichever of the sums specified in paragraph (3) applies in his case.

(2) The conditions of this paragraph are that–

(a) the claimant's earnings which form part of his average weekly income are less than the lower of either his relevant child care charges or whichever of the deductions specified in paragraph (3) otherwise applies in his case; and

(b) that claimant or, if he is a member of a couple either the claimant or his partner, is in receipt of working tax credit or child tax credit.

(3) The maximum deduction to which paragraph (1)(c) above refers shall be–

(a) where the claimant's family includes only one child in respect of whom relevant child care charges are paid, [¹³ £175.00] per week;

(b) where the claimant's family includes more than one child in respect of whom relevant child care charges are paid, [¹³ £300] per week.

Amendments

1. Confirmed by art 20(3) of SI 2006 No 645 and reg 8 of SI 2006 No 217 as from 1.4.06 (3.4.06 where rent payable weekly or at intervals of a week).

2. Confirmed by art 20(2) of SI 2007 No 688 as from 1.4.07 (2.4.07 where rent payable weekly or at intervals of a week).

3. Confirmed by art 20(3) of SI 2008 No 632 as from 1.4.08 (7.4.08 where rent payable weekly or in multiples of a week).

4. Confirmed by art 20(3) of SI 2009 No 497 as from 1.4.09 (6.4.08 where rent payable weekly or in multiples of a week).

5. Confirmed by art 20(2) of SI 2010 No 793 as from 1.4.10 (5.4.10 where rent payable weekly or in multiples of a week).

6. Confirmed by art 21(2) of SI 2011 No 821 as from 1.4.11 (4.4.11 where rent payable weekly or in multiples of a week).

7. Confirmed by art 21(2) of SI 2012 No 780 as from 1.4.11 (2.4.11 where rent payable weekly or in multiples of a week).

8. Confirmed by art 20(2) of SI 2013 No 574 as from 1.4.13.

9. Confirmed by art 18(2) of SI 2014 No 16 as from 1.4.14 (7.4.14 where rent payable weekly or in multiples of a week).

10. Confirmed by art 18(2) of SI 2015 No 547 as from 1.4.15 (6.4.15 where rent payable weekly or in multiples of a week).

11. Confirmed by art 23(2) of SI 2017 No 260 as from 1.4.17 (3.4.17 where rent payable weekly or in multiples of a week).

12. Confirmed by art 24(2) of SI 2018 No 281 as from 1.4.18 (2.4.18 where rent payable weekly or in multiples of a week).

13. Confirmed by art 24(2) of SI 2019 No 480 as from 1.4.19.

General Note

This is, for practical purposes, identical to reg 27 HB Regs (see p423).

Treatment of child care charges

31.–(1)   This regulation applies where a claimant is incurring relevant child care charges and–

(a)   is a lone parent and is engaged in remunerative work;

(b)   is a member of a couple both of whom are engaged in remunerative work; or

(c)   is a member of a couple where one member is engaged in remunerative work and the other–

   (i)   is incapacitated;

   (ii)   is an in-patient in hospital; or

   (iii)   is in prison (whether serving a custodial sentence or remanded in custody awaiting trial or sentence).

(2)   For the purposes of paragraph (1) and subject to paragraph (4), a person to whom paragraph (3) applies shall be treated as engaged in remunerative work for a period not exceeding 28 weeks during which he–

(a)   is paid statutory sick pay;

(b)   is paid short-term incapacity benefit at the lower rate under sections 30A to 30E of the Act;

[² (ba) is paid an employment and support allowance;]

(c)   is paid income support on the grounds of incapacity for work under regulation 4ZA of, and paragraph 7 or 14 of Schedule 1B to, the Income Support Regulations; or

(d)   is credited with earnings on the grounds of incapacity for work [² or limited capability for work] under regulation 8B of the Social Security (Credits) Regulations 1975.

(3)   This paragraph applies to a person who was engaged in remunerative work immediately before–

(a)   the first day of the period in respect of which he was first paid statutory sick pay, short-term incapacity benefit [² , an employment and support allowance] or income support on the grounds of incapacity for work; or

(b)   the first day of the period in respect of which earnings are credited, as the case may be.

(4)   In a case to which paragraph (2)(c) or (d) applies, the period of 28 weeks begins on the day on which the person is first paid income support or on the first day of the period in respect of which earnings are credited, as the case may be.

(5)   Relevant child care charges are those charges for care to which paragraphs (6) and (7) apply, and shall be estimated on a weekly basis in accordance with paragraph (10).

(6)   The charges are paid by the claimant for care which is provided–

(a)   in the case of any child of the claimant's family who is not disabled, in respect of the period beginning on that child's date of birth and ending on the day preceding the first Monday in September following that child's fifteenth birthday; or

(b)   in the case of any child of the claimant's family who is disabled, in respect of the period beginning on that person's date of birth and ending on the day preceding the first Monday in September following that person's sixteenth birthday.

(7)   The charges are paid for care which is provided by one or more of the care providers listed in paragraph (8) and are not paid–

(a)   in respect of the child's compulsory education;

(b)   by a claimant to a partner or by a partner to a claimant in respect of any child for whom either or any of them is responsible in accordance with regulation 20 (circumstances in which a person is treated as responsible or not responsible for another); or

(c)   in respect of care provided by a relative of a child wholly or mainly in the child's home.

(8)   The care to which paragraph (7) refers may be provided–

(a)   out of school hours, by a school on school premises or by a local authority–

      (i)   for children who are not disabled in respect of the period beginning on their eighth birthday and ending on the day preceding the first Monday in September following their fifteenth birthday; or

      (ii)   for children who are disabled in respect of the period beginning on their eighth birthday and ending on the day preceding the first Monday in September following their sixteenth birthday;

(b)   by a child care provider approved by an organisation accredited by the Secretary of State under the scheme established by the Tax Credit (New Category of Child Care Provider) Regulations 1999;

(c)   by persons registered under Part 10A of the Children Act 1989;

[⁶ (d) by a person who is excepted from registration under Part 2 of the Children and Families (Wales) Measure 2010 because the child care that person provides is in a school or establishment referred to in article 11, 12 or 14 of the Child Minding and Day Care Exceptions (Wales) Order 2010;];

[⁷ (e) by–

      (i)   persons registered under section 59(1) of the Public Services Reform (Scotland) Act 2010; or

      (ii)   local authorities registered under section 83(1) of that Act,

where the care provided is childminding or day care of children within the meaning of that Act; or]

(f)   by a person prescribed in regulations made pursuant to section 12(4) of the Tax Credits Act.[⁴ or

(g)   by a person who is registered under Chapter 2 or 3 of Part 3 of the Childcare Act 2006; or

(h)   by any of the schools mentioned in section 34(2) of the Childcare Act 2006 in circumstances where the requirement to register under Chapter 2 of Part 3 of that Act does not apply by virtue of section 34(2) of that Act; or

(i)   by any of the schools mentioned in section 53(2) of the Childcare Act 2006 in circumstances where the requirement to register under Chapter 3 of Part 3 of that Act does not apply by virtue of section 53(2) of that Act; or

(j)   by any of the establishments mentioned in section 18(5) of the Childcare Act 2006 in circumstances where the care is not included in the meaning of "childcare" for the purposes of Part 1 and Part 3 of that Act by virtue of that subsection; or

(k)   by a foster parent [⁵ or kinship carer] under the Fostering Services Regulations 2002, the Fostering Services (Wales) Regulations 2003 or the [⁵ Looked After Children (Scotland) Regulations 2009] in relation to a child other than one whom the foster parent is fostering [⁵ or kinship carer is looking after]; or

(l)   by a domiciliary care worker under the Domiciliary Care Agencies Regulations 2002 or [¹⁸ by a person who is employed, or engaged under a contract for services, to provide care and support by the provider of a domiciliary support service within the meaning of Part 1 of the Regulation and Inspection of Social Care (Wales) Act 2016]; or

(m)   by a person who is not a relative of the child wholly or mainly in the child's home.]

(9)   In paragraphs (6) and (8)(a), "the first Monday in September" means the Monday which first occurs in the month of September in any year.

(10)   Relevant child care charges shall be estimated over such period, not exceeding a year, as is appropriate in order that the average weekly charge may be estimated accurately having regard to information as to the amount of that charge provided by the child minder or person providing the care.

(11)   For the purposes of paragraph (1)(c) the other member of a couple is to be treated as incapacitated where–

(a)   he is aged not less than 80;

(b)   he is aged less than 80 and–

      (i)   the additional conditions specified in paragraph 13 of Schedule 3 to the Housing Benefit Regulations 2006 are treated as applying in his case; and

    (ii)   he satisfies those conditions or would satisfy them but for his being treated as capable of work by virtue of a determination made in accordance with regulations made under section 171E of the Act;

[² (ba) the [¹⁷ other member of the couple would be a member of the support group or] ¹⁶ a member of the work-related activity group] but for that other member being treated as not having limited capability for work by virtue of a determination made in accordance with the Employment and Support Allowance Regulations [¹¹ or the Employment and Support Allowance Regulations 2013];]

(c)   the claimant is, or is treated as, incapable of work and has been so incapable, or has been so treated as incapable, of work in accordance with the provisions of, and regulations made under, Part 12A of the Act (incapacity for work) for a continuous period of not less than 196 days; and for this purpose any two or more separate periods separated by a break of not more than 56 days shall be treated as one continuous period;

[² (ca) the claimant (within the meaning of regulation 2(1)) has, or is treated as having, limited capability for work and has had, or been treated as having, limited capability for work in accordance with the Employment and Support Allowance Regulations [¹¹ or the Employment and Support Allowance Regulations 2013] for a continuous period of not less than 196 days and for this purpose any two or more separate periods separated by a break of not more than 84 days must be treated as one continuous period;]

(d)   there is payable in respect of him one or more of the following–

    (i)   long-term incapacity benefit or short-term incapacity benefit at the higher rate specified in paragraph 2 of Part 1 of Schedule 4 to the Act;

    (ii)   attendance allowance under section 64 of the Act;

    (iii)   severe disablement allowance under section 68 of the Act;

    (iv)   disability living allowance under section 71 of the Act;

    (v)   increase of disablement pension under section 104 of the Act;

    (vi)   a pension increase [³ paid as part of a war disablement pension or under] an industrial injuries scheme which is analogous to an allowance or increase of disablement pension under head (ii), (iv) or (v) above;

[² (vii) main phase employment and support allowance;]

[⁹ (viii) personal independence payment;]

[¹⁰ (ix) armed forces independence payment;]

(e)   a pension [¹² , allowance or payment to which head (ii), (iv), (v), (vi) or (viii)] of sub-paragraph (d) above refers was payable on account of his incapacity but has ceased to be payable in consequence of his becoming a patient within the meaning of regulation 22(5) (applicable amounts);

(f)   [¹ sub-paragraph (d) or (e)] would apply to him if the legislative provisions referred to in those sub-paragraphs were provisions under any corresponding enactment having effect in Northern Ireland; or

(g)   he has an invalid carriage or other vehicle provided to him by the Secretary of State under section 5(2)(a) of and Schedule 2 to the National Health Service Act 1977 or by Scottish Ministers under section 46 of the National Health Service (Scotland) Act 1978 or provided by the Department of Health and Social Services for Northern Ireland under Article 30(1) of the Health and Personal Social Services (Northern Ireland) Order 1972.

(12)   For the purposes of paragraph (11), once paragraph (11)(c) applies to the claimant, if he then ceases, for a period of 56 days or less, to be incapable, or to be treated as incapable, of work, that paragraph shall, on his again becoming so incapable, or so treated as incapable, of work at the end of that period, immediately thereafter apply to him for so long as he remains incapable, or is treated as remaining incapable, of work.

[² (12A)   For the purposes of paragraph (11), once paragraph (11)(ca) applies to the claimant, if he then ceases, for a period of 84 days or less, to have, or to be treated as having, limited capability for work, that paragraph is, on his again having, or being treated as having, limited capability for work at the end of that period, immediately thereafter to apply to him for so long as he has, or is treated as having, limited capability for work.]

(13)   For the purposes of paragraphs (6) and (8)(a), a person is disabled if he is a person–

(a)   in respect of whom disability living allowance is payable, or has ceased to be payable solely because he is a patient;

[¹³ (b) who is certified as severely sight impaired or blind by a consultant ophthalmologist;] [⁹]

(c)   who ceased to be [¹³ certified as severely sight impaired or blind] within the period beginning 28 weeks before the first Monday in September following that person's fifteenth birthday and ending on the day preceding the first Monday in September following that person's sixteenth birthday. [⁹ or]

[⁹ (d) in respect of whom personal independence payment is payable, or [¹² has ceased to be payable solely by virtue of] regulations made under section 86(1) (hospital in-patients) of the 2012 Act][¹⁰; or]

[¹⁰ (e) in respect of whom armed forces independence payment is payable.]

(14)   For the purposes of paragraph (1) a person on maternity leave, paternity leave [¹⁴, adoption leave or shared parental leave] shall be treated as if he is engaged in remunerative work for the period specified in paragraph (15) ("the relevant period") provided that–

(a)   in the week before the period of maternity leave, paternity leave [¹⁴, adoption leave or shared parental leave] began he was in remunerative work;

(b)   the claimant is incurring relevant child care charges within the meaning of paragraph (5); and

(c)   he is entitled to statutory maternity pay under section 164 of the Act,[⁸ [¹⁵] statutory paternity pay by virtue of section 171ZA or 171ZB of the Act, [¹⁵]], statutory adoption pay by virtue of section 171ZL of the Act [¹⁴, statutory shared parental pay by virtue of section 171ZU or 171ZV of the Act] or maternity allowance under section 35 of the Act.

(15)   The relevant period shall begin on the day on which the person's maternity leave, paternity leave or adoption leave commences and shall end on–

(a)   the date that leave ends;

(b)   if no child care element of working tax credit is in payment on the date that entitlement to maternity allowance, statutory maternity pay, [⁸ [¹⁵] statutory paternity pay] [¹⁴, statutory adoption pay or statutory shared parental pay] ends, the date that entitlement ends; or

(c)   if a child care element of working tax credit is in payment on the date that entitlement to maternity allowance, statutory maternity pay, [⁸ [¹⁵] statutory paternity pay] [¹⁴, statutory adoption pay or statutory shared parental pay] ends, the date that entitlement to that award of the child care element of working tax credit ends,

whichever shall occur first.

(16)   In paragraph (15), "child care element" of working tax credit means the element of working tax credit prescribed under section 12 of the Tax Credits Act (child care element).

Modifications

The amendments made by SI 2014 No.3255 which came into force on 5 April 2015 do not have effect in relation to ordinary statutory paternity pay which is paid, additional statutory paternity pay which is paid, a period in respect of which additional statutory paternity pay is payable which begins, or continues, ordinary paternity leave which is taken or additional paternity leave which is taken on or after 5 April 2015. See art 35 of SI 2014 No.3255.

Amendments

1.   Amended by reg 4(5) of SI 2008 No 1042 as from 19.5.08.
2.   Amended by reg 34 of SI 2008 No 1082 as from 27.10.08.
3.   Amended by reg 6(5) of SI 2008 No 3157 as from 5.1.09.
4.   Amended by reg 2 of SI 2008 No 1848 as from 5.8.09.
5.   Inserted by reg 8(2) of SI 2010 No 2429 as from 1.11.10.

6.   Substituted by art 5 and Sch 4 para 11 of SI 2010 No.2582 (W.216)(C.123) as inserted by Art 2 of SI 2011 No.577 (W.82)(C.20) as from 1.4.11.
7.   Substituted by art 2 and Sch 2 para 52 of SI 2011 No 2581 as from 28.10.11.
8.   Amended by reg 8(4) of SI 2012 No 757 as from 1.4.12 (2.4.12 where rent payable weekly or in multiples of a week).
9.   Amended by reg 8 and Sch para 37(4) of SI 2013 No 388 as from 8.4.13.
10.   Amended by art 7 and Sch para 35(4) of SI 2013 No 591 as from 8.4.13.
11.   Amended by reg 36(4) of SI 2013 No 630 as from 29.4.13.
12.   Amended by reg 4(2) of SI 2014 No 213 as from 1.4.14 (7.4.14 where rent payable weekly or in multiples of a week).
13.   Amended by reg 3(6)(a) of SI 2014 No 2888 as from 26.11.14.
14.   Amended by art 18(5)(a), (b), (c)(iii), (d)(ii) and (e)(ii) of SI 2014 No 3255 as from 31.12.14.
15.   Amended by art 18(5)(c)(i) and (ii), (d)(i) and (e)(i) of SI 2014 No 3255 as from 5.4.15.
16.   Amended by Sch 1 para 7(3) of SI 2017 No 204 as from 3.4.17, subject to transitional and savings provisions in Sch 2 paras 1–7.
17.   Amended by reg 7(2) of SI 2017 No 1187 as from 21.12.17.
18.   Amended by reg 10(3) of SI 2018 No 228 as from 2.4.18.

General Note
This is, for practical purposes, identical to reg 28 HB Regs (see p424).

Calculation of average weekly income from tax credits

32.–(1)   This regulation applies where a claimant receives a tax credit.

(2)   Where this regulation applies, the period over which a tax credit is to be taken into account shall be the period set out in paragraph (3).

(3)   Where the instalment in respect of which payment of a tax credit is made is–

(a)   a daily instalment, the period is 1 day, being the day in respect of which the instalment is paid;

(b)   a weekly instalment, the period is 7 days, ending on the day on which the instalment is due to be paid;

(c)   a two weekly instalment, the period is 14 days, commencing 6 days before the day on which the instalment is due to be paid;

(d)   a four weekly instalment, the period is 28 days, ending on the day on which the instalment is due to be paid.

(4)   For the purposes of this regulation "tax credit" means working tax credit.

General Note
This is, for practical purposes, identical to reg 32 HB Regs (see p435).

Calculation of weekly income

33.–(1)   Except where paragraphs (2) [⁴, (2A), (3A)] and (4) apply, for the purposes of calculating the weekly income of the claimant, where the period in respect of which a payment is made–

(a)   does not exceed a week, the whole of that payment shall be included in the claimant's weekly income;

(b)   exceeds a week, the amount to be included in the claimant's weekly income shall be determined–

(i)   in a case where that period is a month, by multiplying the amount of the payment by 12 and dividing the product by 52;

(ii)   in a case where that period is three months, by multiplying the amount of the payment by 4 and dividing the product by 52;

(iii) in a case where that period is a year, by dividing the amount of the payment by 52;

(iv)   in any other case, by multiplying the amount of the payment by 7 and dividing the product by the number of days in the period in respect of which it is made.

(2)   Where–

(a)   the claimant's regular pattern of work is such that he does not work the same hours every week; or

777

(b)   the amount of the claimant's income fluctuates and has changed more than once, the weekly amount of that claimant's income shall be determined–

(i)   if, in a case to which sub-paragraph (a) applies, there is a recognised cycle of work, by reference to his average weekly income over the period of the complete cycle (including, where the cycle involves periods in which the claimant does no work, those periods but disregarding any other absences); or

(ii)   in any other case, on the basis of–

(aa)   the last two payments if those payments are one month or more apart;

(bb)   the last four payments if the last two payments are less than one month apart; or

(cc)   calculating or estimating such other payments as may, in the particular circumstances of the case, enable the claimant's average weekly income to be determined more accurately.

[⁴ (2A)   Income calculated pursuant to paragraph (2) shall be taken into account–

(a)   in the case of a claim, on the date the claim was made or treated as made, and the first day of each benefit week thereafter;

(b)   in the case of a claim or award where the claimant commences employment, the first day of the benefit week following the date the claimant commences that employment, and the first day of each benefit week thereafter; or

(c)   in the case of a claim or award where the claimant's average weekly earnings from employment change, the first day of the benefit week following the date the claimant's earnings from employment change so as to require recalculation under this paragraph, and the first day of each benefit week thereafter,

regardless of whether those earnings were actually received in that benefit week.]

(3)   For the purposes of paragraph (2)(b) the last payments are the last payments before the date the claim was made or treated as made or, if there is a subsequent supersession under paragraph 4 of Schedule 7 to the Child Support, Pensions and Social Security Act 2000, the last payments before the date of the supersession.

[⁴ (3A)   A claimant's earnings from employment as an employed earner not calculated pursuant to paragraph (2) shall be taken into account–

(a)   in the case of a claim, on the date that the claim was made or treated as made and the first day of each benefit week thereafter;

(b)   in the case of a claim or award where the claimant commences employment, the first day of the benefit week following the date the claimant commences that employment, and the first day of each benefit week thereafter; or

(c)   in the case of a claim or award where the claimant's average weekly earnings from employment change, the first day of the benefit week following the date of the change, and the beginning of each benefit week thereafter,

regardless of whether those earnings were actually received in that benefit week.]

(4)   If a claimant is entitled to receive a payment to which paragraph (5) applies, the amount of that payment shall be treated as if made in respect of a period of a year.

(5)   This paragraph applies to–

[³ (a)   royalties or other sums paid as a consideration for the use of, or the right to use, any copyright, design, patent or trade mark;];

[³ (b)   any payment in respect of any–

(i)   book registered under the Public Lending Right Scheme 1982; or

(ii)   work made under any international public lending right scheme that is analogous to the Public Lending Right Scheme 1982; or]

(c)   any payment which is made on an occasional basis.

(6)   The period under which any benefit under the benefit Acts is to be taken into account shall be the period in respect of which that benefit is payable.

(7)   Where payments are made in a currency other than Sterling, the value of the payment shall be determined by taking the Sterling equivalent on the date the payment is made.

(8)   The sums specified in Schedule 4 shall be disregarded in calculating–

(a)   the claimant's earnings; and

[³ (b)   any amount to which paragraph (5) applies where the claimant is the first owner of the copyright, design, patent or trademark, or an original contributor to the book or work referred to in paragraph (5)(b).]

[³ (8A)   For the purpose of paragraph (8)(b), and for that purpose only, the amounts specified in paragraph (5) shall be treated as though they were earnings.]

(9)   Income specified in Schedule 5 is to be disregarded in the calculation of a claimant's income.

[² (10)]

(11)   Schedule 6 shall have effect so that–

(a)   the capital specified in Part 1 shall be disregarded for the purpose of determining a claimant's income; and

(b)   the capital specified in Part 2 shall be disregarded for the purpose of determining a claimant's income under regulation 29(2) (weekly income from capital).

(12)   In the case of any income taken into account for the purpose of calculating a person's income, there shall be disregarded any amount payable by way of tax.

[² (13)]

[² (14)]

Amendments

1.   Inserted by reg 3 of SI 2006 No 2813 as from 20.11.06.
2.   Omitted by reg 6(b) of SI 2007 No 1619 as from 3.7.07.
3.   Amended by reg 7(5) of SI 2009 No 583 as from the first day of the first benefit week for a claimant on or after 6.4.09.
4.   Amended by reg 3 of SI 2015 No 6 as from 9.2.15.

Analysis

Reg 33 contains a number of rules to facilitate the calculation of income on a weekly basis.

Para (1) contains the general rule and is similar in effect to reg 33 HB Regs (see p436). It is subject to the specific circumstances set out in paras (2), (2A), (3A) and (4) (and also para (6), though para (1) does not specifically state this).

Paras (2) and (3) deal with fluctuating income from work, whether employed or self-employed. Where the hours of work are different each week or income flucuates and has changed more than once, the first step is to look for a pattern of work under sub-para (b)(i). The wording is similar to that of reg 6(2)(a) HB Regs and caselaw under that and the equivalent IS and income-based JSA provisions are relevant to the question of whether a cycle exists and, if so, what it is.

In the absence of a cycle, either the last two or four payments may be taken according to their time period. There is also the option of using other means of estimating weekly income under (b)(ii)(cc). It appears that (b)(ii)(cc) is an alternative to (b)(ii)(aa) or (bb).

Paras (2A) and (3A) provide the date earnings from employment are to be taken into account, whether or not they are actually received.

Paras (4) and (5) require royalty payments and Public Lending Right Scheme payments and analogous income, along with any payments made on an "occasional" basis, to be taken into account as referable to a year. It is inherent in the word "occasional" that the payments must be infrequent and irregular.

Para (6) requires payments of benefit to be taken into account over a period equivalent to that in respect of which it is payable. Note that reg 44(3) provides for certain arrears of PC to be treated as capital.

Para (7) requires foreign payments to be converted into Sterling for the purpose of assessment of income. The exchange rate at the date of payment is to be used.

Paras (8) to (9) and (11) bring in the schedules for disregards of income and capital. Note that Sch 6 Part 2 contains capital disregarded for the purposes of generating deemed income under reg 29(2).

Para (12) requires tax liabilities to be ignored when calculating income. "Tax" covers income tax and presumably also national insurance contributions, which are a form of taxation, as well as any other forms of tax that might apply to the particular type of income.

Paras (10), (13) and (14) contained a power to modify the HB scheme so as to disregard war widow's and widower's pensions and certain payments made under the Armed Forces and Reserve Forces (Compensation Scheme) Order 2005. s134(8) SSAA 1992 sets out the circumstances in which modifications can be made. The prescribed pensions are now found in the Schedule to the Housing Benefit and Council Tax Benefit (War Pension Disregards) Regulations 2007 (on p1808). See the commentary to s134(8) (see p79) for a discussion of an authority's powers.

Disregard of changes in tax, contributions etc

34. In calculating the claimant's income the appropriate authority may disregard any legislative change–

(a)   in the basic or other rates of income tax;

[⁴ (aa) in the Scottish basic or other rates of income tax;]

(b)   in the amount of any personal tax [⁴ reliefs under Chapters 2, 3 and 3A of Part 3 of the Income Tax Act 2007];

(c)   in the rates of [¹ national insurance contributions] payable under the Act or in the lower earnings limit or upper earnings limit for Class 1 contributions under that Act, the lower or upper limits applicable to Class 4 contributions under that Act or the amount specified in section 11(4) of the Act ([² small profits threshold] in relation to Class 2 contributions);

(d)   in the amount of tax payable as a result of an increase in the weekly rate of Category A, B, C or D retirement pension or any addition thereto or any graduated pension payable under the Act [³ or a state pension under Part 1 of the Pensions Act 2014]; and

(e)   in the maximum rate of child tax credit or working tax credit,

for a period not exceeding 30 benefit weeks beginning with the benefit week immediately following the date from which the change is effective.

Amendments

1.   Amended by reg 4(3)(a) of SI 2014 No 213 as from 1.4.14 (7.4.14 where rent payable weekly or in multiples of a week).
2.   Amended by reg 34(2) of SI 2015 No 478 as from 6.4.15.
3.   Amended by art 29(3) of SI 2015 No 1985 as from 6.4.16.
4.   Amended by reg 5(3) of SI 2016 No 233 as from 6.4.16.

Definition

"Scottish basic rate" – see reg 2(1).

General Note

This is the equivalent of reg 34 HB Regs (see p437).

SECTION 3
Employed earners

Earnings of employed earners

35.–(1)   Subject to paragraph (2), "earnings" means in the case of employment as an employed earner, any remuneration or profit derived from that employment and includes–

(a)   any bonus or commission;

(b)   any payment in lieu of remuneration except any periodic sum paid to a claimant on account of the termination of his employment by reason of redundancy;

(c)   any payment in lieu of notice;

(d)   any holiday pay;

(e)   any payment by way of a retainer;

(f)   any payment made by the claimant's employer in respect of expenses not wholly, exclusively and necessarily incurred in the performance of the duties of the employment, including any payment made by the claimant's employer in respect of–

(i)   travelling expenses incurred by the claimant between his home and place of employment;

(ii)   expenses incurred by the claimant under arrangements made for the care of a member of his family owing to the claimant's absence from home;

(g)   the amount of any payment by way of a non-cash voucher which has been taken into account in the computation of a person's earnings in accordance with Part 5 of Schedule 3 to the Social Security (Contributions) Regulations 2001;

(h)   statutory sick pay and statutory maternity pay payable by the employer under the Act;

[² (i) [⁵] statutory paternity pay payable under Part 12ZA of the Act;]
[² [⁵ (ia)]]
(j)   statutory adoption pay payable under Part 12ZB of the Act;
[⁴ (ja) statutory shared parental pay payable under Part 12ZC of the Act;]
(k)   any sums payable under a contract of service–
         (i)   for incapacity for work due to sickness or injury; or
         (ii)   by reason of pregnancy or confinement.
(2)   Earnings shall not include–
(a)   subject to paragraph (3), any payment in kind;
(b)   any payment in respect of expenses wholly, exclusively and necessarily incurred
         in the performance of the duties of the employment;
(c)   any occupational pension;
(d)   any lump sum payment made under the Iron and Steel Re-adaptation Benefits
         Scheme;
(e)   any payment of compensation made pursuant to an award by an employment
         tribunal established under the Employment Tribunals Act 1996 in respect of
         unfair dismissal or unlawful discrimination.
[¹ (f) any payment in respect of expenses arising out of the [³ claimant participating
         as a service user].]
(3)   Paragraph (2)(a) shall not apply in respect of any non-cash voucher referred to
in paragraph (1)(g).

Modifications

The amendments made by SI 2014 No.3255 which came into force on 5 April 2015 do not have effect in relation to ordinary statutory paternity pay which is paid, additional statutory paternity pay which is paid, a period in respect of which additional statutory paternity pay is payable which begins, or continues, ordinary paternity leave which is taken or additional paternity leave which is taken on or after 5 April 2015. See art 35 of SI 2014 No.3255.

Amendments

1.   Inserted by reg 7(3) of SI 2009 No 2655 as from 2.11.09.
2.   Substituted by reg 8(5) of SI 2012 No 757 as from 1.4.12 (2.4.12 where rent payable weekly or in multiples of a week).
3.   Amended by reg 9(3) of SI 2014 No 591 as from 28.4.14.
4.   Inserted by art 18(6)(c) of SI 2014 No 3255 as from 31.12.14.
5.   Amended by art 18(6)(a) and (b) of SI 2014 No 3255 as from 5.4.15.

Calculation of net earnings of employed earners

36.–(1)   For the purposes of regulation 30 (calculation of income on a weekly basis), the earnings of a claimant derived or likely to be derived from employment as an employed earner to be taken into account shall, subject to regulation 33(5) and Schedule 4, be his net earnings.
(2)   For the purposes of paragraph (1) net earnings shall, except in relation to any payment to which regulation 33(5) refers, be calculated by taking into account the gross earnings of the claimant from that employment over the assessment period, less–
(a)   any amount deducted from those earnings by way of–
         (i)   income tax;
         (ii)   primary Class 1 contributions under the Act;
(b)   one-half of any sum paid by the claimant by way of a contribution towards an
         occupational pension scheme;
(c)   one-half of the amount calculated in accordance with paragraph (4) in respect of
         any qualifying contribution payable by the claimant; and
(d)   where those earnings include a payment which is payable under any enactment
         having effect in Northern Ireland and which corresponds to statutory sick pay,
         statutory maternity pay, [³ [⁵] statutory paternity pay] [⁴, statutory adoption pay
         or statutory shared parental pay], any amount deducted from those earnings by
         way of any contributions which are payable under any enactment having effect
         in Northern Ireland and which correspond to primary Class 1 contributions
         under the Act.

(3)   In this regulation "qualifying contribution" means any sum which is payable periodically as a contribution towards a personal pension scheme.

(4)   The amount in respect of any qualifying contribution shall be calculated by multiplying the daily amount of the qualifying contribution by the number equal to the number of days in the assessment period; and for the purposes of this regulation the daily amount of the qualifying contribution shall be determined–

(a)   where the qualifying contribution is payable monthly, by multiplying the amount of the qualifying contribution by 12 and dividing the product by 365;

(b)   in any other case, by dividing the amount of the qualifying contribution by the number equal to the number of days in the period to which the qualifying contribution relates.

(5)   Where the earnings of a claimant are determined under sub-paragraph (b) of paragraph (2) of regulation 33 (calculation of weekly income), his net earnings shall be calculated by taking into account those earnings over the assessment period, less–

(a)   an amount in respect of income tax equivalent to an amount calculated by applying to those earnings the [¹ [²] the basic rate [⁶, or in the case of a Scottish taxpayer, the Scottish basic rate,] of tax applicable to the assessment period less only the [⁶ personal reliefs to which the claimant is entitled under Chapters 2, 3 and 3A of the Income Tax Act 2007 as are] appropriate to his circumstances but, if the assessment period is less than a year, the earnings to which the [¹ [² basic] rate] [⁶, or the Scottish basic rate,] of tax is to be applied and the amount of the personal [⁶ reliefs] deductible under this sub-paragraph shall be calculated on a pro rata basis;

(b)   an amount equivalent to the amount of the primary Class 1 contributions that would be payable by him under the Act in respect of those earnings if such contributions were payable; and

(c)   one-half of any sum which would be payable by the claimant by way of a contribution towards an occupational or personal pension scheme, if the earnings so estimated were actual earnings.

Modifications

The amendments made by SI 2014 No.3255 which came into force on 5 April 2015 do not have effect in relation to ordinary statutory paternity pay which is paid, additional statutory paternity pay which is paid, a period in respect of which additional statutory paternity pay is payable which begins, or continues, ordinary paternity leave which is taken or additional paternity leave which is taken on or after 5 April 2015. See art 35 of SI 2014 No.3255.

Amendments

1.   Amended by reg 12(4) of SI 2007 No 2618 as from 1.10.07.
2.   Amended by reg 7(6) of SI 2009 No 583 as from 6.4.09.
3.   Amended by reg 8(6) of SI 2012 No 757 as from 1.4.12 (2.4.12 where rent payable weekly or in multiples of a week).
4.   Inserted by art 18(7)(b) of SI 2014 No 3255 as from 31.12.14.
5.   Amended by art 18(7)(a) of SI 2014 No 3255 as from 5.4.15.
6.   Amended by reg 5(4) of SI 2016 No 233 as from 6.4.16.

Definitions

"Scottish basic rate" – see reg 2(1).
"Scottish taxpayer" – see reg 2(1).

General Note

This is equivalent to reg 36 HB Regs (see p442).

SECTION 4
Self-employed earners

Calculation of earnings of self-employed earners

37.–(1)   Where a claimant's earnings consist of earnings from employment as a self-employed earner, the weekly amount of his earnings shall be determined by reference to his average weekly earnings from that employment–

(a)   over a period of one year; or
(b)   where the claimant has recently become engaged in that employment or there has been a change which is likely to affect the normal pattern of business, over such other period ("computation period") as may, in the particular case, enable the weekly amount of his earnings to be determined more accurately.
(2)   For the purposes of determining the weekly amount of earnings of a claimant to whom paragraph (1)(b) applies, his earnings over the computation period shall be divided by the number equal to the number of days in that period and multiplying the quotient by 7.
(3)   The period over which the weekly amount of a claimant's earnings is calculated in accordance with this regulation shall be his assessment period.

General Note

This has no equivalent in the HB Regs. It simply states that self-employed earners have their weekly earnings calculated from average earnings over a year or where the business has recently started or there has been a change in the pattern of the business, such other period that enables the earnings to be determined more accurately.

Earnings of self-employed earners

38.–(1)   Subject to paragraph (2), "earnings", in the case of employment as a self-employed earner, means the gross receipts of the employment [³].
(2)   "Earnings" in the case of employment as a self-employed earner does not include–
(a)   where a claimant occupies a dwelling as his home and he provides in that dwelling board and lodging accommodation for which payment is made, those payments;
(b)   any payment made by a local authority to a claimant–
   (i)   with whom a person is accommodated by virtue of arrangements made under [⁷ section 22C(2) of the Children Act 1989 (ways in which looked after children are to be accommodated and maintained)] or, as the case may be, [⁷ section 81(2) of the Social Services and Well-being (Wales) Act 2014 (ways in which looked after children are to be accommodated and maintained),] [⁶ section 26 or 26A of the Children (Scotland) Act 1995 (manner of provision of accommodation to child looked afer by local authority and duty to provide continuing care); or]
   [² (ii) with whom a local authority foster a child under the Looked After Children (Scotland) Regulations 2009 or who is a kinship carer under those Regulations;]
(c)   any payment made by a voluntary organisation in accordance with section 59(1)(a) of the Children Act 1989 (provision of accommodation by voluntary organisations);
(d)   any payment made to the claimant or his partner for a person ("the person concerned") who is not normally a member of the claimant's household but is temporarily in his care, by–
   (i)   a health authority;
   (ii)   a local authority, but excluding payments of housing benefit made in respect of the person concerned;
   (iii) a voluntary organisation;
   (iv)   the person concerned pursuant to section 26(3A) of the National Assistance Act 1948; [¹]
   [² (iva) a clinical commissioning group established under section 14D of the National Health Service Act 2006;]
   [² (ivb) the National Health Service Commissioning Board; [⁵]]
   [² (v)]
   [¹ (vi) a Local Health Board established under section 16BA of the National Health Service Act 1977 or established by an order made under section 11 of the National Health Service (Wales) Act 2006;] [⁷]

[⁵ (vii) the person concerned where the payment is for the provision of accommodation in respect of the meeting of that person's needs under section 18 or 19 of the Care Act 2014 (duty and power to meet needs for care and support);] [⁷ or

(viii) the person concerned where the payment is for the provision of accommodation to meet that person's needs for care and support under section 35 or 36 of the Social Services and Well-being (Wales) Act 2014 (duty and power to meet care and support needs of an adult);]

[⁶ (da) any payment or part of a payment made by a local authority in accordance with section 26A of the Children (Scotland) Act 1995 (duty to provide continuing care) to a person ("A") which A passes on to the claimant where A–

    (i)   was formerly in the claimant's care;

    (ii)   is aged 16 or over; and

    (iii) continues to live with the claimant;]

[⁸ (db) any payment made to a claimant under section 73(1)(b) of the Children and Young People (Scotland) Act 2014 (kinship care assistance).]

(e)   any sports award.

Amendments

1.   Amended by reg 6(6) of SI 2008 No 3157 as from 5.1.09.
2.   Substituted by reg 8(3) of SI 2010 No 2429 as from 1.11.10.
3.   Omitted by reg 20(5) of SI 2011 No 2425 as from 31.10.11.
4.   Amended by Sch 2 para 94(3) of SI 2013 No 235 as from 1.4.13.
5.   Amendedby art 2 and Sch para 25(2) of SI 2015 No 643 as from 1.4.15.
6.   Amended by art 7(2) of SI 2016 No 732 as from 5.8.16.
7.   Amended by arts 12(4) and 26(3) of SI 2017 No 901 as from 3.11.17.
8.   Inserted by reg 6 of SI 2017 No 995 as from 7.11.17.

General Note

Para (1) is equivalent to reg 37(1) HB Regs. On para (2)(c) and (d), see Sch 5 paras 26 and 27 HB Regs on p673.

Calculation of net profit of self-employed earners

39.–(1)   For the purposes of regulation 30 (calculation of income on a weekly basis) the earnings of a claimant to be taken into account shall be–

(a)   in the case of a self-employed earner who is engaged in employment on his own account, the net profit derived from that employment;

(b)   in the case of a self-employed earner whose employment is carried on in partnership, his share of the net profit derived from that employment, less–

    (i)   an amount in respect of income tax and of [² national insurance contributions] payable under the Act calculated in accordance with regulation 40 (deduction of tax and contributions for self-employed earners); and

    (ii)   one-half of the amount calculated in accordance with paragraph (10) in respect of any qualifying premium.

(2)   For the purposes of paragraph (1)(a) the net profit of the employment shall, except where paragraph (8) applies, be calculated by taking into account the earnings of the employment over the assessment period less–

(a)   subject to paragraphs (4) to (7), any expenses wholly and exclusively incurred in that period for the purposes of that employment;

(b)   an amount in respect of–

    (i)   income tax; and

    (ii)   [² national insurance contributions] payable under the Act,

    calculated in accordance with regulation 40 (deduction of tax and contributions for self-employed earners); and

(c)   one-half of the amount calculated in accordance with paragraph (10) in respect of any qualifying premium.

(3)   For the purposes of paragraph (1)(b) the net profit of the employment shall be calculated by taking into account the earnings of the employment over the assessment

period less, subject to paragraphs (4) to (7), any expenses wholly and exclusively incurred in that period for the purposes of the employment.

(4)   Subject to paragraph (5), no deduction shall be made under paragraph (2)(a) or (3), in respect of–
(a)   any capital expenditure;
(b)   the depreciation of any capital asset;
(c)   any sum employed or intended to be employed in the setting up or expansion of the employment;
(d)   any loss incurred before the beginning of the assessment period;
(e)   the repayment of capital on any loan taken out for the purposes of the employment; and
(f)   any expenses incurred in providing business entertainment.

(5)   A deduction shall be made under paragraph (2)(a) or (3) in respect of the repayment of capital on any loan used for–
(a)   the replacement in the course of business of equipment or machinery; and
(b)   the repair of an existing business asset except to the extent that any sum is payable under an insurance policy for its repair.

(6)   The relevant authority shall refuse to make a deduction in respect of any expenses under paragraph (2)(a) or (3) where it is not satisfied given the nature and the amount of the expense that it has been reasonably incurred.

(7)   For the avoidance of doubt–
(a)   a deduction shall not be made under paragraph (2)(a) or (3) in respect of any sum unless it has been expended for the purposes of the business;
(b)   a deduction shall be made thereunder in respect of–
(i)   the excess of any value added tax paid over value added tax received in the assessment period;
(ii)   any income expended in the repair of an existing business asset except to the extent that any sum is payable under an insurance policy for its repair;
(iii)   any payment of interest on a loan taken out for the purposes of the employment.

(8)   Where a claimant is engaged in employment as a child minder the net profit of the employment shall be one-third of the earnings of that employment, less–
(a)   an amount in respect of–
(i)   income tax; and
(ii)   [² national insurance contributions] payable under the Act,
        calculated in accordance with regulation 40 (deduction of tax and contributions for self-employed earners); and
(b)   one-half of the amount calculated in accordance with paragraph (10) in respect of any qualifying premium.

(9)   For the avoidance of doubt where a claimant is engaged in employment as a self-employed earner and he is also engaged in one or more other employments as a self-employed or employed earner any loss incurred in any one of his employments shall not be offset against his earnings in any other of his employments.

(10)   The amount in respect of any qualifying premium shall be calculated by multiplying the daily amount of the qualifying premium by the number equal to the number of days in the assessment period; and for the purposes of this regulation the daily amount of the qualifying premium shall be determined–
(a)   where the qualifying premium is payable monthly, by multiplying the amount of the qualifying premium by 12 and dividing the product by 365;
(b)   in any other case, by dividing the amount of the qualifying premium by the number equal to the number of days in the period to which the qualifying premium relates.

(11)   In this regulation, "qualifying premium" means any premium which is payable periodically in respect of [¹] a personal pension scheme and is so payable on or after the date of claim.

Amendments
1. Omitted by reg 5(3) of SI 2007 No 1749 as from 16.7.07.
2. Amended by reg 4(3)(b) of SI 2014 No 213 as from 1.4.14 (7.4.14 where rent payable weekly or in multiples of a week).

General Note
This regulation is equivalent to reg 38 HB Regs (see p445).

Deduction of tax and contributions of self-employed earners

40.–(1)   The amount to be deducted in respect of income tax under regulation 39(1)(b)(i), (2)(b)(i) or (8)(a)(i) (calculation of net profit of self-employed earners) shall be calculated on the basis of the amount of chargeable income and as if that income were assessable to income tax at [²...] the basic rate [⁶ , or in the case of a Scottish taxpayer, the Scottish basic rate,] of tax applicable to the assessment period less only the [⁶ personal reliefs to which the claimant is entitled under Chapters 2, 3 and 3A of the Income Tax Act 2007 as are] appropriate to his circumstances; but, if the assessment period is less than a year, the earnings to which the [¹ [³ basic[rate] [⁶ , or the Scottish basic rate,] of tax is to be applied and the amount of the personal reliefs deductible under this paragraph shall be calculated on a pro rata basis.

(2)   The amount to be deducted in respect of [⁴ national insurance contributions] under regulation 39(1)(b)(i), (2)(b)(ii) or (8)(a)(ii) shall be the total of–
(a)   the amount of Class 2 contributions payable under section [⁵ 11(2)] or, as the case may be, [⁵ 11(8)] of the Act at the rate applicable to the assessment period except where the claimant's chargeable income is less than the amount specified in section 11(4) of the Act ([⁵ small profits threshold]) for the tax year applicable to the assessment period; but if the assessment period is less than a year, the amount specified for that tax year shall be reduced pro rata; and
(b)   the amount of Class 4 contributions (if any) which would be payable under section 15 of the Act (Class 4 contributions recoverable under the Income Tax Acts) at the percentage rate applicable to the assessment period on so much of the chargeable income as exceeds the lower limit but does not exceed the upper limit of profits and gains applicable for the tax year applicable to the assessment period; but if the assessment period is less than a year, those limits shall be reduced pro rata.

(3)   In this regulation "chargeable income" means–
(a)   except where sub-paragraph (b) applies, the earnings derived from the employment less any expenses deducted under paragraph (2)(a) or, as the case may be, (3) of regulation 39;
(b)   in the case of employment as a child minder, one-third of the earnings of that employment.

Amendments
1. Amended by reg 12(5) of SI 2007 No 2618 as from 1.10.07.
2. Omitted by reg 7(6)(a) of SI 2009 No 583 as from 6.4.09.
3. Amended by reg 7(6)(b) of SI 2009 No 583 as from 6.4.09.
4. Amended by reg 4(3)(c) of SI 2014 No 213 as from 1.4.14 (7.4.14 where rent payable weekly or in multiples of a week).
5. Amended by reg 34(3) of SI 2015 No 478 as from 6.4.15.
6. Amended by reg 5(5) of SI 2016 No 233 as from 6.4.16.

Definitions
"Scottish basic rate" – see reg 2(1).
"Scottish taxpayer" – see reg 2(1).

General Note
This is equivalent to reg 39 HB Regs (see p449).

SECTION 5
Other income

Notional income

41.–(1)   A claimant shall be treated as possessing–

(a)   subject to paragraph (2), the amount of any retirement pension income–

   (i)   for which no claim has been made; and

   (ii)   to which he might expect to be entitled if a claim for it were made;

(b)   income from an occupational pension scheme which the claimant elected to defer.

(2)   Paragraph (1)(a) shall not apply to the following where entitlement has been deferred–

(a)   Category A or Category B retirement pension payable under sections 43 to 55 of the Act;

(b)   a shared additional pension payable under section 55A [⁸ or 55AA] of the Act; [⁸]

(c)   graduated retirement benefit payable under sections 36 or 37 of the National Insurance Act 1965; [⁸ and

(d)   a state pension under Part 1 of the Pensions Act 2014.]

(3)   For the purposes of paragraph (2), entitlement has been deferred–

(a)   in the case of a Category A or Category B pension, in the circumstances specified in section 55(3) of the Act;

(b)   in the case of a shared additional pension, in the circumstances specified in section 55C(3) of the Act;

(c)   in the case of graduated retirement benefit, in the circumstances specified in section 36(4) and (4A) of the National Insurance Act 1965;

[⁸ (d)   in the case of a state pension under Part 1 of the Pensions Act 2014, in the circumstances specified in section 17(7) and (8) of that Act.]

[⁴ (4)   This paragraph applies where a person [⁶ who has attained the qualifying age for state pension credit]–

(a)   is entitled to money purchase benefits under an occupational pension scheme or a personal pension scheme;

(b)   fails to purchase an annuity with the funds available in that scheme; and

(c)   either–

   (i)   defers in whole or in part the payment of any income which would have been payable to him by his pension fund holder, or

   (ii)   fails to take any necessary action to secure that the whole of any income which would be payable to him by his pension fund holder upon his applying for it, is so paid, or

   (iii)   income withdrawal is not available to him under that scheme.

(4A)   Where paragraph (4) applies, the amount of any income foregone shall be treated as possessed by that person, but only from the date on which it could be expected to be acquired were an application for it to be made.]

(5)   The amount of any income foregone in a case [⁴ where paragraph (4)(c)(i) or (ii)] applies shall be the [⁹ rate of the annuity which may have been purchased with the fund] and shall be determined by the relevant authority which shall take account of information provided by the pension fund holder in accordance with regulation 67(6) (evidence and information).

(6)   The amount of any income foregone in a case [⁴ where paragraph (4)(c)(iii)] applies shall be the income that the claimant could have received without purchasing an annuity had the funds held under the relevant scheme [⁴] been held under a personal pension scheme or occupational pension scheme where income withdrawal was available and shall be determined in the manner specified in paragraph (5).

(7)   In paragraph (4), "money purchase benefits" has the meaning it has in the Pension Schemes Act 1993.

(8)   [² Subject to paragraph (8A) [⁸, (8BA), (8BB)] [⁵ and (8C)],] a person shall be treated as possessing income of which he has deprived himself for the purpose of securing entitlement to housing benefit or increasing the amount of that benefit.

[² (8A)   Paragraph (8) shall not apply in respect of the amount of an increase of pension or benefit where a person, having made an election in favour of that increase of pension or benefit under Schedule 5 or 5A to the Contributions and Benefits Act or under Schedule 1 to the Graduated Retirement Benefit Regulations, changes that election in accordance with regulations made under Schedule 5 or 5A to that Act in favour of a lump sum.

(8B)   In paragraph (8A), "lump sum" means a lump sum under Schedule 5 or 5A to the Contributions and Benefits Act or under Schedule 1 to the Graduated Retirement Benefit Regulations.]

[⁸ (8BA)   Paragraph (8) shall not apply in respect of the amount of an increase of pension where a person, having made a choice in favour of that increase of pension under section 8(2) of the Pensions Act 2014, alters that choice in accordance with Regulations made under section 8(7) of that Act in favour of a lump sum.

(8BB)   Paragraph (8) shall not apply in respect of the amount of an increase of pension where a person, having made a choice in favour of that increase of pension in accordance with Regulations made under section 10 of the Pensions Act 2014 which include provision corresponding or similar to section 8(2) of that Act, alters that choice in favour of a lump sum, in accordance with Regulations made under section 10 of that Act which include provision corresponding or similar to Regulations made under section 8(7) of that Act.

(8BC)   In paragraph (8BA), "lump sum" means a lump sum under section 8 of the Pensions Act 2014.

(8BD)   In paragraph (8BB), "lump sum" means a lump sum under Regulations made under section 10 of the Pensions Act 2014 which include provision corresponding or similar to section 8 of that Act.]

[⁵ (8C) Paragraph (8) shall not apply in respect of any amount of income other than earnings, or earnings of an employed earner, arising out of the [⁷ claimant participating as a service user].]

(9)   Where a claimant is in receipt of any benefit (other than housing benefit) under the benefit Acts and the rate of that benefit is altered with effect from a date on or after 1st April in any year but not more than 14 days thereafter, the relevant authority shall treat the claimant as possessing such benefit at the altered rate–

(a)   in a case in which the claimant's weekly amount of eligible rent falls to be calculated in accordance with regulation 61(2)(b) [¹ or (c)] (calculation of weekly amounts), from 1st April in that year;

(b)   in any other case, from the first Monday in April in that year,
to the date on which the altered rate is to take effect.

(10)   In the case of a claimant who has, or whose partner has, an award of state pension credit comprising only the savings credit, where a relevant authority treats the claimant as possessing any benefit (other than housing benefit) at the altered rate in accordance with paragraph (9), that authority shall–

(a)   determine the income and capital of that claimant in accordance with regulation 27(1) (calculation of claimant's income in savings credit only cases) where the calculation or estimate of that income and capital is altered with effect from a date on or after 1st April in any year but not more than 14 days thereafter; and

(b)   treat that claimant as possessing such income and capital at the altered rate by reference to the period referred to in paragraph (9)(a) or (b), as the case may be.

[³ (11)   For the purposes of paragraph (8), a person is not to be regarded as depriving himself of income where–

(a)   his rights to benefits under a registered pension scheme are extinguished and in consequence of this he receives a payment from the scheme, and

(b)   that payment is a trivial commutation lump sum within the meaning given by paragraph 7 of Schedule 29 to the Finance Act 2004.

(12) In paragraph (11), "registered pension scheme" has the meaning given in section 150(2) of the Finance Act 2004.]

Amendments

1. Amended by reg 2(7) of SI 2005 No 2502 as amended by Sch 2 para 27 of SI 2006 No 217 as from 1.4.06 (3.4.06 where rent payable weekly or at intervals of a week).
2. Inserted by reg 11(3) of SI 2005 No 2677 and reg 2 of SI 2006 No 217 as from 6.4.06.
3. Amended by reg 16(2) of SI 2006 No 2378 as from 2.10.06.
4. Amended by reg 5(4) of SI 2007 No 1749 as from 16.7.07.
5. Amended by reg 7(4) of SI 2009 No 2655 as from 2.11.09.
6. Amended by reg 9(4) of SI 2010 No 641 as from 6.4.10.
7. Amended by reg 9(4) of SI 2014 No.591 as from 28.4.14.
8. Amended by art 29(4) of SI 2015 No 1985 as from 6.4.16.
9. Amended by reg 12(3) of SI 2017 No 1015 as from 16.11.17.

Analysis

Paras (1) to (3) deal with two types of income.

(1) "Retirement pension income" as defined in s16 SPCA (see reg 29(c)) for which no claim has been made: para (1)(a). Note the phrase "might expect to be entitled if a claim for it were made" in para (1)(a)(ii) which sets a lower burden of proof of availability. Para (1)(a) does not apply where entitlement to the types of pension listed in para (2) has been deferred in the circumstances set out in para (3).

(2) Income from an occupational pension scheme which the claimant has elected to defer: para (1)(b). If a claimant or her/his partner fails to take up income from one of those sources, s/he will be treated as having income of that amount.

Paras (4) to (6) aim to ensure that a claimant aged at least the qualifying age for PC (defined in reg 2(1)) does not deprive her/himself of income available from an occupational or personal pension scheme. The claimant or other relevant person is expected to purchase an annuity with the funds available in the pension scheme. If s/he does not do so, s/he will be treated as possessing the maximum amount that can be withdrawn from the scheme, as assessed under para (5) or (6) as appropriate. *BRG v SSWP (SPC)* [2014] UKUT 246 (AAC) decided that this can apply where the claimant or other person has not yet reached the retirement age which s/he originally selected for the pension, but is the age at which s/he could request benefits to be made available to her/him. The claimant is treated as possessing the income from the date it could be expected to be acquired were an application made for it: para (4A). The provision is only triggered if one of the conditions in heads (4)(c)(i) to (iii) are met.

Paras (8) to (8C). Para (8) is the equivalent of reg 42(1) HB Regs, but here it is subject to paras (8A), (8C) and (11). Under para (8A), where someone defers claiming a pension or benefit opting for an increase in it, then opts to take a lump sum instead, the deprivation rules do not apply to the increase. "Lump sum" is defined in para (8B). Paras (8BA) to (8BD) make equivalent provision in respect of a person who defers claiming state pension. Para (11) concerns trivial lump sum payments made to a claimant in consequence of the ending of her/his right to receive benefits under a registered pension scheme: defined in para (12). The effect of para (11) is that the person cannot be treated as still receiving as income the benefits s/he used to receive under the registered pension scheme. The lump sum payment itself should be treated as capital. See Sch 6 para 26A for a disregard of lump sum payments made under Sch 5 or 5A SSCBA. Para (8C) concerns the payments set out made to claimants in respect of their participation as a service user, defined in reg 2(6) (see p727).

Paras (9) and (10). Para (9) is designed to ease administration connected with the uprating of benefits. The increased amount of benefit is treated as possessed from 1 April each year unless rent is not payable weekly in which case it will apply from the first Monday in April. Where para (9) applies and a claimant or her/his partner has an award of the savings credit of PC only, para (10) tells an authority to redetermine such a claimant's income and capital and to treat the altered rate as the claimant's by reference to the relevant period in para (9).

Income paid to third parties

42.–(1) Any payment of income, other than a payment specified in [² paragraphs (2) or (3)], to a third party in respect of the claimant shall be treated as possessed by the claimant.

(2) Paragraph (1) shall not apply in respect of a payment of income made under an occupational pension scheme [¹, in respect of a pension or other periodical payment made under a personal pension scheme or a payment made by the Board of the Pension Protection Fund] where–

(a) a bankruptcy order has been made in respect of the person in respect of whom the payment has been made or, in Scotland, the estate of that person is subject to sequestration or a judicial factor has been appointed on that person's estate under section 41 of the Solicitors (Scotland) Act 1980;

(b)   the payment is made to the trustee in bankruptcy or any other person acting on behalf of the creditors; and

(c)   the person referred to in sub-paragraph (a) and his partner does not possess, or is not treated as possessing, any other income apart from that payment.

[² (3)   Paragraph (1) shall not apply in respect of any payment of income other than earnings, or earnings derived from employment as an employed earner, arising out of the [³ claimant participating as a service user].]

Amendments

1.   Substituted by reg 10(3) of SI 2006 No 588 as from 6.4.06.

2.   Amended by reg 20(6) of SI 2011 No 2425 as from 31.10.11.

3.   Amended by reg 9(5) of SI 2014 No 591 as from 28.4.14.

Analysis

This is significantly different in effect to the more complex reg 42(6) HB Regs (see p453). Under para (1), any payment of income to a third party in respect of the claimant is treated as possessed by the claimant. Paras (2) and (3) contain the only exceptions. Para (2) is equivalent to reg 42(7)(d) HB Regs. However, as "income" is defined categorically in reg 29(1), reg 42 has only limited impact. Para (3) is equivalent to reg 42(12A).

SECTION 6

Capital

Capital limit

43.   For the purposes of section 134(1) of the Act as it applies to housing benefit (no entitlement to benefit if capital exceeds a prescribed amount), the prescribed amount is £16,000.

General Note

This is equivalent to reg 43 HB Regs (see p462). Note, however, that if a claimant or her/his partner is in receipt of the guarantee credit of PC, income and capital are ignored under reg 26; effectively, such claimants have no capital limit.

Calculation of capital

44.–(1)   For the purposes of Part 7 of the Act as it applies to housing benefit, the capital of a claimant to be taken into account shall, subject to paragraph (2), be the whole of his capital calculated in accordance with this Part.

(2)   There shall be disregarded from the calculation of the claimant's capital under paragraph (1) any capital, where applicable, specified in Schedule 6.

(3)   A claimant's capital shall be treated as including any payment made to him by way of arrears of–

(a)   child tax credit;

(b)   working tax credit;

(c)   state pension credit,

if the payment was made in respect of a period for the whole or part of which housing benefit was paid before those arrears were paid.

General Note

Paras (1) and (2) are equivalent to reg 44 HB Regs (see p462). Para (3) requires arrears of CTC, WTC and PC to be treated as capital if HB was paid to the claimant in respect of the period to which the payment is attributable. This is to avoid the creation of overpayments.

Note that where a claimant or her/his partner is awarded the savings credit of PC but not the guarantee credit, the authority must use the assessment of income and capital the DWP used for PC purposes to calculate HB: reg 27(1) to (6). It is only where such a claimant's capital increases to more than £16,000 during an assessed income period that the authority is required to calculate capital for itself under regs 43 to 49: reg 27(7) and (8).

[¹Calculation of capital in the United Kingdom

45.   Capital which a claimant possesses in the United Kingdom shall be calculated at its current market or surrender value less–

(a)   where there would be expenses attributable to the sale, 10 per cent.; and

(b)   the amount of any encumbrance secured on it.]

Amendment
1.   Substituted by reg 12(6) of SI 2007 No 2618 as from 1.10.07.

General Note
This is equivalent to reg 47 HB Regs (see p464).

Calculation of capital outside the United Kingdom

46.   Capital which a claimant possesses in a country outside the United Kingdom shall be calculated–
   (a)   in a case where there is no prohibition in that country against the transfer to the United Kingdom of an amount equal to its current market or surrender value in that country, at that value;
   (b)   in a case where there is such a prohibition, at the price which it would realise if sold in the United Kingdom to a willing buyer,
less, where there would be expenses attributable to sale, 10 per cent. and the amount of any encumbrance secured on it.

General Note
This is equivalent to reg 48 HB Regs (see p465).

Notional capital

47.–(1)   A claimant shall be treated as possessing capital of which he has deprived himself for the purpose of securing entitlement to housing benefit or increasing the amount of that benefit except to the extent that the capital which he is treated as possessing is reduced in accordance with regulation 48 (diminishing notional capital rule).
   (2)   A person who disposes of capital for the purpose of–
   (a)   reducing or paying a debt owed by the claimant; or
   (b)   purchasing goods or services if the expenditure was reasonable in the circumstances of the claimant's case,
shall be regarded as not depriving himself of it.
   (3)   Where a claimant stands in relation to a company in a position analogous to that of a sole owner or partner in the business of that company, he shall be treated as if he were such sole owner or partner and in such a case–
   (a)   the value of his holding in that company shall, notwithstanding regulation 44 (calculation of capital), be disregarded; and
   (b)   he shall, subject to paragraph (4), be treated as possessing an amount of capital equal to the value or, as the case may be, his share of the value of the capital of that company and the foregoing provisions of this Part shall apply for the purposes of calculating that amount as if it were actual capital which he does possess.
   (4)   For so long as a claimant undertakes activities in the course of the business of the company, the amount which he is treated as possessing under paragraph (3) shall be disregarded.
   (5)   Where under this regulation a person is treated as possessing capital, the amount of that capital shall be calculated in accordance with the provisions of this Part as if it were actual capital which he does possess.

General Note
Para (1) is equivalent to reg 49(1) HB Regs (see p466) and paras (3) to (5) are equivalent to paras (5) to (7) of that regulation.
   Para (2) confirms the existing caselaw. There is no deprivation if the claimant is reducing or paying a debt or buying goods or services. The latter are subject to a test of reasonableness, the former is not.

Diminishing notional capital rule

48.–(1)   Where a claimant is treated as possessing capital under regulation 47(1) (notional capital), the amount which he is treated as possessing–
   (a)   in the case of a week that is subsequent to–

> (i)   the relevant week in respect of which the conditions set out in paragraph (2) are satisfied; or
>
> (ii)   a week which follows that relevant week and which satisfies those conditions,
>
> shall be reduced by an amount determined under paragraph (3);

(b)   in the case of a week in respect of which paragraph (1)(a) does not apply but where–

> (i)   that week is a week subsequent to the relevant week; and
>
> (ii)   that relevant week is a week in which the condition in paragraph (4) is satisfied,
>
> shall be reduced by the amount determined under paragraph (4).

(2)   This paragraph applies to a benefit week where the claimant satisfies the conditions that–

(a)   he is in receipt of housing benefit; and

(b)   but for regulation 47(1), he would have received an additional amount of housing benefit in that week.

(3)   In a case to which paragraph (2) applies, the amount of the reduction for the purposes of paragraph (1)(a) shall be equal to the aggregate of–

(a)   the additional amount to which paragraph (2)(b) refers;

(b)   where the claimant has also claimed state pension credit, the amount of any state pension credit or any additional amount of state pension credit to which he would have been entitled in respect of the benefit week to which paragraph (2) refers but for the application of regulation 21(1) of the State Pension Credit Regulations 2002 (notional capital);

(c)   where the claimant has also claimed council tax benefit, the amount of any council tax benefit or any additional amount of council tax benefit to which he would have been entitled in respect of the benefit week to which paragraph (2) refers but for the application of regulation 39(1) of the Council Tax Benefit Regulations 2006 or regulation 37(1) (notional capital)of the Council Tax Benefit (Persons who have obtained the qualifying age for state pensions credit) Regulations 2006;

(d)   where the claimant has also claimed a jobseeker's allowance, the amount of an income-based jobseeker's allowance to which he would have been entitled in respect of the benefit week to which paragraph (2) refers but for the application of regulation 113 of the Jobseeker's Allowance Regulations (notional capital).

[² (e)   where the claimant has also claimed an employment and support allowance, the amount of an income-related employment and support allowance to which he would have been entitled in respect of the benefit week to which paragraph (2) refers but for the application of regulation 115 of the Employment and Support Allowance Regulations (notional capital).]

(4)   Subject to paragraph (5), for the purposes of paragraph (1)(b) the condition is that the claimant would have been entitled to housing benefit in the relevant week but for regulation 47(1), and in such a case the amount of the reduction shall be equal to the aggregate of–

(a)   the amount of housing benefit to which the claimant would have been entitled in the relevant week but for regulation 47(1) and, for the purposes of this sub-paragraph, if the relevant week is a week to which [¹ regulation 61(3)(a)] refers (calculation of weekly amounts), that amount shall be determined by dividing the amount of housing benefit to which he would have been so entitled by the number of days in that week for which he was liable to make payments in respect of the dwelling he occupies as his home and multiplying the quotient so obtained by 7;

(b)   if the claimant would, but for regulation 21 of the State Pension Credit Regulations 2002, have been entitled to state pension credit in respect of the benefit week, within the meaning of regulation 1(2) of those Regulations (interpretation), which includes the last day of the relevant week, the amount to which he would have been entitled and, for the purposes of this sub-paragraph, if the amount is in respect of a part-week, that amount shall be determined by dividing the amount of the state pension credit to which he would have been so entitled by the number equal to the number of days in the part-week and multiplying the quotient so obtained by 7;

(c) if the claimant would, but for regulation 37(1) of the Council Tax Benefit (Persons who have attained the qualifying age for state pension credit) Regulations 2006, have been entitled to council tax benefit or to an additional amount of council tax benefit in respect of the benefit week which includes the last day of the relevant week, the amount which is equal to–

    (i) in a case where no council tax benefit is payable, the amount to which he would have been entitled; or

    (ii) in any other case, the amount equal to the additional amount of council tax benefit to which he would have been entitled;

and, for the purposes of this sub-paragraph, if the amount is in respect of a part-week, that amount shall be determined by dividing the amount of the council tax benefit to which he would have been so entitled by the number equal to the number of days in the part-week and multiplying the quotient so obtained by 7;

(d) if the claimant would, but for regulation 113 of the Jobseeker's Allowance Regulations, have been entitled to an income-based jobseeker's allowance in respect of the benefit week, within the meaning of regulation 1(3) of those Regulations (interpretation), which includes the last day of the relevant week, the amount to which he would have been entitled and, for the purposes of this sub-paragraph, if the amount is in respect of a part-week, that amount shall be determined by dividing the amount of the income-based jobseeker's allowance to which he would have been so entitled by the number equal to the number of days in the part-week and multiplying the quotient so obtained by 7. [³ and]

[² (e) if the claimant would, but for regulation 115 of the Employment and Support Allowance Regulations, have been entitled to an income-related employment and support allowance in respect of the benefit week, within the meaning of regulation 2(1) of those Regulations (interpretation), which includes the last day of the relevant week, the amount to which he would have been entitled and, for the purposes of this sub-paragraph, if the amount is in respect of a part-week, that amount must be determined by dividing the amount of the income-related employment and support allowance to which he would have been so entitled by the number equal to the number of days in that part-week and multiplying the quotient so obtained by 7.]

(5) The amount determined under paragraph (4) shall be redetermined under that paragraph if the claimant makes a further claim for housing benefit and the conditions in paragraph (6) are satisfied, and in such a case–

(a) sub-paragraphs (a) to (d) of paragraph (4) shall apply as if for the words "relevant week" there were substituted the words "relevant subsequent week"; and

(b) subject to paragraph (7), the amount as redetermined shall have effect from the first week following the relevant subsequent week in question.

(6) The conditions are that–

(a) a further claim is made 26 or more weeks after–

    (i) the date on which the claimant made a claim for housing benefit in respect of which he was first treated as possessing the capital in question under regulation 47(1);

    (ii) in a case where there has been at least one redetermination in accordance with paragraph (5), the date on which he last made a claim for housing benefit which resulted in the weekly amount being redetermined; or

    (iii) the date on which he last ceased to be entitled to housing benefit, whichever last occurred; and

(b) the claimant would have been entitled to housing benefit but for regulation 47(1) of these Regulations or regulation 49(1) of the Housing Benefit Regulations 2006.

(7)   The amount as re-determined pursuant to paragraph (5) shall not have effect if it is less than the amount which applied in that case immediately before the redetermination and in such a case the higher amount shall continue to have effect.

(8)   For the purposes of this regulation–

(a)   "part-week" in paragraph (4)(b) [² (d) and (e)] means–

  (i)   a period of less than a week which is the whole period for which state pension credit [², an income-related employment and support allowance], or, as the case may be, an income-based jobseeker's allowance, is payable; and

  (ii)   any other period of less than a week for which either of those benefits is payable;

(b)   "part-week" in paragraph (4)(c) means a period of less than a week for which council tax benefit is allowed;

(c)   "relevant week" means the benefit week in which the capital in question of which the claimant has deprived himself within the meaning of regulation 47(1)–

  (i)   was first taken into account for the purpose of determining his entitlement to housing benefit; or

  (ii)   was taken into account on a subsequent occasion for the purpose of determining or redetermining his entitlement to housing benefit on that subsequent occasion and that determination or redetermination resulted in his beginning to receive, or ceasing to receive, housing benefit,

and where more than one benefit week is identified by reference to heads (i) and (ii) of this sub-paragraph, means the later or latest such benefit week;

(d)   "relevant subsequent week" means the benefit week which includes the day on which the further claim or, if more than one further claim has been made, the last such claim was made.

Modifications

Para (4)(a) amended by reg 11 Housing Benefit (State Pension Credit) (Local Housing Allowance and Information Sharing) Amendment Regulations 2007 No.2869 as from 7 April 2008, save that for a person to whom reg 1(5) of those regulations applied (see p1814), the amendments came into force on the day on or after 7 April 2008 when the first of the events specified in reg 1(6) applied to her/him, or on 6 April 2009 if none had before that date.

Amendments

1.   Amended by reg 11 of SI 2007 No 2869 as from 7.4.08 (or if reg 1(5) of that SI applies, on the day on or after 7.4.08 when the first of the events specified in reg 1(6) applies, or from 6.4.09 if none have before that date).

2.   Amended by reg 35 of SI 2008 No 1082 as from 27.10.08.

3.   Amended by reg 35 of SI 2008 No 2428 as from 27.10.08.

General Note

This is, for the most part, equivalent to reg 50 HB Regs (see p472). Paras (3) and (4) are different. Only notional entitlements to PC, income-based JSA (defined in reg 2(1) by reference to s1(4) of the Jobseeker's Act 1995 as including joint-claim JSA) and income-related ESA are to be taken into account in calculating diminished notional capital. Note that CTB is also mentioned. CTB was abolished from 1 April 2013.

Capital jointly held

49.   Where a claimant and one or more other persons are beneficially entitled in possession to any capital asset, other than a capital asset disregarded under regulation 47(3), they shall be treated as if each of them were entitled in possession to the whole beneficial interest therein in an equal share and the foregoing provisions of this Part shall apply for the purposes of calculating the amount of capital which the claimant is treated as possessing as if it were actual capital which the claimant does possess.

General Note

This is equivalent to reg 51 HB Regs (see p476).

PART 7
Amount of benefit

[¹ Maximum housing benefit

50. The amount of a person's appropriate maximum housing benefit in any week shall be 100 per cent. of his eligible rent calculated on a weekly basis in accordance with regulation 61 and 62 (calculation of weekly amounts and rent free periods) less any deductions in respect of non-dependants which fall to be made under regulation 55 (non-dependant deductions).]

Modifications

Reg 50 substituted by reg 12 Housing Benefit (State Pension Credit) (Local Housing Allowance and Information Sharing) Amendment Regulations 2007 No.2869 as from 7 April 2008, save that for a person to whom reg 1(5) of those regulations applied (see p1814), the amendments came into force on the day on or after 7 April 2008 when the first of the events specified in reg 1(6) applied to her/him, or on 6 April 2009 if none had before that date.

Amendment

1. Substituted by reg 12 of SI 2007 No 2869 as from 7.4.08 (or if reg 1(5) of that SI applies, on the day on or after 7.4.08 when the first of the events specified in reg 1(6) applies, or from 6.4.09 if none have before that date).

General Note

This regulation is identical to reg 70 HB Regs (see p505).

Housing benefit tapers

51. The prescribed percentages for the purpose of sub-section (3)(b) of section 130 of the Act (percentage of excess of income over applicable amount which is deducted from maximum housing benefit) shall be 65 per cent.

General Note

This regulation is identical to reg 71 HB Regs (see p506).

[¹Amount payable during extended payment period when an extended payment is payable pursuant to regulation 72 or 73 of the Housing Benefit Regulations

52.–(1)   This regulation applies where–
(a)   a claimant became entitled to an extended payment pursuant to regulation 72 of the Housing Benefit Regulations 2006 or an extended payment (qualifying contributory benefits) pursuant to regulation 73 of those Regulations; and
(b)   during the extended payment period, these Regulations become applicable to the claimant or the claimant's partner in accordance with regulation 5 (persons who have attained the qualifying age for state pension credit).

(2)   Where this regulation applies, the amount of the extended payment or extended payment (qualifying contributory benefits) payable to a claimant for any week during the extended payment period shall be the higher of–
(a)   the amount of the extended payment payable in accordance with regulation 72B(1)(a) of the Housing Benefit Regulations 2006 or the extended payment (qualifying contributory benefits) payable in accordance with regulation 73B(1)(a) of those Regulations, as the case may be; or
(b)   the amount of housing benefit to which a claimant would be entitled under the general conditions of entitlement of these Regulations, if regulation 72 (extended payments) or 73 (extended payments (qualifying contributory benefits)) of the Housing Benefit Regulations 2006 did not apply to the claimant; or
(c)   the amount of housing benefit to which the claimant's partner would be entitled under the general conditions of entitlement of these Regulations, if regulation 72 or 73 of the Housing Benefit Regulations 2006 did not apply to the claimant.

(3)   Where this regulation applies, no amount of housing benefit shall be payable by the appropriate authority during the extended payment period to a claimant's partner under these Regulations for any week in the extended payment period.]

Amendment

1.   Substituted by reg 6(3) of SI 2008 No 959 as from 6.10.08.

Analysis

A claimant might claim (and be awarded) HB under these regs for the same period in which s/he is entitled to an extended payment under reg 72 or 73 HB Regs (see p506 and p512). Reg 52 ensures that where an award of HB under the HB(SPC) Regs is made, the amount of the extended payment is effectively offset against the amount of HB payable or the extended payment is topped up to the level of the new HB entitlement; the extended payment is the higher of the amount of the extended payment or the amount of HB which would be payable under these regulations to the claimant or her/his partner: para (2). Para (3) prevents payment of HB to the extended payment claimant's partner during the extended payment period (defined in reg 2(1) on p721).

[²Extended payments (qualifying contributory benefits)

53.–(1)   Except in the case of a claimant who is in receipt of state pension credit, a claimant who is entitled to housing benefit (by virtue of the general conditions of entitlement) shall be entitled to an extended payment (qualifying contributory benefits) where–

(a)   the claimant or the claimant's partner was entitled to a qualifying contributory benefit;

(b)   entitlement to a qualifying contributory benefit ceased because the claimant or the claimant's partner–
(i)   commenced employment as an employed or self-employed earner;
(ii)   increased their earnings from such employment; or
(iii)   increased the number of hours worked in such employment,
and that employment is or, as the case may be, increased earnings or increased number of hours are expected to last five weeks or more;

(c)   the claimant or the claimant's partner had been entitled to and in receipt of a qualifying contributory benefit or a combination of qualifying contributory benefits for a continuous period of at least 26 weeks before the day on which the entitlement to a qualifying contributory benefit ceased;

(d)   the claimant or the claimant's partner was not entitled to and not in receipt of a qualifying income-related benefit in the last benefit week in which the claimant, or the claimant's partner, was entitled to a qualifying contributory benefit.

(2)   A claimant must be treated as entitled to housing benefit by virtue of the general conditions of entitlement where–

(a)   the claimant ceased to be entitled to housing benefit because the claimant vacated the dwelling occupied as the claimant's home;

(b)   the day on which the claimant vacated the dwelling was either in the week in which entitlement to a qualifying contributory benefit ceased, or in the preceding week; and

(c)   entitlement to the qualifying contributory benefit ceased in any of the circumstances listed in paragraph (1)(b).]

Amendments

1.   Amended by reg 13 of SI 2007 No 2869 as from 7.4.08 (or if reg 1(5) of that SI applies, on the day on or after 7.4.08 when the first of the events specified in reg 1(6) applies, or from 6.4.09 if none have before that date).

2.   Substituted by reg 5(2) of SI 2008 No 959 as from 6.10.08.

General Note

This regulation is broadly equivalent in its effect to reg 73 HB Regs (see p512).

[¹ Duration of extended payment period (qualifying contributory benefits)

53A.–(1)   Where a claimant is entitled to an extended payment (qualifying contributory benefits), the extended payment period starts on the first day of the benefit week immediately following the benefit week in which the claimant, or the claimant's partner, ceased to be entitled to a qualifying contributory benefit.

(2)   For the purpose of paragraph (1), a claimant or a claimant's partner ceases to be entitled to a qualifying contributory benefit on the day immediately following the last day of entitlement to that benefit.

(3)   The extended payment period ends–

(a)   at the end of a period of four weeks; or

(b)   on the date on which the claimant to whom the extended payment (qualifying contributory benefits) is payable has no liability for rent, if that occurs first.]

Amendment

1.   Inserted by reg 5(2) of SI 2008 No 959 as from 6.10.08.

General Note

This regulation is identical to reg 73A HB Regs (see p513).

[¹ Amount of extended payment (qualifying contributory benefits)

53B.–(1)   For any week during the extended payment period the amount of the extended payment (qualifying contributory benefits) payable to a claimant shall be the higher of–

(a)   the amount of housing benefit to which the claimant was entitled under the general conditions of entitlement in the last benefit week before the claimant or the claimant's partner ceased to be entitled to a qualifying contributory benefit;

(b)   the amount of housing benefit to which the claimant would be entitled under the general conditions of entitlement for any benefit week during the extended payment period, if regulation 53 (extended payments (qualifying contributory benefits)) did not apply to the claimant; or

(c)   the amount of housing benefit to which the claimant's partner would be entitled under the general conditions of entitlement, if regulation 53 did not apply to the claimant.

(2)   Paragraph (1) is subject to the paragraphs (3) to (6) and does not apply in the case of a mover.

(3)   Where the last benefit week referred to in paragraph (1)(a) fell, in whole or in part, within a rent free period, the last benefit week for the purposes of that paragraph is the last benefit week that did not fall within the rent free period.

(4)   Where–

(a)   a claimant is entitled to an extended payment (qualifying contributory benefit) by virtue of regulation 53(2) (early vacation of dwelling); and

(b)   the last benefit week before the claimant ceased to be entitled to a qualifying contributory benefit was a week in which the claimant's eligible rent was calculated in accordance with regulation 61(3)(c) (calculation of rent for a partial week),

the last benefit week for the purpose of calculating the amount of the extended payment (qualifying contributory benefits) under paragraph (1)(a) shall be the benefit week before the partial week.

(5)   Where–

(a)   a claimant was treated as occupying two dwellings as the claimant's home under regulation 7(6) (liability to make payments in respect of two homes) at the time when the claimant's entitlement to a qualifying contributory benefit ceased; and

(b)   the claimant's liability to pay rent for either of those dwellings ceases during the extended payment period,

the amount of the extended payment (qualifying contributory benefits) for any week shall be reduced by a sum equivalent to the housing benefit which was payable in respect of that dwelling.

(6)   No extended payment (qualifying contributory benefits) is payable for any rent free period as defined in regulation 62(1) (rent free periods).

(7)   Where a claimant is in receipt of an extended payment (qualifying contributory benefits) under this regulation and the claimant's partner makes a claim for housing benefit, no amount of housing benefit shall be payable by the appropriate authority during the extended payment period.]

Amendment

1.   Inserted by reg 5(2) of SI 2008 No 959 as from 6.10.08.

General Note

This regulation is identical to reg 73B HB Regs (see p513).

[¹ Extended payments (qualifying contributory benefits) – movers

53C.–(1)   This regulation applies–

(a)   to a mover; and

(b)   from the Monday following the day of the move.

(2)   The amount of the extended payment (qualifying contributory benefits) payable from the Monday from which this regulation applies until the end of the extended payment period shall be the amount of housing benefit which was payable to the mover for the last benefit week before the mover, or the mover's partner, ceased to be entitled to a qualifying contributory benefit.

(3)   Where a mover's liability to make payments for the new dwelling is to the second authority, the extended payment (qualifying contributory benefits) may take the form of a payment from the appropriate authority to–

(a)   the second authority; or

(b)   the mover directly.

(4)   Where–

(a)   a mover, or the mover's partner, makes a claim for housing benefit to the second authority after the mover, or the mover's partner, ceased to be entitled to a qualifying contributory benefit; and

(b)   the mover, or the mover's partner, is in receipt of an extended payment(qualifying contributory benefits) from the appropriate authority,

the second authority shall reduce the weekly amount of housing benefit that the mover, or the mover's partner, is entitled to by a sum equal to the amount of the extended payment (qualifying contributory benefits) until the end of the extended payment period.

(5)   The reduction of housing benefit made by the second authority under paragraph (4) is subject to any entitlement the claimant may have pursuant to regulation 7(6) (liability to make payments in respect of two homes).

(6)   Where the last benefit week referred to in paragraph (2) fell, in whole or in part, within a rent free period, the last benefit week for the purposes of that paragraph is the last benefit week that did not fall within the rent free period.

(7)   No extended payment (qualifying contributory benefits) is payable for any rent free period as defined in regulation 62(1) (rent free periods).]

Amendment

1.   Inserted by reg 5(2) of SI 2008 No 959 as from 6.10.08.

General Note

This regulation is identical to reg 73C HB Regs (see p515).

[¹ Relationship between extended payment (qualifying contributory benefits) and entitlement to housing benefit under the general conditions of entitlement

53D.–(1)   Where a claimant's housing benefit award would have ended when the claimant ceased to be entitled to a qualifying contributory benefit in the circumstances listed in regulation 53(1)(b), that award will not cease until the end of the extended payment period.

(2)   Part 8 (calculation of weekly amounts and changes of circumstances) shall not apply to any extended payment (qualifying contributory benefits) payable in accordance with regulation 53B(1)(a) or 53C(2) (amount of extended payment – movers).]

Amendment

1.   Inserted by reg 5(2) of SI 2008 No 959 as from 6.10.08.

General Note

This regulation is identical to reg 73D HB Regs (see p515).

Continuing payments where state pension credit claimed

54.–(1)   This regulation applies where–

(a)   the claimant is entitled to housing benefit;

(b)   paragraph (2) is satisfied; and

(c)   either–

   (i)   the claimant has attained the qualifying age for state pension credit [² [¹]]; or

   (ii)   the claimant's partner has actually claimed state pension credit.

(2)   This regulation is only satisfied if the Secretary of State has certified to the relevant authority that the claimant's partner has actually claimed state pension credit or that–

(a)   the claimant's award of–

   (i)   income support has terminated because the claimant has attained the qualifying age for state pension credit; or

   (ii)   income-based jobseeker's allowance [¹ or income-related employment and support allowance] has terminated because the claimant has attained the qualifying age for state pension credit [²]; and

(b)   the claimant has claimed or is treated as having claimed or is required to make a claim for state pension credit.

(3)   Subject to paragraph (4), in a case to which this regulation applies housing benefit shall continue to be paid for the period of 4 weeks beginning on the day following the day the claimant's entitlement to income support [¹, income-related employment and support allowance] or, as the case may be, income-based jobseeker's allowance, ceased, if and for so long as the claimant otherwise satisfies the conditions for entitlement to housing benefit.

(4)   Where housing benefit is paid for the period of 4 weeks in accordance with paragraph (3) above, and the last day of that period falls on a day other than the last day of a benefit week, then housing benefit shall continue to be paid until the end of the benefit week in which the last day of that period falls.

(5)   Throughout the period of 4 weeks specified in paragraph (3) and any further period specified in paragraph (4)–

(a)   the whole of the income and capital of the claimant shall be disregarded;

(b)   subject to paragraph (6) the appropriate maximum housing benefit of the claimant shall be that which was applicable in his case immediately before that period commenced.

(6)   The appropriate maximum housing benefit shall be calculated in accordance with regulation 50 if, since the date it was last calculated–

(a)   the claimant's rent has increased; or

(b)   a change in the deduction under regulation 55 falls to be made.

Amendments

1.   Amended by reg 36 of SI 2008 No 1082 as from 27.10.08.
2.   Amended by reg 7(3) of SI 2017 No 1187 as from 6.12.18.

Analysis

Reg 54 provides a further scheme of extended payments to that in regs 53 to 53D, but are here called "continuing payments". Here, they are designed to ease the transition into retirement. To qualify for continuing payments, two conditions must be fulfilled:

(1)   Either the claimant has attained the qualifying age for PC (defined in reg 2(1) and discussed on p731) or the claimant's partner has claimed PC: para (1).

(2)   The Secretary of State has certified two matters: either that the claimant's partner has claimed PC; or that an award of IS has ceased because the claimant has attained the qualifying age for PC or an award of income-based JSA or income-related ESA has ceased because the claimant has attained the qualifying age for PC. In the latter case, the Secretary of State also certifies that the claimant has claimed (or has been treated as having claimed) PC or is required to make such a claim: para (2).

Income-based JSA includes joint-claim JSA. See the definition of income-based JSA in reg 2(1).

Continuing payments last for four weeks from the day after the day IS, income-based JSA or income-related ESA ceases or if the four-week period ends before the end of a benefit week, until the end of the benefit week in which the end of the four-week period falls: paras (3) and (4). They are paid at the rate of the maximum HB applicable immediately preceding the start of the continuing payments: para (5). They may be adjusted, however, for rent increases or a change in applicable non-dependant deductions: para (6). Other changes of circumstances do not take effect until the first day of the benefit week after continuing payments end: reg 60(8). At the time of writing, no provision had been made for those transferring from universal credit (UC) to PC.

Note that entitlement to HB can continue beyond the end of the continuing payment period under the normal rules of entitlement to HB. This may still be at the rate of maximum HB – eg, if the claimant or her/his partner is entitled to the guarantee credit of PC.

[¹ Non-dependant deductions

55.–(1)   Subject to the following provisions of this regulation, the deductions referred to in regulation 50 (maximum housing benefit) shall be–

(a)   in respect of a non-dependant aged 18 or over who is engaged in remunerative work, [²⁹ £100.65];

(b)   in respect of a non-dependant aged 18 or over to whom sub-paragraph (a) does not apply, [²⁹ £15.60] per week.

(2)   In the case of a non-dependant aged 18 or over to whom paragraph (1)(a) applies because he is in remunerative work, where it is shown to the appropriate authority that his normal weekly gross income is–

(a)   less than [²⁹ £143.00], the deduction to be made under this regulation shall be that specified in paragraph 1(b);

(b)   not less than [²⁹ £143.00] but less than [²⁹ £209.00], the deduction to be made under this regulation shall be [²⁹ £35.85];

(c)   not less than [²⁹ £209.00] but less than [²⁹ £272.00], the deduction to be made under this regulation shall be [²⁹ £49.20];

(d)   not less than [²⁹ £272.00] but less than [²⁹ £363.00], the deduction to be made under this regulation shall be [²⁹ £80.55];

(e)   not less than [²⁹ £363.00] but less than [²⁹ £451.00], the deduction to be made under this regulation shall be [²⁹ £91.70].

(3)   Only one deduction shall be made under this regulation in respect of a couple or, as the case may be, members of a polygamous marriage and, where, but for this paragraph, the amount that would fall to be deducted in respect of one member of a couple or polygamous marriage is higher than the amount (if any) that would fall to be deducted in respect of the other, or any other, member, the higher amount shall be deducted.

(4)   In applying the provisions of paragraph (2) in the case of a couple or, as the case may be, a polygamous marriage, regard shall be had, for the purpose of paragraph (2) to the couple's or, as the case may be, all members of the polygamous marriage's joint weekly gross income.

(5)   Where a person is a non-dependant in respect of more than one joint occupier of a dwelling (except where the joint occupiers are a couple or members of a polygamous marriage), the deduction in respect of that non-dependant shall be apportioned between the joint occupiers (the amount so apportioned being rounded to the nearest penny) having regard to the number of joint occupiers and the proportion of the payments in respect of the dwelling payable by each of them.

(6)   No deduction shall be made in respect of any non-dependants occupying a claimant's dwelling if the claimant or his partner is–

(a)   blind or treated as blind by virtue of paragraph 6(5) of Schedule 3 (severe disability premiums); or

(b)   receiving in respect of himself either–

(i)   attendance allowance; [¹⁵]

(ii)   the care component of the disability living allowance. [¹⁵ [¹⁶]]

[¹⁵ (iii) the daily living component of personal independence payment][¹⁶; or]

[¹⁶ (iv) armed forces independence payment,]

(7)   No deduction shall be made in respect of a non-dependant if–

(a)   although he resides with the claimant, it appears to the appropriate authority that his normal home is elsewhere; or

(b)   he is in receipt of a training allowance paid in connection with [⁵ youth training] established under section 2 of the 1973 Act or section 2 of the Enterprise and New Towns (Scotland) Act 1990; or

[²⁸]

(e)   he is a full-time student [²⁸]; or

(f)   he is not residing with the claimant because he has been a patient for a period in excess of 52 weeks, or a prisoner, and for these purposes–

    (i)   "patient" has the meaning given in paragraph (18) of regulation 7 (circumstances in which a person is or is not to be treated as occupying a dwelling as his home);

    (ii)   where a person has been a patient for two or more distinct periods separated by one or more intervals each not exceeding 28 days, he shall be treated as having been a patient continuously for a period equal in duration to the total of those distinct periods; and

    (iii)   "prisoner" means a person who is detained in custody pending trial or sentence upon conviction or under a sentence imposed by a court other than a person who is detained in hospital under the provisions of the Mental Health Act 1983, or, in Scotland, under the provisions of the Mental Health (Care and Treatment) (Scotland) Act 2003 or the Criminal Procedure (Scotland) Act 1995.

[¹⁴ (g) he is not residing with the claimant because he is a member of the armed forces away on operations.]

(8)   No deduction shall be made in calculating the amount of a rent rebate or allowance in respect of a non-dependant aged less than 25 who is on income support [⁴, an income-based jobseeker's allowance or an income-related employment and support allowance which does not include an amount under section 4(2)(b) of the Welfare Reform Act (the support component [²¹]) [²¹, ²⁴ and where the non-dependant is not a member of the work-related activity group] [¹⁷ or who is entitled to an award of universal credit where the award is calculated on the basis that the person does not have any earned income]].

(9)   No deduction shall be made in respect of a non-dependant who is on state pension credit.

(10)   In the case of a non-dependant to whom paragraph (2) applies because he is in remunerative work, there shall be disregarded from his weekly gross income–

(a)   any attendance allowance [¹⁵, disability living allowance or personal independence payment][¹⁶, armed forces independence payment] received by him;

(b)   any payment made under [⁸ or by] the Macfarlane Trust, the Macfarlane (Special Payments) Trust, the Macfarlane (Special Payments) (No. 2) Trust, the Fund, the Eileen Trust [⁸, MFET Limited] [¹¹, the Skipton Fund, the Caxton Foundation] [²³, the Scottish Infected Blood Support Scheme] [²⁶, an approved blood scheme] [²⁵, the London Emergencies Trust, the We Love Manchester Emergency Fund] or the Independent Living [⁵ Fund (2006)] which had his income fallen to be calculated under regulation 40 (calculation of income other than earnings) of the Housing Benefit Regulations 2006 would have been disregarded under paragraph 23 of Schedule 5 (income in kind) to those Regulations; and

(c)   any payment which had his income fallen to be calculated under regulation 40 of the Housing Benefit Regulations 2006 would have been disregarded under paragraph 35 of Schedule 5 to those Regulations (payments made under certain trusts and certain other payments);]

[²⁶ (d) any payment made under or by a trust, established for the purpose of giving relief and assistance to disabled persons whose disabilities were caused by the fact that during their mother's pregnancy she had taken a preparation containing the drug known as Thalidomide, and which is approved by the Secretary of State.]

[¹⁷ (11)   For the purposes of paragraph (8), "earned income" has the meaning given in regulation 52 of the Universal Credit Regulations 2013.]

Modifications

Reg 55 substituted by reg 14 Housing Benefit (State Pension Credit) (Local Housing Allowance and Information Sharing) Amendment Regulations 2007 No.2869 as from 7 April 2008, save that for a person to whom reg 1(5) of those regulations applied (see p1814), the amendments came into force on the day on or after 7 April 2008 when the first of the events specified in reg 1(6) applied to her/him, or on 6 April 2009 if none had before that date.

Amendments

1.   Substituted by reg 14 of SI 2007 No 2869 as from 7.4.08 (or if reg 1(5) of that SI applies, on the day on or after 7.4.08 when the first of the events specified in reg 1(6) applies, or from 6.4.09 if none have before that date).
2.   Confirmed by art 20(4) of SI 2008 No 632 as from 1.4.08 (7.4.08 where rent payable weekly or in multiples of a week).
3.   Amended by art 20(4) of SI 2008 No 632 as from 1.4.08 (7.4.08 where rent payable weekly or in multiples of a week).
4.   Amended by reg 37 of SI 2008 No 1082 as from 27.10.08.
5.   Amended by reg 7(4) of SI 2008 No 2767 as from 17.11.08.
6.   Confirmed by art 20(4) of SI 2009 No 497 as from 1.4.09 (6.4.08 where rent payable weekly or in multiples of a week).
7.   Amended by art 20(4) of SI 2009 No 497 as from 1.4.09 (6.4.08 where rent payable weekly or in multiples of a week).
8.   Amended by reg 9(3) and (5) of SI 2010 No 641 as from 1.4.10 (5.4.10 where rent payable weekly or in multiples of a week).
9.   Confirmed by art 20(3) of SI 2010 No 793 as from 1.4.10 (5.4.10 where rent payable weekly or in multiples of a week).
10.   Amended by art 21(3) of SI 2011 No 821 as from 1.4.11 (4.4.11 where rent payable weekly or in multiples of a week).
11.   Amended by reg 20(7) of SI 2011 No 2425 as from 31.10.11.
12.   Amended by art 21(3) of SI 2012 No 780 as from 1.4.11 (2.4.11 where rent payable weekly or in multiples of a week).
13.   Amended by art 20(3) of SI 2013 No 574 as from 1.4.13.
14.   Inserted by reg 3(5) of SI 2013 No 665 as from 1.4.13.
15.   Amended by reg 8 and Sch para 37(5) of SI 2013 No 388 as from 8.4.13.
16.   Amended by art 7 and Sch para 35(5) of SI 2013 No 591 as from 8.4.13.
17.   Amended by reg 36(5) of SI 2013 No 630 as from 29.4.13.
18.   Amended by art 18(3) of SI 2014 No 16 as from 1.4.14 (7.4.14 where rent payable weekly or in multiples of a week).
19.   Amended by art 18(3) of SI 2015 No 547 as from 1.4.15 (6.4.15 where rent payable weekly or in multiples of a week).
20.   Amended by reg 6(2) of SI 2016 No 242 as from 1.4.16 (4.4.16 where rent payable weekly or in multiples of a week).
21.   Amended by Sch 1 para 7(4) of SI 2017 No 204 as from 3.4.17, subject to transitional and savings provisions in Sch 2 paras 1–7.
22.   Amended by art 23(3) of SI 2017 No 260 as from 1.4.17 (3.4.17 where rent payable weekly or in multiples of a week).
23.   Amended by reg 7(3)(a) of SI 2017 No 329 as from 3.4.17.
24.   Amended by reg 6(3) of SI 2017 No 581 as from 23.6.17, subject to transitional and savings provision in reg 9.
25.   Amended by reg 7(3)(a) of SI 2017 No 689 as from 19.6.17.
26.   Amended by reg 7(3)(b) and (4) of SI 2017 No 870 as from 23.10.17.
27.   Amended by art 24(3) of SI 2018 No 281 as from 1.4.18 (2.4.18 where rent payable weekly or in multiples of a week).
28.   Amended by reg 7(4) of SI 2017 No 1187 as from 6.12.18.
29.   Amended by art 24(3) of SI 2019 No 480 as from 1.4.19.

General Note

The practical effect of this regulation is identical to that of reg 74 HB Regs (see p516).

Minimum housing benefit

56.   Where housing benefit is payable in the form of a rent rebate or allowance, it shall not be payable where the amount to which a person would otherwise be entitled is less than 50 pence per benefit week.

General Note

This regulation is identical to reg 75 HB Regs (see p521).

PART 8
Calculation of weekly amounts and changes of circumstances

Date on which entitlement is to commence
57.–(1) Subject to paragraph (2), a person who makes a claim for, and is otherwise entitled to, housing benefit shall be entitled to that benefit from the benefit week following the first day in respect of which that claim is made.

[¹ (2) A claimant shall become entitled to housing benefit from the benefit week in which the first day in respect of which his claim is made falls, where he is otherwise entitled to housing benefit and–

(a) he becomes liable in that benefit week, for the first time, to make payments in respect of a dwelling which he occupies as his home; or,

[² (b) he becomes liable in that benefit week to make payments, which fall due on a daily basis, in respect of the accommodation listed in paragraph (3) which he occupies as his home.]]

(3) The accommodation referred to in paragraph (2)(b) is–

(a) a hostel;

(b) board and lodging accommodation where the payments are to an authority under section 206(2) of the Housing Act 1996 or section 35(2)(b) of the Housing (Scotland) Act 1987;

(c) accommodation which the authority holds on a licence agreement where the payments are to an authority under section 206(2) of the Housing Act 1996 or section 35(2)(b) of the Housing (Scotland) Act 1987; or

(d) accommodation outside that authority's Housing Revenue Account which the authority holds on a lease granted for a term not exceeding 10 years.

[³ (4) In this regulation–
"board and lodging accommodation" means–

(a) accommodation provided to a person or, if he is a member of a family, to him or any other member of his family, for a charge which is inclusive of the provision of that accommodation and at least some cooked or prepared meals which both are cooked or prepared (by a person other than a person to whom the accommodation is provided or by a member of his family) and are consumed in that accommodation or associated premises; or

(b) accommodation provided to a person in a hotel, guest house, lodging house or some similar establishment,

but it does not include accommodation in a care home, an Abbeyfield Home, an independent hospital or a hostel; and

"Housing Revenue Account" has the same meaning as for the purposes of Part VIII of the Social Security Administration Act 1992.]

Amendments
1.   Substituted by reg 2(9) of SI 2005 No 2502 as amended by Sch 2 para 27 of SI 2006 No 217 as from 1.4.06 (3.4.06 where rent payable weekly or at intervals of a week).
2.   Substituted by reg 3(2)(a) SI 2007 No 294 as from 1.4.07.
3.   Inserted by reg 3(2)(b) SI 2007 No 294 as from 1.4.07.

Analysis
Para (1) sets the date on which entitlement to HB commences. Unlike under the HB Regs, this is the first day of the benefit week following the first day in respect of which the claim is made, provided the claimant is otherwise entitled to benefit. The earliest the date of entitlement can commence is determined by reg 64(1) – ie, currently three months before the date of claim determined under reg 64(6). See p815 for a discussion of *Leicester CC v LG* [2009] UKUT 155 (AAC), a decision which dealt with the similar provisions under the CTB(SPC) Regs as they were prior to 1 November 2010.

Paras (2) to (4) have the same effect as reg 76(3) to (5) HB Regs (see p532).

[¹**Date on which housing benefit is to end where entitlement to severe disablement allowance or incapacity benefit ceases**
58.]

Amendment

1.   Omitted by reg 6(4)(a) of SI 2008 No 959 as from 6.10.08.

Date on which change of circumstances is to take effect

59.–(1)   Except in cases where regulation 34 (disregard of changes in tax, contributions, etc) [⁶ applies, and subject to regulation 8(3) of the Decisions and Appeals Regulations and] the following provisions of this regulation and to [⁸ regulations 60 and 61(5)], a change of circumstances which affects entitlement to, or the amount of, housing benefit ("change of circumstances") shall take effect from the first day of the benefit week following the date on which the change of circumstances actually occurs, and where that change is cessation of entitlement to any benefit under the benefit Acts, the date on which the change actually occurs shall be the day immediately following the last day of entitlement to that benefit.

[¹ (2)   Subject to paragraph (8) [⁶ and regulation 8(3) of the Decisions and Appeals Regulations] where the change of circumstances is a change in the amount of rent payable in respect of a dwelling, that change shall take effect from the day on which it actually occurs.]

[² (2A)   Subject to paragraphs (8) [⁷ to (9A), except in a case where regulation 8(3) of the Decisions and Appeals Regulations applies, where the change of circumstances is–

(a)   that a person moves into a new dwelling occupied as the home, or

(b)   any other event which–

   (i)   entitles a person to be treated as occupying two dwellings as his home under regulation 7(6), or

   (ii)   brings to an end a person's right to be treated as occupying two dwellings as his home under that regulation, in a case where he has, immediately prior to the event, been treated as occupying two dwellings as his home,

that change of circumstances shall take effect on the day on which it actually occurs.

(2B)   Subject to paragraph (8), where the change of circumstances is the expiry of a maximum period of time, referred to in regulation 7(6), for which a person can be treated as occupying two dwellings as his home, that change shall take effect on the day after the last day of that period]

(3)   Subject to paragraphs (8) [³], where the change of circumstances is an amendment to these Regulations that change, subject to [⁸ regulation 61(5)], shall take effect as follows–

(a)   where the amendment is made by an order under section 150 of the Administration Act (annual up-rating of benefits)–

   (i)   in a case in which the claimant's weekly amount of eligible rent falls to be calculated in accordance with regulation 61(2)(b) [³ or (c)](calculation of weekly amounts), from 1st April;

   (ii)   in any other case, from the first Monday in April,
   in the year in which that order comes into force;

(b)   in respect of any other amendment, from the date on which the amendment of these Regulations comes into force in the particular case.

[¹ (4)   Subject to paragraph (8), if two or more changes of circumstances occurring in the same benefit week would, but for this paragraph, take effect in different benefit weeks in accordance with this regulation, they shall all take effect on the first day of the benefit week in which they occur, unless a change taking effect under paragraphs (2), (2A) or (2B) takes effect in that week, in which case the changes shall all take effect on the day on which that change takes effect.]

(5)   Where, during a benefit week commencing on the first Monday in April–

(a)   a change of circumstances takes effect in accordance with paragraph (3)(a)(ii);

(b)   one or more changes of circumstances occur to which paragraph (1) applies; and

(c)   no other change of circumstances occurs to which this regulation applies,

any change of circumstances to which paragraph (1) applies and which occurs in that benefit week shall take effect from the first day of that benefit week.

(6)   Where the change of circumstances is that income, or an increase in the amount of income, other than a benefit or an increase in the amount of a benefit under the Act [¹⁰ or Part 4 of the 2012 Act] [¹¹ or the Armed Forces and Reserve Forces (Compensation Scheme) Order 2011], is paid in respect of a past period and there was no entitlement to income of that amount during that period, the change of circumstances shall take effect from the first day on which such income, had it been paid in that period at intervals appropriate to that income, would have fallen to be taken into account for the purposes of these Regulations.

(7)   Without prejudice to paragraph (6), where the change of circumstances is the payment of income, or arrears of income, in respect of a past period, the change of circumstances shall take effect from the first day on which such income, had it been timeously paid in that period at intervals appropriate to that income, would have fallen to be taken into account for the purposes of these Regulations.

[¹ (8)   Subject to paragraph (9), where a change of circumstances occurs which has the effect of bringing entitlement to an end it shall take effect on the first day of the benefit week following the benefit week in which that change actually occurs except in a case where a person is liable to make payments, which fall due on a daily basis, [⁵] in which case that change shall take effect on the day on which it actually occurs.

(9)   Where the change of circumstances is that a person moves to a new dwelling and immediately after the move he is treated as occupying his former dwelling as his home in accordance with regulation 7(7) or (10) then that change of circumstances shall take effect on the day after the last day for which he is treated as [⁹ occupying] the former dwelling in accordance with whichever of those regulations applies in his case.]

[⁷ (9A)   Where the change of circumstances is that the person moves to a new dwelling and immediately before the move that person is treated as occupying the new dwelling in accordance with regulation 7(8) then that change of circumstances shall take effect on the first day on which the person is treated as occupying the new dwelling as the home under that regulation.]

(10)   Paragraph (11) applies if–

[¹²]

(b)   either–
    (i)   a non-dependant took up residence in the claimant's dwelling; or
    (ii)   there has been a change of circumstances in respect of a non-dependant so that the amount of the deduction which falls to be made under regulation 55 (non-dependant deductions) increased.

(11)   Where this paragraph applies, the change of circumstances [⁴ referred to in paragraph (10)(b)] shall take effect from the effective date.

(12)   In paragraph (11) but subject to paragraph (13), "the effective date" means–

(a)   where more than one change of a kind referred to in paragraph (10)(b) relating to the same non-dependant has occurred since–
    (i)   the date on which the claimant's entitlement to housing benefit first began; or
    (ii)   the date which was the last effective date in respect of such a change; whichever is the later, the date which falls 26 weeks after the date on which the first such change occurred;

(b)   where sub-paragraph (a) does not apply, the date which falls 26 weeks after the date on which the change referred to in paragraph (10)(b) occurred.

(13)   If in any particular case the date determined under paragraph (12) is not the first day of the benefit week, the effective date in that case shall be the first day of the next benefit week to commence after the date determined under that paragraph.

Modifications

Paras (1) and (3) amended by reg 15(1) Housing Benefit (State Pension Credit) (Local Housing Allowance and Information Sharing) Amendment Regulations 2007 No.2869, as amended by reg 5(6) of SI 2008 No.586, as from 7 April 2008, save that for a person to whom reg 1(5) of those regulations applied (see p1814), the amendments came into force on the day on or after 7 April 2008 when the first of the events specified in reg 1(6) applied to her/him, or on 6 April 2009 if none had before that date.

Reg 59 applies as if para (7) was omitted where a change of circumstances occurs as a result of the payment of arrears of any income which affects a determination or decision in respect of entitlement to, or the amount of, HB or CTB before 6 March 1995. See Sch 3 para 1 HB&CTB(CP) Regs on p1774.

Amendments

1. Substituted by reg 2(10)(b), (e) and, (f) of SI 2005 No 2502 as amended by Sch 2 para 27 of SI 2006 No 217 as from 1.4.06 (3.4.06 where rent payable weekly or at intervals of a week).
2. Inserted by reg 2(10)(c) of SI 2005 No 2502 as amended by Sch 2 para 27 of SI 2006 No 217 as from 1.4.06 (3.4.06 where rent payable weekly or at intervals of a week).
3. Amended by reg 2(10)(d) of SI 2005 No 2502 as amended by Sch 2 para 27 of SI 2006 No 217 as from 1.4.06 (3.4.06 where rent payable weekly or at intervals of a week).
4. Amended by reg 16(3) of SI 2006 No 2378 as from 2.10.06.
5. Amended by reg 3(3) SI 2007 No 294 as from 1.4.07.
6. Substituted by reg 5 of SI 2007 No 2470 as from 24.9.07.
7. Amended by reg 12(7) of SI 2007 No 2618 as from 1.10.07.
8. Amended by reg 15 of SI 2007 No 2869, as amended by reg 5(6) of SI 2008 No 586,as from 7.4.08 (or if reg 1(5) of that SI applies, on the day on or after 7.4.08 when the first of the events specified in reg 1(6) applies, or from 6.4.09 if none have before that date).
9. Substituted by reg 6 of SI 2008 No 2667 as from 30.10.08.
10. Amended by reg 8 and Sch para 37(6) of SI 2013 No 388 as from 8.4.13.
11. Amended by art 7 and Sch para 35(6) of SI 2013 No 591 as from 8.4.13.
12. Omitted by reg 7(5) of SI 2017 No 1187 as from 6.12.18.

General Note

Paras (1)–(9A) of this regulation are equivalent to reg 79 HB Regs (see p535).

Note the exceptions to the normal rules for determining the effective date of changes in circumstance in reg 59, set out in reg 60 immediately below.

Change of circumstances where state pension credit payable

60.–(1) Paragraphs (2) to (4) apply where–
(a) the claimant is also on state pension credit;
(b) the amount of state pension credit awarded to him is changed in consequence of a change in the claimant's circumstances or the correction of an official error; and
(c) the change in the amount of state pension credit payable to the claimant results in a change in the rate of housing benefit payable to the claimant.

(2) Where the change of circumstance is that an increase in the amount of state pension credit payable to the claimant results in–
(a) an increase in the rate at which housing benefit is payable to him, the change shall take effect from the first day of the benefit week in which state pension credit becomes payable at the increased rate; or
(b) a decrease in the rate at which housing benefit is payable to him, the change shall take effect from the first day of the benefit week next following the date on which–
(i) the local authority receives notification from the Secretary of State of the increase in the amount of state pension credit; or
(ii) state pension credit is increased,
whichever is the later.

(3) Where the change of circumstance is that the claimant's state pension credit is reduced and in consequence the rate of housing benefit payable to the claimant reduces–
(a) in a case where the claimant's state pension credit is reduced because the claimant failed to notify the Secretary of State timeously of the change of circumstances, the change shall take effect from the first day of the benefit week from which state pension credit was reduced; or
(b) in any other case the change shall take effect from the first day of the benefit week next following the date on which–
(i) the local authority receives notification from the Secretary of State of the reduction in the amount of state pension credit; or
(ii) state pension credit is reduced,
whichever is the later.

(4)   Where the change of circumstance is that–

(a)   state pension credit is reduced; and

(b)   in consequence of the change the rate of housing benefit payable to the claimant is increased,

the change shall take effect from the first day of the benefit week in which state pension credit becomes payable at the reduced rate.

(5)   Where a change of circumstances occurs in that an award of state pension credit has been made to the claimant or his partner and this would result in a decrease in the rate of housing benefit payable to the claimant, the change shall take effect from the first day of the benefit week next following the date on which–

(a)   the local authority receives notification from the Secretary of State of the award; or

(b)   entitlement to state pension credit begins,
        whichever is the later.

(6)   Where, in the case of a claimant who, or whose partner, is or has been awarded state pension credit comprising only the savings credit, there is–

(a)   a change of circumstances of a kind described in any of paragraphs (2) to (5) which results from a relevant calculation or estimate; and

(b)   a change of circumstances which is a relevant determination,

each of which results in a change in the rate of housing benefit payable to the claimant, the change of circumstances referred to in sub-paragraph (b) shall take effect from the day specified in paragraphs (2), (3), (4) or (5) as the case may be, in relation to the change referred to in sub-paragraph (a).

(7)   Where a change of circumstance occurs in that a guarantee credit has been awarded to the claimant or his partner and this would result in an increase in the rate of housing benefit payable to the claimant, the change shall take effect from the first day of the benefit week next following the date in respect of which the guarantee credit is first payable.

(8)   Where a change of circumstances would but for this paragraph take effect under the preceding provisions of this regulation within the 4 week period specified in regulation 54 (continuing payments where state pension credit claimed), that change shall take effect on the first day of the first benefit week to commence after the expiry of the 4 week period.

(9)   Where the change of circumstances is an amendment of these Regulations, that change, subject to [² regulation 61(5)] (calculation of weekly amounts), shall take effect as follows–

(a)   where the amendment is made by an order under section 150 of the Administration Act (annual uprating of benefits)–

(i)   in a case in which the claimant's weekly amount of eligible rent falls to be calculated in accordance with regulation 61(2)(b) [¹ or (c)], from 1st April;

(ii)   in any other case, from the first Monday in April, in the year in which that order comes into force;

(b)   in respect of any other amendment, from the date on which the amendment of these Regulations comes into force in the particular case.

(10)   In this regulation–

"official error" has the meaning it has in the Decisions and Appeals Regulations by virtue of regulation 1(2) of those Regulations;

"relevant calculation or estimate" means the calculation or estimate made by the Secretary of State of the claimant's or, as the case may be, the claimant's partner's income and capital for the purposes of the award of state pension credit;

"relevant determination" means a change in the determination by the relevant authority of the claimant's income and capital using the relevant calculation or estimate, in accordance with regulation 27(1) (calculation of claimant's income and capital in savings credit only cases).

Modifications
Para (9) amended by reg 15 Housing Benefit (State Pension Credit) (Local Housing Allowance and Information Sharing) Amendment Regulations 2007 No.2869 as from 7 April 2008, save that for a person to whom reg 1(5) of those regulations applied (see p1814), the amendments came into force on the day on or after 7 April 2008 when the first of the events specified in reg 1(6) applied to her/him, or on 6 April 2009 if none had before that date.

Amendments
1. Amended by reg 2(11) of SI 2005 No 2502 as amended by Sch 2 para 27 of SI 2006 No 217 as from 1.4.06 (3.4.06 where rent payable weekly or at intervals of a week).
2. Amended by reg 15 of SI 2007 No 2869 as from 7.4.08 (or if reg 1(5) of that SI applies, on the day on or after 7.4.08 when the first of the events specified in reg 1(6) applies, or from 6.4.09 if none have before that date).

Definition
"person on state pension credit" – see reg 2(1).

General Note
Reg 60 provides exceptions to the normal rules for determining the effective date of changes in circumstance in reg 59. The effect of reg 60 is that overpayments are not created where there has been a delay in the DWP passing information to authorities about a claimant's (or her/his partner's) PC. It applies when PC is awarded or a PC award is changed which in turn requires an HB award to be modified. Where HB increases as a result of the change in entitlement to PC, the change generally takes effect from the week the PC entitlement alters. However, where HB decreases, the change takes effect from the week the authority is notified of the change in entitlement to PC, or the date the PC changes if this is later. Exceptions are found in paras (8) and (9) where continuing payments are being made and where the change is an amendment to the HB(SPC) Regs.

Analysis
Paragraphs (1) to (5) and (7): The general rules
Where HB payable increases because the amount of PC payable increases or decreases due to a change in circumstances or the correction of an official error (defined in para (10) by reference to the D&A Regs), the change generally takes effect from the first day of the benefit week in which the rate of PC is altered: paras (2)(a) and (4). However, where HB increases because an award of guarantee credit of PC is made to the claimant or her/his partner, the change takes effect from the first day of the benefit week after the date the guarantee credit is payable: para (7).
    Where HB payable decreases there are three possibilities. Where:
(1)   a claimant's PC increases due to a change in circumstances or the correction of an official error, the change takes effect from the first day in the benefit week following the later of the date the authority receives notification of the increase from the DWP or the date the PC increases: para (2)(b);
(2)   a claimant's PC decreases, the change takes effect from the first day in the benefit week following the later of the date the authority receives notification of the decreased PC from the DWP or the PC decreases, unless the reduction was due to a failure by the claimant to notify a change to the DWP "timeously". In this case it takes effect from the first day of the benefit week in which the PC decreased: para (3);
(3)   an award of PC is made to the claimant or her/his partner, the change takes effect from the first day of the benefit week following the later of the date the authority receives notification of the award of PC from the DWP or the date entitlement to PC begins: para (5).
Paragraph (6): Savings credit only cases
Where a claimant or her/his partner is getting the savings credit of PC only and the HB payable changes as a result of a change in the DWP assessment of income and capital and a change in the assessment of income and capital by the authority, the change in the authority's assessment takes effect under whichever of paras (2) to (5) applies in relation to the change in PC as a result of the DWP assessment. The definitions of "relevant calculation or estimate" and "relevant determination" are in para (10). Note that from April 2016, the savings credit of PC is being phased out.
Paragraph (8): Where continuing payments are made
By virtue of para (8), a change taking place while continuing payments are being made under reg 54 above takes effect on the first day of the benefit week after continuing payments end.
Paragraph (9): Amendments to regulations
Where the change is an amendment to the HB(SPC) Regs, it takes effect from the date on which the amendment comes into force unless it is an amendment in respect of the annual uprating of benefits. In this case, if rent is payable monthly or daily, the change takes effect from 1 April or, in any other case, from the first Monday in April. Para (9) is subject to reg 61(5).

[¹ Calculation of weekly amounts

61.–(1)   A person's entitlement to housing benefit in any benefit week shall be calculated in accordance with the following provisions of this regulation.

(2)   The weekly amount of a claimant's eligible rent shall be–

(a)   subject to paragraph (3), where rent is payable at intervals of one week or a multiple thereof, the amount of eligible rent payable weekly or, where it is payable at intervals of a multiple of a week, the amount determined by dividing the amount of eligible rent payable by the number equal to the number of weeks in respect of which it is payable; or

(b)   subject to paragraph (3), where the rent is payable at intervals of a calendar month or multiples thereof, the amount determined by dividing the amount payable by the number equal to the number of calendar months in respect of which it is payable, multiplying by 12 and dividing by 52;

(c)   subject to paragraph (3), where the rent is payable at intervals of a day or multiples thereof, the amount determined by dividing the amount payable by the number equal to the number of days in respect of which it is payable and multiplying by 7.

(3)   In a case–

(a)   to which regulation 57(2) (date on which entitlement is to commence) applies, his eligible rent for the benefit week in which he becomes liable to make payments in respect of a dwelling which he occupies as his home shall be calculated by multiplying his daily rent by the number equal to the number of days in that benefit week for which he is liable to make such payments;

(b)   where a change of circumstances takes effect in a benefit week under regulation 59(2A), (but is not a change described in sub-paragraph (c)(ii) of this regulation), (2B), (8) or (9) other than on the Monday of a benefit week then the claimant's eligible rent for that benefit week shall be calculated by multiplying his daily rent by the appropriate number of days in that benefit week;

(c)   where–

   (i)   the amount of eligible rent which the claimant is liable to pay in respect of a dwelling is altered and that change of circumstances takes effect under regulation 59(2); or

   (ii)   the claimant–

      (aa)   moves to a new dwelling occupied as the home,

      (bb)   he is not entitled to be treated, immediately after that move, as occupying two dwellings as his home or as occupying his former dwelling as his home, and

      (cc)   that change of circumstances takes effect under regulation 59(2A),

   other than on the Monday of a benefit week, then the claimant's eligible rent for that benefit week shall be calculated by multiplying his old and new daily rent by the number equal to the number of days in that week which relate respectively to the old and new amounts which he is liable to pay.

(4)   In the case of a claimant whose weekly eligible rent falls to be calculated in accordance with paragraph (3)(a) or (b) by reference to the daily rent in his case, his weekly applicable amount, weekly income, the weekly amount of any non-dependant deductions and the minimum amount payable in his case shall be calculated in the same manner as his weekly eligible rent by reference to the amounts determined in his case in accordance with Parts 5 to 7 (applicable amounts, income and capital, and amount of benefit).

(5)   Where a change in the amount of a claimant's applicable amount, income or non-dependant deductions falls to be taken into account in the same benefit week as a change in his eligible rent to which paragraph (3)(c) applies, it shall be taken into account in that week on a daily basis in the same manner and as if it had occurred on the same day as that change in his eligible rent.

(6)   Any amount determined under these Regulations may, if it is appropriate, be rounded to the nearest whole penny by disregarding any amount less than half a penny and treating any amount of half a penny or more as a whole penny.

[² (7)]

(8)   In this regulation "daily rent" shall mean the amount determined by dividing by 7 the amount determined under whichever sub-paragraph of paragraph (2) is appropriate in each case.

(9)   Where a claimant is entitled to benefit in respect of two (but not more than two) dwellings in accordance with regulation 7(6) his eligible rent shall be calculated in respect of each dwelling in accordance with this regulation.]

Modifications

Reg 61 substituted by reg 16 Housing Benefit (State Pension Credit) (Local Housing Allowance and Information Sharing) Amendment Regulations 2007 No.2869 as from 7 April 2008, save that for a person to whom reg 1(5) of those regulations applied (see p1814), the amendments came into force on the day on or after 7 April 2008 when the first of the events specified in reg 1(6) applied to her/him, or on 6 April 2009 if none had before that date.

Amendments

1.   Substituted by reg 16 of SI 2007 No 2869 as from 7.4.08 (or if reg 1(5) of that SI applies, on the day on or after 7.4.08 when the first of the events specified in reg 1(6) applies, or from 6.4.09 if none have before that date).

2.   Omitted by reg 6(4)(b) of SI 2008 No 959 as from 6.10.08.

General Note

This regulation is equivalent to reg 80 HB Regs (see p538).

[¹ **Rent free periods**

62.–(1)   This regulation applies to a claimant for any period (referred to in this regulation as a rent free period) in, or in respect of, which he is not liable to pay rent except for any period to which regulation 8(1)(d) (waiver of rent by landlord in return for work done) applies.

(2)   In the case of the beginning or ending of a claimant's rent-free period, his eligible rent for the benefit week in which the rent free period begins and ends shall be calculated on a daily basis as if those benefit weeks were weeks to which regulation 61(3) applies.

(3)   For the purpose of determining the weekly applicable amount and income of a claimant to whom this regulation applies, the weekly amount of any non-dependant deductions and the minimum amount payable in his case–

(a)   in a case to which regulation 61(2)(a) applies, the amounts determined in his case in accordance with Parts 5 to 7 (applicable amounts, income and capital, and amount of benefit) shall be multiplied by 52 or 53, whichever is appropriate, and divided by the number equal to the number of weeks in that 52 or 53 week period in respect of which he is liable to pay rent;

(b)   subject to paragraph (4), in a case to which regulation 61(2)(b) or (c) applies, the amounts determined in his case in accordance with Parts 5 to 7 shall be multiplied by 365 or 366, whichever is appropriate and divided by the number of days in that 365 or 366 day period in respect of which he is liable to pay rent.

(4)   In a case to which paragraph (3)(b) applies, where either regulation 61(4) or (5) also applies or it is the beginning or end of a rent-free period, the weekly amounts referred to in paragraph (3) shall first be calculated in accordance with sub-paragraph (b) of that paragraph and then determined on a daily basis in the same manner as the claimant's eligible rent.]

Modifications

Reg 62 substituted by reg 16 Housing Benefit (State Pension Credit) (Local Housing Allowance and Information Sharing) Amendment Regulations 2007 No.2869 as from 7 April 2008, save that for a person to whom reg 1(5) of those regulations applied (see p1814), the amendments came into force on the day on or after 7 April 2008 when the first of the events specified in reg 1(6) applied to her/him, or on 6 April 2009 if none had before that date.

Amendment

1.   Substituted by reg 16 of SI 2007 No 2869 as from 7.4.08 (or if reg 1(5) of that SI applies, on the day on or after 7.4.08 when the first of the events specified in reg 1(6) applies, or from 6.4.09 if none have before that date).

General Note
The practical effect of this regulation is identical to that of reg 81 HB Regs (see p541).

PART 9
Claims

Who may claim

63.–(1)   In the case of a couple or members of a polygamous marriage a claim shall be made by whichever one of them they agree should so claim or, in default of agreement, by such one of them as the relevant authority shall determine.

(2)   Where a person who is liable to make payments in respect of a dwelling is unable for the time being to act, and–

(a)   a [¹ deputy] has been appointed by the Court of Protection with power to claim, or as the case may be, receive benefit on his behalf; or

(b)   in Scotland, his estate is being administered by a judicial factor or any guardian acting or appointed under the Adults with Incapacity (Scotland) Act 2000 who has power to claim or, as the case may be, receive benefit on his behalf; or

(c)   an attorney with a general power or a power to claim or as the case may be, receive benefit, has been appointed by that person under [¹ the Powers of Attorney Act 1971, the Enduring Powers of Attorney Act 1985 or the Mental Capacity Act 2005 or otherwise],

that [¹ deputy], judicial factor, guardian or attorney, as the case may be, may make a claim on behalf of that person.

(3)   Where a person who is liable to make payments in respect of a dwelling is unable for the time being to act and paragraph (2) does not apply to him, the relevant authority may, upon written application made to them by a person who, if a natural person, is over the age of 18, appoint that person to exercise on behalf of the person who is unable to act, any right to which that person might be entitled under the Act and to receive and deal on his behalf with any sums payable to him.

(4)   Where the relevant authority has made an appointment under paragraph (3) or treated a person as an appointee under paragraph (5)–

(a)   it may at any time revoke the appointment;

(b)   the person appointed may resign his office after having given four week's notice in writing to the relevant authority of his intention to do so;

(c)   any such appointment shall terminate when the relevant authority is notified that a receiver or other person to whom paragraph (2)(b) or (c) applies has been appointed.

(5)   Where a person who is liable to make payments in respect of a dwelling is for the time being unable to act and the Secretary of State has appointed a person to act on his behalf for the purposes of the Act the relevant authority may if that person agrees treat him as if he had been appointed by them under paragraph (3).

(6)   Anything required by these Regulations to be done by or to any person who is for the time being unable to act may be done by or to the [¹ deputy], judicial factor, guardian or attorney, if any, or by or to the person appointed or treated as appointed under this regulation and the receipt of any such person so appointed shall be a good discharge to the relevant authority for any sum paid.

[² (7)]

Amendments
1.   Amended by reg 12(8) of SI 2007 No 2618 as from 1.10.07.
2.   Omitted by reg 3(3) of SI 2008 No 2299 as from 1.10.08.

General Note
This regulation is identical to reg 82 HB Regs (see p542).

Time and manner in which claims are to be made

64.–(1)   [¹⁰ Subject to paragraph (1A),] The prescribed time for claiming housing benefit is as regards any day on which, apart from satisfying the condition of making a claim, the claimant is entitled to housing benefit, that day and the period of [⁵ three months] immediately following it.

[¹⁰ (1A)   In any case where paragraph (6)(a) applies, paragraph (1) does not entitle a claimant to claim housing benefit in respect of any day earlier than 3 months before the date on which the claim for state pension credit is made (or treated as made by virtue of any provision of the Social Security (Claims and Payments) Regulations 1987).]

(2)   [¹ Subject to [⁴ paragraphs (5A) to (5BD)],] Every claim shall be in writing and made on a properly completed form approved for the purpose by the relevant authority or in such written form as the relevant authority may accept as sufficient in the circumstances of any particular case or class of cases having regard to the sufficiency of the written information and evidence.

(3)   The forms approved for the purpose of claiming shall be provided free of charge by the relevant authority or such persons as they may authorise or appoint for the purpose.

(4)   Each relevant authority shall notify the Secretary of State of the address to which claims delivered or sent to the appropriate DWP office are to be forwarded.

(5)   A claim [¹ in writing]–

(a)   may be sent or delivered to the appropriate DWP office where the claimant or his partner is also claiming income support, incapacity benefit, state pension credit [⁶, a jobseeker's allowance or an employment and support allowance];

(b)   where it has not been sent or delivered to the appropriate DWP office, shall be sent or delivered to the designated office;

(c)   sent or delivered to the appropriate DWP office, other than one sent on the same form as a claim made to income support, incapacity benefit [⁶, a jobseeker's allowance or an employment and support allowance] and as approved by the Secretary of State for the purpose of the benefits being claimed, shall be forwarded to the relevant authority within two working days of the date of the receipt of the claim at the appropriate DWP office, or as soon as practicable thereafter;

[⁴ (d)]

[⁴ (e)]

(f)   where the claimant has attained the qualifying age for entitlement to state pension credit may be sent or delivered to an authorised office.

[³ (g) may be sent or delivered to the offices of a county council in England if the council has arranged with the relevant authority for claims to be received at their offices ("county offices").]

[¹ (5A)   Where the relevant authority has published a telephone number for the purpose of receiving claims for housing benefit a claim may be made by telephone to that telephone number.

[⁴ (5B)   If the Secretary of State agrees, where–

(a)   a person makes a claim for a benefit referred to in paragraph (5)(a); and

(b)   the Secretary of State has made provision in the Social Security (Claims and Payments) Regulations 1987 for that benefit to be claimed by telephone,

that person may claim housing benefit by telephone to the telephone number specified by the Secretary of State.

(5BA)   A claim for housing benefit may be made in accordance with paragraph (5B) at any time before a decision has been made on the claim for the benefit referred to in paragraph (5)(a).

(5BB)   If the Secretary of State agrees, where a person, in accordance with regulation 32 of the Social Security (Claims and Payments) Regulations 1987 (information to be given and changes to be notified)–

(a)   furnishes the Secretary of State with such information or evidence as he may require; or

(b)   notifies the Secretary of State of any change of circumstances,

that person may claim housing benefit in the same manner in which the information or evidence was furnished or the notification was given.

(5BC)   If the Secretary of State agrees, where a person, in accordance with regulation 24 of the Jobseeker's Allowance Regulations (provision of information and evidence)–

(a) furnishes the Secretary of State with such certificates, documents and other evidence as he may require; or

(b) notifies the Secretary of State of any change of circumstances,

that person may claim housing benefit in the same manner as the certificate, document and other evidence was furnished or the notification was given.

(5BD) A claim for housing benefit may be made in accordance with paragraphs (5BB) or (5BC) at any time before a decision has been made on the award of benefit to which the information, evidence, certificates, documents or notification relates.]

(5C) The relevant authority may determine, in any particular case, that a claim made by telephone [⁴ in accordance with paragraph (5A)] is not a valid claim unless the person making the claim approves a written statement of his circumstances, provided for the purpose by the relevant authority [⁴].

[⁴ (5CA) The relevant authority or the Secretary of State may determine that a claim made by telephone in accordance with paragraphs (5B) to (5BD) is not a valid claim unless the person making the claim approves a written statement of his circumstances, provided for the purpose by the Secretary of State.]

[⁴ (5D) A claim made by telephone in accordance with paragraphs (5A) to (5BD) is defective unless the relevant authority or the Secretary of State is provided with all the information requested during that telephone call.]

(5E) Where a claim made by telephone in accordance with paragraph (5A) [⁴] is defective, the relevant authority [⁴ must] provide the person making it with an opportunity to correct the defect.

[⁴ (5EA) Where a claim made by telephone in accordance with paragraphs (5B) to (5BD) is defective–

(a) the Secretary of State may provide the person making it with an opportunity to correct the defect;

(b) the relevant authority must provide the person making it with an opportunity to correct the defect if the Secretary of State has not already done so unless it considers that it has sufficient information to determine the claim.]

(5F) If the person corrects the defect within one month, or such longer period as the relevant authority considers reasonable, of the date the relevant authority [⁴ or the Secretary of State] last drew attention to it, the relevant authority shall treat the claim as if it had been duly made in the first instance.]

[⁴ (5G) If the person does not correct the defect within one month, or such longer period as the relevant authority considers reasonable, of the date the relevant authority or the Secretary of State last drew attention to it, the relevant authority may treat the claim as if it had been duly made in the first instance, where it considers that it has sufficient information to determine the claim.]

(6) Subject to paragraph (11) [⁴] the date on which a claim is made shall be–

(a) in a case where an award of state pension credit which comprises a guarantee credit has been made to the claimant or his partner and the claim for housing benefit is made within one month of the date on which the claim for state pension credit was received at the appropriate DWP office, the first day of entitlement to state pension credit arising from that claim;

(b) in a case where a claimant or his partner is a person in receipt of a guarantee credit and he becomes liable for the first time to make payments in respect of the dwelling which he occupies as his home, where the claim is received at the designated office or appropriate DWP office within one month of the claimant first becoming liable for such payments, the date he became liable for those payments;

(c) in a case where the claimant is the former partner of a person who was, at the date of his death or their separation, entitled to housing benefit and the claimant makes a claim within one month of the date of the death or the separation, that date;

[⁴ (d) except where sub-paragraph (a), (b) or (c) is satisfied, in a case where a properly completed claim is received in a designated office, an authorised office, county offices or an appropriate DWP office within one month, or such longer period as the relevant authority considers reasonable, of the date on which–

 (i) a claim form was issued to the claimant following the claimant first notifying, by whatever means, a designated office, an authorised office or an appropriate DWP office of an intention to make a claim; or

 (ii) a claimant notifies, by whatever means, a designated office, an authorised office or an appropriate DWP office of an intention to make a claim by telephone in accordance with paragraphs (5A) to (5BD),

the date of first notification;]

(e) in any other case, the date on which the claim is received at the designated office, authorised office [³, county offices] or appropriate DWP office.

(7) Where a claim received at the designated office [⁸ or appropriate DWP office] has not been made in the manner prescribed in paragraph (2), that claim is for the purposes of these Regulations defective.

(8) Where a claim [⁸, which is received by a relevant authority,] is defective because–

(a) it was made on the form approved for the purpose but that form is not accepted by the relevant authority as being properly completed; or

(b) it was made in writing but not on the form approved for the purpose and the relevant authority does not accept the claim as being in a written form which is sufficient in the circumstances of the case having regard to the sufficiency of the written information and evidence,

the relevant authority may, in a case to which sub-paragraph (a) applies, request the claimant to complete the defective claim or, in the case to which sub-paragraph (b) applies, supply the claimant with the approved form or request further information or evidence.

[⁸ (8A) Where a claim is received at an appropriate DWP office and it appears to the Secretary of State that the form has not been properly completed, the Secretary of State may request that the claimant provides the relevant authority with the information required to complete the form.]

[⁸ (9) The relevant authority shall treat a defective claim as if it had been validly made in the first instance if, in any particular case, the conditions specified in sub-paragraph (a), (b) or (c) of paragraph (9A) are satisfied.

(9A) The conditions are that–

(a) where paragraph (8)(a) (incomplete form) applies, the authority receives at the designated office the properly completed claim or the information requested to complete it or the evidence within one month of the request, or such longer period as the relevant authority may consider reasonable; or

(b) where paragraph (8)(b) (claim not on approved form or further information requested by relevant authority) applies–

 (i) the approved form sent to the claimant is received at the designated office properly completed within one month of it having been sent to him; or, as the case may be,

 (ii) the claimant supplies whatever information or evidence was requested under paragraph (8) within one month of the request,

 or, in either case, within such longer period as the relevant authority may consider reasonable; or

(c) where paragraph (8A) (further information requested by Secretary of State) applies, the relevant authority receives at the designated office the properly completed claim or the information requested to complete it within one month of the request by the Secretary of State or within such longer period as the relevant authority considers reasonable.]

(9) The relevant authority shall treat a defective claim as if it had been validly made in the first instance if–

(a) where paragraph (8)(a) applies, the authority receives at the designated office the properly completed claim or the information requested to complete it or the evidence within one month of the request, or such longer period as the relevant authority may consider reasonable; or

(b)   where paragraph (8)(b) applies–

    (i)   the approved form sent to the claimant is received at the designated office properly completed within one month of it having been sent to him; or, as the case may be,

    (ii)   the claimant supplies whatever information or evidence was requested under paragraph (8) within one month of the request,

or within such longer period as the relevant authority may consider reasonable.

(10)   A claim which is made on an approved form for the time being is, for the purposes of this regulation, properly completed if completed in accordance with the instructions on the form, including any instructions to provide information and evidence in connection with the claim.

[² (11)   Except in the case of a claim made by a person from abroad, where the claimant is not entitled to housing benefit in the benefit week immediately following the date of his claim but the relevant authority is of the opinion that unless there is a change of circumstances he will be entitled to housing benefit for a period beginning not later than the seventeenth benefit week following the date on which the claim is made, the relevant authority may treat the claim as made on a date in the benefit week immediately preceding the first benefit week of that period of entitlement and award benefit accordingly.]

(12)   Paragraph (11) applies in the case of a person who has attained, or whose partner has attained, [⁹ the age which is 17 weeks younger than the qualifying age for state pension credit].

[⁷ (13)]

(14)   In this regulation "authorised office" means an office which is nominated by the Secretary of State and authorised by the relevant authority for receiving claims for decision by the relevant authority.

Amendments

    1.   Inserted by reg 3(2) of SI 2006 No 2967 as from 20.12.06.

    2.   Substituted by reg 4 of SI 2007 No 1331 as from 23.5.07.

    3.   Amended by reg 8(2) of SI 2007 No 2911 as from 31.10.07.

    4.   Amended by reg 3(4) of SI 2008 No 2299 as from 1.10.08.

    5.   Substituted by reg 5 of SI 2008 No 2424 as from 6.10.08.

    6.   Amended by reg 38 of SI 2008 No 1082 as from 27.10.08.

    7.   Omitted by reg 8 of SI 2008 No 2824 as from 27.11.08.

    8.   Amended by reg 3(2) of SI 2008 No 2987 as from 22.12.08.

    9.   Amended by reg 30 of SI 2009 No 1488 as from 6.4.10.

    10.   Amended by reg 3(4) of SI 2010 No 2449 as from 1.11.10.

Analysis

This is the equivalent of reg 83 HB Regs (see p544). There are some differences.

Paras (1), (1A) and (6)

Para (1) determines the earliest date of entitlement to HB; it is not a backdating provision as such. Accordingly, all the claimant has to show is that s/he was entitled to HB throughout the relevant three-month period; unlike under the HB Regs (where, also, the claim can now only be treated as made a maximum of one month before it was made – see reg 83 on p544), there is no test of good cause, and so judgements as to why the claimant did not claim previously are irrelevant. If the claimant only qualified under the HB(SPC) Regs for part of the three-month period before the actual claim or was not entitled to HB for all of the three-month period, s/he should still benefit from this rule for that part of the period that s/he was entitled, as long as that period runs continuously up to the date of the actual claim, applying, by analogy, *R(IS) 3/01* and *R(IS) 16/04*. Note: the relevant period was 12 months until 6 October 2008.

Paras (1A) and (6). Para (6) determines the date of claim for HB purposes, which is not necessarily the date the claim is actually received by the authority. The date on which entitlement to HB then commences is determined by reg 57. However, where para 6(a) applies (ie, where there is an award of PC guarantee credit and a claim for HB was made within one month of the claim for PC), a claimant is not entitled to claim HB for any day earlier than three months before the claim for PC was made (or treated as made): para (1A). This would appear to mean that, in such a case, the effective date for HB as determined by reg 57 (ie, the date on which entitlement to HB is to commence) cannot be earlier than the effective date of the PC award because the claimant cannot specify a date from which her/his claim is made that precedes that date.

Prior to 1 November 2010, the combined effect of these provisions and reg 57 could be generous, as shown in *Leicester CC v LG* [2009] UKUT 155 (AAC), an Upper Tribunal decision which dealt with the provisions under the CTB(SPC) Regs, which were effectively the same. A request to the Pension Service to visit the claimant and assist with backdated claims for PC and CTB was made on 4 July 2007. The visit did not take place until 21 February 2008, when claim forms for both benefits were completed at the same time. The claimant was awarded PC with effect from 6 July 2006, based on her claim for PC being accepted as made in July 2007 (at the time a claim for PC could be backdated 12 months). The local authority determined the date of claim for CTB as 26 February 2007, the date 12 months before the date it received the CTB claim form, 12 months being the maximum period a CTB claim could then be "backdated" under regs 53(1ZA) and 56 CTB(SPC) Regs. Judge Jacobs disagreed. He decided that the date of claim for CTB was 6 July 2006 and that the claimant's entitlement to CTB was to be determined from a date 12 months before that date. His analysis of the issues was as follows.

(1)   Once a claim for CTB was made, the date of that claim was determined by reg 53 CTB(SPC) Regs. Reg 53(5) expressly provided what the date of claim was. The HB equivalent is reg 64(6) HB(SPC) Regs. As the claimant had been awarded PC and had claimed CTB within one month of her claim for that benefit, under para (5)(a) her date of claim was the effective date of the PC award – ie, 6 July 2006, the date to which her PC claim had been backdated. The HB equivalent is para (6)(a).

(2)   The earliest date of entitlement to CTB was determined by reg 53(1ZA) which dealt in form with the date of claim but in substance with the start of entitlement to CTB. The HB equivalent is reg 64(1) HB(SPC) Regs. The effect of the provisions is to give the claimant a period of time in which to make a claim from the time when the other conditions of entitlement were satisfied. At the time of the decision this was 12 months (ie, 12 months before the date of claim), but has since been shortened to three months.

(3)   The effective date (ie, the date on which entitlement to CTB was to commence) was determined by reg 48. The HB equivalent is reg 57 HB(SPC) Regs. If the claimant is otherwise entitled, the effective date is the first day of the benefit week following the first day in respect of which the claim was made. "In respect of" caters for the possibility that the claim may have been made in respect of a period before the date of claim. The claimant may specify a date from which the claim is made. If so, that is the effective date, provided the other conditions of entitlement are satisfied. If the claimant does not specify a date, the local authority has two choices. It may ask the claimant to specify the date, or it may take the most favourable date, which for HB is the maximum set by reg 64(1).

Judge Jacobs accepted that this analysis produced an outcome that was very generous to claimants but said that was not a reason for rejecting it. He said: "No one can have missed the publicity about low take up of entitlement to council tax benefit and benefits for pensioners generally. The legislation clearly allows generous periods within which to claim, although they have now been significantly reduced, and my analysis is merely the logical consequence of the provisions."

Para (1A) was inserted from 1 November 2010 to reverse the effect of the decision in *Leicester CC v LG*. Now, in a case where para (6)(a) applies (ie, where there is an award of PC guarantee credit and a claim for HB was made within one month of the claim for PC), a claimant is not entitled to claim HB for any day earlier than three months before the claim for PC was made (or treated as made). This would appear to mean that in such a case, the effective date for HB as determined by reg 57 (ie, the date on which entitlement to HB is to commence) cannot be earlier than the effective date of the PC award because the claimant cannot specify a date from which her/his claim is made that precedes that date.

Paras (11) and (12)

Paras (11) and (12) allow the authority to treat an advance claim for HB as made in the benefit week before the first week of entitlement where the claimant will become entitled to HB in the next 17 weeks if the claimant or her/his partner is 17 weeks (or fewer) younger than the qualifying age for PC (defined in reg 2(1)).

[¹Electronic claims for benefit

64A.   A claim for housing benefit may be made by means of an electronic communication in accordance with Schedule 10.]

Amendment

1.   Inserted by art 3(3) of SI 2006 No 2968 as from 20.12.06.

General Note

This regulation is identical to reg 83A HB Regs (see p554).

[¹ Date of claim where claim sent or delivered to a gateway office 65.]

Amendment

1.   Omitted by reg 3(5) of SI 2008 No 2299 as from 1.10.08.

[¹ **Date of claim where claim sent or delivered to an office of a designated authority 66.**]

Amendment
1.   Omitted by reg 3(6) of SI 2008 No 2299 as from 1.10.08.

Evidence and information

67.–(1)   Subject to [⁴ paragraphs (1A) and (2)] and to paragraph 5 of Schedule A1 (treatment of claims for housing benefit by refugees), a person who makes a claim, or a person to whom housing benefit has been awarded, shall furnish such certificates, documents, information and evidence in connection with the claim or the award, or any question arising out of the claim or the award, as may reasonably be required by the relevant authority in order to determine that person's entitlement to, or continuing entitlement to, housing benefit and shall do so within one month of [⁴ the relevant authority requiring him, or the Secretary of State requesting him, to do so] or such longer period as the relevant authority may consider reasonable.

[⁴ (1A)   Where a person notifies a change of circumstances to the appropriate DWP office under regulation 69(9), the Secretary of State may request that the claimant provides to the relevant authority the information or evidence that the Secretary of State considers the relevant authority may require to determine the claimant's continuing entitlement to housing benefit.]

(2)   Nothing in this regulation shall require a person to furnish any certificates, documents, information or evidence relating to a payment to which paragraph (4) applies.

(3)   Where a request is made under paragraph (1), the relevant authority shall–

(a)   inform the claimant or the person to whom housing benefit has been awarded of his duty under regulation 69 (duty to notify change of circumstances) to notify the designated office of any change of circumstances; and

(b)   without prejudice to the extent of the duty owed under regulation 69, indicate to him either orally or by notice or by reference to some other document available to him on application and without charge, the kind of change or circumstances which is to be notified.

(4)   This paragraph applies to any of the following payments–

(a)   a payment which is–

(i)   disregarded under paragraph 23 of Schedule 5 to the Housing Benefit Regulations 2006 (income in kind) or paragraph 34 of Schedule 6 to those Regulations (certain payments in kind); and

(ii)   made under [⁵ or by] the Macfarlane Trust, the Macfarlane (Special Payments) Trust, the Macfarlane (Special Payments) (No 2) Trust, the Fund, the Eileen Trust [⁵, MFET Limited], the Skipton Fund [⁶, the Caxton Foundation] [⁷, ⁹] [⁸, the London Emergencies Trust, the We Love Manchester Emergency Fund] or the [² London Bombings Relief Charitable Fund];

(b)   a payment which is disregarded under paragraph 35 of Schedule 5 to the Housing Benefit Regulations 2006 or paragraph 24 of Schedule 6 to those Regulations (payments made under certain trusts and certain other payments), other than a payment made under the Independent Living [³ Fund (2006)];

(c)   a payment which is disregarded under regulation 55(10)(b) or (c) (income of non-dependant) other than a payment made under the Independent Living [³ Fund (2006)].

(5)   Where a claimant or a person to whom housing benefit has been awarded or any partner is [⁵ has attained the qualifying age for state pension credit] and is a member of, or a person deriving entitlement to a pension under, a personal pension scheme, [¹] he shall where the relevant authority so requires furnish the following information–

(a)   the name and address of the pension fund holder;

(b)   such other information including any reference or policy number as is needed to enable the personal pension scheme [¹] to be identified.

(6)   Where the pension fund holder receives from a relevant authority a request for details concerning a personal pension scheme [¹] relating to a person or any partner to

whom paragraph (5) refers, the pension fund holder shall provide the relevant authority with any information to which paragraph (7) refers.

(7)   The information to which this paragraph refers is–

(a)   where the purchase of an annuity under a personal pension scheme has been deferred, the amount of any income which is being withdrawn from the personal pension scheme;

(b)   in the case of–

    (i)   a personal pension scheme where income withdrawal is available, the [¹⁰ rate of the annuity which may have been purchased with the funds held under the scheme]; or

    (ii)   a personal pension scheme where income withdrawal is not available, [¹] the [¹⁰ rate of the annuity which might have been purchased with the fund] if the fund were held under a personal pension scheme where income withdrawal was available,

calculated by or on behalf of the pension fund holder by means of tables prepared from time to time by the Government Actuary which are appropriate for this purpose.

Amendments

1.   Amended by reg 5(5) of SI 2007 No 1749 as from 16.7.07.
2.   Amended by reg 4(6) of SI 2008 No 1042 as from 19.5.08.
3.   Amended by reg 7(5(a) of SI 2008 No 2767 as from 17.11.08.
4.   Amended by reg 3(3) of SI 2008 No 2987 as from 22.12.08.
5.   Amended by reg 9(3), (5) and (6) of SI 2010 No 641 as from 1.4.10 (5.4.10 where rent payable weekly or in multiples of a week).
6.   Amended by reg 20(8) of SI 2011 No 2425 as from 31.10.11.
7.   Amended by reg 7(3)(b) of SI 2017 No 329 as from 3.4.17.
8.   Amended by reg 7(3)(b) of SI 2017 No 689 as from 19.6.17.
9.   Amended by reg 7(5) of SI 2017 No 870 as from 23.10.17.
10.   Amended by reg 12(4) of SI 2017 No 1015 as from 16.11.17.

General Note

This regulation is identical to reg 86 HB Regs (see p555).

[² Amendment and withdrawal of claim

[³ **68.**–[⁴ (1)   A person who has made a claim for benefit may amend it at any time before a [² decision] has been made on the claim by notice in writing received at the designated office, by telephone call to a telephone number specified by the relevant authority under regulation 64(5A) (time and manner in which claims are to be made) or by the Secretary of State under regulation 64(5B) or in such other manner as the relevant authority or the Secretary of State may decide or accept.]

[⁴ (2)]

(3)   Any claim amended in accordance with paragraph (1) [⁴] shall be treated as if it had been amended in the first instance.

(4)   A person who has made a claim may withdraw it at any time before a decision has been made on it by notice to the designated office.

(5)   Where the claim was made by telephone in accordance with paragraphs (5B) to (5BD) of regulation 64, the withdrawal may also be made by telephone to the telephone number specified by the Secretary of State.

(6)   Any notice of withdrawal given in accordance with paragraph (4) or (5) shall have effect when it is received.]]

Amendments

1.   Inserted by reg 3(3) of SI 2006 No 2967 as from 20.12.06.
2.   Substituted by reg 7(2) of SI 2007 No 719 as from 2.4.07.
3.   Substituted by reg 3(7) of SI 2008 No 2299 as from 1.10.08.
4.   Amended by reg 12(4) of SI 2013 No 2536 as from 29.10.13.
5.   Amended by reg 4(4) of SI 2014 No 213 as from 1.4.14 (7.4.14 where rent payable weekly or in multiples of a week).

General Note
This regulation is identical to reg 87 HB Regs (see p558).

Duty to notify changes of circumstances

69.–(1)   Subject to paragraphs [³ (3), (6) [⁴, (7) and (9)]], if at any time between the making of a claim and a decision being made on it, or during the award of housing benefit, there is a change of circumstances which the claimant, or any person by whom or on whose behalf sums payable by way of housing benefit are receivable, might reasonably be expected to know might affect the claimant's right to, the amount of or the receipt of housing benefit, that person shall be under a duty to notify that change of circumstances by giving notice [²] to the designated office–

[²[⁵ (a)   in writing; or

(b)   by telephone–

    (i)   where the relevant authority has published a telephone number for that purpose or for the purposes of regulation 64 (time and manner in which claims are to be made) unless the authority determines that in any particular case or class of case notification may not be given by telephone; or

    (ii)   in any case or class of case where the relevant authority determines that notice may be given by telephone; or

(c)   by any other means which the relevant authority agrees to accept in any particular case.]

[³ (2)]

(3)   The duty imposed on a person by paragraph (1) does not extend to changes–

(a)   in the amount of rent payable to a housing authority;

(b)   in the age of the claimant or that of any member of his family or of any non-dependants;

(c)   in these Regulations.

(4)   Notwithstanding paragraph (3)(b) a claimant shall be required by paragraph (1) to notify the designated office of any change in the composition of his family arising from the fact that a person who was a member of his family is now no longer such a person because he ceases to be a child or young person.

[³ (5)]

(6)   A person on housing benefit who is also on state pension credit must report–

(a)   changes to his tenancy, but not changes in the amount of rent payable to a housing authority;

(b)   changes affecting the residence or income of any non-dependant normally residing with the claimant or with whom the claimant normally resides;

(c)   any absence from the dwelling which exceeds or is likely to exceed 13 weeks [⁶ or where the absence is from Great Britain, which exceeds or is likely to exceed 4 weeks].

(7)   In addition to the changes required to be reported under paragraph (6) a person whose state pension credit comprises only a savings credit must also report–

(a)   changes affecting a child living with him which may result in a change in the amount of housing benefit payable in his case, but not changes in the age of the child;

[¹ (b)]

(c)   any change in the amount of the claimant's capital to be taken into account which does or may take the amount of his capital to more than £16,000;

(d)   any change in the income or capital of–

    (i)   a non-dependant whose income and capital are treated as belonging to the claimant in accordance with regulation 24 (circumstances in which income of a non-dependant is to be treated as claimant's); or

    (ii)   a person to whom regulation 27(4)(e) refers,

and whether such a person or, as the case may be, non-dependant stops living or begins or resumes living with the claimant.

(8)   A person who is on housing benefit and on state pension credit need only report to the designated office the changes specified in paragraphs (6) and (7).

[⁴ (9)   Where–
(a)   the claimant or the claimant's partner is in receipt of jobseeker's allowance;
(b)   the change of circumstance is that the claimant or the claimant's partner starts employment; and
(c)   as a result of that change of circumstance either entitlement to that benefit will end or the amount of that benefit will be reduced,
the claimant may discharge the duty in paragraph (1) by notifying the change of circumstance by telephoning the appropriate DWP office if a telephone number has been provided for that purpose.]

Amendments

1.   Omitted by reg 2(14) of SI 2005 No 2502 as amended by Sch 2 para 27 of SI 2006 No 217 as from 1.4.06 (3.4.06 where rent payable weekly or at intervals of a week).
2.   Inserted by reg 3(3) of SI 2006 No 2967 as from 20.12.06.
3.   Amended by reg 3(8) of SI 2008 No 2299 as from 1.10.08.
4.   Amended by reg 3(4) of SI 2008 No 2987 as from 22.12.08.
5.   Amended by reg 3(5) of SI 2010 No 2449 as from 1.11.10.
6.   Amended by reg 7(6) of SI 2017 No 1187 as from 21.12.17.

Analysis

Paras (1) to (5) are identical to reg 88 HB Regs (see p559).

Paras (6) to (8). Paras (6) and (7) set out the only types of change that PC recipients who are also on HB need to report to the local authority: para (8). All PC recipients must report changes relating to the residence or income of non-dependants, absences which exceed (or are likely to exceed) 13 weeks (four weeks if the absence is from Great Britain) and "changes to his tenancy": para (6). This presumably includes changes to the demise, rent-free periods and so on, as well as increases or decreases in rent, other than the rent payable to a housing authority which is specifically excluded.

Para (7) lists further changes to be reported by PC recipients who are only getting savings credit. They must report changes in respect of dependant children (other than age), changes in the income and capital of the non-dependants and partners specified, and changes which may take capital over £16,000. Note that from April 2016, the savings credit of PC is being phased out.

Para (9) differs slightly from reg 88(6) HB Regs. Under para (9) where the claimant or her/his partner is in receipt of JSA and starts employment and as a result entitlement to any type of JSA ends or will be reduced, the claimant can report the change by telephoning the DWP, if a telephone number has been provided for that purpose.

[¹ **Alternative means of notifying changes of circumstances**
69ZA.–(1)   In such cases and subject to such conditions as the Secretary of State may specify, the duty in regulation 69(1) to notify a change of circumstances may be discharged by notifying the Secretary of State–
(a)   where the change of circumstances is a birth or death, through a relevant authority, or a county council in England, by personal attendance at an office specified by that authority or county council, provided the Secretary of State has agreed with that authority or county council for it to facilitate such notification; or
(b)   where the change of circumstances is a death, by telephone to a telephone number specified for that purpose by the Secretary of State.

(2)   Paragraph (1) only applies if the authority administering the claimant's housing benefit agrees with the Secretary of State that notifications may be made in accordance with that paragraph.

(3)   The Secretary of State must forward information received in accordance with paragraph (1) to the authority administering the claimant's housing benefit.]

Amendment

1.   Inserted by reg 6 of SI 2010 No 444 as from 5.4.10.

General Note

This regulation is identical to reg 88ZA HB Regs (see p561).

[¹Notice of changes of circumstances given electronically

[² **69A.**–(1)] A person may give notice of a change of circumstances required to be notified under regulation 69 by means of an electronic communication in accordance with Schedule 10.]

[² (2) Where–
(a) the change of circumstances required to be notified is a death; and
(b) the authority administering the claimant's housing benefit agrees with the Secretary of State that notifications may be made in accordance with regulation 69ZA(1) (alternative means of notifying changes of circumstances),

a person may give notice of the change to the Secretary of State by means of an electronic communication in accordance with the provisions set out in Schedule 9ZC to the Social Security (Claims and Payments) Regulations 1987 (electronic communication).

(3) The provisions set out in that Schedule shall apply for the purposes of paragraph (2) as they apply for the purposes of regulation 32ZA of the Social Security (Claims and Payments) Regulations 1987 (information given electronically).

(4) The Secretary of State must forward information received in accordance with paragraph (2) to the authority administering the claimant's housing benefit.]

Amendments
1. Inserted by art 3(4) of SI 2006 No 2968 as from 20.12.06.
2. Amended by art 7 of SI 2011 No 2943 as from 23.1.12.

General Note
This regulation is identical to reg 88A HB Regs (see p562).

PART 10
Decisions on questions

Decisions by a relevant authority
70.–(1) Unless provided otherwise by these Regulations, any matter required to be determined under these Regulations shall be determined in the first instance by the relevant authority.

(2) The relevant authority shall make a decision on each claim within 14 days of the provisions of regulations 64 and 67 (time and manner in which claims are to be made and evidence and information) being satisfied or as soon as reasonably practicable thereafter.
[¹ (3)]

Amendment
1. Omitted by reg 6(4)(c) of SI 2008 No 959 as from 6.10.08.

General Note
This regulation is identical to reg 89 HB Regs (see p563).

Notification of decision
71.–(1) An authority shall notify in writing any person affected by a decision made by it under these Regulations–
(a) in the case of a decision on a claim, forthwith or as soon as reasonably practicable thereafter;
(b) in any other case, within 14 days of that decision or as soon as reasonably practicable thereafter,

and every notification shall include a statement as to the matters set out in Schedule 8.

(2) A person affected to whom an authority sends or delivers a notification of decision may, by notice in writing signed by him, [¹ within one month of the date of the notification of that decision (or, if the decision was notified before 1st November 2010, before 1st December 2010)] request the authority to provide a written statement setting out the reasons for its decision on any matter set out in the notice.

(3)   For the purposes of paragraph (2), where a person affected who requests a written statement is not a natural person, the notice in writing referred to in that paragraph shall be signed by a person over the age of 18 who is authorised to act on that person's behalf.

(4)   The written statement referred to in paragraph (2) shall be sent to the person requesting it within 14 days or as soon as is reasonably practical thereafter.

Amendment

1.   Amended by reg 3(6) of SI 2010 No 2449 as from 1.11.10.

General Note

This regulation is identical to reg 90 HB Regs (see p564).

PART 11
Payments

Time and manner of payment

72.–(1)   Subject to paragraphs (2) and (3) and regulations 73 to 79 (frequency of payment of rent allowance, payment on account of a rent allowance, payment provisions, offsetting) the relevant authority shall pay housing benefit to which a person is entitled under these Regulations at such time and in such manner as is appropriate, having regard to–

(a)   the times at which and the frequency with which a person's liability to make payment of rent arises; and

(b)   the reasonable needs and convenience of the person entitled thereto.

(2)   Where a person's entitlement to housing benefit is less than £1 weekly the relevant authority may pay that benefit at 6 monthly intervals.

(3)   Subject to regulations 73 to 78 (frequency of payment of and payment on account of rent allowance, payment provisions), every authority shall make the first payment of any housing benefit awarded by it within 14 days of the receipt of the claim at the designated office or, if that is not reasonably practical, as soon as possible thereafter.

Modifications

Reg 72(3) has effect as modified by Sch 3 para 7 HB&CTB(CP) Regs (see p1801) for some claimants entitled to and in receipt of HB in respect of their current home on 6 October 1996 and continuously since that date.

General Note

This regulation is identical to reg 91 HB Regs (see p567).

[¹Cases in which payments to a housing authority are to take the form of a rent allowance

72A.–(1)   Where the occupier of a dwelling is liable to make payments in respect of that dwelling to a housing authority as a result of the making of an order specified in paragraph (2), housing benefit in respect of those payments shall take the form of a rent allowance.

(2)   The orders specified for the purposes of paragraph (1) are–

(a)   a management control order made in accordance with section 74 of the Antisocial Behaviour etc. (Scotland) Act 2004;

(b)   an interim management order made in accordance with section 102 of the Housing Act 2004;

(c)   a final management order made in accordance with section 113 of that Act;

(d)   an interim empty dwelling management order made in accordance with section 133 of that Act; and

(e)   a final empty dwelling management order made in accordance with section 136 of that Act.]

[² (3)   Where–

(a)   the occupier of a caravan, mobile home or houseboat is liable to make payments in respect of that caravan, mobile home or houseboat and housing benefit in relation to those payments takes the form of a rent allowance; and

(b) the occupier is also liable to make payments to a housing authority in respect of the site on which that caravan or mobile home stands, or in respect of the mooring to which the houseboat is attached,

housing benefit in respect of payments to the housing authority shall take the form of a rent allowance.]

Amendments

1. Inserted by reg 3 of SI 2006 No 644 as from 3.4.06.
2. Inserted by reg 3(2) of SI 2008 No 2824 as from 6.4.09.

General Note

This regulation is identical to reg 91A HB Regs (see p568).

Frequency of payment of a rent allowance

73.–(1)   Subject to the following provisions of this regulation any rent allowance other than a payment made in accordance with regulation 72(2) or (3) or 74 (time and manner of payment, payment on account of rent allowance) shall be paid at intervals of 2 or 4 weeks or one month or, with the consent of the person entitled, at intervals greater than one month.

(2)   Except in a case to which paragraph (3) applies, any payment of a rent allowance shall be made, in so far as it is practicable to do so, at the end of the period in respect of which it is made.

(3)   Except in a case to which regulation 77(2) applies and subject to paragraph (4), this paragraph applies where payment of a rent allowance is being made to a landlord (which for these purposes has the same meaning as in regulations 76 and 77 (payments to a landlord)), when that payment shall be made–

(a)   at intervals of 4 weeks; and

(b)   at the end of the period in respect of which it is made.

(4)   Where paragraph (3) applies–

(a)   in a case where the liability in respect of which the rent allowance is paid is monthly, the authority may make payment at intervals of 1 month;

(b)   in a case where the authority is paying a rent allowance to a landlord in respect of more than one claimant, then the first such payment in respect of any claimant may be made to that landlord at such lesser interval as that authority considers is in the best interest of the efficient administration of housing benefit.

(5)   Except in a case to which paragraph (3) applies, where a person's weekly entitlement to a rent allowance is more than £2 he may require payment at two weekly intervals and the relevant authority shall pay at two weekly intervals in such a case.

(6)   Except in a case to which paragraph (3) applies, the relevant authority may pay a rent allowance at weekly intervals where either–

(a)   it considers that unless the rent allowance is paid at weekly intervals an overpayment is likely to occur; or

(b)   the person entitled is liable to pay his rent weekly and it considers that it is in his interest that his allowance be paid weekly.

(7)   Subject to paragraphs (2), (3) and (5), the relevant authority may pay a rent allowance to a student once a term.

Modifications

Reg 73 has effect as modified by Sch 3 para 7 HB&CTB(CP) Regs (see p1801) for some claimants entitled to and in receipt of HB in respect of their current home on 6 October 1996 and continuously since that date.

General Note

This regulation is identical to reg 92 HB Regs (see p569).

Payment on account of a rent allowance

74.–(1)   Where it is impracticable for the relevant authority to make a decision on a claim for a rent allowance within 14 days of the claim for it having been made and that impracticability does not arise out of the failure of the claimant, without good cause, to furnish such information, certificates, documents or evidence as the authority reasonably requires and has requested or which has been requested by the Secretary of State, the authority shall make a payment on account of any entitlement to a rent allowance of such amount as it considers reasonable having regard to–

(a)   such information which may at the time be available to it concerning the claimant's circumstances; and

(b)   any relevant determination made by a rent officer in exercise of the Housing Act functions.

(2)   The notice of award of any payment on account of a rent allowance made under paragraph (1) shall contain a notice to the effect that if on subsequent decision of the claim the person is not entitled to a rent allowance, or is entitled to an amount of rent allowance less than the amount of the payment on account, the whole of the amount paid on account or the excess of that amount over the entitlement to an allowance, as the case may be, will be recoverable from the person to whom the payment on account was made.

(3)   Where on the basis of the subsequent decision the amount of rent allowance payable differs from the amount paid on account under paragraph (1), future payments of rent allowance shall be increased or reduced to take account of any underpayment or, as the case may be, overpayment.

General Note

This regulation is identical to reg 93 HB Regs (see p571).

Payment to be made to a person entitled

75.–(1)   Subject to regulations 76 to 78 (payment to landlords, payment on death) and the following provisions of this regulation, payment of any rent allowance to which a person is entitled shall be made to that person.

(2)   Where a person other than a person who is entitled to a rent allowance made the claim and that first person is a person referred to in regulation 63(2), (3) or (5) (persons appointed to act for a person unable to act), payment may be made to that person.

(3)   A person entitled to a rent allowance, although able to act on his own behalf, may request in writing that the appropriate authority make payments to a person, who if a natural person must be aged 18 or more, nominated by him, and the authority may make payments to that person.

General Note

This regulation is identical to reg 94 HB Regs (see p572).

Circumstances in which payment is to be made to a landlord

76.–(1)   Subject to paragraph (2) and paragraph 8(4) of Schedule A1 (treatment of claims for housing benefit by refugees), a payment of rent allowance shall be made to a landlord (and in this regulation the "landlord" includes a person to whom rent is payable by the person entitled to that allowance)–

(a)   where under Regulations made under the Administration Act an amount of state pension credit payable to the claimant or his partner is being paid direct to the landlord; or

(b)   where sub-paragraph (a) does not apply and the person is in arrears of an amount equivalent to 8 weeks or more of the amount he is liable to pay his landlord as rent, except where it is in the overriding interest of the claimant not to make direct payments to the landlord.

(2)   Any payment of rent allowance made to a landlord pursuant to this regulation or to regulation 77 (circumstances in which payment may be made to a landlord) shall be to discharge, in whole or in part, the liability of the claimant to pay rent to that landlord in respect of the dwelling concerned, except in so far as–

(a)   the claimant had no entitlement to the whole or part of that rent allowance so paid to his landlord; and

(b)   the overpayment of rent allowance resulting was recovered in whole or in part from that landlord.

[¹ (2A)   In a case where–
(a)   a relevant authority has determined a maximum rent (LHA) in accordance with regulation 13D; and
(b)   the rent allowance exceeds the amount which the claimant is liable to pay his landlord by way of rent,
any payment of rent allowance made to a landlord pursuant to this regulation or to regulation 77 may include all or part of any amount by which the rent allowance exceeds the amount which the claimant is liable to pay his landlord as rent but shall not include any amount by which the rent allowance exceeds the amount which the claimant is liable to pay his landlord as rent and arrears of rent.]
(3)   Where the relevant authority is not satisfied that the landlord is a fit and proper person to be the recipient of a payment of rent allowance no such payment shall be made direct to him under paragraph (1).

Amendment

1.   Inserted by reg 17 (1) of SI 2007 No 2869 as from 7.4.08 (or if reg 1(5) of that SI applies, on the day on or after 7.4.08 when the first of the events specified in reg 1(6) applies, or from 6.4.09 if none have before that date).

General Note

This is the equivalent of reg 95 HB Regs (see p573), though here the authority is obliged to make direct payments to the landlord where direct payments of PC are being made towards arrears of rent.

Circumstances in which payment may be made to a landlord

77.–(1)   Subject to paragraph 8(4) of Schedule A1 (treatment of claims for housing benefit by refugees), where regulation 76 (circumstances in which payment is to be made to a landlord) does not apply but subject to [¹ paragraphs (3) and (3A)], a payment of a rent allowance may nevertheless be made to a person's landlord where–
(a)   the person has requested or consented to such payment;
(b)   payment to the landlord is in the interest of the claimant and his family;
(c)   the person has ceased to reside in the dwelling in respect of which the allowance was payable and there are outstanding payments of rent but any payment under this sub-paragraph shall be limited to an amount equal to the amount of rent outstanding.
(2)   Without prejudice to the power in paragraph (1), in any case where in the opinion of the authority–
(a)   the claimant has not already discharged his liability to pay his landlord for the period in respect of which any payment is to be made; and
(b)   it would be in the interests of the efficient administration of housing benefit,
a first payment of a rent allowance following the making of a decision on a claim, or a supersession under paragraph 4 of Schedule 7 to the Child Support, Pensions and Social Security Act 2000 may be made, in whole or in part, [²] to that landlord.
(3)   In a case where the relevant authority is not satisfied that the landlord is a fit and proper person to be the recipient of a claimant's rent allowance, the authority may either–
(a)   not make direct payments to the landlord in accordance with paragraph (1) [², (3A) or (3B)]; or
(b)   make such payments to the landlord where the authority is satisfied that it is nonetheless in the best interests of the claimant and his family that the payments be made.
[¹ (3A)   In a case where a relevant authority has determined a maximum rent in accordance with regulation 13D–
(a)   sub-paragraphs (a) and (b) of paragraph (1) shall not apply; and
(b)   payment of a rent allowance to a person's landlord may be made where–
(i)   the relevant authority considers that the claimant is likely to have difficulty in relation to the management of his financial affairs;
(ii)   the relevant authority considers that it is improbable that the claimant will pay his rent; or

      (iii)   a direct payment has previously been made by the relevant authority to the landlord in accordance with regulation 76 in respect of the current award of housing benefit. [³ or

      (iv)   the relevant authority considers that it will assist the claimant in securing or retaining a tenancy.]

    (3B)   Where the relevant authority suspects that the grounds in paragraph (3A)(b)(i) or (ii) apply and is considering whether to make payments on one of those grounds, it may make a payment of a rent allowance to the person's landlord for a period not exceeding 8 weeks.]

    [³ (4)   In this regulation–

"landlord" has the same meaning as in [⁴ regulation 76] and paragraph (2) of that regulation shall have effect for the purposes of this regulation; and

"tenancy" includes–

    (a)   in Scotland, any other right of occupancy; and

    (b)   in England and Wales, a licence to occupy premises.]

Modifications

Paras (1) and (3) amended and paras (3A) and (3B) inserted by reg 17(2) Housing Benefit (State Pension Credit) (Local Housing Allowance and Information Sharing) Amendment Regulations 2007 No.2869 as from 7 April 2008, save that for a person to whom reg 1(5) of those regulations applied (see p1814), the amendments came into force on the day on or after 7 April 2008 when the first of the events specified in reg 1(6) applied to her/him, or on 6 April 2009 if none had before that date.

Amendments

1.   Amended by reg 17(2) of SI 2007 No 2869 as from 7.4.08 (or if reg 1(5) of that SI applies, on the day on or after 7.4.08 when the first of the events specified in reg 1(6) applies, or from 6.4.09 if none have before that date).

2.   Amended by reg 3(7) of SI 2010 No 2449 as from 1.11.10.

3.   Amended by reg 3(8) of SI 2010 No 2835 as from 1.4.11.

4.   Amended by reg 20(9) of SI 2011 No 2425 as from 31.10.11.

General Note

This regulation is identical to reg 96 HB Regs (see p577).

Payment on death of the person entitled

78.–(1)   Subject to paragraphs (3) and (5) where the person entitled to an allowance has died the relevant authority shall make payment either to his personal representative or, where there is none, his next of kin if aged 16 or over.

    (2)   For the purposes of paragraph (1) "next of kin" means in England and Wales the persons who would take beneficially on an intestacy and in Scotland the persons entitled to the moveable estate on intestacy.

    (3)   A payment under paragraph (1) or (5) shall not be made unless the landlord, the personal representative or the next of kin, as the case may be, makes written application for the payment of any sum of benefit to which the deceased was entitled, and such written application is sent to or delivered to the relevant authority at its designated office within 12 months of the deceased's death or such longer period as the authority may allow in any particular case.

    (4)   The authority may dispense with strict proof of title of any person claiming under paragraph (3) and the receipt of such a person shall be a good discharge to the authority for any sum so paid.

    (5)   Subject to paragraph (3), where the relevant authority determines, before the death of the person first mentioned in paragraph (1), that a rent allowance was payable to his landlord in accordance with regulation 76 or 77, that authority shall pay to that landlord so much of that allowance as does not exceed the amount of rent outstanding at the date of the person's death.

General Note

This regulation is identical to reg 97 HB Regs (see p580).

Offsetting

79.–(1)   Where a person has been paid a sum of housing benefit under a decision which is subsequently revised or [¹ superseded or further revised or superseded], any sum paid in respect of a period covered by a subsequent decision shall be offset against arrears of entitlement under the subsequent decision except to the extent that the sum exceeds the arrears and shall be treated as properly paid on account of them.

(2)   Where an amount has been deducted under regulation 85(1) (sums to be deducted in calculating recoverable overpayments) an equivalent sum shall be offset against any arrears of entitlement under the subsequent decision except to the extent that the sum exceeds the arrears and shall be treated as properly paid on account of them.

(3)   No amount may be offset under paragraph (1) which has been determined to be an overpayment within the meaning of regulation 80 (meaning of overpayment).

Amendment
1.   Amended by reg 5(2)(b) of SI 2012 No 824 as from 17.4.12.

General Note
This regulation is identical to reg 98 HB Regs (see p581).

PART 12
Overpayments

Meaning of overpayment

80.   In this Part, "overpayment" means any amount which has been paid by way of housing benefit and to which there was no entitlement under these Regulations (whether on the initial decision [¹ or as subsequently revised or superseded or further revised or superseded]) and includes any amount paid on account under regulation 74 (payment on account of a rent allowance) which is in excess of the entitlement to housing benefit as subsequently decided.

Amendment
1.   Amended by reg 2 of SI 2005 No 2904 as amended by Sch 2 para 29 of SI 2006 No 217 as from 10.4.06.

Recoverable overpayments

81.–(1)   Any overpayment, except one to which paragraph (2) applies, shall be recoverable.

(2)   Subject to paragraph (4) this paragraph applies to an overpayment [¹ which arose in consequence of] an official error where the claimant or a person acting on his behalf or any other person to whom the payment is made could not, at the time of receipt of the payment or of any notice relating to that payment, reasonably have been expected to realise that it was an overpayment.

(3)   In paragraph (2), "overpayment [¹ which arose in consequence of] official error" means an overpayment caused by a mistake made whether in the form of an act or omission by–

(a)   the relevant authority;

(b)   an officer or person acting for that authority;

(c)   an officer of–
    (i)   the Department for Work and Pensions;
    (ii)   Revenue and Customs,
    acting as such; or

(d)   a person providing services to the Department for Work and Pensions or to the Commissioners for Her Majesty's Revenue and Customs,

where the claimant, a person acting on his behalf or any other person to whom the payment is made, did not cause or materially contribute to that mistake, act or omission.

(4)   Where in consequence of an official error, a person has been awarded a rent rebate to which he was not entitled or which exceeded the benefit to which he was entitled, upon the award being revised [¹ or superseded] any overpayment of benefit,

which remains credited to him by the relevant authority in respect of a period after the date on which the revision [¹ or supersession] took place, shall be recoverable.

Amendment

1.   Amended by reg 4 of SI 2005 No 2904 as amended by Sch 2 para 29 of SI 2006 No 217 as from 10.4.06.

Person from whom recovery may be sought

82.–(1)   For the purposes of section 75(3)(a) of the Administration Act (prescribed circumstances in which an amount recoverable shall not be recovered from the person to whom it was paid), the prescribed circumstance is–

(a)   housing benefit has been paid in accordance with regulation 76 (circumstances in which payment is to be made to the landlord) or regulation 77 (circumstances in which payment may be made to a landlord);

(b)   the landlord has notified the relevant authority or the Secretary of State in writing that he suspects that there has been an overpayment;

[¹ (bb) the relevant authority is satisfied that the overpayment did not occur as a result of any change of dwelling occupied by the claimant as his home;]

(c)   it appears to the relevant authority that, on the assumption that there has been an overpayment–

(i)   there are grounds for instituting proceedings against any person for an offence under section 111A or 112(1) of the Administration (dishonest or false representations for obtaining benefit); or

(ii)   there has been a deliberate failure to report a relevant change of circumstances contrary to the requirement of regulation 69 (duty to notify a change of circumstances) and the overpayment occurred as a result of that deliberate failure; and

(d)   the relevant authority is satisfied that the landlord–

(i)   has not colluded with the claimant so as to cause the overpayment;

(ii)   has not acted, or neglected to act, in such a way so as to contribute to the period, or the amount, of the overpayment.

[² [⁴ (2)   For the purposes of section 75(3)(b) of the Administration Act (recovery from such other person, as well as or instead of the person to whom the overpayment was made), where recovery of an overpayment is sought by a relevant authority–

(a)   subject to paragraph (1) and where sub-paragraph (b) or (c) does not apply, the overpayment is recoverable from the claimant as well as the person to whom the payment was made, if different;

(b)   in a case where an overpayment arose in consequence of a misrepresentation of or a failure to disclose a material fact (in either case, whether fraudulently or otherwise) by or on behalf of the claimant, or by or on behalf of any person to whom the payment was made, the overpayment is only recoverable from any person who misrepresented or failed to disclose that material fact instead of, if different, the person to whom the payment was made; or

(c)   in a case where an overpayment arose in consequence of an official error where the claimant, or a person acting on the claimant's behalf, or any person to whom the payment was paid, or any person acting on their behalf, could reasonably have been expected, at the time of receipt of the payment or of any notice relating to that payment, to realise that it was an overpayment, the overpayment is only recoverable from any such person instead of, if different, the person to whom the payment was made.]]

[³ (2A)   Where an overpayment is made in a case where a relevant authority has determined a maximum rent (LHA) in accordance with regulation 13D (determination of a maximum rent (LHA)), and the housing benefit payable exceeds the amount which the claimant is liable to pay his landlord by way of rent, the relevant authority must not recover from the landlord more than the landlord has received.]

(3)   For the purposes of [³ paragraphs (1) and (2A)], "landlord" shall have the same meaning as it has for the purposes of regulation 76.

[¹ (3A) For the purposes of [⁴ paragraph (2)(c)], "overpayment arose in consequence of an official error" shall have the same meaning as in regulation 81(3) above.]

[⁴ (4)]

Amendments

1.   Inserted by reg 6(2) and (4A) of SI 2005 No 2904 as amended by Sch 2 para 29 of SI 2006 No 217 as from 10.4.06.

2.   Substituted by reg 6(3) and (5) of SI 2005 No 2904 as amended by Sch 2 para 29 of SI 2006 No 217 as from 10.4.06.

3.   Amended by reg 3 of SI 2008 No 586 as from 7.4.08.

4.   Amended by reg 5(2) of SI 2008 No 2824 as from 6.4.09.

Method of recovery

83.–(1)   Without prejudice to any other method of recovery, [¹ a relevant authority] may recover a recoverable overpayment from any person referred to in regulation 82 (persons from whom recovery may be sought) by deduction from any housing benefit to which that person is entitled (including arrears of entitlement after offsetting under regulation 79 (offsetting)) or, where it is unable to do so, may request the Secretary of State to recover any recoverable overpayment from the benefits prescribed in [⁴ regulation 86(1)] (recovery of overpayments from prescribed benefits).

[⁴ (1ZA) Where an overpayment is recoverable from a claimant who has one or more partners, a relevant authority may recover the overpayment by deduction from any housing benefit payable to the claimant's partner, or where it is unable to do so, may request the Secretary of State to recover any recoverable overpayment from the benefits prescribed in regulation 86(1B) (recovery of overpayments from prescribed benefits), provided that the claimant and that partner were a couple both at the time of the overpayment and when the deduction is made.]

[² [⁵]]

(2)   Subject to paragraphs [² [⁵]] (4) and (5), where [¹ a relevant authority] makes deductions permitted by paragraph (1) [⁴ or (1ZA)] from the housing benefit it is paying to a claimant [⁴ or a claimant's partner] (other than deductions from arrears of entitlement), the deduction in respect of a benefit week shall be–

(a)   in a case to which paragraph (3) applies, not more than the amount there specified; and

(b)   in any other case, not more than 3 times five per cent. of the personal allowance for a single claimant aged not less than 25, that five per cent. being, where it is not a multiple of five pence, rounded to the next higher such multiple.

(3)   Where [¹ a relevant authority] makes deductions from housing benefit it is paying to a claimant [⁴ or a claimant's partner, where the claimant has], in respect of the whole or part of the recoverable overpayment–

(a)   been found guilty of an offence whether under a statute or otherwise;

(b)   made an admission after caution of deception or fraud for the purpose of obtaining relevant benefit; or

(c)   agreed to pay a penalty under section 115A of the Administration Act and the agreement has not been withdrawn,

the amount deducted under paragraph (2) shall be not more than [⁶ five times] five per cent. of the personal allowance for a single claimant aged not less than 25, [⁶ that five per cent. being, where it is not a multiple of 5 pence, rounded to the next higher such multiple].

(4)   Where, in the calculation of housing benefit, the amount of earnings or other income falling to be taken into account is reduced by reason of [³ paragraphs 2 to 5 and 7] of Schedule 4 (sums to be disregarded in the calculation of earnings) [⁵, or paragraph 5A of that Schedule in a case where the amount of earnings to be disregarded under that paragraph is the amount referred to in regulation 45(2) of the Employment and Support Allowance Regulations [⁷, regulation 39(1)(a) of the Employment and Support Allowance Regulations 2013] or regulation 17(2) of the Social Security (Incapacity for Work) (General) Regulations 1995,] or paragraph 1 of Schedule 5 (sums to be disregarded in the

calculation of income other than earnings), the deduction under paragraph (2) may be increased by not more than half the amount of the reduction.

(5)　　No deduction made under this regulation [² [⁵]] shall be applied so as to reduce the housing benefit in respect of a benefit week to less than 50 pence.

(6)　　In this regulation–
"admission after caution" means–

(i)　　in England and Wales, an admission after a caution has been administered in accordance with a Code issued under the Police and Criminal Evidence Act 1984;

(ii)　　in Scotland, admission after a caution has been administered, such admission being duly witnessed by two persons; and

"personal allowance for a single claimant aged not less than 25" means the amount specified in paragraph 1(1)(b) of column 2 of Schedule 3 to the Housing Benefit Regulations 2006 (applicable amounts).

(7)　　This regulation shall not apply in respect of an offence committed or an admission after caution or an agreement to pay a penalty made before 2nd October 2000.

Amendments

1.　　Substituted by reg 7(2) of SI 2005 No 2904 as amended by Sch 2 para 29 of SI 2006 No 217 as from 10.4.06.
2.　　Inserted by reg 7(3), (4) and (5) of SI 2005 No 2904 as amended by Sch 2 para 29 of SI 2006 No 217 as from 10.4.06.
3.　　Amended by reg 4(7) of SI 2008 No 1042 as from 19.5.08.
4.　　Amended by reg 5(3) of SI 2008 No 2824 as from 6.4.09.
5.　　Amended by reg 3(3) of SI 2009 No 2608 as from 1.4.10 (5.4.10 where rent payable weekly or in multiples of a week).
6.　　Amended by reg 3(2) of SI 2012 No 645 as from 1.4.12.
7.　　Amended by reg 36(6) of SI 2013 No 630 as from 29.4.13.

Diminution of capital

84.–(1)　　Where, in the case of a recoverable overpayment, in consequence of a misrepresentation or failure to disclose a material fact (in either case whether fraudulent or otherwise) as to a person's capital, or an error, other than one to which regulation 81(2) (effect of official error) refers, as to the amount of a person's capital, the overpayment was in respect of a period ("the overpayment period") of more than 13 benefit weeks, the relevant authority shall, for the purposes only of calculating the amount of that overpayment–

(a)　　at the end of the first 13 benefit weeks of the overpayment period, treat the amount of that capital as having been reduced by the amount of housing benefit overpaid during those 13 weeks;

(b)　　at the end of each subsequent period of 13 benefit weeks, if any, of the overpayment period, treat the amount of that capital as having been further reduced by the amount of housing benefit overpaid during the immediately preceding 13 benefit weeks.

(2)　　Capital shall not be treated as reduced over any period other than 13 benefit weeks or in any circumstances other than those for which paragraph (1) provides.

Sums to be deducted in calculating recoverable overpayments

85.–(1)　　Subject to paragraph (2), in calculating the amount of a recoverable overpayment, the relevant authority shall deduct any amount of housing benefit which should have been determined to be payable [² to the person from whom the overpayment is recoverable or their partner] in respect of the whole or part of the overpayment period–

(a)　　on the basis of the claim as presented to the authority;

(b)　　on the basis of the claim as it would have appeared had any misrepresentation or non-disclosure been remedied before the decision; or

(c)　　on the basis of the claim as it would have appeared if any change of circumstances [¹, except a change of the dwelling which the claimant occupies as his home,] had been notified at the time that change occurred.

(2)   In the case of rent rebate only, in calculating the amount of a recoverable overpayment the relevant authority may deduct so much of any payment by way of rent in respect of the overpayment period which exceeds the amount, if any, which the claimant was liable to pay for that period under the original erroneous determination.

Amendments
1.   Inserted by reg 8 of SI 2005 No 2904 as amended by Sch 2 para 29 of SI 2006 No 217 as from 10.4.06.
2.   Amended by reg 2(2) of SI 2012 No 645 as from 1.4.12.

[¹Sums to be deducted in calculating recoverable overpayments where the claimant has changed dwelling

85A.–(1)   This regulation applies where an overpayment has occurred in the following circumstances–
(a)   a claimant has moved from the dwelling previously occupied as his home ("dwelling A") to another dwelling which he occupies as his home ("dwelling B");
(b)   the claimant has been awarded housing benefit in the form of a rent allowance in respect of dwelling A to which he is not entitled because he is no longer occupying or treated as occupying dwelling A as his home;
(c)   housing benefit is paid to the same person in respect of the claimant's occupation of dwelling B as it was paid to in respect of dwelling A; and
(d)   the same relevant authority is responsible for paying the housing benefit in respect of dwelling A and dwelling B.

(2)   Where this regulation applies, in calculating the amount of the overpayment which is recoverable the relevant authority may at its discretion deduct an amount equal to the claimant's weekly entitlement to housing benefit in respect of dwelling B for the number of benefit weeks equal to the number of weeks during which the claimant was overpaid housing benefit in respect of dwelling A.

(3)   Where a sum has been deducted under paragraph (2), an equivalent sum shall be treated as having been paid in respect of the claimant's entitlement to housing benefit in respect of dwelling B for the number of benefit weeks equal to the number of weeks during which the claimant was overpaid housing benefit in respect of dwelling A.]

Amendment
1.   Inserted by reg 3(4) of SI 2009 No 2608 as from 1.4.10 (5.4.10 where rent payable weekly or in multiples of a week).

Recovery of overpayments from prescribed benefits

86.–(1)   [³ Subject to paragraph (1B),] For the purposes of section 75(4) of the Administration Act (recovery of overpaid housing benefit by deduction from other benefits), the benefits prescribed by this regulation are–
(a)   any benefit except guardian's allowance;
(b)   income support under Part 7 of the Act;
(c)   any benefit payable under the legislation of any member State other than the United Kingdom concerning the branches of social security mentioned in Article 4(1) of Regulation (EEC) No 1408/71 [⁶ ,as amended from time to time,] on the application of social security schemes to employed persons, to self-employed persons and to members of their families moving within the Community, [⁶ or in Article 3(1) of Regulation (EC) No 883/2004 of the European Parliament and of the Council of 29 April 2004, as amended from time to time, on the coordination of social security systems] whether or not the benefit has been acquired by virtue of the provisions of [⁶ either Regulation, as amended from time to time];
(d)   a jobseeker's allowance;
(e)   state pension credit.
[² (f)   an employment and support allowance.]
[⁴ (g)   personal independence payment.]
[⁵ (h)   universal credit.

[³ (1B)   For the purposes of section 75(4) of the Administration Act, where recovery is sought from the claimant's partner under regulation 83(1ZA), the benefits prescribed by this regulation are–
(a)   income support under Part 7 of the Act;
(b)   income-based jobseeker's allowance;
(c)   state pension credit; and
(d)   income-related employment and support allowance.]
[⁴ (e) personal independence payment.]
[⁵ (f) universal credit.]
[¹ (1A)   For the purposes of paragraph (1)(c) the term "member State" shall be understood to include Switzerland in accordance with and subject to the provisions of Annex II of the Agreement between the European Community and its Member States and the Swiss Confederation on the free movement of persons, signed at Brussels on 21st June 1999.]
[³ (2)   The Secretary of State shall, if requested to do so by an authority under regulation 83 (method of recovery), recover a recoverable overpayment by deduction from any of the benefits prescribed in paragraph (1) or (in the case of the claimant's partner) any of the benefits prescribed in paragraph (1B) provided that the Secretary of State is satisfied that–
(a)   a recoverable overpayment has been made in consequence of a misrepresentation of or a failure to disclose a material fact (in either case whether fraudulently or otherwise), by a claimant or any other person to whom a payment of housing benefit has been made; and
(b)   the person from whom it is sought to recover the overpayment is receiving sufficient amounts of any of the benefits prescribed in paragraph (1) or (1B) (as the case may be) to enable deductions to be made for the recovery of the overpayment.]
(2)   Where the Secretary of State is satisfied that–
(a)   a recoverable overpayment of housing benefit has been made, in consequence of a misrepresentation of or failure to disclose a material fact (in either case whether fraudulently or otherwise), by or on behalf of a claimant or any other person to whom a payment of housing benefit has been made; and
(b)   the person who misrepresented that fact or failed to disclose it is receiving a sufficient amount of one or more of the benefits prescribed in paragraph (1) to enable deductions to be made for the recovery of the overpayment,
he shall, if requested to do so by an authority under regulation 83 (method of recovery), recover the overpayment by deduction from any of those benefits.
(3)   In paragraph (1)(a), "benefit" has the meaning it has in section 122(1) of the Act.

Amendments

1.   Inserted by reg 9 of SI 2005 No 2904 as amended by Sch 2 para 29 of SI 2006 No 217 as from 10.4.06.
2.   Amended by reg 39 of SI 2008 No 1082 as from 27.10.08.
3.   Amended by reg 5(4) of SI 2008 No 2824 as from 6.4.09.
4.   Amended by ref 34(2) of SI 2013 No 384 as from 8.4.13.
5.   Amended by reg 34(2) of SI 2013 No 384 as from 29.4.13.
6.   Amended by reg 4 and Sch para 11 of SI 2018 No 1084 as from 15.11.18.

Prescribed benefits

87.–(1)   The benefits prescribed for the purposes of section 75(5) and (7) of the Administration Act (recovery of overpayments) are those set out in the following paragraphs.
(2)   Prescribed benefits within section 75(5)(a) of the Administration Act (benefits to which a landlord or agent is entitled) are–
(a)   housing benefit; and
(b)   those benefits prescribed from time to time in regulation 86(1) (recovery of overpayments from prescribed benefits), but only in cases where–

(i)   an authority has, pursuant to regulation 83 (method of recovery), requested the Secretary of State to recover an overpayment of housing benefit from such benefits; and

(ii)   the Secretary of State is satisfied as to the matters prescribed in paragraph (2)(a) and (b) of regulation 86.

(3)   Housing benefit is prescribed for the purposes of section 75(5)(b) or (c) of the Administration Act (benefits paid to a landlord or agent to discharge an obligation owed by another person).

(4)   Prescribed benefits within section 75(7) of the Administration Act (benefits recoverable from the county court or the sheriff court) are housing benefit and those benefits prescribed from time to time in regulation 86(1).

[¹ Recovery by deduction from earnings

87A.–(1)   Any overpayment which is recoverable by virtue of regulation 81 may be recovered by a relevant authority by deduction from the earnings of the person from whom it is recoverable.

(2)   Part 6 of the Social Security (Overpayments and Recovery) Regulations 2013 applies in relation to the recovery of overpayments by deduction from the earnings of a person specified in paragraph (1) by a relevant authority as it applies to the recovery of recoverable amounts by deduction from the earnings of persons under that Part of those Regulations by an appropriate authority.]

Amendment

1.   Inserted by reg 34(3) of SI 2013 No 384 as from 8.4.13.

Restrictions on recovery of rent and consequent notifications

88.–(1)   Where, pursuant to section 75(5)(b) of the Administration Act, an amount has been recovered by deduction from housing benefit paid to a person (referred to as "the landlord" in this regulation) to discharge (in whole or in part) an obligation owed to him by the person on whose behalf the recoverable amount was paid (referred to as "the tenant" in this regulation) that obligation shall, in a case to which paragraph (2) applies, be taken to be discharged by the amount of the deduction.

(2)   This paragraph applies in a case where the amount recoverable from the landlord relates to an overpayment of housing benefit in relation to which the landlord has–

(a)   agreed to pay a penalty pursuant to section 115A of the Administration Act (penalty as an alternative to prosecution); or

(b)   been convicted of an offence arising under the Act or any other enactment.

(3)   In any case to which paragraph (2) applies or will apply when recovery is made the authority that has determined that there is an overpayment and that it is recoverable from the landlord shall notify both the landlord and the tenant that–

(a)   the overpayment that it has recovered or that it has determined to recover ("the sum") is or will be one to which paragraph (2) applies; and

(b)   the landlord has no right in relation to that sum against the tenant, and that his obligation to the landlord shall be taken to be discharged by the amount so recovered.

PART 13
Information
SECTION 1
Claims and information

Interpretation

89.   In this Section–

[¹ "county council" means a county council in England, but only if the council has made an arrangement in accordance with regulation 64(5)(g) or 90(3);]

"local authority" means an authority administering housing benefit;

"relevant authority" means–

(a)   the Secretary of State;
(b)   a person providing services to the Secretary of State; [¹ or
(c)   a county council;]
"relevant information" means information or evidence relating to the administration of
        claims to or awards of housing benefit.

Amendment
1.   Amended by reg 8(3) of SI 2007 No 2911 as from 31.10.07.

[¹Collection of information

90.–(1)   The Secretary of State, or a person providing services to him, may receive
or obtain relevant information from–
(a)   persons making, or who have made, claims for housing benefit; or
(b)   other persons in connection with such claims.
(2)   In paragraph (1) references to persons who have made claims for housing benefit
include persons to whom awards of benefit have been made on those claims.
(3)   Where a county council has made an arrangement with a local authority, or a
person authorised to exercise any function of a local authority relating to housing benefit
[²], to receive and obtain information and evidence relating to claims for housing benefit,
the council may receive or obtain the information or evidence from–
(a)   persons making claims for housing benefit; or
(b)   other persons in connection with such claims.
(4)   A county council may receive information or evidence relating to an award of
housing benefit which is supplied by–
(a)   the person to whom the award has been made; or
(b)   other persons in connection with the award.]

Amendments
1.   Substituted by reg 8(4) of SI 2007 No 2911 as from 31.10.07.
2.   Amended by reg 3 and Sch 1 of SI 2013 No 458 as from 1.4.13.

[¹Verifying information

90A.   A relevant authority may verify relevant information supplied to, or obtained
by, the authority in accordance with regulation 90.]

Amendment
1.   Inserted by reg 8(5) of SI 2007 No 2911 as from 31.10.07.

[¹Recording and holding information

91.   A relevant authority which obtains relevant information or to whom such
information is supplied–
(a)   shall make a record of such information; and
(b)   may hold that information, whether as supplied or obtained or recorded, for the
        purpose of forwarding it to the person or authority for the time being
        administering housing benefit.]

Amendment
1.   Substituted by reg 8(6) of SI 2007 No 2911 as from 31.10.07.

Forwarding of information

92.   A relevant authority which holds relevant information–
(a)   shall forward it to the person or authority for the time being administering claims
        to or awards of housing benefit to which the relevant information relates, being
        either–
        (i)   a local authority;
        (ii)   a person providing services to a local authority; or
        (iii)   a person authorised to exercise any function of a local authority relating
                to housing benefit; and

[¹ (b) may, if the relevant authority is the Secretary of State or a person providing services to the Secretary of State, continue to hold a record of such information, whether as supplied or obtained or recorded, for such period as he considers appropriate.]

Amendment

1.   Substituted by reg 8(7) of SI 2007 No 2911 as from 31.10.07.

Request for information
93.   A relevant authority which holds information or evidence relating to social security matters shall forward such information or evidence as may be requested to the person or authority making that request, provided that–
- (a)   the request is made by–
  - (i)   a local authority;
  - (ii)   a person providing services to a local authority; or
  - (iii)   a person authorised to exercise any function of a local authority relating to housing benefit; and
- (b)   the information or evidence requested includes relevant information;
- (c)   the relevant authority is able to provide the information or evidence requested in the form in which it was originally supplied or obtained; and
- (d)   provision of the information or evidence requested is considered necessary by the relevant authority to the proper performance by a local authority of its functions relating to housing benefit.

SECTION 2
Evidence and Information

Interpretation
94.   In this Section–
"the notice" means the notice prescribed in regulation 99(1)(b) (circumstances for requiring information);
"relevant information" means such information as is prescribed in regulation 100 (relevant information);
"the requirer" means a person within regulation 98 (requiring information from landlords and agents), who requires information pursuant to that regulation;
"the supplier" means an appropriate person who is required, pursuant to regulations 98 and 99, to supply relevant information and any person who is not so required is not, for the purpose of supplying information pursuant to section 126A of the Administration Act and these Regulations, an appropriate person.

[¹ Information to be provided to rent officers
95A.–(1)   This paragraph applies to every claim for or award of housing benefit in the form of a rent allowance where the eligible rent has been, or is to be determined, in accordance with–
- (a)   regulation 12(3)(a) (rent) or 12C (eligible rent and maximum rent), as the case may require;
- (b)   regulation 12A (eligible rent and the maximum rent (LHA)) or any of regulations 12E to 12K (transitional protection for pathfinder cases), as the case may require; or
- (c)   regulations 12 (rent) and 13 (maximum rent) as set out in paragraph 5 of Schedule 3 to the Consequential Provisions Regulations.

(2)   No earlier than the first, and no later than the fifth, working day of every month a relevant authority shall provide the following information to the rent officer in relation to every claim for or award of housing benefit to which paragraph (1) applied in the preceding month–
- (a)   the address, including any room or unit number, house or flat number or name, and the postcode of the dwelling to which the claim or award relates;

(b)   where the claim or award relates to mooring charges for a houseboat, or payments in respect of the site on which a caravan or mobile home stands, the mooring or plot number and the address of the mooring or site, including the postcode;

(c)   the date on which the tenancy began;

(d)   the amount of rent and the rental period, whether calendar monthly, four weekly, weekly or some other period;

(e)   where the claimant has the use of two or more bedrooms, the number of bedrooms and rooms suitable for living in that there are in the dwelling, and in this sub-paragraph "bedroom" does not include a bedroom which the claimant shares with any person other than a member of his household, a non-dependant of his, or a person who pays rent to him or his partner;

(f)   whether the tenant (together with his partner where he has one) has exclusive use of only one bedroom, and if so, whether they have exclusive use of a kitchen, bathroom, toilet and a room suitable for living in;

(g)   whether the tenant has exclusive use of only one bedroom, and if so, which, if any, of the following the tenancy provides for him to share–
    (i)   a kitchen;
    (ii)   a bathroom;
    (iii)   a toilet; or
    (iv)   a room suitable for living in;

(h)   the date on which entitlement to housing benefit began; and

(i)   where applicable, the date on which entitlement to housing benefit ended.

(3)   Where the relevant authority is required to apply to the rent officer for a board and attendance determination by virtue of regulation 13D(10) (determination of a maximum rent (LHA)), it shall provide the following information in the application to the Rent Officer–

(a)   the address, including any room or unit number, house or flat number or name and the postcode of the dwelling to which the claim or award relates;

(b)   the date on which the tenancy began;

(c)   the length of the tenancy;

(d)   the total amount of those payments referred to in regulation 12(1) (rent) which the claimant is liable to make in respect of the dwelling which he occupies as his home;

(e)   whether those payments include any charges for water, sewerage or allied environmental services or charges in respect of meals or fuel which are ineligible for housing benefit; and

(f)   where those payments include any charges that are ineligible for housing benefit by reason of paragraph 1(a)(iv) and (c) to (f) of Schedule 1 (ineligible service charges), that such charges are included, and the value of those charges as determined by that authority pursuant to regulation 12B(2) and that Schedule.

(4)   where the relevant authority has identified charges to which paragraph (3)(f) applies, it shall–

(a)   deduct those charges from the total amount of those payments which, in accordance with paragraph (3)(d), it has stated that the claimant is liable to make in respect of the dwelling which he occupies as his home; and

(b)   notify that total so reduced to the rent officer in its application.

(5)   Where a relevant authority has received notification from the rent officer that a substantial part of the rent is attributable to board and attendance, it shall provide the information referred to in paragraphs (7) and (8), except for such information as it has already provided in accordance with paragraphs (3) and (4).

(6)   Where the relevant authority is required to apply to the rent officer for a determination by virtue of regulation 14(1) (requirement to refer to rent officers), it shall provide the information referred to in paragraphs (7) to (9) in the application to the rent officer.

(7)   In relation to the dwelling to which the claim or award relates, the relevant authority shall provide the following information–

(a)   the address, including any room or unit number, house or flat number or name and the postcode of the dwelling;

(b)   where the claim or award relates to mooring charges for a houseboat, or payments in respect of the site on which a caravan or mobile home stands, the mooring or plot number and the address of the mooring or site, including the postcode;

(c)   whether the dwelling is–
    (i)   a detached house;
    (ii)   a semi-detached house;
    (iii)   a terraced house;
    (iv)   a maisonette;
    (v)   a detached bungalow;
    (vi)   a semi-detached bungalow;
    (vii)   a flat in a house;
    (viii) a flat in a block;
    (ix)   a flat over a shop;
    (x)   a bedsit or rooms or a studio flat;
    (xi)   a hostel;
    (xii)   a caravan, mobile home or houseboat;
    (xiii) board and lodgings;
    (xiv) a hotel;
    (xv)   a care home;
    (xvi) an independent hospital; or
    (xvii) some other description of dwelling, and if so what;

(d)   whether the dwelling has central heating, a garden, a garage or a parking space;

(e)   how many rooms suitable for living in there are–
    (i)   in the dwelling;
    (ii)   in the dwelling which the claimant shares with any person other than a member of his household, a non-dependant of his, or a person who pays rent to him or his partner;

(f)   how many bedsitting rooms there are in the categories (e)(i) and (ii);

(g)   how many bedrooms there are in the categories (e)(i) and (ii);

(h)   how many bathrooms or toilets there are in the categories (e)(i) and (ii); and

(i)   such other information as the rent officer may reasonably require to make a determination.

(8)   In relation to the tenancy to which the claim or award relates, the relevant authority shall provide the following information–

(a)   the information referred to in paragraphs (3)(d) to (f) and (4);

(b)   if the tenancy is furnished, and if so, to what extent;

(c)   the rental period, whether calendar monthly, four weekly, weekly or some other period;

(d)   the length of the tenancy;

(e)   when the tenancy began and, if appropriate, when it ended;

(h)   the landlord's or letting agent's name;

(i)   the landlord's or letting agent's business address;

(j)   whether the landlord is a housing association [², private registered provider of social housing] or registered social landlord; and

(k)   such other information as the rent officer may reasonably require to make a determination.

(9)   In relation to the claimant and the other occupiers of the dwelling to which the claim or award relates, the relevant authority shall provide the following information–

(a)   such information regarding the relationship of the claimant to the occupiers and the occupiers to each other, as is necessary for the rent officer to make the determination;

(b)   the age and sex of each occupier under 18;

[³ (ba) whether [⁴ any person mentioned in regulation 13D(3A)(a)] is a person who requires overnight care;] and

(c) any other information that is relevant to the rent officer in making the determination, including visits to the dwelling.

(10) Where a rent officer serves a notice under article 5 (insufficient information) of the Rent Officers Order the relevant authority shall supply the further information required under this regulation, or confirm whether information already supplied is correct and, if it is not, supply the correct information.

(11) Where the relevant authority refers a case to the rent officer in accordance with regulation 14 as in force before the coming into force of regulation 8 of the Housing Benefit (State Pension Credit) (Local Housing Allowance and Information Sharing) Amendment Regulations 2007, it shall notify the rent officer that the referral is made in accordance with regulation 14 as in force before the coming into force of regulation 8 of those Regulations.

(12) In this regulation–
"tenancy" includes–
(a) in Scotland, any other right of occupancy; and
(b) in any other case, a licence to occupy premises,
and reference to a tenant, landlord or any other expression appropriate to a tenancy shall be construed accordingly;
"working day" means any day other than a Saturday, a Sunday, Christmas Day, Good Friday or a day which is a bank holiday under the Banking and Financial Dealings Act 1971 in the jurisdiction in which the area of the relevant authority is situated.]

Amendments
1. Inserted by reg 3(2) of SI 2007 No 2869 as from 7.4.08.
2. Amended by art 4 and Sch 1 para 59 of SI 2010 No 671 as from 1.4.10.
3. Inserted by reg 3(9) of SI 2010 No 2835 as from 1.4.11.
4. Amended by reg 5(4) of SI 2017 No 213 as from 1.4.17.

General Note
Reg 5(2)(b) Housing benefit (Local Housing Allowance, Information Sharing and Miscellaneous) Amendment Regulations 2008 SI No.586 says to amend "regulation 114A" inserted by reg 3 Housing Benefit (State Pension Credit) (Local Housing Allowance and Information Sharing) Regulations 2007 SI No.2869. However, reg 3 inserted this regulation (reg 95A). Reg 5(2)(b) says: "in paragraph (1)(b) of the inserted regulation 114A for "regulation 12A" substitute "regulation 12D"".

[¹ **Evidence and information required by rent officers**
95.]

Amendment
1. Omitted by reg 3(3) of SI 2007 No 2869 as from 7.4.08.

[¹**Information to be supplied by an authority to another authority**
96.–(1) This regulation applies for the purposes of section 128A of the Administration Act (duty of an authority to disclose information to another authority).

(2) Information is to be disclosed by one authority to another where–
(a) there is a mover who is or was in receipt of housing benefit from Authority "A";
(b) either the mover's new dwelling is within the area of another Authority "B" or the mover is liable or treated as liable to make payments in respect of the new dwelling to housing authority B; and
(c) the mover is entitled to an extended payment in accordance with regulation 72 of the Housing Benefit Regulations 2006.

(3) Authority A shall disclose to Authority B–
(a) the amount of the extended payment calculated in accordance with regulation 72C(2) of the Housing Benefit Regulations 2006 (amount of extended payment – movers);
(b) the date that entitlement to the extended payment will commence or has commenced;

(c)   the date that entitlement to the extended payment ceased or will cease;

(d)   the date of the move from Authority A to Authority B;

(e)   where the extended payment will be paid by Authority A to Authority B in accordance with regulation 72C(3)(a) of the Housing Benefit Regulations 2006 (payment of extended payment to the second authority)–

    (i)   the amount that Authority A will pay to Authority B in accordance with that paragraph; and

    (ii)   any other information required by Authority B to enable Authority A to make the payment in accordance with that paragraph; and

(f)   if any deduction was being made in respect of a recoverable overpayment.

(4)   Authority B shall disclose to Authority A–

(a)   if a mover's liability to make payments for the new dwelling is to Authority B; and

(b)   where the extended payment will be paid by Authority A to Authority B in accordance with regulation 72C(3)(a) of the Housing Benefit Regulations 2006–

    (i)   any information required by Authority A to enable Authority A to make the payment in accordance with that paragraph; and

    (ii)   the date on which Authority B receives any such payment.]

Amendment

1.   Substituted by reg 5(3) of SI 2008 No 959 as from 6.10.08.

[¹Supply of information – extended payments (qualifying contributory benefits)

97.–(1)   This regulation applies for the purposes of section 122E(3) of the Administration Act (duty of an authority to supply information to another authority).

(2)   Information must be disclosed by one authority to another where–

(a)   there is a mover who is or was in receipt of housing benefit from Authority "A";

(b)   either the mover's new dwelling is within the area of another Authority "B" or the mover is liable or treated as liable to make payments in respect of the new dwelling to housing authority B; and

(c)   the mover is entitled to an extended payment (qualifying contributory benefits) in accordance with regulation 53 of these Regulations or regulation 73 of the Housing Benefit Regulations 2006.

(3)   Authority A shall disclose to Authority B–

(a)   the amount of the extended payment (qualifying contributory benefits) calculated in accordance with regulation 53C(2) of these Regulations or regulation 73C(2) of the Housing Benefit Regulations 2006 (amount of extended payment – movers);

(b)   the date that entitlement to the extended payment will commence or has commenced;

(c)   the date that entitlement to the extended payment ceased or will cease;

(d)   the date of the move from Authority A to Authority B;

(e)   where the extended payment will be paid by Authority A to Authority B in accordance with regulation 53C(3)(a) of these Regulations or regulation 73C(3)(a) of the Housing Benefit Regulations 2006 (payment of the extended payment to the second authority)–

    (i)   the amount that Authority A will pay to Authority B in accordance with that paragraph; and

    (ii)   any other information required by Authority B to enable Authority A to make the payment in accordance with that paragraph; and

(f)   if any deduction was being made in respect of a recoverable overpayment.

(4)   Authority B shall disclose to Authority A–

(a)   if a mover's liability to make payments for the new dwelling is to Authority B; and

(b)   where the extended payment will be paid by Authority A to Authority B in accordance with regulation 53C(3)(a) of these Regulations or regulation 73C(3)(a) of the Housing Benefit Regulations 2006–

      (i)   any information required by Authority A to enable Authority A to make the payment in accordance with that paragraph; and

      (ii)   the date on which Authority B receives any such payment.]

Amendment

1.   Substituted by reg 5(3) of SI 2008 No 959 as from 6.10.08.

Requiring information from landlords and agents

98.   Pursuant to section 126A of the Administration Act, where a claim is made to an authority, on which a rent allowance may be awarded, then, in the circumstances prescribed in regulation 99 (circumstances for requiring information), that authority, or any person authorised to exercise any function of the authority relating to housing benefit, may require an appropriate person to supply to that authority or person relevant information, in the manner prescribed in regulation 101 (manner of supply of information).

Circumstances for requiring information

99.–(1)   A person is required to supply information in the following circumstances–

  (a)   he is an appropriate person in relation to any dwelling in respect of which–

      (i)   housing benefit is being paid to an appropriate person pursuant to regulation 76 or 77 (circumstances in which payment is to be or may be made to a landlord); or

      (ii)   a request has been made by an appropriate person or by the claimant for housing benefit to be so paid; and

  (b)   the requirer serves upon that appropriate person, whether by post or otherwise, a written notice stating that the requirer–

      (i)   suspects that there is or may be an impropriety in relation to a claim in respect of any dwelling wherever situated in relation to which he is an appropriate person; or

      (ii)   is already investigating an allegation of impropriety in relation to that person.

  (2)   Information required to be supplied under paragraph (1) shall be supplied to the requirer at the address specified in the notice.

Relevant information

100.–(1)   The information the supplier is to supply to the requirer is that prescribed in paragraphs (2) and (3) (referred to in this Part as "the relevant information").

  (2)   For a supplier who falls within paragraph (4) or section 126A(2)(b) of the Administration Act ("the landlord"), the information is–

  (a)   where the landlord is a natural person–

      (i)   his appropriate details;

      (ii)   the relevant particulars of any residential property in which he has an interest; and

      (iii) the appropriate details of any body corporate, in which he is a major shareholder or of which he is a director and which has an interest in residential property;

  (b)   where the landlord is a trustee, except a trustee of a charity, in addition to any information that he is required to supply in accordance with sub-paragraph (a) or (c), as the case may be, the relevant particulars of any residential property held by the trust of which he is a trustee and the name and address of any beneficiary under the trust or the objects of that trust, as the case may be;

  (c)   where the landlord is a body corporate or otherwise not a natural person, other than a charity–

      (i)   its appropriate details;

      (ii)   the relevant particulars of any residential property in which it has an interest;

      (iii) the names and addresses of any directors of it;

      (iv) the appropriate details of any person–

       (aa)   who owns 20 per cent. or more of it; or

       (bb)   of whom it owns 20 per cent. or more; and

   (v)   the names and addresses of its major shareholders;

(d)   where the landlord is a charity or is a recognised body the appropriate details relating to the landlord and particulars of the landlord's registration as a charity.

(3)   For a supplier who falls within section 126A(2)(c) of the Administration Act or paragraph (5) ("the agent"), the information is–

(a)   the name and address of any person ("his principal")–

   (i)   to whom the agent has agreed to make payments in consequence of being entitled to receive relevant payments; or

   (ii)   for whom the agent is acting on behalf of or in connection with any aspect of the management of a dwelling,

   as the case may be;

(b)   the relevant particulars of any residential property in respect of which the agent–

   (i)   has agreed to make payments in consequence of being entitled to receive relevant payments; or

   (ii)   is acting on behalf of his principal in connection with any aspect of its management;

(c)   where the agent is a natural person–

   (i)   the relevant particulars of any residential property in which he has an interest;

   (ii)   the appropriate details of any body corporate or any person not a natural person, in which he is a major shareholder or of which he is a director and which has any interest in residential property; or

(d)   where the agent is a body corporate or other than a natural person–

   (i)   the relevant particulars of any residential property in which it has an interest;

   (ii)   the names and addresses of any directors of or major shareholders in the agent; and

   (iii)   the appropriate details of any person–

       (aa)   who owns 20 per cent. or more of the agent; or

       (bb)   of whom the agent owns 20 per cent. or more.

(4)   A supplier falls within this paragraph (landlord receiving rent), if he falls within section 126A(2)(a) of the Administration Act, but does not fall within paragraph (5).

(5)   A supplier falls within this paragraph (agent receiving the rent), if he falls within subsection (2)(a) of section 126A of the Administration Act and has agreed to make payments, in consequence of being entitled to receive relevant payments, to a person falling within subsection (2)(b) of that section.

(6)   For the purposes of this regulation–

"appropriate details" means the name of the person and (in the case of a company) its registered office and, in any case, the full postal address, including post code, of the principal place of business of that person and the telephone and facsimile number (if any) of that place;

"charity" means a charity which is registered under section 3 of the Charities Act 1993 and is not an exempt charity within the meaning of that Act;

"major shareholder" means, where a body corporate is a company limited by shares, any person holding one tenth or more of the issued shares in that company and, in any other case, all the owners of that body;

"recognised body" has the same meaning as in section 1(7) of the Law Reform (Miscellaneous Provisions) (Scotland) Act 1990;

"relevant particulars" means the full postal address, including post code, and number of current lettings of or within that residential property and, if that property includes two or more dwellings, that address and the number of such lettings for each such dwelling;

"residential property" includes any premises, situated within the United Kingdom–

   (i)   used or which has, within the last six months, been used; or

(ii)   which may be used or is adapted for use,

as residential accommodation,

and other expressions used in this regulation and also in the Companies Act 1985 shall have the same meaning in this regulation as they have in that Act.

Manner of supply of information

101.–(1)   Subject to paragraph (2), the relevant information shall be supplied–

(a)   in typewritten or printed form; or

(b)   with the written agreement of the inquirer, in electronic or handwritten form,

within a period of 4 weeks commencing on the date on which the notice was sent or given.

(2)   Where–

(a)   within a period of 4 weeks commencing on the date on which the notice was sent or given, the supplier requests that the time for the supply of the relevant information be extended; and

(b)   the requirer provides written agreement to that request,

the time for the supply of the relevant information shall be extended to a period of 8 weeks commencing on the date on which the notice was sent or given.

Criminal offence

[¹**102.**   Any supplier who fails to supply relevant information to the requirer as, when and how required under regulations 98 to 101 shall be guilty of an offence under section 113 of the Administration Act.]

Amendment

1.   Substituted by reg 3(9) of SI 2008 No 2299 as from 1.10.08.

[¹ Supply of benefit administration information between authorities

102A.–(1)   For the purpose of section 122E(3) of the Administration Act (supply of information between authorities administering benefit) the circumstances in which information is to be supplied and the information to be supplied are set out in paragraph (2).

(2)   Where the functions of an authority ("Authority A") relating to housing benefit are being exercised, wholly or in part, by another authority ("Authority B")–

(a)   Authority A must supply to Authority B any benefit administration information it holds which is relevant to, and necessary for, Authority B to exercise those functions; and

(b)   Authority B must supply to Authority A any benefit administration information it holds which is relevant to, and necessary for, Authority A to exercise those functions.

(3)   The circumstances in which paragraph (2) applies include cases where the authorities have agreed to discharge functions jointly.

(4)   In paragraph (2), "Authority A" and "Authority B" include any person authorised to exercise functions relating to housing benefit on behalf of the authority in question.

(5)   This regulation shall not apply if the person or authority to whom the information is to be supplied agrees that the information need not be supplied.]

Amendment

1.   Inserted by reg 3(10) of SI 2008 No 2299 as from 1.10.08.

[¹ PART 14
Former pathfinder authorities

Modifications in respect of former pathfinder authorities

103.–(1)   In this regulation and in Schedule 9, "former pathfinder authority" means a relevant authority specified in Part 1 of that Schedule.

(2)   The provisions of Part 2 of Schedule 9 apply in relation to the area of a former pathfinder authority.]

Amendment
1.   Substituted by reg 20 of SI 2007 No 2869 as from 7.4.08.

[¹ SCHEDULE A1]
Treatment of claims for housing benefit by refugees

Modifications
Sch A1 was inserted by Sch 4 para 2(2) as modified by Sch 4 para 2(3) HB&CTB(CP) Regs in respect of claims for HB by some refugees. Sch A1 was further modifed by Sch 4 para 4(2) and (3) for some HB claimants who were refugees who claimed asylum on or before 2 April 2000.

Amendment
1.   Lapsed by s12(2)(e) of the Asylum and Immigration (Treatment of Claimants, etc) Act 2004 (for those recorded as refugees after 14.6.07).

SCHEDULE 1

REGULATION 11

Ineligible service charges

PART 1
Service charges other than for fuel

Ineligible service charges
1.   The following service charges shall not be eligible to be met by housing benefit–
(a)   charges in respect of day-to-day living expenses including, in particular, all provision of–
    (i)   subject to paragraph 2 meals (including the preparation of meals or provision of unprepared food);
    (ii)   laundry (other than the provision of premises or equipment to enable a person to do his own laundry);
    [¹ (iii)   leisure items such as either sports facilities (except a children's play area), or television rental, licence and subscription fees (except radio relay charges and charges made in respect of the conveyance and installation and maintenance of equipment for the conveyance of a television broadcasting service);]
    (iv)   cleaning of rooms and windows except cleaning of–
        (aa)   communal areas; or
        (bb)   the exterior of any windows where neither the claimant nor any member of his household is able to clean them himself,
where a payment is not made in respect of such cleaning by a local authority (including, in relation to England, a county council) or the [² Welsh Ministers] to the claimant or his partner, or to another person on their behalf; and
    (v)   transport;
(b)   charges in respect of–
    (i)   the acquisition of furniture or household equipment; and
    (ii)   the use of such furniture or equipment where that furniture or household equipment will become the property of the claimant by virtue of an agreement with the landlord;
(c)   charges in respect of the provision of an emergency alarm system;
(d)   charges in respect of medical expenses (including the cost of treatment or counselling related to mental disorder, mental handicap, physical disablement or past or present alcohol or drug dependence);
(e)   charges in respect of the provision of nursing care or personal care (including assistance at meal-times or with personal appearance or hygiene);
(f)   charges in respect of general counselling or of any other support services, whoever provides those services;
(g)   charges in respect of any services not specified in sub-paragraphs (a) to (f) which are not connected with the provision of adequate accommodation.

Amendments
1.   Substituted by reg 7(3) of SI 2007 No 719 as from 2.4.07.
2.   Amended by reg 6(7) of SI 2008 No 3157 as from 5.1.09.

Amount ineligible for meals

2.–(1)   Where a charge for meals is ineligible to be met by housing benefit under paragraph 1, the amount ineligible in respect of each week shall be the amount specified in the following provisions of this paragraph.

(2)   Subject to sub-paragraph (4), where the charge includes provision for at least three meals a day, the amount shall be–

(a)   for a single claimant, [¹³ £28.55];

(b)   if the claimant is a member of a family–

    (i)   for the claimant and for each member of his family aged 16 or over, [¹³ £28.55];

    (ii)   for each member of his family under age 16, [¹³ £14.50].

(3)   Except where sub-paragraph (5) applies and subject to sub-paragraph (4), where the charge includes provision for less than three meals a day, the amount shall be–

(a)   for a single claimant, [¹³ £19.05];

(b)   if the claimant is a member of a family–

    (i)   for the claimant and for each member of his family aged 16 or over, [¹³ £19.05];

    (ii)   for each member of his family under age 16, [¹³ £9.55].

(4)   For the purposes of sub-paragraphs (2)(b) and (3)(b), a person attains the age of 16 on the first Monday in September following his 16th birthday.

(5)   Where the charge for meals includes the provision of breakfast only, the amount for the claimant and, if he is a member of a family, for the claimant and for each member of his family, shall be [¹³ £3.55].

(6)   Where a charge for meals includes provision for meals for a person who is not a member of the claimant's family sub-paragraphs (2) to (5) shall apply as if that person were a member of the claimant's family.

(7)   For the avoidance of doubt where the charge does not include provision for meals for a claimant or, as the case may be, a member of his family, sub-paragraphs (2) to (5) shall not apply in respect of that person.

Amendments

1.   Amended by art 19(4) of SI 2006 No 645 and reg 8 of SI 2006 No 217 as from 1.4.06 (3.4.06 where rent payable weekly or at intervals of a week).

2.   Amended by art 20(4) of SI 2007 No 688 as from 1.4.07 (2.4.07 where rent payable weekly or at intervals of a week).

3.   Amended by art 20(5) of SI 2008 No 632 as from 1.4.08 (7.4.08 where rent payable weekly or in multiples of a week).

4.   Amended by art 20(5) of SI 2009 No 497 as from 1.4.09 (6.4.09 where rent payable weekly or at intervals of a week).

5.   Amended by art 20(4) of SI 2010 No 793 as from 1.4.10 (5.4.10 where rent payable weekly or in multiples of a week).

6.   Amended by art 21(4) of SI 2011 No 821 as from 1.4.11 (4.4.11 where rent payable weekly or in multiples of a week).

7.   Amended by art 21(4) of SI 2012 No 780 as from 1.4.11 (2.4.11 where rent payable weekly or in multiples of a week).

8.   Amended by art 20(4) of SI 2013 No 574 as from 1.4.13.

9.   Amended by art 18(4) of SI 2014 No16 as from 1.4.14 (7.4.14 where rent payable weekly or in multiples of a week).

10.   Amended by art 18(4) of SI 2015 No 547 as from 1.4.15 (6.4.15 where rent payable weekly or in multiples of a week).

11.   Amended by art 23(4) of SI 2017 No 260 as from 1.4.17 (3.4.17 where rent payable weekly or in multiples of a week).

12.   Amended by art 24(4) of SI 2018 No 281 as from 1.4.18 (2.4.18 where rent payable weekly or in multiples of a week).

13.   Amended by art 24(4) of SI 2019 No 480 as from 1.4.19.

Amount of ineligible charges

3.–(1)   Subject to paragraph 2 where an ineligible service charge is not separated from or separately identified within other payments made by the occupier in respect of the dwelling, the appropriate authority shall apportion such charge as is fairly attributable to the provision of that service, having regard to the cost of comparable services and such portion of those payments shall be ineligible to be met by housing benefit.

(2)   Subject to paragraph 2, where the relevant authority considers that the amount of any ineligible service charge which is separately identified within other payments made by the occupier in respect of the dwelling is unreasonably low having regard to the service provided, it shall substitute a sum for the charge in question which it considers represents the value of the services concerned and the amount so substituted shall be ineligible to be met by housing benefit.

(3)   In sub-paragraph (2) the expression "ineligible service charge" includes any service charge which does not qualify as a periodical payment under regulation 12(1)(e) (rent).

(4)   In any other case, the whole amount of the ineligible service charge shall be ineligible to be met by housing benefit.

Excessive service costs

4. Subject to paragraph 2, where the relevant authority considers that the amount of a service charge to which regulation 12(1)(e) (rent) applies is excessive in relation to the service provided for the claimant or his family, having regard to the cost of comparable services, it shall make a deduction from that charge of the excess and the amount so deducted shall be ineligible to be met by housing benefit.

PART 2
Payments in respect of fuel charges

5. A service charge for fuel except a charge in respect of services for communal areas shall be ineligible to be met by housing benefit.

6.–(1) Where a charge is ineligible to be met by housing benefit under paragraph 5–

(a) in the calculation of entitlement to a rent rebate; or

(b) in the calculation of entitlement to a rent allowance if the amount of the charge is specified or is otherwise readily identifiable (except where the amount of the charge is unrealistically low in relation to the fuel provided or the charge cannot readily be distinguished from a charge for a communal area),

the amount ineligible to be met by housing benefit shall be the full amount of the service charge.

(2) In any other case, subject to sub-paragraphs (3) and (4) and paragraph 7, the amount ineligible to be met by housing benefit shall be the following amounts in respect of each week–

(a) for heating (other than hot water) [¹⁴ £32.70];

(b) for hot water [¹⁴ £3.80];

(c) for lighting [¹⁴ £2.60];

(d) for cooking [¹⁴ £3.80].

(3) Where the accommodation occupied by the claimant or, if he is a member of a family, by the claimant and the members of his family, consists of one room only, the amount ineligible to be met by housing benefit in respect of each week where heating only is, or heating and either hot water or lighting (or both) are, provided, shall be one-half of the aggregate of the amounts specified in sub-paragraphs (2)(a), (b) and (c).

(4) In a case to which sub-paragraph (2) or (3) applies, if a claimant provides evidence on which the actual or approximate amount of the service charge for fuel may be estimated, the amount ineligible to be met by housing benefit under this paragraph shall be that estimated amount.

Amendments

1. Amended by art 19(5) of SI 2006 No 645 and reg 8 of SI 2006 No 217 as from 1.4.06 (3.4.06 where rent payable weekly or at intervals of a week).
2. Amended by art 20(5) of SI 2007 No 688 as from 1.4.07 (2.4.07 where rent payable weekly or at intervals of a week).
3. Confirmed by art 20(6) of SI 2008 No 632 as from 1.4.08 (7.4.08 where rent payable weekly or in multiples of a week).
4. Amended by art 20(6) of SI 2009 No 497 as from 1.4.09 (6.4.09 where rent payable weekly or at intervals of a week).
5. Confirmed by art 20(5) of SI 2010 No 793 as from 1.4.10 (5.4.10 where rent payable weekly or in multiples of a week).
6. Confirmed by art 21(5) of SI 2011 No 821 as from 1.4.11 (4.4.11 where rent payable weekly or in multiples of a week).
7. Amended by art 21(5) of SI 2012 No 780 as from 1.4.11 (2.4.11 where rent payable weekly or in multiples of a week).
8. Amended by art 20(5)(a) of SI 2013 No 574 as from 1.4.13.
9. Confirmed by art 20(5)(b) and (c) of SI 2013 No 574 as from 1.4.13.
10. Amended by art 18(5) of SI 2014 No 16 as from 1.4.14 (7.4.14 where rent payable weekly or in multiples of a week).
11. Amended by art 18(5) of SI 2015 No 547 as from 1.4.15 (6.4.15 where rent payable weekly or in multiples of a week).
12. Confirmed by art 23(5) of SI 2017 No 260 as from 1.4.17 (3.4.17 where rent payable weekly or in multiples of a week).
13. Amended by art 24(5) of SI 2018 No 281 as from 1.4.18 (2.4.18 where rent payable weekly or in multiples of a week).
14. Amended by art 24(5) of SI 2019 No 480 as from 1.4.19.

7.–(1) Where rent is payable other than weekly, any amount ineligible to be met by housing benefit which is specified in this Schedule as a weekly amount shall–

(a) where rent is payable in multiples of a week, be multiplied by the number equal to the number of weeks in respect of which it is payable; or

(b)   in any other case, be divided by 7 and multiplied by the number of days in the period to be used by the relevant authority for the purpose of calculating the claimant's weekly eligible rent under regulation 61 (calculation of weekly amounts).

(2)   In a case to which regulation 62 applies (rent free periods), any amount ineligible to be met by housing benefit which is specified in this Schedule as a weekly amount shall, where appropriate, be converted in accordance with sub-paragraph (1) and shall–

(a)   where rent is payable weekly, or in multiples of a week, be multiplied by 52 or 53, whichever is appropriate, and divided by the number equal to the number of weeks in that 52 or 53 week period in respect of which he is liable to pay rent; or

(b)   in any other case, be multiplied by 365 or 366, whichever is appropriate, and divided by the number of days in that 365 or 366 day period in respect of which he is liable to pay rent.

8.   In this Schedule–

"communal areas" mean areas (other than rooms) of common access (including halls and passageways) and rooms of common use in sheltered accommodation;

"fuel" includes gas and electricity and a reference to a charge for fuel includes a charge for fuel which includes an amount in respect of the facility of providing it other than a specified amount for the provision of a heating system.

[¹ SCHEDULE 2

REGULATION 14

Excluded tenancies

Modifications

Sch 2 substituted by reg 18 Housing Benefit (State Pension Credit) (Local Housing Allowance and Information Sharing) Amendment Regulations 2007 No.2869 as from 7 April 2008, save that for a person to whom reg 1(5) of those regulations applied (see p1812), the amendments came into force on the day on or after 7 April 2008 when the first of the events specified in reg 1(6) applied to her/him, or on 6 April 2009 if none had before that date.

Amendment

1.   Substituted by reg 18 of SI 2007 No 2869 as from 7.4.08 (or if reg 1(5) of that SI applies, on the day on or after 7.4.08 when the first of the events specified in reg 1(6) applies, or from 6.4.09 if none have before that date).

---

1.   An excluded tenancy is any tenancy to which any of the following paragraphs applies.

2.–(1)   Subject to sub-paragraphs (2) to (3), where a rent officer has made a determination, which relates to the tenancy in question or any other tenancy of the same dwelling this paragraph applies to–

(a)   the tenancy in respect of which that determination was made; and

(b)   any other tenancy of the same dwelling on terms which are substantially the same, other than the term relating to the amount of rent, as those terms were at the time of that determination or, if earlier, at the end of the tenancy.

(2)   For the purposes of any claim, notification, request or application under regulation 14(1) ("the later application"), a tenancy shall not be an excluded tenancy by virtue of sub-paragraph (1) by reference to a rent officer's determination made in consequence of an earlier claim, notification, request or application ("the earlier application") where–

(a)   the earlier and later applications were made in respect of the same claimant or different claimants; and

(b)   the earlier application was made more than 52 weeks before the later application was made.

(3)   Sub-paragraph (1) shall not apply where subsequent to the making of the determination mentioned in that sub-paragraph–

(a)   the number of occupiers of the dwelling has changed and that dwelling is not in a hostel;

(b)   there has been a substantial change in the condition of the dwelling (including the making of improvements) or the terms of the tenancy other than a term relating to rent;

(c)   there has been a rent increase under a term of the tenancy and the term under which that increase was made was either included in the tenancy at the time when the application for that determination was made (or was a term substantially the same as such a term) and that determination was not made under paragraph 1(2), 2(2) or 3(3) of Schedule 1 to the Rent Officers Order;

(d)   in a case where the rent officer has made a determination under paragraph 2(2) of Schedule 1 to the Rent Officers Order (size and rent determinations), but since the date of the application for that determination–

(i)   a child, who is a member of the household occupying the dwelling, has attained the age of 10 years;

(ii)   a young person, who is a member of the household occupying that dwelling, has attained the age of 16 years; or

(iii)   there is a change in the composition of the household occupying the dwelling.

[¹⋅⁴ (e) any person mentioned in paragraph 1A(a) of Schedule 2 to the Rent Officer Order becomes or ceases to be a person who requires overnight care where that affects the size criteria, as set out in that Schedule to that Rent Officers Order, applicable in the claimant's case;]

[² (f) the claimant or the claimant's partner becomes, or ceases to be, a qualifying parent or carer where that affects the size criteria, as set out in Schedule 2 to the Rent Officers Order, applicable in the claimant's case.]

[³ (g) an occupier becomes or ceases to be a child who cannot share a bedroom [⁴ or a member of a couple who cannot share a bedroom] where that affects the size criteria, as set out in Schedule 2 to the Rent Officers Order, applicable in the claimant's case.]

[² (4) For the purposes of sub-paragraph (3)(d)(iii) it does not amount to a change in the composition of the household where a son, daughter, step-son or step-daughter of the claimant or the claimant's partner who is the claimant's non-dependant ceases to occupy the dwelling as their home because they become a member of the armed forces away on operations, or subsequently resumes occupying the dwelling as their home on ceasing to be a member of the armed forces away on operations.]

Amendments
1.   Inserted by reg 3(10) of SI 2010 No 2835 as from 1.4.11.
2.   Inserted by reg 3(6) of SI 2013 No 665 as from 1.4.13.
3.   Amended by reg 3(5) of SI 2013 No 2828 as from 4.12.13.
4.   Amended by reg 5(5) of SI 2017 No 213 as from 1.4.17.

[¹**3.**–(1) Subject to [² sub-paragraphs (1A) and (2)], this paragraph applies where the landlord is–
(a)   a registered housing association;
(b)   a county council, with regard to gypsies' and travellers' caravan or mobile home sites and caravans or mobile homes provided on those sites; or
(c)   a housing authority, with regard to caravan or mobile home sites or houseboat moorings, payments in respect of which are to take the form of a rent allowance in accordance with regulation 72A(3).

[² (1A) In relation to a profit-making registered provider of social housing, sub-paragraph (1)(a) only applies to its social housing (within the meaning of sections 68 to 77 of the Housing and Regeneration Act 2008).]

(2)   Sub-paragraph (1) does not apply where the local authority considers that–
(a)   the claimant occupies a dwelling larger than is reasonably required by the claimant and any others who occupy that dwelling (including any non-dependants of the claimant and any person paying rent to the claimant); or
(b)   the rent payable for that dwelling is unreasonably high.
(3)   Where the circumstances set out in head (a) or (b) of sub-paragraph (2) exist, the authority must state this in their application for a determination.
(4)   In this Schedule "gypsies and travellers" means–
(a)   persons with a cultural tradition of nomadism or of living in a caravan; and
(b)   all other persons of a nomadic habit of life, whatever their race or origin, including–
    (i)   such persons who, on grounds only of their own or their family's or dependant's educational or health needs or old age, have ceased to travel temporarily or permanently; and
    (ii)   members of an organised group of travelling show people or circus people (whether or not travelling together as such).]

Amendments
1.   Substituted by reg 3(3) of SI 2008 No 2824 as from 6.4.09.
2.   Amended by art 4 and Sch 1 paras 60 and 61 of SI 2010 No 671 as from 1.4.10.

---

4.   This paragraph applies to a tenancy entered into before–
(a)   in Scotland, 2nd January 1989; and
(b)   in any other case, 15th January 1989.
5.   This paragraph applies to a regulated tenancy within the meaning of–
(a)   in Scotland, the Rent (Scotland) Act 1984; and
(b)   in any other case, the Rent Act 1977.
6.   This paragraph applies to a housing association tenancy which–
(a)   in Scotland, is a tenancy to which Part 6 of the Rent (Scotland) Act 1984 applies; and
(b)   in any other case, is a housing association tenancy to which Part 6 of the Rent Act 1977 applies.
7.   This paragraph applies to a protected occupancy or statutory tenancy within the meaning of the Rent (Agriculture) Act 1976.
8.   This paragraph applies to a tenancy at a low rent within the meaning of Part 1 of the Landlord and Tenant Act 1954 or Schedule 10 to the Local Government and Housing Act 1989.
9.   This paragraph applies to a tenancy of any dwelling which is a bail hostel or probation hostel approved by the Secretary of State under [¹ section 13 of the Offender Management Act 2007].

Amendment

1.   Amended by reg 7(6) of SI 2008 No 2767 as from 17.11.08.

---

10.   This paragraph applies to a tenancy of a housing action trust established under Part 3 of the Housing Act 1988.

11.–(1)   Subject to sub-paragraphs (2) and (3) this paragraph applies to a tenancy–

(a)   in respect of a dwelling comprised in land which has been disposed of under section 32 of the Housing Act 1985 or section 12 of the Housing (Scotland) Act 1987;

(b)   in respect of a dwelling comprised in land which has been disposed of with the consent required by section 43 of the Housing Act 1985 or section 12 of the Housing (Scotland) Act 1987;

(c)   in respect of which the fee simple estate has been acquired, under the right conferred by Chapter 2 of Part 1 of the Housing Act 1996, otherwise than from a housing action trust within the meaning of Part 3 of the Housing Act 1988, or in respect of which the house has been acquired under the right conferred by Part 3 of the Housing (Scotland) Act 1988; or

(d)   in respect of a dwelling disposed of under the New Towns (Transfer of Housing Stock) Regulations 1990 to a person who is an approved person for the purposes of disposal under those Regulations or in respect of a dwelling disposed of pursuant to powers contained in the New Towns (Scotland) Act 1968 to a housing association.

(2)   This paragraph shall not apply to a tenancy to which sub-paragraph (1) refers if–

(a)   there has been an increase in rent since the disposal or acquisition, as the case may be, occurred; and

(b)   the local authority stated in the application for determination that–

(i)   the claimant occupies a dwelling larger than is reasonably required by him and any others who occupy that dwelling (including any non-dependant of his and any person paying rent to him); or

(ii)   the rent payable for that dwelling is unreasonably high.

(3)   Where the disposal or acquisition, as the case may be, took place on or after 7th October 2002, sub-paragraph (2)(b) shall apply to a tenancy to which sub-paragraph (1) refers as if head (i) were omitted.

12.   This paragraph applies to a shared ownership tenancy.

13.   In this Schedule, "rent" shall be construed in accordance with paragraph (8) of regulation 14 (interpretation of "tenancy" and other expressions appropriate to a tenancy) and, subject to that paragraph, has the same meaning–

(a)   in Scotland, as in section 25 of the Housing (Scotland) Act 1988, except that the reference to the house in subsection (3) shall be construed as a reference to the dwelling;

(b)   in any other case, as in section 14 of the Housing Act 1988, except that the reference to the dwelling-house in subsection (4) shall be construed as a reference to the dwelling,

and–

(i)   other expressions have the same meanings as in regulation 14(8);

(ii)   in the case of a determination by a rent officer pursuant to a request for such a determination under regulation 14(1)(e), any reference to a "tenancy" shall be taken as a reference to a prospective tenancy and any reference to an "occupier" or any person "occupying" a dwelling shall, in the case of such a determination, be taken to be a reference to a potential occupier or potential occupation of that dwelling.]

SCHEDULE 3

REGULATION 22

Applicable amounts

General Note to Schedule 3

The amounts of the personal allowances and premiums are different than for those to whom the HB Regs apply.

The adult personal allowances are higher than under the HB Regs and those for single claimants of pensionable age or over and couples where at least one is pensionable age or over are higher than those for claimants and couples under pensionable age: para 1. Of the premiums, only severe disability premium, enhanced disability premium, disabled child premium and carer premium are available: paras 4 to 11. Note also that there is no equivalent to the support component provided in Sch 3 Part 5 HB Regs and no equivalent to the transitional addition provided in Sch 3 Parts 7 and 8 HB Regs. Note: the family premium under para 3 was abolished from 1 May 2016 subject to transitional rules. See the commentary on p634. Note also that, from 6 April 2017, payment of allowances for children or young people is restricted to two per claim, subject to exceptions and transitional rules. See the commentary on p412. The transitional rules in both cases are the same as for those entitled to HB under the HB Regs.

The rules for the severe disability premium are identical to those in the HB Regs: see p642. The enhanced disability premium is only available for specified children or young persons – ie, *not* for the claimant or her/his partner.

For commentary on paras 6 to 11, see the equivalent provisions in the HB Regs on pp641-646.

PART 1
Personal allowances
1.   The amount specified in column (2) below in respect of each person or couple specified in column (1) shall be the amount specified for the purposes of regulation 22–

Column (1) Person, couple or polygamous marriage	Column (2) Amount
(1) Single claimant or lone parent–	(1) –
[¹⁴]	[¹⁴]
(b) [¹⁴ who has attained pensionable age].	(b) [¹⁵ £181.00].
(2) Couple–	(2) –
[¹⁴]	[¹⁴]
(b) one member or both members [¹⁴ who have attained pensionable age].	(b) [¹⁵ £270.60].
[¹⁴]	[¹⁴]
(4) If the claimant is a member of a polygamous marriage and one or more members of the marriage [¹⁴ have attained pensionable age]–	(4) –
(a) for the claimant and the other party to the marriage;	(a) [¹⁵ £270.60];
(b) for each additional spouse who is a member of the same household as the claimant.	(b) [¹⁵ £89.60].

Amendments
1.   Amended by art 20(4) and Sch 8 para 1 of SI 2006 No 645 and reg 8 of SI 2006 No 217 as from 1.4.06 (3.4.06 where rent payable weekly or at intervals of a week).
2.   Amended by art 20(6) and Sch 8 of SI 2007 No 688 as from 1.4.07 (2.4.07 where rent payable weekly or at intervals of a week).
3.   Amended by art 20(7) and Sch 8 of SI 2008 No 632 as from 1.4.08 (7.4.08 where rent payable weekly or in multiples of a week).
4.   Amended by art 20(7) and Sch 7 of SI 2009 No 497 as from 1.4.09 (6.4.09 where rent payable weekly or in multiples of a week).
5.   Amended by art 20(6) and Sch 7 of SI 2010 No 793 as from 1.4.10 (5.4.10 where rent payable weekly or in multiples of a week).
6.   Amended by art 21(6) and Sch 7 of SI 2011 No 821 as from 1.4.11 (4.4.11 where rent payable weekly or in multiples of a week).
7.   Amended by art 21(6) and Sch 7 of SI 2012 No 780 as from 1.4.11 (2.4.11 where rent payable weekly or in multiples of a week).
8.   Amended by art 20(6) and Sch 7 para 1 of SI 2013 No 574 as from 1.4.13.
9.   Amended by art 18(6) and Sch 7 of SI 2014 No 16 as from 1.4.14 (7.4.14 where rent payable weekly or in multiples of a week).
10.   Amended by art 18(6) and Sch 7 para 1 of SI 2015 No 547 as from 1.4.15 (6.4.15 where rent payable weekly or in multiples of a week).
11.   Amended by reg 6(3) of SI 2016 No 242 as from 1.4.16 (4.4.16 where rent payable weekly or in multiples of a week).
12.   Amended by art 23(6) and Sch 7 of SI 2017 No 260 as from 1.4.17 (3.4.17 where rent payable weekly or in multiples of a week).
13.   Amended by art 24(6) and Sch 6 of SI 2018 No 281 as from 1.4.18 (2.4.18 where rent payable weekly or in multiples of a week).
14.   Amended by reg 7(7) of SI 2017 No 1187 as from 6.12.18.
15   Amended by art 24(6)(a) and Sch 4 of SI 2019 No 480 as from 1.4.19. (**Note**: Sch 4 of SI 2019 No 480 purports to amend figures in the table above for persons aged under 65 and persons aged 65 or over. This is an error. As a result of amendments made by art 7(7) of SI 2017 No 1187, the table should refer only to persons who have attained pensionable age. It is understood that this error will be corrected by future uprating orders. In the meantime, the table above has been amended only to show the 2019 uprating as it should have applied.)

2.–(1)   The amounts specified in column (2) below in respect of each person specified in column (1) shall, for the relevant period specified in column (1), be the amounts specified for the purposes of regulation 22–

Column (1) Child or young person	Column (2) Amount
Person in respect of the period–	
(a) beginning on that person's date of birth and ending on the day preceding the first Monday in September following that person's sixteenth birthday;	[¹⁴ £66.90];
(b) beginning on the first Monday in September following that persons 16th birthday and ending on the day preceding that person's [² twentieth] birthday.	[¹⁴ £66.90].

(2)   In column (1) of the Table above, "the first Monday in September" means the Monday which first occurs in the month of September in any year.

Amendments

1.   Amended by art 20(4) and Sch 8 para 2 of SI 2006 No 645 and reg 8 of SI 2006 No 217 as from 1.4.06 (3.4.06 where rent payable weekly or at intervals of a week).
2.   Amended by reg 4(4) of SI 2006 No 718 as from 10.4.06.
3.   Amended by art 20(6) and Sch 8 of SI 2007 No 688 as from 1.4.07 (2.4.07 where rent payable weekly or at intervals of a week).
4.   Amended by art 20(7) and Sch 8 of SI 2008 No 632 as from 1.4.08 (7.4.08 where rent payable weekly or in multiples of a week).
5.   Amended by art 20(7) and Sch 7 of SI 2009 No 497 as from 1.4.09 (6.4.09 where rent payable weekly or in multiples of a week).
6.   Amended by art 20(6) and Sch 7 of SI 2010 No 793 as from 1.4.10 (5.4.10 where rent payable weekly or in multiples of a week).
7.   Amended by art 21(6) and Sch 7 of SI 2011 No 821 as from 1.4.11 (4.4.11 where rent payable weekly or in multiples of a week).
8.   Amended by art 21(6) and Sch 7 of SI 2012 No 780 as from 1.4.11 (2.4.11 where rent payable weekly or in multiples of a week).
9.   Amended by art 20(6) and Sch 7 para 2 of SI 2013 No 574 as from 1.4.13.
10.   Amended by art 18(6) and Sch 7 of SI 2014 No 16 as from 1.4.14 (7.4.14 where rent payable weekly or in multiples of a week).
11.   Amended by art 18(6) and Sch 7 para 2 of SI 2015 No.547 as from 1.4.15 (6.4.15 where rent payable weekly or in multiples of a week).
12.   Confirmed by art 23(6) and Sch 7 of SI 2017 No 260 as from 1.4.17 (3.4.17 where rent payable weekly or in multiples of a week).
13.   Confirmed by art 24(6) and Sch 6 of SI 2018 No 281 as from 1.4.18 (2.4.18 where rent payable weekly or in multiples of a week).
14.   Confirmed by art 24(6)(b) of SI 2019 No 480 as from 1.4.19.

[¹ PART 2]

1.   Omitted by reg 2(2)(b) of SI 2015 No 1857 as from 1.05.16, subject to transitional provision in reg 4 of SI 2015 No 1857.

PART 3
Premiums

4.   The premiums specified in Part 4 shall, for the purposes of regulation 22(1)(e), be applicable to a claimant who satisfies the condition specified in this Part in respect of that premium.

5.–(1)   Subject to sub-paragraph (2), for the purposes of this Part of this Schedule, once a premium is applicable to a claimant under this Part, a person shall be treated as being in receipt of any benefit for–

(a)   in the case of a benefit to which the Social Security (Overlapping Benefits) Regulations 1979 applies, any period during which, apart from the provisions of those Regulations, he would be in receipt of that benefit; and

(b)   any period spent by a person in undertaking a course of training or instruction provided or approved by the Secretary of State under section 2 of the 1973 Act, or by [¹ Skills Development Scotland,] Scottish Enterprise or Highlands and Islands Enterprise under section 2 of the Enterprise and New Towns (Scotland) Act 1990 or for any period during which he is in receipt of a training allowance.

[² (2)   For the purposes of the carer premium under paragraph 9, a person shall be treated as being in receipt of a carer's allowance under section 70 of the Act by virtue of subparagraph (1)(a) only if and for so long as the person in respect of whose care the allowance has been claimed remains in receipt of–

(a)   attendance allowance;

(b)   the care component of disability living allowance at the highest or middle rate prescribed in accordance with section 72(3) of the Act; [³]

(c)   the daily living component of personal independence payment at the standard or enhanced rate in accordance with section 78(3) of the 2012 Act.[³; or]

[³ (d)   armed forces independence payment.]]

Amendments

1.   Amended by reg 7(3)(c) of SI 2009 No 583 as from 6.4.09.
2.   Substituted by reg 8 and Sch para 37(7)(a) of SI 2013 No 388 as from 8.4.13.
3.   Amended by art 7 and Sch para 35(7)(a) of SI 2013 No 591 as from 8.4.13.

Severe disability premium

6.–(1)   The condition is that the claimant is a severely disabled person.

(2)   For the purposes of sub-paragraph (1), a claimant shall be treated as being a severely disabled person if, and only if–

(a)   in the case of a single claimant, lone parent or a claimant who is treated as having no partner in consequence of sub-paragraph (3)–

(i)   he is in receipt of attendance allowance [³, the care component of disability living allowance at the highest or middle rate prescribed in accordance with section 72(3) of the Act or the daily living component of personal independence payment at the standard or enhanced rate in accordance with section 78(3) of the 2012 Act][⁴ or armed forces independence payment]; and

(ii)   subject to sub-paragraph (6), he has no non-dependants aged 18 or over normally residing with him or with whom he is normally residing; and

(iii)   no person is entitled to, and in receipt of, a carer's allowance [⁷ under section 70 of the Act or has an award of universal credit which includes the carer element under regulation 29 of the Universal Credit Regulations 2013] in respect of caring for him;

(b)   in the case of a claimant who has a partner–

(i)   the claimant is in receipt of attendance allowance [³, the care component of disability living allowance at the highest or middle rate prescribed in accordance with section 72(3) of the Act or the daily living component of personal independence payment at the standard or enhanced rate in accordance with section 78(3) of the 2012 Act] [⁴ or armed forces independence payment]; and

(ii)   his partner is also in receipt of such an allowance [³ or payment] or, if the claimant is a member of a polygamous marriage, each other member of that marriage is in receipt of such an allowance [³ or payment]; and

(iii)   subject to sub-paragraph (6), the claimant has no non-dependants aged 18 or over normally residing with him or with whom he is normally residing,

and either a person is entitled to and in receipt of a carer's allowance [⁷ or has an award of universal credit that includes the carer element] in respect of caring for only one of the couple or, if he is a member of a polygamous marriage, for one or more but not all the members of the marriage, or as the case may be, no person is entitled to and in receipt of such an allowance [⁷ or has such an award of universal credit] in respect of caring for either member of a couple or any of the members of the marriage.

(3)   Where a claimant has a partner who does not satisfy the condition in sub-paragraph (2)(b)(ii), and that partner is blind or is treated as blind within the meaning of sub-paragraph (4), that partner shall be treated for the purposes of sub-paragraph (2) as if he were not a partner of the claimant.

[⁶ (4)   For the purposes of sub-paragraph (3), a person is blind if he is certified as severely sight impaired or blind by a consultant ophthalmologist.]

[⁶ (5)   For the purposes of sub-paragraph (4), a person who has ceased to be certified as severely sight impaired or blind on regaining his eyesight shall nevertheless be treated as blind and as satisfying the additional condition set out in that sub-paragraph for a period of 28 weeks following the date on which he ceased to be so certified.]

(6)   For the purposes of sub-paragraph (2)(a)(ii) and (2)(b)(iii) no account shall be taken of–

(a)   a person receiving attendance allowance [³, the care component of disability living allowance at the highest or middle rate prescribed in accordance with section 72(3) of the Act or the daily living component of personal independence payment at the standard or enhanced rate in accordance with section 78(3) of the 2012 Act][⁴ or armed forces independence payment]; or

(b)   a person who is blind or is treated as blind within the meaning of sub-paragraphs (4) and (5).

(7)   For the purposes of sub-paragraph (2)(b) a person shall be treated–

(a)   as being in receipt of attendance allowance, or the care component of disability living allowance at the highest or middle rate prescribed in accordance with section 72(3) of the Act, if he would, but for his being a patient for a period exceeding 28 days, be so in receipt;

(b)   as being entitled to and in receipt of a carer's allowance [⁷ or having an award of universal credit which includes the carer element] if he would, but for the person for whom he was caring being a patient in hospital for a period exceeding 28 days, be so entitled and in receipt [⁷ or have such an award of universal credit].

[³ (c)   as being in receipt of the daily living component of personal independence payment at the standard or enhanced rate in accordance with section 78 of the 2012 Act, if he would, but for [⁵ payment ceasing by virtue of] regulations made under section 86(1) (hospital inpatients) of the 2012 Act, be so in receipt.]

(8)   For the purposes of sub-paragraph (2)(a)(iii) and (2)(b)–

(a)   no account shall be taken of an award of a carer's allowance [⁷ or an award of universal credit which includes the carer element] to the extent that payment of such an award is backdated for a period before [¹ the date on which the award is first paid]; and

(b)   references to a person being in receipt of a carer's allowance [⁷ or as having an award of universal credit which includes the carer element] shall include references to a person who would have been in receipt of that allowance [⁷ or had such an award of universal credit] but for the application of a restriction under section [² 6B or] 7 of the Social Security Fraud Act 2001 (loss of benefit).

Amendments

1.   Amended by reg 7(4) of SI 2007 No 719 as from 2.4.07.
2.   Amended by reg 5 of SI 2010 No 1160 as from 1.4.10.
3.   Amended by reg 8 and Sch para 37(7)(b) of SI 2013 No 388 as from 8.4.13.
4.   Amended by art 7 and Sch para 35(7)(b) of SI 2013 No 591 as from 8.4.13.
5.   Amended by reg 4(5)(a) of SI 2014 No 213 as from 1.4.14 (7.4.14 where rent payable weekly or in multiples of a week).
6.   Amended by reg 3(6)(b) of SI 2014 No 2888 as from 26.11.14.
7.   Inserted by reg 18(2) of SI 2015 No 1754 as from 4.11.15.

Enhanced disability premium

7.–[¹ [³ (1)(1)   Subject to sub-paragraph (2), the condition is that–

(a)   the care component of disability living allowance is, or would, but for a suspension of benefit in accordance with regulations under section 113(2) of the Act or but for an abatement as a consequence of hospitalisation, be payable at the highest rate prescribed under section 72(3) of the Act; or

(b)   the daily living component of personal independence payment is [⁵ payable, or has ceased to be payable by virtue of] regulations made under section 86(1) (hospital in-patients) of the 2012 Act, be payable at the enhanced rate under section 78(2) of the 2012 Act; [⁴ or]

[⁴ (c)   armed forces independence payment is payable,]
in respect of a child or young person who is a member of the claimant's family.]]

[¹ (2)   Where the condition in sub-paragraph (1) ceases to be satisfied because of the death of a child or young person, the condition is that the claimant [² or partner] is entitled to child benefit in respect of that person under section 145A of the Act (entitlement after death of child or qualifying young person).]

Amendments

1.   Amended by reg 13(2) of SI 2011 No 674 as from 1.4.11 (4.4.11 where rent payable weekly or in any multiple of whole weeks).
2.   Inserted by reg 20(10)(b) of SI 2011 No 2425 as from 31.10.11.
3.   Amended by reg 8 and Sch para 37(7)(c) of SI 2013 No 388 as from 8.4.13.
4.   Amended by art 7 and Sch para 35(7)(c) of SI 2013 No 591 as from 8.4.13.
5.   Amended by reg 4(5)(b) of SI 2014 No 213 as from 1.4.14 (7.4.14 where rent payable weekly or in multiples of a week).

Disabled child premium

8.   The condition is that a child or young person for whom the claimant or a partner of his is responsible and who is a member of the claimant's household–

(a)   is in receipt of disability living allowance or is no longer in receipt of such allowance because he is a patient, provided that the child or young person continues to be a member of the family; or

(b)   is blind within the meaning of paragraph 6(4) or is treated as blind in accordance with paragraph 6(5);

[¹ (c)   is a child or young person in respect of whom section 145A of the Act (entitlement after death of child or qualifying young person) applies for the purposes of entitlement to child benefit but only for the period prescribed under that section, and in respect of whom a disabled child premium was included in the claimant's applicable amount immediately before the death of that child or young person, or ceased to be included in the claimant's applicable amount because of that child or young person's death.] [² or]

[² (d)   is a young person who is in receipt of personal independence payment or who would, but for [⁴ payment ceasing by virtue of] regulations made under section 86(1) (hospital in-patients) of the 2012 Act be so in receipt, provided that the young person continues to be a member of the family] [³ ; or]

[³ (e)   is a young person who is in receipt of armed forces independence payment.]

Amendments

1.   Substituted by reg 13(3) of SI 2011 No 674 as from 1.4.11 (4.4.11 where rent payable weekly or in any multiple of whole weeks).
2.   Amended by reg 8 and Sch para 37(7)(d) of SI 2013 No 388 as from 8.4.13.
3.   Amended by art 7 and Sch para 35(7)(d) of SI 2013 No 591 as from 8.4.13.
4.   Amended by reg 4(5)(c) of SI 2014 No 213 as from 1.4.14 (7.4.14 where rent payable weekly or in multiples of a week).

Carer premium

9.–(1)   The condition is that the claimant or his partner is, or both of them are, entitled to a carer's allowance.

(2)   Where a carer premium has been awarded but–

(a)   the person in respect of whose care the carer's allowance has been awarded dies; or

(b)   the person in respect of whom the premium was awarded ceases to be entitled, or ceases to be treated as entitled, to a carer's allowance,

this paragraph shall be treated as satisfied for a period of eight weeks from the relevant date specified in sub-paragraph (3).

(3)   The relevant date for the purposes of sub-paragraph (2) is–

(a)   the Sunday following the death of the person in respect of whose care the carer's allowance has been awarded (or beginning with the date of death if the date occurred on a Sunday);

(b)   where head (a) above does not apply, the date on which that person who was entitled to a carer's allowance ceases to be entitled to it.

(4)   For the purposes of this paragraph, a person shall be treated as being entitled to and in receipt of a carer's allowance for any period not covered by an award but in respect of which a payment is made in lieu of an award.

Persons in receipt of concessionary payments

10.   For the purpose of determining whether a premium is applicable to a person under paragraphs 6 to 9, any concessionary payment made to compensate that person for the non-payment of any benefit mentioned in those paragraphs shall be treated as if it were a payment of that benefit.

Person in receipt of benefit

11.   For the purposes of this Part of this Schedule, a person shall be regarded as being in receipt of any benefit if, and only if, it is paid in respect of him and shall be so regarded only for any period in respect of which that benefit is paid.

PART 4
Amounts of premiums specified in Part 3

Premium	*Amount*
12.–(1) Severe Disability Premium	(1)
(a) where the claimant satisfies the condition in paragraph 6(2)(a);	(a) [¹⁴ £65.85];
(b) where the claimant satisfies the condition in paragraph 6(2)(b)–	
(i) in a case where there is someone in receipt of a carer's allowance [¹¹ or who has an award of universal credit which includes the carer element under regulation 29 of the Universal Credit Regulations 2013,] or if he or any partner satisfies that condition only by virtue of paragraph 6(7);	(b)(i) [¹⁴ £65.85];
(ii) in a case where there is no-one in receipt of such an allowance [¹¹ or such an award of universal credit].	(b) (ii) [¹⁴ £131.70].
(2) Enhanced disability premium.	(2) [¹⁴ £26.04] in respect of each child or young person in respect of whom the conditions specified in paragraph 7 are satisfied.
(3) Disabled child premium.	(3) [¹⁴ £64.19] in respect of each child or young person in respect of whom the condition specified in paragraph 8 is satisfied.
(4) Carer premium.	(4) [¹⁴ £36.85] in respect of each person who satisfies the condition specified in paragraph 9.

Amendments

1.   Amended by art 20(5) and Sch 9 of SI 2006 No 645 and reg 8 of SI 2006 No 217 as from 1.4.06 (3.4.06 where rent payable weekly or at intervals of a week).

2.   Amended by art 20(8) and Sch 9 of SI 2007 No 688 as from 1.4.07 (2.4.07 where rent payable weekly or at intervals of a week).

3.   Amended by art 20(9) and Sch 9 of SI 2008 No 632 as from 1.4.08 (7.4.08 where rent payable weekly or in multiples of a week).

4.   Amended by art 20(9) and Sch 8 of SI 2009 No 497 as from 1.4.09 (6.4.08 where rent payable weekly or in multiples of a week).

5.   Amended by art 20(8) and Sch 8 of SI 2010 No 793 as from 1.4.10 (5.4.10 where rent payable weekly or in multiples of a week).

6.   Amended by art 21(8) and Sch 8 of SI 2011 No 821 as from 1.4.11 (4.4.11 where rent payable weekly or in multiples of a week).

7.   Amended by art 21(8) and Sch 8 of SI 2012 No 780 as from 1.4.11 (2.4.11 where rent payable weekly or in multiples of a week).

8.   Amended by art 20(8) and Sch 8 of SI 2013 No 574 as from 1.4.13.

9.   Amended by art 18(8) and Sch 8 of SI 2014 No 16 as from 1.4.14 (7.4.14 where rent payable weekly or in multiples of a week).

10.   Amended by art 18(8) and Sch 8 of SI 2015 No 547 as from 1.4.15 (6.4.15 where rent payable weekly or in multiples of a week).

11.   Inserted by reg 18(3) of SI 2015 No 1754 as from 4.11.15.

12.   Amended by art 23(8) and Sch 8 of SI 2017 No 260 as from 1.4.17 (3.4.17 where rent payable weekly or in multiples of a week).

13.   Amended by art 24(8) and Sch 7 of SI 2018 No 281 as from 1.4.18 (2.4.18 where rent payable weekly or in multiples of a week).

14.   Amended by art 24(8) and Sch 5 of SI 2019 No 480 as from 1.4.19.

SCHEDULE 4

REGULATION 36(1)

Sums disregarded from claimant's earnings

General Note to Schedule 4

The general rule, found in para 7, is that a single claimant qualifies for an earnings disregard of £5 and a claimant with a partner qualifies for an earnings disregard of £10. However, the earnings disregard for a lone parent is £25 and for certain categories of people is £20. Note the potentially higher earnings disregard in para 5A where the claimant or her/his partner is undertaking "exempt work". See the Analysis of the equivalent Sch 4 para 10A HB Regs on p661.

    The categories of people qualifying for a disregard of £20 are the following.

(1)   Claimants working for the rescue services and reserve armed forces listed: para 3. If the claimant is earning less than £20, any earnings of her/his partner will be disregarded up to that amount.

(2)   Carers who are in employment: para 4. Again, the earnings of both partners may be added together for the purposes of the disregard.

(3)   Certain sick or disabled claimants: para 5(1). Much of para 5(1) is similar to Sch 3 para 13(1) HB Regs, to which reference should be made.

(4)   Claimants who had a £20 disregard in an award of HB in the eight weeks before attaining the qualifying age for PC and where employment continues after the termination of that award: para 5(2). That disregard continues as long as HB entitlement continues: para 5(3).

There are then a number of other disregards. Para 6 requires the disregarding of any balance of parental contributions made to a student which are not disregarded under Sch 5 paras 18 and 19. Para 8 requires earnings derived from employment pre-dating the claim to be ignored, save for royalties and analogous payments. Para 9 is equivalent to Sch 4 para 17 HB Regs, and para 10 is equivalent to Sch 4 para 14 HB Regs.

---

1.   Where two or more of paragraphs 2 to 5 apply in any particular case the overall maximum sum which falls to be disregarded in that case under those paragraphs is restricted to–

(a)   £25 in the case of a lone parent;

(b)   £20 in any other case.

2.   In a case where a claimant is a lone parent, £25 of earnings.

3.–(1)   In a case of earnings from any employment or employments to which sub-paragraph (2) applies, £20.

(2)   This paragraph applies to employment–

[¹ (a)   a part-time fire-fighter employed by a fire and rescue authority under the Fire and Rescue Services Act 2004 or by the Scottish Fire and Rescue Service established under section 1A of the Fire (Scotland) Act 2005;]

[¹ (b)]

(c)   as an auxiliary coastguard in respect of coast rescue activities;

(d)   in the manning or launching of a lifeboat if the employment is part-time;

(e)   as a member of any territorial or reserve force prescribed in Part 1 of Schedule 6 to Social Security (Contributions) Regulations 2001.

(3)   If–

(a)   any of the earnings of the claimant or, if he has a partner, his partner, or both of them, are disregarded under sub-paragraph (1); and

(b)   either of them has, or they both have, other earnings,

so much of those other earnings as would not, in aggregate with the earnings disregarded under that sub-paragraph, exceed £20.

Amendment

1.   Substituted by reg 12(5) of SI 2013 No 2536 as form 29.10.13.

4.–(1)   If the claimant or, if he has a partner, his partner is a carer, or both are carers, £20 of any earnings received from his or their employment.

(2)   Where the carer premium is awarded in respect of the claimant and of any partner of his, their earnings shall for the purposes of this paragraph be aggregated, but the amount to be disregarded in accordance with sub-paragraph (1) shall not exceed £20 of the aggregated amount.

(3)   In this paragraph the claimant or his partner is a carer if paragraph 9 of Part 3 of Schedule 3 (amount applicable for carers) is satisfied in respect of him.

5.–(1)   £20 is disregarded if the claimant or, if he has a partner, his partner–

(a)   is in receipt of–

    (i)   long-term incapacity benefit under Section 30A of the Act;

    (ii)   severe disablement allowance under section 68 of the Act;

    (iii)   attendance allowance;

    (iv)   disability living allowance under sections 71 to 76 of the Act;

    (v)   any mobility supplement under [² article 20 of the Naval, Military and Air Forces Etc. (Disablement and Death) Service Pensions Order 2006] (including such a supplement by virtue of any other scheme or order) or under article 25A of the Personal Injuries (Civilians) Scheme 1983; [¹]

    (vi)   the disability element or the severe disability element of working tax credit under Schedule 2 to the Working Tax Credit Regulations; or

    [¹ (vii) main phase employment and support allowance; [⁵]]

    [⁵ (viii) personal independence payment; [⁶]]

    [⁶ (ix) armed forces independence payment; or]

[⁸ (b)   is or are certified as severely sight impaired or blind by a consultant ophthalmologist; or]

(c)   is, or is treated as, incapable of work in accordance with the provisions of, and regulations made under, Part 12A of the Act (incapacity for work), and has been incapable, or has been treated as incapable, of work for a continuous period of not less than–

    (i)   in the case of a claimant who is terminally ill within the meaning of section 30B(4) of that Act, 196 days;

    (ii)   in any other case, 364 days.[³ or]

[³ (d)   has, or is treated as having, limited capability for work within the meaning of section 1(4) of the Welfare Reform Act or limited capability for work-related activity within the meaning of section 2(5) of that Act and either–

    (i)   the assessment phase as defined in section 24(2) of the Welfare Reform Act has ended; or

    (ii)   regulation 7 of the Employment and Support Allowance Regulations [⁷ or regulation 7 of the Employment and Support Allowance Regulations 2013] (circumstances where the condition that the assessment phase has ended before entitlement to the support component [⁹] arises does not apply) applies.]

(2)   Subject to sub-paragraph (3), £20 is disregarded if the claimant or, if he has a partner, his partner has, within a period of 8 weeks ending on the day in respect of which the claimant or his partner attains the qualifying age for state pension credit, had an award of housing benefit [⁴] and–

(a)   £20 was disregarded in respect of earnings taken into account in that award;

(b)   the person whose earnings qualified for the disregard continues in employment after the termination of that award.

(3)   The disregard of £20 specified in sub-paragraph (2) applies so long as there is no break, other than a break which does not exceed 8 weeks, in a person's entitlement to housing benefit [³] or in employment following the first day in respect of which that benefit is awarded.

(4)   £20 is the maximum amount which may be disregarded under this paragraph, notwithstanding that, where the claimant has a partner, both the claimant and his partner satisfy the requirements of this paragraph.

Amendments

1.   Amended by reg 40 of SI 2008 No 1082 as from 27.10.08.

2.   Amended by reg 6(8) of SI 2008 No 3157 as from 5.1.09.

3.   Amended by reg 7(7)(a) of SI 2009 No 583 as from 1.4.09 (6.4.09 where rent payable weekly or at intervals of a week).

4.   Amended by reg 3 and Sch 1 of SI 2013 No 458 as from 1.4.13.

5.   Amended by reg 8 and Sch para 37(8) of SI 2013 No 388 as from 8.4.13.

6.   Amended by art 7 and Sch para 35(8) of SI 2013 No 591 as from 8.4.13.

7.   Amended by reg 36(7)(a) of SI 2013 No 630 as from 29.4.13.

8.   Amended by reg 3(6)(c) of SI 2014 No 2888 as from 26.11.14.

9.   Amended by Sch 1 para 7(5) of SI 2017 No 204 as from 3.4.17, subject to transitional and savings provisions in Sch 2 paras 1–7.

[¹**5A.**   (1) Where–

(a)   the claimant (or if the claimant is a member of a couple, at least one member of that couple) is a person to whom sub-paragraph (5) applies;

(b)   the Secretary of State is satisfied that that person is undertaking exempt work as defined in sub-paragraph (6); and

(c)   regulation 26 does not apply,
the amount specified in sub-paragraph (7) ("the specified amount").

(2)   Where this paragraph applies, paragraphs 1 to 5 and 7 do not apply; but in any case where the claimant is a lone parent, and the specified amount would be less than the amount specified in paragraph 2, then paragraph 2 applies instead of this paragraph.

(3)   Notwithstanding regulation 23 (calculation of income and capital of members of claimant's family and of a polygamous marriage), if sub-paragraph (1) applies to one member of a couple ("A") it shall not apply to the other member of that couple ("B") except to the extent provided in sub-paragraph (4).

(4)   Where A's earnings are less than the specified amount, there shall also be disregarded so much of B's earnings as would not when aggregated with A's earnings exceed the specified amount; but the amount of B's earnings which may be disregarded under this sub-paragraph is limited to a maximum of £20 unless the Secretary of State is satisfied that B is also undertaking exempt work.

(5)   This sub-paragraph applies to a person who is–
(a)   in receipt of a contributory employment and support allowance;
(b)   in receipt of incapacity benefit;
(c)   in receipt of severe disablement allowance; or
(d)   being credited with earnings on the grounds of incapacity for work or limited capability for work under regulation 8B of the Social Security (Credits) Regulations 1975.

(6)   "Exempt work" means work of the kind described in–
(a)   regulation 45(2), (3) or (4) of the Employment and Support Allowance Regulations [² or regulation 39(1)(a), (b) or (c) of the Employment and Support Allowance Regulations 2013]; or (as the case may be)
(b)   regulation 17(2), (3) or (4) of the Social Security (Incapacity for Work) (General) Regulations 1995,
and, in determining for the purposes of this paragraph whether a claimant or a member of a couple is undertaking any type of exempt work, it is immaterial whether that person or their partner is also undertaking other work.

(7)   The specified amount is the amount of money from time to time mentioned in any provision referred to in sub-paragraph (6) by virtue of which the work referred to in sub-paragraph (1) is exempt (or, where more than one such provision is relevant and those provisions mention different amounts of money, the highest of those amounts).]

Amendments

1.   Inserted by reg 3(5) of SI 2009 No 2608 as from 1.4.10 (5.4.10 where rent payable weekly or in multiples of a week).
2.   Amended by reg 36(7)(b) of SI 2013 No 630 as from 29.4.13.

---

6.   Any amount or the balance of any amount which would fall to be disregarded under paragraph 18 or 19 of Schedule 5 had the claimant's income which does not consist of earnings been sufficient to entitle him to the full disregard thereunder.

7.   Except where the claimant or his partner qualifies for a £20 disregard under the preceding provisions of this Schedule–
(a)   £5 shall be disregarded if a claimant who has no partner has earnings;
(b)   £10 shall be disregarded if a claimant who has a partner has earnings.

8.   Any earnings, other than earnings referred to in regulation 33(8)(b) (copyright [¹ design], patent or trade mark), derived from employment which ended before the day in respect of which the claimant first satisfies the conditions for entitlement to housing benefit.

Amendment

1.   Amended by reg 7(7)(b) of SI 2009 No 583 as from the first day of the first benefit week for a claimant on or after 6.4.09.

9.–(1)   In a case where the claimant is a person who satisfies at least one of the conditions set out in sub-paragraph (2), and his net earnings equal or exceed the total of the amounts set out in sub-paragraph (3), the amount of his earnings that falls to be disregarded under this Schedule shall be increased by [¹⁴ £17.10].

(2)   The conditions of this sub-paragraph are that–
(a)   the claimant, or if he has a partner, either the claimant or his partner, is a person to whom regulation 20(1)(c) of the Working Tax Credit Regulations applies; or
(b)   the claimant–
(i)   is, or any partner of his is, aged at least 25 and is engaged in remunerative work for on average not less than 30 hours per week; or
(ii)   if he is a member of a couple–
(aa)   at least one member of that couple is engaged in remunerative work for on average not less than 16 hours per week; and
[¹¹ (bb) his family includes at least one child or young person;] or
(iii)   is a lone parent who is engaged in remunerative work for on average not less than 16 hours per week; or

(iv)   is, or if he has a partner, one of them is, engaged in remunerative work for on average not less than 16 hours per week, and paragraph 5(1) above is satisfied in respect of that person; or

(c)   the claimant is, or, if he has a partner, one of them is, a person to whom regulation 18(3) of the Working Tax Credit Regulations (eligibility for 50 plus element) applies, or would apply if an application for working tax credit were to be made in his case.

(3)   The following are the amounts referred to in sub-paragraph (1)–

(a)   any amount disregarded under this Schedule;

(b)   the amount of child care charges calculated as deductible under regulation 31(1)(c) (treatment of child care charges); and

(c)   [¹⁴ £17.10].

(4)   The provisions of regulation 6 (remunerative work) shall apply in determining whether or not a person works for on average not less than 30 hours per week, but as if the reference to 16 hours in paragraph (1) of that regulation was a reference to 30 hours.

Amendments

1.   Amended by art 20(7) of SI 2006 No 645 and reg 8 of SI 2006 No 217 as from 1.4.06 (3.4.06 where rent payable weekly or at intervals of a week).

2.   Amended by art 20(9) of SI 2007 No 688 as from 1.4.07 (2.4.07 where rent payable weekly or at intervals of a week).

3.   Amended by art 20(10) of SI 2008 No 632 as from 1.4.08 (7.4.08 where rent payable weekly or in multiples of a week).

4.   Amended by art 20(10) of SI 2009 No 497 as from 1.4.09 (6.4.09 where rent payable weekly or at intervals of a week).

5.   Amended by art 20(9) of SI 2010 No 793 as from 1.4.10 (5.4.10 where rent payable weekly or in multiples of a week).

6.   Confirmed by art 21(9) of SI 2011 No 821 as from 1.4.11 (4.4.11 where rent payable weekly or in multiples of a week).

7.   Confirmed by art 21(9) of SI 2012 No 780 as from 1.4.11 (2.4.11 where rent payable weekly or in multiples of a week).

8.   Confirmed by art 20(9) of SI 2013 No 574 as from 1.4.13.

9.   Confirmed by art 18(9) of SI 2014 No 16 as from 1.4.14 (7.4.14 where rent payable weekly or in multiples of a week).

10.   Confirmed by art 18(9) of SI 2015 No 547 as from 1.4.15 (6.4.15 where rent payable weekly or in multiples of a week).

11.   Substituted by reg 2(2)(c) of SI 2015 No 1857 as from 1.5.16, subject to transitional provision in reg 4 of SI 2015 No 1857.

12.   Confirmed by art 23(9) of SI 2017 No 260 as from 1.4.17 (3.4.17 where rent payable weekly or in multiples of a week).

13.   Confirmed by art 24(9) of SI 2018 No 281 as from 1.4.18 (2.4.18 where rent payable weekly or in multiples of a week).

14.   Confirmed by art 24(9) of SI 2019 No 480 as from 1.4.19.

---

10.   Where a payment of earnings is made in a currency other than Sterling any banking charge or commission payable in converting that payment into Sterling.

SCHEDULE 5

REGULATION 33(9)

Amounts to be disregarded in the calculation of income other than earnings

1.   In addition to any sum which falls to be disregarded in accordance with paragraphs 2 to 6, £10 of any of the following, namely–

(a)   a war disablement pension (except insofar as such a pension falls to be disregarded under paragraph 2 or 3);

[¹ (b)   a war widow's pension or [³ war widower's pension];]

(c)   a pension payable to a person as a widow, widower or surviving civil partner under [²] any power of Her Majesty otherwise than under an enactment to make provision about pensions for or in respect of persons who have been disabled or have died in consequence of service as members of the armed forces of the Crown;

(d)   a guaranteed income payment [² and, if the amount of that payment has been abated to less than £10 by a [³ pension or payment falling within article 31(1)(a) or (b) of the Armed Forces and Reserve Forces (Compensation Scheme) Order 2005], so much of [³ that pension or payment] as would not, in aggregate with the amount of [³ any] guaranteed income payment disregarded, exceed £10];

(e)   a payment made to compensate for the non-payment of such a pension or payment as is mentioned in any of the preceding sub-paragraphs;

(f)   a pension paid by the government of a country outside Great Britain which is analogous to any of the pensions or payments mentioned in sub-paragraphs (a) to (d) above;

[⁴ (g) a pension paid by a government to victims of National Socialist persecution .]

Amendments
1.   Amended by reg 4(8)(a) of SI 2008 No 1042 as from 19.5.08.
2.   Amended by reg 6(9)(a) of SI 2008 No 3157 as from 5.1.09.
3.   Amended by reg 7(5) of SI 2009 No 2655 as from 2.11.09.
4.   Substituted by reg 6(3) of SI 2017 No 174 as from 20.3.17.

Analysis
See Sch 5 para 15 HB Regs (see p669), but note para 2 below.

---

2.   The whole of any amount included in a pension to which paragraph 1 relates in respect of–
(a)   the claimant's need for constant attendance;
(b)   the claimant's exceptionally severe disablement.

Analysis
These are supplements payable in respect of various war pensions for the exceptional needs of a recipient. The whole of such supplements are disregarded.

---

3.   Any mobility supplement under [¹ article 20 of the Naval, Military and Air Forces Etc. (Disablement and Death) Service Pensions Order 2006] (including such a supplement by virtue of any other scheme or order) or under article 25A of the Personal Injuries (Civilians) Scheme 1983 or any payment intended to compensate for the non-payment of such a supplement.

Amendment
1.   Amended by reg 6(9)(b) of SI 2008 No 3157 as from 5.1.09.

Analysis
This is equivalent to Sch 5 para 8 HB Regs (see p667).

[¹4.   Any supplementary pension under article 23(2) of the Naval, Military and Air Forces Etc. (Disablement and Death) Service Pensions Order 2006 (pensions to surviving spouses and surviving civil partners) and any analogous payment made by the Secretary of State for Defence to any person who is not a person entitled under that Order.]

Amendment
1.   Substituted by reg 6(9)(c) of SI 2008 No 3157 as from 5.1.09.

Analysis of paras 4, 5 and 6
Note that under Sch 6 paras 18 and 26B, arrears of supplementary pension disregarded under para 4, and any amount disregarded under paras 5 or 6, are disregarded as capital for one year from the date of receipt.

---

5.   In the case of a pension awarded at the supplementary rate under article 27(3) of the Personal Injuries (Civilians) Scheme 1983 (pensions to widows, widowers or surviving civil partners), the sum specified in paragraph 1(c) of Schedule 4 to that Scheme.

6.–(1)   Any payment which is–
(a)   made under any of the Dispensing Instruments to a widow, widower or surviving civil partner of a person–
       (i)   whose death was attributable to service in a capacity analogous to service as a member of the armed forces of the Crown; and
       (ii)   whose service in such capacity terminated before 31st March 1973; and
[¹ (b) equal to the amount specified in article 23(2) of the Naval, Military and Air Forces Etc. (Disablement and Death) Service Pensions Order 2006.]
(2)   In this paragraph "the Dispensing Instruments" means the Order in Council of 19th December 1881, the Royal Warrant of 27th October 1884 and the Order by His Majesty of 14th January 1922 (exceptional grants of pay, non-effective pay and allowances).

Amendment
1.   Substituted by reg 6(9)(d) of SI 2008 No 3157 as from 5.1.09.

7.   £15 of any widowed parent's allowance to which the claimant is entitled under section 39A of the Act.

8.   £15 of any widowed mother's allowance to which the claimant is entitled under section 37 of the Act.

9.   Where the claimant occupies a dwelling as his home and he provides in that dwelling board and lodging accommodation, an amount, in respect of each person for whom such accommodation is provided for the whole or any part of a week, equal to–

(a)   where the aggregate of any payments made in respect of any one week in respect of such accommodation provided to such person does not exceed £20, 100 per cent. of such payments; or

(b)   where the aggregate of any such payments exceeds £20, £20 and 50 per cent. of the excess over £20.

Analysis
"Board and lodging accommodation" is defined in reg 2(1).

---

10.   If the claimant–

(a)   owns the freehold or leasehold interest in any property or is a tenant of any property; and

(b)   occupies a part of that property; and

(c)   has an agreement with another person allowing that person to occupy another part of that property on payment of rent and–

(i)   the amount paid by that person is less than £20 per week, the whole of that amount; or

(ii)   the amount paid is £20 or more per week, £20.

Analysis
This has no equivalent in Sch 5 HB Regs (but see Sch 5 paras 22 and 42 HB Regs). Up to £20 of rent payable by a lodger may be disregarded whether or not board is also provided.

---

11.   Where a claimant receives income under an annuity purchased with a loan, which satisfies the following conditions–

(a)   that the loan was made as part of a scheme under which not less than 90 per cent. of the proceeds of the loan were applied to the purchase by the person to whom it was made of an annuity ending with his life or with the life of the survivor of two or more persons (in this paragraph referred to as "the annuitants") who include the person to whom the loan was made;

(b)   that at the time the loan was made the person to whom it was made or each of the annuitants had attained the age of 65 [¹ or, if it was higher at that time, pensionable age];

(c)   that the loan was secured on a dwelling in Great Britain and the person to whom the loan was made or one of the annuitants owns an estate or interest in that dwelling;

(d)   that the person to whom the loan was made or one of the annuitants occupies the dwelling on which it was secured as his home at the time the interest is paid; and

(e)   that the interest payable on the loan is paid by the person to whom the loan was made or by one of the annuitants,

the amount, calculated on a weekly basis, equal to–

(i)   where, or insofar as, section 369 of the Income and Corporation Taxes Act 1988 (mortgage interest payable under deduction of tax) applies to the payments of interest on the loan, the interest which is payable after deduction of a sum equal to income tax on such payments at the applicable percentage of income tax within the meaning of section 369(1A) of that Act;

(ii)   in any other case, the interest which is payable on the loan without deduction of such a sum.

Amendment
1.   Amended by reg 7(8) of SI 2017 No 1187 as from 6.12.18.

Analysis
The basic effect of this paragraph is to provide a disregard from the income produced by an annuity under a "Home Income Plan", of an amount equal to the interest payments (net of tax) on the loan used to purchase the annuity.

Sub-paras (a) to (e) set out the conditions which must be satisfied before the disregard can apply and sub-paras (i) and (ii) deal with how much of the annuity can be ignored.

(1)   The person to whom the loan was made (the payee) must have used 90 per cent of it at least to purchase the annuity which must last for the life of the payee or another person (the annuitant): sub-para (a).

(2)   The interest on the loan must be payable by the payee or one of the annuitants: sub-para (e).

(3)   The payee or any annuitant(s) must have been aged at least 65 (or, if it was higher at the time, pensionable age) at the time the loan in question was made: sub-para (b).

(4)   The loan must have been secured on a dwelling in Great Britain which the payee or one of the annuitants owns (or owns an interest in): sub-para (c).

(5) The payee or one of the annuitants must actually occupy the dwelling as her/his home at the time the interest is paid: sub-para (d).

Sub-paras (i) and (ii). s369 Income and Corporation Taxes Act 1988 allows tax relief on certain interest payments; where the section applies, the interest paid net of tax should be disregarded. Otherwise, all of the interest may be disregarded.

12.–(1) Any payment, other than a payment to which sub-paragraph (2) applies, made to the claimant by Trustees in exercise of a discretion exercisable by them.

(2) This sub-paragraph applies to payments made to the claimant by Trustees in exercise of a discretion exercisable by them for the purpose of–
(a) obtaining food, ordinary clothing or footwear or household fuel;
(b) the payment of rent, council tax or water charges for which that claimant or his partner is liable;
(c) meeting housing costs of a kind specified in Schedule 2 to the State Pension Credit Regulations 2002.

(3) In a case to which sub-paragraph (2) applies, £20 or–
(a) if the payment is less than £20, the whole payment;
(b) if, in the claimant's case, £10 is disregarded in accordance with paragraph 1(a) to (g), £10 or the whole payment if it is less than £10; or
(c) if, in the claimant's case, £15 is disregarded under paragraph 7 or paragraph 8 and–
   (i) he has no disregard under paragraph 1(a) to (g), £5 or the whole payment if it is less than £5;
   (ii) he has a disregard under paragraph 1(a) to (g), nil.

(4) For the purposes of this paragraph–
[1 "ordinary clothing or footwear"] means clothing or footwear for normal daily use, but does not include school uniforms, or clothing and footwear used solely for sporting activities; and
"rent" means eligible rent for the purposes of these Regulations less any deductions in respect of non-dependants which fall to be made under regulation 55 (non-dependant deductions).

Amendment
1. Amended by reg 4(8)(b) of SI 2008 No 1042 as from 19.5.08.

Analysis
This paragraph has no equivalent in Sch 5 HB Regs. All payments under a discretionary trust are ignored, except for those which are used for the essentials set out in para (2), which receive only a limited disregard calculated according to the amounts of other disregards.

13. Any increase in [1 pension or allowance under Part 2 or 3 of the Naval, Military and Air Forces Etc. (Disablement and Death) Service Pensions Order 2006] paid in respect of a dependent other than the pensioner's [1] partner.

Amendment
1. Amended by reg 6(9)(e) of SI 2008 No 3157 as from 5.1.09.

Analysis
This paragraph deals with increases in war pensions for dependants, which are to be ignored completely.

14. Any payment ordered by a court to be made to the claimant or the claimant's partner in consequence of any accident, injury or disease suffered by the person or a child of the person to or in respect of whom the payments are made.

15. Periodic payments made to the claimant or the claimant's partner under an agreement entered into in settlement of a claim made by the claimant or, as the case may be, the claimant's partner for an injury suffered by him.

Analysis to paras 14 and 15
The phrase "any accident, injury or disease" used in para 14 is probably wider than the phrase used in reg 42(2)(b) HB Regs "a personal injury". It might, for example, cover wrongful birth claims which can be said to arise from an "accident" such as a negligently carried out sterilisation.
Para 15 does not appear to include payments from an annuity purchased by a defendant's insurer, since those are payments made under the annuity contract rather than under the settlement agreement.

16. Any income which is payable outside the United Kingdom for such period during which there is a prohibition against the transfer to the United Kingdom of that income.

17. Any banking charges or commission payable in converting to Sterling payments of income made in a currency other than Sterling.

18. Where the claimant makes a parental contribution in respect of a student attending a course at an establishment in the United Kingdom or undergoing education in the United Kingdom, which contribution has been assessed for the purposes of calculating–
(a) under, or pursuant to regulations made under powers conferred, by section 1 or 2 of the Education Act 1962, or section 22 of the Teaching and Higher Education Act 1998, that student's award;
(b) under regulations made in exercise of the powers conferred by section 49 of the Education (Scotland) Act 1980, that student's bursary, scholarship, or other allowance under that section or under regulations made in exercise of the powers conferred by section 73 of that Act of 1980, any payment to that student under that section; or
(c) the student's student loan,
an amount equal to the weekly amount of that parental contribution, but only in respect of the period for which that contribution is assessed as being payable.

Analysis
This is equivalent to Sch 5 para 19 HB Regs (see p671).

19.–(1) Where the claimant is the parent of a student aged under 25 in advanced education who either–
(a) is not in receipt of any award, grant or student loan in respect of that education; or
(b) is in receipt of an award under section 2 of the Education Act 1962 (discretionary awards) or an award bestowed by virtue of the Teaching and Higher Education Act 1998, or regulations made thereunder, or a bursary, scholarship or other allowance under section 49(1) of the Education (Scotland) Act 1980, or a payment under section 73 of that Act of 1980,
and the claimant makes payments by way of a contribution towards the student's maintenance, other than a parental contribution falling within paragraph 18, an amount specified in sub-paragraph (2) in respect of each week during the student's term.
(2) For the purposes of sub-paragraph (1), the amount shall be equal to–
(a) the weekly amount of the payments; or
(b) the amount by way of a personal allowance for a single claimant under 25 less the weekly amount of any award, bursary, scholarship, allowance or payment referred to in sub-paragraph (1)(b),
whichever is less.

Analysis
This is equivalent to Sch 5 para 20 HB Regs (see p671).

20.–(1) Where a claimant's [¹² family includes at least one child or young person,] £15 of any payment of maintenance, whether under a court order or not, which is made or due to be made by the claimant's spouse, civil partner, former spouse or former civil partner or the claimant's partner's spouse, civil partner, former spouse, or former civil partner.
(2) For the purposes of sub-paragraph (1), where more than one maintenance payment falls to be taken into account in any week, all such payments shall be aggregated and treated as if they were a single payment.

Analysis
This is equivalent to Sch 5 para 47 HB Regs (see p664), though there is no equivalent to para 47(3). Note that other kinds of maintenance (eg, for a child) do not count as income and are ignored completely: reg 29(1)(o).

21. Except in a case which falls under paragraph 9 of Schedule 4, where the claimant is a person who satisfies [⁴ any of] the conditions of sub-paragraph (2) of that paragraph, any amount of working tax credit up to [¹⁵ £17.10].

1. Amended by art 20(8) of SI 2006 No 645 and reg 8 of SI 2006 No 217 as from 1.4.06 (3.4.06 where rent payable weekly or at intervals of a week).
2. Amended by art 20(10) of SI 2007 No 688 as from 1.4.07 (2.4.07 where rent payable weekly or at intervals of a week).
3. Amended by art 20(11) of SI 2008 No 632 as from 1.4.08 (7.4.08 where rent payable weekly or in multiples of a week).
4. Amended by reg 6(9)(f) of SI 2008 No 3157 as from 5.1.09.
5. Amended by art 20(11) of SI 2009 No 497 as from 1.4.09 (6.4.09 where rent payable weekly or at intervals of a week).
6. Amended by art 20(10) of SI 2010 No 793 as from 1.4.10 (5.4.10 where rent payable weekly or in multiples of a week).
7. Confirmed by art 21(10) of SI 2011 No 821 as from 1.4.11 (4.4.11 where rent payable weekly or in multiples of a week).
8. Confirmed by art 21(10) of SI 2012 No 780 as from 1.4.12 (2.4.12 where rent payable weekly or in multiples of a week).
9. Confirmed by art 20(10) of SI 2013 No 574 as from 1.4.13.

10. Confirmed by art 18(10) of SI 2014 No 16 as from 1.4.14 (7.4.14 where rent payable weekly or in multiples of a week).
11. Confirmed by art 18(10) of SI 2015 No 547 as from 1.4.15 (6.4.15 where rent payable weekly or in multiples of a week).
12. Amended by reg 2(2)(d) of SI 2015 No 1857 as from 1.5.16, subject to transitional provision in reg 4 of SI 2015 No 1857.
13. Confirmed by art 23(10) of SI 2017 No 260 as from 1.4.17 (3.4.17 where rent payable weekly or in multiples of a week).
14. Confirmed by art 24(10) of SI 2018 No 281 as from 1.4.18 (2.4.18 where rent payable weekly or in multiples of a week).
15. Confirmed by art 24(10) of SI 2019 No 480 as from 1.4.19.

Analysis
See the commentary to Sch 4 para 17 HB Regs on p663 and Sch 5 para 56 on p680.

---

22. Except in the case of income from capital specified in Part 2 of Schedule 6, any actual income from capital.

Analysis
The combined effect of reg 29(1)(i) (which defines "income from capital" other than capital disregarded under Sch 6 Part 1 as income) and para 22 is that it is only actual income from any capital not specified in either Part 1 or Part 2 of Sch 6 that is disregarded. Instead, reg 29(2) provides a formula for calculating "deemed" income from the capital. Actual income from capital is only taken into account if the capital is specified in Sch 6 Part 2, but see para 24 below for a partial disregard.

[¹**23.**]

Amendment
1. Omitted by reg 6(9)(g) of SI 2008 No 3157 as from 5.1.09.

[¹**24.** Where the total value of any capital specified in Part 2 (capital disregarded only for the purposes of determining deemed income) of Schedule 6 does not exceed £10,000, any income actually derived from such capital.]

Amendment
1. Substituted by reg 6 of SI 2009 No 1676 as from 2.11.09.

Analysis
Under para 24, actual income from capital listed in Sch 6 Part 2 is disregarded, but only where the total value of the capital does not exceed £10,000. If the total value does exceed that amount, actual income from the capital is taken into account under reg 29(1)(i). See para 22 above for a disregard of actual income from capital not specified in Sch 6 Part 2.

SCHEDULE 6

REGULATION 44(2)

Capital to be disregarded

General Note to Sch 6
Sch 6 sets out the capital that is to be disregarded. It serves more than one purpose.
(1) Capital listed in either Part 1 or Part 2 is not to be taken into account in working out if a claimant's capital exceeds the £16,000 capital limit: regs 43 and 44(2).
(2) The capital specified in Part 1 is disregarded for the purposes of determining a claimant's income: reg 33(11)(a). In any event, actual income from the capital is not to be treated as "income": reg 29(1)(i).
(3) Actual income from capital listed in Part 2 and from any other capital not disregarded under Part 1, is treated as income under reg 29(1)(i). Note, however, it is only taken into account if it is income from capital disregarded under Part 2 and then only if the total value exceeds £10,000: see Sch 5 para 24. Otherwise actual income from the capital is disregarded under Sch 5 para 22.
(4) The capital specified in either Part 1 or Part 2 is disregarded for the purposes of determining "deemed" income: reg 33(11)(a) and (b). Other capital can be deemed to produce a weekly income under reg 29(2).
Note: payments made to qualifying Equitable Life annuitants under the Age Related Payments Regulations 2013 SI No.2980 are disregarded under reg 5 of those regulations (see p1855).

PART 1

General Note

Part 1 of Sch 6 lists capital that can be disregarded generally. If capital is in Part 1, actual income from it does not count as "income": reg 29(1)(i). In addition, the capital is not "deemed" to produce a weekly income under reg 29(2). This is confirmed by reg 33(11)(a).

Capital to be disregarded generally

1.   Any premises acquired for occupation by the claimant which he intends to occupy as his home within 26 weeks of the date of acquisition or such longer period as is reasonable in the circumstances to enable the claimant to obtain possession and commence occupation of the premises.

2.   Any premises which the claimant intends to occupy as his home, and in respect of which he is taking steps to obtain possession and has sought legal advice, or has commenced legal proceedings, with a view to obtaining possession, for a period of 26 weeks from the date on which he first sought such advice or first commenced such proceedings whichever is the earlier, or such longer period as is reasonable in the circumstances to enable him to obtain possession and commence occupation of those premises.

3.   Any premises which the claimant intends to occupy as his home to which essential repairs or alterations are required in order to render them fit for such occupation, for a period of 26 weeks from the date on which the claimant first takes steps to effect those repairs or alterations, or such longer period as is necessary to enable those repairs or alterations to be carried out.

4.   Any premises occupied in whole or in part–

(a)   by a person who is a relative of the claimant or of his partner as his home [¹ where that person has attained the qualifying age for state pension credit or is incapacitated];

(b)   by the former partner of the claimant as his home; but this provision shall not apply where the former partner is a person from whom the claimant is estranged or divorced or with whom he had formed a civil partnership that has been dissolved.

Amendment

1.   Amended by reg 31 of SI 2009 No 1488 as from 6.4.10.

5.   Any future interest in property of any kind, other than land or premises in respect of which the claimant has granted a subsisting lease or tenancy, including sub-leases or sub-tenancies.

6.   Where a claimant has ceased to occupy what was formerly the dwelling occupied as the home following his estrangement or divorce from his former partner or the dissolution of a civil partnership with his former partner, that dwelling for a period of 26 weeks from the date on which he ceased to occupy that dwelling or, where the dwelling is occupied as the home by the former partner who is a lone parent, for so long as it is so occupied.

7.   Any premises where the claimant is taking reasonable steps to dispose of the whole of his interest in those premises, for a period of 26 weeks from the date on which he first took such steps, or such longer period as is reasonable in the circumstances to enable him to dispose of those premises.

Analysis to paras 1 to 7

These are equivalent to HB Regs Sch 6 paras 2, 27, 28, 4, 7, 25 and 26 respectively (see p683).

8.   All personal possessions.

Analysis

This is different to Sch 6 para 12 HB Regs because it contains no exception for possessions purchased in order to reduce capital and increase benefit. Unless the notional capital provision in reg 47 applies, the value of such possessions must be completely ignored.

9.   The assets of any business owned in whole or in part by the claimant and for the purposes of which he is engaged as a self-employed earner or, if he has ceased to be engaged, for such period as may be reasonable in the circumstances to allow for disposal of those assets.

10.   The assets of any business owned in whole or in part by the claimant if–

(a)   he is not engaged as a self-employed earner in that business by reason of some disease or bodily or mental disablement; but

(b)   he intends to become engaged (or, as the case may be, re-engaged) as a self-employed earner in that business as soon as he recovers or is able to become engaged, or re-engaged, in that business,

for a period of 26 weeks from the date on which the claim for housing benefit is made or, if it is unreasonable to expect him to become engaged or re-engaged in that business within that period, for such longer period as is reasonable in the circumstances to enable him to become so engaged or re-engaged.

Analysis to paras 9 and 10

These are equivalent to Sch 6 para 8 HB Regs (see p686).

11. The surrender value of any policy of life insurance.

12. The value of any funeral plan contract; and for this purpose, "funeral plan contract" means a contract under which–

(a) the claimant makes one or more payments to another person ("the provider");

(b) the provider undertakes to provide, or secure the provision of, a funeral in the United Kingdom for the claimant on his death; and

(c) the sole purpose of the plan is to provide or secure the provision of a funeral for the claimant on his death.

Analysis

This has no equivalent in Sch 6 HB Regs but para 12 is self-explanatory.

---

13. Where an ex-gratia payment has been made by the Secretary of State on or after 1st February 2001 in consequence of the imprisonment or internment of–

(a) the claimant;

(b) the claimant's partner;

(c) the claimant's deceased spouse or deceased civil partner; or

(d) the claimant's partner's deceased spouse or deceased civil partner,

by the Japanese during the Second World War, an amount equal to that payment.

14.–(1) Subject to sub-paragraph (2), the amount of any trust payment made to a claimant or a claimant's partner who is–

(a) a diagnosed person;

(b) a diagnosed person's partner or was a diagnosed person's partner at the time of the diagnosed person's death;

(c) a parent of a diagnosed person, a person acting in place of the diagnosed person's parents or a person who was so acting at the date of the diagnosed person's death.

(2) Where a trust payment is made to–

(a) a person referred to in sub-paragraph (1)(a) or (b), that sub-paragraph shall apply for the period beginning on the date on which the trust payment is made and ending on the date on which that person dies;

(b) a person referred to in sub-paragraph (1)(c), that sub-paragraph shall apply for the period beginning on the date on which the trust payment is made and ending two years after that date.

(3) Subject to sub-paragraph (4), the amount of any payment by a person to whom a trust payment has been made or of any payment out of the estate of a person to whom a trust payment has been made, which is made to a claimant or a claimant's partner who is–

(a) the diagnosed person;

(b) a diagnosed person's partner or was a diagnosed person's partner at the date of the diagnosed person's death; or

(c) a parent of a diagnosed person, a person acting in place of the diagnosed person's parents or a person who was so acting at the date of the diagnosed person's death.

(4) Where a payment such as referred to in sub-paragraph (3) is made to–

(a) a person referred to in sub-paragraph (3)(a) or (b), that sub-paragraph shall apply for the period beginning on the date on which the payment is made and ending on the date on which that person dies;

(b) a person referred to in sub-paragraph (3)(c), that sub-paragraph shall apply for the period beginning on the date on which the payment is made and ending two years after that date.

(5) In this paragraph, a reference to a person–

(a) being the diagnosed person's partner;

(b) acting in place of the diagnosed person's parents,

at the date of the diagnosed person's death shall include a person who would have been such a person or a person who would have been so acting, but for the diagnosed person residing in a care home or an independent hospital.

(6) In this paragraph–

"diagnosed person" means a person who has been diagnosed as suffering from, or who, after his death, has been diagnosed as having suffered from, variant Creutzfeldt-Jakob disease;

"relevant trust" means a trust established out of funds provided by the Secretary of State in respect of persons who suffered, or who are suffering, from variant Creutzfeldt-Jakob disease for the benefit of persons eligible for payments in accordance with its provisions;

"trust payment" means a payment under a relevant trust.

15. The amount of any payment, other than a [¹ war pension], to compensate for the fact that the claimant, the claimant's partner, the claimant's deceased spouse or civil partner or the claimant's partner's deceased spouse or civil partner–

(a) was a slave labourer or a forced labourer;

(b) had suffered property loss or had suffered personal injury; or

(c) was a parent of a child who had died,

during the Second World War.

Amendment

1.   Amended by reg 6(10)(a) of SI 2008 No 3157 as from 5.1.09.

16.–(1)   Any payment made under [² or by]–

(a)   the Macfarlane Trust, the Macfarlane (Special Payments) Trust, the Macfarlane (Special Payments) (No. 2) Trust, the Fund, the Eileen Trust [², MFET Limited], the Skipton Fund [³, the Caxton Foundation] [⁴, the Scottish Infected Blood Support Scheme] [⁶, an approved blood scheme] [⁵, the London Emergencies Trust, the We Love Manchester Emergency Fund] or the London Bombings Relief Charitable Fund (collectively referred to in this paragraph as "the Trusts"); or

(b)   the Independent Living [¹ Fund (2006)].

(2)   Any payment by or on behalf of a person who is suffering or who suffered from haemophilia or who is or was a qualifying person, which derives from a payment made under [² or by] any of the Trusts and which is made to or for the benefit of that person's partner or former partner from whom he is not, or where that person has died was not, estranged or divorced or with whom he has formed a civil partnership that has not been dissolved or, where that person has died, had not been dissolved at the time of that person's death.

(3)   Any payment by or on behalf of the partner or former partner of a person who is suffering or who suffered from haemophilia or who is or was a qualifying person provided that the partner or former partner and that person are not, or if either of them has died were not, estranged or divorced or, where the partner or former partner and that person have formed a civil partnership, the civil partnership has not been dissolved or, if either of them has died, had not been dissolved at the time of the death, which derives from a payment made under [² or by] any of the Trusts and which is made to or for the benefit of the person who is suffering from haemophilia or who is a qualifying person.

(4)   Any payment by a person who is suffering from haemophilia or who is a qualifying person, which derives from a payment under [² or by] any of the Trusts, where–

(a)   that person has no partner or former partner from whom he is not estranged or divorced or with whom he has formed a civil partnership that has not been dissolved nor any child who is or had been a member of that person's household; and

(b)   the payment is made either–

    (i)   to that person's parent or step-parent; or

    (ii)   where that person at the date of the payment is a child or a student who has not completed his full-time education and has no parent or step-parent, to any person standing in the place of his parent,

but only for a period from the date of the payment until the end of two years from that person's death.

(5)   Any payment out of the estate of a person who suffered from haemophilia or who was a qualifying person, which derives from a payment under [² or by] any of the Trusts, where–

(a)   that person at the date of his death ("the relevant date") had no partner or former partner from whom he was not estranged or divorced or with whom he had formed a civil partnership that had not been dissolved, nor any child who was or had been a member of his household; and

(b)   the payment is made either–

    (i)   to that person's parent or step-parent; or

    (ii)   where that person at the relevant date was a child or a student who had not completed his full-time education and had no parent or step-parent, to any person standing in place of his parent,

but only for a period of two years from the relevant date.

(6)   In the case of a person to whom or for whose benefit a payment referred to in this paragraph is made, any capital resource which derives from any payment of income or capital made under or deriving from any of the Trusts.

Modifications

References to "step-parent" in sub-paras (4)(b)(i) and (ii) and (5)(b)(i) and (ii) are modified by s246 Civil Partnership Act 2004 (see p1729) and art 3 and Sch para 27 to SI 2005 No 3137 (see p1772).

Amendments

1.   Amended by reg 7(5)(b) of SI 2008 No 2767 as from 17.11.08.

2.   Amended by reg 9(3) and (5) of SI 2010 No 641 as from 1.4.10 (5.4.10 where rent payable weekly or in multiples of a week).

3.   Amended by reg 20(8) of SI 2011 No 2425 as from 31.10.11.

4.   Amended by reg 7(3)(c) of SI 2017 No 329 as from 3.4.17.

5.   Amended by reg 7(3)(c) of SI 2017 No 689 as from 19.6.17.

6.   Amended by reg 7(3)(b) of SI 2017 No 870 as from 23.10.17.

Analysis to paras 13 to 16

These are equivalent to HB Regs Sch 6 paras 54 (although there is no reference to the amount of the payment being £10,000), 55, 56 and 24 respectively (see p683).

17.–(1)   An amount equal to the amount of any payment made in consequence of any personal injury to the claimant or, if the claimant has a partner, to the partner.

(2)   Where the whole or part of the payment is administered–

[¹ (a)   by the High Court or the County Court under Rule 21.11(1) of the Civil Procedure Rules 1998, or the Court of Protection, or on behalf of a person where the payment can only be disposed of by order or direction of any such court;]

(b)   in accordance with an order under Rule 36.14 of the Ordinary Cause Rules 1993 or under Rule 128 of those Rules; or

(c)   in accordance with the terms of a trust established for the benefit of the claimant or his partner,

the whole of the amount so administered.

Amendment

1.   Substituted by reg 16(4) of SI 2006 No 2378 from the first day of the first benefit week to commence on or after 2.10.06.

Analysis

On sub-para (2), see Sch 6 paras 45 and 46 HB Regs on p696. For the words "in consequence of any personal injury", see reg 42(2) HB Regs on p453.

18.   Any amount specified in paragraphs 19, 20 [¹ , 21 or 26B] for a period of one year beginning with the date of receipt.

Amendment

1.   Amended by reg 6(10)(b) of SI 2008 No 3157 as from 5.1.09.

19.   Amounts paid under a policy of insurance in connection with the loss of or damage to the property occupied by the claimant as his home and to his personal possessions.

Analysis

By para 18, the amounts are disregarded for one year from the date of receipt.

20.   So much of any amounts paid to the claimant or deposited in the claimant's name for the sole purpose of–

(a)   purchasing premises which the claimant intends to occupy as his home; or

(b)   effecting essential repairs or alterations to the premises occupied or intended to be occupied by the claimant as his home.

Analysis

By para 18, the amounts are disregarded for one year from the date of receipt.

21.–(1)   Subject to paragraph 22 any amount paid–

(a)   by way of arrears of benefit;

(b)   by way of compensation for the late payment of benefit;

(c)   in lieu of the payment of benefit;

(d)   to rectify, or compensate for, an official error, as defined for the purposes of paragraph 22, being an amount to which that paragraph does not apply;

(e)   by a local authority (including, in relation to England, a county council), or by the National Assembly for Wales, to or on behalf of the claimant or his partner relating to a service which is provided to develop or sustain the capacity of the claimant or his partner to live independently in his accommodation.

[³ (f)   by way of local welfare provision including arrears and payments in lieu of local welfare provision.]

(2)   In sub-paragraph (1), "benefit" means–

(a)   attendance allowance under section 64 of the Act;

(b)   disability living allowance;

[⁴ (ba)   personal independence payment;]

[⁵ (bb)   armed forces independence payment;]

(c)   income support;

(d)   income-based jobseeker's allowance;

(e)   state pension credit;

(f)   housing benefit;

(g)   council tax benefit;

(h)   child tax credit;

(i)   an increase of a disablement pension under section 104 of the Act (increase where constant attendance is needed), and any further increase of such a pension under section 105 of the Act (increase for exceptionally severe disablement);

(j)   any amount included on account of the claimant's exceptionally severe disablement or need for constant attendance in a war disablement pension or a war widow's or widower's pension.

[¹ (k)   any discretionary housing payment paid pursuant to regulation 2(1) of the Discretionary Financial Assistance Regulations 2001; [²]

(l)   working tax credit.] [² [³]

[² (m) income-related employment and support allowance.]

[³ (n)   social fund payments][⁶ ;or]

[⁶ (o)   universal credit]

[⁷ (p)   bereavement support payment under section 30 of the Pensions Act 2014.]

[⁸ (q)   early years assistance given in accordance with section 32 of the Social Security (Scotland) Act 2018.]

[⁹ (r)   funeral expense assistance given in accordance with section 34 of the Social Security (Scotland) Act 2018.]

[¹⁰ (s) maternity allowance under section 35 of the Act (state maternity allowance for employed or self-employed earner).]

Amendments

1.   Inserted by reg 2(17) of SI 2005 No 2502 as amended by Sch 2 para 27 of SI 2006 No 217 as from 1.4.06 (3.4.06 where rent payable weekly or at intervals of a week).

2.   Amended by reg 41 of SI 2008 No 1082 as from 27.10.08.

3.   Amended by reg 8(4)(a) of SI 2013 No 443 as from 2.4.13.

4.   Amended by reg 8 and Sch para 37(9) of SI 2013 No 388 as from 8.4.13.

5.   Amended by art 7 and Sch para 35(9) of SI 2013 No 591 as from 8.4.13.

6.   Inserted by reg 36(8) of SI 2013 No 630 as from 29.4.13.

7.   Inserted by art 26(3)(a) of SI 2017 No 422 as from 6.4.17, subject to transitional provisions in arts 2 and 3.

8.   Inserted by reg 9(3) of SI 2018 No 1138 as from 10.12.18.

9.   Inserted by reg 15(3) of SI 2019 No 1060 as from 16.9.19.

10.   Inserted by reg 6 of SI 2019 No 1314 as from 31.10.19.

Analysis

By para 18, the amounts are disregarded for one year from date of receipt. Para 21 covers arrears, compensatory payments and payments in lieu of benefits or "local welfare provision" (the replacement for certain social fund payments – see the definition in reg 2(1)), certain assistance given under the Social Security (Scotland) Act 2018 and payments relating to a service provided to develop or sustain the capacity of the claimant or her/his partner to live independently in her/his home. "Benefit" is defined in para 21(2). Note that CTB is included. CTB was abolished and replaced by local CTR schemes from 1 April 2013. Note the disregard of payments in consequence of CTR in para 26E.

See also para 22 below where arrears of benefit are paid to compensate for "official error" or error on a point of law.

22.–(1)   Subject to sub-paragraph (3), any payment of £5,000 or more which has been made to rectify, or to compensate for, an official error [⁵ or an error on a point of law] relating to a relevant benefit and has been received by the claimant in full on or after the day on which he became entitled to benefit under these Regulations or the Housing Benefit Regulations 2006.

(2)   Subject to sub-paragraph (3), the total amount of any payments disregarded under–

(a)   paragraph 7(2) of Schedule 10 to the Income Support Regulations;

(b)   paragraph 12(2) of Schedule 8 to the Jobseeker's Allowance Regulations;

(c)   paragraph 9(2) of [¹ Schedule 6] to the Housing Benefit Regulations 2006;

(d)   paragraph 20A of Schedule 5 to the State Pension Credit Regulations 2002,

[² (e)   paragraph 11(2) of Schedule 9 to the Employment and Support Allowance Regulations,]

[⁴ (f)   paragraph 18 of Schedule 10 to the Universal Credit Regulations 2013,]

where the award in respect of which the payments last fell to be disregarded under those Regulations either terminated immediately before the relevant date or is still in existence at that date.

(3)   Any disregard which applies under sub-paragraph (1) or (2) shall have effect until the award comes to an end.

(4)   In this paragraph–

"the award", except in sub-paragraph (2), means–

(a)   the award of benefit under these Regulations during which the relevant sum or, where it is paid in more than one instalment, the first instalment of that sum is received; and

(b)   where that award is followed by one or more further awards which, or each of which, begins immediately after the previous award ends, such further awards until the end of the last such award, provided that, for such further awards, the claimant–

(i)   is the person who received the relevant sum;

(ii)   is the partner of that person; or

       (iii)   was the partner of that person at the date of his death;

"official error" –

    (a)   where the error relates to housing benefit [³], has the meaning given by regulation 1(2) of the Decisions and Appeals Regulations;

    (b)   where the error relates to any other relevant benefit, has the meaning given by regulation 1(3) of the Social Security and Child Support (Decisions and Appeals) Regulations 1999;

"the relevant date" means–

    (a)   in the case of an existing award of benefit under these Regulations or the Housing Benefit Regulations 2006, 6th October 2003; and

    (b)   in any other case, the date on which the claim for benefit under these Regulations or the Housing Benefit Regulations 2006 was made;

"relevant benefit" means any benefit specified in paragraph 21(2); and

"the relevant sum" means the payment referred to in sub-paragraph (1) or the total amount referred to in sub-paragraph (2).

Amendments

1.   Amended by reg 4(9) of SI 2008 No 1042 as from 19.5.08.
2.   Amended by reg 41(b) of SI 2008 No 1082 as from 27.10.08.
3.   Amended by ref 3 and Sch 1 of SI 2013 No 458 as from 1.4.13.
4.   Inserted by reg 12(6) of SI 2013 No.2536 as from 29.10.13.
5.   Amended by reg 6 of SI 2018 No 932 as from 11.9.18.

Analysis

Arrears of relevant benefits (for which see para 21(2)) are disregarded for longer than the year allowed under para 21 if the payment is £5,000 or more and was made to rectify or to compensate for an "official error" (defined in sub-para (4)) or error on a point of law. The arrears must have been received in full on or after the day the claimant became entitled to HB or if paid before then, the current award of HB must follow immediately from a previous award of IS, income-based JSA, income-related ESA, PC, UC or HB, or must still be being disregarded in an award of one of those benefits: paras (1) and (2) and the definition of "relevant date" in para (4). The arrears are disregarded until the award ends: sub-para (3).

---

23.   Where a capital asset is held in a currency other than Sterling, any banking charge or commission payable in converting that capital into Sterling.

24.   The value of the right to receive income from an occupational pension scheme or a personal pension scheme.

[¹**25.**]

Amendment

1.   Omitted by reg 5(6) of SI 2007 No 1749 as from 16.7.07.

---

26.   The dwelling occupied as the home; but only one dwelling shall be disregarded under this paragraph.

[¹**26A.**   Where a person elects to be entitled to a lump sum under Schedule 5 or 5A to the Contributions and Benefits Act or under Schedule 1 to the Graduated Retirement Benefit Regulations, or is treated as having made such an election, and a payment has been made pursuant to that election, an amount equal to–

    (a)   except where sub-paragraph (b) applies, the amount of any payment or payments made on account of that lump sum;

    (b)   the amount of that lump sum,

but only for so long as that person does not change that election in favour of an increase of pension or benefit.]

Amendment

1.   Inserted by reg 11(4) of SI 2005 No 2677 and reg 2 of SI 2006 No 217 as from 6.4.06.

[¹**26AA.**   Where a person chooses a lump sum under section 8(2) of the Pensions Act 2014 or in accordance with Regulations made under section 10 of that Act which include provision corresponding or similar to section 8(2) of that Act, or fails to make a choice, and a lump sum payment has been made, an amount equal to–

    (a)   except where sub-paragraph (b) applies, the amount of any payment or payments made on account of that lump sum;

    (b)   the amount of that lump sum,

but only for so long as that person does not alter that choice in favour of an increase of pension.]

Amendment

1.   Inserted by art 29(5) of SI 2015 No 1985 as from 6.4.16.

[¹**26B.**   Any arrears of supplementary pension which is disregarded under paragraph 4 of Schedule 5 (amounts to be disregarded in the calculation of income other than earnings) or of any amount which is disregarded under paragraph 5 or 6 of that Schedule.]

Amendment

1.   Inserted by reg 6(10)(d) of SI 2008 No 3157 as from 5.1.09.

Analysis

By para 18, the arrears are disregarded for one year from the date of receipt.

[¹**26C.**   Any payment made under Part 8A of the Act (entitlement to health in pregnancy grant).]

Amendment

1.   Inserted by reg 7(8) of SI 2009 No 583 as from 6.4.09.

[¹**26D.**   Any payments made [²]–

(a)   [² by virtue of regulations made under] section 57 of the Health and Social Care Act 2001 (direct payments);

[² (b)   as a direct payment as defined in section 4(2) of the Social Care (Self-directed Support) (Scotland) Act 2003;] [³]

(c)   [² by virtue of regulations made under] sections 12A to 12C of the National Health Service Act 2006 (direct payments for health care).] [⁴]

[³ (d)   as a direct payment under Part 1 of the Care Act 2014 (care and support).] [⁴ or

(e)   by virtue of regulations made under section 50 or 52 of the Social Services and Well-being (Wales) Act 2014 (direct payments).]

Amendments

1.   Inserted by reg 20(11) of SI 2011 No 2425 as from 31.10.11.
2.   Amended by art 2 and Sch para 11 of SI 2014 No 513 as from 1.4.14.
3.   Amended by art 2 and Sch para 25(3) of SI 2015 No 643 as from 1.4.15.
4.   Amended by art 12(5) of SI 2017 No 901 as from 3.11.17.

[¹**26E.**   Any payment in consequence of a reduction of council tax under section 13, 13A or 80 of the Local Government Finance Act 1992 (reduction of liability for council tax), but only for a period of 52 weeks from the date of the receipt of the payment.]

Amendment

1.   Inserted by reg 8(4)(b) of SI 2013 No 443 as from 2.4.13.

Analysis

Among other things, para 26E allows payments in consequence of a local authority's CTR scheme (the replacement for CTB from 1 April 2013) to be disregarded.

Note the disregard of arrears and compensatory payments of CTB in paras 21 and 22.

[¹**26F.**   Any payments to a claimant made under section 49 of the Children and Families Act 2014 (personal budgets and direct payments).]

Amendment

1.   Inserted by reg 21 of SI 2014 No.2103 as from 1.9.14.

[¹**26G.**–(1)   Any payment made by a local authority in accordance with section 26A of the Children (Scotland) Act 1995.

(2)   Subject to sub-paragraph (3), any payment or part of a payment made by a local authority in accordance with section 26A of the Children (Scotland) Act 1995 to a person ("A") which A passes on to the claimant.

(3)   Sub-paragraph (2) only applies where A–

(a)   was formerly in the care of the claimant;

(b)   is aged 16 or over; and

(c)   continues to live with the claimant.]

Amendment

1.   Inserted by art 7(3) of SI 2016 No 732 as from 5.8.16.

[¹**26H.**   Any bereavement support payment in respect of the rate set out in regulations 3(2) or (5) of the Bereavement Support Payment Regulations 2017 (rate of bereavement support payment), but only for a period of 52 weeks from the date of receipt of the payment.

Amendment
1.   Inserted by art 26(3)(b) of SI 2017 No 422 as from 6.4.17, subject to transitional provisions in arts 2 and 3.

[¹**26I.**
Any payment made under or by a trust, established for the purpose of giving relief and assistance to disabled persons whose disabililties were caused by the fact that during their mother's pregnancy she had taken a preparation containing the drug known as Thalidomide, and which is approved by the Secretary of State.]
Amendment
1.   Inserted by reg 7(6) of SI 2017 No 870 as from 23.10.17.

PART 2

General Note
Part 2 lists capital that is disregarded "only for the purposes of determining deemed income" under reg 29(2). See also reg 33(11)(b). However, note that it is also disregarded for the purposes of the capital limit by reg 44(2). If capital is in this list, although it is not treated as producing a weekly deemed income, actual income from the capital can be taken into account, subject to para 24 of Sch 5.

Capital disregarded only for the purposes of determining deemed income
27.   The value of the right to receive any income under a life interest or from a life rent.

Analysis
This is the equivalent, save for the fact that the disregard only operates for the calculation of tariff income and the capital limit, of HB Regs Sch 6 para 15 (see p690).

28.   The value of the right to receive any rent except where the claimant has a reversionary interest in the property in respect of which rent is due.
29.   The value of the right to receive any income under an annuity or the surrender value (if any) of such an annuity.

Analysis
This is the equivalent, save for the fact that the disregard only operates for the calculation of tariff income and the capital limit, of HB Regs Sch 6 para 13 (see p688).

30.   Where property is held under a trust, other than–
(a)   a charitable trust within the meaning of the Charities Act 1993; or
(b)   a trust set up with any payment to which paragraph 16 of this Schedule applies,
and under the terms of the trust, payments fall to be made, or the trustees have a discretion to make payments, to or for the benefit of the claimant or the claimant's partner, or both, that property.

Analysis
Para 30 requires beneficial interests under a trust to be ignored.

[² SCHEDULE 7

Amendments
1.   Amended by reg 19 of SI 2007 No 2869 as from 7.4.08 (or if reg 1(5) of that SI applies, on the day on or after 7.4.08 when the first of the events specified in reg 1(6) applies, or from 6.4.09 if none have before that date).
2.   Omitted by reg 6(4)(d) of SI 2008 No 959 as from 6.10.08.

SCHEDULE 8

REGULATION 71

Matters to be included in decision notice

PART 1
General
1.   The statement of matters to be included in any decision notice issued by a relevant authority to a person, and referred to in regulation 71 (notification of decisions) and in regulation 10 of the Decisions and Appeals Regulations are those matters set out in the following provisions of this Schedule.

2. Every decision notice shall include a statement as to the right of any person affected by that decision to request a written statement under regulation 71(2) (requests for statement of reasons) and the manner and time in which to do so.

3. Every decision notice shall include a statement as to the right of any person affected by that decision to make an application for a revision in accordance with regulation 4(1)(a) of the Decisions and Appeals Regulations and, where appropriate, to appeal against that decision and the manner and time in which to do so.

4. Every decision notice following an application for a revision in accordance with regulation 4(1)(a) of the Decisions and Appeals Regulations shall include a statement as to whether the original decision in respect of which the person made his representations has been confirmed or revised and where the relevant authority has not revised the decision the reasons why not.

5. Every decision notice following an application for a revision in accordance with regulation 4(1)(a) of the Decisions and Appeals Regulations shall, if the original decision has been revised, include a statement as to the right of any person affected by that decision to apply for a revision in accordance with regulation 4(1)(a) of those Regulations and the manner and time in which to do so.

6. An authority may include in the decision notice any other matters not prescribed by this Schedule which it sees fit, whether expressly or by reference to some other document available without charge to the person.

7. Parts 2, 3 and 6 of this Schedule shall apply only to the decision notice given on a claim.

8. Where a decision notice is given following a revision of an earlier decision–

(a) made of the authority's own motion which results in a revision of that earlier decision; or

(b) made following an application for a revision in accordance with regulation 4(1)(a) of the Decisions and Appeals Regulations, whether or not resulting in a revision of that earlier decision,

that notice shall, subject to paragraph 6, contain a statement only as to all the matters revised.

PART 2
Awards where state pension credit [³ or an extended payment (qualifying contributory benefits] is payable

9.–(1) Where a person on state pension credit is awarded housing benefit, the decision notice shall include a statement as to–

(a) his weekly eligible rent, if any; and

(b) the amount and an explanation of any deduction made under paragraph 6(2) or (3) of Schedule 1 (fuel deductions), if any, and that the deduction may be varied if he provides to the authority evidence on which it may estimate the actual or approximate amount of that service charge; and

(c) the amount of and the category of non-dependant deductions made under regulation 55 (non-dependant deductions), if any; and

(d) the normal weekly amount of rent allowance, or rent rebate as the case may be, to which he is entitled; and

(e) in the case of a rent allowance and a [² rent rebate] paid as if it were a rent allowance, the day of payment, and the period in respect of which payment of that allowance is to be made; and

(f) the first day of entitlement to an allowance or rebate; and

(g) his duty to notify any change of circumstances which might affect his entitlement to, or the amount of, housing benefit and (without prejudice to the extent of the duty owed under regulation 69 (duty to notify changes of circumstances)) the kind of change of circumstances which is to be notified, either upon the notice or by reference to some other document available to him on application and without charge.

(2) In a case where a person on state pension credit has entitlement only to the savings credit, the following additional matters shall also be set out–

(a) the applicable amount and the basis of calculation;

(b) the amount of the savings credit [¹] taken into account;

(c) the amount of the person's income and capital as notified to the local authority by the Secretary of State and taken into account for the purposes of the housing benefit assessment;

(d) any modification of the claimant's income or capital made in accordance with regulation 27 (calculation of claimant's income in savings credit only cases); and

(e) the amount of the claimant's capital if paragraph (7) of regulation 27 applies in his case.

[³ (3) Where a claimant is entitled to an extended payment (qualifying contributory benefits) in accordance with regulation 53, the decision notice shall include a statement as to the matters set out in paragraph 9(1).]

Amendments

1. Amended by reg 2(18) of SI 2005 No 2502 as amended by Sch 2 para 27 of SI 2006 No 217 as from 1.4.06 (3.4.06 where rent payable weekly or at intervals of a week).
2. Amended by reg 4(10) of SI 2008 No 1042 as from 19.5.08.
3. Amended by reg 6(5) of SI 2008 No 959 as from 6.10.08.

PART 3
Awards where no state pension credit is payable
10. Where a person is not on state pension credit but is awarded housing benefit, the decision notice shall include a statement as to–
(a) the matters set out in paragraph 9; and
(b) his applicable amount and how it is calculated; and
(c) his weekly earnings; and
(d) his weekly income other than earnings.

PART 4
Awards where direct payments made to landlords
11. Where a decision has been made under regulation 76 or 77 (circumstances in which payment is to be made, or may be made, direct to a landlord), the decision notice shall include a statement–
(a) as to the amount of housing benefit which is to be paid direct to the landlord and the date from which it is to be paid; and
(b) informing the landlord of the duty imposed upon him to notify the local authority of–
    (i) any change in circumstances which might affect the claimant's entitlement to housing benefit, or the amount of housing benefit payable in his case; and
    (ii) the kind of change of circumstances which is to be notified,
and the notice shall be sent both to the claimant and to the landlord; and
(c) informing both landlords and claimants that where a payment of housing benefit is recoverable from a landlord and the recovery is made from housing benefit payable to the landlord to discharge (in whole or in part) an obligation owed to him by a claimant, then, in a case where that claimant is not the person on whose behalf the recoverable amount was paid, that obligation shall nonetheless be taken to be discharged by the amount so recovered.
12. In this Schedule, "landlord" has the same meaning as in regulation 76.

PART 5
Notice where income of non-dependant is treated as claimant's
13. Where an authority makes a decision under regulation 24 (circumstances in which income of non-dependant is to be treated as claimant's) the decision notice shall contain a statement as to–
(a) the fact that a decision has been made by reference to the income and capital of the claimant's non-dependant; and
(b) the relevant authority's reasons for making that decision.

PART 6
Notice where no award is made
14. Where a person is not awarded housing benefit–
(a) either on grounds of income or because the amount of any housing benefit is less than the minimum housing benefit prescribed by regulation 56, the decision notice shall include a statement as to–
    (i) the matters set out in paragraphs 9(1)(a) to (c), and in a case where the amount of entitlement is less than the minimum amount of housing benefit prescribed, paragraph 9(1)(d) also; and
    (ii) the matters set out in paragraphs 10(b) to (d) where the person is not on [¹ state pension credit]; and
    (iii) where the amount of entitlement is less than the minimum amount of housing benefit prescribed, that fact and that such entitlement is not payable;
(b) for any reason other than one mentioned in sub-paragraph (a), the decision notice shall include a statement as to the reason why no award has been made.

Amendment
1.   Amended by reg 7(7) of SI 2008 No 2767 as from 6.4.09.

PART 7
Notice where recoverable overpayment
15.–(1) Where the appropriate authority makes a decision that there is a recoverable overpayment within the meaning of regulation 81 (recoverable overpayments), the decision notice shall include a statement as to–
(a) the fact that there is a recoverable overpayment; and
(b) the reason why there is a recoverable overpayment; and
(c) the amount of the recoverable overpayment; and
(d) how the amount of the recoverable overpayment was calculated; and
(e) the benefit weeks to which the recoverable overpayment relates; and
(f) where recovery of the recoverable overpayment is to be made by deduction from a rent allowance or rebate, as the case may be, that fact and the amount of the deduction.
(2) In a case where it is–
(a) determined that there is a recoverable overpayment;

(b)   determined that that overpayment is recoverable from a landlord; and
(c)   decided that recovery of that overpayment is to be made by deduction from a rent allowance paid to that landlord to discharge (in whole or in part) an obligation owed to him by a claimant ("claimant A"), not being the claimant on whose behalf the recoverable amount was paid,
the decision notice sent to that landlord shall identify both–
  (i)   the person on whose behalf the recoverable amount was paid to that landlord; and
  (ii)   claimant A.

[¹ SCHEDULE 9

REGULATION 103

Former pathfinder authorities

Amendment
1.   Substituted by reg 20(2) of SI 2007 No 2869 as from 7.4.08.

PART 1
Former pathfinder authorities

Argyll and Bute
Blackpool
Brighton and Hove
Conwy
Coventry
East Riding of Yorkshire
Edinburgh
Guildford
Leeds
Lewisham
North East Lincolnshire
Norwich
Pembrokeshire
St Helens
Salford
South Norfolk
Teignbridge
Wandsworth

PART 2
Application of the Regulations
1.   These Regulations shall apply to former pathfinder authorities subject to the provisions of this Part of this Schedule.

Amendment of regulation 2
2.   In regulation 2(1) (interpretation)–
(a)   in the definition of "eligible rent", in sub-paragraph (a) for "or 12D (eligible rent and maximum rent (LHA))" substitute ", 12D (eligible rent and maximum rent (LHA)) or any of regulations 12E to 12K (transitional protection for pathfinder cases)";
(b)   after the definition of "maximum rent (LHA)" insert–
" "maximum rent (standard local rent)" means a maximum rent (standard local rate) determined in accordance with regulation 13A;".

Amendment of regulation 11
3.   In regulation 11(1) (eligible housing costs)–
(a)   in paragraph (c) omit "or"; and
(b)   after sub-paragraph (d) insert–

" ; or
(e)   any of regulations 12E to 12K (transitional protection for pathfinder cases), and regulations 13C (when a maximum rent (LHA) is to be determined) and 13D (determination of a maximum rent (LHA)),".

Amendment of regulation 12B
4.   In regulation 12B(1) (eligible rent) for "or 12D (eligible rent and maximum rent (LHA))" substitute ", 12D (eligible rent and maximum rent (LHA)) or any of regulations 12E to 12K (transitional protection for pathfinder cases)".

Amendment of regulation 12D

5. In regulation 12D (eligible rent and maximum rent (LHA)) before paragraph (1) insert–

" (A1) This regulation shall not apply where any of regulations 12E to 12K (transitional protection for pathfinder cases) apply."

Insertion of regulations 12E to 12K

6. After regulation 12D (eligible rent and maximum rent (LHA)) insert–

"Basic transitional protection for pathfinder cases

12E.–(1) This regulation applies where–

(a) reference was made to a maximum rent (standard local rate) in determining the amount of the eligible rent which applied immediately before 7th April 2008;

(b) on 7th April 2008 the local authority determines a maximum rent (LHA) by virtue of regulation 13C(4A)(a); and

(c) regulations 12F (cases where the claimant enjoyed protection on death before 7th April 2008) and 12G (cases where the claimant enjoyed 13 week protection before 7th April 2008) do not apply.

(2) Where this regulation applies, the claimant's eligible rent is–

(a) the maximum rent (LHA) where that is higher than the eligible rent which applied immediately before 7th April 2008; or

(b) the amount of the eligible rent which applied immediately before 7th April 2008.

(3) Where the eligible rent is the amount of the eligible rent which applied immediately before 7th April 2008, it will continue to apply until, on or after 7th April 2008, the first of the following events occurs–

(a) the relevant authority is required to determine a maximum rent (LHA) by virtue of regulation 13C(2)(d)(i) (change of category of dwelling) because the claimant has become entitled to a larger category of dwelling and the maximum rent (LHA) is higher than that eligible rent;

(b) the relevant authority is required to determine a maximum rent (LHA) by virtue of regulation 13C(2)(d)(i) (change of category of dwelling) because the claimant has become entitled to a smaller category of dwelling;

(c) the relevant authority is required to determine an eligible rent following a change of dwelling;

(d) the relevant authority is required to determine an eligible rent in accordance with regulation 12H (cases where a death occurs in the first year on or after 7th April 2008) following the death of a linked person;

(e) the relevant authority determines a maximum rent (LHA) on 7th April 2009 by virtue of regulation 13C(4A)(b).

(4) Where the eligible rent is the maximum rent (LHA), it shall be treated as if it had been determined in accordance with regulation 12D(2)(a) (eligible rent is maximum rent (LHA)) and shall apply according to the provisions of regulation 12D (eligible rent and maximum rent (LHA)).

Cases where the claimant enjoyed protection on death before 7th April 2008

12F.–(1) This regulation applies where–

(a) immediately before 7th April 2008 the claimant enjoyed protection on death in accordance with regulation 12A(4)(a)(ii) (pathfinder protection on death based on reckonable rent); and

(b) on 7th April 2008 the local authority determines a maximum rent (LHA) by virtue of regulation 13C(4A)(a).

(2) Where this regulation applies, the claimant's eligible rent is–

(a) the maximum rent (LHA) where that is higher than the eligible rent which applied immediately before 7th April 2008; or

(b) the amount of the eligible rent which applied immediately before 7th April 2008.

(3) Where the eligible rent is the amount of the eligible rent which applied immediately before 7th April 2008, it will continue to apply until, on or after 7th April 2008, the first of the following events occurs–

(a) the end of 12 months after the death to which the protection relates;

(b) the relevant authority is required to determine a maximum rent (LHA) by virtue of regulation 13C(2)(d)(i) (change of category of dwelling) and it is higher than that eligible rent;

(c) the relevant authority is required to determine an eligible rent following a change of dwelling;

(d) the relevant authority is required to determine an eligible rent in accordance with regulation 12H (cases where a death occurs in the first year on or after 7th April 2008) following the death of a linked person;

(4) Where the eligible rent ceases to apply because of paragraph (3)(a), the eligible rent will be the maximum rent (LHA) which would have applied but for the transitional protection.

(5) Where the eligible rent is the maximum rent (LHA), it shall be treated as if it had been determined in accordance with regulation 12D(2)(a) (eligible rent is maximum rent (LHA)) and shall apply according to the provisions of regulation 12D (eligible rent and maximum rent (LHA)).

Cases where the claimant enjoyed 13 week protection before 7th April 2008

12G.–(1) This regulation applies where–

(a)   immediately before 7th April 2008 the claimant enjoyed 13 week protection in accordance with regulation 12A(6)(a) (lo cal housing allowance pathfinder 13 week protection); and

(b)   on 7th April 2008 the local authority determines a maximum rent (LHA) by virtue of regulation 13C(4A)(a).

(2)   Where this regulation applies, the claimant's eligible rent is–

(a)   the maximum rent (LHA) where that is higher than the eligible rent which applied immediately before 7th April 2008; or

(b)   the amount of the eligible rent which applied immediately before 7th April 2008.

(3)   Where the eligible rent is the amount of the eligible rent which applied immediately before 7th April 2008, it will continue to apply until, on or after 7th April 2008, the first of the following events occurs–

(a)   the end of the day when the protection expires, namely 13 weeks after the date of the claim;

(b)   the relevant authority is required to determine a maximum rent (LHA) by virtue of regulation 13C(2)(d)(i) (change of category of dwelling) and it is higher than that eligible rent;

(c)   the relevant authority is required to determine an eligible rent following a change of dwelling;

(d)   the relevant authority is required to determine an eligible rent in accordance with regulation 12H (cases where a death occurs in the first year on or after 7th April 2008) following the death of a linked person.

(4)   Where the eligible rent ceases to apply because of paragraph (3)(a), the eligible rent will be the maximum rent (LHA) which would have applied but for the transitional protection.

(5)   Where the eligible rent is the maximum rent (LHA), it shall be treated as if it had been determined in accordance with regulation 12D(2)(a) (eligible rent is maximum rent (LHA)) and shall apply according to the provisions of regulation 12D (eligible rent and maximum rent (LHA)).

Cases where a death occurs in the first year on or after 7th April 2008

12H.–(1) This regulation applies where–

(a)   the eligible rent is that specified in regulation 12E(2)(b) (basic transitional protection for pathfinder cases), 12F(2)(b) (transitional protection where the claimant enjoyed protection on death before 7th April 2008), 12G(2)(b) (transitional protection where the claimant enjoyed 13 week protection before 7th April 2008) or paragraph (2)(b) of this regulation;

(b)   a linked person dies on or after 7th April 2008 and before 7th April 2009;

(c)   the claimant occupies the same dwelling as the linked person at the date of death; and

(d)   the relevant authority determines a maximum rent (LHA) by virtue of regulation 13C(2)(d)(i) or (ii) (change of category of dwelling or death of a linked person).

(2)   Where this regulation applies, the claimant's eligible rent is–

(a)   the maximum rent (LHA) where that is higher than the eligible rent which applied immediately before the date of the death; or

(b)   the amount of the eligible rent which applied immediately before the date of the death.

(3)   Where the eligible rent is the amount of the eligible rent which applied immediately before the date of death, it will continue to apply until, on or after the date of the death, the first of the following events occurs–

(a)   the end of 12 months from the date of the death;

(b)   the relevant authority is required to determine a maximum rent (LHA) by virtue of regulation 13C(2)(d)(i) (change of category of dwelling) and it is higher than that eligible rent;

(c)   the relevant authority is required to determine an eligible rent following a change of dwelling;

(d)   the relevant authority is required to determine an eligible rent in accordance with this regulation following the death of another linked person.

(4)   Where the eligible rent is the maximum rent (LHA), it shall be treated as if it had been determined in accordance with regulation 12D(2)(a) (eligible rent is maximum rent (LHA)) and shall apply according to the provisions of regulation 12D (eligible rent and maximum rent (LHA)).

(5)   For the purposes of paragraph (1)(c), a claimant shall be treated as occupying the dwelling if regulation 7(13) is satisfied and for that purpose paragraph (13) of regulation 7 shall have effect as if sub-paragraph (b) were omitted.

Basic transitional protection in the second year and subsequent years after 7th April 2008

12I.–(1) This regulation applies where–

(a)   immediately before 7th April 2009 the claimant was enjoying basic transitional protection under regulation 12E; and

(b)   the local authority determines a maximum rent (LHA) by virtue of 13C(4A)(b) on 7th April 2009.

(2)   Where this regulation applies, the claimant's eligible rent is–

(a)   the maximum rent (LHA) where it is higher than the eligible rent applying immediately before 7th April 2008; or

(b)   in any other case, the lower of–

(i)   the amount of the eligible rent applying immediately before 7th April 2008; or

(ii)   the amount of the cap rent by reference to which the maximum rent (LHA) was determined [¹].

(3)   Where the claimant's eligible rent is determined in accordance with paragraph (2)(b), it continues to apply until, on or after 7th April 2009, the first of the following events occurs–

(a)   the relevant authority is required to determine a maximum rent (LHA) by virtue of regulation 13C(2)(d)(i) (change of category of dwelling) because the claimant has become entitled to a larger category of dwelling or 13C(3) (anniversary of the LHA date) and the maximum rent (LHA) is higher than that eligible rent;

(b)   the relevant authority is required to determine a maximum rent (LHA) by virtue of regulation 13C(2)(d)(i) (change of category of dwelling) because the claimant has become entitled to a smaller category of dwelling;

(c)   the relevant authority is required to determine an eligible rent following a change of dwelling;

(d)   the relevant authority is required to determine an eligible rent in accordance with regulation 12K (protection on death in the second and subsequent years after 7th April 2008) following the death of a linked person.

(4)   Where the eligible rent is the maximum rent (LHA), it shall be treated as if it had been determined in accordance with regulation 12D(2)(a) (eligible rent is maximum rent (LHA)) and shall apply according to the provisions of regulation 12D (eligible rent and maximum rent (LHA)).

Amendment
1.   Amended by reg 3(11) of SI 2010 No 2835 as from 1.4.11.

Transitional protection in the second year after 7th April 2008 where the claimant is already enjoying protection on death

12J.–(1)   This regulation applies where–
(a)   immediately before 7th April 2009 the claimant was enjoying transitional protection on death under regulation 12H (cases where a death occurs in the first year on or after 7th April 2008); and
(b)   the local authority determines a maximum rent (LHA) by virtue of regulation 13C(4A)(b) on 7th April 2009 .

(2)   Where this regulation applies, the claimant's eligible rent is–
(a)   the maximum rent (LHA) where that is higher than the eligible rent which applied immediately before the date of the death to which the protection relates; or
(b)   the amount of the eligible rent which applied immediately before the date of the death.

(3)   Where the eligible rent which applies is the one that applied immediately before the date of the death, it continues to apply until, on or after the date of the death, the first of the following events occurs–
(a)   the end of 12 months after the date of the death to which the protection relates;
(b)   the relevant authority is required to determine a maximum rent (LHA) by virtue of regulation 13C(2)(d)(i) (change of category of dwelling) and it is higher than that eligible rent;
(c)   the relevant authority is required to determine an eligible rent following a change of dwelling;
(d)   the relevant authority is required to determine an eligible rent in accordance with regulation 12K (protection on death in the second and subsequent years after 7th April 2008) following the death of a linked person.

(4)   Where the eligible rent ceases to apply because of paragraph (3)(a) the eligible rent is the one that would have applied if the relevant authority not determined an eligible rent in accordance with regulation 12H(2)(b) (transitional protection where a death occurs in the first year on or after 7th April 2008).

(5)   Where the eligible rent is the maximum rent (LHA), it shall be treated as if it had been determined in accordance with regulation 12D(2)(a) (eligible rent is maximum rent (LHA)) and shall apply according to the provisions of regulation 12D (eligible rent and maximum rent (LHA)).

Protection on death in the second and subsequent years after 7th April 2008

12K.–(1)   This regulation applies where–
(a)   the claimant's eligible rent is that specified in regulation 12I(2)(b) (basic transitional protection in the second and subsequent years after 7th April 2008), 12J(2)(b) (transitional protection in the second year after 7th April 2008 where the claimant is already enjoying protection on death) or paragraph (2)(b) of this regulation; and
(b)   a linked person dies on or after 7th April 2009;
(c)   the claimant occupies the same dwelling as the linked person at the date of death; and
(d)   the relevant authority determines a maximum rent (LHA) by virtue of regulation 13C(2)(d)(i) or (ii) (change of category of dwelling or death of a linked person).

(2)   Where this regulation applies, the claimant's eligible rent is–
(a)   the maximum rent (LHA) where that is higher than the eligible rent which applied immediately before the date of the death; or
(b)   the amount of eligible rent which applied immediately before the death.

(3)   Where the eligible rent which applies is the one that applied immediately before the date of the death, it will continue to apply until, on or after the date of the death, the first of the following events occurs–
(a)   the end of 12 months from the date of the death;
(b)   the relevant authority is required to determine a maximum rent (LHA) by virtue of regulation 13C(2)(d)(i) or (3) (change of category of dwelling or anniversary of the LHA date) and it is higher than that eligible rent;
(c)   the relevant authority is required to determine an eligible rent following a change of dwelling;

(d)   the relevant authority is required to determine an eligible rent in accordance with this regulation following the death of another linked person.

(4)   Where the eligible rent ceases to apply because of paragraph (3)(a) the eligible rent is the one that would have applied but had the relevant authority not determined an eligible rent in accordance with this regulation.

(5)   Where the eligible rent is the maximum rent (LHA), it shall be treated as if it had been determined in accordance with regulation 12D(2)(a) (eligible rent is maximum rent (LHA)) and shall apply according to the provisions of regulation 12D (eligible rent and maximum rent (LHA)).

(6)   For the purposes of paragraph (1)(c), a claimant shall be treated as occupying the dwelling if regulation 7(13) is satisfied and for that purpose paragraph (13) of regulation 7 shall have effect as if sub-paragraph (b) were omitted.".

Amendment of regulation 13C

7.   In regulation 13C (when a maximum rent (LHA) is to be determined)–

(a)   in paragraph (1) for "paragraphs (2) or (3)" substitute "paragraphs (2), (3) or (4A)";

(b)   in paragraph (3) after "LHA date" insert "except where paragraph (4A)(b) applies";

(c)   after paragraph (4) insert–

"(4A)   This paragraph applies where it is–

(a)   7th April 2008 and reference was made to a maximum rent (standard local rate) in determining the amount of the eligible rent which applied immediately before 7th April 2008; or

(b)   7th April 2009 and the eligible rent which applies on that date was determined in accordance with regulation 12E(2)(b) (basic transitional protection for pathfinder cases) or 12H(2)(b) (transitional protection where a death occurs in the first year on or after 7th April 2008).".

Amendment of regulation 13D

8.   In regulation 13D(12) (determination of a maximum rent (LHA)) in the definition of "relevant date" after sub-paragraph (c) insert–

"(d)   7th April 2008;

(e)   7th April 2009."]

[¹SCHEDULE 10
Electronic Communication

Amendment

1.   Inserted by art 3(5) of SI 2006 No 2968 as from 20.12.06.

PART 1
Introduction

Interpretation

1.   In this Schedule "official computer system" means a computer system maintained by or on behalf of the relevant authority or of the Secretary of State for sending, receiving, processing or storing of any claim, certificate, notice, information or evidence.

PART 2
Electronic Communication – General Provisions

Conditions for the use of electronic communication

2.–(1)   The relevant authority may use an electronic communication in connection with claims for, and awards of, benefit under these Regulations.

(2)   A person other than the relevant authority may use an electronic communication in connection with the matters referred to in sub-paragraph (1) if the conditions specified in sub-paragraphs (3) to (6) are satisfied.

(3)   The first condition is that the person is for the time being permitted to use an electronic communication by an authorisation given by means of a direction of the Chief Executive of the relevant authority.

(4)   The second condition is that the person uses an approved method of–

(a)   authenticating the identity of the sender of the communication;

(b)   electronic communication;

(c)   authenticating any claim or notice delivered by means of an electronic communication; and

(d)   subject to sub-paragraph (7), submitting to the relevant authority any claim, certificate, notice, information or evidence.

(5)   The third condition is that any claim, certificate, notice, information or evidence sent by means of an electronic communication is in a form approved for the purposes of this Schedule.

(6)   The fourth condition is that the person maintains such records in written or electronic form as may be specified in a direction given by the Chief Executive of the relevant authority.

(7)   Where the person uses any method other than the method approved of submitting any claim, certificate, notice, information or evidence, that claim, certificate, notice, information or evidence shall be treated as not having been submitted.

(8)   In this paragraph "approved" means approved by means of a direction given by the Chief Executive of the relevant authority for the purposes of this Schedule.

Use of intermediaries

3.   The relevant authority may use intermediaries in connection with–

(a)   the delivery of any claim, certificate, notice, information or evidence by means of an electronic communication; and

(b)   the authentication or security of anything transmitted by such means,

and may require other persons to use intermediaries in connection with those matters.

PART 3
Electronic Communication – Evidential Provisions

Effect of delivering information by means of electronic communication

4.–(1)   Any claim, certificate, notice, information or evidence which is delivered by means of an electronic communication shall be treated as having been delivered in the manner or form required by any provision of these Regulations, on the day the conditions imposed–

(a)   by this Schedule; and

(b)   by or under an enactment,

are satisfied.

(2)   The relevant authority may, by a direction, determine that any claim, certificate, notice, information or evidence is to be treated as delivered on a different day (whether earlier or later) from the day provided for in sub-paragraph (1).

(3)   Information shall not be taken to have been delivered to an official computer system by means of an electronic communication unless it is accepted by the system to which it is delivered.

Proof of identity of sender or recipient of information

5.   If it is necessary to prove, for the purpose of any legal proceedings, the identity of–

(a)   the sender of any claim, certificate, notice, information or evidence delivered by means of an electronic communication to an official computer system; or

(b)   the recipient of any such claim, certificate, notice, information or evidence delivered by means of an electronic communication from an official computer system,

the sender or recipient, as the case may be, shall be presumed to be the person whose name is recorded as such on that official computer system.

Proof of delivery of information

6.–(1)   If it is necessary to prove, for the purpose of any legal proceedings, that the use of an electronic communication has resulted in the delivery of any claim, certificate, notice, information or evidence this shall be presumed to have been the case where–

(a)   any such claim, certificate, notice, information or evidence has been delivered to the relevant authority, if the delivery of that claim, certificate, notice, information or evidence has been recorded on an official computer system; or

(b)   any such claim, certificate, notice, information or evidence has been delivered by the relevant authority, if the delivery of that certificate, notice, information or evidence has been recorded on an official computer system.

(2)   If it is necessary to prove, for the purpose of any legal proceedings, that the use of an electronic communication has resulted in the delivery of any such claim, certificate, notice, information or evidence, this shall be presumed not to be the case, if that claim, certificate, notice, information or evidence delivered to the relevant authority has not been recorded on an official computer system.

(3)   If it is necessary to prove, for the purpose of any legal proceedings, when any such claim, certificate, notice, information or evidence sent by means of an electronic communication has been received, the time and date of receipt shall be presumed to be that recorded on an official computer system.

Proof of content of information

7.   If it is necessary to prove, for the purpose of any legal proceedings, the content of any claim, certificate, notice, information or evidence sent by means of an electronic communication, the content shall be presumed to be that recorded on an official computer system.]

The Rent Officers (Housing Benefit Functions) Order 1997
(SI 1997 No.1984)

General Note

This order sets out the determinations to be made by rent officers when a tenancy is referred to them under regs 13D(10) or 14 of both the HB and the HB(SPC) Regs by an authority in England and Wales. It also sets out the determinations to be made by rent officers relating to the "local housing allowance" scheme for rent restriction used by authorities to determine eligible rent under regs 12D and 13D of both the HB and the HB(SPC) Regs. The equivalent Order for Scotland is SI 1997 No.1995 (see p909).

The determinations made by rent officers under this order are relevant in two ways. The first concerns the calculation of a claimant's "maximum rent" or "maximum rent (LHA)", and thus the "eligible rent" where HB is paid as a rent allowance (ie, to private sector and some social sector landlord tenants). "Eligible rent" is used to determine "maximum HB" under reg 70 HB Regs and reg 50 HB(SPC) Regs. The second concerns the amount of subsidy received by an authority. As to the first:

(1)   For certain private sector and social sector landlord tenants whose tenancies commenced after 1 January 1996, the rent officers' figures are the basis on which a "maximum rent" is calculated under reg 13 of both the HB and the HB(SPC) Regs: art 3 and Schs 1 and 2.

(2)   For most private sector tenants and the tenants of profit-making registered providers of social housing who live in a dwelling that is not social housing, who claim HB on or after 7 April 2008, or who move while awarded HB on or after that date, the rent officer figures are the basis on which a "maximum rent (LHA)" is calculated under reg 13D of both the HB and the HB(SPC) Regs: art 4B and Sch 3B.

See the commentary to the regulations in Part 3 of the HB Regs for a summary of how "maximum rent" and "maximum rent (LHA)" are calculated (from p348).

See arts 4 and 4A for redetermination of rent officer determinations and redeterminations and substitute determinations and redeterminations respectively. See art 6 for situations in which no determination or redetermination can be made. Art 7 deals with special cases – ie, mooring charges payable for a houseboat, payments for caravan or mobile home sites and payments under rental purchase agreements.

For tenants who live in "exempt accommodation" or "exempt claimants" who have the benefit of the transitional protection set out in Sch 3 paras 4 and 5 HB&CTB(CP) Regs (the "pre-January 1996" rent restriction scheme – see from p1774), a rent officer's determination is not determinative of maximum rent. It is a factor to which an authority may have regard when considering whether the dwelling occupied by the claimant is larger than reasonably required or if the rent is unreasonably high by comparison with the rent payable in respect of suitable alternative accommodation elsewhere: see paras (3)(a) and (b) of the version of reg 13 of both the HB and the HB(SPC) Regs in Sch 3 para 5 HB&CTB(CP) Regs and the Analysis thereto (from p1783).

There is no right of appeal to the First-tier Tribunal against a decision of the rent officer. However, the claimant can appeal the local authority's "outcome" decision on HB entitlement and, as such, can challenge the factual basis upon which the rent officer decision was made – eg, the number of occupiers given to the rent officer by the local authority: *Bexley LB v LD (HB)* [2010] UKUT 79 (AAC).

The role of rent officers in rent allowance subsidy is governed by art 16 of, and Sch 4, to the Income-Related Benefits (Subsidy) Order 1998 (SI 1998 No.562). There are financial incentives resting on local authorities to apply the rent restrictions scheme correctly.

Citation and commencement

1.–(1)   This Order may be cited as the Rent Officers (Housing Benefit Functions) Order 1997.

(2)   This article and articles 8 and 10(1) shall come into force on 18th August 1997 and all the other articles shall come into force on 3rd September 1997.

Interpretation

2.–(1)   In this Order, unless the context otherwise requires–
[^{15} [^{14}]]
"assured tenancy" has the same meaning as in Part I of the Housing Act 1988, except that it includes a tenancy which would be an assured tenancy but for paragraph 2 [^{3}, 8] or 10 of Schedule 1 to that Act and a licence which would be an assured tenancy (within the extended meaning given in this definition) were it a tenancy;
[^{2} "board and attendance determination" means a determination made in accordance with article 4C;]
[^{9} "broad rental market area" has the meaning specified in paragraph 4 of Schedule 3B;]
[^{9} "broad rental market area determination" means a determination made in accordance with article 4B(1A);]

"child" means a person under the age of 16;

"determination" means a determination made in accordance with Part I or IV of Schedule 1 to this Order;

"dwelling" means any residential accommodation whether or not consisting of the whole or part of a building and whether or not comprising separate and self-contained premises;

[¹⁰ "hostel" has the same meaning as in regulation 2(1) of the Housing Benefit Regulations or, as the case may be, regulation 2(1) of the Housing Benefit (State Pension Credit) Regulations;]

[¹¹ "the Housing Benefit Regulations" mean the Housing Benefit Regulations 2006;

"the Housing Benefit (State Pension Credit) Regulations" means the Housing Benefit (Persons who have attained the qualifying age for state pension credit) Regulations 2006;]

"local authority" has the same meaning as in the Social Security Administration Act 1992 in relation to England and in relation to Wales;

[⁹ "local housing allowance determination" means a determination made in accordance with article 4B(2A);]

"occupier" means a person (whether or not identified by name) who is stated, in the application for the determination, to occupy the dwelling as his home;

[⁹]

[¹³ "person who requires overnight care" has the meaning given by regulation 2(1) of the Housing Benefit Regulations and the Housing Benefit (State Pension Credit) Regulations;]

"redetetermination" means a redetermination made in accordance with article 4;

[⁹ "relevant date" means the date specified by a local authority in an application for a local housing allowance determination made in accordance with regulation 13D(7)(a) of the Housing Benefit Regulations or, as the case may be, regulation 13D(7)(a) of the Housing Benefit (State Pension Credit) Regulations;]

[¹ "relevant period" means–
  (a) in relation to a determination, the period of five working days (or, where the determination does not relate to a prospective tenancy and the rent officer intends to inspect the dwelling before making the determination, 25 working days) beginning with–
      (i)   where the rent officer requests further information under article 5, the date on which he receives the information; and
      (ii) in any other case, the date on which he receives the application for the determination; and
  (b) in relation to a redetermination, the period of 20 working days beginning with-
      (i)   where the rent officer requests further information under article 5, the date on which he receives the information; and
      (ii) in any other case, the date on which he receives the application for that redetermination;]

"relevant time" means the time the application for the determination [² or board and attendance determination] is made or, if earlier, the tenancy ends;

[¹⁰ "rent" means any of the periodical payments referred to in regulation 12(1) of the Housing Benefit Regulations or, as the case may be, regulation 12(1) of the Housing Benefit (State Pension Credit) Regulations;]

"size criteria" means the standards relating to bedrooms and rooms suitable for living in specified in Schedule 2 to this Order;

"tenancy" includes–
  (a) a licence; and
  (b) a prospective tenancy or licence; and

references to a tenant, a landlord or any other expression appropriate to a tenancy shall be construed accordingly; and

[⁸ "working day" means any day other than a Saturday, a Sunday, Christmas Day, Good Friday or a day which is a bank holiday in England and Wales under the Banking and Financial Dealings Act 1971.]

[^{12}]
    (2)   In this Order any reference to a notice or application is to a notice or application in writing, except in a case where the recipient consents (whether generally or specifically) to the notice or application being transmitted by electronic means.

Modifications

Some definitions substituted and the definition of "pathfinder authority" omitted by art 6(3) Rent Officers (Housing Benefit Functions) Amendment Order 2007 SI No.2871 as from 7 April 2008, save where art 6(1)(a), (b) or (c) of that order applied (see p931).

    Note that by art 3 of SI 2007 No.2871, those provisions which on 19 March 2008 applied only in relation to the areas of former Pathfinder authorities, apply in the same way to the areas of every local authority in England and Wales.

Amendments

1.   Substituted by art 3 of SI 2000 No 1 as from 3.4.00.
2.   Insertions made by art 2 of SI 2003 No 2398 as from a date specified in Sch 1 to that SI in relation to each individual authority.
3.   Inserted by art 2(1) of SI 2004 No 2101 as from 31.8.04.
4.   Substituted by Sch 1 para 11(2)(a), (c) and (d) of SI 2006 No 217 as from 6.3.06.
5.   Inserted by Sch 1 para 11(2)(b) of SI 2006 No 217 as from 6.3.06.
6.   Omitted by Sch 1 para 11(2)(e) of SI 2006 No 217 as from 6.3.06.
7.   Amended by art 4(1)(a)-(c) of SI 2007 No 2871 as from 20.3.08.
8.   Inserted by art 4(d) of SI 2007 No 2871 as from 20.3.08.
9.   Substituted by art 6(3) of SI 2007 No 2871 as from 7.4.08, save where Art 6(1)(a), (b) or (c) of that order applies.
10.   Substituted by art 10(1) of SI 2007 No 2871 as from 7.4.08.
11.   Inserted by art 10(1) of SI 2007 No 2871 as from 7.4.08.
12.   Omitted by art 10(1) of SI 2007 No 2871 as from 7.4.08.
13.   Amended by art 3(2) of SI 2010 No 2836 as from 1.4.11
14.   Inserted by art 2(2) of SI 2012 No 646 as from 2.4.12.
15.   Omitted by art 2(2) of SI 2013 No 1544 as from 1.9.13.

Analysis

"Assured tenancy". By s1 Housing Act 1988 an "assured tenancy" is a tenancy of a dwelling house let to an individual or individuals as their "only or principal home". It has an extended definition in this order. Sch 1 para 2 of the 1988 Act excludes houses with an annual rent of more than a set amount from the Act, but tenancies of such properties fall within the definition for the purposes of this Order. Sch 1 para 8 excludes certain tenancies granted to students by specified educational institutions or other specified bodies, but again tenancies of such properties fall within the definition for the purposes of this Order. Sch 1 para 10, broadly speaking, excludes properties where the landlord is resident. The very complex provisions of that paragraph and those accompanying it do not arise here either. Licenses also fall within the definition of "assured tenancy", so there will be no issue as to whether or not exclusive possession of the premises has been granted. Note that an assured shorthold tenancy is just a particular type of assured tenancy: see ss19A and 20 of the 1988 Act. Such tenancies therefore also fall within this definition.

    "Occupier". An "occupier" is a person who is stated on the application for the rent officer determination (ie, by the local authority) as occupying the dwelling as a home. This can include people who are not part of the claimant's "family" – eg, non-dependants or live-in carers. It cannot include foster children, who do not count as occupiers for HB purposes (see reg 21(3) of both the HB and the HB(SPC) Regs) although certain foster and kinship carers may be entitled to an additional bedroom under the size criteria in Sch 2. The definition may include people who normally live with the claimant but who are temporarily away: *R(H) 8/09* and *SK v South Hams DC (HB)* [2010] UKUT 129 (AAC); [2010] AACR 40.

    The definition of "occupier" was discussed in *R v Swale BC HBRB ex p Marchant* [1999] 1 FLR 1087, QBD; [2000] 1 FLR 246, CA. The claimant was separated from his wife. Their children spent alternate weeks with the claimant and his wife. She received child benefit for them. The rent officer was instructed by the local authority to assess the claimant's rent on the basis that the children were not "occupiers" of his property. Kay J [1999] 1 FLR 1087 upheld that decision on the basis that as the wife was "responsible" for the children pursuant to reg 14 HB Regs 1987 (now reg 20 of both the HB and the HB(SPC) Regs), they were members of her family. Consequently reg 5(1) HB regs 1987 (now reg 7(1) of both the HB and the HB(SPC) Regs) proceeded on the basis that they were normally occupying the wife's home and that was the proper definition of "occupier" in art 2.

    The Court of Appeal heard and dismissed an appeal from that decision. Potter LJ stated that it was clear that resolution of the questions of with which parent a child normally lived and of whose household the child was a member should also be regarded as determinative of the question of which dwelling a child occupied for the purposes of the Rent Officers (Additional Functions) Order 1995 (which was in identical terms to the 1997 Order).

To permit the children to be taken into account in examining the sizes of both households would lead to an "element of double provision" in the scheme.

It was also confirmed in the judgment of Potter LJ that the decision as to whether or not a person is an "occupier" is one for the local authority. This is made in the "application" to the rent officer pursuant to reg 14(1) of both the HB and the HB(SPC) Regs. See also the discussion of *Stroud DC v JG* [2009] UKUT 67 (AAC); R(H) 8/09 on p627, and the discussion of *MR v North Tyneside Council and SSWP* [2015] UKUT 34 (AAC) on p373.

"Person who requires overnight care". This definition is relevant for both the local housing allowance and the local reference rent schemes for rent restriction. From 1 April 2011, under both schemes, there is a requirement to take account of an additional bedroom for a non-resident carer where a relevant person is a "person who requires overnight care": Sch 2 para 1A of this Order and regs 13 and 13D HB Regs. See p243 for a discussion of the meaning.

"Relevant period". The rent officer must provide a determination within five working days and a redetermination within 20 working days running from the date of receipt of the request for the determination or, if the rent officer has to seek further information, the date on which that information is received. In the case of a determination, the "relevant period" is lengthened to 25 days where the determination sought is not a pre-tenancy determination under reg 14(1)(e) of both the HB and the HB(SPC) Regs and where the rent officer wishes to inspect the home first.

Determinations

3.–(1) Subject to [² articles 3A and 6], where a local authority, in accordance with regulations made under section 136(2) or (3) of the Social Security Administration Act 1992, [¹ or section 122(5) of the Housing Act 1996,] applies to a rent officer for determinations in respect of a tenancy of a dwelling, a rent officer shall–

(a) make the determinations in accordance with Part I of Schedule 1 (determinations);

(b) comply with Part II of Schedule 1 when making the determinations (assumptions etc.); and

(c) give notice in accordance with Part III of Schedule 1 (notifications) [¹ within the relevant period or as soon as is practicable after that period].

(2) A rent officer for each registration area (within the meaning of section 62 of the Rent Act 1977), on the first working day of each month, shall–

(a) make determinations in accordance with Part IV of Schedule 1 (indicative rent levels) in relation to the area of each local authority [⁴] within the registration area;

(b) comply with paragraph 8(2) of Part II of Schedule 1 (assumptions etc.) when making the determinations; and

(c) give to the local authority notice of the determinations relating to its area when they have been made.

Modifications

By art 3 Rent Officers (Housing Benefit Functions) Amendment Order 2007 SI No.2871, those provisions which on 19 March 2008 applied only in relation to the areas of former Pathfinder authorities, apply in the same way to the areas of every other local authority in England and Wales.

Amendments

1. Amended by art 4 of SI 2000 No 1 as from 3.4.00.

2. Amended by reg 3 of SI 2001 No 1325 as from 2.7.01.

3. Insertion made by art 2 of SI 2003 No 2398 as from a date specified in Sch 1 to that SI in relation to each individual authority.

4. Amended by art 5(1) of SI 2007 No 2871 as from 7.4.08.

[¹ Transitional arrangements for determination of Single Room Rents with effect from 2nd July 2001

3A. In a case where the rent officer has made and notified an authority of a determination of a single room rent pursuant to paragraph 5 of Schedule 1 in the period of 12 months before 2nd July 2001 that determination shall cease to have effect on [² ...] 2nd July 2001 and a rent officer shall–

(a) make a new determination of that single room rent in accordance with Part I of Schedule 1;

(b) comply with Part II of Schedule 1; and

(c)   give notice in accordance with Part III of Schedule 1 within the relevant period or as soon as is practicable after that period;

without an application for a determination under [³ [⁴ regulation 14 of the Housing Benefit Regulations or, as the case may be, regulation 14 of the Housing Benefit (State Pension Credit) Regulations] having been made.]]

Amendments
1.   Inserted by reg 3 of SI 2001 No 1325 as from 2.7.01.
2.   Amended by reg 2(2) of SI 2001 No 2317 as from 2.7.01.
3.   Amended by reg 5 and Sch 2 para 11(3) of SI 2006 No 217 as from 6.3.06.
4.   Substituted by art 10(2) of SI 2007 No 2871 as from 7.4.08.

General Note
The definition of the "single room rent" was amended on 2 July 2001 to be more generous to claimants. Art 3A aimed to ensure that those who were affected by this change benefited from it immediately. For further information, see the commentary on p570 of the 18th edition of this book.

[¹ Redeterminations
4.–(1)   Subject to article 6, where the local authority applies to a rent officer for a redetermination of any determination or redetermination in respect of a tenancy of a dwelling the rent officer shall, in accordance with Schedule 3–
(a)   make redeterminations of any effective determinations and any effective redeterminations in respect of that tenancy; and
(b)   give notice within the relevant period or as soon as is practicable after that period.
(2)   For the purposes of paragraph (1)–
(a)   "effective determinations" means any determinations made in accordance with Part I of Schedule 1 which have effect at the date of the application for a redetermination of a determination or redetermination; and
(b)   "effective redeterminations" means any redeterminations made in accordance with Schedule 3 which have effect at that date.
(3)   A rent officer whose advice is sought as provided for in Schedule 3 shall give that advice.

Amendment
1.   Substituted by art 5 of SI 2000 No 1 as from 3.4.00.

General Note
Art 4 makes it clear that only "effective" determinations or redeterminations need to be redetermined – that is those that have effect at the time that the local authority applies for a redetermination.

[¹ Substitute determinations and substitute redeterminations
4A.–(1)   Where a local authority applies to a rent officer for a substitute determination, in accordance with [² [³ regulation 17 of the Housing Benefit Regulations or, as the case may be, regulation 17 of the Housing Benefit (State Pension Credit) Regulations]], the provisions of this Order shall apply to that substitute determination as they apply to a determination, but as if references to the relevant time were references to the date the application for the original determination was made or, if earlier, the date the tenancy ended.
(2)   Where a local authority applies to a rent officer for a substitute redetermination, in accordance with that regulation, the provisions of this Order shall apply to that substitute redetermination as they apply to a redetermination.]

Amendments
1.   Inserted by art 5 of SI 2000 No 1 as from 3.4.00.
2.   Amended by reg 5 and Sch 2 para 11(4) of SI 2006 No 217 as from 6.3.06.
3.   Substituted by art 10(3) of SI 2007 No 2871 as from 7.4.08.

General Note
Art 4A(1) allows for determinations to be substituted on an application under reg 17 of both the HB and the HB(SPC) Regs. Reg 17 permits substitute determinations where either the local authority or the rent officer has made an error in specified circumstances.

[¹Broad rental market area determinations and local housing allowance determinations

4B.–[⁶ (1)]

[⁴ (1A)   [¹⁰ At such times as a rent officer considers appropriate, a rent officer shall, if the Secretary of State agrees], in relation to each local authority–

(a)   determine one or more broad rental market areas which will (during the month which next begins after the determination is made) fall, in whole or in part, within the area of the local authority so that every part of the area of that local authority falls within a broad rental market area and no part of the area of that authority falls within more than one broad rental market area; and

(b)   give to that local authority a notice which–

(i)   specifies the area contained within each broad rental market area as falls, in whole or in part, within the area of that authority, by reference to the postcodes for each such broad rental market area; and

(ii)   identifies such of those postcodes as fall within the area of that authority.]

[¹³ (1B)   The power in paragraph (1A) is not limited by paragraph 2(2A) or (2B) of Schedule 3B.]

[⁶ (2)]

[⁴ (2A)   [¹⁰ [¹¹ In 2014 and in each subsequent year, on the date specified in paragraph (2B),] a rent officer shall–

(a)   for each broad rental market area determine, in accordance with Schedule 3B, a local housing allowance for each of the categories of dwelling set out in paragraph 1 of Schedule 3B; and

(b)   notify each local authority of the local housing allowance determination made in accordance with sub-paragraph (a) for each broad rental market area falling within, in whole or in part, the area of that authority.]]

[¹¹ [¹² (2B)   The date specified for the purposes of paragraph (2A) is the last working day of January.]]

[⁶ (3)]

[⁴ [¹⁰ (3A)   Any broad rental market area determination made in accordance with paragraph (1A) shall take effect–

(a)   on the day the determination is made for the purpose of enabling a rent officer to determine a local housing allowance for that area; and

[¹⁴ (b) for all other purposes–

(i)   on the next 1st April following the day on which the determination is made; or

(ii)   where the next 1st April is within 11 months beginning with the day on which the determination is made, on the next 1st April after that.]

(3B)   Any local housing allowance determination made in accordance with paragraph (2A) shall take effect on the next 1st April following the day on which the determination is made.]]

[⁹ [⁶ (4)]]

[⁹ [⁶ (4A)]]

(5)   Where a rent officer has made a local housing allowance determination in accordance with paragraph (4)–

(a)   he shall give notice of the determination to the [⁶ local authority] that made the application;

[⁶ (b) any local housing allowance determination made in accordance with paragraph (4) shall take effect for the month in which the relevant date falls, except that no such determination can have effect before 7th April 2008; and

(c)   any local housing allowance determination made in accordance with paragraph (4A) shall take effect for the month in which notice is given in accordance with sub-paragraph (a), except that no such determination can have effect before 7th April 2008.]

[⁴ (6)   Where a rent officer has made a local housing allowance determination in accordance with paragraph (2A) [⁵ [⁹]] he shall–

(a)   make an approximate monthly allowance determination in relation to that local housing allowance determination; and

(b)   give notice of the approximate monthly allowance determination to each authority to which he is required to give notice of the local housing allowance determination when he gives notice of that determination.]

Modifications

Paras (1), (2) and (3) omitted, para (4) substituted, para (4A) inserted and para (5) amended by art 6(4) Rent Officers (Housing Benefit Functions) Amendment Order 2007 SI No.2871 as from 7 April 2008, save where art 6(1)(a), (b) or (c) of that order applied (see p931).

Note that by art 3 of SI 2007 No.2871, those provisions which on 19 March 2008 applied only in relation to the areas of former Pathfinder authorities, apply in the same way to the areas of every other local authority in England and Wales.

Amendments

1.   Inserted by at 2(5) of SI 2003 No 2398 as from a date specified in Sch 1 to that SI in relation to each individual authority.
2.   Amended by reg 5 and Sch 2 para 11(5) of SI 2006 No 217 as from 6.3.06.
3.   Amended by art 4(2)(a) of SI 2007 No 2871 as from 20.3.08.
4.   Inserted by art 4(2)(b)–(e) of SI 2007 No 2871 as from 20.3.08.
5.   Amended by art 5(2) of SI 2007 No 2871 as from 7.4.08.
6.   Amended by art 6(4) of SI 2007 No 2871, as amended by art 2(3) of SI 2008 No 587, as from 7.4.08, save where art 6(1)(a), (b) or (c) of that order applies.
7.   Amended by art 2(2) of SI 2008 No 587 as from 7.4.08.
8.   Amended by art 2(2) of SI 2008 No 3156 as from 5.1.09.
9.   Amended by art 2(2) of SI 2010 No 2836 as from 18.3.11.
10. Amended by art 2(3) of SI 2012 No 646 as from 2.4.12.
11. Amended by art 2(3) of SI 2013 No 1544 as from 1.9.13.
12. Substituted by art 2(2) of SI 2014 No 3126 as from 8.1.15.
13. Inserted by art 2(2) of SI 2016 No 1179 as from 23.1.17.
14. Substituted by art 2(2) of SI 2017 No 1323 as from 26.1.18.

Definitions

"broad rental market area" – see art 2.
"determination" – see art 2.
"local authority" – see art 2.

General Note

Art 4B sets out the determinations that a rent officer must make in connection with the "local housing allowance" (LHA) scheme for rent restriction (see regs 12D, 13C and 13D of both the HB and HB(SPC) Regs), and the time frame for these. The rent officer must determine:

(1)   One or more "broad rental market areas" in relation to each local authority, defined in Sch 3B para 4: para (1A). The first such determination was to be made on 20 March 2008 (see the version of para (1A), as inserted by art 4(2) of SI 2007 No.2871, prior to the amendments made on 2 April 2012). Thereafter the rent officer must determine these, if the Secretary of State agrees, as often as s/he considers appropriate. Para (3A) fixes the date the determination takes effect. The power in para (1A) is not limited by Sch 3B para 2(2A) and (2B) which fixes the relevant local housing allowances for the different categories of dwelling.

(2)   A "local housing allowance" for the categories of dwelling set out in Sch 3B para 1: paras (2A) and (2B). The categories are: one-bedroom shared accommodation and one, two, three and four bedroom dwellings. See p391 for a summary of the local housing allowance scheme and the General Note to Sch 3B of the RO Order (on p899) for an explanation of how local housing allowances are determined and the maximum rates.

In both cases, the rent officer is required to notify the local authority as set out. See the discussion of *R (CPAG) v SSWP* [2011] EWHC 2616 (Admin) on p392. See art 7A for when a rent officer believes s/he has made an error (other than in the application of her/his professional judgement).

Since 8 January 2015, LHAs are determined on the last working day of January in any year. The determinations do not, however, take effect until the following 1 April: para (3B).

Note that a challenge on the vires of the amendments made to the RO orders with effect from 2 April 2012 was unsuccessful: *R (Zacchaeus 2000 Trust) v SSWP* [2013] EWHC 233 (Admin).

[¹Board and attendance determinations and notifications

[³4C.–(1) Where a relevant authority makes an application to a rent officer in accordance with regulation 13D(10) of the Housing Benefit Regulations or, as the case may be, regulation 13D(10) of the Housing Benefit (State Pension Credit) Regulations, a rent officer shall determine whether or not a substantial part of the rent under the tenancy at the relevant time is fairly attributable to board and attendance.

(2) Where a rent officer determines that a substantial part of the rent under the tenancy at the relevant time is fairly attributable to board and attendance, he shall–

(a) notify the relevant authority accordingly; and

(b) treat the application as if it had been made in accordance with regulation 14(1) of the Housing Benefit Regulations or, as the case may be regulation 14(1) of the Housing Benefit (State Pension Credit) Regulations.]

(3) Where a rent officer determines that a substantial part of the rent under the tenancy at the relevant time is not fairly attributable to board and attendance, he shall notify the pathfinder authority accordingly.

[⁴ (4) Where an application for a board and attendance determination is treated as if it had been made in accordance with regulation 14(1) of the Housing Benefit Regulations or, as the case may be, regulation 14(1) of the Housing Benefit (State Pension Credit) Regulations, then, for the purposes of paragraph (a)(ii) of the definition of "relevant period" in article 2(1), it shall be treated as having been received on the day on which the further information provided in accordance with regulation 114A(4) of the Housing Benefit Regulations or regulation 95A(4) of the Housing Benefit (State Pension Credit) Regulations is received.]]

Modifications

Paras (1) and (2) substituted by art 6(5) Rent Officers (Housing Benefit Functions) Amendment Order 2007 SI No.2871 as from 7 April 2008, save where art 6(1)(a), (b) or (c) of that order applied (see p931). Para (4) substituted by art 7(2) Rent Officers (Housing Benefit Functions) Amendment Order 2007 SI No.2871 as from 7 April 2008, save where art 7(1) of that order applied (see p931).

Note that by art 3 SI 2007 No.2871, those provisions which on 19 March 2008 applied only in relation to the areas of former Pathfinder authorities, apply in the same way to the areas of every other local authority in England and Wales.

Amendments

1. Inserted by art 2(5) of SI 2003 No 2398 as from a date specified in Sch 1 to that SI in relation to each individual authority.
2. Amended by reg 5 and Sch 2 para 11(6) of SI 2006 No 217 as from 6.3.06.
3. Amended by art 6(5) of SI 2007 No 2871 as from 7.4.08, save where art 6(1)(a), (b) or (c) of that order applies.
4. Amended by art 7(2) of SI 2007 No 2871 as from 7.4.08, save where art 7(1) of that order applies.

General Note

Art 4C deals with the determinations that a rent officer must make when a relevant authority (an authority administering HB) has applied for a board and attendance determination under reg 13D(10) of either the HB Regs or HB(SPC) Regs. Note that if s/he decides that a substantial part of the rent under the tenancy at the "relevant time" (defined in art 2) is fairly attributable to board and attendance, the application is treated as one under reg 14(1) of either the HB or the HB(SPC) Regs. This ensures that the determinations can then be used by the authority as appropriate in calculating maximum rent under reg 13 and then eligible rent under reg 12C. See also arts 4D and 4E for redeterminations and substitute determinations.

[¹Board and attendance redeterminations

4D.–(1) Subject to article 6, where a [² local authority] applies to a rent officer for a redetermination of a board and attendance determination or board and attendance redetermination, the rent officer shall, in accordance with paragraph (2)–

(a) make a redetermination of–

      (i)   the board and attendance determination, provided it was made in accordance with article 4C and had effect at the date of the application for it to be redetermined; or

      (ii)   the board and attendance redetermination provided it was made in accordance with head (i), and had effect at the date of the application for it to be redetermined; and

(b)   notify the [² local authority] of the redetermination.

(2)   When making a board and attendance redetermination under this article, the rent officer shall seek, and have regard to, the advice of one or two other rent officers in relation to the redetermination.

(3)   A rent officer whose advice is sought in accordance with paragraph (2) shall give that advice.

(4)   Article 4C shall apply in relation to a board and attendance redetermination but as if the references to the relevant time were references to the date on which the original application for a board and attendance determination was made, or if earlier, to the date on which the tenancy ended.]

Modifications

Para (1) amended by art 6(6) Rent Officers (Housing Benefit Functions) Amendment Order 2007 SI No.2871 as from 7 April 2008, save where art 6(1)(a), (b) or (c) of that order applied (see p931).

Note that by art 3 SI 2007 No.2871, those provisions which on 19 March 2008 applied only in relation to the areas of former Pathfinder authorities, apply in the same way to the areas of every other local authority in England and Wales.

Amendments

1.   Inserted by art 2(5) of SI 2003 No 2398 as from a date specified in Sch 1 to that SI in relation to each individual authority.

2.   Amended by art 6(6) of SI 2007 No 2871 as from 7.4.08, save where art 6(1)(a), (b) or (c) of that order applies.

[¹Substitute board and attendance determinations and substitute board and attendance redeterminations

4E.–(1)   Where a [³ local authority] applies to a rent officer for a substitute board and attendance determination in accordance with [²[⁴ regulation 17 of the Housing Benefit Regulations or, as the case may be, regulation 17 of the Housing Benefit (State Pension Credit) Regulations]], the provisions of this Order shall apply to that substitute board and attendance determination as they apply to a board and attendance determination but as if references to the relevant time were references to the date on which the original application for a board and attendance determination was made or, if earlier, the date on which the tenancy ended.

(2)   Where a [³ local authority] applies to a rent officer for a substitute board and attendance redetermination in accordance with [² [⁴ regulation 17 of the Housing Benefit Regulations or, as the case may be, regulation 17 of the Housing Benefit (State Pension Credit) Regulations], the provisions of this Order shall apply to that substitute board and attendance redetermination as they apply to a board and attendance redetermination.]]

Modifications

Art 4E amended by art 6(6) Rent Officers (Housing Benefit Functions) Amendment Order 2007 SI No.2871 as from 7 April 2008, save where art 6(1)(a), (b) or (c) of that order applied (see p931).

Note that by art 3 SI 2007 No.2871, those provisions which on 19 March 2008 applied only in relation to the areas of former Pathfinder authorities, apply in the same way to the areas of every other local authority in England and Wales.

Amendments

1.   Inserted by art 2(5) of SI 2003 No 2398 as from a date specified in Sch 1 to that SI in relation to each individual authority.

2.   Amended by reg 5 and Sch 2 para 11(7) of SI 2006 No 217 as from 6.3.06.

3.   Amended by art 6(6) of SI 2007 No 2871 as from 7.4.08, save where art 6(1)(a), (b) or (c) of that order applies.

4.   Substituted by art 10(4) of SI 2007 No 2871 as from 7.4.08.

Insufficient information

5.   If a rent officer needs further information in order to make a determination under article 3(1) [², a redetermination under article 4, a board and attendance determination under article 4C or a board and attendance redetermination under article 4D][³ where the information supplied under regulation 114A of the Housing Benefit Regulations or regulation 95A of the Housing Benefit (State Pension Credit) Regulations was incomplete or incorrect, he shall serve notice on the local authority requesting it to supply the further information required under regulation 114A or regulation 95A, as the case may be, or to confirm whether the information already supplied is correct and, if it is not, to supply the correct information] [¹ ...].

Modifications

Art 5 amended by art 7(3) Rent Officers (Housing Benefit Functions) Amendment Order 2007 SI No.2871 as from 7 April 2008, save where art 7(1) of that order applied (see p931).

Note that by art 3 SI 2007 No.2871, those provisions which on 19 March 2008 applied only in relation to the areas of former Pathfinder authorities, apply in the same way to the areas of every other local authority in England and Wales.

Amendments

1.   Deleted by art 6 of SI 2000 No 1 as from 3.4.00.
2.   Substituted by art 2(6) SI 2003 No 2398 as from a date specified in Sch 1 to that SI in relation to each individual authority.
3.   Amended by art 7(3) of SI 2007 No 2871 as from 7.4.08, save where art 7(1) of that order applies.

Exceptions

6.–(1)   No determination [¹, redetermination, board and attendance determination or board and attendance redetermination] shall be made if the application for it is withdrawn.

(2)   No determination shall be made under paragraph 3, 4 or 5 of Part I of Schedule 1 if the tenancy is of residential accommodation, within the meaning of [² [³ regulation 9(4) of the Housing Benefit Regulations or, as the case may be, regulation 9(4) of the Housing Benefit (State Pension Credit) Regulations]] (registered homes etc.), or in a hostel.

(3)   No determination shall be made under paragraph 5 of Part I of Schedule 1 unless the local authority states in the application that the claimant is, or may be, a young individual (which has the same meaning as in [² [³ the Housing Benefit Regulations and the Housing Benefit (State Pension Credit) Regulations]]).

(4)   If the rent officer becomes aware that an application is not one which gives rise to a duty to make a determination [¹, redetermination, board and attendance determination or a board and attendance redetermination], the rent officer shall give the local authority notice to that effect.

Modifications

Note that by art 3 Rent Officers (Housing Benefit Functions) Amendment Order 2007 SI No.2871, those provisions which on 19 March 2008 applied only in relation to the areas of former Pathfinder authorities, apply in the same way to the areas of every other local authority in England and Wales.

Amendments

1.   Substituted by art 2(7) of SI 2003 No 2398 as from a date specified in Sch 1 to that SI in relation to each individual authority.
2.   Amended by reg 5 and Sch 2 para 11(8) of SI 2006 No 217 as from 6.3.06.
3.   Substituted by art 10(5) of SI 2007 No 2871 as from 7.4.08.

Special cases

7.–(1)   This Order shall apply as specified in Schedule 4 in relation to–
(a)   mooring charges payable for a houseboat;
(b)   payments in respect of the site on which a caravan or mobile home stands; or
(c)   payments under a rental purchase agreement.

(2)   Terms used in paragraph (1) have the same meaning in this article and in Schedule 4 as they have in [² [³ regulation 12(1) of the Housing Benefit Regulations or,

as the case may be, regulation 12(1) of the Housing Benefit (State Pension Credit) Regulations]] (rents).[¹ ...]

Amendments
1.   Omitted by art 7 of SI 2000 No 1 as from 3.4.00.
2.   Amended by reg 5 and Sch 2 para 11(9) of SI 2006 No 217 as from 6.3.06.
3.   Substituted by art 10(6) of SI 2007 No 2871 as from 7.4.08.

[¹Errors

7A.–[² (1)]   If a rent officer is of the opinion that he has made an error (other than in the application of his professional judgement) in relation to a determination or redetermination, he shall notify the local authority which made the application for that determination or redetermination of the error as soon as practicable after he becomes aware of it.]

[² (2)   If a rent officer is of the opinion that he has made an error (other than in the application of his professional judgement) in relation to a board and attendance determination or board and attendance redetermination, he shall notify the [⁵ local authority] which made the application for that board and attendance determination or board and attendance redetermination of the error as soon as practicable after he becomes aware of it.

[⁵ (3)]]

[⁴ (4)   If a rent officer is of the opinion that he has made an error (other than in the application of his professional judgement) in relation to a broad rental market area determination determined in accordance with article 4B(1A) or a local housing allowance determination determined in accordance with article 4B(2A), he shall notify any local authority to which notification of that determination was sent of the error, and the amended determination, as soon as practicable after he becomes aware of it.]

Modifications
Para (2) amended and para (3) omitted by art 6(7) Rent Officers (Housing Benefit Functions) Amendment Order 2007 SI No.2871 as from 7 April 2008, save where art 6(1)(a), (b) or (c) of that order applied (see p931).
    Note that by art 3 of SI 2007 No.2871, those provisions which on 19 March 2008 applied only in relation to the areas of former Pathfinder authorities, apply in the same way to the areas of every other local authority in England and Wales.

Amendments
1.   Inserted by art 8 of SI 2000 No 1 as from 3.4.00.
2.   Inserted by art 2(8) of SI 2003 No 2398 as from a date specified in Sch 1 to that SI in relation to each individual authority.
3.   Amended by art 4(3)(a) of SI 2007 No 2871 as from 20.3.08.
4.   Inserted by art 4(3)(b) of SI 2007 No 2871 as from 20.3.08.
5.   Amended by art 6(7) of SI 2007 No 2871 as from 7.4.08, save where art 6(1)(a), (b) or (c) of that order applies.

General Note
Art 7A requires a rent officer to notify the local authority of an error in relation to determinations or redeterminations, which will then require the local authority to apply under reg 17 HB Regs or HB(SPC) Regs for a substitute determination under art 4A. Likewise, art 7A requires the rent officer to notify the local authority of error in relation to broad rental market area or local housing allowance determinations. In this case, the error, as well as the amended determination, is notified.
    The words in brackets, "other than in the application of his professional judgement", are important. A rent officer may not notify a local authority where s/he has second thoughts about a figure that s/he has assessed for a property. There must be some basic error of fact or law that vitiates the decision, or, for example, a slip of the pen.

Amendment to 1995 Order

8.   The Rent Officers (Additional Functions) Order 1995 shall be amended by the insertion at the end of article 6 (special cases) of the following–
    "(3)   In a case where the local authority states in the application that the rent includes charges for general counselling or any other support services which are eligible for

housing benefit solely by virtue of paragraph 1(f)(iii) of Schedule 1 to the 1987 Regulations (landlord's support services: supported accommodation) or solely by virtue of that provision and paragraph 1(f)(ii) of that Schedule, the rent officer shall assume when making a determination on a redetermination that–
(a)   the services were not to be provided or made available; and
(b)   the rent payable under the tenancy at the relevant time is such amount as is specified in the application as the rent which would have been payable under the tenancy at that time if those items were not to be provided or made available.
(4)   In a case where the local authority states in the application that the rent includes charges for general counselling or any other support services and the charges–
(a)   are eligible for housing benefit by virtue of paragraph 1(f)(iii) of Schedule 1 to the 1987 Regulations (landlord's support services: supported accommodation) or that provision and paragraph 1(f)(ii) of that Schedule; and
(b)   are also eligible for housing benefit by virtue of paragraph 1(f)(i) of that Schedule (support services: other exceptions);
the rent officer shall include in the notice to the local authority, required under article 3(1)(c), a statement of the amount of the rent payable for the tenancy (which has the same meaning as in paragraph 3(1) of Schedule 1 to this Order) which relates to those charges.".

Revocations
9.   The Rent Officers (Additional Functions) Order 1995, the Rent Officers (Additional Functions) (Amendment) Order 1995, the Rent Officers (Additional Functions) (Amendment No. 2) Order 1995, the Rent Officers (Additional Functions) (Amendment) Order 1996 and the Rent Officers (Additional Functions) (Amendment) Order 1997 are hereby revoked.

Application
10.–(1)   The amendment made by article 8 does not have effect in a case where an application for a determination is made before the date that article comes into force.
(2)   The remaining articles of the Order (other than paragraph (1)) do not have effect in a case where an application is made for a determination before the date those articles come into force

---

SCHEDULE 1

ARTICLE 3(1)

Analysis
This Schedule applies for determinations relevant to the "local reference rent scheme" for rent restriction. Note the special rules for houseboats, mobile homes and rental purchase agreements in art 7 and Sch 4. For a summary of the scheme, see the General Note to reg 13 HB Regs on p381.

Part I
Determinations

Significantly high rents
1.–(1)   The rent officer shall determine whether, in his opinion, the rent payable under the tenancy of the dwelling at the relevant time is significantly higher than the rent which the landlord might reasonably have been expected to obtain under the tenancy at that time.
(2)   If the rent officer determines under sub-paragraph (1) that the rent is significantly higher, the rent officer shall also determine the rent which the landlord might reasonably have been expected to obtain under the tenancy at the relevant time.
(3)   When making a determination under this paragraph, the rent officer shall have regard to the level of rent under similar tenancies of similar dwellings in the [¹ vicinity] (or as similar as regards tenancy, dwelling and [¹ vicinity] as is reasonably practicable) and shall assume that no one who would have been entitled to housing benefit had sought or is seeking the tenancy.
[²(4)   For the purposes of this paragraph and paragraph 2 "vicinity" means–
(a)   the area immediately surrounding the dwelling; or
(b)   where, for the purposes of sub-paragraph (2)(c) of paragraph 2, there is no dwelling in the area immediately surrounding the dwelling which satisfies the description in heads (i), (ii) and (iii) of that sub-paragraph, the area nearest to the dwelling where there is such a dwelling.]

Amendments
1.   Amended by art 2(2) of SI 2001 No 3561 as from 6.11.01.
2.   Inserted by art 2(2) of SI 2001 No 3561 as from 6.11.01.

General Note
Significantly high rent (SHR) figures are determined on the basis of rents for tenancies in the *"vicinity"*. Note the extended definition of "tenancy" in art 2. Para 1(4) defines "vicinity" for this para and para 2 in fairly restrictive terms. "Immediately surrounding" must, on any view, connote a limited geographical area. It cannot, of course, be taken literally so as to preclude any comparators other than immediately neighbouring dwellings, but it cannot sensibly be extended to a zone extending further than, say, a few streets away. Only if there are no homes of a comparable size in that area may the "vicinity" be extended, but then only to an area where such homes exist: para 1(4)(b). It is not clear whether the "vicinity" is then expanded for the purpose of calculating the SHR as well as the SizeRR. It would appear from the wording of para 1(4)(b) that it is to be expanded for both purposes. There is still considerable room for judgement here, both as to what the "vicinity" is and the area to which it should be expanded if applicable.

Size and rent
2.–(1)   The rent officer shall determine whether the dwelling, at the relevant time, exceeds the size criteria for the occupiers.
(2)   If the rent officer determines that the dwelling exceeds the size criteria, the rent officer shall also determine the rent which a landlord might reasonably have been expected to obtain, at the relevant time, for a tenancy which is–
(a)   similar to the tenancy of the dwelling;
(b)   on the same terms other than the term relating to the amount of rent; and
(c)   of a dwelling which is in the same [¹ vicinity] as the dwelling, but which–
   (i)   accords with the size criteria for the occupiers;
   (ii)   is in a reasonable state of repair; and
   (iii)   corresponds in other respects, in the rent officer's opinion, as closely as is reasonably practicable to the dwelling.
(3)   When making a determination under sub-paragraph (2), the rent officer shall have regard to the same matter and make the same assumption as specified in paragraph 1(3), except that in judging the similarity of other tenancies and dwellings the comparison shall be with the tenancy of the second dwelling referred to in sub-paragraph (2) and shall assume that no one who would have been entitled to housing benefit had sought or is seeking that tenancy.

Amendment
1.   Amended by art 2(3) of SI 2001 No 3561 as from 6.11.01.

General Note
Size related rent (SizeRR) figures are determined on the basis of rents in the **"vicinity"**. See para 1(4) above for the definition and for commentary.

Exceptionally high rents
3.–(1)   The rent officer shall determine whether, in his opinion, the rent payable for the tenancy of the dwelling at the relevant time is exceptionally high.
(2)   In sub-paragraph (1) "rent payable for the tenancy" means–
(a)   where a determination is made under sub-paragraph (2) of paragraph 2, the rent determined under that sub-paragraph;
(b)   where no determination is so made and a determination is made under sub-paragraph (2) of paragraph 1, the rent determined under that sub-paragraph; and
(c)   in any other case, the rent payable under the tenancy [¹ at the relevant time].
(3)   If the rent officer determines under sub-paragraph (1) that the rent is exceptionally high, the rent officer shall also determine the highest rent, which is not an exceptionally high rent and which a landlord might reasonably have been expected to obtain at the relevant time (on the assumption that no one who would have been entitled to housing benefit had sought or is seeking the tenancy) for an assured tenancy of a dwelling which–
(a)   is in the same [² neighbourhood] as the dwelling;
(b)   has the same number of bedrooms and rooms suitable for living in as the dwelling (or, where the dwelling exceeds the size criteria for the occupiers, accords with the size criteria); and
(c)   is in a reasonable state of repair.
(4)   For the purpose of determining whether a rent is an exceptionally high rent under this paragraph, the rent officer shall have regard to the levels of rent under assured tenancies of dwellings which–
(a)   are in the same [² neighbourhood] as the dwelling (or in as similar a locality as is reasonably practicable); and

(b)   have the same number of bedrooms and rooms suitable for living in as the dwelling (or, in a case where the dwelling exceeds the size criteria for the occupiers, accord with the size criteria).

[³ (5)   For the purposes of this paragraph and paragraph 4(6) "neighbourhood" means-

(a)   where the dwelling is in a town or city, the part of that town or city where the dwelling is located which is a distinct area of residential accommodation; or

(b)   where the dwelling is not in a town or city, the area surrounding the dwelling which is a distinct area of residential accommodation and where there are dwellings satisfying the description in sub-paragraph (4)(b).]

Amendments

1.   Inserted by arts 9 and 10 of SI 2000 No 1 as from 3.4.00.
2.   Amended by art 2(4) of SI 2001 No 3561 as from 6.11.01.
3.   Inserted by art 2(4) of SI 2001 No 3561 as from 6.11.01.

General Note

"Neighbourhood" is used for the purposes of an exceptionally high rent determination. Para 3(5)(a) defines "neighbourhood" in a town or city as the part of that town or city where the home is located that is a "distinct area of residential accommodation". This a vague definition and could cause much dispute, particularly in densely populated inner city areas where affluent areas and deprived areas are mixed freely and closely. And what is a "town or city"? Outside a town or city, the "neighbourhood" is expanded by para 3(5)(b) to as much as is required to incorporate comparator dwellings. Note that para 3(5) says that the definition of "neighbourhood" is also applicable for the purposes of para 4(6), but para 4(6) no longer makes reference to neighbourhood. There is still considerable room for judgement here as to what the "neighbourhood" is.

Local reference rents

4.–(1)   The rent officer shall make a determination of a local reference rent in accordance with the formula–

$$R = \frac{H+L}{2}$$

where–

R is the local reference rent;

H is the highest rent, in the rent officer's opinion–

(a)   which a landlord might reasonably have been expected to obtain, at the relevant time, for an assured tenancy of a dwelling which meets the criteria in sub-paragraph (2); and

(b)   which is not an exceptionally high rent; and

L is the lowest rent, in the rent officer's opinion,–

(a)   which a landlord might reasonably have been expected to obtain, at the relevant time, for an assured tenancy of a dwelling which meets the criteria in sub-paragraph (2); and

(b)   which is not an exceptionally low rent; and

(2)   The criteria are–

(a)   that the dwelling under the assured tenancy–

    (i)   is in the same [⁷ broad rental market area (local reference rent)] as the dwelling;

    (ii)   is in a reasonable state of repair; and

    (iii)   has the same number of bedrooms and rooms suitable for living in as the dwelling (or, in a case where the dwelling exceeds the size criteria for the occupiers, accords with the size criteria); and

(b)   if the tenant does not have the use under the tenancy of the dwelling [¹ at the relevant time] of more than one bedroom or room suitable for living in [⁸ and neither the tenant nor the tenant's partner is a person who requires overnight care]–

    (i)   that under the assured tenancy the tenant does not have the use of more than one bedroom or room suitable for living in;

    (ii)   if the rent under the tenancy [¹ at the relevant time] includes payments for board and attendance and the rent officer considers the amount fairly attributable to board and attendance is a substantial part of the rent, that a substantial part of the rent under the assured tenancy is fairly attributable to board and attendance;

    (iii)   if sub-paragraph (ii) does not apply and the tenant shares a [² kitchen, toilet, bathroom and room suitable for living in] with a person other than a member of his household, a non-dependant or a person who pays rent to the tenant, that the assured tenancy provides for the tenant to share a [² kitchen, toilet, bathroom and room suitable for living in]; and

    (iv)   if sub-paragraphs (ii) and (iii) do not apply, that the circumstances described in sub-paragraphs (ii) and (iii) do not apply in relation to the assured tenancy.

(3)   Where ascertaining H and L under sub-paragraph (1), the rent officer:

(a)   shall assume that no one who would have been entitled to housing benefit had sought or is seeking the tenancy; and

(b)   shall exclude the amount of any rent which, in the rent officer's opinion, is fairly attributable to the provision of services which are ineligible to be met by housing benefit

[⁴ . . .]

(4)   In sub-paragraph (2)(b)–
"bedroom or room suitable for living in" does not include a room which the tenant shares with any person other than–
(a)   a member of his household;
(b)   a non-dependant (as defined in this sub-paragraph); or
(c)   a person who pays rent to the tenant; and
[⁵ [⁶ "non-dependant" means a non-dependant of the tenant within the meaning of regulation 3 of the Housing Benefit Regulations or, as the case may be, regulation 3 of the Housing Benefit (State Pension Credit) Regulations;]]

(5)   In sub-paragraph (3), "services" means services performed or facilities (including the use of furniture) provided for, or rights made available to, the tenant, but not [¹ , in the case of a tenancy where a substantial part of the rent under the tenancy is fairly attributable to board and attendance, the provision of meals (including the preparation of meals or provision of unprepared food).]

[³ [⁷ (6)   For the purposes of this paragraph and paragraph 5 "broad rental market area (local reference rent)" means the area within which a tenant of the dwelling could reasonably be expected to live having regard to facilities and services for the purposes of health, education, recreation, personal banking and shopping, taking account of the distance of travel, by public and private transport, to and from those facilities and services.
(7)   A broad rental market area (local reference rent) must contain–
(a)   residential premises of a variety of types, including such premises held on a variety of tenures; and
(b)   sufficient privately rented residential premises, to ensure that, in the rent officer's opinion, the local reference rents for tenancies in the area are representative of the rents that a landlord might reasonably be expected to obtain in that area.]]

Amendments

1.   Inserted by arts 9 and 10 of SI 2000 No 1 as from 3.4.00.
2.   Amended by reg 2(3) of SI 2001 No 2317 as from 2.7.01.
3.   Amended by art 2(5) of SI 2001 No 3561 as from 6.11.01.
4.   Deleted by art 2 of SI 2003 No 478 as from 1.4.03 (7.4.03 where rent payable weekly or in multiples of a week).
5.   Substituted by reg 5 and Sch 2 para 11(10)(a) of SI 2006 No 217 as from 6.3.06.
6.   Substituted by art 10(7)(a) of SI 2007 No 2871 as from 7.4.08.
7.   Amended by art 2(3)(a) of SI 2008 No 3156 as from 5.1.09.
8.   Amended by art 3(3) of SI 2010 No 2836 as from 1.4.11.

Analysis

A "broad rental market area (local reference rent)" is used for the purposes of the determination of the local reference rent and the single room rent. The definition was inserted and amendments made to paras 4 and 5 from 5 January 2009, to reverse the effect of the House of Lords decision in *R (on the application of Heffernan) (FC) v The Rent Service* [2008] UKHL 58. Para 4(6) and (7) defines a "broad rental market area (local reference rent)" as an area within which a person could reasonably be expected to live having regard to facilities and services for the purposes of health, education, recreation, personal banking and shopping and the travel distance by public and private transport. It must contain a variety of types of residential accommodation and types of lettings, and have sufficient private rented housing to ensure that the local reference rents for tenancies in the area are representative of the rents that a landlord might reasonably be expected to obtain in that area.

Single room rents

5.–(1)   The rent officer shall determine a single room rent in accordance with the following formula–

$$S = \frac{H+L}{2}$$

where–
S is the single room rent;
H is the highest rent, in the rent officer's opinion,–
(a)   which a landlord might reasonably have been expected to obtain, at the relevant time, for an assured tenancy of a dwelling which meets the criteria in sub-paragraph (2); and
(b)   which is not an exceptionally high rent.
L is the lowest rent, in the rent officer's opinion,–
(a)   which a landlord might reasonably have been expected to obtain, at the relevant time, for an assured tenancy of a dwelling which meets the criteria in sub-paragraph (2); and
(b)   which is not an exceptionally low rent.
(2)   The criteria are–
(a)   that the dwelling under the assured tenancy is in the same [⁴ broad rental market area (local reference rent)] as the dwelling and is in a reasonable state of repair;

(b)   that, under the assured tenancy, the tenant–
    (i)   has the exclusive use of one bedroom;
    (ii)   does not have the use of any other bedroom [¹...];
    [¹(iia)   shares the use of a room suitable for living in;]
    (iii)   shares the use of a toilet [¹ and bathroom]; and
    (iv)   shares the use of a kitchen and does not have the exclusive use of facilities for cooking food; and
(c)   that the rent does not include any payment for board and attendance.
(3)   Sub-paragraphs [³ (3) and (5)] of paragraph 4 apply when ascertaining H and L under this sub-paragraph as if the reference in those sub-paragraphs to H and L were to H and L under [³ this paragraph].

Amendments

1.   Amended by reg 4 of SI 2001 No 1325 as from 2.7.01.
2.   Substituted by art 2(9) of SI 2003 No 2398 as from a date specified in Sch 1 to that SI in relation to each individual authority.
3.   Amended by arts 2(1) and 3 of SI 2005 No 236 as from 13.3.05.
4.   Amended by art 2(3)(b) of SI 2008 No 3156 as from 5.1.09.

General Note

The single room rent applies where the claimant is a "young individual" (see the definition in reg 2(1) HB Regs and the commentary to reg 13 HB Regs) which, in broad terms means a single claimant under the age of 35 (there are a number of exceptions). The policy is that HB should not pay for such people to live in self-contained accommodation but only in a single bedroom with shared facilities. Note that the "young individual" age limit was 25 prior to 1 January 2012.

Claim-related rent

[¹**6.**–[² (1)   In this paragraph, and in paragraph 9, "claim-related rent" means the claim-related rent determined by the rent officer in accordance with paragraph (2A).]
[² (2A)   The rent officer shall determine that the claim-related rent is–
(a)   where he makes a determination under sub-paragraph (2) of paragraph 1, sub-paragraph (2) of paragraph 2 and sub-paragraph (3) of paragraph 3, the lowest of the three rents determined under those sub-paragraphs;
(b)   where he makes a determination under only two of the sub-paragraphs referred to in paragraph (a), the lower of the two rents determined under those sub-paragraphs;
(c)   where he makes a determination under only one of the sub-paragraphs referred to in paragraph (a), the rent determined under that sub-paragraph;
(d)   where he does not make a determination under any of the sub-paragraphs referred to in sub-paragraph (a), the rent payable under the tenancy of the dwelling at the relevant time.]
[² (2)]
(3)   [²] the rent officer shall also determine the total amount of ineligible charges, as defined in paragraph 7, which he has not included in the claim-related rent because of the assumptions made in accordance with that paragraph.]

Modifications

Para (1) substituted, para (2A) inserted, para (2) omitted and para (3) is amended by art 9(2) Rent Officers (Housing Benefit Functions) Amendment Order 2007 SI No.2871 as from 7 April 2008, save where art 9(1)(a) or (b) of that order applied (see p932).

Amendments

1.   Substituted by arts 11 and 12 of SI 2000 No 1 as from 3.4.00.
2.   Amended by art 9(2) of SI 2007 No 2871 as from 7.4.08, save where art 9(1) of that order applies.

Analysis

The "claim-related rent" (CRR) is the lowest of the rent officer determinations, or if there are none, the rent payable under the tenancy. It is the lowest of the CRR and the local reference rent (or if relevant, the single room rent) which determines maximum rent under reg 13.

    There is a potential drawback in that claimants do not usually get an opportunity to examine the notifications given by the rent officer to the authority, still less the basis on which the rent officer has reached those calculations. This may make it questionable whether the procedure before the rent officer may infringe art 6 of the European Convention on Human Rights, because the claimant has no effective means of challenging the determination. However, the claimant *can* appeal the local authority's decision on HB entitlement and, as such, can challenge the factual basis upon which the rent officer decision was made: *Bexley LB v LD (HB)* [2010] UKUT 79 (AAC).

Part II
Assumptions

Ineligible charges and support charges

['**7.**–[⁵ (1) "ineligible charges" means service charges which are ineligible to be met by housing benefit by virtue of regulation 12B(2) (rent) of and Schedule 1 (ineligible service charges) to the Housing Benefit Regulations or, as the case may be, regulation 12B(2) of and Schedule 1 to the Housing Benefit (State Pension Credit) Regulations except in the case of a tenancy where the rent includes payments for board and attendance, and the rent officer considers that a substantial part of the rent under the tenancy is fairly attributable to board and attendance, charges specified in paragraph 1(a)(i) of Schedule 1 to the Housing Benefit Regulations or, as the case may be, in paragraph 1(a)(i) of Schedule 1 to the Housing Benefit (State Pension Credit) Regulations (charges for meals)]

(2)   When making a determination under paragraph 1, 2 or 3 of this Schedule, the rent officer shall assume that–

(a)   the items to which the ineligible charges relate;

[² . . .]

were not to be provided or made available.

[⁴ (3)   For the purposes of paragraphs 1, 2, 3, and 6 of Part 1 of this Schedule, the rent officer shall assume that the rent payable under the tenancy at the relevant time is–

(a)   where an amount is notified to the rent officer under regulation 114A(4)(b) of the Housing Benefit Regulations or, as the case may be, regulations 95A(4)(b) of the Housing Benefit (State Pension Credit) Regulations in respect of that tenancy, that notified amount less the total of any ineligible charges included in that amount; or

(b)   in any other case, the total amount stated under regulation 114A(3)(d) of the Housing Benefit Regulations or, as the case may be regulation 95A(3)(d) of the Housing Benefit (State Pension Credit) Regulations less the total of any ineligible charges included in that stated amount.]

(4)   The total of any ineligible charges, referred to in sub-paragraph (3), shall be the total of the amounts (excluding any amount which he considers is negligible) of any charges included in the notified amount or the stated amount, as the case may be, which, in the rent officer's opinion, are at the relevant time fairly attributable to any items to which ineligible charges relate.]

Modifications

Para 7(1) substituted by art 8(2) Rent Officers (Housing Benefit Functions) Amendment Order 2007 SI No.2871 as from 7 April 2008, save where art 8(1)(a) or (b) of that order applied (see p932).

Para 7(3) substituted by art 7(4) of the Rent Officers (Housing Benefit Functions) Amendment Order 2007 SI No.2871 as from 7 April 2008, save where art 7(1) of that order applied (see p931).

Amendments

1.   Substituted by arts 11 and 12 of SI 2000 No 1 as from 3.4.00.
2.   Deleted by art 2 of SI 2003 No 478 as from 1.4.03 (7.4.03 where rent payable weekly or in multiples of a week).
3.   Amended by reg 5 and Sch 2 para 11(10)(b) of SI 2006 No 217 as from 6.3.03.
4.   Substituted by art 7(4) of SI 2007 No 2871 as from 7.4.08, save where art 7(1) of that order applies.
5.   Substituted by art 8(2) of SI 2007 No 2871 as from 7.4.08, save where art 8(1) of that order applies.

Analysis

Para 7 specifies how ineligible charges are dealt with.

"Ineligible charges" are those which are ineligible for HB under reg 12B(2) and Sch 1 of both the HB and the HB(SPC) Regs, with the exception of charges for meals in certain cases. These are where board and attendance are included in the rent and a "substantial" part of the rent is attributable to those elements. "Substantial" will be taken to mean "more than minimal". "Attendance", however, is not defined and it is not precisely clear what it refers to. In context, it is suggested that it must be intended to refer to the cooking and serving of meals, rather than the provision of some sort of physical attendance by way of nursing care or similar.

Para (2) requires the rent officer to leave out of account ineligible charges in making determinations.

Para (3) sets out what the rent officer is to assume the rent payable by the claimant is. The normal rule, set out in sub-para (b), is that the rent is treated as being the amount stated by the local authority minus any ineligible charges. Sub-para (a) applies where the local authority states an amount under reg 114A(4)(b) HB Regs or reg 95A(4)(b) HB(SPC) Regs (or reg 14(9)(b) HB Regs or 14(8)(b) HB(SPC) Regs if art 7(1) of SI 2007 No.2871 applies – see p931).

Para (4) specifies that "ineligible" charges for the purpose of para (3)(b) are those which the rent officer considers to be ineligible under the HB or HB(SPC) Regs.

Housing associations etc.

8.–(1)   In a case where the local authority states in the application that the landlord is a housing association or a charity, the rent officer shall assume that the landlord is not such a body.

(2)   The rent officer shall not take into account the rent under any tenancy where the landlord is a housing association or where the landlord is a charity and the dwelling is provided by the landlord in the pursuit of its charitable purposes.

(3)   In this paragraph–

"charity" has the same meaning as in the Charities Act 1993, except that it includes a Scottish charity (which has the same meaning as in section 1(7) of the Law Reform (Miscellaneous Provisions) (Scotland) Act 1990); and

"housing association" has the same meaning as in the Housing Associations Act 1985.

Part III
Notifications of Part I determinations

Notifications

9.–[¹ (1)   Subject to sub-paragraph (2), the rent officer shall give notice to the local authority of–

(a)   the claim-related rent determined under Part I;

(b)   where the dwelling is not in a hostel, the total amount of ineligible charges determined under paragraph 6(3) in relation to that claim-related rent;

[³ (c)   where that claim-related rent includes an amount which would be ineligible for housing benefit under paragraph 1(a)(i) of Schedule 1 to the Housing Benefit Regulations or, as the case may be, paragraph 1(a)(i) of Schedule 1 to the Housing Benefit (State Pension Credit) Regulations (charges for meals), the inclusion of an ineligible amount in respect of meals;]

(d)   any rent determined by the rent officer under paragraph 4 (local reference rents); and

[³ (da)   where any rent determined under paragraph 4 includes an amount which would be ineligible for housing benefit under the provisions referred to in sub-paragraph (c), the inclusion of an ineligible amount in respect of meals; and]

(e)   any rent determined by the rent officer under paragraph 5 (single room rents).]

(2)   If the rent officer determines a rent under–

(a)   paragraph 4 (local reference rents); or

(b)   paragraph 5 (single room rents);

which is equal to or more than the [¹ claim-related rent], the rent officer shall give notice to the local authority of this in place of giving notice of the determination made under paragraph 4 or, as the case may be, paragraph 5.

[¹ (3)]

Modifications

Para (1) amended by art 9(3) Rent Officers (Housing Benefit Functions) Amendment Order 2007 SI No.2871 as from 7 April 2008, save where art 9(1)(a) or (b) of that order applied (see p932).

Amendments

1.   Amended by art 13 of SI 2000 No 1 as from 3.4.00.
2.   Amended by reg 5 and Sch 2 para 11(10)(c) of SI 2006 No 217 as from 6.3.06.
3.   Amended by art 9(3) of SI 2007 No 2871 as from 7.4.08, save where art 9(1) of that order applies.

[¹**10.**]

Amendment

1.   Omitted by art 13 of SI 2000 No 1 as from 3.4.00.

Part IV
Indicative Rent Levels

11.–(1)   The rent officer shall determine the indicative rent level for each category described in sub-paragraph (3) in accordance with the following formula–

$$I = \frac{H+3L}{4}$$

where–

I is the indicative rent level;

H is the highest rent, in the rent officer's opinion,–

(a)   which a landlord might reasonably be expected to obtain at the time the determination is being made for an assured tenancy of a dwelling meeting the criteria in sub-paragraph (2); and

(b)   which is not an exceptionally high rent; and

L is the lowest rent, in the rent officer's opinion,–

(a)   which a landlord might reasonably be expected to obtain at the time the determination is being made for an assured tenancy of a dwelling meeting the criteria in sub-paragraph (2); and

(b)   which is not an exceptionally low rent.

(2)   The criteria are that–

(a)   the dwelling is in the area of the local authority;

(b)   the dwelling is in a reasonable state of repair; and

(c)   the dwelling and tenancy accord with the category to which the determination relates.

(3)   The categories for the purposes of this paragraph are–

(a)   a dwelling where the tenant does not have use of more than one room where a substantial part of the rent under the tenancy is fairly attributable to board and attendance;

(b)   a dwelling where the tenant does not have use of more than one room, the tenancy provides for him to share a kitchen or toilet and paragraph (a) does not apply;

(c)   a dwelling where the tenant does not have use of more than one room and where paragraphs (a) and (b) do not apply;

(d)   a dwelling where the tenant does not have use of more than two rooms and where none of paragraphs (a) to (c) applies;

(e)   a dwelling where the tenant does not have use of more than three rooms and where none of paragraphs (a) to (d) applies;

(f)   a dwelling where the tenant does not have use of more than four rooms and where none of paragraphs (a) to (e) applies;

(g)   a dwelling where the tenant does not have use of more than five rooms and where none of paragraphs (a) to (f) applies; and

(h)   a dwelling where the tenant does not have use of more than six rooms and where none of paragraphs (a) to (g) applies.

(4)   When ascertaining H and L under sub-paragraph (1), the rent officer:

(a)   shall assume that no one who would have been entitled to housing benefit had sought or is seeking the tenancy; and

(b)   shall exclude the amount of any rent which, in the rent officer's opinion, is fairly attributable to the provision of services which are ineligible to be met by housing benefit

[¹ . . .].]

(5)   In this paragraph–

"room" means a bedroom or room suitable for living in and in paragraphs (a), (b) and (c) of sub-paragraph (3) does not include a room which the tenant shares with any person other than–

(a)   a member of his household;

(b)   a non-dependant of the tenant (within the meaning of [² [³ regulation 3 of the Housing Benefit Regulations or, as the case may be, regulation 3 of the Housing Benefit (State Pension Credit) Regulations]]); or

(c)   a person who pays rent to the tenant; and "services" has the meaning given by paragraph 4(5).

Amendments

1.   Deleted by art 2 of SI 2003 No 478 as from 1.4.03 (7.4.03 where rent payable weekly or in multiples of a week).

2.   Amended by reg 5 and Sch 2 para 11(10)(d) of SI 2006 No 217 as from 6.3.06.

3.   Substituted by art 10(7)(b) of SI 2007 No 2871 as from 7.4.08.

SCHEDULE 2

ARTICLE 2

Size Criteria

1.   One bedroom or room suitable for living in shall be allowed for each of the following categories of occupier (and each occupier shall come within only the first category for which he is eligible)–

[⁵ (za)   a member of a couple who cannot share a bedroom;

(zb)   a member of a couple who can share a bedroom;]

(a)   [¹ a couple] [⁵];

(b)   a person who is not a child;

[⁴ (ba)   a child who cannot share a bedroom;]

(c)   two children of the same sex;

(d)   two children who are less than ten years old;

(e)   a child.

[⁴ but the claimant is only entitled to a bedroom in respect of a child who cannot share a bedroom [⁵ or a member of a couple who cannot share a bedroom] if there is a bedroom in the dwelling occupied as the home that is additional to those to which the claimant would be entitled if the child [⁵ or the member of the couple] were able to share a bedroom.]

[³**1A.**   One additional bedroom is allowed where on the application for the determination–

[⁵ (a)   one or more of the following persons is stated as being a person who requires overnight care–

(i)   the tenant;

(ii)   the tenant's partner;

(iii)   a person (other than the tenant or the tenant's partner) who occupies the dwelling as their home;

(iv)   a child or young person in respect of whom the tenant or the tenant's partner is a qualifying parent or carer;]

(b)   the tenant or the tenant's partner is (or both of them are) stated as being a qualifying parent or carer.]

[³**1B.**   Two additional bedrooms are allowed where sub-paragraphs (a) and (b) of paragraph 1A both apply.]

2.   The number of rooms (excluding any allowed under paragraph 1) suitable for living in allowed are–

(a)   if there are less than four occupiers, one;

(b)   if there are more than three and less than seven occupiers, two; and

(c)   in any other case, three.

[³[⁴**3.**   In this Schedule "child who cannot share a bedroom" [⁵, "couple", "member of a couple who cannot share a bedroom"] and "qualifying parent or carer" have the meaning given by regulation 2(1) of the Housing Benefit Regulations [⁵ and reference to a member of a couple who can share a bedroom is to be construed in accordance with regulation 2(6) of those Regulations].]]

Amendments

1.   Substituted by art 29 of SI 2005 No 2877 as from 5.12.05.
2.   Inserted by art 3(4) of SI 2010 No 2836 as from 1.4.11.
3.   Amended by art 2 of SI 2013 No 666 as from 1.4.13.
4.   Amended by art 2 of SI 2013 No 2827 as from 4.12.13.
5.   Amended by reg 2 of SI 2017 No 213 as from 1.4.17.

General Note

This schedule is relevant for the local reference rent scheme for rent restriction. The rent officer makes a size related rent determination under Sch 1 para 2 if the claimant's dwelling exceeds the size criteria for the number of occupiers found in Sch 2.

Para 1. Under para 1, one bedroom or room suitable for living in is allowed for each category of occupier listed, each coming only into the first category for which s/he is eligible. "Child" is defined in art 2 and is a person under the age of 16. "Occupier" is also defined in art 2. See p881 for a discussion. A "member of a couple who cannot share a bedroom" is defined as in reg 2(1) HB Regs and is a member of a couple receiving higher rate AA, highest or middle rate DLA care component, either rate of the daily living component of PIP or armed forces independence payment and who the local authority is satisfied is not reasonably able to share a bedroom with the other member of the couple by virtue of her/his disability. A "member of a couple who can share a bedroom" is defined as in reg 2(6) and is a member of a couple whose partner is a "member of a couple who cannot share a bedroom".

A "child who cannot share a bedroom" is defined as in reg 2(1) HB Regs and is a child entitled to DLA care component at the highest or middle rate who the local authority is satisfied cannot reasonably share a bedroom with another child by virtue of her/his disability.

Note that an additional bedroom is only allowed for a child or member of a couple who cannot share a bedroom if there is a bedroom in the home additional to those to which the claimant would be entitled if the person were able to share a bedroom. "Room suitable for living in" is not defined, but it is suggested would not include a kitchen, bathroom or toilet.

Paras 1A and 1B. An additional bedroom is allowed under para 1A in the following situations.

(1)   The tenant or her/his partner, or a person (other than the tenant or the tenant's partner) who occupies the dwelling as her/his home (eg a child or young person, or a joint occupier or non-dependant), or a child or young person in respect of whom the tenant or the tenant's partner is a "qualifying parent or carer" is a "person who requires overnight care", defined in art 2 by reference to reg 2 of the HB Regs and the HB(SPC) Regs – ie, an additional bedroom is allowed for a non-resident carer: sub-para (a). See p243 for a discussion. "Qualifying parent or carer" is defined as in reg 2(1) HB Regs. Only one additional room is allowed under this sub-para even if there is more than non-resident carer.

(2)   The tenant or her/his partner is a "qualifying parent or carer" (a specified foster carer or kinship carer as defined in reg 2(1) HB Regs): sub-para (b). See p245 for a discussion. Note that only one additional bedroom is allowed under this sub-para even if the qualifying parent or carer has more than one child or young person placed with her/him.

Two additional bedrooms are allowed if both of the situations in para 1A apply: para 1B.

Para 2. In addition, an extra number of rooms suitable for living in are allowed under para 2, dependant on the total number of occupiers.

Example. A claimant and his partner have two sons aged 12 and 14 and a foster daughter aged 17. The 12 year old is a "child who cannot share a bedroom". The foster daughter is a "person who requires overnight care". The claimant is a "qualifying parent or carer". He is allowed three bedrooms (or rooms suitable for living in) under para 1 – one for him and his partner and one for each of the two sons. He is not allowed a bedroom under para 1 for his foster daughter as she does not count as an occupier (see reg 21(3) HB Regs). He is allowed two additional bedrooms under para 1A and 1B because he is a "qualifying parent or carer" and because his foster daughter is a "person who requires overnight care". There are four occupiers (the foster daughter does not count), so he is allowed two other rooms suitable for living in. Thus they are allowed seven rooms as well as a kitchen, bathroom and toilet.

Note that unlike with the local housing allowance scheme for rent restriction, there is no maximum number of bedrooms (or rooms suitable for living in) that can be allowed under Sch 2.

The size criteria do not expressly include an additional bedroom where this is needed for any other reason. However, see the discussion on p395. Note that prior to 4 December 2013, the size criteria did not include an additional bedroom for a child unable to share because of severe disabilities. However, the government accepted under the "local housing allowance" scheme rules, following the Court of Appeal decision in *Burnip v Birmingham CC and Others* [2012] EWCA Civ 629; [2013] AACR 7 (*Burnip, Trengove* and *Gorry*), that local authorities *should* allow an extra bedroom in such cases. It is suggested that the same would apply here.

SCHEDULE 3

ARTICLE 4

Redeterminations

[¹**1.**   Schedules 1 and 2 shall apply in relation to a redetermination as they apply to a determination, but as if references in those Schedules to the relevant time were references to the date the application for the original determination was made or, if earlier, the date the tenancy ended.]

Amendment
1.   Substituted by SI 2000 No 1 from 3.4.00.

2.   The rent officer making the redetermination shall seek and have regard to the advice of one or two other rent officers in relation to the redetermination.

[² SCHEDULE 3A]

ARTICLES 2(2) AND 4B

Modifications
Schedule 3A omitted by art 6(8) Rent Officers (Housing Benefit Functions) Amendment Order 2007 SI No.2871 as from 7 April 2008, save where art 6(1)(a), (b) or (c) of that order applied (see p931).

Amendments
1.   Schedule inserted by art 2(10) of SI 2003 No 2398 as from a date specified in Sch 1 to that SI in relation to each individual authority.
2.   Omitted by art 6(8) of SI 2007 No 2871 as from 7.4.08, save where art 6(1)(a), (b) or (c) of that order applies.
3.   Substituted by art 10(8) of SI 2007 No 2871 as from 7.4.08.

[¹ SCHEDULE 3B

ARTICLE 4B

Amendment
1.   Schedule inserted by art 4(4) of SI 2007 No 2871 as from 20.3.08.

General Note
This schedule is relevant for the local housing allowance scheme for rent restriction. The rent officer determines local housing allowances (LHAs) in accordance with Sch 3B for each category of dwelling set out in Para 1: art 4B. The authority then uses these to determine maximum rent (LHA) under reg 13D of both the HB and the HB(SPC) Regs.

Para 1 sets out the categories of dwellings. Note that prior to 18 March 2011, the largest category of dwelling was five bedroom accommodation and that a LHA for larger dwellings could be set either because the rent officer believed it was likely to be required, or because the authority applied for one under reg 13D HB Regs. Some transitional protection was provided under reg 12L of both the HB and the HB(SPC) Regs.

Para 2 provides the process by which a LHA is determined, and the presumptions the rent officer is to use.

Para 2(3A) provides the LHA rate for the specified categories of dwelling in the specified broad rental market areas listed in para 5A: para 2(2B)(a). This is the lower of the following figures.

(1)   The LHA last determined for the category of dwelling, or where that determination is amended because the rent officer made an error as specified in art 7A(4) "other than in the application of his professional judgement", the LHA provided in the amended determination, in either case, plus 3 per cent: sub-para (3A)(a). Note that prior to 26 January 2018, the relevant LHA was that determined on 30 January 2015.

(2)   The maximum LHA for the relevant category of dwelling in the table: sub-para (3A)(b).

(3) From 25 January 2019, the rent at the 30th percentile of a list of rents for dwellings let under assured tenancies, payable at the date of the determination: sub-paras (3A)(c) and (4) to (8). The criteria for including an assured tenancy on the list are in sub-para (5)(a).

Para 2(3) provides the LHA rate for all other categories of dwelling: para 2(2A) and (2B)(b). This is the lower of the following figures.

(1) The rent at the 30th percentile of a list of rents for dwellings let under assured tenancies, payable at the date of the determination: sub-paras (3)(b) and (4) to (8). The criteria for including an assured tenancy on the list are in sub-para (5)(a). Note that prior to 18 March 2011, the LHA was the median rent in the list – ie, a higher figure.

(2) The LHA last determined for the category of dwelling, or where that determination is amended because the rent officer made an error as specified in art 7A(4) "other than in the application of his professional judgement", the LHA provided in the amended determination: sub-para (3)(a). Note that prior to 26 January 2018, the relevant LHA was that determined on 30 January 2015.

The rent officer determines LHA rates annually, on the last working day of January in any year and these rates take effect from the following 1 April: art 4B(2A), (2B) and (3A). From 1 April 2015 to 26 January 2018, the LHA rates were effectively capped at the rates determined on 30 January 2015 – ie, they could be lower than that figure, but never higher. The government indicated in its 2015 Summer Budget that it intended LHA rates to be "frozen" for four years from April 2016. However, from 23 January 2017, it allowed for a potential increase, but only for the specified categories of dwelling in the specified broad rental market areas then listed in para 5A.

Note that prior to 2 November 2015, the rules allowed for the LHA rates to increase annually. From 13 January 2014 to 2 November 2015, there were two possibilities. For details of the rules between 13 January and 2 November 2015, see pp831–36 of the 27th edition.

Para 3 deals with situations where the LHA for a category is lower than that for a category with a smaller number of bedrooms.

Paras 4 and 5 define "broad rental market area".

Broad rental market area determinations and local housing allowance determinations

Categories of dwelling
1.–(1) The categories of dwelling for which a rent officer is required to determine a local housing allowance in accordance with [² article 4B(2A)(a)] are–
(a) a dwelling where the tenant has the exclusive use of only one bedroom and where the tenancy provides for him to share the use of one or more of–
    (i) a kitchen;
    (ii) a bathroom;
    (iii) a toilet; or
    (iv) a room suitable for living in;
(b) a dwelling where the tenant (together with his partner where he has one) has the exclusive use of only one bedroom and exclusive use of a kitchen, a bathroom, a toilet and a room suitable for living in;
(c) a dwelling where the tenant has the use of only two bedrooms;
(d) a dwelling where the tenant has the use of only three bedrooms;
(e) a dwelling where the tenant has the use of only four bedrooms;
[¹ (f)]
(2) In–
(a) sub-paragraph (1)(b) "partner" has the same meaning as in regulation 2 of the Housing Benefit Regulations or, as the case may be, regulation 2 of the Housing Benefit (State Pension Credit) Regulations;
(b) sub-paragraph (1)(c) [¹ to (e)] "bedroom" means a bedroom, except for a bedroom which the tenant shares with any person other than–
    (i) a member of his household;
    (ii) a non-dependant of the tenant (within the meaning of regulation 3 of the Housing Benefit Regulations or, as the case may be, regulation 3 of the Housing Benefit (State Pension Credit) Regulations); or
    (iii) a person who pays rent to the tenant.

Amendments
1. Amended by art 2(3)(a) of SI 2010 No 2836 as from 18.3.11.
2. Amended by art 2(4)(a) of SI 2012 No 646 as from 2.4.12.

[⁶ **Local housing allowance for category of dwelling in paragraph 1**
2.–(1) Subject to paragraph 3 (anomalous local housing allowances), the rent officer must determine a local housing allowance for each category of dwelling in paragraph 1 as follows.

[⁸]

[⁹ (2A)   For a broad rental market area not listed in column 1 of the table in paragraph 5A, the local housing allowance for any category of dwelling is the lower of the amounts set out in sub-paragraphs (3)(a) and (b).

(2B)   For a broad rental market area listed in column 1 of the table in paragraph 5A, the local housing allowance–

(a)   for a category of dwelling listed in the corresponding entry in column 2 of that table, is the [¹¹ lowest of the amounts set out in sub-paragraph (3A)(a), (b) and (c)];

(b)   for a category of dwelling not so listed, is the lower of the amounts set out in sub-paragraph (3)(a) and (b).]

[⁸ (3)   [⁹ The amounts referred to in sub-paragraphs (2A) and (2B)(b) are–]

(a)   the local housing allowance [¹⁰ last determined for that category of dwelling] (or, where the determination is amended under article 7A(4) (errors), the allowance provided for in the amended determination); [⁹ and]

(b)   the rent at the 30th percentile determined in accordance with sub-paragraphs (4) to (8) [⁹].]

[⁹ (3A)   The amounts referred to in sub-paragraph (2B)(a) are–

(a)   the local housing allowance [¹⁰ last determined for that category of dwelling] (or, where the determination is amended under article 7A(4) (errors), the allowance provided for in the amended determination), plus 3%; [¹¹]

(b)   the maximum local housing allowance listed in column 2 of the following table for the category of dwelling–

[¹¹ 1. *Category of dwelling as defined in the following paragraphs of this Schedule* and 2. *Maximum local housing allowance for that category of dwelling*]

1. Category of dwelling as defined in the following paragraphs of this Schedule	2. Maximum local housing allowance for that category of dwelling
paragraph 1(1)(a) (one bedroom, shared accommodation)	£276.51
paragraph 1(1)(b) (one bedroom, exclusive use)	£276.51
paragraph 1(1)(c) (two bedrooms)	£320.74
paragraph 1(1)(d) (three bedrooms)	£376.04
paragraph 1(1)(e) (four bedrooms)	£442.42]]

[¹¹; and

(c)   the rent at the 30th percentile determined in accordance with sub-paragraphs (4) to (8).]

(4)   The rent officer must compile a list of rents in ascending order of the rents which, in the rent officer's opinion, are payable–

(a)   for a dwelling let under an assured tenancy for each category of dwelling specified in paragraph 1; and

(b)   in the 12 month period ending on the 30th day of the September preceding the date of the determination.

(5)   In compiling the list of rents, the rent officer must–

(a)   include within it the rent of an assured tenancy in relation to each category of dwelling if–

(i)   the dwelling let under the assured tenancy is in the broad rental market area for which the local housing allowance for that category of dwelling is being determined;

(ii)   the dwelling is in a reasonable state of repair; and

(iii)   the assured tenancy permits the tenant to use exclusively or share the use of, as the case may be, the same number and type of rooms as the category of dwelling in relation to which the list is being compiled;

(b)   include within it any rents which are of the same amount;

(c)   where rent is payable other than weekly, use the figure which would be payable if the rent were to be payable weekly by–

(i)   multiplying the rent by an appropriate figure to obtain the rent for a year;

(ii)   dividing the total in (i) by 365; and

(iii)   multiplying the total in (ii) by 7;

(d)   assume that no one who would have been entitled to housing benefit had sought or is seeking the tenancy; and

(e)   exclude the amount of any rent which, in the rent officer's opinion, is fairly attributable to the provision of services performed for, or facilities (including the use of furniture) provided for, or rights made available to, the tenant which are ineligible to be met by housing benefit.

(6)   Sub-paragraph (7) applies where the rent officer is not satisfied that the list of rents in respect of any category of dwelling would contain sufficient rents, payable in the 12 month period ending on the 30th day of the September preceding the date of the determination for dwellings in the broad rental market area, to enable a local housing allowance to be determined which is representative of the rents that a landlord might reasonably be expected to obtain in that area.

(7)   In a case where this sub-paragraph applies the rent officer may add to the list rents for dwellings in the same category in other areas in which a comparable market exists.

(8)   The rent officer must use the list of rents to determine the rent at the 30th percentile in the list ("R") by–

(a)　　where the number of rents on the list is a multiple of 10, applying the formula–

$$R = \frac{\text{the amount of the rent at P} + \text{the amount of the rent at P1}}{2}$$

Where–
　　(i)　　P is the position on the list found by multiplying the number of rents on the list by 3 and dividing by 10; and
　　(ii)　　P1 is the following position on the list;
(b)　　where the number of rents on the list is not a multiple of 10, applying the formula–

$$R = \text{the amount of the rent at P2}$$

Where–
P2 is the position on the list found by multiplying the number of rents on the list by 3 and dividing by 10 and rounding the result upwards to the nearest whole number.
[8]
(10)　　Where the local housing allowance would otherwise not be a whole number of pence, it must be rounded to the nearest whole penny by disregarding any amount less than half a penny and treating any amount of half a penny or more as a whole penny.]

Amendments
1.　　Omitted by art 2(4)(a) of SI 2008 No 3156 as from 5.1.09.
2.　　Inserted by art 2(2) of SI 2009 No 2459 as from 12.10.09.
3.　　Amended by art 2(3)(b) of SI 2010 No 2836 as from 18.3.11.
4.　　Amended by art 2(4)(b) of SI 2012 No 646 as from 2.4.12.
5.　　Amended by art 2(4) of SI 2013 No 1544 as from 1.9.13.
6.　　Substituted by art 2(2) of SI 2013 No 2978 as from 13.1.14.
7.　　Substituted by art 2(2) of SI 2014 No 3126 as from 8.1.15.
8.　　Amended by art 2(2)(a) and (b) of SI 2015 No 1753 as from 2.11.15.
9.　　Amended by art 2(3)(a) of SI 2016 No 1179 as from 23.1.17.
10.　　Amended by art 2(3) of SI 2017 No 1323 as from 26.1.18.
11.　　Amended by art 2(2) of SI 2018 No 1332 as from 25.1.19.

Anomalous local housing allowances
3.–(1)　　Where–
(a)　　the rent officer has determined the local housing allowance for each of the categories of dwelling in paragraph 1(1) in accordance with the preceding paragraphs of this Schedule; and
(b)　　the local housing allowance for a category of dwelling in paragraph 1(1)(b) [1 to (e)] is lower than the local housing allowance for any of the categories of dwelling which precede it,
that local housing allowance shall be the same as the highest local housing allowance which precedes it.
[1 (2)]

Amendment
1.　　Amended by art 2(3)(c) of SI 2010 No 2836 as from 18.3.11.

Broad rental market area
[14.　　In this Schedule "broad rental market area" means an area within which a person could reasonably be expected to live having regard to facilities and services for the purposes of health, education, recreation, personal banking and shopping, taking account of the distance of travel, by public and private transport, to and from those facilities and services.]

Amendment
1.　　Inserted by art 2(4)(b) of SI 2008 No 3156 as from 5.1.09.

[15.　　A broad rental market area must contain–
(a)　　residential premises of a variety of types, including such premises held on a variety of tenures; and
(b)　　sufficient privately rented residential premises to ensure that, in the rent officer's opinion, the local housing allowance for the categories of dwelling in the area for which the rent officer is required to determine a local housing allowance is representative of the rents that a landlord might reasonably be expected to obtain in that area.]

Amendment
1.　　Inserted by art 2(4)(b) of SI 2008 No 3156 as from 5.1.09.

[¹**5A.** The table referred to in paragraph 2(2A) and (2B) is as follows–

[³ *1. Broad rental market area*	*2. Category of dwelling as defined in the following paragraphs of this Schedule*
Ashford	paragraph 1(1)(a) (one bedroom, shared accommodation)
Ashford	paragraph 1(1)(b) (one bedroom, exclusive use)
Ashford	paragraph 1(1)(c) (two bedrooms)
Ashford	paragraph 1(1)(d) (three bedrooms)
Ashford	paragraph 1(1)(e) (four bedrooms)
Aylesbury	paragraph 1(1)(b) (one bedroom, exclusive use)
Aylesbury	paragraph 1(1)(c) (two bedrooms)
Aylesbury	paragraph 1(1)(d) (three bedrooms)
Basingstoke	paragraph 1(1)(c) (two bedrooms)
Basingstoke	paragraph 1(1)(d) (three bedrooms)
Bath	paragraph 1(1)(b) (one bedroom, exclusive use)
Bath	paragraph 1(1)(c) (two bedrooms)
Bath	paragraph 1(1)(d) (three bedrooms)
Bath	paragraph 1(1)(e) (four bedrooms)
Bedford	paragraph 1(1)(a) (one bedroom, shared accommodation)
Bedford	paragraph 1(1)(b) (one bedroom, exclusive use)
Bedford	paragraph 1(1)(c) (two bedrooms)
Bedford	paragraph 1(1)(d) (three bedrooms)
Bedford	paragraph 1(1)(e) (four bedrooms)
Birmingham	paragraph 1(1)(b) (one bedroom, exclusive use)
Birmingham	paragraph 1(1)(c) (two bedrooms)
Birmingham	paragraph 1(1)(d) (three bedrooms)
Black Country	paragraph 1(1)(d) (three bedrooms)
Blackwater Valley	paragraph 1(1)(b) (one bedroom, exclusive use)
Blaenau Gwent	paragraph 1(1)(a) (one bedroom, shared accommodation)
Bolton and Bury	paragraph 1(1)(a) (one bedroom, shared accommodation)
Bolton and Bury	paragraph 1(1)(d) (three bedrooms)
Bolton and Bury	paragraph 1(1)(e) (four bedrooms)
Bournemouth	paragraph 1(1)(c) (two bedrooms)
Bournemouth	paragraph 1(1)(d) (three bedrooms)
Bradford & South Dales	paragraph 1(1)(a) (one bedroom, shared accommodation)
Brecon and Radnor	paragraph 1(1)(a) (one bedroom, shared accommodation)
Brighton and Hove	paragraph 1(1)(b) (one bedroom, exclusive use)
Brighton and Hove	paragraph 1(1)(c) (two bedrooms)
Brighton and Hove	paragraph 1(1)(d) (three bedrooms)
Brighton and Hove	paragraph 1(1)(e) (four bedrooms)
Bristol	paragraph 1(1)(a) (one bedroom, shared accommodation)
Bristol	paragraph 1(1)(b) (one bedroom, exclusive use)
Bristol	paragraph 1(1)(c) (two bedrooms)
Bristol	paragraph 1(1)(d) (three bedrooms)
Bristol	paragraph 1(1)(e) (four bedrooms)
Bury St. Edmunds	paragraph 1(1)(c) (two bedrooms)
Bury St. Edmunds	paragraph 1(1)(d) (three bedrooms)
Caerphilly	paragraph 1(1)(a) (one bedroom, shared accommodation)
Cambridge	paragraph 1(1)(b) (one bedroom, exclusive use)
Cambridge	paragraph 1(1)(c) (two bedrooms)
Cambridge	paragraph 1(1)(d) (three bedrooms)
Cambridge	paragraph 1(1)(e) (four bedrooms)
Canterbury	paragraph 1(1)(a) (one bedroom, shared accommodation)
Canterbury	paragraph 1(1)(c) (two bedrooms)
Canterbury	paragraph 1(1)(d) (three bedrooms)
Carmarthenshire	paragraph 1(1)(a) (one bedroom, shared accommodation)
Central Greater Manchester	paragraph 1(1)(b) (one bedroom, exclusive use)
Central Greater Manchester	paragraph 1(1)(c) (two bedrooms)
Central Greater Manchester	paragraph 1(1)(d) (three bedrooms)
Central Lancs	paragraph 1(1)(a) (one bedroom, shared accommodation)
Central London	paragraph 1(1)(b) (one bedroom, exclusive use)
Central London	paragraph 1(1)(c) (two bedrooms)
Central London	paragraph 1(1)(d) (three bedrooms)
Central London	paragraph 1(1)(e) (four bedrooms)
Central Norfolk & Norwich	paragraph 1(1)(b) (one bedroom, exclusive use)
Central Norfolk & Norwich	paragraph 1(1)(c) (two bedrooms)
Central Norfolk & Norwich	paragraph 1(1)(d) (three bedrooms)

Chelmsford	paragraph 1(1)(a) (one bedroom, shared accommodation)
Chelmsford	paragraph 1(1)(b) (one bedroom, exclusive use)
Chelmsford	paragraph 1(1)(c) (two bedrooms)
Chelmsford	paragraph 1(1)(d) (three bedrooms)
Chelmsford	paragraph 1(1)(e) (four bedrooms)
Cherwell Valley	paragraph 1(1)(b) (one bedroom, exclusive use)
Cherwell Valley	paragraph 1(1)(d) (three bedrooms)
Chichester	paragraph 1(1)(a) (one bedroom, shared accommodation)
Chichester	paragraph 1(1)(d) (three bedrooms)
Chilterns	paragraph 1(1)(a) (one bedroom, shared accommodation)
Chilterns	paragraph 1(1)(b) (one bedroom, exclusive use)
Chilterns	paragraph 1(1)(c) (two bedrooms)
Chilterns	paragraph 1(1)(d) (three bedrooms)
Colchester	paragraph 1(1)(b) (one bedroom, exclusive use)
Colchester	paragraph 1(1)(c) (two bedrooms)
Colchester	paragraph 1(1)(d) (three bedrooms)
Colchester	paragraph 1(1)(e) (four bedrooms)
Coventry	paragraph 1(1)(a) (one bedroom, shared accommodation)
Coventry	paragraph 1(1)(c) (two bedrooms)
Coventry	paragraph 1(1)(d) (three bedrooms)
Coventry	paragraph 1(1)(e) (four bedrooms)
Crawley & Reigate	paragraph 1(1)(a) (one bedroom, shared accommodation)
Crawley & Reigate	paragraph 1(1)(b) (one bedroom, exclusive use)
Crawley & Reigate	paragraph 1(1)(c) (two bedrooms)
Crawley & Reigate	paragraph 1(1)(d) (three bedrooms)
Crawley & Reigate	paragraph 1(1)(e) (four bedrooms)
Darlington	paragraph 1(1)(a) (one bedroom, shared accommodation)
Dover-Shepway	paragraph 1(1)(a) (one bedroom, shared accommodation)
Dover-Shepway	paragraph 1(1)(b) (one bedroom, exclusive use)
East Cheshire	paragraph 1(1)(a) (one bedroom, shared accommodation)
East Thames Valley	paragraph 1(1)(a) (one bedroom, shared accommodation)
East Thames Valley	paragraph 1(1)(b) (one bedroom, exclusive use)
East Thames Valley	paragraph 1(1)(c) (two bedrooms)
East Thames Valley	paragraph 1(1)(d) (three bedrooms)
Eastbourne	paragraph 1(1)(a) (one bedroom, shared accommodation)
Eastbourne	paragraph 1(1)(b) (one bedroom, exclusive use)
Eastbourne	paragraph 1(1)(c) (two bedrooms)
Eastbourne	paragraph 1(1)(d) (three bedrooms)
Eastern Staffordshire	paragraph 1(1)(b) (one bedroom, exclusive use)
Flintshire	paragraph 1(1)(a) (one bedroom, shared accommodation)
Gloucester	paragraph 1(1)(a) (one bedroom, shared accommodation)
Gloucester	paragraph 1(1)(c) (two bedrooms)
Gloucester	paragraph 1(1)(d) (three bedrooms)
Gloucester	paragraph 1(1)(e) (four bedrooms)
Grantham & Newark	paragraph 1(1)(a) (one bedroom, shared accommodation)
Grantham & Newark	paragraph 1(1)(b) (one bedroom, exclusive use)
Guildford	paragraph 1(1)(a) (one bedroom, shared accommodation)
Guildford	paragraph 1(1)(b) (one bedroom, exclusive use)
Guildford	paragraph 1(1)(e) (four bedrooms)
Harlow and Stortford	paragraph 1(1)(a) (one bedroom, shared accommodation)
Harlow and Stortford	paragraph 1(1)(b) (one bedroom, exclusive use)
Harlow and Stortford	paragraph 1(1)(c) (two bedrooms)
Harlow and Stortford	paragraph 1(1)(d) (three bedrooms)
Herefordshire	paragraph 1(1)(a) (one bedroom, shared accommodation)
Herefordshire	paragraph 1(1)(e) (four bedrooms)
High Weald	paragraph 1(1)(a) (one bedroom, shared accommodation)
High Weald	paragraph 1(1)(b) (one bedroom, exclusive use)
High Weald	paragraph 1(1)(c) (two bedrooms)
Huntingdon	paragraph 1(1)(b) (one bedroom, exclusive use)
Huntingdon	paragraph 1(1)(c) (two bedrooms)
Huntingdon	paragraph 1(1)(d) (three bedrooms)
Huntingdon	paragraph 1(1)(e) (four bedrooms)
Inner East London	paragraph 1(1)(a) (one bedroom, shared accommodation)
Inner East London	paragraph 1(1)(b) (one bedroom, exclusive use)
Inner East London	paragraph 1(1)(c) (two bedrooms)
Inner East London	paragraph 1(1)(d) (three bedrooms)
Inner East London	paragraph 1(1)(e) (four bedrooms)

Inner North London	paragraph 1(1)(a) (one bedroom, shared accommodation)
Inner North London	paragraph 1(1)(b) (one bedroom, exclusive use)
Inner North London	paragraph 1(1)(c) (two bedrooms)
Inner North London	paragraph 1(1)(d) (three bedrooms)
Inner North London	paragraph 1(1)(e) (four bedrooms)
Inner South East London	paragraph 1(1)(b) (one bedroom, exclusive use)
Inner South East London	paragraph 1(1)(c) (two bedrooms)
Inner South East London	paragraph 1(1)(d) (three bedrooms)
Inner South East London	paragraph 1(1)(e) (four bedrooms)
Inner South West London	paragraph 1(1)(a) (one bedroom, shared accommodation)
Inner South West London	paragraph 1(1)(b) (one bedroom, exclusive use)
Inner South West London	paragraph 1(1)(c) (two bedrooms)
Inner South West London	paragraph 1(1)(d) (three bedrooms)
Inner South West London	paragraph 1(1)(e) (four bedrooms)
Inner West London	paragraph 1(1)(a) (one bedroom, shared accommodation)
Inner West London	paragraph 1(1)(c) (two bedrooms)
Inner West London	paragraph 1(1)(d) (three bedrooms)
Inner West London	paragraph 1(1)(e) (four bedrooms)
Ipswich	paragraph 1(1)(a) (one bedroom, shared accommodation)
Ipswich	paragraph 1(1)(b) (onc bcdroom, exclusive use)
Ipswich	paragraph 1(1)(c) (two bedrooms)
Ipswich	paragraph 1(1)(d) (three bedrooms)
Ipswich	paragraph 1(1)(e) (four bedrooms)
Kendal	paragraph 1(1)(c) (two bedrooms)
Kendal	paragraph 1(1)(d) (three bedrooms)
Kernow West	paragraph 1(1)(a) (one bedroom, shared accommodation)
Kings Lynn	paragraph 1(1)(c) (two bedrooms)
Kings Lynn	paragraph 1(1)(d) (three bedrooms)
Kings Lynn	paragraph 1(1)(e) (four bedrooms)
Lancaster	paragraph 1(1)(a) (one bedroom, shared accommodation)
Leicester	paragraph 1(1)(a) (one bedroom, shared accommodation)
Leicester	paragraph 1(1)(d) (three bedrooms)
Lincolnshire Fens	paragraph 1(1)(b) (one bedroom, exclusive use)
Lincolnshire Fens	paragraph 1(1)(c) (two bedrooms)
Lincolnshire Fens	paragraph 1(1)(d) (three bedrooms)
Lincolnshire Fens	paragraph 1(1)(e) (four bedrooms)
Luton	paragraph 1(1)(a) (one bedroom, shared accommodation)
Luton	paragraph 1(1)(b) (one bedroom, exclusive use)
Luton	paragraph 1(1)(c) (two bedrooms)
Luton	paragraph 1(1)(d) (three bedrooms)
Luton	paragraph 1(1)(e) (four bedrooms)
Maidstone	paragraph 1(1)(a) (one bedroom, shared accommodation)
Maidstone	paragraph 1(1)(b) (one bedroom, exclusive use)
Maidstone	paragraph 1(1)(c) (two bedrooms)
Maidstone	paragraph 1(1)(d) (three bedrooms)
Medway & Swale	paragraph 1(1)(b) (one bedroom, exclusive use)
Medway & Swale	paragraph 1(1)(c) (two bedrooms)
Medway & Swale	paragraph 1(1)(d) (three bedrooms)
Medway & Swale	paragraph 1(1)(e) (four bedrooms)
Mendip	paragraph 1(1)(a) (one bedroom, shared accommodation)
Mendip	paragraph 1(1)(e) (four bedrooms)
Merthyr Cynon	paragraph 1(1)(a) (one bedroom, shared accommodation)
Mid & East Devon	paragraph 1(1)(a) (one bedroom, shared accommodation)
Mid & West Dorset	paragraph 1(1)(a) (one bedroom, shared accommodation)
Mid Staffs	paragraph 1(1)(d) (three bedrooms)
Milton Keynes	paragraph 1(1)(b) (one bedroom, exclusive use)
Milton Keynes	paragraph 1(1)(c) (two bedrooms)
Milton Keynes	paragraph 1(1)(d) (three bedrooms)
Milton Keynes	paragraph 1(1)(e) (four bedrooms)
Monmouthshire	paragraph 1(1)(a) (one bedroom, shared accommodation)
Neath Port Talbot	paragraph 1(1)(a) (one bedroom, shared accommodation)
Newbury	paragraph 1(1)(b) (one bedroom, exclusive use)
Newbury	paragraph 1(1)(c) (two bedrooms)
Newbury	paragraph 1(1)(d) (three bedrooms)
Newbury	paragraph 1(1)(e) (four bedrooms)
North Cheshire	paragraph 1(1)(a) (one bedroom, shared accommodation)
North Clwyd	paragraph 1(1)(a) (one bedroom, shared accommodation)

North Cornwall & Devon Borders	paragraph 1(1)(e) (four bedrooms)
North Devon	paragraph 1(1)(a) (one bedroom, shared accommodation)
North West Kent	paragraph 1(1)(a) (one bedroom, shared accommodation)
North West Kent	paragraph 1(1)(b) (one bedroom, exclusive use)
North West Kent	paragraph 1(1)(c) (two bedrooms)
North West Kent	paragraph 1(1)(d) (three bedrooms)
North West Kent	paragraph 1(1)(e) (four bedrooms)
North West London	paragraph 1(1)(a) (one bedroom, shared accommodation)
North West London	paragraph 1(1)(b) (one bedroom, exclusive use)
North West London	paragraph 1(1)(c) (two bedrooms)
North West London	paragraph 1(1)(d) (three bedrooms)
North West Wales	paragraph 1(1)(a) (one bedroom, shared accommodation)
Northampton	paragraph 1(1)(a) (one bedroom, shared accommodation)
Northampton	paragraph 1(1)(b) (one bedroom, exclusive use)
Northampton	paragraph 1(1)(c) (two bedrooms)
Northampton	paragraph 1(1)(d) (three bedrooms)
Northampton	paragraph 1(1)(e) (four bedrooms)
Northants Central	paragraph 1(1)(a) (one bedroom, shared accommodation)
Northants Central	paragraph 1(1)(b) (one bedroom, exclusive use)
Northants Central	paragraph 1(1)(c) (two bedrooms)
Northants Central	paragraph 1(1)(d) (three bedrooms)
Northants Central	paragraph 1(1)(e) (four bedrooms)
Northumberland	paragraph 1(1)(a) (one bedroom, shared accommodation)
Nottingham	paragraph 1(1)(d) (three bedrooms)
Nottingham	paragraph 1(1)(e) (four bedrooms)
Outer East London	paragraph 1(1)(a) (one bedroom, shared accommodation)
Outer East London	paragraph 1(1)(b) (one bedroom, exclusive use)
Outer East London	paragraph 1(1)(c) (two bedrooms)
Outer East London	paragraph 1(1)(d) (three bedrooms)
Outer East London	paragraph 1(1)(e) (four bedrooms)
Outer North East London	paragraph 1(1)(a) (one bedroom, shared accommodation)
Outer North East London	paragraph 1(1)(b) (one bedroom, exclusive use)
Outer North East London	paragraph 1(1)(c) (two bedrooms)
Outer North East London	paragraph 1(1)(d) (three bedrooms)
Outer North East London	paragraph 1(1)(e) (four bedrooms)
Outer North London	paragraph 1(1)(b) (one bedroom, exclusive use)
Outer North London	paragraph 1(1)(c) (two bedrooms)
Outer North London	paragraph 1(1)(d) (three bedrooms)
Outer South East London	paragraph 1(1)(a) (one bedroom, shared accommodation)
Outer South East London	paragraph 1(1)(b) (one bedroom, exclusive use)
Outer South East London	paragraph 1(1)(c) (two bedrooms)
Outer South East London	paragraph 1(1)(d) (three bedrooms)
Outer South East London	paragraph 1(1)(e) (four bedrooms)
Outer South London	paragraph 1(1)(b) (one bedroom, exclusive use)
Outer South London	paragraph 1(1)(c) (two bedrooms)
Outer South London	paragraph 1(1)(e) (four bedrooms)
Outer South West London	paragraph 1(1)(a) (one bedroom, shared accommodation)
Outer South West London	paragraph 1(1)(b) (one bedroom, exclusive use)
Outer West London	paragraph 1(1)(a) (one bedroom, shared accommodation)
Outer West London	paragraph 1(1)(b) (one bedroom, exclusive use)
Outer West London	paragraph 1(1)(c) (two bedrooms)
Outer West London	paragraph 1(1)(e) (four bedrooms)
Oxford	paragraph 1(1)(a) (one bedroom, shared accommodation)
Oxford	paragraph 1(1)(b) (one bedroom, exclusive use)
Pembrokeshire	paragraph 1(1)(a) (one bedroom, shared accommodation)
Peterborough	paragraph 1(1)(b) (one bedroom, exclusive use)
Peterborough	paragraph 1(1)(c) (two bedrooms)
Peterborough	paragraph 1(1)(d) (three bedrooms)
Peterborough	paragraph 1(1)(e) (four bedrooms)
Plymouth	paragraph 1(1)(b) (one bedroom, exclusive use)
Portsmouth	paragraph 1(1)(b) (one bedroom, exclusive use)
Portsmouth	paragraph 1(1)(c) (two bedrooms)
Portsmouth	paragraph 1(1)(d) (three bedrooms)
Reading	paragraph 1(1)(b) (one bedroom, exclusive use)
Reading	paragraph 1(1)(c) (two bedrooms)
Reading	paragraph 1(1)(d) (three bedrooms)
Rotherham	paragraph 1(1)(a) (one bedroom, shared accommodation)

Rugby & East	paragraph 1(1)(a) (one bedroom, shared accommodation)
Rugby & East	paragraph 1(1)(b) (one bedroom, exclusive use)
Rugby & East	paragraph 1(1)(c) (two bedrooms)
Rugby & East	paragraph 1(1)(d) (three bedrooms)
Rugby & East	paragraph 1(1)(e) (four bedrooms)
Salisbury	paragraph 1(1)(a) (one bedroom, shared accommodation)
Salisbury	paragraph 1(1)(b) (one bedroom, exclusive use)
Scarborough	paragraph 1(1)(a) (one bedroom, shared accommodation)
Solihull	paragraph 1(1)(a) (one bedroom, shared accommodation)
South Cheshire	paragraph 1(1)(a) (one bedroom, shared accommodation)
South East Herts	paragraph 1(1)(b) (one bedroom, exclusive use)
South East Herts	paragraph 1(1)(c) (two bedrooms)
South East Herts	paragraph 1(1)(d) (three bedrooms)
South Gwynedd	paragraph 1(1)(a) (one bedroom, shared accommodation)
South West Essex	paragraph 1(1)(a) (one bedroom, shared accommodation)
South West Essex	paragraph 1(1)(b) (one bedroom, exclusive use)
South West Essex	paragraph 1(1)(c) (two bedrooms)
South West Essex	paragraph 1(1)(d) (three bedrooms)
South West Herts	paragraph 1(1)(a) (one bedroom, shared accommodation)
South West Herts	paragraph 1(1)(b) (one bedroom, exclusive use)
South West Herts	paragraph 1(1)(c) (two bedrooms)
South West Herts	paragraph 1(1)(d) (three bedrooms)
Southampton	paragraph 1(1)(b) (one bedroom, exclusive use)
Southampton	paragraph 1(1)(c) (two bedrooms)
Southampton	paragraph 1(1)(d) (three bedrooms)
Southend	paragraph 1(1)(b) (one bedroom, exclusive use)
Southend	paragraph 1(1)(c) (two bedrooms)
Southend	paragraph 1(1)(d) (three bedrooms)
Southend	paragraph 1(1)(e) (four bedrooms)
Southern Greater Manchester	paragraph 1(1)(a) (one bedroom, shared accommodation)
Southern Greater Manchester	paragraph 1(1)(b) (one bedroom, exclusive use)
Southern Greater Manchester	paragraph 1(1)(c) (two bedrooms)
Southern Greater Manchester	paragraph 1(1)(d) (three bedrooms)
Southern Greater Manchester	paragraph 1(1)(e) (four bedrooms)
Staffordshire North	paragraph 1(1)(a) (one bedroom, shared accommodation)
Staffordshire North	paragraph 1(1)(e) (four bedrooms)
Stevenage & North Herts	paragraph 1(1)(b) (one bedroom, exclusive use)
Stevenage & North Herts	paragraph 1(1)(c) (two bedrooms)
Stevenage & North Herts	paragraph 1(1)(d) (three bedrooms)
Stevenage & North Herts	paragraph 1(1)(e) (four bedrooms)
Sunderland	paragraph 1(1)(a) (one bedroom, shared accommodation)
Sussex East	paragraph 1(1)(b) (one bedroom, exclusive use)
Sussex East	paragraph 1(1)(c) (two bedrooms)
Sussex East	paragraph 1(1)(d) (three bedrooms)
Sussex East	paragraph 1(1)(e) (four bedrooms)
Swindon	paragraph 1(1)(a) (one bedroom, shared accommodation)
Swindon	paragraph 1(1)(b) (one bedroom, exclusive use)
Swindon	paragraph 1(1)(c) (two bedrooms)
Swindon	paragraph 1(1)(d) (three bedrooms)
Swindon	paragraph 1(1)(e) (four bedrooms)
Taff Rhondda	paragraph 1(1)(a) (one bedroom, shared accommodation)
Taunton & West Somerset	paragraph 1(1)(a) (one bedroom, shared accommodation)
Thanet	paragraph 1(1)(b) (one bedroom, exclusive use)
Thanet	paragraph 1(1)(c) (two bedrooms)
Thanet	paragraph 1(1)(e) (four bedrooms)
Torfaen	paragraph 1(1)(a) (one bedroom, shared accommodation)
Tyneside	paragraph 1(1)(a) (one bedroom, shared accommodation)
Vale of Glamorgan	paragraph 1(1)(a) (one bedroom, shared accommodation)
Walton	paragraph 1(1)(b) (one bedroom, exclusive use)
Walton	paragraph 1(1)(c) (two bedrooms)
Warwickshire South	paragraph 1(1)(a) (one bedroom, shared accommodation)
Warwickshire South	paragraph 1(1)(b) (one bedroom, exclusive use)
Warwickshire South	paragraph 1(1)(c) (two bedrooms)
Warwickshire South	paragraph 1(1)(d) (three bedrooms)
West Cumbria	paragraph 1(1)(a) (one bedroom, shared accommodation)
West Wiltshire	paragraph 1(1)(a) (one bedroom, shared accommodation)
West Wiltshire	paragraph 1(1)(c) (two bedrooms)

West Wiltshire	paragraph 1(1)(d) (three bedrooms)
West Wiltshire	paragraph 1(1)(e) (four bedrooms)
Weston-Super-Mare	paragraph 1(1)(c) (two bedrooms)
Weston-Super-Mare	paragraph 1(1)(d) (three bedrooms)
Winchester	paragraph 1(1)(a) (one bedroom, shared accommodation)
Winchester	paragraph 1(1)(b) (one bedroom, exclusive use)
Winchester	paragraph 1(1)(e) (four bedrooms)
Worcester South	paragraph 1(1)(b) (one bedroom, exclusive use)
Worcester South	paragraph 1(1)(e) (four bedrooms)
Worthing	paragraph 1(1)(b) (one bedroom, exclusive use)
Worthing	paragraph 1(1)(c) (two bedrooms)
Worthing	paragraph 1(1)(d) (three bedrooms)
Worthing	paragraph 1(1)(e) (four bedrooms)
Yeovil	paragraph 1(1)(d) (three bedrooms)]

Amendments

1.   Inserted by art 2(3)(b) of SI 2016 No 1179 as from 23.1.17.
2.   Substituted by art 2(4) of SI 2017 No 1323 as from 26.1.18.
3.   Substituted by art 2(3) of SI 2018 No 1332 as from 25.1.19

[²**6.**]

Amendments

1.   Inserted by Sch 1 of SI 2014 No 3126 from 8.1.15.
2.   Omitted by art 2(2)(c) of SI 2015 No 1753 as from 2.11.15.

SCHEDULE 4

ARTICLE 7

Special Cases

Houseboats

1.   Where an application for a determination or a redetermination relates in whole or in part to mooring charges for a houseboat, this Order applies in relation to that application (or, as the case may be, to that part which relates to those charges) with the following modifications–

(a)   references to a tenancy, a tenancy of a dwelling or an assured tenancy are references to an agreement under which those charges are payable (and references to a landlord and a tenant shall be construed accordingly); and

(b)   no determination shall be made under paragraph 2 of Part I of Schedule 1 (size criteria) and references to the dwelling exceeding the size criteria shall not apply.

Mobile homes

2.   Where an application for a determination or redetermination relates in whole or in part to payments in respect of the site on which a caravan or a mobile home stands, this Order applies in relation to that application (or, as the case may be, that part which relates to those payments) with the following modifications–

(a)   references to a tenancy, a tenancy of a dwelling or an assured tenancy are references to an agreement under which those payments are payable (and references to a landlord and a tenant shall be construed accordingly); and

(b)   no determination shall be made under paragraph 2 of Part I of Schedule 1 (size criteria) and references to the dwelling exceeding the size criteria shall not apply.

Rental purchase agreements

3.   Where an application for a determination or a redetermination relates to a rental purchase agreement, the agreement is to be treated as if it were a tenancy.

The Rent Officers (Housing Benefit Functions) (Scotland) Order 1997
(SI 1997 No.1995 (S.144))

General Note
This Order is the Scottish equivalent of SI 1997 No.1984 and sets out the determinations to be made by rent officers when a tenancy is referred to them under regs 13D(10) and 14 of both the HB and the HB(SPC) Regs by an authority in Scotland. It also sets out the determinations to be made by rent officers relating to the "local housing allowance" scheme for rent restriction used by authorities to determine eligible rent under regs 12D and 13D of both the HB and the HB(SPC) Regs. See the commentary to SI 1997 No.1984.

Citation and commencement

1.–(1)   This Order may be cited as the Rent Officers (Housing Benefit Functions) (Scotland) Order 1997.

(2)   This Order shall come into force for the purposes of article 8 on 18th August 1997 and for all other purposes on 3rd September 1997.

Interpretation

2.–(1)   In this Order, unless the context otherwise requires–
[¹⁴ [¹⁵]]
"assured tenancy" has the same meaning as in Part II of the Housing (Scotland) Act 1988, except that it includes a tenancy which would be an assured tenancy but for paragraph [³ 7 or] 9 of Schedule 4 to that Act;
[² "board and attendance determination" means a determination made in accordance with article 4C;]
[⁹ "broad rental market area" has the meaning specified in paragraph 4 of Schedule 3B;]
[⁹ "broad rental market area determination" means a determination made in accordance with article 4B(1A);]
"child" means a person under the age of 16;
"determination" means a determination made in accordance with Part I or IV of Schedule 1 to this Order;
"dwelling" means any residential accommodation whether or not consisting of the whole or part of a building and whether or not comprising separate and self-contained premises;
[¹⁰ "hostel" has the same meaning as in regulation 2(1) of the Housing Benefit Regulations or, as the case may be, regulation 2(1) of the Housing Benefit (State Pension Credit) Regulations;]
[¹¹ "the Housing Benefit Regulations" mean the Housing Benefit Regulations 2006;
"the Housing Benefit (State Pension Credit) Regulations" means the Housing Benefit (Persons who have attained the qualifying age for state pension credit) Regulations 2006;]
"local authority" has the same meaning as in the Social Security Administration Act 1992 in relation to England and in relation to Wales;
[⁹ "local housing allowance determination" means a determination made in accordance with article 4B(2A);]
"occupier" means a person (whether or not identified by name) who is stated, in the application for the determination, to occupy the dwelling as his home;
[⁹]
[¹³ "person who requires overnight care" has the meaning given by regulation 2(1) of the Housing Benefit Regulations and the Housing Benefit (State Pension Credit) Regulations;]
"redetermination" means a redetermination made in accordance with article 4;
[⁹ "relevant date" means the date specified by a local authority in an application for a local housing allowance determination made in accordance with regulation 13D(7)(a) of the Housing Benefit Regulations or, as the case may be, regulation 13D(7)(a) of the Housing Benefit (State Pension Credit) Regulations;]
[¹ "relevant period" means–

(a) in relation to a determination, the period of five working days (or, where the determination does not relate to a prospective tenancy and the rent officer intends to inspect the dwelling before making the determination, 25 working days) beginning with–
   (i) where the rent officer requests further information under article 5, the date on which he receives the information; and
   (ii) in any other case, the date on which he receives the application for the determination; and
(b) in relation to a redetermination, the period of 20 working days beginning with–
   (i) where the rent officer requests further information under article 5, the date on which he receives the information; and
   (ii) in any other case, the date on which he receives the application for that redetermination;]

"relevant time" means the time the application for the determination [² or board and attendance determination] is made or, if earlier, the tenancy ends;

[¹⁰ "rent" means any of the periodical payments referred to in regulation 12(1) of the Housing Benefit Regulations or, as the case may be, regulation 12(1) of the Housing Benefit (State Pension Credit) Regulations;]

"size criteria" means the standards relating to bedrooms and rooms suitable for living in specified in Schedule 2 to this Order;

"tenancy" includes any other right of occupancy and a prospective tenancy or right of occupancy and references to a tenant, a landlord or any other expression appropriate to a tenancy shall be construed accordingly; and

[⁸ "working day" means any day other than a Saturday, a Sunday or a day which is a bank holiday in Scotland under the Banking and Financial Dealings Act 1971.]

[¹²]

(2) In this Order any reference to a notice or application is to a notice or application in writing, except in a case where the recipient consents (whether generally or specifically) to the notice or application being transmitted by electronic means.

Modifications

Some definitions substituted and the definition of "pathfinder authority" omitted by art 15(3) Rent Officers (Housing Benefit Functions) Amendment Order 2007 SI No.2871 as from 7 April 2008, save where art 15(1)(a), (b) or (c) of that order applied (see p933).

Note that by art 11 of SI 2007 No.2871, those provisions which on 19 March 2008 applied only in relation to the areas of former Pathfinder authorities, apply in the same way to the areas of every other local authority in Scotland.

Amendments

1. Inserted by art 3 of SI 2000 No 3 as from 3.4.00.
2. Insertions made by art 3 of SI 2003 No 2398 as from a date specified in Sch 1 to that SI in relation to each individual authority.
3. Inserted by art 2(2) of SI 2004 No 2101 as from 31.8.04.
4. Substituted by reg 5 and Sch 2 para 12(2)(a), (c) and (d) of SI 2006 No 217 as from 6.3.06.
5. Inserted by reg 5 and Sch 2 para 12(2)(b) of SI 2006 No 217 as from 6.3.06.
6. Omitted by reg 5 and Sch 2 para 12(2)(e) of SI 2006 No 217 as from 6.3.06.
7. Amended by art 13(1)(a)-(c) of SI 2007 No 2871 as from 20.3.08.
8. Inserted by art 13(1)(d) of SI 2007 No 2871 as from 20.3.08.
9. Amended by art 15(3) of SI 2007 No 2871 as from 7.4.08, save where art 15(1)(a), (b) or (c) of that order applies.
10. Substituted by art 19(1) of SI 2007 No 2871 as from 7.4.08.
11. Inserted by art 19(1) of SI 2007 No 2871 as from 7.4.08.
12. Omitted by art 19(1) of SI 2007 No 2871 as from 7.4.08.
13. Amended by art 5(2) of SI 2010 No 2836 as from 1.4.11.
14. Inserted by art 3(2) of SI 2012 No 646 as from 2.4.12.
15. Omitted by art 3(2) of SI 2013 No 1544 as from 1.9.13.

Determinations

3.–(1) Subject to [² articles 3A and 6], where a local authority, in accordance with regulations made under section 136(2) or (3) of the Social Security Administration Act

1992 [¹ or section 122(5) of the Housing Act 1996], applies to a rent officer for determinations in respect of a tenancy of a dwelling, a rent officer shall–
- (a) make the determinations in accordance with Part I of Schedule 1 (determinations);
- (b) comply with Part II of Schedule 1 when making the determinations (assumptions etc.); and
- (c) give notice in accordance with Part III of Schedule 1 (notifications) [¹ within the relevant period or as soon as is practicable after that period].

(2) A rent officer for each registration area (within the meaning of section 43 of the Rent (Scotland) Act 1984) on the first working day of each month shall–
- (a) make determinations in accordance with Part IV of Schedule 1 (indicative rent levels) in the registration area [⁴ [⁵]];
- (b) comply with paragraph 8(2) of Part II of Schedule 1 (assumptions etc.) when making the determinations; and
- (c) give to the local authority notice of the determinations relating to its area when they have been made.

Modifications

Note that by art 11 Rent Officers (Housing Benefit Functions) Amendment Order 2007 SI No.2871, those provisions which on 19 March 2008 applied only in relation to the areas of former Pathfinder authorities, apply in the same way to the areas of every other local authority in Scotland.

Amendments

1. Amended by art 4 of SI 2000 No 3 as from 3.4.00.
2. Amended by art 3(1) of SI 2001 No 1326 as from 2.7.01.
3. Substitution made by art 3 of SI 2003 No 2398 as from a date specified in Sch 1 to that SI in relation to each individual authority.
4. Amended by art 5(2)(a) of SI 2005 No 236 as from 13.3.05.
5. Omitted by art 14(1) of SI 2007 No 2871 as from 7.4.08.

[¹Transitional arrangements for determination of Single Room Rents with effect from 2nd July 2001

3A. In a case where the rent officer has made and notified an authority of a determination of a single room rent pursuant to paragraph 5 of Schedule 1 in the period of 12 months before 2nd July 2001 that determination shall cease to have effect on [² ...] 2nd July 2001 and a rent officer shall–
- (a) make a new determination of that single room rent in accordance with Part I of Schedule 1;
- (b) comply with Part II of Schedule 1; and
- (c) give notice in accordance with Part III of Schedule 1 within the relevant period or as soon as is practicable after that period;

without an application for a determination under [³ [⁴ regulation 14 of the Housing Benefit Regulations or, as the case may be, regulation 14 of the Housing Benefit (State Pension Credit) Regulations]] having been made.]

Amendments

1. Inserted by art 3(2) of SI 2001 No 1326 as from 2.7.01.
2. Amended by art 2(2) of SI 2001 No 2318 as from 2.7.01.
3. Amended by reg 5 and Sch 2 para 12(3) of SI 2006 No 217 as from 6.3.06.
4. Substituted by art 19(2) of SI 2007 No 2871 as from 7.4.08.

Redeterminations

[¹**4.**–(1) Subject to article 6, where the local authority applies to a rent officer for a redetermination of any determination or redetermination in respect of a tenancy of a dwelling the rent officer shall, in accordance with Schedule 3–
- (a) make redeterminations of any effective determinations and any effective redeterminations in respect of that tenancy; and
- (b) give notice within the relevant period or as soon as is practicable after that period.

(2)   For the purposes of paragraph (1)–
"effective determinations" means any determinations made in accordance with Part I of
        Schedule 1 which have effect at the date of the application for a redetermination
        of a determination or redetermination; and
"effective redeterminations" means any redeterminations made in accordance with
        Schedule 3 which have effect at that date.
(3)   A rent officer whose advice is sought as provided for in Schedule 3 shall give
that advice.]

Amendment
1.   Substituted by art 5 of SI 2000 No 3 as from 3.4.00.

Substitute determinations and substitute redeterminations

[¹**4A.**–(1)   Where a local authority applies to a rent officer for a substitute
determination, in accordance with [² [³ regulation 17 of the Housing Benefit Regulations
or, as the case may be, regulation 17 of the Housing Benefit (State Pension Credit)
Regulations]], the provisions of this Order shall apply to that substitute determination as
they apply to a determination, but as if references to the relevant time were references to
the date the application for the original determination was made or, if earlier, the date the
tenancy ended.
(2)   Where a local authority applies to a rent officer for a substitute redetermination,
in accordance with that regulation, the provisions of this Order shall apply to that
substitute redetermination as they apply to a redetermination.]

Amendments
1.   Inserted by art 5 of SI 2000 No 3 as from 3.4.00.
2.   Amended by reg 5 and Sch 2 para 12(4) of SI 2006 No 217 as from 6.3.06.
3.   Substituted by art 19(3) of SI 2007 No 2871 as from 7.4.08.

[¹Broad rental market area determinations and local housing allowance determinations

4B.   [⁶ (1)]
[⁴ (1A)   [¹⁰ At such times as a rent officer considers appropriate, a rent officer shall,
if the Secretary of State agrees], in relation to each local authority–
(a)   determine one or more broad rental market areas which will (during the month
        which next begins after the determination is made) fall, in whole or in part,
        within the area of the local authority so that every part of the area of that local
        authority falls within a broad rental market area and no part of the area of that
        authority falls within more than one broad rental market area; and
(b)   give to that local authority a notice which–
        (i)   specifies the area contained within each broad rental market area as falls,
               in whole or in part, within the area of that authority, by reference to the
               postcodes for each such broad rental market area; and
        (ii)   identifies such of those postcodes as fall within the area of that authority.]
    [¹³ (1B)   The power in paragraph (1A) is not limited by paragraph 2(2A) or (2B) of
Schedule 3B.]
    [⁶ (2)]
    [¹⁰ [⁴ (2A)   [¹¹ In 2014 and in each subsequent year, on the date specified in paragraph
(2B),] a rent officer shall–
(a)   for each broad rental market area determine, in accordance with Schedule 3B,a
        local housing allowance for each of the categories of dwelling set out in
        paragraph 1 of Schedule 3B; and
(b)   notify each local authority of the local housing allowance determination made
        in accordance with sub-paragraph (a) for each broad rental market area falling
        within, in whole or in part, the area of that authority.]]
    [¹¹ [¹² (2B)   The date specified for the purposes of paragraph (2A) is the last working
day of January.]]
    [⁶ (3)]

[¹⁰ [⁴ (3A)   Any broad rental market area determination made in accordance with paragraph (1A) shall take effect–

(a)   on the day the determination is made for the purpose of enabling a rent officer to determine a local housing allowance for that area; and

[¹⁴ (b) for all other purposes–

(i)   on the next 1st April following the day on which the determination is made; or

(ii)   where the next 1st April is within 11 months beginning with the day on which the determination is made, on the next 1st April after that.]

(3B)   Any local housing allowance determination made in accordance with paragraph (2A) shall take effect on the next 1st April following the day on which the determination is made.]]

[⁹ [⁶ (4)]]

[⁹ [⁶ (4A)]]

(5)   Where a rent officer has made a local housing allowance determination in accordance with paragraph (4)–

(a)   he shall give notice of the determination to the [⁶ local authority] that made the application;

[⁶ (b) any local housing allowance determination made in accordance with paragraph (4) shall take effect for the month in which the relevant date falls, except that no such determination can have effect before 7th April 2008; and

(c)   any local housing allowance determination made in accordance with paragraph (4A) shall take effect for the month in which notice is given in accordance with sub-paragraph (a), except that no such determination can have effect before 7th April 2008.]

[⁴ (6)   Where a rent officer has made a local housing allowance determination in accordance with paragraph (2A) [⁵ [⁹]] he shall–

(a)   make an approximate monthly allowance determination in relation to that local housing allowance determination; and

(b)   give notice of the approximate monthly allowance determination to each authority to which he is required to give notice of the local housing allowance determination when he gives notice of that determination.]

Modifications

Paras (1), (2) and (3) omitted, para (4) substituted, para (4A) inserted and para (5) amended by art 15(4) Rent Officers (Housing Benefit Functions) Amendment Order 2007 SI No.2871 as from 7 April 2008, save where art 15(1)(a), (b) or (c) of that order applied (see p933).

Note that by art 11 of SI 2007 No.2871, those provisions which on 19 March 2008 applied only in relation to the areas of former Pathfinder authorities, apply in the same way to the areas of every other local authority in Scotland.

Amendments

1.   Inserted by art 3(5) of SI 2003 No 2398 as from a date specified in Sch 1 to that SI in relation to each individual authority.

2.   Amended by reg 5 and Sch 2 para 12(5) of SI 2006 No 217 as from 6.3.06.

3.   Amended by art 13(2)(a) of SI 2007 No 2871 as from 20.3.08.

4.   Inserted by art 13(2)(b)-(e) of SI 2007 No 2871 as from 20.3.08.

5.   Amended by art 14(2) of SI 2007 No 2871 as from 7.4.08.

6.   Amended by art 15(4) of SI 2007 No 2871, as amended by art 2(4) of SI 2008 No 587, as from 7.4.08, save where art 15(1)(a), (b) or (c) of that order applies.

7.   Amended by art 2(4) of SI 2008 No 587 as from 7.4.08.

8.   Amended by art 3(2) of SI 2008 No 3156 as from 5.1.09.

9.   Amended by art 4(2) of SI 2010 No 2836 as from 18.3.11.

10.   Amended by art 3(3) of SI 2012 No 646 as from 2.4.12.

11.   Amended by art 3(3) of SI 2013 No 1455 as from 1.9.13.

12.   Substituted by art 3(2) of SI 2014 No 3126 as from 8.1.15.

13.   Inserted by art 3(2) of SI 2016 No 1179 as from 23.1.17.

14.   Substituted by art 3(2) of SI2017 No 1323 as from 26.1.18.

[¹**Board and attendance determinations and notifications**

[³**4C.**–(1)   Where a relevant authority makes an application to a rent officer in accordance with regulation 13D(10) of the Housing Benefit Regulations or, as the case may be, regulation 13D(10) of the Housing Benefit (State Pension Credit) Regulations, a rent officer shall determine whether or not a substantial part of the rent under the tenancy at the relevant time is fairly attributable to board and attendance.

(2)   Where a rent officer determines that a substantial part of the rent under the tenancy at the relevant time is fairly attributable to board and attendance, he shall–

(a)   notify the relevant authority accordingly; and

(b)   treat the application as if it had been made in accordance with regulation 14(1) of the Housing Benefit Regulations or, as the case may be regulation 14(1) of the Housing Benefit (State Pension Credit) Regulations.]

(3)   Where a rent officer determines that a substantial part of the rent under the tenancy at the relevant time is not fairly attributable to board and attendance, he shall notify the pathfinder authority accordingly.

[⁴ (4)   Where an application for a board and attendance determination is treated as if it had been made in accordance with regulation 14(1) of the Housing Benefit Regulations or, as the case may be, regulation 14(1) of the Housing Benefit (State Pension Credit) Regulations, then, for the purposes of paragraph (a)(ii) of the definition of "relevant period" in article 2(1), it shall be treated as having been received on the day on which the further information provided in accordance with regulation 114A(4) of the Housing Benefit Regulations or regulation 95A(4) of the Housing Benefit (State Pension Credit) Regulations is received.]

Modifications

Paras (1) and (2) substituted by art 15(5) Rent Officers (Housing Benefit Functions) Amendment Order 2007 SI No.2871 as from 7 April 2008, save where art 15(1)(a), (b) or (c) of that order applied (see p933). Para (4) substituted by art 16(2) Rent Officers (Housing Benefit Functions) Amendment Order 2007 SI No.2871 as from 7 April 2008, save where art 16(1) of that order applied (see p933).

Note that by art 11 of SI 2007 No.2871, those provisions which on 19 March 2008 applied only in relation to the areas of former Pathfinder authorities, apply in the same way to the areas of every other local authority in Scotland.

Amendments

1.   Inserted by art 3(5) of SI 2003 No 2398 as from a date specified in Sch 1 to that SI in relation to each individual authority.

2.   Amended by reg 5 and Sch 2 para 12(6) of SI 2006 No 217 as from 6.3.06.

3.   Substituted by art 15(5) of SI 2007 No 2871 as from 7.4.08, save where art 15(1)(a), (b) or (c) of that order applies.

4.   Substituted by art 16(2) of SI 2007 No 2871 as from 7.4.08, save where art 16(1) of that order applies.

[¹**Board and attendance redeterminations**

4D.–(1)   Subject to article 6, where a [² local authority] applies to a rent officer for a redetermination of a board and attendance determination or board and attendance redetermination, the rent officer shall, in accordance with paragraph (2)–

(a)   make a redetermination of–

(i)   the board and attendance determination, provided it was made in accordance with article 4C and had effect at the date of the application for it to be redetermined; or

(ii)   the board and attendance redetermination provided it was made in accordance with head (i), and had effect at the date of the application for it to be redetermined; and

(b)   notify the [² local authority] of the redetermination.

(2)   When making a board and attendance redetermination under this article, the rent officer shall seek, and have regard to, the advice of one or two other rent officers in relation to the redetermination.

(3)   A rent officer whose advice is sought in accordance with paragraph (2) shall give that advice.

(4)   Article 4C shall apply in relation to a board and attendance redetermination but as if the references to the relevant time were references to the date on which the original application for a board and attendance determination was made, or if earlier, to the date on which the tenancy ended.]

Modifications

Para (1) amended by art 15(6) Rent Officers (Housing Benefit Functions) Amendment Order 2007 SI No.2871 as from 7 April 2008, save where art 15(1)(a), (b) or (c) of that order applied (see p933).

Note that by art 11 of SI 2007 No.2871, those provisions which on 19 March 2008 applied only in relation to the areas of former Pathfinder authorities, apply in the same way to the areas of every other local authority in Scotland.

Amendments

1.   Inserted by art 3(5) of SI 2003 No 2398 as from a date specified in Sch 1 to that SI in relation to each individual authority.
2.   Amended by art 15(6) of SI 2007 No 2871 as from 7.4.08, save where art 15(1)(a), (b) or (c) of that order applies.

[¹Substitute board and attendance determinations and substitute board and attendance redeterminations

4E.–(1)   Where a [³ local authorit] applies to a rent officer for a substitute board and attendance determination in accordance with [² [³ regulation 17 of the Housing Benefit Regulations or, as the case may be, regulation 17 of the Housing Benefit (State Pension Credit) Regulations]], the provisions of this Order shall apply to that substitute board and attendance determination as they apply to a board and attendance determination but as if references to the relevant time were references to the date on which the original application for a board and attendance determination was made or, if earlier, the date on which the tenancy ended.

(2)   Where a [³ local authority] applies to a rent officer for a substitute board and attendance redetermination in accordance with [² [³ regulation 17 of the Housing Benefit Regulations or, as the case may be, regulation 17 of the Housing Benefit (State Pension Credit) Regulations]], the provisions of this Order shall apply to that substitute board and attendance redetermination as they apply to a board and attendance redetermination.]

Modifications

Paras (1) and (2) amended by art 15(6) Rent Officers (Housing Benefit Functions) Amendment Order 2007 SI No.2871 as from 7 April 2008, save where art 15(1)(a), (b) or (c) of that order applied (see p933).

Note that by art 11 of SI 2007 No.2871, those provisions which on 19 March 2008 applied only in relation to the areas of former Pathfinder authorities, apply in the same way to the areas of every other local authority in Scotland.

Amendments

1.   Inserted by art 3(5) of SI 2003 No 2398 as from a date specified in Sch 1 to that SI in relation to each individual authority.
2.   Amended by reg 5 and Sch 2 para 12(7) of SI 2006 No 217 as from 6.3.06.
3.   Amended by art 15(6) of SI 2007 No 2871 as from 7.4.08, save where art 15(1)(a), (b) or (c) of that order applies.
4.   Substituted by art 19(4) of SI 2007 No 2871 as from 7.4.08.

Insufficient information

5.   If a rent officer needs further information in order to make a determination under article 3(1) or a [² redetermination under article 4, a board and attendance determination under article 4C or a board and attendance redetermination under article 4D], [³ where the information supplied under regulation 114A of the Housing Benefit Regulations or regulation 95A of the Housing Benefit (State Pension Credit) Regulations was incomplete or incorrect, he shall serve notice on the local authority requesting it to supply the further information required under regulation 114A or regulation 95A, as the case may be, or to confirm whether the information already supplied is correct and, if it is not, to supply the correct information.] [¹ ...]

Modifications

Art 5 amended by art 16(3) Rent Officers (Housing Benefit Functions) Amendment Order 2007 SI No.2871 as from 7 April 2008, save where art 16(1) of that order applied (see p933).

Note that by art 11 of SI 2007 No.2871, those provisions which on 19 March 2008 applied only in relation to the areas of former Pathfinder authorities, apply in the same way to the areas of every other local authority in Scotland.

Amendments

1. Deleted by art 6 of SI 2000 No 1 as from 3.4.00.
2. Substituted by art 3(6) of SI 2003 No 2398 as from a date specified in Sch 1 to that SI in relation to each individual authority.
3. Amended by art 16(1) of SI 2007 No 2871 as from 7.4.08, save where art 16(1) of that order applies.

Exceptions

6.–(1)   No determination[¹, redetermination, board and attendance determination or board and attendance redetermination] shall be made if the application for it is withdrawn.

(2)   No determination shall be made under paragraph 3, 4 or 5 of Part I of Schedule 1 if the tenancy is of residential accommodation, within the meaning of [² [³ regulation 9(4) of the Housing Benefit Regulations or, as the case may be, regulation 9(4) of the Housing Benefit (State Pension Credit) Regulations]], or in a hostel.

(3)   No determination shall be made under paragraph 5 of Part I of Schedule 1 unless the local authority states in the application that the claimant is, or may be, a young individual (which has the same meaning as in [² [³ the Housing Benefit Regulations and the Housing Benefit (State Pension Credit) Regulations]]).

(4)   If the rent officer becomes aware that an application is not one which gives rise to a duty to make a determination[¹, redetermination, board and attendance determination or a board and attendance redetermination], the rent officer shall give the local authority notice to that effect.

Modifications

Note that by art 11 Rent Officers (Housing Benefit Functions) Amendment Order 2007 SI No.2871, those provisions which on 19 March 2008 applied only in relation to the areas of former Pathfinder authorities, apply in the same way to the areas of every other local authority in Scotland.

Amendments

1. Substituted by art 3(7) of SI 2003 No 2398 as from a date specified in Sch 1 to that SI in relation to each individual authority.
2. Amended by reg 5 and Sch 2 para 12(8) of SI 2006 No 217 as from 6.3.06.
3. Substituted by art 19(5) of SI 2007 No 2871 as from 7.4.08.

Special cases

7.–(1)   This Order shall apply as specified in Schedule 4 in relation to–

(a)   mooring charges payable for a houseboat;

(b)   payments in respect of the site on which a caravan or a mobile home stands; or

(c)   payments under a rental purchase agreement.

(2)   Terms used in paragraph (1) have the same meaning in this article and in Schedule 4 as they have in [² [³ regulation 12(1) of the Housing Benefit Regulations or, as the case may be, regulation 12(1) of the Housing Benefit (State Pension Credit) Regulations]].

[¹ ...]

Amendments

1. Deleted by art 7 of SI 2000 No 3 as from 3.4.00.
2. Amended by reg 5 and Sch 2 para 12(9) of SI 2006 No 217 as from 6.3.06.
3. Substituted by art 19(6) of SI 2007 No 2871 as from 7.4.08.

[¹Errors

7A.–[² (1)]   If a rent officer is of the opinion that he has made an error (other than in the application of his professional judgement) in relation to a determination or redetermination, he shall notify the local authority which made the application for that determination or redetermination of the error as soon as practicable after he becomes aware of it.]

[² (2)   If a rent officer is of the opinion that he has made an error (other than in the application of his professional judgement) in relation to a board and attendance determination or board and attendance redetermination, he shall notify the [⁵ local authority] which made the application for that board and attendance determination or board and attendance redetermination of the error as soon as practicable after he becomes aware of it.

[⁵ (3)]]

[⁴ (4)   If a rent officer is of the opinion that he has made an error (other than in the application of his professional judgement) in relation to a broad rental market area determination determined in accordance with article 4B(1A) or a local housing allowance determination determined in accordance with article 4B(2A), he shall notify any local authority to which notification of that determination was sent of the error, and the amended determination, as soon as practicable after he becomes aware of it.]

Modifications

Para (2) amended and para (3) omitted by art 15(7) of the Rent Officers (Housing Benefit Functions) Amendment Order 2007 SI No.2871 as from 7 April 2008, save where art 15(1)(a), (b) or (c) of that order applied (see p933).

Note that by art 11 of SI 2007 No. 2871, those provisions which on 19 March 2008 applied only in relation to the areas of former Pathfinder authorities, apply in the same way to the areas of every other local authority in Scotland.

Amendments

1.   Inserted by art 8 of SI 2000 No 3 as from 3.4.00.
2.   Inserted by art 2(8) of SI 2003 No 2398 as from a date specified in Sch 1 to that SI in relation to each individual authority.
3.   Amended by art 13(3)(a) of SI 2007 No 2871 as from 20.3.08.
4.   Inserted by art 13(3)(b) of SI 2007 No 2871 as from 20.3.08.
5.   Amended by art 15(7) of SI 2007 No 2871 as from 7.4.08, save where art 15(1)(a), (b) or (c) of that order applies.

Amendment to 1995 Order

8.–(1)   The Rent Officers (Additional Functions) (Scotland) Order 1995 shall be amended by the insertion at the end of article 6 (special cases) of the following:–

"(3)   In a case where the local authority states in the application that the rent includes charges for general counselling or any other support services which are eligible for housing benefit solely by virtue of paragraph 1(f)(iii) of Schedule 1 to the 1987 Regulations (landlord's support services: supported accommodation) or solely by virtue of that provision and paragraph 1(f)(ii) of that Schedule, the rent officer shall assume when making a determination or a redetermination that–

(a)   the services were not to be provided or made available; and

(b)   the rent payable under the tenancy at the relevant time is such amount as is specified in the application as the rent which would have been payable under the tenancy at that time if those items were not to be provided or made available.

(4)   In a case where the local authority states in the application that the rent includes charges for general counselling or any other support services and the charges–

(a)   are eligible for housing benefit by virtue of paragraph 1(f)(iii) of Schedule 1 to the 1987 Regulations, or that provision and paragraph 1(f)(ii) of that Schedule; and

(b)   are also eligible for housing benefit by virtue of paragraph 1(f)(i) of that Schedule (support services: other exceptions), the rent officer shall include in the notice to the local authority, required under article 3(1)(c), a statement of the amount of the rent payable for the tenancy (which has the same meaning as in paragraph 3(1) of Schedule 1 to this Order) which relates to those charges.".

(2)   The amendment made by paragraph (1) above does not have effect in a case where an application for a determination is made before 18th August 1997.

Revocations and application

9.–(1) Subject to paragraph (2), article 8 of this Order and the Orders specified in Schedule 5 are hereby revoked.

(2) Nothing in articles 2 to 7 has effect in a case where an application for a determination is made before 3rd September 1997 and, in such a case, the Rent Officers (Additional Functions) (Scotland) Order 1995 shall continue to have effect.

SCHEDULE 1

ARTICLE 3(1)(A)

Part I

Determinations

Significantly high rents

1.–(1) The rent officer shall determine whether, in his opinion, the rent payable under the tenancy of the dwelling at the relevant time is significantly higher than the rent which the landlord might reasonably have been expected to obtain under the tenancy at that time.

(2) If the rent officer determines under sub-paragraph (1) that the rent is significantly higher, the rent officer shall also determine the rent which the landlord might reasonably have been expected to obtain under the tenancy at the relevant time.

(3) When making a determination under this paragraph, the rent officer shall have regard to the level of rent under similar tenancies of similar dwellings in the [¹ vicinity] (or as similar as regards tenancy, dwelling and [¹ vicinity] as is reasonably practicable) and shall assume that no one who would have been entitled to housing benefit had sought or is seeking the tenancy.

[²(4) For the purposes of this paragraph and paragraph 2 "vicinity" means–

(a) the area immediately surrounding the dwelling; or

(b) where, for the purposes of sub-paragraph (2)(c) of paragraph 2, there is no dwelling in the area immediately surrounding the dwelling which satisfies the description in heads (i), (ii) and (iii) of that sub-paragraph, the area nearest to the dwelling where there is such a dwelling.]

Amendments

1. Amended by art 3(2) of SI 2001 No 3561 as from 6.11.01.
2. Inserted by art 3(2) of SI 2001 No 3561 as from 6.11.01.

Size and rent

2.–(1) The rent officer shall determine whether the dwelling, at the relevant time, exceeds the size criteria for the occupiers.

(2) If the rent officer determines that the dwelling exceeds the size criteria, the rent officer shall also determine the rent which a landlord might reasonably have been expected to obtain, at the relevant time, for a tenancy which is–

(a) similar to the tenancy of the dwelling;

(b) on the same terms other than the term relating to the amount of rent; and

(c) of a dwelling which is in the same [¹ vicinity] as the dwelling, but which–

(i) accords with the size criteria for the occupiers;

(ii) is in a reasonable state of repair; and

(iii) corresponds in other respects, in the rent officer's opinion, as closely as is reasonably practicable to the dwelling.

(3) When making a determination under sub-paragraph (2), the rent officer shall have regard to the same matter and make the same assumption as specified in paragraph 1(3), except that in judging the similarity of other tenancies and dwellings the comparison shall be with the tenancy of the second dwelling referred to in sub-paragraph (2), and shall assume that no one who would have been entitled to housing benefit had sought or is seeking that tenancy.

Amendment

1. Amended by art 3(3) of SI 2001 No 3561 as from 6.11.01.

Exceptionally high rents

3.–(1) The rent officer shall determine whether, in his opinion, the rent payable for the tenancy of the dwelling at the relevant time is exceptionally high.

(2) In sub-paragraph (1), "rent payable for the tenancy" means–

(a) where a determination is made under sub-paragraph (2) of paragraph 2, the rent determined under that sub-paragraph;

(b) where no determination is so made and a determination is made under sub-paragraph (2) of paragraph 1, the rent determined under that sub-paragraph; and

(c) in any other case, the rent payable under the tenancy [¹ at the relevant time].

(3)   If the rent officer determines under sub-paragraph (1) that the rent is exceptionally high, the rent officer shall also determine the highest rent, which is not an exceptionally high rent and which a landlord might reasonably have been expected to obtain at the relevant time (on the assumption that no one who would have been entitled to housing benefit had sought or is seeking the tenancy) for an assured tenancy of a dwelling which–

(a)   is in the same [² neighbourhood] as the dwelling;

(b)   has the same number of bedrooms and rooms suitable for living in as the dwelling (or, where the dwelling exceeds the size criteria for the occupiers, accords with the size criteria); and

(c)   is in a reasonable state of repair.

(4)   For the purpose of determining whether a rent is an exceptionally high rent under this paragraph, the rent officer shall have regard to the levels of rent under assured tenancies of dwellings which–

(a)   are in the same [² neighbourhood] as the dwelling (or in as similar a locality as is reasonably practicable); and

(b)   have the same number of bedrooms and rooms suitable for living in as the dwelling (or, in a case where the dwelling exceeds the size criteria for the occupiers, accord with the size of criteria).

[³ (5) For the purposes of this paragraph and paragraph 4(6) "neighbourhood" means-

(a)   where the dwelling is in a town or city, the part of that town or city where the dwelling is located which is a distinct area of residential accommodation; or

(b)   where the dwelling is not in a town or city, the area surrounding the dwelling which is a distinct area of residential accommodation and where there are dwellings satisfying the description in sub-paragraph (4)(b).]

Amendments

1.   Amended by art 9 of SI 2000 No 3 as from 3.4.00.
2.   Amended by art 3(4) of SI 2001 No 3561 as from 6.11.01.
3.   Inserted by art 3(4) of SI 2001 No 3561 as from 6.11.01.

Local reference rents

4.–(1)   The rent officer shall make a determination of a local rent in accordance with the formula–

$$R = \frac{H+L}{2}$$

where–

R is the local reference rent;

H is the hughest rent, in the rent officer's opinion–

(a)   which a landlord might reasonably have been expected to obtain, at the relevant time, for an assured tenancy of a dwelling which meets the criteria in sub-paragraph (2); and

(b)   which is not an exceptionally high rent; and

L is the lowest rent, in the rent officer's opinion–

(a)   which a landlord might reasonably have been expected to obtain, at the relevant time, for an assured tenancy of a dwelling which meets the criteria in sub-paragraph (2); and

(b)   which is not an exceptionally low rent.

(2)   The criteria are–

(a)   that the dwelling under the assured tenancy–

(i)   is in the same [⁸ broad rental market area (local reference rent)] as the dwelling;

(ii)   is in a reasonable state of repair; and

(iii)   has the same number of bedrooms and rooms suitable for living in as the dwelling (or, in a case where the dwelling exceeds the size criteria for the occupiers, accords with the size criteria); and

(b)   if the tenant does not have the use under the tenancy of the dwelling [¹ at the relevant time] of more than one bedroom or room suitable for living in [⁹ and neither the tenant nor the tenant's partner is a person who requires overnight care]–

(i)   that under the assured tenancy the tenant does not have the use of more than one bedroom or room suitable for living in;

(ii)   if the rent under the tenancy [¹ at the relevant time] includes payments for board and attendance and the rent officer considers that the amount fairly attributable to board and attendance is a substantial part of the rent, that a substantial part of the rent under the assured tenancy is fairly attributable to board and attendance;

(iii)   if sub-paragraph (ii) does not apply and the tenant shares a [⁴ kitchen, toilet, bathroom and room suitable for living in] with a person other than a member of his household, a non-dependant or a person who pays rent to the tenant, that the assured tenancy provides for the tenant to share a [⁴ kitchen, toilet, bathroom and room suitable for living in]; and

(iv)   if sub-paragraphs (ii) and (iii) do not apply, that the circumstances described in sub-paragraphs (ii) and (iii) do not apply in relation to the assured tenancy.

(3)   When ascertaining H and L under sub-paragraph (1), the rent officer–

(a)   shall assume that no one who would have been entitled to housing benefit had sought or is seeking the tenancy; and

(b)   shall exclude the amount of any rent which, in the rent officer's opinion, is fairly attributable to the provision of services which are ineligible to be met by housing benefit; [⁵. . .]

(4)   In sub-paragraph (2)(b)–
"bedroom or room suitable for living in" does not include a room which the tenant shares with any person other than–

(a)   a member of his household;
(b)   a non-dependant (as defined in this sub-paragraph); or
(c)   a person who pays rent to the tenant; and
[⁶ [⁷ "non-dependant" means a non-dependant of the tenant within the meaning of regulation 3 of the Housing Benefit Regulations or, as the case may be, regulation 3 of the Housing Benefit (State Pension Credit) Regulations;]].

(5)   In sub-paragraph (3), "services" means services performed or facilities (including the use of furniture) provided for, or rights made available to, the tenant, but not [², in the case of a tenancy where a substantial part of the rent under the tenancy is fairly attributable to board and attendance, the provision of meals (including the preparation of meals or provision of unprepared food).]

[³[⁸ (6)   For the purposes of this paragraph and paragraph 5 "broad rental market area (local reference rent)" means the area within which a tenant of the dwelling could reasonably be expected to live having regard to facilities and services for the purposes of health, education, recreation, personal banking and shopping, taking account of the distance of travel, by public and private transport, to and from those facilities and services.

(7)   A broad rental market area (local reference rent) must contain–
(a)   residential premises of a variety of types, including such premises held on a variety of tenures; and
(b)   sufficient privately rented residential premises, to ensure that, in the rent officer's opinion, the local reference rents for tenancies in the area are representative of the rents that a landlord might reasonably be expected to obtain in that area.]]

Amendments

1.   Amended by art 9 of SI 2000 No 3 as from 3.4.00.
2.   Substituted by art 10 of SI 2000 No 3 as from 3.4.00.
3.   Inserted by art 3(5) of SI 2001 No 3561 as from 6.11.01.
4.   Amended by art 2(3) of SI 2001 No2318 as from 2.7.01.
5.   Deleted by art 3 of SI 2003 No 478 as from 1.4.03 (7.4.03 where rent payable weekly or in multiples of a week).
6.   Amended by reg 5 and Sch 2 para 12(10)(a) of SI 2006 No 217 as from 6.3.06.
7.   Substituted by art 19(7(a) of SI 2007 No 2871 as from 7.4.08.
8.   Amended by art 3(3)(a) of SI 2008 No 3156 as from 5.1.09.
9.   Amended by art 5(3) of SI 2010 No 2836 as from 1.4.11.

Single room rents

5.–(1)   The rent officer shall determine a single room rent in accordance with the following formula–

$$S = \frac{H+L}{2}$$

where–
S is the single room rent;
H is the highest rent, in the rent officer's opinion–
(a)   which a landlord might reasonable have been expected to obtain, at the relevant time, for an assured tenancy of a dwelling which meets the criteria in sub-paragraph (2); and
(b)   which is not an exceptionally high rent; and
L is the lowest rent, in the rent officer's opinion–
(a)   which a landlord might reasonably have been expected to obtain, at the relevant time, for an assured tenancy of a dwelling which meets the criteria in sub-paragraph (2); and
(b)   which is not an exceptionally low rent.
(2)   The criteria are–
(a)   that the dwelling under the assured tenancy is in the same [⁴ broad rental market area (local reference rent)] as the dwelling and is in a reasonable state of repair;
(b)   that, under the assured tenancy, the tenant–
(i)   has the exclusive use of one bedroom;
(ii)   does not have the use of any other bedroom [¹ . . .] or room suitable for living in;
[² (iia)   shares the use of a room suitable for living in]
(iii)   shares the use of a toilet [¹ and bathroom]; and
(iv)   shares the use of a kitchen and does not have the exclusive use of facilities for cooking food; and
(c)   that the rent does not include any payment for board and attendance.
(3)   Sub-paragraphs [³ (3) and (5)] of paragraph 4 apply when ascertaining H and L under this sub-paragraph as if the reference in those sub-paragraphs to H and L were to H and L under [³ this paragraph].

Amendments
1.   Amended by reg 4 of SI 2001 No 1326 as from 2.7.01.
2.   Substituted by art 2(9) of SI 2003 No 2398 as from a date specified in Sch 1 to that SI in relation to each individual authority.
3.   Amended by arts 5(1) and 6 of SI 2005 No 236 as from 13.3.05.
4.   Amended by art 3(3)(b) of SI 2008 No 3156 as from 5.1.09.

Claim-related rent

[¹**6.**–[² (1)   In this paragraph, and in paragraph 9, "claim-related rent" means the claim-related rent determined by the rent officer in accordance with paragraph (2A).]

[² (2A)   The rent officer shall determine that the claim-related rent is–
(a)   where he makes a determination under sub-paragraph (2) of paragraph 1, sub-paragraph (2) of paragraph 2 and sub-paragraph (3) of paragraph 3, the lowest of the three rents determined under those sub-paragraphs;
(b)   where he makes a determination under only two of the sub-paragraphs referred to in paragraph (a), the lower of the two rents determined under those sub-paragraphs;
(c)   where he makes a determination under only one of the sub-paragraphs referred to in paragraph (a), the rent determined under that sub-paragraph;
(d)   where he does not make a determination under any of the sub-paragraphs referred to in sub-paragraph (a), the rent payable under the tenancy of the dwelling at the relevant time.]

[² (2)]]
(3)   [²] the rent officer shall also determine the total amount of ineligible charges, as defined in paragraph 7, which he has not included in the claim-related rent because of the assumptions made in accordance with that paragraph.]

Modifications
Para 6(1) substituted, para 6(2A) inserted, para 6(2) omitted and para 6(3) amended by art 18(2) Rent Officers (Housing Benefit Functions) Amendment Order 2007 SI No.2871 as from 7 April 2008, save where art 18(1)(a) or (b) of that order applied (see p934).

Amendments
1.   Substituted by art 11 of SI 2000 No 3 as from 3.4.00.
2.   Amended by art 18(2) of SI 2007 No 2971 as from 7.4.08, save where art 18(1)(a) or (b) of that order applies.

Part II
Assumptions

Ineligible charges and support charges

[¹**7.**[⁵–(1)   "ineligible charges" means service charges which are ineligible to be met by housing benefit by virtue of regulation 12B(2) (rent) of and Schedule 1 (ineligible service charges) to the Housing Benefit Regulations or, as the case may be, regulation 12B(2) of and Schedule 1 to the Housing Benefit (State Pension Credit) Regulations except in the case of a tenancy where the rent includes payments for board and attendance, and the rent officer considers that a substantial part of the rent under the tenancy is fairly attributable to board and attendance, charges specified in paragraph 1(a)(i) of Schedule 1 to the Housing Benefit Regulations or, as the case may be, in paragraph 1(a)(i) of Schedule 1 to the Housing Benefit (State Pension Credit) Regulations (charges for meals).]

        [². . .]
(2)   When making a determination under paragraph 1, 2 or 3 of this Schedule, the rent officer shall assume that–
(a)   the items to which the ineligible charges relate; [² . . .]
        were not to be provided or made available.
[⁴ (3)   For the purposes of paragraphs 1, 2, 3, and 6 of Part 1 of this Schedule, the rent officer shall assume that the rent payable under the tenancy at the relevant time is–
(a)   where an amount is notified to the rent officer under regulation 114A(4)(b) of the Housing Benefit Regulations or, as the case may be, regulations 95A(4)(b) of the Housing Benefit (State Pension Credit) Regulations in respect of that tenancy, that notified amount less the total of any ineligible charges included in that amount; or
(b)   in any other case, the total amount stated under regulation 114A(3)(d) of the Housing Benefit Regulations or, as the case may be regulation 95A(3)(d) of the Housing Benefit (State Pension Credit) Regulations less the total of any ineligible charges included in that stated amount.]
(4)   The total of any ineligible charges, referred to in sub-paragraph (3), shall be the total of the amounts (excluding any amount which he considers is negligible) of any charges included in the notified amount or the stated amount, as the case may be, which, in the rent officer's opinion, are at the relevant time fairly attributable to any items to which ineligible charges relate.]

Modifications

Para 7(3) substituted by art 16(4) Rent Officers (Housing Benefit Functions) Amendment Order 2007 SI No.2871 as from 7 April 2008, save where art 16(1) of that order applied (see p933). Para 7(1) substituted by art 17(2) Rent Officers (Housing Benefit Functions) Amendment Order 2007 SI No.2871 as from 7 April 2008, save where art 17(1) of that order applied (see p933).

Amendments

1. Amended by art 9 of SI 2000 No 3 as from 3.4.00.
2. Deleted by art 3 of SI 2003 No 478 as from 1.4.03 (7.4.03 where rent payable weekly or in multiples of a week).
3. Amended by reg 5 and Sch 2 para 12(10)(b) of SI 2006 No 217 as from 6.3.06.
4. Substituted by art 16(4) of SI 2007 No 2871 as from 7.4.08, save where art 16(1) of that order applies.
5. Substituted by art 17(2) of SI 2007 No 2871 as from 7.4.08, save where art 17(1) of that order applies.

Housing associations etc.

8.–(1) In a case where the local authority states in the application that the landlord is a housing association or a charity, the rent officer shall assume that the landlord is not such a body.

(2) The rent officer shall not take into account the rent under any tenancy where the landlord is a housing association or where the landlord is a charity and the dwelling is provided by the landlord in the pursuit of its charitable purposes.

(3) In this paragraph–

"charity" has the same meaning as in the Charities Act 1993, except that it includes a Scottish charity (which has the same meaning as in section 1(7) of the Law Reform (Miscellaneous Provisions) (Scotland) Act 1990); and

"housing association" has the same meaning as in the Housing Associations Act 1985.

Part III
Notifications of Part I Determinations

Notifications

9.–[¹(1) Subject to sub-paragraph (2), the rent officer shall give notice to the local authority of–

(a) the claim-related rent determined under Part I;

(b) where the dwelling is not in a hostel, the total amount of ineligible charges determined under paragraph 6(3) in relation to that claim-related rent;

[³ (c) where that claim-related rent includes an amount which would be ineligible for housing benefit under paragraph 1(a)(i) of Schedule 1 to the Housing Benefit Regulations or, as the case may be, paragraph 1(a)(i) of Schedule 1 to the Housing Benefit (State Pension Credit) Regulations (charges for meals), the inclusion of an ineligible amount in respect of meals;]

(d) any rent determined by the rent officer under paragraph 4 (local reference rents); and

[³ (da) where any rent determined under paragraph 4 includes an amount which would be ineligible for housing benefit under the provisions referred to in sub-paragraph (c), the inclusion of an ineligible amount in respect of meals;]

(e) any rent determined by the rent officer under paragraph 5 (single room rents).]

(2) If the rent officer determines a rent under–

(a) paragraph 4 (local reference rents); or

(b) paragraph 5 (single room rents),

which is equal to or more than the [¹ claim-related rent], the rent officer shall give notice to the local authority of this in place of giving notice of the determination made under paragraph 4 or, as the case may be, paragraph 5.

Modifications

Para 9(1)(c) substituted and para 9(1)(da) inserted by art 18(3) Rent Officers (Housing Benefit Functions) Amendment Order 2007 SI No.2871 as from 7 April 2008, save where art 18(1)(a) or (b) of that order applied (see p934).

Amendments

1. Amended by art 9 of SI 2000 No 3 as from 3.4.00.
2. Amended by reg 5 and Sch 2 para 12(10)(c) of SI 2006 No 217 as from 6.3.06.
3. Amended by art 18(3) of SI 2007 No 2971 as from 7.4.08, save where art 18(1)(a) or (b) of that order apply.

Part IV

Indicative Rent Levels

11.–(1) The rent officer shall determine the indicative rent level for each category described in sub-paragraph (3) in accordance with the following formula–

$$I = \frac{H+3L}{4}$$

where–

I is the indicative rent level;

H is the highest rent, in the rent officer's opinion–

(a) which a landlord might reasonably be expected to obtain at the time the determination is being made for an assured tenancy of a dwelling meeting the criteria in sub-paragraph (2); and

(b) which is not an exceptionally high rent; and

L is the lowest rent, in the rent officer's opinion–

(a) which a landlord might reasonably be expected to obtain at the time the determination is being made for an assured tenancy of a dwelling meeting the criteria in sub-paragraph (2); and

(b) which is not an exceptionally low rent.

(2) The criteria are that–

(a) the dwelling is in the area of the local authority;

(b) the dwelling is in a reasonable state of repair; and

(c) the dwelling and tenancy accord with the category to which the determination relates.

(3) The categories for the purposes of this paragraph are–

(a) a dwelling where the tenant does not have use of more than one room where a substantial part of the rent under the tenancy is fairly attributable to board and attendance;

(b) a dwelling where the tenant does not have use of more than one room, the tenancy provides for him to share a kitchen or toilet and paragraph (a) does not apply;

(c) a dwelling where the tenant does not have use of more than one room and where paragraphs (a) and (b) do not apply;

(d) a dwelling where the tenant does not have use of more than two rooms and where none of paragraphs (a) to (c) applies;

(e) a dwelling where the tenant does not have use of more than three rooms and where none of paragraphs (a) to (d) applies;

(f) a dwelling where the tenant does not have use of more than four rooms and where none of paragraphs (a) to (e) applies;

(g) a dwelling where the tenant does not have use of more than five rooms and where none of paragraphs (a) to (f) applies; and

(h) a dwelling where the tenant does not have use of more than six rooms and where none of paragraphs (a) to (g) applies.

(4) When ascertaining H and L under sub-paragraph (1), the rent officer–

(a) shall assume that no one who would have been entitled to housing benefit had sought or is seeking the tenancy; and

(b) shall exclude the amount of any rent which, in the rent officer's opinion, is fairly attributable to the provision of services which are ineligible to be met by housing benefit; [¹ . . .]

(5) In this paragraph–

"room" means a bedroom or room suitable for living in and in paragraphs (a), (b) and (c) of sub-paragraph (3) does not include a room which the tenant shares with any person other than–

(a) a member of his household;

(b) a non-dependant of the tenant (within the meaning of [² [³ regulation 3 of the Housing Benefit Regulations or, as the case may be, regulation 3 of the Housing Benefit (State Pension Credit) Regulations]]); or

(c) a person who pays rent to the tenant;

"services" has the meaning given by paragraph 4(5).

Amendments

1. Deleted by art 3 of SI 2003 No 478 as from 1.4.03 (7.4.03 where rent payable weekly or in multiples of a week).

2. Amended by reg 5 and Sch 2 para 12(10)(d) of SI 2006 No 217 as from 6.3.06.

3. Substituted by art 19(7)(b) of SI 2007 No 2871 as from 7.4.08.

SCHEDULE 2

ARTICLE 2

SIZE CRITERIA

1. One bedroom or room suitable for living in shall be allowed for each of the following categories of occupier (and each occupier shall come within only the first category for which he is eligible)–

[⁵ (za) a member of a couple who cannot share a bedroom;

(zb)   a member of a couple who can share a bedroom;]
(a)   [¹ a couple] [⁵];
(b)   a person who is not a child;
[⁴ (ba)   a child who cannot share a bedroom;]
(c)   two children of the same sex;
(d)   two children who are less than ten years old;
(e)   a child.
[⁴ but the claimant is only entitled to a bedroom in respect of a child who cannot share a bedroom [⁵ or a member of a couple who cannot share a bedroom] if there is a bedroom in the dwelling occupied as the home that is additional to those to which the claimant would be entitled if the child [⁵ or the member of the couple] were able to share a bedroom.]

[³**1A.**   One additional bedroom is allowed where on the application for the determination–
[⁵ (a)   one or more of the following persons is stated as being a person who requires overnight care–
(i)   the tenant;
(ii)   the tenant'spartner;
(iii)   a person (other than the tenant or the tenant's partner) who occupies the dwelling as their home;
(iv)   a child or young person in respect of whom the tenant or the tenant's partner is a qualifying parent or carer; or]
(b)   the tenant or the tenant's partner is (or both of them are) stated as being a qualifying parent or carer.]

[³**1B.**   Two additional bedrooms are allowed where sub-paragraphs (a) and (b) of paragraph 1A both apply.]

[²**1A.**   Where the tenant or the tenant's partner is a person who is stated on the application for the determination as being a person who requires overnight care (or in any case where both of them are so stated), one additional bedroom is allowed.]

2.   The number of rooms (excluding any allowed under paragraph 1) suitable for living in allowed are–
(a)   if there are less than four occupiers, one;
(b)   if there are more than three and less than seven occupiers, two; and
(c)   in any other case, three.

[³[⁴**3.**   In this Schedule "child who cannot share a bedroom" [⁵, "couple", "member of a couple who cannot share a bedroom"] and "qualifying parent or carer" have the meaning given by regulation 2(1) of the Housing Benefit Regulations [⁵ and reference to a member of a couple who can share a bedroom is to be construed in accordance with regulation 2(6) of those Regulations].]]

Amendments

  1.   Substituted by art 30 of SI 2005 No 2877 as from 5.12.05.
  2.   Inserted by art 5(4) of SI 2010 No 2836 as from 1.4.11.
  3.   Amended by art 3 of SI 2013 No 666 as from 1.4.13.
  4.   Amended by art 3 of SI 2013 No 2827 as from 4.12.13.
  5.   Amended by reg 3 of SI 2017 No 213 as from 1.4.17.

SCHEDULE 3

ARTICLE 4

REDETERMINATIONS

[¹**1.**   Schedules 1 and 2 shall apply in relation to a redetermination as they apply to a determination, but as if references in those Schedules to the relevant time were references to the date the application for the original determination was made or, if earlier, the date the tenancy ended.]

Amendment

  1.   Substituted by art 12 of SI 2000 No 3 as from 3.4.00.

---

2.   The rent officer making the redetermination shall seek and have regard to the advice of one or two other rent officers in relation to the redetermination.

[² SCHEDULE 3A]

ARTICLES 2(2) AND 4B

Modifications

    Sch 3A omitted by art 15(8) Rent Officers (Housing Benefit Functions) Amendment Order 2007 SI No.2871 as from 7 April 2008, save where art 15(1)(a), (b) or (c) of that order applied (see p933).

Amendments

  1.   Schedule inserted by art 2(10) of SI 2003 No 2398 as from a date specified in Sch 1 to that SI in relation to each individual authority.

2. Omitted by art 15(8) of SI 2007 No 2871 as from 7.4.08, save where Art 15(1)(a), (b) or (c) of that order applies.
3. Substituted by art 19(8) of SI 2007 No 2871 as from 7.4.08.

[¹ SCHEDULE 3B

ARTICLE 4B

Amendment
1. Schedule inserted by art 13(4) of SI 2007 No 2871 as from 20.3.08.

Broad rental market area determinations and local housing allowance determinations

Categories of dwelling
1.–(1) The categories of dwelling for which a rent officer is required to determine a local housing allowance in accordance with [² article 4B(2A)(a)] are–
(a) a dwelling where the tenant has the exclusive use of only one bedroom and where the tenancy provides for him to share the use of one or more of–
    (i)   a kitchen;
    (ii)   a bathroom;
    (iii) a toilet; or
    (iv)   a room suitable for living in;
(b) a dwelling where the tenant (together with his partner where he has one) has the exclusive use of only one bedroom and exclusive use of a kitchen, a bathroom, a toilet and a room suitable for living in;
(c) a dwelling where the tenant has the use of only two bedrooms;
(d) a dwelling where the tenant has the use of only three bedrooms;
(e) a dwelling where the tenant has the use of only four bedrooms;
[¹ (f)]
(2) In–
(a) sub-paragraph (1)(b) "partner" has the same meaning as in regulation 2 of the Housing Benefit Regulations or, as the case may be, regulation 2 of the Housing Benefit (State Pension Credit) Regulations;
(b) sub-paragraph (1)(c) [¹ to (e)] "bedroom" means a bedroom, except for a bedroom which the tenant shares with any person other than–
    (i)   a member of his household;
    (ii)   a non-dependant of the tenant (within the meaning of regulation 3 of the Housing Benefit Regulations or, as the case may be, regulation 3 of the Housing Benefit (State Pension Credit) Regulations); or
    (iii) a person who pays rent to the tenant.

Amendments
1. Amended by art 4(3)(a) of SI 2010 No 2836 as from 18.3.11.
2. Amended by art 3(4)(a) of SI 2012 No 646 as from 2.4.12.

[⁶ Local housing allowance for category of dwelling in paragraph 1
2.–(1) Subject to paragraph 3 (anomalous local housing allowances)(d), the rent officer must determine a local housing allowance for each category of dwelling in paragraph 1 as follows.
[⁸]
[⁹ (2A) For all broad rental market areas [¹¹ not listed in column 1 of the table in paragraph 5A], the local housing allowance for any category of dwelling is the lower of the amounts set out in sub-paragraph (3)(a) and (b).
[¹¹ (2B) For a broad rental market area listed in column 1 of the table in paragraph 5A, the local housing allowance–
(a) for a category of dwelling listed in the corresponding entry in column 2 of that table, is the lowest of the amounts set out in sub-paragraph (3A)(a), (b) and (c);
(b) for a category of dwelling not so listed, is the lower of the amounts set out in sub-paragraph (3)(a) and (b).]
[¹¹]
[⁸ (3) [⁹ The amounts referred to in sub-paragraphs [¹¹ (2A) and (2B)(b)] are–]
(a) the local housing allowance [¹⁰ last determined for that category of dwelling] (or, where the determination is amended under article 7A(4) (errors), the allowance provided for in the amended determination); [⁹ and]
(b) the rent at the 30th percentile determined in accordance with sub-paragraphs (4) to (8)[⁹].]
[⁹ (3A) The amounts referred to in (2B)(a) [¹¹] are–

(a)   the local housing allowance [¹⁰ last determined for that category of dwelling] (or, where the determination is amended under article 7A(4) (errors), the allowance provided for in the amended determination), plus 3%; [¹¹]

[¹¹ (b)   the maximum local housing allowance listed in column 2 of the following table for the category of dwelling–

1. category of accommodation as defined in the following paragraphs of this Schedule	2. Maximum local housing allowance for that category of dwelling
paragraph 1(1)(a) (one bedroom, shared accommodation)	£276.51
paragraph 1(1)(b) (one bedroom, exclusive use)	£276.51
paragraph 1(1)(c) (two bedrooms)	£320.74
paragraph 1(1)(d) (three bedrooms)	£376.04
paragraph 1(1)(ce (four bedrooms)	£442.42]

[¹¹; and

(c)   the rent at the 30th percentile determined in accordance with sub-paragraphs (4) to (8).]

(4)   The rent officer must compile a list of rents in ascending order of the rents which, in the rent officer's opinion, are payable–

(a)   for a dwelling let under an assured tenancy for each category of dwelling specified in paragraph 1; and

(b)   in the 12 month period ending on the 30th day of the September preceding the date of the determination.

(5)   In compiling the list of rents, the rent officer must–

(a)   include within it the rent of an assured tenancy in relation to each category of dwelling if–

    (i)   the dwelling let under the assured tenancy is in the broad rental market area for which the local housing allowance for that category of dwelling is being determined;

    (ii)   the dwelling is in a reasonable state of repair; and

    (iii) the assured tenancy permits the tenant to use exclusively or share the use of, as the case may be, the same number and type of rooms as the category of dwelling in relation to which the list is being compiled;

(b)   include within it any rents which are of the same amount;

(c)   where rent is payable other than weekly, use the figure which would be payable if the rent were to be payable weekly by–

    (i)   multiplying the rent by an appropriate figure to obtain the rent for a year;

    (ii)   dividing the total in (i) by 365; and

    (iii) multiplying the total in (ii) by 7;

(d)   assume that no one who would have been entitled to housing benefit had sought or is seeking the tenancy; and

(e)   exclude the amount of any rent which, in the rent officer's opinion, is fairly attributable to the provision of services performed for, or facilities (including the use of furniture) provided for, or rights made available to, the tenant which are ineligible to be met by housing benefit.

(6)   Sub-paragraph (7) applies where the rent officer is not satisfied that the list of rents in respect of any category of dwelling would contain sufficient rents, payable in the 12 month period ending on the 30th day of the September preceding the date of the determination for dwellings in the broad rental market area, to enable a local housing allowance to be determined which is representative of the rents that a landlord might reasonably be expected to obtain in that area.

(7)   In a case where this sub-paragraph applies the rent officer may add to the list rents for dwellings in the same category in other areas in which a comparable market exists.

(8)   The rent officer must use the list of rents to determine the rent at the 30th percentile in the list ("R") by–

(a)   where the number of rents on the list is a multiple of 10, applying the formula–

$$R = \frac{\text{the amount of the rent at P} + \text{the amount of the rent at P1}}{2}$$

Where–

    (i)   P is the position on the list found by multiplying the number of rents on the list by 3 and dividing by 10; and

    (ii)   P1 is the following position on the list;

(b)   where the number of rents on the list is not a multiple of 10, applying the formula–

$$R = \text{the amount of the rent at P2}$$

Where–

P2 is the position on the list found by multiplying the number of rents on the list by 3 and dividing by 10 and rounding the result upwards to the nearest whole number.

[⁸]

(10)   Where the local housing allowance would otherwise not be a whole number of pence, it must be rounded to the nearest whole penny by disregarding any amount less than half a penny and treating any amount of half a penny or more as a whole penny.]

Amendments
1.   Omitted by art 3(4)(a) of SI 2008 No 3156 as from 5.1.09.
2.   Inserted by art 2(2) of SI 2009 No 2459 as from 12.10.09.
3.   Amended by art 4(3)(b) of SI 2010 No 2836 as from 18.3.11.
4.   Amended by art 3(4)(b) of SI 2012 No 646 as from 2.4.12.
5.   Amended by art 3(4) of SI 2013 No 1544 as from 1.9.13.
6.   Substituted by art 3(2) of SI 2013 No 2978 as from 13.1.14.
7.   Substituted by art 3(3)(a) of SI 2014 No 3126 as from 8.1.15.
8.   Amended by art 3(2)(a) and (b) of SI 2015 No 1753 as from 2.11.15.
9.   Amended by art 3(3) of SI 2016 No 1179 as from 23.1.17.
10.   Amended by art 3(3) of SI 2017 No 1323 as from 26.1.18.
11.   Amended by art 3(2) of SI 2018 No 1332 as from 25.1.19.

Anomalous local housing allowances
3.–(1)   Where–
(a)   the rent officer has determined the local housing allowance for each of the categories of dwelling in paragraph 1(1) in accordance with the preceding paragraphs of this Schedule; and
(b)   the local housing allowance for a category of dwelling in paragraph 1(1)(b) [¹ to (e)] is lower than the local housing allowance for any of the categories of dwelling which precede it,
that local housing allowance shall be the same as the highest local housing allowance which precedes it.
   [¹ (2)]

Amendment
1.   Amended by art 4(3)(c) of SI 2010 No 2836 as from 18.3.11.

Broad rental market area
[¹**4.**   In this Schedule "broad rental market area" means an area within which a person could reasonably be expected to live having regard to facilities and services for the purposes of health, education, recreation, personal banking and shopping, taking account of the distance of travel, by public and private transport, to and from those facilities and services.]

Amendment
1.   Substituted by art 3(4)(b) of SI 2008 No 3156 as from 5.1.09.

[¹**5.**   A broad rental market area must contain–
(a)   residential premises of a variety of types, including such premises held on a variety of tenures; and
(b)   sufficient privately rented residential premises to ensure that, in the rent officer's opinion, the local housing allowance for the categories of dwelling in the area for which the rent officer is required to determine a local housing allowance is representative of the rents that a landlord might reasonably be expected to obtain in that area.]]

Amendment
1.   Inserted by art 3(4)(b) of SI 2008 No 3156 as from 5.1.09.

[³]

Amendments
1.   Inserted by art 3(3) of SI 2013 No 2978 as from 13.1.14.
2.   Substituted by art 3(3)(b) and Sch 2 of SI 2014 No 3126 as from 8.1.15.
3.   Omitted by art 3(2)(c) of SI 2015 No 1753 as from 2.11.15.

[¹**5A.**   The table referred to in paragraph 2(2A) and (2B) is as follows–

1. Broad rental market area	*2. Category of accommodation as defined in the following paragraphs of this Schedule*
East Dunbartonshire	Paragraph 1(1)(c) (two bedrooms)
Fife	Paragraph 1(1)(a) (one bedroom, shared accommodation)
Forth Valley	Paragraph 1(1)(a) (one bedroom, shared accommodation)
Greater Glasgow	Paragraph 1(1)(b) (one bedroom, exclusive use)
Greater Glasgow	Paragraph 1(1)(c) (two bedrooms)
Greater Glasgow	Paragraph 1(1)(e) (four bedrooms)

Highlands and Islands	Paragraph 1(1)(a) (one bedroom, shared accommodation)
Lothian	Paragraph 1(1)(a) (one bedroom, shared accommodation)
Lothian	Paragraph 1(1)(b) (one bedroom, exclusive use)
Lothian	Paragraph 1(1)(c) (two bedrooms)
Lothian	Paragraph 1(1)(d) (three bedrooms)
North Lanarkshire	Paragraph 1(1)(a) (one bedroom, shared accommodation)
Scottish Borders	Paragraph 1(1)(e) (four bedrooms)
South Lanarkshire	Paragraph 1(1)(e) (four bedrooms)
West Lothian	Paragraph 1(1)(c) (two bedrooms)
West Lothian	Paragraph 1(1)(d) (three bedrooms)]

Amendment

1.   Inserted by art 3(3) of SI 2018 No 1332 as from 25.1.19.

SCHEDULE 4

ARTICLE 7

SPECIAL CASES

Houseboats

1.   Where an application for a determination or a redetermination relates in whole or in part to mooring charges for a houseboat, this Order applies in relation to that application (or, as the case may be, to that part which relates to those charges) with the following modifications–

(a)   references to a tenancy, a tenancy of a dwelling or an assured tenancy are references to an agreement under which those charges are payable (and references to a landlord and a tenant shall be construed accordingly); and

(b)   no determination shall be made under paragraph 2 of Part I of Schedule 1 (size criteria) and references to the dwelling exceeding the size criteria shall not apply.

Mobile homes

2.   Where an application for a determination or redetermination relates in whole or in part to payments in respect of the site on which a caravan or a mobile home stands, this Order applies in relation to that application (or, as the case may be, that part which relates to those payments) with the following modifications–

(a)   references to a tenancy, a tenancy of a dwelling or an assured tenancy are references to an agreement under which those payments are payable (and references to a landlord and a tenant shall be construed accordingly); and

(b)   no determination shall be made under paragraph 2 of Part I of Schedule 1 (size criteria) and references to the dwelling exceeding the size criteria shall not apply.

Rental purchase agreements

3.   Where an application for a determination or a redetermination relates to a rental purchase agreement, the agreement is to be treated as if it were a tenancy.

The Rent Officers (Housing Benefit Functions) (Local Housing Allowance) Amendment Order 2003
(SI 2003 No.2398)

General Note

This Order modified the Rent Officers (Housing Benefit Functions) Orders in respect of the implementation of the pilot housing allowance scheme in Pathfinder Authorities. Only the commencement dates are reproduced here.

Citation, commencement and interpretation

1.–(1) This Order may be cited as the Rent Officers (Housing Benefit Functions) (Local Housing Allowance) Amendment Order 2003 and shall come into force in relation to the area of a local authority specified in Schedule 1 to this Order on the date specified in that Schedule in relation to that local authority.

(2) *[Omitted]*

SCHEDULE 1

ARTICLE 1

DATE ON WHICH ORDER COMES INTO FORCE FOR LOCAL AUTHORITY AREAS

Local authority	Date
Blackpool	17th October 2003
Brighton and Hove	19th January 2004
Conwy	19th January 2004
Coventry	15th December 2003
Edinburgh	19th January 2004
Leeds	19th January 2004
Lewisham	17th November 2003
North East Lincolnshire	19th January 2004
Teignbridge	15th December 2003

The Rent Officers (Housing Benefit Functions) (Local Housing Allowance) Amendment Order 2005

(SI 2005 No.236)

Citation, commencement and interpretation

1.–(1) This order may be cited as the Rent Officers (Housing Benefit Functions) (Local Housing Allowance) Amendment Order 2005.

(2) This article and articles 2, 3, 5 and 6 shall come into force on 13th March 2005.

(3) Articles 4 and 7 shall come into force in relation to the area of a local authority specified in the Schedule to this Order on the date specified in that Schedule in relation to that local authority.

(4) In this Order–

(a) "local authority" has the same meaning as in the Social Security Administration Act 1992; and

(b) "the 2003 Order" means the Rent Officers (Housing Benefit Functions) (Local Housing Allowance) Amendment Order 2003.

The Rent Officers (Housing Benefit Functions) Order 1997: additional pathfinder authorities

4. The Rent Officers (Housing Benefit Functions) Order 1997 shall apply in relation to the area of a local authority in England and Wales specified in the Schedule to this Order as it applies in relation to the area of a local authority in England and Wales specified in Schedule 1 to the 2003 Order.

The Rent Officers (Housing Benefit Functions) (Scotland) Order 1997: additional pathfinder authorities

7. The Rent Officers (Housing Benefit Functions) (Scotland) Order 1997 shall apply in relation to the area of a local authority in Scotland specified in the Schedule to this Order as it applies in relation to the area of a local authority in Scotland specified in Schedule 1 to the 2003 Order.

SCHEDULE

ARTICLE 1(5)

DATE ON WHICH ARTICLES 4 AND 7 COME INTO FORCE FOR LOCAL AUTHORITY AREAS

Relevant authority	*Date*
Argyll and Bute	25th April 2005
East Riding of Yorkshire	21st March 2005
Guildford	6th June 2005
Norwich	16th May 2005
Pembrokeshire	23rd May 2005
St Helens	25th April 2005
Salford	20th June 2005
South Norfolk	9th May 2005
Wandsworth	14th March 2005.

The Rent Officers (Housing Benefit Functions) Amendment Order 2007

(SI 2007 No.2871)

Citation, commencement and interpretation

1.–(1)   This Order may be cited as the Rent Officers (Housing Benefit Functions) Amendment Order 2007.

(2)   This article and articles 2 (application of the Rent Officers Order), 3 (amendment of the Rent Officers Order), 11 (application of the Rent Officers (Scotland) Order) and 12 (amendment of the Rent Officers (Scotland) Order) shall come into force on 20th March 2008.

(3)-(4)   *Omitted.*

(5)   In this Order–

"local authority" has the same meaning as in the Social Security Administration Act 1992;

"the Rent Officers Order" means the Rent Officers (Housing Benefit Functions) Order 1997; and

"the Rent Officers (Scotland) Order" means Rent Officers (Housing Benefit Functions) (Scotland) Order 1997.

Application of the Rent Officers Order

2.   Those provisions of the Rent Officers Order which on 19th March 2008 apply only in relation to the area of a local authority listed in the Schedule, shall apply in the same way to the area of every other local authority in England and Wales.

Amendments to the Rent Officers Order relating to the local housing allowance coming into force on 7th April 2008 save for certain purposes

6.–(1)   This article shall not apply where–

(a)   a board and attendance determination, board and attendance redetermination, substitute board and attendance determination or substitute board and attendance redetermination is to be made and the application for the board and attendance determination or original board and attendance determination was made by virtue of regulation 13A(6) of the Housing Benefit Regulations 2006 or, as the case may be, regulation 13A(6) of the Housing Benefit (Persons who have attained the qualifying age for state pension credit) Regulations 2006 as in force immediately before 7th April 2008;

(b)   a local housing allowance determination is to be made and the application was made by virtue of regulation 13A(4) or (5) of the Housing Benefit Regulations 2006 or, as the case may be, regulation 13A(4) or (5) of the Housing Benefit (Persons who have attained the qualifying age for state pension credit) Regulations 2006 as in force immediately before 7th April 2008; or

(c)   an error in relation to a broad rental market area determination, local housing allowance determination, board and attendance determination or a board and attendance redetermination is to be corrected and the original determination was made in accordance with the Rent Officers Order as in force immediately before 7th April 2008.

(2)   For the purpose of sub-paragraph (1)(c) "original determination" means the broad rental market area determination, local housing allowance determination, board and attendance determination or board and attendance redetermination to which the correction of an error relates.

(3)-(8)   *[Omitted]*

Amendments to the Rent Officers Order relating to information sharing coming into force on 7th April 2008 save for certain purposes

7.–(1)   This article shall not apply where information is provided to the rent officer by virtue of regulation 14 or 114 of the Housing Benefit Regulations 2006 or, as the case may be, regulation 14 or 95 of the Housing Benefit (Persons who have attained the qualifying age for state pension credit) Regulations 2006 as in force immediately before 7th April 2008.

(2)-(4) *[Omitted]*

Amendments to the Rent Officers Order relating to ineligible service charges coming into force on 7th April 2008 save for certain purposes

8.–(1) This article shall not apply where the rent officer is required to make a determination under paragraphs 1, 2, 3, or 6 of Part 1 of Schedule 1 to the Rent Officers Order by virtue of–

(a) an application made under–
- (i) regulation 14 of the Housing Benefit Regulations 2006 as in force before the substitution of regulation 14 by virtue of regulation 8 of the Housing Benefit (Local Housing Allowance and Information Sharing) Amendment Regulations 2007; or
- (ii) regulation 14 of the Housing Benefit (Persons who have attained the qualifying age for state pension credit) Regulations 2006 as in force before the substitution of regulation 14 by virtue of regulation 8 of the Housing Benefit (State Pension Credit) (Local Housing Allowance and Information Sharing) Amendment Regulations 2007; or

(b) an application for a redetermination, substitute determination or substitute redetermination relating to a determination to which sub-paragraph (a) applies made under regulation 15, 16 or 17 of the Regulations referred to in sub-paragraph (a)(i) or (ii).

(2) *[Omitted]*

Amendments to the Rent Officers Order relating to claim-related rent coming into force on 7th April 2008 save for certain purposes

9.–(1) This article shall not apply where the rent officer has made a determination under paragraphs 1, 2, 3, 4 or 5 of Part 1 of Schedule 1 to the Rent Officers Order and that determination was made in relation to–

(a) an application under–
- (i) regulation 14 of the Housing Benefit Regulations 2006 as in force before the substitution of regulation 14 by virtue of regulation 8 of the Housing Benefit (Local Housing Allowance and Information Sharing) Amendment Regulations 2007; or
- (ii) regulation 14 of the Housing Benefit (Persons who have attained the qualifying age for state pension credit) Regulations 2006 as in force before the substitution of regulation 14 by virtue of regulation 8 of the Housing Benefit (State Pension Credit) (Local Housing Allowance and Information Sharing) Amendment Regulations 2007; or

(b) an application for a redetermination, substitute determination or substitute redetermination relating to a determination to which sub-paragraph (a) applies made under regulation 15, 16 or 17 of the Regulations referred to in sub-paragraph (a)(i) or (ii).

(2)-(3) *[Omitted]*

Application of the Rent Officers (Scotland) Order

11. Those provisions of the Rent Officers (Scotland) Order which on 19th March 2008 apply only in relation to the areas of the local authority of Argyll and Bute and the local authority of Edinburgh, shall apply in the same way to the area of every other local authority in Scotland.

Amendments to the Rent Officers (Scotland) Order relating to the local housing allowance coming into force on 7th April 2008 save for certain purposes

15.–(1)   This article shall not apply where–
(a)   a board and attendance determination, board and attendance redetermination, substitute board and attendance determination or substitute board and attendance redetermination is to be made and the application for the board and attendance determination or original board and attendance determination was made by virtue of regulation 13A(6) of the Housing Benefit Regulations 2006 or, as the case may be, regulation 13A(6) of the Housing Benefit (Persons who have attained the qualifying age for state pension credit) Regulations 2006 as in force immediately before 7th April 2008;
(b)   a local housing allowance determination is to be made and the application was made by virtue of regulation 13A(4) or (5) of the Housing Benefit Regulations 2006 or, as the case may be, regulation 13A(4) or (5) of the Housing Benefit (Persons who have attained the qualifying age for state pension credit) Regulations 2006 as in force immediately before 7th April 2008; or
(c)   an error in relation to a broad rental market area determination, local housing allowance determination, board and attendance determination or a board and attendance redetermination is to be corrected and the original determination was made in accordance with the Rent Officers (Scotland) Order as in force immediately before 7th April 2008.
(2)   For the purpose of sub-paragraph (1)(c) "original determination" means the broad rental market area determination, local housing allowance determination, board and attendance determination or board and attendance redetermination to which the correction of an error relates.
(3)-(8)   *[Omitted]*

Amendments to the Rent Officers (Scotland) Order relating to information sharing coming into force on 7th April 2008

16.–(1)   where information is provided to the rent officer by virtue of regulation 14 or 114 of the Housing Benefit Regulations 2006 or, as the case may be, regulation 14 or 95 of the Housing Benefit (Persons who have attained the qualifying age for state pension credit) Regulations 2006 as in force immediately before 7th April 2008.
(2)-(4)   *[Omitted]*

Amendments to the Rent Officers (Scotland) Order relating to ineligible service charges coming into force on 7th April 2008 save for certain purposes

17.–(1)   This article shall not apply where the rent officer is required to make a determination under paragraphs 1, 2, 3, or 6 of Part 1 of Schedule 1 to the Rent Officers (Scotland) Order by virtue of–
(a)   an application made under–
(i)   regulation 14 of the Housing Benefit Regulations 2006 as in force before the substitution of regulation 14 by virtue of regulation 8 of the Housing Benefit (Local Housing Allowance and Information Sharing) Amendment Regulations 2007; or
(ii)   regulation 14 of the Housing Benefit (Persons who have attained the qualifying age for state pension credit) Regulations 2006 as in force before the substitution of regulation 14 by virtue of regulation 8 of the Housing Benefit (State Pension Credit) (Local Housing Allowance and Information Sharing) Amendment Regulations 2007; or
(b)   an application for a redetermination, substitute determination or substitute redetermination relating to a determination to which sub-paragraph (a) applies made under regulation 15, 16 or 17 of the Regulations referred to in sub-paragraph (a)(i) or (ii).
(2)   *[Omitted]*

Amendments to the Rent Officers (Scotland) Order relating to claim-related rent coming into force on 7th April 2008 save for certain purposes

18.–(1)   This article shall not apply where the rent officer has made a determination under paragraphs 1, 2, 3, 4 or 5 of Part 1 of Schedule 1 to the Rent Officers (Scotland) Order and that determination was made in relation to–

(a)   an application under–

    (i)   regulation 14 of the Housing Benefit Regulations 2006 as in force before the substitution of regulation 14 by virtue of regulation 8 of the Housing Benefit (Local Housing Allowance and Information Sharing) Amendment Regulations 2007; or

    (ii)   regulation 14 of the as in force before the substitution of regulation 14 by virtue of regulation 8 of the Housing Benefit (State Pension Credit) (Local Housing Allowance and Information Sharing) Amendment Regulations 2007; or

(b)   an application for a redetermination, substitute determination or substitute redetermination relating to a determination to which sub-paragraph (a) applies made under regulation 15, 16 or 17 of the Regulations referred to in sub-paragraph (a)(i) or (ii).

(2)-(3)   *[Omitted]*

SCHEDULE

ARTICLE 2

LISTED AUTHORITIES

Blackpool
Brighton and Hove
Conwy
Coventry
East Riding of Yorkshire
Guildford
Leeds
Lewisham
North East Lincolnshire
Norwich
Pembrokeshire
St Helens
Salford
South Norfolk
Teignbridge
Wandsworth

Part 3:

Decision making and appeals – housing benefit

The Housing Benefit and Council Tax Benefit (Decisions and Appeals) Regulations 2001
(SI 2001 No.1002)

PART I

General

1. Citation, commencement and interpretation
2. Service of notices or documents
3. Person treated as a person affected by a decision

PART II

Revisions and supersessions

4. Revision of decisions
5. Late application for a revision
6. Date from which a revision takes effect
7. Decisions superseding earlier decisions
8. Date from which a decision superseding an earlier decision takes effect
9. Effective date for late notification of change of circumstances
10. Notice of a decision against which an appeal lies

PART III

Suspension and termination of benefit and other matters

11. Cases where a relevant authority may suspend
12. Making or restoring of payments or reductions suspended
13. Suspension for failure to furnish information etc.
14. Termination in cases of a failure to furnish information
15. Decisions involving issues that arise on appeal in other cases

PART IV

Rights of appeal and procedure for bringing appeals

16. Decisions against which no appeal lies
17. Appeal against a decision which has been revised
18. Time within which an appeal is to be brought
19. Late appeals
20. Making of appeals and applications
21. Death of a party to an appeal

PART V

Appeal Tribunals

22. Composition of appeal tribunals
23. Procedure in connection with appeals

SCHEDULE

Decisions against which no appeal lies

PART I

General

Citation, commencement and interpretation

1.–(1)   These Regulations may be cited as the Housing Benefit and Council Tax Benefit (Decisions and Appeals) Regulations 2001 and shall come into force on 2nd July 2001.

(2)   In these Regulations, unless the context otherwise requires–

"the Act" means the Child Support, Pensions and Social Security Act 2000;

[³ "the 1998 Act" means the Social Security Act 1998;]

"the Administration Act" means the Social Security Administration Act 1992;

"appeal" means an appeal to [⁸ the First-tier Tribunal];

"appropriate relevant authority" has the meaning it has in paragraph 4 of Schedule 7 to the Act;

"benefit week" means a period of seven consecutive days commencing on a Monday and ending on a Sunday;

"claimant" means a person claiming housing benefit or council tax benefit or both;

[⁸]

[⁶ "Council Tax Benefit Regulations" means the Council Tax Benefit Regulations 2006;]

[⁶ "Council Tax Benefit (State Pension Credit) Regulations" means the Council Tax Benefit (Persons who have attained the qualifying age for state pension credit) Regulations 2006;]

[⁴]]

[¹⁰ "couple" means–
   (a)   two people who are married to, or civil partners of, each other and are members of the same household; or
   (b)   two people who are not married to, or civil partners of, each other but are living together as a married couple;]

[¹¹ "couple" means–
   (a)   two people who are married to, or civil partners of, each other and are members of the same household; or
   (b)   two people who are not married to, or civil partners of, each other but are living together as a married couple;]

"Decisions and Appeals Regulations 1999" means the Social Security and Child Support (Decisions and Appeals) Regulations 1999;

[² . . .]

[³ "family" has the same meaning as in section 137 of the Social Security Contributions and Benefits Act 1992;]

[⁸]

[⁶ "Housing Benefit Regulations" means the Housing Benefit Regulations 2006;]

[⁶ "Housing Benefit (State Pension Credit) Regulations" means the Housing Benefit (Persons who have attained the qualifying age for state pension credit) Regulations 2006;]

[⁸]

"official error" means an error made by–
   (a)   a relevant authority or a person–
         (i)   authorised to carry out any function of a relevant authority relating to housing benefit or council tax benefit; or
         (ii)   providing services relating to housing benefit or council tax benefit directly or indirectly to a relevant authority;
   [¹ (b)   an officer of–
         (i)   the Department for Work and Pensions; or
         (ii)   the Commissioners of Inland Revenue,
         acting as such;]–
   [²(c) . . .]
         but excludes any error caused wholly or partly by any person or body not specified in [⁹ sub-paragraph (a) or (b)] of this definition and any error of law which is shown to have been an error only by virtue of a subsequent decision of [⁸ the Upper Tribunal] or the court;

[⁸]

"partner" means–
   (a)   where a claimant is a member of [⁵ a couple], the other member of that couple; or
   (b)   where a claimant is polygamously married to two or more members of his household, any such member;

"person affected" shall be construed in accordance with regulation 3;

[⁸]
"principal parties" has the same meaning as in paragraph 7(4) of Schedule 7 to the Act;
"relevant authority" has the same meaning as in paragraph 1(1) of Schedule 7 to the Act;
"relevant decision" has the same meaning as in paragraph 1(2) of Schedule 7 to the Act;
[⁷ "the Welfare Reform Act" means the Welfare Reform Act 2007.]
[² . . .]
[² . . .]

    (3)   In these Regulations, unless the context otherwise requires, a reference–

    (a)   to a numbered regulation is to the regulation in these Regulations bearing that number;

    (b)   in a regulation to a numbered paragraph is to the paragraph in that regulation bearing that number.

Amendments

1.   Amended by reg 23 of SI 2002 No 1379 as from 20.5.02.
?   Deleted by Sch 2 para 8 (a) of SI 2002 No 1703 as from 30.9.02.
3.   Inserted by reg 5(2)(a) of SI 2003 No 2275 as from 6.10.03.
4.   Inserted by reg 9(2)(a) of SI 2005 No 2878 as from 5.12.05.
5.   Substituted by reg 9(b) of SI 2005 No 2878 as from 5.12.05.
6.   Amended by reg 5 and Sch 2 para 17(2) of SI 2006 No 217 as from 6.3.06.
7.   Inserted by reg 3 of SI 2008 No 1082, as substituted by reg 26 of SI 2008 No 2428, as from 27.10.08.
8.   Amended by Sch 1 para 149 of SI 2008 No 2683 as from 3.11.08.
9.   Amended reg 19 of SI 2012 No 757 as from 1.4.12.
10.   Substituted (in England and Wales only) by art 2 and Sch 1 para 30 of SI 2014 No 107 as from 13.3.14.
11.   Substituted (in Scotland only) by art 29 and Sch 6 para 21 of SI 2014 No 3229 as from 16.12.14.

Analysis

"Official error" is a ground for revision under reg 4(2)(a). It is an error wholly caused by one of the named categories of people. Those falling into sub-paras (a) and (b) are equivalent to the categories in sub-paras (a) to (c) of reg 100(3) HB Regs and reference should be made to the commentary to that provision on p584. Since 30 September 2002, "official error" has no longer included errors made by someone employed by an authority acting on behalf of the relevant HB authority for the area: sub-para (c) deleted.

The tailpiece excludes an error caused by a person not falling within the categories listed in the definition. That person may be wholly or only partly to blame for the error occurring.

Official errors include errors of law. However, an error of law is not an official error if it is "shown to have been" a mistake by a subsequent decision of the Upper Tribunal or a court. "Court" is not defined but will inevitably be interpreted to cover all superior courts in England, Scotland and Wales. If, however, as often occurs, there is a pre-existing commissioner's decision which gives a ruling on the point but the significance of which was not fully appreciated at the time, the failure to follow that decision will still be an official error. Before 3 November 2008, the reference to "the Upper Tribunal" was to "a Commissioner". The way in which the regulation has been amended appears to have the effect that where, on or after 3 November 2008, an authority or a tribunal is considering an error of law that is "shown to have been" a mistake by a decision of a commissioner before that date, the exclusion from the definition of official error no longer applies. In order to reflect what was almost certainly the policy intention, the words "a Commissioner" should have been replaced by the words "a Commissioner or the Upper Tribunal" rather than merely "the Upper Tribunal". However, the error (if it is one) was not corrected at the same time as similar errors in the rules for supersession were corrected retrospectively by s103 and Sch 12 WRA 2012.

It is suggested that official error also includes situations where there is specific evidence which the authority or person had but which was not taken into account even though it was relevant, and where there is documentary or other written evidence of entitlement which the authority had but failed to give to the person making the decision at the time it was made.

Note that the difference in wording in sub-para (a) means that the restrictive reasoning in *R(I) 5/02* – error of law made by an adjudication officer on a decision made prior to the inception of the SSA 1998 does not fall within the definition and so that decision cannot ever be revised for "official error" – has no application to HB decisions. Note, in any case, that in *CG 2122/2001* Commissioner Mesher was reluctant to accept the tribunal's reasoning on this point in *R(I) 5/02* and in *R(CS) 3/04* Commissioner Turnbull decided that *R(I) 5/02* was wrongly decided on this point and he did not need to follow it. The meaning of "official error" was also considered by the Upper Tribunal in *FW v SSWP (DLA)* [2011] UKUT 88 (AAC).

Service of notices or documents

2. Where, by, or in consequence of, any provision of these Regulations or Schedule 7 to the Act–

(a) any notice or other document is required to be given or sent to [¹] the Secretary of State or the relevant authority, that notice or document shall be treated as having been so given or sent on the day that it is received by [¹] the Secretary of State or the relevant authority, as the case may be; and

(b) any notice (including notification of a decision of a relevant authority) or other document is required to be given or sent to any person other than [¹] the Secretary of State or the relevant authority, as the case may be, that notice or document shall, if sent by post to that person's last known address, be treated as having been so given or sent on the day it was posted.

Amendment

1. Amended by Sch 1 para 150 of SI 2008 No 2683 as from 3.11.08.

General Note

Reg 2 governs when notices and other documents are to be treated as having been served. It applies to all documents that are "required to be given or sent" by, or in consequence of, "any provision of these Regulations or Schedule 7" to CSPSSA.

There are two rules:

(1) Under para (a), documents sent to the local authority are served when they are received.

(2) Under para (b), a document sent to other parties (eg, by a local authority to a claimant) is deemed to be served on the day that it is posted.

Analysis

Para (a). The fact that a document given/sent to a local authority is only treated as having been given/sent when it is actually received is a constant source of dispute, and a trap for claimants who are often placed in the position of having to establish that it was more likely than not that a document was received by an authority when all the evidence relevant to that issue lies in the hands of the authority. The best advice for claimants is to either deliver all documents in person and obtain a receipt or send them by recorded delivery so that the Royal Mail can be approached for evidence of delivery if necessary. Unfortunately, that advice will often be impracticable either in terms of time (the claimant may well be in full-time low-waged work) or money (as recorded delivery greatly increases the cost of posting a letter and many letters may be necessary during the course of a claim). A compromise may be to advise claimants to send letters by ordinary post but obtain a free certificate of posting from the Post Office counter: proof of posting may help persuade a tribunal that it is more likely than not that the authority received the letter and subsequently misplaced it. But even if it does not, a claimant who can prove that s/he committed a document to the post is in a much stronger position to argue for any necessary extension of time if that document subsequently goes astray.

Local authorities are under a duty to ensure that those who are entitled to benefit receive it as well as to ensure that those with no entitlement do not. As entitlement may depend upon when they receive a particular document, it is important that all authorities should have rigorous and documented procedures for the opening of post. It is not unusual for the First-tier Tribunal to question presenting officers in detail about such procedures.

Documents sent by fax can raise particular difficulties. Provided a fax is sent prior to midnight – or 5.00 pm if the fax is to the First-tier Tribunal or the Upper Tribunal (see r12(1) of the TP(FT) Rules and the TP(UT) Rules) – and successfully transmitted, it will have been "received" on that day: *CDLA 4895/2001* (para 7). This issue was further considered in *R(DLA) 3/05*, in the context of a request for a statement of the appeal tribunal's reasons for its decision being faxed to a tribunal venue within the relevant time limit, but where that faxed request had not been picked up by the clerk to the tribunal – to whom such applications had to be made, see the former reg 53(4) SSCS D&A Regs – until after that time limit had expired, because the venue was not used on a daily basis. Commissioner Jacobs decided that, in such circumstances, an application is made when it is received by a fax machine, and that this is the case regardless of when the clerk actually collects the fax from the machine, which may be hours or days later (para 18). However, the fax machine used must relate in some way to the case to which the application relates, and at the very least it must be a fax machine within the relevant Tribunals Service Region (para 19). Nor is it sufficient to send an application to a fax machine at a casual venue, such as a town hall, as the fax machine there will belong to the owner or occupier of the premises and not the tribunal (para 20). In this case the application had been made to a dedicated appeals venue (albeit one that was not used for appeals each and every day), where the claimant's appeal had been heard and where the fax number for that venue had been made available to those with appeals at that venue. In these circumstances, and in the absence of any directions to the contrary, service on that fax machine was good service, and so the request for the statement of reasons had been made within time.

Para (b). The effect of this is that where on service of a document, a time limit begins to run, it runs from the date of posting, not date of receipt of the document. This presumes that if the document was sent to the correct address, it has been delivered. Extensions of time ought readily to be granted where a document is lost in the post or has been sent to an incorrect address. As Commissioner Williams pointed out in *CH 3009/2002*, there is no matching presumption that a document which it was intended to be posted was actually posted. He said that where, as in this case, an appellant challenges whether something has been posted for good reason, evidence of office practice is required to show that on the balance of probabilities, the document was posted: paras 12 and 13.

Before 3 November 2008, reg 2 also applied to documents sent to and by the clerk to an appeal tribunal. Sending and delivery of documents in proceedings before the First-tier Tribunal is now governed by r13 TP(FT) Rules 2008 (see p1000).

The divergent treatment of documents sent to local authorities and documents sent to other parties to the appeal would seem to raise issues about the "equality of arms" (see the commentary to Art 6 European Convention on Human Rights on p124). Reg 2 means that the risk of documents going astray in the post is always borne by the claimant or appellant, never by the local authority, and that, in the event of a dispute, the claimant or appellant either has to prove that s/he did not receive the document (which involves proving a negative) or that the authority did receive the document (which involves proving a fact when all the potential evidence for that fact is in the possession of the other party). The harsh effects of reg 2 will often, but not always, be mitigated by the possibility of obtaining an extension of time. Nevertheless, it is wrong in principle for procedural rules to favour one party over another overtly. That is particularly so when the advantaged party is the more powerful (in this case, the state) and the disadvantaged the less powerful (in this case, the citizen).

Person treated as a person affected by a decision

3.–(1)   For the purposes of Schedule 7 to the Act and subject to paragraph (2), a person is to be treated as a person affected by a relevant decision of a relevant authority where that person is–

(a) a claimant;

(b) in the case of a person who is liable to make payments in respect of a dwelling and is unable for the time being to act–

 (i) a [² deputy] appointed by the Court of Protection with power to claim, or as the case may be, receive benefit on his behalf,

 (ii) in Scotland, a tutor, curator, judicial factor or other guardian acting or appointed in terms of law administering that person's estate, or

 (iii) an attorney with a general power or a power to receive benefit appointed by the person liable to make those payments under [² the Powers of Attorney Act 1971, the Enduring Powers of Attorney Act 1985 or the Mental Capacity Act 2005 or otherwise];

[¹ (c) a person appointed by the relevant authority under regulation 82(3) of the Housing Benefit Regulations, regulation 63(3) of the Housing Benefit (State Pension Credit) Regulations, regulation 68(3) of the Council Tax Benefit Regulations or, as the case may be, regulation 52(3) of the Council Tax Benefit (State Pension Credit) Regulations (appointments for persons unable to act);

(d) a person from whom the relevant authority determines that–

 (i) an overpayment is recoverable in accordance with Part 13 of the Housing Benefit Regulations or Part 12 of the Housing Benefit (State Pension Credit) Regulations; or

 (ii) excess benefit is recoverable in accordance with Part 11 of the Council Tax Benefit Regulations or Part 10 of the Council Tax Benefit (State Pension Credit) Regulations; or

(e) a landlord or agent acting on behalf of that landlord and that decision is made under–

 (i) regulation 95 (circumstances in which payment is to be made to the landlord) of the Housing Benefit Regulations;

 (ii) regulation 96 (circumstances in which payment may be made to the landlord) of those Regulations;

 (iii) regulation 76 (circumstances in which payment is to be made to the landlord) of the Housing Benefit (State Pension Credit) Regulations;

 (iv) regulation 77 (circumstances in which payment may be made to the landlord) of those Regulations.]

(2)   Paragraph (1) only applies in relation to a person referred to in paragraph (1) where the rights, duties or obligations of that person are affected by a relevant decision.

Amendments

1.   Substituted by reg 5 and Sch 2 para 17(3) of SI 2006 No 217 as from 6.3.06.
2.   Amended by reg 9 of SI 2007 No 2618 as from 1.10.07.

Analysis

Para (1) sets out the categories of "person affected". This definition is important, since it is a "person affected" who has the right to challenge decisions and appeal under Sch 7 CSPSSA and these regulations. The categories are:

(1)   The claimant: sub-para (a).

(2)   A deputy or attorney in England and Wales, or the Scottish equivalents, who is acting on behalf of the person who is liable to make payments: sub-para (b). The deemed non-liability in regs 9(1) and 10(1) of both the HB and the HB(SPC) Regs and reg 56(1) HB Regs will not preclude such a person acting on an appeal against such a decision.

(3)   An appointee appointed by the relevant authority: sub-para (c).

(4)   A person from whom it is decided that an overpayment is recoverable: sub-para (d). This could be a landlord. In *CH 3679/2002* (para 3) it was held that a landlord would be a "person affected" in relation to an appeal by a claimant against a decision that an overpayment was recoverable from a landlord. The failure to notify the landlord of the appeal rendered the decision erroneous in law.

(5)   A landlord or her/his agent, where the decision relates to direct payments (including a decision that the landlord is not a "fit and proper person" – see commentary to regs 95 and 96 HB Regs on p574 and p578: sub-para (e)).

That list is exhaustive (see the decision of the Court of Appeal in *Wirral MBC v Salisbury Independent Living* [2012] EWCA 84; [2012] AACR 37 (Maurice Kay, Hughes and Lewison LJJ) overruling *CH 3817/2004* on this point).

   Para (2) provides that a person will only be a "person affected" if her/his rights, duties and obligations are affected by the decision in question. However, as the list in para (1) is exhaustive, this will always be the case. The rights of the claimant are affected by a decision to pay HB directly to a landlord or agent, or to recover an overpayment from such a person, because (in the former case) the entitlement to benefit is the claimant's and s/he is *prima facie* entitled to receive payment (see reg 94 HB Regs and reg 75 HB(SPC) Regs) and (in the latter) because recovery of an HB overpayment from the landlord or agent will create a debt from the claimant to the recoveree and (at least if reg 95(2)(b) HB Regs and reg 76(2)(b) of the HB(SPC) Regs are validly made) reg 95(2)(b) will create arrears of rent that could lead to eviction (see p574). The rights of deputies (etc) and appointees (para (1)(b) and (c)) are affected because they are acting in the place of the claimant.

PART II
Revisions and Supersessions

General Note on Part II

Pt II contains the rules for revisions and supersessions, which are two of the three means by which a decision can be altered. The third is for the decision to be reversed or varied on appeal.

   Reference should be made to Sch 7 paras 3 and 4 for the enabling provisions governing revisions and supersessions. Regs 4 to 6 contain the detailed provisions for the operation of revisions under Sch 7 para 4 CSPSSA. Reg 4 deals with grounds on which a revision can be made and the procedure for doing so. Reg 5 deals with applications for revision made outside the time limit in reg 4(1), and reg 6 deals with the effective date of a decision which has been revised. Regs 7 and 8 deal with the grounds and procedure (reg 7) and the effective date (reg 8) of a supersession. Reg 9 deals with late notifications of changes of circumstances (which are under reg 7(2)(a) grounds for a supersession) and reg 10 deals with notifications of decisions generally.

Revision of decisions

4.–(1)   Subject to the provisions in this regulation, a relevant decision ("the original decision") may be revised or further revised by the relevant authority which made the decision where–

(a)   [² subject to regulation 10A(3),] the person affected makes an application for a revision within–

   (i)   one month of the date of notification of the original decision; or

   (ii)   such extended time as the relevant authority may allow under regulation 5;

(b)   within one month of the date of notification of the original decision that authority has information which is sufficient to show that the original decision was made in ignorance of, or was based upon a mistake as to, some material fact; or

(c)   an appeal is made under paragraph 6 of Schedule 7 to the Act against the original decision within the time prescribed [¹⁰ by Tribunal Procedure Rules] but the appeal has not been determined.

(2)   An original decision may be revised or further revised by the relevant authority which made the decision, at any time by that authority, where that decision–

(a)   arose from anofficial error; or

(b)   was made in ignorance of, or was based upon a mistake as to, some material fact and as a result of that ignorance of or mistake as to that fact, the decision was more advantageous to the person affected than it would otherwise have been but for that ignorance or mistake.

(3)   Notwithstanding the provisions in paragraph (1), a relevant decision which adopts a rent officer's determination [⁶ , board and attendance determination, broad rental market area determination or local housing allowance determination] may be revised or further revised by the relevant authority which made the decision at any time in consequence of a rent officer's redetermination, substitute determination [⁶substitute redetermination, board and attendance redetermination, substitute board and attendance determination, substitute board and attendance redetermination, amended broad rental market area determination or amended local housing allowance determination] made under the Rent Officers (Housing Benefit Functions) Order 1997 or the Rent Officers (Housing Benefit Functions) (Scotland) Order 1997 which resulted in an increase in the amount which represents the rent for the purposes of calculating entitlement to benefit.

(4)   For the purposes of calculating the period in paragraph (1)(a)(i), where a written statement is requested under regulation 10, no account shall be taken of any period beginning with the day on which the relevant authority received the request for a statement and ending with the day on which that statement was provided to that person.

(5)   Where the relevant authority requires further evidence or information in order to consider all the issues raised by an application under paragraph (1)(a) ("the original application"), that authority shall notify the applicant that further evidence or information is required and, if it does so, the decision may be revised–

(a)   where the evidence or information so requested is provided within one month of the date of the notification or such longer period as the relevant authority may allow; or

(b)   where such evidence or information is not provided within the period referred to in sub-paragraph (a), on the basis of the original application.

(6)   A relevant decision that is prescribed under paragraph 6(2)(e) or (4)(a) of Schedule 7 to the Act may be revised at any time.

(7)   A relevant decision made in respect of a claim or an award may be revised where–

(a)   a decision in respect of that claim or that award is given by [¹⁰ the First-tier Tribunal, Upper Tribunal] or court on appeal against a decision ("decision A");

(b)   the relevant decision was made after decision A; and

(c)   the relevant decision would have been made differently had the relevant authority been aware of that appeal decision at the time it made the relevant decision.

[¹[¹¹ (7A)   Where–

(a)   a restriction is imposed on a person under section 6B, 7, 8 or 9 of the Social Security Fraud Act 2001 (loss of benefit provisions) as a result of the person–

    (i)   being convicted of an offence by a court; or

    (ii)   agreeing to pay a penalty as an alternative to prosecution under section 115A of the Administration Act or section 109A of the Social Security Administration (Northern Ireland) Act 1992, and

(b)   that conviction is quashed or set aside by that or any other court, or the person withdraws his agreement to pay a penalty, a decision of the relevant authority made in accordance with regulation 7(2)(g) or (h) may be revised at any time.]]

[⁴ (7B)   Where–

(a)   the relevant authority makes an original decision awarding housing benefit or council tax benefit to a claimant; and

(b)   entitlement to a relevant benefit within the meaning of section 8(3) of the 1998 Act or to an increase in the rate of that relevant benefit is awarded to the claimant or a member of his family for a period which includes the date on which the original decision took effect,

the relevant authority may revise or further revise that original decision at any time.

(7C)   Where entitlement to housing benefit or council tax benefit has ceased ("decision A") because entitlement to a relevant benefit within the meaning of section 8(3) of the 1998 Act has ceased ("decision B"), decision A may be revised at any time if the entitlement to the relevant benefit to which decision B applies has been reinstated in consequence of a decision made under [⁵ section 9 or 10 of the 1998 Act or on an appeal under section 12 of that Act.]]

[⁸ (7D)   Where–

(a)   a person elects for an increase of–

(i)   a Category A or Category B retirement pension in accordance with paragraph A1 or 3C of Schedule 5 to the Contributions and Benefits Act (pension increase or lump sum where entitlement to retirement pension is deferred);

(ii)   a shared additional pension in accordance with paragraph 1 of Schedule 5A to that Act (pension increase or lump sum where entitlement to shared additional pension is deferred); or, as the case may be,

(iii)   graduated retirement benefit in accordance with paragraph 12 or 17 of Schedule 1 to the Social Security (Graduated Retirement Benefit) Regulations 2005 (further provisions replacing section 36(4) of the National Insurance Act 1965: increases of graduated retirement benefit and lump sums);

(b)   the relevant authority decides that the person or his partner is entitled to housing benefit or council tax benefit and takes into account the increase of pension or benefit in making or superseding that decision; and

(c)   the person's election for an increase is changed so that he is entitled to a lump sum,

the relevant authority may revise the housing benefit or council tax benefit decision.]

[¹³ (7DA)   Where–

(a)   a person chooses to be paid a state pension under section 9 of the Pensions Act 2014 in accordance with section 8(2) of that Act;

(b)   the relevant authority decides that the person or his partner is entitled to housing benefit and takes into account the state pension under section 9 of that Act in making or superseding that decision; and

(c)   the person alters their choice under section 8(2) of that Act in accordance with Regulations made under section 8(7),

the relevant authority may revise the housing benefit decision.

(7DB)   Where–

(a)   a person, in accordance with Regulations made under section 10 of the Pensions Act 2014 which include provision corresponding or similar to section 8(2) of that Act, chooses to be paid a survivor's pension based on inheritance of deferred graduated retirement benefit;

(b)   the relevant authority decides that the person or his partner is entitled to housing benefit and takes into account the survivor's pension in sub-paragraph (a) in making or superseding that decision; and

(c)   the person alters their choice to be paid the survivor's pension in sub-paragraph (a) in accordance with Regulations made under section 10 of the Pensions Act 2014 which include provision corresponding or similar to section 8(2) of that Act, the relevant authority may revise the housing benefit decision.]

[⁹ (7E)   Where a court makes an order under section 71 of the Antisocial Behaviour etc. (Scotland) Act 2004 and that order is set aside by the sheriff principal following an appeal under section 72(1) of that Act, a decision made in accordance with regulation 7(2)(a) may be revised at any time.

(7F)   Where a local authority has served a notice in accordance with section 94 of the Antisocial Behaviour etc. (Scotland) Act 2004 and that notice is set aside by a court following an appeal under section 97(1) of that Act, a decision made in accordance with regulation 7(2)(a) may be revised at any time.]

[(7G)   See Modifications below]

[¹² (7H)   Where a relevant authority has reduced housing benefit as a consequence of regulation 75D of the Housing Benefit Regulations, that decision may be revised at any time.]

(8)   An application for a revision shall be made in writing and delivered, by whatever means, to the relevant authority [³ . . .]

(9)   The relevant authority may treat an application for a supersession as an application for a revision.

(10)   Paragraph (1) shall not apply in respect of a change of circumstances which occurred since the decision [⁷ had effect] or where the relevant authority has evidence or information which indicates that a relevant change of circumstances will occur.

Modifications

Reg 4 was modified in respect of people to whom the Housing Benefit (Loss of Benefit) (Pilot Scheme) (Supplementary) Regulations 2007 SI No.2474 applied. See pp1188–92 of the 22nd edition. Para (7G) was inserted. The modification applied until 31 October 2009.

Amendments

1.   Inserted by reg 9(a) of SI 2002 No 490 as from 1.4.02.
2.   Amended by reg 24 of SI 2002 No 1379 as from 20.5.02.
3.   Deleted by Sch 2 para 8(b) of SI 2002 No 1703 as from 30.9.02.
4.   Inserted by reg 5(3) of SI 2003 No 2275 as from 6.10.03.
5.   Amended by reg 2 of SI 2003 No 2526 as from 5.10.03.
6.   Inserted by reg 16 of SI 2003 No 2399 as from a date specified in Sch 8 in relation to each particular authority.
7.   Amended by reg 3(2) of SI 2005 No 337 as from 18.3.05.
8.   Inserted by Reg 10(2) of SI 2005 No 2677 as from 6.4.06.
9.   Inserted by Reg 4 of SI 2006 No 644 as from 3.4.06.
10.   Amended by Sch 1 para 151 of SI 2008 No 2683 as from 3.11.08.
11.   Substituted by reg 9(2) of SI 2010 No 1160 as from 1.4.10.
12.   Inserted by reg 3(2) of SI 2012 No 2994 as from 15.4.13.
13.   Inserted by art 20(2) of SI 2015 No 1985 as from 6.4.16.

Definition

"family" – see reg 1(2) and s137(1) SSCBA 1992.

General Note

A decision can be revised by a relevant authority following an application made by a "person affected" (defined in reg 3 – see p941) on any ground: para (1)(a). A decision can also be revised by a relevant authority in specific circumstances.

Under paras (1)(a)–(c), a revision is only possible within a specific time frame. Under paras (2), (3), (6), (7) and (7A)–(7H) a revision is only possible if specific grounds apply – referred to here as "any time revisions".

Authorities may treat an application for a supersession as one for revision: para (9).

Authorities cannot, in general, supersede a decision where it can be revised: see reg 7(4) – the exception is where there are grounds for revision and further grounds for supersession that are not also grounds for a revision – eg, a subsequent change of circumstances. In considering any application for revision or supersession, a local authority should therefore first ask whether a revision under para (1) is possible, including whether an extension of time for the application can be granted under reg 5. If this is not possible, a revision under any of the other grounds provided by reg 4 should be considered before consideration of any grounds for supersession under reg 7.

If an authority supersedes an earlier decision, or revises it in circumstances that give rise to a right of appeal, it must give notice of the new decision to every "person affected": see reg 10. In the past, reg 18(3) provided that where an authority revises, or – following an in-time application for revision – does not revise, a decision, the one-month time limit for appealing begins to run from the date on which notice is given of the revised decision or the decision not to revise. From 1 September 2009, that is again the position (see r23 TP(FT) Rules 2008 and Sch 7 para 3(5) CSPSSA 2000). For the position between 3 November 2008 and 1 September 2009, see p1036 of the 21st edition.

On an appeal against a decision that has been revised (or, in cases where revision has been refused, against the original decision), the First-tier Tribunal has power to make any decision that the authority could have taken. This includes "considering in appropriate cases whether a claim should be considered as a request for a revision or supersession of a decision on a previous claim, subject to time limits and other statutory provisions": *CH 3009/ 2002* (para 21) following *R(IB) 2/04* (para 25). However, there will be some cases in which the decision under appeal has "so little coherence or connection to legal powers" that it does not amount to a decision under CSPSSA Sch 7 para 3 at all (see *R(IB) 2/04* (paras 72 and 192)). In such cases, the decision should be set aside and the case remitted to the authority for a lawful decision to be taken. There is no power for a local authority to revise a decision made by a tribunal. That is the case even if the tribunal's decision was to confirm the decision made by the authority, because the tribunal's decision replaces the authority's decision even if it is in the same terms: see *VW v London Borough of Hackney (HB)* [2014] UKUT 277 (AAC) at paras 23–25.

Analysis

In *CIS 6249/1999* (paras 21–25) – a case decided under the system of social security adjudication that was in place before SSA 1998 – the commissioner decided that if it would be so unfair to a claimant to "review" a decision that it would be an abuse of process to do so, the Secretary of State (and, on appeal, an appeal tribunal) could decline to do so. This also applies to the revision of decisions under SSA 1998 or Sch 7 CSPSSA. However, it will be a rare case where it will be legitimate for an authority to refrain from revising an earlier decision on this ground. See also the commentary to paras (2), (3), (6), (7) and (7A)–(7H). The use of the word 'may' in paras (1) and (2) does not mean that an HB authority has a general discretion to refuse to revise a decision. Where the grounds of revision are made out, particularly where the ground is 'official error', the authority must usually revise: *R(IS) 15/04*.

Paragraphs (1)(a), (4) and (5): Applications for revision

Para (1)(a) sets out circumstances in which a person affected can apply for a revision on "any grounds". A person affected may apply for a revision within one month of the date of notification of the decision which is sought to be revised. If an accidental error in a decision has been corrected under reg 10A, any day falling before the day on which notice of the correction is given must be ignored in calculating the one-month period. For the date of notification, see reg 2. Where something must be done "within" a certain period of time, time runs from the day after notification: *R(IB) 4/02* (para 15). An act is done "within" a certain period of time if it is done at midnight on the last day of the period: *Manorlike Ltd v Le Vitas Travel Agency and Consultancy Services Ltd* [1986] 1 All ER 573 at 575e-h, 576b-d, CA.

Where a request is made for a written statement of reasons for a decision under reg 10(2), para (4) stops the clock in respect of the one-month time limit for seeking a revision. The period from the date on which the request is received until the date on which the statement of reasons is provided to the person affected must be ignored in calculating whether an application was made within the one-month time limit. Reg 10 obliges authorities to "provide" a written statement to a claimant who has requested one. The use of the word "provide" (and the phrase "provided to" in para (4)) is to be contrasted with the words "given or sent to" in reg 2. It is suggested that the effect is that the deemed service rules in reg 2 do not apply and that the written statement of reasons will not have been "provided to" the claimant until s/he has actually received it: something is not "provided" to a person until it is actually in the possession of that person. If that is correct, the one-month period will not start running until the date of receipt. In practical terms, however, it will often be difficult for a claimant to prove the date of receipt. To avoid unnecessary disputes, it will – where possible – be preferable for a claimant to seek a revision on the basis that the written statement was "provided" on the date it was sent out by the authority.

Although a person affected may believe a written statement of reasons has not been included with a decision or that what has been provided is inadequate, the local authority could disagree. If there is any doubt, it is advisable for the claimant to presume the clock has not stopped and to apply for a revision within a month of the date on which the decision was sent to her/him.

The time limit can be extended in the restricted circumstances set out in reg 5.

Where a decision carries a right of appeal, revision is only one of the two means of disputing the decision, the other being an appeal under Sch 7 para 6 CSPSSA. Unlike for other benefits, for disputes about HB, revision is not a mandatory step that must be taken prior to an appeal. A "person affected" can exercise her/his right of appeal without having first sought a revision. Authorities can then revise a decision, if appropriate, pending determination of that appeal: see para (1)(c) below. However, an appeal should not be held up while this is done as appears to be the practice with some local authorities. The Local Government Ombudsman has made it clear in a report in Complaint No.01/C/13400 against Scarborough BC that authorities should aim to refer all appeals to the First-tier Tribunal within 28 days.

Para (5) gives an authority a power to require further evidence or information to be furnished within one month or a further period that may be allowed. If the evidence or information is not forthcoming, a decision as to whether to revise must be made on the existing material before the authority.

Paragraph (1)(b): Revision of decisions made on basis of incorrect facts
A local authority may revise a decision if, within one month of the date of notification of the original decision, it has information before it showing that the original decision was made on the wrong factual basis. There will be some overlap between this provision and revision for official error under para (2)(a). After the one-month period, a revision under para (2)(b) or a supersession under reg 7(2)(b) may be appropriate instead.

In *Saker v Secretary of State for Social Security* [1988] 16 January *The Times*, CA (reported as *R(I) 2/88*)) – decided under the old "review" regime in place prior to the SSA 1998 – it was held that a material fact is one which may affect the extent of entitlement. However, under the SSA 1998 and the CSPSSA 2000, as explained by the Court of Appeal in *Wood v SSWP* [2003] EWCA Civ 53; reported as *R(DLA) 1/03*, for a revision or supersession to be made the award must change. In the tribunal of commissioners' decision *R(IB) 2/04*, the commissioners further explained *Wood* by stating that: (i) there can be no revision or supersession unless one of the grounds for revision or supersession is actually found to exist, and (ii) that ground forms the basis of the revision or supersession decision, in the sense that the original decision can only be altered in a way which follows from that ground. Therefore, a fact is not material unless it "would justify a different outcome": a material fact is "a fact that makes a difference" (*CIS 3655/2007* para 29).

A distinction must be drawn between facts and the inferences to be drawn from those facts. Again, if the authority simply changes its mind about how it sees the evidence, the original determination is not open to revision on the ground of a mistake of fact: *R(S) 4/86* (para 6).

A distinction also needs to be drawn between mistakes of fact and law, though the distinction is not always easy to make. In addition, if a fact did not exist at the time a decision was made, that decision cannot be said to have been taken in ignorance of that fact: *Chief Adjudication Officer v Combe* [1998] SLT 15; reported as *R(IS) 8/98*. Supersession will be appropriate instead in such a situation.

For the rights of appeal where an authority exercises its powers of revision and supersession, see the commentary to Sch 7 para 1 CSPSSA on p149.

Paragraph (1)(c): Revision while appeal pending
An authority may revise a decision which has been appealed within the time limit, where the appeal is still pending. The process of deciding whether to revise pending an appeal has, confusingly, been termed "reconsideration" by the DWP and local authorities, and is carried out as a matter of course whenever an appeal is made. An appeal will lapse if a revision is carried out and the new decision is more advantageous to the appellant: see Sch 7 para 3 CSPSSA on p142 and reg 17 on p971.

At least in the past, some local authorities have abused the possibility of "reconsideration" created by para (1)(c) to delay, sometimes virtually indefinitely, the submission of the appeal to the tribunal. The technique involves asking a large number of supplementary questions, often in tendentious terms, so that the "reconsideration" can be carried out. If the questions are not answered, or information is not supplied, the appellant is told – quite unlawfully – that the claim has been treated as withdrawn or that the award has been terminated. If the questions are answered, further questions are asked seeking to exploit supposed inconsistencies with information previously given. In extreme cases, the claimant is then told that a decision has been taken not to change the original decision and that as this is a "revision" (which it is not: see the commentary to para 3 Sch 7 CSPSSA on p149) the appeal has therefore lapsed (which is also wrong because there has not in fact been a revision and, anyway, the new decision is not more advantageous to the claimant than the old: see the commentary to reg 17 on p971). The hapless appellant then makes a fresh appeal and the whole sorry process starts all over again.

The primary duty on a local authority that receives an appeal is to prepare a submission and send it to the First-tier Tribunal without delay. The Local Government Ombudsman requires that this should normally be done within 28 days. Where there is delay (which would, in practice, have to be considerably longer than 28 days) or wilful refusal to submit an appeal the tribunal has a residual power to hear the appeal without such a submission: see *R(H) 1/07*.

If, in the course of preparing the response to the appeal, it becomes clear that the decision was wrong then the authority should, of course, revise it under para (1)(c). But if all that can be said is that there are unanswered questions that, if answered, might make a difference to the decision, then the best practice is for the authority to list those questions in the submission (so that the appellant will be aware of the type of further evidence that might be relevant) and, in an appropriate case, to apply for an interlocutory direction from the tribunal that the appellant should produce such evidence.

KD v SSWP (DLA) [2013] UKUT 23 (AAC), at para 46, holds that the equivalent provision for SSWP administered benefits to para (1)(c), is a freestanding power to revise: it is not necessary for the decision maker to identify any error of law or mistake of fact in the original decision – thus a revision decision can be made where an appeal is pending simply on the basis that the decision maker takes a different view of the facts based on the same evidence.

Paragraphs (2), (3), (6), (7) and (7A)–(7H): "Any time" revisions
There are several further grounds for revision which can be applied by the authority at any time. They apply in the following circumstances.

(1)   Where the decision "arose from an official error": para (2)(a). For the definition of "official error", see reg 1(2) on p937. The official error must have influenced the outcome of the decision in question.

(2)   The decision was made on the wrong factual basis and was more advantageous to a person affected as a result: para (2)(b). For the meaning of "material fact" see the commentary to para (1)(b). Reg 17(2) does not specifically apply to para (2)(b) but will no doubt give a good guide as to the types of case where a decision is more "advantageous". It will include situations where on the correct factual basis, the claimant was not entitled to as much benefit as originally determined. This ground will therefore often be used in overpayment cases. In other circumstances, revision is possible under para (1)(b) or supersession is possible under reg 7(2)(b).

(3)   Where a rent officer's redetermination or other subsequent decision has resulted in an *increase* in "the rent for the purposes of calculating entitlement to benefit": para (3). The latter phrase must refer to the maximum rent under reg 13 of both the HB and the HB(SPC) Regs. A reduction in the maximum rent is grounds for a supersession under reg 7(2)(c).

(4)   Where the decision revised is one against which there is no right of appeal: para (6). See the Schedule on p980 for decisions against which an appeal does not lie to a tribunal.

(5)   Where an appeal is made against a decision to the First-tier Tribunal or Upper Tribunal or a court and after its decision (decision A), a fresh claim is decided or the decision is changed, for example, by a supersession (decision B): para (7). However, a revision is only possible on this ground if decision B would have been made differently had the relevant authority been aware of decision A at the time it made its decision. It does not appear that this ground can apply where the decision maker was aware of the decision but did not appreciate its significance. However, such an approach would constitute an "official error" and a revision could be made under para (2)(a) instead. Before 3 November 2008, this ground for revision applied where decision A was made by an appeal tribunal or a commissioner. The amendments made from that date appear to have the effect that there is no longer any power to revise in those circumstances. This is unfortunate. Even after 3 November 2008, there could still be circumstances in which it is desirable to revise a relevant decision made before that date in ignorance of a "decision A" that were both made before that date. Once again, the amendment should have substituted the words "an appeal tribunal or the First-tier Tribunal" for the words "an appeal tribunal" and the words "Commissioner or the Upper Tribunal" for the word "Commissioner". However, the error (if it is one) was not corrected at the same time as similar errors in the rules for supersession were corrected retrospectively by s103 and Sch 12 WRA 2012.

(6)   Where a conviction resulted in benefit being restricted under ss7, 8 or 9 Social Security Fraud Act 2001 (loss of benefit provisions) and that conviction has since been quashed or set aside: para (7A). Only decisions made in accordance with regs 7(2)(g) or (h) (grounds for supersession) can be revised on this ground.

(7)   Where a local authority awards HB and, for a period which includes the date that award took effect, the claimant or a member of her/his family is awarded a "relevant benefit" or an increase in its rate: para (7B). "Relevant benefit" is defined in s8(3) SSA 1998 as any benefit under Parts II to V SSCBA 1992, JSA, UC, ESA, PIP, PC, IS, a social fund grant for maternity or funeral expenses, child benefit and other benefits which may be prescribed. This is a welcome addition of what is known as a "qualifying benefit" rule. It allows HB awards to be increased and arrears to be paid back to the date the awards took effect where a relevant benefit is awarded or its rate is increased for a period including that date – eg, where an award of DLA (a relevant benefit) is made to a claimant and thus a disability premium should be included in her/his HB applicable amount. Where entitlement to a relevant benefit or an increase in its rate commences *after* the date the HB award took effect, the decision awarding HB can instead be superseded under reg 7(2)(i).

This ground for revision is only available where there is an existing award of HB. Where there is no entitlement to HB until an award of a relevant benefit (or increase in its rate) is made, a claimant will be wise to make a claim for HB while the claim for the relevant benefit is being considered, asking the local authority to delay making a decision until the claim for the relevant benefit is determined – known as "stockpiling" a claim. If a decision maker fails to delay making a decision until the result of the claim for a relevant benefit is known, *CG 1479/1999* and *CIS 217/1999* suggest that this may be an error of law, giving rise to a ground for revision under para (2)(a). Alternatively, a claim for backdated HB is required under reg 83(12) and (12A) HB Regs or reg 64(1) HB(SPC) Regs as the case may be. See also para (7C) for the situation where HB ceases when entitlement to a relevant benefit ceases.

(8)   Where entitlement to HB ceases because entitlement to a "relevant benefit" ceases, and the relevant benefit is re-instated in consequence of a revision or supersession decision or an appeal: para (7C). For the definition of "relevant benefit", see the commentary to para (7B). In some cases, a claimant is only entitled to HB because s/he or a member of her/his family is entitled to a relevant benefit – eg, where s/he would not be entitled to HB but for the fact that a carer premium should be included in her/his applicable amount because s/he is entitled to carer's allowance (a relevant benefit). In such a situation, if entitlement to the relevant benefit ceases, so does the entitlement to HB. However, where the relevant benefit is re-instated because of a revision, a supersession or an appeal, para (7C) allows the decision ceasing entitlement to HB to be revised. The effect of this is that HB can be reinstated and arrears paid back to the date from which entitlement ceased.

(9)   Where the claimant or her/his partner deferred claiming Category A or B retirement pension, shared additional pension or graduated retirement benefit and originally opted for an increase in the pension, but then opts for a lump sum instead: para (7D). This only applies where the authority has made a decision on her/his entitlement to HB and takes the increase in pension or benefit into account in making or superseding that decision.

(10)   Where a court makes an order under s71 Antisocial Behaviour etc (Scotland) Act 2004 (or a local authority has served a notice in accordance with s94 of that Act) and that order is set aside by the sheriff principal (or that notice is set aside by a court) following an appeal: paras (7E) and (7F). Since 30 April 2006, in Scotland, where a local authority serves an anti-social behaviour notice on a landlord and s/he has failed to take reasonable management steps to deal with the behaviour, the local authority can ask a court to make a "no rent payable order" or a management control order (in the latter case rent then becomes payable to the local authority under reg 91A HB Regs or reg 72A HB(SPC) Regs). In addition, if a landlord fails to register with the local authority, it can serve a notice stating that no rent is payable on the property – known as a "no rent payable" notice. Where the order or notice is then set aside following an appeal, paras (7E) and (7D) enable a decision ending HB entitlement under reg 7(2)(a) below to be revised. In practice, this means that a claimant does not have to make a fresh claim for HB in these circumstnaces. A helpful explanation of the Antisocial Behaviour etc (Scotland) Act 2004 provisions and their impact on HB is available in Circular HB/CTB A10/2006.

(11)   A decision to reduce HB by virtue of the benefit cap may be revised at any time: para (7H).

Is an authority obliged to carry out an "any time" revision?
The above grounds all confer, on the face of it, a discretion on the local authority as to whether it goes ahead and revises. However, a HB authority does not have a general discretion to refuse to revise a decision. Where the grounds of revision are made out, particularly where the ground is 'official error', the authority must revise: *R(IS) 15/04* (para 39). Sometimes the person affected will not want the revision to be made, because it will inevitably be less advantageous. However, sometimes it may benefit the person affected, but s/he will not be able to apply for a revision under para (1) and will wish the authority to exercise its power to carry out the revision.

If the application cannot be treated as made within the time limit under para (1), an authority may simply reject the application as being out of time under that provision or refuse to extend the time for applying under reg 5. That rejection or refusal would not be a decision giving rise to a right of appeal. The only remedy is judicial review.

Paragraphs (8), (9) and (10): Procedural matters
Applications for revision are to be made in writing to the authority "by whatever means", for the significance of which, see the commentary to reg 20(1) on p976.

Para (9) confers the power to treat an application for supersession as an application for revision. For the power to treat an application for revision as an application for supersession, see reg 7(6) on p951.

A decision can only be revised under para (1) on the basis of the circumstances at the time the decision had effect: para (10). Where a change of circumstances occurs after the decision took effect or the authority has evidence or information that indicates a change is due to take place, supersession under reg 7(2)(a) is appropriate instead. An application for revision on such grounds should be treated as an application for supersession under reg 7(6).

Late application for a revision

5.–(1)   The time limit for making an application for a revision specified in regulation 4 may be extended where the conditions specified in the following paragraphs of this regulation are satisfied.

(2)   An application for an extension of time ("the application") shall be made in writing by the person affected by a relevant decision.

(3)   The application shall–

(a)   contain particulars of the grounds on which the extension of time is sought and shall contain sufficient details of the decision which it is sought to have revised to enable that decision to be identified;

(b)   [² subject to regulation 4(4)] be made within 13 months of the date of notification of the decision which it is sought to have revised; and

(c)   be delivered, by whatever means, to the relevant authority [¹ . . .].

(4)   The application shall not be granted unless the person affected satisfies the relevant authority that–

(a)   it is reasonable to grant the application;

(b)   the application for revision has merit; and

(c)   special circumstances are relevant to the application and as a result of those special circumstances it was not practicable for the application to be made within the time limit specified in regulation 4.

(5)   In determining whether it is reasonable to grant the application for an extension of time, no account shall be taken of the following–

(a)   that the person affected was unaware of or misunderstood the law applicable to his case (including ignorance or misunderstanding of the time limits imposed by these Regulations); or

(b)   that [³ the Upper Tribunal] or a court has taken a different view of the law from that previously understood and applied.

(6)   In determining whether it is reasonable to grant an application, the relevant authority shall have regard to the principle that the greater the amount of time that has elapsed between the expiration of the time specified in regulation 4 for applying for a revision and the making of the application for an extension of time, the more compelling should be the special circumstances on which the application is based.

(7)   An application under this regulation for an extension of time which has been refused may not be renewed.

Amendments

1.   Deleted by Sch 2 para 8(c) of SI 2002 No 1703 as from 30.9.02.
2.   Amended by reg 3(3) of SI 2005 No 337 as from 18.3.05.
3.   Amended by Sch 1 para 152 of SI 2008 No 2683 as from 3.11.08.

Analysis

Reg 5 deals with extensions of time for making an application for a revision under reg 4(1)(a).

It refers to the authority "determining" the question of whether an extension of time should be granted. The ruling is not a "decision" and no appeal to a tribunal lies against it. What is appealable is the original decision made under Sch 7 para 2 or 4 CSPSSA, either as revised under para 3, or – if no extension of time is granted – as originally made.

In *R(TC) 1/05*, Commissioner Turnbull said that an appeal tribunal does not have any jurisdiction to determine whether a decision maker ought to have exercised the power to extend time for applying for a revision and that a refusal or failure to extend the time was not a decision capable of being appealed. That reasoning was in the context of reg 4 SSCS D&A Regs, but would seem to apply four square to the rule in reg 5.

If, by the time an extension has been refused, fewer than 13 months have passed since the original decision, the person affected should consider applying to the tribunal for an extension of time in which to appeal against that decision. The rules for admitting late appeals in rr23(4) and (5) and 5(3)(a) TP(FT) Rules are less stringent than the rules for a late revision in para (4) and it may be to the advantage of the claimant to have the decision taken by an independent tribunal judge rather than an officer of the authority that made the original decision.

If, on the other hand, more than 13 months have passed since the original decision, the only remedy is judicial review.

Paras (2) and (3) set out the procedural requirements. An application must be made in writing with sufficient detail of the decision under attack to enable it to be identified and the grounds on which the late application is made. It must be made within 13 months of the date of notification of the decision (subject to reg 4(4) which extends the normal time limit where a written statement of reasons is requested). See p946 on the meaning of "within". It must be delivered to the authority "by whatever means": see the commentary to reg 20(1) on p976.

Paras (4) to (6) set out the criteria under which a late revision may be carried out. Under para (4), there are four principal conditions that must be met.

(1)   It must be reasonable to grant the application. Paras (5) and (6) are similar to reg 19(8) and (9): see the commentary on p975.

(2)   There must be merit in the application for revision. It need not be certain to succeed, but it must be shown that a serious issue is raised for consideration.

(3)   There are "special circumstances" relevant to the application. "Special circumstances" are not defined, but are likely to be interpreted in a similar way to "special reasons" under the former reg 78(3) HB Regs 1987.

(4)   It was not practicable, as a result of the circumstances, to make the application within the time limit. Reg 19(6) contains similar wording, see p974.

Para (7) appears to prevent a second bite at the cherry of an extension of time for applying for a revision. However, *CIS 93/1992*, held (at para 16) that reg 3(4) Social Security Adjudication Regulations 1986, which was in similar terms, "does not ... prohibit a reconsideration by the chairman. It merely provides that a chairman is not *obliged* to consider a renewed application for extension of time". Although that was necessary to prevent repeated applications, if the chairman did consider a further application for extension of time after an earlier refusal of such extension, then s/he was entitled to do so and to change her/his mind if s/he wished. It is nevertheless important that all relevant matters are placed before the authority on the initial application.

Date from which a revision takes effect

6. Where, on a revision under paragraph 3 of Schedule 7 to the Act, the relevant authority decides that the date from which a relevant decision ("the original decision") took effect was erroneous, the decision under that paragraph shall take effect on the date the original decision would have taken effect had the error not been made.

Analysis

The general rule is that a revised decision has effect from the same date as the original decision took effect, regardless of how long ago the original decision was made: Sch 7 para 3(3) CSPSSA. Where the reason, or one of the reasons, for the revision it is decided that the effective date of the original decision was wrong, the correct date will be used.

Decisions superseding earlier decisions

7.–(1) Subject to the provisions in this regulation, the prescribed cases and circumstances in which a decision may be made under paragraph 4 of Schedule 7 to the Act (decisions superseding earlier decisions) are as set out in paragraph (2).

(2) The appropriate relevant authority may make a decision under paragraph 4 of Schedule 7 to the Act upon its own initiative or on an application made for the purpose on the basis that the decision to be superseded is adecision–

(a) in respect of which–
   (i) there has been a change of circumstances [³ since the decision had effect]; or
   (ii) it is anticipated that a change of circumstances will occur;

(b) which is erroneous in point of law or made in ignorance of, or was based upon a mistake as to, some material fact provided that the decision–
   (i) cannot be revised on the basis of that error, ignorance or mistake; and
   (ii) is not a decision prescribed in regulations under paragraph 6(2)(e) or (4)(a) of Schedule 7 to the Act;

(c) which adopts a rent officer's determination [⁶, board and attendance determination, broad rental market area determination or local housing allowance determination] and in consequence of a rent officer's redetermination, substitute determination, [⁶ substitute redetermination, board and attendance redetermination, substitute board and attendance determination, substitute board and attendance redetermination, amended broad rental market area determination or amended local housing allowance determination] made under the Rent Officers (Housing Benefit Functions) Order 1997 or the Rent Officers (Housing Benefit Functions) (Scotland) Order 1997 the amount which represents the rent for the purposes of calculating entitlement to benefit is reduced;

[³ (d) of [¹⁴ [¹⁸an appeal tribunal, the First-tier Tribunal, the Upper Tribunal or of a Commissioner]]–
   (i) that was made in ignorance of, or was based upon a mistake as to, some material fact; or
   (ii) that was made in accordance with paragraph 17(4)(b) of Schedule 7 to the Act, in a case where paragraph 17(5) of that Schedule to the Act applies;]

(e) which is prescribed in regulations made under paragraph 6(2)(e) or (4)(a) of Schedule 7 to the Act;

[² (f)]

[¹ (g) which is affected by a decision of the Secretary of State that a sanctionable benefit payable to a claimant ceases to be payable or falls to be reduced under section [¹⁵ 6B,] 7 or 9 of the Social Security Fraud Act 2001 and for this purpose "sanctionable benefit" has the [¹⁵ meaning given in section 6A] of that Act; or

(h) which is affected by a decision of the Secretary of State that a joint-claim jobseeker's allowance ceases to be payable or falls to be reduced under section 8 of the Social Security Fraud Act 2001.]

[⁵ (i) [¹³ except where sub-paragraph (o) [¹⁶, (p) [²⁰, (q) or (s)]] applies,] where–
   (i) the claimant has been awarded entitlement to housing benefit or council tax benefit; and

    (ii)   subsequent to the first day of the period to which that entitlement relates, the claimant or a member of his family becomes entitled to an award of a relevant benefit within the meaning of section 8(3) of the 1998 Act or an increase in the rate of that relevant benefit.]

[⁹ (j) where–

    (i)   the claimant or his partner makes, or is treated as having made, an election for a lump sum in accordance with–

      (aa) paragraph A1 or 3C of Schedule 5 to the Contributions and Benefits Act;

      (bb) paragraph 1 of Schedule 5A to that Act; or, as the case may be,

      (cc) paragraph 12 or 17 of Schedule 1 to the Social Security (Graduated Retirement Benefit) Regulations 2005; or

    (ii) such a lump sum is repaid in consequence of an application to change an election for a lump sum in accordance with regulation 5 of the Social Security (Deferral of Retirement Pensions, Shared Additional Pension and Graduated Retirement Benefit) (Miscellaneous Provisions) Regulations 2005 or, as the case may be, paragraph 20D of Schedule 1 to the Social Security (Graduated Retirement Benefit) Regulations 2005.]

[²¹ (ja) where–

    (i)   the claimant or his partner chooses to be paid a lump sum under section 8(2) of the Pensions Act 2014, or fails to choose, and is entitled to a lump sum under section 8(4) of that Act; or

    (ii) such a lump sum is repaid in consequence of a decision to alter that choice, being a decision made in accordance with Regulations made under section 8(7) of that Act;

(jb) where–

    (i)   the claimant or his partner chooses to be paid a lump sum under Regulations made under section 10 of the Pensions Act 2014 which include provision corresponding or similar to section 8(2) of that Act, or fails to choose, and is entitled to a lump sum under Regulations made under section 10 of that Act which include provision corresponding or similar to section 8(4) of that Act; or

    (ii) such a lump sum is repaid in consequence of a decision to alter that choice, being a decision made in accordance with Regulations made under section 10 of the Pensions Act 2014 which include provision corresponding or similar to Regulations made under section 8(7) of that Act;]

[(k)-(n) See Modifications below]

[¹³ (o) where–

    (i)   the claimant has been awarded entitlement to housing benefit or council tax benefit;

    (ii) the claimant or the claimant's partner has made a claim for employment and support allowance;

    (iii) subsequent to the first day of the period to which entitlement to housing benefit or council tax benefit relates, the Secretary of State has decided that the claimant or the claimant's partner has, or is to be treated as having, limited capability for work within the meaning of section 1(4) of the Welfare Reform Act or limited capability for work-related activity within the meaning of section 2(5) of that Act; and

    (iv) either–

      (aa) the assessment phase as defined in section 24(2) of the Welfare Reform Act has ended; or

      (bb) regulation 7 of the Employment and Support Allowance Regulations 2008 (circumstances where the condition that the assessment phase has ended before entitlement to the support component [²²] arises does not apply) applies.]

[¹⁶ (p) where–
    (i)   the claimant has been awarded entitlement to housing benefit or council tax benefit;
    (ii)   the claimant or the claimant's partner has had an award of benefit converted to an employment and support allowance in accordance with regulation 5(2)(a) of the Employment and Support Allowance (Transitional Provisions, Housing Benefit and Council Tax Benefit) (Existing Awards) Regulations 2010; and
    (iii) subsequent to the first day of the period to which that entitlement to housing benefit or council tax benefit relates, the Secretary of State makes a decision to supersede the award of employment and support allowance to award a different component;
  (q) where the claimant has been awarded entitlement to housing benefit or council tax benefit and subsequent to the first day of the period to which that entitlement relates–
    (i)   a conversion decision of the kind set out in regulation 5(2)(a) of the Employment and Support Allowance (Transitional Provisions, Housing Benefit and Council Tax Benefit) (Existing Awards) Regulations 2010 takes effect in respect of the claimant or the claimant's partner; or
    (ii)   [¹⁷ the claimant or the claimant's partner is appealing a conversion decision] as described in regulation 5(2)(b) of the Employment and Support Allowance (Transitional Provisions, Housing Benefit and Council Tax Benefit) (Existing Awards) Regulations 2010 and is treated as having limited capability for work by virtue of regulation 30 of the Employment and Support Allowance Regulations 2008 as modified by the Employment and Support Allowance (Transitional Provisions, Housing Benefit and Council Tax Benefit) (Existing Awards) Regulations 2010.]
[¹⁹ (r) which as a consequence of regulation 75D of the Housing Benefit Regulations reduces housing benefit to apply the benefit cap or increases or decreases such a reduction (including a decrease to nil).]
[²⁰ (s) which is affected by the award of personal independence payment under Part 4 of the Welfare Reform Act 2012 where–
    (i)   the claimant, the claimant's partner or a member of the claimant's family ("P") was entitled to disability living allowance under section 71 of the Social Security Contributions and Benefits Act 1992; and
    (ii)   subsequent to the first day of the period to which the claimant's entitlement to housing benefit relates, P becomes entitled to personal independence payment as a transfer claimant (within the meaning of regulation 2(1) of the Personal Independence Payment (Transitional Provisions) Regulations 2013.]
[¹² [⁷ (2ZA)]]
[⁸ [¹¹ (2A)]]
[¹² [⁶ (2B)]]
[¹² [⁶ (2C)]]
  (3)   The reference to a change of circumstances in paragraph (2)(a) shall include changes of circumstances specified in [¹⁰ [¹²], regulation 74(3) of the Council Tax Benefit Regulations or regulation 59(3) of the Council Tax Benefit (State Pension Credit) Regulations (changes of circumstances which do not need to be notified)].
  (4)   A decision which may be revised under regulation 4 may not be superseded under this regulation except where–
  (a) circumstances arise in which the appropriate relevant authority may revise that decision under regulation 4; and
  (b) further circumstances arise in relation to that decision which are not specified in regulation 4 but are specified in paragraph (2) or (5).
  (5)   Where the appropriate relevant authority requires further evidence or information from the applicant in order to consider all the issues raised by an application under paragraph (2) ("the original application"), the authority shall notify the applicant that

further evidence or information is required and, if it does so, the decision may be superseded–

(a)   where the applicant provides further relevant evidence or information within one month of the date of notification or such longer period of time as the appropriate relevant authority may allow; or

(b)   where the applicant does not provide such evidence or information within the time allowed under sub-paragraph (a), on the basis of the original application.

(6)   The appropriate relevant authority may treat an application for a revision or a notification of a change of circumstances as an application for a supersession.

(7)   An application under this regulation shall be made in writing and delivered, by whatever means, to the relevant authority [^{2} . . .].

Modifications

Paras (2ZA), (2B) and (2C) omitted and para (3) amended by reg 4(2) Housing Benefit (Local Housing Allowance, Miscellaneous and Consequential) Amendment Regulations 2007 SI No.2870 as from 7 April 2008, save that for a person to whom reg 1(3) of those regulations applied (see p1816), the amendments came into force on the day on or after 7 April 2008 when the first of the events specified in reg 1(4) applied to her/him, or on 6 April 2009 if none had before that date.

Sub-paras (2)(k) to (n) were inserted but only in respect of people to whom the Housing Benefit (Loss of Benefit) (Pilot Scheme) (Supplementary) Regulations 2007 SI No.2474 applied and only until 31 October 2009.

Amendments

1.   Inserted by reg 9(b) of SI 2002 No 490 as from 1.4.02.
2.   Deleted by Sch 2 para 8(d) of SI 2002 No 1703 as from 30.9.02.
3.   Amended by reg 4(1) of SI 2003 No 1050 as from 5.5.03.
4.   Amended by reg 24(1) of SI 2003 No 1338 as from 6.10.03.
5.   Amended by reg 5(4) of SI 2003 No 2275 as from 6.10.03.
6.   Inserted by reg 16 of SI 2003 No 2399 as from a date specified in Sch 8 in relation to each particular authority.
7.   Inserted by reg 34(1) of SI 2004 No 14 as from 5.4.04.
8.   Revoked by reg 33 of SI 2004 No 14 as from 5.4.04.
9.   Inserted by reg 10(3) of SI 2005 No 2677 as from 6.4.06.
10.   Amended by reg 5 and sch 2 para 17(3) of SI 2006 No 217 as from 6.3.06.
11.   Revoked by reg 8 of SI 2007 No 2470 as from 24.9.07.
12.   Omitted by reg 4(2) of SI 2007 No 2870 as from 7.4.08 (or if reg 1(3) of that SI applies, on the day on or after 7.4.08 when the first of the events specified in reg 1(4) applies, or from 6.4.09 if none have before that date).
13.   Amended by reg 3(3) of SI 2008 No 1082, as substituted by reg 26 of SI 2008 No 2428, as from 27.10.08.
14.   Amended by Sch 1 para 153 of SI 2008 No 2683 as from 3.11.08.
15.   Amended by reg 9(3) of SI 2010 No 1160 as from 1.4.10.
16.   Amended by reg 27 and Sch 5 para 3(2) of SI 2010 No 1907 as amended by reg 15 of SI 2010 No 2430 as from 1.10.10.
17.   Amended by reg 20 of SI 2010 No 2430 as from 1.11.10.
18.   Amended by reg 5(2) of SI 2012 No 1267 as from 4.6.12, but having effect from 3.11.08.
19.   Inserted by reg 3(3) of SI 2012 No 2994 as from 15.4.13.
20.   Amended by reg 2(2) of SI 2014 No 213 as from 31.3.14.
21.   Inserted by art 20(3) of SI 2015 No 1985 as from 6.4.16.
22.   Amended by Sch 1 para 4 of SI 2017 No 204 as from 3.4.17, subject to transitional and savings provisions in Sch 2 paras 1–7.

Definition

"family" – see reg 1(2) and s137(1) SSCBA 1992.

General Note

A decision can be superseded by a relevant authority on its own initiative or following an application made by a "person affected" by it (defined in reg 3). There must be grounds for supersession: para (2). See *Wood v SSWP* [2003] EWCA Civ 53; reported as *R(DLA) 1/03* for an authoritative analysis of the supersession scheme. *Wood* was further explained by the tribunal of commissioners in *R(IB) 2/04*. The commissioners ruled that: (i) there can be no supersession unless one of the grounds for supersession is actually found to exist; and (ii) that ground forms the basis of the supersession decision, in the sense that the original decision can only be altered in a way which follows from that ground: and see further *CIS 3655/2007*. See also the commentary to reg 90 HB Regs on p565 for consideration of the question of whether a decision is rendered invalid by virtue of a failure to revise or supersede or where there is a defective attempt at revision or supersession.

There is no time limit for applying for a supersession. However, where the ground for supersession is a change in circumstances (para (2)(a)) and the superseding decision is to the advantage of the claimant, the change must be reported within one month of it occurring (or any longer period allowed by the authority) for full arrears of benefit to be paid. See regs 8(3) and 9.

Authorities may treat an application for a revision as one for supersession: para (6).

By virtue of reg 7(4), there is no power to supersede a decision that could be revised except where there are grounds for revision and further grounds for supersession that are not also grounds for revision – eg, a subsequent change of circumstances. In those circumstances, local authorities that receive an application to supersede a decision should first consider whether a revision under reg 4(1) is possible, including whether an extension of time for the application can be granted under reg 5. If this is not possible, a revision under any of the other grounds provided by reg 4 should be considered before consideration of any grounds for supersession under reg 7.

On an appeal against a superseding decision (or a refusal to supersede), the First-tier Tribunal has power to make any decision that the authority could have taken. This includes "considering in appropriate cases whether a claim should be considered as a request for a revision or supersession of a decision on a previous claim, subject to time limits and other statutory provisions": *CH 3009/2002* (para 21) following *R(IB) 2/04* (para 25). However, there will be some cases in which the decision under appeal has "so little coherence or connection to legal powers" that it does not amount to a decision under CSPSSA Sch 7 para 4 at all (see *R(IB) 2/04* paras 72 and 192). In such cases the decision should be set aside and the case remitted to the authority for a lawful decision to be taken.

Analysis
Paragraph (2): Grounds for supersession
Para (2) sets out the various bases on which a supersession of a decision can be made.

(1)   Where there has been a change of circumstances since the decision had effect, or where such a change is expected in the future: sub-para (a). The words added with effect from 5 May 2003 confirm that a supersession of a decision can be made not only where there has been a change of circumstances since the decision was made, but also after it took effect.

The wording omits the word "relevant" that was formerly present in reg 79(1)(a) HB Regs 1987, but nothing turns on this. As the superseding decision has to follow the ground for supersession (see the discussion of *Wood* above), the change of circumstance referred to in para (2)(a) must be one which affects claimant's entitlement to HB, the extent of entitlement or to whom it should be paid. A change in the law is a change of circumstances, but a court decision that changes the authority's view of the law is not: *Chief Adjudication Officer v McKiernon* [1993] 3 July, CA (reported as *R(I) 2/94*). Such issues are dealt with under sub-para (b) or by way of revision. Furthermore, the fact that an officer of the authority disagrees with the inferences to be drawn from the evidence is not a relevant change of circumstances, but if new evidence shows that there has been a change in the claimant's status, there can be a supersession: *R(S) 4/86* (para 5). For council tax benefit (abolished on 1 April 2013), a change of circumstances includes the types of changes which need not be disclosed: para (3). For the position with changes that need not be disclosed for HB, see reg 7A(4).

(2)   Where the decision is based on incorrect facts or a mistake as to the law: sub-para (b). For the meaning of "material fact", see the commentary to reg 4(1)(b). This ground is subject to two qualifications. Head (i) prohibits its use if a revision is possible on the same grounds (see reg 4(1)(b) and (2)(b)) and head (ii) renders it non-available where no appeal lies against the decision (see the Schedule). In the latter case, sub-para (e) can apply instead.

(3)   Where a rent officer's redetermination or other further determination has resulted in a *reduction* in "the rent for the purposes of calculating entitlement to benefit": sub-para (c). The latter phrase must refer to the maximum rent under reg 13 of both the HB and the HB(SPC) Regs. An increase in the maximum rent is grounds for a revision: see reg 4(3).

(4)   Where a decision of the First-tier Tribunal or Upper Tribunal (or an appeal tribunal or a commissioner) was based on incorrect facts or was made pending a "test case" under Sch 7 para 17(4)(b) CSPSSA where the "test case" has subsequently been decided: sub-para (d). However, the latter of these grounds for supersession is not currently relevant as Sch 7 para 17 is not yet in force. It is understood that the government does not intend to bring it into force. Superseding a First-tier Tribunal or Upper Tribunal decision on the basis that it was made in ignorance of, or was based upon a mistake as to, some material fact involves identifying on the evidence a fact which the First-tier Tribunal or Upper Tribunal was not aware of and that fact *would* justify a different outcome decision: *CIS 3655/2007* (at para 29, following *Wood* above and, in effect, restoring *R(I) 56/54* to orthodoxy). The decision of the Court of Appeal in *R(I)*

2/88, in which it was held that a fact was "material" if it might make a difference to the decision being sought to be reviewed is, accordingly, no longer applicable.

The retrospective changes to sub-para (2)(d) by SI 2012 No.1267 (which was made under powers conferred by s103 and Sch 12 WRA 2012) correct the error, first identified in the 21st edition of this book and confirmed by the Upper Tribunal in *DN v Leicester City Council (HB)* [2010] UKUT 253 (AAC), which, from 3 November 2008, made it legally impossible to supersede decisions of the former appeal tribunals and social security commissioners. For the position before the amendments, see pp1040–41 of the 24th edition.

(5)   Where the decision is one against which there is no right of appeal: sub-para (e). See the Schedule on p980 for details of the decisions against which an appeal does not lie to the First-tier Tribunal.

(6)   Where a decision is affected by a DWP decision stopping or restricting benefit under ss7 or 9 Social Security Fraud Act 2001 (loss of benefit provisions): sub-paras (g) and (h).

(7)   Where a local authority awards HB and, after the first day of the period of that award, the claimant or a member of her/his family becomes entitled to a "relevant benefit" or an increase in its rate: sub-para (i). "Relevant benefit" is defined in s8(3) SSA 1998 as any benefit under Parts II to V SSCBA 1992, JSA, UC, ESA, PIP, PC, IS, a social fund grant for maternity or funeral expenses, child benefit and other benefits which may be prescribed. This allows HB awards to be increased and arrears to be paid back to the date of entitlement to a relevant benefit or an increase in its rate – eg, where an award of DLA is made to a claimant and thus a disability premium should be included in her/his HB applicable amount. Note that a supersession under sub-para (i) is not permitted where sub-paras (o), (p), (q) or (s) applies. Where the claimant or family member is awarded a relevant benefit or an increase in its rate for a period which includes the date the HB award took effect, the decision awarding HB can instead be revised under reg 4(7B). See the commentary to reg 4(7B) for the situation when there is no entitlement to HB until an award of a relevant benefit (or an increase in its rate) is made.

(8)   Where the claimant or her/his partner deferred claiming Category A or B retirement pension, shared additional pension or graduated retirement benefit and originally opted (or is treated as opting) for and is paid a lump sum or repays a lump sum because she opts instead for an increase in the pension: sub-para (j).

(9)   Where the local authority awards HB, the claimant or her/his partner claims ESA and, after the first day of the period of the HB award, the DWP decides that the claimant (or partner) has, or is to be treated as having, limited capability for work: sub-para (o). This only applies if the assessment phase (normally the first 13 weeks of entitlement to ESA) has ended or if the claimant (or partner) is someone to whom reg 7 of the ESA Regs 2008 applies. Those regulations set out situations when an ESA claimant can qualify for an ESA work-related activity component or support component before the end of the assessment phase – eg, if s/he is terminally ill. Sub-para (o) therefore allows for the HB award to be superseded to include one of the components in Sch 3 para 25 or 26. A separate ground of supersession is needed in this case so that there can be special rules about the date on which the superseding decision takes effect in those circumstances: see reg 8(14D). Note this provision was not amended to include reference to the similar provision in the ESA Regs 2013.

(10)   Where the local authority awards HB, the claimant or her/his partner's benefit (ie, IS, IB or SDA) had been converted to ESA and after the first day of the period of the HB award the DWP supersedes that award of ESA to include a different component (eg, where a work-related activity component was included in the converted award), but the ESA claimant is now entitled to a support component: sub-para (p). A separate ground of supersession is needed in this case so that there can be special rules about the date on which the superseding decision takes effect in those circumstances: see reg 8(14D).

(11)   Where the local authority awards HB and after the first day of the the period of the HB award, the DWP decides to convert the claimant's or her/his partner's benefit (ie, IS, IB or SDA) to ESA, or the claimant or partner is appealing a conversion decision (ie, one refusing to convert a benefit to ESA) and is treated as having limited capability for work under reg 30 ESA Regs 2008: sub-para (q). A separate ground of supersession is needed in this case so that there can be special rules about the date on which the superseding decision takes effect in those circumstances: see reg 8(14F).

(12)   Where the original decision was to reduce HB under the benefit cap or to increase or decrease such a reduction (including a decrease to nil): sub-para (r).

(13)   Where the claimant, or a member of the claimant's family, who was entitled to DLA is transferred to PIP under the Personal Independence Payment (Transitional Provisions) Regulations 2013: sub-para (s). A separate ground of supersession is needed in this case so that there can be special rules about the date on which the superseding decision takes effect in those circumstances: see reg 8(14G).

Paragraph (4): Relationship between revision and supersession

Para (4) provides that if a revision is possible as well as supersession, a revision must be carried out unless there are grounds for supersession which are not covered by the revision rules in reg 4. On receiving an application for revision or supersession, an authority should therefore first consider whether a revision under reg 4 is possible. It may be necessary to carry out a supersession at the same time as a revision, if some of the matters raised can be the subject matter of a revision but not all of them.

Paragraphs (5) to (7): Procedure

Paras (5) and (7) are in similar terms to reg 4(5) and (8). Para (6) entitles an authority to treat an application for revision or a notification of a change in circumstances as being an application for a supersession.

[¹ Decisions superseding earlier decisions in accordance with paragraph 4(4A) of Schedule 7 to the Act

7A.–(1)   The prescribed cases and circumstances in which a decision must be made under paragraph 4 of Schedule 7 to the Act (decisions superseding earlier decisions) are set out in paragraphs (2) to (4).

(2)   The appropriate relevant authority must make a decision superseding an earlier decision where it is required to determine a maximum rent (LHA) in accordance with [² regulation 13C(3)] of the Housing Benefit Regulations and [² regulation 13C(3)] of the Housing Benefit (State Pension Credit) Regulations (when a maximum rent (LHA) is to be determined).

(3)   The appropriate relevant authority must make a decision superseding an earlier decision in any case to which regulation 14(1)(f) or (g) or the Housing Benefit Regulations or regulation 14(1)(f) or (g) of the Housing Benefit (State Pension Credit) Regulations (requirement to refer to rent officers) applies.

(4)   The appropriate relevant authority must make a decision superseding an earlier decision where a change of circumstances specified in regulation 88(3) of the Housing Benefit Regulations or regulation 69(3) of the Housing Benefit (State Pension Credit) Regulations (changes of circumstances which do not need to be notified) occurs.]

Modifications

Reg 7A inserted by reg 4(3) Housing Benefit (Local Housing Allowance, Miscellaneous and Consequential) Amendment Regulations 2007 SI No.2870, as amended by reg 6(2)(a) of SI 2008 No.586, as from 7 April 2008, save that for a person to whom reg 1(3) of those regulations applied (see p1816), the amendments came into force on the day on or after 7 April 2008 when the first of the events specified in reg 1(4) applied to her/him, or on 6 April 2009 if none had before that date.

Amendments

1.   Inserted by reg 4(3) of SI 2007 No 2870 as from 7.4.08 (or if reg 1(3) of that SI applies, on the day on or after 7.4.08 when the first of the events specified in reg 1(4) applies, or from 6.4.09 if none have before that date).
2.   Amended by reg 6(2)(a) of SI 2008 No 586 as from 7.4.08.

Date from which a decision superseding an earlier decision takes effect

8.–(1)   A decision made by virtue of paragraph 4 of Schedule 7 to the Act ("the superseding decision") shall take effect on a date other than the date on which it is made or the date on which the application was made in the cases or circumstances prescribed in paragraphs (2) to (7).

(2)   Subject to paragraphs (3) and (6), where the superseding decision is made on the ground that there has been, or it is anticipated that there will be, a change of circumstances, the superseding decision shall take effect on the date on which the change of circumstances is to take effect [¹⁰ in accordance with–
  (a)   regulation 79 of the Housing Benefit Regulations;
  (b)   regulation 59 or 60 of the Housing Benefit (State Pension Credit) Regulations;
  (c)   regulation 67 of the Council Tax Benefit Regulations; or
  (d)   regulation 50 or 51 of the Council Tax Benefit (State Pension Credit) Regulations as the case may be.]

(3)   For the purposes of determining the date on which a superseding decision is to take effect in accordance with paragraph (2), in a case where–
  (a)   the change of circumstances is a change of circumstances that is required by regulations to be notified, other than any change of circumstances to which regulation 68A [² or 68B] of the Housing Benefit Regulations or regulation 59A [² or 59B] of the Council Tax Benefit Regulations applies; and
  (b)   that change of circumstances is notified more than one month after it occurs, or such longer period as may be allowed under regulation 9; and

   (c)   the superseding decision is advantageous to the claimant,
the date of notification of the change of circumstances shall be treated as the date on which the change of circumstances occurred.

   (4)   Where the superseding decision is advantageous to the claimant and is made on the ground that the superseded decision was made in ignorance of, or was based upon a mistake as to, some material fact, the superseding decision shall take effect from the first day of the benefit week in which–
   (a)   except where sub-paragraph (b) applies, the appropriate relevant authority first has information which is sufficient to show that the superseded decision was made in ignorance of, or was based upon a mistake as to, some material fact;
   (b)   where the superseding decision was made pursuant to an application, that application was received by the appropriate relevant authority.

   (5)   For the purpose of paragraphs (3)(c) and (4), the reference to the decision which is advantageous to the claimant includes a decision specified in regulation 17(2).

   (6)   A superseding decision made in consequence of a rent officer's redetermination, substitute determination, [⁶ substitute redetermination, board and attendance redetermination, substitute board and attendance determination, substitute board and attendance redetermination, amended broad rental market area determination or amended local housing allowance determination] under the Rent Officers (Housing Benefit Functions) Order 1997 or the Rent Officers (Housing Benefit Functions) (Scotland) Order 1997 shall take effect on the date on which a change of circumstances is to take effect in accordance with [¹⁸ regulation 79 of the Housing Benefit Regulations or, as the case may be, regulation 59 or 60 of the Housing Benefit (State Pension Credit) Regulations] as if that determination or redetermination were the relevant change of circumstances.

   [⁷ (6A)   Except in a case where entitlement to housing benefit ceases, where a rent officer has made a determination in exercise of the Housing Act functions pursuant to an application by a relevant authority under [¹⁰ regulation 14(1)(f) or (g) of the Housing Benefit Regulations or, as the case may be, regulation 14(1)(f) or (g) of the Housing Benefit (State Pension Credit) Regulations, any decision to which [¹² regulation 7A(3)] applies which adopts that determination shall take effect from–
   (a)   in a case where the amount of the rent officer's determination has increased or remains unchanged, and–
      (i)   rent is payable weekly or in multiples of weeks, the first day of the benefit week in which the day following the last day of the period mentioned in [¹⁰ regulation 14(1)(f) or (g) of the Housing Benefit Regulations or, as the case may be, regulation 14(1)(f) or (g) of the Housing Benefit (State Pension Credit) Regulations] occurs;
      (ii)   rent is payable other than in accordance with head (i), the first day following the last day of the period mentioned in [¹⁰ regulation 14(1)(f) or (g) of the Housing Benefit Regulations or, as the case may be, regulation 14(1)(f) or (g) of the Housing Benefit (State Pension Credit) Regulations];
   (b)   in a case where the amount of the rent officer's determination has decreased, the first day of the benefit week following the date on which that determination was received by a relevant authority;

   (6B)   For the purposes of paragraph (6A) "Housing Act functions" has the same meaning as in regulation 2(1) of the Housing Benefit Regulations [¹⁰ or, as the case may be, regulation 2(1) of the Housing Benefit (State Pension Credit) Regulations.].]

   (7)   Where a decision is made superseding a decision of [¹⁵ [¹⁹ an appeal tribunal, the First-tier Tribunal, the Upper Tribunal or of a Commissioner]] ("the appeal decision") which–
   (a)   was made in ignorance of, or was based upon a mistake as to, some material fact; and
   (b)   was more advantageous to the claimant than it would otherwise have been but for that ignorance or mistake,
that superseding decision shall take effect on the date on which the appeal decision took or was to take effect.

(8)   A superseding decision made as a consequence of a determination which is a relevant determination for the purposes of paragraph 18 of Schedule 7 to the Act (restrictions on entitlement to benefit in certain cases of error) shall take effect from the date of the relevant determination.

[¹(9)   A decision to which regulation 7(2)(g) or (h) applies shall take effect from the first day of the disqualification period prescribed for the purposes of section [¹⁶ 6B or] 7 of the Social Security Fraud Act 2001.]

[³ (10)   Where the decision is superseded in accordance with regulation 7(2)(a)(i) and the relevant circumstances are that there has been a change in the legislation in relation to housing benefit or council tax benefit, the superseding decision shall take effect from the date on which that change in the legislation had effect.

(11)   Where a superseding decision is made in a case to which regulation 7(2)(d)(ii) applies the superseding decision shall take effect from the date on which [¹⁹] [¹⁵ [¹⁹ the decision of the appeal tribunal, the First-tier Tribunal, the Upper Tribunal or the Commissioner]] [¹⁹] would have taken effect had it been decided in accordance with the determination of the [¹⁵ Upper Tribunal] [¹⁹, the Commissioner] or the court in the appeal referred to in paragraph 17(1)(b) of Schedule 7 to the Act.]

[⁸ [¹¹ (12)]]

[⁸ [¹¹ (13)]]

[⁵ (14)   Where the decision is superseded in accordance with regulation 7(2)(i) the superseding decision shall take effect from the date on which entitlement arises to the relevant benefit referred to in regulation 7(2)(i)(ii) or to an increase in the rate of that relevant benefit.]

[⁹ (14A)   Where a decision is superseded in accordance with regulation 7(2)(j), [²³ (ja) or (jb),] the superseding decision shall take effect from the day on which a lump sum, or a payment on account of a lump sum, is paid or repaid if that day is the first day of the benefit week but, if it is not, from the next following such day.]

[(14B)-(14C)   See Modifications below]

[¹⁴ (14D)   Where the decision is superseded in accordance with regulation 7(2)(o) [¹⁷ or (p)], the decision shall take effect from–

(a)   the first day of entitlement to an amount in consequence of the decision of the Secretary of State referred to in regulation 7(2)(o)(iii) [¹⁷ or (p)(iii)]; or

(b)   the first day that there would have been such entitlement had the claimant or the claimant's partner been entitled to an employment and support allowance by virtue of section 1 of the Welfare Reform Act,

if that day is the first day of the benefit week but, if it is not, from the next following such day.]

[¹⁷ (14E)   Where a decision is superseded in accordance with regulation 7(2)(q) the decision shall take effect–

(a)   where the decision made in accordance with the Employment and Support Allowance (Transitional Provisions, Housing Benefit and Council Tax Benefit) (Existing Awards) Regulations 2010 takes effect on or after 1st April in any year but before 16th April of that year–

(i)   from 1st April for a council tax benefit award;

(ii)   from 1st April for a housing benefit award in which the claimant's weekly amount of eligible rent falls to be calculated in accordance with regulation 80(2)(b) or (c) of the Housing Benefit Regulations or, as the case may be, regulation 61(2)(b) or (c) of the Housing Benefit (State Pension Credit) Regulations;

(iii)   from the first Monday in April for a housing benefit award to which sub-paragraph (a)(ii) does not apply;

(b)   in any other case, from the day the decision made in accordance with the Employment and Support Allowance (Transitional Provisions, Housing Benefit and Council Tax Benefit) (Existing Awards) Regulations 2010 takes effect.]

[²¹ (14F)   Where a decision is superseded in accordance with regulation 7(2)(r), the superseding decision shall take effect–

(a)   on the date the superseding decision is made where the decision results in the application of the benefit cap or an increase in a reduction; and

(b)   where the decision results in the benefit cap ceasing to apply or a decrease in a reduction, on the date from which the welfare benefit (within the meaning of [²⁴ section 96(10) of the Welfare Reform Act 2012 (benefit cap)]) is reduced.]

[²² (14G)   A superseding decision made in consequence of regulation 7(2)(s) shall take effect–

(a)   on 1st April in a case where–
    (i)   the claimant's weekly amount of eligible rent falls to be calculated in accordance with regulation 80(2)(b) or (c) of the Housing Benefit Regulations or, as the case may be, regulation 61(2)(b) or (c) of the Housing Benefit (State Pension Credit) Regulations; and
    (ii)   the decision to award personal independence payment takes effect in the same benefit week as the 1st April;

(b)   on the first Monday in April in a case where–
    (i)   the claimant's weekly amount of eligible rent falls to be calculated in accordance with regulation 80(2)(a) of the Housing Benefit Regulations or, as the case may be, regulation 61(2)(a) of the Housing Benefit (State Pension Credit) Regulations; and
    (ii)   the decision to award personal independence payment takes effect in the same benefit week as the first Monday in April;

(c)   in ay other case, on the day after the last day of entitlement to disability living allowance.]

[¹² [¹³ [²⁰ (15)   A decision to which regulation 7A(2) applies shall take effect–

(a)   from 1st April in a case where the claimant's weekly amount of eligible rent falls to be calculated in accordance with regulation 80(2)(b) or (c) of the Housing Benefit Regulations or, as the case may be, regulation 61(2)(b) or (c) of the Housing Benefit (State Pension Credit) Regulations; and

(b)   in any other case, from the first Monday in April.]]]

Modifications

Para (6A) amended and para (15) substituted by reg 4(4) Housing Benefit (Local Housing Allowance, Miscellaneous and Consequential) Amendment Regulations 2007 SI No.2870, as amended by reg 6(2)(b) of SI 2008 No.586, as from 7 April 2008, save that for a person to whom reg 1(3) of those regulations applied (see p1816), the amendments came into force on the day on or after 7 April 2008 when the first of the events specified in reg 1(4) applied to her/him, or on 6 April 2009 if none had before that date.

Reg 8 was modified in respect of people to whom the Housing Benefit (Loss of Benefit) (Pilot Scheme) (Supplementary) Regulations 2007 SI No.2474 applied. See pp1188–92 of the 22nd edition. Paras (14B) and (14C) were inserted. The modification applied until 31 October 2009.

Amendments

1.   Inserted by reg 9(c) of SI 2002 No 490 as from 1.4.02.
2.   Amended by reg 28(a) of SI 2003 No 325 as from 6.10.03.
3.   Inserted by reg 4(2) of SI 2003 No 1050 as from 5.5.03.
4.   Amended by reg 24(2) of SI 2003 No 1338 as from 6.10.03.
5.   Amended by reg 5(5) of SI 2003 No 2275 as from 6.10.03.
6.   Inserted by reg 16 of SI 2003 No 2399 as from a date specified in Sch 8 in relation to each particular authority.
7.   Inserted by reg 34(2) of SI 2004 No 14 as from 5.4.04.
8.   Revoked by reg 33 of SI 2004 No 14 as from 5.4.04.
9.   Inserted by Reg 10(4) of SI 2005 No 2677 as from 6.4.06.
10.   Amended by reg 5 and sch 2 para 17(3) of SI 2006 No 217 as from 6.3.06.
11.   Revoked by reg 8 of SI 2007 No 2470 as from 24.9.07.
12.   Amended by reg 4(4) of SI 2007 No 2870 as from 7.4.08 (or if reg 1(3) of that SI applies, on the day on or after 7.4.08 when the first of the events specified in reg 1(4) applies, or from 6.4.09 if none have before that date).
13.   Substituted by reg 6(2)(b) of SI 2008 No 286 as from 7.4.08.
14.   Inserted by reg 3(4) of SI 2008 No 1082, as substituted by reg 26 of SI 2008 No 2428, as from 27.10.08.
15.   Amended by Sch 1 para 154 of SI 2008 No 2683 as from 3.11.08.
16.   Amended by reg 9(4) of SI 2010 No 1160 as from 1.4.10.

17. Amended by reg 27 And Sch 5 para 3(3) of SI 2010 No 1907 as amended by reg 15 of SI 2010 No 2430 as from 1.10.10.
18. Amended by reg 6(2) of SI 2010 No 2449 as from 1.11.10.
19. Amended by reg 5(3) of SI 2012 No 1267 as from 4.6.12, but having effect from 3.11.08.
20. Substituted by reg 2 of SI 2012 No 3040 as from 1.1.13.
21. Inserted by reg 3(4) of SI 2012 No 2994 as from 15.4.13.
22. Inserted by reg 2(3) of SI 2014 No 213 as from 31.3.14.
23. Amended by art 20(4) of SI 2015 No 1985 as from 6.4.16.
24. Amended by reg 4 of SI 2016 No 909 as from 7.11.16.

Analysis

Paragraph (1): The general rule

Para (1) reflects the general rule as set out in Sch 7 para 4(5) CSPSSA, namely that a supersession takes effect on the date that the superseding decision was made or the date of the application, as the case may be. Exceptions to the general rule are found in paras (2) to (15).

Paragraphs (2), (3), (6) and (10): Changes of circumstances

Para (2) provides that superseding decisions made on the ground of change of circumstances generally take effect from the date on which the change falls to be taken into account under reg 79 HB Regs or regs 50 or 60 HB(SPC) Regs. See the commentary to those provisions. Similarly, under para (6), where a rent officer has made a redetermination or other altering decision, that will be treated as a change of circumstances and will have similar effect.

Where a change of circumstances is one which someone is required to report (other than one under the regulations listed), para (3) effectively sets a one-month time limit for reporting the change, if the resulting superseding decision is to the advantage of the claimant. Note that regs 68A HB Regs and reg 59A CTB Regs were revoked in September 2002 subject to savings and transitional protection. Note also that by reg 2(4) HB&CTB(CP) Regs, the references to reg 68B HB Regs and reg 59B CTB Regs should be read as reg 60 HB(SPC) Regs and reg 51 CTB(SPC) Regs.

If such a change is reported within one month, the decision takes effect in accordance with para (2). The day of the change will be excluded, so a change occurring on 25 May and notified on 25 June is notified within the time period. Where notification of a change is made more than a month after it occurs and the new decision is advantageous to the claimant, the date of notification is treated as the date the change occurred: para (3). In such a case, this will normally be less beneficial to the claimant. An "advantageous" decision includes where it falls within reg 17(2): see para (5). The one-month period can be extended under reg 9. Note also that it was held in *CIS 1277/2002* (paras 13–15) that "notified to an appropriate office" in reg 7(2)(a)(ii) SSCS D&A Regs could include a case where a different office of the DWP passed the information to the office dealing with the relevant claim as well as a case where the claimant made the notification. Since that provision is in different form to reg 8(2), it is open to argument as to whether that analysis can be applied here, although there is nothing explicit to prevent its application.

Para (10) provides that where the change of circumstances is that there has been a change in the legislation in relation to HB/CTB, the superseding decision takes effect from the date the change in legislation has effect. Note that art 3 Civil Partnership (Pensions, Social Security and Child Support) (Consequential, etc. Provisions) Order 2005 disapplied para (10) and provided transitional provisions for setting the effective date of a supersession for some claimants who were members of a couple who lived together as if they are civil partners on or after 5 December 2005, and had an award of HB or CTB on 5 December 2005.

For the possibility of carrying out a "closed period" supersession where there has been more than one change of circumstance with the consequence that the claimant ceased to be entitled to benefit for a fixed period but has regained entitlement before the date on which the superseding decision is taken, see p142.

Paragraph (4): Decisions based on incorrect facts and supersession advantageous to the claimant

In such a case, the superseding decision has effect from the first day of the benefit week in which an application for a supersession was received *or* the authority had the relevant information justifying the supersession before it.

An "advantageous" decision includes where it falls within reg 17(2): see para (5).

Paragraphs (6A) and (6B): Supersession where rent officer determination required

Paras (6A) and (6B) deal with supersessions made under reg 7A(3). Except where entitlement to HB ceases, where a rent officer has made a determination following a local authority application under reg 14(1)(f) or (g) of either the HB or the HB(SPC) Regs, a supersession decision which adopts that determination takes effect as follows:

(1) If the determination is the same or has increased and rent is payable weekly or in multiples of weeks, it takes effect from the first day of the benefit week which includes the day after the end of the period covered by the previous determinations: sub-para (a)(i).

(2) If the determination is the same or has increased and rent is payable at intervals of other than a week, it takes effect from the day after the end of the period covered by the previous determinations: sub-para (a)(ii).

(3)   If the determination has decreased, it takes effect from the first day of the week after the local authority receives it: sub-para (b).

Paragraph (7): Erroneous appeal decisions
If a First-tier Tribunal or Upper Tribunal decision (or a decision of an appeal tribunal or social security commissioner) was based on incorrect facts and was more advantageous to the claimant than it would otherwise have been, a decision superseding it takes effect from the date on which the appeal decision took (or was to take) effect.

Note that if an *authority's* decision was based on incorrect facts and was more advantageous to the claimant, it can be revised at any time under reg 4(2)(b), taking effect from the date of the original decision: reg 6.

Paragraph (8): Supersession following a "test case"
If a decision is being superseded because of a decision by the Upper Tribunal or a court in a "test case" (a relevant determination for the purposes of Sch 7 para 18 CSPSSA), the supersession is effective from the date of the Upper Tribunal's or court's decision.

Paragraph (9): Supersession where decision affected by "loss of benefit" provisions
Where a decision is affected by a DWP decision stopping or restricting benefit and is superseded under reg 7(2)(g) or (h), the supersession is effective from the first day of the disqualification period.

Paragraph (11): Supersession where decision made pending a "test case"
The ground for supersession in reg 7(2)(d)(ii) is not currently relevant for the reasons stated in the commentary on p955.

Paragraph (14): Supersession on entitlement to a "relevant benefit" or an increase in its rate
Where a decision is superseded under reg 7(2)(i), the superseding decision has effect from the date of entitlement to the relevant benefit or the increase in its rate.

Paragraph (14A): Supersession on opting for or repaying a lump sum on deferring claiming pension
Where a decision is superseded under reg 7(2)(j), the superseding decision has effect from the day on which a lump sum (or a payment on account of a lump sum) is paid or repaid if that day is the first day of the benefit week. If not, it takes effect from the first day of the following benefit week.

Paragraph (14D): Supersession where ESA component included or changed
Where a decision is superseded under reg 7(2)(o) or (p), the superseding decision takes effect from the first date of entitlement to an ESA componenet (or to a different ESA component), or the first day there would have been such entitlement had the claimant or her/his partner been entitled to ESA (eg, where the claimant or partner is entitled to NI credits only).

Paragraph (14E): Supersession where an award of benefit is converted to ESA, or an appeal is made against a decision not to convert a benefit to ESA
Where a decision is superseded under reg 7(2)(q), the superseding decision normally takes effect from the date the DWP decision on ESA takes effect. However, if the DWP decision is made between 31 March and 16 April in any year, for HB the superseding decision takes effect from the first Monday in April, or if rent is payable calendar monthly or daily (or in multiples thereof), on 1 April.

Paragraph (14F): Supersession of benefit cap decisions
Where a decision is superseded under reg 7(2)(r), the effective date of the superseding decision depends on whether its effect is to apply the benefit cap (or increase the amount by which HB is reduced under the benefit cap) or to cease to apply the benefit cap (or decrease the amount by which HB is reduced). In the former case, the superseding decision takes effect on the day on which it is made. In the latter, it takes effect from the date that the claimant's total amount of welfare benefits (and therefore the amount by which the total amount of welfare benefits exceeds the benefit cap relevant amount:see reg 75D) reduced.

Paragraph (14G): Supersession where DLA claimant becomes entitled to personal independence payment
Where the claimant, or a member of the claimant's family, who was entitled to DLA is transferred to PIP under the Personal Independence Payment (Transitional Provisions) Regulations 2013, a decision awarding HB may be superseded under reg 7(2)(s). If that change occurs at the same time as an increase in rent or as the annual uprating of benefits, the technical rules about when changes in circumstances take effect can lead to claimants losing entitlement to the HB premiums that are linked to DLA entitlement for a short period. Para (14G) is intended to ensure that entitlement to those premiums is continuous.

Effective date for late notification of change of circumstances

9.–(1)   For the purposes of making a decision under paragraph 4 of Schedule 7 to the Act a longer period of time may be allowed for the notification of a change of circumstances in so far as it affects the effective date of the change where the conditions specified in the following provisions of this regulation are satisfied.

(2)   An application for the purposes of paragraph (1) shall–

(a)   include particulars of the change of circumstances and the reasons for the failure to notify the change of circumstances on an earlier date; and

(b)   be made within 13 months of the date on which the change occurred.

(3)   An application for the purposes of paragraph (1) shall not be granted unless the appropriate relevant authority is satisfied that–

(a)   it is reasonable to grant the application;

(b)   the change of circumstances notified by the applicant is relevant to the decision which is to be superseded; and

(c)   special circumstances are relevant and as a result of those special circumstances it was not practicable for the applicant to notify the change of circumstances within one month of the change occurring.

(4)   In determining whether it is reasonable to grant the application, the appropriate relevant authority shall have regard to the principle that the greater the amount of time that has elapsed between the date one month after the change of circumstances occurred and the date the application for a superseding decision is made, the more compelling should be the special circumstances on which the application is based.

(5)   In determining whether it is reasonable to grant an application, no account shall be taken of the following–

(a)   that the applicant was unaware of, or misunderstood, the law applicable to his case (including ignorance or misunderstanding of the time limits imposed by these Regulations); or

(b)   that [¹ the Upper Tribunal] or a court has taken a different view of the law from that previously understood and applied.

(6)   An application under this regulation which has been refused may not be renewed.

Amendment

1.   Amended by Sch 1 para 155 of SI 2008 No 2683 as from 3.11.08.

Analysis

Reg 9 deals with the circumstances in which a notification of a change of circumstances made more than one month after it occurs may nonetheless be treated as if made in time. In this situation a superseding decision takes effect as set out in reg 8(2) rather than in reg 8(3), to the advantage of the claimant. The structure of reg 9 is similar to that of reg 5.

Para (2) deals with applications for an extension of time to report a change of circumstances and is similar to reg 5(3), save that the operative decision need not be identified and there is no provision for the place at which disclosure must be made (which is dealt with by reg 88 HB Regs and reg 69 HB(SPC) Regs). An application must be made within 13 months of the date the change of circumstances occurred.

Para (3) is similar to reg 5(4), save that there is no need for the application to have merit – instead, the change of circumstances must be relevant. Practicability "involves a test of feasibility, not a test of desirability or convenience or anything of that sort": *CH 282/2006* applying *Singh v Post Office* [1973] ICR 437 at 440. Moreover, as the impracticability must result from the special circumstances, those circumstances must in some way relate to or affect the practicability of reporting the change of time within one month.

Paras (4), (5) and (6) are comparable to paras (6), (5) and (7) of reg 5 respectively.

Notice of a decision against which an appeal lies

10.–(1)   A person affected who has a right of appeal against a relevant decision shall be given written notice–

(a)   of the decision against which the appeal lies;

(b)   in a case where that notice does not include a statement of reasons for the decision, that he may [¹ , within one month of the date of notification of that decision (or, if the decision was notified before 1st November 2010, before 1st December 2010),] request the relevant authority to provide him with a written statement of the reasons for that decision; and

(c)   of his right of appeal against that decision.

(2)   Where a written statement of the reasons for the decision is not included in the written notice of the decision and is requested under paragraph (1)(b), the relevant authority shall, so far as practicable, provide that statement within 14 days.

Amendment

1.   Amended by reg 6(3) of SI 2010 No 2449 as from 1.11.10.

Definition

"person affected" – see reg 3.

Analysis

If there is a right of appeal against a decision, written notice of it must be given of it to a person affected by the decision. It must contain information as specified in paras (b) and (c). "Person affected" is defined in reg 3. The obligation in reg 10(1) is additional to those set out in Sch 9 HB Regs and Sch 8 HB(SPC) Regs.

If a request for a written statement of reasons is made (where not already provided), the local authority must provide one within 14 days if this is practicable. The onus to provide a statement of reasons within 14 days if "practicable" is a heavy one. Days between the date a request is received by the authority and the date on which it is provided are ignored when calculating the one-month time limits for seeking a revision and appealing: see commentary to reg 4(4) on p946. Since 1 November 2010, any request for a statement of reasons for a decision must be made within a month of the date on which the decision was notified or, if the decision was made before 1 November 2010, by 1 December 2010. The effect, taken together with the changes to Sch 1 TP(FT) Rules, is to close the loophole by which it was possible to circumvent the 13-month time limit for appealing (see p994 and p1039 of the 22nd edition).

[¹ Correction of accidental errors

10A.–(1)   Accidental errors in a relevant decision, or a revised decision, or the record of such a decision, may be corrected by the relevant authority at any time.

(2)   A correction made to a relevant decision, or a revised decision, or the record of such a decision, shall be deemed to be part of the decision, or of that record, and the relevant authority shall give a written notice of the correction as soon as practicable to the claimant.

(3)   In calculating the time within which an application can be made under regulation 4(1)(a) for a relevant decision to be revised [²] there shall be disregarded any day falling before the day on which notice was given of a correction of the decision or to the revision or record thereof under paragraph (2).

Definition

"relevant decision" – see reg 1(2) above and Sch 7 para 19(2) CSPSSA.

Amendments

1.   Inserted by reg 25 of SI 2002 No 1379 as from 20.5.02.
2.   Amended by Sch 1 para 156 of SI 2008 No 2683 as from 3.11.08.

General Note

Accidental errors in decisions can be corrected under reg 10A. Written notice of the correction must be given to the claimant as soon as it is practicable. In calculating the time limit for seeking a revision under reg 4(1)(a), days before the day on which notice is given of the correction must be ignored.

PART III

Suspension and Termination of Benefit and Other Matters

Cases where a relevant authority may suspend

11.–(1)   A relevant authority may suspend, in whole or in part–

(a)   any payment of housing benefit or council tax benefit;

(b)   any reduction (by way of council tax benefit) in the amount that a person is or will become liable to pay in respect of council tax,

in the circumstances prescribed in paragraph (2).

(2)   The prescribed circumstances are where–

(a)   it appears to the relevant authority that an issue arises whether–

    (i)   the conditions for entitlement to housing benefit or council tax benefit are or were fulfilled; or

    (ii)   a decision as to an award of such a benefit should be revised under paragraph 3 of Schedule 7 to the Act or superseded under paragraph 4 of that Schedule;

(b)   an appeal is pending against–

    (i)   a decision of [² the First-tier Tribunal, the Upper Tribunal] or a court; or

    (ii)   a decision given by [² the Upper Tribunal] or a court in a different case,

and it appears to the relevant authority that if the appeal were to be determined in a particular way an issue would arise whether the award of housing benefit or council tax benefit in the case itself ought to be revised or superseded; or

(c)   an issue arises whether–
>   (i)   an amount of housing benefit is recoverable under section 75 (overpayments) of the Administration Act or regulations made under that section; or
>   (ii)   an excess payment of council tax benefit under section 76 of the Administration Act or regulations made under that section has occurred.

[¹ (3)   For the purposes of paragraph 13(3)(c) of Schedule 7 to the Act the prescribed circumstances are that a decision of an appeal tribunal, a Commissioner or a court has been made and the relevant authority–
>   (a)   is waiting to receive that decision, or in the case of an appeal tribunal decision, is considering whether to apply for a statement of reasons for it, or has applied for such a statement and is waiting to receive it; or
>   (b)   has received that decision or, in the case of an appeal tribunal decision, the statement of reasons for it, and is considering whether to apply for leave to appeal, or where leave to appeal has been granted, is considering whether to appeal,

and the relevant authority shall as soon as reasonably practicable give written notice of its intention to apply for a statement of the reasons for a tribunal decision, to apply for leave to appeal, or to appeal.]

Amendments

1.   Inserted by reg 4(2) of SI 2008 No 2667 as from 30.10.08.
2.   Amended by Sch 1 para 157 of SI 2008 No 2683 as from 3.11.08.

General Note

Reg 11 is made under Sch 7 para 13 CSPSSA (see p152). Reg 12 sets out the situations in which a suspension must be lifted.

Analysis

Para (1) specifies that the power to suspend may be exercised in the whole amount of the benefit payable or only part thereof. Payments of HB (whether or not made to the claimant) may be suspended.

Suspension is discretionary, and the discretion must be exercised reasonably even if one of the specified circumstances exists. Thus if, for example, an issue arises as to whether a few hundred pounds of benefit was overpaid and the claimant has capital of that sum, it might not be reasonable for the authority to suspend ongoing entitlement to benefit under para (2)(c) if it could readily be recovered. However, as there is no right of appeal against a decision to suspend (see Schedule para 5) the claimant's only remedy against an unreasonable suspension is judicial review. It is often quicker, easier and less expensive to seek to provide the authority with the information and evidence it needs to resolve the question that has arisen.

Para (2) specifies the circumstances in which a suspension can be made. There is a degree of overlap between the provisions.

(1)   There may be a suspension where current or past entitlement is in issue, or when a revision or supersession is being considered: sub-para (a). It need not be clear that an existing decision was incorrect; all that is required is that "an issue arises" through a reasonable doubt existing as to the correctness of a decision. The power to suspend where an issue arises cannot be used merely to check the accuracy of an existing award where there are no particular grounds for doubting that it is correct. In *CH 2995/2006*, the commissioner stated:

>   "26.   The second of the two situations I mentioned earlier as the ones that I presume were envisaged by Parliament is where a local authority has no particular doubt, or only a weak doubt, about the claimant's entitlement to ... benefit but, as a matter of good administration, wishes the claimant to provide information and evidence in order, in effect, to update the information and evidence provided on the original claim and check its accuracy. Parliament seems to have expected that there would be no suspension of payment while that information was awaited but, if it was not forthcoming within the time allowed, there would be a suspension and, if the information was still not forthcoming, there would eventually be a termination of entitlement".

(2)   Pending appeals may give rise to a suspension under sub-para (b).

The appeals referred to in head (i) must, by implication, be appeals involving the claimant whose benefit is to be suspended. Note that the appeal must be pending: see Sch 7 para 13(3) CSPSSA on p152 for the extended definition of "pending". It includes cases where an application for permission to appeal has been lodged or where the time limit for applying for permission or lodging an appeal has not expired. It does not, however, appear to extend to a situation where a statement of reasons has been requested under reg 53 SSCS D&A Regs, though it may be arguable that sub-para (a)(i) can apply in such a situation. It would not be reasonable to continue a suspension where a decision had been taken by an authority not to pursue an appeal.

Under head (ii), appeals in other cases may also result in a suspension. However, this power only applies to an appeal *from* the Upper Tribunal or a court. It does not, therefore, apply where an appeal is pending *to* the Upper Tribunal. For discussion of "different case", see Sch 7 para 13(4) CSPSSA and the commentary on p152.

(3) Suspected overpayments may also give rise to a right to suspend: sub-para (c). Again, "an issue arises" means it need not be clear that an overpayment has occurred. All that is necessary is reasonable grounds to suspect that too much benefit has been paid.

Making or restoring of payments or reductions suspended

12.–(1)   Subject to paragraph (2), the prescribed circumstances for the purposes of paragraph 13(1)(c) of Schedule 7 to the Act (the subsequent making, or restoring, of any or all of the payments or reductions so suspended) are–

(a)   in a case to which regulation 11(2)(a) applies, where the relevant authority is satisfied that the benefit so suspended is properly payable and no outstanding issues remain to be resolved;

(b)   in a case to which regulation 11(2)(b) applies, an appeal is no longer pending and the benefit suspended remains payable following the determination of that appeal.

(2)   Where any of the circumstances in paragraph (1) is satisfied, the relevant authority shall, so far as practicable, make the payment, or as the case may be, restore the reduction within 14 days of the decision to make or restore that payment or reduction.

Analysis

Reg 12 deals with the circumstances in which a suspension must be lifted under Sch 7 para 13(1)(c) CSPSSA. It is not well drafted.

Para (1) sub-para (a) requires that accrued arrears be paid where any issues referred to in reg 11(2)(a) have been resolved. Note that there must be "no outstanding issues" and so if an authority has been satisfied that its initial concerns had no basis but further issues have arisen as a result of its inquiries, the suspension can remain in force.

Sub-para (b) deals with suspension pending appeals. For the question of when an appeal is "pending", see Sch 7 para 13(3) CSPSSA on p152 and reg 11(2)(b) above. The phrase "determination of that appeal" is inapt in the context of a suspension having been imposed during the period when the time limit for applying for permission or appealing has yet to expire but no application for permission has actually been made. In that situation, it is suggested that the "determination" of the appeal occurs once a final decision is taken not to pursue an appeal.

Para (2) requires an authority to make good a suspension which is brought to an end under para (1). Curiously, there is no specific provision governing suspensions under reg 11(2)(c) for suspected overpayments. However, if a suspension is revoked, it is suggested that the ordinary provisions as to payment in the HB and HB(SPC) Regs would then become enforceable by a claimant by way of a debt action or a claim for judicial review.

Suspension for failure to furnish information etc.

13.–(1)   The relevant authority may suspend in whole or in part–

(a)   any payment of housing benefit or council tax benefit;

(b)   any reduction (by way of council tax benefit) in the amount that a person is or will become liable to pay in respect of council tax,

in relation to persons who fail to comply with the information requirements (as defined in paragraph 14 of Schedule 7 to the Act) as provided for in regulations made pursuant to section 5(1)(hh) and 6(1)(hh) of the Administration Act (person required to satisfy the information provisions).

(2)   For the purposes of section 5(1)(hh) in so far as it applies to housing benefit and section 6(1)(hh) of the Administration Act the prescribed persons are–

(a)   a person in respect of whom payment of benefit or a reduction has been suspended under regulation 11(2)(a);

(b)   a person who has made an application for a decision of the relevant authority to be revised or superseded;

(c)   a person in respect of whom a question has arisen in connection with his award of benefit and who fails to comply with the requirement in [¹ regulation 86 of the Housing Benefit Regulations, regulation 67 of the Housing Benefit (State

Pension Credit) Regulations, regulation 72 of the Council Tax Benefit Regulations or regulation 57 of the Council Tax Benefit (State Pension Credit) Regulations] to furnish information or evidence needed for a determination whether a decision on an award should be revised under paragraph 3 or superseded under paragraph 4 of Schedule 7 to the Act.

(3)   The relevant authority shall notify any person to whom paragraph (2) refers of the requirements of this regulation.

(4)   A person to whom paragraph (2) refers must–

(a)   furnish the information or evidence needed within a period of–

    (i)   one month beginning with the date on which the notification under paragraph (3) was sent to him; or

    (ii)   such longer period as the relevant authority considers necessary in order to enable him to comply with the requirement; or

(b)   satisfy the relevant authority within the period provided for in paragraph (4)(a) that–

    (i)   the information or evidence so required does not exist; or

    (ii)   it is not possible for him to obtain the information or evidence so required.

(5)   Where a person satisfies the requirements in paragraph (4), the relevant authority shall, so far as practicable, make, or as the case may be restore, the payment within 14 days of the decision to make or restore that payment.

Amendment

1.   Amended by reg 5 and Sch 2 para 17(3) of SI 2006 No 217 as from 6.3.06.

Analysis

Reg 13 provides a power to suspend which is additional to those set out in reg 11. It deals with cases in which a person is required to provide information to an authority. The relationship between regs 11 and 13 was explained by Commissioner Rowland in *CH 2995/2006* as follows:

"21.   The 2001 Regulations make adequate, albeit complicated, provision for the ... [situation]...where a local authority considers that there may be a question as to the claimant's continued entitlement to benefit and perhaps also as to his or her entitlement in the past. In those circumstances, payments may be suspended under reg 11(1) and (2)(a) while investigations are carried out. When the investigations have been concluded, the local authority must either restore the payments under regulation 12 or else revise or supersede the decision awarding benefit. If, as part of the investigation, the local authority asks the claimant for further information or evidence, the case falls within regulation 13(2)(a) and the claimant must be given the notice required by regulation 13(3) and in particular must be informed of the time within which the information must be provided under regulation 13(4)(a). If the claimant then fails to provide the information within the time allowed under regulation 13(4)(a), the local authority may, instead of restoring the payments or revising or superseding the award on any other ground, terminate the award under regulation 14 with effect from the date of the suspension under regulation 11(1) and (2)(a)."

The commissioner also notes (at para 24) that paras (2) to (4) "apply where there has been a suspension under reg 11(1) and (2)(a) just as much as where there has been a suspension under regulation 13(1)".

Paras (1) and (2) set out the situation in which the power to suspend may be exercised. The two provisions in the SSAA referred to give power to require information during the currency of a claim. The extended versions of reg 86(1) HB Regs, reg 67(1) HB(SPC) Regs, reg 72(1) CTB Regs and reg 57(1) CTB(SPC) Regs are made under ss5(1)(hh) and 6(1)(hh) SSAA respectively.

In order for a suspension to be lawful, the authority must show that the person of whom information is required falls into one of the categories in para (2).

In *AA v Hounslow LB* [2008] UKUT 13 (AAC), the judge decided that the requirement to supply information (eg, under reg 86 HB Regs) must actually have been communicated to the person in question; proof of posting to the last known address is not sufficient.

There cannot be any suspension under para (1) until there has been at least one failure to comply with a request for information (although suspension may still be possible under reg 11). However, the suggestion in the 21st edition that para 2(c) might require a failure to comply with two requests is wrong for the reasons given by Deputy Judge Ovey in *AA v Leicester City Council* [2009] UKUT 86 (AAC). Note that a refusal to allow a home visit does not amount to a failure to comply with an information requirement (see *CH 2995/2006* (para 35)) although in some circumstances, it might give rise to a question about entitlement that would justify suspension under reg 11. The same would, presumably, be true of a failure to attend an interview under caution.

Paras (3) to (5) deal with the procedure for operating the regulation. The first step is for the authority to give the person notice under para (3) of "the requirements of this regulation". Failure to do so invalidates any subsequent termination: *AA v Hounslow LB* [2008] UKUT 13 (AAC) and *VW v London Borough of Hackney (HB)* [2014] UKUT 277 (AAC) at para 5. Those requirements are set out in para (4) and are as follows.

(1)   **The information or evidence that is needed**. It is suggested that the information or evidence required by the authority must be specified in sufficient detail for the person to know what is required and for it to be possible to demonstrate whether or not the requirement has been complied with for the purposes of reg 14. For example, telling the person to telephone the benefits office is not, in itself, a request for information or evidence.

(2)   **The time limit for the provision of the evidence**. The clamant must be given a "firm deadline" for the provision of the information (*CH 2995/2006* para 43) and that deadline must be at least one month after the date on which the notification is sent (para (4)(a)). Despite the fact that the one-month time limit is explicitly set out in the regulations, many local authorities purport to impose shorter periods in practice. Time limits of seven and 14 days that have no basis in law and appear to have been plucked from the air by optimistic benefit officers – or, more probably, by the companies responsible for their computer software – are particularly common. As Upper Tribunal Judge Wikeley stated in *SS v North East Lincolnshire Council (HB)* [2011] UKUT 300 (AAC) (at para 21): "the one month time limit is mandatory under regulation 13(4)(a) – it cannot simply be abridged at the whim of the local authority...A failure to provide a one month time limit will necessarily invalidate any subsequent termination of benefit under regulation 14."

The notice should also advise the person of the possibility of applying for an extension of time under para (4)(a)(ii) if s/he needs longer than a month in which to comply with the requirement: see *SS v North East Lincolnshire Council (HB)* (at para 21) and *VW v London Borough of Hackney (HB)* (at para 5).

(3)   **Evidence that does not exist or cannot be obtained**. As an alternative to providing the information within the one-month (or longer) time limit, the person may instead seek to persuade the authority that that information does not exist or that it is not possible for her/him to obtain it. The standard-form notices issued by many authorities fail to mention this alternative and the deputy judge in *AA v Leicester City Council* [2009] UKUT 86 (AAC) held (at paras 54–56) that the failure invalidated the subsequent termination. That consequence has subsequently confirmed in *VW v Hackney LB (HB)* (at para 5).

Alternatively, it could be argued that a person who does not provide information that does not exist, or that s/he cannot obtain, does not "fail" to comply with an information requirement for the purposes of reg 14(1) but merely omits to comply with that requirement. The word "failure" carries connotations of breach of duty (see, for example, *B v SSWP* [2005] EWCA Civ 929, [2005] 1 WLR 3796; reported as *R(IS) 9/06*) and tribunals should be slow to find that a person is under a duty to perform the impossible.

Unfortunately, it is not all that uncommon to find authorities purporting to impose information requirements with which claimants obviously cannot comply: an example is demanding that a claimant who has just started work and is paid monthly should produce her/his "three most recent pay slips" within a month.

Para (3) does not require an authority to tell the person that her/his entitlement to benefit may be terminated under reg 14 if the information requirement is not satisfied. However, it is good practice to do so. By definition, the person's benefit has already been suspended (which a claimant is likely to see as "stopped"). S/he may therefore not understand the serious consequences of failing to comply unless these are explained. In those circumstances, it is in the authority's interests as well as the claimant's to give the explanation: a claimant who understands the nature of the penalty for non-compliance is more likely to comply.

In *CH 2995/2006*, the commissioner left open the possibility that some failures to comply with para (3) might not be fatal to a subsequent termination (para 43). However, it is suggested that that possibility has since been closed by the decisions in *AA v Hounslow LB*, *SS v North East Lincolnshire Council*, *AA v Leicester City Council* and *VW v Hackney LB*. That is unsurprising. As the commissioner in *CH 2995/2006* acknowledged, reg 14 imposes a procedural penalty for failing to provide information on a person who may well be otherwise entitled to benefit. In general terms, all para (3) requires is that, before such a penalty is imposed, the authority must tell the person in sufficient detail what s/he has to do and when s/he has to do it by. It is very difficult to imagine cases in which it would be just to impose a penalty where that information had not been given.

Under para (5), once the person has satisfied the requirements of para (4), the suspension imposed under reg 13 must be lifted.

Termination in cases of a failure to furnish information

14.–(1)   A person in respect of whom payment of benefit or a reduction has been suspended–

(a)   under regulation 11 and who subsequently fails to comply with an information requirement; or

(b)   under regulation 13 for failing to comply with such a requirement,

shall cease to be entitled to the benefit from the date on which the payments or reduction were so suspended, or such earlier date on which entitlement to benefit ceases.

(2)   Paragraph (1) does not apply–

[¹ (a) subject to sub-paragraph (b), before the end of the period under regulation 13(4) for the provision of information;]

(b) where payment of benefit or a reduction has been suspended in part under regulation 11 or regulation 13.

Amendment

1. Substituted by reg 4 of SI 2005 No 2894 as from 10.11.05.

Analysis

Under reg 14, a claimant ceases to be entitled to benefit if, following suspension under regs 11 or 13, s/he fails to comply with a request for information.

There must be a failure to comply with "an information requirement". To be an information requirement for these purposes, the request must be for documents which are reasonably required by the local authority to determine the claimant's continuing entitlement to benefit: *R(H) 1/09*. Further, if a document which is the subject of an information requirement does not exist at the time that the information requirement is notified to the claimant an omission to produce it is not a "failure" for the purposes of reg 14. There is no power to terminate an award under reg 14 for failure to provide evidence or information relating to the method by which HB is to be paid (ie, as opposed to whether the conditions of entitlement are satisfied): see *CH v Plymouth City Council and DE (HB)* [2018] UKUT 215 (AAC).

Decisions made by virtue of reg 14 are "decisions superseding earlier decisions" within Sch 7 para 4 CSPSSA: *R(H) 4/08*. It follows that they can be revised under Sch 7 para 3 CSPSSA and that they carry a right of appeal to a tribunal: *R(H) 4/08* and *CH 2995/2006*. That right is expressly preserved by para 5 of the Schedule to these regulations. Given the decision of the ECtHR in *Tsfayo v United Kingdom* (2009) 48 EHRR 18, any other arrangement would be an infringement of the claimant's Convention Rights.

It also follows that any person affected by the decision to terminate must be properly notified of that decision and of her/his right to appeal against it. In the absence of such a notification, the time for bringing an appeal will not normally begin to run.

The view expressed in previous editions that termination is "a third mechanism for altering decisions to add to revision and supersession" is wrong: *CH 2995/2006* (para 22). So is the DWP advice in Circular HB/CTB A2/2006 that "decisions given under Regulations 11–14 of the HB/CTB Decision and Appeals Regulations are made outside the normal revision/supersession rules" and instead are "administrative decisions" that do not carry a right of appeal: *R(H) 4/08* (in particular para 24). The word "termination" (which only appears in the heading to reg 14, and not in the operative words) describes the *outcome* of the process established by regs 11, 13 and 14 and not the process itself.

The scope of the appeal against a decision under reg 14 is less clear. It is certainly open to the claimant to argue that s/he did not "cease to be entitled to benefit" because the original decision to suspend was invalid, or because mandatory procedural requirements (particularly in reg 13) have not been observed, or because s/he did not in fact fail to comply with an information requirement. It is suggested, however, that where a claimant accepts (or the tribunal finds) that that the procedure in regs 11–14 was validly operated, and that the claimant did not produce the necessary information and evidence at the time, the tribunal has no power to reinstate benefit on the basis that, by the time of the appeal hearing, the necessary information and evidence has been supplied. This is because, whatever might have been the case if the claimant had produced the information or evidence on time, the fact that s/he did not do so caused her/his entitlement to cease from the date on which payments were suspended. The position is therefore different from an appeal against a decision where the authority does not rely on the Part III procedure, but instead draws an adverse inference against the claimant and supersedes on the basis that entitlement has ended on substantive, rather than procedural, grounds: *CH 3736/2006* (para 27).

As decisions under reg 14 are superseding decisions, and the First-tier Tribunal has power to perfect superseding decisions on appeal (see *R(IB) 2/04*), it is open to a tribunal to decide that, even though the decision to terminate is ineffective, the decision awarding HB falls to be superseded on other grounds: *VW v London Borough of Hackney (HB)* [2014] UKUT 277 (AAC) (at para 10). The tribunal would need to ensure that the claimant had sufficient notice that other grounds for supersession would be considered and, unless it could be said that the issue was one that was raised by the appeal, the tribunal would have to consciously consider whether to exercise its discretion under Sch 7 para 6(9)(a) CSPSSA to consider the issue: see further the commentary to para 6(9)(a).

It is suggested that the only remedy open to a claimant whose entitlement has been validly terminated under reg 14 but who is subsequently in a position to provide the information and evidence requested, is to ask the authority to extend time for the production of that information and evidence under reg 13(4)(a)(ii) and then to revise the termination decision. A refusal to revise the termination decision may, in some circumstances, give rise to a technical right of appeal against that decision but that right may be of little practical value because the tribunal has no jurisdiction to interfere with the authority's refusal to extend time under reg 13: see Sch para 5 on p981.

Para (1). Termination can take place in two circumstances. First, there are cases where there has been a suspension under reg 11 and then a failure to comply with a requirement to supply information: see the definition of "information requirement" in Sch 7 para 14(3) CSPSSA on p153. The latter must have taken place "subsequently". If a reg 11 suspension is imposed as a result of a failure to provide information (when reg 13 could have been used instead), then a further chance would have to be given to the claimant before reg 14 can operate.

Secondly, there are cases where a requirement imposed by reg 13 is not complied with.

It is important for authorities to ensure (and, on appeal, for tribunals to satisfy themselves) that all the procedural safeguards (particularly in reg 13(3)) have been complied with. A failure to give a valid notice under reg 13(3) will almost always be fatal to a termination under reg 14. In particular, the claimant must be given a "firm deadline" by which to provide the evidence and information: *CH 2995/2006* (paras 43 and 44). See further the commentary to reg 13 on p968.

CH 2995/2006 also confirms (para 41) that termination under reg 14 cannot be effective from any date before the date on which the decision to suspend was made. Para (1) appears to allow the possibility that termination might take effect from "such earlier date on which entitlement to benefit ceases" but those words are either meaningless or *ultra vires*. From a formal point of view, the provision is circular: stripped of irrelevant words it states that: "A person ... shall cease to be entitled to the benefit ... from such earlier date on which entitlement to benefit ceases". That proposition conveys no useful information whatsoever. Secondly, if entitlement to benefit ceases from some "earlier date" then that can only be because there are substantive grounds on which to revise or supersede the decision awarding benefit with effect from that earlier date. An authority that had such grounds would not need to rely upon reg 14 in the first place. Finally, reg 14 is made under para 15 Sch 7 CSPSSA, which only empowers the Secretary of State to make regulations that bring entitlement to HB to an end "not earlier than the date on which payments were suspended". It follows that, if reg 14 did permit a termination from an earlier date, it would be *ultra vires*: *CH 3736/2006* (para 27). At best, the words "or such earlier date on which entitlement to benefit ceases" should be interpreted as confirming that the possibility of a termination under reg 14 does not prevent an authority from making a substantive revision or supersession with effect from an earlier date where there are grounds upon which to do so.

An example demonstrates this. Benefit is awarded on 1 February, but on 1 June a question arises about the award, a reg 11 suspension is imposed and the claimant is required to supply information. By 1 September, the claimant has failed to comply with the information requirement. Entitlement can be terminated from 1 June, but in order to deprive the claimant of the award from any earlier date, grounds for revision or supersession must be shown. In other words, it is not possible for a decision under reg 14 to give rise to an overpayment of HB.

Para (2) prevents termination of an award in two situations: where the suspension was only partial: sub-para (b), and before the end of the period specified in reg 13(4) for the provision of information: sub-para (a). Although an authority is not obliged to accept information late, it is suggested that it will rarely, if ever, be appropriate for an authority to proceed to terminate entitlement in circumstances in which the information requirement is complied with a few days late. This will be a trap for many authorities which were prone to reject or 'cancel' claims automatically if a claimant was even one day late with supplying information.

Decisions involving issues that arise on appeal in other cases

15.–(1)   For the purposes of paragraph 16(3)(b) of Schedule 7 to the Act (prescribed cases and circumstances in which a decision may be made) the prescribed cases and circumstances are those in which the claimant would be entitled to benefit to which the decision which falls to be made relates, even if the appeal in the other case referred to in paragraph 16(1)(b) of that Schedule were decided in the way which is most unfavourable to him.

(2)   For the purposes of paragraph 16(3)(b) of Schedule 7 to the Act (prescribed basis) the prescribed basis on which the relevant authority may make a decision is as if–

(a)   the appeal in the other case referred to in paragraph 16(1)(b) of that Schedule 7 had already been determined; and

(b)   the appeal had been decided in the way which is most unfavourable to the claimant.

Analysis

Sch 7 para 16 CSPSSA generally excuses an authority from making a decision where there is an appeal pending in a test case. Sch 7 para 16(3) gives a discretion to issue a decision where regulations so prescribe. Reg 15 exercises that power. If it chooses to issue a decision, the authority must make its decision on the assumption that the appeal is decided in the way most unfavourable to the claimant: para (2)(b).

The discretion conferred by Sch 7 para 16(3) and reg 15 must be exercised reasonably. Where it is clear that the claimant is entitled to a substantial award of HB whatever the outcome of the appeal, it would not be reasonable to refuse to make a decision. Persons affected will, however, have to ensure that they then appeal against the authority's decision in order to protect their interests.

PART IV
Rights of Appeal and Procedure for Bringing Appeals

Decisions against which no appeal lies

16.–(1)   No appeal shall lie against a decision specified in the Schedule to these Regulations.

[¹ (2)]

(3)   In this regulation references to a decision include references to a determination embodied in or necessary to a decision.

Amendment

1.   Amended by Sch 1 para 158 of SI 2008 No 2683 as from 3.11.08.

Analysis

See p980 for those decisions which are excluded from the appeal regime. All other decisions may be appealed, but note that an appeal may only lie against an "outcome decision": see the commentary to Sch 7 para 6(1) CSPSSA on p145. Reg 16(3) reflects the distinction between decisions and determinations referred to in that commentary. The effect of para (3) is to confirm that it is not possible to appeal against a determination embodied in a decision which falls within the Schedule.

Appeal against a decision which has been revised

17.–(1)   An appeal against a decision of the relevant authority shall not lapse where the decision is revised under paragraph 3 of Schedule 7 to the Act before the appeal is determined and the decision as revised is not more advantageous to the appellant than the decision before it was so revised.

(2)   For the purposes of this regulation, a decision which is more advantageous includes any decision where–

(a)   any housing benefit or council tax benefit paid or any reduction in the amount that a person is liable to pay in respect of council tax is greater or is awarded for a longer period in consequence of a decision made under paragraph 3 of Schedule 7 to the Act;

(b)   the amount of housing benefit or council tax benefit in payment or reduction in the amount a person is liable to pay in respect of council tax would have been greater but for the operation of the Administration Act in suspending the payment of, or disqualifying a claimant from receiving, some or all of the benefit;

(c)   as a result of the decision, a denial of, or disqualification for the receiving of, housing benefit or council tax benefit is lifted, wholly or in part; or

(d)   in consequence of the revised decision, housing benefit or council tax benefit paid is not recoverable by virtue of or as a consequence of section 75 or 76 of the Administration Act, or an amount so recoverable is reduced.

(3)   Where a decision as revised under paragraph 3 of Schedule 7 to the Act is not more advantageous to the appellant than the decision before it was revised, the appeal shall be treated as though it had been brought against the decision as revised.

(4)   The appellant shall have a period of one month from the date of notification of the decision as revised to make further representations as to the appeal.

(5)   After the expiration of the period specified in paragraph (4), or within that period if the appellant consents in writing, the appeal to the [¹ First-tier Tribunal] shall proceed except where, in the light of further representations from the appellant, the relevant authority further revises its decision and that decision is more advantageous to the appellant than the decision before it was revised.

Amendment

1.   Amended by Sch 1 para 159 of SI 2008 No 2683 as from 3.11.08.

Analysis

Sch 7 para 3(6) CSPSSA provides that if a decision is revised while an appeal against it is pending, the appeal lapses except in the circumstances prescribed by regulations. Reg 17 is made under that power.

Note that it is only a revising decision that can cause an appeal to lapse. A superseding decision that changes the decision under appeal from a later date does not have that effect: see *MS v SSWP (DLA)* [2012] UKUT 463 (AAC) at para 10.

Para (1) sets out the general rule, which is that an appeal will only lapse if the decision is "more advantageous" to the claimant than the appealed decision was. The claimant has a fresh right of appeal against the decision as revised: see Sch 7 para 6(1) CSPSSA on p145. However, it is inevitable that some claimants will find the procedures confusing and will assume that their appeal is still pending. Authorities ought to emphasise that the appeal is no longer proceeding in their correspondence with a claimant in these circumstances. The time limit for appealing runs from the date of notification of the new decision: Sch 7 para 3(5) CSPSSA.

If the fresh appeal is late then, as long as 13 months have not passed since the revision, an extension of time is possible under reg 19(5A) or rr23(2), (4) and (5) and 5(3)(a) TP(FT) Rules. The fact (if it be) that the local authority had failed to advise the appellant that the previous appeal had lapsed and/or of the need to make a fresh appeal would probably amount to a "special circumstance" within reg19(6)(b). If, however, the local authority had correctly advised the appellant but the appellant failed to make the appeal on time because s/he misunderstood, or disbelieved, that advice, that would not be a circumstance that could be taken into account (see reg 19(9)(a)). Note, however, that the First-tier Tribunal's power to extend time under r5(3)(a) is not constrained by regs 19(6)-(9).

In some circumstances, particularly where an appeal has already been part-heard and adjourned and where the revision will not give the appellant everything s/he seeks from the appeal, it will often be preferable for the authority to make a supplementary submission to the tribunal, asking the tribunal to substitute the proposed new decision rather than to issue the revised decision itself so as to cause the appeal to lapse and force the appellant to re-start the process from the beginning.

Para (2) offers a partial definition of "more advantageous". It only "includes" the four comparisons set out in sub-paras (a) to (d) and so if other changes make a decision better for a claimant, they may also fall within para (1). The best approach is to look at the result in pure money terms: is the claimant entitled to and/or receiving more money as a result of the revised decision? – see *AJ v SSWP (ESA)* [2014] UKUT 208 (AAC) which (in connection with the similar rule in reg 30 Social Security and Child Support (Decisions and Appeals) Regulations 1999) confirms that a decision with no financial consequences is not "more advantageous" for the purposes of the lapsing rule. Another way of putting this would be to say, by analogy with the decision of the Court of Appeal in *Wood v SSWP* [2003] EWCA Civ 53; reported as *R(DLA) 1/03*, that to revise a decision is to change it. Where there is no change in the outcome decision, there has been no revision and therefore Sch 7 para 3(6) CSPSSA does not apply and reg 17 cannot provide an exception to it. However the argument is put, it is suggested that *AJ v SSWP (ESA)* is correct and *DP v Mid Suffolk DC (HB)* [2013] UKUT 93 (AAC) (which is to the contrary effect: see pp892–93 of the 26th edition) was wrongly decided. That is also the implication of *GM v SSWP (JSA)* [2014] UKUT 57 (AAC) in which the Upper Tribunal appears to have accepted (eg, at para 10) that "merely substituting one ground for disallowance for another should not cause an appeal to lapse".

Sub-para (a) deals with the most common situation, which is an increase in the amount of benefit payable or period for which it is awarded. Sub-para (b) deals with the same situation where the claimant's right to receive benefit is suspended. Revisions which lift disqualifications and reduce or eliminate recoverable overpayments are also "more advantageous".

However, at least in overpayment cases, it is important to have regard to the period covered by the revising decision. Suppose a local authority decides that there is a recoverable overpayment of £5,200 covering a period of two years (104 weeks at £50 a week). The claimant appeals and, having considered the appeal, the local authority accepts that, for the last four weeks, the overpayment was caused by official error and is irrecoverable. It revises its original decision so as to reduce the recoverable overpayment to £5,000. That decision is more advantageous to the appellant than the decision that was originally appealed but there remains a substantial dispute. Is the effect of reg 17 that the appeal lapses and the claimant has to appeal again? That issue was considered by a Tribunal of Commissioners in *R(IS) 2/08*. It was decided that the appeal only lapsed in respect of the period for which the original decision had been revised. The tribunal stated (at para 31):

"It is true that section 9(6) of the 1998 Act [equivalent to para 3(6) of Sch 7 CSPSSA] provides that an appeal lapses if the decision under appeal is revised save where regulations otherwise provide and that regulation 30 of the 1999 Regulations [equivalent to reg 17] provides that an appeal does not lapse only where the revised decision is not more advantageous than the original decision. It is also true that regulation 30(2)(a) [equivalent to reg 17(2)(a)] provides that decisions that are more advantageous include those where "any benefit paid to the appellant is greater or is awarded for a longer period in consequence of the decision made under section 9". However, where a period before the date of the original decision is in issue and a revision affects only part of that period, it seems to us that there are many circumstances in which it can be appropriate to regard the decision as being more advantageous to the appellant only in respect of that part of the period and not the remainder of the period. This is particularly so where the Secretary of State knows very well that the revision does not deal with the main issue raised by the appeal and that it would be a waste of time to treat the appeal as having lapsed and to require the appellant to start all over again."

Therefore, in the example given above, the appeal lapses but only as regards the final four weeks of the overpayment period. However, *R(IS) 2/08* is not authority for the proposition that an appeal only lapses if the revising decision given the appellant everything s/he could have obtained from the appeal: see *Islington LB v JM (HB)* [2014] UKUT 23 (AAC) at para 42.

Para (3) confirms that where the appeal does not lapse, it continues as if it was against the original decision as revised.

Paras (4) to (5) provide that an appeal will proceed after the claimant has a period of one month to make further representations. It is suggested that it will be open to a claimant to raise new issues for consideration if s/he wishes. At the end of the one-month period (or earlier if the appellant agrees in writing), the appeal must proceed unless the decision is further revised and is then more advantageous.

It is sometimes disputed whether the First-tier Tribunal and Upper Tribunal have jurisdiction to second-guess a decision by a local authority that an appeal has lapsed. The answer is that they do (and, indeed, the decision in *R(IS) 2/08* could not have been given if it were otherwise). As Judge Rowland put it in *GM v SSWP (JSA)* (at para 7):

"A ruling that an appeal has lapsed is in principle appealable (see *LS v LB Lambeth (HB)* [2010] UKUT 461 (AAC); [2011] AACR 27). I agree with the Secretary of State that the First-tier Tribunal has no power to decide whether or not an appeal *should* lapse, because lapsing occurs automatically…However, if there is a dispute as to whether an appeal has, by operation of law, lapsed, the First-tier Tribunal must rule on the issue and such a ruling is appealable." (added emphasis)

Similarly, in *Islington LB v JM (HB)*, it was stated (at para 38) that it is "ultimately for the tribunal to decide whether – and to what extent – revision has occurred". It might also have been said that it is for the First-tier Tribunal to decide whether the effect of a revising decision is "more advantageous".

[² Time within which an appeal is to be brought
18.]

Amendments
1. Amended by reg 26 of SI 2002 No 1379 as from 20.5.02.
2. Omitted by Sch 1 para 160 of SI 2008 No 2683 as from 3.11.08.

Late appeals
19.–[⁵ (1)]

[⁵ (2)]

[⁵ (3)]

[⁵ (4)]

[² [⁵ (5) Where a dispute arises as to whether an appeal was brought within the time specified under Tribunal Procedure Rules the dispute shall be referred to, and determined by, the First-tier Tribunal.

(5A)   The relevant authority may treat a late appeal as made in time in accordance with Tribunal Procedure Rules if the relevant authority is satisfied that it is in the interests of justice.];

(6)   For the purposes of paragraph [⁵ (5)], it is not in the interests of justice to [⁵ treat the appeal as made in time unless the relevant authority] is satisfied that–

(a)   any of the special circumstances specified in paragraph (7) are relevant [⁵]; or

(b)   some other special circumstances exist which are wholly exceptional and relevant [⁵],

and as a result of those special circumstances, it was not practicable for the [⁵ appeal notice to be submitted in accordance with Tribunal Procedure Rules.]

(7)   For the purposes of paragraph (6)(a), the special circumstances are–

(a)   the [⁵ appellant] or a partner or dependant of the [⁵ appellant] has died or suffered serious illness;

(b)   the [⁵ appellant] is not resident in the United Kingdom; or

(c)   normal postal services were disrupted.

(8)   In determining whether it is in the interests of justice to [⁵ treat the appeal as made in time], [⁴ regard shall be had] to the principle that the greater the amount of time that has elapsed between the expiration of the time [⁵ limit under Tribunal Procedure Rules and the submission of the notice of appeal, the more compelling should be the special circumstances.]

(9)   In determining whether it is in the interests of justice to [⁵ treat the appeal as made in time], no account shall be taken of the following–

(a)   that the applicant was unaware of or misunderstood the law applicable to his case (including ignorance or misunderstanding of the time limits imposed by [⁵ Tribunal Procedure Rules]); or

(b)   that [⁵ the Upper Tribunal] or a court has taken a different view of the law from that previously understood and applied.

[⁵ (10)-(12)]

Definition

"partner" – see reg 1(2).

Amendments

1.   Amended by reg 27(a) of SI 2002 No 1379 as from 20.5.02.
2.   Substituted by reg 27(b) of SI 2002 No 1379 as from 20.5.02.
3.   Amended by reg 27(c) of SI 2002 No 1379 as from 20.5.02.
4.   Amended by reg 27(d) of SI 2002 No 1379 as from 20.5.02.
5.   Amended by Sch 1 para 161 of SI 2008 No 2683 as from 3.11.08.

Analysis

Paragraph (5)

As the appeal must be delivered to the authority (see r23(1) and (2) TP(FT) Rules), the authority must first decide whether to treat a late appeal as made in time under paras (5A) to (9). If the authority does not treat the appeal as made in time (and "objects" to the First-tier Tribunal doing so: see below), then the dispute must be referred to the First-tier Tribunal under para (5). This must be done immediately (see r23(7) on p1006).

If the authority grants an extension, section 4 of its submission to the First-tier Tribunal should include a statement to that effect (Code of Appeals Procedure para 2060).

Paragraphs (5A) to (9): Criteria for late appeals

These set out the criteria by reference to which an authority may "treat a late appeal as made in time in accordance with the Tribunal Procedure Rules". The reference to the Tribunal Procedure Rules is puzzling because those rules do not require a decision maker to make a positive decision to treat a late appeal as made in time. Rather r23(4) provides that where an appeal is late "it will be treated [ie, treated by the First-tier Tribunal, not the decision maker] as having been made in time if the decision maker ... does not object". The position therefore appears to be that even if the authority cannot treat the decision as having been made in time (ie, because the criteria in paras (6)-(9) are not satisfied), it may nevertheless force the First-tier Tribunal to do so, simply by not objecting. That interpretation is confirmed by CAP Bulletin 03/08, para 16.

Under para (5A), the authority must be satisfied that it is "in the interests of justice" before it can treat the appeal as made in time. Paras (6) to (9) qualify that test. The reference in para (6) to "paragraph (5)" is an obvious drafting error for "paragraph (5A)".

"the interests of justice". The meaning of this phrase is extensively modified by paras (6) to (9). However, once any relevant modifications made by those rules have been taken into account, it will still be necessary for the local authority or panel member to stand back and consider the overall interests of justice. Given the highly deserving nature of the "special circumstances" that need to be shown under paras (6) and (7), however, it will be a rare case where such circumstances exist and yet an extension of time is refused.

Paras (6) and (7) set up an exclusionary rule. An appellant must bring her/himself within either sub-para (a) or (b) in para (6). Effectively, this means that one of the following must be shown:

(1)   The appellant, her/his partner or a dependant has died or suffered serious illness: paras (6)(a) and (7)(a). Whether an illness is "serious" is a question of fact and degree. "Partner" is defined in reg 1(2).

(2)   The appellant is not resident in the UK: paras (6)(a) and (7)(b). On first impression, this is an odd provision in regulations dealing with benefits where, to be entitled at all, the claimant must (for HB) occupy a dwelling in Great Britain as her/his home (s130(1)(a) SSCBA). It is suggested that the provision might apply to landlords who are resident abroad but in receipt of direct payments of HB or where an appellant was resident in the UK at the time of the events that gave rise to the appeal but has since become resident elsewhere. Absence from the country that does not amount to residing abroad may amount to a special circumstance within para (6)(b), as to which see below.

(3)   Normal postal services were disrupted: paras (6)(a) and (7)(c). Strike action need not be shown; it will be sufficient if there is some delay in a decision letter or a letter of appeal reaching its destination. The caselaw on reg 19(7)(c) SSCS D&A Regs, which is in similar terms, will also be relevant here. See, in particular, the decisions of Commissioner Angus in *CIS 4901/2002* and Deputy Commissioner Poynter in *CJSA 3960/2006.* For postal delays over the Christmas period, see *R(IS) 16/04.*

(4)   There are some other special circumstances which are "wholly exceptional" and "relevant to the application": para (6)(b). "Wholly" emphasises the need for the circumstances to be unusual in nature, though not necessarily unique to the appellant. "Relevant" must simply mean that the circumstances are relevant to the question of whether it is in the interests of justice to admit the appeal. "Special

circumstances" are not defined, but are likely to be interpreted in a similar way to "special reasons" under the former reg 78(3) HB Regs 1987.

Once it is shown that the appellant can bring her/himself within one of the four situations above, s/he must also show that it was not practicable for the appeal to be made within the reg 18 time limit as a result of the circumstances. "Practicable" is a stiffer test than "reasonably practicable", but the phrase "as a result" does not require that the circumstances should be the sole cause of the delay, though it will have to be a substantial cause. Questions of reasonableness may well enter into consideration – eg, was it reasonable to expect an appellant to deal with an appeal even though her/his partner was in hospital? In considering such matters, it may be legitimate for the local authority or panel member to consider other deserving factors even where these do not fall within any of the categories set out above.

It is suggested that there is no rigid rule that every single day of delay after the one-month period must be explained, in the way that good cause for a late claim must be shown. All that is necessary is that the additional period of delay was broadly caused by the special circumstances on which reliance is placed. Some support for this approach can be seen in para (8).

Para (8) requires the common-sense approach that the later the appeal is, the more compelling the special circumstances must be for it to be regarded as being in the interests of justice to admit the appeal.

Para (9) requires two factors, which would otherwise be relevant, to be left out of account. First, under sub-para (a), ignorance of, or mistakes as to, the law on the part of the appellant (or, it is suggested, her/his adviser) cannot be taken into account. This includes ignorance of the time limit. The rule applies, on the face of it, irrespective of the reasonableness of the mistake. However, it is suggested that the view expressed in previous editions that it might prevent an extension of time even where the appellant's mistake arose from incorrect advice given by a local authority officer is itself mistaken. In such a case, the incorrect advice would be the cause of the delay, would amount to a special circumstance under para (6)(b) and would not be excluded from consideration under para (9).

Second, under sub-para (b), the fact that the Upper Tribunal or a court has interpreted the law in a different way than previously "understood and applied" cannot be taken into account. This aims to prevent a torrent of late appeals relying on a favourable "test case" decision of a commissioner or a court. However, "understood and applied" will cause difficulties. Understood and applied by whom? It is likely that the phrase refers to the views of the local authorities and DWP practice, though this cannot be regarded as certain. And what about cases where a provision is not being applied consistently?

The 3 November 2008 amendments (substituting the words "the Upper Tribunal" for the words "a commissioner") have the effect that where a social security commissioner (as opposed to the Upper Tribunal) has taken a different view of the law from that previously understood and applied, that can now be taken into account even though it could not have been taken into account before that date.

An appellant who is refused an extension of time by the authority should always insist that the application be referred to the tribunal under para (3).

[² **Notice of appeal**]

20.–[² (1) A notice of appeal made in accordance with Tribunal Procedure Rules must be made on a form approved by the relevant authority, or in such other format as the relevant authority may accept, and sent or delivered to the relevant authority.]

[² (2) Except where paragraph (3) applies, where a form does not contain the information required under Tribunal Procedure Rules the form may be returned by the relevant authority to the sender for completion in accordance with the Tribunal Procedure Rules.]

(3) Where the relevant authority is satisfied that the form, although not completed in accordance with the instructions on it, includes sufficient information to enable the appeal [²] to proceed, it may treat the form as satisfying the requirements of [² Tribunal Procedure Rules].

(4) Where [² a notice of appeal] is made in writing otherwise than on the approved form ("the letter"), and the letter includes sufficient information to enable the appeal [²] to proceed, the relevant authority may treat the letter as satisfying the requirements of [² Tribunal Procedure Rules].

(5) Where the letter does not include sufficient information to enable the appeal [²] to proceed, the relevant authority may request, in writing, further particulars.

(6) Where a person to whom a form is returned or from whom further particulars are requested duly completes and returns the form or sends the further particulars and the form or particulars, as the case may be, are received by the relevant authority within–

(a) 14 days of the date on which the form was returned to him, the time for making the appeal shall be extended by 14 days from the date on which the form was returned;

(b)   14 days of the date on which the relevant authority's request was made, the time for making the appeal shall be extended by 14 days from the date of the request;

(c)   such longer period as the relevant authority may direct, the time for making the appeal shall be extended by a period equal to that longer period directed by the relevant authority.

(7)   Where a person to whom a form is returned or from whom further particulars are requested does not complete and return the form or send further particulars within the period of time specified in paragraph (6)–

(a)   the relevant authority shall forward a copy of the form, or as the case may be, the letter, together with any other relevant documents or evidence to [² the First-tier Tribunal]; and

(b)   the [² First-tier Tribunal] shall determine whether the form or the letter satisfies the requirements of [² Tribunal Procedure Rules.]

(8)   Where–

(a)   a form is duly completed and returned or further particulars are sent after the expiry of the period of time allowed in accordance with paragraph (6); and

(b)   no decision has been made under paragraph (7) at the time the form or the further particulars are received by the relevant authority,

the form or further particulars shall also be forwarded to the [² First-tier Tribunal which] shall take into account any further information or evidence set out in the form or further particulars.

(9)   The relevant authority may discontinue action on an appeal where [² the notice of appeal] has not been forwarded to the [² First-tier Tribunal] and the appellant or an authorised representative of the appellant has given written notice that the appellant does not wish the appeal to continue.

Amendments

1.   Deleted by Sch 2 para 8(e) of SI 2002 No 1703 as from 30.9.02.
2.   Amended by Sch 1 para 162 of SI 2008 No 2683 as from 3.11.08.

General Note

Reg 20 contains the rules for making appeals. The requirements for a valid appeal are found in para (1). Where an appeal does not meet the requirements or does not contain sufficient information, paras (2) to (8) allow an authority to give an appellant an opportunity to put things right. It is important to note that although a local authority can treat an appeal as validly made under paras (3) and (4), only the First-tier Tribunal can reject an appeal as invalidly made: para (7)(b).

However, the Local Government Ombudsman has made it clear in *Complaint No 01/C/13400 against Scarborough BC* that authorities should aim to refer all appeals to the tribunal within 28 days. The power to revise a decision under reg 4(1)(c) is still available to authorities after an appeal has been referred to the tribunal, until such time as the appeal has been determined.

In *CH 3497/2005*, there had been serious delay in the local authority's referral of a claimant's appeals to the tribunal. Deputy Commissioner Mark pointed out that under Article 6 of the European Convention on Human Rights, a claimant is entitled to have her/his appeal heard within a reasonable time by an appeal tribunal and that this could be particularly important in HB appeals, where delay could cost claimants their homes. Under s6(1) HRA 1998, it is unlawful for a public authority to act in a way which is incompatible with a Convention right. By s6(6), "an act" includes a failure to act – eg, a failure to refer an appeal to HMCTS in a reasonable time. The deputy commissioner said at para 6 of his decision:

"In any event, it is wholly unacceptable to the proper operation of the system of appeals in housing benefit and council tax benefit appeals that delays of this sort should occur. If a local authority receives an appeal, it must be processed promptly and passed to the Appeals Service without delay. This applies also in cases where there is an issue which requires to be dealt with by a legally qualified panel member under regulation 20(7) or (8) of the 2001 Regulations."

What if a local authority does not refer an appeal to the tribunal? In *R(H) 1/07*, Commissioner Jacobs considered whether, in such a case, a tribunal has power to deal with the appeal until it is referred. The local authority argued that where an appeal is not referred to the tribunal, the claimant had to apply for judicial review of the local authority's failure or refusal to refer. The commissioner disagreed. He said that the usual principle is exclusivity of jurisdiction; if an issue is allocated to a judicial body, only that body has jurisdiction over it. A tribunal has power to determine whether it has jurisdiction and any challenge should be by appeal to the commissioners and from them to the Court of Appeal. Reg 20 does not deal with a challenge by the local authority to the tribunal's jurisdiction. However, its structure is relevant to whether a tribunal can deal with an appeal when it has not been referred to it by the local authority. The commissioner said:

"31. . . .
    First, so long as regulation 20(1) is satisfied, the appeal tribunal has jurisdiction. Second, the only role of the local authority is to receive the appeal documents and to ensure, as far as it can, that they contain the necessary information. It has no power to decide whether the information provided is sufficient. That is for the legally qualified panel member and there is an express duty to refer the issue to that member. The local authority's function is essentially administrative.

33.   If the appeal were lodged with the tribunal, there would be no problem. However, as the appeal is lodged elsewhere, there has to be a procedure by which it comes to the notice of the clerk or the tribunal. It is possible for legislation expressly to provide for an appeal that is lodged with one body to be referred to the tribunal. In the case of housing benefit, there is no express provision. The referral is but one of the many necessary administrative steps that have to be taken to bring a case before a tribunal. Others include the notification of sittings to the members of a tribunal and the photocopying and sending of the papers to the members. Most of these tasks are not spelt out in the legislation. They are assumed as necessary to allow the statutory powers and duties of the tribunal to operate. In legal terms, that assumption takes effect by implication, either as a general duty and power or as a series of specific duties and powers. It is not rational to interpret the legislation as making the tribunal's jurisdiction depend on a particular exercise of these administrative tasks. That would be incompatible with their function, which is to ensure that the tribunal established by the legislation can discharge its statutory function and do so efficiently and effectively. They are supportive not jurisdictional.

34.   In other words, an administrative task need not be performed by a particular person or in a particular way. So long as there is an appeal that satisfies the conditions of regulation 20(1), the tribunal has jurisdiction to deal with any issues that arise in respect of it, regardless of how they are brought to the tribunal's attention. This does not mean that the parties are free to disregard the usual procedures at will. Claimants cannot simply bypass the local authority and lodge appeals with the tribunal. Likewise, they cannot usually expect the tribunal to deal with a case before the local authority has had a chance to prepare the submission and assemble the papers for the parties and the tribunal. But what the tribunal is free to do is to allow matters to be handled differently if circumstances require it. The circumstances of this case did require it for two reasons. First, the local authority was refusing to refer the cases to the tribunal on the basis of an issue which the tribunal had (perhaps exclusive) jurisdiction to decide. Second, the local authority was trying to force the claimant to embark on an expensive legal procedure, which was risky in that the Administrative Court might not accept jurisdiction."

Analysis

Para (1). To be valid, the appeal must be made in writing, either on a form approved by the authority or "in such other format as the … authority may accept". It must be sent or delivered to the authority (see also r23(1) TP(FT) Rules on p1006).

Paras (2) and (3) apply where the appeal has been made on the approved form. If that form has not been completed in accordance with the instructions on it, then under para (3), the authority may nevertheless treat it as satisfying the requirements of the Tribunal Procedure Rules (ie, r23(6)) if it is satisfied that it "includes sufficient information to enable the appeal to proceed". Otherwise, para (2) applies and the authority "may" – which, in practice, means "must" – return the form to the sender "for completion in accordance with the Tribunal Procedure Rules". It is implicit in the difference in wording between the two paragraphs (ie, "does not contain the information required by the Tribunal Procedure Rules" and "not completed in accordance with the instructions on it") that the authority may not reject a form that contains the information required by the Rules even if (as is all too common) it has drafted its approved form so that the instructions on it require additional information. A form that complies with r23(6) will inevitably include sufficient information to enable the appeal to proceed.

Paras (4) and (5) apply where the appellant has appealed in writing but has not used the approved form. Where the letter of appeal includes sufficient information, the authority may – and, again, this means "must" – treat it as satisfying the Tribunal Procedure Rules under para (4). Where it does not include sufficient information, the authority should request "further particulars" under para (5). The further particulars an authority requires should be clearly set out in a letter to the appellant.

Paras (6)–(8). If the form is returned for completion or the further particulars are sought, an extension of time for appealing of 14 days is automatically conferred if the completed form or further particulars are received back by the authority within 14 days. An authority may grant a longer period, which then allows an equivalent extension of time: sub-para (c). This need not be done at the same time that the form is returned or particulars sought and it is suggested that it may be done after the 14-day period has expired.

If the authority's request is not complied with, it is required under para (7) to send all relevant documentation to the First-tier Tribunal, which will then decide whether the appeal has been validly made. If the completed form or further particulars are received by the authority after the time limit has expired, they must be sent to the First-tier Tribunal under para (8) for consideration. Any further details provided must be taken into account. If the First-tier Tribunal refuses to admit the appeal, it remains to be decided whether there is a further right of appeal to the Upper Tribunal: see the commentary on s11 TCEA 2007 on p176.

Para (9). If an appeal has not yet been passed to the First-tier Tribunal, an authority is absolved from taking action on it where it is withdrawn by a notice in writing. An "authorised representative" can withdraw an appeal on behalf of an appellant. A representative is only "authorised" where there is a validly given authorisation to act on behalf of the person affected. If an appeal is withdrawn but subsequently a second appeal on the same or similar grounds is made within the time limit, there seems to be no reason why the withdrawal of the first appeal affects the validity of the second appeal.

An appeal that has been passed to the First-tier Tribunal can be withdrawn under r17 TP(FT) Rules.

Death of a party to an appeal

21.–(1)   In any proceedings, on the death of a party to those proceedings, the relevant authority may appoint such person as it thinks fit to proceed with the appeal in the place of the deceased.

(2)   A grant of probate, confirmation or letters of administration in respect of the deceased, whenever taken out, shall have no effect on an appointment made under paragraph (1).

(3)   Where a person appointed under paragraph (1) has, prior to the date of such appointment, taken any action in relation to the appeal on behalf of the deceased, the effective date of appointment shall be treated as the day immediately prior to the first day on which such action was taken.

[¹ (4)   For the purposes of this regulation only, "appeal" means an appeal to an appeal tribunal, a Commissioner or a court.]

Amendment

1.   Inserted by reg 4(3) of SI 2008 No 2667 as from 30.10.08.

Analysis

Where an appellant dies in the course of an appeal to a tribunal, the local authority has power to appoint another person to act in her/his place. If, following reasonable enquiries, no one is available to be appointed then the First-tier Tribunal or Upper Tribunal may direct that the appeal should abate.

Unfortunately, reg 21 is unclear in parts and, where it is clear, it is less helpful than would be desirable. To understand the problems, it is necessary to go back a stage to the claim for benefit and the authority's decision on that claim. It is not possible for a new claim for HB to be made on behalf of someone who is dead (see, by analogy, *R(IS) 3/04*: reg 30 Social Security (Claims and Payments) Regulations 1987, and in particular, reg 30(5), probably does not extend to HB). But if a claimant dies after having made a claim, it is possible for the authority to pay any benefit due to her/his personal representative or next of kin under reg 97 HB Regs and reg 78 HB(SPC) Regs. Unfortunately, those regulations contain no provision equivalent to reg 30(1) Social Security (Claims and Payments) Regulations 1987, which allows the Secretary of State to appoint a person "to proceed with the claim" of someone who has died.

This probably does not matter too much in a case where the authority needs further information before it is able to reach a decision. The personal representative or next of kin cannot be compelled to produce the necessary information (because, at this stage s/he is neither a "person who makes a claim" or "a person to whom ... benefit has been awarded" for the purposes of reg 86 HB Regs etc or a "person by whom .... sums payable by way of ... benefit are receivable" for the purposes of reg 88 HB Regs etc). But if s/he does not do so, the authority will take a decision on the basis of the information it does have. That decision will inevitably be to refuse the claim on the basis that the claimant has not established entitlement.

It does, however, matter where the personal representative or next of kin wishes to appeal against the authority's decision. Reg 97 HB Regs etc does not expressly give them standing to appeal and reg 21 does not assist because the opening words "In any proceedings" and the phrase "*proceed* with the appeal" (emphasis added) show that an appeal must already exist before the power of appointment can be exercised. It might be possible for the personal representative or next of kin to make an appeal even though s/he had no standing to do so, seek appointment under para (1) and then rely on para (3) to validate the appeal retrospectively but such a solution would be unsatisfactory because of the circularity involved: the appeal would not become valid until the appointment was made and the appointment could not be made in the absence of a valid appeal.

Even if that hurdle can be surmounted, there are still problems with reg 21. As noted by Commissioner Levenson in *CH 3631/2007* (at para 13):

(1)   It is unclear whether the authority's power to appoint "such person as it thinks fit" includes the power to appoint someone who does not consent to be appointed and may refuse to act under the appointment.

(2)   It is also unclear whether a power to appoint a person "to proceed with the appeal" includes a power to appoint someone to act as respondent to an appeal brought by the local authority.

Question 2 can only arise on an appeal to the Upper Tribunal (local authorities having no right of appeal to the First-tier Tribunal against their own decisions).

Since 3 November 2008, there has also been problem about whether reg 21 applies to appeals to the First-tier Tribunal. This is because of the addition of para (4) from 30 October 2008. Para (4) provides that for the purposes of reg 21 "appeal" means an appeal to "an appeal tribunal, a Commissioner or a court". The change was made to reverse the decision in *CH 3631/2007* that the regulation did not apply to appeals to the commissioner because the word "appeal" in the phrase "proceed with the appeal" was defined by reg 1(2) as meaning "an appeal to an appeal tribunal". The problem arises because, four days later, on 3 November 2008 appeal tribunals and commissioners were abolished by TCEA 2007 but the wording of para (4) has not been updated to reflect that (although, the definition in reg 1(2) – which no longer applies – was). The result is that the regulation now definitely applies to appeals to the Upper Tribunal which is a court (see s3(5) TCEA 2007). However, as there does not appear to be any relevant transitional provision, and nothing in the Interpretation Act 1978 requires the reference to "an appeal tribunal" to be read as if it were a reference to "the First-tier Tribunal", reg 21 will only apply to the First-tier Tribunal if that tribunal is also a "court". In contrast to the position for the Upper Tribunal, there is no statutory provision declaring the First-tier Tribunal to be a court. However, some support for the view that it is a court may be found in *IB v Information Commissioner* [2011] UKUT 370 (AAC); [2012] AACR 26.

In *CH 3631/2007* (a case concerning the recovery of an overpayment), the commissioner held, following *R(IS) 6/01*, that the estate of a deceased claimant is not itself a legal person and cannot be a party to an appeal. In the absence of a grant of probate or letters of administration, there was no one with power to represent the estate before the commissioner and the appeal to the commissioner therefore abated. Although the commissioner's reasoning about the status of the deceased's estate is uncontroversial, the conclusion that the appeal must therefore abate may require further consideration. The authorities relied on by the commissioner at paras 14 and 15 are all cases in which the appeal abated on the death of the *appellant* and *R(SB) 25/84* states expressly that abatement is not appropriate where the deceased is the respondent to the appeal and the appellant is not willing to withdraw it. However, as abatement does not bring the appeal permanently to an end but merely suspends it, leaving open the possibility that it will be revived in the future (eg, by a grant of probate or letters of administration – see *R(I) 7/62* and *R(I) 2/83*), it may be that nothing turns on what procedure is followed.

Local authorities who wish to recover overpayments from unrepresented estates may consider applying for a grant of limited representation under s116 Senior Courts Act 1981 (formerly the Supreme Court Act 1981) – see *R(IS) 6/01* (para 38).

Abatement is not automatic. It is for the tribunal to declare whether an appeal has abated, and it may decide instead to dismiss or allow the appeal. In *Torbay BC v BW (HB)* [2011] UKUT 305 (AAC), Judge Rowland stated that he was prepared to assume, without deciding, that the tribunal had no power to direct an authority to exercise the power of appointment conferred by reg 21(1) and continued:

"… the question arises whether an appeal tribunal was entitled to hear an appeal in the absence of an appointment. In my view it was, provided that it was satisfied that justice would be better served by hearing the appeal rather than declaring it to be abated. As the appeal tribunal in these cases reasoned, the authorities show that abatement is not the only course of action that may be taken and, if dismissal may sometimes be appropriate (as accepted in R(I) 2/83), there is no reason in principle why allowing an appeal may not also be appropriate in some cases. Before considering the merits of an appeal where no-one had been appointed to act on behalf of the appellant, an appeal tribunal would have had to be satisfied that there was some practical purpose in hearing the appeal and that it was unlikely that the interests of any person would be overlooked. It would have been entitled to bear in mind that no payment could be made in the light of the appeal unless the local authority was satisfied that there was someone to whom it could properly make the payment."

PART V
Appeal Tribunals

[² Composition of appeal tribunals
22.]

Amendments

1. Omitted by reg 3(2) of SI 2004 No 3368 as from 21.12.04.
2. Omitted by Sch 1 para 163 of SI 2008 No 2683 as from 3.11.08.

[⁵ Procedure in connection with appeals
23.]

Amendments

1. Amended by reg 28 of SI 2002 No 1379 as from 20.5.02.
2. Amended by reg 3(3) of SI 2004 No 3368 as from 21.12.04.
3. Amended by reg 3(4) of SI 2005 No 337 as from 18.3.05.
4. Substituted by reg 9(3) of SI 2005 No 2878 as from 5.12.05.
5. Omitted by Sch 1 para 163 of SI 2008 No 2683 as from 3.11.08.

SCHEDULE

REGULATION 16(1)

Decisions Against which no Appeal Lies

General Note

The Schedule, made under reg 16, sets out the categories of decisions which would otherwise fall within the right of appeal but which cannot be subject to an appeal to a tribunal. See the commentary to reg 16 (see p971) and Sch 7 para 6(1) CSPSSA (see p145) for discussion of the types of decisions that can be appealed.

Note that certain exclusions of the right of appeal may infringe Art 6 of the European Convention on Human Rights: see *R(IS) 6/04*, discussed in the commentary to Art 6 on p124.

1. No appeal shall lie against a decision made by virtue of, or as a consequence of, any of the provisions in Part X (claims), Part XII (payments) and Part XIII (overpayments) of the Housing Benefit Regulations except a decision under–

[² (a) regulations 83 (time and manner in which claims are to be made), 84(1) and 85(1) and (4) (date of claim);
(b) regulation 93(3) (adjustments to payments to take account of underpayment or overpayment on account of rent allowance);
(c) regulation 95 (circumstances in which payment is to be made to a landlord);
(d) regulation 96 (circumstances in which payment may be made to a landlord);
(e) regulation 100 (recoverable overpayments);
(f) regulation 101 (person from whom recovery may be sought);
(g) regulation 103 (diminution of capital); or
(h) regulation 104 (sums to be deducted in calculating recoverable overpayments).]

Amendments

1.   Substituted by reg 3(4)(a) of SI 2004 No 3368 as from 21.12.04.
2.   Substituted by reg 5 and para 17(3) of SI 2006 No 217 as from 6.3.06.

[¹**1A.** No appeal shall lie against a decision made by virtue of, or as a consequence of, any of the provisions in Part 9 (claims), Part 11 (payments) and Part 12 (overpayments) of the Housing Benefit (State Pension Credit) Regulations except a decision under–

(a) regulations 64 (time and manner in which claims are to be made), 65(1) and 66(1) and (4) (date of claim);
(b) regulation 74(3) (adjustments to payments to take account of underpayment or overpayment on account of rent allowance);
(c) regulation 76 (circumstances in which payment is to be made to a landlord);
(d) regulation 77 (circumstances in which payment may be made to a landlord);
(e) regulation 81 (recoverable overpayments);
(f) regulation 84 (diminution of capital); or
(g) regulation 85 (sums to be deducted in calculating recoverable overpayments).]

Amendment

1.   Inserted by reg 5 and sch 2 para 17(3)(e)(ii) of SI 2006 No 217 as from 6.3.06.

2. No appeal shall lie against a decision made by virtue of, or as a consequence of, any of the provisions in Part VIII (claims), Part X (awards or payments of benefit) and Part XI (excess benefit) of the Council Tax Benefit Regulations except a decision under–

[² (a) regulations 69 (time and manner in which claims are to be made), 69(1) and 70(1) and (4) (date of claim);
(b) regulation 83 (recoverable excess benefit);
(c) regulation 85 (persons from whom recovery may be sought);
(d) regulation 88 (diminution of capital); or
(e) regulation 89 (sums to be deducted in calculating recoverable excess benefit).]

Amendments

1.   Substituted by reg 3(4)(b) of SI 2004 No 3368 as from 21.12.04.
2.   Substituted by reg 5 and Sch 2 para 17(3)(e) of SI 2006 No 217 as from 6.3.06

[¹**2A.** No appeal shall lie against a decision made by virtue of, or as a consequence of, any of the provisions in Part 7 (claims), Part 9 (awards or payments of benefit) and Part 10 (excess benefit) of the Council Tax Benefit (State Pension Credit) Regulations except a decision under–

(a) regulations 53 (time and manner in which claims are to be made), 54(1) and 55(1) and (4) (date of claim);
(b) regulation 68 (recoverable excess benefit);

(c)   regulation 70 (persons from whom recovery may be sought);
(d)   regulation 73 (diminution of capital); or
(e)   regulation 74 (sums to be deducted in calculating recoverable excess benefit).]

Amendment

1.   Inserted by reg 5 and Sch 2 para 17(3)(e)(iv) of SI 2006 No 217 as from 6.3.06.

Analysis

Paras 1, 1A, 2 and 2A effectively reverse the presumption that an appeal lies against any "decision" not within the scope of the Schedule and provide that in relation to decisions on claims, payments and overpayment, an appeal only lies against the decisions listed. They are:

(1)   A decision as to the time and manner in which a claim was made and the date on which a claim was made.

(2)   A decision as to whether a claim should be backdated for good cause.

(3)   A decision to make, or not to make, adjustments to ongoing payments of HB to reflect underpayments or overpayments made where payments on account under reg 93(3) HB Regs or 74(3) HB(SPC) Regs are made.

(4)   A decision as to whether direct payments of HB should be made to a landlord. This includes decisions on whether a landlord is a "fit and proper person" to receive direct payments.

(5)   A decision as to whether an overpayment is recoverable, and if so how much is recoverable.

(6)   A decision as to from whom an overpayment is recoverable. See also the commentary to para 3.

(7)   A decision as to the amount of a recoverable overpayment taking into account the diminishing capital rule and the rules in reg 104 HB Regs or reg 85 HB(SPC) Regs.

---

3.   Subject to paragraphs 1(f) and 2(c), no appeal shall lie against a decision as to the exercise of discretion to recover an overpayment of housing benefit or, as the case may be, excess council tax benefit.

Analysis

Whatever the correctness of the Court of Appeal's decision in *SSWP v Chiltern DC* [2003] EWCA Civ 508 (reported as *R(H) 2/03*) and the tribunal of commissioner's decision in *R(H) 3/04* in respect of the regime in place prior to October 2001 (and the correctness of the Court of Appeal's decision is strongly doubted in *R(H) 6/06*), the tribunal of commissioner's decision in *R(H) 6/06* holds that rights of appeal only attach to decisions going to the recoverability of an overpayment and do not attach to decisions concerning the recovery (or enforcement) of such recoverable overpayment decisions. As the tribunal of commissioners said:

"under the legislation in force from 1 October 2001 to 9 April 2006, an overpayment of housing benefit is always recoverable from any person within the scope of reg 101(2) as well as, if different, the person to whom the overpayment was made, except where reg 101(1) applies in which case it is recoverable only from any person within the scope of reg 101(2). No non-justiciable issues fall within the scope of the right of appeal and so there is no longer any need to apply *R(H) 3/04* and construe that right as being limited to points of law."

So the only appealable point (apart from whether there has in fact been an overpayment and whether it is recoverable) under s75(3) SSAA 1992 and reg 101 HB Regs is whether the person does in fact fall within reg 101. Once that point has been finally decided, *R(H) 6/06* makes it clear that no appeal right attaches to the enforcement decision of the local authority as to from whom the recoverable overpayment should actually be recovered.

---

4.   No appeal shall lie against a decision of a relevant authority under paragraph 16(3)(a) or (b) and (4) of Schedule 7 to the Act (decisions involving issues that arise on appeal in other cases).

Analysis

Sch 7 para 16(3) CSPSSA and reg 15 of these regulations permit an authority to postpone a decision pending a decision in a "test case", while giving it a discretion to issue a decision in certain cases. Para 4 confirms that there is no appeal against a decision to issue, or not to issue, a decision. The only remedy is judicial review.

---

5.   No appeal shall lie against a decision under Part III of these Regulations of a relevant authority relating to—

(a)   suspension of a payment of benefit or of a reduction; or

(b)   restoration following a suspension of payment of benefit or of a reduction,

except a decision that entitlement to benefit is terminated under regulation 14.

Analysis

There is no appeal against a decision to suspend or restore benefit under Part III of these regulations. There is, however, an appeal against a termination of benefit under reg 14: see *R(H) 4/08*.

[¹**6.** No appeal shall lie against the calculation or estimate of the claimant's, or the claimant's partner's, income or capital used by a relevant authority in accordance with [² regulation 27(1) of the Housing Benefit (State Pension Credit) Regulations or regulation 17(1) of the Council Tax Benefit (State Pension Credit) Regulations] (calculation of claimant's income in savings credit only cases), as modified, in both cases, by the Housing Benefit and Council Tax Benefit (State Pension Credit) Regulations 2003.]

Amendments

1.   Inserted by reg 3 of SI 2003 No 1581 as from 18.6.03.
2.   Amended by reg 5 and sch 2 para 17(3)(e) of SI 2006 No 217 as from 6.3.06.

Analysis

Reg 27(1) HB(SPC) Regs provides for local authorities to use the calculation or estimate of a claimant's (or her/his partner's) income and capital provided by the DWP (known as the "assessed income figure") where there is entitlement to the "savings credit" of pension credit only. There is no appeal against the local authority use of the DWP calculation or estimate of income and capital. An appeal would need to be made against the DWP income/capital decision instead. Note that from 6 April 2016, mixed-age couples (ie, couples where one member is at least pensionable age and the other is not) will no longer qualify for savings credit other than in transitional cases: s3ZA SPCA 2002 and reg 7A State Pension Credit Regulations 2002 SI No.1792.

Note that if the local authority modifies the "assessed income figure" under reg 27(4) HB(SPC) Regs, there *is* a right of appeal against the modification. There is therefore a potential for appeals against both the income/capital decision made by the DWP and the modification decision made by the local authority. It is suggested that it would be good practice to deal with both appeals together and that the former appeal should be dealt with first.

If a claimant wrongly lodges an appeal against the DWP income/capital decision with the local authority, the DWP's former *Housing Benefit and Council Tax Benefit Pension Credit Handbook* (at Part 1 para 1103) reminded a local authority what it should do – ie, that the local authority should advise the claimant to lodge an appeal with the DWP. It should also advise the claimant that the appeal lodged with the local authority will be processed as "out of jurisdiction" and could therefore be struck out (see r8(2) TP(FTT) Rules). The guidance rightly suggested that if the situation is ambiguous, claimants should be advised to consider lodging an appeal with the DWP as well as with the local authority.

The Tribunal Procedure (First-tier Tribunal) (Social Entitlement Chamber) Rules 2008
2008 No.2685 (L.13)

PART 1
Introduction
1.   Citation, commencement, application and interpretation
2.   Overriding objective and parties' obligation to co-operate with the Tribunal
3.   Alternative dispute resolution and arbitration

PART 2
General powers and provisions
4.   Delegation to staff
5.   Case management powers
6.   Procedure for applying for and giving directions
7.   Failure to comply with rules etc.
8.   Striking out a party's case
9.   Substitution and addition of parties
10. No power to award costs
11. Representatives
12. Calculating time
13. Sending and delivery of documents
14. Use of documents and information
15. Evidence and submissions
16. Summoning or citation of witnesses and orders to answer questions or produce documents
17. Withdrawal
18. Lead cases
19. Confidentiality in [social security and child support] cases
21. Expenses in social security and child support cases

PART 3
Proceedings before the Tribunal
CHAPTER 1
Before the hearing
22. Cases in which the notice of appeal is to be sent to the Tribunal
23. Cases in which the notice of appeal is to be sent to the decision maker
24. Responses and replies

CHAPTER 2
Hearings
27. Decision with or without a hearing
28. Entitlement to attend a hearing
29. Notice of hearings
30. Public and private hearings
31. Hearings in a party's absence

CHAPTER 3
Decisions
32. Consent orders
33. Notice of decisions
34. Reasons for decisions

PART 4
Correcting, setting aside, reviewing and appealing Tribunal decisions
35.   Interpretation
36.   Clerical mistakes and accidental slips or omissions
37.   Setting aside a decision which disposes of proceedings
38.   Application for permission to appeal
39.   Tribunal's consideration of application for permission to appeal
40.   Review of a decision
41.   Power to treat an application as a different type of application

SCHEDULE 1
Time limits for providing notices of appeal in social security and child support cases where mandatory reconsideration does not apply

PART 1
Introduction

General Note on TP(FTT) Rules

Each chamber of the First-tier Tribunal has its own procedural rules. These rules govern all appeals assigned to the Social Entitlement Chamber and, therefore, HB appeals.

In addition to social security appeals, the Social Entitlement Chamber deals with appeals relating to child support, child trust funds, childcare payments, vaccine damage payments, national insurance credits, asylum support, criminal injuries compensation, diffuse mesothelioma payments, saving gateway accounts and decisions in relation to NHS charges. See the First-tier Tribunal and Upper Tribunal (Chambers) Order 2010 SI No.2655 on p1065. Where a rule applies solely to one of those other jurisdictions, it has been omitted for reasons of space. However, there may be other rules which, while technically applicable to HB appeals, are designed for use in one or more of the other jurisdictions and are best understood in that context.

The rules are made by the Tribunal Procedure Committee, which is constituted by s22 and Sch 5 TCEA 2007. One of the major benefits of the November 2008 reforms is that procedural rules are now made by an independent body with a majority of judicial members, rather than by the Secretary of State who, through the subsidy system, is responsible for paying any HB that may be awarded as a result of a successful appeal. However, under Sch 5 para 28 (not reproduced in this book) the rules must be submitted to the Lord Chancellor who may allow or disallow them. The Lord Chancellor also has power to require the Committee to make rules to achieve a specified purpose (Sch 5 para 29). There is therefore scope for the DWP (and other government departments) to influence the content of the rules by making representations to the Lord Chancellor (who, since the Constitutional Reform Act 2005, is a government minister and no longer the head of the judiciary). One may speculate that certain aspects of the Rules, notably the requirement in r23 that HB appeals should be made to the decision maker rather than the First-tier Tribunal itself and the absence of any meaningful time limit for the decision maker to respond to the appeal once it has been received (r24(1A)), reflect such influence.

Citation, commencement, application and interpretation
1.–(1)   These Rules may be cited as the Tribunal Procedure (First-tier Tribunal) (Social Entitlement Chamber) Rules 2008 and come into force on 3rd November 2008.

[² (2)   These Rules apply to proceedings before the the Social Entitlement Chamber of the First-tier Tribunal.]

(3)   In these Rules–

"the 2007 Act" means the Tribunals, Courts and Enforcement Act 2007;

"appeal" includes an application under section 19(9) of the Tax Credits Act 2002;

"appellant" means a person who makes an appeal to the Tribunal, or a person substituted as an appellant under rule 9(1) (substitution of parties);

"decision maker" means the maker of a decision against which an appeal has been brought;

"dispose of proceedings" includes, unless indicated otherwise, disposing of a part of the proceedings;

"document" means anything in which information is recorded in any form, and an obligation under these Rules to provide or allow access to a document or a copy of a document for any purpose means, unless the Tribunal directs otherwise, an obligation to provide or allow access to such document or copy in a legible form or in a form which can be readily made into a legible form;

"hearing" means an oral hearing and includes a hearing conducted in whole or in part by video link, telephone or other means of instantaneous two-way electronic communication;

"legal representative" means [¹ a person who, for the purposes of the Legal Services Act 2007, is an authorised person in relation to an activity which constitutes the exercise of a right of audience or the conduct of litigation within the meaning of that Act], an advocate or solicitor in Scotland or a barrister or solicitor in Northern Ireland;

"party" means–

(a) a person who is an appellant or respondent in proceedings before the Tribunal;

(b)-(c) *[Omitted]*

(d) if the proceedings have been concluded, a person who was a party under paragraph (a), (b) or (c) when the Tribunal finally disposed of all issues in the proceedings;

"practice direction" means a direction given under section 23 of the 2007 Act;

"respondent" means–

(a) in an appeal against a decision, the decision maker and any person other than the appellant who had a right of appeal against the decision;

(b)-(c) *[Omitted]*

([⁵ (cc) *[Omitted]* or;]

(d) a person substituted or added as a respondent under rule 9 (substitution and addition of parties);

[³]

"social security and child support case" means any case allocated to the Social Entitlement Chamber [⁴ of the First-tier Tribunal] except an asylum support case or a criminal injuries compensation case;

"Tribunal" means the First-tier Tribunal.

Amendments

1. Amended by r3 of SI 2010 No 43 as from 18.1.10.
2. Substituted by r5(2) of SI 2010 No 2653 as from 29.11.10.
3. Omitted by r4(2)(a) of SI 2011 No 651(L.6) as from 1.4.11.
4. Amended by r4(2)(b) of SI 2011 No 651 (L.6) as from 1.4.11.
5. Inserted by r12 of SI 2015 No 1510 as from 21.8.15.

General Note

Rule 1 defines words and phrases that are used elsewhere in the Rules. Where appropriate, an analysis of those definitions will be given in the commentary to the individual rules.

Note that the definition of "respondent" is not confined to the local authority but includes "any person other than the appellant who had a right of appeal against the decision". A person has such a right if s/he is a "person affected" as defined by reg 3 D&A Regs (see the commentary on p942). In HB appeals there will often be more than one person affected. In particular, the claimant is always a person affected and so will automatically be a respondent to an appeal by her/his landlord even if s/he has not appealed her/himself. Landlords will automatically be respondents to appeals by claimants in cases involving direct payment of benefit and recovery of overpayments from the landlord and may also be respondents in other cases.

Overriding objective and parties' obligation to co-operate with the Tribunal

2.–(1) The overriding objective of these Rules is to enable the Tribunal to deal with cases fairly and justly.

(2) Dealing with a case fairly and justly includes–

(a) dealing with the case in ways which are proportionate to the importance of the case, the complexity of the issues, the anticipated costs and the resources of the parties;

(b) avoiding unnecessary formality and seeking flexibility in the proceedings;

(c) ensuring, so far as practicable, that the parties are able to participate fully in the proceedings;

(d) using any special expertise of the Tribunal effectively; and

(e) avoiding delay, so far as compatible with proper consideration of the issues.

(3) The Tribunal must seek to give effect to the overriding objective when it–

(a)   exercises any power under these Rules; or
(b)   interprets any rule or practice direction.
(4)   Parties must–
(a)   help the Tribunal to further the overriding objective; and
(b)   co-operate with the Tribunal generally.

General Note

The overriding objective of the rules is that the First-tier Tribunal should deal with appeals "fairly and justly": para (1). Under para (3), the tribunal must seek to give effect to that objective when it exercises any power conferred by the Rules or interprets any rule or practice direction.

"Fairly and justly" is probably best regarded as a composite phrase that does not gain from being broken down into its individual words – "just and equitable" in relation to child support variations would be another example. However, if further analysis is required it is tentatively suggested that "fairly" requires the tribunal to adopt a fair procedure and "justly" to achieve the correct outcome in accordance with the law. A "just" outcome is, of course, more likely if a "fair" procedure is followed.

The overriding objective was considered by the Upper Tribunal in *MA v SSWP* [2009] UKUT 211 (AAC), a case concerning the refusal of an adjournment. Judge Jacobs confirmed (para 10) that the principles listed in rule 2(2) are "illustrative, not comprehensive". He continued:

"11.   It is unlikely that these principles will dictate the decision for the tribunal. In the majority of cases, there will be factors pointing both for and against a proposed adjournment. The nature of the decision is likely to require the tribunal to undertake a balancing exercise between competing considerations. And it is the nature of such an exercise that different tribunals might properly make different assessments of the factors. On appeal, the Upper Tribunal will not find an error of law simply because it would have made a different assessment …

12.   The introduction of the overriding objective into the rules of procedure governing social security cases frees tribunals from the binding effect of previous authorities. They may continue to be relevant, but only to the extent that their principles are compatible with the overriding objective (*Albon (trading as NA Carriage Co) v Naza Motor Trading Sdn Bhd (No 5)* [2008] 1 WLR 2380 at [18])."

Para (2) contains a non-exhaustive list of the factors that are included in dealing with a case fairly and justly. They are largely self-explanatory and, as the tribunal is required to have regard to them by virtue of para (3), appellants, their representatives and presenting officers will be well advised to address them in any submission about how the tribunal should exercise its case management powers.

Some of the factors are similar to those in the list in r1.1 Civil Procedure Rules (CPR) 1998. However, the overriding objective in the civil courts is differently worded ("justly" rather than "fairly and justly") and the two lists are not identical. Caution must therefore be exercised when applying authorities relating to the overriding objective under the CPR to the First-tier Tribunal. In particular, para (2) (unlike r1.1(2)(e) CPR) does not oblige the tribunal to allot a share of the tribunal's resources to an appeal, while taking into account the need to allot resources to other cases.

There is, however, one way in which comparison with the CPR is instructive. Rule 1.1(2)(c)(i) and (ii) CPR mentions both "the amount of money involved" and "the importance of the case" as factors to be taken into account when deciding what is proportionate. It is to be inferred that "the importance of the case" and "the amount of money involved" are not the same thing.

Para (2)(a) while directing the tribunal to have regard to (among other things) "the importance of the case" makes no mention of "the amount of money involved". This is significant for social security appeals, including those relating to HB. Such appeals can involve large amounts of money – often so large that the County Court would not have jurisdiction over a civil dispute of the same size without the consent of the parties. In other cases, however, the amount of money involved is so small that the expense of holding a hearing to decide the appeal will inevitably exceed the potential benefit to the claimant. If the amount of money involved were a relevant factor, it might be argued that considering the appeal at all – or at any rate devoting any significant resources to it – was disproportionate. However, as it is not a relevant factor, there is no scope for such an argument. Claimants have a statutory right of appeal even in the smallest cases and it is the First-tier Tribunal's duty to decide such appeals in accordance with the law. To take any other approach would be to give decision makers carte blanche to make wrong decisions whenever the sum of money at stake was small and thus would ultimately undermine the rule of law.

The comparison between para (2)(a) and r1.1(2)(c)(i) and (ii) CPR also raises the question of what is meant by "the importance of the case" if it is not related to the amount of money involved. It is suggested that the case is important if it involves a point of law of general application (particularly if it has been selected as a lead case under r18). Any other interpretation inevitably raises the question, "Important to whom?" And answering that question will almost inevitably force the tribunal to consider the amount of money involved. An appeal involving, say, an alleged HB overpayment of £100 is likely to be more important to a single claimant under 25 with a JSA entitlement of £57.90 a week than it is to an authority with a budget of millions of pounds. However, it has already been established that the amount of money involved is a separate factor and one that is not relevant under para (2)(a).

The parties to an appeal have always been under an obligation to obey directions given by a tribunal: see, for example, *Davies v Child Support Commissioner and Child Support Agency* [2008] EWHC 334 (Admin), QBD, (Black J), in which (at paras 11–14) a refusal by the Secretary of State for Work and Pensions to obey a direction to give disclosure of a CSA file was formally declared to be irrational. However, that obligation is now spelled out in para (4). The parties must help the tribunal to further the overriding objective and co-operate with the tribunal generally. A failure to comply with directions can lead to the appeal (or part of it) being struck out or, in the case of a failure by a respondent, to her/his being barred from taking further part in the proceedings (r8). A failure to co-operate can lead to a strike out or a barring order even if no directions have been disobeyed, if that failure has the effect that the tribunal cannot deal with the proceedings fairly and justly (r8(3)(b) and (7)).

The parties' duty to co-operate with the tribunal generally involves "ensuring as far as possible that their case is ready by the time of the hearing" (see *MA v SSWP* above).

In *RF v CMEC (CSM)* [2010] UKUT 41 (AAC), the Upper Tribunal considered how the duty to co-operate affected the obligation on respondents to arrange for a presenting officer to attend a hearing when directed to do so. The judge stated:

"12.   The appeal tribunal directed that a presenting officer attend. … One was not sent. That was wrong. The tribunal had given a direction and the parties were under a duty to obey it. That duty is now incorporated into the duty on all parties 'to co-operate with the Tribunal generally' … . They do so by complying with the direction. If a party is unable to comply or finds it difficult to do so, the proper course is to apply under rule 6(5) for the tribunal to amend, suspend and set aside its direction. A party is not entitled to disregard a direction."

Alternative dispute resolution and arbitration

3.–(1)   The Tribunal should seek, where appropriate–

(a)   to bring to the attention of the parties the availability of any appropriate alternative procedure for the resolution of the dispute; and

(b)   if the parties wish and provided that it is compatible with the overriding objective, to facilitate the use of the procedure.

(2)   Part 1 of the Arbitration Act 1996 does not apply to proceedings before the Tribunal.

General Note

At present, r3 is easy to apply to HB. There is no alternative dispute resolution (ADR) procedure for HB appeals and therefore the tribunal cannot bring the parties' attention to such a procedure. Rule 3 does, however, raise issues about the possible role of ADR in the social security decision making and appeals system. It is suggested that the scope for any such role is limited. To begin with tribunals are themselves a form of ADR. The average HB appeal is dealt with in a single hearing lasting about 50 minutes and held within three or four months of the appeal being submitted to HM Courts and Tribunals Service. It is unlikely that a civil court would be able to deal with the same issues in so short a time and with such a relatively short delay. Moreover, generalist judges in the civil courts would be unlikely to possess the specialist knowledge that allows tribunals to adopt an enabling role, thereby reducing the need for representation.

Diverting the appeal into ADR risks taking up a disproportionate amount of the time of a tribunal judge (which could be used simply to decide the appeal at a hearing) and if ADR is unsuccessful, it will have added to the delay. There is no reason to suppose that there will be an improved outcome to the appeal in return for those disadvantages. In January 2010, a report to the Ministry of Justice, *Early neutral evaluation pilot in the Social Security and Child Support Tribunal* (available from the Ministry of Justice website) concluded that a scheme piloting "early neutral evaluation" (a form of ADR) did not achieve swifter resolution of cases and was less cost-effective than the traditional tribunal process.

In addition, while ADR (and, in particular, mediation) may be a useful aid to settling disputes between citizens, it is doubted whether it can be appropriate for disputes between the citizen and the state that relate to specified statutory entitlements. Given the facts of an individual case, a claimant is either entitled to a prescribed amount of HB or s/he is not entitled at all. Particularly given the vast disparity of bargaining power between the state and the citizen, it is not appropriate to involve the latter in any procedure in which s/he may either feel under pressure to accept less than full entitlement in order to avoid the perceived risks of a hearing or may, in effect, be bribed to give up an appeal by being offered more than s/he is strictly entitled to. The purpose of the social security decision making and appeals system is not to make disputes go away but to ensure that those who are entitled to benefit receive that entitlement and those who are not entitled do not. To be appropriate for social security appeals, any system of ADR adopted must not compromise that principle.

PART 2

General powers and provisions

Delegation to staff

4.–(1)   Staff appointed under section 40(1) of the 2007 Act (tribunal staff and services) may, with the approval of the Senior President of Tribunals, carry out functions of a judicial nature permitted or required to be done by the Tribunal.

(2)   The approval referred to at paragraph (1) may apply generally to the carrying out of specified functions by members of staff of a specified description in specified circumstances.

(3)   Within 14 days after the date on which the Tribunal sends notice of a decision made by a member of staff under paragraph (1) to a party, that party may apply in writing to the Tribunal for that decision to be considered afresh by a judge.

General Note

The Senior President of Tribunals has issued seven practice statements under r4. The current practice statement is in the following terms:

> *"Practice Statement authorising Tribunal Caseworkers First-tier Tribunal (Social Entitlement Chamber) to carry out functions of a judicial nature*
>
> Having evaluated the performance of the Tribunals Caseworker delegation scheme in the First-tier Tribunal (Social Entitlement Chamber), I am content that the delegations should remain in place, subject to periodic reviews to be led by the Chamber President at intervals agreed by him.
>
> 1.   The Senior President of Tribunals hereby approves that an appropriately trained member of staff appointed under section 40(1) of the Tribunals, Courts and Enforcement Act 2007 and designated as a 'Tribunal Caseworker' by the Chamber President, may carry out the functions of the Tribunal Procedure (First-tier Tribunal) (Social Entitlement Chamber) Rules 2008 set out in paragraph 3 below.
> 2.   A Tribunal Caseworker must have been authorised by the Chamber President to exercise those functions. All functions must be exercised under the supervision of a judge and in accordance with guidance issued by the Chamber President.
> 3.   A Tribunal Caseworker may make all decisions that a judge assigned to the Social Security and Child Support/Criminal Injuries Compensation jurisdiction may make under the Tribunal Procedure (First Tier Tribunal) (Social Entitlement Chamber) Rules 2008 save those which are substantive final decisions.
> 4.   In accordance with rule 4(3) of the Tribunal Procedure (First Tier Tribunal) (Social Entitlement Chamber) Rules 2008, within 14 days after the date that the Tribunal sends notice of a decision made by a Tribunal Caseworker pursuant to an approval under paragraph 1 above that party may apply in writing to the Tribunal for the decision to be considered afresh by a judge.
>
> The Rt. Hon. Sir Ernest Ryder
> Senior President of Tribunal
> 16 July 2018"

The 14-day limit in r4(3) and para 4 of the Practice Statement is likely to be too short in practice. Up to seven of those 14 days may have expired before the parties receive the tribunal caseworker's direction. If the party is a claimant, s/he may then have to take advice and in some cases will also have to have the direction translated into another language. However, the time limit can be extended under r5(3)(a). Note also that, under r5(2), the tribunal has a general power (that is without limit of time as long as the final decision has not been given) to give a direction "amending, suspending or setting aside an earlier direction". An application to amend, suspend or set aside an earlier direction made by a tribunal caseworker may be referred to the tribunal casework concerned. However, if s/he refuses to change the direction, it will then be possible to apply to have *that* decision considered afresh by a judge.

Where a tribunal caseworker or registrar refuses a postponement, that issue must normally be reconsidered by the tribunal at the start of the hearing. For the principles that apply in those circumstances, see *JC v SSWP (PIP)* [2018] UKUT 110 (AAC).

Rule 4(3) which allows a party to apply within 14 days for a decision made by a member of staff to be reconsidered by a judge, has the effect that, where a postponement has been refused by a tribunal caseworker or registrar, the appeal cannot be listed for hearing during the next 14 days: see *T v SSWP (ESA)* [2019] UKUT 59 (AAC). Case management decisions cannot lawfully deprive a party of a right conferred by the TP(FTT) Rules unless that is provided for in those rules.

Case management powers

5.–(1)   Subject to the provisions of the 2007 Act and any other enactment, the Tribunal may regulate its own procedure.

(2)   The Tribunal may give a direction in relation to the conduct or disposal of proceedings at any time, including a direction amending, suspending or setting aside an earlier direction.

(3)   In particular, and without restricting the general powers in paragraphs (1) and (2), the Tribunal may–

(a)   extend or shorten the time for complying with any rule, practice direction or direction;

[² [¹]]

(b)   consolidate or hear together two or more sets of proceedings or parts of proceedings raising common issues, or treat a case as a lead case (whether in accordance with rule 18 (lead cases) or otherwise);

(c)   permit or require a party to amend a document;

(d)   permit or require a party or another person to provide documents, information, evidence or submissions to the Tribunal or a party;

(e)   deal with an issue in the proceedings as a preliminary issue;

(f)   hold a hearing to consider any matter, including a case management issue;

(g)   decide the form of any hearing;

(h)   adjourn or postpone a hearing;

(i)   require a party to produce a bundle for a hearing;

(j)   stay (or, in Scotland, sist) proceedings;

(k)   transfer proceedings to another court or tribunal if that other court or tribunal has jurisdiction in relation to the proceedings and–

(i)   because of a change of circumstances since the proceedings were started, the Tribunal no longer has jurisdiction in relation to the proceedings; or

(ii)   the Tribunal considers that the other court or tribunal is a more appropriate forum for the determination of the case; or

(l)   suspend the effect of its own decision pending the determination by the Tribunal or the Upper Tribunal of an application for permission to appeal against, and any appeal or review of, that decision.

Amendments

1.   Inserted by r23 of SI 2013 No 2067 as from 1.11.13.
2.   Omitted by r13 of SI 2015 No 1510 as from 21.8.15.

General Note

The case management provisions in r5 are the heart of the First-tier Tribunal's powers under the Rules.

By r5(1), the tribunal may regulate its own procedure except that it may not do anything that conflicts with TCEA 2007 or any other enactment. In doing so (and in exercising the case management powers in r5(2) and (3)) it must seek to give effect to the overriding objective.

It is important for the tribunal to ensure that case management directions are carefully, and accurately, drafted: see, for example, *EM v SSWP (DLA)* [2011] UKUT 320 (AAC). The parties to an appeal are entitled to know that any application they make has been considered, and any direction has been given, by a judge (or by a tribunal caseworker in cases where delegation is permitted by r4). Therefore, in all but the most urgent cases, a direction or a decision on an application should be communicated to the parties in the form of an order signed by a judge (or tribunal caseworker) and not in the form of an administrative summary contained in a letter: see *JP v SSWP (ESA)* [2016] UKUT 48 (AAC) and *Camden LB v FG (SEN)* [2010] 249 (AAC).

The powers conferred by r5(2) and (3) are self-explanatory. It is, however, worth pointing out that, before 3 November 2008, appeal tribunals did not have the following powers:

(1)   to shorten a time limit;

(2)   to consolidate appeals or treat an appeal as a lead case;

(3)   to stay (or sist) proceedings;

(4)   to transfer proceedings to another court or tribunal;

(5)   to suspend the effect of a decision pending appeal.

Representatives and presenting officers should make themselves familiar with the full range of the First-tier Tribunal's case management powers and be prepared to ask the tribunal to use them in an appropriate case.

When exercising the power to extend time for appealing (r5(3)(a)), the First-tier Tribunal need not have regard to the considerations listed in Rule 3.9(1) of the Civil Proceedings Rules, which apply when a court is considering whether to apply a sanction for a breach of procedural rules (see *CD v First-tier Tribunal (SEC) (CIC)* [2010] UKUT 181 (AAC).

In *MA v SSWP* [2009] UKUT 211 (AAC), the Upper Tribunal gives helpful guidance on the approach to be taken by the First-tier Tribunal when considering an application for adjournment in the context of the overriding objective in rule 2. Judge Jacobs stated that it was likely the tribunal's inquiries would focus on three issues: (1) what would be the benefit of an adjournment; (2) why was the party not ready to proceed; and (3) what impact will an adjournment have on the other party and the operation of the tribunal system? As regards (1), the application to adjourn had been to obtain further evidence. The judge advised that:

"A tribunal is always entitled to consider whether further evidence is likely to be helpful. In making its assessment, it is relevant to take into account: (i) the evidence that is already before the tribunal; (ii) the evidence that is likely to be obtained if the proceedings are adjourned; (iii) how long it will take to obtain it; and (iv) whether the tribunal could use its expertise to compensate for the lack of additional evidence."

As regards (2), the parties' duty is to co-operate with the tribunal generally under rule 2(4)(b). That involves ensuring as far as possible that their case is ready by the time of the hearing. It will be relevant to consider the advice given to claimants by the tribunal when an appeal is lodged. In relation to (3), the Secretary of State's interest in the appeal (and, by analogy, the interest of a local authority) is not contentious and, except in an overpayment case when the Secretary of State may be concerned to avoid delaying tactics, is limited to "assisting the tribunal to ensure that it makes the correct decision in fact and law on the claimant's entitlement to benefit". The interests of the functioning of the tribunal system as a whole are unlikely to be of great significance in most cases and it will be "exceptional" for an adjournment that would otherwise be granted to be refused solely on account of the needs of the system as a whole.

The power in r5(3)(h) to adjourn a hearing does not permit the First-tier Tribunal to give a "peremptory adjournment" – ie, when granting an adjournment, the tribunal may not "seek to bind the hands of a future tribunal by directing that an appeal 'must proceed when next listed' or that a future tribunal may not grant a further adjournment; or by giving any other direction with a similar effect": see *LJT v SSWP (PIP)* [2019] UKUT 21 (AAC).

For guidance on the considerations that are relevant where a party asks the First-tier Tribunal to exercise its power under r5(3)(h) to postpone or adjourn a hearing because of a conflicting appointment, see *BV v SSWP (PIP)* [2018] UKUT 444 (AAC); [2019] 1 WLR 3185 at paras 9–12 and 25–26. The tribunal has an inquisitorial jurisdiction and when it lacks relevant information, it should usually ask for it. A claimant seeking a postponement because of a conflicting appointment, is not usually asserting that the appointment is more important than her/his appeal, but only that it is more urgent.

The decision of Judge Jacobs in *JC v SSWP (PIP)* [2018] UKUT 110 (AAC) includes further discussion of the principles to be applied when considering whether it is fair and just to grant an adjournment and reiterates that where a postponement has been refused, whether by a registrar or a judge, "tribunals should be alert to the possibility that reconsideration [*i.e.,* of an adjournment] at their own initiative may be appropriate".

In particular, there is no absolute rule that judicial proceedings take precedence over other appointments (see *FR v Broadland DC* [2012] UKUT 449 (AAC) at paras 9 and 10). In that case, the claimant could not attend the hearing because he was committed to a series of meetings with a view to launching a business and coming off benefits. Upper Tribunal Judge Mark held that two decisions of the First-tier Tribunal not to postpone or adjourn the hearing of the appeal and a subsequent decision not to set aside the First-tier Tribunal's substantive decision on the appeal were "patently ... perverse". Relevant factors included that the date of the hearing had been fixed at relatively short notice without reference to the claimant, that he had indicated his availability to attend a restored hearing at any time in the following two months, that the application to postpone had been made promptly and some time before the date fixed for the hearing and that the disputed benefit remained in the local authority's hands unless and until the claimant won his appeal (so that he had no incentive to delay matters). It was not proportionate to the importance of the case to insist on a hearing on a date of which the claimant had been given relatively short notice, if that might put at risk reasonable efforts to get off and stay off benefits, when the claimant had offered a wide range of alternative dates. *FR* also emphasises (at para 6) the importance of a judge who decides a written application for a postponement reading that application rather than relying upon a second-hand account of it.

The power in para (3)(b) to treat a case as a lead case may be delegated to a Regional Tribunal Judge but not a District Tribunal Judge (see para 10 of the Senior President's Practice Statement on the Composition of Tribunals on p1063).

If the First-tier Tribunal decides an issue in the proceedings as a preliminary issue under r5(3)(e), its decision on that issue is binding (subject to any appeal or application under Part 4 of the TP(FTT) Rules) on the parties and on any tribunal that subsequently decides other issues in the same proceedings even if that tribunal is differently constituted from the tribunal that decided the preliminary issue. It is to be contrasted with an interim decision in which the First-tier Tribunal or Upper Tribunal makes a decision on some of the issues – or in respect of part of the period – before it, but adjourns the other issues – or periods – to be decided by the same tribunal on a later date.

There is some dispute whether it is possible for the First-tier Tribunal to decide an issue as a preliminary issue without there first having been a formal direction that the issue should be dealt with in that way. The answer depends upon whether r5(3) is read as giving examples of the type of directions that may be given under r5(2) or whether it is a read as giving examples of the ways in which the First-tier Tribunal may regulate its own procedure under r5(1), some – but not necessarily all – of which will require directions to be given under r5(2). The latter is the better view, particularly as r5(3) is expressed as not restricting the general powers conferred by both rr5(1) and (2). However, the dispute is academic because even if – contrary to the view expressed in the previous sentence – a direction is necessary, r5(2) provides that the necessary direction can be given "at any time". So a tribunal that decided in the course of a hearing that it was appropriate to deal with an issue as a preliminary issue could give the necessary direction there and then, subject to its being in accordance with the overriding objective to do so.

The more important question is whether it is ever appropriate for the First-tier Tribunal to proceed in that way. In *R (SB and others) v First-tier Tribunal and CICA* [2014] UKUT 497 (AAC) (a judicial review of a number of decisions of the First-tier Tribunal relating to criminal injuries compensation) a three-judge panel of the Upper Tribunal suggests that it might be. The panel states:

"104.   We recognise, however, that if the terms of a CICA review decision were to encompass determinations in respect of eligibility and the level of compensation then on an appeal against such a decision a FtT may be required to decide both issues… In such an example we can see that in some circumstances it may be sensible for the FtT to hold separate hearings on the two issues under appeal. We are cautious about seeking to give detailed guidance as to how the FtT should approach such a scenario given it is hypothetical and none of the parties made detailed or contested arguments on this issue. We therefore confine ourselves to drawing attention to the provisions of rule 5(3)(e) of the FtT's procedure rules – "the Tribunal may deal with an issue in the proceedings as a preliminary issue" – and observe that if this rule is invoked and the preliminary issue decided then the time limit for judicial review of that decision would run from the date of the decision or written reasons being given for it: per r.28(2) and (3)(a) of the Tribunal Procedure (Upper Tribunal) Rules 2008.

105.   Care may therefore need to be taken by the FtT when faced with deciding more than one issue on an appeal. In the case of Ms Barrett it was (and is) possible that determining the tariff and loss of earnings levels of compensation could be addressed separately at different hearings. If the appeal hearing genuinely goes part heard (e.g. the FtT intended to address both issues but simply runs out of time), and it is therefore adjourned to be heard by the same FtT members (and doing so would not unnecessarily delay the final resolution of the appeal), then it would seem to us that, whatever preliminary view the FtT may have come to on the first issue (e.g. the level of the tariff award), no decision would be made until the further hearing has taken place. The time limit for applying for judicial review would therefore not begin to run until the decision made at the second (or final) hearing.

106.   On the other hand, it may be clear at the outset of the first hearing, or even during the course of that hearing, that only one issue can sensibly be determined, and the FtT may then wish to use the r.5(3)(e) power to finally decide that issue (e.g. where it may not be possible to reconvene the same tribunal membership within an appropriate time)."

However, there is a tension between that approach and what has been said about the use of preliminary issues by judges of the House of Lords in *Tilling v Whiteman* [1980] AC 1 at 17F-18A and 25B-C, of the Court of Appeal in *McLoughlin and Jones* [2002] QB 1312 at para 66, and of the High Court in *Steele v Steele* [2001] CP Rep 106. In particular, in *McLoughlin v Jones*, David Steel J stated:

"66.   In my judgment, the right approach to preliminary issues should be as follows. (a) Only issues which are decisive or potentially decisive should be identified. (b) The questions should usually be questions of law. (c) They should be decided on the basis of a schedule of agreed or assumed facts. (d) They should be triable without significant delay, making full allowance for the implications of a possible appeal. (e) Any order should be made by the court following a case management conference."

As noted by Judge Jacobs, writing extra-judicially in *Tribunal Practice and Procedure* (Third Edition, Legal Action Group, 2014) at p317 para 7.172 (Courts and Enforcement Act 2007), the final requirement may be less appropriate in the tribunal context. However, the approach set out in the first four requirements is very different to the approach of the Upper Tribunal in *SB* and others under which, it is contemplated that it may be appropriate to decide a preliminary issue merely to avoid going part-heard.

A tribunal that decides a preliminary issue following a direction under r5(3)(e), should consider giving a direction that the one-month period for applying for permission to appeal should run from the date of the decision that disposes of all issues in the proceedings (ie, under r38(3A)). To do so means that anyone aggrieved by the decision on the preliminary issue can wait to see whether s/he is happy with the outcome of the appeal as a whole before deciding whether to appeal to the Upper Tribunal.

Procedure for applying for and giving directions

6.–(1)   The Tribunal may give a direction on the application of one or more of the parties or on its own initiative.

(2)   An application for a direction may be made–

(a)   by sending or delivering a written application to the Tribunal; or

(b)   orally during the course of a hearing.

(3)   An application for a direction must include the reason for making that application.

(4)   Unless the Tribunal considers that there is good reason not to do so, the Tribunal must send written notice of any direction to every party and to any other person affected by the direction.

(5)   If a party or any other person sent notice of the direction under paragraph (4) wishes to challenge a direction which the Tribunal has given, they may do so by applying for another direction which amends, suspends or sets aside the first direction.

General Note

The tribunal may give directions on its own initiative and need not wait for an application from the parties: para (1). Under para (2), an application by a party must be in writing unless it is made at a hearing in which case it can be made by word of mouth. In either case, reasons must be given: para (3) and also simple common sense.

The requirement that an application be in writing is unnecessarily bureaucratic. Taken literally, it prevents an appellant (or a presenting officer) who is taken ill on the day of the hearing from telephoning the tribunal and requesting a postponement (because the "application" is neither in writing nor made at a hearing). It is hoped that the tribunal would exercise its powers under r7(2)(a) to waive the requirement for writing in such circumstances.

There is no requirement that the tribunal should seek the views of the parties before giving a direction. Once a direction has been made, however, any party may challenge it by applying for another direction which amends, suspends or sets aside the first direction. It cannot be over-emphasised that unless and until the first direction is amended, suspended or set aside, it must be obeyed.

If the tribunal gives a direction, a copy must normally be sent to every party: para (4).

Failure to comply with rules etc.

7.–(1)   An irregularity resulting from a failure to comply with any requirement in these Rules, a practice direction or a direction, does not of itself render void the proceedings or any step taken in the proceedings.

(2)   If a party has failed to comply with a requirement in these Rules, a practice direction or a direction, the Tribunal may take such action as it considers just, which may include–

(a)   waiving the requirement;

(b)   requiring the failure to be remedied;

(c)   exercising its power under rule 8 (striking out a party's case); or

(d)   exercising its power under paragraph (3).

(3)   The Tribunal may refer to the Upper Tribunal, and ask the Upper Tribunal to exercise its power under section 25 of the 2007 Act in relation to, any failure by a person to comply with a requirement imposed by the Tribunal–

(a)   to attend at any place for the purpose of giving evidence;

(b)   otherwise to make themselves available to give evidence;

(c)   to swear an oath in connection with the giving of evidence;

(d)   to give evidence as a witness;

(e)   to produce a document; or

(f)   to facilitate the inspection of a document or any other thing (including any premises).

General Note

A failure to comply with a rule, practice direction or direction has no practical consequences unless and until the tribunal decides to take action under para (2). Having regard to the overriding objective and, in particular, to the aim of "avoiding unnecessary formality and seeking flexibility in the proceedings" (r2(2)(b)) it will often be appropriate to waive the requirement, as long as this can be done without prejudicing the other party. The discretion to waive an irregularity conferred by r7(2)(a) must be consciously exercised and reasons given (at least if requested): *MT v SSWP (IS)* [2010] UKUT 382 (AAC).

Under s25 TCEA 2007, the Upper Tribunal has the same powers as the High Court or the Court of Session in relation to the attendance and examination of witnesses, the production and inspection of documents and all other matters incidental to its functions. In principle, this includes power to punish for contempt of court. In practice, it is suspected that any prospect of a party going to prison for failure to comply with a requirement imposed by the First-tier Tribunal is an illusion.

The powers of the Upper Tribunal under s25 TCEA 2007 were considered by a three-judge panel in *PA v CMEC* [2009] UKUT 283 (AAC) and *MR v CMEC* [2009] UKUT 284 (AAC), [2009] UKUT 285 (AAC), [2010] UKUT 38 (AAC). In the former case, the tribunal stated:

"In our judgement these provisions [ie, rr7(3) and (4) of the TP(UT) Rules] mean that the Upper Tribunal can only exercise its powers under section 25 upon a referral by the First-tier Tribunal in respect of the requirement imposed by that tribunal. It is not open to the Upper Tribunal to impose a different requirement in substitution for that imposed by the First-tier Tribunal. It is the First-tier tribunal that knows what issues arise in the appeal and what material is required to assist in its resolution. It is therefore of the first importance that the First-tier tribunal consider carefully the terms of any direction to produce documents. Plainly any such documents require to be relevant to the resolution of the issues before it. The Direction Notice should articulate with precision what documents it requires and the period for which they are required. In the case of bank statements, for example, the dates specified must be related to the subject matter of the appeal before the First-tier tribunal."

Further consideration was given by a three-judge panel of the Upper Tribunal in *MD v SSWP (Enforcement Reference)* [2010] UKUT 202 (AAC); [2011] AACR 5. The panel stressed the importance of complying with procedural requirements in contempt cases (in that case the letter serving the summons misspelled the name of the person to whom it was addressed and contained no indication of the address to which it had been sent, and the summons made no provision for the payment of expenses as required by rule 16(2)(b)). It is also important that the First-tier Tribunal should investigate for itself whether there has actually been a breach of an order (rather than, for example, a failure of communication) before making the reference. The panel also pointed out that under para 10 of the Senior President's Practice Statement on the Composition of Tribunals, the power to refer to the Upper Tribunal is reserved to the Chamber President. That power may be delegated to a Regional Tribunal Judge (though not a District Tribunal Judge) but, at least at the time of the decision, no such delegation had actually been made.

For an example (in the context of special educational needs) of the exercise of by the Upper Tribunal of the power to punish for contempt of court under s25 TCEA 2007, see *CB v Suffolk CC* [2010] UKUT 413 (AAC); [2011] AACR 22.

Striking out a party's case

8.–(1)   The proceedings, or the appropriate part of them, will automatically be struck out if the appellant has failed to comply with a direction that stated that failure by a party to comply with the direction would lead to the striking out of the proceedings or that part of them.

(2)   The Tribunal must strike out the whole or a part of the proceedings if the Tribunal–

(a)   does not have jurisdiction in relation to the proceedings or that part of them; and

(b)   does not exercise its power under rule 5(3)(k)(i) (transfer to another court or tribunal) in relation to the proceedings or that part of them.

(3)   The Tribunal may strike out the whole or a part of the proceedings if–

(a)   the appellant has failed to comply with a direction which stated that failure by the appellant to comply with the direction could lead to the striking out of the proceedings or part of them;

(b)   the appellant has failed to co-operate with the Tribunal to such an extent that the Tribunal cannot deal with the proceedings fairly and justly; or

(c)   the Tribunal considers there is no reasonable prospect of the appellant's case, or part of it, succeeding.

(4)   The Tribunal may not strike out the whole or a part of the proceedings under paragraph (2) or (3)(b) or (c) without first giving the appellant an opportunity to make representations in relation to the proposed striking out.

(5)   If the proceedings, or part of them, have been struck out under paragraph (1) or (3)(a), the appellant may apply for the proceedings, or part of them, to be reinstated.

(6)   An application under paragraph (5) must be made in writing and received by the Tribunal within 1 month after the date on which the Tribunal sent notification of the striking out to the appellant.

(7)   This rule applies to a respondent as it applies to an appellant except that–

(a)   a reference to the striking out of the proceedings is to be read as a reference to the barring of the respondent from taking further part in the proceedings; and

(b)   a reference to an application for the reinstatement of proceedings which have been struck out is to be read as a reference to an application for the lifting of the bar on the respondent from taking further part in the proceedings.

(8)   If a respondent has been barred from taking further part in proceedings under this rule and that bar has not been lifted, the Tribunal need not consider any response or other submission made by that respondent [¹ and may summarily determine any or all issues against that respondent].

Amendment
1.   Amended by r5(3) of SI 2010 No 2653 as from 29.11.10.

General Note
Rule 8 sets out the tribunal's powers to strike out all or part of an appeal (and to bar a respondent from participating in the proceedings). In the past, striking out was most common under reg 46(1)(d) of the former SS D&A Regs – ie, where an appellant did not return the TAS1 questionnaire that was sent out at the beginning of an appeal and which asked for information (eg, does the appellant want a hearing, does s/he need an interpreter) that is then used for listing purposes. However, from 3 November 2008, such appeals are no longer automatically struck out. Instead they are referred to a tribunal judge who may decide to list them for hearing or (as, in the absence of an Enquiry Form (as the TAS1 is now called), it is probable that no party will have objected to a decision without a hearing) decide them without a hearing under r27. The tribunal judge may also strike out the appeal under reg 8(3)(a). However, there is no power to strike out an appeal merely because the appellant has not completed and returned the enquiry form. That form (available at http://hmctsformfinder.justice.gov.uk/HMCTS/FormFinder.do) tells the appellant "Please complete in block capitals and return this form to us within 14 days". That is not, by any stretch of the imagination, a direction within r8(3)(a). That rule is referring to a direction given by the tribunal in relation to an individual case. By contrast, the quoted part of the form is a general administrative instruction (and is issued by HM Courts and Tribunals Service rather than by the First-tier Tribunal itself or of any individual tribunal judge); it uses the language of request rather than direction; and it does not "state that failure to comply could lead to the striking out of the proceedings or part of them" as is required by r8(3)(a). In any case, the exercise of that power is subject to the overriding objective and it is not immediately apparent how striking out the proceedings thereby depriving the claimant of access to the tribunal is a "fair and just" response to a failure to return an administrative form. Deciding such appeals rather than striking them out will sometimes be an unnecessary use of the resources of the tribunal. But the tribunal's resources, as opposed to the resources of the parties, are not listed as a relevant factor in r2(2). It might also be argued that deciding, rather than striking out, appeals in which the appellant may have lost interest will produce delay. However, under r2(2)(e) avoiding delay is only part of the overriding objective to the extent that it is "compatible with proper consideration of the issues": striking out the appeal prevents the issues from being considered at all, let alone properly.

See further *DTM v Kettering Borough Council (CTB)* [2013] UKUT 625 (AAC).

Analysis
Failure to comply with Directions: paras (1), (3)(a), (5) and (6)
Paras (1) and (3)(a) both provide for an appeal, or part of it, to be struck out where the appellant has failed to comply with a direction. Which paragraph applies depends upon the warning that was given as part of the direction that has been disobeyed. If the direction states that a failure to comply "will" lead to the striking out of the proceedings, then those proceedings will automatically be struck out under para (1) as soon as the time limit for compliance has expired. If, however, the warning said that the proceedings "could" be struck out (or, presumably, used some similar word such as "can", "might" or "may"), the tribunal has a discretion to strike out under para (3)(a).

The power to strike out in para (3)(a) must be exercised in accordance with the overriding objective. As para (1) does not confer a power, no consideration is given to the overriding objective before the proceedings are automatically struck out. However, the tribunal judge who gave the original direction (ie, the direction containing the warning that failure to comply would lead to an automatic strike out) must have been satisfied that it was in the interests of the overriding objective to include such a warning in the first place.

In a social security appeal (including HB), the circumstances in which it will be appropriate to strike out an appeal under paras (1) or (3)(a) will be exceptional. In *DTM v Kettering Borough Council (CTB)*, Judge Poynter stated:

"57.   The First-tier Tribunal's jurisdiction in relation to social security appeals is inquisitorial. When it is seised of an appeal, its primary duty is to decide that appeal on its merits. That is because giving a decision on the merits is usually the fairest and most just way of disposing of the proceedings. It is implicit in the requirement to seek to give effect to the overriding objective when exercising the power to strike out that that power should only be used in cases where striking out is a fairer, or more just, way of dealing with the appeal than giving a substantive decision.

58.   The fact that the Tribunal's jurisdiction is inquisitorial means that the issues in a social security appeal are likely to be less clearly defined than they would be in adversarial proceedings. There are no pleadings and the Tribunal exercises an "enabling role". What that means is that claimants are entitled to rely upon the special expertise of the Tribunal to ensure that the law is correctly applied to the facts of their case even if they themselves do not raise all the issues which arise from the evidence (see the decision of the Court of Appeal of Northern Ireland in *Mongan v Department of Social Development* [2005] NICA 16 (reported as *R 4/01(IS)*) and endorsed by the Court of Appeal of England and Wales in *Hooper v Secretary of State for Work and Pensions* [2007] EWCA Civ 495 at paragraphs 25–28).

59. Given the complexity of the social security system, a just outcome would be impossible in many appeals if the Tribunal did not perform that role. Its existence is often cited as a reason why it is not necessary to extend legal aid to social security appeals (e.g., *Tribunals for Users: One System, One Service, the report of the review of tribunals by Sir Andrew Leggatt*, The Stationery Office, London, 2001).

60. The fact that claimants may rely upon the Tribunal's enabling role means that they are permitted to use the appellate process to ask the Tribunal to check whether a decision about their benefits is correct. Claimants will often, and understandably, be unaware of the detailed rules about entitlement to benefits and the respondent's decision-making procedures. They will often be unable to identify with any precision why they believe a decision is wrong. Rule 23(6)(e) of the Procedure Rules requires that an appeal should state the grounds on which the appellant relies, so claimants must give the best explanation they can, but, once they have done so, the rules do not require them to participate any further in the process unless the Tribunal so directs.

61. So if a claimant sets out his or her case in the notice of appeal and then waits for the Tribunal to give its decision, that is a legitimate use of the Tribunal's procedures – and, in particular, its enabling role – not a basis for striking out the appeal. A claimant who does so is not misusing those procedures in the same way as claimants in adversarial proceedings misuse the procedures of a court if they commence proceedings and then do not pursue them.

62. A further aspect of the Tribunal's inquisitorial jurisdiction in social security appeals is that the role of the respondent is not adverse to the claimant (see Diplock J. (as he then was) in *R. v Medical Appeal Tribunal (North Midland Region), ex parte Hubble* [1958] 2 QB 228 at 240 as approved by the House of Lords in *Kerr v Department of Social Development*, [2004] UKHL 23 (also reported as R 1/04 (SF)) at para.61). That is so whether the respondent is the Secretary of State, HM Revenue & Customs or a local authority.

63. Entitlement to social security benefits is conferred by Parliament as a matter of right on claimants who satisfy the conditions of entitlement. The authorities that administer those benefits must do their best to ensure that such claimants receive their proper entitlement. If they do not do so, the purpose of the legislation conferring the right to benefit is frustrated as much as it is if benefits are awarded to those who are not entitled to them. The role of a respondent to a social security appeal is therefore to help the Tribunal arrive at the correct decision. There is no legitimate interest in the maintenance of the decision under appeal if that decision is incorrect and usually no unfairness, or injustice, to the respondent if the First-tier Tribunal checks that the decision is correct rather than striking out the appeal without consideration of the issues."

For examples of the practical problems that can result from use of the power of automatic strike out under para (1), see *DTM v Kettering Borough Council (CTB)* at paras 40–43 and 84 and *SL v SSWP and KL-D* [2014] UKUT 128 (AAC) at paras 12–15.

Where the proceedings have been struck out under paras (1) or (3)(a), the appellant may apply under para (5) for them to be reinstated. Under para (6) that application must be in writing. The tribunal is unlikely to grant the application unless, belatedly, the appellant complies with the original direction or, possibly, explains why it is not practicable to do so. Any application to reinstate must be received by the tribunal within a month after notice of the striking out was sent to the parties. That time limit can be extended under reg 5(3)(a) if it is in accordance with the overriding objective to do so.

Out of jurisdiction appeals: paras (2) and (4)

Where the First-tier Tribunal does not have jurisdiction, it must either transfer the appeal to another court or tribunal under r5(3)(k)(i) (para (2)(b)) or strike it out. An appeal may be out of jurisdiction either because it is not a decision that carries a right of appeal under Sch 7 para 6 TCEA 2007, or because it is listed in the Schedule to the D&A Regs or because it is out of time and no decision has been made to treat it as in time under r23 or reg 19 D&A Regs or to extend time under r5(3)(a).

Before striking an appeal out under para (2), the tribunal must give the appellant an opportunity to make representations in relation to the proposed striking out: para (4). When seeking representations, the tribunal should bear in mind that an unrepresented appellant may not understand that an appeal that is "struck out", will not continue – ie, that the outcome will be as if the appellant had lost: see *AM v Information Commissioner* [2014] UKUT 239 (AAC) (at paras 31 and 65). The tribunal may (r5(3)(f)), but does not have to (r27(3)), hold a hearing to give the appellant that opportunity. The discretion to hold a hearing must be consciously exercised and, at least if a written statement of reasons is requested, reasons must be given: see *AM v Information Commissioner* (above) (at paras 3 and 61) and the earlier cases referred to in that decision. In that case, it was held that Guidance Notes issued by the tribunal which, as the Upper Tribunal held, contained "a clear representation that if one party to an appeal chose an oral hearing (as the appellant had done), there would be an oral hearing" was relevant to the exercise of the discretion.

There is no power to reinstate an appeal that has been struck out under para (2). However, the decision to strike out may be appealed to the Upper Tribunal (subject to permission being granted): see the decision of the three-judge panel in *LS v Lambeth LB (HB)* [2010] UKUT 461 (AAC); [2011] AACR 27. This means that, once an application for permission to appeal has been made, the First-tier Tribunal has power to review the decision under s9 TCEA and r40. A decision to strike out an appeal also disposes of the proceedings and may therefore be set aside under r37 in an appropriate case.

Failure to co-operate: paras (3)(b) and (4)

Under para (3)(b), the tribunal may strike out the appeal if the appellant has "failed to co-operate with the tribunal to such an extent that the tribunal cannot deal with the proceedings fairly and justly". It is difficult to envisage circumstances in which such a failure to co-operate did not involve a failure to comply with a specific direction (in which case, the proceedings would be more safely struck out under paras (1) or (3)(a)). One possible example may be where an appellant misconducts her/himself during a hearing to an extent that makes it impossible to continue with the hearing. However, the power in para (3)(b) is subject to the obligation in para (4) to give the appellant an opportunity to make representations in relation to the proposed striking out. It is unclear how the tribunal could give the appellant that opportunity without first adjourning. If the tribunal has to adjourn in any event, it may be preferable to give a direction under rule 30(5)(a) excluding the appellant from future hearings.

For guidance on the exercise of the power conferred by para (3)(b), see *AD v Information Commissioner and Devon CC* [2013] UKUT 550 (AAC).

There is no power to reinstate an appeal that has been struck out under para (3)(b). However, as with out-of-jurisdiction appeals, there is a right of appeal to the Upper Tribunal and the decision to strike out may be set aside for procedural reasons under r37.

No reasonable prospects of success: paras (3)(c) and (4)

Rule 8(3)(c) is permissive, not mandatory. The tribunal may, not must, strike out the appeal, if it has no reasonable prospect of success: see Judge Lane in *NT v FtT (CIC)* [2014] UKUT 210 (AAC) (at para 17).

It is suggested that the power in para (3)(c) should be exercised sparingly. Almost every tribunal judge will have experience of appeals which, on the papers, could not possibly succeed but, in the event, did so. There is also little to gain administratively from striking such appeals out. Once again, the power cannot be exercised without giving the appellant an opportunity to make representations in relation to the proposed striking out (para (4)) and making those representations may involve holding a hearing: rr5(3)(f) and 27(3). If, having received those representations, the tribunal is satisfied that the appeal has no reasonable prospects of success then the better course is to give a decision disallowing it on the merits rather than striking it out.

In *R(AM) v First-tier Tribunal (CIC)* [2013] UKUT 333 (AAC), Judge Rowland said (at para 11):

"The effect of striking a case out under rule 8(3)(c) is to deprive a person of an oral hearing and it should therefore be used to weed out hopeless cases but not cases that are merely weak. Moreover, it is important that it is not used in a way that prejudices those better at expressing themselves orally than in writing and in particular so that those with mental health problems are not prejudiced."

and (at paragraph 19):

"In the Social Entitlement Chamber of the First-tier Tribunal, where substantive hearings are usually very short, there can be few occasions when there is any point in striking a case out under rule 8(3)(c) at a hearing rather than proceeding to hear the substantive appeal ..."

In *AW v Information Commissioner and Blackpool City Council* [2013] UKUT 30 (AAC), Judge Wikeley approved the summary of the law in Jacobs, *Tribunal Practice and Procedure*, Legal Action Group, 2nd edn, 2011, at para 12.39 to the effect that striking out an appeal as having no reasonable prospects of success: "is only appropriate if the outcome of the case is, realistically and for practical purposes, clear and incontestable. It is not usually appropriate if facts relevant to the ultimate outcome of the case are disputed".

An application to strike out an appeal as having no prospects of success should normally be accompanied by a full response, complying with r24(4), and that response must be copied to the claimant by the decision maker: see *JT v HMRC (TC)* [2015] UKUT 81 (AAC) at para 22 where Judge Rowland stated:

"22.   An application for the striking out of an appeal can be distinguished from a response to an appeal but, except where providing a full response would clearly be disproportionate, there are several reasons why an application for the striking out of an appeal under rule 8(3)(c) on the ground that it has no prospects of success should be accompanied by a full response and should be copied to the claimant. First, it is obviously difficult for the First-tier Tribunal to decide whether an appeal has any prospects of success unless it has a substantial amount of information about the merits of the appeal. Secondly, rule 8(4) requires the First-tier Tribunal to give the appellant an opportunity to make representations in relation to the proposed striking out and the claimant needs a copy of the application in order to make effective representations. Striking an appeal out rather than determining it is not likely to be justified unless there will be a saving of time and money and requiring the First-tier Tribunal to send the claimant the application rather than the decision maker doing it is likely to be both time-consuming and more costly. Thirdly, and again in the interests of saving time and money, the provision of a response with an application for striking out enables the First-tier Tribunal to proceed to list the case for determination straightaway if not minded to strike it out."

There is no power to reinstate an appeal that has been struck out under para (3)(c). However, the decision to strike out carries the same right of appeal to the Upper Tribunal (and gives rise to the same possibilities of review and procedural set aside) as a decision to strike out for lack of jurisdiction or failure to co-operate.

Barring respondents from further participation in the proceedings: paras (7) and (8)
One innovation of the November 2008 changes is that a respondent may now be barred from taking further part in the proceedings in the same circumstances as an appellant's appeal may be struck out. The power to bar respondents from further participation in the proceedings "is a draconian provision, and it should be used only in the most blatant cases of disregard on the part of a party to the proceedings": see *FC v Suffolk CC (SEN)* [2010] UKUT 368 (AAC). So far as practicable, the overriding objective requires the tribunal to ensure that the parties are able to participate fully in proceedings. The same is presumably true of the power to strike out an appeal under r8(3) TP(FTT) Rules or to give a direction that may lead to an automatic strike out under r8(1).

The tribunal may lift a bar in the same circumstances as it may reinstate an appeal that has been struck out. A decision to bar a respondent and a decision to lift, or not to lift the bar, carries the same right of appeal as a decision to strike out (and to reinstate, or not to reinstate) an appeal. The decision to determine all or any issues against a barred respondent disposes of proceedings and may therefore be set aside under r37, although it is arguable that a barred respondent has no right to apply for a set aside.

Barring a respondent should be a matter of last resort. The tribunal should consider whether more proportionate means are available to the same end. If, for example, a local authority is in default of a direction to produce evidence, a witness summons – or the threat of one – addressed to the Chief Executive or the Leader of the Council can work wonders. Often the tribunal needs the participation of the respondent which may be the only party with relevant evidence.

A respondent who has been barred nevertheless remains a party to the appeal and is entitled to attend any hearing held by the First-tier Tribunal (unless excluded under r30(5)), although s/he cannot take part in the hearing: see *CW v SSWP and another (CSM)* [2014] UKUT 290 (AAC) (at paras 35–38). In addition, s/he retains the right of appeal to the Upper Tribunal and, as part of that right, the right to request a written statement of reasons under r34 – the word "proceedings" in r8 does not refer to all stages of the First-tier Tribunal proceedings and, in particular, not the post-decision stages of the appeal (which only occur after the proceedings have been "disposed of"): *CW v SSWP and another* (above) (at paras 53–59). However, the fact that the respondent has been barred may be relevant to what need be included in that statement: see *ZB v SSWP (CSM)* [2013] UKUT 367 (AAC).

In *SL v SSWP and KL-D*, Judge Jacobs gave detailed guidance about the effects of barring a respondent as follows.

"17.   Rule 8 bars a party from taking further part in the proceedings. It does not operate retrospectively to render that which has already been done nugatory or invalid: rule 7(1). Evidence submitted and submissions made remain before the tribunal and have to be taken into account. When it provides that 'the Tribunal need not consider any response or other submission made by that respondent' it means any future response or submission.

18.   Rule 8(8) provides that the tribunal 'may summarily determine any or all issues against that respondent.' This is not a penal provision. The tribunal cannot simply accept the appellant's case if the respondent is barred. It must still act in accordance with the overriding objective when considering whether to exercise this power. And it is, on basic principle as part of its duty to act fairly, required to act rationally on material of probative value in making its decision: *Mahon v New Zealand Ltd* [1984] AC 808 at 820-821 (Lord Diplock). This requires it to give proper consideration to submissions made and to take account of evidence submitted. The key word in rule 8(8) is summarily. It allows the tribunal to deal with the respondent's case rather more briefly than would otherwise be required.

19.   The effect of rule 8 is to bar a respondent from participating in the proceedings. It does not remove that person as a party.

20.   That means that a respondent barred from participating retains the right to appeal to the Upper Tribunal: section 11(2).

21.   An application to the First-tier Tribunal for permission to appeal to the Upper Tribunal is a separate proceeding from the appeal itself: *Harkness v Bell's Asbestos and Engineering Ltd* [1967] 2 QB 729 at 735 (Lord Denning MR) and 736 (Diplock LJ). To put it another way, barring only applies to the proceedings on the appeal. A party who is barred from participating may, therefore, nonetheless apply to the First-tier Tribunal for permission to appeal.

22.   Even if that is wrong, barring under rule 8 applies only to the proceedings before the First-tier Tribunal: rule 1(2). It has no effect on the Upper Tribunal, which has power to waive any irregularity in its own rules as a result of a party's inability to apply for permission from the First-tier Tribunal: rule 7(2)(a).

23.   When the Upper Tribunal sets aside a decision of the First-tier Tribunal and remits the case for reconsideration, the proceedings before the First-tier Tribunal are fresh proceedings. Any barring or strike out no longer operates. This follows from the rules of procedure, the nature of a rehearing and practical considerations.

24.   As to the rules of procedure, they envisage that there comes a point at which proceedings on appeal are concluded. They do so by attaching consequences to the (final) disposal of the proceedings or of all the issues in the proceedings. See the definition of 'party' in rule 1(2), rule 17(1)(a) (withdrawal), rule 27(3) (striking out without a hearing), rule 33 (notice of decision), rule 34 (reasons for decision) and rule 37 (setting aside).

25.   As to the nature of a rehearing, there is no provision for proceedings to revive following a successful appeal, whether in statute, in the rules of procedure, or on the general principles on the operation of appeals. If a case is remitted, the First-tier Tribunal considers the case afresh. The earlier proceedings are now past …"

Substitution and addition of parties

9.–(1)   The Tribunal may give a direction substituting a party if–

(a)   the wrong person has been named as a party; or

(b)   the substitution has become necessary because of a change in circumstances since the start of proceedings.

(2)   The Tribunal may give a direction adding a person to the proceedings as a respondent.

(3)   If the Tribunal gives a direction under paragraph (1) or (2) it may give such consequential directions as it considers appropriate.

General Note

Before considering whether to add a person as a respondent to the appeal under r9(2), the tribunal should consider whether s/he is already a respondent by operation of law: see the General Note to r1(2) on p985 and in particular, *Salisbury Independent Living v Wirral MBC (HB)* [2011] UKUT 44 (AAC) (although that decision has been reversed on other grounds by the Court of Appeal – see *Wirral MBC v Salisbury Independent Living* [2012] EWCA 84; [2012] AACR 37). For the approach to be adopted in adding respondents who are not already parties by operation of law, see *CM v HMRC (TC)* [2014] UKUT 272 (AAC).

No power to award costs

10.   The Tribunal may not make any order in respect of costs (or, in Scotland, expenses).

Representatives

11.–(1)   A party may appoint a representative (whether a legal representative or not) to represent that party in the proceedings.

(2)   Subject to paragraph (3), if a party appoints a representative, that party (or the representative if the representative is a legal representative) must send or deliver to the Tribunal written notice of the representative's name and address.

(3)   In a case to which rule 23 (cases in which the notice of appeal is to be sent to the decision maker) applies, if the appellant (or the appellant's representative if the representative is a legal representative) provides written notification of the appellant's representative's name and address to the decision maker before the decision maker provides its response to the Tribunal, the appellant need not take any further steps in order to comply with paragraph (2).

(4)   If the Tribunal receives notice that a party has appointed a representative under paragraph (2), it must send a copy of that notice to each other party.

(5)   Anything permitted or required to be done by a party under these Rules, a practice direction or a direction may be done by the representative of that party, except signing a witness statement.

(6)   A person who receives due notice of the appointment of a representative–

(a)   must provide to the representative any document which is required to be provided to the represented party, and need not provide that document to the represented party; and

(b)   may assume that the representative is and remains authorised as such until they receive written notification that this is not so from the representative or the represented party.

(7)   At a hearing a party may be accompanied by another person whose name and address has not been notified under paragraph (2) or (3) but who, with the permission of the Tribunal, may act as a representative or otherwise assist in presenting the party's case at the hearing.

(8)   Paragraphs (2) to (6) do not apply to a person who accompanies a party under paragraph (7).

General Note

A party may appoint a representative who need not be legally qualified: para (1). Appointment is effected by sending written notice of the representative's name and address to the tribunal (para (2)) or, if the party appointing the representative is the appellant, by giving such notice to the decision maker before the decision maker provides the tribunal with a response to the appeal under r24: para (3). If the tribunal receives notice under para (2), it must send a copy to all the other parties: para (4).

Once appointed, the representative may do anything permitted or required to be done by the party s/he represents except signing a witness statement: para (5). However, it is doubted that para (5) entitles a representative to give oral evidence at a hearing instead of an appellant. Once the tribunal and the other parties have been notified that a representative has been appointed, they may deal with her/him instead of the appellant and may continue to do so until notified that the representative has ceased to act. In particular, they must provide the representative with any relevant document and need not also provide a copy to the appellant. As many representative organisations are unable to attend hearings for funding reasons, the effect of the rule about documents is likely to be that more appellants attend tribunal hearings without the papers. Representatives who are unable to attend hearings themselves should ensure that they give the appeal papers to the appellant in good time and tell the appellant to take those papers to the hearing.

The decision of Judge Williams in *BB v SSWP (ESA)* [2014] UKUT 55 (AAC) highlights, perhaps unintentionally, an ambiguity in the wording of r11(6). The rule appears to operate prospectively – ie, any person who is given notice that a representative has been appointed must *in future* send any document that s/he would otherwise be required to send to the represented party to the representative instead. The additional provision that the person 'need not provide the document to the represented party' is otiose if the rule covers documents that have already been provided to that party in the past.

However, Judge Williams appears (the decision is brief and it is not entirely clear) to have interpreted the rule as meaning that documents that have been sent in the past to the party must be sent again to the representative. The judge stated that "all relevant documents **must** be given to the representative once due notice is received" (original emphasis).

If that is what was intended, then it is doubted whether the decision is correct. The rule does not state that "all relevant documents" must be provided to the representative. It says that documents which are "required to be provided to the represented party" must be so provided. Where a document has been provided to a party in the past, any requirement to provide it ceases to exist. So, any document that has already been provided to the party before the appointment of the representative is no longer a document which is required to be provided to the represented party and therefore need not be provided to the representative.

Nevertheless, the decision in *BB v SSWP (ESA)* exists and may be of assistance to representatives who need to obtain duplicate copies of documents from the First-tier Tribunal.

In *MP v SSWP (DLA)* [2010] UKUT 103 (AAC), the Upper Tribunal considered the position where under r11(3), the appellant notifies the decision maker of the details of her/his representative before the decision maker delivers the response to the First-tier Tribunal. Judge Turnbull stated:

"The Tribunals Service would therefore have been justified, under the express terms of Rule 11(6)(b), in sending the Enquiry Form to the solicitors only, but I do not think that there was any procedural irregularity in it being sent (and sent only, it appears) to the Claimant. The Enquiry Form does not appear to have been a document which was required to be provided, within the meaning of Rule 11(3)(a) *[sic, an obvious typographical error for 11(6)(a)]*, and so there was strictly no breach of the Rules in it being sent only to the Claimant. Nor do I think that the sending of it to the Claimant, rather than to the solicitors, involved a breach of natural justice. The Claimant of course had the opportunity to complete the Enquiry Form properly, and the fact that a paper hearing took place without her solicitors' knowledge was caused by the fact that she did not complete it properly. One might nevertheless question whether, in cases where the Tribunals Service is notified by the decision maker, in accordance with the procedure in Rule 11, that a representative has been appointed, it is sensible for the Tribunals Service to send the Enquiry Form to the claimant rather than to the representative. (I have examined the files in a number of other cases, and that does indeed appear to be the general practice of the Tribunals Service.) In many cases where a representative is appointed initially the reason may be that the claimant is hampered in dealing with his or her affairs, and there is therefore the potential for errors of the nature which occurred in this case to result. But it seems to me that the safeguard, if an error which causes unfairness does occur, lies in the power to set aside in Rule 37, and at the end of the day no harm should therefore result."

There is no absolute rule that representatives can only give evidence of matters within their personal knowledge: see *PM v SSWP (IS)* [2014] UKUT 474 (AAC) (applying what was said by Judge Jacobs about the evidence of submission writers and presenting officers in *Walsall MBC v PL (HB)* [2009] UKUT 27 (AAC)).

In the vast majority of cases, the First-tier Tribunal is entitled to accept that a representative's factual assertions, especially those of a professional representative, are made on a claimant's instruction so that they may be treated as part of the body of evidence. However, there may be cases in which the "representative's factual assertions and other arguments [are] so bizarre" that the tribunal should consider whether it is the representative rather than the claimant who might not be reliable: see *DI v SSWP (PIP)* [2018] UKUT 350 (AAC) at paras 22 and 23.

Calculating time

12.–(1)   Except in asylum support cases, an act required by these Rules, a practice direction or a direction to be done on or by a particular day must be done by 5pm on that day.

(2)   If the time specified by these Rules, a practice direction or a direction for doing any act ends on a day other than a working day, the act is done in time if it is done on the next working day.

(3)   In this rule "working day" means any day except a Saturday or Sunday, Christmas Day, Good Friday or a bank holiday under section 1 of the Banking and Financial Dealings Act 1971.

General Note

Para (1) provides that time for doing anything required by the Rules, a practice direction or a direction expires at 5.00 pm on the day in question.

Paras (2) and (3) provide that a time limit can only expire on a working day.

Sending and delivery of documents

13.–(1)   Any document to be provided to the Tribunal under these Rules, a practice direction or a direction must be–

(a)   sent by pre-paid post or delivered by hand to the address specified for the proceedings;

(b)   sent by fax to the number specified for the proceedings; or

(c)   sent or delivered by such other method as the Tribunal may permit or direct.

(2)   Subject to paragraph (3), if a party provides a fax number, email address or other details for the electronic transmission of documents to them, that party must accept delivery of documents by that method.

(3)   If a party informs the Tribunal and all other parties that a particular form of communication (other than pre-paid post or delivery by hand) should not be used to provide documents to that party, that form of communication must not be so used.

(4)   If the Tribunal or a party sends a document to a party or the Tribunal by email or any other electronic means of communication, the recipient may request that the sender provide a hard copy of the document to the recipient. The recipient must make such a request as soon as reasonably practicable after receiving the document electronically.

(5)   The Tribunal and each party may assume that the address provided by a party or its representative is and remains the address to which documents should be sent or delivered until receiving written notification to the contrary.

Use of documents and information

14.–(1)   The Tribunal may make an order prohibiting the disclosure or publication of–

(a)   specified documents or information relating to the proceedings; or

(b)   any matter likely to lead members of the public to identify any person whom the Tribunal considers should not be identified.

(2)   The Tribunal may give a direction prohibiting the disclosure of a document or information to a person if–

(a)   the Tribunal is satisfied that such disclosure would be likely to cause that person or some other person serious harm; and

(b)   the Tribunal is satisfied, having regard to the interests of justice, that it is proportionate to give such a direction.

(3)   If a party ("the first party") considers that the Tribunal should give a direction under paragraph (2) prohibiting the disclosure of a document or information to another party ("the second party"), the first party must–

(a)   exclude the relevant document or information from any documents that will be provided to the second party; and

(b)   provide to the Tribunal the excluded document or information, and the reason for its exclusion, so that the Tribunal may decide whether the document or information should be disclosed to the second party or should be the subject of a direction under paragraph (2).

(4)   The Tribunal must conduct proceedings as appropriate in order to give effect to a direction given under paragraph (2).

(5)   If the Tribunal gives a direction under paragraph (2) which prevents disclosure to a party who has appointed a representative, the Tribunal may give a direction that the documents or information be disclosed to that representative if the Tribunal is satisfied that–

(a)   disclosure to the representative would be in the interests of the party; and

(b)   the representative will act in accordance with paragraph (6).

(6)   Documents or information disclosed to a representative in accordance with a direction under paragraph (5) must not be disclosed either directly or indirectly to any other person without the Tribunal's consent.

Evidence and submissions

15.–(1)   Without restriction on the general powers in rule 5(1) and (2) (case management powers), the Tribunal may give directions as to–

(a)   issues on which it requires evidence or submissions;

(b)   the nature of the evidence or submissions it requires;

(c)   whether the parties are permitted or required to provide expert evidence;

(d)   any limit on the number of witnesses whose evidence a party may put forward, whether in relation to a particular issue or generally;

(e)   the manner in which any evidence or submissions are to be provided, which may include a direction for them to be given–

(i)   orally at a hearing; or

(ii)   by written submissions or witness statement; and

(f)   the time at which any evidence or submissions are to be provided.

(2)   The Tribunal may–

(a)   admit evidence whether or not–

(i)   the evidence would be admissible in a civil trial in the United Kingdom; or

(ii)   the evidence was available to a previous decision maker; or

(b)   exclude evidence that would otherwise be admissible where–

(i)   the evidence was not provided within the time allowed by a direction or a practice direction;

(ii)   the evidence was otherwise provided in a manner that did not comply with a direction or a practice direction; or

(iii)   it would otherwise be unfair to admit the evidence.

(3)   The Tribunal may consent to a witness giving, or require any witness to give, evidence on oath, and may administer an oath for that purpose.

General Note

Para (1) confers supplementary case management powers on the tribunal in relation to evidence and submissions.

Para (2)(a) provides that the tribunal "may" admit evidence whether or not the evidence would be admissible in a civil trial or was available to the decision maker. Predecessors to the First-tier Tribunal (eg, social security appeal tribunals) were not bound by the rules on admissibility of evidence (see, for example, *CDLA 2014/2004* and the list of cases cited in para 10 of that decision): the only evidential issues were whether the evidence was relevant and, if so, how much weight to attach to it. Given that background, it is suggested that, unless para (2)(b) applies, the tribunal not only "may" but "must" admit all evidence that is relevant to the issues it has to decide.

It is also suggested that the First-tier Tribunal should be slow to exercise the power in para (2)(b) to exclude evidence. The overriding objective is unlikely to be served by excluding relevant evidence and, while the late production of evidence is an irritating obstacle to the smooth running of the tribunal's list, it is rare for late evidence to prejudice the other parties to the appeal or, indeed, to affect its outcome. If so, why create a collateral ground of appeal by refusing to consider it? And in those cases where the late evidence is determinative, it is unjust to exclude it and thereby reach the wrong result.

Para (3) permits the tribunal to take evidence on oath. Tribunal judges hold differing views on how helpful this is. However, it would be rare for the tribunal to refuse to allow a party or witness who wanted to give evidence on oath to do so.

Summoning or citation of witnesses and orders to answer questions or produce documents

16.–(1)   On the application of a party or on its own initiative, the Tribunal may–

(a)   by summons (or, in Scotland, citation) require any person to attend as a witness at a hearing at the time and place specified in the summons or citation; or

(b)   order any person to answer any questions or produce any documents in that person's possession or control which relate to any issue in the proceedings.

(2)   A summons or citation under paragraph (1)(a) must–

(a)   give the person required to attend 14 days' notice of the hearing or such shorter period as the Tribunal may direct; and

(b)   where the person is not a party, make provision for the person's necessary expenses of attendance to be paid, and state who is to pay them.

(3)   No person may be compelled to give any evidence or produce any document that the person could not be compelled to give or produce on a trial of an action in a court of law in the part of the United Kingdom where the proceedings are due to be determined.

(4)   A summons, citation or order under this rule must–

(a)   state that the person on whom the requirement is imposed may apply to the Tribunal to vary or set aside the summons, citation or order, if they have not had an opportunity to object to it; and

(b)   state the consequences of failure to comply with the summons, citation or order.

General Note

The power in r16(1)(b) to order any person to produce documents does not extend to the production of documents that are subject to legal professional privilege, see *LM v Lewisham LB* [2009] UKUT 204 (AAC); [2010] AACR 12.

Withdrawal

17.–(1)   Subject to paragraph (2), a party may give notice of the withdrawal of its case, or any part of it–

(a)   [¹] by sending or delivering to the Tribunal a written notice of withdrawal; or

(b)   orally at a hearing.

(2)   In the circumstances described in paragraph (3), a notice of withdrawal will not take effect unless the Tribunal consents to the withdrawal.

(3)   The circumstances referred to in paragraph (2) are where a party gives notice of withdrawal–

(a)   [¹] in a criminal injuries compensation case; [¹]

[¹ (b)   in a social security and child support case where the Tribunal has directed that notice of withdrawal shall take effect only with the Tribunal's consent; or

(c)   at a hearing.]

[² (4)   An application for a withdrawn case to be reinstated may be made by–

(a)   the party who withdrew the case;

(b)   where an appeal in a social security and child support case has been withdrawn, a respondent.]

[² (5)   An application under paragraph (4) must be made in writing and be received by the Tribunal within 1 month after the earlier of–

(a)   the date on which the applicant was sent notice under paragraph (6) that the withdrawal had taken effect; or

(b)   if the applicant was present at the hearing when the case was withdrawn orally under paragraph (1)(b), the date of that hearing.]

(6)   The Tribunal must notify each party in writing [¹ that a withdrawal has taken effect] under this rule.

Amendments

1.   Amended by r24 of SI 2013 No 477 as from 8.4.13.

2.   Substituted by r14 of SI 2015 No 1510 as from 21.8.15.

General Note

A party may withdraw its case by giving written notice of withdrawal or by word of mouth at a hearing. In HB appeals, withdrawal is only relevant to parties to the appeal other than the local authority – eg, the claimant, or her/his landlord if relevant. An authority that became persuaded that the grounds of appeal were correct should instead revise the decision against which the appeal was brought, thereby causing the appeal to lapse.

From 8 April 2013, the withdrawal of the appeal is effected by giving the notice specified in r17(1) and does not require the consent of the tribunal unless a direction has previously been given under r17(3)(b) (ie, that notice of withdrawal shall take effect only with the tribunal's consent). Such directions will be rare in practice, not least because most appeals in the Social Entitlement Chamber are not reviewed by a judge before the hearing. As with all other powers conferred by the Rules, the power to direct that withdrawal shall take effect only with the tribunal's consent must be exercised so as to further the overriding objective in r2. It will not usually be appropriate to give that direction. Even if the tribunal has decided that the correct decision will be more disadvantageous to the appellant than the decision s/he has appealed against, the withdrawal of the appeal will not normally prevent the authority from revising its decision to the appellant's detriment after the withdrawal. An exception might be in three-party appeals where the claimant has not exercised her/his right of appeal because the landlord has done so. Even then it might only be appropriate if there was a risk that the claimant would be unable to make her/his own appeal because of the time limits.

Paras (4) and (5) contain a power for the tribunal to reinstate a withdrawn appeal. Note that since 21 August 2015, it is not only the party who withdrew the appeal who can apply for it to be reinstated. A respondent can also do so. The time limit in para (5) may be extended under rule 5(3)(a) if it is in accordance with the overriding objective to do so.

For guidance on the factors that may be relevant on an application under r17(4) to reinstate an appeal that has been withdrawn with consent, see the decision of the Upper Tribunal in a mental health appeal: *JS v South London and Maudsley NHS Foundation Trust and the Secretary of State for Justice* [2019] UKUT 172 (AAC).

Lead cases

18.–(1)   This rule applies if–
(a)   two or more cases have been started before the Tribunal;
(b)   in each such case the Tribunal has not made a decision disposing of the proceedings; and
(c)   the cases give rise to common or related issues of fact or law.
(2)   The Tribunal may give a direction–
(a)   specifying one or more cases falling under paragraph (1) as a lead case or lead cases; and
(b)   staying (or, in Scotland, sisting) the other cases falling under paragraph (1) ("the related cases").
(3)   When the Tribunal makes a decision in respect of the common or related issues–
(a)   the Tribunal must send a copy of that decision to each party in each of the related cases; and
(b)   subject to paragraph (4), that decision shall be binding on each of those parties.
(4)   Within 1 month after the date on which the Tribunal sent a copy of the decision to a party under paragraph (3)(a), that party may apply in writing for a direction that the decision does not apply to, and is not binding on the parties to, a particular related case.
(5)   The Tribunal must give directions in respect of cases which are stayed or sisted under paragraph (2)(b), providing for the disposal of or further directions in those cases.
(6)   If the lead case or cases lapse or are withdrawn before the Tribunal makes a decision in respect of the common or related issues, the Tribunal must give directions as to–
(a)   whether another case or other cases are to be specified as a lead case or lead cases; and
(b)   whether any direction affecting the related cases should be set aside or amended.

General Note

For the first time, r18 establishes a formal procedure for dealing with related or "lookalike" appeals. Note that, under paras 9 and 10 of the Senior President's Practice Statement *Composition of Tribunals in Social Security and Child Support Cases in the Social Entitlement Chamber on or after 1 August 2013*, the decision to treat a case as a lead case (whether under r18 or otherwise) can only be made by the Chamber President.

[¹ Confidentiality in social security and child support cases

19.–(1)   Paragraph (4) applies to–
(a)   *[Omitted]*;
(b)   proceedings where the parties to the appeal include former joint claimants who are no longer living together in the circumstances described in paragraph (3).

(2)   *[Omitted]*

(3)   The circumstances referred to in paragraph (1)(b) are that one of the former joint claimants would like their address to be kept confidential and has given notice to that effect–

(a)   in the notice of appeal or when notifying the decision maker or the tribunal of any subsequent change of address; or

(b)   within 14 days after an enquiry is made by the recipient of the notice of appeal or the notification referred to in sub-paragraph (a).

(4)   Where this paragraph applies, the Secretary of State or other decision maker and the Tribunal must take appropriate steps to secure the confidentiality of the address and of any information which could reasonably be expected to enable a person to identify the address, to the extent that the address or that information is not already known to each other party.

(5)   In this rule–

"absent parent", "non-resident parent" and "person with care" *[Omitted]*;

"joint claimants" means the persons who made a joint claim for a jobseeker's allowance under the Jobseekers Act 1995, a tax credit under the Tax Credits Act 2002 or in relation to whom an award of universal credit is made under Part 1 of the Welfare Reform Act 2012.]

Amendment

1.   Substituted by r35 of SI 2014 No 2128 as from 20.10.14.

Expenses in social security and child support cases

21.–(1)   This rule applies only to social security and child support cases.

(2)   The Secretary of State may pay such travelling and other allowances (including compensation for loss of remunerative time) as the Secretary of State may determine to any person required to attend a hearing in proceedings under section 20 of the Child Support Act 1991, section 12 of the Social Security Act 1998 or paragraph 6 of Schedule 7 to the Child Support, Pensions and Social Security Act 2000.

PART 3

Proceedings before the Tribunal

CHAPTER 1

Before the hearing

Cases in which the notice of appeal is to be sent to the Tribunal

22.–[¹ (1)   This rule applies to all cases except those to which–

(a)   rule 23 (cases in which the notice of appeal is to be sent to the decision maker), or

(b)   rule 26 (social security and child support cases started by reference or information in writing), applies.]

(2)   An appellant must start proceedings by sending or delivering a notice of appeal to the Tribunal so that it is received–

(a)   in asylum support cases, within 3 days after the date on which the appellant received written notice of the decision being challenged;

(b)   in criminal injuries compensation cases, within 90 days after the date of the decision being challenged [¹;

(c)   in appeals under the Vaccine Damage Payments Act 1979(c), at any time;

(d)   in other cases–

(i)   if mandatory reconsideration applies, within 1 month after the date on which the appellant was sent notice of the result of mandatory reconsideration;

(ii)   if mandatory reconsideration does not apply, within the time specified in Schedule 1 to these Rules [⁴ (time limits for providing notices of appeal in social security and child support cases where mandatory reconsideration does not apply)]].

(3)   The notice of appeal must be in English or Welsh, must be signed by the appellant and must state–

(a)   the name and address of the appellant;

(b)   the name and address of the appellant's representative (if any);

(c)   an address where documents for the appellant may be sent or delivered;

(d)   the name and address of any respondent [¹ other than the decision maker];

[¹ (e)] and

(f)   the grounds on which the appellant relies.

(4)   The appellant must provide with the notice of appeal–

[¹ (a) a copy of–

    (i)   the notice of the result of mandatory reconsideration, in any social security and child support case to which mandatory reconsideration applies;

    (ii)   the decision being challenged, in any other case;]

(b)   any statement of reasons for that decision that the appellant has [¹; and];

(c)   any documents in support of the appellant's case which have not been supplied to the respondent; [¹]

[¹ (d)]

(5)   In asylum support cases the notice of appeal must also–

(a)   state whether the appellant will require an interpreter at any hearing, and if so for which language or dialect; and

(b)   state whether the appellant intends to attend or be represented at any hearing.

(6)   If the appellant provides the notice of appeal to the Tribunal later than the time required by paragraph (2) or by an extension of time allowed under rule 5(3)(a) [² [³]] (power to extend time)–

(a)   the notice of appeal must include a request for an extension of time and the reason why the notice of appeal was not provided in time; and

(b)   [¹ subject to paragraph (8)] unless the Tribunal extends time for the notice of appeal under rule 5(3)(a) [² [³]] (power to extend time) the Tribunal must not admit the notice of appeal.

(7)   The Tribunal must send a copy of the notice of appeal and any accompanying documents to each other party–

(a)   in asylum support cases, on the day that the Tribunal receives the notice of appeal, or (if that is not reasonably practicable) as soon as reasonably practicable on the following day;

(b)   in [¹ all other], as soon as reasonably practicable after the Tribunal receives the notice of appeal.

[⁴ (7A)   *[Omitted]*]

[¹ (8)   Where an appeal in a social security and child support case is not made within the time specified in paragraph (2)–

(a)   it will be treated as having been made in time, unless the Tribunal directs otherwise, if it is made within not more than 12 months of the time specified and neither the decision maker nor any other respondent objects;

(b)   the time for bringing the appeal may not be extended under rule 5(3)(a) by more than 12 months.

[⁴ (9)   For the purposes of this rule, mandatory reconsideration applies where–

(a)   the notice of the decision being challenged includes a statement to the effect that there is a right of appeal in relation to the decision only if the decision-maker has considered an application for the revision, reversal, review or reconsideration (as the case may be) of the decision being challenged; or

(b)   *[Omitted]*]

Amendments

1.   Amended by r25 of SI 2013 No 477 as from 8.4.13.

2.   Amended by r25 of SI 2013 No 2067 as from 1.11.13.

3.   Amended by r22 of SI 2014 No 514 as from 6.4.14.

4.   Amended by r15 of SI 2015 No 1510 as from 21.8.15.

Cases in which the notice of appeal is to be sent to the decision maker

23.–[¹ (1)   This rule applies to [⁴ appeals under paragraph 6 of Schedule 7 to the Child Support, Pensions and Social Security Act 2000 (housing benefit and council tax benefit: revisions and appeals) or under section 22 of the Child Trust Funds Act 2004]]

(2)   An appellant must start proceedings by sending or delivering a notice of appeal to the decision maker so that it is received [⁴ [⁵]–

(a)   in a housing benefit or council tax benefit case [⁵, no later than the latest of]–

    (i)   one month after the date on which notice of the decision being challended was sent to the appellant;

    (ii)   if a written statement of reasons for the decision was requested within that month, 14 days after the later of–

        (aa)   the end of that month; or

        (ab)   the date on which the written statement of reasons was provided; or

    (iii)   if the appellant made an application for a revision of the decision under regulation 4(1)(a) of the Housing Benefit and Council Tax Benefit (Decisions and Appeals) Regulations 2001 and that application was unsuccessful, one month after the date on which notice that the decision would not be revised was sent to the appellant;

(b)   *[Omitted]*].

(3)   If the appellant provides the notice of appeal to the decision maker later than the time required by [⁴ paragraph (2)(a)] the notice of appeal must include the reason why the notice of appeal was not provided in time.

(4)   Subject to paragraph (5), where an appeal is not made within the time specified in [⁴ paragraph (2)], it will be treated as having been made in time [² if neither the decision maker nor any other respondent objects].

(5)   No appeal may be made more than 12 months after the time specified in [⁴ paragraph (2)].

(6)   The notice of appeal must be in English or Welsh, must be signed by the appellant and must state–

(a)   the name and address of the appellant;

(b)   the name and address of the appellant's representative (if any);

(c)   an address where documents for the appellant may be sent or delivered;

(d)   details of the decision being appealed; and

(e)   the grounds on which the appellant relies.

(7)   The decision maker must refer the case to the Tribunal immediately if–

(a)   the appeal has been made after the time specified in [⁴ paragraph (2)] and the decision maker [² or any other respondent] objects to it being treated as having been made in time; or

(b)   the decision maker considers that the appeal has been made more than 12 months after the time specified in [⁴ paragraph (2)].

[¹ (8) Notwithstanding rule 5(3)(a) [⁴] (case management powers) and rule 7(2) (failure to comply with rules etc.), the Tribunal must not extend the time limit in paragraph (5).]

Amendments

    1.   Inserted by r3 of SI 2009 No 1975 as from 1.9.09.

    2.   Amended by r4(2) of SI 2012 No 500 as from 6.4.12.

    3.   Substituted by r26 of SI 2013 No 477 as from 8.4.13.

    4.   Amended by r16 of SI 2015 No 1510 as from 21.8.15.

    5.   Amended by r2 of SI 2018 No 1053 as from 30.10.18.

General Note

The TP(FTT) Rules were amended from 21 August 2015 to clarify, among other things, which appeals are to be lodged at the First-tier Tribunal, and which are to be lodged with the decision maker. Thus, r23 now only applies to HB (and CTB) appeals, and appeals under s22 Child Trust Funds Act 2004.

Paras (1), (2) and (7). HB appeals must be made by sending or delivering a notice of appeal to the decision maker (ie, the local authority) within the time limit specified in para (2)(a). Broadly speaking, this is one month from the date on which notice of the decision being appealed was sent to the claimant: para(2)(a)(i). However, where the appellant requests a written statement of reasons for the decision under appeal (ie, under reg 90(2) HB Regs or reg 71 HB(SPC) Regs) within that one-month period, the time limit for appealing is extended until 14 days after the one-month period or 14 days after the date on which the statement of reasons was provided: para (2)(a)(ii). Para (2)(a)(iii) provides the time limit if the appellant applied for a revision of the disputed decision under reg 4(1)(a) D&A Regs and the application was unsuccessful. In this case, the appeal must be made no later than one month after notice that the decision would not be revised was sent to the appellant.

Note that until 21 August 2015, the time limit for appealing in HB cases was in Sch 1 of these rules. Before 1 November 2010, the effect of Sch 1 para (b) (now r23(2)(a)(ii)) was to circumvent the (supposedly) absolute 13-month time limit (see p1039 of the 22nd edition). Before 1 September 2009, the drafting of Sch 1 para (c) (now r23(2)(a)(iii) of these rules) was also defective. See p1101 of the 21st edition for details.

If the appeal is late, the notice of appeal must explain why: para (3). Note, however, that in an appropriate case, the tribunal may waive that requirement under r7(2)(a).

No appeal may be made more than 12 months after the time limit specified in para (2): para (5). Subject to that absolute limit:

(1)   The decision maker may treat a late appeal as having been made in time if the criteria in reg 19(6)–(9) D&A Regs are satisfied.

(2)   If the decision maker cannot treat the appeal as having been made in time, the tribunal must nevertheless do so as long as the decision maker does not object: para (4).

(3)   If the decision maker does object, the tribunal may still extend the time for appealing under rule 5(3)(a) if it is in accordance with the overriding objective to do so.

Under para (7) the decision maker must refer the appeal to the tribunal immediately if it considers that it has been made outside the absolute time limit or if, although made within that limit, the authority objects to the appeal being treated as having been made in time.

Para (6) sets out the requirements for a valid appeal.

(1)   The notice must be in English or Welsh.

(2)   The notice must be signed by the appellant.

This requirement is also met if the notice is signed by the appellant's solicitor: see *CO v LB Havering (CH)* [2015] UKUT 28 (AAC) at paras 22–31. In *R v Lambeth LBC ex p Crookes* (1998) 31 HLR 59, QBD, the High Court had held that an equivalent requirement in reg 79(2) of the Housing Benefit (General) Regulations 1987 could only be satisfied by the personal signature of the claimant. However, as noted in previous editions, the decision in *Crookes* strongly relied upon the decision of the Court of Appeal in *re Prince Blucher* [1931] 2 Ch D 70, which was held to have been wrongly decided by the Privy Council in *General Legal Council ex p Basil Whitter v Barrington Earl Frankson* [2006] UKPC 42. In those circumstances, Upper Tribunal Judge Wikeley declined to follow *Crookes* in *CO* and that decision is now binding on the First-tier Tribunal.

Where the notice is signed by a representative who does not hold a professional qualification, such as a Citizens Advice adviser or a local authority welfare rights worker, the position is more complex. If the representative provides a letter of authority signed by the claimant then "for the purposes of rule 26(3) they are, in practical terms, in the same position as a solicitor who writes on the instructions of their client": see *CO* at para 30. If no authority is provided, it cannot always be assumed that the representative is acting on the claimant's instructions. However, it is suggested that where subsequent investigation establishes that the representative did have authority, it will usually be appropriate for the tribunal to waive the failure to comply with the requirement for the claimant's signature under r7 TP(FTT) Rules.

(3)   The notice must state the appellant's name and address, the name and address of any representative, an address for service of documents, details of the decision being appealed and the grounds of appeal.

(4)   The details of the decision being appealed must be sufficient for that decision to be identified. The grounds of appeal need only be in general terms (the requirement is to state the "grounds on which the appellant relies", not to give particulars of those grounds). It is unrealistic to expect an unrepresented appellant to identify all the relevant points with precision. Simply to say "I want to appeal" is insufficient, but, for example, "I disagree with your decision that I have no liability for rent" is probably sufficient, since that raises questions of fact and law. Authorities may well want to seek further details of the challenge on an informal basis in order to respond to the appeal.

Appellants and their representatives are advised to remember that under Sch 7 para 6(9a) CSPSSA, the tribunal "need not consider any issue that is not raised by the appeal" (see p147). It is therefore important to raise all possible issues at the earliest opportunity.

Useful guidance on the question of how decision makers should approach the issue of whether the notice of appeal gives "details of the decision being appealed" as is required by r23(6)(d) is given by Judge Warren in *CS v SSWP (DLA)* 2011 UKUT 509 AAC (at para 18):

"18.   I agree that the tribunal were correct to treat the appeal as being against both the entitlement decision and the overpayment decision. Appellants often have difficulty in identifying the decision or decisions which they should appeal. I note in this case that the official form used by the appellant asked her to indicate the "date at the top of the letter about the decision" and that the box provided for this purpose was not large enough for two dates to be entered. This case also demonstrates the injustice that an inflexible approach might cause. By the time of the First Tier Tribunal hearing the overpayment decision was more than 13 months old. It was therefore no longer possible for another appeal to be lodged, even with an extension of time. In my judgement the approach to be adopted, is that, once the appellant has expressed a grievance in the letter of appeal, it is then for those more knowledgeable with the process, by they officers of the DWP or tribunal judges to identify the decision or the decisions which are the source of the appellant's grievance and then to treat the letter of appeal accordingly. This approach accords with the spirit of Kerr. It is also in line with that adopted by Judge Jacobs, then a social security commissioner, in CJSA/714/2004 when he held that a tribunal should have considered not just whether a second claim should have been backdated but also whether an earlier one had been correctly refused."

Sch 1 contains the time limits for appealing. In social security cases, the limit is normally one month from the date on which the decision being appealed was sent to the appellant: para (a). However, where the appellant requests a written statement of reasons for the decision under appeal (ie, under reg 90(2) HB Regs or reg 71 HB(SPC) Regs) within that one-month period, the time limit for appealing is extended until 14 days after the one-month period or 14 days after the date on which the statement of reasons was provided. Until 1 November 2010, the effect of para (b) was to circumvent the (supposedly) absolute 13-month time limit (see p1039 of the 22nd edition). Until 1 September 2009, the drafting of para (c) was also defective. See p1101 of the 21st edition for details.

Responses and replies

24.–[¹ (1) When a decision maker receives a copy of a notice of appeal from the Tribunal under rule 22(7), the decision maker must send or deliver a response to the Tribunal–

(a)-(b) *[Omitted]*; and

(c) in other cases, within 28 days after the date on which the decision maker received the copy of the notice of appeal.

(1A) Where a decision maker receives a notice of appeal from an appellant under rule 23(2), the decision maker must send or deliver a response to the Tribunal so that it is received as soon as reasonably practicable after the decision maker received the notice of appeal.]

(2) The response must state–

(a) the name and address of the decision maker;

(b) the name and address of the decision maker's representative (if any);

(c) an address where documents for the decision maker may be sent or delivered;

(d) the names and addresses of any other respondents and their representatives (if any);

(e) whether the decision maker opposes the appellant's case and, if so, any grounds for such opposition which are not set out in any documents which are before the Tribunal; and

(f) any further information [¹] required by a practice direction or direction.

(3) The response may include a submission as to whether it would be appropriate for the case to be disposed of without a hearing.

(4) The decision maker must provide with the response–

(a) a copy of any written record of the decision under challenge, and any statement of reasons for that decision, if they were not sent with the notice of appeal;

(b) copies of all documents relevant to the case in the decision maker's possession, unless a practice direction or direction states otherwise; and

(c) in cases to which rule 23 (cases in which the notice of appeal is to be sent to the decision maker) applies, a copy of the notice of appeal, any documents provided by the appellant with the notice of appeal and (if they have not otherwise been provided to the Tribunal) the name and address of the appellant's representative (if any).

(5) The decision maker must provide a copy of the response and any accompanying documents to each other party at the same time as it provides the response to the Tribunal.

(6) The appellant and any other respondent may make a written submission and supply further documents in reply to the decision maker's response.

(7) Any submission or further documents under paragraph (6) must be provided to the Tribunal within 1 month after the date on which the decision maker sent the response to the party providing the reply, and the Tribunal must send a copy to each other party.

Amendment

1.   Amended by r27 of SI 2014 No 477 as from 1.10.14.

General Note

An authority that receives a notice of appeal under r23 must prepare a response and send it to the tribunal "as soon as reasonably practicable after the decision maker received the notice of appeal": para (1A).

The "response" is, in effect, the document that was referred to colloquially as the "submission" in appeals to the former appeal tribunals. It must contain the information specified in para (2) and be accompanied by the documents specified in para (4), namely:

Head (a): a copy of the written record of the decision under challenge, and any statement of reasons for that decision. The reference in head (a) to "if they were not sent with the notice of appeal" applies to appeals (not HB appeals) which are commenced by sending the notice of appeal to the tribunal rather than to the decision maker. Setting out in black and white that the decision maker must let the tribunal know the precise terms of the decision it is considering might be thought superfluous. Unfortunately, experience with HB/CTB appeals since 2001 shows that it is not. Being required to tell the tribunal what decisions they have made will involve a significant change of culture at some authorities.

Head (b): copies of all documents relevant to the case in the decision maker's possession. "Document" is defined by r1(3) and means "anything in which information is recorded in any form", including, for example, recordings of telephone calls which recorded information: see *AG v HMRC (TC)* [2013] UKUT 530 (AAC).

The important words here are "relevant to the case". Relevant documents must be produced even if the decision maker does not wish to rely upon them and even if – one might say particularly if – they do not assist the authority's case. The obligation to provide copies of relevant documents is not "cut down by consideration of what the appellant might have in his or her possession and be able to put before the tribunal": see *ST v SSWP (ESA)* [2012] UKUT 469 (AAC) at para 25.

In *FI v HMRC (CHB)* [2018] UKUT 226 (AAC), HMRC submitted that Head (b) did not require it to provide copies of departmental records that "indicate the claimant may be self-employed but do not on the balance of probabilities show that she is" with the response. The Upper Tribunal (Judge Mitchell) rejected that submission as confusing its responsibilities as a party to proceedings with those of the First-tier Tribunal. He continued:

"17.   … It is not for the public authority respondent to an appeal to determine whether a document proves a particular fact…That is the function of the First-tier Tribunal. The approach advocated by HMRC would involve it usurping the constitutional role that Parliament has entrusted to the First-tier Tribunal.

18.   Rule 24 of the First-tier Tribunal's rules required HMRC to supply all "relevant" documents. The evaluation of a document's relevance must be carried out in a manner that respects the constitutional role of the First-tier Tribunal. On an appeal, the tribunal is the (judicial) body charged with determining whether a piece of evidence proves any fact on a balance of probabilities. A document should be considered relevant, and hence disclosed, if the Tribunal could (not would) rely on it to make any relevant finding of fact. Applying that test, on the description of the evidence given by HMRC in these proceedings they were required to supply the documentation to the First-tier Tribunal."

It will be particularly important for the authorities to comply with head (b) in overpayment cases. Submissions to the tribunal in such cases regularly fail to include the decision notices for the original (ie, allegedly incorrect) awards and a proper schedule explaining how the alleged overpayment has been calculated. The tribunal has an inquisitorial role. Without the former information it can be difficult for the tribunal to understand how the overpayment is said to have arisen and – more importantly – verify that the original decision has been properly revised or superseded so that there is an overpayment in the first place. In overpayment cases where there has been an interview under caution, the transcript of that interview is a relevant document and must be produced to the tribunal by the local authority: see *LM v LB Southwark (HB)* [2015] UKUT 86 (AAC) at paras 35–43.

Head (c): again, one might have thought it would be unnecessary to make regulations requiring authorities to include a copy of the notice of appeal in the appeal papers. For a minority of authorities, however, head (c) will be a useful reminder.

The requirement in rule 24(2)(c) for the response to state any grounds for opposing the appeal "must include not only an explanation for [the local authority's] findings of fact but also an explanation of the legal basis for [its] decision". It is "obviously arguable" that rule 24(2)(e), taken together with rule 2(2)(c) and (4)(a), and read with the decision of the Court of Appeal in *R (Gudanaviciene) v Director of Legal Aid Casework* [2014] EWCA Civ 1622 at [46], "require the [respondent] to set out his grounds for opposing an appeal in a manner that has regard to his duty to enable the First-tier Tribunal to ensure, so far as is practicable, that the claimant is able to participate fully in the proceedings under conditions that do not place him or her at a substantial disadvantage vis-a-vis the [respondent]": see the decision of Judge Rowland in *LH v SSWP (PIP)* [2018] UKUT 57 (AAC) at paras 27 and 32–34. Judge Rowland continued:

"35.   In my judgment, it is the combination of the duty to give reasons for opposing the appeal and the duty to act fairly that require the Secretary of State to take a different approach in proceedings before the First-tier Tribunal from the approach he takes to his own decision-making. In making decisions himself, he may be entitled to investigate a claim by giving a claimant opportunities to provide information without fully explaining what information might be relevant …. However, proceedings before the First-tier Tribunal are judicial and judicial standards of fairness apply."

"As soon as reasonably practicable". Decision makers in social security and child support cases are the only parties that are not required by the rules to comply with a proper time limit – ie, expressed by reference to a finite period of time. Even the time limit imposed on the tribunal – which in practice means a judge, not a party to the appeal – is subject to a primary time limit of one month in which to produce a statement of reasons under r34(5). This exemption of government departments and local authorities, from the rules that apply to ordinary citizens is an unfortunate anomaly in the rules and may raise issues of "equality of arms" under Art 6 of the ECHR. It may be argued that the exemption is necessary because it takes longer to produce a response (which has to be properly structured and argued and be accompanied by all relevant documents) than it does to produce an appeal (which need only say, for example, "I do not agree with your decision that my tenancy is uncommercial"). But even if one accepts that point, it only justifies there being a longer time limit for decision makers than exists for claimants and landlords. It does not justify an indefinite time limit.

The leading authority on what is "practicable" in the context of social security law is *R v Secretary of State for Social Services ex p CPAG* [1990] 2 QB 540, CA, (Balcombe, Woolf and Russell LJJ). The Court was considering s99(1) Social Security Act 1975 which provided that an "adjudication officer to whom a claim or question is submitted … shall take …, so far as practicable, dispose of it …, within 14 days of its submission to him." The Court held that:

"[t]here is nothing in the language of section 99(1) which means that it is not permissible to look at factors other than those involved in an individual claim in deciding whether it was practicable to come to a decision within 14 days. Section 99(1) does not require matters independent of the claim to be ignored in deciding what is practical. The volume of claims awaiting determination and the number of investigating officers available to deal with the claims are examples of matters which can be relevant to the decision as to whether or not it was practicable to come to a determination within the 14 day period".

Except, perhaps, in the case of a flagrant delay, it will therefore be difficult for a claimant to show that an authority has taken longer than is "reasonably practicable" to produce a response because s/he will have no information as to the resources available to the decision maker or what other demands there are on those resources.

In *MB v Wychavon DC (HB)* [2013] UKUT 67 (AAC) there had been a long delay in preparing the appeal (the facts were not clear but it was either approximately six months or approximately one year). The Upper Tribunal comments include reference to the views of the Local Government Ombudsman to the effect that 28 days should be the time within which authorities attempt to prepare the response:

"8.   […] According to the claimant in his submissions to the First-tier Tribunal, during the period of delay Wychavon continually stated to him that they could take as long as they liked in submitting the appeal and that their internal resources were such that they had to externally source the preparation of the tribunal application. Whatever the truth of this, and Wychavon has not had the opportunity to respond to this claim, the delay by Wychavon in notifying the appeal to the tribunal was wholly unacceptable. I also note from the bundle of documents submitted by the claimant to the tribunal at the tribunal hearing that the reference to the tribunal only occurred after intervention by the claimant's MP in November 2011.

9.   There is no excuse whatsoever for such delay by Wychavon. Claimants can suffer severe hardship if a claim for benefit is refused. The duty to initiate the appeal proceedings that might lead to the amelioration of that hardship is placed on the council whose decision is being appealed. Independently of any special provision in the regulations, there is a duty on them to act with reasonable speed in forwarding notification of the appeal to the tribunal. They cannot simply do it as and when they please and while some allowance may be made for temporary staff shortages or similar problems, a delay even from late December to July would be unacceptable, let alone one until the following November which is then only remedied after the local MP has intervened.

10.   The Local Government Ombudsman has made it clear in *Complaint No 01/C/13400* against Scarborough BC that authorities should aim to refer all appeals to HMCTS within 28 days. As I also pointed out in *CH/3497/2005*, a claimant is entitled under Article 6 of the European Convention on Human Rights to have his or her appeal heard within a reasonable time, and this could be particularly important in housing benefit cases where a delay could cost a tenant his home. It is unlawful for a local authority or any other public authority to act (which includes a failure to act) in a way which is incompatible with a Convention right (Human Rights Act 1998, s.6(1), (6)). The conduct of Wychavon in this case was wholly unacceptable and inconsistent with the proper conduct of this appeal."

It is unclear whether the tribunal can shorten the authority's time for producing a response by giving a direction under its power (in r5(3)(a)) to "shorten the time for complying with any rule". To do so the tribunal would either have to direct the authority to deliver the response "sooner than reasonably practicable" or within a specified number of days. The former would probably be perverse. The latter does not involve "shortening" (or "extending") a time limit as much as substituting a definite time limit for an indefinite one or, arguably, imposing a time limit where none previously existed. However, such difficulties do not mean that the tribunal is powerless in the face of local authority delay. As is clear from *R(H) 1/07*, as long as a valid appeal has been made, the tribunal has jurisdiction over it even if it has not been registered. Under r5(1), the tribunal may regulate its own procedure. In an appropriate case, it may therefore decide the appeal in the absence of a response (possibly waiving the requirement to provide one under r7) as long as it is satisfied that the authority has had a reasonable opportunity to provide one. Alternatively, it could use its case management powers under rr5 and (in particular) 15 to direct the authority to make submissions and produce evidence equivalent (in substance, if not in name) to a response. A finite time limit may be imposed as part of such directions and, ultimately, an authority may be barred from further participation under r8(7) if those time limits are not met.

Provision of response to other parties: para (5). In the absence of a direction to the contrary in an individual case, the local authority must always send a copy of the response to the other parties as well as to the First-tier Tribunal: see *TM v HMRC (TC)* [2013] UKUT 444 (AAC) at paras 5–7. If an authority wishes to absolve itself of its duty to provide its written appeal response to an appellant (or her/his representative or any other party to the appeal), it must first makes its case to the First-tier Tribunal and obtain a direction to that effect. It would be extremely rare for such a direction to be given.

Further submissions: paras (6) and (7). Other parties may make a submission in reply and supply further documents within one month from the date the response is sent to them. It is suggested that the effect of these provisions is that (unless it expressly shortens the time limit) the tribunal cannot decide the appeal – or, at least, decide it in a manner that is adverse to the appellant or a respondent other than the decision maker – without giving a month for further comment. It does not mean that no further documents can be produced (or written submissions made) after the one-month limit has expired unless the tribunal gives leave. Even if that interpretation is wrong, the power to exclude evidence under r15(2) does not apply to evidence that is late merely because the limit in para (7) has expired. That power applies where "the evidence was not provided within the time allowed by a **direction or practice direction**" (emphasis added). It does not apply to evidence produced later than is allowed by a **rule**. And if the tribunal has no power to exclude such evidence, it inevitably follows that, provided the evidence is relevant, the tribunal must consider it.

CHAPTER 2
Hearings

Decision with or without a hearing

27.–(1) Subject to the following paragraphs, the Tribunal must hold a hearing before making a decision which disposes of proceedings unless–
- (a) each party has consented to, or has not objected to, the matter being decided without a hearing; and
- (b) the Tribunal considers that it is able to decide the matter without a hearing.

(2) This rule does not apply to decisions under Part 4.

(3) The Tribunal may in any event dispose of proceedings without a hearing under rule 8 (striking out a party's case).

(4)-(6) *[Omitted]*

General Note

"Hearing" is defined by r1(2) as meaning "an oral hearing". That phrase includes hearings conducted by telephone, video link or other means of instantaneous two-way electronic communication. Before the establishment of the First-tier Tribunal, it was common to refer colloquially to the process of deciding an appeal by considering only the written submissions and documentary evidence as a "paper hearing". That terminology will probably continue but, given the definition in r1(2), a "paper hearing" is now a contradiction in terms and the phrase "oral hearing" is tautologous.

Under r5(3)(f), the tribunal may hold a hearing in relation to any matter. Rule 27 is concerned with when the tribunal must hold a hearing. It says that, with four exceptions, the tribunal must hold a hearing "before making a decision which disposes of proceedings" – ie, a final decision of the appeal. Those four exceptions are: consent of all the parties (para (1)(a)); absence of objection from any party (para (1)(a)); post-hearing interlocutory decisions (para (2)) and striking out under rule 8 (para (3)). The first two of those exceptions only apply if, *in addition*, the tribunal considers it is able to decide the matter without a hearing (para (1)(b)). Therefore, the tribunal must over-rule the parties' wishes (or lack of objection) unless it considers, having regard to the overriding objective, that a hearing is not necessary.

In *TMcG v SSWP (ESA)* [2013] UKUT 411 (AAC), the claimant attended the hearing venue on the day of the hearing. The claimant, while he was in the waiting room, was told that his appeal had been allowed and he did not need to attend. Unfortunately, although he had won his appeal, he had not achieved everything he could have done via the decision of the tribunal. The Upper Tribunal set aside the First-tier tribunal decision on the basis the claimant had been denied a right to a hearing. The decision is a useful warning: where a tribunal has taken a preliminary view the appeal will succeed it should still ensure that the appellant goes into the tribunal room (and so the right to a hearing is respected albeit that the procedure can be brief).

The decision of Judge Mesher in *MM v SSWP (ESA)* [2011] UKUT 334 (AAC) holds that the discretion not to hold a hearing must be consciously exercised and, if a statement of reasons is requested, it should record that fact and include reasons for the exercise of the discretion. Failure to do so will amount to an error of law.

It may also be a procedural irregularity which might justify the decision's being set aside under r37.

Any reasons given for the tribunal's substantive decision must not undermine the reasons given for deciding not to hold a hearing: see *JP v SSWP (IB)* [2011] UKUT 459 (AAC) (at paras 16–20) in which the tribunal had decided to proceed without holding a hearing and then held the appellant's absence against her when weighing her evidence.

The duty to hold a hearing unless the appeal can be decided fairly and justly without one continues throughout the case and cannot be decided as a preliminary issue: see *KO v SSWP (ESA)* [2013] UKUT 544 (AAC) and *DT v SSWP (UC)* [2019] UKUT 268 (AAC). In effect, the First-tier Tribunal cannot decide finally whether a hearing is needed until it knows what that decision would be and its reasons for reaching it. In cases where a claimant has asked for a decision on the papers because s/he is unable to attend a hearing in person (eg, for reasons of ill-health such as agoraphobia), the overriding objective may require the tribunal to attempt to overcome that inability "by considering whether her participation in the hearing could have been facilitated, for instance by offering to her/him the opportunity to participate by telephone or skype, or explaining to her/him that taxi fares could be reimbursed": see *LC v SSWP (DLA)* [2015] UKUT 100 (AAC) at para 10.

In *FY v SSWP (ESA)* [2017] UKUT 501 (AAC), the First-tier Tribunal had decided that it was able to decide the appeal without holding a hearing because it considered it had "adequate information to come to a reasoned decision". Judge Hemingway emphasises (at paras 9–10) that the test is not whether the First-tier Tribunal has sufficient evidence to make a decision without a hearing, but whether it is fair and just to do so: "there is not necessarily a connection between what is fair and just and an ability to reason out a decision on the available documents".

The fact that rule 27(1)(a) gives the respondent an automatic right to a hearing even if the appellant does not want – and cannot attend – one does not infringe the principle of "equality of arms" and, therefore, complies with Art 6 ECHR: see *FY v SSWP (RP)* [2018] UKUT 146 (AAC).

Before proceeding with a hearing in absence, on the basis that an appellant does not wish to attend a hearing, tribunals should check the claimant's address and read her/his correspondence with HMCTS: see *TA v SSWP (PIP)* [2018] UKUT 26 (AAC).

In some cases, rule 27(1)(a) will require the First-tier Tribunal to consider expressly whether a telephone hearing is desirable: see *JM v SSWP (PIP)* [2018] UKUT 108 (AAC) at paras 4–7.

Consent is not the same thing as the absence of objection and there must be evidence that it has been positively given: see *IB v Information Commissioner and Dorset Police* [2013] UKUT 582 (AAC). Before reaching a decision without a hearing in a case where there has been no positive consent to that course, it is necessary for the tribunal to consider carefully on the facts of each individual case whether a claimant has "not objected" to a decision without a hearing: *SB v SSWP (ESA)* [2012] UKUT 249 (AAC).

Once an authority has prepared a response to the appeal, it must submit it to HMCTS accompanied by a covering sheet (Form AT37). That form requires the authority to state whether it requires a hearing of the appeal. HMCTS then sends the response to the appellant (and any other respondent) together with an Enquiry Form (the former TAS1). The Enquiry Form asks "Do you want to have a hearing where you and your representative, if you have one, can meet the Tribunal and put your case?"

It is very important that appellants should answer 'yes' to that question and should attend the hearing that will then be held. Many people do not like the prospect of having to attend a hearing but the advantages of doing so are clear as the Guidance Notes to the Enquiry Form state:

"The advantage of a hearing is that you have an opportunity to speak to the Tribunal and the Tribunal has an opportunity to learn more about your case than it could gather from the appeal papers alone. Most people who appeal opt for a hearing. Statistically, *more than twice as many* appeals are successful with a hearing." (emphasis added).

Why is it that an appeal is more than twice as likely to succeed if there is a hearing? There are a number of factors:

(1)   In most cases, it is ultimately for the appellant to prove that s/he is entitled to the benefit s/he has claimed and not for the authority to prove that s/he is not. This means that the authority, not the appellant gets the benefit of any doubt. If the appeal papers leave the tribunal in doubt – eg, if they fail to mention a necessary fact, the appellant will lose unless there is a hearing and the tribunal can ask questions to elicit the missing evidence.

(2)   It is quite likely that an appellant will not include all the necessary facts in the papers. Social security law is complex and – at least where s/he is unrepresented – the appellant may simply not realise that a particular fact is relevant and needs to be mentioned.

(3)   Experience suggests that appellants tend to overestimate their powers of written explanation. (The same is also true of local authorities but that is not relevant to this discussion.) Their case is clear to them and they therefore assume it will be clear to everybody. Often, however, an appellant's explanation of her/his case assumes background knowledge that the tribunal does not share and will never learn unless the appellant comes to a hearing and answers the tribunal's questions. Most tribunal judges (and other

members) will be able to give examples of appeals that seemed hopeless on paper, but which eventually succeeded because the appellant attended a hearing.

(4) Many appeals turn on an assessment of credibility – ie, on whether the tribunal accepts that the appellant is telling the truth. Except for cases in which the appellant's case is wholly implausible, it is often difficult for the tribunal to assess who is telling the truth without being able to ask questions. Again, the appellant will not usually get the benefit of any doubt.

The procedure at a tribunal hearing is more formal than, say, at most meetings an appellant will attend, but it is much less formal than a court. The tribunal judge and other members will not wear robes and will normally sit on the other side of a table from the parties, rather than on a raised "bench". The tribunal has an enabling role and, although it must remain impartial, will try to help appellants put their cases in the best way possible. The tribunal (and any presenting officer from the authority) will want to ask the appellant questions (and appellants should not assume that their version of events will automatically be accepted) but hostile cross-examination of the type portrayed in television "court-room dramas" is strongly discouraged. Finally, hearings are normally held in public: if an appellant is concerned about attending a hearing or wants to know what happens at a hearing s/he can go to the local tribunal venue and sit in on a hearing as an observer before her/his own appeal is heard.

If, nevertheless, the appellant answers that s/he does not want a hearing, the Enquiry Form advises that "we will go ahead on the basis that you have no objection to your appeal being decided by the Tribunal in your absence. You can still write to us with anything you would like the Tribunal to take into consideration, but please do so within the next 14 days". The 14 day time limit is not consistent with r24(6) and (7) which allows a minimum of one month in which to reply to the response unless that time limit is shortened by a case management direction under r5(3)(a) – ie, a direction made by a judge in an individual case not an administrator as part of a general form. Even if the Enquiry Form is returned on the last day of the 14-day period that is allowed, a further 14 days will expire 28 days from the date on which the response was sent to the appellant. Except for February (and even then only three times every four years) 28 days is less than a month. Nevertheless, an appellant who requests a decision without a hearing but cannot obtain all the evidence s/he wants to submit within the 14 day period would be well advised to write in within that time limit and request an extension.

Where the appellant does not return the Enquiry Form at all, the appeal will be submitted to a tribunal judge for case management directions or a decision. In such cases the appellant will not have "objected to" a decision without a hearing and the tribunal judge may therefore decide the appeal there and then, request further evidence and submissions, or list the decision for a hearing. In *RM v SSWP* [2009] UKUT 256 (AAC), the Upper Tribunal allowed a DLA appeal where the First-tier Tribunal had refused the appeal without a hearing. The appellant suffered from fits and told the First-tier Tribunal that she could not attend a hearing because she was scared that lights would trigger her fits off. Judge Williams stated:

"In my view this is precisely the sort of case where a tribunal's decision to hear the case on paper creates a danger of prejudging the outcome decision. The appellant clearly wanted to attend a hearing, and clearly knew it was to her advantage to do so, but felt unable to do so for precisely the reason she was claiming the allowance. There is no indication that the tribunal considered the reasons why the appellant stated that she could not attend the hearing and therefore did not. It did not consider whether it should adjourn for a domiciliary visit or for further evidence. But there was the clearest evidence from both the appellant and from her general practitioner of the reasons why she could not attend a tribunal where there was a risk that the lights would set off a fit. So do crowds of people. Nor, in common experience, could a tribunal hearing be held in the normal way in conditions that involved no such risks. So the appellant's approach to not attending the tribunal was entirely consistent with her claim for the allowance. In my view this is one of those rare cases where the inquisitorial function of the tribunal required that it consider whether it was being fair in taking no steps to deal with this justified fear of the appellant about attempting to attend the tribunal hearing."

Even when an appellant does not object to the appeal being decided without a hearing, s/he is still entitled to at least a month in which to make a written submission and supply further documents in response to the decision maker's response (see rr24(6) and (7)). Unless the appellant indicates that s/he does not have anything further to say or wishes to produce further evidence, a decision made within that period will be liable to be set aside under r37(2)(d) (see *MP v SSWP (DLA)* [2010] UKUT 103 (AAC)).

'Post-hearing' decisions: para (2)
The tribunal may make a decision under Part 4 of the Rules to correct, set aside, or review a decision (or not to correct it, set it aside or review it) and to grant or refuse permission to appeal without holding a hearing.

Striking out: para (3)
In most cases, the whole point of striking out an appeal will be to bring it to an end without the trouble and expense of a hearing. Para (3) therefore excludes decisions under r8 from the requirement to hold a hearing before disposing of proceedings.

Rule 32(2)
Note, finally, that the tribunal need not hold a hearing if it disposes of the appeal by a consent order under r32.

Entitlement to attend a hearing

28. Subject to rule 30(5) (exclusion of a person from a hearing), each party to proceedings is entitled to attend a hearing.

Notice of hearings

29.–(1)   The Tribunal must give each party entitled to attend a hearing reasonable notice of the time and place of the hearing (including any adjourned or postponed hearing) and any changes to the time and place of the hearing.

(2)   The period of notice under paragraph (1) must be at least 14 days except that–

(a)   *[Omitted]*; and

(b)   the Tribunal may give shorter notice–

    (i)   with the parties' consent; or

    (ii)   in urgent or exceptional circumstances.

General Note

The tribunal must "give" the parties "reasonable notice" of the date, time and place of the hearing. Under para (2), that period of notice must normally be at least 14 days but the primary requirement of "reasonable notice" in para (1) leaves open the possibility that in some cases the parties may be entitled to more than 14 days' notice.

The Rules contain no equivalent to reg 2(2) D&A Regs under which notice sent to a claimant by post is deemed to have been "given" on the date it is posted. In those circumstances, the date on which notice of the hearing is given would appear to be governed by s7 Interpretation Act 1978 which is in the following terms:

"References to service by post.

> 7.   Where an Act authorises or requires any document to be served by post (whether the expression "serve" or the expression "give" or "send" or any other expression is used) then, unless the contrary intention appears, the service is deemed to be effected by properly addressing, pre-paying and posting a letter containing the document and, unless the contrary is proved, to have been effected at the time at which the letter would be delivered in the ordinary course of post."

Para (2)(b) allows the tribunal to give less than 14 days' notice if the parties consent or in urgent or exceptional cases. It is suggested that it will be rare for a social security case to be so urgent that a hearing is required in less than 14 days even when the parties do not consent.

Para (1) does not merely entitle the parties to reasonable notice of the time and place of the hearing but also to "any changes to the time and place of the hearing". It is, at the very least, arguable that the 14-day period in para (2) applies to changes in the time or place of the hearing as it does to the initial notification of that hearing. Nevertheless, it is not uncommon for tribunals to telephone the parties to rearrange the time of a hearing on the day of the hearing or the day before. This practice was considered (without reference to r29) by Judge Wikeley in *GK v SSWP (ESA)* [2016] UKUT 465 (AAC). Judge Wikeley stressed (at para 9) that any alteration to the listing arrangements for the day is a case management decision for the tribunal judge and, therefore, subject to the overriding objective. The judge then continued:

> "10.   There are a number of other reasons why considerable caution may need to be exercised about moving an appeal listed hearing time on the day. Just because an appellant lives relatively near to the venue does not mean s/he does not have other commitments. The hearing time may have been scheduled by the regional listing team following consultation with the appellant for a given time for a particular reason which may not be immediately evident from the file. There is a clear risk that a revised starting time on the day may put the appellant at some inconvenience but he or she may still feel obliged to agree to a new start time for the hearing, not wishing to upset the panel. Much may depend on how the clerk put any such request to the appellant. There is a world of difference between a clerk telephoning and saying "The Tribunal can now see you at 2 pm today, are you free to come along early?" and saying "Your hearing is fixed at 4 pm. If it is convenient to you, but only if it is, in fact the Tribunal could hear your appeal at 2 pm today. Please do not feel obliged to change the time; the Tribunal will of course see you as agreed at 4 pm if that is better for you."
>
> 11.   There may, of course, be some cases where an appellant is genuinely only too happy to agree to an earlier hearing slot on the day. It may reduce (rather than heighten) their sense of anxiety. It may fit in better with their domestic commitments, e.g. the school run. But tribunals should be very wary of making assumptions in this regard. As a starting point, tribunals would be well advised to start from the position that there should be a good reason to change a previously notified hearing start time. A last minute change in the listing arrangements – which, in the context of an appeal that may have been pending several months, a change on the day amounts to – is likely to add to (rather than detract from) an individual's general sense of anxiety about the hearing. The convenience of the tribunal panel members can hardly be regarded as a pressing reason in terms of the overriding objective."

It also follows from the fact that altering listing arrangements is a case management decision, that it is not something that can properly be done by the clerk to the tribunal on her/his own initiative.

Public and private hearings

30.–(1)   Subject to the following paragraphs, all hearings must be held in public.

(2)   *[Omitted]*

(3)   The Tribunal may give a direction that a hearing, or part of it, is to be held in private.

(4)   Where a hearing, or part of it, is to be held in private, the Tribunal may determine who is permitted to attend the hearing or part of it.

(5)   The Tribunal may give a direction excluding from any hearing, or part of it–

(a)   any person whose conduct the Tribunal considers is disrupting or is likely to disrupt the hearing;

(b)   any person whose presence the Tribunal considers is likely to prevent another person from giving evidence or making submissions freely;

(c)   any person who the Tribunal considers should be excluded in order to give effect to a direction under rule 14(2) (withholding information likely to cause harm); or

(d)   any person where the purpose of the hearing would be defeated by the attendance of that person.

(6)   The Tribunal may give a direction excluding a witness from a hearing until that witness gives evidence.

General Note

The general rule is that hearings must be in public: para (1). However, the tribunal may give a direction in an individual case that the hearing, or part of it, should be private (para (3)) and as to who may attend it (para (4)). In addition, the tribunal may exclude witnesses who have yet to give evidence (para (6)) and anyone (including a party – see r28) who is disrupting or likely to disrupt the hearing or who is likely inhibit others from giving evidence or making submissions or to give effect to a direction under r14(2). The minimum requirement of a public hearing is that it takes place within reasonable office hours and at a publicly recognised court or tribunal hearing centre. It is not necessary for the hearing to be publicised in advance or for a list of scheduled public hearings to be on display at that centre, except where the absence of publicity can be shown to be a stratagem to deprive a claimant of a public hearing in a particular case: see *DF v SSWP (ESA)* [2015] UKUT 143 (AAC).

For guidance on who may attend a hearing, the First-tier Tribunal's powers of exclusion and the role of the tribunal clerk, see *KM v SSWP and DM (CSM)* [2019] UKUT 48 (AAC). Note in particular: "... it is not for the clerk to decide who should be in the hearing. Nor is it for the clerk to decide the capacity in which a person who is not a party attends the hearing, for example as witness or to give moral support or both. It is the tribunal which bears ultimate responsibility for acting in accordance with natural justice and providing a fair hearing, not the clerk. That is why any decisions about people in the hearing, and their role in that hearing, must ultimately be for the tribunal" per Judge Poole QC at para 13.

Hearings in a party's absence

31.   If a party fails to attend a hearing the Tribunal may proceed with the hearing if the Tribunal–

(a)   is satisfied that the party has been notified of the hearing or that reasonable steps have been taken to notify the party of the hearing; and

(b)   considers that it is in the interests of justice to proceed with the hearing.

General Note

The tribunal may proceed with a hearing in the absence of a party if two conditions are met.

The first condition is that the tribunal is satisfied that the party has been notified of the hearing or that reasonable steps have been taken to notify the party of the hearing. The record of proceedings produced by HMCTS's "GAPS2" computer system will state the date on which notice is recorded as having been sent. However, it will be good practice for the tribunal to ask the clerk to check GAPS2 for the copies of the letters that were sent to ensure they were correctly addressed. GAPS2 should also contain notes of any telephone calls that may have been made to HMCTS's call centre explaining an appellant's non-attendance.

The second condition is that the tribunal considers that it is in the interests of justice to proceed with the hearing. *JF v SSWP (IS)* [2010] UKUT 267 (AAC) holds that "decision on whether it is in the interests of justice to proceed requires an exercise of judicial discretion". By analogy with *MM v SSWP (ESA)* [2011] UKUT 334 (AAC), that discretion must be consciously and expressly exercised taking into account the overriding objective.

The test under r31(b) is whether it is in the "interests of justice" to proceed with a hearing in the absence of a party, not whether the tribunal has sufficient evidence to make a decision: see *LJT v SSWP (PIP)* [2019] UKUT 21 (AAC) at paras 27 and 28 and *BV v SSWP (PIP)* [2018] UKUT 444 (AAC); [2019] 1 WLR 3185 at paras 28–31, where Judge Poynter stated:

"27.   The Tribunal's decision to proceed in the claimant's absence also involved an error of law.

28.   Paragraph 7 of the statement ... explains that the Tribunal made that decision because it had "sufficient evidence" to do so. However, the test under rule 31 of the [TP(FTT) Rules] is not whether there is

sufficient evidence to make a decision in the absence of a party, but whether it is in the interests of justice to do so. That requires the Tribunal to consider what is fair. And if a statement of reasons is requested, it also requires the Tribunal to explain its decision that the course it chose was in the interests of justice.

29.   It will often not be possible to decide whether it is fair to proceed to a decision in a party's absence without knowing what that decision will be. It is not difficult to think of circumstances in which it would be in the interests of justice to decide an appeal in favour of an absent party when it would not be in the interests of justice to decide it against her.

30.   In other words, the question that rule 31 requires the Tribunal to ask itself is not "Can we make a decision in the party's absence?" but "Would it be fair for us to make this particular decision in the party's absence?""

The satisfaction of the r31 criteria does not prevent the tribunal's decision being set aside under r37 on the basis of non-attendance of a party or preclude an appeal to the Upper Tribunal on the ground that there has been a breach of the duty to act fairly: see *KH v CMEC (CSM)* [2012] UKUT 329 (AAC). The tribunal is entitled to take those factors into consideration when considering whether it is in the interests of justice to proceed (*KH* at para 28). For the factors that are relevant to the decision to proceed in a party's absence, and guidance as to the practice to be followed before doing so, see *GJ v SSWP, JG and SW* [2012] UKUT 447 (AAC) and *CH v SSWP (DLA)* [2012] UKUT 427 (AAC).

Where the first-tier agency fails to provide a presenting officer after having been directed to do so, and the First-tier Tribunal decides to proceed in the presenting officer's absence it must – if it is asked for a written statement of reasons – explain why it did so: *TJ v SSWP (ESA)* [2014] UKUT 445 (AAC).

Where a claimant or presenting officer is late, the First-tier Tribunal will normally wait for 10, or sometimes 15 minutes, before proceeding in the absence of the party. However, where the tribunal knows that the party is on her/his way but has been delayed, it may be disproportionate and unfair to proceed to a decision before s/he arrives: see the decision of the Upper Tribunal on appeal from a Traffic Commissioner in *N Warwickshire Travel Ltd and Michael James* [2018] UKUT 11 (AAC) (in which the appellant had attended a hearing that was listed before the Traffic Commissioner at 10.00 am by 10.30 am only to find that the decision had been made in his absence at 10.25 am). Appeals before the Social Entitlement Chamber are heavily listed and there would not usually be sufficient spare time in the list to permit the tribunal either to wait for half an hour or hear a party who arrived half an hour late. However, the observations made by the Upper Tribunal in *N Warwickshire Travel Ltd* may assist claimants who came late to a hearing and who wish the First-tier Tribunal to set aside its decision under r.37. The case also illustrates how important it is for parties who are running late to telephone the hearing venue to let the tribunal clerk know about the delay. When this happens, it is also a good idea to keep any itemised mobile phone bill (or to print it off if billed online) to show that the calls were made. If it was impossible to phone (because, for example, the party was travelling to the hearing by an underground railway), that should be explained.

The discretion whether or not to proceed in the absence of a party (and therefore also the power to adjourn where the decision is not to proceed) is conferred by rule 31 and paragraph 4 of the Practice Statement: Composition of Tribunals in Social Security and Child Support Cases in the Social Entitlement Chamber on or after 1 August 2013 on the tribunal before which the appeal is listed. That discretion cannot be exercised in advance by another tribunal or by a single judge giving case management decisions: see *LJT v SSWP (PIP)* [2019] UKUT 21 (AAC) at paras 32–35.

CHAPTER 3
Decisions

Consent orders

32.–(1)   The Tribunal may, at the request of the parties but only if it considers it appropriate, make a consent order disposing of the proceedings and making such other appropriate provision as the parties have agreed.

(2)   Notwithstanding any other provision of these Rules, the Tribunal need not hold a hearing before making an order under paragraph (1), or provide reasons for the order.

General Note

A consent order under r32 is a "decision" which can be reviewed under s9 TCEA and to which the rules in Part 4 on correcting, setting aside, reviewing and appealing tribunal decisions apply; see *R (LR by ER) v FtT (HESC) & Hertfordshire CC* [2012] UKUT 213 (AAC), a decision on the similar rules for the Health Education and Social Care Chamber.

Notice of decisions

33.–(1)   The Tribunal may give a decision orally at a hearing.

(2)   Subject to rule 14(2) (withholding information likely to cause harm), the Tribunal must provide to each party as soon as reasonably practicable after making [[1] a

decision (other than a decision under Part 4) which finally disposes of all issues in the proceedings or of a preliminary issue dealt with following a direction under rule 5(3)(e)]–

(a)   a decision notice stating the Tribunal's decision;

(b)   where appropriate, notification of the right to apply for a written statement of reasons under rule 34(3); and

(c)   notification of any right of appeal against the decision and the time within which, and the manner in which, such right of appeal may be exercised.

(3)   *[Omitted]*

Amendment

1.   Amended by r28 of SI 2013 No 477 as from 8.4.13.

General Note

There is no longer any obligation for a tribunal with more than one member to state on the decision notice whether its decision is unanimous or by a majority. However, it is still permissible to do so. If – but only if – the decision notice indicates that the decision is by a majority, any statement of reasons must include reasons for the minority decision: see *SSWP v SS (DLA)* [2010] UKUT 384 (AAC); [2011] AACR 24. Multi-member tribunals are rare at First-tier Tribunal level in HB appeals but may occur if two tribunal judges are sitting together to provide further experience for the additional judge or if an accountant is sitting (see para 7 of the Practice Statement "Composition of Tribunals in Social Security and Child Support Cases in the Social Entitlement Chamber on or after 1 August 2013").

Reasons for decisions

34.–(1)   *[Omitted]*

(2)   In all other cases the Tribunal may give reasons for a decision which disposes of proceedings (except a decision under Part 4)–

(a)   orally at a hearing; or

(b)   in a written statement of reasons to each party.

(3)   Unless the Tribunal has already provided a written statement of reasons under paragraph (2)(b), a party may make a written application to the Tribunal for such statement following a decision [¹ which finally disposes of–

(a)   all issues in the proceedings; or

(b)   a preliminary issue dealt with following a direction under rule 5(3)(e).]

(4)   An application under paragraph (3) must be received within 1 month of the date on which the Tribunal sent or otherwise provided to the party a decision notice relating to the decision [¹].

(5)   If a party makes an application in accordance with paragraphs (3) and (4) the Tribunal must, subject to rule 14(2) (withholding information likely to cause harm), send a written statement of reasons to each party within 1 month of the date on which it received the application or as soon as reasonably practicable after the end of that period.

Amendment

1.   Amended by r29 of SI 2013 No 477 as from 8.4.13.

General Note

The tribunal may give its reasons orally at a hearing (para (2)(a)) and by issuing a written statement of reasons on its own initiative: para (2)(b). If it does not issue a written statement under para (2)(b), any party may make a written application for one under para (3) within one month: para (4). Note that this right exists in relation to "a decision which finally disposes of all issues in the proceedings" and therefore applies to decisions to strike out under r8 as well as decisions on the merits of the appeal. However, reasons for decisions to strike out are likely to be brief.

However, r.34 does not impose a "statutory requirement to provide reasons for interlocutory rulings and such reasons as are given may well be concise": see *FY v SSWP (RP)* [2018] UKUT 146 (AAC) at para 74 and *KP v Hertfordshire CC (SEN)* [2010] UKUT 233 (AAC) at para 28.

From 8 April 2013, there is also an immediate right to a written statement of reasons for the tribunal's decision on a preliminary issue dealt with following a direction under r5(3)(e). Previously, there was no right to a written statement until all issues had been disposed of. "It is axiomatic that the First-tier Tribunal's decision notice and (if requested) its statement of reasons should be capable of being read together so that the parties (and, if called upon, the Upper Tribunal) can understand what the Tribunal decided and why." Therefore, a conflict between the decision notice and the written statement of reasons will amount to an error of law: see *SSWP v CO'N (ESA)* [2018] UKUT 80 (AAC).

The tribunal must then send the statement to the parties within one month of receiving the application "or as soon as reasonably practicable after the end of that period". For "reasonably practicable", see the General Note to r24 on p1009.

If an application for permission to appeal is made when no written statement of reasons has been issued, then the tribunal must treat the application as being for a statement of reasons: r38(7)(a).

The one-month time limit for applying for a statement can be extended under r5(3)(a). The principles on which the discretion to extend time should be exercised in this context were considered by the Upper Tribunal in *SD v SSWP (ESA)* [2017] UKUT 278 (AAC). At para 11, Judge Bano referred to the summary of those principles given by McCowan LJ in *Norwich and Peterborough Building Society v Steed* [1991] 1 WLR 449:

"The matters which this court takes into account in deciding whether to grant an extension of time are first, the length of the delay; secondly, the reasons for the delay; thirdly the chances of the appeal succeeding if the application is granted; and fourthly the degree of prejudice to the respondent if the application is granted."

In *SD v SSWP*, the First-tier Tribunal judge had not evaluated the extent to which the delay was excusable in the light of the reasons for delay put forward by each of the claimants – there is no requirement for it to have been impossible to apply for a statement of reasons within the permitted time – and had relied upon the absence of corroborative evidence of the reasons for delay where there was no requirement for such evidence to be provided. In a case in which a statement of reasons is being requested in order to consider an appeal, it will be difficult to gauge the strength of any possible such appeal without the reasons and, although the prejudice resulting from delay in requesting statements of reasons was expressed in general terms, there was no investigation of whether preparation of full reasons would in fact be hampered by the delay in these cases, as might occur if the case papers had been destroyed.

A decision to refuse an extension of the time limit in r34(4) – and, by implication, also decision to grant one – is a decision within s11 TCEA and can therefore be appealed to the Upper Tribunal and set aside under s9, if it is made in error of law. The TP(FTT) Rules do not require a judge who refuses – or grants – an extension of time to provide reasons for that decision. However, any reasons in fact given can be taken into account when deciding whether there has been an error of law: see *HP v SSWP (ESA)* [2014] UKUT 491 (AAC), *RU v SSWP (ESA)* [2014] UKUT 532 (AAC) and *SD v SSWP* (above). In *SD v SSWP*, Judge Bano also – in reliance on the decision of the ECtHR in *Mansur v Turkey* (1995) Series A No. 319-B – raised the possibility that it might be a ground for appeal if any reasons given by the judge were formulaic and indicated that he or she had not considered the individuals facts and circumstances of the case fully.

A respondent who has been barred from taking further part in the proceedings under r8(7) retains of the right to apply for a written statement of reasons under r34(3): see *ZB v SSWP (CSM)* [2013] UKUT 367 (AAC), *CW v SSWP and another (CSM)* [2014] UKUT 290 (AAC) and the commentary to r8.

PART 4
Correcting, setting aside, reviewing and appealing Tribunal decisions

---

Interpretation
35. In this Part–
"appeal" means the exercise of a right of appeal–
   (a)-(b) *[Omitted]*
   (c)   on a point of law under section 11 of the 2007 Act; and
"review" means the review of a decision by the Tribunal under section 9 of the 2007 Act.

Clerical mistakes and accidental slips or omissions
36. The Tribunal may at any time correct any clerical mistake or other accidental slip or omission in a decision, direction or any document produced by it, by–
   (a)   sending notification of the amended decision or direction, or a copy of the amended document, to all parties; and
   (b)   making any necessary amendment to any information published in relation to the decision, direction or document.

General Note

Rule 36 contains what is known colloquially as the "slip-rule". It allows the tribunal to correct a decision notice, directions notice or a statement of reasons where as a result of "any clerical mistake or other accidental slip or omission" the notice or statement fails to reflect the decision (or directions) the tribunal intended to make or the reasons it intended to give.

It is common for unsuccessful appellants – and sometimes also authorities – to apply for a tribunal's decision to be "corrected" because the tribunal decided against them and was "incorrect" to do so. The slip rule cannot be used for that purpose. Parties who are dissatisfied with the tribunal's substantive decision must apply for permission to appeal against it.

Neither can the power be used by the First-tier Tribunal to amend or supplement its reasons: see *AS v SSWP (ESA)* [2011] UKUT 159 (AAC) in which Judge Jacobs stated:

"16.   Rule 36 is by its contents a species of slip rule and should be interpreted in accordance with the nature of that type of provision. As such, it deals with matters that were in the judge's mind when writing but for some reason did not find their way onto the page. Typical examples are the typing error that produces the wrong date or a momentary lapse of concentration that results in the word 'not' being omitted. The rule does not cover matters that the judge had planned to mention but forgot to include. Obviously, it is difficult for the Upper Tribunal to know what was in the judge's mind, but the extent of the changes are an indication. It is difficult to classify the omission of a total of nine lines of explanation as in the same category of mistake as a typing error or a momentary lapse of concentration. For that reason, I decide that the changes made by the presiding judge were not authorised by rule 36."

See also *CG v SSWP (DLA)* [2011] UKUT 453 (AAC) in which it was held that r36 did not permit the tribunal to "amplify" its reasons to address matters that had been raised in an application for permission to appeal. In *SC v SSWP (ESA)* [2012] UKUT 98 (AAC) 11, the Upper Tribunal drew the attention of the First-tier Tribunal to what the Court of Appeal said in *Brewer v Mann* [2012] EWCA Civ 246 at para 31 as follows:

"…where a judge has received no request from the parties to reconsider his judgment or add to his reasons, and has not demonstrated the need in conscience to revisit his judgment, but on the contrary has received grounds of appeal and an application for permission to appeal on the basis of the alleged inadequacies of his judgment, then it would be most unwise for him to rewrite his judgment (other than purely editorially) and it would take the most extraordinary reasons, if any, to justify such a course on his part."

For the power to amend a statement of reasons on review under s9 TCEA, see the commentary to r40.

Setting aside a decision which disposes of proceedings

37.–(1)   The Tribunal may set aside a decision which disposes of proceedings, or part of such a decision, and re-make the decision, or the relevant part of it, if–

(a)   the Tribunal considers that it is in the interests of justice to do so; and

(b)   one or more of the conditions in paragraph (2) are satisfied.

(2)   The conditions are–

(a)   a document relating to the proceedings was not sent to, or was not received at an appropriate time by, a party or a party's representative;

(b)   a document relating to the proceedings was not sent to the Tribunal at an appropriate time;

(c)   a party, or a party's representative, was not present at a hearing related to the proceedings; or

(d)   there has been some other procedural irregularity in the proceedings.

(3)   A party applying for a decision, or part of a decision, to be set aside under paragraph (1) must make a written application to the Tribunal so that it is received no later than 1 month after the date on which the Tribunal sent notice of the decision to the party.

General Note

The setting aside procedure provides an expeditious alternative to appealing where there has been some procedural difficulty, but it is important to bear in mind that setting aside is not a substitute for an appeal in all cases and to consider carefully which course is appropriate. If a set aside is refused, an application for leave to appeal to the Upper Tribunal can still be made and under r38(3)(c) the time limit for applying for permission to appeal is extended to one month from the date on which the tribunal notifies the party that the application to set aside has been unsuccessful, but only where that application was made in time: reg 38(4).

In *MP v SSWP (DLA)* [2010] UKUT 103 (AAC), Upper Tribunal Judge Turnbull accepted a concession from the Secretary of State for Work and Pensions that a refusal to set aside a decision of the Social Entitlement Chamber of the First-tier Tribunal under r37 TP(FTT) Rules was appealable. In that case, the Upper Tribunal set aside the First-tier Tribunal's substantive decision. However, it stated that, had it not done so, it would have set aside the refusal to set aside and re-made that decision by setting aside the substantive decision. See also *GA v Southwark LB (HB)* [2013] UKUT 170 (AAC).

Rule 37 is limited to procedural errors and does not allow a decision to be set aside for matters that relate to the substance of the decision: see *R (LR by ER) v FtT (HESC) & Hertfordshire CC* [2012] UKUT 213 (AAC) at para 47. The fact that the First-tier Tribunal has complied with r31 before proceeding with a hearing in the absence of a party does not prevent its decision subsequently being set aside under r37(2)(c): see *KH v CMEC (CSM)* [2012] UKUT 329 (AAC).

Setting aside for procedural reasons under this rule must be distinguished from setting aside on review under s9 TCEA 2007 and r40: see, for example, *Worcestershire CC v JJ (SEN)* [2014] UKUT 406 (AAC).

Analysis

Paras (1) and (2): Grounds for setting aside

Under para (1) there are two grounds for setting aside. Both must be satisfied. The first is that "the Tribunal considers that it is in the interests of justice" to set the decision aside and the second is that one of the conditions in para (2) is satisfied.

The conditions

The first two of those conditions relate to missing documents. This could be a notice of hearing that went astray or a piece of evidence that was missing. It could also be documents relevant to the production of a statement of reasons for a tribunal's decision (under r34(3) and (4)) going astray after the decision has been given: *CDLA 1685/2004*. The grounds will be made out if the document was not received by the applicant, her/his representative or was not sent to the tribunal. This includes where an appellant does not complete and return the Enquiry Form asking whether s/he wishes there to be a hearing of the appeal (see the commentary to r27). Comparison of paras 2(a) and (b) shows that, by a curious quirk of drafting, there is no power to set aside under those paras where a document is sent to the tribunal but not received by it. However, that circumstance would probably constitute "some other procedural irregularity in the proceedings" within para (2)(d). The document must be one that existed at the appropriate time, rather than one which has, for example, been brought into existence in response to the tribunal's decision. It is not possible to send or receive a non-existent document.

Para (2)(c) applies where the party or representative "was not present at a hearing related to the proceedings". If there has been a hearing, this condition is self-explanatory. A "necessary concomitant to a robust approach by Tribunals to going ahead in an Appellant's absence [*ie,* under rule 31] is a greater preparedness to set aside decisions where appropriate": see *MK v SSWP (ESA)* [2018] UKUT 33 (AAC) at para 9 and also *Cooke v Glenrose Fish Company* [2004] ICR 1188, *PS v SSWP* [2017] UKUT 55 (AAC) and *SA v SSWP (PIP)* [2017] UKUT 224 (AAC), which are referred to in that paragraph.

But what if there has been no hearing because the neither party asked for one, or both asked for the appeal to be decided without a hearing? Contrary to the view expressed below, the Upper Tribunal has decided that para (2)(c) does not apply in those circumstances (see *JC v SSWP (DLA)* [2013] UKUT 171 (AAC)). Judge Turnbull stated:

> "13. In her submission in this appeal the Secretary of State's representative submits that Rule 37(2)(c) applies even where there has been no oral hearing because the Claimant elected for a paper hearing, and that the chairman of the First-tier Tribunal therefore went wrong in law in refusing the application to set aside on the ground which she did. The Secretary of State further submits that I should set aside the substantive decision of 18 August 2011 on the ground that it would be in the interests of justice to do so.
>
> 14. However, reg. 1(3) of the 2008 Rules provides that in the Rules ""hearing" means an oral hearing and includes a hearing conducted in whole or in part by video link, telephone or other means of instantaneous two-way electronic communication." I therefore think that it is clear that I was wrong, at the time of giving permission to appeal, in stating that Rule 37(2)(c) applied. It is in my view clear that it did not apply, because there was no oral hearing. That would plainly have been so if this had been a type of case heard by a First-tier Tribunal Judge alone. In a case, such as the present, where the Tribunal comprises more than one member, there must in a sense be a hearing, but where the case is determined without any of the parties being entitled to be present, because a paper hearing has been elected for, there is in my judgment no "hearing" within Rule 37(2)(c)."

Although the decision in *JC v SSWP (DLA)* is binding on the First-tier Tribunal, the view expressed below is maintained. With respect to the judge, the point is not just whether "hearing" in rule 37(2)(c) means "oral hearing" (which, for the reasons given by the judge, it clearly does). The point is rather whether one can be "present" at an oral hearing which does not take place (which one equally clearly cannot). The salaried First-tier Tribunal judge to whom the application is referred must therefore ask her/himself, "Was the relevant party or representative present at a hearing related to the proceedings?" If no hearing has taken place, the answer to that question must be no, in which case why does the paragraph not apply?

This is not merely semantics. Interpreting para (2)(c) in the way the First-tier Tribunal is now bound to do creates an undesirable lack of flexibility in the application of the rule. Most salaried judges will have come across circumstances in which procedural injustice has occurred because a party has ill-advisedly chosen to have a decision without a hearing but in which there has been no procedural irregularity within para (2)(d). The most obvious example occurs when the appellant (whose command of English may not be perfect) accidentally ticks the wrong box on the enquiry form, but there are many others. Reading para (2)(c) as if it said "there has been a hearing related to the proceedings and a party, or a party's representative was not present at it", prevents the tribunal from doing justice in such circumstances, because there will be no ground for setting the decision aside, no matter how much it is in the interests of justice to do so.

Further, the decision in *JC v SSWP (DLA)* creates perverse incentives for appellants not to co-operate with the tribunal. An appellant who would prefer a decision without a hearing would now be well-advised not to return the enquiry form at all, rather than to return it saying that s/he did not want an oral hearing. If something subsequently goes wrong, taking the latter course of action will now prevent the tribunal from setting aside its decision. The former course of action will mean that "a document relating to the proceedings was not sent to the Tribunal at an appropriate time" so that para (2)(b) will apply.

It is suggested that adopting a broad construction of para (2)(c) carries no risks that First-tier Tribunal decisions will be set aside merely because an unsuccessful appellant who requested a decision without a hearing now regrets that choice and wants a second bite at the cherry. Before the decision can be set aside, the judge must also be satisfied that "it is in the interests of justice to do so" and the appellant's original choice of hearing will be a factor – and sometimes the determining factor – in that decision."

Para (2)(d) allows the tribunal to set aside a decision where there has been "some other procedural irregularity in the proceedings". This wording is deliberately wide so as to allow justice to be done in a wide range of individual cases. It has some similarity with the old ground for setting aside "where the interests of justice so require" under reg 86(1)(c) HB Regs 1987 (revoked on 2 July 2001). One difference, however, is that the tribunal now has an express power to waive procedural irregularities under r7(2)(a). Presumably, an irregularity that has been waived under that rule cannot subsequently form the basis of a decision to set aside under r37(2)(d).

It is suggested that a failure by the First-tier Tribunal consciously to exercise its discretion under r27(1)(b) to decide a case without holding a hearing, or under r31(b) to proceed with a hearing in the absence of a party, or to give reasons for such a decision (see, generally, *MM v SSWP (ESA)* [2011] UKUT 334 (AAC)), may amount to a procedural irregularity for the purposes of r37(2)(d).

A procedural irregularity that affected, or might have affected, the outcome of the appeal will also be an error of law and may therefore form the basis of an appeal to the Upper Tribunal.

The interests of justice

Even if one or more of the para (2) conditions are satisfied, the tribunal may only set the decision aside if it considers it to be "in the interests of justice to do so". This will not always be so. For example, the applicant may have made a deliberate decision not to attend the hearing, or a procedural mistake may have made no difference to the outcome. For discussions of when it will and will not be in the interests of justice to set aside see *SOA v Ealing LB (HB)* [2012] UKUT 437 (AAC) and *GA v Southwark LB (HB)*.

Procedure

There has recently been a difference of view between Upper Tribunal judges about whether the First-tier Tribunal can exercise the r37 power on its own initiative (or, as lawyers sometimes say, "on its own motion") – ie, without an application from a one of the parties. In *RR v SSWP (ESA)* [2017] UKUT 403 (AAC), Judge Gray held, following Judge Mitchell in *DC v SSWP (ESA)* [2015] UKUT 150 (AAC), that, unless there is some other power within the rules or other statutory provision for the judge to act on her/his own initiative, the r37 power is limited by para (3) "which provides that there must be a written application for such a set-aside". However, in *MQ v SSWP and SQ (CS)* [2017] UKUT 392 (AAC), Judge Wikeley stated that (at para 28):

"It also appears from the drafting of rule 37 that the First-tier Tribunal may exercise the power to set aside of its own initiative, without an application from any party, and indeed in principle may do so at any time. The one-month time limit for making a set aside request in rule 37(3) by definition applies only to applications by parties."

The better view is that Judge Wikeley is correct. Rule 37(3) sets out the procedure to be followed *if* a party wishes to make an application to set aside, rather than requiring such an application before the power is exercised. Where the rules require an application, they say so expressly – eg, r40(2)(a). Further, if r37 is ambiguous, the overriding objective requires that it be interpreted so as to promote the overriding objective (r2(3)(b)) including the requirement in r2(2)(b) of "avoiding unnecessary formality and seeking flexibility in the proceedings". In practice, the First-tier Tribunal often use r37 in the absence of an application from the parties and the ability to do so is an important tool in providing flexible justice and preventing injustice.

Where an application is made, para (3) provides that it must be made in writing and received by the tribunal within one month of the decision notice. That limit may be extended under r5(3)(a) where to do so would further the overriding objective.

Note that an application for a written statement of reasons under r34(3) does not automatically extend the time for applying to set the decision aside. This is a change from the former reg 57 SSD&A Regs. Moreover, the tribunal's express power under r41 to treat certain applications as other applications does not permit an application to set aside to be treated as an application under r34(3) or vice versa (see *RR v SSWP (ESA)*, above). However, if the tribunal chooses to do so, it may (r34(2)) issue a written statement on its own initiative at any time.

Application for permission to appeal

38.–(1) This rule does not apply to asylum support cases or criminal injuries compensation cases.

(2) A person seeking permission to appeal must make a written application to the Tribunal for permission to appeal.

(3) An application under paragraph (2) must be sent or delivered to the Tribunal so that it is received no later than 1 month after the latest of the dates that the Tribunal sends to the person making the application–

[¹ (za) the relevant decision notice;]

(a) written reasons for the decision [¹, if the decision disposes of–
(i) all issues in the proceedings; or
(ii) subject to paragraph (3A), a preliminary issue dealt with following a direction under rule 5(3)(e);];
(b) notification of amended reasons for, or correction of, the decision following a review; or
(c) notification that an application for the decision to be set aside has been unsuccessful.

[(3A)   The Tribunal may direct that the 1 month within which a party may send or deliver an application for permission to appeal against a decision that disposes of a preliminary issue shall run from the date of the decision that disposes of all issues in the proceedings.]

(4)   The date in paragraph (3)(c) applies only if the application for the decision to be set aside was made within the time stipulated in rule 37 (setting aside a decision which disposes of proceedings) or any extension of that time granted by the Tribunal.

(5)   If the person seeking permission to appeal sends or delivers the application to the Tribunal later than the time required by paragraph (3) or by any extension of time under rule 5(3)(a) (power to extend time)–
(a) the application must include a request for an extension of time and the reason why the application was not provided in time; and
(b) unless the Tribunal extends time for the application under rule 5(3)(a) (power to extend time) the Tribunal must not admit the application.

(6)   An application under paragraph (2) must–
(a) identify the decision of the Tribunal to which it relates;
(b) identify the alleged error or errors of law in the decision; and
(c) state the result the party making the application is seeking.

(7)   If a person makes an application under paragraph (2) [¹ in respect of a decision that disposes of proceedings or of a preliminary issue dealt with following a direction under rule 5(3)(e)] when the Tribunal has not given a written statement of reasons for its decision–
(a) if no application for a written statement of reasons has been made to the Tribunal, the application for permission must be treated as such an application;
(b) unless the Tribunal decides to give permission and directs that this sub-paragraph does not apply, the application is not to be treated as an application for permission to appeal; and
(c) if an application for a written statement of reasons has been, or is, refused because of a delay in making the application, the Tribunal must only admit the application for permission if the Tribunal considers that it is in the interests of justice to do so.

Amendment

1.   Inserted by r30 of SI 2013 No 477 as from 8.4.13.

General Note

An application for permission to appeal must be in writing: para (2). By para (6) it must identify the tribunal decision which the applicant wishes to appeal, identify the alleged error or errors of law and state the result the applicant is seeking – ie, how s/he wishes the Upper Tribunal to exercise its powers under s12 TCEA 2007.

The application must be received by the tribunal within one month from the latest of the dates on which the tribunal sent the applicant the decision, the written statement of reasons under r34, notification that the decision (or the reasons for it) has been amended following review under s9 TCEA 2007 and r40, or notice that an in-time application to set aside has been refused: paras (3) and (4). That time limit may be extended under r5(3)(a) either on an application under para (5) or (by waiving para (5) under r7(2)(a)) on the tribunal's own initiative.

Para (7) sets out what should happen when, as is common, an application for permission to appeal is made when no written statement of reasons has been made under r34. The application must be treated as being for a statement of reasons. It will also be treated as not being an application for permission to appeal unless the tribunal is prepared to give permission to appeal and directs that para (7)(2) should not apply. Where there is no written statement of reasons because of delay in applying for one, the tribunal may only admit the application for permission to appeal where it is in the interests of justice to do so.

In practice, it will be difficult for the tribunal to be persuaded that a decision contains an arguable error of law where no statement of reasons has been given. Rule 38(7)(c) requires the tribunal to consider whether or not to admit the application for permission to appeal in all cases in which there is no written statement of reasons because of delay in applying for one: see *HP v SSWP (ESA)* [2014] UKUT 491 (AAC) at paras 23–25.

Tribunal's consideration of application for permission to appeal

39.–(1)   On receiving an application for permission to appeal the Tribunal must first consider, taking into account the overriding objective in rule 2, whether to review the decision in accordance with rule 40 (review of a decision).

(2)   If the Tribunal decides not to review the decision, or reviews the decision and decides to take no action in relation to the decision, or part of it, the Tribunal must consider whether to give permission to appeal in relation to the decision or that part of it.

(3)   The Tribunal must send a record of its decision to the parties as soon as practicable.

(4)   If the Tribunal refuses permission to appeal it must send with the record of its decision–

(a)   a statement of its reasons for such refusal; and

(b)   notification of the right to make an application to the Upper Tribunal for permission to appeal and the time within which, and the method by which, such application must be made.

(5)   The Tribunal may give permission to appeal on limited grounds, but must comply with paragraph (4) in relation to any grounds on which it has refused permission.

General Note

The tribunal must first consider whether to review the decision under s9 TCEA 2007 and r40: para (1). If it decides not to review the decision, or reviews the decision but does not take any action in respect of it, it must consider the application for permission to appeal: para (2). Reasons must be given for any refusal: para (4). A decision to review the tribunal's decision but take no action implies that the reviewing judge considers that the decision contained an error of law (see r40(2)(b)). Therefore, any subsequent refusal of permission to appeal should be based on the discretion not to grant permission to appeal where there is an error of law rather than on the absence of an error of law: see *VH v Suffolk CC* [2010] UKUT 203 (AAC). Permission to appeal may be given on limited grounds, in which case reasons must be given for the refusal of any other grounds: para (5). At least where the appellant is competently represented, a failure by the First-tier Tribunal to notify the appellant that s/he can apply to the Upper Tribunal for permission to appeal on any ground not included in a grant of limited permission to appeal, does not vitiate the proceedings. If no such application is made, the Upper Tribunal is bound by the limited grant of permission: see *AW v SSWP (IB)* [2012] UKUT 104 (AAC).

It is not unlawful for a judge of the First-tier Tribunal to consider an application for permission to appeal from her/his own decision: see *AA v Cheshire and Wirral Partnership NHS Foundation Trust* [2009] UKUT 195 (AAC); [2011] AACR 37 (paras 26–27) and *DL v LB Redbridge* [2010] UKUT 293 (AAC).

Reasons given for refusing permission to appeal may not add to the tribunal's reasons in order to bolster its decision in the light of the grounds of appeal.

Review of a decision

40.–(1)   This rule does not apply to asylum support cases or criminal injuries compensation cases.

(2)   The Tribunal may only undertake a review of a decision–

(a)   pursuant to rule 39(1) (review on an application for permission to appeal); and

(b)   if it is satisfied that there was an error of law in the decision.

(3)   The Tribunal must notify the parties in writing of the outcome of any review, and of any right of appeal in relation to the outcome.

(4)   If the Tribunal takes any action in relation to a decision following a review without first giving every party an opportunity to make representations, the notice under paragraph (3) must state that any party that did not have an opportunity to make representations may apply for such action to be set aside and for the decision to be reviewed again.

General Note

This rule establishes the procedure under which the tribunal may review its decision under s9 TCEA 2007.

Para (2) provides that the power to review may only be exercised on an application for permission to appeal (which presumably includes an application treated as an application for permission to appeal under r41) and where the original decision contains an error of law. A three-judge panel of the Upper Tribunal has held that the power to review should only be exercised where the decision is clearly wrong in law so as not to usurp the Upper Tribunal's function of deciding contentious points of law. The power of review was not intended to enable the judge to take a different view on the law from that previously reached when both views are tenable: see *R (RB) v First-tier Tribunal (Review)* [2010] UKUT 160 (AAC); [2010] AACR 41.

The view, expressed in previous editions, that the requirement that there should be an application for permission to appeal is *ultra vires* is incorrect: see *JS v Kingston upon Hull City Council (HB)* [2014] UKUT 43 (AAC). Rule 40(2)(a) is authorised by s22 and Sch 5 para 6 TCEA. The First-tier Tribunal has no power to review its decisions on its own initiative.

By para 11 of the Senior President's Practice Statement on the Composition of Tribunals in Child Support and Social Security Cases in the Social Entitlement Chamber (see pp1062–1063), the review must be carried out by a salaried tribunal judge. Where the judge who constituted or chaired the tribunal was a salaried judge, s/he must carry out the review unless it would be impracticable or cause undue delay. *AA v Cheshire and Wirral Partnership NHS Foundation Trust* [2009] UKUT 195 (AAC); [2011] AACR 37 (paras 26–27) confirms that it is not unlawful for a tribunal judge to carry out a review of her/his own decision.

The first step the reviewing judge must take is to consider whether there was an error of law in the original decision. Until such an error has been identified, no review can be carried out and the powers listed in s9(4) TCEA 2007 do not arise see *SE v SSWP* [2009] UKUT 163 (AAC) and *AM v SSWP* [2009] UKUT 224 (AAC). The purported exercise of the powers before an error of law has been identified, renders the review a nullity (*AM v SSWP* at para 15).

In *LM v SSWP* [2009] UKUT 185 (AAC), the tribunal judge made a bizarre attempt to pre-empt the exercise of the review power by purporting to consider when the original decision was made whether it was wrong in law, concluding (unsurprisingly!) that it was not, and then declaring that the issue was *res judicata* (ie, that it was an issue that had been finally determined by the tribunal and could not be re-opened). The decision of the Upper Tribunal confirms that this is not permissible.

On the assumption that the original decision did contain an error of law, the salaried tribunal judge may review it and may (under s9(4) TCEA 2007) correct accidental errors in the decision, amend the decision, or set the decision aside. Those powers are cumulative and not exclusive so that the First-tier Tribunal may exercise more than one of them on a review (*AM v SSWP* at para 7).

Particular problems arise in relation to the amendment of statements of reasons. To begin with, the reviewing judge will probably not be the same judge who heard (or presided over) the appeal and wrote the statement. In *AM v SSWP*, Judge Agnew of Locknaw considered those circumstances and gave the following advice:

"11.   If, following representations, the salaried judge determines that the tribunal should be given such an opportunity, then the appeal should be remitted to the fee-paid chairman to determine whether or not to amend the Statement of Reasons together with a note of any representations made to the salaried judge. In light of the Practice Statement, the salaried chairman having received any proposed amendments to the Statement of Reasons from the fee-paid judge, if so advised, the salaried chairman should the take the action to amend the Statement of Reasons."

However, the problems are not just procedural. Issues also arise as to the extent of the power and as to whether the statement of reasons ought to be amended even when there is power to do so.

Judge White gave guidance on the former issue in *SE v SSWP*:

"28.   In cases where (as in this case) the tribunal which decided the case consisted of a panel of three, any subsequent variation of the statement of reasons must reflect issues which were discussed by all three members of the tribunal, but which were then inadvertently not included in the statement written by the chair of the tribunal. If this is not the case, then the decision will not be that of the tribunal which heard the case, but in part that of just one of its members. It would follow that in such cases the chair in revising the statement of reasons should state explicitly (1) that the issue which is the subject of revision was expressly considered and discussed by all members of the tribunal, and (2) what is now added to the statement of reasons represents actual conclusions of the whole tribunal (rather than something which the chair thinks they would have concluded if they had considered the point in issue).

29.   It would not be right in my view for the power in rule 40 to be used in some informal way as a means of adding to the reasons when prompted by an application for permission to appeal, and in order to address issues raised in the application which had not been fully considered by the tribunal in its deliberations."

Paragraph 28 above was quoted with approval in *AM v SSWP*.

As to the latter issue Judge Agnew stated:

"21.   Section 9(4)(b) of the 2007 Act does give the tribunal a power to amend a Statement of Reasons and therefore supersedes Mr Levenson's decision in CA/4297/2004 that it was not competent to amend a Statement of Reasons. The issue therefore is the circumstances in which such a power ought to be exercised. Considerable guidance is given in both *Barke v SEETEC Business Technology Centre Ltd* [2005] EWCA Civ 578 and *English v Emerty Reimgold & Strick Ltd* [2002] 1 WLR 2409. It is clear from those cases that a tribunal that has failed to give reasons or failed to deal with a particular point may deal with such a lacuna and provide those reasons. I consider the same approach applies to a tribunal, which will generally be expected to act professionally in amending a Statement of Reasons and therefore may, as the tribunal purported to do in this case, deal with the lacuna....

22. However, a tribunal that has to decide whether or not to exercise the power to amend a Statement of Reasons should consider whether or not in the particular circumstances it ought to do so. Where a Statement of Reasons deals with a point, but in retrospect can be seen to have dealt with it inadequately or unclearly, then it may be reasonable to amend the reasons to amplify or clarify the point. If an argument is not dealt with in the Statement of Reasons at all, then more careful consideration might have to be given to whether or not the lacuna should be filled by new material in the Statement of Reasons on this point. The length of time since the hearing might be relevant, as might be the availability of contemporary material showing what was the decision and the reasons of the tribunal at the time. These are all matters upon which the parties might want to make representations, which could be of assistance to the tribunal in determining whether or not to consider amending the Statement of Reasons."

If the judge sets the decision aside, the tribunal must either re-make the decision or refer it to the Upper Tribunal: s9(5). As almost all HB appeals are decided by a single judge sitting alone, this will probably mean that the judge who carries out the review also re-decides the appeal. Appeals involving other benefits (eg, employment and support allowance) are decided by a judge sitting with at least one other member. The reviewing judge will therefore refer the reviewed appeal to an appropriately constituted panel to be re-decided.

For the procedural safeguards which must be observed on a review, particularly where the proposed outcome is amended reasons for the same result, see *SE v SSWP* [2009] UKUT 163 (AAC). Where (as is the case with HB decisions) the decision is one that may be heard by a single tribunal judge, the tribunal may re-make the decision immediately and may make new findings of fact: s9(8). In some other social security cases, the appeal will be listed before a two- or three-member panel for decision.

Where the decision is referred to the Upper Tribunal, it must re-decide the matter (s9(6)) and may make any decision the First-tier Tribunal could have made: s9(7).

Para (4) of r40 provides that where the tribunal takes any action in relation to a decision following a review without first giving every party an opportunity to make representations, then the notice of the review decision must inform the parties that any party who did not have an opportunity to make representations may apply for the action taken following the review decision to be set aside and for the decision to be reviewed again.

This rule can probably be reconciled with s9(10) TCEA 2007 which provides that a decision of the tribunal may not be reviewed more than once by drawing a distinction between the review itself (the formal process of re-considering the decision) and the action taken following that review (ie, the steps listed in s9(4) TCEA): although the review cannot be set aside, the consequential action can.

In *SE v SSWP* and *AM v SSWP* (above), the Upper Tribunal held that a failure to follow the procedure in r40(4) renders the review a nullity. This partially solves any problem that might be thought to exist despite the previous paragraph: where the First-tier Tribunal does not either seek representations from the parties before the review or inform them of the possibility that the action taken following the review may be set aside, then the first review will be a nullity and s9(10) therefore has no application. However, in a case where the tribunal does not seek representations before the review but *does* give the notice required by r40(4), the review is not a nullity and the problem remains.

In those circumstances, it is suggested that the tribunal should usually seek representations from all parties before taking any action under s9(4).

The Upper Tribunal, sitting as a three judge panel, delivered a further judgment on the proper use of the review procedure, and in particular, the power to amend reasons, in *JS v SSWP (DLA)* [2013] UKUT 100 (AAC); [2013] AACR 30. The Upper Tribunal holds (para 45) that the power should only be used in cases which properly fulfil its purpose (avoiding unnecessary appeals while still allowing the tribunal to give the actual reasons for the decision: para 40 to 42) and in a way which minimises the risks of unfairness, or its perception, that attends its use (particularly the risk that the amended reasons will be justification or defence of the decision rather than reasons for it). Although the Upper Tribunal declined to give an exhaustive list of when, those principles should result in the power to amend being exercised, it does give a useful indication at paras 47 to 50 of examples at either end of the spectrum:

"47. A clear example of a permissible amendment would be an issue that had been expressly raised on the appeal and explored at the hearing, but not mentioned in the written reasons. In such a case, it would be clear that part of the tribunal's reasoning was missing by oversight, and there would be no danger of the judge writing a justification by reference to the grounds of appeal.

48. Another example of a permissible amendment would be a passage that was ambiguous or otherwise unclear in what it was saying. In such a case, it would be clear that something had gone wrong with the composition of the reasons and there would be limited scope for the judge to drift away from the task of explaining what the passage meant.

49. In both these examples, amending the reasons would not undermine the parties' confidence in the judicial decision-making process and the finality of decisions. The amendment would be directed to and might avoid the need for an appeal.

50. At the other extreme, an example of an impermissible amendment would be a passage that gave a poor explanation of a tribunal's analysis of a piece of evidence. In such a case, it would not be self-

evident that something had gone wrong, and there would be an effectively unavoidable risk that the judge, in seeking to bolster the reasons already given, would drift into supplementing the tribunal's actual reasons and, perhaps, into justification. And both those dangers would undermine confidence in the judicial decision-making process and in the finality of decisions. It is unlikely that the amendment would avoid the desire to appeal.

51.   In our judgment, it is likely that many inadequacies identified in a tribunal's reasons will be at or towards this end of the spectrum and so not appropriate for amendment."

The Upper Tribunal goes on to give detailed guidance about how procedurally the power should be exercised, including noting that where the judge conducting the review is not the judge who dealt with the case (who is being asked to amend the reasons), then in general the latter judge should not be shown the application for permission to appeal.

Power to treat an application as a different type of application

41.   The Tribunal may treat an application for a decision to be corrected, set aside or reviewed, or for permission to appeal against a decision, as an application for any other one of those things.

General Note

It will often be unclear what application an unrepresented appellant intends to make. In such circumstances, the tribunal, in the exercise of its enabling jurisdiction, should interpret what has been written as being whatever application gives the claimant the best chance of achieving what s/he wants under the TP(FTT) Rules. It may sometimes be necessary to seek clarification from the claimant about what s/he is asking for.

Rule 41 serves a different purpose. Even where a party has unequivocally applied for a particular remedy under Part 4 of the Rules, the tribunal may treat that application as being for a different remedy. So, for example, if a party has applied for permission to appeal to the Upper Tribunal, but the judge considering that application decides that the conditions in r37 for the First-tier Tribunal's decision to be set aside on procedural grounds are satisfied, s/he may instead treat the application as being for the decision to be set aside. As with all discretionary powers under the rules, this power must be exercised having regard to the overriding objective of dealing with cases fairly and justly. It is, therefore, necessary for the judge to consider whether or not to treat the application as being a different application in every case in which a post-hearing application is made and there will be occasions on which the overriding objective will require the judge to take that course: see *DC v SSWP (ESA)* [2015] UKUT 150 (AAC) at paras 26–33.

[⁴ SCHEDULE 1

RULE 23

Time limits for providing notices of appeal in social security and child support cases where mandatory reconsideration does not apply [³]

Type of proceedings
[² 1-4 *Omitted*
5 Cases other than those listed above

Time for providing notice of appeal
[² The latest of–
    (a) one month after the date on which notice of the decision being challenged was sent to the appellant;
    (b) if a written statement of reasons for the decision was requested within that month, 14 days after the later of–
        (i) the end of that month; or
        (ii) the date on which the written statement of reasons was provided;
    [³ (c) *Omitted*]

Amendments

1.   Substituted by r4 of SI 2009 No 1975 as from 1.9.09.
2.   Substituted by r5(4) of SI 2010 No 2653 as from 29.11.10.
3.   Amended by r31 of SI 2013 No 477 as from 8.4.13.
4.   Substituted by r17 of SI 2015 No 1510 as from 21.8.15.

General Note

From 21 August 2015, Sch 1 only contains the time limits for appealing where the notice of appeal is to be sent to the tribunal under r22. Thus it no longer has application for HB (and CTB) appeals which must be sent to the decision maker under r23. The time limit for these appeals is now in r23(2). See the commentary to that provision on p1006. Prior to 21 August 2015, Sch 1 did provide the time limit for appealing in an HB (or CTB) case. Note that until 1 November 2010, the effect of Sch 1 para (b) was to circumvent the (supposedly) absolute 13-month time limit (see p1039 of the 22nd edition). Until 1 September 2009, the drafting of Sch 1 para (c) was also defective. See p1101 of the 21st edition for details.

The Qualifications for Appointment of Members to the First-tier Tribunal and Upper Tribunal Order 2008

2008 No.2692

1.–(1)   This Order may be cited as the Qualifications for Appointment of Members to the First-tier Tribunal and Upper Tribunal Order 2008 and shall come into force on 3rd November 2008.

[¹ (2)   In this Order "registered medical practitioner" means a fully registered person within the meaning of the Medical Act 1983 whether or not they hold a licence to practise under that Act.]

Amendment
1.   Amended by Art 3 of SI 2009 No 1592 as from 16.11.09.

2.–(1)   A person is eligible for appointment as a member of the First-tier Tribunal or the Upper Tribunal who is not a judge of those tribunals if paragraph (2), (3) or (4) applies.

(2)   This paragraph applies to a person who is–
(a)   a registered medical practitioner;
(b)   a registered nurse;
(c)   a registered dentist;
[¹ (ca) a registered optometrist;]
(d)   a clinical psychologist;
(e)   an educational psychologist;
(f)   a pharmacologist;
(g)   a veterinary surgeon or a veterinary practitioner registered under the Veterinary Surgeons Act 1966;
(h)   a Member or Fellow of the Royal Institution of Chartered Surveyors; or
(i)   an accountant who is a member of–
    (i)   the Institute of Chartered Accountants in England and Wales;
    (ii)   the Institute of Chartered Accountants in Scotland;
    (iii)   the Institute of Chartered Accountants in Ireland;
    (iv)   the Institute of Certified Public Accountants in Ireland;
    (v)   the Association of Chartered Certified Accountants;
    (vi)   the Chartered Institute of Management Accountants; or
    (vii) the Chartered Institute of Public Finance and Accountancy.

(3)   This paragraph applies to a person [¹] who is experienced in dealing with the physical or mental needs of disabled persons because they–
(a)   work with disabled persons in a professional or voluntary capacity; or
(b)   are themselves disabled.

[¹ (3A)   A person is not eligible for appointment under paragraph (3) if they are a registered medical practitioner.]

(4)   This paragraph applies to a person who has substantial experience–
(a)   of service in Her Majesty's naval, military, or air forces;
(b)   of educational, child care, health, or social care matters;
(c)   of dealing with victims of violent crime;
(d)   in transport operations and its law and practice;
(e)   in the regulatory field;
(f)   in consumer affairs;
(g)   in an industry, trade or business sector and the matters that are likely to arise as issues in the course of disputes with regulators of such industries, trades or businesses;
(h)   in tax matters and related tax procedures;
(i)   in a business, trade [¹, charity] or not-for-profit organisation.
[¹ (j)   in immigration services or the law and procedure relating to immigration;
(k)   of data protection;

   (l)   of freedom of information (including environmental information) rights;
   (m) of service as a Member or Senior Officer of a local authority in England.]
[(n) in environmental matters.]
[³ (o) in the drainage of land;
   (p)   in farming and the ownership or management of agricultural property;
   (q)   in relation to housing or housing conditions;
   (r)   in matters relating to landlord and tenant relationships;
   (s)   in valuation]

Amendments
1.   Amended by art 4 of SI 2009 No 1592 as from 1.9.09.
2.   Amended by art 3 of SI 2012 No 897 as from 16.4.12.
3.   Inserted by art 3 of SI 2013 No 1185 as from 1.7.13.

The Tribunal Procedure (Upper Tribunal) Rules 2008
No.2698 (L.15)

PART 1
Introduction
1.   Citation, commencement, application and interpretation
2.   Overriding objective and parties' obligation to co-operate with the Upper Tribunal
3.   Alternative dispute resolution and arbitration

PART 2
General powers and provisions
4.   Delegation to staff
5.   Case management powers
6.   Procedure for applying for and giving directions
7.   Failure to comply with rules etc.
8.   Striking out a party's case
9.   Addition, substitution and removal of parties
10.   Orders for costs
11.   Representatives
12.   Calculating time
13.   Sending and delivery of documents
14.   Use of documents and information
15.   Evidence and submissions
16.   Summoning or citation of witnesses and orders to answer questions or produce documents
17.   Withdrawal
17A.   Appeal treated as abandoned or finally determined in an asylum case or an immigration case
18.   Notice of funding of legal services
19.   Confidentiality in social security and child support cases
20.   Power to pay expenses and allowances
20A.   Procedure for applying for a stay of a decision pending an appeal

PART 3
Procedure for cases in the Upper Tribunal
21.   Application to the Upper Tribunal for permission to appeal
22.   Decision in relation to permission to appeal
23.   Notice of appeal
24.   Response to the notice of appeal
25.   Appellant's reply
26A.   Cases transferred or referred to the Upper Tribunal, applications made directly to the Upper Tribunal and proceedings without notice to a respondent

PART 4
Judicial review proceedings in the Upper Tribunal
27.   Application of this Part to judicial review proceedings transferred to the Upper Tribunal
28.   Applications for permission to bring judicial review proceedings
28A.   Special provisions for immigration judicial review proceedings
29.   Acknowledgment of service
30.   Decision on permission or summary dismissal, and reconsideration of permission or summary dismissal at a hearing
31.   Responses

32.   Applicant seeking to rely on additional grounds
33.   Right to make representations
33A.   Amendments and additional grounds resulting in transfer of proceedings to the High Court in England and Wales

PART 5
Hearings
34.   Decision with or without a hearing
35.   Entitlement to attend a hearing
36.   Notice of hearings
36A.   Special time limits for hearing an appeal in a fast-track case
37.   Public and private hearings
38.   Hearings in a party's absence

PART 6
Decisions
39.   Consent orders
40.   Decisions

PART 7
Correcting, setting aside, reviewing and appealing decisions of the Upper Tribunal
41.   Interpretation
42.   Clerical mistakes and accidental slips or omissions
43.   Setting aside a decision which disposes of proceedings
44.   Application for permission to appeal
45.   Upper Tribunal's consideration of application for permission to appeal
46.   Review of a decision
47.   Setting aside a decision in proceedings under the Forfeiture Act 1982
48.   Power to treat an application as a different type of application

PART 1
Introduction

Citation, commencement, application and interpretation

1.–(1)   These Rules may be cited as the Tribunal Procedure (Upper Tribunal) Rules 2008 and come into force on 3rd November 2008.

(2)   These Rules apply to proceedings before the Upper Tribunal [² except proceedings in the Lands Chamber].

(3)   In these Rules–

"the 2007 Act" means the Tribunals, Courts and Enforcement Act 2007;

[¹ "appellant" means–
   (a)   a person who makes an appeal, or applies for permission to appeal, to the Upper Tribunal;
   (b)   in proceedings transferred or referred to the Upper Tribunal from the First-tier Tribunal, a person who started the proceedings in the First-tier Tribunal; or
   (c)   a person substituted as an appellant under rule 9(1) (substitution and addition of parties);]

[³ "applicant" means–
   (a)   a person who applies for permission to bring, or does bring, judicial review proceedings before the Upper Tribunal and, in judicial review proceedings transferred to the Upper Tribunal from a court, includes a person who was a claimant or petitioner in the proceedings immediately before they were transferred; or
   (b)   a person who refers a financial services case [⁷ or a wholesale energy case] to the Upper Tribunal;]

[² "appropriate national authority" means, in relation to an appeal, the Secretary of State, the Scottish Ministers [⁵, the Department of the Environment in Northern Ireland] or the Welsh Ministers, as the case may be;

[⁵ "authorised person" *[Omitted]*]

[⁸ "disability educational needs case" *[Omitted]*]

"dispose of proceedings" includes, unless indicated otherwise, disposing of a part of the proceedings;

"document" means anything in which information is recorded in any form, and an obligation under these Rules or any practice direction or direction to provide or allow access to a document or a copy of a document for any purpose means, unless the Upper Tribunal directs otherwise, an obligation to provide or allow access to such document or copy in a legible form or in a form which can be readily made into a legible form;

"hearing" means an oral hearing and includes a hearing conducted in whole or in part by video link, telephone or other means of instantaneous two-way electronic communication;

"interested party" means–
   (a)   a person who is directly affected by the outcome sought in judicial review proceedings, and has been named as an interested party under rule 28 or 29 (judicial review), or has been substituted or added as an interested party under rule 9 [⁴ (addition, substitution and removal of parties)]; [⁴]
   (b)   in judicial review proceedings transferred to the Upper Tribunal under section 25A(2) or (3) of the Judicature (Northern Ireland) Act 1978 or section 31A(2) or (3) of the Supreme Court Act 1981, a person who was an interested party in the proceedings immediately before they were transferred to the Upper Tribunal; [⁴ and
   (c)-(d) *[Omitted]*
   [¹¹ (e) *[Omitted]*]

"judicial review proceedings" means proceedings within the jurisdiction of the Upper Tribunal pursuant to section 15 or 21 of the 2007 Act, whether such proceedings are started in the Upper Tribunal or transferred to the Upper Tribunal;

[¹]

"party" means a person who is an appellant, an applicant, a respondent or an interested party in proceedings before the Upper Tribunal, a person who has referred a question [⁴ or matter] to the Upper Tribunal or, if the proceedings have been concluded, a person who was an appellant, an applicant, a respondent or an interested party when the [⁶ Upper] Tribunal finally disposed of all issues in the proceedings;

"permission" includes leave in cases arising under the law of Northern Ireland;

"practice direction" means a direction given under section 23 of the 2007 Act;

[⁹ "QCS Board" *[Omitted]*

"quality contracts scheme" *[Omitted]*

"quality contracts scheme case" *[Omitted]*]

"respondent" means–
   (a)   in an appeal, or application for permission to appeal, against a decision of another tribunal, any person other than the appellant who–
         (i)   was a party before that other tribunal;
         [¹ (ii)]
         (iii) otherwise has a right of appeal against the decision of the other tribunal and has given notice to the Upper Tribunal that they wish to be a party to the appeal;
   [¹⁰ (b) in any other application for permission to appeal, or any other appeal except a road transport case, the person who made the decision that has been challenged;]
   (c)   in judicial review proceedings–
         (i)   in proceedings started in the Upper Tribunal, the person named by the applicant as the respondent;

(ii) in proceedings transferred to the Upper Tribunal under section 25A(2) or (3) of the Judicature (Northern Ireland) Act 1978 or section 31A(2) or (3) of the Supreme Court Act 1981, a person who was a defendant in the proceedings immediately before they were transferred;

(iii) in proceedings transferred to the Upper Tribunal under section 20(1) of the 2007 Act, a person to whom intimation of the petition was made before the proceedings were transferred, or to whom the Upper Tribunal has required intimation to be made.

[[5,11] "road transport case" *[Omitted]*]

[[8] "special educational needs case" *[Omitted]*]

[[11] "TRA" *[Omitted]*"trade remedies case" *[Omitted]*]

[[1] (ca) in proceedings transferred or referred to the Upper Tribunal from the First-tier Tribunal, a person who was a respondent in the proceedings in the First-tier Tribunal;]

(d) *[Omitted]*; [[4]

(da) *[Omitted]*;]

[[7] (db) *[Omitted]*]

(e) a person substituted or added as a respondent under rule 9 (substitution and addition of parties);

[[2] "tribunal" does not include a traffic commissioner;]

[[7] "wholesale energy case" *[Omitted]*]

"working day" means any day except a Saturday or Sunday, Christmas Day, Good Friday or a bank holiday under section 1 of the Banking and Financial Dealings Act 1971.

Amendments

1. Amended by r5 of SI 2009 No 274 as from 1.4.09.
2. Amended by r8 of SI 2009 No 1975 as from 1.9.09.
3. Substituted by r4(a) of SI 2010 No 747 as from 6.4.10.
4. Amended by r4(c)-(f) of SI 2010 No 747 as from 6.4.10.
5. Amended by r5 of SI 2012 No.1363 as from 1.7.12.
6. Amended by r4 of SI 2013 No 2067 as from 1.11.13.
7. Amended by r4 of SI 2014 No 514 as from 6.4.14.
8. Amended by r4 of SI 2014 No 2128 as from 1.9.14.
9. Inserted by r3(a) of SI 2015 No 1510 as from 21.8.15.
10. Substituted by r3(2)(b) of SI 2018 No 1053 as from 30.10.18.
11. Amended by r2(2) of SI 2019 No 925 as from 3.6.19, subject to transitional provision until the Trade Remedies Authority is established.

Overriding objective and parties' obligation to co-operate with the Upper Tribunal

2.–(1) The overriding objective of these Rules is to enable the Upper Tribunal to deal with cases fairly and justly.

(2) Dealing with a case fairly and justly includes–

(a) dealing with the case in ways which are proportionate to the importance of the case, the complexity of the issues, the anticipated costs and the resources of the parties;

(b) avoiding unnecessary formality and seeking flexibility in the proceedings;

(c) ensuring, so far as practicable, that the parties are able to participate fully in the proceedings;

(d) using any special expertise of the Upper Tribunal effectively; and

(e) avoiding delay, so far as compatible with proper consideration of the issues.

(3) The Upper Tribunal must seek to give effect to the overriding objective when it–

(a) exercises any power under these Rules; or

(b) interprets any rule or practice direction.

(4) Parties must–

(a) help the Upper Tribunal to further the overriding objective; and

(b) co-operate with the Upper Tribunal generally.

General Note
See the commentary to r2 TP(FTT) Rules 2008 on p985.

Alternative dispute resolution and arbitration

3.–(1)   The Upper Tribunal should seek, where appropriate–

(a)   to bring to the attention of the parties the availability of any appropriate alternative procedure for the resolution of the dispute; and

(b)   if the parties wish and provided that it is compatible with the overriding objective, to facilitate the use of the procedure.

(2)   Part 1 of the Arbitration Act 1996 does not apply to proceedings before the Upper Tribunal.

PART 2

General powers and provisions

Delegation to staff

4.–(1)   Staff appointed under section 40(1) of the 2007 Act (tribunal staff and services) may, with the approval of the Senior President of Tribunals, carry out functions of a judicial nature permitted or required to be done by the Upper Tribunal.

(2)   The approval referred to at paragraph (1) may apply generally to the carrying out of specified functions by members of staff of a specified description in specified circumstances.

(3)   Within 14 days after the date on which the Upper Tribunal sends notice of a decision made by a member of staff under paragraph (1) to a party, that party may apply in writing to the Upper Tribunal for that decision to be considered afresh by a judge.

General Note
Certain case management powers of the Upper Tribunal have been delegated to Registrars (the former "legal officers").

The relevant parts of the Practice Statement, Delegation of Functions to Staff on or after 3 November 2008 are in the following terms.

ADMINISTRATIVE APPEALS CHAMBER OF THE UPPER TRIBUNAL
1.   The Senior President of Tribunals hereby approves that the following functions of the Upper Tribunal under the Tribunal Procedure (Upper Tribunal) Rules 2008 may be carried out by those legally qualified members of staff appointed under section 40(1) of the Tribunals, Courts and Enforcement Act 2007 who, for the purpose of exercising those functions, shall be known as Registrars–

a. Exercising any case management powers under rule 5 except–

i. Extending time under rule 5(3)(a) in relation to the time limits for appeals referred to in rules 21(3), (6), 22(5), 23(2), (5), 44(3), (4), (6) or in relation to the time limits for judicial review proceedings referred to in rules 28(2), (3), (7) and 30(5);

ii. Suspending a decision under rule 5(3)(l) or (m);

iii. Requiring a tribunal to provide reasons for its decision under rule 5(3)(n);

b. Dealing with irregularities under rule 7(2) (except taking action under rule 7(2)(d) or (4));

c. Striking out under rule 8(1) or (3)(a) and reinstating proceedings under rule 8(5);

d. Giving directions substituting or adding parties under rule 9;

e. Summarily assessing costs under rule 10(6)(a);

f. Making orders prohibiting disclosure or publication of documents and information under rule 14;

g. Giving directions in relation to evidence and submissions under rule 15(1);

h. Summoning (or, in Scotland, citing) witnesses and issuing orders to persons to answer questions and produce documents under rule 16;

i. Giving consent to withdraw a case and reinstating a case under rule 17.

2.   In this Practice Statement "legally qualified" means being a solicitor or barrister, or in Scotland, a solicitor or advocate.

3.   In accordance with rule 4(3) of the Tribunal Procedure (Upper Tribunal) Rules 2008, within 14 days after the date that the Upper Tribunal sends notice of a decision made by a Registrar pursuant to an approval under paragraph 1 above to a party, that party may apply in writing to the Upper Tribunal for that decision to be considered afresh by a judge.

Registrars also undertake research for the Upper Tribunal. However, they do not grant or refuse permission to appeal or decide appeals.

Case management powers

5.–(1)   Subject to the provisions of the 2007 Act and any other enactment, the Upper Tribunal may regulate its own procedure.

(2)   The Upper Tribunal may give a direction in relation to the conduct or disposal of proceedings at any time, including a direction amending, suspending or setting aside an earlier direction.

(3)   In particular, and without restricting the general powers in paragraphs (1) and (2), the Upper Tribunal may–

(a)   extend or shorten the time for complying with any rule, practice direction or direction;

(b)   consolidate or hear together two or more sets of proceedings or parts of proceedings raising common issues, or treat a case as a lead case;

(c)   permit or require a party to amend a document;

(d)   permit or require a party or another person to provide documents, information, evidence or submissions to the Upper Tribunal or a party;

(e)   deal with an issue in the proceedings as a preliminary issue;

(f)   hold a hearing to consider any matter, including a case management issue;

(g)   decide the form of any hearing;

(h)   adjourn or postpone a hearing;

(i)   require a party to produce a bundle for a hearing;

(j)   stay (or, in Scotland, sist) proceedings;

(k)   transfer proceedings to another court or tribunal if that other court or tribunal has jurisdiction in relation to the proceedings and–

(i)   because of a change of circumstances since the proceedings were started, the Upper Tribunal no longer has jurisdiction in relation to the proceedings; or

(ii)   the Upper Tribunal considers that the other court or tribunal is a more appropriate forum for the determination of the case;

(l)   suspend the effect of its own decision pending an appeal or review of that decision;

(m)   in an appeal, or an application for permission to appeal, against the decision of another tribunal, suspend the effect of that decision pending the determination of the application for permission to appeal, and any appeal;

[[1] (n) require any person, body or other tribunal whose decision is the subject of proceedings before the Upper Tribunal to provide reasons for the decision, or other information or documents in relation to the decision or any proceedings before that person, body or tribunal.]

[(4)-(7)   *[Omitted]*]]

Amendment

1.   Substituted by r9 of SI 2009 No 1975 as from 1.9.09.

General Note

See the commentary to r5 TP(FTT) Rules 2008 on p988.

Procedure for applying for and giving directions

6.–(1)   The Upper Tribunal may give a direction on the application of one or more of the parties or on its own initiative.

(2)   An application for a direction may be made–

(a)   by sending or delivering a written application to the Upper Tribunal; or

(b)   orally during the course of a hearing.

(3)   An application for a direction must include the reason for making that application.

(4)   Unless the Upper Tribunal considers that there is good reason not to do so, the Upper Tribunal must send written notice of any direction to every party and to any other person affected by the direction.

(5)   If a party or any other person sent notice of the direction under paragraph (4) wishes to challenge a direction which the Upper Tribunal has given, they may do so by applying for another direction which amends, suspends or sets aside the first direction.

General Note
    See the commentary to r6 TP(FTT) Rules 2008 on p992.

Failure to comply with rules etc.

7.–(1) An irregularity resulting from a failure to comply with any requirement in these Rules, a practice direction or a direction, does not of itself render void the proceedings or any step taken in the proceedings.

(2) If a party has failed to comply with a requirement in these Rules, a practice direction or a direction, the Upper Tribunal may take such action as it considers just, which may include–

(a) waiving the requirement;

(b) requiring the failure to be remedied;

(c) exercising its power under rule 8 (striking out a party's case); or

(d) except in [¹ a mental health case, an asylum case or an immigration case], restricting a party's participation in the proceedings.

(3) Paragraph (4) applies where the First-tier Tribunal has referred to the Upper Tribunal a failure by a person to comply with a requirement imposed by the First-tier Tribunal–

(a) to attend at any place for the purpose of giving evidence;

(b) otherwise to make themselves available to give evidence;

(c) to swear an oath in connection with the giving of evidence;

(d) to give evidence as a witness;

(e) to produce a document; or

(f) to facilitate the inspection of a document or any other thing (including any premises).

(4) The Upper Tribunal may exercise its power under section 25 of the 2007 Act (supplementary powers of the Upper Tribunal) in relation to such non-compliance as if the requirement had been imposed by the Upper Tribunal.

Amendment
    1.   Amended by r5 of SI 2010 No 44 as from 15.2.10.

General Note
    See the commentary to r7 TP(FTT) Rules 2008 on p992.

Striking out a party's case

8.–[(1A)   *[Omitted]*]

[² (1)   The proceedings, or the appropriate part of them, will automatically be struck out–

(a) if the appellant or applicant has failed to comply with a direction that stated that failure by the appellant or applicant to comply with the direction would lead to the striking out of the proceedings or part of them; or

(b) *[Omitted]*

(2) The Upper Tribunal must strike out the whole or a part of the proceedings if the Upper Tribunal–

(a) does not have jurisdiction in relation to the proceedings or that part of them; and

(b) does not exercise its power under rule 5(3)(k)(i) (transfer to another court or tribunal) in relation to the proceedings or that part of them.

(3) The Upper Tribunal may strike out the whole or a part of the proceedings if–

(a) the appellant or applicant has failed to comply with a direction which stated that failure by the appellant or applicant to comply with the direction could lead to the striking out of the proceedings or part of them;

(b) the appellant or applicant has failed to co-operate with the Upper Tribunal to such an extent that the Upper Tribunal cannot deal with the proceedings fairly and justly; or

(c) in proceedings which are not an appeal from the decision of another tribunal or judicial review proceedings, the Upper Tribunal considers there is no reasonable prospect of the appellant's or the applicant's case, or part of it, succeeding.

(4)   The Upper Tribunal may not strike out the whole or a part of the proceedings under paragraph (2) or (3)(b) or (c) without first giving the appellant or applicant an opportunity to make representations in relation to the proposed striking out.

(5)   If the proceedings have been struck out under paragraph (1) or (3)(a), the appellant or applicant may apply for the proceedings, or part of them, to be reinstated.

(6)   An application under paragraph (5) must be made in writing and received by the Upper Tribunal within 1 month after the date on which the Upper Tribunal sent notification of the striking out to the appellant or applicant.

(7)   This rule applies to a respondent [¹ or an interested party] as it applies to an appellant or applicant except that–

(a)   a reference to the striking out of the proceedings is to be read as a reference to the barring of the respondent [¹ or an interested party] from taking further part in the proceedings; and

(b)   a reference to an application for the reinstatement of proceedings which have been struck out is to be read as a reference to an application for the lifting of the bar on the respondent [¹ or an interested party] [¹] taking further part in the proceedings.

(8)   If a respondent [¹ or an interested party] has been barred from taking further part in proceedings under this rule and that bar has not been lifted, the Upper Tribunal need not consider any response or other submission made by that respondent [¹ or interested party, and may summarily determine any or all issues against that respondent or interested party].

Amendments

1.   Amended by r6 of SI 2009 No 274 as from 1.4.09.

2.   Substituted by r5 of SI 2011 No 2343 as from 17.10.11.

General Note

See the commentary to r8 TP(FTT) Rules 2008 on p993.

The requirements for permission to appeal, and permission to apply for judicial review, should ensure that appeals and judicial review proceedings before the Upper Tribunal are never liable to be struck out as having no reasonable prospects of success. Rule 8(1)(c) of the TP(UT) Rules 2008 is therefore worded differently from the equivalent provision of the TP(FTT) Rules 2008. However, it remains possible that, for example, an application for permission to appeal might itself have no reasonable prospects of success. In *AD v Information Commissioner* [2016] UKUT 273 (AAC), *Martyres v Information Commissioner and Chief Constable of Cambridgeshire Police* [2016] UKUT 471 (AAC) and *Gaskin v Information Commissioner and Norwich City Council* [2016] UKUT 382 (AAC), Judge Mitchell (*AD*) and Judge Wikeley (*Martyres* and *Gaskin*) struck out applications for permission under r8(3)(c). However, the applications in those cases were for permission to appeal against decisions of the General Regulatory Chamber of the First-tier Tribunal, in circumstances where r22(3) and (4) give a person who has been refused permission to appeal without a hearing the right to apply for the application to be reconsidered at a hearing. There is no equivalent right where the application is for permission to appeal against a decision of the Social Entitlement Chamber. It is therefore unlikely that the power to strike out such an application will ever be used in connection with a HB case. It will almost always be simpler, as well as being more fair and more just, to refuse the application for permission to appeal on the merits.

Substitution and addition of parties

[¹ **9.**–(1)   The Upper Tribunal may give a direction adding, substituting or removing a party as an appellant, a respondent or an interested party.

(2)   If the Upper Tribunal gives a direction under paragraph (1) it may give such consequential directions as it considers appropriate.

(3)   A person who is not a party may apply to the Upper Tribunal to be added or substituted as a party.

(4)   If a person who is entitled to be a party to proceedings by virtue of another enactment applies to be added as a party, and any conditions applicable to that entitlement have been satisfied, the Upper Tribunal must give a direction adding that person as a respondent or, if appropriate, as an appellant.]

[(5)   *[Omitted]*

(6)   *[Omitted]*]

Amendment
1.   Substituted by r10 of SI 2009 No 1975 as from 1.9.09.

[¹ Orders for costs

10.–(1)   The Upper Tribunal may not make an order in respect of costs (or, in Scotland, expenses) in proceedings [² transferred or referred by, or on appeal from,] another tribunal except–

[(aa) *[Omitted]*]
(a)   in proceedings [² transferred by, or on appeal from,] the Tax Chamber of the First-tier Tribunal; or
(b)   to the extent and in the circumstances that the other tribunal had the power to make an order in respect of costs (or, in Scotland, expenses).

[(1A)   *[Omitted]*]
(2)   The Upper Tribunal may not make an order in respect of costs or expenses under section 4 of the Forfeiture Act 1982.
(3)   In other proceedings, the Upper Tribunal may not make an order in respect of costs or expenses except–
(a)   in judicial review proceedings;
[² (b)]
(c)   under section 29(4) of the 2007 Act (wasted costs) [⁴ and costs incurred in applying for such costs]; [³]
(d)   if the Upper Tribunal considers that a party or its representative has acted unreasonably in bringing, defending or conducting the proceedings.[³ or
(e)   *[Omitted]*]
(4)   The Upper Tribunal may make an order for costs (or, in Scotland, expenses) on an application or on its own initiative.
(5)   A person making an application for an order for costs or expenses must–
(a)   send or deliver a written application to the Upper Tribunal and to the person against whom it is proposed that the order be made; and
(b)   send or deliver with the application a schedule of the costs or expenses claimed sufficient to allow summary assessment of such costs or expenses by the Upper Tribunal.
(6)   An application for an order for costs or expenses may be made at any time during the proceedings but may not be made later than 1 month after the date on which the Upper Tribunal sends–
(a)   a decision notice recording the decision which finally disposes of all issues in the proceedings; or
[⁴ (b) notice under rule 17(5) that a withdrawal which ends the proceedings has taken effect].
(7)   The Upper Tribunal may not make an order for costs or expenses against a person (the "paying person") without first–
(a)   giving that person an opportunity to make representations; and
(b)   if the paying person is an individual and the order is to be made under paragraph (3)(a), (b) or (d), considering that person's financial means.
(8)   The amount of costs or expenses to be paid under an order under this rule may be ascertained by–
(a)   summary assessment by the Upper Tribunal;
(b)   agreement of a specified sum by the paying person and the person entitled to receive the costs or expenses ("the receiving person"); or
(c)   assessment of the whole or a specified part of the costs or expenses [⁴, including the cvosts or expenses of the assessment,] incurred by the receiving person, if not agreed.
(9)   Following an order for assessment under paragraph (8)(c), the paying person or the receiving person may apply–
(a)   in England and Wales, to the High Court or the Costs Office of the Supreme Court (as specified in the order) for a detailed assessment of the costs on the standard basis or, if specified in the order, on the indemnity basis; and the Civil

Procedure Rules 1998(6) shall apply, with necessary modifications, to that application and assessment as if the proceedings in the tribunal had been proceedings in a court to which the Civil Procedure Rules 1998 apply;

(b) in Scotland, to the Auditor of the Court of Session for the taxation of the expenses according to the fees payable in that court; or

(c) in Northern Ireland, to the Taxing Office of the High Court of Northern Ireland for taxation on the standard basis or, if specified in the order, on the indemnity basis.]

[⁴ (10) Upon making an order for the assessment of costs, the [⁵ Upper] Tribunal may order an amount to be paid on account before the costs or expenses are assessed.]

Amendments

1. Substituted by r7 of SI 2009 No 274 as from 1.4.09.
2. Amended by r11 of SI 2009 No 1975 as from 1.9.09.
3. Amended by r6 of SI 2010 No 747 as from 6.4.10.
4. Amended by rr50 to 53 of SI 2013 No 477 as from 1.4.13.
5. Amended by r6 of SI 2013 No 2067 as from 1.11.13.

Representatives

11.–(1) [⁴ Subject to paragraph (5A),] A party may appoint a representative (whether a legal representative or not) to represent that party in the proceedings [³ save that a party in an asylum or immigration case may not be represented by any person prohibited from representing by section 84 of the Immigration and Asylum Act 1999].

(2) If a party appoints a representative, that party (or the representative if the representative is a legal representative) must send or deliver to the Upper Tribunal [¹] written notice of the representative's name and address.

[¹ (2A) If the Upper Tribunal receives notice that a party has appointed a representative under paragraph (2), it must send a copy of that notice to each other party.]

(3) Anything permitted or required to be done by a party under these Rules, a practice direction or a direction may be done by the representative of that party, except signing a witness statement.

(4) A person who receives due notice of the appointment of a representative–

(a) must provide to the representative any document which is required to be provided to the represented party, and need not provide that document to the represented party; and

(b) may assume that the representative is and remains authorised as such until they receive written notification that this is not so from the representative or the represented party.

(5) [⁴ Subject to paragraph (5B),] At a hearing a party may be accompanied by another person whose name and address has not been notified under paragraph (2) but who, subject to paragraph (8) and with the permission of the Upper Tribunal, may act as a representative or otherwise assist in presenting the party's case at the hearing.

[⁴ (5A) *Omitted*

(5B) *Omitted*]

(6) Paragraphs (2) to (4) do not apply to a person who accompanies a party under paragraph (5).

(7)-(8) *[Omitted]*

[¹ (9) In this rule "legal representative" means [² a person who, for the purposes of the Legal Services Act 2007, is an authorised person in relation to an activity which constitutes the exercise of a right of audience or the conduct of litigation within the meaning of that Act,][³ a qualified person as defined in section 84(2) of the Immigration and Asylum Act 1999,] an advocate or solicitor in Scotland or a barrister or solicitor in Northern Ireland.]

[(10) *[Omitted]*]]

Amendments

1. Amended by r8 of SI 2009 No 274 as from 1.4.09.
2. Amended by r8 of SI 2010 No 43 as from 18.1.10.

3. Amended by r8 of SI 2010 No 44 as from 15.2.10.
4. Amended by r6 of SI 2011 No 2343 as from 17.10.11.

General Note
See the commentary to r11 TP(FTT) Rules 2008 on p999.

Calculating time

12.–(1)   An act required by these Rules, a practice direction or a direction to be done on or by a particular day must be done by 5pm on that day.

(2)   If the time specified by these Rules, a practice direction or a direction for doing any act ends on a day other than a working day, the act is done in time if it is done on the next working day.

(3)-(4)   *[Omitted]*

General Note
See the commentary to rule 12 TP(FTT) Rules 2008 on p1000.

Sending and delivery of documents

13.–(1)   Any document to be provided to the Upper Tribunal under these Rules, a practice direction or a direction must be–

(a)   sent by pre-paid post or [¹ by document exchange, or delivered by hand,] to the address specified for the proceedings;

(b)   sent by fax to the number specified for the proceedings; or

(c)   sent or delivered by such other method as the Upper Tribunal may permit or direct.

(2)   Subject to paragraph (3), if a party provides a fax number, email address or other details for the electronic transmission of documents to them, that party must accept delivery of documents by that method.

(3)   If a party informs the Upper Tribunal and all other parties that a particular form of communication, other than pre-paid post or delivery by hand, should not be used to provide documents to that party, that form of communication must not be so used.

(4)   If the Upper Tribunal or a party sends a document to a party or the Upper Tribunal by email or any other electronic means of communication, the recipient may request that the sender provide a hard copy of the document to the recipient. The recipient must make such a request as soon as reasonably practicable after receiving the document electronically.

(5)   The Upper Tribunal and each party may assume that the address provided by a party or its representative is and remains the address to which documents should be sent or delivered until receiving written notification to the contrary.

[² (6)   Subject to paragraph (7), if a document submitted to the Upper Tribunal is not written in English, it must be accompanied by an English translation.

(7)   In proceedings that are in Wales or have a connection with Wales, a document or translation may be submitted to the [³ Upper] Tribunal in Welsh.]

Amendments
1. Amended by r10 of SI 2009 No 274 as from 1.4.09.
2. Inserted by r10 of SI 2010 No 44 as from 15.2.10.
3. Amended by r8 of SI 2013 No 2067 as from 1.11.13.

Use of documents and information

14.–(1)   The Upper Tribunal may make an order prohibiting the disclosure or publication of–

(a)   specified documents or information relating to the proceedings; or

(b)   any matter likely to lead members of the public to identify any person whom the Upper Tribunal considers should not be identified.

(2)   The Upper Tribunal may give a direction prohibiting the disclosure of a document or information to a person if–

(a)   the Upper Tribunal is satisfied that such disclosure would be likely to cause that person or some other person serious harm; and

(b)   the Upper Tribunal is satisfied, having regard to the interests of justice, that it is proportionate to give such a direction.

(3)   If a party ("the first party") considers that the Upper Tribunal should give a direction under paragraph (2) prohibiting the disclosure of a document or information to another party ("the second party"), the first party must–

(a)   exclude the relevant document or information from any documents that will be provided to the second party; and

(b)   provide to the Upper Tribunal the excluded document or information, and the reason for its exclusion, so that the Upper Tribunal may decide whether the document or information should be disclosed to the second party or should be the subject of a direction under paragraph (2).

[¹ (4)]

(5)   If the Upper Tribunal gives a direction under paragraph (2) which prevents disclosure to a party who has appointed a representative, the Upper Tribunal may give a direction that the documents or information be disclosed to that representative if the Upper Tribunal is satisfied that–

(a)   disclosure to the representative would be in the interests of the party; and

(b)   the representative will act in accordance with paragraph (6).

(6)   Documents or information disclosed to a representative in accordance with a direction under paragraph (5) must not be disclosed either directly or indirectly to any other person without the Upper Tribunal's consent.

(7)   Unless the Upper Tribunal gives a direction to the contrary, information about mental health cases and the names of any persons concerned in such cases must not be made public.

[¹ (8)   The Upper Tribunal may, on its own initiative or on the application of a party, give a direction that certain documents or information must or may be disclosed to the Upper Tribunal on the basis that the Upper Tribunal will not disclose such documents or information to other persons, or specified other persons.

[² (8A)   *[Omitted]*]

(9)   A party making an application for a direction under paragraph (8) may withhold the relevant documents or information from other parties until the Upper Tribunal has granted or refused the application.

(10)   In a case involving matters relating to national security, the Upper Tribunal must ensure that information is not disclosed contrary to the interests of national security.

(11)   The Upper Tribunal must conduct proceedings and record its decision and reasons appropriately so as not to undermine the effect of an order made under paragraph (1), a direction given under paragraph (2) or (8) or the duty imposed by paragraph (10).]

Amendments

1.   Amended by r13 of SI 2009 No 1975 as from 1.9.09.

2.   Inserted by r2(3) of SI 2019 No 925 as from 3.6.19, subject to transitional provision until the Trade Remedies Authority is established.

Evidence and submissions

15.–(1)   Without restriction on the general powers in rule 5(1) and (2) (case management powers), the Upper Tribunal may give directions as to–

(a)   issues on which it requires evidence or submissions;

(b)   the nature of the evidence or submissions it requires;

(c)   whether the parties are permitted or required to provide expert evidence, and if so whether the parties must jointly appoint a single expert to provide such evidence;

(d)   any limit on the number of witnesses whose evidence a party may put forward, whether in relation to a particular issue or generally;

(e)   the manner in which any evidence or submissions are to be provided, which may include a direction for them to be given–

(i) orally at a hearing; or

(ii) by written submissions or witness statement; and

(f) the time at which any evidence or submissions are to be provided.

(2) The Upper Tribunal may–

(a) admit evidence whether or not–

(i) the evidence would be admissible in a civil trial in the United Kingdom; or

(ii) the evidence was available to a previous decision maker; or

(b) exclude evidence that would otherwise be admissible where–

(i) the evidence was not provided within the time allowed by a direction or a practice direction;

(ii) the evidence was otherwise provided in a manner that did not comply with a direction or a practice direction; or

(iii) it would otherwise be unfair to admit the evidence.

[(2A) *[Omitted]*]

(3) The Upper Tribunal may consent to a witness giving, or require any witness to give, evidence on oath, and may administer an oath for that purpose.

General Note

See the commentary to r15 TP(FTT) Rules 2008 on p1001.

Summoning or citation of witnesses and orders to answer questions or produce documents

16.–(1) On the application of a party or on its own initiative, the Upper Tribunal may–

(a) by summons (or, in Scotland, citation) require any person to attend as a witness at a hearing at the time and place specified in the summons or citation; or

(b) order any person to answer any questions or produce any documents in that person's possession or control which relate to any issue in the proceedings.

(2) A summons or citation under paragraph (1)(a) must–

(a) give the person required to attend 14 days' notice of the hearing or such shorter period as the Upper Tribunal may direct; and

(b) where the person is not a party, make provision for the person's necessary expenses of attendance to be paid, and state who is to pay them.

(3) No person may be compelled to give any evidence or produce any document that the person could not be compelled to give or produce on a trial of an action in a court of law in the part of the United Kingdom where the proceedings are due to be determined.

[¹ (4) A person who receives a summons, citation or order may apply to the Upper Tribunal for it to be varied or set aside if they did not have an opportunity to object to it before it was made or issued.

(5) A person making an application under paragraph (4) must do so as soon as reasonably practicable after receiving notice of the summons, citation or order.

(6) A summons, citation or order under this rule must–

(a) state that the person on whom the requirement is imposed may apply to the Upper Tribunal to vary or set aside the summons, citation or order, if they did not have an opportunity to object to it before it was made or issued; and

(b) state the consequences of failure to comply with the summons, citation or order.]

Amendment

1.   Substituted by r11 of SI 2009 No 274 as from 1.4.09.

Withdrawal

17.–(1) Subject to paragraph (2), a party may give notice of the withdrawal of its case, or any part of it–

(a) [¹] by sending or delivering to the Upper Tribunal a written notice of withdrawal; or

(b) orally at a hearing.

(2)   Notice of withdrawal will not take effect unless the Upper Tribunal consents to the withdrawal except in relation to an application for permission to appeal.

(3)   A party which has withdrawn its case may apply to the Upper Tribunal for the case to be reinstated.

(4)   An application under paragraph (3) must be made in writing and be received by the Upper Tribunal within 1 month after–

(a)   the date on which the Upper Tribunal received the notice under paragraph (1)(a); or

(b)   the date of the hearing at which the case was withdrawn orally under paragraph (1)(b).

(5)   The Upper Tribunal must notify each party in writing [¹ that a withdrawal has taken effect] under this rule.

[(6)   *[Omitted]*]

Amendment
1.   Amended by r54 of SI 2013 No 477 as from 1.4.13.

General Note
See the commentary to r17 TP(FTT) Rules 2008 on p1002.

Notice of funding of legal services

18.   If a party is granted funding of legal services at any time, that party must as soon as practicable–

(a)(i) if [¹ civil legal services (within the meaning of section 8 of the Legal Aid, Sentencing and Punishment of Offenders Act 2012) are provided under arrangements made for the purposes of Part 1 of that Act or by] the Northern Ireland Legal Services Commission, send a copy of the [¹ certificate or] funding notice to the Upper Tribunal; or

(ii)   if funding is granted by the Scottish Legal Aid Board, send a copy of the legal aid certificate to the Upper Tribunal; and

(b)   notify every other party in writing that funding has been granted.

Amendment
1.   Amended by r55 of SI 2013 No 477 as from 1.4.13.

General Note
In *CSG 336/2003*, the commissioner (at para 10) expressed concern that what he described as "responsible solicitors" had made a request for an oral hearing when they were unsure whether they would be able to appear at such a hearing due to funding considerations. He suggested that it would be good practice for solicitors appearing in appeals to the commissioners for claimants to indicate, when applying for oral hearings, whether they had applied for legal aid (or other funding) and the outcome of that funding application. Thereafter, it would also be good practice for such solicitors to keep the Commissioners' Office up to date with the progress of any such applications for funding, and inform that Office of any other reasons why they may not be able to appear at the oral hearing.

Now r18 sets out what an appellant must do if granted funding of legal services by the Legal Services Commission (the Legal Aid Board in Scotland). A copy of the funding notice (or legal aid certificate) must be sent to the Upper Tribunal and notice that funding has been granted must be given to all other parties.

[¹ Confidentiality in social security and child support cases

19.–(1)   Paragraph (4) applies to–

(a)   *[Omitted]*;

(b)   proceedings where the parties to the appeal include former joint claimants who are no longer living together in the circumstances described in paragraph (3).

(2)   *[Omitted]*

(3)   The circumstances referred to in paragraph (1)(b) are that one of the former joint claimants would like their address to be kept confidential and has given notice to that effect–

(a)   in the notice of appeal or when notifying the decision maker or the tribunal of any subsequent change of address; or

(b)   within 14 days after an enquiry is made by the recipient of the notice of appeal or the notification referred to in sub-paragraph (a).

(4)   Where this paragraph applies, the Secretary of State or other decision maker and the Tribunal must take appropriate steps to secure the confidentiality of the address and of any information which could reasonably be expected to enable a person to identify the address, to the extent that the address or that information is not already known to each other party.

(5)   In this rule–

"absent parent", "non-resident parent" and "person with care" *[Omitted]*;

"joint claimants" means the persons who made a joint claim for a jobseeker's allowance under the Jobseekers Act 1995, a tax credit under the Tax Credits Act 2002 or in relation to whom an award of universal credit is made under Part 1 of the Welfare Reform Act 2012.]

Amendment

1.   Substituted by r7 of SI 2014 No 2128 as from 20.10.14.

Power to pay expenses and allowances

20.–(1)   *[Omitted]*

(2)   Paragraph (3) applies to proceedings on appeal from a decision of–

(a)   the First-tier Tribunal in proceedings under the Child Support Act 1991, section 12 of the Social Security Act 1998 or paragraph 6 of Schedule 7 to the Child Support, Pensions and Social Security Act 2000;

(b)-(c) *[Omitted]*

(3)   The Lord Chancellor (or, in Scotland, the Secretary of State) may pay to any person who attends any hearing such travelling and other allowances, including compensation for loss of remunerative time, as the Lord Chancellor (or, in Scotland, the Secretary of State) may determine.

[¹ Procedure for applying for a stay of a decision pending an appeal

20A.–(1)   This rule applies where another enactment provides in any terms for the Upper Tribunal to stay or suspend, or to lift a stay or suspension of, a decision which is or may be the subject of an appeal to the Upper Tribunal ("the substantive decision") pending such appeal.

(2)   A person who wishes the Upper Tribunal to decide whether the substantive decision should be stayed or suspended must make a written application to the Upper Tribunal which must include–

(a)   the name and address of the person making the application;

(b)   the name and address of any representative of that person;

(c)   the address to which documents for that person should be sent or delivered;

(d)   the name and address of any person who will be a respondent to the appeal;

(e)   details of the substantive decision and any decision as to when that decision is to take effect, and copies of any written record of, or reasons for, those decisions; and

(f)   the grounds on which the person making the application relies.

(3)   *[Omitted]*

(4)   If the Upper Tribunal grants a stay or suspension following an application under this rule–

(a)   the Upper Tribunal may give directions as to the conduct of the appeal of the substantive decision; and

(b)   the Upper Tribunal may, where appropriate, grant the stay or suspension subject to conditions.

(5)   Unless the Upper Tribunal considers that there is good reason not to do so, the Upper Tribunal must send written notice of any decision made under this rule to each party.]

Amendment

1.   Inserted by r14 of SI 2009 No 1975 as from 1.9.09.

PART 3

[¹ *Procedure for cases in]* the Upper Tribunal

Amendment

1.   Amended by r13 of SI 2009 No 274 as from 1.4.09.

Application to the Upper Tribunal for permission to appeal

21.–[¹ (1)]

(2)   A person may apply to the Upper Tribunal for permission to appeal to the Upper Tribunal against a decision of another tribunal only if–

(a)   they have made an application for permission to appeal to the tribunal which made the decision challenged; and

(b)   that application has been refused or has not been admitted [² or has been granted only on limited grounds].

(3)   An application for permission to appeal must be made in writing and received by the Upper Tribunal no later than–

(a)-(aa) *[Omitted]*;

(b)   otherwise, a month after the date on which the tribunal that made the decision under challenge sent notice of its refusal of permission to appeal, or refusal to admit the application for permission to appeal, to the appellant.

[(3A)]

(4)   The application must state–

(a)   the name and address of the appellant;

(b)   the name and address of the representative (if any) of the appellant;

(c)   an address where documents for the appellant may be sent or delivered;

(d)   details (including the full reference) of the decision challenged;

(e)   the grounds on which the appellant relies; and

(f)   whether the appellant wants the application to be dealt with at a hearing.

(5)   The appellant must provide with the application a copy of–

(a)   any written record of the decision being challenged;

(b)   any separate written statement of reasons for that decision; and

(c)   if the application is for permission to appeal against a decision of another tribunal, the notice of refusal of permission to appeal, or notice of refusal to admit the application for permission to appeal, from that other tribunal.

(6)   If the appellant provides the application to the Upper Tribunal later than the time required by paragraph (3) or by an extension of time allowed under rule 5(3)(a) (power to extend time)–

(a)   the application must include a request for an extension of time and the reason why the application was not provided in time; and

(b)   unless the Upper Tribunal extends time for the application under rule 5(3)(a) (power to extend time) the Upper Tribunal must not admit the application.

(7)   If the appellant makes an application to the Upper Tribunal for permission to appeal against the decision of another tribunal, and that other tribunal refused to admit the appellant's application for permission to appeal because the application for permission or for a written statement of reasons was not made in time–

(a)   the application to the Upper Tribunal for permission to appeal must include the reason why the application to the other tribunal for permission to appeal or for a written statement of reasons, as the case may be, was not made in time; and

(b)   the Upper Tribunal must only admit the application if the Upper Tribunal considers that it is in the interests of justice for it to do so.

[²(8)   In this rule, a reference to notice of a refusal of permission to appeal is to be taken to include a reference to notice of a grant of permission to appeal on limited grounds.]

Amendments

1.   Omitted by r15 of SI 2009 No 1975 as from 1.9.09.

2.   Amended by r7 of SI 2014 No 514 as from 6.4.14.

General Note

    A party who wishes to appeal to the Upper Tribunal must first apply to the First-tier Tribunal for permission to appeal under r38 TP(FT) Rules 2008. If the First-tier Tribunal refuses permission (or refuses to admit the application) a further application may be made to the Upper Tribunal: para (2). The application to the Upper Tribunal must be in writing (para (3)), include the information specified in para (4) and be accompanied by the documents specified in para (5) (and, if applicable, paras (6)(a) and (7)(a)).

    The Upper Tribunal must receive the application no later than a month from the date on which notice of the First-tier Tribunal's decision to refuse permission to appeal (or to admit the application) was sent to the appellant: para (3)(b). That limit may be extended under r5(3)(a) either on an application under para (6) or of its own initiative by waiving para (6) under r7(2)(a). Where the application for permission to appeal to the First-tier Tribunal was late and the First-tier Tribunal refused to admit it on that ground, the Upper Tribunal may only admit the application if it is in the interests of justice to do so. There has been some disagreement whether the requirement in r21(2)(a) that a party must first have applied to the First-tier Tribunal for permission to appeal before applying to the Upper Tribunal can be waived under r7. The better view is that it can: see *ZN, BB, JHS v Redbridge LB (HB)* [2013] UKUT 503 (AAC) at paras 8–19 and the decisions discussed in those paragraphs.

Decision in relation to permission to appeal

22.–(1)   [¹ [³ Except where rule 22A (special procedure for providing notice of a refusal of permission to appeal in an asylum case) applies]] If the Upper Tribunal refuses permission to appeal [² or refuses to admit a late application for permission], it must send written notice of the refusal and of the reasons for the refusal to the appellant.

(2)   If the Upper Tribunal gives permission to appeal–

(a)   the Upper Tribunal must send written notice of the permission, and of the reasons for any limitations or conditions on such permission, to each party;

(b)   subject to any direction by the Upper Tribunal, the application for permission to appeal stands as the notice of appeal and the Upper Tribunal must send to each respondent a copy of the application for permission to appeal and any documents provided with it by the appellant; and

(c)   the Upper Tribunal may, with the consent of the appellant and each respondent, determine the appeal without obtaining any further response.

(3)-(5)   *[Omitted]*

Amendments

1.   Inserted by r8 of SI 2014 No 514 as from 6.4.14.

2.   Inserted by r3 of SI 2014 No 1505 as from 30.6.14.

3.   Amended by r9 of SI 2014 No 2128 as from 20.10.14.

Definitions

"appellant" – see r1(3).

"respondent" – see r1(3).

General Note

    Rule 22(2)(b) provides for the continuation of the long-standing practice of treating the application for permission to appeal as the notice of appeal once permission is granted.

    Rule 22(2)(c) gives the Upper Tribunal a power to finally determine an appeal once permission is granted without obtaining any further response, provided that the appellant and all respondents consent.

Notice of appeal

23.–[¹ (1)   This rule applies–

(a)   to proceedings on appeal to the Upper Tribunal for which permission to appeal is not required, except proceedings to which rule 26A [² or 26B] applies;

(b)   if another tribunal has given permission for a party to appeal to the Upper Tribunal; or

(c)   subject to any other direction by the Upper Tribunal, if the Upper Tribunal has given permission to appeal and has given a direction that the application for permission to appeal does not stand as the notice of appeal.

[(1A)   *[Omitted]*

(2)   The appellant must provide a notice of appeal to the Upper Tribunal so that it is received within 1 month after–

(a)   the date that the tribunal that gave permission to appeal sent notice of such permission to the appellant; or

[³ (b) if permission to appeal is not required, the date on which notice of decision to which the appeal relates–

(i)   was sent to the appellant; or

(ii)   *[Omitted]*]

[⁵ (iii) *[Omitted]*]

(3)   The notice of appeal must include the information listed in rule 21(4)(a) to (e) (content of the application for permission to appeal) and, where the Upper Tribunal has given permission to appeal, the Upper Tribunal's case reference.

(4)   If another tribunal has granted permission to appeal, the appellant must provide with the notice of appeal a copy of–

(a)   any written record of the decision being challenged;

(b)   any separate written statement of reasons for that decision; and

(c)   the notice of permission to appeal.

(5)   If the appellant provides the notice of appeal to the Upper Tribunal later than the time required by paragraph (2) or by an extension of time allowed under rule 5(3)(a) (power to extend time)–

(a)   the notice of appeal must include a request for an extension of time and the reason why the notice was not provided in time; and

(b)   unless the Upper Tribunal extends time for the notice of appeal under rule 5(3)(a) (power to extend time) the Upper Tribunal must not admit the notice of appeal.

[¹ (6)   When the Upper Tribunal receives the notice of appeal it must send a copy of the notice and any accompanying documents–

(a)   to each respondent; or

(b)   *[Omitted]*]

[⁵ (c) *[Omitted]*

(6A)   *[Omitted]*]

[⁴ (7)   *[Omitted]*]

Amendments

1.   Substituted by r17 of SI 2009 No 1975 as from 1.9.09.
2.   Amended by r8 of SI 2010 No 747 as from 6.4.10.
3.   Substituted by r4(a) of SI 2015 No 1510 as from 21.8.15.
4.   Inserted by r4(b) of SI 2015 No 1510 as from 21.8.15.
5.   Inserted by r2(4) of SI 2019 No 925 as from 3.6.19, subject to transitional provision until the Trade Remedies Authority is established.

General Note

Where the First-tier Tribunal gives permission to appeal (or where the Upper Tribunal gives permission but gives a direction under r22(2)(b) that the application for permission should not stand as the notice of appeal), the appellant must provide a notice of appeal meeting the requirements of para (3) and (4) within one month from notice of the grant of permission. The one-month limit may be extended: para (5) and rr5(3)(a) and 7(2)(a).

Response to the notice of appeal

24.–[²,⁵ (1)   *[Omitted]*

(1A)   Subject to any direction given by the Upper Tribunal, a respondent may provide a response to a notice of appeal.]

(2)   Any response provided under paragraph [³ (1A)] must be in writing and must be sent or delivered to the Upper Tribunal so that it is received–

[⁴ (a) if an application for permission to appeal stands as the notice of appeal, no later than one month after the date on which the respondent was sent notice that permission to appeal had been granted;] [⁴]

[(aa) *[Omitted]]*

[(ab) *[Omitted]]*

(b)   in any other case, no later than 1 month after the date on which the Upper Tribunal sent a copy of the notice of appeal to the respondent.

(3)　　The response must state–
(a)　　the name and address of the respondent;
(b)　　the name and address of the representative (if any) of the respondent;
(c)　　an address where documents for the respondent may be sent or delivered;
(d)　　whether the respondent opposes the appeal;
(e)　　the grounds on which the respondent relies, including [² (in the case of an appeal against the decision of another tribunal)] any grounds on which the respondent was unsuccessful in the proceedings which are the subject of the appeal, but intends to rely in the appeal; and
(f)　　whether the respondent wants the case to be dealt with at a hearing.

(4)　　If the respondent provides the response to the Upper Tribunal later than the time required by paragraph (2) or by an extension of time allowed under rule 5(3)(a) (power to extend time), the response must include a request for an extension of time and the reason why the [¹ response] was not provided in time.

(5)　　When the Upper Tribunal receives the response it must send a copy of the response and any accompanying documents to the appellant and each other party.

[⁶ (6)　　*[Omitted]*]

Amendments

1.　　Amended by Art 15 of SI 2009 No 274 as from 1.4.09.
2.　　Amended by r18 of SI 2009 No 1975 as from 1.9.09.
3.　　Amended by r9 of SI 2010 No 43 as from 18.1.10.
4.　　Amended by r15 of SI 2010 No 44 as from 15.2.10.
5.　　Amended by r5(a) of SI 2015 No 1510 as from 21.8.15.
6.　　Inserted by r5(b) of SI 2015 No 1510 as from 21.8.15.

General Note

See the commentary to r24 TP(FTT) Rules 2008 on p1009 (except that, in the Upper Tribunal, there is a proper time limit of one month in which to provide a response to the appeal).

Appellant's reply

25.–(1)　　Subject to any direction given by the Upper Tribunal, the appellant may provide a reply to any response provided under rule 24 (response to the notice of appeal).

(2)　　[¹ Subject to paragraph (2A), any] reply provided under paragraph (1) must be in writing and must be sent or delivered to the Upper Tribunal so that it is received within one month after the date on which the Upper Tribunal sent a copy of the response to the appellant.

[(2A)　　*[Omitted]*]
[² (2B)　　*[Omitted]*]

(3)　　When the Upper Tribunal receives the reply it must send a copy of the reply and any accompanying documents to each respondent.

[² (4)　　*[Omitted]*]

Amendments

1.　　Amended by r16 of SI 2010 No 44 as from 15.2.10.
2.　　Inserted by r6 of SI 2015 No 1510 as from 21.8.15.

General Note

The appellant has a month in which to reply to the response.

[¹ Cases transferred or referred to the Upper Tribunal, applications made directly to the Upper Tribunal[⁴*[Omitted]*] and proceedings without notice to a respondent

26A.–[² (1)　　Paragraphs (2) and (3) apply to–
(a)　　a case transferred or referred to the Upper Tribunal from the First-tier Tribunal; [⁴]
(b)　　a case, other than an appeal or a case to which rule 26 (references under the Forfeiture Act 1982) applies, which is started by an application made directly to the Upper Tribunal.] [⁴ or
(c)　　*[Omitted]*]

(2)　In a case to which this paragraph applies–
(a)　the Upper Tribunal must give directions as to the procedure to be followed in the consideration and disposal of the proceedings; [³
(aa)　*[Omitted]*]
(b)　the preceding rules in this Part will only apply to the proceedings to the extent provided for by such directions.
(3)　If a case or matter to which this paragraph applies is to be determined without notice to or the involvement of a respondent–
(a)　any provision in these Rules requiring a document to be provided by or to a respondent; and
(b)　any other provision in these Rules permitting a respondent to participate in the proceedings
does not apply to that case or matter.]
(4)　*[Omitted]*

Amendments
1.　Inserted by Art 16 of SI 2009 No 274 as from 1.4.09.
2.　Substituted by r19 of SI 2009 No 1975 as from 1.9.09.
3.　Amended by r5 of SI 2012 No 500 as from 6.4.12.
4.　Amended by r2(5) of SI 2019 No 925 as from 3.6.19.

PART 4
Judicial review proceedings in the Upper Tribunal

General Note on Part 4
See the General Note to ss15–21 TCEA 2007 on p190.

Application of this Part to judicial review proceedings transferred to the Upper Tribunal
27.–(1)　When a court transfers judicial review proceedings to the Upper Tribunal, the Upper Tribunal–
(a)　must notify each party in writing that the proceedings have been transferred to the Upper Tribunal; and
(b)　must give directions as to the future conduct of the proceedings.
(2)　The directions given under paragraph (1)(b) may modify or disapply for the purposes of the proceedings any of the provisions of the following rules in this Part.
(3)　In proceedings transferred from the Court of Session under section 20(1) of the 2007 Act, the directions given under paragraph (1)(b) must–
(a)　if the Court of Session did not make a first order specifying the required intimation, service and advertisement of the petition, state the Upper Tribunal's requirements in relation to those matters;
(b)　state whether the Upper Tribunal will consider summary dismissal of the proceedings; and
(c)　where necessary, modify or disapply provisions relating to permission in the following rules in this Part.

Applications for permission to bring judicial review proceedings
28.–(1)　A person seeking permission to bring judicial review proceedings before the Upper Tribunal under section 16 of the 2007 Act must make a written application to the Upper Tribunal for such permission.
(2)　Subject to paragraph (3), an application under paragraph (1) must be made promptly and, unless any other enactment specifies a shorter time limit, must be sent or delivered to the Upper Tribunal so that it is received no later than 3 months after the date of the decision [¹ , action or omission] to which the application relates.
(3)　An application for permission to bring judicial review proceedings challenging a decision of the First-tier Tribunal may be made later than the time required by paragraph (2) if it is made within 1 month after the date on which the First-tier Tribunal sent–
(a)　written reasons for the decision; or

(b)   notification that an application for the decision to be set aside has been unsuccessful, provided that that application was made in time.

(4)   The application must state–

(a)   the name and address of the applicant, the respondent and any other person whom the applicant considers to be an interested party;

(b)   the name and address of the applicant's representative (if any);

(c)   an address where documents for the applicant may be sent or delivered;

(d)   details of the decision challenged (including the date, the full reference and the identity of the decision maker);

(e)   that the application is for permission to bring judicial review proceedings;

(f)   the outcome that the applicant is seeking; and

(g)   the facts and grounds on which the applicant relies.

(5)   If the application relates to proceedings in a court or tribunal, the application must name as an interested party each party to those proceedings who is not the applicant or a respondent.

(6)   The applicant must send with the application–

(a)   a copy of any written record of the decision in the applicant's possession or control; and

(b)   copies of any other documents in the applicant's possession or control on which the applicant intends to rely.

(7)   If the applicant provides the application to the Upper Tribunal later than the time required by paragraph (2) or (3) or by an extension of time allowed under rule 5(3)(a) (power to extend time)–

(a)   the application must include a request for an extension of time and the reason why the application was not provided in time; and

(b)   unless the Upper Tribunal extends time for the application under rule 5(3)(a) (power to extend time) the Upper Tribunal must not admit the application.

(8)   [² Except where rule 28A(2)(a) (special provisions for [³ immigration judicial review] proceedings) applies,] when the Upper Tribunal receives the application it must send a copy of the application and any accompanying documents to each person named in the application as a respondent or interested party.

Amendments

1.   Amended by r17 of SI 2009 No 274 as from 1.4.09.

2.   Amended by r7 of SI 2011 No 2343 as from 17.10.11.

3.   Amended by r10 of SI 2013 No 2067 as from 1.11.13.

Acknowledgment of service

29.–(1)   A person who is sent [⁴ or provided with] a copy of an application for permission under rule 28(8) (application for permission to bring judicial review proceedings) [⁴ or rule 28A(2)(a) (special provisions for [⁵ immigration judicial review] proceedings)] and wishes to take part in the proceedings must [⁴ provide] to the Upper Tribunal an acknowledgment of service so that it is received no later than 21 days after the date on which the Upper Tribunal sent [⁴, or in [⁵ immigration judicial review] proceedings the applicant provided,] a copy of the application to that person.

(2)   An acknowledgment of service under paragraph (1) must be in writing and state–

(a)   whether the person intends to [¹ support or] oppose the application for permission;

(b)   their grounds for any [¹ support or] opposition under sub-paragraph (a), or any other submission or [² information which they consider may] assist the Upper Tribunal; and

(c)   the name and address of any other person not named in the application as a respondent or interested party whom the person providing the acknowledgment considers to be an interested party.

[⁴ (2A)   *Omitted*]

(3)   A person who is [⁴ provided with] a copy of an application for permission under rule 28(8) [⁴ or 28A(2)(a)] but does not provide an acknowledgment of service [⁴ to the

Upper Tribunal] may not take part in the application for permission [³ unless allowed to do so by the Upper Tribunal], but may take part in the subsequent proceedings if the application is successful.

Amendments
1.   Amended by r18 of SI 2009 No 274 as from 1.4.09.
2.   Amended by correction slip 9.09.
3.   Amended by r8(3) of SI 2011 No 651 (L.6) as from 1.4.11.
4.   Amended by r9 of SI 2011 No 2343 as from 17.10.11.
5.   Amended by r12 of SI 2013 No 2067 as from 1.11.13.

Decision on permission or summary dismissal, and reconsideration of permission or summary dismissal at a hearing

30.–(1)   The Upper Tribunal must send to the applicant, each respondent and any other person who provided an acknowledgment of service to the Upper Tribunal, and may send to any other person who may have an interest in the proceedings, written notice of–

(a)   its decision in relation to the application for permission; and

[³ (b)   the reasons for any–

(i)   refusal of the application or refusal to admit the late application, or

(ii)   limitations or conditions on permission.]

(2)   In proceedings transferred from the Court of Session under section 20(1) of the 2007 Act, where the Upper Tribunal has considered whether summarily to dismiss of the proceedings, the Upper Tribunal must send to the applicant and each respondent, and may send to any other person who may have an interest in the proceedings, written notice of–

(a)   its decision in relation to the summary dismissal of proceedings; and

(b)   the reasons for any decision summarily to dismiss part or all of the proceedings, or any limitations or conditions on the continuation of such proceedings.

(3)   Paragraph (4) applies where the Upper Tribunal, without a hearing–

[³ (a)   determines an application for permission to bring judicial review proceedings by–

(i)   refusing permission or refusing to admit the late application, or

(ii)   giving permission on limited grounds or subject to conditions]; or

(b)   in proceedings transferred from the Court of Session, summarily dismisses part or all of the proceedings, or imposes any limitations or conditions on the continuation of such proceedings.

(4)   [² Subject to paragraph (4A), in] the circumstances specified in paragraph (3) the applicant may apply for the decision to be reconsidered at a hearing.

[² (4A)   *[Omitted]]*

(5)   An application under paragraph (4) must be made in writing and must be sent or delivered to the Upper Tribunal so that it is received within 14 days [¹, or in [² immigration judicial review] proceedings 9 days] after the date on which the Upper Tribunal sent written notice of its decision regarding the application to the applicant.

Amendments
1.   Amended by r10 of SI 2011 No 2343 as from 17.10.11.
2.   Amended by r13 of SI 2013 No 2067 as from 1.11.13.
3.   Amended by r11 of SI 2014 No 514 as from 6.4.14.

Responses

31.–(1)   Any person to whom the Upper Tribunal has sent notice of the grant of permission under rule 30(1) (notification of decision on permission), and who wishes to contest the application or support it on additional grounds, must provide detailed grounds for contesting or supporting the application to the Upper Tribunal.

(2)   Any detailed grounds must be provided in writing and must be sent or delivered to the Upper Tribunal so that they are received not more than 35 days after the Upper Tribunal sent notice of the grant of permission under rule 30(1).

Applicant seeking to rely on additional grounds

32. The applicant may not rely on any grounds, other than those grounds on which the applicant obtained permission for the judicial review proceedings, without the consent of the Upper Tribunal.

Right to make representations

33. Each party and, with the permission of the Upper Tribunal, any other person, may–

(a) submit evidence, except at the hearing of an application for permission;

(b) make representations at any hearing which they are entitled to attend; and

(c) make written representations in relation to a decision to be made without a hearing.

[¹ Amendments and additional grounds resulting in transfer of proceedings to the High Court in England and Wales

33A.–(1) This rule applies only to judicial review proceedings arising under the law of England and Wales.

(2) In relation to such proceedings–

(a) the powers of the Upper Tribunal to permit or require amendments under rule 5(3)(c) extend to amendments which would, once in place, give rise to an obligation or power to transfer the proceedings to the High Court in England and Wales under section 18(3) of the 2007 Act or paragraph (3);

(b) except with the permission of the Upper Tribunal, additional grounds may not be advanced, whether by an applicant or otherwise, if they would give rise to an obligation or power to transfer the proceedings to the High Court in England and Wales under section 18(3) of the 2007 Act or paragraph (3).

(3) Where the High Court in England and Wales has transferred judicial review proceedings to the Upper Tribunal under any power or duty and subsequently the proceedings are amended or any party advances additional grounds–

(a) if the proceedings in their present form could not have been transferred to the Upper Tribunal under the relevant power or duty had they been in that form at the time of the transfer, the Upper Tribunal must transfer the proceedings back to the High Court in England and Wales;

(b) subject to sub-paragraph (a), where the proceedings were transferred to the Upper Tribunal under section 31A(3) of the Senior Courts Act 1981(a)(power to transfer judicial review proceedings to the Upper Tribunal), the Upper Tribunal may transfer proceedings back to the High Court in England and Wales if it appears just and convenient to do so.]

Amendment

1.   Inserted by r11 of SI 2011 No 2343 as from 17.10.11.

PART 5
Hearings

Decision with or without a hearing

34.–(1) Subject to [¹ paragraphs (2) and (3)], the Upper Tribunal may make any decision without a hearing.

(2) The Upper Tribunal must have regard to any view expressed by a party when deciding whether to hold a hearing to consider any matter, and the form of any such hearing.

[¹ (3)-(4) *[Omitted]*]]

Amendment

1.   Amended by r14 of SI 2013 No 2067 as from 1.11.13.

General Note
> The Upper Tribunal is not obliged to hold a hearing of the appeal. The decision whether to hold one is made by judge of the Upper Tribunal who must have regard to the parties' views. It is probable that the former practice (ie, in appeals to the commissioner) will continue to apply and that the Upper Tribunal will hold a hearing if any of the parties requests one, unless the judge considers that the appeal can be determined properly without one. The Upper Tribunal may also hold a hearing even if no party has requested it.

Entitlement to attend a hearing

35.[¹–(1)]   Subject to rule 37(4) (exclusion of a person from a hearing), each party is entitled to attend a hearing.

[¹ (2)   *[Omitted]*]

Amendment
1.   Amended by r11 of SI 2010 No 43 as from 18.1.10.

Notice of hearings

36.–(1)   The Upper Tribunal must give each party entitled to attend a hearing reasonable notice of the time and place of the hearing (including any adjourned or postponed hearing) and any change to the time and place of the hearing.

(2)   The period of notice under paragraph (1) must be at least 14 days except that–

(a)   in applications for permission to bring judicial review proceedings, the period of notice must be at least 2 working days; [¹]

[(aa)   *[Omitted]*]

(b)   [¹ in any case other than a fast-track case] the Upper Tribunal may give shorter notice–

(i)   with the parties' consent; or

(ii)   in urgent or exceptional cases.

Amendment
1.   Amended by r17 of SI 2010 No 44 as from 15.2.10.

General Note
> See the commentary to r29 TP(FTT) Rules 2008 on p1014. In a judicial review case, only two working days' notice is required.

Public and private hearings

37.–(1)   Subject to the following paragraphs, all hearings must be held in public.

(2)   The Upper Tribunal may give a direction that a hearing, or part of it, is to be held in private.

(2A)   *[Omitted]*

(3)   Where a hearing, or part of it, is to be held in private, the Upper Tribunal may determine who is entitled to attend the hearing or part of it.

(4)   The Upper Tribunal may give a direction excluding from any hearing, or part of it–

(a)   any person whose conduct the Upper Tribunal considers is disrupting or is likely to disrupt the hearing;

(b)   any person whose presence the Upper Tribunal considers is likely to prevent another person from giving evidence or making submissions freely;

(c)   any person who the Upper Tribunal considers should be excluded in order to give effect to [² the requirement at rule 14(11) (prevention of disclosure or publication of documents and information)] ; [¹]

(d)   any person where the purpose of the hearing would be defeated by the attendance of that person. [¹; or

(e)   a person under [³ 18, other than a young person who is a party in a special educational needs case or a disability discrimination in schools case].]

(5)   The Upper Tribunal may give a direction excluding a witness from a hearing until that witness gives evidence.

Amendments
1.   Amended by r19 of SI 2009 No 274 as from 1.4.09.
2.   Amended by r20 of SI 2009 No 1975 as from 1.9.09.
3.   Amended by r13 of SI 2014 No 2128 as from 1.9.14.

General Note
See the commentary to r30 TP(FTT) Rules 2008 on p1014.

Hearings in a party's absence
38. If a party fails to attend a hearing, the Upper Tribunal may proceed with the hearing if the Upper Tribunal–
(a)   is satisfied that the party has been notified of the hearing or that reasonable steps have been taken to notify the party of the hearing; and
(b)   considers that it is in the interests of justice to proceed with the hearing.

PART 6
Decisions

Consent orders
39.–(1)   The Upper Tribunal may, at the request of the parties but only if it considers it appropriate, make a consent order disposing of the proceedings and making such other appropriate provision as the parties have agreed.
(2)   Notwithstanding any other provision of these Rules, the [² Upper] Tribunal need not hold a hearing before making an order under paragraph (1) [¹].

Amendments
1.   Amended by r20 of SI 2009 No 274 as from 1.4.09.
2.   Amended by r15 of SI 2013 No 2067 as from 1.11.13.

Decisions
40.–(1)   The Upper Tribunal may give a decision orally at a hearing.
(1A)-(1B)   *[Omitted]*
(2)   [¹] [³ Except where [⁵ rule 22 (decision in relation to permission to appeal) or rule 22A (special procedure for providing notice of a refusal of permission to appeal in an asylum case)] applies,] the Upper Tribunal must provide to each party as soon as reasonably practicable after making [⁴ a decision (other than a decision under Part 7) which finally disposes of all issues in the proceedings or of a preliminary issue dealt with following a direction under rule 5(3)(e)]–
(a)   a decision notice stating the [⁴ Upper] Tribunal's decision; and
(b)   notification of any rights of review or appeal against the decision and the time and manner in which such rights of review or appeal may be exercised.
(3)   [¹ Subject to rule [² 14(11) (prevention of disclosure or publication of documents and information)] ,] The Upper Tribunal must provide written reasons for its decision with a decision notice provided under paragraph (2)(a) unless–
(a)   the decision was made with the consent of the parties; or
(b)   the parties have consented to the Upper Tribunal not giving written reasons.
(4)   The [² Upper] Tribunal may provide written reasons for any decision to which paragraph (2) does not apply.
(5)   *[Omitted]*

Amendments
1.   Amended by r21 of SI 2009 No 274 as from 1.4.09.
2.   Amended by r21 of SI 2009 No 1975 as from 1.9.09.
3.   Amended by r19 of SI 2010 No 44 as from 15.2.10.
4.   Amended by r56 of SI 2013 No 477 as from 1.4.13.
5.   Amended by r14 of SI 2014 No 2128 as from 20.10.14.

General Note

The Upper Tribunal may give its decision by word of mouth (para (1)) but must then provide a written notice (para (2)(a)) and a written statement of reasons: para (3). There is no obligation to give reasons where the decision is made by consent or all parties have consented to a decision without reasons: para (3)(a) and (b).

PART 7
Correcting, setting aside, reviewing and appealing decisions of the Upper Tribunal

Interpretation
41. In this Part–

"appeal" [¹, except in rule 44(2) (application for permission to appeal),] means the exercise of a right of appeal under section 13 of the 2007 Act; and

"review" means the review of a decision by the Upper Tribunal under section 10 of the 2007 Act.

Amendment

1.   Amended by art 22 of SI 2009 No 274 as from 1.4.09.

Clerical mistakes and accidental slips or omissions
42. The Upper Tribunal may at any time correct any clerical mistake or other accidental slip or omission in a decision or record of a decision by–
  (a)   sending notification of the amended decision, or a copy of the amended record, to all parties; and
  (b)   making any necessary amendment to any information published in relation to the decision or record.

General Note

See the commentary to r36 TP(FTT) Rules 2008 on p1018.

The reference to "a decision or record of a decision" is wide enough to allow the Upper Tribunal to correct clerical mistakes and other accidental slips or omissions in its reasons as well as its formal decisions: *AF (Afghanistan) v Secretary of State for the Home Department* [2019] EWCA Civ 208.

Setting aside a decision which disposes of proceedings
43.–(1)   The Upper Tribunal may set aside a decision which disposes of proceedings, or part of such a decision, and re-make the decision or the relevant part of it, if–
  (a)   the Upper Tribunal considers that it is in the interests of justice to do so; and
  (b)   one or more of the conditions in paragraph (2) are satisfied.
  (2)   The conditions are–
  (a)   a document relating to the proceedings was not sent to, or was not received at an appropriate time by, a party or a party's representative;
  (b)   a document relating to the proceedings was not sent to the Upper Tribunal at an appropriate time;
  (c)   a party, or a party's representative, was not present at a hearing related to the proceedings; or
  (d)   there has been some other procedural irregularity in the proceedings.
  (3)   [¹ Except where paragraph (4) applies,] A party applying for a decision, or part of a decision, to be set aside under paragraph (1) must make a written application to the Upper Tribunal so that it is received no later than 1 month after the date on which the [² Upper] Tribunal sent notice of the decision to the party.
  [(4)-(5)   *[Omitted]*]

Amendments

1.   Amended by r21 of SI 2010 No 44 as from 15.2.10.
2.   Amended by r17 of SI 2013 No 2067 as from 1.11.13.

General Note

See the commentary to r37 TP(FTT) Rules 2008 on p1019.

There is no right of appeal to the Court of Appeal against a decision made by the Upper Tribunal under r43: see *Samuda v Secretary of SSWP* [2014] EWCA Civ 1, as applied by Singh LJ in *Alcorn v SSWP*, unreported, 12 April 2019.

Application for permission to appeal

44.–(1)   [³ Subject to [⁴ paragraphs (4A) and (4B)],] A person seeking permission to appeal must make a written application to the Upper Tribunal for permission to appeal.

(2)   Paragraph (3) applies to an application under paragraph (1) in respect of a decision–

(a)   on an appeal against a decision in a social security and child support case (as defined in the Tribunal Procedure (First-tier Tribunal) (Social Entitlement Chamber) Rules 2008;

(b)-(c) *[Omitted]*

(3)   Where this paragraph applies, the application must be sent or delivered to the Upper Tribunal so that it is received within 3 months after the date on which the Upper Tribunal sent to the person making the application–

(a)   written notice of the decision;

(b)   notification of amended reasons for, or correction of, the decision following a review; or

(c)   notification that an application for the decision to be set aside has been unsuccessful.

[(3A)-(3D)   *[Omitted]*]

(4)   Where paragraph (3) [¹ [², (3A) [⁴, (3D) or (4C)]]] does not apply, an application under paragraph (1) must be sent or delivered to the Upper Tribunal so that it is received within 1 month after the latest of the dates on which the Upper Tribunal sent to the person making the application–

(a)   written reasons for the decision;

(b)   notification of amended reasons for, or correction of, the decision following a review; or

(c)   notification that an application for the decision to be set aside has been unsuccessful.

[(4A)-(4C)]   *[Omitted]*

(5)   The date in paragraph (3)(c) or (4)(c) applies only if the application for the decision to be set aside was made within the time stipulated in rule 43 (setting aside a decision which disposes of proceedings) or any extension of that time granted by the Upper Tribunal.

(6)   If the person seeking permission to appeal provides the application to the Upper Tribunal later than the time required by paragraph (3) [¹, (3A)][², (3D)] or (4), or by any extension of time under rule 5(3)(a) (power to extend time)–

(a)   the application must include a request for an extension of time and the reason why the application notice was not provided in time; and

(b)   unless the Upper Tribunal extends time for the application under rule 5(3)(a) (power to extend time) the Upper Tribunal must refuse the application.

(7)   An application under paragraph (1) [³ or (4A)(a)] must–

(a)   identify the decision of the [⁴ Upper] Tribunal to which it relates;

(b)   identify the alleged error or errors of law in the decision; and

(c)   state the result the party making the application is seeking.

Amendments

1.   Amended by r22 of SI 2010 No 44 as from 15.2.10.
2.   Amended by r10 of SI 2010 No 747 as from 6.4.10.
3.   Amended by r3 of SI 2012 No.2890 as from 11.12.12.
4.   Amended by r18 of SI 2013 No 2067 as from 1.11.13.

General Note

Rule 44 deals with applications for permission to appeal from the Upper Tribunal to the Court of Appeal or Court of Session. The application for permission to appeal must be in writing (para (1)) and made within three months of the latest of the decisions listed in para (3). That time limit may be extended under para (6) and rr5(3)(a) and 7(2)(a).

Upper Tribunal's consideration of application for permission to appeal

45.–(1)   On receiving an application for permission to appeal the Upper Tribunal may review the decision in accordance with rule 46 (review of a decision), but may only do so if–

(a)   when making the decision the Upper Tribunal overlooked a legislative provision or binding authority which could have had a material effect on the decision; or

(b)   since the Upper Tribunal's decision, a court has made a decision which is binding on the Upper Tribunal and which, had it been made before the Upper Tribunal's decision, could have had a material effect on the decision.

(2)   If the Upper Tribunal decides not to review the decision, or reviews the decision and decides to take no action in relation to the decision or part of it, the Upper Tribunal must consider whether to give permission to appeal in relation to the decision or that part of it.

(3)   The Upper Tribunal must [¹ provide] a record of its decision to the parties as soon as practicable.

(4)   If the Upper Tribunal refuses permission to appeal it must [¹ provide] with the record of its decision–

(a)   a statement of its reasons for such refusal; and

(b)   notification of the right to make an application to the relevant appellate court for permission to appeal and the time within which, and the method by which, such application must be made.

(5)   The Upper Tribunal may give permission to appeal on limited grounds, but must comply with paragraph (4) in relation to any grounds on which it has refused permission.

Amendment

1.   Amended by r19 of SI 2013 No 2067 as from 1.11.13.

General Note

See the commentary to r39 TP(FTT) Rules 2008 on p1023. The grounds upon which the Upper Tribunal may review its decision in response to an application for permission to appeal are restricted to those in para (1)(a) and (b).

Review of a decision

46.–[¹ (1)   The Upper Tribunal may only undertake a review of a decision pursuant to rule 45(1) (review on an application for permission to appeal).]

(2)   The Upper Tribunal must notify the parties in writing of the outcome of any review and of any rights of review or appeal in relation to the outcome.

(3)   If the Upper Tribunal decides to take any action in relation to a decision following a review without first giving every party an opportunity to make representations, the notice under paragraph (2) must state that any party that did not have an opportunity to make representations may apply for such action to be set aside and for the decision to be reviewed again.

Amendment

1.   Substituted by r12 of SI 2011 No 2343 as from 17.10.11.

General Note

See the commentary to r40 TP(FTT) Rules 2008 on p1023. The relevant provision of the TCEA 2007 is s10.

[¹ Power to treat an application as a different type of application

48.   The [² Upper] Tribunal may treat an application for a decision to be corrected, set aside or reviewed, or for permission to appeal against a decision, as an application for any other one of those things.]

Amendments

1.   Inserted by r8 of SI 2010 No 2653 as from 29.11.10.

2.   Amended by r20 of SI 2013 No 2067 as from 1.11.13.

The Transfer of Tribunal Functions Order 2008
(2008 No.2833)

Citation, commencement, interpretation and extent

1.–(1) This Order may be cited as the Transfer of Tribunal Functions Order 2008 and comes into force on 3rd November 2008.

(2) A reference in this Order to a Schedule by a number alone is a reference to the Schedule so numbered in this Order.

(3) Subject as follows, this Order extends to England and Wales, Scotland and Northern Ireland.

(4) Except as provided by paragraph (5) or (6), an amendment, repeal or revocation of any enactment by any provision of Schedule 3 extends to the part or parts of the United Kingdom to which the enactment extends.

(5)-(6) *[Omitted]*.

Transfer of functions of certain tribunals

3.–(1) Subject to paragraph (3), the functions of the tribunals listed in Table 1 of Schedule 1 are transferred to the First-tier Tribunal.

(2) Subject to paragraph (3), the functions of the tribunals listed in Table 2 of Schedule 1 are transferred to the Upper Tribunal.

(3) *[Omitted]*

Abolition of tribunals transferred under section 30(1)

4. The tribunals listed in Table 1 and Table 2 of Schedule 1 are abolished except for–

(a)-(b) *[Omitted]*

Transfer of persons into the First-tier Tribunal and the Upper Tribunal

5.–(1) A person holding an office listed in a table in Schedule 2 who was, was a member of, or was an authorised decision-maker for, a tribunal listed in the corresponding table in Schedule 1 immediately before the functions of that tribunal were transferred under article 3 shall hold the corresponding office or offices.

(2) In paragraph (1) "corresponding" means appearing in the corresponding entry in the table below.

Table in Schedule 1	Table in Schedule 2	Office or offices
Table 1	Table 1	Transferred-in judge of the First-tier Tribunal
Table 1	Table 2	Transferred-in other member of the First-tier Tribunal
Table 1	Table 3	Transferred in judge of the First-tier Tribunal and deputy judge of the Upper Tribunal
Table 2	Table 4	Transferred-in judge of the Upper Tribunal
Table 1 or 2	Table 5	Transferred-in other member of the Upper Tribunal

SCHEDULE 1

ARTICLES 3, 4 AND 5

Functions transferred to the First-tier Tribunal and Upper Tribunal

Table 1: Functions transferred to the First-tier Tribunal

Tribunal	Enactment
Appeal tribunal	Chapter 1 of Part 1 of the Social Security Act 1998 (c.14)

Table 2: Functions transferred to the Upper Tribunal

Tribunal	Enactment
Social Security Commissioner	Schedule 4 to the Social Security Act 1998 (c.14)

SCHEDULE 2

ARTICLE 5

Persons transferred as judges and members of the First-tier Tribunal and Upper Tribunal

Table 1: Members becoming transferred-in judges of the First-tier Tribunal

Tribunal Member	Enactment
A legally qualified panel member	Section 6 of the Social Security Act 1998 (c.14)

Table 2: Members becoming transferred-in other members of the First-tier Tribunal

Tribunal Member	Enactment
A financially qualified panel member, a medically qualified panel member or a panel member with a disability qualification	Section 6 of the Social Security Act 1998 (c.14)

Table 3: Members becoming transferred-in judges of the First-tier Tribunal and deputy judges of the Upper Tribunal

Tribunal Member	Enactment
The President	Section 5 of the Social Security Act 1998 (c.14)
A deputy Commissioner	Paragraph 1(2) of Schedule 4 to the Social Security Act 1998 (c.14)

Table 4: Members becoming transferred-in judges of the Upper Tribunal

Tribunal Member	Enactment
The Chief Social Security Commissioner or a Social Security Commissioner	Paragraph 1 of Schedule 4 to the Social Security Act 1998 (c.14)

SCHEDULE 4

ARTICLE 6

Transitional provisions

1.   Subject to article 3(3)(a) any proceedings before a tribunal listed in Table 1 of Schedule 1 which are pending immediately before 3rd November 2008 shall continue on and after 3rd November 2008 as proceedings before the First-tier Tribunal.

2.   Subject to article 3(3)(b) any proceedings before a tribunal listed in Table 2 of Schedule 1 which are pending immediately before 3rd November 2008 shall continue on and after 3rd November 2008 as proceedings before the Upper Tribunal.

3.–(1)   The following sub-paragraphs apply where proceedings are continued in the First-tier Tribunal or Upper Tribunal by virtue of paragraph 1 or 2.

(2)   Where a hearing began before 3rd November 2008 but was not completed by that date, the First-tier Tribunal or the Upper Tribunal, as the case may be, must be comprised for the continuation of that hearing of the person or persons who began it.

(3)   The First-tier Tribunal or Upper Tribunal, as the case may be, may give any direction to ensure that proceedings are dealt with fairly and, in particular, may–

(a)   apply any provision in procedural rules which applied to the proceedings before 3rd November 2008; or

(b)   disapply provisions of Tribunal Procedure Rules.

(4)   In sub-paragraph (3) "procedural rules" means provision (whether called rules or not) regulating practice or procedure before a tribunal.

(5)   Any direction or order given or made in proceedings which is in force immediately before 3rd November 2008 remains in force on and after that date as if it were a direction or order of the First-tier Tribunal or Upper Tribunal, as the case may be.

(6)   A time period which has started to run before 3rd November 2008 and which has not expired shall continue to apply.

(7)   An order for costs may only be made if, and to the extent that, an order could have been made before 3rd November 2008.

4.   Subject to article 3(3)(a) and (b) where an appeal lies to a Child Support or Social Security Commissioner from any decision made before 3rd November 2008 by a tribunal listed in Table 1 of Schedule 1, section 11 of the 2007 Act (right to appeal to Upper Tribunal) shall apply as if the decision were a decision made on or after 3rd November 2008 by the First-tier Tribunal.

5.   Subject to article 3(3)(b) where an appeal lies to a court from any decision made before 3rd November 2008 by a Child Support or Social Security Commissioner, section 13 of the 2007 Act (right to appeal to Court of Appeal etc.) shall apply as if the decision were a decision made on or after 3rd November 2008 by the Upper Tribunal.

6.   Subject to article 3(3)(a) and (b) any case to be remitted by a court on or after 3rd November 2008 in relation to a tribunal listed in Schedule 1 shall be remitted to the First-tier Tribunal or Upper Tribunal as the case may be.

The Appeals from the Upper Tribunal to the Court of Appeal Order 2008

(SI 2008 No.2834)

1. This Order may be cited as the Appeals from the Upper Tribunal to the Court of Appeal Order 2008 and shall come into force on 3rd November 2008.

2. Permission to appeal to the Court of Appeal in England and Wales or leave to appeal to the Court of Appeal in Northern Ireland shall not be granted unless the Upper Tribunal or, where the Upper Tribunal refuses permission, the relevant appellate court, considers that–

(a) the proposed appeal would raise some important point of principle or practice; or

(b) there is some other compelling reason for the relevant appellate court to hear the appeal.

The First-tier Tribunal and Upper Tribunal (Composition of Tribunal) Order 2008
(2008 No.2835)

Citation and commencement
1. This Order may be cited as the First-tier Tribunal and Upper Tribunal (Composition of Tribunal) Order 2008 and comes into force on 3rd November 2008.

[¹ Interpretation
1A. In this Order–
"practice direction" means a direction made under section 23 of the Tribunals, Courts and Enforcement Act 2007 as to the practice and procedure of the First-tier Tribunal or the Upper Tribunal that contains criteria for determining which members of the First-tier Tribunal or Upper Tribunal may be chosen to decide particular categories of matter.]

Amendment

1.   Inserted by art 2 of SI 2018 No 606 as from 18.05.18.

Number of members of the First-tier Tribunal
[¹**2.**–(1)   The number of members of the tribunal who are to decide any matter that falls to be decided by the First-tier Tribunal must be determined by the Senior President of Tribunals in a practice direction in accordance with paragraphs (2) and (3) below.

(2)   The Senior President of Tribunals must determine whether the tribunal consists of one, two or three members.

(3)   The Senior President of Tribunals must have regard to–

(a)   the nature of the matter that falls to be decided and the means by which it is to be decided; and

(b)   the need for members of tribunals to have particular expertise, skills or knowledge.]

Amendment

1.   Substituted by art 3 of SI 2018 No 606 as from 18.05.18 (subject to saving provision in art 5 of SI 2018 No 606 that provides that any arrangement for the determination of the number of members of the tribunal made by the Senior President under the previous version of art 2(1) before 18.05.18 continues to apply to the extent that it is not superseded by a practice direction made under the substituted version of art 2(1)).

Number of members of the Upper Tribunal
3.–(1)   The number of members of the tribunal who are to decide any matter that falls to be decided by the Upper Tribunal is one unless determined otherwise under paragraph (2).

(2)   The tribunal may consist of two or three members if the Senior President of Tribunals so determines [¹ in a practice direction].

Amendment

1.   Amended by art 4 of SI 2018 No 606 as from 18.05.18 (subject to saving provision in art 5 of SI 2018 No 606 that provides that any arrangement for the determination of the number of members of the tribunal made by the Senior President under art 3 before 18.05.18 continues to apply to the extent that it is not superseded by a practice direction made under the amended version of art 3).

Tribunal consisting of single member
4.–(1)   Where a matter is to be decided by a single member of a tribunal, it must be decided by a judge of the tribunal unless paragraph (2) applies.

(2)   The matter may be decided by one of the other members of the tribunal if the Senior President of Tribunals so determines.

Tribunal consisting of two or more members

5.   The following articles apply where a matter is to be decided by two or more members of a tribunal.

6.   The number of members who are to be judges of the tribunal and the number of members who are to be other members of the tribunal must be determined by the Senior President of Tribunals.

7.   The Senior President of Tribunals must select one of the members (the "presiding member") to chair the tribunal.

8.   If the decision of the tribunal is not unanimous, the decision of the majority is the decision of the tribunal; and the presiding member has a casting vote if the votes are equally divided.

General Note

The Senior President has exercised the powers under Art 2(1) to make the Practice Statement Composition of Tribunals in Social Security and Child Support Cases in the Social Entitlement Chamber on or after 1 August 2013 as follows.

1.   In this Practice Statement;

a. "the 2008 Order" means the First-tier Tribunal and Upper Tribunal (Composition of Tribunal) Order 2008;

b. "the Qualifications Order" means the Qualifications for Appointment of Members to the First-tier Tribunal and Upper Tribunal Order 2008;

c. "the 2008 Rules" means the Tribunal Procedure (First-tier Tribunal) (Social Entitlement Chamber) Rules 2008;

d. "social security and child support case" has the meaning given in rule 1(3) of the 2008 Rules.

2.   In exercise of the powers conferred by the 2008 Order the Senior President of Tribunals makes the following determinations and supplementary provision–

3.   The number of members of the Tribunal must not exceed three.

4.   Where the appeal relates to an attendance allowance or a disability living allowance under Part III of the Social Security Contributions and Benefits Act 1992, or to personal independence payment under Part 4 of the Welfare Reform Act 2012, the Tribunal must, subject to paragraphs 8 to 13, consist of a Tribunal Judge, a Tribunal Member who is a registered medical practitioner, and a Tribunal Member who has a disability qualification as set out in article 2(3) of the Qualifications Order.

5.   Where–

a. the appeal involves the personal capability assessment, as defined in regulation 2(1) of the Social Security (Incapacity for Work) (General) Regulations 1995;

b. the appeal involves the limited capability for work assessment under Part 5 of the Employment and Support Allowance Regulations 2008, under Part 5 of the Universal Credit Regulations 2013 or under Part 4 of the Employment and Support Allowance Regulations 2013;

c. the appeal involves the limited capability for work-related activity assessment under Part 6 of the Employment and Support Allowance Regulations 2008, under Part 5 of the Universal Credit Regulations 2013 or under Part 5 of the Employment and Support Allowance Regulations 2013;

d. the appeal is made under section 11(1)(b) of the Social Security (Recovery of Benefits) Act 1997;

e. the appeal raises issues relating to severe disablement allowance under section 68 of the Social Security Contributions and Benefits Act 1992 or industrial injuries benefit under Part V of that Act (except for an appeal where the only issue is whether there should be a declaration of an industrial accident under section 29(2) of the Social Security Act 1998);

f. the appeal is made under section 4 of the Vaccine Damage Payments Act 1979;

g. the appeal is against a certificate of NHS charges under section 157(1) of the Health and Social Care (Community Health and Standards) Act 2003;

h. the appeal arises under Part IV of the Child Maintenance and Other Payments Act 2008; the Tribunal must, subject to paragraphs 7 to 14, consist of a Tribunal Judge and a Tribunal Member who is a registered medical practitioner.

6.   In any other case the Tribunal must consist of a Tribunal Judge.

7.   The Chamber President may determine that the Tribunal constituted under paragraph 5 or 6 must also include–

a. a Tribunal Member who is an accountant within the meaning of Article 2(i) of the Qualifications Order, where the appeal may require the examination of financial accounts;

b. an additional Member who is a registered medical practitioner, where the complexity of the medical issues in the appeal so demands; c. such an additional Tribunal Judge or Member as he considers appropriate for the purposes of providing further experience for that additional Judge or Member or for assisting the Chamber President in the monitoring of standards of decision-making.

8.   Where the Chamber President considers, in a particular case, that a matter that would otherwise be decided in accordance with paragraphs 4 or 5 only raises questions of law and the expertise of any of the other members is not necessary to decide the matter, the Chamber President may direct that the Tribunal must consist of a Tribunal Judge, or a Tribunal Judge and any Tribunal Member whose experience and qualifications are necessary to decide the matter.

9.   The powers of the Chamber President referred to in paragraphs 7, 8, 10 and 12 may be delegated to a Regional Tribunal Judge and those referred to in paragraphs 7, 8 and 12 may be delegated to a District Tribunal Judge.

10.   A decision, including a decision to give a direction or make an order, made under, or in accordance with, rules 5 to 9, 11, 14 to 19, 25(3), 30, 32, 36, 37 or 41 of the 2008 Rules may be made by a Tribunal Judge, except that a decision made under, or in accordance, with rule 7(3) or rule 5(3)(b) to treat a case as a lead case (whether in accordance with rule 18 (lead cases) or otherwise) of the 2008 Rules must be made by the Chamber President.

11.   The determination of an application for permission to appeal under rule 38 of the 2008 Rules and the exercise of the power of review under section 9 of the Tribunals, Courts and Enforcement Act 2007 must be carried out–

a. where the Judge who constituted or was a member of the Tribunal that made the decision was a fee-paid Judge, by a Judge who holds or has held salaried judicial office; or

h where the Judge who constituted or was a member of the Tribunal that made the decision was a salaried Judge, by that Judge or, if it would be impracticable or cause undue delay, by another salaried Tribunal Judge, save that, where the decision is set aside under section 9(4)(c) of the Act, the matter may only be re-decided under section 9(5)(a) by a Tribunal composed in accordance with paragraph 4, 5 or 6 above.

12.   Where the Tribunal consists of a Tribunal Judge and one or two Tribunal Members, the Tribunal Judge shall be the presiding member. Where the Tribunal comprises more than one Tribunal Judge, the Chamber President must select the presiding member. The presiding member may regulate the procedure of the Tribunal.

13.   Under rule 34(2) of the 2008 Rules it will be for the presiding member to give any written statement of reasons.

14.   In rule 25(2) (Medical and physical examination in appeals under section 12 of the Social Security Act 1998) of the 2008 Rules "an appropriate member" of the Tribunal is a Tribunal Member who is a registered medical practitioner.

SIR JEREMY SULLIVAN SENIOR PRESIDENT OF TRIBUNALS
31 July 2013

The effect is that HB appeals will almost always be heard by a single tribunal judge.

For a discussion of the legal issues arising out of the Practice Statement, see *MB and others v SSWP (ESA and DLA)* [2013] UKUT 111 (AAC); [2014] AACR 1.

It is an error of law for a tribunal to decide an appeal when it is not properly constituted to do so: see *PJ v SSWP (ESA)* [2011] UKUT 224 (AAC), *GC v SSWP (ESA)* [2012] UKUT 60 (AAC) and *ET v SSWP (II)* [2014] UKUT 417 (AAC).

Where the decision of a tribunal is made by a majority, see *SSWP v SS (DLA)* [2010] UKUT 384 (AAC); [2011] AACR 24 and the General Note to r33 TP(FTT) Rules on p1017.

The Contracting Out (Administrative Work of Tribunals) Order 2009

(2009 No.121)

1. This Order may be cited as the Contracting Out (Administrative Work of Tribunals) Order 2009 and comes into force on 2nd March 2009.

2. The Lord Chancellor may enter into such contracts with other persons for the provision, by them or their sub-contractors, of staff to carry out the administrative work of–

(a) the First-tier Tribunal;

(b) the Upper Tribunal;

(c)-(e) *[Omitted]*

The First-tier Tribunal and Upper Tribunal (Chambers) Order 2010
(2010 No.2655)

Citation, commencement and revocations

1.–(1)   This Order may be cited as the First-tier Tribunal and Upper Tribunal (Chambers) Order 2010 and comes into force on 29th November 2010.

(2)   The Orders listed in the first column of the Schedule to this Order are revoked to the extent specified in the second column.

First-tier Tribunal Chambers

2.   The First-tier Tribunal shall be organised into the following chambers–
(a)   the General Regulatory Chamber;
(b)   the Health, Education and Social Care Chamber;
(c)   the Immigration and Asylum Chamber;
[¹ (cc) the Property Chamber;]
(d)   the Social Entitlement Chamber;
(e)   the Tax Chamber;
(f)   the War Pensions and Armed Forces Compensation Chamber.

Amendment
1.   Amended by art 3 of SI 2013 No 1187 as from 1.7.13.

Functions of the Immigration and Asylum Chamber of the First-tier Tribunal

5.   To the Immigration and Asylum Chamber of the First-tier Tribunal are allocated all functions related to immigration and asylum matters, with the exception of matters allocated to–
(a)   the Social Entitlement Chamber by article 6(a);
(b)   *Omitted*

Functions of the Social Entitlement Chamber

6.   To the Social Entitlement Chamber are allocated all functions related to appeals–
(a)   in cases regarding support for asylum seekers, failed asylum seekers, persons designated under section 130 of the Criminal Justice and Immigration Act 2008, or the dependants of any such persons;
(b)   in criminal injuries compensation cases;
(c)   regarding entitlement to, payments of, or recovery or recoupment of payments of, social security benefits, child support, vaccine damage payments, health in pregnancy grant and tax credits, with the exception of–
    (i)   appeals under section 11 of the Social Security Contributions (Transfer of Functions, etc.) Act 1999 (appeals against decisions of Her Majesty's Revenue and Customs);
    (ii)   appeals in respect of employer penalties or employer information penalties (as defined in section 63(11) and (12) of the Tax Credits Act 2002);
    (iii)   appeals under regulation 28(3) of the Child Trust Funds Regulations 2004;
(d)   regarding saving gateway accounts with the exception of appeals against requirements to account for an amount under regulations made under section 14 of the Saving Gateway Accounts Act 2009;
(e)   regarding child trust funds with the exception of appeals against requirements to account for an amount under regulations made under section 22(4) of the Child Trust Funds Act 2004 in relation to section 13 of that Act;
[¹ (ea) *Omitted*]
(f)   regarding payments in consequence of diffuse mesothelioma;
(g)   regarding a certificate or waiver decision in relation to NHS charges;
(h)   regarding entitlement to be credited with earnings or contributions;
(i)   against a decision as to whether an accident was an industrial accident.

Amendment
1.   Inserted by SI 2015 No 1563 as from 1.10.15.

Upper Tribunal Chambers
   9.   The Upper Tribunal shall be organised into the following chambers–
   (a)   the Administrative Appeals Chamber;
   (b)   the Immigration and Asylum Chamber of the Upper Tribunal;
   (c)   the Lands Chamber;
   (d)   the Tax and Chancery Chamber.

Functions of the Administrative Appeals Chamber
   10.   To the Administrative Appeals Chamber are allocated all functions related to–
   (a)   an appeal–
         (i)   against a decision made by the First-tier Tribunal, except an appeal allocated to the Tax and Chancery Chamber by article 13(a) or the Immigration and Asylum Chamber of the Upper Tribunal by article 11(a);
         (ii)-(vi) *Omitted*
         (vii)   transferred to the Upper Tribunal from the First-tier Tribunal under Tribunal Procedure Rules, except an appeal allocated to the Tax and Chancery Chamber by article 13(1)(e);
         [² (viii) *Omitted*]
   (b)   an application, except an application allocated to another chamber by article 11(c) [¹ [⁴ , (d) or (e)]], 12(c) or 13(g), for the Upper Tribunal–
         (i)   to grant the relief mentioned in section 15(1) of the Tribunals, Courts and Enforcement Act 2007 (Upper Tribunal's "judicial review" jurisdiction);
         (ii)   to exercise the powers of review under section 21(2) of that Act (Upper Tribunal's "judicial review" jurisdiction: Scotland);
   (c)   a matter referred to the Upper Tribunal by the First-tier Tribunal–
         (i)   under section 9(5)(b) of the Tribunals, Courts and Enforcement Act 2007 (review of decision of First-tier Tribunal), or
         (ii)   under Tribunal Procedure Rules relating to non-compliance with a requirement of the First-tier Tribunal,
         except where the reference is allocated to another chamber by article 11(b) or 13(f);
   (d)   a determination or decision under section 4 of the Forfeiture Act 1982;
   (e)   proceedings, or a preliminary issue, transferred under Tribunal Procedure Rules to the Upper Tribunal from the First-tier Tribunal, except those allocated to [³ the Lands Chamber by article 12(cc) or to] the Tax and Chancery Chamber by article 13(1)(e).

Amendments
1.   Amended by art 3 of SI 2011 No.2342 as from 17.10.11.
2.   Substituted by art 3 of SI 2012 No.1673 as from 20.7.12.
3.   Amended by art 5 of SI 2013 No 1187 as from 1.7.13.
4.   Amended by art 3 of SI 2013 No 2068 as from 1.11.13.

General Note

All HB appeals are assigned to the Social Entitlement Chamber of the First-tier Tribunal. Since 29 November 2010, the Upper Tribunal has consisted of four chambers: the Administrative Appeals Chamber, the Immigration and Asylum Chamber, the Tax and Chancery Chamber and the Lands Chamber. Appeals relating to social security benefits (including HB) are assigned to the Administrative Appeals Chamber.

Resolution of doubt or dispute as to chamber
   14.   If there is any doubt or dispute as to the chamber in which a particular matter is to be dealt with, the Senior President of Tribunals may allocate that matter to the chamber which appears to the Senior President of Tribunals to be most appropriate.

Re-allocation of a case to another chamber

15.   At any point in the proceedings, the Chamber President of the chamber to which a case or any issue in that case has been allocated by or under this Order may, with the consent of the corresponding Chamber President, allocate that case or that issue to another chamber within the same tribunal, by giving a direction to that effect.

Part 4

Main primary legislation – council tax reduction schemes

Local Government Finance Act 1992
(1992 c14)

General Note to the Act

This Act introduced the council tax and council tax benefit (CTB) to replace the former community charge (or poll tax) and community charge benefit. From 1 April 2013, on the abolition of CTB, it sets the conditions for the local provision of council tax reduction (CTR) schemes. The council tax itself is outside the scope of this work – see CPAG's *Council Tax Handbook*. The parts of the Act reproduced below are those which are most necessary for a full understanding of the CTR schemes.

PART I
Council Tax: England and Wales
Chapter I: Main ProvisionsLiability to tax

Persons liable to pay council tax

6.–(1)   The person who is liable to pay council tax in respect of any chargeable dwelling and any day is the person who falls within the first paragraph of subsection (2) below to apply, taking paragraph (a) of that subsection first, paragraph (b) next, and so on.

(2)   A person falls within this subsection in relation to any chargeable dwelling and any day if, on that day–

(a)   he is a resident of the dwelling and has a freehold interest in the whole or any part of it;

(b)   he is such a resident and has a leasehold interest in the whole or any part of the dwelling which is not inferior to another such interest held by another such resident;

(c)   he is both such a resident and a statutory [¹...secure or introductory tenant] of the whole or any part of the dwelling;

(d)   he is such a resident and has a contractual licence to occupy the whole or any part of the dwelling;

(e)   he is such a resident; or

(f)   he is the owner of the dwelling.

(3)   Where, in relation to any chargeable dwelling and any day, two or more persons fall within the first paragraph of subsection (2) above to apply, they shall be jointly and severally liable to pay the council tax payable in respect of that dwelling and that day.

(4)   Subsection (3) above shall not apply as respects any day on which one or more of the persons there mentioned fall to be disregarded for the purposes of discount by virtue of [³ paragraph 2 (severely mentally impaired) or 4 (students etc.) of Schedule 1 to this Act] and one or more of them do not; and liability to pay the council tax in respect of the dwelling and that day shall be determined as follows–

(a)   if only one of those persons does not fall to be so disregarded, he shall be solely liable;

(b)   if two or more of those persons do not fall to be so disregarded, they shall be jointly and severally liable.

(5)   In this Part, unless the context otherwise requires–
"owner", in relation to any dwelling, means the person as regards whom the following conditions are fulfilled–

(a)   he has a material interest in the whole or any part of the dwelling; and

(b)   at least part of the dwelling or, as the case may be, of the part concerned is not subject to a material interest inferior to his interest;

"resident", in relation to any dwelling, means an individual who has attained the age of 18 years and has his sole or main residence in the dwelling

(6)   In this section–
[² "introductory tenant" means a tenant under an introductory tenancy within the meaning of Chapter I of Part V of the Housing Act 1996]
"material interest" means a freehold interest or a leasehold interest which was granted for a term of six months or more;

"secure tenant" means a tenant under a secure tenancy within the meaning of Part IV of the Housing Act 1985;

"statutory tenant" means a statutory tenant within the meaning of the Rent Act 1977 or the Rent (Agriculture) Act 1976.

Amendments
1. Substituted by art 2 and Sch para 8(a) of SI 1997 No 74 as from 12.2.97.
2. Substituted by art 2 and Sch para 8(b) of SI 1997 No 74 as from 12.2.97.
3. Amended by Local Government Act 2003 s74(1) (for financial years beginning on or after 1.4.04).

Amounts of tax payable

Discounts

11.–(1)   The amount of council tax payable in respect of any chargeable dwelling and any day shall be subject to a discount equal to the appropriate percentage of that amount if on that day–

(a)   there is only one resident of the dwelling and he does not fall to be disregarded for the purposes of discount; or

(b)   there are two or more residents of the dwelling and each of them except one falls to be disregarded for those purposes.

(2)   Subject to [¹ sections 11A and 12] below, the amount of council tax payable in respect of any chargeable dwelling and any day shall be subject to a discount equal to twice the appropriate percentage of that amount if on that day–

(a)   there is no resident of the dwelling; or

(b)   there are one or more residents of the dwelling and each of them falls to be disregarded for the purposes of discount.

(3)   In this section [²] "the appropriate percentage" means 25 per cent. or, if the Secretary of State by order so provides in relation to the financial year in which the day falls, such other percentage as may be specified in the order.

(4)   No order under subsection (3) above shall be made unless a draft of the order has been laid before and approved by resolution of the House of Commons.

(5)   Schedule 1 to this Act shall have effect for determining who shall be disregarded for the purposes of discount.

Amendments
1. Amended by Local Government Act 2003 s127(1) and Sch 7 para 41 (18.11.03).
2. Repealed by Local Government Act 2003 s127(2) and Part 1 Sch 8 (18.11.03).

Reduced Amounts

13.–(1)   The Secretary of State may make regulations as regards any case where–

(a)   a person is liable to pay an amount to a billing authority in respect of council tax for any financial year which is prescribed; and

(b)   prescribed conditions are fulfilled.

(2)   The regulations may provide that the amount he is liable to pay shall be an amount which–

(a)   is less than the amount it would be apart from the regulations; and

(b)   is determined in accordance with prescribed rules.

(3)   This section applies whether the amount mentioned in subsection (1) above is determined under section 10 above or under that section read with section 11[¹, 11A] or 12 above.

(4)   The conditions mentioned in subsection (1) above may be prescribed by reference to such factors as the Secretary of State thinks fit; and in particular such factors may include the making of an application by the person concerned and all or any of–

(a)   the factors mentioned in subsection (5) below; or

(b)   the factors mentioned in subsection (6) below.

(5)   The factors referred to in subsection (4)(a) above are–

(a)   community charges for a period before 1st April 1993;

(b)   the circumstances of, or other matters relating to, the person concerned;

(c)   an amount relating to the authority concerned and specified, or to be specified, for the purposes of the regulations in a report laid, or to be laid, before the House of Commons;

(d)   such other amounts as may be prescribed or arrived at in a prescribed manner.

(6)   The factors referred to in subsection (4)(b) above are–

(a)   a disabled person having his sole or main residence in the dwelling concerned;

(b)   the circumstances of, or other matters relating to, that persons;

(c)   the physical characteristics of, or other matters relating to, that dwelling.

(7)   The rules mentioned in subsection (2) above may be prescribed by reference to such factors as the Secretary of State thinks fit; and in particular such factors may include all or any of the factors mentioned in subsection (5) or subsection (6)(b) or (c) above.

(8)   Without prejudice to the generality of section 113(2) below, regulations under this section may include–

(a)   provision requiring the Secretary of State to specify in a report, for the purposes of the regulations, an amount in relation to each billing authority;

(b)   provision requiring him to lay the report before the House of Commons;

(c)   provision for the review of any prescribed decision of a billing authority relating to the application or operation of the regulations;

(d)   provision that no appeal may be made to a valuation tribunal in respect of such a decision, notwithstanding section 16(1) below.

(9)   To the extent that he would not have power to do so apart from this subsection, the Secretary of State may–

(a)   include in regulations under this section such amendments of any social security instrument as he thinks expedient in consequence of the regulations under this section;

(b)   include in any social security instrument such provision as he thinks expedient in consequence of regulations under this section.

(10)   In subsection (9) above "social security instrument" means

[2(a)] an order or regulations made, or falling to be made, by the Secretary of State under the Social Security Acts, that is to say, the Social Security Contributions and Benefits Act 1992 and the Social Security Administration Act 1992. [2 or]

[2 (b) regulations made, or falling to be made, under Part 4 of the Welfare Reform Act 2012.]

Amendments

1.   Amended by Local Government Act 2003 s127(1) and Sch 7 para 42 (18.11.03).

2.   Amended by reg 8 and Sch para 7(2) of SI 2013 No 388 as from 8.4.13.

[1[2 **Reductions by billing authority**

13A.–(1)   The amount of council tax which a person is liable to pay in respect of any chargeable dwelling and any day (as determined in accordance with sections 10 to 13)–

(a)   in the case of a dwelling situated in the area of a billing authority in England, is to be reduced to the extent, if any, required by the authority's council tax reduction scheme (see subsection (2));

(b)   in the case of a dwelling situated in the area of a billing authority in Wales, is to be reduced to the extent, if any, required by any council tax reduction scheme made under regulations under subsection (4) that applies to that dwelling;

(c)   in any case, may be reduced to such extent (or, if the amount has been reduced under paragraph (a) or (b), such further extent) as the billing authority for the area in which the dwelling is situated thinks fit.

(2)   Each billing authority in England must make a scheme specifying the reductions which are to apply to amounts of council tax payable, in respect of dwellings situated in its area, by–

(a)   persons whom the authority considers to be in financial need, or

(b)   persons in classes consisting of persons whom the authority considers to be, in general, in financial need.

(3)   Schedule 1A (which contains provisions about schemes under subsection (2)) has effect.

(4)   The Welsh Ministers may by regulations–

(a)   require a person or body specified in the regulations to make a scheme specifying the reductions which are to apply to amounts of council tax payable, in respect of dwellings to which the scheme applies, by persons to whom the scheme applies,

(b)   impose requirements on that person or body regarding the matters which must be included in that scheme, and

(c)   make other provision for and in connection with such schemes.

(5)   Schedule 1B (which contains further provisions about regulations under subsection (4) and about schemes under those regulations) has effect.

(6)   The power under subsection (1)(c) includes power to reduce an amount to nil.

(7)   The power under subsection (1)(c) may be exercised in relation to particular cases or by determining a class of case in which liability is to be reduced to an extent provided by the determination.

(8)   No regulations under subsection (4) are to be made unless a draft of the statutory instrument containing them has been laid before, and approved by a resolution of, the National Assembly for Wales.

(9)   In this Part "council tax reduction scheme" means a scheme under subsection (2) or regulations under subsection (4).]]

Amendments

1.   Inserted by Local Government Act 2003 s76 (18.11.03).
2.   Substituted by Local Government Finance Act 2012 s10 (31.10.12).

Analysis

Local council tax reduction schemes

This section, as substituted by the LGFA 2012, requires billing authorities in England to make a CTR scheme: s13A(2) and (3). It also enables the Welsh Ministers to make regulations for CTR schemes in Wales: s13A(4). Then, under s13A(1), the amount of council tax which a person is liable to pay must be reduced in accordance with the scheme: s13A(1)(a) (England); s13A(1)(b) (Wales). See Sch 1A (for England) and Sch 1B (for Wales) for more detailed scheme provisions.

Sub-section 13A(1) therefore encapsulates an important difference between CTR and the previous system of council tax benefit. Council tax benefit was a benefit paid to cover some or all of a person's council tax liability, whereas CTR is a reduction in a person's liability to pay council tax.

One consequence of this distinction was highlighted in a case before Vice President Dickie of the Valuation Tribunal for England (VTE): *DG v Liverpool City Council (Appeal No.43 10M140277/CTR)*. Changes in DG's financial circumstances had resulted in Liverpool City Council reassessing her entitlement to CTR – including her entitlement for a past period – and increasing the amount of council tax she was liable to pay. DG appealed on the grounds that the 'overpayment' of CTR which had occurred for the past period was not recoverable from her as she had informed the billing authority of her change of circumstances in a timely manner and could not have reasonably known she was being overpaid. The VTE issued DG with a notice of intention to strike out her appeal under reg 10(3)(c) of the Valuation Tribunal for England (Council Tax and Rating Appeals) (Procedure) Regulations 2009 No.2269 (see p1671) – ie, on the ground that her appeal had no reasonable prospect of succeeding. An oral hearing was then held to decide the preliminary issue of whether the appeal should be struck out. DG was represented at the hearing but the council was not and its written submissions only concerned the merits of its decision as to the calculation of council tax liability. (There was no dispute that DG had been awarded the correct amount of CTR under the billing authority's CTR scheme following the reassessment.) Vice President Dickie stated that as there was no entitlement under the legislation to a payment of CTR as such, there can be no overpayment – the entitlement is to a reduction in council tax liability and the decision to make a downward adjustment in the CTR awarded resulted in council tax liability being greater than previously notified. She indicated that in CTR legislation there also is no such thing as "official error". It followed, therefore, that as Liverpool City Council's CTR scheme did not include provision for restricting the retrospective adjustment of CTR in the case of official error, DG's appeal had no prospect of succeeding on this ground. A further argument made on behalf of DG that, in these circumstances, the VTE should consider awarding her discretionary CTR despite her not having made an application to the council for a discretionary reduction and not having raised the issue of a discretionary reduction in the grounds she gave when appealing, also failed. For further details on this point, see below. Vice President Dickie, therefore, decided that the appeal should be struck out.

DG was free to apply to the council for a discretionary reduction in council tax liability under s13A(1)(c) to cover the increased council tax liability, and to appeal to the VTE if she did not agree with the billing authority's decision on her application.

It is worth noting that, although not required to do so under the CTR legislation, a billing authority in England or Wales is at liberty to include in its CTR scheme provisions prescribing circumstances when it will not claw back, through an increase in council tax liability, excess CTR that has already been awarded. If an authority's scheme includes such provisions, then a failure to follow them could be successfully challenged by way of s16. *DG v Liverpool City Council* was decided on the basis that the council's scheme included no such provisions. In Scotland, such a provision, in cases of official error, is contained in the CTR schemes for both pensioners and non-pensioners from 1 April 2019: reg 20A CTR(S) Regs and reg 19A CTR(SPC)(S) Regs.

While decisions of the Valuation Tribunal are not binding, those made by the President or Vice Presidents of the Valuation Tribunal on a point of law are normally followed in later cases and a significant number of other appeals were stayed pending the decision in *DG v Liverpool City Council*.

England. Section 10(4) LGFA 2012 required each billing authority in England to make a CTR scheme under s13A(2) no later than 31 January 2013, to begin on 1 April 2013.

Under s13A(2), billing authorities are required to make a scheme specifying reductions in council tax payable by people the authority "considers to be in financial need", or classes of people it considers in general to be in financial need. Sch 1A para 2 sets out minimum requirements.

In *R (Winder and others) v Sandwell MBC* [2014] EWHC 2617 (Admin), Hickinbottom J concluded that Sandwell Council did not have the power to include a residence requirement within its CTR scheme. The council had restricted its CTR scheme for non-pensioners to those who had lived in the borough for the previous two years and argued that, under s13A(2)(b), a billing authority could determine classes of people who may qualify for CTR on grounds unrelated to financial need. The judge rejected this argument, stating that:

"the class must be defined by reference to financial need, albeit by reference to criteria which the authority considers identify those who are, in general, in financial need. There is therefore considerable discretion in the authority as to the criteria adopted to identify financial need. However, criteria which do not identify those who are at least more likely to be in financial need fall outside the powers granted to an authority by Parliament."

He said that even if the council had had the power to include a residence requirement, he would have found the requirement unlawful on other grounds. Specifically, in adopting the requirement:

–   the council failed to take into account the material considerations of the government's policy objectives and the wider consequence of other authorities adopting a similar requirement;

–   the council failed to consult on the requirement;

–   the residence requirement was a barrier to freedom of movement within the EU and was indirectly discriminatory (and the council had failed to justify the impact of the measure); *and*

–   the council failed in its duty under s149 Equality Act 2010.

The Secretary of State has the power to make regulations prescribing other requirements for schemes, which are not necessarily related to financial need: Sch 1A para 2(8) and (9). Regulations have been made under para 2(8) prescribing these further requirements: The Council Tax Reduction Schemes (Prescribed Requirements) (England) Regulations 2012 SI No.2885 (see p1103).

Under Sch 1A para 4, the Secretary of State had to prescribe a scheme (a "default scheme") which applied for the financial year beginning on 1 April 2013 if a billing authority had not made its own scheme. The default scheme is in the Council Tax Reduction Schemes (Default Scheme) (England) Regulations 2012 SI No.2886, for which see p1060 of the 26th edition. For financial years from 1 April 2014, authorities must have their own CTR scheme which may or may not be based on the default scheme, but must comply with the requirements in the LGFA and CTRS(PR)(E) Regs.

Wales. Under s13A(4) and Sch 1B, the Welsh Ministers have made regulations. The prescribed requirements that apply for financial years from 1 April 2014 are found in the Council Tax Reduction Schemes and Prescribed Requirements (Wales) Regulations 2013 SI No.3029 (W.301) (see p1190). The Council Tax Reduction Schemes and Prescribed Requirements (Wales) Regulations 2012 SI No.3144 (W.316) (see p1171 of the 26th edition) applied in relation to the financial year starting on 1 April 2013 but were revoked on 1 April 2014 subject to the saving provision in reg 36(2) CTRSPR(W) Regs (see p1215).

Under Sch 1B para 6(e), the Welsh Ministers have also made a default scheme which applies for financial years from 1 April 2014, found in the Council Tax Reduction Schemes (Default Scheme) (Wales) Regulations 2013 SI No.3035 (W.303) (see p1333). For the financial year starting on 1 April 2013, the default scheme was contained in the Council Tax Reduction Schemes (Default Scheme) (Wales) Regulations 2012 SI No.3145 (W.317) (see p1293 of the 26th edition).

Discretionary council tax reductions

Section 13A(1)(c) gives a billing authority (in both England and Wales) the discretion to reduce the amount of council tax which a person is liable to pay as it thinks fit. See sub-section (7) for how the power in s13A(1)(c) may be exercised.

In England, the authority's CTR scheme must state the procedure by which a person can apply for a discretionary reduction under s13A(1)(c): Sch 1A para 2(7) LGFA 1992. The ways in which such an application may be made, or treated as made, are detailed in Sch 7 para 9 CTRS(PR)(E) Regs and must be included in an authority's scheme. In Wales, the Welsh Ministers, using their powers under s13A(4) and Sch 1B para 5(c), also require an authority's scheme to state the means by which an application for a discretionary reduction must be made or may be treated as made: Sch 12 para 11 CTRSPR(W) Regs.

An application for discretionary council tax reduction may be made for council tax liability for any year, not just years since the CTR scheme was introduced. In *Morgan v Warwick DC* [2015] RVR 224, it was argued for the billing authority that a person could not rely on s13A(1)(c) ("the discretionary relief provision") to gain a reduction in council tax for years prior to 1 April 2013 (when the replacement of council tax benefit with CTR came into effect). The VTE President, rejecting the argument, stated: "all that s13A(1)(c) requires is that there exists 'an amount of council tax which a person is liable to pay in respect of any chargeable dwelling and any day'. There is no requirement that the liability must have been incurred post-March 2013. It is enough that there is a liability at the time the application is made and an application has been made under the discretionary relief provision."

If an applicant's council tax liability has been reduced by an award of CTR under s13A(1)(a) in England, or (b) in Wales, it may be further reduced by an award of discretionary council tax reduction (an authority in England or Wales has the power under 13A(1)(c) to reduce council tax liability to zero: s13A(6)). Discretionary council tax reduction also may be awarded even if there is no entitlement to CTR under s13A(1)(a) or (b), although in *Morgan v Warwick District Council* the VTE President observed: "Obviously, where a person would qualify for a reduction under the CTR scheme, that route should be pursued before seeking to invoke discretionary relief."

Authorities must consider each application for discretionary council tax reduction on its merits. A decision to refuse to reduce council tax under s13A(1)(c) can be appealed as can a decision on the amount of, or the duration of, the discretionary reduction: *SC v East Riding of Yorkshire Council* [2014] EW Misc B46 (VT), para 14; *Consolidated Practice Statement for the Valuation Tribunal for England 2017* (as amended) (VTE CPS 2017 (as amended)) PS10, para 1.

In *SC v East Riding of Yorkshire Council,* the VTE President stated that his initial view on the extent of the tribunal's powers on such appeals, expressed in an earlier version of *Practice Statement A11*, was incorrect. That initial view was that a tribunal should only be concerned with whether the authority's discretion had been exercised lawfully in a public law sense (ie, that the tribunal should apply the same principles for making its determination as would be applied by a court on an application for judicial review) and it should not normally substitute its own view but instead remit the matter back to the billing authority for reconsideration. Practice Statement A11 was therefore amended to state that a tribunal is not restricted to inquiring whether the billing authority has exercised its discretion lawfully and reasonably but must consider an appeal on its merits and may substitute its view for that of the authority (if there are sound reasons for doing so): *Practice Statement A11*, para 28; see also *SC v East Riding of Yorkshire Council*, para 24. This revised version of Practice Statement A11 was replaced by *VTE CPS* 2017. This has since been amended and the above information has been reproduced in *VTE CPS* 2017 (as amended), PS10, para 2.

The President outlined a number of points "designed to assist billing authorities, council tax payers and Tribunal members and clerks in dealing with these appeals": *SC v East Riding of Yorkshire Council*, para 25.

"(1) The focus of an appeal as opposed to a review is fundamentally different: full appeal reaches further and assesses the actual merits of the decision reached.

(2) Some deference should, however, be paid to the view of the original decision-maker and an effort made to understand how that decision was arrived at, but that cannot prevent the Tribunal from substituting its view for that of the authority provided that the Tribunal can articulate cogently why it is doing so and how it has arrived at its conclusion.

(3) The authority's decision does not have to be unreasonable in the Wednesbury sense before it can be set aside, but the Tribunal should intervene only where there are strong grounds for doing so.

(4) It may not be an exact parallel, but the Court of Appeal will allow an appeal against sentence only where the sentence is wrong in principle. This suggests that some restraint should be exhibited by the Tribunal before disturbing a billing authority's decision.

(5) Procedural defects may recede in importance, or be completely effaced, since the Tribunal will be chiefly concerned with the actual merits of the decision. Earlier defects in process may therefore be cured or superseded by the appeal, and a decision may be adjudged correct despite defects in process.

(6) Although a scheme or policy is not required by statute, it is difficult to see how such an open-ended discretion can be satisfactorily exercised in the absence of one.

(7) Any such policy should be scrutinised by the authority's lawyers before promulgation.

(8) Compliance with a formal published policy or scheme, if there is one, cannot preclude the Tribunal from allowing an appeal.

(9) Any such scheme is not immune from challenge in the Tribunal as, for example, is a council tax reduction scheme (see para. 13 above). It is not the Tribunal's business to impugn any scheme as such but rather that its own powers cannot be inhibited or circumscribed by a scheme.

(10) Failure to comply with a substantive element of a scheme to the detriment of the applicant is likely to lead to the overturning of the decision unless there are good reasons for having departed from it.

(11) However, compliance with a scheme or policy may help in persuading the Tribunal that the original decision was correct.

(12)   The Tribunal should be slow to interfere with a decision that properly flows from a determination made under section 13A(7).

(13)   An authority cannot as a matter of law fetter its discretion and must therefore consider every application on its merits whatever the policy or scheme says.

(14)   Suppose, for example, there is a provision that non-essential expenditure should be disregarded when calculating legitimate outgoings and determining disposable income. The Tribunal could conclude that the item was wrongly so characterised and should be included. Or that on its specific facts it should be included. Thus, mobile phones might normally be treated as a luxury but might become a necessity if the appellant is a carer who might need to be contacted urgently when not at home. Or a subscription to a satellite television service might have to be accepted if the appellant is locked into a contract that pre-dates his financial difficulties.

(15)   A factor which cannot have any relevance for the Tribunal is an overall budget created by the authority for the totality of discretionary applications in a given year so that any application will be considered in relation to the available budget and once that sum is exhausted no further applications can be granted. I do not see how in law this can be a cash-limited exercise. The merits of an appeal cannot be affected by the existence of any such budget. A "budget" is in any event a somewhat artificial concept in view of the fact that the authority is forgoing income and not spending existing funds.

(16)   Where the Tribunal is minded to allow the appeal and order a recalculation but is unsure of the actual amount to substitute, the appeal may either be adjourned for the parties to supply whatever further information is needed to reach a decision or it may conclude the appeal by quashing the calculation and ordering the authority to recalculate properly. The former is likely to be the better course in most cases."

For appeals under s16(1)(b) LGFA 1992, the President considers that reg 38(1)(d) Valuation Tribunal for England (Council Tax and Rating Appeals) (Procedure) Regulations 2009 No.2269 (see p1680) applies and the tribunal, therefore, has the power to require that a calculation be quashed and the amount recalculated. A billing authority must comply with such an order within two weeks: reg 38(9) SI 2009 No.2269.

In a case in which the council tax payer had not requested that the billing authority consider awarding her discretionary CTR, the billing authority had not made a decision on whether she should be awarded discretionary CTR and, when the council tax payer appealed under s16, she had not indicated that she was aggrieved that she had not been awarded discretionary CTR, a Vice President of the VTE concluded that the VT did not have jurisdiction to consider whether a council tax payer should be awarded discretionary CTR under s13A(1)(c): *DG v Liverpool City Council* (see above). Vice President Dickie indicated that if a billing authority has expressly refused to grant discretionary CTR in the absence of a specific application, then the council tax payer's appeal may not need to make explicit reference to the discretionary power in the grounds for the grievance as this could be implied. However, in cases where the billing authority has communicated no decision on the exercise of the power to award discretionary CTR (whether or not an application for it had been made) the Vice President indicated that the council tax payer's appeal must sufficiently clearly refer to that power in the matters and grounds relied on. The appeal was struck out.

Most applications for discretionary CTR will involve an assessment of an applicant's financial circumstances and her/his ability to pay the council tax otherwise due. Decisions of the VTE indicate the importance, when appealing against a refusal of discretionary CTR, of providing detailed information on, and evidence of, an applicant's financial situation, including her/his capital, income and expenditure, any efforts made by the applicant to improve her/his financial situation and any exceptional circumstances which apply. This was underlined by Ms Dickie, Vice President of the VTE, in *Appellant v Basingstoke and Deane BC* (1705M219033/176C). The appellant had a range of disabilities, had been diagnosed with cancer and suffered from anxiety and depression. She had been unable to work since 2014 and applied for discretionary CTR for the years 2014/15 onwards. She did not dispute that she had savings in excess of £16,000 but stated her savings were "ring-fenced for cancer treatment and mental ill-health treatment" and said she had no surplus of income over expenditure and lived a frugal lifestyle. Basingstoke and Deane BC refused her application.

Vice President Dickie noted that although the appellant provided a breakdown of her expenditure, most of it (including her credit card expenditure) was not itemised and there was no supporting evidence (such a bank or credit card statements), and no medical evidence in relation to expenditure said to be medically necessary. Vice President Dickie stated (at para 20):

"The authority was entitled to take the appellant's means into account, as am I. Council tax relief is public money and in the present case it is proper to consider whether that there is evidence of a clear financial need. That does not affect the billing authority's ability to take exceptional steps to determine a class for exemption where there is none (e.g. in the case of a natural disaster)."

She was not persuaded that the appellant did not have the funds to pay her council tax and stated (at para 25):

"The evidence of income and expenditure is not substantiated or sufficiently reliable, and the existence of unquantified savings above £16,000 which are said to be required for treatments that are not medically supported by evidence. Accordingly I refuse this appeal."

In *R (Hardy) v Sandwell MBC* [2015] EWHC 890 (Admin), which concerned discretionary housing payments (DHPs), the High Court decided that Sandwell Council acted unlawfully in including Mr and Mrs Hardy's DLA care components in the assessment of their income when determining whether to award DHPs (DLA mobility component had been ignored in accordance with s73(14) SSCBA, 1992). See also p1752 for commentary on the case.

In relation to discretionary CTR, Vice President Young considered there was sufficient cause to direct a review of a VTE decision on an application for discretionary CTR on the basis that the principle established in *Hardy* may have been relevant in considering the application, and the case was not considered at the original hearing: *Appellant v Folkestone and Hythe DC* (Appeal No.2250M213194/084C). The original tribunal had decided that as the council tax payer's income was higher than his expenditure there was insufficient cause or evidence to justify the granting of discretionary CTR. It included the PIP he received in its assessment of his income. Vice President Young directed a review of the case under reg 40(2) and Sch 11 para A16 LGFA 1988 (which allows the President of the VTE to delegate his/her functions to another member of the VTE). Folkestone and Hythe Council conceded that, following the principle established *Hardy*, the applicant's PIP should not be counted as available income when considering his application for discretionary CTR. Vice President Young therefore set aside the original tribunal's decision without hearing argument on the applicability of *Hardy*, and allowed the council tax payer's appeal. As the billing authority had already reduced the council tax liability to nil, no order was required to be made.

In *Hardy*, Mr Justice Phillips concluded that Sandwell Council's policy of always taking DLA care component into account when calculating an applicant's income for DHPs failed to have regard to the DWP's DHPs Guidance Manual and Good Practice Guide and represented an unlawful fetter on the Council's discretion. Furthermore it was:

"an example of indirect or Thlimmenos discrimination because it treats disabled applicants and their disability-related income in exactly the same way as it treats others and their non-disability related incomes, giving rise to unfavourable treatment to the disabled applicants. DLA(c) is not the same as any other income, but is awarded specially to enable disabled persons in need of personal care to cope better with their disabilities in the way they see fit. Equally, the pattern of expenditure of a disabled person may well be different and more difficult to predict than that of an applicant without a disability…" (para 58)

As the discriminatory effect did not have an objective and reasonable justification, it was contrary to Art 14 of the European Convention on Human Rights. Mr Justice Phillips decided that Art 14 was engaged because DHPs form an integral part of HB entitlements for disabled people – without them, the social sector size criteria rules discriminate against people with disabilities – it is therefore appropriate to consider them in the context of the HB scheme as a whole and, in such circumstances, DHPs come within the ambit of Art 1 Protocol 1 (A1P1) of the ECHR. He also considered that decisions on the award of DHPs to applicants with disabilities are sufficiently related to Art 8 rights to engage Art 14.

The question therefore arises in relation to CTR and discretionary CTR – which are reductions in liability to pay council tax rather than payments – would Art 14 be engaged? In *R (Winder and others) v Sandwell MBC* [2014] EWHC 2617 (Admin), it was argued that the CTR scheme engages A1P1 because it involves compulsory taxation. In *R (Logan) v LB of Havering* [2015] EWHC 3193 (Admin), which concerned the legality of Havering's CTR scheme and the way it was adopted (see p1092), Mr Justice Blake stated:

"I have some doubts whether eligibility for council tax support is a possession for the purpose of A1P1 of the ECHR and accordingly whether any difference of treatment falls within the scope of Article 14 taken with other substantive Articles of the Convention. In R (Winder and others) v Sandwell Metropolitan Borough Council [2014] EWHC 2617 (Admin) [2015] PTSR 34 at [86] Hickinbottom J made the assumption in favour of the claimant that the support scheme is to be seen as an adjunct of a taxation measure that deprives someone of the possession of that portion of their income or resources they must spend on paying the tax. I will do the same …" (para 34)

An additional argument put forward in *Hardy*, also potentially relevant to CTR and discretionary CTR, was that Sandwell council failed in its duty not to do anything that constitutes discrimination in the exercise of a public function. Section 29(6) EA 2010 states:

"(6)   A person must not, in the exercise of a public function that is not the provision of a service to the public or a section of the public, do anything that constitutes discrimination, harassment or victimisation."

On this issue, Mr Justice Phillips stated: "It seems clear that a decision as to the award of DHPs is a public function within that section…the approach of local authorities to making discretionary awards would seem to fall squarely within the above provisions of the 2010 Act" (para 53). Regarding the scope of the duty not to discriminate, he stated: "The question which arises under section 15 of the 2010 Act is whether the treatment is "a proportionate means of achieving a legitimate aim" (para 61). On this he said:

"Given that the discriminatory effect of the HB size criteria on disabled persons is only justified by the availability of DHPs to "plug the gap", and given that paragraph 2.7 the Good Practice Guide refers to additional funding having been allocated for this purposes, it is difficult to see any reasonable justification for the Council's approach, nor that it is a means of achieving a legitimate aim, let alone a proportionate one. Having analysed the effect of Burnip and MA, Stuart-Smith J in Rutherford took the view that a decision to withhold DHPs in that case "would appear to be unjustifiable" and, more generally, that councils were acting "wrongly" by including DLA(c) in household income: I fully agree with that conclusion." (para 62)

He stated that the Sandwell council's approach to including the care component as income in calculating DHPs was therefore in breach of s29(6) of EA 2010.

In *Appellants v Bury Council* (Appeal No.4210M139633/254C), Vice President Young of the VTE decided that there is nothing in s11B LGFA 1992 to prevent a local authority from awarding a discretionary CTR for a long-term empty dwelling (s11B LGFA 1992 allows a billing authority to increase the council tax charged on such properties). Therefore, Bury Council was wrong to refuse the appellants application for a payment under s13A(1)(c) on the ground that there was no provision for any discretionary element to the council tax charged on long-term empty dwellings. Instead, such applications should be considered on their merits (as *SC v East Riding of Yorkshire Council* applied). In addition to the factors set out in *SC v East Riding of Yorkshire Council* para 25, the Vice President stated that the details of how and why the dwelling had lain empty for so long, as opposed to being let or sold, were important factors in deciding cases where discretionary reduction is sought for a long-term empty dwelling.

Administration and appeals

Appeals General

16.–(1)   A person may appeal to a valuation tribunal if he is aggrieved by–

(a)   any decision of a billing authority that a dwelling is a chargeable dwelling, or that he is liable to pay council tax in respect of such a dwelling; or

(b)   any calculation made by such an authority of an amount which he is liable to pay to the authority in respect of council tax.

(2)   In subsection (1) above the reference to any calculation of an amount includes a reference to any estimate of the amount.

(3)   Subsection (1) above shall not apply where the grounds on which the person concerned is aggrieved fall within such category or categories as may be prescribed.

(4)   No appeal may be made under subsection (1) above unless–

(a)   the aggrieved person serves a written notice under this subsection; and

(b)   one of the conditions mentioned in subsection (7) below is fulfilled.

(5)   A notice under subsection (4) above must be served on the billing authority concerned.

(6)   A notice under subsection (4) above must state the matter by which and the grounds on which the person is aggrieved.

(7)   The conditions are that–

(a)   the aggrieved person is notified in writing, by the authority on which he served the notice, that the authority believes the grievance is not well founded, but the person is still aggrieved;

(b)   the aggrieved person is notified in writing, by the authority on which he served the notice, that steps have been taken to deal with the grievance, but the person is still aggrieved;

(c)   the period of two months, beginning with the date of service of the aggrieved person's notice, has ended without his being notified under paragraph (a) or (b) above.

(8)   Where a notice under subsection (4) above is served on an authority, the authority shall–

(a)   consider the matter to which the notice relates;

(b)   include in any notification under subsection (7)(a) above the reasons for the belief concerned;

(c)   include in any notification under subsection (7)(b) above a statement of the steps taken.

Modifications

Section 16(1) does not apply where the ground on which the person concerned is aggrieved is that any assumption as to the future that is required by Part V of the Council Tax (Administration and Enforcement) Regulations 1992 SI No.613 to be made in the calculation of an amount may prove to be inaccurate: reg 30 SI 1992 No.613.

General Note

Section 16 applies only in England and Wales. For appeals in Scotland, see p1082.

For schemes in England, Sch 1A para 2(6) of this Act requires an authority to state the procedure by which a person can appeal under s16 (ie, to a Valuation Tribunal) against any decision of the authority which affects either the person's entitlement to CTR under its scheme or the amount of any reduction to which s/he is entitled. This procedure is set out in Sch 7 Part 2 CTRS(PR)(E) Regs (see p1176).

For schemes in Wales, regulations made under s13A(4) and Sch 1B para 5(1)(b) of this Act give the procedure for an appeal to the valuation tribunal (on the same grounds) under s16: Sch 12 Part 2 CTRSPR(W) Regs (see p1322).

Note that, in *SC v East Riding of Yorkshire Council* [2014] EW Misc B46 (VT), the President of the Valuation Tribunal for England (VTE) said that an authority's decision on entitlement to a discretionary reduction under s13A(1)(c) (including a decision on the amount of, or the duration of, such a reduction) can be appealed to a valuation tribunal under s16(1)(b). See p1075 for further commentary on such appeals.

However, in both England and Wales, a challenge to the lawfulness of the contents of an authority's CTR scheme or to the procedure by which it was adopted cannot be made to a valuation tribunal but can only be made by way of judicial review: s66.

In accordance with reg 57(1) Council Tax (Administration and Enforcement) Regulations 1992 No.613, matters which fall under s16 cannot be considered by magistrates as part of enforcement proceedings before a magistrates' court but must be appealed to the valuation tribunal. As was confirmed in *Wiltshire Council v Piggin* [2014] EWHC 4386 (Admin) and *Yang v The Official Receiver and others* [2013] EWHC 3577 (Ch), magistrates have no jurisdiction to hear them (see also *Okun v London Borough of Lewisham* [2016] EWHC 864 (Ch)).

A person who is affected by a decision made under a CTR scheme, who has been sent a decision notice or has had one delivered to her/him by the authority, has the right to request a written statement from the authority setting out the reasons for its decision. The request for the written statement must be made within one month of the date of the notification of that decision: Sch 8 para 12(5) CTRS(PR)(E) Regs; Sch 13 para 9(5) CTRSPR(W) Regs. For who counts as a "person affected" under English schemes, see Sch 8 para 12(7) and (8) CTRS(PR)(E) Regs and under Welsh schemes, see Sch 13 para 9(7) and (8) CTRSPR(W) Regs. The written statement must be sent within 14 days or as soon as reasonably practicable after that: Sch 8 para 12(6) CTRS(PR)(E) Regs; Sch 13 para 9(6) CTRSPR(W) Regs. While in some cases it may prove useful, it is not necessary to obtain a written statement before appealing.

In both England and Wales, before someone can appeal to a valuation tribunal, s/he must first serve notice on the authority stating her/his grievance (ie, giving details of the decision s/he thinks is wrong and her/his reasons for disputing it): s16(4)(a), (5) and (6); Sch 7 para 8(1) CTRS(PR)(E) Regs; Sch 12 para 8(1) CTRSPR(W) Regs. In England, there is no time limit for serving this notice: Sch 7 para 8 CTRS(PR)(E) Regs. If an English authority includes a time limit for serving the notice in its scheme, the authority nevertheless should consider the grievance even if it is received outside the stated time limit. If it refuses to do so, an appeal can be made to the valuation tribunal relying on s16(7)(c). This also applied in Wales but only in respect of decisions under CTR schemes for the financial year beginning on 1 April 2013 as there was no time limit included in Sch 12 paras 8 to 10 CTRSPR(W) Regs 2012. In Wales, for financial years beginning on or after 1 April 2014, a person's written notice of her/his grievance must be served on the authority within one month of the date of service of the notification of the authority's decision or, if s/he has requested a written statement of the reasons for the authority's decision within the time limit, within one month of the service of the statement of reasons: Sch 12 para 8(2) and Sch 13 para 9(5) CTRSPR(W) Regs.

This is effectively a request for a reconsideration, and the authority has two months from the date of service of the notice to notify the applicant in writing either: that the ground for grievance is not well founded, giving reasons, or that steps have been taken to deal with the grievance, stating what has been done. If the person is still aggrieved or if the authority does not notify her/him of its decision within the time limit, s/he then can appeal to the valuation tribunal under s16. The procedure for such appeals is contained in the Valuation Tribunal for England (Council Tax and Rating Appeals) (Procedure) Regulations 2009 SI No.2269 and the Valuation Tribunal for Wales Regulations 2010 SI No.713 (W.69). The appeal must be initiated within the time limit set out in reg 21 SI 2009 SI No.2269 (p1677) or reg 29 SI 2010 SI No.713 (p1687). An appeal is initiated by serving on the valuation tribunal a written notice of the appeal which must include the information set out in reg 20A(2) SI 2009 SI No.2269 or reg 30 2010 SI No.713.

However, in *MM v Medway Council* (Appeal No.2280M157095/084C) – an appeal against a decision not to award discretionary council tax reduction under s13A(1)(c) – one argument put forward by the council tax payer was that his appeal should be allowed and his council tax reduced to nil because the billing authority had not dealt with his application within the time limits stated in its own policy. Vice President Young of the VTE did not accept this argument, stating that there was no provision in the legislation, nor in the billing authority's policy, which meant that an application for discretionary reduction had to be granted if it was not dealt with within the time limits given in the policy. The Vice President reasoned: "it is now plain enough that an application for a discretionary reduction in council tax takes effect as a notice under section 16(4) of the 1992 Act because, in seeking that reduction, the applicant is aggrieved at the calculation of council tax he has otherwise been found liable to pay. That application, by way of notice, must comply with sections 16(5) and (6). Then, if the billing authority does not give notification of its decision, in accordance with section 16(7)(a) or (b), within two months the aggrieved person, or appellant, may appeal to the Tribunal in accordance with section 16(4) and (7)(c)." The Vice President said: "Parliament has provided the remedy for delay in dealing with these applications, which is not that they should be granted by default when time limits expire."

In England, at the request of the VTE President and with the approval of the Senior President of Tribunals, a member of the First-tier Tribunal may sit as a member of the Valuation Tribunal to hear appeals relating to CTR: Sch 11 para A18A(1) and (2) LGFA 1988. The President may only request this if s/he thinks that the First-tier Tribunal member is likely to have expertise relevant to the determination of the appeal, or to appeals of its kind.

In addition, complex cases, including those that raise a "novel, important or contentious point of law", should be referred to the registrar who consults with the President about whether it should be listed for hearing by the President, a Vice President or a VTE panel including a member with specialist skills in accordance with the Consolidated Practice Statement for the Valuation Tribunal for England 2017 (as amended) (VTE CPS 2017 (as amended)), PS3.

Other CTR appeals are listed before a panel normally consisting of two members of the valuation tribunal.

In Wales, three members of the valuation tribunal normally hear appeals (or, with agreement of all the parties appearing at the hearing, two members): reg 37 SI 2010 SI No.713 (W.69).

An appeal against a decision or order of the VTE or VTW on CTR lies to the High Court on a point of law: reg 43 SI 2009 No.2269; reg 42 SI 2010 SI No.713 (W.69).

Section 16 does not apply in Scotland and determinations on CTR in Scotland cannot be appealed to a Valuation Appeal Committee, the Scottish equivalent of a valuation tribunal: s80(8)(c) and (d); reg 90A(1) CTR(S) Regs; reg 70A(1) CTR(SPC)(S) Regs. Instead, further reviews are conducted by the Council Tax Reduction Review Panel, see regs 90B to 90D CTR(S) Regs and 70B and 70C CTR(SPC)(S) Regs.

Chapter III: Setting of Council Tax

Substituted amount

31.–(1)   Where a billing authority has set amounts for a financial year under section 30 above and at any later time–

(a)   it makes substitute calculations under section [²36A,] 37 or 60 below;

[¹ (aa) substitute calculations it has made under section 52ZF below have effect by virtue of section 52ZH or 52ZI below; or]

(b)   it is issued with a precept for the year (originally or by way of substitute) by a major precepting authority,

it shall as soon as reasonably practicable after that time set amounts in substitution so as to give effect to those calculations or that precept.

(2)   Any amount set in substitution under subsection (1) above must be set in accordance with section 30 above, but subsection (6) of that section shall be ignored for this purpose.

(3)   Where a billing authority sets any amount in substitution under subsection (1) above (a new amount), anything paid to it by reference to the amount from which it is substituted (the old amount) shall be treated as paid by reference to the new amount.

(4)   If the old amount exceeds the new amount, the following shall apply as regards anything paid if it would not have been paid had the old amount been the same as the new amount–

(a)   it shall be repaid if the person by whom it was paid so requires;

(b)   in any other case it shall (as the billing authority determines) either be repaid or be credited against any subsequent liability of the person to pay in respect of any council tax set by the authority in accordance with section 30 above.

[¹ (4A)   Subject to any provision made by regulations under subsection (6) below, where an authority sets amounts in substitution under subsection (1)(a) above in the circumstances described in section 52ZO(6) or 52ZP(6) or (8) below, it may recover from the local precepting authority in question administrative expenses incurred by it in, or in consequence of, so doing.]

(5)   [¹Subject to any provision made by regulations under subsection (6) below,] Where an authority sets amounts in substitution under subsection (1)(b) above, it may recover from the major precepting authority administrative expenses incurred by it in, or in consequence of, so doing.

[¹ (6)   The Secretary of State may by regulations make provision for cases in which–

(a)   subsection (4A) or (5) above does not apply, or

(b)   that subsection applies with modifications.]

Amendments

1.   Amended by s72 and Sch 6 para 2 Localism Act 2011 (3.12.11).
2.   Amended by s79 and Sch 7 para 9 Localism Act 2011 (3.12.11).

Chapter VI: Incidental and supplemental

Judicial review

66.–(1) The matters mentioned in subsection (2) below shall not be questioned except by an application for judicial review.

(2) The matters are–

(a)-(b) *[Omitted]*

[¹ (ba) a council tax reduction scheme, or any revision of such a scheme;]

(c)-(e) *[Omitted]*

(3) If on an application for judicial review the court decides to grant relief in respect of any of the matters mentioned in subsection (2) [² (b) or (c) to (e)] above, it shall quash the determination, calculation, setting or precept (as the case may be).

Amendments

1.   Inserted by Sch 4 para 5(2) Local Government Finance Act 2012 (31.10.12).
2.   Amended by Sch 4 para 5(3) Local Government Finance Act 2012 (31.10.12).

General Note

In England and Wales, any challenge to the lawfulness of the contents of an authority's CTR scheme, including the procedure by which it is adopted, replaced or revised, must be made by way of judicial review, rather than by an appeal under s16 to a valuation tribunal.

    Such a challenge was made to Sandwell Metropolitan Borough Council's decision to include a residence requirement in its CTR scheme. The High Court ruled that the council did not have the power to include a two-year residence requirement in its scheme and that the scheme was therefore unlawful: *R (Winder and others) v Sandwell MBC* [2014] EWHC 2617 (Admin) (see p1075 for a discussion of this case).

    For a discussion of the procedures that must be followed when preparing, revising or replacing a CTR scheme, see the analysis of Sch 1A para 3 on p1091. Similar requirements as to preparation, revision or replacement of a CTR scheme in Wales are included in reg 16 and 17 of CTRSPR(W) Regs.

PART II
Council Tax: Scotland
Liability to tax

Persons liable to pay council tax

75.–(1) The person who is liable to pay council tax in respect of any chargeable dwelling and any day is the person who falls within the first paragraph of subsection (2) below to apply, taking paragraph (a) of that subsection first, paragraph (b) next, and so on.

(2) A person falls within this subsection in relation to any chargeable dwelling and any day if, on that day–

(a) he is the resident owner of the whole or any part of the dwelling;

(b) he is a resident tenant of the whole or any part of the dwelling;

(c) he is a resident statutory tenant, resident statutory assured tenant or resident [² Scottish] secure tenant of the whole or any part of the dwelling;

(d) he is a resident sub-tenant of the whole or any part of the dwelling;

(e) he is a resident of the dwelling;

(f) he is any of the following–

    (i) the sub-tenant of the whole or any part of the dwelling under a sub-lease granted for a term of 6 months or more;

    (ii) the tenant, under a lease granted for a term of 6 months or more, of any part of the dwelling which is not subject to a sub-lease granted for a term of 6 months or more;

    (iii) the owner of any part of the dwelling which is not subject to a lease granted for a term of 6 months or more.

(3)　Where, in relation to any chargeable dwelling and any day, two or more persons fall within the first paragraph of subsection (2) above to apply, they shall be jointly and severally liable to pay the council tax payable in respect of that dwelling and that day.

(4)　Subsection (3) above shall not apply as respects any day on which one or more of the persons there mentioned fall to be disregarded for the purposes of discount [¹ either] by virtue of paragraph 2 of Schedule 1 to this Act (the severely mentally impaired) [¹ or, being a student, by virtue of paragraph 4 of that Schedule] and one or more of them do not; and liability to pay the council tax in respect of the dwelling and that day shall be determined as follows–

(a)　if only one of those persons does not fall to be so disregarded, he shall be solely liable;

(b)　if two or more of those persons do not fall to be so disregarded, they shall be jointly and severally liable.

(5)　In this section–

[² "Scottish secure tenant" means a tenant under a Scottish secure tenancy within the meaning of the Housing (Scotland) Act 2001 (asp 10)];

"statutory tenant" means a statutory tenant within the meaning of the Rent (Scotland) Act 1984;

"statutory assured tenant" means a statutory assured tenant within the meaning of the Housing (Scotland) Act 1988.

Amendments
1.　Amended by Education (Graduate Endowment and Student Support) Act 2001 s4 (1.6.01).
2.　Amended by Housing (Scotland) Act 2001 Sch 10 para 19 (30.9.02).

Amounts of tax payable

Discounts

79.–(1)　The amount of council tax payable in respect of any chargeable dwelling and any day shall be subject to a discount equal to the appropriate percentage of that amount if on that day–

(a)　there is only one resident of the dwelling and he does not fall to be disregarded for the purposes of discount; or

(b)　there are two or more residents of the dwelling and each of them except one falls to be disregarded for those purposes.

(2)　The amount of council tax payable in respect of any chargeable dwelling and any day shall be subject to a discount equal to twice the appropriate percentage of that amount if on that day–

[¹ (a)]

(b)　there are one or more residents of the dwelling and each of them falls to be disregarded for the purposes of discount.

(3)　In this section "the appropriate percentage" means 25 per cent. or, if the Secretary of State by order so provides in relation to the financial year in which the day falls, such other percentage as may be specified in the order.

(4)　No order under subsection (3) above shall be made unless a draft of the order has been laid before and approved by resolution of the House of Commons.

(5)　Schedule 1 to this Act shall have effect for determining who shall be disregarded for the purposes of discount.

Amendment
1.　Repealed by reg 2 of SI 2005 No 51 as from 1.4.05.

Reduced amounts

80.–(1)　The Secretary of State may make regulations as regards any case where–

(a)　a person is liable to pay an amount to a [¹ ...local] authority in respect of council tax for any financial year which is prescribed; and

(b)　prescribed conditions are fulfilled.

(2)   The regulations may provide that the amount he is liable to pay shall be an amount which–

(a)   is less than the amount it would be apart from the regulations; and

(b)   is determined in accordance with prescribed rules.

(3)   This section applies whether the amount mentioned in subsection (1) above is determined under section 78 above or under that section read with section 79 above.

(4)   The conditions mentioned in subsection (1) above may be prescribed by reference to such factors as the Secretary of State thinks fit; and in particular such factors may include the making of an application by the person concerned and all or any or–

(a)   the factors mentioned in subsection (5) below; or

(b)   the factors mentioned in subsection (6) below.

(5)   The factors mentioned in subsection (4)(a) above are–

(a)   community charges for a period before 1st April 1993;

(b)   the circumstances of, or other matters relating to, the person concerned;

(c)   an amount–

[²(i)   relating to the local authority whose council tax constitutes the amount referred to in subsection (1) above;] and

(ii)   which is specified, or is to be specified, in a report laid, or to be laid, before the House of Commons;

(6)   The factors referred to in subsection (4)(b) above are–

(a)   a disabled person having his sole or main residence in the dwelling concerned;

(b)   the circumstances of, or other matters relating to, that person;

(c)   the physical characteristics of, or other matters relating to, that dwelling.

(7)   The rules mentioned in subsection (2) above may be prescribed by reference to such factors as the Secretary of State thinks fit; and in particular such factors may include all or any of the factors mentioned in subsection (5) or subsection (6)(b) or (c) above.

(8)   Without prejudice to the generality of section 113(2) below, regulations under this section may include–

(a)   provision requiring the Secretary of State to specify in a report, for the purposes of the regulations, an amount in relation to each local authority;

(b)   provision requiring him to lay the report before the House of Commons;

(c)   provision for the review of any prescribed decision of a [¹ ...local] authority relating to the application or operation of the regulations;

(d)   provision that no appeal may be made to a valuation appeal committee in respect of such a decision, notwithstanding section 81(1) below.

(9)   To the extent that he would not have power to do so apart from this subsection, the Secretary of State may–

(a)   include in regulations under this section such amendments of any social security instrument as he thinks expedient in consequence of the regulations under this section;

(b)   include in any social security instrument such provision as he thinks expedient in consequence of regulations under this section.

(10)   In subsection (9) above "social security instrument" means

[³ (a)] an order or regulations made, or falling to be made, by the Secretary of State under the Social Security Acts. [³ or]

[³ (b) regulations made, or falling to be made, under Part 4 of the Welfare Reform Act 2012.]

Amendments

1.   Substituted by Local Government Etc (Scotland) Act 1994 c.39 s180(1) and Sch 13 para 176(4)(a) (1.4.96).

2.   Substituted by Local Government Etc (Scotland) Act 1994 c.39 s180(1) and Sch 13 para 176(4)(b) (1.4.96).

3.   Amended by reg 8 and Sch para 7(2) of SI 2013 No 388 as from 8.4.13.

General Note
Among other things, this section provides the power for the Scottish Ministers to make regulations setting up CTR schemes. Two national schemes were set up with effect from 1 April 2013, on the abolition of CTB. The scheme for working-age people is in the Council Tax Reduction (Scotland) Regulations 2012 SSI No.303 (see p1452). The scheme for pension credit aged people is in the Council Tax Reduction (State Pension Credit) (Scotland) Regulations 2012 SSI No.319 (see p1574).

Setting of the tax

Substituted and reduced settings

94.–(1) Subject to subsection (3) below, a local authority may set, in substitution for an amount of council tax already set or deemed to have been set, a lesser amount of council tax for the same financial year.

(2) Schedule 7 to this Act has effect for the purpose of making provision as to the reduction of council tax where the Secretary of State is satisfied, in accordance with that Schedule, that the total estimated expenses mentioned in section 93(3) above of a local authority are excessive or that an increase in those expenses is excessive.

(3) A local authority may not set a substitute amount of council tax during the period between the approval by the House of Commons of a report in respect of that authority made by the Secretary of State under paragraph 1 of that Schedule and the setting or deemed setting of a reduced amount of council tax under paragraph 3 of that Schedule.

(4) Section 93(2) above shall not apply for the purposes of this section.

(5) A local authority who, in respect of any financial year, set (or are deemed to have set) a substituted or reduced council tax shall neither wholly nor partially offset the difference between–

(a) the amount produced by that substituted or reduced setting; and

(b) the amount which would have been produced had they not substituted or reduced their setting,

with sums advanced from their loans fund established under Schedule 3 to the 1975 Act: Provided that such offsetting may nevertheless be permitted by the Secretary of State in any case on such terms and conditions as he considers appropriate.

(6) If the Secretary of State is of the opinion that subsection (5) above, or any term or condition imposed under the proviso thereto, has been contravened, the local authority shall, on such opinion being intimated to them, reimburse their loans fund forthwith or within such time as the Secretary of State may allow.

(7) Anything paid by reference to one setting of council tax shall be treated as paid by reference to a substitute setting by virtue of paragraph 3 of Schedule 7 to this Act.

(8) Where a person has paid by reference to one setting of council tax more than is due under a substituted or reduced setting–

(a) the balance shall be repaid to the person if s/he so requires;

(b) in any other case the balance shall (as the [¹ ...local] authority determine) either be repaid to the person or be credited against any subsequent liability of the person to pay in respect of any council tax due to the authority.

(9) Where–

(a) a substitute amount of council tax has been set under subsection (1) above; or

(b) a reduced amount of council tax has been set or been deemed to have been set under paragraph 3 of that Schedule,

the regional council shall levy and collect that substituted or reduced amount in place of the previous amount of council tax and may recover from the district council any administrative expenses incurred in so doing in relation to a substituted or reduced amount of district council tax.

Amendment
1.   Substituted by Local Government Etc. (Scotland) Act 1994 c.39 s180(1) and Sch 13 para 176(9) (1.4.96).

SCHEDULE 1

SECTIONS 11(5) AND 79(5)

Persons disregarded for purposes of discount

Persons in detention

1.–(1)   A person shall be disregarded for the purposes of discount on a particular day if on the day–

(a)   he is detained in a prison, a hospital or any other place by virtue of an order [³ or award] to which sub-paragraph (2) below applies;

(b)   he is detained under paragraph 2 of Schedule 3 to the Immigration Act 1971 (deportation);

(c)   he is detained under Part II or section 46, 47, 48 or 136 of the Mental Health Act 1983; or

(d)   he is detained under [² Parts 5, 6 and 7 or sections 136 or 297 of the Mental Health (Care and Treatment) (Scotland) Act 2003 or sections 52D or 52M of the Criminal Procedure (Scotland) Act 1995;].

[³ (2)   This sub-paragraph applies to–

(a)   an order of a court in the United Kingdom;

(b)   an order or award (whether or not of a court) made (anywhere) in proceedings in respect of a service offence within the meaning of the Armed Forces Act 2006.

(3)   If a person–

(a)   is temporarily discharged under section 28 of the Prison Act 1952, or temporarily released under rules under section 47(5) of that Act; [³]

[³ (aa)   is temporarily released under rules under section 300 of the Armed Forces Act 2006; or]

(b)   is temporarily discharged under section 27 of the Prisons (Scotland) Act 1989, or temporarily released under rules under section 39(6) or that Act,

for the purposes of sub-paragraph (1) above he shall be treated as detained.

(4)   Sub-paragraph (1) above does not apply where the person–

(a)   is detained under regulations made under paragraph 8 of Schedule 4 to this Act;

(b)   is detained under section 76 of the Magistrates' Courts Act 1980, or [¹ section 108 of the Powers of Criminal Courts (Sentencing) Act 2000], for default in payment of a fine; or

(c)   is detained only under section 407 of the Criminal Procedure (Scotland) Act 1975.

(5)   In sub-paragraph (1) above "order" includes a sentence, direction, warrant or other means of giving effect to the decision of the court concerned.

(6)   The Secretary of State may by order provide that a person shall be disregarded for the purposes of discount on a particular day if–

(a)   on the day he is [³ in service custody; and]

(b)   such conditions as may be prescribed by the order are fulfilled.

Amendments

1.   Amended by Sch 9 para 152 Powers of Criminal Courts (Sentencing) Act 2000 as from 25.8.00.

2.   Amended by Sch 1 para 22(2)(a) of SSI 2005 No 465 as from 27.9.05.

3.   Amended by Sch 16 para 123 Armed Forces Act 2006 as from 31.10.09.

The severely mentally impaired

2.–(1)   A person shall be disregarded for the purposes of discount on a particular day if

(a)   on the day he is severely mentally impaired;

(b)   as regards any period which includes the day he is stated in a certificate of a registered medical practitioner to have been or to be likely to be severely mentally impaired; and

(c)   as regards the day he fulfils such conditions as may be prescribed by order made by the Secretary of State.

(2)   For the purposes of this paragraph a person is severely mentally impaired if he has a severe impairment of intelligence and social functioning (however caused) which appears to be permanent.

(3)   The Secretary of State may by order substitute another definition for the definition in sub-paragraph (2) above as for the time being effective for the purposes of this paragraph.

Persons in respect of whom child benefit is payable

3.–(1)   A person shall be disregarded for the purposes of discount on a particular day if on the day he–

(a)   has attained the age of 18 years; but

(b)   is a person in respect of whom another person is entitled to child benefit, or would be so entitled but for paragraph 1(c) of Schedule 9 to the Social Security Contributions and Benefits Act 1992.

(2)   The Secretary of State may by order substitute another provision for sub-paragraph (1)(b) above as for the time being effective for the purposes of this paragraph.

Students etc

4.–(1)   A person shall be disregarded for the purposes of discount on a particular day if–

(a)   on the day he is a student, student nurse, apprentice or youth training trainee; and

(b)   such conditions as may be prescribed by order made by the Secretary of State are fulfilled.

(2)   In this paragraph "apprentice", "student", "student nurse" and "youth training trainee" have the meanings for the time being assigned to them by order made by the Secretary of State.

5.–(1)   An institution shall, on request, supply a certificate under this paragraph to any person who is following or, subject to sub-paragraph (3) below, has followed a course of education at that institution as a student or student nurse.

(2)   A certificate under this paragraph shall contain such information about the person to whom it refers as may be prescribed by order made by the Secretary of State.

(3)   An institution may refuse to comply with a request made more than one year after the person making it has ceased to follow a course of education at that institution.

(4)   In this paragraph–

"institution" means any such educational establishment or other body as may be prescribed by order made by the Secretary of State; and

"student" and "student nurse" have the same meanings as in paragraph 4 above.

Hospital patients

6.–(1)   A person shall be disregarded for the purposes of discount on a particular day if on the day he is a patient who has his sole or main residence in a hospital.

(2)   In this paragraph "hospital" means–

(a)   a health service hospital within the meaning of the [¹ National Health Service Act 2006, the National Health Service (Wales) Act 2006] or section 108(1) (interpretation) of the National Health Service (Scotland) Act 1978; and

(b)   a military, air-force or naval unit or establishment at or in which medical or surgical treatment is provided for persons [² subject to service law within the meaning of the Armed Forces Act 2006.].

(3)   The Secretary of State may by order substitute another definition for the definition in sub-paragraph (2) above as for the time being effective for the purposes of this paragraph.

Amendments

1.   Amended by the National Health Service (Consequential Provisions) Act 2006 s2 and Sch 1 para 152 as from 1.3.07.

2.   Amended by Sch 16 para 123 Armed Forces Act 2006 as from 31.10.09.

Patients in homes in England and Wales

7.–(1)   A person shall be disregarded for the purposes of discount on a particular day if on the day–

(a)   he has his sole or main residence in a [¹ care home, independent hospital] or hostel in England and Wales; and

(b)   he is receiving care or treatment (or both) in the home [¹, hospital] or hostel.

[¹ (2)   In this paragraph–

"care home" means–

(a)   a care home within the meaning of the Care Standards Act 2000; or

[⁴ (b)   a building or part of a building in which accommodation is provided for an adult under Part 4 of the Social Services and Well-being (Wales) Act 2014]; [³ or

(c)   a building or part of a building in which accommodation is provided under Part 1 of the Care Act 2014;]

"hostel" means anything which falls within any definition of hostel for the time being prescribed by order made by the Secretary of State under this sub-paragraph;

[² "independent hospital"–

(a)   in relation to England, means a hospital as defined by section 275 of the National Health Service Act 2006 that is not a health service hospital as defined by that section; and

(b)   in relation to Wales, has the same meaning as in the Care Standards Act 2000.]

(3)   The Secretary of State may by order substitute another definition for any definition of [¹ "care home" or "independent hospital"] for the time being effective for the purposes of this paragraph.

Amendments

1.   Amended by the Care Standards Act 2000 Sch 4 para 20 as from 1.4.02.

2.   Substituted by art 9 of SI 2010 No 813 as from 1.10.10.

3.   Inserted by art 2 and Sch para 55 of SI 2015 No 914 as from 1.4.15.

4.   Substituted by reg 141 of SI 2016 No 413 (W.131) as from 6.4.16.

Patients in homes in Scotland

8.–(1)   A person shall be disregarded for the purposes of discount on a particular day if on the day–

[¹ (a)   either–

(i)   he has as his sole or main residence a private hospital in Scotland; or

(ii)   a care home service provides, in Scotland, accommodation which is his sole or main residence; and

(b)   he is receiving care or treatment (or both) in the hospital or in the accommodation so provided.]
(2)   In this paragraph–
[¹ "care home service" has the same meaning as in the Regulation of Care (Scotland) Act 2001 (asp 8); and]
    [¹ ...]
[² "private hospital" means an independent health care service as defined in section 329(1) of the Mental Health
    (Care and Treatment) (Scotland) Act 2003;]
    [¹ ...]
(3)   [¹ ...]
(4)   The Secretary of State may by order substitute another definition for any definition of [¹ ...] "private
hospital" or [¹ "care home service"] for the time being effective for the purposes of this paragraph.

Amendments
1.   Amended by the Regulation of Care (Scotland) Act 2001 Sch 3 para 18 as from 1.4.02.
2.   Substituted by Sch 1 para 22(2)(b) of SSI 2005 No 465 as from 27.9.05.

Care workers

9.–(1)   A person shall be disregarded for the purposes of discount on a particular day if–
(a)   on the day he is engaged in providing care or support (or both) to another person or other persons;
       and
(b)   such conditions as may be prescribed are fulfilled.
(2)   Without prejudice to the generality of sub-paragraph (1)(b) above the conditions may–
(a)   require the care or support (or both) to be provided on behalf of a charity or a person fulfilling some
       other description;
(b)   relate to the period for which the person is engaged in providing care of support (or both);
(c)   require his income for a prescribed period (which contains the day concerned) not to exceed a
       prescribed amount;
(d)   require his capital not to exceed a prescribed amount;
(e)   require him to be resident in prescribed premises;
(f)   require him not to exceed a prescribed age;
(g)   require the other person or persons to fulfil a prescribed description (whether relating to age,
       disablement or otherwise).

Residents of certain dwellings

10.–(1)   A person shall be disregarded for the purposes of discount on a particular day if on the day he has
his sole or main residence in a dwelling to which sub-paragraph (2) below applies.
(2)   This sub-paragraph applies to any dwelling if–
(a)   it is for the time being providing residential accommodation, whether as a hostel or night shelter or
       otherwise; and
(b)   the accommodation is predominantly provided–
       (i)   otherwise than in separate and self-contained sets of premises;
       (ii)   for persons of no fixed abode and no settled way of life; and
       (iii)   under licences to occupy which do not constitute tenancies.

Persons of other descriptions

11.   A person shall be disregarded for the purposes of discount on a particular day if–
(a)   on the day he falls within such descriptions as may be prescribed; and
(b)   such conditions as may be prescribed are fulfilled.

[¹ SCHEDULE 1A

Amendment
1.   Inserted by Local Government Finance Act 2012 s10 and Sch 4 (31.10.12).

SECTION 13A

COUNCIL TAX REDUCTION SCHEMES: ENGLAND

Interpretation
1.   In this Schedule–
(a)   "scheme" means council tax reduction scheme under section 13A(2), and
(b)   in relation to a scheme, "the authority" means the billing authority which made the scheme or is
       under a duty to make it.

Matters to be included in schemes
2.–(1)   A scheme must state the classes of person who are to be entitled to a reduction under the scheme.
(2)   The classes may be determined by reference to, in particular–

(a)   the income of any person liable to pay council tax to the authority in respect of a dwelling;

(b)   the capital of any such person;

(c)   the income and capital of any other person who is a resident of the dwelling;

(d)   the number of dependants of any person within paragraph (a) or (c);

(e)   whether the person has made an application for the reduction.

(3)   A scheme must set out the reduction to which persons in each class are to be entitled; and different reductions may be set out for different classes.

(4)   A reduction may be–

(a)   a discount calculated as a percentage of the amount which would be payable apart from the scheme,

(b)   a discount of an amount set out in the scheme or to be calculated in accordance with the scheme,

(c)   expressed as an amount of council tax to be paid (lower than the amount which would be payable apart from the scheme) which is set out in the scheme or is to be calculated in accordance with it, or

(d)   the whole amount of council tax (so that the amount payable is nil).

(5)   A scheme must state the procedure by which a person may apply for a reduction under the scheme.

(6)   A scheme must state the procedure by which a person can make an appeal under section 16 against any decision of the authority which affects–

(a)   the person's entitlement to a reduction under the scheme, or

(b)   the amount of any reduction to which the person is entitled.

(7)   A scheme must state the procedure by which a person can apply to the authority for a reduction under section 13A(1)(c).

(8)   The Secretary of State may by regulations prescribe other requirements for schemes.

(9)   under sub-paragraph (8) may in particular–

(a)   require other matters to be included in a scheme;

(b)   prescribe classes of person which must or must not be included in a scheme;

(c)   prescribe reductions, including minimum or maximum reductions, which must be applicable to persons in prescribed classes;

(d)   prescribe requirements which must be met by the procedure mentioned in sub-paragraph (5).

(10)   Regulations under sub-paragraph (8) may in particular set out provision to be included in a scheme that is equivalent to–

(a)   provision made by a relevant enactment, or

(b)   that is capable of being made under a relevant enactment,

with such modifications as the Secretary of State thinks fit.

(11)   Subject to compliance with regulations under sub-paragraph (8), a scheme may make provision that is equivalent to–

(a)   provision made by a relevant enactment, or

(b)   provision that is capable of being made under a relevant enactment,

with such modifications as the authority thinks fit.

(12)   For the purposes of sub-paragraphs (10) and (11), each of the following enactments as it had effect on the day on which the Local Government Finance Act 2012 was passed is a "relevant enactment"–

(a)   sections 131 to 133 of the Social Security Contributions and Benefits Act 1992 (council tax benefit);

(b)   sections 134 to 137 of that Act (general provisions about income-related benefits) so far as applying in relation to council tax benefit;

(c)   section 1 of the Social Security Administration Act 1992 (entitlement to benefit dependent on claim) so far as applying in relation to council tax benefit;

(d)   section 6 of that Act (regulations about council tax benefit administration);

(e)   sections 32 to 34 of the Welfare Reform Act 2007 (benefit for persons taking up employment) so far as applying in relation to council tax benefit.

Analysis

Paragraph 2 describes what must be included in a billing authority's CTR scheme.

A scheme must state:

–   the classes of people who are entitled to a reduction: sub para (1). Such classes may be determined by reference to the factors described in sub para (2) (for more on this see the commentary to s13A LGFA 1992 on p1074);

–   the reduction to which each these classes of people are entitled: sub para (3). This may be calculated in one of the ways given in sub para (4);

–   the procedure by which someone may apply for a CTR: sub para (5);

–   the procedure by which someone can appeal against a decision on her/his entitlement to CTR or the amount of any reduction: sub para (6); *and*

–   the procedure for applying for a discretionary council tax reduction under s13A(1)(c) LGFA: sub para (7).

The Secretary of State has the power to prescribe other requirements for the scheme, such as the classes of people who must or must not be included in the scheme and the reductions, including the minimum or maximum reductions, which apply to people in those classes: sub para (8)–(10). The requirements that have been prescribed are contained in the CTRS(PR)(E) Regs. The classes of people who must not be included in a scheme are described in regs 12 and 13 of those regulations. The classes of people who must be included in an authority's scheme are the classes of pensioner (other than pensioners with capital of over £16,000) who are described in

Sch 1 paras 2–4 CTRS(PR)(E) Regs (see p1121) and the amount of reduction to which they are entitled is calculated in accordance with para 10 of that schedule. See reg 3 CTRS(PR)(E) Regs for the meaning of 'pensioner'.

Provided they do not fall within the classes of people who cannot be included in the scheme, an authority is free to include other classes of people in its scheme (eg, classes of people who are not pensioners), as long as the class is defined by reference to financial need: s13A(2)(b) LGFA 1992; *R (Winder and others) v Sandwell MBC* [2014] EWHC 2617 (Admin), para 53. The authority is free also to specify reductions that apply to other individuals it considers to be in financial need in its scheme: s13A(2)(a) LGFA 1992. Many billing authorities have, in including classes of people who are not pensioners in their schemes, specified that a standard percentage reduction is to be applied to the maximum council tax reduction when calculating their entitlement to CTR. This creates a situation where an applicant who is not a pensioner has to pay at least a proportion of her/his council tax even if on a very low income. Research by New Policy Institute states that for the tax year from April 2018, only 36 of the 326 billing authorities in England continued to provide the levels of support available under the former council tax benefit scheme& (figures from https://counciltaxreduction.org/schemes/).

South Tyneside Council v Aitkin [2014] EWHC 4163 (Admin) concerned an applicant for CTR who was not a pensioner. Mr Aitkin, who lived with his wife, was entitled to, and receiving, DLA and ESA and received the support component within his ESA as he had limited capability for work-related activity. South Tyneside Council had adopted the Council Tax Reduction Schemes (Default Scheme) (England) Regulations 2012 (for which see p1060 of the 26th edition) as its council tax support scheme with some amendments. Of relevance to the case was that it had reduced the amount of CTR a person falling into Class D of that scheme could receive, to the maximum CTR minus a standard percentage reduction of 30 per cent. This standard percentage reduction did not apply if an applicant was in receipt of a disability, severe disability or disabled child premium, or if the family had a child under 5. The rules regarding the premiums in Sch 3 CTRS(DS)(E) Regs had been adopted without amendment. According to those rules, Mr Aitkin (who fell into Class D) was entitled to an enhanced disability premium but not a disability premium (because he had limited capability for work and Sch 3 para 10(8) CTRS(DS)(E) Regs therefore applied). He was also not entitled to a severe disability premium. The council therefore restricted his CTR to his maximum CTR minus 30 per cent. He had successfully appealed to the valuation tribunal which decided that the standard percentage reduction should not apply to him because of his disability. South Tyneside Council's appeal against the valuation tribunal's decision was allowed. The standard percentage reduction was found to apply to Mr Aitkin. Mr Justice Ouseley, indicating that the valuation tribunal had misinterpreted the way statute intended "limited" in "limited capability for work" to be understood, decided that an applicant who satisfies the condition for the enhanced disability premium in Sch 3 para 12 CTRS(DS)(E) Regs could not qualify for the disability premium by virtue of para 10(8) of that Schedule and stated:

"30.   The tribunal is not concerned with whether someone has a capability to work. It is sufficient, notwithstanding the language of the paragraphs, for them to see what the individual is receiving. The conditions are not ones which they themselves have to be satisfied apply, if the Secretary of State is providing the relevant sum of money. The position therefore, was concluded by the fact that the appellant was in receipt of ESA."

In cases similar to this, when an applicant gets ESA and is a member of a couple, it may be important to assess whether s/he would be better off if her/his partner instead became the applicant for CTR (see p640 for a discussion of the considerations that apply for HB, some of which may be relevant to such a calculation).

Preparation of a scheme

3.–(1)   Before making a scheme, the authority must (in the following order)–

(a)   consult any major precepting authority which has power to issue a precept to it,

(b)   publish a draft scheme in such manner as it thinks fit, and

(c)   consult such other persons as it considers are likely to have an interest in the operation of the scheme.

(2)   The fact that this paragraph was not in force when any step described in sub-paragraph (1) was taken is to be disregarded in determining whether there has been compliance with that subparagraph.

(3)   Having made a scheme, the authority must publish it in such manner as the authority thinks fit.

(4)   The Secretary of State may make regulations about the procedure for preparing a scheme.

(5)   Regulations under sub-paragraph (4) may in particular–

(a)   require the authority to produce documents of a particular description in connection with the preparation of a scheme;

(b)   include requirements as to the form and content of documents produced in connection with the preparation of a scheme;

(c)   include requirements (in addition to sub-paragraphs (1)(b) and (3)) about the manner in which such documents must be published;

(d)   require the authority to make copies of such documents available for inspection by members of the public, or to supply copies of such documents to them;

(e)   include provision about the making of reasonable charges for the supply of copies of such documents to members of the public.

Analysis

This paragraph sets out the procedure that must be followed by a billing authority before making a CTR scheme (in accordance with para 5(5) the procedure also applies when an authority revises its scheme).

(1)   It must consult with any major precepting authority which has power to issue a precept. Major precepting authorities are defined in s39 and include, in England, county councils and the Greater London Authority.

(2)   It must publish a draft scheme in a manner which it thinks fit.

(3)   It must consult people it considers are likely to have an interest in the operation of the scheme.

(4)   Once the scheme has been made, it must publish it in a manner it thinks fit.

The duty of an authority under para 3(1)(c) to "consult such other persons as it considers are likely to have an interest in the operation of the scheme" was considered by the Supreme Court in *R (on the application of Moseley (in substitution of Stirling Deceased)) v London Borough of Haringey* [2014] UKSC 56.

Haringey's draft scheme proposed to limit the maximum CTR available to applicants who were not pensioners to about 80 per cent of their council tax to deal with the shortfall between the amount that had been spent on CTB and the amount of funding available to the authority from central government for CTR. Haringey conducted its consultation by posting a consultation document online, with an invitation to all residents to respond, and sending a copy of the document and a questionnaire with a covering letter to 36,000 households eligible for CTB. The consultation document and covering letter gave as an established fact that the shortfall would be met by a cutback in CTR for non-pensioners – the only issue was how that cut should be distributed.

The Court unanimously decided that Haringey's consultation was unlawful as it had failed to refer to alternative means of absorbing the shortfall and had not given the reasons why such alternatives had been rejected by the authority. However, the Court did not order Haringey to conduct a fresh consultation on the ground that this would be disproportionate in the circumstances.

Lord Wilson, who gave the main judgment, said that irrespective of whether the duty to consult arose by statute (as here) or by the common law duty of a public authority to act fairly, the same duty of procedural fairness applies to the way the consultation is conducted. He endorsed the four basic requirements of a fair consultation, set out in *R v Brent LBC ex p Gunning* [1986] 84 LGR 168 and approved by the Court of Appeal in *R v North and East Devon Health Authority ex p Coughlan* [2001] QB 213, which are that to be proper:

–   consultation must be undertaken at a time when proposals are still at a formative stage;

–   it must include sufficient reasons for particular proposals to allow those consulted to give intelligent consideration and an intelligent response;

–   it must give adequate time for this consideration and response; *and*

–   the results of the consultation must be conscientiously taken into account when the ultimate decision is taken.

He said that fairness demanded that brief reference should have been made in the consultation document to other ways of absorbing the shortfall and to the reasons why Haringey had concluded that they were unacceptable: para 29. The consultation document made no such reference and accordingly Lord Wilson concluded that the consultation was unfair and therefore unlawful.

Lord Reed gave slightly different reasons for ruling the consultation unlawful. He said that when there is a statutory duty to consult, the content of that duty will vary according to the particular provision in question, the particular context and the purpose for which the consultation is carried out. In the case of consultation under para 3(1)(c), he said the purpose of the consultation is not to ensure procedural fairness in the treatment of people whose legally protected interests may be adversely affected, as the common law seeks to do, but to ensure public participation in the local authority's decision-making process. To achieve that objective, the consultation must provide information about the draft scheme, an outline of realistic alternatives and an indication of the main reasons for the authority's adoption of the draft scheme. Enough must be said about realistic alternatives, and the reasons for the local authority's preferred choice, to enable the consultees to make an intelligent response in respect of the scheme on which their views are sought. Haringey had not met those requirements.

The Court also ruled that Haringey's failure to extend its consultation to refer to the government's transitional grant scheme, which was announced less than five weeks before Haringey's consultation period ended and in light of which it did not propose to alter its scheme, was not unlawful. For a discussion of *Mosely*, see *R (on the application of T) v Trafford MBC* [2015] EWHC 369 (Admin).

In *R (Winder and others) v Sandwell MBC* [2014] EWHC 2617 (Admin), which was decided before the Supreme Court's ruling in *Moseley*, one ground for the challenge to Sandwell's decision to include a requirement in its CTR scheme that, to qualify, working-age taxpayers must have lived in the borough for the previous two years, was that the council had failed to consult on this aspect of its scheme. The council added the two-year residence requirement after it had conducted its consultation on its draft scheme for 2013/14 and, when it reviewed its scheme for 2014/15, it put a link on its website to a page seeking the public's views on the scheme on which it referred to the residence requirement and stated: "Consultation on the scheme took place during the period August to October 2012. Sandwell Council is proposing to make no changes to its [CTR Scheme] for 2014-15 and is now seeking your views and feedback on the scheme…". The council stated it had received no responses to this consultation. Although it was not determinative of the claim, which succeeded on another ground, Hickinbottom J said of the 2013/14 consultation: "A complete absence of consultation cannot arguably be sufficient consultation." He also considered that the 2014/15 consultation had not been a fair consultation on the residence requirement. Quoting from *R (JL and AT Baird) v Environment Agency* [2011] EWHC 939 (Admin), in which Sullivan LJ said "a conclusion that a consultation process has been so unfair as to be unlawful is likely to be based on a factual finding that something has gone clearly and radically wrong", Hickinbottom J said: "In my view, here, in each year, something did go clearly and radically wrong: as a result, there was no fair consultation, in either year, in respect of this fundamental requirement."

In *R (Buckley and others) v Sheffield City Council* [2013] EWHC 512 (Admin), similar arguments were put forward to support the contention that Sheffield's consultation process was unfair and, therefore, unlawful, to those used in *R (Sarah Stirling) v LB Haringey* [2013] EWCA Civ 116. These were rejected by Supperston J, who was bound by the decision of the Court of Appeal in that case (the Court of Appeal's decision has since been overturned by the Supreme Court: *Moseley*). A further argument was that Sheffield acted in breach of its duty under s149 Equality Act 2010. s149(1) of that Act states:

> (1) A public authority must, in the exercise of its functions, have due regard to the need to–
> (a) eliminate discrimination, harassment, victimisation and any other conduct that is prohibited by or under this Act;
> (b) advance equality of opportunity between persons who share a relevant protected characteristic and persons who do not share it;
> (c) foster good relations between persons who share a relevant protected characteristic and persons who do not share it.

Section 149(7) lists the relevant protected characteristics which include age and disability.

It was argued that Sheffield failed to comply with the obligation to have 'due regard' to the requirements of s149(1) with respect to disabled people and children but this argument failed. The scheme Sheffield proposed was to restrict reductions of council tax for working-age residents to a maximum of 80 per cent and to maintain an extra hardship fund to help residents in severe financial hardship. Supperstone J considered that the council had had due regard to the impact of the proposals on people with protected characteristics and had therefore complied with its duty under s149. He did not accept that to have 'due regard' the council had to identify the number of children and disabled persons affected by the proposal, analyse the impact on them and consider whether any negative impact could be avoided or mitigated. He said the impact on people who share a relevant protected characteristic is not uniform but depends on individual circumstances. He stated: "The Council were entitled to conclude that the impact on disabled people and children was not uniform; and that in the circumstances the creation and operation of the hardship fund is the best way to help those in severe financial hardship".

The legality of London Borough of Havering's revised CTR scheme ("the 2015 scheme") and how it was adopted was challenged by way of judicial review in *R (Logan) v LB of Havering* [2015] EWHC 3193 (Admin). Prior to the revision to the CTR scheme, Mr Logan, whose income was below his applicable amount and who had multiple health problems and received the higher rates of both the care and mobility components of DLA and was in the ESA support group, qualified for CTR of 100 per cent of his full liability. After the revision, he could only qualify for the maximum CTR of 85 per cent of his full liability although he was also awarded a discretionary CTR under s13A(1)(c) of the LGFA 1992 to cover the remaining 15 per cent.

The legality of the public consultation on the revised scheme was not at issue but whether the full council had due regard to their public sector equality duty (PSED) under s149 of the Equality Act 2010 when adopting the revised scheme was. Hard copies of the Equality Impact Assessment (EIA) had not been circulated to all members of the council, although they could have accessed the documents electronically. The High Court held that for a local authority to meet its PSED:

> "There must be conscientious consideration of the impact of the proposals on the relevant groups, whether by diligent reading of the EIA or some other evidence based assessment. In my judgment, the EIA was adequate to enable members who read it to have due regard to the PSED, but there was insufficient evidence to indicate that the decision makers had accessed the EIA attached to the officers' report or had understood the importance of reading it in order to discharge their statutory obligation. It is not sufficient to assume that they could have done so and therefore would have done so. The procedure whereby the 2015 scheme was adopted was accordingly defective even though I have concluded that the scheme itself was not unlawful by reason of discrimination." (para 53).

Mr Logan, who was 55 years old, had also contended that Havering's revised scheme was discriminatory on the grounds of disability and age contrary to Article 14 of the European Convention on Human Rights, taken together with Article 1 of Protocol 1 (the right to peaceful enjoyment of possessions), and indirectly discriminatory on the grounds of disability and age contrary to the Equality Act 2010. Age discrimination was argued on the basis that the maximum CTR available to pensioners on low incomes was 100 per cent of their council tax as provided by the Council Tax Reduction Schemes (Prescribed Requirements) (England) Regs 2012 No.2885 whereas Mr Logan, despite having no prospect of being able to work again, was only eligible for CTR of 85 per cent of his council tax. These arguments failed. Mr Justice Blake expressed doubts about whether eligibility for CTR is a possession for the purpose of Article 1 of Protocol 1 of the ECHR, but even if making an assumption that it is, he did not consider the 2015 scheme amounted to discrimination stating:

> "First, this was a scheme that applied to all people of working age and whose income fell beneath the applicable amount; it was thus overtly neutral with respect to age or disability. Although retirement age is an age based criterion, it was not Havering's scheme that excluded pensioners from the 100% scheme but the

primary legislation... The discretion afforded to billing authorities to promote a scheme reducing council tax support is limited to people of working age. I do not accept that the prohibition on discrimination means that there is an implicit requirement that the billing authority must always exercise its discretion to treat certain classes who are subject to the discretionary scheme, in the same way as those who are statutorily excluded from it." (para 35)

And distinguishing the case from *Burnip v Birmingham CC and Others* [2012] EWCA Civ 629; [2013] AACR 7, which related to the restriction of the amount of rent used for the assessment of HB as a result of the size criteria under the local housing allowance rules (see p369), he stated:

"39.   ...I do not read the Burnip decision as stating that it is always discriminatory to expect the disabled poor to meet ordinary living expenses out of benefits that are provided because they are disabled. Council tax liability is a general charge on living expenses in the same way as any other item of expenditure that the able bodied and disabled poor both have to make out of their subsistence budgets....

40.   Once it is recognised that different rules have been established for the disabled in calculating the applicable amount, I do not see why it constitutes either a difference in treatment or an unlawful failure to treat people differently who are situated differently, to expect that a modest percentage of council tax support will be absorbed in the subsistence budgets of the poor generally, even if the benefits forming that budget are provided because of eligibility through the disability gateway. Further in the light of the above and with the existence of a discretionary scheme to address exceptional hardship I consider that any indirect difference in treatment on the grounds of age or disability is justified; in particular maintaining the distinction in the statutory scheme of people above and below retirement age is justified."

See also p1075 for commentary on disability benefits and discretionary CTR.

Default scheme

4.–(1)   The Secretary of State must by regulations prescribe a scheme ("the default scheme") for the purposes of this paragraph.

(2)   The first financial year to which the default scheme relates must be the year beginning with 1 April 2013 (or such other year as is specified in section 10(4) of the Local Government Finance Act 2012).

(3)   The default scheme must comply with the requirements of–

(a)   paragraph 2(1) to (7), and

(b)   any regulations under paragraph 2(8).

(4)   The default scheme may in particular make provision that is equivalent to–

(a)   provision made by a relevant enactment, or

(b)   provision that is capable of being made under a relevant enactment,

with such modifications as the Secretary of State thinks fit.

(5)   For the purposes of sub-paragraph (4), each of the following enactments as it had effect on the day on which the Local Government Finance Act 2012 was passed is a "relevant enactment"–

(a)   sections 131 to 133 of the Social Security Contributions and Benefits Act 1992 (council tax benefit);

(b)   sections 134 to 137 of that Act (general provisions about income-related benefits) so far as applying in relation to council tax benefit;

(c)   section 1 of the Social Security Administration Act 1992 (entitlement to benefit dependent on claim) so far as applying in relation to council tax benefit;

(d)   section 6 of that Act (regulations about council tax benefit administration);

(e)   sections 32 to 34 of the Welfare Reform Act 2007 (benefit for persons taking up employment) so far as applying in relation to council tax benefit.

(6)   The default scheme is to take effect, in respect of dwellings situated in the area of a billing authority, if the authority fails to make a scheme on or before 31 January 2013 (or such other date as is specified in section 10(4) of the Local Government Finance Act 2012).

(7)   If the default scheme takes effect in the area of a billing authority, this Part applies to the default scheme as if it had been made by the authority.

General Note

The default scheme, which applied if a billing authority in England did not have its own scheme in place by 31 January 2013, was set out in the schedule to the Council Tax Reduction Schemes (Default Scheme) (England) Regulations 2012 No.2886 and related to the financial year beginning on 1 April 2013: Sch para 1 CTRS(DS)(E) Regs. For the CTRS(DS)(E) Regs see the 26th edition. Billing authorities in England have had to have their own scheme in place for tax years from 2014/15 but have been free to adopt the default scheme, with or without amendment, as their own CTR scheme. A scheme must meet the requirements contained in this schedule, including the requirements for the preparation and any revision or replacement of the scheme in paras 3 and 5, and the requirements contained in the CTRS(PR)(E) Regs.

Revisions to and replacement of scheme

5.–(1)   For each financial year, each billing authority must consider whether to revise its scheme or to replace it with another scheme.

(2)   The authority must make any revision to its scheme, or any replacement scheme, no later than [¹ 11 March] in the financial year preceding that for which the revision or replacement scheme is to have effect.

(3)   The Secretary of State may by order amend sub-paragraph (2) by substituting a different date.

(4)   If any revision to a scheme, or any replacement scheme, has the effect of reducing or removing a reduction to which any class of persons is entitled, the revision or replacement must include such transitional provision relating to that reduction or removal as the authority thinks fit.

(5)   Paragraph 3 applies to an a uthority when revising a scheme as it applies to an authority when making a scheme.

(6)   References in this Part to a scheme include a replacement scheme.

Amendment
1.   Amended by reg 2 of SI 2017 No 1305 as from 12.1.18.

General Note
Prior to the amendment contained in SI 2017 No 1305, which came into force on 12 January 2018, if a billing authority intended to amend or replace its CTR scheme, it had to do so by the 31 January falling before the tax year to which the new or amended CTR scheme related. The amendment of this deadline to 11 March gives billing authorities more time to follow the consultation process required by para 3: para 5(2) and (5). The removal of the 31 January deadline and its replacement with a March deadline was one of the recommendations in the Ollerenshaw review: *Three Years On: An Independent Review of Local Council Tax Support,* conducted in accordance with s9 LGFA 2012 (see p1097). The review highlighted the broad consensus between billing authorities that the January deadline was arbitrarily early, out of sync with their financial cycles and hindered efficiency.

Arrangements to deal with shortfall in council tax receipts
6.–(1)   In this paragraph "scheme authority" means, in relation to a scheme and a year–

(a)   the billing authority which made the scheme, and

(b)   any major precepting authority with power to issue a precept to that billing authority in relation to that year.

(2)   Two or more scheme authorities may make arrangements which are to have effect if, as a result of the operation of the scheme–

(a)   there is a deficit in the billing authority's collection fund for that year, or

(b)   the billing authority estimates that there will be such a deficit.

(3)   Arrangements under this paragraph may include–

(a)   the making of payments by one scheme authority to another scheme authority;

(b)   the variation of any payment or instalment of a payment which is required to be made under regulations under section 99 of the 1988 Act (regulations about funds) that make provision in relation to council tax.

Provision of information to the Secretary of State
7.–(1)   The Secretary of State may serve on a billing authority in England a notice requiring it to supply to the Secretary of State such information as is specified in the notice and required by the Secretary of State for the purpose of exercising, or of deciding whether to exercise, any function relating to schemes.

(2)   The authority must supply the information required if it is in its possession or control, and must do so in such form and manner and at such time as the Secretary of State specifies in the notice.

(3)   If an authority fails to comply with sub-paragraph (2), the Secretary of State may exercise the function on the basis of such assumptions and estimates as the Secretary of State thinks fit.

(4)   In exercising, or deciding whether to exercise, any function relating to schemes, the Secretary of State may also take into account any other available information, whatever its source and whether or not obtained under a provision contained in or made under this or any other Act.

Guidance
8.   In exercising any function relating to schemes, a billing authority must have regard to any guidance issued by the Secretary of State.

Transitional provision
9.–(1)   The Secretary of State may by regulations make such transitional provision regarding the commencement of schemes as the Secretary of State thinks fit.

(2)   Such provision may include, in particular, provision for and in connection with treating a person who is or was in receipt of council tax benefit, or who makes or has made a claim for that benefit, as having made an application for a reduction under a scheme.]

[¹ SCHEDULE 1B

Amendment
1.   Inserted by Local Government Finance Act 2012 s10 and Sch 4 (31.10.12).

SECTION 13A

COUNCIL TAX REDUCTION SCHEMES: WALES

Interpretation
1. In this Schedule–
(a) "the regulations" means regulations under section 13A(4);
(b) "scheme" means council tax reduction scheme under the regulations;
(c) "specified" means specified in the regulations;
(d) "specified authority" means a person or body required by the regulations to make a scheme (and, in relation to a particular scheme, means the authority which made the scheme or is under a duty to make it).

Application of schemes
2.–(1) The regulations may–
(a) prescribe, for each scheme that is to be made, the dwellings to which that scheme is to apply;
(b) require each scheme to state the dwellings to which it is to apply.
(2) The regulations may prescribe–
(a) the date by which each scheme is to be made, and
(b) the first financial year to which it must relate.

Persons entitled to reductions
3.–(1) The regulations may prescribe–
(a) classes of person who are to be entitled to a reduction under schemes;
(b) classes of person who must not be entitled to a reduction under schemes.
(2) The regulations may–
(a) allow specified authorities to determine (subject to regulations under sub-paragraph (1)) classes of person who are to be entitled to a reduction under schemes, or
(b) provide that specified authorities may not determine such classes.
(3) The regulations may require each scheme to state the classes of person (prescribed under sub-paragraph (1)(a) or determined under sub-paragraph (2)(a)) who are to be entitled to a reduction under the scheme.
(4) Any class of person prescribed under sub-paragraph (1)(a) may be determined by reference to, in particular, the matters listed in subparagraph (7).
(5) The regulations may require any class of person determined under sub-paragraph (2)(a) to be determined by reference to specified matters (which may include those listed in sub-paragraph (7)).
(6) If the regulations do not require a class of person to be determined as mentioned in sub-paragraph (5), the specified authority may determine that class by reference to, in particular, the matters listed in sub-paragraph (7).
(7) Those matters are–
(a) whether the Welsh Ministers consider, or the specified authority considers, any person to be in financial need;
(b) the income of any person liable to pay council tax in respect of any dwelling to which a scheme is to apply;
(c) the capital of any such person;
(d) whether any such person is in receipt of any specified benefit;
(e) the income and capital of any other person who is a resident of the dwelling, or whether any such person is in receipt of any specified benefit;
(f) number of dependants of any person within paragraph (b) or (e);
(g) whether the person has made an application for the reduction.

Reductions
4.–(1) The regulations may prescribe reductions, including minimum and maximum reductions, to which persons in each class (whether prescribed under paragraph 3(1)(a) or determined under paragraph 3(2)(a)) are to be entitled under schemes.
(2) The regulations may–
(a) allow specified authorities to determine (subject to regulations under sub-paragraph (1)) reductions to which persons in each class set out in the scheme are to be entitled, or
(b) provide that specified authorities may not determine such reductions.
(3) The regulations may require each scheme to set out the reductions (whether prescribed under sub-paragraph (1) or determined under sub-paragraph (2)(a)) to which persons in each class set out in the scheme are to be entitled.
(4) Different reductions may be set out for different classes.
(5) A reduction under a scheme may be–
(a) a discount calculated as a percentage of the amount which would be payable apart from the scheme,
(b) a discount of an amount set out in the scheme or to be calculated in accordance with the scheme,

(c) expressed as an amount of council tax to be paid (lower than the amount which would be payable apart from the scheme) which is set out in the scheme or is to be calculated in accordance with it, or

(d) the whole amount of council tax (so that the amount payable is nil).

Other matters

5.–(1) The regulations may require each scheme to state–

(a) the procedure by which a person may apply for a reduction under the scheme;

(b) the procedure by which a person can make an appeal under section 16 against any decision which affects the person's entitlement to a reduction under the scheme or the amount of any reduction to which the person is entitled;

(c) the procedure by which a person can apply to the relevant billing authority for a reduction under section 13A(1)(c).

(2) In sub-paragraph (1)(c), the relevant billing authority for any dwelling to which the scheme applies is the billing authority in whose area the dwelling is situated.

(3) The regulations may prescribe requirements which must be met by the procedure mentioned in sub-paragraph (1)(a) or (b).

6.–(1) The regulations may–

(a) require other matters to be included in schemes;

(b) allow schemes to make provision that is equivalent to provision made by a relevant enactment, or provision that is capable of being made under a relevant enactment, with such modifications as specified authorities think fit;

(c) prescribe the procedure which a specified authority must follow when making a scheme (including requirements regarding consultation and other steps to be taken before and after making the scheme);

(d) require or allow functions conferred by the regulations to be exercised by specified authorities jointly with other authorities;

(e) prescribe a default scheme which is to take effect, if a specified authority fails to make a scheme in accordance with the regulations, in respect of dwellings to which that scheme would have applied;

(f) impose requirements on specified authorities relating to the review, revision or replacement of schemes;

(g) enable specified authorities to make reasonable charges for the supply of copies of documents relating to schemes;

(h) require specified authorities to provide to the Welsh Ministers information about schemes.

(2) In particular, the regulations may under sub-paragraph (1)(a) set out provision to be included in schemes, and a default scheme prescribed under sub-paragraph (1)(e) may make provision, that is equivalent to–

(a) provision made by a relevant enactment, or

(b) provision that is capable of being made under a relevant enactment,

with such modifications as the Welsh Ministers think fit.

(3) For the purposes of sub-paragraphs (1)(b) and (2), each of the following enactments as it had effect on the day on which the Local Government Finance Act 2012 was passed is a "relevant enactment"–

(a) sections 131 to 133 of the Social Security Contributions and Benefits Act 1992 (council tax benefit);

(b) sections 134 to 137 of that Act (general provisions about income-related benefits) so far as applying in relation to council tax benefit;

(c) section 1 of the Social Security Administration Act 1992 (entitlement to benefit dependent on claim) so far as applying in relation to council tax benefit;

(d) section 6 of that Act (regulations about council tax benefit administration);

(e) sections 32 to 34 of the Welfare Reform Act 2007 (benefit for persons taking up employment) so far as applying in relation to council tax benefit.

Transitional provision

7.–(1) The regulations may make such transitional provision regarding the commencement of schemes as the Welsh Ministers think fit.

(2) Such provision may include, in particular, provision for and in connection with treating a person who is or was in receipt of council tax benefit, or who makes or has made a claim for that benefit, as having made an application for a reduction under a scheme.

Guidance

8. In exercising any function relating to schemes, a specified authority must have regard to any guidance issued by the Welsh Ministers.]

Local Government Finance Act 2012
(2012 c17)

Council tax

Council tax reduction schemes: review

9.–(1)   The Secretary of State shall make provision for an independent review of all council tax reduction schemes made under the provisions of this Act–

(a)   to consider their effectiveness, efficiency, fairness and transparency and their impact on the localism agenda, and

(b)   to make recommendations as to whether such schemes should be brought within universal credit.

(2)   A review under subsection (1) shall take place within three years after this Act comes into effect.

Commentary

As required by s9, an independent review of CTR schemes was conducted and the report of that review, *Three Years on: An Independent Review of Local Council Tax Support Schemes* by Eric Ollerenshaw OBE, was published in March 2016. The report focuses mainly on English CTR schemes (in part because the Welsh government had undertaken its own comprehensive review of CTR each year since its introduction) and includes recommendations for both government and councils. The recommendations for government include the following.

(1)   The government removes the 31 January deadline for billing authorities to agree their CTR schemes and replace it with a requirement that schemes are agreed and in place by the end of March each year.

(2)   Billing authorities only be required to review their schemes at Full Council when changes to the scheme are proposed.

(3)   The government clarifies the requirements to consult on proposed schemes.

(4)   The Department for Communities and Local Government [now the Ministry of Housing, Communities and Local Government] issues updates to the prescribed regulations sooner in the year, so as to inform local consultation, which could be by way of a two-stage process, with policy intent provided in summer, and details and updates to regulations confirmed after the Autumn Statement.

(5)   Tax payers be allowed to agree to a voluntary attachment of benefits to recover council tax arrears without the billing authority first getting a liability order from the magistrates court and that safeguards should be put in place to ensure council tax payers have time, information and capacity to make an informed decision.

(6)   The government works closely with councils to rectify data-sharing issues between council systems and universal credit systems, and to address concerns about how critical government-held data will be shared with councils as universal credit is rolled out to CTR recipients.

(7)   The government considers localising at least part of the CTR scheme for pensioners to allow billing authorities to decide on the amount of support they provide for all low-income residents.

(8)   The government considers granting more local flexibility over other nationally-set council tax discounts, such as the single person discount.

(9)   The government takes steps to better understand the impact of CTR on individuals and councils, widening the data it holds on CTR to enable future policy evaluation.

(10)   The government commissions academic research on the impact of CTR within the context of other welfare and socio-economic changes.

(11)   The government confirms that CTR will remain localised and that it will not be rolled into universal credit.

The government responded to these recommendations in January 2018 (*The Government Response to an Independent Review of Local Council Tax Support Schemes*, January 2018, Ministry of Housing, Communities and Local Government). Its responses to the recommendations above can be summarised as follows.

(1)   It would change the deadline for billing authorities to agree CTR schemes from 31 January to 11 March. This amendment was made by SI 2017 No.1305 and came into force on 12 January 2018.

(2)   No change would be made regarding reviewing schemes as it states the obligation on billing authorities is just to 'consider' whether to revise or replace a scheme and, save for changes necessary as a result of amendments to the CTRS(PS)(E) Regs, billing authorities are not required to revise or replace their CTR schemes each year.

(3)   It will not issue separate guidance on consultation – councils are free to use the Cabinet Office's general guidance for public authorities on conducting consultations.

(4)   It will "make every effort to minimise delays and will work closely with stakeholder groups when preparing and implementing the necessary changes to the regulations".

(5)   It will not introduce a voluntary attachment of benefit as it states a liability order provides a clear arbitration that the debt is correctly assessed and the individual is liable for the debt. The recommendation on this

point contained in the Ollerenshaw review was based on recognition of the cost normally passed on to the council tax payer when a liability order is issued which, particularly for CTR recipients, can be disproportionate to the amount owed, the length of time the process takes during which arrears continue to build up, and the additional costs to the council and to the court system in general. Given that other debts, such as those for housing costs and water, may be collected through an attachment of benefit without court action being necessary to ensure the debt is correctly assessed and to confirm liability, the government's reasoning for rejecting this recommendation seems incomplete.

(6)   It accepts the need for better data sharing with local authorities and introduced a technical data-sharing solution to support this in May 2016. It states it will continue to work with local authorities to refine the solution.

(7)   It has no plans to allow local authorities increased discretion over the provision of CTR for pensioners.

(8)   It has no plans to change single person discounts, student discounts for full time students, disabled person discounts, discounts for properties that are annexes and used together with the main property, second home discounts and job-related second home discounts.

(9)   It will explore options for data gathering and analysis to better understand the impact of CTR on individuals and decide on the next steps "in due course".

(10)   It will explore options, including the potential for undertaking a feasibility study, before deciding whether to commission additional research on the impact of CTR within the context of other welfare and socio-economic changes.

(11)   It considers it is right that CTR is a localised benefit and has no plans to roll it into UC.

Council tax reduction schemes
10.–(1)-(3)   *[Omitted]*

(4)   Each billing authority in England must make a council tax reduction scheme under section 13A(2) of the LGFA 1992 no later than 31 January 2013; and the first financial year to which that scheme relates must be the year beginning with 1 April 2013.

(5)   But the Secretary of State may by order made by statutory instrument amend subsection (4) by substituting a different date or a later financial year (or both).

General

Interpretation
19.   In this Act–
"financial year" means a period of 12 months beginning with 1 April;
"the LGFA 1988" means the Local Government Finance Act 1988;
"the LGFA 1992" means the Local Government Finance Act 1992.

Power to make transitional, consequential etc provision
20.–(1)   The Secretary of State may by order made by statutory instrument make such transitory or transitional provision, or savings, as the Secretary of State considers appropriate in connection with the coming into force of any provision of this Act.

(2)   The Secretary of State may by order made by statutory instrument make such consequential provision (including provision amending, repealing or revoking any legislation passed or made before, or in the same Session as, this Act) as the Secretary of State considers appropriate in connection with any provision of this Act.

(3)   A statutory instrument containing an order under subsection (2) that amends or repeals any of the following may not be made unless a draft of the instrument has been laid before, and approved by a resolution of, each House of Parliament–
(a)   an Act of Parliament;
(b)   an Act of the Scottish Parliament;
(c)   an Act or Measure of the National Assembly for Wales;
(d)   Northern Ireland legislation as defined in section 24 of the Interpretation Act 1978.

(4)   Any other statutory instrument containing an order under subsection (2) is subject to annulment in pursuance of a resolution of either House of Parliament.

(5)   The powers under subsections (1) and (2) include power to make different provision for different cases or descriptions of case, including different provision for different areas or different authorities.

Financial provisions

    21.   There is to be paid out of money provided by Parliament–

    (a)   any expenditure incurred by the Secretary of State in consequence of this Act, and

    (b)   any increase attributable to this Act in the sums payable under any other Act out of money so provided.

Extent and short title

    22.–(1)   This Act extends to England and Wales only, subject to subsections (2) and (3).

    (2)   Section 17 extends also to Scotland.

    (3)   Sections 18 and 20 extend to England and Wales, Scotland and Northern Ireland.

    (4)   This Act may be cited as the Local Government Finance Act 2012.

Part 5

Main secondary legislation – council tax reduction schemes

The Council Tax Reduction Schemes (Prescribed Requirements) (England) Regulations 2012
(2012 No.2885)

PART 1
General
1.   Citation, commencement and application
2.   Interpretation
3.   Meaning of "pensioner" and "person who is not a pensioner"
4.   Meaning of "couple"
5.   Polygamous marriages
6.   Meaning of "family"
7.   Circumstances in which a person is to be treated as responsible or not responsible for another
8.   Households
9.   Non-dependants
10.   Remunerative work

PART 2
Prescribed classes of persons
11.   Pensioners
12.   Persons treated as not being in Great Britain
13.   Persons subject to immigration control

PART 3
Matters that must be included in an authority's scheme
14.   Provision for pensioners
15.   Provision for all applicants

SCHEDULE 1
Pensioners: matters that must be included in an authority's scheme
PART 1
1.   Classes of persons entitled to a reduction under an authority's scheme
2.   Class A: pensioners whose income is less than the applicable amount
3.   Class B: pensioners whose income is greater than the applicable amount
4.   Class C: alternative maximum council tax reduction
5.   Periods of absence from a dwelling

PART 2
6.   Applicable amounts

PART 3
7.   Maximum council tax reduction amount under an authority's scheme
8.   Non-dependant deductions

PART 4
9.   Alternative maximum council tax reduction under a scheme

PART 5
10.   Amount of reduction under a scheme: classes A to C

PART 6
CHAPTER 1
11.   Calculation of income and capital: applicant's family and polygamous marriages
12.   Circumstances in which income and capital of non-dependant is to be treated as applicant's

CHAPTER 2

13. Applicant in receipt of guarantee credit
14. Calculation of applicant's income in savings credit only cases
15. Calculation of income and capital where state pension credit is not payable
16. Meaning of "income"
17. Calculation of weekly income
18. Earnings of employed earners
19. Calculation of net earnings of employed earners
20. Calculation of earnings of self-employed earners
21. Earnings of self-employers earners
22. Notional income
23. Income paid to third parties
24. Calculation of income on a weekly basis
25. Treatment of child care charges
26. Additional condition referred to in paragraph 25(10)(b)(i): disability
27. Calculation of average weekly income from tax credits
28. Disregard of changes in tax, contributions etc
29. Calculation of net profit of self-employed earners
30. Calculation of deduction of tax and contributions of self-employed earners

CHAPTER 3

31. Calculation of capital
32. Calculation of capital in the United Kingdom
33. Calculation of capital outside the United Kingdom
34. Notional capital
35. Diminishing notional capital rule
36. Capital jointly held
37. Calculation of tariff income from capital

PART 7

38. Extended reductions (qualifying contributory benefits)
39. Duration of extended reduction period (qualifying contributory benefits)
40. Amount of extended reduction (qualifying contributory benefits)
41. Extended reductions (qualifying contributory benefits): movers
42. Relationship between extended reduction (qualifying contributory benefits) and entitlement to a reduction by virtue of classes A to C
43. Continuing reductions where state pension credit claimed
44. Extended reductions: movers into an authority's area

PART 8
When entitlement begins and change of circumstances

45. Date on which entitlement begins
46. Date on which change of circumstances is to take effect
47. Change of circumstances where state pension credit in payment

SCHEDULE 2
Applicable amounts
PART 1 Personal allowances
PART 2 Family premium
PART 3 Premiums
PART 4 Amounts of premium specified in Part 3

SCHEDULE 3
Amount of alternative maximum council tax reduction

SCHEDULE 4
Sums disregarded from applicant's earnings

SCHEDULE 5
Amounts to be disregarded in the calculation of income other than earnings

SCHEDULE 6
Capital Disregards

SCHEDULE 7
All applicants: matters that must be included in an authority's scheme – procedural matters
PART 1 Applications
PART 2 Appeals
PART 3 Discretionary reductions
PART 4 Electronic communications

SCHEDULE 8
All applicants: matters that must be included in an authority's scheme – other matters
PART 1 Extended reductions: persons who are not pensioners
PART 2 Further provision about applications and duty to notify a change of circumstances
PART 3 Decisions by an authority
PART 4 Circumstances in which a payment may be made

PART 1
General

Citation, commencement and application
1.–(1)   These Regulations may be cited as the Council Tax Reduction Schemes (Prescribed Requirements) (England) Regulations 2012 and come into force on 27th November 2012.
(2)   These Regulations apply in relation to billing authorities in England.
(3)   These Regulations apply in relation to council tax reduction schemes made by billing authorities for financial years beginning on or after 1st April 2013.

Interpretation
2.–(1)   In these Regulations–
"the 1992 Act" means the Local Government Finance Act 1992;
"Abbeyfield Home" means an establishment run by the Abbeyfield Society including all bodies corporate or unincorporated which are affiliated to that society;
"adoption leave" means a period of absence from work on ordinary or additional adoption leave by virtue of section 75A or 75B of the Employment Rights Act 1996;
"AFIP" means an armed forces independence payment payable in accordance with an armed and reserve forces compensation scheme established under section 1(2) of the Armed Forces(Pensions and Compensation) Act 2004;
"alternative maximum council tax reduction" means the amount determined in accordance with Part 4 of Schedule 1 and Schedule 3;
"applicable amount" means the amount calculated in accordance with paragraph 6 of Schedule 1 and Schedule 2;
"applicant" means a person who has made an application;
"application" means an application for a reduction under a scheme;
[¹⁰ "approved blood scheme" means a scheme established or approved by the Secretary of State, or trust established with funds provided by the Secretary of State, for the purpose of providing compensation in respect of a person having been infected from contaminated blood products;]
"assessment period" means–
    (a)   in relation to the earnings of a self-employed earner, the period determined in accordance with paragraph 20 of Schedule 1 for the purpose of calculating the weekly earnings of the applicant; or

    (b)   in relation to any other income, the period determined in accordance with paragraph 17 of Schedule 1 for the purpose of calculating the weekly income of the applicant;

"attendance allowance" means–

    (a)   an attendance allowance under Part 3 of the SSCBA;

    (b)   an increase of disablement pension under section 104 or 105 of that Act;

    (c)   a payment by virtue of article 14, 15, 16, 43 or 44 of the Personal Injuries (Civilians) Scheme 1983 or any analogous payment; or

    (d)   any payment based on need for attendance which is paid as part of a war disablement pension;

"basic rate" has the meaning given by the Income Tax Act 2007;

"the benefit Acts" means the SSCBA, the Jobseekers Act 1995, the State Pension Credit Act 2002 [⁶ , the Welfare Reform Act 2007 and the Pensions Act 2014];

"board and lodging accommodation" means accommodation provided to a person or, if he is a member of a family, to him or any other member of his family, for a charge which is inclusive of the provision of that accommodation and at least some cooked or prepared meals which both are cooked or prepared (by a person other than the person to whom the accommodation is provided or a member of his family) and are consumed in that accommodation or associated premises;

"care home" [¹¹ in England] has the meaning given by section 3 of the Care Standards Act 2000 and in Scotland means a care home service within the meaning given by section 2(3) of the Regulation of Care (Scotland) Act 2001 and in Northern Ireland means a nursing home within the meaning of Article 11 of the Health and Personal Social Services (Quality, Improvement and Regulation) (Northern Ireland) Order 2003 or a residential care home within the meaning of Article 10 of that Order [¹¹ , and in Wales means a care home service, within the meaning of Part 1 of the Regulation and Inspection of Social Care (Wales) Act 2016, which is provided wholly or mainly to adults];

"the Caxton Foundation" means the charitable trust of that name established on 28th March 2011 out of funds provided by the Secretary of State for the benefit of certain persons suffering from hepatitis C and other persons eligible for payment in accordance with its provisions;

"child" means a person under the age of 16;

"child benefit" has the meaning given by section 141 of the SSCBA;

"child tax credit" means a child tax credit under section 8 of the Tax Credits Act 2002;

"close relative" means a parent, parent-in-law, son, son-in-law, daughter, daughter-in-law, step-parent, step-son, step-daughter, brother, sister, or if any of the preceding persons is one member of a couple, the other member of that couple;

"concessionary payment" means a payment made under arrangements made by the Secretary of State with the consent of the Treasury which is charged either to the National Insurance Fund or to a Departmental Expenditure Vote to which payments of benefit or tax credits under the benefit Acts or the Tax Credits Act 2002 are charged;

[³ "contributory employment and support allowance" means an allowance under Part 1 of the Welfare Reform Act 2007 as amended by the provisions of Schedule 3, and Part 1 of Schedule 14, to the Welfare Reform Act 2012 that remove references to an income-related allowance and a contributory allowance under Part 1 of the Welfare Reform Act 2007 as that Part has effect apart from those provisions;]

"council tax benefit" means council tax benefit under Part 7 of the SSCBA;

"couple" has the meaning given by regulation 4 of these Regulations;

"Default Scheme Regulations" means the Council Tax Reduction Schemes (Default Scheme) (England) Regulations 2012;

"designated office" means the office of an authority designated by it for the receipt of applications–

    (a)   by notice upon or with a form supplied by it for the purpose of making an application;

(b) by reference upon or with such a form to some other document from it and sent by electronic means or otherwise on application and without charge; or

(c) by any combination of the provisions set out in paragraphs (a) and (b);

"disability living allowance" means a disability living allowance under section 71 of the SSCBA;

"earnings" has the meaning given by paragraph 18, 20 or 21 of Schedule 1 as the case may be;

"the Eileen Trust" means the charitable trust of that name established on 29th March 1993 out of funds provided by the Secretary of State for the benefit of persons eligible for payment in accordance with its provisions;

"electronic communication" has the same meaning as in section 15(1) of the Electronic Communications Act 2000;

"employed earner" is to be construed in accordance with section 2(1)(a) of the SSCBA and also includes a person who is in receipt of a payment which is payable under any enactment having effect in Northern Ireland and which corresponds to statutory sick pay or statutory maternity pay;

"enactment" includes an enactment comprised in, or in an instrument made under, an Act of the Scottish Parliament [¹ or the National Assembly of Wales];

"extended reduction" means a reduction under a scheme for which a person is eligible under Part 7 of Schedule 1 or paragraph 2 of Schedule 8;

"extended reduction period" means the period for which a person is in receipt of an extended reduction in accordance with paragraph 39 of Schedule 1;

"extended reduction (qualifying contributory benefits)" means a reduction under Schedule 1 by which a person is eligible pursuant to paragraph 38 or 41 of Schedule 1;

"family" has the meaning given by regulation 6 of these Regulations;

"the Fund" means moneys made available from time to time by the Secretary of State for the benefit of persons eligible for payment in accordance with the provisions of a scheme established by the Secretary of State on 24th April 1992 or, in Scotland, on 10th April 1992;

"guarantee credit" is to be construed in accordance with sections 1 and 2 of the State Pension Credit Act 2002;

"a guaranteed income payment" means a payment made under article 15(1)(c) or 29(1)(a) of the Armed Forces and Reserve Forces (Compensation Scheme) Order 2011;

"housing benefit" means housing benefit under Part 7 of the SSCBA;

"an income-based jobseeker's allowance" and "a joint-claim jobseeker's allowance" have the meanings given by section 1(4) of the Jobseekers Act 1995;

"income-related employment and support allowance" means an income-related allowance under Part 1 of the Welfare Reform Act 2007;

"independent hospital"–

(a) in England means a hospital as defined by section 275 of the National Health Service Act 2006 that is not a health service hospital as defined by that section;

(b) in Wales has the meaning given by section 2 of the Care Standards Act 2000; and

(c) in Scotland means an independent health care service as defined by section 10F of the National Health Service (Scotland) Act 1978;

"the Independent Living Fund (2006)" means the Trust of that name established by a deed dated 10th April 2006 and made between the Secretary of State for Work and Pensions of the one part and Margaret Rosemary Cooper, Michael Beresford Boyall and Marie Theresa Martin of the other part;

"invalid carriage or other vehicle" means a vehicle propelled by a petrol engine or by electric power supplied for use on the road and to be controlled by the occupant;

"the London Bombings Relief Charitable Fund" means the company limited by guarantee (number 5505072), and registered charity of that name established on 11th July 2005 for the purpose of (amongst other things) relieving sickness, disability or financial need of victims (including families or dependants of victims) of the terrorist attacks carried out in London on 7th July 2005;

[[10] "the London Emergencies Trust" means the compay of that name (number 09928465) incororated on 23rd December 2015 and the registered charity of that name (number 1172307) established on 28th March 2017;]

"lone parent" means a person who has no partner and who is responsible for and a member of the same household as a child or young person;

"the Macfarlane (Special Payments) Trust" means the trust of that name, established on 29th January 1990 partly out of funds provided by the Secretary of State, for the benefit of certain persons suffering from haemophilia;

"the Macfarlane (Special Payments) (No 2) Trust" means the trust of that name, established on 3rd May 1991 partly out of funds provided by the Secretary of State, for the benefit of certain persons suffering from haemophilia and other beneficiaries;

"the Macfarlane Trust" means the charitable trust, established partly out of funds provided by the Secretary of State to the Haemophilia Society, for the relief of poverty or distress among those suffering from haemophilia;

"main phase employment and support allowance" means an employment and support allowance where the calculation of the amount payable in respect of the applicant includes a component under section 2(1)(b) or 4(2)(b) of the Welfare Reform Act 2007 [[10] or the applicant is a member of the work-related activity group];

"maternity leave" means a period during which a woman is absent from work because she is pregnant or has given birth to a child, and at the end of which she has a right to return to work either under the terms of her contract of employment or under Part 8 of the Employment Rights Act 1996;

"maximum council tax reduction amount" means the amount determined in accordance with paragraph 7 of Schedule 1.

"member of a couple" means a member of a married or unmarried couple;

[[9] "member of the work-related activity group" means a [[10] person] who has or is treated as having limited capability for work under either–

(a) Part 5 of the Employment and Support Allowance Regulations 2008 other than by virtue of regulation 30 of those Regulations; or

(b) Part 4 of the Employment and Support Allowance Regulations 2013 other than by virtue of regulation 26 of those Regulations;]

"MFET Limited" means the company limited by guarantee (number 7121661) of that name, established for the purpose in particular of making payments in accordance with arrangements made with the Secretary of State to persons who have acquired HIV as a result of treatment by the NHS with blood or blood products;

"mobility supplement" means a supplement to which paragraph 5(1)(a)(vii) of Schedule 4 refers;

"mover" means an applicant who changes the dwelling in which the applicant is resident, and in respect of which the applicant is liable to pay council tax, from a dwelling in the area of one authority to a dwelling in the area of a second authority;

"net earnings" means such earnings as are calculated in accordance with paragraph 19 of Schedule 1;

"net profit" means such profit as is calculated in accordance with paragraph 29 of Schedule 1;

"new dwelling" means, for the purposes of the definition of "second authority" and paragraph 41 of Schedule 1, the dwelling to which an applicant has moved, or is about to move, in which the applicant will be resident;

"non-dependant" has the meaning given by regulation 9;

"occupational pension" means any pension or other periodical payment under an occupational pension scheme but does not include any discretionary payment out of a fund established for relieving hardship in particular cases;

"partner", in relation to a person, means–

(a) where that person is a member of a couple, the other member of that couple; or

(b) where that person is polygamously married to two or more members of his household, any such member to whom he is married;

"paternity leave" means a period of absence from work on [⁴] paternity leave by virtue of section 80A or 80B of the Employment Rights Act 1996 [⁴];

"pension fund holder" means with respect to a personal pension scheme or an occupational pension scheme, the trustees, managers or scheme administrators, as the case may be, of the scheme concerned;

"pensionable age" has the meaning given by the rules in paragraph 1 of Schedule 4 to the Pensions Act 1995;

"pensioner" has the meaning given by regulation 3(a);

"person on income support" means a person in receipt of income support;

"person treated as not being in Great Britain" has the meaning given by regulation 12;

"person who is not a pensioner" has the meaning given by regulation 3(b);

"personal independence payment" has the meaning given by Part 4 of the Welfare Reform Act 2012;

"personal pension scheme" means–

(a)   a personal pension scheme as defined by section 1 of the Pension Schemes Act 1993;

(b)   an annuity contract or trust scheme approved under section 620 or 621 of the Income and Corporation Taxes Act 1988 or a substituted contract within the meaning of section 622(3) of that Act which is treated as having become a registered pension scheme by virtue of paragraph 1(1)(f) of Schedule 36 to the Finance Act 2004;

(c)   a personal pension scheme approved under Chapter 4 of Part 14 of the Income and Corporation Taxes Act 1988 which is treated as having become a registered pension scheme by virtue of paragraph 1(1)(g) of Schedule 36 to the Finance Act 2004;

"policy of life insurance" means any instrument by which the payment of money is assured on death (except death by accident only) or the happening of any contingency dependent on human life, or any instrument evidencing a contract which is subject to payment of premiums for a term dependent on human life;

"polygamous marriage" means any marriage to which regulation 5 applies;

"qualifying age for state pension credit" means (in accordance with section 1(2)(b) and (6) of the State Pension Credit Act 2002)–

(a)   in the case of a woman, pensionable age; or

(b)   in the case of a man, the age which is pensionable age in the case of a woman born on the same day as the man;

"qualifying contributory benefit" means–

(a)   severe disablement allowance;

(b)   incapacity benefit;

(c)   contributory employment and support allowance;

"qualifying income-related benefit" means–

(a)   income support;

(b)   income-based jobseeker's allowance;

(c)   income-related employment and support allowance;

"qualifying course" means a qualifying course as defined for the purposes of Parts 2 and 4 of the Job Seeker's Allowance Regulations 1996;

"qualifying person" means a person in respect of whom payment has been made from the Fund, the Eileen Trust, MFET Limited, the Skipton Fund, the Caxton Foundation [¹⁰,the Scottish Infected Blood Support Scheme, an approved blood scheme, the London Emergencies Trust, the We Love Manchester Emergency Fund] or the London Bombings Relief Charitable Fund;

"reduction week" means a period of seven consecutive days beginning with a Monday and ending with a Sunday;

"relative" means a close relative, grandparent, grandchild, uncle, aunt, nephew or niece;

"relevant week", in relation to any particular day, means the week within which the day in question falls;

"remunerative work" has the meaning given by regulation 10;

"rent" means "eligible rent" to which regulation 12 of the Housing Benefit (Persons who have acquired the qualifying age for state pension credit) Regulations 2006 refer, less any deductions in respect of non-dependants which fall to be made under paragraph 8 of Schedule 1 (non-dependant deductions);

"savings credit" is to be construed in accordance with sections 1 and 3 of the State Pension Credit Act 2002;

[8 "Scottish basic rate" means the rate of income tax of that name calculated in accordance with section 6A of the Income Tax Act 2007;

"Scottish taxpayer" has the same meaning as in Chapter 2 of Part 4A of the Scotland Act 1998;]

[10 "the Scottish Infected Blood Support Scheme" means the scheme of that name administered by the Common Services Agency (constituted under section 10 of the National Health Service (Scotland) Act 1978);]

"second authority" means the authority to which a mover is liable to make payments for the new dwelling;

"self-employed earner" is to be construed in accordance with section 2(1)(b) of the SSCBA;

[3]

[2 "shared parental leave" means leave under section 75E or 75G of the Employment Rights Act 1996;]

"single applicant" means an applicant who neither has a partner nor is a lone parent;

"the Skipton Fund" means the ex-gratia payment scheme administered by the Skipton Fund Limited, incorporated on 25th March 2004, for the benefit of certain persons suffering from hepatitis C and other persons eligible for payment in accordance with the scheme's provisions;

"sports award" means an award made by one of the Sports Councils named in section 23(2) of the National Lottery etc. Act 1993 out of sums allocated to it for distribution under that section;

"the SSCBA" means the Social Security Contributions and Benefits Act 1992;

"state pension credit" means state pension credit under the State Pension Credit Act 2002;

"student" means a person, other than a person in receipt of a training allowance, who is attending or undertaking–

(a)   a course of study at an educational establishment; or

(b)   a qualifying course;

"tax year" means a period beginning with 6th April in one year and ending with 5th April in the next;

"training allowance" means an allowance (whether by way of periodical grants or otherwise) payable–

(a)   out of public funds by a Government department or by or on behalf of the Secretary of State, Skills Development Scotland, Scottish Enterprise or Highlands and Islands Enterprise[5] or the Welsh Ministers;

(b)   to a person for his maintenance or in respect of a member of his family; and

(c)   for the period, or part of the period, during which he is following a course of training or instruction provided by, or in pursuance of arrangements made with, that department or approved by that department in relation to him or so provided or approved by or on behalf of the Secretary of State, Skills Development Scotland, Scottish Enterprise or Highlands and Islands Enterprise or the Welsh Ministers,

but it does not include an allowance paid by any Government department to or in respect of a person by reason of the fact that he is following a course of full-time education, other than under arrangements made under section 2 of the Employment and Training Act 1973, or is training as a teacher;

"the Trusts" (except where the context otherwise requires) means the Macfarlane Trust, the Macfarlane (Special Payments) Trust and the Macfarlane (Special Payments) (No 2) Trust and "Trustees" is to be construed accordingly;

"universal credit" has the meaning given by section 1 of the Welfare Reform Act 2012;

"voluntary organisation" means a body, other than a public or local authority, the
    activities of which are carried on otherwise than for profit;
"war disablement pension" means any retired pay or pension or allowance payable in
    respect of disablement under an instrument specified in section 639(2) of the
    Income Tax (Earnings and Pensions) Act 2003;
"war pension" means a war disablement pension, a war widow's pension or a war
    widower's pension;
"war widow's pension" means any pension or allowance payable to a woman as a widow
    under an instrument specified in section 639(2) of the Income Tax (Earnings
    and Pensions) Act 2003 in respect of the death or disablement of any person;
"war widower's pension" means any pension or allowance payable to a man as a widower
    or to a surviving civil partner under an instrument specified in section 639(2) of
    the Income Tax (Earnings and Pensions) Act 2003 in respect of the death or
    disablement of any person;
"water charges" means–
    (a)   as respects England and Wales, any water and sewerage charges under Chapter
           1 of Part 5 of the Water Industry Act 1991,
    (b)   as respects Scotland, any water and sewerage charges established by Scottish
           Water under a charges scheme made under section 29A of the Water Industry
           (Scotland) Act 2002,
in so far as such charges are in respect of the dwelling which a person occupies as his
home;
[[10] "the We Love Manchester Emergency Fund" means the registered charity of that
    name (number 1173260) established on 30th May 2017;]
"working tax credit" means a working tax credit under section 10 of the Tax Credits Act
    2002;
"young person" means a person who falls within the definition of qualifying young
    person in section 142 of the SSCBA.
    (2)   In these Regulations, where an amount is to be rounded to the nearest penny, a
fraction of a penny must be disregarded if it is less than half a penny and must otherwise
be treated as a whole penny.
    (3)   For the purpose of these Regulations, a person is on an income-based jobseeker's
allowance on any day in respect of which an income-based jobseeker's allowance is
payable to him and on any day–
    (a)   in respect of which he satisfies the conditions for entitlement to an income-based
           jobseeker's allowance but where the allowance is not paid because of a reduction
           in accordance with section 19 or 19A or regulations made under section 17A or
           19B of the Jobseekers Act 1995 (circumstances in which a jobseeker's allowance
           is not payable);
    (b)   which is a waiting day for the purposes of paragraph 4 of Schedule 1 to that Act
           and which falls immediately before a day in respect of which an income-based
           jobseeker's allowance is payable to him or would be payable to him but for
           section 19 or 19A or regulations made under section 17A or 19B of that Act; or
    (c)   in respect of which an income-based jobseeker's allowance would be payable
           but for a restriction imposed pursuant to section 6B, 7, 8 or 9 of the Social
           Security Fraud Act 2001 (loss of benefit provisions).
    (4)   For the purposes of these Regulations, a person is on an income-related
employment and support allowance on any day in respect of which an income-related
employment and support allowance is payable to him and on any day–
    (a)   in respect of which he satisfies the conditions for entitlement to an income-
           related employment and support allowance but where the allowance is not paid
           in accordance with section 18 of the Welfare Reform Act 2007 (disqualification);
           or
    (b)   which is a waiting day for the purposes of paragraph 2 of Schedule 2 to that Act
           and which falls immediately before a day in respect of which an income-related
           employment and support allowance is payable to him or would be payable to
           him but for section 18 of that Act.

(5)   For the purposes of these Regulations, two persons shall be taken to be estranged only if their estrangement constitutes a breakdown of the relationship between them.

(6)   In these Regulations, references to any person in receipt of state pension credit includes a person who would be in receipt of state pension credit but for regulation 13 of the State Pension Credit Regulations 2002 (small amounts of state pension credit).

(7)   In these Regulations, references to a person in class A, B or C (as the case may be) is a reference to class A, B or C described in paragraphs 2 to 4 of Schedule 1.

[³ (8)   References in these Regulations to an applicant participating as a service user are to–

(a)   a person who is being consulted by or on behalf of–

    (i)   a body which has a statutory duty to provide services in the field of health, social care or social housing; or

    (ii)   a body which conducts research or undertakes monitoring for the purpose of planning or improving such services, in their capacity as a user, potential user, carer of a user or person otherwise affected by the provision of those services;

[⁷ (aa)   a person who is being consulted by or on behalf of–

    (i)   the Secretary of State in relation to any of the Secretary of State's functions in the field of social security or child support or under section 2 of the Employment and Training Act 1973; or

    (ii)   a body which conducts research or undertakes monitoring for the purpose of planning or improving such functions,

in their capacity as a person affected or potentially affected by the exercise of those functions or the carer of such a person;] or

(b)   the carer of a person consulted as described in [⁷ sub-paragraph (a) or (aa)] where the carer is not being consulted as described in that sub-paragraph.]

Modifications

The amendments made by SI 2014 No.3255 which came into force on 5 April 2015 did not have effect in relation to ordinary statutory paternity pay or additional statutory paternity pay which was paid on or after 5 April 2015, or to a period in respect of which additional statutory paternity pay was payable which began, or continued on or after 5 April 2015, or to ordinary paternity leave or additional paternity leave which was taken on or after 5 April 2015. See art 35 of SI 2014 No.3255.

Amendments

1.   Amended by reg 2(2) of SI 2013 No.3181, applying to schemes for financial years beginning on or after 1.1.14.
2.   Inserted by art 27(2)(b) of SI 2014 No 3255 as from 31.12.14.
3.   Amended by reg 2(2) of SI 2014 No 3312 as from 12.1.15, in relation to schemes made for financial years starting on or after 1.4.15.
4.   Amended by art 27(2)(a) of SI 2014 No 3255 as from 5.4.15.
5.   Amended by art 2 and Sch 3 para 23 of SI 2015 No 971 as from 26.5.15.
6.   Amended by art 39(2) of SI 2015 No 1985 as from 6.4.16.
7.   Inserted by reg 2(2) of SI 2015 No 2041 as from 14.1.16, in relation to schemes made for financial years starting on or after 1.4.16.
8.   Inserted by reg 2(2) of SI 2016 No 1262 as from 15.1.17, in relation to schemes made for financial years starting on or after 1.4.17.
9.   Inserted by Sch 1 para 8(2) of SI 2017 No 204 as from 3.4.17, subject to transitional and savings provisions in Sch 2 paras 1–7.
10.   Amended by reg 4 of SI 2017 No 1305 as from 12.1.18, in relation to schemes made for financial years starting on or after 1.4.18.
11.   Amended by Sch 1 para 28(2) of SI 2018 No 48 (W.15) as from 2.4.18.

General Note

Much of reg 2, including many of the definitions in reg 2(1), corresponds with reg 2 HB Regs. See p239 for commentary.

In relation to the definition of "lone parent", "partner" is defined later in this regulation, as is "child" (someone aged under 16) and "young person" (someone who counts as a "qualifying young person" for child benefit purposes – see s142 SSCBA 1992 and regs 2 to 8 Child Benefit (General) Regulations 2006). See also reg 7 for the circumstances in which a person is treated as responsible for a child or young person and reg 8 for circumstances in which people are treated or not treated as members of the same household. See commentary on s137 SSCBA on p14 for discussion of the definition of "couple".

Meaning of "pensioner" and "person who is not a pensioner"
3.   In these Regulations a person is–
(a)   a "pensioner" if–
    (i)   he has attained the qualifying age for state pension credit; and
    (ii)   [¹ he is not and] if he has a partner, his partner is not–
        (aa)   a person on income support, on an income-based jobseeker's allowance or on an income-related employment and support allowance; or
        (bb)   a person with an award of universal credit; and
(b)   a "person who is not a pensioner" if–
    (i)   he has not attained the qualifying age for state pension credit; or
    (ii)   he has attained the qualifying age for state pension credit and he, or if he has a partner, his partner, is–
        (aa)   a person on income support, on income-based jobseeker's allowance or an income-related employment and support allowance; or
        (bb)   a person with an award of universal credit.

Amendment
1.   Amended by reg 2(3) of SI 2013 No 3181, applying to schemes for financial years beginning on or after 1.1.14.

General Note
Whether an applicant is "a pensioner" or a "person who is not a pensioner" is relevant to how entitlement to CTR is assessed. If an applicant or her/his partner is "on" IS, income-based JSA or income-related ESA or has an award of UC, then, even if the applicant has reached the qualifying age for PC, s/he must be classed as a "person who is not a pensioner". A "person on income support" is defined in reg 2 as a person in receipt of IS. Reg 2(3) deals with when a person is on an income-based JSA and reg 2(4) with when a person is on income-related ESA. In effect, a person who is a pensioner broadly corresponds with someone to whom the HB(SPC) Regs would apply should s/he claim HB (see reg 5 HB(SPC) Regs on p733) and a person who is not a pensioner with someone to whom the HB Regs would apply (see reg 5 HB Regs on p252).

[¹ Meaning of "couple"
4.   In these Regulations, "couple" means–
(a)   two people who are married to, or civil partners of, each other and are members of the same household; or
(b)   two people who are not married to, or civil partners of, each other but are living together as a married couple.]

Amendment
1.   Substituted by art 2 and Sch 1 para 54 of SI 2014 No 107 as from 13.3.14.

General Note
This definition is almost identical to the definition of couple in s137 SSCBA (see p14 and its analysis). A person can be treated as a member of the same household despite temporary absences (see reg 8).

Polygamous marriages
5.–(1)   This regulation applies to any case where–
(a)   a person is a husband or wife by virtue of a marriage entered into under a law which permits polygamy; and
(b)   either party to the marriage has for the time being any spouse additional to the other party.
(2)   For the purposes of regulation 4 neither party to the marriage is to be taken to be a member of a couple.

Meaning of "family"
6.–(1)   In these Regulations "family" means–
(a)   a couple;
(b)   a couple and a member of the same household for whom one of them is or both are responsible and who is a child or a young person; or

(c)   a person who is not a member of a couple and a member of the same household for whom that person is responsible and who is a child or a young person.

(2)   The references to a child or young person in sub-paragraph (1)(b) and (c) include a child or young person in respect of whom section 145A of the SSCBA applies for the purposes of entitlement to child benefit, but only for the period prescribed under section 145A(1).

(3)   The references to a young person in paragraph (1)(b) and (c) do not include a young person who is–

(a)   on income support, an income-based jobseeker's allowance or an income-related employment and support allowance; [¹]

(b)   a person to whom section 6 of the Children (Leaving Care) Act 2000 (exclusion from benefits) applies [¹; or]

[¹ (c)   entitled to an award of universal credit.].

Amendment

1.   Amended by reg 2(3) of SI 2014 No 3312 as from 12.1.15, in relation to schemes made for financial years starting on or after 1.4.15.

General Note

The definition of "family" in para (1) is similar to that in s137 SSCBA (see p12 and p17). The definition in s137 uses the term "person of a prescribed description" in place of "young person" which is used in this regulation. Both terms, however, mean a "qualifying young person" for child benefit purposes (as defined by s142 SSCBA 1992).

Para (2) allows a child or young person to continue to be treated as a member of a family, notwithstanding that s/he has died, for the period prescribed under s145A(1) SSCBA.

See p406 for commentary on reg 19(1) and (3) HB Regs which is relevant here.

Circumstances in which a person is to be treated as responsible or not responsible for another

7.–(1)   A person is to be treated as responsible for a child or young person who is normally living with him, including a child or young person to whom regulation 6(2) applies.

(2)   Where a child or young person spends equal amounts of time in different households, or where there is a question as to which household he is living in, the child or young person must be treated for the purposes of paragraph (1) as normally living with–

(a)   the person who is receiving child benefit in respect of that child or young person, or

(b)   if there is no such person–

(i)   where only one claim for child benefit has been made in respect of him, the person who made that claim, or

(ii)   in any other case the person who has the primary responsibility for him.

(3)   For the purposes of these Regulations a child or young person is the responsibility of only one person in any reduction week and any person other than the one treated as responsible for the child or young person under this regulation is to be treated as not so responsible.

General Note

Regulation 7 is almost identical to reg 20 HB Regs. For commentary on that regulation, see p408.

Households

8.–(1)   Subject to paragraphs (2) and (3), an applicant and any partner and, where the applicant or his partner is treated (by virtue of regulation 7) as responsible for a child or young person, that child or young person and any child of that child or young person, are to be treated as members of the same household notwithstanding that any of them is temporarily absent from that household.

(2)   A child or young person is not to be treated as a member of the applicant's household where he is–

(a) placed with the applicant or his partner by a local authority under section 22C [²
] of the Children Act 1989 or by a voluntary organisation under section 59(1)(a)
of that Act, [³ or section 81(2) of the Social Services and Well-being (Wales)
Act 2014 (ways in which looked after children are to be accommodated and
maintained)] or in Scotland boarded out [¹ or placed] with the applicant or his
partner under a relevant enactment [² or in Wales, placed with the applicant or
the applicant's partner by a local authority under section 81 of the Social
Services and Well-being (Wales) Act 2014 or by a voluntary organisation under
section 59(1)(a) of the Children Act 1989]; or

(b) placed, or in Scotland boarded out, with the applicant or his partner prior to
adoption; or

(c) placed for adoption with the applicant or his partner in accordance with the
Adoption and Children Act 2002, the Adoption Agencies (Scotland) Regulations
2009 or the Adoption (Northern Ireland) Order 1987.

(3) Subject to paragraph (4), paragraph (1) does not apply to a child or young person
who is not living with the applicant and who–

(a) is being looked after by, or in Scotland is in the care of, a local authority under
a relevant enactment; or

(b) has been placed, or in Scotland boarded out, with a person other than the
applicant prior to adoption; or

(c) has been placed for adoption in accordance with the Adoption and Children Act
2002 or the Adoption Agencies (Scotland) Regulations 2009.

(4) An authority must treat a child or young person to whom paragraph (3)(a)
applies as being a member of the applicant's household in any reduction week where–

(a) that child or young person lives with the applicant for part or all of that reduction
week; and

(b) the authority considers that it is reasonable to do so taking into account the
nature and frequency of that child's or young person's visits.

(5) In this regulation "relevant enactment" means–

(a) the Army Act 1955;
(b) the Air Force Act 1955;
(c) the Naval Discipline Act 1957;
(d) the Matrimonial Proceedings (Children) Act 1958;
(e) the Social Work (Scotland) Act 1968;
(f) the Family Law Reform Act 1969;
(g) the Children and Young Persons Act 1969;
(h) the Matrimonial Causes Act 1973;
(i) the Children Act 1975;
(j) the Domestic Proceedings and Magistrates' Courts Act 1978;
(k) the Adoption and Children (Scotland) Act 2007;
(l) the Family Law Act 1986;
(m) the Children Act 1989;
(n) the Children (Scotland) Act 1995; [¹]
[¹ (na) the Children's Hearings (Scotland) Act 2011; and]
(o) the Legal Aid, Sentencing and Punishment of Offenders Act 2012.

Amendments

1.   Amended by reg 2(4) of SI 2013 No.3181, applying to schemes for financial years beginning on or after
     1.1.14.
2.   Amended by Sch 3 para 134 of SI 2016 No 211 (W.84) as from 6.4.16.
3.   Amended by reg 5 of SI 2017 No 1305 as from 12.1.18, in relation to schemes made for financial years
     starting on or after 1.4.18.

General Note

This is almost identical to reg 11 CTR(S) Regs (for commentary, see p1473). See also p410 for the commentary
on reg 21 HB Regs which is similar.

Non-dependants

9.–(1)   In these Regulations, "non-dependant" means any person, except someone to whom paragraph (2) applies, who normally resides with an applicant or with whom an applicant normally resides.

(2)   This paragraph applies to–

(a)   any member of the applicant's family;

(b)   if the applicant is polygamously married, any partner of his and any child or young person who is a member of his household and for whom he or one of his partners is responsible;

(c)   a child or young person who is living with the applicant but who is not a member of his household by virtue of regulation 8 (households);

(d)   subject to paragraph (3), any person who, with the applicant, is jointly and severally liable to pay council tax in respect of a dwelling for any day under section 6 or 7 of the 1992 Act (persons liable to pay council tax);

(e)   subject to paragraph (3), any person who is liable to make payments on a commercial basis to the applicant or the applicant's partner in respect of the occupation of the dwelling;

(f)   a person who lives with the applicant in order to care for him or a partner of his and who is engaged by a charitable or voluntary organisation which makes a charge to the applicant or his partner for the services provided by that person.

(3)   Excepting persons to whom sub-paragraph (2)(a) to (c) and (f) refer, a person to whom any of the following paragraphs applies is a non-dependant–

(a)   a person who resides with the person to whom he is liable to make payments in respect of the dwelling and either–

(i)   that person is a close relative of his or his partner; or

(ii)   the tenancy or other agreement between them is other than on a commercial basis;

(b)   a person whose liability to make payments in respect of the dwelling appears to the authority to have been created to take advantage of a scheme except someone who was, for any period within the eight weeks prior to the creation of the agreement giving rise to the liability to make such payments, otherwise liable to make payments of rent in respect of the same dwelling;

(c)   a person who becomes jointly and severally liable with the applicant for council tax in respect of a dwelling and who was, at any time during the period of eight weeks prior to his becoming so liable, a non-dependant of one or more of the other residents in that dwelling who are so liable for the tax, unless the change giving rise to the new liability was not made to take advantage of a scheme.

General Note

A "non-dependant" is someone who normally resides with an applicant, or is someone with whom an applicant normally resides, and who does not come within one of the descriptions in para (2). In respect of applicants who are "pensioners" (for which see reg 3), Sch 1 para 7 provides that an applicant's "maximum CTR" – which is used to assess the amount of any entitlement to CTR – is calculated by ascertaining her/his daily liability for council tax for the dwelling and deducting from this figure any deductions for non-dependants that fall to be made under Sch 1 para 8, known as "non-dependant deductions". This regulation is similar to reg 3 CTR(S) Regs and to reg 3 HB Regs (see p1466 and p249 for commentary).

Remunerative work

10.–(1)   Subject to the following provisions of this regulation, a person must be treated for the purposes of these Regulations as engaged in remunerative work if he is engaged, or, where his hours of work fluctuate, he is engaged on average, for not less than 16 hours a week, in work for which payment is made or which is done in expectation of payment.

(2)   Subject to sub-paragraph (3), in determining the number of hours for which a person is engaged in work where his hours of work fluctuate, regard must be had to the average of hours worked over–

(a)   if there is a recognisable cycle of work, the period of one complete cycle (including, where the cycle involves periods in which the person does no work, those periods but disregarding any other absences);

(b)   in any other case, the period of 5 weeks immediately prior to the date of application, or such other length of time as may, in the particular case, enable the person's weekly average hours of work to be determined more accurately.

(3)   Where, for the purposes of paragraph (2)(a), a person's recognisable cycle of work at a school, other educational establishment or other place of employment is one year and includes periods of school holidays or similar vacations during which he does not work, those periods and any other periods not forming part of such holidays or vacations during which he is not required to work must be disregarded in establishing the average hours for which he is engaged in work.

(4)   Where no recognisable cycle has been established in respect of a person's work, regard must be had to the number of hours or, where those hours will fluctuate, the average of the hours, which he is expected to work in a week.

(5)   A person must be treated as engaged in remunerative work during any period for which he is absent from work referred to in paragraph (1) if the absence is either without good cause or by reason of a recognised, customary or other holiday.

(6)   A person on income support, an income-based jobseeker's allowance or an income-related employment and support allowance for more than 3 days in any reduction week must be treated as not being in remunerative work in that week.

(7)   A person must not be treated as engaged in remunerative work on any day on which the person is on maternity leave, paternity leave [¹, shared parental leave] or adoption leave, or is absent from work because he is ill.

(8)   A person must not be treated as engaged in remunerative work on any day on which he is engaged in an activity in respect of which–

(a)   a sports award has been made, or is to be made, to him; and

(b)   no other payment is made or is expected to be made to him.

Amendment

1.   Amended by art 27(3) of SI 2014 No 3255 as from 31.12.14.

General Note

Reg 10 is almost identical to reg 6 HB regs (see p253 for commentary).

PART 2
Prescribed classes of persons

General Note to Part 2

Under s13A(2) LGFA 1992, each English billing authority must make a scheme stipulating reductions in the council tax payable by those it considers are in financial need or by those within classes of people it considers are, in general, in financial need. The amount of council tax to be paid is then reduced to the extent, if any, required by that scheme. A scheme must state the classes of people entitled to a reduction under the scheme: Sch 1A para 2(1) LGFA 1992. The Secretary of State may prescribe classes of people who must, or must not, be included in an authority's scheme: Sch 1A para 2(8) and (9)(b) LGFA 1992. This Part prescribes those classes. Those who must be included in an authority's scheme are the classes of pensioners described in Sch 1 Part 1 apart from pensioners with over £16,000 capital (see below).

The classes of people prescribed as people who must not be included in a scheme are:

–   pensioners who have over £16,000 capital (calculated in accordance with Sch 1 Part 6): reg 11(2) and (3);

–   people treated as not being in Great Britain: reg 12; *and*

–   people "subject to immigration control": reg 13.

An authority is free to include other classes of people within its scheme provided they do not fall into classes of people who are specifically excluded from a scheme by these regulations and provided they are either people the authority considers to be in financial need or the class is defined "by reference to criteria which the authority considers identify those who are, in general, in financial need": *R (Winder and others) v Sandwell MBC* [2014] EWHC 2617 (Admin), para 53.

Pensioners

11.–(1)   Subject to paragraph (2), the classes of pensioners described in paragraph 1 of Schedule 1 are classes of person prescribed for the purposes of paragraph 2(9)(b) of Schedule 1A to the 1992 Act and which must be included in an authority's scheme.

(2)   Pensioners whose capital exceeds £16,000 are a class of person prescribed for the purposes of that paragraph and which must not be included in an authority's scheme.

(3)   Capital for the purposes of paragraph (2) is to be calculated in accordance with Part 6 of Schedule 1.

General Note

In calculating whether a pensioner has capital of over £16,000, it is the combined capital of both the pensioner and her/his partner, if s/he has one, which is counted, calculated in accordance with Sch 1 Part 6: Sch 1 para 11. In limited circumstances, the capital of a non-dependant is counted rather than that of the applicant, see Sch 1 para 12 (p1131).

Note that if an applicant or her/his partner is in receipt of the guarantee credit of PC, all of her/his income and capital are disregarded under Sch 1 para 13 (p1132) with the effect that the capital limit does not apply.

Persons treated as not being in Great Britain

12.–(1)   Persons treated as not being in Great Britain are a class of person prescribed for the purposes of paragraph 2(9)(b) of Schedule 1A to the 1992 Act and which must not be included in an authority's scheme.

(2)   Except where a person falls within paragraph (5) or (6), a person is to be treated as not being in Great Britain if the person is not habitually resident in the United Kingdom, the Channel Islands, the Isle of Man or the Republic of Ireland.

(3)   A person must not be treated as habitually resident in the United Kingdom, the Channel Islands, the Isle of Man or the Republic of Ireland unless the person has a right to reside in one of those places.

(4)   For the purposes of paragraph (3), a right to reside does not include a right which exists by virtue of, or in accordance with–

(a)   regulation 13 of the EEA Regulations(1) or Article 6 of Council Directive 2004/38/EC;

[¹ (aa) regulation 14 of the EEA Regulations, but only in a case where the right exists under that regulation because the person is–

   (i)   a jobseeker for the purpose of the definition of "qualified person" in regulation 6(1) of those Regulations, or

   (ii)   a family member (within the meaning of regulation 7 of those Regulations) of such a jobseeker;

(ab)   Article 45 of the Treaty on the functioning of the European Union (in a case where the person is seeking work in the United Kingdom, the Channel Islands, the Isle of Man or the Republic of Ireland);] or

(b)   regulation 15A(1) of the EEA Regulations, but only in a case where the right exists under that regulation because the applicant satisfies the criteria in paragraph (4A) of that regulation or Article 20 of the Treaty on the Functioning of the European Union (in a case where the right to reside arises because a British citizen would otherwise be deprived of the genuine enjoyment of their rights as a European Union citizen).

(5)   A person falls within this paragraph if the person is–

(a)   a qualified person for the purposes of regulation 6 of the EEA Regulations as a worker or a self-employed person;

(b)   a family member of a person referred to in sub-paragraph (a) within the meaning of regulation 7(1)(a), (b) or (c) of the EEA Regulations;

(c)   a person who has a right to reside permanently in the United Kingdom by virtue of regulation 15(1)(c), (d) or (e) of the EEA Regulations;

(d)   a person recorded by the Secretary of State as a refugee within the definition in Article 1 of the Convention relating to the Status of Refugees done at Geneva on 28th July 1951, as extended by Article 1(2) of the Protocol relating to the Status of Refugees done at New York on 31st January 1967;

[¹(e) a person who has been granted, or who is deemed to have been granted, leave outside the rules made under section 3(2) of the Immigration Act 1971 where that leave is–
(i) discretionary leave to enter or remain in the United Kingdom,
(ii) leave to remain under the Destitution Domestic Violence concession which came into effect on 1st April 2012, or
(iii) leave deemed to have been granted by virtue of regulation 3 of the Displaced Persons (Temporary Protection) Regulations 2005;]
(f) a person who has humanitarian protection granted under those rules; [¹]
(g) a person who is not a person subject to immigration control within the meaning of section 115(9) of the Immigration and Asylum Act 1999 and who is in the United Kingdom as a result of his deportation, expulsion or other removal by compulsion of law from another country to the United Kingdom.
[¹ (h) in receipt of income support [²] or on an income-related employment and support allowance; [²]
[² (ha) in receipt of an income-based jobseeker's allowance and has a right to reside other than a right to reside falling within paragraph (4); or]
(i) a person who is treated as a worker for the purpose of the definition of "qualified person" in regulation 6(1) of the EEA Regulations pursuant to regulation 5 of the Accession of Croatia (Immigration and Worker Authorisation) Regulations 2013 (right of residence of a Croatian who is an "accession State national subject to worker authorisation")]

(6) A person falls within this paragraph if the person is a Crown servant or member of Her Majesty's forces posted overseas.

(7) A person mentioned in sub-paragraph (6) is posted overseas if the person is performing overseas the duties of a Crown servant or member of Her Majesty's forces and was, immediately before the posting or the first of consecutive postings, habitually resident in the United Kingdom.

(8) In this regulation–
"claim for asylum" has the same meaning as in section 94(1) of the Immigration and Asylum Act 1999;
"Crown servant" means a person holding an office or employment under the Crown;
"EEA Regulations" means the Immigration (European Economic Area) Regulations 2006; and
"Her Majesty's forces" has the same meaning as in the Armed Forces Act 2006.

Modifications

The amendment made to reg 12(5) by SI 2014 No.3312 does not apply to a person who is entitled to income-based JSA and who on 31 March 2015 is liable to pay council tax at a reduced rate by virtue of a council tax reduction under an authority's scheme: reg 3 of SI 2014 No.3312. The transitional protection applies until the earliest of two specified events – ie, (1) the person makes a new application for CTR or (2) the person ceases to be entitled to income-based JSA.

Amendments

1. Amended by reg 2(5) of SI 2013 No 3181, applying to schemes for financial years beginning on or after 1.1.14.
2. Amended by reg 2(4) of SI 2014 No 3312 as from 12.1.15, in relation to schemes made for financial years starting on or after 1.4.15.

General Note

Reg 12 defines a class of person excluded from entitlement to CTR – those who are treated as not in GB. A person is treated as not in GB if s/he is not habitually resident in the UK, Channel Islands, Isle of Man or Republic of Ireland, unless s/he comes within para (5) or (6). People covered by para (5) or (6) are therefore exempt from this habitual residence test and are not excluded from CTR under this regulation. Others cannot be treated as habitually resident unless they have a right to reside in the UK, Channel Islands, Isle of Man or Republic of Ireland: para (3). However, a right to reside does not include a right held in accordance the provisions in para (4). Therefore, a person who is not exempt under para (5) or (6) and who either does not have a right to reside or only has a right to reside under para (4), is treated as not habitually resident and so does not qualify for CTR. If s/he does have a right to reside and that right is not solely a right under para (4), s/he has to satisfy the habitual residence test to qualify.

Reg 12 is similar to reg 10 HB Regs although, for HB, the rule is framed in terms of who is a "person from abroad" rather than who is treated as not in GB (a "person from abroad" is treated as not liable to make payments in respect of a dwelling, even if s/he is making such a payment, and so cannot qualify for HB). See p299 for relevant commentary. However, amendments made to reg 10 HB Regs which clarify the position for those granted limited leave to enter or remain under the EU Settlement Scheme and reflect the fact that the Immigration (European Economic Area) Regulations 2006 have been revoked and replaced by the Immigration (European Economic Area) Regulations 2016, have not, at the time of writing, been replicated in this regulation.

Persons subject to immigration control

13.–(1)   [¹ Subject to paragraph (1A),] Persons subject to immigration control are a class of person prescribed for the purposes of paragraph 2(9)(b) of Schedule 1A to the 1992 Act and which must not be included in an authority's scheme.

[¹ (1A)   A person who is a national of a state which has ratified the European Convention on Social and Medical Assistance (done in Paris on 11th December 1953) or a state which has ratified the Council of Europe Social Charter (signed in Turin on 18th October 1961) and who is lawfully present in the United Kingdom is not a person subject to immigration control for the purpose of paragraph (1).]

(2)   "Person subject to immigration control" has the same meaning as in section 115(9) of the Immigration and Asylum Act 1999.

Amendment

1.   Amended by reg 2(6) of SI 2013 No 3181, applying to schemes for financial years beginning on or aftr 1.1.14.

General Note

A "person subject to immigration control" is not entitled to CTR. Someone covered by para (1A) is not a person subject to immigration control and, therefore, is not excluded from entitlement by this regulation. For commentary relevant to para (1A), see the analysis of Sch para 4 Social Security (Immigration and Asylum) Consequential Amendments Regs on p1750. See also the commentary to s115(9) IAA on p1707 on who is a "person subject to immigration control".

PART 3
Matters that must be included in an authority's scheme

Provision for pensioners

14.–(1)   A scheme must make provision in respect of pensioners.

(2)   Schedules 1 to 6, which contain those matters that must be included in a scheme in respect of pensioners, have effect.

General Note

Using the power afforded by Sch 1A para 2(9)(b) LGFA 1992, the Secretary of State has prescribed that the classes of pensioners who meet the descriptions of Classes A, B or C in Sch 1 paras 2–4 must be included in an English billing authority's scheme: reg 11. In accordance with Sch 1 para 1, such pensioners are entitled to CTR. Pensioners with more than £16,000 capital, as calculated in accordance with Sch 1 Part 6, are not entitled to CTR as they are a class which is explicitly to be excluded from an authority's scheme and who therefore do not fit the description of pensioners who come within Class A, B or C: reg 11(2) and (3) and Sch 1 paras 2(d), 3(d), 4(1)(d). A pensioner who is in receipt of guarantee credit of pension credit, or whose partner is in receipt of it, will not be caught by this exclusion because her/his income and capital are ignored. Unless excluded on another ground, s/he will come within Class A: Sch 1 para 13. Pensioners who are treated as not being in Great Britain under reg 12, or who are 'subject to immigration control' under reg 13, must also be excluded from an authority's scheme and do not fit the description of pensioners who come within Classes A, B and C: Sch 1 para 2(d), 3(d) and 4(1)(d). It is worth noting that regs 12 and 13, in defining classes of people who must not be included in an authority's scheme, apply to both pensioners and non-pensioners. For who counts as a pensioner and who does not, see reg 3. This regulation stipulates that an English authority's scheme must contain the matters set out in Schedules 1 to 6 – these schedules relate to pensioners only, and set out the rules for calculating a pensioner's entitlement to CTR.

Provision for all applicants

15.–(1)   A scheme must include the provisions set out in Schedules 7 and 8.

(2)   The provisions mentioned in paragraph (1) must apply to all applicants (both persons who are pensioners and persons who are not pensioners) unless otherwise provided.

SCHEDULE 1
Pensioners: matters that must be included in an authority's scheme

Amendment
1.   Amended by reg 2(7)(a) of SI 2013 No.3181 for schemes for financial years beginning on or after 1.4.14.

PART 1

General Note to Part 1

People falling into any one of the three sets of conditions (called "classes") outlined in paras 2 to 4 must be entitled to a reduction under an authority"s scheme. All three classes, Classes A to C, relate to pensioners. Pensioners are defined in reg 3.

The three classes have certain qualifying conditions in common. These are that on any day the pensioner:

(1)   must be liable to pay council tax for a dwelling of which s/he is a resident (for "resident" see s6 LGFA, 1992). This is similar to the condition for CTR in Scotland where an applicant must be liable to pay council tax for a dwelling in which s/he resides as her/his sole or main residence – see the commentary on reg 14(3)(a) CTR(S) Regs on p1475 which is relevant here;

(2)   must not be absent from the dwelling throughout the day (although see para 5 for circumstances in which a person is treated as not absent during "periods of temporary absence");

(3)   must be someone in respect of whom a maximum CTR amount can be calculated. For how this is calculated, see para 7;

(4)   must not be someone who falls within the classes of people described in regs 11(2), 12 and 13, who are excluded from entitlement to CTR; *and*

(5)   must have "made an application".

Classes of persons entitled to a reduction under an authority's scheme

1.–(1)   The classes of pensioners described in paragraphs 2 to 4 are entitled to a reduction under an authority's scheme.

(2)   In those paragraphs, references to an applicant's income or capital include, in a case where that income or capital cannot accurately be determined, references to the applicant's estimated income or capital.

Class A: pensioners whose income [¹ is no greater than] the applicable amount

2.   On any day class A consists of any person who is a pensioner–

(a)   who is for that day liable to pay council tax in respect of a dwelling of which he is a resident;

(b)   who, subject to paragraph 5 (periods of absence from a dwelling), is not absent from the dwelling throughout the day;

(c)   in respect of whom a maximum council tax reduction amount can be calculated;

(d)   who does not fall within a class of persons prescribed for the purposes of paragraph 2(9) of Schedule 1A to the 1992 Act as a class of person which must not be included in an authority's scheme;

(e)   whose income (if any) for the relevant week does not exceed his applicable amount; and

(f)   who has made an application.

Amendment
1.   Amended by reg 2(7)(a) of SI 2013 No 3181 for schemes for financial years beginning on or after 1.4.14.

General Note

To fall within class A (and therefore be entitled to CTR) a pensioner's income for the relevant week must be equal to or less than her/his applicable amount. For how her/his applicable amount is calculated, see para 6. S/he must also satisfy the conditions outlined in paras 2(a)–(d) and (f) (for which see the commentary at the start of this Schedule). Relevant week is defined in reg 2. If the applicant or her/his partner is in receipt of the guarantee credit of PC, all their income and capital is disregarded and so the applicant automatically meets the requirement of para 2(e) and s/he is not excluded from CTR on the ground that her/his capital is over £16,000: Sch 1 para 13. If an applicant falls within Class A, the amount of CTR equals the amount of her/his maximum CTR: para 10(2). For how this is calculated, see para 7.

Class B: pensioners whose income is greater than the applicable amount

3.   On any day class B consists of any person who is a pensioner–

(a)   who is for that day liable to pay council tax in respect of a dwelling of which he is a resident;

(b)   who, subject to paragraph 5, is not absent from the dwelling throughout the day;

(c)   in respect of whom a maximum council tax reduction amount can be calculated;

(d)   who does not fall within a class of person prescribed for the purposes of paragraph 2(9) of Schedule 1A to the 1992 Act as a class of person which must not be included in an authority's scheme;

(e)   whose income for the relevant week is greater than his applicable amount;

(f)   in respect of whom amount A exceeds amount B where–
     (i)   amount A is the maximum council tax reduction in respect of the day in the applicant's case; and
     (ii)   amount B is 2 6/7 per cent of the difference between his income for the relevant week and his applicable amount; and

(g)   who has made an application.

General Note

A pensioner (as defined in reg 3) whose income is more than her/his applicable amount (determined under Parts 2 and 6 of this Sch) is entitled to CTR if, as well as satisfying the conditions in paras (a)–(d) and (g) (for which see the commentary at the start of this Schedule), her/his income is sufficiently low. The calculation in para (f) is formulated to assess this on a daily basis (in line with para 7 and s13A LGFA 1992) – two and six-sevenths equates to a weekly amount of 20 per cent. If the amount of the applicant's maximum CTR in respect of the day (Amount A) is greater than the specified percentage of the difference between her/his income (for the week in which the day falls) and her/his applicable amount (Amount B), s/he will qualify. The amount of CTR s/he qualifies for is the amount by which her/his maximum CTR exceeds the percentage amount (para 10(3)). This is essentially the same as the calculation that was used for council tax benefit (CTB); for an analysis of the CTB calculation, see *IB v Barnsley MBC* [2009] UKUT 279 (AAC).

Class C: alternative maximum council tax reduction

4.–(1)   On any day class C consists of any person who is a pensioner–
(a)   who is for that day liable to pay council tax in respect of a dwelling of which he is a resident;
(b)   who, subject to paragraph 5, is not absent from the dwelling throughout the day;
(c)   in respect of whom a maximum council tax reduction amount can be calculated;
(d)   who does not fall within a class of person prescribed for the purposes of paragraph 2(9) of Schedule 1A to the 1992 Act as a class of person which must not be included in an authority's scheme;
(e)   who has made an application; and
(f)   in relation to whom the condition in sub-paragraph (2) is met.

(2)   The condition referred to in sub-paragraph (1)(f) is that no other resident of the dwelling is liable to pay rent to the applicant in respect of the dwelling and there is an alternative maximum council tax reduction in respect of the day in the case of that person which is derived from the income, or aggregate incomes, of one or more residents to whom this sub-paragraph applies.

(3)   Sub-paragraph (2) applies to any other resident of the dwelling who–
(a)   is not a person who, in accordance with Schedule 1 to the 1992 Act, falls to be disregarded for the purposes of discount;
(b)   is not a person who is liable for council tax solely in consequence of the provisions of section 9 of the 1992 Act (spouse's or civil partner's joint and several liability for tax);
(c)   is not a person who is residing with a couple or with the members of a polygamous marriage where the applicant is a member of that couple or of that marriage and–
     (i)   in the case of a couple, neither member of that couple is a person who, in accordance with Schedule 1 to the 1992 Act, falls to be disregarded for the purposes of discount; or
     (ii)   in the case of a polygamous marriage, two or more members of that marriage are not persons who, in accordance with Schedule 1 to the 1992 Act, fall to be disregarded for the purposes of discount;
(d)   is not a person who jointly with the applicant falls within the same paragraph of section 6(2)(a) to (e) of the 1992 Act (persons liable to pay council tax) as applies in the case of the applicant; or
(e)   is not a person who is residing with two or more persons both or all of whom fall within the same paragraph of section 6(2)(a) to (e) of the 1992 Act where two or more of those persons are not persons who, in accordance with Schedule 1 to the 1992 Act, fall to be disregarded for the purposes of discount.

General Note

This paragraph describes the rules for entitlement to alternative maximum CTR for pensioners, which must be included in the CTR scheme of each English authority. An authority is free to include alternative maximum CTR for people who are not pensioners in its scheme, but is not required to do so. Alternative maximum CTR is sometimes known as the "second adult rebate".

To understand whether a pensioner can qualify for alternative maximum CTR, it is necessary also to refer to para 9 and Sch 3. Note that if a pensioner falls within both Class C and either Class A or B, s/he is entitled to whichever is higher: the CTR s/he qualifies for under Class A or B, or the CTR s/he qualifies for under Class C: para 10(5) and (6). To fall within Class C, a pensioner must, in addition to satisfying the conditions in paras 4(1)(a) to (e) (for which see the commentary at the start of this Schedule), have at least one "second adult" residing with her/him. A "second adult" is someone to whom sub-para (2) applies, as defined by sub-para (3). Alternative maximum CTR takes the form of a percentage reduction in council tax and entitlement to it, and the amount of the percentage reduction, is dependent on the income of the second adult(s): para 9(1) and Sch 3. Para 4(3) restricts the categories of people who effectively count as "second adults" and whose income can be taken into account for para (2). So, for example, someone who is jointly and severally liable with the pensioner for the council tax for the dwelling under s6(2)(a)–(e) of the LGFA 1992 cannot count as a second adult for the purpose of sub-para (2): para 4(3)(d). The combined effect of ss6 and 9 of the LGFA 1992 and para 4(3)(a), (b) and (d) is that a spouse, civil partner or partner of the applicant who is resident in the same dwelling with her/him also cannot count as a second adult for the purpose of sub-para (2). Furthermore, if the pensioner is a member of a couple (see reg 4) someone residing with her/him and her/his/partner cannot count as a second adult unless the applicant or her/his partner is disregarded for the purpose of a council tax discount under Sch 1 LGFA 1992. For details of who else cannot count as a second adult for the purpose of sub-para (2), see sub-para (3).

A pensioner cannot qualify for alternative maximum CTR if another resident in the dwelling is liable to pay rent to her/him in respect of the dwelling: sub-para (2). This only applies to residents who fall within sub-para (3). If the pensioner is jointly and severally liable for the council tax for the dwelling, the amount of any alternative maximum CTR is divided by the number of people who are jointly and severally liable for the council tax: para 9(2), (each liable person is expected to make her/his own application for a share of the alternative maximum CTR). Note, however, that this does not apply if the pensioner is only jointly and severally liable with her/his spouse, civil partner or partner under s9 LGFA 1992: para 9(3). For additional commentary, see the similar provisions for Scotland: regs 14(6) and (7) and 79 CTR(S) Regs on p1475 and p1530.

Periods of absence from a dwelling

5.–(1)   A person is not absent from a dwelling in relation to any day which falls within a period of temporary absence from that dwelling.

(2)   In sub-paragraph (1), a "period of temporary absence" means–

(a)   a period of absence not exceeding 13 weeks, beginning with the first whole day on which a person resides in residential accommodation [¹ in Great Britain] where and for so long as–
   (i)   the person resides in that accommodation;
   (ii)   the part of the dwelling in which he usually resided is not let or sub-let; and
   (iii)   that period of absence does not form part of a longer period of absence from the dwelling of more than 52 weeks,

where he has entered the accommodation for the purpose of ascertaining whether it suits his needs and with the intention of returning to the dwelling if it proves not to suit his needs;

(b)   [¹ subject to sub-paragraph (2B), a period of absence within Great Britain] not exceeding 13 weeks, beginning with the first whole day of absence from the dwelling, where and for so long as–
   (i)   the person intends to return to the dwelling;
   (ii)   the part of the dwelling in which he usually resided is not let or sub-let; and
   (iii)   that period is unlikely to exceed 13 weeks; [¹]

(c)   [¹ subject to sub-paragrah (2D), a period of absence within Great Britain] not exceeding 52 weeks, beginning with the first whole day of that absence, where and for so long as–
   (i)   the person intends to return to the dwelling;
   (ii)   the part of the dwelling in which he usually resided is not let or sub-let;
   (iii)   the person is a person to whom sub-paragraph (3) applies; and
   (iv)   the period of absence is unlikely to exceed 52 weeks or, in exceptional circumstances, is unlikely substantially to exceed that period [¹ ; and

(d)   subject to sub-paragraphs (2F), (3C), (3E) and (3G) and where sub-paragraph (2E) applies, a period of absence outside Great Britain not exceeding 4 weeks, beginning with the first day of that absence from Great Britain and for so long as–
   (i)   the person intends to return to the dwelling;
   (ii)   the part of the dwelling in which he usually resides is not let or sub-let; and
   (iii)   the period of absence from Great Britain is unlikely to exceed 4 weeks.

(2A)   The period of 13 weeks referred to in sub-paragraph (2)(b) shall run or continue to run during any period of absence from Great Britain.

(2B)   Where–
(a)   a person returns to Great Britain after a period of absence from Great Britain (period A);
(b)   that person has been absent from the dwelling, including any absence within Great Britain, for less than 13 weeks beginning with the first day of absence from that dwelling; and
(c)   at the outset of, or during, period A, period A ceased to be treated as a period of temporary absence, then any day that follows period A and precedes the person's return to the dwelling, shall not be treated as a period of temporary absence under sub-paragraph (2)(b).

(2C)   The period of 52 weeks referred to in sub-paragraph (2)(c) shall run or continue to run during any period of absence from Great Britain.

(2D)   Where–
(a)   a person returns to Great Britain after a period of absence from Great Britain (period A);
(b)   that person has been absent from the dwelling, including any absence within Great Britain, for less than 52 weeks beginning with the first day of absence from that dwelling; and
(c)   at the outset of, or during, period A, period A ceased to be treated as a period of temporary absence, then any day that follows period A and precedes the person's return to the dwelling, shall not be treated as a period of temporary absence under sub-paragraph (2)(c).

(2E)   This sub-paragraph applies where–
(a)   a person is temporarily absent from Great Britain;
(b)   immediately before that period of absence from Great Britain, the person was not absent from the dwelling.
(2F)   If the temporary absence referred to in sub-paragraph (2)(d) is in connection with the death of–
(a)   the person's partner or a child or young person for whom the person or the person's partner is responsible;
(b)   the person's close relative;
(c)   the close relative of the person's partner; or
(d)   the close relative of a child or young person for whom the person or the person's partner is responsible,
         then the period of 4 weeks in the opening words of sub-paragraph (2)(d) may be extended by up to 4 further weeks if the relevant authority considers it unreasonable to expect the person to return to Great Britain within the first 4 weeks (and the reference in sub-paragraph (iii) of that paragraph to a period of 4 weeks shall, where the period is extended, be taken as referring to the period as so extended).]
(3)   This sub-paragraph applies to a person who–
[¹ (a) is a person to whom sub-paragraph (3A) applies;]
         (i)   in a dwelling, other than the dwelling referred to in sub-paragraph (1), or
         (ii)   in premises approved under section 13 of the Offender Management Act 2007,
         or is detained in custody pending sentence upon conviction;
(b)   is resident in a hospital or similar institution as a patient;
(c)   is undergoing, or whose partner or dependent child is undergoing [¹] medical treatment, or medically approved convalescence, in accommodation other than residential accommodation;
(d)   is following [¹] a training course;
(e)   is undertaking medically approved care of a person [¹];
(f)   is undertaking the care of a child whose parent or guardian is temporarily absent from the dwelling normally occupied by that parent or guardian for the purpose of receiving medically approved care or medical treatment;
(g)   is [¹] receiving medically approved care provided in accommodation other than residential accommodation;
(h)   is a student;
(i)   is receiving care provided in residential accommodation and is not a person to whom sub-paragraph (2)(a) applies; or
(j)   has left the dwelling he resides in through fear of violence, in that dwelling, or by a person who was formerly a member of the family of the person first mentioned.
[¹ (3A) This sub-paragraph applies to a person ("P") who is–
(a)   detained in custody on remand pending trial;
(b)   detained pending sentence upon conviction; or
(c)   as a condition of bail required to reside–
         (i)   in a dwelling, other than a dwelling P occupies as P's home; or
         (ii)   in premises approved under section 13 of the Offender Management Act 2007,
         and who is not also detained in custody following sentence upon conviction.
(3B)   This sub-paragraph applies where–
(a)   a person is temporarily absent from Great Britain;
(b)   the person is a member of Her Majesty's forces posted overseas, a mariner or a continental shelf worker;
(c)   immediately before that period of absence from Great Britain, the person was not absent from the dwelling.
(3C)   Where sub-paragraph (3B) applies, a period of absence from Great Britain not exceeding 26 weeks, beginning with the first day of absence from Great Britain, shall be treated as a period of temporary absence where and for so long as–
(a)   the person intends to return to the dwelling;
(b)   the part of the dwelling in which he usually resided is not let or sub-let;
(c)   the period of absence from Great Britain is unlikely to exceed 26 weeks.
(3D)   This sub-paragraph applies where–
(a)   a person is temporarily absent from Great Britain;
(b)   the person is a person described in any of paragraphs (b), (c), (g) or (j) of sub-paragraph (3);
(c)   immediately before that period of absence from Great Britain, the person was not absent from the dwelling.
(3E)   Where sub-paragraph (3D) applies, a period of absence from Great Britain not exceeding 26 weeks, beginning with the first day of absence from Great Britain, shall be treated as a period of temporary absence where and for so long as–
(a)   the person intends to return to the dwelling;
(b)   the part of the dwelling in which he usually resided is not let or sub-let;
(c)   the period of absence is unlikely to exceed 26 weeks, or in exceptional circumstances, is unlikely substantially to exceed that period.

(3F)   This sub-paragraph applies where–
(a)   a person is temporarily absent from Great Britain;
(b)   the person is a person described in any of paragraphs (a), (d), (e), (f), (h) or (i) of sub-paragraph (3);
(c)   immediately before that period of absence from Great Britain, the person was not absent from the dwelling.
(3G)   Where sub-paragraph (3F) applies, a period of absence from Great Britain not exceeding 4 weeks, beginning with the first day of absence from Great Britain, shall be treated as a period of temporary absence where and for so long as–
(a)   the person intends to return to the dwelling;
(b)   the part of the dwelling in which he usually resided is not let or sub-let;
(c)   the period of absence is unlikely to exceed 4 weeks, or in exceptional circumstances, is unlikely substantially to exceed that period.]
(4)   This sub-paragraph applies to a person who is–
(a)   detained in custody pending sentence upon conviction or under a sentence imposed by a court (other than a person who is detained in hospital under the provisions of the Mental Health Act 1983, or, in Scotland, under the provisions of the Mental Health (Care and Treatment) (Scotland) Act 2003 or the Criminal Procedure (Scotland) Act 1995 or in Northern Ireland under Article 4 or 12 of the Mental Health (Northern Ireland) Order 1986); and
(b)   on temporary release from detention in accordance with Rules made under the provisions of the Prison Act 1952 or the Prisons (Scotland) Act 1989.
(5)   Where sub-paragraph (4) applies to a person, then, for any day when he is on temporary release–
(a)   if such temporary release was immediately preceded by a period of temporary absence under sub-paragraph (2)(b) or (c), he must be treated, for the purposes of sub-paragraph (1), as if he continues to be absent from the dwelling, despite any return to the dwelling;
(b)   for the purposes of sub-paragraph (3)(a), he must be treated as if he remains in detention;
(c)   if he does not fall within paragraph (a), he is not to be considered to be a person who is liable to pay council tax in respect of a dwelling of which he is a resident.
(6)   In this paragraph–
[¹ "continental shelf worker" means a person who is employed, whether under a contract of service or not, in a designated area or a prescribed area in connection with any of the activities mentioned in section 11(2) of the Petroleum Act 1998;
"designated area" means any area which may from time to time be designated by Order in Council under the Continental Shelf Act 1964 as an area within which the rights of the United Kingdom with respect to the seabed and subsoil and their natural resources may be exercised;
"mariner" means a person who is employed under a contract of service either as a master or member of the crew of any ship or vessel, or in any other capacity on board any ship or vessel, where–
(a)   the employment in that capacity is for the purposes of that ship or vessel or its crew or any passengers or cargo or mails carried by the ship or vessel; and
(b)   the contract is entered into in the United Kingdom with a view to its performance (in whole or in part) while the ship or vessel is on its voyage;]
"medically approved" means certified by a medical practitioner;
[¹ "member of Her Majesty's forces posted overseas" means a person who is a member of the regular forces or the reserve forces (within the meaning of section 374 of the Armed Forces Act 2006), who is absent from the main dwelling because the person has been posted outside of Great Britain to perform the duties of a member of Her Maesty's regular forces or reserve forces;]
"patient" means a person who is undergoing medical or other treatment as an in-patient in any hospital or similar institution;
[¹ "prescribed area" means any area over which Norway or any member State (other than the United Kingdom) exercises sovereign rights for the purpose of exploring the seabed and subsoil and exploiting their natural resources, being an area outside the territorial sea of Norway or such member State, or any other area which is from time to time specified under section 10(8) of the Petroleum Act 1998;]
"residential accommodation" means accommodation which is provided in–
(a)   a care home;
(b)   an independent hospital;
(c)   an Abbeyfield Home; or
(d)   an establishment managed or provided by a body incorporated by Royal Charter or constituted by Act of Parliament other than a local social services authority;
"training course" means a course of training or instruction provided wholly or partly by or on behalf of or in pursuance of arrangements made with, or approved by or on behalf of, Skills Development Scotland, Scottish Enterprise, Highlands and Islands Enterprise, a government department or the Secretary of State.

Amendment
1.   Amended by reg 2(3)(a) of SI 2016 No 1262 as from 15.1.17, in relation to schemes made for financial years starting on or after 1.4.17, subject to transitional provision in reg 3.

General Note

To come within one of the classes of people who must be entitled to CTR on any day under an authority's scheme, an applicant must not be absent from home throughout that day. However, in accordance with this paragraph, days of absence that fall within "a period of temporary absence" must be ignored. Subject to the transitional provision in reg 3 of SI 2016 No.1262, "a period of temporary absence" is defined in sub-para (2) and means, for example, that if the specified conditions are met, periods of up to 4, 13 or 52 weeks' absence can be ignored. In some but not all respects, this is similar to the provisions in reg 7(11), (13), (13A)–(13(G), (14), (15) and (16) HB regs – see the commentary on p263 for a discussion of some of the terms that are common to both this regulation and reg 7 HB Regs, but note that for CTR the period of temporary absence begins on the first whole day of absence, and the rules relate to the dwelling in which an applicant usually resides rather than normally occupies.

PART 2

Applicable amounts for the purposes of calculating eligibility for a reduction under an authority's scheme and amount of reduction

---

Applicable amounts

6.–(1) The applicable amount for a pensioner for a week is the aggregate of such of the following amounts as apply in his case–

(a) an amount in respect of his personal allowance, determined in accordance with paragraph 1 of Schedule 2 to these Regulations;

[² (b) an amount determined in accordance with paragraph 2 of that Schedule in respect of up to two individuals who are either children or young persons and who are members of his family;]

(c) if he is a member of a family of which at least one member is a child or young person, an amount determined in accordance with paragraph 3 of that Schedule (family premium);

(d) the amount of any premiums which may be applicable to him, determined in accordance with Parts 3 and 4 of that Schedule (premiums).

[² (1A) For the purposes of sub-paragraph (1)(b) as it applies apart from sub-paragraph (1C), where the family includes more than two individuals who are either children or young persons and under paragraph 2 of that Schedule a different amount applies to different individuals, the two amounts to be included in the applicable amount shall be those that result in the greatest possible total amount.

(1B) Sub-paragraph (1C) applies where–

(a) (whether or not as part of a tax credit couple as defined in section 3(5A) of the Tax Credits Act 2002) the applicant has an award of child tax credit (whether or not any amount is payable by way of such credit) in respect of a child or young person who is a member of his family; and

(b) the total amount to be included in the applicable amount under sub-paragraph (1)(b) as substituted by sub-paragraph (1C) would be higher than the total amount that would be included under paragraph (1)(b) apart from sub-paragraph (1C).

(1C) Where this paragraph applies, for sub-paragraph (1)(b) substitute–

(b) an amount determined in accordance with paragraph 2 of that Schedule in respect of any child or young person who is a member of his family and in respect of whom the individual element of child tax credit has been included in the determination of the maximum rate of that credit;]

(2) In Schedule 2–

[² "additional spouse" means a spouse of either party to the marriage who is additional to the other party to the marriage;]

"patient" means a person (other than a person who is serving a sentence of imprisonment or detention in a youth custody institution) who is regarded as receiving free in-patient treatment within the meaning of regulation 2(4) and (5) of the Social Security (Hospital In-Patients) Regulations 2005.

Amendments

1. Amended by reg 2(7)(b) of SI 2013 No 3181 in relation to schemes made for financial years beginning on or after 1.4.14.

2. Amended by reg 7 of SI 2017 No 1305 as from 12.1.18, in relation to schemes made for financial years starting on or after 1.4.18 and subject to transitional provisions in reg 17.

General Note

This paragraph is broadly equivalent to reg 22 HB(SPC) Regs. See p765 for commentary.

Sub-para 1(b).

A child allowance is included for each child (we use the term "child" to cover both a child under 16 and a young person of 16 or over who meets the definition of "young person" in reg 2) who is a member of a pensioner applicant's family (for which see reg 6). However, for tax years from 1 April 2018, subject to the exceptions described below, the maximum number of child allowances that can be included in the applicable amount is limited to two. This is known as the "two-child limit". The exceptions to the two-child limit apply if:

(1) an applicant has an award of child tax credit (CTC) in respect of a child who is a member of the applicant's family (whether or not CTC is actually payable). In such circumstances, a child allowance can be included

in the applicable amount for CTR for each child for whom a child element is included in the assessment of maximum CTC, if this would result in a higher amount than would otherwise be paid under sub-para (1)(b): paras (1B) and (1C). CTC can be awarded for three or more children in certain circumstances. However, it is now only possible to make a new claim for CTC in limited circumstances. Note that the Court of Appeal dismissed an appeal against the High Court's decision in *SC & Ors v SSWP & Ors* [2018] EWHC 864 (Admin), determining that the High Court was correct to hold that the imposition of a two-child limit in CTC and UC is not incompatible with the claimants' rights under Arts 8, 12 or 14 of the ECHR: *SC & Ors v SSWP & Ors* [2019] EWCA Civ 615. See p412 for commentary;

(2)   a pensioner's liability to pay council tax was reduced by entitlement to CTR on 31 March 2018 and s/he has not made a new application for CTR since that date. However, even in this circumstance, a third or subsequent child allowance will not be included in the applicable amount for any child who becomes a member of the applicant's household after 31 March 2018, unless the exception in the above para (1) applies: reg 17 of SI 2017 No.1305.

The wording of sub-para 1(b) is similar to reg 22(1)(b) HB Regs (for which see p411 and the commentary that follows it) and the wording of the transitional provisions in reg 17 of SI 2017 No.1305 (p1188) is similar to reg 9 of SI 2017 No.376 (for which see p1894).

Sub-para (1)(c). This sub-para refers to the circumstances in which a family premium can be included in a pensioner's applicable amount, but for reduction weeks starting on or after 2 May 2016, the family premium is nil, unless an applicant is covered by the transitional provision in reg 3 of the Council Tax Reduction Schemes (Prescribed Requirements) (England) (Amendment) Regulations 2015 No.2041 (see the commentary on of Sch 2 para 3 on p1158).

PART 3

Maximum council tax reduction for the purposes of calculating eligibility for a reduction under an authority's scheme and amount of reduction

---

Maximum council tax reduction amount under an authority's scheme

7.–(1)   Subject to sub-paragraphs (2) to (4), a person's maximum council tax reduction amount in respect of a day is 100 per cent of the amount A/B where–

(a)   A is the amount set by the authority as the council tax for the relevant financial year in respect of the dwelling in which he is a resident and for which he is liable, subject to any discount which may be appropriate to that dwelling under the 1992 Act; and

(b)   B is the number of days in that financial year,

less any deductions in respect of non-dependants which fall to be made under paragraph 8 (non-dependant deductions).

(2)   In calculating a person's maximum council tax reduction under the authority's scheme any reduction in the amount that person is liable to pay in respect of council tax, which is made in consequence of any enactment in, or made under, the 1992 Act (other than a reduction under that authority's scheme), is to be taken into account.

(3)   Subject to sub-paragraph (4), where an applicant is jointly and severally liable for council tax in respect of a dwelling in which he is resident with one or more other persons in determining the maximum council tax reduction in his case in accordance with sub-paragraph (1), the amount A is to be divided by the number of persons who are jointly and severally liable for that tax.

(4)   Where an applicant is jointly and severally liable for council tax in respect of a dwelling with only his partner, sub-paragraph (3) does not apply in his case.

(5)   The reference in sub-paragraph (3) to a person with whom an applicant is jointly and severally liable for council tax does not include a student to whom paragraph 75(1) of the Schedule to the Default Scheme Regulations applies.

(6)   In this paragraph "relevant financial year" means, in relation to any particular day, the financial year within which the day in question falls.

General Note

Although it is structured slightly differently, this paragraph is similar to reg 66 CTR(S) Regs. See p1522 for commentary.

Non-dependant deductions

8.–(1)   Subject to the following provisions of this paragraph, the non-dependant deductions in respect of a day referred to in paragraph 7 are–

(a)   in respect of a non-dependant aged 18 or over in remunerative work, [⁹ £12.20] 1/7;

(b)   in respect of a non-dependant aged 18 or over to whom paragraph (a) does not apply, [⁹ £4.00] 1/7.

(2)   In the case of a non-dependant aged 18 or over to whom sub-paragraph (1)(a) applies, where it is shown to the appropriate authority that his normal gross weekly income is–

(a)   less than [⁹ £207.70] the deduction to be made under this paragraph is that specified in sub-paragraph (1)(b);

(b)   not less than [⁹ £207.70] but less than [⁹ £360.10], the deduction to be made under this paragraph is [⁹ £8.10 x 1/7];

(c)   not less than [⁹ £360.10] but less than [⁹ £447.40], the deduction to be made under this paragraph is [⁹ £10.20 x 1/7].

(3)   Only one deduction is to be made under this paragraph in respect of a couple or, as the case may be, members of a polygamous marriage and, where, but for this paragraph, the amount that would fall to be deducted in respect of one member of a couple or polygamous marriage is higher than the amount (if any) that would fall to be deducted in respect of the other, or any other, member, the higher amount shall be deducted.

(4)   In applying the provisions of sub-paragraph (2) in the case of a couple or, as the case may be, a polygamous marriage, regard must be had, for the purpose of that sub-paragraph, to the couple's or, as the case may be, all members of the polygamous marriage's joint weekly gross income.

(5)   Where in respect of a day–

(a)   a person is a resident in a dwelling but is not himself liable for council tax in respect of that dwelling and that day;

(b)   other residents in that dwelling (the liable persons) have joint and several liability for council tax in respect of that dwelling and that day otherwise than by virtue of section 9 of the 1992 Act (liability of spouses and civil partners); and

(c)   the person to whom paragraph (a) refers is a non-dependant of two or more of the liable persons, the deduction in respect of that non-dependant must be apportioned equally between those liable persons.

(6)   No deduction is to be made in respect of any non-dependants occupying an applicant's dwelling if the applicant or his partner is–

(a)   [⁴ severely sight-impaired or] blind or treated as [⁴ such] by virtue of sub-paragraphs (12) or (13) below; or

(b)   receiving in respect of himself either–

    (i)   attendance allowance, or would be receiving that allowance but for–

        (aa)   a suspension of benefit in accordance with regulations under section 113(2) of the SSCBA; or

        (bb)   an abatement as a result of hospitalisation; or

    (ii)   the care component of the disability living allowance, or would be receiving that component, but for–

        (aa)   a suspension of benefit in accordance with regulations under section 113(2) of the SSCBA; or

        (bb)   an abatement as a result of hospitalisation; or

    (iii)   the daily living component of personal independence payment, or would be receiving that allowance but for a suspension of benefit in accordance with regulations under section 86 of the Welfare Reform Act 2012 (hospital in-patients); or

    (iv)   an AFIP, or would be receiving that payment but for a suspension of it in accordance with any terms of the armed and reserve forces compensation scheme which allow for a suspension because a person is undergoing medical treatment in a hospital or similar institution.

(7)   No deduction is to be made in respect of a non-dependant if–

(a)   although he resides with the applicant, it appears to the authority that his normal home is elsewhere; or

(b)   he is in receipt of a training allowance paid in connection with youth training established under section 2 of the Employment and Training Act 1973 or section 2 of the Enterprise and New Towns (Scotland) Act 1990; or

(c)   he is a full-time student within the meaning of Part 11 of the Schedule to the Default Scheme Regulations (students); or

(d)   he is not residing with the applicant because he has been a patient for a period in excess of 52 weeks, and for these purposes–

    (i)   "patient" has the meaning given in paragraph 5(6) of this Schedule, and

    (ii)   where a person has been a patient for two or more distinct periods separated by one or more intervals each not exceeding 28 days, he is to be treated as having been a patient continuously for a period equal in duration to the total of those distinct periods.

[² (e)   he is not residing with the applicant because he is a member of the regular forces or the reserve forces (within the meaning of section 374 of the Armed Forces Act 2006) who is absent, while on operations, from the dwelling usually occupied as their home.]

(8)   No deduction is to be made in respect of a non-dependant–

(a)   who is on income support, state pension credit, an income-based jobseeker's allowance or an income-related employment and support allowance; [³]

(b)   to whom Schedule 1 to the 1992 Act applies (persons disregarded for purposes of discount) but this paragraph does not apply to a non-dependant who is a student to whom paragraph 4 of that Schedule refers.[³ ; or]

[³ (c) who is entitled to an award of universal credit where the award is calculated on the basis that the person does not have any earned income.]

(9)   In the application of sub-paragraph (2) there is to be disregarded from the non-dependent's weekly gross income–

(a)   any attendance allowance, disability living allowance, personal independence payment or AFIP received by him;

(b)   any payment made under or by the Trusts, the Fund, the Eileen Trust, MFET Limited, the Skipton Fund, the Caxton Foundation [⁸, the Scottish Infected Blood Support Scheme, an approved blood scheme, the London Emergencies Trust, the We Love Manchester Emergency Fund] or the Independent Living Fund (2006) which are paid as income in kind (see sub-paragraph (13)); and

(c)   the payments set out in sub-paragraph (10).

(10)   The payments mentioned in sub-paragraph (9) are–

(a)   any payment made under or by the Trusts, the Fund, the Eileen Trust, MFET Limited, the Skipton Fund, the Caxton Foundation [⁸ the Scottish Infected Blood Support Scheme, an approved blood scheme, the London Emergencies Trust, the We Love Manchester Emergency Fund]or the Independent Living Fund (2006);

(b)   any payment by or on behalf of a person who is suffering or who suffered from haemophilia or who is or was a qualifying person, which derives from a payment made under or by any of the Trusts to which paragraph (a) refers and which is made to or for the benefit of–

(i)   that person's partner or former partner from whom he is not, or where that person has died was not, estranged or divorced or with whom he has formed a civil partnership that has not been dissolved or, where that person has died, had not been dissolved at the time of that person's death;

(ii)   any child who is a member of that person's family or who was such a member and who is a member of the applicant's family; or

(iii)   any young person who is a member of that person's family or who was such a member and who is a member of the applicant's family;

(c)   any payment by or on behalf of the partner or former partner of a person who is suffering or who suffered from haemophilia or who is or was a qualifying person provided that the partner or former partner and that person are not, or if either of them has died were not, estranged or divorced or, where the partner or former partner and that person have formed a civil partnership, the civil partnership has not been dissolved or, if either of them has died, had not been dissolved at the time of the death, which derives from a payment made under or by any of the Trusts to which paragraph (a) refers and which is made to or for the benefit of–

(i)   the person who is suffering from haemophilia or who is a qualifying person;

(ii)   any child who is a member of that person's family or who was such a member and who is a member of the applicant's family; or

(iii)   any young person who is a member of that person's family or who was such a member and who is a member of the applicant's family;

(d)   any payment by a person who is suffering from haemophilia or who is a qualifying person, which derives from a payment under or by any of the Trusts to which paragraph (a) refers, where–

(i)   that person has no partner or former partner from whom he is not estranged or divorced or with whom he has formed a civil partnership that has not been dissolved, nor any child or young person who is or had been a member of that person's family; and

(ii)   the payment is made either–

(aa)   to that person's parent or step-parent, or

(bb)   where that person at the date of the payment is a child, a young person or a student who has not completed his full-time education and has no parent or step-parent, to his guardian,

but only for a period from the date of the payment until the end of two years from that person's death;

(e)   any payment out of the estate of a person who suffered from haemophilia or who was a qualifying person, which derives from a payment under or by any of the Trusts to which paragraph (a) refers, where–

(i)   that person at the date of his death (the relevant date) had no partner or former partner from whom he was not estranged or divorced or with whom he has formed a civil partnership that has not been dissolved, nor any child or young person who was or had been a member of his family; and

(ii)   the payment is made either–

(aa)   to that person's parent or step-parent, or

(bb)   where that person at the relevant date was a child, a young person or a student who had not completed his full-time education and had no parent or step-parent, to his guardian,

but only for a period of two years from the relevant date;

(f)   in the case of a person to whom or for whose benefit a payment referred to in this sub-paragraph is made, any income which derives from any payment of income or capital made under or deriving from any of the Trusts.

[⁸ (g)   any payment made under, or by, a trust which is approved by the Secretary of State and which is established for the purpose of giving relief and assistance to a disabled person whose disability was caused by their mother having taken a preparation containing the drug known as Thalidomide during her pregnancy.]

[⁴ (11)   An applicant or his partner is severely sight-impaired or blind or treated as such for the purposes of sub-paragraph (6)(a) if the applicant or his partner–

[⁶ (a)   is registered as severely sight-impaired in a register kept by a local authority in Wales under section 18(1) of the Social Services and Well-being (Wales) Act 2014;] or

(b)   is registered as severely sight-impaired in a register kept by a local authority in England under section 77(1) of the Care Act 2014 (registers of sight-impaired adults); or

(c)   in Scotland, has been certified as blind and in consequence he is registered in a register maintained by or on behalf of a council constituted under section 2 of the Local Government (Scotland) Act 1994.]

[³ (11A)   For the purposes of sub-paragraph (8), "earned income" has the meaning given in regulation 52 of the Universal Credit Regulations 2013.]

(12)   For the purposes of sub-paragraph (11), a person who has ceased to be registered as [⁵ severely sight-impaired or] blind on regaining his eyesight is nevertheless to be treated as [⁵ such] for a period of 28 weeks following the date on which he ceased to be so registered.

(13)   The reference in sub-paragraph (9)(b) to "income in kind" does not include a payment to a third party made in respect of the applicant which is used by the third party to provide benefits in kind to the applicant.

Amendments

1.   Amended by reg 3 of SI 2012 No 3085 as from 10.1.13.
2.   Amended by reg 2(7)(c) of SI 2013 No 3181 for schemes for financial years beginning on or after 1.4.14.
3.   Amended by reg 2(5)(a) of SI 2014 No 3312 as from 12.1.15, in relation to schemes made for financial years starting on or after 1.4.15.
4.   Amended by art 2 and Sch para 36(2) of SI 2015 No 643 as from 1.4.15.
5.   Amended by reg 2(3)(a) of SI 2015 No 2041 as from 14.1.16, in relation to schemes made for financial years starting on or after 1.4.16.
6.   Substituted by Sch 3 para 135(2) of SI 2016 No 211 (W.84) as from 6.4.16.
7.   Amended by reg 2(3)(b) of SI 2016 No 1262 as from 15.1.17, in relation to schemes made for financial years starting on or after 1.4.17,
8.   Amended by reg 8 of SI 2017 No 1305 as from 12.1.18, in relation to schemes made for financial years starting on or after 1.4.18.
9.   Amended by reg 3(a) of SI 2018 No 1346 as from 14.1.19, in relation to schemes made for financial years starting on or after 1.4.19.

General Note

This paragraph gives the amounts of any non-dependant deductions that fall to be made from a pensioner applicant's daily liability for council tax for a dwelling in which s/he is resident when calculating her/his 'maximum CTR' under para 7. If the applicant or her/his partner satisfy the conditions in sub-para 8(6), no non-dependant deduction is made. In relation to sub-para 8(6)(a), see sub-para 8(11) and (12) for provisions relating to who counts as severely sight impaired or who can be treated as such (it appears that the reference in sub-para (8)(6)(a) to sub-para (13) may be a drafting error). Also, no non-dependant deduction is made for any non-dependant that comes within sub-para (7) or to whom sub-para (8) applies. For who counts as a non-dependant, see reg 9.

Paragraph 8 is similar to reg 67 CTR(S) Regs (for commentary, see p1524) and reg 74 HB Regs (for commentary, see p519). However, for pensioners in England, no non-dependant deduction is made if payment of any of the benefits specified in para 8(b) are suspended because the applicant is an in-patient in a hospital or similar institution or, in respect of AA and DLA, is abated because of hospitalisation.

The income disregarded in reg 67(9)(c) CTR(S) Regs and 74(9)(c) HB Regs is broadly equivalent to that covered in sub-para (10) of this paragraph.

PART 4

Alternative maximum council tax reduction for the purposes of calculating eligibility for a reduction under an authority's scheme and amount of reduction

Alternative maximum council tax reduction under a scheme

9.–(1)   Subject to sub-paragraphs (2) and (3), the alternative maximum council tax reduction in respect of a day where the conditions set out in paragraph 4 (alternative maximum council tax reduction) are fulfilled, is the amount determined in accordance with Schedule 3 (amount of alternative maximum council tax reduction).

(2)   Subject to sub-paragraph (3), where an applicant is jointly and severally liable for council tax in respect of a dwelling in which he is resident with one or more other persons, in determining the alternative maximum council tax reduction in his case, the amount determined in accordance with Schedule 3 must be divided by the number of persons who are jointly and severally liable for that tax.

(3)   Where an applicant is jointly and severally liable for council tax in respect of a dwelling with only his partner, solely by virtue of section 9 of the 1992 Act (liability of spouses and civil partners), sub-paragraph (2) does not apply in his case.

General Note
This is equivalent to reg 78 CTR(S) Regs. See the analysis of that regulation on p1529.

PART 5
Amount of reduction under an authority's scheme

Amount of reduction under a scheme: classes A to C
10.–(1)   Where a person is entitled to a reduction under an authority's scheme in respect of a day, the amount of the reduction to which he is entitled is as follows.
(2)   Where the person is within class A, that amount is the maximum council tax reduction amount in respect of the day in the applicant's case.
(3)   Where the person is within class B, that amount is the amount found by deducting amount B from amount A, where "amount A" and "amount B" have the meanings given in paragraph 3 (income greater than applicable amount).
(4)   Where the person is within class C, that amount is the amount which is the alternative maximum council tax reduction in respect of the day in the applicant's case.
(5)   Sub-paragraph (6) applies where both–
(a)   sub-paragraph (2) or sub-paragraph (3), and
(b)   sub-paragraph (4),
apply to a person.
(6)   The amount of the reduction to which he is entitled is whichever is the greater of–
(a)   the amount of the reduction given by sub-paragraph (2) or sub-paragraph (3), as the case may be, and
(b)   the amount of the reduction given by sub-paragraph (4).

General Note
This sets out how the amount of CTR should be calculated. If an applicant falls within Class A (those covered by para 2), the amount of CTR in respect of a day is the "maximum CTR amount" for that day. For how the maximum CTR amount is calculated, see para 7. If an applicant falls within Class B, the amount of CTR s/he qualifies for is obtained by deducting the percentage difference (as defined in para 3(f)(ii)) between her/his income for the week in which the day falls and her/his applicable amount (Amount B) from her/his maximum CTR for the day (Amount A). If the applicant falls within Class C, the amount of CTR in respect of a day is the amount of the alternative maximum CTR for that day (for the amount of alternative maximum CTR, see para 9 and Sch 3).
    If an applicant falls within both Class C and either Class A or B, s/he is entitled to whichever is higher: the CTR s/he qualifies for under Class A or B, or the CTR s/he qualifies for under Class C: sub-paras (5) and (6).

PART 6
Income and capital for the purposes of calculating eligibility for a reduction under an authority's scheme and amount of reduction
CHAPTER 1
General

Calculation of income and capital: applicant's family and polygamous marriages
11.–(1)   The income and capital of–
(a)   an applicant; and
(b)   any partner of that applicant,
is to be calculated in accordance with the provisions of this Part.
(2)   The income and capital of any partner of the applicant is to be treated as income and capital of the applicant, and in this Part any reference to the applicant applies equally to any partner of the applicant.
(3)   Where an applicant or the partner of an applicant is married polygamously to two or more members of his household–
(a)   the applicant must be treated as possessing capital and income belonging to each such member; and
(b)   the income and capital of that member must be calculated in accordance with the following provisions of this Part in like manner as for the applicant.

General Note
If an applicant has a partner (for definition see regs 2 and 4), s/he is treated as possessing the income and capital of her/his partner in addition her/his own. Any reference to the applicant's income and capital in this Part is to be read as including that of her/his partner. If an applicant is polygamously married, s/he is treated as possessing the income and capital of all the partners in the marriage with whom she shares a household (sub-para (3)).
    See p17 for a discussion of caselaw concerning membership of a household.

Circumstances in which income and capital of non-dependant is to be treated as applicant's
12.–(1)   Sub-paragraph (2) applies where it appears to an authority that a non-dependant and an applicant have entered into arrangements in order to take advantage of the authority's scheme and the non-dependant has more income and capital than the applicant.

(2)   Except where the applicant is on a guarantee credit the authority must treat the applicant as possessing income and capital belonging to that non-dependant and, in such a case, any income and capital which the applicant does possess must be disregarded.

(3)   Where an applicant is treated as possessing income and capital belonging to a non-dependant under sub-paragraph (2) the income and capital of that non-dependant must be calculated in accordance with the following provisions of this Part in like manner as for the applicant and, except where the context otherwise requires, any reference to the "applicant" is to be construed for the purposes of this Part as if it were a reference to that non-dependant.

General Note

This is similar to reg 26 HB Regs and reg 24 HB(SPC) Regs. See the commentary on reg 26 HB Regs for analysis (p422) but note that under this paragraph a non-dependant's income and capital cannot be treated as the income and capital of the applicant if the applicant is on guarantee credit of PC (the same exception for people on IS, income-based JSA or income-related ESA contained in reg 26 HB Regs does not apply here as, under these regulations, s/he would not count as a pensioner).

CHAPTER 2
Income

Applicant in receipt of guarantee credit

13.   In the case of an applicant who is in receipt, or whose partner is in receipt, of a guarantee credit, the whole of his capital and income must be disregarded.

Calculation of applicant's income in savings credit only cases

14.–(1)   In determining the income and capital of an applicant who has, or whose partner has, an award of state pension credit comprising only the savings credit, subject to the following provisions of this paragraph, an authority must use the calculation or estimate of the applicant's or as the case may be, the applicant's partner's income and capital made by the Secretary of State for the purpose of determining the award of state pension credit.

(2)   Where the calculation or estimate provided by the Secretary of State includes the amount taken into account in that determination in respect of net income, the authority may only adjust that amount so far as necessary to take into account–

(a)   the amount of any savings credit payable;

(b)   in respect of any dependent children of the applicant, child care charges taken into account under paragraph 24(1)(c) (calculation of income on a weekly basis);

(c)   the higher amount disregarded under this Schedule in respect of–

    (i)   lone parent's earnings; or

    (ii)   payments of maintenance, whether under a court order or not, which are made or due to be made by–

        (aa)   the applicant's former partner, or the applicant's partner's former partner; or

        (bb)   he parent of a child or young person where that child or young person is a member of the applicant's family except where that parent is the applicant or the applicant's partner;

(d)   any amount to be disregarded by virtue of paragraph 10(1) of Schedule 4 (sums disregarded from earnings);

(e)   the income and capital of any partner of the applicant who is treated as a member of the applicant's household under regulation 8, to the extent that it is not taken into account in determining the net income of the person claiming state pension credit;

(f)   paragraph 12 (circumstances in which income of a non-dependant is to be treated as applicant's), if the authority determines that that provision applies in the applicant's case;

(g)   such further reduction (if any) as the authority thinks fit under section 13A(1)(c) of the 1992 Act;

(h)   any amount to be disregarded by virtue of paragraph 6 of Schedule 4.

(3)   Paragraphs 16 to 36 of this Schedule do not apply to the amount of the net income to be taken into account under sub-paragraph (1), but do apply (so far as relevant) for the purpose of determining any adjustments to that amount which the authority makes under sub-paragraph (2).

(4)   If sub-paragraph (5) applies, the authority must calculate the applicant's capital in accordance with paragraphs 31 to 36 of this Schedule.

(5)   This sub-paragraph applies if–

(a)   the Secretary of State notifies the authority that the applicant's capital has been determined as being £16,000 or less;

(b)   subsequent to that determination the applicant's capital rises to more than £16,000; and

(c)   the increase occurs whilst there is in force an assessed income period within the meaning of sections 6 and 9 of the State Pension Credit Act 2002.

General Note

This is similar to reg 27 HB(SPC) regs. See p767 for the commentary.

Calculation of income and capital where state pension credit is not payable

    15.   Where neither paragraph 13 (applicant in receipt of guarantee credit) nor 14 (calculation of income in savings credit only cases) applies in the applicant's case, his income and capital is to be calculated or estimated in accordance with paragraphs 16 to 21, 24, 25, 27 to 29 and chapter 3 (capital) of this Part.

Meaning of "income"

    16.–(1)   For the purposes of classes A to C, "income" means income of any of the following descriptions–
- (a)   earnings;
- (b)   working tax credit;
- (c)   retirement pension income within the meaning of the State Pension Credit Act 2002;
- (d)   income from annuity contracts (other than retirement pension income);
- (e)   a war disablement pension or war widow's or widower's pension;
- (f)   a foreign war disablement pension or war widow's or widower's pension;
- (g)   a guaranteed income payment;
- (h)   a payment made under article 29(1)(c) of the Armed Forces and Reserve Forces (Compensation Scheme) Order 2011, in any case where article 31(2)(c) applies;
- (i)   income from capital other than capital disregarded under Part 1 of Schedule 6 (capital disregards);
- (j)   social security benefits, other than retirement pension income or any of the following benefits–
  - (i)   disability living allowance;
  - (ii)   personal independence payment;
  - (iii)   an AFIP;
  - (iv)   attendance allowance payable under section 64 of the SSCBA;
  - (v)   an increase of disablement pension under section 104 or 105 of that Act;
  - (vi)   child benefit;
  - (vii)   any guardian's allowance payable under section 77 of the SSCBA;
  - (viii)   any increase for a dependant, other than the applicant's partner, payable in accordance with Part 4 of that Act;
  - (ix)   any–
    - (aa)   social fund payment made under Part 8 of that Act, or
    - (bb)   occasional assistance;
  - (x)   Christmas bonus payable under Part 10 of that Act;
  - (xi)   housing benefit;
  - (xii)   council tax benefit;
  - [³ (xiii) bereavement support payment under section 30 of the Pensions Act 2014;]
  - (xiv)   statutory sick pay;
  - (xv)   statutory maternity pay;
  - (xvi)   [²] statutory paternity pay payable under Part 12ZA of the SSCBA;
  - [¹ (xvia) statutory shared parental pay under Part 12ZC of that Act;]
  - [² (xvii)]
  - (xviii)   statutory adoption pay payable under Part 12ZB of that Act;
  - (xix)   any benefit similar to those mentioned in the preceding provisions of this paragraph payable under legislation having effect in Northern Ireland;
  - [⁵ (xx) carer's allowance supplement payable under section 81 of the Social Security (Scotland) Act 2018;]
- (k)   all foreign social security benefits which are similar to the social security benefits mentioned above;
- (l)   a payment made–
  - (i)   under article 30 of the Naval, Military and Air Forces Etc (Disablement and Death) Service Pensions Order 2006, in any case where article 30(1)(b) applies; or
  - (ii)   under article 12(8) of that Order, in any case where sub-paragraph (b) of that article applies;
- [⁴ (m)   a pension paid by a government to victims of National Socialist persecution ;]
- (n)   payments under a scheme made under the Pneumoconiosis etc (Workers' Compensation) Act 1979;
- (o)   payments made towards the maintenance of the applicant by his spouse, civil partner, former spouse or former civil partner or towards the maintenance of the applicant's partner by his spouse, civil partner, former spouse or former civil partner, including payments made–
  - (i)   under a court order;
  - (ii)   under an agreement for maintenance; or
  - (iii)   voluntarily;
- (p)   payments due from any person in respect of board and lodging accommodation provided by the applicant;
- (q)   royalties or other sums paid as a consideration for the use of, or the right to use, any copyright, design, patent or trade mark;
- (r)   any payment in respect of any–
  - (i)   book registered under the Public Lending Right Scheme 1982; or
  - (ii)   work made under any international public lending right scheme that is analogous to the Public Lending Right Scheme 1982;

(s)   any payment, other than a payment ordered by a court or made in settlement of a claim, made by or on behalf of a former employer of a person on account of the early retirement of that person on grounds of ill-health or disability;

(t)   any sum payable by way of pension out of money provided under–
  (i)   the Civil List Act 1837,
  (ii)   the Civil List Act 1937,
  (iii) the Civil List Act 1952,
  (iv)   the Civil List Act 1972, or
  (v)   the Civil List Act 1975;

(u)   any income in lieu of that specified in paragraphs (a) to (r);

(v)   any payment of rent made to an applicant who–
  (i)   owns the freehold or leasehold interest in any property or is a tenant of any property;
  (ii)   occupies part of the property; and
  (iii) has an agreement with another person allowing that person to occupy that property on payment of rent;

(w)   any payment made at regular intervals under an equity release scheme;

(x)   PPF periodic payments within the meaning of section 17(1) of the State Pension Credit Act 2002.

(2)   Where the payment of any social security benefit referred to in sub-paragraph (1) [⁴, or retirement pension income to which section 16(1)(za) to (e) of the State Pension Cedit Act 2002 applies,] is subject to any deduction (other than an adjustment specified in sub-paragraph (4)) the amount to be taken into account under sub-paragraph (1) is to be the amount before the deduction is made.

(3)   Where an award of any working tax credit or child tax credit is subject to a deduction by way of recovery of an overpayment of working tax credit or child tax credit which arose in a previous tax year the amount to be taken into account under sub-paragraph (1) shall be the amount of working tax credit or child tax credit awarded less the amount of that deduction.

(4)   The adjustments specified in this paragraph are those made in accordance with–
(a)   the Social Security (Overlapping Benefits) Regulations 1979;
(b)   the Social Security (Hospital In-Patients) Regulations 1975;
(c)   section 30DD or section 30E of the SSCBA (reductions in incapacity benefit in respect of pensions and councillor's allowances);
(d)   section 3 of the Welfare Reform Act 2007 (deductions from contributory employment and support allowance in respect of pensions and councillor's allowances) and regulations made under it.
[⁴ (e)   section 14 of the Pensions Act 2014 (pension sharing: reduction in sharer's section 4 pension);
(f)   section 45B or 55B of the Social Security Contributions and Benefits Act 1992 (reduction in additional pension in Category A retirement pension and shared additional pension: pension sharing).]

(5)   In sub-paragraph (1)–
(a)   in paragraph (w) an "equity release scheme" means a loan–
  (i)   made between a person ("the lender") and the applicant;
  (ii)   by means of which a sum of money is advanced by the lender to the applicant by way of payments at regular intervals; and
  (iii) which is secured on a dwelling in which the applicant owns an estate or interest and which he occupies as his home; and
(b)   in paragraph (J)(ix) "occasional assistance" means any payment or provision made by a local authority, the Welsh Ministers or the Scottish Ministers for the purposes of–
  (i)   meeting, or helping to meet an immediate short-term need–
    (aa)   arising out of an exceptional event or exceptional circumstances, or
    (bb)   that needs to be met to avoid a risk to the well-being of an individual; and
  (ii)   enabling qualifying individuals to establish or maintain a settled home, and "qualifying individuals" means individuals who have been, or without the assistance might otherwise be–
    (aa)   in prison, hospital, an establishment providing residential care or other institution, or
    (bb)   homeless or otherwise living an unsettled way of life.

(6)   In sub-paragraph (5)(b) "local authority" means a local authority in England within the meaning of the Local Government Act 1972.

Modifications

The amendments made by SI 2014 No.3255 which came into force on 5 April 2015 do not have effect in relation to ordinary statutory paternity pay which is paid, additional statutory paternity pay which is paid, a period in respect of which additional statutory paternity pay is payable which begins, or continues, ordinary paternity leave which is taken or additional paternity leave which is taken on or after 5 April 2015. See art 35 of SI 2014 No.3255.

Amendments

1.   Inserted by art 27(4)(a)(iii) of SI 2014 No 3255 as from 31.12.14.
2.   Amended by art 27(4)(a)(i) and (ii) of SI 2014 No 3255 as from 5.4.15.
3.   Substituted by art 41 of SI 2017 No 422 as from 6.4.17, subject to transitional provisions in arts 2 and 3.

4. Amended by reg 9(a) of SI 2017 No 1305 as from 12.1.18, in relation to schemes made for financial years starting on or after 1.4.18.
5. Inserted by reg 3(b) of SI 2018 No 1346 as from 14.1.19, in relation to schemes made for financial years starting on or after 1.4.19.

General Note
This is similar to reg 29 HB(SPC) Regs. See p771 for the commentary. Note, however, there is no equivalent to reg 29(1)(j)(iv) and (v) HB(SPC) Regs in this regulation as those sub-paras relate to payments and increases payable in respect of old cases of industrial injuries and diseases under Sch 8 SSCBA 1992 which has been repealed, Also, at the time of writing, this regulation does not include the Scottish benefits: early years assistance and funeral expenses assistance as benefits which cannot be counted as income in CTR schemes for pensioners. These are included in the HB(SPC) Regs at reg 29(1)(j)(xviic) and (xviid).

Calculation of weekly income
17.–(1) Except in a case within [¹ sub-paragraph (2), (3A), (4A) or (5)], for the purposes of calculating the weekly income of an applicant, where the period in respect of which payment is made–
(a) does not exceed a week, the whole of that payment must be included in the applicant's weekly income;
(b) exceeds a week, the amount to be included in the applicant's weekly income is to be determined–
  (i) in a case where that period is a month, by multiplying the amount of the payment by 12 and dividing the product by 52;
  (ii) in a case where that period is three months, by multiplying the amount of the payment by 4 and dividing the product by 52;
  (iii) in a case where that period is a year, by dividing the amount of the payment by 52;
  (iv) in any other case, by multiplying the amount of the payment by 7 and dividing the product by the number of days in the period in respect of which it is made.
(2) Sub-paragraph (3) applies where–
(a) the applicant's regular pattern of work is such that he does not work the same hours every week; or
(b) the amount of the applicant's income fluctuates and has changed more than once.
(3) The weekly amount of that applicant's income is to be determined–
(a) if, in a case to which sub-paragraph (2)(a) applies, there is a recognised cycle of work, by reference to his average weekly income over the period of the complete cycle (including, where the cycle involves periods in which the applicant does no work, those periods but disregarding any other absences); or
(b) in any other case, on the basis of–
  (i) the last two payments if those payments are one month or more apart;
  (ii) the last four payments if the last two payments are less than one month apart; or
  (iii) calculating or estimating such other payments as may, in the particular circumstances of the case, enable the applicant's average weekly income to be determined more accurately.
[¹ (3A) Income calculated pursuant to sub-paragraphs (2) and (3) must be taken into account–
(a) in the case of an application, on the date on which the application was made or treated as made, and the first day of each reduction week thereafter;
(b) in the case of an application or a reduction under a scheme where the applicant commences employment, the first day of the reduction week following the date the applicant commences that employment, and the first day of each reduction week thereafter; or
(c) in the case of an application or a reduction under a scheme where the applicant's average weekly earnings from employment change, the first day of the reduction week following the date the applicant's earnings from employment change so as to require recalculation under this paragraph, and the first day of each reduction week thereafter,
regardless of whether those earnings were actually received in that reduction week.]
(4) For the purposes of sub-paragraph (3)(b) the last payments are the last payments before the date the application was made or treated as made.
[¹ (4A) An applicant's earnings from employment as an employed earner not calculated pursuant to sub-paragraphs (2) and (3) must be taken into account–
(a) in the case of an application, on the date on which the application was made or treated as made, and the first day of each reduction week thereafter;
(b) in the case of an application or a reduction under a scheme where the applicant commences employment, the first day of the reduction week following the date the applicant commences that employment, and the first day of each reduction week thereafter; or
(c) in the case of an application or a reduction under a scheme where the applicant's average weekly earnings from employment change, the first day of the reduction week following the date of the change, and the beginning of each reduction week thereafter,
regardless of whether those earnings were actually received in that reduction week.]
(5) If the applicant is entitled to receive a payment to which sub-paragraph (6) applies, the amount of that payment is to be treated as if made in respect of a period of a year.

(6) This sub-paragraph applies to–
(a) royalties or other sums paid as a consideration for the use of, or the right to use, any copyright, design, patent or trade mark;
(b) any payment in respect of any–
    (i) book registered under the Public Lending Right Scheme 1982; or
    (ii) work made under any international public lending right scheme that is analogous to the Public Lending Right Scheme 1982; and
(c) any payment which is made on an occasional basis.
(7) The period under which any benefit under the benefit Acts is to be taken into account is to be the period in respect of which that benefit is payable.
(8) Where payments are made in a currency other than Sterling, the value of the payment is to be determined by taking the Sterling equivalent on the date the payment is made.
(9) The sums specified in Schedule 4 (sums disregarded from earnings) are to be disregarded in calculating–
(a) an applicant's earnings; and
(b) any amount to which sub-paragraph (6) applies where an applicant is the first owner of the copyright, design, patent or trademark, or an original contributor to the book or work referred to in sub-paragraph (6)(b).
(10) For the purposes of sub-paragraph (9)(b), and for that purpose only, the amounts specified in sub-paragraph (6) are to be treated as though they were earnings.
(11) Income specified in Schedule 5 (amount disregarded in calculation of amounts other than earnings) is to be disregarded in the calculation of an applicant's income.
(12) Schedule 6 (capital disregards) has effect so that–
(a) the capital specified in Part 1 is disregarded for the purpose of determining an applicant's income; and
(b) the capital specified in Part 2 is disregarded for the purpose of determining an applicant's income under paragraph 37 (calculation of tariff income from capital).
(13) In the case of any income taken into account for the purpose of calculating a person's income any amount payable by way of tax is disregarded.

Amendment
1. Inserted by reg 2(3)(b) of SI 2015 No 2041 as from 14.1.16, in relation to schemes made for financial years starting on or after 1.4.16.

General Note
This is similar to reg 33 HB(SPC) Regs. See p779 for the commentary.

Earnings of employed earners
18.–(1) Subject to sub-paragraph (2), "earnings" in the case of employment as an employed earner, means any remuneration or profit derived from that employment and includes–
(a) any bonus or commission;
(b) any payment in lieu of remuneration except any periodic sum paid to an applicant on account of the termination of his employment by reason of redundancy;
(c) any payment in lieu of notice;
(d) any holiday pay;
(e) any payment by way of a retainer;
(f) any payment made by the applicant's employer in respect of expenses not wholly, exclusively and necessarily incurred in the performance of the duties of the employment, including any payment made by the applicant's employer in respect of–
    (i) travelling expenses incurred by the applicant between his home and place of employment;
    (ii) expenses incurred by the applicant under arrangements made for the care of a member of his family owing to the applicant's absence from home;
(g) the amount of any payment by way of a non-cash voucher which has been taken into account in the computation of a person's earnings in accordance with Part 5 of Schedule 3 to the Social Security (Contributions) Regulations 2001;
(h) statutory sick pay payable by the employer under the SSCBA;
(i) statutory maternity pay payable by the employer under that Act;
(j) [³] statutory paternity pay payable under Part 12ZA of that Act;
[¹ (ja) statutory shared parental pay under Part 12ZC of that Act;]
[³ (k)]
(l) statutory adoption pay payable under Part 12ZB of that Act;
(m) any sums payable under a contract of service–
    (i) for incapacity for work due to sickness or injury; or
    (ii) by reason of pregnancy or confinement.
(2) Earnings does not include–
(a) subject to sub-paragraph (3), any payment in kind;

(b)   any payment in respect of expenses wholly, exclusively and necessarily incurred in the performance of the duties of the employment;

(c)   any occupational pension;

(d)   any lump sum payment made under the Iron and Steel Re-adaptation Benefits Scheme;

(e)   any payment of compensation made pursuant to an award by an employment tribunal established under the Employment Tribunals Act 1996 in respect of unfair dismissal or unlawful discrimination;

(f)   any payment in respect of expenses arising out of the [² applicant participating as a service user].

(3)   Sub-paragraph (2)(a) does not apply in respect of any non-cash voucher referred to in sub-paragraph (1)(g).

Amendments

1.   Inserted by art 27(4)(b)(iii) of SI 2014 No 3255 as from 31.12.14.
2.   Amended by reg 2(5)(b) of SI 2014 No 3312 as from 12.1.15, in relation to schemes made for financial years starting on or after 1.4.15.
3.   Amended by art 27(4)(b)(i) and (ii) of SI 2014 No 3255 as from 5.4.15.

General Note

This is similar to reg 35 HB Regs. See p439 for the commentary.

Calculation of net earnings of employed earners

19.–(1)   For the purposes of paragraph 24 (calculation of income on a weekly basis), the earnings of an applicant derived or likely to be derived from employment as an employed earner to be taken into account must, subject to paragraph 17(5) and Schedule 4 (sums disregarded from earnings), be his net earnings.

(2)   For the purposes of sub-paragraph (1) net earnings must, except where sub-paragraph (5) applies, be calculated by taking into account the gross earnings of the applicant from that employment over the assessment period, less–

(a)   any amount deducted from those earnings by way of–
    (i)   income tax;
    (ii)   primary Class 1 contributions under the SSCBA;

(b)   one-half of any sum paid by the applicant by way of a contribution towards an occupational pension scheme;

(c)   one-half of the amount calculated in accordance with sub-paragraph (4) in respect of any qualifying contribution payable by the applicant; and

(d)   where those earnings include a payment which is payable under any enactment having effect in Northern Ireland and which corresponds to statutory sick pay, statutory maternity pay, [¹ statutory paternity pay, statutory shared parental pay] or statutory adoption pay, any amount deducted from those earnings by way of any contributions which are payable under any enactment having effect in Northern Ireland and which correspond to primary Class 1 contributions under the SSCBA.

(3)   In this regulation "qualifying contribution" means any sum which is payable periodically as a contribution towards a personal pension scheme.

(4)   The amount in respect of any qualifying contribution is to be calculated by multiplying the daily amount of the qualifying contribution by the number equal to the number of days in the assessment period; and for the purposes of this paragraph the daily amount of the qualifying contribution is to be determined–

(a)   where the qualifying contribution is payable monthly, by multiplying the amount of the qualifying contribution by 12 and dividing the product by 365;

(b)   in any other case, by dividing the amount of the qualifying contribution by the number equal to the number of days in the period to which the qualifying contribution relates.

(5)   Where the earnings of an applicant are determined under paragraph 17(2)(b) (calculation of weekly income) his net earnings are to be calculated by taking into account those earnings over the assessment period, less–

(a)   an amount in respect of income tax equivalent to an amount calculated by applying to those earnings the basic rate [², or in the case of a Scottish taxpayer, the Scottish basic rate,] of tax applicable to the assessment period less only the [² personal reliefs to which the applicant is entitled under Chapters 2, 3 and 3A of Part 3 of the Income Tax Act 2007 as are] appropriate to his circumstances but, if the assessment period is less than a year, the earnings to which the basic rate [², or the Scottish basic rate,] of tax is to be applied and the amount of the personal [² reliefs] deductible under this sub-paragraph is to be calculated on a pro rata basis;

(b)   an amount equivalent to the amount of the primary Class 1 contributions that would be payable by him under the SSCBA in respect of those earnings if such contributions were payable; and

(c)   one-half of any sum which would be payable by the applicant by way of a contribution towards an occupational or personal pension scheme, if the earnings so estimated were actual earnings.

Amendments

1.   Amended by art 27(4)(c) of SI 2014 No 3255 as from 31.12.14.
2.   Amended by reg 2(3)(c) of SI 2016 No 1262 as from 15.1.17, in relation to schemes made for financial years starting on or after 1.4.17.

General Note

This is similar to reg 36 HB Regs. See p443 for the commentary.

Calculation of earnings of self-employed earners

20.–(1) Where the earnings of an applicant consist of earnings from employment as a self-employed earner, the weekly amount of his earnings must be determined by reference to his average weekly earnings from that employment–

(a)   over a period of one year; or

(b)   where the applicant has recently become engaged in that employment or there has been a change which is likely to affect the normal pattern of business, over such other period ("computation period") as may, in the particular case, enable the weekly amount of his earnings to be determined more accurately.

(2)   For the purposes of determining the weekly amount of earnings of an applicant to whom sub-paragraph (1)(b) applies, his earnings over the computation period are to be divided by the number equal to the number of days in that period and the product multiplied by 7.

(3)   The period over which the weekly amount of an applicant's earnings is calculated in accordance with this paragraph will be his assessment period.

General Note

This paragraph corresponds with reg 37 HB(SPC) Regs – see p783.

Earnings of self-employers earners

21.–(1) Subject to sub-paragraph (2), "earnings", in the case of employment as a self-employed earner, means the gross income of the employment.

(2)   "Earnings" in the case of employment as a self-employed earner does not include–

(a)   where an applicant occupies a dwelling as his home and he provides in that dwelling board and lodging accommodation for which payment is made, those payments;

(b)   any payment made by a local authority to an applicant–

(i)   with whom a person is accommodated by virtue of arrangements made under sections 22C [²] of the Children Act 1989 or, as the case may be, [³ section 26 or 26A] of the Children (Scotland) Act 1995 [² or in Wales placed with the applicant or the applicant's partner by a local authority under section 81 of the Social Services and Well-being (Wales) Act 2014;] or

(ii)   with whom a local authority fosters a child under the Looked After Children (Scotland) Regulations 2009 or who is a kinship carer under those Regulations;

(c)   any payment made by a voluntary organisation in accordance with section 59(1)(a) of the Children Act 1989;

(d)   any payment made to the applicant or his partner for a person ("the person concerned") who is not normally a member of the applicant's household but is temporarily in his care, by–

(i)   a local authority but excluding payments of housing benefit made in respect of the person concerned;

(ii)   a voluntary organisation;

(iii)   the person concerned [¹ where the payment is for the provision of accommodation in respect of the meeting of that person's needs under section 18 or 19 of the Care Act 2014 (duty and power to meet needs for care and support)];

(iv)   the National Health Service Commissioning Board or a clinical commissioning group established under section 14D of the National Health Service Act 2006; [³]

(v)   a Local Health Board established by an order made under section 11 of the National Health Service (Wales) Act 2006 [³ or

(vi)   the persons concerned where the payment is for the provision of accommodation to meet that person's needs for care and support under section 35 or 36 of the Social Services and Well-being (Wales) Act 2014 (respectively, duty and power to meet care and support needs of an adult);

(da)   any payment or part of a payment made by a local authority in accordance with section 26A of the Children (Scotland) Act 1995 (duty to provide continuing care) to a person ("A") which A passes on the the applicant where A–

(i)   was formerly in the applicant's care;

(ii)   is aged 16 or over;

(iii)   continues to live with the applicant;

(db)   any payments made to an applicant under section 73(1)(b) of the Children and Young People (Scotland) Act 2014 (kinship care assistance: further provisions);];

(e)   any sports award.

Amendments

1.   Amended by art 2 and Sch para 36(3) of SI 2015 No 643 as from 1.4.15.

2.   Amended by Sch 3 para 135(3) of SI 2016 No 211 (W.84) as from 6.4.16.

3.　　Amended by reg 9(b) of SI 2017 No 1305 as from 12.1.18, in relation to schemes made for financial years starting on or after 1.4.18.

General Note

Para 21(1) is equivalent to reg 37(1) HB Regs (see commentary on p783). Sub-paras 21(2)(b) and (c) broadly correspond with Sch 5 para 26 HB Regs (p673), sub-para 21(2)(d) corresponds with Sch 5 para 27 HB Regs (p673) and sub-para 21(2)(db) is similar to Sch 5 para 28A HB Regs (p674).

Notional income

22.–(1)　　An applicant is to be treated as possessing–

(a)　　subject to sub-paragraph (2), the amount of any retirement pension income–
　　(i)　　for which no claim has been made; and
　　(ii)　　to which he might expect to be entitled if a claim for it were made;

(b)　　income from an occupational pension scheme which the applicant elected to defer.

(2)　　Sub-paragraph (1)(a) does not apply to the following where entitlement has been deferred–

(a)　　a Category A or Category B retirement pension payable under sections 43 to 55 of the SSCBA;

(b)　　a shared additional pension payable under section 55A [² or 55AA] of the SSCBA;

(c)　　graduated retirement benefit payable under sections 36 and 37 of the National Insurance Act 1965;

[² (d)　　a state pension under Part 1 of the Pensions Act 2014.]

(3)　　For the purposes of sub-paragraph (2), entitlement has been deferred–

(a)　　in the case of a Category A or Category B pension, in the circumstances specified in section 55(3) of the SSCBA;

(b)　　in the case of a shared additional pension, in the circumstances specified in section 55C(3) of the SSCBA; [²]

(c)　　in the case of graduated retirement benefit, in the circumstances specified in section 36(4) and (4A) of the National Insurance Act 1965;

[² (d)　　in the case of a state pension under Part 1 of the Pensions Act 2014, in the circumstances specified in section 17(7) and (8) of that Act.]

(4)　　This sub-paragraph applies where a person who has attained the qualifying age for state pension credit–

(a)　　is entitled to money purchase benefits under an occupational pension scheme or a personal pension scheme;

(b)　　fails to purchase an annuity with the funds available in that scheme; and

(c)　　either–
　　(i)　　defers in whole or in part the payment of any income which would have been payable to him by his pension fund holder, or
　　(ii)　　fails to take any necessary action to secure that the whole of any income which would be payable to him by his pension fund holder upon his applying for it, is so paid, or
　　(iii)　　income withdrawal is not available to him under that scheme.

(5)　　Where sub-paragraph (4) applies, the amount of any income foregone is to be treated as possessed by that person, but only from the date on which it could be expected to be acquired were an application for it to be made.

(6)　　The amount of any income foregone in a case where sub-paragraph (4)(c)(i) or (ii) applies is to be the [³ rate of the annuity which may have been purchased with the fund] and must be determined by the authority, taking account of information provided by the pension fund holder.

(7)　　The amount of any income foregone in a case where sub-paragraph (4)(c)(iii) applies is to be the income that the applicant could have received without purchasing an annuity had the funds held under the relevant scheme been held under a personal pension scheme or occupational pension scheme where income withdrawal was available and is to be determined in the manner specified in sub-paragraph (6).

(8)　　In sub-paragraph (4), "money purchase benefits" has the same meaning as in the Pensions Scheme Act 1993.

(9)　　Subject to sub-paragraphs (10) [², (11A), (11B)] and (12), a person will be treated as possessing income of which he has deprived himself for the purpose of securing entitlement to a reduction under the authority's scheme or increasing the amount of the reduction.

(10)　　Sub-paragraph (9) does not apply in respect of the amount of an increase of pension or benefit where a person, having made an election in favour of that increase of pension or benefit under Schedule 5 or 5A to the SSCBA or under Schedule 1 to the Social Security (Graduated Retirement Benefit) Regulations 2005, changes that election in accordance with regulations made under Schedule 5 or 5A to that Act in favour of a lump sum.

(11)　　In sub-paragraph (10), "lump sum" means a lump sum under Schedule 5 or 5A to the SSCBA or under Schedule 1 to the Social Security (Graduated Retirement Benefit) Regulations 2005.

[² (11A)　　Sub-paragraph (9) does not apply in respect of the amount of an increase of pension where a person, having made a choice in favour of that increase of pension under section 8(2) of the Pensions Act 2014, alters that choice in accordance with Regulations made under section 8(7) of that Act in favour of a lump sum.

(11B)　　Sub-paragraph (9) does not apply in respect of the amount of an increase of pension where a person, having made a choice in favour of that increase of pension in accordance with Regulations made under section 10 of the Pensions Act 2014, which include provision corresponding or similar to section 8(2) of that Act, alters that choice in favour of a lump sum, in accordance with Regulations made under section 10 of that Act, which include provision corresponding or similar to Regulations made under section 8(7) of that Act.

(11C)   In sub-parragraph (11A), "lump sum" means a lump sum under section 8 of the Pensions Act 2014.

(11D)   In sub-paragraph (11B), "lump sum" means a lump sum under Regulations made under section 10 of the Pensions Act 2014 which including provision corresponding or similar to section 8 of that Act.]

(12)   Sub-paragraph (9) does not apply in respect of any amount of income other than earnings, or earnings of an employed earner, arising out of the [¹ applicant participating as a service user].

(13)   Where an applicant is in receipt of any benefit under the benefit Acts and the rate of that benefit is altered with effect from a date on or after 1st April in any year but not more than 14 days thereafter, the authority must treat the applicant as possessing such benefit at the altered rate from either 1st April or the first Monday in April in that year, whichever date the authority selects to apply, to the date on which the altered rate is to take effect.

(14)   In the case of an applicant who has, or whose partner has, an award of state pension credit comprising only the savings credit, where the authority treats the applicant as possessing any benefit at the altered rate in accordance with paragraph (13), the authority must–

(a)   determine the income and capital of that applicant in accordance with paragraph 14(1) (calculation of applicant's income in savings credit only cases) where the calculation or estimate of that income and capital is altered with effect from a date on or after 1st April in any year but not more than 14 days thereafter; and

(b)   treat that applicant as possessing such income and capital at the altered rate by reference to the date selected by the relevant authority to apply in its area, for the purposes of establishing the period referred to in sub-paragraph (13).

(15)   For the purposes of sub-paragraph (9), a person is not to be regarded as depriving himself of income where–

(a)   his rights to benefits under a registered pension scheme are extinguished and in consequence of this he receives a payment from that scheme, and

(b)   that payment is a trivial commutation lump sum within the meaning given by paragraph 7 of Schedule 29 to the Finance Act 2004.

(16)   In sub-paragraph (15), "registered pension scheme" has the meaning given in section 150(2) of the Finance Act 2004.

Amendments

1.   Amended by reg 2(5)(b) of SI 2014 No 3312 as from 12.1.15, in relation to schemes made for financial years starting on or after 1.4.15.

2.   Amended by art 39(3)(a) of SI 2015 No 1985 as from 6.4.16.

3.   Amended by reg 9(c) of SI 2017 No 1305 as from 12.1.18, in relation to schemes made for financial years starting on or after 1.4.18.

General Note

This paragraph is equivalent to 41 HB(SPC) Regs. See the commentary on p453. Under CTR schemes in England, it is for the authority to decide whether it takes the annual uprating of benefit into account either from 1 April or the first Monday in April in that year: sub-para (13) (for HB the date used depends on the frequency of rental payments).

Income paid to third parties

23.–(1)   Any payment of income, other than a payment specified in sub-paragraph (2) or (3), to a third party in respect of an applicant is to be treated as possessed by the applicant.

(2)   Sub-paragraph (1) does not apply in respect of a payment of income made under an occupational pension scheme, in respect of a pension or other periodical payment made under a personal pension scheme or a payment made by the Board of the Pension Protection Fund where–

(a)   a bankruptcy order has been made in respect of the person in respect of whom the payment has been made or, in Scotland, the estate of that person is subject to sequestration or a judicial factor has been appointed on that person's estate under section 41 of the Solicitors (Scotland) Act 1980;

(b)   the payment is made to the trustee in bankruptcy or any other person acting on behalf of the creditors; and

(c)   the person referred to in paragraph (a) and his partner do not possess, or are not treated as possessing, any other income apart from that payment.

(3)   Sub-paragraph (1) does not apply in respect of any payment of income other than earnings, or earnings derived from employment as an employed earner, arising out of the [¹ applicant participating as a service user].

Amendment

1.   Amended by reg 2(5)(b) of SI 2014 No 3312 as from 12.1.15, in relation to schemes made for financial years starting on or after 1.4.15.

General Note
This paragraph is equivalent to reg 42 HB(SPC) Regs. See the commentary under that regulation on p457.

Calculation of income on a weekly basis

24.–(1) Subject to paragraph 28 (disregard of changes in tax, etc), the income of an applicant is to be calculated on a weekly basis–

(a) by estimating the amount which is likely to be his average weekly income in accordance with this Part;

(b) by adding to that amount the weekly income calculated under paragraph 37 (calculation of tariff income from capital); and

(c) deducting from the sum of paragraphs (a) and (b) any relevant child care charges to which paragraph 25 (treatment of child care charges) applies from any earnings which form part of the average weekly income or, in a case where the conditions in sub-paragraph (2) are met, from those earnings plus whichever credit specified in paragraph (b) of that sub-paragraph is appropriate, up to a maximum deduction in respect of the applicant's family of whichever of the sums specified in sub-paragraph (3) applies in his case.

(2) The conditions of this paragraph are that–

(a) the applicant's earnings which form part of his average weekly income are less than the lower of either his relevant child care charges or whichever of the deductions specified in paragraph (3) otherwise applies in his case; and

(b) that applicant or, if he is a member of a couple either the applicant or his partner, is in receipt of either working tax credit or child tax credit.

(3) The maximum deduction to which sub-paragraph (1)(c) refers is to be–

(a) where the applicant's family includes only one child in respect of whom relevant child care charges are paid, £175.00 per week;

(b) where the applicant's family includes more than one child in respect of whom relevant child care charges are paid, £300 per week.

General Note
This paragraph is equivalent to reg 30 HB(SPC) Regs and is broadly the same as reg 27 HB Regs (see p424 for commentary on reg 27).

Treatment of child care charges

25.–(1) This paragraph applies where an applicant is incurring relevant child care charges and–

(a) is a lone parent and is engaged in remunerative work;

(b) is a member of a couple both of whom are engaged in remunerative work; or

(c) is a member of a couple where one member is engaged in remunerative work and the other–

(i) is incapacitated;

(ii) is an in-patient in hospital; or

(iii) is in prison (whether serving a custodial sentence or remanded in custody awaiting trial or sentence).

(2) For the purposes of sub-paragraph (1) and subject to sub-paragraph (4), a person to whom sub-paragraph (3) applies must be treated as engaged in remunerative work for a period not exceeding 28 weeks during which he–

(a) is paid statutory sick pay;

(b) is paid short-term incapacity benefit at the lower rate under sections 30A to 30E of the SSCBA;

(c) is paid an employment and support allowance;

(d) is paid income support on the grounds of incapacity for work under regulation 4ZA of, and paragraph 7 or 14 of Schedule 1B to, the Income Support (General) Regulations 1987; or

(e) is credited with earnings on the grounds of incapacity for work or limited capability for work under regulation 8B of the Social Security (Credits) Regulations 1975.

(3) This sub-paragraph applies to a person who was engaged in remunerative work immediately before–

(a) the first day of the period in respect of which he was first paid statutory sick pay, short-term incapacity benefit, an employment and support allowance or income support on the grounds of incapacity for work; or

(b) the first day of the period in respect of which earnings are credited,

as the case may be.

(4) In a case to which sub-paragraph (2)(d) or (e) applies, the period of 28 weeks begins on the day on which the person is first paid income support or on the first day of the period in respect of which earnings are credited, as the case may be.

(5) Relevant child care charges are those charges for care to which sub-paragraphs (6) and (7) apply, and are to be calculated on a weekly basis in accordance with sub-paragraph (9).

(6) The charges are paid by the applicant for care which is provided–

(a) in the case of any child of the applicant's family who is not disabled, in respect of the period beginning on that child's date of birth and ending on the day preceding the first Monday in September following that child's fifteenth birthday; or

(b)   in the case of any child of the applicant's family who is disabled, in respect of the period beginning on that person's date of birth and ending on the day preceding the first Monday in September following that person's sixteenth birthday.

(7)   The charges are paid for care which is provided by one or more of the care providers listed in sub-paragraph (8) and are not paid–

(a)   in respect of the child's compulsory education;

(b)   by an applicant to a partner or by a partner to an applicant in respect of any child for whom either or any of them is responsible in accordance with regulation 7 (circumstances in which a person is treated as responsible or not responsible for another); or

(c)   in respect of care provided by a relative of the child wholly or mainly in the child's home.

(8)   The care to which sub-paragraph (7) refers may be provided–

(a)   out of school hours, by a school on school premises or by a local authority–

    (i)   for children who are not disabled in respect of the period beginning on their eighth birthday and ending on the day preceding the first Monday in September following their fifteenth birthday; or

    (ii)   for children who are disabled in respect of the period beginning on their eighth birthday and ending on the day preceding the first Monday in September following their sixteenth birthday; or

(b)   by a child care provider approved in accordance with the Tax Credit (New Category of Child Care Provider) Regulations 1999; or

(c)   by persons registered under Part 2 of the Children and Families (Wales) Measure 2010; or

(d)   by a person who is excepted from registration under Part 2 of the Children and Families (Wales) Measure 2010 because the child care that person provides is in a school or establishment referred to in article 11, 12 or 14 of the Child Minding and Day Care Exceptions (Wales) Order 2010; or

(e)   by–

    (i)   persons registered under section 59(1) of the Public Services Reform (Scotland) Act 2010; or

    (ii)   local authorities registered under section 83(1) of that Act,

    where the care provided is child minding or day care of children within the meaning of that Act; or

(f)   by a person prescribed in regulations made pursuant to section 12(4) of the Tax Credits Act 2002; or

(g)   by a person who is registered under Chapter 2 or 3 of Part 3 of the Childcare Act 2006; or

(h)   by any of the schools mentioned in section 34(2) of the Childcare Act 2006 in circumstances where the requirement to register under Chapter 2 of Part 3 of that Act does not apply by virtue of section 34(2) of that Act; or

(i)   by any of the schools mentioned in section 53(2) of the Childcare Act 2006 in circumstances where the requirement to register under Chapter 3 of Part 3 of that Act does not apply by virtue of section 53(2) of that Act; or

(j)   by any of the establishments mentioned in section 18(5) of the Childcare Act 2006 in circumstances where the care is not included in the meaning of "childcare" for the purposes of Part 1 and Part 3 of that Act by virtue of that subsection; or

(k)   by a foster parent or kinship carer under the Fostering Services (England) Regulations 2011, the [10] or the Looked After Children (Scotland) Regulations 2009 in relation to a child other than one whom the foster parent is fostering or kinship carer is looking after; or

[10 (ka)   by a foster parent under the Fostering Panels (Establishment and Functions) (Wales) Regulations 2018 or a person with whom a child is placed under regulation 26 of the Care Planning, Placement and Case Review (Wales) Regulations 2015 (temporary approval of a relative, friend or other person connected with the child) or regulation 28 of those Regulations (temporary approval of a particular prospective adopter) in relation to a child other than one whom the foster parent is fostering or the person is looking after; or]

(l)   by a provider of personal care within the meaning of paragraph 1 of Schedule 1 to the Health and Social Care Act 2008 (Regulated Activities) Regulations 2010 and being a regulated activity prescribed by those Regulations [9 or by a person who is employed, or engaged under a contract for services, to provide care and support by the provider of a domiciliary support service within the meaning of Part 1 of the Regulation and Inspection of Socal Care (Wales) Act 2016]; or

(m)   by a person who is not a relative of the child wholly or mainly in the child's home.

(9)   Relevant child care charges are to be estimated over such period, not exceeding a year, as is appropriate in order that the average weekly charge may be estimated accurately having regard to information as to the amount of that charge provided by the child minder or person providing the care.

(10)   For the purposes of sub-paragraph (1)(c) the other member of a couple is incapacitated where–

(a)   he is aged not less than 80;

(b)   he is aged less than 80, and–

    (i)   an additional condition specified in paragraph 26 is treated as applying in his case; and

    (ii)   he satisfies that condition or would satisfy it but for his being treated as capable of work by virtue of a determination made in accordance with regulations made under section 171E of the SSCBA;

(c)   the [⁸ other member of the couple would be a member of the support group or] [⁷ a member of the work-related activity group] but for that other member being treated as not having limited capability for work by virtue of a determination made in accordance with the Employment and Support Allowance Regulations 2008 [³ or the Employment and Support Allowance Regulations 2013];

(d)   he is, or is treated as, incapable of work and has been so incapable, or has been so treated as incapable, of work in accordance with the provisions of, and regulations made under, Part 12A of the SSCBA (incapacity for work) for a continuous period of not less than 196 days; and for this purpose any two or more separate periods separated by a break of not more than 56 days must be treated as one continuous period;

(e)   he is, or is treated as having, limited capability for work and has had, or been treated as having, limited capability for work in accordance with the Employment and Support Allowance Regulations 2008 [³ or the Employment and Support Allowance Regulations 2013] for a continuous period of not less than 196 days and for this purpose any two or more separate periods separated by a break of not more than 84 days must be treated as one continuous period;

(f)   there is payable in respect of him one or more of the following pensions or allowances–

     (i)   long-term incapacity benefit or short-term incapacity benefit at the higher rate under Schedule 4 to the SSCBA;

     (ii)   attendance allowance under section 64 of the SSCBA;

     (iii)   severe disablement allowance under section 68 of the SSCBA;

     (iv)   disability living allowance;

     (v)   personal independence payment;

     (vi)   an AFIP;

     (vii)   increase of disablement pension under section 104 of the SSCBA;

     (viii)   a pension increase paid as part of a war disablement pension or under an industrial injuries scheme which is analogous to an allowance or increase of disablement pension under sub-paragraph (ii), (iv), (v) or (vii) above;

     (ix)   main phase employment and support allowance;

(g)   a pension [³ or allowance or payment to which sub-paragraph (v), (vii) or (viii)] of paragraph (f) above refers was payable on account of his incapacity but has ceased to be payable in consequence of his becoming a patient, which in this paragraph means a person (other than a person who is serving a sentence of imprisonment or detention in a youth custody institution) who is regarded as receiving free in-patient treatment within the meaning of regulation 2(4) and (5) of the Social Security (Hospital In-Patients) Regulations 2005;

(h)   an attendance allowance under section 64 of the SSCBA or disability living allowance would be payable to that person but for–

     (i)   a suspension of benefit in accordance with regulations made under section 113(2) of the SSCBA; or

     (ii)   an abatement as a consequence of hospitalisation;

(i)   the daily living component of personal independence payment would be payable to that person but for a suspension of benefit in accordance with regulations under section 86 of the Welfare Reform Act 2012 (hospital in-patients);

(j)   an AFIP would be payable to that person but for a suspension of payment in accordance with any terms of the armed and reserve forces compensation scheme which allow for a suspension because a person is undergoing medical treatment in a hospital or similar institution.

(k)   paragraph (f), (g), (h) or (i) would apply to him if the legislative provisions referred to in those paragraphs were provisions under any corresponding enactment having effect in Northern Ireland; or

(l)   he has an invalid carriage or other vehicle provided to him by the Secretary of State or a clinical commissioning group under paragraph 9 of Schedule 1 to the National Health Service Act 2006 or under section 46 of the National Health Service (Scotland) Act 1978 or provided by the Department of Health, Social Services and Public Safety in Northern Ireland under Article 30(1) of the Health and Personal Social Services (Northern Ireland) Order 1972.

(11)   For the purposes of sub-paragraph (10), once sub-paragraph (10)(d) applies to the person, if he then ceases, for a period of 56 days or less, to be incapable, or to be treated as incapable, of work, that paragraph is to, on his again becoming so incapable, or so treated as incapable, of work at the end of that period, immediately thereafter apply to him for so long as he remains incapable, or is treated as remaining incapable, of work.

(12)   For the purposes of sub-paragraph (10), once sub-paragraph (10)(e) applies to the person, if he then ceases, for a period of 84 days or less, to have, or to be treated as having, limited capability for work, that paragraph is to, on his again having, or being treated as having, limited capability for work at the end of that period, immediately thereafter apply to him for so long as he has, or is treated as having, limited capability for work.

(13)   For the purposes of sub-paragraphs (6) and (8)(a), a person is disabled if he is a person–

(a)   to whom an attendance allowance or care component of disability allowance is payable or would be payable but for–

     (i)   a suspension of benefit in accordance with regulations under section 113(2) of the SSCBA; or

     (ii)   an abatement as a consequence of hospitalisation;

(b)   to whom the daily living component of personal independence payment is payable or [³ has ceased to be payable by virtue of] a suspension of benefit in accordance with regulations under section 86 of the Welfare Reform Act 2012 (hospital in-patients);

(c)   who is registered as [⁶] [⁵ severely sight-impaired in a register kept under section 77(1) of the Care Act 2014 (registers of sight-impaired adults)] [⁶], in Scotland, has been certified as blind and in consequence he is registered as blind in a register maintained by or on behalf of a council constituted under section 2 of the Local Government (Scotland) Act 1994 [⁶ or is registered as severely sight-impaired in a register kept by a local authority in Wales under section 18(1) of the Social Services and Well-being (Wales) Act 2014]; or

(d)   who ceased to be registered as blind [⁵ or severely sight-impaired] in such a register within the period beginning 28 weeks before the first Monday in September following that person's fifteenth birthday and ending on the day preceding that person's sixteenth birthday.

(14)   For the purposes of sub-paragraph (1) a person on maternity leave, paternity leave [², shared parental leave] or adoption leave is to be treated as if he is engaged in remunerative work for the period specified in [¹ sub-paragraph (15)] ("the relevant period") provided that–

(a)   in the week before the period of maternity leave, paternity leave [², shared parental leave] or adoption leave began he was in remunerative work;

(b)   the applicant is incurring relevant child care charges within the meaning of sub-paragraph (5); and

(c)   he is entitled to either statutory maternity pay under section 164 of the SSCBA, [⁴] statutory paternity pay by virtue of section 171ZA or 171ZB of that Act, [⁴], statutory adoption pay by virtue of section 171ZL of that Act, maternity allowance under section 35 of that Act [², statutory shared parental pay by virtue of section 171ZU or 171ZV of that Act] or qualifying support.

(15)   For the purposes of sub-paragraph (14) the relevant period begins on the day on which the person's maternity, paternity leave [², shared parental leave] or adoption leave commences and ends on–

(a)   the date that leave ends;

(b)   if no child care element of working tax credit is in payment on the date that entitlement to maternity allowance, qualifying support, statutory maternity pay, ordinary or additional statutory paternity pay [² statutory shared paternity pay or statutory adoption pay ends], the date that entitlement ends; or

(c)   if a child care element of working tax credit is in payment on the date that entitlement to maternity allowance or qualifying support, statutory maternity pay, ordinary or additional statutory paternity pay [² statutory shared paternity pay or statutory adoption pay ends], the date that entitlement to that award of the child care element of the working tax credit ends,

whichever shall occur first.

(16)   In sub-paragraphs (14) and (15)–

(a)   "qualifying support" means income support to which that person is entitled by virtue of paragraph 14B of Schedule 1B to the Income Support (General) Regulations 1987; and

(b)   "child care element" of working tax credit means the element of working tax credit prescribed under section 12 of the Tax Credits Act 2002 (child care element).

(17)   In sub-paragraphs (6), (8)(a) and (13)(d), "the first Monday in September" means the Monday which first occurs in the month of September in any year.

Amendments

1.   Amended by reg 2(7)(d) of SI 2013 No 3181 for schemes for financial years beginning on or after 1.4.14.
2.   Amended by art 27(4)(d)(i) and (iv) and (e) of SI 2014 No 3255 as from 31.12.14.
3.   Amended by reg 2(5)(c) of SI 2014 No 3312 as from 12.1.15, in relation to schemes made for financial years starting on or after 1.4.15.
4.   Amended by art 27(4)(d)(ii) and (iii) of SI 2014 No 3255 as from 5.4.15.
5.   Amended by art 2 and Sch para 36(4) of SI 2015 No 643 as from 1.4.15.
6.   Amended by Sch 3 para 135(4) of SI 2016 No 211 (W.84) as from 6.4.16.
7.   Amended by Sch 1 para 8(3) of SI 2017 No 204 as from 3.4.17, subject to transitional and savings provisions in Sch 2 paras 1–7.
8.   Amended by reg 9(d) of SI 2017 No 1305 as from 12.1.18, in relation to schemes made for financial years starting on or after 1.4.18.
9.   Amended by reg 3(c) of SI 2018 No 1346 as from 14.1.19, in relation to schemes made for financial years starting on or after 1.4.19.
10.   Amended by Sch 1 para 21 of SI 2019 No 237 as from 29.4.19.

General Note

This paragraph is broadly the same as reg 28 HB Regs. See p429 for commentary, but note that there is no equivalent to reg 28(11)(a) and (b) in this paragraph (as the disability premium does not apply here).

Additional condition referred to in paragraph 25(10)(b)(i): disability

26.–(1)   Subject to sub-paragraph (2), the additional condition referred to in paragraph 25(10)(b)(i) is that either–

(a)   the applicant or, as the case may be, the other member of the couple–

    (i)   is in receipt of one or more of the following benefits: attendance allowance, disability living allowance, personal independence payment, an AFIP, the disability element or the severe disability element of working tax credit as specified in regulation 20(1)(b) and (f) of the Working Tax Credit (Entitlement and Maximum Rate) Regulations 2002, mobility supplement, long-term incapacity benefit under Part 2 of the SSCBA or severe disablement allowance under Part 3 of that Act but, in the case of long-term incapacity benefit or severe disablement allowance, only where it is paid in respect of him; or

    (ii)   was in receipt of long-term incapacity benefit under Part 2 of the SSCBA when entitlement to that benefit ceased on account of the payment of a retirement pension under that Act [² or a state pension under Part 1 of the Pensions Act 2014] and the applicant has since remained continuously entitled to council tax benefit (for the period prior to 1st April 2013) or a reduction under an authority's scheme (for the period on or after 1st April 2013) and, if the long-term incapacity benefit was payable to his partner, the partner is still a member of the family; or

    (iii)   was in receipt of attendance allowance or disability living allowance but payment of benefit has been suspended in accordance with regulations made under section 113(2) of the SSCBA or otherwise abated as a consequence of the applicant or his partner becoming a patient within the meaning of paragraph 25(10)(g) (treatment of child care charges); or

    (iv)   was in receipt of personal independence payment, but payment of that benefit has been suspended in accordance with section 86 of the Welfare Reform Act 2012 as a consequence of the applicant becoming a patient within the meaning of paragraph 25(10)(g); or

    (v)   was in receipt of an AFIP but its payment has been suspended in accordance with any terms of the armed and reserve forces compensation scheme which allow for a suspension because a person is undergoing medical treatment in a hospital or similar institution; or

    (vi)   is provided by the Secretary of State or a clinical commissioning group with an invalid carriage or other vehicle under paragraph 9 of Schedule 1 to the National Health Service Act 2006 or, in Scotland, under section 46 of the National Health Service (Scotland) Act 1978 (provision of services by Scottish Ministers) or receives payments by way of grant from the Secretary of State under paragraph 10(3) of Schedule 1 to the Act of 2006 or, in Scotland, by Scottish Ministers under section 46 of the Act of 1978; or

    (vii)   [³] [¹ is registered as severely sight-impaired in a register kept by a local authority in England under section 77(1) of the Care Act 2014 (registers of sight-impaired adults)] [³], in Scotland, has been certified as blind and in consequence he is registered in a register maintained by or on behalf of a council constituted under section 2 of the Local Government (Scotland) Act 1994 [³ or is registered as severely sight-impaired in a register kept by a local authority in Wales under section 18(1) of the Social Services and Well-being (Wales) Act 2014]; or

(b)   the applicant, or as the case may be, the other member of the couple–

    (i)   is, or is treated as, incapable of work in accordance with the provisions of, and regulations made under, Part 12A of the SSCBA (incapacity for work); and

    (ii)   has been incapable, or has been treated as incapable, of work for a continuous period of not less than–

        (aa)   in the case of an applicant who is terminally ill within the meaning of section 30B(4) of the SSCBA, 196 days;

        (bb)   in any other case, 364 days.

(2)   For the purposes of sub-paragraph (1)(a)(vii), a person who has ceased to be registered as blind [¹ or severely sight-impaired] on regaining his eyesight is nevertheless to be treated as [¹ such] and as satisfying the additional condition set out in that sub-paragraph for a period of 28 weeks following the date on which he ceased to be so registered.

(3)   For the purposes of sub-paragraph (1)(b), where any two or more periods of incapacity are separated by a break of not more than 56 days, those periods must be treated as one continuous period.

(4)   For the purposes of this paragraph, a reference to a person who is or was in receipt of long-term incapacity benefit includes a person who is or was in receipt of short-term incapacity benefit at a rate equal to the long-term rate by virtue of section 30B(4)(a) of the SSCBA (short-term incapacity benefit for a person who is terminally ill), or who would be or would have been in receipt of short-term incapacity benefit at such a rate but for the fact that the rate of short-term incapacity benefit already payable to him is or was equal to or greater than the long-term rate.

(5)   In the case of a person who is a welfare to work beneficiary (a person to whom regulation 13A(1) of the Social Security (Incapacity for Work) (General) Regulations 1995 applies, and who again becomes incapable of work for the purposes of Part 12A of the SSCBA) the reference to a period of 56 days in sub-paragraph (3) must be treated as a reference to a period of 104 weeks.

Amendments

    1.   Amended by art 2 and Sch para 36(5) of SI 2015 No 643 as from 1.4.15.

2.   Amended by art 39(3)(b) of SI 2015 No 1985 as from 6.4.16.
3.   Amended by Sch 3 para 135(5) of SI 2016 No 211 (W.84) as from 6.4.16.

General Note
This paragraph is similar to Sch 3 para 13 HB Regs (which describes the additional conditions for the disability premium). See p638 for commentary. Here, it defines when someone can be treated as incapacitated under paragraph 25(10)(b)(i) for the purpose of child care charges.

Calculation of average weekly income from tax credits

27.–(1)   This paragraph applies where an applicant receives a tax credit.

(2)   Where this paragraph applies, the period over which a tax credit is to be taken into account is the period set out in sub-paragraph (3).

(3)   Where the instalment in respect of which payment of a tax credit is made is–

(a)   a daily instalment, the period is 1 day, being the day in respect of which the instalment is paid;

(b)   a weekly instalment, the period is 7 days, ending on the day on which the instalment is due to be paid;

(c)   a two weekly instalment, the period is 14 days, commencing 6 days before the day on which the instalment is due to be paid;

(d)   a four weekly instalment, the period is 28 days, ending on the day on which the instalment is due to be paid.

(4)   For the purposes of this paragraph "tax credit" means child tax credit or working tax credit.

General Note
This paragraph mirrors reg 32 HB Regs. See p435 for commentary.

Disregard of changes in tax, contributions etc.

28.   In calculating the applicant's income an authority may disregard any legislative change–

(a)   in the basic or other rates of income tax;

[⁴ (aa)   in the Scottish basic or other rates of income tax;]

(b)   in the amount of any personal tax [⁴ reliefs under Chapters 2, 3 and 3A of Part 3 of the Income Tax Act 2007];

(c)   in the rates of [¹ national insurance contributions] payable under the SSCBA or in the lower earnings limit or upper earnings limit for Class 1 contributions under that Act, the lower or upper limits applicable to Class 4 contributions under that Act or the amount specified in section 11(4) of that Act ([³ small profits threshold] in relation to Class 2 contributions);

(d)   in the amount of tax payable as a result of an increase in the weekly rate of Category A, B, C or D retirement pension or any addition thereto or any graduated pension payable under the SSCBA [² or a state pension under Part 1 of the Pensions Act 2014];

(e)   in the maximum rate of child tax credit or working tax credit,

for a period not exceeding 30 reduction weeks beginning with the reduction week immediately following the date from which the change is effective.

Amendments
1.   Amended by reg 2(5)(d) of SI 2014 No 3312 as from 12.1.15, in relation to schemes made for financial years starting on or after 1.4.15.
2.   Amended by art 39(3)(c) of SI 2015 No 1985 as from 6.4.16.
3.   Amended by reg 2(3)(c) of SI 2015 No 2041 as from 14.1.16, in relation to schemes made for financial years starting on or after 1.4.16.
4.   Amended by reg 2(3)(d) of SI 2016 No 1262 as from 15.1.17, in relation to schemes made for financial years starting on or after 1.4.17,

General Note
This paragraph assists billing authorities in the administration of CTR by effectively giving them the discretion to ignore an increase or decrease in an applicant's income that arises from the legislative changes listed in sub-paras (a)–(e) for up to 30 reduction weeks, starting with the reduction week after the change in the legislation comes into force. If a billing authority exercises its discretion under this paragraph an applicant may qualify for a higher or lower amount of CTR than s/he would otherwise receive over those weeks. As the amount of CTR awarded for the period would have been correctly assessed, the change in income over the period would not result in a change in council tax liability. This paragraph is almost identical to reg 34 HB Regs (p437).

Calculation of net profit of self-employed earners

29.–(1)   For the purposes of paragraph 24 (calculation of income on a weekly basis) the earnings of an applicant to be taken into account are–

(a)   in the case of a self-employed earner who is engaged in employment on his own account, the net profit derived from that employment;

(b)　in the case of a self-employed earner whose employment is carried on in partnership, his share of the net profit derived from that employment, less–
- (i)　an amount in respect of income tax and of [¹ national insurance contributions] payable under the SSCBA calculated in accordance with paragraph 30 (deduction of tax and contributions of self-employed earners); and
- (ii)　one-half of the amount calculated in accordance with sub-paragraph (11) in respect of any qualifying premium;

(2)　For the purposes of sub-paragraph (1)(a) the net profit of the employment must, except where sub-paragraph (8) applies, be calculated by taking into account the earnings of the employment over the assessment period less–
- (a)　subject to sub-paragraphs (4) to (7), any expenses wholly and exclusively incurred in that period for the purposes of that employment;
- (b)　an amount in respect of–
  - (i)　income tax; and
  - (ii)　[¹ national insurance contributions] payable under the SSCBA, calculated in accordance with paragraph 30; and
- (c)　one-half of the amount calculated in accordance with sub-paragraph (10) in respect of any qualifying premium.

(3)　For the purposes of sub-paragraph (1)(b) the net profit of the employment is to be calculated by taking into account the earnings of the employment over the assessment period less, subject to sub-paragraphs (4) to (7), any expenses wholly and exclusively incurred in that period for the purposes of the employment.

(4)　Subject to sub-paragraph (5), no deduction is to be made under sub-paragraph (2)(a) or (3), in respect of–
- (a)　any capital expenditure;
- (b)　the depreciation of any capital asset;
- (c)　any sum employed or intended to be employed in the setting up or expansion of the employment;
- (d)　any loss incurred before the beginning of the assessment period;
- (e)　the repayment of capital on any loan taken out for the purposes of the employment; and
- (f)　any expenses incurred in providing business entertainment.

(5)　A deduction must be made under sub-paragraph (2)(a) or (3) in respect of the repayment of capital on any loan used for–
- (a)　the replacement in the course of business of equipment or machinery; or
- (b)　the repair of an existing business asset except to the extent that any sum is payable under an insurance policy for its repair.

(6)　An authority must refuse to make a deduction in respect of any expenses under sub-paragraph (2)(a) or (3) where it is not satisfied given the nature and the amount of the expense that it has been reasonably incurred.

(7)　For the avoidance of doubt–
- (a)　a deduction must not be made under sub-paragraph (2)(a) or (3) in respect of any sum unless it has been expended for the purposes of the business;
- (b)　a deduction must be made thereunder in respect of–
  - (i)　the excess of any value added tax paid over value added tax received in the assessment period;
  - (ii)　any income expended in the repair of an existing business asset except to the extent that any sum is payable under an insurance policy for its repair;
  - (iii)　any payment of interest on a loan taken out for the purposes of the employment.

(8)　Where an applicant is engaged in employment as a child minder the net profit of the employment is to be one-third of the earnings of that employment, less–
- (a)　an amount in respect of–
  - (i)　income tax; and
  - (ii)　[¹ national insurance contributions] payable under the SSCBA, calculated in accordance with paragraph 30; and
- (b)　one-half of the amount calculated in accordance with sub-paragraph (10) in respect of any qualifying premium.

(9)　For the avoidance of doubt where an applicant is engaged in employment as a self-employed earner and he is also engaged in one or more other employments as a self-employed or employed earner any loss incurred in any one of his employments must not be offset against his earnings in any other of his employments.

(10)　The amount in respect of any qualifying premium is to be calculated by multiplying the daily amount of the qualifying premium by the number equal to the number of days in the assessment period; and for the purposes of this paragraph the daily amount of the qualifying premium is to be determined–
- (a)　where the qualifying premium is payable monthly, by multiplying the amount of the qualifying premium by 12 and dividing the product by 365;
- (b)　in any other case, by dividing the amount of the qualifying premium by the number equal to the number of days in the period to which the qualifying premium relates.

(11)　In this paragraph, "qualifying premium" means any premium which is payable periodically in respect of a personal pension scheme and is so payable on or after the date of claim.

Amendment

1.   Amended by reg 2(5)(d) of SI 2014 No.3312 as from 12.1.15, in relation to schemes made for financial years starting on or after 1.4.15.

General Note

This is broadly the same as reg 38 HB Regs. See p447 for commentary. Note the difference between reg 38(1)(b) in that it refers to share fishermen, and sub-para (1)(b) above, and that there is no equivalent to reg 38(2) or (5)(g) in this paragraph.

Calculation of deduction of tax and contributions of self-employed earners

30.–(1)   The amount to be deducted in respect of income tax under paragraph 29(1)(b)(i), (2)(b)(i) or (8)(a)(i) (calculation of net profit of self-employed earners) is to be calculated–

(a)   on the basis of the amount of chargeable income; and

(b)   as if that income were assessable to income tax at the basic rate [³, or in the case of a Scottish taxpayer, the Scottish basic rate,] of tax applicable to the assessment period less only the [³ personal reliefs to which the applicant is entitled under Chapters 2, 3 and 3A of Part 3 of the Income Tax Act 2007 as are] appropriate to his circumstances.

(2)   But, if the assessment period is less than a year, the earnings to which the basic rate [³, or the Scottish basic rate] of tax is to be applied and the amount of the personal reliefs deductible under this paragraph must be calculated on a pro rata basis.

(3)   The amount to be deducted in respect of [¹ national insurance contributions] under paragraph 29(1)(b)(i), (2)(b)(ii) or (8)(a)(ii) is the total of–

(a)   the amount of Class 2 contributions payable under section [² 11(2)] or, as the case may be, [² 11(8)] of the SSCBA at the rate applicable to the assessment period except where the applicant's chargeable income is less than the amount specified in section 11(4) of that Act ([² small profits threshold]) for the tax year applicable to the assessment period; but if the assessment period is less than a year, the amount specified for that tax year must be reduced pro rata; and

(b)   the amount of Class 4 contributions (if any) which would be payable under section 15 of the SSCBA (Class 4 contributions recoverable under the Income Tax Acts) at the percentage rate applicable to the assessment period on so much of the chargeable income as exceeds the lower limit but does not exceed the upper limit of profits and gains applicable for the tax year applicable to the assessment period; but if the assessment period is less than a year, those limits must be reduced pro rata.

(4)   In this paragraph "chargeable income" means–

(a)   except where paragraph (b) applies, the earnings derived from the employment less any expenses deducted under sub-paragraph (3)(a) or, as the case may be, (3) of paragraph 29;

(b)   in the case of employment as a child minder, one-third of the earnings of that employment.

Amendments

1.   Amended by reg 2(5)(d) of SI 2014 No 3312 as from 12.1.15, in relation to schemes made for financial years starting on or after 1.4.15.

2.   Amended by reg 2(3)(d) of SI 2015 No 2041 as from 14.1.16, in relation to schemes made for financial years starting on or after 1.4.16.

3.   Amended by reg 2(3)(e) of SI 2016 No 1262 as from 15.1.17, in relation to schemes made for financial years starting on or after 1.4.17.

General Note

This paragraph is equivalent to reg 39 HB Regs. See p450 for commentary. Note, however, that the reference to sub-para (3)(a) in sub-para (4)(a) above may be a drafting error. The similar reference in reg 39(3)(a) HB Regs refers to the equivalent of sub-para (2)(a) of para 29. A similar discrepancy in Sch 1 para 24 CTRSPR(W) Regs was corrected by amendment.

CHAPTER 3
Capital

Calculation of capital

31.–(1)   The capital of an applicant to be taken into account must, subject to sub-paragraph (2), be the whole of his capital calculated in accordance with this Part.

(2)   There must be disregarded from the calculation of an applicant's capital under sub-paragraph (1), any capital, where applicable, specified in Schedule 6 (capital disregards).

(3)   An applicant's capital is to be treated as including any payment made to him by way of arrears of–

(a)   child tax credit;

(b)   working tax credit;

(c)   state pension credit,

if the payment was made in respect of a period for the whole or part of which a reduction under an authority's scheme was allowed before those arrears were paid.

General Note
This paragraph is similar to reg 44 HB(SPC) Regs. See p463 for commentary.

Calculation of capital in the United Kingdom
32. Capital which an applicant possesses in the United Kingdom is to be calculated at its current market or surrender value less–
(a) where there would be expenses attributable to the sale, 10 per cent; and
(b) the amount of any encumbrance secured on it.

General Note
This paragraph is equivalent to reg 47 HB Regs. See p465 for commentary.

Calculation of capital outside the United Kingdom
33. Capital which an applicant possesses in a country outside the United Kingdom is to be calculated–
(a) in a case where there is no prohibition in that country against the transfer to the United Kingdom of an amount equal to its current market or surrender value in that country, at that value;
(b) in a case where there is such a prohibition, at the price which it would realise if sold in the United Kingdom to a willing buyer,
less, where there would be expenses attributable to sale, 10 per cent and the amount of any encumbrances secured on it.

General Note
This paragraph is equivalent to reg 48 HB Regs. See p466 for commentary.

Notional capital
34.–(1) An applicant is to be treated as possessing capital of which he has deprived himself for the purpose of securing entitlement to a reduction under an authority's scheme or increasing the amount of that reduction except to the extent that that capital is reduced in accordance with paragraph 35 (diminishing notional capital rule).
(2) A person who disposes of capital for the purpose of–
(a) reducing or paying a debt owed by the applicant; or
(b) purchasing goods or services if the expenditure was reasonable in the circumstances of the applicant's case,
is to be regarded as not depriving himself of it.
(3) Where an applicant stands in relation to a company in a position analogous to that of a sole owner or partner in the business of that company, he may be treated as if he were such sole owner or partner and in such a case–
(a) the value of his holding in that company must, notwithstanding paragraph 31 (calculation of capital) be disregarded; and
(b) he must, subject to sub-paragraph (4), be treated as possessing an amount of capital equal to the value or, as the case may be, his share of the value of the capital of that company and the foregoing provisions of this Chapter apply for the purposes of calculating that amount as if it were actual capital which he does possess.
(4) For so long as the applicant undertakes activities in the course of the business of the company, the amount which he is treated as possessing under sub-paragraph (3) is to be disregarded.
(5) Where an applicant is treated as possessing capital under sub-paragraph (1) the foregoing provisions of this Chapter apply for the purposes of calculating its amount as if it were actual capital which he does possess.

General Note
Sub-para (1) is equivalent to reg 49(1) HB Regs and sub-paras (3) to (5) are equivalent to reg 49(5) to (7). See p468 for commentary.
Sub-para (2) is equivalent to reg 47(2) HB(SPC) Regs (see p791 for commentary).

Diminishing notional capital rule
35.–(1) Where an applicant is treated as possessing capital under paragraph 34(1) (notional capital), the amount which he is treated as possessing–
(a) in the case of a week that is subsequent to–
(i) the relevant week in respect of which the conditions set out in sub-paragraph (2) are satisfied; or
(ii) a week which follows that relevant week and which satisfies those conditions,
is to be reduced by an amount determined under sub-paragraph (3);

(b)   in the case of a week in respect of which sub-paragraph (1)(a) does not apply but where–

       (i)   that week is a week subsequent to the relevant week; and

       (ii)   that relevant week is a week in which the condition in sub-paragraph (4) is satisfied,

    is to be reduced by the amount determined under sub-paragraph (5).

(2)   This sub-paragraph applies to a reduction week where the applicant satisfies the conditions that–

(a)   he is in receipt of a reduction under an authority's scheme; and

(b)   but for paragraph 34(1), he would have received a greater reduction under that scheme in that week.

(3)   In a case to which sub-paragraph (2) applies, the amount of the reduction in the amount of capital he is treated as possessing for the purposes of sub-paragraph (1)(a) is to be equal to the aggregate of–

(a)   an amount equal to the additional amount of the reduction in council tax to which sub-paragraph (2)(b) refers;

(b)   where the applicant has also claimed state pension credit, the amount of any state pension credit or any additional amount of state pension credit to which he would have been entitled in respect of the reduction week to which sub-paragraph (2) refers but for the application of regulation 21(1) of the State Pension Credit Regulations 2002 (notional capital);

(c)   where the applicant has also claimed housing benefit, the amount of any housing benefit or any additional amount of housing benefit to which he would have been entitled in respect of the whole or part of that reduction week to which sub-paragraph (2) refers but for the application of regulation 47(1) of the Housing Benefit (Persons who have attained the qualifying age for state pension credit) Regulations 2006 (notional capital);

(d)   where the applicant has also claimed a jobseeker's allowance, the amount of an income-based jobseeker's allowance to which he would have been entitled in respect of the reduction week to which sub-paragraph (2) refers but for the application of regulation 113 of the Jobseeker's Allowance Regulations 1996 (notional capital); and

(e)   where the applicant has also claimed an employment and support allowance, the amount of an income-related employment and support allowance to which he would have been entitled in respect of the reduction week to which sub-paragraph (2) refers but for the application of regulation 115 of the Employment and Support Allowance Regulations 2008 (notional capital).

(4)   Subject to sub-paragraph (7), for the purposes of sub-paragraph (1)(b), the condition is that the applicant would have been entitled to a reduction in council tax under the authority's scheme in the relevant week but for paragraph 34(1).

(5)   In such a case the amount of reduction in the amount of the capital which he is treated as possessing for the purposes of sub-paragraph (1)(b) is equal to the aggregate of–

(a)   the amount of the reduction in council tax to which the applicant would have been entitled in the relevant week but for paragraph 34(1);

(b)   if the applicant would, but for regulation 21 of the State Pension Credit Regulations 2002, have been entitled to state pension credit in respect of the benefit week, within the meaning of regulation 1(2) of those Regulations (interpretation), which includes the last day of the relevant week, the amount to which he would have been entitled;

(c)   if the applicant would, but for regulation 47(1) of the Housing Benefit (Persons who have attained the qualifying age for state pension credit) Regulations 2006, have been entitled to housing benefit or to an additional amount of housing benefit in respect of the benefit week, within the meaning of regulation 2 of those Regulations (interpretation), which includes the last day of the relevant week, the amount which is equal to–

       (i)   in a case where no housing benefit is payable, the amount to which he would have been entitled; or

       (ii)   in any other case, the amount equal to the additional amount of housing benefit to which he would have been entitled,

(d)   if the applicant would, but for regulation 113 of the Jobseeker's Allowance Regulations 1996, have been entitled to an income-based jobseeker's allowance in respect of the benefit week, within the meaning of regulation 1(3) of those Regulations (interpretation), which includes the last day of the relevant week, the amount to which he would have been entitled; and

(e)   if the applicant would, but for regulation 115 of the Employment and Support Allowance Regulations 2008, have been entitled to an income-related employment and support allowance in respect of the benefit week, within the meaning of regulation 2(1) of those Regulations (interpretation), which includes the last day of the relevant week, the amount to which he would have been entitled.

(6)   But if the amount mentioned in paragraph (a), (b), (c), (d), or (e) of sub-paragraph (5) ("the relevant amount") is in respect of a part-week, the amount that is to be taken into account under that paragraph is to be determined by–

(a)   dividing the relevant amount by the number equal to the number of days in that part-week, and

(b)   multiplying the result of that calculation by 7.

(7)   The amount determined under sub-paragraph (5) must be re-determined under that sub-paragraph if the applicant makes a further application for a reduction in council tax under the authority's scheme and the conditions in sub-paragraph (8) are satisfied, and in such a case–

(a)   paragraphs (a) to (e) of sub-paragraph (5) apply as if for the words "relevant week" there were substituted the words "relevant subsequent week"; and

(b)   subject to sub-paragraph (9), the amount as re-determined has effect from the first week following the relevant subsequent week in question.

(8)   The conditions are that–

(a)   a further application is made 26 or more weeks after–

    (i)   the date on which the applicant made an application in respect of which he was first treated as possessing the capital in question under paragraph 34(1);

    (ii)   in a case where there has been at least one re-determination in accordance with sub-paragraph (5), the date on which he last made an application which resulted in the weekly amount being re-determined, or

    (iii)   the date on which he last ceased to be entitled to a reduction in council tax under the authority's scheme,

whichever last occurred; and

(b)   the applicant would have been entitled to a reduction under the authority's scheme but for paragraph 34(1).

(9)   The amount as re-determined pursuant to sub-paragraph (7) does not have effect if it is less than the amount which applied in that case immediately before the re-determination and in such a case the higher amount must continue to have effect.

(10)   For the purposes of this paragraph–

"part-week"–

(a)   in relation to an amount mentioned in sub-paragraph (5)(a) means a period of less than a week for which a reduction in council tax under an authority's scheme is allowed;

(b)   in relation to an amount mentioned in sub-paragraph (5)(b) means a period of less than a week for which housing benefit is payable;

(c)   in relation to an amount mentioned in sub-paragraph (5)(c), (d) or (e) means–

    (i)   a period of less than a week which is the whole period for which income support, an income-related employment and support allowance or, as the case may be, an income-based jobseeker's allowance is payable; and

    (ii)   any other period of less than a week for which it is payable;

"relevant week" means the reduction week or part-week in which the capital in question of which the applicant has deprived himself within the meaning of paragraph 34(1)–

(a)   was first taken into account for the purpose of determining his entitlement to a reduction under an authority's scheme; or

(b)   was taken into account on a subsequent occasion for the purpose of determining or re-determining his entitlement to a reduction on that subsequent occasion and that determination or re-determination resulted in his beginning to receive, or ceasing to receive, a reduction under that authority's scheme,

and where more than one reduction week is identified by reference to paragraphs (a) and (b) of this definition the later or latest such reduction week or, as the case may be, the later or latest such part-week of the relevant week;

"relevant subsequent week" means the reduction week or part-week which includes the day on which the further application or, if more than one further application has been made, the last such application was made.

General Note

This is broadly equivalent to reg 50 HB Regs. The differences between the two provisions are due to the fact that this paragraph applies to pensioners and so sub-paras (3) and (5) are slightly different to the equivalent HB paras (reg 50(3) and (4)), and that CTR can be awarded for part of a week (unlike HB) and consequently the definitions of "part-week", "relevant week" and "relevant subsequent week" in sub-para (10) are slightly different to those in reg 50(8) HB Regs. See p475 for commentary on reg 50 HB Regs but note that para 35(4) to (6) is similar to reg 50(4), para 35(7) is equivalent to reg 50(5) HB Regs, and para 35(8) to (10) is broadly equivalent to reg 50(6) to (8) HB Regs.

Capital jointly held

36.   Except where an applicant possesses capital which is disregarded under paragraph 34(4) (notional capital), where an applicant and one or more persons are beneficially entitled in possession to any capital asset they must be treated, in the absence of evidence to the contrary, as if each of them were entitled in possession to the whole beneficial interest therein in an equal share and the foregoing provisions of this Chapter apply for the purposes of calculating the amount of capital which the applicant is treated as possessing as if it were actual capital which the applicant does possess.

General Note

This paragraph is similar, but not identical, to reg 51 HB Regs. See p476 for commentary.

Calculation of tariff income from capital

37.   The capital of an applicant, calculated in accordance with this Part, is to be treated as if it were a weekly income of–

(a)   £1 for each £500 in excess of £10,000 but not exceeding £16,000; and

(b)   £1 for any excess which is not a complete £500.

General Note
This paragraph concerns income that is deemed to be derived from capital ("tariff income"). Tariff income is assumed for capital which is in excess of £10,000 but not over £16,000 (as an applicant with capital of over £16,000 cannot be entitled to CTR under reg 11(2)). Each £500 (or part of £500) capital in excess of £10,000 is deemed to give rise to £1 income.

The amount of capital is assessed in accordance with this Part (and so, for example, it includes the capital of the applicant's partner, if s/he has one, and does not include capital that is disregarded under Sch 6).

PART 7
Extended reductions

Extended reductions (qualifying contributory benefits)

38.–(1)   Except in the case of an applicant who is in receipt of state pension credit, an applicant who is entitled to a reduction under a scheme (by virtue of falling within any of classes A to C) is entitled to an extended reduction (qualifying contributory benefits) where–
(a)   the applicant or the applicant's partner was entitled to a qualifying contributory benefit;
(b)   entitlement to a qualifying contributory benefit ceased because the applicant or the applicant's partner–
   (i)   commenced employment as an employed or self-employed earner;
   (ii)   increased their earnings from such employment; or
   (iii)   increased the number of hours worked in such employment,
   and that employment is or, as the case may be, increased earnings or increased number of hours are, expected to last five weeks or more;
(c)   the applicant or the applicant's partner had been entitled to and in receipt of a qualifying contributory benefit or a combination of qualifying contributory benefits for a continuous period of at least 26 weeks before the day on which the entitlement to a qualifying contributory benefit ceased; and
(d)   the applicant or the applicant's partner was not entitled to and not in receipt of a qualifying income-related benefit in the last reduction week in which the applicant, or the applicant's partner, was entitled to a qualifying contributory benefit.
(2)   An applicant must be treated as entitled to a reduction under an authority's scheme by virtue of falling within any of classes A to C where–
(a)   the applicant ceased to be entitled to a reduction under the authority's scheme because the applicant vacated the dwelling in which the applicant was resident;
(b)   the day on which the applicant vacated the dwelling was either in the week in which entitlement to a qualifying contributory benefit ceased, or in the preceding week; and
(c)   entitlement to the qualifying contributory benefit ceased in any of the circumstances listed in sub-paragraph (1)(b).

General Note

This is similar to Sch 1 para 32 CTRSPR(W) Regs (see p1241 for commentary) but note that this paragraph also covers extended reductions for applicants who are entitled to CTR by virtue of falling within Class C – ie, who are entitled to alternative maximum CTR (for which there is no equivalent in the CTRSPR(W) Regs). This rule is also similar to reg 73 HB Regs (see p512).

Duration of extended reduction period (qualifying contributory benefits)

39.–(1)   Where an applicant is entitled to an extended reduction (qualifying contributory benefits), the extended reduction period starts on the first day of the reduction week immediately following the reduction week in which the applicant, or the applicant's partner, ceased to be entitled to a qualifying contributory benefit.
(2)   For the purpose of sub-paragraph (1), an applicant or an applicant's partner ceases to be entitled to a qualifying contributory benefit on the day immediately following the last day of entitlement to that benefit.
(3)   The extended reduction period ends–
(a)   at the end of a period of four weeks; or
(b)   on the date on which the applicant who is receiving the extended reduction (qualifying contributory benefits) has no liability for council tax, if that occurs first.

Amount of extended reduction (qualifying contributory benefits)

40.–(1)   For any week during the extended reduction period the amount of the extended reduction (qualifying contributory benefits) the applicant is entitled to is the greater of–
(a)   the amount of reduction under the authority's scheme to which the applicant was entitled by virtue of falling within any of classes A to C in the last reduction week before the applicant or the applicant's partner ceased to be entitled to a qualifying contributory benefit;
(b)   the amount of reduction under the authority's scheme to which the applicant would be entitled by virtue of falling within any of classes A to C for any reduction week during the extended reduction period, if paragraph 38 (extended reductions (qualifying contributory benefits)) did not apply to the applicant; or

(c)   the amount of reduction under the authority's scheme to which the applicant's partner would be entitled by virtue of falling within any of classes A to C, if paragraph 38 did not apply to the applicant.

(2)   Sub-paragraph (1) does not apply in the case of a mover.

(3)   Where an applicant is in receipt of an extended reduction (qualifying contributory benefits) under this paragraph and the applicant's partner makes an application for a reduction under the authority's scheme, no reduction is to be awarded during the extended reduction period.

Extended reductions (qualifying contributory benefits): movers

41.–(1)   This paragraph applies–

(a)   to a mover; and

(b)   from the Monday following the day of the move.

(2)   The amount of the extended reduction (qualifying contributory benefit) awarded from the Monday from which this paragraph applies until the end of the extended reduction period is the amount of reduction under the authority's ("the first authority") scheme which was payable to the mover for the last reduction week before the mover, or the mover's partner, ceased to be entitled to a qualifying contributory benefit.

(3)   Where a mover's liability to pay council tax in respect of the new dwelling is to a second authority, the extended reduction (qualifying contributory benefits) may take the form of a payment from the first authority to–

(a)   the second authority; or

(b)   the mover directly.

Definitions

"mover" – see reg 2(1).
"authority" – see reg 2(1).
"partner" – see reg 2(1).
"qualifying contributory benefit" – see reg 2(1).
"new dwelling" – see reg 2(1).
"second authority" – see reg 2(1).

General Note

A "mover" is defined in reg 2 as an applicant who changes the dwelling in which s/he is resident and for which s/he is liable to pay council tax, from an area covered by one authority (the "first authority") to an area covered by a different authority, so this paragraph only applies to applicants who have moved between authorities rather than within an authority's area. Note that para 40(1) does not apply to movers: para 40(2), and the amount of the extended reduction in the case of a mover is determined in accordance with para 41(2) for the period from the Monday after the move until the end of the extended reduction period (as determined by para 39). The amount of the extended reduction is not affected by a change of circumstance during the extended reduction period: para 42(2). The mover can still apply to the new authority for CTR – but in accordance with para 44, the amount of any extended reduction to which s/he is entitled from the first authority is deducted from her/his CTR entitlement for the same period and only any remainder is paid.

Relationship between extended reduction (qualifying contributory benefits) and entitlement to a reduction by virtue of classes A to C

42.–(1)   Where an applicant's reduction under an authority's scheme would have ended when the applicant ceased to be entitled to a qualifying contributory benefit in the circumstances listed in paragraph 38(1)(b) (extended reductions: qualifying contributory benefits), that reduction does not cease to have effect until the end of the extended reduction period.

(2)   Part 9 (period of entitlement and changes of circumstances) does not apply to any extended reduction (qualifying contributory benefits) payable in accordance with paragraph 40(1)(a) or paragraph 41(2) (amount of extended reduction: movers).

Continuing reductions where state pension credit claimed

43.–(1)   This paragraph applies where–

(a)   the applicant is entitled to a reduction under an authority's scheme;

(b)   sub-paragraph (2) is satisfied; and

(c)   either–

    (i)   the applicant has attained the qualifying age for state pension credit [¹]; or

    (ii)   the applicant's partner has actually claimed state pension credit.

(2)   This sub-paragraph is only satisfied if the Secretary of State has certified to the authority that the applicant's partner has actually claimed state pension credit or that–

(a)   the applicant's award of–

    (i)   income support has terminated because the applicant has attained the qualifying age for state pension credit; or

(ii)   income-based jobseeker's allowance or income-related employment and support allowance has terminated because the applicant has attained the qualifying age for state pension credit [¹]; and

(b)   the applicant has claimed or is treated as having claimed or is required to make a claim for state pension credit.

(3)   Subject to sub-paragraph (4), in a case to which this paragraph applies, a person continues to be entitled to a reduction under an authority's scheme for the period of 4 weeks beginning on the day following the day on which the applicant's entitlement to income support or, as the case may be, income-based jobseeker's allowance or, income-related employment and support allowance, ceased, if and for so long as the applicant otherwise satisfies the conditions for entitlement to a reduction under the scheme.

(4)   Where a reduction under that scheme is awarded for the period of 4 weeks in accordance with sub-paragraph (3), and the last day of that period falls on a day other than the last day of a reduction week, then a reduction under the scheme must continue to be awarded until the end of the reduction week in which the last day of that period falls.

(5)   Throughout the period of 4 weeks specified in sub-paragraph (3) and any further period specified in sub-paragraph (4)–

(a)   the whole of the income and capital of the applicant is to be disregarded;

(b)   the maximum council tax reduction amount of the applicant is to be that which was applicable in his case immediately before that period commenced.

(6)   The appropriate maximum council tax reduction amount is to be calculated in accordance with paragraph 7(1) if, since the date it was last calculated–

(a)   the applicant's council tax liability has increased; or

(b)   a change in the deduction under paragraph 8 (non-dependent deductions) falls to be made.

Amendment
1.   Amended by reg 10 of SI 2017 No 1305 as from 6.12.18 in relation to schemes made for financial years starting on or after 1.4.18.

General Note
This paragraph, which provides for a "continuing reduction" for a period of four weeks, is equivalent to reg 54 HB(SPC) Regs. See p799 for commentary on that regulation.

Extended reductions: movers into an authority's area
44.   Where–

(a)   an application is made to an authority ("the current authority") for a reduction under its scheme, and

(b)   the applicant, or the partner of the applicant, is in receipt of an extended reduction from–

(i)   another billing authority in England; or

(ii)   a billing authority in Wales,

the current authority must reduce any reduction to which the applicant is entitled under its scheme by the amount of that extended reduction.

PART 8
When entitlement begins and change of circumstances

Date on which entitlement begins
45.–(1)   Subject to sub-paragraph (2), any person by whom or in respect of whom an application for a reduction under an authority's scheme is made and who is otherwise entitled to that reduction is so entitled from the reduction week following the date on which that application is made or is treated as made.

(2)   Where a person is otherwise entitled to a reduction under an authority's scheme and becomes liable for the first time for the authority's council tax in respect of a dwelling of which he is a resident in the reduction week in which his application is made or is treated as made, he shall be so entitled from that reduction week.

General Note
This paragraph stipulates when entitlement to CTR commences and is similar to reg 76(1) and (2) HB Regs. See p533 for commentary.

Date on which change of circumstances is to take effect
46.–(1)   Except in cases where paragraph 28 (disregard of changes in tax, contributions, etc) applies and subject to the following provisions of this paragraph and paragraph 47 (change of circumstances when state pension credit in payment), a change of circumstances which affects entitlement to, or the amount of, a reduction under an authority's scheme ("change of circumstances"), takes effect from the first day of the reduction week following the date on which the change actually occurs.

(2)   Where that change is cessation of entitlement to any benefit under the benefit Acts, the date on which the change actually occurs is the day immediately following the last day of entitlement to that benefit.

(3)　　Subject to sub-paragraph (4), where the change of circumstances is a change in the amount of council tax payable, it takes effect from the day on which it actually occurs.

(4)　　Where the change of circumstances is a change in the amount a person is liable to pay in respect of council tax in consequence of regulations under section 13 of the 1992 Act (reduced amounts of council tax) or changes in the discount to which a dwelling may be subject under sections 11 or 11A (discounts) of that Act, it takes effect from the day on which the change in amount has effect.

(5)　　Where the change of circumstances is the applicant's acquisition of a partner, the change takes effect on the day on which the acquisition takes place.

(6)　　Where the change of circumstances is the death of an applicant's partner or their separation, it takes effect on the day the death or separation occurs.

(7)　　If two or more changes of circumstances occurring in the same reduction week would, but for this paragraph, take effect in different reduction weeks in accordance with sub-paragraphs (1) to (6) they take effect from the day to which the appropriate sub-paragraph from (3) to (6) above refers, or, where more than one day is concerned, from the earlier day.

(8)　　Where the change of circumstances is that income, or an increase in the amount of income, other than a benefit or an increase in the amount of a benefit under the SSCBA, is paid in respect of a past period and there was no entitlement to income of that amount during that period, the change of circumstances takes effect from the first day on which such income, had it been paid in that period at intervals appropriate to that income, would have fallen to be taken into account for the purposes of the authority's scheme.

(9)　　Without prejudice to sub-paragraph (8), where the change of circumstances is the payment of income, or arrears of income, in respect of a past period, the change of circumstances takes effect from the first day on which such income, had it been timeously paid in that period at intervals appropriate to that income, would have fallen to be taken into account for the purposes of the authority's scheme.

(10)　　Sub-paragraph (11) applies if–

[¹]

(b)　　either–
  (i)　　a non-dependant took up residence in the applicant's dwelling; or
  (ii)　　there has been a change of circumstances in respect of a non-dependant so that the amount of the deduction which falls to be made under paragraph 8 (non-dependent deductions) increased.

(11)　　Where this sub-paragraph applies, the change of circumstances referred to in sub-paragraph (10)(b) takes effect from the effective date.

(12)　　In sub-paragraph (11), but subject to sub-paragraph (13), "the effective date" means–
(a)　　where more than one change of a kind referred to in sub-paragraph (10)(b) relating to the same non-dependant has occurred since–
  (i)　　the date on which the applicant's entitlement to a reduction under the authority's scheme first began; or
  (ii)　　the date which was the last effective date in respect of such a change,
  whichever is the later, the date which falls 26 weeks after the date on which the first such change occurred;
(b)　　where paragraph (a) does not apply, the date which falls 26 weeks after the date on which the change referred to in sub-paragraph (10)(b) occurred.

(13)　　If in any particular case the date determined under sub-paragraph (12) is not the first day of a reduction week, the effective date in that case is the first day of the next reduction week to commence after the date determined under that sub-paragraph.

Amendment

1.　　Omitted by reg 11 of SI 2017 No 1305 as from 6.12.18 in relation to schemes made for financial years starting on or after 1.4.18.

General Note

The general rule contained in para 46(1) is that a change of circumstance which affects whether an applicant is entitled to CTR or the amount of CTR to which s/he is entitled, takes effect from the first day of the reduction week (ie, from the Monday) which follows the day on which the change occurs. This general rule does not apply to certain legislative changes which can be disregarded for a period of up to 30 reduction weeks: para 28. Para 46(1) is also subject to para 47 and sub-paras (2) to (8) which set out exceptions to the general rule.

Change of circumstances where state pension credit in payment

47.–(1)　　Sub-paragraphs (2) and (3) apply where–
(a)　　an applicant is in receipt of state pension credit;
(b)　　the amount of state pension credit awarded to him is changed in consequence of a change in the applicant's circumstances or the correction of an official error; and
(c)　　the change in the amount of state pension credit payable to the applicant results in a change in the amount of a reduction he receives under an authority's scheme.

(2)　　Where the change of circumstance is that an increase in the amount of state pension credit payable to the applicant results in–
(a)　　an increase in the reduction he receives under that scheme, the change takes effect from the first day of the reduction week in which state pension credit becomes payable at the increased rate; or

    (b)   a decrease in the reduction he receives under that scheme, the change takes effect from the first day of the reduction week next following the date on which–

        (i)   the authority receives notification from the Secretary of State of the increase in the amount of state pension credit; or

        (ii)   state pension credit is increased,

        whichever is the later.

    (3)   Where the change of circumstance ("the relevant change") is that the applicant's state pension credit has been reduced and in consequence the reduction the applicant receives under the authority's scheme reduces–

    (a)   in a case where the applicant's state pension credit has been reduced because the applicant failed to notify the Secretary of State timeously of a change of circumstances, the relevant change takes effect from the first day of the reduction week from which state pension credit was reduced; or

    (b)   in any other case the relevant change takes effect from the first day of the reduction week next following the date on which–

        (i)   the authority receives notification from the Secretary of State of the reduction in the amount of state pension credit; or

        (ii)   state pension credit is reduced,

        whichever is the later.

    (4)   Where the change of circumstance is that state pension credit is reduced and in consequence of the change, the amount of a reduction the applicant receives under the authority's scheme is increased, the change takes effect from the first day of the reduction week in which state pension credit becomes payable at the reduced rate.

    (5)   Where a change of circumstance occurs in that an award of state pension credit has been made to the applicant or his partner and this would result in a decrease in the amount of reduction he receives under the authority's scheme, the change takes effect from the first day of the reduction week next following the date on which–

    (a)   the authority receives notification from the Secretary of State of the award of state pension credit; or

    (b)   entitlement to state pension credit begins,

whichever is the later.

    (6)   Where, in the case of an applicant who, or whose partner, is or has been awarded state pension credit comprising only the savings credit, there is–

    (a)   a change of circumstances of a kind described in any of sub-paragraphs (2) to (5) which results from a relevant calculation or estimate; and

    (b)   a change of circumstances which is a relevant determination,

each of which results in a change in the amount of reduction the applicant receives under the authority's scheme, the change of circumstances referred to in paragraph (b) takes effect from the day specified in sub-paragraph (2), (3), (4) or (5) as the case may be, in relation to the change referred to in paragraph (a).

    (7)   Where a change of circumstance occurs in that a guarantee credit has been awarded to the applicant or his partner and this would result in an increase in the amount of a reduction the applicant receives under the authority's scheme, the change takes effect from the first day of the reduction week next following the date in respect of which the guarantee credit is first payable.

    (8)   Where a change of circumstances would, but for this sub-paragraph, take effect under the preceding provisions of this paragraph within the 4 week period specified in paragraph 43 (continuing reductions where state pension credit claimed), that change takes effect on the first day of the first reduction week to commence after the expiry of the 4 week period.

    (9)   In this paragraph "official error" means an error made by–

    (a)   an authority or a person–

        (i)   authorised to carry out any function of an authority relating to its scheme; or

        (ii)   providing services relating to its scheme directly or indirectly to the authority; or

    (b)   an officer of–

        (i)   the Department for Work and Pensions; or

        (ii)   the Commissioners of Inland Revenue,

        acting as such, but excludes any error caused wholly or partly by any person or body not specified in paragraph (a) or (b) of this definition and any error of law which is shown to have been an error only by virtue of a subsequent decision of the court;

"relevant calculation or estimate" means the calculation or estimate made by the Secretary of State of the applicant's or, as the case may be, the applicant's partner's income and capital for the purposes of the award of state pension credit;

"relevant determination" means a change in the determination by the authority of the applicant's income and capital using the relevant calculation or estimate, in accordance with paragraph 14(1) (calculation of applicant's income in savings credit only cases).

General Note

    This paragraph is similar to reg 60 HB(SPC) Regs. It provides an exception to the general rule in para 40(1). See p808 for commentary.

SCHEDULE 2

General Note
This Schedule is equivalent to Sch 3 HB(SPC) Regs. See p848 for commentary on that schedule and its relationship to the HB Regs, but note that, for CTR, the restriction on the number of children for whom a 'pensioner' applicant can receive an amount under Sch 2 para 2 – ie, the so called "two-child limit" applies from 1 April 2018 (see the commentary under Sch 1 para 6, on p1126, for further details and exceptions to the two-child limit). Certain paragraphs also correspond to paragraphs in Sch 3 HB Regs, and cross references to commentary on these paragraphs are given below.

Applicable amounts

PART 1
Personal allowances

Personal allowance
[⁸**1.** The amount specified in column (2) below is respect of each person or couple specified in column (1) is the amount specified for the purposes of paragraph 6(1)(a) of Schedule 1.

Column (1) *Person or couple*	*Column (2)* *Amount*
(1) Single applicant or lone parent who has attained pensionable age	£181.00.
(2) Couple where one or both members have attained pensionable age	£270.60.
(3) If the applicant is a member of a polygamous marriage and one or more members of the marriage have attained pensionable age–	
(a) for the applicant and the other party to the marriage;	(a)£270.60;
(b) for each additional spouse who is a member of the same household as the applicant.	(b) £89.60.]

Amendments
1.   Amended by reg 4(a) of SI 2012 No 3085 as from 10.1.13.
2.   Amended by reg 2(8)(a) of SI 2013 No.3181 for schemes for financial years beginning on or after 1.4.14.
3.   Amended by reg 2 of SI 2014 No 488 for schemes for financial years beginning on or after 1.4.14.
4.   Amended by reg 2(6)(a) of SI 2014 No 3312 as from 12.1.15, for schemes made for financial years starting on or after 1.4.15.
5.   Amended by reg 2(4)(a) of SI 2015 No 2041 as from 14.1.16, in relation to schemes made for financial years starting on or after 1.4.16.
6.   Amended by reg 2(4)(a) of SI 2016 No 1262 as from 15.1.17, in relation to schemes made for financial years starting on or after 1.4.17.
7.   Substituted by reg 12(a) of SI 2017 No 1305 as from 12.1.18 in relation to schemes made for financial years starting on or after 1.4.18.
8.   Substituted by reg 4(a) of SI 2018 No 1346 as from 14.1.19, in relation to schemes made for financial years starting on or after 1.4.19.

Child or young person amounts
2.–(1)   The amounts specified in column (2) below in respect of each person specified in column (1) are the amounts, for the relevant period specified in column (1), specified for the purposes of paragraph 6(1)(b) of Schedule 1.

Column (1) *Child or young person*	*Column (2)* *Amount*
Person in respect of the period–	
(a) beginning on that person's date of birth and ending on the day preceding the first Monday in September following that person's sixteenth birthday;	(a) [³£66.90];
(b) beginning on the first Monday in September following that person's sixteenth birthday and ending on the day preceding that person's twentieth birthday.	(b) [³£66.90].

(2)   In column (1) of the table "the first Monday in September" means the Monday which first occurs in the month of September in any year.

Amendments
1.   Amended by reg 4(b) of SI 2012 No 3085 as from 10.1.13.
2.   Amended by reg 2(8)(b) of SI 2013 No 3181 for schemes for financial years beginning on or after 1.4.14.
3.   Amended by reg 2(6)(b) of SI 2014 No 3312 as from 12.1.15, for schemes made for financial years starting on or after 1.4.15.

PART 2
Family premium

Family premium

[¹**3.** The amount for the purposes of paragraph 6(1)(c) of Schedule 1 in respect of a family of which at least one member is a child or young person–

(a) is £17.45 in respect of a reduction week which begins in the period beginning with 1st April 2016 and ending with 30th April 2016;

(b) is nil in respect of a reduction week which begins after 1st May 2016].

Amendment

1. Substituted by reg 2(4)(b) of SI 2015 No 2041 as from 14.1.16, in relation to schemes made for financial years starting on or after 1.4.16, subject to transitional provision in reg 3 of SI 2015 No 2041.

General Note

If a 'pensioner' applicant is a member of a family which includes a child or young person, her/his applicable amount must include an amount determined by this paragraph (a family premium): Sch 1 para 6(1)(c). In respect of reduction weeks starting on or after Monday 2 May 2016, unless the pensioner is covered by the transitional provision in reg 3 Council Tax Reduction Schemes (Prescribed Requirements) (England) (Amendment) Regulations 2015 No.2041 (see p1187), the amount of the family premium is nil. This effectively means that for reduction weeks starting on or after 2 May 2016, the family premium is abolished for pensioners who are not covered by the transitional provision. Arguably, a billing authority is still free to include in its CTR scheme some provision allowing a higher discount or a discounted amount for applicants (including applicants who are not pensioners) whose family includes a child or young person if it chooses to do so. However, in accordance with reg 3 of SI 2015 No.2041, a billing authority's scheme is now only required to include a family premium of £17.45 in the applicable amount of a pensioner applicant if, on 30 April 2016, the applicant was liable to pay a reduced amount of council tax because s/he was entitled to CTR under the authority's CTR scheme and was either:

(1) a member of a family which includes at least one child or young person; *or*

(2) a partner in a polygamous marriage and either s/he, or another partner of the polygamous marriage, was responsible for a child or young person who was a member of the same household.

An applicant's entitlement to the £17.45 family premium ends either when the above condition (1) or (2) no longer applies to her/him or when s/he makes a new CTR application.

'Pensioner' is defined in reg 3 and 'family' is defined in reg 6. To ascertain who is 'partner in a polygamous marriage' see reg 5 and the definition of 'partner' in reg 2. 'Child' and 'young person' are defined in reg 2 and reg 7 explains when someone can be treated as responsible for a child or young person.

PART 3
Premiums

4. The premiums specified in Part 4 are, for the purposes of paragraph 6(1)(d) of Schedule 1, applicable to an applicant who satisfies the condition specified in this Part in respect of that premium.

5. Subject to sub-paragraph (2), for the purposes of this Part, once a premium is applicable to an applicant under this Part, a person is to be treated as being in receipt of any benefit for–

(a) in the case of a benefit to which the Social Security (Overlapping Benefits) Regulations 1979 applies, any period during which, apart from the provision of those Regulations, he would be in receipt of that benefit; and

(b) any period spent by a person in undertaking a course of training or instruction provided or approved by the Secretary of State under section 2 of the Employment and Training Act 1973, or by Skills Development Scotland, Scottish Enterprise or Highland and Islands Enterprise under section 2 of the Enterprise and New Towns (Scotland) Act 1990 or for any period during which he is in receipt of a training allowance.

(2) For the purposes of the carer premium under paragraph 9, a person is to be treated as being in receipt of a carer's allowance by virtue of sub-paragraph (1)(a) only if and for so long as the person in respect of whose care the allowance has been claimed remains in receipt of attendance allowance, or the care component of disability living allowance at the highest or middle rate prescribed in accordance with section 72(3) of the SSCBA or the daily living component of personal independence payment paid at either rate prescribed in accordance with Part 4 of the Welfare Reform Act 2012 or an AFIP.

General Note

This paragraph is equivalent to Sch 3 para 7 HB Regs. See p635 for commentary.

Severe disability premium

6.–(1) The condition is that the applicant is a severely disabled person.

(2) For the purposes of sub-paragraph (1), an applicant is to be treated as being a severely disabled person if, and only if–

(a)   in the case of a single applicant, a lone parent or an applicant who is treated as having no partner in consequence of sub-paragraph (3)–

  (i)   he is in receipt of attendance allowance, or the care component of disability living allowance at the highest or middle rate prescribed in accordance with section 72(3) of the SSCBA, or the daily living component of personal independence payment paid at either rate prescribed in accordance with Part 4 of the Welfare Reform Act 2012, or an AFIP; and

  (ii)   subject to sub-paragraph (6), he has no non-dependants aged 18 or over normally residing with him or with whom he is normally residing; and

  (iii)   no person is entitled to, and in receipt of, a carer's allowance [² under section 70 of the SSCBA or has an award of universal credit which includes the carer element under regulation 29 of the Universal Credit Regulations 2013] in respect of caring for him;

(b)   in the case of an applicant who has a partner–

  (i)   the applicant is in receipt of attendance allowance, or the care component of disability living allowance at the highest or middle rate prescribed in accordance with section 72(3) of the SSCBA, or the daily living component of personal independence payment paid at either rate prescribed in accordance with Part 4 of the Welfare Reform Act 2012, or an AFIP;

  (ii)   his partner is also in receipt of such an allowance or, if he is a member of a polygamous marriage, each other member of that marriage is in receipt of such an allowance; and

  (iii)   subject to sub-paragraph (6), the applicant has no non-dependants aged 18 or over normally residing with him or with whom he is normally residing,

and either a person is entitled to and in receipt of a carer's allowance [² or has an award of universal credit that includes the carer element] in respect of caring for only one of the couple or, if he is a member of a polygamous marriage, for one or more but not all the members of the marriage, or as the case may be, no person is entitled to and in receipt of such an allowance [² or has such an award of universal credit] in respect of caring for either member of a couple or any of the members of the marriage.

(3)   Where an applicant has a partner who does not satisfy the condition in sub-paragraph (2)(b)(ii), and that partner is blind [¹ or severely sight-impaired] or is treated as [¹ such] within the meaning of sub-paragraph (4), that partner is to be treated for the purposes of sub-paragraph (2) as if he were not a partner of the applicant.

(4)   For the purposes of sub-paragraph (3), a person is blind [¹ or severely sight-impaired] if he is registered [³] [¹as severely sight-impaired in a register kept by a local authority in England under section 77(1) of the Care Act 2014 (registers of sight-impaired adults)] [³], in Scotland, has been certified as blind and in consequence he is registered in a register maintained by or on behalf of a council constituted under section 2 of the Local Government (Scotland) Act 1994 [³ or is registered as severely sight-impaired in a register kept by a local authority in Wales under section 18(1) of the Social Services and Well-being (Wales) Act 2014].

(5)   For the purposes of sub-paragraph (4), a person who has ceased to be registered as blind [¹ or severely sight-impaired] on regaining his eyesight is nevertheless to be treated as [¹ such] and as satisfying the additional condition set out in that sub-paragraph for a period of 28 weeks following the date on which he ceased to be so registered.

(6)   For the purposes of sub-paragraph (2)(a)(ii) and (2)(b)(iii) no account is to be taken of–

(a)   a person receiving attendance allowance, or the care component of disability living allowance at the highest or middle rate prescribed in accordance with section 72(3) of the SSCBA, or the daily living component of personal independence payment paid at either rate prescribed in accordance with Part 4 of the Welfare Reform Act 2012, or an AFIP; or

(b)   a person who is blind or is treated as blind within the meaning of sub-paragraphs (4) and (5).

(7)   For the purposes of sub-paragraph (2)(b) a person is to be treated–

(a)   as being in receipt of attendance allowance, or the care component of disability living allowance at the highest or middle rate prescribed in accordance with section 72(3) of the SSCBA, if he would, but for his being a patient for a period exceeding 28 days, be so in receipt;

(b)   as being in receipt of the daily living component of personal independence payment paid at the rate prescribed in accordance with Part 4 of the Welfare Reform Act 2012 if he would, but for his being a patient for a period exceeding 28 days, be so entitled and in receipt notwithstanding section 86 of that Act and regulations made thereunder;

(c)   as being in receipt of an AFIP, if he would, but for any suspension of payment in accordance with any terms of the armed and reserve forces compensation scheme which allow for a suspension because a person is undergoing medical treatment in a hospital or similar institution;

(d)   as being entitled to and in receipt of a carer's allowance [² or having an award of universal credit which includes the carer element] if he would, but for the person for whom he was caring being a patient in hospital for a period exceeding 28 days, be so entitled [² or have such an award of universal credit] and in receipt.

(8)   For the purposes of sub-paragraph (2)(a)(iii) and (2)(b)–

(a)   no account is to be taken of an award of carer's allowance to the extent that payment of such an award is back-dated for a period before the date on which the award is first paid; and

(b)   a reference to a person being in receipt of a carer's allowance [² or as having an award of universal credit which includes the carer element] is to include reference to a person who would have been in receipt of that allowance [² or had such an award of universal credit] but for the application of a restriction under section 6B or 7 of the Social Security Fraud Act 2001 (loss of benefit).

Amendments
1. Amended by art 2 and Sch para 36(6) of SI 2015 No.643 as from 1.4.15.
2. Amended by reg 2(4)(c) of SI 2015 No 2041 as from 14.1.16, in relation to schemes made for financial years starting on or after 1.4.16.
3. Amended by Sch 3 para 136 of SI 2016 No 211 (W.84) as from 6.4.16.

General Note
This paragraph is broadly equivalent to Sch 3 para 14 HB Regs (although the wording of sub-para (7)(b) is slightly different than the equivalent in Sch 3 HB Regs – para 14(5)(c) – in that it includes the words "so entitled"). See p642 for commentary.

Enhanced disability premium
  7.–(1) The condition is that–
  (a) the care component of disability living allowance is, or would, but for a suspension of benefit in accordance with regulations under section 113(2) of the SSCBA or but for an abatement as a consequence of hospitalisation, be payable at the highest rate prescribed under section 73(2) of that Act; or
  (b) (as the case may be) the daily living component of personal independence payment is, or would, but for a suspension of payment in accordance with regulations under section 86 of the Welfare Reform Act 2012, be payable at the enhanced rate under section 78(2) of that Act,
in respect of a child or young person who is a member of the applicant's family.
  (2) Where the condition in sub-paragraph (1) ceases to be satisfied because of the death of a child or young person, the condition is that the applicant or partner is entitled to child benefit in respect of that person under section 145A of the SSCBA (entitlement after death of child or qualifying young person).

General Note
It appears s73(2) SSCBA has been referred to in sub-para (1)(a) in error, and that the intended reference is likely to have been to 72(3) SSCBA.

Disabled child premium
  8. The condition is that a child or young person for whom the applicant or a partner of his is responsible and who is a member of the applicant's household–
  (a) is in receipt of disability living allowance or personal independence payment or is no longer in receipt of such allowance because he is a patient, provided that the child or young person continues to be a member of the family; or
  (b) is blind within the meaning of paragraph 6(4) of this Schedule or treated as blind in accordance with paragraph 6(5); or
  (c) is a child or young person in respect of whom section 145A of the SSCBA (entitlement after death of child or qualifying young person) applies for the purposes of entitlement to child benefit but only for the period prescribed under that section, and in respect of whom a disabled child premium was included in the applicant's applicable amount immediately before the death of that child or young person, or ceased to be included in the applicant's applicable amount because of that child or young person's death.

General Note
This paragraph is equivalent to Sch 3 para 16 HB Regs (although there is no equivalent to sub-para 16(e) which provides another route to qualification for a disabled child premium – a young person's receipt of AFIP). See p644 for commentary.

Carer premium
  9.–(1) The condition is that the applicant or his partner is, or both of them are, entitled to a carer's allowance.
  (2) Where a carer premium has been awarded but–
  (a) the person in respect of whose care the carer's allowance has been awarded dies; or
  (b) the person in respect of whom the premium was awarded ceases to be entitled, or ceases to be treated as entitled, to a carer's allowance,
this paragraph shall be treated as satisfied for a period of eight weeks from the relevant date specified in sub-paragraph (3).
  (3) The relevant date for the purposes of sub-paragraph (2) is–
  (a) in a case within sub-paragraph (2)(a) the Sunday following the death of the person in respect of whose care the carer's allowance has been awarded (or beginning with the date of death if the date occurred on a Sunday);
  (b) in a case within sub-paragraph (2)(b), the date on which that person who was entitled to a carer's allowance ceases to be entitled to it.

(4)   For the purposes of this paragraph, a person is to be treated as being entitled to and in receipt of a carer's allowance for any period not covered by an award but in respect of which a payment is made in lieu of an award.

General Note

This paragraph is similar to Sch 3 para 17(3) HB Regs. See p645 for commentary.

Persons in receipt of concessionary payments
    10.   For the purpose of determining whether a premium is applicable to a person under paragraphs 6 to 9 of this Schedule, any concessionary payment made to compensate that person for the non-payment of any benefit mentioned in those paragraphs is to be treated as if it were a payment of that benefit.

Person in receipt of benefit
    11.   For the purposes of this Part, a person is to be regarded as being in receipt of any benefit if, and only if, it is paid in respect of him and is to be so regarded only for any period in respect of which that benefit is paid.

General Note

This paragraph is equivalent to Sch 3 para 19 HB Regs. See p646 for commentary.

PART 4
Amounts of premium specified in Part 3

Provision	Amount
(1) Severe Disability Premium–	
(a) where the applicant satisfies the condition in paragraph 6(2)(a);	(a) [⁶£65.85];
(b) where the applicant satisfies the condition in paragraph 6(2)(b)–	
(i) in a case where there is someone in receipt of a carer's allowance [⁴ or who has an award of universal credit which includes the carer element under regulation 29 of the Universal Credit Regulations 2013] or if he or any partner satisfies that condition only by virtue of paragraph 6(7);	(i) [⁶£65.85];
(ii) in a case where there is no-one in receipt of such an allowance [⁴ or such an award of universal credit].	(ii) [⁶£131.70].
(2) Enhanced disability premium.	(2) [⁶£26.04] in respect of each child or young person in respect of whom the conditions specified in paragraph 7 are satisfied.
(3) Disabled Child Premium.	(3) [⁶£64.19] in respect of each child or young person in respect of whom the condition specified in paragraph 8 is satisfied
(4) Carer Premium.	(4) [⁶£36.85] in respect of each person who satisfies the condition specified in paragraph 9.

Amendments
1.   Amended by reg 4(c) of SI 2012 No 3085 as from 10.1.13.
2.   Amended by reg 2(8)(c) of SI 2013 No 3181 for schemes for financial years beginning on or after 1.4.14.
3.   Amended by reg 2(6)(c) of SI 2014 No 3312 as from 12.1.15, for schemes made for financial years starting on or after 1.4.15.
4.   Amended by reg 2(4)(d) of SI 2015 No 2041 as from 14.1.16, in relation to schemes made for financial years starting on or after 1.4.16.
5.   Amended by reg 12(b) of SI 2017 No 1305 as from 12.1.18 in relation to schemes made for financial years starting on or after 1.4.18.
6.   Amended by reg 4(b) of SI 2018 No 1346 as from 14.1.19, in relation to schemes made for financial years starting on or after 1.4.19.

SCHEDULE 3

General Note

This is similar to Sch 2 CTR(S) Regs. See p1552 for commentary on that Schedule.

Amount of alternative maximum council tax reduction

1.–(1)   Subject to paragraphs 2 and 3, the alternative maximum council tax reduction in respect of a day for the purpose of paragraph 9 of Schedule 1 is determined in accordance with the following Table and in this Table–

(a)   "second adult" means any person or persons residing with the applicant to whom paragraph 4(2) of Schedule 1 applies (class C); and

(b)   "person to whom paragraph 75(1) of Schedule 1 to the Default Scheme Regulations applies" includes any person to whom that paragraph would apply were they, and their partner if they had one, below the qualifying age for state pension credit.

(2)   In this Schedule "council tax due in respect of that day" means the council tax payable under section 10 of the 1992 Act less–

(a)   any reductions made in consequence of any enactment in, or under, the 1992 Act (other than a reduction under an authority's scheme); and

(b)   in a case to which sub-paragraph (c) in column (1) of the table below applies, the amount of any discount which may be appropriate to the dwelling under the 1992 Act.

(1) Second adult	(2) Alternative maximum council tax reduction
(a) Where the second adult or all second adults are in receipt of income support, an income-related employment and support allowance or state pension credit or are persons on an income-based jobseeker's allowance;	(a) 25 per cent of the council tax due in respect of that day;
(b) where the gross income of the second adult or, where there is more than one second adult, their aggregate gross income disregarding any income of persons on income support, an income-related employment and support allowance, state pension credit or an income-based jobseeker's allowance–	
(i) is less than [⁷£206.00] per week;	(i) 15 per cent of the council tax due in respect of that day;
(ii) is not less than [⁷£206.00] per week but less than [⁷£266.00] per week;	(ii) 7.5 per cent of the council tax due in respect of that day;
(c) where the dwelling would be wholly occupied by one or more persons to whom paragraph 73(1) of Schedule 1 to the Default Scheme Regulations applies but for the presence of one or more second adults who are in receipt of income support, state pension credit, an income-related employment and support allowance or are persons on an income-based jobseeker's allowance.	(c) 100 per cent of the council tax due in respect of that day.

Amendments

1.   Amended by reg 5 of SI 2012 No 3085 as from 10.1.13.

2.   Amended by reg 2(9) of SI 2013 No 3181 for schemes for financial years beginning on or after 1.4.14.

3.   Amended by reg 2(7) of SI 2014 No 3312 as from 12.1.15, for schemes made for financial years starting on or after 1.4.15.

4.   Amended by reg 2(5) of SI 2015 No 2041 as from 14.1.16, in relation to schemes made for financial years starting on or after 1.4.16.

5.   Amended by reg 2(5) of SI 2016 No 1262 as from 15.1.17, in relation to schemes made for financial years starting on or after 1.4.17.

6.   Amended by reg 13 of SI 2017 No 1305 as from 12.1.18 in relation to schemes made for financial years starting on or after 1.4.18.

7.   Amended by reg 5 of SI 2018 No 1346 as from 14.1.19, in relation to schemes made for financial years starting on or after 1.4.19.

2.   In determining a second adult's gross income for the purposes of this Schedule, the following must be disregarded from that income–

(a)   any attendance allowance, or any disability living allowance or any personal independence payment under Part 4 of the Welfare Reform Act 2012 or an AFIP; and

(b)   any payment to which paragraph 8(9)(b) or (10) of Schedule 1 to these Regulations refers (and sub-paragraph (13) of paragraph 8 applies to this paragraph as it applies in relation to that paragraph).

3.   Where there are two or more second adults residing with the applicant and any such second adult falls to be disregarded for the purposes of discount in accordance with Schedule 1 to the 1992 Act, his income is to be disregarded in determining the amount of any alternative maximum council tax reduction, unless that second adult is a member of a couple and his partner does not fall to be disregarded for the purposes of discount.

SCHEDULE 4

General Note
This is broadly equivalent to Sch 4 HB(SPC) Regs, see p854 for commentary but note that under para 5(2) and (3) of this Schedule, £20 can be disregarded from earnings if an applicant had such a disregard in an award of CTR, HB or CTB in the circumstances outlined.

Sums disregarded from applicant's earnings

1.   Where two or more of paragraphs 2 to 5 apply in any particular case the overall maximum sum which falls to be disregarded in that case under those paragraphs is restricted to–
(a)   £25 in the case of a lone parent;
(b)   £20 in any other case.

2.   In a case where an applicant is a lone parent, £25 of earnings.
3.–(1)   In a case of earnings from any employment or employments to which sub-paragraph (2) applies, £20.
(2)   This paragraph applies to employment–
(a)   as a part-time fire-fighter employed by a fire and rescue authority constituted by a scheme under section 2 of the Fire and Rescue Services Act 2004 or a scheme to which section 4 of that Act applies;
[² (ab)   as a part-time fire-fighter employed by a fire and rescue authority created by an order under section 4A of the Fire and Rescue Services Act 2004;]
[¹ (b)   a part-time fire-fighter employed by the Scottish Fire and Rescue Service established under section 1A of the Fire (Scotland) Act 2005;]
(c)   as an auxiliary coastguard in respect of coast rescue activities;
(d)   in the manning or launching of a lifeboat if the employment is part-time;
(e)   as a member of any territorial or reserve force prescribed in Part I of Schedule 6 to the Social Security (Contributions) Regulations 2001.
(3)   If–
(a)   any of the earnings of the applicant or, if he has a partner, his partner, or both of them, are disregarded under sub-paragraph (1); and
(b)   either of them has, or both of them have, other earnings,
so much of those other earnings as would not, in the aggregate with the earnings disregarded under that sub-paragraph, exceed £20.

Amendments
1.   Substituted by reg 2(10) of SI 2013 No 3181 for schemes for financial years beginning on or after 1.4.14.
2.   Inserted by Sch 2 para 8 of SI 2017 No 863 as from 1.10.17 for schemes for financial years beginning on or after 1.4.18.

4.–(1)   If the applicant or, if he has a partner, his partner is a carer, or both are carers, £20 of any earnings received from his or their employment.
(2)   Where the carer premium is awarded in respect of the applicant and of any partner of his, their earnings must for the purposes of this paragraph be aggregated, but the amount to be disregarded in accordance with sub-paragraph (1) must not exceed £20 of the aggregated amount.
(3)   In this paragraph the applicant or his partner is a carer if paragraph 9 of Part 3 of Schedule 2 (amount applicable for carers) is satisfied in respect of him.
5.–(1)   £20 is disregarded if the applicant or, if he has a partner, his partner–
(a)   is in receipt of–
    (i)   long-term incapacity benefit under section 30A of the SSCBA;
    (ii)   severe disablement allowance under section 68 of that Act;
    (iii)   attendance allowance under sections 64 to 70 of that Act;
    (iv)   disability living allowance;
    (v)   personal independence payment;
    (vi)   an AFIP;
    (vii)   any mobility supplement under article 20 of the Naval, Military and Air Forces Etc (Disablement and Death) Service Pensions Order 2006 (including such a supplement by virtue of any other scheme or order) or under article 25A of the Personal Injuries (Civilians) Scheme 1983;

    (viii)   the disability element or the severe disability element of working tax credit under Schedule 2 to the Working Tax Credit (Entitlement and Maximum Rate) Regulations 2002; or

    (ix)   main phase employment and support allowance; or

(b)   is or are registered [^{3}] [^{2} as severely sight-impaired in a register kept by a local authority in England under section 77(1) of the Care Act 2014 (registers of sight-impaired adults)] [^{3}], in Scotland, has been certified as blind and in consequence is registered in a register maintained by or on behalf of a council constituted under section 2 of the Local Government (Scotland) Act 1994 [^{3} or is registered as severely sight-impaired in a register kept by a local authority in Wales under section 18(1) of the Social Services and Well-being (Wales) Act 2014]; or

(c)   is, or is treated as, incapable of work in accordance with the provisions of, and regulations made under, Part 12A of the SSCBA (incapacity for work), and has been incapable, or has been treated as incapable, of work for a continuous period of not less than–

    (i)   in the case of an applicant who is terminally ill within the meaning of section 30B(4) of the SSCBA, 196 days;

    (ii)   in any other case, 364 days; or

(d)   has, or is treated as having, limited capacity for work within the meaning of section 1(4) of the Welfare Reform Act 2007 or limited capability for work-related activity within the meaning of section 2(5) of that Act and either–

    (i)   the assessment phase as defined in section 24(2) of the Welfare Reform Act 2007 has ended; or

    (ii)   regulation 7 of the Employment and Support Allowance Regulations 2008 [^{1} or regulation 7 of the Employment and Support Allowance Regulations 2013] (circumstances where the condition that the assessment phase has ended before entitlement to the support component [^{4}] arising does not apply) applies.

(2)   Subject to sub-paragraph (3), £20 is disregarded if the applicant or, if he has a partner, his partner has, within a period of 8 weeks ending on the day in respect of which the applicant or his partner attains the qualifying age for state pension credit, had an award of housing benefit or council tax benefit or was in receipt of a reduction under an authority's scheme (including under another authority's scheme) and–

(a)   £20 was disregarded in respect of earnings taken into account in that award; and

(b)   the person whose earnings qualified for the disregard continues in employment after the termination of that award.

(3)   The disregard of £20 specified in sub-paragraph (2) applies so long as there is no break, other than a break which does not exceed 8 weeks, in a person's–

(a)   entitlement to housing benefit; or

(b)   receipt of a reduction under an authority's (including under another authority's) scheme; or

(c)   employment,

following the first day in respect of which that benefit is awarded or the reduction given under that scheme.

(4)   £20 is the maximum amount which may be disregarded under this paragraph, notwithstanding that, where the applicant has a partner, both the applicant and his partner satisfy the requirements of this paragraph.

Amendments

1.   Amended by reg 2(8)(a) of SI 2014 No 3312 as from 12.1.15, for schemes made for financial years starting on or after 1.4.15.

2.   Amended by art 2 and Sch para 36(7) of SI 2015 No 643 as from 1.4.15.

3.   Amended by Sch 3 para 137 of SI 2016 No 211 (W.84) as from 6.4.16.

4.   Amended by Sch 1 para 8(4) of SI 2017 No 204 as from 3.4.17, subject to transitional and savings provisions in Sch 2 paras 1–7.

6.–(1)   Where–

(a)   the applicant (or if the applicant is a member of a couple, at least one member of that couple) is a person to whom sub-paragraph (5) applies;

(b)   the Secretary of State is satisfied that that person is undertaking exempt work as defined in sub-paragraph (6); and

(c)   paragraph 13 of Schedule 1 does not apply,

the amount specified in sub-paragraph (7) ("the specified amount").

(2)   Where this paragraph applies, paragraphs 1 to 5 and 7 do not apply; but in any case where the applicant is a lone parent, and the specified amount would be less than the amount specified in paragraph 2, then paragraph 2 applies instead of this paragraph.

(3)   Notwithstanding paragraph 11 of Schedule 1 (calculation of income and capital of members applicant's family and of a polygamous marriage), if sub-paragraph (1) applies to one member of a couple ("A") it shall not apply to the other member of that couple ("B") except to the extent provided in sub-paragraph (4).

(4)   Where A's earnings are less than the specified amount, there must also be disregarded so much of B's earnings as would not when aggregated with A's earnings exceed the specified amount; but the amount of B's earnings which may be disregarded under this sub-paragraph is limited to a maximum of £20 unless the Secretary of State is satisfied that B is also undertaking exempt work.

(5)   This sub-paragraph applies to a person who is–

(a)   in receipt of a contributory employment and support allowance;

(b)   in receipt of incapacity benefit;

(c)   in receipt of severe disablement allowance;

(d)   being credited with earnings on the grounds of incapacity for work or limited capability for work under regulation 8B of the Social Security (Credits) Regulations 1975.

(6)   "Exempt work" means work of the kind described in–

(a)   regulation 45(2), (3) or (4) of the Employment and Support Allowance Regulations 2008 [¹ or regulation 39(1)(a), (b) or (c) of the Employment and Support Allowance Regulations 2013]; or (as the case may be)

(b)   regulation 17(2), (3) or (4) of the Social Security (Incapacity for Work) (General) Regulations 1995, and, in determining for the purposes of this paragraph whether an applicant or a member of a couple is undertaking any type of exempt work, it is immaterial whether that person or their partner is also undertaking other work.

(7)   The specified amount is the amount of money from time to time mentioned in any provision referred to in sub-paragraph (6) by virtue of which the work referred to in sub-paragraph (1) is exempt (or, where more than one such provision is relevant and those provisions mention different amounts of money, the highest of those amounts).

Amendment

1.   Amended by reg 2(8)(b) of SI 2014 No 3312 as from 12.1.15, for schemes made for financial years starting on or after 1.4.15.

---

7.   Any amount or the balance of any amount which would fall to be disregarded under paragraph 18 or 19 of Schedule 5 to these Regulations had the applicant's income which does not consist of earnings been sufficient to entitle him to the full disregarded thereunder.

8.   Except where the applicant or his partner qualifies for a £20 disregard under the preceding provisions of this Schedule–

(a)   £5 must be disregarded if an applicant who has no partner has earnings;

(b)   £10 must be disregarded if an applicant who has a partner has earnings.

9.   Any earnings, other than earnings referred to in paragraph 17(9)(b) of Schedule 1, derived from employment which ended before the day in respect of which the applicant first satisfies the conditions for entitlement to a reduction under an authority's scheme.

10.–(1)   In a case where the applicant is a person who satisfies at least one of the conditions set out in sub-paragraph (2), and his net earnings equal or exceed the total of the amounts set out in sub-paragraph (3), the amount of his earnings that falls to be disregarded under this Schedule must be increased by £17.10.

(2)   The conditions of this sub-paragraph are that–

(a)   the applicant, or if he has a partner, either the applicant or his partner, is a person to whom regulation 20(1)(c) of the Working Tax Credit (Entitlement and Maximum Rate) Regulations 2002 applies; or

(b)   the applicant–

(i)   is, or any partner of his is, aged at least 25 and is engaged in remunerative work for on average not less than 30 hours per week; or

(ii)   if he is a member of a couple–

(aa)   at least one member of that couple is engaged in remunerative work for on average not less than 16 hours per week; and

[¹ (bb)   his family includes at least one child or young person;] or

(iii)   is a lone parent who is engaged in remunerative work for on average not less than 16 hours per week; or

(iv)   is, or if he has a partner, one of them is, engaged in remunerative work for on average not less than 16 hours per week and paragraph 5(1) above is satisfied in respect of that person.

(3)   The following are the amounts referred to in sub-paragraph (1)–

(a)   any amount disregarded under this Schedule;

(b)   the amount of child care charges calculated as deductible under paragraph 24(1)(c) of Schedule 1 (calculation of income on a weekly basis); and

(c)   £17.10.

(4)   The provisions of regulation 10 (remunerative work) are to apply in determining whether or not a person works for on average not fewer than 30 hours per week, but as if the reference to 16 hours in paragraph (1) of that regulation was a reference to 30 hours.

Amendment

1.   Substituted by reg 2(6) of SI 2015 No 2041 as from 14.1.16, in relation to schemes made for financial years starting on or after 1.4.16.

---

11.   Where a payment of earnings is made in a currency other than Sterling, any banking charge or commission payable in converting to that payment into Sterling.

SCHEDULE 5

General Note
This is similar to the HB equivalent (see p857).

Amounts to be disregarded in the calculation of income other than earnings

1.   In addition to any sum which falls to be disregarded in accordance with paragraphs 2 to 6, £10 of any of the following, namely–
   (a)   a war disablement pension (except insofar as such a pension falls to be disregarded under paragraph 2 or 3);
   (b)   a war widow's pension or war widower's pension;
   (c)   a pension payable to a person as a widow, widower or surviving civil partner under any power of Her Majesty otherwise than under an enactment to make provision about pensions for or in respect of persons who have been disabled or have died in consequence of service as members of the armed forces of the Crown;
   (d)   a guaranteed income payment and, if the amount of that payment has been adjusted to less than £10 by a pension or payment falling within article 39(1)(a) or (b) of the Armed Forces and Reserve Forces (Compensation Scheme) Order 2011, so much of that pension or payment as would not, in aggregate with the amount of any guaranteed income payment disregarded, exceed £10;
   (e)   a payment made to compensate for the non-payment of such a pension or payment as is mentioned in any of the preceding sub-paragraphs;
   (f)   a pension paid by the government of a country outside Great Britain which is analogous to any of the pensions or payments mentioned in sub-paragraphs (a) to (d) above;
   [¹ (g) a pension paid by a government to victims of National Socialist persecution.]

Amendment
1.   Substituted by reg 14(a) of SI 2017 No 1305 as from 12.1.18 in relation to schemes made for financial years starting on or after 1.4.18.

2.   The whole of any amount included in a pension to which paragraph 1 relates in respect of–
   (a)   the applicant's need for constant attendance;
   (b)   the applicant's exceptionally severe disablement.
3.   Any mobility supplement under article 20 of the Naval, Military and Air Forces Etc (Disablement and Death) Service Pensions Order 2006 (including such a supplement by virtue of any other scheme or order) or under article 25A of the Personal Injuries (Civilians) Scheme 1983 or any payment intended to compensate for the non-payment of such a supplement.
4.   Any supplementary pension under article 23(2) of the Naval, Military and Air Forces Etc (Disablement and Death) Service Pensions Order 2006 (pensions to surviving spouses and surviving civil partners) and any analogous payment made by the Secretary of State for Defence to any person who is not a person entitled under that Order.
5.   In the case of a pension awarded at the supplementary rate under article 27(3) of the Personal Injuries (Civilians) Scheme 1983 (pensions to widows, widowers or surviving civil partners), the sum specified in paragraph 1(c) of Schedule 4 to that Scheme.
6.–(1) Any payment which is–
   (a)   made under any of the Dispensing Instruments to a widow, widower or surviving civil partner of a person–
      (i)   whose death was attributable to service in a capacity analogous to service as a member of the armed forces of the Crown; and
      (ii)   whose service in such capacity terminated before 31st March 1973; and
   (b)   equal to the amount specified in article 23(2) of the Naval, Military and Air Forces Etc (Disablement and Death) Service Pensions Order 2006.
   (2)   In this paragraph "the Dispensing Instruments" means the Order in Council of 19th December 1881, the Royal Warrant of 27th October 1884 and the Order by His Majesty of 14th January 1922 (exceptional grants of pay, non-effective pay and allowances).
7.   £15 of any widowed parent's allowance to which the applicant is entitled under section 39A of the SSCBA.
8.   £15 of any widowed mother's allowance to which the applicant is entitled under section 37 of the SSCBA.
9.   Where the applicant occupies a dwelling as his home and he provides in that dwelling board and lodging accommodation, an amount, in respect of each person for whom such accommodation is provided for the whole or any part of a week, equal to–
   (a)   where the aggregate of any payments made in respect of any one week in respect of such accommodation provided to such person does not exceed £20, 100 per cent. of such payments; or
   (b)   where the aggregate of any such payments exceeds £20, £20 and 50 per cent. of the excess over £20.

10. If the applicant–
(a) owns the freehold or leasehold interest in any property or is a tenant of any property; and
(b) occupies a part of that property; and
(c) has an agreement with another person allowing that person to occupy another part of that property on payment of rent and–
   (i) the amount paid by that person is less than £20 per week, the whole of that amount; or
   (ii) the amount paid is £20 or more per week, £20.

11. Where an applicant receives income under an annuity purchased with a loan, which satisfies the following conditions–
(a) that the loan was made as part of a scheme under which not less than 90 per cent. of the proceeds of the loan were applied to the purchase by the person to whom it was made of an annuity ending with his life or with the life of the survivor of two or more persons (in this paragraph referred to as "the annuitants") who include the person to whom the loan was made;
(b) that at the time the loan was made the person to whom it was made or each of the annuitants had attained the age of 65 [¹ or, if it was higher at the time, pensionable age];
(c) that the loan was secured on a dwelling in Great Britain and the person to whom the loan was made or one of the annuitants owns an estate or interest in that dwelling;
(d) that the person to whom the loan was made or one of the annuitants occupies the dwelling on which it was secured as his home at the time the interest is paid; and
(e) that the interest payable on the loan is paid by the person to whom the loan was made or by one of the annuitants,
the amount, calculated on a weekly basis, equal to–
   (i) where, or insofar as, section 369 of the Income and Corporation Taxes Act 1988 (mortgage interest payable under deduction of tax) applies to the payments of interest on the loan, the interest which is payable after deduction of a sum equal to income tax on such payments at the applicable percentage of income tax within the meaning of section 369(1A) of that Act;
   (ii) in any other case, the interest which is payable on the loan without deduction of such a sum.

Amendment
1. Amended by reg 14(b) of SI 2017 No 1305 as from 6.12.18 in relation to schemes made for financial years starting on or after 1.4.18.

12.–(1) Any payment, other than a payment to which sub-paragraph (2) applies, made to the applicant by Trustees in exercise of a discretion exercisable by them.
(2) This sub-paragraph applies to payments made to the applicant by Trustees in exercise of a discretion exercisable by them for the purpose of–
(a) obtaining food, ordinary clothing or footwear or household fuel;
(b) the payment of rent, council tax or water charges for which that applicant or his partner is liable;
(c) meeting housing costs of a kind specified in Schedule 2 to the State Pension Credit Regulations 2002.
(3) In a case to which sub-paragraph (2) applies, £20 or–
(a) if the payment is less than £20, the whole payment;
(b) if, in the applicant's case, £10 is disregarded in accordance with paragraph 1(a) to (g), £10 or the whole payment if it is less than £10; or
(c) if, in the applicant's case, £15 is disregarded under paragraph 7 or paragraph 8 and–
   (i) he has no disregard under paragraph 1(a) to (g), £5 or the whole payment if it is less than £5;
   (ii) he has a disregard under paragraph 1(a) to (g), nil.
(4) For the purposes of this paragraph, "ordinary clothing or footwear" means clothing or footwear for normal daily use, but does not include school uniforms, or clothing and footwear used solely for sporting activities.

13. Any increase in pension or allowance under Part 2 or 3 of the Naval, Military and Air Forces Etc (Disablement and Death) Service Pensions Order 2006 paid in respect of a dependent other than the pensioner's partner.

14. Any payment ordered by a court to be made to the applicant or the applicant's partner in consequence of any accident, injury or disease suffered by the person or a child of the person to or in respect of whom the payments are made.

15. Periodic payments made to the applicant or the applicant's partner under an agreement entered into in settlement of a claim made by the applicant or, as the case may be, the applicant's partner for an injury suffered by him.

16. Any income which is payable outside the United Kingdom for such period during which there is a prohibition against the transfer to the United Kingdom of that income.

17. Any banking charges or commission payable in converting to Sterling payments of income made in a currency other than Sterling.

18. Where the applicant makes a parental contribution in respect of a student attending a course at an establishment in the United Kingdom or undergoing education in the United Kingdom, which contribution has been assessed for the purposes of calculating–

(a)   under, or pursuant to regulations made under powers conferred by section 22 of the Teaching and Higher Education Act 1998, that student's award;

(b)   under regulations made in exercise of the powers conferred by section 49 of the Education (Scotland) Act 1980, that student's bursary, scholarship, or other allowance under that section or under regulations made in exercise of the powers conferred by section 73 of that Act of 1980, any payment to that student under that section; or

(c)   the student's student loan,

an amount equal to the weekly amount of that parental contribution, but only in respect of the period for which that contribution is assessed as being payable.

19.–(1)   Where the applicant is the parent of a student aged under 25 in advanced education who either–

(a)   is not in receipt of any award, grant or student loan in respect of that education; or

(b)   is in receipt of an award bestowed by virtue of the Teaching and Higher Education Act 1998, or regulations made thereunder, or a bursary, scholarship or other allowance under section 49(1) of the Education (Scotland) Act 1980, or a payment under section 73 of that Act of 1980,

and the applicant makes payments by way of a contribution towards the student's maintenance, other than a parental contribution falling within paragraph 18, an amount specified in sub-paragraph (2) in respect of each week during the student's term.

(2)   For the purposes of sub-paragraph (1), the amount is to be equal to–

(a)   the weekly amount of the payments; or

[¹(b)   [³ £57.90] less the weekly amount of any award, bursary, scholarship, allowance or payment referred to in sub-paragraph (1)(b),]

whichever is less.

(3)   In this paragraph and paragraph 18 a reference to a "student loan" or a "grant" is a reference to a student loan or a grant within the meaning of Part 11 of the Schedule to the Default Scheme Regulations.

Amendments

1.   Amended by reg 6 of SI 2012 No 3085 as from 10.1.13.

2.   Amended by reg 2(11) of SI 2013 No 3181 for schemes for financial years beginning on or after 1.4.14.

3.   Amended by reg 2(9) of SI 2014 No 3312 as from 12.1.15, for schemes made for financial years starting on or after 1.4.15.

20.–(1)   [¹ Where an applicant's family includes at least one child or young person] £15 of any payment of maintenance, whether under a court order or not, which is made or due to be made by the applicant's spouse, civil partner, former spouse or former civil partner or the applicant's partner's spouse, civil partner, former spouse, or former civil partner.

(2)   For the purposes of sub-paragraph (1), where more than one maintenance payment falls to be taken into account in any week, all such payments must be aggregated and treated as if they were a single payment.

Amendment

1.   Amended by reg 2(7) of SI 2015 No 2041 as from 14.1.16, in relation to schemes made for financial years starting on or after 1.4.16.

---

21.   Except in a case which falls under paragraph 10 of Schedule 4, where the applicant is a person who satisfies any of the conditions of sub-paragraph (2) of that paragraph, any amount of working tax credit up to £17.10.

22.   Where the total value of any capital specified in Part 2 (capital disregarded only for the purposes of determining deemed income) of Schedule 6 does not exceed £10,000, any income actually derived from such capital.

23.   Except in the case of income from capital specified in Part 2 of Schedule 6 (capital disregards), any actual income from capital.

24.   Where the applicant, or the person who was the partner of the applicant on 31st March 2003, was entitled on that date to income support or an income-based jobseeker's allowance but ceased to be so entitled on or before 5th April 2003 by virtue only of regulation 13 of the Housing Benefit (General) Amendment (No 3) Regulations 1999 as in force at that date, the whole of his income.

SCHEDULE 6

General Note

This schedule, which is similar to Sch 6 of the HB(SPC) Regs (see p862), sets out the capital that must be disregarded when assessing a pensioner's entitlement to CTR: Sch 1 para 31(2).

In accordance with Sch 1 paras 11 and 12, a partner's capital and, in some cases, a non-dependant's capital, is treated as the applicant's capital and, as it is treated as such, it is also subject to the disregards in this Schedule. Similarly, if an applicant is polygamously married to two or more members of her/his household, the capital of each member is also treated as the applicant's.

If a single pensioner applicant (or, in the case of a couple, a pensioner applicant or her/his partner) receives the guarantee credit of PC the whole of the applicant's capital (and income), including any capital that s/he is treated as having under Sch 1 para 11 or 12, is disregarded: Sch 1 para 13.

If a single pensioner applicant (or in the case of a couple a pensioner applicant or her/his partner) receives only the savings credit of PC and not guarantee credit, a billing authority must usually use the amount of capital calculated or estimated by the DWP for the purpose of the savings credit calculation to assess entitlement to CTR: Sch 1 para 14.

It is, therefore, only in other cases – when capital has to be assessed by a billing authority – that this Schedule comes into play. If, after any capital disregarded under Parts 1 or 2 of this Schedule is deducted, a pensioner has capital of over £16,000, s/he cannot qualify for CTR unless s/he or her/his partner is in receipt of the guarantee credit of pension credit. This is because s/he comes within a class of person who must not be included in a billing authority's CTR scheme: Sch 1A para 2(9)(b) and reg 11.

Although the definition of 'income' for pensioner applicants includes income from any capital that is not disregarded under Part 1 of this Schedule, actual income from that capital is ignored when calculating entitlement to CTR with the one exception mentioned below: Sch 1 para 16(1)(i) and Sch 5 para 23. Instead, if the value of the applicant's capital (after disregarding capital listed in Parts 1 and 2 of this Schedule) is over £10,000, s/he is deemed to have a specified amount of income arising from it. This is known as tariff income and is calculated in accordance with Sch 1 para 37.

The one exception is that actual income from the capital listed in Part 2 of this Schedule is included in the assessment of a pensioner applicant's income (unless s/he or her/his partner receives guarantee credit of PC), and is just ignored for the purpose of calculating deemed income (to avoid it being counted twice): Sch 1 para 17(12)(b).

See Sch 1 paras 31–37 for how the value of capital is calculated.

Capital Disregards
PART 1
Capital to be disregarded

1.   Any premises acquired for occupation by the applicant which he intends to occupy as his home within 26 weeks of the date of acquisition or such longer period as is reasonable in the circumstances to enable the applicant to obtain possession and commence occupation of the premises.

2.   Any premises which the applicant intends to occupy as his home, and in respect of which he is taking steps to obtain possession and has sought legal advice, or has commenced legal proceedings, with a view to obtaining possession, for a period of 26 weeks from the date on which he first sought such advice or first commenced such proceedings whichever is the earlier, or such longer period as is reasonable in the circumstances to enable him to obtain possession and commence occupation of those premises.

3.   Any premises which the applicant intends to occupy as his home to which essential repairs or alterations are required in order to render them fit for such occupation, for a period of 26 weeks from the date on which the applicant first takes steps to effect those repairs or alterations, or such longer period as is necessary to enable those repairs or alterations to be carried out.

4.   Any premises occupied in whole or in part–

(a)   by a person who is a relative of the applicant or his partner as his home where that person has attained the qualifying age for state pension credit or is incapacitated;

(b)   by the former partner of the applicant as his home; but this provision does not apply where the former partner is a person from whom the applicant is estranged or divorced or with whom he had formed a civil partnership that has been dissolved.

5.   Any future interest in property of any kind, other than land or premises in respect of which the applicant has granted a subsisting lease or tenancy, including sub-leases or sub-tenancies.

6.   Where an applicant has ceased to occupy what was formerly the dwelling occupied as the home following his estrangement or divorce from his former partner or the dissolution of a civil partnership with his former partner, that dwelling for a period of 26 weeks from the date on which he ceased to occupy that dwelling or, where the dwelling is occupied as the home by the former partner who is a lone parent, for so long as it is so occupied.

7.   Any premises where the applicant is taking reasonable steps to dispose of the whole of his interest in those premises, for a period of 26 weeks from the date on which he first took such steps, or such longer period as is reasonable in the circumstances to enable him to dispose of those premises.

8.   All personal possessions.

9.   The assets of any business owned in whole or in part by the applicant and for the purposes of which he is engaged as a self-employed earner or, if he has ceased to be so engaged, for such period as may be reasonable in the circumstances to allow for disposal of those assets.

10.   The assets of any business owned in whole or in part by the applicant if–

(a)   he is not engaged as a self-employed earner in that business by reason of some disease or bodily or mental disablement; but

(b)   he intends to become engaged (or, as the case may be, re-engaged) as a self-employed earner in that business as soon as he recovers or is able to become engaged, or re-engaged, in that business, for a period of 26 weeks from the date on which the application for a reduction under an authority's scheme is made or, if it is unreasonable to expect him to become engaged or re-engaged in that business within that period, for such longer period as is reasonable in the circumstances to enable him to become so engaged or re-engaged.

11. The surrender value of any policy of life insurance.

12. The value of any funeral plan contract; and for this purpose, "funeral plan contract" means a contract under which–

(a) the applicant makes one or more payments to another person ("the provider");

(b) the provider undertakes to provide, or secure the provision of, a funeral in the United Kingdom for the applicant on his death; and

(c) the sole purpose of the plan is to provide or secure the provision of a funeral for the applicant on his death.

13. Where an ex-gratia payment has been made by the Secretary of State on or after 1st February 2001 in consequence of the imprisonment or internment of–

(a) the applicant;

(b) the applicant's partner;

(c) the applicant's deceased spouse or deceased civil partner; or

(d) the applicant's partner's deceased spouse or deceased civil partner,

by the Japanese during the Second World War, an amount equal to that payment.

14.–(1) Subject to sub-paragraph (2), the amount of any trust payment made to an applicant or an applicant's partner who is–

(a) a diagnosed person;

(b) a diagnosed person's partner or was a diagnosed person's partner at the time of the diagnosed person's death; or

(c) a parent of a diagnosed person, a person acting in place of the diagnosed person's parents or a person who was so acting at the date of the diagnosed person's death.

(2) Where a trust payment is made to–

(a) a person referred to in sub-paragraph (1)(a) or (b), that sub-paragraph is to apply for the period beginning on the date on which the trust payment is made and ending on the date on which that person dies;

(b) a person referred to in sub-paragraph (1)(c), that sub-paragraph shall apply for the period beginning on the date on which the trust payment is made and ending two years after that date.

(3) Subject to sub-paragraph (4), the amount of any payment by a person to whom a trust payment has been made or of any payment out of the estate of a person to whom a trust payment has been made, which is made to an applicant or an applicant's partner who is–

(a) the diagnosed person;

(b) a diagnosed person's partner or was a diagnosed person's partner at the date of the diagnosed person's death; or

(c) a parent of a diagnosed person, a person acting in place of the diagnosed person's parents or a person who was so acting at the date of the diagnosed person's death.

(4) Where a payment such as referred to in sub-paragraph (3) is made to–

(a) a person referred to in sub-paragraph (3)(a) or (b), that sub-paragraph applies for the period beginning on the date on which the payment is made and ends on the date on which that person dies;

(b) a person referred to in sub-paragraph (3)(c), that sub-paragraph is to apply for the period beginning on the date on which the payment is made and ending two years after that date.

(5) In this paragraph, a reference to a person–

(a) being the diagnosed person's partner;

(b) acting in place of the diagnosed person's parents,

at the date of the diagnosed person's death includes a person who would have been such a person or a person who would have been so acting, but for the diagnosed person residing in a care home or an independent hospital.

(6) In this paragraph–

"diagnosed person" means a person who has been diagnosed as suffering from, or who, after his death, has been diagnosed as having suffered from, variant Creutzfeldt-Jakob disease;

"relevant trust" means a trust established out of funds provided by the Secretary of State in respect of persons who suffered, or who are suffering, from variant Creutzfeldt-Jakob disease for the benefit of persons eligible for payments in accordance with its provisions;

"trust payment" means a payment under a relevant trust.

15. The amount of any payment, other than a war pension, to compensate for the fact that the applicant, the applicant's partner, the applicant's deceased spouse or civil partner or the applicant's partner's deceased spouse or civil partner–

(a) was a slave labourer or a forced labourer;

(b) had suffered property loss or had suffered personal injury; or

(c) was a parent of a child who had died,

during the Second World War.

16.–(1)   Any payment made under or by–

(a)   the Macfarlane Trust, the Macfarlane (Special Payments) Trust, the Macfarlane (Special Payments) (No 2) Trust, the Fund, the Eileen Trust, MFET Limited, the Skipton Fund, the Caxton Foundation, [¹ the Scottish Infected Blood Support Scheme, an approved blood scheme, the London Emergencies Trust, the We Love Manchester Emergency Fund] or the London Bombings Relief Charitable Fund (collectively referred to in this paragraph as "the Trusts"); or

(b)   the Independent Living Fund (2006).

(2)   Any payment by or on behalf of a person who is suffering or who suffered from haemophilia or who is or was a qualifying person, which derives from a payment made under or by any of the Trusts and which is made to or for the benefit of that person's partner or former partner–

(a)   from whom he is not, or where that person has died was not, estranged or divorced, or

(b)   with whom he has formed a civil partnership that has not been dissolved or, where that person has died, had not been dissolved at the time of that person's death.

(3)   Any payment by or on behalf of the partner or former partner of a person who is suffering or who suffered from haemophilia or who is or was a qualifying person which derives from a payment made under or by any of the Trusts and which is made to or for the benefit of the person who is suffering from haemophilia or who is a qualifying person.

(4)   Sub-paragraph (3) does not apply if–

(a)   the partner or former partner and that person are not, or if either of them has died were not, estranged or divorced, or

(b)   where the partner or former partner and that person have formed a civil partnership, the civil partnership has not been dissolved or, if either of them has died, had not been dissolved at the time of the death.

(5)   Any payment by a person who is suffering from haemophilia or who is a qualifying person, which derives from a payment under or by any of the Trusts, where–

(a)   that person has no partner or former partner from whom he is not estranged or divorced or with whom he has formed a civil partnership that has not been dissolved, nor any child who is or had been a member of that person's household; and

(b)   the payment is made either–

(i)   to that person's parent or step-parent; or

(ii)   where that person at the date of the payment is a child or a student who has not completed his full-time education and has no parent or step-parent, to any person standing in the place of his parent,

but only for a period from the date of the payment until the end of two years from that person's death.

(6)   Any payment out of the estate of a person who suffered from haemophilia or who was a qualifying person, which derives from a payment under or by any of the Trusts, where–

(a)   that person at the date of his death ("the relevant date") had no partner or former partner from whom he was not estranged or divorced or with whom he had formed a civil partnership that had not been dissolved, nor any child who was or had been a member of his household; and

(b)   the payment is made either–

(i)   to that person's parent or step-parent; or

(ii)   where that person at the relevant date was a child or a student who had not completed his full-time education and had no parent or step-parent, to any person standing in place of his parent,

but only for a period of two years from the relevant date.

(7)   In the case of a person to whom or for whose benefit a payment referred to in this paragraph is made, any capital resource which derives from any payment of income or capital made under or deriving from any of the Trusts.

Amendment

1.   Amended by reg 15(a) of SI 2017 No 1305 as from 12.1.18 in relation to schemes made for financial years starting on or after 1.4.18.

[¹**16A.**–(1)   Any payment made under, or by, a trust which is approved by the Secretary of State and which is established for the purpose of giving relief and assistance to a disabled person whose disabilities were caused by their mother having taken a preparation containing the drug known as Thalidomide during her pregnancy.]

Amendment

1.   Inserted by reg 15(b) of SI 2017 No 1305 as from 12.1.18 in relation to schemes made for financial years starting on or after 1.4.18.

17.–(1) An amount equal to the amount of any payment made in consequence of any personal injury to the applicant or, if the applicant has a partner, to the partner.

(2) Where the whole or part of the payment is administered–

(a) by the High Court or the County Court under Rule 21.11(1) of the Civil Procedure Rules 1998, or the Court of Protection, or on behalf of a person where the payment can only be disposed of by order or direction of any such court;

(b) in accordance with an order made under Rule 36.14 of the Ordinary Cause Rules 1993 or under Rule 128 of those Rules; or

(c) in accordance with the terms of a trust established for the benefit of the applicant or his partner, the whole of the amount so administered.

18. Any amount specified in paragraph 19, 20, 21 or 25 of this Schedule for a period of one year beginning with the date of receipt.

19. Amounts paid under a policy of insurance in connection with the loss of or damage to the property occupied by the applicant as his home and to his personal possessions.

20. So much of any amounts paid to the applicant or deposited in the applicant's name for the sole purpose of–

(a) purchasing premises which the applicant intends to occupy as his home; or

(b) effecting essential repairs or alterations to the premises occupied or intended to be occupied by the applicant as his home.

21.–(1) Subject to paragraph 22 any amount paid–

(a) by way of arrears of benefit;

(b) by way of compensation for the late payment of benefit;

(c) in lieu of the payment of benefit;

(d) to rectify, or compensate for, an official error, as defined for the purposes of paragraph 22, being an amount to which that paragraph does not apply;

(e) by a local authority out of funds provided under either section 93 of the Local Government Act 2000 under a scheme known as "Supporting People" or section 91 of the Housing (Scotland) Act 2001.

[¹ (f) by way of occasional assistance including arrears and payments in lieu of occasional assistance (and in this paragraph "occasional assistance" has the same meaning as in paragraph 16 of Schedule 1)]

(2) In sub-paragraph (1), "benefit" means–

(a) attendance allowance under section 64 of the SSCBA;

(b) disability living allowance;

(c) personal independence payment

(d) an AFIP;

(e) income support;

(f) income-based jobseeker's allowance;

(g) state pension credit;

(h) housing benefit;

(i) council tax benefit;

(j) child tax credit;

(k) an increase of a disablement pension under section 104 of the SSCBA (increase where constant attendance is needed), and any further increase of such a pension under section 105 of that Act (increase for exceptionally severe disablement);

(l) any amount included on account of the applicant's exceptionally severe disablement or need for constant attendance in a war disablement pension or a war widow's or widower's pension;

(m) any discretionary housing payment paid pursuant to regulation 2(1) of the Discretionary Financial Assistance Regulations 2001;

(n) working tax credit; [¹]

(o) income-related employment and support allowance.[³ [²]]

[¹ (p) social fund payments under Part 8 of the SSCBA.][³ or]

[³ (q) universal credit.]

Amendments

1. Amended by reg 2(12)(a) of SI 2013 No 3181 for schemes for financial years beginning on or after 1.4.14.

2. Amended by reg 2(10)(a) of SI 2014 No 3312 as from 12.1.15, for schemes made for financial years starting on or after 1.4.15.

Analysis

Certain payments relating to the benefits specified in para 21(2) must be ignored as capital for one year from the date of receipt under a local authority's scheme for pensioners. These include payments of arrears of the specified benefits, payment compensating for the late payment of the benefits or payment made in lieu of the benefits (see paras 21(1) and 22 for all of the types of payments that can be ignored). In England, unlike in Wales and Scotland, bereavement support payment is not included in the list of specified benefits and so, for example, a local authority's scheme does not have to include provision to disregard capital that arises from a payment of arrears of bereavement support payment when calculating CTR entitlement for pensioners (or non-pensioners).

In contrast, arrears of bereavement support payment are ignored for one year after they are received when calculating both pensioners' and non-pensioners' capital for CTR in Wales (Sch 5 para 21(2)(r) and Sch 10 para 12(1)(h) CTRS(PR)(W) Regs) and in Scotland (Sch 5 para 11(1)(g) CTR(S) Regs and Sch 4 para 21(2)(aa) CTR(SPC)(S) Regs) and when calculating HB for pensioners and non-pensioners (Sch 6 para 9 HB Regs and Sch 6 para 21 HB(SPC) Regs).

Note also that the lump sum payment made for the first month of entitlement to bereavement support payment, under reg 3(2) or (5) of the Bereavement Support Payment Regs 2017 No 410, is not included in this Schedule as capital that must be disregarded. In Wales and Scotland, it must be ignored for 52 weeks from the date of its receipt: Sch 5 para 28C and Sch 10 para 65 CTRSPR(W) Regs; Sch 5 para 65 CTR(S) Regs and Sch 4 para 30B CTR(SPC)(S) Regs.

22.–(1) Subject to sub-paragraph (3), any payment of £5,000 or more which has been made to rectify, or to compensate for, an official error [³ or an error on a point of law] relating to a relevant benefit and has been received by the applicant in full on or after the day on which he became entitled to a reduction under an authority's scheme.

(2) Subject to sub-paragraph (3), the total amount of any payments disregarded under–

(a) paragraph 7(2) of Schedule 10 to the Income Support (General) Regulations 1987;

(b) paragraph 12(2) of Schedule 8 to the Jobseeker's Allowance Regulations [²1996];

(c) paragraph 9(2) of Schedule 5 to the Council Tax Benefit Regulations 2006;

(d) paragraph 20A of Schedule 5 to the State Pension Credit Regulations 2002,

(e) paragraph 11(2) of Schedule 9 to the Employment and Support Allowance Regulations [² 2008],

[¹ (f) paragraph 18 of Schedule 10 to the Universal Credit Regulations 2013;]

where the award in respect of which the payments last fell to be disregarded under those Regulations either terminated immediately before the relevant date or is still in existence at that date.

(3) Any disregard which applies under sub-paragraph (1) or (2) is to have effect until the award comes to an end.

(4) In this paragraph–

"the award", except in sub-paragraph (2), means–

(a) the award of a reduction u~ an authority's scheme during which the relevant sum or, where it is paid in more than one instalment, the first instalment of that sum is received; and

(b) where that award is followed by one or more further awards which, or each of which, begins immediately after the previous award ends, such further awards until the end of the last such award, provided that, for such further awards, the applicant–

(i) is the person who received the relevant sum;

(ii) is the partner of that person; or

(iii) was the partner of that person at the date of his death;

"official error" means–

(a) where the error relates to housing benefit or council tax benefit (in respect of any period before 1st April 2013), has the meaning given by regulation 1(2) of the Housing Benefit and the Council Tax Benefit (Decisions and Appeals) Regulations 2001; and

(b) where the error relates to any other relevant benefit, has the meaning given by regulation 1(3) of the Social Security and Child Support (Decisions and Appeals) Regulations 1999;

"the relevant date" means the date on which an application for a reduction under the authority's scheme was made;

"relevant benefit" means any benefit specified in paragraph 21(2); and

"the relevant sum" means the payment referred to in sub-paragraph (1) or the total amount referred to in sub-paragraph (2).

Amendments

1. Amended by reg 2(12)(b) of SI 2013 No 3181 for schemes for financial years beginning on or after 1.4.14.

2. Amended by reg 2(10)(b) and (c) of SI 2014 No 3312 as from 12.1.15, for schemes made for financial years starting on or after 1.4.15.

3. Amended by reg 6 of SI 2018 No 1346 as from 14.1.19, in relation to schemes made for financial years starting on or after 1.4.19.

---

23. Where a capital asset is held in a currency other than Sterling, any banking charge or commission payable in converting that capital into Sterling.

24. The value of the right to receive income from an occupational pension scheme or a personal pension scheme.

25. Any arrears of supplementary pension which is disregarded under paragraph 4 of Schedule 5 (amounts to be disregarded in the calculation of income other than earnings) or of any amount which is disregarded under paragraph 5 or 6 of that Schedule.

26. The dwelling occupied as the home; but only one dwelling may be disregarded under this paragraph.

27.–(1) Subject to sub-paragraph (2) where an applicant falls within class C (alternative maximum council tax reduction), the whole of his capital.

(2)   Sub-paragraph (1) does not apply, where an applicant falls within class B (income greater than applicable amount) and class C.

28.   Where a person elects to be entitled to a lump sum under Schedule 5 or 5A to the SSCBA or under Schedule 1 to the Social Security (Graduated Retirement Benefit) Regulations 2005, or is treated as having made such an election, and a payment has been made pursuant to that election, an amount equal to–

(a)   except where sub-paragraph (b) applies, the amount of any payment or payments made on account of that lump sum; or

(b)   the amount of that lump sum,

but only for so long as that person does not change that election in favour of an increase of pension or benefit.

[¹**28A.**   Where a person chooses a lump sum under section 8(2) of the Pensions Act 2014 or in accordance with Regulations made under section 10 of that Act which include provision corresponding or similar to section 8(2) of that Act, or fails to make a choice, and a lump sum payment has been made, an amount equal to–

(a)   except where sub-paragraph (b) applies, the amount of any payment or payments made on account of that lump sum; or

(b)   the amount of that lump sum,

but only for so long as that person does not alter that choice in favour of an increase of pension.]

Amendment

1.   Inserted by art 39(4) of SI 2015 No 1985 as from 6.4.16.

---

29.   Any payments made [²]–

(a)   [² by virtue of regulations made under] section 57 of the Health and Social Care Act 2001 (direct payments);

[¹ (b)]

(c)   [² by virtue of regulations made under] sections 12A to 12C of the National Health Service Act 2006 (direct payments for health care);

(d)   [² by virtue of regulations made under] Article 15 of the Health and Personal Social Services (Northern Ireland) Order 1972 (general social welfare); [²]

(e)   [² by virtue of regulations made under]] section 8 of the Carers and Direct Payments Act (Northern Ireland) 2002 (direct payments). [³]

[² (f)   under sections 31 to 33 of the Care Act 2014 (direct payments).] [³ ; or

(g)   by virtue of regulations made under section 50 or 52 of the Social Services and Well-being (Wales) Act 2014 (direct payments).]

Amendments

1.   Omitted by art 2 and Sch para 22(a) of SI 2014 No 513 as from 1.4.14.

2.   Amended by art 2 and Sch para 36(8) of SI 2015 No 643 as from 1.4.15.

3.   Amended by reg 15(c) of SI 2017 No 1305 as from 12.1.18 in relation to schemes made for financial years starting on or after 1.4.18.

[¹**29ZA.**   Any payment made as a direct payment as defined in section 4(2) of the Social Care (Self-directed Support) (Scotland) Act 2013.]

Amendment

1.   Inserted by Art 2 and Sch para 22(b) of SI 2014 No 513 as from 1.4.14.

[¹**29A.**   A payment made under the Age-Related Payments Regulations 2013(c).]

Amendment

1.   Inserted by reg 2(12)(c) of SI 2013 No 3181 for schemes for financial years beginning on or after 1.4.14.

[¹**29B.**   Any payments to an applicant made under section 49 of the Children and Families Act 2014 (pesonal budgets and direct payments).]

Amendment

1.   Inserted by reg 2(78 of SI 2015 No 2041 as from 14.1.16, in relation to schemes made for financial years starting on or after 1.4.16.

[¹**29C.**–(1)   Any payment made by a local authority in accordance with section 26A of the Children (Scotland) Act 1995 (duty to provide continuing care).

(2)   Any payment or part of payment made by a local authority in accordance with that section to a person ("A") which A passes on to the applicant where A–

(a)   was formerly in the applicants care;

(b)   is aged 16 or over; and

(c)   continues to live with the applicant.]

Amendment

1.   Inserted by reg 15(d) of SI 2017 No 1305 as from 12.1.18 in relation to schemes made for financial years starting on or after 1.4.18.

PART 2
Capital disregarded only for the purposes of determining deemed income

30.   The value of the right to receive any income under a life interest or from a life rent.

31.   The value of the right to receive any rent except where the applicant has a reversionary interest in the property in respect of which rent is due.

32.   The value of the right to receive any income under an annuity or the surrender value (if any) of such an annuity.

33.   Where property is held under a trust, other than–

(a)   a charitable trust within the meaning of the Charities Act 1993; or

(b)   a trust set up with any payment to which paragraph 16 of this Schedule applies,

and under the terms of the trust, payments fall to be made, or the trustees have a discretion to make payments, to or for the benefit of the applicant or the applicant's partner, or both, that property.

SCHEDULE 7
All applicants: matters that must be included in an authority's scheme – procedural matters

PART 1
Applications

General Note on Parts 1 and 4

The provisions in this Schedule and the one that follows it apply to all applicants to an English authority's scheme (ie, to both people who are pensioners and people who are not pensioners), unless stated otherwise: reg 15. Reg 83(1), (2), (4A)–(4D), (7) and (9) of the HB Regs are similar to paras 2(a) and (c), 3, 4, 6 and 7 of this Schedule. See p549 for commentary on reg 83 HB Regs. Para 2(b) and Part 4 of this Schedule are similar to reg 83A and Sch 11 of the HB Regs (see p554 for commentary). For the meaning of "designated office", see reg 2(1) of these regs.

Procedure by which a person may apply for a reduction under an authority's scheme

1.   Paragraphs 2 to 7 apply to an application made under an authority's scheme.

2.   An application may be made–

(a)   in writing,

(b)   by means of an electronic communication in accordance with Part 4 of this Schedule, or

(c)   where an authority has published a telephone number for the purpose of receiving such applications, by telephone.

3.–(1)   An application which is made in writing must be made to the designated office on a properly completed form.

(2)   The form must be provided free of charge by the authority for the purpose.

4.   Where an application made in writing is defective because–

(a)   it was made on the form supplied for the purpose but that form is not accepted by the authority as being properly completed; or

(b)   it was made in writing but not on the form approved for the purpose and the authority does not accept the application as being in a written form which is sufficient in the circumstances of the case having regard to the sufficiency of the written information and evidence,

the authority may, in a case to which sub-paragraph (a) applies, request the applicant to complete the defective application or, in the case to which sub-paragraph (b) applies, supply the applicant with the approved form or request further information and evidence.

(2)   An application made on a form provided by an authority is properly completed if it is completed in accordance with the instructions on the form, including any instructions to provide information and evidence in connection with the application.

5.–(1)   If an application made by electronic communication is defective an authority must provide the person making the application with an opportunity to correct the defect.

(2)   An application made by electronic communication is defective if the applicant does not provide all the information the authority requires.

6.   In a particular case an authority may determine that an application made by telephone is only valid if the person making the application approves a written statement of his circumstances provided by the authority.

7.–(1)   If an application made by telephone is defective an authority must provide the person making the application with an opportunity to correct the defect.

(2)   An application made by telephone is defective if the applicant does not provide all the information the authority requests during the telephone call.

PART 2
Appeals

Procedure by which a person may appeal against certain decisions of the authority
   8.–(1) A person who is aggrieved by a decision of an authority which affects–
   (a)   the person's entitlement to a reduction under its scheme, or
   (b)   the amount of any reduction to which that person is entitled,
may serve a written notice on that authority stating the matter by which, and the grounds on which, he is aggrieved.
   (2)   The authority must–
   (a)   consider the matter to which the notice relates;
   (b)   notify the aggrieved person in writing–
        (i)   that the ground is not well founded, giving reasons for that belief; or
        (ii)   that steps have been taken to deal with the grievance, stating the steps taken.
   (3)   Where, following notification under sub-paragraph (2)(b)(i) or (ii), the person is still aggrieved, or if the authority fails to notify the person aggrieved in accordance with sub-paragraph (2)(b) within two months of the service of his notice, he may appeal to a valuation tribunal under section 16 of the 1992 Act.

PART 3
Discretionary reductions

Procedure for an application to the authority for a reduction under section 13A(1)(c) of the 1992 Act
   9.–(1) An application to an authority for a reduction under section 13A(1)(c) of the 1992 Act may be made–
   (a)   in writing,
   (b)   by means of an electronic communication in accordance with Part 4 of this Schedule, or
   (c)   where the authority has published a telephone number for the purpose of receiving such applications, by telephone.
   (2)   Where–
   (a)   the authority has made a determination under section 13A(1)(c) in relation to a class of case in which liability is to be reduced; and
   (b)   a person in that class would otherwise be entitled to a reduction under its scheme,
that person's application for a reduction under the authority's scheme may also be treated as an application for a reduction under section 13A(1)(c).

PART 4
Electronic communication

Interpretation
   10.   In this Part–
"information" includes an application, a certificate, notice or other evidence; and
"official computer system" means a computer system maintained by or on behalf of an authority for sending, receiving, processing or storing of any information.

Conditions for the use of electronic communication
   11.–(1) An authority may use an electronic communication in connection with applications for, and awards of, reductions under its scheme.
   (2)   A person other than that authority may use an electronic communication in connection with the matters referred to in sub-paragraph (1) if the conditions specified in sub-paragraphs (3) to (6) are satisfied.
   (3)   The first condition is that the person is for the time being permitted to use an electronic communication by an authorisation given by means of a direction of the Chief Executive of the authority.
   (4)   The second condition is that the person uses an approved method of–
   (a)   authenticating the identity of the sender of the communication;
   (b)   electronic communication;
   (c)   authenticating any application or notice delivered by means of an electronic communication; and
   (d)   subject to sub-paragraph (7), submitting to the authority any information.
   (5)   The third condition is that any information sent by means of an electronic communication is in a form approved for the purposes of this Part.
   (6)   The fourth condition is that the person maintains such records in written or electronic form as may be specified in a direction given by the Chief Executive of the authority.
   (7)   Where the person uses any method other than the method approved of submitting any information, that information is to be treated as not having been submitted.
   (8)   In this paragraph "approved" means approved by means of a direction given by the Chief Executive of the authority for the purposes of this Part.

Use of intermediaries
    12.   The authority may use intermediaries in connection with–
    (a)   the delivery of any information by means of an electronic communication; and
    (b)   the authentication or security of anything transmitted by such means,
and may require other persons to use intermediaries in connection with those matters.

Effect of delivering information by means of electronic communication
    13.–(1)   Any information which is delivered by means of an electronic communication is to be treated as having been delivered in the manner or form required by any provision of an authority's scheme on the day the conditions imposed–
    (a)   by this Part; and
    (b)   by or under an enactment,
are satisfied.
    (2)   An authority may determine that any information is to be treated as delivered on a different day (whether earlier or later) from the day provided for in sub-paragraph (1).
    (3)   Information may not be taken to have been delivered to an official computer system by means of an electronic communication unless it is accepted by the system to which it is delivered.

Proof of identity of sender or recipient of information
    14.   If it is necessary to prove, for the purpose of any legal proceedings, the identity of–
    (a)   the sender of any information delivered by means of an electronic communication to an official computer system; or
    (b)   the recipient of any such information delivered by means of an electronic communication from an official computer system,
the sender or recipient, as the case may be, is to be presumed to be the person whose name is recorded as such on that official computer system.

Proof of delivery of information
    15.–(1)   If it is necessary to prove, for the purpose of any legal proceedings, that the use of an electronic communication has resulted in the delivery of any information this is presumed to have been the case where–
    (a)   any such information has been delivered to the relevant authority, if the delivery of that information has been recorded on an official computer system; or
    (b)   any such information has been delivered by the relevant authority, if the delivery of that information has been recorded on an official computer system.
    (2)   If it is necessary to prove, for the purpose of any legal proceedings, that the use of an electronic communication has resulted in the delivery of any such information, this is presumed not to be the case, if that information delivered to the relevant authority has not been recorded on an official computer system.
    (3)   If it is necessary to prove, for the purpose of any legal proceedings, when any such information sent by means of an electronic communication has been received, the time and date of receipt is presumed to be that recorded on an official computer system.

Proof of content of information
    16.   If it is necessary to prove, for the purpose of any legal proceedings, the content of any information sent by means of an electronic communication, the content is presumed to be that recorded on an official computer system.

SCHEDULE 8
All applicants: matters that must be included in an authority's scheme – other matters

PART 1
Extended reductions: persons who are not pensioners

    1.   Paragraph 2 applies only in relation to persons who are not pensioners.

Extended reductions: movers into an authority's area
    2.   Where–
    (a)   an application is made to an authority ("the current authority") for a reduction under its scheme, and
    (b)   the applicant or the partner of the applicant, is in receipt of an extended reduction from–
        (i)   another billing authority in England; or
        (ii)   a billing authority in Wales,
the current authority must reduce any reduction to which the applicant is entitled under its scheme by the amount of that extended reduction.

PART 2
Further provision about applications and duty to notify a change of circumstances

    3.   Except for paragraph 6 (which applies to persons who are pensioners only), paragraphs 4 to 9 apply to persons who are pensioners and persons who are not pensioners.

Making an application

4.–(1)   In the case of a couple or members of a polygamous marriage an application is to be made by whichever one of them they agree should so apply or, in default of agreement, by such one of them as the authority determines.

(2)   Where a person who is liable to pay council tax in respect of a dwelling is unable for the time being to act, and–

(a)   a deputy has been appointed by the Court of Protection with power to claim, or as the case may be, receive benefit on his behalf; or

(b)   in Scotland, his estate is being administered by a judicial factor or any guardian acting or appointed under the Adults with Incapacity (Scotland) Act 2000 who has power to apply or, as the case may be, receive benefit on his behalf; or

(c)   an attorney with a general power or a power to apply or, as the case may be, receive benefit, has been appointed by that person under the Powers of Attorney Act 1971, the Enduring Powers of Attorney Act 1985 or the Mental Capacity Act 2005 or otherwise,

that deputy, judicial factor, guardian or attorney, as the case may be, may make an application on behalf of that person.

(3)   Where a person who is liable to pay council tax in respect of a dwelling is unable for the time being to act and sub-paragraph (2) does not apply to him, an authority may, upon written application made to them by a person who, if a natural person, is over the age of 18, appoint that person to exercise on behalf of the person who is unable to act, any right to which that person might be entitled under the authority's scheme and to receive and deal on his behalf with any sums payable to him.

(4)   Where a person who is liable to pay council tax in respect of a dwelling is for the time being unable to act and the Secretary of State has appointed a person to act on his behalf under regulation 33 of the Social Security (Claims and Payments) Regulations 1987 (persons unable to act), the authority may if that person agrees, treat him as if he had been appointed by them under sub-paragraph (3).

(5)   Where the authority has made an appointment under sub-paragraph (3) or treated a person as an appointee under sub-paragraph (4)–

(a)   it may at any time revoke the appointment;

(b)   the person appointed may resign his office after having given 4 weeks notice in writing to the authority of his intention to do so;

(c)   any such appointment terminates when the authority is notified of the appointment of a person mentioned in sub-paragraph (2).

(6)   Anything required by an authority's scheme to be done by or to any person who is for the time being unable to act may be done by or to the persons mentioned in sub-paragraph (2) above or by or to the person appointed or treated as appointed under this paragraph and the receipt of any such person so appointed shall be a good discharge to the authority for any sum paid.

(7)   The authority must–

(a)   inform any person making an application of the duty imposed by paragraph 9(1)(a);

(b)   explain the possible consequences (including prosecution) of failing to comply with that duty; and

(c)   set out the circumstances a change in which might affect entitlement to the reduction or its amount.

General Note

This is similar to the HB equivalent. See the commentary on p543.

Date on which an application is made

5.–(1)   Subject to sub-paragraph (7), the date on which an application is made is–

(a)   in a case where–

(i)   an award of state pension credit which comprises a guarantee credit has been made to the applicant or his partner, and

(ii)   the application for a reduction is made within one month of the date on which the claim for that state pension credit which comprises a guarantee credit was received at the appropriate DWP office,

the first day of entitlement to state pension credit which comprises a guarantee credit arising from that claim;

(b)   in a case where–

(i)   an applicant or his partner is a person in receipt of a guarantee credit,

(ii)   the applicant becomes liable for the first time to pay council tax in respect of the dwelling he occupies as his home, and

(iii)   the application is received at the designated office within one month of the date of the change,

the date on which the change takes place;

(c)   in a case where–

(i)   an award of income support, an income-based jobseeker's allowance or an income-related employment and support allowance or an award of universal credit has been made to the applicant or his partner, and

(ii)   the application is made within one month of the date on which the claim for that income support, jobseeker's allowance, employment and support allowance or universal credit was received,

the first day of entitlement to income support, an income-based jobseeker's allowance, an income-related employment and support allowance or universal credit arising from that claim;

(d)   in a case where–

    (i)   an applicant or his partner is a person on income support, an income-based jobseeker's allowance or an income-related employment and support allowance or has an award of universal credit,

    (ii)   the applicant becomes liable for the first time to pay council tax in respect of the dwelling which he occupies as his home, and

    (iii)   the application is received at the designated office within one month of the date of the change,

the date on which the change takes place;

(e)   in a case where–

    (i)   an applicant is the former partner of a person who was, at the date of his death or their separation, entitled to a reduction under an authority's scheme, and

    (ii)   the applicant makes an application for a reduction under that scheme within one month of the date of the death or the separation,

the date of the death or separation;

(f)   except where paragraph (a), (b) or (e) is satisfied, in a case where a properly completed application is received within one month (or such longer period as an authority considers reasonable) of the date on which an application form was issued to an applicant following the applicant first notifying, by whatever means, the authority of an intention to make an application, the date of first notification;

(g)   in any other case, the date on which an application is received at the designated office.

(2)   For the purposes only of sub-paragraph (1)(c) a person who has been awarded an income-based jobseeker's allowance or an income-related employment and support allowance is to be treated as entitled to that allowance for any days which immediately precede the first day in that award and on which he would, but for regulations made under–

(a)   in the case of income-based jobseeker's allowance, paragraph 4 of Schedule 1 to the Jobseekers Act 1995 (waiting days); or

(b)   in the case of income-related employment and support allowance, paragraph 2 of Schedule 2 to the Welfare Reform Act 2007 (waiting days),

have been entitled to that allowance.

(3)   Where the defect referred to in paragraph 7 of Schedule 7 (applications by telephone)–

(a)   is corrected within one month (or such longer period as the authority considers reasonable) of the date the authority last drew attention to it, the authority must treat the application as if it had been duly made in the first instance;

(b)   is not corrected within one month (or such longer period as the authority considers reasonable) of the date the authority last drew attention to it, the authority must treat the application as if it had been duly made in the first instance where it considers it has sufficient information to decide the application.

(4)   An authority must treat a defective application as if it had been validly made in the first instance if, in any particular case, the conditions specified in sub-paragraph (5)(a), (b) or (c) are satisfied.

(5)   The conditions are that–

(a)   where paragraph 4(a) of Schedule 7 (incomplete form) applies, the authority receives at its designated office the properly completed application or the information requested to complete it or the evidence within one month of the request, or such longer period as the authority may consider reasonable; or

(b)   where paragraph 4(b) of Schedule 7 (application not on approved form or further information requested by authority) applies–

    (i)   the approved form sent to the applicant is received at the designated office properly completed within one month of it having been sent to him; or, as the case may be,

    (ii)   the applicant supplies whatever information or evidence was requested under paragraph 4 of that Schedule within one month of the request,

or, in either case, within such longer period as the authority may consider reasonable; or

(c)   where the authority has requested further information, the authority receives at its designated office the properly completed application or the information requested to complete it within one month of the request or within such longer period as the authority considers reasonable.

(6)   Except in the case of an application made by a person treated as not being in Great Britain, where a person has not become liable for council tax to an authority but it is anticipated that he will become so liable within the period of 8 weeks (the relevant period), he may apply for a reduction under that authority's scheme at any time in that period in respect of that tax and, provided that liability arises within the relevant period, the authority must treat the application as having been made on the day on which the liability for the tax arises.

(7)   Except in the case of an application made by a person treated as not being in Great Britain, where the applicant is not entitled to a reduction under an authority's scheme in the reduction week immediately

following the date of his application but the authority is of the opinion that unless there is a change of circumstances he will be entitled to a reduction under its scheme for a period beginning not later than–

(a) in the case of an application made by–

    (i) a pensioner, or

    (ii) a person who has attained, or whose partner has attained, the age which is 17 weeks younger than the qualifying age for state pension credit,

    the seventeenth reduction week following the date on which the application is made, or

(b) in the case of an application made by a person who is not a pensioner, the thirteenth reduction week following the date on which the application is made,

the authority may treat the application as made on a date in the reduction week immediately preceding the first reduction week of that period of entitlement and award a reduction accordingly.

(8) In this paragraph "appropriate DWP office" means an office of the Department for Work and Pensions dealing with state pension credit or an office which is normally open to the public for the receipt of claims of income support, a job seekers allowance or an employment and support allowance.

General Note
This is similar to the HB equivalent. See the commentary on p549 and p815.

Back-dating of applications
    6.–(1) This paragraph applies only to persons who are pensioners.

(2) Subject to sub-paragraph (3), the time for the making of an application under an authority's scheme is as regards any day on which, apart from satisfying the condition of making an application, the applicant is entitled to such a reduction, that day and the period of three months immediately following it.

(3) In any case where paragraph 5(1)(a) (date on which application made: state pension credit comprising guarantee credit) applies, sub-paragraph (2) does not entitle a person to apply for a reduction under an authority's scheme in respect of any day earlier than three months before the date on which the claim for state pension credit is made (or treated as made by virtue of any provision of the Social Security (Claims and Payments) Regulations 1987).

General Note
This is similar to reg 64(1) and (1A) HB Regs. See the commentary on p815.

Paragraph 6 applies only to pensioners. Regulation 3 defines the meaning of "pensioner" and "person who is not a pensioner". In England, unlike in Wales, there is no requirement for CTR schemes to include provision for the backdating of applications for a person who is not a pensioner. Billing authorities are free to include backdating provisions for such applicants in their schemes but do not have to. (For Wales: see Sch 13 para 4 of the Council Tax Reduction Schemes and Prescribed Requirements (Wales) Regulations 2013 No.3029; in Scotland: see reg 85(7) and (8) of the Council Tax Reduction (Scotland) Regs 2012 No.303.)

In England, for couples in which one member of couple has reached the qualifying age for PC but the other has not, it can, in some circumstances, be worth giving careful thought to which partner makes the application for CTR. If either member of the couple is on IS, income-based JSA, income-related ESA or have an award of UC (for more on this see p1113), neither of them will be a 'pensioner' and they cannot benefit from the 'backdating' provision in para 6. However, when neither of them are on IS, income-based JSA or income-related ESA, and neither has an award of UC, if the CTR application is made by the partner who has reached the qualifying age for PC, they can benefit from the rule in para 6; while if the application is made by the other partner they cannot. Working out whether it would be financially beneficial for one partner to make the CTR application rather than the other will also require an assessment of any eligibility for backdating under the authority's CTR scheme.

Information and evidence
    7.–(1) Subject to sub-paragraph (3), a person who makes an application for a reduction under an authority's scheme must satisfy sub-paragraph (2) in relation both to himself and to any other person in respect of whom he is making the application.

(2) This sub-paragraph is satisfied in relation to a person if–

(a) the application is accompanied by–

    (i) a statement of the person's national insurance number and information or evidence establishing that that number has been allocated to the person; or

    (ii) information or evidence enabling the authority to ascertain the national insurance number that has been allocated to the person; or

(b) the person has made an application for a national insurance number to be allocated to him and the application for the reduction is accompanied by–

    (i) evidence of the application for a national insurance number to be so allocated; and

    (ii) the information or evidence enabling it to be so allocated.

(3) Sub-paragraph (2) does not apply–

(a) in the case of a child or young person in respect of whom an application for a reduction is made;

(b) to a person who–

    (i) is a person treated as not being in Great Britain for the purposes of these Regulations;

(ii)   is subject to immigration control within the meaning of section 115(9)(a) of the Immigration and Asylum Act 1999; and

(iii)   has not previously been allocated a national insurance number.

(4)   Subject to sub-paragraph (5), a person who makes an application, or a person to whom a reduction under an authority's scheme has been awarded, must furnish such certificates, documents, information and evidence in connection with the application or the award, or any question arising out of the application or the award, as may reasonably be required by that authority in order to determine that person's entitlement to, or continuing entitlement to a reduction under its scheme and must do so within one month of the authority requiring him to do so or such longer period as the authority may consider reasonable.

(5)   Nothing in this paragraph requires a person who is a pensioner to furnish any certificates, documents, information or evidence relating to a payment to which sub-paragraph (7) applies.

(6)   Where an authority makes a request under sub-paragraph (4), it must–

(a)   inform the applicant or the person to whom a reduction under its scheme has been awarded of his duty under paragraph 9 (duty to notify change of circumstances) to notify the authority of any change of circumstances; and

(b)   without prejudice to the extent of the duty owed under paragraph 9, indicate to him either orally or by notice or by reference to some other document available to him on application and without charge, the kind of change of circumstances which must be notified.

(7)   This sub-paragraph applies to any of the following payments–

(a)   a payment which is made under or by the Trusts, the Fund, the Eileen Trust, MFET Limited, the Skipton Fund, the Caxton Foundation [¹ , the London Emergencies Trust, the We Love Manchester Emergency Fund] or the London Bombings Relief Charitable Fund;

(b)   a payment which is disregarded under paragraph 16 of Schedule 6 (payments made under certain trusts and certain other payments), other than a payment under the Independent Living Fund (2006);

(c)   a payment which is disregarded under paragraph 8(10) of Schedule 1.

(8)   Where an applicant or a person to whom a reduction under an authority's scheme has been awarded or any partner has attained the qualifying age for state pension credit and is a member of, or a person deriving entitlement to a pension under, a personal pension scheme, he must where the authority so requires furnish the following information–

(a)   the name and address of the pension fund holder;

(b)   such other information including any reference or policy number as is needed to enable the personal pension scheme to be identified.

Amendment

1.   Amended by reg 16(a) of SI 2017 No 1305 as from 12.1.18 in relation to schemes made for financial years starting on or after 1.4.18.

Analysis

This is similar to the HB equivalent. See the commentary on p556.

Para 7(4), (5) and (7)

The obligation imposed under para 7(4) was considered by the High Court in *Francois v LB Waltham Forest* [2017] EWHC 2252 (Admin). Mrs Francois had placed in trust money awarded as compensation for a personal injury. Under Waltham Forest's CTR scheme, non-pensioners with capital over £6,000 were not entitled to CTR. The scheme also provided that the value of trusts set up from payments for personal injury to applicants and their partners, and the value of the right to receive payments from such trusts, were disregarded as capital. Waltham Forest had requested information from Mrs Francois regarding her bank accounts and the personal injury trust. She had given Waltham Forest a copy of a letter from her solicitors which confirmed the compensation payment had been placed in a personal injury trust and both Mrs Francois and the solicitors invited Waltham Forest to contact the solicitors should more information be required. They did not do so but decided, as Mrs Francois had failed to provide the further information they had requested, that she had capital of over £6,000 and so was not entitled to CTR. Following her appeal to the VTE, the VTE issued directions requesting Mrs Francois provide details of her bank accounts and a statement giving details of all transactions relating to the Trust but Mrs Francois did not comply with the order. The VTE concluded that the solicitor's letter was not enough in itself and the onus was on Mrs Francois to provide the information requested by the local authority. The VTE decided that as she had not done so the council was entitled to conclude that she had capital of more than £6,000 and therefore was not entitled to CTR. Mrs Francois appealed to the High Court.

The High Court dismissed Ms Francois's appeal stating that there was no error of law in the VTE's decision, and confirmed the applicability of *Kerr v Department for Social Development* [2004] UKHL 23; reported as *R 1/04 (SF)* (which concerned entitlement to a funeral payment) and *Jeleniewicz v SSWP* [2008] EWCA Civ 1163 (which concerned entitlement of a Polish national to income support) to cases concerning entitlement to CTR.

The High Court quoted Baroness Hale in *Kerr* who stated:

"62.   What emerges from all this is a co-operative process of investigation in which both the claimant and the department play their part. The department is the one which knows what questions it needs to ask and what information it needs to have in order to determine whether the conditions of entitlement have been met. The claimant is the one who generally speaking can and must supply that information.

But where the information is available to the department rather than the claimant, then the department must take the necessary steps to enable it to be traced.

63.   If that sensible approach is taken, it will rarely be necessary to resort to concepts taken from adversarial litigation such as the burden of proof. The first question will be whether each partner in the process has played their part. If there is still ignorance about a relevant matter then generally speaking it should be determined against the one who has not done all they reasonably could to discover it. As Mr Commissioner Henty put it in decision CIS/5321/1998: "a claimant must to the best of his or her ability give such information to the AO as he reasonably can, in default of which a contrary inference can always be drawn." The same should apply to information which the department can reasonably be expected to discover for itself."

The Court went on to quote Mummery LJ in *Jeleniewicz*, who concluded:

30.   "First, as to the process adopted by the Commissioner on the hearing of the appeal, there was no error of law as Baroness Hale observed in Kerr [at paragraph 62, quoted supra] the claimant is the person, who generally speaking, can and must supply the information needed to determine whether the conditions of entitlement had been met…In my judgment, this is true in determining whether the conditions of entitlement have ceased to be satisfied as it is when determining whether the conditions have been satisfied."

The High Court stated (para 28): "These cases establish that when considering an entitlement to a benefit, which would include a reduction in council tax, the principle is that the person who has knowledge or access to information that supports their claim should provide it."

The duty is to provide such information and evidence etc "as may reasonably be required" by the authority. For commentary, see p557. Note that the duty does not require a pensioner to provide information relating to the payments listed in para (7), which would be disregarded as capital: para (5).

Amendment and withdrawal of application

8.–(1)   A person who has made an application may amend it at any time before a decision has been made on it by a notice in writing delivered or sent to the designated office.

(2)   Where the application was made by telephone in accordance with Part 1 of Schedule 7, the amendment may also be made by telephone.

(3)   Any application amended in accordance with sub-paragraph (1) or (2) is to be treated as if it had been amended in the first instance.

(4)   A person who has made an application may withdraw it by notice to the designated office at any time before a decision has been made on it.

(5)   Where the application was made by telephone in accordance with Part 1 of Schedule 7, the withdrawal may also be made by telephone.

(6)   Any notice of withdrawal given in accordance with sub-paragraph (4) or (5) has effect when it is received.

(7)   Where a person, by telephone, amends or withdraws an application the person must (if required to do so by the authority) confirm the amendment or withdrawal by a notice in writing delivered or sent to the designated office.

General Note

This is similar to the HB equivalent. See the commentary on p558.

Duty to notify changes of circumstances

9.–(1)   [¹ Subject to sub-paragraphs (3) and (9)], an applicant (or any person acting on his behalf) must comply with sub-paragraph (2) if there is a relevant change of circumstances at any time–

(a)   between the making of an application and a decision being made on it, or

(b)   after the decision is made (where the decision is that the applicant is entitled to a reduction under an authority's scheme) including at any time while the applicant is in receipt of such a reduction.

(2)   The applicant (or any person acting on his behalf) must notify any change of circumstances which the applicant (or that person) might reasonably be expected to know might affect his entitlement to, or the amount of, a reduction under the authority's scheme (a "relevant change of circumstances") by giving notice to the authority–

(a)   in writing; or

(b)   by telephone–

    (i)   where the authority has published a telephone number for that purpose or for the purposes of Part 1 of Schedule 7 unless the authority determines that in any particular case or class of case notification may not be given by telephone; or

    (ii)   in any case or class of case where the authority determines that notice may be given by telephone; or

(c)   by any other means which the authority agrees to accept in any particular case,

within a period of 21 days beginning with the day on which the change occurs, or as soon as reasonably practicable after the change occurs, whichever is later.

(3)   The duty imposed on a person by sub-paragraph (1) does not extend to notifying–

(a)   changes in the amount of council tax payable to the authority;

(b)   changes in the age of the applicant or that of any member of his family;

(c)   in the case of an applicant in receipt of a relevant benefit, changes in circumstances which affect the amount of the benefit but not the amount of the reduction under the authority's scheme to which he is entitled, other than the cessation of that entitlement to the benefit.

(4)   For the purposes of sub-paragraph (3)(c) "relevant benefit" means income support, an income-based jobseeker's allowance or an income-related employment and support allowance or universal credit.

(5)   Notwithstanding sub-paragraph (3)(b) or (c) an applicant is required by sub-paragraph (1) to notify the authority of any change in the composition of his family arising from the fact that a person who was a member of his family is now no longer such a person because he has ceased to be a child or young person.

(6)   The duty imposed on a person by sub-paragraph (1) includes in the case of a person falling within class C (pensioners: alternative maximum council tax reduction), giving written notice to the authority of changes which occur in the number of adults in the dwelling or in their total gross incomes and, where any such adult ceases to be in receipt of state pension credit, the date when this occurs.

(7)   A person who has been awarded a reduction under an authority's scheme who is also on state pension credit must report–

(a)   changes affecting the residence or income of any non-dependant normally residing with the applicant or with whom the applicant normally resides;

(b)   any absence from the dwelling which exceeds or is likely to exceed 13 weeks [² or where the absence is from Great Britain, which exceeds or is likely to exceed 4 weeks].

(8)   In addition to the changes required to be reported under sub-paragraph (7), a person whose state pension credit comprises only a savings credit must also report–

(a)   changes affecting a child living with him which may result in a change in the amount of reduction under the authority's scheme allowed in his case, but not changes in the age of the child;

(b)   any change in the amount of the applicant's capital to be taken into account which does or may take the amount of his capital to more than £16,000;

(c)   any change in the income or capital of–

(i)   a non-dependant whose income and capital are treated as belonging to the applicant in accordance with paragraph 12 of Schedule 1 (circumstances in which income of a non-dependant is to be treated as applicant's); or

(ii)   a person to whom paragraph 14(2)(e) of Schedule 1 refers (partner treated as member of the household under regulation 8),

and whether such a person or, as the case may be, non-dependant stops living or begins or resumes living with the applicant.

(9)   A person who is entitled to a reduction under an authority's scheme and on state pension credit need only report to the authority the changes specified in sub-paragraphs (7) and (8).

Amendments

1.   Amended by reg 2(13) of SI 2013 No.3181 for schemes for financial years beginning on or after 1.4.14.

2.   Amended by reg 16(b) of SI 2017 No 1305 as from 12.1.18 in relation to schemes made for financial years starting on or after 1.4.18.

General Note

This is similar to the HB equivalent. See the commentary on p819.

PART 3
Decisions by an authority

10.   This Part applies to persons who are pensioners and persons who are not pensioners.

Decision by authority

11.   An authority must make a decision on an application under its scheme within 14 days of paragraphs 4 and 7 and Part 1 of Schedule 7 being satisfied, or as soon as reasonably practicable thereafter.

General Note

This is similar to the HB equivalent. See the commentary on p563.

Notification of decision

12.–(1)   An authority must notify in writing any person affected by a decision made by it under its scheme–

(a)   in the case of a decision on an application, forthwith or as soon as reasonably practicable thereafter;

(b)   in any other case, within 14 days of that decision or as soon as reasonably practicable thereafter.

(2)   Where the decision is to award a reduction, the notification under sub-paragraph (1) must include a statement–

(a)   informing the person affected of the duty imposed by paragraph 9(1);

(b)   explaining the possible consequences (including prosecution) of failing to comply with that duty; and

(c)   setting out the circumstances a change in which might affect entitlement to the reduction or its amount.

(3)   Where the decision is to award a reduction, the notification under sub-paragraph (1) must include a statement as to how that entitlement is to be discharged.

(4)   In any case, the notification under sub-paragraph (1) must inform the person affected of the procedure by which an appeal may be made and must refer the person to the provisions in the authority's scheme relating to the procedure for making an appeal.

(5)   A person affected to whom an authority sends or delivers a notification of decision may, within one month of the date of the notification of that decision request in writing the authority to provide a written statement setting out the reasons for its decision on any matter set out in the notice.

(6)   The written statement referred to in sub-paragraph (5) must be sent to the person requesting it within 14 days or as soon as reasonably practicable thereafter.

(7)   For the purposes of this paragraph a person is to be treated as a person affected by a decision of an authority under its scheme where the rights, duties or obligations of that person are affected by that decision and the person falls within sub-paragraph (8).

(8)   This sub-paragraph applies to–

(a)   the applicant;

(b)   in the case of a person who is liable to pay council tax in respect of a dwelling and is unable for the time being to act–

(i)   a deputy appointed by the Court of Protection with power to claim, or as the case may be, receive benefit on his behalf; or

(ii)   in Scotland, a judicial factor or any guardian acting or appointed under the Adults with Incapacity (Scotland) Act 2000 who has power to apply or, as the case may be, receive benefit on the person's behalf; or

(iii)   an attorney with a general power or a power to apply or, as the case may be, receive benefit, has been appointed by that person under the Powers of Attorney Act 1971, the Enduring Powers of Attorney Act 1985 or the Mental Capacity Act 2005 or otherwise,

(c)   a person appointed by an authority under paragraph 4(3) (persons appointed to act for a person unable to act).

General Note
This is similar to the HB equivalent. See the commentary on p564.

PART 4
Circumstances in which a payment may be made

13.   This part applies to persons who are pensioners and persons who are not pensioners.

Payment where there is joint and several liability
14.–(1)   Where–

(a)   a person is entitled to a reduction under an authority's scheme in respect of his liability for the authority's council tax as it has effect in respect of a chargeable financial year;

(b)   the person entitled to the reduction is jointly and severally liable for the council tax; and

(c)   the authority determines that discharging his entitlement by reducing the amount of his liability to which regulation 20(2) of the Council Tax (Administration and Enforcement) Regulations 1992 refers would be inappropriate,

it may make a payment to him of the amount of the reduction to which he is entitled, rounded where necessary to the nearest penny.

(2)   Subject to sub-paragraph (3) any payment made under sub-paragraph (1) must be made to the person who is entitled to the reduction.

(3)   Where a person other than a person who is entitled to a reduction under an authority's scheme made the application and that first person is a person acting pursuant to an appointment under paragraph 4(3) or is treated as having been so appointed by virtue of paragraph 4(4), the amount of the reduction may be paid to that person.

The Council Tax Reduction Schemes (Transitional Provision) (England) Regulations 2013

(2013 No.215)

Citation, commencement, application and interpretation

1.–(1)   These Regulations may be cited as the Council Tax Reduction Schemes (Transitional Provision) (England) Regulations 2013 and come into force on 6th March 2013.

(2)   These Regulations apply in relation to billing authorities in England and for the purposes of the commencement of schemes on 1st April 2013.

(3)   In these Regulations–

"council tax benefit" means council tax benefit under Part 7 of the Social Security Contributions and Benefits Act 1992;

"relevant billing authority" in relation to a person means the billing authority in whose area the dwelling in which the person is resident is situated.

Persons to be treated as having made an application for a council tax reduction

2.–(1)   A person who is resident in a dwelling in England and who falls within paragraph (2) is to be treated as having made an application for a reduction under the relevant billing authority's scheme.

(2)   The persons referred to in paragraph (1) are any person who on or after the date these Regulations come into force–

(a)   has made a claim for council tax benefit which has not been determined;

(b)   is in receipt of council tax benefit;

(c)   is a person whose payments of council tax benefit have been suspended under regulation 11 or 13 of the Housing Benefit and Council Tax Benefit (Decisions and Appeals) Regulations 2001.

Date on which change of circumstances is to take effect

3.–(1)   Where–

(a)   by virtue of regulation 2(1) a person (P) is treated as having made an application for a reduction under a scheme;

(b)   on a day before 1st April 2013, P becomes a person to whom paragraphs (10) to (13) of regulation 50 of the Council Tax Benefit (Persons who have attained the qualifying age for state pension credit) Regulations 2006 (change of circumstances in connection with non-dependants) apply; and

(c)   the effective date for the change of circumstances in accordance with the provisions referred to in sub-paragraph (b) is a date after 31st March 2013 (D date),

the effective date for the purposes of the relevant provisions is the same as D date and no account is to be taken of those change of circumstances in determining the application for the reduction until that date.

(2)   In paragraph (1) "the relevant provisions" means–

(a)   a provision contained in the authority's scheme by virtue of paragraph 46(10) to (13) of Schedule 1 to the Council Tax Reduction Schemes (Prescribed Requirements) (England) Regulations 2012;

(b)   paragraph 107(10) to (13) of the scheme prescribed in the Schedule to the Council Tax Reduction Schemes (Default Scheme) (England) Regulations 2012.

Notification of change of circumstances

4.–(1)   This regulation applies in relation to a person who is treated by virtue of regulation 2(1) as having made an application for a reduction under a scheme.

(2)   Where this regulation applies, the following provisions in the relevant billing authority's scheme do not apply in relation to that person's application–

(a)   a provision contained in the authority's scheme by virtue of paragraph 4(7) of Schedule 8 to the Council Tax Reduction Schemes (Prescribed Requirements) (England) Regulations 2012; or

(b)   paragraph 109(7) of the scheme prescribed in the Schedule to the Council Tax Reduction Schemes (Default Scheme) (England) Regulations 2012.

The Council Tax Reduction Schemes (Prescribed Requirements) (England) (Amendment) Regulations 2015
(2015 No.2041)

Citation, commencement and application

1.–(1) These Regulations may be cited as the Council Tax Reduction Schemes (Prescribed Requirements) (England) (Amendment) Regulations 2015 and come into force on 14th January 2016.

(2) These Regulations apply in relation to council tax reduction schemes made by billing authorities for financial years beginning on or after 1st April 2016.

Transitional provision

3.–(1) Subject to paragraph (2), the amendment in regulation 2(4)(b) does not apply to a person who, on 30th April 2016, is liable to pay council tax at a reduced rate by virtue of a council tax reduction under an authority's scheme established under section 13A(2) of the Act and is–

(a) a member of a family of which at least one member is a child or young person; or

(b) a partner in a polygamous marriage, where he or she, or another partner of the polygamous marriage, is responsible for a child or young person who is a member of the same household.

(2) Paragraph (1) does not apply if–

(a) sub-paragraph (a) or (b) of that paragraph ceases to apply; or

(b) the person makes a new application for a reduction under an authority's scheme under section 13A(2) of the Act.

(3) For the purposes of this regulation–

(a) "the Act" means the Local Government Finance Act 1992;

(b) "child", "family", "partner", "polygamous marriage" and "young person" have the meanings given by regulation 2 of the Council Tax Reduction Schemes (Prescribed Requirements) (England) Regulations 2012.

The Council Tax Reduction Schemes (Amendment) (England) Regulations 2017

(2017 No.1305)

Citation, commencement and application

1.–(1) These Regulations may be cited as the Council Tax Reduction Schemes (Amendment) (England) Regulations 2017 and, save as provided in paragraph (2), come into force on 12th January 2018.

(2) Regulations 10, 11 and 14(b) come into force on 6th December 2018.

(3) Parts 3 and 4 of these Regulations apply in relation to council tax reduction schemes(2) made by billing authorities(3) for financial years beginning on or after 1st April 2018.

Transitional provisions for restrictions on amounts for children and young persons

17.–(1) This regulation applies where–

(a) on 31st March 2018, a person is liable to pay council tax at a reduced rate by virtue of a council tax reduction under an authority's scheme established under section 13A(2) of the Local Government Finance Act 1992 ("a section 13A(2) scheme"); and

(b) the person is, or the person and the person's partner are between them, responsible for more than two individuals who are either children or young persons and who are members of the same household (each such individual is referred to as a "protected individual").

(2) Where this regulation applies, the amendments made by regulation 7 do not apply to the person entitled to a council tax reduction referred to in paragraph (1) until–

(a) the person makes a new application for a reduction under an authority's section 13A(2) scheme; or

(b) the person or the person's partner (if any) becomes responsible for a new individual,

whichever is the first to occur.

(3) Paragraphs (4) to (8) apply where–

(a) the amendments made by regulation 7 apply by virtue of paragraph (2)(b);

(b) the child tax credit provisions do not apply; and

(c) the person has not made a new application for a reduction under an authority's scheme for a reduction under an authority's section 13A(2) scheme.

(4) Notwithstanding the default provisions, a child amount shall be included in the applicable amount in relation to any protected individual, in relation to any time when the person or the person's partner (if any) is responsible for the individual and the individual is a member of the same household.

(5) Paragraph (6) applies where–

(a) the person or the person's partner (if any) is responsible for one or more protected individuals who are members of the same household; and

(b) either of them is responsible for one or more new individuals who are members of the same household.

(6) Where this paragraph applies, any protected individual for whom the person or the person's partner is responsible is to be counted for the purpose of deciding whether, under the default provisions, an additional child amount is to be included in the applicable amount with respect to the new individual or individuals referred to in paragraph (5)(b).

(7) Paragraph (8) applies where–

(a) the number of protected individuals for whom either the person or the person's partner (if any) is responsible, and who are members of the same household, is one;

(b) the number of new individuals for whom either the person or the person's partner is responsible, and who are members of the same household, is two or more; and

(c) a different child amount would apply to different individuals.

(8)   Where this paragraph applies, the child amounts to be included in the applicable amount shall be–

(a)   the child amount in relation to the protected individual; and

(b)   a child amount in relation to such one of the new individuals as will result in the greatest possible total amount.

(9)   Under paragraph (3), for the purposes of determining whether the child tax credit provisions apply, by virtue of paragraph 6(1B) of Schedule 1 to the 2012 Regulations, where the person or the person's partner is responsible for one or more protected individuals, the total amount that would be included in the applicable amount under the default provisions shall be taken to be the total that would be included under paragraphs (4), (6) and (8).

(10)   For the purposes of this regulation–

(a)   "the 2012 Regulations" means the Council Tax Reduction Schemes (Prescribed Requirements) (England) Regulations 2012;

(b)   "applicable amount", "child", "partner" and "young person" have the same meanings as in the 2012 Regulations;

(c)   "child amount" means the amount determined under paragraph 2 of Schedule 2 to the 2012 Regulations;

(d)   "child tax credit provisions" means the provisions of paragraph 6(1)(b) of Schedule 1 to the 2012 Regulations (as substituted by paragraph 6(1C) of that Schedule);

(e)   "default provisions" means the provisions of paragraph 6(1)(b) of Schedule 1 to the 2012 Regulations (as substituted by paragraph 6(1C) of that Schedule);

(f)   "new individual" means a child or young person who is not a protected individual;

(g)   any reference to an individual being part of the same household means being part of the same household with the person who is entitled to a reduction under an authority's section 13A(2) scheme and the person's partner (if any);

(h)   a person is to be treated as responsible for a child or young person in the circumstances set out in regulation 7 of the 2012 Regulations.

The Council Tax Reduction Schemes and Prescribed Requirements (Wales) Regulations 2013

(SI 2013 No.3029)

PART 1
General
1. Title, commencement and application
2. Interpretation
3. Meaning of "pensioner" and "person who is not a pensioner"
4. Meaning of "couple"
5. Polygamous marriages
6. Meaning of "family"
7. Circumstances in which a person is to be treated as responsible or not responsible for another
8. Households
9. Non-dependants
10. Remunerative work

PART 2
Council tax reduction schemes
11. Schemes
12. Duty to make schemes and exercise of functions by authorities
13. First financial year of schemes
14. Scheme requirements in relation to classes of persons
15. Scheme requirements in relation to reductions
16. Scheme procedural requirements
17. Preparation of a scheme
18. Revisions to and replacement of schemes
19. Notice requiring provision of information to the Welsh Ministers
20. Supply of documents

PART 3
Prescribed classes of person who must be included in an authority's scheme
21. Classes of person who must be included in a scheme
22. Class A: pensioners whose income is less than the applicable amount
23. Class B: pensioners whose income is greater than the applicable amount
24. Class C: persons who are not pensioners whose income is less than the applicable amount
25. Class D: persons who are not pensioners whose income is greater than the applicable amount
26. Periods of absence from a dwelling

PART 4
Prescribed classes of person who must not be included in an authority's scheme
27. Classes of person who must not be included in a scheme
28. Persons treated as not being in Great Britain
29. Persons subject to immigration control
30. Persons whose capital exceeds £16,000
31. Students

PART 5
Other matters that must be included in an authority's scheme
32. Provision for pensioners
33. Provision for persons who are not pensioners
34. Provision for pensioners and persons who are not pensioners

PART 6
Revocation, transitional and savings provisions

35.   Interpretation
36.   Revocation and savings
37.   Persons to be treated as having made an application for a reduction
38.   Applications received between 15 February 2014 and 31 March 2014
39.   Date on which change of circumstances is to take effect
40.   Notification relating to change of circumstances

SCHEDULES

1.   Determining eligibility for a reduction under an authority's scheme, amount
         of reduction and calculation of income and capital: pensioners
2.   Applicable amounts: pensioners
3.   Sums disregarded from applicant's earnings: pensioners
4.   Amounts to be disregarded in the calculation of income other than earnings:
         pensioners
5.   Capital disregards: pensioners
6.   Determining eligibility for a reduction under an authority's scheme, amount
         of reduction and calculation of income and capital: persons who are not
         pensioners
7.   Applicable amounts: persons who are not pensioners
8.   Sums disregarded in the calculation of earnings: persons who are not
         pensioners
9.   Sums disregarded in the calculation of income other than earnings: persons
         who are not pensioners
10.   Capital disregards: persons who are not pensioners
11.   Students
12.   All applicants: matters that must be included in an authority's scheme –
         procedural matters
13.   All applicants: matters that must be included in an authority's scheme –
         other matters
14.   Matters to be included in a notification

Part 1
General

Title, commencement and application
     1.–(1)   The title of these Regulations is the Council Tax Reduction Schemes and
Prescribed Requirements (Wales) Regulations 2013.
     (2)   These Regulations come into force on the day after the day on which they are
made and apply in relation to Wales.
     (3)   These Regulations apply in relation to council tax reduction schemes made by
authorities for financial years beginning on or after 1 April 2014.

Interpretation
     2.–(1)   In these Regulations–
"the 1992 Act" ("Deddf 1992") means the Local Government Finance Act 1992;
"Abbeyfield Home" ("Cartref Abbeyfield") means an establishment run by the Abbeyfield
          Society including all bodies corporate or unincorporated which are affiliated to
          that society;
"adoption leave" ("absenoldeb mabwysiadu") means a period of absence from work
          onordinary or additional adoption leave by virtue of section 75A or 75B of the
          Employment Rights Act 1996;
"AFIP" ("TALIA") means an armed forces independence payment payable in accordance
          with an armed and reserve forces compensation scheme established under
          section 1(2) of the ArmedForces (Pensions and Compensation) Act 2004;
"applicable amount" ("swm cymwysadwy") means–

    (a)   in relation to a pensioner, the amount calculated in accordance with paragraph 1 of Schedule 1 and Schedule 2; and

    (b)   in relation to a person who is not a pensioner, the amount calculated in accordance with–

        (i)   paragraphs 1 and 2 of Schedule 6 and Schedule 7; or

        (ii)   paragraph 3 of Schedule 6,

as the case may be;

"applicant" ("ceisydd") means a person applying for a reduction under an authority's scheme;

"application" ("cais") means an application for a reduction under an authority's scheme;

"appropriate DWP office" ("swyddfa briodol yr Adran Gwaith a Phensiynau") means an office of the Department for Work and Pensions dealing with state pension credit or an office which is normally open to the public for the receipt of claims for income support, a jobseeker's allowance or an employment and support allowance;

[⁵ "approved blood scheme" ("cynllun gwaed cymeradwy") means–

    (a)   a scheme established or approved by the Secretary of State, or a trust established with funds provided by the Secretary of State, for the purpose of providing compensation in respect of a person having been infected from contaminated blood products; or

    (b)   a scheme established under sections 1 to 3 of the National Health Service (Wales) Act 2006 and administered by the Velindre Trust for the purpose of making payments and providing support to, or in respect of, individuals infected with Hepatitis C, HIV or both, through contaminated blood or blood products used by the NHS;]

"assessment period" ("cyfnod asesu") means the period determined–

    (a)   in relation to pensioners–

        (i)   in relation to the earnings of a self-employed earner, in accordance with paragraph14 of Schedule 1 for the purpose of calculating the weekly earnings of the applicant;or

        (ii)   in relation to any other income, in accordance with paragraph 11 of Schedule 1 for the purpose of calculating the weekly income of the applicant;

    (b)   in relation to persons who are not pensioners, such period as is set out in paragraphs 10 to 12 of Schedule 6 over which income falls to be calculated;

"attendance allowance" ("lwfans gweini") means–

    (a)   an attendance allowance under Part 3 of the SSCBA(4);

    (b)   an increase of disablement pension under section 104 or 105 of the SSCBA;

    (c)   a payment by virtue of article 14, 15, 16, 43 or 44 of the Personal Injuries (Civilians) Scheme 1983 or any analogous payment; or

    (d)   any payment based on need for attendance which is paid as part of a war disablement pension;

"the authority" ("yr awdurdod") means a billing authority in relation to whose area a scheme has effect in accordance with regulation 12;

"basic rate" ("cyfradd sylfaenol") has the meaning given by the Income Tax Act 2007;

"the benefit Acts" ("y Deddfau budd-dal") means the SSCBA, the Jobseekers Act 1995, the State Pension Credit Act 2002[⁴,] the Welfare Reform Act 2007 [⁴ and the Pensions Act 2014];

"board and lodging accommodation" ("prydau bwyd a llety") means accommodation provided to a person, or if that person is a member of a family, to that person or any other member of that person's family, for a charge which is inclusive of the provision of that accommodation and at least some cooked or prepared meals which both are cooked or prepared (by a person other than the person to whom the accommodation is provided or a member of that person's family) and are consumed in that accommodation or associated premises;

[⁵ "care home" ("cartref gofal")–

    (a)   in England has the meaning given by section 3 of the Care Standards Act 2000;

(b)   in Wales means a place at which a care home service, within the meaning of Part 1 of the Regulation and Inspection of Social Care (Wales) Act 2016, is provided wholly or mainly to adults;

(c)   in Scotland means a care home service within the meaning given by paragraph 2 of Schedule 12 to the Public Services Reform (Scotland) Act 2010; and

(d)   in Northern Ireland means a nursing home within the meaning of article 11 of the Health and Personal Social Services (Quality, Improvement and Regulation) (Northern Ireland) Order 2003 or a residential care home within the meaning of article 10 of that Order;]

"the Caxton Foundation" ("Sefydliad Caxton") means the charitable trust of that name established on 28 March 2011 out of funds provided by the Secretary of State for the benefit of certain persons suffering from hepatitis C and other persons eligible for payment in accordance with its provisions;

"child" ("plentyn") means a person under the age of 16;

"child benefit" ("budd-dal plant") has the meaning given by section 141 of the SSCBA;

"child tax credit" ("crcdyd treth plant") means a child tax credit under section 8 of the Tax Credits Act 2002;

"close relative" ("perthynas agos") means a parent, parent-in-law, son, son-in-law, daughter, daughter-in-law, step-parent, step-son, step-daughter, brother, sister, or if any of the preceding persons is one member of a couple, the other member of that couple;

"concessionary payment" ("taliad consesiynol") means a payment made under arrangements made by the Secretary of State with the consent of the Treasury which is charged either to the National Insurance Fund or to a Departmental Expenditure Vote to which payments of benefit or tax credits under the benefit Acts or the Tax Credits Act 2002 are charged;

[² "contributory employment and support allowance" ("lwfans cyflogaeth a chymorth cyfrannol") means an allowance under Part 1 of the Welfare Reform Act 2007 as amended by the provisions of Schedule 3, and Part 1 of Schedule 14, to the Welfare Reform Act 2012 that remove references to an income-related allowance, and a contributory allowance under Part 1 of the Welfare Reform Act 2007 as that Part has effect apart from those provisions;]

"council tax benefit" ("budd-dal treth gyngor") means council tax benefit under Part 7 of the SSCBA;

"couple" ("cwpl") has the meaning given by regulation 4;

"designated office" ("swyddfa ddynodedig") means the office of an authority designated by it for the receipt of applications–

(a)   by notice upon or with a form supplied by the authority for the purposes of making anapplication; or

(b)   by reference upon or with such a form to some other document available from it and sent by electronic means or otherwise on application and without charge; or

(c)   by any combination of the provisions set out in paragraphs (a) and (b);

"disability living allowance" ("lwfans byw i'r anabl") means a disability living allowance under section 71 of the SSCBA;

"dwelling" ("annedd") has the meaning given by section 3 of the 1992 Act;

"earnings" ("enillion") has the meaning given by paragraphs 12, 14 and 15 of Schedule 1 and paragraph 14 or 16 of Schedule 6 as the case may be;

"the Eileen Trust" ("Ymddiriedolaeth Eileen") means the charitable trust of that name established on 29 March 1993 out of funds provided by the Secretary of State for the benefit of persons eligible for payment in accordance with its provisions;

"electronic communication" ("cyfathrebiad electronig") has the same meaning as in section 15(1) of the Electronic Communications Act 2000;

"employed earner" ("enillydd cyflogedig") is to be construed in accordance with section 2(1)(a) of the SSCBA and also includes a person who is in receipt of a payment which is payable under any enactment having effect in Northern Ireland and which corresponds to statutory sick pay or statutory maternity pay;

"the Employment, Skills and Enterprise Scheme" ("y Cynllun Cyflogaeth, Sgiliau a Menter") means a scheme under section 17A (schemes for assisting persons to obtain employment: "work for your benefit" schemes etc.) of the Jobseekers Act 1995 known by that name and provided pursuant to arrangements made by the Secretary of State that is designed to assist claimants for job-seekers allowance to obtain employment, including self-employment, and which may include for any individual work-related activity (including work experience or job search);

"employment zone" ("parth cyflogaeth") means an area within Great Britain designated for the purposes of section 60 of the Welfare Reform and Pensions Act 1999 and an "employment zone programme" ("rhaglen parth cyflogaeth") means a programme established for such an area or areas designed to assist claimants for a jobseeker's allowance to obtain sustainable employment;

"employment zone contractor" ("contractwr parth cyflogaeth") means a person who is undertaking the provision of facilities in respect of an employment zone programme on behalf of the Secretary of State for Work and Pensions;

"enactment" ("deddfiad") includes an enactment comprised in, or in an instrument made under, an Act of the Scottish Parliament or an Act or Measure of the National Assembly for Wales;

"extended reduction" ("gostyngiad estynedig") means a reduction under a scheme to which a person is eligible under Part 5 of Schedule 1 and Part 5 of Schedule 6;

"extended reduction period" ("cyfnod gostyngiad estynedig") means the period for which a person is in receipt of an extended reduction in accordance with paragraph 33 of Schedule 1 and paragraph 35 of Schedule 6 or paragraph 40 of Schedule 6;

"extended reduction (qualifying contributory benefits)" ("gostyngiad estynedig (budd-daliadau cyfrannol cymwys)") means a reduction under a scheme for which a person is eligible pursuant to paragraph 32 of Schedule 1 and paragraph 39 of Schedule 6;

"family" ("teulu") has the meaning given by regulation 6;

"the Fund" ("y Gronfa") means moneys made available from time to time by the Secretaryof State for the benefit of persons eligible for payment in accordance with the provisions of a scheme established by the Secretary of State on 24 April 1992 or, in Scotland, on 10 April 1992;

"guarantee credit" ("credyd gwarant") is to be construed in accordance with sections 1 and 2 of the State Pension Credit Act 2002;

"a guaranteed income payment" ("taliad incwm gwarantedig") means a payment made under article 15(1)(c) or article 29(1)(a) of the Armed Forces and Reserve Forces (Compensation Scheme) Order 2011;

"housing benefit" ("budd-dal tai") means housing benefit under Part 7 of the SSCBA;

"an income-based jobseeker's allowance" ("lwfans ceisio gwaith ar sail incwm") and "a joint-claim jobseeker's allowance" ("lwfans ceisio gwaith cyd-hawliad") have the meanings given by section 1(4) of the Jobseekers Act 1995;

"income-related employment and support allowance" ("lwfans cyflogaeth a chymorth ar sailincwm") means an income-related allowance under Part 1 of the Welfare Reform Act 2007;

"independent hospital" ("ysbyty annibynnol")–

(a)   in England means a hospital as defined by section 275 of the National Health Service Act 2006 that is not a health service hospital as defined by that section;

(b)   in Wales has the meaning given by section 2 of the Care Standards Act 2000; and

(c)   [¹ in Scotland means an independent hospital or a private psychiatric hospital as defined by section 10F(2) of the National Health Service (Scotland) Act 1978;]

"the Independent Living Fund (2006)" ("y Gronfa Byw'n Annibynnol (2006)") means the Trust of that name established by a deed dated 10 April 2006 and made between the Secretary of State for Work and Pensions of the one part and Margaret Rosemary Cooper, Michael Beresford Boyall and Marie Theresa Martin of the other part;

"invalid carriage or other vehicle" ("cerbyd ar gyfer pobl anabl neu fath arall o gerbyd") means a vehicle propelled by a petrol engine or by electric power supplied for use on the road andto be controlled by the occupant;

"the London Bombings Relief Charitable Fund" ("Cronfa Gymorth Elusennol Bomiau Llundain") means the company limited by guarantee (number 5505072), and registered charity of that name established on 11 July 2005 for the purpose of (amongst other things) relieving sickness, disability or financial need of victims (including families or dependants of victims) of the terrorist attacks carried out in London on 7 July 2005;

[⁵ "the London Emergencies Trust" ("Ymddiriedolaeth Argyfyngau Llundain") means the company of that name (number 09928465) incorporated on 23 December 2015 and the registered charity of that name (number 1172307) established on 28 March 2017;]

"lone parent" ("unig riant") means a person who has no partner and who is responsible for and a member of the same household as a child or young person;

"the Macfarlane (Special Payments) Trust" ("Ymddiriedolaeth Macfarlane (Taliadau Arbennig)") means the trust of that name, established on 29 January 1990 partly out of funds provided by the Secretary of State, for the benefit of certain persons suffering from haemophilia;

"the Macfarlane (Special Payments) (No 2) Trust" ("Ymddiriedolaeth Macfarlane (TaliadauArbennig) (Rhif 2)") means the trust of that name, established on 3 May 1991 partly out of funds provided by the Secretary of State, for the benefit of certain persons suffering from haemophilia and other beneficiaries;

"the Macfarlane Trust" ("Ymddiriedolaeth Macfarlane") means the charitable trust,established partly out of funds provided by the Secretary of State to the Haemophilia Society, for the relief of poverty or distress among those suffering from haemophilia;

[⁵ "main phase employment and support allowance" ("lwfans cyflogaeth a chymorth prif wedd"), except in Part 1 of Schedule 7, means an employment and support allowance where–

(a)   the calculation of the amount payable in respect of the applicant includes a component under section 2(1)(b) or 4(2)(b) of the Welfare Reform Act 2007; or

(b)   the applicant is a member of the work-related activity group;]

"maternity leave" ("absenoldeb mamaeth") means a period during which a woman is absent from work because the woman is pregnant or has given birth to a child, and at the end of which the woman has a right to return to work either under the terms of the woman's contract of employment or under Part 8 of the Employment Rights Act 1996;

"maximum council tax reduction amount" ("uchafswm gostyngiad treth gyngor") means the amount determined in accordance with paragraph 2 of Schedule 1 and paragraph 4 of Schedule 6;

"member of a couple" ("aelod o gwpl") means a member of a married or unmarried couple;

[⁵ "member of the work-related activity group" ("aelod o'r grwp gweithgaredd perthynol i waith") means a person who has or is treated as having limited capability for work under either–

(a)   Part 5 of the Employment and Support Allowance Regulations 2008 other than by virtue of regulation 30 of those Regulations; or

(b)   Part 4 of the Employment and Support Allowance Regulations 2013 other than by virtue of regulation 26 of those Regulations;]

"MFET Limited" ("MFET Limited") means the company limited by guarantee (number 7121661) of that name, established for the purpose in particular of making payments in accordance with arrangements made with the Secretary of State to persons who have acquired HIV as a result of treatment by the NHS with blood or blood products;

"mobility supplement" ("atodiad symudedd") means–

(a)   in relation to pensioners, a supplement to which paragraph 5(1)(a)(vii) of Schedule 3 refers;

(b)   in relation to persons who are not pensioners, a supplement to which paragraph 13 of Schedule 9 refers;

"mover" ("symudwr") means an applicant who changes the dwelling in which the applicant is resident, and in respect of which the applicant is liable to pay council tax, from a dwelling in the area of one authority to a dwelling in the area of a second authority;

"net earnings" ("enillion net") means such earnings as are calculated in accordance with paragraph 13 of Schedule 1 or paragraph 15 of Schedule 6, as the case may be;

"net profit" ("elw net") means such profit as is calculated in accordance with paragraph 23 of Schedule 1 or paragraph 24 of Schedule 6, as the case may be;

"new dwelling" ("annedd newydd") means, for the purposes of the definition of "second authority" and paragraph 35 of Schedule 1, paragraphs 37 and 42 of Schedule 6, the dwelling to which an applicant has moved, or is about to move, in which the applicant will be resident;

"non-dependant" ("annibynnydd") has the meaning given by regulation 9;

"occasional assistance" ("cymorth achlysurol") means any payment or provision made by a local authority, the Welsh Ministers or the Scottish Ministers for the purposes of–

(a)   meeting, or helping to meet an immediate short-term need–

    (i)   arising out of an exceptional event or exceptional circumstance, or

    (ii)   that needs to be met to avoid a risk to the well-being of an individual, and

(b)   enabling qualifying individuals to establish or maintain a settled home, and–

    (i)   "local authority" ("awdurdod lleol") has the meaning given by section 270(1) of the Local Government Act 1972; and

    (ii)   "qualifying individuals" ("unigolion cymwys") means individuals who have been, or without the assistance might otherwise be–

        (aa)   in prison, hospital, an establishment providing residential care or other institution, or

        (bb)   homeless or otherwise living an unsettled way of life;

"occupational pension" ("pensiwn galwedigaethol") means any pension or other periodical payment under an occupational pension scheme but does not include any discretionary payment out of a fund established for relieving hardship in particular cases;

"occupational pension scheme" ("cynllun pensiwn galwedigaethol") has the same meaning as in section 1 of the Pension Schemes Act 1993;

"ordinary clothing and footwear" ("dillad ac esgidiau cyffredin") means clothing or footwear for normal daily use, but does not include school uniforms, or clothing or footwear used solely for sporting activities;

"partner" ("partner"), in relation to a person, means–

(a)   where that person is a member of a couple, the other member of that couple; or

(b)   subject to paragraph (c), where that person is polygamously married to two or more members of that person's household, any such member to whom that person is married; or

(c)   where that person is polygamously married and has an award of universal credit with the other party to the earliest marriage that still subsists, that other party to the earliest marriage;

"paternity leave" ("absenoldeb tadolaeth") means a period of absence from work on leave by virtue of section 80A or 80B of the Employment Rights Act 1996 or on additional paternity leave by virtue of regulations made under section 80AA or 80BB of that Act;

"pension fund holder" ("deiliad cronfa bensiwn") means with respect to a personal pension scheme or an occupational pension scheme, the trustees, managers or scheme administrators, as the case may be, of the scheme concerned;

"pensionable age" ("oedran pensiynadwy") has the meaning given by the rules in paragraph 1 of Schedule 4 to the Pensions Act 1995;

"pensioner" ("pensiynwr") has the meaning given by regulation 3(a);

"person on income support" ("person ar gymhorthdal incwm") means a person in receipt of income support;

"person who is not a pensioner" ("person nad yw'n bensiynwr") has the meaning given by regulation 3(b);

"persons treated as not being in Great Britain" ("personau a drinnir fel pe na baent ym Mhrydain Fawr") has the meaning given by regulation 28;

"personal independence payment" ("taliad annibynniaeth bersonol") has the meaning given by Part 4 of the Welfare Reform Act 2012;

"personal pension scheme" ("cynllun pensiwn personol") means–

(a) a personal pension scheme as defined by section 1 of the Pension Schemes Act 1993;

(b) an annuity contract or trust scheme approved under section 620 or 621 of the Income and Corporation Taxes Act 1988 or a substituted contract within the meaning of section 622(3) of that Act which is treated as having become a registered pension scheme by virtue of paragraph 1 of Schedule 36 to the Finance Act 2004;

(c) a personal pension scheme approved under Chapter 4 of Part 14 of the Income and Corporation Taxes Act 1988 which is treated as having become a registered pension scheme by virtue of paragraph 1 of Schedule 36 to the Finance Act 2004;

"policy of life insurance" ("polisi yswiriant bywyd") means any instrument by which the payment of money is assured on death (except death by accident only) or the happening of any contingency dependent on human life, or any instrument evidencing a contract which is subject to payment of premiums for a term dependent on human life;

"polygamous marriage" ("priodas amlbriod") means any marriage to which regulation 5 applies;

"public authority" ("awdurdod cyhoeddus") includes any person whose functions are functions of a public nature;

"qualifying age for state pension credit" ("oedran cymhwyso ar gyfer credyd pensiwn ywladwriaeth") means (in accordance with section 1(2)(b) and (6) of the State Pension Credit Act 2002)–

(a) in the case of a woman, pensionable age; or

(b) in the case of a man, the age which is pensionable age in the case of a woman born on the same day as the man;

"qualifying contributory benefit" ("budd-dal cyfrannol cymwys") means–

(a) severe disablement allowance;

(b) incapacity benefit;

(c) contributory employment and support allowance;

"qualifying income-related benefit" ("budd-dal cymwys ar sail incwm") means–

(a) income support;

(b) income-based jobseeker's allowance;

(c) income-related employment and support allowance;

"qualifying person" ("person cymwys") means a person in respect of whom payment has been made from the Fund, the Eileen Trust, MFET Limited, the Skipton Fund, the Caxton Foundation [⁵ , an approved blood scheme, the Scottish Infected Blood Support Scheme, the London Emergencies Trust, the We Love Manchester Emergency Fund]or the London Bombings Relief Charitable Fund;

"reduction week" ("wythnos ostyngiad") means a period of seven consecutive days beginning with a Monday and ending with a Sunday;

"relative" ("perthynas") means a close relative, grandparent, grandchild, uncle, aunt, nephewor niece;

"relevant week" ("wythnos berthnasol"), in relation to any particular day, means the week within which the day in question falls;

"remunerative work" ("gwaith am dâl") has the meaning given by regulation 10;

"rent" ("rhent") means "eligible rent" to which [¹ regulation 12B] of the Housing Benefit (Persons who have acquired the qualifying age for state pension credit) Regulations 2006 refers, less any deductions in respect of non-dependants which fall to be made under paragraph 3 of Schedule 1 and paragraph 5 of Schedule 6 (non-dependent deductions) under an authority's scheme;

"resident" ("preswylydd") has the meaning given by Part 1 of the 1992 Act;

"savings credit" ("credyd cynilion") is to be construed in accordance with sections 1 and 3 of the State Pension Credit Act 2002;

"scheme" ("cynllun") means a council tax reduction scheme as prescribed within Parts 2 to 5 of these Regulations;

[⁵ "the Scottish Infected Blood Support Scheme" ("Cynllum Cymorth Gwaed Heintiedig yr Alban") means the scheme of that name administered by the Common Services Agency (constituted by section 10 of the National Health Service (Scotland) Act 1978;]

"second authority" ("ail awdurdod") means the authority to which a mover is liable to make payments for a new dwelling;

"self-employed earner" ("enillydd hunangyflogedig") is to be construed in accordance with section 2(1)(b) of the SSCBA;

"self-employment route" ("llwybr hunangyflogaeth") means assistance in pursuing self-employed earner's employment whilst participating in–

(a)   an employment zone programme;

(b)   a programme provided by or under arrangements made pursuant to section 2 of the Employment and Training Act 1973 (functions of the Secretary of State) or section 2 of the Enterprise and New Towns (Scotland) Act 1990 (functions in relation totraining for employment, etc); or

(c)   the Employment, Skills and Enterprise Scheme;

"service user group" ("grwp defnyddwyr gwasanaeth") means a group of individuals that is consulted by or on behalf of–

(a)   a Health Board, Special Health Board or the Common Services Agency for Scottish Health in consequence of a function under section 2B of the National Health Service(Scotland) Act 1978,

(b)   a landlord authority in consequence of a function under section 105 of the Housing Act 1985,

(c)   a public authority in Northern Ireland in consequence of a function under section 49A of the Disability Discrimination Act 1995,

(d)   a public authority in consequence of a function under section 149 of the Equality Act 2010 (public authority general duty),

(e)   a best value authority in consequence of a function under section 3 of the Local Government Act 1999,

(f)   a Welsh improvement authority in consequence of a function under section 5 of the Local Government (Wales) Measure 2009,

(g)   a local authority landlord or registered social landlord in consequence of a function under section 53 of the Housing (Scotland) Act 2001,

(h)   a relevant English body or a relevant Welsh body in consequence of a function undersection 242 of the National Health Service Act 2006,

(i)   a Local Health Board in consequence of a function under section 183 of the National Health Service (Wales) Act 2006,

(j)   the Care Quality Commission in exercise of a function under sections 4 or 5 of the Health and Social Care Act 2008,

(k)   the regulator or a private registered provider of social housing in consequence of a function under sections 98, 193 or 196 of the Housing and Regeneration Act 2008, or

(l)   a public or local authority in Great Britain in consequence of a function conferred under any other enactment,

for the purposes of monitoring and advising on a policy of that body or authority which affects or may affect persons in the group, or of monitoring or advising on services provided by that body or authority which are used (or may potentially be used) by those persons;

[² "shared parental leave" ("absenoldeb rhiant a rennir") means leave by virtue of regulations made under section 75E or 75G of the Employment Rights Act 1996;]

"single applicant" ("ceisydd sengl") means an applicant who neither has a partner nor is a lone parent;

"the Skipton Fund" ("Cronfa Skipton") means the ex-gratia payment scheme administered by the Skipton Fund Limited, incorporated on 25 March 2004, for the benefit of certain persons suffering from hepatitis C and other persons eligible for payment in accordance with the scheme's provisions;

"sports award" ("dyfarniad chwaraeon") means an award made by one of the Sports Councils named in section 23(2) of the National Lottery etc Act 1993 out of sums allocated to it for distribution under that section;

"the SSCBA" ("DCBNC") means the Social Security Contributions and Benefits Act 1992;

"state pension credit" ("credyd pensiwn y wladwriaeth") means state pension credit under the State Pension Credit Act 2002;

"student" ("myfyriwr") has the meaning prescribed within paragraph 1 of Schedule 11;

"subsistence allowance" ("lwfans cynhaliaeth") means an allowance which an employment zone contractor has agreed to pay to a person who is participating in an employment zone programme;

"tax year" ("blwyddyn dreth") means a period beginning with 6 April in one year and ending with 5 April in the next;

"training allowance" ("lwfans hyfforddi") means an allowance (whether by way of periodical grants or otherwise) payable–

(a)   out of public funds by a Government department or by or on behalf of the Secretary of State, Skills Development Scotland, Scottish Enterprise or Highlands and Islands Enterprise [³] or the Welsh Ministers;

(b)   to a person for that person's maintenance or in respect of a member of that person's family; and

(c)   for the period, or part of the period, during which that person is following a course of training or instruction provided by, or in pursuance of arrangements made with, that department or approved by that department in relation to that person or so provided or approved by or on behalf of the Secretary of State, Skills Development Scotland, Scottish Enterprise or Highlands and Islands Enterprise or the Welsh Ministers,

but it does not include an allowance paid by any Government department to or in respect of a person by reason of the fact that that person is following a course of full-time education, other than under arrangements made under section 2 of the Employment and Training Act 1973 or is training as a teacher;

"the Trusts" ("yr Ymddiriedolaethau") means the Macfarlane Trust, the Macfarlane (Special Payments) Trust and the Macfarlane (Special Payments) (No 2) Trust;

"universal credit" ("credyd cynhwysol") has the meaning given by section 1 of the Welfare Reform Act 2012;

"voluntary organisation" ("sefydliad gwirfoddol") means a body, other than a public or local authority, the activities of which are carried on otherwise than for profit;

"war disablement pension" ("pensiwn anabledd rhyfel") means any retired pay or pension or allowance payable in respect of disablement under an instrument specified in section 639(2) of the Income Tax (Earnings and Pensions) Act 2003;

"war pension" ("pensiwn rhyfel") means a war disablement pension, a war widow's pension or a war widower's pension;

"war widow's pension" ("pensiwn rhyfel gwraig weddw") means any pension or allowance payable to a woman as a widow under an instrument specified in section 639(2) of the Income Tax (Earnings and Pensions) Act 2003 in respect of the death or disablement of any person;

"war widower's pension" ("pensiwn rhyfel gwr gweddw") means any pension or allowance payable to a man as a widower or to a surviving civil partner under an instrument specified in section 639(2) of the Income Tax (Earnings and Pensions) Act 2003 in respect of the death or disablement of any person;

"water charges" ("taliadau dwr") means–

(a) as respects England and Wales, any water and sewerage charges under Chapter 1 of Part 5 of the Water Industry Act 1991,

(b) as respects Scotland, any water and sewerage charges established by Scottish Water under a charges scheme made under section 29A of the Water Industry (Scotland) Act 2002,

in so far as such charges are in respect of the dwelling which a person occupies as that person's home;

[⁵ "the We Love Manchester Emergency Fund" ("Cronfa Argyfwng We Love Manchester") means the registered charity of that name (number 1173260) established on 30 May 2017;]

"working tax credit" ("credyd treth gwaith") means a working tax credit under section 10 of the Tax Credits Act 2002;

"young person" ("person ifanc") means a person who falls within the definition of qualifying young person in section 142 of the SSCBA.

(2) In these Regulations, where an amount is to be rounded to the nearest penny, a fraction of a penny must be disregarded if it is less than half a penny and must otherwise be treated as a whole penny.

(3) For the purpose of these Regulations, a person is on an income-based jobseeker's allowance on any day in respect of which an income-based jobseeker's allowance is payable to that person and on any day–

(a) in respect of which that person satisfies the conditions for entitlement to an income-based jobseeker's allowance but where the allowance is not paid because of a reduction in accordance with section 19 or 19A or regulations made under section 17A or 19B of the Jobseeker's Act 1995 (circumstances in which jobseeker's allowance is not payable);

(b) which is a waiting day for the purposes of paragraph 4 of Schedule 1 to that Act and which falls immediately before a day in respect of which an income-based jobseeker's allowance is payable to that person or would be payable to that person but for section 19 or 19A or regulations made under section 17A or 19B of that Act; or

(c) in respect of which an income-based jobseeker's allowance would be payable but for a restriction imposed pursuant to section 6B, 7, 8 or 9 of the Social Security Fraud Act 2001 (loss of benefit provisions).

(4) For the purposes of these Regulations, a person is on an income-related employment and support allowance on any day in respect of which an income-related employment and support allowance is payable to that person and on any day–

(a) in respect of which that person satisfies the conditions for entitlement to an income-related employment and support allowance but where the allowance is not paid in accordance with section 18 of the Welfare Reform Act 2007 (disqualification); or

(b) which is a waiting day for the purposes of paragraph 2 of Schedule 2 to that Act (employment and support allowance: supplementary provisions) and which falls immediately before a day in respect of which an income-related employment and support allowance is payable to that person or would be payable to that person but for section 18 of that Act.

(5) For the purposes of these Regulations, two persons must be taken to be estranged only if their estrangement constitutes a breakdown of the relationship between them.

(6) In these Regulations, references to any person in receipt of state pension credit includes a person who would be in receipt of state pension credit but for regulation 13 of the State Pension Credit Regulations 2002 (small amounts of state pension credit).

Amendments
1. Amended by reg 3 of SI 2014 No 66 (W.6) as from 15.1.14.
2. Amended by reg 3 of SI 2015 No 44 (W.3) as from 21.1.15, for schemes made for a financial year starting on or after 1.4.15.
3. Amended by art 2 and Sch 3 para 30(2) of SI 2015 No 971 as from 26.5.15.
4. Amended by reg 3 of SI 2016 No 50 (W.21) as from 20.1.16, for schemes made for a financial year starting on or after 1.4.16.
5. Amended by reg 3 of SI 2018 No 14 (W.7) as from 10.1.18, for schemes made for a financial year starting on or after 1.4.18.

General Note

Much of reg 2, including many of the definitions in reg 2(1), corresponds with reg 2 HB Regs. See p239 for commentary.

In relation to the definition of **"lone parent"**, "partner" is defined in this regulation, as is "child" (someone aged under 16) and "young person" (someone who counts as a "qualifying young person" for child benefit purposes – see s142 SSCBA 1992 and regs 2–8 Child Benefit (General) Regulations 2006). See also reg 7 for the circumstances in which a person is treated as responsible for a child or young person and reg 8 for circumstances in which people are treated or not treated as members of the same household.

Meaning of "pensioner" and "person who is not a pensioner"

3. In these Regulations a person is–
(a) a "pensioner" ("pensiynwr") if–
    (i) that person has attained the qualifying age for state pension credit; and
    (ii) that person is not, and, if that person has a partner, that person's partner is not–
        (aa) a person on income support, on an income-based jobseeker's allowance or on an income-related employment and support allowance, or
        (bb) a person with an award of universal credit; and
(b) a "person who is not a pensioner" ("person nad yw'n bensiynwr") if–
    (i) that person has not attained the qualifying age for state pension credit; or
    (ii) that person has attained the qualifying age for state pension credit and that person, or if that person has a partner, that person's partner, is–
        (aa) a person on income support, on an income-based jobseeker's allowance or on an income-related employment and support allowance, or
        (bb) a person with an award of universal credit.

General Note

Whether an applicant is "a pensioner" or a "person who is not a pensioner" is relevant to how CTR entitlement is assessed. If an applicant or her/his partner is "on" IS, income-based JSA or income-related ESA or has an award of UC, then, even if the applicant has reached the qualifying age for PC, s/he must be classed as a "person who is not a pensioner". A "person on income support" is defined in reg 2 as a person in receipt of IS. Reg 2(3) deals with when a person is on an income-based JSA and reg 2(4) with when a person is on an income-related ESA. In effect, a person who is a pensioner broadly corresponds with someone to whom the HB(SPC) Regs would apply should they claim HB (see reg 5 of those regulations on p733) and a person who is not a pensioner with someone to whom the HB Regs would apply (see reg 5 of those regulations on p252).

Meaning of "couple"

4. In these Regulations "couple" ("cwpl") means–
(a) two people who are either married to, or civil partners of, each other and who are members of the same household;
(b) two people who are living together as if they are a married couple.

General Note

This definition is similar to the definition of couple in s137 SSCBA (see the analysis on p12). You can be treated as a member of the same household despite temporary absences (see reg 8).

Polygamous marriages

5.–(1)   This regulation applies to any case where–

(a)   a person is a husband or wife by virtue of a marriage entered into under a law which permits polygamy; and

(b)   either party to the marriage has for the time being any spouse additional to the other party.

(2)   For the purposes of regulation 4 neither party to the marriage is to be taken to be a member of a couple.

Meaning of "family"

6.–(1)   In these Regulations "family" ("teulu") means–

(a)   a couple;

(b)   a couple and a member of the same household for whom one of them is or both are responsible and who is a child or a young person; or

(c)   a person who is not a member of a couple and a member of the same household for whom that person is responsible and who is a child or a young person.

(2)   The references to a child or young person in paragraph (1)(b) and (c) include a child or young person in respect of whom section 145A of the SSCBA applies for the purposes of entitlement to child benefit, but only for the period prescribed under section 145A(1).

(3)   The references to a young person in paragraph (1)(b) and (c) do not include a young person who is–

(a)   on income support, an income-based jobseeker's allowance or an income-related employment and support allowance or has an award of universal credit; or

(b)   a person to whom section 6 of the Children (Leaving Care) Act 2000 (exclusion from benefits) applies.

General Note

The definition of "family" in para (1) is similar to that in s137 SSCBA (see p12 and p17 for analysis). The definition in s137 uses the term "person of a prescribed description" in place of "young person" which is used in this regulation. Both terms, however, mean a "qualifying young person" for child benefit purposes (as defined by s142 SSCBA 1992): reg 2; reg 19 HB Regs.

Para (2) allows a child or young person to continue to be treated as a member of a family, notwithstanding that s/he has died, for the period prescribed under s145A(1) SSCBA. Reg 20 Child Benefit (General) Regulations 2006 sets out the prescribed period in this situation.

See p406 for commentary on reg 19 HB Regs which is relevant here.

Circumstances in which a person is to be treated as responsible or not responsible for another

7.–(1)   A person is to be treated as responsible for a child or young person who is normally living with that person, including a child or young person to whom regulation 6(2) applies.

(2)   Where a child or young person spends equal amounts of time in different households, or where there is a question as to which household the child or young person is living in, the child or young person must be treated for the purposes of paragraph (1) as normally living with–

(a)   the person who is receiving child benefit in respect of that child or young person, or

(b)   if there is no such person–

(i)   where only one claim for child benefit has been made in respect of that child or young person, the person who made that claim, or

(ii)   in any other case the person who has the primary responsibility for that child or young person.

(3)   For the purposes of these Regulations a child or young person is the responsibility of only one person in any reduction week and any person other than the one treated as responsible for the child or young person under this regulation is to be treated as not so responsible.

General Note

Regulation 7 is almost identical to reg 20 HB Regs. For commentary on that regulation, see p408.

Households

8.–(1) Subject to paragraphs (2) and (3), an applicant and any partner and, where the applicant or the applicant's partner is treated (by virtue of regulation 7) as responsible for a child or young person, that child or young person and any child of that child or young person, are to be treated as members of the same household notwithstanding that any of them is temporarily absent from that household.

(2) A child or young person is not be treated as a member of the applicant's household where that child or young person is–

(a) placed with the applicant or the applicant's partner by a local authority under section 22C or 23(2)(a) of the Children Act 1989 or by a voluntary organisation under section 59(1)(a) of that Act, or in Scotland boarded out [¹ or placed] with the applicant or the applicant's partner under a relevant enactment; or

[² (aa) placed with the applicant or the applicant's partner by a local authority under section 81 of the Social Services and Well-being (Wales) Act 2014; or]

(b) placed, or in Scotland boarded out, with the applicant or the applicant's partner prior to adoption; or

(c) placed for adoption with the applicant or the applicant's partner in accordance with the Adoption and Children Act 2002 or the Adoption Agencies (Scotland) Regulations 2009, or the Adoption (Northern Ireland) Order 1987.

(3) Subject to paragraph (4), paragraph (1) does not apply to a child or young person who is not living with the applicant and who–

(a) is being looked after by, or in Scotland is in the care of, a local authority under a relevant enactment; or

(b) has been placed, or in Scotland boarded out, with a person other than the applicant prior to adoption; or

(c) has been placed for adoption in accordance with the Adoption and Children Act 2002 or the Adoption Agencies (Scotland) Regulations 2009, or the Adoption (Northern Ireland) Order 1987.

(4) An authority must treat a child or young person to whom paragraph (3)(a) applies as being a member of the applicant's household in any reduction week where–

(a) that child or young person lives with the applicant for part or all of that reduction week; and

(b) the authority considers that it is reasonable to do so taking into account the nature and frequency of that child's or young person's visits.

(5) In this paragraph "relevant enactment" ("deddfiad perthnasol") means–

(a) the Army Act 1955;

(b) the Air Force Act 1955;

(c) the Naval Discipline Act 1957;

(d) the Matrimonial Proceedings (Children) Act 1958;

(e) the Social Work (Scotland) Act 1968;

(f) the Family Law Reform Act 1969;

(g) the Children and Young Persons Act 1969;

(h) the Matrimonial Causes Act 1973;

(i) the Children Act 1975;

(j) the Domestic Proceedings and Magistrates' Courts Act 1978;

(k) the Adoption and Children (Scotland) Act 2007;

(l) the Family Law Act 1986;

(m) the Children Act 1989;

(n) The Children (Scotland) Act 1995;

(o) the Armed Forces Act 2006; [¹]

[¹ (oa) the children's Hearings (Scotland) Act 2011; and]

(p) the Legal Aid, Sentencing and Punishment of Offenders Act 2012.

Amendments

1.   Amended by reg 4 of SI 2014 No 66 (W.6) as from 15.1.14.

2.   Amended by reg 4 of SI 2016 No 50 (W.21) as from 20.1.16, for schemes made for a financial year starting on or after 1.4.16.

General Note
This is almost identical to reg 11 CTR(S) Regs (for commentary, see p1473). See also p410 for the commentary on reg 21 HB Regs which is similar. It seems likely that "In this paragraph" at the beginning of para (5) is a drafting error and that the definition of "relevant enactment" was intended to apply to the regulation as a whole.

Non-dependants

9.–(1)   In these Regulations, "non-dependant" ("annibynnydd") means any person, except someone to whom paragraph (2) applies, who normally resides with an applicant or with whom an applicant normally resides.

(2)   This paragraph applies to–

(a)   any member of the applicant's family;

(b)   if the applicant is polygamously married, any partner of the applicant and any child or young person who is a member of the applicant's household and for whom the applicant or one of the applicant's partners is responsible;

(c)   a child or young person who is living with the applicant but who is not a member of the applicant's household by virtue of regulation 8 (households);

(d)   subject to paragraph (3), any person who, with the applicant, is jointly and severally liable to pay council tax in respect of a dwelling for any day under sections 6 or 7 of the 1992 Act (persons liable to pay council tax);

(e)   subject to paragraph (3), any person who is liable to make payments on a commercial basis to the applicant or the applicant's partner in respect of the occupation of the dwelling;

(f)   a person who lives with the applicant in order to care for the applicant or a partner of the applicant, and who is engaged by a charitable or voluntary organisation which makes a charge to the applicant or the applicant's partner for the services provided by that person.

(3)   Excepting persons to whom paragraph (2)(a) to (c) and (f) refer, a person to whom any of the following sub-paragraphs apply is a non-dependant–

(a)   a person (P) who resides with the person (O) to whom P is liable to make payments in respect of the dwelling and either–

(i)   O is a close relative of P's or P's partner; or

(ii)   the tenancy or other agreement between them is other than on a commercial basis;

(b)   a person whose liability to make payments in respect of the dwelling appears to the authority to have been created to take advantage of a council tax reduction scheme except someone who was, for any period within the eight weeks prior to the creation of the agreement giving rise to the liability to make such payments, otherwise liable to make payments of rent in respect of the same dwelling;

(c)   a person who becomes jointly and severally liable with the applicant for council tax in respect of a dwelling and who was, at any time during the period of eight weeks prior to that person becoming so liable, a non-dependent of one or more of the other residents in that dwelling who are so liable for the tax, unless the change giving rise to the new liability was not made to take advantage of a council tax reduction scheme.

General Note
Just as in reg 9 of the CTR(PR)(E) Regs, a 'non-dependant' is defined as someone who normally resides with an applicant, or is someone with whom an applicant normally resides, and who does not come within one of the descriptions in para (2). In accordance with Sch 1 para 2 (for pensioners) and Sch 6 para 4 (for non-pensioners), an applicant's 'maximum CTR' – which is used to assess the amount of any entitlement to CTR – is calculated by ascertaining her/his daily liability for council tax for the dwelling and deducting from this figure any deductions for non dependants that fall to be made under para 3 and 5 of those schedules, respectively. Such deductions are known as 'non-dependant deductions'.

This regulation is similar to reg 3 CTR(S) Regs and to reg 3 HB Regs (see p1466 and p249 for commentary).

Remunerative work

10.–(1)   Subject to the following provisions of this regulation, a person must be treated for the purposes of these Regulations as engaged in remunerative work if that person is engaged, or, where that person's hours of work fluctuate, that person is engaged on average, for not less than 16 hours a week, in work for which payment is made or which is done in expectation of payment.

(2)   Subject to paragraph (3), in determining the number of hours for which a person is engaged in work where that person's hours of work fluctuate, regard must be had to the average of hours worked over–

(a)   if there is a recognisable cycle of work, the period of one complete cycle (including, where the cycle involves periods in which the person does no work, those periods but disregarding any other absences);

(b)   in any other case, the period of 5 weeks immediately prior to the date of application, or such other length of time as may, in the particular case, enable the person's weekly average hours of work to be determined more accurately.

(3)   Where, for the purposes of paragraph (2)(a), a person's recognisable cycle of work at a school, other educational establishment or other place of employment is one year and includes periods of school holidays or similar vacations during which that person does not work, those periods and any other periods not forming part of such holidays or vacations during which that person is not required to work must be disregarded in establishing the average hours for which that person is engaged in work.

(4)   Where no recognisable cycle has been established in respect of a person's work, regard must be had to the number of hours or, where those hours will fluctuate, the average of the hours, which that person is expected to work in a week.

(5)   A person must be treated as engaged in remunerative work during any period for which that person is absent from work referred to in paragraph (1) if the absence is either without good cause or by reason of a recognised, customary or other holiday.

(6)   A person on income support, an income-based jobseeker's allowance or an income-related employment and support allowance for more than 3 days in any reduction week must be treated as not being in remunerative work in that week.

(7)   A person must not be treated as engaged in remunerative work on any day on which that person is on maternity leave, paternity leave [' , shared parental leave] or adoption leave, or is absent from work because that person is ill.

(8)   A person must not be treated as engaged in remunerative work on any day on which that person is engaged in an activity in respect of which–

(a)   a sports award has been made, or is to be made, to that person; and

(b)   no other payment is made or is expected to be made to that person.

Amendment

1.   Amended by reg 4 of SI 2015 No 44 (W.3) as from 21.1.15, for schemes made for a financial year starting on or after 1.4.15.

General Note

Reg 10 is almost identical to reg 6 HB regs (see p253 for relevant commentary).

PART 2
Council tax reduction schemes

Schemes

11.   An authority in Wales is a specified authority for the purposes of section 13A(4)(a) of the1992 Act.

Duty to make schemes and exercise of functions by authorities

12.–(1)   Each authority in Wales must make a scheme specifying the reductions which are to apply to the amounts of council tax payable by persons to whom the scheme applies in respect of dwellings situated in its area.

(2)   The function of making a scheme required by these Regulations is not to be the responsibility of an executive of an authority under executive arrangements.

(3)   Section 101 of the Local Government Act 1972 (arrangements for discharge of functions by local authorities) does not apply with respect to the discharge of the function mentioned in paragraph (1).

(4)   In this regulation, references to "executive" ("gweithrediaeth") and "executive arrangements" ("trefniadau gweithredol") have the same meaning given by Part 2 of the Local Government Act 2000 or an instrument made under that Part of that Act.

First financial year of schemes

13.   Each authority in Wales must make a scheme no later than the 31 January 2014, and the first financial year to which that scheme relates must be the year beginning 1 April 2014.

Scheme requirements in relation to classes of persons

14.   A scheme must–
(a)   state the classes of persons who are to be entitled to a reduction;
(b)   include those classes of persons prescribed in regulations 22 to 25;
(c)   not include those classes of persons prescribed in regulations 28 to 31.

Scheme requirements in relation to reductions

15.–(1)   A scheme must set out the reduction to which persons in each class are to be entitled.
(2)   The classes of persons prescribed in regulations 22 and 23, are to be entitled under a scheme to the reductions prescribed in Part 3 of Schedule 1 (pensioners).
(3)   The classes of persons prescribed in regulations 24 and 25, are to be entitled under a scheme to the reductions prescribed in Part 3 of Schedule 6 (persons who are not pensioners).

Scheme procedural requirements

16.   A scheme must state–
(a)   the procedure by which a person may apply for a reduction under a scheme;
(b)   the procedure by which a person may appeal against a decision of an authority with respect to–
(i)   a person's entitlement to a reduction under a scheme; or
(ii)   the amount of any reduction to which the person is entitled.
(c)   the procedure by which a person may apply to an authority for a reduction under section 13A(1)(c) of the 1992 Act.

Preparation of a scheme

17.–(1)   Before making a scheme an authority must–
(a)   publish a draft scheme in such manner as it thinks fit, and
(b)   consult any persons it considers are likely to have an interest in the operation of its scheme.
(2)   Having made a scheme, the authority must publish that scheme in such manner as it thinks fit.

General Note

This is similar to the requirements placed on English authorities under Sch 1A para 3 LGFA. See p1091 for relevant commentary.

Revisions to and replacement of schemes

18.–(1)   For each financial year, an authority must consider whether to revise its scheme or to replace it with another scheme.
(2)   An authority must make any revision to its scheme, or any replacement scheme, no later than 31 January in the financial year preceding that for which the revision or replacement scheme is to have effect.
(3)   If any revision to a scheme, or any replacement scheme, has the effect of reducing or removing a reduction to which any class of persons is entitled, the revision or replacement scheme must include such transitional provision relating to that reduction or removal as the authority thinks fit.

(4)   [¹ Subject to paragraph (6), regulation 17] applies to an authority when revising a scheme as it applies to an authority when making a scheme.

(5)   References in this Part to a scheme include a replacement scheme.

[¹(6)   Regulation 17(1) does not apply where a scheme is revised in consequence only of one or more amendments made to these Regulations.]

Amendment

1.   Amended by reg 5 of SI 2015 No 44 (W.3) as from 21.1.15, for schemes made for a financial year starting on or after 1.4.15.

Notice requiring provision of information to the Welsh Ministers

19.–(1)   The Welsh Ministers may serve a notice on an authority in Wales requiring it to supply to them such information as is specified in the notice and required by them for the purpose of exercising, or deciding whether to exercise, any function relating to schemes.

(2)   The authority must supply the information required if it is in its possession or control, and must do so in such form and manner and at such time as specified in the notice.

(3)   If an authority fails to comply with paragraph (2), the Welsh Ministers may exercise the function on the basis of such assumptions and estimates as they think fit.

(4)   In exercising, or deciding whether to exercise, any function relating to schemes, the Welsh Ministers may also take into account any other available information, whatever its source and whether or not obtained under a provision contained in or made under these Regulations or any Act.

Supply of documents

20.   Subject to regulation 19, an authority may make a reasonable charge for the supply of copies of documents relating to its scheme.

PART 3
Prescribed classes of person who must be included in an authority's scheme

Classes of person who must be included in a scheme

21.   The classes of persons described in regulations 22 to 25 are classes of person prescribed for the purposes of paragraph 3(1)(a) of Schedule 1B to the 1992 Act and who must be included in and entitled to a reduction under an authority's scheme.

General Note to regulations 21 to 25

People falling into any one of the four sets of conditions (called classes) outlined in regulations 22–25 must be entitled to a reduction. Classes A and B relate to pensioners; classes C and D to people who are not pensioners (who is or is not a pensioner is defined in reg 3).

The four classes have certain qualifying conditions in common. These are that on any day a person:

(1)   must be liable to pay council tax for a dwelling in which s/he is resident (this is similar although not identical to the condition for CTR in Scotland where an applicant must be liable to pay council tax for a dwelling in which s/he resides as her/his sole or main residence – see the commentary on reg 14(3)(a) CTR(S) Regs on p1475 which is relevant here);

(2)   must not be absent from the dwelling throughout the day (although see reg 26 for circumstances in which a person is treated as not absent during "periods of temporary absence");

(3)   must be someone in respect of whom a maximum CTR amount can be calculated;

(4)   must not be someone who falls within the classes of people described in regs 28 to 31, and who are therefore excluded from entitlement to CTR. Regs 28 to 31, broadly speaking, cover people who are not habitually resident in the UK, the Channel Islands, Isle of Man or Republic of Ireland (who are treated as not being in GB), people "subject to immigration control", people with more than £16,000 capital and "students" (see commentary under those regulations for more detail); *and*

(5)   must have "made an application for a reduction under an authority's scheme".

Class A: pensioners whose income is less than the applicable amount

22. On any day class A consists of any person who is a pensioner–

(a) who is for that day liable to pay council tax in respect of a dwelling of which that person is a resident;

(b) who, subject to regulation 26 (periods of absence from a dwelling), is not absent from the dwelling throughout the day;

(c) in respect of whom a maximum council tax reduction amount can be calculated;

(d) who does not fall within a class of person prescribed in regulations 28 to 31 and excluded from entitlement under a scheme;

(e) whose income (if any) for the relevant week does not exceed that person's applicable amount calculated in accordance with paragraph 1 of Part 1 of Schedule 1 and Schedule 2 (applicable amounts : pensioners); and

(f) who has made an application for a reduction under an authority's scheme.

General Note

To fall within class A (and therefore be entitled to CTR) the applicant must be a pensioner (as defined in reg 3) and her/his income for the relevant week must be equal to or less than her/his applicable amount determined in accordance with Sch 1 para 1 and Sch 2: para (e). S/he must also satisfy the conditions outlined in paras (a)–(d) and (f) (for which see the commentary for reg 21). Relevant week is defined in reg 2. If the applicant or her/his partner is in receipt of the guarantee credit of PC, all their income and capital is disregarded under Sch 1 paras 5(2) and 7, and so the applicant automatically meets the requirement of reg 22(e) and is not excluded from CTR even if the actual capital held is over £16,000. In accordance with Sch 1 para 4(2), if an applicant falls within class A the amount of CTR equals the amount of her/his maximum CTR (see Sch 1 para 2 for how this is calculated).

Class B: pensioners whose income is greater than the applicable amount

23. On any day class B consists of any person who is a pensioner–

(a) who is for that day liable to pay council tax in respect of a dwelling of which that person is a resident;

(b) who, subject to regulation 26 (periods of absence from a dwelling), is not absent from the dwelling throughout the day;

(c) in respect of whom a maximum council tax reduction amount can be calculated;

(d) who does not fall within a class of person prescribed in regulations 28 to 31 and excluded from entitlement under a scheme;

(e) whose income for the relevant week is greater than that person's applicable amount calculated in accordance with paragraph 1 of Part 1 of Schedule 1 and Schedule 2 (applicable amounts : pensioners);

(f) in respect of whom amount A exceeds amount B where–

(i) amount A is the maximum council tax reduction in respect of the day in that person's case; and

(ii) amount B is 2 6/7 per cent of the difference between that person's income for the relevant week and that person's applicable amount; and

(g) who has made an application for a reduction under an authority's scheme.

General Note

A pensioner (as defined in reg 3) whose income is more than her/his applicable amount (determined under Sch 1 para 1 and Sch 2) is entitled to CTR if, as well as satisfying the conditions in paras (a)–(d) and (g) (for which see the commentary for reg 21), her/his income is sufficiently low. The calculation in para (f) is formulated to assess this on a daily basis (in line with s13A LGFA 1992 and Sch 1 para 2) – two and six sevenths equates to a weekly amount of 20 per cent. If the amount of the applicant's maximum CTR in respect of the day (Amount A) is greater than the specified percentage of the difference between her/his income (for the week in which the day falls) and her/his applicable amount (Amount B), s/he will qualify. The amount of CTR s/he qualifies for is the amount by which her/his maximum CTR exceeds the percentage amount :Sch 1 para 4(3). This is essentially the same as the calculation that was used for council tax benefit; for an analysis of the CTB calculation, see *IB v Barnsley MBC* [2009] UKUT 279 (AAC).

Class C: persons who are not pensioners whose income is less than the applicable amount

24. On any day class C consists of any person who is not a pensioner–

(a) who is for that day liable to pay council tax in respect of a dwelling of which that person is a resident;

(b) who, subject to regulation 26 (periods of absence from a dwelling), is not absent from the dwelling throughout the day;

(c) in respect of whom a maximum council tax reduction amount can be calculated;

(d) who does not fall within a class of person prescribed in regulations 28 to 31 and excluded from entitlement under a scheme;

(e) whose income (if any) for the relevant week is less than that person's applicable amount calculated in accordance with paragraph 1 of Part 1 of Schedule 6 and Schedule 7 (applicable amounts: persons who are not pensioners); and

(f) who has made an application for a reduction under an authority's scheme.

General Note

This is the equivalent of class A (reg 22) for people who are not pensioners with one significant difference (for who is defined as "not a pensioner" see reg 3). In this case, if a person who is not a pensioner satisfies the conditions in paras (a)–(d) and (f) (for which see the commentary for reg 21) and if her/his income in the relevant week (defined in reg 2) is *less than* her/his applicable amount, s/he qualifies for CTR (para (e)).

In accordance with Sch 6 para 6, the amount of CTR s/he qualifies for is equal to the amount of her/his maximum CTR. See Sch 6 para 4 for how maximum CTR is calculated.

To fall within class A, a pensioner must have income that is *equal to or less than* her/his applicable amount. The wording of regs 24(e) and 25(e) leave open the question of how someone who is not a pensioner and whose income is equal to her/his applicable amount will be dealt with. Clearly the intention must be that s/he will qualify for CTR at a rate which is equal to her/his maximum CTR, as this would be the result whether s/he fell within class C or D, but this is not provided for.

Class D: persons who are not pensioners whose income is greater than the applicable amount

25. On any day class D consists of any person who is not a pensioner–

(a) who is for that day liable to pay council tax in respect of a dwelling of which that person is a resident;

(b) who, subject to regulation 26 (periods of absence from a dwelling), is not absent from the dwelling throughout the day;

(c) in respect of whom a maximum council tax reduction amount can be calculated;

(d) who does not fall within a class of person prescribed in regulations 28 to 31 and excluded from entitlement under a scheme;

(e) whose income for the relevant week is greater than that person's applicable amount calculated in accordance with paragraph 1 of Part 1 of Schedule 6 and Schedule 7 (applicable amounts: persons who are not pensioners);

(f) in respect of whom amount A exceeds amount B where–

    (i) amount A is the maximum council tax reduction in respect of the day in that person's case; and

    (ii) amount B is 2 6/7 per cent of the difference between that person's income for the relevant week and that person's applicable amount; and

(g) who has made an application for a reduction under an authority's scheme.

General Note

Class D is the equivalent to class B but is for people who are not pensioners (for the definition, see reg 3). See commentary under reg 23 but note that Sch 6 para 4 explains the calculation of maximum CTR for people who are not pensioners and Sch 6 para 6(3) details how the amount of CTR is calculated for people coming within class D.

Periods of absence from a dwelling

26.–(1) A person is not absent from a dwelling in relation to any day which falls within a period of temporary absence from that dwelling.

(2) In paragraph (1), a "period of temporary absence" ("cyfnod o absenoldeb dros dro") means–

(a)   a period of absence not exceeding 13 weeks, beginning with the first whole day on which a person resides in residential accommodation where and for so long as–

      (i)   that person resides in that accommodation;

      (ii)   the part of the dwelling in which that person usually resides is not let or sub-let; and

      (iii)   that period of absence does not form part of a longer period of absence from the dwelling of more than 52 weeks,

      (iv)   where that person has entered the accommodation for the purpose of ascertaining whether it suits the person's needs and with the intention of returning to the dwelling if it proves not to suit the person's needs;

(b)   a period of absence not exceeding 13 weeks, beginning with the first whole day of absence from the dwelling, where and for so long as–

      (i)   the person intends to return to the dwelling;

      (ii)   the part of the dwelling in which that person usually resides is not let or sub-let; and

      (iii)   that period is unlikely to exceed 13 weeks; and

(c)   a period of absence not exceeding 52 weeks, beginning with the first whole day of that absence, where and for so long as –

      (i)   the person intends to return to the dwelling;

      (ii)   the part of the dwelling in which the person usually resides is not let or sub-let;

      (iii)   the person is a person to whom paragraph (3) applies; and

      (iv)   the period of absence is unlikely to exceed 52 weeks or, in exceptional circumstances, is unlikely substantially to exceed that period.

(3)   This paragraph applies to a person who–

(a)   is detained in custody on remand pending trial or required, as a condition of bail, to reside–

      (i)   in a dwelling, other than the dwelling referred to in paragraph (1), or

      (ii)   in premises approved under section 13 of the Offender Management Act 2007,

      or is detained in custody pending sentence upon conviction;

(b)   is resident in a hospital or similar institution as a patient;

(c)   is undergoing, or whose partner or dependent child is undergoing, in the United Kingdom or elsewhere, medical treatment, or medically approved convalescence, in accommodation other than residential accommodation;

(d)   is following, in the United Kingdom or elsewhere, a training course;

(e)   is undertaking medically approved care of a person residing in the United Kingdom or elsewhere;

(f)   is undertaking the care of a child whose parent or guardian is temporarily absent from the dwelling normally occupied by that parent or guardian for the purpose of receiving medically approved care or medical treatment;

(g)   is in the United Kingdom or elsewhere, receiving medically approved care provided in accommodation other than residential accommodation;

(h)   is a student;

(i)   is receiving care provided in residential accommodation and is not a person to whom paragraph (2)(a) applies; or

(j)   has left the dwelling the person resides in through fear of violence, in that dwelling, or by a person who was formerly a member of the family of that person.

(4)   This paragraph applies to a person who is–

(a)   detained in custody pending sentence upon conviction or under a sentence imposed by a court (other than a person who is detained in hospital under the provisions of the Mental Health Act 1983, or, in Scotland, under the provisions of the Mental Health (Care andTreatment) (Scotland) Act 2003 or the Criminal Procedure (Scotland) Act 1995 or in Northern Ireland under article 4 or 12 of the Mental Health (Northern Ireland) Order1986); and

(b)   on temporary release from detention in accordance with Rules made under the provisions of the Prison Act 1952 or the Prisons (Scotland) Act 1989.

(5)   Where paragraph (4) applies to a person, then, for any day when that person is on temporary release–

(a)   if such temporary release was immediately preceded by a period of temporary absence under paragraph (2)(b) or (c), that person is to be treated, for the purposes of paragraph (1), as if that person continues to be absent from the dwelling, despite any return to the dwelling;

(b)   for the purposes of paragraph (3)(a), that person is to be treated as if that person remains in detention;

(c)   if that person does not fall within sub-paragraph (a), that person is not to be considered to be a person who is liable to pay council tax in respect of a dwelling of which that person is a resident.

(6)   In this regulation–

"medically approved" ("a gymeradwywyd yn feddygol") means certified by a medical practitioner;

"patient" ("claf") means a person who is undergoing medical or other treatment as an in-patient in any hospital or similar institution;

"residential accommodation" ("llety preswyl") means accommodation which is provided in–

(a)   a care home;

(b)   an independent hospital;

(c)   an Abbeyfield Home; or

(d)   an establishment managed or provided by a body incorporated by Royal Charter or constituted by Act of Parliament other than a local social services authority;

"training course" ("cwrs hyfforddi") means a course of training or instruction provided wholly or partly by or on behalf of or in pursuance of arrangements made with, or approved by or on behalf of, Skills Development Scotland, Scottish Enterprise, Highlands and Islands Enterprise, a government department, the Welsh Ministers or the Secretary of State.

General Note

To come within one of the classes of people who must be entitled to CTR on any day under an authority's scheme, an applicant must not be absent from home throughout that day. However, in accordance with this paragraph, days of absence that fall within "a period of temporary absence" must be ignored. "A period of temporary absence" is defined in sub-para (2) and means, for example, that if the specified conditions are met, periods of up to 13 or 52 weeks' absence can be ignored. In some, but not all, respects, this is similar to the provisions in reg 7(11), (13), (14), (15) and (16) HB regs – see the commentary on p269 for a discussion of the terms that are common to both this regulation and reg 7 HB Regs, but note that for CTR the period of temporary absence begins on the first whole day of absence, there is not the same distinction between periods of absence within Great Britain or outside Great Britain for CTR in Wales, and the rules relate to the dwelling in which an applicant usually resides rather than normally occupies.

PART 4
Prescribed classes of person who must not be included in an authority's scheme

Classes of person who must not be included in a scheme

27.   The classes of persons described in regulations 28 to 31 are classes of person prescribed for the purposes of paragraph 3(1)(b) of Schedule 1B of the 1992 Act and who must not be included in nor entitled to a reduction under an authority's scheme.

Persons treated as not being in Great Britain

28.–(1)   The class of person described in this regulation consists of any person treated as not being in Great Britain.

(2)   Except where a person falls within paragraph (5) or (6), a person is to be treated as not being in Great Britain if the person is not habitually resident in the United Kingdom, the Channel Islands, the Isle of Man or the Republic of Ireland.

(3)   A person must not be treated as habitually resident in the United Kingdom, the Channel Islands, the Isle of Man or the Republic of Ireland unless the person has a right to reside in one of those places.

(4)   For the purposes of paragraph (3), a right to reside does not include a right which exists by virtue of, or in accordance with–

(a)   regulation 13 of the EEA Regulations or Article 6 of Council Directive No.2004/ 38/EC;

(b)   regulation 14 of the EEA Regulations, but only in a case where the right exists under that regulation because the person is–

    (i)   a jobseeker for the purpose of the definition of "qualified person" in regulation 6(1) of those Regulations, or

    (ii)   a family member (within the meaning of regulation 7 of those Regulations) of such a jobseeker;

(c)   Article 45 of the Treaty on the Functioning of the European Union (in a case where the person is seeking work in the United Kingdom, the Channel Islands, the Isle of Man or the Republic of Ireland); or

(d)   regulation 15A(1) of the EEA Regulations, but only in a case where the right exists under that regulation because the applicant satisfies the criteria in paragraph (4A) of that regulation or Article 20 of the Treaty on the Functioning of the European Union (in a case where the right to reside arises because a British citizen would otherwise be deprived ofthe genuine enjoyment of their rights as a European Union citizen).

(5)   A person falls within this paragraph if the person is–

(a)   a qualified person for the purposes of regulation 6 of the EEA Regulations as a worker or a self-employed person;

(b)   a family member of a person referred to in sub-paragraph (a) within the meaning of regulation 7(1)(a), (b) or (c) of the EEA Regulations;

(c)   a person who has a right to reside permanently in the United Kingdom by virtue of regulation 15(1)(c), (d) or (e) of the EEA Regulations;

(d)   a person recorded by the Secretary of State as a refugee within the definition in Article 1of the Convention relating to the Status of Refugees adopted at Geneva on 28 July 1951, as extended by Article 1(2) of the Protocol relating to the Status of Refugees adopted at New York on 31 January 1967;

[¹(e)   a person who has been granted, or who is deemed to have been granted, leave outside the rules made under section 3(2) of the Immigration Act 1971 where that leave is–

    (i)   discretionary leave to enter or remain in the United Kingdom,

    (ii)   leave to remain under the Destitution Domestic Violence concession, or

    (iii)   leave deemed to have been granted by virtue of regulation 3 of the Displaced Persons (Temporary Protection) Regulations 2005;]

(f)   a person who has humanitarian protection granted under those rules;

(g)   a person who is not a person subject to immigration control within the meaning of section 115(9) of the Immigration and Asylum Act 1999 and who is in the United Kingdom as a result of the person's deportation, expulsion or other removal by compulsion of law from another country to the United Kingdom;

[¹(h)]

[¹ (i)]

(j)   a person who is in receipt of income support [²] or on an income-related employment and support allowance.

[¹ (k)   a person who is treated as a worker for the purposes of the definition of "qualified person" in regulation 6(1) of the EEA Regulations pursuant to regulation 5 of the Accession of Croatia (Immigration and Worker Authorisation) Regulations 2013 (right of residence of a Croatian who is an "accession State national subject to worker authorisation")[²]][²;]

[² (l)   in receipt of an income-based jobseeker's allowance and has a right to reside other than a right to reside falling within paragraph (4)(a) to (d).]

(6)   A person falls within this paragraph if the person is a Crown servant or member of Her Majesty's forces posted overseas.

(7)   A person mentioned in paragraph (6) is posted overseas if the person is performing overseas the duties of a Crown servant or member of Her Majesty's forces and was, immediately before the posting or the first of consecutive postings, habitually resident in the United Kingdom.

(8)   In this regulation–

"claim for asylum" ("hawliad am loches") has the same meaning as in section 94(1) of the Immigration and Asylum Act 1999;

"EEA Regulations" ("Rheoliadau AEE") means the Immigration (European Economic Area) Regulations 2006.

Amendments

1.   Amended by reg 5 of SI 2014 No 66 (W.6) as from 15.1.14.
2.   Amended by reg 6 of SI 2015 No 44 (W.3) as from 21.1.15, for schemes made for a financial year starting on or after 1.4.15.

Modifications

The amendments made by SI 2014 No.44 do not apply to a person who, on 31 March 2015, was liable to pay council tax at a reduced rate by virtue of a CTR scheme and was entitled to income-based JSA, until the earliest of the date s/he makes a new application for CTE or the date s/he ceases to be entitled to income-based JSA.

General Note

Reg 28 defines a class of person excluded from entitlement to CTR – those who are treated as not in GB.

A person is treated as not in GB if s/he is not habitually resident in the UK, Channel Islands, Isle of Man or Republic of Ireland, unless s/he comes within para (5) or (6). People covered by para (5) or (6) are therefore exempt from this habitual residence test and are not excluded from CTR under reg 28. Others cannot be treated as habitually resident unless they have a right to reside in the UK, Channel Islands, Isle of Man or Republic of Ireland (reg 28(3)). However, a right to reside does not include a right held in accordance the provisions in para (4). Therefore, a person who is not exempt under para (5) or (6) and who either does not have a right to reside or only has a right to reside under para (4), is treated as not habitually resident and so does not qualify for CTR. If s/he does have a right to reside and that right is not solely a right under para (4), s/he has to satisfy the habitual residence test to qualify.

This is similar to reg 10 HB Regs although, for HB, the rule is framed in terms of who is a "person from abroad" rather than who is treated as not in GB (a "person from abroad" is treated as not liable to make payments in respect of a dwelling, even if s/he is making such a payment, and so cannot qualify for HB). Also, amendments made to reg 10 HB Regs which clarify the position for those granted limited leave to enter or remain under the EU Settlement Scheme and reflect the fact that the Immigration (European Economic Area) Regulations 2006 have been revoked and replaced by the Immigration (European Economic Area) Regulations 2016, have not, at the time of writing, been replicated in this regulation. See p299 for relevant commentary.

Persons subject to immigration control

29.–(1)   Subject to paragraph (2), the class of person described in this regulation consists of any person who is subject to immigration control.

(2)   A person who is a national of a state which has ratified the European Convention on Social and Medical Assistance (adopted in Paris on 11 December 1953) or a state which has ratified the Council of Europe Social Charter (signed in Turin on 18 October 1961) and who is lawfully present in the United Kingdom is not a person subject to immigration control for the purposes of paragraph (1).

(3)   "Person subject to immigration control" ("person sy'n ddarostyngedig i reolaeth fewnfudo") has the meaning given in section 115(9) of the Immigration and Asylum Act 1999.

General Note

A "person subject to immigration control" is not entitled to CTR: reg 27 and 29. Someone covered by para (2) is not a person subject to immigration control and therefore is not excluded from entitlement by reg 29. For commentary relevant to paragraph (2), see the analysis of Sch para 4 Social Security (Immigration and Asylum) Consequential Amendments Regs on p1750. See also the commentary to s115(9) IAA on p1707 on who is a "person subject to immigration control".

Persons whose capital exceeds £16,000

30.–(1)   The class of person described in this regulation consists of any person whose capital exceeds £16,000.

(2)   Capital for the purposes of paragraph (1) is to be calculated in accordance with Schedule 1 (pensioners) or Schedule 6 (persons who are not pensioners).

General Note

In accordance with reg 27, a class of person described by this regulation is not entitled to a CTR under an authority's scheme. Note that if a person or her/his partner is in receipt of the guarantee credit of PC, income and capital are disregarded under Sch 1 para 7 (p1220) with the effect that such applicants are not caught by this regulation.

Students

31.–(1)   The class of person described in this regulation consists of any person who is a student.

(2)   In this regulation "student" ("myfyriwr") has the meaning given by paragraph 1 of Part 1 of Schedule 11.

(3)   Schedule 11, which contains matters that must be included in a scheme in respect of students has effect.

PART 5
Other matters that must be included in an authority's scheme

Provision for pensioners

32.–(1)   A scheme must make provision in respect of the classes of persons referred to in regulations 22 and 23 (classes A and B).

(2)   Schedules 1 to 5, which contain matters that must be included in a scheme in respect of those classes of person, have effect.

(3)   For the purposes of this regulation, the provisions in paragraph 33 of Schedule 1 (duration of extended reduction period) are minimum requirements.

Provision for persons who are not pensioners

33.–(1)   A scheme must make provision in respect of the classes of persons referred to in regulations 24 and 25 (classes C and D).

(2)   Schedules 6 to 10, which contain matters that must be included in a scheme in respect of those classes of person, have effect.

(3)   For the purposes of this regulation, the provisions in paragraphs 35 (duration of extended reduction period) and 40 (duration of extended reduction period (qualifying contributory benefits)) of Schedule 6 are minimum requirements.

Provision for pensioners and persons who are not pensioners

34.–(1)   A scheme must include the provisions set out within Schedules 12 to 14.

(2)   The provisions mentioned in paragraph (1) must apply to all applications for a council tax reduction unless otherwise provided.

(3)   Schedules 12 to 14, which contain matters that must be included in a scheme in respect of all applicants for a council tax reduction, unless otherwise provided, have effect.

(4)   For the purposes of this regulation, the provisions in paragraphs 3 and 4 of Schedule 13 (backdating) are minimum requirements.

(5)   For the purposes of this regulation, the amount to be disregarded in accordance with paragraph1(a) and (b) of Schedule 4 (amounts to be disregarded for war disablement pension, war widow's pension and war widower's pension: pensioners) and paragraph 20(a) and (b) of Schedule 9 (amounts to be disregarded for war disablement pension, war widow's pension and war widower's pension; persons who are not pensioners) is a minimum amount.

PART 6
Revocation, transitional and savings provisions

Interpretation
35. In this Part of the Regulations–

"2012 Regulations" ("Rheoliadau 2012") means the Council Tax Reduction Schemes and Prescribed Requirements (Wales) Regulations 2012;

"2013 scheme" ("cynllun 2013") means a scheme made by a billing authority in accordance with the 2012 Regulations or which applies in default on 1 April 2013 in accordance with paragraph 6(1)(e) of Schedule 1B to the Local Government Finance Act 1992;

"relevant authority" ("awdurdod perthnasol") means an authority administering a 2013 scheme or a scheme;

"scheme" ("cynllun") means a scheme made by a billing authority in accordance with these Regulations or which applies in default on 1 April 2014 in accordance with paragraph 6(1)(e) of Schedule 1B to the Local Government Finance Act 1992.

Revocation and savings
36.–(1) Subject to paragraph (2) the 2012 Regulations are revoked on 1 April 2014.

(2) The 2012 Regulations continue to apply to any applications made and any reductions awarded in accordance with the provisions of a 2013 scheme.

Persons to be treated as having made an application for a reduction
37.–(1) A person who falls within one of the categories of person described in paragraph (2) is to be treated as having made an application for a reduction under a scheme on 15 February 2014.

(2) A person referred to in paragraph (1) is a person who–

(a) is in receipt of a reduction under a 2013 scheme on 15 February 2014;

(b) has made an application for a reduction under a 2013 scheme which is not determined immediately before 15 February 2014;

(c) has served a written notice upon a relevant authority regarding a decision of the authority in relation to a claim for a reduction under a 2013 scheme, and whose decision in respect of the written notice is pending immediately before 15 February 2014;

(d) has appealed to the Valuation Tribunal for Wales against a decision of a relevant authority in relation to a claim for a reduction under a 2013 scheme, and whose appeal or decision in respect of the appeal is pending immediately before 15 February 2014;

(e) has appealed against the decision of the Valuation Tribunal for Wales in relation to claim for a reduction under a 2013 scheme, and whose appeal is pending immediately before 15 February 2014.

(3) For the purposes of paragraph (2)(e) an appeal against a decision relating to a claim for a reduction under a 2013 scheme is pending if–

(a) an appeal against the decision has been brought but not determined; or

(b) an application for permission to appeal against the decision has been made but not determined.

General Note
These regulations revoke and replace the Council Tax Reduction Schemes and Prescribed Requirements (Wales) Regulations 2012 No.3144 from 1 April 2014: regs 1 and 36. This regulation and regs 38 to 40 set out transitional provisions consequent on this change. People covered by regs 37(2) or 38 do not need to make a new application but instead are treated as having made an application for CTR under a scheme made either in accordance with these regulations or in accordance with the default scheme.

Applications received between 15 February 2014 and 31 March 2014
38. A person who makes a claim for a reduction under a 2013 scheme on any day during the period beginning on 15 February 2014 and ending on 31 March 2014 is to be treated as having made an application for a reduction under a scheme on the same day.

Date on which change of circumstances is to take effect
39.–(1)   Where a person (P) by virtue of regulation 37(1) or 38 is treated as having made an application for a reduction under a scheme and–
- (a)   on 15 February 2014 P is, or on any day during the period beginning on 15 February 2014 and ending on 31 March 2014 becomes, a person to whom the relevant provisions apply; and
- (b)   the effective date for the change of circumstances in accordance with the relevant provisions is a date after 31 March 2014,

the application is to be determined as though the change of circumstances has not taken place, but is to be re-determined upon the effective date to take account of the change of circumstances.

(2)   In paragraph (1) "relevant provisions" ("darpariaethau perthnasol") means–
- (a)   a provision contained within a 2013 scheme by virtue of regulation 30(2) of, and paragraph 40(10) to (12) of Schedule 1 to, the 2012 Regulations (date on which change of circumstances is to take effect: pensioners);
- (b)   provision contained within a 2013 scheme by virtue of regulation 31(2) of, and paragraph 46(10) to (12) of Schedule 6 to, the 2012 Regulations (date on which change of circumstances is to take effect: persons who are not pensioners); or
- (c)   paragraph 105(10) to (12) of the scheme prescribed in the Schedule to the Council Tax Reduction Schemes (Default Scheme) (Wales) Regulations 2012 (date on which change of circumstances is to take effect).

Notification relating to change of circumstances
40.   Where by virtue of regulation 37(1) or 38 a person is treated as having made an application under a scheme, the following provisions in a relevant authority's scheme do not apply in relation to that person's application–
- (a)   a provision contained in a scheme by virtue of regulation 33(3) of, and paragraph 1(7) of Schedule 13 to these Regulations (who may make an application); or
- (b)   paragraph 107(7) of the scheme prescribed in the Schedule to the Council Tax Reduction Schemes (Default Scheme) (Wales) Regulations 2013 (who may make an application).

SCHEDULE 1

REGULATION 32(2)

Determining eligibility for a reduction under an authority's scheme, amount of reduction and calculation of income and capital: pensioners

PART 1

Applicable amounts for the purposes of calculating eligibility for a reduction under an authority's scheme and amount of reduction: pensioners

Applicable amounts: pensioners (including pensioners in polygamous marriages)
1.–(1)   The applicable amount for a pensioner for a week is the aggregate of such of the following amounts as apply in that person's case–
- (a)   an amount in respect of the person's personal allowance or if that person is a member of a couple, an amount in respect of both of them, determined in accordance with paragraph 1 of Schedule 2 (personal allowance);
- (b)   an amount in respect of any child or young person who is a member of the person's family, determined in accordance with paragraph 2 of that Schedule (child or young person amounts);
- (c)   if the person is a member of a family of which at least one member is a child or young person, an amount determined in accordance with paragraph 3 of that Schedule (family premium);
- (d)   the amount of any premiums which may be applicable to the person, determined in accordance with Parts 3 and 4 of that Schedule (premiums).

(2)   In Schedule 2–
"additional spouse" ("priod ychwanegol") means a spouse of either party to the marriage who is additional to the other party to the marriage;
"patient" ("claf") means a person (other than a person who is serving a sentence of imprisonment or detention in a youth custody institution) who is regarded as receiving free in-patient treatment within the meaning of regulation 2(4) and (5) of the Social Security (Hospital In-Patients) Regulations 2005.

General Note
This paragraph is almost identical to reg 22 HB(SPC) Regs. See p765 for commentary but note that CTR schemes in Wales should not place a restriction on the number of children for whom an applicant can receive an allowance within her/his applicable amount under Sch 2 para 2 – ie, the so-called "two-child limit", which in some circumstances applies to HB and CTR in England, does not apply to CTR in Wales. Also, a family premium is included in the assessment of the applicable amount in Wales if at least one child or young person (as defined by reg 2) is a member of the applicant's family. Unless transitional rules apply, a family premium is no longer included in the assessment of the applicable amount for HB.

PART 2

Maximum council tax reduction for the purposes of calculating eligibility for a reduction under an authority's scheme and amount of reduction: pensioners

Maximum council tax reduction under an authority's scheme: pensioners
2.–(1)   Subject to sub-paragraphs (2) to (4), the amount of a person's maximum council tax reduction in respect of a day is 100 per cent of the amount A/B where–
    (a)   A is the amount set by the authority as the council tax for the relevant financial year in respect of the dwelling in which the person is a resident and for which the person is liable, subject to any discount which may be appropriate to that dwelling under the 1992 Act; and
    (b)   B is the number of days in that financial year,
less any deductions in respect of non-dependants which fall to be made under paragraph 3 (non-dependant deductions: pensioners).
    (2)   In calculating a person's maximum council tax reduction under an authority's scheme any reduction in the amount that person is liable to pay in respect of council tax, which is made in consequence of any enactment in, or made under, the 1992 Act (other than a reduction under an authority's scheme), is to be taken into account.
    (3)   Subject to sub-paragraph (4), where an applicant is jointly and severally liable for council tax in respect of a dwelling in which the applicant is resident with one or more other persons, in determining the maximum council tax reduction in the applicant's case in accordance with sub-paragraph (1), the amount A is to be divided by the number of persons who are jointly and severally liable for that tax.
    (4)   Where an applicant is jointly and severally liable for council tax in respect of a dwelling with only a partner, sub-paragraph (3) does not apply in that applicant's case.
    (5)   The reference in sub-paragraph (3) to a person with whom an applicant is jointly and severally liable for council tax does not include a student to whom paragraph 3 of Schedule 11 (students who are excluded from entitlement to a reduction under an authority's scheme) applies.
    (6)   In this paragraph "relevant financial year" ("blwyddyn ariannol berthnasol") means, in relation to any particular day, the financial year within which the day in question falls.

General Note
Although it is structured slightly differently, this is similar to reg 66 CTR(S) Regs. See p1522 for commentary.

Non-dependant deductions: pensioners
3.–(1)   Subject to the following provisions of this paragraph, the non-dependant deductions in respect of a day referred to in paragraph 2 are–
    (a)   in respect of a non-dependant aged 18 or over in remunerative work, [⁶ £13.75] x 1/7;
    (b)   in respect of a non-dependant aged 18 or over to whom paragraph (a) does not apply, [⁶ £4.55] x 1/7.
    (2)   In the case of a non-dependant aged 18 or over to whom sub-paragraph (1)(a) applies, where it is shown to the authority that that non-dependant's normal gross weekly income is–
    (a)   less than [⁶ £210.00], the deduction to be made under this paragraph is that specified in sub-paragraph (1)(b);
    (b)   not less than [⁶ £210.00] but less than [⁶ £365.00], the deduction to be made under this paragraph is [⁶ £9.15] x 1/7;
    (c)   not less than [⁶ £365.00] but less than [⁶ £450.00], the deduction to be made under this paragraph is [⁶ £11.50] x 1/7.
    (3)   Only one deduction is to be made under this paragraph in respect of a couple or, as the case may be, members of a polygamous marriage and, where, but for this paragraph, the amount that would fall to be deducted in respect of one member of a couple or polygamous marriage is higher than the amount (if any) that would fall to be deducted in respect of the other, or any other, member, the higher amount is to be deducted.
    (4)   In applying the provisions of sub-paragraph (2) in the case of a couple or, as the case may be, a polygamous marriage, regard must be had, for the purpose of that sub-paragraph, to the couple's or, as the case may be, all members of the polygamous marriage's joint weekly gross income.
    (5)   Where in respect of a day–
    (a)   a person is a resident in a dwelling but that person is not liable for council tax in respect of that dwelling and that day;

(b)   other residents in that dwelling (the liable persons) have joint and several liability for council tax in respect of that dwelling and that day otherwise than by virtue of section 9 of the 1992 Act (liability of spouses and civil partners); and

(c)   the person to whom paragraph (a) refers is a non-dependant of two or more of the liable persons, the deduction in respect of that non-dependant must be apportioned equally between those liable persons.

(6)   No deduction is to be made in respect of any non-dependants occupying an applicant's dwelling if the applicant or the applicant's partner is–

(a)   [3[³ blind or severely sight-impaired or is treated as such] by virtue of paragraph 20 of Schedule 1 (additional condition for the disability premium); or

(b)   receiving in respect of the applicant–

      (i)   attendance allowance or would be receiving that allowance but for–

            (aa)   a suspension of benefit in accordance with regulations under section 113(2)of the SSCBA; or

            (bb)   an abatement as a result of hospitalisation; or

      (ii)   the care component of the disability living allowance, or would be receiving that component but for–

            (aa)   a suspension of benefit in accordance with regulations under section 113(2)of the SSCBA; or

            (bb)   an abatement as a result of hospitalisation; or

      (iii)   the daily living component of personal independence payment or would be receiving that allowance but for a suspension of benefit in accordance with regulations under section 86 of the Welfare Reform Act 2012 (hospital in-patients); or

      (iv)   an AFIP, or would be receiving that payment but for a suspension of it in accordance with any terms of the armed and reserve forces compensation scheme which allow for a suspension because a person is undergoing medical treatment in a hospital or similar institution.

(7)   No deduction is to be made in respect of a non-dependant if–

(a)   although that non-dependant resides with the applicant, it appears to the authority that that non-dependant's normal home is elsewhere; or

(b)   the non-dependant is in receipt of a training allowance paid in connection with youth training established under section 2 of the Employment and Training Act 1973 or section 2 of the Enterprise and New Towns (Scotland) Act 1990; or

(c)   the non-dependant is a full-time student within the meaning of Schedule 11 (Students); or

(d)   the non-dependant is not residing with the applicant because the non-dependant has been a patient for a period in excess of 52 weeks, and for these purposes–

      (i)   "patient" ("claf") has the meaning given in [¹ regulation 26(6)], and

      (ii)   where a person has been a patient for two or more distinct periods separated by one or more intervals each not exceeding 28 days, that person is to be treated as having been a patient continuously for a period equal in duration to the total of those distinct periods.

(8)   No deduction is to be made in respect of a non-dependant–

(a)   who is on income support, state pension credit, an income-based jobseeker's allowance or an income related employment and support allowance [⁵ and where the non-dependent is not a member of the work-related activity group]; [²]

(b)   to whom Schedule 1 to the 1992 Act applies (persons disregarded for purposes of discount); but this paragraph does not apply to a non-dependant who is a student to whom paragraph 4 of that Schedule refers.[²;]

[² (c)   who is entitled to an award of universal credit where the award is calculated on the basis that the person does not have any earned income.]

[⁵ (9)   In the application of sub-paragraph (2) there is to be disregarded from the non-dependant's weekly gross income–

(a)   any attendance allowance, disability living allowance, personal independence payment or AFIP received by the non-dependant;

(b)   any payment made by or under a trust, established for the purpose of giving relief and assistance to disabled persons whose disabilities were caused by the fact that during their mother's pregnancy she had taken a preparation containing the drug known as Thalidomide, and which is approved by the Secretary of State.]

[² (10)   For the purposes of sub-paragraph (8), "earned income" ("incwm a enillir") has the meaning given in regulation 52 of the Universal Credit Regulations 2013.]

Amendments

1.   Amended by reg 6 of SI 2014 No 66 (W.6) as from 15.1.14.

2.   Amended by reg 7(a) of SI 2015 No 44 (W.3) as from 21.1.15, for schemes made for a financial year starting on or after 1.4.15.

3.   Amended by reg 5(a) of SI 2016 No 50 (W.21) as from 20.1.16, for schemes made for a financial year starting on or after 1.4.16.

4.   Amended by reg 3(a) of SI 2017 No 46 (W.20) as from 19.1.17, for schemes made for a financial year starting on or after 1.4.17.

5.   Amended by reg 4(a) of SI 2018 No 14 (W.7) as from 10.1.18, for schemes made for a financial year starting on or after 1.4.18.
6.   Amended by reg 3(a) of SI 2019 No 11 (W.5) as from 9.1.19, for schemes made for a financial year starting on or after 1.4.19.

Definitions

"non-dependant" – see reg 9.
"couple" – see reg 4.
"polygamous marriage" – see reg 2(1).
"AFIP" – see reg 2(1).
"applicant" – see reg 2(1).

General Note

Paragraph 3 is similar to reg 67 CTR(S) Regs (for commentary see p1524) and reg 74 HB Regs (for commentary see p519). For who counts as a non-dependant, see reg 9. Note that both reg 67(6)(b) CTR(S) Regs and reg 74(6)(b) HB Regs provide that no deduction is made if either *the applicant or her/his partner* is in receipt of one of the specified benefits. However, sub-para (6)(b) of this Schedule provides that no non-dependent deduction is to be made if the applicant or her/his partner receives *in respect of the applicant* one of the specified benefits. Therefore, it seems that a Welsh authority's scheme need not preclude a non-dependant deduction if the applicant or the partner receives one of the specified benefits in respect of the applicant's partner. This suggests that in some cases, if only one member of a couple receives one of the specified benefits, it may be beneficial for that person to become the applicant.
    Note also that under Welsh schemes.
(1)   No non-dependant deduction is made if:
(a)   payment of any of the specified benefits is suspended because the applicant is an in-patient in a hospital or similar institution or, in respect of AA and DLA, is abated because of hospitalisation;
(b)   the non-dependant is on IS, income-based JSA, income-related ESA (or PC), provided the non-dependant is not in the work–related activity group. Unlike the rules for housing benefit, this applies even if the non-dependant is over 25, and even if the non-dependant is getting the support component within her/his income-related ESA;
(c)   the non-dependant is entitled to UC on the basis that s/he does not have earned income, whatever her/his age. For HB, this only applies if the non-dependant is under 25;
(d)   the non-dependant is a "full-time student". "Full-time student" is defined as a person attending or undertaking a full time course of study and includes a student on a sandwich course: Sch 11 para 1(1). (For the definition of a "full time course of study", see Sch 11 para 1(1) and for when a student is to be regarded as attending or undertaking a full time course of study, see Sch 11 para 1(2)). In contrast to the HB rules, no non-dependant deduction is made during the student's summer vacation even if the non-dependant is in remunerative work during that vacation;
(e)   the non-dependant is someone who is disregarded for the purpose of a council tax discount under Sch 1 LGFA 1992, other than someone who is a student disregarded under para 4 of that schedule.
(2)   There is no equivalent to the HB rule that states no non-dependant deduction should be made if the non-dependant is not residing with the claimant because s/he a member of the armed forces away on operations: reg 55(7)(g) HB(SPC) Regs and reg 75(7)(g) HB Regs.
(3)   The only income which must be disregarded when calculating the non-dependant's gross weekly income for the purpose of sub-para (2) is AA, DLA, PIP and AFIP and payments made by or under a trust set up for people who were disabled as a result of their mother taking Thalidomide while pregnant: para 3(9). Certain other income is also disregarded for HB under reg 74(9) HB Regs and for CTR in Scotland under reg 67(9) CTR(S) Regs.
(4)   In respect of CTR for pensioners in Wales, the amounts deducted for non-dependants are not the same as the amounts deducted in England and Scotland.
For when a non-dependant's income can be treated as the applicant's, see para 6.

PART 3
Amount of reduction under an authority's scheme: pensioners

Amount of reduction under an authority's scheme: Classes A and B
    4.–(1)   Where a pensioner is entitled to a reduction under an authority's scheme in respect of a day, the amount of the reduction to which that pensioner is to be entitled is as follows.
    (2)   Where the person is within class A, that amount is the amount which is the maximum council tax reduction in respect of the day in the person's case.
    (3)   Where the person is within class B, that amount is the amount found by deducting amount B from amount A, where "amount A" and "amount B" have the meanings given in regulation 23.

PART 4
Income and capital for the purposes of calculating eligibility for a reduction under an authority's scheme and amount of reduction: pensioners
CHAPTER 1
General: pensioners

Calculation of income and capital: applicant's family and polygamous marriages: pensioners

5.–(1)   The income and capital of–

(a)   an applicant; and

(b)   any partner of that applicant,

is to be calculated in accordance with the provisions of this Part.

(2)   The income and capital of any partner of the applicant is to be treated as income and capital of the applicant, and in this Part any reference to the applicant applies equally to any partner of that applicant.

(3)   Where an applicant or the partner of an applicant is married polygamously to two or more members of the applicant's household–

(a)   the applicant must be treated as possessing capital and income belonging to each such member; and

(b)   the income and capital of that member is to be calculated in accordance with the following provisions of this Part in like manner as for the applicant.

Definitions

"applicant" – see reg 2(1).

"partner" – see reg 2(1).

"polygamous marriage" – see reg 2(1).

General Note

This provides that an applicant's income and capital are to be treated as including the income and capital of her/his partner, and that any reference to the applicant's income and capital in this Part is to be read accordingly. If an applicant is polygamously married, s/he is treated as possessing the income and capital of all the partners in the marriage with whom s/he shares a household (sub-para (3)). See p17 for a discussion of caselaw concerning membership of a household.

Circumstances in which capital and income of non-dependant is to be treated as applicant's: pensioners

6.–(1)   Sub-paragraph (2) applies where it appears to the authority that a non-dependant and an applicant have entered into arrangements in order to take advantage of an authority's scheme and the non-dependant has more income and capital than the applicant.

(2)   Except where–

(a)   the applicant is a pensioner and is on a guarantee credit, or

(b)   the applicant is not a pensioner and is on income support, an income-based jobseeker's allowance or an income-related employment and support allowance,

the authority must treat the applicant as possessing income and capital belonging to that non-dependant and, in such a case, any capital and income which the applicant does possess is to be disregarded.

(3)   Where an applicant is treated as possessing capital and income belonging to a non-dependant under sub-paragraph (2) the capital and income of that non-dependant must be calculated in accordance with the following provisions of this Part in like manner as for the applicant and, except where the context otherwise requires, any reference to the "applicant" ("ceisydd") is to be construed for the purposes of this Part as if it were a reference to that non-dependant.

Definitions

"non-dependant" – see reg 9.

"applicant" – see reg 2(1).

"pensioner" – see reg 3.

General Note

This is similar to reg 26 HB Regs and reg 24 HB(SPC) Regs. See the analysis of reg 26 HB Regs on p422 but note that under this paragraph a non-dependant's income and capital cannot be treated as the income and capital of the applicant if the applicant is on guarantee credit of PC.

CHAPTER 2
Income: pensioners in receipt of guarantee credit or savings credit: pensioners

Pensioners in receipt of guarantee credit

7.   In the case of an applicant who is a pensioner and who is in receipt, or whose partner is in receipt, of a guarantee credit, the whole of the applicant's capital and income must be disregarded.

Calculation of pensioner's income in savings credit only cases

8.–(1)   In determining the income and capital of an applicant who is a pensioner and who has, or whose partner has, an award of state pension credit comprising only the savings credit, subject to the following provisions of this paragraph, an authority must use the calculation or estimate of the applicant's or as the case may be, the applicant's partner's income and capital made by the Secretary of State for the purpose of determining the award of state pension credit.

(2)   Where the calculation or estimate provided by the Secretary of State includes an amount taken into account in that determination in respect of net income, the authority may only adjust that amount so far as necessary to take into account–

(a)   the amount of any savings credit payable;

(b)   in respect of any dependent children of the applicant, child care charges taken into account under paragraph 18 (calculation of income on a weekly basis);

(c)   the higher amount disregarded under an authority's scheme in respect of–

   (i)   lone parent's earnings; or

   (ii)   payments of maintenance, whether under a court order or not, which is made or due to be made by–

      (aa)   the applicant's former partner, or the applicant's partner's former partner; or

      (bb)   the parent of a child or young person where that child or young person is a member of the applicant's family except where that parent is the applicant or the applicant's partner;

(d)   any amount to be disregarded by virtue of paragraph 10(1) of Schedule 3 (sums disregarded from applicant's earnings);

(e)   the income and capital of any partner of the applicant who is treated as a member of the applicant's household under regulation 8, to the extent that it is not taken into account in determining the net income of the person claiming state pension credit;

(f)   paragraph 6 (circumstances in which capital and income of a non-dependant is to be treated as applicant's), if the authority determines that that provision applies in the applicant's case;

(g)   such further reduction (if any) as the authority thinks fit under section 13A(1)(c) of the 1992 Act;

(h)   any amount to be disregarded by virtue of paragraph 6 of Schedule 3 (sums to be disregarded from applicant's income: pensioners).

(3)   Paragraphs 10 to 30 of this Schedule do not apply to the amount of the net income to be taken into account under sub-paragraph (1), but do apply (so far as relevant) for the purpose of determining any adjustments to that amount which the authority makes under sub-paragraph (2).

(4)   If sub-paragraph (5) applies, the authority must calculate the applicant's capital in accordance with paragraphs 25 to 30 (calculation of capital: pensioners).

(5)   This sub-paragraph applies if–

(a)   the Secretary of State notifies the authority that the applicant's capital has been determined as being £16,000 or less or the authority determines the applicant's capital as being £16,000 or less;

(b)   subsequent to that determination the applicant's capital rises to more than £16,000; and

(c)   the increase occurs whilst there is in force an assessed income period within the meaning of sections 6 and 9 of the State Pension Credit Act 2002.

General Note

This paragraph is similar to reg 27 HB(SPC) Regs although there is no equivalent here to reg 27(2), (3) or (6).

For pensioners, the general rule is that if an applicant or her/his partner has an award of the savings credit of PC (and not the guarantee credit), in determining entitlement to CTR the authority must use the income and capital figures which the DWP used to work out the savings credit award, subject to the modifications in paras 8(2) to (5). See the analysis of reg 27(1), (4) and (5) HB(SPC) Regs on p767, which seem to apply here, but note the following.

(1)   The earnings disregarded for HB purposes under Sch 4 para 5A HB(SPC) Regs (reg 27(4)(d) HB(SPC) Regs) is equivalent to the amount disregarded under Sch 3 para 6 of these regulations: para 8(2)(h).

(2)   Section 13A(1)(c) LGFA mentioned in the above para 8(2)(g), gives the billing authority power to reduce, or further reduce, the amount of an individual's council tax to the extent that the authority thinks fit.

(3)   The wording of para 8(5)(a) is slightly different from the HB counterpart (reg 27(8)(a) HB(SPC) Regs), although the effect is similar. For CTR in Wales, the authority must determine the amount of capital rather than using the DWP's assessment of the amount if, within the "assessed income period" for PC, the amount of the applicant's capital has increased to over £16,000 and this has happened since the DWP determined it was £16,000 or less for the purpose of the savings credit of PC or since the authority determined it was £16,000 or less (presumably where the authority has relied on para 8(2) and (3) to make such a determination). Amendments in ss28 and 29 of the Pensions Act 2014, which at the time of writing are not yet in force, are intended to ensure that no new assessed income periods are set for PC claimants from 6 April 2016, and that any remaining assessed income periods of five years or less will be gradually phased out from that date.

CHAPTER 3
Income: other pensioners

Calculation of income and capital where state pension credit is not payable: pensioners
  9.   Where neither paragraph 7 (pensioner in receipt of guarantee credit) nor 8 (calculation of pensioner's income in savings credit only cases) applies in the applicant's case, the applicant's income and capital is to be calculated or estimated in accordance with paragraphs 10 to 19 and 21 to 24 (calculation of income) and paragraphs 25 to 31 (calculation of capital).

Meaning of "income": pensioners
  10.–(1)   For the purposes of classes A and B "income" ("incwm") means income of any of the following descriptions–
  (a)   earnings;
  (b)   working tax credit;
  (c)   retirement pension income within the meaning of the State Pension Credit Act 2002;
  (d)   income from annuity contracts (other than retirement pension income);
  (e)   a war disablement pension or war widow's or widower's pension;
  (f)   a foreign war disablement pension or war widow's or widower's pension;
  (g)   a guaranteed income payment;
  (h)   a payment made under article 29(1)(c) of the Armed Forces and Reserve Forces (Compensation Scheme) Order 2011, in any case where article 31(2)(c) applies;
  (i)   income from capital other than capital disregarded under Part 1 of Schedule 5;
  (j)   social security benefits, other than retirement pension income or any of the following benefits–
        (i)   disability living allowance;
        (ii)   personal independence payment;
        (iii)   an AFIP;
        (iv)   attendance allowance payable under section 64 of the SSCBA (entitlement to attendance allowance);
        (v)   an increase of disablement pension under section 104 (increase for constant attendance) or 105 (increase for exceptionally severe disablement) of the SSCBA;
        (vi)   child benefit;
        (vii)   any guardian's allowance payable under section 77 of the SSCBA (guardian's allowance);
        (viii)   any increase for a dependant, other than the applicant's partner, payable in accordance with Part 4 of the SSCBA (increases for dependants);
        (ix)   any–
        (aa) social fund payment made under Part 8 of the SSCBA (the social fund); or
        (bb)   occasional assistance;
        (x)   Christmas bonus payable under Part 10 of the SSCBA (Christmas bonus for pensioners);
        (xi)   housing benefit;
        (xii)   council tax benefit;
        [² (xiii) bereavement and support payment under section 30 of the Pensions Act 2014;]
        (xiv)   statutory sick pay;
        (xv)   statutory maternity pay;
        (xvi)   [¹] statutory paternity pay payable under Part 12ZA of the SSCBA (statutory paternity pay);
        [¹(xvia) statutory shared parental pay payable under Part 12ZC of the SSCBA;]
        (xvii)   additional statutory paternity pay payable under Part 12ZA of the SSCBA;
        (xviii)   statutory adoption pay payable under Part 12ZB of the SSCBA (statutory adoption pay);
        (xix)   any benefit similar to those mentioned in the preceding provisions of this paragraph payable under legislation having effect in Northern Ireland;
  (k)   all foreign social security benefits which are similar to the social security benefits prescribed above;
  (l)   a payment made–
        (i)   under article 30 of the Naval, Military and Air Forces Etc (Disablement and Death) Service Pensions Order 2006, in any case where article 30(1)(b) applies; or
        (ii)   under article 12(8) of that Order, in any case where sub-paragraph (b) of article 12(8) applies;
  [² (m)   a pension paid by a Government to victims of National Socialist persecution;]
  (n)   payments under a scheme made under the Pneumoconiosis etc (Workers' Compensation) Act 1979;
  (o)   payments made towards the maintenance of the applicant by the applicant's spouse, civil partner, former spouse or former civil partner or towards the maintenance of the applicant's partner by that person's spouse, civil partner, former spouse or former civil partner, including payments made–
        (i)   under a court order;
        (ii)   under an agreement for maintenance; or
        (iii)   voluntarily;
  (p)   payments due from any person in respect of board and lodging accommodation provided by the applicant;
  (q)   Royalties or other sums paid as a consideration for the use of, or the right to use, any copyright, design, patent or trade mark;

(r)   any payment in respect of any–
      (i)   book registered under the Public Lending Right Scheme 1982; or
      (ii)   work made under any international public lending right scheme that is analogous to the Public Lending Right Scheme 1982;

(s)   any payment, other than a payment ordered by a court or made in settlement of a claim, made by or on behalf of a former employer of a person on account of the early retirement of that person on grounds of ill-health or disability;

(t)   any sum payable by way of pension out of money provided under–
      (i)   the Civil List Act 1837,
      (ii)   the Civil List Act 1937,
      (iii) the Civil List Act 1952,
      (iv) the Civil List Act 1972, or
      (v)   the Civil List Act 1975;

(u)   any income in lieu of that specified in paragraphs (a) to (r);

(v)   any payment of rent made to an applicant who–
      (i)   owns the freehold or leasehold interest in any property or is a tenant of any property;
      (ii)   occupies part of the property; and
      (iii) has an agreement with another person allowing that person to occupy that property on payment of rent;

(w)   any payment made at regular intervals under an equity release scheme;

(x)   PPF periodic payments within the meaning of section 17(1) of the State Pension Credit Act 2002.

(2)   Where the payment of any social security benefit referred to in sub-paragraph (1) is subject to any deduction (other than an adjustment specified in sub-paragraph (4)) the amount to be taken into account under sub-paragraph (1) is to be the amount before the deduction is made.

(3)   Where an award of any working tax credit or child tax credit is subject to a deduction by way of recovery of an overpayment of working tax credit or child tax credit which arose in a previous tax year the amount to be taken into account under sub-paragraph (1) is to be the amount of working tax credit or child tax credit awarded less the amount of that deduction.

(4)   The adjustments specified in this sub-paragraph are those made in accordance with–

(a)   the Social Security (Overlapping Benefits) Regulations 1979;

(b)   the Social Security (Hospital In-Patients) Regulations 2005;

(c)   section 30DD or section 30E of the SSCBA (reductions in incapacity benefit in respect of pensions and councillor's allowances);

(d)   section 3 of the Welfare Reform Act 2007 (deductions from contributory employment and support allowance in respect of pensions and councillor's allowances) and regulations made under it.

(5)   In sub-paragraph (1)(w), "equity release scheme" ("cynllun rhyddau ecwiti") means a loan–

(a)   made between a person ("the lender") and the applicant;

(b)   by means of which a sum of money is advanced by the lender to the applicant by way of payments at regular intervals; and

(c)   which is secured on a dwelling in which the applicant owns an estate or interest and which the applicant occupies as the applicant's home.

Amendments

1.   Amended by reg 7(b) of SI 2015 No 44 (W.3) as from 21.1.15, for schemes made for a financial year starting on or after 1.4.15.

2.   Amended by reg 4(b) of SI 2018 No 14 (W.7) as from 10.1.18, for schemes made for a financial year starting on or after 1.4.18.

General Note

This paragraph is almost identical to reg 29 HB(SPC) Regs. See p771 for commentary on that regulation but note that there is no equivalent to para 10(1)(j)(ix)(bb) in reg 29 of HB(SPC) Regs. This states that any occasional payment (as defined in reg 2(1) of these regs) is treated as income. Also tariff income from capital mentioned in the commentary (reg 29(2) HB(SPC) Regs) is not covered in this paragraph but in para 31.

Calculation of weekly income: pensioners

11.–(1)   Except in a case where [¹ sub-paragraph (2), (3A), (4A) or (5)] apply, for the purposes of calculating the weekly income of an applicant who is a pensioner, where the period in respect of which a payment is made–

(a)   does not exceed a week, the whole of that payment is to be included in the applicant's weekly income;

(b)   exceeds a week, the amount to be included in the applicant's weekly income is to be determined–
      (i)   in a case where that period is a month, by multiplying the amount of the payment by 12 and dividing the product by 52;
      (ii)   in a case where that period is three months, by multiplying the amount of the payment by 4 and dividing the product by 52;
      (iii) in a case where that period is a year, by dividing the amount of the payment by 52;

        (iv)   in any other case, by multiplying the amount of the payment by 7 and dividing the product by the number of days in the period in respect of which it is made.

(2)   Sub-paragraph (3) applies where–

(a)   the applicant's regular pattern of work is such that the applicant does not work the same hours every week; or

(b)   the amount of the applicant's income fluctuates and has changed more than once.

(3)   The weekly amount of that applicant's income is to be determined–

(a)   if, in a case to which sub-paragraph (2)(a) applies, there is a recognised cycle of work, by reference to the applicant's average weekly income over the period of the complete cycle (including, where the cycle involves periods in which the applicant does no work, those periods but disregarding any other absences); or

(b)   in any other case, on the basis of–

        (i)   the last two payments if those payments are one month or more apart;

        (ii)   the last four payments if the last two payments are less than one month apart; or

        (iii)   calculating or estimating such other payments as may, in the particular circumstances of the case, enable the applicant's average weekly income to be determined more accurately.

[¹ (3A)   Income calculated pursuant to sub-paragraphs (2) and (3) must be taken into account–

(a)   in the case of an application, on the date on which the application was made or treated as made, and the first day of each reduction week thereafter, [² regardless of when those earnings were actually received];

[² (b)   in the case of an application or a reduction under a scheme where the applicant commences employment, the day on which applicant commences that employment, and the first day of each reduction week thereafter, regardless of when those earnings were actually received; or

(c)   in the case of an application or a reduction under a scheme where the applicant's average weekly earnings from employment change, the day on which the applicant's earnings change, so as to require recalculation under this paragraph, and the first day of each reduction week thereafter, regardless of when those earnings were actually received .]]

(4)   For the purposes of sub-paragraph (3)(b) the last payments are the last payments before the date the application was made or treated as made.

[¹ (4A)   An applicant's earnings from employment as an employed earner not calculated pursuant to sub-paragraphs (2) and (3) must be taken into account–

(a)   in the case of an application, on the date on which the application was made or treated as made, and the first day of each reduction week thereafter, [² regardless of when those earnings were actually received];

[² (b)   in the case of an application or a reduction under a scheme where the applicant commences employment, the day on which the applicant commences that employment, and the first day of each reduction week thereafter, regardless of when those earnings were actually received; or

(c)   in the case of an application or a reduction under a scheme where the applicant's average weekly earnings from employment change, the day on which applicant's earnings from employment change and the first day of each reduction week thereafter, regardless of when those earnings were actually received.]]

(5)   If the applicant is entitled to receive a payment to which sub-paragraph (6) applies, the amount of that payment is to be treated as if made in respect of a period of a year.

(6)   This sub-paragraph applies to–

(a)   royalties or other sums paid as a consideration for the use of, or the right to use, any copyright, design, patent or trade mark;

(b)   any payment in respect of any–

        (i)   book registered under the Public Lending Right Scheme 1982; or

        (ii)   work made under any international public lending right scheme that is analogous to the Public Lending Right Scheme 1982; and

(c)   any payment which is made on an occasional basis.

(7)   The period under which any benefit under the benefit Acts is to be taken into account is to be the period in respect of which that benefit is payable.

(8)   Where payments are made in a currency other than sterling, the value of the payment is to be determined by taking the sterling equivalent on the date the payment is made.

(9)   The sums specified in Schedule 3 are to be disregarded in calculating–

(a)   the applicant's earnings; and

(b)   any amount to which sub-paragraph (6) applies where the applicant is the first owner of the copyright, design, patent or trademark, or an original contributor to the book or work referred to in sub-paragraph (6)(b).

(10)   For the purposes of sub-paragraph (9)(b), and for those purposes only, the amounts specified in sub-paragraph (6) are to be treated as though they were earnings.

(11)   Income specified in Schedule 4 is to be disregarded in the calculation of the applicant's income.

(12)   Schedule 5 has effect so that–

(a)   the capital specified in Part 1 of that Schedule is disregarded for the purpose of determining an applicant's income; and

(b)   the capital specified in Part 2 of that Schedule is disregarded for the purpose of determining an applicant's income under paragraph 31 (calculation of tariff income from capital: pensioners).

(13)   In the case of any income taken into account for the purpose of calculating a person's income any amount payable by way of tax is disregarded.

Amendments

1.   Amended by reg 3(b) of SI 2017 No 46 (W.20) as from 19.1.17. for schemes made for a financial year starting on or after 1.4.17.
2.   Amended by reg 4(c) of SI 2018 No 14 (W.7) as from 10.1.18, for schemes made for a financial year starting on or after 1.4.18.

General Note

This paragraph is similar to reg 33 HB(SPC) Regs. See p779 for commentary on that regulation but note that provisions in reg 33(2) HB(SPC) Regs are contained in sub-paras (2) and (3) of this paragraph. Thus the numbering of these and subsequent sub-paragraphs does not correspond with the numbering in the commentary. Also note the differences between reg 33(3) HB(SPC) Regs and para 11(4) above.

Earnings of employed earners: pensioners

12.–(1)   Subject to sub-paragraph (2), "earnings" ("enillion"), in the case of employment as an employed earner who is a pensioner, means any remuneration or profit derived from that employment and includes–
(a)   any bonus or commission;
(b)   any payment in lieu of remuneration except any periodic sum paid to an applicant on account of the termination of that applicant's employment by reason of redundancy;
(c)   any payment in lieu of notice;
(d)   any holiday pay;
(e)   any payment by way of a retainer;
(f)   any payment made by the applicant's employer in respect of expenses not wholly, exclusively and necessarily incurred in the performance of the duties of the employment, including any payment made by the applicant's employer in respect of–
    (i)   travelling expenses incurred by the applicant between the applicant's home and place of employment;
    (ii)   expenses incurred by the applicant under arrangements made for the care of a member of the applicant's family owing to the applicant's absence from home;
(g)   the amount of any payment by way of a non-cash voucher which has been taken into account in the computation of a person's earnings in accordance with Part 5 of Schedule 3 to the Social Security (Contributions) Regulations 2001;
(h)   statutory sick pay and statutory maternity pay payable by the employer under the SSCBA;
(i)   statutory paternity pay payable under Part 12ZA of the SSCBA;
(j)   statutory adoption pay payable under Part 12ZB of the SSCBA;
[¹ (ja)   statutory shared parental pay payable under Part 12ZC of the SSCBA;]
(k)   any sums payable under a contract of service–
    (i)   for incapacity for work due to sickness or injury; or
    (ii)   by reason of pregnancy or confinement.
(2)   Earnings does not include–
(a)   subject to sub-paragraph (3), any payment in kind;
(b)   any payment in respect of expenses wholly, exclusively and necessarily incurred in the performance of the duties of the employment;
(c)   any occupational pension;
(d)   any lump sum payment made under the Iron and Steel Re-adaptation Benefits Scheme;
(e)   any payment of compensation made pursuant to an award by an employment tribunal established under the Employment Tribunals Act 1996 in respect of unfair dismissal or unlawful discrimination;
(f)   any payment in respect of expenses arising out of the applicant's participation in a service user group.
(3)   Sub-paragraph (2)(a) does not apply in respect of any non-cash voucher referred to in sub-paragraph (1)(g).

Amendment

1.   Inserted by reg 7(c) of SI 2015 No 44 (W.3) as from 21.1.15, for schemes made for a financial year starting on or after 1.4.15.

General Note

This paragraph is similar to reg 35 HB Regs but has some significant differences. See the commentary on that regulation on p439 but note the exclusion from the definition of "earnings" for CTR of any lump sum payment made under the Iron and Steel Re-adaptation Benefits Scheme and of any payment of compensation awarded by an employment tribunalfor unfair dismissal or unlawful discrimination (sub-para (2)(d) and (e)). Note also that reg 35(1)(g) and (gg) HB Regs are not reproduced in this para.

Calculation of net earnings of employed earners: pensioners

13.–(1) For the purposes of paragraph 18 (calculation of income on a weekly basis: pensioners), the earnings of an applicant derived or likely to be derived from employment as an employed earner to be taken into account must, subject to paragraph 11(4) and Schedule 3, (calculation of weekly income: pensioners) be that applicant's net earnings.

(2) For the purposes of sub-paragraph (1) net earnings must, except where sub-paragraph (5) applies, be calculated by taking into account the gross earnings of the applicant from that employment over the assessment period, less–

(a) any amount deducted from those earnings by way of–
  (i) income tax;
  (ii) primary Class 1 contributions under the SSCBA;

(b) one-half of any sum paid by the applicant by way of a contribution towards an occupational pension scheme;

(c) one-half of the amount calculated in accordance with sub-paragraph (4) in respect of any qualifying contribution payable by the applicant; and

(d) where those earnings include a payment which is payable under any enactment having effect in Northern Ireland and which corresponds to statutory sick pay, statutory maternity pay, [¹] statutory paternity pay [¹, statutory shared parental pay] or statutory adoption pay, any amount deducted from those earnings by way of any contributions which correspond to primary Class 1 contributions under the SSCBA.

(3) In this paragraph "qualifying contribution" ("cyfraniad cymwys") means any sum which is payable periodically as a contribution towards a personal pension scheme.

(4) The amount in respect of any qualifying contribution is to be calculated by multiplying the daily amount of the qualifying contribution by the number equal to the number of days in the assessment period; and for the purposes of this paragraph the daily amount of the qualifying contribution is to be determined–

(a) where the qualifying contribution is payable monthly, by multiplying the amount of the qualifying contribution by 12 and dividing the product by 365;

(b) in any other case, by dividing the amount of the qualifying contribution by the number equal to the number of days in the period to which the qualifying contribution relates.

(5) Where the earnings of an applicant are determined under paragraph 11(2)(b) (calculation of weekly income: classes A and B) that applicant's net earnings are to be calculated by taking into account those earnings over the assessment period, less–

(a) an amount in respect of income tax equivalent to an amount calculated by applying to those earnings the basic rate of tax applicable to the assessment period less only the [² personal reliefs to which the applicant is entitled under Chapters 2, 3 and 3A of Part 3] of the Income Tax Act 2007 [²] as is appropriate to the applicant's circumstances but, if the assessment period is less than a year, the earnings to which the basic rate of tax is to be applied and the amount of the personal [² reliefs] deductible under this sub-paragraph is to be calculated on a pro rata basis;

(b) an amount equivalent to the amount of the primary Class 1 contributions that would be payable by the applicant under the SSCBA in respect of those earnings if such contributions were payable; and

(c) one-half of any sum which would be payable by the applicant by way of a contribution towards an occupational or personal pension scheme, if the earnings so estimated were actual earnings.

Amendments

1. Amended by reg 7(d) of SI 2015 No 44 (W.3) as from 21.1.15, for schemes made for a financial year starting on or after 1.4.15.

2. Amended by reg 3(c) of SI 2017 No 46 (W.20) as from 19.1.17, for schemes made for a financial year starting on or after 1.4.17.

General Note

This paragraph is almost identical to reg 36 HB Regs. For commentary, see p443.

Calculation of earnings self-employed earners: pensioners

14.–(1) Where the earnings of an applicant who is a pensioner consist of earnings from employment as a self employed earner, the weekly amount of that applicant's earnings is to be determined by reference to the applicant's average weekly earnings from that employment–

(a) over a period of one year; or

(b) where the applicant has recently become engaged in that employment or there has been a change which is likely to affect the normal pattern of business, over such other period ("computation period") as may, in the particular case, enable the weekly amount of the applicant's earnings to be determined more accurately.

(2) For the purposes of determining the weekly amount of earnings of an applicant to whom sub-paragraph (1)(b) applies, the applicant's earnings over the computation period are to be divided by the number equal to the number of days in that period and the quotient multiplied by 7.

(3) The period over which the weekly amount of an applicant's earnings is calculated in accordance with this paragraph is to be the applicant's assessment period.

General Note

This paragraph corresponds with reg 37 HB(SPC) Regs. For commentary, see p783.

Earnings of self-employed earners: pensioners

15.–(1)   Subject to sub-paragraph (2), "earnings" ("enillion"), in the case of employment as a self-employed earner who is a pensioner, means the gross income of the employment.

(2)   "Earnings" in the case of employment as a self-employed earner does not include–

(a)   where an applicant occupies a dwelling as the applicant's home and the applicant provides in that dwelling board and lodging accommodation for which payment is made, those payments;

(b)   any payment made by a local authority to an applicant–

    (i)   with whom a person is accommodated by virtue of arrangements made under section 22C or 23(2)(a) of the Children Act 1989 (provision of accommodation and maintenance for a child whom they are looking after) or, as the case may be, section 26(1) of the Children (Scotland) Act 1995 [¹ , or section 81 of the Social Services and Well-being (Wales) Act 2014 (accommodation and maintenance of looked after children)]; or

    (ii)   with whom a local authority fosters a child under the Looked After Children (Scotland) Regulations 2009 or who is a kinship carer under those Regulations;

(c)   any payment made by a voluntary organisation in accordance with section 59(1)(a) of the Children Act 1989 (provision of accommodation by voluntary organisations);

(d)   any payment made to the applicant or the applicant's partner for a person ("the person concerned") who is not normally a member of the applicant's household but is temporarily in the applicant's care, by–

    (i)   a local authority but excluding payments of housing benefit made in respect of the person concerned;

    (ii)   a voluntary organisation;

    (iii)   the person concerned pursuant to section 26(3A) of the National Assistance Act 1948;

    (iv)   the National Health Service Commissioning Board or a clinical commissioning group established under section 14D of the National Health Service Act 2006; [¹]

    (v)   a Local Health Board established by an order made under section 11 of the National Health Service (Wales) Act 2006;

    [¹ (vi)   the person concerned where the payment is for the provision of accommodation to meet that person's needs for care and support arranged pursuant to section 35 or 36 of the Social Services and Well-being (Wales) Act 2014; or

    (vii)   the person concerned where the payment is for the provision of accommodation to meet that person's needs for care and support arranged pursuant to section 18 or 19 of the Care Act 2014;]

(e)   any sports award.

Amendment

1.   Amended by reg 5(b) of SI 2016 No 50 (W.21) as from 20.1.16, for schemes made for a financial year starting on or after 1.4.16.

General Note

This paragraph is broadly equivalent to reg 38 HB(SPC) Regs. Para 15(1) also corresponds with reg 37(1) HB Regs (see commentary on p445). Para 15(2)(b) and (c) is similar to Sch 5 para 26 HB Regs (p673) and para 15(2)(d) corresponds with Sch 5 para 27 HB Regs (p674).

Notional income: pensioners

16.–(1)   An applicant who is a pensioner is to be treated as possessing–

(a)   subject to sub-paragraph (2), the amount of any retirement pension income–

    (i)   for which no claim has been made; and

    (ii)   to which that applicant might expect to be entitled if a claim for it were made;

(b)   income from an occupational pension scheme which the applicant elected to defer.

(2)   Sub-paragraph (1)(a) does not apply to the following where entitlement has been deferred–

(a)   a Category A or Category B retirement pension payable under sections 43 to 55 of the SSCBA;

(b)   a shared additional pension payable under [¹ sections 55A and 55AA] of the SSCBA;

(c)   graduated retirement benefit payable under sections 36 and 37 of the National Insurance Act 1965 [¹ ;]

[¹ (d)   a state pension under Part 1 of the Pensions Act 2014.]

(3)   For the purposes of sub-paragraph (2), entitlement has been deferred–

(a)   in the case of a Category A or Category B pension, in the circumstances specified in section 55(3) of the SSCBA;

(b)   in the case of a shared additional pension, in the circumstances specified in section 55C(3) of the SSCBA; [¹]

(c)   in the case of graduated retirement benefit, in the circumstances specified in section 36(4) and (4A) of the National Insurance Act 1965 [¹ ; and]

[¹ (d)   in the case of a state pension under Part 1 of the Pensions Act 2014, in the circumstances specified in section 17(7) and (8) of that Act.]

(4)   This sub-paragraph applies where a person who has attained the qualifying age for state pension credit–

(a)   is entitled to money purchase benefits under an occupational pension scheme or a personal pension scheme;

(b)   fails to purchase an annuity with the funds available in that scheme; and

(c)   either–

(i)   defers in whole or in part the payment of any income which would have been payable to that person by that person's pension fund holder, or

(ii)   fails to take any necessary action to secure that the whole of any income which would be payable to that person by that person's pension fund holder upon that person applying for it, is so paid, or

(iii)   is a person to whom income withdrawal is not available under that scheme.

(5)   Where sub-paragraph (4) applies, the amount of any income foregone is to be treated as possessed by that person, but only from the date on which it could be expected to be acquired were an application for it to be made.

(6)   The amount of any income foregone in a case where sub-paragraph (4)(c)(i) or (ii) applies is to be the maximum amount of income which may be withdrawn from the fund and must be determined by the authority, taking account of information provided by the pension fund holder.

(7)   The amount of any income foregone in a case where sub-paragraph (4)(c)(iii) applies is to be the income that the applicant could have received without purchasing an annuity had the funds held under the relevant scheme been held under a personal pension scheme or occupational pension scheme where income withdrawal was available and is to be determined in the manner specified in sub-paragraph (6).

(8)   In sub-paragraph (4), "money purchase benefits" ("buddion pryniant ariannol") has the same meaning as in the Pension Schemes Act 1993.

(9)   Subject to sub-paragraphs (10) [¹, (11A), (11B)] and (12), a person is to be treated as possessing income of which that person has deprived himself or herself for the purpose of securing entitlement to a reduction under an authority's scheme or increasing the amount of the reduction.

(10)   Sub-paragraph (9) does not apply in respect of the amount of an increase of pension or benefit where a person, having made an election in favour of that increase of pension or benefit under Schedule 5 or 5A to the SSCBA or under Schedule 1 to the Social Security (Graduated Retirement Benefit) Regulations 2005, changes that election in accordance with regulations made under Schedule 5 or 5A to that Act in favour of a lump sum.

(11)   In sub-paragraph (10), "lump sum" ("cyfandaliad") means a lump sum under Schedule 5 or 5A to the SSCBA or under Schedule 1 to the Social Security (Graduated Retirement Benefit) Regulations 2005.

[¹ (11A)   Sub-paragraph (9) does not apply in respect of the amount of an increase of pension where a person, having made an election in favour of that increase in pension under section 8(2) of the Pensions Act 2014, changes that election in accordance with regulations made under section 8(7) of that Act in favour of a lump sum.

(11B)   Sub-paragraph (9) does not apply in respect of the amount of an increase of pension where a person, having made an election in favour of that increase in pension in accordance with regulations made under section 10 of the Pensions Act 2014, which include provision corresponding or similar to provision made by section 8(2) of that Act, changes that election in favour of a lump sum, in accordance with regulations made under section 10 of that Act which include provision corresponding or similar to provision made by regulations made under section 8(7).

(11C)   In sub-paragraph (11A), "lump sum" ("cyfandaliad") means a lump sum under section 8 of the Pensions Act 2014.

(11D)   In sub-paragraph (11B), "lump sum" ("cyfandaliad") means a lump sum under section 10 of the Pensions Act 2014.]

(12)   Sub-paragraph (9) does not apply in respect of any amount of income other than earnings, or earnings of an employed earner, arising out of the applicant's participation in a service user group.

(13)   Where an applicant is in receipt of any benefit under the benefit Acts and the rate of that benefit is altered with effect from a date on or after 1 April in any year but not more than 14 days thereafter, the authority must treat the applicant as possessing such benefit at the altered rate from either 1 April or the first Monday in April in that year, whichever date the authority selects to apply, to the date on which the altered rate is to take effect.

(14)   In the case of an applicant who has, or whose partner has, an award of state pension credit comprising only the savings credit, where the authority treats the applicant as possessing any benefit at the altered rate in accordance with sub-paragraph (13), the authority must–

(a)   determine the income and capital of that applicant in accordance with paragraph 8 (calculation of pensioner's income in savings credit only cases) where the calculation or estimate of that income and capital is altered with effect from a date on or after 1 April in any year but not more than 14 days thereafter; and

(b)   treat that applicant as possessing such income and capital at the altered rate by reference to the date selected by the authority to apply in its area, for the purposes of establishing the period referred to in sub-paragraph (13).

(15)   For the purposes of sub-paragraph (9), a person is not to be regarded as depriving himself or herself of income where–

(a)   that person's rights to benefits under a registered pension scheme are extinguished and in consequence of this that person receives a payment from the scheme, and

(b)   that payment is a trivial commutation lump sum within the meaning given by paragraph 7 of Schedule 29 to the Finance Act 2004.

(16)   In sub-paragraph (15), "registered pension scheme" ("cynllun pensiwn cofrestredig") has the meaning given in section 150(2) of the Finance Act 2004.

Amendment

1.   Amended by reg 5(c) of SI 2016 No 50 (W.21) as from 20.1.16, for schemes made for a financial year starting on or after 1.4.16.

General Note

This paragraph is equivalent to 41 HB(SPC) Regs. See the commentary on that regulation on p789. Under CTR schemes in Wales, it is for the authority to decide whether it takes the annual uprating of benefit into account either from 1 April or the first Monday in April in that year: sub-para (13). For HB, the date used depends on the frequency of rental payments.

Income paid to third parties: pensioners

17.–(1)   Any payment of income, other than a payment specified in sub-paragraph (2) or (3), to a third party in respect of the applicant is to be treated as possessed by the applicant.

(2)   Sub-paragraph (1) does not apply in respect of a payment of income made under an occupational pension scheme, in respect of a pension or other periodical payment made under a personal pension scheme or a payment made by the Board of the Pension Protection Fund where–

(a)   a bankruptcy order has been made in respect of the person in respect of whom the payment has been made or, in Scotland, the estate of that person is subject to sequestration or a judicial factor has been appointed on that person's estate under section 41 of the Solicitors (Scotland) Act 1980;

(b)   the payment is made to the trustee in bankruptcy or any other person acting on behalf of the creditors; and

(c)   the person referred to in paragraph (a) and that person's partner does not possess, or is not treated as possessing, any other income apart from that payment.

(3)   Sub-paragraph (1) does not apply in respect of any payment of income other than earnings, or earnings derived from employment as an employed earner, arising out of the applicant's participation in a service user group.

General Note

This paragraph is equivalent to 42 HB(SPC) Regs. See the commentary on p790.

Calculation of income on a weekly basis: pensioners

18.–(1)   Subject to paragraph 22 (disregard of changes in tax contributions, etc), the income of an applicant is to be calculated on a weekly basis–

(a)   by estimating the amount which is likely to be the applicant's average weekly income in accordance with this Part;

(b)   by adding to that amount the weekly income calculated under paragraph 31 (calculation of tariff income from capital); and

(c)   by then deducting any relevant child care charges to which paragraph 19 (treatment of child care charges) applies from any earnings which form part of the average weekly income or, in a case where the conditions in sub-paragraph (2) are met, from those earnings plus whichever credit specified in paragraph (b) of that sub-paragraph is appropriate, up to a maximum deduction in respect of the applicant's family of whichever of the sums specified in sub-paragraph (3) applies in the applicant's case.

(2)   The conditions of this paragraph are that–

(a)   the applicant's earnings which form part of the applicant's average weekly income are less than the lower of either the applicant's relevant child care charges or whichever of the deductions specified in sub-paragraph (3) otherwise applies in the applicant's case; and

(b)   that applicant or, if the applicant is a member of a couple either the applicant or the applicant's partner, is in receipt of either working tax credit or child tax credit.

(3)   The maximum deduction to which sub-paragraph (1)(c) above refers is to be–

(a)   where the applicant's family includes only one child in respect of whom relevant child care charges are paid, £175 week;

(b)   where the applicant's family includes more than one child in respect of whom relevant child care charges are paid, £300 per week.

General Note
This paragraph equivalent to reg 30 HB(SPC) Regs and is broadly the same as reg 27 HB Regs. See the commentary on p424.

Treatment of child care charges: pensioners
19.–(1)   This paragraph applies where an applicant (within the meaning of this paragraph) is incurring relevant child care charges and–
    (a)   is a lone parent and is engaged in remunerative work;
    (b)   is a member of a couple both of whom are engaged in remunerative work; or
    (c)   is a member of a couple where one member is engaged in remunerative work and the other–
        (i)   is incapacitated;
        (ii)   is an in-patient in hospital; or
        (iii)   is in prison (whether serving a custodial sentence or remanded in custody awaiting trial or sentence).
(2)   For the purposes of sub-paragraph (1) and subject to sub-paragraph (4), a person to whom sub-paragraph (3) applies must be treated as engaged in remunerative work for a period not exceeding 28 weeks during which the person–
    (a)   is paid statutory sick pay;
    (b)   is paid short-term incapacity benefit at the lower rate under sections 30A to 30E of the SSCBA;
    (c)   is paid an employment and support allowance;
    (d)   is paid income support on the grounds of incapacity for work under regulation 4ZA of, and paragraph 7 or 14 of Schedule 1B to, the Income Support (General) Regulations 1987; or
    (e)   is credited with earnings on the grounds of incapacity for work or limited capability for work under regulation 8B of the Social Security (Credits) Regulations 1975.
(3)   This sub-paragraph applies to a person who was engaged in remunerative work immediately before–
    (a)   the first day of the period in respect of which the person was first paid statutory sick pay, short-term incapacity benefit, an employment and support allowance or income support on the grounds of incapacity for work; or
    (b)   the first day of the period in respect of which earnings are credited,
as the case may be.
(4)   In a case to which sub-paragraph (2)(d) or (e) applies, the period of 28 weeks begins on the day on which the person is first paid income support or on the first day of the period in respect of which earnings are credited, as the case may be.
(5)   Relevant child care charges are those charges for care to which sub-paragraphs (6) and (7) apply, and are to be calculated on a weekly basis in accordance with sub-paragraph (10).
(6)   The charges are paid by the applicant for care which is provided–
    (a)   in the case of any child of the applicant's family who is not disabled, in respect of the period beginning on that child's date of birth and ending on the day preceding the first Monday in September following that child's fifteenth birthday; or
    (b)   in the case of any child of the applicant's family who is disabled, in respect of the period beginning on that child's date of birth and ending on the day preceding the first Monday in September following that child's sixteenth birthday.
(7)   The charges are paid for care which is provided by one or more of the care providers listed in sub-paragraph (8) and are not paid–
    (a)   in respect of the child's compulsory education;
    (b)   by an applicant to a partner or by a partner to an applicant in respect of any child for whom either or any of them is responsible in accordance with regulation 7 (circumstances in which a person is treated as responsible or not responsible for another); or
    (c)   in respect of care provided by a relative of the child wholly or mainly in the child's home.
(8)   The care to which sub-paragraph (7) refers may be provided–
    (a)   out of school hours, by a school on school premises or by a local authority–
        (i)   for children who are not disabled in respect of the period beginning on their eighth birthday and ending on the day preceding the first Monday in September following their fifteenth birthday; or
        (ii)   for children who are disabled in respect of the period beginning on their eighth birthday and ending on the day preceding the first Monday in September following their sixteenth birthday; or
    (b)   by a child care provider approved in accordance with the Tax Credit (New Category of Child Care Provider) Regulations 1999; or
    (c)   by persons registered under Part 2 of the Children and Families (Wales) Measure 2010; or
    (d)   by a person who is excepted from registration under Part 2 of the Children and Families (Wales) Measure 2010 because the child care that person provides is in a school or establishment referred to in article 11, 12 or 14 of the Child Minding and Day Care Exceptions (Wales) Order 2010; or
    (e)   by–
        (i)   persons registered under section 59(1) of the Public Services Reform (Scotland) Act 2010; or

(ii)   local authorities registered under section 83(1) of that Act,

where the care provided is child minding or day care of children within the meaning of that Act; or

(f)   by a person prescribed in regulations made pursuant to section 12(4) of the Tax Credits Act 2002; or

(g)   by a person who is registered under Chapter 2 or 3 of Part 3 of the Childcare Act 2006;or

(h)   by any of the schools mentioned in section 34(2) of the Childcare Act 2006 in circumstances where the requirement to register under Chapter 2 of Part 3 of that Act does not apply by virtue of section 34(2) of that Act; or

(i)   by any of the schools mentioned in section 53(2) of the Childcare Act 2006 in circumstances where the requirement to register under Chapter 3 of Part 3 of that Act does not apply by virtue of section 53(2) of that Act; or

(j)   by any of the establishments mentioned in section 18(5) of the Childcare Act 2006 in circumstances where the care is not included in the meaning of "childcare" for the purposes of Part 1 and Part 3 of that Act by virtue of section 18(5) of that Act; or

(k)   by a foster parent or kinship carer under the Fostering Services (England) Regulations 2011, the [⁵ Fostering Services (Wales) Regulations 2003 or any regulations made under sections 87 and 93 of the Social Services and Well-being (Wales) Act 2014 which make provision for the approval of local authority foster parents] or the Looked After Children (Scotland) Regulations 2009 in relation to a child other than one whom the foster parent is fostering or kinship carer is looking after; or

[⁴ (l)   by a person who is employed, or engaged under a contract for services, to provide care and support by the provider of a domiciliary support service, within the meaning of Part 1 of the Regulation and Inspection of Social Care (Wales) Act 2016;] or

(m)   by a person who is not a relative of the child wholly or mainly in the child's home.

(9)   In sub-paragraphs (6) and (8)(a), "the first Monday in September" ("y dydd Llun cyntaf ym Medi") means the Monday which first occurs in the month of September in any year.

(10)   Relevant child care charges must be estimated over such period, not exceeding a year, as is appropriate in order that the average weekly charge may be estimated accurately having regard to information as to the amount of that charge provided by the child minder or person providing the care.

(11)   For the purposes of sub-paragraph (1)(c) the other member of a couple is incapacitated where–

(a)   the applicant is a pensioner and the other member of the couple is aged not less than 80;

(b)   the applicant is a pensioner and the other member of the couple is aged less than 80, and–

(i)   an additional condition specified in paragraph 20 (additional condition for the disability premium) is treated as applying in the other member of the couple's case; and

(ii)   the other member of the couple satisfies those conditions or would satisfy them but for that member of the couple being treated as capable of work by virtue of a determination made in accordance with regulations made under section 171E of the SSCBA;

(c)   the applicant's applicable amount would include the support component or the work-related activity component on account of the other member having limited capability for work [⁴ or the other member of the couple would be a member of the work-related activity group] but for that other member being treated as not having limited capability for work by virtue of a determination made in accordance with the Employment and Support Allowance Regulations 2008 [² or the Employment and Support Allowance Regulations 2013];

(d)   the applicant is, or is treated as, incapable of work and has been so incapable, or has been so treated as incapable, of work in accordance with the provisions of, and regulations made under, Part 12A of the SSCBA (incapacity for work) for a continuous period of not less than 196 days; and for this purpose any two or more separate periods separated by a break of not more than 56 days must be treated as one continuous period;

(e)   the applicant has, or is treated as having, limited capability for work and has had, or been treated as having, limited capability for work in accordance with the Employment and Support Allowance Regulations 2008 [² or the Employment and Support Allowance Regulations 2013] for a continuous period of not less than 196 days and for this purpose any two or more separate periods separated by a break of not more than 84 days must be treated as one continuous period;

(f)   there is payable in respect of the other member one or more of the following pensions or allowances–

(i)   long-term incapacity benefit or short-term incapacity benefit at the higher rate under Schedule 4 to the SSCBA;

(ii)   attendance allowance under section 64 of the SSCBA;

(iii)   severe disablement allowance under section 68 of the SSCBA;

(iv)   disability living allowance under section 71 of the SSCBA;

(v)   personal independence payment under Part 4 of the Welfare Reform Act 2012;

(vi)   an AFIP;

(vii)   increase of disablement pension under section 104 of the SSCBA;

(viii)   a pension increase paid as part of a war disablement pension or under an industrial injuries scheme which is analogous to an allowance or increase of disablement pension under sub-paragraph (ii), (iv), (v) or (vi) above;

(ix)   main phase employment and support allowance;

(g)   a pension or allowance to which sub-paragraph (vi) or (vii) of paragraph (f) refers was payable on account of the other member's incapacity but has ceased to be payable in consequence of that other member becoming a patient, which in this paragraph means a person (other than a person who is serving a sentence of imprisonment or detention in a youth custody institution) who is regarded as receiving free in-patient treatment within the meaning of regulation 2(4) and (5) of the Social Security (Hospital In-Patients) Regulations 2005;

(h)   an attendance allowance under section 64 of the SSCBA or disability living allowance under section 71 of that Act would be payable to that person but for–

    (i)   a suspension of benefit in accordance with regulations under section 113(2) of the SSCBA; or .

    (ii)   an abatement as a consequence of hospitalisation;

(i)   the daily living component of personal independence payment would be payable to that person but for a suspension of benefit in accordance with regulations under section 86 of the Welfare Reform Act 2012 (hospital in-patients);

(j)   an AFIP would be payable to that person but for a suspension of payment in accordance with any terms of the armed and reserve forces compensation scheme which allow for a suspension because a person is undergoing medical treatment in a hospital or similar institution;

(k)   paragraph (f), (g), (h) or (i) would apply to the other member if the legislative provisions referred to in those paragraphs were provisions under any corresponding enactment having effect in Northern Ireland; or

(l)   the other member has an invalid carriage or other vehicle provided to the other member by the Secretary of State under paragraph 9 of Schedule 1 to the National Health Service Act 2006 or under section 46 of the National Health Service (Scotland) Act 1978, or provided by the Department of Health, Social Services and Public Safety in Northern Ireland under article 30(1) of the Health and Personal Social Services (Northern Ireland) Order 1972, or provided by the Welsh Ministers under section 5 of, and Schedule 1 to the National Health Service (Wales) Act 2006.

(12)   For the purposes of sub-paragraph (11), once sub-paragraph (11)(d) applies to the applicant, if the applicant then ceases, for a period of 56 days or less, to be incapable, or to be treated as incapable, of work, that sub-paragraph is, on the applicant again becoming so incapable, or so treated as incapable, of work at the end of that period, to immediately thereafter apply to the applicant for so long as the applicant remains incapable, or is treated as remaining incapable, of work.

(13)   For the purposes of sub-paragraph (11), once sub-paragraph (11)(e) applies to the applicant, if the applicant then ceases, for a period of 84 days or less, to have, or to be treated as having, limited capability for work, that sub-paragraph is, on the applicant again having, or being treated as having limited capability for work at the end of that period, immediately thereafter to apply to the applicant for so long as the applicant has, or is treated as having, limited capability for work.

(14)   For the purposes of sub-paragraphs (6) and (8)(a), a person is disabled if that person is a person–

(a)   to whom an attendance allowance or the care component of disability allowance is payable or would be payable but for–

    (i)   a suspension of benefit in accordance with regulations under section 113(2) of the SSCBA; or

    (ii)   an abatement as a consequence of hospitalisation;

(b)   to whom the daily living component of personal independence payment is payable or would be payable but for a suspension of benefit in accordance with regulations under section 86 of the Welfare Reform Act 2012 (hospital in-patients);

[³ (c)   who–

    (i)   is registered as blind in a register compiled under section 29 of the National Assistance Act 1948 (welfare services);

    (ii)   is registered as severely sight-impaired in a register established and maintained by a local authority under section 18(1) of the Social Services and Well-being (Wales) Act 2014;

    (iii)   is registered as severely sight-impaired in a register established and maintained by a local authority under section 77(1) of the Care Act 2014; or

    (iv)   in Scotland, has been certified as blind and in consequence that person is registered as blind in a register maintained by or on behalf of a council constituted under section 2 of the [¹ Local Government etc. (Scotland) Act 1994];]

(d)   who ceased to be registered as blind [³ or severely sight-impaired] in such a register within the period beginning 28 weeks before the first Monday in September following that person's fifteenth birthday and ending on the day preceding that person's sixteenth birthday; or

(e)   to whom AFIP is payable.

(15)   For the purposes of sub-paragraph (1) a person on maternity leave, paternity leave [², shared parental leave] or adoption leave is to be treated as if engaged in remunerative work for the period specified in sub-paragraph (16) ("the relevant period") provided that–

(a)   in the week before the period of maternity leave, paternity leave [², shared parental leave] or adoption leave began the person was in remunerative work;

(b)   the person is incurring relevant child care charges within the meaning of sub-paragraph (5); and

(c)   the person is entitled to either statutory maternity pay under section 164 of the SSCBA, [²] statutory paternity pay by virtue of section 171ZA or 171ZB of that Act, additional statutory paternity pay by virtue of section 171ZEA or 171ZEB of that Act, statutory adoption pay by virtue of section 171ZL of that Act, maternity allowance under section 35 of that Act [², statutory shared parental pay by virtue of section 171ZU or 171ZV of that Act] or qualifying support.

(16)   For the purposes of sub-paragraph (15) the relevant period begins on the day on which the person's maternity leave, paternity leave [², shared parental leave] or adoption leave commences and ends on–
(a)   the date that leave ends;
(b)   if no child care element of working tax credit is in payment on the date that entitlement to maternity allowance, qualifying support (if relevant), statutory maternity pay, [²] statutory paternity pay [², statutory shared parental pay] or statutory adoption pay ends, the date that entitlement ends; or
(c)   if a child care element of working tax credit is in payment on the date that entitlement to maternity allowance or qualifying support, statutory maternity pay, [²]statutory paternity pay [², statutory shared parental pay] or statutory adoption pay ends, the date that entitlement to that award of the child care element of the working tax credit ends;
whichever occurs first.
(17)   In sub-paragraphs (15) and (16)–
(a)   "qualifying support" ("cymhorthdal cymwys") means income support to which that person is entitled by virtue of paragraph 14B of Schedule 1B to the Income Support (General) Regulations 1987; and
(b)   "child care element" ("elfen gofal plant") of working tax credit means the element of working tax credit prescribed under section 12 of the Tax Credits Act 2002 (child care element).
(18)   In this paragraph "applicant" ("ceisydd") does not include an applicant–
(a)   who has, or
(b)   who (jointly with a partner) has,
an award of universal credit.

Amendments
1.   Amended by reg 6(e) of SI 2014 No 66 (W.6) as from 15.1.14.
2.   Amended by reg 7(e) of SI 2015 No 44 (W.3) as from 21.1.15, for schemes made for a financial year starting on or after 1.4.15.
3.   Amended by reg 5(d) of SI 2016 No 50 (W.21) as from 20.1.16, for schemes made for a financial year starting on or after 1.4.16.
4.   Amended by reg 4(d) of SI 2018 No 14 (W.7) as from 10.1.18, for schemes made for a financial year starting on or after 1.4.18.
5.   Amended by reg 3(b) of SI 2019 No 11 (W.5) as from 9.1.19, for schemes made for a financial year starting on or after 1.4.19.

General Note
This paragraph is almost the same as reg 28 HB Regs. See p429 for commentary on reg 28 but note that there is no equivalent to reg 28(11)(a) and (b) in this paragraph, and that sub-paras (11)(c), (11)(f)(viii) and (g) and (14) are slightly different to their HB counterparts. For commentary on the need to register as blind or severely sight impaired to satisfy sub-para (14)(c), see the General Note to Sch 2 para 6 (p1248).

Sub-para (18) states that this para does not apply if an applicant has an award of UC or a joint award with her/his partner, but such an applicant would not come within the definition of pensioner by virtue of reg 3(a)(ii)(bb).

Additional condition referred to in paragraph 19(11)(b)(i): disability : pensioners
20.–(1)   Subject to sub-paragraph (2), the additional condition referred to in paragraph 19(11)(b)(i) is that either–
(a)   the applicant or, as the case may be, the applicant's partner–
(i)   is in receipt of one or more of the following benefits: attendance allowance, disability living allowance, personal independence payment, an AFIP, the disability element or the severe disability element of working tax credit as specified in regulation 20(1)(b) and (f) of the Working Tax Credit (Entitlement and Maximum Rate) Regulations 2002, mobility supplement, long-term incapacity benefit under Part 2 of the SSCBA or severe disablement allowance under Part 3 of that Act but, in the case of long-term incapacity benefit or severe disablement allowance, only where it is paid in respect of the applicant; or
(ii)   was in receipt of long-term incapacity benefit under Part 2 of the SSCBA when entitlement to that benefit ceased on account of the payment of a retirement pension under that Act [¹ or a state pension under Part 1 of the Pensions Act 2014] and the applicant has since remained continuously entitled to council tax benefit (for the period prior to 1 April 2013) or a reduction under an authority's scheme (for the period after 1 April 2013) and, if the long-term incapacity benefit was payable to the applicant's partner, the partner is still a member of the family; or
(iii)   was in receipt of attendance allowance or disability living allowance but payment of benefit has been suspended in accordance with regulations made under section 113(2) of the SSCBA or otherwise abated as a consequence of the applicant or the applicant's partner becoming a patient within the meaning of paragraph 19(11)(g) (treatment of child care charges); or

       (iv)   was in receipt of personal independence payment, but payment of that benefit has been suspended in accordance with section 86 of the Welfare Reform Act 2012 as a consequence of the applicant becoming a patient within the meaning of paragraph19(11)(g) (treatment of child care charges); or

       (v)   was in receipt of an AFIP but its payment has been suspended in accordance with any terms of the armed and reserve forces compensation scheme which allow for a suspension because a person is undergoing medical treatment in a hospital or similar institution; or

       (vi)   is provided by the Secretary of State or a clinical commissioning group with an invalid carriage or other vehicle under paragraph 9 of Schedule 1 to the National Health Service Act 2006 or, in Scotland, under section 46 of the National Health Service (Scotland) Act 1978 (provision of services by Scottish Ministers), or in Wales, under section 5 and Schedule 1 to the National Health Service (Wales) Act 2006, or in Northern Ireland, is provided with an invalid carriage or other vehicle by the Department of Health, Social Services and Public Safety under article 30(1) of the Health and Personal Social Services (Northern Ireland) Order 1972, or receives payments by way of grant from the Secretary of State under paragraph 10(3) of Schedule 1 to the Act of 2006 (provision of vehicles for disabled persons) or, in Scotland, by Scottish Ministers under section 46 of the Act of 1978; or

      [1 (vii)   is blind or severely sight-impaired and in consequence is registered in a register compiled under section 29 of the National Assistance Act 1948 (welfare services), or is registered as severely sight-impaired in a register established and maintained by a local authority under section 18(1) of the Social Services and Well-being (Wales) Act 2014 or section 77(1) of the Care Act 2014, or, in Scotland has been certified as blind and in consequence is registered in a register maintained by or on behalf of a council constituted under section 2 of the Local Government etc. (Scotland) Act 1994; or]

   (b)   the applicant–

       (i)   is, or is treated as, incapable of work in accordance with the provisions of, and regulations made under, Part 12A of the SSCBA (incapacity for work); and

       (ii)   has been incapable, or has been treated as incapable, of work for a continuous period of not less than–

          (aa)   in the case of an applicant who is terminally ill within the meaning of section 30B(4) of the SSCBA, 196 days;

          (bb)   in any other case, 364 days.

   (2)   For the purposes of sub-paragraph (1)(a)(vii), a person who has ceased to be registered as blind [1 or severely sight-impaired] on that person regaining that person's eyesight is nevertheless to be treated as blind [1 or severely sight-impaired] and as satisfying the additional condition set out in that sub-paragraph for a period of 28 weeks following the date on which that person ceased to be so registered.

   (3)   For the purposes of sub-paragraph (1)(b), where any two or more periods of incapacity are separated by a break of not more than 56 days, those periods must be treated as one continuous period.

   (4)   For the purposes of this paragraph, a reference to a person who is or was in receipt of long-term incapacity benefit includes a person who is or was in receipt of short-term incapacity benefit at a rate equal to the long-term rate by virtue of section 30B(4)(a) of the SSCBA (short-term incapacity benefit for a person who is terminally ill), or who would be or would have been in receipt of short-term incapacity benefit at such a rate but for the fact that the rate of short-term incapacity benefit already payable to the person is or was equal to or greater than the long term rate.

   (5)   In the case of an applicant who is a welfare to work beneficiary (a person to whom regulation 13A(1) of the Social Security (Incapacity for Work) (General) Regulations 1995 applies, and who again becomes incapable of work for the purposes of Part 12A of the SSCBA) the reference to a period of 56 days in sub-paragraph (3) must be treated as a reference to a period of 104 weeks.

Amendment

   1.   Amended by reg 5(e) of SI 2016 No 50 (W.21) as from 20.1.16, for schemes made for a financial year starting on or after 1.4.16.

General Note

This paragraph is similar to Sch 3 para 13 HB Regs (which describes the additional conditions for the disability premium). See p638 for commentary. Here, it defines when someone can be treated as incapacitated under para 19(11)(b) for the purpose of child care charges. For commentary on the need to register as blind or severely sight impaired to satisfy sub-para (1)(a)(vii), see the General Note to Sch 2 para 6 (p1248).

Calculations of average weekly income from tax credits

   21.–(1)   This paragraph applies where an applicant receives a tax credit.

   (2)   Where this paragraph applies, the period over which a tax credit is to be taken into account must be the period set out in sub-paragraph (3).

   (3)   Where the instalment in respect of which payment of a tax credit is made is–

   (a)   a daily instalment, the period is 1 day, being the day in respect of which the instalment is paid;

(b)   a weekly instalment, the period is 7 days, ending on the day on which the instalment is due to be paid;

(c)   a two weekly instalment, the period is 14 days, commencing 6 days before the day on which the instalment is due to be paid;

(d)   a four weekly instalment, the period is 28 days, ending on the day on which the instalment is due to be paid.

(4)   For the purposes of this paragraph "tax credit" ("credyd treth") means child tax credit or working tax credit.

General Note

This paragraph mirrors reg 32 HB Regs. See p435 for commentary.

Disregard of changes in tax, contributions etc

22.–(1)   In calculating the applicant's income an authority may disregard any legislative change–

(a)   in the basic or other rates of income tax;

(b)   in the amount of any personal tax [² reliefs under Chapters 2, 3 and 3A of Part 3 of the Income Tax Act 2007];

(c)   in the rates of social security contributions payable under the SSCBA or in the lower earnings limit or upper earnings limit for Class 1 contributions under that Act, the lower or upper limits applicable to Class 4 contributions under that Act or the amount specified in section 11(4) of that Act ([¹ small profits threshold] in relation to Class 2 contributions);

(d)   in the amount of tax payable as a result of an increase in the weekly rate of Category A, B, C or D retirement pension or any addition thereto or any graduated pension payable under the SSCBA [¹ or a state pension under Part 1 of the Pensions Act 2014];

(e)   in the maximum rate of child tax credit or working tax credit,

for a period not exceeding 30 reduction weeks beginning with the reduction week immediately following the date from which the change is effective.

Amendments

1.   Amended by reg 5(f) of SI 2016 No 50 (W.21) as from 20.1.16, for schemes made for a financial year starting on or after 1.4.16.

2.   Substituted by reg 3(d) of SI 2017 No 46 (W.20) as from 19.1.17, for schemes made for a financial year starting on or after 1.4.17.

General Note

This paragraph is almost identical to reg 34 HB Regs. See p437 for commentary.

Calculation of net profit of self-employed earners

23.–(1)   For the purposes of paragraph 18 (calculation of income on a weekly basis) the earnings of an applicant to be taken into account are–

(a)   in the case of a self-employed earner who is engaged in employment on that person's own account, the net profit derived from that employment;

(b)   in the case of a self-employed earner who is a pensioner whose employment is carried on in partnership, that person's share of the net profit derived from that employment, less–

    (i)   an amount in respect of income tax and of social security contributions payable under the SSCBA calculated in accordance with paragraph 24 (calculation of deduction of tax and contributions of self-employed earners); and

    (ii)   one-half of the amount calculated in accordance with sub-paragraph (11) in respect of any qualifying premium.

(2)   For the purposes of sub-paragraph (1)(a) the net profit of the employment must, except where sub-paragraph (8) applies, be calculated by taking into account the earnings of the employment over the assessment period less–

(a)   subject to sub-paragraphs (4) to (7), any expenses wholly and exclusively incurred in that period for the purposes of that employment;

(b)   an amount in respect of–

    (i)   income tax; and

    (ii)   social security contributions payable under the SSCBA,

    calculated in accordance with paragraph 24 (calculation of deduction of tax and contributions of self-employed earners); and

(c)   one-half of the amount calculated in accordance with sub-paragraph (10) in respect of any qualifying premium.

(3)   For the purposes of sub-paragraph (1)(b) the net profit of the employment is to be calculated by taking into account the earnings of the employment over the assessment period less, subject to sub-paragraphs (4) to (7), any expenses wholly and exclusively incurred in that period for the purposes of the employment.

(4)   Subject to sub-paragraph (5), no deduction is to be made under paragraph (2)(a) or (3), in respect of–

    (a)   any capital expenditure;

    (b)   the depreciation of any capital asset;

    (c)   any sum employed or intended to be employed in the setting up or expansion of the employment;

    (d)   any loss incurred before the beginning of the assessment period;

    (e)   the repayment of capital on any loan taken out for the purposes of the employment; and

    (f)   any expenses incurred in providing business entertainment.

    (5)   A deduction is to be made under sub-paragraph (2)(a) or (3) in respect of the repayment of capital on any loan used for–

    (a)   the replacement in the course of business of equipment or machinery; or

    (b)   the repair of an existing business asset except to the extent that any sum is payable under an insurance policy for its repair.

    (6)   The authority must refuse to make a deduction in respect of any expenses under sub-paragraph (2)(a) or (3) where it is not satisfied given the nature and the amount of the expense that it has been reasonably incurred.

    (7)   For the avoidance of doubt–

    (a)   a deduction must not be made under sub-paragraph (2)(a) or (3) in respect of any sum unless it has been expended for the purposes of the business;

    (b)   a deduction must be made thereunder in respect of–

        (i)   the excess of any value added tax paid over value added tax received in the assessment period;

        (ii)   any income expended in the repair of an existing business asset except to the extent that any sum is payable under an insurance policy for its repair;

        (iii)   any payment of interest on a loan taken out for the purposes of the employment.

    (8)   Where an applicant is engaged in employment as a child minder the net profit of the employment is to be one-third of the earnings of that employment, less–

    (a)   an amount in respect of–

        (i)   income tax; and

        (ii)   social security contributions payable under the SSCBA,

calculated in accordance with paragraph 24 (calculation of deduction of tax and contributions for self-employed earners); and

    (b)   one-half of the amount calculated in accordance with sub-paragraph (10) in respect of any qualifying premium.

    (9)   For the avoidance of doubt where an applicant is engaged in employment as a self-employed earner and the applicant is also engaged in one or more other employments as a self-employed or employed earner any loss incurred in any one of the applicant's employments must not be offset against the applicant's earnings in any other of the applicant's employments.

    (10)   The amount in respect of any qualifying premium is to be calculated by multiplying the daily amount of the qualifying premium by the number equal to the number of days in the assessment period; and for the purposes of this paragraph the daily amount of the qualifying premium must be determined–

    (a)   where the qualifying premium is payable monthly, by multiplying the amount of the qualifying premium by 12 and dividing the product by 365;

    (b)   in any other case, by dividing the amount of the qualifying premium by the number equal to the number of days in the period to which the qualifying premium relates.

    (11)   In this paragraph, "qualifying premium" ("premiwm cymwys") means any premium which is payable periodically in respect of a personal pension scheme and is so payable on or after the date of application.

General Note

This paragraph is broadly the same as reg 38 HB Regs. See p447 for commentary on reg 38 but note the difference between reg 38(1)(b) and sub-para (1)(b) above, and that there is no equivalent to reg 38(2) or 38(5)(g) in this paragraph.

Calculation of deduction of tax and contributions of self-employed earners

    24.–(1)   The amount to be deducted in respect of income tax under paragraph 23(1)(b)(i), (2)(b)(i) or (8)(a)(i) (calculation of net profit of self-employed earners) must be calculated–

    (a)   on the basis of the amount of chargeable income, and

    (b)   as if that income were assessable to income tax at the basic rate of tax applicable to the assessment period less only the [³ personal reliefs to which the applicant is entitled under Chapters 2, 3 and 3A of Part 3] of the Income Tax Act 2007 as is appropriate to the applicant's circumstances.

    (2)   But, if the assessment period is less than a year, the earnings to which the basic rate of tax is to be applied and the amount of the personal reliefs deductible under this paragraph must be calculated on a pro rata basis.

    (3)   The amount to be deducted in respect of social security contributions under paragraph 23(1)(b)(i), (2)(b)(ii) or (8)(a)(ii) is the total of–

    (a)   the amount of Class 2 contributions payable under section 11(1) or, as the case may be, 11(3) of the SSCBA at the rate applicable to the assessment period except where the applicant's chargeable income is less than the amount specified in section 11(4) of that Act ([² small profits threshold]) for the tax year applicable to the assessment period; but if the assessment period is less than a year, the amount specified for that tax year must be reduced pro rata; and

(b)   the amount of Class 4 contributions (if any) which would be payable under section 15 of the SSCBA (Class 4 contributions recoverable under the Income Tax Acts) at the percentage rate applicable to the assessment period on so much of the chargeable income as exceeds the lower limit but does not exceed the upper limit of profits and gains applicable for the tax year applicable to the assessment period; but if the assessment period is less than a year, those limits must be reduced pro rata.

(4)   In this paragraph "chargeable income" ("incwm trethadwy") means–

(a)   except where paragraph (b) applies, the earnings derived from the employment less any expenses deducted under [¹ paragraph 23(2)(a) or, as the case may be, paragraph 23(3)];

(b)   in the case of employment as a child minder, one-third of the earnings of that employment.

Amendments

1.   Amended by reg 6(f) of SI 2014 No 66 (W.6) as from 15.1.14.
2.   Amended by reg 5(g) of SI 2016 No 50 a(W.21) s from 20.1.16, for schemes made for a financial year starting on or after 1.4.16.
3.   Amended by reg 3(e) of SI 2017 No 46 (W.20) as from 19.1.17. for schemes made for a financial year starting on or after 1.4.17.

General Note

This paragraph is equivalent to reg 39 HB Regs. See p450 for commentary.

CHAPTER 4
Capital

Calculation of Capital

25.–(1)   The capital of an applicant to be taken into account must be, subject to sub-paragraph (2), the whole of the applicant's capital calculated in accordance with this Part.

(2)   There must be disregarded from the calculation of an applicant's capital under sub-paragraph (1), any capital, where applicable, specified in Schedule 5 (capital disregards), in relation to pensioners.

(3)   In the case of an applicant who is a pensioner, the applicant's capital is to be treated as including any payment made to the applicant by way of arrears of–

(a)   child tax credit;
(b)   working tax credit;
(c)   state pension credit,

if the payment was made in respect of a period for the whole or part of which a reduction under an authority's scheme was allowed before those arrears were paid.

General Note

This paragraph is similar to reg 44 HB(SPC) Regs. See p790 for commentary.

Calculation of capital in the United Kingdom

26.   Capital which an applicant possesses in the United Kingdom is to be calculated at its current market or surrender value less–

(a)   where there would be expenses attributable to the sale, 10 per cent; and
(b)   the amount of any encumbrance secured on it.

General Note

This paragraph is equivalent to reg 47 HB Regs. See p465 for commentary.

Calculation of capital outside the United Kingdom

27.   Capital which an applicant possesses in a country outside the United Kingdom is to be calculated–

(a)   in a case where there is no prohibition in that country against the transfer to the United Kingdom of an amount equal to its current market or surrender value in that country, at that value;
(b)   in a case where there is such a prohibition, at the price which it would realise if sold in the United Kingdom to a willing buyer,

less, where there would be expenses attributable to sale, 10 per cent and the amount of any encumbrances secured on it.

General Note

This paragraph is equivalent to reg 48 HB Regs. See p466 for commentary.

Notional capital

28.–(1)   An applicant is to be treated as possessing capital of which the applicant has deprived himself or herself for the purpose of securing entitlement to a reduction or increasing the amount of that reduction except to the extent that that capital is reduced in accordance with paragraph 29 (diminishing notional capital rule).

(2)   An applicant who is a pensioner who disposes of capital for the purpose of–
(a)   reducing or paying a debt owed by the applicant; or
(b)   purchasing goods or services if the expenditure was reasonable in the circumstances of the applicant's case,
is to be regarded as not depriving himself or herself of it.

(3)   Where an applicant stands in relation to a company in a position analogous to that of a sole owner or partner in the business of that company, the applicant may be treated as if the applicant were such sole owner or partner and in such a case–
(a)   the value of the applicant's holding in that company must, notwithstanding paragraph 25 (calculation of capital) be disregarded; and
(b)   the applicant must, subject to sub-paragraph (4), be treated as possessing an amount of capital equal to the value or, as the case may be, the applicant's share of the value of the capital of that company and the foregoing provisions of this Chapter apply for the purposes of calculating that amount as if it were actual capital which the applicant does possess.

(4)   For so long as the applicant undertakes activities in the course of the business of the company, the amount which the applicant is treated as possessing under sub-paragraph (3) is to be disregarded.

(5)   Where an applicant is treated as possessing capital under sub-paragraph (1), the foregoing provisions of this Chapter apply for the purposes of calculating its amount as if it were actual capital which the applicant does possess.

General Note
Sub-para (1) is equivalent to reg 49(1) HB Regs and sub-paras (3) to (5) are equivalent to reg 49(5) to (7). See p468 for commentary. Sub-para (2) is equivalent to reg 47(2) HB(SPC) Regs (see p791 for commentary).

Diminishing notional capital rule: pensioners

29.–(1)   Where an applicant who is a pensioner is treated as possessing capital under paragraph 28(1) (notional capital), the amount which the applicant is treated as possessing–
(a)   in the case of a week that is subsequent to–
  (i)   the relevant week in respect of which the conditions set out in sub-paragraph (2) are satisfied; or
  (ii)   a week which follows that relevant week and which satisfies those conditions,
  is to be reduced by an amount determined under sub-paragraph (3);
(b)   in the case of a week in respect of which sub-paragraph (1)(a) does not apply but where–
  (i)   that week is a week subsequent to the relevant week; and
  (ii)   that relevant week is a week in which the condition in sub-paragraph (4) is satisfied,
  is to be reduced by the amount determined under sub-paragraph (5).

(2)   This sub-paragraph applies to a reduction week where the applicant satisfies the conditions that–
(a)   the applicant is in receipt of a reduction in council tax under an authority's scheme; and
(b)   but for paragraph 28(1), the applicant would have received a greater reduction in council tax under an authority's scheme in that week.

(3)   In a case to which sub-paragraph (2) applies, the amount of the reduction in the amount of capital the applicant is treated as possessing for the purposes of sub-paragraph (1)(a) must be equal to the aggregate of–
(a)   an amount equal to the additional amount of the reduction in council tax to which sub-paragraph (2)(b) refers;
(b)   where the applicant has also claimed state pension credit, the amount of any state pension credit or any additional amount of state pension credit to which the applicant would have been entitled in respect of the reduction week to which sub-paragraph (2) refers but for the application of regulation 21(1) of the State Pension Credit Regulations 2002 (notional capital);
(c)   where the applicant has also claimed housing benefit, the amount of any housing benefit or any additional amount of housing benefit to which the applicant would have been entitled in respect of the whole or part of the reduction week to which sub-paragraph (2) refers but for the application of regulation 47(1) of the Housing Benefit (Persons who have attained the qualifying age for state pension credit) Regulations 2006 (notional capital);
(d)   where the applicant has also claimed a jobseeker's allowance, the amount of an income-based jobseeker's allowance to which the applicant would have been entitled in respect of the reduction week to which sub-paragraph (2) refers but for the application of regulation 113 of the Jobseeker's Allowance Regulations 1996 (notional capital); and
(e)   where the applicant has also claimed an employment and support allowance, the amount of an income related employment and support allowance to which the applicant would have been entitled in respect of the reduction week to which sub-paragraph (2) refers but for the application of regulation 115 of the Employment and Support Allowance Regulations 2008 (notional capital).

(4)   Subject to sub-paragraph (7), for the purposes of sub-paragraph (1)(b) the condition is that the applicant is a pensioner and would have been entitled to a reduction in council tax under an authority's scheme in the relevant week but for paragraph 28(1).

(5)   In such a case the amount of the reduction in the amount of capital the applicant is treated as possessing for the purposes of sub-paragraph (1)(b) is equal to the aggregate of–

(a)   the amount of the reduction in council tax to which the applicant would have been entitled in the relevant week but for paragraph 28(1);

(b)   if the applicant would, but for regulation 21 of the State Pension Credit Regulations 2002, have been entitled to state pension credit in respect of the benefit week, within the meaning of regulation 1(2) of those Regulations (interpretation), which includes the last day of the relevant week, the amount to which the applicant would have been entitled;

(c)   if the applicant would, but for regulation 47(1) of the Housing Benefit (Persons who have attained the qualifying age for state pension credit) Regulations 2006, have been entitled to housing benefit or to an additional amount of housing benefit in respect of the benefit week which includes the last day of the relevant week, the amount which is equal to–

    (i)   in a case where no housing benefit is payable, the amount to which the applicant would have been entitled; or

    (ii)   in any other case, the amount equal to the additional amount of housing benefit to which the applicant would have been entitled;

(d)   if the applicant would, but for regulation 113 of the Jobseeker's Allowance Regulations 1996, have been entitled to an income-based jobseeker's allowance in respect of the benefit week, within the meaning of regulation 1(3) of those Regulations (interpretation), which includes the last day of the relevant week, the amount to which the applicant would have been entitled; and

(e)   if the applicant would, but for regulation 115 of the Employment and Support Allowance Regulations 2008, have been entitled to an income-related employment and support allowance in respect of the benefit week, within the meaning of regulation 2(1) of those Regulations (interpretation), which includes the last day of the relevant week, the amount to which the applicant would have been entitled.

(6)   But if the amount mentioned in paragraph (a), (b), (c), (d) or (e) of sub-paragraph (5) ("the relevant amount") is in respect of a part-week, the amount that is to be taken into account under that paragraph is to be determined by–

(a)   dividing the relevant amount by the number equal to the number of days in that part-week, and

(b)   multiplying the result of that calculation by 7.

(7)   The amount determined under sub-paragraph (5) is to be re-determined under that sub-paragraph if the applicant makes a further application for a reduction in council tax and the conditions in sub-paragraph (8) are satisfied, and in such a case–

(a)   paragraphs (a) to (e) of sub-paragraph (5) apply as if for the words "relevant week" there were substituted the words "relevant subsequent week"; and

(b)   subject to sub-paragraph (9), the amount as re-determined has effect from the first week following the relevant subsequent week in question.

(8)   The conditions are that–

(a)   a further application is made 26 or more weeks after–

    (i)   the date on which the applicant made an application for a reduction in council tax in respect of which the applicant was first treated as possessing the capital in question under paragraph 28(1);

    (ii)   in a case where there has been at least one re-determination in accordance with sub-paragraph (7), the date on which the applicant last made an application for a reduction in council tax which resulted in the weekly amount being re-determined, or

    (iii)   the date on which the applicant last ceased to be entitled to a reduction in council tax under the authority's scheme,

    whichever last occurred; and

(b)   the applicant would have been entitled to a reduction in council tax under an authority's scheme but for paragraph 28(1).

(9)   The amount as re-determined pursuant to sub-paragraph (7) must not have effect if it is less than the amount which applied in that case immediately before the re-determination and in such a case the higher amount must continue to have effect.

(10)   For the purposes of this paragraph–

"part-week" ("rhan-wythnos")–

(a)   in relation to an amount mentioned in sub-paragraph (5)(a), means a period of less than a week for which a reduction in council tax under an authority's scheme is allowed;

(b)   in relation to an amount mentioned in sub-paragraph (5)(b), means a period of less than a week for which housing benefit is payable;

(c)   in relation to an amount mentioned in sub-paragraph (5)(c), (d) or (e), means–

    (i)   a period of less than a week which is the whole period for which income support, an income-related employment and support allowance or, as the case may be, an income-based jobseeker's allowance is payable; and

    (ii)   any other period of less than a week for which it is payable;

"relevant week" ("wythnos berthnasol") means the reduction week or part-week in which the capital in question of which the applicant has deprived himself or herself within the meaning of paragraph 28(1)–

(a)   was first taken into account for the purpose of determining the applicant's entitlement to a reduction under an authority's scheme; or

(b)   was taken into account on a subsequent occasion for the purpose of determining or re-determining the applicant's entitlement to a reduction on that subsequent occasion and that determination or redetermination resulted in the applicant beginning to receive, or ceasing to receive, a reduction under an authority's scheme;

and where more than one reduction week is identified by reference to paragraphs (a) and (b)of this definition, the later or latest such reduction week or, as the case may be, the later or latest such part-week is the relevant week;

"relevant subsequent week" ("wythnos ddilynol berthnasol") means the reduction week or part-week which includes the day on which the further application or, if more than one further application has been made, the last such application was made.

General Note

This is broadly equivalent to reg 50 HB Regs. The differences between the two provisions are due to the fact that this paragraph applies to pensioners and so sub-paras (3) and (5) are slightly different to the equivalent HB paras (reg 50(3) and (4)), and that CTR can be awarded for part of a week (unlike HB) and consequently the definitions of "part-week", "relevant week" and "relevant subsequent week" in sub-para (10) are slightly different to those in reg 50(8) HB Regs. See p475 for commentary on reg 50 HB Regs but note that para 29(4) to (6) is similar to reg 50(4), para 29(7) is equivalent to reg 50(5) HB Regs, and para 29(8) to (10) is broadly equivalent to reg 50(6) to (8) HB Regs.

Capital jointly held: pensioners

30.   Except where an applicant possesses capital which is disregarded under paragraph 28(3) (notional capital), where an applicant and one or more persons are beneficially entitled in possession to any capital asset they must be treated, in the absence of evidence to the contrary, as if each of them were entitled in possession to the whole beneficial interest therein in an equal share and the foregoing provisions of this Chapter apply for the purposes of calculating the amount of capital which the applicant is treated as possessing as if it were actual capital which the applicant does possess.

General Note

This paragraph is similar, but not identical, to reg 51 HB Regs (see p476 for commentary on that regulation).

Calculation of tariff income from capital: pensioners

31.   The capital of an applicant who is a pensioner, calculated in accordance with this Schedule, is to be treated as if it were a weekly income of–

(a)   £1 for each £500 in excess of £10,000 but not exceeding £16,000; and

(b)   £1 for any excess which is not a complete £500.

General Note

This paragraph concerns income that is deemed to be derived from capital ("tariff income"). Tariff income is assumed for capital which is in excess of £10,000 but not over £16,000 (as an applicant with capital of over £16,000 cannot be entitled to CTR under regs 27 and 30). Each £500 (or part of £500) capital in excess of £10,000 is deemed to give rise to £1 weekly income. The amount of capital is assessed in accordance with this Schedule (and so does not include, for example, capital that is disregarded under Sch 5).

PART 5
Extended reductions: pensioners

Extended reductions (qualifying contributory benefits): pensioners

32.–(1)   Except in the case of an applicant who is in receipt of state pension credit, an applicant who is entitled to a reduction under an authority's scheme (by virtue of the falling within class A or B) is to be entitled to an extended reduction (qualifying contributory benefits) where–

(a)   the applicant or the applicant's partner was entitled to a qualifying contributory benefit;

(b)   entitlement to a qualifying contributory benefit ceased because the applicant or the applicant's partner–

      (i)   commenced employment as an employed or self-employed earner;

      (ii)   increased their earnings from such employment; or

      (iii) increased the number of hours worked in such employment,

      and that employment is or, as the case may be, those increased earnings or increased number of hours are expected to last five weeks or more;

(c)   the applicant or the applicant's partner had been entitled to and in receipt of a qualifying contributory benefit or a combination of qualifying contributory benefits for a continuous period of at least 26 weeks before the day on which the entitlement to a qualifying contributory benefit ceased; and

(d)   the applicant or the applicant's partner was not entitled to and not in receipt of a qualifying income-related benefit in the last reduction week in which the applicant, or the applicant's partner, was entitled to a qualifying contributory benefit.

(2)   An applicant must be treated as entitled to a reduction under an authority's scheme by virtue of falling within class A or B where–

(a)   the applicant ceased to be entitled to a reduction under the authority's scheme because the applicant vacated the dwelling in which the applicant was resident;

(b)   the day on which the applicant vacated the dwelling was either in the week in which entitlement to a qualifying contributory benefit ceased, or in the preceding week; and

(c)   entitlement to the qualifying contributory benefit ceased in any of the circumstances listed in sub-paragraph (1)(b).

General Note

This paragraph allows an applicant, who is entitled to CTR on the basis of falling within class A or B (regs 22 and 23), to be entitled to payment for an extended period, called an extended reduction (akin to an extended payment of HB), in circumstances in which an applicant or her/his partner were entitled a qualifying contributory benefit (defined in reg 2 as contributory ESA, IB or SDA) and were entitled to and receiving the qualifying contributory benefit (or a combination of any of them) for a continuous period of 26 weeks before entitlement ended as a result of starting work, or increased hours of work or earnings from work. To qualify, the work, or increased hours or earnings, must be expected to last at least five weeks. Someone who is not a pensioner who qualifies for CTR on the basis of falling within class C or D may be entitled to an extended reduction if the conditions of Sch 6 para 34 are met (p1283).

This paragraph does not apply if the applicant is in receipt of PC (s/he still counts as receiving PC if it would have been payable had it not been an award of less than 10 pence a week: reg 2(6)). Note that entitlement to an extended reduction is not affected if it is only the applicant's partner who receives PC. Sub-para 1(d) ensures there is no entitlement to an extended reduction under this paragraph if an applicant or her/his partner was entitled to, or in receipt of, a qualifying income-related benefit (defined in reg 2 as IS, income-based JSA or income-related ESA) in the last reduction week in which the applicant or her/his partner was entitled to a qualifying contributory benefit. However, receipt of such a qualifying income-related benefit means the applicant would not have been classed as a "pensioner" under reg 3 and therefore would not have been able to get CTR by virtue of falling within class A or B, even if s/he had reached the qualifying age for PC. Instead, s/he may have qualified by virtue of falling within class C (reg 24). A question then arises – can such an applicant, who becomes a "pensioner" under reg 3 once s/he and her/his partner are no longer on the qualifying income-related benefit, get an extended reduction? If the requirements of Sch 6 para 34 are met it would seem that s/he can, on the basis that para 38(1) of that Schedule allows the applicant's entitlement to a reduction under class C or D to continue until the end of the reduction period. See also para 37 of this Schedule for the circumstances in which entitlement to a CTR can continue (a "continuing reduction") if the applicant's partner has claimed PC or the applicant has either claimed PC, or can be treated as having claimed it or is required to make a claim for it.

This rule has some similarities to reg 73 HB Regs (see p512).

Duration of extended reduction period (qualifying contributory benefits): pensioners

33.–(1)   Where an applicant is entitled to an extended reduction (qualifying contributory benefits), the extended reduction period starts on the day immediately following the day in which the applicant, or the applicant's partner, ceased to be entitled to a qualifying contributory benefit.

(2)   The extended reduction period ends–

(a)   at the end of a period of four weeks; or

(b)   on the date on which the applicant who is receiving the extended reduction (qualifying contributory benefits) has no liability for council tax, if that occurs first.

Amount of extended reduction (qualifying contributory benefits): pensioners

34.–(1)   For any week during the extended reduction period the amount of the extended reduction (qualifying contributory benefits) the applicant is entitled to is the greater of–

(a)   the amount of council tax reduction to which the applicant was entitled by virtue of falling within class A or B in the last reduction week before the applicant or the applicant's partner ceased to be entitled to a qualifying contributory benefit;

(b)   the amount of reduction under an authority's scheme to which the applicant would be entitled by virtue of falling within class A or B for any reduction week during the extended reduction period, if paragraph 32 (extended reductions (qualifying contributory benefits): pensioners) did not apply to the applicant; or

(c)   the amount of reduction under an authority's scheme to which the applicant's partner would be entitled by virtue of falling within class A or B, if paragraph 32 did not apply to the applicant.

(2)   Sub-paragraph (1) does not apply in the case of a mover.

(3)   Where an applicant is in receipt of an extended reduction (qualifying contributory benefits) under this paragraph and the applicant's partner makes an application for a reduction under an authority's scheme, an authority must not award a reduction in pursuance of that application during the extended reduction period.

Extended reductions (qualifying contributory benefits) – movers: pensioners

35.–(1)   This paragraph applies–

(a)   to a mover; and

(b)   from the Monday following the day of the move.

(2)   The amount of the extended reduction (qualifying contributory benefit) awarded from the Monday from which this paragraph applies until the end of the extended reduction period is the amount of reduction under the authority's ("the first authority") scheme which was awarded to the m over for the last reduction week before the mover, or the mover's partner, ceased to be entitled to a qualifying contributory benefit.

(3)   Where a mover's liability to pay council tax in respect of the new dwelling is to a second authority, the extended reduction (qualifying contributory benefits) may take the form of a payment from the first authority to–

(a)   the second authority; or

(b)   the mover directly.

Definitions

"mover" – see reg 2(1).

"authority" – see reg 2(1).

"partner" – see reg 2(1).

"qualifying contributory benefit" – see reg 2(1).

"new dwelling" – see reg 2(1).

"second authority" – see reg 2(1).

General Note

A "mover" is defined in reg 2 as an applicant who changes the dwelling in which s/he is resident and for which s/he is liable to pay council tax, from an area covered by one authority (the "first authority") to an area covered by a different authority, so this paragraph only applies in respect of pensioners who have moved between authorities rather than within an authority's area. Note that para 34(1) does not apply to movers: para 34(2), and the amount of the extended reduction in the case of a mover is determined in accordance with para 35(2) for the period from the Monday after the move until the end of the extended reduction period (as determined by para 33). The amount of the extended reduction is not affected by a change of circumstance during the extended reduction period (para 36(2)). The mover can still apply to the new authority for CTR – but in accordance with para 38, the amount of any extended reduction to which s/he is entitled from the first authority is deducted from her/his CTR entitlement for the same period and only any remainder is paid.

Relationship between extended reduction (qualifying contributory benefits) and entitlement to a council tax reduction by virtue of falling within class A or B: pensioners

36.–(1)   Where an applicant's reduction under an authority's scheme would have ended when the applicant ceased to be entitled to a qualifying contributory benefit in the circumstances listed in paragraph 32(1)(b), that reduction does not cease to have effect until the end of the extended reduction period.

(2)   Part 6 (period of entitlement and changes of circumstances) will not apply to any extended reduction (qualifying contributory benefits) payable in accordance with paragraph 34(1)(a) or paragraph 35 (amount of extended reduction – movers: pensioners).

Continuing reductions where state pension credit claimed: pensioners

37.–(1)   This paragraph applies where–

(a)   the applicant is entitled to a reduction under an authority's scheme;

(b)   sub-paragraph (2) is satisfied; and

(c)   either–

    (i)   the applicant has attained the qualifying age for state pension credit or, if the applicant's entitlement to income-based jobseeker's allowance or income-related employment and support allowance continued beyond that age, has attained the age of 65; or

    (ii)   the applicant's partner has actually claimed state pension credit.

(2)   This sub-paragraph is only satisfied if the Secretary of State has certified to the authority that the applicant's partner has actually claimed state pension credit or that–

(a)   the applicant's award of–

    (i)   income support has terminated because the applicant has attained the qualifying age for state pension credit; or

    (ii)   income-based jobseeker's allowance or income-related employment and support allowance has terminated because the applicant has attained the qualifying age for state pension credit or the age of 65; and

(b)   the applicant has claimed or is treated as having claimed or is required to make a claim for state pension credit.

(3)   Subject to sub-paragraph (4), in a case to which this paragraph applies, a reduction under an authority's scheme is to continue to be awarded for the period of 4 weeks beginning on the day following the day the applicant's entitlement to income support or, as the case may be, income-based jobseeker's allowance, or income related employment and support allowance, ceased, if and for so long as the applicant otherwise satisfies the conditions for entitlement to a reduction under an authority's scheme.

(4)   Where a reduction under an authority's scheme is awarded for the period of 4 weeks in accordance with sub-paragraph (3) above, and the last day of that period falls on a day other than the last day of a reduction week, then the reduction under the scheme is to continue to be awarded until the end of the reduction week in which the last day of that period falls.

(5)   Throughout the period of 4 weeks specified in sub-paragraph (3) and any further period specified in sub-paragraph (4)–

(a)   the whole of the income and capital of the applicant is to be disregarded;

(b)   the applicant's maximum council tax reduction is to be that which was applicable in the applicant's case immediately before that period commenced.

(6)   The maximum council tax reduction is to be calculated in accordance with paragraph 2(1) if, since the date it was last calculated–

(a)   the applicant's council tax liability has increased; or

(b)   a change in the deduction under paragraph 3 (non-dependant deductions) falls to be made.

General Note

This paragraph, which provides for a "continuing reduction" for a period of four weeks, is equivalent to reg 54 HB(SPC) Regs. See p799 for commentary.

Extended reductions: movers into an authority's area

38.–(1)   Where–

(a)   an application is made to an authority for a reduction under an authority's scheme, and

(b)   the applicant, or the partner of the applicant, is in receipt of an extended reduction from–

(i)   another billing authority in Wales;

(ii)   a billing authority in England;

(iii)   a local authority in Scotland, or

(iv)   a local authority in Northern Ireland,

the billing authority must reduce any reduction to which the applicant is entitled under its scheme by the amount of that extended reduction.

(2)   For the purposes of this paragraph "billing authority" ("awdurdod bilio") means a billing authority as defined in section 1 of the 1992 Act.

PART 6

Period of entitlement and change of circumstances

Date on which entitlement begins

39.   Any person by whom or in respect of whom an application for a reduction under an authority's scheme is made and who is otherwise entitled to that reduction is to be so entitled from the date on which the application is treated as made in accordance with paragraph 2 of Schedule 13 (date on which application is made).

General Note

This paragraph stipulates when entitlement to CTR commences (ie, as long as the applicant is otherwise entitled to it) from the date on which the application is treated as made in accordance with Sch 13 para 2. See also Sch 13 para 3 for the time, of up to three months, which an applicant has for making an application.

Date on which change of circumstances is to take effect

40.–(1)   Except in cases where paragraph 22 (disregard of changes in tax, contributions, etc) applies and subject to the following provisions of this paragraph and paragraph 41 (change of circumstances where state pension credit in payment), a change of circumstances which affects entitlement to, or the amount of, a reduction under an authority's scheme ("change of circumstances"), takes effect from the first day on which the change actually occurs.

(2)   Where that change is cessation of entitlement to any benefit under the benefit Acts, the date on which the change actually occurs will be the day immediately following the last day of entitlement to that benefit.

(3)   Subject to sub-paragraph (4), where the change of circumstances is a change in the amount of council tax payable, it takes effect from the day on which it actually occurs.

(4)   Where the change of circumstances is a change in the amount a person is liable to pay in respect of council tax in consequence of regulations under section 13 of the 1992 Act (reduced amounts of council tax) or changes in the discount to which a dwelling may be subject under section 11 or 12 of that Act, it is to take effect from the day on which the change in amount has effect.

(5)   Where the change of circumstances is the applicant's acquisition of a partner, the change takes effect on the day on which the acquisition takes place.

(6)   Where the change of circumstances is the death of an applicant's partner or their separation, it takes effect on the day the death or separation occurs.

(7)   Where the change of circumstances is that income, or an increase in the amount of income, other than a benefit or an increase in the amount of a benefit under the SSCBA, is paid in respect of a past period and

there was no entitlement to income of that amount during that period, the change of circumstances is to take effect from the first day on which such income, had it been paid in that period at intervals appropriate to that income, would have fallen to be taken into account for the purposes of an authority's scheme.

(8)   Without prejudice to sub-paragraph (7), where the change of circumstances is the payment of income, or arrears of income, in respect of a past period, the change of circumstances takes effect from the first day on which such income, had it been timeously paid in that period at intervals appropriate to that income, would have fallen to be taken into account for the purposes of an authority's scheme.

General Note

The general rule applying to pensioners contained in para 40(1) is that a change of circumstance which affects whether an applicant is entitled to CTR or the amount of CTR to which s/he is entitled takes effect from the first day on which the change occurs. This general rule does not apply to certain legislative changes which can be disregarded for a period of up to 30 reduction weeks: para 22. Para 40(1) is also subject to para 41 and sub-paras (2) to (8) which set out exceptions to the general rule.

Change of circumstances where the state pension credit payment in payment

41.–(1)   Sub-paragraphs (2) to (4) apply where–
(a)   the applicant is in receipt of state pension credit;
(b)   the amount of state pension credit awarded to the applicant is changed in consequence of a change in the applicant's circumstances or the correction of an official error; and
(c)   the change in the amount of state pension credit payable to the applicant results in a change in the amount of a reduction the applicant receives under an authority's scheme.

(2)   Where the change of circumstance is that an increase in the amount of state pension credit payable to the applicant results in–
(a)   an increase in the reduction the applicant receives under an authority's scheme, the change takes effect on the day on which the state pension credit becomes payable at the increased rate; or
(b)   a decrease in the reduction the applicant receives under an authority's scheme, the change takes effect on the day on which–
    (i)   state pension credit becomes payable at the increased rate; or
    (ii)   the authority receives notification from the Secretary of State of the increase in the amount of state pension credit,
whichever is the later.

(3)   Where the change of circumstance ("the relevant change") is that the applicant's state pension credit has been reduced and in consequence the reduction the applicant receives under an authority's scheme reduces–
(a)   in a case where the applicant's state pension credit has been reduced because the applicant failed to notify the Secretary of State timeously of a change of circumstances, the relevant change takes effect on the day on which state pension credit was reduced; or
(b)   in any other case the relevant change takes effect from the first day on which–
    (i)   the state pension credit is reduced; or
    (ii)   the authority receives notification from the Secretary of State of the reduction in the amount of state pension credit,
whichever is the later.

(4)   Where the change of circumstance is that the applicant's state pension credit is reduced and in consequence of the change, the amount of reduction the applicant receives under an authority's scheme is increased, the change takes effect on the day on which state pension credit becomes payable at the reduced rate.

(5)   Where a change of circumstance occurs in that an award of state pension credit has been made to the applicant or the applicant's partner and this would result in a decrease in the amount of reduction the applicant receives under an authority's scheme, the change takes effect on the day on which –
(a)   entitlement to state credit pension begins; or
(b)   the authority receives notification from the Secretary of State of the award of state pension credit, whichever is the later.

(6)   Where, in the case of an applicant who, or whose partner, is or has been awarded state pension credit comprising only the savings credit, there is–
(a)   a change of circumstances of a kind described in any of sub-paragraphs (2) to (5) which results from a relevant calculation or estimate; and
(b)   a change of circumstances which is a relevant determination,
each of which results in a change in the amount of reduction the applicant receives under an authority's scheme, the change of circumstances referred to in paragraph (b) takes effect from the day specified in sub-paragraph (2), (3), (4) or (5) as the case may be, in relation to the change referred to in paragraph (a).

(7)   Where a change of circumstance occurs in that a guarantee credit has been awarded to the applicant or the applicant's partner and this would result in an increase in the amount of a reduction the applicant receives under an authority's scheme, the change takes effect on the day on which the guarantee credit is first payable.

(8)   Where a change of circumstances would, but for this sub-paragraph, take effect under the preceding provisions of this paragraph within the 4 week period specified in paragraph 37 (continuing reductions where state pension credit claimed), that change takes effect on the first day after the expiry of the 4 week period.

(9)   In this paragraph–

"official error" ("camgymeriad swyddogol") means an error made by–

(a)   the authority or a person–
(i)   authorised to carry out any function of the authority relating to its scheme; or
(ii)   providing services relating to an authority's scheme directly or indirectly to the authority; or

(b)   an officer of–
(i)   the Department for Work and Pensions; or
(ii)   the Commissioners for Revenue and Customs,

acting as such, but excludes any error caused wholly or partly by any person or body not specified in paragraph (a) or (b) of this definition and any error of law which is shown to have been an error only by virtue of a subsequent decision of the court;

"relevant calculation or estimate" ("cyfrifiad neu amcangyfrif perthnasol") means the calculation or estimate made by the Secretary of State of the applicant's or, as the case maybe, the applicant's partner's income and capital for the purposes of the award of state pension credit;

"relevant determination" ("penderfyniad perthnasol") means a change in the determination by the authority of the applicant's income and capital using the relevant calculation or estimate, in accordance with paragraph 8(1).

General Note

This paragraph is similar to reg 60 HB(SPC) Regs. It provides an exception to the general rule in para 40(1) on when a change in circumstance takes effect. It applies to applicants who are in receipt of PC, if the amount of CTR an applicant receives changes as a result of an award of PC or a change in the amount of PC awarded. See p808 for commentary on reg 60 HB(SPC) Regs but note that a significant difference between this paragraph and reg 60 is that the effective dates of such changes to CTR do not correlate with the start of a reduction week.

SCHEDULE 2

REGULATION 32(2)

Applicable amounts: pensioners

General Note to Schedule 2

This Schedule is broadly equivalent to Sch 3 HB(SPC) Regs. See p848 for commentary on that Schedule and its relationship to the HB Regs. Certain paragraphs in this schedule also correspond to paragraphs in Sch 3 HB Regs, and cross references to commentary on these paragraphs are given below.

PART 1
Personal allowances

Personal allowance

1.   The amount specified in column (2) below in respect of each person or couple specified in column (1) is the amount specified for the purposes of paragraph 1(1)(a) of Schedule 1.

Column (1) *Person, couple or polygamous marriage*	*Column (2)* *Amount*
(1) Single applicant or lone parent–	
(a) aged under 65;	[⁶ £167.25];
(b) aged 65 or over.	[⁶ £181.00].
(2) Couple–	
(a) Both members aged under 65;	[⁶ £255.25];
(b) one or both members aged 65 or over	[⁶ £270.60].
(3) If the applicant is a member of a polygamous marriage and none of the members of the marriage has attained the age of 65–	
(a) for the applicant and the other party to the marriage;	[⁶ £255.25];
(b) for each additional spouse who is a member of the same household as the applicant.	[⁶ £88.00]
(4) If the applicant is a member of a polygamous marriage and one or more members of the marriage are aged 65 or over–	
(a) for the applicant and the other party to the marriage;	[⁶ £270.60];
(b) for each additional spouse who is a member of the same household as the applicant.	[⁶ £89.60].

Amendments

1.   Amended by reg 7(a) of SI 2014 No 66 (W.6) as from 15.1.14.
2.   Amended by reg 8(a) of SI 2015 No 44 (W.3) as from 21.1.15, for schemes made for a financial year starting on or after 1.4.15.

3.   Amended by reg 6(a) of SI 2016 No 50 (W.21) as from 20.1.16, for schemes made for a financial year starting on or after 1.4.16.

4.   Amended by reg 4(a) of SI 2017 No 46 (W.20) as from 19.1.17, for schemes made for a financial year starting on or after 1.4.17.

5.   Amended by reg 5(a) of SI 2018 No 14 (W.7) as from 10.1.18, for schemes made for a financial year starting on or after 1.4.18.

6.   Amended by reg 4(a) of SI 2019 No 11 (W.5) as from 9.1.19, for schemes made for a financial year starting on or after 1.4.19.

Child or young person amounts

2.–(1)   The amounts specified in column (2) below in respect of each person specified in column (1) are the amounts, for the relevant period specified in column (1), specified for the purposes of paragraph 1(1)(b) of Schedule 1.

Column (1) *Child or young person*	*Column (2)* *Amount*
Person in respect of the period–	
(a) beginning on that person's date of birth and ending on the day preceding the first Monday in September following that person's sixteenth birthday;	[² £66.90];
(b) beginning on the first Monday in September following that person's sixteenth birthday and ending on the day preceding that person's twentieth birthday.	[² £66.90].

(2)   In column (1) of the table in sub-paragraph (1) "the first Monday in September" ("y dydd Llun cyntaf ym Medi") means the Monday which first occurs in the month of September in any year.

Amendments

1.   Amended by reg 7(b) of SI 2014 No 66 (W.6) as from 15.1.14.
2.   Amended by reg 8(b) of SI 2015 No 44 (W.3) as from 21.1.15, for schemes made for a financial year starting on or after 1.4.15.

General Note

Note that CTR schemes in Wales do not place a restriction on the number of children (or young people, as defined in reg 2) for whom an allowance can be included in an applicant's applicable amount under this paragraph – ie, the so-called "two-child limit", which in some circumstances applies to HB and CTR in England, does not apply to CTR in Wales.

PART 2
Family premium

Family premium

3.   The amount for the purposes of paragraph 1(1)(c) of Schedule 1 in respect of a family of which at least one member is a child or young person is [¹ £17.45].

Amendment

1.   Amended by reg 8(c) of SI 2015 No 44 (W.3) as from 21.1.15, for schemes made for a financial year starting on or after 1.4.15.

General Note

Unlike in England, it is still a requirement that Welsh billing authorities include in their CTR schemes provision ensuring *all* applicants whose family includes a child or young person are entitled to a family premium within their applicable amount: Sch 1 para 1(1)(c). (For applicants who are not pensioners, see Sch 6 para 1(1)(c) and Sch 7 para 4.) For the rules in England, see p1158 and in Scotland, see p1543 and p1644. For the meaning of "family", see reg 6.

PART 3

Premiums

4.   The premiums specified in Part 4 are, for the purposes of paragraph 1(1)(d) of Schedule 1, to be applicable to an applicant who satisfies the condition specified in this Part in respect of that premium.

5.–(1)   Subject to sub-paragraph (2), for the purposes of this Part of this Schedule, once a premium is applicable to an applicant under this Part, a person is to be treated as being in receipt of any benefit for–

(a)   in the case of a benefit to which the Social Security (Overlapping Benefits) Regulations 1979 applies, any period during which, apart from the provision of those Regulations, that person would be in receipt of that benefit; and

(b)   any period spent by a person in undertaking a course of training or instruction provided or approved by the Secretary of State or the Welsh Ministers under section 2 of the Employment and Training Act 1973, or by Skills Development Scotland, Scottish Enterprise or Highland and Islands Enterprise under section 2 of the Enterprise and New Towns (Scotland) Act 1990 or for any period during which that person is in receipt of a training allowance.

(2)   For the purposes of the carer premium under paragraph 9, a person is to be treated as being in receipt of a carer's allowance by virtue of sub-paragraph (1)(a) only if and for so long as the person in respect of whose care the allowance has been claimed remains in receipt of attendance allowance, or the care component of disability living allowance at the highest or middle rate prescribed in accordance with section 72(3) of the SSCBA, or the daily living component of personal independence payment paid at either rate prescribed in accordance with Part 4 of the Welfare Reform Act 2012 or an AFIP.

General Note

This paragraph is equivalent to Sch 3 para 7 HB Regs. See p642 for commentary.

Severe disability premium

6.–(1)   The condition is that the applicant is a severely disabled person.

(2)   For the purposes of sub-paragraph (1), an applicant is to be treated as being a severely disabled person if, and only if–

(a)   in the case of a single applicant, a lone parent or an applicant who is treated as having no partner in consequence of sub-paragraph (3)–

    (i)   the applicant is in receipt of attendance allowance, or the care component of disability living allowance at the highest or middle rate prescribed in accordance with section 72(3) of the SSCBA, or the daily living component of personal independence payment paid at either rate prescribed in accordance with Part 4 of the Welfare Reform Act 2012 or an AFIP; and

    (ii)   subject to sub-paragraph (6), the applicant has no non-dependants aged 18 or over normally residing with the applicant or with whom the applicant is normally residing; and

    (iii)   no person is entitled to, and in receipt of, a carer's allowance [² under section 7 of the SSCBA or has an award of universal credit which includes the carer element under regulation 29 of the Universal Credit Regulations 2013] in respect of caring for the applicant;

(b)   in the case of an applicant who has a partner–

    (i)   the applicant is in receipt of attendance allowance, or the care component of disability living allowance at the highest or middle rate prescribed in accordance with section 72(3) of the SSCBA, or the daily living component of personal independence payment paid at either rate prescribed in accordance with Part 4 of the Welfare Reform Act 2012, or an AFIP;

    (ii)   the applicant's partner is also in receipt of such an allowance or, if the applicant is a member of a polygamous marriage, each other member of that marriage is in receipt of such an allowance; and

    (iii)   subject to sub-paragraph (6), the applicant has no non-dependants aged 18 or over normally residing with the applicant or with whom the applicant is normally residing,

and either a person is entitled to and in receipt of a carer's allowance [² or has an award of universal credit which includes the carer element] in respect of caring for only one of the couple or, if the applicant is a member of a polygamous marriage, for one or more but not all the members of the marriage, or as the case may be, no person is entitled to and in receipt of such an allowance [² or has such an award of universal credit] in respect of caring for either member of a couple or any of the members of the marriage.

(3)   Where an applicant has a partner who does not satisfy the condition in sub-paragraph (2)(b)(ii), and that partner [¹ is blind or severely sight-impaired or is treated as such] within the meaning of sub-paragraph (4), that partner is to be treated for the purposes of sub-paragraph (2) as if that partner were not a partner of the applicant.

[¹ (4)   For the purposes of sub-paragraph (3), a person is blind or severely sight-impaired if that person–

(a)   is registered as blind in a register compiled under section 29 of the National Assistance Act 1948 (welfare services);

(b)   is registered as severely sight-impaired in a register established and maintained by a local authority under section 18(1) of the Social Services and Well-being (Wales) Act 2014;

(c)   is registered as severely sight-impaired in a register established and maintained by a local authority under section 77(1) of the Care Act 2014; or,

(d)   in Scotland, has been certified as blind and in consequence is registered in a register maintained by or on behalf of a council constituted under section 2 of the Local Government etc. (Scotland) Act 1994.]

(5)   For the purposes of sub-paragraph (4), a person who has ceased to be registered as blind [¹ or severely sight-impaired] on regaining that person's eyesight is nevertheless to be treated as blind [¹ or severely sight-impaired] and as satisfying the additional condition set out in that sub-paragraph for a period of 28 weeks following the date on which that person ceased to be so registered.

(6)   For the purposes of sub-paragraph (2)(a)(ii) and (2)(b)(iii) no account is to be taken of–

(a)   a person receiving attendance allowance, or the care component of disability living allowance at the highest or middle rate prescribed in accordance with section 72(3) of the SSCBA, or the daily living component of personal independence payment paid at either rate prescribed in accordance with Part 4 of the Welfare Reform Act 2012, or an AFIP; or

(b)   a person who [¹ is blind or severely sight-impaired or is treated as such] within the meaning of sub-paragraphs (4) and (5).

(7)   For the purposes of sub-paragraph (2)(b) a person is to be treated–

(a)   as being in receipt of attendance allowance, or the care component of disability living allowance at the highest or middle rate prescribed in accordance with section 72(3) of the SSCBA, if that person would, but for that person's being a patient for a period exceeding 28 days, be so in receipt;

(b)   as being in receipt of the daily living component of personal independence payment paid at the rate prescribed in accordance with Part 4 of the Welfare Reform Act 2012 if that person would, but for that person's being a patient for a period exceeding 28 days, be so in receipt, notwithstanding section 86 of that Act and regulations made thereunder;

(c)   as being in receipt of AFIP if the person would be so in receipt but for a suspension of payment in accordance with any terms of the armed and reserve forces compensation scheme which allow for suspension because a person is undergoing medical treatment in a hospital or similar institution;

(d)   as being entitled to and in receipt of a carer's allowance [² or having an award of universal credit which includes the carer element] if that person would, but for the person for whom that person was caring being a patient in hospital for a period exceeding 28 days, be so entitled and in receipt [² or have such an award of universal credit].

(8)   For the purposes of sub-paragraph (2)(a)(iii) and (2)(b)–

(a)   no account is to be taken of an award of carer's allowance [² or an award of universal credit which includes the carer element] to the extent that payment of such an award is back-dated for a period before the date on which the award is first paid; and

(b)   references to a person being in receipt of a carer's allowance [² or having an award of universal credit which includes the carer element] are to include references to a person who would have been in receipt of that allowance [² or has such an award of universal credit] but for the application of a restriction under section 6B or 7 of the Social Security Fraud Act 2001 (loss of benefit provisions).

Amendments

1.   Amended by reg 6(b) of SI 2016 No 50 (W.21) as from 20.1.16, for schemes made for a financial year starting on or after 1.4.16.

2.   Amended by reg 4(b) of SI 2017 No 46 (W.20) as from 19.1.17, for schemes made for a financial year starting on or after 1.4.17.

General Note

This paragraph is equivalent to Sch 3 para 14 HB Regs (although there is no equivalent to sub-para 6(7)(c) in para 14), see p642 for commentary. A person who is severely sight impaired or blind is defined in the HB Regs as someone "certified as such by a consultant ophthalmologist" whereas in this para (and elsewhere in these regulations) the definition is that given in sub-para (4). In practice, the terms "severely sight impaired" and "blind" mean the same thing as far as certification is concerned. A consultant ophthalmologist completes a Certificate of Vision Impairment (in England and Wales) or a Form BP1 (in Scotland) which certifies someone as either severely sight impaired (blind) or sight impaired (partially sighted). A copy of the certificate is sent to the person's local authority. The local authority (or someone acting on its behalf) then contacts the person to ask if s/he would like to be placed on the register of people who are severely sight impaired and sight impaired in their area. It would seem that for HB purposes, for someone to be considered severely sight impaired/blind this second stage of being registered as such with the local authority is not necessary, but for CTR it is.

Enhanced disability premium

7.–(1)   The condition is that–

(a)   the care component of disability living allowance is, or would, but for a suspension of benefit in accordance with regulations under section 113(2) of the SSCBA or but for an abatement as a consequence of hospitalisation, be payable at the highest rate prescribed under section 72(3) of that Act;

(b)   the daily living component of personal independence payment is, or would, but for a suspension of benefit in accordance with regulations under section 86 of the Welfare Reform Act 2012, be payable at the enhanced rate prescribed in accordance with section 78(2) of that Act; or

(c)   AFIP is payable,

in respect of a child or young person who is a member of the applicant's family.

(2)   Where the condition in sub-paragraph (1) ceases to be satisfied because of the death of a child or young person, the condition is that the applicant or partner is entitled to child benefit in respect of the child or young person under section 145A of the SSCBA (entitlement after death of child or qualifying young person).

Disabled child premium

8.   The condition is that a child or young person for whom the applicant or a partner of the applicant is responsible and who is a member of the applicant's household–

(a)   is in receipt of disability living allowance or personal independence payment or is no longer in receipt of such allowance or payment because the child or young person is a patient, provided that the child or young person continues to be a member of the family; or

(b)   [¹ is blind or severely sight-impaired] within the meaning of paragraph 6(4) or treated [¹ as such] in accordance with paragraph 6(5); or

(c)   is a child or young person in respect of whom section 145A of the SSCBA (entitlement after death of child or qualifying young person) applies for the purposes of entitlement to child benefit but only for the period prescribed under that section, and in respect of whom a disabled child premium was included in the applicant's applicable amount immediately before the death of that child or young person, or ceased to be included in the applicant's applicable amount because of that child or young person's death.

Amendment

1.   Amended by reg 6(c) of SI 2016 No 50 (W.21) as from 20.1.16, for schemes made for a financial year starting on or after 1.4.16.

General Note

This paragraph is equivalent to Sch 3 para 16 HB Regs (although here there is no equivalent to sub-para 16(e) which provides another route to qualification for a disabled child premium – a young person's receipt of AFIP). See p645 for commentary. See also the General Note to para 6, above, for commentary on the definition of "blind or severely sight-impaired".

Carer premium

9.–(1)   The condition is that the applicant or the applicant's partner is, or both of them are, entitled to a carer's allowance.

(2)   Where a carer premium has been awarded but–

(a)   the person in respect of whose care the carer's allowance has been awarded dies; or

(b)   the person in respect of whom the premium was awarded ceases to be entitled, or ceases to be treated as entitled, to a carer's allowance,

this paragraph is to be treated as satisfied for a period of eight weeks from the relevant date specified in sub-paragraph (3).

(3)   The relevant date for the purposes of sub-paragraph (2) is–

(a)   in a case within sub-paragraph (2)(a), the Sunday following the death of the person in respect of whose care the carer's allowance has been awarded (or the date of death if the death occurred on a Sunday);

(b)   in a case within sub-paragraph (2)(b), the date on which that person who was entitled to a carer's allowance ceases to be entitled to it.

(4)   For the purposes of this paragraph, a person is to be treated as being entitled to and in receipt of a carer's allowance for any period not covered by an award but in respect of which a payment is made in lieu of an award.

General Note

This paragraph is similar to Sch 3 para 17 HB Regs. See p645 for commentary.

Persons in receipt of concessionary payments

10.   For the purpose of determining whether a premium is applicable to a person under paragraphs 6 to 9, any concessionary payment made to compensate that person for the non-payment of any benefit mentioned in those paragraphs is to be treated as if it were a payment of that benefit.

General Note

This paragraph is equivalent to Sch 3 para 18 HB Regs. See p645 for commentary.

Person in receipt of benefit

11.   For the purposes of this Part of this Schedule, a person is to be regarded as being in receipt of any benefit if, and only if, it is paid in respect of that person and is to be so regarded only for any period in respect of which that benefit is paid.

General Note

This paragraph is equivalent to Sch 3 para 19 HB Regs. See p646 for commentary.

PART 4
Amounts of premium specified in Part 3

Premium	Amount
12.–(1) Severe Disability Premium–	
(a) where the applicant satisfies the condition in paragraph 6(2)(a);	[⁵ £65.85];
(b) where the applicant satisfies the condition in paragraph 6(2)(b)–	
(i) in a case where there is someone in receipt of a carer's allowance [³ or who has an award of universal credit which includes the carer element under regulation 29 of the Universal Credit Regulations 2013] or if that person or any partner satisfies that condition only by virtue of paragraph 6(7);	[⁵ £65.85];
(ii) in a case where there is no-one in receipt of such an allowance [³ or such an award of universal credit].	[⁵ £131.70]
(2) Enhanced Disability Premium.	(2) [⁵ £26.04] in respect of each child or young person in respect of whom the conditions specified in paragraph 7 are satisfied.
(3) Disabled Child Premium.	(3) [⁵ £64.19] in respect of each child or young person in respect of whom the condition specified in paragraph 8 is satisfied.
(4) Carer Premium.	(4) [⁵ £36.85] in respect of each person who satisfies the condition specified in paragraph 9.

Amendments

1. Amended by reg 7(c) of SI 2014 No 66 (W.6) as from 15.1.14.
2. Amended by reg 8(d) of SI 2015 No 44 a(W.3) s from 21.1.15, for schemes made for a financial year starting on or after 1.4.15.
3. Amended by reg 4(c) of SI 2017 No 46 (W.20) as from 19.1.17, for schemes made for a financial year starting on or after 1.4.17.
4. Amended by reg 5(b) of SI 2018 No 14 (W.7) as from 10.1.18, for schemes made for a financial year starting on or after 1.4.18.
5. Amended by reg 4(b) of SI 2019 No 11 (W.5) as from 9.1.19, for schemes made for a financial year starting on or after 1.4.19.

SCHEDULE 3

REGULATION 32(2)

General Note to Schedule 3

This Schedule is equivalent to Sch 4 HB(SPC) Regs. See p854 for commentary, but note that under para 5(2) and (3) of this Schedule, £20 can be disregarded from earnings if an applicant had such a disregard in an award of CTR or HB in the circumstances described. For commentary on the need to register as blind or severely sight impaired to satisfy sub-para (5)(1)(b), see the General Note to Sch 2 para 6 (p1248).

Sums disregarded from applicant's earnings: pensioners

1.   Where two or more of paragraphs 2 to 5 apply in any particular case the overall maximum sum which falls to be disregarded in that case under those paragraphs is restricted to–
(a)   £25 in the case of a lone parent;
(b)   £20 in any other case.
2.   In a case where an applicant is a lone parent, £25 of earnings.
3.–(1)   In a case of earnings from any employment or employments to which sub-paragraph (2) applies, £20.
(2)   This paragraph applies to employment–
(a)   as a part-time fire-fighter employed by a fire and rescue authority constituted by a scheme under section 2 of the Fire and Rescue Services Act 2004 or a scheme to which section 4 of that Act applies;
(b)   as a part-time fire-fighter employed by the Scottish Fire and Rescue Service;
(c)   as an auxiliary coastguard in respect of coast rescue activities;
(d)   in the manning or launching of a lifeboat if the employment is part-time;
(e)   as a member of any territorial or reserve force prescribed in Part I of Schedule 6 to the Social Security (Contributions) Regulations 2001.

(3)   If–

(a)   any of the earnings of the applicant or, if the applicant has a partner, the applicant's partner, or both of them, are disregarded under sub-paragraph (1); and

(b)   either of them has, or both of them have, other earnings,

so much of those other earnings as would not, in the aggregate with the earnings disregarded under that sub-paragraph, exceed £20.

4.–(1)   If the applicant or, if the applicant has a partner, the applicant's partner is a carer, or both are carers, £20 of any earnings received from the applicant's or their employment.

(2)   Where the carer premium is awarded in respect of the applicant and of any partner of the applicant, their earnings are for the purposes of this paragraph to be aggregated, but the amount to be disregarded in accordance with sub-paragraph (1) is not to exceed £20 of the aggregated amount.

(3)   In this paragraph the applicant or the applicant's partner is a carer if paragraph 9 of Part 3 of Schedule 2 (carer premium) is satisfied in respect of the applicant.

5.–(1)   £20 is disregarded if the applicant or, if the applicant has a partner, the applicant's partner–

(a)   is in receipt of–

(i)   long-term incapacity benefit under section 30A of the SSCBA;

(ii)   severe disablement allowance under section 68 of that Act;

(iii)   attendance allowance under section 64 of that Act;

(iv)   disability living allowance;

(v)   personal independence payment

(vi)   an AFIP;

(vii)   any mobility supplement under article 20 of the Naval, Military and Air Forces Etc (Disablement and Death) Service Pensions Order 2006 (including such a supplement by virtue of any other scheme or order) or under article 25A of the Personal Injuries (Civilians) Scheme 1983;

(viii)   the disability element or the severe disability element of working tax credit under Schedule 2 to the Working Tax Credit (Entitlement and Maximum Rate) Regulations 2002; or

(ix)   main phase employment and support allowance; or

[² (b)   is or are registered as blind in a register compiled under section 29 of the National Assistance Act 1948 (welfare services), or registered as severely sight-impaired in a register established and maintained by a local authority under section 18(1) of the Social Services and Well-being (Wales) Act 2014 or section 77(1) of the Care Act 2014, or in Scotland has or have been certified as blind and in consequence are registered in a register maintained by or on behalf of a council constituted under section 2 of the Local Government etc. (Scotland) Act 1994; or]

(c)   is, or is treated as, incapable of work in accordance with the provisions of, and regulations made under, Part 12A of the SSCBA (incapacity for work), and has been incapable, or has been treated as incapable, of work for a continuous period of not less than–

(i)   in the case of an applicant who is terminally ill within the meaning of section 30B(4) of the SSCBA, 196 days;

(ii)   in any other case, 364 days; or

(d)   has, or is treated as having, limited capacity for work within the meaning of section 1(4) of the Welfare Reform Act 2007 or limited capability for work-related activity within the meaning of section 2(5) of that Act and either–

(i)   the assessment phase as defined in section 24(2) of the Welfare Reform Act 2007 has ended; or

(ii)   regulation 7 of the Employment and Support Allowance Regulations 2008 [¹ or regulation 7 of the Employment and Support Allowance Regulations 2013] (circumstances where the condition that the assessment phase has ended before entitlement to the support component [³ arises] does not apply) applies.

(2)   Subject to sub-paragraph (3), £20 is disregarded if the applicant or, if the applicant has a partner, the applicant's partner has, within a period of 8 weeks ending on the day on which the applicant or the applicant's partner attains the qualifying age for state pension credit, had an award of housing benefit or been in receipt of a reduction under an authority's scheme and–

(a)   £20 was disregarded in respect of earnings taken into account in that award; and

(b)   the person whose earnings qualified for the disregard continues in employment after the termination of that award.

(3)   The disregard of £20 specified in sub-paragraph (2) applies so long as there is no break, other than a break which does not exceed 8 weeks, in a person's–

(a)   entitlement to housing benefit; or

(b)   receipt of a reduction under an authority's scheme; or

(c)   employment,

following the first day in respect of which that benefit or reduction is awarded under an authority's scheme.

(4)   £20 is the maximum amount which may be disregarded under this paragraph, notwithstanding that, where the applicant has a partner, both the applicant and the applicant's partner satisfy the requirements of this paragraph.

Amendments

1. Amended by reg 9(a) of SI 2015 No 44 (W.3) as from 21.1.15, for schemes made for a financial year starting on or after 1.4.15.
2. Amended by reg 7 of SI 2016 No 50 (W.21) as from 20.1.16, for schemes made for a financial year starting on or after 1.4.16.
3. Amended by reg 6 of SI 2018 No 14 (W.7) as from 10.1.18, for schemes made for a financial year starting on or after 1.4.18.

6.–(1) Where–

(a) the applicant (or if the applicant is a member of a couple, at least one member of that couple) is a person to whom sub-paragraph (5) applies;

(b) the Secretary of State is satisfied that that person is undertaking exempt work as defined in sub-paragraph (6); and

(c) paragraph 7 of Schedule 1 (pensioners in receipt of guarantee credit) does not apply,

the amount specified in sub-paragraph (7) ("the specified amount").

(2) Where this paragraph applies, paragraphs 1 to 5 and 8 do not apply; but in any case where the applicant is a lone parent, and the specified amount would be less than the amount specified in paragraph 2, then paragraph 2 applies instead of this paragraph.

(3) Notwithstanding paragraph 5 of Schedule 1 (calculation of income and capital: applicant's family and polygamous marriages: pensioners), if sub-paragraph (1) applies to one member of a couple ("A") it is not to apply to the other member of that couple ("B") except to the extent provided in sub-paragraph (4).

(4) Where A's earnings are less than the specified amount, there is also to be disregarded so much of B's earnings as would not when aggregated with A's earnings exceed the specified amount; but the amount of B's earnings which may be disregarded under this sub-paragraph is limited to a maximum of £20 unless the Secretary of State is satisfied that B is also undertaking exempt work.

(5) This sub-paragraph applies to a person who is–

(a) in receipt of a contributory employment and support allowance;

(b) in receipt of incapacity benefit;

(c) in receipt of severe disablement allowance;

(d) being credited with earnings on the grounds of incapacity for work or limited capability for work under regulation 8B of the Social Security (Credits) Regulations 1975.

(6) "Exempt work" ("gwaith esempt") means work of the kind described in–

(a) regulation 45(2), (3) or (4) of the Employment and Support Allowance Regulations 2008 [¹ or regulation 39(1)(a), (b) or (c) of the Employment and Support Allowance Regulations 2013]; or (as the case may be)

(b) regulation 17(2), (3) or (4) of the Social Security (Incapacity for Work) (General) Regulations 1995,

and, in determining for the purposes of this paragraph whether an applicant or a member of a couple is undertaking any type of exempt work, it is immaterial whether that person or that person's partner is also undertaking other work.

(7) The specified amount is the amount of money from time to time mentioned in any provision referred to in sub-paragraph (6) by virtue of which the work referred to in sub-paragraph (1) is exempt (or, where more than one such provision is relevant and those provisions mention different amounts of money, the highest of those amounts).

Amendment

1. Amended by reg 9(b) of SI 2015 No 44 (W.3) as from 21.1.15, for schemes made for a financial year starting on or after 1.4.15.

---

7. Any amount or the balance of any amount which would fall to be disregarded under paragraph 18 or 19 of Schedule 4 had the applicant's income which does not consist of earnings been sufficient to entitle the applicant to the full amount disregarded thereunder.

8. Except where the applicant or the applicant's partner qualifies for a £20 disregard under the preceding provisions of this Schedule–

(a) £5 is to be disregarded if an applicant who has no partner has earnings;

(b) £10 is to be disregarded if an applicant who has a partner has earnings.

9. Any earnings, other than earnings referred to in paragraph 11(9)(b) of Schedule 1 (calculation of weekly income: pensioners), derived from employment which ended before the day on which the applicant first satisfies the conditions for entitlement to a reduction under an authority's scheme.

10.–(1) In a case where the applicant is a person who satisfies at least one of the conditions set out in sub-paragraph (2), and the applicant's net earnings equal or exceed the total of the amounts set out in sub-paragraph (3), the amount of the applicant's earnings that falls to be disregarded under this Schedule is to be increased by £17.10.

(2) The conditions of this sub-paragraph are that–

(a) the applicant, or if the applicant has a partner, either the applicant or the applicant's partner, is a person to whom regulation 20(1)(c) of the Working Tax Credit (Entitlement and Maximum Rate) Regulations 2002 applies; or

(b) the applicant–
  (i) is, or any partner of the applicant's is, aged at least 25 and is engaged in remunerative work for on average not less than 30 hours per week; or
  (ii) if the applicant is a member of a couple–
    (aa) at least one member of that couple is engaged in remunerative work for on average not less than 16 hours per week; and
    (bb) the applicant's applicable amount includes a family premium under paragraph 3 of Schedule 2; or
  (iii) is a lone parent who is engaged in remunerative work for on average not less than 16 hours per week; or
  (iv) is, or if the applicant has a partner, one of them is, engaged in remunerative work for on average not less than 16 hours per week and paragraph 5(1) is satisfied in respect of that person.
(3) The following are the amounts referred to in sub-paragraph (1)–
(a) any amount disregarded under this Schedule;
(b) the amount of child care charges calculated as deductible under paragraph 18(1)(c) of Schedule 1 (calculation of income on a weekly basis: pensioners); and
(c) £17.10.
(4) The provisions of regulation 10 (remunerative work) are to apply in determining whether or not a person works for on average not less than 30 hours per week, but as if the reference to 16 hours in sub-paragraph (1) of that regulation was a reference to 30 hours.
11. Where a payment of earnings is made in a currency other than sterling, any banking charge or commission payable in converting that payment into sterling.

SCHEDULE 4

REGULATION 32(2)

Amounts to be disregarded in the calculation of income other than earnings: pensioners
1. In addition to any sum which falls to be disregarded in accordance with paragraphs 2 to 6, £10 of any of the following–
(a) a war disablement pension (except insofar as such a pension falls to be disregarded under paragraph 2 or 3);
(b) a war widow's pension or war widower's pension;
(c) a pension payable to a person as a widow, widower or surviving civil partner under any power of Her Majesty otherwise than under an enactment to make provision about pensions for or in respect of persons who have been disabled or have died in consequence of service as members of the armed forces of the Crown;
(d) a guaranteed income payment and, if the amount of that payment has been abated to less than £10 by a pension or payment falling within article 39(1)(a) or (b) of the Armed Forces and Reserve Forces (Compensation Scheme) Order 2011, so much of that pension or payment as would not, in aggregate with the amount of any guaranteed income payment disregarded, exceed £10;
(e) a payment made to compensate for the non-payment of such a pension or payment as is mentioned in any of the preceding sub-paragraphs;
(f) a pension paid by the government of a country outside Great Britain which is analogous to any of the pensions or payments mentioned in sub-paragraphs (a) to (d) above;
[¹ (g) a pension paid by a government to victims of National Socialist persecution.]

Amendment
1. Substituted by reg 7 of SI 2018 No 14 (W.7) as from 10.1.18, for schemes made for a financial year starting on or after 1.4.18.

2. The whole of any amount included in a pension to which paragraph 1 relates in respect of–
(a) the applicant's need for constant attendance;
(b) the applicant's exceptionally severe disablement.
3. Any mobility supplement under article 20 of the Naval, Military and Air Forces Etc (Disablement and Death) Service Pensions Order 2006 (including such a supplement by virtue of any other scheme or order) or under article 25A of the Personal Injuries (Civilians) Scheme 1983 or any payment intended to compensate for the non-payment of such a supplement.
4. Any supplementary pension under article 23(2) of the Naval, Military and Air Forces Etc (Disablement and Death) Service Pensions Order 2006 (pensions to surviving spouses and surviving civil partners) and any analogous payment made by the Secretary of State for Defence to any person who is not a person entitled under that Order.
5. In the case of a pension awarded at the supplementary rate under article 27(3) of the Personal Injuries (Civilians) Scheme 1983 (pensions to surviving spouses and surviving civil partners), the sum specified in paragraph 1(c) of Schedule 4 to that Scheme.

6.–(1) Any payment which is–

(a) made under any of the Dispensing Instruments to a widow, widower or surviving civil partner of a person–

    (i) whose death was attributable to service in a capacity analogous to service as a member of the armed forces of the Crown; and

    (ii) whose service in such capacity terminated before 31 March 1973; and

(b) equal to the amount specified in article 23(2) of the Naval, Military and Air Forces Etc (Disablement and Death) Service Pensions Order 2006.

(2) In this paragraph "the Dispensing Instruments" ("yr Offerynnau Dosbarthu") means the Order in Council of 19 December 1881, the Royal Warrant of 27 October 1884 and the Order by His Majesty of 14 January 1922 (exceptional grants of pay, non-effective pay and allowances).

7. £15 of any widowed parent's allowance to which the applicant is entitled under section 39A of the SSCBA.

8. £15 of any widowed mother's allowance to which the applicant is entitled under section 37 of the SSCBA.

9. Where the applicant occupies a dwelling as the applicant's home and the applicant provides in that dwelling board and lodging accommodation, an amount, in respect of each person for whom such accommodation is provided for the whole or any part of a week, equal to–

(a) where the aggregate of any payments made in respect of any one week in respect of such accommodation provided to such person does not exceed £20, 100 per cent of such payments; or

(b) where the aggregate of any such payments exceeds £20, £20 and 50 per cent of the excess over £20.

10. If the applicant–

(a) owns the freehold or leasehold interest in any property or is a tenant of any property; and

(b) occupies a part of that property; and

(c) has an agreement with another person allowing that person to occupy another part of that property on payment of rent and–

    (i) the amount paid by that person is less than £20 per week, the whole of that amount; or

    (ii) the amount paid is £20 or more per week, £20.

11. Where an applicant receives income under an annuity purchased with a loan, which satisfies the following conditions–

(a) that the loan was made as part of a scheme under which not less than 90 per cent of the proceeds of the loan were applied to the purchase by the person to whom it was made of an annuity ending with that person's life or with the life of the survivor of two or more persons (in this paragraph referred to as "the annuitants") who include the person to whom the loan was made;

(b) that at the time the loan was made the person to whom it was made or each of the annuitants had attained the age of 65;

(c) that the loan was secured on a dwelling in Great Britain and the person to whom the loan was made or one of the annuitants owns an estate or interest in that dwelling;

(d) that the person to whom the loan was made or one of the annuitants occupies the dwelling on which it was secured as that person's or annuitant's home at the time the interest is paid; and

(e) that the interest payable on the loan is paid by the person to whom the loan was made or by one of the annuitants,

the amount, calculated on a weekly basis, equal to–

    (i) where, or insofar as, section 369 of the Income and Corporation Taxes Act 1988 (mortgage interest payable under deduction of tax) applies to the payments of interest on the loan, the interest which is payable after deduction of a sum equal to income tax on such payments at the applicable percentage of income tax within the meaning of section 369(1A) of that Act;

    (ii) in any other case, the interest which is payable on the loan without deduction of such a sum.

12.–(1) Any payment, other than a payment to which sub-paragraph (2) applies, made to the applicant by Trustees in exercise of a discretion exercisable by them.

(2) This sub-paragraph applies to payments made to the applicant by Trustees in exercise of a discretion exercisable by them for the purpose of–

(a) obtaining food, ordinary clothing or footwear or household fuel;

(b) the payment of rent, council tax or water charges for which that applicant or the applicant's partner is liable;

(c) meeting housing costs of a kind specified in Schedule 2 to the State Pension Credit Regulations 2002.

(3) In a case to which sub-paragraph (2) applies, £20 or–

(a) if the payment is less than £20, the whole payment;

(b) if, in the applicant's case, £10 is disregarded in accordance with paragraph 1(a) to (g), £10 or the whole payment if it is less than £10; or

(c) if, in the applicant's case, £15 is disregarded under paragraph 7 or paragraph 8 and–

    (i) the applicant has no disregard under paragraph 1(a) to (g), £5 or the whole payment if it is less than £5;

    (ii) the applicant has a disregard under paragraph 1(a) to (g), nil.

13.   Any increase in pension or allowance under Part 2 or 3 of the Naval, Military and Air Forces Etc (Disablement and Death) Service Pensions Order 2006 paid in respect of a dependent other than the pensioner's partner.

14.   Any payment ordered by a court to be made to the applicant or the applicant's partner in consequence of any accident, injury or disease suffered by the person or a child of the person to or in respect of whom the payment is made.

15.   Periodic payments made to the applicant or the applicant's partner under an agreement entered into in settlement of a claim made by the applicant or, as the case may be, the applicant's partner for an injury suffered by the applicant or the applicant's partner.

16.   Any income which is payable outside the United Kingdom for such period during which there is a prohibition against the transfer to the United Kingdom of that income.

17.   Any banking charges or commission payable in converting to sterling payments of income made in a currency other than sterling.

18.   Where the applicant makes a parental contribution in respect of a student attending a course at an establishment in the United Kingdom or undergoing education in the United Kingdom, which contribution has been assessed for the purposes of calculating–

(a)   under, or pursuant to regulations made under powers conferred by section 22 of the Teaching and Higher Education Act 1998, that student's award;

(b)   under regulations made in exercise of the powers conferred by section 49 of the Education (Scotland) Act 1980, that student's bursary, scholarship, or other allowance under that section or under regulations made in exercise of the powers conferred by section 73 of that Act of 1980, any payment to that student under that section; or

(c)   the student's student loan,

an amount equal to the weekly amount of that parental contribution, but only in respect of the period for which that contribution is assessed as being payable.

19.–(1)   Where the applicant is the parent of a student aged under 25 in advanced education who either–

(a)   is not in receipt of any award, grant or student loan in respect of that education; or

(b)   is in receipt of an award bestowed by virtue of the Teaching and Higher Education Act 1998, or regulations made thereunder, or a bursary, scholarship or other allowance under section 49(1) of the Education (Scotland) Act 1980, or a payment under section 73 of that Act of 1980,

and the applicant makes payments by way of a contribution towards the student's maintenance, other than a parental contribution falling within paragraph 18, an amount specified in sub-paragraph (2) in respect of each week during the student's term.

(2)   For the purposes of sub-paragraph (1), the amount is to be equal to–

(a)   the weekly amount of the payments; or

(b)   the amount by way of a personal allowance for a single applicant under 25 less the weekly amount of any award, bursary, scholarship, allowance or payment referred to in sub-paragraph (1)(b),

whichever is less.

(3)   In this paragraph and paragraph 18 a reference to a "student loan" or a "grant" is a reference to a student loan or a grant within the meaning of Schedule 11.

20.–(1)   Where an applicant's applicable amount includes an amount by way of a family premium, £15 of any payment of maintenance, whether under a court order or not, which is made or due to be made by the applicant's spouse, civil partner, former spouse or former civil partner or the applicant's partner's spouse, civil partner, former spouse, or former civil partner.

(2)   For the purposes of sub-paragraph (1), where more than one maintenance payment falls to be taken into account in any week, all such payments are to be aggregated and treated as if they were a single payment.

21.   Except in a case which falls under paragraph 10 of Schedule 3, where the applicant is a person who satisfies any of the conditions of sub-paragraph (2) of that paragraph, any amount of working tax credit up to £17.10.

22.   Where the total value of any capital specified in Part 2 of Schedule 5 (capital disregarded only for the purposes of determining deemed income) does not exceed £10,000, any income actually derived from such capital.

23.   Except in the case of income from capital specified in Part 2 of Schedule 5, any actual income from capital.

24.   Where the applicant, or the person who was the partner of the applicant on 31 March 2003, was entitled on that date to income support or an income-based jobseeker's allowance but ceased to be so entitled on or before 5 April 2003 by virtue only of regulation 13 of the Housing Benefit (General) Amendment (No 3) Regulations 1999 as in force at that date, the whole of the applicant's income.

SCHEDULE 5

REGULATION 32(2)

Capital disregards: pensioners

PART 1

General Note

This is similar to Sch 6 of the CTR(PR)(E) Regs. For commentary, see p1168.

Capital to be disregarded

    1.   Any premises acquired for occupation by the applicant which the applicant intends to occupy as the applicant's home within 26 weeks of the date of acquisition or such longer period as is reasonable in the circumstances to enable the applicant to obtain possession and commence occupation of the premises.

    2.   Any premises which the applicant intends to occupy as the applicant's home, and in respect of which the applicant is taking steps to obtain possession and has sought legal advice, or has commenced legal proceedings, with a view to obtaining possession, for a period of 26 weeks from the date on which the applicant first sought such advice or first commenced such proceedings whichever is the earlier, or such longer period as is reasonable in the circumstances to enable the applicant to obtain possession and commence occupation of those premises.

    3.   Any premises which the applicant intends to occupy as the applicant's home to which essential repairs or alterations are required in order to render the premises fit for such occupation, for a period of 26 weeks from the date on which the applicant first takes steps to effect those repairs or alterations, or such longer period as is necessary to enable those repairs or alterations to be carried out.

    4.   Any premises occupied in whole or in part–

    (a)   by a person who is a relative of the applicant or the applicant's partner as that person's home where that person has attained the qualifying age for state pension credit or is incapacitated;

    (b)   by the former partner of the applicant as that person's home; but this provision does not apply where the former partner is a person from whom the applicant is estranged or divorced or with whom the applicant had formed a civil partnership that has been dissolved.

    5.   Any future interest in property of any kind, other than land or premises in respect of which the applicant has granted a subsisting lease or tenancy, including sub-leases or sub-tenancies.

    6.   Where an applicant has ceased to occupy what was formerly the dwelling occupied as the home following the applicant's estrangement or divorce from the applicant's former partner or the dissolution of a civil partnership with the applicant's former partner, that dwelling for a period of 26 weeks from the date on which the applicant ceased to occupy that dwelling or, where the dwelling is occupied as the home by the former partner who is a lone parent, for so long as it is so occupied.

    7.   Any premises where the applicant is taking reasonable steps to dispose of the whole of the applicant's interest in those premises, for a period of 26 weeks from the date on which the applicant first took such steps, or such longer period as is reasonable in the circumstances to enable the applicant to dispose of those premises.

    8.   All personal possessions.

    9.   The assets of any business owned in whole or in part by the applicant and for the purposes of which the applicant is engaged as a self-employed earner or, if the applicant has ceased to be so engaged, for such period as may be reasonable in the circumstances to allow for disposal of those assets.

    10.   The assets of any business owned in whole or in part by the applicant if–

    (a)   the applicant is not engaged as a self-employed earner in that business by reason of some disease or bodily or mental disablement; but

    (b)   the applicant intends to become engaged (or, as the case may be, re-engaged) as a self-employed earner in that business as soon as the applicant recovers or is able to become engaged, or re-engaged, in that business,

for a period of 26 weeks from the date on which the application for a reduction under an authority's scheme is made or, if it is unreasonable to expect the applicant to become engaged or re-engaged in that business within that period, for such longer period as is reasonable in the circumstances to enable the applicant to become so engaged or re-engaged.

    11.   The surrender value of any policy of life insurance.

    12.   The value of any funeral plan contract; and for this purpose, "funeral plan contract" ("contractcynllum angladd") means a contract under which–

    (a)   the applicant makes one or more payments to another person ("the provider");

    (b)   the provider undertakes to provide, or secure the provision of, a funeral in the United Kingdom for the applicant on the applicant's death; and

    (c)   the sole purpose of the plan is to provide or secure the provision of a funeral for the applicant on the applicant's death.

    13.   Where an ex-gratia payment has been made by the Secretary of State on or after 1 February 2001 in consequence of the imprisonment or internment of–

    (a)   the applicant;

    (b)   the applicant's partner;

(c)   the applicant's deceased spouse or deceased civil partner; or

(d)   the applicant's partner's deceased spouse or deceased civil partner,

by the Japanese during the Second World War, an amount equal to that payment.

14.–(1)   Subject to sub-paragraph (2), the amount of any trust payment made to an applicant or an applicant's partner who is–

(a)   a diagnosed person;

(b)   a diagnosed person's partner or was a diagnosed person's partner at the time of the diagnosed person's death; or

(c)   a parent of a diagnosed person, a person acting in place of the diagnosed person's parents or a person who was so acting at the date of the diagnosed person's death.

(2)   Where a trust payment is made to–

(a)   a person referred to in sub-paragraph (1)(a) or (b), that sub-paragraph is to apply for the period beginning on the date on which the trust payment is made and ending on the date on which that person dies;

(b)   a person referred to in sub-paragraph (1)(c), that sub-paragraph is to apply for the period beginning on the date on which the trust payment is made and ending two years after that date.

(3)   Subject to sub-paragraph (4), the amount of any payment by a person to whom a trust payment has been made or of any payment out of the estate of a person to whom a trust payment has been made, which is made to an applicant or an applicant's partner who is–

(a)   the diagnosed person;

(b)   a diagnosed person's partner or was a diagnosed person's partner at the date of the diagnosed person's death; or

(c)   a parent of a diagnosed person, a person acting in place of the diagnosed person's parents or a person who was so acting at the date of the diagnosed person's death.

(4)   Where a payment such as referred to in sub-paragraph (3) is made to–

(a)   a person referred to in sub-paragraph (3)(a) or (b), that sub-paragraph is to apply for the period beginning on the date on which the payment is made and ending on the date on which that person dies;

(b)   a person referred to in sub-paragraph (3)(c), that sub-paragraph is to apply for the period beginning on the date on which the payment is made and ending two years after that date.

(5)   In this paragraph, a reference to a person–

(a)   being the diagnosed person's partner;

(b)   acting in place of the diagnosed person's parents,

at the date of the diagnosed person's death is to include a person who would have been such a person or a person who would have been so acting, but for the diagnosed person residing in a care home or an independent hospital.

(6)   In this paragraph–

"diagnosed person" ("person â diagnosis") means a person who has been diagnosed as suffering from, or who, after that person's death, has been diagnosed as having suffered from, variant Creutzfeldt-Jakob disease;

"relevant trust" ("ymddiriedolaeth berthnasol") means a trust established out of funds provided by the Secretary of State in respect of persons who suffered, or who are suffering, from variant Creutzfeldt-Jakob disease for the benefit of persons eligible for payments in accordance with its provisions;

"trust payment" ("taliad ymddiriedolaeth") means a payment under a relevant trust.

15.   The amount of any payment, other than a war pension, to compensate for the fact that the applicant, the applicant's partner, the applicant's deceased spouse or civil partner or the applicant's partner's deceased spouse or civil partner–

(a)   was a slave labourer or a forced labourer;

(b)   had suffered property loss or had suffered personal injury; or

(c)   was a parent of a child who had died,

during the Second World War.

16.–(1)   Any payment made under or by–

(a)   the Trusts, the Fund, the Eileen Trust, MFET Limited, the Skipton Fund, the Caxton Foundation, [¹ an approved blood scheme, the Scottish Infected Blood Support Scheme, the London Emergencies Trust, the We Love Manchester Emergency Fund] or the London Bombings Relief Charitable Fund (collectively referred to in this paragraph as "the Trusts"); or

(b)   the Independent Living Fund (2006).

(2)   Any payment by or on behalf of a person who is suffering or who suffered from haemophilia or who is or was a qualifying person, which derives from a payment made under or by any of the Trusts and which is made to or for the benefit of that person's partner or former partner–

(a)   from whom that person is not, or where that person has died was not, estranged or divorced, or

(b)   with whom that person has formed a civil partnership that has not been dissolved or, where that person has died, had not been dissolved at the time of that person's death.

(3)   Any payment by or on behalf of the partner or former partner of a person who is suffering or who suffered from haemophilia or who is or was a qualifying person which derives from a payment made under or by any of the Trusts and which is made to or for the benefit of the person who is suffering from haemophilia or who is a qualifying person.

    (4)   Sub-paragraph (3) does not apply if–

(a)   the partner or former partner and that person are not, or if either of them has died were not, estranged or divorced, or

(b)   where the partner or former partner and that person have formed a civil partnership, the civil partnership has not been dissolved or, if either of them has died, had not been dissolved at the time of the death.

    (5)   Any payment by a person who is suffering from haemophilia or who is a qualifying person, which derives from a payment under or by any of the Trusts, where–

(a)   that person has no partner or former partner from whom that person is not estranged or divorced or with whom that person has formed a civil partnership that has not been dissolved, nor any child who is or had been a member of that person's household; and

(b)   the payment is made either–

    (i)   to that person's parent or step-parent; or

    (ii)   where that person at the date of the payment is a child or a student who has not completed full-time education and has no parent or step-parent, to any person standing in the place of that child or young person's parent or that student's parent,

but only for a period from the date of the payment until the end of two years from that person's death.

    (6)   Any payment out of the estate of a person who suffered from haemophilia or who was a qualifying person, which derives from a payment under or by any of the Trusts, where–

(a)   that person at the date of that person's death ("the relevant date") had no partner or former partner from whom that person was not estranged or divorced or with whom that person had formed a civil partnership that had not been dissolved, nor any child who was or had been a member of that person's household; and

(b)   the payment is made either–

    (i)   to that person's parent or step-parent; or

    (ii)   where that person at the relevant date was a child or a student who had not completed full-time education and had no parent or step-parent, to any person standing in place of that child or young person's parent or that student's parent,

but only for a period of two years from the relevant date.

    (7)   In the case of a person to whom or for whose benefit a payment referred to in this paragraph is made, any capital resource which derives from any payment of income or capital made under or deriving from any of the Trusts.

Amendment

1.   Amended by reg 8(a) of SI 2018 No 14 (W.7) as from 10.1.18, for schemes made for a financial year starting on or after 1.4.18.

17.–(1)   An amount equal to the amount of any payment made in consequence of any personal injury to the applicant or, if the applicant has a partner, to the partner.

    (2)   Where the whole or part of the payment is administered–

(a)   by the High Court or the County Court under Rule 21.11(1) of the Civil Procedure Rules 1998, or the Court of Protection, or on behalf of a person where the payment can only be disposed of by order or direction of any such court;

(b)   in accordance with an order made under Rule 36.14 of the Ordinary Cause Rules 1993 or under Rule 128 of those Rules; or

(c)   in accordance with the terms of a trust established for the benefit of the applicant or the applicant's partner,

the whole of the amount so administered.

18.   Any amount specified in paragraph 19, 20, 21 or 25 for a period of one year beginning with the date of receipt.

19.   Amounts paid under a policy of insurance in connection with the loss of or damage to the property occupied by the applicant as the applicant's home and to the applicant's personal possessions.

20.   So much of any amounts paid to the applicant or deposited in the applicant's name for the sole purpose of–

(a)   purchasing premises which the applicant intends to occupy as the applicant's home; or

(b)   effecting essential repairs or alterations to the premises occupied or intended to be occupied by the applicant as the applicant's home.

21.–(1)   Subject to paragraph 22 any amount paid–

(a)   by way of arrears of benefit;

(b)   by way of compensation for the late payment of benefit;

(c)   in lieu of the payment of benefit;

(d)   to rectify, or compensate for, an official error, as defined for the purposes of paragraph 22, being an amount to which that paragraph does not apply;

(e)   by a local authority out of funds provided under either section 93 of the Local Government Act 2000 under a scheme known as "Supporting People" or section 91 of the Housing (Scotland) Act 2001 [¹ ;]

[¹ (f)   by way of occasional assistance including arrears and payments in lieu of occasional assistance.]
(2)   In sub-paragraph (1), "benefit" ("budd-dal") means–
(a)   attendance allowance under section 64 of the SSCBA;
(b)   disability living allowance;
(c)   personal independence payment;
(d)   an AFIP;
(e)   income support;
(f)   income-based jobseeker's allowance;
(g)   state pension credit;
(h)   housing benefit;
(i)   council tax benefit;
(j)   child tax credit;
(k)   an increase of a disablement pension under section 104 of the SSCBA (increase where constant attendance is needed), and any further increase of such a pension under section 105 of the SSCBA (increase for exceptionally severe disablement);
(l)   any amount included on account of the applicant's exceptionally severe disablement or need for constant attendance in a war disablement pension or a war widow's or widower's pension;
(m)   any discretionary housing payment paid pursuant to regulation 2(1) of the Discretionary Financial Assistance Regulations 2001;
(n)   working tax credit; [¹]
(o)   income-related employment and support allowance [¹;]
[¹ (p)   social fund payments under Part 8 of the SSCBA; [²]
(q)   universal credit] [² ; or
(r)   bereavement support payment under section 30 of the Pensions Act 2014,]

Amendments
1.   Amended by reg 8(a) of SI 2014 No 66 (W.6) as from 15.1.14.
2.   Amended by reg 5(a) of SI 2019 No 11 (W.5) as from 9.1.19, for schemes made for a financial year starting on or after 1.4.19.

22.–(1)   Subject to sub-paragraph (3), any payment of £5,000 or more which has been made to rectify, or to compensate for, an official error relating to a relevant benefit and which has been received by the applicant in full on or after the day on which the applicant became entitled to a reduction under an authority's scheme.
(2)   Subject to sub-paragraph (3), the total amount of any payments disregarded under–
(a)   paragraph 7(2) of Schedule 10 to the Income Support (General) Regulations 1987);
(b)   paragraph 12(2) of Schedule 8 to the Jobseeker's Allowance Regulations 1996;
(c)   paragraph 9(2) of Schedule 5 to the Council Tax Benefit Regulations 2006;
(d)   paragraph 20A of Schedule 5 to the State Pension Credit Regulations 2002;
(e)   paragraph 11(2) of Schedule 9 to the Employment and Support Allowance Regulations 2008 [¹;]
[¹ (f)   paragraph 18 of Schedule 10 to the Universal Credit Regulations 2013,]
where the award in respect of which the payments last fell to be disregarded under those Regulations either terminated immediately before the relevant date or is still in existence at that date.
(3)   Any disregard which applies under sub-paragraph (1) or (2) is to have effect until the award comes to an end.
(4)   In this paragraph–
"the award" ("y dyfarniad"), except in sub-paragraph (2), means–
(a)   the award of a reduction under an authority's scheme during which the relevant sum or, where it is paid in more than one instalment, the first instalment of that sum is received; and
(b)   where that award is followed by one or more further awards which, or each of which, begins immediately after the previous award ends, such further awards until the end of the last such award, provided that, for such further awards, the applicant–
(i)   is the person who received the relevant sum;
(ii)   is the partner of that person; or
(iii)   was the partner of that person at the date of that person's death;
"official error" ("camgymeriad swyddogol")–
(a)   where the error relates to housing benefit, or council tax benefit (in respect of any period before 1 April 2013), has the meaning given by regulation 1(2) of the Housing Benefit and Council Tax Benefit (Decisions and Appeals) Regulations 2001; and
(b)   where the error relates to any other relevant benefit, has the meaning given by regulation 1(3) of the Social Security and Child Support (Decisions and Appeals) Regulations 1999;
"relevant benefit" ("budd-dal perthnasol") means any benefit specified in paragraph 21(2);
"the relevant date" ("y dyddiad perthnasol") means the date on which the application for a reduction under an authority's scheme was made; and
"the relevant sum" ("y swm perthnasol") means the payment referred to in sub-paragraph (1) or the total amount referred to in sub-paragraph (2).

Amendment

1.   Amended by reg 8(b) of SI 2014 No 66 (W.6) as from 15.1.14.

---

23.   Where a capital asset is held in a currency other than sterling, any banking charge or commission payable in converting that capital into sterling.

24.   The value of the right to receive income from an occupational pension scheme or a personal pension scheme.

25.   Any arrears of supplementary pension which is disregarded under paragraph 4 of Schedule 4 (amounts to be disregarded in the calculation of income other than earnings: pensioners) or of any amount which is disregarded under paragraph 5 or 6 of that Schedule.

26.   The dwelling occupied as the home; but only one dwelling is to be disregarded under this paragraph.

27.   Where a person elects to be entitled to a lump sum under Schedule 5 or 5A to the SSCBA or under Schedule 1 to the Social Security (Graduated Retirement Benefit) Regulations 2005, or is treated as having made such an election, and a payment has been made pursuant to that election, an amount equal to–

(a)   except where sub-paragraph (b) applies, the amount of any payment or payments made on account of that lump sum; or

(b)   the amount of that lump sum,

but only for so long as that person does not change that election in favour of an increase of pension or benefit.

[¹ 27A.   Where a person elects to be entitled to a lump sum under section 8(2) of the Pensions Act 2014 or in accordance with regulations made under section 10 of that Act, or fails to make an election, and a lump sum payment has been made, an amount equal to–

(a)   except where sub-paragraph (b) applies, the amount of any payment or payments made on account of that lump sum; or

(b)   the amount of that lump sum,

but only for so long as that person does not change that election in favour of an increase of pension.]

Amendment

1.   Inserted by reg 8(a) of SI 2016 No 50 (W.21) as from 20.1.16, for schemes made for a financial year starting on or after 1.4.16.

---

28.   Any payments made by virtue of regulations made under–

(a)   section 57 of the Health and Social Care Act 2001 (direct payments);

[¹ (b)]

(c)   sections 12A to 12C of the National Health Service Act 2006 (direct payments for health care);

(d)   article 15 of the Health and Personal Social Services (Northern Ireland) Order 1972 (general social welfare); [²]

(e)   section 8 of the Carers and Direct Payments Act (Northern Ireland) 2002 (direct payments) [² ;]

[² (f)   sections 50 to 53 of the Social Services and Well-being (Wales) Act 2014; or

(g)   section 33 of the Care Act 2014.]

Amendments

1.   Amended by art 2 and Sch para 25(2) of SI 2014 No 513 as from 1.4.14.

2.   Amended by reg 8(b) of SI 2016 No 50 (W.21) as from 20.1.16, for schemes made for a financial year starting on or after 1.4.16.

[¹28A.   Any payment made as a direct payment as defined in section 4(2) of the Social Care (Self-directed Support) (Scotland) Act 2013.]

Amendment

1.   Inserted by art 2 and Sch para 25(3) of SI 2014 No 513 as from 1.4.14.

[¹28B.   Any payment made under or by a trust, established for the purpose of giving relief and assistance to disabled persons whose disabilities were caused by the fact that during their mother's pregnancy she had taken a preparation containing the drug known as Thalidomide, and which is approved by the Secretary of State.]

Amendment

1.   Inserted by reg 8(b) of SI 2018 No 14 (W.7) as from 10.1.18, for schemes made for a financial year starting on or after 1.4.18.

[¹28C.   Any bereavement support payment in respect of the rate set out in regulation 3(2) or (5) of the Bereavement Support Payment Regulations 2017 (rate of bereavement support payment), but only for a period of 52 weeks from the date of receipt of the payment.]

Amendment
1.   Inserted by reg 5(b) of SI 2019 No 11 (W.5) as from 9.1.19, for schemes made for a financial year starting on or after 1.4.19.

PART 2

Capital disregarded only for the purpose of determining deemed income
29.   The value of the right to receive any income under a life interest or from a life rent.
30.   The value of the right to receive any rent except where the applicant has a reversionary interest in the property in respect of which rent is due.
31.   The value of the right to receive any income under an annuity or the surrender value (if any) of such an annuity.
32.   Where property is held under a trust, other than–
(a)   a charitable trust within the meaning of the Charities Act 2011; or
(b)   a trust set up with any payment to which paragraph 16 applies,
and under the terms of the trust, payments fall to be made, or the trustees have a discretion to make payments, to or for the benefit of the applicant or the applicant's partner, or both, that property.
[¹**33.**   Any payment made by the Treasury to the applicant or the applicant's partner under the Age Related Payments Regulations 2013 (Equitable Life) as a qualifying Equitable Life annuitant.]

Amendment
1.   Inserted by reg 8(c) of SI 2014 No 66 (W.6) as from 15.1.14.

SCHEDULE 6

Regulation 33(2)

Determining eligibility for a reduction under an authority's scheme, amount of reduction and calculation of income and capital: persons who are not pensioners

PART 1
Applicable amounts for the purposes of calculating eligibility for a reduction under an authority's scheme and amount of reduction: persons who are not pensioners

Applicable amounts: persons who are not pensioners
1.–(1)   Subject to paragraphs 2 and 3, the applicable amount for a week for a person who is not a pensioner is the aggregate of such of the following amounts as may apply in the person's case–
(a)   an amount in respect of the person or, if that person is a member of a couple, an amount in respect of both of them, determined in accordance with paragraph 1 of Schedule 7 (personal allowances);
(b)   an amount in respect of any child or young person who is a member of the person's family, determined in accordance with paragraph 3 of Schedule 7 (child or young person amounts);
(c)   if the person is a member of a family of which at least one member is a child or young person, an amount determined in accordance with Part 2 of Schedule 7 (family premium);
(d)   the amount of any premiums which may be applicable to the person, determined in accordance with Parts 3 and 4 of Schedule 7 (premiums);
(e)   the amount of either the–
(i)   work-related activity component; or
(ii)   support component,
which may be applicable to the person in accordance with Parts 5 and 6 of that Schedule (the components);
(f)   the amount of any transitional addition which may be applicable to the person in accordance with Parts 7 and 8 of Schedule 7 (transitional addition).
(2)   In Schedule 7–
"additional spouse" ("priod ychwanegol") means a spouse of either party to the marriage who is additional to the other party to the marriage;
"converted employment and support allowance" ("lwfans cyflogaeth a chymorth a droswyd") means an employment and support allowance which is not income-related and to which a person is entitled as a result of a conversion decision within the meaning of the Employment and Support Allowance Regulations 2008;
"patient" ("claf") means a person (other than a person who is serving a sentence of imprisonment or detention in a youth custody institution) who is regarded as receiving free in-patient treatment within the meaning of regulation 2(4) and (5) of the Social Security (Hospital In-Patients) Regulations 2005.

General Note
This paragraph is almost identical to reg 22 HB Regs. See p412 for commentary but note that CTR schemes in Wales should not place a restriction on the number of children for whom an applicant can receive an allowance within her/his applicable amount under Sch 7 para 3 – ie, the so-called "two-child limit", which in some

circumstances applies to HB and CTR in England, does not apply to CTR in Wales. Also, a family premium is included in the assessment of the applicable amount in Wales if at least one child or young person (as defined by reg 2) is a member of the applicant's family. Unless transitional rules apply, a family premium is no longer included in the assessment of the applicable amount for HB.

Polygamous marriages: persons who are not pensioners

2.–(1)   This paragraph applies where an applicant who is not a pensioner is a member of a polygamous marriage and does not have (alone or jointly with a party to a marriage), an award of universal credit.

(2)   The applicable amount for a week of an applicant where this paragraph applies is the aggregate of such of the following amounts as may apply in that applicant's case–

(a)   the amount applicable to the applicant and one of the applicant's partners determined in accordance with paragraph 1(3) of Schedule 7 (couple) as if the applicant and that partner were a couple;

(b)   an amount equal to the difference between the amounts specified in sub-paragraphs (3) and (1)(b) of paragraph 1 of Schedule 7 in respect of each of the applicant's other partners;

(c)   an amount determined in accordance with paragraph 3 of Schedule 7 (child or young person amounts) in respect of any child or young person for whom the applicant or a partner of the applicant is responsible and who is a member of the same household;

(d)   if the applicant or another partner of the polygamous marriage is responsible for a child or young person who is a member of the same household, the amount specified in Part 2 of Schedule 7 (family premium);

(e)   the amount of any premiums which may be applicable to the applicant determined in accordance with Parts 3 and 4 of Schedule 7 (premiums);

(f)   the amount of either the–

(i)   work-related activity component; or

(ii)   support component;

which may be applicable to the applicant in accordance with Parts 5 and 6 of that Schedule (the components);

(g)   the amount of any transitional addition which may be applicable to the applicant in accordance with Parts 7 and 8 of that Schedule (transitional addition).

Applicable amount: persons who are not pensioners who have an award of universal credit

3.–(1)   Subject to sub-paragraph (2), in determining the applicable amount for a week of an applicant who is not a pensioner–

(a)   who has, or

(b)   who (jointly with a partner) has,

an award of universal credit, the authority will use the calculation or estimate of the maximum amount of the applicant, or the applicant and the applicant's partner jointly (as the case may be), subject to the adjustment described in sub-paragraph (3).

(2)   In determining the applicable amount for a week of an applicant who is a member of a polygamous marriage, the fact that two people are husband and wife is to be disregarded if–

(a)   one of them is a party to an earlier marriage that still subsists; and

(b)   the other party to that earlier marriage is living in the same household.

(3)   The adjustment referred to in sub-paragraph (1) is, to multiply the maximum amount by 12 and divide the product by 52.

(4)   In this paragraph "maximum amount" ("swm uchaf") means the maximum amount calculated by the Secretary of State in accordance with section 8(2) of the Welfare Reform Act 2012.

PART 2

Maximum council tax reduction for the purposes of calculating eligibility for a reduction under an authority's scheme and amount of reduction

Maximum council tax reduction under an authority's scheme: persons who are not pensioners

4.–(1)   Subject to sub-paragraphs (2) to (4), the amount of a person's maximum council tax reduction in respect of a day is 100 per cent of the amount A/B where–

(a)   A is the amount set by the authority as the council tax for the relevant financial year in respect of the dwelling in which the person is a resident and for which the person is liable, subject to any discount which may be appropriate to that dwelling under the 1992 Act; and

(b)   B is the number of days in that financial year,

less any deductions in respect of non-dependants which fall to be made under paragraph 5 (non-dependant deductions).

(2)   In calculating a person's maximum council tax reduction under an authority's scheme any reduction in the amount that person is liable to pay in respect of council tax, which is made in consequence of any enactment in, or made under, the 1992 Act (other than a reduction under an authority's scheme), is to be taken into account.

(3)   Subject to sub-paragraph (4), where an applicant is jointly and severally liable for council tax in respect of a dwelling in which the applicant is resident with one or more other persons, in determining the

maximum council tax reduction in the applicant's case in accordance with sub-paragraph (1), the amount A is to be divided by the number of persons who are jointly and severally liable for that tax.

(4)   Where an applicant is jointly and severally liable for council tax in respect of a dwelling with only a partner, sub-paragraph (3) does not apply in that applicant's case.

(5)   The reference in sub-paragraph (3) to a person with whom an applicant is jointly and severally liable for council tax does not include a student to whom paragraph 3 of Schedule 11 (students who are excluded from entitlement to a reduction under an authority's scheme) applies.

(6)   In this paragraph "relevant financial year" ("blwyddyn ariannol berthnasol") means, in relation to any particular day, the financial year within which the day in question falls.

Non-dependant deductions: persons who are not pensioners

5.–(1)   Subject to the following provisions of this paragraph, the non-dependant deductions in respect of a day referred to in paragraph 4 are–
(a)   in respect of a non-dependant aged 18 or over in remunerative work, [⁶ £13.75] x 1/7;
(b)   in respect of a non-dependant aged 18 or over to whom paragraph (a) does not apply, [⁶ £4.55] x 1/7.

(2)   In the case of a non-dependant aged 18 or over to whom sub-paragraph (1)(a) applies, where it is shown to the appropriate authority that that non-dependant's normal gross weekly income is–
(a)   less than [⁶ £210.00], the deduction to be made under this paragraph is that specified in sub-paragraph (1)(b);
(b)   not less than [⁶ £210.00] but less than [⁶ £365.00], the deduction to be made under this paragraph is [⁶ £9.15] x 1/7;
(c)   not less than [⁶ £365.00] but less than [⁶ £450.00], the deduction to be made under this paragraph is [⁶ £11.50] x 1/7.

(3)   Only one deduction is to be made under this paragraph in respect of a couple or, as the case may be, members of a polygamous marriage (other than where there is an award of universal credit) and, where, but for this paragraph, the amount that would fall to be deducted in respect of one member of a couple or polygamous marriage is higher than the amount (if any) that would fall to be deducted in respect of the other, or any other, member, the higher amount is to be deducted.

(4)   In applying the provisions of sub-paragraph (2) in the case of a couple or, as the case may be, a polygamous marriage, regard must be had, for the purpose of that sub-paragraph, to the couple's or, as the case may be, all members of the polygamous marriage's joint weekly gross income.

(5)   Where in respect of a day–
(a)   a person is a resident in a dwelling but that person is not liable for council tax in respect of that dwelling and that day;
(b)   other residents in that dwelling (the liable persons) have joint and several liability for council tax in respect of that dwelling and that day otherwise than by virtue of section 9 of the 1992 Act (liability of spouses and civil partners); and
(c)   the person to whom paragraph (a) refers is a non-dependant of two or more of the liable persons,
the deduction in respect of that non-dependant must be apportioned equally between those liable persons.

(6)   No deduction is to be made in respect of any non-dependants occupying an applicant's dwelling if the applicant or the applicant's partner is–
(a)   [³ blind or severely sight-impaired or treated as such] by virtue of paragraph 10 of Schedule 7 (additional condition for the disability premium); or
(b)   is receiving in respect of the applicant–
  (i)   attendance allowance or would be receiving that allowance but for–
    (aa)   a suspension of benefit in accordance with regulations under section 113(2) of the SSCBA; or
    (bb)   an abatement as a result of hospitalisation; or
  (ii)   the care component of the disability living allowance, or would be receiving that component but for–
    (aa)   a suspension of benefit in accordance with regulations under section 113(2) of the SSCBA; or
    (bb)   an abatement as a result of hospitalisation; or
  (iii)   the daily living component of personal independence payment or would be receiving that allowance but for a suspension of benefit in accordance with regulations under section 86 of the Welfare Reform Act 2012 (hospital in-patients); or
  (iv)   an AFIP, or would be receiving that payment but for a suspension of it in accordance with any terms of the armed and reserve forces compensation scheme which allows for a suspension because a person is undergoing medical treatment in a hospital or similar institution.

(7)   No deduction is to be made in respect of a non-dependant if–
(a)   although that non-dependant resides with the applicant, it appears to the authority that that non-dependant's normal home is elsewhere; or
(b)   the non-dependant is in receipt of a training allowance paid in connection with youth training established under section 2 of the Employment and Training Act 1973 or section 2 of the Enterprise and New Towns (Scotland) Act 1990; or

(c)   the non-dependant is a full-time student within the meaning of Schedule 11 (students); or

(d)   the non-dependant is not residing with the applicant because the non-dependant has been a patient for a period in excess of 52 weeks, and for these purposes–

     (i)   "patient" ("claf") has the meaning given in [¹ regulation 26(6)], and

     (ii)   where a person has been a patient for two or more distinct periods separated by one or more intervals each not exceeding 28 days, that person is to be treated as having been a patient continuously for a period equal in duration to the total of those distinct periods.

(8)   No deduction is to be made in respect of a non-dependant–

[⁶ (a)   who isnot a member of the work-related activity group, and is on income support, state pension credit, an income-based jobseeker's allowance or an income related employment and support allowance;] [²]

(b)   to whom Schedule 1 to the 1992 Act applies (persons disregarded for purposes of discount); but this paragraph does not apply to a non-dependant who is a student to whom paragraph 4 of that Schedule refers.[²; or]

[² (c)   who is entitled to an award of universal credit where the award is calculated on the basis that the person does not have any earned income.]

(9)   In the application of sub-paragraph (2) there is to be disregarded from the non-dependant's weekly gross income–

(a)   any attendance allowance, disability living allowance or personal independence payment or AFIP received by the non-dependant;

(b)   any payment made under or by the Trusts, the Fund, the Eileen Trust, MFET Limited, the Skipton Fund, the Caxton Foundation [⁵, an approved blood scheme, the Scottish Infected Blood Support Scheme, the London Emergencies Trust, the We Love Manchester Emergency Fund] or the Independent Living Fund (2006) which, had the non-dependant's income fallen to be calculated under paragraph 17 (calculation of income other than earnings), would have been disregarded under paragraph 28 of Schedule 9 (income in kind);

(c)   any payment which, had the non-dependant's income fallen to be calculated under paragraph 17 (calculation of income other than earnings), would have been disregarded under paragraph 41 of Schedule 9 (payments made under certain trusts and certain other payments)[⁵ ;

(d)   any payment made under or by a trust, established for the purpose of giving relief and assistance to disabled persons whose disabilities were caused by the fact that during their mother's pregnancy she had taken a preparation containing the drug known as Thalidomide, and which is approved by the Secretary of State.]

[² (10)   For the purposes of sub-paragraph (8), "earned income" ("incwm a enillir") has the meaning given in regulation 52 of the Universal Credit Regulations 2013.]

Amendments

1.   Amended by reg 9(a) of SI 2014 No 66 (W.6) as from 15.1.14.

2.   Amended by reg 10(a) of SI 2015 No 44 (W.3) as from 21.1.15, for schemes made for a financial year starting on or after 1.4.15.

3.   Amended by reg 9(a) of SI 2016 No 50 (W.21) as from 20.1.16, for schemes made for a financial year starting on or after 1.4.16.

4.   Amended by reg 5(a) of SI 2017 No 46 (W.20) as from 19.1.17, for schemes made for a financial year starting on or after 1.4.17.

5.   Amended by reg 9(a) of SI 2018 No 14 (W.7) as from 10.1.18, for schemes made for a financial year starting on or after 1.4.18.

6.   Amended by reg 6(a) of SI 2019 No 11 (W.5) as from 9.1.19, for schemes made for a financial year starting on or after 1.4.19.

General Note

The rules on non-dependant deductions for applicants who are not pensioners are largely the same as those for pensioners which are contained in Sch 1 para 3 of these regulations. See p1219 for relevant commentary.

PART 3
Amount of reduction under an authority's scheme

Amount of reduction under an authority's scheme: Classes C and D

6.–(1)   Where a person is entitled to a reduction under an authority's scheme in respect of a day, the amount of the reduction to which that person is entitled is as follows.

(2)   Where the person is within class C, that amount is the amount which is the maximum council tax reduction in respect of the day in the person's case.

(3)   Where the person is within class D, that amount is the amount found by deducting amount B from amount A, where "amount A" and "amount B" have the meanings given in regulation 25.

PART 4
Income and capital for the purposes of calculating eligibility for a reduction under an authority's scheme and
amount of reduction
CHAPTER 1
Income and capital: general

Calculation of income and capital: applicant's family and polygamous marriages: persons who are not pensioners

7.–(1)   The income and capital of–
(a)   an applicant; and
(b)   any partner of that applicant,
is to be calculated in accordance with the provisions of this Part.

(2)   The income and capital of any partner of the applicant is to be treated as income and capital of the applicant, and in this Part any reference to the applicant applies equally to any partner of that applicant.

(3)   Where an applicant or the partner of an applicant is married polygamously to two or more members of the applicant's household–
(a)   the applicant must be treated as possessing capital and income belonging to each such member; and
(b)   the income and capital of that member is to be calculated in accordance with the following provisions of this Part in like manner as for the applicant.

General Note
This is equivalent to Sch 1 para 5. See commentary on p1220.

Circumstances in which capital and income of non dependant is to be treated as applicant's: persons who are not pensioners

8.–(1)   Sub-paragraph (2) applies where it appears to an authority that a non-dependant and an applicant have entered into arrangements in order to take advantage of the authority's scheme and the non-dependant has more income and capital than the applicant.

(2)   Except where the applicant is on income support, an income-based jobseeker's allowance or an income related employment and support allowance, the authority must treat the applicant as possessing income and capital belonging to that non-dependant and, in such a case, any capital and income which the applicant does possess is to be disregarded.

(3)   Where an applicant is treated as possessing capital and income belonging to a non-dependant under sub-paragraph (2) the income and capital of that non-dependant must be calculated in accordance with the following provisions of this Part in like manner as for the applicant and, except where the context otherwise requires, any reference to the "applicant" is to be construed for the purposes of this Part as if it were a reference to that non-dependant.

CHAPTER 2
Income and capital where there is an award of universal credit

Calculation of income and capital: persons who are not pensioners who have an award of universal credit

9.–(1)   In determining the income of an applicant–
(a)   who has, or
(b)   who (jointly with a partner) has,
an award of universal credit the authority must, subject to the following provisions of this paragraph, use the calculation or estimate of the income of the applicant, or the applicant and the applicant's partner jointly (as the case may be), made by the Secretary of State for the purpose of determining the award of universal credit.

(2)   The authority must adjust the amount of the income referred to in sub-paragraph (1) by multiplying the amount by 12 and dividing the product by 52.

(3)   The authority must only adjust the amount of the income as adjusted in accordance with sub-paragraph (2) so far as is necessary to take into account–
(a)   the amount of the award of universal credit determined in accordance with sub-paragraph (4);
(b)   paragraph 8 (income and capital of non-dependant to be treated as applicant's), if the authority determines that the provision applies in the applicant's case;
(c)   such further reduction (if any) as the authority thinks fit under section 13A(1)(c) of the 1992 Act (power of billing authority to reduce amount of council tax payable).

(4)   The amount for the award of universal credit is to be taken into account for the purposes of sub-paragraph (3)(a) is to be determined by multiplying the amount of the award of universal credit by 12 and dividing the product by 52.

(5)   Paragraph 8 (income and capital of non-dependant to be treated as applicant's) applies for the purposes of determining any adjustments which fall to be made to the figure for income under sub-paragraph (3).

(6)   In determining the capital of an applicant–
(a)   who has, or

(b)   who (jointly with a partner) has,

an award of universal credit, the authority must use the calculation or estimate of the capital of the applicant, or the applicant and the applicant's partner jointly (as the case may be), made by the Secretary of State for the purpose of determining the award of universal credit.

Analysis

Paragraph 9 sets out how an applicant's income and capital are calculated for the purpose of assessing CTR entitlement, if the applicant has, or the applicant and her/his partner jointly have, an award of universal credit (UC).

Unless para 8 applies (see below), the income used in the CTR calculation is:

(1)   the applicant's income, or the applicant's and the applicant's partner's income jointly, as calculated or estimated by the DWP for the purpose of determining the UC award (converted into a weekly figure by multiplying the amount by 12 and dividing by 52). However the billing authority has the discretion to adjust this amount to take account of any discretionary council tax reduction awarded: sub-paras (1), (2) and (3)(c); *plus*

(2)   the amount of the award of UC (converted into a weekly figure by multiplying the amount by 12 and dividing by 52): sub-paras (3)(a) and (4).

Note that the income of an applicant's non-dependant is used instead of that of the applicant if the circumstances in para 8 apply – ie, if it appears to the billing authority that the applicant and non-dependant have made arrangements so as to take advantage of the council tax reduction scheme and the non-dependant has more income and capital than the applicant: sub-para (3)(b) and para 8.

The capital used in the CTR calculation is the applicant's capital, or the applicant's and the applicant's partner's capital, as calculated or estimated by the DWP for the purpose of determining the UC award: sub-para (6).

CHAPTER 3
Income: persons who are not pensioners

Average weekly earnings of employed earners: persons who are not pensioners

10.–(1)   Where the income of an applicant who is not a pensioner consists of earnings from employment as an employed earner the applicant's average weekly earnings must be estimated by reference to the applicant's earnings from that employment–

(a)   over a period immediately preceding the reduction week in which the application is made or treated as made and being a period of–

(i)   5 weeks, if the applicant is paid weekly; or

(ii)   2 months, if the applicant is paid monthly; or

(b)   whether or not paragraph (a)(i) or (ii) applies, where an applicant's earnings fluctuate, over such other period preceding the reduction week in which the application is made or treated as made as may, in any particular case, enable the applicant's average weekly earnings to be estimated more accurately.

(2)   Where the applicant has been in employment for less than the period specified in sub-paragraph (1)(a)(i) or (ii)–

(a)   if the applicant has received any earnings [¹ or expects to receive an amount of earnings] for the period that the applicant has been in that employment and those earnings are likely to represent the applicant's average weekly earnings from that employment the applicant's average weekly earnings must be estimated by reference to those earnings;

(b)   in any other case, the authority must estimate the applicant's average weekly earnings.

(3)   Where the amount of an applicant's earnings changes the authority must estimate the applicant's average weekly earnings by reference to the applicant's likely earnings from the employment over such period as is appropriate in order that the applicant's average weekly earnings may be estimated accurately but the length of the period must not in any case exceed 52 weeks.

(4)   For the purposes of this paragraph the applicant's earnings are to be calculated in accordance with paragraphs 14 and 15 (earnings of employed earners).

Amendment

1.   Amended by reg 5(b) of SI 2017 No 46 (W.20) as from 19.1.17, for schemes made for a financial year starting on or after 1.4.17.

[¹**Date on which income consisting of earnings from employment as an employed earner are taken into account: persons who are not pensioners**

10A.   An applicant's average weekly earnings from employment estimated pursuant to paragraph 10 (average weekly earnings of employed earners: persons who are not pensioners) and paragraphs 14 and 15 (earnings of employed earners: persons who are not pensioners) of this Schedule must be taken into account–

(a)   in the case of an application, on the date on which the application was made or treated as made, and the first day of each reduction week thereafter, [² regardless of when those earnings were actually received];

[² (b)   in the case of an application or a reduction under a scheme where the applicant commences employment, the day on which the applicant commences that employment, and the first day of each reduction week thereafter, regardless of when those earnings were actually received; or

(c)   in the case of an application or reduction under a scheme where the applicant's average weekly earnings from employment change, the day on which the applicant's earnings from employment change, and the first day of each reduction week thereafter, regardless of when those earnings were actually received.]]

Amendments
1.   Inserted by reg 5(c) of SI 2017 No 46 (W.20) as from 19.1.17, for schemes made for a financial year starting on or after 1.4.17.
2.   Amended by reg 9(b) of SI 2018 No 14 (W.7) as from 10.1.18, for schemes made for a financial year starting on or after 1.4.18.

Average weekly earnings of self-employed earners: persons who are not pensioners
11.–(1)   Where the income of an applicant who is not a pensioner consists of earnings from employment as a self-employed earner that applicant's average weekly earnings must be estimated by reference to that applicant's earnings from that employment over such period as is appropriate in order that that applicant's average weekly earnings may be estimated accurately but the length of the period must not in any case exceed 52 weeks.

(2)   For the purposes of this paragraph the applicant's earnings must be calculated in accordance with paragraphs 16, 24 and 25 (earnings and net profit of self-employed earners).

Average weekly income other than earnings: persons who are not pensioners
12.–(1)   The income of an applicant who is not a pensioner which does not consist of earnings must, except where sub-paragraph (2) applies, be estimated over such period as is appropriate in order that that applicant's average weekly income may be estimated accurately but the length of the period must not in any case exceed 52 weeks; and nothing in this paragraph authorises an authority to disregard any such income other than that specified in Schedule 9 (sums disregarded in the calculation of income other than earnings).

(2)   The period over which any benefit under the benefit Acts is to be taken into account is to be the period in respect of which that benefit is payable.

(3)   For the purposes of this paragraph income other than earnings is to be calculated in accordance with paragraph 17 (calculation of income other than earnings).

Calculation of weekly income of employed earners: persons who are not pensioners
13.–(1)   For the purposes of paragraphs 10 (average weekly earnings of employed earners), 12 (average weekly income other than earnings) and 22 (calculation of average weekly income from tax credits), where the period in respect of which a payment is made–
(a)   does not exceed a week, the weekly amount is to be the amount of that payment;
(b)   exceeds a week, the weekly amount is to be determined–
    (i)   in a case where that period is a month, by multiplying the amount of the payment by 12 and dividing the product by 52;
    (ii)   in any other case, by dividing the amount of the payment by the number equal to the number of days in the period to which it relates and multiplying the quotient by 7.

(2)   For the purposes of paragraph 11 (average weekly earnings of self-employed earners) the weekly amount of earnings of an applicant is to be determined by dividing the applicant's earnings over the assessment period by the number equal to the number of days in that period and multiplying the quotient by 7.

Earnings of employed earners: persons who are not pensioners
14.–(1)   Subject to sub-paragraph (2), "earnings" ("*enillion*"), in the case of employment as an employed earner of a person who is not a pensioner, means any remuneration or profit derived from that employment and includes–
(a)   any bonus or commission;
(b)   any payment in lieu of remuneration except any periodic sum paid to an applicant on account of the termination of the applicant's employment by reason of redundancy;
(c)   any payment in lieu of notice or any lump sum payment intended as compensation for the loss of employment but only in so far as it represents loss of income;
(d)   any holiday pay except any payable more than 4 weeks after termination or interruption of the employment;
(e)   any payment by way of a retainer;
(f)   any payment made by the applicant's employer in respect of expenses not wholly, exclusively and necessarily incurred in the performance of the duties of the employment, including any payment made by the applicant's employer in respect of–

(i)   travelling expenses incurred by the applicant between the applicant's home and place of employment;

(ii)   expenses incurred by the applicant under arrangements made for the care of a member of the applicant's family owing to the applicant's absence from home;

(g)   any award of compensation made under section 112(4) or 117(3)(a) of the Employment Rights Act 1996 (remedies and compensation for unfair dismissal);

(h)   any payment or remuneration made under section 28, 34, 64, 68 or 70 of the Employment Rights Act 1996 (right to guarantee payments, remuneration on suspension on medical or maternity grounds, complaints to employment tribunals);

(i)   any such sum as is referred to in section 112 of the SSCBA (certain sums to be earnings for social security purposes);

(j)   any statutory sick pay, statutory maternity pay, statutory paternity pay [¹, statutory shared parental pay] or statutory adoption pay, or a corresponding payment under any enactment having effect in Northern Ireland;

(k)   any remuneration paid by or on behalf of an employer to the applicant who for the time being is on maternity leave, paternity leave [¹, shared parental leave] or adoption leave or is absent from work because the applicant is ill;

(l)   the amount of any payment by way of a non-cash voucher which has been taken into account in the computation of a person's earnings in accordance with Part 5 of Schedule 3 to the Social Security (Contributions) Regulations 2001.

(2)   Earnings does not include–

(a)   subject to sub-paragraph (3), any payment in kind;

(b)   any payment in respect of expenses wholly, exclusively and necessarily incurred in the performance of the duties of the employment;

(c)   any occupational pension;

(d)   any payment in respect of expenses arising out of the applicant's participation in a service user group.

(3)   Sub-paragraph (2)(a) does not apply in respect of any non-cash voucher referred to in sub-paragraph (1)(l).

Amendment

1.   Amended by reg 10(b) of SI 2015 No 44 (W.3) as from 21.1.15, for schemes made for a financial year starting on or after 1.4.15.

Calculation of net earnings of employed earners: persons who are not pensioners

15.–(1)   For the purposes of paragraph 10 (average weekly earnings of employed earners: persons who are not pensioners), the earnings of an applicant derived or likely to be derived from employment as an employed earner to be taken into account must, subject to sub-paragraph (2), be the applicant's net earnings.

(2)   There is to be disregarded from an applicant's net earnings, any sum, where applicable, specified in paragraphs 1 to 18 of Schedule 8 (sums disregarded in the calculation of earnings).

(3)   For the purposes of sub-paragraph (1) net earnings must, except where sub-paragraph (6) applies, be calculated by taking into account the gross earnings of the applicant from that employment over the assessment period, less–

(a)   any amount deducted from those earnings by way of–

(i)   income tax;

(ii)   primary Class 1 contributions under the SSCBA;

(b)   one-half of any sum paid by the applicant by way of a contribution towards an occupational pension scheme;

(c)   one-half of the amount calculated in accordance with sub-paragraph (5) in respect of any qualifying contribution payable by the applicant; and

(d)   where those earnings include a payment which is payable under any enactment having effect in Northern Ireland and which corresponds to statutory sick pay, statutory maternity pay, [¹] statutory paternity pay [¹, statutory shared parental pay] or statutory adoption pay, any amount deducted from those earnings by way of any contributions which correspond to primary Class 1 contributions under the SSCBA.

(4)   In this paragraph "qualifying contribution" ("cyfraniad cymwys") means any sum which is payable periodically as a contribution towards a personal pension scheme.

(5)   The amount in respect of any qualifying contribution is to be calculated by multiplying the daily amount of the qualifying contribution by the number equal to the number of days in the assessment period; and for the purposes of this paragraph the daily amount of the qualifying contribution is to be determined–

(a)   where the qualifying contribution is payable monthly, by multiplying the amount of the qualifying contribution by 12 and dividing the product by 365;

(b)   in any other case, by dividing the amount of the qualifying contribution by the number equal to the number of days in the period to which the qualifying contribution relates.

(6)   Where the earnings of an applicant are estimated under paragraph 10 (average weekly earnings of employed earners: persons who are not pensioners), the applicant's net earnings are to be calculated by taking into account those earnings over the assessment period, less–

(a)   an amount in respect of income tax equivalent to an amount calculated by applying to those earnings the basic rate of tax applicable to the assessment period less only the [² personal reliefs to which the applicant is entitled under Chapters 2, 3 and 3A of Part 3] of the Income Tax Act2007 [²] as is appropriate to the applicant's circumstances but, if the assessment period is less than a year, the earnings to which the basic rate of tax is to be applied and the amount of the personal [² reliefs] deductible under this sub- paragraph is to be calculated on a pro rata basis;

(b)   an amount equivalent to the amount of the primary Class 1 contributions that would be payable by the applicant under the SSCBA in respect of those earnings if such contributions were payable; and

(c)   one-half of any sum which would be payable by the applicant by way of a contribution towards an occupational or personal pension scheme, if the earnings so estimated were actual earnings.

Amendments

1.   Amended by reg 10(c) of SI 2015 No 44 (W.3) as from 21.1.15, for schemes made for a financial year starting on or after 1.4.15.

2.   Amended by reg 5(d) of SI 2017 No 46 (W.20) as from 19.1.17, for schemes made for a financial year starting on or after 1.4.17.

Earnings of self-employed earners: persons who are not pensioners

16.–(1)   Subject to sub-paragraph (2), "earnings" ("enillion"), in the case of employment as a self-employed earner of a person who is not a pensioner, means the gross income of the employment.

(2)   "Earnings" does not include any payment to which paragraph 31 or 32 of Schedule 9 refers (payments in respect of a person accommodated with the applicant under arrangements made by a local authority or voluntary organisation and payments made to the applicant by a health authority, local authority or voluntary organisation in respect of persons temporarily in the applicant's care) nor does it include any sports award.

(3)   This paragraph applies to–

(a)   royalties or other sums paid as a consideration for the use of, or the right to use, any copyright, design, patent or trade mark; or

(b)   any payment in respect of any–
        (i)   book registered under the Public Lending Right Scheme 1982; or
        (ii)   work made under any international public lending right scheme that is analogous to the Public Lending Right Scheme 1982,

where the applicant is the first owner of the copyright, design, patent or trade mark, or an original contributor to the book or work concerned.

(4)   Where the applicant's earnings consist of any items to which sub-paragraph (3) applies, those earnings must be taken into account over a period equal to such number of weeks as is equal to the number obtained (and any fraction is to be treated as a corresponding fraction of a week) by dividing the earnings by–

(a)   the amount of reduction under an authority's scheme to which the applicant would have been entitled had the payment not been made, plus

(b)   an amount equal to the total of the sums which would fall to be disregarded from the payment under Schedule 8 (sums disregarded in the calculation of earnings) as appropriate in the applicant's case.

Calculation of income other than earnings: persons who are not pensioners

17.–(1)   For the purposes of paragraph 12 (average weekly income other than earnings: persons who are not pensioners; persons who are not pensioners), the income of an applicant who is not a pensioner which does not consist of earnings to be taken into account must, subject to sub-paragraphs (2) to (6), be that applicant's gross income and any capital treated as income under paragraph 18 (capital treated as income; persons who are not pensioners).

(2)   There is to be disregarded from the calculation of an applicant's gross income under sub-paragraph (1), any sum, where applicable, specified in Schedule 9.

(3)   Where the payment of any benefit under the benefit Acts is subject to any deduction by way of recovery the amount to be taken into account under sub-paragraph (1) must be the gross amount payable.

(4)   Where the applicant or, where the applicant is a member of a couple, the applicant's partner is receiving a contributory employment and support allowance and that benefit has been reduced under regulation 63 of the Employment and Support Allowance Regulations 2008 [¹ or section 11J of the Welfare Reform Act 2007], the amount of that benefit to be taken into account is the amount as if it had not been reduced.

(5)   Where an award of any working tax credit or child tax credit under the Tax Credits Act 2002 is subject to a deduction by way of recovery of an overpayment of working tax credit or child tax credit which arose in a previous tax year the amount to be taken into account under sub-paragraph (1) is to be the amount of working tax credit or child tax credit awarded less the amount of that deduction.

(6)   Sub-paragraphs (7) and (8) apply where–

(a)   a relevant payment has been made to a person in an academic year; and

(b)   that person abandons, or is dismissed from, that person's course of study before the payment to that person of the final instalment of the relevant payment.

(7)   Where a relevant payment is made quarterly, the amount of a relevant payment to be taken into account for the assessment period for the purposes of sub-paragraph (1) in respect of a person to whom sub-paragraph (6) applies, is to be calculated by applying the formula–

$$\frac{(A - (B \times C))}{D}$$

where–

A = the total amount of the relevant payment which that person would have received had that person remained a student until the last day of the academic term in which that person abandoned, or was dismissed from, the course, less any deduction under paragraph 9(5) of Schedule 11 (costs of travel, books and equipment);

B = the number of reduction weeks from the reduction week immediately following that which includes the first day of that academic year to the reduction week which includes the day on which the person abandoned, or was dismissed from, the course;

C = the weekly amount of the relevant payment, before the application of the £10 disregard, which would have been taken into account as income under paragraph 9(2) of Schedule 11 (treatment of student loans) had the person not abandoned or been dismissed from, the course and, in the case of a person who was not entitled to a reduction under an authority's scheme immediately before that person abandoned or was dismissed from the course, had that person, at that time, been entitled to housing benefit;

D = the number of reduction weeks in the assessment period.

(8)   Where a relevant payment is made by two or more instalments in a quarter, the amount of a relevant payment to be taken into account for the assessment period for the purposes of sub-paragraph (1) in respect of a person to whom sub-paragraph (6) applies, is to be calculated by applying the formula in sub-paragraph (7) but as if–

A= the total amount of relevant payments which that person received, or would have received, from the first day of the academic year to the day the person abandoned the course, or was dismissed from it, less any deduction under paragraph 9(5) of Schedule 11.

(9)   In this paragraph–

"academic year" ("blwyddyn academaidd") and "student loan" ("benthyciad myfyriwr") have the same meanings as in Schedule 11 (students);

"assessment period" ("cyfnod asesu") means–

(a)   in a case where a relevant payment is made quarterly, the period beginning with the reduction week which includes the day on which the person abandoned, or was dismissed from, the course and ending with the reduction week which includes the last day of the last quarter for which an instalment of the relevant payment was payable to that person;

(b)   in a case where the relevant payment is made by two or more instalments in a quarter, the period beginning with the reduction week which includes the day on which the person abandoned, or was dismissed from, the course and ending with the reduction week which includes–

(i)   the day immediately before the day on which the next instalment of the relevant payment would have been due had the payments continued; or

(ii)   the last day of the last quarter for which an instalment of the relevant payment was payable to that person,

whichever of those dates is earlier;

"quarter" ("chwarter") in relation to an assessment period means a period in that year beginning on–

(a)   1 January and ending on 31 March;

(b)   1 April and ending on 30 June;

(c)   1 July and ending on 31 August; or

(d)   1 September and ending on 31 December;

"relevant payment" ("taliad perthnasol") means either a student loan or an amount intended for the maintenance of dependants referred to in paragraph 4(7) of Schedule 11 or both.

(10)   For the avoidance of doubt there must be included as income to be taken into account under sub-paragraph (1)–

(a)   any payment to which paragraph 14(2) (payments not earnings) applies; or

(b)   in the case of an applicant who is receiving support under section 95 or 98 of the Immigration and Asylum Act 1999 including support provided by virtue of regulations made under Schedule 9 to that Act, the amount of such support provided in respect of essential living needs of the applicant and the applicant's dependants (if any) as is specified in regulations made under paragraph 3 of Schedule 8 to the Immigration and Asylum Act 1999.

Amendment

1.   Amended by reg 10(d) of SI 2015 No 44 (W.3) as from 21.1.15, for schemes made for a financial year starting on or after 1.4.15.

Capital treated as income: persons who are not pensioners

18.–(1)   Any capital payable by instalments which are outstanding at the date on which the application is made or treated as made, or, at the date of any subsequent revision or supersession, must, if the aggregate of the instalments outstanding and the amount of the applicant's capital otherwise calculated in accordance with paragraphs 26 to 33 of this Schedule exceeds £16,000, be treated as income.

(2)   Any payment received under an annuity is to be treated as income.

(3)   Any earnings to the extent that they are not a payment of income is to be treated as income.

(4)   Any Career Development Loan paid pursuant to section 2 of the Employment and Training Act 1973 is to be treated as income.

(5)   Where an agreement or court order provides that payments must be made to the applicant in consequence of any personal injury to the applicant and that such payments are to be made, wholly or partly, by way of periodic payments, any such periodic payments received by the applicant (but not a payment which is treated as capital by virtue of this Part), is to be treated as income.

Notional income: persons who are not pensioners

19.–(1)   An applicant who is not a pensioner is to be treated as possessing income of which that applicant has deprived himself or herself for the purpose of securing entitlement to a reduction or increasing the amount of the reduction.

(2)   Except in the case of–

(a)   a discretionary trust;

(b)   a trust derived from a payment made in consequence of a personal injury;

(c)   a personal pension scheme, occupational pension scheme or a payment made by the Board of the Pension Protection Fund where the applicant has not attained the qualifying age for state pension credit;

(d)   any sum to which paragraph 48(2)(a) of Schedule 10 (capital to be disregarded) applies which is administered in the way referred to in paragraph 48(1)(a) of that Schedule;

(e)   any sum to which paragraph 49(a) of Schedule 10 refers;

(f)   rehabilitation allowance made under section 2 of the Employment and Training Act 1973;

(g)   child tax credit;

(h)   working tax credit, or

(i)   any sum to which sub-paragraph (11) applies,

any income which would become available to the applicant upon application being made, but which has not been acquired by the applicant, is to be treated as possessed by the applicant but only from the date on which it could be expected to be acquired were an application made.

(3)   Any payment of income, other than a payment of income specified in sub-paragraph (4), made–

(a)   to a third party in respect of a single applicant or a member of the family (but not a member of the third party's family) must, where that payment is a payment of an occupational pension, a pension or other periodical payment made under a personal pension scheme or a payment made by the Board of the Pension Protection Fund, be treated as possessed by that single applicant or, as the case may be, by that member;

(b)   to a third party in respect of a single applicant or in respect of a member of the family (but not a member of the third party's family) must, where it is not a payment referred to in paragraph (a), be treated as possessed by that single applicant or by that member to the extent that it is used for the food, ordinary clothing or footwear, household fuel or rent of that single applicant or, as the case may be, of any member of that family or is used for any council tax or water charges for which that applicant or member is liable;

(c)   to a single applicant or a member of the family in respect of a third party (but not in respect of another member of that family) must be treated as possessed by that single applicant or, as the case may be, that member of the family to the extent that it is kept or used by that single applicant or used by or on behalf of any member of the family.

(4)   Sub-paragraph (3) does not apply in respect of a payment of income made–

(a)   under or by the Trusts, the Fund, the Eileen Trust, MFET Limited, the Skipton Fund, the Caxton Foundation [², an approved blood scheme, the Scottish Infected Blood Support Scheme, the London Emergencies Trust, the We Love Manchester Emergency Fund] or the Independent Living Fund (2006);

(b)   pursuant to section 19(1)(a) of the Coal Industry Act 1994 (concessionary coal);

(c)   pursuant to section 2 of the Employment and Training Act 1973 in respect of a person's participation–

(i)   in an employment programme specified in regulation 75(1)(a) of the Jobseeker's Allowance Regulations 1996;

(ii)   in a training scheme specified in regulation 75(1)(b) of those Regulations; or

(iii)   in a qualifying course within the meaning specified in regulation 17A(7) of those Regulations;

(d)   in respect of a person's participation in the Work for Your Benefit Pilot Scheme;

(e)   in respect of a person's participation in the Mandatory Work Activity Scheme;

(f)   in respect of an applicant's participation in the Employment, Skills and Enterprise Scheme;

(g)   under an occupational pension scheme, in respect of a pension or other periodical payment made under a personal pension scheme or a payment made by the Board of the Pension Protection Fund where–

(i)   a bankruptcy order has been made in respect of the person in respect of whom the payment has been made or, in Scotland, the estate of that person is subject to sequestration or a judicial factor has been appointed on that person's estate under section 41 of the Solicitors (Scotland) Act 1980;

(ii)   the payment is made to the trustee in bankruptcy or any other person acting on behalf of the creditors; and

(iii)   the person referred to in sub-paragraph (i) and any member of that person's family does not possess, or is not treated as possessing, any other income apart from that payment.

(5)   Where an applicant is in receipt of any benefit under the benefit Acts and the rate of that benefit is altered with effect from a date on or after 1 April in any year but not more than 14 days thereafter, the authority must treat the applicant as possessing such benefit at the altered rate from either 1 April or the first Monday in April in that year, whichever date the authority selects, to the date on which the altered rate is to take effect.

(6)   Subject to sub-paragraph (7), where–

(a)   an applicant performs a service for another person; and

(b)   that person makes no payment of earnings or pays less than that paid for a comparable employment in the area,

the authority must treat the applicant as possessing such earnings (if any) as is reasonable for that employment unless the applicant satisfies the authority that the means of that person are insufficient for that person to pay or to pay more for the service.

(7)   Sub-paragraph (6) does not apply–

(a)   to an applicant who is engaged by a charitable or voluntary organisation or who is a volunteer if the authority is satisfied in any of those cases that it is reasonable for the applicant to provide those services free of charge; or

(b)   in a case where the service is performed in connection with–

(i)   the applicant's participation in an employment or training programme in accordance with regulation 19(1)(q) of the Jobseeker's Allowance Regulations 1996; or

(ii)   the applicant's or the applicant's partner's participation in an employment or training programme as defined in regulation 19(3) of those Regulations for which a training allowance is not payable or, where such an allowance is payable, it is payable for the sole purpose of reimbursement of travelling or meal expenses to the person participating in that programme; or

(c)   to an applicant who is participating in a work placement approved by the Secretary of State (or a person providing services to the Secretary of State) before the placement starts.

(8)   In sub-paragraph (7)(c) "work placement" ("lleoliad gwaith") means practical work experience which is not undertaken in expectation of payment.

(9)   Where an applicant is treated as possessing any income under any of sub-paragraphs (1) to (8), the foregoing provisions of this Part apply for the purposes of calculating the amount of that income as if a payment had actually been made and as if it were actual income which that applicant does possess.

(10)   Where an applicant is treated as possessing any earnings under sub-paragraph (6) the foregoing provisions of this Part apply for the purposes of calculating the amount of those earnings as if a payment had actually been made and as if they were actual earnings which that applicant does possess except that paragraph 15(3) (calculation of net earnings of employed earners: persons who are not pensioners) does not apply and that applicant's net earnings are to be calculated by taking into account those earnings which that applicant is treated as possessing, less–

(a)   an amount in respect of income tax equivalent to an amount calculated by applying to those earnings the basic rate of tax applicable to the assessment period less only the [¹ personal relief to which the applicant is entitled under Chapters 2, 3 and 3A of Part 3] of the Income Tax Act 2007 [¹] as is appropriate to the applicant's circumstances; but, if the assessment period is less than a year, the earnings to which the basic rate of tax is to be applied and the amount of the personal [¹ reliefs] deductible under this sub-paragraph is to be calculated on a pro rata basis;

(b)   an amount equivalent to the amount of the primary Class 1 contributions that would be payable by the applicant under the SSCBA in respect of those earnings if such contributions were payable; and

(c)   one-half of any sum payable by the applicant by way of a contribution towards an occupational or personal pension scheme.

(11)   Sub-paragraphs (1), (2), (3) and (6) do not apply in respect of any amount of income other than earnings, or earnings of an employed earner, arising out of the applicant's participation in a service user group.

Amendments

1.   Amended by reg 5(e) of SI 2017 No 46 (W.20) as from 19.1.17, for schemes made for a financial year starting on or after 1.4.17.

2.   Amended by reg 9(c) of SI 2018 No 14 (W.7) as from 10.1.18, for schemes made for a financial year starting on or after 1.4.18.

CHAPTER 5
Income: persons who are not pensioners

Calculation of income on a weekly basis

20.–(1)   Subject to paragraph 23 (disregard of changes in tax, etc), the income of an applicant is to be calculated on a weekly basis–

(a)   by estimating the amount which is likely to be the applicant's average weekly income in accordance with this Part;

(b)   by adding to that amount the weekly income calculated under paragraph 33 (tariff income); and

(c)   by then deducting any relevant child care charges to which paragraph 21 (treatment of child care charges) applies from any earnings which form part of the average weekly income or, in a case where the conditions in sub-paragraph (2) are met, from those earnings plus whichever credit specified in paragraph (b) of that sub-paragraph is appropriate, up to a maximum deduction in respect of the applicant's family of whichever of the sums specified in sub-paragraph (3) applies in the applicant's case.

(2)   The conditions of this paragraph are that–

(a)   the applicant's earnings which form part of the applicant's average weekly income are less than the lower of either the applicant's relevant child care charges or whichever of the deductions specified in paragraph (3) otherwise applies in the applicant's case; and

(b)   that applicant or, if the applicant is a member of a couple either the applicant or the applicant's partner, is in receipt of either working tax credit or child tax credit.

(3)   The maximum deduction to which paragraph (1)(c) above refers is to be–

(a)   where the applicant's family includes only one child in respect of whom relevant child care charges are paid, £175 per week;

(b)   where the applicant's family includes more than one child in respect of whom relevant child care charges are paid, £300 per week.

Treatment of child care charges

21.–(1)   This paragraph applies where an applicant (within the meaning of this paragraph) is incurring relevant child care charges and–

(a)   is a lone parent and is engaged in remunerative work;

(b)   is a member of a couple both of whom are engaged in remunerative work; or

(c)   is a member of a couple where one member is engaged in remunerative work and the other–

     (i)   is incapacitated;

     (ii)   is an in-patient in hospital; or

     (iii)   is in prison (whether serving a custodial sentence or remanded in custody awaiting trial or sentence).

(2)   For the purposes of sub-paragraph (1) and subject to sub-paragraph (4), a person to whom sub-paragraph (3) applies must be treated as engaged in remunerative work for a period not exceeding 28 weeks during which the person–

(a)   is paid statutory sick pay;

(b)   is paid short-term incapacity benefit at the lower rate under sections 30A to 30E of the SSCBA;

(c)   is paid an employment and support allowance;

(d)   is paid income support on the grounds of incapacity for work under regulation 4ZA of, and paragraph 7 or 14 of Schedule 1B to, the Income Support (General) Regulations 1987; or

(e)   is credited with earnings on the grounds of incapacity for work or limited capability for work under regulation 8B of the Social Security (Credits) Regulations 1975.

(3)   This sub-paragraph applies to a person who was engaged in remunerative work immediately before–

(a)   the first day of the period in respect of which the person was first paid statutory sick pay, short-term incapacity benefit, an employment and support allowance or income support on the grounds of incapacity for work; or

(b)   the first day of the period in respect of which earnings are credited,

as the case may be.

(4)   In a case to which sub-paragraph (2)(d) or (e) applies, the period of 28 weeks begins on the day on which the person is first paid income support or on the first day of the period in respect of which earnings are credited, as the case may be.

(5)   Relevant child care charges are those charges for care to which sub-paragraphs (6) and (7) apply, and are to be calculated on a weekly basis in accordance with sub-paragraph (10).

(6)   The charges are paid by the applicant for care which is provided–

(a)   in the case of any child of the applicant's family who is not disabled, in respect of the period beginning on that child's date of birth and ending on the day preceding the first Monday in September following that child's fifteenth birthday; or

(b)   in the case of any child of the applicant's family who is disabled, in respect of the period beginning on that child's date of birth and ending on the day preceding the first Monday in September following that child's sixteenth birthday.

(7)   The charges are paid for care which is provided by one or more of the care providers listed in sub-paragraph (8) and are not paid–

(a)   in respect of the child's compulsory education;

(b)   by an applicant to a partner or by a partner to an applicant in respect of any child for whom either or any of them is responsible in accordance with regulation 7 (circumstances in which a person is treated as responsible or not responsible for another); or

(c)   in respect of care provided by a relative of the child wholly or mainly in the child's home.

(8)   The care to which sub-paragraph (7) refers may be provided–

(a)   out of school hours, by a school on school premises or by a local authority–
    (i)   for children who are not disabled in respect of the period beginning on their eighth birthday and ending on the day preceding the first Monday in September following their fifteenth birthday; or
    (ii)   for children who are disabled in respect of the period beginning on their eighth birthday and ending on the day preceding the first Monday in September following their sixteenth birthday; or
(b)   by a child care provider approved in accordance with the Tax Credit (New Category of Child Care Provider) Regulations 1999; or
(c)   by persons registered under Part 2 of the Children and Families (Wales) Measure 2010; or
(d)   by a person who is excepted from registration under Part 2 of the Children and Families (Wales) Measure 2010 because the child care that person provides is in a school or establishment referred to in article 11, 12 or 14 of the Child Minding and Day Care Exceptions (Wales) Order 2010; or
(e)   by–
    (i)   persons registered under section 59(1) of the Public Services Reform (Scotland) Act 2010; or
    (ii)   local authorities registered under section 83(1) of that Act,
    where the care provided is child minding or day care of children within the meaning of that Act; or
(f)   by a person prescribed in regulations made pursuant to section 12(4) of the Tax Credits Act 2002; or
(g)   by a person who is registered under Chapter 2 or 3 of Part 3 of the Childcare Act 2006; or
(h)   by any of the schools mentioned in section 34(2) of the Childcare Act 2006 in circumstances where the requirement to register under Chapter 2 of Part 3 of that Act does not apply by virtue of section 34(2) of that Act; or
(i)   by any of the schools mentioned in section 53(2) of the Childcare Act 2006 in circumstances where the requirement to register under Chapter 3 of Part 3 of that Act does not apply by virtue of section 53(2) of that Act; or
(j)   by any of the establishments mentioned in section 18(5) of the Childcare Act 2006 in circumstances where the care is not included in the meaning of "childcare" for the purposes of Part 1 and Part 3 of that Act by virtue of section 18(5) of that Act; or
(k)   by a foster parent or kinship carer under the Fostering Services (England) Regulations 2011, the [⁴ Fostering Services (Wales) Regulations 2003 or any regulations made under sections 87 and 93 of the Social Services and Well-being (Wales) Act 2014 which make provision for the approval of local authority foster parents] or the Looked After Children (Scotland) Regulations 2009 in relation to a child other than one whom the foster parent is fostering or kinship carer is looking after; or
[³ (l)   by a person who is employed, or engaged under a contract for services, to provide care and support by the provider of a domiciliary support service, within the meaning of Part 1 of the Regulation and Inspection of Social Care (Wales) Act 2016; or]
(m)   by a person who is not a relative of the child wholly or mainly in the child's home.
(9)   In sub-paragraphs (6) and (8)(a), "the first Monday in September" ("y dydd Llun cyntaf ym Medi") means the Monday which first occurs in the month of September in any year.
(10)   Relevant child care charges must be estimated over such period, not exceeding a year, as is appropriate in order that the average weekly charge may be estimated accurately having regard to information as to the amount of that charge provided by the child minder or person providing the care.
(11)   For the purposes of sub-paragraph (1)(c) the other member of a couple is incapacitated where–
(a)   the applicant's applicable amount includes a disability premium on account of the other member's incapacity or the support component or the work-related activity component [³ or the other member would be a member of the work-related activity group] on account of the other member's having limited capability for work;
(b)   the applicant's applicable amount would include a disability premium on account of the other member's incapacity but for that other member being treated as capable of work by virtue of a determination made in accordance with regulations made under section 171E of the SSCBA;
(c)   the applicant's applicable amount would include the support component or the work-related activity component [³ or the other member would be a member of the work-related activity group] on account of the other member having limited capability for work but for that other member being treated as not having limited capability for work by virtue of a determination made in accordance with the Employment and Support Allowance Regulations 2008 [¹or the Employment and Support Allowance Regulations 2013];
(d)   the applicant is, or is treated as, incapable of work and has been so incapable, or has been so treated as incapable, of work in accordance with the provisions of, and regulations made under, Part 12A of the SSCBA (incapacity for work) for a continuous period of not less than 196 days; and for this purpose any two or more separate periods separated by a break of not more than 56 days must be treated as one continuous period;
(e)   the applicant has, or is treated as having, limited capability for work and has had, or been treated as having, limited capability for work in accordance with the Employment and Support Allowance Regulations 2008 [¹or the Employment and Support Allowance Regulations 2013] for a continuous

period of not less than 196 days and for this purpose any two or more separate periods separated by a break of not more than 84 days must be treated as one continuous period;

(f) there is payable in respect of the other member one or more of the following pensions or allowances–
    (i)   long-term incapacity benefit or short-term incapacity benefit at the higher rate under Schedule 4 to the SSCBA;
    (ii)   attendance allowance under section 64 of the SSCBA;
    (iii) severe disablement allowance under section 68 of the SSCBA;
    (iv) disability living allowance under section 71 of the SSCBA;
    (v)   personal independence payment under Part 4 of the Welfare Reform Act 2012;
    (vi) an AFIP;
    (vii) increase of disablement pension under section 104 of the SSCBA;
    (viii) a pension increase paid as part of a war disablement pension or under an industrial injuries scheme which is analogous to an allowance or increase of disablement pension under sub-paragraph (ii), (iv), (v) or (vii) above;
    (ix) main phase employment and support allowance;

(g) a pension or allowance to which sub-paragraph (vi) or (vii) of paragraph (f) refers was payable on account of the other member's incapacity but has ceased to be payable in consequence of that other member becoming a patient, which in this paragraph means a person (other than a person who is serving a sentence of imprisonment or detention in a youth custody institution) who is regarded as receiving free in-patient treatment within the meaning of regulation 2(4) and (5) of the Social Security (Hospital In-Patients) Regulations 2005;

(h) an attendance allowance under section 64 of the SSCBA or disability living allowance under section 71 of that Act would be payable to that person but for–
    (i)   a suspension of benefit in accordance with regulations under section 113(2) of the SSCBA; or
    (ii)   an abatement as a consequence of hospitalisation;

(i) the daily living component of personal independence payment would be payable to that person but for a suspension of benefit in accordance with regulations under section 86 of the Welfare Reform Act 2012 (hospital in-patients);

(j) an AFIP would be payable to that person but for any suspension of payment in accordance with any terms of the armed and reserve forces compensation scheme which allow for a suspension because a person is undergoing medical treatment in a hospital or similar institution;

(k) paragraph (f), (g), (h) or (i) would apply to the other member if the legislative provisions referred to in those paragraphs were provisions under any corresponding enactment having effect in Northern Ireland; or

(l) the other member has an invalid carriage or other vehicle provided to the other member by the Secretary of State under paragraph 9 of Schedule 1 to the National Health Service Act 2006 or under section 46 of the National Health Service (Scotland) Act 1978,or provided by the Department of Health, Social Services and Public Safety in Northern Ireland under article 30(1) of the Health and Personal Social Services (Northern Ireland) Order 1972, or provided by the Welsh Ministers under section 5 of, and Schedule 1 to the National Health Service (Wales) Act 2006.

(12) For the purposes of sub-paragraph (11), once sub-paragraph (11)(d) applies to the applicant, if the applicant then ceases, for a period of 56 days or less, to be incapable, or to be treated as incapable, of work, that sub-paragraph is, on the applicant again becoming so incapable, or so treated as incapable, of work at the end of that period, to immediately thereafter apply to the applicant for so long as the applicant remains incapable, or is treated as remaining incapable, of work.

(13) For the purposes of sub-paragraph (11), once sub-paragraph (11)(e) applies to the applicant, if the applicant then ceases, for a period of 84 days or less, to have, or to be treated as having, limited capability for work, that sub-paragraph is, on the applicant again having, or being treated as having limited capability for work at the end of that period, immediately thereafter to apply to the applicant for so long as the applicant has, or is treated as having, limited capability for work.

(14) For the purposes of sub-paragraphs (6) and (8)(a), a person is disabled if that person is a person–

(a) to whom an attendance allowance or the care component of disability allowance is payable or would be payable but for–
    (i)   a suspension of benefit in accordance with regulations under section 113(2) of the SSCBA; or
    (ii)   an abatement as a consequence of hospitalisation;

(b) to whom the daily living component of personal independence payment is payable or would be payable but for a suspension of benefit in accordance with regulations under section 86 of the Welfare Reform Act 2012 (hospital in-patients);

[² (c) who–
    (i)   is registered as blind in a register compiled under section 29 of the National Assistance Act 1948 (welfare services);
    (ii)   is registered as severely sight-impaired in a register established and maintained by a local authority under section 18(1) of the Social Services and Well-being (Wales) Act 2014;
    (iii) is registered as severely sight-impaired in a register established and maintained by a local authority under section 77(1) of the Care Act 2014; or,

(iv)   in Scotland, has been certified as blind and in consequence is registered as blind in a register maintained by or on behalf of a council constituted under section 2 of the Local Government etc. (Scotland) Act 1994;]

(d)   who ceased to be registered as blind [² or severely sight-impaired] in such a register within the period beginning 28weeks before the first Monday in September following that person's fifteenth birthday and ending on the day preceding that person's sixteenth birthday; or

(e)   to whom AFIP is payable.

(15)   For the purposes of sub-paragraph (1) a person on maternity leave, paternity leave [¹, shared parental leave] or adoption leave is to be treated as if engaged in remunerative work for the period specified in sub-paragraph (16) ("the relevant period") provided that–

(a)   in the week before the period of maternity leave, paternity leave [¹, shared parental leave] or adoption leave began the person was in remunerative work;

(b)   the person is incurring relevant child care charges within the meaning of sub-paragraph (5); and

(c)   the person is entitled to either statutory maternity pay under section 164 of the SSCBA, [¹] statutory paternity pay by virtue of section 171ZA or 171ZB of that Act, additional statutory paternity pay by virtue of section 171ZEA or 171ZEB of that Act, statutory adoption pay by virtue of section 171ZL of that Act, maternity allowance under section 35 of that Act [¹, statutory shared parental pay under section 171ZU or 171ZV of that Act] or qualifying support.

(16)   For the purposes of sub-paragraph (15) the relevant period begins on the day on which the person's maternity leave, paternity leave [¹, shared parental leave] or adoption leave commences and ends on–

(a)   the date that leave ends;

(b)   if no child care element of working tax credit is in payment on the date that entitlement to maternity allowance, qualifying support (if relevant), statutory maternity pay, [¹] statutory paternity pay [¹, statutory shared parental pay] or statutory adoption pay ends, the date that entitlement ends; or

(c)   if a child care element of working tax credit is in payment on the date that entitlement to maternity allowance or qualifying support, statutory maternity pay, [¹] statutory paternity pay [¹, statutory shared parental pay] or statutory adoption pay ends, the date that entitlement to that award of the child care element of the working tax credit ends,

whichever occurs first.

(17)   In sub-paragraphs (15) and (16)–

(a)   "qualifying support" ("cymhorthdal cymwys") means income support to which that person is entitled by virtue of paragraph 14B of Schedule 1B to the Income Support (General) Regulations 1987; and

(b)   "child care element" ("elfen gofal plant") of working tax credit means the element of working tax credit prescribed under section 12 of the Tax Credits Act 2002 (child care element).

(18)   In this paragraph "applicant" ("ceisydd") does not include an applicant–

(a)   who has, or

(b)   who (jointly with a partner) has,

an award of universal credit.

Amendments

1.   Amended by reg 10(e) of SI 2015 No 44 (W.3) as from 21.1.15, for schemes made for a financial year starting on or after 1.4.15.

2.   Amended by reg 9(b) of SI 2016 No 50 (W.21) as from 20.1.16, for schemes made for a financial year starting on or after 1.4.16.

3.   Amended by reg 9(d) of SI 2018 No 14 (W.7) as from 10.1.18, for schemes made for a financial year starting on or after 1.4.18.

4.   Amended by reg 6(b) of SI 2019 No 11 (W.5) as from 9.1.19, for schemes made for a financial year starting on or after 1.4.19.

Calculations of average weekly income from tax credits

22.–(1)   This paragraph applies where an applicant receives a tax credit.

(2)   Where this paragraph applies, the period over which a tax credit is to be taken into account must be the period set out in sub-paragraph (3).

(3)   Where the instalment in respect of which payment of a tax credit is made is–

(a)   a daily instalment, the period is 1 day, being the day in respect of which the instalment is paid;

(b)   a weekly instalment, the period is 7 days, ending on the day on which the instalment is due to be paid;

(c)   a two weekly instalment, the period is 14 days, commencing 6 days before the day on which the instalment is due to be paid;

(d)   a four weekly instalment, the period is 28 days, ending on the day on which the instalment is due to be paid.

(4)   For the purposes of this paragraph "tax credit" ("credyd treth") means child tax credit or working tax credit.

Disregard of changes in tax, contributions etc

23.   In calculating the applicant's income an authority may disregard any legislative change–

(a)   in the basic or other rates of income tax;

(b)   in the amount of any personal tax [² reliefs under Chapters 2, 3 and 3A of Part 3 of the Income Tax Act 2007];

(c)   in the rates of social security contributions payable under the SSCBA or in the lower earnings limit or upper earnings limit for Class 1 contributions under that Act, the lower or upper limits applicable to Class 4 contributions under that Act or the amount specified in section 11(4) of that Act ([¹ small profits threshold] in relation to Class 2 contributions);

(d)   in the amount of tax payable as a result of an increase in the weekly rate of Category A, B, C or D retirement pension or any addition thereto or any graduated pension payable under the SSCBA [¹ or a state pension under Part 1 of the Pensions Act 2014];

(e)   in the maximum rate of child tax credit or working tax credit,

for a period not exceeding 30 reduction weeks beginning with the reduction week immediately following the date from which the change is effective.

Amendments

1.   Amended by reg 9(c) of SI 2016 No 50 (W.21) as from 20.1.16, for schemes made for a financial year starting on or after 1.4.16.

2.   Amended by reg 5(f) of SI 2017 No 46 (W.20) as from 19.1.17, for schemes made for a financial year starting on or after 1.4.17.

Calculation of net profit of self-employed earners

24.–(1)   For the purposes of paragraph 11 (average weekly earnings of self-employed earners) the earnings of an applicant to be taken into account must be–

(a)   in the case of a self-employed earner who is engaged in employment on that person's own account, the net profit derived from that employment;

(b)   in the case of a self-employed earner who is a pensioner whose employment is carried on in partnership, that person's share of the net profit derived from that employment, less–

    (i)   an amount in respect of income tax and of social security contributions payable under the SSCBA calculated in accordance with paragraph 25 (calculation of deduction of tax and contributions of self-employed earners); and

    (ii)   one-half of the amount calculated in accordance with sub-paragraph (11) in respect of any qualifying premium;

(c)   in the case of a self-employed earner who is not a pensioner whose employment is carried on in partnership or is that of a share fisherman within the meaning of the Social Security (Mariners' Benefits) Regulations 1975, that person's share of the net profit derived from that employment, less–

    (i)   an amount in respect of income tax and of social security contributions payable under the SSCBA calculated in accordance with paragraph 25 (calculation of deduction of tax and contributions for self-employed earners); and

    (ii)   one-half of the amount calculated in accordance with sub-paragraph (11) in respect of any qualifying premium.

(2)   There must be disregarded from the net profit of an applicant who is not a pensioner, any sum, where applicable, specified in paragraphs 1 to 16 of Schedule 8 (sums disregarded in the calculation of earnings).

(3)   For the purposes of sub-paragraph (1)(a) the net profit of the employment must, except where sub-paragraph (9) applies, be calculated by taking into account the earnings of the employment over the assessment period less–

(a)   subject to sub-paragraphs (5) to (8), any expenses wholly and exclusively incurred in that period for the purposes of that employment;

(b)   an amount in respect of–

    (i)   income tax; and

    (ii)   social security contributions payable under the SSCBA,

calculated in accordance with paragraph 25 (calculation of deduction of tax and contributions for self-employed earners); and

(c)   one-half of the amount calculated in accordance with sub-paragraph (11) in respect of any qualifying premium.

(4)   For the purposes of sub-paragraph (1)(b) the net profit of the employment is to be calculated by taking into account the earnings of the employment over the assessment period less, subject to sub-paragraphs (5) to (8), any expenses wholly and exclusively incurred in that period for the purposes of the employment.

(5)   Subject to sub-paragraph (6), no deduction is to be made under paragraph (3)(a) or (4), in respect of–

(a)   any capital expenditure;

(b)   the depreciation of any capital asset;

(c)   any sum employed or intended to be employed in the setting up or expansion of the employment;

(d)   any loss incurred before the beginning of the assessment period;

(e)   the repayment of capital on any loan taken out for the purposes of the employment;

(f)   any expenses incurred in providing business entertainment; and

    (g)   in the case of an applicant who is not a pensioner, any debts, except bad debts proved to be such, but this paragraph does not apply to any expenses incurred in the recovery of a debt.

    (6)   A deduction is to be made under sub-paragraph (3)(a) or (4) in respect of the repayment of capital on any loan used for–

    (a)   the replacement in the course of business of equipment or machinery; or

    (b)   the repair of an existing business asset except to the extent that any sum is payable under an insurance policy for its repair.

    (7)   The authority must refuse to make a deduction in respect of any expenses under sub-paragraph (3)(a) or (4) where it is not satisfied given the nature and the amount of the expense that it has been reasonably incurred.

    (8)   For the avoidance of doubt–

    (a)   a deduction must not be made under sub-paragraph (3)(a) or (4) in respect of any sum unless it has been expended for the purposes of the business;

    (b)   a deduction must be made thereunder in respect of–

        (i)   the excess of any value added tax paid over value added tax received in the assessment period;

        (ii)   any income expended in the repair of an existing business asset except to the extent that any sum is payable under an insurance policy for its repair;

        (iii)   any payment of interest on a loan taken out for the purposes of the employment.

    (9)   Where an applicant is engaged in employment as a child minder the net profit of the employment is to be one-third of the earnings of that employment, less–

    (a)   an amount in respect of–

        (i)   income tax; and

        (ii)   social security contributions payable under the SSCBA,

        calculated in accordance with paragraph 25 (calculation of deduction of tax and contributions for self-employed earners); and

    (b)   one-half of the amount calculated in accordance with sub-paragraph (11) in respect of any qualifying premium.

    (10)   For the avoidance of doubt where an applicant is engaged in employment as a self-employed earner and the applicant is also engaged in one or more other employments as a self-employed or employed earner any loss incurred in any one of the applicant's employments must not be offset against the applicant's earnings in any other of the applicant's employments.

    (11)   The amount in respect of any qualifying premium is to be calculated by multiplying the daily amount of the qualifying premium by the number equal to the number of days in the assessment period; and for the purposes of this paragraph the daily amount of the qualifying premium must be determined–

    (a)   where the qualifying premium is payable monthly, by multiplying the amount of the qualifying premium by 12 and dividing the product by 365;

    (b)   in any other case, by dividing the amount of the qualifying premium by the number equal to the number of days in the period to which the qualifying premium relates.

    (12)   In this paragraph, "qualifying premium" ("premiwm cymwys") means any premium which is payable periodically in respect of a personal pension scheme and is so payable on or after the date of application.

Calculation of deduction of tax and contributions of self-employed earners

25.–(1)   The amount to be deducted in respect of income tax under paragraph 24(1)(b)(i), (3)(b)(i) or (9) (a)(i) (calculation of net profit of self-employed earners) must be calculated–

    (a)   on the basis of the amount of chargeable income, and

    (b)   as if that income were assessable to income tax at the basic rate of tax applicable to the assessment period less only the [³ personal reliefs to which the applicant is entitled under Chapters 2, 3 and 3A of Part 3] of the Income Tax Act 2007 [³] as is appropriate to the applicant's circumstances.

    (2)   But, if the assessment period is less than a year, the earnings to which the basic rate of tax is to be applied and the amount of the personal reliefs deductible under this paragraph must be calculated on a pro rata basis.

    (3)   The amount to be deducted in respect of social security contributions under paragraph 24(1)(b)(i), (3)(b)(ii) or (9)(a)(ii) is the total of–

    (a)   the amount of Class 2 contributions payable under section 11(1) or, as the case may be, 11(3) of the SSCBA at the rate applicable to the assessment period except where the applicant's chargeable income is less than the amount specified in section 11(4) of that Act ([² small profits threshold]) for the tax year applicable to the assessment period; but if the assessment period is less than a year, the amount specified for that tax year must be reduced pro rata; and

    (b)   the amount of Class 4 contributions (if any) which would be payable under section 15 of the SSCBA (Class 4 contributions recoverable under the Income Tax Acts) at the percentage rate applicable to the assessment period on so much of the chargeable income as exceeds the lower limit but does not exceed the upper limit of profits and gains applicable for the tax year applicable to the assessment period; but if the assessment period is less than a year, those limits must be reduced pro rata.

    (4)   In this paragraph "chargeable income" ("incwm trethadwy") means–

    (a)   except where paragraph (b) applies, the earnings derived from the employment less any expenses deducted under [¹ sub-paragraph (3)(a) or, as the case may be, (4) of paragraph 24];

    (b)   in the case of employment as a child minder, one-third of the earnings of that employment.

Amendments

1.   Amended by reg 9(b) of SI 2014 No 66 (W.6) as from 15.1.14.
2.   Amended by reg 9(d) of SI 2016 No 50 (W.21) as from 20.1.16, for schemes made for a financial year starting on or after 1.4.16.
3.   Amended by reg 5(g) of SI 2017 No 46 (W.20) as from 19.1.17, for schemes made for a financial year starting on or after 1.4.17.

CHAPTER 3

Capital: persons who are not pensioners

Calculation of capital: persons who are not pensioners

26.–(1)   The capital of an applicant to be taken into account must be, subject to sub-paragraph (2), the whole of the applicant's capital calculated in accordance with this Part and any income treated as capital under paragraph 27 (income treated as capital: persons who are not pensioners).

(2)   There must be disregarded from the calculation of an applicant's capital under sub-paragraph (1), any capital, where applicable, specified in Schedule 10 in relation to persons who are not pensioners.

(3)   The capital of a child or young person who is a member of the family of an applicant who is not a pensioner must not be treated as capital of the applicant.

Income treated as capital: persons who are not pensioners

27.–(1)   This paragraph applies in relation to persons who are not pensioners.

(2)   Any bounty derived from employment to which paragraph 9 of Schedule 8 (sums disregarded in the calculation of earnings), applies and paid at intervals of at least one year is to be treated as capital.

(3)   Any amount by way of a refund of income tax deducted from profits or emoluments chargeable to income tax under Schedule D or E is to be treated as capital.

(4)   Any holiday pay which is not earnings under paragraph 14 (earnings of employed earners) is to be treated as capital.

(5)   Except any income derived from capital disregarded under paragraphs 4, 5, 7, 11, 17, 30 to 33, 48 or 49 of Schedule 10 (capital disregards), any income derived from capital is to be treated as capital but only from the date it is normally due to be credited to the applicant's account.

(6)   In the case of employment as an employed earner, any advance of earnings or any loan made by the applicant's employer is to be treated as capital.

(7)   Any charitable or voluntary payment which is not made or due to be made at regular intervals, other than a payment which is made under or by the Trusts, the Fund, the Eileen Trust, MFET Limited, the Skipton Fund, the Caxton Foundation, [¹ an approved blood scheme, the Scottish Infected Blood Support Scheme, the London Emergencies Trust, the We Love Manchester Emergency Fund,] the Independent Living Fund (2006) or the London Bombings Charitable Relief Fund, is to be treated as capital.

(8)   There is to be treated as capital the gross receipts of any commercial activity carried on by a person in respect of which assistance is received under the self-employment route, but only in so far as those receipts were payable into a special account during the period in which that person was receiving such assistance.

(9)   Any arrears of subsistence allowance which are paid to an applicant as a lump sum must be treated as capital.

(10)   Any arrears of working tax credit or child tax credit must be treated as capital.

Amendment

1.   Amended by reg 9(e) of SI 2018 No 14 (W.7) as from 10.1.18, for schemes made for a financial year starting on or after 1.4.18.

Calculation of capital in the United Kingdom: persons who are not pensioners

28.   Capital which an applicant possesses in the United Kingdom is to be calculated at its current market or surrender value less–

(a)   where there would be expenses attributable to the sale, 10 per cent; and

(b)   the amount of any encumbrance secured on it.

Calculation of capital outside the United Kingdom: persons who are not pensioners

29.   Capital which an applicant possesses in a country outside the United Kingdom is to be calculated–

(a)   in a case where there is no prohibition in that country against the transfer to the United Kingdom of an amount equal to its current market or surrender value in that country, at that value;

(b)   in a case where there is such a prohibition, at the price which it would realise if sold in the United Kingdom to a willing buyer,

less, where there would be expenses attributable to sale, 10 per cent and the amount of any encumbrances secured on it.

Notional capital: persons who are not pensioners

30.–(1)   An applicant is to be treated as possessing capital of which the applicant has deprived himself or herself for the purpose of securing entitlement to a reduction or increasing the amount of that reduction except to the extent that that capital is reduced in accordance with paragraph 31(diminishing notional capital rule).

(2)   Except in the case of–

(a)   a discretionary trust; or

(b)   a trust derived from a payment made in consequence of a personal injury; or

(c)   any loan which would be obtained only if secured against capital disregarded under Schedule 10; or

(d)   a personal pension scheme, occupational pension scheme or a payment made by the Board of the Pension Protection Fund; or

(e)   any sum to which paragraph 48(2)(a) of Schedule 10 (capital disregards) applies which is administered in the way referred to in paragraph 48(1)(a) of that Schedule; or

(f)   any sum to which paragraph 49(a) of Schedule 10 refers; or

(g)   child tax credit; or

(h)   working tax credit,

any capital which would become available to the applicant upon application being made, but which has not been acquired by the applicant, is to be treated as possessed by the applicant but only from the date on which it could be expected to be acquired were an application made.

(3)   Any payment of capital, other than a payment of capital specified in sub-paragraph (4), made–

(a)   to a third party in respect of a single applicant or a member of the family (but not a member of the third party's family) must, where that payment is a payment of an occupational pension, a pension or other periodical payment made under a personal pension scheme or a payment made by the Board of the Pension Protection Fund, be treated as possessed by that single applicant or, as the case may be, by that member;

(b)   to a third party in respect of a single applicant or a member of the family (but not a member of the third party's family) must, where it is not a payment referred to in paragraph (a), be treated as possessed by that single applicant or by that member to the extent that it is used for the food, ordinary clothing or footwear, household fuel or rent of that single applicant or, as the case may be, of any member of that family or is used for any council tax or water charges for which that applicant or member is liable;

(c)   to a single applicant or a member of the family in respect of a third party (but not in respect of another member of the family) must be treated as possessed by that single applicant or, as the case may be, that member of the family to the extent that it is kept or used by the single applicant or used by or on behalf of any member of the family.

(4)   Sub-paragraph (3) does not apply in respect of a payment of capital made–

(a)   under or by any of the Trusts, the Fund, the Eileen Trust, MFET Limited, the Independent Living Fund (2006), the Skipton Fund, the Caxton Foundation, [¹ an approved blood scheme, the Scottish Infected Blood Support Scheme, the London Emergencies Trust, the We Love Manchester Emergency Fund] or the London Bombings Relief Charitable Fund;

(b)   pursuant to section 2 of the Employment and Training Act 1973 in respect of a person's participation–

(i)   in an employment programme specified in regulation 75(1)(a) of the Jobseeker's Allowance Regulations 1996;

(ii)   in a training scheme specified in regulation 75(1)(b) of those Regulations; or

(iii)   in a qualifying course within the meaning specified in regulation 17A(7) of those Regulations;

(c)   in respect of a person's participation in the Work for Your Benefit Pilot Scheme;

(d)   in respect of a person's participation in the Mandatory Work Activity Scheme;

(e)   in respect of an applicant's participation in the Employment, Skills and Enterprise Scheme;

(f)   under an occupational pension scheme, in respect of a pension or other periodical payment made under a personal pension scheme or a payment made by the Board of the Pension Protection Fund where–

(i)   a bankruptcy order has been made in respect of the person in respect of whom the payment has been made or, in Scotland, the estate of that person is subject to sequestration or a judicial factor has been appointed on that person's estate under section 41 of the Solicitors (Scotland) Act 1980;

(ii)   the payment is made to the trustee in bankruptcy or any other person acting on behalf of the creditors; and

(iii)   the person referred to in sub-paragraph (i) and any member of that person's family does not possess, or is not treated as possessing, any other income apart from that payment.

(5)   Where an applicant stands in relation to a company in a position analogous to that of a sole owner or partner in the business of that company, the applicant may be treated as if the applicant were such sole owner or partner and in such a case–

(a)   the value of the applicant's holding in that company must, notwithstanding paragraph 26 (calculation of capital) be disregarded; and

(b)   the applicant must, subject to sub-paragraph (6), be treated as possessing an amount of capital equal to the value or, as the case may be, the applicant's share of the value of the capital of that company and the foregoing provisions of this Chapter apply for the purposes of calculating that amount as if it were actual capital which the applicant does possess.

(6)   For so long as the applicant undertakes activities in the course of the business of the company, the amount which the applicant is treated as possessing under sub-paragraph (5) is to be disregarded.

(7)   Where an applicant is treated as possessing capital under any of sub-paragraphs (1), (2) or (3) the foregoing provisions of this Chapter apply for the purposes of calculating its amount as if it were actual capital which the applicant does possess.

Amendment

1.   Amended by reg 9(f) of SI 2018 No 14 (W.7) as from 10.1.18, for schemes made for a financial year starting on or after 1.4.18.

Diminishing notional capital rule: persons who are not pensioners

31.–(1)   Where an applicant who is not a pensioner is treated as possessing capital under paragraph 30(1) (notional capital), the amount which the applicant is treated as possessing–

(a)   in the case of a week that is subsequent to–
 (i)   the relevant week in respect of which the conditions set out in sub-paragraph (2) are satisfied; or
 (ii)   a week which follows that relevant week and which satisfies those conditions,
 is to be reduced by an amount determined under sub-paragraph (3);

(b)   in the case of a week in respect of which sub-paragraph (1)(a) does not apply but where–
 (i)   that week is a week subsequent to the relevant week; and
 (ii)   that relevant week is a week in which the condition in sub-paragraph (4) is satisfied,
 is to be reduced by the amount determined under sub-paragraph (5).

(2)   This sub-paragraph applies to a reduction week where the applicant satisfies the conditions that–

(a)   the applicant is in receipt of a reduction in council tax under an authority's scheme; and

(b)   but for paragraph 30(1) the applicant would have received a greater reduction in council tax under an authority's scheme in that week.

(3)   In a case to which sub-paragraph (2) applies, the amount of the reduction in the amount of capital the applicant is treated as possessing for the purposes of sub-paragraph (1)(a) is equal to the aggregate of–

(a)   an amount equal to the additional amount of the reduction in council tax to which sub-paragraph (2)(b) refers;

(b)   where the applicant has also claimed housing benefit, the amount of any housing benefit or any additional amount of that benefit to which the applicant would have been entitled in respect of the whole or part of the reduction week to which sub-paragraph (2) refers but for the application of regulation 49(1) of the Housing Benefit Regulations 2006 (notional capital);

(c)   where the applicant has also claimed income support, the amount of income support to which the applicant would have been entitled in respect of the whole or part of the reduction week to which sub-paragraph (2) refers but for the application of regulation 51(1) of the Income Support (General) Regulations 1987 (notional capital);

(d)   where the applicant has also claimed a jobseeker's allowance, the amount of an income-based jobseeker's allowance to which the applicant would have been entitled in respect of the whole or part of the reduction week to which sub-paragraph (2) refers but for the application of regulation 113 of the Jobseeker's Allowance Regulations 1996 (notional capital); and

(e)   where the applicant has also claimed an employment and support allowance, the amount of an income related employment and support allowance to which the applicant would have been entitled in respect of the whole or part of the reduction week to which sub-paragraph (2) refers but for the application of regulation 115 of the Employment and Support Allowance Regulations 2008 (notional capital).

(4)   Subject to sub-paragraph (7), for the purposes of sub-paragraph (1)(b) the condition is that the applicant is not a pensioner and would have been entitled to a reduction in council tax in the relevant week but for paragraph 30(1).

(5)   In such a case the amount of the reduction in the amount of capital the applicant is treated as possessing must be equal to the aggregate of–

(a)   the amount of council tax benefit to which the applicant would have been entitled in the relevant week but for paragraph 30(1);

(b)   if the applicant would, but for regulation 49(1) of the Housing Benefit Regulations 2006, have been entitled to housing benefit or to an additional amount of housing benefit in respect of the benefit week which includes the last day of the relevant week, the amount which is equal to–
 (i)   in a case where no housing benefit is payable, the amount to which the applicant would have been entitled; or
 (ii)   in any other case, the amount equal to the additional amount of housing benefit to which the applicant would have been entitled;

(c)   if the applicant would, but for regulation 51(1) of the Income Support (General) Regulations 1987, have been entitled to income support in respect of the benefit week, within the meaning of regulation 2(1) of those Regulations (interpretation), which includes the last day of the relevant week, the amount to which the applicant would have been entitled;

(d)   if the applicant would, but for regulation 113 of the Jobseeker's Allowance Regulations 1996, have been entitled to an income-based jobseeker's allowance in respect of the benefit week, within the meaning of regulation 1(3) of those Regulations (interpretation), which includes the last day of the relevant week, the amount to which the applicant would have been entitled; and

(e)   if the applicant would, but for regulation 115 of the Employment and Support Allowance Regulations 2008, have been entitled to an income-related employment and support allowance in respect of the benefit week, within the meaning of regulation 2(1) of those Regulations (interpretation), which includes the last day of the relevant week, the amount to which the applicant would have been entitled.

(6)   But if the amount mentioned in paragraph (a), (b), (c), (d) or (e) of sub-paragraph (5) ("the relevant amount") is in respect of a part-week, the amount that is to be taken into account under that paragraph is to be determined by–

(a)   dividing the relevant amount by the number equal to the number of days in that part-week, and

(b)   multiplying the result of that calculation by 7.

(7)   The amount determined under sub-paragraph (5) is to be re-determined under the appropriate sub-paragraph if the applicant makes a further application for a reduction in council tax and the conditions in sub-paragraph (8) are satisfied, and in such a case–

(a)   paragraphs (a) to (e) of sub-paragraph (5) apply as if for the words "relevant week" there were substituted the words "relevant subsequent week"; and

(b)   subject to sub-paragraph (9), the amount as re-determined has effect from the first week following the relevant subsequent week in question.

(8)   The conditions are that–

(a)   a further application is made 26 or more weeks after–

    (i)   the date on which the applicant made an application for a reduction in council tax in respect of which the applicant was first treated as possessing the capital in question under paragraph 30(1);

    (ii)   in a case where there has been at least one re-determination in accordance with sub-paragraph (7), the date on which the applicant last made an application for a reduction in council tax which resulted in the weekly amount being re-determined, or

    (iii)   the date on which the applicant last ceased to be entitled to a reduction in council tax, whichever last occurred; and

(b)   the applicant would have been entitled to a reduction in council tax under an authority's scheme but for paragraph 30(1).

(9)   The amount as re-determined pursuant to sub-paragraph (7) must not have effect if it is less than the amount which applied in that case immediately before the re-determination and in such a case the higher amount must continue to have effect.

(10)   For the purposes of this paragraph–

"part-week" ("rhan-wythnos")–

(a)   in relation to an amount mentioned in sub-paragraph (5)(a), means a period of less than a week for which a reduction in council tax under an authority's scheme is allowed;

(b)   in relation to an amount mentioned in sub-paragraph (5)(b), means a period of less than a week for which housing benefit is payable;

(c)   in relation to an amount mentioned in sub-paragraph (5)(c), (d) or (e), means–

    (i)   a period of less than a week which is the whole period for which income support, an income-related employment and support allowance or, as the case may be, an income-based jobseeker's allowance is payable; and

    (ii)   any other period of less than a week for which it is payable;

"relevant week" ("wythnos berthnasol") means the reduction week or part-week in which the capital in question of which the applicant has deprived himself or herself within the meaning of paragraph 30(1)–

(a)   was first taken into account for the purpose of determining the applicant's entitlement to a reduction; or

(b)   was taken into account on a subsequent occasion for the purpose of determining or re-determining the applicant's entitlement to a reduction on that subsequent occasion and that determination or redetermination resulted in the applicant beginning to receive, or ceasing to receive, a reduction,

and where more than one reduction week is identified by reference to paragraphs (a) and (b)of this definition, the later or latest such reduction week or, as the case may be, the later or latest such part-week is the relevant week;

"relevant subsequent week" ("wythnos ddilynol berthnasol") means the reduction week or part-week which includes the day on which the further application or, if more than one further application has been made, the last such application was made.

Capital jointly held: persons who are not pensioners

32.   Except where an applicant possesses capital which is disregarded under paragraph 30(5) (notional capital), where an applicant and one or more persons are beneficially entitled in possession to any capital asset they must be treated, in the absence of evidence to the contrary, as if each of them were entitled in possession to the whole beneficial interest therein in an equal share and the foregoing provisions of this Chapter apply for the purposes of calculating the amount of capital which the applicant is treated as possessing as if it were actual capital which the applicant does possess.

Calculation of tariff income: persons who are not pensioners

    33.   The capital of an applicant who is not a pensioner, calculated in accordance with this Schedule, is to be treated as if it were a weekly income of–

    (a)   £1 for each complete £250 in excess of £6,000 but not exceeding £16,000;

    (b)   £1 for any excess which is not a complete £250.

PART 5

Extended reductions: persons who are not pensioners

Extended reductions: persons who are not pensioners

    34.–(1)   An applicant who is entitled to a reduction under an authority's scheme (by virtue of falling within class C or D) is to be entitled to an extended reduction where–

    (a)   the applicant or the applicant's partner was entitled to a qualifying income-related benefit;

    (b)   entitlement to a qualifying income-related benefit ceased because the applicant or the applicant's partner–

        (i)   commenced employment as an employed or self-employed earner;

        (ii)   increased their earnings from such employment; or

        (iii)   increased the number of hours worked in such employment,

    and that employment is or, as the case may be, those increased earnings or increased number of hours arc cxpcctcd to last fivc wccks or more; and

    (c)   the applicant or the applicant's partner had been entitled to and in receipt of a qualifying income-related benefit, jobseeker's allowance or a combination of those benefits for a continuous period of at least 26 weeks before the day on which the entitlement to a qualifying income-related benefit ceased.

    (2)   For the purpose of sub-paragraph (1)(c), an applicant or an applicant's partner is to be treated as having been entitled to and in receipt of a qualifying income-related benefit or jobseeker's allowance during any period of less than five weeks in respect of which the applicant or the applicant's partner was not entitled to any of those benefits because the applicant or the applicant's partner was engaged in remunerative work as a consequence of their participation in an employment zone programme.

    (3)   For the purpose of this paragraph, where an applicant or an applicant's partner is entitled to and in receipt of joint-claim jobseeker's allowance they are to be treated as being entitled to and in receipt of jobseeker's allowance.

    (4)   An applicant must be treated as entitled to a reduction under an authority's scheme by virtue of falling within class C or D where–

    (a)   the applicant ceased to be entitled to a reduction under an authority's scheme because the applicant vacated the dwelling in which the applicant was resident;

    (b)   the day on which the applicant vacated the dwelling was either in the week in which entitlement to a qualifying income-related benefit ceased, or in the preceding week; and

    (c)   entitlement to the qualifying income-related benefit ceased in any of the circumstances listed in sub-paragraph (1)(b).

    (5)   This paragraph does not apply where, on the day before an applicant's entitlement to income support ceased, regulation 6(5) of the Income Support (General) Regulations 1987 (remunerative work: housing costs) applied to that applicant.

Duration of extended reduction: persons who are not pensioners

    35.–(1)   Where an applicant is entitled to an extended reduction, the extended reduction period starts on the day immediately following the day on which the applicant, or the applicant's partner, ceased to be entitled to a qualifying income-related benefit.

    (2)   The extended reduction period ends–

    (a)   at the end of a period of four weeks; or

    (b)   on the date on which the applicant to whom the extended reduction is payable has no liability for council tax, if that occurs first.

Amount of extended reduction: persons who are not pensioners

    36.–(1)   For any week during the extended reduction period the amount of the extended reduction to which an applicant is entitled is to be the greater of the amount of the reduction under an authority's scheme to which–

    (a)   the applicant was entitled by virtue of falling within class C or D in the last reduction week before the applicant or the applicant's partner ceased to be entitled to a qualifying income-related benefit;

    (b)   the applicant would be entitled by virtue of falling within class C or D for any reduction week during the extended reduction period, if paragraph 34 (extended reductions: persons who are not pensioners) did not apply to the applicant; or

    (c)   the applicant's partner would be entitled by virtue of falling within class C or D, if paragraph 34 did not apply to the applicant.

    (2)   Sub-paragraph (1) does not apply in the case of a mover.

    (3)   Where an applicant is in receipt of an extended reduction under this paragraph and the applicant's partner makes an application for a reduction under an authority's scheme, no amount of reduction under an authority's scheme is to be awarded by the authority during the extended reduction period.

Extended reductions-movers: persons who are not pensioners

37.–(1) This paragraph applies–

(a) to a mover; and

(b) from the Monday following the day of the move.

(2) The amount of the extended reduction awarded from the Monday from which this paragraph applies until the end of the extended reduction period is to be the amount of reduction under the authority's ("the first authority") scheme to which the mover would have been entitled had the mover, or the mover's partner, not ceased to be entitled to a qualifying income-related benefit.

(3) Where a mover's liability to pay council tax in respect of the new dwelling is to a second authority, the extended reduction (qualifying contributory benefits) may take the form of a payment from the first authority to–

(a) the second authority; or

(b) the mover directly.

Relationship between extended reduction and entitlement to reduction by virtue of falling within class C or D

38.–(1) Where an applicant's reduction under an authority's scheme would have ended when the applicant ceased to be entitled to a qualifying income-related benefit in the circumstances listed in paragraph 34(1)(b), that entitlement does not cease until the end of the extended reduction period.

(2) Paragraphs 45 and 46 (period of entitlement and change of circumstances) do not apply to any extended reduction payable in accordance with paragraph 36(1)(a) or 37(2) (amount of extended reduction-movers: persons who are not pensioners).

Extended reductions (qualifying contributory benefits): persons who are not pensioners

39.–(1) An applicant who is entitled to a reduction under an authority's scheme (by virtue of falling within class C or D) will be entitled to an extended reduction (qualifying contributory benefits) where–

(a) the applicant or the applicant's partner was entitled to a qualifying contributory benefit;

(b) entitlement to a qualifying contributory benefit ceased because the applicant or the applicant's partner–

(i) commenced employment as an employed or self-employed earner;

(ii) increased their earnings from such employment; or

(iii) increased the number of hours worked in such employment,

and that employment is or, as the case may be, those increased earnings or increased number of hours are expected to last five weeks or more;

(c) the applicant or the applicant's partner had been entitled to and in receipt of a qualifying contributory benefit or a combination of qualifying contributory benefits for a continuous period of at least 26 weeks before the day on which the entitlement to a qualifying contributory benefit ceased; and

(d) the applicant or the applicant's partner was not entitled to and not in receipt of a qualifying income-related benefit in the last reduction week in which the applicant, or the applicant's partner, was entitled to a qualifying contributory benefit.

(2) An applicant must be treated as entitled to a reduction under an authority's scheme by virtue of falling within class C or D where–

(a) the applicant ceased to be entitled to a reduction under an authority's scheme because the applicant vacated the dwelling in which the applicant was resident;

(b) the day on which the applicant vacated the dwelling was either in the week in which entitlement to a qualifying contributory benefit ceased, or in the preceding week; and

(c) entitlement to the qualifying contributory benefit ceased in any of the circumstances listed in sub-paragraph (1)(b).

Duration of extended reduction period (qualifying contributory benefits): persons who are not pensioners

40.–(1) Where an applicant is entitled to an extended reduction (qualifying contributory benefits), the extended reduction period starts on the day immediately following the day on which the applicant, or the applicant's partner, ceased to be entitled to a qualifying contributory benefit.

(2) The extended reduction period ends–

(a) at the end of a period of four weeks; or

(b) on the date on which the applicant entitled to the extended reduction (qualifying contributory benefits) has no liability for council tax, if that occurs first.

Amount of extended reduction (qualifying contributory benefits): persons who are not pensioners

41.–(1) For any week during the extended reduction period the amount of the extended reduction (qualifying contributory benefits) payable to an applicant is to be the greater of the amount of reduction under an authority's scheme–

(a) to which the applicant was entitled by virtue of falling within class C or D in the last reduction week before the applicant or the applicant's partner ceased to be entitled to a qualifying contributory benefit;

(b)   to which the applicant would be entitled by virtue of falling within class C or D for any reduction week during the extended reduction period, if paragraph 39 (extended reductions (qualifying contributory benefits): persons who are not pensioners) did not apply to the applicant; or

(c)   to which the applicant's partner would be entitled by virtue of falling within class C or D, if paragraph 39 did not apply to the applicant.

(2)   Sub-paragraph (1) does not apply in the case of a mover.

(3)   Where an applicant is in receipt of an extended reduction (qualifying contributory benefits) under this paragraph and the applicant's partner makes an application for a reduction under an authority's scheme, no amount of reduction under an authority's scheme is to be awarded by the authority during the extended reduction period.

Extended reductions (qualifying contributory benefits)-movers: persons who are not pensioners

42.–(1)   This paragraph applies–

(a)   to a mover; and

(b)   from the Monday following the day of the move.

(2)   The amount of the extended reduction (qualifying contributory benefits) awarded from the Monday from which this paragraph applies until the end of the extended reduction period is to be the amount of reduction under the authority's (the first authority's) scheme which was awarded to the mover for the last reduction week before the mover, or the mover's partner, ceased to be entitled to a qualifying contributory benefit.

(3)   Where a mover's liability to pay council tax in respect of the new dwelling is to a second billing authority, the extended reduction (qualifying contributory benefits) may take the form of a payment from the first authority to–

(a)   that second authority; or

(b)   the mover directly.

Relationship between extended reduction (qualifying contributory benefits) and entitlement to reduction by virtue of falling within class C or D

43.–(1)   Where an applicant's reduction under an authority's scheme would have ended when the applicant ceased to be entitled to a qualifying contributory benefit in the circumstances listed in paragraph 39(1)(b), that reduction does not cease until the end of the extended reduction period.

(2)   Paragraphs 45 and 46 (period of entitlement and change of circumstances) do not apply to any extended reduction (qualifying contributory benefits) payable in accordance with paragraphs 41(1)(a) or 42(2) (amount of extended reduction-movers: persons who are not pensioners).

Extended reductions: movers into the authority's area: persons who are not pensioners

44.–(1)   Where–

(a)   an application is made to an authority for a reduction under its scheme, and

(b)   the applicant, or the partner of the applicant, is in receipt of an extended reduction from–

    (i)   another billing authority in Wales;

    (ii)   a billing authority in England;

    (iii)   a local authority in Scotland; or

    (iv)   a local authority in Northern Ireland,

the authority must reduce any reduction to which the applicant is entitled under its scheme by the amount of that extended reduction.

(2)   For the purposes of this paragraph "billing authority" ("awdurdod bilio") means a billing authority as defined in section 1 of the 1992 Act.

PART 6
Period of entitlement and change of circumstances

Date on which entitlement begins: persons who are not pensioners

45.   Any person by whom or in respect of whom an application for a reduction under an authority's scheme is made and who is otherwise entitled to that reduction is to be so entitled from the date on which the application is treated as made in accordance with paragraph 2 of Schedule 13.

Date on which change of circumstances is to take effect: persons who are not pensioners

46.–(1)   Except in cases where paragraph 23 (disregard of changes in tax, contributions, etc) applies and subject to the following provisions of this paragraph a change of circumstances which affects entitlement to, or the amount of, a reduction under an authority's scheme ("change of circumstances"), takes effect from the first day on which the change actually occurs.

(2)   Where that change is cessation of entitlement to any benefit under the benefit Acts, the date on which the change actually occurs will be the day immediately following the last day of entitlement to that benefit.

(3)   Subject to sub-paragraph (4), where the change of circumstances is a change in the amount of council tax payable, it takes effect from the day on which it actually occurs.

(4)   Where the change of circumstances is a change in the amount a person is liable to pay in respect of council tax in consequence of regulations under section 13 of the 1992 Act (reduced amounts of council tax) or changes in the discount to which a dwelling may be subject under section 11 or 12 of that Act, it is to take effect from the day on which the change in amount has effect.

(5)   Where the change of circumstances is the applicant's acquisition of a partner, the change takes effect on the day on which the acquisition takes place.

(6)   Where the change of circumstances is the death of an applicant's partner or their separation, it takes effect on the day the death or separation occurs.

(7)   Where the change of circumstances is that income, or an increase in the amount of income, other than a benefit or an increase in the amount of a benefit under the SSCBA, is paid in respect of a past period and there was no entitlement to income of that amount during that period, the change of circumstances is to take effect from the first day on which such income, had it been paid in that period at intervals appropriate to that income, would have fallen to be taken into account for the purposes of an authority's scheme.

(8)   Without prejudice to sub-paragraph (7), where the change of circumstances is the payment of income, or arrears of income, in respect of a past period, the change of circumstances takes effect from the first day on which such income, had it been timeously paid in that period at intervals appropriate to that income, would have fallen to be taken into account for the purposes of an authority's scheme.

SCHEDULE 7

REGULATION 33(2)

Applicable amounts: persons who are not pensioners

PART 1

Personal allowances

1.   The amounts specified in column (2) below in respect of each person or couple specified in column (1) are to be the amounts specified for the purposes of paragraphs 1(1)(a) and 2(2)(a) and (b) of Schedule 6.

Column (1) Person or couple	Column (2) Amount
(1) A single applicant who–	
(a) is entitled to main phase employment and support allowance;	[5 £77.90];
(b) is aged not less than 25;	[5 £77.90];
(c) is aged not less than 18 but less than 25.	[5 £61.70].
(2) Lone parent.	[5 £77.90].
(3) Couple.	[5 £122.35].

Amendments

1.   Amended by reg 10(a) of SI 2014 No 66 (W.6) as from 15.1.14.
2.   Amended by reg 11(a) of SI 2015 No 44 (W.3) as from 21.1.15, for schemes made for a financial year starting on or after 1.4.15.
3.   Amended by reg 6(a) of SI 2017 No 46 (W.20) as from 19.1.17, for schemes made for a financial year starting on or after 1.4.17.
4.   Amended by reg 10(a) of SI 2018 No 14 (W.7) as from 10.1.18, for schemes made for a financial year starting on or after 1.4.18.
5.   Amended by reg 7(a) of SI 2019 No 11 (W.5) as from 9.1.19, for schemes made for a financial year starting on or after 1.4.19.

---

2.   For the purposes of paragraph 1, an applicant is entitled to main phase employment and support allowance if–

(a)   paragraph 18 is satisfied in relation to the applicant [1 or the applicant is a member of the work-related activity group]; or

(b)   the applicant is entitled to a converted employment and support allowance.

Amendment

1.   Amended by reg 10(b) of SI 2018 No 14 (W.7) as from 10.1.18, for schemes made for a financial year starting on or after 1.4.18.

3.–(1)   The amounts specified in column (2) below in respect of each person specified in column (1) are, for the relevant period specified in column (1), be the amounts specified for the purposes of paragraphs 1(1)(b) and 2(2)(c) of Schedule 6.

Column (1)   *Column (2)*
Child or Young person   *Amount*
Person in respect of the period–
(a) beginning on that person's date of birth and ending on the day preceding the   [² £66.90];
first Monday in September following that person's sixteenth birthday;
(b) beginning on the first Monday in September following that person's   [² £66.90].
sixteenth birthday and ending on the day preceding that person's twentieth
birthday.

(2)   In column (1) of the table in sub-paragraph (1), "the first Monday in September" ("y dydd Llun cyntaf ym Medi") means the Monday which first occurs in the month of September in any year.

Amendments
1.   Amended by reg 10(b) of SI 2014 No 66 (W.6) as from 15.1.14.
2.   Amended by reg 11(b) of SI 2015 No 44 (W.3) as from 21.1.15, for schemes made for a financial year starting on or after 1.4.15.

General Note
Note that CTR schemes in Wales do not place a restriction on the number of children (or young people, as defined in reg 2) for whom an allowance can be included in an applicant's applicable amount under this paragraph – ie, the so-called "two-child limit", which in some circumstances applies to HB and CTR in England, does not apply to CTR in Wales.

PART 2

Family premium
   4.–(1)   The amount for the purposes of paragraphs 1(1)(c) and (2)(d) of Schedule 6 in respect of a family of which at least one member is a child or young person is to be–
  (a)   where the applicant is a lone parent to whom sub-paragraph (2) applies, £22.20;
  (b)   in any other case, [¹ £17.45].
  (2)   The amount in sub-paragraph (1)(a) is to be applicable to a lone parent–
  (a)   who was entitled to council tax benefit on 5 April 1998 and whose applicable amount on that date included the amount applicable under paragraph 3(1) of Schedule 1 to the Council Tax Benefit (Persons who have attained the qualifying age for state pension credit) Regulations 2006 as in force on that date; or
  (b)   on becoming entitled to council tax benefit where that lone parent–
     (i)   had been treated as entitled to that benefit in accordance with sub-paragraph (3) as at the day before the date of claim for that benefit; and
     (ii)   was entitled to housing benefit as at the date of claim for council tax benefit or would have been entitled to housing benefit as at that date had that day not fallen during a rent free period as defined in regulation 81 of the Housing Benefit Regulations 2006,
      and in respect of whom, all of the conditions specified in sub-paragraph (3) have continued to apply.
  (3)   The conditions specified for the purposes of sub-paragraph (2) are that, in respect of the period commencing on 6 April 1998–
  (a)   the applicant has not ceased to be entitled, or has not ceased to be treated as entitled, to–
     (i)   council tax benefit (in relation to the period prior to 1 April 2013), and
     (ii)   a reduction under an authority's scheme (in relation to the period commencing on 1 April 2013);
  (b)   the applicant has not ceased to be a lone parent;
  (c)   where the applicant was entitled to income support or to an income-based jobseeker's allowance on 5 April 1998, the applicant has continuously, since that date, been entitled to income support, an income-based jobseeker's allowance or income-related employment and support allowance or a combination of those benefits;
  (d)   where the applicant was not entitled to income support or to an income-based jobseeker's allowance on 5 April 1998, the applicant has not become entitled to income support, an income-based jobseeker's allowance or an income-related employment and support allowance; and
  (e)   a premium under paragraph 9, or a component under paragraph 21 or 22, has not become applicable to the applicant.
  (4)   For the purposes of sub-paragraphs (2)(b)(i) and (3)(a), an applicant is to be treated as entitled to council tax benefit during any period where the applicant was not, or had ceased to be, so entitled and–
  (a)   throughout that period, the applicant had been awarded housing benefit and the applicant's applicable amount included the amount applicable under paragraph 3(1)(a) of Schedule 3 to the Housing Benefit Regulations 2006 (lone parent rate of family premium); or
  (b)   the applicant would have been awarded housing benefit during that period had that period not been a rent free period as defined in regulation 81 of the Housing Benefit Regulations 2006 and the applicant's applicable amount throughout that period would have included the amount applicable under paragraph 3(1)(a) of Schedule 3 to those Regulations.

Amendment

1.   Amended by reg 11(c) of SI 2015 No 44 (W.3) as from 21.1.15, for schemes made for a financial year starting on or after 1.4.15.

PART 3

Premiums

5.   Except as provided in paragraph 6, the premiums specified in Part 4 are, for the purposes of paragraphs 1(1)(d) and 2(e) of Schedule 6, to be applicable to an applicant who satisfies the condition specified in paragraphs 9 to 14 in respect of that premium.

6.   Subject to paragraph 7, where an applicant satisfies the conditions in respect of more than one premium in this Part of this Schedule, only one premium is to be applicable to the applicant and, if they are different amounts, the higher or highest amount is to apply.

7.   The following premiums, namely–

(a)   a severe disability premium to which paragraph 11 applies;

(b)   an enhanced disability premium to which paragraph 12 applies;

(c)   a disabled child premium to which paragraph 13 applies; and

(d)   a carer premium to which paragraph 14 applies,

may be applicable in addition to any other premium which may apply under this Schedule.

8.–(1)   Subject to sub-paragraph (2), for the purposes of this Part of this Schedule, once a premium is applicable to an applicant under this Part, a person is to be treated as being in receipt of any benefit for–

(a)   in the case of a benefit to which the Social Security (Overlapping Benefits) Regulations 1979 applies, any period during which, apart from the provisions of those Regulations, that person would be in receipt of that benefit; and

(b)   any period spent by a person in undertaking a course of training or instruction provided or approved by the Secretary of State or the Welsh Ministers under section 2 of the Employment and Training Act 1973 or by Skills Development Scotland, Scottish Enterprise or Highlands and Islands Enterprise under section 2 of the Enterprise and New Towns (Scotland) Act 1990 or for any period during which that person is in receipt of a training allowance.

(2)   For the purposes of the carer premium under paragraph 14, a person is to be treated as being in receipt of carer's allowance by virtue of sub-paragraph (1)(a) only if and for so long as the person in respect of whose care the allowance has been claimed remains in receipt of attendance allowance, or the care component of disability living allowance at the highest or middle rate prescribed in accordance with section 72(3) of the SSCBA or the daily living component of personal independence payment payable under Part 4 of the Welfare Reform Act 2012, or AFIP.

Disability premium

9.   The condition is that–

(a)   where the applicant is a single applicant or a lone parent, the applicant has not attained the qualifying age for state pension credit and the additional condition specified in paragraph 10 is satisfied; or

(b)   where the applicant has a partner, either–

(i)   the applicant has not attained the qualifying age for state pension credit and the additional condition specified in paragraph 10(1)(a) or (b) is satisfied by the applicant; or

(ii)   the applicant's partner has not attained the qualifying age for state pension credit and the additional condition specified in paragraph 10(1)(a) is satisfied by the applicant's partner.

Additional condition for the disability premium

10.–(1)   Subject to sub-paragraph (2) and paragraph 8, the additional condition referred to in paragraph 9 is that either–

(a)   the applicant or, as the case may be, the applicant's partner–

(i)   is in receipt of one or more of the following benefits: attendance allowance, disability living allowance, personal independence payment, AFIP, the disability element or the severe disability element of working tax credit as specified in regulation 20(1)(b) and (f) of the Working Tax Credit (Entitlement and Maximum Rate) Regulations 2002, mobility supplement, long-term incapacity benefit under Part 2 of the SSCBA or severe disablement allowance under Part 3 of that Act but, in the case of long-term incapacity benefit or severe disablement allowance, only where it is paid in respect of the applicant; or

(ii)   was in receipt of long-term incapacity benefit under Part 2 of the SSCBA when entitlement to that benefit ceased on account of the payment of a retirement pension under that Act [² or a state pension under Part 1 of the Pensions Act 2014] and the applicant has since remained continuously entitled to–

(aa)   council tax benefit (in relation to the period to 1 April 2013), or

(bb)   a reduction under an authority's scheme (in relation to the period commencing 1 April 2013), and

if the long-term incapacity benefit was payable to the applicant's partner, the partner is still a member of the family; or

    (iii)   was in receipt of attendance allowance or disability living allowance but payment of benefit has been suspended in accordance with regulations made under section 113(2) of the SSCBA or otherwise abated as a consequence of the applicant or the applicant's partner becoming a patient within the meaning of paragraph 21(11)(i) of Schedule 6 (treatment of child care charges); or

    (iv)   was in receipt of personal independence payment, but payment of that benefit has been suspended in accordance with section 86 of the Welfare Reform Act 2012 as a consequence of the applicant becoming a patient within the meaning of paragraph 21 of Schedule 6 (treatment of child care charges); or

    (v)   was in receipt of AFIP, but payment has been suspended in accordance with any terms of the armed and reserve forces compensation scheme which allow for suspension because a person is undergoing medical treatment in a hospital or similar institution; or

    (vi)   is provided with an invalid carriage or other vehicle by the Secretary of State or a clinical commissioning group under paragraph 9 of Schedule 1 to the National Health Service Act 2006 or, in Scotland, under section 46 of the National Health Service (Scotland) Act 1978 (provision of services by Scottish Ministers) or, in Wales, under section 5 of, and Schedule 1 to the National Health Service (Wales) Act 2006 or, in Northern Ireland, is provided with an invalid carriage or other vehicle by the Department of Health, Social Services and Public Safety under article 30(1) of the Health and Personal Social Services (Northern Ireland) Order 1972, or receives payments by way of grant from the Secretary of State under paragraph 10(3) of Schedule 1 to the Act of 2006 (provision of vehicles for disabled persons) or, in Scotland by the Scottish Ministers under section 46 of the Act of 1978; or

    [² (vii)   is blind and in consequence is registered as blind in a register compiled under section 29 of the National Assistance Act 1948 (welfare services), or is severely sight-impaired and in consequence is registered as severely sight-impaired in a register established and maintained by a local authority under section 18(1) of the Social Services and Well-being (Wales) Act 2014 or section 77(1) of the Care Act 2014, or in Scotland has been certified as blind and in consequence is registered in a register maintained by or on behalf of a council constituted under section 2 of the Local Government etc. (Scotland) Act 1994; or]

    (b)   the applicant–

    (i)   is, or is treated as, incapable of work in accordance with the provisions of, and regulations made under, Part 12A of the SSCBA (incapacity for work); and

    (ii)   has been incapable, or has been treated as incapable, of work for a continuous period of not less than–

    (aa)   in the case of an applicant who is terminally ill within the meaning of section 30B(4) of the SSCBA, 196 days;

    (bb)   in any other case, 364 days.

(2)   For the purposes of [¹ sub-paragraph (1)(a)(vii)], a person who has ceased to be registered as blind [² or severely sight-impaired] on regaining that person's eyesight is nevertheless to be treated as blind [² or severely sight-impaired] and as satisfying the additional condition set out in that sub-paragraph for a period of 28 weeks following the date on which that person ceased to be so registered.

(3)   For the purposes of sub-paragraph (1)(b), once the disability premium is applicable to an applicant by virtue of the applicant's satisfying the additional condition specified in that provision, if the applicant then ceases, for a period of 8 weeks or less, to be treated as incapable of work or to be incapable of work the applicant is, on again becoming so incapable of work, to immediately thereafter be treated as satisfying the condition in sub-paragraph (1)(b).

(4)   For the purposes of sub-paragraph (1)(b), once the disability premium is applicable to an applicant by virtue of the applicant satisfying the additional condition specified in that provision, the applicant is to continue to be treated as satisfying that condition for any period spent by the applicant in undertaking a course of training provided under section 2 of the Employment and Training Act 1973 or section 2 of the Enterprise and New Towns (Scotland) Act 1990 or for any period during which the applicant is in receipt of a training allowance.

(5)   For the purposes of sub-paragraph (1)(b), where any two or more periods of incapacity are separated by a break of not more than 56 days, those periods are to be treated as one continuous period.

(6)   For the purposes of this paragraph, a reference to a person who is or was in receipt of long-term incapacity benefit includes a person who is or was in receipt of short-term incapacity benefit at a rate equal to the long-term rate by virtue of section 30B(4)(a) of the SSCBA (short-term incapacity benefit for a person who is terminally ill), or who would be or would have been in receipt of short-term incapacity benefit at such a rate but for the fact that the rate of short-term incapacity benefit already payable to that person is or was equal to or greater than the long-term rate.

(7)   In the case of an applicant who is a welfare to work beneficiary (a person to whom regulation 13A(1) of the Social Security (Incapacity for Work) (General) Regulations 1995 applies, and who again becomes incapable of work for the purposes of Part 12A of the SSCBA)–

    (a)   the reference to a period of 8 weeks in sub-paragraph (3); and

    (b)   the reference to a period of 56 days in sub-paragraph (5),

is in each case to be treated as a reference to a period of 104 weeks.

(8)   The applicant is not entitled to the disability premium if the applicant has, or is treated as having, limited capability for work.

Amendments
1.   Amended by reg 10(c) of SI 2014 No 66 (W.6) as from 15.1.14.
2.   Amended by reg 10(a) of SI 2016 No 50 (W.21) as from 20.1.16, for schemes made for a financial year starting on or after 1.4.16.

Severe disability premium
    11.–(1)   The condition is that the applicant is a severely disabled person.
    (2)   For the purposes of sub-paragraph (1), an applicant is to be treated as being a severely disabled person if, and only if–
    (a)   in the case of a single applicant, a lone parent or an applicant who is treated as having no partner in consequence of sub-paragraph (3)–
        (i)   the applicant is in receipt of attendance allowance, or the care component of disability living allowance at the highest or middle rate prescribed in accordance with section 72(3) of the SSCBA or the daily living component of personal independence payment payable at either rate under Part 4 of the Welfare Reform Act 2012, or AFIP; and
        (ii)   subject to sub-paragraph (4), the applicant has no non-dependants aged 18 or over normally residing with the applicant with whom the applicant is normally residing; and
        (iii)   no person is entitled to, and in receipt of, a carer's allowance under section 70 of the SSCBA [² or has an award of universal credit which includes the carer element under regulation 29 of the Universal Credit Regulations 2013] in respect of caring for the applicant;
    (b)   in the case of an applicant who has a partner–
        (i)   the applicant is in receipt of attendance allowance, or the care component of disability living allowance at the highest or middle rate prescribed in accordance with section 72(3) of the SSCBA or the daily living component of personal independence payment payable at either rate under Part 4 of the Welfare Reform Act 2012, or AFIP; and
        (ii)   the applicant's partner is also in receipt of such an allowance or, if the applicant is a member of a polygamous marriage, all the members of that marriage are in receipt of such an allowance; and
        (iii)   subject to sub-paragraph (4), the applicant has no non-dependants aged 18 or over normally residing with the applicant or with whom the applicant is normally residing,
and either a person is entitled to and in receipt of a carer's allowance [² or has an award of universal credit which includes the carer element] in respect of caring for only one member of a couple or, in the case of a polygamous marriage, for one or more but not all the members of the marriage, or as the case may be, no person is entitled to and in receipt of such an allowance [² or has such an award of universal credit] in respect of caring for either member of a couple or any member of a polygamous marriage.
    (3)   Where an applicant has a partner who does not satisfy the condition in sub-paragraph (2)(b)(ii), and that partner [¹ is blind or severely sight-impaired or is treated as such] within the meaning of paragraph 10(1)(a)(vii) and(2), that partner is to be treated for the purposes of sub-paragraph (2)(b)(ii) as if that person were not a partner of the applicant.
    (4)   For the purposes of sub-paragraph (2)(a)(ii) and (2)(b)(iii) no account is to be taken of–
    (a)   a person receiving attendance allowance, or disability living allowance by virtue of the care component at the highest or middle rate prescribed in accordance with section 72(3) of the SSCBA, or the daily living component of personal independence at either rate prescribed in accordance with Part 4 of the Welfare Reform Act 2012, or AFIP; or
    (b)   a person who [¹ is blind or severely sight-impaired or is treated as such] within the meaning of paragraph 10(1)(a)(vii) and (2).
    (5)   For the purposes of sub-paragraph (2)(b) a person is to be treated–
    (a)   as being in receipt of attendance allowance, or the care component of disability living allowance at the highest or middle rate prescribed in accordance with section 72(3) of the SSCBA or the daily living component of personal independence payment payable at either rate under Part 4 of the Welfare Reform Act 2012, or AFIP, if that person would, but for that person's being a patient for a period exceeding 28 days, be so in receipt;
    (b)   as being entitled to and in receipt of a carer's allowance [² or having an award of universal credit which includes the carer element] if that person would, but for the person for whom that person was caring being a patient in hospital for a period exceeding 28 days, be so entitled and in receipt [² or have such an award of universal credit].
    (6)   For the purposes of sub-paragraph (2)(a)(iii) and (2)(b), no account is to be taken of an award of carer's allowance [² or an award of universal credit which includes the carer element] to the extent that payment of such an award is back-dated for a period before the date on which the award is first paid.
    (7)   In sub-paragraph (2)(a)(iii) and (b), references to a person being in receipt of a carer's allowance [² or having an award of universal credit which includes the carer element] are to include references to a person who would have been in receipt of that allowance [2 or had such an award of universal credit] but for the application of a restriction under section 6B or 7 of the Social Security Fraud Act 2001 (loss of benefit provisions).

Amendments
1.   Amended by reg 10(b) of SI 2016 No 50 (W.21) as from 20.1.16, for schemes made for a financial year starting on or after 1.4.16.
2.   Inserted by reg 6(b) of SI 2017 No 46 (W.20) as from 19.1.17, for schemes made for a financial year starting on or after 1.4.17.

Enhanced disability premium

12.–(1)   Subject to sub-paragraph (2), the condition is that–
(a)   the Secretary of State has decided that the applicant has, or is to be treated as having, limited capability for work-related activity; or
(b)   the care component of disability living allowance is, or would be payable at the highest rate prescribed under section 72(3) of the SSCBA, but for a suspension of benefit in accordance with regulations made under section 113(2) of the SSCBA or but for an abatement as a consequence of hospitalisation, in respect of–
  (i)   the applicant; or
  (ii)   a member of the applicant's family,
  who has not attained the qualifying age for state pension credit; or
(c)   the daily living component of personal independence payment is, or would be payable at the enhanced rate prescribed in accordance with section 78(2) of the Welfare Reform Act 2012, but for a suspension of benefit in accordance with section 86 of the Welfare Reform Act 2012 in respect of–
  (i)   the applicant; or
  (ii)   a member of the applicant's family,
  who has not attained the qualifying age for state pension credit: or
(d)   AFIP is payable in respect of–
  (i)   the applicant; or
  (ii)   a member of the applicant's family,
  who has not attained the qualifying age for state pension credit.
(2)   Where the condition in sub-paragraph (1) ceases to be satisfied because of the death of a child or young person, the condition is that the applicant or partner is entitled to child benefit in respect of that child or young person under section 145A of the SSCBA (entitlement after death of child or qualifying young person).
(3)   The condition is not satisfied if the person to whom sub-paragraph (1) refers is–
(a)   an applicant who–
  (i)   is not a member of a couple or a polygamous marriage; and
  (ii)   is a patient within the meaning of paragraph 21(11)(g) of Schedule 6 (treatment of child care charges) and has been for a period of more than 52 weeks; or
(b)   a member of a couple or a polygamous marriage where each member is a patient within the meaning of paragraph 21(11)(g) of Schedule 6 and has been for a period of more than 52 weeks.

Disabled child premium

13.   The condition is that a child or young person for whom the applicant or a partner of the applicant is responsible and who is a member of the applicant's household–
(a)   is in receipt of disability living allowance or personal independence payment or is no longer in receipt of such allowance because the child or young person is a patient, provided that the child or young person continues to be a member of the family; or
(b)   [¹ is blind or severely sight-impaired or is treated as such] within the meaning of paragraph 10; or
(c)   is a child or young person in respect of whom section 145A of the SSCBA (entitlement after death of child or qualifying young person) applies for the purposes of entitlement to child benefit but only for the period prescribed under that section, and in respect of whom a disabled child premium was included in the applicant's applicable amount immediately before the death of that child or young person, or ceased to be included in the applicant's applicable amount because of that child or young person's death; or
(d)   is in receipt of AFIP.

Amendment
1.   Amended by reg 10(c) of SI 2016 No 50 (W.21) as from 20.1.16, for schemes made for a financial year starting on or after 1.4.16.

Carer premium

14.–(1)   The condition is that the applicant or the applicant's partner is, or both of them are, entitled to a carer's allowance under section 70 of the SSCBA.
(2)   Where a carer premium is awarded but–
(a)   the person in respect of whose care the carer's allowance has been awarded dies; or
(b)   in any other case the person in respect of whom a carer premium has been awarded ceases to be entitled to a carer's allowance,
the condition for the award of the premium is to be treated as satisfied for a period of eight weeks from the relevant date specified in sub-paragraph (3).

(3)   The relevant date for the purposes of sub-paragraph (2) is to be–

(a)   where sub-paragraph (2)(a) applies, the Sunday following the death of the person in respect of whose care a carer's allowance has been awarded or the date of death if the death occurred on a Sunday;

(b)   in any other case, the date on which the person who has been entitled to a carer's allowance ceases to be entitled to that allowance.

(4)   Where a person who has been entitled to a carer's allowance ceases to be entitled to that allowance and makes an application for a reduction, the condition for the award of the carer premium is to be treated as satisfied for a period of eight weeks from the date on which–

(a)   the person in respect of whose care the carer's allowance has been awarded dies;

(b)   in any other case, the person who has been entitled to a carer's allowance ceased to be entitled to that allowance.

Persons in receipt of concessionary payments

15.   For the purpose of determining whether a premium is applicable to a person under paragraphs 10 to 14, any concessionary payment made to compensate that person for the non-payment of any benefit mentioned in those paragraphs is to be treated as if it were a payment of that benefit.

Persons in receipt of benefit for another

16.   For the purposes of this Part of this Schedule, a person is to be regarded as being in receipt of any benefit if, and only if, it is paid in respect of that person and is to be so regarded only for any period in respect of which that benefit is paid.

PART 4
Amounts of premiums specified in Part 3

Premium	*Amount*
17.–(1) Disability Premium–	
(a) where the applicant satisfies the condition in paragraph 9(a);	[⁵ £34.35];
(b) where the applicant satisfies the condition in paragraph 9(b)	[⁵ £48.95].
(2) Severe Disability Premium–	
(a) where the applicant satisfies the condition in paragraph 11(2)(a);	[⁵ £65.85];
(b) where the applicant satisfies the condition in paragraph 11(2)(b)–	
(i) in a case where there is someone in receipt of a carer's allowance [³ or who has an award of universal credit which includes the carer element under regulation 29 of the Universal Credit Regulations 2013] or if that person or any partner satisfies that condition only by virtue of paragraph 11(5);	[⁵ £65.85];
(ii) in a case where there is no-one in receipt of such an allowance [³ or such an award of universal credit].	[⁵ £131.70].
(3) Disabled Child Premium.	[⁵ £64.19] in respect of each child or young person in respect of whom the condition specified in paragraph 13 of Part 3 is satisfied.
(4) Carer Premium.	[⁵ £36.85] in respect of each person who satisfies the condition specified in paragraph 14.
(5) Enhanced Disability Premium.	(a) [⁵ £26.04] in respect of each child or young person in respect of whom the conditions specified in paragraph 12 are satisfied;
	(b) [⁵ £16.80] in respect of each person who is neither–
	(i) a child or young person; nor
	(ii) member of a couple or a polygamous marriage;
	(iii) in respect of whom the conditions specified in paragraph 12 are satisfied;
	(c) [⁵ £24.10] where the applicant is a member of a couple or a polygamous marriage and the conditions specified in paragraph 12 are satisfied in respect of a member of that couple or polygamous marriage.

Amendments
1. Amended by reg 10(d) of SI 2014 No 66 (W.6) as from 15.1.14.
2. Amended by reg 11(d) of SI 2015 No 44 (W.3) as from 21.1.15, for schemes made for a financial year starting on or after 1.4.15.
3. Amended by reg 6(c) of SI 2017 No 46 (W.20) as from 19.1.17, for schemes made for a financial year starting on or after 1.4.17.
4. Amended by reg 10(c) of SI 2018 No 14 (W.7) as from 10.1.18, for schemes made for a financial year starting on or after 1.4.18.
5. Amended by reg 7(b) of SI 2019 No 11 (W.5) as from 9.1.19, for schemes made for a financial year starting on or after 1.4.19.

PART 5

The components

18. Subject to paragraph 20 the applicant is entitled to one, but not both, of the components in paragraph 21 or 22 if–

(a) the applicant or the applicant's partner has made a claim for employment and support allowance;

(b) the Secretary of State has decided that the applicant or the applicant's partner has, or is to be treated as having, limited capability for work or limited capability for work-related activity; and

(c) either–

    (i) the assessment phase as defined in section 24(2) of the Welfare Reform Act 2007 has ended; or

    (ii) regulation 7 of the Employment and Support Allowance Regulations 2008 [¹ or regulation 7 of the Employment and Support Allowance Regulations 2013] circumstances where the condition that the assessment phase has ended before entitlement to the support component [²] arises does not apply) applies.

Amendments
1. Amended by reg 11(e) of SI 2015 No 44 (W.3) as from 21.1.15, for schemes made for a financial year starting on or after 1.4.15.
2. Amended by reg 10(d) of SI 2018 No 14 (W.7) as from 10.1.18, for schemes made for a financial year starting on or after 1.4.18.

19. Subject to paragraph 20, the applicant is entitled to one, but not both, of the components in paragraphs 21 and 22 if the applicant or the applicant's partner is entitled to a converted employment and support allowance.

20.–(1) The applicant has no entitlement under paragraph 21 or 22 if the applicant is entitled to the disability premium under paragraphs 9 and 10.

(2) Where the applicant and the applicant's partner each satisfy paragraph 21 or 22, the component to be included in the applicant's applicable amount is that which relates to the applicant.

The work-related activity component

21. The applicant is entitled to the work-related activity component if the Secretary of State has decided that the applicant or the applicant's partner has, or is to be treated as having, limited capability for work.

The support component

22. The applicant is entitled to the support component if the Secretary of State has decided that the applicant or the applicant's partner has, or is to be treated as having, limited capability for work-related activity.

PART 6

Amount of components

23. The amount of the work-related activity component is [³ £29.35].

Amendments
1. Amended by reg 10(e) of SI 2014 No 66 (W.6) as from 15.1.14.
2. Amended by reg 11(f) of SI 2015 No 44 (W.3) as from 21.1.15, for schemes made for a financial year starting on or after 1.4.15.
3. Amended by reg 6(d) of SI 2017 No 46 (W.20) as from 19.1.17, for schemes made for a financial year starting on or after 1.4.17.

24. The amount of the support component is [⁵ £38.55].

Amendments
1. Amended by reg 10(f) of SI 2014 No 66 (W.6) as from 15.1.14.
2. Amended by reg 11(g) of SI 2015 No 44 (W.3) as from 21.1.15, for schemes made for a financial year starting on or after 1.4.15.
3. Amended by reg 6(e) of SI 2017 No 46 (W.20) as from 19.1.17, for schemes made for a financial year starting on or after 1.4.17.
4. Amended by reg 10(e) of SI 2018 No 14 (W.7) as from 10.1.18, for schemes made for a financial year starting on or after 1.4.18.
5. Amended by reg 7(c) of SI 2019 No 11 (W.5) as from 9.1.19, for schemes made for a financial year starting on or after 1.4.19.

PART 7

Transitional addition

25.–(1)   The applicant is entitled to the transitional addition calculated in accordance with paragraph 28 where the applicant or the applicant's partner ("the relevant person")–
(a)   is entitled to a converted employment and support allowance; or
(b)   is appealing a conversion decision as described in regulation 5(2)(b) of the Employment and Support Allowance (Transitional Provisions, Housing Benefit and Council Tax Benefit) (Existing Awards) (No 2) Regulations 2010 and–
    (i)   is treated as having limited capability for work by virtue of regulation 30 of the Employment and Support Allowance Regulations 2008 as modified by the Employment and Support Allowance (Transitional Provisions, Housing Benefit and Council Tax Benefit) (Existing Awards) (No 2) Regulations 2010 [¹ or regulation 26 of the Employment and Support Allowance Regulations 2013]; and
    (ii)   is not in receipt of an income-related employment and support allowance,
unless the amount of the transitional addition calculated in accordance with paragraph 28 would be nil.

(2)   The applicant's entitlement to a transitional addition by virtue of this paragraph ends on any of the following–
(a)   the reduction of the transitional addition to nil in accordance with paragraph 29;
(b)   the termination of the applicant's award of reduction under an authority's scheme;
(c)   the relevant person ceasing to meet the requirements of sub-paragraph (1)(a) or (b), as the case may be;
(d)   the applicant or the applicant's partner becoming entitled to an income-related employment and support allowance, an income-based jobseeker's allowance or income support;
(e)   5 April 2020.

Amendment
1. Amended by reg 11(h) of SI 2015 No 44 (W.3) as from 21.1.15, for schemes made for a financial year starting on or after 1.4.15.

26.–(1)   This paragraph applies where–
(a)   the applicant's entitlement to a transitional addition, ends by virtue of the termination of the applicant's award of reduction, under–
    (i)   paragraph 25(2)(b);
    (ii)   sub-paragraph (3)(b) of this paragraph; or
    (iii)   paragraph 27(3)(b);
(b)   within 12 weeks of that termination but before 5 April 2020 the applicant again becomes entitled to a reduction under an authority's scheme;
(c)   in the reduction week in which the applicant again becomes entitled to a reduction under an authority's scheme the relevant person is entitled to an employment and support allowance which is not income related; and
(d)   at the date on which the applicant again becomes entitled to a reduction under an authority's scheme, neither the applicant nor the applicant's partner is entitled to an income-related employment and support allowance, an income-based jobseeker's allowance or income support.

(2)   Where this paragraph applies, the applicant is entitled, with effect from the day on which the applicant again becomes entitled to a reduction under an authority's scheme, to a transitional addition of the amount of the transitional addition that would have applied had the applicant's entitlement to a transitional addition not ended (but taking account of the effect which any intervening change of circumstances would have had by virtue of paragraph 29), unless the amount of the transitional addition would be nil.

(3)   The applicant's entitlement to a transitional addition by virtue of this paragraph ends on any of the following–
(a)   the reduction of the transitional addition to nil in accordance with paragraph 29;
(b)   the termination of the applicant's award of a reduction under an authority's scheme;
(c)   the relevant person no longer being entitled to the employment and support allowance referred to in sub-paragraph (1)(c);

(d) the applicant or the applicant's partner becoming entitled to an income-related employment and support allowance, an income-based jobseeker's allowance or income support;

(e) 5 April 2020.

27.–(1) This paragraph applies where–

(a) the applicant's entitlement to a transitional addition ends, by virtue of the relevant person ceasing to be entitled to an employment and support allowance, under–

    (i) paragraph 25(2)(c);

    (ii) paragraph 26(3)(c); or

    (iii) sub-paragraph (3)(c);

(b) before 5 April 2020 the relevant person again becomes entitled to an employment and support allowance which is not income-related;

(c) at the date on which the relevant person again becomes entitled to an employment and support allowance which is not income-related, regulation 145(1) of the Employment and Support Allowance Regulations 2008 [¹ or regulation 86 of the Employment and Support Allowance Regulations 2013] applies to the relevant person; and

(d) at the date on which the relevant person again becomes entitled to an employment and support allowance which is not income-related, neither the applicant nor the applicant's partner is entitled to an income-related employment and support allowance, an income-based jobseeker's allowance or income support.

(2) Where this paragraph applies, the applicant is entitled, with effect from the day that the relevant person's entitlement to employment and support allowance takes effect for the purposes of a reduction under an authority's scheme, to a transitional addition of the amount of the transitional addition that would have applied had the applicant's entitlement to a transitional addition not ended (but taking account of the effect which any intervening change of circumstances would have had by virtue of paragraph 29), unless the amount of the transitional addition would be nil.

(3) The applicant's entitlement to a transitional addition by virtue of this paragraph ends on any of the following–

(a) the reduction of the transitional addition to nil in accordance with paragraph 29;

(b) the termination of the applicant's award of a reduction under an authority's scheme;

(c) the relevant person no longer being entitled to the employment and support allowance referred to in sub-paragraph (1)(b);

(d) the applicant or the applicant's partner becoming entitled to an income-related employment and support allowance, an income-based jobseeker's allowance or income support;

(e) 5 April 2020.

Amendment

1. Amended by reg 11(i) of SI 2015 No 44 (W.3) as from 21.1.15, for schemes made for a financial year starting on or after 1.4.15.

PART 8

Amount of transitional addition

28.–(1) Subject to paragraph 29, the amount of the transitional addition is the amount by which Amount A exceeds Amount B.

(2) Where a conversion decision as described in regulation 5(2)(a) of the Employment and Support Allowance (Transitional Provisions, Housing Benefit and Council Tax Benefit) (Existing Awards) (No. 2) Regulations 2010 ("the 2010 Regulations") is made in respect of the relevant person–

(a) Amount A is the basic amount that would have applied on the day that decision took effect had that decision not been made; and

(b) Amount B is the basic amount that applied on that day as a result of that decision.

(3) Where the relevant person is appealing a conversion decision as described in regulation 5(2)(b) of the 2010 Regulations and is treated as having limited capability for work by virtue of regulation 30 of the Employment and Support Allowance Regulations 2008 as modified by the 2010 Regulations–

(a) Amount A is the basic amount that would have applied on the day the relevant person was first treated as having limited capability for work if the relevant person had not been so treated; and

(b) Amount B is the basic amount that applied on that day as a result of the relevant person being so treated.

(4) In this paragraph and paragraph 29, "basic amount" ("swm sylfaenol") means the aggregate of such amounts as may apply in the applicant's case in accordance with paragraph 1(1)(a) to (e) or paragraph (2)(2)(a) to (f) of Schedule 6.

29.–(1) Subject to sub-paragraph (2), where there is a change of circumstances which leads to an increase in the applicant's basic amount, the transitional addition that applies immediately before the change of circumstances is to be reduced by the amount by which Amount C exceeds Amount D.

(2) If Amount C exceeds Amount D by more than the amount of the transitional addition that applies immediately before the change of circumstances, that transitional addition is to be reduced to nil.

(3) Amount C is the basic amount that applies as a result of the increase.

(4) Amount D is the basic amount that applied immediately before the increase.

SCHEDULE 8

Regulation 33(2)

Sums disregarded in the calculation of earnings: persons who are not pensioners

1.   In the case of an applicant who has been engaged in remunerative work as an employed earner or, had the employment been in Great Britain, would have been so engaged–

(a)   where–

(i)   the employment has been terminated because of retirement; and

(ii)   on retirement the applicant is entitled to a retirement pension under the SSCBA [¹ or a state pension under Part 1 of the Pensions Act 2014], or is not so entitled solely because of the applicant's failure to satisfy the contribution conditions [¹ or to have the minimum number of qualifying years],

any earnings paid or due to be paid in respect of that employment, but only for a period commencing on the day immediately after the date on which the employment was terminated;

(b)   where before the first day of entitlement to a reduction under an authority's scheme the employment has been terminated otherwise than because of retirement, any earnings paid or due to be paid in respect of that employment except–

(i)   any payment of the nature described in–

(aa)   paragraph 14(1)(e) of Schedule 6 to these Regulations, or

(bb)   section 28, 64 or 68 of the Employment Rights Act 1996 (guarantee payments, suspension from work on medical or maternity grounds); and

(ii)   any award, sum or payment of the nature described in–

(aa)   paragraph 14(1)(g) or (i) of Schedule 6 to these Regulations, or

(bb)   section 34 or 70 of the Employment Rights Act 1996 (guarantee payments and suspension from work: complaints to employment tribunals),

including any payment made following the settlement of a complaint to an employment tribunal or of court proceedings;

(c)   where before the first day of entitlement to a reduction under an authority's scheme–

(i)   the employment has not been terminated, but

(ii)   the applicant is not engaged in remunerative work,

any earnings paid or due to be paid in respect of that employment except any payment or remuneration of the nature described in paragraph 1(b)(i) or (ii)(bb) or paragraph 14(1)(j) of Schedule 6.

Amendment

1.   Amended by reg 11 of SI 2016 No 50 (W.21) as from 20.1.16, for schemes made for a financial year starting on or after 1.4.16.

2.   In the case of an applicant who, before the first day of entitlement to a reduction under an authority's scheme–

(a)   has been engaged in part-time employment as an employed earner or, where the employment has been outside Great Britain, would have been so engaged had the employment been in Great Britain; and

(b)   has ceased to be engaged in that employment, whether or not that employment has been terminated, any earnings paid or due to be paid in respect of that employment except–

(i)   where that employment has been terminated, any payment of the nature described in paragraph 1(b)(i) or (ii)(bb);

(ii)   where that employment has not been terminated, any payment or remuneration of the nature described in paragraph 1(b)(i) or (ii)(bb) or paragraph 14(1)(j) of Schedule 6.

3.   In the case of an applicant who has been engaged in remunerative work or part-time employment as a self employed earner or, had the employment been in Great Britain, would have been so engaged and who has ceased to be so employed, from the date of the cessation of the applicant's employment, any earnings derived from that employment except earnings to which paragraph 16(3) of Schedule 6 (earnings of self-employed earners) apply.

4.–(1)   In a case to which this paragraph applies and paragraph 5 does not apply, £20; but notwithstanding paragraph 7 of Schedule 6 (calculation of income and capital of members of an applicant's family and of a polygamous marriage) if this paragraph applies to an applicant it is not to apply to the applicant's partner except where, and to the extent that, the earnings of the applicant which are to be disregarded under this paragraph are less than £20.

(2)   This paragraph applies where the applicant's applicable amount includes an amount by way of the disability premium, severe disability premium, work-related activity component or support component under Schedule 7 (applicable amounts: persons who are not pensioners) [¹ or where the applicant or the applicant's partner is a member of the work-related activity group].

(3) This paragraph applies where–

(a) the applicant is a member of a couple and the applicant's applicable amount includes an amount by way of the disability premium under Schedule 7; and

(b) the applicant or the applicant's partner has not attained the qualifying age for state pension credit and at least one is engaged in employment.

Amendment

1. Amended by reg 11(a) of SI 2018 No 14 (W.7) as from 10.1.18, for schemes made for a financial year starting on or after 1.4.18.

---

5. In a case where the applicant is a lone parent, £25.

6.–(1) In a case to which neither paragraph 4 nor paragraph 5 applies to the applicant and, subject to sub-paragraph (2), where the applicant's applicable amount includes an amount by way of the carer premium under Schedule 7 (applicable amounts: persons who are not pensioners), £20 of the earnings of the person who is, or at any time in the preceding eight weeks was, in receipt of carer's allowance or treated in accordance with paragraph 14(2) of that Schedule as being in receipt of carer's allowance.

(2) Where the carer premium is awarded in respect of the applicant and of any partner of the applicant's, their earnings are for the purposes of this paragraph to be aggregated, but the amount to be disregarded in accordance with sub-paragraph (1) is not to exceed £20 of the aggregated amount.

7. Where the carer premium is awarded in respect of an applicant who is a member of a couple and whose earnings are less than £20, but is not awarded in respect of the other member of the couple, and that other member is engaged in an employment–

(a) specified in paragraph 9(1), so much of the other member's earnings as would not when aggregated with the amount disregarded under paragraph 6 exceed £20;

(b) other than one specified in paragraph 9(1), so much of the other member's earnings from such other employment up to £10 as would not when aggregated with the amount disregarded under paragraph 6 exceed £20.

8. In a case where paragraphs 4, 6, 7 and 9 do not apply to the applicant and the applicant is one of a couple and a member of that couple is in employment, £10; but, notwithstanding paragraph 7 of Schedule 6 (calculation of income and capital of members of applicant's family and of a polygamous marriage), if this paragraph applies to an applicant it is not to apply to the applicant's partner except where, and to the extent that, the earnings of the applicant which are to be disregarded under this paragraph are less than £10.

9.–(1) In a case where paragraphs 4, 6, 7 and 9 do not apply to the applicant, £20 of earnings derived from one or more employments as–

(a) a part-time fire-fighter employed by a fire and rescue authority constituted by a scheme under section 2 of the Fire and Rescue Services Act 2004 or a scheme to which section 4 of that Act applies;

(b) a part-time fire-fighter employed by the Scottish Fire and Rescue Service;

(c) an auxiliary coastguard in respect of coast rescue activities;

(d) a person engaged part-time in the manning or launching of a life boat;

(e) a member of any territorial or reserve force prescribed in Part I of Schedule 6 to the Social Security (Contributions) Regulations 2001;

but, notwithstanding paragraph 7 of Schedule 6 (calculation of income and capital of members of applicant's family and of a polygamous marriage), if this paragraph applies to an applicant it is not to apply to that applicant's partner except to the extent specified in sub-paragraph (2).

(2) If the applicant's partner is engaged in employment–

(a) specified in sub-paragraph (1), so much of the applicant's partner's earnings as would not in aggregate with the amount of the applicant's earnings disregarded under this paragraph exceed £20;

(b) other than one specified in sub-paragraph (1), so much of the applicant's partner's earnings from that employment up to £10 as would not in aggregate with the applicant's earnings disregarded under this paragraph exceed £20.

10. Where the applicant is engaged in one or more employments specified in paragraph 9(1), but the applicant's earnings derived from such employments are less than £20 in any week and the applicant is also engaged in any other employment, so much of the applicant's earnings from that other employment, up to £5 if the applicant is a single applicant, or up to £10 if the applicant has a partner, as would not in aggregate with the amount of the applicant's earnings disregarded under paragraph 9 exceed £20.

11. In a case to which none of the paragraphs 4 to 10 applies, £5.

12.–(1) Where–

(a) the applicant (or if the applicant is a member of a couple, at least one member of that couple) is a person to whom sub-paragraph (5) applies;

(b) the Secretary of State is satisfied that that person is undertaking exempt work as defined in sub-paragraph (6); and

(c) paragraph 14 does not apply,

the amount specified in sub-paragraph (7) ("the specified amount").

(2) Where this paragraph applies, paragraphs 4 to 11 do not apply; but in any case where the applicant is a lone parent, and the specified amount would be less than the amount specified in paragraph 5, then paragraph 5 applies instead of this paragraph.

(3)   Notwithstanding paragraph 7 of Schedule 6 (calculation of income and capital of members of applicant's family and of a polygamous marriage), if sub-paragraph (1) applies to one member of a couple ("A") it is not to apply to the other member of that couple ("B") except to the extent provided in sub-paragraph (4).

(4)   Where A's earnings are less than the specified amount, there is also to be disregarded so much of B's earnings as would not when aggregated with A's earnings exceed the specified amount; but the amount of B's earnings which may be disregarded under this sub-paragraph is limited to a maximum of £20 unless the Secretary of State is satisfied that B is also undertaking exempt work.

(5)   This sub-paragraph applies to a person who is–

(a)   in receipt of a contributory employment and support allowance;

(b)   in receipt of incapacity benefit;

(c)   in receipt of severe disablement allowance; or

(d)   being credited with earnings on the grounds of incapacity for work or limited capability for work under regulation 8B of the Social Security (Credits) Regulations 1975.

(6)   "Exempt work" ("gwaith esempt") means work of the kind described in–

(a)   regulation 45(2), (3) or (4) of the Employment and Support Allowance Regulations 2008 [¹or regulation 39(1)(a), (b) or (c) of the Employment and Support Allowance Regulations 2013]; or (as the case may be)

(b)   regulation 17(2), (3) or (4) of the Social Security (Incapacity for Work) (General) Regulations 1995,

and, in determining for the purposes of this paragraph whether an applicant or a member of a couple is undertaking any type of exempt work, it is immaterial whether that person or that person's partner is also undertaking other work.

(7)   The specified amount is the amount of money from time to time mentioned in any provision referred to in sub-paragraph (6) by virtue of which the work referred to in sub-paragraph (1) is exempt (or, where more than one such provision is relevant and those provisions mention different amounts of money, the highest of those amounts).

Amendment

1.   Amended by reg 12 of SI 2015 No 44 (W.3) as from 21.1.15, for schemes made for a financial year starting on or after 1.4.15.

---

13.   Any amount or the balance of any amount which would fall to be disregarded under paragraph 23 or 24 of Schedule 9 had the applicant's income which does not consist of earnings been sufficient to entitle the applicant to the full disregard thereunder.

14.   Where an applicant is on income support, an income-based jobseeker's allowance or an income-related employment and support allowance, the applicant's earnings.

15.   Any earnings derived from employment which are payable in a country outside the United Kingdom for such period during which there is a prohibition against the transfer to the United Kingdom of those earnings.

16.   Where a payment of earnings is made in a currency other than sterling, any banking charge or commission payable in converting that payment into sterling.

17.   Any earnings of a child or young person.

18.–(1)   In a case where the applicant is a person who satisfies at least one of the conditions set out in sub-paragraph (2), and the applicant's net earnings equal or exceed the total of the amounts set out in sub-paragraph (3), the amount of the applicant's earnings that falls to be disregarded under paragraphs 4 to 12, is to be increased by £17.10.

(2)   The conditions of this sub-paragraph are that–

(a)   the applicant, or if the applicant is a member of a couple, either the applicant or the applicant's partner, is a person to whom regulation 20(1)(c) of the Working Tax Credit (Entitlement and Maximum Rate) Regulations 2002 applies; or

(b)   the applicant–

(i)   is, or if the applicant is a member of a couple, at least one member of that couple is aged at least 25 and is engaged in remunerative work for on average not less than 30 hours per week; or

(ii)   is a member of a couple and–

(aa)   at least one member of that couple, is engaged in remunerative work for on average not less than 16 hours per week; and

(bb)   the applicant's applicable amount includes a family premium under paragraph 4 of Schedule 7; or

(iii)   is a lone parent who is engaged in remunerative work for on average not less than 16 hours per week; or

[² (iv)   not being a member of a couple, is engaged in remunerative work for on average not less than 16 hours per week and–

(aa)   the applicant's applicable amount includes a disability premium under paragraph 9 of Schedule 7 or the support component under paragraph 22 of Schedule 7; or

(bb)   the applicant is a member of the work-related activity group, or

(v) is a member of a couple and at least one member of that couple is engaged in remunerative work for on average not less than 16 hours per week and that member of the couple–

    (aa) satisfies the qualifying conditions for the disability premium under paragraph 9 of Schedule 7 or the support component under paragraph 22 of Schedule 7; or

    (bb) is a member of the work-related activity group.]

(3) The following are the amounts referred to in sub-paragraph (1)–

(a) the amount calculated as disregardable from the applicant's earnings under paragraphs 4 to 12;

(b) the amount of child care charges calculated as deductible under paragraph 20(1)(c) of Schedule 6 (calculation of income on a weekly basis: persons who are not pensioners); and

(c) £17.10.

(4) The provisions of regulation 10 (remunerative work) are to apply in determining whether or not a person works for on average not less than 30 hours per week, but as if the reference to 16 hours in paragraph (1) of that regulation were a reference to 30 hours.

Amendments

1. Amended by reg 11(b) of SI 2018 No 14 (W.7) as from 10.1.18, for schemes made for a financial year starting on or after 1.4.18.

2. Amended by reg 8 of SI 2019 No 11 (W.5) as from 9.1.19, for schemes made for a financial year starting on or after 1.4.19.

---

19. In this Schedule "part-time employment" ("cyflogaeth ran-amser") means employment in which the person is engaged on average for less than 16 hours a week.

SCHEDULE 9

Regulation 33(2)

Sums disregarded in the calculation of income other than earnings: persons who are not pensioners

1. Any payment made to the applicant in respect of any child care, travel or other expenses incurred, or to be incurred, by the applicant in respect of the applicant's participation in the Work for Your Benefit Pilot Scheme.

2. Any payment made to the applicant in respect of any travel or other expenses incurred, or to be incurred, by the applicant in respect of the applicant's participation in the Mandatory Work Activity Scheme.

3. Any payment made to the applicant in respect of any travel or other expenses incurred, or to be incurred, by the applicant in respect of the applicant's participation in the Employment, Skills and Enterprise Scheme.

4. Any amount paid by way of tax on income which is to be taken into account under paragraph 17 of Schedule 6 (calculation of income other than earnings).

5. Any payment in respect of any expenses incurred or to be incurred by an applicant who is–

(a) engaged by a charitable or voluntary organisation, or

(b) a volunteer,

if that applicant otherwise derives no remuneration or profit from the employment and is not to be treated as possessing any earnings under paragraph 19(5) of Schedule 6 (notional income: persons who are not pensioners).

6. Any payment in respect of expenses arising out of the applicant's participation in a service user group.

7. In the case of employment as an employed earner, any payment in respect of expenses wholly, exclusively and necessarily incurred in the performance of the duties of the employment.

8. Where an applicant is on income support, an income-based jobseeker's allowance or an income-related employment and support allowance, the whole of the applicant's income.

9. Where the applicant is a member of a joint-claim couple for the purposes of the Jobseekers Act 1995 and the applicant's partner is on an income-based jobseeker's allowance, the whole of the applicant's income.

10. Where the applicant, or the person who was the partner of the applicant on 31 March 2003, was entitled on that date to income support or an income-based jobseeker's allowance but ceased to be so entitled on or before 5 April 2003 by virtue only of regulation 13 of the Housing Benefit (General) Amendment (No 3) Regulations 1999 as in force at that date, the whole of the applicant's income.

11. Any disability living allowance, personal independence payment, or AFIP.

12. Any concessionary payment made to compensate for the non-payment of–

(a) any payment specified in paragraph 11 or 14;

(b) income support;

(c) an income-based jobseeker's allowance;

(d) an income-related employment and support allowance.

13. Any mobility supplement under article 20 of the Naval, Military and Air Forces Etc (Disablement and Death) Service Pensions Order 2006 (including such a supplement by virtue of any other scheme or order) or under article 25A of the Personal Injuries (Civilians) Scheme 1983 or any payment intended to compensate for the non-payment of such a supplement.

14. Any attendance allowance.

15.   Any payment to the applicant as holder of the Victoria Cross or of the George Cross or any analogous payment.

16.–(1)   Any payment–

(a)   by way of an education maintenance allowance made pursuant to–

    (i)   regulations made under section 518 of the Education Act 1996 (payment of school expenses; grant of scholarships etc);

    (ii)   regulations made under section 49 or 73(f) of the Education (Scotland) Act 1980 (power to assist persons to take advantage of educational facilities);

    (iii)   directions made under section 73ZA of the Education (Scotland) Act 1980 and paid under section 12(2)(c) of the Further and Higher Education (Scotland) Act 1992;

(b)   corresponding to such an education maintenance allowance, made pursuant to–

    (i)   section 14 or section 181 of the Education Act 2002 (power of Secretary of State and the Welsh Ministers to give financial assistance for purposes related to education or childcare, and allowances in respect of education or training); or

    (ii)   regulations made under section 181 of that Act; or

(c)   in England and Wales, by way of financial assistance made pursuant to section 14 of the Education Act 2002.

(2)   Any payment, other than a payment to which sub-paragraph (1) applies, made pursuant to–

(a)   regulations made under section 518 of the Education Act 1996;

(b)   regulations made under section 49 of the Education (Scotland) Act 1980; or

(c)   directions made under section 73ZA of the Education (Scotland) Act 1980 and paid under section 12(2)(c) of the Further and Higher Education (Scotland) Act 1992,

in respect of a course of study attended by a child or a young person or a person who is in receipt of an education maintenance allowance or other payment made pursuant to any provision specified in sub-paragraph (1).

17.   Any payment made to the applicant by way of a repayment under regulation 11(2) of the Education (Teacher Student Loans) (Repayment etc) Regulations 2003.

18.–(1)   Any payment made pursuant to section 2 of the Employment and Training Act 1973 or section 2 of the Enterprise and New Towns (Scotland) Act 1990 except a payment–

(a)   made as a substitute for income support, a jobseeker's allowance, incapacity benefit, severe disablement allowance or an employment and support allowance;

(b)   of an allowance referred to in section 2(3) of the Employment and Training Act 1973 or section 2(5) of the Enterprise and New Towns (Scotland) Act 1990; or

(c)   intended to meet the cost of living expenses which relate to any one or more of the items specified in sub-paragraph (2) whilst an applicant is participating in an education, training or other scheme to help the applicant enhance the applicant's employment prospects unless the payment is a Career Development Loan paid pursuant to section 2 of the 1973 Act and the period of education or training or the scheme, which is supported by that loan, has been completed.

(2)   The items specified in this sub-paragraph for the purposes of sub-paragraph (1)(c) are food, ordinary clothing or footwear, household fuel or rent of the applicant or, where the applicant is a member of a family, any other member of the applicant's family, or any council tax or water charges for which that applicant or member is liable.

19.–(1)   Subject to sub-paragraph (2), any of the following payments–

(a)   a charitable payment;

(b)   a voluntary payment;

(c)   a payment (not falling within paragraph (a) or (b)) from a trust whose funds are derived from a payment made in consequence of any personal injury to the applicant;

(d)   a payment under an annuity purchased–

    (i)   pursuant to any agreement or court order to make payments to the applicant; or

    (ii)   from funds derived from a payment made,

in consequence of any personal injury to the applicant; or

(e)   a payment (not falling within paragraphs (a) to (d)) received by virtue of any agreement or court order to make payments to the applicant in consequence of any personal injury to the applicant.

(2)   Sub-paragraph (1) is not to apply to a payment which is made or due to be made by–

(a)   a former partner of the applicant, or a former partner of any member of the applicant's family; or

(b)   the parent of a child or young person where that child or young person is a member of the applicant's family.

20.   Subject to paragraph 40, £10 of any of the following, namely–

(a)   a war disablement pension (except insofar as such a pension falls to be disregarded under paragraph 13 or 14);

(b)   a war widow's pension or war widower's pension;

(c)   a pension payable to a person as a widow, widower or surviving civil partner under any power of Her Majesty otherwise than under an enactment to make provision about pensions for or in respect of persons who have been disabled or have died in consequence of service as members of the armed forces of the Crown;

(d)   a guaranteed income payment and, if the amount of that payment has been abated to less than £10 by a pension or payment falling within article 39(1)(a) or (b) of the Armed Forces and Reserve

Forces (Compensation Scheme) Order 2011, so much of that pension or payment as would not, in aggregate with the amount of any guaranteed income payment disregarded, exceed £10;

(e) a payment made to compensate for the non-payment of such a pension or payment as is mentioned in any of the preceding sub-paragraphs;

(f) a pension paid by the government of a country outside Great Britain which is analogous to any of the pensions or payments mentioned in sub-paragraphs (a) to (d) above;

[¹ (g) a pension paid by a government to victims of National Socialist persecution.]

Amendment

1.   Substituted by reg 12(a) of SI 2018 No 14 (W.7) as from 10.1.18, for schemes made for a financial year starting on or after 1.4.18.

---

21.   Subject to paragraph 40, £15 of any–
(a)   widowed mother's allowance paid pursuant to section 37 of the SSCBA;
(b)   widowed parent's allowance paid pursuant to section 39A of the SSCBA.

22.–(1)   Any income derived from capital to which the applicant is or is treated under paragraph32 of Schedule 6 (capital jointly held) as beneficially entitled but, subject to sub-paragraph (2), not income derived from capital disregarded under paragraphs 4, 5, 7, 11, 17 or 30 to 33 of Schedule 10.

(2)   Income derived from capital disregarded under paragraphs 5, 7 or 30 to 33 of Schedule 10 but only to the extent of–
(a)   any mortgage repayments made in respect of the dwelling or premises in the period during which that income accrued; or
(b)   any council tax or water charges which the applicant is liable to pay in respect of the dwelling or premises and which are paid in the period during which that income accrued.

(3)   The definition of "water charges" ("taliadau dwr") in regulation 2(1) applies to sub-paragraph (2) of this paragraph with the omission of the words "in so far as such charges are in respect of the dwelling which a person occupies as that person's home".

23.   Where the applicant makes a parental contribution in respect of a student attending a course at an establishment in the United Kingdom or undergoing education in the United Kingdom, which contribution has been assessed for the purposes of calculating–
(a)   under, or pursuant to regulations made under powers conferred by section 22 of the Teaching and Higher Education Act 1998, that student's award;
(b)   under regulations made in exercise of the powers conferred by section 49 of the Education (Scotland) Act 1980, that student's bursary, scholarship, or other allowance under that section or under regulations made in exercise of the powers conferred by section 73 of that Act of 1980, any payment to that student under that section; or
(c)   the student's student loan,
an amount equal to the weekly amount of that parental contribution, but only in respect of the period for which that contribution is assessed as being payable.

24.–(1)   Where the applicant is the parent of a student aged under 25 in advanced education who either–
(a)   is not in receipt of any award, grant or student loan in respect of that education; or
(b)   is in receipt of an award bestowed by virtue of the Teaching and Higher Education Act 1998, or regulations made thereunder, or a bursary, scholarship or other allowance under section 49(1) of the Education (Scotland) Act 1980, or a payment under section 73 of that Act of 1980,
and the applicant makes payments by way of a contribution towards the student's maintenance, other than a parental contribution falling within paragraph 23, an amount specified in sub-paragraph (2) in respect of each week during the student's term.

(2)   For the purposes of sub-paragraph (1), the amount is to be equal to–
(a)   the weekly amount of the payments; or
(b)   the amount by way of a personal allowance for a single applicant under 25 less the weekly amount of any award, bursary, scholarship, allowance or payment referred to in sub-paragraph (1)(b),
whichever is less.

25.   Any payment made to the applicant by a child or young person or a non-dependant.

26.   Where the applicant occupies a dwelling as the applicant's home and the dwelling is also occupied by a person other than one to whom paragraph 25 or 27 refers and there is a contractual liability to make payments to the applicant in respect of the occupation of the dwelling by that person or a member of that person's family–
(a)   where the aggregate of any payments made in respect of any one week in respect of the occupation of the dwelling by that person or a member of that person's family, or by that person and a member of that person's family, is less than £20, the whole of that amount; or
(b)   where the aggregate of any such payments is £20 or more per week, £20.

27.   Where the applicant occupies a dwelling as the applicant's home and the applicant provides in that dwelling board and lodging accommodation, an amount, in respect of each person for which such accommodation is provided for the whole or any part of a week, equal to–
(a)   where the aggregate of any payments made in respect of any one week in respect of such accommodation provided to such person does not exceed £20, 100 per cent of such payments;
(b)   where the aggregate of any such payments exceeds £20, £20 and 50 per cent of the excess over £20.

28.–(1)   Any income in kind, except where paragraph 17(10)(b) of Schedule 6 (provision of support under section 95 or 98 of the Immigration and Asylum Act 1999 in the calculation of income other than earnings) applies.

(2)   The reference in sub-paragraph (1) to "income in kind" ("incwm mewn nwyddau neu wasanaethau") does not include a payment to a third party made in respect of the applicant which is used by the third party to provide benefits in kind to the applicant.

29.   Any income which is payable in a country outside the United Kingdom for such period during which there is a prohibition against the transfer to the United Kingdom of that income.

30.–(1)   Any payment made to the applicant in respect of a person who is a member of the applicant's family–

(a)   pursuant to regulations under section 2(6)(b), 3 or 4 of the Adoption and Children Act 2002 or in accordance with a scheme approved by the Scottish Ministers under section 71 of the Adoption and Children (Scotland) Act 2007 (adoption allowances schemes);

(b)   which is a payment made by a local authority in pursuance of section 15(1) of, and paragraph 15 of Schedule 1 to, the Children Act 1989 (local authority contribution to a child's maintenance where the child is living with a person as a result of a [¹child arrangements] order) or in Scotland section 50 of the Children Act 1975 (payments towards maintenance of children);

(c)   which is a payment made by an authority, as defined in article 2 of the Children (Northern Ireland) Order 1995, in pursuance of article 15 of, and paragraph 17 of Schedule 1 to, that Order (contribution by an authority to child's maintenance);

(d)   in accordance with regulations made pursuant to section 14F of the Children Act 1989 (special guardianship support services).

(2)   Any payment, other than a payment to which sub-paragraph (1)(a) applies, made to the applicant pursuant to regulations under section 2(6)(b), 3 or 4 of the Adoption and Children Act 2002.

Amendment

1.   Amended by art 25 of SI 2014 No 852 as from 22.4.14.

---

31.   Any payment made to an applicant with whom a person is accommodated by virtue of arrangements made–

(a)   by a local authority under–

(i)   section 23(2)(a) [¹ or 22C] of the Children Act 1989 (provision of accommodation and maintenance for a child whom they are looking after),

(ii)   section 26 of the Children (Scotland) Act 1995 (manner of provision of accommodation to child looked after by local authority), [1]

(iii)   regulation 33 or 51 of the Looked After Children (Scotland) Regulations 2009 (fostering and kinship care allowances and fostering allowances)[¹ ,]

[¹ (iv)   section 81 of the Social Services and Well-being (Wales) Act 2014, or]

(b)   by a voluntary organisation under section 59(1)(a) of the Children Act 1989 (provision of accommodation by voluntary organisations).

Amendment

1.   Amended by reg 12(a) of SI 2016 No 50 (W.21) as from 20.1.16, for schemes made for a financial year starting on or after 1.4.16.

---

32.   Any payment made to the applicant or the applicant's partner for a person ("the person concerned"), who is not normally a member of the applicant's household but is temporarily in the applicant's care, by–

(a)   a health authority;

(b)   a local authority but excluding payments of housing benefit made in respect of the person concerned;

(c)   a voluntary organisation;

(d)   the person concerned pursuant to section 26(3A) of the National Assistance Act 1948;

(e)   a primary care trust established under section 16A of the National Health Service Act 1977 or established by an order made under section 18(2)(c) of the National Health Service Act 2006;[1]

(f)   a Local Health Board established under section 11 of the National Health Service (Wales) Act 2006 [¹ ;]

[¹ (g)   the person concerned where the payment is for the provision of accommodation to meet that person's needs for care and support arranged pursuant to section 35 or 36 of the Social Services and Well-being (Wales) Act 2014; or

(h)   the person concerned where the payment is for the provision of accommodation to meet that person's needs for care and support arranged pursuant to section 18 or 19 of the Care Act 2014.]

Amendment

1.   Amended by reg 12(b) of SI 2016 No 50 (W.21) as from 20.1.16, for schemes made for a financial year starting on or after 1.4.16.

[¹**33.** Any payment made by a local authority in accordance with–
(a) section 17, 23B, 23C or 24A of the Children Act 1989;
(b) section 12 of the Social Work (Scotland) Act 1968;
(c) section 22, 29 or 30 of the Children (Scotland) Act 1995; or
(d) section 37, 38, 109, 110 or 114 of the Social Services and Well-being (Wales) Act 2014, but excluding any direct payments made under that Act.]

Amendment
1. Substituted by reg 12(c) of SI 2016 No 50 (W.21) as from 20.1.16, for schemes made for a financial year starting on or after 1.4.16.

34.–[¹ (1) Subject to sub-paragraph (2), any payment (or part payment) made by a local authority to a person ("A") which A passes on to the applicant, where the payment is made in accordance with–
(a) section 23C of the Children Act 1989;
(b) section 29 of the Children (Scotland) Act 1995; or
(c) section 110 of the Social Services and Well-being (Wales) Act 2014.]
(2) Sub-paragraph (1) applies only where A–
(a) was formerly in the applicant's care, and
(b) is aged 18 or over, and
(c) continues to live with the applicant.

Amendment
1. Substituted by reg 12(d) of SI 2016 No 50 (W.21) as from 20.1.16, for schemes made for a financial year starting on or after 1.4.16.

35.–(1) Subject to sub-paragraph (2), any payment received under an insurance policy taken out to insure against the risk of being unable to maintain repayments–
(a) on a loan which is secured on the dwelling which the applicant occupies as the applicant's home; or
(b) under a regulated agreement as defined for the purposes of the Consumer Credit Act 1974 or under a hire-purchase agreement or a conditional sale agreement as defined for the purposes of Part 3 of the Hire-Purchase Act 1964.
(2) A payment referred to in sub-paragraph (1) is only to be disregarded to the extent that the payment received under that policy does not exceed the amounts, calculated on a weekly basis, which are used to–
(a) maintain the repayments referred to in sub-paragraph (1)(a) or, as the case may be, (1)(b); and
(b) meet any amount due by way of premiums on–
(i) that policy; or
(ii) in a case to which sub-paragraph (1)(a) applies, an insurance policy taken out to insure against loss or damage to any building or part of a building which is occupied by the applicant as the applicant's home and which is required as a condition of the loan referred to in sub-paragraph (1)(a).
36. Any payment of income which by virtue of paragraph 27 of Schedule 6 (income treated as capital: persons who are not pensioners) is to be treated as capital.
37. Any–
(a) social fund payment made pursuant to Part 8 of the SSCBA (the social fund); or
(b) occasional assistance.
38. Any payment under Part 10 of the SSCBA (Christmas bonus for pensioners).
39. Where a payment of income is made in a currency other than sterling, any banking charge or commission payable in converting that payment into sterling.
40. The total of an applicant's income or, if the applicant is a member of a family, the family's income and the income of any person which that applicant is treated as possessing under paragraph 7(3) of Schedule 6 (calculation of income and capital of members of applicant's family and of a polygamous marriage) to be disregarded under paragraph 5(2)(b) and paragraph 6(1)(d) of Schedule 11 (calculation of covenant income where a contribution is assessed, covenant income where no grant income or no contribution is assessed), paragraph 9(2) of Schedule 11 (treatment of student loans), paragraph 11(3) of Schedule 11 (treatment of payments from access funds) and paragraphs 20 and 21, is in no case to exceed £20 per week.
41.–(1) Any payment made under or by any of the Trusts, the Fund, the Eileen Trust, MFET Limited, the Skipton Fund, the Caxton Foundation [¹ , an approved blood scheme, the Scottish Infected Blood Support Scheme, the London Emergencies Trust, the We Love Manchester Emergency Fund] or the Independent Living Fund (2006).
(2) Any payment by or on behalf of a person who is suffering or who suffered from haemophilia or who is or was a qualifying person, which derives from a payment made under or by any of the Trusts to which sub-paragraph (1) refers and which is made to or for the benefit of–
(a) that person's partner or former partner from whom that person is not, or where that person has died was not, estranged or divorced or with whom that person has formed a civil partnership that has not been dissolved or, where that person has died, had not been dissolved at the time of that person's death;

(b)　any child who is a member of that person's family or who was such a member and who is a member of the applicant's family; or

(c)　any young person who is a member of that person's family or who was such a member and who is a member of the applicant's family.

(3)　Any payment by or on behalf of the partner or former partner of a person who is suffering or who suffered from haemophilia or who is or was a qualifying person provided that the partner or former partner and that person are not, or if either of them has died were not, estranged or divorced or, where the partner or former partner and that person have formed a civil partnership, the civil partnership has not been dissolved or, if either of them has died, had not been dissolved at the time of the death, which derives from a payment made under or by any of the Trusts to which sub-paragraph (1) refers and which is made to or for the benefit of–

(a)　the person who is suffering from haemophilia or who is a qualifying person;

(b)　any child who is a member of that person's family or who was such a member and who is a member of the applicant's family; or

(c)　any young person who is a member of that person's family or who was such a member and who is a member of the applicant's family.

(4)　Any payment by a person who is suffering from haemophilia or who is a qualifying person, which derives from a payment under or by any of the Trusts to which sub-paragraph (1) refers, where–

(a)　that person has no partner or former partner from whom that person is not estranged or divorced or with whom that person has formed a civil partnership that has not been dissolved, nor any child or young person who is or had been a member of that person's family; and

(b)　the payment is made either–

(i)　to that person's parent or step-parent, or

(ii)　where that person at the date of the payment is a child, a young person or a student who has not completed full-time education and that person has no parent or step-parent, to that person's guardian,

but only for a period from the date of the payment until the end of two years from that person's death.

(5)　Any payment out of the estate of a person who suffered from haemophilia or who was a qualifying person, which derives from a payment under or by any of the Trusts to which sub-paragraph (1) refers, where–

(a)　that person at the date of that person's death (the relevant date) had no partner or former partner from whom that person was not estranged or divorced or with whom that person has formed a civil partnership that has not been dissolved, nor any child or young person who was or had been a member of that person's family; and

(b)　the payment is made either–

(i)　to that person's parent or step-parent, or

(ii)　where that person at the relevant date was a child, a young person or a student who had not completed full-time education and that person had no parent or step-parent, to that person's guardian,

but only for a period of two years from the relevant date.

(6)　In the case of a person to whom or for whose benefit a payment referred to in this paragraph is made, any income which derives from any payment of income or capital made under or deriving from any of the Trusts.

(7)　For the purposes of sub-paragraphs (2) to (6), any reference to the Trusts is to be construed as including a reference to the Fund, the Eileen Trust, MFET Limited, the Skipton Fund, the Caxton Foundation [¹, an approved blood scheme, the Scottish Infected Blood Support Scheme, the London Emergencies Trust, the We Love Manchester Emergency Fund] and the London Bombings Relief Charitable Fund.

Amendment

1.　Amended by reg 12(b) of SI 2018 No 14 (W.7) as from 10.1.18, for schemes made for a financial year starting on or after 1.4.18.

42.　Any housing benefit.

43.　Any payment made by the Secretary of State to compensate for the loss (in whole or in part) of entitlement to housing benefit.

44.　Any payment to a juror or witness in respect of attendance at a court other than compensation for loss of earnings or for the loss of a benefit payable under the benefit Acts.

45.　Any payment in consequence of a reduction of council tax under section 13A(1)(c) of the 1992 Act (reduction of liability for council tax).

46.–(1)　Any payment or repayment made–

(a)　as respects England, under regulation 5, 6 or 12 of the National Health Service (Travel Expenses and Remission of Charges) Regulations 2003 (travelling expenses and health service supplies);

(b)　as respects Wales, under regulation 5, 6 or 11 of the National Health Service (Travelling Expenses and Remission of Charges) (Wales) Regulations 2007 (travelling expenses and health service supplies);

(c)　as respects Scotland, under regulation 3, 5 or 11 of the National Health Service (Travelling Expenses and Remission of Charges) (Scotland) (No 2) Regulations 2003 (travelling expenses and health service supplies).

(2)   Any payment or repayment made by the Secretary of State for Health [¹ and Social Care], the Scottish Ministers or the Welsh Ministers which is analogous to a payment or repayment mentioned in sub-paragraph (1).

Amendment

1.   Amended by reg 9(a) of SI 2019 No 11 (W.5) as from 9.1.19, for schemes made for a financial year starting on or after 1.4.19.

---

47.   Any payment made to such persons entitled to receive benefits as may be determined by or under a scheme made pursuant to section 13 of the Social Security Act 1988 in lieu of vouchers or similar arrangements in connection with the provision of those benefits (including payments made in place of healthy start vouchers, milk tokens or the supply of vitamins).

48.   Any payment made by either the Secretary of State for Justice or by the Scottish Ministers under a scheme established to assist relatives and other persons to visit persons in custody.

49.–(1)   Where an applicant's applicable amount includes an amount by way of family premium, £15 of any payment of maintenance, other than child maintenance, whether under a court order or not, which is made or due to be made by the applicant's former partner, or the applicant's partner's former partner.

(2)   For the purpose of sub-paragraph (1) where more than one maintenance payment falls to be taken into account in any week, all such payments are to be aggregated and treated as if they were a single payment.

(3)   A payment made by the Secretary of State in lieu of maintenance is, for the purpose of sub-paragraph (1), to be treated as a payment of maintenance made by a person specified in sub-paragraph (1).

50.–(1)   Any payment of child maintenance made or derived from a liable relative where the child or young person in respect of whom the payment is made is a member of the applicant's family, except where the person making the payment is the applicant or the applicant's partner.

(2)   In sub-paragraph (1)–

"child maintenance" ("cynhaliaeth plant") means any payment towards the maintenance of a child or young person, including any payment made voluntarily and payments made under–

(a)   the Child Support Act 1991;

(b)   the Child Support (Northern Ireland) Order 1991;

(c)   a court order;

(d)   a consent order;

(e)   a maintenance agreement registered for execution in the Books of Council and Session or the sheriff court books;

"liable relative" ("perthynas atebol") means a person listed in regulation 54 (interpretation) of the Income Support (General) Regulations 1987, other than a person falling within sub-paragraph (d) of that definition.

51.   Any payment (other than a training allowance) made, whether by the Secretary of State or any other person, under the Disabled Persons (Employment) Act 1944 to assist disabled persons to obtain or retain employment despite their disability.

52.   Any guardian's allowance.

53.–(1)   If the applicant is in receipt of any benefit under Part 2, 3 or 5 of the SSCBA, any increase in the rate of that benefit arising under Part 4 (increases for dependants) or section 106(a) (unemployability supplement) of that Act, where the dependant in respect of whom the increase is paid is not a member of the applicant's family.

(2)   If the applicant is in receipt of any pension or allowance under Part 2 or 3 of the Naval, Military and Air Forces Etc (Disablement and Death) Service Pensions Order 2006, any increase in the rate of that pension or allowance under that Order, where the dependant in respect of whom the increase is paid is not a member of the applicant's family.

54.   Any supplementary pension under article 23(2) of the Naval, Military and Air Forces Etc (Disablement and Death) Service Pensions Order 2006 (pensions to surviving spouses and surviving civil partners) and any analogous payment made by the Secretary of State for Defence to any person who is not a person entitled under that Order.

55.   In the case of a pension awarded at the supplementary rate under article 27(3) of the Personal Injuries (Civilians) Scheme 1983 (pensions to surviving spouses and surviving civil partners), the sum specified in paragraph 1(c) of Schedule 4 to that Scheme.

56.–(1)   Any payment which is–

(a)   made under any of the Dispensing Instruments to a widow, widower or surviving civil partner of a person–

(i)   whose death was attributable to service in a capacity analogous to service as a member of the armed forces of the Crown; and

(ii)   whose service in such capacity terminated before 31 March 1973; and

(b)   equal to the amount specified in article 23(2) of the Naval, Military and Air Forces Etc (Disablement and Death) Service Pensions Order 2006.

(2)   In this paragraph "the Dispensing Instruments" ("yr Offerynnau Dosbarthu") means the Order in Council of 19 December 1881, the Royal Warrant of 27 October 1884 and the Order by His Majesty of 14 January 1922 (exceptional grants of pay, non-effective pay and allowances).

57.   Any reduction under an authority's scheme to which the applicant is entitled.

58. Except in a case which falls under sub-paragraph (1) of paragraph 18 of Schedule 8, where the applicant is a person who satisfies any of the conditions of sub-paragraph (2) of that paragraph, any amount of working tax credit up to £17.10.

[¹**59.** Any payment made–
(a) as a direct payment as defined in section 4(2) of the Social Care (Self-directed Support) (Scotland) Act 2013;
(b) under sections 12A to 12D of the National Health Service Act 2006 (direct payments for health care);
(c) under regulations made under section 57 of the Health and Social Care Act 2001 (direct payments);
(d) under regulations made under sections 50 to 53 of the Social Services and Well-being (Wales) Act 2014 (direct payments); or
(e) under regulations made under section 33 of the Care Act 2014 (direct payments).]

Amendment
1. Substituted by reg 12(e) of SI 2016 No 50 (W.21) as from 20.1.16, for schemes made for a financial year starting on or after 1.4.16.

60.–(1) Subject to sub-paragraph (2), in respect of a person who is receiving, or who has received, assistance under the self-employment route, any payment to that person–
(a) to meet expenses wholly and necessarily incurred whilst carrying on the commercial activity;
(b) which is used or intended to be used to maintain repayments on a loan taken out by that person for the purpose of establishing or carrying on the commercial activity,
in respect of which such assistance is or was received.
(2) Sub-paragraph (1) is to apply only in respect of payments which are paid to that person from the special account.

61.–(1) Any payment of a sports award except to the extent that it has been made in respect of any one or more of the items specified in sub-paragraph (2).
(2) The items specified for the purposes of sub-paragraph (1) are food, ordinary clothing or footwear, household fuel or rent of the applicant or where the applicant is a member of a family, any other member of the applicant's family, or any council tax or water charges for which that applicant or member is liable.
(3) For the purposes of sub-paragraph (2) "food" ("bwyd") does not include vitamins, minerals or other special dietary supplements intended to enhance the performance of the person in the sport in respect of which the award was made.

62. Where the amount of subsistence allowance paid to a person in a reduction week exceeds the amount of income-based jobseeker's allowance that person would have received in that reduction week had it been payable to that person, less 50p, that excess amount.

63. In the case of an applicant participating in an employment zone programme, any discretionary payment made by an employment zone contractor to the applicant, being a fee, grant, loan or otherwise.

64. Any discretionary housing payment paid pursuant to regulation 2(1) of the Discretionary Financial Assistance Regulations 2001.

65. Any payment made by a local authority or by the Welsh Ministers, to or on behalf of the applicant or the applicant's partner relating to a service which is provided to develop or sustain the capacity of the applicant or the applicant's partner to live independently in the applicant's accommodation.

66. Any payment of child benefit.

[¹**67.** Any bereavement support payment under section 30 of the Pensions Act 2014 (bereavement support payment) except any such payment which is disregarded as capital under paragraph 12(1)(h) or 65 of Schedule 10.]

Amendment
1. Amended by reg 9(b) of SI 2019 No 11 (W.5) as from 9.1.19, for schemes made for a financial year starting on or after 1.4.19.

SCHEDULE 10

Regulation 33(2)

Capital disregards: persons who are not pensioners

1. Any payment made to the applicant in respect of any child care, travel or other expenses incurred, or to be incurred, by the applicant in respect of the applicant's participation in the Work for Your Benefit Pilot Scheme but only for 52 weeks beginning with the date of receipt of the payment.

2. Any payment made to the applicant in respect of any travel or other expenses incurred, or to be incurred, by the applicant in respect of the applicant's participation in the Mandatory Work Activity Scheme but only for 52 weeks beginning with the date of receipt of the payment.

[¹ **2A.** Any payment made to the applicant in respect of any travel or other expenses incurred, or to be incurred, by the applicant in respect of the applicant's participation in a scheme prescribed in regulation 3 of the Jobseeker's Allowance (Schemes for Assisting Persons to Obtain Employment) Regulations 2013 but only for 52 weeks beginning with the date of receipt of the payment.]

Amendment

1.　　Inserted by reg 11(a) of SI 2014 No 66 (W.6) as from 15.1.14.

3.　　Any payment made to the applicant in respect of any travel or other expenses incurred, or to be incurred, by the applicant in respect of the applicant's participation in the Employment, Skills and Enterprise Scheme but only for 52 weeks beginning with the date of receipt of the payment.

4.　　The dwelling together with any garage, garden and outbuildings, normally occupied by the applicant as the applicant's home including any premises not so occupied which it is impracticable or unreasonable to sell separately, but, notwithstanding paragraph 7 of Schedule 6 (calculation of income and capital of members of applicant's family and of a polygamous marriage), only one dwelling is to be disregarded under this paragraph.

5.　　Any premises acquired for occupation by the applicant which the applicant intends to occupy as the applicant's home within 26 weeks of the date of acquisition or such longer period as is reasonable in the circumstances to enable the applicant to obtain possession and commence occupation of the premises.

6.　　Any sum directly attributable to the proceeds of sale of any premises formerly occupied by the applicant as the applicant's home which is to be used for the purchase of other premises intended for such occupation within 26 weeks of the date of sale or such longer period as is reasonable in the circumstances to enable the applicant to complete the purchase.

7.　　Any premises occupied in whole or in part–

(a)　　by a partner or relative of a single applicant or any member of the family as that person's home where that person has attained the qualifying age for state pension credit or is incapacitated;

(b)　　by the former partner of the applicant as that person's home; but this provision is not to apply where the former partner is a person from whom the applicant is estranged or divorced or with whom the applicant had formed a civil partnership that has been dissolved.

8.　　Where an applicant is on income support, an income-based jobseeker's allowance or an income-related employment and support allowance, the whole of the applicant's capital.

9.　　Where the applicant is a member of a joint-claim couple for the purposes of the Jobseekers Act 1995 and the applicant's partner is on income-based jobseeker's allowance, the whole of the applicant's capital.

10.　　Any future interest in property of any kind, other than land or premises in respect of which the applicant has granted a subsisting lease or tenancy, including sub-leases or sub-tenancies.

11.–(1)　　The assets of any business owned in whole or in part by the applicant and for the purposes of which the applicant is engaged as a self-employed earner, or if the applicant has ceased to be so engaged, for such period as may be reasonable in the circumstances to allow for disposal of any such asset.

(2)　　The assets of any business owned in whole or in part by the applicant where–

(a)　　the applicant is not engaged as a self-employed earner in that business by reason of some disease or bodily or mental disablement; but

(b)　　the applicant intends to become engaged or, as the case may be, re-engaged as a self-employed earner in that business as soon as the applicant recovers or is able to become engaged or re-engaged in that business,

for a period of 26 weeks from the date on which the application for a reduction under an authority's scheme is made, or is treated as made, or, if it is unreasonable to expect the applicant to become engaged or re-engaged in that business within that period, for such longer period as is reasonable in the circumstances to enable the applicant to become so engaged or re-engaged.

(3)　　In the case of a person who is receiving assistance under the self-employment route, the assets acquired by that person for the purpose of establishing or carrying on the commercial activity in respect of which such assistance is being received.

(4)　　In the case of a person who has ceased carrying on the commercial activity in respect of which assistance was received as specified in sub-paragraph (3), the assets relating to that activity for such period as may be reasonable in the circumstances to allow for disposal of any such asset.

12.–(1)　　Subject to sub-paragraph (2), any arrears of, or any concessionary payment made to compensate for arrears due to the non-payment of–

(a)　　any payment specified in paragraphs 11, 13 or 14 of Schedule 9;

(b)　　an income-related benefit under Part 7 of the SSCBA;

(c)　　an income-based jobseeker's allowance;

(d)　　any discretionary housing payment paid pursuant to regulation 2(1) of the Discretionary Financial Assistance Regulations 2001;

(e)　　working tax credit and child tax credit;

(f)　　an income-related employment and support allowance [¹ ;]

[¹ (g)　　universal credit][² ;

(h)　　bereavement support payment under section 30 of the Pensions Act 2014,]

but only for a period of 52 weeks from the date of the receipt of arrears or of the concessionary payment.

(2)　　In a case where the total of any arrears and, if appropriate, any concessionary payment referred to in sub-paragraph (1) relating to one of the specified payments, benefits or allowances amounts to £5,000 or more (referred to in this sub-paragraph and in sub-paragraph (3) as "the relevant sum") and is–

(a)　　paid in order to rectify or to compensate for, an official error as defined in regulation 1(2) of the Housing Benefit and Council Tax Benefit (Decisions and Appeals) Regulations 2001; and

(b)   received by the applicant in full on or after 14 October 2001,
sub-paragraph (1) is to have effect in relation to such arrears or concessionary payment either for a period of 52 weeks from the date of receipt, or, if the relevant sum is received in its entirety during the period of an award of a reduction under an authority's scheme, for the remainder of that period if that is a longer period.

(3)   For the purposes of sub-paragraph (2), "the period of an award of a reduction under an authority's scheme" ("cyfnod dyfarniad o ostyngiad o dan gynllun awdurdod") means–

(a)   the award in which the relevant sum is first received (or the first part thereof where it is paid in more than one instalment); and

(b)   where that award is followed by one or more further awards which, or each of which, begins immediately after the end of the previous award, such further award provided that for that further award the applicant–

(i)   is the person who received the relevant sum; or

(ii)   is the partner of the person who received the relevant sum, or was that person's partner at the date of that person's death.

Amendments

1.   Amended by reg 11(b) of SI 2014 No 66 (W.6) as from 15.1.14.

2.   Inserted by reg 10(a) of SI 2019 No 11 (W.5) as from 9.1.19, for schemes made for a financial year starting on or after 1.4.19.

---

13.   Any sum–

(a)   paid to the applicant in consequence of damage to, or loss of the home or any personal possession and intended for its repair or replacement; or

(b)   acquired by the applicant (whether as a loan or otherwise) on the express condition that it is to be used for effecting essential repairs or improvement to the home,

which is to be used for the intended purpose, for a period of 26 weeks from the date on which it was so paid or acquired or such longer period as is reasonable in the circumstances to effect the repairs, replacement or improvement.

14.   Any sum–

(a)   deposited with a housing association as defined in section 1(1) of the Housing Associations Act 1985 as a condition of occupying the home;

(b)   which was so deposited and which is to be used for the purchase of another home,

for the period of 26 weeks or such longer period as may be reasonable in the circumstances to enable the applicant to complete the purchase.

15.   Any personal possessions except those which have been acquired by the applicant with the intention of reducing the applicant's capital in order to secure entitlement to a reduction under an authority's scheme or to increase the amount of that reduction.

16.   The value of the right to receive any income under an annuity or the surrender value (if any) of such an annuity.

17.   Where the funds of a trust are derived from a payment made in consequence of any personal injury to the applicant or applicant's partner, the value of the trust fund and the value of the right to receive any payment under that trust.

18.–(1)   Any payment made to the applicant or the applicant's partner in consequence of any personal injury to the applicant or, as the case may be, the applicant's partner.

(2)   But sub-paragraph (1)–

(a)   applies only for the period of 52 weeks beginning with the day on which the applicant first receives any payment in consequence of that personal injury;

(b)   does not apply to any subsequent payment made to the applicant in consequence of that injury (whether it is made by the same person or another);

(c)   ceases to apply to the payment or any part of the payment from the day on which the applicant no longer possesses it;

(d)   does not apply to any payment from a trust where the funds of the trust are derived from a payment made in consequence of any personal injury to the applicant.

(3)   For the purposes of sub-paragraph (2)(c), the circumstances in which an applicant no longer possesses a payment or a part of it include where the applicant has used a payment or part of it to purchase an asset.

(4)   References in sub-paragraphs (2) and (3) to the applicant are to be construed as including references to the applicant's partner (where applicable).

19.   The value of the right to receive any income under a life interest or from a life rent.

20.   The value of the right to receive any income which is disregarded under paragraph 15 of Schedule 8 or paragraph 29 of Schedule 9.

21.   The surrender value of any policy of life insurance.

22.   Where any payment of capital falls to be made by instalments, the value of the right to receive any outstanding instalments.

[¹]**23.**   Any payment made by a local authority in accordance with–

(a)   section 17, 23B, 23C or 24A of the Children Act 1989;

(b)   section 12 of the Social Work (Scotland) Act 1968;

(c)   sections 22, 29 or 30 of the Children (Scotland) Act 1995; or
(d)   section 37, 38, 109, 110 or 114 of the Social Services and Well-being (Wales) Act 2014, but excluding any direct payments made under that Act.]

Amendment
1.   Substituted by reg 13(a) of SI 2016 No 50 (W.21) as from 20.1.16, for schemes made for a financial year starting on or after 1.4.16.

24.–[¹ (1)   Subject to sub-paragraph (2), any payment (or part payment) made by a local authority to a person ("A") which A passes on to the applicant, where the payment is made in accordance with–
(a)   section 23C of the Children Act 1989;
(b)   section 29 of the Children (Scotland) Act 1995; or
(c)   section 110 of the Social Services and Well-being (Wales) Act 2014.]
(2)   Sub-paragraph (1) applies only where A–
(a)   was formerly in the applicant's care, and
(b)   is aged 18 or over, and
(c)   continues to live with the applicant.

Amendment
1.   Substituted by reg 13(b) of SI 2016 No 50 (W.21) as from 20.1.16, for schemes made for a financial year starting on or after 1.4.16.

25.   Any–
(a)   social fund payment made pursuant to Part 8 of the SSCBA (the social fund); or
(b)   occasional assistance.
26.   Any refund of tax which falls to be deducted under section 369 of the Income and Corporation Taxes Act 1988 (deduction of tax from certain loan interest) on a payment of relevant loan interest for the purpose of acquiring an interest in the home or carrying out repairs or improvements to the home.
27.   Any capital which by virtue of paragraph 18 of Schedule 6 (capital treated as income) or paragraph 9 of Schedule 11 (treatment of student loans) is to be treated as income.
28.   Where any payment of capital is made in a currency other than sterling, any banking charge or commission payable in converting that payment into sterling.
29.–(1)   Any payment made under or by the Trusts, the Fund, the Eileen Trust, MFET Limited, the Independent Living Fund (2006), the Skipton Fund, the Caxton Foundation [¹, an approved blood scheme, the Scottish Infected Blood Support Scheme, the London Emergencies Trust, the We Love Manchester Emergency Fund] or the London Bombings Relief Charitable Fund.
(2)   Any payment by or on behalf of a person who is suffering or who suffered from haemophilia or who is or was a qualifying person, which derives from a payment made under or by any of the Trusts to which sub-paragraph (1) refers and which is made to or for the benefit of–
(a)   that person's partner or former partner from whom that person is not, or where that person has died was not, estranged or divorced or with whom that person has formed a civil partnership that has not been dissolved or, where that person has died, had not been dissolved at the time of that person's death;
(b)   any child who is a member of that person's family or who was such a member and who is a member of the applicant's family; or
(c)   any young person who is a member of that person's family or who was such a member and who is a member of the applicant's family.
(3)   Any payment by or on behalf of the partner or former partner of a person who is suffering or who suffered from haemophilia or who is or was a qualifying person provided that the partner or former partner and that person are not, or if either of them has died were not, estranged or divorced or, where the partner or former partner and that person have formed a civil partnership, the civil partnership has not been dissolved, or if either of them has died, had not been dissolved at the time of the death, which derives from a payment made under or by any of the Trusts to which sub-paragraph (1) refers and which is made to or for the benefit of–
(a)   the person who is suffering from haemophilia or who is a qualifying person;
(b)   any child who is a member of that person's family or who was such a member and who is a member of the applicant's family; or
(c)   any young person who is a member of that person's family or who was such a member and who is a member of the applicant's family.
(4)   Any payment by a person who is suffering from haemophilia or who is a qualifying person, which derives from a payment under or by any of the Trusts to which sub-paragraph (1) refers, where–
(a)   that person has no partner or former partner from whom that person is not estranged or divorced or with whom that person has formed a civil partnership that has not been dissolved, nor any child or young person who is or had been a member of that person's family; and
(b)   the payment is made either–
(i)   to that person's parent or step-parent; or

(ii)   where that person at the date of the payment is a child, a young person or a student who has not completed full-time education and has no parent or step-parent, to that child or young person's guardian or that student's guardian,

but only for a period from the date of the payment until the end of two years from that person's death.

(5)   Any payment out of the estate of a person who suffered from haemophilia or who was a qualifying person, which derives from a payment under or by any of the Trusts to which sub-paragraph (1) refers, where–

(a)   that person at the date of that person's death (the relevant date) had no partner or former partner from whom that person was not estranged or divorced or with whom that person had formed a civil partnership that had not been dissolved, nor any child or young person who was or had been a member of that person's family; and

(b)   the payment is made either–

(i)   to that person's parent or step-parent; or

(ii)   where that person at the relevant date was a child, a young person or a student who had not completed full-time education and had no parent or step-parent, to that child or young person's guardian or that student's guardian,

but only for a period of two years from the relevant date.

(6)   In the case of a person to whom or for whose benefit a payment referred to in this paragraph is made, any capital resource which derives from any payment of income or capital made under or deriving from any of the Trusts.

(7)   For the purposes of sub-paragraphs (2) to (6), any reference to the Trusts is to be construed as including a reference to the Fund, the Eileen Trust, MFET Limited, the Skipton Fund, the Caxton Foundation, [¹ an approved blood scheme, the Scottish Infected Blood Support Scheme, the London Emergencies Trust, the We Love Manchester Emergency Fund] and the London Bombings Relief Charitable Fund.

Amendment

1.   Amended by reg 13(a) of SI 2018 No 14 (W.7) as from 10.1.18, for schemes made for a financial year starting on or after 1.4.18.

30.–(1)   Where an applicant has ceased to occupy what was formerly the dwelling occupied as the home following the applicant's estrangement or divorce from, or dissolution of the applicant's civil partnership with, the applicant's former partner, that dwelling for a period of 26 weeks from the date on which the applicant ceased to occupy that dwelling or, where the dwelling is occupied as the home by the former partner who is a lone parent, for so long as it is so occupied.

(2)   In this paragraph "dwelling" ("annedd") includes any garage, garden and outbuildings, which were formerly occupied by the applicant as the applicant's home and any premises not so occupied which it is impracticable or unreasonable to sell separately, in particular, in Scotland, any croft land on which the dwelling is situated.

31.   Any premises where the applicant is taking reasonable steps to dispose of those premises, for a period of 26 weeks from the date on which the applicant first took such steps, or such longer period as is reasonable in the circumstances to enable the applicant to dispose of those premises.

32.   Any premises which the applicant intends to occupy as the applicant's home, and in respect of which the applicant is taking steps to obtain possession and has sought legal advice, or has commenced legal proceedings, with a view to obtaining possession, for a period of 26 weeks from the date on which the applicant first sought such advice or first commenced such proceedings whichever is the earlier, or such longer period as is reasonable in the circumstances to enable the applicant to obtain possession and commence occupation of those premises.

33.   Any premises which the applicant intends to occupy as the applicant's home to which essential repairs or alterations are required in order to render them fit for such occupation, for a period of 26 weeks from the date on which the applicant first takes steps to effect those repairs or alterations, or such longer period as is necessary to enable those repairs or alterations to be carried out.

34.   Any payment made by the Secretary of State to compensate for the loss (in whole or in part) of entitlement to housing benefit.

35.   The value of the right to receive an occupational or personal pension.

36.   The value of any funds held under a personal pension scheme.

37.   The value of the right to receive any rent except where the applicant has a reversionary interest in the property in respect of which rent is due.

38.   Any payment in kind made by a charity or under or by the Trusts, the Fund, MFET Limited, the Skipton Fund, the Caxton Foundation [¹, an approved blood scheme, the Scottish Infected Blood Support Scheme, the London Emergencies Trust, the We Love Manchester Emergency Fund] or the Independent Living Fund (2006).

Amendment

1.   Amended by reg 13(b) of SI 2018 No 14 (W.7) as from 10.1.18, for schemes made for a financial year starting on or after 1.4.18.

39. Any payment made pursuant to section 2 of the Employment and Training Act 1973 or section 2 of the Enterprise and New Towns (Scotland) Act 1990, but only for the period of 52 weeks beginning on the date of receipt of the payment.

40. Any payment in consequence of a reduction of council tax under section 13 of the 1992 Act, (reduction of liability for council tax), but only for a period of 52 weeks from the date of the receipt of the payment.

41. Any grant made in accordance with a scheme made under section 129 of the Housing Act 1988 or section 66 of the Housing (Scotland) Act 1988 (schemes for payments to assist local housing authority and local authority tenants to obtain other accommodation) which is to be used–

(a) to purchase premises intended for occupation as the applicant's home; or

(b) to carry out repairs or alterations which are required to render premises fit for occupation as the applicant's home,

for a period of 26 weeks from the date on which the applicant received such a grant or such longer period as is reasonable in the circumstances to enable the purchase, repairs or alterations to be completed and the applicant to commence occupation of those premises as the applicant's home.

42. Any arrears of supplementary pension which is disregarded under paragraph 53 of Schedule 9 (sums to be disregarded in the calculation of income other than earnings) or of any amount which is disregarded under paragraph 54 or 55 of that Schedule, but only for a period of 52 weeks from the date of receipt of the arrears.

43.–(1) Any payment or repayment made–

(a) as respects England, under regulation 5, 6 or 12 of the National Health Service (Travel Expenses and Remission of Charges) Regulations 2003 (travelling expenses and health service supplies);

(b) as respects Wales, under regulation 5, 6 or 11 of the National Health Service (Travelling Expenses and Remission of Charges) (Wales) Regulations 2007 (travelling expenses and health service supplies);

(c) as respects Scotland, under regulation 3, 5 or 11 of the National Health Service (Travelling Expenses and Remission of Charges) (Scotland) (No 2) Regulations 2003 (travelling expenses and health service supplies),

but only for a period of 52 weeks from the date of receipt of the payment or repayment.

(2) Any payment or repayment made by the Secretary of State for Health [¹ and Social Care], the Scottish Ministers or the Welsh Ministers which is analogous to a payment or repayment mentioned in sub-paragraph (1), but only for a period of 52 weeks from the date of receipt of the payment or repayment.

Amendment

1. Amended by reg 10(b) of SI 2019 No 11 (W.5) as from 9.1.19, for schemes made for a financial year starting on or after 1.4.19.

---

44. Any payment made to such persons entitled to receive benefits as may be determined by or under a scheme made pursuant to section 13 of the Social Security Act 1988 in lieu of vouchers or similar arrangements in connection with the provision of those benefits (including payments made in place of healthy start vouchers, milk tokens or the supply of vitamins), but only for a period of 52 weeks from the date of receipt of the payment.

45. Any payment made either by the Secretary of State for Justice or by Scottish Ministers under a scheme established to assist relatives and other persons to visit persons in custody, but only for a period of 52 weeks from the date of the receipt of the payment.

46. Any payment (other than a training allowance) made, whether by the Secretary of State or any other person, under the Disabled Persons (Employment) Act 1944 to assist disabled persons to obtain or retain employment despite their disability.

[¹**47.**–(1) Any payment made by a local authority under section 3 of the Disabled Persons (Employment) Act 1958 to homeworkers assisted under a blind homeworkers' scheme.

(2) Any payment made by a local authority under Part 4 of the Social Services and Well-being (Wales) Act 2014 to homeworkers assisted under a blind homeworkers' scheme.]

Amendment

1. Substituted by reg 13(c) of SI 2016 No 50 (W.21) as from 20.1.16, for schemes made for a financial year starting on or after 1.4.16.

48.–(1) Any sum of capital to which sub-paragraph (2) applies and–

(a) which is administered on behalf of a person by the High Court or the County Court under Rule 21.11(1) of the Civil Procedure Rules 1998 or by the Court of Protection;

(b) which can only be disposed of by order or direction of any such court; or

(c) where the person concerned is under the age of 18, which can only be disposed of by order or direction prior to that person attaining age 18.

(2) This sub-paragraph applies to a sum of capital which is derived from–

(a) an award of damages for a personal injury to that person; or

(b) compensation for the death of one or both parents where the person concerned is under the age of 18.

49. Any sum of capital administered on behalf of a person in accordance with an order made under section 13 of the Children (Scotland) Act 1995, or under Rule 36.14 of the Act of Sederunt (Sheriff Court Ordinary Cause Rules) 1993 or under Rule 128 of those Rules, where such sum derives from–
(a) an award of damages for a personal injury to that person; or
(b) compensation for the death of one or both parents where the person concerned is under the age of 18.

50. Any payment to the applicant as holder of the Victoria Cross or George Cross.

51. In the case of a person who is receiving, or who has received, assistance under the self-employment route, any sum of capital which is acquired by that person for the purpose of establishing or carrying on the commercial activity in respect of which such assistance is or was received but only for a period of 52 weeks from the date on which that sum was acquired.

52.–(1) Any payment of a sports award for a period of 26 weeks from the date of receipt of that payment except to the extent that it has been made in respect of any one or more of the items specified in sub-paragraph (2).

(2) The items specified for the purposes of sub-paragraph (1) are food, ordinary clothing or footwear, household fuel or rent of the applicant or, where the applicant is a member of a family, any other member of the applicant's family, or any council tax or water charges for which that applicant or member is liable.

(3) For the purposes of sub-paragraph (2) "food" ("bwyd") does not include vitamins, minerals or other special dietary supplements intended to enhance the performance of the person in the sport in respect of which the award was made.

53.–(1) Any payment–
(a) by way of an education maintenance allowance made pursuant to–
(i) regulations made under section 518 of the Education Act 1996;
(ii) regulations made under section 49 or 73(f) of the Education (Scotland) Act 1980;
(iii) directions made under section 73ZA of the Education (Scotland) Act 1980 and paid under section 12(2)(c) of the Further and Higher Education (Scotland) Act 1992;
(b) corresponding to such an education maintenance allowance, made pursuant to–
(i) section 14 or section 181 of the Education Act 2002 (power of Secretary of State and Welsh Ministers to give financial assistance for purposes related to education or childcare, and allowances in respect of education or training); or
(ii) regulations made under section 181 of that Act; or
(c) in England and Wales, by way of financial assistance made pursuant to section 14 of the Education Act 2002.

(2) Any payment, other than a payment to which sub-paragraph (1) applies, made pursuant to–
(a) regulations made under section 518 of the Education Act 1996;
(b) regulations made under section 49 of the Education (Scotland) Act 1980; or
(c) directions made under section 73ZA of the Education (Scotland) Act 1980 and paid under section 12(2)(c) of the Further and Higher Education (Scotland) Act 1992,
in respect of a course of study attended by a child or a young person or a person who is in receipt of an education maintenance allowance or other payment made pursuant to any provision specified in sub-paragraph (1).

54. In the case of an applicant participating in an employment zone programme, any discretionary payment made by an employment zone contractor to the applicant, being a fee, grant, loan or otherwise, but only for the period of 52 weeks from the date of receipt of the payment.

55. Any arrears of subsistence allowance paid as a lump sum but only for the period of 52 weeks from the date of receipt of the payment.

56. Where an ex-gratia payment of £10,000 has been made by the Secretary of State on or after 1 February 2001 in consequence of the imprisonment or interment of–
(a) the applicant;
(b) the applicant's partner;
(c) the applicant's deceased spouse or deceased civil partner; or
(d) the applicant's partner's deceased spouse or deceased civil partner,
by the Japanese during the Second World War, £10,000.

57.–(1) Subject to sub-paragraph (2), the amount of any trust payment made to an applicant or a member of an applicant's family who is–
(a) a diagnosed person;
(b) the diagnosed person's partner or the person who was the diagnosed person's partner at the date of the diagnosed person's death;
(c) a parent of a diagnosed person, a person acting in place of the diagnosed person's parents or a person who was so acting at the date of the diagnosed person's death; or
(d) a member of the diagnosed person's family (other than that person's partner) or a person who was a member of the diagnosed person's family (other than that person's partner) at the date of the diagnosed person's death.

(2) Where a trust payment is made to–
(a) a person referred to in sub-paragraph (1)(a) or (b), that sub-paragraph is to apply for the period beginning on the date on which the trust payment is made and ending on the date on which that person dies;

(b)   a person referred to in sub-paragraph (1)(c), that sub-paragraph is to apply for the period beginning on the date on which the trust payment is made and ending two years after that date;

(c)   a person referred to in sub-paragraph (1)(d), that sub-paragraph is to apply for the period beginning on the date on which the trust payment is made and ending–

    (i)   two years after that date; or

    (ii)   on the day before the day on which that person–

        (aa)   ceases receiving full-time education; or

        (bb)   attains the age of 20,

whichever is the latest.

(3)   Subject to sub-paragraph (4), the amount of any payment by a person to whom a trust payment has been made or of any payment out of the estate of a person to whom a trust payment has been made, which is made to an applicant or a member of an applicant's family who is–

(a)   the diagnosed person's partner or the person who was the diagnosed person's partner at the date of the diagnosed person's death;

(b)   a parent of a diagnosed person, a person acting in place of the diagnosed person's parents or a person who was so acting at the date of the diagnosed person's death; or

(c)   a member of the diagnosed person's family (other than that person's partner) or a person who was a member of the diagnosed person's family (other than that person's partner) at the date of the diagnosed person's death,

but only to the extent that such payments do not exceed the total amount of any trust payments made to that person.

(4)   Where a payment as referred to in sub-paragraph (3) is made to–

(a)   a person referred to in sub-paragraph (3)(a), that sub-paragraph is to apply for the period beginning on the date on which that payment is made and ending on the date on which that person dies;

(b)   a person referred to in sub-paragraph (3)(b), that sub-paragraph is to apply for the period beginning on the date on which that payment is made and ending two years after that date; or

(c)   a person referred to in sub-paragraph (3)(c), that sub-paragraph is to apply for the period beginning on the date on which that payment is made and ending–

    (i)   two years after that date; or

    (ii)   on the day before the day on which that person–

        (aa)   ceases receiving full-time education; or

        (bb)   attains the age of 20,

whichever is the latest.

(5)   In this paragraph, a reference to a person–

(a)   being the diagnosed person's partner;

(b)   being a member of a diagnosed person's family;

(c)   acting in place of the diagnosed person's parents,

at the date of the diagnosed person's death is to include a person who would have been such a person or a person who would have been so acting, but for the diagnosed person residing in a care home, an Abbeyfield Home or an independent hospital on that date.

(6)   In this paragraph–

"diagnosed person" ("person â diagnosis") means a person who has been diagnosed as suffering from, or who, after that person's death, has been diagnosed as having suffered from, variant Creutzfeld-Jakob disease;

"relevant trust" ("ymddiriedolaeth berthnasol") means a trust established out of funds provided by the Secretary of State in respect of persons who suffered, or who are suffering, from variant Creutzfeld-Jakob disease for the benefit of persons eligible for payments in accordance with its provisions;

"trust payment" ("taliad ymddiriedolaeth") means a payment under a relevant trust.

58.   The amount of any payment, other than a war pension, to compensate for the fact that the applicant, the applicant's partner, the applicant's deceased spouse or deceased civil partner or the applicant's partner's deceased spouse or deceased civil partner–

(a)   was a slave labourer or a forced labourer;

(b)   had suffered property loss or had suffered personal injury; or

(c)   was a parent of a child who had died,

during the Second World War.

59.   Any payment made by a local authority, or by the Welsh Ministers, to or on behalf of the applicant or the applicant's partner relating to a service which is provided to develop or sustain the capacity of the applicant or the applicant's partner to live independently in the applicant's accommodation.

[²**60.**   Any payment made

(a)   under regulations made under section 57 of the Health and Social Care Act 2001 (direct payments);

(b)   as a direct payment as defined in section 4(2) of the Social Care (Self-directed Support) (Scotland) Act 2013;

(c)   under sections 12A to 12D of the National Health Service Act 2006 (direct payments for health care);

(d)   under regulations made under section 50 to 53 or the Social Services and Well-being (Wales) Act 2014 (direct payments); or

(e)   under regulations made under section 33 of the Care Act 2014 (direct payments).]

Amendments
1.   Amended by art 2 and Sch para 25(4) of SI 2014 No 513 as from 1.4.14.
2.   Substituted by reg 13(d) of SI 2016 No 50 (W.21) as from 20.1.16, for schemes made for a financial year starting on or after 1.4.16.

61.   Any payment made to the applicant pursuant to regulations under section 2(6)(b), 3 or 4 of the Adoption and Children Act 2002.
62.   Any payment made to the applicant in accordance with regulations made pursuant to section 14F of the Children Act 1989 (special guardianship support services).
[¹**63.**   Any payment made by the Treasury to the applicant or the applicant's partner under the Age-Related Payments Regulations 2013 (Equitable Life) as a qualifying Equitable Life annuitant.]

Amendment
1.   Inserted by reg 11(c) of SI 2014 No 66 (W.6) as from 15.1.14.

[¹**64.**   Any payment made by or under a trust, established for the purpose of giving relief and assistance to disabled persons whose disabilities were caused by the fact that during their mother's pregnancy she had taken a preparation containing the drug known as Thalidomide, and which is approved by the Secretary of State.]

Amendment
1.   Inserted by reg 13(c) of SI 2018 No 14 (W.7) as from 10.1.18, for schemes made for a financial year starting on or after 1.4.18.

[¹**65.**   Any bereavement support payment in respect of the rate set out in regulation 3(2) or (5) of the Bereavement Support Payment Regulations 2017 (rate of bereavement support payment), but only for a period of 52 weeeks from the date of receipt of the payment.]

Amendment
1.   Inserted by reg 10(c) of SI 2019 No 11 (W.5) as from 9.1.19, for schemes made for a financial year starting on or after 1.4.19.

SCHEDULE 11

REGULATION 31(3)

Students

PART 1
General

Interpretation
1.–(1)   In this Schedule–
"academic year" ("blwyddyn academaidd") means the period of twelve months beginning on 1 January, 1 April, 1 July or 1 September according to whether the course in question begins in the winter, the spring, the summer or the autumn respectively but if students are required to begin attending the course during August or September and to continue attending through the autumn, the academic year of the course is to be considered to begin in the autumn rather than the summer;
"access funds" ("cronfeydd mynediad") means–
(a)   grants made under section 68 of the Further and Higher Education Act 1992 for the purpose of providing funds on a discretionary basis to be paid to students;
(b)   grants made under sections 73(a) and (c) and 74(1) of the Education (Scotland) Act 1980;
(c)   grants made under article 30 of the Education and Libraries (Northern Ireland) Order 1993 or grants, loans or other payments made under article 5 of the Further Education (Northern Ireland) Order 1997 in each case being grants, or grants, loans or other payments as the case may be, for the purpose of assisting students in financial difficulties;
(d)   discretionary payments, known as "learner support funds", which are made available to students in further education by institutions out of funds provided by the Secretary of State in relation to England or the Welsh Ministers in relation to Wales under section 14 of the Education Act 2002 or [¹ the Secretary of State] under sections 100 and 101 of the Apprenticeships, Skills, Children and Learning Act 2009; or
(e)   Financial Contingency Funds made available by the Welsh Ministers;
"college of further education" ("coleg addysg bellach") means a college of further education within the meaning of Part 1 of the Further and Higher Education (Scotland) Act 1992;
"contribution" ("cyfraniad") means–

(a) any contribution in respect of the income of a student or any person which the Secretary of State, the Welsh Ministers, the Scottish Ministers or an education authority takes into account in ascertaining the amount of a student's grant or student loan; or

(b) any sums, which in determining the amount of a student's allowance or bursary in Scotland under the Education (Scotland) Act 1980, the Scottish Ministers or education authority take into account being sums which the Scottish Ministers or education authority considers that it is reasonable for the following persons to contribute towards the holder's expenses–

    (i) the holder of the allowance or bursary;

    (ii) the holder's parents;

    (iii) the holder's parent's spouse, civil partner or a person ordinarily living with the holder's parent as if that person were the spouse or civil partner of that parent; or

    (iv) the holder's spouse or civil partner;

"course of study" ("cwrs astudio") means any course of study, whether or not it is a sandwich course and whether or not a grant is made for attending or undertaking it;

"covenant income" ("incwm cyfamod") means the gross income payable to a full-time student under a Deed of Covenant by that student's parent;

"education authority" ("awdurdod addysg") means a government department, a local authority as defined in section 579 of the Education Act 1996 (interpretation), a local education authority as defined in section 123 of the Local Government (Scotland) Act 1973, an education and library board established under article 3 of the Education and Libraries (Northern Ireland) Order 1986, any body which is a research council for the purposes of the Science and Technology Act 1965 or any analogous government department, authority, board or body, of the Channel Islands, Isle of Man or any other country outside Great Britain;

"full-time course of study" ("cwrs astudio amser llawn") means a full-time course of study which–

(a) is not funded in whole or in part by the Secretary of State in relation to England or the Welsh Ministers in relation to Wales under section 14 of the Education Act 2002, or [¹ the Secretary of State under section 100 of the Apprenticeship, Skills, Children and Learning Act 2009], or a full-time course of study which is not funded in whole or in part by the Scottish Ministers at a college of further education or a full-time course of study which is a course of higher education and is funded in whole or in part by the Scottish Ministers;

(b) is funded in whole or in part by the Secretary of State in relation to England or the Welsh Ministers in relation to Wales under section 14 of the Education Act 2002, or [¹ the Secretary of State under section 100 of the Apprenticeship, Skills, Children and Learning Act 2009] if it involves more than 16 guided learning hours per week for the student in question, according to the number of guided learning hours per week for that student set out–

    (i) in the case of a course funded by the Secretary of State [¹], in the student's learning agreement signed on behalf of the establishment which is funded by [¹ the Secretary of State] for the delivery of that course; or

    (ii) in the case of a course funded by the Welsh Ministers, in a document signed on behalf of the establishment which is funded by the Welsh Ministers for the delivery of that course; or

(c) is not higher education and is funded in whole or in part by the Scottish Ministers at a college of further education and involves–

    (i) more than 16 hours per week of classroom-based or workshop-based programmed learning under the direct guidance of teaching staff according to the number of hours set out in a document signed on behalf of the college; or

    (ii) 16 hours or less per week of classroom-based or workshop-based programmed learning under the direct guidance of teaching staff and additional hours using structured learning packages supported by the teaching staff where the combined total of hours exceeds 21 hours per week, according to the number of hours set out in a document signed on behalf of the college;

"full-time student" ("myfyriwr amser llawn") means a person attending or undertaking a full-time course of study and includes a student on a sandwich course;

"grant" ("grant") (except in the definition of "access funds") means any kind of educational grant or award and includes any scholarship, studentship, exhibition, allowance or bursary but does not include a payment from access funds or any payment to which paragraph 16 of Schedule 9 or paragraph 53 of Schedule 10 applies;

"grant income" ("incwm grant") means–

(a) any income by way of a grant;

(b) any contribution whether or not it is paid;

"higher education" ("addysg uwch") means higher education within the meaning of Part 2 of the Further and Higher Education (Scotland) Act 1992;

"last day of the course" ("diwrnod olaf y cwrs") means–

(a) in the case of a qualifying course, the date on which the last day of that course falls or the date on which the final examination relating to that course is completed, whichever is the later;

(b) in any other case, the date on which the last day of the final academic term falls in respect of the course in which the student is enrolled;

"period of study" ("cyfnod astudio") means–

(a)   in the case of a course of study for one year or less, the period beginning with the start of the course and ending with the last day of the course;

(b)   in the case of a course of study for more than one year, in the first or, as the case may be, any subsequent year of the course, other than the final year of the course, the period beginning with the start of the course or, as the case may be, that year's start and ending with either–

  (i)   the day before the start of the next year of the course in a case where the student's grant or loan is assessed at a rate appropriate to the student's studying throughout the year or, if the student does not have a grant or loan, where a loan would have been assessed at such a rate had the student had one; or

  (ii)   in any other case, the day before the start of the normal summer vacation appropriate to the student's course;

(c)   in the final year of a course of study of more than one year, the period beginning with that year's start and ending with the last day of the course;

"periods of experience" ("cyfnodau o brofiad") means periods of work experience which form part of a sandwich course;

"qualifying course" ("cwrs cymwys") means a qualifying course as defined for the purposes of Parts 2 and 4 of the Jobseeker's Allowance Regulations 1996;

"sandwich course" ("cwrs rhyngosod") has the meaning prescribed in regulation 2(10) of the Education (Student Support) Regulations 2011, regulation 2(6) of the Education (Student Support) (Wales) Regulations 2012, regulation 4(2) of the Education (Student Loans) (Scotland) Regulations 2007 or regulation 2(10) of the Education (Student Support) (No. 2) Regulations (Northern Ireland) 2009, as the case may be;

"standard maintenance grant" ("grant cynhaliaeth safonol") means–

(a)   except where paragraph (b) or (c) applies, in the case of a student attending or undertaking a course of study at the University of London or an establishment within the area comprising the City of London and the Metropolitan Police District, the amount specified for the time being in paragraph 2(2)(a) of Schedule 2 to the Education (Mandatory Awards) Regulations 2003 ("the 2003 Regulations") for such a student;

(b)   except where paragraph (c) applies, in the case of a student residing at that student's parent's home, the amount specified in paragraph 3 of Schedule 2 to the 2003 Regulations;

(c)   in the case of a student receiving an allowance or bursary under the Education (Scotland) Act 1980, the amount of money specified as "standard maintenance allowance" for the relevant year appropriate for the student set out in the Student Support in Scotland Guide issued by the Student Awards Agency for Scotland, or its nearest equivalent in the case of a bursary provided by a college of further education or a local education authority;

(d)   in any other case, the amount specified in paragraph 2(2) of Schedule 2 to the 2003 Regulations other than the amounts specified in sub-paragraph (2)(a) or (b) thereof;

"student" ("myfyriwr") means a person, other than a person in receipt of a training allowance, who is attending or undertaking–

(a)   a course of study at an educational establishment; or

(b)   a qualifying course;

"student loan" ("benthyciad myfyriwr") means a loan towards a student's maintenance pursuant to any regulations made under section 22 of the Teaching and Higher Education Act 1998, section 73 of the Education (Scotland) Act 1980 or article 3 of the Education (Student Support) (Northern Ireland) Order 1998 and includes, in Scotland, a young student's bursary paid under regulation 4(1)(c) of the Students' Allowances (Scotland) Regulations 2007.

(2)   For the purposes of the definition of "full-time student" in sub-paragraph (1), a person must be regarded as attending or, as the case may be, undertaking a full-time course of study or as being on a sandwich course–

(a)   subject to sub-paragraph (3), in the case of a person attending or undertaking a part of a modular course which would be a full-time course of study for the purposes of this Part, for the period beginning on the day on which that part of the course starts and ending–

  (i)   on the last day on which the person is registered with the educational establishment as attending or undertaking that part as a full-time course of study; or

  (ii)   on such earlier date (if any) as the person finally abandons the course or is dismissed from it;

(b)   in any other case, throughout the period beginning on the date on which the person starts attending or undertaking the course and ending on the last day of the course or on such earlier date (if any) as the person finally abandons it or is dismissed from it.

(3)   For the purposes of paragraph (a) of sub-paragraph (2), the period referred to in that paragraph includes–

(a)   where a person has failed examinations or has failed to successfully complete a module Relating to a period when the person was attending or undertaking a part of the course as a full-time course of study, any period in respect of which the person attends or undertakes the course for the purpose of retaking those examinations or that module;

(b)   any period of vacation within the period specified in that paragraph or immediately following that period except where the person has registered with the educational establishment to attend or undertake the final module in the course and the vacation immediately follows the last day on which the person is required to attend or undertake the course.

(4)   In sub-paragraph (2), "modular course" ("cwrs modiwlaidd") means a course of study which consists of two or more modules, the successful completion of a specified number of which is required before a person is considered by the educational establishment to have completed the course.

Amendment

1.   Amended by art 2 and Sch 3 para 30(3) of SI 2015 No 971 as from 26.5.15.

Treatment of Students

2.   An authority's scheme is to have effect in relation to students subject to regulation 31 (persons excluded from an authority's scheme; students) and the following provisions of this Schedule.

Students who are excluded from entitlement to a council tax reduction under an authority's scheme

3.–(1)   The students who are excluded from entitlement to a reduction under an authority's scheme are–

(a)   students who are pensioners; and

(b)   subject to sub-paragraphs (2) and (7)–

    (i)   full-time students, and

    (ii)   students who are persons treated as not being in Great Britain.

(2)   Sub-paragraph (1)(b) does not apply to a student–

(a)   who is a person on income support, an income-based jobseeker's allowance or an income-related employment and support allowance;

(b)   who is a lone parent;

(c)   whose applicable amount would, but for this paragraph, include the disability premium or severe disability premium;

(d)   whose applicable amount would include the disability premium but for the student being treated as capable of work by virtue of a determination made in accordance with regulations made under section 171E of the SSCBA;

(e)   who is, or is treated as, incapable of work and has been so incapable, or has been so treated as incapable, of work in accordance with the provisions of, and regulations made under Part 12A of the SSCBA (incapacity for work) for a continuous period of not less than 196 days; and for this purpose any two or more separate periods separated by a break of not more than 56 days must be treated as one continuous period;

(f)   who has, or is treated as having, limited capability for work and has had, or been treated as having, limited capability for work in accordance with the Employment and Support Allowance Regulations 2008 [¹or the Employment and Support Allowance Regulations 2013] for a continuous period of not less than 196 days and for this purpose any two or more separate periods separated by a break of not more than 84 days must be treated as one continuous period;

(g)   who has a partner who is also a full-time student, if the student or that partner is treated as responsible for a child or young person;

(h)   who is a single applicant with whom a child is placed by a local authority or voluntary organisation within the meaning of the Children Act 1989 or, in Scotland, boarded out within the meaning of the Social Work (Scotland) Act 1968;

(i)   who is–

    (i)   aged under 21 and whose course of study is not a course of higher education,

    (ii)   aged 21 and attained that age during a course of study which is not a course of higher education, or

    (iii)   a qualifying young person or child within the meaning of section 142 of the SSCBA (child and qualifying young person);

(j)   in respect of whom–

    (i)   a supplementary requirement has been determined under paragraph 9 of Part 2 of Schedule 2 to the Education (Mandatory Awards) Regulations 2003;

    (ii)   an allowance, or as the case may be, bursary has been granted which includes a sum under regulation 4 of the Students' Allowances (Scotland) Regulations 2007 or, as the case may be, under the Education Authority (Bursaries) (Scotland) Regulations 2007, in respect of expenses incurred;

    (iii)   a payment has been made under section 2 of the Education Act 1962 or under or by virtue of regulations made under the Teaching and Higher Education Act 1998;

    (iv)   a grant has been made under regulation 13 of the Education (Student Support) Regulations 2005, regulation 13 of the Education (Student Support) Regulations (Northern Ireland) 2000, or regulation 41 of the Education(Student Support) (No. 2) Regulations (Northern Ireland) 2009; or

    (v)   a supplementary requirement has been determined under paragraph 9 of Schedule 6 to the Students Awards Regulations (Northern Ireland) 2003 or a payment has been made under article 50(3) of the Education and Libraries (Northern Ireland) Order 1986,

on account of the student's disability by reason of deafness.

(3)   Sub-paragraph (2)(i)(ii) only applies to an applicant until the end of the course during which the applicant attained the age of 21.

(4)   For the purposes of sub-paragraph (2), once sub-paragraph (2)(e) applies to a full-time student, if that student then ceases, for a period of 56 days or less, to be incapable, or to be treated as incapable, of work, that sub-paragraph must, on that student again becoming so incapable, or so treated as incapable, of work at the end of that period, immediately thereafter apply to that student for so long as that student remains incapable or is treated as remaining incapable, of work.

(5)   In sub-paragraph (2)(i) the reference to a course of higher education is a reference to a course of any description mentioned in Schedule 6 to the Education Reform Act 1988.

(6)   A full-time student to whom paragraph (i) of sub-paragraph (2) applies must be treated as satisfying that sub-paragraph from the date on which that student made a request for the supplementary requirement, allowance, bursary or payment as the case may be.

(7)   Sub-paragraph (1)(b) does not apply to a full-time student for the period specified in sub-paragraph (8) if–

(a)   at any time during an academic year, with the consent of the relevant educational establishment, the student ceases to attend or undertake a course because the student is–
   (i)   engaged in caring for another person; or
   (ii)   ill;
(b)   the student has subsequently ceased to be engaged in caring for that person or, as the case may be, the student has subsequently recovered from that illness; and
(c)   the student is not eligible for a grant or a student loan in respect of the period specified in sub-paragraph (8).

(8)   The period specified for the purposes of sub-paragraph (7) is the period, not exceeding one year, beginning on the day on which the student ceased to be engaged in caring for that person or, as the case may be, the day on which the student recovered from that illness and ending on the day before–
(a)   the day on which the student resumes attending or undertaking the course; or
(b)   the day from which the relevant educational establishment has agreed that the student may resume attending or undertaking the course,
whichever first occurs.

Amendment
1.   Amended by reg 13 of SI 2015 No 44 (W.3) as from 21.1.15, for schemes made for a financial year starting on or after 1.4.15.

PART 2
Income

Calculation of grant income
4.–(1)   The amount of a student's grant income to be taken into account in assessing the student's income must, subject to sub-paragraphs (2) and (3), be the whole of the student's grant income.

(2)   There must be excluded from a student's grant income any payment–
(a)   intended to meet tuition fees or examination fees;
(b)   in respect of the student's disability;
(c)   intended to meet additional expenditure connected with term time residential study away from the student's educational establishment;
(d)   on account of the student maintaining a home at a place other than that at which the student resides during the student's course;
(e)   on account of any other person but only if that person is residing outside the United Kingdom and there is no applicable amount in respect of that person;
(f)   intended to meet the cost of books and equipment;
(g)   intended to meet travel expenses incurred as a result of the student's attendance on the course;
(h)   intended for the child care costs of a child dependant;
(i)   of higher education bursary for care leavers made under Part 3 of the Children Act 1989 [¹ ;
(j)   of higher education bursary for category 3 and category 4 young persons made under section 110 or 112 of the Social Services and Well-being (Wales) Act 2014, and in accordance with regulations made under section 116 of that Act.

(2A)   In sub-paragraph (2)(j) "category 3 young person" and "category 4 young person" have the meaning given in section 104(2) of the Social Services and Well-being (Wales) Act 2014.]

(3)   Where a student does not have a student loan and is not treated as possessing such a loan, there must be excluded from the student's grant income–
(a)   the sum of £303 per academic year in respect of travel costs; and
(b)   the sum of £390 per academic year towards the costs of books and equipment,
whether or not any such costs are incurred.

(4)   There must also be excluded from a student's grant income the grant for dependants known as the parents' learning allowance paid pursuant to regulations made under article 3 of the Education (Student Support) (Northern Ireland) Order 1998 or section 22 of the Teaching and Higher Education Act 1998.

(5)   Subject to sub-paragraphs (6) and (7), a student's grant income must be apportioned–
(a)   subject to sub-paragraph (8), in a case where it is attributable to the period of study, equally between the weeks in that period beginning with the reduction week, the first day of which coincides with, or immediately follows, the first day of the period of study and ending with the reduction week, the last day of which coincides with, or immediately precedes, the last day of the period of study;
(b)   in any other case, equally between the weeks in the period beginning with the reduction week, the first day of which coincides with, or immediately follows, the first day of the period for which it is payable and ending with the reduction week, the last day of which coincides with, or immediately precedes, the last day of the period for which it is payable.
(6)   Any grant in respect of dependants paid under section 63(6) of the Health Services and Public Health Act 1968 (grants in respect of the provision of instruction to officers of hospital authorities) and any amount intended for the maintenance of dependants under Part 3 of Schedule 2 to the Education (Mandatory Awards) Regulations 2003 must be apportioned equally over the period of 52 weeks or, if there are 53 reduction weeks (including part weeks) in the year, 53 weeks.
(7)   In a case where a student is in receipt of a student loan or where the student could have acquired a student loan by taking reasonable steps but had not done so, any amount intended for the maintenance of dependants to which neither sub-paragraph (6) nor paragraph 8(2) (other amounts to be disregarded) applies, must be apportioned over the same period as the student's loan is apportioned or, as the case may be, would have been apportioned.
(8)   In the case of a student on a sandwich course, any periods of experience within the period of study must be excluded and the student's grant income must be apportioned equally between the weeks in the period beginning with the reduction week, the first day of which immediately follows the last day of the period of experience and ending with the reduction week, the last day of which coincides with, or immediately precedes, the last day of the period of study.

Amendment
1.   Inserted by reg 14 of SI 2016 No 50 (W.21) as from 20.1.16, for schemes made for a financial year starting on or after 1.4.16.

Calculation of covenant income where a contribution is assessed
    5.–(1)   Where a student is in receipt of income by way of a grant during a period of study and a contribution has been assessed, the amount of the student's covenant income to be taken into account for that period and any summer vacation immediately following must be the whole amount of the covenant income less, subject to sub-paragraph (3), the amount of the contribution.
(2)   The weekly amount of the student's covenant income must be determined–
(a)   by dividing the amount of income which falls to be taken into account under sub-paragraph (1) by 52 or 53, whichever is reasonable in the circumstances; and
(b)   by disregarding £5 from the resulting amount.
(3)   For the purposes of sub-paragraph (1), the contribution must be treated as increased by the amount (if any) by which the amount excluded under paragraph 4(2)(g) (calculation of grant income) falls short of the amount specified in paragraph 7(2) of Schedule 2 to the Education (Mandatory Awards) Regulations 2003 (travel expenditure).

Covenant income where no grant income or no contribution is assessed
    6.–(1)   Where a student is not in receipt of income by way of a grant the amount of the student's covenant income must be calculated as follows–
(a)   any sums intended for any expenditure specified in paragraph 4(2)(a) to (e) (calculation of grant income) necessary as a result of the student's attendance on the course must be disregarded;
(b)   any covenant income, up to the amount of the standard maintenance grant, which is not so disregarded, must be apportioned equally between the weeks of the period of study;
(c)   there must be disregarded from the amount so apportioned the amount which would have been disregarded under paragraph 4(2)(f) and (3) (calculation of grant income) had the student been in receipt of the standard maintenance grant; and
(d)   the balance, if any, must be divided by 52 or 53 whichever is reasonable in the circumstances and treated as weekly income of which £5 must be disregarded.
(2)   Where a student is in receipt of income by way of a grant and no contribution has been assessed, the amount of the student's covenanted income must be calculated in accordance with paragraphs (a) to (d) of sub-paragraph (1), except that–
(a)   the value of the standard maintenance grant must be abated by the amount of such grant income less an amount equal to the amount of any sums disregarded under paragraph 4(2)(a) to (e); and
(b)   the amount to be disregarded under sub-paragraph (1)(c) must be abated by an amount equal to the amount of any sums disregarded under paragraph 4(2)(f) and (g) and (3).

Relationship with amounts to be disregarded under Schedule 9
    7.   No part of a student's covenant income or grant income is to be disregarded under paragraph 19 of Schedule 9 (disregard of certain charitable and voluntary, etc., payments).

Other amounts to be disregarded

8.–(1)   For the purposes of ascertaining income other than grant income, covenant income and loans treated as income in accordance with paragraph 9 (treatment of student loans), any amounts intended for any expenditure specified in paragraph 4(2) (calculation of grant income), necessary as a result of the student's attendance on the course are to be disregarded.

(2)   But sub-paragraph (1) applies only if, and to the extent that, the necessary expenditure exceeds or is likely to exceed the amount of the sums disregarded under paragraph 4(2) or (3), 5(3), 6(1)(a) or (c) or 9(5) (calculation of grant income, covenant income and treatment of student loans) on like expenditure.

Treatment of student loans

9.–(1)   A student loan is to be treated as income.

(2)   In calculating the weekly amount of the loan to be taken into account as income–

(a)   in respect of a course that is of a single academic year's duration or less, a loan which is payable in respect of that period is to be apportioned equally between the weeks in the period beginning with–

    (i)   except in a case where sub-paragraph (ii) applies, the reduction week, the first day of which coincides with, or immediately follows, the first day of the single academic year;

    (ii)   where the student is required to start attending the course in August or where the course is less than an academic year's duration, the reduction week, the first day of which coincides with, or immediately follows, the first day of the course,

and ending with the reduction week, the last day of which coincides with, or immediately precedes, the last day of the course;

(b)   in respect of an academic year of a course which starts other than on 1 September, a loan which is payable in respect of that academic year is to be apportioned equally between the weeks in the period–

    (i)   beginning with the reduction week, the first day of which coincides with or immediately follows, the first day of that academic year; and

    (ii)   ending with the reduction week, the last day of which coincides with or immediately precedes, the last day of that academic year,

but excluding any reduction weeks falling entirely within the quarter during which, in the opinion of the authority, the longest of any vacation is taken [¹];

(c)   in respect of the final academic year of a course (not being a course of a single year's duration), a loan which is payable in respect of that final academic year is to be apportioned equally between the weeks in the period beginning with–

    (i)   except in a case where sub-paragraph (ii) applies, the reduction week, the first day of which coincides with, or immediately follows, the first day of that academic year;

    (ii)   where the final academic year starts on 1 September, the reduction week, the first day of which coincides with, or immediately follows, the earlier of 1 September or the first day of the autumn term,

and ending with the reduction week, the last day of which coincides with, or immediately precedes, the last day of the course;

(d)   in any other case, the loan is to be apportioned equally between the weeks in the period beginning with the earlier of–

    (i)   the first day of the first reduction week in September; or

    (ii)   the reduction week, the first day of which coincides with, or immediately follows the first day of the autumn term,

and ending with the reduction week, the last day of which coincides with, or immediately precedes, the last day of June, and, in all cases, from the weekly amount so apportioned there is to be disregarded £10.

(3)   A student is to be treated as possessing a student loan in respect of an academic year where–

(a)   a student loan has been made to the student in respect of that year; or

(b)   the student could acquire such a loan in respect of that year by taking reasonable steps to do so.

(4)   Where a student is treated as possessing a student loan under sub-paragraph (3), the amount of the student loan to be taken into account as income must be, subject to sub-paragraph (5)–

(a)   in the case of a student to whom a student loan is made in respect of an academic year, a sum equal to–

    (i)   the maximum student loan the student is able to acquire in respect of that year by taking reasonable steps to do so; and

    (ii)   any contribution whether or not it has been paid to the student;

(b)   in the case of a student to whom a student loan is not made in respect of an academic year, the maximum student loan that would be made to the student if–

    (i)   the student took all reasonable steps to obtain the maximum student loan that student is able to acquire in respect of that year; and

    (ii)   no deduction in that loan was made by virtue of the application of a means test.

(5)   There must be deducted from the amount of income taken into account under sub-paragraph (4)–

(a)   the sum of £303 per academic year in respect of travel costs; and

(b)   the sum of £390 per academic year towards the cost of books and equipment,

whether or not any such costs are incurred.

[¹ (6)   For the purposes of this paragraph "quarter" ("chwarter") in relation to an academic year means a period in that year–
(a)   beginning on 1 January and ending on 31 March;
(b)   beginning on 1 April and ending on 30 June;
(c)   beginning on 1 July and ending on 31 August; or
(d)   beginning on 1 September and ending on 31 December.]

Amendment
1.   Amended by reg 12(a) of SI 2014 No 66 (W.6) as from 15.1.14.

Treatment of fee loans

10.   A loan for fees, known as a fee loan or a fee contribution loan, made pursuant to regulations made under article 3 of the [¹ Education (Student Support) (Northern Ireland) Order 1998], section 22 of the Teaching and Higher Education Act 1998 or section 73 (f) of the Education (Scotland) Act 1980, must be disregarded as income.

Amendment
1.   Amended by reg 12(b) of SI 2014 No 66 (W.6) as from 15.1.14.

Treatment of payments from access funds

11.–(1)   This paragraph applies to payments from access funds that are not payments to which paragraph 14(2) or (3) (income treated as capital) applies.
(2)   A payment from access funds, other than a payment to which sub-paragraph (3) applies, must be disregarded as income.
(3)   Subject to sub-paragraph (4) of this paragraph and paragraph 40 of Schedule 9–
(a)   any payments from access funds which are intended and used for an item of food, ordinary clothing or footwear, household fuel, or rent of a single applicant or, as the case may be, of the applicant or any other member of the applicant's family, and
(b)   any payments from access funds which are used for any council tax or water charges for which that applicant or any other member of the applicant's family is liable,
must be disregarded as income to the extent of £20 per week.
(4)   Where a payment from access funds is made–
(a)   on or after 1 September or the first day of the course, whichever first occurs, but before receipt of any student loan in respect of that year and that payment is intended for the purpose of bridging the period until receipt of the student loan; or
(b)   before the first day of the course to a person in anticipation of that person becoming a student,
that payment must be disregarded as income.

Disregard of contribution

12.   Where the applicant or the applicant's partner is a student and, for the purposes of assessing a contribution to the student's grant or student loan, the other partner's income has been taken into account, an amount equal to that contribution must be disregarded for the purposes of assessing that other partner's income.

Further disregard of student's income

13.   Where any part of a student's income has already been taken into account for the purposes of assessing that student's entitlement to a grant or student loan, the amount taken into account must be disregarded in assessing that student's income.

Income treated as capital

14.–(1)   Any amount by way of a refund of tax deducted from a student's covenant income must be treated as capital.
(2)   An amount paid from access funds as a single lump sum must be treated as capital.
(3)   An amount paid from access funds as a single lump sum which is intended and used for an item other than food, ordinary clothing or footwear, household fuel or rent, or which is used for an item other than any council tax or water charges for which that applicant or any other member of the applicant's family is liable, must be disregarded as capital but only for a period of 52 weeks from the date of the payment.

Disregard of changes occurring during summer vacation

15.   In calculating a student's income an authority must disregard any change in the standard maintenance grant, occurring in the recognised summer vacation appropriate to the student's course, if that vacation does not form part of the student's period of study from the date on which the change occurred to the end of that vacation.

SCHEDULE 12

REGULATION 34(3)

All applicants: matters that must be included in an authority's scheme – procedural matters

PART 1

Procedure for an application for a reduction under an authority's scheme

Procedure by which a person may apply for a reduction under an authority's scheme

1.　　Paragraphs 2 to 7 apply to an application for a reduction under an authority's scheme.

2.　　An application may be made–

(a)　　in writing,

(b)　　by means of an electronic communication in accordance with Part 4, or

(c)　　where the authority has published a telephone number for the purpose of receiving such applications, by telephone.

3.–(1)　　An application which is made in writing must be made to the designated office and be–

(a)　　on a properly completed form approved by the authority for the purposes of making an application in writing; or

(b)　　in such written form as the authority accepts as sufficient in the circumstances of any particular case (or class of cases) having regard to the sufficiency of the written information and evidence.

(2)　　Where an application in writing is not made in the form described in paragraph 3(1)(a) or (b) it is defective.

(3)　　Any form provided by the authority for the purposes of making an application in writing must be provided free of charge.

4.–(1)　　Where an application made in writing is defective because–

(a)　　it was made on the form approved for the purpose but that form is not accepted by the authority as being properly completed, the authority may request the applicant to complete the defective application; or

(b)　　it was made in writing but not on the form approved for the purpose and the authority does not accept the application as being in a written form which is sufficient in the circumstances of the case having regard to the sufficiency of the written information and evidence, the authority may supply the applicant with the approved form or request further information or evidence.

(2)　　An application made on an approved form is properly completed if it is completed in accordance with the instructions on the form, including any instructions to provide information and evidence in connection with the application.

5.–(1)　　If an application made by electronic communication is defective the authority must provide the person making the application with an opportunity to correct the defect.

(2)　　An application made by electronic communication is defective if the applicant does not provide all the information the authority requires.

6.　　In a particular case the authority may determine that an application made by telephone is only valid if the person making the application approves a written statement of that person's circumstances provided by the authority.

7.–(1)　　If an application made by telephone is defective the authority must provide the person making the application with an opportunity to correct the defect.

(2)　　An application made by telephone is defective if the applicant does not provide all the information the authority requests during the telephone call.

PART 2

Procedure for making an appeal

Procedure by which a person may make an appeal against certain decisions of the authority

8.–(1)　　A person who is aggrieved by a decision of an authority which affects–

(a)　　that person's entitlement to a reduction under an authority's scheme; or

(b)　　the amount of any reduction under an authority's scheme,

may serve a written notice on the authority stating the matter by which, and the grounds on which, the person is aggrieved.

(2)　　A notice under sub-paragraph (1) must be served within one month of the date of service of the notification of the decision of the authority, or where a person has made a request for a written statement in accordance with paragraph 9(5) of Schedule 13 (request for statement of written reasons), within one month of the date of service of the statement of reasons.

9.　　The authority must–

(a)　　consider the matter to which the notice relates;

(b)　　notify the aggrieved person in writing–

(i)　　that the ground is not well founded, giving reasons for that belief; or

(ii)　　that steps have been taken to deal with the grievance, stating the steps taken.

10.   Where, following notification under paragraph 9(b)(i) or (ii), the person is still aggrieved, or if the authority fails to notify the person aggrieved in accordance with paragraph 9(b) within two months of the service of the person's notice, the person may appeal to the valuation tribunal under section 16 of the 1992 Act.

PART 3
Procedure for applying for a discretionary reduction

Procedure for an application to an authority for a reduction under section 13A(1)(c) of the1992 Act
11.   An application to an authority for a reduction under section 13A(1)(c) of the 1992 Act must be made–
(a)   in writing,
(b)   by means of an electronic communication in accordance with Part 4, or
(c)   where the authority has published a telephone number for the purpose of receiving such applications, by telephone.
(2)   Where–
(a)   the authority has made a determination under section 13A(1)(c) in relation to a class of case in which liability is to be reduced; and
(b)   a person in that class would otherwise be entitled to a reduction under the authority's scheme,
that person's application for a reduction under the authority's scheme may also be treated as an application for a reduction under section 13Λ(1)(c).

PART 4
Electronic communication

Interpretation
12.   In this Part of this Schedule–
"information" ("gwybodaeth") includes an application for a reduction under an authority's scheme, a certificate, notice or other evidence;
"official computer system" ("system gyfrifiadurol swyddogol") means a computer system maintained by or on behalf of an authority for the sending, receiving, processing or storing of any information.

Conditions for the use of electronic communication
13.–(1)   An authority may use an electronic communication in connection with an application for, and an award of, a reduction under its scheme.
(2)   A person other than the authority may use an electronic communication in connection with the matters referred to in sub-paragraph (1) if the conditions specified in sub-paragraphs (3) to (6) are satisfied.
(3)   The first condition is that the person is for the time being permitted to use an electronic communication by an authorisation given by means of a direction of the Chief Executive of the authority.
(4)   The second condition is that the person uses an approved method of–
(a)   authenticating the identity of the sender of the communication;
(b)   electronic communication;
(c)   authenticating any application or notice delivered by means of an electronic communication; and
(d)   subject to sub-paragraph (7), submitting to the authority any information.
(5)   The third condition is that any information sent by means of an electronic communication is in a form approved for the purposes of this Part.
(6)   The fourth condition is that the person maintains such records in written or electronic form as may be specified in a direction given by the Chief Executive of the authority.
(7)   Where the person uses any method other than the method approved of submitting any information, that information is to be treated as not having been submitted.
(8)   In this paragraph "approved" ("cymeradwy") means approved by means of a direction give by the Chief Executive of the authority for the purposes of this Part.

Use of intermediaries
14.   An authority may use intermediaries in connection with–
(a)   the delivery of any information by means of an electronic communication; and
(b)   the authentication or security of anything transmitted by such means,
and may require other persons to use intermediaries in connection with those matters.

Effect of delivering information by means of electronic communication
15.–(1)   Any information which is delivered by means of an electronic communication is to be treated as having been delivered in the manner or form required by any provision of an authority's scheme, on the day the conditions imposed–
(a)   by this Part; and
(b)   by or under an enactment,
are satisfied.

(2)   An authority may determine that any information is to be treated as delivered on a different day (whether earlier or later) from the day provided for in sub-paragraph (1).

(3)   Information is not to be taken to have been delivered to an official computer system by means of an electronic communication unless it is accepted by the system to which it is delivered.

Proof of identity of sender or recipient of information
  16.   If it is necessary to prove, for the purpose of any legal proceedings, the identity of–
  (a)   the sender of any information delivered by means of an electronic communication to an official computer system; or
  (b)   the recipient of any such information delivered by means of an electronic communication from an official computer system,
the sender or recipient, as the case may be, is to be presumed to be the person whose name is recorded as such on that official computer system.

Proof of delivery of information
  17.–(1)   If it is necessary to prove, for the purpose of any legal proceedings, that the use of an electronic communication has resulted in the delivery of any information this is to be presumed to have been the case where–
  (a)   any such information has been delivered to the authority, if the delivery of that information has been recorded on an official computer system; or
  (b)   any such information has been delivered by the authority, if the delivery of that information has been recorded on an official computer system.

(2)   If it is necessary to prove, for the purpose of any legal proceedings, that the use of an electronic communication has resulted in the delivery of any such information, this is to be presumed not to be the case, if that information delivered to the authority has not been recorded on an official computer system.

(3)   If it is necessary to prove, for the purpose of any legal proceedings, when any such information sent by means of an electronic communication has been received, the time and date of receipt is to be presumed to be that recorded on an official computer system.

Proof of content of information
  18.   If it is necessary to prove, for the purpose of any legal proceedings, the content of any information sent by means of an electronic communication, the content is to be presumed to be that recorded on an official computer system.

SCHEDULE 13

REGULATION 34(3)

All applicants: matters that must be included in an authority's scheme – other matters

PART 1
Applications

Who may make an application
  1.–(1)   In the case of–
  (a)   a couple or (subject to paragraph (b)) members of a polygamous marriage, an application is to be made by whichever one of them they agree should so apply or, in default of agreement, by such one of them as the authority determines; or
  (b)   members of a polygamous marriage to whom paragraph 9 of Schedule 6 (income and capital: award of universal credit) applies, an application is to be made by whichever one of the parties to the earliest marriage that still subsists they agree should so apply or, in default of agreement, by such one of them as the authority determines.

(2)   Where a person who is liable to pay council tax in respect of a dwelling is unable for the time being to act, and–
  (a)   a deputy has been appointed by the Court of Protection with power to claim, or as the case may be, receive benefit on that person's behalf; or
  (b)   in Scotland, that person's estate is being administered by a judicial factor or any guardian acting or appointed under the Adults with Incapacity (Scotland) Act 2000 who has power to apply or, as the case may be, receive benefit on that person's behalf; or
  (c)   an attorney with a general power or a power to apply or, as the case may be, receive benefit, has been appointed by that person under the Powers of Attorney Act 1971, the Enduring Powers of Attorney Act 1985 or the Mental Capacity Act 2005 or otherwise,
that deputy, judicial factor, guardian or attorney, as the case may be, may make an application on behalf of that person.

(3)   Where a person who is liable to pay council tax in respect of a dwelling is unable for the time being to act and sub-paragraph (2) does not apply to that person, the authority may, upon written application made to it by a person who, if a natural person, is over the age of 18, appoint that person to exercise on behalf of the

person who is unable to act, any right to which the person who is unable to act might be entitled under an authority's scheme, and to receive and deal on that person's behalf with any sums payable to that person.

(4)   Where a person who is liable to pay council tax in respect of a dwelling is for the time being unable to act and the Secretary of State has appointed a person to act on that person's behalf under regulation 33 of the Social Security (Claims and Payments) Regulations 1987 (persons unable to act), the authority may if the person so appointed agrees, treat that person as if that person had been appointed by it under sub-paragraph (3).

(5)   Where the authority has made an appointment under sub-paragraph (3) or treated a person as an appointee under sub-paragraph (4)–

(a)   it may at any time revoke the appointment;

(b)   the person appointed may resign that person's office after having given 4 weeks notice in writing to the authority of that person's intention to do so;

(c)   any such appointment must terminate when the authority is notified of the appointment of a person mentioned in sub-paragraph (2).

(6)   Anything required by an authority's scheme to be done by or to any person who is for the time being unable to act may be done by or to the persons mentioned in sub-paragraph (2) or by or to the person appointed or treated as appointed under this paragraph and the receipt of any such person so appointed is to be a good discharge to the authority for any sum paid.

(7)   The authority must–

(a)   inform any person making an application of the duty imposed by paragraph 7(1)(a) (duty to notify change of circumstances);

(b)   explain the possible consequences (including prosecution) of failing to comply with that duty; and

(c)   set out the circumstances a change in which might affect entitlement to a reduction or its amount.

Date on which an application is made

2.–(1)   Subject to sub-paragraph (7), the date on which an application is made is–

(a)   in a case where–

(i)   an award of state pension credit which comprises a guarantee credit has been made to the applicant or the applicant's partner, and

(ii)   the application for a reduction under an authority's scheme is made within one month of the date on which the claim for that state pension credit which comprises a guarantee credit was received at the appropriate DWP office,

the first day of entitlement to state pension credit which comprises a guarantee credit arising from that claim;

(b)   in a case where–

(i)   an applicant or the applicant's partner is a person in receipt of a guarantee credit,

(ii)   the applicant becomes liable for the first time to pay council tax in respect of the dwelling which the applicant occupies as the applicant's home, and

(iii)   the application to the authority is received at the designated office within one month of the date of the change,

the date on which the change takes place;

(c)   in a case where–

(i)   an award of income support, an income-based jobseeker's allowance or an income-related employment and support allowance or an award of universal credit has been made to the applicant or the applicant's partner, and

(ii)   the application for a reduction under an authority's scheme is made within one month of the date on which the claim for that income support, jobseeker's allowance, employment and support allowance or universal credit was received,

the first day of entitlement to income support, an income-based jobseeker's allowance, an income-related employment and support allowance or universal credit arising from that claim;

(d)   in a case where–

(i)   an applicant or the applicant's partner is a person on income support, an income-based jobseeker's allowance or an income-related employment and support allowance or has an award of universal credit,

(ii)   the applicant becomes liable for the first time to pay council tax in respect of the dwelling which the applicant occupies as the applicant's home, and

(iii)   the application to the authority is received at the designated office within one month of the date of the change,

the date on which the change takes place;

(e)   in a case where–

(i)   the applicant is the former partner of a person who was, at the date of that person's death or the separation of the applicant and that person, entitled to a reduction under an authority's scheme, and

(ii)   where the applicant makes an application for a reduction under an authority's scheme within one month of the date of the death or the separation,

the date of the death or separation;

(f)   except where paragraph (a), (b) or (e) is satisfied, in a case where a properly completed application is received at the designated office within one month (or such longer period as the authority considers reasonable) of the date on which an application form was issued to the applicant following the applicant first notifying, by whatever means, the authority of an intention to make an application, the date of first notification;

(g)   in any other case, the date on which the application is received at the designated office.

(2)   For the purposes only of sub-paragraph (1)(c) a person who has been awarded an income-based jobseeker's allowance or an income-related employment and support allowance is to be treated as entitled to that allowance for any days which immediately precede the first day in that award and on which the person would, but for regulations made under–

(a)   in the case of income-based jobseeker's allowance, paragraph 4 of Schedule 1 to the Jobseekers Act 1995 (waiting days); or

(b)   in the case of income-related employment and support allowance, paragraph 2 of Schedule 2 to the Welfare Reform Act 2007 (waiting days),

have been entitled to that allowance.

(3)   Where the defect referred to in paragraph 7 of Schedule 12 (telephone application)–

(a)   is corrected within one month (or such longer period as an authority considers reasonable) of the date the authority last drew attention to it, the authority is to treat the application as if it had been duly made in the first instance;

(b)   is not corrected within one month (or such longer period as an authority considers reasonable) of the date the authority last drew attention to it, the authority is to treat the application as if it had been duly made in the first instance where it considers it has sufficient information to decide on the application.

(4)   An authority is to treat a defective application as if it had been validly made in the first instance if, in any particular case, the conditions specified in sub-paragraph (5)(a), (b) or (c) are satisfied.

(5)   The conditions are that–

(a)   where paragraph 4(1)(a) of Schedule 12 (incomplete form) applies, the authority receives at the designated office the properly completed application or the information requested to complete it or the evidence within one month of the request, or such longer period as the authority considers reasonable; or

(b)   where paragraph 4(1)(b) of Schedule 12 (application not on approved form or further information requested by authority) applies–

    (i)   the approved form sent to the applicant is received at the designated office properly completed within one month of it having been sent to the applicant; or, as the case may be,

    (ii)   the applicant supplies whatever information or evidence was requested under paragraph 4 of Schedule 12 within one month of the request,

    or, in either case, within such longer period as the authority considers reasonable; or

(c)   where the authority has requested further information, the authority receives at the designated office the properly completed application or the information requested within one month of the request or within such longer period as the authority considers reasonable.

(6)   Except in the case of an application made by a person treated as not being in Great Britain, where a person has not become liable for council tax to an authority but it is anticipated that the person will become so liable within the period of 13 weeks (the relevant period), the person may apply for a reduction under an authority's scheme at any time in that period in respect of that tax and, provided that liability arises within the relevant period, the authority is to treat the application as having been made on the day on which the liability for the tax arises.

(7)   Except in the case of an application made by a person treated as not being in Great Britain, where the applicant is not entitled to a reduction under an authority's scheme at the time that the application is received by an authority but the authority is of the opinion that, unless there is a change of circumstances, the applicant will be entitled to a reduction under its scheme for a period beginning not later than the thirteenth reduction week following the date on which the application is made (or such other period as the authority considers reasonable), the authority may treat the application as made on a date in the reduction week immediately preceding the first reduction week of that period of entitlement and award a reduction accordingly.

Back-dating of applications: pensioners

3.–(1)   Subject to sub-paragraph (2), the time for the making of an application for a reduction under an authority's scheme by a pensioner is, as regards any day on which, apart from satisfying the condition of making an application, the applicant is entitled to such a reduction, that day and the period of three months immediately following it.

(2)   In any case where paragraph 2(1)(a) applies, sub-paragraph (1) does not entitle a person to apply for a reduction under an authority's scheme in respect of any day earlier than 3 months before the date on which the claim for state pension credit is made (or treated as made by virtue of any provision of the Social Security (Claims and Payments) Regulations 1987).

Back-dating of applications: persons who are not pensioners

4.–(1)   Where an applicant who is a person who is not a pensioner–

(a)   makes an application under an authority's scheme which includes (or which the applicant subsequently requests should include) a period before the application is made; and

(b)   from a day in that period, up to the date the applicant made the application (or subsequently requested that the application should include a past period), the applicant had continuous good cause for failing to make an application (or request that the application should include that period),

the application is to be treated as made on the date determined in accordance with sub-paragraph (2).

(2)   That date is the latest of–

(a)   the first day from which the applicant had continuous good cause;

(b)   the day 3 months before the date the application was made;

(c)   the day 3 months before the date when the applicant requested that the application should include a past period.

Evidence and information

5.–(1)   Subject to sub-paragraph (3), a person who makes an application for a reduction under an authority's scheme must satisfy sub-paragraph (2) in relation both to the person making the application and to any other person in respect of whom the person is making the application.

(2)   This sub-paragraph is satisfied in relation to a person if–

(a)   the application is accompanied by–

    (i)   a statement of the person's national insurance number and information or evidence establishing that that number has been allocated to the person; or

    (ii)   information or evidence enabling an authority to ascertain the national insurance number that has been allocated to the person; or

(b)   the person has made an application for a national insurance number to be allocated to that person and the application for the reduction is accompanied by–

    (i)   evidence of the application for a national insurance number to be so allocated; and

    (ii)   the information or evidence enabling it to be so allocated.

(3)   Sub-paragraph (2) does not apply–

(a)   in the case of a child or young person in respect of whom an application for a reduction is made;

(b)   to a person who–

    (i)   is treated as not being in Great Britain for the purposes of that scheme;

    (ii)   is subject to immigration control within the meaning of section 115(9)(a) of the Immigration and Asylum Act 1999; and

    (iii)   has not previously been allocated a national insurance number.

(4)   Subject to sub-paragraph (5), a person who makes an application, or a person to whom a reduction under an authority's scheme has been awarded, must furnish such certificates, documents, information and evidence in connection with the application or the award, or any question arising out of the application or award, as may reasonably be required by the authority in order to determine that person's entitlement to, or continuing entitlement to a reduction under its scheme and must do so within one month of the authority requiring the person to do so or such longer period as the authority considers reasonable.

(5)   Nothing in this paragraph requires a person to furnish any certificates, documents, information or evidence relating to a payment to which sub-paragraph (7) applies.

(6)   Where a request is made under sub-paragraph (4), the authority must–

(a)   inform the applicant or the person to whom a reduction under its scheme has been awarded of the applicant's duty under paragraph 7 (duty to notify changes of circumstances) to notify the authority of any change of circumstances; and

(b)   without prejudice to the extent of the duty owed under paragraph 7, indicate to the person either orally or by notice or by reference to some other document available to the person on application and without charge, the kind of change of circumstances which is to be notified to the authority.

(7)   This sub-paragraph applies to any of the following payments–

(a)   a payment which is–

    (i)   disregarded under paragraph 28 of Schedule 9 (sums disregarded in the calculation of income other than earnings: persons who are not pensioners) or paragraph 38 of Schedule 10 (capital disregards: persons who are not pensioners); or

    (ii)   made under or by the Trusts, the Fund, the Eileen Trust, MFET Limited, the Skipton Fund, the Caxton Foundation [¹, an approved blood scheme, the Scottish Infected Blood Support Scheme, the London Emergencies Trust, the We Love Manchester Emergency Fund] or the London Bombings Relief Charitable Fund;

(b)   a payment which is disregarded under paragraph 16 of Schedule 5 (payments made under certain trusts and certain other payments) other than a payment under the Independent Living Fund (2006);

(c)   a payment which is disregarded under paragraph 5(9)(b) or (c) of Schedule 6 (non-dependent deductions; persons who are not pensioners) other than a payment made under the Independent Living Fund (2006).

(8)   Where an applicant or a person to whom a reduction under an authority's scheme has been awarded or any partner has attained the qualifying age for state pension credit and is a member of, or a person deriving entitlement to a pension under a personal pension scheme, the person must where the authority so requires furnish the following information–

(a)   the name and address of the pension fund holder;

(b)   such other information including any reference or policy number as is needed to enable the personal pension scheme to be identified.

Amendment

1.   Amended by reg 14 of SI 2018 No 14 (W.7) as from 10.1.18, for schemes made for a financial year starting on or after 1.4.18.

General Note

This is similar to reg 86 HB Regs in some respects. See p556 for the commentary. Para 5(4) is also similar to Sch 8 para 7(4) of CTRS(PR)(E) Regs, see p1181 for commentary.

Amendment and withdrawal of application

6.–(1)   A person who has made an application may amend it at any time before a decision has been made on it by a notice in writing delivered or sent to the designated office.

(2)   Where the application was made by telephone in accordance with Part 1 of Schedule 12, the amendment may also be made by telephone.

(3)   Any application amended in accordance with sub-paragraph (1) or (2) is to be treated as if it had been amended in the first instance.

(4)   A person who has made an application may withdraw it by notice to the designated office at any time before a decision has been made on it.

(5)   Where the application was made by telephone in accordance with Part 1 of Schedule 12 the withdrawal may also be made by telephone.

(6)   Any notice of withdrawal given in accordance with sub-paragraph (4) or (5) is to have effect when it is received.

(7)   Where a person, by telephone, amends or withdraws an application the person must (if required to do so by the authority) confirm the amendment or withdrawal by a notice in writing delivered or sent to the designated office.

Duty to notify changes of circumstances

7.–(1)   Subject to sub-paragraphs (3) and (8), the applicant (or any person acting on the applicant's behalf) must comply with sub-paragraph (2) if there is a relevant change of circumstances at any time–

(a)   between the making of an application and a decision being made on it, or

(b)   after the decision is made (where the decision is that the applicant is entitled to a reduction under an authority's scheme) including at any time while the applicant is in receipt of such a reduction.

(2)   The applicant (or any person acting on the applicant's behalf) must notify any change of circumstances which the applicant (or that person) might reasonably be expected to know might affect the applicant's entitlement to, or the amount of, a reduction under the authority's scheme (a "relevant change of circumstances") by giving notice to the authority–

(a)   in writing; or

(b)   by telephone–

    (i)   where the authority has published a telephone number for that purpose or for the purposes of Part 1 of Schedule 12 unless the authority determines that in any particular case or class of case notification may not be given by telephone; or

    (ii)   in any case or class of case where the authority determines that notice may be given by telephone; or

(c)   by any other means which the authority agrees to accept in any particular case,

within a period of 21 days beginning with the day on which the change occurs, or as soon as reasonably practicable after the change occurs, whichever is the later.

(3)   The duty imposed on a person by sub-paragraph (1) does not extend to notifying–

(a)   changes in the amount of council tax payable to the authority;

(b)   changes in the age of the applicant or that of any member of the applicant's family;

(c)   in the case of an applicant in receipt of a relevant benefit, changes in circumstances which affect the amount of the benefit but not the amount of the reduction under the authority's scheme to which the applicant is entitled, other than the cessation of that entitlement to the benefit.

(4)   For the purposes of sub-paragraph (3)(c) "relevant benefit" ("budd-dal perthnasol") means income support, an income-based jobseeker's allowance or an income-related employment and support allowance or universal credit.

(5)   Notwithstanding sub-paragraph (3)(b) or (c) an applicant is required by sub-paragraph (1) to notify the authority of any change in the composition of the applicant's family arising from the fact that a person who was a member of the applicant's family is now no longer such a person because that person has ceased to be a child or young person.

(6)   A person who has been granted a reduction under an authority's scheme who is also on state pension credit must report–

(a)   changes affecting the residence or income of any non-dependant normally residing with the applicant or with whom the applicant normally resides;

(b)   any absence from the dwelling which exceeds or is likely to exceed 13 weeks.

(7)   A person whose state pension credit comprises only a savings credit must also report–

(a)   changes affecting a child living with that person which may result in a change in the amount of reduction under the authority's scheme allowed in that person's case, but not changes in the age of the child;

(b)   any change in the amount of that person's capital to be taken into account which does or may take the amount of that person's capital to more than £16,000;

(c)   any change in the income or capital of–

    (i)   a non-dependant whose income and capital are treated as belonging to the applicant in accordance with paragraph 6 of Schedule 1 or paragraph 8 of Schedule 6(circumstances in which income of a nondependent is to be treated as applicant's); or

    (ii)   a person to whom paragraph 8(2)(e) of Schedule 1 (partner treated as member of the household under paragraph 8) refers,

and whether such a person or, as the case may be, non-dependant stops living or begins or resumes living with the applicant.

(8)   A person who is entitled to a reduction under an authority's scheme and on state pension credit need only report to the authority the changes specified in sub-paragraphs (6) and (7).

PART 2
Decisions by an authority

Decision by an authority

8.   An authority must make a decision on an application for a reduction under its scheme within 14 days of paragraphs 2 and 5 being satisfied, or as soon as reasonably practicable thereafter.

Notification of decision

9.–(1)   An authority must notify in writing any person affected by a decision made by it under its scheme–

(a)   in the case of a decision on an application, forthwith or as soon as reasonably practicable thereafter;

(b)   in any other case, within 14 days of that decision or as soon as reasonably practicable thereafter.

(2)   Where the decision is to award a reduction the notification under sub-paragraph (1) must include a statement–

(a)   informing the person affected of the duty imposed by paragraph 7 (duty to notify change of circumstances);

(b)   explaining the possible consequences (including prosecution) of failing to comply with that duty; and

(c)   setting out the circumstances a change in which might affect entitlement to the reduction or its amount.

(3)   Where the decision is to award a reduction, the notification under sub-paragraph (1) must include a statement as to how that entitlement is to be discharged.

(4)   The notification under sub-paragraph (1) must also include a statement as to the matters set out in Schedule 14.

(5)   A person affected to whom the authority sends or delivers a notification of decision may, within one month of the date of the notification of that decision request in writing the authority to provide a written statement setting out the reasons for its decision on any matter set out in the notice.

(6)   The written statement referred to in sub-paragraph (5) must be sent to the person requesting it within 14 days or as soon as reasonably practicable thereafter.

(7)   For the purposes of this paragraph a person is to be treated as a person affected by a decision of an authority under its scheme where the rights, duties or obligations of that person are affected by that decision and the person falls within sub-paragraph (8).

(8)   This sub-paragraph applies to–

(a)   the applicant;

(b)   in the case of a person who is liable to pay council tax in respect of a dwelling and is unable for the time being to act–

    (i)   a deputy appointed by the Court of Protection with power to claim, or as the case may be, receive benefit on the person's behalf; or

    (ii)   in Scotland, a judicial factor or any guardian acting or appointed under the Adults with Incapacity (Scotland) Act 2000 who has power to apply or, as the case may be, receive benefit on the person's behalf; or

    (iii)   an attorney with a general power or a power to apply or, as the case may be, receive benefit, has been appointed by that person under the Powers of Attorney Act 1971, the Enduring Powers of Attorney Act 1985 or the Mental Capacity Act 2005 or otherwise;

(c)   a person appointed by the authority under paragraph 1(3).

PART 3
Award or payment of reduction

The award or payment of a reduction under a scheme

10.–(1)   Subject to sub-paragraph (2), where a person is entitled to a reduction under an authority's scheme in respect of that person's liability for council tax as it has effect in respect of a financial year, the authority must discharge that person's entitlement by reducing, so far as possible, the amount of that person's liability to which regulation 20(2) of the Council Tax (Administration and Enforcement) Regulations 1992 refers.

(2)   Where–

(a)   a person is entitled to a reduction under an authority's scheme in respect of that person's liability for the authority's council tax as it has effect in respect of a financial year;

(b)   the person entitled to the reduction is joint and severally liable for the council tax; and

(c)   the authority determines that discharging that person's entitlement by reducing the amount of that person's liability to which regulation 20(2) of the Council Tax (Administration and Enforcement) Regulations 1992 refers would be inappropriate,

it may make a payment to that person of the amount of reduction to which that person is entitled, rounded where necessary to the nearest penny.

(3)   Subject to sub-paragraph (4) any payment made under sub-paragraphs (1) or (2) must be made to the person who is entitled to the reduction.

(4)   Where a person other than the person who is entitled to the reduction under an authority's scheme made the application for the reduction and that first person is a person acting pursuant to an appointment under paragraph 1(3) (persons appointed to act for a person unable to act) or is treated as having been so appointed by virtue of paragraph 1(4), the amount of the reduction may be paid to that person.

SCHEDULE 14

REGULATION 34(3)

Matters to be included in a notification

PART 1

General

1.   The matters to be included in any notification issued by an authority in accordance with paragraph 9 of Schedule 13 (notification of decision) are the matters set out in the following provisions of this Schedule.

2.   Every notification must include a statement as to the right of any person affected by the decision to request a written statement under paragraph 9(5) of Schedule 13 (requests for statement of reasons), and the manner and time in which to do so.

3.   Every notification must include a statement as to the right of any person affected by the decision to appeal against the decision in accordance with paragraphs 8 and 10 of Schedule 12 (procedure by which a person may make an appeal against certain decisions of the authority), and the manner and time in which to do so.

PART 2

Awards of reductions where state pension credit or extended reduction (qualifying contributory benefits) is payable: pensioners

4.–(1)   Where a pensioner who is in receipt of state pension credit is awarded a reduction under an authority's scheme, the notification must include a statement as to–

(a)   the normal weekly amount of council tax the person would be liable to pay before any reduction is awarded under an authority's scheme, rounded to the nearest penny;

(b)   the maximum weekly amount of reduction the person could be entitled to under an authority's scheme, rounded to the nearest penny;

(c)   the normal weekly amount of reduction the authority has determined the person is entitled to under its scheme, rounded to the nearest penny;

(d)   the amount and category of any non-dependant deductions made in accordance with the authority's scheme, if any; and

(e)   the first day that the person is entitled to a reduction under the authority's scheme,

and in any case where the amount to which paragraphs (a) to (c) refers disregards fractions of a penny, the notice must include a statement to that effect.

(2)   In a case where a pensioner who is in receipt of state pension credit has entitlement only to the savings credit, the notification must also set out the following matters–

(a)   the person's applicable amount and the basis of the calculation;

(b)   the amounts of the savings credit taken into account;

(c)   the amount of the person's income and capital as notified to the authority by the Secretary of State and taken into account for the purposes of the determination of the reduction under the authority's scheme;

(d)   any modification made to the person's income or capital (paragraph 8 of Schedule 1 (calculation of pensioner's income in savings credit only cases) refers); and

(e)   the amount of the person's capital in that case.

(3)   Where a pensioner is entitled to an extended reduction (qualifying contributory benefits) (paragraph 32 of Schedule 1 refers), the notification must include a statement as to the matters set out in paragraph 4(1).

PART 3

Awards of reductions where state pension credit not in payment: pensioners
    5.   Where a pensioner who is not in receipt of state pension credit is awarded a reduction under an authority's scheme, the notification must include a statement as to–
(a)   the matters set out in paragraph 4(1);
(b)   the pensioner's applicable amount and how it is calculated;
(c)   the pensioner's weekly earnings; and
(d)   the pensioner's income and other earnings.

PART 4

Notification where no award of a reduction is made: pensioners
    6.   Where a pensioner is not awarded a reduction under an authority's scheme–
(a)   on the ground of income, the notification must include a statement as to–
    (i)   the matters set out in paragraph 4(1)(a), and
    (ii)   the matters set out in paragraph 5(b) to (d) where the pensioner is not on state pension credit;
(b)   for any other reason, the notification must include a statement as to the reason why no award has been made.

PART 5

Awards of reductions where income support, income-based jobseeker's allowance, income related employment and support allowance, an extended reduction or an extended reduction (qualifying contributory benefits) is payable: persons who are not pensioners
    7.–(1)   Where a person who is not a pensioner and who is on income support, an income-based jobseeker's allowance, or an income-related employment and support allowance is awarded a reduction under an authority's scheme, the notification must include a statement as to–
(a)   the normal weekly amount of council tax the person would be liable to pay before any reduction is awarded under an authority's scheme, rounded to the nearest penny;
(b)   the maximum weekly amount of reduction the person could be entitled to under the authority's scheme, rounded to the nearest penny;
(c)   the normal weekly amount of reduction the authority has determined the person is entitled to under its scheme, rounded to the nearest penny;
(d)   the amount and category of any non-dependant deductions made in accordance with the authority's scheme, if any; and
(e)   the first day that the person is entitled to a reduction under the authority's scheme,
and in any case where the amount to which paragraphs (a) to (c) refers disregards fractions of a penny, the notice must include a statement to that effect.
    (2)   Where a person who is not a pensioner is entitled to an extended reduction or an extended reduction (qualifying contributory benefits) in accordance with an authority's scheme, the notification must include a statement as to the matters set out in paragraph 7(1).

PART 6

Awards of reduction where universal credit is payable: persons who are not pensioners
    8.   Where a person who is not a pensioner and who has an award of universal credit is awarded a reduction under an authority's scheme, the notification must include a statement as to–
(a)   the matters set out in paragraph 7(1);
(b)   the person's applicable amount (paragraph 3 of Schedule 6 (applicable amount: persons who are not pensioners who have an award of universal credit) refers); and
(c)   the person's income (paragraph 9 of Schedule 6 (calculation of income and capital; persons who are not pensioners who have an award of universal credit) refers).

PART 7

Awards of reduction where no income support, income-based jobseeker's allowance, income related employment and support allowance or universal credit is payable: persons who are not pensioners
    9.   Where a person who is not a pensioner and who is not on income support, income-based jobseeker's allowance, income-related employment and support allowance or universal credit is awarded a reduction under an authority's scheme, the notification must include a statement as to–
(a)   the matters set out in paragraph 7(1);
(b)   the person's applicable amount and how it is calculated;
(c)   the person's weekly earnings; and
(d)   the person's weekly income other than earnings.

PART 8

Notification where no award of a reduction is made: persons who are not pensioners

10.   Where a person who is not a pensioner is not awarded a reduction under an authority's scheme–

(a)   on the ground of income, the notification must include a statement as to–

     (i)   the matters set out in paragraph 7(1)(a); and

     (ii)   the matters set out in paragraph 8(b) and (c) where the person is not on income support, an income based jobseeker's allowance, an income-related employment and support allowance, or universal credit;

(b)   for any other reason, the notification must include a statement as to the reason why no award has been made.

PART 9

Notification where income of non-dependant is treated as applicant's income: pensioners and persons who are not pensioners

11.   Where an authority makes a decision under its scheme to treat the capital and income of a non-dependant as the applicant's, (paragraph 6 of Schedule 1 and paragraph 8 of Schedule 6 refer), the notification must contain a statement as to–

(a)   the fact that a decision has been made by reference to the income and capital of the applicant's non-dependant, and

(b)   the authority's reason for making that decision.

The Council Tax Reduction Schemes (Default Scheme) (Wales) Regulations 2013
(SI 2013 No.3035)

Title, commencement, application and revocation

1.–(1)   The title of these Regulations is the Council Tax Reduction Schemes (Default Scheme)(Wales) Regulations 2013.

(2)   These Regulations come into force on the day after the day on which they are made.

(3)   These Regulations apply in relation to billing authorities in Wales, and the first financial year to which the scheme set out in the Schedule to these Regulations relates is the year beginning 1 April 2014.

(4)   The Council Tax Reduction Schemes (Default Scheme) (Wales) Regulations 2012 are revoked.

Default scheme

2.   The scheme set out in the Schedule to these Regulations is the scheme prescribed for the purposes of paragraph 6 of Schedule 1B to the Local Government Finance Act 1992.

SCHEDULE

REGULATION 2

Council Tax Reduction Schemes (Default Scheme) (Wales)

PART 1

INTRODUCTION

1.   Title

PART 2

INTERPRETATION

2.   Interpretation
3.   Application of scheme: pensioners and persons who are not pensioners
4.   Meaning of "couple"
5.   Polygamous marriages
6.   Meaning of "family"
7.   Circumstances in which a person is to be treated as responsible or not responsible for another
8.   Households
9.   Non-dependants
10.   Remunerative work

PART 3

PROCEDURAL MATTERS

11.   Procedure for reduction applications and appeals against reduction decisions

PART 4

CLASSES OF PERSON ENTITLED TO A REDUCTION UNDER THIS SCHEME

12.   Classes of person entitled to a reduction under this scheme
13.   Class A: pensioners whose income is less than the applicable amount
14.   Class B: pensioners whose income is greater than the applicable amount
15.   Class C: persons who are not pensioners whose income is less than the applicable amount
16.   Class D: persons who are not pensioners whose income is greater than the applicable amount
17.   Periods of absence from a dwelling

PART 5
CLASSES OF PERSON EXCLUDED FROM THIS SCHEME

18. Classes of person excluded from this scheme
19. Class of person excluded from this scheme: persons treated as not being in Great Britain
20. Class of person excluded from this scheme: persons subject to immigration control
21. Class of person excluded from this scheme: capital limit
22. Class of person excluded from this scheme: students

PART 6
APPLICABLE AMOUNTS FOR THE PURPOSES OF CALCULATING ELIGIBILITY FOR A REDUCTION UNDER THIS SCHEME AND AMOUNT OF REDUCTION

23. Applicable amounts: pensioners (including pensioners in polygamous marriages)
24. Applicable amounts: persons who are not pensioners
25. Polygamous marriages: persons who are not pensioners
26. Applicable amount: persons who are not pensioners who have an award of universal credit

PART 7
MAXIMUM COUNCIL TAX REDUCTION FOR THE PURPOSES OF CALCULATING ELIGIBILITY FOR A REDUCTION UNDER THIS SCHEME AND AMOUNT OF REDUCTION

27. Maximum council tax reduction under this scheme: pensioners and persons who are not pensioners
28. Non-dependant deductions: pensioners and persons who are not pensioners

PART 8
AMOUNT OF REDUCTION UNDER THIS SCHEME

29. Amount of reduction under this scheme: Classes A to D

PART 9
INCOME AND CAPITAL FOR THE PURPOSES OF CALCULATING ELIGIBILITY FOR A REDUCTION UNDER THIS SCHEME AND AMOUNT OF REDUCTION
CHAPTER 1
Income and capital: general

30. Calculation of income and capital: applicant's family and polygamous marriages
31. Circumstances in which capital and income of non-dependant is to be treated as applicant's

CHAPTER 2
Income and capital: pensioners in receipt of guarantee credit or savings credit

32. Pensioners in receipt of guarantee credit
33. Calculation of pensioner's income in savings credit only cases

CHAPTER 3
Income and capital where there is an award of universal credit

34. Calculation of income and capital: persons who are not pensioners who have an award of universal credit

CHAPTER 4
Income: other pensioners

35. Calculation of income and capital where state pension credit is not payable: pensioners
36. Meaning of "income": pensioners
37. Calculation of weekly income: pensioners

38.   Earnings of employed earners: pensioners
39.   Calculation of net earnings of employed earners: pensioners
40.   Calculation of earnings of self-employed earners: pensioners
41.   Earnings of self-employed earners: pensioners
42.   Notional income: pensioners
43.   Income paid to third parties: pensioners

CHAPTER 5
Income: persons who are not pensioners
44.   Average weekly earnings of employed earners: persons who are not pensioners
44A.   Date on which income consisting of earnings from employment as an empoyed earner are taken into account: persons who are not pensioners
45.   Average weekly earnings of self-employed earners: persons who are not pensioners
46.   Average weekly income other than earnings: persons who are not pensioners
47.   Calculation of weekly income of employed earners: persons who are not pensioners
48.   Earnings of employed earners: persons who are not pensioners
49.   Calculation of net earnings of employed earners: persons who are not pensioners
50.   Earnings of self-employed earners: persons who are not pensioners
51.   Calculation of income other than earnings: persons who are not pensioners
52.   Capital treated as income: persons who are not pensioners
53.   Notional income: persons who are not pensioners

CHAPTER 6
Income: pensioners and persons who are not pensioners
54.   Calculation of income on a weekly basis
55.   Treatment of child care charges
56.   Calculation of average weekly income from tax credits
57.   Disregard of changes in tax, contributions etc
58.   Calculation of net profit of self-employed earners
59.   Calculation of deduction of tax and contributions of self-employed earners

CHAPTER 7
Capital
60.   Calculation of capital
61.   Income treated as capital: persons who are not pensioners
62.   Calculation of capital in the United Kingdom
63.   Calculation of capital outside the United Kingdom
64.   Notional capital
65.   Diminishing notional capital rule: pensioners
66.   Diminishing notional capital rule: persons who are not pensioners
67.   Capital jointly held
68.   Calculation of tariff income from capital: pensioners
69.   Calculation of tariff income from capital: persons who are not pensioners

PART 10
STUDENTS
CHAPTER 1
General
70.   Interpretation
71.   Treatment of students
72.   Students who are excluded from entitlement to a council tax reduction under this scheme

CHAPTER 2
Income
73. Calculation of grant income
74. Calculation of covenant income where a contribution is assessed
75. Covenant income where no grant income or no contribution is assessed
76. Relationship with amounts to be disregarded under Schedule 7
77. Other amounts to be disregarded
78. Treatment of student loans
79. Treatment of fee loans
80. Treatment of payments from access funds
81. Disregard of contribution
82. Further disregard of student's income
83. Income treated as capital
84. Disregard of changes occurring during summer vacation

PART 11
EXTENDED REDUCTIONS
85. Extended reductions: pensioners
86. Extended reductions (qualifying contributory benefits): pensioners
87. Duration of extended reduction period (qualifying contributory benefits): pensioners
88. Amount of extended reduction (qualifying contributory benefits): pensioners
89. Extended reductions (qualifying contributory benefits)-movers: pensioners
90. Relationship between extended reduction (qualifying contributory benefits) and entitlement to a reduction by virtue of falling within class A or B
91. Continuing reductions where state pension credit claimed: pensioners
92. Extended reductions: persons who are not pensioners (general)
93. Extended reductions: persons who are not pensioners
94. Duration of extended reduction period: persons who are not pensioners
95. Amount of extended reduction: persons who are not pensioners
96. Extended reductions-movers: persons who are not pensioners
97. Relationship between extended reduction and entitlement to reduction by virtue of falling within class C or D
98. Extended reductions (qualifying contributory benefits): persons who are not pensioners
99. Duration of extended reduction period (qualifying contributory benefits): persons who are not pensioners
100. Amount of extended reduction (qualifying contributory benefits): persons who are not pensioners
101. Extended reductions (qualifying contributory benefits)-movers: persons who are not pensioners
102. Relationship between extended reduction (qualifying contributory benefits) and entitlement to reduction by virtue of falling within class C or D
103. Extended reductions: movers into the authority's area: persons who are not pensioners

PART 12
PERIOD OF ENTITLEMENT AND CHANGE OF CIRCUMSTANCES
104. Date on which entitlement begins
105. Date on which change of circumstances is to take effect
106. Change of circumstances where state pension credit in payment

PART 13
APPLICATIONS
107. Who may make an application
108. Date on which an application is made
109. Back-dating of applications: pensioners

110.   Back-dating of applications: persons who are not pensioners
111.   Evidence and information
112.   Amendment and withdrawal of application
113.   Duty to notify changes of circumstances

PART 14
DECISIONS BY AUTHORITY
114.   Decision by authority
115.   Notification of decision

PART 15
AWARD OR PAYMENT OF REDUCTION
116.   The award or payment of a reduction under this scheme

SCHEDULES
1   Procedural matters
2   Applicable amounts: pensioners
3   Applicable amounts: persons who are not pensioners
4   Sums disregarded from applicant's earnings: pensioners
5   Amounts to be disregarded in the calculation of income other than earnings: pensioners
6   Sums disregarded in the calculation of earnings: persons who are not pensioners
7   Sums disregarded in the calculation of income other than earnings: persons who are not pensioners
8   Capital disregards: pensioners
9   Capital disregards: persons who are not pensioners
10   Matters to be included in the notification

PART 1
Introduction

Title
1.   The title of this scheme is the Council Tax Reduction Schemes (Default Scheme) (Wales).

PART 2
Interpretation

Interpretation
2.–(1)   In this scheme–
"the 1992 Act" ("Deddf 1992") means the Local Government Finance Act 1992;
"Abbeyfield Home" ("Cartref Abbeyfield") means an establishment run by the Abbeyfield Society including all bodies corporate or unincorporated which are affiliated to that society;
"adoption leave" ("absenoldeb mabwysiadu") means a period of absence from work on ordinary or additional adoption leave by virtue of section 75A or 75B of the Employment Rights Act 1996;
"AFIP" ("TALIA") means an armed forces independence payment payable in accordance with an armed and reserve forces compensation scheme established under section 1(2) of the Armed Forces (Pensions and Compensation) Act 2004;
"applicable amount" ("swm cymwysadwy") means–
   (a)   in relation to a pensioner, the amount calculated in accordance with paragraph 23 and Schedule 2; and
   (b)   in relation to a person who is not a pensioner, the amount calculated in accordance with–
          (i)   paragraph 24 and Schedule 3; or
          (ii)   paragraph 26,
as the case may be;
"applicant" ("ceisydd") means a person applying for a reduction under this scheme;
"application" ("cais") means an application for a reduction under this scheme;
[⁵ "approved blood scheme" ("cynllun gwaed cymeradwy") means–
   (a)   a scheme established or approved by the Secretary of State, or a trust established with funds provided by the Secretary of State, for the purpose of providing compensation in respect of a person having been infected from contaminated blood products; or

    (b)   a scheme established under sections 1 to 3 of the National Health Service (Wales) Act 2006 and administered by Velindre Trust for the purpose of making payments and providing support to, or in respect of, individuals infected with Hepatitis C, HIV or both, through contaminated blood or blood products used by the NHS;]

"assessment period" ("cyfnod asesu") means–
    (a)   in relation to pensioners–
        (i)   in relation to the earnings of a self-employed earner, the period determined in accordance with paragraph 40 of this scheme for the purpose of calculating the weekly earnings of the applicant; or
        (ii)   in relation to any other income, the period determined in accordance with paragraph 37 of this scheme for the purpose of calculating the weekly income of the applicant;
    (b)   in relation to persons who are not pensioners, such period as is set out in paragraphs 44 to 46 of this scheme over which income falls to be calculated;

"attendance allowance" ("lwfans gweini") means–
    (a)   an attendance allowance under Part 3 of the SSCBA;
    (b)   an increase of disablement pension under section 104 or 105 of the SSCBA;
    (c)   a payment by virtue of article 14, 15, 16, 43 or 44 of the Personal Injuries (Civilians) Scheme 1983 or any analogous payment; or
    (d)   any payment based on need for attendance which is paid as part of a war disablement pension;

"the authority" ("yr awdurdod") means a billing authority in relation to whose area this scheme has effect;

"basic rate" ("cyfradd sylfaenol") has the meaning given by the Income Tax Act 2007;

"the benefit Acts" ("y Deddfau budd-dal") means the SSCBA, the Jobseekers Act 1995, the State Pension Credit Act 2002 [⁴,] the Welfare Reform Act 2007 [⁴ and the Pensions Act 2014];

"board and lodging accommodation" ("prydau bwyd a llety") means accommodation provided to a person, or if that person is a member of a family, to that person or any other member of that person's family, for a charge which is inclusive of the provision of that accommodation and at least some cooked or prepared meals which both are cooked or prepared (by a person other than the person to whom the accommodation is provided or a member of that person's family) and are consumed in that accommodation or associated premises;

[⁵ "care home" ("cartref gofal")–
    (a)   in England has the meaning given by section 3 of the Care Standards Act 2000;
    (b)   in Wales means a place at which a care home service, within the meaning of Part 1 of the Regulation and Inspection of Social Care (Wales) Act 2016, is provided wholly or mainly to adults;
    (c)   in Scotland means a care home service within the meaning given by paragraph 2 of Schedule 12 to the Public Services Reform (Scotland) Act 2010; and
    (d)   in Northern Ireland means a nursing home within the meaning of article 11 of the Health and Personal Social Services (Quality, Improvement and Regulation) (Northern Ireland) Order 2003 or a residential care home within the meaning of article 10 of that Order;]

"the Caxton Foundation" ("sefydliad Caxton") means the charitable trust of that name established on 28 March 2011 out of funds provided by the Secretary of State for the benefit of certain persons suffering from hepatitis C and other persons eligible for payment in accordance with its provisions;

"child" ("plentyn") means a person under the age of 16;

"child benefit" ("budd-dal plant") has the meaning given by section 141 of the SSCBA;

"child tax credit" ("credyd treth plant") means a child tax credit under section 8 of the Tax Credits Act 2002;

"close relative" ("perthynas agos") means a parent, parent-in-law, son, son-in-law, daughter,daughter-in-law, step-parent, step-son, step-daughter, brother, sister, or if any of the preceding persons is one member of a couple, the other member of that couple;

"concessionary payment" ("taliad consesiynol") means a payment made under arrangements made by the Secretary of State with the consent of the Treasury which is charged either to the National Insurance Fund or to a Departmental Expenditure Vote to which payments of benefit or tax credits under the benefit Acts or the Tax Credits Act 2002 are charged;

[² "contributory employment and support allowance" ("lwfans cyflogaeth a chymorth cyfrannol") means an allowance under Part 1 of the Welfare Reform Act 2007 as amended by the provisions of Schedule 3 and Part 1 of Schedule 14, to the Welfare Reform Act 2012 that remove references to an income-related allowance, and a contributory allowance under Part 1 of the Welfare Reform Act 2007 as that Part has effect apart from those provisions;]

"council tax benefit" ("budd-dal treth gyngor") means council tax benefit under Part 7 of the SSCBA;

"couple" ("cwpl") has the meaning given by paragraph 4 of this scheme;

"designated office" ("swyddfa ddynodedig") means the office of the authority designated by it for the receipt of applications–
    (a)   by notice upon or with a form supplied by the authority for the purposes of making anapplication; or
    (b)   by reference upon or with such a form to some other document available from it and sent by electronic means or otherwise on application and without charge; or
    (c)   by any combination of the provisions set out in paragraphs (a) and (b);

"disability living allowance" ("lwfans byw anabl") means a disability living allowance under section 71 of the SSCBA;

"dwelling" ("annedd") has the meaning given by section 3 of the 1992 Act;

"earnings" ("enillion") has the meaning given by paragraph 38, 40, 41, 48 or 50 of this scheme as the case may be;

"the Eileen Trust" ("Ymddiriedolaeth Eileen") means the charitable trust of that name established on 29 March 1993 out of funds provided by the Secretary of State for the benefit of persons eligible for payment in accordance with its provisions;

"electronic communication" ("cyfathrebiad electronig") has the same meaning as in section 15(1) of the Electronic Communications Act 2000;

"employed earner" ("enillydd cyflogedig") is to be construed in accordance with section 2(1)(a) of the SSCBA and also includes a person who is in receipt of a payment which is payable under any enactment having effect in Northern Ireland and which corresponds to statutory sick pay or statutory maternity pay;

"the Employment, Skills and Enterprise Scheme" ("y Cynllun Cyflogaeth, Sgiliau a Menter") means a scheme under section 17A (schemes for assisting persons to obtain employment: "work for your benefit" schemes etc.) of the Jobseekers Act 1995 known by that name and provided pursuant to arrangements made by the Secretary of State that is designed to assist claimants for job-seekers allowance to obtain employment, including self-employment, and which may include for any individual work-related activity (including work experience or jobsearch);

"employment zone" ("parth cyflogaeth") means an area within Great Britain designated for the purposes of section 60 of the Welfare Reform and Pensions Act 1999 and an "employment zone programme" ("rhaglen parth cyflogaeth") means a programme established for such an area or areas designed to assist claimants for a jobseeker's allowance to obtain sustainable employment;

"employment zone contractor" ("contractwr parth cyflogaeth") means a person who is undertaking the provision of facilities in respect of an employment zone programme on behalf of the Secretary of State for Work and Pensions;

"enactment" ("deddfiad") includes an enactment comprised in, or in an instrument made under, an Act of the Scottish Parliament or an Act or Measure of the National Assembly for Wales;

"extended reduction" ("gostyngiad estynedig") means a reduction under this scheme for which a person is eligible under Part 11 of this scheme;

"extended reduction period" ("cyfnod gostyngiad estynedig") means the period for which a person is in receipt of an extended reduction in accordance with paragraph 87, 94 or 99 of this scheme;

"extended reduction (qualifying contributory benefits)" ("gostyngedig estynedig (budd-daliadau cyfrannol cymwys)") means a reduction under this scheme for which a person is eligible pursuant to paragraph 86 or 98 of this scheme;

"family" ("teulu") has the meaning given by paragraph 6 of this scheme;

"the Fund" ("y Gronfa") means moneys made available from time to time by the Secretary of State for the benefit of persons eligible for payment in accordance with the provisions of a scheme established by the Secretary of State on 24 April 1992 or, in Scotland, on 10 April 1992;

"guarantee credit" ("credyd gwarant") is to be construed in accordance with sections 1 and 2 of the State Pension Credit Act 2002;

"a guaranteed income payment" ("taliad incwm gwarantedig") means a payment made under article 15(1)(c) or article 29(1)(a) of the Armed Forces and Reserve Forces (Compensation Scheme) Order 2011;

"housing benefit" ("budd-dal tai") means housing benefit under Part 7 of the SSCBA;

"an income-based jobseeker's allowance" ("lwfans ceisio gwaith ar sail incwm") and "a joint-claim jobseeker's allowance" ("lwfans ceisio gwaith cyd-hawliad") have the meanings given by section 1(4) of the Jobseekers Act 1995;

"income-related employment and support allowance" ("lwfans cyflogaeth a chymorth ar sail incwm") means an income-related allowance under Part 1 of the Welfare Reform Act 2007;

"independent hospital" ("ysbyty annibynnol")–

(a)   in England means a hospital as defined by section 275 of the National Health Service Act 2006 that is not a health service hospital as defined by that section;

(b)   in Wales has the meaning given by section 2 of the Care Standards Act 2000; and

[¹ (c)   in Scotland means an independent hospital or a private psychiatric hospital as defined by section 10F(2) of the National Health Service (Scotland) Act 1978;]

"the Independent Living Fund (2006)" ("y Gronfa Byw'n Annibynnol (2006)") means the Trust of that name established by a deed dated 10 April 2006 and made between the Secretary of State for Work and Pensions of the one part and Margaret Rosemary Cooper, Michael Beresford Boyall and Marie Theresa Martin of the other part;

"invalid carriage or other vehicle" ("cerbyd ar gyfer pobl anabl neu fath arall o gerbyd") means a vehicle propelled by a petrol engine or by electric power supplied for use on the road and to be controlled by the occupant;

"the London Bombings Relief Charitable Fund" ("Cronfa Gymorth Elusennol Bomiau Llundain") means the company limited by guarantee (number 5505072), and registered charity of that name established on 11 July 2005 for the purpose of (amongst other things) relieving sickness, disability or financial need of victims (including families or dependants of victims) of the terrorist attacks carried out in London on 7 July 2005;

[⁵ "the London Emergencies Trust" ("Ymddiriedolaeth Argyfyngau Llundain") means the company of that name (number 09928465) incorporated on 23 December 2015 and the registered charity of that name (number 1172307) established on 28 March 2017;]

"lone parent" ("unig riant") means a person who has no partner and who is responsible for and a member of the same household as a child or young person;

"the Macfarlane (Special Payments) Trust" ("Ymddiriedolaeth Macfarlane (Taliadau Arbennig)") means the trust of that name, established on 29 January 1990 partly out of funds provided by the Secretary of State, for the benefit of certain persons suffering from haemophilia;

"the Macfarlane (Special Payments) (No.2) Trust" ("Ymddiriedolaeth Macfarlane (Taliadau Arbennig) (Rhif 2)") means the trust of that name, established on 3 May 1991 partly out of funds provided by the Secretary of State, for the benefit of certain persons suffering from haemophilia and other beneficiaries;

"the Macfarlane Trust" ("Ymddiriedolaeth Macfarlane") means the charitable trust, established partly out of funds provided by the Secretary of State to the Haemophilia Society, for the relief of poverty or distress among those suffering from haemophilia;

[⁵ "main phase employment and support allowance" ("lwfans cyflogaeth a chymorth prif wedd"), except in Part 1 of Schedule 3, means an employment and support allowance where–
- (a) the calculation of the amount payable in respect of the applicant includes a component under section 2(1)(b) or 4(2)(b) of the Welfare Reform Act 2007; or
- (b) the applicant is a member of the work-related activity group;]

"maternity leave" ("cyfnod mamolaeth") means a period during which a woman is absent from work because the woman is pregnant or has given birth to a child, and at the end of which the woman has a right to return to work either under the terms of the woman's contract of employment or under Part 8 of the Employment Rights Act 1996;

"maximum council tax reduction amount" ("uchafswm gostyngiad treth gyngor") means the amount determined in accordance with paragraph 27 of this scheme;

"member of a couple" ("aelod o gwpl") means a member of a married or unmarried couple;

[⁵ "member of the work-related activity group" ("aelod o'r grwp gweithgaredd perthynol i waith") means a person who has or is treated as having limited capability for work under either–
- (a) Part 5 of the Employment and Support Allowance Regulations 2008 other than by virtue of regulation 30 of those Regulations; or
- (b) Part 4 of the Employment and Support Allowance Regulations 2013 other than by virtue of regulation 26 of those Regulations;]

"MFET Limited" ("MFET Limited") means the company limited by guarantee (number 7121661) of that name, established for the purpose in particular of making payments in accordance with arrangements made with the Secretary of State to persons who have acquired HIV as a result of treatment by the NHS with blood or blood products;

"mobility supplement" ("atodiad symudedd") means–
- (a) in relation to pensioners, a supplement to which paragraph 5(1)(a)(vii) of Schedule 4 to this scheme refers;
- (b) in relation to persons who are not pensioners, a supplement to which paragraph 13 of Schedule 7 refers;

"mover" ("symudwr") means an applicant who changes the dwelling in which the applicant is resident, and in respect of which the applicant is liable to pay council tax, from a dwelling in the area of the authority to a dwelling in the area of a second authority;

"net earnings" ("enillion net") means such earnings as are calculated in accordance with paragraph 39 or 49 of this scheme, as the case may be;

"net profit" ("elw net") means such profit as is calculated in accordance with paragraph 58 of this scheme;

"new dwelling" ("annedd newydd") means, for the purposes of the definition of "second authority" and paragraphs 89, 96 and 101 of this scheme, the dwelling to which an applicant has moved, or is about to move, in which the applicant will be resident;

"non-dependant" ("annibynnydd") has the meaning given by paragraph 9 of this scheme;

"occasional assistance" ("cymorth achlysurol") means any payment or provision made by a local authority, the Welsh Ministers or the Scottish Ministers for the purposes of–
- (a) meeting, or helping to meet an immediate short-term need–
  - (i) arising out of an exceptional event or exceptional circumstance, or
  - (ii) that needs to be met to avoid a risk to the well-being of an individual, and
- (b) enabling qualifying individuals to establish or maintain a settled home, and–
  - (i) "local authority" ("awdurdod lleol") has the meaning given by section 270(1) of the Local Government Act 1972; and
  - (ii) "qualifying individuals" ("unigolion cymwys") means individuals who have been, or without the assistance might otherwise be–
    - (aa) in prison, hospital, an establishment providing residential care or other institution, or
    - (bb) homeless or otherwise living an unsettled way of life;

"occupational pension" ("pensiwn galwedigaethol") means any pension or other periodical payment under an occupational pension scheme but does not include any discretionary payment out of a fund established for relieving hardship in particular cases;

"occupational pension scheme" ("cynllun pensiwn galwedigaethol") has the same meaning as in section 1 of the Pension Schemes Act 1993;

"ordinary clothing and footwear" ("dillad ac esgidiau cyffredin") means clothing or footwear for normal daily use, but does not include school uniforms, or clothing or footwear used solely for sporting activities;

"partner" ("partner"), in relation to a person, means–

(a)   where that person is a member of a couple, the other member of that couple;

(b)   subject to paragraph (c), where that person is polygamously married to two or more members of that person's household, any such member to whom that person is married; or

(c)   where that person is polygamously married and has an award of universal credit with the other party to the earliest marriage that still subsists, that other party to the earliest marriage;

"paternity leave" ("absenoldeb tadolaeth") means a period of absence from work on [²] leave by virtue of section 80A or 80B of the Employment Rights Act 1996 or on additional paternity leave by virtue of section 80AA or 80BB of that Act;

"pension fund holder" ("deiliad cronfa bensiwn") means with respect to a personal pension scheme or an occupational pension scheme, the trustees, managers or scheme administrators, as the case may be, of the scheme concerned;

"pensionable age" ("oedran pensiynadwy") has the meaning given by the rules in paragraph 1 of Schedule 4 to the Pensions Act 1995;

"pensioner" ("pensiynwr") has the meaning given by paragraph 3(2)(a) of this scheme;

"person on income support" ("person ar gymhorthdal incwm") means a person in receipt of income support;

"person who is not a pensioner" ("person nad yw'n bensiynwr") has the meaning given by paragraph 3(2)(b) of this scheme;

"persons treated as not being in Great Britain" ("personal a drinnir fel pe na baent ym Mhrydain Fawr") has the meaning given by paragraph 19 of this scheme;

"personal independence payment" ("taliad annibyniaeth bersonol") has the meaning given by Part 4 of the Welfare Reform Act 2012;

"personal pension scheme" ("cynllun pensiwn personol") means–

(a)   a personal pension scheme as defined by section 1 of the Pension Schemes Act 1993;

(b)   an annuity contract or trust scheme approved under section 620 or 621 of the Income and Corporation Taxes Act 1988 or a substituted contract within the meaning of section 622(3) of that Act which is treated as having become a registered pension scheme by virtue of paragraph 1 of Schedule 36 to the Finance Act 2004;

(c)   a personal pension scheme approved under Chapter 4 of Part 14 of the Income and Corporation Taxes Act 1988 which is treated as having become a registered pension scheme by virtue of paragraph 1 of Schedule 36 to the Finance Act 2004;

"policy of life insurance" ("polisi yswiriant bywyd") means any instrument by which the payment of money is assured on death (except death by accident only) or the happening of any contingency dependent on human life, or any instrument evidencing a contract which is subject to payment of premiums for a term dependent on human life;

"polygamous marriage" ("priodas amlbriod") means any marriage to which paragraph 5 of this scheme applies;

"public authority" ("awdurdod cyhoeddus") includes any person whose functions are of a public nature;

"qualifying age for state pension credit" ("oedran cymhwyso ar gyfer credyd pensiwn y wladwriaeth") means (in accordance with section 1(2)(b) and (6) of the State Pension Credit Act 2002)–

(a)   in the case of a woman, pensionable age; or

(b)   in the case of a man, the age which is pensionable age in the case of a woman born on the same day as the man;

"qualifying contributory benefit" ("budd-dal cyfrannol cymwys") means–

(a)   severe disablement allowance;

(b)   incapacity benefit;

(c)   contributory employment and support allowance;

"qualifying income-related benefit" ("budd-dal cymwys ar sail incwm") means–

(a)   income support;

(b)   income-based jobseeker's allowance;

(c)   income-related employment and support allowance;

"qualifying person" ("person cymwys") means a person in respect of whom payment has been made from the Fund, the Eileen Trust, MFET Limited, the Skipton Fund, the Caxton Foundation [⁵, an approved blood scheme, the Scottish Infected Blood Support Scheme, the London Emergencies Trust, the We Love Manchester Emergency Fund] or the London Bombings Relief Charitable Fund;

"reduction week" ("wythnos ostyngiad") means a period of seven consecutive days beginning with a Monday and ending with a Sunday;

"relative" ("perthynas") means a close relative, grandparent, grandchild, uncle, aunt, nephew or niece;

"relevant week" ("wythnos berthnasol"), in relation to any particular day, means the week within which the day in question falls;

"remunerative work" ("gwaith am dâl") has the meaning given by paragraph 10 of this scheme;

"rent" ("rhent") means "eligible rent" to which [¹ regulation 12B] of the Housing Benefit (Persons who have acquired the qualifying age for state pension credit) Regulations 2006 refers, less any deductions in respect of non-dependants which fall to be made under paragraph 28 (non-dependant deductions) of this scheme;

"resident" ("preswylydd") has the meaning given by Part 1 of the 1992 Act;

"savings credit" ("credyd cynilion") is to be construed in accordance with sections 1 and 3 of the State Pension Credit Act 2002;

[⁵ "the Scottish Infected Blood Support Scheme" ("Cynllun Cymorth Gwaed Heintiedig yr Alban") means the scheme of that name administered by the Common Services Agency (constituted by section 10 of the National Health Service (Scotland) Act 1978;]

"second authority" ("ail awdurdod") means the authority to which a mover is liable to make payments for the new dwelling;

"self-employed earner" ("enillydd hunangyflogaeth") is to be construed in accordance with section 2(1)(b) of the SSCBA;

"self-employment route" ("llwybr hunangyflogaeth") means assistance in pursuing self-employed earner's employment whilst participating in–

(a)   an employment zone programme;

(b)   a programme provided by or under arrangements made pursuant to section 2 of the Employment and Training Act 1973 (functions of the Secretary of State) or section 2 of the Enterprise and New Towns (Scotland) Act 1990 (functions in relation to training for employment, etc); or

(c)   the Employment, Skills and Enterprise Scheme;

"service user group" ("grwp defnyddwyr gwasanaeth") means a group of individuals that is consulted by or on behalf of–

(a)   a Health Board, Special Health Board or the Common Services Agency for Scottish Health in consequence of a function under section 2B of the National Health Service (Scotland) Act 1978;

(b)   a landlord authority in consequence of a function under section 105 of the Housing Act 1985;

(c)   a public authority in Northern Ireland in consequence of a function under section 49A of the Disability Discrimination Act 1995;

(d)   a public authority in consequence of a function under section 149 of the Equality Act 2010 (public authority general duty);

(e)   a best value authority in consequence of a function under section 3 of the Local Government Act 1999;

(f)   a Welsh improvement authority in consequence of a function under section 5 of the Local Government (Wales) Measure 2009;

(g)   a local authority landlord or registered social landlord in consequence of a function under section 53 of the Housing (Scotland) Act 2001;

(h)   a relevant English body or a relevant Welsh body in consequence of a function under section 242 of the National Health Service Act 2006;

(i)   a Local Health Board in consequence of a function under section 183 of the National Health Service (Wales) Act 2006;

(j)   the Care Quality Commission in exercise of a function under sections 4 or 5 of the Health and Social Care Act 2008;

(k)   the regulator or a private registered provider of social housing in consequence of a function under sections 98, 193 or 196 of the Housing and Regeneration Act 2008; or

(l)   a public or local authority in Great Britain in consequence of a function conferred under any other enactment,

for the purposes of monitoring and advising on a policy of that body or authority which affects or may affect persons in the group, or of monitoring or advising on services provided by that body or authority which are used (or may potentially be used) by those persons;

[² "shared parental leave" ("absenoldeb rhiant a rennir") means leave by virtue of section 75E or 75G of the Employment Rights Act 1996;]

"single applicant" ("ceisydd sengl") means an applicant who neither has a partner nor is a lone parent;

"the Skipton Fund" ("Cronfa Skipton") means the ex-gratia payment scheme administered by the Skipton Fund Limited, incorporated on 25 March 2004, for the benefit of certain persons suffering from hepatitis C and other persons eligible for payment in accordance with the scheme's provisions;

"sports award" ("dyfarniad chwaraeon") means an award made by one of the Sports Councils named in section 23(2) of the National Lottery etc Act 1993 out of sums allocated to it for distribution under that section;

"the SSCBA" ("DCBNC") means the Social Security Contributions and Benefits Act 1992;

"state pension credit" ("credyd pensiwn y wladwriaeth") means state pension credit under the State Pension Credit Act 2002;

"student" ("myfyriwr") has the meaning given by paragraph 70 of this scheme;

"subsistence allowance" ("lwfans cynhaliaeth") means an allowance which an employment zone contractor has agreed to pay to a person who is participating in an employment zone programme;

"tax year" ("blwyddyn dreth") means a period beginning with 6 April in one year and ending with 5 April in the next;

"training allowance" ("lwfans hyfforddi") means an allowance (whether by way of periodical grants or otherwise) payable–

(a) out of public funds by a Government department or by or on behalf of the Secretary of State, Skills Development Scotland, Scottish Enterprise or Highlands and Islands Enterprise [³] or the Welsh Ministers;

(b) to a person for that person's maintenance or in respect of a member of that person's family; and

(c) for the period, or part of the period, during which that person is following a course of training or instruction provided by, or in pursuance of arrangements made with, that department or approved by that department in relation to that person or so provided or approved by or on behalf of the Secretary of State, Skills Development Scotland, Scottish Enterprise or Highlands and Islands Enterprise or the Welsh Ministers,

but it does not include an allowance paid by any Government department to or in respect of a person by reason of the fact that that person is following a course of full-time education, other than under arrangements made under section 2 of the Employment and Training Act 1973 or is training as a teacher;

"the Trusts" ("yr Ymddiriedolaethau") means the Macfarlane Trust, the Macfarlane (Special Payments) Trust and the Macfarlane (Special Payments) (No 2) Trust;

"universal credit" ("credyd cynhwysol") has the meaning given by section 1 of the Welfare Reform Act 2012;

"voluntary organisation" ("sefydliad gwirfoddol") means a body, other than a public or local authority, the activities of which are carried on otherwise than for profit;

"war disablement pension" ("pensiwn anabledd rhyfel") means any retired pay or pension or allowance payable in respect of disablement under an instrument specified in section 639(2) of the Income Tax (Earnings and Pensions) Act 2003;

"war pension" ("pensiwn rhyfel") means a war disablement pension, a war widow's pension or a war widower's pension;

"war widow's pension" ("pensiwn rhyfel gwraig weddw") means any pension or allowance payable to a woman as a widow under an instrument specified in section 639(2) of the Income Tax (Earnings and Pensions) Act 2003 in respect of the death or disablement of any person;

"war widower's pension" ("pensiwn rhyfel gwr gweddw") means any pension or allowance payable to a man as a widower or to a surviving civil partner under an instrument specified in section 639(2) of the Income Tax (Earnings and Pensions) Act 2003 in respect of the death or disablement of any person;

"water charges" ("taliadau dwr") means–

(a) as respects England and Wales, any water and sewerage charges under Chapter 1 of Part 5 of the Water Industry Act 1991;

(b) as respects Scotland, any water and sewerage charges established by Scottish Water under a charges scheme made under section 29A of the Water Industry (Scotland) Act 2002,

in so far as such charges are in respect of the dwelling which a person occupies as that person's home;

[⁵ "the We Love Manchester Emergency Fund" ("Cronfa Argyfwng We Love Manchester") means the registered charity of that name (number 1173260) established on 30 May 2017;]

"working tax credit" ("credyd treth gwaith") means a working tax credit under section 10 of the Tax Credits Act 2002;

"young person" ("person ifanc") means a person who falls within the definition of qualifying young person in section 142 of the SSCBA.

(2) In this scheme, where an amount is to be rounded to the nearest penny, a fraction of a penny must be disregarded if it is less than half a penny and must otherwise be treated as a whole penny.

(3) For the purpose of this scheme, a person is on an income-based jobseeker's allowance on any day in respect of which an income-based jobseeker's allowance is payable to that person and on any day–

(a) in respect of which that person satisfies the conditions for entitlement to an income-based jobseeker's allowance but where the allowance is not paid because of a reduction in accordance with section 19 or 19A or regulations made under section 17A or 19B of the Jobseekers Act 1995 (circumstances in which a jobseeker's allowance is not payable);

(b) which is a waiting day for the purposes of paragraph 4 of Schedule 1 to that Act and which falls immediately before a day in respect of which an income-based jobseeker's allowance is payable to that person or would be payable to that person but for section 19 or 19A or regulations made under section 17A or 19B of that Act; or

(c) in respect of which an income-based jobseeker's allowance would be payable but for a restriction imposed pursuant to section 6B, 7, 8 or 9 of the Social Security Fraud Act 2001 (loss of benefit provisions).

(4) For the purposes of this scheme, a person is on an income-related employment and support allowance on any day in respect of which an income-related employment and support allowance is payable to that person and on any day–

(a) in respect of which that person satisfies the conditions for entitlement to an income-related employment and support allowance but where the allowance is not paid in accordance with section 18 of the Welfare Reform Act 2007 (disqualification); or

(b) which is a waiting day for the purposes of paragraph 2 of Schedule 2 to that Act (employment and support allowance: supplementary provisions) and which falls immediately before a day in respect of which an income-related employment and support allowance is payable to that person or would be payable to that person but for section 18of that Act.

(5) For the purposes of this scheme, two persons must be taken to be estranged only if their estrangement constitutes a breakdown of the relationship between them.

(6)   In this scheme, references to any person in receipt of state pension credit include a person who would be in receipt of state pension credit but for regulation 13 of the State Pension Credit Regulations 2002 (small amounts of state pension credit).

Amendments

1.   Amended by reg 14 of SI 2014 No 66 (W.6) as from 15.1.14.
2.   Amended by reg 15 of SI 2015 No 44 (W.3) as from 21.1.15, for schemes made for a financial year starting on or after 1.4.15.
3.   Amended by art 2 and Sch 3 para 31(2) of SI 2015 No 971 as from 26.5.15.
4.   Amended by reg 16 of SI 2016 No 50 (W.21) as from 20.1.16, for schemes made for a financial year starting on or after 1.4.16.
5.   Amended by reg 16 of SI 2018 No 14 (W.7) as from 10.1.18, for schemes made for a financial year starting on or after 1.4.18.

Application of scheme: pensioners and persons who are not pensioners
3.–(1)   This scheme applies to–
(a)   pensioners who fall within class A or B; and
(b)   persons who are not pensioners who fall within class C or D.
(2)   In this scheme–
(a)   a person is a "pensioner" ("pensiynwr") if–
          (i)   that person has attained the qualifying age for state pension credit; and
          (ii)   that person is not, and, if that person has a partner, that person's partner is not–
                    (aa)   a person on income support, on an income-based jobseeker's allowance or on an income-related employment and support allowance, or
                    (bb)   a person with an award of universal credit; and
(b)   a person is a "person who is not a pensioner" ("person nad yw'n bensiynwr") if–
          (i)   that person has not attained the qualifying age for state pension credit; or
          (ii)   that person has attained the qualifying age for state pension credit and that person, or if that person has a partner, that person's partner, is–
                    (aa)   a person on income support, on an income-based jobseeker's allowance or on an income-related employment and support allowance, or
                    (bb)   a person with an award of universal credit.

Meaning of "couple"
4.   In this scheme "couple" ("cwpl") means–
(a)   two people who are either married to, or civil partners of, each other and who are members of the same household;
(b)   two people who are living together as if they are a married couple.

Polygamous marriages
5.–(1)   This paragraph applies to any case where–
(a)   a person is a husband or wife by virtue of a marriage entered into under a law which permits polygamy; and
(b)   either party to the marriage has for the time being any spouse additional to the other party.
(2)   For the purposes of paragraph 4 (meaning of "couple") neither party to the marriage is to be taken to be a member of a couple.

Meaning of "family"
6.–(1)   In this scheme "family" ("teulu") means–
(a)   a couple;
(b)   a couple and a member of the same household for whom one of them is or both are responsible and who is a child or a young person; or
(c)   a person who is not a member of a couple and a member of the same household for whom that person is responsible and who is a child or a young person.
(2)   The references to a child or young person in sub-paragraph (1)(b) and (c) include a child or young person in respect of whom section 145A of the SSCBA applies for the purposes of entitlement to child benefit, but only for the period prescribed under section 145A(1).
(3)   The references to a young person in sub-paragraph (1)(b) and (c) do not include a young person who is–
(a)   on income support, an income-based jobseeker's allowance or an income-related employment and support allowance or has an award of universal credit; or
(b)   a person to whom section 6 of the Children (Leaving Care) Act 2000 (exclusion from benefits) applies.

Circumstances in which a person is to be treated as responsible or not responsible for another

7.–(1)   A person is to be treated as responsible for a child or young person who is normally living with that person, including a child or young person to whom paragraph 6(2) applies.

(2)   Where a child or young person spends equal amounts of time in different households, or where there is a question as to which household the child or young person is living in, the child or young person must be treated for the purposes of sub-paragraph (1) as normally living with–

(a)   the person who is receiving child benefit in respect of that child or young person, or

(b)   if there is no such person–

(i)   where only one claim for child benefit has been made in respect of that child or young person, the person who made that claim; or

(ii)   in any other case the person who has the primary responsibility for that child or young person.

(3)   For the purposes of this scheme a child or young person is the responsibility of only one person in any reduction week and any person other than the one treated as responsible for the child or young person under this paragraph is to be treated as not so responsible.

Households

8.–(1)   Subject to sub-paragraphs (2) and (3), an applicant and any partner and, where the applicant or the applicant's partner is treated (by virtue of paragraph 7) as responsible for a child or young person, that child or young person and any child of that child or young person, are to be treated as members of the same household notwithstanding that any of them is temporarily absent from that household.

(2)   A child or young person is not be treated as a member of the applicant's household where that child or young person is–

(a)   placed with the applicant or the applicant's partner by a local authority under section 22C or 23(2)(a) of the Children Act 1989 or by a voluntary organisation under section 59(1)(a) of that Act, or in Scotland boarded out [¹ or placed] with the applicant or the applicant's partner under a relevant enactment; or

[² (aa)   placed with the applicant or the applicant's partner under section 81 of the Social Services and Well-being (Wales) Act 2014; or]

(b)   placed, or in Scotland boarded out, with the applicant or the applicant's partner prior to adoption; or

(c)   placed for adoption with the applicant or the applicant's partner in accordance with the Adoption and Children Act 2002, or the Adoption Agencies (Scotland) Regulations 2009, or the Adoption (Northern Ireland) Order 1987.

(3)   Subject to sub-paragraph (4), sub-paragraph (1) does not apply to a child or young person who is not living with the applicant and who–

(a)   is being looked after by, or in Scotland is in the care of, a local authority under a relevant enactment; or

(b)   has been placed, or in Scotland boarded out, with a person other than the applicant prior to adoption; or

(c)   has been placed for adoption in accordance with the Adoption and Children Act 2002 or the Adoption Agencies (Scotland) Regulations 2009, or the Adoption (Northern Ireland) Order 1987.

(4)   An authority must treat a child or young person to whom sub-paragraph (3)(a) applies as being a member of the applicant's household in any reduction week where–

(a)   that child or young person lives with the applicant for part or all of that reduction week; and

(b)   the authority considers that it is reasonable to do so taking into account the nature and frequency of that child's or young person's visits.

(5)   In this paragraph "relevant enactment" ("deddfiad perthnasol") means–

(a)   the Army Act 1955;

(b)   the Air Force Act 1955;

(c)   the Naval Discipline Act 1957:

(d)   the Matrimonial Proceedings (Children) Act 1958;

(e)   the Social Work (Scotland) Act 1968;

(f)   the Family Law Reform Act 1969;

(g)   the Children and Young Persons Act 1969;

(h)   the Matrimonial Causes Act 1973;

(i)   the Children Act 1975:

(j)   the Domestic Proceedings and Magistrates' Courts Act 1978;

(k)   the Adoption and Children (Scotland) Act 2007;

(l)   the Family Law Act 1986;

(m)   the Children Act 1989;

(n)   the Children (Scotland) Act 1995;

(o)   the Armed Forces Act 2006; [¹]

[¹ (oa)   the Children's Hearings (Scotland) Act 2011; and]

(p)   the Legal Aid, Sentencing and Punishment of Offenders Act 2012.

Amendments
1. Amended by reg 15 of SI 2014 No 66 (W.6) as from 15.1.14.
2. Inserted by reg 17 of SI 2016 No 50 (W.21) as from 20.1.16, for schemes made for a financial year starting on or after 1.4.16.

Non-dependants
   9.–(1)   In this scheme, "non-dependant" ("annibynnydd") means any person, except someone to whom sub-paragraph (2) applies, who normally resides with an applicant or with whom an applicant normally resides.
   (2)   This sub-paragraph applies to–
   (a)   any member of the applicant's family;
   (b)   if the applicant is polygamously married, any partner of the applicant and any child or young person who is a member of the applicant's household and for whom the applicant or one of the applicant's partners is responsible;
   (c)   a child or young person who is living with the applicant but who is not a member of the applicant's household by virtue of paragraph 8 (households);
   (d)   subject to sub-paragraph (3), any person who, with the applicant, is jointly and severally liable to pay council tax in respect of a dwelling for any day under sections 6 or 7 of the 1992 Act (persons liable to pay council tax);
   (e)   subject to sub-paragraph (3), any person who is liable to make payments on a commercial basis to the applicant or the applicant's partner in respect of the occupation of the dwelling;
   (f)   a person who lives with the applicant in order to care for the applicant or a partner of the applicant, and who is engaged by a charitable or voluntary organisation which makes a charge to the applicant or the applicant's partner for the services provided by that person.
   (3)   Excepting persons to whom sub-paragraph (2)(a) to (c) and (f) refer, a person to whom any of the following paragraphs applies is a non-dependant–
   (a)   a person (P) who resides with the person (O) to whom P is liable to make payments in respect of the dwelling and either–
   (i)   O is a close relative of P's or P's partner; or
   (ii)   the tenancy or other agreement between them is other than on a commercial basis;
   (b)   a person whose liability to make payments in respect of the dwelling appears to the authority to have been created to take advantage of a council tax reduction scheme except someone who was, for any period within the eight weeks prior to the creation of the agreement giving rise to the liability to make such payments, otherwise liable to make payments of rent in respect of the same dwelling;
   (c)   a person who becomes jointly and severally liable with the applicant for council tax in respect of a dwelling and who was, at any time during the period of eight weeks prior to that person becoming so liable, a nondependent of one or more of the other residents in that dwelling who are so liable for the tax, unless the change giving rise to the new liability was not made to take advantage of a council tax reduction scheme.

Remunerative work
   10.–(1)   Subject to the following provisions of this paragraph, a person must be treated for the purposes of this scheme as engaged in remunerative work if that person is engaged, or, where that person's hours of work fluctuate, that person is engaged on average, for not less than 16 hours a week, in work for which payment is made or which is done in expectation of payment.
   (2)   Subject to sub-paragraph (3), in determining the number of hours for which a person is engaged in work where that person's hours of work fluctuate, regard must be had to the average of hours worked over–
   (a)   if there is a recognisable cycle of work, the period of one complete cycle (including, where the cycle involves periods in which the person does no work, those periods but disregarding any other absences);
   (b)   in any other case, the period of 5 weeks immediately prior to the date of application, or such other length of time as may, in the particular case, enable the person's weekly average hours of work to be determined more accurately.
   (3)   Where, for the purposes of sub-paragraph (2)(a), a person's recognisable cycle of work at a school, other educational establishment or other place of employment is one year and includes periods of school holidays or similar vacations during which that person does not work, those periods and any other periods not forming part of such holidays or vacations during which that person is not required to work must be disregarded in establishing the average hours for which that person is engaged in work.
   (4)   Where no recognisable cycle has been established in respect of a person's work, regard must be had to the number of hours or, where those hours will fluctuate, the average of the hours, which that person is expected to work in a week.
   (5)   A person must be treated as engaged in remunerative work during any period for which that person is absent from work referred to in sub-paragraph (1) if the absence is either without good cause or by reason of a recognised, customary or other holiday.
   (6)   A person on income support, an income-based jobseeker's allowance or an income-related employment and support allowance for more than 3 days in any reduction week is to be treated as not being in remunerative work in that week.

(7)   A person must not be treated as engaged in remunerative work on any day on which that person is on maternity leave, paternity leave [¹ ,shared parental leave] or adoption leave, or is absent from work because that person is ill.

(8)   A person must not be treated as engaged in remunerative work on any day on which that person is engaged in an activity in respect of which–

(a)   a sports award has been made, or is to be made, to that person; and

(b)   no other payment is made or is expected to be made to that person.

Amendment

1.   Amended by reg 16 of SI 2015 No 44 (W.3) as from 21.1.15, for schemes made for a financial year starting on or after 1.4.15.

PART 3
Procedural matters

Procedure for reduction applications and appeals against reduction decisions

11.   Schedule 1 contains provisions about the procedure–

(a)   by which a person may apply for a reduction under this scheme;

(b)   by which a person may make an appeal against certain decisions of the authority;

(c)   by which a person can apply to the authority for a reduction under section 13A(1)(c) of the 1992 Act.

PART 4
Classes of person entitled to a reduction under this scheme

Classes of person entitled to a reduction under this scheme

12.–(1)   The classes of person described in paragraphs 13 to 16 are entitled to a reduction under this scheme.

(2)   In those paragraphs, references to the applicant's income or capital include, in a case where that income or capital cannot accurately be determined, references to the applicant's estimated income or capital.

Class A: pensioners whose income is less than the applicable amount

13.   On any day class A consists of any person who is a pensioner–

(a)   who is for that day liable to pay council tax in respect of a dwelling of which the person is a resident;

(b)   who, subject to paragraph 17 (periods of absence from a dwelling), is not absent from the dwelling throughout the day;

(c)   in respect of whom a maximum council tax reduction amount can be calculated;

(d)   who does not fall within a class of person not entitled to a reduction under this scheme;

(e)   whose income (if any) for the relevant week does not exceed the person's applicable amount; and

(f)   who has made an application.

Class B: pensioners whose income is greater than the applicable amount

14.   On any day class B consists of any person who is a pensioner–

(a)   who is for that day liable to pay council tax in respect of a dwelling of which the person is a resident;

(b)   who, subject to paragraph 17 (periods of absence from a dwelling), is not absent from the dwelling throughout the day;

(c)   in respect of whom a maximum council tax reduction amount can be calculated;

(d)   who does not fall within a class of person not entitled to a reduction under this scheme;

(e)   whose income for the relevant week is greater than the person's applicable amount;

(f)   in respect of whom amount A exceeds amount B where–

(i)   amount A is the maximum council tax reduction in respect of the day in the person's case; and

(ii)   amount B is 2 6/7 per cent of the difference between the person's income for the relevant week and the person's applicable amount; and

(g)   who has made an application.

Class C: persons who are not pensioners whose income is less than the applicable amount

15.   On any day class C consists of any person who is not a pensioner–

(a)   who is for that day liable to pay council tax in respect of a dwelling of which the person is a resident;

(b)   who, subject to paragraph 17 (periods of absence from a dwelling), is not absent from the dwelling throughout the day;

(c)   in respect of whom a maximum council tax reduction amount can be calculated;

    (d)   who does not fall within a class of person not entitled to a reduction under this scheme;

    (e)   whose income (if any) for the relevant week is less than the person's applicable amount; and

    (f)   who has made an application.

Class D: persons who are not pensioners whose income is greater than the applicable amount

    16.   On any day class D consists of any person who is not a pensioner–

    (a)   who is for that day liable to pay council tax in respect of a dwelling of which the person is a resident;

    (b)   who, subject to paragraph 17 (periods of absence from a dwelling), is not absent from the dwelling throughout the day;

    (c)   in respect of whom a maximum council tax reduction amount can be calculated;

    (d)   who does not fall within a class of person not entitled to a reduction under this scheme;

    (e)   whose income for the relevant week is greater than the person's applicable amount;

    (f)   in respect of whom amount A exceeds amount B where–

        (i)   amount A is the maximum council tax reduction in respect of the day in the person's case; and

        (ii)   amount B is 2 6/7 per cent of the difference between the person's income for the relevant week and the person's applicable amount; and

    (g)   who has made an application.

Periods of absence from a dwelling

    17.–(1)   A person is not absent from a dwelling in relation to any day which falls within a period of temporary absence from that dwelling.

    (2)   In sub-paragraph (1), a "period of temporary absence" ("cyfnod o absenoldeb") means–

    (a)   a period of absence not exceeding 13 weeks, beginning with the first whole day on which a person resides in residential accommodation where and for so long as–

        (i)   the person resides in that accommodation;

        (ii)   the part of the dwelling in which the person usually resides is not let or sub-let; and

        (iii)   that period of absence does not form part of a longer period of absence from the dwelling of more than 52 weeks,

    (b)   where the person has entered the accommodation for the purpose of ascertaining whether it suits the person's needs and with the intention of returning to the dwelling if it proves not to suit the person's needs;

    (c)   a period of absence not exceeding 13 weeks, beginning with the first whole day of absence rom the dwelling, where and for so long as–

        (i)   the person intends to return to the dwelling;

        (ii)   the part of the dwelling in which the person usually resided is not let or sub-let; and

        (iii)   that period is unlikely to exceed 13 weeks; and

    (d)   a period of absence not exceeding 52 weeks, beginning with the first whole day of that absence, where and for so long as–

        (i)   the person intends to return to the dwelling;

        (ii)   the part of the dwelling in which the person usually resided is not let or sub-let;

        (iii)   the person is a person to whom sub-paragraph (3) applies; and

        (iv)   the period of absence is unlikely to exceed 52 weeks or, in exceptional circumstances, is unlikely substantially to exceed that period.

    (3)   This sub-paragraph applies to a person who–

    (a)   is detained in custody on remand pending trial or required, as a condition of bail, to reside–

        (i)   in a dwelling, other than the dwelling referred to in sub-paragraph (1); or

        (ii)   in premises approved under section 13 of the Offender Management Act 2007;

        or is detained in custody pending sentence upon conviction;

    (b)   is resident in a hospital or similar institution as a patient;

    (c)   is undergoing, or whose partner or dependent child is undergoing, in the United Kingdom or elsewhere, medical treatment, or medically approved convalescence, in accommodation other than residential accommodation;

    (d)   is following, in the United Kingdom or elsewhere, a training course;

    (e)   is undertaking medically approved care of a person residing in the United Kingdom or elsewhere;

    (f)   is undertaking the care of a child whose parent or guardian is temporarily absent from the dwelling normally occupied by that parent or guardian for the purpose of receiving medically approved care or medical treatment;

    (g)   is, in the United Kingdom or elsewhere, receiving medically approved care provided in accommodation other than residential accommodation;

    (h)   is a student;

    (i)   is receiving care provided in residential accommodation and is not a person to whom sub-paragraph (2)(a) applies; or

    (j)   has left the dwelling the person resides in through fear of violence, in that dwelling, or by a person who was formerly a member of the family of that person.

    (4)   This sub-paragraph applies to a person who is–

(a)   detained in custody pending sentence upon conviction or under a sentence imposed by a court (other than a person who is detained in hospital under the provisions of the Mental Health Act 1983, or, in Scotland, under the provisions of the Mental Health (Care and Treatment) (Scotland) Act 2003 or the Criminal Procedure (Scotland) Act 1995, or in Northern Ireland, under Article 4 or 12 of the Mental Health (Northern Ireland) Order1986; and

(b)   on temporary release from detention in accordance with Rules made under the provisions of the Prison Act 1952 or the Prisons (Scotland) Act 1989.

(5)   Where sub-paragraph (4) applies to a person, then, for any day when that person is on temporary release–

(a)   if such temporary release was immediately preceded by a period of temporary absence under sub-paragraph (2)(b) or (c), that person must be treated, for the purposes of sub-paragraph (1), as if that person continues to be absent from the dwelling, despite any return to the dwelling;

(b)   for the purposes of sub-paragraph (3)(a), that person must be treated as if that person remains in detention;

(c)   if that person does not fall within paragraph (a), that person is not to be considered to be a person who is liable to pay council tax in respect of a dwelling of which that person is a resident.

(6)   In this paragraph–

"medically approved" ("a gymeradwywyd yn feddygol") means certified by a medical practitioner;

"patient" ("claf") means a person who is undergoing medical or other treatment as an in-patient in any hospital or similar institution;

"residential accommodation" ("llety preswyl") means accommodation which is provided in–

(a)   a care home;

(b)   an independent hospital;

(c)   an Abbeyfield Home; or

(d)   an establishment managed or provided by a body incorporated by Royal Charter or constituted by Act of Parliament other than a local social services authority;

"training course" ("cwrs hyfforddi") means a course of training or instruction provided wholly or partly by or on behalf of or in pursuance of arrangements made with, or approved by or on behalf of, Skills Development Scotland, Scottish Enterprise, Highlands and Islands Enterprise, a government department, the Welsh Ministers or the Secretary of State.

PART 5
Classes of person excluded from this scheme

Classes of person excluded from this scheme

18.   The classes of person described in paragraphs 19 to 22 are not entitled to a reduction under this scheme.

Class of person excluded from this scheme: persons treated as not being in Great Britain

19.–(1)   The class of person described in this paragraph consists of any person treated as not being in Great Britain.

(2)   Except where a person falls within sub-paragraph (5) or (6), a person is to be treated as not being in Great Britain if the person is not habitually resident in the United Kingdom, the Channel Islands, the Isle of Man or the Republic of Ireland.

(3)   A person must not be treated as habitually resident in the United Kingdom, the Channel Islands, the Isle of Man or the Republic of Ireland unless the person has a right to reside in one of those places.

(4)   For the purposes of sub-paragraph (3), a right to reside does not include a right which exists by virtue of, or in accordance with–

(a)   regulation 13 of the EEA Regulations or Article 6 of Council Directive No.2004/38/EC;

(b)   regulation 14 of the EEA Regulations, but only in a case where the right exists under that regulation because the person is–

(i)   a jobseeker for the purpose of the definition of "qualified person" in regulation 6(1) of those Regulations, or

(ii)   a family member (within the meaning of regulation 7 of those Regulations) of such a jobseeker;

(c)   Article 45 of the Treaty on the Functioning of the European Union (in a case where the person is seeking work in the United Kingdom, the Channel Islands, the Isle of Man or the Republic of Ireland); or

(d)   regulation 15A(1) of the EEA Regulations, but only in a case where the right exists under that regulation because the applicant satisfies the criteria in paragraph (4A) of that regulation or Article 20 of the Treaty on the Functioning of the European Union (in a case where the right to reside arises because a British citizen would otherwise be deprived of the genuine enjoyment of their rights as a European Union citizen).

(5)   A person falls within this sub-paragraph if the person is–

(a)   a qualified person for the purposes of regulation 6 of the EEA Regulations as a worker or a self-employed person;

(b)   a family member of a person referred to in paragraph (a) within the meaning of regulation 7(1)(a), (b) or (c) of the EEA Regulations;

(c)   a person who has a right to reside permanently in the United Kingdom by virtue of regulation 15(1)(c), (d) or (e) of the EEA Regulations;

(d)   a person recorded by the Secretary of State as a refugee within the definition in Article 1of the Convention relating to the Status of Refugees adopted at Geneva on 28th July 1951,as extended by Article 1(2) of the Protocol relating to the Status of Refugees adopted at New York on 31 January 1967;

[¹ (e)   a person who has been granted, or who is deemed to have been granted, leave outside the rules made under section 3(2) of the Immigration Act 1971 where that leave is–

  (i)   discretionary leave to enter or remain in the United Kingdom,

  (ii)   leave to remain under the Destitution Domestic Violence concession, or

  (iii)   leave deemed to have been granted by virtue of regulation 3 of the Displaced Persons (Temporary Protection) Regulations 2005;]

(f)   a person who has humanitarian protection granted under those rules;

(g)   a person who is not a person subject to immigration control within the meaning of section 115(9) of the Immigration and Asylum Act 1999 and who is in the United Kingdom as a result of the person's deportation, expulsion or other removal by compulsion of law from another country to the United Kingdom;

[¹ (h)]

[¹ (i)]

(j)   a person who is in receipt of income support [²] or on an income-related employment and support allowance.

[¹ (k)   a person who is treated as a worker for the purposes of the definition of "qualified person" in regulation 6(1) of the EEA Regulations pursuant to regulation 5 of the Accession of Croatia (Immigration and Worker Authorisation) Regulations 2013 (right of residence of a Croatian who is an "accession State national subject to worker authorisation")[²]] [² ; or]

[² (l)   in receipt of an income-based jobseeker's allowance and has a right to reside other than a right to reside falling within sub-paragraph (4)(a) to (d).]

(6)   A person falls within this sub-paragraph if the person is a Crown servant or member of Her Majesty's forces posted overseas.

(7)   A person mentioned in sub-paragraph (6) is posted overseas if the person is performing oversees the duties of a Crown servant or member of Her Majesty's forces and was, immediately before the posting or the first of consecutive postings, habitually resident in the United Kingdom.

(8)   In this paragraph–

"claim for asylum" ("hawliad am loches") has the same meaning as in section 94(1) of the Immigration and Asylum Act 1999;

"EEA Regulations" ("Rheoliadau AEE") means the Immigration (European Economic Area) Regulations 2006.

Modification

The amendments made by SI 2014 No.44 do not apply to a person who, on 31 March 2015 was liable to pay council tax at a reduced rate by virtue of a CTR scheme and was entitled to income-based JSA, until the earliest of the date s/he makes a new application for CTR or the date s/he ceases to be entitled to income-based JSA.

Amendments

1.   Amended by reg 16 of SI 2014 No 66 (W.6) as from 15.1.14.

2.   Amended by reg 17 of SI 2015 No 44 (W.3) as from 21.1.15, for schemes made for a financial year starting on or after 1.4.15.

General Note

Paragraph 19 is equivalent to reg 28 CTRSPR(W) Regs. See p1213 for commentary.

Class of person excluded from this scheme: persons subject to immigration control

20.–(1)   Subject to sub-paragraph (2), persons subject to immigration control are not entitled to a reduction under this scheme.

(2)   A person who is a national of a state which has ratified the European Convention on Social and Medical Assistance (adopted in Paris on 11 December 1953) or a state which has ratified the Council of Europe Social Charter (signed in Turin on 18 October 1961) and who is lawfully present in the United Kingdom is not a person subject to immigration control for the purposes of sub-paragraph (1).

(3)   "Person subject to immigration control" ("person sy'n ddarostyngedig i reolaeth fewnfudo") has the meaning given in section 115(9) of the Immigration and Asylum Act 1999.

Class of person excluded from this scheme: capital limit

21.–(1)   The class of person described in this paragraph consists of any person whose capital exceeds £16,000.

(2)   Capital for the purposes of sub-paragraph (1) is to be calculated in accordance with Part 9 of this scheme.

Class of person excluded from this scheme: students
22.   The class of person described in this paragraph consists of any student to whom paragraph 72(1) of this scheme applies.

PART 6
Applicable amounts for the purposes of calculating eligibilityfor a reduction under this scheme and amount of reduction

Applicable amounts: pensioners (including pensioners in polygamous marriages)
23.–(1)   The applicable amount for a pensioner for a week is the aggregate of such of the following amounts as apply in that person's case–
- (a)   an amount in respect of the person, or if that person is a member of a couple, an amount in respect of both of them, determined in accordance with paragraph 1 of Schedule 2 (personal allowance);
- (b)   an amount in respect of any child or young person who is a member of the person's family, determined in accordance with paragraph 2 of that Schedule (child or young person amounts);
- (c)   if the person is a member of a family of which at least one member is a child or young person, an amount determined in accordance with paragraph 3 of that Schedule (family premium);
- (d)   the amount of any premiums which may be applicable to the person, determined in accordance with Parts 3 and 4 of that Schedule (premiums).

(2)   In Schedule 2–
"additional spouse" ("priod ychwanegol") means a spouse of either party to the marriage who is additional to the other party to the marriage;
"patient" ("claf") means a person (other than a person who is serving a sentence of imprisonment or detention in a youth custody institution) who is regarded as receiving free in-patient treatment within the meaning of regulation 2(4) and (5) of the Social Security (Hospital In-Patients) Regulations 2005.

Applicable amounts: persons who are not pensioners
24.–(1)   Subject to paragraphs 25 and 26, the applicable amount for a week for a person who is not a pensioner is the aggregate of such of the following amounts as may apply in the person's case–
- (a)   an amount in respect of the person or, if that person is a member of a couple, an amount in respect of both of them, determined in accordance with paragraph 1 of Schedule 3 (personal allowances);
- (b)   an amount in respect of any child or young person who is a member of the person's family, determined in accordance with paragraph 3 of that Schedule (child or young person amounts);
- (c)   if the person is a member of a family of which at least one member is a child or young person, an amount determined in accordance with Part 2 of that Schedule (family premium);
- (d)   the amount of any premiums which may be applicable to the person, determined in accordance with Parts 3 and 4 of that Schedule (premiums);
- (e)   the amount of either the–
    - (i)   work-related activity component; or
    - (ii)   support component,
- (f)   which may be applicable to the person in accordance with Parts 5 and 6 of that Schedule (the components);
- (g)   the amount of any transitional addition which may be applicable to the person in accordance with Parts 7 and 8 of that Schedule (transitional addition).

(2)   In Schedule 3–
"additional spouse" ("priod ychwanegol") means a spouse of either party to the marriage who is additional to the other party to the marriage;
"converted employment and support allowance" ("lwfans cyflogaeth a chymorth a droswyd") means an employment and support allowance which is not income-related and to which a person is entitled as a result of a conversion decision within the meaning of the Employment and Support Allowance (Existing Awards) Regulations 2008;
"patient" ("claf") means a person (other than a person who is serving a sentence of imprisonment or detention in a youth custody institution) who is regarded as receiving free in-patient treatment within the meaning of regulation 2(4) and (5) of the Social Security (Hospital In-Patients) Regulations 2005.

Polygamous marriages: persons who are not pensioners
25.–(1)   This paragraph applies where an applicant who is not a pensioner is a member of a polygamous marriage and does not have (alone or jointly with a party to a marriage), an award of universal credit.

(2)   The applicable amount for a week of an applicant where this paragraph applies is the aggregate of such of the following amounts as may apply in that applicant's case–
- (a)   the amount applicable to the applicant and one of the applicant's partners determined in accordance with paragraph 1(3) of Schedule 3 (couple) as if the applicant and that partner were a couple;
- (b)   an amount equal to the difference between the amounts specified in sub-paragraphs (3) and (1)(b) of paragraph 1 of that Schedule in respect of each of the applicant's other partners;

(c)   an amount determined in accordance with paragraph 3 of that Schedule (child or young person amounts) in respect of any child or young person for whom the applicant or a partner of the applicant is responsible and who is a member of the same household;

(d)   if the applicant or another partner of the polygamous marriage is responsible for a child or young person who is a member of the same household, the amount specified in Part 2 of that Schedule (family premium);

(e)   the amount of any premiums which may be applicable to the applicant determined in accordance with Parts 3 and 4 of that Schedule (premiums);

(f)   the amount of either the–
    (i)   work-related activity component; or
    (ii)   support component,
    which may be applicable to the applicant in accordance with Parts 5 and 6 of that Schedule (the components);

(g)   the amount of any transitional addition which may be applicable to the applicant in accordance with Parts 7 and 8 of that Schedule (transitional addition).

Applicable amount: persons who are not pensioners who have an award of universal credit

26.–(1)   Subject to sub-paragraph (2), in determining the applicable amount for a week of an applicant who is not a pensioner–

(a)   who has, or

(b)   who (jointly with a partner) has,

an award of universal credit, the authority will use the calculation or estimate of the maximum amount of the applicant, or the applicant and the applicant's partner jointly (as the case may be), subject to the adjustment described in sub-paragraph (3).

(2)   In determining the applicable amount for a week of an applicant who is a member of a polygamous marriage, the fact that two people are husband and wife is to be disregarded if–

(a)   one of them is a party to an earlier marriage that still subsists; and

(b)   the other party to that earlier marriage is living in the same household.

(3)   The adjustment referred to in sub-paragraph (1) is to multiply the maximum amount by 12 and divide the product by 52.

(4)   In this paragraph "maximum amount" ("swm uchaf") means the maximum amount calculated by the Secretary of State in accordance with section 8(2) of the Welfare Reform Act 2012.

PART 7
Maximum council tax reduction for the purposes of calculatingeligibility for a reduction under this scheme and amount of reduction

Maximum council tax reduction under this scheme: pensioners and persons who are not pensioners

27.–(1)   Subject to sub-paragraphs (2) to (4), the amount of a person's maximum council tax reduction in respect of a day is 100 per cent of the amount A/B where–

(a)   A is the amount set by the authority as the council tax for the relevant financial year in respect of the dwelling in which the person is a resident and for which the person is liable, subject to any discount which may be appropriate to that dwelling under the 1992 Act; and

(b)   B is the number of days in that financial year,

less any deductions in respect of non-dependants which fall to be made under paragraph 28 (non-dependant deductions: pensioners and persons who are not pensioners).

(2)   In calculating a person's maximum council tax reduction under this scheme any reduction in the amount that person is liable to pay in respect of council tax, which is made in consequence of any enactment in, or made under, the 1992 Act (other than a reduction under this scheme), is to be taken into account.

(3)   Subject to sub-paragraph (4), where an applicant is jointly and severally liable for council tax in respect of a dwelling in which the applicant is resident with one or more other persons, in determining the maximum council tax reduction in the applicant's case in accordance with sub-paragraph (1), the amount A is to be divided by the number of persons who are jointly and severally liable for that tax.

(4)   Where an applicant is jointly and severally liable for council tax in respect of a dwelling with only a partner, sub-paragraph (3) does not apply in that applicant's case.

(5)   The reference in sub-paragraph (3) to a person with whom an applicant is jointly and severally liable for council tax, where the applicant is a person who is not a pensioner, does not include a student to whom paragraph 72(1) (students who are excluded from entitlement to a reduction under this scheme) applies.

(6)   In this paragraph "relevant financial year" ("blwyddyn ariannol berthnasol") means, in relation to any particular day, the financial year within which the day in question falls.

Non-dependant deductions: pensioners and persons who are not pensioners

28.–(1)   Subject to the following provisions of this paragraph, the non-dependant deductions in respect of a day referred to in paragraph 27 are–

(a)   in respect of a non-dependant aged 18 or over in remunerative work, [⁶ £13.75] x 1/7;

(b)   in respect of a non-dependant aged 18 or over to whom paragraph (a) does not apply, [⁶ £4.55] x 1/7.

(2)   In the case of a non-dependant aged 18 or over to whom sub-paragraph (1)(a) applies, where it is shown to the authority that that non-dependant's normal gross weekly income is–

(a)   less than [⁶ £210.00], the deduction to be made under this paragraph is that specified in sub-paragraph (1)(b);

(b)   not less than [⁶ £210.00] but less than [⁶ £365.00], the deduction to be made under this paragraph is [⁶ £9.15] x 1/7;

(c)   not less than [⁶ £365.00] but less than [⁶ £450.00], the deduction to be made under this paragraph is [⁶ £11.50] x 1/7.

(3)   Only one deduction is to be made under this paragraph in respect of a couple or, as the case may be, members of a polygamous marriage (other than where there is an award of universal credit) and, where, but for this paragraph, the amount that would fall to be deducted in respect of one member of a couple or polygamous marriage is higher than the amount (if any) that would fall to be deducted in respect of the other, or any other, member, the higher amount is to be deducted.

(4)   In applying the provisions of sub-paragraph (2) in the case of a couple or, as the case may be, a polygamous marriage, regard must be had, for the purpose of that sub-paragraph, to the couple's or, as the case may be, all members of the polygamous marriage's joint weekly gross income.

(5)   Where in respect of a day–

(a)   a person is a resident in a dwelling but that person is not liable for council tax in respect of that dwelling and that day;

(b)   other residents in that dwelling (the liable persons) have joint and several liability for council tax in respect of that dwelling and that day otherwise than by virtue of section 9of the 1992 Act (liability of spouses and civil partners); and

(c)   the person to whom paragraph (a) refers is a non-dependant of two or more of the liable persons, the deduction in respect of that non-dependant must be apportioned equally between those liable persons.

(6)   No deduction is to be made in respect of any non-dependants occupying an applicant's dwelling if the applicant or the applicant's partner is–

(a)   [³ blind or severely sight-impaired or treated as such] by virtue of paragraph 10 of Schedule 3 (additional condition for the disability premium); or

(b)   receiving in respect of the applicant–

    (i)   attendance allowance, or would be receiving that allowance but for–

        (aa)   a suspension of benefit in accordance with regulations under section 113(2) of the SSCBA; or

        (bb)   an abatement as a result of hospitalisation; or

    (ii)   the care component of the disability living allowance, or would be receiving that component but for–

        (aa)   a suspension of benefit in accordance with regulations under section 113(2) of the SSCBA; or

        (bb)   an abatement as a result of hospitalisation; or

    (iii)   the daily living component of personal independence payment, or would be receiving that allowance but for a suspension of benefit in accordance with regulations under section 86 of the Welfare Reform Act 2012 (hospital in-patients);or

    (iv)   an AFIP, or would be receiving that payment but for a suspension of it in accordance with any terms of the armed and reserve forces compensation scheme which allows for a suspension because a person is undergoing medical treatment in a hospital or similar institution.

(7)   No deduction is to be made in respect of a non-dependant if–

(a)   although that non-dependant resides with the applicant, it appears to the authority that that non-dependant's normal home is elsewhere; or

(b)   the non-dependant is in receipt of a training allowance paid in connection with youth training established under section 2 of the Employment and Training Act 1973 or section 2 of the Enterprise and New Towns (Scotland) Act 1990; or

(c)   the non-dependant is a full-time student within the meaning of Part 10 (Students); or

(d)   the non-dependant is not residing with the applicant because the non-dependant has been a patient for a period in excess of 52 weeks, and for these purposes–

    (i)   "patient" ("claf") has the meaning given in paragraph 17(6) of this scheme, and

    (ii)   where a person has been a patient for two or more distinct periods separated by one or more intervals each not exceeding 28 days, that person is to be treated as having been a patient continuously for a period equal in duration to the total of those distinct periods.

(8)   No deduction is to be made in respect of a non-dependant–

(a)   who is on income support, state pension credit, an income-based jobseeker's allowance or an income related employment and support allowance [⁵ and where the non-dependant is not a member of the work-related activity group]; [²]

(b)   to whom Schedule 1 to the 1992 Act applies (persons disregarded for purposes of discount); but this paragraph does not apply to a non-dependant who is a student to whom paragraph 4 of that Schedule refers.[²; or]

[² (c)   who is entitled to an award of universal credit where the award is calculated on the basis that the person does not have any earned income.]

(9)   In the application of sub-paragraph (2) there is to be disregarded from the non-dependant's weekly gross income–

(a)   any attendance allowance, disability living allowance, personal independence payment or AFIP received by the non-dependant;

(b)   any payment made under or by the Trusts, the Fund, the Eileen Trust, MFET Limited, the Skipton Fund, the Caxton Foundation [⁵, an approved blood scheme, the Scottish Infected Blood Support Scheme, the London Emergencies Trust, the We Love Manchester Emergency Fund] or the Independent Living Fund (2006) which, had the non-dependant's income fallen to be calculated under paragraph 51 (calculation of income other than earnings: persons who are not pensioners), would have been disregarded under paragraph 28 of Schedule 7 (income in kind); and

(c)   any payment which, had the non-dependant's income fallen to be calculated under paragraph 51 (calculation of income other than earnings: persons who are not pensioners), would have been disregarded under paragraph 41 of Schedule 7 (payments made under certain trusts and certain other payments)[⁵ ; and

(d)   any payment made under or by a trust, established for the purpose of giving relief and assistance to disabled persons whose disabilities were caused by the fact that during their mother's pregnancy she had taken a preparation containing the drug known as Thalidomide, and which is approved by the Secretary of State.]

[² (10)   For the purposes of sub-paragraph (8), "earned income" ("incwm a enillir") has the meaning given in regulation 52 of the Universal Credit Regulations 2013.]

Amendments

1.   Amended by reg 17 of SI 2014 No 66 (W.6) as from 15.1.14.
2.   Amended by reg 18 of SI 2015 No 44 (W.3) as from 21.1.15, for schemes made for a financial year starting on or after 1.4.15.
3.   Amended by reg 18 of SI 2016 No 50 (W.21) as from 20.1.16, for schemes made for a financial year starting on or after 1.4.16.
4.   Amended by reg 8 of SI 2017 No 46 (W.20) as from 19.1.17, for schemes made for a financial year starting on or after 1.4.17.
5.   Amended by reg 17 of SI 2018 No 14 (W.7) as from 10.1.18, for schemes made for a financial year starting on or after 1.4.18.
6.   Amended by reg 12 of SI 2019 No 11 (W.5) as from 9.1.19, for schemes made for a financial year starting on or after 1.4.19.

PART 8
Amount of reduction under this scheme

Amount of reduction under this scheme: Classes A to D

29.–(1)   Where a person is entitled to a reduction under this scheme in respect of a day, the amount of the reduction to which that person is entitled is as follows.

(2)   Where the person is within class A or C, that amount is the amount which is the maximum council tax reduction in respect of the day in the person's case.

(3)   Where the person is within class B or D, that amount is the amount found by deducting amount B from amount A, where "amount A" and "amount B" have the meanings given in paragraph 14(f) or 16(f), as the case may be.

PART 9
Income and capital for the purposes of calculating eligibilityfor a reduction under this scheme and amount of reduction

CHAPTER 1
Income and capital: general

Calculation of income and capital: applicant's family and polygamous marriages

30.–(1)   The income and capital of–

(a)   an applicant; and
(b)   any partner of that applicant,

is to be calculated in accordance with the provisions of this Part.

(2)   The income and capital of any partner of the applicant is to be treated as income and capital of the applicant, and in this Part any reference to the applicant applies equally to any partner of that applicant.

(3)   Where an applicant or the partner of an applicant is married polygamously to two or more members of the applicant's household–

(a)   the applicant must be treated as possessing capital and income belonging to each such member; and

(b)   the income and capital of that member is to be calculated in accordance with the following provisions of this Part in like manner as for the applicant.

General Note
This is equivalent to Sch 1 para 5 CTRSPR(W) Regs. See commentary on p1220.

Circumstances in which capital and income of non-dependant is to be treated as applicant's

31.–(1)   Sub-paragraph (2) applies where it appears to the authority that a non-dependant and an applicant have entered into arrangements in order to take advantage of this scheme and the non-dependant has more income and capital than the applicant.

(2)   Except where–

(a)   the applicant is a pensioner and is on a guarantee credit, or

(b)   the applicant is not a pensioner and is on income support, an income-based jobseeker's allowance or an income-related employment and support allowance,

the authority must treat the applicant as possessing income and capital belonging to that non-dependant and, in such a case, any capital and income which the applicant does possess is to be disregarded.

(3)   Where an applicant is treated as possessing capital and income belonging to a non-dependant under sub-paragraph (2) the capital and income of that non-dependant will be calculated in accordance with the following provisions of this Part in like manner as for the applicant and, except where the context otherwise requires, any reference to the "applicant" ("ceisydd") is to be construed for the purposes of this Part as if it were a reference to that non-dependant.

CHAPTER 2
Income and capital: pensioners in receipt of guarantee credit or savings credit

---

Pensioners in receipt of guarantee credit

32.   In the case of an applicant who is a pensioner and who is in receipt, or whose partner is in receipt, of a guarantee credit, the whole of the applicant's capital and income must be disregarded.

Calculation of pensioner's income in savings credit only cases

33.–(1)   In determining the income and capital of an applicant who is a pensioner and who has, or whose partner has, an award of state pension credit comprising only the savings credit, subject to the following provisions of this paragraph, the authority will use the calculation or estimate of the applicant's or as the case may be, the applicant's partner's income and capital made by the Secretary of State for the purpose of determining the award of state pension credit.

(2)   Where the calculation or estimate provided by the Secretary of State includes an amount taken into account in that determination in respect of net income, the authority may only adjust that amount so far as necessary to take into account–

(a)   the amount of any savings credit payable;

(b)   in respect of any dependent children of the applicant, child care charges taken into account under paragraph 54(1)(c) (calculation of income on a weekly basis);

(c)   the higher amount disregarded under this scheme in respect of–

(i)   lone parent's earnings; or

(ii)   payments of maintenance, whether under a court order or not, which is made or due to be made by–

(aa)   the applicant's former partner, or the applicant's partner's former partner; or

(bb)   the parent of a child or young person where that child or young person is a member of the applicant's family except where that parent is the applicant or the applicant's partner;

(d)   any amount to be disregarded by virtue of paragraph 10(1) of Schedule 4 (sums disregarded from applicant's earnings);

(e)   the income and capital of any partner of the applicant who is treated as a member of the applicant's household under paragraph 8 (households), to the extent that it is not taken into account in determining the net income of the person claiming state pension credit;

(f)   paragraph 31 (circumstances in which capital and income of a non-dependant is to be treated as applicant's), if the authority determines that that provision applies in the applicant's case;

(g)   such further reduction (if any) as the authority thinks fit under section 13A(1)(c) of the 1992 Act (power of billing authority to reduce amount of council tax payable);

(h)   any amount to be disregarded by virtue of paragraph 6 of Schedule 4 (sums to be disregarded from applicant's income: pensioners).

(3)   Paragraphs 37 to 42 (calculation of income: pensioners), and 54 to 58 (calculation of income: pensioners and persons who are not pensioners) do not apply to the amount of the net income to be taken into account under sub-paragraph (1), but do apply (so far as relevant) for the purpose of determining any adjustments to that amount which the authority makes under sub-paragraph (2).

(4)   If sub-paragraph (5) applies, the authority must calculate the applicant's capital in accordance with paragraphs 60, 62 to 65 and 67 of this scheme (calculation of capital: pensioners).

(5)   This sub-paragraph applies if–

(a)   the Secretary of State notifies the authority that the applicant's capital has been determined as being £16,000 or less or the authority determines the applicant's capital as being £16,000 or less;

(b)   subsequent to that determination the applicant's capital rises to more than £16,000; and

(c)   the increase occurs whilst there is in force an assessed income period within the meaning of sections 6 and 9 of the State Pension Credit Act 2002.

CHAPTER 3
Income and capital where there is an award of universal credit

---

Calculation of income and capital: persons who are not pensioners who have an award of universal credit

34.–(1)   In determining the income of an applicant–

(a)   who has, or

(b)   who (jointly with a partner) has,

an award of universal credit the authority must, subject to the following provisions of this paragraph, use the calculation or estimate of the income of the applicant, or the applicant and the applicant's partner jointly (as the case may be), made by the Secretary of State for the purpose of determining the award of universal credit.

(2)   The authority must adjust the amount of the income referred to in sub-paragraph (1) by multiplying the amount by 12 and dividing the product by 52.

(3)   The authority must only adjust the amount of the income as adjusted in accordance with sub-paragraph (2) so far as necessary to take into account–

(a)   the amount of the award of universal credit, determined in accordance with sub-paragraph (4);

(b)   paragraph 31 (income and capital of non-dependant to be treated as applicant's), if the authority determines that the provision applies in the applicant's case;

(c)   such further reduction (if any) as the authority thinks fit under section 13A(1)(c) of the 1992 Act (power of billing authority to reduce amount of council tax payable).

(4)   The amount for the award of universal credit to be taken into account for the purposes of sub-paragraph (3)(a) is to be determined by multiplying the amount of the award of universal credit by12 and dividing the product by 52.

(5)   Paragraph 31 (income and capital of non-dependant to be treated as applicant's) applies for the purpose of determining any adjustments which fall to be made to the figure for income under sub-paragraph (3).

(6)   In determining the capital of an applicant–

(a)   who has, or

(b)   who (jointly with a partner) has,

an award of universal credit, the authority must use the calculation or estimate of the capital of the applicant, or the applicant and the applicant's partner jointly (as the case may be), made by the Secretary of State for the purpose of determining the award of universal credit.

General Note

This paragraph is equivalent to Sch 6 para 9 CTRSPR(W) Regs. See p1266 for commentary.

CHAPTER 4
Income: other pensioners

Calculation of income and capital where state pension credit is not payable: pensioners

35.   Where neither paragraph 32 (pensioner in receipt of guarantee credit) nor 33 (applicant in receipt of savings credit only: pensioners) applies in the applicant's case, the applicant's income and capital is to be calculated or estimated in accordance with paragraphs 36 to 43, and 54 to 59 (calculations of income) and Chapter 7 of this Part (calculation of capital).

Meaning of "income": pensioners

36.–(1)   For the purposes of classes A and B in this scheme, "income" ("incwm") means income of any of the following descriptions–

(a)   earnings;

(b)   working tax credit;

(c)   retirement pension income within the meaning of the State Pension Credit Act 2002;

(d)   income from annuity contracts (other than retirement pension income);

(e)   a war disablement pension or war widow's or widower's pension;

(f)   a foreign war disablement pension or war widow's or widower's pension;

(g)   a guaranteed income payment;

(h)   a payment made under article 29(1)(c) of the Armed Forces and Reserve Forces (Compensation Scheme) Order 2011, in any case where article 31(2)(c) applies;

(i)   income from capital other than capital disregarded under Part 1 of Schedule 8;

(j)   social security benefits, other than retirement pension income or any of the following benefits–

        (i)   disability living allowance;

        (ii)   personal independence payment;

        (iii)   an AFIP;

        (iv)   attendance allowance payable under section 64 of the SSCBA (entitlement to attendance allowance);

        (v)   an increase of disablement pension under section 104 (increase for constant attendance) or 105 of the SSCBA (increase for exceptionally severe disablement);

        (vi)   child benefit;

        (vii)   any guardian's allowance payable under section 77 of the SSCBA (guardian's allowance);

        (viii) any increase for a dependant, other than the applicant's partner, payable in accordance with Part 4 of the SSCBA (increases for dependants);

        (ix)   any–

             (aa)   social fund payment made under Part 8 of the SSCBA (the social fund); or

             (bb)   occasional assistance;

        (x)   Christmas bonus payable under Part 10 of the SSCBA (Christmas bonus for pensioners);

        (xi)   housing benefit;

        (xii)   council tax benefit;

        [² (xiii) bereavement support payment under section 30 of the Pensions Act 2014;]

        (xiv) statutory sick pay;

        (xv)   statutory maternity pay;

        (xvi) [¹] statutory paternity pay payable under Part 12ZA of the SSCBA (statutory paternity pay);

        [¹ (xvia) statutory shared parental pay payable under Part 12ZC of the SSCBA;]

        (xvii) additional statutory paternity pay payable under Part 12ZA of the SSCBA;

        (xviii) statutory adoption pay payable under Part 12ZB of the SSCBA (statutory adoption pay);

        (xix) any benefit similar to those mentioned in the preceding provisions of this paragraph payable under legislation having effect in Northern Ireland;

(k)   all foreign social security benefits which are similar to the social security benefits prescribed above;

(l)   a payment made–

        (i)   under article 30 of the Naval, Military and Air Forces Etc (Disablement and Death) Service Pensions Order 2006, in any case where article 30(1)(b) applies; or

        (ii)   under article 12(8) of that Order (unemployability allowances: children who have reached the child's age limit), in any case where sub-paragraph (b) of article 12(8)applies;

[² (m)   a pension paid by a government to victims of National Socialist persecution;]

(n)   payments under a scheme made under the Pneumoconiosis etc (Worker's Compensation) Act 1979;

(o)   payments made towards the maintenance of the applicant by the applicant's spouse, civil partner, former spouse or former civil partner or towards the maintenance of the applicant's partner by that person's spouse, civil partner, former spouse or former civil partner, including payments made–

        (i)   under a court order;

        (ii)   under an agreement for maintenance; or

        (iii)   voluntarily;

(p)   payments due from any person in respect of board and lodging accommodation provided by the applicant;

(q)   royalties or other sums paid as a consideration for the use of, or the right to use, any copyright, design, patent or trade mark;

(r)   any payment in respect of any–

        (i)   book registered under the Public Lending Right Scheme 1982; or

        (ii)   work made under any international public lending right scheme that is analogous to the Public Lending Right Scheme 1982;

(s)   any payment, other than a payment ordered by a court or made in settlement of a claim, made by or on behalf of a former employer of a person on account of the early retirement of that person on grounds of ill-health or disability;

(t)   any sum payable by way of pension out of money provided under–

        (i)   the Civil List Act 1837;

        (ii)   the Civil List Act 1937;

        (iii)   the Civil List Act 1952;

        (iv)   the Civil List Act 1972; or

        (v)   the Civil List Act 1975;

(u)   any income in lieu of that specified in paragraphs (a) to (r);

(v)   any payment of rent made to an applicant who–

        (i)   owns the freehold or leasehold interest in any property or is a tenant of any property;

        (ii)   occupies part of the property; and

        (iii)   has an agreement with another person allowing that person to occupy that property on payment of rent;

(w)   any payment made at regular intervals under an equity release scheme;

(x)   PPF periodic payments within the meaning of section 17(1) of the State Pension Credit Act 2002.

(2)   Where the payment of any social security benefit referred to in sub-paragraph (1) is subject to any deduction (other than an adjustment specified in sub-paragraph (4)) the amount to be taken into account under sub-paragraph (1) is to be the amount before the deduction is made.

(3)   Where an award of any working tax credit or child tax credit is subject to a deduction by way of recovery of an overpayment of working tax credit or child tax credit which arose in a previous tax year the amount to be taken into account under sub-paragraph (1) is to be the amount of working tax credit or child tax credit awarded less the amount of that deduction.

(4)   The adjustments specified in this sub-paragraph are those made in accordance with–

(a)   the Social Security (Overlapping Benefits) Regulations 1979;

(b)   the Social Security (Hospital In-Patients) Regulations 2005;

(c)   section 30DD or section 30E of the SSCBA (reductions in incapacity benefit in respect of pensions and councillor's allowances);

(d)   section 3 of the Welfare Reform Act 2007 (deductions from contributory employment and support allowance in respect of pensions and councillor's allowances) and regulations made under it.

(5)   In sub-paragraph (1)(w), "equity release scheme" ("cynllun rhyddhau ecwiti") means a loan–

(a)   made between a person ("the lender") and the applicant;

(b)   by means of which a sum of money is advanced by the lender to the applicant by way of payments at regular intervals; and

(c)   which is secured on a dwelling in which the applicant owns an estate or interest and which the applicant occupies as the applicant's home.

Amendments

1.   Amended by reg 19 of SI 2015 No 44 (W.3) as from 21.1.15, for schemes made for a financial year starting on or after 1.4.15.

2.   Substituted by reg 18 of SI 2018 No 14 (W.7) as from 10.1.18, for schemes made for a financial year starting on or after 1.4.18.

Calculation of weekly income: pensioners

37.–(1)   Except in a case where [¹ sub-paragraph (2), (3A), (4A) or (5)] applies, for the purposes of calculating the weekly income of an applicant who is a pensioner, where the period in respect of which a payment is made–

(a)   does not exceed a week, the whole of that payment is to be included in the applicant's weekly income;

(b)   exceeds a week, the amount to be included in the applicant's weekly income is to be determined–

(i)   in a case where that period is a month, by multiplying the amount of the payment by 12 and dividing the product by 52;

(ii)   in a case where that period is three months, by multiplying the amount of the payment by 4 and dividing the product by 52;

(iii)   in a case where that period is a year, by dividing the amount of the payment by 52;

(iv)   in any other case, by multiplying the amount of the payment by 7 and dividing the product by the number of days in the period in respect of which it is made.

(2)   Sub-paragraph (3) applies where–

(a)   the applicant's regular pattern of work is such that the applicant does not work the same hours every week; or

(b)   the amount of the applicant's income fluctuates and has changed more than once.

(3)   The weekly amount of that applicant's income is to be determined–

(a)   if, in a case to which sub-paragraph (2)(a) applies, there is a recognised cycle of work, by reference to the applicant's average weekly income over the period of the complete cycle (including, where the cycle involves periods in which the applicant does no work, those periods but disregarding any other absences); or

(b)   in any other case, on the basis of–

(i)   the last two payments if those payments are one month or more apart;

(ii)   the last four payments if the last two payments are less than one month apart; or

(iii)   calculating or estimating such other payments as may, in the particular circumstances of the case, enable the applicant's average weekly income to be determined more accurately.

[¹ (3A)   Income calculated pursuant to sub-paragraphs (2) and (3) must be taken into account–

(a)   in the case of an application, on the date on which the application was made or treated as made, and the first day of each reduction week thereafter, [² regardless of when those earnings were actually received];

[² (b)   in the case of an application or a reduction under a scheme where the applicant commences employment, the day on which the applicant commences that employment, and the first day of each reduction week thereafter, regardless of when those earnings were actually received ; or

(c)   in the case of an application or a reduction under a scheme where the applicant 's average weekly earnings from employment change, the day on which the applicant's earnings from employment change, so as to require recalculation under this paragraph, and the first day of each reduction week thereafter, regardless of when those earnings were actually received .]]

(4)   For the purposes of sub-paragraph (3)(b) the last payments are the last payments before the date the application was made or treated as made.

[¹ (4A)   An applicant's earnings from employment as an employed earner not calculated pursuant to sub-paragraphs (2) and (3) must be taken into account–

(a)   in the case of an application, on the date on which the application was made or treated as made, and the first day of each reduction week thereafter, [² regardless of when those earnings were actually received];

[² (b)   in the case of an application or a reduction under a scheme where the applicant commences employment, the day on which the applicant commences that employment, and the first day of each reduction week thereafter, regardless of when those earnings were actually received ; or

(c)   in the case of an application or a reduction under a scheme where the applicant's average weekly earnings from employment change, the day on which the applicant's earnings from employment change and the first day of each reduction week thereafter, regardless of when those earnings were actually received .]]

(5)   If the applicant is entitled to receive a payment to which sub-paragraph (6) applies, the amount of that payment is to be treated as if made in respect of a period of a year.

(6)   This sub-paragraph applies to–

(a)   royalties or other sums paid as a consideration for the use of, or the right to use, any copyright, design, patent or trade mark;

(b)   any payment in respect of any–
    (i)   book registered under the Public Lending Right Scheme 1982; or
    (ii)   work made under any international public lending right scheme that is analogous to the Public Lending Right Scheme 1982; and

(c)   any payment which is made on an occasional basis.

(7)   The period under which any benefit under the benefit Acts is to be taken into account is to be the period in respect of which that benefit is payable.

(8)   Where payments are made in a currency other than Sterling, the value of the payment is to be determined by taking the Sterling equivalent on the date the payment is made.

(9)   The sums specified in Schedule 4 are to be disregarded in calculating–

(a)   the applicant's earnings; and

(b)   any amount to which sub-paragraph (6) applies where the applicant is the first owner of the copyright, design, patent or trademark, or an original contributor to the book or work referred to in sub-paragraph (6)(b).

(10)   For the purposes of sub-paragraph (9)(b), and for that purpose only, the amounts specified in sub-paragraph (6) are to be treated as though they were earnings.

(11)   Income specified in Schedule 5 is to be disregarded in the calculation of the applicant's income.

(12)   Schedule 8 (capital disregards: pensioners) has effect so that–

(a)   the capital specified in Part 1 is disregarded for the purpose of determining an applicant's income; and

(b)   the capital specified in Part 2 is disregarded for the purpose of determining an applicant's income under paragraph 68 (calculation of tariff income from capital: pensioners).

(13)   In the case of any income taken into account for the purpose of calculating a person's income any amount payable by way of tax is disregarded.

Amendments

1.   Amended by reg 9 of SI 2017 No 46 (W.20) as from 19.1.17, for schemes made for a financial year starting on or after 1.4.17.

2.   Amended by reg 19 of SI 2018 No 14 (W.7) as from 10.1.18, for schemes made for a financial year starting on or after 1.4.18.

Earnings of employed earners: pensioners

38.–(1)   Subject to sub-paragraph (2), "earnings" ("enillion"), in the case of employment as an employed earner who is a pensioner, means any remuneration or profit derived from that employment and includes–

(a)   any bonus or commission;

(b)   any payment in lieu of remuneration except any periodic sum paid to an applicant on account of the termination of that applicant's employment by reason of redundancy;

(c)   any payment in lieu of notice;

(d)   any holiday pay;

(e)   any payment by way of a retainer;

(f)   any payment made by the applicant's employer in respect of expenses not wholly, exclusively and necessarily incurred in the performance of the duties of the employment, including any payment made by the applicant's employer in respect of–
    (i)   travelling expenses incurred by the applicant between the applicant's home and place of employment;
    (ii)   expenses incurred by the applicant under arrangements made for the care of a member of the applicant's family owing to the applicant's absence from home;

(g)   the amount of any payment by way of a non-cash voucher which has been taken into account in the computation of a person's earnings in accordance with Part 5 of Schedule 3 to the Social Security (Contributions) Regulations 2001;

(h)   statutory sick pay and statutory maternity pay payable by the employer under the SSCBA;

(i)   statutory paternity pay payable under Part 12ZA of the SSCBA;

(j)   statutory adoption pay payable under Part 12ZB of the SSCBA;

[¹ (ja)   statutory shared parental pay payable under Part 12ZC of the SSCBA;]

(k)   any sums payable under a contract of service–

    (i)   for incapacity for work due to sickness or injury; or

    (ii)   by reason of pregnancy or confinement.

(2)   Earnings does not include–

(a)   subject to sub-paragraph (3), any payment in kind;

(b)   any payment in respect of expenses wholly, exclusively and necessarily incurred in the performance of the duties of the employment;

(c)   any occupational pension;

(d)   any lump sum payment made under the Iron and Steel Re-adaptation Benefits Scheme;

(e)   any payment of compensation made pursuant to an award by an employment tribunal established under the Employment Tribunals Act 1996 in respect of unfair dismissal or unlawful discrimination;

(f)   any payment in respect of expenses arising out of the applicant's participation in a service user group.

(3)   Sub-paragraph (2)(a) does not apply in respect of any non-cash voucher referred to in sub-paragraph (1)(g).

Amendment

1.   Amended by reg 20 of SI 2015 No 44 (W.3) as from 21.1.15, for schemes made for a financial year starting on or after 1.4.15.

Calculation of net earnings of employed earners: pensioners

39.–(1)   For the purposes of paragraph 54 (calculation of income on a weekly basis), the earnings of an applicant derived or likely to be derived from employment as an employed earner to be taken into account must, subject to paragraph 37(4) (calculation of weekly income: pensioners) and Schedule 4, be that applicant's net earnings.

(2)   For the purposes of sub-paragraph (1) net earnings must, except where sub-paragraph (5) applies, be calculated by taking into account the gross earnings of the applicant from that employment over the assessment period, less–

(a)   any amount deducted from those earnings by way of–

    (i)   income tax;

    (ii)   primary Class 1 contributions under the SSCBA;

(b)   one-half of any sum paid by the applicant by way of a contribution towards an occupational pension scheme;

(c)   one-half of the amount calculated in accordance with sub-paragraph (4) in respect of any qualifying contribution payable by the applicant; and

(d)   where those earnings include a payment which is payable under any enactment having effect in Northern Ireland and which corresponds to statutory sick pay, statutory maternity pay, ordinary or additional statutory paternity pay [¹, statutory shared parental pay] or statutory adoption pay, any amount deducted from those earnings by way of any contributions which correspond to primary Class 1 contributions under the SSCBA.

(3)   In this paragraph "qualifying contribution" ("cyfraniad cymwys") means any sum which is payable periodically as a contribution towards a personal pension scheme.

(4)   The amount in respect of any qualifying contribution is to be calculated by multiplying the daily amount of the qualifying contribution by the number equal to the number of days in the assessment period; and for the purposes of this paragraph the daily amount of the qualifying contribution is to be determined–

(a)   where the qualifying contribution is payable monthly, by multiplying the amount of the qualifying contribution by 12 and dividing the product by 365;

(b)   in any other case, by dividing the amount of the qualifying contribution by the number equal to the number of days in the period to which the qualifying contribution relates.

(5)   Where the earnings of an applicant are determined under paragraph 37(2)(b) (calculation of weekly income: pensioners) that applicant's net earnings are to be calculated by taking into account those earnings over the assessment period, less–

(a)   an amount in respect of income tax equivalent to an amount calculated by applying to those earnings the basic rate of tax applicable to the assessment period less only the [² personal reliefs to which the applicant is entitled under Chapters 2, 3 and 3A of Part 3] of the Income Tax Act 2007 [²] as is appropriate to the applicant's circumstances but, if the assessment period is less than a year, the earnings to which the basic rate of tax is to be applied and the amount of the personal [² reliefs] deductible under this sub-paragraph is to be calculated on a pro rata basis;

(b)   an amount equivalent to the amount of the primary Class 1 contributions that would be payable by the applicant under the SSCBA in respect of those earnings if such contributions were payable; and

(c)   one-half of any sum which would be payable by the applicant by way of a contribution towards an occupational or personal pension scheme, if the earnings so estimated were actual earnings.

Amendments
1.   Amended by reg 21 of SI 2015 No 44 (W.3) as from 21.1.15, for schemes made for a financial year starting on or after 1.4.15.
2.   Amended by reg 10 of SI 2017 No 46 (W.20) as from 19.1.17, for schemes made for a financial year starting on or after 1.4.17.

Calculation of earnings of self-employed earners: pensioners
40.–(1)   Where the earnings of an applicant who is a pensioner consist of earnings from employment as a self-employed earner, the weekly amount of that applicant's earnings is to be determined by reference to the applicant's average weekly earnings from that employment–
(a)   over a period of one year; or
(b)   where the applicant has recently become engaged in that employment or there has been a change which is likely to affect the normal pattern of business, over such other period ("computation period") as may, in the particular case, enable the weekly amount of the applicant's earnings to be determined more accurately.
(2)   For the purposes of determining the weekly amount of earnings of an applicant to whom sub-paragraph (1)(b) applies, the applicant's earnings over the computation period are to be divided by the number equal to the number of days in that period and the product multiplied by 7.
(3)   The period over which the weekly amount of an applicant's earnings is calculated in accordance with this paragraph is to be the applicant's assessment period.

Earnings of self-employed earners: pensioners
41.–(1)   Subject to sub-paragraph (2), "earnings" ("enillion"), in the case of employment as a self-employed earner who is a pensioner, means the gross income of the employment.
(2)   "Earnings" in the case of employment as a self-employed earner does not include–
(a)   where an applicant occupies a dwelling as the applicant's home and the applicant provides in that dwelling board and lodging accommodation for which payment is made, those payments;
(b)   any payment made by a local authority to an applicant–
         (i)   with whom a person is accommodated by virtue of arrangements made under section 22C or 23(2)(a) of the Children Act 1989 (provision of accommodation and maintenance for a child whom they are looking after) or, as the case may be, section 26(1) of the Children (Scotland) Act 1995 [¹, or section 81 of the Social Services and Well-being (Wales) Act 2014]; or
         (ii)   with whom a local authority fosters a child under the Looked After Children (Scotland) Regulations 2009 or who is a kinship carer under those Regulations;
(c)   any payment made by a voluntary organisation in accordance with section 59(1)(a) of the Children Act 1989 (provision of accommodation by voluntary organisations);
(d)   any payment made to the applicant or the applicant's partner for a person ("the person concerned") who is not normally a member of the applicant's household but is temporarily in the applicant's care, by–
         (i)   a local authority but excluding payments of housing benefit made in respect of the person concerned;
         (ii)   a voluntary organisation;
         (iii)   the person concerned pursuant to section 26(3A) of the National Assistance Act 1948;
         (iv)   the National Health Service Commissioning Board or a clinical commissioning group established under section 14D of the National Health Service Act 2006; [¹]
         (v)   a Local Health Board established under section 11 of the National Health Service (Wales) Act 2006;
         [¹ (vi)   the person concerned where the payment is for the provision of accommodation to meet the person's needs for care and support arranged pursuant to section 35 or 36 of the Social Services and Well-being (Wales) Act 2014; or
         (vii)   the person concerned where the payment is for the provision of accommodation to meet the person's needs for care and support arranged pursuant to section 18 or 19 of the Care Act 2014;]
(e)   any sports award.

Amendment
1.   Amended by reg 19 of SI 2016 No 50 (W.21) as from 20.1.16, for schemes made for a financial year starting on or after 1.4.16.

Notional income: pensioners
42.–(1)   An applicant who is a pensioner is to be treated as possessing–
(a)   subject to sub-paragraph (2), the amount of any retirement pension income–
         (i)   for which no claim has been made; and

(ii)   to which that applicant might expect to be entitled if a claim for it were made;

(b)   income from an occupational pension scheme which the applicant elected to defer.

(2)   Sub-paragraph (1)(a) does not apply to the following where entitlement has been deferred–

(a)   a Category A or Category B retirement pension payable under sections 43 to 55 of the SSCBA;

(b)   a shared additional pension payable under [¹ sections 55A and 55AA] of the SSCBA;

(c)   graduated retirement benefit payable under sections 36 and 37 of the National Insurance Act 1965 [¹ ;

(d)   a state pension under Part 1 of the Pensions Act 2014.]

(3)   For the purposes of sub-paragraph (2), entitlement has been deferred–

(a)   in the case of a Category A or Category B pension, in the circumstances specified in section 55(3) of the SSCBA;

(b)   in the case of a shared additional pension, in the circumstances specified in section 55C(3) of the SSCBA; [¹]

(c)   in the case of graduated retirement benefit, in the circumstances specified in section 36(4) and (4A) of the National Insurance Act 1965 [¹ and

(d)   in the case of a state pension under Part 1 of the Pensions Act 2014, in the circumstances specified in section 17(7) and (8) of that Act.]

(4)   This sub-paragraph applies where a person who has attained the qualifying age for state pension credit–

(a)   is entitled to money purchase benefits under an occupational pension scheme or a personal pension scheme;

(b)   fails to purchase an annuity with the funds available in that scheme; and

(c)   either–

(i)   defers in whole or in part the payment of any income which would have been payable to that person by that person's pension fund holder, or

(ii)   fails to take any necessary action to secure that the whole of any income which would be payable to that person by that person's pension fund holder upon that person applying for it, is so paid, or

(iii)   is a person to whom income withdrawal is not available under that scheme.

(5)   Where sub-paragraph (4) applies, the amount of any income foregone is to be treated as possessed by that person, but only from the date on which it could be expected to be acquired were an application for it to be made.

(6)   The amount of any income foregone in a case where sub-paragraph (4)(c)(i) or (ii) applies is to be the maximum amount of income which may be withdrawn from the fund and must be determined by the authority, taking account of information provided by the pension fund holder.

(7)   The amount of any income foregone in a case where sub-paragraph (4)(c)(iii) applies is to be the income that the applicant could have received without purchasing an annuity had the funds held under the relevant scheme been held under a personal pension scheme or occupational pension scheme where income withdrawal was available and is to be determined in the manner specified in sub-paragraph (6).

(8)   In sub-paragraph (4), "money purchase benefits" ("buddion pryniant ariannol") has the same meaning as in the Pension Schemes Act 1993.

(9)   Subject to sub-paragraphs (10) [¹, (11A), (11B)] and (12), a person is to be treated as possessing income of which that person has deprived himself or herself for the purpose of securing entitlement to a reduction under this scheme or increasing the amount of the reduction.

(10)   Sub-paragraph (9) does not apply in respect of the amount of an increase of pension or benefit where a person, having made an election in favour of that increase of pension or benefit under Schedule 5 or 5A to the SSCBA or under Schedule 1 to the Social Security (Graduated Retirement Benefit) Regulations 2005, changes that election in accordance with regulations made under Schedule 5 or 5A to that Act in favour of a lump sum.

(11)   In sub-paragraph (10), "lump sum" ("cyfandaliad") means a lump sum under Schedule 5 or 5A to the SSCBA or under Schedule 1 to the Social Security (Graduated Retirement Benefit) Regulations 2005.

[¹ (11A)   Sub-paragraph (9) does not apply in respect of the amount of an increase of pension where a person, having made an election in favour of that increase in pension under section 8(2) of the Pensions Act 2014, changes that election in accordance with regulations made under section 8(7) of that Act in favour of a lump sum.

(11B)   Sub-paragraph (9) does not apply in respect of the amount of an increase of pension where a person, having made an election in favour of that increase in pension in accordance with regulations made under section 10 of the Pensions Act 2014, which include provision corresponding or similar to provision made by section 8(2) of that Act, changes that election in favour of a lump sum, in accordance with regulations made under section 10 of that Act which include provision corresponding or similar to provision made by regulations made under section 8(7).

(11C)   In sub-paragraph (11A), "lump sum" ("cyfandaliad") means a lump sum under section 8 of the Pensions Act 2014.

(11D)   In sub-paragraph (11B), "lump sum" ("cyfandaliad") means a lump sum under section 10 of the Pensions Act 2014.]

(12)   Sub-paragraph (9) does not apply in respect of any amount of income other than earnings, or earnings of an employed earner, arising out of the applicant's participation in a service user group.

(13)   Where an applicant is in receipt of any benefit under the benefit Acts and the rate of that benefit is altered with effect from a date on or after 1 April in any year but not more than 14 days thereafter, the authority must treat the applicant as possessing such benefit at the altered rate from either 1 April or the first Monday in April in that year, whichever date the authority selects to apply, to the date on which the altered rate is to take effect.

(14)   In the case of an applicant who has, or whose partner has, an award of state pension credit comprising only the savings credit, where the authority treats the applicant as possessing any benefit at the altered rate in accordance with sub-paragraph (13), the authority must–

(a)   determine the income and capital of that applicant in accordance with paragraph 33(1) (calculation of pensioner's income in savings credit only cases) where the calculation or estimate of that income and capital is altered with effect from a date on or after 1 April in any year but not more than 14 days thereafter; and

(b)   treat that applicant as possessing such income and capital at the altered rate by reference to the date selected by the authority to apply in its area, for the purposes of establishing the period referred to in sub-paragraph (13).

(15)   For the purposes of sub-paragraph (9), a person is not to be regarded as depriving himself or herself of income where–

(a)   that person's rights to benefits under a registered pension scheme are extinguished and in consequence of this that person receives a payment from the scheme; and

(b)   that payment is a trivial commutation lump sum within the meaning given by paragraph 7 of Schedule 29 to the Finance Act 2004.

(16)   In sub-paragraph (15), "registered pension scheme" ("cynllun pensiwn cofrestredig") has the meaning given in section 150(2) of the Finance Act 2004.

Amendment

1.   Amended by reg 20 of SI 2016 No 50 (W.21) as from 20.1.16, for schemes made for a financial year starting on or after 1.4.16.

Income paid to third parties: pensioners

43.–(1)   Any payment of income, other than a payment specified in sub-paragraph (2) or (3), to a third party in respect of the applicant is to be treated as possessed by the applicant.

(2)   Sub-paragraph (1) does not apply in respect of a payment of income made under an occupational pension scheme, in respect of a pension or other periodical payment made under a personal pension scheme or a payment made by the Board of the Pension Protection Fund where–

(a)   a bankruptcy order has been made in respect of the person in respect of whom the payment has been made or, in Scotland, the estate of that person is subject to sequestration or a judicial factor has been appointed on that person's estate under section 41 of the Solicitors (Scotland) Act 1980;

(b)   the payment is made to the trustee in bankruptcy or any other person acting on behalf of the creditors; and

(c)   the person referred to in paragraph (a) and that person's partner does not possess, or is not treated as possessing, any other income apart from that payment.

(3)   Sub-paragraph (1) does not apply in respect of any payment of income other than earnings, or earnings derived from employment as an employed earner, arising out of the applicant's participation in a service user group.

CHAPTER 5
Income: persons who are not pensioners

Average weekly earnings of employed earners: persons who are not pensioners

44.–(1)   Where the income of an applicant who is not a pensioner consists of earnings from employment as an employed earner the applicant's average weekly earnings must be estimated by reference to the applicant's earnings from that employment–

(a)   over a period immediately preceding the reduction week in which the application is made or treated as made and being a period of–
     (i)   5 weeks, if the applicant is paid weekly; or
     (ii)   2 months, if the applicant is paid monthly; or

(b)   whether or not paragraph (a)(i) or (ii) applies, where an applicant's earnings fluctuate, over such other period preceding the reduction week in which the application is made or treated as made as may, in any particular case, enable the applicant's average weekly earnings to be estimated more accurately.

(2)   Where the applicant has been in employment for less than the period specified in sub-paragraph (1)(a)(i) or (ii)–

(a)   if the applicant has received any earnings [¹ or expects to receive an amount of earnings] for the period that the applicant has been in that employment and those earnings are likely to represent the applicant's average weekly earnings from that employment the applicant's average weekly earnings must be estimated by reference to those earnings;

(b)   in any other case, the authority must estimate the applicant's average weekly earnings.

(3)   Where the amount of an applicant's earnings changes the authority must estimate the applicant's average weekly earnings by reference to the applicant's likely earnings from the employment over such period as is appropriate in order that the applicant's average weekly earnings may be estimated accurately but the length of the period must not in any case exceed 52 weeks.

(4)   For the purposes of this paragraph the applicant's earnings are to be calculated in accordance with paragraphs 48 and 49 (earnings of employed earners: persons who are not pensioners).

Amendment

1.   Amended by reg 11 of SI 2017 No 46 (W.20) as from 19.1.17, for schemes made for a financial year starting on or after 1.4.17.

[1, 2 Date on which income consisting of earnings from employment as an employed earner are taken into account: persons who are not pensioners

44A.   An applicant's average weekly earnings from employment estimated pursuant to paragraph 44 (average weekly earnings of employed earners: persons who are not pensioners) must be taken into account–

(a)   in the case of an application, on the date on which the application was made or treated as made, and the first day of each reduction week thereafter, regardless of when those earnings were actually received ;

(b)   in the case of an application or a reduction under a scheme where the applicant commences employment, the day on which the applicant commences that employment and the first day of each reduction week thereafter, regardless of when those earnings were actually received; or

(c)   in the case of an application or reduction under a scheme where the applicant's average weekly earnings from employment change, the day on which the applicant's earnings from employment change and the first day of each reduction week thereafter, regardless of when those earnings were actually received.]

Amendments

1.   Inserted by reg 12 of SI 2017 No 46 (W.20) as from 19.1.17, for schemes made for a financial year starting on or after 1.4.17.

2.   Substituted by reg 20 of SI 2018 No 14 (W.7) as from 10.1.18, for schemes made for a financial year starting on or after 1.4.18.

Average weekly earnings of self-employed earners: persons who are not pensioners

45.–(1)   Where the income of an applicant who is not a pensioner consists of earnings from employment as a self-employed earner that applicant's average weekly earnings must be estimated by reference to that applicant's earnings from that employment over such period as is appropriate in order that that applicant's average weekly earnings may be estimated accurately but the length of the period must not in any case exceed 52 weeks.

(2)   For the purposes of this paragraph the applicant's earnings must be calculated in accordance with paragraphs 50, 58 and 59 (earnings and net profit of self-employed earners).

Average weekly income other than earnings: persons who are not pensioners

46.–(1)   The income of an applicant who is not a pensioner which does not consist of earnings must, except where sub-paragraph (2) applies, be estimated over such period as is appropriate in order that that applicant's average weekly income may be estimated accurately but the length of the period must not in any case exceed 52 weeks; and nothing in this paragraph authorises an authority to disregard any such income other than that specified in Schedule 7 (sums disregarded in the calculation of income other than earnings: persons who are not pensioners).

(2)   The period over which any benefit under the benefit Acts is to be taken into account is to be the period in respect of which that benefit is payable.

(3)   For the purposes of this paragraph income other than earnings is to be calculated in accordance with paragraph 51 (calculation of income other than earnings: persons who are not pensioners).

Calculation of weekly income of employed earners: persons who are not pensioners

47.–(1)   For the purposes of paragraphs 44 (average weekly earnings of employed earners), 46 (average weekly income other than earnings) and 56 (calculation of average weekly income from tax credits), where the period in respect of which a payment is made–

(a)   does not exceed a week, the weekly amount is to be the amount of that payment;

(b)   exceeds a week, the weekly amount is to be determined–

(i)   in a case where that period is a month, by multiplying the amount of the payment by 12 and dividing the product by 52;

(ii)   in any other case, by dividing the amount of the payment by the number equal to the number of days in the period to which it relates and multiplying the quotient by 7.

(2)   For the purposes of paragraph 45 (average weekly earnings of self-employed earners) the weekly amount of earnings of an applicant is to be determined by dividing the applicant's earnings over the assessment period by the number equal to the number of days in that period and multiplying the quotient by 7.

Earnings of employed earners: persons who are not pensioners

48.–(1)   Subject to sub-paragraph (2), "earnings" ("enillion"), in the case of employment as an employed earner of a person who is not a pensioner, means any remuneration or profit derived from that employment and includes–

(a)   any bonus or commission;

(b)   any payment in lieu of remuneration except any periodic sum paid to an applicant on account of the termination of the applicant's employment by reason of redundancy;

(c)   any payment in lieu of notice or any lump sum payment intended as compensation for the loss of employment but only in so far as it represents loss of income;

(d)   any holiday pay except any payable more than 4 weeks after termination or interruption of the employment;

(e)   any payment by way of a retainer;

(f)   any payment made by the applicant's employer in respect of expenses not wholly, exclusively and necessarily incurred in the performance of the duties of the employment, including any payment made by the applicant's employer in respect of–

    (i)   travelling expenses incurred by the applicant between the applicant's home and place of employment;

    (ii)   expenses incurred by the applicant under arrangements made for the care of a member of the applicant's family owing to the applicant's absence from home;

(g)   any award of compensation made under section 112(4) or 117(3)(a) of the Employment Rights Act 1996 (remedies and compensation for unfair dismissal);

(h)   any payment or remuneration made under section 28, 34, 64, 68 or 70 of the Employment Rights Act 1996 (right to guarantee payments, remuneration on suspension on medical or maternity grounds, complaints to employment tribunals);

(i)   any such sum as is referred to in section 112 of the SSCBA (certain sums to be earnings for social security purposes);

(j)   any statutory sick pay, statutory maternity pay, statutory paternity pay [¹, statutory shared parental pay] or statutory adoption pay, or a corresponding payment under any enactment having effect in Northern Ireland;

(k)   any remuneration paid by or on behalf of an employer to the applicant who for the time being is on maternity leave, paternity leave [¹ , shared parental leave] or adoption leave or is absent from work because the applicant is ill;

(l)   the amount of any payment by way of a non-cash voucher which has been taken into account in the computation of a person's earnings in accordance with Part 5 of Schedule 3 to the Social Security (Contributions) Regulations 2001.

(2)   Earnings does not include–

(a)   subject to sub-paragraph (3), any payment in kind;

(b)   any payment in respect of expenses wholly, exclusively and necessarily incurred in the performance of the duties of the employment;

(c)   any occupational pension;

(d)   any payment in respect of expenses arising out of the applicant's participation in a service user group.

(3)   Sub-paragraph (2)(a) does not apply in respect of any non-cash voucher referred to in sub-paragraph (1)(l).

Amendment

1.   Amended by reg 22 of SI 2015 No 44 (W.3) as from 21.1.15, for schemes made for a financial year starting on or after 1.4.15.

Calculation of net earnings of employed earners: persons who are not pensioners

49.–(1)   For the purposes of paragraph 44 (average weekly earnings of employed earners: persons who are not pensioners), the earnings of an applicant derived or likely to be derived from employment as an employed earner to be taken into account must, subject to sub-paragraph (2), be the applicant's net earnings.

(2)   There is to be disregarded from an applicant's net earnings, any sum, where applicable, specified in paragraphs 1 to 18 of Schedule 6 (sums disregarded in the calculation of earnings: persons who are not pensioners).

(3)   For the purposes of sub-paragraph (1) net earnings must, except where sub-paragraph (6) applies, be calculated by taking into account the gross earnings of the applicant from that employment over the assessment period, less–

(a)   any amount deducted from those earnings by way of–

    (i)   income tax;

    (ii)   primary Class 1 contributions under the SSCBA;

(b)   one-half of any sum paid by the applicant by way of a contribution towards an occupational pension scheme;

(c)   one-half of the amount calculated in accordance with sub-paragraph (5) in respect of any qualifying contribution payable by the applicant; and

(d)   where those earnings include a payment which is payable under any enactment having effect in Northern Ireland and which corresponds to statutory sick pay, statutory maternity pay, [¹] statutory paternity pay [¹, statutory shared parental pay] or statutory adoption pay, any amount deducted from those earnings by way of any contributions which correspond to primary Class 1 contributions under the SSCBA.

(4)   In this regulation "qualifying contribution" ("cyfraniad cymwys") means any sum which is payable periodically as a contribution towards a personal pension scheme.

(5)   The amount in respect of any qualifying contribution is to be calculated by multiplying the daily amount of the qualifying contribution by the number equal to the number of days in the assessment period; and for the purposes of this paragraph the daily amount of the qualifying contribution is to be determined–

(a)   where the qualifying contribution is payable monthly, by multiplying the amount of the qualifying contribution by 12 and dividing the product by 365;

(b)   in any other case, by dividing the amount of the qualifying contribution by the number equal to the number of days in the period to which the qualifying contribution relates.

(6)   Where the earnings of an applicant are estimated under paragraph 44(2)(b) (average weekly earnings of employed earners: persons who are not pensioners), the applicant's net earnings are to be calculated by taking into account those earnings over the assessment period, less–

(a)   an amount in respect of income tax equivalent to an amount calculated by applying to those earnings the basic rate of tax applicable to the assessment period less only the [² personal reliefs to which the applicant is entitled under Chapters 2, 3 and 3A of Part 3] of the Income Tax Act 2007 [²] as is appropriate to the applicant's circumstances but, if the assessment period is less than a year, the earnings to which the basic rate of tax is to be applied and the amount of the personal [² reliefs] deductible under this sub-paragraph is tobe calculated on a pro rata basis;

(b)   an amount equivalent to the amount of the primary Class 1 contributions that would be payable by the applicant under the SSCBA in respect of those earnings if such contributions were payable; and

(c)   one-half of any sum which would be payable by the applicant by way of a contribution towards an occupational or personal pension scheme, if the earnings so estimated were actual earnings.

Amendments

1.   Amended by reg 23 of SI 2015 No 44 (W.3) as from 21.1.15, for schemes made for a financial year starting on or after 1.4.15.

2.   Amended by reg 13 of SI 2017 No 46 (W.20) as from 19.1.17, for schemes made for a financial year starting on or after 1.4.17.

Earnings of self-employed earners: persons who are not pensioners

50.–(1)   Subject to sub-paragraph (2), "earnings" ("enillion"), in the case of employment as a self-employed earner of a person who is not a pensioner, means the gross income of the employment.

(2)   "Earnings" does not include any payment to which paragraph 31 or 32 of Schedule 7 refers (payments in respect of a person accommodated with the applicant under arrangements made by a local authority or voluntary organisation and payments made to the applicant by a health authority, local authority or voluntary organisation in respect of persons temporarily in the applicant's care) nor does it include any sports award.

(3)   This paragraph applies to–

(a)   royalties or other sums paid as a consideration for the use of, or the right to use, any copyright, design, patent or trade mark; or

(b)   any payment in respect of any–

(i)   book registered under the Public Lending Right Scheme 1982; or

(ii)   work made under any international public lending right scheme that is analogous to the Public Lending Right Scheme 1982,

where the applicant is the first owner of the copyright, design, patent or trade mark, or an original contributor to the book or work concerned.

(4)   Where the applicant's earnings consist of any items to which sub-paragraph (3) applies, those earnings must be taken into account over a period equal to such number of weeks as is equal to the number obtained (and any fraction is to be treated as a corresponding fraction of a week) by dividing the earnings by–

(a)   the amount of reduction under this scheme to which the applicant would have been entitled had the payment not been made, plus

(b)   an amount equal to the total of the sums which would fall to be disregarded from the payment under Schedule 6 (sums disregarded in the calculation of earnings; persons who are not pensioners) as appropriate in the applicant's case.

Calculation of income other than earnings: persons who are not pensioners

51.–(1)   For the purposes of paragraph 46 (average weekly income other than earnings: persons who are not pensioners), the income of an applicant who is not a pensioner which does not consist of earnings to be taken into account must, subject to sub-paragraphs (2) to (6), be that applicant's gross income and any capital treated as income under paragraph 52 (capital treated as income: persons who are not pensioners).

(2)   There is to be disregarded from the calculation of an applicant's gross income under sub-paragraph (1), any sum, where applicable, specified in Schedule 7.

(3)   Where the payment of any benefit under the benefit Acts is subject to any deduction by way of recovery the amount to be taken into account under sub-paragraph (1) must be the gross amount payable.

(4)   Where the applicant or, where the applicant is a member of a couple, the applicant's partner is receiving a contributory employment and support allowance and that benefit has been reduced under regulation 63 of the Employment and Support Allowance Regulations 2008 [¹ or section 11J of the Welfare Reform Act 2007], the amount of that benefit to be taken into account is the amount as if it had not been reduced.

(5)   Where an award of any working tax credit or child tax credit under the Tax Credits Act 2002 is subject to a deduction by way of recovery of an overpayment of working tax credit or child tax credit which arose in a previous tax year the amount to be taken into account under sub-paragraph (1) is to be the amount of working tax credit or child tax credit awarded less the amount of that deduction.

(6)   Sub-paragraphs (7) and (8) apply where–

(a)   a relevant payment has been made to a person in an academic year; and

(b)   that person abandons, or is dismissed from, that person's course of study before the payment to that person of the final instalment of the relevant payment.

(7)   Where a relevant payment is made quarterly, the amount of a relevant payment to be taken into account for the assessment period for the purposes of sub-paragraph (1) in respect of a person to whom sub-paragraph (6) applies, is to be calculated by applying the formula–

$$\frac{(A - (B \times C))}{D}$$

where–

A = the total amount of the relevant payment which that person would have received had that person remained a student until the last day of the academic term in which that person abandoned, or was dismissed from, the course, less any deduction under paragraph 78(5) (costs of travel, books and equipment);

B = the number of reduction weeks from the reduction week immediately following that which includes the first day of that academic year to the reduction week which includes the day on which the person abandoned, or was dismissed from, the course;

C = the weekly amount of the relevant payment, before the application of the £10 disregard, which would have been taken into account as income under paragraph 78(2) (treatment of student loans) had the person not abandoned or been dismissed from, the course and, in the case of a person who was not entitled to a reduction under this scheme immediately before that person abandoned or was dismissed from the course, had that person, at that time, been entitled to housing benefit;

D = the number of reduction weeks in the assessment period.

(8)   Where a relevant payment is made by two or more instalments in a quarter, the amount of a relevant payment to be taken into account for the assessment period for the purposes of sub-paragraph (1) in respect of a person to whom sub-paragraph (6) applies, is to be calculated by applying the formula in sub-paragraph (7) but as if–

A = the total amount of relevant payments which that person received, or would have received, from the first day of the academic year to the day the person abandoned the course, or was dismissed from it, less any deduction under paragraph 78(5).

(9)   In this paragraph–

"academic year" ("blwyddyn academaidd") and "student loan" ("benthyciad myfyriwr") have the same meanings as in Part 10 (students);

"assessment period" ("cyfnod asesu") means–

(a)   in a case where a relevant payment is made quarterly, the period beginning with the reduction week which includes the day on which the person abandoned, or was dismissed from, the course and ending with the reduction week which includes the last day of the last quarter for which an instalment of the relevant payment was payable to that person;

(b)   in a case where the relevant payment is made by two or more instalments in a quarter, the period beginning with the reduction week which includes the day on which the person abandoned, or was dismissed from, the course and ending with the reduction week which includes–

(i)   the day immediately before the day on which the next instalment of the relevant payment would have been due had the payments continued; or

(ii)   the last day of the last quarter for which an instalment of the relevant payment was payable to that person,

whichever of those dates is earlier;

"quarter" ("chwarter") in relation to an assessment period means a period in that year beginning on–

(c)   1 January and ending on 31 March;

(d)   1 April and ending on 30 June;

(e)   1 July and ending on 31 August; or
(f)   1 September and ending on 31 December;
"relevant payment" ("taliad perthnasol") means either a student loan or an amount intended for the maintenance of dependants referred to in paragraph 73(7) or both.
(10)   For the avoidance of doubt there must be included as income to be taken into account under sub-paragraph (1)–
(a)   any payment to which paragraph 48(2) (payments not earnings) applies; or
(b)   in the case of an applicant who is receiving support under section 95 or 98 of the Immigration and Asylum Act 1999 including support provided by virtue of regulations made under Schedule 9 to that Act, the amount of such support provided in respect of essential living needs of the applicant and the applicant's dependants (if any) as is specified in regulations made under paragraph 3 of Schedule 8 to the Immigration and Asylum Act 1999.

Amendment

1.   Amended by reg 24 of SI 2015 No 44 (W.3) as from 21.1.15, for schemes made for a financial year starting on or after 1.4.15.

Capital treated as income: persons who are not pensioners

52.–(1)   Any capital payable by instalments which are outstanding at the date on which the application is made or treated as made, or, at the date of any subsequent revision or supersession, must, if the aggregate of the instalments outstanding and the amount of the applicant's capital otherwise calculated in accordance with Chapter 7 of this Part exceeds £16,000, be treated as income.
(2)   Any payment received under an annuity is to be treated as income.
(3)   Any earnings to the extent that they are not a payment of income is to be treated as income.
(4)   Any Career Development Loan paid pursuant to section 2 of the Employment and Training Act 1973 is to be treated as income.
(5)   Where an agreement or court order provides that payments must be made to the applicant in consequence of any personal injury to the applicant and that such payments are to be made, wholly or partly, by way of periodic payments, any such periodic payments received by the applicant (but not a payment which is treated as capital by virtue of this Part), is to be treated as income.

Notional income: persons who are not pensioners

53.–(1)   An applicant who is not a pensioner is to be treated as possessing income of which that applicant has deprived himself or herself for the purpose of securing entitlement to a reduction or increasing the amount of the reduction.
(2)   Except in the case of–
(a)   a discretionary trust;
(b)   a trust derived from a payment made in consequence of a personal injury;
(c)   a personal pension scheme, occupational pension scheme or a payment made by the Board of the Pension Protection Fund where the applicant has not attained the qualifying age for state pension credit;
(d)   any sum to which paragraph 48(2)(a) of Schedule 9 (capital disregards: persons who are not pensioners) applies which is administered in the way referred to in paragraph 48(1)(a) of that Schedule;
(e)   any sum to which paragraph 49(a) of Schedule 9 refers;
(f)   rehabilitation allowance made under section 2 of the Employment and Training Act 1973;
(g)   child tax credit;
(h)   working tax credit; or
(i)   any sum to which sub-paragraph (11) applies,
any income which would become available to the applicant upon application being made, but which has not been acquired by the applicant, is to be treated as possessed by the applicant but only from the date on which it could be expected to be acquired were an application made.
(3)   Any payment of income, other than a payment of income specified in sub-paragraph (4),made–
(a)   to a third party in respect of a single applicant or a member of the family (but not a member of the third party's family) must, where that payment is a payment of an occupational pension, a pension or other periodical payment made under a personal pension scheme or a payment made by the Board of the Pension Protection Fund, be treated as possessed by that single applicant or, as the case may be, by that member;
(b)   to a third party in respect of a single applicant or in respect of a member of the family (but not a member of the third party's family) must, where it is not a payment referred to in paragraph (a), be treated as possessed by that single applicant or by that member to the extent that it is used for the food, ordinary clothing or footwear, household fuel or rent of that single applicant or, as the case may be, of any member of that family or is used for any council tax or water charges for which that applicant or member is liable;
(c)   to a single applicant or a member of the family in respect of a third party (but not in respect of another member of that family) must be treated as possessed by that single applicant or, as the case

may be, that member of the family to the extent that it is kept or used by that single applicant or used by or on behalf of any member of the family.

(4) Sub-paragraph (3) does not apply in respect of a payment of income made–

(a) under or by the Trusts, the Fund, the Eileen Trust, MFET Limited, the Skipton Fund, the Caxton Foundation [², an approved blood scheme, the Scottish Infected Blood Support Scheme, the London Emergencies Trust, the We Love Manchester Emergency Fund] or the Independent Living Fund (2006);

(b) pursuant to section 19(1)(a) of the Coal Industry Act 1994 (concessionary coal);

(c) pursuant to section 2 of the Employment and Training Act 1973 in respect of a person's participation–

    (i) in an employment programme specified in regulation 75(1)(a) of the Jobseeker's Allowance Regulations 1996;

    (ii) in a training scheme specified in regulation 75(1)(b) of those Regulations; or

    (iii) in a qualifying course within the meaning specified in regulation 17A(7) of those Regulations;

(d) in respect of a person's participation in the Work for Your Benefit Pilot Scheme;

(e) in respect of a person's participation in the Mandatory Work Activity Scheme;

(f) in respect of an applicant's participation in the Employment, Skills and Enterprise Scheme;

(g) under an occupational pension scheme, in respect of a pension or other periodical payment made under a personal pension scheme or a payment made by the Board of the Pension Protection Fund where–

    (i) a bankruptcy order has been made in respect of the person in respect of whom the payment has been made or, in Scotland, the estate of that person is subject to sequestration or a judicial factor has been appointed on that person's estate under section 41 of the Solicitors (Scotland) Act 1980;

    (ii) the payment is made to the trustee in bankruptcy or any other person acting on behalf of the creditors; and

    (iii) the person referred to in sub-paragraph (i) and any member of that person's family does not possess, or is not treated as possessing, any other income apart from that payment.

(5) Where an applicant is in receipt of any benefit under the benefit Acts and the rate of that benefit is altered with effect from a date on or after 1 April in any year but not more than 14 days thereafter, the authority must treat the applicant as possessing such benefit at the altered rate from either 1 April or the first Monday in April in that year, whichever date the authority selects, to the date on which the altered rate is to take effect.

(6) Subject to sub-paragraph (7), where–

(a) an applicant performs a service for another person; and

(b) that person makes no payment of earnings or pays less than that paid for a comparable employment in the area,

the authority must treat the applicant as possessing such earnings (if any) as is reasonable for that employment unless the applicant satisfies the authority that the means of that person are insufficient for that person to pay or to pay more for the service.

(7) Sub-paragraph (6) does not apply–

(a) to an applicant who is engaged by a charitable or voluntary organisation or who is a volunteer if the authority is satisfied in any of those cases that it is reasonable for the applicant to provide those services free of charge; or

(b) in a case where the service is performed in connection with–

    (i) the applicant's participation in an employment or training programme in accordance with regulation 19(1)(q) of the Jobseeker's Allowance Regulations 1996; or

    (ii) the applicant's or the applicant's partner's participation in an employment or training programme as defined in regulation 19(3) of those Regulations for which a training allowance is not payable or, where such an allowance is payable, it is payable for the sole purpose of reimbursement of travelling or meal expenses to the person participating in that programme; or

(c) to an applicant who is participating in a work placement approved by the Secretary of State(or a person providing services to the Secretary of State) before the placement starts.

(8) In sub-paragraph (7)(c) "work placement" ("lleoliad gwaith") means practical work experience which is not undertaken in expectation of payment.

(9) Where an applicant is treated as possessing any income under any of sub-paragraphs (1) to(8), the foregoing provisions of this Part apply for the purposes of calculating the amount of that income as if a payment had actually been made and as if it were actual income which that applicant does possess.

(10) Where an applicant is treated as possessing any earnings under sub-paragraph (6) the foregoing provisions of this Part apply for the purposes of calculating the amount of those earnings as if a payment had actually been made and as if they were actual earnings which that applicant does possess except that paragraph 39(2) or 49(3) (calculation of net earnings of employed earners: pensioners and persons who are not pensioners, respectively) do not apply and that applicant's net earnings are to be calculated by taking into account those earnings which that applicant is treated as possessing, less–

(a) an amount in respect of income tax equivalent to an amount calculated by applying to those earnings the basic rate of tax applicable to the assessment period less only the [¹ personal reliefs to which the applicant is entitled under Chapters 2, 3 and 3A] of Part 3 of the Income Tax Act 2007 [¹] as is appropriate to the applicant's circumstances; but, if the assessment period is less than a year, the earnings to which the basic rate of tax is to be applied and the amount of the personal [¹ reliefs] deductible under this sub-paragraph is to be calculated on a pro rata basis;

(b)   an amount equivalent to the amount of the primary Class 1 contributions that would be payable by the applicant under the SSCBA in respect of those earnings if such contributions were payable; and

(c)   one-half of any sum payable by the applicant by way of a contribution towards an occupational or personal pension scheme.

(11)   Sub-paragraphs (1), (2), (3) and (6) do not apply in respect of any amount of income other than earnings, or earnings of an employed earner, arising out of the applicant's participation in a service user group.

Amendments

1.   Amended by reg 14 of SI 2017 No 46 (W.20) as from 19.1.17, for schemes made for a financial year starting on or after 1.4.17.

2.   Amended by reg 21 of SI 2018 No 14 (W.7) as from 10.1.18, for schemes made for a financial year starting on or after 1.4.18.

CHAPTER 6

Income: pensioners and persons who are not pensioners

Calculation of income on a weekly basis

54.–(1)   Subject to paragraph 57 (disregard of changes in tax, contributions etc), the income of an applicant is to be calculated on a weekly basis–

(a)   by estimating the amount which is likely to be the applicant's average weekly income in accordance with this Part;

(b)   by adding to that amount the weekly income calculated–

    (i)   if the applicant is a pensioner, under paragraph 68 (tariff income: pensioners);

    (ii)   if the applicant is a person who is not a pensioner, under paragraph 69 (tariff income: persons who are not pensioners); and

(c)   by then deducting any relevant child care charges to which paragraph 55 (treatment of child care charges) applies from any earnings which form part of the average weekly income or, in a case where the conditions in sub-paragraph (2) are met, from those earnings plus whichever credit specified in paragraph (b) of that sub-paragraph is appropriate, up to a maximum deduction in respect of the applicant's family of whichever of the sums specified in sub-paragraph (3) applies in the applicant's case.

(2)   The conditions of this paragraph are that–

(a)   the applicant's earnings which form part of the applicant's average weekly income are less than the lower of either the applicant's relevant child care charges or whichever of the deductions specified in paragraph (3) otherwise applies in the applicant's case; and

(b)   that applicant or, if the applicant is a member of a couple either the applicant or the applicant's partner, is in receipt of either working tax credit or child tax credit.

(3)   The maximum deduction to which paragraph (1)(c) above refers is to be–

(a)   where the applicant's family includes only one child in respect of whom relevant child care charges are paid, £175 per week;

(b)   where the applicant's family includes more than one child in respect of whom relevant child care charges are paid, £300 per week.

Treatment of child care charges

55.–(1)   This paragraph applies where an applicant (within the meaning of this paragraph) is incurring relevant child care charges and–

(a)   is a lone parent and is engaged in remunerative work;

(b)   is a member of a couple both of whom are engaged in remunerative work; or

(c)   is a member of a couple where one member is engaged in remunerative work and the other–

    (i)   is incapacitated;

    (ii)   is an in-patient in hospital; or

    (iii)   is in prison (whether serving a custodial sentence or remanded in custody awaiting trial or sentence).

(2)   For the purposes of sub-paragraph (1) and subject to sub-paragraph (4), a person to whom sub-paragraph (3) applies must be treated as engaged in remunerative work for a period not exceeding 28 weeks during which the person–

(a)   is paid statutory sick pay;

(b)   is paid short-term incapacity benefit at the lower rate under sections 30A to 30E of the SSCBA;

(c)   is paid an employment and support allowance;

(d)   is paid income support on the grounds of incapacity for work under regulation 4ZA of, and paragraph 7 or 14 of Schedule 1B to, the Income Support (General) Regulations 1987; or

(e)   is credited with earnings on the grounds of incapacity for work or limited capability for work under regulation 8B of the Social Security (Credits) Regulations 1975.

(3)   This sub-paragraph applies to a person who was engaged in remunerative work immediately before–

(a)   the first day of the period in respect of which the person was first paid statutory sick pay, short-term incapacity benefit, an employment and support allowance or income support on the grounds of incapacity for work; or

(b)   the first day of the period in respect of which earnings are credited,

as the case may be.

(4)   In a case to which sub-paragraph (2)(d) or (e) applies, the period of 28 weeks begins on the day on which the person is first paid income support or on the first day of the period in respect of which earnings are credited, as the case may be.

(5)   Relevant child care charges are those charges for care to which sub-paragraphs (6) and (7) apply, and are to be calculated on a weekly basis in accordance with sub-paragraph (10).

(6)   The charges are paid by the applicant for care which is provided–

(a)   in the case of any child of the applicant's family who is not disabled, in respect of the period beginning on that child's date of birth and ending on the day preceding the first Monday in September following that child's fifteenth birthday; or

(b)   in the case of any child of the applicant's family who is disabled, in respect of the period beginning on that child's date of birth and ending on the day preceding the first Monday in September following that child's sixteenth birthday.

(7)   The charges are paid for care which is provided by one or more of the care providers listed in sub-paragraph (8) and are not paid–

(a)   in respect of the child's compulsory education;

(b)   by an applicant to a partner or by a partner to an applicant in respect of any child for whom either or any of them is responsible in accordance with paragraph 7 (circumstances in which a person is treated as responsible or not responsible for another); or

(c)   in respect of care provided by a relative of the child wholly or mainly in the child's home.

(8)   The care to which sub-paragraph (7) refers may be provided–

(a)   out of school hours, by a school on school premises or by a local authority–

(i)   for children who are not disabled in respect of the period beginning on their eighth birthday and ending on the day preceding the first Monday in September following their fifteenth birthday; or

(ii)   for children who are disabled in respect of the period beginning on their eighth birthday and ending on the day preceding the first Monday in September following their sixteenth birthday; or

(b)   by a child care provider approved in accordance with the Tax Credit (New Category of Child Care Provider) Regulations 1999; or

(c)   by persons registered under Part 2 of the Children and Families (Wales) Measure 2010; or

(d)   by a person who is excepted from registration under Part 2 of the Children and Families (Wales) Measure 2010 because the child care that person provides is in a school or establishment referred to in article 11, 12 or 14 of the Child Minding and Day Care Exceptions (Wales) Order 2010; or

(e)   by–

(i)   persons registered under section 59(1) of the Public Services Reform (Scotland) Act 2010; or

(ii)   local authorities registered under section 83(1) of that Act,

         where the care provided is child minding or day care of children within the meaning of that Act; or

(f)   by a person prescribed in regulations made pursuant to section 12(4) of the Tax Credits Act 2002; or

(g)   by a person who is registered under Chapter 2 or 3 of Part 3 of the Childcare Act 2006; or

(h)   by any of the schools mentioned in section 34(2) of the Childcare Act 2006 in circumstances where the requirement to register under Chapter 2 of Part 3 of that Act does not apply by virtue of section 34(2) of that Act; or

(i)   by any of the schools mentioned in section 53(2) of the Childcare Act 2006 in circumstances where the requirement to register under Chapter 3 of Part 3 of that Act does not apply by virtue of section 53(2) of that Act; or

(j)   by any of the establishments mentioned in section 18(5) of the Childcare Act 2006 in circumstances where the care is not included in the meaning of "childcare" for the purposes of Part 1 and Part 3 of that Act by virtue of section 18(5) of that Act; or

(k)   by a foster parent or kinship carer under the Fostering Services (England) Regulations 2011, the [⁵ Fostering Services (Wales) Regulations 2003 or any regulations made under sections 87 and 93 of the Social Services and Well-being (Wales) Act 2014 which make provision for the approval of local authority foster parents] or the Looked After Children (Scotland) Regulations 2009 in relation to a child other than one whom the foster parent is fostering or kinship carer is looking after; or

[⁴ (l) by a person who is employed, or engaged under a contract for services, to provide care and support by the provider of a domiciliary support service, within the meaning of Part 1 of the Regulation and Inspection of Social Care (Wales) Act 2016; or]

(m)   by a person who is not a relative of the child wholly or mainly in the child's home.

(9)   In sub-paragraphs (6) and (8)(a), "the first Monday in September" ("y dydd Llun cyntaf ym Medi") means the Monday which first occurs in the month of September in any year.

(10)   Relevant child care charges must be estimated over such period, not exceeding a year, as is appropriate in order that the average weekly charge may be estimated accurately having regard to information as to the amount of that charge provided by the child minder or person providing the care.

(11)   For the purposes of sub-paragraph (1)(c) the other member of a couple is incapacitated where–

(a)   the applicant is a pensioner and the other member of the couple is aged not less than 80;

(b)   the applicant is a pensioner and the other member of the couple is aged less than 80, and–

    (i)   the additional condition specified in paragraph 10 of Schedule 3 (additional condition for the disability premium) to this scheme is treated as applying in the other member of the couple's case; and

    (ii)   the other member of the couple satisfies those conditions or would satisfy them but for the other member of the couple being treated as capable of work by virtue of a determination made in accordance with regulations made under section 171E of the SSCBA;

(c)   the applicant is not a pensioner, the applicant's applicable amount includes a disability premium on account of the other member's incapacity or the support component or the work-related activity component [⁴ or the other member would be a member of the work-related activity group] on account of the other member's having limited capability for work;

(d)   the applicant is not a pensioner, the applicant's applicable amount would include a disability premium on account of the other member's incapacity but for that other member being treated as capable of work by virtue of a determination made in accordance with regulations made under section 171E of the SSCBA;

(e)   the applicant's applicable amount would include the support component or the work-related activity component [⁴ or the other member of the couple would be a member of the work-related activity group] on account of the other member having limited capability for work but for that other member being treated as not having limited capability for work by virtue of a determination made in accordance with the Employment and Support Allowance Regulations 2008 [² or the Employment and Support Allowance Regulations 2013];

(f)   the applicant is, or is treated as, incapable of work and has been so incapable, or has been so treated as incapable, of work in accordance with the provisions of, and regulations made under, Part 12A of the SSCBA (incapacity for work) for a continuous period of not less than 196 days; and for this purpose any two or more separate periods separated by a break of not more than 56 days must be treated as one continuous period;

(g)   the applicant has, or is treated as having, limited capability for work and has had, or been treated as having, limited capability for work in accordance with the Employment and Support Allowance Regulations 2008 [² or the Employment and Support Allowance Regulations 2013] for a continuous period of not less than 196 days and for this purpose any two or more separate periods separated by a break of not more than 84 days must be treated as one continuous period;

(h)   there is payable in respect of the other member one or more of the following pensions or allowances–

    (i)   long-term incapacity benefit or short-term incapacity benefit at the higher rate under Schedule 4 to the SSCBA;

    (ii)   attendance allowance under section 64 of the SSCBA;

    (iii)   severe disablement allowance under section 68 of the SSCBA;

    (iv)   disability living allowance under section 71 of the SSCBA;

    (v)   personal independence payment under Part 4 of the Welfare Reform Act 2012;

    (vi)   an AFIP;

    (vii)   increase of disablement pension under section 104 of the SSCBA;

    (viii)   a pension increase paid as part of a war disablement pension or under an industrial injuries scheme which is analogous to an allowance or increase of disablement pension under sub-paragraph (ii), (iv), (v) or (vii) above;

    (ix)   main phase employment and support allowance;

(i)   a pension or allowance to which sub-paragraph (vi) or (vii) of paragraph (h) above refers was payable on account of the other member's incapacity but has ceased to be payable in consequence of that other member becoming a patient, which in this paragraph means a person (other than a person who is serving a sentence of imprisonment or detention in a youth custody institution) who is regarded as receiving free in-patient treatment within the meaning of regulation 2(4) and (5) of the Social Security (Hospital In-Patients)Regulations 2005;

(j)   an attendance allowance under section 64 of the SSCBA or disability living allowance under section 71 of that Act would be payable to that person but for–

    (i)   a suspension of benefit in accordance with regulations under section 113(2) of the SSCBA; or

    (ii)   an abatement as a consequence of hospitalisation;

(k)   the daily living component of personal independence payment would be payable to that person but for a suspension of benefit in accordance with regulations under section 86 of the Welfare Reform Act 2012 (hospital in-patients);

(l)   an AFIP would be payable to that person but for any suspension of payment in accordance with any terms of the armed and reserve forces compensation scheme which allow for a suspension because a person is undergoing medical treatment in a hospital or similar institution;

(m)   paragraph (h), (i), (j) or (k) would apply to the other member if the legislative provisions referred to in those paragraphs were provisions under any corresponding enactment having effect in Northern Ireland; or

(n)   the other member has an invalid carriage or other vehicle provided to the other member by the Secretary of State under paragraph 9 of Schedule 1 to the National Health Service Act 2006 or under section 46 of the National Health Service (Scotland) Act 1978, or provided by the Department of Health, Social Services and Public Safety in Northern Ireland under Article 30(1) of the Health and Personal Social Services (Northern Ireland) Order 1972, or provided by the Welsh Ministers under section 5 of, and Schedule 1 to the National Health Service (Wales) Act 2006.

(12)   For the purposes of sub-paragraph (11), once sub-paragraph (11)(f) applies to the applicant, if the applicant then ceases, for a period of 56 days or less, to be incapable, or to be treated as incapable, of work, that sub-paragraph is, on the applicant again becoming so incapable, or so treated as incapable, of work at the end of that period, to immediately thereafter apply to the applicant for so long as the applicant remains incapable, or is treated as remaining incapable, of work..

(13)   For the purposes of sub-paragraph (11), once sub-paragraph (11)(g) applies to the applicant, if the applicant then ceases, for a period of 84 days or less, to have, or to be treated as having, limited capability for work, that paragraph is, on the applicant again having, or being treated as having limited capability for work at the end of that period, immediately thereafter to apply to the applicant for so long as the applicant has, or is treated as having, limited capability for work.

(14)   For the purposes of sub-paragraphs (6) and (8)(a), a person is disabled if that person is a person–

(a)   to whom an attendance allowance or the care component of disability allowance is payable or would be payable but for–

    (i)   a suspension of benefit in accordance with regulations under section 113(2) of the SSCBA; or

    (ii)   an abatement as a consequence of hospitalisation;

(b)   to whom the daily living component of personal independence payment is payable or would be payable but for a suspension of benefit in accordance with regulations under section 86 of the Welfare Reform Act 2012 (hospital in-patients);

[³ (c)   who–

    (i)   is registered as blind in a register compiled under section 29 of the National Assistance Act 1948 (welfare services);

    (ii)   is registered as severely sight-impaired in a register established and maintained by a local authority under section 18(1) of the Social Services and Well-being (Wales) Act 2014;

    (iii)   is registered as severely sight-impaired in a register established and maintained by a local authority under section 77(1) of the Care Act 2014; or,

    (iv)   in Scotland, has been certified as blind and in consequence is registered as blind in a register maintained by or on behalf of a council constituted under section 2 of the Local Government etc. (Scotland) Act 1994;]

(d)   who ceased to be registered as blind [³ or severely sight-impaired] in such a register within the period beginning 28 weeks before the first Monday in September following that person's fifteenth birthday and ending on the day preceding that person's sixteenth birthday; or

(e)   to whom AFIP is payable.

(15)   For the purposes of sub-paragraph (1) a person on maternity leave, paternity leave [², shared parental leave] or adoption leave is to be treated as if engaged in remunerative work for the period specified in sub-paragraph (16) ("the relevant period") provided that–

(a)   in the week before the period of maternity leave, paternity leave[², shared parental leave] or adoption leave began the person was in remunerative work;

(b)   the person is incurring relevant child care charges within the meaning of sub-paragraph (5); and

(c)   the person is entitled to either statutory maternity pay under section 164 of the SSCBA, [²] statutory paternity pay by virtue of section 171ZA or 171ZB of that Act, additional statutory paternity pay by virtue of section 171ZEA or 171ZEB of that Act, statutory adoption pay by of section 171ZL of that Act, maternity allowance under section 35 of that Act [², statutory shared parental pay under section 171ZU or 171ZV of that Act] or qualifying support.

(16)   For the purposes of sub-paragraph (15) the relevant period begins on the day on which the person's maternity, paternity leave [², shared parental leave] or adoption leave commences and ends on–

(a)   the date that leave ends;

(b)   if no child care element of working tax credit is in payment on the date that entitlement to maternity allowance, qualifying support (if relevant), statutory maternity pay, [²] statutory paternity pay [², statutory shared parental pay] or statutory adoption pay ends, the date that entitlement ends; or

(c)   if a child care element of working tax credit is in payment on the date that entitlement to maternity allowance or qualifying support, statutory maternity pay, [²] statutory paternity pay [², statutory shared parental pay] ends or statutory adoption pay ends, the date that entitlement to that award of the child care element of the working tax credit ends,

whichever occurs first.

(17)   In sub-paragraphs (15) and (16)–
(a)   "qualifying support" ("cymhorthdal cymwys") means income support to which that person is entitled by virtue of paragraph 14B of Schedule 1B to the Income Support (General) Regulations 1987; and
(b)   "child care element" ("elfen gofal plant") of working tax credit means the element of working tax credit prescribed under section 12 of the Tax Credits Act 2002 (child care element).
(18)   In this paragraph "applicant" ("ceisydd") does not include an applicant–
(a)   who has, or
(b)   who (jointly with a partner) has,
an award of universal credit.

Amendments
1.   Amended by reg 18 of SI 2014 No 66 (W.6) as from 15.1.14.
2.   Amended by reg 25 of SI 2015 No 44 (W.3) as from 21.1.15, for schemes made for a financial year starting on or after 1.4.15.
3.   Inserted by reg 21 of SI 2016 No 50 (W.21) as from 20.1.16, for schemes made for a financial year starting on or after 1.4.16.
4.   Amended by reg 22 of SI 2018 No 14 (W.7) as from 10.1.18, for schemes made for a financial year starting on or after 1.4.18.
5.   Amended by reg 13 of SI 2019 No 11 (W.5) as from 9.1.19, for schemes made for a financial year starting on or after 1.4.19.

Calculation of average weekly income from tax credits
56.–(1)   This paragraph applies where an applicant receives a tax credit.
(2)   Where this paragraph applies, the period over which a tax credit is to be taken into account must be the period set out in sub-paragraph (3).
(3)   Where the instalment in respect of which payment of a tax credit is made is–
(a)   a daily instalment, the period is 1 day, being the day in respect of which the instalment is paid;
(b)   a weekly instalment, the period is 7 days, ending on the day on which the instalment is due to be paid;
(c)   a two weekly instalment, the period is 14 days, commencing 6 days before the day on which the instalment is due to be paid;
(d)   a four weekly instalment, the period is 28 days, ending on the day on which the instalment is due to be paid.
(4)   For the purposes of this paragraph "tax credit" ("credyd treth") means child tax credit or working tax credit.

Disregard of changes in tax, contributions etc
57.   In calculating the applicant's income the authority may disregard any legislative change–
(a)   in the basic or other rates of income tax;
(b)   in the amount of any personal tax [² reliefs under Chapters 2, 3 and 3A of Part 3 of the Income Tax Act 2007];
(c)   in the rates of social security contributions payable under the SSCBA or in the lower earnings limit or upper earnings limit for Class 1 contributions under that Act, the lower or upper limits applicable to Class 4 contributions under that Act or the amount specified in section 11(4) of that Act ([¹ small profits threshold] in relation to Class 2 contributions);
(d)   in the amount of tax payable as a result of an increase in the weekly rate of Category A, B, C or D retirement pension or any addition thereto or any graduated pension payable under the SSCBA [¹ or a state pension under Part 1 of the Pensions Act 2014];
(e)   in the maximum rate of child tax credit or working tax credit,
for a period not exceeding 30 reduction weeks beginning with the reduction week immediately following the date from which the change is effective.

Amendments
1.   Amended by reg 22 of SI 2016 No 50 (W.21) as from 20.1.16, for schemes made for a financial year starting on or after 1.4.16.
2.   Amended by reg 15 of SI 2017 No 46 (W.20) as from 19.1.17, for schemes made for a financial year starting on or after 1.4.17.

Calculation of net profit of self-employed earners
58.–(1)   For the purposes of paragraphs 45 (average weekly earnings of self-employed earners: persons who are not pensioners) and 54 (calculation of income on a weekly basis) the earnings of an applicant to be taken into account must be–
(a)   in the case of a self-employed earner who is engaged in employment on that person's own account, the net profit derived from that employment;

   (b)   in the case of a self-employed earner who is a pensioner whose employment is carried on in partnership, that person's share of the net profit derived from that employment, less–

        (i)   an amount in respect of income tax and of social security contributions payable under the SSCBA calculated in accordance with paragraph 59 (deduction of tax and contributions of self-employed earners); and

        (ii)   one-half of the amount calculated in accordance with sub-paragraph (11) in respect of any qualifying premium;

   (c)   in the case of a self-employed earner who is not a pensioner whose employment is carried on in partnership or is that of a share fisherman within the meaning of the Social Security (Mariners' Benefits) Regulations 1975, that person's share of the net profit derived from that employment, less–

        (i)   an amount in respect of income tax and of social security contributions payable under the SSCBA calculated in accordance with paragraph 59 (deduction of tax and contributions of self-employed earners); and

        (ii)   one-half of the amount calculated in accordance with sub-paragraph (11) in respect of any qualifying premium.

   (2)   There must be disregarded from the net profit of an applicant who is not a pensioner, any sum, where applicable, specified in paragraphs 1 to 16 of Schedule 6 (sums disregarded in the calculation of earnings: persons who are not pensioners).

   (3)   For the purposes of sub-paragraph (1)(a) the net profit of the employment must, except where sub-paragraph (9) applies, be calculated by taking into account the earnings of the employment over the assessment period less–

   (a)   subject to sub-paragraphs (5) to (8), any expenses wholly and exclusively incurred in that period for the purposes of that employment;

   (b)   an amount in respect of–

        (i)   income tax; and

        (ii)   social security contributions payable under the SSCBA,

        calculated in accordance with paragraph 59 (deduction of tax and contributions of self-employed earners); and

   (c)   one-half of the amount calculated in accordance with sub-paragraph (11) in respect of any qualifying premium.

   (4)   For the purposes of sub-paragraph (1)(b) the net profit of the employment is to be calculated by taking into account the earnings of the employment over the assessment period less, subject to sub-paragraphs (5) to (8), any expenses wholly and exclusively incurred in that period for the purposes of the employment.

   (5)   Subject to sub-paragraph (6), no deduction is to be made under paragraph (3)(a) or (4), in respect of–

   (a)   any capital expenditure;

   (b)   the depreciation of any capital asset;

   (c)   any sum employed or intended to be employed in the setting up or expansion of the employment;

   (d)   any loss incurred before the beginning of the assessment period;

   (e)   the repayment of capital on any loan taken out for the purposes of the employment;

   (f)   any expenses incurred in providing business entertainment; and

   (g)   in the case of an applicant who is not a pensioner, any debts, except bad debts proved to be such, but this paragraph does not apply to any expenses incurred in the recovery of a debt.

   (6)   A deduction is to be made under sub-paragraph (3)(a) or (4) in respect of the repayment of capital on any loan used for–

   (a)   the replacement in the course of business of equipment or machinery; or

   (b)   the repair of an existing business asset except to the extent that any sum is payable under an insurance policy for its repair.

   (7)   The authority must refuse to make a deduction in respect of any expenses under sub-paragraph (3)(a) or (4) where it is not satisfied given the nature and the amount of the expense that it has been reasonably incurred.

   (8)   For the avoidance of doubt–

   (a)   a deduction must not be made under sub-paragraph (3)(a) or (4) in respect of any sum unless it has been expended for the purposes of the business;

   (b)   a deduction must be made thereunder in respect of–

        (i)   the excess of any value added tax paid over value added tax received in the assessment period;

        (ii)   any income expended in the repair of an existing business asset except to the extent that any sum is payable under an insurance policy for its repair;

        (iii) any payment of interest on a loan taken out for the purposes of the employment.

   (9)   Where an applicant is engaged in employment as a child minder the net profit of the employment is to be one-third of the earnings of that employment, less–

   (a)   an amount in respect of–

        (i)   income tax; and

        (ii)   social security contributions payable under the SSCBA,

        calculated in accordance with paragraph 59 (deduction of tax and contributions of self-employed earners); and

(b)   one-half of the amount calculated in accordance with sub-paragraph (11) in respect of any qualifying premium.

(10)   For the avoidance of doubt where an applicant is engaged in employment as a self-employed earner and the applicant is also engaged in one or more other employments as a self-employed or employed earner any loss incurred in any one of the applicant's employments must not be offset against the applicant's earnings in any other of the applicant's employments.

(11)   The amount in respect of any qualifying premium is to be calculated by multiplying the daily amount of the qualifying premium by the number equal to the number of days in the assessment period; and for the purposes of this paragraph the daily amount of the qualifying premium must be determined–

(a)   where the qualifying premium is payable monthly, by multiplying the amount of the qualifying premium by 12 and dividing the product by 365;

(b)   in any other case, by dividing the amount of the qualifying premium by the number equal to the number of days in the period to which the qualifying premium relates.

(12)   In this paragraph, "qualifying premium" ("premiwm cymwys") means any premium which is payable periodically in respect of a personal pension scheme and is so payable on or after the date of application.

Calculation of deduction of tax and contributions of self-employed earners

59.–(1)   The amount to be deducted in respect of income tax under paragraph 58(1)(b)(i), (3)(b)(i) or (9)(a)(i) (calculation of net profit of self-employed earners) must be calculated–

(a)   on the basis of the amount of chargeable income, and

(b)   as if that income were assessable to income tax at the basic rate of tax applicable to the assessment period less only the [³ personal reliefs to which the applicant is entitled under Chapters 2, 3 and 3A of Part 3] of the Income Tax Act 2007 [³] as is appropriate to the applicant's circumstances.

(2)   But, if the assessment period is less than a year, the earnings to which the basic rate of tax is to be applied and the amount of the personal reliefs deductible under this paragraph must be calculated on a pro rata basis.

(3)   The amount to be deducted in respect of social security contributions under paragraph 58 (1)(b)(i), (3)(b)(ii) or (9)(a)(ii) is the total of–

(a)   the amount of Class 2 contributions payable under section 11(1) or, as the case may be, 11(3) of the SSCBA at the rate applicable to the assessment period except where the applicant's chargeable income is less than the amount specified in section 11(4) of that Act ([² small profits threshold]) for the tax year applicable to the assessment period; but if the assessment period is less than a year, the amount specified for that tax year must be reduced pro rata; and

(b)   the amount of Class 4 contributions (if any) which would be payable under section 15 of the SSCBA (Class 4 contributions recoverable under the Income Tax Acts) at the percentage rate applicable to the assessment period on so much of the chargeable income as exceeds the lower limit but does not exceed the upper limit of profits and gains applicable for the tax year applicable to the assessment period; but if the assessment period is less than a year, those limits must be reduced pro rata.

(4)   In this paragraph "chargeable income" ("incwm trethadwy") means–

(a)   except where paragraph (b) applies, the earnings derived from the employment less any expenses deducted under [¹ sub-paragraph (3)(a) or, as the case may be, (4) of paragraph 58];

(b)   in the case of employment as a child minder, one-third of the earnings of that employment.

Amendments

1.   Amended by reg 19 of SI 2014 No 66 (W.6) as from 15.1.14.

2.   Amended by reg 23 of SI 2016 No 50 (W.21) as from 20.1.16, for schemes made for a financial year starting on or after 1.4.16.

3.   Amended by reg 16 of SI 2017 No 46 (W.20) as from 19.1.17, for schemes made for a financial year starting on or after 1.4.17.

CHAPTER 7
Capital

Calculation of capital

60.–(1)   The capital of an applicant to be taken into account must be, subject to sub-paragraph (2), the whole of the applicant's capital calculated in accordance with this Part and (in the case of persons who are not pensioners) any income treated as capital under paragraph 61 (income treated as capital: persons who are not pensioners).

(2)   There must be disregarded from the calculation of an applicant's capital under sub-paragraph (1), any capital, where applicable, specified in–

(a)   Schedule 8, in relation to pensioners;

(b)   Schedule 9, in relation to persons who are not pensioners.

(3)   In the case of an applicant who is a pensioner, the applicant's capital is to be treated as including any payment made to the applicant by way of arrears of–

(a)   child tax credit;

(b)   working tax credit;

(c)   state pension credit,

if the payment was made in respect of a period for the whole or part of which a reduction under this scheme was allowed before those arrears were paid.

(4)   The capital of a child or young person who is a member of the family of an applicant who is not a pensioner must not be treated as capital of the applicant.

Income treated as capital: persons who are not pensioners

61.–(1)   This paragraph applies in relation to persons who are not pensioners.

(2)   Any bounty derived from employment to which paragraph 9 of Schedule 6 (sums disregarded in the calculation of earnings: persons who are not pensioners) applies and paid at intervals of at least one year is to be treated as capital.

(3)   Any amount by way of a refund of income tax deducted from profits or emoluments chargeable to income tax under Schedule D or E is to be treated as capital.

(4)   Any holiday pay which is not earnings under paragraph 38(1)(d) or 48(1)(d) (earnings of employed earners) is to be treated as capital.

(5)   Except any income derived from capital disregarded under paragraphs 4, 5, 7, 11, 17, 30 to 33, 48 or 49 of Schedule 9 (capital disregards: persons who are not pensioners), any income derived from capital is to be treated as capital but only from the date it is normally due to be credited to the applicant's account.

(6)   In the case of employment as an employed earner, any advance of earnings or any loan made by the applicant's employer is to be treated as capital.

(7)   Any charitable or voluntary payment which is not made or due to be made at regular intervals, other than a payment which is made under or by the Trusts, the Fund, the Eileen Trust, MFET Limited, the Skipton Fund, the Caxton Foundation [¹, an approved blood scheme, the Scottish Infected Blood Support Scheme, the London Emergencies Trust, the We Love Manchester Emergency Fund], the Independent Living Fund (2006) or the London Bombings Relief Charitable Fund, is to be treated as capital.

(8)   There is to be treated as capital the gross receipts of any commercial activity carried on by a person in respect of which assistance is received under the self-employment route, but only in so far as those receipts were payable into a special account during the period in which that person was receiving such assistance.

(9)   Any arrears of subsistence allowance which are paid to an applicant as a lump sum must be treated as capital.

(10)   Any arrears of working tax credit or child tax credit must be treated as capital.

Amendment

1.   Amended by reg 23(a) of SI 2018 No 14 (W.7) as from 10.1.18, for schemes made for a financial year starting on or after 1.4.18.

Calculation of capital in the United Kingdom

62.   Capital which an applicant possesses in the United Kingdom is to be calculated at its current market or surrender value less–

(a)   where there would be expenses attributable to the sale, 10 per cent; and

(b)   the amount of any encumbrance secured on it.

Calculation of capital outside the United Kingdom

63.   Capital which an applicant possesses in a country outside the United Kingdom is to be calculated–

(a)   in a case where there is no prohibition in that country against the transfer to the United Kingdom of an amount equal to its current market or surrender value in that country, at that value;

(b)   in a case where there is such a prohibition, at the price which it would realise if sold in the United Kingdom to a willing buyer,

less, where there would be expenses attributable to sale, 10 per cent and the amount of any encumbrances secured on it.

Notional capital

64.–(1)   An applicant is to be treated as possessing capital of which the applicant has deprived himself or herself for the purpose of securing entitlement to a reduction or increasing the amount of that reduction except to the extent that that capital is reduced in accordance with paragraphs 65 and 66 (diminishing notional capital rule).

(2)   An applicant who is a pensioner who disposes of capital for the purpose of–

(a)   reducing or paying a debt owed by the applicant; or

(b)   purchasing goods or services if the expenditure was reasonable in the circumstances of the applicant's case,

is to be regarded as not depriving himself or herself of it.

(3)   Sub-paragraphs (4) to (6) apply in relation to applicants who are not pensioners.

(4)   Except in the case of–

(a)   a discretionary trust; or

(b)   a trust derived from a payment made in consequence of a personal injury; or

(c)   any loan which would be obtained only if secured against capital disregarded under Schedule 9; or

(d)   a personal pension scheme, occupational pension scheme or a payment made by the Board of the Pension Protection Fund; or

(e)   any sum to which paragraph 48(2)(a) of Schedule 9 (capital disregards: persons who are not pensioner) applies which is administered in the way referred to in [¹ paragraph 49(a)] of that Schedule; or

(f)   any sum to which paragraph 49(a) of Schedule 9 refers; or

(g)   child tax credit; or

(h)   working tax credit,

any capital which would become available to the applicant upon application being made, but which has not been acquired by the applicant, is to be treated as possessed by the applicant but only from the date on which it could be expected to be acquired were an application made.

(5)   Any payment of capital, other than a payment of capital specified in sub-paragraph (6), made–

(a)   to a third party in respect of a single applicant or a member of the family (but not a member of the third party's family) must, where that payment is a payment of an occupational pension, a pension or other periodical payment made under a personal pension scheme or a payment made by the Board of the Pension Protection Fund, be treated as possessed by that single applicant or, as the case may be, by that member;

(b)   to a third party in respect of a single applicant or in respect of a member of the family (but not a member of the third party's family) must, where it is not a payment referred to in paragraph (a), be treated as possessed by that single applicant or by that member to the extent that it is used for the food, ordinary clothing or footwear, household fuel or rent of that single applicant or, as the case may be, of any member of that family or is used for any council tax or water charges for which that applicant or member is liable;

(c)   to a single applicant or a member of the family in respect of a third party (but not in respect of another member of the family) must be treated as possessed by that single applicant or, as the case may be, that member of the family to the extent that it is kept or used by the single applicant or used by or on behalf of any member of the family.

(6)   Sub-paragraph (5) does not apply in respect of a payment of capital made–

(a)   under or by any of the Trusts, the Fund, the Eileen Trust, MFET Limited, the Independent Living Fund (2006), the Skipton Fund, the Caxton Foundation [², an approved blood scheme, the Scottish Infected Blood Support Scheme, the London Emergencies Trust, the We Love Manchester Emergency Fund], or the London Bombings Relief Charitable Fund;

(b)   pursuant to section 2 of the Employment and Training Act 1973 in respect of a person's participation–

    (i)   in an employment programme specified in regulation 75(1)(a) of the Jobseeker's Allowance Regulations 1996;

    (ii)   in a training scheme specified in regulation 75(1)(b) of those Regulations; or

    (iii)   in a qualifying course within the meaning specified in regulation 17A(7) of those Regulations;

(c)   in respect of a person's participation in the Work for Your Benefit Pilot Scheme;

(d)   in respect of a person's participation in the Mandatory Work Activity Scheme;

(e)   in respect of an applicant's participation in the Employment, Skills and Enterprise Scheme;

(f)   under an occupational pension scheme, in respect of a pension or other periodical payment made under a personal pension scheme or a payment made by the Board of the Pension Protection Fund where–

    (i)   a bankruptcy order has been made in respect of the person in respect of whom the payment has been made or, in Scotland, the estate of that person is subject to sequestration or a judicial factor has been appointed on that person's estate under section 41 of the Solicitors (Scotland) Act 1980;

    (ii)   the payment is made to the trustee in bankruptcy or any other person acting on behalf of the creditors; and

    (iii)   the person referred to in sub-paragraph (i) and any member of that person's family do not possess, or are not treated as possessing, any other income apart from that payment.

(7)   Where an applicant stands in relation to a company in a position analogous to that of a sole owner or partner in the business of that company, the applicant may be treated as if the applicant were such sole owner or partner and in such a case–

(a)   the value of the applicant's holding in that company must, notwithstanding paragraph 60 (calculation of capital) be disregarded; and

(b)   the applicant must, subject to sub-paragraph (8), be treated as possessing an amount of capital equal to the value or, as the case may be, the applicant's share of the value of the capital of that company and the foregoing provisions of this Chapter apply for the purposes of calculating that amount as if it were actual capital which the applicant does possess.

(8)   For so long as the applicant undertakes activities in the course of the business of the company, the amount which the applicant is treated as possessing under sub-paragraph (7) is to be disregarded.

(9)   Where an applicant is treated as possessing capital under any of sub-paragraphs (1), (4) or (5) the foregoing provisions of this Chapter apply for the purposes of calculating its amount as if it were actual capital which the applicant does possess.

Amendments
1. Amended by reg 20 of SI 2014 No 66 (W.6) as from 15.1.14.
2. Amended by reg 23(b) of SI 2018 No 14 (W.7) as from 10.1.18, for schemes made for a financial year starting on or after 1.4.18.

Diminishing notional capital rule: pensioners
65.–(1)   Where an applicant who is a pensioner is treated as possessing capital under paragraph 64(1) (notional capital), the amount which the applicant is treated as possessing–
  (a)   in the case of a week that is subsequent to–
    (i)   the relevant week in respect of which the conditions set out in sub-paragraph (2) are satisfied; or
    (ii)   a week which follows that relevant week and which satisfies those conditions,
  is to be reduced by an amount determined under sub-paragraph (3);
  (b)   in the case of a week in respect of which sub-paragraph (1)(a) does not apply but where–
    (i)   that week is a week subsequent to the relevant week; and
    (ii)   that relevant week is a week in which the condition in sub-paragraph (4) is satisfied,
  is to be reduced by the amount determined under sub-paragraph (5).
  (2)   This sub-paragraph applies to a reduction week where the applicant satisfies the conditions that–
  (a)   the applicant is in receipt of a reduction in council tax under this scheme; and
  (b)   but for paragraph 64(1), the applicant would have received a greater reduction in council tax under this scheme in that week.
  (3)   In a case to which sub-paragraph (2) applies, the amount of the reduction in the amount of capital the applicant is treated as possessing for the purposes of sub-paragraph (1)(a) must be equal to the aggregate of–
  (a)   an amount equal to the additional amount of the reduction in council tax to which sub-paragraph (2)(b) refers;
  (b)   where the applicant has also claimed state pension credit, the amount of any state pension credit or any additional amount of state pension credit to which the applicant would have been entitled in respect of the reduction week to which sub-paragraph (2) refers but for the application of regulation 21(1) of the State Pension Credit Regulations 2002 (notional capital);
  (c)   where the applicant has also claimed housing benefit, the amount of any housing benefit or any additional amount of housing benefit to which the applicant would have been entitled in respect of the whole or part of the reduction week to which sub-paragraph (2) refers but for the application of regulation 47(1) of the Housing Benefit (Persons who have attained the qualifying age for state pension credit) Regulations 2006 (notional capital);
  (d)   where the applicant has also claimed a jobseeker's allowance, the amount of an income-based jobseeker's allowance to which the applicant would have been entitled in respect of the reduction week to which sub-paragraph (2) refers but for the application of regulation 113 of the Jobseeker's Allowance Regulations 1996 (notional capital); and
  (e)   where the applicant has also claimed an employment and support allowance, the amount of an income related employment and support allowance to which the applicant would have been entitled in respect of the reduction week to which sub-paragraph (2) refers but for the application of regulation 115 of the Employment and Support Allowance Regulations 2008 (notional capital).
  (4)   Subject to sub-paragraph (7), for the purposes of sub-paragraph (1)(b) the condition is that the applicant is a pensioner and would have been entitled to a reduction in council tax under this scheme in the relevant week but for paragraph 64(1).
  (5)   In such a case the amount of the reduction in the amount of capital the applicant is treated as possessing for the purposes of sub-paragraph (1)(b) is equal to the aggregate of–
  (a)   the amount of the reduction in council tax to which the applicant would have been entitled in the relevant week but for paragraph 64(1);
  (b)   if the applicant would, but for regulation 21 of the State Pension Credit Regulations 2002, have been entitled to state pension credit in respect of the benefit week, within the meaning of regulation 1(2) of those Regulations (interpretation), which includes the last day of the relevant week, the amount to which the applicant would have been entitled;
  (c)   if the applicant would, but for regulation 47(1) of the Housing Benefit (Persons who have attained the qualifying age for state pension credit) Regulations 2006, have been entitled to housing benefit or to an additional amount of housing benefit in respect of the benefit week which includes the last day of the relevant week, the amount which is equal to–
    (i)   in a case where no housing benefit is payable, the amount to which the applicant would have been entitled; or
    (ii)   in any other case, the amount equal to the additional amount of housing benefit to which the applicant would have been entitled;
  (d)   if the applicant would, but for regulation 113 of the Jobseeker's Allowance Regulations 1996, have been entitled to an income-based jobseeker's allowance in respect of the benefit week, within the meaning of regulation 1(3) of those Regulations (interpretation), which includes the last day of the relevant week, the amount to which the applicant would have been entitled; and

(e)   if the applicant would, but for regulation 115 of the Employment and Support Allowance Regulations 2008, have been entitled to an income-related employment and support allowance in respect of the benefit week, within the meaning of regulation 2(1) of those Regulations (interpretation), which includes the last day of the relevant week, the amount to which the applicant would have been entitled.

(6)   But if the amount mentioned in paragraph (a), (b), (c), (d) or (e) of sub-paragraph (5) ("the relevant amount") is in respect of a part-week, the amount that is to be taken into account under that paragraph is to be determined by–

(a)   dividing the relevant amount by the number equal to the number of days in that part-week; and

(b)   multiplying the result of that calculation by 7.

(7)   The amount determined under sub-paragraph (5) is to be re-determined under that sub-paragraph if the applicant makes a further application for a reduction in council tax and the conditions in sub-paragraph (8) are satisfied, and in such a case–

(a)   paragraphs (a) to (e) of sub-paragraph (5) apply as if for the words "relevant week" there were substituted the words "relevant subsequent week"; and

(b)   subject to sub-paragraph (9), the amount as re-determined has effect from the first week following the relevant subsequent week in question.

(8)   The conditions are that–

(a)   a further application is made 26 or more weeks after–

    (i)   the date on which the applicant made an application for a reduction in council tax in respect of which the applicant was first treated as possessing the capital in question under paragraph 64(1);

    (ii)   in a case where there has been at least one re-determination in accordance with sub-paragraph (7), the date on which the applicant last made an application for a reduction in council tax which resulted in the weekly amount being re-determined; or

    (iii)   the date on which the applicant last ceased to be entitled to a reduction in council tax, whichever last occurred; and

(b)   the applicant would have been entitled to a reduction in council tax under this scheme but for paragraph 64(1).

(9)   The amount as re-determined pursuant to sub-paragraph (7) must not have effect if it is less than the amount which applied in that case immediately before the re-determination and in such a case the higher amount must continue to have effect.

(10)   For the purposes of this paragraph–

"part-week" ("rhan-wythnos")–

(a)   in relation to an amount mentioned in sub-paragraph (5)(a), means a period of less than a week for which a reduction in council tax under this scheme is allowed;

(b)   in relation to an amount mentioned in [¹ sub-paragraph (5)(c)], means a period of less than a week for which housing benefit is payable;

(c)   in relation to an amount mentioned in sub-paragraph (5)(c), (d) or (e), means–

    (i)   a period of less than a week which is the whole period for which income support, an income-related employment and support allowance or, as the case may be, an income-based jobseeker's allowance is payable; and

    (ii)   any other period of less than a week for which it is payable;

"relevant week" ("wythnos berthnasol") means the reduction week or part-week in which the capital in question of which the applicant has deprived himself or herself within the meaning of paragraph 64(1)–

(a)   was first taken into account for the purpose of determining the applicant's entitlement to a reduction; or

(b)   was taken into account on a subsequent occasion for the purpose of determining or re-determining the applicant's entitlement to a reduction on that subsequent occasion and that determination or redetermination resulted in the applicant beginning to receive, or ceasing to receive, a reduction;

and where more than one reduction week is identified by reference to paragraphs (a) and (b) of this definition, the later or latest such reduction week or, as the case may be, the later or latest such part-week is the relevant week;

"relevant subsequent week" ("wythnos ddilynol berthnasol") means the reduction week or part-week which includes the day on which the further application or, if more than one further application has been made, the last such application was made.

Amendment

1.   Amended by reg 21 of SI 2014 No 66 (W.6) as from 15.1.14.

Diminishing notional capital rule: persons who are not pensioners

66.–(1)   Where an applicant who is not a pensioner is treated as possessing capital under paragraph 64(1) (notional capital), the amount which the applicant is treated as possessing–

(a)   in the case of a week that is subsequent to–

    (i)   the relevant week in respect of which the conditions set out in sub-paragraph (2) are satisfied; or

       (ii)   a week which follows that relevant week and which satisfies those conditions,
is to be reduced by an amount determined under sub-paragraph (3);

(b)   in the case of a week in respect of which sub-paragraph (1)(a) does not apply but where–

       (i)   that week is a week subsequent to the relevant week; and

       (ii)   that relevant week is a week in which the condition in sub-paragraph (4) is satisfied,

is to be reduced by the amount determined under sub-paragraph (5).

(2)   This sub-paragraph applies to a reduction week (or, in the case of persons who are not pensioners, part-week) where the applicant satisfies the conditions that–

(a)   the applicant is in receipt of a reduction in council tax under this scheme; and

(b)   but for paragraph 64(1), the applicant would have received a greater reduction in council tax under this scheme in that week.

(3)   In a case to which sub-paragraph (2) applies, the amount of the reduction in the amount of capital the applicant is treated as possessing for the purposes of sub-paragraph (1)(a) is equal to the aggregate of–

(a)   an amount equal to the additional amount of the reduction in council tax to which sub-paragraph (2)(b) refers;

(b)   where the applicant has also claimed housing benefit, the amount of any housing benefit or any additional amount of that benefit to which the applicant would have been entitled in respect of the whole or part of the reduction week to which sub-paragraph (2) refers but for the application of regulation 49(1) of the Housing Benefit Regulations 2006 (notional capital);

(c)   where the applicant has also claimed income support, the amount of income support to which the applicant would have been entitled in respect of the whole or part of the reduction week to which sub-paragraph (2) refers but for the application of regulation 51(1) of the Income Support (General) Regulations 1987 (notional capital);

(d)   where the applicant has also claimed a jobseeker's allowance, the amount of an income-based jobseeker's allowance to which the applicant would have been entitled in respect of the whole or part of the reduction week to which sub-paragraph (2) refers but for the application of regulation 113 of the Jobseeker's Allowance Regulations 1996 (notional capital); and

(e)   where the applicant has also claimed an employment and support allowance, the amount of an income related employment and support allowance to which the applicant would have been entitled in respect of the whole or part of the reduction week to which sub-paragraph (2) refers but for the application of regulation 115 of the Employment and Support Allowance Regulations 2008 (notional capital).

(4)   Subject to sub-paragraph (7), for the purposes of sub-paragraph (1)(b) the condition is that the applicant is not a pensioner and would have been entitled to a reduction in council tax in the relevant week but for paragraph 64(1).

(5)   In such a case the amount of the reduction in the amount of capital the applicant is treated as possessing must be equal to the aggregate of–

(a)   the amount of council tax benefit to which the applicant would have been entitled in the relevant week but for paragraph 64(1);

(b)   if the applicant would, but for regulation 49(1) of the Housing Benefit Regulations 2006, have been entitled to housing benefit or to an additional amount of housing benefit in respect of the benefit week which includes the last day of the relevant week, the amount which is equal to–

       (i)   in a case where no housing benefit is payable, the amount to which the applicant would have been entitled; or

       (ii)   in any other case, the amount equal to the additional amount of housing benefit to which the applicant would have been entitled;

(c)   if the applicant would, but for regulation 51(1) of the Income Support (General) Regulations 1987, have been entitled to income support in respect of the benefit week, within the meaning of regulation 2(1) of those Regulations (interpretation), which includes the last day of the relevant week, the amount to which the applicant would have been entitled;

(d)   if the applicant would, but for regulation 113 of the Jobseeker's Allowance Regulations 1996, have been entitled to an income-based jobseeker's allowance in respect of the benefit week, within the meaning of regulation 1(3) of those Regulations (interpretation), which includes the last day of the relevant week, the amount to which the applicant would have been entitled; and

(e)   if the applicant would, but for regulation 115 of the Employment and Support Allowance Regulations 2008, have been entitled to an income-related employment and support allowance in respect of the benefit week, within the meaning of regulation 2(1) of those Regulations (interpretation), which includes the last day of the relevant week, the amount to which the applicant would have been entitled.

(6)   But if the amount mentioned in paragraph (a), (b), (c), (d) or (e) of sub-paragraph (5) ("the relevant amount") is in respect of a part-week, the amount that is to be taken into account under that paragraph is to be determined by–

(a)   dividing the relevant amount by the number equal to the number of days in that part-week; and

(b)   multiplying the result of that calculation by 7.

(7)   The amount determined under sub-paragraph (5) is to be re-determined under the appropriate sub-paragraph if the applicant makes a further application for a reduction in council tax and the conditions in sub-paragraph (8) are satisfied, and in such a case–

(a)   paragraphs (a) to (e) of sub-paragraph (5) apply as if for the words "relevant week" there were substituted the words "relevant subsequent week"; and

(b)   subject to sub-paragraph (9), the amount as re-determined has effect from the first week following the relevant subsequent week in question.

(8)   The conditions are that–

(a)   a further application is made 26 or more weeks after–

  (i)   the date on which the applicant made an application for a reduction in council tax in respect of which the applicant was first treated as possessing the capital in question under paragraph 64(1);

  (ii)   in a case where there has been at least one re-determination in accordance with sub-paragraph (7), the date on which the applicant last made an application for a reduction in council tax which resulted in the weekly amount being re-determined; or

  (iii)   the date on which the applicant last ceased to be entitled to a reduction in council tax, whichever last occurred; and

(b)   the applicant would have been entitled to a reduction in council tax under this scheme but for paragraph 64(1).

(9)   The amount as re-determined pursuant to sub-paragraph (7) must not have effect if it is less than the amount which applied in that case immediately before the re-determination and in such a case the higher amount must continue to have effect.

(10)   For the purposes of this paragraph–

"part-week" ("rhan-wythnos")–

(a)   in relation to an amount mentioned in sub-paragraph (5)(a), means a period of less than a week for which a reduction in council tax under this scheme is allowed;

(b)   in relation to an amount mentioned in sub-paragraph (5)(b), means a period of less than a week for which housing benefit is payable;

(c)   in relation to an amount mentioned in sub-paragraph (5)(c), (d) or (e), means–

  (i)   a period of less than a week which is the whole period for which income support, an income-related employment and support allowance or, as the case may be, an income-based jobseeker's allowance is payable; and

  (ii)   any other period of less than a week for which it is payable;

"relevant week" ("wythnos berthnasol") means the reduction week or part-week in which the capital in question of which the applicant has deprived himself or herself within the meaning of paragraph 64(1)–

(a)   was first taken into account for the purpose of determining the applicant's entitlement to a reduction; or

(b)   was taken into account on a subsequent occasion for the purpose of determining or re-determining the applicant's entitlement to a reduction on that subsequent occasion and that determination or redetermination resulted in the applicant beginning to receive, or ceasing to receive, a reduction,

and where more than one reduction week is identified by reference to paragraphs (a) and (b) of this definition, the later or latest such reduction week or, as the case may be, the later or latest such part-week is the relevant week;

"relevant subsequent week" ("wythnos ddilynol berthnasol") means the reduction week or part-week which includes the day on which the further application or, if more than one further application has been made, the last such application was made.

Capital jointly held

67.   Except where an applicant possesses capital which is disregarded under paragraph 64(7) (notional capital), where an applicant and one or more persons are beneficially entitled in possession to any capital asset they must be treated, in the absence of evidence to the contrary, as if each of them were entitled in possession to the whole beneficial interest therein in an equal share and the foregoing provisions of this Chapter apply for the purposes of calculating the amount of capital which the applicant is treated as possessing as if it were actual capital which the applicant does possess.

Calculation of tariff income from capital: pensioners

68.   The capital of an applicant who is a pensioner, calculated in accordance with this Part, is to be treated as if it were a weekly income of–

(a)   £1 for each £500 in excess of £10,000 but not exceeding £16,000; and

(b)   £1 for any excess which is not a complete £500.

Calculation of tariff income from capital: persons who are not pensioners

69.   The capital of an applicant who is not a pensioner, calculated in accordance with this Part, is to be treated as if it were a weekly income of–

(a)   £1 for each complete £250 in excess of £6,000 but not exceeding £16,000;

(b)   £1 for any excess which is not a complete £250.

PART 10
Students

CHAPTER 1
General

Interpretation
70.–(1)   In this Part–
"academic year" ("blwyddyn academaidd") means the period of twelve months beginning on 1 January, 1 April, 1 July or 1 September according to whether the course in question begins in the winter, the spring, the summer or the autumn respectively but if students are required to begin attending the course during August or September and to continue attending through the autumn, the academic year of the course is to be considered to begin in the autumn rather than the summer;
"access funds" ("cronfeydd mynediad") means–
(a)   grants made under section 68 of the Further and Higher Education Act 1992 for the purpose of providing funds on a discretionary basis to be paid to students;
(b)   grants made under sections 73(a) and (c) and 74(1) of the Education (Scotland) Act 1980;
(c)   grants made under Article 30 of the Education and Libraries (Northern Ireland) Order 1993 or grants, loans or other payments made under Article 5 of the Further Education (Northern Ireland) Order 1997 in each case being grants, or grants, loans or other payments as the case may be, for the purpose of assisting students in financial difficulties;
(d)   discretionary payments, known as "learner support funds", which are made available to students in further education by institutions out of funds provided by the Secretary of State in relation to England or the Welsh Ministers in relation to Wales under section 14 of the Education Act 2002 or [² the Secretary of State] under sections 100 and 101 of the Apprenticeships, Skills, Children and Learning Act 2009; or
(e)   Financial Contingency Funds made available by the Welsh Ministers;
"college of further education" ("coleg addysg bellach")_means a college of further education within the meaning of Part 1 of the Further and Higher Education (Scotland) Act 1992;
"contribution" ("cyfraniad") means–
(a)   any contribution in respect of the income of a student or any person which the Secretary of State, the Welsh Ministers, the Scottish Ministers or an education authority takes into account in ascertaining the amount of a student's grant or student loan; or
(b)   any sums, which in determining the amount of a student's allowance or bursary in Scotland under the Education (Scotland) Act 1980, the Scottish Ministers or education authority takes into account being sums which the Scottish Ministers or education authority considers that it is reasonable for the following persons to contribute towards the holder's expenses–
(i)   the holder of the allowance or bursary;
(ii)   the holder's parents;
(iii)   the holder's parent's spouse, civil partner or a person ordinarily living with the holder's parent as if that person were the spouse or civil partner of that parent; or
(iv)   the holder's spouse or civil partner;
"course of study" ("cwrs astudio") means any course of study, whether or not it is a sandwich course and whether or not a grant is made for attending or undertaking it;
"covenant income" ("incwm cyfamod") means the gross income payable to a full-time student under a Deed of Covenant by that student's parent;
"education authority" ("awdurdod addysg") means a government department, a local authority as defined in section 579 of the Education Act 1996 (interpretation), a local education authority as defined in section 123 of the Local Government (Scotland) Act 1973, an education and library board established under Article 3 of the Education and Libraries (Northern Ireland) Order 1986, any body which is a research council for the purposes of the Science and Technology Act 1965 or any analogous government department, authority, board or body, of the Channel Islands, Isle of Man or any other country outside Great Britain;
"full-time course of study" ("cwrs astudio llawn amser") means a full-time course of study which–
(a)   is not funded in whole or in part by the Secretary of State in relation to England or the Welsh Ministers in relation to Wales under section 14 of the Education Act 2002 or [² the Secretary of State under section 100 of the Apprenticeships, Skills, Children and Learning Act 2009], or a full-time course of study which is not funded in whole or in part by the Scottish Ministers at a college of further education or a full-time course of study which is a course of higher education and is funded in whole or in part by the Scottish Ministers;
(b)   is funded in whole or in part by the Secretary of State in relation to England or the Welsh Ministers in relation to Wales under section 14 of the [¹ Education Act 2002] or [² the Secretary of State under section 100 of the Apprenticeships, Skills, Children and Learning Act 2009] if it involves more than 16 guided learning hours per week for the student in question, according to the number of guided learning hours per week for that student set out–

        (i)   in the case of a course funded by the Secretary of State [²], in the student's learning agreement signed on behalf of the establishment which is funded by [² the Secretary of State] for the delivery of that course; or

        (ii)   in the case of a course funded by the Welsh Ministers, in a document signed on behalf of the establishment which is funded by the Welsh Ministers for the delivery of that course; or

(c)   is not higher education and is funded in whole or in part by the Scottish Ministers at a college of further education and involves–

        (i)   more than 16 hours per week of classroom-based or workshop-based programmed learning under the direct guidance of teaching staff according to the number of hours set out in a document signed on behalf of the college; or

        (ii)   16 hours or less per week of classroom-based or workshop-based programmed learning under the direct guidance of teaching staff and additional hours using structured learning packages supported by the teaching staff where the combined total of hours exceeds 21 hours per week, according to the number of hours set out in a document signed on behalf of the college;

"full-time student" ("myfyriwr amser llawn") means a person attending or undertaking a full-time course of study and includes a student on a sandwich course;

"grant" ("grant") (except in the definition of "access funds") means any kind of educational grant or award and includes any scholarship, studentship, exhibition, allowance or bursary but does not include a payment from access funds or any payment to which paragraph 16 of Schedule 7 or paragraph 53 of Schedule 9 (allowances and payments for courses of study) applies;

"grant income" ("incwm grant") means–

(a)   any income by way of a grant;

(b)   any contribution whether or not it is paid;

"higher education" ("addysg uwch") means higher education within the meaning of Part 2 of the Further and Higher Education (Scotland) Act 1992;

"last day of the course" ("diwrnod olaf y cwrs") means–

(a)   in the case of a qualifying course, the date on which the last day of that course falls or the date on which the final examination relating to that course is completed, whichever is the later;

(b)   in any other case, the date on which the last day of the final academic term falls in respect of the course in which the student is enrolled;

"period of study" ("cyfnod astudio") means–

(a)   in the case of a course of study for one year or less, the period beginning with the start of the course and ending with the last day of the course;

(b)   in the case of a course of study for more than one year, in the first or, as the case may be, any subsequent year of the course, other than the final year of the course, the period beginning with the start of the course or, as the case may be, that year's start and ending with either–

        (i)   the day before the start of the next year of the course in a case where the student's grant or loan is assessed at a rate appropriate to the student's studying throughout the year or, if the student does not have a grant or loan, where a loan would have been assessed at such a rate had the student had one; or

        (ii)   in any other case, the day before the start of the normal summer vacation appropriate to the student's course;

(c)   in the final year of a course of study of more than one year, the period beginning with that year's start and ending with the last day of the course;

"periods of experience" ("cyfnodau o brofiad") means periods of work experience which form part of a sandwich course;

"qualifying course" ("cwrs cymwys") means a qualifying course as defined for the purposes of Parts 2 and 4 of the Jobseeker's Allowance Regulations 1996;

"sandwich course" ("cwrs rhyngosod") has the meaning prescribed in regulation 2(10) of the Education (Student Support) Regulations 2011, regulation 2(6) of the Education (Student Support) (Wales) Regulations 2012, regulation 4(2) of the Education (Student Loans) (Scotland) Regulations 2007, or regulation 2(10) of the Education (Student Support) (No. 2) Regulations (Northern Ireland) 2009, as the case may be;

"standard maintenance grant" ("grant cynhaliaeth safonol") means–

(a)   except where paragraph (b) or (c) applies, in the case of a student attending or undertaking a course of study at the University of London or an establishment within the area comprising the City of London and the Metropolitan Police District, the amount specified for the time being in paragraph 2(2)(a) of Schedule 2 to the Education (Mandatory Awards) Regulations 2003 ("the 2003 Regulations") for such a student;

(b)   except where paragraph (c) applies, in the case of a student residing at that student's parent's home, the amount specified in paragraph 3 of Schedule 2 to the 2003 Regulations;

(c)   in the case of a student receiving an allowance or bursary under the Education (Scotland) Act 1980, the amount of money specified as "standard maintenance allowance" for the relevant year appropriate for the student set out in the Student Support in Scotland Guide issued by the Student Awards Agency for Scotland, or its nearest equivalent in the case of a bursary provided by a college of further education or a local education authority;

(d)   in any other case, the amount specified in paragraph 2(2) of Schedule 2 to the 2003 Regulations other than in sub-paragraph (2)(a) or (b) thereof;

"student" ("myfyriwr") means a person, other than a person in receipt of a training allowance, who is attending or undertaking–

(a)   a course of study at an educational establishment; or

(b)   a qualifying course;

"student loan" ("benthyciad myfyriwr") means a loan towards a student's maintenance pursuant to any regulations made under section 22 of the Teaching and Higher Education Act 1998, section 73 of the Education (Scotland) Act 1980 or Article 3 of the Education (Student Support) (Northern Ireland) Order 1998 and includes, in Scotland, a young student's bursary paid under regulation 4(1)(c) of the Students' Allowances (Scotland) Regulations 2007.

(2)   For the purposes of the definition of "full-time student" ("myfyriwr amser llawn") in sub-paragraph (1), a person must be regarded as attending or, as the case may be, undertaking a full-time course of study or as being on a sandwich course–

(a)   subject to sub-paragraph (3), in the case of a person attending or undertaking a part of a modular course which would be a full-time course of study for the purposes of this Part, for the period beginning on the day on which that part of the course starts and ending–

(i)   on the last day on which the person is registered with the educational establishment as attending or undertaking that part as a full-time course of study; or

(ii)   on such earlier date (if any) as the person finally abandons the course or is dismissed from it;

(b)   in any other case, throughout the period beginning on the date on which the person starts attending or undertaking the course and ending on the last day of the course or on such earlier date (if any) as the person finally abandons it or is dismissed from it.

(3)   For the purposes of paragraph (a) of sub-paragraph (2), the period referred to in that paragraph includes–

(a)   where a person has failed examinations or has failed to successfully complete a module relating to a period when the person was attending or undertaking a part of the course as a full-time course of study, any period in respect of which the person attends or undertakes the course for the purpose of retaking those examinations or that module;

(b)   any period of vacation within the period specified in that paragraph or immediately following that period except where the person has registered with the educational establishment to attend or undertake the final module in the course and the vacation immediately follows the last day on which the person is required to attend or undertake the course.

(4)   In sub-paragraph (2), "modular course" ("cwrs modiwlaidd") means a course of study which consists of two or more modules, the successful completion of a specified number of which is required before a person is considered by the educational establishment to have completed the course.

Amendments

1.   Amended by reg 22 of SI 2014 No 66 (W.6) as from 15.1.14.

2.   Amended by art 2 and Sch 3 para 31(3) of SI 2015 No 971 as from 26.5.15.

Treatment of students

71.   This scheme has effect in relation to students subject to paragraph 72 (students excluded from entitlement to a council tax reduction under this scheme) and the following provisions of this Part.

Students who are excluded from entitlement to a council tax reduction under this scheme

72.–(1)   The students who are excluded from entitlement to a reduction under this scheme are–

(a)   students who are pensioners; and

(b)   subject to sub-paragraphs (2) and (7)–

(i)   full-time students, and

(ii)   students who are persons treated as not being in Great Britain.

(2)   Sub-paragraph (1)(b) does not apply to a student–

(a)   who is a person on income support, an income-based jobseeker's allowance or an income-related employment and support allowance;

(b)   who is a lone parent;

(c)   whose applicable amount would, but for this paragraph, include the disability premium or severe disability premium;

(d)   whose applicable amount would include the disability premium but for the student being treated as capable of work by virtue of a determination made in accordance with regulations made under section 171E of the SSCBA;

(e)   who is, or is treated as, incapable of work and has been so incapable, or has been so treated as incapable, of work in accordance with the provisions of, and regulations made under, Part 12A of the SSCBA (incapacity for work) for a continuous period of not less than 196 days; and for this purpose any two or more separate periods separated by a break of not more than 56 days must be treated as one continuous period;

(f)   who has, or is treated as having, limited capability for work and has had, or been treated as having, limited capability for work in accordance with the Employment and Support Allowance Regulations 2008 [¹ or the Employment and Support Allowance Regulations 2013] for a continuous period of not less than 196 days, and for this purpose any two or more separate periods separated by a break of not more than 84 days must be treated as one continuous period;

(g)   who has a partner who is also a full-time student, if the student or that partner is treated as responsible for a child or young person;

(h)   who is a single applicant with whom a child is placed by a local authority or voluntary organisation within the meaning of the Children Act 1989 or, in Scotland, boarded out within the meaning of the Social Work (Scotland) Act 1968;

(i)   who is–

      (i)   aged under 21 and whose course of study is not a course of higher education,

      (ii)   aged 21 and attained that age during a course of study which is not a course of higher education, or

      (iii)   a qualifying young person or child within the meaning of section 142 of the SSCBA (child and qualifying young person);

(j)   in respect of whom–

      (i)   a supplementary requirement has been determined under paragraph 9 of Part 2 of Schedule 2 to the Education (Mandatory Awards) Regulations 2003;

      (ii)   an allowance, or as the case may be, bursary has been granted which includes a sum under regulation 4 of the Students' Allowances (Scotland) Regulations 2007 or, as the case may be, under the Education Authority (Bursaries) (Scotland) Regulations 2007, in respect of expenses incurred;

      (iii)   a payment has been made under section 2 of the Education Act 1962 or by virtue of regulations made under the Teaching and Higher Education Act 1998;

      (iv)   a grant has been made under regulation 13 of the Education (Student Support) Regulations 2005, regulation 13 of the Education (Student Support) Regulations (Northern Ireland) 2000, or regulation 41 of the Education (Student Support) (No. 2) Regulations (Northern Ireland) 2009; or

      (v)   a supplementary requirement has been determined under paragraph 9 of Schedule 6 to the Students Awards Regulations (Northern Ireland) 2003 or a payment has been made under Article 50(3) of the Education and Libraries (Northern Ireland) Order 1986,

      on account of the student's disability by reason of deafness.

(3)   Sub-paragraph (2)(i)(ii) only applies to an applicant until the end of the course during which the applicant attained the age of 21.

(4)   For the purposes of sub-paragraph (2), once sub-paragraph (2)(e) applies to a full-time student, if that student then ceases, for a period of 56 days or less, to be incapable, or to be treated as incapable, of work, that sub-paragraph must, on that student again becoming so incapable, or so treated as incapable, of work at the end of that period, immediately thereafter apply to that student for so long as that student remains incapable or is treated as remaining incapable, of work..

(5)   In sub-paragraph (2)(i) the reference to a course of higher education is a reference to a course of any description mentioned in Schedule 6 to the Education Reform Act 1988.

(6)   A full-time student to whom sub-paragraph (2)(i) applies must be treated as satisfying that sub-paragraph from the date on which that student made a request for the supplementary requirement, allowance, bursary or payment as the case may be.

(7)   Sub-paragraph (1)(b) does not apply to a full-time student for the period specified in sub-paragraph (8) if–

(a)   at any time during an academic year, with the consent of the relevant educational establishment, the student ceases to attend or undertake a course because the student is–

      (i)   engaged in caring for another person; or

      (ii)   ill;

(b)   the student has subsequently ceased to be engaged in caring for that person or, as the case may be, the student has subsequently recovered from that illness; and

(c)   the student is not eligible for a grant or a student loan in respect of the period specified in sub-paragraph (8).

(8)   The period specified for the purposes of sub-paragraph (7) is the period, not exceeding one year, beginning on the day on which the student ceased to be engaged in caring for that person or, as the case may be, the day on which the student recovered from that illness and ending on the day before–

(a)   the day on which the student resumes attending or undertaking the course; or

(b)   the day from which the relevant educational establishment has agreed that the student may resume attending or undertaking the course,

whichever first occurs.

Amendment

1.   Amended by reg 26 of SI 2015 No 44 (W.3) as from 21.1.15, for schemes made for a financial year starting on or after 1.4.15.

CHAPTER 2
Income

Calculation of grant income
73.–(1)   The amount of a student's grant income to be taken into account in assessing the student's income must, subject to sub-paragraphs (2) and (3), be the whole of the student's grant income.
(2)   There must be excluded from a student's grant income any payment–
(a)   intended to meet tuition fees or examination fees;
(b)   in respect of the student's disability;
(c)   intended to meet additional expenditure connected with term time residential study away from the student's educational establishment;
(d)   on account of the student maintaining a home at a place other than that at which the student resides during the student's course;
(e)   on account of any other person but only if that person is residing outside the United Kingdom and there is no applicable amount in respect of that person;
(f)   intended to meet the cost of books and equipment;
(g)   intended to meet travel expenses incurred as a result of the student's attendance on the course;
(h)   intended for the child care costs of a child dependant;
(i)   of higher education bursary for care leavers made under Part 3 of the Children Act 1989 [¹ ;
(j)   of higher education bursary for category 3 and category 4 young persons made under section 110 or 112 of the Social Services and Well-being (Wales) Act 2014, and in accordance with regulations made under section 116 of that Act.
(2A)   In sub-paragraph (2)(j) "category 3 young person" and "category 4 young person" have the meaning given in section 104(2) of the Social Services and Well-being (Wales) Act 2014.]
(3)   Where a student does not have a student loan and is not treated as possessing such a loan, there must be excluded from the student's grant income–
(a)   the sum of £303 per academic year in respect of travel costs; and
(b)   the sum of £390 per academic year towards the costs of books and equipment, whether or not any such costs are incurred.
(4)   There must also be excluded from a student's grant income the grant for dependants known as the parents' learning allowance paid pursuant to regulations made under Article 3 of the Education (Student Support) (Northern Ireland) Order 1998 or section 22 of the Teaching and Higher Education Act 1998.
(5)   Subject to sub-paragraphs (6) and (7), a student's grant income must be apportioned–
(a)   subject to sub-paragraph (8), in a case where it is attributable to the period of study, equally between the weeks in that period beginning with the reduction week, the first day of which coincides with, or immediately follows, the first day of the period of study and ending with the reduction week, the last day of which coincides with, or immediately precedes, the last day of the period of study;
(b)   in any other case, equally between the weeks in the period beginning with the reduction week, the first day of which coincides with, or immediately follows, the first day of the period for which it is payable and ending with the reduction week, the last day of which coincides with, or immediately precedes, the last day of the period for which it is payable.
(6)   Any grant in respect of dependants paid under section 63(6) of the Health Services and Public Health Act 1968 (grants in respect of the provision of instruction to officers of hospital authorities) and any amount intended for the maintenance of dependants under Part 3 of Schedule 2 to the Education (Mandatory Awards) Regulations 2003 must be apportioned equally over the period of 52 weeks or, if there are 53 reduction weeks (including part-weeks) in the year, 53 weeks.
(7)   In a case where a student is in receipt of a student loan or where the student could have acquired a student loan by taking reasonable steps but had not done so, any amount intended for the maintenance of dependants to which neither sub-paragraph (6) nor paragraph 77(2) (other amounts to be disregarded) applies, must be apportioned over the same period as the student's loan is apportioned or, as the case may be, would have been apportioned.
(8)   In the case of a student on a sandwich course, any periods of experience within the period of study must be excluded and the student's grant income must be apportioned equally between the weeks in the period beginning with the reduction week, the first day of which immediately follows the last day of the period of experience and ending with the reduction week, the last day of which coincides with, or immediately precedes, the last day of the period of study.

Amendment
1.   Amended by reg 24 of SI 2016 No 50 (W.21) as from 20.1.16, for schemes made for a financial year starting on or after 1.4.16.

Calculation of covenant income where a contribution is assessed
74.–(1)   Where a student is in receipt of income by way of a grant during a period of study and a contribution has been assessed, the amount of the student's covenant income to be taken into account for that period and any summer vacation immediately following must be the whole amount of the covenant income less, subject to sub-paragraph (3), the amount of the contribution.

(2)   The weekly amount of the student's covenant must be determined–

(a)   by dividing the amount of income which falls to be taken into account under sub-paragraph (1) by 52 or 53, whichever is reasonable in the circumstances; and

(b)   by disregarding £5 from the resulting amount.

(3)   For the purposes of sub-paragraph (1), the contribution must be treated as increased by the amount (if any) by which the amount excluded under paragraph 73(2)(g) (calculation of grant income) falls short of the amount specified in paragraph 7(2) of Schedule 2 to the Education (Mandatory Awards) Regulations 2003 (travel expenditure).

Covenant income where no grant income or no contribution is assessed

75.–(1)   Where a student is not in receipt of income by way of a grant the amount of the student's covenant income must be calculated as follows–

(a)   any sums intended for any expenditure specified in paragraph 73(2)(a) to (e) (calculation of grant income) necessary as a result of the student's attendance on the course must be disregarded;

(b)   any covenant income, up to the amount of the standard maintenance grant, which is not so disregarded, must be apportioned equally between the weeks of the period of study;

(c)   there must be disregarded from the amount so apportioned the amount which would have been disregarded under paragraph 73(2)(f) and (3) (calculation of grant income) had the student been in receipt of the standard maintenance grant; and

(d)   the balance, if any, must be divided by 52 or 53 whichever is reasonable in the circumstances and treated as weekly income of which £5 must be disregarded.

(2)   Where a student is in receipt of income by way of a grant and no contribution has been assessed, the amount of the student's covenanted income must be calculated in accordance with paragraphs (a) to (d) of sub-paragraph (1), except that–

(a)   the value of the standard maintenance grant must be abated by the amount of such grant income less an amount equal to the amount of any sums disregarded under paragraph 73(2)(a) to (e); and

(b)   the amount to be disregarded under sub-paragraph (1)(c) must be abated by an amount equal to the amount of any sums disregarded under paragraph 73(2)(f) and (g) and (3).

Relationship with amounts to be disregarded under Schedule 7

76.   No part of a student's covenant income or grant income is to be disregarded under paragraph 19 of Schedule 7 (disregard of certain charitable and voluntary, etc., payments).

Other amounts to be disregarded

77.–(1)   For the purposes of ascertaining income other than grant income, covenant income and loans treated as income in accordance with paragraph 78 (treatment of student loans), any amounts intended for any expenditure specified in paragraph 73(2) (calculation of grant income), necessary as a result of the student's attendance on the course is to be disregarded.

(2)   But sub-paragraph (1) applies only if, and to the extent that, the necessary expenditure exceeds or is likely to exceed the amount of the sums disregarded under paragraph 73(2) or (3), 74(3), 75(1)(a) or (c) or 78(5) (calculation of grant income, covenant income and treatment of student loans) on like expenditure.

Treatment of student loans

78.–(1)   A student loan is to be treated as income.

(2)   In calculating the weekly amount of the loan to be taken into account as income–

(a)   in respect of a course that is of a single academic year's duration or less, a loan which is payable in respect of that period is to be apportioned equally between the weeks in the period beginning with–

(i)   except in a case where sub-paragraph (ii) applies, the reduction week, the first day of which coincides with, or immediately follows, the first day of the single academic year;

(ii)   where the student is required to start attending the course in August or where the course is less than an academic year's duration, the reduction week, the first day of which coincides with, or immediately follows, the first day of the course,

and ending with the reduction week, the last day of which coincides with, or immediately precedes, the last day of the course;

(b)   in respect of an academic year of a course which starts other than on 1 September, a loan which is payable in respect of that academic year is to be apportioned equally between the weeks in the period–

(i)   beginning with the reduction week, the first day of which coincides with or immediately follows, the first day of that academic year; and

(ii)   ending with the reduction week, the last day of which coincides with or immediately precedes, the last day of that academic year,

but excluding any reduction weeks falling entirely within the quarter during which, in the opinion of the authority, the longest of any vacation is taken [¹];

(c)   in respect of the final academic year of a course (not being a course of a single year's duration), a loan which is payable in respect of that final academic year is to be apportioned equally between the weeks in the period beginning with–

(i)   except in a case where sub-paragraph (ii) applies, the reduction week, the first day of which coincides with, or immediately follows, the first day of that academic year;

(ii)   where the final academic year starts on 1 September, the reduction week, the first day of which coincides with, or immediately follows, the earlier of 1 September or the first day of the autumn term,

and ending with the reduction week, the last day of which coincides with, or immediately precedes, the last day of the course;

(d)   in any other case, the loan is to be apportioned equally between the weeks in the period beginning with the earlier of–

(i)   the first day of the first reduction week in September; or

(ii)   the reduction week, the first day of which coincides with, or immediately follows the first day of the autumn term,

and ending with the reduction week, the last day of which coincides with, or immediately precedes, the last day of June, and, in all cases, from the weekly amount so apportioned there is to be disregarded £10.

(3)   A student is to be treated as possessing a student loan in respect of an academic year where–

(a)   a student loan has been made to the student in respect of that year; or

(b)   the student could acquire such a loan in respect of that year by taking reasonable steps to do so.

(4)   Where a student is treated as possessing a student loan under sub-paragraph (3), the amount of the student loan to be taken into account as income must be, subject to sub-paragraph (5)–

(a)   in the case of a student to whom a student loan is made in respect of an academic year, a sum equal to–

(i)   the maximum student loan the student is able to acquire in respect of that year by taking reasonable steps to do so; and

(ii)   any contribution whether or not it has been paid to the student;

(b)   in the case of a student to whom a student loan is not made in respect of an academic year, the maximum student loan that would be made to the student if–

(i)   the student took all reasonable steps to obtain the maximum student loan that student is able to acquire in respect of that year; and

(ii)   no deduction in that loan was made by virtue of the application of a means test.

(5)   There must be deducted from the amount of income taken into account under sub-paragraph (4)–

(a)   the sum of £303 per academic year in respect of travel costs; and

(b)   the sum of £390 per academic year towards the cost of books and equipment,

whether or not any such costs are incurred.

[¹ (6)   For the purposes of this paragraph "quarter" ("chwarter") in relation to an academic year means a period in that year–

(a)   beginning on 1 January and ending on 31 March;

(b)   beginning on 1 April and ending on 30 June;

(c)   beginning on 1 July and ending on 31 August; or

(d)   beginning on 1 September and ending on 31 December]]

Amendment

1.   Amended by reg 23 of SI 2014 No 66 (W.6) as from 15.1.14.

Treatment of fee loans

79.   A loan for fees, known as a fee loan or a fee contribution loan, made pursuant to regulations made under Article 3 of the [¹ Education (Student Support) (Northern Ireland) Order 1998], section 22 of the Teaching and Higher Education Act 1998 or section 73(f) of the Education (Scotland) Act 1980, will be disregarded as income.

Amendment

1.   Amended by reg 24 of SI 2014 No 66 (W.6) as from 15.1.14.

Treatment of payments from access funds

80.–(1)   This paragraph applies to payments from access funds that are not payments to which paragraph 83(2) or (3) (income treated as capital) applies.

(2)   A payment from access funds, other than a payment to which sub-paragraph (3) applies, must be disregarded as income.

(3)   Subject to sub-paragraph (4) of this paragraph and paragraph 40 of Schedule 7 (disregards in the calculation of income other than earnings: persons who are not pensioners)–

(a)   any payments from access funds which are intended and used for an item of food, ordinary clothing or footwear, household fuel, or rent of a single applicant or, as the case may be, of the applicant or any other member of the applicant's family; and

(b)   any payments from access funds which are used for any council tax or water charges for which that applicant or any other member of the applicant's family is liable,

must be disregarded as income to the extent of £20 per week.

(4)   Where a payment from access funds is made–

(a)   on or after 1 September or the first day of the course, whichever first occurs, but before receipt of any student loan in respect of that year and that payment is intended for the purpose of bridging the period until receipt of the student loan; or

(b)   before the first day of the course to a person in anticipation of that person becoming a student,

that payment must be disregarded as income.

Disregard of contribution

81.   Where the applicant or the applicant's partner is a student and, for the purposes of assessing a contribution to the student's grant or student loan, the other partner's income has been taken into account, an amount equal to that contribution must be disregarded for the purposes of assessing that other partner's income.

Further disregard of student's income

82.   Where any part of a student's income has already been taken into account for the purposes of assessing that student's entitlement to a grant or student loan, the amount taken into account must be disregarded in assessing that student's income.

Income treated as capital

83.–(1)   Any amount by way of a refund of tax deducted from a student's covenant income must be treated as capital.

(2)   An amount paid from access funds as a single lump sum must be treated as capital.

(3)   An amount paid from access funds as a single lump sum which is intended and used for an item other than food, ordinary clothing or footwear, household fuel or rent, or which is used for an item other than any council tax or water charges for which that applicant or any other member of the applicant's family is liable, must be disregarded as capital but only for a period of 52 weeks from the date of the payment.

Disregard of changes occurring during summer vacation

84.   In calculating a student's income the authority must disregard any change in the standard maintenance grant, occurring in the recognised summer vacation appropriate to the student's course, if that vacation does not form part of the student's period of study from the date on which the change occurred to the end of that vacation.

PART 11
Extended reductions

Extended reductions: pensioners

85.   Paragraphs 86 to 91 apply in relation to applicants who are pensioners.

Extended reductions (qualifying contributory benefits): pensioners

86.–(1)   Except in the case of an applicant who is in receipt of state pension credit, an applicant who is entitled to a reduction under this scheme (by virtue of falling within class A or B) must be entitled to an extended reduction (qualifying contributory benefits) where–

(a)   the applicant or the applicant's partner was entitled to a qualifying contributory benefit;

(b)   entitlement to a qualifying contributory benefit ceased because the applicant or the applicant's partner–

(i)   commenced employment as an employed or self-employed earner;

(ii)   increased their earnings from such employment; or

(iii)   increased the number of hours worked in such employment,

and that employment is or, as the case may be, those increased earnings or increased number of hours are expected to last five weeks or more;

(c)   the applicant or the applicant's partner had been entitled to and in receipt of a qualifying contributory benefit or a combination of qualifying contributory benefits for a continuous period of at least 26 weeks before the day on which the entitlement to a qualifying contributory benefit ceased; and

(d)   the applicant or the applicant's partner was not entitled to and not in receipt of a qualifying income-related benefit in the last reduction week in which the applicant, or the applicant's partner, was entitled to a qualifying contributory benefit.

(2)   An applicant must be treated as entitled to a reduction under this scheme by virtue of falling within class A or B where–

(a)   the applicant ceased to be entitled to a reduction under this scheme because the applicant vacated the dwelling in which the applicant was resident;

(b)   the day on which the applicant vacated the dwelling was either in the week in which entitlement to a qualifying contributory benefit ceased, or in the preceding week; and

(c)   entitlement to the qualifying contributory benefit ceased in any of the circumstances listed in sub-paragraph (1)(b).

Duration of extended reduction period (qualifying contributory benefits): pensioners
87.–(1)   Where an applicant is entitled to an extended reduction (qualifying contributory benefits), the extended reduction period starts on the day immediately following the day on which the applicant, or the applicant's partner, ceased to be entitled to a qualifying contributory benefit.
(2)   The extended reduction period ends–
(a)   at the end of a period of four weeks; or
(b)   on the date on which the applicant who is receiving the extended reduction (qualifying contributory benefits) has no liability for council tax, if that occurs first.

Amount of extended reduction (qualifying contributory benefits): pensioners
88.–(1)   For any week during the extended reduction period the amount of the extended reduction (qualifying contributory benefits) the applicant is entitled to is the greater of–
(a)   the amount of council tax reduction to which the applicant was entitled by virtue of falling within class A or B in the last reduction week before the applicant or the applicant's partner ceased to be entitled to a qualifying contributory benefit;
(b)   the amount of reduction under this scheme to which the applicant would be entitled by virtue of falling within class A or B for any reduction week during the extended reduction period, if paragraph 86 (extended reductions (qualifying contributory benefits): pensioners) did not apply to the applicant; or
(c)   the amount of reduction under this scheme to which the applicant's partner would be entitled by virtue of falling within class A or B, if paragraph 86 did not apply to the applicant.
(2)   Sub-paragraph (1) does not apply in the case of a mover.
(3)   Where an applicant is in receipt of an extended reduction (qualifying contributory benefits) under this paragraph and the applicant's partner makes an application for a reduction under this scheme, the authority will not award a reduction in pursuance of that application during the extended reduction period.

Extended reductions (qualifying contributory benefits)-movers: pensioners
89.–(1)   This paragraph applies–
(a)   to a mover; and
(b)   from the Monday following the day of the move.
(2)   The amount of the extended reduction (qualifying contributory benefit) awarded from the Monday from which this paragraph applies until the end of the extended reduction period is to be the amount of reduction under this scheme which was awarded to the mover for the last reduction week before the mover, or the mover's partner, ceased to be entitled to a qualifying contributory benefit.
(3)   Where a mover's liability to pay council tax in respect of the new dwelling is to a second authority, the extended reduction (qualifying contributory benefits) may take the form of a payment from this authority to–
(a)   the second authority; or
(b)   the mover directly.

Relationship between extended reduction (qualifying contributory benefits) and entitlement to a reduction by virtue of falling within class A or B
90.–(1)   Where an applicant's reduction under this scheme would have ended when the applicant ceased to be entitled to a qualifying contributory benefit in the circumstances listed in paragraph 86(1)(b) (extended reductions (qualifying contributory benefits): pensioners), that reduction does not cease to have effect until the end of the extended reduction period.
(2)   Part 12 (period of entitlement and changes of circumstances) will not apply to any extended reduction (qualifying contributory benefits) payable in accordance with paragraph 88(1)(a) or paragraph 89(2) (amount of extended reduction – movers: pensioners).

Continuing reductions where state pension credit claimed: pensioners
91.–(1)   This paragraph applies where–
(a)   the applicant is entitled to a reduction under this scheme;
(b)   sub-paragraph (2) is satisfied; and
(c)   either–
(i)   the applicant has attained the qualifying age for state pension credit or, if the applicant's entitlement to income-based jobseeker's allowance or income-related employment and support allowance continued beyond that age, has attained the age of 65; or
(ii)   the applicant's partner has actually claimed state pension credit.
(2)   This sub-paragraph is only satisfied if the Secretary of State has certified to the authority that the applicant's partner has actually claimed state pension credit or that–
(a)   the applicant's award of–
(i)   income support has terminated because the applicant has attained the qualifying age for state pension credit; or
(ii)   income-based jobseeker's allowance or income-related employment and support allowance has terminated because the applicant has attained the qualifying age for state pension credit or the age of 65; and

    (b)   the applicant has claimed or is treated as having claimed or is required to make a claim for state pension credit.

    (3)   Subject to sub-paragraph (4), in a case to which this paragraph applies, a person continues to be entitled to a reduction under this scheme for the period of 4 weeks beginning on the day following the day the applicant's entitlement to income support or, as the case may be, income-based jobseeker's allowance, income-related employment and support allowance, ceased, if and for so long as the applicant otherwise satisfies the conditions for entitlement to a reduction under this scheme.

    (4)   Where a reduction under this scheme is awarded for the period of 4 weeks in accordance with sub-paragraph (3) above, and the last day of that period falls on a day other than the last day of a reduction week, then a reduction under this scheme is to continue to be awarded until the end of the reduction week in which the last day of that period falls.

    (5)   Throughout the period of 4 weeks specified in sub-paragraph (3) and any further period specified in sub-paragraph (4)–

    (a)   the whole of the income and capital of the applicant is to be disregarded;

    (b)   the applicant's maximum council tax reduction is to be that which was applicable in the applicant's case immediately before that period commenced.

    (6)   The maximum council tax reduction is to be calculated in accordance with paragraph 27(1) if, since the date it was last calculated–

    (a)   the applicant's council tax liability has increased; or

    (b)   a change in the deduction under paragraph 28 (non-dependant deductions) falls to be made.

Extended reductions: persons who are not pensioners (general)

    92.   Paragraphs 93 to 102 apply in relation to applicants who are not pensioners.

Extended reductions: persons who are not pensioners

    93.–(1)   An applicant who is entitled to a reduction under this scheme (by virtue of falling within class C or D) is to be entitled to an extended reduction where–

    (a)   the applicant or the applicant's partner was entitled to a qualifying income-related benefit;

    (b)   entitlement to a qualifying income-related benefit ceased because the applicant or the applicant's partner–

        (i)   commenced employment as an employed or self-employed earner;

        (ii)   increased their earnings from such employment; or

        (iii)   increased the number of hours worked in such employment,

        and that employment is or, as the case may be, those increased earnings or increased number of hours are expected to last five weeks or more; and

    (c)   the applicant or the applicant's partner had been entitled to and in receipt of a qualifying income-related benefit, jobseeker's allowance or a combination of those benefits for a continuous period of at least 26 weeks before the day on which the entitlement to a qualifying income-related benefit ceased.

    (2)   For the purpose of sub-paragraph (1)(c), an applicant or an applicant's partner is to be treated as having been entitled to and in receipt of a qualifying income-related benefit or jobseeker's allowance during any period of less than five weeks in respect of which the applicant or the applicant's partner was not entitled to any of those benefits because the applicant or the applicant's partner was engaged in remunerative work as a consequence of their participation in an employment zone programme.

    (3)   For the purpose of this paragraph, where an applicant or an applicant's partner is entitled to and in receipt of joint-claim jobseeker's allowance they are to be treated as being entitled to and in receipt of jobseeker's allowance.

    (4)   An applicant must be treated as entitled to a reduction under this scheme by virtue of falling within class C or D where–

    (a)   the applicant ceased to be entitled to a reduction under this scheme because the applicant vacated the dwelling in which the applicant was resident;

    (b)   the day on which the applicant vacated the dwelling was either in the week in which entitlement to a qualifying income-related benefit ceased, or in the preceding week; and

    (c)   entitlement to the qualifying income-related benefit ceased in any of the circumstances listed in sub-paragraph (1)(b).

    (5)   This paragraph does not apply where, on the day before an applicant's entitlement to income support ceased, regulation 6(5) of the Income Support (General) Regulations 1987 (remunerative work: housing costs) applied to that applicant.

Duration of extended reduction period: persons who are not pensioners

    94.–(1)   Where an applicant is entitled to an extended reduction, the extended reduction period starts on the day immediately following the day on which the applicant, or the applicant's partner, ceased to be entitled to a qualifying income-related benefit.

    (2)   The extended reduction period ends–

    (a)   at the end of a period of four weeks; or

    (b)   on the date on which the applicant to whom the extended reduction is payable has no liability for council tax, if that occurs first.

Amount of extended reduction: persons who are not pensioners

95.–(1) For any week during the extended reduction period the amount of the extended reduction to which an applicant is entitled is to be the greater of the amount of reduction under this scheme to which–

(a) the applicant was entitled by virtue of falling within class C or D in the last reduction week before the applicant or the applicant's partner ceased to be entitled to a qualifying income-related benefit;

(b) the applicant would be entitled by virtue of falling within class C or D for any reduction week during the extended reduction period, if paragraph 93 (extended reductions: persons who are not pensioners) did not apply to the applicant; or

(c) the applicant's partner would be entitled by virtue of falling within class C or D, if paragraph 93 did not apply to the applicant.

(2) Sub-paragraph (1) does not apply in the case of a mover.

(3) Where an applicant is in receipt of an extended reduction under this paragraph and the applicant's partner makes an application for a reduction under this scheme, no amount of reduction under this scheme is to be awarded by the authority during the extended reduction period.

Extended reductions-movers: persons who are not pensioners

96.–(1) This paragraph applies–

(a) to a mover; and

(b) from the Monday following the day of the move.

(2) The amount of the extended reduction awarded from the Monday from which this paragraph applies until the end of the extended reduction period is to be the amount of reduction under this scheme to which the mover would have been entitled had the mover, or the mover's partner, not ceased to be entitled to a qualifying income-related benefit.

(3) Where a mover's liability to pay council tax in respect of the new dwelling is to a second authority, the extended reduction (qualifying contributory benefits) may take the form of a payment from this authority to–

(a) the second authority; or

(b) the mover directly.

Relationship between extended reduction and entitlement to reduction by virtue of falling within class C or D

97.–(1) Where an applicant's reduction under this scheme would have ended when the applicant ceased to be entitled to a qualifying income-related benefit in the circumstances listed in paragraph 93(1)(b) (extended reductions: persons who are not pensioners), that entitlement does not cease until the end of the extended reduction period.

(2) Paragraphs 104 and 105 (period of entitlement and change of circumstances) do not apply to any extended reduction payable in accordance with paragraph 95(1)(a) or 96(2) (amount of extended reduction-movers: persons who are not pensioners).

Extended reductions (qualifying contributory benefits): persons who are not pensioners

98.–(1) An applicant who is entitled to a reduction under this scheme by virtue of falling within class C or D will be entitled to an extended reduction (qualifying contributory benefits) where–

(a) the applicant or the applicant's partner was entitled to a qualifying contributory benefit;

(b) entitlement to a qualifying contributory benefit ceased because the applicant or the applicant's partner–

(i) commenced employment as an employed or self-employed earner;

(ii) increased their earnings from such employment; or

(iii) increased the number of hours worked in such employment,

and that employment is or, as the case may be, those increased earnings or increased number of hours are expected to last five weeks or more;

(c) the applicant or the applicant's partner had been entitled to and in receipt of a qualifying contributory benefit or a combination of qualifying contributory benefits for a continuous period of at least 26 weeks before the day on which the entitlement to a qualifying contributory benefit ceased; and

(d) the applicant or the applicant's partner was not entitled to and not in receipt of a qualifying income-related benefit in the last reduction week in which the applicant, or the applicant's partner, was entitled to a qualifying contributory benefit.

(2) An applicant must be treated as entitled to a reduction under this scheme by virtue of falling within class C or D where–

(a) the applicant ceased to be entitled to a reduction under this scheme because the applicant vacated the dwelling in which the applicant was resident;

(b) the day on which the applicant vacated the dwelling was either in the week in which entitlement to a qualifying contributory benefit ceased, or in the preceding week; and

(c) entitlement to the qualifying contributory benefit ceased in any of the circumstances listed in sub-paragraph (1)(b).

Duration of extended reduction period (qualifying contributory benefits): persons who are not pensioners

99.–(1)   Where an applicant is entitled to an extended reduction (qualifying contributory benefits), the extended reduction period starts on the day immediately following the day on which the applicant, or the applicant's partner, ceased to be entitled to a qualifying contributory benefit.

(2)   The extended reduction period ends–

(a)   at the end of a period of four weeks; or

(b)   on the date on which the applicant entitled to the extended reduction (qualifying contributory benefits) has no liability for council tax, if that occurs first.

Amount of extended reduction (qualifying contributory benefits): persons who are not pensioners

100.–(1)   For any week during the extended reduction period the amount of the extended reduction (qualifying contributory benefits) payable to an applicant is to be the greater of the amount of reduction under this scheme–

(a)   to which the applicant was entitled by virtue of falling within class C or D in the last reduction week before the applicant or the applicant's partner ceased to be entitled to a qualifying contributory benefit;

(b)   to which the applicant would be entitled by virtue of falling within class C or D for any reduction week during the extended reduction period, if paragraph 98 (extended reductions (qualifying contributory benefits): persons who are not pensioners) did not apply to the applicant; or

(c)   to which the applicant's partner would be entitled by virtue of falling within class C or D, if paragraph 98 did not apply to the applicant.

(2)   Sub-paragraph (1) does not apply in the case of a mover.

(3)   Where an applicant is in receipt of an extended reduction (qualifying contributory benefits) under this paragraph and the applicant's partner makes an application for a reduction under this scheme, no amount of reduction under this scheme is to be awarded by the authority during the extended reduction period.

Extended reductions (qualifying contributory benefits)-movers: persons who are notpensioners

101.–(1)   This paragraph applies–

(a)   to a mover; and

(b)   from the Monday following the day of the move.

(2)   The amount of the extended reduction (qualifying contributory benefits) awarded from the Monday from which this paragraph applies until the end of the extended reduction period is to be the amount of reduction under this scheme which was awarded to the mover for the last reduction week before the mover, or the mover's partner, ceased to be entitled to a qualifying contributory benefit.

(3)   Where a mover's liability to pay council tax in respect of the new dwelling is to a second authority, the extended reduction (qualifying contributory benefits) may take the form of a payment from this authority to–

(a)   that second authority; or

(b)   the mover directly.

Relationship between extended reduction (qualifying contributory benefits) andentitlement to reduction by virtue of falling within class C or D

102.–(1)   Where an applicant's reduction under this scheme would have ended when the applicant ceased to be entitled to a qualifying contributory benefit in the circumstances listed in paragraph 98(1)(b) (extended reductions (qualifying contributory benefits): persons who are not pensioners), that reduction does not cease until the end of the extended reduction period.

(2)   Paragraphs 104 and 105 (period of entitlement and change of circumstances) do not apply to any extended reduction (qualifying contributory benefits) payable in accordance with paragraphs 100(1)(a) or 101(2) (amount of extended reduction-movers: persons who are not pensioners).

[¹ Extended reductions: movers into the authority's area: pensioners and persons who are not pensioners]

103.–(1)   Where–

(a)   an application is made to the authority for a reduction under this scheme, and

(b)   the applicant, or the partner of the applicant, is in receipt of an extended reduction from–

(i)   another billing authority in Wales;

(ii)   a billing authority in England;

(iii)   a local authority in Scotland, or

(iv)   a local authority in Northern Ireland,

the authority must reduce any reduction to which the applicant is entitled under this scheme by the amount of that extended reduction.

(2)   For the purposes of this paragraph "billing authority" ("awdurdod bilio") means a billing authority as defined in section 1 of the 1992 Act.

Amendment

1.   Amended by reg 26 of SI 2014 No 66 (W.6) as from 15.1.14.

PART 12
Period of entitlement and change of circumstances

Date on which entitlement begins

104. Any person by whom or in respect of whom an application for a reduction under this scheme is made and who is otherwise entitled to that reduction is to be so entitled from the date on which the application is treated as made in accordance with paragraph 108 (date on which application is made).

Date on which change of circumstances is to take effect

105.–(1) Except in cases where paragraph 57 (disregard of changes in tax, contributions, etc) applies and subject to the following provisions of this paragraph and (in the case of applicants who are pensioners) paragraph 106 (change of circumstances where state pension credit in payment), a change of circumstances which affects entitlement to, or the amount of, a reduction under this scheme ("change of circumstances"), takes effect from the first day on which the change actually occurs.

(2) Where that change is cessation of entitlement to any benefit under the benefit Acts, the date on which the change actually occurs will be the day immediately following the last day of entitlement to that benefit.

(3) Subject to sub-paragraph (4), where the change of circumstances is a change in the amount of council tax payable, it takes effect from the day on which it actually occurs.

(4) Where the change of circumstances is a change in the amount a person is liable to pay in respect of council tax in consequence of regulations under section 13 of the 1992 Act (reduced amounts of council tax) or changes in the discount to which a dwelling may be subject under section 11 or 12 of that Act, it is to take effect from the day on which the change in amount has effect.

(5) Where the change of circumstances is the applicant's acquisition of a partner, the change takes effect on the day on which the acquisition takes place.

(6) Where the change of circumstances is the death of an applicant's partner or their separation, it takes effect on the day the death or separation occurs.

(7) Where the change of circumstances is that income, or an increase in the amount of income, other than a benefit or an increase in the amount of a benefit under the SSCBA, is paid in respect of a past period and there was no entitlement to income of that amount during that period, the change of circumstances is to take effect from the first day on which such income, had it been paid in that period at intervals appropriate to that income, would have fallen to be taken into account for the purposes of this scheme.

(8) Without prejudice to sub-paragraph (7), where the change of circumstances is the payment of income, or arrears of income, in respect of a past period, the change of circumstances takes effect from the first day on which such income, had it been timeously paid in that period at intervals appropriate to that income, would have fallen to be taken into account for the purposes of this scheme.

Change of circumstances where state pension credit in payment

106.–(1) Sub-paragraphs (2) to (4) apply where–
(a) the applicant is in receipt of state pension credit;
(b) the amount of state pension credit awarded to the applicant is changed in consequence of a change in the applicant's circumstances or the correction of an official error; and
(c) the change in the amount of state pension credit payable to the applicant results in a change in the amount of a reduction the applicant receives under this scheme.

(2) Where the change of circumstance is that an increase in the amount of state pension credit payable to the applicant results in–
(a) an increase in the reduction the applicant receives under this scheme, the change takes effect on the day on which the state pension credit becomes payable at the increased rate; or
(b) a decrease in the reduction the applicant receives under this scheme, the change takes effect on the day on which–
(i) state pension credit becomes payable at the increased rate; or
(ii) the authority receives notification from the Secretary of State of the increase in the amount of state pension credit,
whichever is the later.

(3) Where the change of circumstance ("the relevant change") is that the applicant's state pension credit has been reduced and in consequence the reduction the applicant receives under this scheme reduces–
(a) in a case where the applicant's state pension credit has been reduced because the applicant failed to notify the Secretary of State timeously of a change of circumstances, the relevant change takes effect on the day on which state pension credit was reduced; or
(b) in any other case the relevant change takes effect from the first day on which–
(i) the state pension credit is reduced; or
(ii) the authority receives notification from the Secretary of State of the reduction in the amount of state pension credit,
whichever is the later.

(4)	Where the change of circumstance is that the applicant's state pension credit is reduced and in consequence of the change, the amount of reduction the applicant receives under this scheme is increased, the change takes effect on the day on which state pension credit becomes payable at the reduced rate.

(5)	Where a change of circumstance occurs in that an award of state pension credit has been made to the applicant or the applicant's partner and this would result in a decrease in the amount of reduction the applicant receives under this scheme, the change takes effect on the day on which–
(a)	entitlement to state credit pension begins; or
(b)	the authority receives notification from the Secretary of State of the award of state pension credit,
(c)	whichever is the later.

(6)	Where, in the case of an applicant who, or whose partner, is or has been awarded state pension credit comprising only the savings credit, there is–
(a)	a change of circumstances of a kind described in any of sub-paragraphs (2) to (5) which results from a relevant calculation or estimate; and
(b)	a change of circumstances which is a relevant determination,
(c)	each of which results in a change in the amount of reduction the applicant receives under this scheme, the change of circumstances referred to in paragraph (b) takes effect from the day specified in sub-paragraph (2), (3), (4) or (5) as the case may be, in relation to the change referred to in paragraph (a).

(7)	Where a change of circumstance occurs in that a guarantee credit has been awarded to the applicant or the applicant's partner and this would result in an increase in the amount of a reduction the applicant receives under this scheme, the change takes effect on the day on which the guarantee credit is first payable.

(8)	Where a change of circumstances would, but for this sub-paragraph, take effect under the preceding provisions of this paragraph within the 4 week period specified in paragraph 91 (continuing reductions where state pension credit claimed: pensioners), that change takes effect on the first day after the expiry of the 4 week period.

(9)	In this paragraph–
"official error" ("camgymeriad swyddogol") means an error made by–
(a)	the authority or a person–
(i)	authorised to carry out any function of the authority relating to this scheme; or
(ii)	providing services relating to this scheme directly or indirectly to the authority; or
(b)	an officer of–
(i)	the Department for Work and Pensions; or
(ii)	the Commissioners for Revenue and Customs,
acting as such, but excludes any error caused wholly or partly by any person or body not specified in paragraph (a) or (b) of this definition and any error of law which is shown to have been an error only by virtue of a subsequent decision of the court;
"relevant calculation or estimate" ("cyfrifiad neu amcangyfrif perthnasol") means the calculation or estimate made by the Secretary of State of the applicant's or, as the case may be, the applicant's partner's income and capital for the purposes of the award of state pension credit;
"relevant determination" ("penderfyniad perthnasol") means a change in the determination by the authority of the applicant's income and capital using the relevant calculation or estimate, in accordance with paragraph 33(1) (calculation of pensioner's income in savings credit only cases).

PART 13
Applications

Who may make an application
107.–(1)	In the case of–
(a)	a couple or (subject to paragraph (b)) members of a polygamous marriage an application is to be made by whichever one of them they agree should so apply or, in default of agreement, by such one of them as the authority determines; or
(b)	members of a polygamous marriage to whom paragraph 34 (calculation of income and capital: persons who are not pensioners who have an award of universal credit) applies, an application is to be made by whichever one of the parties to the earliest marriage that still subsists they agree should so apply or, in default of agreement, by such one of them as the authority determines.

(2)	Where a person who is liable to pay council tax in respect of a dwelling is unable for the time being to act, and–
(a)	a deputy has been appointed by the Court of Protection with power to claim, or as the case may be, receive benefit on that person's behalf; or
(b)	in Scotland, that person's estate is being administered by a judicial factor or any guardian acting or appointed under the Adults with Incapacity (Scotland) Act 2000 who has power to apply or, as the case may be, receive benefit on that person's behalf; or
(c)	an attorney with a general power or a power to apply or, as the case may be, receive benefit, has been appointed by that person under the Powers of Attorney Act 1971, the Enduring Powers of Attorney Act 1985 or the Mental Capacity Act 2005 or otherwise,
that deputy, judicial factor, guardian or attorney, as the case may be, may make an application on behalf of that person.

(3)   Where a person who is liable to pay council tax in respect of a dwelling is unable for the time being to act and sub-paragraph (2) does not apply to that person, the authority may, upon written application made to it by a person who, if a natural person, is over the age of 18, appoint that person to exercise on behalf of the person who is unable to act, any right to which the person who is unable to act might be entitled under this scheme, and to receive and deal on that person's behalf with any sums payable to that person.

(4)   Where a person who is liable to pay council tax in respect of a dwelling is for the time being unable to act and the Secretary of State has appointed a person to act on that person's behalf under regulation 33 of the Social Security (Claims and Payments) Regulations 1987 (persons unable to act), the authority may if the person so appointed agrees, treat that person as if that person had been appointed by it under sub-paragraph (3).

(5)   Where the authority has made an appointment under sub-paragraph (3) or treated a person as an appointee under sub-paragraph (4)–

(a)   it may at any time revoke the appointment;

(b)   the person appointed may resign that person's office after having given 4 weeks notice in writing to the authority of that person's intention to do so;

(c)   any such appointment must terminate when the authority is notified of the appointment of a person mentioned in sub-paragraph (2).

(6)   Anything required by this scheme to be done by or to any person who is for the time being unable to act may be done by or to the persons mentioned in sub-paragraph (2) above or by or to the person appointed or treated as appointed under this paragraph and the receipt of any such person so appointed is to be a good discharge to the authority for any sum paid.

(7)   The authority must–

(a)   inform any person making an application of the duty imposed by paragraph 113(1)(a) of this scheme (duty to notify change of circumstances);

(b)   explain the possible consequences (including prosecution) of failing to comply with that duty; and

(c)   set out the circumstances a change in which might affect entitlement to a reduction or its amount.

Date on which an application is made

108.–(1)   Subject to sub-paragraph (7), the date on which an application is made is–

(a)   in a case where–

(i)   an award of state pension credit which comprises a guarantee credit has been made to the applicant or the applicant's partner, and

(ii)   the application for a reduction under this scheme is made within one month of the date on which the claim for that state pension credit which comprises a guarantee credit was received at the appropriate DWP office,

the first day of entitlement to state pension credit which comprises guarantee credit arising from that claim;

(b)   in a case where–

(i)   an applicant or the applicant's partner is a person in receipt of guarantee credit,

(ii)   the applicant becomes liable for the first time to pay council tax in respect of the dwelling which the applicant occupies as the applicant's home, and

(iii)   the application to the authority is received at the designated office within one month of the date of the change,

the date on which the change takes place;

(c)   in a case where–

(i)   an award of income support, an income-based jobseeker's allowance or an income-related employment and support allowance or an award of universal credit has been made to the applicant or the applicant's partner, and

(ii)   the application for a reduction under this scheme is made within one month of the date on which the claim for that income support, jobseeker's allowance, employment and support allowance or universal credit was received,

the first day of entitlement to income support, an income-based jobseeker's allowance, an income-related employment and support allowance or universal credit arising from that claim;

(d)   in a case where–

(i)   an applicant or the applicant's partner is a person on income support, an income-based jobseeker's allowance or an income-related employment and support allowance or has an award of universal credit,

(ii)   the applicant becomes liable for the first time to pay council tax in respect of the dwelling which the applicant occupies as the applicant's home, and

(iii)   the application to the authority is received at the designated office within one month of the date of the change,

the date on which the change takes place;

(e)   in a case where–

(i)   the applicant is the former partner of a person who was, at the date of that person's death or the separation of the applicant and that person, entitled to a reduction under this scheme, and

(ii)   where the applicant makes an application for a reduction under this scheme within one month of the date of the death or the separation,

the date of the death or the separation;

(f) except where paragraph (a), (b) or (e) is satisfied, in a case where a properly completed application is received at the designated office within one month (or such longer period as the authority considers reasonable) of the date on which an application form was issued to the applicant following the applicant first notifying, by whatever means, the authority of an intention to make an application, the date of first notification;

(g) in any other case, the date on which the application is received at the designated office.

(2) For the purposes only of sub-paragraph (1)(c), a person who has been awarded an income-based jobseeker's allowance or an income-related employment and support allowance is to be treated as entitled to that allowance for any days which immediately precede the first day in that award and on which the person would, but for the regulations made under–

(a) in the case of income-based jobseeker's allowance, paragraph 4 of Schedule 1 to the Jobseekers Act 1995 (waiting days); or

(b) in the case of income-related employment and support allowance, paragraph 2 of Schedule 2 to the Welfare Reform Act 2007 (waiting days),

have been entitled to that allowance.

(3) Where the defect referred to in paragraph 7 of Schedule 1 to this scheme (telephone application)–

(a) is corrected within one month (or such longer period as the authority considers reasonable) of the date the authority last drew attention to it, the authority is to treat the application as if it had been duly made in the first instance;

(b) is not corrected within one month (or such longer period as the authority considers reasonable) of the date the authority last drew attention to it, the authority is to treat the application as if it had been duly made in the first instance where it considers it has sufficient information to decide on the application.

(4) The authority is to treat a defective application as if it had been validly made in the first instance if, in any particular case, the conditions specified in sub-paragraph (5)(a), (b) or (c) are satisfied.

(5) The conditions are that–

(a) where paragraph 4(1)(a) of Schedule 1 (incomplete form) applies, the authority receives at the designated offices the properly completed application or the information requested to complete it or the evidence within one month of the request, or such longer period as the authority considers reasonable; or

(b) where paragraph 4(1)(b) of Schedule 1 (application not on approved form or further information requested by authority) applies–

(i) the approved form sent to the applicant is received at the designated office properly completed within one month of it having been sent to the applicant; or, as the case may be,

(ii) the applicant supplies whatever information or evidence was requested under paragraph 4 of that Schedule within one month of the request,

or, in either case, within such longer period as the authority considers reasonable; or

(c) where the authority has requested further information, the authority receives at its designated office the properly completed application or the information requested within one month of the request or within such longer period as the authority considers reasonable.

(6) Except in the case of an application made by a person treated as not being in Great Britain, where a person has not become liable for council tax to the authority but it is anticipated that the person will become so liable within the period of 13 weeks (the relevant period), the person may apply for a reduction under this scheme at any time in that period in respect of that tax and, provided that liability arises within the relevant period, the authority is to treat the application as having been made on the day on which the liability for the tax arises.

(7) Except in the case of an application made by a person treated as not being in Great Britain, where the applicant is not entitled to a reduction under this scheme at the time that the application is received by the authority but the authority is of the opinion that, unless there is a change of circumstances, the applicant will be entitled to a reduction under this scheme for a period beginning not later than the thirteenth reduction week following the date on which the application is made (or such other period as the authority considers reasonable), the authority may treat the application as made on a date in the reduction week immediately preceding the first reduction week of that period of entitlement and award a reduction accordingly.

(8) In this paragraph "appropriate DWP office" ("swyddfa briodol yr Adran Gwaith a Phensiynau") means an office of the Department of Work and Pensions dealing with state pension credit or an office which is normally open to the public for the receipt of claims for income support, a jobseeker's allowance or an employment and support allowance.

Back-dating of applications: pensioners

109.–(1) Subject to sub-paragraph (2), the time for the making of an application under this scheme by a pensioner is as regards any day on which, apart from satisfying the condition of making an application, the applicant is entitled to such a reduction, that day and the period of three months immediately following it.

(2) In any case where paragraph 108(1)(a) applies (date on which application is made), sub-paragraph (1) does not entitle a person to apply for a reduction under this scheme in respect of any day earlier than 3 months before the date on which the claim for state pension credit is made (or treated as made by virtue of any provision of the Social Security (Claims and Payments) Regulations 1987).

Back-dating of applications: persons who are not pensioners

110.–(1)   Where an applicant who is a person who is not a pensioner–

(a)   makes an application under this scheme which includes (or which the applicant subsequently requests should include) a period before the application is made; and

(b)   from a day in that period, up to the date the applicant made the application (or subsequently requested that the application should include a past period), the applicant had continuous good cause for failing to make an application (or request that the application should include that period),

the application is to be treated as made on the date determined in accordance with sub-paragraph (2).

(2)   That date is the latest of–

(a)   the first day from which the applicant had continuous good cause;

(b)   the day 3 months before the date the application was made;

(c)   the day 3 months before the date when the applicant requested that the application should include a past period.

Evidence and information

111.–(1)   Subject to sub-paragraph (3), a person who makes an application for a reduction under this scheme must satisfy sub-paragraph (2) in relation both to the person making the application and to any other person in respect of whom the person is making the application.

(2)   This sub-paragraph is satisfied in relation to a person if–

(a)   the application is accompanied by–

(i)   a statement of the person's national insurance number and information or evidence establishing that that number has been allocated to the person; or

(ii)   information or evidence enabling the authority to ascertain the national insurance number that has been allocated to the person; or

(b)   the person has made an application for a national insurance number to be allocated to that person and the application for the reduction is accompanied by–

(i)   evidence of the application for a national insurance number to be so allocated; and

(ii)   the information or evidence enabling it to be so allocated.

(3)   Sub-paragraph (2) does not apply–

(a)   in the case of a child or young person in respect of whom an application for a reduction is made;

(b)   to a person who–

(i)   is treated as not being in Great Britain for the purposes of this scheme;

(ii)   is subject to immigration control within the meaning of section 115(9)(a) of the Immigration and Asylum Act 1999; and

has not previously been allocated a national insurance number.

(4)   Subject to sub-paragraph (5), a person who makes an application, or a person to whom a reduction under this scheme has been awarded, must furnish such certificates, documents, information and evidence in connection with the application or the award, or any question arising out of the application or award, as may reasonably be required by the authority in order to determine that person's entitlement to, or continuing entitlement to a reduction under this scheme and must do so within one month of the authority requiring the person to do so or such longer period as the authority considers reasonable.

(5)   Nothing in this paragraph requires a person to furnish any certificates, documents, information or evidence relating to a payment to which sub-paragraph (7) applies.

(6)   Where a request is made under sub-paragraph (4), the authority must–

(a)   inform the applicant or the person to whom a reduction under this scheme has been awarded of the applicant's or that other person's duty under paragraph 113 (duty to notify changes of circumstances) to notify the authority of any change of circumstances; and

(b)   without prejudice to the extent of the duty owed under paragraph 113, indicate to the person either orally or by notice or by reference to some other document available to the person on application and without charge, the kind of change of circumstances which is to be notified to the authority.

(7)   This sub-paragraph applies to any of the following payments–

(a)   a payment which is–

(i)   disregarded under paragraph 28 of Schedule 7 (sums disregarded in the calculation of income other than earnings: persons who are not pensioners) or paragraph 38 of Schedule 9 (capital disregards: persons who are not pensioners); or

(ii)   made under or by the Trusts, the Fund, the Eileen Trust, MFET Limited, the Skipton Fund, the Caxton Foundation [', an approved blood scheme, the Scottish Infected Blood Support Scheme, the London Emergencies Trust, the We Love Manchester Emergency Fund] or the London Bombings Relief Charitable Fund;

(b)   a payment which is disregarded under paragraph 16 of Schedule 8 (payments made under certain trusts and certain other payments), other than a payment under the Independent Living Fund (2006);

(c)   a payment which is disregarded under paragraph 28(9)(b) or (c) (non-dependant deductions) other than a payment under the Independent Living Fund (2006).

(8)   Where an applicant or a person to whom a reduction under this scheme has been awarded or any partner has attained the qualifying age for state pension credit and is a member of, or a person deriving entitlement to a pension under a personal pension scheme, the person must where the authority so requires furnish the following information–

(a)   the name and address of the pension fund holder;

(b)   such other information including any reference or policy number as is needed to enable the personal pension scheme to be identified.

Amendment

1.   Amended by reg 23(c) of SI 2018 No 14 (W.7) as from 10.1.18, for schemes made for a financial year starting on or after 1.4.18.

Amendment and withdrawal of application

112.–(1)   A person who has made an application may amend it at any time before a decision has been made on it by a notice in writing delivered or sent to the designated office.

(2)   Where the application was made by telephone in accordance with Part 1 of Schedule 1, the amendment may also be made by telephone.

(3)   Any application amended in accordance with sub-paragraph (1) or (2) is to be treated as if it had been amended in the first instance.

(4)   A person who has made an application may withdraw it by notice to the designated office at any time before a decision has been made on it.

(5)   Where the application was made by telephone in accordance with Part 1 of Schedule 1, the withdrawal may also be made by telephone.

(6)   Any notice of withdrawal given in accordance with sub-paragraph (4) or (5) is to have effect when it is received.

(7)   Where a person, by telephone, amends or withdraws an application the person must (if required to do so by the authority) confirm the amendment or withdrawal by a notice in writing delivered or sent to the designated office.

Duty to notify changes of circumstances

113.–(1)   Subject to sub-paragraphs (3) and (7), the applicant (or any person acting on the applicant's behalf) must comply with sub-paragraph (2) if there is a relevant change of circumstances at any time–

(a)   between the making of an application and a decision being made on it; or

(b)   after the decision is made (where the decision is that the applicant is entitled to a reduction under this scheme) including at any time while the applicant is in receipt of such a reduction.

(2)   The applicant (or any person acting on the applicant's behalf) must notify any change of circumstances which the applicant (or that person) might reasonably be expected to know might affect the applicant's entitlement to, or the amount of, a reduction under this scheme (a "relevant change of circumstances") by giving notice to the authority–

(a)   in writing; or

(b)   by telephone–

    (i)   where the authority has published a telephone number for that purpose or for the purposes of Part 1 of Schedule 1 unless the authority determines that in any particular case or class of case notification may not be given by telephone; or

    (ii)   in any case or class of case where the authority determines that notice may be given by telephone; or

(c)   by any other means which the authority agrees to accept in any particular case,

within a period of 21 days beginning with the day on which the change occurs, or as soon as reasonably practicable after the change occurs, whichever is the later.

(3)   The duty imposed on a person by sub-paragraph (1) does not extend to notifying–

(a)   changes in the amount of council tax payable to the authority;

(b)   changes in the age of the applicant or that of any member of the applicant's family;

(c)   in the case of an applicant in receipt of a relevant benefit, changes in circumstances which affect the amount of the benefit but not the amount of the reduction under this scheme to which the applicant is entitled, other than the cessation of that entitlement to the benefit.

(4)   For the purposes of sub-paragraph (3)(c) "relevant benefit" ("budd-dal perthnasol") means income support, an income-based jobseeker's allowance or an income-related employment and support allowance or universal credit.

(5)   Notwithstanding sub-paragraph (3)(b) or (c) an applicant is required by sub-paragraph (1) to notify the authority of any change in the composition of the applicant's family arising from the fact that a person who was a member of the applicant's family is now no longer such a person because that person has ceased to be a child or young person.

(6)   A person who has been awarded a reduction under this scheme who is also on state pension credit must report–

(a)   changes affecting the residence or income of any non-dependant normally residing with the applicant or with whom the applicant normally resides;

(b)   any absence from the dwelling which exceeds or is likely to exceed 13 weeks.

(7)   A person whose state pension credit comprises only a savings credit must also report–

(a)   changes affecting a child living with that person which may result in a change in the amount of reduction under this scheme allowed in that person's case, but not changes in the age of the child;

(b) any change in the amount of the person's capital to be taken into account which does or may take the amount of that person's capital to more than £16,000;

(c) any change in the income or capital of–

    (i) a non-dependant whose income and capital are treated as belonging to the applicant in accordance with paragraph 31 (circumstances in which capital and income of a non-dependant is to be treated as applicant's); or

    (ii) a person to whom paragraph 33(2)(e) (partner treated as member of the household under paragraph 8) refers,

and whether such a person or, as the case may be, non-dependant stops living or begins or resumes living with the applicant.

(8) A person who is entitled to a reduction under this scheme and on state pension credit need only report to the authority the changes specified in sub-paragraphs (6) and (7).

PART 14
Decisions by authority

Decision by authority

114. The authority must make a decision on an application for a reduction under this scheme within 14 days of paragraphs 108 and 111 and Part 1 of Schedule 1 being satisfied, or as soon as reasonably practicable thereafter.

Notification of decision

115.–(1) The authority must notify in writing any person affected by a decision made by it under this scheme–

(a) in the case of a decision on an application, forthwith or as soon as reasonably practicable thereafter;

(b) in any other case, within 14 days of that decision or as soon as reasonably practicable thereafter.

(2) Where the decision is to award a reduction the notification under sub-paragraph (1) must include a statement–

(a) informing the person affected of the duty imposed by paragraph 113(1)(b) (duty to notify change of circumstances);

(b) explaining the possible consequences (including prosecution) of failing to comply with that duty; and

(c) setting out the circumstances a change in which might affect entitlement to the reduction or its amount.

(3) Where the decision is to award a reduction, the notification under sub-paragraph (1) must include a statement as to how that entitlement is to be discharged.

(4) The notification under sub-paragraph (1) must also include a statement as to the matters set out in Schedule 10.

(5) A person affected to whom the authority sends or delivers a notification of decision may, within one month of the date of the notification of that decision request in writing the authority to provide a written statement setting out the reasons for its decision on any matter set out in the notice.

(6) The written statement referred to in sub-paragraph (5) must be sent to the person requesting it within 14 days or as soon as reasonably practicable thereafter.

(7) For the purposes of this paragraph a person is to be treated as a person affected by a decision of the authority under this scheme where the rights, duties or obligations of that person are affected by that decision and the person falls within sub-paragraph (8).

(8) This sub-paragraph applies to–

(a) the applicant;

(b) in the case of a person who is liable to pay council tax in respect of a dwelling and is unable for the time being to act–

    (i) a deputy appointed by the Court of Protection with power to claim, or as the case may be, receive benefit on the person's behalf; or

    (ii) in Scotland, a judicial factor or any guardian acting or appointed under the Adults with Incapacity (Scotland) Act 2000 who has power to apply or, as the case may be, receive benefit on the person's behalf; or

    (iii) an attorney with a general power or a power to apply or, as the case may be, receive benefit, has been appointed by that person under the Powers of Attorney Act 1971, the Enduring Powers of Attorney Act 1985 or the Mental Capacity Act 2005 or otherwise,

(c) a person appointed by the authority under paragraph 107(3).

PART 15
Award or payment of reduction

The award or payment of a reduction under this scheme

116.–(1) Subject to sub-paragraph (2) where a person is entitled to a reduction under this scheme in respect of that person's liability for council tax as it has effect in respect of a financial year, the authority must discharge that person's entitlement by reducing, so far as possible, the amount of that person's liability to which regulation 20(2) of the Council Tax (Administration and Enforcement) Regulations 1992 refers.

(2)   Where–

(a)   a person is entitled to a reduction under this scheme in respect of that person's liability for the authority's council tax as it has effect in respect of a financial year;

(b)   the person entitled to the reduction is joint and severally liable for the council tax; and

(c)   the authority determines that discharging that person's entitlement by reducing the amount of that person's liability to which regulation 20(2) of the Council Tax (Administration and Enforcement) Regulations 1992 refers would be inappropriate,

it may make a payment to that person of the amount of reduction to which that person is entitled, rounded where necessary to the nearest penny.

(3)   Subject to sub-paragraph (4) any payment made under sub-paragraphs (1) or (2) must be made to the person who is entitled to the reduction.

(4)   Where a person other than the person who is entitled to the reduction under this scheme made the application for the reduction and that first person is a person acting pursuant to an appointment under paragraph 107(3) (persons appointed to act for a person unable to act) or is treated as having been so appointed by virtue of paragraph 107(4), the amount of the reduction may be paid to that person.

SCHEDULE 1
Procedural matters

PART 1
Procedure for an application for a reduction under this scheme

Procedure by which a person may apply for a reduction under this scheme

1.   Paragraphs 2 to 7 of this Schedule apply to an application for a reduction under this scheme.

2.   An application may be made–

(a)   in writing;

(b)   by means of an electronic communication in accordance with Part 4 of this Schedule; or

(c)   where the authority has published a telephone number for the purpose of receiving such applications, by telephone.

3.–(1)   An application which is made in writing must be made to the designated office and be–

(a)   on a properly completed form approved by the authority for the purposes of making an application in writing; or

(b)   in such written form as the authority accepts as sufficient in the circumstances of any particular case (or class of cases) having regard to the sufficiency of the written information and evidence.

(2)   Where an application in writing is not made in the form described in paragraph 3(1)(a) or (b) it is defective.

(3)   Any form provided by the authority for the purposes of making an application in writing must be provided free of charge.

4.–(1)   Where an application made in writing is defective because–

(a)   it was made on the form approved for the purpose but that form is not accepted by the authority as being properly completed, the authority may request the applicant to complete the defective application; or

(b)   it was made in writing but not on the form approved for the purpose and the authority does not accept the application as being in a written form which is sufficient in the circumstances of the case having regard to the sufficiency of the written information and evidence, the authority may supply the applicant with the approved form or request further information or evidence.

(2)   An application made on an approved form is properly completed if it is completed in accordance with the instructions on the form, including any instructions to provide information and evidence in connection with the application.

5.–(1)   If an application made by electronic communication is defective the authority must provide the person making the application with an opportunity to correct the defect.

(2)   An application made by electronic communication is defective if the applicant does not provide all the information the authority requires.

6.   In a particular case the authority may determine that an application made by telephone is only valid if the person making the application approves a written statement of that person's circumstances provided by the authority.

7.–(1)   If an application made by telephone is defective the authority must provide the person making the application with an opportunity to correct the defect.

(2)   An application made by telephone is defective if the applicant does not provide all the information the authority requests during the telephone call.

PART 2
Procedure for making an appeal

Procedure by which a person may make an appeal against certain decisions of the authority
    8.–(1)   A person who is aggrieved by a decision of the authority which affects–
  (a)   a person's entitlement to a reduction under this scheme; or
  (b)   the amount of any reduction under this scheme,
  (c)   may serve a written notice on the authority stating the matter by which, and the grounds on which, the person is aggrieved.
    (2)   A notice under sub-paragraph (1) must be served within one month of the date of service of the notification of the decision of the authority, or where a person has made a request for a written statement in accordance with paragraph 115(5) of this scheme (request for statement of written reasons), within one month of the date of service of the statement of reasons.
    9.   The authority must–
  (a)   consider the matter to which the notice relates;
  (b)   notify the aggrieved person in writing–
      (i)   that the ground is not well founded, giving reasons for that belief; or
      (ii)   that steps have been taken to deal with the grievance, stating the steps taken.
    10.   Where, following notification under paragraph 9(b)(i) or (ii), the person is still aggrieved, or if the authority fails to notify the person aggrieved in accordance with paragraph 9(b) within two months of the service of the person's notice, the person may appeal to a valuation tribunal under section 16 of the 1992 Act.

PART 3
Procedure for applying for a discretionary reduction

Procedure for an application to the authority for a reduction under section 13A(1)(c) of the 1992 Act
    11.–(1)   An application to the authority for a reduction under section 13A(1)(c) of the 1992 Act may be made–
  (a)   in writing;
  (b)   by means of an electronic communication in accordance with Part 4 of this Schedule; or
  (c)   where the authority has published a telephone number for the purposes of receiving such applications, by telephone.
    (2)   Where–
  (a)   the authority has made a determination under section 13A(1)(c) in relation to a class of case in which liability is to be reduced; and
  (b)   a person in that class would otherwise be entitled to a reduction under this scheme,
    that person's application for a reduction under this scheme may also be treated as an application for a reduction under section 13A (1)(c).

PART 4
Electronic communication

Interpretation
    12.   In this Part of this Schedule–
"information" ("gwybodaeth") includes an application for a reduction under this scheme and a certificate, notice or other evidence;
"official computer system" ("system gyfrifiadurol swyddogol") means a computer system maintained by or on behalf of the authority for the sending, receiving, processing or storing of any information.

Conditions for the use of electronic communication
    13.–(1)   The authority may use an electronic communication in connection with applications for, and awards of, reductions under this scheme.
    (2)   A person other than the authority may use an electronic communication in connection with the matters referred to in sub-paragraph (1) if the conditions specified in sub-paragraphs (3) to (6) are satisfied.
    (3)   The first condition is that the person is for the time being permitted to use an electronic communication by an authorisation given by means of a direction of the Chief Executive of the authority.
    (4)   The second condition is that the person uses an approved method of–
  (a)   authenticating the identity of the sender of the communication;
  (b)   electronic communication;
  (c)   authenticating any application or notice delivered by means of an electronic communication; and
  (d)   subject to sub-paragraph (7), submitting to the authority any information.
    (5)   The third condition is that any information sent by means of an electronic communication is in a form approved for the purposes of this Part of this Schedule.
    (6)   The fourth condition is that the person maintains such records in written or electronic form as may be specified in a direction given by the Chief Executive of the authority.

(7)   Where the person uses any method other than the method approved of submitting any information, that information is to be treated as not having been submitted.

(8)   In this paragraph "approved" ("cymeradwy") means approved by means of a direction given by the Chief Executive of the authority for the purposes of this Part of this Schedule.

Use of intermediaries
   14.   The authority may use intermediaries in connection with–
   (a)   the delivery of any information by means of an electronic communication; and
   (b)   the authentication or security of anything transmitted by such means,
and may require other persons to use intermediaries in connection with those matters.

Effect of delivering information by means of electronic communication
   15.–(1)   Any information which is delivered by means of an electronic communication is to be treated as having been delivered in the manner or form required by any provision of this scheme, on the day the conditions imposed–
   (a)   by this Part of this Schedule; and
   (b)   by or under an enactment,
are satisfied.

   (2)   The authority may determine that any information is to be treated as delivered on a different day (whether earlier or later) from the day provided for in sub-paragraph (1).

   (3)   Information is not to be taken to have been delivered to an official computer system by means of an electronic communication unless it is accepted by the system to which it is delivered.

Proof of identity of sender or recipient of information
   16.   If it is necessary to prove, for the purpose of any legal proceedings, the identity of–
   (a)   the sender of any information delivered by means of an electronic communication to an official computer system; or
   (b)   the recipient of any such information delivered by means of an electronic communication from an official computer system,
the sender or recipient, as the case may be, is to be presumed to be the person whose name is recorded as such on that official computer system.

Proof of delivery of information
   17.–(1)   If it is necessary to prove, for the purpose of any legal proceedings, that the use of an electronic communication has resulted in the delivery of any information this is to be presumed to have been the case where–
   (a)   any such information has been delivered to the authority, if the delivery of that information has been recorded on an official computer system; or
   (b)   any such information has been delivered by the authority, if the delivery of that information has been recorded on an official computer system.

   (2)   If it is necessary to prove, for the purpose of any legal proceedings, that the use of an electronic communication has resulted in the delivery of any such information, this is to be presumed not to be the case, if that information delivered to the authority has not been recorded on an official computer system.

   (3)   If it is necessary to prove, for the purpose of any legal proceedings, when any such information sent by means of an electronic communication has been received, the time and date of receipt is to be presumed to be that recorded on an official computer system.

Proof of content of information
   18.   If it is necessary to prove, for the purpose of any legal proceedings, the content of any information sent by means of an electronic communication, the content is to be presumed to be that recorded on an official computer system.

SCHEDULE 2
Applicable amounts: pensioners

PART 1
Personal allowances

Personal allowance
   1.   The amount specified in column (2) below in respect of each person or couple specified in column (1) is the amount specified for the purposes of paragraph 23(1)(a) of this scheme.

Column (1) Person, Couple or polygamous marriage	Column (2) Amount
(1) Single applicant or lone parent–	
(a) aged under 65;	[⁶ £167.25];
(b) aged 65 or over.	[⁶ £181.00].
(2) Couple–	
(c) both members aged under 65;	[⁶ £255.25];
(d) one or both members aged 65 or over	[⁶ £270.60].
(3) If the applicant is a member of a polygamous marriage and none of the members of the marriage has attained the age of 65–	
(e) for the applicant and the other party to the marriage;	[⁶ £255.25];
(f) for each additional spouse who is a member of the same household as the applicant.	[⁶ £88.00].
(4) If the applicant is a member of a polygamous marriage and one or more members of the marriage are aged 65 or over–	
(g) for the applicant and the other party to the marriage;	[⁶ £270.60];
(h) for each additional spouse who is a member of the same household as the applicant.	[⁶ £89.60].

Amendments

1. Amended by reg 27(a) of SI 2014 No 66 (W.6) as from 15.1.14.
2. Amended by reg 27(a) of SI 2015 No 44 (W.3) as from 21.1.15, for schemes made for a financial year starting on or after 1.4.15.
3. Amended by reg 25(a) of SI 2016 No 50 (W.21) as from 20.1.16, for schemes made for a financial year starting on or after 1.4.16.
4. Amended by reg 17(a) of SI 2017 No 46 (W.20) as from 19.1.17, for schemes made for a financial year starting on or after 1.4.17.
5. Amended by reg 24(a) of SI 2018 No 14 (W.7) as from 10.1.18, for schemes made for a financial year starting on or after 1.4.18.
6. Amended by reg 14(a) of SI 2019 No 11 (W.5) as from 9.1.19, for schemes made for a financial year starting on or after 1.4.19.

Child or young person amounts

2.–(1) The amounts specified in column (2) below in respect of each person specified in column (1) are the amounts, for the relevant period specified in column (1), specified for the purposes of paragraph 23(1)(b) of this scheme.

Column (1) Child or Young Person	Column (2) Amount
Person in respect of the period–	
(i) beginning on that person's date of birth and ending on the day preceding the first Monday in September following that person's sixteenth birthday;	[² £66.90];
(j) beginning on the first Monday in September following that person's sixteenth birthday and ending on the day preceding that person's twentieth birthday.	[² £66.90].

(2) In column (1) of the table "the first Monday in September" ("y dydd Llun cyntaf ym Medi") means the Monday which first occurs in the month of September in any year.

Amendments

1. Amended by reg 27(b) of SI 2014 No 66 (W.6) as from 15.1.14.
2. Amended by reg 27(b) of SI 2015 No 44 (W.3) as from 21.1.15, for schemes made for a financial year starting on or after 1.4.15.

PART 2
Family premium

Family premium

3. The amount for the purposes of paragraph 23(1)(c) of this scheme in respect of a family of which at least one member is a child or young person is [¹ £17.45].

Amendment

1. Amended by reg 27(c) of SI 2015 No 44 (W.3) as from 21.1.15, for schemes made for a financial year starting on or after 1.4.15.

PART 3

Premiums

4. The premiums specified in Part 4 are, for the purposes of paragraph 23(1)(d) of this scheme, to be applicable to an applicant who satisfies the condition specified in this Part in respect of that premium.

5.–(1) Subject to sub-paragraph (2), for the purposes of this Part of this Schedule, once a premium is applicable to an applicant under this Part, a person is to be treated as being in receipt of any benefit for–

(a) in the case of a benefit to which the Social Security (Overlapping Benefits) Regulations 1979 applies, any period during which, apart from the provision of those Regulations, that person would be in receipt of that benefit; and

(b) any period spent by a person in undertaking a course of training or instruction provided or approved by the Secretary of State or the Welsh Ministers under section 2 of the Employment and Training Act 1973, or by Skills Development Scotland, Scottish Enterprise or Highland and Islands Enterprise under section 2 of the Enterprise and New Towns (Scotland) Act 1990 or for any period during which that person is in receipt of a training allowance.

(2) For the purposes of the carer premium under paragraph 9 of this Schedule, a person is to be treated as being in receipt of a carer's allowance by virtue of sub-paragraph (1)(a) only if and for so long as the person in respect of whose care the allowance has been claimed remains in receipt of attendance allowance, or the care component of disability living allowance at the highest or middle rate prescribed in accordance with section 72(3) of the SSCBA, or the daily living component of personal independence payment paid at either rate prescribed in accordance with Part 4 of the Welfare Reform Act 2012 or AFIP.

Severe disability premium

6.–(1) The condition is that the applicant is a severely disabled person.

(2) For the purposes of sub-paragraph (1), an applicant is to be treated as being a severely disabled person if, and only if–

(a) in the case of a single applicant, a lone parent or an applicant who is treated as having no partner in consequence of sub-paragraph (3)–

    (i) the applicant is in receipt of attendance allowance, or the care component of disability living allowance at the highest or middle rate prescribed in accordance with section 72(3) of the SSCBA, or the daily living component of personal independence payment paid at either rate prescribed in accordance with Part 4 of the Welfare Reform Act 2012, or AFIP; and

    (ii) subject to sub-paragraph (6), the applicant has no non-dependants aged 18 or over normally residing with the applicant or with whom the applicant is normally residing; and

    (iii) no person is entitled to, and in receipt of, a carer's allowance [² under section 70 of the SSCBA or has an award of universal credit which includes the carer element under regulation 29 of the Universal Credit Regulations 2013] in respect of caring for the applicant;

(b) in the case of an applicant who has a partner–

    (i) the applicant is in receipt of attendance allowance, or the care component of disability living allowance at the highest or middle rate prescribed in accordance with section 72(3) of the SSCBA, or the daily living component of personal independence payment paid at either rate prescribed in accordance with Part 4 of the Welfare Reform Act 2012, or AFIP;

    (ii) the applicant's partner is also in receipt of such an allowance or, if the applicant is a member of a polygamous marriage, each other member of that marriage is in receipt of such an allowance; and

    (iii) subject to sub-paragraph (6), the applicant has no non-dependants aged 18 or over normally residing with the applicant or with whom the applicant is normally residing,

and either a person is entitled to and in receipt of a carer's allowance [² or has an award of universal credit which includes the carer element] in respect of caring for only one of the couple or, if the applicant is a member of a polygamous marriage, for one or more but not all the members of the marriage, or as the case may be, no person is entitled to and in receipt of such an allowance [² or has such an award of universal credit] in respect of caring for either member of a couple or any of the members of the marriage.

(3) Where an applicant has a partner who does not satisfy the condition in sub-paragraph (2)(b)(ii), and that partner [¹ is blind or severely sight-impaired or is treated as such] within the meaning of sub-paragraph (4), that partner is to be treated for the purposes of sub-paragraph (2) as if that partner were not a partner of the applicant.

[¹ (4) For the purposes of sub-paragraph (3), a person is blind or severely sight-impaired if that person–

(a) is registered as blind in a register compiled under section 29 of the National Assistance Act 1948 (welfare services);

(b) is registered as severely sight-impaired in a register established and maintained by a local authority under section 18(1) of the Social Services and Well-being (Wales) Act 2014;

(c) is registered as severely sight-impaired in a register established and maintained by a local authority under section 77(1) of the Care Act 2014; or,

(d) in Scotland, has been certified as blind and in consequence is registered in a register maintained by or on behalf of a council constituted under section 2 of the Local Government etc. (Scotland) Act 1994.]

(5)   For the purposes of sub-paragraph (4), a person who has ceased to be registered as blind [¹ or severely sight-impaired] on regaining that person's eyesight is nevertheless to be treated as blind [¹ or severely sight-impaired] and as satisfying the additional condition set out in that sub-paragraph for a period of 28 weeks following the date on which that person ceased to be so registered.

(6)   For the purposes of sub-paragraph (2)(a)(ii) and (2)(b)(iii) no account is to be taken of–

(a)   a person receiving attendance allowance, or the care component of disability living allowance at the highest or middle rate prescribed in accordance with section 72(3) of the SSCBA, or the daily living component of personal independence payment paid at either rate prescribed in accordance with Part 4 of the Welfare Reform Act 2012, or AFIP; or

(b)   a person who [¹ is blind or severely sight-impaired or is treated as such] within the meaning of sub-paragraphs (4) and (5).

(7)   For the purposes of sub-paragraph (2)(b) a person is to be treated–

(a)   as being in receipt of attendance allowance, or the care component of disability living allowance at the highest or middle rate prescribed in accordance with section 72(3) of the SSCBA, if that person would, but for that person's being a patient for a period exceeding 28 days, be so in receipt;

(b)   as being in receipt of the daily living component of personal independence payment paid at the rate prescribed in accordance with Part 4 of the Welfare Reform Act 2012 if that person would, but for that person's being a patient for a period exceeding 28 days, be so in receipt, notwithstanding section 86 of that Act and regulations made thereunder;

(c)   as being in receipt of AFIP if the person would be so in receipt but for a suspension of payment in accordance with any terms of the armed and reserve forces compensation scheme which allow for suspension because a person is undergoing medical treatment in a hospital or similar institution;

(d)   as being entitled to and in receipt of a carer's allowance [² or having an award of universal credit which includes the carer element] if that person would, but for the person for whom that person was caring being a patient in hospital for a period exceeding 28 days, be so entitled and in receipt [² or have such an award of universal credit].

(8)   For the purposes of sub-paragraph (2)(a)(iii) and (2)(b)–

(a)   no account is to be taken of an award of carer's allowance [² or an award of universal credit which includes the carer element] to the extent that payment of such an award is back-dated for a period before the date on which the award is first paid; and

(b)   references to a person being in receipt of a carer's allowance [² or having an award of universal credit which includes the carer element] are to include references to a person who would have been in receipt of that allowance [² or had such an award of universal credit] but for the application of a restriction under section 6B or 7 of the Social Security Fraud Act 2001 (loss of benefit provisions).

Amendments

1.   Amended by reg 25(b) of SI 2016 No 50 (W.21) as from 20.1.16, for schemes made for a financial year starting on or after 1.4.16.

2.   Amended by reg 17(b) of SI 2017 No 46 (W.20) as from 19.1.17, for schemes made for a financial year starting on or after 1.4.17.

Enhanced disability premium

7.–(1)   The condition is that–

(a)   the care component of disability living allowance is, or would, but for a suspension of benefit in accordance with regulations under section 113(2) of the SSCBA or but for an abatement as a consequence of hospitalisation, be payable at the highest rate prescribed under section 73(2) of that Act;

(b)   the daily living component of personal independence payment is, or would, but for a suspension of benefit in accordance with regulations under section 86 of the Welfare Reform Act 2012, be payable at the enhanced rate prescribed in accordance with section 78(2) of that Act; or

(c)   AFIP is payable,

(d)   in respect of a child or young person who is a member of the applicant's family.

(2)   Where the condition in sub-paragraph (1) ceases to be satisfied because of the death of a child or young person, the condition is that the applicant or partner is entitled to child benefit in respect of the child or young person under section 145A of the SSCBA (entitlement after death of child or qualifying young person).

Disabled child premium

8.   The condition is that a child or young person for whom the applicant or a partner of the applicant is responsible and who is a member of the applicant's household–

(a)   is in receipt of disability living allowance or personal independence payment or is no longer in receipt of such allowance or payment because the child or young person is a patient, provided that the child or young person continues to be a member of the family; or

(b)   [¹ is blind or severely sight-impaired] within the meaning of paragraph 6(4) of this Schedule or treated [¹ as such] in accordance with paragraph 6(5); or

(c)   is a child or young person in respect of whom section 145A of the SSCBA (entitlement after death of child or qualifying young person) applies for the purposes of entitlement to child benefit but only for the period prescribed under that section, and in respect of whom a disabled child premium was included in the applicant's applicable amount immediately before the death of that child or young person, or ceased to be included in the applicant's applicable amount because of that child or young person's death.

Amendment

1.   Amended by reg 25(c) of SI 2016 No 50 (W.21) as from 20.1.16, for schemes made for a financial year starting on or after 1.4.16.

Carer premium

9.–(1)   The condition is that the applicant or the applicant's partner is, or both of them are, entitled to a carer's allowance.

(2)   Where a carer premium has been awarded but–

(a)   the person in respect of whose care the carer's allowance has been awarded dies; or

(b)   the person in respect of whom the premium was awarded ceases to be entitled, or ceases to be treated as entitled, to a carer's allowance,

this paragraph is to be treated as satisfied for a period of eight weeks from the relevant date specified in sub-paragraph (3).

(3)   The relevant date for the purposes of sub-paragraph (2) is–

(a)   in a case within sub-paragraph (2)(a), the Sunday following the death of the person in respect of whose care the carer's allowance has been awarded (or beginning with the date of death if the date occurred on a Sunday);

(b)   in a case within sub-paragraph (2)(b), the date on which that person who was entitled to a carer's allowance ceases to be entitled to it.

(4)   For the purposes of this paragraph, a person is to be treated as being entitled to and in receipt of a carer's allowance for any period not covered by an award but in respect of which a payment is made in lieu of an award.

Persons in receipt of concessionary payments

10.   For the purpose of determining whether a premium is applicable to a person under paragraphs 6 to 9 of this Schedule, any concessionary payment made to compensate that person for the non-payment of any benefit mentioned in those paragraphs is to be treated as if it were a payment of that benefit.

Person in receipt of benefit

11.   For the purposes of this Part of this Schedule, a person is to be regarded as being in receipt of any benefit if, and only if, it is paid in respect of that person and is to be so regarded only for any period in respect of which that benefit is paid.

PART 4
Amounts of premium specified in Part 3

Provision	*Amount*
12.–(1) Severe Disability Premium–	
(a) where the applicant satisfies the condition in paragraph 6(2)(a);	[⁵ £65.85];
(b) where the applicant satisfies the condition in paragraph 6(2)(b)–	
(i) in a case where there is someone in receipt of a carer's allowance [³ or who has an award of universal credit which includes the carer element under regulation 29 of the Universal Credit Regulations 2013] or if that person or any partner satisfies that condition only by virtue of paragraph 6(7);	[⁵ £65.85];
(ii) in a case where there is no-one in receipt of such an allowance [³ or such an award of universal credit].	[⁵ £131.70].
(2) Enhanced Disability Premium.	[⁵ £26.04] in respect of each child or young person in respect of whom the conditions specified in paragraph 7 of this Schedule are satisfied.
(3) Disabled Child Premium.	[⁵ £64.19] in respect of each child or young person in respect of whom the condition specified in paragraph 8 of this Schedule is satisfied
(4) Carer Premium.	[⁵ £36.85] in respect of each person who satisfies the condition specified in paragraph 9 of this Schedule.

Amendments
1.   Amended by reg 27(c) of SI 2014 No 66 (W.6) as from 15.1.14.
2.   Amended by reg 27(d) of SI 2015 No 44 (W.3) as from 21.1.15, for schemes made for a financial year starting on or after 1.4.15.
3.   Amended by reg 17(c) of SI 2017 No 46 (W.20) as from 19.1.17, for schemes made for a financial year starting on or after 1.4.17.
4.   Amended by reg 24(b) of SI 2018 No 14 (W.7) as from 10.1.18, for schemes made for a financial year starting on or after 1.4.18.
5.   Amended by reg 14(b) of SI 2019 No 11 (W.5) as from 9.1.19, for schemes made for a financial year starting on or after 1.4.19.

SCHEDULE 3
Applicable amounts: persons who are not pensioners

PART 1

Personal allowances
1.   The amounts specified in column (2) below in respect of each person or couple specified in column (1) are the amounts specified for the purposes of paragraphs 24(1)(a) and 25(2)(a) and (b)of this scheme–

Column (1)	*Column (2)*
Person or couple	*Amount*
(1) A single applicant who–	
(a) is entitled to main phase employment and support allowance;	[⁵ £77.90];
(b) is aged not less than 25;	[⁵ £77.90];
(c) is aged not less than 18 but less than 25.	[⁵ £61.70].
(2) Lone parent.	[⁵ £77.90].
(3) Couple.	[⁵ £122.35]

Amendments
1.   Amended by reg 28(a) of SI 2014 No 66 (W.6) as from 15.1.14.
2.   Amended by reg 28(a) of SI 2015 No 44 (W.3) as from 21.1.15, for schemes made for a financial year starting on or after 1.4.15.
3.   Amended by reg 18(a) of SI 2017 No 46 (W.20) as from 19.1.17, for schemes made for a financial year starting on or after 1.4.17.
4.   Amended by reg 25(a) of SI 2018 No 14 (W.7) as from 10.1.18, for schemes made for a financial year starting on or after 1.4.18.
5.   Amended by reg 15(a) of SI 2019 No 11 (W.5) as from 9.1.19, for schemes made for a financial year starting on or after 1.4.19.

2.   For the purposes of paragraph 1 of this Schedule an applicant is entitled to main phase employment and support allowance if–
(a)   paragraph 18 of this Schedule is satisfied in relation to the applicant [¹ or the applicant is a member of the work-related activity group]; or
(b)   the applicant is entitled to a converted employment and support allowance.

Amendment
1.   Amended by reg 25(b) of SI 2018 No 14 (W.7) as from 10.1.18, for schemes made for a financial year starting on or after 1.4.18.

3.–(1)   The amounts specified in column (2) below in respect of each person specified in column (1) are, for the relevant period specified in column (1), the amounts specified for the purposes of paragraphs 24(1)(b) and 25(2)(c) of this scheme–

Column (1)	*Column (2)*
Child or young person	*Amount*
Person in respect of the period–	
(a) beginning on that person's date of birth and ending on the day preceding the first Monday in September following that person's sixteenth birthday;	[² £66.90];
(b) beginning on the first Monday in September following that person's sixteenth birthday and ending on the day preceding that person's twentieth birthday.	[² £66.90].

(2)   In column (1) of the table in sub-paragraph (1), "the first Monday in September" ("y dydd Llun cyntaf ym Medi") means the Monday which first occurs in the month of September in any year.

Amendments
1. Amended by reg 28(b) of SI 2014 No 66 (W.6) as from 15.1.14.
2. Amended by reg 28(b) of SI 2015 No 44 (W.3) as from 21.1.15, for schemes made for a financial year starting on or after 1.4.15.

PART 2
Family premium

4.–(1)   The amount for the purposes of paragraphs 24(1)(c) and 25(2)(d) in respect of a family of which at least one member is a child or young person is–
(a)   where the applicant is a lone parent to whom sub-paragraph (2) applies, £22.20;
(b)   in any other case, [¹ £17.45].
(2)   The amount in sub-paragraph (1)(a) is to be applicable to a lone parent–
(a)   who was entitled to council tax benefit on 5 April 1998 and whose applicable amount on that date included the amount applicable under paragraph 3(1) of Schedule 1 to the Council Tax Benefit (Persons who have attained the qualifying age for state pension credit) Regulations 2006 as in force on that date; or
(b)   on becoming entitled to council tax benefit where that lone parent–
(i)   had been treated as entitled to that benefit in accordance with sub-paragraph (3) as at the day before the date of claim for that benefit; and
(ii)   was entitled to housing benefit as at the date of claim for council tax benefit or would have been entitled to housing benefit as at that date had that day not fallen during a rent free period as defined in regulation 81 of the Housing Benefit Regulations2006,
and in respect of whom, all of the conditions specified in sub-paragraph (3) have continued to apply.
(3)   The conditions specified for the purposes of sub-paragraph (2) are that, in respect of the period commencing on 6 April 1998–
(a)   the applicant has not ceased to be entitled, or has not ceased to be treated as entitled, to–
(i)   council tax benefit (in relation to the period prior to 1 April 2013), and
(ii)   a reduction under this scheme (in relation to the period commencing on 1 April 2013);
(b)   the applicant has not ceased to be a lone parent;
(c)   where the applicant was entitled to income support or to an income-based jobseeker's allowance on 5 April 1998, the applicant has continuously, since that date, been entitled to income support, an income-based jobseeker's allowance or income-related employment and support allowance or a combination of those benefits;
(d)   where the applicant was not entitled to income support or to an income-based jobseeker's allowance on 5 April 1998, the applicant has not become entitled to income support, an income-based jobseeker's allowance or an income-related employment and support allowance; and
(e)   a premium under paragraph 9 of this Schedule or a component under paragraph 21 or 22 of this Schedule has not become applicable to the applicant.
(4)   For the purposes of sub-paragraphs (2)(b)(i) and (3)(a), an applicant is to be treated as entitled to council tax benefit during any period where the applicant was not, or had ceased to be, so entitled and–
(a)   throughout that period, the applicant had been awarded housing benefit and the applicant's applicable amount included the amount applicable under paragraph 3(1)(a) of Schedule 3 to the Housing Benefit Regulations 2006 (lone parent rate of family premium); or
(b)   the applicant would have been awarded housing benefit during that period had that period not been a rent free period as defined in regulation 81 of the Housing Benefit Regulations 2006 and the applicant's applicable amount throughout that period would have included the amount applicable under paragraph 3(1)(a) of Schedule 3 to those Regulations.

Amendment
1. Amended by reg 28(c) of SI 2015 No 44 (W.3) as from 21.1.15, for schemes made for a financial year starting on or after 1.4.15.

PART 3
Premiums

5.   Except as provided in paragraph 6 of this Schedule, the premiums specified in Part 4 of this Schedule are, for the purposes of paragraphs 24(1)(d) and 25(2)(e) of this scheme, to be applicable to an applicant who satisfies the condition specified in paragraphs 9 to 14 of this Schedule in respect of that premium.
6.   Subject to paragraph 7 of this Schedule, where an applicant satisfies the conditions in respect of more than one premium in this Part of this Schedule, only one premium is to be applicable to the applicant and, if they are different amounts, the higher or highest amount is to apply.
7.   The following premiums, namely–
(a)   a severe disability premium to which paragraph 11 of this Schedule applies;
(b)   an enhanced disability premium to which paragraph 12 of this Schedule applies;
(c)   a disabled child premium to which paragraph 13 of this Schedule applies; and

(d)   a carer premium to which paragraph 14 of this Schedule applies,

may be applicable in addition to any other premium which may apply under this Schedule.

8.–(1)   Subject to sub-paragraph (2), for the purposes of this Part of this Schedule, once a premium is applicable to an applicant under this Part, a person is to be treated as being in receipt of any benefit for–

(a)   in the case of a benefit to which the Social Security (Overlapping Benefits) Regulations 1979 applies, any period during which, apart from the provisions of those Regulations, that person would be in receipt of that benefit; and

(b)   any period spent by a person in undertaking a course of training or instruction provided or approved by the Secretary of State or the Welsh Ministers under section 2 of the Employment and Training Act 1973 or by Skills Development Scotland, Scottish Enterprise or Highlands and Islands Enterprise under section 2 of the Enterprise and New Towns (Scotland) Act 1990 or for any period during which that person is in receiptof a training allowance.

(2)   For the purposes of the carer premium under paragraph 14 of this Schedule, a person is to be treated as being in receipt of carer's allowance by virtue of sub-paragraph (1)(a) only if and for so long as the person in respect of whose care the allowance has been claimed remains in receipt of attendance allowance, or the care component of disability living allowance at the highest or middle rate prescribed in accordance with section 72(3) of the SSCBA or the daily living component of personal independence payment payable under Part 4 of the Welfare Reform Act 2012, or AFIP.

Disability premium

9.   The condition is that–

(a)   where the applicant is a single applicant or a lone parent, the applicant has not attained the qualifying age for state pension credit and the additional condition specified in paragraph 10 of this Schedule is satisfied; or

(b)   where the applicant has a partner, either–

(i)   the applicant has not attained the qualifying age for state pension credit and the additional condition specified in paragraph 10(1)(a) or (b) is satisfied by the applicant; or

(ii)   the applicant's partner has not attained the qualifying age for state pension credit and the additional condition specified in paragraph 10(1)(a) is satisfied by the applicant's partner.

Additional condition for the disability premium

10.–(1)   Subject to sub-paragraph (2) and paragraph 8 of this Schedule, the additional condition referred to in paragraph 9 of this Schedule is that either–

(a)   the applicant or, as the case may be, the applicant's partner–

(i)   is in receipt of one or more of the following benefits: attendance allowance, disability living allowance, personal independence payment, AFIP, the disability element or the severe disability element of working tax credit as specified in regulation 20(1)(b) and (f) of the Working Tax Credit (Entitlement and Maximum Rate) Regulations 2002, mobility supplement, long-term incapacity benefit under Part 2 of the SSCBA or severe disablement allowance under Part 3 of that Act but, in the case of long-term incapacity benefit or severe disablement allowance, only where it is paid in respect of the applicant; or

(ii)   was in receipt of long-term incapacity benefit under Part 2 of the SSCBA when entitlement to that benefit ceased on account of the payment of a retirement pension under that Act [² or a state pension under Part 1 of the Pensions Act 2014]and the applicant has since remained continuously entitled to–

(aa)   council tax benefit (in relation to the period to 1 April 2013), and

(bb)   a reduction under this scheme (in relation to the period commencing on 1 April 2013), and

if the long-term incapacity benefit was payable to the applicant's partner, the partner is still a member of the family; or

(iii)   was in receipt of attendance allowance or disability living allowance but payment of benefit has been suspended in accordance with regulations made under section 113(2) of the SSCBA or otherwise abated as a consequence of the applicant or the applicant's partner becoming a patient within the meaning of paragraph 55(11)(i) (treatment of child care charges); or

(iv)   was in receipt of personal independence payment, but payment of that benefit has been suspended in accordance with section 86 of the Welfare Reform Act 2012 as a consequence of the applicant becoming a patient within the meaning of paragraph 55(11)(i) (treatment of child care charges);

(v)   was in receipt of AFIP, but payment has been suspended in accordance with any terms of the armed and reserve forces compensation scheme which allow for suspension because a person is undergoing medical treatment in a hospital or similar institution; or

(vi)   is provided with an invalid carriage or other vehicle by the Secretary of State or a clinical commissioning group under paragraph 9 of Schedule 1 to the National Health Service Act 2006 or, in Scotland, under section 46 of the National Health Service (Scotland) Act 1978 (provision of services by Scottish Ministers) or, in Wales, under section 5 of, and Schedule 1 to the National Health Service (Wales) Act 2006 or, in Northern Ireland, is provided with an invalid carriage or other vehicle by the Department of Health, Social Services and Public

Safety under article 30(1) of the Health and Personal Social Services (Northern Ireland) Order 1972, or receives payments by way of grant from the Secretary of State under paragraph 10(3) of Schedule 1 to the Act of 2006 (provision of vehicles for disabled persons) or, in Scotland by the Scottish Ministers under section 46 of the Act of 1978; or

[² (vii) is blind and in consequence is registered as blind in a register compiled under section 29 of the National Assistance Act 1948 (welfare services), or is severely sight-impaired and in consequence is registered as severely sight-impaired in a register established and maintained by a local authority under section 18(1) of the Social Services and Well-being (Wales) Act 2014 or section 77(1) of the Care Act 2014, or in Scotland has been certified as blind and in consequence is registered as blind in a register maintained by or on behalf of a council constituted under section 2 of the Local Government etc. (Scotland) Act 1994; or]

    (b)   the applicant–

        (i)   is, or is treated as, incapable of work in accordance with the provisions of, and regulations made under, Part 12A of the SSCBA (incapacity for work); and

        (ii)   has been incapable, or has been treated as incapable, of work for a continuous period of not less than–

            (aa)   in the case of an applicant who is terminally ill within the meaning of section 30B(4) of the SSCBA, 196 days;

            (bb)   in any other case, 364 days.

    (2)   For the purposes of [¹ sub-paragraph (1)(a)(vii)], a person who has ceased to be [² registered as blind or severely sight-impaired] on regaining that person's eyesight is nevertheless to be [² treated as such] and as satisfying the additional condition set out in that sub-paragraph for a period of 28 weeks following the date on which that person ceased to be so registered.

    (3)   For the purposes of sub-paragraph (1)(b), once the disability premium is applicable to an applicant by virtue of the applicant's satisfying the additional condition specified in that provision, if the applicant then ceases, for a period of 8 weeks or less, to be treated as incapable of work or to be incapable of work the applicant is, on again becoming so incapable of work, to immediately thereafter be treated as satisfying the condition in sub-paragraph (1)(b).

    (4)   For the purposes of sub-paragraph (1)(b), once the disability premium is applicable to an applicant by virtue of the applicant satisfying the additional condition specified in that provision, the applicant is to continue to be treated as satisfying that condition for any period spent by the applicant in undertaking a course of training provided under section 2 of the Employment and Training Act 1973 or section 2 of the Enterprise and New Towns (Scotland) Act 1990 or for any period during which the applicant is in receipt of a training allowance.

    (5)   For the purposes of sub-paragraph (1)(b), where any two or more periods of incapacity are separated by a break of not more than 56 days, those periods are to be treated as one continuous period.

    (6)   For the purposes of this paragraph, a reference to a person who is or was in receipt of long-term incapacity benefit includes a person who is or was in receipt of short-term incapacity benefit at a rate equal to the long-term rate by virtue of section 30B(4)(a) of the SSCBA (short-term incapacity benefit for a person who is terminally ill), or who would be or would have been in receipt of short-term incapacity benefit at such a rate but for the fact that the rate of short-term incapacity benefit already payable to that person is or was equal to or greater than the long-term rate.

    (7)   In the case of an applicant who is a welfare to work beneficiary (a person to whom regulation 13A(1) of the Social Security (Incapacity for Work) (General) Regulations 1995 applies, and who again becomes incapable of work for the purposes of Part 12A of the SSCBA)–

    (a)   the reference to a period of 8 weeks in sub-paragraph (3); and

    (b)   the reference to a period of 56 days in sub-paragraph (5),

    (c)   is in each case to be treated as a reference to a period of 104 weeks.

    (8)   The applicant is not entitled to the disability premium if the applicant has, or is treated as having, limited capability for work.

Amendments

1.   Amended by reg 28(c) of SI 2014 No 66 (W.6) as from 15.1.14.
2.   Amended by reg 26(a) of SI 2016 No 50 (W.21) as from 20.1.16, for schemes made for a financial year starting on or after 1.4.16.

Severe disability premium

    11.–(1)   The condition is that the applicant is a severely disabled person.

    (2)   For the purposes of sub-paragraph (1), an applicant is to be treated as being a severely disabled person if, and only if–

    (a)   in the case of a single applicant, a lone parent or an applicant who is treated as having no partner in consequence of sub-paragraph (3)–

        (i)   the applicant is in receipt of attendance allowance, or the care component of disability living allowance at the highest or middle rate prescribed in accordance with section 72(3) of the SSCBA or the daily living component of personal independence payment payable at either rate under Part 4 of the Welfare Reform Act 2012, or AFIP; and

(ii) subject to sub-paragraph (4), the applicant has no non-dependants aged 18 or over normally residing with the applicant with whom the applicant is normally residing; and

(iii) no person is entitled to, and in receipt of, a carer's allowance under section 70 of the SSCBA [² or has an award of universal credit which includes the carer element under regulation 29 of the Universal Credit Regulations 2013] in respect of caring for the applicant;

(b) in the case of an applicant who has a partner–

    (i) the applicant is in receipt of attendance allowance, or the care component of disability living allowance at the highest or middle rate prescribed in accordance with section 72(3) of the SSCBA or the daily living component of personal independence payment payable at either rate under Part 4 of the Welfare Reform Act 2012, or AFIP; and

    (ii) the applicant's partner is also in receipt of such an allowance or, if the applicant is a member of a polygamous marriage, all the members of that marriage are in receipt of such an allowance; and

    (iii) subject to sub-paragraph (4), the applicant has no non-dependants aged 18 or over normally residing with the applicant or with whom the applicant is normally residing,

and either a person is entitled to and in receipt of a carer's allowance [² or has an award of universal credit which includes the carer element] in respect of caring for only one member of a couple or, in the case of a polygamous marriage, for one or more but not all the members of the marriage, or as the case may be, no person is entitled to and in receipt of such an allowance [² or has such an award of universal credit] in respect of caring for either member of a couple or any member of a polygamous marriage.

(3) Where an applicant has a partner who does not satisfy the condition in sub-paragraph (2)(b)(ii), and that partner [¹ is blind or severely sight-impaired or is treated as such] within the meaning of paragraph 10(1)(a)(vii) and(2) of this Schedule, that partner is to be treated for the purposes of sub-paragraph (2)(b)(ii) as if that person were not a partner of the applicant.

(4) For the purposes of sub-paragraph (2)(a)(ii) and (2)(b)(iii) no account is to be taken of–

(a) a person receiving attendance allowance, or disability living allowance by virtue of the care component at the highest or middle rate prescribed in accordance with section 72(3)of the SSCBA, or the daily living component of personal independence payment payable at either rate prescribed in accordance with Part 4 of the Welfare Reform Act 2012, or AFIP; or

(b) a person [¹ who is blind or severely sight-impaired or is treated as such] within the meaning of paragraph 10(1)(a)(vii)and (2).

(5) For the purposes of sub-paragraph (2)(b) a person is to be treated–

(a) as being in receipt of attendance allowance, or the care component of disability living allowance at the highest or middle rate prescribed in accordance with section 72(3) of the SSCBA or the daily living component of personal independence payment payable at either rate under Part 4 of the Welfare Reform Act 2012, or AFIP, if that person would, but for that person's being a patient for a period exceeding 28 days, be so in receipt;

(b) as being entitled to and in receipt of a carer's allowance [² or having an award of universal credit which includes the carer element] if that person would, but for the person for whom that person was caring being a patient in hospital for a period exceeding 28 days, be so entitled and in receipt [² or have such an award of universal credit].

(6) For the purposes of sub-paragraph (2)(a)(iii) and (2)(b), no account is to be taken of an award of carer's allowance [² or an award of universal credit which includes the carer element] to the extent that payment of such an award is back-dated for a period before the date on which the award is first paid.

(7) In sub-paragraph (2)(a)(iii) and (b), references to a person being in receipt of a carer's allowance [² or having an award of universal credit which includes the carer element] are to include references to a person who would have been in receipt of that allowance [² or had such an award of universal credit] but for the application of a restriction under section 6B or 7 of the Social Security Fraud Act 2001 (loss of benefit provisions).

Amendments

1. Amended by reg 26(b) of SI 2016 No 50 (W.21) as from 20.1.16, for schemes made for a financial year starting on or after 1.4.16.
2. Amended by reg 18(b) of SI 2017 No 46 (W.20) as from 19.1.17, for schemes made for a financial year starting on or after 1.4.17.

Enhanced disability premium

12.–(1) Subject to sub-paragraph (2), the condition is that–

(a) the Secretary of State has decided that the applicant has, or is to be treated as having, limited capability for work-related activity; or

(b) the care component of disability living allowance is, or would be payable at the highest rate prescribed under section 72(3) of the SSCBA, but for a suspension of benefit in accordance with regulations made under section 113(2) of the SSCBA or but for an abatement as a consequence of hospitalisation, in respect of–

    (i) the applicant; or

       (ii)   a member of the applicant's family,
       who has not attained the qualifying age for state pension credit; or
(c)   the daily living component of personal independence payment is, or would be payable at the enhanced rate prescribed in accordance with section 78(2) of the Welfare Reform Act 2012, but for a suspension of benefit in accordance with section 86 of the Welfare Reform Act 2012 in respect of–
       (i)   the applicant; or
       (ii)   a member of the applicant's family,
       who has not attained the qualifying age for state pension credit; or
(d)   AFIP is payable in respect of–
       (i)   the applicant; or
       (ii)   a member of the applicant's family,
       who has not attained the qualifying age for state pension credit.
     (2)   Where the condition in sub-paragraph (1) ceases to be satisfied because of the death of a child or young person, the condition is that the applicant or partner is entitled to child benefit in respect of that child or young person under section 145A of the SSCBA (entitlement after death of child or qualifying young person).
     (3)   The condition is not satisfied if the person to whom sub-paragraph (1) refers is–
(a)   an applicant who–
       (i)   is not a member of a couple or a polygamous marriage; and
       (ii)   is a patient within the meaning of paragraph 55(11)(e) of this scheme (treatment of child care charges) and has been for a period of more than 52 weeks; or
(b)   a member of a couple or a polygamous marriage where each member is a patient within the meaning of paragraph 55(11)(e) and has been for a period of more than 52 weeks.

Disabled child premium
13.   The condition is that a child or young person for whom the applicant or a partner of the applicant is responsible and who is a member of the applicant's household–
(a)   is in receipt of disability living allowance or personal independence payment or is no longer in receipt of such allowance because the child or young person is a patient, provided that the child or young person continues to be a member of the family; or
(b)   [¹ is blind or severely sight-impaired or treated as such] within the meaning of paragraph 10 of this Schedule; or
(c)   is a child or young person in respect of whom section 145A of the SSCBA (entitlement after death of child or qualifying young person) applies for the purposes of entitlement to child benefit but only for the period prescribed under that section, and in respect of whom a disabled child premium was included in the applicant's applicable amount immediately before the death of that child or young person, or ceased to be included in the applicant's applicable amount because of that child or young person's death; or
(d)   is in receipt of AFIP.

Amendment
1.   Amended by reg 26(c) of SI 2016 No 50 (W.21) as from 20.1.16, for schemes made for a financial year starting on or after 1.4.16.

Carer premium
14.–(1)   The condition is that the applicant or the applicant's partner is, or both of them are, entitled to a carer's allowance under section 70 of the SSCBA.
     (2)   Where a carer premium is awarded but–
(a)   the person in respect of whose care the carer's allowance has been awarded dies; or
(b)   in any other case the person in respect of whom a carer premium has been awarded ceases to be entitled to a carer's allowance,
the condition for the award of the premium is to be treated as satisfied for a period of eight weeks from the relevant date specified in sub-paragraph (3).
     (3)   The relevant date for the purposes of sub-paragraph (2) is–
(a)   where sub-paragraph (2)(a) applies, the Sunday following the death of the person in respect of whose care a carer's allowance has been awarded or the date of death if the death occurred on a Sunday;
(b)   in any other case, the date on which the person who has been entitled to a carer's allowance ceases to be entitled to that allowance.
     (4)   Where a person who has been entitled to a carer's allowance ceases to be entitled to that allowance and makes an application for a reduction, the condition for the award of the carer premium is to be treated as satisfied for a period of eight weeks from the date on which–
(a)   the person in respect of whose care the carer's allowance has been awarded dies;
(b)   in any other case, the person who has been entitled to a carer's allowance ceased to be entitled to that allowance.

Persons in receipt of concessionary payments
    15.   For the purpose of determining whether a premium is applicable to a person under paragraphs 10 to 14 of this Schedule, any concessionary payment made to compensate that person for the non-payment of any benefit mentioned in those paragraphs is to be treated as if it were a payment of that benefit.

Persons in receipt of benefit for another
    16.   For the purposes of this Part of this Schedule, a person is to be regarded as being in receipt of any benefit if, and only if, it is paid in respect of that person and is to be so regarded only for any period in respect of which that benefit is paid.

PART 4
Amounts of Premiums Specified in Part 3

Premium	Amount
17.–(1)Disability Premium–	
(a) where the applicant satisfies the condition in paragraph 9(a) of this Schedule;	[⁵ £34.35];
(b) where the applicant satisfies the condition in paragraph 9(b) of this Schedule.	[⁵ £48.95].
(2) Severe Disability Premium–	
(a) where the applicant satisfies the condition in paragraph 11(2)(a) of this Schedule;	[⁵ £65.85];
(b) where the applicant satisfies the condition in paragraph 11(2)(b) of this Schedule–	
(i) in a case where there is someone in receipt of a carer's allowance [³ or who has an award of universal credit which includes the carer element under regulation 29 of the Universal Credit Regulations 2013] or if that person or any partner satisfies that condition only by virtue of paragraph 11(5) of this Schedule;	[⁵ £65.85];
(ii) in a case where there is no-one in receipt of such an allowance [³ or such an award of universal credit].	[⁵ £131.70].
(3) Disabled Child Premium.	[⁵ £64.19] in respect of each child or young person in respect of whom the condition specified in paragraph 13 of Part 3 of this Schedule is satisfied.
(4) Carer Premium.	[⁵ £36.85] in respect of each person who satisfies the condition specified in paragraph 14 of this Schedule.
(5) Enhanced Disability Premium.	(a) [⁵ £26.04] in respect of each child or young person in respect of whom the conditions specified in paragraph 12 of this Schedule are satisfied; (b) [⁵ £16.80] in respect of each person who is neither– (i) a child or young person; nor (ii) a member of a couple or a polygamous marriage, in respect of whom the conditions specified in paragraph 12 of this Schedule are satisfied; (c) [⁵ £24.10] where the applicant is a member of a couple or a polygamous marriage and the conditions specified in paragraph 12 of this Schedule are satisfied in respect of a member of that couple or polygamous marriage.

Amendments
    1.   Amended by reg 28(d) of SI 2014 No 66 (W.6) as from 15.1.14.
    2.   Amended by reg 28(d) of SI 2015 No 44 (W.3) as from 21.1.15, for schemes made for a financial year starting on or after 1.4.15.
    3.   Amended by reg 18(c) of SI 2017 No 46 (W.20) as from 19.1.17, for schemes made for a financial year starting on or after 1.4.17.
    4.   Amended by reg 25(c) of SI 2018 No 14 (W.7) as from 10.1.18, for schemes made for a financial year starting on or after 1.4.18.
    5.   Amended by reg 15(b) of SI 2019 No 11 (W.5) as from 9.1.19, for schemes made for a financial year starting on or after 1.4.19.

PART 5
The components

18. Subject to paragraph 20 of this Schedule the applicant is entitled to one, but not both, of the components in paragraph 21 or 22 of this Schedule if–

(a) the applicant or the applicant's partner has made a claim for employment and support allowance;

(b) the Secretary of State has decided that the applicant or the applicant's partner has, or is to be treated as having, limited capability for work or limited capability for work-related activity; and

(c) either–

    (i) the assessment phase as defined in section 24(2) of the Welfare Reform Act 2007 has ended; or

    (ii) regulation 7 of the Employment and Support Allowance Regulations 2008 [1 or regulation 7 of the Employment and Support Allowance Regulations 2013] (circumstances where the condition that the assessment phase has ended before entitlement to the support component [2] arises does not apply) applies.

Amendments

1. Amended by reg 28(e) of SI 2015 No 44 (W.3) as from 21.1.15, for schemes made for a financial year starting on or after 1.4.15.

2. Amended by reg 25(d) of SI 2018 No 14 (W.7) as from 10.1.18, for schemes made for a financial year starting on or after 1.4.18.

19. Subject to paragraph 20, the applicant is entitled to one, but not both, of the components in paragraphs 21 and 22 if the applicant or the applicant's partner is entitled to a converted employment and support allowance.

20.–(1) The applicant has no entitlement under paragraph 21 or 22 if the applicant is entitled to the disability premium under paragraphs 9 and 10 of this Schedule.

(2) Where the applicant and the applicant's partner each satisfy paragraph 21 or 22, the component to be included in the applicant's applicable amount is that which relates to the applicant.

The work-related activity component

21. The applicant is entitled to the work-related activity component if the Secretary of State has decided that the applicant or the applicant's partner has, or is to be treated as having, limited capability for work.

The support component

22. The applicant is entitled to the support component if the Secretary of State has decided that the applicant or the applicant's partner has, or is to be treated as having, limited capability for work-related activity.

PART 6
Amount of Components

23. The amount of the work-related activity component is [3 £29.35].

Amendments

1. Amended by reg 28(e) of SI 2014 No 66 (W.6) as from 15.1.14.

2. Amended by reg 28(f) of SI 2015 No 44 (W.3) as from 21.1.15, for schemes made for a financial year starting on or after 1.4.15.

3. Amended by reg 18(d) of SI 2017 No 46 (W.20) as from 19.1.17, for schemes made for a financial year starting on or after 1.4.17.

24. The amount of the support component is [5 £38.55].

Amendments

1. Amended by reg 28(f) of SI 2014 No 66 as from 15.1.14.

2. Amended by reg 28(g) of SI 2015 No 44 as from 21.1.15, for schemes made for a financial year starting on or after 1.4.15.

3. Amended by reg 18(e) of SI 2017 No 46 (W.20) as from 19.1.17, for schemes made for a financial year starting on or after 1.4.17.

4. Amended by reg 25(e) of SI 2018 No 14 as from 10.1.18, for schemes made for a financial year starting on or after 1.4.18.

5. Amended by reg 15(c) of SI 2019 No 11 (W.5) as from 9.1.19, for schemes made for a financial year starting on or after 1.4.19.

PART 7
Transitional Addition

25.–(1)   The applicant is entitled to the transitional addition calculated in accordance with paragraph 28 where the applicant or the applicant's partner ("the relevant person")–

(a)   is entitled to a converted employment and support allowance; or

(b)   is appealing a conversion decision as described in regulation 5(2)(b) of the Employment and Support Allowance (Transitional Provisions, Housing Benefit and Council Tax Benefit) (Existing Awards) (No 2) Regulations 2010 and–

    (i)   is treated as having limited capability for work by virtue of regulation 30 of the Employment and Support Allowance Regulations 2008 as modified by the Employment and Support Allowance (Transitional Provisions, Housing Benefit and Council Tax Benefit) (Existing Awards) (No 2) Regulations 2010 [¹ or regulation 26 of the Employment and Support Allowance Regulations 2013]; and

    (ii)   is not in receipt of an income-related employment and support allowance,

unless the amount of the transitional addition calculated in accordance with paragraph 28 of this Schedule would be nil.

(2)   The applicant's entitlement to a transitional addition by virtue of this paragraph ends on any of the following–

(a)   the reduction of the transitional addition to nil in accordance with paragraph 29 of this Schedule;

(b)   the termination of the applicant's award of reduction under this scheme;

(c)   the relevant person ceasing to meet the requirements of sub-paragraph (1)(a) or (b), as the case may be;

(d)   the applicant or the applicant's partner becoming entitled to an income-related employment and support allowance, an income-based jobseeker's allowance or income support;

(e)   5 April 2020.

Amendment

1.   Amended by reg 28(h) of SI 2015 No 44 (W.3) as from 21.1.15, for schemes made for a financial year starting on or after 1.4.15.

26.–(1)   This paragraph applies where–

(a)   the applicant's entitlement to a transitional addition ends, by virtue of the termination of the applicant's award of reduction, under–

    (i)   paragraph 25(2)(b) of this Schedule;

    (ii)   sub-paragraph (3)(b) of this paragraph; or

    (iii)   paragraph 27(3)(b) of this Schedule;

(b)   within 12 weeks of that termination but before 5 April 2020 the applicant again becomes entitled to a reduction under this scheme;

(c)   in the reduction week in which the applicant again becomes entitled to a reduction under this scheme the relevant person is entitled to an employment and support allowance which is not income-related; and

(d)   at the date on which the applicant again becomes entitled to a reduction under this scheme, neither the applicant nor the applicant's partner is entitled to an income-related employment and support allowance, an income-based jobseeker's allowance or income support.

(2)   Where this paragraph applies, the applicant is entitled, with effect from the day on which the applicant again becomes entitled to a reduction under this scheme, to a transitional addition of the amount of the transitional addition that would have applied had the applicant's entitlement to a transitional addition not ended (but taking account of the effect which any intervening change of circumstances would have had by virtue of paragraph 29), unless the amount of the transitional addition would be nil.

(3)   The applicant's entitlement to a transitional addition by virtue of this paragraph ends on any of the following–

(a)   the reduction of the transitional addition to nil in accordance with paragraph 29 of this Schedule;

(b)   the termination of the applicant's award of a reduction under this scheme;

(c)   the relevant person no longer being entitled to the employment and support allowance referred to in sub-paragraph (1)(c);

(d)   the applicant or the applicant's partner becoming entitled to an income-related employment and support allowance, an income-based jobseeker's allowance or income support;

(e)   5 April 2020.

27.–(1)   This paragraph applies where–

(a)   the applicant's entitlement to a transitional addition ends, by virtue of the relevant person ceasing to be entitled to an employment and support allowance, under–

    (i)   paragraph 25(2)(c) of this Schedule;

    (ii)   paragraph 26(3)(c) of this Schedule; or

    (iii)   sub-paragraph (3)(c) of this paragraph;

(b)   before 5 April 2020 the relevant person again becomes entitled to an employment and support allowance which is not income-related;

(c)   at the date on which the relevant person again becomes entitled to an employment and support allowance which is not income-related, regulation 145(1) of the Employment and Support Allowance Regulations 2008 applies to the relevant person; and

(d)   at the date on which the relevant person again becomes entitled to an employment and support allowance which is not income-related, neither the applicant nor the applicant's partner is entitled to an income-related employment and support allowance, an income-based jobseeker's allowance or income support.

(2)   Where this paragraph applies, the applicant is entitled, with effect from the day that the relevant person's entitlement to employment and support allowance takes effect for the purposes of a reduction under this scheme, to a transitional addition of the amount of the transitional addition that would have applied had the applicant's entitlement to a transitional addition not ended (but taking account of the effect which any intervening change of circumstances would have had by virtue of paragraph 29 of this Schedule), unless the amount of the transitional addition would be nil.

(3)   The applicant's entitlement to a transitional addition by virtue of this paragraph ends on any of the following–

(a)   the reduction of the transitional addition to nil in accordance with paragraph 29 of this Schedule;

(b)   the termination of the applicant's award of a reduction under this scheme;

(c)   the relevant person no longer being entitled to the employment and support allowance referred to in sub-paragraph (1)(b);

(d)   the applicant or the applicant's partner becoming entitled to an income-related employment and support allowance, an income-based jobseeker's allowance or income support;

(e)   5 April 2020.

PART 8
Amount of Transitional Addition

28.–(1)   Subject to paragraph 29 of this Schedule, the amount of the transitional addition is the amount by which Amount A exceeds Amount B.

(2)   Where a conversion decision as described in regulation 5(2)(a) of the Employment and Support Allowance (Transitional Provisions, Housing Benefit and Council Tax Benefit) (Existing Awards) (No. 2) Regulations 2010 ("the 2010 Regulations") is made in respect of the relevant person–

(a)   Amount A is the basic amount that would have applied on the day that decision took effect had that decision not been made; and

(b)   Amount B is the basic amount that applied on that day as a result of that decision.

(3)   Where the relevant person is appealing a conversion decision as described in regulation 5(2)(b) of the 2010 Regulations and is treated as having limited capability for work by virtue of regulation 30 of the Employment and Support Allowance Regulations 2008 as modified by the 2010 Regulations–

(a)   Amount A is the basic amount that would have applied on the day the relevant person was first treated as having limited capability for work if the relevant person had not been so treated; and

(b)   Amount B is the basic amount that applied on that day as a result of the relevant person being so treated.

(4)   In this paragraph and paragraph 29, "basic amount" ("swm sylfaenol") means the aggregate of such amounts as may apply in the applicant's case in accordance with paragraph 24(1)(a) to (e) or paragraph 25(2)(a) to (f) of this scheme.

29.–(1)   Subject to sub-paragraph (2), where there is a change of circumstances which leads to an increase in the applicant's basic amount, the transitional addition that applies immediately before the change of circumstances is to be reduced by the amount by which Amount C exceeds Amount D.

(2)   If Amount C exceeds Amount D by more than the amount of the transitional addition that applies immediately before the change of circumstances, that transitional addition is to be reduced to nil.

(3)   Amount C is the basic amount that applies as a result of the increase.

(4)   Amount D is the basic amount that applied immediately before the increase.

SCHEDULE 4
Sums disregarded from applicant's earnings: pensioners

1.   Where two or more of paragraphs 2 to 5 of this Schedule apply in any particular case the overall maximum sum which falls to be disregarded in that case under those paragraphs is restricted to–

(a)   £25 in the case of a lone parent;

(b)   £20 in any other case.

2.   In a case where an applicant is a lone parent, £25 of earnings.

3.–(1)   In a case of earnings from any employment or employments to which sub-paragraph (2) applies, £20.

(2)   This paragraph applies to employment–

(a)   as a part-time fire-fighter employed by a fire and rescue authority constituted by a scheme under section 2 of the Fire and Rescue Services Act 2004 or a scheme to which section 4 of that Act applies;

(b)   a part-time fire-fighter employed by the Scottish Fire and Rescue Service;

(c)   as an auxiliary coastguard in respect of coast rescue activities;

(d)   in the manning or launching of a lifeboat if the employment is part-time;

(e)   as a member of any territorial or reserve force prescribed in Part I of Schedule 6 to the Social Security (Contributions) Regulations 2001.

(3)   If–

(a)   any of the earnings of the applicant or, if the applicant has a partner, the applicant's partner, or both of them, are disregarded under sub-paragraph (1); and

(b)   either of them has, or both of them have, other earnings,

(c)   so much of those other earnings as would not, in the aggregate with the earnings disregarded under that sub-paragraph, exceed £20.

4.–(1)   If the applicant or, if the applicant has a partner, the applicant's partner is a carer, or both are carers, £20 of any earnings received from the applicant's or their employment.

(2)   Where the carer premium is awarded in respect of the applicant and of any partner of the applicant, their earnings are for the purposes of this paragraph to be aggregated, but the amount to be disregarded in accordance with sub-paragraph (1) is not to exceed £20 of the aggregated amount.

(3)   In this paragraph the applicant or the applicant's partner is a carer if paragraph 14 of Part 3 of Schedule 3 (amount applicable for carers) is satisfied in respect of the applicant.

5.–(1)   £20 is disregarded if the applicant or, if the applicant has a partner, the applicant's partner–

(a)   is in receipt of

    (i)   long-term incapacity benefit under section 30A of the SSCBA;

    (ii)   severe disablement allowance under section 68 of the SSCBA;

    (iii)   attendance allowance under section 64 of the SSCBA;

    (iv)   disability living allowance;

    (v)   personal independence payment;

    (vi)   an AFIP;

    (vii)   any mobility supplement under article 20 of the Naval, Military and Air Forces Etc (Disablement and Death) Service Pensions Order 2006 (including such a supplement by virtue of any other scheme or order) or under article 25A of the Personal Injuries (Civilians) Scheme 1983;

    (viii)   the disability element or the severe disability element of working tax credit under Schedule 2 to the Working Tax Credit (Entitlement and Maximum Rate) Regulations 2002; or

    (ix)   main phase employment and support allowance; or

[² (b)   is or are registered as blind in a register compiled under section 29 of the National Assistance Act 1948 (welfare services), or registered as severely sight-impaired in a registerestablished and maintained by a local authority under section 18(1) of the Social Services and Well-being (Wales) Act 2014 or section 77(1) of the Care Act 2014, or in Scotland, has or have been certified as blind and in consequence is or registered as blind in a register maintained by or on behalf of a council constituted under section 2 of the Local Government etc. (Scotland) Act 1994; or]

(c)   is, or is treated as, incapable of work in accordance with the provisions of, and regulations made under, Part 12A of the SSCBA (incapacity for work), and has been incapable, or has been treated as incapable, of work for a continuous period of not less than–

    (i)   in the case of an applicant who is terminally ill within the meaning of section 30B(4) of the SCCBA, 196 days;

    (ii)   in any other case, 364 days; or

(d)   has, or is treated as having, limited capacity for work within the meaning of section 1(4) of the Welfare Reform Act 2007 or limited capability for work-related activity within the meaning of section 2(5) of that Act and either–

    (i)   the assessment phase as defined in section 24(2) of the Welfare Reform Act 2007 has ended; or

    (ii)   regulation 7 of the Employment and Support Allowance Regulations 2008 [¹ or regulation 7 of the Employment and Support Allowance Regulations 2013] (circumstances where the condition that the assessment phase has ended before entitlement to the support component [³ arises] does not apply) applies.

(2)   Subject to sub-paragraph (3), £20 is disregarded if the applicant or, if the applicant has a partner, the applicant's partner has, within a period of 8 weeks ending on the day in respect of which the applicant or the applicant's partner attains the qualifying age for state pension credit, had an award of housing benefit or council tax benefit or been in receipt of a reduction under this scheme and–

(a)   £20 was disregarded in respect of earnings taken into account in that award; and

(b)   the person whose earnings qualified for the disregard continues in employment after the termination of that award.

(3)   The disregard of £20 specified in sub-paragraph (2) applies so long as there is no break, other than a break which does not exceed 8 weeks, in a person's–

(a)   entitlement to housing benefit; or

(b)   receipt of a reduction under this scheme; or

(c)   employment,

following the first day in respect of which that benefit or reduction under this scheme is awarded.

(4)   £20 is the maximum amount which may be disregarded under this paragraph, notwithstanding that, where the applicant has a partner, both the applicant and the applicant's partner satisfy the requirements of this paragraph.

Amendments

1.   Amended by reg 29(a) of SI 2015 No 44 (W.3) as from 21.1.15, for schemes made for a financial year starting on or after 1.4.15.
2.   Substituted by reg 27 of SI 2016 No 50 (W.21) as from 20.1.16, for schemes made for a financial year starting on or after 1.4.16.
3.   Amended by reg 26 of SI 2018 No 14 (W.7) as from 10.1.18, for schemes made for a financial year starting on or after 1.4.18.

6.–(1)   Where–
(a)   the applicant (or if the applicant is a member of a couple, at least one member of that couple) is a person to whom sub-paragraph (5) applies;
(b)   the Secretary of State is satisfied that that person is undertaking exempt work as defined in sub-paragraph (6); and
(c)   paragraph 32 of this scheme (pensioners in receipt of guarantee credit) does not apply,
the amount specified in sub-paragraph (7) ("the specified amount").
(2)   Where this paragraph applies, paragraphs 1 to 5 and 8 of this Schedule do not apply; but in any case where the applicant is a lone parent, and the specified amount would be less than the amount specified in paragraph 2, then paragraph 2 applies instead of this paragraph.
(3)   Notwithstanding paragraph 30 (calculation of income and capital: applicant's family and polygamous marriages), if sub-paragraph (1) applies to one member of a couple ("A") it is not to apply to the other member of that couple ("B") except to the extent provided in sub-paragraph (4).
(4)   Where A's earnings are less than the specified amount, there is also to be disregarded so much of B's earnings as would not when aggregated with A's earnings exceed the specified amount; but the amount of B's earnings which may be disregarded under this sub-paragraph is limited to a maximum of £20 unless the Secretary of State is satisfied that B is also undertaking exempt work.
(5)   This sub-paragraph applies to a person who is–
(a)   in receipt of a contributory employment and support allowance;
(b)   in receipt of incapacity benefit;
(c)   in receipt of severe disablement allowance;
(d)   being credited with earnings on the grounds of incapacity for work or limited capability for work under regulation 8B of the Social Security (Credits) Regulations 1975.
(6)   "Exempt work" ("gwaith esempt") means work of the kind described in–
(a)   regulation 45(2), (3) or (4) of the Employment and Support Allowance Regulations 2008 [¹ or regulation 39(1)(a), (b) or (c) of the Employment and Support Allowance Regulations 2013]; or (as the case may be);
(b)   regulation 17(2), (3) or (4) of the Social Security (Incapacity for Work) (General) Regulations 1995, and, in determining for the purposes of this paragraph whether an applicant or a member of a couple is undertaking any type of exempt work, it is immaterial whether that person or that person's partner is also undertaking other work.
(7)   The specified amount is the amount of money from time to time mentioned in any provision referred to in sub-paragraph (6) by virtue of which the work referred to in sub-paragraph (1) is exempt (or, where more than one such provision is relevant and those provisions mention different amounts of money, the highest of those amounts).

Amendment

1.   Amended by reg 29(b) of SI 2015 No 44 (W.3) as from 21.1.15, for schemes made for a financial year starting on or after 1.4.15.

---

7.   Any amount or the balance of any amount which would fall to be disregarded under paragraph 18 or 19 of Schedule 5 had the applicant's income which does not consist of earnings been sufficient to entitle the applicant to the full amount disregarded thereunder.
8.   Except where the applicant or the applicant's partner qualifies for a £20 disregard under the preceding provisions of this Schedule–
(a)   £5 is to be disregarded if an applicant who has no partner has earnings;
(b)   £10 is to be disregarded if an applicant who has a partner has earnings.
9.   Any earnings, other than earnings referred to in paragraph 37(9)(b) of this scheme (calculation of weekly income: pensioners), derived from employment which ended before the day in respect of which the applicant first satisfies the conditions for entitlement to a reduction under this scheme.
10.–(1)   In a case where the applicant is a person who satisfies at least one of the conditions set out in sub-paragraph (2), and the applicant's net earnings equal or exceed the total of the amounts set out in sub-paragraph (3), the amount of the applicant's earnings that falls to be disregarded under this Schedule is to be increased by £17.10.

(2)   The conditions of this sub-paragraph are that–

(a)   the applicant, or if the applicant has a partner, either the applicant or the applicant's partner, is a person to whom regulation 20(1)(c) of the Working Tax Credit (Entitlement and Maximum Rate) Regulations 2002 applies; or

(b)   the applicant–

     (i)   is, or any partner of the applicant's is, aged at least 25 and is engaged in remunerative work for on average not less than 30 hours per week; or

     (ii)   if the applicant is a member of a couple–

          (aa)   at least one member of that couple is engaged in remunerative work for on average not less than 16 hours per week; and

          (bb)   the applicant's applicable amount includes a family premium under paragraph 3 of Schedule 2; or

     (iii)   is a lone parent who is engaged in remunerative work for on average not less than 16 hours per week; or

     (iv)   is, or if the applicant has a partner, one of them is, engaged in remunerative work for on average not less than 16 hours per week and paragraph 5(1) above is satisfied in respect of that person.

(3)   The following are the amounts referred to in sub-paragraph (1)–

(a)   any amount disregarded under this Schedule;

(b)   the amount of child care charges calculated as deductible under paragraph 54(1)(c) of this scheme (calculation of income on a weekly basis: pensioners and persons who are not pensioners); and

(c)   £17.10.

(4)   The provisions of paragraph 10 (remunerative work) of this scheme are to apply in determining whether or not a person works for on average not less than 30 hours per week, but as if the reference to 16 hours in sub-paragraph (1) of that paragraph was a reference to 30 hours.

11.   Where a payment of earnings is made in a currency other than Sterling, any banking charge or commission payable in converting to that payment into Sterling.

SCHEDULE 5
Amounts to be disregarded in the calculation of income other than earnings: pensioners

1.   In addition to any sum which falls to be disregarded in accordance with paragraphs 2 to 6 of this Schedule, £10 of any of the following–

(a)   a war disablement pension (except insofar as such a pension falls to be disregarded under paragraph 2 or 3 of this Schedule);

(b)   a war widow's pension or war widower's pension;

(c)   a pension payable to a person as a widow, widower or surviving civil partner under any power of Her Majesty otherwise than under an enactment to make provision about pensions for or in respect of persons who have been disabled or have died in consequence of service as members of the armed forces of the Crown;

(d)   a guaranteed income payment and, if the amount of that payment has been abated to less than £10 by a pension or payment falling within Article 39(1)(a) or (b) of the Armed Forces and Reserve Forces (Compensation Scheme) Order 2011, so much of that pension or payment as would not, in aggregate with the amount of any guaranteed income payment disregarded, exceed £10;

(e)   a payment made to compensate for the non-payment of such a pension or payment as is mentioned in any of the preceding sub-paragraphs;

(f)   a pension paid by the government of a country outside Great Britain which is analogous to any of the pensions or payments mentioned in sub-paragraphs (a) to (d) above;

[¹ (g)   a pension paid by a government to victims of National Socialist persecution.]

Amendment

1.   Substituted by reg 27 of SI 2018 No 14 (W.7) as from 10.1.18, for schemes made for a financial year starting on or after 1.4.18.

---

2.   The whole of any amount included in a pension to which paragraph 1 relates in respect of–

(a)   the applicant's need for constant attendance;

(b)   the applicant's exceptionally severe disablement.

3.   Any mobility supplement under article 20 of the Naval, Military and Air Forces Etc (Disablement and Death) Service Pensions Order 2006 (including such a supplement by virtue of any other scheme or order) or under article 25A of the Personal Injuries (Civilians) Scheme1983 or any payment intended to compensate for the non-payment of such a supplement.

4.   Any supplementary pension under article 23(2) of the Naval, Military and Air Forces Etc (Disablement and Death) Service Pensions Order 2006 (pensions to surviving spouses and surviving civil partners) and any analogous payment made by the Secretary of State for Defence to any person who is not a person entitled under that Order.

5. In the case of a pension awarded at the supplementary rate under article 27(3) of the Personal Injuries (Civilians) Scheme 1983 (pensions to surviving spouses and surviving civil partners), the sum specified in paragraph 1(c) of Schedule 4 to that Scheme.

6.–(1) Any payment which is–

(a) made under any of the Dispensing Instruments to a widow, widower or surviving civil partner of a person–

    (i) whose death was attributable to service in a capacity analogous to service as a member of the armed forces of the Crown; and

    (ii) whose service in such capacity terminated before 31 March 1973; and

(b) equal to the amount specified in article 23(2) of the Naval, Military and Air Forces Etc (Disablement and Death) Service Pensions Order 2006.

(2) In this paragraph "the Dispensing Instruments" ("yr Offerynnau Dosbarthu") means the Order in Council of 19 December 1881, the Royal Warrant of 27 October 1884 and the Order by His Majesty of 14 January 1922 (exceptional grants of pay, non-effective pay and allowances).

7. £15 of any widowed parent's allowance to which the applicant is entitled under section 39A of the SSCBA.

8. £15 of any widowed mother's allowance to which the applicant is entitled under section 37 of the SSCBA.

9. Where the applicant occupies a dwelling as the applicant's home and the applicant provides in that dwelling board and lodging accommodation, an amount, in respect of each person for whom such accommodation is provided for the whole or any part of a week, equal to–

(a) where the aggregate of any payments made in respect of any one week in respect of such accommodation provided to such person does not exceed £20, 100 per cent of such payments; or

(b) where the aggregate of any such payments exceeds £20, £20 and 50 per cent of the excess over £20.

10. If the applicant–

(a) owns the freehold or leasehold interest in any property or is a tenant of any property; and

(b) occupies a part of that property; and

(c) has an agreement with another person allowing that person to occupy another part of that property on payment of rent and–

    (i) the amount paid by that person is less than £20 per week, the whole of that amount; or

    (ii) the amount paid is £20 or more per week, £20.

11. Where an applicant receives income under an annuity purchased with a loan, which satisfies the following conditions–

(a) that the loan was made as part of a scheme under which not less than 90 per cent of the proceeds of the loan were applied to the purchase by the person to whom it was made of an annuity ending with that person's life or with the life of the survivor of two or more persons (in this paragraph referred to as "the annuitants") who include the person to whom the loan was made;

(b) that at the time the loan was made the person to whom it was made or each of the annuitants had attained the age of 65;

(c) that the loan was secured on a dwelling in Great Britain and the person to whom the loan was made or one of the annuitants owns an estate or interest in that dwelling;

(d) that the person to whom the loan was made or one of the annuitants occupies the dwelling on which it was secured as that person's or annuitant's home at the time the interest is paid; and

(e) that the interest payable on the loan is paid by the person to whom the loan was made or by one of the annuitants;

(f) the amount, calculated on a weekly basis, equal to–

    (i) where, or insofar as, section 369 of the Income and Corporation Taxes Act 1988 (mortgage interest payable under deduction of tax) applies to the payments of interest on the loan, the interest which is payable after deduction of a sum equal to income tax on such payments at the applicable percentage of income tax within the meaning of section 369(1A) of that Act;

    (ii) in any other case, the interest which is payable on the loan without deduction of such a sum.

12.–(1) Any payment, other than a payment to which sub-paragraph (2) applies, made to the applicant by Trustees in exercise of a discretion exercisable by them.

(2) This sub-paragraph applies to payments made to the applicant by Trustees in exercise of a discretion exercisable by them for the purpose of–

(a) obtaining food, ordinary clothing or footwear or household fuel;

(b) the payment of rent, council tax or water charges for which that applicant or the applicant's partner is liable;

(c) meeting housing costs of a kind specified in Schedule 2 to the State Pension Credit Regulations 2002.

(3) In a case to which sub-paragraph (2) applies, £20 or–

(a) if the payment is less than £20, the whole payment;

(b) if, in the applicant's case, £10 is disregarded in accordance with paragraph 1(a) to (g) of this Schedule, £10 or the whole payment if it is less than £10; or

(c) if, in the applicant's case, £15 is disregarded under paragraph 7 or paragraph 8 of this Schedule and–

    (i) the applicant has no disregard under paragraph 1(a) to (g) of this Schedule , £5 or the whole payment if it is less than £5;

(ii)   the applicant has a disregard under paragraph 1(a) to (g) of this Schedule, nil.

13.   Any increase in pension or allowance under Part 2 or 3 of the Naval, Military and Air Forces Etc (Disablement and Death) Service Pensions Order 2006 paid in respect of a dependent other than the pensioner's partner.

14.   Any payment ordered by a court to be made to the applicant or the applicant's partner in consequence of any accident, injury or disease suffered by the person or a child of the person to or in respect of whom the payments are made.

15.   Periodic payments made to the applicant or the applicant's partner under an agreement entered into in settlement of a claim made by the applicant or, as the case may be, the applicant's partner for an injury suffered by the applicant or the applicant's partner.

16.   Any income which is payable outside the United Kingdom for such period during which there is a prohibition against the transfer to the United Kingdom of that income.

17.   Any banking charges or commission payable in converting to Sterling payments of income made in a currency other than Sterling.

18.   Where the applicant makes a parental contribution in respect of a student attending a course at an establishment in the United Kingdom or undergoing education in the United Kingdom, which contribution has been assessed for the purposes of calculating–

(a)   under, or pursuant to regulations made under powers conferred by section 22 of the Teaching and Higher Education Act 1998, that student's award;

(b)   under regulations made in exercise of the powers conferred by section 49 of the Education (Scotland) Act 1980, that student's bursary, scholarship, or other allowance under that section or under regulations made in exercise of the powers conferred by section 73of that Act of 1980, any payment to that student under that section; or

(c)   the student's student loan,

an amount equal to the weekly amount of that parental contribution, but only in respect of the period for which that contribution is assessed as being payable.

19.–(1)   Where the applicant is the parent of a student aged under 25 in advanced education who either–

(a)   is not in receipt of any award, grant or student loan in respect of that education; or

(b)   is in receipt of an award bestowed by virtue of the Teaching and Higher Education Act 1998, or regulations made thereunder, or a bursary, scholarship or other allowance under section 49(1) of the Education (Scotland) Act 1980, or a payment under section 73 of that Act of 1980,

and the applicant makes payments by way of a contribution towards the student's maintenance, other than a parental contribution falling within paragraph 18, an amount specified in sub-paragraph (2) in respect of each week during the student's term.

(2)   For the purposes of sub-paragraph (1), the amount is to be equal to–

(a)   the weekly amount of the payments; or

(b)   the amount by way of a personal allowance for a single applicant under 25 less the weekly amount of any award, bursary, scholarship, allowance or payment referred to in sub-paragraph (1)(b),

whichever is less.

(3)   In this paragraph and paragraph 18 a reference to a "student loan" ("benthyciad myfyriwr") or a "grant" ("grant") is a reference to a student loan or a grant within the meaning of Part 10 of this scheme.

20.–(1)   Where an applicant's applicable amount includes an amount by way of a family premium, £15 of any payment of maintenance, whether under a court order or not, which is made or due to be made by the applicant's spouse, civil partner, former spouse or former civil partner or the applicant's partner's spouse, civil partner, former spouse, or former civil partner.

(2)   For the purposes of sub-paragraph (1), where more than one maintenance payment falls to be taken into account in any week, all such payments are to be aggregated and treated as if they were a single payment.

21.   Except in a case which falls under paragraph 10 of Schedule 4, where the applicant is a person who satisfies any of the conditions of sub-paragraph (2) of that paragraph, any amount of working tax credit up to £17.10.

22.   Where the total value of any capital specified in Part 2 (capital disregarded only for the purposes of determining deemed income) of Schedule 8 does not exceed £10,000, any income actually derived from such capital.

23.   Except in the case of income from capital specified in Part 2 of Schedule 8, any actual income from capital.

24.   Where the applicant, or the person who was the partner of the applicant on 31 March 2003, was entitled on that date to income support or an income-based jobseeker's allowance but ceased to be so entitled on or before 5 April 2003 by virtue only of regulation 13 of the Housing Benefit (General) Amendment (No 3) Regulations 1999 as in force at that date, the whole of the applicant's income.

SCHEDULE 6
Sums disregarded in the calculation of earnings: persons who are not pensioners

1.   In the case of an applicant who has been engaged in remunerative work as an employed earner or, had the employment been in Great Britain, would have been so engaged–

(a)   where–

       (i)   the employment has been terminated because of retirement; and

       (ii)   on retirement the applicant is entitled to a retirement pension under the SSCBA [¹ or a state pension under Part 1 of the Pensions Act 2014], or is not so entitled solely because of the applicant's failure to satisfy the contribution conditions [¹ or to have the minimum number of qualifying years],

any earnings paid or due to be paid in respect of that employment, but only for a period commencing on the day immediately after the date on which the employment was terminated;

(b)   where before the first day of entitlement to a reduction under this scheme the employment has been terminated otherwise than because of retirement, any earnings paid or due to be paid in respect of that employment except–

       (i)   any payment of the nature described in–

           (aa)   paragraph 48(1)(e) of this scheme, or

           (bb)   section 28, 64 or 68 of the Employment Rights Act 1996 (guarantee payments, suspension from work on medical or maternity grounds); and

       (ii)   any award, sum or payment of the nature described in–

           (aa)   paragraph 48(1)(g) or (i) of this scheme, or

           (bb)   section 34 or 70 of the Employment Rights Act 1996 (guarantee payments and suspension from work: complaints to employment tribunals),

including any payment made following the settlement of a complaint to an employment tribunal or of court proceedings;

(c)   where before the first day of entitlement to a reduction under this scheme–

       (i)   the employment has not been terminated, but

       (ii)   the applicant is not engaged in remunerative work,

any earnings paid or due to be paid in respect of that employment except any payment or remuneration of the nature described in paragraph 1(b)(i) or (ii)(bb) of this Schedule or paragraph 48(1)(j) of this scheme.

Amendment

1.   Inserted by reg 28 of SI 2016 No 50 (W.21) as from 20.1.16, for schemes made for a financial year starting on or after 1.4.16.

---

2.   In the case of an applicant who, before the first day of entitlement to a reduction under this scheme–

(a)   has been engaged in part-time employment as an employed earner or, where the employment has been outside Great Britain, would have been so engaged had the employment been in Great Britain; and

(b)   has ceased to be engaged in that employment, whether or not that employment has been terminated,

(c)   any earnings paid or due to be paid in respect of that employment except–

       (i)   where that employment has been terminated, any payment of the nature described in paragraph 1(b)(i) or (ii)(bb) of this Schedule;

       (ii)   where that employment has not been terminated, any payment or remuneration of the nature described in paragraph 1(b)(i) or (ii)(bb) of this Schedule or paragraph 48(1)(j) of this scheme.

3.   In the case of an applicant who has been engaged in remunerative work or part-time employment as a self employed earner or, had the employment been in Great Britain, would have been so engaged and who has ceased to be so employed, from the date of the cessation of the applicant's employment, any earnings derived from that employment except earnings to which paragraph 50(3) and (4) of this Scheme (earnings of self-employed earners: persons who are not pensioners) apply.

4.–(1)   In a case to which this paragraph applies and paragraph 5 does not apply, £20; but notwithstanding paragraph 30 of this scheme (calculation of income and capital: applicant's family and polygamous marriages) if this paragraph applies to an applicant it is not to apply to the applicant's partner except where, and to the extent that, the earnings of the applicant which are to be disregarded under this paragraph are less than £20.

(2)   This paragraph applies where the applicant's applicable amount includes an amount by way of the disability premium, severe disability premium, work-related activity component or support component under Schedule 3 (applicable amounts: persons who are not pensioners) [¹ or where the applicant or the applicant's partner is a member of the work-related activity group].

(3)   This paragraph applies where–

(a)   the applicant is a member of a couple and the applicant's applicable amount includes an amount by way of the disability premium under Schedule 3; and

(b)   the applicant or the applicant's partner has not attained the qualifying age for state pension credit and at least one is engaged in employment.

Amendment

1.   Amended by reg 28(a) of SI 2018 No 14 (W.7) as from 10.1.18, for schemes made for a financial year starting on or after 1.4.18.

---

5.   In a case where the applicant is a lone parent, £25.

6.–(1)   In a case to which neither paragraph 4 nor paragraph 5 of this Schedule applies to the applicant and, subject to sub-paragraph (2), where the applicant's applicable amount includes an amount by way of the carer premium under Schedule 3 (applicable amounts: persons who are not pensioners), £20 of the earnings of the person who is, or at any time in the preceding eight weeks was, in receipt of carer's allowance or treated in accordance with paragraph 14(2) of that Schedule as being in receipt of carer's allowance.

(2)   Where the carer premium is awarded in respect of the applicant and of any partner of the applicant's, their earnings are for the purposes of this paragraph to be aggregated, but the amount to be disregarded in accordance with sub-paragraph (1) is not to exceed £20 of the aggregated amount.

7.   Where the carer premium is awarded in respect of an applicant who is a member of a couple and whose earnings are less than £20, but is not awarded in respect of the other member of the couple, and that other member is engaged in an employment–

(a)   specified in paragraph 9(1) of this Schedule, so much of the other member's earnings as would not when aggregated with the amount disregarded under paragraph 6 of this Schedule exceed £20;

(b)   other than one specified in paragraph 9(1) of this Schedule, so much of the other member's earnings from such other employment up to £10 as would not when aggregated with the amount disregarded under paragraph 5 exceed £20.

8.   In a case where [¹ paragraphs 4,5, 6 and 7] of this Schedule do not apply to the applicant and the applicant is one of a couple and a member of that couple is in employment, £10; but, not withstanding paragraph 30 of this scheme (calculation of income and capital: applicant's family and polygamous marriages), if this paragraph applies to an applicant it is not to apply to the applicant's partner except where, and to the extent that, the earnings of the applicant which are to be disregarded under this paragraph are less than £10.

9.–(1)   In a case where paragraphs 4, 6, 7 and 9 of this Schedule do not apply to the applicant, £20 of earnings derived from one or more employments as–

(a)   a part-time fire-fighter employed by a fire and rescue authority constituted by a scheme under section 2 of the Fire and Rescue Services Act 2004 or a scheme to which section 4 of that Act applies;

(b)   a part-time fire-fighter employed by the Scottish Fire and Rescue Service;

(c)   an auxiliary coastguard in respect of coast rescue activities;

(d)   a person engaged part-time in the manning or launching of a life boat;

(e)   a member of any territorial or reserve force prescribed in Part I of Schedule 6 to the Social Security (Contributions) Regulations 2001;

but, notwithstanding paragraph 30 of this scheme (calculation of income and capital: applicant's family and polygamous marriages), if this paragraph applies to an applicant it is not to apply to that applicant's partner except to the extent specified in sub-paragraph (2).

(2)   If the applicant's partner is engaged in employment–

(a)   specified in sub-paragraph (1), so much of the applicant's partner's earnings as would not in aggregate with the amount of the applicant's earnings disregarded under this paragraph exceed £20;

(b)   other than one specified in sub-paragraph (1), so much of the applicant's partner's earnings from that employment up to £10 as would not in aggregate with the applicant's earnings disregarded under this paragraph exceed £20.

Amendment

1.   Amended by reg 29 of SI 2014 No 66 (W.6) as from 15.1.14.

---

10.   Where the applicant is engaged in one or more employments specified in paragraph 9(1) of this Schedule, but the applicant's earnings derived from such employments are less than £20 in any week and the applicant is also engaged in any other employment, so much of the applicant's earnings from that other employment, up to £5 if the applicant is a single applicant, or up to £10 if the applicant has a partner, as would not in aggregate with the amount of the applicant's earnings disregarded under paragraph 9 exceed £20.

11.   In a case to which none of the paragraphs 4 to 10 of this Schedule applies, £5.

12.–(1)   Where–

(a)   the applicant (or if the applicant is a member of a couple, at least one member of that couple) is a person to whom sub-paragraph (5) applies;

(b)   the Secretary of State is satisfied that that person is undertaking exempt work as defined in sub-paragraph (6); and

(c)   paragraph 14 of this Schedule does not apply,

the amount specified in sub-paragraph (7) ("the specified amount").

(2)   Where this paragraph applies, paragraphs 4 to 11 of this Schedule do not apply; but in any case where the applicant is a lone parent, and the specified amount would be less than the amount specified in paragraph 5, of this Schedule then paragraph 5 applies instead of this paragraph.

(3)   Notwithstanding paragraph 30 of this scheme (calculation of income and capital: applicant's family and polygamous marriages), if sub-paragraph (1) applies to one member of a couple ("A") it is not to apply to the other member of that couple ("B") except to the extent provided in sub-paragraph (4).

(4)   Where A's earnings are less than the specified amount, there is also to be disregarded so much of B's earnings as would not when aggregated with A's earnings exceed the specified amount; but the amount of B's earnings which may be disregarded under this sub-paragraph is limited to a maximum of £20 unless the Secretary of State is satisfied that B is also undertaking exempt work.

(5)   This sub-paragraph applies to a person who is–
(a)   in receipt of a contributory employment and support allowance;
(b)   in receipt of incapacity benefit;
(c)   in receipt of severe disablement allowance; or
(d)   being credited with earnings on the grounds of incapacity for work or limited capability for work under regulation 8B of the Social Security (Credits) Regulations 1975.
(6)   "Exempt work" ("gwaith esempt") means work of the kind described in–
(a)   regulation 45(2), (3) or (4) of the Employment and Support Allowance Regulations 2008 [¹ or regulation 39(1)(a), (b) or (c) of the Employment and Support Allowance Regulations 2013]; or (as the case may be)
(b)   regulation 17(2), (3) or (4) of the Social Security (Incapacity for Work) (General) Regulations 1995, and, in determining for the purposes of this paragraph whether an applicant or a member of a couple is undertaking any type of exempt work, it is immaterial whether that person or that person's partner is also undertaking other work.
(7)   The specified amount is the amount of money from time to time mentioned in any provision referred to in sub-paragraph (6) by virtue of which the work referred to in sub-paragraph (1) is exempt (or, where more than one such provision is relevant and those provisions mention different amounts of money, the highest of those amounts).

Amendment
1.   Amended by reg 30 of SI 2015 No 44 (W.3) as from 21.1.15, for schemes made for a financial year starting on or after 1.4.15.

---

13.   Any amount or the balance of any amount which would fall to be disregarded under paragraph23 or 24 of Schedule 7 had the applicant's income which does not consist of earnings been sufficient to entitle the applicant to the full disregard thereunder.
14.   Where an applicant is on income support, an income-based jobseeker's allowance or an income-related employment and support allowance, the applicant's earnings.
15.   Any earnings derived from employment which are payable in a country outside the United Kingdom for such period during which there is a prohibition against the transfer to the United Kingdom of those earnings.
16.   Where a payment of earnings is made in a currency other than Sterling, any banking charge or commission payable in converting that payment into Sterling.
17.   Any earnings of a child or young person.
18.–(1)   In a case where the applicant is a person who satisfies at least one of the conditions set out in sub-paragraph (2), and the applicant's net earnings equal or exceed the total of the amounts set out in sub-paragraph (3), the amount of the applicant's earnings that falls to be disregarded under paragraphs 4 to 12 of this Schedule is to be increased by £17.10.
(2)   The conditions of this sub-paragraph are that–
(a)   the applicant, or if the applicant is a member of a couple, either the applicant or the applicant's partner, is a person to whom regulation 20(1)(c) of the Working Tax Credit (Entitlement and Maximum Rate) Regulations 2002 applies; or
(b)   the applicant–
        (i)   is, or if the applicant is a member of a couple, at least one member of that couple is aged at least 25 and is engaged in remunerative work for on average not less than 30 hours per week; or
        (ii)   is a member of a couple and–
                (aa)   at least one member of that couple, is engaged in remunerative work for on average not less than 16 hours per week; and
                (bb)   the applicant's applicable amount includes a family premium under paragraph 4 of Schedule 3; or
        (iii)   is a lone parent who is engaged in remunerative work for on average not less than 16 hours per week; or
        [² (iv)   not being a member of a couple, is engaged in remunerative work for on average not less than 16 hours per week and–
                (aa)   the applicant's applicable amount includes a disability premium under paragraph 9 of Schedule 3 or the support component under paragraph 22 of Schedule 3; or
                (bb)   the applicant is a member of the work-related activity group; or
        (v)   is a member of a couple and at least one member of that couple is engaged in remunerative work for on average not less than 16 hours per week and that member of the couple–
                (aa)   satisfies the qualifying conditions for the disability premium under paragraph 9 of Schedule 3 or the support component under paragraph 22 of Schedule 3; or
                (bb)   is a member of the work-related activity group.]
(3)   The following are the amounts referred to in sub-paragraph (1)–
(a)   the amount calculated as disregardable from the applicant's earnings under paragraphs 4 to 12 of this Schedule;
(b)   the amount of child care charges calculated as deductible under paragraph 54(1)(c) of this scheme (calculation of income on a weekly basis: persons who are not pensioners); and

(c)   £17.10.

(4)   The provisions of paragraph 10 (remunerative work) of this scheme are to apply in determining whether or not a person works for on average not less than 30 hours per week, but as if the reference to 16 hours in sub-paragraph (1) of that paragraph were a reference to 30 hours.

Amendments

1.   Amended by reg 28(b) of SI 2018 No 14 (W.7) as from 10.1.18, for schemes made for a financial year starting on or after 1.4.18.

2.   Amended by reg 16 of SI 2019 No 11 (W.5) as from 9.1.19, for schemes made for a financial year starting on or after 1.4.19.

---

19.   In this Schedule "part-time employment" ("cyflogaeth ran-amser") means employment in which the person is engaged on average for less than 16 hours a week.

SCHEDULE 7
Sums disregarded in the calculation of income other than earnings: persons who are not pensioners

1.   Any payment made to the applicant in respect of any child care, travel or other expenses incurred, or to be incurred, by the applicant in respect of the applicant's participation in the Work for Your Benefit Pilot Scheme.

2.   Any payment made to the applicant in respect of any travel or other expenses incurred, or to be incurred, by the applicant in respect of the applicant's participation in the Mandatory Work Activity Scheme.

3.   Any payment made to the applicant in respect of any travel or other expenses incurred, or to be incurred, by the applicant in respect of the applicant's participation in the Employment, Skills and Enterprise Scheme.

4.   Any amount paid by way of tax on income which is to be taken into account under paragraph 51 of this scheme (calculation of income other than earnings: persons who are not pensioners).

5.   Any payment in respect of any expenses incurred or to be incurred by an applicant who is–

(a)   engaged by a charitable or voluntary organisation, or

(b)   a volunteer,

if that applicant otherwise derives no remuneration or profit from the employment and is not to be treated as possessing any earnings under paragraph 53(5) of this scheme (notional income: persons who are not pensioners).

6.   Any payment in respect of expenses arising out of the applicant's participation in a service user group.

7.   In the case of employment as an employed earner, any payment in respect of expenses wholly, exclusively and necessarily incurred in the performance of the duties of the employment.

8.   Where an applicant is on income support, an income-based jobseeker's allowance or an income-related employment and support allowance, the whole of the applicant's income.

9.   Where the applicant is a member of a joint-claim couple for the purposes of the Jobseekers Act 1995 and the applicant's partner is on an income-based jobseeker's allowance, the whole of the applicant's income.

10.   Where the applicant, or the person who was the partner of the applicant on 31st March 2003, was entitled on that date to income support or an income-based jobseeker's allowance but ceased to be so entitled on or before 5 April 2003 by virtue only of regulation 13 of the Housing Benefit (General) Amendment (No 3) Regulations 1999 as in force at that date, the whole of the applicant's income.

11.   Any disability living allowance, personal independence payment or AFIP.

12.   Any concessionary payment made to compensate for the non-payment of–

(a)   any payment specified in paragraph 11 or 14 of this Schedule;

(b)   income support;

(c)   an income-based jobseeker's allowance;

(d)   an income-related employment and support allowance.

13.   Any mobility supplement under article 20 of the Naval, Military and Air Forces Etc (Disablement and Death) Service Pensions Order 2006 (including such a supplement by virtue of any other scheme or order) or under article 25A of the Personal Injuries (Civilians) Scheme 1983 or any payment intended to compensate for the non-payment of such a supplement.

14.   Any attendance allowance.

15.   Any payment to the applicant as holder of the Victoria Cross or of the George Cross or any analogous payment.

16.–(1)   Any payment–

(a)   by way of an education maintenance allowance made pursuant to–

    (i)   regulations made under section 518 of the Education Act 1996(273) (payment of school expenses; grant of scholarships etc);

    (ii)   regulations made under section 49 or 73(f) of the Education (Scotland) Act 1980 (power to assist persons to take advantage of educational facilities);

     (iii)   directions made under section 73ZA of the Education (Scotland) Act 1980 and paid under section 12(2)(c) of the Further and Higher Education (Scotland) Act1992;

(b)   corresponding to such an education maintenance allowance, made pursuant to–

     (i)   section 14 or section 181 of the Education Act 2002 (power of Secretary of State and the Welsh Ministers to give financial assistance for purposes related to education or childcare, and allowances in respect of education or training); or

     (ii)   regulations made under section 181 of that Act; or

(c)   in England and Wales, by way of financial assistance made pursuant to section 14 of the Education Act 2002.

(2)   Any payment, other than a payment to which sub-paragraph (1) applies, made pursuant to–

(a)   regulations made under section 518 of the Education Act 1996;

(b)   regulations made under section 49 of the Education (Scotland) Act 1980; or

(c)   directions made under section 73ZA of the Education (Scotland) Act 1980 and paid under section 12(2)(c) of the Further and Higher Education (Scotland) Act 1992,

in respect of a course of study attended by a child or a young person or a person who is in receipt of an education maintenance allowance or other payment made pursuant to any provision specified in sub-paragraph (1).

17.   Any payment made to the applicant by way of a repayment under regulation 11(2) of the Education (Teacher Student Loans) (Repayment etc) Regulations 2003.

18.–(1)   Any payment made pursuant to section 2 of the Employment and Training Act 1973 or section 2 of the Enterprise and New Towns (Scotland) Act 1990 except a payment–

(a)   made as a substitute for income support, a jobseeker's allowance, incapacity benefit, severe disablement allowance or an employment and support allowance;

(b)   of an allowance referred to in section 2(3) of the Employment and Training Act 1973 or section 2(5) of the Enterprise and New Towns (Scotland) Act 1990; or

(c)   intended to meet the cost of living expenses which relate to any one or more of the items specified in sub-paragraph (2) whilst an applicant is participating in an education, training or other scheme to help the applicant enhance the applicant's employment prospects unless the payment is a Career Development Loan paid pursuant to section 2 of the 1973 Act and the period of education or training or the scheme, which is supported by that loan, has been completed.

(2)   The items specified in this sub-paragraph for the purposes of sub-paragraph (1)(c) are food, ordinary clothing or footwear, household fuel or rent of the applicant or, where the applicant is a member of a family, any other member of the applicant's family, or any council tax or water charges for which that applicant or member is liable.

19.–(1)   Subject to sub-paragraph (2), any of the following payments–

(a)   a charitable payment;

(b)   a voluntary payment;

(c)   a payment (not falling within paragraph (a) or (b) above) from a trust whose funds are derived from a payment made in consequence of any personal injury to the applicant;

(d)   a payment under an annuity purchased–

     (i)   pursuant to any agreement or court order to make payments to the applicant; or

     (ii)   from funds derived from a payment made,

    in consequence of any personal injury to the applicant; or

(e)   a payment (not falling within paragraphs (a) to (d)) received by virtue of any agreement or court order to make payments to the applicant in consequence of any personal injury to the applicant.

(2)   Sub-paragraph (1) is not to apply to a payment which is made or due to be made by–

(a)   a former partner of the applicant, or a former partner of any member of the applicant's family; or

(b)   the parent of a child or young person where that child or young person is a member of the applicant's family.

20.   Subject to paragraph 40 of this Schedule, £10 of any of the following, namely–

(a)   a war disablement pension (except insofar as such a pension falls to be disregarded under paragraph 13 or 14 of this Schedule);

(b)   a war widow's pension or war widower's pension;

(c)   a pension payable to a person as a widow, widower or surviving civil partner under any power of Her Majesty otherwise than under an enactment to make provision about pensions for or in respect of persons who have been disabled or have died in consequence of service as members of the armed forces of the Crown;

(d)   a guaranteed income payment and, if the amount of that payment has been abated to less than £10 by a pension or payment falling within article 39(1)(a) or (b) of the Armed Forces and Reserve Forces (Compensation Scheme) Order 2011, so much of that pension or payment as would not, in aggregate with the amount of any guaranteed income payment disregarded, exceed £10;

(e)   a payment made to compensate for the non-payment of such a pension or payment as is mentioned in any of the preceding sub-paragraphs;

(f)   a pension paid by the government of a country outside Great Britain which is analogous to any of the pensions or payments mentioned in paragraphs (a) to (d) above;

[¹ (g)   a pension paid by a government to victims of National Socialist persecution.]

Amendment
1.   Substituted by reg 29(a) of SI 2018 No 14 (W.7) as from 10.1.18, for schemes made for a financial year starting on or after 1.4.18.

21.   Subject to paragraph 40 of this Schedule, £15 of any–
(a)   widowed mother's allowance paid pursuant to section 37 of the SSCBA;
(b)   widowed parent's allowance paid pursuant to section 39A of the SSCBA.
22.–(1)   Any income derived from capital to which the applicant is or is treated under paragraph67 of this scheme (capital jointly held) as beneficially entitled but, subject to sub-paragraph (2), not income derived from capital disregarded under paragraphs 4, 5, 7, 11, 17 or 30 to 33 of Schedule 9.
(2)   Income derived from capital disregarded under paragraphs 5, 7 or 30 to 33 of Schedule 9 but only to the extent of–
(a)   any mortgage repayments made in respect of the dwelling or premises in the period during which that income accrued; or
(b)   any council tax or water charges which the applicant is liable to pay in respect of the dwelling or premises and which are paid in the period during which that income accrued.
(3)   The definition of "water charges" ("taliadau dwr") in paragraph 2(1) of this scheme applies to sub-paragraph (2) of this paragraph with the omission of the words "in so far as such charges are in respect of the dwelling which a person occupies as that person's home".
23.   Where the applicant makes a parental contribution in respect of a student attending a course at an establishment in the United Kingdom or undergoing education in the United Kingdom, which contribution has been assessed for the purposes of calculating–
(a)   under, or pursuant to regulations made under powers conferred by section 22 of the Teaching and Higher Education Act 1998, that student's award;
(b)   under regulations made in exercise of the powers conferred by section 49 of the Education (Scotland) Act 1980, that student's bursary, scholarship, or other allowance under that section or under regulations made in exercise of the powers conferred by section 73 of that Act of 1980, any payment to that student under that section; or
(c)   the student's student loan,
an amount equal to the weekly amount of that parental contribution, but only in respect of the period for which that contribution is assessed as being payable.
24.–(1)   Where the applicant is the parent of a student aged under 25 in advanced education who either–
(a)   is not in receipt of any award, grant or student loan in respect of that education; or
(b)   is in receipt of an award bestowed by virtue of the Teaching and Higher Education Act 1998, or regulations made thereunder, or a bursary, scholarship or other allowance under section 49(1) of the Education (Scotland) Act 1980, or a payment under section 73 of that Act of 1980,
and the applicant makes payments by way of a contribution towards the student's maintenance, other than a parental contribution falling within paragraph 23 of this Schedule, an amount specified in sub-paragraph (2) in respect of each week during the student's term.
(2)   For the purposes of sub-paragraph (1), the amount is to be equal to–
(a)   the weekly amount of the payments; or
(b)   the amount by way of a personal allowance for a single applicant under 25 less the weekly amount of any award, bursary, scholarship, allowance or payment referred to in sub-paragraph (1)(b),
whichever is less.
25.   Any payment made to the applicant by a child or young person or a non-dependant.
26.   Where the applicant occupies a dwelling as the applicant's home and the dwelling is also occupied by a person other than one to whom paragraph 25 or 27 of this Schedule refers and there is a contractual liability to make payments to the applicant in respect of the occupation of the dwelling by that person or a member of that person's family–
(a)   where the aggregate of any payments made in respect of any one week in respect of the occupation of the dwelling by that person or a member of that person's family, or by that person and a member of that person's family, is less than £20, the whole of that amount; or
(b)   where the aggregate of any such payments is £20 or more per week, £20.
27.   Where the applicant occupies a dwelling as the applicant's home and the applicant provides in that dwelling board and lodging accommodation, an amount, in respect of each person for which such accommodation is provided for the whole or any part of a week, equal to–
(a)   where the aggregate of any payments made in respect of any one week in respect of such accommodation provided to such person does not exceed £20, 100 per cent of such payments;
(b)   where the aggregate of any such payments exceeds £20, £20 and 50 per cent of the excess over £20.
28.–(1)   Any income in kind, except where paragraph 51(10)(b) of this scheme (provision of support under section 95 or 98 of the Immigration and Asylum Act 1999 in the calculation of income other than earnings) applies.
(2)   The reference in sub-paragraph (1) to "income in kind" ("incwm mewn nwyddau neu wasanaethau") does not include a payment to a third party made in respect of the applicant which is used by the third party to provide benefits in kind to the applicant.
29.   Any income which is payable in a country outside the United Kingdom for such period during which there is a prohibition against the transfer to the United Kingdom of that income.

30.–(1) Any payment made to the applicant in respect of a person who is a member of the applicant's family–

(a) pursuant to regulations under section 2(6)(b), 3 or 4 of the Adoption and Children Act 2002 or in accordance with a scheme approved by the Scottish Ministers under section 71 of the Adoption and Children (Scotland) Act 2007 (adoption allowances schemes);

(b) which is a payment made by a local authority in pursuance of section 15(1) of, and paragraph 15 of Schedule 1 to, the Children Act 1989 (local authority contribution to a child's maintenance where the child is living with a person as a result of a [¹child arrangements] order) or in Scotland section 50 of the Children Act 1975 (payments towards maintenance of children);

(c) which is a payment made by an authority, as defined in Article 2 of the Children (Northern Ireland) Order 1995, in pursuance of Article 15 of, and paragraph 17 of Schedule 1 to, that Order (contribution by an authority to child's maintenance);

(d) in accordance with regulations made pursuant to section 14F of the Children Act 1989 (special guardianship support services);

(2) Any payment, other than a payment to which sub-paragraph (1)(a) applies, made to the applicant pursuant to regulations under section 2(6)(b), 3 or 4 of the Adoption and Children Act 2002.

Amendment

1. Amended by art 26 of SI 2014 No 852 as from 22.4.14.

31. Any payment made to the applicant with whom a person is accommodated by virtue of arrangements made–

(a) by a local authority under–
   (i) section 23(2)(a) [¹ or 22C] of the Children Act 1989 (provision of accommodation and maintenance for a child whom they are looking after);
   (ii) section 26 of the Children (Scotland) Act 1995 (manner of provision of accommodation to child looked after by local authority); [¹]
   (iii) regulations 33 or 51 of the Looked After Children (Scotland) Regulations 2009 (fostering and kinship care allowances and fostering allowances); [¹
   (iv) section 81 of the Social Services and Well-being (Wales) Act 2014; or]

(b) by a voluntary organisation under section 59(1)(a) of the Children Act 1989 (provision of accommodation by voluntary organisations).

Amendment

1. Amended by reg 29(a) of SI 2016 No 50 (W.21) as from 20.1.16, for schemes made for a financial year starting on or after 1.4.16.

32. Any payment made to the applicant or the applicant's partner for a person ("the person concerned"), who is not normally a member of the applicant's household but is temporarily in the applicant's care, by–

(a) a health authority;

(b) a local authority but excluding payments of housing benefit made in respect of the person concerned;

(c) a voluntary organisation;

(d) the person concerned pursuant to section 26(3A) of the National Assistance Act 1948;

(e) a primary care trust established under section 16A of the National Health Service Act 1977 or established by an order made under [¹ section 18(2)(c)] of the National Health Service Act 2006; [²]

(f) a Local Health Board established under section 11 of the National Health Service (Wales) Act 2006 [² ;

(g) the person concerned where the payment is for the provision of accommodation to meet that person's needs for care and support arranged pursuant to section 35 or 36 of the Social Services and Well-being (Wales) Act 2014; or

(h) the person concerned where the payment is for the provision of accommodation to meet that person's needs for care and support arranged pursuant to section 18 or 19 of the Care Act 2014.]

Amendments

1. Amended by reg 30(a) of SI 2014 No 66 (W.6) as from 15.1.14.

2. Amended by reg 29(b) of SI 2016 No 50 (W.21) as from 20.1.16, for schemes made for a financial year starting on or after 1.4.16.

[¹**33.** Any payment made by a local authority in accordance with–

(a) section 17, 23B, 23C or 24A of the Children Act 1989;

(b) section 12 of the Social Work (Scotland) Act 1968;

(c) section 22, 29 or 30 of the Children (Scotland) Act 1995; or

(d) section 37, 38, 109, 100 or 114 of the Social Services and Well-being (Wales) Act 2014, but excluding any direct payments under that Act.]

Amendment
1. Substituted by reg 29(c) of SI 2016 No 50 (W.21) as from 20.1.16, for schemes made for a financial year starting on or after 1.4.16.

34.–[¹ (1) Subject to sub-paragraph (2), any payment (or part payment) made by a local authority to a person ("A") which A passes on to the applicant, where the payment is made in accordance with–
(a) section 23C of the Children Act 1989;
(b) section 29 of the Children (Scotland) Act 1995; or
(c) section 110 of the Social Services and Well-being (Wales) Act 2014.]
(2) Sub-paragraph (1) applies only where A–
(a) was formerly in the applicant's care, and
(b) is aged 18 or over, and
(c) continues to live with the applicant.

Amendment
1. Substituted by reg 29(d) of SI 2016 No 50 (W.21) as from 20.1.16, for schemes made for a financial year starting on or after 1.4.16.

35.–(1) Subject to sub-paragraph (2), any payment received under an insurance policy taken out to insure against the risk of being unable to maintain repayments–
(a) on a loan which is secured on the dwelling which the applicant occupies as the applicant's home; or
(b) under a regulated agreement as defined for the purposes of the Consumer Credit Act 1974 or under a hire purchase agreement or a conditional sale agreement as defined for the purposes of Part 3 of the Hire-Purchase Act 1964.
(2) A payment referred to in sub-paragraph (1) is only to be disregarded to the extent that the payment received under that policy does not exceed the amounts, calculated on a weekly basis, which are used to–
(a) maintain the repayments referred to in sub-paragraph (1)(a) or, as the case may be, (1)(b); and
(b) meet any amount due by way of premiums on–
   (i) that policy; or
   (ii) in a case to which sub-paragraph (1)(a) applies, an insurance policy taken out to insure against loss or damage to any building or part of a building which is occupied by the applicant as the applicant's home and which is required as a condition of the loan referred to in sub-paragraph (1)(a).

36. Any payment of income which by virtue of paragraph 61 of this scheme (income treated as capital: persons who are not pensioners) is to be treated as capital.

37. Any–
(a) social fund payment made pursuant to Part 8 of the SSCBA (the social fund); or
(b) occasional assistance.

38. Any payment under Part 10 of the SSCBA (Christmas bonus for pensioners).

39. Where a payment of income is made in a currency other than sterling, any banking charge or commission payable in converting that payment into sterling.

40. The total of an applicant's income or, if the applicant is a member of a family, the family's income and the income of any person which that applicant is treated as possessing under paragraph 30(3) (calculation of income and capital: applicant's family and polygamous marriages) to be disregarded under paragraph 74(2)(b) and paragraph 75(1)(d) of this scheme (calculation of covenant income where a contribution assessed, covenant income where no grant income or no contribution is assessed), paragraph 78(2) of this scheme (treatment of student loans), [¹ paragraph 80(3)] of this scheme (treatment of payments from access funds) and paragraphs 20 and 21 of this Schedule is in no case to exceed £20 per week.

Amendment
1. Amended by reg 30(b) of SI 2014 No 66 (W.6) as from 15.1.14.

41.–(1) Any payment made under or by any of the Trusts, the Fund, the Eileen Trust, MFET Limited, the Skipton Fund, the Caxton Foundation [¹, an approved blood scheme, the Scottish Infected Blood Support Scheme, the London Emergencies Trust, the We Love Manchester Emergency Fund] or the Independent Living Fund (2006).
(2) Any payment by or on behalf of a person who is suffering or who suffered from haemophilia or who is or was a qualifying person, which derives from a payment made under or by any of the Trusts to which sub-paragraph (1) refers and which is made to or for the benefit of–
(a) that person's partner or former partner from whom that person is not, or where that person has died was not, estranged or divorced or with whom that person has formed a civil partnership that has not been dissolved or, where that person has died, had not been dissolved at the time of that person's death;
(b) any child who is a member of that person's family or who was such a member and who is a member of the applicant's family; or

(c)   any young person who is a member of that person's family or who was such a member and who is a member of the applicant's family.

(3)   Any payment by or on behalf of the partner or former partner of a person who is suffering or who suffered from haemophilia or who is or was a qualifying person provided that the partner or former partner and that person are not, or if either of them has died were not, estranged or divorced or, where the partner or former partner and that person have formed a civil partnership, the civil partnership has not been dissolved or, if either of them has died, had not been dissolved at the time of the death, which derives from a payment made under or by any of the Trusts to which sub-paragraph (1) refers and which is made to or for the benefit of–

(a)   the person who is suffering from haemophilia or who is a qualifying person;

(b)   any child who is a member of that person's family or who was such a member and who is a member of the applicant's family; or

(c)   any young person who is a member of that person's family or who was such a member and who is a member of the applicant's family.

(4)   Any payment by a person who is suffering from haemophilia or who is a qualifying person, which derives from a payment under or by any of the Trusts to which sub-paragraph (1) refers, where–

(a)   that person has no partner or former partner from whom that person is not estranged or divorced or with whom that person has formed a civil partnership that has not been dissolved, nor any child or young person who is or had been a member of that person's family; and

(b)   the payment is made either–

      (i)   to that person's parent or step-parent, or

      (ii)   where that person at the date of the payment is a child, a young person or a student who has not completed full-time education and has no parent or step-parent, to the child or young person's parent or that student's guardian,

but only for a period from the date of the payment until the end of two years from that person's death.

(5)   Any payment out of the estate of a person who suffered from haemophilia or who was a qualifying person, which derives from a payment under or by any of the Trusts to which sub-paragraph (1) refers, where–

(a)   that person at the date of that person's death (the relevant date) had no partner or former partner from whom that person was not estranged or divorced or with whom that person has formed a civil partnership that has not been dissolved, nor any child or young person who was or had been a member of that person's family; and

(b)   the payment is made either–

      (i)   to that person's parent or step-parent, or

      (ii)   where that person at the relevant date was a child, a young person or a student who had not completed full-time education and had no parent or step-parent, to that child or young person's parent or that student's guardian,

but only for a period of two years from the relevant date.

(6)   In the case of a person to whom or for whose benefit a payment referred to in this paragraph is made, any income which derives from any payment of income or capital made under or deriving from any of the Trusts.

(7)   For the purposes of sub-paragraphs (2) to (6), any reference to the Trusts is to be construed as including a reference to the Fund, the Eileen Trust, MFET Limited, the Skipton Fund, the Caxton Foundation [¹, an approved blood scheme, the Scottish Infected Blood Support Scheme, the London Emergencies Trust, the We Love Manchester Emergency Fund] and the London Bombings Relief Charitable Fund.

Amendment

1.   Amended by reg 29(b) of SI 2018 No 14 (W.7) as from 10.1.18, for schemes made for a financial year starting on or after 1.4.18.

---

42.   Any housing benefit.

43.   Any payment made by the Secretary of State to compensate for the loss (in whole or in part) of entitlement to housing benefit.

44.   Any payment to a juror or witness in respect of attendance at a court other than compensation for loss of earnings or for the loss of a benefit payable under the benefit Acts.

45.   Any payment in consequence of a reduction of council tax under section 13A(1)(c) of the 1992 Act (reduction of liability for council tax).

46.–(1)   Any payment or repayment made–

(a)   as respects England, under regulation 5, 6 or 12 of the National Health Service (Travel Expenses and Remission of Charges) Regulations 2003 (travelling expenses and health service supplies);

(b)   as respects Wales, under regulation 5, 6 or 11 of the National Health Service (Travelling Expenses and Remission of Charges) (Wales) Regulations 2007 (travelling expenses and health service supplies);

(c)   as respects Scotland, under regulation 3, 5 or 11 of the National Health Service (Travelling Expenses and Remission of Charges) (Scotland) (No 2) Regulations 2003 (travelling expenses and health service supplies).

(2)   Any payment or repayment made by the Secretary of State for Health [¹ and Social Care], the Scottish Ministers or the Welsh Ministers which is analogous to a payment or repayment mentioned in sub-paragraph (1).

Amendment

1.   Amended by reg 17(a) of SI 2019 No 11 (W.5) as from 9.1.19, for schemes made for a financial year starting on or after 1.4.19.

---

47.   Any payment made to such persons entitled to receive benefits as may be determined by or under a scheme made pursuant to section 13 of the Social Security Act 1988 in lieu of vouchers or similar arrangements in connection with the provision of those benefits (including payments made in place of healthy start vouchers, milk tokens or the supply of vitamins).

48.   Any payment made by either the Secretary of State for Justice or by the Scottish Ministers under a scheme established to assist relatives and other persons to visit persons in custody.

49.–(1)   Where an applicant's applicable amount includes an amount by way of family premium,£15 of any payment of maintenance, other than child maintenance, whether under a court order or not, which is made or due to be made by the applicant's former partner, or the applicant's partner's former partner.

(2)   For the purpose of sub-paragraph (1) where more than one maintenance payment falls to be taken into account in any week, all such payments are to be aggregated and treated as if they were a single payment.

(3)   A payment made by the Secretary of State in lieu of maintenance is, for the purpose of sub-paragraph (1), to be treated as a payment of maintenance made by a person specified in sub-paragraph (1).

50.–(1)   Any payment of child maintenance made or derived from a liable relative where the child or young person in respect of whom the payment is made is a member of the applicant's family, except where the person making the payment is the applicant or the applicant's partner.

(2)   In sub-paragraph (1)–

"child maintenance" ("cynhaliaeth plant") means any payment towards the maintenance of a child or young person, including any payment made voluntarily and payments made under–

(a)   the Child Support Act 1991;

(b)   the Child Support (Northern Ireland) Order 1991;

(c)   a court order;

(d)   a consent order;

(e)   a maintenance agreement registered for execution in the Books of Council and Session or the sheriff court books;

"liable relative" ("perthynas atebol") means a person listed in regulation 54 (interpretation) of the Income Support (General) Regulations 1987, other than a person falling within sub-paragraph (d) of that definition.

51.   Any payment (other than a training allowance) made, whether by the Secretary of State or any other person, under the Disabled Persons (Employment) Act 1944 to assist disabled persons to obtain or retain employment despite their disability.

52.   Any guardian's allowance.

53.–(1)   If the applicant is in receipt of any benefit under Part 2, 3 or 5 of the SSCBA, any increase in the rate of that benefit arising under Part 4 (increases for dependants) or section 106(a) (unemployability supplement) of that Act, where the dependant in respect of whom the increase is paid is not a member of the applicant's family.

(2)   If the applicant is in receipt of any pension or allowance under Part 2 or 3 of the Naval, Military and Air Forces Etc (Disablement and Death) Service Pensions Order 2006, any increase in the rate of that pension or allowance under that Order, where the dependant in respect of whom the increase is paid is not a member of the applicant's family.

54.   Any supplementary pension under article 23(2) of the Naval, Military and Air Forces Etc (Disablement and Death) Service Pensions Order 2006 (pensions to surviving spouses and surviving civil partners) and any analogous payment made by the Secretary of State for Defence to any person who is not a person entitled under that Order.

55.   In the case of a pension awarded at the supplementary rate under article 27(3) of the Personal Injuries (Civilians) Scheme 1983 (pensions to surviving spouses and surviving civil partners), the sum specified in paragraph 1(c) of Schedule 4 to that Scheme.

56.–(1)   Any payment which is–

(a)   made under any of the Dispensing Instruments to a widow, widower or surviving civil partner of a person–

(i)   whose death was attributable to service in a capacity analogous to service as a member of the armed forces of the Crown; and

(ii)   whose service in such capacity terminated before 31 March 1973; and

(b)   equal to the amount specified in article 23(2) of the Naval, Military and Air Forces Etc (Disablement and Death) Service Pensions Order 2006.

(2)   In this paragraph "the Dispensing Instruments" ("yr Offerynnau Dosbarthu") means the Order in Council of 19 December 1881, the Royal Warrant of 27 October 1884 and the Order by His Majesty of 14 January 1922 (exceptional grants of pay, non-effective pay and allowances).

57.   Any reduction under this scheme to which the applicant is entitled.

58.   Except in a case which falls under sub-paragraph (1) of paragraph 18 of Schedule 6, where the applicant is a person who satisfies any of the conditions of sub-paragraph (2) of that paragraph, any amount of working tax credit up to £17.10.

[²**59.**   Any payment made–
(a)   as a direct payment as defined in section 4(2) of the Social Care (Self-directed Support) (Scotland) Act 2013;
(b)   under sections 12A to 12D of the National Health Service Act 2006 (direct payments for health care);
(c)   under regulations made under section 57 of the Health and Social Care Act 2001 (direct payments);
(d)   under regulations made under sections 50 to 53 of the Social Services and Well-being (Wales) Act 2014 (direct payments); or
(e)   under regulations made under section 33 of the Care Act 2014 (direct payments).]

Amendments
1.   Amended by Art 2 and Sch para 26(2) of SI 2014 No 513 as from 1.4.14.
2.   Substituted by reg 29(e) of SI 2016 No 50 (W.21) as from 20.1.16, for schemes made for a financial year starting on or after 1.4.16.

60.–(1)   Subject to sub-paragraph (2), in respect of a person who is receiving, or who has received, assistance under the self-employment route, any payment to that person–
(a)   to meet expenses wholly and necessarily incurred whilst carrying on the commercial activity;
(b)   which is used or intended to be used to maintain repayments on a loan taken out by that person for the purpose of establishing or carrying on the commercial activity,
(c)   in respect of which such assistance is or was received.
(2)   Sub-paragraph (1) is to apply only in respect of payments which are paid to that person from the special account.

61.–(1)   Any payment of a sports award except to the extent that it has been made in respect of any one or more of the items specified in sub-paragraph (2).
(2)   The items specified for the purposes of sub-paragraph (1) are food, ordinary clothing or footwear, household fuel or rent of the applicant or where the applicant is a member of a family, any other member of the applicant's family, or any council tax or water charges for which that applicant or member is liable.
(3)   For the purposes of sub-paragraph (2) "food" ("bwyd") does not include vitamins, minerals or other special dietary supplements intended to enhance the performance of the person in the sport in respect of which the award was made.

62.   Where the amount of subsistence allowance paid to a person in a reduction week exceeds the amount of income-based jobseeker's allowance that person would have received in that reduction week had it been payable to that person, less 50p, that excess amount.

63.   In the case of an applicant participating in an employment zone programme, any discretionary payment made by an employment zone contractor to the applicant, being a fee, grant, loan or otherwise.

64.   Any discretionary housing payment paid pursuant to regulation 2(1) of the Discretionary Financial Assistance Regulations 2001.

65.   Any payment made by a local authority or by the Welsh Ministers, to or on behalf of the applicant or the applicant's partner relating to a service which is provided to develop or sustain the capacity of the applicant or the applicant's partner to live independently in the applicant's accommodation.

66.   Any payment of child benefit.

[¹**67.**   Any bereavement support payment under section 30 of the Pensions Act 2014 (bereavement support payment) except any such payment which is disregarded as capital under paragraph 12(1)(h) of Schedule 9 or paragraph 65 of Schedule 9.]

Amendment
1.   Inserted by reg 17(b) of SI 2019 No 11 (W.5) as from 9.1.19, for schemes made for a financial year starting on or after 1.4.19.

SCHEDULE 8
Capital disregards: pensioners

PART 1
Capital to be disregarded

1.   Any premises acquired for occupation by the applicant which the applicant intends to occupy as the applicant's home within 26 weeks of the date of acquisition or such longer period as is reasonable in the circumstances to enable the applicant to obtain possession and commence occupation of the premises.

2.   Any premises which the applicant intends to occupy as the applicant's home, and in respect of which the applicant is taking steps to obtain possession and has sought legal advice, or has commenced legal proceedings, with a view to obtaining possession, for a period of 26 weeks from the date on which the applicant first sought such advice or first commenced such proceedings whichever is the earlier, or such longer period as is reasonable in the circumstances to enable the applicant to obtain possession and commence occupation of those premises.

3.   Any premises which the applicant intends to occupy as the applicant's home to which essential repairs or alterations are required in order to render the premises fit for such occupation, for a period of 26 weeks from the date on which the applicant first takes steps to effect those repairs or alterations, or such longer period as is necessary to enable those repairs or alterations to be carried out.

4.   Any premises occupied in whole or in part–

(a)   by a person who is a relative of the applicant or the applicant's partner as that person's home where that person has attained the qualifying age for state pension credit or is incapacitated;

(b)   by the former partner of the applicant as that person's home; but this provision is not to apply where the former partner is a person from whom the applicant is estranged or divorced or with whom the applicant had formed a civil partnership that has been dissolved.

5.   Any future interest in property of any kind, other than land or premises in respect of which the applicant has granted a subsisting lease or tenancy, including sub-leases or sub-tenancies.

6.   Where an applicant has ceased to occupy what was formerly the dwelling occupied as the home following the applicant's estrangement or divorce from the applicant's former partner or the dissolution of a civil partnership with the applicant's former partner, that dwelling for a period of 26 weeks from the date on which the applicant ceased to occupy that dwelling or, where the dwelling is occupied as the home by the former partner who is a lone parent, for so long as it is so occupied.

7.   Any premises where the applicant is taking reasonable steps to dispose of the whole of the applicant's interest in those premises, for a period of 26 weeks from the date on which the applicant first took such steps, or such longer period as is reasonable in the circumstances to enable the applicant to dispose of those premises.

8.   All personal possessions.

9.   The assets of any business owned in whole or in part by the applicant and for the purposes of which the applicant is engaged as a self-employed earner or, if the applicant has ceased to be so engaged, for such period as may be reasonable in the circumstances to allow for disposal of those assets.

10.   The assets of any business owned in whole or in part by the applicant if–

(a)   the applicant is not engaged as a self-employed earner in that business by reason of some disease or bodily or mental disablement; but

(b)   the applicant intends to become engaged (or, as the case may be, re-engaged) as a self-employed earner in that business as soon as the applicant recovers or is able to become engaged, or re-engaged, in that business,

for a period of 26 weeks from the date on which the application for a reduction under this scheme is made or, if it is unreasonable to expect the applicant to become engaged or re-engaged in that business within that period, for such longer period as is reasonable in the circumstances to enable the applicant to become so engaged or re-engaged.

11.   The surrender value of any policy of life insurance.

12.   The value of any funeral plan contract; and for this purpose, "funeral plan contract" ("contract cynllun angladd ") means a contract under which–

(a)   the applicant makes one or more payments to another person ("the provider");

(b)   the provider undertakes to provide, or secure the provision of, a funeral in the United Kingdom for the applicant on the applicant's death; and

(c)   the sole purpose of the plan is to provide or secure the provision of a funeral for the applicant on the applicant's death.

13.   Where an ex-gratia payment has been made by the Secretary of State on or after 1 February 2001 in consequence of the imprisonment or internment of–

(a)   the applicant;

(b)   the applicant's partner;

(c)   the applicant's deceased spouse or deceased civil partner; or

(d)   the applicant's partner's deceased spouse or deceased civil partner,

by the Japanese during the Second World War, an amount equal to that payment.

14.–(1)   Subject to sub-paragraph (2), the amount of any trust payment made to an applicant or an applicant's partner who is–

(a)   a diagnosed person;

(b)   a diagnosed person's partner or was a diagnosed person's partner at the time of the diagnosed person's death; or

(c)   a parent of a diagnosed person, a person acting in place of the diagnosed person's parents or a person who was so acting at the date of the diagnosed person's death.

(2)   Where a trust payment is made to–

(a)   a person referred to in sub-paragraph (1)(a) or (b), that sub-paragraph is to apply for the period beginning on the date on which the trust payment is made and ending on the date on which that person dies;

(b)   a person referred to in sub-paragraph (1)(c), that sub-paragraph is to apply for the period beginning on the date on which the trust payment is made and ending two years after that date.

(3)　Subject to sub-paragraph (4), the amount of any payment by a person to whom a trust payment has been made or of any payment out of the estate of a person to whom a trust payment has been made, which is made to an applicant or an applicant's partner who is–

(a)　the diagnosed person;

(b)　a diagnosed person's partner or was a diagnosed person's partner at the date of the diagnosed person's death; or

(c)　a parent of a diagnosed person, a person acting in place of the diagnosed person's parents or a person who was so acting at the date of the diagnosed person's death.

(4)　Where a payment such as referred to in sub-paragraph (3) is made to–

(a)　a person referred to in sub-paragraph (3)(a) or (b), that sub-paragraph is to apply for the period beginning on the date on which the payment is made and ending on the date on which that person dies;

(b)　a person referred to in sub-paragraph (3)(c), that sub-paragraph is to apply for the period beginning on the date on which the payment is made and ending two years after that date.

(5)　In this paragraph, a reference to a person–

(a)　being the diagnosed person's partner;

(b)　acting in place of the diagnosed person's parents,

at the date of the diagnosed person's death is to include a person who would have been such a person or a person who would have been so acting, but for the diagnosed person residing in a care home or an independent hospital.

(6)　In this paragraph–

"diagnosed person" ("person â diagnosis") means a person who has been diagnosed as suffering from, or who, after that person's death, has been diagnosed as having suffered from, variant Creutzfeldt-Jakob disease;

"relevant trust" ("ymddiriedolaeth berthnasol") means a trust established out of funds provided by the Secretary of State in respect of persons who suffered, or who are suffering, from variant Creutzfeldt-Jakob disease for the benefit of persons eligible for payments in accordance with its provisions;

"trust payment" ("taliad ymddiriedolaeth") means a payment under a relevant trust.

15.　The amount of any payment, other than a war pension, to compensate for the fact that the applicant, the applicant's partner, the applicant's deceased spouse or civil partner or the applicant's partner's deceased spouse or civil partner–

(a)　was a slave labourer or a forced labourer;

(b)　had suffered property loss or had suffered personal injury; or

(c)　was a parent of a child who had died,

during the Second World War.

16.–(1)　Any payment made under or by–

(a)　the Trusts, the Fund, the Eileen Trust, MFET Limited, the Skipton Fund, the Caxton Foundation, [¹ an approved blood scheme, the Scottish Infected Blood Support Scheme, the London Emergencies Trust, the We Love Manchester Emergency Fund] or the London Bombings Relief Charitable Fund (collectively referred to in this paragraph as "the Trusts"); or

(b)　the Independent Living Fund (2006).

(2)　Any payment by or on behalf of a person who is suffering or who suffered from haemophilia or who is or was a qualifying person, which derives from a payment made under or by any of the Trusts and which is made to or for the benefit of that person's partner or former partner–

(a)　from whom that person is not, or where that person has died was not, estranged or divorced; or

(b)　with whom that person has formed a civil partnership that has not been dissolved or, where that person has died, had not been dissolved at the time of that person's death.

(3)　Any payment by or on behalf of the partner or former partner of a person who is suffering or who suffered from haemophilia or who is or was a qualifying person which derives from a payment made under or by any of the Trusts and which is made to or for the benefit of the person who is suffering from haemophilia or who is a qualifying person.

(4)　Sub-paragraph (3) does not apply if–

(a)　the partner or former partner and that person are not, or if either of them has died were not, estranged or divorced; or

(b)　where the partner or former partner and that person have formed a civil partnership, the civil partnership has not been dissolved or, if either of them has died, had not been dissolved at the time of the death.

(5)　Any payment by a person who is suffering from haemophilia or who is a qualifying person, which derives from a payment under or by any of the Trusts, where–

(a)　that person has no partner or former partner from whom that person is not estranged or divorced or with whom that person has formed a civil partnership that has not been dissolved, nor any child who is or had been a member of that person's household; and

(b)　the payment is made either–

(i)　to that person's parent or step-parent; or

(ii)　where that person at the date of the payment is a child or a student who has not completed full-time education and has no parent or step-parent, to any person standing in the place of that child or young person's parent or that student's parent, but only for a period from the date of the payment until the end of two years from that person's death.

(6)   Any payment out of the estate of a person who suffered from haemophilia or who was a qualifying person, which derives from a payment under or by any of the Trusts, where–

(a)   that person at the date of that person's death ("the relevant date") had no partner or former partner from whom that person was not estranged or divorced or with whom that person had formed a civil partnership that had not been dissolved, nor any child who was or had been a member of that person's household; and

(b)   the payment is made either–

(i)   to that person's parent or step-parent; or

(ii)   where that person at the relevant date was a child or a student who had not completed full-time education and had no parent or step-parent, to any person standing in place of that child or young person's parent or that student's parent,

but only for a period of two years from the relevant date.

(7)   In the case of a person to whom or for whose benefit a payment referred to in this paragraph is made, any capital resource which derives from any payment of income or capital made under or deriving from any of the Trusts.

Amendment

1.   Amended by reg 30(a) of SI 2018 No 14 (W.7) as from 10.1.18, for schemes made for a financial year starting on or after 1.4.18.

17.–(1)   An amount equal to the amount of any payment made in consequence of any personal injury to the applicant or, if the applicant has a partner, to the partner.

(2)   Where the whole or part of the payment is administered–

(a)   by the High Court or the County Court under Rule 21.11(1) of the Civil Procedure Rules 1998, or the Court of Protection, or on behalf of a person where the payment can only be disposed of by order or direction of any such court;

(b)   in accordance with an order made under Rule 36.14 of the Ordinary Cause Rules 1993 or under Rule 128 of those Rules; or

(c)   in accordance with the terms of a trust established for the benefit of the applicant or the applicant's partner,

(d)   the whole of the amount so administered.

18.   Any amount specified in paragraph 19, 20, 21 or 25 of this Schedule for a period of one year beginning with the date of receipt.

19.   Amounts paid under a policy of insurance in connection with the loss of or damage to the property occupied by the applicant as the applicant's home and to the applicant's personal possessions.

20.   So much of any amounts paid to the applicant or deposited in the applicant's name for the sole purpose of–

(a)   purchasing premises which the applicant intends to occupy as the applicant's home; or

(b)   effecting essential repairs or alterations to the premises occupied or intended to be occupied by the applicant as the applicant's home.

21.–(1)   Subject to paragraph 22 of this Schedule any amount paid–

(a)   by way of arrears of benefit;

(b)   by way of compensation for the late payment of benefit;

(c)   in lieu of the payment of benefit;

(d)   to rectify, or compensate for, an official error, as defined for the purposes of paragraph 22, being an amount to which that paragraph does not apply;

(e)   by a local authority out of funds provided under either section 93 of the Local Government Act 2000 under a scheme known as "Supporting People" or section 91 of the Housing (Scotland) Act 2001 [¹;]

[¹ (f)   by way of occasional assistance including arrears and payments in lieu of occasional assistance.]

(2)   In sub-paragraph (1), "benefit" ("budd-dal") means–

(a)   attendance allowance under section 64 of the SSCBA;

(b)   disability living allowance;

(c)   personal independence payment;

(d)   an AFIP;

(e)   income support;

(f)   income-based jobseeker's allowance;

(g)   state pension credit;

(h)   housing benefit;

(i)   council tax benefit;

(j)   child tax credit;

(k)   an increase of a disablement pension under section 104 of the SSCBA (increase where constant attendance is needed), and any further increase of such a pension under section 105 of the SSCBA (increase for exceptionally severe disablement);

(l)   any amount included on account of the applicant's exceptionally severe disablement or need for constant attendance in a war disablement pension or a war widow's or widower's pension;

(m) any discretionary housing payment paid pursuant to regulation 2(1) of the Discretionary Financial Assistance Regulations 2001;

(n) working tax credit; [¹]

(o) income-related employment and support allowance [¹;]

[¹ (p) fund payments under Part 8 of the SSCBA; [²]]

[¹ (q) universal credit][² ; or

(r) bereavement support payment under section 30 of the Pensions Act 2014.]

Amendments

1. Amended by reg 31(a) of SI 2014 No 66 (W.6) as from 15.1.14.

2. Amended by reg 18(a) of SI 2019 No 11 (W.5) as from 9.1.19, for schemes made for a financial year starting on or after 1.4.19.

22.–(1)   Subject to sub-paragraph (3), any payment of £5,000 or more which has been made to rectify, or to compensate for, an official error relating to a relevant benefit and which has been received by the applicant in full on or after the day on which the applicant became entitled to a reduction under this scheme.

(2)   Subject to sub-paragraph (3), the total amount of any payments disregarded under–

(a) paragraph 7(2) of Schedule 10 to the Income Support (General) Regulations 1987;

(b) paragraph 12(2) of Schedule 8 to the Jobseeker's Allowance Regulations 1996;

(c) paragraph 9(2) of Schedule 5 to the Council Tax Benefit Regulations 2006;

(d) paragraph 20A of Schedule 5 to the State Pension Credit Regulations 2002 [¹;]

(e) paragraph 11(2) of Schedule 9 to the Employment and Support Allowance Regulations 2008 [¹;]

[¹ (f) paragraph 18 of Schedule 10 to the Universal Credit Regulations 2013,]

where the award in respect of which the payments last fell to be disregarded under those Regulations either terminated immediately before the relevant date or is still in existence at that date.

(3)   Any disregard which applies under sub-paragraph (1) or (2) is to have effect until the award comes to an end.

(4)   In this paragraph–

"the award" ("y dyfarniad"), except in sub-paragraph (2), means–

(a) the award of a reduction under this scheme during which the relevant sum or, where it is paid in more than one instalment, the first instalment of that sum is received; and

(b) where that award is followed by one or more further awards which, or each of which, begins immediately after the previous award ends, such further awards until the end of the last such award, provided that, for such further awards, the applicant–

   (i) is the person who received the relevant sum;

   (ii) is the partner of that person; or

   (iii) was the partner of that person at the date of that person's death;

"official error" ("camgymeriad swyddogol")–

(a) where the error relates to housing benefit, or council tax benefit (in respect of any period before 1 April 2013), has the meaning given by regulation 1(2) of the Housing Benefit and Council Tax Benefit (Decisions and Appeals) Regulations 2001; and

(b) where the error relates to any other relevant benefit, has the meaning given by regulation 1(3) of the Social Security and Child Support (Decisions and Appeals) Regulations 1999;

"relevant benefit" ("budd-dal perthnasol") means any benefit specified in paragraph 21(2);

"the relevant date" ("y dyddiad perthnasol") means the date on which the application for a reduction under this scheme was made; and

"the relevant sum" ("y swm perthnasol") means the payment referred to in sub-paragraph (1) or the total amount referred to in sub-paragraph (2).

Amendment

1. Amended by reg 31(b) of SI 2014 No.66 (W.6) as from 15.1.14.

---

23.   Where a capital asset is held in a currency other than Sterling, any banking charge or commission payable in converting that capital into Sterling.

24.   The value of the right to receive income from an occupational pension scheme or a personal pension scheme.

25.   Any arrears of supplementary pension which is disregarded under paragraph 4 of Schedule 5 (amounts to be disregarded in the calculation of income other than earnings: pensioners) or of any amount which is disregarded under paragraph 5 or 6 of that Schedule.

26.   The dwelling occupied as the home; but only one dwelling is to be disregarded under this paragraph.

27.   Where a person elects to be entitled to a lump sum under Schedule 5 or 5A to the SSCBA or under Schedule 1 to the Social Security (Graduated Retirement Benefit) Regulations 2005, or is treated as having made such an election, and a payment has been made pursuant to that election, an amount equal to–

(a) except where sub-paragraph (b) applies, the amount of any payment or payments made on account of that lump sum;

(b)   the amount of that lump sum,
but only for so long as that person does not change that election in favour of an increase of pension or benefit.

[¹**27A.**   Where a person elects to be entitled to a lump sum under section 8(2) of the Pensions Act 2014 or in accordance with regulations made under section 10 of that Act, or fails to make an election, and a lump sum payment has been made, an amount equal to–

(a)   except where sub-paragraph (b) applies, the amount of any payment or payments made on account of that lump sum; or

(b)   the amount of that lump sum,
but only for so long as that person does not change that election in favour of an increase of pension.]

Amendment
1.   Inserted by reg 30(a) of SI 2016 No 50 (W.21) as from 20.1.16, for schemes made for a financial year starting on or after 1.4.16.

---

28.   Any payments made by virtue of regulations made under–

(a)   section 57 of the Health and Social Care Act 2001 (direct payments);

[¹ (b)]

(c)   sections 12A to 12C of the National Health Service Act 2006 (direct payments for health care);

(d)   Article 15 of the Health and Personal Social Services (Northern Ireland) Order 1972; [² or];

(e)   section 8 of the Carers and Direct Payments Act (Northern Ireland) 2002 (direct payments) [²;

(f)   sections 50 to 53 of the Social Services and Well-being (Wales) Act 2014; or

(g)   section 33 of the Care Act 2014.]

Amendments
1.   Amended by art 2 and Sch para 26(3) of SI 2014 No 513 as from 1.4.14.
2.   Amended by reg 30(b) of SI 2016 No 50 (W.21) as from 20.1.16, for schemes made for a financial year starting on or after 1.4.16.

[¹**28A.**   Any payment made as a direct payment as defined in section 4(2) of the Social Care (Self-directed Support) (Scotland) Act 2013.]

Amendment
1.   Inserted by art 2 and Sch para 26(4) of SI 2014 No 513 as from 1.4.14.

[¹**28B.**   Any payment made under or by a trust, established for the purpose of giving relief and assistance to disabled persons whose disabilities were caused by the fact that during their mother's pregnancy she had taken a preparation containing the drug known as Thalidomide, and which is approved by the Secretary of State.]

Amendment
1.   Inserted by reg 30(b) of SI 2018 No 14 (W.7) as from 10.1.18, for schemes made for a financial year starting on or after 1.4.18.

[¹**28C.**   Any bereavement support payment in respect of the rate set out in regulation 3(2) or (5) of the Bereavement Support Payment Regulations 2017 (rate of bereavement support payment), but only for a period of 52 weeks from the date of receipt of the payment.]

Amendment
1.   Inserted by reg 18(b) of SI 2019 No 11 (W.5) as from 9.1.19, for schemes made for a financial year starting on or after 1.4.19.

PART 2
Capital disregarded only for the purposes of determining deemed income

29.   The value of the right to receive any income under a life interest or from a life rent.

30.   The value of the right to receive any rent except where the applicant has a reversionary interest in the property in respect of which rent is due.

31.   The value of the right to receive any income under an annuity or the surrender value (if any) of such an annuity.

32.   Where property is held under a trust, other than–

(a)   a charitable trust within the meaning of the Charities Act 2011; or

(b)   a trust set up with any payment to which paragraph 16 of this Schedule applies,
and under the terms of the trust, payments fall to be made, or the trustees have a discretion to make payments, to or for the benefit of the applicant or the applicant's partner, or both, that property.

[¹**33.**   Any payment made by the Treasury to the applicant or the applicant's partner under the Age-Related Payments Regulations 2013 (Equitable Life) as a qualifying Equitable Life annuitant.]

Amendment
1.   Inserted by reg 31(c) of SI 2014 No 66 (W.6) as from 15.1.14.

SCHEDULE 9
Capital disregards: persons who are not pensioners

1.   Any payment made to the applicant in respect of any child care, travel or other expenses incurred, or to be incurred, by the applicant in respect of the applicant's participation in the Work for Your Benefit Pilot Scheme but only for 52 weeks beginning with the date of receipt of the payment.

2.   Any payment made to the applicant in respect of any travel or other expenses incurred, or to be incurred, by the applicant in respect of the applicant's participation in the Mandatory Work Activity Scheme but only for 52 weeks beginning with the date of receipt of the payment.

[¹**(2A).**   Any payment made to the applicant in respect of any travel or other expenses incurred, or to be incurred, by the applicant in respect of the applicant's participation in a scheme prescribed in regulation 3 of the Jobseeker's Allowance (Schemes for Assisting Persons to Obtain Employment) Regulations 2013 but only for 52 weeks beginning with the date of receipt of the payment.]

Amendment
1.   Inserted by reg 32(a) of SI 2014 No 66 (W.6) as from 15.1.14.

3.   Any payment made to the applicant in respect of any travel or other expenses incurred, or to be incurred, by the applicant in respect of the applicant's participation in the Employment, Skills and Enterprise Scheme but only for 52 weeks beginning with the date of receipt of the payment.

4.   The dwelling together with any garage, garden and outbuildings, normally occupied by the applicant as the applicant's home including any premises not so occupied which it is impracticable or unreasonable to sell separately, but, notwithstanding paragraph 30 of this scheme (calculation of income and capital: applicant's family and polygamous marriages), only one dwelling is to be disregarded under this paragraph.

5.   Any premises acquired for occupation by the applicant which the applicant intends to occupy as the applicant's home within 26 weeks of the date of acquisition or such longer period as is reasonable in the circumstances to enable the applicant to obtain possession and commence occupation of the premises.

6.   Any sum directly attributable to the proceeds of sale of any premises formerly occupied by the applicant as the applicant's home which is to be used for the purchase of other premises intended for such occupation within 26 weeks of the date of sale or such longer period as is reasonable in the circumstances to enable the applicant to complete the purchase.

7.   Any premises occupied in whole or in part–
(a)   by a partner or relative of a single applicant or any member of the family as that person's home where that person has attained the qualifying age for state pension credit or is incapacitated;
(b)   by the former partner of the applicant as that person's home; but this provision is not to apply where the former partner is a person from whom the applicant is estranged or divorced or with whom the applicant had formed a civil partnership that has been dissolved.

8.   Where an applicant is on income support, an income-based jobseeker's allowance or an income-related employment and support allowance, the whole of the applicant's capital.

9.   Where the applicant is a member of a joint-claim couple for the purposes of the Jobseekers Act 1995 and the applicant's partner is on income-based jobseeker's allowance, the whole of the applicant's capital.

10.   Any future interest in property of any kind, other than land or premises in respect of which the applicant has granted a subsisting lease or tenancy, including sub-leases or sub-tenancies.

11.–(1)   The assets of any business owned in whole or in part by the applicant and for the purposes of which the applicant is engaged as a self-employed earner, or if the applicant has ceased to be so engaged, for such period as may be reasonable in the circumstances to allow for disposal of any such asset.

(2)   The assets of any business owned in whole or in part by the applicant where–
(a)   the applicant is not engaged as a self-employed earner in that business by reason of some disease or bodily or mental disablement; but
(b)   the applicant intends to become engaged or, as the case may be, re-engaged as a self-employed earner in that business as soon as the applicant recovers or is able to become engaged or re-engaged in that business,
for a period of 26 weeks from the date on which the application for a reduction under this scheme is made, or is treated as made, or, if it is unreasonable to expect the applicant to become engaged or re-engaged in that business within that period, for such longer period as is reasonable in the circumstances to enable the applicant to become so engaged or re-engaged.

(3)   In the case of a person who is receiving assistance under the self-employment route, the assets acquired by that person for the purpose of establishing or carrying on the commercial activity in respect of which such assistance is being received.

(4)   In the case of a person who has ceased carrying on the commercial activity in respect of which assistance was received as specified in sub-paragraph (3), the assets relating to that activity for such period as may be reasonable in the circumstances to allow for disposal of any such asset.

12.–[² (1)   Subject to sub-paragraph (2), any arrears of, or any concessionary payment made to compensate for arrears due to the non-payment of the following, but only for a period of 52 weeks from the date of the receipt of the arrears or of the concessionary payment–

(a)   any payment specified in paragraphs 11, 13 or 14 of Schedule 7;
(b)   an income-related benefit under Part 7 of the SSCBA;
(c)   an income-based jobseeker's allowance;
(d)   any discretionary housing payment paid pursuant to regulation 2(1) of the Discretionary Financial Assistance Regulations 2001;
(e)   working tax credit and child tax credit;
(f)   an income-related employment and support allowance;
(g)   universal credit;
(h)   bereavement support payment under section 30 of the Pensions Act 2014.]

(2)   In a case where the total of any arrears and, if appropriate, any concessionary payment referred to in sub-paragraph (1) relating to one of the specified payments, benefits or allowances amounts to £5,000 or more (referred to in this sub-paragraph and in sub-paragraph (3) as "the relevant sum") and is–

(a)   paid in order to rectify or to compensate for, an official error as defined in regulation 1(2) of the Housing Benefit and Council Tax Benefit (Decisions and Appeals) Regulations 2001; and
(b)   received by the applicant in full on or after 14th October 2001,
(c)   sub-paragraph (1) is to have effect in relation to such arrears or concessionary payment either for a period of 52 weeks from the date of receipt, or, if the relevant sum is received in its entirety during the period of an award of a reduction under this scheme, for the remainder of that period if that is a longer period.

(3)   For the purposes of sub-paragraph (2), "the period of an award of a reduction under this scheme" ("cyfnod dyfarniad o ostyngiad o dan gynllun awdurdod") means–

(a)   the award in which the relevant sum is first received (or the first part thereof where it is paid in more than one instalment); and
(b)   where that award is followed by one or more further awards which, or each of which, begins immediately after the end of the previous award, such further award provided that for that further award the applicant–
(i)   is the person who received the relevant sum; or
(ii)   is the partner of the person who received the relevant sum, or was that person's partner at the date of that person's death.

Amendments
1.   Amended by reg 32(b) of SI 2014 No 66 (W.6) as from 15.1.14.
2.   Substituted by reg 19(a) of SI 2019 No 11 (W.5) as from 9.1.19, for schemes made for a financial year starting on or after 1.4.19.

---

13.   Any sum–
(a)   paid to the applicant in consequence of damage to, or loss of the home or any personal possession and intended for its repair or replacement; or
(b)   acquired by the applicant (whether as a loan or otherwise) on the express condition that it is to be used for effecting essential repairs or improvement to the home,
(c)   which is to be used for the intended purpose, for a period of 26 weeks from the date on which it was so paid or acquired or such longer period as is reasonable in the circumstances to effect the repairs, replacement or improvement.

14.   Any sum–
(a)   deposited with a housing association as defined in section 1(1) of the Housing Associations Act 1985 as a condition of occupying the home;
(b)   which was so deposited and which is to be used for the purchase of another home,
for the period of 26 weeks or such longer period as may be reasonable in the circumstances to enable the applicant to complete the purchase.

15.   Any personal possessions except those which have been acquired by the applicant with the intention of reducing the applicant's capital in order to secure entitlement to a reduction under this scheme or to increase the amount of that reduction.

16.   The value of the right to receive any income under an annuity or the surrender value (if any) of such an annuity.

17.   Where the funds of a trust are derived from a payment made in consequence of any personal injury to the applicant or applicant's partner, the value of the trust fund and the value of the right to receive any payment under that trust.

18.–(1)   Any payment made to the applicant or the applicant's partner in consequence of any personal injury to the applicant or, as the case may be, the applicant's partner.

(2)   But sub-paragraph (1)–

(a)   applies only for the period of 52 weeks beginning with the day on which the applicant first receives any payment in consequence of that personal injury;

(b)   does not apply to any subsequent payment made to the applicant in consequence of that injury (whether it is made by the same person or another);

(c)   ceases to apply to the payment or any part of the payment from the day on which the applicant no longer possesses it;

(d)   does not apply to any payment from a trust where the funds of the trust are derived from a payment made in consequence of any personal injury to the applicant.

(3)   For the purposes of sub-paragraph (2)(c), the circumstances in which an applicant no longer possesses a payment or a part of it include where the applicant has used a payment or part of it to purchase an asset.

(4)   References in sub-paragraphs (2) and (3) to the applicant are to be construed as including references to the applicant's partner (where applicable).

19.   The value of the right to receive any income under a life interest or from a life rent.

20.   The value of the right to receive any income which is disregarded under paragraph 15 of Schedule 6 or paragraph 29 of Schedule 7.

21.   The surrender value of any policy of life insurance.

22.   Where any payment of capital falls to be made by instalments, the value of the right to receive any outstanding instalments.

[¹**23.**   Any payment made by a local authority in accordance with–

(a)   section 17, 23B, 23C or 24A of the Children Act 1989;

(b)   section 12 of the Social Work (Scotland) Act 1968;

(c)   sections 22, 29 or 30 of the Children (Scotland) Act 1995; or

(d)   section 37, 38, 109, 110 or 114 of the Social Services and Well-being (Wales) Act 2014, but excluding any direct payments under that Act.]

Amendment

1.   Substituted by reg 31(a) of SI 2016 No 50 (W.21) as from 20.1.16, for schemes made for a financial year starting on or after 1.4.16.

24.–(1)   Subject to sub-paragraph (2), any payment (or part of a payment) made by a local authority in accordance with section 23C of the Children Act 1989 or section 29 of the Children (Scotland) Act 1995 (local authorities' duty to promote welfare of children and powers to grant financial assistance to persons in, or formerly in, their care) to a person ("A") which A passes on to the applicant.

(2)   Sub-paragraph (1) applies only where A–

(a)   was formerly in the applicant's care; and

(b)   is aged 18 or over; and

(c)   continues to live with the applicant.

25.   Any–

(a)   social fund payment made pursuant to Part 8 of the SSCBA (the social fund); or

(b)   occasional assistance.

26.   Any refund of tax which falls to be deducted under section 369 of the Income and Corporation Taxes Act 1988 (deduction of tax from certain loan interest) on a payment of relevant loan interest for the purpose of acquiring an interest in the home or carrying out repairs or improvements to the home.

27.   Any capital which by virtue of paragraphs 52 or 78 of this scheme (capital treated as income, treatment of student loans) is to be treated as income.

28.   Where any payment of capital is made in a currency other than sterling, any banking charge or commission payable in converting that payment into sterling.

29.–(1)   Any payment made under or by the Trusts, the Fund, the Eileen Trust, MFET Limited, the Independent Living Fund (2006), the Skipton Fund, the Caxton Foundation [¹, an approved blood scheme, the Scottish Infected Blood Support Scheme, the London Emergencies Trust, the We Love Mancheser Emergency Fund] or the London Bombings Relief Charitable Fund.

(2)   Any payment by or on behalf of a person who is suffering or who suffered from haemophilia or who is or was a qualifying person, which derives from a payment made under or by any of the Trusts to which sub-paragraph (1) refers and which is made to or for the benefit of–

(a)   that person's partner or former partner from whom that person is not, or where that person has died was not, estranged or divorced or with whom that person has formed a civil partnership that has not been dissolved or, where that person has died, had not been dissolved at the time of that person's death;

(b)   any child who is a member of that person's family or who was such a member and who is a member of the applicant's family; or

(c)   any young person who is a member of that person's family or who was such a member and who is a member of the applicant's family.

(3)   Any payment by or on behalf of the partner or former partner of a person who is suffering or who suffered from haemophilia or who is or was a qualifying person which derives from a payment made under or by any of the Trusts to which sub-paragraph (1) refers and which is made to or for the benefit of–

(a)   the person who is suffering from haemophilia or who is a qualifying person;

(b)   any child who is a member of that person's family or who was such a member and who is a member of the applicant's family; or

(c)   any young person who is a member of that person's family or who was such a member and who is a member of the applicant's family.

(4)   Sub-paragraph (3) does not apply if–

(a)   the partner or former partner and that person are not, or if either of them has died were not, estranged or divorced, or

(b)   where the partner or former partner and that person have formed a civil partnership, the civil partnership has not been dissolved or, if either of them has died, had not been dissolved at the time of the death.

(5)   Any payment by a person who is suffering from haemophilia or who is a qualifying person, which derives from a payment under or by any of the Trusts to which sub-paragraph (1) refers, where–

(a)   that person has no partner or former partner from whom that person is not estranged or divorced or with whom that person has formed a civil partnership that has not been dissolved, nor any child or young person who is or had been a member of that person's family; and

(b)   the payment is made either–

(i)   to that person's parent or step-parent; or

(ii)   where that person at the date of the payment is a child, a young person or a student who has not completed full-time education and has no parent or step-parent, to that child or young person's guardian or that student's guardian,

but only for a period from the date of the payment until the end of two years from that person's death.

(6)   Any payment out of the estate of a person who suffered from haemophilia or who was a qualifying person, which derives from a payment under or by any of the Trusts to which sub-paragraph (1) refers, where–

(a)   that person at the date of that person's death (the relevant date) had no partner or former partner from whom that person was not estranged or divorced or with whom that person had formed a civil partnership that had not been dissolved, nor any child or young person who was or had been a member of that person's family; and

(b)   the payment is made either–

(i)   to that person's parent or step-parent; or

(ii)   where that person at the relevant date was a child, a young person or a student who had not completed full-time education and had no parent or step-parent, to that child or young person's guardian or that student's guardian,

but only for a period of two years from the relevant date.

(7)   In the case of a person to whom or for whose benefit a payment referred to in this paragraph is made, any capital resource which derives from any payment of income or capital made under or deriving from any of the Trusts.

(8)   For the purposes of sub-paragraphs (2) to (7), any reference to the Trusts is to be construed as including a reference to the Fund, the Eileen Trust, MFET Limited, the Skipton Fund, the Caxton Foundation, [¹ an approved blood scheme, the Scottish Infected Blood Support Scheme, the London Emergencies Trust, the We Love Mancheser Emergency Fund] and the London Bombings Relief Charitable Fund.

Amendment

1.   Amended by reg 31(a) and (b) of SI 2018 No 14 (W.7) as from 10.1.18, for schemes made for a financial year starting on or after 1.4.18.

30.–(1)   Where an applicant has ceased to occupy what was formerly the dwelling occupied as the home following the applicant's estrangement or divorce from, or dissolution of the applicant's civil partnership with, the applicant's former partner, that dwelling for a period of 26 weeks from the date on which the applicant ceased to occupy that dwelling or, where the dwelling is occupied as the home by the former partner who is a lone parent, for so long as it is so occupied.

(2)   In this paragraph "dwelling" ("annedd") includes any garage, garden and outbuildings, which were formerly occupied by the applicant as the applicant's home and any premises not so occupied which it is impracticable or unreasonable to sell separately, in particular, in Scotland, any croft land on which the dwelling is situated.

31.   Any premises where the applicant is taking reasonable steps to dispose of those premises, for a period of 26 weeks from the date on which the applicant first took such steps, or such longer period as is reasonable in the circumstances to enable the applicant to dispose of those premises.

32.   Any premises which the applicant intends to occupy as the applicant's home, and in respect of which the applicant is taking steps to obtain possession and has sought legal advice, or has commenced legal proceedings, with a view to obtaining possession, for a period of 26 weeks from the date on which the applicant first sought such advice or first commenced such proceedings whichever is the earlier, or such longer period as is reasonable in the circumstances to enable the applicant to obtain possession and commence occupation of those premises.

33.   Any premises which the applicant intends to occupy as the applicant's home to which essential repairs or alterations are required in order to render them fit for such occupation, for a period of 26 weeks from the date on which the applicant first takes steps to effect those repairs or alterations, or such longer period as is necessary to enable those repairs or alterations to be carried out.

34.   Any payment made by the Secretary of State to compensate for the loss (in whole or in part) of entitlement to housing benefit.

35.   The value of the right to receive an occupational or personal pension.

36.   The value of any funds held under a personal pension scheme.

37.   The value of the right to receive any rent except where the applicant has a reversionary interest in the property in respect of which rent is due.

38.   Any payment in kind made by a charity or under or by the Trusts, the Fund, MFET Limited, the Skipton Fund, the Caxton Foundation [¹, an approved blood scheme, the Scottish Infected Blood Support Scheme, the London Emergencies Trust, the We Love Mancheser Emergency Fund] or the Independent Living Fund (2006).

Amendment

1.   Amended by reg 31(c) of SI 2018 No 14 (W.7) as from 10.1.18, for schemes made for a financial year starting on or after 1.4.18.

---

39.   Any payment made pursuant to section 2 of the Employment and Training Act 1973 Act or section 2 of the Enterprise and New Towns (Scotland) Act 1990, but only for the period of 52 weeks beginning on the date of receipt of the payment.

40.   Any payment in consequence of a reduction of council tax under section 13 of the 1992 Act, (reduction of liability for council tax), but only for a period of 52 weeks from the date of the receipt of the payment.

41.   Any grant made in accordance with a scheme made under section 129 of the Housing Act 1988 or section 66 of the Housing (Scotland) Act 1988 schemes for payments to assist local housing authority and local authority tenants to obtain other accommodation) which is to be used–

(a)   to purchase premises intended for occupation as the applicant's home; or

(b)   to carry out repairs or alterations which are required to render premises fit for occupation as the applicant's home,

for a period of 26 weeks from the date on which the applicant received such a grant or such longer period as is reasonable in the circumstances to enable the purchase, repairs or alterations to be completed and the applicant to commence occupation of those premises as the applicant's home.

42.   Any arrears of supplementary pension which is disregarded under paragraph 53 of Schedule 7 (sums disregarded in the calculation of income other than earnings) or of any amount which is disregarded under paragraph 54 or 55 of that Schedule, but only for a period of 52 weeks from the date of receipt of the arrears.

43.–(1)   Any payment or repayment made–

(a)   as respects England, under regulation 5, 6 or 12 of the National Health Service (Travel Expenses and Remission of Charges) Regulations 2003 (travelling expenses and health service supplies);

(b)   as respects Wales, under regulation 5, 6 or 11 of the National Health Service (Travelling Expenses and Remission of Charges) (Wales) Regulations 2007 (travelling expenses and health service supplies);

(c)   as respects Scotland, under regulation 3, 5 or 11 of the National Health Service (Travelling Expenses and Remission of Charges) (Scotland) (No 2) Regulations 2003 (travelling expenses and health service supplies),

but only for a period of 52 weeks from the date of receipt of the payment or repayment.

(2)   Any payment or repayment made by the Secretary of State for Health [¹ and Social Care], the Scottish Ministers or the Welsh Ministers which is analogous to a payment or repayment mentioned in sub-paragraph (1), but only for a period of 52 weeks from the date of receipt of the payment or repayment.

Amendment

1.   Amended by reg 19(b) of SI 2019 No 11 (W.5) as from 9.1.19, for schemes made for a financial year starting on or after 1.4.19.

---

44.   Any payment made to such persons entitled to receive benefits as may be determined by or under a scheme made pursuant to section 13 of the Social Security Act 1988 in lieu of vouchers or similar arrangements in connection with the provision of those benefits (including payments made in place of healthy start vouchers, milk tokens or the supply of vitamins), but only for a period of 52 weeks from the date of receipt of the payment.

45.   Any payment made either by the Secretary of State for Justice or by Scottish Ministers under a scheme established to assist relatives and other persons to visit persons in custody, but only for a period of 52 weeks from the date of the receipt of the payment.

46.   Any payment (other than a training allowance) made, whether by the Secretary of State or any other person, under the Disabled Persons (Employment) Act 1944 to assist disabled persons to obtain or retain employment despite their disability.

[¹**47.**–(1)   Any payment made by a local authority under section 3 of the Disabled Persons (Employment) Act 1958 to homeworkers assisted under a blind homeworkers' scheme.

(2)   Any payment made by a local authority under Part 4 of the Social Services and Well-being (Wales) Act 2014 to homeworkers assisted under a blind homeworkers' scheme.]

Amendment

1.   Substituted by reg 31(b) of SI 2016 No 50 (W.21) as from 20.1.16, for schemes made for a financial year starting on or after 1.4.16.

48.–(1)   Any sum of capital to which sub-paragraph (2) applies and–

(a)   which is administered on behalf of a person by the High Court or the County Court under Rule 21.11(1) of the Civil Procedure Rules 1998 or by the Court of Protection;

(b)   which can only be disposed of by order or direction of any such court; or

(c)   where the person concerned is under the age of 18, which can only be disposed of by order or direction prior to that person attaining age 18.

(2)   This sub-paragraph applies to a sum of capital which is derived from–

(a)   an award of damages for a personal injury to that person; or

(b)   compensation for the death of one or both parents where the person concerned is under the age of 18.

49.   Any sum of capital administered on behalf of a person in accordance with an order made under section 13 of the Children (Scotland) Act 1995, or under Rule 36.14 of the Act of Sederunt (Sheriff Court Ordinary Cause Rules) 1993 or under Rule 128 of those Rules, where such sum derives from–

(a)   award of damages for a personal injury to that person; or

(b)   compensation for the death of one or both parents where the person concerned is under the age of 18.

50.   Any payment to the applicant as holder of the Victoria Cross or George Cross.

51.   In the case of a person who is receiving, or who has received, assistance under the self-employment route, any sum of capital which is acquired by that person for the purpose of establishing or carrying on the commercial activity in respect of which such assistance is or was received but only for a period of 52 weeks from the date on which that sum was acquired.

52.–(1)   Any payment of a sports award for a period of 26 weeks from the date of receipt of that payment except to the extent that it has been made in respect of any one or more of the items specified in sub-paragraph (2).

(2)   The items specified for the purposes of sub-paragraph (1) are food, ordinary clothing or footwear, household fuel or rent of the applicant or, where the applicant is a member of a family, any other member of the applicant's family, or any council tax or water charges for which that applicant or member is liable.

(3)   For the purposes of sub-paragraph (2) "food" ("bwyd") does not include vitamins, minerals or other special dietary supplements intended to enhance the performance of the person in the sport in respect of which the award was made.

53.–(1)   Any payment–

(a)   by way of an education maintenance allowance made pursuant to–

    (i)   regulations made under section 518 of the Education Act 1996;

    (ii)   regulations made under section 49 or 73(f) of the Education (Scotland) Act1980;

    (iii) directions made under section 73ZA of the Education (Scotland) Act 1980 and paid under section 12(2)(c) of the Further and Higher Education (Scotland) Act1992;

(b)   corresponding to such an education maintenance allowance, made pursuant to–

    (i)   section 14 or section 181 of the Education Act 2002 (power of Secretary of State and Welsh Ministers to give financial assistance for purposes related to education or childcare, and allowances in respect of education or training); or

    (ii)   regulations made under section 181 of that Act; or

(c)   in England and Wales, by way of financial assistance made pursuant to section 14 of the Education Act 2002.

(2)   Any payment, other than a payment to which sub-paragraph (1) applies, made pursuant to–

(a)   regulations made under section 518 of the Education Act 1996;

(b)   regulations made under section 49 of the Education (Scotland) Act 1980; or

(c)   directions made under section 73ZA of the Education (Scotland) Act 1980 and paid under section 12(2)(c) of the Further and Higher Education (Scotland) Act 1992,

in respect of a course of study attended by a child or a young person or a person who is in receipt of an education maintenance allowance or other payment made pursuant to any provision specified in sub-paragraph (1).

54.   In the case of an applicant participating in an employment zone programme, any discretionary payment made by an employment zone contractor to the applicant, being a fee, grant, loan or otherwise, but only for the period of 52 weeks from the date of receipt of the payment.

55.   Any arrears of subsistence allowance paid as a lump sum but only for the period of 52 weeks from the date of receipt of the payment.

56.   Where an ex-gratia payment of £10,000 has been made by the Secretary of State on or after 1 February 2001 in consequence of the imprisonment or interment of–

(a)   the applicant;

(b)   the applicant's partner;

(c)   the applicant's deceased spouse or deceased civil partner; or

(d)   the applicant's partner's deceased spouse or deceased civil partner,

by the Japanese during the Second World War, £10,000.

57.–(1)   Subject to sub-paragraph (2), the amount of any trust payment made to an applicant or a member of an applicant's family who is–

(a)   a diagnosed person;

(b)   the diagnosed person's partner or the person who was the diagnosed person's partner at the date of the diagnosed person's death;

(c)   a parent of a diagnosed person, a person acting in place of the diagnosed person's parents or a person who was so acting at the date of the diagnosed person's death; or

(d)   a member of the diagnosed person's family (other than that person's partner) or a person who was a member of the diagnosed person's family (other than that person's partner) at the date of the diagnosed person's death.

(2)   Where a trust payment is made to–

(a)   a person referred to in sub-paragraph (1)(a) or (b), that sub-paragraph is to apply for the period beginning on the date on which the trust payment is made and ending on the date on which that person dies;

(b)   a person referred to in sub-paragraph (1)(c), that sub-paragraph is to apply for the period beginning on the date on which the trust payment is made and ending two years after that date;

(c)   a person referred to in sub-paragraph (1)(d), that sub-paragraph is to apply for the period beginning on the date on which the trust payment is made and ending–

(i)   two years after that date; or

(ii)   on the day before the day on which that person–

(aa)   ceases receiving full-time education; or

(bb)   attains the age of 20,

whichever is the latest.

(3)   Subject to sub-paragraph (4), the amount of any payment by a person to whom a trust payment has been made or of any payment out of the estate of a person to whom a trust payment has been made, which is made to an applicant or a member of an applicant's family who is–

(a)   the diagnosed person's partner or the person who was the diagnosed person's partner at the date of the diagnosed person's death;

(b)   a parent of a diagnosed person, a person acting in place of the diagnosed person's parents or a person who was so acting at the date of the diagnosed person's death; or

(c)   a member of the diagnosed person's family (other than that person's partner) or a person who was a member of the diagnosed person's family (other than that person's partner) at the date of the diagnosed person's death,

but only to the extent that such payments do not exceed the total amount of any trust payments made to that person.

(4)   Where a payment as referred to in sub-paragraph (3) is made to–

(a)   a person referred to in sub-paragraph (3)(a), that sub-paragraph is to apply for the period beginning on the date on which that payment is made and ending on the date on which that person dies;

(b)   a person referred to in sub-paragraph (3)(b), that sub-paragraph is to apply for the period beginning on the date on which that payment is made and ending two years after that date; or

(c)   person referred to in sub-paragraph (3)(c), that sub-paragraph is to apply for the period beginning on the date on which that payment is made and ending–

(i)   two years after that date; or

(ii)   on the day before the day on which that person–

(aa)   ceases receiving full-time education; or

(bb)   attains the age of 20,

whichever is the latest.

(5)   In this paragraph, a reference to a person–

(a)   being the diagnosed person's partner;

(b)   being a member of a diagnosed person's family;

(c)   acting in place of the diagnosed person's parents,

at the date of the diagnosed person's death is to include a person who would have been such a person or a person who would have been so acting, but for the diagnosed person residing in a care home, an Abbeyfield Home or an independent hospital on that date.

(6)   In this paragraph–

"diagnosed person" ("person â diagnosis") means a person who has been diagnosed as suffering from, or who, after that person's death, has been diagnosed as having suffered from, variant Creutzfeld-Jakob disease;

"relevant trust" ("ymddiriedolaeth berthnasol") means a trust established out of funds provided by the Secretary of State in respect of persons who suffered, or who are suffering, from variant Creutzfeld-Jakob disease for the benefit of persons eligible for payments in accordance with its provisions;

"trust payment" ("taliad ymddiriedolaeth") means a payment under a relevant trust.

58.   The amount of any payment, other than a war pension, to compensate for the fact that the applicant, the applicant's partner, the applicant's deceased spouse or deceased civil partner or the applicant's partner's deceased spouse or deceased civil partner–

(a)   was a slave labourer or a forced labourer;

(b)   had suffered property loss or had suffered personal injury; or

(c)   was a parent of a child who had died,
(d)   during the Second World War.

59.   Any payment made by a local authority, or by the Welsh Ministers, to or on behalf of the applicant or the applicant's partner relating to a service which is provided to develop or sustain the capacity of the applicant or the applicant's partner to live independently in the applicant's accommodation.

[¹**60.**   Any payment made–
(a)   under regulations made under section 57 of the Health and Social Care Act 2001 (direct payments);
(b)   as a direct payment as defined in section 4(2) of the Social Care (Self-directed Support) (Scotland) Act 2013;
(c)   under sections 12A to 12D of the National Health Service Act 2006 (direct payments for health care);
(d)   under regulations made under sections 50 to 53 of the Social Services and Well-being (Wales) Act 2014 (direct payments); or
(e)   under regulations made under section 33 of the Care Act 2014 (direct payments).]

Amendment
1.   Substituted by reg 31(c) of SI 2016 No 50 (W.21)as from 20.1.16, for schemes made for a financial year starting on or after 1.4.16.

---

61.   Any payment made to the applicant pursuant to regulations under section 2(6)(b), 3 or 4 of the Adoption and Children Act 2002.

62.   Any payment made to the applicant in accordance with regulations made pursuant to section 14F of the Children Act 1989 (special guardianship support services).

[¹**63.**   Any payment made by the Treasury to the applicant or the applicant's partner under the Age-Related Payments Regulations 2013 (Equitable Life) as a qualifying Equitable Life annuitant.]

Amendment
1.   Inserted by reg 32(c) of SI 2014 No 66 (W.6) as from 15.1.14.

[¹**64.**   Any payment made under or by a trust, established for the purpose of giving relief and assistance to disabled persons whose disabilities were caused by the fact that during their mother's pregnancy she had taken a preparation containing the drug known as Thalidomide, and which is approved by the Secretary of State.]

Amendment
1.   Inserted by reg 30(b) of SI 2018 No 14 (W.7) as from 10.1.18, for schemes made for a financial year starting on or after 1.4.18.

[¹**65.**   Any bereavement support payment in respect of the rate set out in regulation 3(2) or (5) of the Bereavement Support Payment Regulations 2017 (rate of bereavement support payment), but only for a period of 52 weeks from the date of receipt of the payment.]

Amendment
1.   Inserted by reg 19(c) of SI 2019 No 11 (W.5) as from 9.1.19, for schemes made for a financial year starting on or after 1.4.19.

SCHEDULE 10
Matters to be included in a notification

PART 1
General

1.   The statement of matters to be included in any notification issued by the authority in accordance with paragraph 115 of this scheme (notification of decision) are the matters set out in the following provisions of this Schedule.

2.   Every notification must include a statement as to the right of any person affected by the decision to request a written statement under paragraph 115(5) of this scheme (requests for statement of reasons), and the manner and time in which to do so.

3.   Every notification must include a statement as to the right of any person affected by the decision to appeal against the decision in accordance with paragraphs 8 and 10 of Schedule 1 to this scheme (procedure by which a person may make an appeal against certain decisions of the authority), and the manner and time in which to do so.

PART 2

Awards of reductions where state pension credit or extended payment (qualifying contributory benefits) is payable: pensioners

4.–(1) 'Where a pensioner who is in receipt of state pension credit is awarded a reduction under this scheme, the notification must include a statement as to–

(a) the normal weekly amount of council tax the person would be liable to pay before any reduction is awarded under this scheme, rounded to the nearest penny;

(b) the maximum weekly amount of reduction the person could be entitled to under this scheme, rounded to the nearest penny;

(c) the normal weekly amount of reduction the authority has determined the person is entitled to under this scheme, rounded to the nearest penny;

(d) the amount and category of any non-dependant deductions made under paragraph 30 (calculation of income and capital: applicant's family and polygamous marriages) of this scheme, if any; and

(e) the first day that the person is entitled to a reduction under this scheme,

and in any case where the amount to which paragraphs (a) to (c) refers disregards fractions of a penny, the notice must include a statement to that effect.

(2) In a case where a pensioner who is in receipt of state pension credit has entitlement only to the savings credit, the notification must also set out the following matters–

(a) the person's applicable amount and the basis of the calculation;

(b) the amount of the savings credit taken into account;

(c) the amount of the person's income and capital as notified to the authority by the Secretary of State and taken into account for the purposes of the determination of the reduction under this scheme;

(d) any modification of the person's income or capital made in accordance with paragraph 33 of this scheme (calculation of pensioner's income in savings credit only cases); and

(e) the amount of the person's capital if paragraph 33(4) applies in that person's case.

(3) Where a pensioner is entitled to an extended payment (qualifying contributory benefits) in accordance with paragraph 86 (extended reduction (qualifying contributory benefits): pensioners) of this scheme, the notification must include a statement as to the matters set out in paragraph 4(1).

PART 3

Awards of reductions where state pension credit not in payment: pensioners

5. Where a pensioner who is not in receipt of state pension credit is awarded a reduction under this scheme, the notification must include a statement as to–

(a) the matters set out in paragraph 4(1);

(b) the pensioner's applicable amount and how it is calculated;

(c) the pensioner's weekly earnings; and

(d) the pensioner's income and other earnings.

PART 4

Notification where no award of a reduction is made: pensioners

6. Where a pensioner is not awarded a reduction under this scheme–

(a) on the ground of income, the notification must include a statement as to–

(i) the matters set out in paragraph 4(1)(a), and

(ii) the matters set out in paragraph 5(b) to (d) where the pensioner is not on state pension credit;

(b) for any other reason, the notification must include a statement as to the reason why no award has been made.

PART 5

Awards of reductions where income support, income-based jobseeker's allowance, income-related employment and support allowance, an extended payment or an extended payment (qualifying contributory benefits) is payable: persons who are not pensioners

7.–(1) Where a person who is not a pensioner and who is on income support, an income-based jobseeker's allowance, or an income-related employment and support allowance is awarded a reduction under this scheme, the notification must include a statement as to–

(a) the normal weekly amount of council tax the person would be liable to pay before any reduction is awarded under this scheme, rounded to the nearest penny;

(b) the maximum weekly amount of reduction the person could be entitled to under this scheme, rounded to the nearest penny;

(c) the normal weekly amount of reduction the authority has determined the person is entitled to under this scheme, rounded to the nearest penny;

(d) the amount and category of any non dependant deductions made under paragraph 30 (calculation of income and capital: applicant's family and polygamous marriages) of this scheme, if any; and

(e) the first day that the person is entitled to a reduction under this scheme,

(f)   and in any case where the amount to which paragraphs (a) to (c) refers disregards fractions of a penny, the notice must include a statement to that effect.

(2)   Where a person who is not a pensioner is entitled to an extended payment in accordance with paragraph 93 of this scheme (extended reductions: persons who are not pensioners), or an extended payment (qualifying contributory benefits) in accordance with paragraph 98 of this scheme (extended reductions (qualifying contributory benefits): persons who are not pensioners), the notification must include a statement as to the matters set out in paragraph 7(1).

PART 6
Awards of reduction where universal credit is payable: persons who are not pensioners

8.   Where a person who is not a pensioner and who has an award of universal credit is awarded a reduction under this scheme, the notification must include a statement as to–
(a)   the matters set out in paragraph 7(1);
(b)   the person's applicable amount as determined in accordance with paragraph 26 of this scheme (applicable amount: persons who are not pensioners who have an award of universal credit); and
(c)   the person's income as determined in accordance with paragraph 34 of this scheme (calculation of income and capital: persons who are not pensioners who have an award of universal credit).

PART 7
Awards of reduction where no income support, income-based jobseeker's allowance, income- related employment and support allowance or universal credit is payable: persons who are not pensioners

9.   Where a person who is not a pensioner and who is not on income support, income-based jobseeker's allowance, income-related employment and support allowance or universal credit is awarded a reduction under this scheme, the notification must include a statement as to–
(a)   the matters set out in paragraph 7(1);
(b)   the person's applicable amount and how it is calculated;
(c)   the person's weekly earnings; and
(d)   the person's weekly income other than earnings.

PART 8
Notification where no award of a reduction is made: persons who are not pensioners

10.   Where a person who is not a pensioner is not awarded a reduction under this scheme–
(a)   on the ground of income, the notification must include a statement as to–
     (i)   the matters set out in paragraph 7(1)(a); and
     (ii)   the matters set out in paragraph 8(b) and (c) where the person is not on income support, an income-based jobseeker's allowance, an income-related employment and support allowance, or universal credit;
(b)   for any other reason, the notification must include a statement as to the reason why no award has been made.

PART 9
Notification where income of non-dependant is treated as applicant's income: pensioners and persons who are not pensioners

11.   Where the authority makes a decision under paragraph 31 of this scheme (circumstances in which capital and income of non-dependant is to be treated as applicant's) the notification must contain a statement as to–
(a)   the fact that a decision has been made by reference to the income and capital of the applicant's non-dependant, and
(b)   the authority's reason for making that decision."

The Council Tax Reduction Schemes (Transitional Provisions) (Wales) Regulations 2013

(2013 No.111 (W. 16))

Title, commencement and application

1.–(1) The title of these Regulations is the Council Tax Reduction Schemes (Transitional Provisions) (Wales) Regulations 2013.

(2) These Regulations come into force on the day after the day on which they were made and apply in relation to Wales.

Interpretation

2. In these Regulations–

"council tax benefit" means council tax benefit under Part 7 of the Social Security Contributions and Benefits Act 1992;

"council tax reduction scheme" means a scheme made by a billing authority in accordance with the Council Tax Reduction Schemes and Prescribed Requirements (Wales) Regulations 2012 or which applies in default in accordance with paragraph 6(1)(e) of Schedule 1B to the Local Government Finance Act 1992;

"relevant decision" has the same meaning as in paragraph 1(2) of Schedule 7 to the Child Support, Pensions and Social Security Act 2000;

"relevant authority" means an authority administering council tax benefit;

"specified day" means the day on which these Regulations come into force;

"suspended" means suspended in accordance with regulation 11 or 13 of the Housing Benefit and Council Tax Benefit (Decisions and Appeals) Regulations 2001.

Transitional provisions

3.–(1) A person who falls within one of the categories of person described in paragraph (2) is deemed to have made an application for a reduction under a council tax reduction scheme on the specified day.

(2) A person referred to in paragraph (1) is a person–

(a) who is in receipt of council tax benefit on the specified day;

(b) who made a claim for council tax benefit which is not determined immediately before the specified day;

(c) whose payments of council tax benefit have been wholly or partly suspended immediately before the specified day;

(d) other than a person described in sub-paragraphs (a) or (c), who has applied for a revision of a relevant decision by a relevant authority and whose decision in respect of that revision is pending immediately before the specified day;

(e) other than a person described in sub-paragraphs (a) or (c), who has appealed against a decision of the First-tier Tribunal, the Upper Tribunal or a court in relation to a claim for council tax benefit and whose appeal is pending immediately before the specified day.

(2) For the purposes of sub-paragraph (2)(d) a revision of a relevant decision relating to a claim for council tax benefit is pending if–

(a) an application for a revision has been made but not been determined;

(b) the time within which an application for a revision may be made as prescribed in regulations 4 and 5 of the Housing Benefit and Council Tax Benefit (Decisions and Appeals) Regulations 2001 has not expired.

(3) For the purposes of sub-paragraph (2)(e) an appeal against a decision relating to a claim for council tax benefit is pending if–

(a) an appeal against the decision has been brought but not been determined;

(b) an application for permission to appeal against the decision has been made but not determined; or

(c) the time within which–

(i) an application for permission to appeal may be made; or

(ii)   an appeal against the decision may be brought,

has not expired and one of the circumstances prescribed in regulations 11(3) of the Housing Benefit and Council Tax Benefit (Decisions and Appeals) Regulations 2001 apply.

4.   A person who makes a claim for council tax benefit on any day during the period beginning on the specified day and ending on the 31st March 2013 is deemed to have made an application for a reduction under a council tax reduction scheme on the same day.

5.   Where an application for a reduction under a council tax reduction scheme is deemed to have been made in accordance with regulation 3(1) and–

(a)   on the specified day, the person by whom the application is deemed to have been made is a person to whom paragraphs (10) to (12) of regulation 50 of the Council Tax Benefit (Persons who have attained the qualifying age for state pension credit) Regulations 2006 (change of circumstances in connection with non-dependants) apply; and

(b)   the effective date for the change of circumstances is a date after 31st March 2013, that application is to be determined as though the change of circumstances has not taken place, but is to be redetermined upon the effective date to take account of the change of circumstances.

(2)   Where an application for a reduction under a council tax reduction scheme is deemed to have been made in accordance with regulation 3(1) or 4 and–

(a)   on a day in the period beginning with the day after the specified day and ending with the 31st March 2013, the person by whom the application is deemed to have been made becomes a person to whom paragraphs (10) to (12) of regulation 50 of the Council Tax Benefit (Persons who have attained the qualifying age for state pension credit) Regulations 2006 (change of circumstances in connection with non-dependants) apply; and

(b)   the effective date for the change of circumstances is a date after 31st March 2013,

that application is to be determined to take account of the person's circumstances on the date the application for a reduction is deemed to have been made, but is to be re-determined upon the effective date to take account of the change of circumstances.

6.   Where an application for a reduction under a council tax reduction scheme is deemed to have been made in accordance with regulation 3(1) or 4, the following provisions in a council tax reduction scheme do not apply in relation to that application–

(a)   a provision contained in the authority's scheme by virtue of regulation 32(3) of, and paragraph 1(7) of Schedule 13 to, the Council Tax Reduction Schemes and Prescribed Requirements (Wales) Regulations 2012; or

(b)   paragraph 107(7) of the scheme prescribed in the Schedule to the Council Tax Reduction Schemes (Default Scheme) (Wales) Regulations 2012.

The Council Tax Reduction (Scotland) Regulations 2012
(2012 No.303)

PART 1
General
1. Citation and commencement
2. Interpretation
3. Non-dependants
4. Young persons
5. Occupation of a dwelling as a home
6. Remunerative work

PART 2
Families
7. Entitlement of only one member of a family
8. Couples: polygamous marriages
9. Applicant in receipt of income-related benefit
10. Responsibility for another person
11. Membership of a household

PART 3
Application of the Regulations
12. Application
13. Prescribed years

PART 4
Entitlement to council tax reduction
14. Conditions of entitlement to council tax reduction
14A. Conditions of entitlement to council tax reduction – dwellings in bands E to H
15. Persons not entitled to council tax reduction: absentees
16. Persons not entitled to council tax reduction: persons treated as not being in Great Britain
17. Persons treated as being in Great Britain
18. Temporary absence from Great Britain
19. Persons not entitled to council tax reduction: persons subject to immigration control
20. Persons not entitled to council tax reduction: students
20A. Non-recovery of council tax arrears caused by official error

PART 5
Applicable amount
21. Applicable amount
22. Applicable amount: polygamous marriages
23. Applicable amount: persons who have an award of universal credit

PART 6
Income and capital
CHAPTER 1
General
24. Calculation of income and capital of members of applicant's family and of a polygamous marriage
25. Circumstances in which capital and income of non-dependant is to be treated as applicant's

CHAPTER 2
Income and capital where there is an award of universal credit

26. Calculation of income and capital: persons who have an award of universal credit

CHAPTER 3
Income

27. Calculation of income on a weekly basis
28. Treatment of child care charges
29. Average weekly earnings of employed earners
30. Average weekly earnings of self-employed earners
31. Average weekly income other than earnings
32. Calculation of average weekly income from working tax credits
33. Calculation of weekly income

CHAPTER 4
Employed earners

34. Earnings of employed earners
35. Calculation of net earnings of employed earners

CHAPTER 5
Self-employed earners

36. Earnings of self-employed earners
37. Calculation of net profit of self-employed earners
38. Deduction of tax and contributions of self-employed earners

CHAPTER 6
Other income

39. Calculation of income other than earnings
40. Capital treated as income
41. Notional income

CHAPTER 7
Capital

42. Capital limit
43. Calculation of capital
44. Disregard of capital of child and young person
45. Income treated as capital
46. Calculation of capital in the United Kingdom
47. Calculation of capital outside the United Kingdom
48. Notional capital
49. Diminishing notional capital
50. Capital jointly held
51. Calculation of tariff income from capital

PART 7
Students
CHAPTER 1
General

52. Interpretation: students
53. Treatment of students

CHAPTER 2
Income

54. Calculation of grant income
55. Calculation of covenant income where a contribution is assessed
56. Covenant income where no grant income or no contribution is assessed

57.   Relationship with amounts to be disregarded under Schedule 4
58.   Other amounts to be disregarded
59.   Treatment of student loans
60.   Treatment of fee loans
61.   Treatment of payments from access funds
62.   Disregard of contribution
63.   Further disregard of student's income
64.   Income treated as capital
65.   Disregard of changes occurring during summer vacation

PART 8
Amount of reduction

66.   Maximum council tax reduction
67.   Non-dependant deductions
68.   Extended council tax reduction
69.   Duration of period of entitlement to extended council tax reduction
70.   Amount of extended council tax reduction
71.   Extended council tax reduction: movers
72.   Relationship between council tax reduction and extended council tax reduction
73.   Extended council tax reduction (qualifying contributory benefits)
74.   Duration of extended council tax reduction (qualifying contributory benefits)
75.   Amount of extended council tax reduction (qualifying contributory benefits)
76.   Extended council tax reduction (qualifying contributory benefits): movers
77.   Relationship between council tax reduction and extended council tax reduction (qualifying contributory benefits)
78.   Alternative maximum council tax reduction
79.   Residents of a dwelling to whom regulation 14(6) does not apply

PART 9
Effective date

80.   Date on which entitlement is to begin
81.   Date on which a change of circumstances is to take effect

PART 10
Applications

82.   Who may apply
83.   Written applications
84.   Telephone applications
85.   Date on which an application is made
86.   Evidence and information
87.   Amendment of applications
88.   Withdrawal of applications

PART 11
Notification of changes of circumstances

89.   Duty to notify changes of circumstances
90.   Alternative means of notifying changes of circumstances

PART 11A
Reviews

90A.   Review of determination on an application
90B.   Request for further review
90C.   Panel to conduct further reviews
90D.   Conduct of further reviews

PART 12
Electronic communications

91.   Sending documents by electronic communication

PART 13
Consequential and transitional provisions

92.   Transitional provision
93.   Savings provision
94.   Consequential amendments

SCHEDULES

1.   Applicable amount
2.   Amount of alternative maximum council tax reduction
3.   Sums to be disregarded in the calculation of earnings
4.   Sums to be disregarded in the calculation of income other than earnings
5.   Capital to be disregarded
6.   Savings provisions
7.   Consequential amendments

PART 1
General

Citation and commencement

1.   These Regulations may be cited as the Council Tax Reduction (Scotland) Regulations 2012 and come into force on 28th January 2013.

Interpretation

2.–(1)   In these Regulations, unless the context otherwise requires–

"the 1973 Act" means the Employment and Training Act 1973;

"the 1992 Act" means the Social Security Contributions and Benefits Act 1992;

"Abbeyfield Home" means an establishment run by the Abbeyfield Society including all bodies corporate or unincorporated which are affiliated to that Society;

"academic year" means the period of 12 months beginning on 1st January, 1st April, 1st July or 1st September according to whether the course in question begins in the winter, the spring, the summer or the autumn respectively but if students are required to begin attending the course during August or September and to continue attending through the autumn, the academic year of the course is to be considered to begin in the autumn rather than the summer;

"the Act" means the Local Government Finance Act 1992;

[⁷]

"adoption leave" means a period of absence from work on ordinary or additional adoption leave by virtue of section 75A or 75B of the Employment Rights Act 1996;

"alternative maximum council tax reduction" means the amount calculated in accordance with regulation 78 (alternative maximum council tax reduction) and Schedule 2;

"applicable amount" means the amount calculated in accordance with Part 5 and Schedule 1;

"applicant" means a person applying for council tax reduction or, as the case may be, a person who is entitled to council tax reduction whose entitlement is or may be subject to re-assessment by the relevant authority;

"application" means an application for council tax reduction;

"appropriate maximum council tax reduction" means the maximum council tax reduction applicable to a person calculated in accordance with regulation 66;

[³"armed forces independence payment" means armed forces independence payment under the Armed Forces and Reserve Forces (Compensation Scheme) Order 2011;]

"assessment period" means a period described in regulations 29 (average weekly earnings of employed earners), 30 (average weekly earnings of self-employed earners) and 31 (average weekly income other than earnings) over which income falls to be calculated;

"attendance allowance" means–

    (a)   an attendance allowance under Part 3 of the 1992 Act;

    (b)   an increase of disablement pension under section 104 or 105 of the 1992 Act;

    (c)   [²...]

    (d)   [²...]

    (e)   a payment by virtue of article 14, 15, 16, 43 or 44 of the Personal Injuries (Civilians) Scheme 1983 or any analogous payment; or

    (f)   any payment based on need for attendance which is paid as part of a war disablement pension;

"basic rate" has the meaning given by section 989 of Income Tax Act 2007;

"the benefit Acts" means the 1992 Act, [³the Armed Forces (Pensions and Compensation) Act 2004 insofar as it relates to armed forces independence payment, Part 4 (personal independence payment) of the Welfare Reform Act 2012,] the Jobseekers Act [⁹, the Welfare Reform Act and the Pensions Act 2014];

"the Board of the Pension Protection Fund" means the body corporate established under section 107 of the Pensions Act 2004;

"care home" in Scotland means a care home service within the meaning given by paragraph 2 of schedule 12 to the Public Services Reform (Scotland) Act 2010 and in England and Wales has the meaning given by section 3 of the Care Standards Act 2000;

"carer's allowance" means an allowance under section 70 of the 1992 Act;

"the Caxton Foundation" means the charitable trust of that name established on 28th March 2011 out of funds provided by the Secretary of State for the benefit of certain persons suffering from hepatitis C and other persons eligible for payment in accordance with its provisions;

"child" means a person under the age of 16 [⁴ and where section 145A of the 1992 Act (entitlement after death of a child or qualifying young person) applies, then during the period prescribed under subsection (1) of that section (and only during that period)–

    (a)   references in these Regulations to a child include the child in respect of whom there is entitlement under that section; and

    (b)   for the purposes of these Regulations the circumstances pertaining to the child at the date of their death are deemed to continue throughout that period];

"child benefit" means child benefit under section 141 of the 1992 Act;

[⁴]

"child tax credit" means a child tax credit under section 8 of the Tax Credits Act 2002;

"civil partnership" means a civil partnership which exists under or by virtue of the Civil Partnership Act 2004, and "civil partner" is to be construed accordingly;

"close relative" means a parent, parent-in-law, son, son-in-law, daughter, daughter-in-law, step-parent, step-son, step-daughter, brother, sister or, if any of the preceding persons is one member of a couple, the other member of that couple;

"concessionary payment" means a payment made under arrangements made by the Secretary of State with the consent of the Treasury which is charged either to the National Insurance Fund or to a Departmental Expenditure Vote to which payments of benefit or tax credits under the benefit Acts or the Tax Credits Act 2002 are charged;

"contributory employment and support allowance" means a contributory allowance under Part 1 of the Welfare Reform Act;

"converted employment and support allowance" means an employment and support allowance which is not income-related and to which a person is entitled as a result of a conversion decision within the meaning of the Employment and Support Allowance (Existing Awards) Regulations;

"council tax benefit" means council tax benefit under the Council Tax Benefit Regulations 2006;

"council tax reduction" means a reduction in liability for council tax calculated in accordance with these Regulations;

[⁶ "couple" means–
  (a) two people who are married to each other and are members of the same household, but not if the marriage is a polygamous marriage;
  (b) two people who are civil partners of each other and are members of the same household; or
  (c) two people who are neither married to each other nor civil partners of each other but who are living together as if they were married to each other;]

"course of study" means any course of study, whether or not it is a sandwich course and whether or not a grant is made for attending or undertaking it;

"date of application" means the date on which the application is made, or treated as made, for the purposes of regulation 5(9) (occupation of a dwelling as a home) and regulation 85 (date on which an application is made);

"designated office" means the office designated by the relevant authority as the office to which applications should be sent;

"disability living allowance" means a disability living allowance under section 71 of the 1992 Act;

"discount" means discount under section 79 of the Act (discount of the amount of council tax payable);

"earnings" has the meaning given by regulation 34 (earnings of employed earners) or, as the case may be, regulation 36 (earnings of self-employed earners);

"educational establishment" has the meaning given by section 135(1) of the Education (Scotland) Act 1980;

"the Eileen Trust" means the charitable trust of that name established on 29th March 1993 out of funds provided by the Secretary of State for the benefit of persons eligible for payment in accordance with its provisions;

"employed earner" is to be construed in accordance with section 2(1)(a) of the 1992 Act and also includes a person who is in receipt of a payment which is payable under any enactment having effect in Northern Ireland and which corresponds to statutory sick pay or statutory maternity pay;

"employment and support allowance" means employment and support allowance under Part 1 of the Welfare Reform Act;

"Employment and Support Allowance Regulations" means the Employment and Support Allowance Regulations 2008;

"Employment and Support Allowance (Existing Awards) Regulations" means the Employment and Support Allowance (Transitional Provisions, Housing Benefit and Council Tax Benefit) (Existing Awards) (No. 2) Regulations 2010;

"the Employment, Skills and Enterprise Scheme" means a scheme under section 17A of the Jobseekers Act 1995 (schemes for assisting persons to obtain employment: "work for your benefit" schemes etc.) known by that name and provided pursuant to arrangements made by the Secretary of State that is designed to assist applicants to obtain employment, including self-employment, and which may include for any individual work-related activity (including work experience or job search);

"employment zone" means an area within Great Britain designated for the purposes of section 60 of the Welfare Reform and Pensions Act 1999 and an "employment zone programme" means a programme established for such an area or areas designed to assist applicants for a jobseeker's allowance to obtain sustainable employment;

"employment zone contractor" means a person who is undertaking the provision of facilities in respect of an employment zone programme on behalf of the Secretary of State;

"enactment" includes an enactment contained in, or in an instrument made under, an Act of the Scottish Parliament;

"extended council tax reduction" means an extension of a period of entitlement to council
tax reduction under regulation 68 (extended council tax reduction);
"extended council tax reduction (qualifying contributory benefits)" means an extension
of a period of entitlement to council tax reduction under regulation 73 (extended
council tax reduction (qualifying contributory benefits));
"family" means–
  (a)   a couple;
  (b)   a couple and a member of the same household for whom one of them is, or both
         are, responsible and who is a child or young person; or
  (c)   subject to regulation 25 (circumstances in which the income and capital of a
         non-dependant is to be treated as the applicant's), a person who is not a member
         of a couple and a member of the same household for whom the person is
         responsible and who is a child or young person.
"first authority" means the relevant authority to which a mover was liable to pay council
         tax for the dwelling that person resided in immediately before moving to the
         dwelling in the area of the second authority;
"full-time course of study" means a full-time course of study which–
  (a)   is not funded in whole or in part by the Scottish Ministers at a college of further
         education or by the Young People's Learning Agency for England, [⁸ the
         Secretary of State] or by the Welsh Ministers;
  (b)   is a course of higher education and is funded in whole or in part by the Scottish
         Ministers;
  (c)   is not higher education and is funded in whole or in part by the Scottish Ministers
         at a college of further education and involves–
         (i)   more than 16 hours per week of classroom-based or workshop-based
                programmed learning under the direct guidance of teaching staff according
                to the number of hours set out in a document signed on behalf of the
                college; or
         (ii)   16 hours or less per week of classroom-based or workshop-based
                programmed learning under the direct guidance of teaching staff and it
                involves additional hours using structured learning packages supported by
                the teaching staff where the combined total of hours exceeds 21 hours per
                week, according to the number of hours set out in a document signed on
                behalf of the college; or
  (d)   is funded in whole or in part by the Young People's Learning Agency for
         England, [⁸ the secretary of State] or by the Welsh Ministers if it involves more
         than 16 guided learning hours per week for the student in question, according to
         the number of guided learning hours per week for that student set out–
         (i)   in the case of a course funded by the Young People's Learning Agency
                for England or [⁸ the Secretary of State], in the student's learning
                agreement signed on behalf of the establishment which is funded by either
                of those bodies for the delivery of that course; or
         (ii)   in the case of a course funded by the Welsh Ministers, in a document
                signed on behalf of the establishment which is funded by the Welsh
                Ministers for the delivery of that course;
"full-time student" means a person attending or undertaking a full-time course of study;
"the Fund" means moneys made available from time to time by the Secretary of State for
         the benefit of persons eligible for payment in accordance with the provisions of
         a scheme established by the Secretary of State on 10th or 24th April 1992, as
         the case may be;
"guaranteed income payment" means a payment made under article 15(1)(c) or 29(1)(a)
         of the Armed Forces and Reserve Forces (Compensation Scheme) Order 2011;
"higher education" means higher education within the meaning of Part 2 of the Further
         and Higher Education (Scotland) Act 1992;
"housing benefit" means housing benefit under section 130 of the 1992 Act;
"the Housing Benefit Regulations" means the Housing Benefit Regulations 2006;
[⁴]

[⁹ "ILF Scotland" means the company limited by guarantee under the name ILF Scotland, registered under number SC500075;]

"Immigration and Asylum Act" means the Immigration and Asylum Act 1999;

"incapacity benefit" means incapacity benefit under section 30A, 40 or 41 of the 1992 Act;

"an income-based jobseeker's allowance" and "a joint-claim jobseeker's allowance" have the same meaning as they have in the Jobseekers Act by virtue of section 1(4) of that Act;

"income-related employment and support allowance" means an income-related allowance under Part 1 of the Welfare Reform Act;

"income support" means income support under section 124 of the 1992 Act;

"Income Support Regulations" means the Income Support (General) Regulations 1987;

"independent hospital" –

(a)   in Scotland, means an independent health care service as defined in section 10F(1)(a) and (b) of the National Health Service (Scotland) Act 1978;

(b)   in England, means a hospital as defined by section 275 of the National Health Service Act 2006 that is not a health service hospital as defined by that section; and

(c)   in Wales, has the meaning assigned to it by section 2 of the Care Standards Act 2000;

[¹⁰ "infected blood payment scheme" means a scheme established by, or under arrangements made with, the Scottish Ministers, the Secretary of State, the Welsh Ministers or the Department of Health in Northern Ireland for making *ex gratia* payments to or in respect of persons who have acquired HIV or hepatitis C as a result of treatment with blood or blood products within the national health service;]

[⁹]

"invalid carriage or other vehicle" means a vehicle propelled by a petrol engine or by electric power supplied for use on the road and to be controlled by the occupant;

"Jobseekers Act" means the Jobseekers Act 1995;

"Jobseeker's Allowance Regulations" means the Jobseeker's Allowance Regulations 1996;

"limited capability for work" has the meaning given in section 1(4) of the Welfare Reform Act;

"limited capability for work-related activity" has the meaning given in section 2(5) of the Welfare Reform Act;

"local authority" in Scotland means a council constituted by section 2 of the Local Government etc. (Scotland) Act 1994;

"the London Bombings Relief Charitable Fund" means the company limited by guarantee (number 5505072) and registered charity of that name established on 11th July 2005 for the purpose of (amongst other things) relieving sickness, disability or financial need of victims (including families or dependants of victims) of the terrorist attacks carried out in London on 7th July 2005;

[¹¹ "the London Emergencies Trust" means the company of that name (number 09928465) incorporated on 23rd December 2015 and registered charity of that name (number 1172307) established on 28th March 2017 for the purpose of (amongst other things) relieving sickness, disability or financial need of victims of emergency incidents occurring in Greater London;]

"lone parent" means a person who has no partner and who is responsible for and a member of the same household as a child or young person;

"the Macfarlane (Special Payments) Trust" means the trust of that name, established on 29th January 1990 partly out of funds provided by the Secretary of State, for the benefit of certain persons suffering from haemophilia;

"the Macfarlane (Special Payments) (No. 2) Trust" means the trust of that name, established on 3rd May 1991 partly out of funds provided by the Secretary of State, for the benefit of certain persons suffering from haemophilia and other beneficiaries;

"the Macfarlane Trust" means the charitable trust, established partly out of funds provided by the Secretary of State to the Haemophilia Society, for the relief of poverty or distress among those suffering from haemophilia;

"the Mandatory Work Activity Scheme" means a scheme within section 17A (schemes for assisting persons to obtain employment: "work for your benefit" schemes etc.) of the Jobseekers Act 1995 known by that name and provided pursuant to arrangements made by the Secretary of State that is designed to provide work or work-related activity for up to 30 hours per week over a period of 4 consecutive weeks with a view to assisting applicants to improve their prospects of obtaining employment;

"maternity leave" means a period during which a woman is absent from work because she is pregnant or has given birth to a child, and at the end of which she has a right to return to work either under the terms of her contract of employment or under Part 8 of the Employment Rights Act 1996;

"medically approved" means certified by a medical practitioner;

"MFET Limited" means the company limited by guarantee (number 7121661) of that name, established for the purpose in particular of making payments in accordance with arrangements made with the Secretary of State to persons who have acquired HIV as a result of treatment by the NHS with blood or blood products;

"mobility supplement" means a supplement to which paragraph 12 of Schedule 4 refers;

"mover" means a person who moves from a dwelling in which the person is resident, and in respect of which the person is liable to pay council tax to the first authority, to reside in a dwelling in the area of the second authority and any reference to a mover is to be construed as including a reference to the mover's partner;

"net earnings" means earnings calculated in accordance with regulation 35 (calculation of net earnings of employed earners);

"new dwelling" means, for the purposes of the definition of "second authority" and regulations 71 (extended council tax reduction: movers) and 76 (extended council tax reduction (qualifying contributory benefits): movers) the dwelling to which an applicant has moved, or is about to move, in which the applicant is or will be resident;

"non-dependant" has the meaning given by regulation 3 (non-dependants);

"occupational pension" means any pension or other periodical payment under an occupational pension scheme but does not include any discretionary payment out of a fund established for relieving hardship in particular cases;

"ordinary clothing or footwear" means clothing or footwear for normal daily use, but does not include school uniforms, or clothing or footwear used solely for sporting activities;

[7]

"partner" means–
  (a) where a person is a member of a couple, the other member of that couple; or
  (b) where a person is polygamously married to two or more members of the person's household, any such member to whom the person is married;

"paternity leave" means a period of absence from work on [7] paternity leave by virtue of section 80A or 80B of the Employment Rights Act 1996 [7];

"patient" means a person who is undergoing medical or other treatment as an in-patient in any hospital or similar institution;

"payment" includes part of a payment;

"personal independence payment" has the meaning given by Part 4 of the Welfare Reform Act 2012;

"personal pension scheme" means–
  (a) a personal pension scheme as defined by section 1 of the Pension Schemes Act 1993;
  (b) an annuity contract or trust scheme approved under section 620 or 621 of the Income and Corporation Taxes Act 1988 or a substituted contract within the meaning of section 622(3) of that Act which is treated as having become a

registered pension scheme by virtue of paragraph 1(1)(f) of Schedule 36 to the Finance Act 2004; or

(c) a personal pension scheme approved under chapter 4 of Part 14 of the Income and Corporation Taxes Act 1988 which is treated as having become a registered pension scheme by virtue of paragraph 1(1)(g) of Schedule 36 to the Finance Act 2004;

"polygamous marriage" means any marriage during the subsistence of which a party to it is married to more than one person and the ceremony of marriage took place under the law of a country which permits polygamy, and cognate expressions are to be construed accordingly;

"qualifying age for state pension credit" means (in accordance with section 1(2)(b) and (6) of the State Pension Credit Act 2002)–

(a) in the case of a woman, pensionable age; or

(b) in the case of a man, the age which is pensionable age in the case of a woman born on the same day as the man;

"qualifying contributory benefit" means–

(a) severe disablement allowance under section 68 of the 1992 Act;

(b) incapacity benefit; or

(c) contributory employment and support allowance;

"qualifying course" has the same meaning as it has in regulation 17A of the Jobseeker's Allowance Regulations;

"qualifying income-related benefit" means–

(a) income support;

(b) income-based jobseeker's allowance; or

(c) income-related employment and support allowance;

"qualifying person" means a person in respect of whom payment has been made from the Fund, the Eileen Trust, MFET Limited, the Skipton Fund, the Caxton Foundation [¹¹, the London Bombings Relief Charitable Fund, the London Emergencies Trust or the We Love Manchester Emergency Fund];

"reduction week" means a period of 7 consecutive days commencing on a Monday and ending on a Sunday;

"relative" means a close relative, grandparent, grandchild, uncle, aunt, nephew or niece;

"relevant authority" means a local authority administering council tax reduction;

"relevant child care charges" has the meaning given by regulation 28(5) (treatment of child care charges);

"remunerative work" has the meaning given by regulation 6 (remunerative work);

"rent" means "eligible rent" to which regulation 12B of the Housing Benefit Regulations refers less any deductions in respect of non-dependants to be made under regulation 74 (non-dependant deductions) of those Regulations;

"residential accommodation" means accommodation which is provided in–

(a) a care home;

(b) an independent hospital;

(c) an Abbeyfield home; or

(d) an establishment managed or provided by a body incorporated by Royal charter or constituted by Act of Parliament or by Act of the Scottish Parliament other than a local social services authority;

"sandwich course" has the meaning prescribed in regulation 4(2) of the Education (Student Loans) (Scotland) Regulations 2007, regulation 2(10) of the Education (Student Support) Regulations 2011 or regulation 2(10) of the Education (Student Support) (No. 2) Regulations (Northern Ireland) 2009, as the case may be;

"second adult" has the meaning given to it in Schedule 2 (amount of alternative maximum council tax reduction);

"second authority" means the local authority to which a mover is liable to pay council tax for the new dwelling;

"self-employed earner" has the meaning given by section 2(1)(b) of the 1992 Act (categories of earners);

"self-employment route" means assistance in pursuing self-employed earner's employment whilst participating in–

(a)   an employment zone programme;

(b)   a programme provided or other arrangements made pursuant to section 2 of the Enterprise and New Towns (Scotland) Act 1990 (functions in relation to training for employment, etc.) or section 2 of the 1973 Act (functions of the Secretary of State); or

(c)   the Employment, Skills and Enterprise Scheme;

"service user group" means a group of individuals consulted by or on behalf of–

(a)   a Health Board, Special Health Board or the Common Services Agency for the Scottish Health Service in consequence of a function under section 2B of the National Health Service (Scotland) Act 1978;

(b)   a landlord authority in consequence of a function under section 105 of the Housing Act 1985;

(c)   a public authority in consequence of a function under section 149 of the Equality Act 2010 or section 49A of the Disability Discrimination Act 1995;

(d)   a best value authority in consequence of a function under section 3 of the Local Government Act 1999;

(e)   a local authority landlord or registered social landlord in consequence of a function under section 53 of the Housing (Scotland) Act 2001;

(f)   a relevant English body or a relevant Welsh body in consequence of a function under section 242 of the National Health Service Act 2006;

(g)   a Local Health Board in consequence of a function under section 183 of the National Health Service (Wales) Act 2006;

(h)   the Commission in consequence of a function under sections 4 or 5 of the Health and Social Care Act 2008;

(i)   the regulator or a private registered provider of social housing in consequence of a function under sections 98, 193 or 196 of the Housing and Regeneration Act 2008; or

(j)   a public or local authority in Great Britain in consequence of a function conferred under any other enactment,

for the purposes of monitoring and advising on a policy of that body or authority which affects or may affect persons in the group, or of monitoring or advising on services provided by that body or authority which are used (or may potentially be used) by those persons;

[⁵ "shared parental leave" means leave by virtue of section 75E or 75G of the Employment Rights Act 1996;]

"the Skipton Fund" means the ex-gratia payment scheme administered by the Skipton Fund Limited, incorporated on 25th March 2004, for the benefit of certain persons suffering from hepatitis C and other persons eligible for payment in accordance with the scheme's provisions;

"special account" means an account as defined for the purposes of chapter 4A of Part 8 of the Jobseeker's Allowance Regulations or chapter 5 of Part 10 of the Employment and Support Allowance Regulations;

"sports award" means an award made by one of the Sports Councils named in section 23(2) of the National Lottery etc Act 1993 out of sums allocated to it for distribution under that section;

[¹"state pension credit" means state pension credit under the State Pension Credit Act 2002;]

"statutory adoption pay" means statutory adoption pay under section 171ZL of the 1992 Act;

"statutory maternity pay" means statutory maternity pay under section 164 of the 1992 Act;

"statutory paternity pay" means statutory paternity pay payable under Part 12ZA of the 1992 Act;

[⁵ "statutory shared parental pay" means statutory shared parental pay under section 171ZU or 171ZV of the 1992 Act;]

"statutory sick pay" means statutory sick pay under section 151 of the 1992 Act;

"student" means a person, other than a person in receipt of a training allowance, who is attending or undertaking–

(a)   a course of study at an educational establishment; or

(b)   a qualifying course;

"student loan" means a loan towards a student's maintenance pursuant to section 73 of the Education (Scotland) Act 1980, any regulations made under section 22 of the Teaching and Higher Education Act 1998 or article 3 of the Education (Student Support) (Northern Ireland) Order 1998 and includes a young student's bursary paid under regulation 4(1)(c) of the Students' Allowances (Scotland) Regulations 2007;

"subsistence allowance" means an allowance which an employment zone contractor has agreed to pay to a person who is participating in an employment zone programme;

[[12] "the Thalidomide Trust" means the registered charity of that name (number 266220) established for the purpose of giving relief and assistance to disabled persons whose disabilities were caused by the fact that their mother had taken a preparation containing the drug known as Thalidomide during pregnancy;]

"training allowance" means an allowance (whether by way of periodical grants or otherwise) payable–

(a)   out of public funds by a Government department or by or on behalf of Skills Development Scotland, Scottish Enterprise or Highlands and Islands Enterprise, the Secretary of State, the Young People's Learning Agency for England [[8]] or the Welsh Ministers;

(b)   to a person for that person's maintenance or in respect of a member of the person's family; and

(c)   for the period, or part of the period, during which the person is following a course of training or instruction provided by, or in pursuance of arrangements made with, that department or approved by that department in relation to the person or so provided or approved by or on behalf of the Secretary of State, Skills Development Scotland, Scottish Enterprise or Highlands and Islands Enterprise or the Welsh Ministers,

but it does not include an allowance paid by any Government department to or in respect of a person by reason of the fact that that person is following a course of full-time education, other than under arrangements made under section 2 of the 1973 Act, or is training as a teacher;

"training course" means a course of training or instruction provided wholly or partly by or on behalf of or in pursuance of arrangements made with, or approved by or on behalf of, Skills Development Scotland, Scottish Enterprise, Highlands and Islands Enterprise, a government department or the Secretary of State;

"the Trusts" means the Macfarlane Trust, the Macfarlane (Special Payments) Trust and the Macfarlane (Special Payments) (No. 2) Trust;

"universal credit" has the meaning given by section 1 of the Welfare Reform Act 2012;

"voluntary organisation" means a body, other than a public or local authority, the activities of which are carried on otherwise than for profit;

"war disablement pension" means any retired pay or pension or allowance payable in respect of disablement under an instrument specified in section 639(2) of the Income Tax (Earnings and Pensions) Act 2003;

"war widow's pension" means any pension or allowance payable to a woman as a widow or surviving civil partner under an instrument specified in section 639(2) of the Income Tax (Earnings and Pensions) Act 2003 in respect of the death or disablement of any person;

"war widower's pension" means any pension or allowance payable to a man as a widower or surviving civil partner under an instrument specified in section 639(2) of the Income Tax (Earnings and Pensions) Act 2003 in respect of the death or disablement of any person;

"water charges" means–

(a) as respects Scotland, any water and sewerage charges established by Scottish Water under a charges scheme made under section 29A of the Water Industry (Scotland) Act 2002, in so far as such charges are in respect of the dwelling which a person occupies as a home; and

(b) as respects England and Wales, any water and sewerage charges under chapter 1 of Part 5 of the Water Industry Act 1991;

[¹¹ "the We Love Manchester Emergency Fund" means the registered charity of that name (number 1173260) established on 30th May 2017 for the purpose of (amongst other things) relieving sickness, disability or financial need of victims (including families or dependants of victims) of the bombing at Manchester Arena on 22nd May 2017;]

[⁹ "welfare fund" means any fund maintained by a local authority in terms of section 1 of the Welfare Funds (Scotland) Act 2015;]

"Welfare Reform Act" means the Welfare Reform Act 2007;

"working tax credit" means a working tax credit under section 10 of the Tax Credits Act 2002;

"Working Tax Credit Regulations" means the Working Tax Credit (Entitlement and Maximum Rate) Regulations 2002; and

"young person" has the meaning given by regulation 4 (young persons).

(2) For the purposes of the definition of "full-time student" in paragraph (1), a person is to be regarded as attending or, as the case may be, undertaking a full-time course of study–

(a) subject to paragraph (3), in the case of a person attending or undertaking a part of a modular course which would be a full-time course of study for the purposes of this Part, for the period beginning on the day on which that part of the course starts and ending–

    (i) on the last day on which that person is registered with the educational establishment as attending or undertaking that part as a full-time course of study; or

    (ii) on such earlier date (if any) as the person finally abandons the course or is dismissed from it; and

(b) in any other case, throughout the period beginning on the date on which that person starts attending or undertaking the course and ending on the last day of the course or on such earlier date, if any, as the person finally abandons the course or is dismissed from it.

(3) The period referred to in paragraph (2)(a) includes–

(a) where a person has failed examinations or has failed to successfully complete a module relating to a period when the person was attending or undertaking a part of the course as a full-time course of study, any period in respect of which the person attends or undertakes the course for the purpose of retaking those examinations or that module; and

(b) any period of vacation within the period specified in that paragraph or immediately following that period except where the person has registered with the educational establishment to attend or undertake the final module in the course and the vacation immediately follows the last day on which the person is required to attend or undertake the course.

(4) In paragraph (2), "modular course" means a course of study which consists of two or more modules, the successful completion of a specified number of which is required before a person is considered by the educational establishment to have completed the course.

(5) For the purposes of these Regulations, a person is on an income-based jobseeker's allowance on any day in respect of which an income-based jobseeker's allowance is payable to that person and on any day–

(a) in respect of which the person satisfies the conditions for entitlement to an income-based jobseeker's allowance but where the allowance is not paid as a consequence of section 19 or 19A or regulations made under section 17A of the Jobseekers Act (circumstances in which a jobseeker's allowance is not payable);

(b) which is a waiting day for the purposes of paragraph 4 of Schedule 1 to that Act and which falls immediately before a day in respect of which an income-based jobseeker's allowance is payable to the person or would be payable to the person but for section 19 or 19A or regulations made under section 17A of that Act;

(c) in respect of which the person is a member of a joint-claim couple for the purposes of the Jobseekers Act and no joint-claim jobseeker's allowance is payable in respect of that couple as a consequence of either member of the couple being subject to sanctions for the purposes of section 19 or 19A of that Act; or

(d) in respect of which an income-based jobseeker's allowance or a joint-claim jobseeker's allowance would be payable but for a restriction imposed pursuant to section 6B, 7, 8 or 9 of the Social Security Fraud Act 2001 (loss of benefit provisions).

(6) For the purposes of these Regulations, a person is on an income-related employment and support allowance on any day in respect of which an income-related employment and support allowance is payable to the person and on any day–

(a) in respect of which the person satisfies the conditions for entitlement to an income-related employment and support allowance but where the allowance is not paid as a consequence of section 18 of the Welfare Reform Act (disqualification); or

(b) which is a waiting day for the purposes of paragraph 2 of Schedule 2 to that Act and which falls immediately before a day in respect of which an income-related employment and support allowance is payable to the person or would be payable to the person but for section 18 of that Act.

(7) In these Regulations, where an amount is to be rounded to the nearest penny, a fraction of a penny is to be disregarded if it is less than half a penny and is if it is a half penny or more to be treated as a whole penny.

(8) For the purposes of these Regulations, two persons are to be taken to be estranged only if their estrangement constitutes a breakdown of the relationship between them.

(9) In these Regulations, references to any person in receipt of state pension credit includes a person who would be in receipt of state pension credit but for regulation 13 of the State Pension Credit Regulations 2002 (small amounts of state pension credit).

Modifications

The amendments made by SI 2014 No.3255 which came into force on 5 April 2015 do not have effect in relation to ordinary statutory paternity pay which is paid, additional statutory paternity pay which is paid, a period in respect of which additional statutory paternity pay is payable which begins, or continues, ordinary paternity leave which is taken or additional paternity leave which is taken on or after 5 April 2015. See art 35 of SI 2014 No.3255.

Amendments

1. Inserted by reg 3 of SSI 2013 No 48 as from 18.3.13.
2. Omitted by reg 3 of SSI 2013 No 48 as from 18.3.13.
3. Inserted by reg 11(2) of SSI 2013 No 142 as from 11.6.13.
4. Amended by reg 3 of SSI 2013 No 287 as from 25.11.13.
5. Inserted by art 23(2)(d) of SI 2014 No 3255 as from 31.12.14.
6. Substituted by reg 3 of SSI 2015 No 46 as from 1.4.15.
7. Amended by art 23(2)(a)-(c) of SI 2014 No 3255 as from 5.4.15.
8. Amended by art 2 and Sch 3 para 18(2) of SI 2015 No 971 as from 26.5.15.
9. Amended by regs 4(1) and 9 of SSI 2016 No 81 as from 1.4.16.
10. Inserted by reg 3 of SSI 2017 No 41 as from 1.4.17.
11. Inserted by regs 3 and 4(a) of SSI 2017 No 326 as from 20.11.17.
12. Inserted by reg 4 of SSI 2018 No 69 as from 1.4.18.

General Note

This is similar to the HB equivalent. See p239 for the commentary.

Non-dependants

3.–(1)   In these Regulations, "non-dependant" means any person, except someone to whom paragraph (2) applies, who normally resides with an applicant or with whom an applicant normally resides.

(2)   This paragraph applies to–

(a)   any member of the applicant's family;

(b)   if the applicant is polygamously married, any partner of the applicant and any child or young person who is a member of the applicant's household and for whom the applicant or one of the applicant's partners is responsible;

(c)   a child or young person who is living with the applicant but who is not a member of the applicant's household by virtue of regulation 11 (membership of a household);

(d)   subject to paragraph (3), any person who, with the applicant, is jointly and severally liable to pay council tax in respect of a dwelling for any day under section 75 of the Act (persons liable to pay council tax);

(e)   subject to paragraph (3), any person who is liable to make payments on a commercial basis to the applicant or any partner of the applicant in respect of the occupation of the dwelling; or

(f)   any person who lives with the applicant in order to care for the applicant or any partner of the applicant, or both of them, and who is engaged by a charitable or voluntary organisation which makes a charge to the applicant or the applicant's partner or both of them, for the services provided by that person.

(3)   Excepting persons to whom paragraph (2)(a) to (c) and (f) refer, a person to whom any of the following sub-paragraphs applies is a non-dependant for the purpose of these Regulations–

(a)   a person who resides with another person to whom the first mentioned person is liable to make payments in respect of the dwelling and either–

(i)   that another person is a close relative of the first mentioned person or of the first mentioned person's partner; or

(ii)   the tenancy or other agreement between them is other than on a commercial basis;

(b)   a person whose liability to make payments in respect of the dwelling appears to the relevant authority to have been created to take advantage of the council tax reduction scheme, except someone who was, for any period within the 8 weeks prior to the creation of the agreement giving rise to the liability to make the payments, otherwise liable to make payments of rent in respect of the same dwelling; or

(c)   a person who becomes jointly and severally liable with the applicant for council tax in respect of a dwelling and who was, at any time during the period of 8 weeks prior to becoming liable, a non-dependant of one or more of the other residents in that dwelling who are liable for the council tax, unless the relevant authority is satisfied that the change giving rise to the new liability was not made to take advantage of the council tax reduction scheme.

Analysis

This regulation is similar to reg 3 HB Regs, but there are a number of important differences.

(1)   Sub-para (2)(d) is different in that it exempts those who are jointly and severally liable to pay the council tax with the applicant instead of those who have a legal joint right of occupation: see Analysis to reg 3(2)(d) HB Regs on p250. In reality, these are usually the same people.

(2)   There is no equivalent of reg 3(4) HB Regs.

(3)   There is no equivalent of reg 3(2)(e)(ii) and (iii) HB Regs. It follows that resident landlords and their families may be treated as non-dependants.

(4)   The deeming provision in para (3) is similar, but again not identical. A person whose liability to pay rent to the applicant would fall foul of reg 9(1)(a) HB Regs if s/he claimed HB, would count as a non-dependant for CTR purposes, just as s/he is for HB purposes: sub-para (a) (unless any of sub-paras (2)(a)-(c) or (f) applies to her/him). However, sub-paras (b) and (c) refer to a liability created to take advantage of the CTR scheme rather than the HB scheme. It does not follow that an arrangement that falls foul of reg 9(1)(l) HB Regs will also have been created to take advantage of the CTR scheme. In most cases, the

parties will probably not even have considered the council tax implications of the agreement. It is suggested that unless it can be shown that the dominant purpose of the parties was to secure CTR, as opposed to HB, the deeming provision in sub-para (b) cannot be satisfied: see the Analysis on p282.

Young persons

4.–(1)   In these Regulations "young person" means a person who falls within the definition of "qualifying young person" in section 142 of the 1992 Act (child and qualifying young person).

(2)   Paragraph (1) does not apply to a person who–

(a)   is on income support, an income-based jobseeker's allowance or an income-related employment and support allowance or has an award of universal credit; or

(b)   is a person to whom section 6 of the Children (Leaving Care) Act 2000 (exclusion from benefits) applies.

(3)   [¹][² Where section 145A of the 1992 Act (entitlement after death of a child or qualifying young person) applies, then during the period prescribed under subsection (1) of that section (and only during that period)–

(a)   references in these Regulations to a young person include the young person in respect of whom there is entitlement under that section; and

(b)   for the purposes of these Regulations the circumstances pertaining to the young person at the date of their death are deemed to continue throughout that period.]

Amendments

1.   Omitted by reg 4 of SSI 2013 No 48 as from 18.3.13.
2.   Amended by reg 4 of SSI 2013 No 287 as from 25.11.13.

General Note

This is similar to the HB equivalent. See p406 for the commentary.

Occupation of a dwelling as a home

5.–(1)   Subject to the following provisions of this regulation, a person is to be treated as occupying as a home the dwelling normally occupied as a home–

(a)   by that person or, if the person is a member of a family, by the person and that family; or

(b)   if the person is polygamously married, by the person, the person's partners and any child or young person for whom the person or any of the partners is responsible and who is a member of that same household,

and is not to be treated as occupying any other dwelling as a home.

(2)   In determining whether a dwelling is the dwelling normally occupied as a person's home for the purpose of paragraph (1) regard must be had to any other dwelling occupied by the person or any other person referred to in that paragraph whether or not that dwelling is in Scotland.

(3)   Where a lone parent or a person who does not have a partner and is not a lone parent is a student, other than a full-time student to whom regulation 20 applies (persons not entitled to council tax reduction: students), or is on a training course, and is liable to make payments in respect of either–

(a)   the dwelling which that person occupies for the purpose of attending a course of study or a training course; or

(b)   the dwelling which the person occupies when not attending the course,

the person is to be treated as occupying as a home the dwelling in respect of which the person is liable to make those payments.

(4)   Where a person has required to move into temporary accommodation because of the carrying out of essential repairs to the dwelling normally occupied as that person's home, and the person is liable to make payments in respect of either the dwelling which the person normally occupies as a home or the temporary accommodation, the person is to be treated as occupying as a home the dwelling in respect of which the person is liable to make payments.

(5)   Where a person is required to reside in a dwelling which is a bail hostel or probation hostel approved by the Secretary of State under section 13 of the Offender Management Act 2007, that person is not to be treated as occupying that dwelling as a home.

(6)   Where a person is liable to make payments in respect of two (but not more than two) dwellings, that person is to be treated as occupying both dwellings as a home–

(a)   for a period not exceeding 52 weeks, where the person left and remains absent from the former dwelling occupied as a home and for which the person is liable to make payments through fear of violence in that dwelling or by a former member of the person's family and–

    (i)   the relevant authority is satisfied that it is reasonable that the person should be entitled to council tax reduction in respect of the former dwelling and the present dwelling occupied as a home; and

    (ii)   the person intends to return to occupy the former dwelling as a home;

(b)   in the case of a person who is a member of a couple or a member of a polygamous marriage, where the person or one partner is a student, other than a full-time student to whom regulation 20(1) (persons not entitled to council tax reduction: students) applies, or is on a training course, and–

    (i)   it is unavoidable that the partners should occupy two separate dwellings; and

    (ii)   the local authority is satisfied that it is reasonable that the person should be entitled to council tax reduction in respect of both dwellings;

(c)   where, because of the number of persons in a family referred to in paragraph (1)(a) or (b), those persons have been housed by a housing authority in two separate dwellings;

(d)   where a person has moved into a new dwelling occupied as a home, except where paragraph (4) applies, for a period not exceeding 4 reduction weeks from the date on which that person moved if the person could not reasonably have avoided liability in respect of two dwellings; or

(e)   where a person–

    (i)   is treated by virtue of paragraph (8) as occupying a dwelling as that person's home and paragraph 8(c)(i) applies; and

    (ii)   the person has occupied another dwelling as a home on any day within the period of 4 weeks immediately preceding the date the person moved to the new dwelling,

for a period not exceeding 4 reduction weeks immediately preceding the date on which the person moved.

(7)   Where–

(a)   a person has moved into a dwelling for which that person is not liable to make payments ("the new dwelling");

(b)   immediately before that move, the person was liable to make payments for the dwelling previously occupied as a home ("the former dwelling"); and

(c)   that liability continues after the person has moved into the new dwelling,

the person is to be treated as occupying the former dwelling as a home for a period not exceeding 4 reduction weeks if the person could not reasonably have avoided liability in respect of the former dwelling.

(8)   Where–

(a)   a person moved into a dwelling and was liable to make payments in respect of that dwelling before moving in; and

(b)   either–

    (i)   that person applied for council tax reduction before moving in and no decision has been made or it was refused but a further application was made or treated as made within 4 weeks of the date on which the person moved into the new dwelling to occupy it as a home; or

    (ii)   the person notified the move to the new dwelling as a change of circumstances under regulation 89 (duty to notify changes of circumstances) before the move; and

(c)   the delay in moving into the dwelling was reasonable and–
    (i)   that delay was necessary in order to adapt the dwelling to meet the disability needs of the person or any member of the person's family;
    (ii)   the move was delayed pending the outcome of an application–
        (aa)   under Part 8 of the 1992 Act for a social fund payment;
        [¹ (bb) to a welfare fund for a payment;]
        (cc)   to a local authority in exercise of the power in section 1 of the Localism Act 2011 (local authority's general power of competence) using funds provided by the Secretary of State, and in this sub-head local authority means a local authority within the meaning of section 8 of that Act; or
        (dd)   to the Welsh Ministers, or to a person acting on their behalf, for a payment made in exercise of the power in section 60 of the Government of Wales Act 2006 (promotion etc. of well-being),
to meet a need arising out of the move or in connection with setting up the home in the dwelling and either a member of the applicant's family is aged 5 or under or the applicant's applicable amount includes a premium under paragraph 9 (disability premium), paragraph 11 (severe disability premium) or 13 (disabled child premium) of Schedule 1 (applicable amounts) or a component under paragraph 21 (work-related activity component) or 22 (support component) of that Schedule; or
    (iii)   the applicant became liable to make payments in respect of the dwelling while a patient or in residential accommodation,
the person is to be treated as occupying the dwelling as a home for any period not exceeding 4 weeks immediately prior to the date on which the person moved into the dwelling.

(9)   Where a person is treated by virtue of paragraph (8) as occupying a dwelling as a home in respect of the period before moving in, the person's application for council tax reduction in respect of that dwelling is to be treated as having been made on the latest of–

(a)   in the case of an application in respect of which a decision has not yet been made, the date that application is or is treated as made in accordance with regulation 85 (date on which an application is made);

(b)   in the case of an application which was refused and a further application was or was treated as made in accordance with regulation 85 within 4 weeks of the date on which the person moved into the dwelling, the date on which the claim was refused or was treated as made; or

(c)   the date from which the person is treated as occupying the dwelling as a home by virtue of paragraph (8).

(10)   Where a person to whom neither paragraph (6)(a) or (16)(c)(x) applies–

(a)   formerly occupied a dwelling but left and remains absent from it through fear of violence in the dwelling or by a person who was formerly a member of the family of that person; and

(b)   has an unavoidable liability to make payments in respect of that dwelling,
the person is to be treated as occupying the dwelling as a home for a period not exceeding 4 reduction weeks.

(11)   This paragraph applies to a person who enters residential accommodation–

(a)   for the purpose of ascertaining whether the accommodation suits that person's needs;

(b)   with the intention of returning to the dwelling which is normally occupied by the person as a home should the residential accommodation prove not to suit the person's needs; and

(c)   while the part of the dwelling which is normally occupied by the person as a home is not let, or as the case may be, sublet.

(12)   A person to whom paragraph (11) applies is to be treated as occupying the dwelling normally occupied as the person's home for a period not exceeding 13 weeks beginning from the first day the person enters residential accommodation, but a person is

not to be treated as occupying that dwelling as a home if the total of all periods in residential accommodation exceeds 52 weeks.

(13)   Subject to paragraph (17), a person is to be treated as occupying a dwelling as a home while that person is temporarily absent from the dwelling for a period not exceeding 13 weeks beginning from the first day of that absence from the home if–

(a)   the person intends to return to occupy the dwelling as a home;

(b)   the part of the dwelling normally occupied by the person has not been let or, as the case may be, sublet; and

(c)   the period of absence is unlikely to exceed 13 weeks.

(14)   This paragraph applies to a person who is–

(a)   detained in custody pending sentence upon conviction or under a sentence imposed by a court, other than a person who is detained in hospital under the provisions of the Mental Health (Care and Treatment) (Scotland) Act 2003, the Criminal Procedure (Scotland) Act 1995, the Mental Health Act 1983 or the Mental Health (Northern Ireland) Order 1986; and

(b)   on temporary release from a detention referred to in sub-paragraph (a) in accordance with rules made under the provisions of the Prisons (Scotland) Act 1989, the Prison Act 1952 or the Prison Act (Northern Ireland) 1953.

(15)   Where paragraph (14) applies to a person, for any day when that person is on temporary release–

(a)   if the temporary release was immediately preceded by a period of temporary absence under paragraph (13) or (16), the person is to be treated as if continuing to be absent from the dwelling, despite any occupation of the dwelling;

(b)   for the purposes of paragraph (16)(c)(i), the person is to be treated as if remaining in detention; and

(c)   if the person does not fall within sub-paragraph (a), the person is to be treated as if not occupying a dwelling as a home despite any occupation of the dwelling.

(16)   This paragraph applies to a person who is temporarily absent from the dwelling normally occupied by that person as a home and–

(a)   that person intends to return to occupy the dwelling as a home;

(b)   the part of the dwelling which is normally occupied by the person has not been let or, as the case may be, sublet;

(c)   the person is–

   (i)   detained in custody on remand pending trial or, as a condition of bail, required to reside–

      (aa)   in a dwelling other than the dwelling the person occupies as a home;

      (bb)   in premises approved under section 13 of the Offender Management Act 2007; or

      (cc)   detained pending sentence upon conviction;

   (ii)   resident in a hospital or similar institution as a patient;

   (iii)   undergoing, or as the case may be, any partner of the person or dependant child of the person is undergoing, in the United Kingdom or elsewhere, medical treatment, or medically approved convalescence, in accommodation other than residential accommodation;

   (iv)   following, in the United Kingdom or elsewhere, a training course;

   (v)   undertaking medically approved care of a person residing in the United Kingdom or elsewhere;

   (vi)   undertaking the care of a child whose parent or guardian is temporarily absent from the dwelling normally occupied by that parent or guardian for the purpose of receiving medically approved care or medical treatment;

   (vii)   in the United Kingdom or elsewhere, receiving medically approved care provided in accommodation other than residential accommodation;

   (viii)   a student to whom paragraph (3) or (6)(b) does not apply;

   (ix)   receiving care provided in residential accommodation other than a person to whom paragraph (11) applies; or

(x)   a person to whom paragraph (6)(a) does not apply and who left the dwelling occupied as that person's home through fear of violence in that dwelling or by a former member of the person's family; and

(d)   the period of absence is unlikely to exceed 52 weeks or, in exceptional circumstances, is unlikely substantially to exceed that period.

(17)   A person to whom paragraph (16) applies is to be treated as occupying the dwelling normally occupied as a home during any period of temporary absence, but the period during which the person is treated as occupying the dwelling must not exceed 52 weeks beginning from the first day of temporary absence.

Amendment

1.   Substituted by reg 4(3) of SSI 2016 No 81 as from 1.4.16.

General Note

Reg 5 is in some respects similar to reg 7 HB Regs, to which reference should be made for many of the principles to be applied (see p263 for commentary on reg 7 HB Regs). One significant difference is that in this regulation there is not the same distinction between periods of temporary absence within Great Britain or outside it as there is in reg 7 HB Regs. However, reg 5 is not relevant to the question of whether or not an applicant is entitled to CTR. To qualify for CTR, the applicant must be liable to pay council tax in respect of a dwelling in which s/he resides as her/his sole or main residence, or from which s/he is only temporarily absent, for which see regs 14 and 15. Reg 5 is, in some cases, relevant for the calculation of an applicant's capital (see, for example, Sch 5 paras 3 to 5, 13 and 30).

Remunerative work

6.–(1)   Subject to the following provisions of this regulation, a person is to be treated for the purposes of these Regulations as engaged in remunerative work if that person is engaged, or, where hours of work fluctuate, is engaged on average, for not less than 16 hours a week, in work for which payment is made or which is done in expectation of payment.

(2)   Subject to paragraph (3), in determining the number of hours for which a person is engaged in work where that person's hours of work fluctuate, regard is to be had to the average of hours worked over–

(a)   if there is a recognisable cycle of work, the period of one complete cycle (including, where the cycle involves periods in which the person does no work, those periods but disregarding any other absences); and

(b)   in any other case, the period of 5 weeks immediately prior to the date of application, or any other length of time as may, in the particular case, enable the person's weekly average hours of work to be determined more accurately.

(3)   Where, for the purposes of paragraph (2)(a), a person's recognisable cycle of work at a school, other educational establishment or other place of employment is one year and includes periods of school holidays or similar vacations during which that person does not work, those periods and any other periods not forming part of such holidays or vacations during which the person is not required to work are to be disregarded in establishing the average hours for which the person is engaged in work.

(4)   Where no recognisable cycle has been established in respect of a person's work, regard must be had to the number of hours or, where those hours will fluctuate, the average of the hours which the person is expected to work in a week.

(5)   A person is to be treated as engaged in remunerative work during any period for which the person is absent from work referred to in paragraph (1) if the absence is either without good cause or by reason of a recognised, customary or other holiday.

(6)   A person on income support, an income-based jobseeker's allowance or an income-related employment and support allowance for more than 3 days in any reduction week is to be treated as not being in remunerative work in that week.

(7)   A person is not to be treated as engaged in remunerative work on any day on which that person is on maternity leave, paternity leave [¹, shared parental leave] or adoption leave or is absent from work because the person is ill.

(8)   A person is not to be treated as engaged in remunerative work on any day on which the person is engaged in an activity in respect of which–

(a)   a sports award has been made, or is to be made, to the person; and

(b)   no other payment is made or is expected to be made to the person.

Amendment
   1.   Amended by art 23(3) of SI 2014 No 3255 as from 31.12.14.

General Note
This is similar to the HB equivalent. See p253 for the commentary.

PART 2
Families

Entitlement of only one member of a family
   7.   The entitlement of one member of a family to council tax reduction in respect of a dwelling excludes entitlement to that reduction in respect of that dwelling for any other member of the family for the same period.

Couples: polygamous marriages
   8.   Where a person is a party to a polygamous marriage no party to the marriage is to be taken to be a member of a couple for the purposes of these Regulations.

Applicant in receipt of income-related benefit
   9.   Where an applicant in receipt of an income-related benefit is a member of a family, the income and capital of any member of that family is to be treated as the income and capital of the applicant.

Responsibility for another person
   10.–(1)   Subject to the following provisions of this regulation a person is to be treated as responsible for a child or a young person who normally lives with that person.

   (2)   Where a child or young person spends equal amounts of time in different households, or where there is a question as to which household the child or young person is living in, the child or young person is to be treated for the purposes of paragraph (1) as normally living with–

   (a)   the person who is receiving child benefit in respect of the child or young person; or

   (b)   if there is no such person–
        (i)   where only one claim for child benefit has been made in respect of the child or young person, the person who made that claim; or
        (ii)   in any other case the person who has the primary responsibility for the child or young person.

   (3)   For the purposes of these Regulations a child or young person can be the responsibility of only one person in any reduction week and any person other than the one treated as responsible for the child or young person under this regulation is to be treated as not responsible for the child or young person.

General Note
This is similar to the HB equivalent. See p408 for the commentary.

Membership of a household
   11.–(1)   Subject to paragraphs (2) and (3), the applicant and any partner of the applicant and, where the applicant or the applicant's partner is treated as responsible for a child or young person by virtue of regulation 10 (responsibility for another person) that child or young person and any child of that child or young person, are to be treated as members of the same household even if temporarily absent from that household.

   (2)   A child or young person is not to be treated as a member of the applicant's household where that child or young person is–

   (a)   boarded out with the applicant or any partner of the applicant under a relevant enactment or placed with the applicant or any partner of the applicant by a local authority under section 22C(5) and (6)(a) or (b) or section 23(2)(a) of the

Children Act 1989 or by a voluntary organisation under section 59(1)(a) of that Act;

(b)   boarded out or placed with the applicant or any partner of the applicant prior to adoption; or

(c)   placed for adoption with the applicant or any partner of the applicant in accordance with the Adoption and Children Act 2002 or the Adoption Agencies (Scotland) Regulations 2009.

(3)   Subject to paragraph (4), paragraph (1) does not apply to a child or young person who is not living with the applicant and the child or young person–

(a)   is in the care of, or is being looked after by, a local authority under a relevant enactment;

(b)   has been boarded out or placed with a person other than the applicant prior to adoption; or

(c)   has been placed for adoption in accordance with the Adoption and Children Act 2002 or the Adoption Agencies (Scotland) Regulations 2009.

(4)   A child or young person to whom paragraph (3)(a) applies is to be treated as being a member of the applicant's household in any reduction week where–

(a)   that child or young person lives with the applicant for part or all of that reduction week; and

(b)   the relevant authority considers that it is reasonable to do so taking into account the nature and frequency of that child's or young person's visits.

(5)   In this regulation "relevant enactment" means the Social Work (Scotland) Act 1968, the Family Law Reform Act 1969, the Children and Young Persons Act 1969, the Children Act 1975, the Domestic Proceedings and Magistrates' Courts Act 1978, the Family Law Act 1986, the Children Act 1989, the Armed Forces Act 1991 and the Children (Scotland) Act 1995.

General Note

This is similar to reg 21 HB Regs (see p409). The difference is that in relation to reg 21, when someone does not count as "temporarily living away" from the family is defined, whereas no definition of when someone does not count as "temporarily absent" from the household is given here. This means that authorities have more discretion in relation to CTR than they do in relation to HB in this respect.

This regulation does not define household but sets out the situations in which a member of a household will continue to be treated as such, despite physical absence from it.

Para (1) sets out the general rule that applicants, their partner(s), any child or young person for whom they are responsible, and any child of such a child or young person, shall continue to be treated as members of the same household even when one or more of them is "temporarily absent" from the household. "Child" is defined in reg 2(1) and "young person" in regs 2(1) and 4.

Para (2) excludes certain children and young people from the applicant's household even when they actually live there.

Para (3) excludes certain children and young people who are absent from the household and living in the circumstances set out in para (3)(a) to (c) from being treated as a member of the household, but para (4) itself provides an exception to para (3)(a). This means that children or young people to whom both paras (3)(a) and (4) apply *are* to be treated as members of the claimant's household despite their absence – ie, certain children or young people who are being "looked after" but are living with the claimant for part or all of certain reduction weeks provided, given the nature and frequency of their visits, the local authority considers it reasonable to treat them as such. "Reduction week" is defined in reg 2(1).

Para (5) defines "relevant enactment" for these purposes.

PART 3
Application of the Regulations

Application

12.–(1)   These Regulations apply to a person who–

(a)   has not attained the qualifying age for state pension credit; or

(b)   has attained the qualifying age for state pension credit if that person, or any partner of that person, is a person on income support, [¹ universal credit,] an income-based jobseeker's allowance or an income-related employment and support allowance.

(2)   Except as provided in paragraph (1)(b), these Regulations do not apply in relation to a person whose partner has attained the qualifying age for state pension credit.

Amendment

1.   Amended by reg 5 of SSI 2013 No 287 as from 25.11.13.

General Note

The CTR(S) Regs apply where neither the applicant nor her/his partner has reached the qualifying age for PC or if either have reached that age, where one of them is in receipt of IS, UC, income-based JSA or income-related ESA. "Qualifying age for state pension credit" is defined in reg 2(1). This is the same definition in reg 2(1) HB Regs. See p244 for a discussion. Where the claimant or her/his partner has reached the qualifying age for PC and neither are in receipt of UC, IS, income-based JSA or income-related ESA, the CTR(SPC)(S) Regs instead apply (see p1574).

Prescribed years

13.   The financial year commencing 1st April 2013 and each subsequent financial year are prescribed as the years for which these Regulations apply.

PART 4

Entitlement to council tax reduction

Conditions of entitlement to council tax reduction

14.–(1)   A person who is liable to pay council tax under section 75 of the Act ("relevant person") is entitled to council tax reduction [² under this regulation] in respect of a day if the conditions set out in [² paragraphs (3) and (3A)] are satisfied and–

(a)   each of the conditions set out in paragraphs (4) and (5) is satisfied; or

(b)   the condition set out in paragraph (6) is satisfied.

(2)   A relevant person is not entitled to council tax reduction in respect of any day before the day on which that person's entitlement to council tax reduction commences in accordance with regulation 80 (date on which entitlement is to begin).

(3)   The conditions referred to in paragraph (1) are that the relevant person–

(a)   is for the day liable to pay council tax in respect of a dwelling in which that person resides [¹as their sole or main residence];

(b)   is not a person to whom regulation 15 (persons not entitled to council tax reduction: absentees), 16 (persons not entitled to council tax reduction: persons treated as not being in Great Britain, 19 (persons not entitled to council tax reduction: persons subject to immigration control) or 20 (persons not entitled to council tax reduction: students) applies; and

(c)   makes an application for council tax reduction in accordance with Part 10 (applications).

[² (3A)   The condition referred to in paragraph (1) is that the amount of council tax reduction calculated under this regulation is not less than the amount of council tax reduction calculated under regulation 14A.]

(4)   The condition referred to in paragraph (1)(a) is that there is an appropriate maximum council tax reduction in the case of the relevant person.

(5)   The condition referred to in paragraph (1)(a) is that–

(a)   the day falls within a week in respect of which–

    (i)   the relevant person has no income; or

    (ii)   the relevant person's income does not exceed the applicable amount; or

(b)   neither paragraph (a)(i) or (ii) applies to the relevant person but amount A exceeds amount B where–

    (i)   amount A is the appropriate maximum council tax reduction in the relevant person's case; and

    (ii)   amount B is 2 6/7 per cent of the difference between the person's income in respect of the week in which the day falls and the applicable amount.

(6)   The condition referred to in paragraph (1)(b) is that–

(a)   no other resident of the dwelling is liable to pay rent to the relevant person in respect of the dwelling; and

(b)   the relevant person is entitled to alternative maximum council tax reduction because of the income or aggregate incomes of one or more residents of the dwelling.

(7)   For the purpose of paragraph (6) a resident of the dwelling other than the relevant person does not include a resident who–

(a)   falls to be disregarded for the purposes of discount in accordance with Schedule 1 to the Act; or

(b)   is a person described in regulation 79 (residents of a dwelling to whom regulation 14(6) does not apply).

(8)   Subject to paragraph (9) below, where a relevant person is entitled to council tax reduction in respect of a day, the amount to which the person is entitled is–

(a)   if paragraph (5)(a) applies, the amount which is the appropriate maximum council tax reduction in that person's case;

(b)   if paragraph (5)(b) applies, the amount found by deducting amount B from amount A, where "amount A" and "amount B" have the meanings given by that paragraph; and

(c)   if paragraph (6) applies, the amount which is the appropriate alternative maximum council tax reduction in that person's case.

(9)   Where a relevant person is entitled to council tax reduction in respect of a day and paragraphs (5) and (6) apply, the amount to which the person is entitled is whichever is the greater of–

(a)   the amount referred to in paragraph (8)(a) or, as the case may be, paragraph (8)(b); or

(b)   the amount referred to in paragraph (8)(c).

Amendments

1.   Inserted by reg 3 of SSI 2013 No 218 as from 1.10.13.
2.   Amended by reg 3 of SSI 2016 No 253 as from 1.4.17.

General Note

In Scotland, the council tax valuation band multipliers for properties in bands E, F, G and H (relative to band D properties) were increased from 1 April 2017, increasing the council tax charged for those properties before any discount and/or reduction is applied.

From that date this regulation was amended and a new regulation 14A inserted by the Council Tax Reduction (Scotland) Amendment (No. 2) Regulations 2016 No.253. These amendments and an associated amendment to reg 66 introduced a new, alternative, formula for calculating CTR for applicants who are liable for council tax in a property in which they reside, as their sole or main residence, which is in band E to H, if their entitlement under that formula would be more than their CTR entitlement calculated under reg 14. As the CTR calculated under reg 14 is the greater of 'main CTR' or the 'alternative maximum CTR' (see below), this represents a third comparator. The alternative formula in reg 14A compares an applicant's income to one of two threshold amounts (the lesser of the two threshold amounts applies if the applicant is single and is not responsible for a child or young person). The threshold amounts are based on the median net income for the same kind of household, and the introduction of the alternative formula aims to ensure that applicants with income equal to or below the median are no worse off following the introduction of the higher amount for bands E to H.

Analysis

Reg 14, together with reg 14A, sets out the basic conditions of entitlement to CTR. This entitlement is calculated on a daily basis. Note that regs 14 and 14A are supplemented by regs 15 to 20.

Subsections (1) and (3) to (7): Conditions of entitlement

Under reg 14, there are two types of CTR: that known as "main" CTR and the "alternative maximum" CTR, sometimes referred to as "second adult rebate". Para (1) provides that in order to be entitled to either type of CTR, a person must always fulfil the conditions in para (3) and (3A). Then, to qualify for main CTR, both conditions in paras (4) and (5) must be fulfilled and, for alternative maximum CTR, the conditions in para (6) must be fulfilled.

The general conditions

To be entitled to CTR for any day under reg 14:

(1)   The applicant must be liable to pay council tax for that day in respect of a dwelling in which s/he resides as her/his sole or main residence: para (3)(a). Liability for council tax is defined by the LGFA 1992 and secondary legislation made thereunder. It is a subject outside the scope of this book: see CPAG's *Council Tax Handbook*. The principal section that defines liability, s75 (in Scotland), is set out in the extracts from

the LGFA 1992 (see p1082). Being "resident" in relation to any chargeable dwelling means where an individual has her/his "sole or main residence", which is a question of fact and degree in every case: *Frost v Feltham* [1981] 1 WLR 455. Accordingly, where a family had to occupy two flats in one building because of the number of members of the family, and the father was liable for council tax in respect of both flats, the tribunal erred in holding the claimant not to be resident in both dwellings (and so not eligible for CTB for the second flat): *R(H) 3/08*. The tribunal had erred in law by conflating the meaning of "dwelling" with "residence". Commissioner Howell noted in *R(H) 3/08* (para 9) that if a person is a resident of a chargeable dwelling so as to be liable for council tax on it, then s/he must also meet the condition of being a resident of that dwelling to qualify for CTB. There was therefore a legal inconsistency in the local authority's case in, on the one hand, holding the claimant to be liable for council tax for the second flat because he was resident in it, but, on the other, hand denying him CTB on the basis that he was not resident in the second flat. Although these were decisions in respect of CTB, the same would apply for CTR. For a detailed discussion of the terminology, see below.

(2)   The applicant must not be a person to whom any of regs 15, 16, 19 or 20 applies: para (3)(b). There are four categories. A person is not entitled to CTR in respect of any day on which s/he is any of the following.

–   **Absent from the dwelling** in which s/he resides, unless it is part of a "period of temporary absence": reg 15.

–   **Treated as not in Great Britain** – ie, if s/he is not "habitually resident" in the United Kingdom, the Channel Islands, the Isle of Man or the Republic of Ireland: reg 16. Certain temporary absences are disregarded for a period: reg 18. Note that a person can be treated as in Great Britain in specified circumstances: reg 17.

–   A **"person subject to immigration control"** within the meaning of s115(9) Immigration and Asylum Act 1999: reg 19.

–   An **excluded student**. Specified students are excluded from entitlement to main CTR: reg 20. They are not, however, excluded from entitlement to alternative maximum CTR.

(3)   The applicant must apply for CTR in accordance witht he rules in Part 10: para (3)(c).

(4)   The amount of CTR to which an applicant is entitled under reg 14 for that day must be equal to or more than the CTR s/he would be entitled to under reg 14A (if it is less, reg 14A determines entitlement): para (3A). Note that reg 14A can only apply if the dwelling in which the applicant resides is in council tax band E, F, G or H (see the General Note, above).

Main CTR

The additional conditions for main CTR under reg 14 are as follows.

(1)   There is an appropriate maximum CTR: para (4). See reg 66.

(2)   The applicant's income is sufficiently low: para (5). Income is calculated under Part 6 and applicable amounts under Part 5. If the day falls in a week in which the applicant's income is lower than or equal to the applicable amount, s/he qualifies under sub-para 5(a)(i) or (ii). If it is higher, s/he qualifies under sub-para 5(b) where the maximum CTR exceeds a figure obtained by applying the specified percentage to the difference between the income and the applicable amount. The daily percentage is two and six-sevenths per cent.

Maximum CTR is calculated under reg 66 on a daily basis. The weekly equivalent of the taper is 2 and 6/7 per cent times 7, which is 20 per cent. For a detailed analysis of the CTB calculation, which is the same as the CTR calculation, see *IB v Barnsley MBC* [2009] UKUT 279 (AAC).

Alternative maximum CTR

The additional conditions for alternative maximum CTR are as follows.

(1)   No other resident of the dwelling is liable to pay rent to the "relevant person" (the applicant): para (6)(a). Note that this only applies to residents who are not excluded by para (7). Note also that the phrase "liable to pay rent" is used rather than the phrase "liable to make payments in respect of the dwelling" as used for HB, for example, in s130(1)(a) SSCBA. It would seem to follow from the difference in the wording that the liability must be in respect of rent in the strict sense, that is payment made under a tenancy. Thus if the person liable is not a tenant but is a licensee or some other form of occupant, because s/he either does not have exclusive possession of any part of the property or because the nature of the occupancy is inconsistent with the nature of a tenancy, the applicant is not excluded from alternative maximum CTR. There is a great deal of caselaw on whether an occupant is a tenant or not. See *Street v Mountford* [1995] AC 809, HL and any standard textbook on landlord and tenant law for general guidance.

(2)   The applicant is entitled to alternative maximum CTR because of the income of one or more residents ("second adults") in the dwelling: para (6)(b). See reg 78 and Sch 2. This is based on the income of the "second adults", not the income of the applicant. The aim of alternative maximum CTR is to deal with cases of multiple occupancy where some residents have low incomes and others have higher incomes. Para (7) restricts the categories of people who count as "second adults".

Para (2): Period of entitlement

For the dates on which entitlement begins, see reg 80 on p1530.

Paras (8) and (9): Amount of CTR

The amount of CTR to which an applicant is entitled under reg 14 is either that calculated under para (8)(a) or (b) (main CTR) or that calculated under para 8(c) (alternative maximum CTR), whichever is higher.

An applicant who has no income, or whose income is equal to or less than her/his applicable amount, is entitled to the maximum CTR: para (8)(a). For how maximum CTR is calculated, see reg 66.

If the applicant's income is more than her/his applicable amount, entitlement to main CTR is calculated by deducting the percentage of the difference between the applicant's income and applicable amount from the maximum CTR: para 8(b).

If an applicant is entitled to alternative maximum CTR, the amount is calculated in accordance with reg 78 and Sch 2: para (6) and para 8(c).

If an applicant qualifies for both main CTR and alternative maximum CTR, s/he is awarded the higher amount of the two, commonly referred to by local authorities as the "best buy": para (9).

From 1 April 2017, if the applicant's sole or main residence is in a dwelling in the council tax band E, F, G or H a further calculation is done. This is the calculation of entitlement under reg 14A. If the applicant's entitlement under regulation 14 is equal to or higher than her/his entitlement under reg 14A, s/he will be entitled to the amount calculated in accordance with reg 14(8) and (9). If entitlement under reg 14A is higher than that under reg 14 s/he will be entitled to the amount calculated in accordance with reg 14A: para (3A) and reg 14A(1)(b).

Terminology

"Dwelling". In Scotland, by s72 of the 1992 Act a "dwelling" means any lands and heritages which fulfil the following criteria.

(1)   It consists of one or more dwelling houses with any garden, yard, garage, outhouse or pertinent other area belonging to and occupied with such dwelling house or dwelling houses.

(2)   It would, but for the fact that it is a dwelling, be entered separately in the valuation roll. The valuation roll now only records the details of non-domestic and part residential subjects.

The Scottish dwelling includes the residential part of part residential subjects and that part of any premises which has been apportioned, as at 1 April 1989, as a dwelling house. It includes caravans but only if they are the sole or main residence. Certain types of property are explicitly included in or excluded from the Scottish definition of a dwelling by statutory instruments – eg, women's refuges by SI 1992 No.2955.

"Sole or main residence" is not defined in the regulations, but there is a body of caselaw in relation to council tax and the community charge, which uses the same expression. In *Stevenson v Rogers* [1992] SLT 558, IH, it was said that the principal consideration in identifying a person's "main residence" was the length of time s/he spent in each place. This has to be read with the Court of Appeal decision in *Williams v Horsham DC* [2004] EWCA Civ 39, which, drawing on *Frost v Feltham* [1981] 1 WLR 455 (and the latter's apparent acceptance that "main" means "principal" or "most important"), concludes that "sole or main residence" refers to premises in which a person actually resides rather than the dwelling itself. The Court of Appeal went on to state that it is probably impossible to produce a definition of "main residence" that will provide the appropriate test in all circumstances. However, the Court of Appeal said that usually a person's main residence will be the dwelling that a reasonable onlooker, with knowledge of the material facts, would regard as the person's home at the material time. Arguably, the factors identified in the cases below may now be seen as material facts which the hypothetical reasonable onlooker would be expected to have regard to under the *Williams* test.

Ownership of a dwelling is not equivalent to residence, and an owner of a dwelling is not, without more, resident in it: *Parry v Derbyshire Dales DC* [2006] EWHC 988 (Admin), 5 May, unreported.

That case also decides (a) (see immediately following paragraph) that security of tenure may be relevant to the question whether the property is the person's main residence but is not relevant to whether s/he in fact resides there and (b) (see last but one paragraph below) that Mr Parry ceased to reside in the property in question when he went abroad for a protracted period and let the property for two years.

The question of whether different accommodation was rented or owned was said in *Stevenson* to be irrelevant, though a comparison of security of tenure at two competing properties may be: *Ward v Kingston upon Hull CC* [1993] RA 71, QBD.

However, the authority is also entitled to take into account where the claimant's family live and where her/his children go to school: *Codner v Wiltshire Valuation and Community Charge Tribunal* [1994] 34 RVR 169, QBD; *Cox v London (South West) Valuation and Community Charge Tribunal* [1994] 34 RVR 171, QBD. A person who owns a property and continues a relationship with a person living in another may be found to be mainly resident in the latter: *Mullaney v Watford BC* [1997] RA 225, QBD.

There is conflicting authority on the position where a person maintains a home in this country and works for long periods outside the jurisdiction. In *Ward*, the fact that the charge payer worked for most of the year in Saudi Arabia did not prevent him being mainly resident here. Merchant seamen have also given rise to litigation: in *Bradford MBC v Anderton* [1991] RA 45, QBD it was said that the home had to be the main residence because a ship could not be a residence. In *Cameron v Henry* [1992] SLT 586, IH, the Court of Session reached the opposite conclusion and held that when the charge payer was at sea, he was not mainly resident on the mainland. Some of the "habitual residence" caselaw may also be helpful: see the commentary from p301. Note also that an applicant may be excluded from entitlement to CTR if s/he is treated as not being in Great Britain: reg 16.

Practically, "sole or main residence" ought never to be an issue for CTR purposes. If someone is not a "solely or mainly resident", s/he is not liable for council tax and has no need to claim CTR. If someone is a "solely or mainly resident", and hence liable for council tax, s/he ought also to be treated as a such for the purposes of CTR. This was confirmed in *R(H) 3/08*. The claimant and his family occupied two properties as a home. He was liable for council tax on both dwellings, but the authority only awarded CTB in respect of one of them. The issue was whether a person could be a "resident", in terms of s6(5) of the 1992 Act, in two properties being occupied and used together as one combined residence, when they were listed separately on the valuation list as two hereditaments and were taxed as two chargeable dwellings rather than a single one. The commissioner said that although the question of what is a person's "sole or main residence" is always a question of fact and degree for the tribunal of first instance to determine on the evidence, there is a material difference between the kind of case (such as *Mullaney*) where a person is dividing her/his time between two distinct homes and a decision has to be made on which is the "main" one, and cases such as this, where a person is occupying contiguous premises as a single combined home. Whereas it is true that a person can only have one "sole or main" *residence*, it did not follow that this always had to be identified with one single "chargeable dwelling".

Conditions of entitlement to council tax reduction – dwellings in bands E to H

[¹ **14A.**–(1)   A person who is liable to pay council tax under section 75 of the Act ("relevant person") is entitled to council tax reduction under this regulation in respect of a day if–

(a)   the conditions set out in paragraph (3) to (5) are satisfied; and

(b)   the amount of council tax reduction calculated under this regulation is greater than the amount of council tax reduction calculated under regulation 14.

(2)   A relevant person is not entitled to council tax reduction in respect of any day before the day on which that person's entitlement to council tax reduction commences in accordance with regulation 80 (date on which entitlement is to begin).

(3)   The conditions referred to in paragraph (1)(a) are that the relevant person–

(a)   is for the day liable to pay council tax in respect of a dwelling in valuation band E, F, G or H in which that person resides as their sole or main residence;

(b)   is not a person to whom regulation 15 (persons not entitled to council tax reduction: absentees), 16 (persons not entitled to council tax reduction: persons treated as not being in Great Britain), 19 (persons not entitled to council tax reduction: persons subject to immigration control) or 20 (persons not entitled to council tax reduction: students) applies; and

(c)   makes an application for council tax reduction in accordance with Part 10 (applications).

(4)   The condition referred to in paragraph (1)(a) is that there is an appropriate maximum council tax reduction in the case of the relevant person.

(5)   The condition referred to in paragraph (1)(a) is that–

(a)   the day falls within a week in respect of which–

(i)   the relevant person has no income; or

(ii)   the relevant person's income does not exceed–

(aa)   £321, in the case of a person to whom paragraph (6) applies;

(bb)   £479 in any other case; or

(b)   neither sub-paragraph (a)(i) or (ii) applies to the relevant person but amount A exceeds amount B where–

(i)   amount A is the appropriate maximum council tax reduction in the relevant person's case; and

(ii)   amount B is 2 6/7 per cent of the difference between the person's income in respect of the week in which the day falls and the amount stated in sub-paragraph (a)(ii)(aa) or (bb) (as the case may be).

(6)   This paragraph applies to a person who–

(a)   is not a member of a couple or of a polygamous marriage; and

(b)   is not responsible for a child or young person (within the meaning of regulation 10).

(7)   Where a relevant person is entitled to council tax reduction in respect of a day, the amount to which the person is entitled is–

(a)   if paragraph (5)(a) applies, the amount which is the appropriate maximum council tax reduction in that person's case;

(b)   if paragraph (5)(b) applies, the amount found by deducting amount B from amount A, where "amount A" and "amount B" have the meanings given by that paragraph.]

Amendment

1.   Inserted by reg 4 of SSI 2016 No 253 as from 1.4.17.

Analysis

See the general note under reg 14 for the interplay between this regulation and reg 14.

Entitlement to CTR is calculated on a daily basis.

To be entitled to CTR for any day under reg 14A, just as for reg 14 the following conditions must be met.

(1)   The applicant must be liable to pay council tax for that day in respect of a dwelling in which s/he resides as her/his sole or main residence: paras (1) and (3)(a). For a discussion of the meaning of 'dwelling' and 'sole or main residence', see p1477.

(2)   The applicant must not be a person to whom any of regs 15, 16, 19 or 20 applies – see the analysis of this on p1476: para (3)(b).

(3)   The applicant must apply for CTR in accordance with the rules in Part 10: para (3)(c).

(4)   There must be an appropriate maximum council tax reduction: para (4), see reg 66.

(5)   The applicant's income must be sufficiently low. For reg 14A, this means the day falls in a week in which:

(a) if s/he is single, her/his weekly income is not more than the threshold amount of £321: para (5)(a); or

(b) if s/he is a member of a couple, a polygamous marriage or, in accordance with reg 10, is responsible for a child or young person, her/his weekly income is not more than the threshold amount or £479: para (5)(a); or

(c) if neither (a) nor (b) apply, her/his appropriate maximum council tax is higher than a figure obtained by applying the specified percentage to the difference between the applicant's income and the threshold amount of either £321 or £479, whichever applies: para (5)(b). The specified percentage is two and sixth sevenths per cent a day, equivalent to 20 per cent a week.

In addition, for an applicant to be entitled to CTR under reg 14A:

(1)   The dwelling for which she is liable to pay council tax must be in council tax valuation band E, F, G or H. If it is not, entitlement is determined under reg 14: para (3)(a).

(2)   The amount of CTR to which the applicant is entitled under reg 14A must be more than the amount to which s/he would be entitled under reg 14: para (1)(b).

If an applicant is entitled to CTR under reg 14A, the amount to which s/he is entitled is calculated in accordance with para (7).

For the date on which entitlement begins, see reg 80 on p1530: para (2).

Persons not entitled to council tax reduction: absentees

15.–(1)   Subject to paragraph (2), a person is not entitled to council tax reduction in respect of a day and a dwelling of which the person is a resident if the person is throughout that day absent from the dwelling.

(2)   Paragraph (1) does not include a person whose absence from the dwelling is part of a period of temporary absence.

(3)   In paragraph (2) a "period of temporary absence" means–

(a)   a period of absence not exceeding 13 weeks, beginning with the first whole day on which a person resides in residential accommodation and for so long as–

(i)   the person resides in that accommodation;

(ii)   the part of the dwelling in which the person usually resides is not let or sub-let; and

(iii)   that period of absence does not form part of a longer period of absence from the dwelling of more than 52 weeks,

where the person has entered the accommodation for the purpose of ascertaining whether it suits the person's needs and with the intention of returning to the dwelling if it proves not to suit the person's needs;

(b)   a period of absence not exceeding 13 weeks, beginning with the first whole day of absence from the dwelling and for so long as–

(i)   the person intends to return to the dwelling;

(ii)   the part of the dwelling in which the person usually resides is not let or sub-let; and .

(iii)   that period is unlikely to exceed 13 weeks;

(c)   a period of absence not exceeding 52 weeks, beginning with the first whole day of that absence and for so long as–

       (i)   the person intends to return to the dwelling;

      (ii)   the part of the dwelling in which the person usually resides is not let or sub-let;

    (iii)   the person is a person to whom paragraph (4) applies; and

    (iv)   the period of absence is unlikely to exceed 52 weeks or, in exceptional circumstances, is unlikely substantially to exceed 52 weeks.

(4)   This paragraph applies to a person who is–

(a)   (i) detained in custody on remand pending trial or required, as a condition of bail, to reside–

        (aa)   in a dwelling other than the dwelling referred to in paragraph (1); or

        (bb)   in premises approved under section 13 of the Offender Management Act 2007; or

      (ii)   detained in custody pending sentence upon conviction;

(b)   resident in a hospital or similar institution as a patient;

(c)   undergoing, or who has a partner or dependent child who is undergoing, in the United Kingdom or elsewhere, medical treatment or medically approved convalescence in accommodation other than residential accommodation;

(d)   following, in the United Kingdom or elsewhere, a training course;

(e)   undertaking medically approved care of a person residing in the United Kingdom or elsewhere;

(f)   undertaking the care of a child whose parent or guardian is temporarily absent from the dwelling normally occupied by that parent or guardian for the purpose of receiving medically approved care or medical treatment;

(g)   receiving medically approved care, in the United Kingdom or elsewhere, provided in accommodation other than residential accommodation;

(h)   a student;

(i)   receiving care provided in residential accommodation other than a person to whom paragraph (3)(a) applies; or

(j)   a person who has left the dwelling the person resides in through fear of violence in that dwelling or by a person who was formerly a member of the person's family.

(5)   This paragraph applies to a person who is–

(a)   detained in custody pending sentence upon conviction or under a sentence imposed by a court (other than a person who is detained in hospital under the provisions of the Mental Health Act 1983, the Criminal Procedure (Scotland) Act 1995 or the Mental Health (Care and Treatment) (Scotland) Act 2003); and

(b)   on temporary release from detention in accordance with Rules made under the provisions of the Prisons (Scotland) Act 1989 or the Prison Act 1952.

(6)   Where paragraph (5) applies to a person, for any day when the person is on temporary release–

(a)   if that temporary release was immediately preceded by a period of temporary absence under paragraph (3)(b) or (c)–

      (i)   for the purposes of paragraph (1), the person is to be treated as if still absent from the dwelling; and

      (ii)   for the purposes of paragraph (4)(a), the person is to be treated as if still in detention;

(b)   if sub-paragraph (a) does not apply the person is to be treated as absent from the dwelling for the purpose of paragraph (1).

Analysis

Except during periods of temporary absence, as defined in paragraph (3), an applicant is not entitled to CTR for any day throughout which s/he is absent from home. In some, but not all, respects reg 15 is similar in effect to reg 7(13), (16) and (17) HB Regs (ie, enabling entitlement to be retained if temporarily absent from the dwelling for up to 13 or 52 weeks in certain specified circumstances), to which reference should be made for the principles to be applied. But note that for CTR in Scotland, unlike for HB (and CTR in England), there is not the distinction between periods of absence within Great Britain and outside Great Britain. Also for CTR, in working out whether a period of absence exceeds 13 or 52 weeks, the period is to be taken as beginning on the first whole day of absence: reg 15(3).

Persons not entitled to council tax reduction: persons treated as not being in Great Britain

16.–(1)   Subject to paragraph (5), a person is not entitled to council tax reduction in respect of a day and a dwelling of which the person is a resident if the person is throughout that day treated as not being in Great Britain in accordance with this regulation.

(2)   Subject to paragraph (5), a person is to be treated as not being in Great Britain if that person is not habitually resident in the United Kingdom, the Channel Islands, the Isle of Man or the Republic of Ireland.

(3)   A person is not to be treated as habitually resident in the United Kingdom, the Channel Islands, the Isle of Man or the Republic of Ireland unless the person has a right to reside in one of those places.

(4)   For the purposes of paragraph (3), a right to reside does not include a right which exists by virtue of, or in accordance with–

(a)   regulation 13 of the 2006 Regulations; or

(b)   Article 6 of Directive 2004/38/EC of the European Parliament and of the Council on the rights of citizens of the Union and their family members to move and reside within the territory of the Member States.

(5)   A person is not to be treated as not being in Great Britain if that person is–

(a)   a qualified person for the purposes of regulation 6 of the 2006 Regulations as a worker or a self-employed person;

(b)   a family member of a person referred to in paragraph (a) within the meaning of regulation 7 of the 2006 Regulations;

(c)   a person who has a right to reside permanently in the United Kingdom by virtue of regulation 15(1)(c), (d) or (e) of the 2006 Regulations;

(d)   a refugee within the definition in Article 1 of the Convention relating to the Status of Refugees done at Geneva on 28th July 1951, as extended by Article 1(2) of the Protocol relating to the Status of Refugees done at New York on 31st January 1967;

[¹ (e) a person who has been granted, or who is deemed to have been granted, leave outside the rules made under section 3(2) of the Immigration Act 1971 where that leave is–

(i)   discretionary leave to enter or remain in the United Kingdom;

(ii)   leave to remain under the Destitution Domestic Violence concession; or

(iii) leave deemed to have been granted by virtue of regulation 3 of the Displaced Persons (Temporary Protection) Regulations 2005;]

(f)   a person who has humanitarian protection granted under the rules referred to in sub-paragraph (e); [¹]

(g)   a person who is not a person subject to immigration control within the meaning of section 115(9) of the Immigration and Asylum Act and who is in the United Kingdom as a result of that person's deportation, expulsion or other removal by compulsion of law from another country to the United Kingdom.

[¹ (h) in receipt of income support, an income-based jobseeker's allowance or on an income-related employment and support allowance; or]

[¹ (i) a person who is treated as a worker for the purpose of the definition of "qualified person" in regulation 6(1) of the 2006 Regulations pursuant to regulation 5 of the Accession of Croatia (Immigration and Worker Authorisation) Regulations 2013 (right of residence of a Croatian who is an accession State national subject to worker authorisation).]

(6)   In this regulation "the 2006 Regulations" means the Immigration (European Economic Area) Regulations 2006.

Amendment

1.   Amended by reg 4 of SSI 2015 No 46 as from 1.4.15.

General Note

This is similar to the HB equivalent. However, amendments made to reg 10 HB Regs which clarify the position for those granted limited leave to enter or remain under the EU Settlement Scheme and reflect the fact that the

Immigration (European Economic Area) Regulations 2006 have been revoked and replaced by the Immigration (European Economic Area) Regulations 2016, have not, at the time of writing, been replicated in this regulation. See p299 for commentary.

Persons treated as being in Great Britain

17.–(1) A person to whom paragraph (2) or (3) applies is to be treated as being in Great Britain, unless the person is to be treated as not in Great Britain under regulation 16.

(2) This paragraph applies to a person who is outside Great Britain in that person's capacity as–

(a) an aircraft worker;

(b) a continental shelf worker who is in a designated area or a prescribed area;

(c) a Crown servant;

(d) a mariner; or

(e) a member of her Majesty's forces.

(3) This paragraph applies to a person if–

(a) that person is a member of a couple and the other member of the couple is a person to whom paragraph (2) applies; and

(b) the person is outside Great Britain by reason only of the fact that the person is living with the other member of the couple.

(4) In this regulation–

(a) "aircraft worker" means a person who is employed under a contract of service as a pilot, commander, navigator or other member of the crew of any aircraft or in any other capacity on board any aircraft where–

(i) the employment in that other capacity is for the purposes of the aircraft or its crew or of any passengers or cargo or mail carried on that aircraft; and

(ii) the contract is entered into in the United Kingdom with a view to its performance (in whole or in part) while the aircraft is in flight;

(b) "continental shelf worker" means a person who is employed, whether under a contract of service or not, in a designated area or a prescribed area in connection with any activity mentioned in section 11(2) of Petroleum Act 1998;

(c) "Crown servant" means a person employed by or under the Crown;

(d) "designated area" means any area which may from time to time be designated by Order in Council under the Continental Shelf Act 1964 as an area within which the rights of the United Kingdom with respect to the seabed and subsoil and their natural resources may be exercised;

(e) "mariner" means a person who is employed under a contract of service as a master or member of the crew of any ship or vessel or in any other capacity on board any ship or vessel where–

(i) the employment in that other capacity is for the purposes of that ship or vessel or its crew or any passengers or cargo or mails carried by the ship or vessel; and

(ii) the contract is entered into in the United Kingdom with a view to its performance (in whole or in part) while the ship or vessel is on its voyage; and

(f) "prescribed area" means any area over which Norway or any member State of the European Union (other than the United Kingdom) exercises sovereign rights for the purpose of exploring the seabed and subsoil and exploiting their natural resources, being an area outside the territorial seas of Norway or that member State, or any other area which is from time to time specified under section 10(8) of the Petroleum Act 1998.

Temporary absence from Great Britain

18.–(1) For the purposes of determining whether a person is in Great Britain, a person's temporary absence from Great Britain is disregarded–

(a) for the first month of the temporary absence if paragraph (2) applies; or

(b) for the first 6 months of the temporary absence if paragraph (3) applies.

(2)   This pa...

(a)   the person ...
of the period c...

(SI 2012 No.303, reg 20)

(b)   the person has no...
weeks, starting from the first day...

(3)   This paragraph applies where–

...ly before the beginning
...the previous 52
...sence.

(a)   the person was entitled to council tax reduction immediately ...he previous
of the period of temporary absence; and

(b)   the absence is solely in connection with–

    (i)   the treatment of the person for an illness or physical or mental disability by, or under the supervision of, a person appropriately qualified to carry out that treatment;

    (ii)   the person accompanying a person described in paragraph (5) for the treatment of the person so described for an illness or physical or mental disability by, or under the supervision of, a person appropriately qualified to carry out that treatment; or

    (iii)   the person undergoing medically approved convalescence or care as a result of treatment for an illness or physical or mental disability, where the person had that illness or disability before leaving Great Britain.

(4)   The period in paragraph (1)(a) may be extended by up to a one month if–

(a)   the temporary absence is in connection with the death of–

    (i)   a person described in paragraph (5); or

    (ii)   a close relative of the person or a close relative of a person described in paragraph (5); and

(b)   the relevant authority is satisfied that it would be unreasonable to expect the person to return to Great Britain within the first month.

(5)   A person described by this paragraph is–

(a)   where the person is a member of a couple, the other member of the couple; or

(b)   a child or young person for whom the person, or where the person is a member of a couple, the other member of the couple, is responsible.

(6)   In this regulation "appropriately qualified" means qualified to provide medical treatment or physiotherapy or a form of treatment which is similar to, or related to, either of those forms of treatment.

Persons not entitled to council tax reduction: persons subject to immigration control

19.[¹ –(1)]   A person is not entitled to council tax reduction in respect of a day and a dwelling of which the person is a resident if the person is throughout that day a person subject to immigration control [¹]

[¹ (2)   In paragraph (1) "a person subject to immigration control" has the meaning given in section 115(9) of the Immigration and Asylum Act, but does not include a person who is–

(a)   a national of a state which has ratified the European Convention on Social and Medical Assistance (done in Paris on 11th December 1953) or a state which has ratified the Council of Europe Social Charter (signed in Turin on 18th October 1961); and

(b)   lawfully present in the United Kingdom.]

Amendment

1.   Amended by reg 5 of SSI 2015 No 46 as from 1.4.15.

General Note

See the commentary to s115(9) IAA 1999 on p1707 on who is a "person subject to immigration control".

Persons not entitled to council tax reduction: students

20.–(1)   Except to the extent that a student may be entitled to an alternative maximum council tax reduction by virtue of regulation 14 (conditions of entitlement to council tax

...es is not entitled to council tax reduction
...en that student is resident.

...) and (7), this paragraph applies to a full-time student
...ed as not being in Great Britain in accordance with regulation
...tled to council tax reduction: persons treated as not being in Great

(a)   who is a person on income support, an income-based jobseeker's allowance or
      an income-related employment and support allowance or who has an award of
      universal credit;
(b)   who is a lone parent;
(c)   whose applicable amount would, but for this regulation, include disability
      premium under paragraph 9 of Schedule 1 or severe disability premium under
      paragraph 11 of that Schedule;
(d)   whose applicable amount would include the disability premium but for the
      student being treated as capable of work by virtue of a determination made in
      accordance with regulations made under section 171E of the 1992 Act;
(e)   who is, or is treated as, incapable of work and has been so incapable, or has
      been so treated as incapable, of work in accordance with the provisions of, and
      regulations made under, Part 12A of the 1992 Act (incapacity for work) for a
      continuous period of not less than 196 days; and for this purpose any two or
      more separate periods separated by a break of not more than 56 days is to be
      treated as one continuous period;
(f)   who has, or is treated as having, limited capability for work and has had, or been
      treated as having, limited capability for work in accordance with the Employment
      and Support Allowance Regulations for a continuous period of not less than 196
      days, and for this purpose any two or more separate periods separated by a break
      of not more than 84 days are to be treated as one continuous period;
(g)   who has a partner who is also a full-time student, if the student or that partner is
      treated as responsible for a child or young person;
(h)   who is a single applicant with whom a child is placed by a local authority or
      voluntary organisation within the meaning of the Children Act 1989 or, in
      Scotland, boarded out within the meaning of the Social Work (Scotland) Act
      1968;
(i)   who is–
      (i)   aged under 21 and whose course of study is not a course of higher
             education; or
      [²(ia) aged 21 and attained that age during a course of study which is not a
             course of higher education;]
      (ii)   a qualifying young person or child within the meaning of section 142 of
             the 1992 Act (child and qualifying young person);
(j)   in respect of whom–
      (i)   a supplementary requirement has been determined under paragraph 9 of
             Part 2 of Schedule 2 to the Education (Mandatory Awards) Regulations
             2003;
      (ii)   an allowance, or as the case may be, bursary has been granted which
             includes a sum under regulation 4(1)(d) of the Students' Allowances
             (Scotland) Regulations 2007 in respect of expenses incurred;
      (iii) a payment has been made under section 2 of the Education Act 1962 or
             under or by virtue of regulations made under the Teaching and Higher
             Education Act 1998;
      (iv)   a grant has been made under regulation 38 of the Education (Student
             Support) Regulations 2011, regulation 25 of the Assembly Learning
             Grants and Loans (Higher Education) (Wales) (No. 2) Regulations 2011
             [¹or] regulation 5 of the Education (Student Support) (No. 2) Regulations
             (Northern Ireland) 2009; or

(v) a supplementary requirement has been determined under paragraph 9 of Schedule 6 to the Students Awards Regulations (Northern Ireland) 2003 or a payment has been made under Article 50(3) of the Education and Libraries (Northern Ireland) Order 1986 on account of the student's disability by reason of deafness.

(4) Where paragraph (3)(e) applies to a full-time student and the student ceases, for a period of 56 days or less, to be incapable or to be treated as incapable of work, on the student again becoming incapable or treated as incapable of work, paragraph (3)(e) applies for so long as the student remains incapable or is treated as remaining incapable of work.

(5) [³In paragraph (3)(i)]–

[⁴(a) head (ia) only applies to an applicant until the end of the course during which the applicant attained the age of 21;] and

(b) [³a reference] to a course of higher education is a reference to a course of any description mentioned in Schedule 6 to the Education Reform Act 1988.

(6) A full-time student to whom paragraph (3)(j) applies, is to be treated as satisfying that sub-paragraph from the date on which the student made a request for the supplementary requirement, allowance, bursary or payment as the case may be.

(7) Paragraph (2) does not apply to a full-time student for the period specified in paragraph (8) if–

(a) at any time during an academic year, with the consent of the relevant educational establishment, the student ceases to attend or undertake a course of study because the student is–

(i) engaged in caring for another person; or

(ii) ill;

(b) the student has subsequently ceased to be engaged in caring for the person or, as the case may be, has subsequently recovered from that illness; and

(c) the student is not eligible for a grant or a student loan in respect of the period specified in paragraph (8).

(8) The period specified for the purposes of paragraph (7) is the period, not exceeding one year, beginning on the day on which the student ceased to be engaged in caring for the person or, as the case may be, the day on which the student recovered from that illness and ending on the day before the earliest of–

(a) the day on which the student resumes attending or undertaking the course of study; or

(b) the day from which the relevant educational establishment agrees that the student may resume attending or undertaking the course of study.

Amendments

1. Amended by reg 5 of SSI 2013 No 48 as from 18.3.13.
2. Inserted by reg 4(a) of SSI 2013 No 218 as from 1.10.13.
3. Amended by reg 4(b)(i) and (iii) of SSI 2013 No 218 as from 1.10.13.
4. Substituted by reg 4(b)(ii) of SSI 2013 No 218 as from 1.10.13.

General Note

This regulation is similar to reg 56 HB Regs (see p487) in that it operates to exclude those students specified in para (2) from entitlement to CTR, though this is done simply by exclusion from entitlement rather than treating them as not liable to make payments on their homes: para (1). Full-time students are *not* precluded from entitlement to an alternative maximum CTR – known as "second adult rebate": reg 20(1). This should be assessed in the normal way. The general exclusion of full-time students from CTR does not prevent a claimant whose partner is a student from claiming CTR.

Excluded from entitlement to CTR are full-time students (defined in reg 2(1)) and students who are treated as not being in Great Britain under reg 16. The latter has no equivalent in reg 56 HB Regs, which merely bars full-time students. Para (2) confirms that even a part-time student is excluded from entitlement to CTR if s/he is treated as not being in Great Britain. The end result is the same, since reg 16 excludes such a student in any case.

The categories of students entitled to CTR are specified in para (3). These are the same as those entitled to HB in reg 56(2), save that there is no equivalent of reg 56(2)(j) here, which is spent in any case. See the commentary to reg 56 on p490.

In some cases, it does not matter that a student cannot qualify for CTR as some dwellings occupied by students are exempt from council tax (eg, dwellings where all of the residents are students and unoccupied dwellings owned by students): the Council Tax (Exempt Dwellings) (Scotland) Order 1997 (for Scotland). Where a dwelling is not exempt from council tax, students who share with non-students are not jointly and severally liable for council tax with the non-students: ss75 and 77 Local Government Finance Act 1992 as amended by s4 Education (Graduate Endowment and Student Support) (Scotland) Act 2001 (for Scotland). The definition of student is different for these purposes than for CTR: Sch 1 para 4(2) Local Government Finance Act 1992.

Note: where a non-student applies for CTR and s/he is sharing with a liable person who is a student excluded from CTR, the student is ignored in working out maximum CTR under reg 66. Alternatively, if the non-student is on IS, income-based JSA, income-related ESA or PC, the student will qualify for 100 per cent alternative maximum CTR: Sch 2 para 1.

[¹ Non-recovery of council tax arrears caused by official error

20A.–(1) Arrears of council tax are not recoverable if they arise in consequence of an over-entitlement to council tax reduction as described in paragraph (2).

(2) This paragraph applies to an over-entitlement which arises in consequence of an official error where the claimant or a person acting on their behalf or any other person to whom the council tax reduction is awarded could not have reasonably been expected to realise that it was an over-entitlement at the time it arose or upon any subsequent notification of entitlement.

(3) In this regulation, "over-entitlement" means an amount of council tax reduction which was awarded and to which there was no entitlement (whether on the initial decision or as subsequently reviewed or superseded or further reviewed or superseded).

(4) In this regulation, "official error" means a mistake, whether in the form of an act or omission, by–

(a) the relevant authority,

(b) an officer or person acting for the relevant authority, or

(c) a person providing services to the relevant authority,

where the claimant, a person acting on their behalf or any other person to whom the council tax reduction is awarded, did not cause or materially contribute to that mistake.]

Amendment
1. Inserted by reg 3 of SSI 2019 No 29 as from 1.4.19.

Analysis
As council tax reduction is a reduction in liability for council tax, rather than a benefit paid to offset council tax liability, there can be no "overpayment" in the way there was for council tax benefit and is for HB. In England, this was confirmed in a case before a VTE Vice President: *DG v Liverpool City Council* (for a discussion of the case see p1074).

An award of CTR for any given year will result in a matching reduction in council tax liability for that year. If an award of CTR for a tax year is later adjusted, the council tax liability for that tax year will be adjusted accordingly. If such an adjustment is to reduce the amount of CTR for the year, the council tax liability will increase.

Rules such as those for HB – which set out when an overpayment of HB cannot be recovered from a claimant – are not replicated in the CTR legislation in England or Wales (for more on which see p1075) nor until 1 April 2019, in Scotland.

Regulaton 20A introduces such a provision in Scotland from 1 April 2019. From that date, any arrears of council tax liability arising from an adjustment to CTR are, in the following circumstances, not recoverable. Absent those circumstances, the council tax arrears arising from the adjustment are recoverable from the council tax payer.

Under reg 20A, for arrears of council tax not to be recoverable **all** of the following circumstances must apply.

(1) There must have been an amount of CTR awarded to which the applicant has been found not to have been entitled (whether on the initial decision, or following a revision or supersession), here called an "over-entitlement".

(2) The arrears of council tax must have arisen as a result of this over-entitlement.

(3) The over-entitlement must have been caused by an official error, ie, a mistake (which can be in the form of an act or omission) by the billing authority, an officer acting on its behalf or someone providing services to the billing authority.

(4) The applicant, person acting on her/his behalf or person to whom the CTR is awarded must not have caused or materially contributed to the official error.

(5)   The applicant, person acting on her/his behalf or person to whom the CTR is awarded could not have reasonably been expected to realise that it was an over-entitlement at the time the overentitlement arose, or on any subsequent notification of entitlement.

Many of the terms used in this regulation are identical to those used in regs 99 and 100 HB Regs. See the commentary on p583 for a helpful analysis.

PART 5
Applicable amount

General Note

Ascertaining an applicant's applicable amount is a necessary step in calculating whether s/he qualifies for CTR and the amount to which s/he is entitled – as set out in regs 14 and 14A.

Reg 22 specifies the constituent parts of the applicable amount if the applicant is a member of a polygamous marriage (as defined in reg 2(1)), reg 23 explains how the applicable amount is calculated if the applicant or her/his partner "have an award of universal credit" or if they jointly have such an award, and reg 21 sets out the constituent parts of the applicable amount in all other cases. Under regs 21 and 22 the applicable amount is the sum of the amounts for the following elements, whichever apply.

−   "Personal allowances". The amount of an applicant's personal allowance depends on whether s/he is single, a lone parent or a member of a couple. Single applicants qualify for a higher personal allowance if they are 25 or over or entitled to "main phase ESA" as defined in Sch 1 para 2. Personal allowances also include an amount for each child or young person who is a member of the applicant's family. A child is someone under 16, a young person is defined in reg 4 and family is defined in reg 2(1). Unlike in England, there is no limit on the number of children or young people for whom such an amount can be included.

−   Any premiums for which the applicant qualifies, for which see Parts 3 and 4 of Sch 1.

−   Either a work-related activity component or a support component, if an applicant meets the conditions described in Part 5 of Sch 1. Note that although, subject to transitional rules, the work-related activity component is no longer included in the HB applicable amount for claims made on or after 3 April 2017, this does not apply to CTR in Scotland. Unlike for HB, the work-related activity component can still be included in a working-age applicant's applicable amount provided the conditions in Part 5 of Sch 1 are met.

−   A transitional addition if the applicant qualifies for this. The qualifying conditions are set out in Part 6 of Sch 1.

The amount attributable to each of these elements is set out in Sch 1.

For an applicant who has an award of universal credit, or if s/he is a member of a couple, whose partner does, or if they jointly have such an award the applicable amount is calculated differently – see the General Note to reg 23.

Applicable amount

21.   Subject to regulations 22 (applicable amount: polygamous marriages) and 23 (applicable amount: persons who have an award of universal credit) an applicant's weekly applicable amount is the aggregate of each of the following amounts which apply in the applicant's case–

(a)   an amount in respect of the applicant or, if the applicant is a member of a couple, an amount in respect of both of them, determined in accordance with paragraph 1 of Schedule 1 (personal allowances);

(b)   an amount determined in accordance with paragraph 3 of Schedule 1 in respect of any child or young person who is a member of the applicant's family;

[¹]

(d)   the amount of any premiums which may be applicable to the applicant, determined in accordance with Parts 3 and 4 of Schedule 1 (disability premiums);

(e)   the amount of either the–
    (i)   work-related activity component; or
    (ii)   support component,
    which may be applicable to the applicant in accordance with Part 5 of Schedule 1 (components); and

(f)   the amount of any transitional addition which may be applicable to the applicant in accordance with Part 6 of Schedule 1 (transitional addition).

Amendment

1.   Omitted by reg 5(1) of SSI 2016 No 81 as from 1.5.16, subject to transitional provision in reg 2 of SSI 2016 No 81.

General Note

See the general note under Part 5 on p1487.

This is similar to reg 22(1) HB Regs. See p412 for the commentary but note that there is no restriction on the number of children who can receive an amount under Sch 1 para 3 (ie, the so called 'two-child limit', which in some circumstances applies to HB, does not apply to CTR) and a work-related activity component can be included in the applicable amount for CTR under these regulations provided the conditions in Sch 1 Part 5 are met.

Applicable amount: polygamous marriages.

22. Where an applicant is a member of a polygamous marriage, the applicant's weekly applicable amount is the aggregate of each of the following amounts which apply in the applicant's case–

(a) the amount applicable to the applicant and one of the applicant's partners determined in accordance with paragraph 1(3) of Schedule 1 (personal allowances) as if the applicant and that partner were a couple;

(b) an amount equal to the difference between the amounts specified in paragraph 1(1)(b) and (3) of Schedule 1 (personal allowances) in respect of each of the applicant's other partners;

(c) an amount determined in accordance with paragraph 3 of Schedule 1 (personal allowances) in respect of any child or young person for whom the applicant or a partner of the applicant is responsible and who is a member of the same household;

[¹]

(e) the amount of any premium which may be applicable to the applicant determined in accordance with Parts 3 and 4 of Schedule 1 (disability premiums);

(f) the amount of either the–

(i) work-related activity component; or

(ii) support component,

which may be applicable to the applicant in accordance with Part 5 of Schedule 1 (components); and

(g) the amount of any transitional addition which may be applicable to the applicant in accordance with Part 6 of Schedule 1 (transitional addition).

Amendment

1. Omitted by reg 5(2) of SSI 2016 No 81 as from 1.5.16, subject to transitional provision in reg 2 of SSI 2016 No 81.

General Note

See the general note to Part 5 on p1487.

This is similar to reg 23(1) HB Regs. See p414 for the commentary but note that there is no restriction on the number of children who can receive an amount under Sch 1 para 3 (ie, the so called 'two-child limit', which in some circumstances applies to HB, does not apply to CTR) and a work-related activity component can be included in the applicable amount for CTR under these regulations, provided the conditions in Part 5 of Sch 1 are met.

Applicable amount: persons who have an award of universal credit

23.–(1) Where an applicant or an applicant's partner has, or the partners jointly have, an award of universal credit, in determining the weekly applicable amount for the applicant the relevant authority must use the calculation or estimate of the maximum amount of the applicant, or the applicant's partner, or partners jointly (as the case may be), subject to the [¹[² [⁴ adjustments] described in paragraph] (2A)].

[² (2)]

[²,³,⁴ (2A) The adjustments referred to in paragraph (1) are–

(a) to multiply the maximum amount by 12 and divide the product by 52; [⁵]

(b)   to add to the weekly applicable amount the sum of £16.73 in respect of each child or young person who is a member of the applicant's family.] [⁵, and

(c)   to add to the weekly applicable amount the sum of £53.47 in respect of each child or young person for whom no amount has been included in the calculation or estimate of the maximum amount as a result of the operation of section 10(1A) of the Welfare Reform Act 2012 (amounts usually to be available in respect of a maximum of two children or qualifying young persons),]

(3)   In paragraph (1) "maximum amount" means the maximum amount calculated by the Secretary of State in accordance with section 8(2) of the Welfare Reform Act 2012.

Amendments

1.   Amended by reg 6(a) of SSI 2013 No 48 as from 18.3.13.
2.   Inserted by reg 6(b) of SSI 2013 No 48 as from 18.3.13.
3.   Amended by SSI 2013 No 287 as from 25.11.13.
4.   Amended by reg 4 of SSI 2017 No 41 as from 1.4.17.
5.   Amended by reg 2(a) of SSI 2019 No 325 as from 26.11.19.

General Note

See the general note to Part 5 on p1487.

This regulation explains the method by which the applicable amount of an applicant is calculated if the applicant or her/his partner, or both of them jointly, has an award of universal credit. In such cases, the applicable amount is the sum of the following elements:

–   the UC maximum amount, as calculated or estimated by the DWP, converted into a weekly figure by multiplying the amount by 12 and dividing by 52; *and*

–   the amount of £16.73 for each child or young person who is a member of the applicant's family; *and*

–   the amount of £53.47 for each child or young person for whom an amount has not been included in calculation or estimate of the UC maximum amount because of the "two-child limit".

As the two-child limit does not apply to CTR in Scotland (see the commentary on reg 21 on p1487), sub-para (2A)(c), in force from 26 November 2019, is intended to protect CTR applicants from the application of the two-child limit to a UC award. Note that if an amount for a particular child or young person who is a member of the applicant's family has not been included in the UC maximum amount because of the UC two-child limit, when calculating the applicable amount for CTR the amount added to the weekly equivalent of the UC maximum amount for that child or young person is the sum of the amounts in sub-paras (2A)(b) and (c).

For the definition of "partner", see reg 2(1). A child is defined as someone under 16, a young person is defined in reg 4 and family is defined in reg 2(1).

Reg 26 specifies how income and capital are determined in such cases.

PART 6
Income and capital
Chapter 1
General

Calculation of income and capital of members of applicant's family and of a polygamous marriage

24.–(1)   The income and capital of an applicant's partner is to be treated as income and capital of the applicant and is to be calculated or estimated in accordance with the provisions of this Part in the same way the applicant's income and capital is calculated or estimated and any reference to the "applicant" is, except where the context otherwise requires, to be construed for the purposes of this Part as if it included a reference to the applicant's partner.

(2)   Where an applicant or the partner of an applicant is polygamously married to two or more members of their household–

(a)   the applicant is to be treated as possessing capital and income belonging to each of those members; and

(b)   the income and capital of each of those members is to be calculated in accordance with the provisions of this Part as if the member was the applicant.

(3)   The income and capital of a child or young person is not to be treated as the income and capital of the applicant.

General Note

This is similar to the HB equivalent. See p421 for the commentary.

Chapter 2
Income and capital where there is an award of universal credit

Circumstances in which capital and income of non-dependant is to be treated as applicant's

25.–(1)   Where it appears to the relevant authority that a non-dependant and the applicant have entered into arrangements in order to take advantage of the council tax reduction scheme set out in these Regulations and the non-dependant has more capital and income than the applicant, the authority must, except where the applicant is on income support, an income-based jobseeker's allowance or an income-related employment and support allowance, treat the applicant as possessing the capital and income of the non-dependant and must disregard any capital and income which the applicant does possess.

(2)   Where an applicant is treated as possessing the capital and income of a non-dependant under paragraph (1) the capital and income of that non-dependant is to be calculated or estimated in accordance with the provisions of this Part as if it was the capital and income of the applicant and any reference to the "applicant" is, except where the context otherwise requires, to be construed for the purposes of this Part as if it were a reference to that non-dependant.

General Note

This is similar to the HB equivalent. See p422 for the commentary.

[³Calculation of income and capital: persons who have an award of universal credit

26.–(1)   Where an applicant or an applicant's partner has, or the partners jointly have, an award of universal credit, in determining the income of the applicant, the relevant authority must use either–

(a)   the calculation or estimate of the income of the applicant, the applicant's partner or the partners jointly (as the case may be), made by the Secretary of State for the purpose of determining that award; or

(b)   where the income of the applicant, the applicant's partner or the partners jointly (as the case may be) is subject to frequent change during a period of entitlement to council tax reduction, an estimate of the income of that person or persons over a period that is appropriate to allow the average weekly income to be estimated accurately but the length of the period is not in any case to exceed 52 weeks.

(2)   For the purposes of paragraph (1), any deduction made from an award of universal credit for payment to a third party must be regarded as income of the person or persons awarded universal credit.

(3)   If the local authority uses the figure for income provided by the Secretary of State under paragraph (1)(a) it must convert that figure into a weekly amount using the adjustment set out in regulation 23(2A)(a) and must then modify the weekly amount to take into account–

(a)   as income, the amount of any universal credit payable converted into a weekly amount using the adjustment set out in regulation 23(2A)(a); and

(b)   regulation 25 (circumstances in which capital and income of non-dependant is to be treated as applicant's) if the relevant authority determines that the provision applies in the applicant's case.

(4)   If the local authority uses the figure for income estimated in accordance with paragraph (1)(b) it must modify that amount to take into account–

(a)   as income, the estimate of the universal credit payable made under paragraph (5), converted into a weekly amount using the adjustment set out in regulation 23(2A)(a); and

(b)   regulation 25 if the relevant authority determines that the provision applies in the applicant's case.

(5)   For the purposes of paragraph (4)(a) the universal credit payable must be estimated by the local authority with reference to the figure for income estimated in accordance with paragraph (1)(b).

[⁴ (5A) In using the figure for income under paragraph (3) or (4), the local authority must not regard as income of the applicant any amount of universal credit paid as a consequence of a determination under schedule 2 of the Universal Credit (Transitional Provisions) Regulations 2014 (transitional severe disability premium payments).]

(6) Where an applicant or an applicant's partner has, or the partners jointly have, an award of universal credit, in determining the capital of the applicant, the applicant's partner or the partners jointly (as the case may be), the relevant authority must use the calculation or estimate of the capital of the applicant, the applicant's partner, or the partners jointly (as the case may be) made by the Secretary of State for the purpose of determining that award.]

Amendments

1. Amended by reg 7 of SSI 2013 No 287 as from 25.11.13.
2. Inserted by reg 10 of SSI 2016 No 81 as from 1.4.16.
3. Substituted by reg 3 of SSI 2018 No 69 as from 1.4.18.
4. Inserted by reg 2(b) of SSI 2019 No 325 as from 26.11.19.

Analysis

Reg 26 sets out how the income and capital of the applicant are calculated for the purpose of assessing CTR entitlement, if the applicant or her/his partner (or the applicant and her/his partner jointly) has an award of universal credit (UC).

Unless reg 25 applies (see below), the income used in the CTR calculation is either:

(1) the applicant's and/or the applicant's partner's income, as calculated or estimated by the DWP for the purpose of determining the UC award (converted into a weekly figure by multiplying the amount by 12 and dividing by 52) *plus* the amount of any UC payable (converted into a weekly figure in the same way): sub-paras (1)(a) and (3)(a); *or*

(2) if the income of the applicant and/or her/his partner fluctuates frequently during the CTR entitlement period, an estimate of the income over an appropriate period *plus* the billing authority's estimate of the UC that would be payable based on the estimated income. An appropriate period is one that allows an accurate estimate of the average weekly income, but must be a period of no more than 52 weeks: sub-paras (1)(b), (4)(a) and (5).

In either case:

– any amount of UC awarded to compensate for the loss of severe disability premium is not included in the assessment of income: sub-para (5A); *and*

– any amount deducted from the UC award for payment to a third party is counted as income (eg, if the housing element of UC is deducted from the UC award and paid direct to the landlord it should still be counted as income): sub-para (2).

Note that the income of the applicant's non-dependant is used instead of that of the applicant if the circumstances in regulation 25 apply – ie, if it appears to the billing authority that the applicant is taking advantage of the CTR scheme and the non-dependant has more income and capital than the applicant: sub-para (3)(b) and (4)(b) and reg 25.

The capital used for CTR is the applicant's and/or the applicant's partner's capital, as calculated or estimated by the DWP for the purpose of determining the UC award: sub-para (6).

Chapter 3
Income

Calculation of income on a weekly basis

27.–(1) For the purposes of regulation 14(5) [¹ or 14A(5)] (conditions of entitlement to council tax reduction) the income of an applicant is to be calculated on a weekly basis–

(a) by estimating the amount which is likely to be the applicant's average weekly income in accordance with this chapter and chapters 4 to 6 of this Part and Part 5;

(b) by adding to that amount the weekly income calculated under regulation 51 (calculation of tariff income from capital); and

(c) by then deducting any relevant child care charges to which regulation 28 (treatment of child care charges) applies from any earnings which form part of the average weekly income or, in a case where the conditions in paragraph (2) are met, from those earnings plus whichever credit specified in paragraph (2)(b) is appropriate, up to a maximum deduction in respect of the applicant's family of whichever of the sums specified in paragraph (3) applies in the applicant's case.

(2)   The conditions referred in paragraph (1)(c) are that–

(a)   the applicant's earnings which form part of the applicant's average weekly income are less than the lower of the relevant child care charges or whichever of the deductions specified in paragraph (3) otherwise applies; and

(b)   the applicant or, if the applicant is a member of a couple, either the applicant or the other member of the couple, is in receipt of working tax credit or child tax credit.

(3)   The maximum deduction to which paragraph (1)(c) refers is–

(a)   where the applicant's family includes only one child in respect of whom relevant child care charges are paid, £175.00 per week; and

(b)   where the applicant's family includes more than one child in respect of whom relevant child care charges are paid, £300 per week.

(4)   For the purposes of paragraph (1), "income" includes capital treated as income under regulation 40 (capital treated as income) and income which an applicant is treated as possessing under regulation 41 (notional income).

Amendment

1.   Amended by reg 5 of SSI 2016 No 253 as from 1.4.17.

General Note

This is similar to the HB equivalent. See p424 for the commentary.

Treatment of child care charges

28.–(1)   [¹ Subject to paragraph (1A),] This regulation applies where an applicant is incurring relevant child care charges and–

(a)   is a lone parent and is engaged in remunerative work;

(b)   is a member of a couple where both are engaged in remunerative work; or

(c)   is a member of a couple where one member is engaged in remunerative work and the other–

(i)   is incapacitated as described in paragraph (11);

(ii)   is a patient; or

(iii)   is in prison (whether serving a custodial sentence or remanded in custody awaiting trial or sentence).

[¹ (1A)   This regulation does not apply where an applicant or an applicant's partner has, or the partners jointly have, an award of universal credit.]

(2)   For the purposes of paragraph (1) and subject to paragraph (4), a person to whom paragraph (3) applies is to be treated as engaged in remunerative work for a period not exceeding 28 weeks during which the person–

(a)   is paid statutory sick pay;

(b)   is paid short-term incapacity benefit at the lower rate under section 30A of the 1992 Act;

(c)   is paid an employment and support allowance;

(d)   is paid income support on the grounds of incapacity for work under regulation 4ZA of, and paragraph 7 or 14 of Schedule 1B to, the Income Support Regulations; or

(e)   is credited with earnings on the grounds of incapacity for work or limited capability for work under regulation 8B of the Social Security (Credits) Regulations 1975.

(3)   This paragraph applies to a person who was engaged in remunerative work immediately before as the case may be–

(a)   the first day of the period in respect of which the person was first paid statutory sick pay, short-term incapacity benefit, an employment and support allowance or income support on the grounds of incapacity for work; or

(b)   the first day of the period in respect of which earnings are credited.

(4) In a case to which paragraph (2)(d) or (e) applies, the period of 28 weeks begins on the day on which the person is first paid income support or on the first day of the period in respect of which earnings are credited, as the case may be.

(5) Relevant child care charges are the charges for care referred to in paragraphs (6) and (7) and they must be calculated on a weekly basis in accordance with paragraph (10).

(6) The charges referred to in paragraph (5) are charges for care which is provided–

(a) in the case of any child of the applicant's family who is not disabled, in respect of the period beginning on that child's date of birth and ending on the day preceding the first Monday in September following that child's fifteenth birthday; or

(b) in the case of any child of the applicant's family who is disabled, in respect of the period beginning on that child's date of birth and ending on the day preceding the first Monday in September following their sixteenth birthday.

(7) The charges referred to in paragraph (5) are charges for care which is provided by one or more of the care providers listed in paragraph (8) and not paid–

(a) in respect of the child's compulsory education;

(b) by an applicant to a partner or by a partner to an applicant in respect of any child for whom either or any of them is responsible in accordance with regulation 10 (responsibility for another person); or

(c) in respect of care provided by a relative of the child wholly or mainly in the child's home.

(8) The care to which paragraph (7) refers may be provided–

(a) out of school hours, by a school on school premises or by a local authority–

 (i) for a child who is not disabled, in respect of the period beginning on the child's eighth birthday and ending on the day preceding the first Monday in September following the child's fifteenth birthday; or

 (ii) for a child who is disabled, in respect of the period beginning on the child's eighth birthday and ending on the day preceding the first Monday in September following their sixteenth birthday;

(b) by a child care provider approved in accordance with the Tax Credit (New Category of Child Care Provider) Regulations 1999;

(c) by persons registered under Part 2 of the Children and Families (Wales) Measure 2010;

(d) by a person who is excepted from registration under Part 2 of the Children and Families (Wales) Measure 2010 because the child care the person provides is in a school or establishment referred to in article 11, 12 or 14 of the Child Minding and Day Care Exceptions (Wales) Order 2010;

(e) by–

 (i) persons registered under section 59(1) of the Public Services Reform (Scotland) Act 2010;

 (ii) local authorities registered under section 83(1) of that Act, where the care provided is child minding or day care of children within the meaning of that Act;

(f) by a person prescribed in regulations made pursuant to section 12(4) of the Tax Credits Act 2002;

(g) by a person who is registered under chapter 2 or 3 of Part 3 of the Childcare Act 2006;

(h) by any of the schools mentioned in section 34(2) of the Childcare Act 2006 in circumstances where the requirement to register under chapter 2 of Part 3 of that Act does not apply by virtue of that subsection;

(i) by any of the schools mentioned in section 53(2) of the Childcare Act 2006 in circumstances where the requirement to register under chapter 3 of Part 3 of that Act does not apply by virtue of that subsection;

(j) by any of the establishments mentioned in section 18(5) of the Childcare Act 2006 in circumstances where the care is not included in the meaning of "childcare" for the purposes of Parts 1 and 3 of that Act by virtue of that subsection; .

(k)   by a foster carer or kinship carer approved under the Looked After Children (Scotland) Regulations 2009 in relation to a child other than a child who has been placed with that carer–

    (i)   by virtue of a requirement of the children's hearing under section 70(3)(a) of the Children (Scotland) Act 1995;

    (ii)   by a local authority exercising the right to determine the residence of a child in respect of whom a permanence order has been granted under section 81 of the Adoption and Children (Scotland) Act 2007; or

    (iii)   in accordance with the Looked After Children (Scotland) Regulations 2009;

(l)   by a foster parent under the Fostering Services (England) Regulations 2011 or the Fostering Services (Wales) Regulations 2003 in relation to a child other than one whom the foster parent is fostering;

(m)   by a carer under the Health and Social Care Act 2008 (Regulated Activities) Regulations 2010 or the Domiciliary Care Agencies (Wales) Regulations 2004; or

(n)   by a person who is not a relative of the child wholly or mainly in the child's home.

(9)   In paragraphs (6) and (8)(a) "the first Monday in September" means the Monday which first occurs in the month of September in any year.

(10)   Relevant child care charges must be estimated over a period, not exceeding a year, that is appropriate to allow the average weekly charge to be estimated accurately having regard to information about the amount of that charge provided by the person providing the care.

(11)   For the purposes of paragraph (1)(c), the other member of a couple is incapacitated where–

(a)   the applicant's applicable amount includes a disability premium under paragraph 9 of Schedule 1 on account of the other member's incapacity or the work-related activity component under paragraph 21 of that Schedule or the support component under paragraph 22 of that Schedule on account of that other member having limited capability for work;

(b)   the applicant's applicable amount would include a disability premium under paragraph 9 of Schedule 1 on account of the other member's incapacity but for that other member being treated as capable of work by virtue of a determination made in accordance with regulations made under section 171E of the 1992 Act;

(c)   the applicant's applicable amount would include the support component under paragraph 22 of Schedule 1 or the work-related activity component under paragraph 21 of Schedule 1 on account of the other member having limited capability for work but for that other member being treated as not having limited capability for work by virtue of a determination made in accordance with the Employment and Support Allowance Regulations;

(d)   the applicant is, or is treated as, incapable of work and has been incapable, or treated as incapable, of work in accordance with the provisions of, and regulations made under, Part 12A of the 1992 Act (incapacity for work) for a continuous period of not less than 196 days, and for this purpose any two or more separate periods separated by a break of not more than 56 days are to be treated as one continuous period;

(e)   the applicant has, or is treated as having, limited capability for work and has had, or been treated as having, limited capability for work in accordance with the Employment and Support Allowance Regulations for a continuous period of not less than 196 days, and for this purpose any two or more separate periods separated by a break of not more than 84 days are to be treated as one continuous period;

(f)   there is payable in respect of the other member one or more of the following pensions or allowances–

    (i)   long-term incapacity benefit or short-term incapacity benefit at the higher rate under Schedule 4 to the 1992 Act;

(ii)   attendance allowance under section 64 of the 1992 Act;
(iii)   severe disablement allowance under section 68 of the 1992 Act;
(iv)   disability living allowance;
[¹(iva) armed forces independence payment;]
(v)   personal independence payment;
(vi)   increase of disablement pension under section 104 of the 1992 Act;
(vii) a pension increase paid as part of a war disablement pension or under an industrial injuries scheme which is analogous to an allowance or increase of disablement pension under head (ii), (iv), (v) or (vi) above; or
(viii) main phase employment and support allowance;

(g)   a pension or allowance to which sub-paragraph (f)(ii), (iv), (v)[², (vi) or (vii)] refers was payable on account of the other member's incapacity but has ceased to be payable in consequence of the other member becoming a patient, which in this regulation means a person (other than a person who is serving a sentence of imprisonment or detention in a youth custody institution) who is regarded as receiving free in-patient treatment within the meaning of regulation 2(4) and (5) of the Social Security (Hospital In-Patients) Regulations 2005;

(h)   sub-paragraph (f) or (g) would apply to the other member if the legislative provisions referred to in those sub-paragraphs were provisions under any corresponding enactment having effect in Northern Ireland; or

(i)   the other member has an invalid carriage or other vehicle provided under section 46 of the National Health Service (Scotland) Act 1978, paragraph 9(1) of Schedule 1 to the National Health Service Act 2006 or article 30(1) of the Health and Personal Social Services (Northern Ireland) Order 1972.

(12)   Where paragraph (11)(d) applies and the applicant ceases to be, or to be treated as, incapable of work but within a period of 56 days or less of that cessation the applicant is, or is treated as, incapable of work, paragraph 11(d) applies from the time the applicant is again, or is again treated as, incapable of work for so long as the applicant is, or is treated as, incapable of work.

(13)   Where paragraph (11)(e) applies and the applicant ceases, to have, or to be treated as having, limited capability for work but within a period of 84 days or less of that cessation the applicant has, or is treated as having, limited capability for work, paragraph 11(e) applies from the time the applicant has again, or is again treated as having, limited capability for work for so long as that situation continues.

(14)   For the purposes of paragraphs (6) and (8)(a), a person is disabled if the person is a person–
(a)   in respect of whom disability living allowance or personal independence payment is payable, or has ceased to be payable solely because the person is a patient[¹, or in respect of whom armed forces independence payment is payable];
(b)   who has been certified as blind and in consequence is registered as blind in a register maintained by or on behalf of a local authority in Scotland or is registered as blind in a register compiled under section 29 of the National Assistance Act 1948 (welfare services) [⁶ or is registered as severely sight-impaired in a register kept by a local authority in Wales under section 18(1)(a) of the Social Services and Well-being (Wales) Act 2014]; or
(c)   who ceased to be registered as blind in such a register within the period beginning 28 weeks before the first Monday in September following the person's fifteenth birthday and ending on the day preceding the person's sixteenth birthday.

(15)   For the purposes of paragraph (1) a person on maternity leave, paternity leave [⁴, shared parental leave] or adoption leave is to be treated as if engaged in remunerative work for the period specified in paragraph (16) ("the relevant period") provided that–
(a)   in the week before the period of maternity leave, paternity leave[⁴, shared parental leave] or adoption leave began the person was in remunerative work;
(b)   the person is incurring relevant child care charges; and
(c)   the person is entitled to either statutory maternity pay under section 164 of the 1992 Act, [⁵] statutory paternity pay] by virtue of section 171ZA or 171ZB of

the 1992 Act[5], [4 statutory shared parental pay, statutory adoption pay] by virtue of section 171ZL of the 1992 Act, maternity allowance under section 35 of the 1992 Act or qualifying support.

(16) For the purposes of paragraph (15) the relevant period begins on the day on which the person's maternity leave, paternity leave [4, shared parental leave] or adoption leave commences and ends on the earliest of the following dates–

(a) the date that leave ends;

(b) if no child care element of working tax credit is in payment on the date that entitlement to maternity allowance, qualifying support, statutory maternity pay,[5] statutory paternity pay [4 or statutory shared parental pay or statutory adoption pay ends], the date that entitlement ends; or

(c) if a child care element of working tax credit is in payment on the date that entitlement to maternity allowance or qualifying support, statutory maternity pay, ordinary or additional statutory paternity pay [4 or statutory shared parental pay or statutory adoption pay ends], the date that entitlement to that award of the child care element of the working tax credit ends.

(17) In this regulation–

(a) "qualifying support" means income support to which the person is entitled by virtue of paragraph 14B of Schedule 1B to the Income Support Regulations; and

(b) "child care element of working tax credit" means the element of working tax credit prescribed under section 12 of the Tax Credits Act 2002 (child care element).

Modifications

The amendments made by SI 2014 No.3255 which came into force on 5 April 2015 do not have effect in relation to ordinary statutory paternity pay which is paid, additional statutory paternity pay which is paid, a period in respect of which additional statutory paternity pay is payable which begins, or continues, ordinary paternity leave which is taken or additional paternity leave which is taken on or after 5 April 2015. See art 35 of SI 2014 No.3255.

Amendments

1. Inserted by reg 11(3) of SSI 2013 No. 142 as from 11.6.13.
2. Amended by reg 5 of SSI 2013 No 218 as from 1.10.13.
3. Amended by reg 8 of SSI 2013 No 287 as from 25.11.13.
4. Amended by art 23(4(a)(i) and (iv) and (b)(i)(and (iii) of SI 2014 No 3255 as from 31.12.14.
5. Amended by art 23(4)(a)(ii) and (iii) and (b)(ii) of SI 2014 No 3255 as from 5.4.15.
6. Inserted by reg 6(1) of SSI 2016 No 81 as from 6.4.16.

General Note

This is similar to the HB equivalent. See p429 for the commentary. For commentary on the need to register as blind or severely sight impaired to satisfy sub-para (14)(b), see the General Note to Sch 2 para 6 of The Council Tax Reduction Schemes and Prescribed Requirements (Wales) Regulations 2013 No.3029 on p1248.

This regulation does not apply if the applicant or her/his partner, or the applicant and her/his partner jointly, has an award of UC. This is because, in such cases, the applicable amount for CTR is based on the UC maximum amount, subject to the adjustments in reg 23(2A), and the UC maximum amount includes a childcare costs element if the conditions in regs 31–33 of the UC Regs are met. See reg 25 for how income and capital are calculated if there is an award of UC.

Average weekly earnings of employed earners

29.–(1) Where an applicant's income consists of earnings from employment as an employed earner the applicant's average weekly earnings are to be estimated by reference to the earnings from that employment–

(a) over a period immediately preceding the reduction week in which the application is made or treated as made and being a period of–

(i) 5 weeks, if the applicant is paid weekly; or

(ii) 2 months, if the applicant is paid monthly; or

(b) whether or not sub-paragraph (a)(i) or (ii) applies, where an applicant's earnings fluctuate, over such other period preceding the reduction week in which the application is made or treated as made as may, in any particular case, enable the applicant's average weekly earnings to be estimated more accurately.

(2)   Where the applicant has been in that employment for less than the period specified in paragraph (1)(a)(i) or (ii)–

(a)   and has received earnings for the period that the applicant has been in that employment and those earnings are likely to represent the average weekly earnings from that employment the applicant's average weekly earnings are to be estimated by reference to those earnings; and

(b)   in any other case, the relevant authority must require the applicant's employer to furnish an estimate of the applicant's likely weekly earnings over such period as the relevant authority may require and the applicant's average weekly earnings are to be estimated by reference to that estimate.

(3)   Where the amount of an applicant's earnings changes during a period of entitlement to council tax reduction average weekly earnings are to be estimated by reference to the applicant's likely earnings from the employment over a period that is appropriate to allow the average weekly earnings to be estimated accurately but the length of the period is not in any case to exceed 52 weeks.

(4)   For the purposes of this regulation the applicant's earnings are to be calculated in accordance with chapter 4 of this Part.

General Note
This is similar to the HB equivalent. See p432 for the commentary.

Average weekly earnings of self-employed earners

30.–(1)   Where an applicant's income consists of earnings from employment as a self-employed earner the applicant's average weekly earnings are to be estimated by reference to the earnings from that employment over such period as is appropriate in order that the applicant's average weekly earnings may be estimated accurately but the length of the period is not in any case to exceed 52 weeks.

(2)   For the purposes of this regulation the applicant's earnings are to be calculated in accordance with chapter 5 of this Part.

General Note
This is similar to the HB equivalent. See p434 for the commentary.

Average weekly income other than earnings

31.–(1)   An applicant's income which does not consist of earnings must, except where paragraph (2) applies, be estimated over a period that is appropriate to allow the applicant's average weekly income to be estimated accurately but the length of the period is not in any case to exceed 52 weeks and nothing in this paragraph authorises a relevant authority to disregard any income other than that specified in Schedule 4.

(2)   The period over which any benefit under the benefit Acts is to be taken into account is the period in respect of which that benefit is payable.

(3)   For the purposes of this regulation income other than earnings is to be calculated in accordance with chapter 6 of this Part.

General Note
This is similar to the HB equivalent. See p434 for the commentary.

Calculation of average weekly income from [¹] tax credits

32.–(1)   This regulation applies where an applicant receives a working tax credit [¹ or child tax credit].

(2)   [¹] the period over which [¹ that] tax credit is to be taken into account is the period set out in paragraph (3).

(3)   Where the instalment in respect of which payment of [¹ that] tax credit is made is–

(a)   a daily instalment, the period is one day, being the day in respect of which the instalment is paid;

(b)   a weekly instalment, the period is 7 days, ending on the day on which the instalment is due to be paid;

(c)   a 2 weekly instalment, the period is 14 days, commencing 6 days before the day on which the instalment is due to be paid; or

(d)   a 4 weekly instalment, the period is 28 days, ending on the day on which the instalment is due to be paid.

Amendment

1.   Amended by regs 9 and 10 of SSI 2013 No 287 as from 25.11.13.

General Note

This is similar to the HB equivalent. See p435 for the commentary.

Calculation of weekly income

33.–(1)   For the purposes of regulations 29 (average weekly earnings of employed earners), 31 (average weekly income other than earnings) and 32 (calculation of average weekly income from tax credits), where the period in respect of which a payment of income is made–

(a)   does not exceed a week, the weekly amount is the amount of that payment;

(b)   exceeds a week, the weekly amount is to be determined–

(i)   in a case where that period is a month, by multiplying the amount of the payment by 12 and dividing the product by 52;

(ii)   in any other case, by dividing the amount of the payment by the number equal to the number of days in the period to which it relates and multiplying the quotient by 7.

(2)   For the purposes of regulation 30 (average weekly earnings of self-employed earners) the weekly amount of earnings of an applicant is to be determined by dividing the applicant's earnings over the assessment period by the number equal to the number of days in that period and multiplying the quotient by 7.

General Note

This is similar to the HB equivalent. See p437 for the commentary.

Chapter 4
Employed earners

Earnings of employed earners

34.–(1)   Subject to paragraph (2), "earnings" means in the case of employment as an employed earner any remuneration or profit derived from that employment and includes–

(a)   any bonus or commission;

(b)   any payment in lieu of remuneration except any periodic sum paid to an applicant on account of the termination of the applicant's employment by reason of redundancy;

(c)   any payment in lieu of notice or any lump sum payment intended as compensation for the loss of employment but only in so far as it represents loss of income;

(d)   any holiday pay except any payable more than 4 weeks after termination or interruption of the employment;

(e)   any payment by way of a retainer;

(f)   any payment made by an applicant's employer in respect of expenses not wholly, exclusively and necessarily incurred in the performance of the duties of the employment, including any payment made by the applicant's employer in respect of–

(i)   travelling expenses incurred by the applicant between the applicant's home and place of employment; or

(ii)   expenses incurred by the applicant under arrangements made for the care of a member of the applicant's family owing to the applicant's absence from home;

(g)   any award of compensation made under section 112(4) or 117(3)(a) of the Employment Rights Act 1996 (remedies and compensation for unfair dismissal);

(h)   any payment or remuneration made under section 28, 34, 64, 68 or 70 of the Employment Rights Act 1996 (right to guarantee payments, remuneration on suspension on medical or maternity grounds, complaints to employment tribunals);

(i)   any such sum as is referred to in section 112 of the 1992 Act (certain sums to be earnings for social security purposes);

(j)   any statutory sick pay, statutory maternity pay, [²] statutory paternity pay[², statutory shared parental pay or statutory adoption pay], or a corresponding payment under any enactment having effect in Northern Ireland;

(k)   any remuneration paid by or on behalf of an employer to an applicant who for the time being is on maternity leave, paternity leave [¹, shared parental leave] or adoption leave or is absent from work because the applicant is ill; and

(l)   the amount of any payment by way of a non-cash voucher which has been taken into account in the computation of a person's earnings in accordance with Part 5 of Schedule 3 to the Social Security (Contributions) Regulations 2001.

(2)   Earnings do not include–

(a)   subject to paragraph (3), any payment in kind;

(b)   any payment in respect of expenses wholly, exclusively and necessarily incurred in the performance of the duties of the employment;

(c)   any occupational pension; or

(d)   any payment in respect of expenses arising out of the applicant's participation in a service user group.

(3)   Paragraph (2)(a) does not apply in respect of any non-cash voucher referred to in paragraph (1)(l).

Modifications
The amendments made by SI 2014 No.3255 which came into force on 5 April 2015 do not have effect in relation to ordinary statutory paternity pay which is paid, additional statutory paternity pay which is paid, a period in respect of which additional statutory paternity pay is payable which begins, or continues, ordinary paternity leave which is taken or additional paternity leave which is taken on or after 5 April 2015. See art 35 of SI 2014 No.3255.

Amendments
1.   Amended by art 23(5)((b) of SI 2014 No 3255 as from 31.12.14.
2.   Amended by art 23(5)(a) of SI 2014 No 3255 as from 5.4.15.

General Note
This is similar to the HB equivalent. See p439 for the commentary.

Calculation of net earnings of employed earners
35.–(1)   For the purposes of regulation 29 (average weekly earnings of employed earners), the earnings of an applicant derived or likely to be derived from employment as an employed earner to be taken into account are, subject to paragraph (2), the applicant's net earnings.

(2)   Any sum, where applicable, specified in Schedule 3 is to be disregarded when calculating an applicant's net earnings.

(3)   For the purposes of paragraph (1) net earnings are, except where paragraph (6) applies, to be calculated by taking into account the gross earnings of the applicant from that employment over the assessment period, less–

(a)   any amount deducted from those earnings by way of–

    (i)   income tax;

    (ii)   primary Class 1 contributions under the 1992 Act;

(b)   one-half of any sum paid by the applicant by way of a contribution towards an occupational pension scheme;

(c)   one-half of the amount calculated in accordance with paragraph (5) in respect of any qualifying contribution payable by the applicant; and

(d)   where those earnings include a payment which is payable under any enactment having effect in Northern Ireland and which corresponds to statutory sick pay, statutory maternity pay, [²] statutory paternity pay [¹, statutory shared parental pay or statutory adoption pay], any amount deducted from those earnings by way of any contributions which are payable under any enactment having effect in Northern Ireland and which correspond to primary Class 1 contributions under the 1992 Act.

(4)   In this regulation "qualifying contribution" means any sum which is payable periodically as a contribution towards a personal pension scheme.

(5)   The amount in respect of any qualifying contribution is to be calculated by multiplying the daily amount of the qualifying contribution by the number equal to the number of days in the assessment period; and for the purposes of this regulation the daily amount of the qualifying contribution is to be determined–

(a)   where the qualifying contribution is payable monthly, by multiplying the amount of the qualifying contribution by 12 and dividing the product by 365; and

(b)   in any other case, by dividing the amount of the qualifying contribution by the number equal to the number of days in the period to which the qualifying contribution relates.

(6)   Where the earnings of an applicant are estimated under regulation 29(2)(b) (average weekly earnings of employed earners), the applicant's net earnings are to be calculated by taking into account those earnings over the assessment period, less–

(a)   an amount in respect of income tax equivalent to an amount calculated by applying to those earnings the basic rate of tax applicable to the assessment period less only the personal relief to which the applicant is entitled under section 35(1) of the Income Tax Act 2007 (personal allowance for those aged under 65) as is appropriate to the applicant's circumstances but, if the assessment period is less than a year, the earnings to which the basic rate of tax is to be applied and the amount of the personal relief deductible under this sub-paragraph are to be calculated on a pro rata basis;

(b)   an amount equivalent to the amount of the primary Class 1 contributions that would be payable by the applicant under the 1992 Act in respect of those earnings if such contributions were payable; and

(c)   one-half of any sum which would be payable by the applicant by way of a contribution towards an occupational or personal pension scheme, if the earnings so estimated were actual earnings.

Modifications

The amendments made by SI 2014 No.3255 which came into force on 5 April 2015 do not have effect in relation to ordinary statutory paternity pay which is paid, additional statutory paternity pay which is paid, a period in respect of which additional statutory paternity pay is payable which begins, or continues, ordinary paternity leave which is taken or additional paternity leave which is taken on or after 5 April 2015. See art 35 of SI 2014 No.3255.

Amendments

1.   Amended by art 23(6)((b) of SI 2014 No 3255 as from 31.12.14.
2.   Amended by art 23(6)(a) of SI 2014 No 3255 as from 5.4.15.

General Note

This is similar to the HB equivalent. See p443 for the commentary.

Chapter 5
Self-employed earners

Earnings of self-employed earners

36.–(1)   Subject to paragraph (2), "earnings" means in the case of employment as a self-employed earner, the gross income of the employment.

(2)   "Earnings" does not include any payment to which paragraph 30 or 31 of Schedule 4 refers (payments in respect of a person accommodated with the applicant under arrangements made by a local authority or voluntary organisation and payments made to the applicant by a health authority, local authority or voluntary organisation in respect of persons temporarily in the applicant's care) nor does it include any sports award.

(3)   This paragraph applies to–
(a)   royalties or other sums paid as a consideration for the use of, or the right to use, any copyright, design, patent or trade mark; and
(b)   any payment in respect of any–
   (i)   book registered under the Public Lending Right Scheme 1982; or
   (ii)   work made under any international public lending right scheme that is analogous to the Public Lending Right Scheme 1982,
where the applicant is the first owner of the copyright, design, patent or trade mark, or an original contributor to the book or work concerned.

(4)   Where the applicant's earnings consist of any items to which paragraph (3) applies, those earnings are to be taken into account over a period equal to the number of weeks equal to the number obtained (and any fraction is to be treated as a corresponding fraction of a week) by dividing the earnings by the amount of council tax reduction to which the applicant would have been entitled had the payment not been made plus an amount equal to the total of the sums which would fall to be disregarded from the payment under Schedule 3 (sums to be disregarded in the calculation of earnings) as appropriate in the applicant's case.

General Note
This is similar to the HB equivalent. See p445 for the commentary.

Calculation of net profit of self-employed earners

37.–(1)   For the purposes of regulation 30 (average weekly earnings of self-employed earners) the earnings of an applicant to be taken into account are–
(a)   in the case of a self-employed earner who is engaged in employment on that earner's own account, the net profit derived from that employment;
(b)   in the case of a self-employed earner whose employment is carried on in partnership or is that of a share fisherman within the meaning of the Social Security (Mariners' Benefits) Regulations 1975, that earner's share of the net profit derived from that employment, less–
   (i)   an amount in respect of income tax and social security contributions payable under the 1992 Act calculated in accordance with regulation 38 (deduction of tax and contributions for self-employed earners); and
   (ii)   one-half of the amount calculated in accordance with paragraph (11) in respect of any qualifying premium.

(2)   Any sum, where applicable, specified in Schedule 3 is to be disregarded when calculating a self-employed earner's net profit.

(3)   For the purposes of paragraph (1)(a) the net profit of the employment is, except where paragraph (9) applies, to be calculated by taking into account the earnings of the employment over the assessment period less–
(a)   subject to paragraphs (5) to (8), any expenses wholly and exclusively incurred in that period for the purposes of that employment;
(b)   an amount in respect of–
   (i)   income tax; and
   (ii)   social security contributions payable under the 1992 Act; and
(c)   one-half of the amount calculated in accordance with paragraph (11) in respect of any qualifying premium.

(4)   For the purposes of paragraph (1)(b) the net profit of the employment is to be calculated by taking into account the earnings of the employment over the assessment period less, subject to paragraphs (5) to (8), any expenses wholly and exclusively incurred in that period for the purposes of the employment.

(5)   Subject to paragraph (6), no deduction is to be made under paragraph (3)(a) or (4), in respect of–
(a)   any capital expenditure;
(b)   the depreciation of any capital asset;
(c)   any sum employed or intended to be employed in the setting up or expansion of the employment;

(d)   any loss incurred before the beginning of the assessment period;

(e)   the repayment of capital on any loan taken out for the purposes of the employment;

(f)   any expenses incurred in providing business entertainment; or

(g)   any debts, except bad debts proved to be bad, but this sub-paragraph does not apply to any expenses incurred in the recovery of a debt.

(6)   A deduction is to be made under paragraph (3)(a) or (4) in respect of the repayment of capital on any loan used for–

(a)   the replacement in the course of business of equipment or machinery; and

(b)   the repair of an existing business asset except to the extent that any sum is payable under an insurance policy for its repair.

(7)   The relevant authority is to refuse to make a deduction in respect of any expenses under paragraph (3)(a) or (4) where it is not satisfied given the nature and the amount of the expense that it has been reasonably incurred.

(8)   For the avoidance of doubt–

(a)   a deduction is not to be made under paragraph (3)(a) or (4) in respect of any sum unless it has been expended for the purposes of the employment;

(b)   a deduction is to be made under paragraph (3)(a) or (4) in respect of–

    (i)   the excess of any value added tax paid over value added tax received in the assessment period;

    (ii)   any income expended in the repair of an existing business asset except to the extent that any sum is payable under an insurance policy for its repair; and

    (iii)   any payment of interest on a loan taken out for the purposes of the employment.

(9)   Where an applicant is engaged in employment as a child minder the net profit of the employment is to be one-third of the earnings of that employment, less–

(a)   an amount in respect of–

    (i)   income tax; and

    (ii)   social security contributions payable under the 1992 Act;

    calculated in accordance with regulation 38 (deduction of tax and contributions of self-employed earners); and

(b)   one-half of the amount calculated in accordance with paragraph (11) in respect of any qualifying premium.

(10)   For the avoidance of doubt where an applicant is engaged in employment as a self-employed earner and is also engaged in one or more other employments as a self-employed or employed earner any loss incurred in any one of those employments is not to be offset against earnings in any other of the applicant's employments.

(11)   The amount in respect of any qualifying premium is to be calculated by multiplying the daily amount of the qualifying premium by the number equal to the number of days in the assessment period, and for the purposes of this regulation the daily amount of the qualifying premium is to be determined–

(a)   where the qualifying premium is payable monthly, by multiplying the amount of the qualifying premium by 12 and dividing the product by 365; and

(b)   in any other case, by dividing the amount of the qualifying premium by the number equal to the number of days in the period to which the qualifying premium relates.

(12)   In this regulation "qualifying premium" means any premium which is payable periodically in respect of a personal pension scheme and is payable on or after the date of the application.

General Note

This is similar to the HB equivalent. See p447 for the commentary.

Deduction of tax and contributions of self-employed earners

38.–(1)   The amount to be deducted in respect of income tax under regulation 37(1)(b)(i), (3)(b)(i) or (9)(a)(i) (calculation of net profit of self-employed earners) is to be calculated on the basis of the amount of chargeable income and as if that income was assessable to income tax at the basic rate of tax applicable to the assessment period less only the personal relief to which the applicant is entitled under section 35(1) of the Income Tax Act 2007 (personal allowance for those aged under 65) as is appropriate to the applicant's circumstances, but, if the assessment period is less than one year the earnings to which the basic rate of tax is to be applied and the amount of the personal reliefs deductible under this paragraph are to be calculated on a pro rata basis.

(2)   The amount to be deducted in respect of social security contributions under regulation 37(1)(b)(i), (3)(b)(ii) or (9)(a)(ii) is the total of–

(a)   the amount of Class 2 contributions payable under section [¹ 11(2)] or, as the case may be, [¹ 11(8)] of the 1992 Act at the rate applicable to the assessment period except where the applicant's chargeable income is less than the amount specified in section 11(4) of that Act (¹ small profits threshold]) for the tax year applicable to the assessment period, but if the assessment period is less than one year, the amount specified for that tax year is to be reduced pro rata; and

(b)   the amount of Class 4 contributions (if any) which would be payable under section 15 of the 1992 Act (Class 4 contributions recoverable under the Income Tax Acts) at the percentage rate applicable to the assessment period on so much of the chargeable income as exceeds the lower limit but does not exceed the upper limit of profits and gains applicable for the tax year applicable to the assessment period, but if the assessment period is less than one year those limits are to be reduced pro rata.

(3)   In this regulation "chargeable income" means–

(a)   except where sub-paragraph (b) applies, the earnings derived from the employment less any expenses deducted under regulation 37(3)(a) or, as the case may be, (4); and

(b)   in the case of employment as a child minder, one-third of the earnings of that employment.

Amendments

1.   Amended by reg 11 of SSI 2016 No 81 as from 1.4.16.

General Note

This is similar to the HB equivalent. See p450 for the commentary.

Chapter 6
Other income

Calculation of income other than earnings

39.–(1)   For the purposes of regulation 31 (average weekly income other than earnings), the income of an applicant which does not consist of earnings to be taken into account is, subject to paragraphs (2) to (6), the applicant's gross income and any capital treated as income under regulation 40 (capital treated as income).

[¹ (1A)   This regulation does not apply where an applicant or an applicant's partner has, or the partners jointly have, an award of universal credit (see regulation 26).]

(2)   Any sum, where applicable, specified in Schedule 4 is to be disregarded when calculating an applicant's gross income under paragraph (1).

(3)   Where the payment of any benefit under the benefit Acts is subject to any deduction by way of recovery the amount to be taken into account under paragraph (1) is the gross amount payable.

(4)   Where the applicant or any partner of the applicant is receiving a contributory employment and support allowance and that allowance has been reduced under regulation 63 of the Employment and Support Allowance Regulations the amount of that allowance to be taken into account is the amount as if it had not been reduced.

(5)   Where an award of any working tax credit or child tax credit under the Tax Credits Act 2002 is subject to a deduction by way of recovery of an overpayment of working tax credit or child tax credit which arose in a previous tax year the amount to be

taken into account under paragraph (1) is the amount of working tax credit or child tax credit awarded less the amount of that deduction.

(6)   In paragraph (5), "tax year" means a period beginning on 6th April in one year and ending on 5th April in the next.

(7)   Paragraphs (8) and (9) apply where–

(a)   a relevant payment has been made to a person in an academic year; and

(b)   the person abandons, or is dismissed from, the relevant course of study before payment is made of the final instalment of the relevant payment.

(8)   Where a relevant payment is made quarterly, the amount of a relevant payment to be taken into account for the assessment period for the purposes of paragraph (1) in respect of a person to whom paragraph (7) applies, is to be calculated by applying the formula–

$$\frac{A - (B \times C)}{D}$$

where–

(a)   A = the total amount of the relevant payment which the person would have received had the person remained a student until the last day of the academic term in which the person abandoned, or was dismissed from, the relevant course of study, less any deduction under regulation 59(6) (treatment of student loans);

(b)   B = the number of reduction weeks from the reduction week immediately following that which includes the first day of that academic year to the reduction week which includes the day on which the person abandoned, or was dismissed from, the relevant course of study;

(c)   C = the weekly amount of the relevant payment, before the application of the £10 disregard, which would have been taken into account as income under regulation 59(2) (treatment of student loans)–

(i)   had the person not abandoned, or been dismissed from, the relevant course of study; and

(ii)   in the case of a person who was not entitled to council tax reduction immediately before abandonment of or dismissal from the course of study, had the person, at that time, been entitled to housing benefit; and

(d)   D = the number of reduction weeks in the assessment period.

(9)   Where a relevant payment is made by two or more instalments in a quarter, the amount of a relevant payment to be taken into account for the assessment period for the purposes of paragraph (1) in respect of a person to whom paragraph (7) applies, is to be calculated by applying the formula in paragraph (8) but as if–

A = the total amount of relevant payments which the person received, or would have received, from the first day of the academic year to the day the person abandoned the course, or was dismissed from it, less any deduction under regulation 59(6) (treatment of student loans).

(10)   In this regulation–

"assessment period" means–

(a)   in a case where a relevant payment is made quarterly, the period beginning with the reduction week which includes the day on which the person abandoned, or was dismissed from, the relevant course of study and ending with the reduction week which includes the last day of the last quarter for which an instalment of the relevant payment was payable to that person;

(b)   in a case where the relevant payment is made by two or more instalments in a quarter, the period beginning with the reduction week which includes the day on which the person abandoned, or was dismissed from, the relevant course of study and ending with the reduction week which includes the earlier of–

(i)   the day immediately before the day on which the next instalment of the relevant payment would have been due had the payments continued; or

(ii)   the last day of the last quarter for which an instalment of the relevant payment was payable to the person;

"quarter" in relation to an assessment period means a period beginning on–
(a)   1st January and ending on 31st March;
(b)   1st April and ending on 30th June;
(c)   1st July and ending on 31st August; or
(d)   1st September and ending on 31st December; and
"relevant payment" means either a student loan or an amount intended for the maintenance
of dependants referred to in regulation 54(7) (calculation of grant income) or
both.
(11)   For the avoidance of doubt the following is income to be taken into account
under paragraph (1)–
(a)   any payment to which regulation 34(2) (payments which are not earnings of
employed earners) applies; or
(b)   in the case of an applicant who is receiving support under section 95 or 98 of
the Immigration and Asylum Act, including support provided by virtue of
regulations made under Schedule 9 to that Act, the amount of support provided
in respect of essential living needs of the applicant and the applicant's dependants
(if any) as specified in regulations made under paragraph 3 of Schedule 8 to the
Immigration and Asylum Act.

Amendment
1.   Inserted by reg 12 of SSI 2016 No 81 as from 1.4.16.

General Note
This is similar to the HB equivalent. See p452 for the commentary.

Capital treated as income
40.–(1)   Any capital payable by instalments which are outstanding at the date on
which the application is made or treated as made, or, at the date of any subsequent
revision or supersession, is, if the aggregate of the instalments outstanding and the
amount of the applicant's capital otherwise calculated in accordance with chapter 7 of
this Part (capital) exceeds £16,000, to be treated as income.
(2)   Any payment received under an annuity is to be treated as income.
(3)   Any earnings to the extent that they are not a payment of income are to be
treated as income.
(4)   Any Career Development Loan paid pursuant to section 2 of the 1973 Act is to
be treated as income.
(5)   Where an agreement or court order provides that [¹a payment] is to be made to
the applicant in consequence of any personal injury to the applicant and that the [¹payment
is] to be made, wholly or partly, by way of periodic payments, any periodic payment
received by the applicant (but not a payment which is treated as capital by virtue of this
Part) is to be treated as income.

Amendment
1.   Amended by reg 7 of SSI 2013 No 48 as from 18.3.13.

General Note
This is similar to the HB equivalent. See p453 for the commentary.

Notional income
41.–(1)   Where a relevant authority is of the opinion that an applicant has been
deprived of income as a result of actings by that applicant carried out for the purpose of
securing entitlement to council tax reduction or increasing the amount of that reduction,
that income is to be treated as income of the applicant.
(2)   Except in the case of–
(a)   a discretionary trust;
(b)   a trust derived from a payment made in consequence of a personal injury;

(c)   a personal pension scheme or a payment made by the Board of the Pension Protection Fund where the applicant has not attained the qualifying age for state pension credit;

(d)   any sum to which paragraph 51(2)(a) of Schedule 5 (capital to be disregarded) applies which is administered in the way referred to in paragraph 50(1)(a) of that Schedule;

(e)   any sum to which paragraph 50(a) of Schedule 5 refers;

(f)   rehabilitation allowance under section 2 of the 1973 Act;

(g)   child tax credit;

(h)   working tax credit; or

(i)   any income, other than earnings or earnings of an employed earner, arising out of the applicant's participation in a service user group,

any income which would become available to the applicant upon application being made, but which has not been acquired by the applicant, is to be treated as possessed by the applicant from the date on which it could be expected to be acquired if application was made.

(3)   Subject to paragraph (4) any payment of income made–

(a)   to a third party in respect of a single applicant or in respect of a member of the applicant's family (but not a member of the third party's family) is, where that payment is a payment of an occupational pension, a pension or other periodical payment made under a personal pension scheme or a payment made by the Board of the Pension Protection Fund, to be treated as possessed by that applicant or, as the case may be, by that family member;

(b)   to a third party in respect of a single applicant or in respect of a member of the applicant's family (but not a member of the third party's family) is, where it is not a payment referred to in sub-paragraph (a), to be treated as possessed by that applicant or by that family member to the extent that it is used for the food, ordinary clothing or footwear, household fuel or rent of that single applicant or, as the case may be, of any member of that family or is used for any council tax or water charges for which that applicant or family member is liable; or

(c)   to a single applicant or a member of the applicant's family in respect of a third party (but not in respect of another member of that family) is to be treated as possessed by that applicant or, as the case may be, that family member to the extent that it is kept or used by that applicant or used by or on behalf of any member of the family.

(4)   Paragraph (3) does not apply in respect of a payment of income made–

(a)   under or by the Trusts, the Fund, the Eileen Trust, MFET Limited, the Skipton Fund, the Caxton Foundation, [³ another infected blood payment scheme,] [² ILF Scotland] [⁴, the London Bombings Relief Charitable Fund, the London Emergencies Trust or the We Love Manchester Emergency Fund];

(b)   pursuant to section 19(1)(a) of the Coal Industry Act 1994 (concessionary coal);

(c)   pursuant to section 2 of the 1973 Act in respect of a person's participation in a qualifying course within the meaning given by regulation 17A(7) of [¹the Jobseeker's Allowance Regulations];

(d)   in respect of a person's participation in the Mandatory Work Activity Scheme;

(e)   in respect of an applicant's participation in the Employment, Skills and Enterprise Scheme; or

(f)   under an occupational pension scheme, in respect of a pension or other periodical payment made under a personal pension scheme or a payment made by the Board of the Pension Protection Fund where–

     (i)   the estate of the person in respect of whom the payment has been made is subject to sequestration, a judicial factor has been appointed on the person's estate under section 41 of the Solicitors (Scotland) Act 1980, the person has entered a protected trust deed within the meaning of section 73(1) of the Bankruptcy Act 1985 or a bankruptcy order within the meaning of section 381(1) of the Insolvency Act 1986 has been made in respect of the person;

  (ii) the payment is made to the trustee in bankruptcy or any other person acting on behalf of the creditors; and

  (iii) the person referred to in head (i) and any member of the person's family does not possess, or is not treated as possessing, any other income apart from that payment.

 (5) Where an applicant is in receipt of any benefit under the benefit Acts and the rate of that benefit is altered with effect from a date on or after 1st April in any year, but not more than 14 days after that date, the applicant is to be treated as possessing that benefit at the altered rate from either 1st April or the first Monday in April in that year, whichever date the relevant authority selects to apply in its area, to the date on which the altered rate is to take effect.

 (6) Subject to paragraph (7), where–

 (a) an applicant performs a service for another person; and

 (b) the person makes no payment of earnings or pays less than that paid for a comparable employment in the area,

the applicant is to be treated as possessing the amount of earnings (if any) that would be reasonable for that employment unless the applicant satisfies the relevant authority that the means of the person are insufficient to pay, or to pay more, for the service.

 (7) Paragraph (6) does not apply–

 (a) to an applicant who is engaged by a charitable or voluntary organisation or who is a volunteer if the relevant authority is satisfied in any of those cases that it is reasonable for the applicant to provide those services free of charge; or

 (b) in a case where the service is performed in connection with–

  (i) the applicant's participation in an employment or training programme in accordance with regulation 19(1)(q) of the Jobseeker's Allowance Regulations; or

  (ii) the applicant's participation or the participation of any partner of the applicant in an employment or training programme as defined in regulation 19(3) of those Regulations for which a training allowance is not payable or, where such an allowance is payable, it is payable for the sole purpose of reimbursement of travelling or meal expenses to the person participating in that programme; or

 (c) to an applicant who is participating in a work placement approved by the Scottish Ministers or the Secretary of State (or by a person providing services to the Scottish Ministers or the Secretary of State) before the placement starts.

 (8) In paragraph (7)(c) "work placement" means practical work experience which is not undertaken in expectation of payment.

 (9) Where an applicant is treated as possessing income under any of paragraphs (1) to (5), the foregoing provisions of this Part apply for the purposes of calculating the amount of that income as if a payment had been made and as if it was income possessed by the applicant.

 (10) Where an applicant is treated as possessing any earnings under paragraph (6) the foregoing provisions of this Part apply for the purposes of calculating the amount of those earnings as if a payment had been made and as if they were earnings the applicant possessed except that regulation 35(3) (calculation of net earnings of employed earners) does not apply and the applicant's net earnings are to be calculated by taking into account the earnings which the applicant is treated as possessing, less–

 (a) an amount in respect of income tax equivalent to an amount calculated by applying to those earnings the starting rate or, as the case may be, the starting rate and the basic rate of tax applicable to the assessment period less the personal relief to which the applicant is entitled under section 35(1) of the Income Tax Act 2007 (personal allowance for those aged under 65) as is appropriate to the applicant's circumstances, but, if the assessment period is less than one year, the earnings to which the starting rate of tax is to be applied and the amount of the personal relief deductible under this sub-paragraph are to be calculated on a pro rata basis;

(b)   an amount equivalent to the amount of the primary Class 1 contributions that would be payable by the applicant under the 1992 Act in respect of those earnings if such contributions were payable; and

(c)   one-half of any sum payable by the applicant by way of a contribution towards an occupational or personal pension scheme.

(11)   Paragraphs (1), (2), (3) and (6) do not apply in respect of any income, other than earnings or earnings of an employed earner, arising out of the applicant's participation in a service user group.

Amendments
1.   Amended by reg 8 of SSI 2013 No 48 as from 18.3.13.
2.   Substituted by reg 4(2)(a) of SSI 2016 No 81 as from 1.4.16.
3.   Amended by reg 5 of SSI 2017 No 41 as from 1.4.17.
4.   Amended by reg 4(b) of SSI 2017 No 326 as from 20.11.17.

General Note
This is similar to the HB equivalent. See p457 for the commentary.

Chapter 7
Capital

Capital limit
42.   No person is entitled to council tax reduction if that person's capital exceeds £16,000.

General Note
This is similar to the HB equivalent. See p462 for the commentary.

Calculation of capital
43.–(1)   Subject to paragraph (2), the capital of an applicant to be taken into account when calculating entitlement to council tax reduction is the whole of the applicant's capital calculated in accordance with this Part and any income treated as capital under regulation 45 (income treated as capital).

(2)   Any capital, where applicable, specified in Schedule 5 is to be disregarded when calculating an applicant's capital.

General Note
This is similar to the HB equivalent. See p463 for the commentary.

Disregard of capital of child and young person
44.   The capital of a child or young person who is a member of the applicant's family is not to be treated as capital of the applicant.

General Note
This is similar to the HB equivalent. See p463 for the commentary.

Income treated as capital
45.–(1)   Any earnings derived from employment to which paragraph 9 of Schedule 3 applies and paid at intervals of at least one year is to be treated as capital.

(2)   Any amount by way of a refund of income tax deducted from profits or emoluments chargeable to income tax under Schedule D or E of the Income and Corporation Taxes Act 1988 is to be treated as capital.

(3)   Any holiday pay which is not earnings under regulation 34(1)(d) (earnings of employed earners) is to be treated as capital.

(4)   Except any income derived from capital disregarded under paragraphs 3, 4, 6, 10, 16, 30 to 33, 50 or 51 of Schedule 5, any income derived from capital is to be treated as capital, but only from the date it is normally due to be credited to the applicant's account.

(5)   In the case of employment as an employed earner, any advance of earnings or any loan made by the applicant's employer is to be treated as capital.

(6)   Any charitable or voluntary payment which is not made or due to be made at regular intervals, other than a payment which is made under or by the Trusts, the Fund, the Eileen Trust, MFET Limited, the Skipton Fund, the Caxton Foundation, [² another infected blood payment scheme,] [¹ ILF Scotland] [³, the London Bombings Relief Charitable Fund, the London Emergencies Trust or the We Love Manchester Emergency Fund], is to be treated as capital.

(7)   The gross receipts of any commercial activity carried on by a person in respect of which assistance is received under the self-employment route is to be treated as capital, but only in so far as those receipts were payable into a special account during the period in which the person was receiving such assistance.

(8)   Any arrears of subsistence allowance paid as a lump sum is to be treated as capital.

(9)   Any arrears of working tax credit or child tax credit is to be treated as capital.

Amendments

1.   Substituted by reg 4(2)(b) of SSI 2016 No 81 as from 1.4.16.
2.   Amended by reg 6 of SSI 2017 No 41 as from 1.4.17.
3.   Amended by reg 4(c) of SSI 2017 No 326 as from 20.11.17.

General Note

This is similar to the HB equivalent. See p464 for the commentary.

Calculation of capital in the United Kingdom

46.   Capital which an applicant possesses in the United Kingdom is to be calculated at its current market or surrender value less–

(a)   where there would be expenses attributable to the sale, 10 per cent; and
(b)   the amount of any encumbrance secured on it.

General Note

This is similar to the HB equivalent. See p465 for the commentary.

Calculation of capital outside the United Kingdom

47.   Capital which an applicant possesses in a country outside the United Kingdom is to be calculated–

(a)   in a case where there is no prohibition in that country against the transfer to the United Kingdom of an amount equal to its current market or surrender value in that country, at that value; and
(b)   in a case where there is a prohibition, at the price it would realise if sold in the United Kingdom to a willing buyer,

less, where there would be expenses attributable to sale, 10 per cent and the amount of any encumbrances secured on it.

General Note

This is similar to the HB equivalent. See p466 for the commentary.

Notional capital

48.–(1)   Where an applicant has been deprived of capital as a result of actings by that applicant carried out for the purpose of securing entitlement to council tax reduction or increasing the amount of that reduction that capital is to be treated as capital of the applicant except to the extent that it is reduced in accordance with regulation 49 (diminishing notional capital).

(2)   Except in the case of–

(a)   a discretionary trust;
(b)   a trust derived from a payment made in consequence of a personal injury;
(c)   any loan which would be obtained only if secured against capital disregarded under Schedule 5;

(d)   a personal pension scheme or a payment made by the Board of the Pension Protection Fund;

(e)   any sum to which paragraph 51(2)(a) of Schedule 5 (capital to be disregarded) applies which is administered in the way referred to in paragraph 51(1)(a) of that Schedule;

(f)   any sum to which paragraph 50(a) of Schedule 5 refers;

(g)   child tax credit; or

(h)   working tax credit,

any capital which would become available to the applicant upon application being made, but which has not been acquired by the applicant, is to be treated as possessed by the applicant from the date on which it could be expected to be acquired if an application was made.

(3)   Subject to paragraph (4) any payment of capital, made–

(a)   to a third party in respect of a single applicant or in respect of a member of the applicant's family (but not a member of the third party's family) is, where that payment is a payment of an occupational pension, a pension or other periodical payment made under a personal pension scheme or a payment made by the Board of the Pension Protection Fund, to be treated as possessed by that applicant or, as the case may be, by that family member;

(b)   to a third party in respect of a single applicant or in respect of a member of the applicant's family (but not a member of the third party's family) is, where it is not a payment referred to in sub-paragraph (a), to be treated as possessed by that applicant or by that family member to the extent that it is used for the food, ordinary clothing or footwear, household fuel or rent of that applicant or, as the case may be, of any member of that family or is used for any council tax or water charges for which that applicant or family member is liable; or

(c)   to a single applicant or a member of the applicant's family in respect of a third party (but not in respect of another member of the family) is to be treated as possessed by that single applicant or, as the case may be, that family member to the extent that it is kept or used by the applicant or used by or on behalf of any member of the family.

(4)   Paragraph (3) does not apply in respect of a payment of capital made–

(a)   under or by the Trusts, the Fund, the Eileen Trust, MFET Limited, the Skipton Fund, the Caxton Foundation, [³ another infected blood payment scheme,] [² ILF Scotland] [⁴, the London Bombings Relief Charitable Fund, the London Emergencies Trust or the We Love Manchester Emergency Fund];

(b)   pursuant to section 2 of the 1973 Act in respect of a person's participation in a qualifying course within the meaning specified in regulation 17A(7) of [¹the Jobseeker's Allowance Regulations];

(c)   in respect of a person's participation in the Mandatory Work Activity Scheme;

(d)   in respect of an applicant's participation in the Employment, Skills and Enterprise Scheme; or

(e)   under an occupational pension scheme, in respect of a pension or other periodical payment made under a personal pension scheme or a payment made by the Board of the Pension Protection Fund where–

(i)   the estate of the person in respect of whom the payment has been made is subject to sequestration, a judicial factor has been appointed on the person's estate under section 41 of the Solicitors (Scotland) Act 1980, the person has entered a protected trust deed within the meaning of section 73(1) of the Bankruptcy Act 1985 or a bankruptcy order within the meaning of section 381(1) of the Insolvency Act 1986 has been made in respect of the person;

(ii)   the payment is made to the trustee in bankruptcy or any other person acting on behalf of the creditors; and

(iii)   the person referred to in head (i) and any member of the person's family does not possess, or is not treated as possessing, any other income apart from that payment.

(5)   Where an applicant stands in relation to a company in a position analogous to that of a sole owner or partner in the business of that company, the applicant is to be treated as sole owner or partner and in such a case–

(a)   the value of the applicant's actual holding in that company must be disregarded notwithstanding regulation 43 (calculation of capital); and

(b)   subject to paragraph (6), the applicant is to be treated as possessing an amount of capital equal to what would have been the applicant's share of the value of the capital of that company if the applicant had been sole owner or partner.

(6)   For so long as the applicant undertakes activities in the course of the business of the company, the amount which the applicant is treated as possessing under paragraph (5) is to be disregarded.

(7)   Where an applicant is treated as possessing capital under any of paragraphs (1) to (3) the provisions of this chapter apply for the purposes of calculating the amount of the capital as if it were actual capital possessed by the applicant.

Amendments
    1.   Amended by reg 9 of SSI 2013 No 48 as from 18.3.13.
    2.   Substituted by reg 4(2)(c) of SSI 2016 No 81 as from 1.4.16.
    3.   Amended by reg 7 of SSI 2017 No 41 as from 1.4.17.
    4.   Amended by reg 4(d) of SSI 2017 No 326 as from 20.11.17.

General Note
    This is similar to the HB equivalent. See p468 for the commentary.

Diminishing notional capital

49.–(1)   Where an applicant is treated as possessing capital under regulation 48(1) (notional capital), the amount which the applicant is treated as possessing–

(a)   in the case of a week that is subsequent to–

(i)   the relevant week in respect of which the conditions set out in paragraph (2) are satisfied; or

(ii)   a week which follows that relevant week and which satisfies those conditions,

is to be reduced by the amount determined under paragraph (3);

(b)   in the case of a week in respect of which paragraph (1)(a) does not apply but where–

(i)   that week is a week subsequent to the relevant week; and

(ii)   that relevant week is a week in which the condition in paragraph (4) is satisfied,

is to be reduced by the amount determined under paragraph (4).

(2)   This paragraph applies to a reduction week or part-week where the applicant satisfies the conditions that–

(a)   the applicant is in receipt of council tax reduction; and

(b)   but for regulation 48(1), the applicant would have received an additional amount of council tax reduction in that week.

(3)   In a case to which paragraph (2) applies, the amount of the reduction for the purposes of paragraph (1)(a) is equal to the aggregate of–

(a)   the additional amount to which paragraph (2)(b) refers;

(b)   where the applicant has also claimed housing benefit, the amount of any housing benefit or any additional amount of that benefit to which the applicant would have been entitled in respect of the whole or part of the reduction week to which paragraph (2) refers but for the application of regulation 49(1) of the Housing Benefit Regulations (notional capital);

(c)   where the applicant has also claimed income support, the amount of income support to which the applicant would have been entitled in respect of the whole or part of the reduction week to which paragraph (2) refers but for the application of regulation 51(1) of the Income Support Regulations (notional capital);

(d)   where the applicant has also claimed a jobseeker's allowance, the amount of an income-based jobseeker's allowance to which the applicant would have been entitled in respect of the whole or part of the reduction week to which paragraph (2) refers but for the application of regulation 113 of the Jobseeker's Allowance Regulations (notional capital); and

(e)   where the applicant has also claimed an employment and support allowance, the amount of an income-related employment and support allowance to which the applicant would have been entitled in respect of the whole or part of reduction week to which paragraph (2) refers but for the application of regulation 115 of the Employment and Support Allowance Regulations (notional capital).

(4)   Subject to paragraph (5), for the purposes of paragraph (1)(b) the condition is that the applicant would have been entitled to council tax reduction in the relevant week but for regulation 48(1) (notional capital), and in such a case the amount of the reduction is to be equal to the aggregate of–

(a)   the amount of council tax reduction to which the applicant would have been entitled in the relevant week but for regulation 48(1), and for the purposes of this sub-paragraph if the amount is in respect of a part-week, that amount is to be determined by dividing the amount of council tax reduction to which the applicant would have been entitled by the number equal to the number of days in the part-week and multiplying the quotient by 7;

(b)   if the applicant would, but for regulation 49(1) of the Housing Benefit Regulations, have been entitled to housing benefit or to an additional amount of housing benefit in respect of the reduction week which includes the last day of the relevant week, the amount which is equal to–

(i)   in a case where no housing benefit is payable, the amount to which the applicant would have been entitled; or

(ii)   in any other case, the amount equal to the additional amount of housing benefit to which the applicant would have been entitled, and, for the purposes of this sub-paragraph, if the amount is in respect of a part-week, that amount is to be determined by dividing the amount of housing benefit to which the applicant would have been entitled by the number equal to the number of days in the part-week and multiplying the quotient by 7;

(c)   if the applicant would, but for regulation 51(1) of the Income Support Regulations, have been entitled to income support in respect of the benefit week (within the meaning of regulation 2(1) of those Regulations) which includes the last day of the relevant week, the amount to which the applicant would have been entitled and, for the purposes of this sub-paragraph, if the amount is in respect of a part-week, that amount is to be determined by dividing the amount of the income support to which the applicant would have been entitled by the number equal to the number of days in the part-week and multiplying the quotient by 7;

(d)   if the applicant would, but for regulation 113 of the Jobseeker's Allowance Regulations, have been entitled to an income-based jobseeker's allowance in respect of the benefit week (within the meaning of regulation 1(3) of those Regulations) which includes the last day of the relevant week, the amount to which the applicant would have been entitled and, for the purposes of this sub-paragraph, if the amount is in respect of a part-week, that amount is to be determined by dividing the amount of the income-based jobseeker's allowance to which the applicant would have been entitled by the number equal to the number of days in the part-week and multiplying the quotient by 7; and

(e)   if the applicant would, but for regulation 115 of the Employment and Support Allowance Regulations, have been entitled to an income-related employment and support allowance in respect of the benefit week (within the meaning of regulation 2(1) of those Regulations) which includes the last day of the relevant week, the amount to which the applicant would have been entitled and, for the purposes of this sub-paragraph, if the amount is in respect of a part-week, that amount is to be determined by dividing the amount of the income-related employment and support allowance to which the applicant would have been entitled by the number equal to the number of days in that part-week and multiplying the quotient by 7.

(5)	The amount determined under paragraph (4) is to be re-determined under that paragraph if the applicant makes a further application for council tax reduction and the conditions in paragraph (6) are satisfied, and in such a case–

(a)	paragraph (4)(a) to (e) applies as if for "relevant week" there was substituted "relevant subsequent week"; and

(b)	subject to paragraph (7), the amount as re-determined has effect from the first week following the relevant subsequent week in question.

(6)	The conditions are that–

(a)	a further application is made 26 or more weeks after the latest of–

(i)	the date on which the applicant made an application for council tax reduction in respect of which the applicant was first treated as possessing the capital in question under regulation 48(1) (notional capital);

(ii)	in a case where there has been at least one re-determination in accordance with paragraph (5), the date on which the applicant last made an application for council tax reduction which resulted in the weekly amount being re-determined; or

(iii)	the date on which the applicant last ceased to be entitled to council tax reduction; and

(b)	the applicant would have been entitled to council tax reduction but for regulation 48(1).

(7)	The amount as re-determined under paragraph (5) is not to have effect if it is less than the amount which applied in that case immediately before the re-determination, and in that case the higher amount continues to have effect.

(8)	In this regulation–

(a)	"part-week"–

(i)	in paragraph (4)(a) means a period of less than a week during which a person is entitled to council tax reduction;

(ii)	in paragraph (4)(b) means a period of less than a week for which housing benefit is payable;

(iii)	in paragraph (4)(c), (d) and (e) means–

(aa)	a period of less than a week which is the whole period for which income support, an income-related employment and support allowance or, as the case may be, an income-based jobseeker's allowance is payable; and

(bb)	any other period of less than a week for which it is payable;

(b)	"relevant week" means the reduction week or part-week in which the capital in question of which the applicant has been deprived within the meaning of regulation 48(1)–

(i)	was first taken into account for the purpose of determining the applicant's entitlement to council tax reduction; or

(ii)	was taken into account on a subsequent occasion for the purpose of determining or re-determining the applicant's entitlement to council tax reduction on that subsequent occasion and that determination or re-determination resulted in the applicant beginning to receive, or ceasing to receive, council tax reduction,

and where more than one reduction week or part-week is identified by reference to heads (i) and (ii) the later or latest reduction week or, as the case may be, the later or latest part-week; and

(c)	"relevant subsequent week" means the reduction week or part-week which includes the day on which the further application or, if more than one further application has been made, the last application was made.

General Note

This is similar to the HB equivalent. See p475 for the commentary.

Capital jointly held

50. Except where an applicant possesses capital which is disregarded under regulation 48(5) (notional capital) where an applicant and one or more other persons are beneficially entitled in possession to any capital asset the applicant and the person or those persons are to be treated as if each of them were entitled in possession to the whole beneficial interest in an equal share and the provisions of this chapter apply for the purposes of calculating the amount of capital which the applicant is treated as possessing as if it were actual capital possessed by applicant.

General Note
This is similar to the HB equivalent. See p476 for the commentary.

Calculation of tariff income from capital

51.–(1) Subject to paragraph (2), where the applicant's capital calculated in accordance with this Part exceeds £6,000 it is to be treated as equivalent to a weekly tariff income of £1 for each complete £250 [¹in excess of £6,000.]

(2) Where any part of the excess is not a complete £250 that part is to be treated as equivalent to a weekly tariff income of £1.

Amendment
1.   Amended by reg 6 of SSI 2013 No 218 as from 1.10.13.

General Note
This is similar to the HB equivalent. See p479 for the commentary.

PART 7
Students

Chapter 1
General

General Note
Most full-time students are excluded from entitlement to CTR: reg 20. Exceptions to the rule are found in reg 20(3). Full-time students are not precluded from claiming the alternative maximum CTR (second adult rebate): reg 20(1).
    Even if a student is not excluded from entitlement to CTR, s/he must still satisfy the other rules set out in this Part before qualifying. The general rule is that claims by students are decided in the same way as claims by non-students, subject to the special income and capital rules found in regs 54–65.
    The general exclusion of full-time students from CTR does not prevent a claimant whose partner is a student from qualifying for CTR.
    There are no comparable rules for students in the CTR(SPC)(S) Regs so claimants covered by those regulations are not excluded from entitlement to CTR for being students. In addition, student loan and grant income is ignored; it does not come within the definition of "income" in reg 27 CTR(SPC)(S) Regs.

Interpretation: students

52. In this Part–
"access funds" means–
(a)   grants made under section 68 of the Further and Higher Education Act 1992 for the purpose of providing funds on a discretionary basis to be paid to students;
(b)   grants made under sections 73(a) and (c) and 74(1) of the Education (Scotland) Act 1980;
(c)   grants made under article 30 of the Education and Libraries (Northern Ireland) Order 1993 or grants, loans or other payments made under article 5 of the Further Education (Northern Ireland) Order 1997, in each case being grants, or grants, loans or other payments as the case may be, for the purpose of assisting students in financial difficulties;
(d)   discretionary payments, known as "learner support funds", which are made available to students in further education by institutions out of funds provided by the Young People's Learning Agency for England under sections 61 and 62

of the Apprenticeships, Skills, Children and Learning Act 2009 or [¹ the
Secretary of State under section 14 of the Education Act 2002 or section 100 of
the Apprenticeships, Skills, Children and Learning Act 2009]; or
   (e)   Financial Contingency Funds made available by the Welsh Ministers;
"college of further education" means a college of further education within the meaning
of Part 1 of the Further and Higher Education (Scotland) Act 1992;
"contribution" means–
   (a)   any contribution in respect of the income of a student or any person which the
         Scottish Ministers, the Secretary of State or an education authority takes into
         account in ascertaining the amount of a student's grant or student loan; or
   (b)   any sums, which in determining the amount of a student's allowance or bursary
         in Scotland under the Education (Scotland) Act 1980, the Scottish Ministers or
         education authority takes into account being sums which the Scottish Ministers
         or education authority consider that it is reasonable for the following persons to
         contribute towards the holder's expenses–
         (i)   the holder of the allowance or bursary;
         (ii)   the holder's parents;
         (iii) the holder's parent's spouse, civil partner or a person ordinarily living
                with the holder's parent as if the person was the spouse or civil partner of
                that parent; or
         (iv)   the holder's spouse or civil partner;
"covenant income" means the gross income payable to a full-time student under a deed
of covenant by the student's parent;
"education authority" means a government department (including any Minister of the
Crown, any part of the Scottish Administration, the National Assembly for
Wales, the Northern Ireland Assembly, any Northern Ireland Minister or
Northern Ireland junior Minister and any Northern Ireland department), a local
education authority as defined in section 123 of the Local Government (Scotland)
Act 1973, a local authority as defined in section 579 of the Education Act 1996
(interpretation), an education and library board established under article 3 of the
Education and Libraries (Northern Ireland) Order 1986, any body which is a
Research Council for the purposes of the Science and Technology Act 1965 or
any analogous government department, authority, board or body, of the Channel
Islands, Isle of Man or any other country outside Great Britain;
"grant" (except in the definition of "access funds") means any kind of educational grant
or award and includes any scholarship, studentship, exhibition, allowance or
bursary but does not include a payment from access funds or any payment to
which paragraph 15 of Schedule 4 or paragraph 55 of Schedule 5 (disregard of
financial assistance with regard to education) applies;
"grant income" means–
   (a)   any income by way of a grant; or
   (b)   any contribution whether or not it is paid;
"last day of the course" means–
   (a)   in the case of a qualifying course, the date on which the last day of that course
         falls or the date on which the final examination relating to that course is
         completed, whichever is the later; and
   (b)   in any other case, the date on which the last day of the final academic term falls
         in respect of the course in which the student is enrolled;
"period of study" means–
   (a)   in the case of a course of study for one year or less, the period beginning with
         the start of the course and ending with the last day of the course;
   (b)   in the case of a course of study for more than one year, in the first or, as the case
         may be, any subsequent year of the course, other than the final year of the
         course, the period beginning with the start of the course or, as the case may be,
         that year's start and ending with either–
         (i)   the day before the start of the next year of the course in a case where the
                student's grant or loan is assessed at a rate appropriate to studying

throughout the year or, if the student does not have a grant or loan, where a loan would have been assessed at such a rate had the student had one; or

    (ii)   in any other case, the day before the start of the normal summer vacation appropriate to the student's course; and

    (c)   in the final year of a course of study of more than one year, the period beginning with that year's start and ending with the last day of the course;

"periods of experience" means periods of work experience which form part of a sandwich course; and

"standard maintenance grant" means–

    (a)   in the case of a student receiving an allowance or bursary under the Education (Scotland) Act 1980, the amount of money specified as "standard maintenance allowance" for the relevant year appropriate for the student set out in the Student Support in Scotland Guide issued by the Student Awards Agency for Scotland, or its nearest equivalent in the case of a bursary provided by a college of further education or a local education authority;

    (b)   except where paragraph (a) or (c) applies in the case of a student attending or undertaking a course of study at the University of London or an establishment within the area comprising the City of London and the Metropolitan Police District, the amount specified for the time being in paragraph 2(2)(a) of Schedule 2 to the Education (Mandatory Awards) Regulations 2003 ("the 2003 Regulations") for that student;

    (c)   except where paragraph (a) applies, in the case of a student residing at that student's parents' home, the amount specified in paragraph 3 of Schedule 2 to the 2003 Regulations; and

    (d)   in any other case, the amount specified in paragraph 2(2) of Schedule 2 to the 2003 Regulations, other than in paragraph 2(2)(a) or (b) of that Schedule.

Amendment

1.   Amended by art 2 and Sch 3 para 18(3) of SI 2015 No 971 as from 26.5.15.

General Note

See the commentary to reg 53 HB Regs on p480 for the definitions of "access funds", "contribution", "covenant income", "education authority", "grant", "grant income", "last day of the course", "period of study" and "periods of experience". Further relevant definitions are in reg 2(1) – ie, "academic year", "course of study", "full-time course of study", "full-time student", "qualifying course", "sandwich course" and "student". For commentary on these, also see the commentary to reg 53 HB Regs.

Treatment of students

53.   These Regulations have effect in relation to students subject to the provisions of this Part.

General Note

This is similar to the HB equivalent. See p484 for the commentary.

Chapter 2
Income

Calculation of grant income

54.–(1) The amount of a student's grant income to be taken into account is, subject to paragraphs (2) and (3), the whole of that student's grant income.

    (2)   There must be excluded from a student's grant income any payment–

    (a)   intended to meet tuition fees or examination fees;

    (b)   in respect of any disability of that student;

    (c)   intended to meet additional expenditure connected with term time residential study away from the student's educational establishment;

    (d)   on account of the student maintaining a home at a place other than that at which the student resides during the course;

(e)   on account of any other person but only if the person is residing outside of the United Kingdom and there is no applicable amount in respect of the person;

(f)   intended to meet the cost of books and equipment;

(g)   intended to meet travel expenses incurred as a result of the student's attendance on the course;

(h)   intended for the child care costs of a child dependant; [¹]

(i)   of higher education bursary for care leavers made under Part III of the Children Act 1989 [¹]; or

(j)   of higher education bursary for a category 3 or category 4 young person, as defined by section 104(2) of the Social Services and Well-being (Wales) Act 2014, made under section 110 or section 112 of that Act].

(3)   Where a student does not have a student loan and is not treated as possessing a student loan, there must be excluded from the student's grant income–

(a)   the sum of £303 per academic year in respect of travel costs; and

(b)   the sum of £390 per academic year towards the costs of books and equipment, whether or not any costs are incurred.

(4)   There must be excluded from a student's grant income the grant for dependants known as the parents' learning allowance paid pursuant to regulations made under article 3 of the Education (Student Support) (Northern Ireland) Order 1998 or section 22 of the Teaching and Higher Education Act 1998.

(5)   Subject to paragraphs (6) and (7), a student's grant income is to be apportioned–

(a)   subject to paragraph (8), in a case where it is attributable to the period of study, equally between the weeks in that period beginning with the reduction week, the first day of which coincides with, or immediately follows, the first day of the period of study and ending with the reduction week, the last day of which coincides with, or immediately precedes, the last day of the period of study; and

(b)   in any other case, equally between the weeks in the period beginning with the reduction week, the first day of which coincides with, or immediately follows, the first day of the period for which it is payable and ending with the reduction week, the last day of which coincides with, or immediately precedes, the last day of the period for which it is payable.

(6)   Any grant in respect of dependants paid under section 63(6) of the Health Services and Public Health Act 1968 (grants in respect of the provision of instruction to officers of hospital authorities) and any amount intended for the maintenance of dependants under Part 3 of Schedule 2 to the Education (Mandatory Awards) Regulations 2003 is to be apportioned equally over the period of 52 weeks or, if there are 53 reduction weeks (including part-weeks) in the year, 53.

(7)   In a case where a student is in receipt of a student loan or where the student could have acquired a student loan by taking reasonable steps but had not done so, any amount intended for the maintenance of dependants to which paragraph (6) does not apply, is to be apportioned over the same period as the student's loan is apportioned or, as the case may be, would have been apportioned.

(8)   In the case of a student on a sandwich course, any periods of experience within the period of study are to be excluded and the student's grant income is to be apportioned equally between the weeks in the period beginning with the reduction week, the first day of which immediately follows the last day of the period of experience and ending with the reduction week, the last day of which coincides with, or immediately precedes, the last day of the period of study.

Amendment

1.   Amended by reg 6(2) of SSI 2016 No 81 as from 6.4.16.

General Note

This is similar to the HB equivalent. See p497 for the commentary.

Calculation of covenant income where a contribution is assessed

55.–(1)   Where a student is in receipt of income by way of a grant during a period of study and a contribution has been assessed, the amount of the student's covenant income to be taken into account for that period and any summer vacation immediately following is the whole amount of the covenant income less, subject to paragraph (3), the amount of the contribution.

(2)   The weekly amount of the student's covenant is to be determined–

(a)   by dividing the amount of income which falls to be taken into account under paragraph (1) by 52 or 53, whichever is reasonable in the circumstances; and

(b)   by disregarding £5 from the resulting amount.

(3)   For the purposes of paragraph (1), the contribution is to be treated as increased by the amount (if any) by which the amount excluded under regulation 54(2)(g) (calculation of grant income) falls short of the amount specified in paragraph 7(2) of Schedule 2 to the Education (Mandatory Awards) Regulations 2003 (travel expenditure).

General Note
This is similar to the HB equivalent. See p498 for the commentary.

Covenant income where no grant income or no contribution is assessed

56.–(1)   Where a student is not in receipt of income by way of a grant the amount of the student's covenant income is to be calculated as follows–

(a)   any sums intended for any expenditure specified in regulation 54(2)(a) to (e) (calculation of grant income) necessary as a result of the student's attendance on the course is to be disregarded;

(b)   any covenant income, up to the amount of the standard maintenance grant, which is not disregarded, is to be apportioned equally between the weeks of the period of study;

(c)   there is to be disregarded from the amount apportioned the amount which would have been disregarded under regulation 54(2)(f) and (3) had the student been in receipt of the standard maintenance grant; and

(d)   the balance, if any, is to be divided by 52 or 53 whichever is reasonable in the circumstances and treated as weekly income of which £5 is to be disregarded.

(2)   Where a student is in receipt of income by way of a grant and no contribution has been assessed, the amount of the student's covenanted income is to be calculated in accordance with paragraph (1), except that–

(a)   the value of the standard maintenance grant is to be abated by the amount of the grant income less an amount equal to the amount of any sums disregarded under regulation 54(2)(a) to (e); and

(b)   the amount to be disregarded under paragraph (1)(c) is to be abated by an amount equal to the amount of any sums disregarded under regulation 54(2)(f) and (g) and (3).

General Note
This is similar to the HB equivalent. See p499 for the commentary.

Relationship with amounts to be disregarded under Schedule 4

57.   No part of a student's covenant income or grant income is to be disregarded under paragraph 18 of Schedule 4.

General Note
This is similar to the HB equivalent. See p499 for the commentary.

Other amounts to be disregarded

58.   For the purposes of ascertaining income other than grant income, covenant income and loans treated as income in accordance with regulation 59 (treatment of student loans), any amount intended for any expenditure specified in regulation 54(2) (calculation of grant income), necessary as a result of the student's attendance on the course is to be disregarded but only if, and to the extent that, the necessary expenditure exceeds or is likely to exceed the amount of the sums disregarded under regulation 54(2) or (3), 55(3), 56(1)(a) or (c) or 59(5) (calculation of grant income, covenant income and treatment of student loans) on like expenditure.

Treatment of student loans

59.–(1)   A student loan is to be treated as income in accordance with the provisions of this regulation.

(2)   Subject to paragraph (3), when calculating the weekly amount of the loan to be taken into account as income–

(a)   in respect of a course that is of a single academic year's duration or less, a loan payable in respect of that period is to be apportioned equally between the weeks in the period beginning with–

(i)   except in a case where head (ii) applies, the reduction week, the first day of which coincides with, or immediately follows, the first day of the single academic year; and

(ii)   where the student is required to start attending the course in August or where the course is less than an academic year's duration, the reduction week, the first day of which coincides with, or immediately follows, the first day of the course,

and ending with the reduction week, the last day of which coincides with, or immediately precedes, the last day of the course;

(b)   in respect of an academic year of a course which starts other than on 1st September, a loan which is payable in respect of that academic year is to be apportioned equally between the weeks in the period beginning with the reduction week, the first day of which coincides with or immediately follows, the first day of that academic year and ending with the reduction week, the last day of which coincides with or immediately precedes, the last day of that academic year but excluding any reduction weeks falling entirely within the quarter during which, in the opinion of, as the case may be, the Scottish Ministers, the Secretary of State, the Welsh Ministers or the Department for Employment and Learning in Northern Ireland, the longest of any vacation is taken;

(c)   in respect of the final academic year of a course (not being a course of a single year's duration), a loan which is payable in respect of that final academic year is to be apportioned equally between the weeks in the period beginning with–

(i)   except in a case where head (ii) applies, the reduction week, the first day of which coincides with, or immediately follows, the first day of that academic year; and

(ii)   where the final academic year starts on 1st September, the reduction week, the first day of which coincides with, or immediately follows, the earlier of 1st September or the first day of the autumn term,

and ending with the reduction week, the last day of which coincides with, or immediately precedes, the last day of the course; and

(d)   in any other case, the loan is to be apportioned equally between the weeks in the period beginning with the earlier of–

(i)   the first day of the first reduction week in September; or

(ii)   the reduction week, the first day of which coincides with, or immediately follows the first day of the autumn term, and ending with the reduction week, the last day of which coincides with, or immediately precedes, the last day of June.

(3)   When calculating the weekly amount of the loan to be taken into account as income £10 is to be disregarded from the weekly amounts apportioned in accordance with paragraph (2).

(4)   A student is to be treated as possessing a student loan in respect of an academic year where–

(a)   a student loan has been made to the student in respect of that year; or

(b)   the student could acquire a student loan in respect of that year by taking reasonable steps to do so.

(5)   Where a student is treated as possessing a student loan under paragraph (4), the amount of the student loan to be taken into account as income is, subject to paragraph (6)–

(a)   in the case of a student to whom a student loan is made in respect of an academic year, a sum equal to–

(i)   the maximum student loan the student is able to acquire in respect of that year by taking reasonable steps to do so; and

(ii)   any contribution whether or not it has been paid to the student; and

(b)   in the case of a student to whom a student loan is not made in respect of an academic year, the maximum student loan that would be made to the student if–

(i)   the student took all reasonable steps to obtain the maximum student loan able to be acquired in respect of that year; and

(ii)   no deduction in that loan was made by virtue of the application of a means test.

(6)   There is to be deducted from the amount of income taken into account under paragraph (5), whether or not any costs are incurred–

(a)   the sum of £303 per academic year in respect of travel costs; and

(b)   the sum of £390 per academic year towards the cost of books and equipment.

(7)   For the purposes of this regulation "quarter" in relation to an academic year means a period in that year–

(a)   beginning on 1st January and ending on 31st March;

(b)   beginning on 1st April and ending on 30th June;

(c)   beginning on 1st July and ending on 31st August; or

(d)   beginning on 1st September and ending on 31st December.

General Note

This is similar to the HB equivalent. See p501 for the commentary.

Treatment of fee loans

60.   A loan for fees, known as a fee loan or a fee contribution loan, made pursuant to regulations made under section 73(f) of the Education (Scotland) Act 1980, section 22 of the Teaching and Higher Education Act 1998 or article 3 of the Education (Student Support) (Northern Ireland) Order 1998 is to be disregarded as income.

General Note

This is similar to the HB equivalent. See p503 for the commentary.

Treatment of payments from access funds

61.–(1)   This regulation applies to payments from access funds that are not payments to which regulation 64(2) or (3) (income treated as capital) applies.

(2)   A payment from access funds, other than a payment to which paragraph (3) applies, is to be disregarded as income.

(3)   Subject to paragraph (4) and paragraph 40 of Schedule 4, any payments from access funds which are intended and used for an item of food, ordinary clothing or footwear, household fuel, or rent of a single applicant or, as the case may be, of the applicant or any other member of the applicant's family and any payments from access funds which are used for any council tax or water charges for which that applicant or member is liable, are to be disregarded as income to the extent of £20 per week.

(4)   Any payment from access funds is to be disregarded as income where that payment is made–

(a)   on or after 1st September or the first day of the course of study, whichever occurs first, but before receipt of any student loan in respect of that year and that payment is intended for the purpose of bridging the period until receipt of the student loan; or

(b)   before the first day of the course to a person in anticipation of the person becoming a student.

Disregard of contribution

62. Where the applicant or any partner of the applicant is a student and, for the purposes of assessing a contribution to the student's grant or student loan, the other partner's income has been taken into account, an amount equal to that contribution is to be disregarded for the purposes of assessing the other partner's income.

Further disregard of student's income

63. Where any part of a student's income has already been taken into account for the purposes of assessing the student's entitlement to a grant or student loan, the amount taken into account must be disregarded in assessing the student's income.

Income treated as capital

64.–(1) Any amount by way of a refund of tax deducted from a student's covenant income is to be treated as capital.

(2) Any amount paid from access funds as a single lump sum is to be treated as capital.

(3) Any amount paid from access funds as a single lump sum which is intended and used for an item other than food, ordinary clothing or footwear, household fuel or rent, or which is used for an item other than any council tax or water charges for which that applicant or a member of the applicant's [¹family] is liable, is to be disregarded as capital but only for a period of 52 weeks from the date of the payment.

Amendment
1.   Inserted by reg 10 of SSI 2013 No 48 as from 18.3.13.

Disregard of changes occurring during summer vacation

65. In calculating a student's income any change in the standard maintenance grant occurring in the recognised summer vacation appropriate to the student's course is to be disregarded if that vacation does not form part of the student's period of study from the date on which the change occurred to the end of that vacation.

PART 8
Amount of reduction

Maximum council tax reduction

66.–(1) Subject to paragraphs (2) and (3) [¹ for the purposes of regulation 14], the amount of a person's maximum council tax reduction in respect of a day for which the person is liable to pay council tax is 100 per cent of the amount A/B where–

(a) A is the amount set by the relevant authority as the council tax for the relevant financial year in respect of the dwelling in which the person is a resident and for which the person is liable, subject to–

(i) any discount which may be appropriate to that dwelling; and

   (ii) any reduction in liability for council tax under regulations made under section 80 of the Act or under a scheme established under section 80A of the Act, other than a reduction under these Regulations; and

 (b) B is the number of days in that financial year,

less any deductions in respect of non-dependants which fall to be made under regulation 67 (non-dependant deductions).

[¹ (1A) Subject to paragraphs (2) and (3), for the purposes of regulation 14A the amount of a person's maximum council tax reduction in respect of a day for which the person is liable to pay council tax is 100% of the amount–

$$\frac{A - A/C}{B}$$

less any deductions in respect of non-dependants which fall to be made under regulation 67.

 (1B) In paragraph (1A)–

 (a) A and B have the same meanings as in paragraph (1); and

 (b) C is–

   (i) 1.075 if the relevant dwelling is in valuation band E;

   (ii) 1.125 if the relevant dwelling is in valuation band F;

   (iii) 1.175 if the relevant dwelling is in valuation band G;

   (iv) 1.225 if the relevant dwelling is in valuation band H.]

 (2) Subject to paragraph (3), where an applicant is jointly and severally liable for council tax in respect of a dwelling in which the person is resident with one or more other persons, but excepting any person residing with the applicant who is a student to whom regulation 20(2) (persons not entitled to council tax reduction: students) applies, in determining the maximum council tax reduction in the person's case in accordance with paragraph (1) [¹ or (1A)] amount A is to be divided by the number of persons who are jointly and severally liable for that tax.

 (3) Where an applicant is jointly and severally liable for council tax in respect of a dwelling with only the applicant's partner, paragraph (2) does not apply.

Amendment

1. Amended by reg 6 of SSI 2016 No 253 as from 1.4.17.

General Note

In Scotland, the council tax valuation band multipliers for properties in bands E, F, G and H (relative to band D properties) was increased from 1 April 2017 increasing the council tax charged for those properties before any discount and/or reduction is applied.

 From that date, reg 66 is amended to reflect the inclusion of an alternative calculation of CTR, and an alternative calculation of the maximum amount, for applicants residing in properties in these valuation bands. See the commentary under the general note to reg 14 for further details.

Analysis

Reg 66 provides the basis for establishing a claimant's maximum CTR. The starting point is the net liability for council tax after reductions (other than under these regulations) and discounts have been applied, less non-dependant deductions applicable under reg 67: paras (1) and (1A).

 Where the applicant is jointly and severally liable for council tax with one or more other persons (excluding any liable person residing with her/him who is a student not entitled to CTR), such person not being her/his partner, her/his benefit is calculated only in respect of the appropriate proportion of the maximum: paras (2) and (3). This gives rise, potentially, to hardship in that, under the 1992 Act, a person who is jointly and severally liable can be pursued for the full amount of the tax due on the property while receiving CTR only on her/his "share".

Non-dependant deductions

67.–(1) Subject to the following provisions of this regulation, the non-dependant deductions in respect of a day referred to in regulation 66 (maximum council tax reduction) are–

 (a) in respect of a non-dependant aged 18 or over in remunerative work, [⁹£12.55] x 1/7; and

(b) in respect of a non-dependant aged 18 or over to whom sub-paragraph (a) does not apply, [⁹£4.15] x 1/7.

(2) In the case of a non-dependant aged 18 or over to whom paragraph (1)(a) applies, where it is shown to the relevant authority that the person's normal gross weekly income is–

(a) less than [⁹£209.00], the deduction to be made is that specified in paragraph (1)(b);

[⁶ (b) not less than [⁹ £209.00] but less than [⁹ £363.00], the deduction to be made is [⁹ £8.30] x 1/7; or

(c) not less than [⁹ £363.00] but less than [⁹ £451.00], the deduction to be made is [⁹ £10.50] x 1/7.]

(3) Only one deduction is to be made in respect of a couple or, as the case may be, members of a polygamous marriage and where, but for this paragraph, the amount that would fall to be deducted in respect of one member of a couple or polygamous marriage is higher than the amount (if any) that would fall to be deducted in respect of the other, or any other, member, the higher amount is to be deducted.

(4) In applying the provisions of paragraph (2) in the case of a couple or, as the case may be, a polygamous marriage, regard must be had, for the purpose of that paragraph, to the couple's or, as the case may be, all members of the polygamous marriage's, joint weekly gross income.

(5) Where in respect of a day–

(a) a person is a resident in a dwelling but is not liable for council tax in respect of that dwelling on that day;

(b) other residents in that dwelling (the liable persons) have joint and several liability for council tax in respect of that dwelling on that day otherwise than by virtue of section 77 or 77A of the Act (liability of spouses and civil partners); and

(c) the person to whom sub-paragraph (a) refers is a non-dependant of two or more of the liable persons,

the deduction in respect of that non-dependant is to be apportioned equally between those liable persons.

(6) No deduction is to be made in respect of any non-dependants occupying an applicant's dwelling if the applicant or the applicant's partner is–

(a) blind or treated as blind by virtue of paragraph 10 of Schedule 1 (additional condition for the disability premium); or

(b) receiving in respect of the applicant or the applicant's partner as the case may be either–

(i) attendance allowance;

(ii) the care component of the disability living allowance; or

[²(iia) armed forces independence payment;]

(iii) the daily living component of personal independence payment.

(7) No deduction is to be made in respect of a non-dependant if–

(a) although residing with the applicant, it appears to the relevant authority that the non-dependant's normal home is elsewhere; or

(b) the non-dependant is in receipt of a training allowance paid in connection with youth training established under section 2 of the 1973 Act or section 2 of the Enterprise and New Towns (Scotland) Act 1990; or

(c) the non-dependant is a full-time student; or

(d) the non-dependent is not residing with the applicant because the non-dependant has been a patient for a period in excess of 52 weeks, and for these purposes where a person has been a patient for two or more distinct periods separated by one or more intervals, each not exceeding 28 days, the person is to be treated as having been a patient continuously for a period equal in duration to the total of those distinct periods [⁴; or]

[⁴ (e) the non-dependant is not residing with the applicant because the non-dependant is a member of the regular forces or the reserve forces (within the meaning of section 374 of the Armed Forces Act 2006) who is absent, while on operations, from the dwelling usually occupied as that person's home.]

(8)   No deduction is to be made in respect of a non-dependant–

(a)   who is on income support, state pension credit, an income-based jobseeker's allowance or an income-related employment and support allowance; [⁵]

(b)   to whom Schedule 1 to the Act applies (persons disregarded for purposes of discount) but this sub-paragraph does not apply to a non-dependant who is a student to whom paragraph 4 of that Schedule refers [⁵; or

(c)   who is entitled to an award of universal credit where the award is calculated on the basis that the non-dependant does not have any earned income, within the meaning given by regulation 52 of the Universal Credit Regulations 2013.]

(9)   In the application of paragraph (2) there is to be disregarded from the person's weekly gross income–

(a)   any attendance allowance, disability living allowance[², armed forces independence payment] or personal independence payment received by the person;

(b)   any payment made under or by the Trusts, the Fund, the Eileen Trust, MFET Limited, the Skipton Fund, the Caxton Foundation, [⁶ another infected blood payment scheme] [⁵ ILF Scotland] [⁷, the London Bombings Relief Charitable Fund, the London Emergencies Trust or the We Love Manchester Emergency Fund] which, had the person's income fallen to be calculated under regulation 39 (ca,lculation of income other than earnings), would have been disregarded under paragraph 27 of Schedule 4 (income in kind); [⁸]

(c)   any payment which, had the person's income fallen to be calculated under regulation 39, would have been disregarded under paragraph 41 of Schedule 4 (payments made under certain trusts and certain other payments)[⁸ ; and

(d)   any payment made under or by the Thalidomide Trust].

Amendments

1.   Amended by reg 11 of SSI 2013 No 48 as from 18.3.13.
2.   Inserted by reg 11(4) of SSI 2013 No 142 as from 11.6.13.
3.   Amended by reg 3 of SSI 2014 No 35 as from 1.4.14.
4.   Amended by reg 6 of SSI 2015 No 46 as from 1.4.15.
5.   Amended by regs 4(2)(d) and 13 of SSI 2016 No 81 as from 1.4.16.
6.   Amended by reg 8 of SSI 2017 No 41 as from 1.4.17.
7.   Amended by reg 4(e) of SSI 2017 No 326 as from 20.11.17.
8.   Amended by regs 5 and 8 of SSI 2018 No 69 as from 1.4.18.
9.   Amended by reg 4 of SSI 2019 No 29 as from 1.4.19.

Analysis

For the meaning on "non-dependant", see reg 3 on p1466. The rules on non-dependant deductions for CTR purposes are broadly the same as those for HB (see reg 74 on p516). However, there are some differences in when no non-dependant deduction is to be made: paras (7) and (8).

(1)   No deduction is made for any non-dependant on IS, income-based JSA, income-related ESA or UC (in the circumstances in sub-para (8)(c)), not just those under 25: para (8)(a) and (c). For CTR, unlike for HB, no deduction is made for a non-dependant on income-related ESA who is in the work related activity group or whose income-related ESA includes a support component.

(2)   No deduction is made for non-dependants to whom Sch 1 LGFA 1992 applies (although students covered by para 4 of Sch 1 are excluded from this particular rule): para (8)(b). These are people with what are known as "status discounts" – ie, people who are disregarded for the purpose of working out whether a council tax payer qualifies for a council tax discount, and include, for example, those 18 or over for whom child benefit is payable and certain recent school and college-leavers, student nurses, apprentices, certain foreign spouses, civil partners or dependants of students, people who are "severely mentally impaired" (defined in Sch 1 para 2 LGFA 1992), people in detention, certain carers and members of visiting armed forces, international headquarters and defence organisations and their dependants. See Sch 1 LGFA 1992 (p1086), the Council Tax (Discounts) (Scotland) Regulations 1992 No.1409 and the Council Tax (Discounts) (Scotland) Consolidation and Amendment Order 2003 No.176 for details of who has a status discount. For further information on status discounts, see CPAG's *Council Tax Handbook*.

(3)   No deduction is made for a non-dependant who is a full-time student, defined in reg 2 as "a person attending or undertaking a full-time course of study", even if s/he works during the summer vacation: para (7)(c). For the definition of full-time course of study see reg 2(1) and for details of when a person is to be regarded as attending or undertaking a full-time course of study see reg 2(2).

Extended council tax reduction

68.–(1)   Subject to regulation 71 (extended council tax reduction: movers), a person who is entitled to council tax reduction by virtue of the general conditions of entitlement is entitled to extended council tax reduction where–

(a)   the person or any partner of the person was entitled to a qualifying income-related benefit;

(b)   entitlement to a qualifying income-related benefit ceased because the person or the person's partner–

    (i)   commenced employment as an employed or self-employed earner;

    (ii)   increased their earnings from employment as an employed or self-employed earner; or

    (iii)   increased the number of hours worked in employment as an employed or self-employed earner,

and that employment is, or the increased earnings or increased number of hours are, expected to last 5 weeks or more; and

(c)   the person or the person's partner had been entitled to and in receipt of a qualifying income-related benefit, jobseeker's allowance or a combination of those benefits for a continuous period of at least 26 weeks before the day on which the entitlement to a qualifying income-related benefit ceased.

(2)   For the purpose of paragraph (1)(c), a person or any partner of the person is to be treated as having been entitled to and in receipt of a qualifying income-related benefit or jobseeker's allowance during any period of less than 5 weeks in respect of which the person or the person's partner was not entitled to any of those benefits because the person or the person's partner was engaged in remunerative work as a consequence of their participation in an employment zone programme.

(3)   For the purposes of this regulation, where a person or any partner of the person is entitled to and in receipt of joint-claim jobseeker's allowance the person or the person's partner, as the case may be, is to be treated as being entitled to and in receipt of jobseeker's allowance.

(4)   For the purposes of this regulation, a person is entitled to council tax reduction by virtue of the general conditions of entitlement where–

(a)   the person ceased to be entitled to council tax reduction on vacating the dwelling in which the person was resident;

(b)   the day on which the person vacated the dwelling was either in the week in which entitlement to a qualifying income-related benefit ceased, or in the preceding week; and

(c)   entitlement to the qualifying income-related benefit ceased in any of the circumstances listed in paragraph (1)(b).

(5)   This regulation does not apply where, on the day before a person's entitlement to income support ceased, regulation 6(5) of the Income Support Regulations (remunerative work: housing costs) applied to that person.

General Note

This is similar to the HB equivalent. See the p507 for the commentary.

Duration of period of entitlement to extended council tax reduction

69.–(1)   Subject to regulation 71 (extended council tax reduction: movers), where a person is entitled to extended council tax reduction, the period of entitlement starts on the first day of the reduction week immediately following the reduction week in which the person, or any partner of the person, ceased to be entitled to a qualifying income-related benefit.

(2)   For the purpose of paragraph (1), a person or a person's partner ceases to be entitled to a qualifying income-related benefit on the day immediately following the last day of entitlement to that benefit.

(3)   The period of entitlement to extended council tax reduction ends on the earliest of–

(a)   the end of a period of 4 weeks of that entitlement; or

(b)   the first day on which the person who is entitled to extended council tax reduction has no liability for council tax.

General Note
This is similar to the HB equivalent. See p513 for the commentary.

Amount of extended council tax reduction

70.–(1)   For any week during the period of entitlement to extended council tax reduction the amount of council tax reduction to which the person is entitled is the higher of–

(a)   the amount of council tax reduction to which the person was entitled in the last reduction week before the person or the person's partner ceased to be entitled to a qualifying income-related benefit;

(b)   the amount of council tax reduction to which the person would be entitled for any reduction week during the period of entitlement to extended council tax reduction if regulation 68 (extended council tax reduction) did not apply to the person; or

(c)   the amount of council tax reduction to which the person's partner would be entitled if regulation 68 did not apply to the person.

(2)   Paragraph (1) does not apply in the case of a mover.

(3)   Where a person is entitled to extended council tax reduction under this regulation and the person's partner applies for council tax reduction, that partner is not entitled to council tax reduction during the other partner's period of entitlement to extended council tax reduction.

General Note
This is similar to the HB equivalent. See p514 for the commentary.

Extended council tax reduction: movers

71.–(1)   Where a mover who is entitled to extended council tax reduction in respect of liability to pay council tax to the first authority moves to reside in a dwelling in the area of the second authority that mover is entitled to extended council tax reduction in respect of any liability to pay council tax to the second authority of an amount calculated in accordance with paragraph (2).

(2)   The amount of extended council tax reduction to which the mover is entitled is the amount of council tax reduction to which the mover was entitled for the last reduction week before the mover ceased to be entitled to a qualifying income-related benefit.

(3)   The period of entitlement to extended council tax reduction in respect of liability to pay council tax to the first authority ends on the earliest of–

(a)   the first Sunday after the move; or

(b)   the day on which the mover's liability to pay council tax to the first authority ends.

(4)   The period of entitlement to extended council tax reduction granted by virtue of paragraph (1)–

(a)   starts on the Monday following the day of the move; and

(b)   ends on the expiry of the period of entitlement to extended council tax reduction which would have applied had the mover not moved from the area of the first authority.

Analysis
The rules for extended CTR are broadly the same as those for extended payments of HB (see regs 72 to 72D HB Regs on p506). However, the rules for "movers" differ. Reg 71 deals with the amount of extended CTR paid to "movers", and the period of entitlement following the move. Movers, as defined by reg 2(1), are claimants who change the dwelling in which they are resident from the area of one authority (the "first authority") to a dwelling in the area of a "second authority". "First authority" is defined in reg 2(1) as the authority to which a mover was liable to pay council tax for the dwelling s/he resided in immediately before moving to the dwelling in the the area of the "second authority". "Second authority" is defined in reg 2(1) as the authority "to which" a mover is liable to pay council tax for the new dwelling.

Relationship between council tax reduction and extended council tax reduction

72.–(1)   Where a person's entitlement to council tax reduction would have ended when the applicant ceased to be entitled to a qualifying income-related benefit in the circumstances listed in regulation 68(1)(b) (extended council tax reduction), that eligibility will not cease until the end of the period of eligibility for extended council tax reduction.

(2)   Part 9 (effective date) does not apply to any extended council tax reduction granted in accordance with regulation 70(1)(a) (amount of extended council tax reduction) or 71(2) (extended council tax reduction: movers).

General Note

This is similar to the HB equivalent. See p512 for the commentary.

Extended council tax reduction (qualifying contributory benefits)

73.–(1)   A person who is entitled to council tax reduction by virtue of the general conditions of entitlement is entitled to extended council tax reduction (qualifying contributory benefits) where–

(a)   the person or any partner of the person was entitled to a qualifying contributory benefit;

(b)   entitlement to a qualifying contributory benefit ceased because the person or the person's partner–

   (i)   commenced employment as an employed or self-employed earner;

   (ii)   had an increase in earnings from such employment; or

   (iii)   increased the number of hours worked in such employment,

and that employment is or, as the case may be, increased earnings or increased number of hours are expected to last 5 weeks or more;

(c)   the person or the person's partner had been entitled to and in receipt of a qualifying contributory benefit or a combination of qualifying contributory benefits for a continuous period of at least 26 weeks before the day on which the entitlement to a qualifying contributory benefit ceased; and

(d)   the person or the person's partner was not entitled to and not in receipt of a qualifying income-related benefit in the last reduction week in which the person or the person's partner was entitled to a qualifying contributory benefit.

(2)   For the purposes of this regulation, a person is entitled to council tax reduction by virtue of the general conditions of entitlement where–

(a)   the person ceased to be entitled to council tax reduction because the person vacated the dwelling in which the person was resident;

(b)   the day on which the person vacated the dwelling was either in the week in which entitlement to a qualifying contributory benefit ceased, or in the preceding week; and

(c)   entitlement to the qualifying contributory benefit ceased in any of the circumstances listed in paragraph (1)(b).

General Note

This is similar to the HB equivalent. See p513 for the commentary.

Duration of extended council tax reduction (qualifying contributory benefits)

74.–(1)   Subject to regulation 76 (extended council tax reduction (qualifying contributory benefits: movers), where a person is entitled to extended council tax reduction (qualifying contributory benefits), the period of entitlement starts on the first day of the reduction week immediately following the reduction week in which the person or the person's partner ceased to be entitled to a qualifying contributory benefit.

(2)   For the purpose of paragraph (1), a person or a person's partner ceases to be entitled to a qualifying contributory benefit on the day immediately following the last day of entitlement to that benefit.

(3)   The period of entitlement to council tax reduction (qualifying contributory benefits) ends on the earliest of–

(a)   the end of a period of 4 weeks of entitlement; or

(b)   the day on which the entitled person's liability for council tax ends.

Amount of extended council tax reduction (qualifying contributory benefits)

75.–(1) For any week during the period of entitlement to council tax reduction (qualifying contributory benefits) the amount of council tax reduction (qualifying contributory benefits) is the higher of–

(a) the amount of council tax reduction to which the person was entitled in the last reduction week before the person or the person's partner ceased to be entitled to a qualifying contributory benefit;

(b) the amount of council tax reduction to which the person would be entitled for any reduction week during the extended payment period, if regulation 73 (extended council tax reduction (qualifying contributory benefits)) did not apply to the person; or

(c) the amount of council tax reduction to which the person's partner would be entitled if regulation 74 (duration of extended council tax reduction (qualifying contributory benefits)) did not apply to the person.

(2) Paragraph (1) does not apply in the case of a mover.

(3) Where a person is entitled to extended council tax reduction (qualifying contributory benefits) under this regulation and the person's partner applies for council tax reduction, that partner is not entitled to council tax reduction during the person's period of entitlement to extended council tax reduction (qualifying contributory benefits).

Extended council tax reduction (qualifying contributory benefits): movers

76.–(1) Where a mover who is entitled to extended council tax reduction (qualifying contributory benefits) in respect of liability to pay council tax to the first authority moves to reside in a dwelling in the area of the second authority that mover is entitled to extended council tax reduction in respect of any liability to pay council tax to the second authority of an amount calculated in accordance with paragraph (2).

(2) The amount of extended council tax reduction (qualifying contributory benefit) to which the mover is entitled is the amount of council tax reduction to which the mover was entitled for the last reduction week before the mover ceased to be entitled to a qualifying contributory benefit.

(3) The period of entitlement to extended council tax reduction (qualifying contributory benefit) in respect of liability to pay council tax to the first authority ends on the earliest of–

(a) the first Sunday after the move; or

(b) the day on which the mover's liability to pay council tax to the first authority ends.

(4) The period of entitlement to extended council tax reduction (qualifying contributory benefits) granted by virtue of paragraph (1)–

(a) starts on the Monday following the day of the move; and

(b) ends on the expiry of the period of extended council tax reduction (qualifying contributory benefits) which would have applied had the mover not moved from the area of the first authority.

Relationship between council tax reduction and extended council tax reduction (qualifying contributory benefits)

77.–(1) Where a person's entitlement to council tax reduction would have ended when the person ceased to be entitled to a qualifying contributory benefit in the circumstances listed in regulation 68(1)(b), that entitlement does not cease until the end of the period of entitlement to extended council tax reduction.

(2) Part 9 (effective date) does not apply to any extended council tax reduction (qualifying contributory benefits) granted in accordance with regulation 70(1)(a) (amount of extended council tax reduction) or 71(2) (amount of extended council tax reduction: movers).

Alternative maximum council tax reduction

78.–(1) Subject to paragraphs (2) and (3), the alternative maximum council tax reduction where the conditions set out in regulation 14(3) and (6) (conditions of entitlement to council tax reduction) are fulfilled is the amount determined in accordance with Schedule 2.

(2)   Subject to paragraph (3), where an applicant is jointly and severally liable for council tax in respect of a dwelling in which the applicant is resident with one or more other persons, in determining the alternative maximum council tax reduction in the applicant's case the amount determined in accordance with Schedule 2 must be divided by the number of persons who are jointly and severally liable for that tax.

(3)   Where an applicant is jointly and severally liable for council tax in respect of a dwelling with only the applicant's partner paragraph (2) does not apply.

General Note

Even if the applicant does not qualify for CTR under reg 14(4) and (5) (eg, because s/he has too much income or capital), s/he still may qualify for CTR under reg 14(3) and (6) based on the income of second adult(s) residing with her/him. Alternative maximum CTR is sometimes referred to as "second adult rebate". If the applicant would be entitled to main CTR under reg 14(4) and (5) *and* alternative maximum CTR, the amount s/he is entitled to under reg 14 is whichever is the higher amount, sometimes referred to by local authorities as the "best buy": reg 14(9). However, if the amount of CTR an applicant would be entitled to under reg 14A is more than the amount s/he would be entitled to under reg 14, reg 14A determines entitlement.

Where an applicant satisfies the reg 14(3) and (6) conditions, the whole of her/his capital is disregarded under Sch 5 para 49. This means that even where an applicant has capital in excess of the limit provided by reg 42, s/he is treated as having capital below that limit. The claimant's income makes no difference to entitlement to the alternative maximum CTR as the amount of this is calculated under Sch 2 by reference only to the income of the second adult(s).

Reference should also be made to regs 14(3) and (6) and 79 and Sch 2 (see p1474, below and p1551).

Analysis

Para (1)

An applicant can only qualify for alternative maximum CTR if there is at least one other adult resident in the dwelling (a "second adult") and no other resident is liable to pay the applicant rent: reg 14(6)(a). Note, however, that a resident liable to pay the applicant rent who is excluded from consideration by reg 14(7) does not preclude entitlement to alternative maximum CTR. Entitlement to alternative maximum CTR depends on the income of the second adult. Certain income can be disregarded. If there is more than one other person resident in the dwelling to whom reg 14(6)(b) applies, their income may be aggregated (see Sch 2). Regs 14(7)(a) and 79 restrict the categories of people whose income can be used for these purposes (see Analysis on p1530). The combined effect of reg 14 and this regulation is that non-dependant deductions do not apply in the calculation of alternative maximum CTR.

Perhaps the most common example of when there is potential entitlement to alternative maximum CTR is where the applicant is a single person and has a non-dependant young person or an elderly relative on a low income, living rent-free with her/him.

Paras (2) and (3)

Where there is a joint and several liability for council tax, an applicant's entitlement is calculated by dividing the alternative maximum CTR by the number of people who are jointly and severally liable. In effect, every liable person is expected to make her/his own application for a share of the alternative maximum CTR: para (2). This potentially raises the same difficulty as reg 66(2) (see Analysis on p1522). However, where the joint liability is only with a partner, the applicant receives the full alternative maximum CTR: para (3).

Residents of a dwelling to whom regulation 14(6) does not apply

79.   Regulation 14(6) (conditions of entitlement to council tax reduction: alternative maximum council tax reduction) does not apply in respect of–

(a)   a person who is liable for council tax solely in consequence of the provisions of section 77 or 77A of the Act (spouse's or civil partner's joint and several liability for tax);

(b)   a person who is residing with a couple or with the members of a polygamous marriage where the applicant for council tax reduction is a member of that couple or of that marriage and–

    (i)   in the case of a couple, neither member of that couple is a person who, in accordance with Schedule 1 to the Act, falls to be disregarded for the purposes of discount; or

    (ii)   in the case of a polygamous marriage, two or more members of that marriage are not persons who, in accordance with Schedule 1 to the Act, fall to be disregarded for the purposes of discount;

    (c)   a person who jointly with the applicant falls within the same sub-paragraph of section 75(2)(a) to (e) of the Act (persons liable to pay council tax) as applies in the case of the applicant; or

    (d)   a person who is residing with two or more persons both or all of whom fall within the same sub-paragraph of section 75(2)(a) to (e) of the Act (persons liable to pay council tax) and two or more of those persons are not persons who, in accordance with Schedule 1 to the Act, fall to be disregarded for the purposes of discount.

Analysis

Reg 79 should be read together with reg 78 and the Analysis on p1529. Reg 14(7) restricts the categories of people who count as "second adults" and hence whose income can be used as a basis for the alternative maximum CTR. This regulation provides further restrictions.

    Sub-para (a). The spouse, civil partner or partner of a person who is liable for the council tax for a dwelling will also be liable, if s/he would not otherwise be so, by virtue of s77 or s77A LGFA 1992, provided s/he is also a resident of the dwelling (ie, they will both be jointly and severally liable). If s/he is liable for council tax for the dwelling by virtue of s77 or s77A, s/he will not count as a second adult for the purpose of reg 14(6). Although joint and several liability cannot arise under ss77 and 77A if the spouse, civil partner or partner qualifies for a 'discount disregard' under Sch 1 para 2 or 4 LGFA 1992, if such circumstances apply s/he still would not count as a second adult by virtue of reg 14(7)(a). Note that a spouse, civil partner or partner who is jointly and severally liable for the council tax with the applicant under s75(2)(a)-(e) and (3) will not count as a second adult by virtue of subpara (c) of this regulation.

    Sub-para (b) excludes any person residing with a couple or partners in a polygamous marriage, where the applicant is a member of the couple or the polygamous marriage. Such a person does not count as a second adult for the purpose of reg 14(6) unless at least one of the couple is disregarded under Sch 1 LGFA 1992 (discounts) or unless all the partners in the polygamous marriage who are residing with her/him are disregarded under Sch 1 LGFA 1992, or all of them except one are.

    Sub-para (c) excludes people who are joint owners or joint tenants, or otherwise share the same status as the applicant under s75(2)(a)–(e) LGFA 1992. Note that although such a person would not count as a second adult, s/he might her/himself qualify for main CTR for her share of the council tax bill under reg 14(4) and (5). However, if two people who are jointly liable are a couple only one of them can apply for CTR: reg 7.

    Sub-para (d) excludes any person residing with two or more people who share the same status under s75(2)(a)–(e) (and who are, therefore, jointly liable for the council tax) unless all of those liable are eligible for a discount disregard under Sch 1 LGFA 1992, or all except one are.

PART 9
Effective date

Date on which entitlement is to begin

    80.–(1)   Subject to paragraph (2), where a person–

    (a)   makes, or is treated as making, an application; and

    (b)   fulfils the conditions of entitlement to council tax reduction in regulation 14 [¹ or 14A],

that person is entitled to council tax reduction from the first Monday after the date on which the application is made or treated as made.

    (2)   Where, a person–

    (a)   becomes liable for the first time for council tax in respect of a dwelling in which the person resides;

    (b)   makes, or is treated as making, an application in the reduction week in which the person first becomes liable for council tax in respect of that dwelling; and

    (c)   fulfils the conditions of entitlement to council tax reduction in regulation 14 [¹ or 14A],

that person is entitled to council tax reduction from the day on which the person first becomes liable for council tax.

Amendment

    1.   Amended by reg 7 of SSI 2016 No 253 as from 1.4.17.

General Note

This is similar to the HB equivalent. See p533 for the commentary.

Date on which a change of circumstances is to take effect

81.–(1)   Subject to the provisions of this regulation, a change of circumstances which affects entitlement to council tax reduction is to take effect for the purpose of calculating entitlement to council tax reduction from the first day of the reduction week ['starting immediately after] the date on which the change actually occurs, and where that change is cessation of entitlement to any benefit under the benefit Acts, the date on which the change actually occurs is the day immediately following the last day of entitlement to that benefit.

(2)   Subject to paragraph (3), where the change of circumstances is a change in the amount of council tax payable, it takes effect for the purpose of calculating entitlement to council tax reduction from the day on which it actually occurs.

(3)   Where the change of circumstances is a change in the amount a person is liable to pay in respect of council tax in consequence of regulations under section 80 of the Act (reduced amounts of council tax) or changes in the discount to which a dwelling may be subject under sections 79 of that Act, it takes effect for the purpose of calculating entitlement to council tax reduction from the day on which the change in amount has effect.

(4)   Where the change of circumstances is an amendment to these Regulations, it takes effect for the purpose of calculating entitlement to council tax reduction from the date on which the amendment to these Regulations comes into force.

(5)   Where the change of circumstances is the applicant's acquisition of a partner, it takes effect for the purpose of calculating entitlement to council tax reduction on the day on which the acquisition takes place.

(6)   Where the change of circumstances is the death of an applicant's partner or their separation, it takes effect for the purpose of calculating entitlement to council tax reduction on the day the death or separation occurred.

(7)   If two or more changes of circumstances occurring in the same reduction week would, but for this paragraph, take effect for the purpose of calculating entitlement to council tax reduction in different reduction weeks in accordance with paragraphs (1) to (6) they take effect from the day to which the appropriate paragraph from (2) to (6) refers, or, where more than one day is concerned, from the earlier day.

(8)   Where the change of circumstances is that income, or an increase in the amount of income, other than a benefit or an increase in the amount of a benefit under the 1992 Act[², Part 4 of the Welfare Reform Act 2012 or article 24A of the Armed Forces and Reserve Forces (Compensation Scheme) Order 2011], is paid in respect of a past period and there was no entitlement to income of that amount during that period, it takes effect for the purpose of calculating entitlement to council tax reduction from the first day on which the income, had it been paid in that period at intervals appropriate to that income, would have been taken into account for the purposes of these Regulations.

(9)   Without prejudice to paragraph (8), where the change of circumstances is the payment of income or arrears of income in respect of a past period, it takes effect for the purpose of calculating entitlement to council tax reduction from the first day on which the income, had it been timeously paid in that period at intervals appropriate to that income, would have been taken into account for the purposes of these Regulations.

['(10)   Where the change of circumstances is that–

(a)   a conversion decision within the meaning of regulation 5(2)(a) of the Employment and Support Allowance (Existing Awards) Regulations has been made in relation to the applicant or the applicant's partner; or

(b)   the applicant or the applicant's partner is appealing a conversion decision within the meaning of regulation 5(2)(b) of the Employment and Support Allowance (Existing Awards) Regulations and is treated as having limited capability for work by virtue of regulation 30 of the Employment and Support Allowance Regulations as modified by the Employment and Support Allowance (Existing Awards) Regulations,

for the purpose of calculating entitlement to council tax reduction it takes effect, where the conversion decision takes effect on or after 1st April in any year but before 16th April of that year, from 1st April and in any other case from the day the conversion decision takes effect.]

Amendments

1. Inserted by reg 12 of SSI 2013 No 48 as from 18.3.13.
2. Inserted by reg 11(5) of SSI 2013 No 142 as from 11.6.13.

General Note

This is similar to the HB equivalent. See p537 for the commentary.

PART 10
Applications

Who may apply

82.   In the case of a couple or members of a polygamous marriage an application is to be made by whichever one of them they agree should apply or, in default of agreement, by whichever one of them the relevant authority determines is to make the application.

General Note

This is similar to the HB equivalent. See p543 and p815 for the commentary.

Written applications

83.–(1)   Subject to regulation 84 (telephone applications), an application must be sent to the designated office in writing and–

(a) made on a properly completed form approved for the purposes by the relevant authority; or

(b) in such written form as the relevant authority accepts as sufficient in the circumstances of any particular case or class of cases having regard to the sufficiency of the written information and evidence.

(2)   Where an application is not made in the form described in paragraph (1)(a) or (b) it is defective.

(3)   Where an application is defective because–

(a) it was made on the form approved for the purpose but that form is not accepted by the relevant authority as being properly completed the relevant authority may request the applicant to complete the defective application; or

(b) it was made in writing but not on the form approved for the purpose and the relevant authority does not accept the application as being in a written form which is sufficient in the circumstances of the case, having regard to the sufficiency of the written information and evidence, the relevant authority may supply the applicant with the approved form or request further information or evidence.

(4)   A defective application is to be treated as if it had been validly made in the first instance if, in any particular case, one of the conditions specified in paragraph (5) is satisfied.

(5)   The conditions are that–

(a) where paragraph (3)(a) (incomplete form) applies, the relevant authority receives the properly completed application, the information requested to complete it or the evidence within one month of the authority's request, or any longer period the relevant authority considers reasonable; or

(b) where paragraph (3)(b) (application not on approved form or further information requested by relevant authority) applies–

   (i) the approved form sent to the applicant is received by the relevant authority properly completed within one month of it having been sent to the applicant, or any longer period the relevant authority considers reasonable; or

   (ii) the applicant supplies whatever information or evidence was requested under paragraph (3) within one month of the request, or any longer period the relevant authority considers reasonable.

(6)   An application made on an approved form is for the purposes of these Regulations properly completed if completed in accordance with the instructions on the form, including any instructions to provide information and evidence in connection with the application.

General Note

This is similar to the HB equivalent. See p549 for the commentary.

Telephone applications

84.–(1)   Where the relevant authority has published a telephone number for the purpose of receiving applications for council tax reduction, an application may be made by telephone to that telephone number.

(2)   The relevant authority may determine that an application made by telephone is not a valid application unless the applicant approves a written statement of the person's circumstances, provided by the relevant authority.

(3)   An application made by telephone in accordance with paragraph (1) is defective unless the relevant authority is provided with all the information requested by it during the telephone call.

(4)   Where an application made by telephone in accordance with paragraph (1) is defective, the applicant must be given an opportunity to correct the defect.

(5)   If the applicant corrects the defect referred to in paragraph (4) within one month, or any longer period the relevant authority considers reasonable, of the date the authority last drew attention to the defect, the application is to be treated as if it had been validly made in the first instance.

(6)   If the person does not correct the defect within one month, or any longer period the relevant authority considers reasonable, of the date the authority last drew attention to the defect, the application may be treated as if it had not been defective if the relevant authority considers that it has sufficient information to determine the application.

General Note

This is similar to the HB equivalent. See p549 for the commentary.

Date on which an application is made

85.–(1)   Subject to paragraph (3) and regulation 5(9) (occupation of a dwelling as a home) the date on which an application is made is–

(a)   where an award of income support, universal credit, an income-based jobseeker's allowance or an income-related employment and support allowance has been made to the applicant or the applicant's partner and the application for council tax reduction is made within one month of the date on which the claim for that income support, universal credit jobseeker's allowance or employment and support allowance was received at the appropriate DWP office, the first day of entitlement to that income support, universal credit, jobseeker's allowance or employment and support allowance arising from that claim;

(b)   where an applicant or the applicant's partner is a person on income support, universal credit, an income-based jobseeker's allowance or an income-related employment and support allowance and the applicant becomes liable for the first time to pay council tax in respect of the dwelling which the applicant occupies as a home, where the application is received by the relevant authority within one month of the date on which the applicant first became liable to pay council tax, the date on which the applicant first became so liable;

(c)   where the applicant is the former partner of a person who was, at the date of that partner's death or the partners' separation, entitled to council tax reduction and where the applicant makes an application for council tax reduction within one month of the date of the death or the separation, that date;

(d)   except where sub-paragraph (a), (b) or (c) is satisfied, in a case where a properly completed application is received within one month, or any longer period the relevant authority considers reasonable, of the date on which–

(i)   an application form was issued to the applicant following the applicant first notifying, by whatever means, the relevant authority of an intention to make an application; or

(ii)   the applicant notifies, by whatever means, the relevant authority of an intention to make an application by telephone in accordance with regulation 84 (telephone applications),

the date of first notification; and

(e)   in any other case, the date on which the application is received by the relevant authority.

(2)   For the purpose of paragraph (1)(a), a person who has been awarded an income-based jobseeker's allowance or an income-related employment and support allowance is to be treated as entitled to that allowance for any days which immediately precede the first day of that award and on which the person would, but for regulations made under–

(a)   in the case of income-based jobseeker's allowance, paragraph 4 of Schedule 1 to the Jobseekers Act (waiting days); or

(b)   in the case of income-related employment and support allowance, paragraph 2 of Schedule 2 to the Welfare Reform Act (waiting days),

have been entitled to that allowance.

(3)   Except in the case of an application made by a person living abroad, where a person has not become liable for council tax to a relevant authority but it is anticipated that the person will become liable within the period of 8 weeks, the person may apply for council tax reduction at any time in that period and, provided that liability arises within that 8 week period, the relevant authority is to treat the application as having been made on the day on which the liability for council tax arises.

(4)   Where a relevant authority has not set or imposed its council tax by the beginning of the financial year, if an application for council tax reduction is properly made or treated as made and–

(a)   the date on which the application is made or treated as made is in the period from 1st April of the current year and ending one month after the date on which the authority sets or imposes the tax; and

(b)   if the tax had been determined, the applicant would have been entitled to council tax reduction either from–

(i)   the reduction week in which 1st April of the current year fell; or

(ii)   a reduction week falling after the date specified in head (i) but before the application was made,

the relevant authority must treat the application as made in the reduction week immediately preceding the reduction week in which such entitlement would have commenced.

(5)   Except in the case of an application made by a person living abroad, where the applicant is not entitled to council tax reduction in the reduction week immediately following the date of the application but the relevant authority is of the opinion that unless there is a change of circumstances the applicant will be entitled to council tax reduction for a period beginning not later than the thirteenth reduction week following the date on which the application is made, the relevant authority may treat the application as made on a date in the reduction week immediately preceding the first reduction week of that period of entitlement and grant entitlement to council tax reduction accordingly.

(6)   In the case of a person who has attained, or whose partner has attained, the age which is 17 weeks younger than the qualifying age for state pension credit, paragraph (5) applies as if for the reference to the thirteenth reduction week, there was substituted a reference to the seventeenth reduction week.

(7)   Where an applicant ("C")–

(a)   makes an application which includes (or which C subsequently requests should include) a period before the application is made; and

(b)   from a day in that period, up to the date when C made the application (or subsequently requested that the application should include a past period), C had continuous good cause for failing to make an application (or request that the application should include that period), the application is to be treated as made on the date determined in accordance with paragraph (8).

(8)　The date referred to in paragraph (7) is the latest of–

(a)　the first day from which C had continuous good cause;

(b)　the day [[1, 2] 6 months] before the date the application was made; or

(c)　the day [[1, 2] 6 months] before the date when C requested that the application should include a past period.

(9)　In this regulation "appropriate DWP office" means an office of the Department for Work and Pensions dealing with state pension credit or claim office which is normally open to the public for the receipt of claims for income support, a jobseeker's allowance or an employment and support allowance.

Amendments

1.　　Substituted by reg 7 of SSI 2016 No 81 as from 1.4.16.

2.　　Amended by reg 7 of SSI 2018 No 69 as from 1.4.18.

General Note

This is similar to reg 83 HB Regs. However, note that, from 1 April 2018, the maximum period of backdating allowed by paras (7) and (8) is extended from one month to six, having been six months prior to the amendment made by SSI 2016 No 81. In the corresponding HB provision (reg 83(12) and (12A) HB Regs), the maximum period of backdating is one month. See p549 for the commentary on reg 83 HB regs.

Evidence and information

86.–(1)　Subject to paragraphs (2) and (3) an applicant must furnish any certificates, documents, information and evidence in connection with an application for council tax reduction or existing entitlement to council tax reduction as may reasonably be required by the relevant authority in order to determine that person's entitlement to, or continuing entitlement to, council tax reduction and must do so within one month of the authority requiring the applicant to do so, or any longer period the authority considers reasonable.

(2)　Nothing in this regulation requires a person to furnish any certificates, documents, information or evidence relating to a payment to which paragraph (3) applies.

(3)　This paragraph applies to–

(a)　a payment which is–

(i)　disregarded under paragraph 27 of Schedule 4 (sums to be disregarded in the calculation of income other than earnings – income in kind) or paragraph 38 of Schedule 5 (capital to be disregarded – certain payments in kind);

(ii)　made under or by the Trusts, the Fund, the Eileen Trust, MFET Limited, the Skipton Fund, the Caxton Foundation [[2, another infected blood payment scheme] [[3, the London Bombings Relief Charitable Fund, the London Emergencies Trust or the We Love Manchester Emergency Fund];

(b)　a payment which is disregarded under paragraph 41 of Schedule 4 (sums to be disregarded in the calculation of income other than earnings: payments made under certain trusts and certain other payments) or under paragraph 29 of Schedule 5 (capital to be disregarded – payments made under certain trusts and certain other payments), other than a payment [[1] by ILF Scotland]; and

(c)　a payment which is disregarded under regulation 67(9)(b) or (c) (non-dependant deductions) or paragraph 2(b) or (c) of Schedule 2 (amount of alternative maximum council tax reduction: second adult's gross income), other than a payment [[1] by ILF Scotland].

(4)　Where a request is made under paragraph (1) the relevant authority must–

(a)　inform the applicant of the duty under regulation 89 to notify the authority of any change of circumstances; and

(b)　without prejudice to the extent of the duty owed under regulation 89, indicate to the applicant, either orally or by notice or by reference to some other document available to that applicant, on application and without charge, the kind of changes of circumstances which are to be notified.

(5)   Where an applicant or any partner of that applicant has attained the qualifying age for state pension credit and is a member of, or a person deriving entitlement to a pension under, a personal pension scheme, the applicant must, where the relevant authority so requires, furnish the following information–

(a)   the name and address of the pension fund holder; and

(b)   any other information including any reference or policy number as is needed to enable the personal pension scheme to be identified.

(6)   In this regulation "pension fund holder" means the trustees, managers or scheme administrators, as the case may be, of the scheme concerned.

Amendments

1.   Substituted by reg 4(4) of SSI 2016 No 81 as from 1.4.16.
2.   Amended by reg 9 of SSI 2017 No 41 as from 1.4.17.
3.   Amended by reg 4(f) of SSI 2017 No 326 as from 20.11.17.

General Note

This is similar to the HB equivalent. See p556 for the commentary. Reg 86(1) is also similar to Sch 8 para 7(4) of CTRS(PR)(E) Regs (see p1181 for commentary).

Amendment of applications

87.–(1)   Subject to paragraph (2), at any time before a relevant authority has made a determination on an application the applicant may amend the application by notice in writing sent to the designated office.

(2)   Where an application is made by telephone in accordance with regulation 84 (telephone applications) an amendment may be made by telephone to the telephone number specified by the relevant authority for the purpose of that regulation.

(3)   Any application amended in accordance with paragraph (1) or (2) is to be treated as if it had been in its amended state when it was first made.

General Note

This is similar to the HB equivalent. See p559 for the commentary.

Withdrawal of applications

88.–(1)   An applicant may withdraw the application at any time by notice in writing delivered or sent to the designated office before the relevant authority has determined the application.

(2)   Where the application was made by telephone in accordance with regulation 84, the withdrawal may be made by telephone to the telephone number specified by the relevant authority for the purpose of that regulation.

(3)   Any notice of withdrawal given in accordance with paragraph (1) or (2) has effect when it is received by the relevant authority.

General Note

This is similar to the HB equivalent. See p559 for the commentary.

PART 11
Notification of changes of circumstances

Duty to notify changes of circumstances

89.–(1)   Subject to paragraphs (3) and (4) and regulation 90 (alternative means of notifying changes of circumstances), if at any time between the making of an application and it being determined or during a period of entitlement to council tax reduction, there is a change of circumstances which an applicant might reasonably be expected to know might affect entitlement to council tax reduction that applicant must notify that change of circumstances by giving notice to the relevant authority–

(a)   in writing; or

(b)   by telephone–
    (i)   where the relevant authority has published a telephone number for that purpose or for the purposes of regulation 84 (telephone applications), unless the authority determines that in any particular case, or class of case, notification of a change of circumstances may not be given by telephone; or
    (ii)   in any case, or class of case, where the relevant authority determines that notice of a change of circumstances may be given by telephone; or

(c)   by any other means the relevant authority agrees to in any particular case.

(2)   Subject to paragraph (3), the duty imposed by paragraph (1) does not extend to notifying changes–

(a)   in the amount of council tax payable to the relevant authority;

(b)   in the age of the applicant or of any member of the applicant's family;

(c)   to these Regulations; or

(d)   in the case of an applicant who has an award of income support, universalcredit, an income-based jobseeker's allowance or an income-related employment and support allowance, in circumstances which affect the amount of the award but not the amount of council tax reduction to which the applicant is or would be entitled, other than the cessation of that entitlement to income support, universal credit, an income-based jobseeker's allowance or an income-related employment and support allowance.

(3)   Notwithstanding paragraph (2)(b) or (d) an applicant is required by paragraph (1) to notify the relevant authority of any change in the composition of the applicant's family arising from the fact that a person who was a member of the family is now no longer a member of the family because that person ceased to be a child or young person.

(4)   Where the amount of an council tax reduction is the alternative maximumcouncil tax reduction applicable to the applicant calculated in accordance with regulation 78 (alternative maximum council tax reduction), the applicant is under a duty to give written notice to the relevant authority of changes which occur in the number of adults in the dwelling or in their total gross incomes which might reasonably be expected to change the applicant's entitlement to council tax reduction and where any of those adults ceases to be in receipt of state pension credit, income support, universal credit, an income-based jobseeker's allowance or an income-related employment and support allowance the date when this occurs.

General Note
This is similar to the HB equivalent. See p560 for the commentary.

Alternative means of notifying changes of circumstances

90.   Where a change of circumstances described in regulation 89(1) (duty to notify changes of circumstances) is a birth or death the relevant authority may determine for a particular class of case that the duty in that regulation to notify a change in circumstances may be discharged by personal attendance at an office specified by that authority.

General Note
This is similar to the HB equivalent. See p562 for the commentary.

[¹PART 11A
Reviews]

Amendment
1.   Inserted by reg 7 of SSI 2013 No 218 as from 1.10.13.

[¹Review of determination on an application

90A.–(1)   A determination on an application may not be appealed to a valuation appeal committee.

(2)   An applicant who is aggrieved by a determination on an application may serve a written notice on the relevant authority requesting that it review its determination.

(3)   The notice under paragraph (2) must be served within two months of the determination it relates to and must state the matter by which, and the grounds on which, the applicant is aggrieved.

(4)   Where a notice under paragraph (2) is served on a relevant authority, that authority must–

(a)   consider the matter to which the notice relates;

(b)   within two months of receipt of the notice, redetermine the application or decide that no alteration of the determination is to be made;

(c)   notify the applicant in writing of its decision and that if the applicant remains aggrieved then a request for further review may be made within 42 days of the notification, with the address to which any such a request is to be sent.]

Amendment

1.   Inserted by reg 7 of SSI 2013 No 218 as from 1.10.13 but for transitional provisions, see reg 17 of SSI 2013 No 218.

[¹Request for further review

90B.–(1)   A request for further review of a determination on an application must be made in writing within 42 days of the notification by the relevant authority under sub-paragraph (c) of regulation 90A(4) and be served at the address notified under that sub-paragraph.

(2)   A request for further review of a determination on an application may also be made where a relevant authority has not notified the applicant of a decision on a request for review under regulation 90A(2) and more than two months have elapsed since the notice requesting review was served.

(3)   A request under paragraph (2)–

(a)   must be made in writing and be served on the relevant authority; and

(b)   prevents the relevant authority from notifying a decision on the request for review under regulation 90A(2).

(4)   A request for further review must state the matter by which, and the grounds on which, the applicant is aggrieved.

(5)   Where a relevant authority is served with a notice requesting further review it must, as soon as possible, forward it to the panel appointed by the Scottish Ministers under regulation 90C.]

Amendment

1.   Inserted by reg 7 of SSI 2013 No 218 as from 1.10.13.

[¹Panel to conduct further reviews

90C.–(1)   The Scottish Ministers must appoint a panel of persons ("the panel") to conduct further review of determinations on applications [¹ and must appoint one of the persons to act as senior reviewer].

(2)   A person may only be appointed to the panel if that person–

(a)   is a solicitor or advocate in Scotland of at least 5 years' standing;

(b)   has a five year general qualification within the meaning of section 71 of the Courts and Legal Services Act 1990; or

(c)   is a member of the Bar of Northern Ireland, or a solicitor of the Court of Judicature of Northern Ireland, of at least 5 years' standing.

(3)   A person may not be appointed to the panel, and if appointed must immediately be removed from the panel, if that person–

(a)   is a member or employee of a local authority in Scotland;

(b)   is a member of Parliament, of the Scottish Parliament or of the European Parliament.

(4)   The Scottish Ministers may remove a person from the panel if they consider that the person is unable to discharge the functions of a panel member or is unsuitable to serve on the panel.

(5)   A member of the panel is entitled to receive payment of such allowances as the Scottish Ministers may determine in respect of performance of the functions of a panel member.]

Amendments
1.   Inserted by reg 7 of SSI 2013 No 218 as from 1.10.13.
2.   Amended by reg 7 of SSI 2015 No 46 as from 1.4.15.

[¹Conduct of further reviews

90D.–(1)   A further review of a determination on an application is to be undertaken by one member of the panel appointed under regulation 90C(1), except as set out in paragraph (8).

(2)   A further review is to include an oral hearing unless the parties and the member of the panel who is undertaking the review agree that the review is to be disposed of by written representations.

(3)   A party to a further review must, if requested, advise the member of the panel who is undertaking the review–

(a)   whether that party agrees that the review may be disposed of by written representations;

(b)   whether the applicant has appealed any application for housing benefit that may be relevant to the consideration of the further review, and if so whether that appeal has been determined (insofar as these matters are within the party's knowledge).

(4)   Where either party to a further review is requested by the member of the panel who is undertaking the further review to provide documents or information and fails to respond to that request within such timescale as the member considers reasonable, such inferences may be drawn from the failure as the member sees fit, including the inference that the further review should be allowed or refused.

(5)   A request for further review that has been validly made in accordance with regulation 90B may not be withdrawn other than with leave of the [² senior reviewer].

(6)   The member of the panel who is undertaking the further review–

(a)   is to decide the procedure for that review [², having regard to any guidance issued by the senior reviewer];

(b)   may hold any oral hearing in public or private, as the member sees fit;

(c)   may request, but has no power to require, the production of documents or the attendance of any person as a witness;

(d)   if satisfied that there are good and sufficient reasons for doing so, may refuse to permit a particular person to represent a party at an oral hearing; [²]

(e)   may uphold or reject the request for that review, in full or in part, but must remit any calculation of the amount of an applicant's entitlement to a council tax reduction to the relevant authority.

[² (f)   must give full reasons for the decision to uphold or reject the request for review, if asked to do so by a party to that review within 14 days of the date on which the decision was given.]

[² (6A)   A member of the panel may set aside a decision disposing of a request for further review if satisfied that it is in the interests of justice to do so.]

[² (6B)   Where a decision is set aside the further review must be undertaken again.]

[² (6C)   A request to set aside a decision must–

(a)   be made within 14 days of the date on which the decision was given, and

(b)   give reasons for the request.]

(7)   The relevant authority must implement the decision of the member of the panel disposing of a request for further review of a determination as soon as is reasonably practicable, including any calculation of the amount of an applicant's entitlement to a council tax reduction that is required.

(8)   In the circumstances of a particular case the Scottish Ministers may consider it appropriate for three members of the panel appointed under regulation 90C(1) to undertake the further review, and in such a case references in this regulation to anything

being done or decided by a member of the panel refer to it being done or decided by all three members, or by two of them should they not be agreed.]

Amendments

1. Inserted by reg 7 of SSI 2013 No 218 as from 1.10.13.
2. Amended by reg 8 of SSI 2015 No 46 as from 1.4.15.

PART 12
Electronic communication

Sending documents by electronic communication

91.–(1)   For the purpose of these Regulations, an applicant may send a document by electronic communication–

(a)   in a form approved by the relevant authority for the purposes of this regulation;

(b)   to an address notified by the relevant authority for the purpose of this regulation; and

(c)   by the method set out in paragraph (4).

(2)   An applicant sending a document to a relevant authority by electronic communications is taken to have agreed–

(a)   to the use of electronic communications for all purposes relating to the application which are capable of being carried out electronically; and

(b)   that the address for the purpose of such communications is the address incorporated into, or otherwise logically associated with, that communication.

(3)   Deemed agreement referred to in paragraph (2) subsists until the applicant gives notice to revoke the agreement, and the notice takes effect from the date specified in it, being a date not less than 7 working days after the date on which the notice is given.

(4)   An electronic communication must be–

(a)   capable of being accessed by the recipient;

(b)   legible in all other material respects; and

(c)   sufficiently permanent to be used for subsequent reference.

(5)   Unless the contrary is proved a document sent by the method specified in paragraph (3) is, for the purposes of any legal proceedings, to be regarded as having been–

(a)   delivered where the document has been delivered to or by the relevant authority and the delivery of the document has been recorded on an official computer system; and

(b)   received at the time and date of receipt recorded in an official computer system.

(6)   In this regulation–

"address" includes any number or address used for the purpose of electronic communications or storage;

"document" includes an application, notice, certificate, information and evidence;

"electronic communication" has the same meaning as in section 15(1) of the Electronic Communications Act 2000;

"legible in all material respects" means that the information contained in the document is available to the recipient to no lesser extent than it would be if sent or given by means of a document in printed form; and

"official computer system" means a computer system maintained by or on behalf of the relevant authority for the sending, receiving, processing or storing of an application.

PART 13
Consequential and transitional provisions

Transitional provision

92.–(1)   A person described in paragraph (2) is deemed to have made an application for council tax reduction on 1st April 2013.

(2)   A person referred to in paragraph (1) is a person–

(a) who is entitled to council tax benefit on 31st March 2013;

(b) who made an application for council tax benefit which is not determined before 1st April 2013;

(c) whose entitlement to council tax benefit is wholly or partly suspended immediately before 1st April 2013;

[¹(ca) other than a person described in sub-paragraph (a) or (c), who has applied for a revision of a decision by a relevant authority under regulation 4(1) (revision of decisions) or 5(1) (late application for a revision) of the Housing Benefit and Council Tax Benefit (Decisions and Appeals) Regulations 2001 and whose application is pending immediately before 1st April 2013.]

(d) other than a person described in sub-paragraphs (a) or (c), who has appealed against a decision of the First-tier Tribunal, the Upper Tribunal or a court in relation to a claim for council tax benefit and whose appeal is pending immediately before 1st April 2013.

[¹(2A) For the purposes of sub-paragraph (2)(ca) a revision of a decision relating to a claim for council tax benefit is pending if an application for a revision has been made but not been determined.]

(3) For the purpose of paragraph (2)(d) an appeal against a decision relating to a claim for council tax benefit is pending if–

(a) an appeal against the decision has been brought but not determined;

(b) an application for permission to appeal against the decision has been made but not determined; or

(c) the time within which–

    (i) an application for permission to appeal may be made; or

    (ii) an appeal against the decision may be brought,

has not expired and one of the circumstances prescribed in regulation 11(3) of the Housing Benefit and Council Tax Benefit (Decisions and Appeals) Regulations 2001 apply.

Amendment

1.   Inserted by reg 13 of SSI 2013 No 48 as from 18.3.13.

Savings provision

93. Schedule 6 has effect.

Consequential amendments

94. The amendments in Schedule 7 have effect.

SCHEDULE 1

Applicable amount

Regulations 21 and 22

General Note

This Schedule, together with regs 21 and 22, determines the amount of an applicant's applicable amount. It is not relevant if an applicant or her/his partner (as defined in reg 2(1)) has an award of UC, or if they jointly have such an award, as in such cases the applicable amount is determined in accordance with reg 23.

This Schedule is broadly equivalent to Sch 3 to the HB Regs although there are some significant differences. For CTR, there isno 'two-child limit' for personal allowances for children and young people, as there is in some circumstances for HB and CTR in England. Instead, an applicant's applicable amount includes an allowance for each child or young person who is a member of the applicant's family. In addition, although subject to transitional rules, the work-related activity component is no longer included in the HB applicable amount for claims made on or after 3 April 2017, this does not apply to CTR in Scotland. Unlike for HB, the work-related activity component can still be included in a working-age applicant's applicable amount provided the conditions in Part 5 of Sch 1 are met. One further difference of substance is the transitional protection in para 4(2) for those who were entitled to the CTB family premium at the lone parent rate prior to the enactment of the Social Security (Lone Parents) Regulations 1998. In these Regulations, broadly, a person is deemed to be entitled to CTR for a period during which s/he was getting HB or would have been but for the fact that s/he was then in a rent-free period for the purposes of reg 81 HB Regs.

From 1 May 2016, an applicant in Scotland can now only be entitled to a family premium within the assessment of her/ his applicable amount for CTR if s/he is covered by the transitional provision reg 2 of The Council Tax Reduction (Scotland) Amendment Regulations 2016 No.81. See the commentary below regarding para 4 for further details.

For commentary on the need to register as blind or severely sight impaired to satisfy para10(1)(a)(v) and therefore paras 11(3) and (4)(b) and 13(b), see the General Note to Sch 2, para 6 of The Council Tax Reduction Schemes and Prescribed Requirements (Wales) Regulations 2013 No.3029 (p1248).

From 1 April 2017, the amount included for a child or young person who is a member of the applicant's family specified in para 3 of this Schedule was increased by 25 per cent.

PART 1
Personal Allowances

1. The amount specified in column (2) below in respect of each person or couple specified in column (1) is the amount specified for the purposes of regulations 21(a) (applicable amount) and 22(a) and (b) (applicable amount: polygamous marriages)–

Column (1)	Column (2)
Person or couple	Amount
(1) A single applicant who–	
(a) is entitled to main phase employment and support allowance;	[³£73.10]
(b) is aged not less than 25;	[³£73.10]
(c) is aged not less than 18 but less than 25.	[³£57.90]
(2) A lone parent.	[³£73.10]
(3) A couple.	[³£114.85]

Amendments
1. Substituted by reg 14(a) of SSI 2013 No 48 as from 18.3.13.
2. Amended by reg 4(a) of SSI 2014 No 35 as from 1.4.14.
3. Amended by reg 9(a) of SSI 2015 No 46 as from 1.4.15.

---

2. For the purposes of paragraph 1 an applicant is entitled to main phase employment and support allowance if–
(a) paragraph [¹18 (components)] is satisfied in relation to the applicant; or
(b) the applicant is entitled to a converted employment and support allowance [², or would be entitled but for the application of section 1A of the Welfare Reform Act (duration of contributory allowance)]

Amendments
1. Amended by reg 14(b)(i) of SSI 2013 No 48 as from 18.3.13.
2. Inserted by reg 14(b)(ii) of SSI 2013 No 48 as from 18.3.13.

---

3. The amounts specified in column (2) below in respect of each person specified in column (1) are, for the relevant period specified in column (1), the amounts specified for the purposes of regulations 21(b) and 22(c)–

Column (1)	Column (2)
Child or Young Person	Amount
A person in respect of the period–	
(a) beginning on that person's date of birth and ending on the day preceding the first Monday in September following that person's sixteenth birthday;	[⁴£83.63]
(b) beginning on the first Monday in September following that person's sixteenth birthday and ending on the day preceding that person's twentieth birthday.	[⁴£83.63]

Amendments
1. Substituted by reg 14(c) of SSI 2013 No 48 as from 18.3.13.
2. Amended by reg 4(b) of SSI 2014 No 35 as from 1.4.14.
3. Amended by reg 9(b) of SSI 2015 No 46 as from 1.4.15.
4. Substituted by reg 8 of SSI 2016 No 253 as from 1.4.17.

[³ PART 2]

Amendments
1.   Amended by reg 14(d) of SSI 2013 No 48 as from 18.3.13.
2.   Amended by reg 4(c) of SSI 2014 No 35 as from 1.4.14.
3.   Omitted by reg 5(3) of SSI 2016 No 81 as from 1.5.16, subject to transitional provision in reg 2 of SSI 2016 No 81.

General Note
Paragraph 4 covered the rules for the family premium. This could be included in an applicant's applicable amount if a child or young person was a member of her/his family. The family premium has been abolished for most applicants from 1 May 2016. From that date only those covered by the transitional provision in reg 2 of the Council Tax Reduction (Scotland) Amendment Regulations 2016 No.81 can be entitled to it. Under reg 2, an applicant can still qualify for a family premium if, on 30 April 2016, s/he was entitled to CTR and was:
(1)   a member of a family which included at least one child or young person; or
(2)   a partner in a polygamous marriage and either s/he, or another partner of the polygamous marriage, was responsible for a child or young person who was a member of the same household.
An applicant covered by this transitional provision will only stop being entitled to a family premium either when the above condition (1) or (2) ceases to apply to her/him or when s/he makes a new CTR application. A reassessment of an existing award does not count as a new CTR application. An applicant who is still entitled to the family premium under the above rules can continue to be awarded a higher rate of the premium on the basis that s/he is a lone parent if s/he satisfies the conditions for it which were contained in para 4(2). See p1433 and p1434 of the 28th edition of this book for para 4 and commentary on it.
   'Family', 'partner', 'polygamous marriage' and 'child' are defined in reg 2. The meaning of 'young person' is defined in reg 4. Reg 10 explains when someone can be treated as responsible for a child or young person and reg 11 deals with when someone is treated as a member of the same household.

PART 3
Disability premiums
   5.   Except as provided in paragraph 6, a premium specified in Part 4 of this Schedule is, for the purposes of regulations 21(d) (applicable amount) and 22(e) (applicable amount: polygamous marriages), applicable to an applicant who satisfies the conditions specified in paragraphs 9 to 14 which relate to that premium.
   6.   Subject to paragraph 7, where an applicant satisfies the conditions in respect of more than one premium in this Part of this Schedule, only one premium is applicable to the applicant and, if they are of different amounts, the higher or highest amount applies.
   7.   The following premiums, namely–
   (a)   a severe disability premium to which paragraph 11 applies;
   (b)   an enhanced disability premium to which paragraph 12 applies;
   (c)   a disabled child premium to which paragraph 13 applies; and
   (d)   a carer premium to which paragraph 14 applies,
may be applicable in addition to any other premium which may apply under this Schedule.
   8.–(1)   Subject to sub-paragraph (2), for the purposes of this Part of this Schedule, once a premium is applicable to an applicant under this Part, a person is to be treated as being in receipt of any benefit for–
   (a)   in the case of a benefit to which the Social Security (Overlapping Benefits) Regulations 1979 applies, any period during which, apart from the provisions of those Regulations, the person would be in receipt of that benefit; and
   (b)   any period spent by a person in undertaking a course of training or instruction provided or approved by Skills Development Scotland, Scottish Enterprise or Highlands and Islands Enterprise under section 2 of the Enterprise and New Towns (Scotland) Act 1990 or the Secretary of State under section 2 of the 1973 Act for any period during which the person is in receipt of a training allowance.
   (2)   For the purposes of the carer premium under paragraph 14, a person is to be treated as being in receipt of carer's allowance by virtue of sub-paragraph (1)(a) only for so long as the person in respect of whose care the allowance has been claimed remains in receipt of attendance allowance, the care component of disability living allowance at the highest or middle rate prescribed in accordance with section 72(3) of the 1992 Act [¹, armed forces independence payment] or the daily living component of personal independence payment.

Amendment
1.   Inserted by reg 11(6)(a) of SSI 2013 No 142 as from 11.6.13.

Disability premium
   9.   With regard to disability premium the condition referred to in paragraph 5 is that–
   (a)   where the applicant is a single applicant or a lone parent, the applicant has not attained the qualifying age for state pension credit and the additional condition specified in paragraph 10(1) is satisfied; or
   (b)   where the applicant has a partner, either–

        (i)   the applicant has not attained the qualifying age for state pension credit and the additional condition specified in paragraph 10(1) is satisfied by the applicant; or

        (ii)   the applicant's partner has not attained the qualifying age for state pension credit and the additional condition specified in paragraph 10(1)(a) is satisfied by the applicant's partner.

Additional condition for the disability premium

10.–(1)   Subject to sub-paragraph (2) and paragraph 8, the additional condition referred to in paragraph 9 is that either–

(a)   the applicant or, as the case may be, the applicant's partner–

        (i)   is in receipt of one or more of the following benefits: attendance allowance, disability living allowance, [¹armed forces independence payment,] personal independence payment, the disability element or the severe disability element of working tax credit as specified in regulation 20(1)(b) and (f) of the Working Tax Credit Regulations, mobility supplement, long-term incapacity benefit or severe disablement allowance under Part 3 of the 1992 Act but, in the case of long-term incapacity benefit or severe disablement allowance, only where it is paid in respect of the applicant;

        (ii)   was in receipt of long-term incapacity benefit when entitlement to that benefit ceased on account of the payment of a retirement pension under that Act [² or a state pension under Part 1 of the Pensions Act 2014] and the applicant remained continuously entitled to council tax benefit under the Council Tax Benefit (General) Regulations 1992 or the Council Tax Benefit Regulations 2006 before 1st April 2013 and to council tax reduction from that date, and, if the long-term incapacity benefit was payable to the applicant's partner, the partner is still a member of the family;

        (iii)   was in receipt of attendance allowance, disability living allowance or personal independence payment, but payment of the benefit has been suspended in accordance with regulations made under section 113(2) of the 1992 Act or section 86(1) of the Welfare Reform Act 2012 or otherwise abated as a consequence of the applicant or the applicant's partner becoming a patient within the meaning of regulation 28(11)(g) (treatment of child care charges);

        (iv)   is provided with an invalid carriage or other vehicle under section 46 of the National Health Service (Scotland) Act 1978 ("the 1978 Act"), paragraph 9(1) of Schedule 1 to the National Health Service Act 2006 ("the 2006 Act") or article 30(1) of the Health and Personal Social Services (Northern Ireland) Order 1972 or receives payments by way of grant from the Scottish Ministers under section 46 of the 1978 Act or the Secretary of State under paragraph 9(3) of Schedule 1 to the 2006 Act; or

        (v)   has been certified as blind and in consequence the applicant or the applicant's partner is registered as blind in a register maintained by or on behalf of a local authority in Scotland or has been registered as blind, in a register compiled under section 29 of the National Assistance Act 1948 (welfare services) [³ or is registered as severely sight impaired in a register kept by a local authority in Wales under section 18(1)(a) of the Social Services and Well-being (Wales) Act 2014]; or

(b)   the applicant–

        (i)   is, or is treated as, incapable of work in accordance with the provisions of, and regulations made under, Part 12A of the 1992 Act (incapacity for work); and

        (ii)   has been incapable, or has been treated as incapable, of work for a continuous period of not less than–

            (aa)   in the case of an applicant who is terminally ill within the meaning of section 30B(4) of the 1992 Act, 196 days; and

            (bb)   in any other case, 364 days.

(2)   For the purposes of sub-paragraph (1)(a)(v), a person who has ceased to be registered as blind on that person regaining eyesight is nevertheless to be treated as blind and as satisfying the additional condition set out in that sub-paragraph for a period of 28 weeks following the date on which the person ceased to be registered as blind.

(3)   For the purposes of sub-paragraph (1)(b), once the disability premium is applicable to an applicant by virtue of the applicant satisfying the additional condition specified in that provision, if the applicant then ceases, for a period of 8 weeks or less, to be treated as incapable of work or to be incapable of work, on again becoming incapable of work the applicant is immediately to be treated as satisfying the condition in that sub-paragraph.

(4)   For the purposes of sub-paragraph (1)(b), once the disability premium is applicable to an applicant by virtue of the applicant satisfying the additional condition specified in that provision, the applicant is to continue to be treated as satisfying that condition for any period spent by the applicant in undertaking a course of training provided under section 2 of the 1973 Act or section 2 of the Enterprise and New Towns (Scotland) Act 1990 or for any period during which the applicant is in receipt of a training allowance.

(5)   For the purposes of sub-paragraph (1)(b), where any two or more periods of incapacity are separated by a break of not more than 56 days, those periods are to be treated as one continuous period.

(6)   For the purposes of sub-paragraph (1)(b), once the disability premium is applicable to an applicant by virtue of the applicant satisfying the additional condition specified in that provision, the applicant is to continue to be treated as satisfying that condition for any period spent by the applicant in undertaking a course

of training provided under section 2 of the Enterprise and New Towns (Scotland) Act 1990 or section 2 of the 1973 Act.

(7) For the purposes of this paragraph, a reference to a person who is or was in receipt of long-term incapacity benefit includes a person who is or was in receipt of short-term incapacity benefit at a rate equal to the long-term rate by virtue of section 30B(4)(a) of the 1992 Act (short-term incapacity benefit for a person who is terminally ill) or who would be or would have been in receipt of short-term incapacity benefit at such a rate but for the fact that the rate of short-term incapacity benefit already payable to the person is or was equal to or greater than the long-term rate.

(8) In the case of an applicant who is a welfare to work beneficiary (a person to whom regulation 13A(1) of the Social Security (Incapacity for Work) (General) Regulations 1995 applies, and who again becomes incapable of work for the purposes of Part 12A of the 1992 Act)–
(a) the reference to a period of 8 weeks in sub-paragraph (3); and
(b) the reference to a period of 56 days in sub-paragraph (5),
is in each case to be treated as a reference to a period of 104 weeks.

(9) The applicant is not entitled to the disability premium if the applicant has, or is treated as having, limited capability for work.

(10) In this paragraph "invalid carriage or other vehicle" means a vehicle propelled by a petrol engine or by electric power supplied for use on the road and to be controlled by the occupant.

Amendments
1. Inserted by reg 11(6)(b) of SSI 2013 No 142 as from 11.6.13.
2. Amended by art 36(2) of SI 2015 No 1985 as from 6.4.16.
3. Insertedby reg 6(3) of SSI 2016 No 81 as from 6.4.16.

Severe disability premium
11.–(1) With regard to severe disability premium the condition referred to in paragraph 5 is that the applicant is a severely disabled person.

(2) For the purposes of sub-paragraph (1), an applicant is to be treated as being a severely disabled person if–
(a) in the case of a single applicant, a lone parent or an applicant who is treated as having no partner in consequence of sub-paragraph (3)–
(i) the applicant is in receipt of attendance allowance, the care component of disability living allowance at the highest or middle rate prescribed in accordance with section 72(3) of the 1992 Act [1, armed forces independence payment] or the daily living component of personal independence payment; and
(ii) subject to sub-paragraph (4), the applicant has no non-dependants aged 18 or over normally residing with the applicant or with whom the applicant normally resides; and
(iii) no person is in receipt of a carer's allowance under section 70 of the 1992 Act [2, or has an award of universal credit which includes the carer element under regulation 29 of the Universal Credit Regulations 2013,] in respect of caring for the applicant; or
(b) in the case of an applicant who has a partner–
(i) the applicant is in receipt of attendance allowance or the care component of disability living allowance at the highest or middle rate prescribed in accordance with section 72(3) of the 1992 Act [1, armed forces independence payment] or the daily living component of personal independence payment;
(ii) the applicant's partner is also in receipt of attendance allowance, the care component of disability living allowance at the highest or middle rate prescribed in accordance with section 72(3) of the 1992 Act [1, armed forces independence payment] or the daily living component of personal independence payment or, if the applicant is a member of a polygamous marriage, all the partners of that marriage are in receipt of such an allowance or payment;
(iii) subject to sub-paragraph (4), the applicant has no non-dependants aged 18 or over normally residing with the applicant or with whom the applicant normally resides,
and either a person is entitled to and in receipt of a carer's allowance [2, or has an award of universal credit which includes the carer element,] in respect of caring for only one of the couple or, in the case of a polygamous marriage, for one or more but not all the partners of the marriage, or as the case may be, no person is entitled to and in receipt of a carer's allowance [2, or has an award of universal credit which includes the carer element,] in respect of caring for either member of the couple or any partner of the polygamous marriage.

(3) Where an applicant has a partner who does not satisfy the condition in sub-paragraph (2)(b)(ii), and that partner is blind or is treated as blind within the meaning of paragraph 10(1)(a)(v) and (2), that partner is to be treated for the purposes of sub-paragraph (2)(b)(ii) as if the partner was not a partner of the applicant.

(4) For the purposes of sub-paragraph (2)(a)(ii) and (2)(b)(iii) no account is to be taken of–
(a) a person receiving attendance allowance, disability living allowance by virtue of the care component at the highest or middle rate prescribed in accordance with section 72(3) of the 1992 Act [1, armed forces independence payment] or the daily living component of personal independence payment; or
(b) a person who is blind or is treated as blind within the meaning of paragraph 10(1)(a)(v) and (2).

(5) For the purposes of sub-paragraph (2)(b) a person is to be treated–

(a)   as being in receipt of attendance allowance, the care component of disability living allowance at the highest or middle rate prescribed in accordance with section 72(3) of the 1992 Act or the daily living component of personal independence payment if the person would, but for being a patient in hospital for a period exceeding 28 days, be in receipt of that allowance or payment;

(b)   as being entitled to and in receipt of a carer's allowance [² or as having an award of universal credit which includes the carer element] if the person would, but for the person being cared for being a patient in hospital for a period exceeding 28 days, be entitled to and in receipt of a carer's allowance [² or would have an award of universal credit which includes the carer element].

(6)   For the purposes of sub-paragraph (2)(a)(iii) and (2)(b), no account is to be taken of an award of carer's allowance [², or of universal credit which includes the carer element,] to the extent that payment of the award is back-dated for a period before the date on which the award is first paid.

(7)   In sub-paragraph (2)(a)(iii) and (b), references to a person being in receipt of a carer's allowance [² or as having an award of universal credit which includes the carer element] include references to a person who would have been in receipt of that allowance [² or award] but for the application of a restriction under section 6B or 7 of the Social Security Fraud Act 2001 (loss of benefit provisions).

Amendments

1.   Inserted by reg 11(6)(c) of SSI 2013 No 142 as from 11.6.13.
2.   Inserted by reg 14(a) of SSI 2016 No 81 as from 1.4.16.

Enhanced disability premium

12.–(1)   With regard to enhanced disability premium and subject to sub-paragraph [¹(3)] the condition referred to in paragraph 5 is that–

(a)   the Secretary of State has decided that the applicant has, or is to be treated as having, limited capability for work-related activity;

(b)   the care component of disability living allowance is, or would, but for a suspension of benefit in accordance with regulations made under section 113(2) of the 1992 Act or an abatement as a consequence of hospitalisation, be payable at the highest rate prescribed under section 72(3) of the 1992 Act in respect of–
        (i)   the applicant; or
        (ii)   a member of the applicant's family,
        who has not attained the qualifying age for state pension credit; or

[³(ba) armed forces independence payment is payable in respect of the applicant or a member of the applicant's family who has not attained the qualifying age for state pension credit;]

(c)   the daily living component of personal independence payment [²at the enhanced rate] is, or would, but for a suspension of benefit in accordance with regulations made under section 86(1) of the Welfare Reform Act 2012 or an abatement as a consequence of hospitalisation, be payable in respect of the applicant or a member of the applicant's family who has not attained the qualifying age for state pension credit.

(2)   Where the condition in sub-paragraph (1) ceases to be satisfied because of the death of a child or young person, the condition is that the applicant or the applicant's partner is entitled to child benefit in respect of child or young person under section 145A of the 1992 Act (entitlement after death of child or qualifying young person).

(3)   The condition is not satisfied if the person to whom sub-paragraph (1) refers is–

(a)   an applicant who–
        (i)   is not a member of a couple or a polygamous marriage; and
        (ii)   is a patient within the meaning of regulation 28(11)(g) (treatment of child care charges: patients) and has been for a period of more than 52 weeks; or

(b)   a member of a couple or a polygamous marriage where each member is a patient within the meaning of regulation 28(11)(g) and has been for a period of more than 52 weeks.

Amendments

1.   Amended by reg 14(e)(i) of SSI 2013 No 48 as from 18.3.13.
2.   Inserted by reg 14(e)(ii) of SSI 2013 No 48 as from 18.3.13.
3.   Inserted by reg 11(6)(d) of SSI 2013 No 142 as from 11.6.13.

Disabled child premium

13.   With regard to disabled child premium the condition referred to in paragraph 5 is that a child or young person for whom the applicant or the applicant's partner is responsible and who is a member of the applicant's household–

(a)   is in receipt of disability living allowance or personal independence payment or is no longer in receipt of such allowance because the child or young person is a patient, provided that the child or young person continues to be a member of the family; or

(b)   is blind or treated as blind within the meaning of paragraph 10(1)(a)(v) and (2) (disability premium);

[¹(ba) is a young person who is in receipt of armed forces independence payment;] or

(c)   is a child or young person in respect of whom section 145A of the 1992 Act (entitlement after death of child or qualifying young person) applies for the purposes of entitlement to child benefit but only for the period prescribed under that section, and in respect of whom a disabled child premium was included in the applicant's applicable amount immediately before the death of that child or young person, or ceased to be included in the applicant's applicable amount because of that child or young person's death.

Amendment

1.   Inserted by reg 11(6)(e) of SSI 2013 No 142 as from 11.6.13.

___

Carer premium

14.–(1)   With regard to carer premium the condition referred to in paragraph 5 is that the applicant or the applicant's partner is, or both of them are, entitled to a carer's allowance.

(2)   Where a carer premium is awarded but–

(a)   the person in respect of whose care the carer's allowance has been awarded dies; or

(b)   in any other case the person in respect of whom a carer premium has been awarded ceases to be entitled to a carer's allowance,

the condition for the award of the premium is to be treated as satisfied for a period of 8 weeks from the relevant date specified in sub-paragraph (3).

(3)   The relevant date for the purposes of sub-paragraph (2) is–

(a)   where sub-paragraph (2)(a) applies, the Sunday following the death of the person in respect of whose care a carer's allowance has been awarded or the date of death if the death occurred on a Sunday; and

(b)   in any other case, the date on which the person who has been entitled to a carer's allowance ceases to be entitled to that allowance.

(4)   Where a person who has been entitled to a carer's allowance ceases to be entitled to that allowance and makes an application for council tax reduction, the condition for the award of the carer premium is to be treated as satisfied for a period of eight weeks from the date on which–

(a)   the person in respect of whose care the carer's allowance has been awarded dies; and

(b)   in any other case, the person who has been entitled to a carer's allowance ceased to be entitled to that allowance.

Persons in receipt of concessionary payments

15.   For the purpose of determining whether a premium is applicable to a person under paragraphs 10 to 14, any concessionary payment made to compensate that person for the non-payment of any benefit mentioned in those paragraphs is to be treated as if it were a payment of that benefit.

Persons in receipt of benefit for another

16.   For the purposes of this Part of this Schedule, a person is to be regarded as being in receipt of any benefit only if it is paid in respect of the person and is to be regarded as being in receipt of the benefit only for any period in respect of which that benefit is paid.

PART 4
Amounts of disability premiums

17.   The premiums referred to in regulation 21(d) (applicable amount) and 22(e) (applicable amount: polygamous marriages) and paragraph 5 of this Schedule are set out in the following table.

Premium	Amount
Disability premium–	
(a) where the applicant satisfies the condition in paragraph 9(a);	[⁷£34.35]
(b) where the applicant satisfies the condition in paragraph 9(b).	[⁷£48.95]
Severe disability premium–	
(a) where the applicant satisfies the condition in paragraph 11(2)(a);	[⁷£65.85]
(b) where the applicant satisfies the condition in paragraph 11(2)(b)–	
(i) in a case where there is someone in receipt of a carer's allowance [⁴, or who has an award of universal credit which includes the carer element under regulation 29 of the Universal Credit Regulations 2013,] or if the applicant or the applicant's partner satisfies that condition only by virtue of paragraph 11(5);	[⁷£65.85]
(ii) in a case where there is no-one in receipt of a carer's allowance [⁴ or an award of universal credit which includes the carer element].	[⁷£131.70]
Disabledchild premium.	[⁷£64.19] in respect of each child or young person in respect of whom the condition specified in paragraph 13 is satisfied.

Carer premium.	[7£36.85] in respect of each person who satisfies the condition specified in paragraph 14.
Enhanceddisability premium.	(a) [7£26.04] in respect of each child or young person in respect of whom the conditions specified in paragraph 12 are satisfied; (b) [7£16.80] in respect of each person who is neither– (i) a child or young person; nor (ii) a member of a couple or a polygamous marriage, in respect of whom the conditions specified in paragraph 12 are satisfied; (c) [7£24.10] where the applicant is a member of a couple or a polygamous marriage and the conditions specified in paragraph 12 are satisfied in respect of a member of that couple or polygamous marriage.

Amendments
1. Substituted by reg 14(f) of SSI 2013 No 48 as from 18.3.13.
2. Amended by reg 4(d) of SSI 2014 No 35 as from 1.4.14.
3. Amended by reg 9(c) of SSI 2015 No 46 as from 1.4.15.
4. Inserted by reg 14(b) of SSI 2016 No 81 as from 1.4.16.
5. Amended by reg 10(a) of SSI 2017 No 41 as from 1.4.17.
6. Amended by reg 9(a) of SSI 2018 No 69 as from 1.4.18.
7. Amended by reg 5(a) of SSI 2019 No 29 as from 1.4.19.

PART 5
Components

Components
    18.   Subject to paragraph 20 the applicant is entitled to one, but not both, of the components in paragraph 21 or 22 if–
    (a)   the applicant or the applicant's partner has made a claim for employment and support allowance;
    (b)   the Secretary of State has decided that the applicant or the applicant's partner has, or is to be treated as having, limited capability for work or limited capability for work-related activity; and
    (c)   either–
        (i)   the assessment phase as defined in section 24(2) of the Welfare Reform Act has ended; or
        (ii)   regulation 7 of the Employment and Support Allowance Regulations (circumstances where the condition that the assessment phase has ended before entitlement to the support component or the work related activity component arises does not apply) applies.
    19.   Subject to paragraph 20, the applicant is entitled to one, but not both, of the components in paragraphs 21 and 22 if the applicant or the applicant's partner is entitled to a converted employment and support allowance [1, or would be entitled but for the application of section 1A of the Welfare Reform Act (duration of contributory allowance)].

Amendment
1. Inserted by reg 14(g) of SSI 2013 No 48 as from 18.3.13.

    20.–(1)   The applicant has no entitlement under paragraph 21 or 22 if the applicant is entitled to the disability premium under paragraphs 9 and 10.
    (2)   Where the applicant and the applicant's partner each satisfies paragraph 21 or 22, the component to be included in the applicant's applicable amount is that which relates to the applicant.

Work-related activity component
    21.   The applicant is entitled to the work-related activity component if the Secretary of State has decided that the applicant or the applicant's partner has, or is to be treated as having, limited capability for work.

Support component
    22.   The applicant is entitled to the support component if the Secretary of State has decided that the applicant or the applicant's partner has, or is to be treated as having, limited capability for work-related activity.

Amount of components

23.   The amount of the work-related activity component is [³£29.05].

Amendments

1.   Amended by reg 14(h) of SSI 2013 No 48 as from 18.3.13.
2.   Amended by reg 4(e) of SSI 2014 No 35 as from 1.4.14.
3.   Amended by reg 9(d) of SSI 2015 No 46 as from 1.4.15.

24.   The amount of the support component is [⁶£38.55].

Amendments

1.   Amended by reg 14(i) of SSI 2013 No 48 as from 18.3.13.
2.   Amended by reg 4(f) of SSI 2014 No 35 as from 1.4.14.
3.   Amended by reg 9(e) of SSI 2015 No 46 as from 1.4.15.
4.   Amended by reg 10(b) of SSI 2017 No 41 as from 1.4.17.
5.   Amended by reg 9(b) of SSI 2018 No 69 as from 1.4.18.
6.   Amended by reg 5(b) of SSI 2019 No 29 as from 1.4.19.

PART 6
Transitional addition

25.–(1)   The applicant is entitled to a transitional addition calculated in accordance with paragraph 28 where the applicant or the applicant's partner–
(a)   is entitled to a converted employment and support allowance[¹, or would be entitled but for the application of section 1A of the Welfare Reform Act (duration of contributory allowance)]; or
(b)   is appealing a conversion decision as described in regulation 5(2)(b) of the Employment and Support Allowance (Existing Awards) Regulations and–
    (i)   is treated as having limited capability for work by virtue of regulation 30 of the Employment and Support Allowance Regulations as modified by the Employment and Support Allowance (Existing Awards) Regulations; and
    (ii)   is not in receipt of an income-related employment and support allowance, unless the amount of the transitional addition calculated in accordance with paragraph 28 would be nil.
(2)   The applicant's entitlement to a transitional addition by virtue of this paragraph ends on any of the following–
(a)   the reduction of the transitional addition to nil in accordance with paragraph 29;
(b)   the end of the applicant's entitlement to council tax reduction;
(c)   [²the relevant person] ceasing to meet the requirements of sub-paragraph (1)(a) or (b), as the case may be;
(d)   the applicant or the applicant's partner becoming entitled to an income-related employment and support allowance, an income-based jobseeker's allowance or income support; or
(e)   5th April 2020.

Amendments

1.   Inserted by reg 14(j)(i) of SSI 2013 No 48 as from 18.3.13.
2.   Amended by reg 14(j)(ii) of SSI 2013 No 48 as from 18.3.13.

26.–(1)   This paragraph applies where–
(a)   the applicant's entitlement to a transitional addition ends because of the ending of the applicant's entitlement to council tax reduction under–
    (i)   paragraph 25(2)(b);
    (ii)   paragraph 27(3)(b);
    (iii)   sub-paragraph (3)(b) of this paragraph; or
(b)   within [¹12] weeks of that termination but before 5th April 2020 the applicant again becomes entitled to council tax reduction;
(c)   in the reduction week in which the applicant again becomes entitled to council tax reduction [¹the relevant person] is entitled to an employment and support allowance which is not income-related;
(d)   [²...]; and
(e)   at the date on which the applicant again becomes entitled to council tax reduction neither the applicant nor the applicant's partner is entitled to an income-related employment and support allowance, an income-based jobseeker's allowance or income support.
(2)   Where this paragraph applies, the applicant is entitled, with effect from the day on which the applicant again becomes entitled to council tax reduction, to a transitional addition of the amount of the transitional addition that would have applied had the applicant's entitlement to a transitional addition not ended (but taking account of the effect which any intervening change of circumstances would have had by virtue of paragraph 29), unless the amount of the transitional addition would be nil.

(3)   The applicant's entitlement to a transitional addition by virtue of this paragraph ends on any of the following–
(a)   the reduction of the transitional addition to nil in accordance with paragraph 29;
(b)   the end of the applicant's entitlement to council tax reduction;
(c)   ['the relevant person] no longer being entitled to the employment and support allowance referred to in sub-paragraph (1)(c);
(d)   the applicant or the applicant's partner becoming entitled to an income-related employment and support allowance, an income-based jobseeker's allowance or income support; or
(e)   5th April 2020.

Amendments
1.   Amended by reg 14(k)(i), (ii) and (iv) of SSI 2013 No 48 as from 18.3.13.
2.   Omitted by reg 14(k)(iii) of SSI 2013 No 48 as from 18.3.13.

27.–(1)   This paragraph applies where–
(a)   the applicant's entitlement to a transitional addition ends by virtue of ['the relevant person] ceasing to be entitled to an employment and support allowance under–
(i)   paragraph 25(2)(c);
(ii)   paragraph 26(3)(c); or
(iii)   sub-paragraph (3)(c) of this paragraph;
(b)   before 5th April 2020 ['the relevant person] again becomes entitled to an employment and support allowance which is not income-related;
[²(c)   at the date on which the relevant person again becomes entitled to an employment and support allowance which is not income-related, regulation 145(1) of the Employment and Support Allowance Regulations applies to the relevant person;]
        and
(d)   at the date on which ['the relevant person] again becomes entitled to an employment and support allowance which is not income-related, neither the applicant nor the applicant's partner is entitled to an income-related employment and support allowance, an income-based jobseeker's allowance or income support.
(2)   Where this paragraph applies, the applicant is entitled, with effect from the day that ['the relevant person's] entitlement to employment and support allowance takes effect for council tax reduction purposes, to a transitional addition of the amount of the transitional addition that would have applied had the applicant's entitlement to a transitional addition not ended (but taking account of the effect which any intervening change of circumstances would have had by virtue of paragraph 29), unless the amount of the transitional addition would be nil.
(3)   The applicant's entitlement to a transitional addition by virtue of this paragraph ends on any of the following–
(a)   the reduction of the transitional addition to nil in accordance with paragraph 29;
(b)   the end of the applicant's entitlement to council tax reduction;
(c)   ['the relevant person] no longer being entitled to the employment and support allowance referred to in sub-paragraph (1)(b);
(d)   the applicant or the applicant's partner becoming entitled to an income-related employment and support allowance, an income-based jobseeker's allowance or income support; or
(e)   5th April 2020.

Amendments
1.   Amended by reg 14(l)(i), (iii) and (iv) of SSI 2013 No 48 as from 18.3.13.
2.   Substituted by reg 14(l)(ii) of SSI 2013 No 48 as from 18.3.13.

Amount of transitional addition
28.–(1)   Subject to paragraph 29, the amount of the transitional addition is the amount by which Amount A exceeds Amount B.
(2)   Where a conversion decision as described in regulation 5(2)(a) of the Employment and Support Allowance (Existing Awards) Regulations is made in respect of ['the relevant person]–
(a)   Amount A is the basic amount that would have applied on the day that decision took effect had that decision not been made; and
(b)   Amount B is the basic amount that applied on that day as a result of that decision.
(3)   Where ['the relevant person] is appealing a conversion decision as described in regulation 5(2)(b) of the Employment and Support Allowance (Existing Awards) Regulations (a decision that an existing award does not qualify for conversion into an award of employment and support allowance) and is treated as having limited capability for work by virtue of regulation 30 of the Employment and Support Allowance Regulations as modified by the Employment and Support Allowance (Existing Awards) Regulations–
(a)   Amount A is the basic amount that would have applied on the day ['the relevant person] was first treated as having limited capability for work if [²the relevant person had not been so treated] as having limited capability for work; and

(b)   Amount B is the basic amount that applied on that day as a result of [¹the relevant person] being [²so treated] as having limited capability for work.

(4)   In this paragraph and paragraph 29, "basic amount" means the aggregate of the amounts applying in the applicant's case in accordance with regulation 21(a) to (e) (applicable amount) or regulation 22(a) to (f) (applicable amount: polygamous marriages).

Amendments

1.   Amended by reg 14(m) of SSI 2013 No 48 as from 18.3.13.
2.   Amended by reg 8 of SSI 2013 No 218 as from 1.10.13.

29.–(1)   Subject to sub-paragraph (2), where there is a change of circumstances which leads to an increase in the applicant's basic amount, the transitional addition that applies immediately before the change of circumstances is to be reduced by the amount by which Amount C exceeds Amount D.

(2)   If Amount C exceeds Amount D by more than the amount of the transitional addition that applies immediately before the change of circumstances, that transitional addition is to be reduced to nil.

(3)   Amount C is the basic amount that applies as a result of the increase.

(4)   Amount D is the basic amount that applied immediately before the increase.

[¹**Interpretation of Part 6**
30.   In this Part "relevant person" means the person who meets the requirements of paragraph 25(1)(a) or (b), as the case may be, by virtue of which the applicant is entitled to a transitional addition under that paragraph.]

Amendment

1.   Inserted by reg 14(n) of SSI 2013 No 48 as from 18.3.13.

SCHEDULE 2
Amount of alternative maximum council tax reduction

1.   Subject to paragraphs 2 and 3, the alternative maximum council tax reduction in respect of a day for the purpose of regulation 78 is to be determined in accordance with the following table.

(1) Second adult	(2) Alternative maximum council tax reduction
(a) Where the second adult or all second adults are in receipt of income support, an income-related employment and support allowance or state pension credit or are persons on an income-based jobseeker's allowance [²];	25 per cent of the council tax due in respect of that day;
(b) where the gross income of the second adult or, where there is more than one second adult, their aggregate gross income disregarding any income of persons on income support, an income-related employment and support allowance, state pension credit or an income-based jobseeker's allowance–	
(i) is less than [⁸ £205.00] per week;	15 per cent of the council tax due in respect of that day;
(ii) is not less than [⁸ £205.00] per week but is less than [⁸ £268.00] per week.	7.5 per cent of the council tax due in respect of that day.
(c) where the dwelling would be wholly occupied by one or more persons to whom regulation 20(2) applies but for the presence of one or more second adults who are in receipt of income support, an income-related employment and support allowance or state pension credit or are persons on an income-based jobseeker's allowance.	100 per cent of the council tax due in respect of that day.

Amendments

1.   Substituted by reg 15 of SSI 2013 No 48 as from 18.3.13.
2.   Amended by reg 11 of SSI 2013 No 287 as from 25.11.13.
3.   Amended by reg 5 of SSI 2014 No 35 as from 1.4.14.
4.   Amended by reg 10 of SSI 2015 No 46 as from 1.4.15.
5.   Amended by reg 15 of SSI 2016 No 81 as from 1.4.16.
6.   Amended by reg 11(a) of SSI 2017 No 41 as from 1.4.17.
7.   Amended by reg 10 of SSI 2018 No 69 as from 1.4.18.
8.   Amended by reg 6 of SSI 2019 No 29 as from 1.4.19.

General Note

The amount of the alternative maximum CTR is the relevant percentage (as set out in the table) of gross council tax liability minus the reductions and discounts listed in the definition of "council tax due in respect of that day": para 4. Note that this is not the same figure used for main CTR. See also the commentary to reg 78 on p1529.

Para (a) of the table is self explanatory.

Under para (b) of the table, the combined gross income of all the second adults not on IS, income-based JSA, income-related ESA or PC is used. For the extended definitions of person on an income-based JSA or on an income-related ESA, see reg 2(5) and (6). Paras 2 and 3 provide for some gross income to be disregarded.

Para (c) of the table applies to dwellings which would be occupied wholly by students excluded from entitlement to main CTR but for the presence of one or more second adults receiving IS, income-based JSA, income-related ESA or PC. Such a dwelling would not be exempt from council tax (as dwellings occupied wholly by students are), but the CTR applicant(s) will be entitled to 100 per cent alternative maximum CTR. For these purposes, someone counts as a student excluded from entitlement to main CTR if s/he would be so excluded were s/he (or her/his partner) under the qualifying age for PC: definition of "person to whom regulation 20(2) applies" in para 4. See the General Note to reg 20 on p1485 where the non-student is liable for council tax on a dwelling shared with students.

---

2.   In determining a second adult's gross income for the purposes of this Schedule, there must be disregarded from that income–
(a)   any attendance allowance, disability living allowance [¹, armed forces independence payment] or personal independence payment;
(b)   any payment made under or by the Trusts, the Fund, the Eileen Trust, MFET Limited, the Skipton Fund, the Caxton Foundation, [³ another infected blood payment scheme,] [² ILF Scotland] [⁴, the London Bombings Relief Charitable Fund, the London Emergencies Trust or the We Love Manchester Emergency Fund] which had the second adult's income fallen to be calculated under regulation 39 (calculation of income other than earnings) would have been disregarded under paragraph 27 of Schedule 4 (income in kind); and .
(c)   any payment which had the second adult's income fallen to be calculated under regulation 39 (calculation of earnings other than income) would have been disregarded under paragraph 41 of Schedule 4 (payments made under certain trusts and certain other payments).

Amendments
1.   Inserted by reg 11(7) of SSI 2013 No 142 as from 11.6.13.
2.   Substituted by reg 4(2)(e) of SSI 2016 No 81 as from 1.4.16.
3.   Amended by reg 11(b) of SSI 2017 No 41 as from 1.4.17.
4.   Amended by reg 5 of SSI 2017 No 326 as from 20.11.17.

---

3.   Where there are two or more second adults residing with the applicant and any of those second adults falls to be disregarded for the purposes of discount in accordance with Schedule 1 of the Act, that second adult's income is to be disregarded in determining the amount of any alternative maximum council tax reduction, unless that second adult is a member of a couple and the other partner does not fall to be disregarded for the purposes of discount.

General Note

For Sch 1 Local Government Finance Act 1992, see p1086.

---

4.   In this Schedule–
"council tax due in respect of that day" means the council tax payable under section 78 of the Act less–
(a)   any reductions in liability for council tax under regulations made under section 80 of the Act or under a scheme established under section 80A of the Act, other than a reduction under these Regulations; and
(b)   in a case to which item (c) in column (1) of the table above applies, the amount of any discount which may be appropriate to the dwelling under the Act;
"persons to whom regulation 20(2) applies" includes any person to whom that regulation would apply if that person, and any partner of that person, was below the qualifying age for state pension credit; and
"second adult" means any person or persons residing with the applicant to whom regulation 14(6) (conditions of entitlement to council tax reduction) applies.

SCHEDULE 3
Sums to be disregarded in the calculation of earnings

General Note

This is similar to the Sch 4 HB Regs (see p655).

1. In the case of an applicant who has been engaged in remunerative work as an employed earner or, where the employment has been outside Great Britain, would have been so engaged had the employment been in Great Britain–
- (a) where–
    - (i) the employment has been terminated because of retirement; and
    - (ii) on retirement the applicant is entitled to a retirement pension under the 1992 Act, or is not entitled solely because of the applicant's failure to satisfy the contribution conditions, any earnings paid or due to be paid in respect of that employment, but only for a period commencing on the day immediately after the date on which the employment was terminated;
- [² (aa) where–
    - (i) the employment has been terminated because of retirement; and
    - (ii) on retirement the applicant is entitled to a state pension under Part 1 of the Pensions Act 2014, or is not so entitled solely because the applicant does not have the minimum number of qualifying years,

    any earnings paid or due to be paid in respect of that employment, but only for a period commencing on the day immediately after the date the employment was terminated;]
- (b) where before the first day of entitlement to council tax reduction the employment has been terminated otherwise than because of retirement, any earnings paid or due to be paid in respect of that employment except–
    - (i) any payment of the nature described in–
        - (aa) regulation 34(1)(e) (earnings of employed earners); or
        - (bb) section 28, 64 or 68 of the Employment Rights Act 1996 (guarantee payments, suspension from work on medical or maternity grounds); and
    - (ii) any award, sum or payment of the nature described in–
        - (aa) regulation 34(1)(g) or (i), or
        - (bb) section 34 or 70 of the Employment Rights Act 1996 (guarantee payments and suspension from work: complaints to employment tribunals), including any payment made following the settlement of a complaint to an employment tribunal or court proceedings;
- (c) where before the first day of entitlement to council tax reduction–
    - (i) the employment has not been terminated; but
    - (ii) the applicant is not engaged in remunerative work,

any earnings paid or due to be paid in respect of that employment except any payment or remuneration of the nature described in paragraph 1(b)(i) or (ii)(bb) or regulation 34(1)(i) or (j) any earnings in respect of that employment except earnings to which regulation 34(1)(d), (e), (i) and (j) applies.

2. In the case of an applicant who, before the first day of entitlement to council tax reduction–
- (a) has been engaged in part-time employment as an employed earner or, where the employment has been outside Great Britain, would have been so engaged had the employment been in Great Britain; and
- (b) has ceased to be engaged in that employment, whether or not that employment has been terminated,

any earnings paid or due to be paid in respect of that employment except–
- (i) where that employment has been terminated, any payment of the nature described in paragraph 1(b)(i) or (ii)(bb); or
- (ii) where that employment has not been terminated, any payment or remuneration of the nature described in paragraph 1(b)(i) or (ii)(bb) or regulation 34(1)(j) or (k) (earnings of employed earners).

3. In the case of an applicant who has been engaged in remunerative work or part-time employment as a self-employed earner or, where the employment has been outside Great Britain, would have been so engaged had the employment been in Great Britain and who has ceased to be so employed, from the date of the cessation of the applicant's employment, any earnings derived from that employment except earnings to which regulation 36(3) and (4) (earnings of self-employed earners) apply.

4.–(1) In a case to which this paragraph applies and paragraph 5 does not apply, £20, but notwithstanding regulation 24 (calculation of income and capital of members of an applicant's family and of a polygamous marriage) if this paragraph applies to an applicant it does not apply to the applicant's partner except where, and to the extent that, the earnings of the applicant which are to be disregarded under this paragraph are less than £20.

(2) This paragraph applies where the applicant's applicable amount includes an amount by way of disability premium, severe disability premium, work-related activity component or support component under Schedule 1 (applicable amounts).

(3) This paragraph applies where–
- (a) the applicant is a member of a couple and the applicant's applicable amount includes an amount by way of the disability premium under Schedule 1; and
- (b) the applicant or the applicant's partner has not attained the qualifying age for state pension credit and at least one of them is engaged in employment.

5. In a case where the applicant is a lone parent, £25.

6.–(1) In a case to which neither paragraph 4 nor paragraph 5 applies to the applicant and, subject to sub-paragraph (2), where the applicant's applicable amount includes an amount by way of the carer premium under

Schedule 1 (applicable amounts), £20 of the earnings of the person who is, or at any time in the preceding 8 weeks was, in receipt of carer's allowance or treated in accordance with paragraph 14(2) of that Schedule as being in receipt of carer's allowance.

(2)   Where the carer premium is awarded in respect of the applicant and the applicant's partner, their earnings are for the purposes of this paragraph to be aggregated, but the amount to be disregarded in accordance with sub-paragraph (1) must not exceed £20 of the aggregated amount.

7.   Where the carer premium is awarded in respect of an applicant who is a member of a couple and whose earnings are less than £20, but is not awarded in respect of the other member of the couple, and that other member is engaged in an employment–

(a)   specified in paragraph 9(1), so much of the other member's earnings as would not when aggregated with the amount disregarded under paragraph 6 exceed £20;

(b)   other than one specified in paragraph 9(1), so much of the other member's earnings from such other employment up to £10 as would not when aggregated with the amount disregarded under paragraph 6 exceed £20.

8.   In a case where paragraphs 4, 6, 7 and 9 do not apply to the applicant and the applicant is one of a couple and a member of that couple is in employment, £10; but, notwithstanding regulation 24 (calculation of income and capital of members of applicant's family and of a polygamous marriage), if this paragraph applies to an applicant it does not apply to the applicant's partner except where, and to the extent that, the earnings of the applicant which are to be disregarded under this paragraph are less than £10.

9.–(1)   In a case where paragraphs 4, 5, 6 and 7 do not apply to the applicant, £20 of earnings derived from one or more employments as–

[¹ (a)   a part-time fire-fighter employed by the Scottish Fire and Rescue Service established under section 1A of the Fire (Scotland) Act 2005;]

(b)   a part-time fire-fighter employed by a fire and rescue authority constituted by a scheme under section 2 of the Fire and Rescue Services Act 2004 or a scheme to which section 4 of that Act applies;

(c)   an auxiliary coastguard in respect of coast rescue activities;

(d)   a person engaged part-time in the manning or launching of a life boat;

(e)   a member of any territorial or reserve force prescribed in Part I of Schedule 6 to the Social Security (Contributions) Regulations 2001,

but, notwithstanding regulation 24 (calculation of income and capital of members of applicant's family and of a polygamous marriage), if this paragraph applies to an applicant it does not apply to the applicant's partner except to the extent specified in sub-paragraph (2).

(2)   If the applicant's partner is engaged in employment–

(a)   specified in sub-paragraph (1), so much of the partner's earnings as would not in aggregate with the amount of the applicant's earnings disregarded under this paragraph exceed £20;

(b)   other than an employment specified in sub-paragraph (1), so much of the partner's earnings from that employment up to £10 as would not in aggregate with the applicant's earnings disregarded under this paragraph exceed £20.

Amendments

1.   Substituted by reg 11 of SSI 2015 No 46 as from 1.4.15.
2.   Inserted by art 36(3) of SI 2015 No 1985 as from 6.4.16.

---

10.   Where the applicant is engaged in one or more employments specified in paragraph 9(1), but the applicant's earnings derived from such employments are less than £20 in any week and the applicant is also engaged in any other employment so much of the applicant's earnings from that other employment, up to £5 if the applicant is a single applicant, or up to £10 if the applicant has a partner, as would not in aggregate with the amount of the applicant's earnings disregarded under paragraph 9 exceed £20.

11.   In a case to which none of paragraphs 4 to 10 applies, £5.

12.–(1)   Where–

(a)   the applicant (or if the applicant is a member of a couple, at least one member of that couple) is a person to whom sub-paragraph (5) applies;

(b)   the relevant authority is satisfied that that person is undertaking exempt work; and

(c)   paragraph 14 does not apply,

the amount specified in sub-paragraph (7) ("the specified amount").

(2)   Where this paragraph applies, paragraphs 4 to 11 do not apply, but in any case where the applicant is a lone parent and the specified amount would be less than the amount specified in paragraph 5, paragraph 5 applies instead of this paragraph.

(3)   Notwithstanding regulation 24 (calculation of income and capital of members of applicant's family and of a polygamous marriage), if sub-paragraph (1) applies to one member of a couple ("A") it does not apply to the other member of that couple ("B") except to the extent provided for in sub-paragraph (4).

(4)   Where A's earnings are less than the specified amount, there must also be disregarded so much of B's earnings as would not when aggregated with A's earnings exceed the specified amount, but the amount of B's earnings which may be disregarded under this sub-paragraph is limited to a maximum of £20 unless the relevant authority is satisfied that B is also undertaking exempt work.

(5)   This sub-paragraph applies to a person who is–

(a)   in receipt of a contributory employment and support allowance;

(b)   in receipt of incapacity benefit under Section 30A, 40 or 41 of the 1992 Act;

(c)   in receipt of severe disablement allowance; or

(d)   being credited with earnings on the grounds of incapacity for work or limited capability for work under regulation 8B of the Social Security (Credits) Regulations 1975.

(6)   In this paragraph "exempt work" means work of the kind described in–

(a)   regulation 45(2), (3) or (4) of the Employment and Support Allowance Regulations; or (as the case may be);

(b)   regulation 17(2), (3) or (4) of the Social Security (Incapacity for Work) (General) Regulations 1995, and, in determining for the purposes of this paragraph whether an applicant or a member of a couple is undertaking any type of exempt work, it is immaterial whether that person or their partner is also undertaking other work.

(7)   The specified amount is the amount of money from time to time mentioned in any provision referred to in sub-paragraph (6) by virtue of which the work referred to in sub-paragraph (1) is exempt (or, where more than one of those provisions is relevant and those provisions mention different amounts of money, the highest of those amounts).

13.   Any amount or the balance of any amount which would fall to be disregarded under paragraph 22 or 23 (students: parental contributions) of Schedule 4 had the applicant's income which does not consist of earnings been sufficient to entitle the applicant to the full disregard under those paragraphs.

14.   Where an applicant is on income support, an income-based jobseeker's allowance or an income-related employment and support allowance, the applicant's earnings.

15.   Any earnings derived from employment which are payable in a country outside the United Kingdom for such period during which there is a prohibition against the transfer to the United Kingdom of those earnings.

16.   Where a payment of earnings is made in a currency other than sterling, any banking charge or commission payable in converting that payment into sterling.

17.   Any earnings of a child or young person.

18.–(1)   In a case where the applicant is a person who satisfies at least one of the conditions set out in sub-paragraph (2), and the applicant's net earnings equal or exceed the total of the amounts set out in sub-paragraph (3), the amount of the applicant's earnings to be disregarded under paragraphs 4 to 12 is to be increased by £17.10.

(2)   The conditions are that–

(a)   the applicant, or if the applicant is a member of a couple, either the applicant or the other member of that couple, is a person to whom regulation 20(1)(c) of the Working Tax Credit Regulations applies; or

(b)   the applicant–

    (i)   is, or if the applicant is a member of a couple, at least one member of that couple is, aged at least 25 and is engaged in remunerative work for on average not less than 30 hours per week;

    (ii)   is a member of a couple and–

        (aa)   at least one member of that couple, is engaged in remunerative work for on average not less than 16 hours per week; and

        [¹ (bb)   the applicant's family includes at least one child or young person;]

    (iii)   is a lone parent who is engaged in remunerative work for on average not less than 16 hours per week; or

    (iv)   is, or if the applicant is a member of a couple, at least one member of that couple is, engaged in remunerative work for on average not less than 16 hours per week and–

        (aa)   the applicant's applicable amount includes a disability premium under paragraph 9 of Schedule 1 the work-related activity component under paragraph 21 of that Schedule or the support component under paragraph 22 of that Schedule; and

        (bb)   where the applicant is a member of a couple, at least one member of that couple satisfies the qualifying conditions for the disability premium or either of the components referred to in sub-head (aa) and is engaged in remunerative work for on average not less than 16 hours per week.

(3)   The following are the amounts referred to in sub-paragraph (1)–

(a)   the amount calculated as disregardable from the applicant's earnings under paragraphs 4 to 12;

(b)   the amount of child care charges calculated as deductible under regulation 27(1)(c) (calculation of income on a weekly basis); and

(c)   £17.10.

(4)   The provisions of regulation 6 (remunerative work) apply in determining whether or not a person works for on average not less than 30 hours per week, but as if the reference to 16 hours in paragraph (1) of that regulation was a reference to 30 hours.

Amendment

1.   Substituted by reg 5(4) of SSI 2016 No 81 as from 1.5.16, subject to transitional provision in reg 2 of SSI 2016 No 81.

19.   In this Schedule "part-time employment" means employment in which the person is engaged on average for less than 16 hours a week.

SCHEDULE 4
Sums to be disregarded in the calculation of income other than earnings

General Note

This is similar to Sch 5 HB Regs (see p664).

1. Any payment made to the applicant in respect of any travel or other expenses incurred, or to be incurred, by the applicant in respect of participation in the Mandatory Work Activity Scheme.

2. Any payment made to the applicant in respect of any travel or other expenses incurred, or to be incurred, by the applicant in respect of participation in the Employment, Skills and Enterprise Scheme.

3. Any amount paid by way of tax on income which is to be taken into account under regulation 39 (calculation of income other than earnings).

4. Any payment in respect of any expenses incurred or to be incurred by an applicant who is–

(a) engaged by a charitable or voluntary organisation; or

(b) volunteer,

if the applicant otherwise derives no remuneration or profit from the employment and is not to be treated as possessing any earnings under regulation 41(5) (notional income).

5. Any payment in respect of expenses arising out of the applicant's participation in a service user group.

6. In the case of employment as an employed earner, any payment in respect of expenses wholly, exclusively and necessarily incurred in the performance of the duties of the employment.

7. Where the applicant is on income support, an income-based jobseeker's allowance or an income-related employment and support allowance, the whole of the applicant's income.

8. Where the applicant is a member of a joint-claim couple for the purposes of the Jobseekers Act and the applicant's partner is on an income-based jobseeker's allowance, the whole of the applicant's income.

9. Where the applicant, or a person who was the applicant's partner on 31st March 2003, was entitled on that date to income support or an income-based jobseeker's allowance but ceased to be entitled on or before 5th April 2003 by virtue only of regulation 13 of the Housing Benefit (General) Amendment (No. 3) Regulations 1999 as in force at that date, the whole of the applicant's income.

General Note

This disregard of the whole of the applicant's income is necessary to ensure that those whose entitlement to IS or income-based JSA ceased because help with housing costs within those benefits no longer included charges for support services continue to be passported to full CTR. It only applies if the claimant was entitled to IS or income-based JSA on 31 March 2003 (or someone who was her/his partner on that date was entitled to one of those benefits) and that entitlement ceased on or before 5 April 2003.

10. Any disability living allowance[1, armed forces independence payment] or personal independence payment.

Amendment

1. Inserted by reg 11(8) of SSI 2013 No 142 as from 11.6.13.

11. Any concessionary payment made to compensate for the non-payment of–

(a) any payment specified in paragraph 10 or 13;

(b) income support;

(c) an income-based jobseeker's allowance;

(d) an income-related employment and support allowance.

12. Any mobility supplement under article 20 of the Naval, Military and Air Forces Etc. (Disablement and Death) Service Pensions Order 2006 (including a mobility supplement under any other scheme or order) or under article 25A of the Personal Injuries (Civilians) Scheme 1983 or any payment intended to compensate for the non-payment of such a supplement.

13. Any attendance allowance.

14. Any payment as holder of the Victoria Cross or of the George Cross or any analogous payment.

15.–(1) Any payment–

(a) by way of an education maintenance allowance made pursuant to–

    (i) regulations made under section 49 or 73(f) of the Education (Scotland) Act 1980 (power to assist persons to take advantage of educational facilities);

    (ii) directions made under section 73ZA of the Education (Scotland) Act 1980 and paid under section 12(2)(c) of the Further and Higher Education (Scotland) Act 1992; or

    (iii) regulations made under section 518 of the Education Act 1996 (payment of school expenses: grant of scholarships etc);

(b) corresponding to an education maintenance allowance made pursuant to–

    (i) section 14 or section 181 of the Education Act 2002 (power of Secretary of State and National Assembly for Wales to give financial assistance for purposes related to education or childcare, and allowances in respect of education or training); or

(ii)   regulations made under section 181 of that Act; or
(c)   by way of financial assistance made pursuant to section 14 of the Education Act 2002.
(2)   Any payment, other than a payment to which sub-paragraph (1) applies, made pursuant to–
(a)   regulations made under section 49 of the Education (Scotland) Act 1980;
(b)   directions made under section 73ZA of the Education (Scotland) Act 1980 and paid under section 12(2)(c) of the Further and Higher Education (Scotland) Act 1992; or
(c)   regulations made under section 518 of the Education Act 1996,
in respect of a course of study attended by a child or a young person or a person who is in receipt of an education maintenance allowance or other payment made pursuant to any provision specified in sub-paragraph (1).

16.   Any payment made by way of a repayment under regulation 11(2) of the Education (Teacher Student Loans) (Repayment etc) Regulations 2003.

17.–(1)   Any payment made pursuant to section 2 of the 1973 Act or section 2 of the Enterprise and New Towns (Scotland) Act 1990 except a payment–
(a)   made as a substitute for income support, a jobseeker's allowance, incapacity benefit under section 30A, 40 or 41 of the 1992 Act, severe disablement allowance or an employment and support allowance;
(b)   of an allowance referred to in section 2(3) of the 1973 Act or section 2(5) of the Enterprise and New Towns (Scotland) Act 1990; or
(c)   intended to meet the cost of living expenses which relate to any one or more of the items specified in sub-paragraph (2) whilst an applicant is participating in an education, training or other scheme to enhance the applicant's employment prospects unless the payment is a Career Development Loan paid pursuant to section 2 of the 1973 Act and the period of education or training or the scheme, which is supported by that loan, has been completed.
(2)   The items specified in this sub-paragraph for the purposes of sub-paragraph (1)(c) are food, ordinary clothing or footwear, household fuel or rent of the applicant or, where the applicant is a member of a family, any other member of the applicant's family, or any council tax or water charges for which that applicant or member is liable.

18.–(1)   Subject to sub-paragraph (2), any of the following payments–
(a)   a charitable payment;
(b)   a voluntary payment;
(c)   a payment not falling within head (a) or (b) from a trust whose funds are derived from a payment made in consequence of any personal injury to the applicant;
(d)   a payment under an annuity purchased–
    (i)   pursuant to any agreement or court order to make payments to the applicant; or
    (ii)   from funds derived from a payment made, in consequence of any personal injury to the applicant; or
(e)   a payment not falling within heads (a) to (d) received by virtue of any agreement or court order to make payments to the applicant in consequence of any personal injury to the applicant.
(2)   Sub-paragraph (1) does not apply to a payment which is made or due to be made by–
(a)   a former partner of the applicant, or a former partner of any member of the applicant's family; or
(b)   the parent of a child or young person where that child or young person is a member of the applicant's family.

19.   Any of the following payments–
(a)   a war disablement pension except insofar as that pension is to be disregarded under paragraph 12 (mobility supplement) or 13 (attendance allowance);
(b)   a war widow's pension or war widower's pension;
(c)   a pension payable to a person as a widow, widower or surviving civil partner under any power of Her Majesty otherwise than under an enactment to make provision about pensions for or in respect of persons who have been disabled or have died in consequence of service as members of the armed forces of the Crown;
(d)   a guaranteed income payment and, if the amount of that payment has been abated to less than £10 by a pension or payment falling within article 39(3)(a) or (b) of the Armed Forces and Reserve Forces (Compensation Scheme) Order 2011, so much of that pension or payment as would not, in aggregate with the amount of any guaranteed income payment disregarded, exceed £10;
(e)   a payment made to compensate for the non-payment of a pension or payment mentioned in any of heads (a) to (d);
(f)   a pension paid by the government of a country outside Great Britain which is analogous to any of the pensions or payments mentioned in heads (a) to (d); or
(g)   a pension paid to victims of National Socialist persecution under any special provision made by the law of the Federal Republic of Germany, or any part of it, or of the Republic of Austria.

20.   Subject to paragraph 40, £15 of any–
(a)   widowed mother's allowance paid pursuant to section 37 of the 1992 Act;
(b)   widowed parent's allowance paid pursuant to section 39A of the 1992 Act.

[¹**20A.**   Any payment of bereavement support payment under section 30 of the Pensions Act 2014 (bereavement support payment) except any such payment which is disregarded as capital under paragraph 11(1)(g) or 65 of schedule 5.]

Amendment
1.   Inserted by reg 7(a) of SSI 2017 No 326 as from 20.11.17.

21.–(1)   Any income derived from capital to which the applicant is or is treated under regulation 50 (capital jointly held) as beneficially entitled but, subject to sub-paragraph (2), not income derived from capital disregarded under paragraphs 3, 4, 6, 10, 16 or 30 to 33 of Schedule 5.

(2)   Income derived from capital disregarded under paragraphs 4, 6 or 30 to 33 of Schedule 5 but only to the extent of–

(a)   any mortgage repayments made in respect of the dwelling or premises in the period during which that income accrued; or

(b)   any council tax or water charges which the applicant is liable to pay in respect of the dwelling or premises and which are paid in the period during which that income accrued.

(3)   The definition of "water charges" in regulation 2(1) (interpretation) applies to sub-paragraph (2) with the omission of the words "in so far as such charges are in respect of the dwelling which a person occupies as a home".

22.   Where the applicant makes a parental contribution in respect of a student attending a course at an establishment in the United Kingdom or undergoing education in the United Kingdom, which contribution has been assessed for the purposes of calculating–

(a)   under regulations made under section 49 of the Education (Scotland) Act 1980, that student's bursary, scholarship or other allowance under that section or under regulations made under section 73 of that Act, any payment to that student under that section;

(b)   the student's student loan, an amount equal to the weekly amount of that parental contribution, but only in respect of the period for which that contribution is assessed as being payable; or

(c)   under or pursuant to regulations made under sections 1 or 2 of the Education Act 1962 or section 22 of the Teaching and Higher Education Act 1998, that student's award.

23.–(1)   Where the applicant is the parent of a student aged under 25 in advanced education who either–

(a)   is not in receipt of any award, grant or student loan in respect of that education; or

(b)   is in receipt of–

(i)   a bursary, scholarship or other allowance under section 49(1) of the Education (Scotland) Act 1980 (power of education authorities to assist pupils to take advantage of educational facilities) or a payment under section 73 of that Act; or

(ii)   an award under section 2 of the Education Act 1962 (discretionary awards) or an award bestowed by virtue of the Teaching and Higher Education Act 1998 or regulations made under that Act,

and the applicant makes payments by way of a contribution towards the student's maintenance, other than a parental contribution falling within paragraph 22, an amount specified in sub-paragraph (2) in respect of each week during the student's term.

(2)   For the purposes of sub-paragraph (1), the amount is a sum equal to the lesser of–

(a)   the weekly amount of the payments; or

(b)   the amount by way of a personal allowance for a single applicant aged under 25 less the weekly amount of any award, bursary, scholarship, allowance or payment referred to in sub-paragraph (1)(b).

24.   Any payment made to the applicant by a child or young person or a non-dependant.

25.   Where the applicant occupies a dwelling as the applicant's home and the dwelling is also occupied by a person other than one to whom paragraph 24 or 26 refers and there is a contractual liability to make payments to the applicant in respect of the occupation of the dwelling by that person or a member of that person's family–

(a)   where the aggregate of any payments made in respect of any one week in respect of the occupation of the dwelling by that person or a member of that person's family, or by that person and a member of that person's family, is less than £20, the whole of that amount; or

(b)   where the aggregate of any such payments is £20 or more per week, £20.

26.–(1)   Where the applicant occupies a dwelling as the applicant's home and the applicant provides in that dwelling board and lodging accommodation, an amount in respect of each person for which the accommodation is provided for the whole or any part of a week equal to–

(a)   where the aggregate of any payments made in respect of any one week in respect of the accommodation provided to such a person does not exceed £20, 100 per cent of the aggregate of the payments; and

(b)   where the aggregate of any payments exceeds £20, £20 and 50 per cent of the excess of the aggregate payment over £20.

(2)   In this paragraph "board and lodging accommodation" means accommodation provided to a person or, if the person is a member of a family, to the person or any other member of the person's family, for a charge which is inclusive of the provision of that accommodation and at least some cooked or prepared meals which are cooked or prepared (by a person other than the person to whom the accommodation is provided or a member of the family of the person to whom the accommodation is provided) and are consumed in that accommodation or associated premises.

27.–(1)   Any income in kind, except where regulation 39(11)(b) (calculation of income other than earnings) applies.

(2)   In sub-paragraph (1) "income in kind" does not include a payment to a third party made in respect of the applicant which is used by the third party to provide benefits in kind to the applicant.

28.   Any income which is payable in a country outside the United Kingdom for such period during which there is a prohibition against the transfer to the United Kingdom of that income.

29.–(1)   Any payment made in respect of a person who is a member of the applicant's family–
(a)   in accordance with an adoption allowance scheme made under section 71 of the Adoption and Children (Scotland) Act 2007 (adoption allowances schemes) or pursuant to regulations under section 2(6)(b), 3 or 4 of the Adoption and Children Act 2002;
(b)   which is a payment made by a local authority in pursuance of section 50 of the Children Act 1975 (payments towards maintenance of children) or section 15(1) of, and paragraph 15 of Schedule 1 to, the Children Act 1989 (local authority contribution to a child's maintenance where the child is living with a person as a result of a residence order);
(c)   which is a payment made by an authority, as defined in article 2 of the Children (Northern Ireland) Order 1995, in pursuance of article 15 of, and paragraph 17 of Schedule 1 to, that Order (contribution by an authority to child's maintenance); or
(d)   in accordance with regulations made pursuant to section 14F of the Children Act 1989 (special guardianship support services).

(2)   Any payment, other than a payment to which sub-paragraph (1)(a) applies, made to the applicant pursuant to regulations under section 2(6)(b), 3 or 4 of the Adoption and Children Act 2002.

30.   Any payment made to the applicant by virtue of arrangements made–
(a)   by a local authority under–
    (i)   regulations 33 or 51 of the Looked After Children (Scotland) Regulations 2009 (fostering and kinship care allowances and fostering allowances); [¹]
    (ii)   section 22C(5) and (6)(a) or (b) or section 23(2)(a) of the Children Act 1989 (provision of accommodation and maintenance for a child whom they are looking after) [¹; or
    (iii)   article 4(b)(ii), (d)(ii), (e)(ii), (f)(ii) or (g)(ii) of the Kinship Care Assistance (Scotland) Order 2016]; or
(b)   by a voluntary organisation under section 59(1)(a) of the Children Act 1989 (provision of accommodation by voluntary organisations).

Amendment
1.   Amended by reg 8 of SSI 2016 No 81 as from 1.4.16.

---

31.   Any payment for a person ("the person concerned"), who is not normally a member of the applicant's household but is placed temporarily in the applicant's care, by–
(a)   a health authority;
(b)   a local authority but excluding payments of housing benefit made in respect of the person concerned;
(c)   a voluntary organisation;
(d)   the person concerned pursuant to section 26(3A) of the National Assistance Act 1948;
[² (da)   the person concerned where the payment is for the provision of accommodation to meet that person's needs for care and support arranged pursuant to section 35 or section 36 of the Social Services and Well-being (Wales) Act 2014;]
[¹(e)   the National Health Service Commissioning Board established by section 1H of the National Health Service Act 2006 or a clinical commissioning group established under section 14D of the National Health Service Act 2006;] or
(f)   a Local Health Board established under section 16BA of the National Health Service Act 1977 or established by an order made under section 11 of the National Health Service (Wales) Act 2006.

Amendments
1.   Substituted by reg 16 of SSI 2013 No 48 as from 18.3.13.
2.   Inserted by reg 6(4)(a) of SSI 2016 No 81 as from 6.4.16.

---

32.   Any payment made by a local authority in accordance with section 12 of the Social Work (Scotland) Act 1968, section 22, 29 or 30 of the Children (Scotland) Act 1995 (provision of services for children and their families and advice and assistance to certain children) [¹, section 17,] 23B, 23C or 24A of the Children Act 1989 [¹ or sections 37, 38, 109, 110 or 114 of the Social Services and Well-being (Wales) Act 2014, but excluding any payment under that last-mentioned Act that is a direct payment within the meaning of sections 50 to 53 of that Act].

Amendment
1.   Amended by reg 6(4)(b) of SSI 2016 No 81 as from 6.4.16.

33.–(1)   Subject to sub-paragraph (2), any payment (or part of a payment) made by a local authority in accordance with section 29 of the Children (Scotland) Act 1995 (local authorities' duty to promote welfare of children and powers to grant financial assistance to persons in, or formerly in, their care) [¹, section 23C] of the

Children Act 1989 [¹ or section 110 of the Social Services and Well-being (Wales) Act 2014, in each case where that payment is made] to a person ("A") which A passes on to the applicant.

(2)   Sub-paragraph (1) applies only where A–

(a)   was formerly in the applicant's care;

(b)   is aged 18 or over; and

(c)   continues to live with the applicant.

Amendment

1.   Amended by reg 6(4)(c) of SSI 2016 No 81 as from 6.4.16.

34.–(1)   Subject to sub-paragraph (2), any payment received under an insurance policy taken out to insure against the risk of being unable to maintain repayments–

(a)   on a loan which is secured on the dwelling which the applicant occupies as the applicant's home; or

(b)   under a regulated agreement as defined for the purposes of the Consumer Credit Act 1974 or under a hire-purchase agreement or a conditional sale agreement as defined for then purposes of Part 3 of the Hire-Purchase Act 1964.

(2)   A payment referred to in sub-paragraph (1) is only to be disregarded to the extent that the payment received under that policy does not exceed the amounts, calculated on a weekly basis, which are used to–

(a)   maintain the repayments referred to in sub-paragraph (1)(a) or (b); and

(b)   meet any amount due by way of premiums on–

(i)   that policy; or

(ii)   in a case to which sub-paragraph (1)(a) applies, an insurance policy taken out to insure against loss or damage to any building or part of a building which is occupied by the applicant as the applicant's home and which is required as a condition of the loan referred to in that sub-paragraph.

35.   Any payment of income which by virtue of regulation 45 (income treated as capital) is to be treated as capital.

36.   Any social fund payment made pursuant to Part 8 of the 1992 Act.

37.   A crisis payment made for the purpose of meeting an immediate short term need or a payment made for the purpose of meeting a need for community care–

[¹ (a)   from a welfare fund;]

(b)   by a local authority in exercise of the power in section 1 of the Localism Act 2011 (local authority's general power of competence) and using funds provided by the Secretary of State, and in this sub-paragraph local authority means a local authority within the meaning of section 8 of that Act; or

(c)   by, or on behalf of, the Welsh Ministers in exercise of the power in section 60 of the Government of Wales Act 2006 (promotion etc. of well-being).

Amendment

1.   Substituted by reg 4(5) of SSI 2016 No 81 as from 1.4.16.

---

38.   Any payment under Part 10 of the 1992 Act (Christmas bonus for pensioners).

39.   Where a payment of income is made in a currency other than sterling, any banking charge or commission payable in converting that payment into sterling.

40.   The total of an applicant's income or, if the applicant is a member of a family, the family's income and the income of any person which the applicant is treated as possessing under regulation 24(2) (calculation of income and capital of members of applicant's family and of a polygamous marriage) to be disregarded under regulation 55(2)(b) (calculation of covenant income where a contribution is assessed), regulation 56(1)(d) (calculation of covenant income where no grant income or no contribution is assessed) regulation 59(2) (treatment of student loans), regulation 61(3) (treatment of payments from access funds) and paragraph 20 (widowed mother's allowance and widowed parent's allowance) must in no case exceed £20 per week.

41.–(1)   Any payment made under or by the Trusts, the Fund, the Eileen Trust, MFET Limited, the Skipton Fund, the Caxton Foundation, [² another infected blood payment scheme,] [¹ ILF Scotland] [³, the London Bombings Relief Charitable Fund, the London Emergencies Trust or the We Love Manchester Emergency Fund].

(2)   Any payment by or on behalf of a person who is suffering or who suffered from haemophilia or who is or was a qualifying person, which derives from a payment made under or by any of the Trusts to which sub-paragraph (1) refers and which is made to or for the benefit of–

(a)   that person's partner or former partner from whom the person is not, or where the person has died was not, estranged or divorced or with whom the person has formed a civil partnership that has not been dissolved or, where the person has died, had not been dissolved at the time of the person's death;

(b)   any child who is a member of the person's family or who was a member and who is a member of the applicant's family; or

(c)   any young person who is a member of the person's family or who was a member and who is a member of the applicant's family.

(3)   Any payment by or on behalf of the partner or former partner of a person who is suffering or who suffered from haemophilia or who is or was a qualifying person provided that the partner or former partner and

that person are not, or if either of them has died were not, estranged or divorced or, where the partner or former partner and that person have formed a civil partnership, the civil partnership has not been dissolved or, if either of them has died, had not been dissolved at the time of the death, which derives from a payment made under or by any of the Trusts to which sub-paragraph (1) refers and which is made to or for the benefit of–

(a)   the person who is suffering from haemophilia or who is a qualifying person;

(b)   any child who is a member of the person's family or who was a member and who is a member of the applicant's family; or

(c)   any young person who is a member of the person's family or who was a member and who is a member of the applicant's family.

(4)   Any payment by a person who is suffering from haemophilia or who is a qualifying person, which derives from a payment under or by any of the Trusts to which sub-paragraph (1) refers, where–

(a)   the person has no partner or former partner from whom the person is not estranged or divorced or with whom the person has formed a civil partnership that has not been dissolved, nor any child or young person who is or had been a member of the person's family; and

(b)   the payment is made either–

(i)   to the person's parent or step-parent; or

(ii)   where the person at the date of the payment is a child, a young person or a student who has not completed full-time education and has no parent or step-parent, to the person's guardian, but only for a period from the date of the payment until the end of two years from the person's death.

(5)   Any payment out of the estate of a person who suffered from haemophilia or who was a qualifying person, which derives from a payment under or by any of the Trusts to which sub-paragraph (1) refers, where–

(a)   the person at the date of death (the relevant date) had no partner or former partner from whom the person was not estranged or divorced or with whom the person has formed a civil partnership that has not been dissolved, nor any child or young person who was or had been a member of the person's family; and

(b)   the payment is made either–

(i)   to the person's parent or step-parent; or

(ii)   where the person at the relevant date was a child, a young person or a student who had not completed full-time education and had no parent or step-parent, to the person's guardian, but only for a period of two years from the relevant date.

(6)   In the case of a person to whom or for whose benefit a payment referred to in this paragraph is made, any income which derives from any payment of income or capital made under or deriving from any of the Trusts.

(7)   For the purposes of sub-paragraphs (2) to (6), any reference to the Trusts is to be construed as including a reference to the Fund, the Eileen Trust, MFET Limited, the Skipton Fund, the Caxton Foundation, [² another infected blood payment scheme,] [¹ ILF Scotland] [³, the London Bombings Relief Charitable Fund, the London Emergencies Trust and the We Love Manchester Emergency Fund].

Amendments

1.   Substituted by reg 4(2)(f) of SSI 2016 No 81 as from 1.4.16.

2.   Amended by reg 12 of SSI 2017 No 41 as from 1.4.17.

3.   Amended by regs 4(g) and 6(a) of SSI 2017 No 326 as from 20.11.17.

Analysis

Note that, unlike for HB, there is a definition of "estranged". It is found in reg 2(8).

---

42.   Any housing benefit.

43.   Any payment made by the Secretary of State to compensate for the loss (in whole or in part) of entitlement to housing benefit.

44.   Any payment in consequence of a reduction of council tax under section 13 or 80 of the Act.

45.–(1)   Any payment or repayment made–

(a)   under regulation 3, 5 or 11 of the National Health Service (Travelling Expenses and Remission of Charges) (Scotland) (No. 2) Regulations 2003 (travelling expenses and health service supplies);

(b)   under regulation 5, 6 or 12 of the National Health Service (Travel Expenses and Remission of Charges) Regulations 2003 (travelling expenses and health service supplies); or

(c)   under regulation 5, 6 or 11 of the National Health Service (Travelling Expenses and Remission of Charges) (Wales) Regulations 2007 (travelling expenses and health service supplies).

(2)   Any payment or repayment made by the Scottish Ministers, the Secretary of State for Health or the Welsh Ministers which is analogous to a payment or repayment mentioned in sub-paragraph (1).

46.   Any payment made to such persons entitled to receive benefits as may be determined by or under a scheme made pursuant to section 13 of the Social Security Act 1988 in lieu of vouchers or similar arrangements in connection with the provision of those benefits (including payments made in place of healthy start vouchers, milk tokens or the supply of vitamins).

47.   Any payment made by the Scottish Ministers or the Secretary of State under a scheme established to assist relatives and other persons to visit persons in custody.

48.–(1)   Where an applicant's [¹ family includes at least one child or young person], £15 of any payment of aliment or maintenance, other than child maintenance, whether under a court order or not, which is made or due to be made by the applicant's former partner or the applicant's partner's former partner.

(2)   For the purpose of sub-paragraph (1) where more than one aliment or maintenance payment is to be taken into account in any week, all the payments are to be aggregated and treated as if they were a single payment.

(3)   A payment made by the Secretary of State in lieu of maintenance is, for the purpose of sub-paragraph (1), to be treated as a payment of maintenance made by a person specified in sub-paragraph (1).

Amendment

1.   Substituted by reg 5(5) of SSI 2016 No 81 as from 1.5.16, subject to transitional provision in reg 2 of SSI 2016 No 81.

49.–(1)   Any payment of child aliment or maintenance made by or derived from a liable relative where the child or young person in respect of whom the payment is made is a member of the applicant's family, except where the person making the payment is the applicant or the applicant's partner.

(2)   In paragraph (1)–

"child aliment or maintenance" means any payment towards the maintenance of a child or young person, including any payment made voluntarily and payments made under–

(a)   the Child Support Act 1991;

(b)   the Child Support (Northern Ireland) Order 1991;

(c)   a court order;

(d)   a consent order under the Civil Partnership Act 2004, the Matrimonial and Family Proceedings Act 1984 or the Matrimonial Causes Act 1973;

(e)   a maintenance agreement registered for execution in the Books of Council and Session or the sheriff court books; and

"liable relative" means a person listed in regulation 54 (interpretation) of the Income Support (General) Regulations 1987, other than a person falling within sub-paragraph (d) of that definition.

50.   Any payment (other than a training allowance) made, whether by the Secretary of State or any other person, under the Disabled Persons (Employment) Act 1944 to assist disabled persons to obtain or retain employment despite their disability.

51.   Any guardian's allowance payable under section 77 of the 1992 Act.

52.–(1)   If the applicant is in receipt of any benefit under Part 2, 3 or 5 of the 1992 Act, any increase in the rate of that benefit arising under Part 4 (increases for dependants) or section 106(a) (unemployability supplement) of the 1992 Act, where the dependant in respect of whom the increase is paid is not a member of the applicant's family.

(2)   If the applicant is in receipt of any pension or allowance under Part 2 or 3 of the Naval, Military and Air Forces Etc. (Disablement and Death) Service Pensions Order 2006, any increase in the rate of that pension or allowance under that Order, where the dependant in respect of whom the increase is paid is not a member of the applicant's family.

53.   Any supplementary pension under article 23(2) of the Naval, Military and Air Forces Etc. (Disablement and Death) Service Pensions Order 2006 (pensions to surviving spouses and surviving civil partners) and any analogous payment made by the Secretary of State for Defence to any person who is not a person entitled under that Order.

54.   In the case of a pension awarded at the supplementary rate under article 27(3) of the Personal Injuries (Civilians) Scheme 1983 (pensions to widows, widowers or surviving civil partners), the sum specified in paragraph 1(c) of Schedule 4 to that Scheme.

55.–(1)   Any payment which is–

(a)   made under any of the Dispensing Instruments to a widow, widower or surviving civil partner of a person–

(i)   whose death was attributable to service in a capacity analogous to service as a member of the armed forces of the Crown; and

(ii)   whose service in such capacity terminated before 31st March 1973; and

(b)   equal to the amount specified in article 23(2) of the Naval, Military and Air Forces Etc. (Disablement and Death) Service Pensions Order 2006.

(2)   In this paragraph "the Dispensing Instruments" means the Order in Council of 19th December 1881, the Royal Warrant of 27th October 1884 and the Order by His Majesty of 14th January 1922 (exceptional grants of pay, non-effective pay and allowances).

56.   Except in a case which falls under paragraph 18(1) of Schedule 3, where the applicant is a person who satisfies any of the conditions of paragraph 18(2) of that Schedule, any amount of working tax credit up to £17.10.

57.   Any payment made [¹as a direct payment as defined in section 4(2) of the Social Care (Self-directed Support) (Scotland) Act 2013], [² under sections 12A to 12D] of the National Health Service Act 2006 (direct payments for health care) or under regulations made under section 57 of the Health and Social Care Act 2001 (direct payments) [³ or under sections 50 to 53 of the Social Services and Well-being (Wales) Act 2014 (direct payments)].

Modification

The amendment made to Sch 4 para 57 by SSI 2014 No.90, which replaced "under section 12B of the Social Work (Scotland) Act 1968", does not have effect in respect of any payment made under s12B Social Work (Scotland) Act 1968 after 1.4.14.

Amendments

1. Amended by art 2(3) and Sch Part 3 of SSI 2014 No.90 as from 1.4.14 subject to the saving provision in art 3 of that SSI.
2. Amended by reg 12 of SSI 2015 No 46 as from 1.4.15.
3. Inserted by reg 6(4)(d) of SSI 2016 No 81 as from 6.4.16.

58.–(1) Subject to sub-paragraph (2), in respect of a person who is receiving, or who has received, assistance under the self-employment route, any payment to that person–

(a) to meet expenses wholly and necessarily incurred whilst carrying on the commercial activity; or

(b) which is used or intended to be used to maintain repayments on a loan taken out by that person for the purpose of establishing or carrying on the commercial activity,

in respect of which such assistance is or was received.

(2) Sub-paragraph (1) applies only in respect of payments which are paid to that person from the special account.

59.–(1) Any payment of a sports award except to the extent that it has been made in respect of any one or more of the items specified in sub-paragraph (2).

(2) The items specified for the purposes of sub-paragraph (1) are food, ordinary clothing or footwear, household fuel or rent of the applicant or where the applicant is a member of a family, any other member of the applicant's family, or any council tax or water charges for which that applicant or member is liable.

(3) For the purposes of sub-paragraph (2) "food" does not include vitamins, minerals or other special dietary supplements intended to enhance the performance of the person in the sport in respect of which the award was made.

60. Where the amount of subsistence allowance paid to a person in a reduction week exceeds the amount of income-based jobseeker's allowance that person would have received in that reduction week had it been payable, that excess amount less 50 pence.

61. In the case of an applicant participating in an employment zone programme, any discretionary payment made by an employment zone contractor to the applicant, being a fee, grant, loan or otherwise.

62. Any discretionary housing payment paid pursuant to [² regulation 2(1) of the Discretionary Financial Assistance Regulations 2001 or] [¹ Part 5 of the Social Security (Scotland) Act 2018.]

Amendments

1. Amended by reg 7 of SSI 2019 No 29 as from 1.4.19.
2. Amended by reg 2(a) of SSI 2019 No 133 as from 1.6.19.

63.–(1) Any payment made by a local authority or by the Welsh Ministers, to or on behalf of the applicant or the applicant's partner relating to a service which is provided to develop or sustain the capacity of the applicant or the applicant's partner to live independently in the applicant's accommodation.

(2) For the purposes of sub-paragraph (1) "local authority" includes, in England, a county council.

64. Any payment of child benefit.

[¹**65.** Any carer's allowance supplement made under section 81 of the Social Security (Scotland) Act 2018.]

Amendment

1. Inserted by reg 3 of SSI 2018 No 211 as from 27.10.18.

General Note

Carer's allowance supplement, a Scottish benefit which is paid twice yearly to claimants who live in Scotland and are receiving carer's allowance on the relevant qualifying dates, is not counted as income for CTR.

[¹**66.** Any early years assistance given under section 24, section 32 and schedule 6 of the Social Security (Scotland) Act 2018.]

Amendment

1. Inserted by reg 3 of SSI 2018 No 295 as from 28.11.18.

[¹ **67.** Any funeral expense assistance given under section 24, section 34 and schedule 8 of the Social Security (Scotland) Act 2018.

Amendment

1. Inserted by reg 3 of SSI 2018 No 295 as from 28.11.18.

[¹68.   Any payment made under the Carer's Assistance (Young Carer Grants) (Scotland) Regulations 2019.]

Amendment

1.   Inserted by reg 2(c) of SSI 2019 No 325 as from 26.11.19.

[¹69.   Any payment or interest on a payment made under, or in connection with, the Windrush Compensation Scheme administered by the Home Office.]

Amendment

1.   Inserted by reg 2(c) of SSI 2019 No 325 as from 26.11.19.

SCHEDULE 5
Capital to be disregarded

General Note

This is similar to the HB equivalent. See p684 for the commentary.

1.   Any payment made to the applicant in respect of any travel or other expenses incurred, or to be incurred, by the applicant in respect of the applicant's participation in the Mandatory Work Activity Scheme, but only for a period of 52 weeks, beginning with the date of receipt of the payment.

2.   Any payment made to the applicant in respect of any travel or other expenses incurred, or to be incurred, by the applicant in respect of the applicant's participation in the Employment, Skills and Enterprise Scheme, but only for a period of 52 weeks beginning with the date of receipt of the payment.

3.   The dwelling together with any garage, garden and outbuildings, normally occupied by the applicant as the applicant's home including any premises not so occupied which it is impracticable or unreasonable to sell separately, in particular, any croft land on which the dwelling is situated, but, notwithstanding regulation 24 (calculation of income and capital of members of applicant's family and of a polygamous marriage), only one dwelling is to be disregarded under this paragraph.

4.   Any premises acquired for occupation by the applicant which the applicant intends to occupy as the applicant's home within 26 weeks of the date of acquisition or such longer period as is reasonable in the circumstances to enable the applicant to obtain possession and commence occupation of the premises.

5.   Any sum directly attributable to the proceeds of sale of any premises formerly occupied by the applicant as the applicant's home which is to be used for the purchase of other premises intended for such occupation within 26 weeks of the date of sale or such longer period as is reasonable in the circumstances to enable the applicant to complete the purchase.

6.   Any premises occupied in whole or in part–

(a)   by a partner or relative of a single applicant or any member of the family as that person's home where that person has attained the qualifying age for state pension credit or is incapacitated; or

(b)   by the former partner of the applicant as that person's home, but this provision does not apply where the former partner is a person from whom the applicant is estranged or divorced or with whom the applicant had formed a civil partnership that has been dissolved.

7.   Where an applicant is on income support, an income-based jobseeker's allowance or an income-related employment and support allowance, the whole of the applicant's capital.

8.   Where the applicant is a member of a joint-claim couple for the purposes of the Jobseekers Act 1995 and the applicant's partner is on income-based jobseeker's allowance, the whole of the applicant's capital.

9.   Any future interest in property of any kind, other than land or premises in respect of which the applicant has granted a subsisting lease or tenancy, including sub-leases or sub-tenancies.

10.–(1)   The assets of any business owned in whole or in part by the applicant and for the purposes of which the applicant is engaged as a self-employed earner, or if the applicant has ceased to be engaged as a self-employed earner, for a period that is reasonable in the circumstances to allow for disposal of any asset.

(2)   The assets of any business owned in whole or in part by the applicant where–

(a)   the applicant is not engaged as a self-employed earner in that business by reason of some disease or bodily or mental disablement; but

(b)   the applicant intends to become engaged or, as the case may be, re-engaged as a self-employed earner in that business as soon as the applicant recovers or is able to become engaged or re-engaged in that business,

for a period of 26 weeks from the date on which the application for council tax reduction is made, or is treated as made, or, if it is unreasonable to expect the applicant to become engaged or re-engaged in that business within that period, for a longer period that is reasonable in the circumstances to enable the applicant to become engaged or re-engaged as a self-employed earner in that business.

(3)   In the case of a person who is receiving assistance under the self-employment route, the assets acquired by that person for the purpose of establishing or carrying on the commercial activity in respect of which the assistance is being received.

(4)   In the case of a person who has ceased carrying on the commercial activity in respect of which assistance was received as specified in sub-paragraph (3), the assets relating to that activity for a period which is reasonable in the circumstances to allow for disposal of any such asset.

11.–(1)   Subject to sub-paragraph (2), any arrears of or any concessionary payment made to compensate for arrears due to the non-payment of–

(a)   any payment specified in paragraphs 10, 12 or 13 of Schedule 4;

[⁶ (aa)   a maternity allowance under section 35 of the 1992 Act,]

(b)   an income-related benefit under Part 7 of the 1992 Act;

(c)   an income-based jobseeker's allowance;

(d)   any discretionary housing payment paid pursuant to [⁵ regulation 2(1) of the Discretionary Financial Assistance Regulations 2001 or] [⁴ Part 5 of the Social Security (Scotland) Act 2018,]

(e)   working tax credit and child tax credit; [¹]

(f)   an income-related employment and support allowance, [¹; [²]

(g)   bereavement support payment under section 30 of the Pensions Act 2014] [²; or

(h)   carer's allowance supplement under section 81 of the Social Security (Scotland) Act 2018]

but only for a period of 52 weeks from the date of the receipt of arrears or of the concessionary payment.

(2)   In a case where the total of any arrears and, if appropriate, any concessionary payment referred to in sub-paragraph (1) relating to one of the specified payments, benefits or allowances amounts to £5,000 or more ("the relevant sum") and is–

[³ (a)   paid in order to rectify, or compensate for–

(i)   an official error as defined in regulation 1(3) of the Social Security and Child Support (Decisions and Appeals) Regulations 1999;

[⁴ (ii)   an error on a point of law made by an officer, person or body described in sub-paragraph (a) or (b) of the definition of "official error" in regulation 1(3) of those Regulations,]

(iii)   any error made by a member of staff of the Scottish Administration involved in the administration of social security benefits to which no person outside the Scottish Government or the Department for Work and Pensions materially contributed; and]

(b)   received by the applicant in full on or after 14th October 2001,

sub-paragraph (1) has effect in relation to the arrears or concessionary payment either for a period of 52 weeks from the date of receipt, or, if the relevant sum is received in its entirety during the period of entitlement to council tax reduction, for the remainder of that period if it is a longer period.

(3)   For the purposes of sub-paragraph (2), "the period of entitlement to council tax reduction" means–

(a)   the period of entitlement to council tax reduction in which the relevant sum is first received (or the first part of the relevant sum where it is paid in more than one instalment); and

(b)   where that period of entitlement is followed by one or more periods of entitlement which, or each of which, begins immediately after the end of the previous period, such further period provided that for that further period the applicant–

(i)   is the person who received the relevant sum; or

(ii)   is the partner of the person who received the relevant sum, or was that person's partner at the date of the partner's death[³]

Amendments

1.   Amended by reg 8(a) of SSI 2017 No 326 as from 20.11.17.
2.   Amended by reg 4 of SSI 2018 No 211 as from 27.10.18.
3.   Amended by reg 4 of SSI 2018 No 295 as from 28.11.18.
4.   Amended by reg 7(a) and (b) of SSI 2019 No 29 as from 1.4.19.
5.   Amended by reg 2(b) of SSI 2019 No 133 as from 1.6.19.
6.   Inserted by reg 2(d)(i) of SSI 2019 No 325 as from 26.11.19.

[¹**11A.**–(1)   The total amount of any payments disregarded under paragraph 18 of Schedule 10 to the Universal Credit Regulations 2013, where the award in respect of which the payments last fell to be disregarded under those Regulations is in existence on the date on which the application for a council tax reduction is made or terminated immediately before that date.

(2)   Any disregard which applies under sub-paragraph (1) has effect until expiry of the period of entitlement to council tax reduction, which period is to be determined in accordance with paragraph 11(3).]

Amendment

1.   Inserted by reg 13 of SSI 2015 No 46 as from 1.4.15.

12.   Any sum–

(a)   paid to the applicant in consequence of damage to, or loss of the home or any personal possession and intended for its repair or replacement; or

(b)   acquired by the applicant (whether as a loan or otherwise) on the express condition that it is to be used for effecting essential repairs or improvement to the home,

which is to be used for the intended purpose, for a period of 26 weeks from the date on which it was so paid or acquired or such longer period as is reasonable in the circumstances to effect the repairs, replacement or improvement.

13. Any sum–

(a) deposited with a housing association as defined in section 1(1) of the Housing Associations Act 1985 or section 338(1) of the Housing (Scotland) Act 1987 as a condition of occupying the home; and

(b) which was so deposited and which is to be used for the purchase of another home,

for the period of 26 weeks or such longer period as may be reasonable in the circumstances to enable the applicant to complete the purchase.

14. Any personal possessions except those acquired by the applicant with the intention of reducing the applicant's capital in order to secure entitlement to council tax reduction or to increase the amount of that reduction.

15. The value of the right to receive any income under an annuity or the surrender value (if any) of such an annuity.

16. Where the funds of a trust are derived from a payment made in consequence of any personal injury to the applicant or applicant's partner, the value of the trust fund and the value of the right to receive any payment under that trust.

17.–(1) Any payment made to the applicant or the applicant's partner in consequence of any personal injury to the applicant or, as the case may be, the applicant's partner.

(2) But sub-paragraph (1)–

(a) applies only for the period of 52 weeks beginning with the day on which the applicant or as the case may be the applicant's partner first receives any payment in consequence of that personal injury;

(b) does not apply to any subsequent payment made to the applicant or as the case may be the applicant's partner in consequence of that injury (whether it is made by the same person or another);

(c) ceases to apply to the payment or any part of the payment from the day on which the applicant or as the case may be the applicant's partner no longer possesses it; and

(d) does not apply to any payment from a trust where the funds of the trust are derived from a payment made in consequence of any personal injury to the applicant or as the case may be the applicant's partner.

(3) For the purposes of sub-paragraph (2)(c), the circumstances in which an applicant or an applicant's partner no longer possesses a payment or a part of it include where the applicant or as the case may be the applicant's partner has used a payment or part of it to purchase an asset.

18. The value of the right to receive any income under a life interest or from a life rent.

19. The value of the right to receive any income which is disregarded under paragraph 15 of Schedule 3 or paragraph 28 of Schedule 4.

20. The surrender value of any instrument by which the payment of money is assured on death (except death by accident only) or the happening of any contingency dependent on human life, or any instrument evidencing a contract which is subject to payment of premiums for a term dependent on human life.

21. Where any payment of capital falls to be made by instalments, the value of the right to receive any outstanding instalments.

22. Any payment made by a local authority in accordance with section 12 of the Social Work (Scotland) Act 1968 (general social welfare services of local authorities), sections 22, 29 or 30 of the Children (Scotland) Act 1995 (provision of services for children and their families and advice and assistance) [¹, sections 17], 23B, 23C or 24A of the Children Act 1989 (provision of services for children and their families and advice and assistance) [¹ or sections 37, 38, 109, 110 or 114 of the Social Services and Well-being (Wales) Act 2014, but excluding any payment under that last-mentioned Act that is a direct payment within the meaning of sections 50 to 53 of that Act].

Amendment

1. Amended by reg 6(5)(a) of SSI 2016 No 81 as from 6.4.16.

23.–(1) Subject to sub-paragraph (2), any payment (or part of a payment) made by a local authority in accordance with section 29 of the Children (Scotland) Act 1995 (local authorities' duty to promote welfare of children and powers to grant financial assistance to persons in, or formerly in, their care) [¹, section 23C] of the Children Act 1989 [¹ or section 110 of the Social Services and Well-being (Wales) Act 2014, in each case where that payment is made] to a person ("A") which A passes on to the applicant.

(2) Sub-paragraph (1) applies only where A–

(a) was formerly in the applicant's care;

(b) is aged 18 or over; and

(c) continues to live with the applicant.

Amendment

1. Amended by reg 6(5)(b) of SSI 2016 No 81 as from 6.4.16.

---

24. Any social fund payment made pursuant to Part 8 of the 1992 Act.

25. Any crisis payment made for the purpose of meeting an immediate short term need or a payment made for the purpose of meeting a need for community care–

[¹ (a) from a welfare fund;]

(b)   by a local authority in exercise of the power in section 1 of the Localism Act 2011 (local authority's general power of competence) and using funds provided by the Secretary of State, and in this sub-paragraph local authority means a local authority within the meaning of section 8 of that Act; or

(c)   by, or on behalf of, the Welsh Ministers in exercise of the power in section 60 of the Government of Wales Act 2006 (promotion etc. of well-being).

Amendment

1.   Substituted by reg 4(6) of SSI 2016 No 81 as from 1.4.16.

---

26.   Any refund of tax which falls to be deducted under section 369 of the Income and Corporation Taxes Act 1988 (deduction of tax from certain loan interest) on a payment of relevant loan interest for the purpose of acquiring an interest in the home or carrying out repairs or improvements to the home.

27.   Any capital which by virtue of regulation 40 (capital treated as income) or 59 (treatment of student loans) is to be treated as income.

28.   Where any payment of capital is made in a currency other than sterling, any banking charge or commission payable in converting that payment into sterling.

29.–(1)   Any payment made under or by any of the Trusts, the Fund, the Eileen Trust, MFET Limited, the Skipton Fund, the Caxton Foundation, [¹ ILF Scotland] [², the London Bombings Relief Charitable Fund, the London Emergencies Trust or the We Love Manchester Emergency Fund].

(2)   Any payment by or on behalf of a person who is suffering or who suffered from haemophilia or who is or was a qualifying person, which derives from a payment made under or by any of the Trusts to which sub-paragraph (1) refers and which is made to or for the benefit of–

(a)   the person's partner or former partner from whom the person is not, or where the person has died was not, estranged or divorced or with whom the person has formed a civil partnership that has not been dissolved or, where the person has died, had not been dissolved at the time of the person's death;

(b)   any child who is a member of the person's family or who was such a member and who is a member of the applicant's family; or

(c)   any young person who is a member of the person's family or who was such a member and who is a member of the applicant's family.

(3)   Any payment by or on behalf of the partner or former partner of a person who is suffering or who suffered from haemophilia or who is or was a qualifying person provided that the partner or former partner and the person are not, or if either of them has died were not, estranged or divorced or, where the partner or former partner and the person have formed a civil partnership, the civil partnership has not been dissolved or, if either of them has died, had not been dissolved at the time of the death, which derives from a payment made under or by any of the Trusts to which sub-paragraph (1) refers and which is made to or for the benefit of–

(a)   the person who is suffering from haemophilia or who is a qualifying person;

(b)   any child who is a member of the person's family or who was such a member and who is a member of the applicant's family; or

(c)   any young person who is a member of the person's family or who was such a member and who is a member of the applicant's family.

(4)   Any payment by a person who is suffering from haemophilia or who is a qualifying person, which derives from a payment under or by any of the Trusts to which sub-paragraph (1) refers, where–

(a)   the person has no partner or former partner from whom the person is not estranged or divorced or with whom the person has formed a civil partnership that has not been dissolved, nor any child or young person who is or had been a member of the person's family; and

(b)   the payment is made either–

     (i)   to the person's parent or step-parent; or

     (ii)   where the person at the date of the payment is a child, a young person or a student who has not completed full-time education and has no parent or step-parent, to the person's guardian,

but only for a period from the date of the payment until the end of two years from the person's death.

(5)   Any payment out of the estate of a person who suffered from haemophilia or who was a qualifying person, which derives from a payment under or by any of the Trusts to which sub-paragraph (1) refers, where–

(a)   that person at the date of death had no partner or former partner from whom the person was not estranged or divorced or with whom the person had formed a civil partnership that had not been dissolved, nor any child or young person who was or had been a member of the person's family; and

(b)   the payment is made either–

     (i)   to that person's parent or step-parent; or

     (ii)   where that person at the relevant date was a child, a young person or a student who had not completed full-time education and had no parent or step-parent, to the person's guardian,

but only for a period of two years from the person's death.

(6)   In the case of a person to whom or for whose benefit a payment referred to in this paragraph is made, any capital resource which derives from any payment of income or capital made under or deriving from any of the Trusts.

(7)   For the purposes of sub-paragraphs (2) to (6), any reference to the Trusts is to be construed as including a reference to the Fund, the Eileen Trust, MFET Limited, the Skipton Fund, the Caxton Foundation,

[¹ ILF Scotland] [² , the London Bombings Relief Charitable Fund, the London Emergencies Trust and the We Love Manchester Emergency Fund].

Amendments
1. Substituted by reg 4(2)(g) of SSI 2016 No 81 as from 1.4.16.
2. Amended by regs 4(h) and 6(b) of SSI 2017 No 326 as from 20.11.17.

30.–(1) Where an applicant has ceased to occupy what was formerly the dwelling occupied as the applicant's home following estrangement or divorce from the applicant's former partner or dissolution of a civil partnership with the applicant's former partner, that dwelling for a period of 26 weeks from the date on which the applicant ceased to occupy it or, where the dwelling is occupied as a home by the former partner who is a lone parent, for so long as it is so occupied.

(2) In this paragraph "dwelling" includes any garage, garden and outbuildings pertaining to the home formerly occupied by the applicant and any premises not so occupied which it is impracticable or unreasonable to sell separately, in particular, any croft land on which the dwelling is situated.

Analysis
Note that unlike for HB, there is a definition of "estranged". It is found in reg 2(8).

---

31. Any premises where the applicant is taking reasonable steps to dispose of the whole of the applicant's interest in those premises, for a period of 26 weeks from the date on which the applicant first took those steps, or any longer period as is reasonable in the circumstances to enable the applicant to dispose of the premises.

32. Any premises which the applicant intends to occupy as the applicant's home, and in respect of which the applicant is taking steps to obtain possession and has sought legal advice, or has commenced legal proceedings, with a view to obtaining possession, for a period of 26 weeks from the earlier of the date on which the applicant first sought that advice or the date on which the applicant first commenced those proceedings, or any longer period as is reasonable in the circumstances to enable the applicant to obtain possession and commence occupation of those premises.

33. Any premises which the applicant intends to occupy as the applicant's home to which essential repairs or alterations are required in order to render them fit for occupation, for a period of 26 weeks from the date on which the applicant first takes steps to effect those repairs or alterations, or any longer period as is necessary to enable those repairs or alterations to be carried out.

34. Any payment made by the Secretary of State to compensate for the loss (in whole or in part) of entitlement to housing benefit.

35. The value of the right to receive an occupational or personal pension.

36. The value of any funds held under a personal pension scheme.

37. The value of the right to receive any rent except where the applicant has a reversionary interest in the property in respect of which rent is due.

38. Any payment in kind made by a charity or under or by the Trusts, the Fund, MFET Limited, the Skipton Fund, the Caxton Foundation, [² another infected blood payment scheme,] [¹ ILF Scotland] [, the London Bombings Relief Charitable Fund, the London Emergencies Trust or the We Love Manchester Emergency Fund].

Amendments
1. Substituted by reg 4(2)(g) of SSI 2016 No 81 as from 1.4.16.
2. Amended by reg 13 of SSI 2017 No 41 as from 1.4.17.
3. Amended by reg 4(h) of SSI 2017 No 326 as from 20.11.17.

---

39. Any payment made pursuant to section 2 of the Enterprise and New Towns (Scotland) Act 1990 or section 2 of the 1973 Act, but only for the period of 52 weeks beginning on the date of receipt of the payment.

40. Any payment in consequence of a reduction of council tax under section 13 or 80 of the Act (reduction of liability for council tax), but only for a period of 52 weeks from the date of the receipt of the payment.

41. Any grant made in accordance with a scheme made under section 129 of the Housing Act 1988 or section 66 of the Housing (Scotland) Act 1988 (schemes for payments to assist local housing authority and local authority tenants to obtain other accommodation) which is to be used–

(a) to purchase premises intended for occupation as the applicant's home; or

(b) to carry out repairs or alterations which are required to render premises fit for occupation as the applicant's home,

for a period of 26 weeks from the date on which the applicant received the grant or any longer period as is reasonable in the circumstances to enable the purchase, repairs or alterations to be completed and the applicant to commence occupation of the premises as a home.

42. Any arrears of supplementary pension which is disregarded under paragraph 53 (supplementary armed forces pension) of Schedule 4 (sums to be disregarded in the calculation of income other than earnings) or of any amount which is disregarded under paragraph 54 (pensions under the Personal Injuries (Civilians)

Scheme 1983) or 55 (older armed forces pensions) of that Schedule, but only for a period of 52 weeks from the date of receipt of the arrears.

43.–(1) Any payment or repayment made–
(a) under regulation 3, 5 or 11 of the National Health Service (Travelling Expenses and Remission of Charges) (Scotland) (No. 2) Regulations 2003 (travelling expenses and health service supplies);
(b) under regulation 5, 6 or 12 of the National Health Service (Travel Expenses and Remission of Charges) Regulations 2003 (travelling expenses and health service supplies); and
(c) under regulation 5, 6 or 11 of the National Health Service (Travelling Expenses and Remission of Charges) (Wales) Regulations 2007 (travelling expenses and health service supplies),
but only for a period of 52 weeks from the date of receipt of the payment or repayment.

(2) Any payment or repayment made by the Scottish Ministers, the Secretary of State for Health or the Welsh Ministers which is analogous to a payment or repayment mentioned in sub-paragraph (1), but only for a period of 52 weeks from the date of receipt of the payment or repayment.

44. Any payment made to those persons entitled to receive benefits as determined by or under a scheme made pursuant to section 13 of the Social Security Act 1988 in lieu of vouchers or similar arrangements in connection with the provision of those benefits (including payments made in place of healthy start vouchers, milk tokens or the supply of vitamins), but only for a period of 52 weeks from the date of receipt of the payment.

45. Any payment made under Part 8A of the 1992 Act (entitlement to health in pregnancy grant).

46. Any payment made by the Scottish Ministers or the Secretary of State under a scheme established to assist relatives and other persons to visit persons in custody, but only for a period of 52 weeks from the date of the receipt of the payment.

47. Any payment (other than a training allowance) made, whether by the Secretary of State or any other person, under the Disabled Persons (Employment) Act 1944 to assist disabled persons to obtain or retain employment despite their disability.

48. Any payment made by a local authority under section 3 of the Disabled Persons (Employment) Act 1958 to homeworkers assisted under the Blind Homeworkers' Scheme.

49.–(1) Subject to sub-paragraph (2), where an applicant satisfies the conditions in regulation 14(3) and (6) (conditions of entitlement to council tax reduction), the whole of the applicant's capital.

(2) Where in addition to satisfying the conditions in regulation 14(3) and (6) the applicant also satisfies the conditions in regulation 14(4) and (5) (entitlement to the maximum council tax reduction), sub-paragraph (1) does not have effect.

50. Any sum of capital administered on behalf of a person in accordance with an order made under section 13 of the Children (Scotland) Act 1995, or under Rule 36.14 of the Ordinary Cause Rules 1993 in Schedule 1 to the Sheriff Courts (Scotland) Act 1907 or under Rule 128 of those Rules, where such sum derives from–
(a) an award of damages for a personal injury to that person; or
(b) compensation for the deathof one or both parents where the person concerned is under the age of 18.

51.–(1) Any sum of capital to which sub-paragraph (2) applies and–
(a) which is administered on behalf of a person by the High Court or the County Court under Rule 21.11(1) of the Civil Procedure Rules 1998 or by the Court of Protection;
(b) which can only be disposed of by order or direction of one of those courts; or
(c) where the person concerned is under the age of 18, which can only be disposed of by order or direction prior to that person attaining the age of 18.
(2) This sub-paragraph applies to a sum of capital which is derived from–
(a) an award of damages for a personal injury to that person; or
(b) compensation for the death of one or both parents where the person is under the age of 18.

52. Any payment to the applicant as holder of the Victoria Cross or George Cross.

53. In the case of a person who is receiving, or who has received, assistance under the self-employment route, any sum of capital which is acquired by the person for the purpose of establishing or carrying on the commercial activity in respect of which the assistance is or was received, but only for a period of 52 weeks from the date on which the sum was acquired.

54.–(1) Any payment of a sports award for a period of 26 weeks from the date of receipt of that payment except to the extent that it has been made in respect of any of the items specified in sub-paragraph (2).

(2) The items specified for the purposes of sub-paragraph (1) are food, ordinary clothing or footwear, household fuel or rent of the applicant or, where the applicant is a member of a family, any other member of the applicant's family, or any council tax or water charges for which the applicant or member of the applicant's family is liable.

(3) For the purposes of sub-paragraph (2) "food" does not include vitamins, minerals or other special dietary supplements intended to enhance the performance of the person in the sport in respect of which the award was made.

55.–(1) Any payment–
(a) by way of an education maintenance allowance made pursuant to–
(i) regulations made under section 49 or 73(f) of the Education (Scotland) Act 1980;
(ii) directions made under section 73ZA of the Education (Scotland) Act 1980 and paid under section 12(2)(c) of the Further and Higher Education (Scotland) Act 1992; or

       (iii)   regulations made under section 518 of the Education Act 1996; or

(b)   corresponding to an education maintenance allowance made pursuant to–
       (i)   section 14 or section 181 of the Education Act 2002 (power of Secretary of State and National Assembly for Wales to give financial assistance for purposes related to education or childcare, and allowances in respect of education or training); or
       (ii)   regulations made under section 181 of that Act.

(2)   Any payment, other than a payment to which sub-paragraph (1) applies, made pursuant to–

(a)   regulations made under section 49 of the Education (Scotland) Act 1980;

(b)   directions made under section 73ZA of the Education (Scotland) Act 1980 and paid under section 12(2)(c) of the Further and Higher Education (Scotland) Act 1992; or

(c)   regulations made under section 518 of the Education Act 1996,

in respect of a course of study attended by a child or a young person or a person who is in receipt of an education maintenance allowance made pursuant to any provision specified in sub-paragraph (1).

56.   In the case of an applicant participating in an employment zone programme, any discretionary payment made by an employment zone contractor to the applicant, being a fee, grant, loan or otherwise, but only for the period of 52 weeks from the date of receipt of the payment.

57.   Any arrears of subsistence allowance paid as a lump sum but only for the period of 52 weeks from the date of receipt of the payment.

58.   Where an ex-gratia payment of £10,000 has been made by the Secretary of State on or after 1st February 2001 in consequence of the imprisonment or interment of–

(a)   the applicant;

(b)   the applicant's partner;

(c)   the applicant's deceased spouse or deceased civil partner; or

(d)   the applicant's partner's deceased spouse or deceased civil partner,

by the Japanese during the Second World War, £10,000.

59.–(1)   Subject to sub-paragraph (2), the amount of any trust payment made to an applicant or a member of an applicant's family who is–

(a)   a diagnosed person;

(b)   the diagnosed person's partner or the person who was the diagnosed person's partner at the date of the diagnosed person's death;

(c)   a parent of a diagnosed person, a person acting in place of the diagnosed person's parents or a person who was acting in place of the diagnosed person's parents at the date of the diagnosed person's death; or

(d)   a member of the diagnosed person's family (other than the diagnosed person's partner) or a person who was a member of the diagnosed person's family (other than the diagnosed person's partner) at the date of the diagnosed person's death.

(2)   Where a trust payment is made to–

(a)   a person referred to in sub-paragraph (1)(a) or (b), that sub-paragraph applies for the period beginning on the date on which the trust payment is made and ending on the date on which that person dies;

(b)   a person referred to in sub-paragraph(1)(c), that sub-paragraph applies for the period beginning on the date on which the trust payment is made and ending two years after that date;

(c)   a person referred to in sub-paragraph (1)(d), that sub-paragraph applies for the period beginning on the date on which the trust payment is made and ending on the latest of–
       (i)   two years after that date; or
       (ii)   on the day before the day the person ceases receiving full-time education; or
       (iii)   on the day before the day the person attains the age of 20.

(3)   Subject to sub-paragraph (4), the amount of any payment by a person to whom a trust payment has been made or of any payment out of the estate of a person to whom a trust payment has been made, which is made to an applicant or a member of an applicant's family who is–

(a)   a diagnosed person's partner or the person who was the diagnosed person's partner at the date of the diagnosed person's death;

(b)   a parent of a diagnosed person, a person acting in place of the diagnosed person's parents or a person who was acting in place of the diagnosed person's parents at the date of the diagnosed person's death; or

(c)   a member of a diagnosed person's family (other than the diagnosed person's partner) or a person who was a member of the diagnosed person's family (other than the diagnosed person's partner) at the date of the diagnosed person's death,

but only to the extent that the payments do not exceed the total amount of any trust payments made to that person.

(4)   Where a payment referred to in sub-paragraph (3) is made to–

(a)   a person referred to in sub-paragraph (3)(a), that sub-paragraph applies for the period beginning on the date on which the payment is made and ending on the date on which that person dies;

(b)   a person referred to in sub-paragraph (3)(b), that sub-paragraph applies for the period beginning on the date on which the payment is made and ending two years after that date; or

(c)   person referred to in sub-paragraph (3)(c), that sub-paragraph applies for the period beginning on the date on which that payment is made and ending on the latest of–

(i)   two years after that date;

(ii)   on the day before the day on which the person ceases receiving full-time education; or

(iii)   on the day before the day the person attains the age of 20.

(5)   In this paragraph, a reference to a person–

(a)   being the diagnosed person's partner;

(b)   being a member of a diagnosed person's family; or

(c)   acting in place of the diagnosed person's parents,

at the date of the diagnosed person's death includes a person who would have been such a person or a person who would have been so acting, but for the diagnosed person residing in a care home, an Abbeyfield Home or an independent hospital on that date.

(6)   In this paragraph–

"diagnosed person" means a person who has been diagnosed as suffering from, or who after death has been diagnosed as having suffered from, variant Creutzfeld-Jakob disease; and

"trust payment" means a payment under a trust established out of funds provided by the Secretary of State in respect of persons who suffered from, or who are suffering from, variant Creutzfeld-Jakob disease for the benefit of persons eligible for payments in accordance with its provisions.

60.   The amount of any payment, other than a war disablement pension, a war widow's pension or a war widower's pension to compensate for the fact that the applicant, the applicant's partner, the applicant's deceased spouse or deceased civil partner or the applicant's partner's deceased spouse or deceased civil partner–

(a)   was a slave labourer or a forced labourer;

(b)   suffered property loss or suffered personal injury; or

(c)   was a parent of a child who had died,

during the Second World War.

61.–(1)   Any payment made by a local authority, or by the Welsh Ministers, to or on behalf of the applicant or the applicant's partner relating to a service which is provided to develop or sustain the capacity of the applicant or the applicant's partner to live independently in their accommodation.

(2)   For the purposes of sub-paragraph (1) "local authority" includes in England a county council.

62.   Any payment made under regulations made under [1] section 57 of the Health and Social Care Act 2001 or sections 12A to 12D of the National Health Service Act 2006 (direct payments for health care) [2or as a direct payment as defined in section 4(2) of the Social Care (Self-directed Support) (Scotland) Act 2013].

Modification

The amendment made to Sch 5 para 62 by SSI 2014 No.90, which omitted "section 12B of the Social Work (Scotland) Act 1968," and inserted the reference to the Social Care (Self-directed Support) (Scotland) Act 2013, does not have effect in respect of any payment made under s12B Social Work (Scotland) Act 1968 after 1.4.14.

Amendments

1.   Omitted by art 2(3) and Sch Part 3 of SSI 2014 No 90 as from 1.4.14 subject to the saving provision in art 3 of that SSI.

2.   Inserted by art 2(3) and Sch Part 3 of SSI 2014 No 90 as from 1.4.14 subject to the saving provision in art 3 of that SSI.

3.   Inserted by reg 6(5)(c) of SSI 2016 No 81 as from 6.4.16.

63.   Any payment made to the applicant under regulations under section 2(6)(b), 3 or 4 of the Adoption and Children Act 2002.

64.   Any payment made to the applicant under regulations made under section 14F of the Children Act 1989 (special guardianship support services).

[1**65.**   Any bereavement support payment in respect of the rate set out in regulation 3(2) or (5) of the Bereavement Support Payment Regulations 2017 (rate of bereavement support payment), but only for a period of 52 weeks from the date of receipt of the payment.]

Amendment

1.   Inserted by reg 8(b) of SSI 2017 No 326 as from 20.11.17.

[1**66.**   Any payment made under or by the Thalidomide Trust.]

Amendment

1.   Inserted by reg 6 of SSI 2018 No 69 as from 1.4.18.

[1**67.**   Any early years assistance given in accordance with section 24, section 32 and schedule 6 of the Social Security (Scotland) Act 2018.]

Amendment

1.   Inserted by reg 8(c) of SSI 2019 No 29 as from 1.4.19.

[1**68.**   Funeral expense assistance given in accordance with section 24, section 34 and schedule 8 of the Social Security (Scotland) Act 2018.]

Amendment

1.   Inserted by reg 8(c) of SSI 2019 No 29 as from 1.4.19.

[¹69.   Any payment made under the Carer's Assistance (Young Carer Grants) (Scotland) Regulations 2019.]

Amendment

1.   Inserted by reg 2(d)(ii) of SSI 2019 No 325 as from 26.11.19.

[¹70.   Any payment or interest on a payment made under, or in connection with, the Windrush Compensation Scheme administered by the Home Office.]

Amendment

1.   Inserted by reg 2(d)(ii) of SSI 2019 No 325 as from 26.11.19.

SCHEDULE 6
Savings provisions

1.–(1)   Where, on 12th April 1995, a person was entitled to disability premium by virtue of paragraph 13(1)(b) of Schedule 1 to the 1992 Regulations the person is to be treated as entitled to disability premium by virtue of paragraph 10(1)(b) of Schedule 1 to these Regulations for so long as the person is incapable of work in accordance with the provisions of, and regulations made under, Part 12A of the 1992 Act (incapacity for work).

(2)   Where, on 12th April 1995, a person was entitled to disability premium by virtue of paragraph 13(1)(b) of Schedule 1 to the 1992 Regulations and in the period from 13th April 1995 to 1st October 1995 entitlement to that disability premium ceased, if–

(a)   for the period when that disability premium did not apply the person was incapable of work or was treated as incapable of work in accordance with the provisions of, and regulations made under, Part 12A of the 1992 Act; and

(b)   any break in the period of incapacity did not exceed a period of 56 continuous days,

for so long as the person is incapable of work or is treated as incapable of work, the disability premium under 10(1)(b) of Schedule 1 to these Regulations is applicable in the person's case.

(3)   Paragraphs (1) and (2) do not apply to a person who ceases to be incapable of work or ceases to be treated as incapable of work in accordance with the provisions of, and regulations made under Part 12A of the 1992 Act (incapacity for work) for a period of more than 56 continuous days.

(4)   Where, in any period immediately preceding 13th April 1995, the circumstances mentioned in paragraph 13(6) of Schedule 1 to the 1992 Regulations, as in force on 12th April 1995, applied to a person to whom the disability premium was not applicable, that person is to be treated for the purposes of regulations 20(3)(e) (persons not entitled to council tax reduction: students) and 28(11)(g) (treatment of childcare charges) and paragraph 10(1)(b) (additional condition for the disability premium) of Schedule 1 as if the person had been incapable of work in accordance with the provisions of, and regulations made under, Part 12A of the 1992 Act (incapacity for work) throughout that period.

2.–(1)   Where the higher pensioner premium was applicable to a person on 12th April 1995, or at any time during the 56 days immediately preceding that date, by virtue of paragraph 13(1)(a)(ii) of Schedule 1 to the 1992 Regulations, as in force on that date, paragraph 10 of Schedule 1 to these Regulations, in so far as it applies to the person, applies subject to the modifications in sub-paragraph (2).

(2)   The modifications are–

(a)   in paragraph 10(1)(a)(i), for the words "long-term incapacity benefit" where they first appear, substitute "an invalidity pension" and for the words "in the case of long-term incapacity benefit", substitute "in the case of invalidity pension";

(b)   in paragraph 10(1)(a)(ii) for the words "long-term incapacity benefit" substitute "invalidity pension";

(c)   for paragraph 10(1)(b), substitute–

"(b)   the circumstances of the applicant fall, and have fallen, in respect of a continuous period of not less than 28 weeks, within sub-paragraph (5) or, if the person was in Northern Ireland for the whole or part of that period, within one or more comparable Northern Irish provisions.";

(d)   in paragraph 10(3), for the words "or to be incapable of work", substitute "for the purposes of the provisions specified in that provision";

(e)   for sub-paragraphs (6) and (7), substitute–

"(6)   For the purposes of sub-paragraph (1)(b) the circumstances of an applicant fall within this sub-paragraph if–

(a)   the applicant provides evidence of incapacity in accordance with regulation 2 of the Social Security (Medical Evidence) Regulations 1976 (evidence of incapacity for work) in support of a claim for sickness benefit, invalidity pension or severe disablement allowance within the meaning of sections

31, 33 or 68 of the 1992 Act, provided that an adjudication officer has not determined the applicant is not incapable of work, or

(b)   the applicant is in receipt of statutory sick pay within the meaning of Part 11 of the 1992 Act.".

Interpretation

3.   In this Schedule "the 1992 Regulations" means the Council Tax Benefit (General) Regulations 1992.

General Note

The Housing Benefit and Council Tax Benefit (Miscellaneous Amendments) (No.2) Regulations 1995 SI No.626 introduced amendments to the conditions for qualifying for various premiums payable as part of HB and CTB. For CTR purposes, the transitional and savings provisions for those receiving the disability or higher pensioner premium on 12 April 1995 are now in paras 1 and 2. These provisions are broadly the same as those the transitional and savings provisions for HB. For Analysis of those, see p1775.

SCHEDULE 7
Consequential amendments

1.–(1)   The Council Tax (Administration and Enforcement) (Scotland) Regulations 1992 are amended in accordance with this paragraph.

(2)   In regulation 1(2) (interpretation), after the definition of "chargeable amount" insert–

""council tax reduction" means council tax reduction under the Council Tax Reduction (Scotland) Regulations 2012 or the Council Tax Reduction (State Pension Credit) (Scotland) Regulations 2012;".

(3)   In regulation 28A (matters not to be shown on demand notices) omit paragraph (b).

(4)   In paragraph 5 of Schedule 2 (contents of demand notices)–

(a)   for sub-paragraph (iii) substitute–

    "(iii)   council tax reduction";

(b)   in sub-paragraph (vi) for "benefit" where it appears for the second time substitute "reduction"; and

(c)   after sub-paragraph (vi) insert–

    "(vii)   any excess council tax reduction being recovered otherwise than by allowing, for the purpose of calculating the total amount payable under the notice, a smaller amount of council tax reduction than would have been applicable but for the excess council tax reduction;".

(5)   For paragraph 8(a)(iv) of Schedule 2 substitute–

    "(iv)   a person may be entitled to council tax reduction;".

2.   In the Council Tax (Reductions for Disabilities) (Scotland) Regulations 1992, in regulation 4(2)(b) (calculation of amount payable) for "council tax benefit" substitute "council tax reduction under the Council Tax Reduction (Scotland) Regulations 2012 or the Council Tax Reduction (State Pension Credit) (Scotland) Regulations 2012".

3.   In the Council Tax (Alteration of Lists and Appeals) (Scotland) Regulations 1993, in regulation 21 (appeals in relation to estimates or benefit matters) omit–

"; or

(b)   the calculation of an amount payable as council tax fails to take proper account of the provisions of the Council Tax Benefit (General) Regulations 1992.".

4.   In the Council Tax (Reduction of Liability) (Scotland) Regulations 1994, for regulation 4(c) (calculation of amount payable) substitute–

"(c)   the Council Tax Reduction (Scotland) Regulations 2012;

(ca)   the Council Tax Reduction State Pension Credit (Scotland) Regulations 2012;".

5.   In the Council Tax (Administration and Enforcement) (Scotland) Amendment Regulations 1996, omit regulation 18 (regulation 28A of the principal Regulations).

The Council Tax Reduction (State Pension Credit) (Scotland) Regulations 2012

(2012 No.319)

PART 1
General

1. Citation and commencement
2. Interpretation
3. Non-dependants
4. Young persons
5. Occupation of a dwelling as a home
6. Remunerative work

PART 2
Families

7. Entitlement of only one member of a family
8. Couples: polygamous marriages
9. Applicant in receipt of income-related benefit
10. Responsibility for another person
11. Membership of a household

PART 3
Application of the Regulations

12. Application
13. Prescribed years

PART 4
Entitlement to council tax reduction

14. Conditions of entitlement to council tax reduction
14A. Conditions of entitlement to council tax reduction – dwellings in bands E to H
15. Persons not entitled to council tax reduction: absentees
16. Persons not entitled to council tax reduction: persons treated as not being in Great Britain
17. Persons treated as being in Great Britain
18. Temporary absence from Great Britain
19. Persons not entitled to council tax reduction: persons subject to immigration control
19A. Non-recovery of council tax arrears caused by official error

PART 5

20. Applicable amount

PART 6
CHAPTER 1

21. Calculation of income and capital of members of applicant's family and of a polygamous marriage
22. Circumstances in which capital and income of non-dependant is to be treated as applicant's

CHAPTER 2

23. Calculation of income and capital
24. Applicant in receipt of guarantee credit
25. Calculation of income in savings credit only cases
26. Calculation of income and capital where state pension credit is not payable
27. Meaning of "income"

28. Calculation of income on a weekly basis
29. Treatment of child care charges
30. Calculation of average weekly income from working tax credits
31. Calculation of weekly income

CHAPTER 3
32. Earnings of employed earners
33. Calculation of net earnings of employed earners

CHAPTER 4
34. Calculation of earnings of self-employed earners
35. Earnings of self-employed earners
36. Calculation of net profit of self-employed earners
37. Deduction of tax and contributions of self-employed earners

CHAPTER 5
38. Notional income
39. Income paid to third parties

CHAPTER 6
40. Capital limit
41. Calculation of capital
42. Calculation of capital in the United Kingdom
43. Calculation of capital outside the United Kingdom
44. Notional capital
45. Diminishing notional capital
46. Capital jointly held

PART 7
47. Maximum council tax reduction
48. Non-dependant deductions
49. Extended council tax reduction (qualifying contributory benefits)
50. Duration of period of entitlement to extended council tax reduction (qualifying contributory benefits)
51. Amount of extended council tax reduction (qualifying contributory benefits)
52. Extended council tax reduction (qualifying contributory benefits): movers
53. Relationship between council tax reduction and extended council tax reduction (qualifying contributory benefits)
54. Entitlement to extended council tax reduction or extended council tax reduction (qualifying contributory benefits) under the Council Tax Reduction Regulations
55. Continuing payments where state pension credit claimed
56. Alternative maximum council tax reduction
57. Residents of a dwelling to whom regulation 14(6) does not apply

PART 8
58. Date on which entitlement begins
59. Date on which a change of circumstances is to take effect
60. Change of circumstances where state pension credit is in payment

PART 9
61. Who may apply
62. Time limit for making an application
63. Written applications
64. Telephone applications
65. Date on which an application is made
66. Evidence and information

67.   Amendment of applications
68.   Withdrawal of applications

PART 10
69.   Duty to notify changes of circumstances
70.   Alternative means of notifying changes of circumstances

PART 10A
70A.   Review of determination on an application
70B.   Request for further review
70C.   Conduct of further reviews

PART 11
71.   Electronic communication

PART 12
72.   Transitional provision

SCHEDULES
1.   Applicable amount
2.   Sums to be disregarded in the calculation of earnings
3.   Sums to be disregarded in the calculation of income other than earnings
4.   Capital disregards
5.   Amount of alternative maximum council tax reduction

PART 1
General

Citation and commencement
   1.   These Regulations may be cited as the Council Tax Reduction (State Pension Credit) (Scotland) Regulations 2012 and come into force on 28th January 2013.

Interpretation
   2.–(1)   In these Regulations, unless the context otherwise requires–
"the 1973 Act" means the Employment and Training Act 1973;
"the 1980 Act" means the Education (Scotland) Act 1980;
"the 1992 Act" means the Social Security Contributions and Benefits Act 1992;
"the 2006 Order" means the Naval, Military and Air Forces Etc. (Disablement and Death)
        Service Pensions Order 2006;
"Abbeyfield Home" means an establishment run by the Abbeyfield Society including all
        bodies corporate or unincorporate which are affiliated to that Society;
"the Act" means the Local Government Finance Act 1992;
[⁶]
"adoption leave" means a period of absence from work on ordinary or additional adoption
        leave by virtue of section 75A or 75B of the Employment Rights Act 1996;
"alternative maximum council tax reduction" means the amount of council tax reduction
        calculated in accordance with regulation 56 and Schedule 5;
"applicable amount" means the amount calculated in accordance with regulation 20 and
        Schedule 1;
"applicant" means a person applying for council tax reduction or, as the case may be, a
        person who is entitled to council tax reduction whose entitlement is or may be
        subject to re-assessment by the relevant authority;
"application" means an application for council tax reduction;
"appropriate maximum council tax reduction" means the maximum council tax reduction
        applicable to a person calculated in accordance with regulation 47;

[²"armed forces independence payment" means armed forces independence payment under the Armed Forces and Reserve Forces (Compensation Scheme) Order 2011;]

"assessment period" means a period described in regulation 31 (calculation of weekly income) or 34 (calculation of earnings of self-employed earners) over which income falls to be calculated;

"attendance allowance" means–

   (a)   an attendance allowance under Part 3 of the 1992 Act;

   (b)   an increase of disablement pension under section 104 or 105 of the 1992 Act;

   (c)   [¹...];

   (d)   a payment by virtue of article 14, 15, 16, 43 or 44 of the Personal Injuries (Civilians) Scheme 1983 or any analogous payment; or

   (e)   any payment based on need for attendance which is paid as part of a war disablement pension;

"basic rate" has the same meaning as in section 989 of the Income Tax Act 2007;

"the benefit Acts" means the 1992 Act, [²the Armed Forces (Pensions and Compensation) Act 2004 insofar as it relates to armed forces independence payment, Part 4 (personal independence payment) of the Welfare Reform Act 2012,] [⁸ the Pensions Act 2014,] the Jobseekers Act 1995, the Welfare Reform Act 2007 and the State Pension Credit Act 2002;

"board and lodging accommodation" means accommodation provided to a person, or if that person is a member of a family, to that person or any other member of that person's family, for a charge which is inclusive of the provision of that accommodation and at least some cooked or prepared meals which are cooked or prepared (by a person other than the person to whom the accommodation is provided or a member of that person's family) and consumed in that accommodation or associated premises;

"care home" in Scotland means a care home service within the meaning given by paragraph 2 of schedule 12 to the Public Services Reform (Scotland) Act 2010 and in England and Wales has the meaning given by section 3 of the Care Standards Act 2000;

"carer's allowance" means an allowance under section 70 of the 1992 Act;

"the Caxton Foundation" means the charitable trust of that name established on 28th March 2011 out of funds provided by the Secretary of State for the benefit of certain persons suffering from hepatitis C and other persons eligible for payment in accordance with its provisions;

"child" means a person under the age of 16 [³ and where section 145A of the 1992 Act (entitlement after death of a child or qualifying young person) applies, then during the period prescribed under subsection (1) of that section (and only during that period)–

   (a)   references in these Regulations to a child include the child in respect of whom there is entitlement under that section; and

   (b)   for the purposes of these Regulations the circumstances pertaining to the child at the date of their death are deemed to continue throughout that period];

"child benefit" means child benefit under section 141 of the 1992 Act;

"child tax credit" means a child tax credit under section 8 of the Tax Credits Act 2002;

"civil partnership" means a civil partnership which exists under or by virtue of the Civil Partnership Act 2004 (and "civil partner" is to be construed accordingly);

"close relative" means a parent, parent-in-law, son, son-in-law, daughter, daughter-in-law, step-parent, step-son, step-daughter, brother, sister or, if any of the preceding persons is one member of a couple, the other member of that couple;

"contributory employment and support allowance" means a contributory allowance under Part 1 of the Welfare Reform Act 2007;

"council tax benefit" means council tax benefit under the Council Tax Benefit (Persons who have attained the qualifying age for state pension credit) Regulations 2006;

"council tax reduction" means a reduction in liability for council tax calculated in accordance with these Regulations;

"the Council Tax Reduction Regulations" means the Council Tax Reduction (Scotland) Regulations 2012;

[⁵ "couple" means–

(a) two people who are married to each other and are members of the same household, but not if the marriage is a polygamous marriage;

(b) two people who are civil partners of each other and are members of the same household; or

(c) two people who are neither married to each other nor civil partners of each other but who are living together as if they were married to each other;]

"course of study" means any course of study, whether or not it is a sandwich course and whether or not an educational grant or award is made for attending or undertaking it;

"date of application" means the date on which the application is made, or treated as made, for the purposes of regulation 5(9) (occupation of a dwelling as a home) and regulation 65 (date on which an application is made);

"designated office" means the office designated by the relevant authority as the office to which applications should be sent;

"disability living allowance" means a disability living allowance under section 71 of the 1992 Act;

"discount" means discount under section 79 of the Act (discount of the amount of council tax payable);

"earnings" has the meaning given by regulation 32 (earnings of employed earners) or, as the case may be, regulation 35 (earnings of self-employed earners);

"educational establishment" has the meaning given by section 135(1) of the Education (Scotland) Act 1980;

"the Eileen Trust" means the charitable trust of that name established on 29th March 1993 out of funds provided by the Secretary of State for the benefit of persons eligible for payment in accordance with its provisions;

"employed earner" is to be construed in accordance with section 2(1)(a) of the 1992 Act and also includes a person who is in receipt of a payment which is payable under any enactment having effect in Northern Ireland and which corresponds to statutory sick pay or statutory maternity pay;

"employment and support allowance" means employment and support allowance under Part 1 of the Welfare Reform Act 2007;

"Employment and Support Allowance Regulations" means the Employment and Support Allowance Regulations 2008;

"enactment" includes an enactment contained in, or in an instrument made under, an Act of the Scottish Parliament;

"extended council tax reduction (qualifying contributory benefits)" means an extension of a period of entitlement to council tax reduction under regulation 49;

"family" means–

(a) a couple;

(b) a couple and a member of the same household for whom one of them is, or both are, responsible and who is a child or young person; or

(c) subject to regulation 22 (circumstances in which capital and income of non-dependant is to be treated as applicant's), a person who is not a member of a couple and a member of the same household for whom the person is responsible and who is a child or a young person;

"first authority" means the relevant authority to which a mover was liable to pay council tax for the dwelling that person resided in immediately before moving to the dwelling in the area of the second authority;

"full-time student" means a person attending or undertaking a full-time course of study;

"the Fund" means moneys made available from time to time by the Secretary of State for the benefit of persons eligible for payment in accordance with the provisions of a scheme established by the Secretary of State on 10th or 24th April 1992, as the case may be;

"guarantee credit" is to be construed in accordance with sections 1 and 2 of the State Pension Credit Act 2002;

"guaranteed income payment" means a payment referred to in article 15(1)(c) or 29(1)(a) of the Armed Forces and Reserve Forces (Compensation Scheme) Order 2011 and determined in accordance with article 24 of that Order;

"housing benefit" means housing benefit under section 130 of the 1992 Act;

[⁸ "ILF Scotland" means the company limited by guarantee under the name ILF Scotland, registered under number SC 500075;]

"incapacity benefit" means incapacity benefit under section 30A, 40 or 41 of the 1992 Act;

"income" has the meaning given by regulation 27 (meaning of "income");

"an income-based jobseeker's allowance" and "a joint-claim jobseeker's allowance" have the same meaning as they have in the Jobseekers Act 1995 by virtue of section 1(4) of that Act;

"income-related employment and support allowance" means an income-related allowance under Part 1 of the Welfare Reform Act 2007;

"income support" means income support under section 124 of the 1992 Act;

"Income Support Regulations" means the Income Support (General) Regulations 1987;

"independent hospital" –

(a) in Scotland, means an independent health care service as defined in section 10F(1)(a) and (b) of the National Health Service (Scotland) Act 1978;

(b) in England, means a hospital as defined by section 275 of the National Health Service Act 2006 that is not a health service hospital as defined by that section; and

(c) in Wales, has the meaning assigned to it by section 2 of the Care Standards Act 2000;

[⁹ "infected blood payment scheme" means a scheme established by, or under arrangements made with, the Scottish Ministers, the Secretary of State, the Welsh Ministers or the Department of Health in Northern Ireland for making ex gratia payments to or in respect of persons who have acquired HIV or hepatitis C as a result of treatment with blood or blood products within the national health service;]

[⁸]

"invalid carriage or other vehicle" means a vehicle propelled by a petrol engine or by electric power supplied for use on the road and to be controlled by the occupant;

"limited capability for work" has the meaning given by section 1(4) of the Welfare Reform Act 2007;

"local authority" in Scotland means a council constituted by section 2 of the Local Government etc. (Scotland) Act 1994;

"the London Bombings Relief Charitable Fund" means the company limited by guarantee (number 5505072) and registered charity of that name established on 11th July 2005 for the purpose of (amongst other things) relieving sickness, disability or financial need of victims (including families or dependants of victims) of the terrorist attacks carried out in London on 7th July 2005;

[¹⁰ the London Emergencies Trust" means the company of that name (number 09928465) incorporated on 23rd December 2015 and registered charity of that name (number 1172307) established on 28th March 2017 for the purpose of (amongst other things) relieving sickness, disability or financial need of victims of emergency incidents occurring in Greater London;]

"lone parent" means a person who has no partner and who is responsible for and a member of the same household as a child or young person;

"the Macfarlane (Special Payments) Trust" means the trust of that name, established on 29th January 1990 partly out of funds provided by the Secretary of State, for the benefit of certain persons suffering from haemophilia;

"the Macfarlane (Special Payments) (No. 2) Trust" means the trust of that name, established on 3rd May 1991 partly out of funds provided by the Secretary of State, for the benefit of certain persons suffering from haemophilia and other beneficiaries;

"the Macfarlane Trust" means the charitable trust, established partly out of funds provided by the Secretary of State, for the relief of poverty or distress among those suffering from haemophilia;

"main phase employment and support allowance" means an employment and support allowance where the calculation of the amount payable in respect of the applicant includes a component under section 2(1)(b) or 4(2)(b) of the Welfare Reform Act 2007 [¹¹ or the applicant is a member of the work-related activity group];

"maternity leave" means a period during which a woman is absent from work because she is pregnant or has given birth to a child, and at the end of which she has a right to return to work under the terms of her contract of employment or under Part 8 of the Employment Rights Act 1996;

"medically approved" means certified by a medical practitioner;

"member of a couple" means a member of a married or unmarried couple;

[¹¹ "member of the work-related activity group" means a person who has or is treated as having limited capability for work under either–

   (a)   Part 5 of the Employment and Support Allowance Regulations 2008 other than by virtue of regulation 30 of those Regulations; or

   (b)   Part 4 of the Employment and Support Allowance Regulations 2013 other than by virtue of regulation 26 of those Regulations;]

"MFET Limited" means the company limited by guarantee (number 7121661) of that name, established for the purpose in particular of making payments in accordance with arrangements made with the Secretary of State to persons who have acquired HIV as a result of treatment by the NHS with blood or blood products;

"mover" means a person who moves from a dwelling in which the person is resident, and in respect of which the person is liable to pay council tax to the first authority, to reside in a dwelling in the area of the second authority and any reference to a mover is to be construed as including a reference to the mover's partner;

"net earnings" means earnings calculated in accordance with regulation 33 (calculation of net earnings of employed earners);

"net profit" means profit calculated in accordance with regulation 36 (calculation of net profit of self-employed earners);

"new dwelling" means, for the purposes of the definition of "second authority" and regulation 52 (extended council tax reduction (qualifying contributory benefits): movers), the dwelling to which an applicant has moved, or is about to move, in which the applicant is or will be resident;

"non-dependant" has the meaning given by regulation 3 (non-dependants);

"non-dependant deduction" means a deduction that is to be made under regulation 48 (non-dependant deductions);

"occupational pension" means any pension or other periodical payment under an occupational pension scheme but does not include any discretionary payment out of a fund established for relieving hardship in particular cases;

"official error" means an error made by an officer of the Department for Work and Pensions acting as such which no person outside the Department caused or to which no person outside the Department materially contributed to but excludes any error of law which is shown to have been an error by virtue of a subsequent decision of the Upper Tribunal [¹or a court];

[⁶]

"partner" means–

   (a)   where an applicant is a member of a couple, the other member of that couple; or

   (b)   where an applicant is polygamously married to two or more members of the applicant's household, any such member to whom the applicant is married;

"paternity leave" means a period of absence from work on [⁶] paternity leave by virtue of sections 80A or 80B of the Employment Rights Act 1996 [⁶];

"patient" means a person who is undergoing medical or other treatment as an in-patient in any hospital or similar institution;

"payment" includes part of a payment;

"pension fund holder" means with respect to a personal pension scheme or an occupational pension scheme, the trustees, managers or scheme administrators, as the case may be, of the scheme concerned;

"personal independence payment" has the meaning given by Part 4 of the Welfare Reform Act 2012;

"personal pension scheme" means–

(a) a personal pension scheme as defined by section 1 of the Pension Schemes Act 1993;

(b) an annuity contract or trust scheme approved under section 620 or 621 of the Income and Corporation Taxes Act 1988 or a substituted contract within the meaning of section 622(3) of that Act which is treated as having become a registered pension scheme by virtue of paragraph 1(1)(f) of Schedule 36 to the Finance Act 2004; or

(c) a personal pension scheme approved under Chapter 4 of Part 14 of the Income and Corporation Taxes Act 1988 which is treated as having become a registered pension scheme by virtue of paragraph 1(1)(g) of Schedule 36 to the Finance Act 2004;

"policy of life insurance" means any instrument by which the payment of money is assured on death (except death by accident only) or the happening of any contingency dependent on human life, or any instrument evidencing a contract which is subject to payment of premiums for a term dependent on human life;

"polygamous marriage" means any marriage during the subsistence of which a party to it is married to more than one person and the ceremony of marriage took place under the law of a country which permits polygamy, and cognate expressions are to be construed accordingly;

"public authority" includes any person certain of whose functions are functions of a public nature;

"qualifying age for state pension credit" means (in accordance with section 1(2)(b) and (6) of the State Pension Credit Act 2002)–

(a) in the case of a woman, pensionable age; or

(b) in the case of a man, the age which is pensionable age in the case of a woman born on the same day as the man;

"qualifying contributory benefit" means–

(a) severe disablement allowance under section 68 of the 1992 Act;

(b) incapacity benefit; or

(c) contributory employment and support allowance;

"qualifying income-related benefit" means–

(a) income support;

(b) income-based jobseeker's allowance; or

(c) income-related employment and support allowance;

"reduction week" means a period of 7 consecutive days commencing on a Monday and ending on a Sunday;

"relative" means a close relative, grandparent, grandchild, uncle, aunt, nephew or niece;

"relevant authority" means a local authority administering council tax reduction;

"relevant child care charges" has the meaning given by regulation 29(5) (treatment of child care charges);

"remunerative work" has the meaning given by regulation 6 (remunerative work);

"rent" means "eligible rent" to which regulation 12B of the Housing Benefit (Persons who have attained the qualifying age for state pension credit) Regulations 2006 refers, less any deductions in respect of non-dependants to be made under regulation 55 (non-dependant deductions) of those Regulations;

"residential accommodation" means accommodation which is provided in–

(a) a care home;

(b) an independent hospital;

(c) an Abbeyfield Home; or

(d) an establishment managed or provided by a body incorporated by Royal Charter or constituted by Act of Parliament or by Act of the Scottish Parliament other than a local social services authority;

"retirement pension income" means retirement pension income within the meaning of section 16 of the State Pension Credit Act 2002;

"sandwich course" has the meaning prescribed in regulation 4(2) of the Education (Student Loans) (Scotland) Regulations 2007, regulation 2(10) of the Education (Student Support) Regulations 2011 or regulation 2(10) of the Education (Student Support) (No.2) Regulations (Northern Ireland) 2009, as the case may be;

"savings credit" is to be construed in accordance with sections 1 and 3 of the State Pension Credit Act 2002;

"second adult" has the meaning given to it in Schedule 5;

"second authority" means the authority to which a mover is liable to make payments for the new dwelling;

"self-employed earner" is to be construed in accordance with section 2(1)(b) of the 1992 Act;

"service user group" means a group of individuals that is consulted by or on behalf of–

(a) a Health Board, Special Health Board or the Agency in consequence of a function under section 2B of the National Health Service (Scotland) Act 1978;

(b) a landlord authority in consequence of a function under section 105 of the Housing Act 1985;

(c) a public authority in consequence of a function under section 149 of the Equality Act 2010 or section 49A of the Disability Discrimination Act 1995;

(d) a best value authority in consequence of a function under section 3 of the Local Government Act 1999;

(e) a local authority landlord or registered social landlord in consequence of a function under section 53 of the Housing (Scotland) Act 2001;

(f) a relevant English body or a relevant Welsh body in consequence of a function under section 242 of the National Health Service Act 2006;

(g) a Local Health Board in consequence of a function under section 183 of the National Health Service (Wales) Act 2006;

(h) the Commission in consequence of a function under sections 4 or 5 of the Health and Social Care Act 2008;

(i) the regulator or a private registered provider of social housing in consequence of a function under sections 98, 193 or 196 of the Housing and Regeneration Act 2008; or

(j) a public or local authority in Great Britain in consequence of a function conferred under any other enactment,

for the purposes of monitoring and advising on a policy of that body or authority which affects or may affect persons in the group, or of monitoring or advising on services provided by that body or authority which are used (or may potentially be used) by those persons;

[4 "shared parental leave" means leave under section 75E or 75G of the Employment Rights Act 1996;]

"single applicant" means an applicant who does not have a partner and who is not a lone parent;

"the Skipton Fund" means the ex-gratia payment scheme administered by the Skipton Fund Limited, incorporated on 25th March 2004, for the benefit of certain persons suffering from hepatitis C and other persons eligible for payment in accordance with the scheme's provisions;

"sports award" means an award made by one of the Sports Councils named in section 23(2) of the National Lottery etc Act 1993 out of sums allocated to it for distribution under that section;

"state pension credit" means state pension credit under the State Pension Credit Act 2002;

"statutory adoption pay" means statutory adoption pay payable under section 171ZL of the 1992 Act;

"statutory maternity pay" means statutory maternity pay payable under section 164 of the 1992 Act;

[6 "statutory paternity pay" means statutory paternity pay under section 171ZA or 171ZB of the 1992 Act;]

[4 "statutory shared parental pay" means statutory shared parental pay under section 171ZU or 171ZV of the 1992 Act;]

"statutory sick pay" means statutory sick pay under section 151 of the 1992 Act;

"student" means a person, other than a person in receipt of a training allowance, who is attending or undertaking–
    (a)   a course of study at an educational establishment; or
    (b)   a qualifying course as defined for the purposes of Parts 2 and 4 of the Jobseeker's Allowance Regulations 1996;

"student loan" means a loan towards a student's maintenance pursuant to section 73 of the 1980 Act, any regulations made under section 22 of the Teaching and Higher Education Act 1998 or article 3 of the Education (Student Support) (Northern Ireland) Order 1998 and includes a young student's bursary paid under regulation 4(1)(c) of the Students' Allowances (Scotland) Regulations 2007;

"training allowance" means an allowance (whether by way of periodical grants or otherwise) payable–

[12 "the Thalidomide Trust" means the registered charity of that name (number 266220) established for the purpose of giving relief and assistance to disabled persons whose disabilities were caused by the fact that their mother had taken a preparation containing the drug known as Thalidomide during pregnancy;]
    (a)   out of public funds by a Government department or by or on behalf of the Secretary of State, Skills Development Scotland, Scottish Enterprise or Highlands and Islands Enterprise, the Young People's Learning Agency for England [7] or the Welsh Ministers;
    (b)   to a person for the person's maintenance or in respect of a member of the person's family; and
    (c)   for the period, or part of the period, during which the person is following a course of training or instruction provided by, or in pursuance of arrangements made with, that department or approved by that department in relation to the person or so provided or approved by or on behalf of the Secretary of State, Skills Development Scotland, Scottish Enterprise or Highlands and Islands Enterprise or the Welsh Ministers,

but it does not include an allowance paid by any Government department to or in respect of a person by reason of the fact that the person is following a course of full-time education, other than under arrangements made under section 2 of the 1973 Act, or is training as a teacher;

"the Trusts" means the Macfarlane Trust, the Macfarlane (Special Payments) Trust and the Macfarlane (Special Payments) (No. 2) Trust;

["universal credit" has the meaning given by section 1 of the Welfare Reform Act 2012;]

"voluntary organisation" means a body, other than a public or local authority, the activities of which are carried on otherwise than for profit;

"war disablement pension" means any retired pay or pension or allowance payable in respect of disablement under an instrument specified in section 639(2) of the Income Tax (Earnings and Pensions) Act 2003;

"war widow's pension" means any pension or allowance payable to a woman as a widow or surviving civil partner under an instrument specified in section 639(2) of the Income Tax (Earnings and Pensions) Act 2003 in respect of the death or disablement of any person;

"war widower's pension" means any pension or allowance payable to a man as a widower or surviving civil partner under an instrument specified in section 639(2) of the Income Tax (Earnings and Pensions) Act 2003 in respect of the death or disablement of any person;

[¹⁰ "the We Love Manchester Emergency Fund" means the registered charity of that name (number 1173260) established on 30th May 2017 for the purpose of (amongst other things) relieving sickness, disability or financial need of victims (including families or dependants of victims) of the bombing at Manchester Arena on 22nd May 2017;]

[⁸ "welfare fund" means any fund maintained by a local authority in terms of section 1 of the Welfare Funds (Scotland) Act 2015;]

"working tax credit" means a working tax credit under section 10 of the Tax Credits Act 2002;

"Working Tax Credit Regulations" means the Working Tax Credit (Entitlement and Maximum Rate) Regulations 2002; and

"young person" has the meaning given by regulation 4 (young persons).

(2)   For the purposes of the definition of "full-time student" in paragraph (1), a person is to be regarded as attending or, as the case may be, undertaking a full-time course of study–

(a)   subject to paragraph (3), in the case of a person attending or undertaking a part of a modular course which would be a full-time course of study for the purposes of this Part, for the period beginning on the day on which that part of the course starts and ending–

(i)   on the last day on which that person is registered with the educational establishment as attending or undertaking that part as a full-time course of study; or

(ii)   on such earlier date, if any, as the person finally abandons the course or is dismissed from it; and

(b)   in any other case, throughout the period beginning on the date on which that person starts attending or undertaking the course and ending on the last day of the course or on such earlier date (if any) as the person finally abandons the course or is dismissed from it.

(3)   The period referred to in paragraph (2)(a) includes–

(a)   where a person has failed examinations or has failed to successfully complete a module relating to a period when the person was attending or undertaking a part of the course as a full-time course of study, any period in respect of which the person attends or undertakes the course for the purpose of retaking those examinations or that module; and

(b)   any period of vacation within the period specified in that paragraph or immediately following that period except where the person has registered with the educational establishment to attend or undertake the final module in the course and the vacation immediately follows the last day on which the person is required to attend or undertake the course.

(4)   In paragraph (2), "modular course" means a course of study which consists of two or more modules, the successful completion of a specified number of which is required before a person is considered by the educational establishment to have completed the course.

(5)   For the purposes of these Regulations, a person is on an income-based jobseeker's allowance on any day in respect of which an income-based jobseeker's allowance is payable to that person and on any day–

(a)   in respect of which the person satisfies the conditions for entitlement to an income-based jobseeker's allowance but where the allowance is not paid as a consequence of regulation section 19 or 19A or regulations made under section 17A of the Jobseekers Act 1995 (circumstances in which a jobseeker's allowance is not payable);

(b)   which is a waiting day for the purposes of paragraph 4 of Schedule 1 to that Act and which falls immediately before a day in respect of which an income-based jobseeker's allowance is payable to the person or would be payable to the person but for section 19 or 19A or regulations made under section 17A of that Act;

(c)   in respect of which the person is a member of a joint-claim couple for the purposes of the Jobseekers Act 1995 and no joint-claim jobseeker's allowance is payable in respect of that couple as a consequence of either member of the couple being subject to sanctions for the purposes of section 19 or 19A of that Act; or

(d) in respect of which an income-based jobseeker's allowance or a joint-claim jobseeker's allowance would be payable but for a restriction imposed pursuant to section 6B, 7, 8 or 9 of the Social Security Fraud Act 2001 (loss of benefit provisions).

(6) For the purposes of these Regulations, a person is on an income-related employment and support allowance on any day in respect of which an income-related employment and support allowance is payable to the person and on any day–

(a) in respect of which the person satisfies the conditions for entitlement to an income-related employment and support allowance but where the allowance is not paid as a consequence of section 18 of the Welfare Reform Act 2007 (disqualification); or

(b) which is a waiting day for the purposes of paragraph 2 of Schedule 2 to that Act and which falls immediately before a day in respect of which an income related employment and support allowance is payable to the person or would be payable to the person but for section 18 of that Act.

(7) In these Regulations, where an amount is to be rounded to the nearest penny, a fraction of a penny is to be disregarded if it is less than half a penny and if it is a half penny or more it is to be treated as a whole penny.

(8) For the purposes of these Regulations, two persons are to be taken to be estranged only if their estrangement constitutes a breakdown of the relationship between them.

(9) In these Regulations references to any person in receipt of a guarantee credit, a savings credit or state pension credit includes a reference to a person who would be in receipt of that credit but for regulation 13 of the State Pension Credit Regulations 2002 (small amounts of state pension credit).

Modifications

The amendments made by SI 2014 No.3255 which came into force on 5 April 2015 do not have effect in relation to ordinary statutory paternity pay which is paid, additional statutory paternity pay which is paid, a period in respect of which additional statutory paternity pay is payable which begins, or continues, ordinary paternity leave which is taken or additional paternity leave which is taken on or after 5 April 2015. See art 35 of SI 2014 No.3255.

Amendments

1. Amended by reg 3 of SSI 2013 No 49 as from 18.3.13.
2. Inserted by reg 12(2) of SSI 2013 No 142 as from 11.6.13.
3. Amended by reg 13 of SSI 2013 No 287 as from 25.11.13.
4. Inserted by art 24(2(d)(i) and (iii) of SI 2014 No 3225 as from 31.12.14.
5. Substituted by reg 15 of SSI 2015 No 46 as from 1.4.15.
6. Amended by art 24(2)(a), (b), (c) and (d)(ii) of SI 2014 No 3255 as from 5.4.15.
7. Amended by art 2 and Sch 3 para 19 of SI 2015 No 971 as from 26.5.15.
8. Amended by regs 17(1) and 21 of SSI 2016 No 81 as from 1.4.16.
9. Inserted by reg 15 of SSI 2017 No 41 as from 1.4.17.
10. Inserted by reg 10 of SSI 2017 No 326 as from 20.11.17.
11. Inserted by reg 15 of SSI 2017 No 326 as from 20.11.17.
12. Inserted by reg 12 of SSI 2018 No 69 as from 1.4.18.

General Note

This is similar to the HB equivalent. See p731 for the commentary.

Non-dependants

3.–(1) In these Regulations, "non-dependant" means any person, except someone to whom paragraph (2) applies, who normally resides with the applicant or with whom the applicant normally resides.

(2) This paragraph applies to–

(a) any member of the applicant's family;

(b)   if the applicant is polygamously married, any partner of the applicant and any child or young person who is a member of the applicant's household and for whom the applicant or one of the applicant's partners is responsible;

(c)   a child or young person who is living with the applicant but who is not treated as a member of the applicant's household by virtue of regulation 11 (membership of a household);

(d)   subject to paragraph (3), any person who, with the applicant, is jointly and severally liable to pay council tax in respect of a dwelling for any day under section 75 of the Act(1) (persons liable to pay council tax);

(e)   subject to paragraph (3), any person who is liable to make payments on a commercial basis to the applicant or any partner of the applicant in respect of the person's occupation of the dwelling; and

(f)   any person who lives with the applicant in order to care for the applicant or any partner of the applicant, or both of them, and who is engaged by a charitable or voluntary organisation which makes a charge to the applicant or the applicant's partner, or both of them, for the services provided by that person.

(3)   Excepting persons to whom paragraph (2)(a) to (c) and (f) refer, a person to whom any of the following sub-paragraphs applies is a non-dependant for the purpose of these Regulations–

(a)   a person who resides with another person to whom the first mentioned person is liable to make payments in respect of the dwelling and either–

(i)   that other person is a close relative of the first mentioned person or of the first mentioned person's partner; or

(ii)   the tenancy or other agreement between them is other than on a commercial basis;

(b)   a person whose liability to make payments in respect of the dwelling appears to the relevant authority to have been created to take advantage of the council tax reduction scheme set out in these Regulations, except someone who was, for any period within the 8 weeks prior to the creation of the agreement giving rise to the liability to make the payments, otherwise liable to make payments of rent in respect of the same dwelling; and

(c)   a person who becomes jointly and severally liable with the applicant for council tax in respect of a dwelling and who was, at any time during the period of 8 weeks prior to becoming liable, a non-dependant of one or more of the other residents in that dwelling who are liable for the council tax, unless the relevant authority is satisfied that the change giving rise to the new liability was not made to take advantage of the council tax reduction scheme set out in these Regulations.

General Note

This regulation is similar to reg 3 HB Regs. For the important differences, see the analysis to reg 3 CTR(S) Regs on p1466.

Young persons

4.–(1)   In these Regulations "young person" means a person who falls within the definition of "qualifying young person" in section 142 of the 1992 Act (child and qualifying young person).

(2)   Paragraph (1) does not apply to a person who is–

(a)   on income support, an income-based jobseeker's allowance or an income-related employment and support allowance; or

(b)   a person to whom section 6 of the Children (Leaving Care) Act 2000 (exclusion from benefits) applies.

(3)   [1...][2 Where section 145A of the 1992 Act (entitlement after death of a child or qualifying young person) applies, then during the period prescribed under subsection (1) of that section (and only during that period)–

(a)   references in these Regulations to a young person include the young person in respect of whom there is entitlement under that section; and

(b)   for the purposes of these Regulations the circumstances pertaining to the young person at the date of their death are deemed to continue throughout that period.]

Amendments
1.   Amended by reg 4 of SSI 2013 No 49 as from 18.3.13.
2.   Amended by reg 14 of SSI 2013 No 287 as from 25.11.13.

General Note
This is similar to the HB equivalent. See p406 for the commentary.

Occupation of a dwelling as a home

5.–(1)   Subject to the following provisions of this regulation, a person is to be treated as occupying as that person's home the dwelling normally occupied as a home–

(a)   by the person or, if the person is a member of a family, by the person and that family; or

(b)   if the person is polygamously married, by the person, the person's partners and any child or young person for whom the person or any of the partners is responsible and who is a member of that same household,

and is not to be treated as occupying any other dwelling as the person's home.

(2)   In determining whether a dwelling is the dwelling normally occupied as a person's home for the purpose of paragraph (1) regard must be had to any other dwelling occupied by the person or any other person referred to in that paragraph whether or not that dwelling is in Scotland.

(3)   Where a single person or a lone parent is a student, other than a full-time student to whom regulation 20 of the Council Tax Reduction Regulations applies (persons not entitled to council tax reduction: students), or is on a training course, and is liable to make payments in respect of either

(a)   the dwelling which that person occupies for the purpose of attending a course of study or a training course; or

(b)   the dwelling which the person occupies when not attending the course,

the person is to be treated as occupying as a home the dwelling in respect of which the person is liable to make those payments.

(4)   Where a person has required to move into temporary accommodation because of the carrying out of essential repairs to the dwelling normally occupied as that person's home, and the person is liable to make payments in respect of either the dwelling which the person normally occupies as a home or the temporary accommodation, the person is to be treated as occupying as a home the dwelling in respect of which the person is liable to make payments.

(5)   Where a person is required to reside in a dwelling which is a bail hostel or probation hostel approved by the Secretary of State under section 13 of the Offender Management Act 2007, that person is not to be treated as occupying that dwelling as a home.

(6)   Where a person is liable to make payments in respect of two (but not more than two) dwellings, that person is to be treated as occupying both dwellings as a home–

(a)   for a period not exceeding 52 weeks, where the person left and remains absent from the former dwelling occupied as a home and for which the person is liable to make payments through fear of violence in that dwelling or by a former member of the person's family and–

(i)   the relevant authority is satisfied that it is reasonable that the person should be entitled to council tax reduction in respect of the former dwelling and the present dwelling occupied as a home, and

(ii)   the person intends to return to occupy the former dwelling as a home;

(b)   in the case of a person who is a member of a couple or a member of a polygamous marriage, where the person or one partner is a student, other than a full-time student to whom regulation 20 of the Council Tax Reduction Regulations (persons not entitled to council tax reduction: students) applies, or is on a training course, and it is–

(i)   unavoidable that the partners should occupy two separate dwellings; and

(ii)   reasonable that the person should be entitled to council tax reduction in respect of both dwellings;

(c)   where, because of the number of persons in a family referred to in paragraph (1)(a) or (b), those persons have been housed by a housing authority in two separate dwellings;

(d)   where a person has moved and occupies the second dwelling as a home, except where paragraph (4) applies, for a period not exceeding 4 reduction weeks from the date on which that person moved if the person could not reasonably have avoided liability in respect of two dwellings; or

(e)   where a person–
    (i)   is treated by virtue of paragraph (8) as occupying a dwelling as that person's home and paragraph (8)(c)(i) applies; and
    (ii)   the person has occupied another dwelling as a home on any day within the period of 4 weeks immediately preceding the date the person moved to the new dwelling,

for a period not exceeding 4 reduction weeks immediately preceding the date on which the person moved.

(7)   Where–

(a)   a person moves into a dwelling for which that person is not liable to make payments ("the new dwelling");

(b)   immediately before that move, the person was liable to make payments for the dwelling previously occupied as a home ("the former dwelling"); and

(c)   that liability continues after the person moves into the new dwelling,

the person is to be treated as occupying the former dwelling as a home for a period not exceeding 4 reduction weeks if the person could not reasonably have avoided liability in respect of the former dwelling.

(8)   Where–

(a)   a person moved into a dwelling and was liable to make payments in respect of that dwelling before moving in; and

(b)   either–
    (i)   that person applied for council tax reduction before moving in and no decision has been made or it was refused but a further application was made or treated as made within 4 weeks of the date on which the person moved into the new dwelling to occupy it as a home; or .
    (ii)   the person notified the move to the new dwelling as a change of circumstances under regulation 69 (duty to notify changes of circumstances) before the move;

(c)   the delay in moving into the dwelling was reasonable and–
    (i)   that delay was necessary in order to adapt the dwelling to meet the disablement needs of the person or any member of the person's family;
    (ii)   the move was delayed pending the outcome of an application–
       (aa)   under Part 8 of the 1992 Act for a social fund payment;
       [¹ (bb) to a welfare fund for a payment;]
       (cc)   to a local authority in exercise of the power in section 1 of the Localism Act 2011 (local authority's general power of competence) using funds provided by the Secretary of State, and in this sub-head local authority means a local authority within the meaning of section 8 of that Act;
       (dd)   to the Welsh Ministers, or to a person acting on their behalf, for a payment made in exercise of the power in section 60 of the Government of Wales Act 2006 (promotion etc. of well-being),
       to meet a need arising out of the move or in connection with setting up the home in the dwelling and either a member of the applicant's family is aged 5 or under or the applicant's applicable amount includes a premium under paragraph 7 (severe disability premium) or 9 (disabled child premium) of Schedule 1 (applicable amounts); or
    (iii)   the applicant became liable to make payments in respect of the dwelling while a patient or in residential accommodation,

the person is to be treated as occupying the dwelling as a home for any period not exceeding 4 weeks immediately prior to the date on which the person moved into the dwelling.

(9)   Where a person is treated by virtue of paragraph (8) as occupying a dwelling as a home in respect of the period before moving in, the person's application for council tax reduction in respect of that dwelling is to be treated as having been made on the latest of–

(a)   in the case of an application in respect of which a decision has not yet been made, the date that application is or is treated as made in accordance with regulation 65 (date on which an application is made);

(b)   in the case of an application which was refused and a further application was or was treated as made in accordance with regulation 65 within 4 weeks of the date on which the person moved into the dwelling, the date on which the application was refused or was treated as made; or

(c)   the date from which the person is treated as occupying the dwelling as a home by virtue of paragraph (8).

(10)   Where a person to whom neither paragraph (6)(a) or (16)(c)(x) applies–

(a)   formerly occupied a dwelling but left and remains absent from it through fear of violence in the dwelling, or by a person who was formerly a member of the family of the person; and

(b)   has a liability to make payments in respect of that dwelling which is unavoidable, the person is to be treated as occupying the dwelling as a home for a period not exceeding 4 reduction weeks.

(11)   This paragraph applies to a person who enters residential accommodation–

(a)   for the purpose of ascertaining whether the accommodation suits that person's needs;

(b)   with the intention of returning to the dwelling which is normally occupied by the person as a home should the residential accommodation prove not to suit the person's needs; and

(c)   while the part of the dwelling which is normally occupied by the person as a home is not let, or as the case may be, sublet.

(12)   A person to whom paragraph (11) applies is to be treated as occupying the dwelling normally occupied as the person's home for a period not exceeding 13 weeks beginning from the first day the person enters residential accommodation, but a person is not to be treated as occupying that dwelling as a home if the total of all periods in residential accommodation exceeds 52 weeks.

(13)   Subject to paragraph (17), a person is to be treated as occupying a dwelling as a home while that person is temporarily absent from the dwelling for a period not exceeding 13 weeks beginning from the first day of that absence from the home if–

(a)   the person intends to return to occupy the dwelling as a home;

(b)   the part of the dwelling normally occupied by the person has not been let or, as the case may be, sublet; and

(c)   the period of absence is unlikely to exceed 13 weeks.

(14)   This paragraph applies to a person who is–

(a)   detained in custody pending sentence upon conviction or under a sentence imposed by a court, other than a person who is detained in hospital under the provisions of the Mental Health (Care and Treatment) (Scotland) Act 2003, the Criminal Procedure (Scotland) Act 1995, the Mental Health Act 1983 or the Mental Health (Northern Ireland) Order 1986; and

(b)   on temporary release from a detention referred to in sub-paragraph (a) in accordance with rules made under the provisions of the Prisons (Scotland) Act 1989, the Prison Act 1952 or the Prison Act (Northern Ireland) 1953.

(15)   Where paragraph (14) applies to a person, for any day when the person is on temporary release–

(a)   if the temporary release was immediately preceded by a period of temporary absence under paragraph (13) or (16), the person is to be treated as if continuing to be absent from the dwelling, despite any occupation of the dwelling;

(b)   for the purposes of paragraph (16)(c)(i), the person is to be treated as if remaining in detention; and

(c)   if the person does not fall within sub-paragraph (a), the person is to be treated as if not occupying a dwelling as a home despite any occupation of the dwelling.

(16)   This paragraph applies to a person who is temporarily absent from the dwelling normally occupied by that person as a home and–

(a)   that person intends to return to occupy the dwelling as a home;

(b)   the part of the dwelling which is normally occupied by the person has not been let or, as the case may be, sublet;

(c)   the person is–

    (i)   detained in custody on remand pending trial or, as a condition of bail, required to reside–

        (aa)   in a dwelling, other than the dwelling the person occupies as a home;

        (bb)   in premises approved under section 13 of the Offender Management Act 2007; or

        (cc)   detained pending sentence upon conviction;

    (ii)   resident in a hospital or similar institution as a patient;

    (iii)   or any partner of the person or the person's dependant child is undergoing, in the United Kingdom or elsewhere, medical treatment, or medically approved convalescence, in accommodation other than residential accommodation;

    (iv)   following, in the United Kingdom or elsewhere, a training course;

    (v)   undertaking medically approved care of a person residing in the United Kingdom or elsewhere;

    (vi)   undertaking the care of a child whose parent or guardian is temporarily absent from the dwelling normally occupied by that parent or guardian for the purpose of receiving medically approved care or medical treatment;

    (vii)   in the United Kingdom or elsewhere, receiving medically approved care provided in accommodation other than residential accommodation;

    (viii)   a student to whom paragraph (3) or (6)(b) does not apply;

    (ix)   receiving care provided in residential accommodation other than a person to whom paragraph (11) applies; or

    (x)   a person to whom paragraph (6)(a) does not apply and who has left the dwelling occupied as the person's home through fear of violence in that dwelling or by a former member of the person's family; and

(d)   the period of absence is unlikely to exceed 52 weeks or, in exceptional circumstances, is unlikely substantially to exceed that period.

(17)   A person to whom paragraph (16) applies is to be treated as occupying the dwelling normally occupied as a home during any period of temporary absence, but the period during which the person is treated as occupying the dwelling must not exceed 52 weeks beginning from the first day of temporary absence.

Amendment

1.   Substituted by reg 17(3) of SSI 2016 No 81 as from 1.4.16.

General Note

See the General Note to reg 5 CTR(S) Regs on p1471.

Remunerative work

6.–(1)   Subject to the following provisions of this regulation, a person is to be treated for the purposes of these Regulations as engaged in remunerative work if that person is engaged, or, where hours of work fluctuate, is engaged on average, for not less than 16 hours a week, in work for which payment is made or which is done in expectation of payment.

(2)   Subject to paragraph (3), in determining the number of hours for which a person is engaged in work where that person's hours of work fluctuate, regard is to be had to the average of hours worked over–

(a)   if there is a recognisable cycle of work, the period of one complete cycle (including, where the cycle involves periods in which the person does no work, those periods but disregarding any other absences); and

(b)   in any other case, the period of 5 weeks immediately prior to the date of application, or any other length of time as may, in the particular case, enable the person's weekly average hours of work to be determined more accurately.

(3)   Where, for the purposes of paragraph (2)(a), a person's recognisable cycle of work at a school, other educational establishment or other place of employment is one year and includes periods of school holidays or similar vacations during which that person does not work, those periods and any other periods not forming part of such holidays or vacations during which the person is not required to work are to be disregarded in establishing the average hours for which the person is engaged in work.

(4)   Where no recognisable cycle has been established in respect of a person's work, regard must be had to the number of hours or, where those hours will fluctuate, the average of the hours which the person is expected to work in a week.

(5)   A person is to be treated as engaged in remunerative work during any period for which the person is absent from work referred to in paragraph (1) if the absence is either without good cause or by reason of a recognised, customary or other holiday.

(6)   A person on income support, an income-based jobseeker's allowance or an income-related employment and support allowance for more than 3 days in any reduction week is to be treated as not being in remunerative work in that week.

(7)   A person is not to be treated as engaged in remunerative work on any day on which the person is on maternity leave, paternity leave [¹, shared parental leave] or adoption leave or is absent from work because the person is ill.

(8)   A person is not to be treated as engaged in remunerative work on any day on which the person is engaged in an activity in respect of which–

(a)   a sports award has been made, or is to be made, to the person; and

(b)   no other payment is made or is expected to be made to the person.

Amendment

1.   Amended by art 24(3) of SI 2014 No 225 as from 31.12.14.

General Note

This is similar to the HB equivalent. See p253 for the commentary.

PART 2
Families

Entitlement of only one member of a family

7.   The entitlement of one member of a family to council tax reduction in respect of a dwelling excludes entitlement to that reduction in respect of that dwelling for any other member of the family for the same period.

Couples: polygamous marriages

8.   Where a person is a party to a polygamous marriage, no party to the marriage is to be taken to be a member of a couple for the purposes of these Regulations.

Applicant in receipt of income-related benefit

9.   Where an applicant in receipt of an income-related benefit is a member of a family, the income and capital of any member of that family is to be treated as the income and capital of the applicant.

Responsibility for another person

10.–(1)   Subject to the following provisions of this regulation, a person is to be treated as responsible for a child or a young person who normally lives with that person.

(2)   Where a child or young person spends equal amounts of time in different households, or where there is a question as to which household the child or young person

is living in, the child or young person is to be treated for the purposes of paragraph (1) as normally living with–

(a)   the person who is receiving child benefit in respect of the child or young person; or

(b)   if there is no such person–

    (i)   where only one claim for child benefit has been made in respect of the child or young person, the person who made that claim; or

    (ii)   in any other case the person who has the primary responsibility for the child or young person.

(3)   For the purposes of these Regulations a child or young person can be the responsibility of only one person in any reduction week and any person other than the one treated as responsible for the child or young person under this regulation is to be treated as not responsible for the child or young person.

General Note

This is similar to the HB equivalent. See p408 for the commentary.

Membership of a household

11.–(1)   Subject to paragraphs (2) and (3), the applicant and any partner of the applicant and, where the applicant or the applicant's partner is treated as responsible for a child or young person by virtue of regulation 10 (responsibility for another person), that child or young person and any child of that child or young person, are to be treated as members of the same household even if temporarily absent from that household.

(2)   A child or young person is not to be treated as a member of the applicant's household where that child or young person is–

(a)   boarded out with the applicant or any partner of the applicant under a relevant enactment or placed with the applicant or any partner of the applicant by a local authority under section 22C(5) and (6)(a) or (b) or section 23(2)(a) of the Children Act 1989 or by a voluntary organisation under section 59(1)(a) of that Act;

(b)   boarded out or placed with the applicant or any partner of the applicant prior to adoption; or

(c)   placed for adoption with the applicant or any partner of the applicant in accordance with the Adoption and Children Act 2002 or the Adoption Agencies (Scotland) Regulations 2009.

(3)   Subject to paragraph (4), paragraph (1) does not apply to a child or young person who is not living with the applicant and the child or young person–

(a)   is in the care of, or is being looked after by, a local authority under a relevant enactment;

(b)   has been boarded out or placed with a person other than the applicant prior to adoption; or

(c)   has been placed for adoption in accordance with the Adoption and Children Act 2002 or the Adoption Agencies (Scotland) Regulations 2009.

(4)   A child or young person to whom paragraph (3)(a) applies is to be treated as being a member of the applicant's household in any reduction week where–

(a)   that child or young person lives with the applicant for part or all of that reduction week; and

(b)   the relevant authority considers that it is reasonable to do so taking into account the nature and frequency of that child's or young person's visits.

(5)   In this regulation "relevant enactment" means the Social Work (Scotland) Act 1968, the Family Law Reform Act 1969, the Children and Young Persons Act 1969, the Children Act 1975, the Domestic Proceedings and Magistrates' Courts Act 1978, the Family Law Act 1986, the Children Act 1989, the Armed Forces Act 1991 and the Children (Scotland) Act 1995.

General Note

See the General Note to reg 11 CTR(S) Regs on p1473.

PART 3
Application of the Regulations

Application
12.–(1)   Subject to paragraph (2), these Regulations apply to a person who has attained the qualifying age for state pension credit.
(2)   These Regulations do not apply to a person if that person, or any partner of that person, is a person on income support, [¹ universal credit,] an income-based jobseeker's allowance or an income-related employment and support allowance.

Amendment
1.   Amended by reg 15 of SSI 2013 No 287 as from 25.11.13.

General Note
The CTR(SPC)(S) Regs apply where the applicant has reached the qualifying age for PC unless s/he or her/his partner is in receipt of IS, UC, income-based JSA or income-related ESA. "Qualifying age for state pension credit" is defined in reg 2(1). This is the same definition as that in reg 2(1) HB Regs. See p244 for a discussion.

Prescribed years
13.   The financial year commencing 1st April 2013 and each subsequent financial year are prescribed as the years for which these Regulations apply.

PART 4
Entitlement to council tax reduction

Conditions of entitlement to council tax reduction
14.–(1)   A person who is liable to pay council tax under section 75 of the Act ("relevant person") is entitled to council tax reduction [² under this regulation] in respect of a day if the conditions set out in [² paragraphs (3) and (3A)] are satisfied and–
(a)   each of the conditions set out in paragraphs (4) and (5) is satisfied; or
(b)   the condition set out in paragraph (6) is satisfied.
(2)   A relevant person is not entitled to council tax reduction in respect of any day before the day on which that person's entitlement to council tax reduction commences in accordance with regulation 58 (date on which entitlement begins);
(3)   The conditions referred to in paragraph (1) are that the relevant person–
(a)   is for the day liable to pay council tax in respect of a dwelling in which that person resides [¹as their sole or main residence];
(b)   is not a person to whom regulation 15 (persons not entitled to council tax reduction: absentees), regulation 16 (persons not entitled to council tax reduction: persons treated as not being in Great Britain) or 19 (persons not entitled to council tax reduction: persons subject to immigration control) applies; and
(c)   makes an application for council tax reduction in accordance with Part 9 (applications).
[² (3A)   The condition referred to in paragraph (1) is that the amount of council tax reduction calculated under this regulation is not less than the amount of council tax reduction calculated under regulation 14A.]
(4)   The condition referred to in paragraph (1)(a) is that there is an appropriate maximum council tax reduction in the case of the relevant person.
(5)   The condition referred to in paragraph (1)(a) is that–
(a)   the day falls within a week in respect of which–
(i)   the relevant person has no income; or
(ii)   the relevant person's income does not exceed the applicable amount; or
(b)   neither paragraph (a)(i) or (ii) applies to the relevant person but amount A exceeds amount B where–
(i)   amount A is the appropriate maximum council tax reduction in the relevant person's case; and
(ii)   amount B is 2 6/7 per cent of the difference between the person's income in respect of the week in which the day falls and the applicable amount.

(6)   The condition referred to in paragraph (1)(b) is that–

(a)   no other resident of the dwelling is liable to pay rent to the relevant person in respect of the dwelling; and

(b)   the relevant person is entitled to alternative maximum council tax reduction because of the income or aggregate incomes of one or more residents of the dwelling.

(7)   For the purpose of paragraph (6) a resident of the dwelling other than the relevant person does not include a resident who–

(a)   falls to be disregarded for the purposes of discount in accordance with Schedule 1 to the Act; or

(b)   is a person described in regulation 57 (residents of a dwelling to whom regulation 14(6) does not apply).

(8)   Subject to paragraph (9) below, where a relevant person is entitled to council tax reduction in respect of a day, the amount to which the person is entitled is–

(a)   if paragraph (5)(a) applies, the amount which is the appropriate maximum council tax reduction in that person's case;

(b)   if paragraph (5)(b) applies, the amount found by deducting amount B from amount A, where "amount A" and "amount B" have the meanings given by that paragraph; and

(c)   if paragraph (6) applies, the amount which is the appropriate alternative maximum council tax reduction in that person's case.

(9)   Where a relevant person is entitled to council tax reduction in respect of a day and paragraphs (5) and (6) apply, the amount to which the person is entitled is whichever is the greater of–

(a)   the amount referred to in paragraph (8)(a) or, as the case may be, paragraph (8)(b); or

(b)   the amount referred to in paragraph (8)(c).

Amendments

1.   Inserted by reg 10 of SSI 2013 No 218 as from 1.10.13.

2.   Amended by reg 10 of SSI 2016 No 253 as from 1.4.17.

General Note

In Scotland, the council tax valuation band multipliers for properties in bands E, F, G and H (relative to band D properties) were increased from 1 April 2017, increasing the council tax charged for those properties before any discount and/or reduction is applied.

From that date, this regulation is amended and a new reg 14A inserted by the Council Tax Reduction (Scotland) Amendment (No.2) Regulations 2016 No.253. These amendments and an associated amendment to reg 47 introduced a new, alternative, formula for calculating CTR for applicants who are liable for council tax in a property in which they reside, as their sole or main residence, which is in band E to H, if their entitlement under that formula would be more than their CTR entitlement calculated under reg 14. As the CTR calculated under reg 14 is the greater of 'main CTR' or the 'alternative maximum CTR', this represents a third comparator. The alternative formula in reg 14A compares an applicant's income to one of two threshold amounts (the lesser of the two threshold amounts applies if the applicant is single and is not responsible for a child or young person). The threshold amounts are based on the median net income for the same kind of household, and the introduction of the alternative, formula aims to ensure that applicants with income equal to or below the median are no worse off following the introduction of the higher amount for bands E to H.

Analysis

See the Analysis to reg 14 CTR(S) Regs on p1475.

Conditions of entitlement to council tax reduction – dwellings in bands E to H

[¹ **14A.**–(1)   A person who is liable to pay council tax under section 75 of the Act ("relevant person") is entitled to council tax reduction under this regulation in respect of a day if–

(a)   the conditions set out in paragraph (3) to (5) are satisfied; and

(b)   the amount of council tax reduction calculated under this regulation is greater than the amount of council tax reduction calculated under regulation 14.

(2)   A relevant person is not entitled to council tax reduction in respect of any day before the day on which that person's entitlement to council tax reduction commences in accordance with regulation 58 (date on which entitlement is to begin).

(3)   The conditions referred to in paragraph (1)(a) are that the relevant person–

(a)   is for the day liable to pay council tax in respect of a dwelling in valuation band E, F, G or H in which that person resides as their sole or main residence;

(b)   is not a person to whom regulation 15 (persons not entitled to council tax reduction: absentees), 16 (persons not entitled to council tax reduction: persons treated as not being in Great Britain) or 19 (persons not entitled to council tax reduction: persons subject to immigration control) applies; and

(c)   makes an application for council tax reduction in accordance with Part 9 (applications).

(4)   The condition referred to in paragraph (1)(a) is that there is an appropriate maximum council tax reduction in the case of the relevant person.

(5)   The condition referred to in paragraph (1)(a) is that–

(a)   the day falls within a week in respect of which–

  (i)   the relevant person has no income; or

  (ii)   the relevant person's income does not exceed–

    (aa)   £321, in the case of a person to whom paragraph (6) applies;

    (bb)   £479 in any other case; or

(b)   neither sub-paragraph (a)(i) or (ii) applies to the relevant person but amount A exceeds amount B where–

  (i)   amount A is the appropriate maximum council tax reduction in the relevant person's case; and

  (ii)   amount B is 2 6/7 per cent of the difference between the person's income in respect of the week in which the day falls and the amount stated in sub-paragraph (a)(ii)(aa) or (bb) (as the case may be).

(6)   This paragraph applies to a person who–

(a)   is not a member of a couple or of a polygamous marriage; and

(b)   is not responsible for a child or young person (within the meaning of regulation 10).

(7)   Where a relevant person is entitled to council tax reduction in respect of a day, the amount to which the person is entitled is–

(a)   if paragraph (5)(a) applies, the amount which is the appropriate maximum council tax reduction in that person's case;

(b)   if paragraph (5)(b) applies, the amount found by deducting amount B from amount A, where "amount A" and "amount B" have the meanings given by that paragraph.]

Amendment

1.   Inserted by reg 11 of SSI 2016 No 253 as from 1.4.17.

General Note

See the General Note under reg 14 for the interplay between this regulation and reg 14. See the General Note to reg 14A CTR(S) Regs which is also relevant.

Persons not entitled to council tax reduction: absentees

15.–(1)   Subject to paragraph (2), a person is not entitled to council tax reduction in respect of a day and a dwelling of which the person is a resident if the person is throughout that day absent from the dwelling.

(2)   Paragraph (1) does not include a person whose absence from the dwelling is part of a period of temporary absence.

(3)   In paragraph (2) a "period of temporary absence" means–

(a)   a period of absence not exceeding 13 weeks, beginning with the first whole day on which a person resides in residential accommodation and for so long as–

  (i)   the person resides in that accommodation;

  (ii)   the part of the dwelling in which the person usually resides is not let or sub-let; and

    (iii)   that period of absence does not form part of a longer period of absence from the dwelling of more than 52 weeks, where the person has entered the accommodation for the purpose of ascertaining whether it suits the person's needs and with the intention of returning to the dwelling if it proves not to suit the person's needs;

(b)   a period of absence not exceeding 13 weeks, beginning with the first whole day of absence from the dwelling and for so long as–

    (i)   the person intends to return to the dwelling;

    (ii)   the part of the dwelling in which the person usually resides is not let or sub-let; and

    (iii)   that period of absence is unlikely to exceed 13 weeks; or

(c)   a period of absence not exceeding 52 weeks, beginning with the first whole day of that absence and for so long as–

    (i)   the person intends to return to the dwelling;

    (ii)   the part of the dwelling in which the person usually resides is not let or sub-let;

    (iii)   the person is a person to whom paragraph (4) applies; and

    (iv)   the period of absence is unlikely to exceed 52 weeks or, in exceptional circumstances, is unlikely substantially to exceed 52 weeks.

(4)   This paragraph applies to a person who is–

(a)   (i) detained in custody on remand pending trial or required, as a condition of bail, to reside–

       (aa)   in a dwelling, other than the dwelling referred to in paragraph (1); or

       (bb)   in premises approved under section 13 of the Offender Management Act 2007; or

    (ii)   detained in custody pending sentence upon conviction;

(b)   resident in a hospital or similar institution as a patient;

(c)   undergoing, or who has a partner or dependent child who is undergoing, in the United Kingdom or elsewhere, medical treatment or medically approved convalescence in accommodation other than residential accommodation;

(d)   following, in the United Kingdom or elsewhere, a training course;

(e)   undertaking medically approved care of a person residing in the United Kingdom or elsewhere;

(f)   undertaking the care of a child whose parent or guardian is temporarily absent from the dwelling normally occupied by that parent or guardian for the purpose of receiving medically approved care or medical treatment;

(g)   receiving medically approved care in the United Kingdom or elsewhere, provided in accommodation other than residential accommodation;

(h)   a student;

(i)   receiving care provided in residential accommodation other than a person to whom paragraph (3)(a) applies; or

(j)   a person who left the dwelling the person resides in through fear of violence in that dwelling or by a former member of the person's family.

(5)   This paragraph applies to a person who is–

(a)   detained in custody pending sentence upon conviction or under a sentence imposed by a court (other than a person who is detained in hospital under the provisions of the Mental Health Act 1983, the Criminal Procedure (Scotland) Act 1995 or the Mental Health (Care and Treatment) (Scotland) Act 2003); or

(b)   on temporary release from detention in accordance with Rules made under the provisions of the Prisons (Scotland) Act 1989 or the Prison Act 1952.

(6)   Where paragraph (5) applies to a person, for any day when the person is on temporary release–

(a)   if that temporary release was immediately preceded by a period of temporary absence under paragraph (3)(b) or (c)–

    (i)   for the purposes of paragraph (1) the person is to be treated as if still absent from the dwelling; and

(ii)   for the purposes of paragraph (4)(a), the person is to be treated as if still in detention;

(b)   if sub-paragraph (a) does not apply the person is to be treated as absent from the dwelling for the purpose of paragraph (1).

General Note

Reg 15 is broadly similar in effect to reg 7(13), (16) and (17) HB Regs, but see the Analysis to reg 15 CTR(S) Regs on p1480 for an important difference.

Persons not entitled to council tax reduction: persons treated as not being in Great Britain

16.–(1)   Subject to paragraph (5), a person is not entitled to council tax reduction in respect of a day and a dwelling of which the person is a resident if the person is throughout that day treated as not being in Great Britain in accordance with this regulation.

(2)   Subject to paragraph (5), a person is to be treated as not being in Great Britain if that person is not habitually resident in the United Kingdom, the Channel Islands, the Isle of Man or the Republic of Ireland.

(3)   A person is not to be treated as habitually resident in the United Kingdom, the Channel Islands, the Isle of Man or the Republic of Ireland unless the person has a right to reside in one of those places.

(4)   For the purposes of paragraph (3), a right to reside does not include a right which exists by virtue of, or in accordance with,–

(a)   regulation 13 of the 2006 Regulations; or

(b)   Article 6 of Directive 2004/38/EC of the European Parliament and of the Council on the rights of citizens of the Union and their family members to move and reside within the territory of the Member States.

(5)   A person is not to be treated as not being in Great Britain if that person is–

(a)   a qualified person for the purposes of regulation 6 of the 2006 Regulations as a worker or a self-employed person;

(b)   a family member of a person referred to in paragraph (a) within the meaning of regulation 7 of the 2006 Regulations;

(c)   a person who has a right to reside permanently in the United Kingdom by virtue of regulation 15(1)(c), (d) or (e) of the 2006 Regulations;

(d)   a refugee within the definition in Article 1 of the Convention relating to the Status of Refugees done at Geneva on 28th July 1951, as extended by Article 1(2) of the Protocol relating to the Status of Refugees done at New York on 31st January 1967;

[¹(e)   a person who has been granted, or who is deemed to have been granted, leave outside the rules made under section 3(2) of the Immigration Act 1971 where that leave is–

(i)   discretionary leave to enter or remain in the United Kingdom;

(ii)   leave to remain under the Destitution Domestic Violence concession; or

(iii)   leave deemed to have been granted by virtue of regulation 3 of the Displaced Persons (Temporary Protection) Regulations 2005;]

(f)   a person who has humanitarian protection granted under the rules referred to in sub-paragraph (e); [¹]

(g)   a person who is not a person subject to immigration control within the meaning of section 115(9) of the Immigration and Asylum Act 1999 and who is in the United Kingdom as a result of that person's deportation, expulsion or other removal by compulsion of law from another country to the United Kingdom [¹;]

[¹(h)   in receipt of income support, an income-based jobseeker's allowance or on an income-related employment and support allowance; or]

[¹(i)   a person who is treated as a worker for the purpose of the definition of "qualified person" in regulation 6(1) of the 2006 Regulations pursuant to regulation 5 of the Accession of Croatia (Immigration and Worker Authorisation) Regulations 2013 (right of residence of a Croatian who is an accession State national subject to worker authorisation).]

(6)   In this regulation "the 2006 Regulations" means the Immigration (European Economic Area) Regulations 2006.

Amendment

1.   Amended by reg 16 of SSI 2015 No 46 as from 1.4.15.

General Note

This is similar to the HB equivalent. However, amendments made to reg 10 HB Regs which clarify the position for those granted limited leave to enter or remain under the EU Settlement Scheme and reflect the fact that the Immigration (European Economic Area) Regulations 2006 have been revoked and replaced by the Immigration (European Economic Area) Regulations 2016, have not, at the time of writing, been replicated in this regulation. See p299 for commentary.

Persons treated as being in Great Britain

17.–(1)   A person to whom paragraph (2) or (3) applies is to be treated as being in Great Britain, unless the person is to be treated as not in Great Britain under regulation 16.

(2)   This paragraph applies to a person who is outside Great Britain in that person's capacity as–
(a)   an aircraft worker;
(b)   a continental shelf worker who is in a designated area or a prescribed area;
(c)   a Crown servant;
(d)   a mariner; or
(e)   a member of Her Majesty's forces.

(3)   This paragraph applies to a person if–
(a)   that person is a member of a couple and the other member of the couple is a person to whom paragraph (2) applies; and
(b)   the person is outside Great Britain by reason only of the fact that the person is living with the other member of the couple.

(4)   In this regulation–
(a)   "aircraft worker" means a person who is employed under a contract of service as a pilot, commander, navigator or other member of the crew of any aircraft or in any other capacity on board any aircraft where–
(i)   the employment in that other capacity is for the purposes of the aircraft or its crew or of any passengers or cargo or mail carried on that aircraft; and
(ii)   the contract is entered into in the United Kingdom with a view to its performance (in whole or in part) while the aircraft is in flight;
(b)   "continental shelf worker" means a person who is employed, whether under a contract of service or not, in a designated area or a prescribed area in connection with any activity mentioned in section 11(2) of Petroleum Act 1998;
(c)   "Crown servant" means a person employed by or under the Crown;
(d)   "designated area" means any area which may from time to time be designated by Order in Council under the Continental Shelf Act 1964 as an area within which the rights of the United Kingdom with respect to the seabed and subsoil and their natural resources may be exercised;
(e)   "mariner" means a person who is employed under a contract of service as a master or member of the crew of any ship or vessel or in any other capacity on board any ship or vessel where–
(i)   the employment in that other capacity is for the purposes of that ship or vessel or its crew or any passengers or cargo or mails carried by the ship or vessel; and
(ii)   the contract is entered into in the United Kingdom with a view to its performance (in whole or in part) while the ship or vessel is on its voyage; and
(f)   "prescribed area" means any area over which Norway or any member State of the European Union (other than the United Kingdom) exercises sovereign rights for the purpose of exploring the seabed and subsoil and exploiting their natural resources, being an area outside the territorial seas of Norway or that member

State, or any other area which is from time to time specified under section 10(8) of the Petroleum Act 1998.

Temporary absence from Great Britain

18.–(1)   For the purposes of determining whether a person is in Great Britain, a person's temporary absence from Great Britain is disregarded–

(a)   for the first month of the temporary absence if paragraph (2) applies; or

(b)   for the first 6 months of the temporary absence if paragraph (3) applies.

(2)   This paragraph applies where–

(a)   the person was entitled to council tax reduction immediately before the beginning of the period of temporary absence; and

(b)   the person has not been absent on more than 2 occasions in the previous 52 weeks, starting from the first day of the current period of temporary absence.

(3)   This paragraph applies where–

(a)   the person was entitled to council tax reduction immediately before the beginning of thc period of tcmporary absence; and

(b)   the absence is solely in connection with–

(i)   the treatment of the person for an illness or physical or mental disability by, or under the supervision of, a person appropriately qualified to carry out that treatment;

(ii)   the person accompanying a person described in paragraph (5) for the treatment of the person so described for an illness or physical or mental disability by, or under the supervision of, a person appropriately qualified to carry out that treatment; or

(iii)   the person undergoing medically approved convalescence or care as a result of treatment for an illness or physical or mental disability, where the person had that illness or disability before leaving Great Britain.

(4)   The period in paragraph (1)(a) may be extended by up to a one month if–

(a)   the temporary absence is in connection with the death of–

(i)   a person described in paragraph (5); or

(ii)   a close relative of the person or a close relative of a person described in paragraph (5); and

(b)   the relevant authority is satisfied that it would be unreasonable to expect the person to return to Great Britain within the first month.

(5)   A person described by this paragraph is–

(a)   where the person is a member of a couple, the other member of the couple; or

(b)   a child or young person for whom the person, or where the person is a member of a couple, the other member of the couple, is responsible.

(6)   In this regulation "appropriately qualified" means qualified to provide medical treatment or physiotherapy or a form of treatment which is similar to, or related to, either of those forms of treatment.

Persons not entitled to council tax reduction: persons subject to immigration control

19.–[¹(1)   A person is not entitled to council tax reduction in respect of a day and a dwelling of which the person is a resident if the person is throughout that day a person subject to immigration control [¹].

[¹ (2)   In paragraph (1) "a person subject to immigration control" has the meaning given in section 115(9) of the Immigration and Asylum Act 1999, but does not include a person who–

(a)   is a national of a state which has ratified the European Convention on Social and Medical Assistance (done in Paris on 11th December 1953) or a state which has ratified the Council of Europe Social Charter (signed in Turin on 18th October 1961); and

(b)   is lawfully present in the United Kingdom.]

Amendment

1.   Amended by reg 17 of SSI 2015 No 46 as from 1.4.15.

General Note

See the commentary to s115(9) IAA on p1707.

[¹ Non-recovery of council tax arrears caused by official error

19A.–(1)   Arrears of council tax are not recoverable if they arise in consequence of an over-entitlement to council tax reduction as described in paragraph (2).

(2)   This paragraph applies to an over-entitlement which arises in consequence of an official error where the claimant or a person acting on their behalf or any other person to whom the council tax reduction is awarded could not have reasonably been expected to realise that it was an over-entitlement at the time it arose or upon any subsequent notification of entitlement.

(3)   In this regulation, "over-entitlement" means an amount of council tax reduction which was awarded and to which there was no entitlement (whether on the initial decision or as subsequently reviewed or superseded or further reviewed or superseded).

(4)   In this regulation, "official error" means a mistake, whether in the form of an act or omission, by–

(a)   the relevant authority,

(b)   an officer or person acting for the relevant authority, or

(c)   a person providing services to the relevant authority,

where the claimant, a person acting on their behalf or any other person to whom the council tax reduction is awarded, did not cause or materially contribute to that mistake.]

Amendment

1.   Inserted by reg 10 of SSI 2019 No 29 as from 1.4.19.

General Note

Reg 19A, in force from 1 April 2019, is identical to reg 20A CTR(S) Regs. See p1486 for commentary.

PART 5
Applicable amount

Applicable amount

20.   An applicant's applicable amount is the aggregate of each of the following amounts which apply in the applicant's case–

(a)   an amount in respect of the applicant's personal allowance, determined in accordance with paragraph 2 of Schedule 1;

(b)   an amount in respect of any child or young person who is a member of the applicant's family, determined in accordance with paragraph 3 of Schedule 1 (personal allowances);

[¹]

(d)   the amount of any premium which may be applicable to the applicant, determined in accordance with Parts 3 and 4 of Schedule 1 (disability premiums).

Amendment

1.   Omitted by reg 18(1) of SSI 2016 No 81 as from 1.5.16, subject to transitional provision in reg 2 of SSI 2016 No 81.

General Note

This is similar to the HB equivalent, but one significant difference is that there is no restriction on the number of children for whom you can receive an amount under Sch 1 para 3 (ie, the so called 'two-child limit', which in some circumstances applies to HB and to CTR in England, does not apply to CTR in Scotland). See p765 for the commentary.

PART 6
Income and Capital

Chapter 1
General

Calculation of income and capital of members of applicant's family and of a polygamous marriage

21.–(1)   The income and capital of an applicant's partner is to be treated as income and capital of the applicant and is to be calculated or estimated in accordance with the provisions of this Part in the same way as the applicant's income and capital is calculated or estimated and any reference to the "applicant" is, except where the context otherwise requires, to be construed for the purposes of this Part as if it included a reference to the applicant's partner.

(2)   Where an applicant or the partner of an applicant is married polygamously to two or more members of their household–

(a)   the applicant is to be treated as possessing capital and income belonging to each of those members; and

(b)   the income and capital of each of those members is to be calculated in accordance with the provisions of this Part as if the member was the applicant.

(3)   The income and capital of a child or young person is not to be treated as the income and capital of the applicant.

General Note

This is similar to the HB equivalent. See p421 for the commentary.

Circumstances in which capital and income of non-dependant is to be treated as applicant's

22.–(1)   Where it appears to the relevant authority that a non-dependant and the applicant have entered into arrangements in order to take advantage of the council tax reduction scheme set out in these Regulations and the non-dependant has more capital and income than the applicant, the authority must, except where the applicant is on a guarantee credit, treat the applicant as possessing the capital and income of the non-dependant and must disregard any capital and income which the applicant does possess.

(2)   Where an applicant is treated as possessing the capital and income of a non-dependant under paragraph (1) the capital and income of that non-dependant is to be calculated or estimated in accordance with the provisions of this Part as if it was the capital and income of the applicant and any reference to the "applicant" is, except where the context otherwise requires, to be construed for the purposes of this Part as if it was a reference to the non-dependant.

General Note

This is similar to reg 26 HB Regs and reg 24 HB(SPC) Regs. See the commentary on reg 26 HB Regs for analysis (p422) but note that under this regulation a non-dependant's income and capital cannot be treated as the income and capital of the applicant if the applicant is on guarantee credit of PC (the same exception for people on IS, income-based JSA or income-related ESA contained in reg 26 HB Regs is not included here as being on one of these benefits would mean that these regulations would not apply: reg 12).

Chapter 2
Income and Capital

Calculation of income and capital

23.   The income and capital of the applicant is to be calculated in accordance with this Chapter.

Applicant in receipt of guarantee credit

24.   In the case of an applicant who is in receipt, or whose partner is in receipt, of a guarantee credit, the whole of the applicant's capital and income is to be disregarded.

Calculation of income in savings credit only cases

25.–(1)   Where the applicant, or any partner of the applicant, has an award of state pension credit comprising only the savings credit, subject to the following provisions of this regulation, the calculation or estimate of the applicant's or as the case may be, the applicant's partner's, income and capital by the Secretary of State for the purpose of determining that award is to be used to determine the income and capital of the applicant.

(2)   The amount of the net income calculated or estimated by the Secretary of State is to be modified only in so far as necessary to take into account–

(a)   the amount of any savings credit payable;

(b)   in respect of any dependent children of the applicant, child care charges taken into account under regulation 28(1)(c) (calculation of income on a weekly basis);

(c)   the higher amount disregarded under these Regulations in respect of–

   (i)   lone parent's earnings; or

   (ii)   a payment of aliment or maintenance, whether under a court order or not, which is made or due to be made by–

      (aa)   the applicant's former partner or the applicant's partner's former partner; or

      (bb)   the parent of a child or young person where that child or young person is a member of the applicant's family, except where that parent is the applicant or the applicant's partner;

(d)   any amount to be disregarded by virtue of paragraph 10(1) of Schedule 2 (sums to be disregarded in the calculation of earnings);

(e)   the income and capital of any partner of the applicant who is treated as a member of the applicant's household under regulation 11 (membership of a household) to the extent that it is not taken into account in determining the net income of the person claiming state pension credit;

(f)   regulation 22 (circumstances in which capital and income of non-dependant is to be treated as applicant's) if the relevant authority determines that this provision applies in the applicant's case; or

(g)   any amount to be disregarded by virtue of paragraph 6 of Schedule 2 (sums to be disregarded in the calculation of earnings).

(3)   Regulations 27 (meaning of "income") to 46 (capital jointly held) do not apply to the amount of the net income to be taken into account under paragraph (1), but do apply (so far as relevant) for the purpose of determining any modifications which fall to be made to that amount under paragraph (2).

(4)   Subject to paragraph (5), if the Secretary of State determines that the applicant's capital is more than £16,000 regulation 40 (capital limit) applies.

(5)   If paragraph (6) applies, the applicant's capital is to be calculated in accordance with regulations 40 (capital limit) to 46 (capital jointly held).

(6)   This paragraph applies if–

(a)   the determination of the Secretary of State referred to in paragraph (1) is that the applicant's capital is £16,000 or less;

(b)   subsequent to that determination the applicant's capital rises to more than £16,000; and

(c)   the increase occurs whilst there is in force an assessed income period within the meaning of sections 6 and 9 of the State Pension Credit Act 2002.

General Note

This is similar to the HB equivalent. See p767 for the commentary.

Calculation of income and capital where state pension credit is not payable

26.   Where neither regulation 24 (applicant in receipt of guarantee credit) nor 25 (calculation of applicant's income in savings credit only cases) applies in the applicant's case, the income and capital of the applicant is to be calculated or estimated in accordance with regulations 27 (meaning of "income") to 46 (capital jointly held).

Meaning of "income"

27.–(1) For the purposes of these Regulations "income" means income of any of the following descriptions

(a) earnings;

(b) working tax credit;

(c) retirement pension income;

(d) income from annuity contracts (other than retirement pension income);

(e) a war disablement pension, war widow's pension or war widower's pension;

(f) a foreign war disablement pension, foreign war widow's pension or foreign widower's pension within the meaning of section 17 of the State Pension Credit Act 2002 (other interpretation provisions);

(g) a guaranteed income payment;

(h) a payment made under article 29(1)(c) of the Armed Forces and Reserve Forces (Compensation Scheme) Order 2011 in any case where article 31(2)(c) of that Order applies;

(i) income from capital other than capital disregarded under Part 1 of Schedule 4;

(j) social security benefits other than–

　(i) retirement pension income,

　(ii) disability living allowance;

　[²(iia) armed forces independence payment;]

　(iii) personal independence payment;

　(iv) attendance allowance payable under section 64 of the 1992 Act;

　(v) an increase of disablement pension under section 104 or 105 of the 1992 Act;

　(vi) [³...]

　(vii) child benefit;

　(viii) any guardian's allowance payable under section 77 of the 1992 Act;

　(ix) any increase for a dependant, other than the applicant's partner, payable in accordance with Part 4 of the 1992 Act;

　(x) any social fund payment made under Part 8 of the 1992 Act;

　(xi) any crisis payment made for the purpose of meeting an immediate short term need or a payment made for the purpose of meeting a need for community care–

　　[⁶ (aa) from a welfare fund]

　　(bb) by a local authority in exercise of the power in section 1 of the Localism Act 2011 (local authority's general power of competence) and using funds provided by the Secretary of State, and in this sub-paragraph local authority means a local authority within the meaning of section 8 of that Act; or

　　(cc) by, or on behalf of, the Welsh Ministers in exercise of the power in section 60 of the Government of Wales Act 2006 (promotion etc. of well-being);

　(xii) Christmas bonus payable under Part 10 of the 1992 Act;

　(xiii) housing benefit;

　(xiv) council tax benefit;

　(xv) bereavement payment under section 36 of the 1992 Act;

　[⁷ (xva) bereavement support payment under section 30 of the Pensions Act 2014;]

　(xvi) statutory sick pay;

　(xvii) statutory maternity pay;

　(xviii) [⁵ statutory paternity pay];

　[⁴ (xviiia statutory shared parental pay;]

　(xix) statutory adoption pay; [⁸]

　(xx) any benefit similar to those mentioned in the preceding provisions of this paragraph payable under legislation having effect in Northern Ireland; [⁸; and

        (xxi) carer's allowance supplement made under section 81 of the Social Security (Scotland) Act 2018]

(k)   all foreign social security benefits which are similar to the social security benefits described above;

(l)   a payment made under–
     (i)   article 30 of the 2006 Order in any case where article 30(1)(b) of that Order applies; or
     (ii)   article 12(8) of the 2006 Order in any case where article 12(8)(b) of that Order applies;

(m)   a pension paid to victims of National Socialist persecution under any special provision made by the law of the Federal Republic of Germany, or any part of it, or of the Republic of Austria;

(n)   payments under a scheme made under the Pneumoconiosis etc. (Worker's Compensation) Act 1979;

(o)   payments made towards the maintenance of the applicant by the applicant's spouse, civil partner, former spouse or former civil partner or towards the maintenance of the applicant's partner by the applicant's partner's spouse, civil partner, former spouse or former civil partner, including payments made–
     (i)   under a court order;
     (ii)   under an agreement for aliment or maintenance; or
     (iii) voluntarily;

(p)   payments due from any person in respect of board and lodging accommodation provided by the applicant;

(q)   royalties or other sums paid as a consideration for the use of, or the right to use, any copyright, design, patent or trade mark;

(r)   any payment in respect of any–
     (i)   book registered under the Public Lending Right Scheme 1982; or
     (ii)   work made under any international public lending right scheme that is analogous to the Public Lending Right Scheme 1982;

(s)   any payment, other than a payment ordered by a court or made in settlement of a claim, made by or on behalf of a former employer of a person on account of the early retirement of that person on grounds of ill-health or disability;

(t)   any sum payable by way of pension out of money provided under the Civil List Act 1837, the Civil List Act 1937, the Civil List Act 1952, the Civil List Act 1972 or the Civil List Act 1975;

(u)   any income in lieu of that specified in sub-paragraphs (a) to (r);

(v)   any payment of rent made to an applicant who–
     [1(i)   owns, owns the freehold or leasehold interest in or is a tenant of the property in respect of which the rent is paid;]
     (ii)   occupies part of the property; and
     (iii) has an agreement with another person allowing that other person to occupy the property on payment of rent;

(w)   any payment made at regular intervals under an equity release scheme; and

(x)   PPF periodic payments within the meaning of section 17 of the State Pension Credit Act 2002.

(2)   For the purposes of these Regulations and subject to regulations 31(11)(b) (calculation of weekly income: capital disregards) and 41(2) (calculation of capital: capital to be disregarded), an applicant's capital is to be treated as if it was a weekly income of–

(a)   £1 for each £500 in excess of £10,000; and

(b)   £1 for any part of that excess which is not a complete £500.

(3)   Where the payment of any social security benefit referred to paragraph (1) is subject to any deduction (other than an adjustment specified in paragraph (5)) the amount to be taken into account under paragraph (1) is the amount before the deduction is made.

(4)   Where an award of any working tax credit or child tax credit is subject to a deduction by way of recovery of an overpayment of working tax credit or child tax credit made in a previous tax year the amount to be taken into account under paragraph (1) is

the amount of working tax credit or child tax credit awarded less the amount of that deduction.

   (5)   The adjustments specified in this paragraph are those made in accordance with–

(a)   the Social Security (Overlapping Benefits) Regulations 1979;

(b)   the Social Security (Hospital In-Patients) Regulations 2005;

(c)   section 30DD or section 30E of the 1992 Act (reductions in incapacity benefit in respect of pensions and councillor's allowances); or

(d)   section 3 of the Welfare Reform Act 2007 (deductions from contributory employment and support allowance in respect of pensions and councillor's allowances) and regulations made under it.

   (6)   In this regulation "equity release scheme" means a loan–

(a)   made between a person ("the lender") and the applicant;

(b)   by means of which a sum of money is advanced by the lender to the applicant by way of payments at regular intervals; and

(c)   which is secured on a dwelling in which the applicant owns an interest and occupies as a home.

Amendments

1.   Amended by reg 5 of SSI 2013 No 49 as from 18.3.13.
2.   Inserted by reg 12(3) of SSI 2013 No 142 as from 11.6.13.
3.   Omitted by reg 11 of SSI 2013 No 3218 as from 1.10.13.
4.   Inserted by art 24(4)(b) of SI 2014 No 255 as from 31.12.14.
5.   Amended by art 24(4)(a) of SI 2014 No.3255 as from 5.4.15.
6.   Substituted by reg 17(4) of SSI 2016 No 81 as from 1.4.16.
7.   Inserted by reg 13 of SSI 2017 No 326 as from 20.11.17.
8.   Amended by reg 6 of SSI 2018 No 211 as from 27.10.18.

Modifications

The amendments made by SI 2014 No.3255 which came into force on 5 April 2015 do not have effect in relation to ordinary statutory paternity pay which is paid, additional statutory paternity pay which is paid, a period in respect of which additional statutory paternity pay is payable which begins, or continues, ordinary paternity leave which is taken or additional paternity leave which is taken on or after 5 April 2015. See art 35 of SI 2014 No.3255.

General Note

This is similar to the HB equivalent. See p771 for the commentary. From 27 October 2018, carer's allowance supplement, a Scottish benefit which is paid twice yearly to claimants who live in Scotland and are receiving carer's allowance on the relevant qualifying dates, is not counted as income for CTR: sub-para (1)(j)(xxi).

Calculation of income on a weekly basis

   28.–(1)   For the purposes of regulation 14(5) [¹ or 14A(5)] (conditions of entitlement to council tax reduction) the income of an applicant is to be calculated on a weekly basis by–

(a)   calculating or estimating the amount which is likely to be the applicant's average weekly income in accordance with this Part;

(b)   adding to that amount the weekly income calculated under regulation 27(2) (meaning of "income": calculation of tariff income from capital); and

(c)   then deducting any relevant child care charges to which regulation 29 (treatment of child care charges) applies from any earnings which form part of the average weekly income or, in a case where the conditions in paragraph (2) are met, from those earnings plus whichever credit specified in paragraph (2)(b) is appropriate, up to a maximum deduction in respect of the applicant's family of whichever of the sums specified in paragraph (3) applies in the applicant's case.

   (2)   The conditions referred to in paragraph (1)(c) are that–

(a)   the applicant's earnings which form part of the applicant's average weekly income are less than the lower of the relevant child care charges or whichever of the deductions specified in paragraph (3) otherwise applies; and

(b)   the applicant or, if the applicant is a member of a couple, either of them is in receipt of working tax credit or child tax credit.

   (3)   The maximum deduction to which paragraph (1)(c) refers is–

(a)   where the applicant's family includes only one child in respect of whom relevant child care charges are paid, £175 per week; and

(b)   where the applicant's family includes more than one child in respect of whom relevant child care charges are paid, £300 per week.

Amendment

1.   Amended by reg 12 of SSI 2016 No 253 as from 1.4.17.

General Note

This is similar to the HB equivalent. See p424 for the commentary.

Treatment of child care charges

29.–(1)   This regulation applies where an applicant is incurring relevant child care charges and–

(a)   is a lone parent and is engaged in remunerative work;

(b)   is a member of a couple where both are engaged in remunerative work; or

(c)   is a member of a couple where one member is engaged in remunerative work and the other is–

(i)   incapacitated as described in paragraph (11);

(ii)   a patient; or

(iii)   in prison (whether serving a custodial sentence or remanded in custody awaiting trial or sentence).

(2)   For the purposes of paragraph (1) and subject to paragraph (4), a person to whom paragraph (3) applies is to be treated as engaged in remunerative work for a period not exceeding 28 weeks during which the person is–

(a)   paid statutory sick pay;

(b)   paid short-term incapacity benefit at the lower rate under section 30A of the 1992 Act;

(c)   paid an employment and support allowance;

(d)   paid income support on the grounds of incapacity for work under regulation 4ZA of, and paragraph 7 or 14 of Schedule 1B to, the Income Support Regulations; or

(e)   credited with earnings on the grounds of incapacity for work or limited capability for work under regulation 8B of the Social Security (Credits) Regulations 1975.

(3)   This paragraph applies to a person who was engaged in remunerative work immediately before, as the case may be–

(a)   the first day of the period in respect of which the person was first paid statutory sick pay, short-term incapacity benefit, an employment and support allowance or income support on the grounds of incapacity for work; or

(b)   the first day of the period in respect of which earnings are credited.

(4)   In a case to which paragraph (2)(d) or (e) applies, the period of 28 weeks begins on the day on which the person is first paid income support or on the first day of the period in respect of which earnings are credited, as the case may be.

(5)   Relevant child care charges are the charges for care referred to in paragraphs (6) and (7) and they must be calculated on a weekly basis in accordance with paragraph (10).

(6) The charges referred to in paragraph (5) are charges for care which is provided–

(a)   in the case of any child of the applicant's family who is not disabled, in respect of the period beginning on that child's date of birth and ending on the day preceding the first Monday in September following that child's fifteenth birthday; or

(b)   in the case of any child of the applicant's family who is disabled, in respect of the period beginning on that child's date of birth and ending on the day preceding the first Monday in September following their sixteenth birthday.

(7)   The charges referred to in paragraph (5) are charges for care which is provided by one or more of the care providers listed in paragraph (8) and not paid–

(a)   in respect of the child's compulsory education;

(b)   by an applicant to a partner or by a partner to an applicant in respect of any child for whom either or any of them is responsible in accordance with regulation 10 (responsibility for another person); or

(c)   in respect of care provided by a relative of the child wholly or mainly in the child's home.

(8)   The care to which paragraph (7) refers may be provided–

(a)   out of school hours, by a school on school premises or by a local authority–

  (i)   for a child who is not disabled, in respect of the period beginning on the child's eighth birthday and ending on the day preceding the first Monday in September following the child's fifteenth birthday; or

  (ii)   for a child who is disabled, in respect of the period beginning on the child's eighth birthday and ending on the day preceding the first Monday in September following their sixteenth birthday;

(b)   by a child care provider approved in accordance with the Tax Credit (New Category of Child Care Provider) Regulations 1999;

(c)   by persons registered under Part 2 of the Children and Families (Wales) Measure 2010;

(d)   by a person who is excepted from registration under Part 2 of the Children and Families (Wales) Measure 2010 because the child care the person provides is in a school or establishment referred to in article 11, 12 or 14 of the Child Minding and Day Care Exceptions (Wales) Order 2010;

(e)   by–

  (i)   persons registered under section 59(1) of the Public Services Reform (Scotland) Act 2010; or

  (ii)   local authorities registered under section 83(1) of that Act, where the care provided is child minding or day care of children within the meaning of that Act;

(f)   by a person prescribed in regulations made pursuant to section 12(4) of the Tax Credits Act 2002;

(g)   by a person who is registered under Chapter 2 or 3 of Part 3 of the Childcare Act 2006;

(h)   by any of the schools mentioned in section 34(2) of the Childcare Act 2006 in circumstances where the requirement to register under Chapter 2 of Part 3 of that Act does not apply by virtue of that sub-section;

(i)   by any of the schools mentioned in section 53(2) of the Childcare Act 2006 in circumstances where the requirement to register under Chapter 3 of Part 3 of that Act does not apply by virtue of that sub-section;

(j)   by any of the establishments mentioned in section 18(5) of the Childcare Act 2006 in circumstances where the care is not included in the meaning of "childcare" for the purposes of Parts 1 and 3 of that Act by virtue of that subsection;

(k)   by a foster carer or kinship carer approved under the Looked After Children (Scotland) Regulations 2009 in relation to a child other than a child who has been placed with that carer–

  (i)   by virtue of a requirement of the children's hearing under section 70(3)(a) of the Children (Scotland) Act 1995;

  (ii)   by a local authority exercising the right to determine the residence of a child in respect of whom a permanence order has been granted under section 81 of the Adoption and Children (Scotland) Act 2007; or

  (iii) in accordance with the Looked After Children (Scotland) Regulations 2009;

(l)   by a foster parent under the Fostering Services (England) Regulations 2011 or the Fostering Services (Wales) Regulations 2003 in relation to a child other than one whom the foster parent is fostering;

(m)   by a carer under the Health and Social Care Act 2008 (Regulated Activities) Regulations 2010 or the Domiciliary Care Agencies (Wales) Regulations 2004; or

(n)   by a person who is not a relative of the child wholly or mainly in the child's home.

(9)   In paragraphs (6) and (8)(a) "the first Monday in September" means the Monday which first occurs in the month of September in any year.

(10)   Relevant child care charges must be estimated over a period, not exceeding a year, that is appropriate to allow the average weekly charge to be estimated accurately having regard to information about the amount of that charge provided by the person providing the care.

(11)   For the purposes of paragraph (1)(c), the other member of a couple is incapacitated where–

(a)   that other member is aged 80 or more; or

(b)   that other member is aged less than 80 and–

    (i)   an additional condition specified in paragraph 10 of Schedule 1 to the Council Tax Reduction (Scotland) Regulations 2012 (additional condition for the disability premium) is treated as applying in that other member's case; and

    (ii)   that other member satisfies that additional condition or would but for the other member being treated as capable of work by virtue of a determination made in accordance with regulations made under section 171E of the 1992 Act;

(c)   had the applicant's applicable amount fallen to be calculated under the Council Tax Reduction Regulations it would include the support component or the work-related activity component on account of the other member having limited capability for work but for that other member being treated as not having limited capability for work by virtue of a determination made in accordance with the Employment and Support Allowance Regulations;

(d)   the applicant is, or is treated as, incapable of work and has been incapable, or treated as incapable, of work in accordance with the provisions of, and regulations made under, Part 12A of the 1992 Act (incapacity for work) for a continuous period of not less than 196 days, and for this purpose any two or more separate periods separated by a break of not more than 56 days are to be treated as one continuous period;

(e)   the applicant is, or is treated as having, limited capability for work and has had, or been treated as having, limited capability for work in accordance with the Employment and Support Allowance Regulations for a continuous period of not less than 196 days and for this purpose any two or more separate periods separated by a break of not more than 84 days are to be treated as one continuous period;

(f)   there is payable in respect of the other member one or more of the following pensions or allowances–

    (i)   long-term incapacity benefit or short-term incapacity benefit at the higher rate under Schedule 4 to the 1992 Act;

    (ii)   attendance allowance under section 64 of the 1992 Act;

    (iii)   severe disablement allowance under section 68 of the 1992 Act;

    (iv)   disability living allowance;

    [[1](iva) armed forces independence payment;]

    (v)   personal independence payment;

    (vi)   an increase of disablement pension under section 104 of the 1992 Act;

    (vii)   a pension increase paid as part of a war disablement pension or under an industrial injuries scheme which is analogous to an allowance or increase of disablement pension under head (ii), (iv) or (vi) above; or

    (viii)   main phase employment and support allowance;

(g)   a pension or allowance to which sub-paragraph (f)(ii), (iv), [[2](v),] (vi) or (vii) refers was payable on account of the other member's incapacity but has ceased to be payable in consequence of the other member becoming a patient within the meaning of Schedule 1 (applicable amount);

(h)   sub-paragraph (f) or (g) would apply to the other member if the legislative provisions referred to in those sub-paragraphs were provisions under any corresponding enactment having effect in Northern Ireland; or

(i)   the other member has an invalid carriage or other vehicle provided under section 46 of the National Health Service (Scotland) Act 1978, paragraph 9(1) of Schedule 1 to the National Health Service Act 2006 or article 30(1) of the Health and Personal Social Services (Northern Ireland) Order 1972.

(12)   Where paragraph (11)(d) applies and the applicant ceases to be, or to be treated as, incapable of work but within a period of 56 days or less of that cessation the applicant is, or is treated as, incapable of work, paragraph 11(d) applies from the time the applicant is again, or is again treated as, incapable of work for so long as the applicant is, or is treated as, incapable of work.

(13)   Where paragraph (11)(e) applies and the applicant ceases to have, or to be treated as having, limited capability for work but within a period of 84 days or less of that cessation the applicant has, or is treated as having, limited capability for work, paragraph 11(e) applies from the time the applicant has again, or is again treated as having, limited capability for work for so long as that situation continues.

(14)   For the purposes of paragraphs (6) and (8)(a), a person is disabled if the person is a person–

(a)   in respect of whom disability living allowance or personal independence payment is payable, or has ceased to be payable solely because the person is a patient [¹, or in respect of whom armed forces independence payment is payable];

(b)   who has been certified as blind and in consequence is registered as blind in a register maintained by or on behalf of a local authority in Scotland or is registered as blind in a register compiled under section 29 of the National Assistance Act 1948 (welfare services) [⁵, or is registered as severely sight-impaired in a register kept by a local authority in Wales under section 18(1)(a) of the Social Services and Well-being (Wales) Act 2014]; or

(c)   who ceased to be registered as blind in a register referred to in sub-paragraph (b) within the period beginning 28 weeks before the first Monday in September following the person's fifteenth birthday and ending on the day preceding the person's sixteenth birthday.

(15)   For the purposes of paragraph (1) a person on maternity leave, paternity leave [³, shared parental leave] or adoption leave is to be treated as if engaged in remunerative work for the period specified in paragraph (16) ("the relevant period") provided that–

(a)   in the week before the period of maternity leave, paternity leave [³, shared parental leave] or adoption leave began the person was in remunerative work;

(b)   the person is incurring relevant child care charges; and

(c)   the person is entitled to statutory maternity pay, [⁴ statutory paternity pay] [⁴], [³ statutory shared parental pay, statutory adoption pay] or maternity allowance under section 35 of the 1992 Act;

(16)   For the purposes of paragraph (15) the relevant period begins on the day on which the person's maternity leave, paternity leave [³ , shared parental leave] or adoption leave commences and ends on the earliest of–

(a)   the date that leave ends;

(b)   if no child care element of working tax credit is in payment on the date that entitlement to maternity allowance, statutory maternity pay, [⁴ statutory paternity pay] [⁴] [³, statutory shared parental pay or statutory adoption pay ends], the date that entitlement ends; or

(c)   if a child care element of working tax credit is in payment on the date that entitlement to maternity allowance, statutory maternity pay, [⁴ statutory paternity pay] [⁴] [³, statutory shared parental pay or statutory adoption pay ends], the date that entitlement to the child care element of the working tax credit ends.

(17)   In this regulation–

(a)   "child care element of working tax credit" means the element of working tax credit prescribed under section 12 of the Tax Credits Act 2002 (child care element); and

(b)   "invalid carriage or other vehicle" means a vehicle propelled by a petrol engine or by electric power supplied for use on the road and to be controlled by the occupant.

Amendments

1.   Inserted by reg 12(4) of SSI 2013 No 142 as from 11.6.13.
2.   Inserted by reg 12 of SSI 2013 No 218 as from 1.10.13.
3.   Amended by art 24(5)(a)(i) and (iv) and (b)(i) and (iv) of SI 2014 No 3255 as from 31.12.14.
4.   Amended by art 24(5)(a)(ii) and (iii) and (b)(ii) of SI 2014 No 3255 as from 5.4.15.
5.   Inserted by reg 19(1) of SSI 2016 No 81 as from 6.4.16.

Modifications

The amendments made by SI 2014 No.3255 which came into force on 5 April 2015 do not have effect in relation to ordinary statutory paternity pay which is paid, additional statutory paternity pay which is paid, a period in respect of which additional statutory paternity pay is payable which begins, or continues, ordinary paternity leave which is taken or additional paternity leave which is taken on or after 5 April 2015. See art 35 of SI 2014 No.3255.

General Note

This is similar to the HB equivalent. See p429 for the commentary. For commentary on the need to register as blind or severely sight impaired to satisfy sub para (14)(b), see the General Note to Sch 2 para 6 of The Council Tax Reduction Schemes and Prescribed Requirements (Wales) Regulations 2013 No.3029 (p1248).

Calculation of average weekly income from [¹] tax credits

30.–(1)   This regulation applies where an applicant receives a working tax credit [¹ or child tax credit].

(2)   [¹] the period over which [¹ that] tax credit is to be taken into account is the period set out in paragraph (3).

(3)   Where the instalment in respect of which payment of [¹ that] tax credit is made is–

(a)   a daily instalment, the period is one day, being the day in respect of which the instalment is paid;

(b)   a weekly instalment, the period is 7 days, ending on the day on which the instalment is due to be paid;

(c)   a two weekly instalment, the period is 14 days, commencing 6 days before the day on which the instalment is due to be paid; and

(d)   a 4 weekly instalment, the period is 28 days, ending on the day on which the instalment is due to be paid.

Amendment

1.   Amended by regs 16 and 17 of SSI 2013 No 287 as from 25.11.13.

General Note

This is similar to the HB equivalent. See p435 for the commentary.

Calculation of weekly income

31.–(1)   Except where paragraphs (2) and (4) apply, for the purposes of calculating the weekly income of the applicant, where the period in respect of which a payment of income is made–

(a)   does not exceed a week, the whole of that payment is to be included in the applicant's weekly income; and

(b)   exceeds a week, the weekly amount is to be determined–

(i)   in a case where that period is a month, by multiplying the amount of the payment by 12 and dividing the product by 52;

(ii)   in a case where that period is 3 months, by multiplying the amount of the payment by 4 and dividing the product by 52;

(iii)   in a case where that period is a year, by dividing the amount of the payment by 52; and

(iv)   in any other case, by multiplying the amount of the payment by 7 and dividing the product by the number of days in the period in respect of which it is made.

(2) The weekly amount of the applicant's income is to be determined–

(a) where the applicant's regular pattern of work is such that the applicant does not work the same hours every week and there is a recognised cycle of work, by reference to the applicant's average weekly income over the period of the complete cycle (including, where the cycle involves periods in which the applicant does no work, those periods but disregarding any other absences); or

(b) if the applicant's income fluctuates and has changed more than once, on the basis of–

(i) the last two payments if those payments are one month or more apart;

(ii) the last 4 payments if the last two payments are less than one month apart; or

(iii) calculating or estimating any other payments that may, in the particular circumstances of the case, enable the applicant's average weekly income to be determined more accurately.

(3) For the purposes of paragraph (2)(b) the last payments are the last payments before the date the application was made or treated as made or, if there is a subsequent supersession under paragraph 4 of Schedule 7 to the Child Support, Pensions and Social Security Act 2000, the last payments before the date of the supersession.

(4) If an applicant is entitled to receive a payment to which paragraph (5) applies, the amount of that payment is to be treated as if made in respect of a period of a year.

(5) This paragraph applies to–

(a) royalties or other sums paid as a consideration for the use of, or the right to use, any copyright, design, patent or trade mark;

(b) any payment in respect of any–

(i) book registered under the Public Lending Right Scheme 1982; or

(ii) work made under any international public lending right scheme that is analogous to the Public Lending Right Scheme 1982; and

(c) any payment made on an occasional basis.

(6) The period under which any benefit under the benefit Acts is to be taken into account is the period in respect of which that benefit is payable.

(7) Where payments are made in a currency other than sterling, the value of the payment is to be determined by taking the sterling equivalent on the date the payment is made.

(8) The sums specified in Schedule 2 (sums to be disregarded in the calculation of earnings) must be disregarded when calculating–

(a) the applicant's earnings; and

(b) any amount to which paragraph (5) applies where the applicant is the first owner of the copyright, design, patent or trademark or an original contributor to a book or work referred to in paragraph (5)(b).

(9) For the purposes of paragraph (8)(b) only, the amounts specified in paragraph (5) are to be treated as though they were earnings.

(10) Income specified in Schedule 3 (sums to be disregarded in the calculation of income other than earnings) is to be disregarded in the calculation of an applicant's income.

(11) Schedule 4 (capital disregards) has effect so that–

(a) the capital specified in Part 1 must be disregarded for the purpose of determining an applicant's income; and

(b) the capital specified in Part 2 must be disregarded for the purpose of determining an applicant's income under regulation 27(2) (meaning of "income": deemed income").

(12) In the case of any income taken into account for the purpose of calculating a person's income, any amount payable by way of tax must be disregarded.

General Note

This is similar to the HB equivalent. See p429 for the commentary.

Chapter 3
Employed earners

Earnings of employed earners

32.–(1)   Subject to paragraph (2), "earnings" means in the case of employment as an employed earner any remuneration or profit derived from that employment and includes–

(a)   any bonus or commission;

(b)   any payment in lieu of remuneration except any periodic sum paid to an applicant on account of the termination of the applicant's employment by reason of redundancy;

(c)   any payment in lieu of notice or any lump sum payment intended as compensation for the loss of employment but only so far as it represents loss of income;

(d)   any holiday pay except any payable more than 4 weeks after termination or interruption of the employment;

(e)   any payment by way of a retainer;

(f)   any payment made by the applicant's employer in respect of expenses not wholly, exclusively and necessarily incurred in the performance of the duties of the employment, including any payment made by the applicant's employer in respect of–

(i)   travelling expenses incurred by the applicant between the applicant's home and place of employment; or

(ii)   expenses incurred by the applicant under arrangements made for the care of a member of the applicant's family owing to the applicant's absence from home;

(g)   the amount of any payment by way of a non-cash voucher which has been taken into account in the computation of a person's earnings in accordance with Part 5 of Schedule 3 to the Social Security (Contributions) Regulations 2001;

(h)   statutory sick pay and statutory maternity pay;

(i)   [² statutory paternity pay];

[¹(ia)   statutory shared parental pay;]

(j)   statutory adoption pay; and

(k)   any sums payable under a contract of service–

(i)   for incapacity for work due to sickness or injury; or

(ii)   by reason of pregnancy or confinement.

(2)   Earnings do not include–

(a)   subject to paragraph (3), any payment in kind;

(b)   any payment in respect of expenses wholly, exclusively and necessarily incurred in the performance of the duties of the employment;

(c)   any occupational pension;

(d)   any lump sum payment made under the Iron and Steel Re-adaptation Benefits Scheme;

(e)   any payment of compensation made pursuant to an award by an employment tribunal established under the Employment Tribunals Act 1996 in respect of unfair dismissal or unlawful discrimination; and

(f)   any payment in respect of expenses arising out of the applicant's participation in a service user group.

(3)   Paragraph (2)(a) does not apply in respect of any non-cash voucher referred to in paragraph (1)(g).

Modifications

The amendments made by SI 2014 No.3255 which came into force on 5 April 2015 do not have effect in relation to ordinary statutory paternity pay which is paid, additional statutory paternity pay which is paid, a period in respect of which additional statutory paternity pay is payable which begins, or continues, ordinary paternity leave which is taken or additional paternity leave which is taken on or after 5 April 2015. See art 35 of SI 2014 No.3255.

Amendments

1.   Inserted by art 24(6)(b) of SI 2014 No 3255 as from 31.12.14.

2.   Amended by art 24(6)(a) of SI 2014 No 3255 as from 5.4.15.

General Note
This is similar to the HB equivalent. See the p439 for the commentary.

Calculation of net earnings of employed earners

33.–(1)   For the purposes of regulation 28 (calculation of income on a weekly basis), the earnings of an applicant derived or likely to be derived from employment as an employed earner to be taken into account, subject to regulation 31(4) (calculation of weekly income) and Schedule 2 (sums to be disregarded in the calculation of earnings), are the applicant's net earnings.

(2)   For the purposes of paragraph (1) net earnings must, except where paragraph (4) applies, be calculated by taking into account the gross earnings of the applicant from the employment over the assessment period, less–

(a)   any amount deducted from those earnings by way of–

   (i)   income tax; or

   (ii)   primary Class 1 contributions under the 1992 Act;

(b)   one-half of any sum paid by the applicant by way of a contribution towards an occupational pension scheme;

(c)   one-half of the amount calculated in accordance with paragraph (3) in respect of any qualifying contribution payable by the applicant; and

(d)   where those earnings include a payment which is payable under any enactment having effect in Northern Ireland and which corresponds to statutory sick pay, statutory maternity pay, [² statutory paternity pay] [²] [¹ statutory shared parental pay or statutory adoption pay], any amount deducted from those earnings by way of any contributions which are payable under any enactment having effect in Northern Ireland and which correspond to primary Class 1 contributions under the 1992 Act.

(3)   The amount in respect of any qualifying contribution must be calculated by multiplying the daily amount of the qualifying contribution by the number of days in the assessment period, and for the purposes of this regulation the daily amount of the qualifying contribution must be determined–

(a)   where the qualifying contribution is payable monthly, by multiplying the amount of the qualifying contribution by 12 and dividing the product by 365; and

(b)   in any other case, by dividing the amount of the qualifying contribution by the number equal to the number of days in the period to which the qualifying contribution relates.

(4)   Where the earnings of an applicant are determined under regulation 31(2)(b) (calculation of weekly income), the net earnings are to be calculated by taking into account those earnings over the assessment period, less–

(a)   an amount in respect of income tax equivalent to an amount calculated by applying to those earnings the basic rate of tax applicable to the assessment period less only the personal relief to which the applicant is entitled under sections 36 or 37 of the Income Tax Act 2007 (personal allowances) as is appropriate to the applicant's circumstances but if the assessment period is less than a year the earnings to which the basic rate of tax is to be applied and the amount of the personal relief deductible under this sub-paragraph are to be calculated on a pro rata basis;

(b)   an amount equivalent to the amount of the primary Class 1 contributions that would be payable by the applicant under the 1992 Act in respect of those earnings if primary Class 1 contributions were payable; and

(c)   one-half of any sum which would be payable by the applicant by way of a contribution towards an occupational pension scheme or personal pension scheme if the estimated earnings were actual earnings.

(5)   In this regulation "qualifying contribution" means any sum which is payable periodically as a contribution towards a personal pension scheme.

Modifications
The amendments made by SI 2014 No.3255 which came into force on 5 April 2015 do not have effect in relation to ordinary statutory paternity pay which is paid, additional statutory paternity pay which is paid, a period in

respect of which additional statutory paternity pay is payable which begins, or continues, ordinary paternity leave which is taken or additional paternity leave which is taken on or after 5 April 2015. See art 35 of SI 2014 No.3255.

Amendments

1.   Amended by art 24(7)(c) of SI 2014 No 3255 as from 31.12.14.
2.   Amended by art 24(7)(a) and (b) of SI 2014 No 3255 as from 5.4.15.

General Note

This is similar to the HB equivalent. See p443 for the commentary.

Chapter 4
Self-employed earners

Calculation of earnings of self-employed earners

34.–(1)   Where an applicant's earnings consist of earnings from employment as a self-employed earner the weekly amount of the applicant's earnings are to be determined by reference to the applicant's average weekly earnings from that employment–

(a)   over a period of one year; or

(b)   where the applicant has recently become engaged in that employment or there has been a change which is likely to affect the normal pattern of business, over any other period ("computation period") as may, in the particular case, enable the weekly amount of the applicant's earnings to be determined more accurately.

(2)   For the purposes of determining the weekly amount of earnings of an applicant to whom paragraph (1)(b) applies, the applicant's earnings over the computation period must be divided by the number of days in that period and the quotient must be multiplied by 7.

(3)   The period over which the weekly amount of an applicant's earnings must be calculated in accordance with this regulation is the applicant's assessment period.

General Note

This is similar to the HB equivalent. See p783 for the commentary.

Earnings of self-employed earners

35.–(1)   Subject to paragraph (2), "earnings" in the case of employment as a self-employed earner means the gross income of the employment.

(2)   Earnings in the case of employment as a self-employed earner do not include–

(a)   where an applicant occupies a dwelling as the applicant's home and the applicant provides in that dwelling board and lodging accommodation for which payment is made, those payments;

(b)   any payment made to an applicant by a local authority under–

(i)   regulations 33 or 51 of the Looked After Children (Scotland) Regulations 2009 (fostering and kinship care allowances and fostering allowances);

[³ (ia) article 4(b)(ii), (d)(ii), (e)(ii), (f)(ii) or (g)(ii) of the Kinship Care Assistance (Scotland) Order 2016;] or

(ii)   section 22C(5) and (6)(a) or (b) or section 23(2)(a) of the Children Act 1989 (provision of accommodation and maintenance for a child whom they are looking after);

(c)   any payment made to an applicant by a voluntary organisation under section 59(1)(a) of the Children Act 1989 (provision of accommodation by voluntary organisations);

(d)   any payment made to the applicant or the applicant's partner for a person ("the relevant person"), who is not normally a member of the applicant's household but is temporarily in the applicant's care, by–

(i)   a health authority;

(ii)   a local authority but excluding payments of housing benefit made in respect of the relevant person;

(iii)   a voluntary organisation;

(iv) the relevant person pursuant to section 26(3A) of the National Assistance Act 1948;

[² (iva) the relevant person where the payment is for the provision of accommodation to meet that person's needs for care and support arranged pursuant to section 35 or section 36 of the Social Services and Well-being (Wales) Act 2014;]

[¹(v) the National Health Service Commissioning Board established by section 1H of the National Health Service Act 2006 or a clinical commissioning group established under section 14D of the National Health Service Act 2006;] or

(vi) a Local Health Board established under section 16BA of the National Health Service Act 1977 or established by an order made under section 11 of the National Health Service (Wales) Act 2006; or

(e) any sports award.

Amendments

1. Amended by reg 6 of SSI 2013 No 49 as from 18.3.13.
2. Inserted by reg 19(2) of SSI 2016 No 81 as from 6.4.16.
3. Inserted by reg 20 of SSI 2016 No 81 as from 1.4.16.

General Note

This is similar to the HB equivalent. See p445 and p784 for the commentary.

Calculation of net profit of self-employed earners

36.–(1) For the purposes of regulation 28 (calculation of income on a weekly basis) the earnings of an applicant to be taken into account are–

(a) in the case of a self-employed earner who is engaged in employment on that earner's own account, the net profit derived from that employment;

(b) in the case of a self-employed earner whose employment is carried on in partnership, that earner's share of the net profit derived from that employment, less–

(i) an amount in respect of income tax and of social security contributions payable under the 1992 Act calculated in accordance with regulation 37 (deduction of tax and contributions of self-employed earners); and

(ii) one-half of the amount calculated in accordance with paragraph (10) in respect of any qualifying premium.

(2) For the purposes of paragraph (1)(a) the net profit of the employment is, except where paragraph (8) applies, to be calculated by taking into account the earnings of the employment over the assessment period less–

(a) subject to paragraphs (4) to (7), any expenses wholly and exclusively incurred in that period for the purposes of that employment;

(b) an amount in respect of–

(i) income tax; and

(ii) social security contributions payable under the 1992 Act,

calculated in accordance with regulation 37 (deduction of tax and contributions of self-employed earners); and

(c) one-half of the amount calculated in accordance with paragraph (10) in respect of any qualifying premium.

(3) For the purposes of paragraph (1)(b), the net profit of the employment is to be calculated by taking into account the earnings of the employment over the assessment period less, subject to paragraphs (4) to (7), any expenses wholly and exclusively incurred in that period for the purposes of the employment.

(4) Subject to paragraph (5), no deduction is to be made under paragraph (2)(a) or (3), in respect of–

(a) any capital expenditure;

(b) the depreciation of any capital asset;

(c) any sum employed or intended to be employed in the setting up or expansion of the employment;

    (d)   any loss incurred before the beginning of the assessment period;

    (e)   the repayment of capital on any loan taken out for the purposes of the employment; and

    (f)   any expenses incurred in providing business entertainment.

    (5)   A deduction is to be made under paragraph (2)(a) or (3) in respect of the repayment of capital on any loan used for–

    (a)   the replacement in the course of business of equipment or machinery; or

    (b)   the repair of an existing business asset except to the extent that any sum is payable under an insurance policy for its repair.

    (6)   A deduction in respect of any expenses under paragraph (2)(a) or (3) must not be made unless the relevant authority is satisfied, given the nature and the amount of the expense, that it has been reasonably incurred.

    (7)   For the avoidance of doubt–

    (a)   a deduction must not be made under paragraph (2)(a) or (3) in respect of any sum unless it has been expended for the purposes of the employment;

    (b)   a deduction must be made under paragraph (2)(a) or (3) in respect of–

        (i)   the excess of any value added tax paid over value added tax received in the assessment period;

        (ii)   any income expended in the repair of an existing business asset except to the extent that any sum is payable under an insurance policy for its repair; and

        (iii)   any payment of interest on a loan taken out for the purposes of the employment.

    (8)   Where an applicant is engaged in employment as a child minder the net profit of the employment is one-third of the earnings of that employment, less–

    (a)   an amount in respect of–

        (i)   income tax; and

        (ii)   social security contributions payable under the 1992 Act,

        calculated in accordance with regulation 37 (deduction of tax and contributions of self-employed earners); and

    (b)   one-half of the amount calculated in accordance with paragraph (10) in respect of any qualifying premium.

    (9)   For the avoidance of doubt where an applicant is engaged in employment as a self-employed earner and the applicant is also engaged in one or more other employments as a self-employed or employed earner any loss incurred in any one of the applicant's employments must not be offset against the applicant's earnings in any other of the applicant's employments.

    (10)   The amount in respect of any qualifying premium must be calculated by multiplying the daily amount of the qualifying premium by the number of days in the assessment period, and for the purposes of this regulation the daily amount of the qualifying premium must be determined–

    (a)   where the qualifying premium is payable monthly, by multiplying the amount of the qualifying premium by 12 and dividing the product by 365; and

    (b)   in any other case, by dividing the amount of the qualifying premium by the number of days in the period to which the qualifying premium relates.

    (11)   In this regulation, "qualifying premium" means any premium which is payable periodically in respect of a personal pension scheme and which is payable on or after the date of the application.

General Note

This is similar to the HB equivalent. See p447 for the commentary.

Deduction of tax and contributions of self-employed earners

    37.–(1)   The amount to be deducted in respect of income tax under regulation 36(1)(b)(i), (2)(b)(i) or (8)(a)(i) (calculation of net profit of self-employed earners) must be calculated on the basis of the amount of chargeable income and as if that income was assessable to income tax at the basic rate of tax applicable to the assessment period less only the personal relief to which the applicant is entitled under sections 36 or 37 of the Income Tax Act 2007 (personal allowances) as is appropriate to the applicant's circumstances, but if the assessment period is less than a year the earnings to which the basic rate of tax is to be applied and the amount of the personal reliefs deductible under this paragraph must be calculated on a pro rata basis.

(2) The amount to be deducted in respect of social security contributions under regulation 37(1)(b)(i), (2)(b)(ii) or (8)(a)(ii) is the total of–

(a) the amount of Class 2 contributions payable under section [¹ 11(2)] or, as the case may be, [¹ 11(8)] of the 1992 Act at the rate applicable to the assessment period except where the applicant's chargeable income is less than the amount specified in section 11(4) of that Act ([¹ small profits threshold]) for the tax year applicable to the assessment period, but if the assessment period is less than a year the amount specified for that tax year must be reduced pro rata; and

(b) the amount of Class 4 contributions (if any) which would be payable under section 15 of the 1992 Act at the percentage rate applicable to the assessment period on so much of the chargeable income as exceeds the lower limit but does not exceed the upper limit of profits and gains applicable for the tax year applicable to the assessment period, but if the assessment period is less than a year those limits must be reduced pro rata.

(3) In this regulation "chargeable income" means–

(a) except where sub-paragraph (b) applies, the earnings derived from the employment less any expenses deducted under regulation 36(2)(a) or (3) (calculation of net profit of self-employed earners); and

(b) in the case of employment as a child minder, one third of the earnings of that employment.

Amendment

1. Amended by reg 22 of SSI 2016 No 81 as from 1.4.16.

General Note

This is similar to the HB equivalent. See p450 for the commentary.

Chapter 5
Other income

Notional income

38.–(1) An applicant is to be treated as possessing–

(a) subject to paragraph (2), the amount of any retirement pension income–
    (i) for which no claim has been made; and
    (ii) to which the applicant could be expected to be entitled if a claim was made; and

(b) income from an occupational pension scheme which the applicant elected to defer.

(2) Paragraph (1)(a) does not apply to the following pensions or benefit where entitlement has been deferred–

(a) a Category A or Category B retirement pension payable under sections 43 to 55 of the 1992 Act;

(b) a shared additional pension payable under section 55A [¹ or 55AA] of the 1992 Act; [¹]

(c) graduated retirement benefit payable under sections 36 and 37 of the National Insurance Act 1965; [¹ and

(d) a state pension under Part 1 of the Pensions Act 2014.]

(3) For the purposes of paragraph (2) entitlement has been deferred–

(a) in the case of a Category A or Category B retirement pension, in the circumstances specified in section 55(3) of the 1992 Act;

(b) in the case of a shared additional pension, in the circumstances specified in section 55C(3) of the 1992 Act; [¹]

    (c)   in the case of graduated retirement benefit, in the circumstances specified in section 36(4) and (4A) of the National Insurance Act 1965; [¹ and

    (d)   in the case of a state pension under Part 1 of the Pensions Act 2014,in the circumstances specified in section 1797) and (8) of that Act.]

    (4)   This paragraph applies where a person who has attained the qualifying age for state pension credit–

    (a)   is entitled to money purchase benefits under an occupational pension scheme or a personal pension scheme;

    (b)   fails to purchase an annuity with the funds available in that scheme; and

    (c)   (i) defers in whole or in part the payment of any income that would have been payable to that person by the pension fund holder;

        (ii)   fails to take any necessary action to secure that the whole of any income that would be payable to the person by the pension fund holder upon the person applying for it, is paid; or

        (iii)   is not able to withdraw income under the rules of that scheme.

    (5)   Where paragraph (4) applies, the amount of any income foregone must be treated as possessed by that person from the date it could be expected to be acquired if an application for it was to be made.

    (6)   The amount of any income foregone in a case where paragraph (4)(c)(i) or (ii) applies is the maximum amount of income that may be withdrawn from the fund.

    (7)   The amount of any income foregone in a case where paragraph (4)(c)(iii) applies is the income that the applicant could have received without purchasing an annuity had the funds held under the relevant scheme been held under a personal pension scheme or occupational pension scheme where income withdrawal was available and is the maximum amount of income that could have been withdrawn from the pension scheme fund.

    (8)   Subject to paragraphs (9) [¹, (9A), (9B)] and (10), where a person has been deprived of income as a result of actings by that person carried out for the purpose of securing entitlement to council tax reduction or increasing the amount of that reduction, that income is to be treated as income of that person.

    (9)   Paragraph (8) does not apply in respect of the amount of an increase of pension or benefit where a person, having made an election in favour of that increase of pension or benefit under Schedule 5 or 5A to the 1992 Act or under Schedule 1 to the Social Security (Graduated Retirement Benefit) Regulations 2005, changes that election in accordance with regulations made under Schedule 5 or 5A to the 1992 Act in favour of a lump sum.

    [¹ (9A)   Paragraph (8) does not apply in respect of the amount of an increase of pension where a person, having made a choice in favour of that increase of pension under section 8(2) of the Pensions Act 2014, alters that choice in accordance with Regulations made under section 8(7) of that Act in favour of a lump sum.

    (9B)   Paragraph (8) does not apply in respect of the amount of an increase of pension where a person, having made a choice in favour of that increase of pension in accordance with Regulations made under section 10 of the Pensions Act 2014 which include provision corresponding or similar to section 8(2) of that Act, alters that choice in favour of a lump sum, in accordance with Regulations made under section 10 of that Act which include provision corresponding or similar to Regulations made under section 8(7) of that Act.]

    (10)   Paragraph (8) does not apply in respect of any amount of income other than earnings, or earnings of an employed earner, arising out of the person's participation in a service user group.

    (11)   Where an applicant is in receipt of any benefit under the benefit Acts and the rate of that benefit is altered with effect from a date on or after 1st April in any year but not more than 14 days after that date, the relevant authority must treat the applicant as possessing that benefit at the altered rate from 1st April or the first Monday in April in that year, whichever date the relevant authority selects to apply in its area, to the date on which the altered rate is to take effect.

    (12)   In the case of an applicant who has, or whose partner has, an award of state pension credit comprising only the savings credit, where a relevant authority treats the

applicant as possessing any benefit under the benefit Acts at the altered rate in accordance with paragraph (11), that authority must–
- (a) determine the income and capital of that applicant in accordance with regulation 25(1) (calculation of income in savings credit only cases) where the calculation or estimate of that income and capital is altered with effect from a date on or after 1st April in any year but not more than 14 days after that date; and
- (b) treat that applicant as possessing that income and capital at the altered rate from the date selected by the relevant authority to apply in its area for the purposes of establishing the period referred to in paragraph (11).

(13) For the purposes of paragraph (8), a person is not to be regarded as having carried out a deprivation of income where–
- (a) the applicant's rights to benefits under a registered pension scheme are extinguished and in consequence of this the applicant receives a payment from the scheme; and
- (b) that payment is a trivial commutation lump sum within the meaning given by paragraph 7 of Schedule 29 to the Finance Act 2004.

(14) In this regulation–
- (a) "money purchase benefits" has the meaning given by section 181(1) of the Pension Schemes Act 1993; and
- (b) "registered pension scheme" has the meaning given in section 150(2) of the Finance Act 2004.

Amendment

1. Amended by art 37 of SI 2015 No 1985 as from 6.4.16.

General Note

This is similar to the HB equivalent. See p789 for the commentary.

Income paid to third parties

39.–(1) Any payment of income, other than a payment specified in paragraphs (2) or (3), to a third party in respect of the applicant is to be treated as possessed by the applicant.

(2) Paragraph (1) does not apply to a payment of income made under an occupational pension scheme, a pension or other periodical payment made under a personal pension scheme or a payment made by the Board of the Pension Protection Fund where–
- (a) the estate of the applicant is subject to sequestration, a judicial factor has been appointed on the applicant's estate under section 41 of the Solicitors (Scotland) Act 1980, the person has entered a protected trust deed within the meaning of section 73(1) of the Bankruptcy Act 1985 or a bankruptcy order within the meaning of section 381(1) of the Insolvency Act 1986 has been made in respect of the applicant;
- (b) the payment is made to the trustee in bankruptcy or any other person acting on behalf of the creditors; and
- (c) neither the applicant nor the applicant's partner possesses, or is treated as possessing, any other income apart from that payment.

(3) Paragraph (1) does not apply in respect of any payment of income other than earnings, or earnings derived from employment as an employed earner, arising out of the applicant's participation in a service user group.

(4) In this regulation "the Board of the Pension Protection Fund" means the body corporate established under section 107 of the Pensions Act 2004.

General Note

This is similar to the HB equivalent. See p790 for the commentary.

Chapter 6
Capital

Capital limit

40. No person is entitled to council tax reduction if that person's capital exceeds £16,000.

General Note
This is similar to the HB equivalent. See p462 and p790 for the commentary.

Calculation of capital

41.–(1) Subject to paragraph (2), the capital of an applicant to be taken into account when calculating entitlement to council tax reduction is the whole of the applicant's capital calculated in accordance with this Part.

(2) Any capital specified in Part 1 of Schedule 4 (capital disregards) is to be disregarded when calculating an applicant's capital.

(3) An applicant's capital is to be treated as including any payment made to the applicant by way of arrears of–

(a) child tax credit;
(b) working tax credit; or
(c) state pension credit,

if the payment was made in respect of a period for the whole or part of which the applicant was entitled to council tax reduction.

General Note
This is similar to the HB equivalent. See p790 for the commentary.

Calculation of capital in the United Kingdom

42. Capital which an applicant possesses in the United Kingdom is to be calculated at its current market or surrender value less–

(a) where there would be expenses attributable to the sale, 10 per cent; and
(b) the amount of any encumbrance secured on it.

General Note
This is similar to the HB equivalent. See p465 for the commentary.

Calculation of capital outside the United Kingdom

43. Capital which an applicant possesses in a country outside the United Kingdom is to be calculated–

(a) in a case where there is no prohibition in that country against the transfer to the United Kingdom of an amount equal to its current market or surrender value in that country, at that value; and
(b) in a case where there is such a prohibition, at the price it would realise if sold in the United Kingdom to a willing buyer,

less, where there would be expenses attributable to sale, 10 per cent and the amount of any encumbrance secured on it.

General Note
This is similar to the HB equivalent. See p466 for the commentary.

Notional capital

44.–(1) Where an applicant has been deprived of capital as a result of actings by that applicant carried out for the purpose of securing entitlement to council tax reduction or increasing the amount of that reduction that capital is to be treated as capital of the applicant except to the extent that it is reduced in accordance with regulation 45 (diminishing notional capital).

(2) An applicant who disposes of capital for the purpose of–

(a) reducing or paying a debt owed by the applicant; or

(b)   purchasing goods or services if the expenditure was reasonable in the circumstances of the applicant's case,
is not to be regarded as having made a deprivation under paragraph (1).

(3)   Where an applicant stands in relation to a company in a position analogous to that of a sole owner or partner in the business of that company, the applicant is to be treated as sole owner or partner and in that case–

(a)   the value of the applicant's actual holding in that company must be disregarded notwithstanding regulation 41 (calculation of capital); and

(b)   subject to paragraph (4), the applicant is be treated as possessing an amount of capital equal to what would have been the applicant's share of the value of the capital of that company if the applicant had been sole owner or partner.

(4)   For so long as an applicant undertakes activities in the course of the business of the company, the amount which the applicant is treated as possessing under paragraph (3) is to be disregarded.

(5)   Where an applicant is treated as possessing capital under this regulation, the amount of that capital is to be calculated in accordance with the provisions of this Part as if it were actual capital possessed by the applicant.

General Note
This is similar to the HB equivalent. See p791 for the commentary.

Diminishing notional capital

45.–(1)   Where an applicant is treated as possessing capital under regulation 44(1) (notional capital), the amount which the applicant is treated as possessing–

(a)   in the case of a week that is subsequent to–
    (i)   the relevant week in respect of which the conditions set out in paragraph (2) are satisfied; or
    (ii)   a week which follows that relevant week and which satisfies those conditions,
    is to be reduced by the amount determined under paragraph (3);

(b)   in the case of a week in respect of which paragraph (1)(a) does not apply but where–
    (i)   that week is a week subsequent to the relevant week; and
    (ii)   that relevant week is a week in which the condition in paragraph (4) is satisfied,
    is to be reduced by the amount determined under paragraph (4).

(2)   This paragraph applies to a reduction week or part-week where the applicant satisfies the conditions that–

(a)   the applicant is in receipt of council tax reduction; and

(b)   but for regulation 44(1), the applicant would have received an additional amount of council tax reduction in that week.

(3)   In a case to which paragraph (2) applies, the amount of the reduction for the purposes of paragraph (1)(a) is equal to the aggregate of–

(a)   the additional amount to which paragraph (2)(b) refers;

(b)   where the applicant has also claimed state pension credit, the amount of any state pension credit or any additional amount of state pension credit to which the applicant would have been entitled in respect of the reduction week to which paragraph (2) refers but for the application of regulation 21(1) of the State Pension Credit Regulations 2002 (notional capital);

(c)   where the applicant has also claimed housing benefit, the amount of any housing benefit or any additional amount of housing benefit to which the applicant would have been entitled in respect of the whole or part of that reduction week to which paragraph (2) refers but for the application of regulation 47(1) of the Housing Benefit (Persons who have attained the qualifying age for state pension credit) Regulations 2006 (notional capital);

(d)   where the applicant has also claimed a jobseeker's allowance, the amount of an income-based jobseeker's allowance to which the applicant would have been entitled in respect of the reduction week or part-week to which paragraph (2) refers but for the application of regulation 113 of the Jobseeker's Allowance Regulations 1996 (notional capital); and

(e)   where the applicant has also claimed an employment and support allowance, the amount of an income-related employment and support allowance to which the applicant would have been entitled in respect of the reduction week or part-week to which paragraph (2) refers but for the application of regulation 115 of the Employment and Support Allowance Regulations (notional capital).

(4)   Subject to paragraph (5), for the purposes of paragraph (1)(b) the condition is that the applicant would have been entitled to council tax reduction in the relevant week but for regulation 44(1) (notional capital), and in such a case the amount of the reduction is to be equal to the aggregate of–

(a)   the amount of council tax reduction to which the applicant would have been entitled in the relevant week but for regulation 44(1), and for the purposes of this sub-paragraph if the amount is in respect of a part-week that amount is to be determined by dividing the amount of council tax reduction to which the applicant would have been entitled by the number equal to the number of days in the part-week and multiplying the quotient by 7;

(b)   if the applicant would, but for regulation 21 of the State Pension Credit Regulations 2002, have been entitled to state pension credit in respect of the benefit week (within the meaning of regulation 1(2) of those Regulations) which includes the last day of the relevant week, the amount to which the applicant would have been entitled and, for the purposes of this sub-paragraph, if the amount is in respect of a part-week, that amount is to be determined by dividing the amount of the state pension credit to which the applicant would have been entitled by the number equal to the number of days in the part-week and multiplying the quotient by 7;

(c)   if the applicant would, but for regulation 47(1) of the Housing Benefit (Persons who have attained the qualifying age for state pension credit) Regulations 2006, have been entitled to housing benefit or to an additional amount of housing benefit in respect of the reduction week which includes the last day of the relevant week, the amount which is equal to–

    (i)   in a case where no housing benefit is payable, the amount to which the applicant would have been entitled; or

    (ii)   in any other case, the amount equal to the additional amount of housing benefit to which the applicant would have been entitled,

and, for the purposes of this sub-paragraph, if the amount is in respect of a part-week, that amount is to be determined by dividing the amount of the housing benefit to which the applicant would have been so entitled by the number equal to the number of days in the part-week and multiplying the quotient by 7;

(d)   if the applicant would, but for regulation 113 of the Jobseeker's Allowance Regulations 1996, have been entitled to an income-based jobseeker's allowance in respect of the benefit week (within the meaning of regulation 1(3) of those Regulations) which includes the last day of the relevant week, the amount to which the applicant would have been entitled and, for the purposes of this sub-paragraph, if the amount is in respect of a part-week, that amount is to be determined by dividing the amount of the income-based jobseeker's allowance to which the applicant would have been so entitled by the number equal to the number of days in the part-week and multiplying the quotient by 7; and

(e)   if the applicant would, but for regulation 115 of the Employment and Support Allowance Regulations, have been entitled to an income-related employment and support allowance in respect of the benefit week (within the meaning of regulation 2(1) of those Regulations) which includes the last day of the relevant week, the amount to which the applicant would have been entitled and, for the purposes of this sub-paragraph, if the amount is in respect of a part-week, that amount must be determined by dividing the amount of the income-related employment and support allowance to which the applicant would have been so entitled by the number equal to the number of days in that part-week and multiplying the quotient by 7.

(5)   The amount determined under paragraph (4) is to be re-determined under that paragraph if the applicant makes a further application for council tax reduction and the conditions in paragraph (6) are satisfied, and in such a case–

(a)   paragraph (4)(a) to (e) applies as if for "relevant week" there was substituted "relevant subsequent week"; and

(b)   subject to paragraph (7), the amount as re-determined has effect from the first week following the relevant subsequent week in question.

(6)   The conditions are that–

(a)   a further application is made 26 or more weeks after the latest of–

(i)   the date on which the applicant made an application for council tax reduction in respect of which the applicant was first treated as possessing the capital in question under regulation 44(1) (notional capital);

(ii)   in a case where there has been at least one re-determination in accordance with paragraph (5), the date on which the applicant last made an application for council tax reduction which resulted in the weekly amount being re-determined; or

(iii)   the date on which the applicant last ceased to be entitled to council tax reduction; and

(b)   the applicant would have been entitled to council tax reduction but for regulation 44(1).

(7)   The amount as re-determined under paragraph (5) is not to have effect if it is less than the amount which applied in that case immediately before the re-determination, and in that case the higher amount continues to have effect.

(8)   In this regulation–

(a)   "part-week" –

(i)   in paragraph (4)(a) means a period of less than a week during which a person is entitled to council tax reduction;

(ii)   in paragraph (4)(b), (d) and (e) means–

(aa)   a period of less than a week which is the whole period for which state pension credit, an income-related employment and support allowance, or, as the case may be, an income-based jobseeker's allowance, is payable; and

(bb)   any other period of less than a week for which either of those benefits is payable; and

(iii)   in paragraph (4)(c) means a period of less than a week for which housing benefit is payable;

(b)   "relevant week" means the reduction week or part-week in which the capital in question of which the applicant has been deprived within the meaning of regulation 44(1)–

(i)   was first taken into account for the purpose of determining the applicant's entitlement to council tax reduction; or

(ii)   was taken into account on a subsequent occasion for the purpose of determining or re-determining the applicant's entitlement to council tax reduction on that subsequent occasion and that determination or re-determination resulted in the applicant beginning to receive, or ceasing to receive, council tax reduction,

and where more than one reduction week or part-week is identified by reference to heads (i) and (ii) the later or latest reduction week or, as the case may be, the later or latest part-week; and

(c)   "relevant subsequent week" means the reduction week or part-week which includes the day on which the further application or, if more than one further application has been made, the last application was made.

General Note
This is similar to the HB equivalent. See p794 for the commentary.

Capital jointly held

46. Except where an applicant possesses capital which is disregarded under regulation 44(4) (notional capital), where an applicant and one or more other persons are beneficially entitled in possession to any capital asset the applicant and the person or those persons are to be treated as if each of them were entitled in possession to the whole beneficial interest in an equal share and the provisions of this Chapter apply for the purposes of calculating the amount of capital which the applicant is treated as possessing as if it were actual capital possessed by the applicant.

General Note
This is similar to the HB equivalent. See p476 for the commentary.

PART 7
Amount of reduction

Maximum council tax reduction

47.–(1) Subject to paragraphs (2) and (3) [¹ for the purposes of regulation 14], the amount of a person's maximum council tax reduction in respect of a day for which the person is liable to pay council tax is 100 per cent of the amount A/B where–
- (a) A is the amount set by the relevant authority as the council tax for the relevant financial year in respect of the dwelling in which the person is a resident and for which the person is liable, subject to–
  - (i) any discount which may be appropriate to that dwelling; and
  - (ii) any reduction in liability for council tax under regulations made under section 80 of the Act or under a scheme established under section 80A of the Act, other than a reduction in liability under these Regulations; and
- (b) B is the number of days in that financial year,

less any deductions in respect of non-dependants which fall to be made under regulation 48 (non-dependant deductions).

[¹(1A) Subject to paragraphs (2) and (3), for the purposes of regulation 14A the amount of a person's maximum council tax reduction in respect of a day for which the person is liable to pay council tax is 100% of the amount–

$$\frac{A - \frac{A}{C}}{B}$$

less any deductions in respect of non-dependants which fall to be made under regulation 48.

(1B) In paragraph (1A)–
- (a) A and B have the same meanings as in paragraph (1); and
- (b) C is–
  - (i) 1.075 if the relevant dwelling is in valuation band E;
  - (ii) 1.125 if the relevant dwelling is in valuation band F;
  - (iii) 1.175 if the relevant dwelling is in valuation band G;
  - (iv) 1.225 if the relevant dwelling is in valuation band H.]

(2) Subject to paragraph (3), where an applicant is jointly and severally liable for council tax in respect of a dwelling in which the person is resident with one or more other persons, but excepting any person residing with the applicant who is a student to whom regulation 20(2) of the Council Tax Reduction Regulations (persons not entitled to council tax reduction: students) applies, in determining the maximum council tax reduction in the person's case in accordance with paragraph (1) [¹ or (1A)] the amount A is to be divided by the number of persons who are jointly and severally liable for that tax.

(3) Where an applicant is jointly and severally liable for council tax in respect of a dwelling with only the applicant's partner, paragraph (2) does not apply.

Amendment
1.   Amended by reg 13 of SSI 2016 No 253 as from 1.4.17.

General Note

In Scotland, the council tax valuation band multipliers for properties in bands E, F, G and H (relative to band D properties) were increased from 1 April 2017 increasing the council tax charged for those properties before any discount and/or reduction is applied.

From that date, reg 47 is amended to reflect the inclusion of a new alternative calculation of CTR, and an alternative calculation of the maximum amount, for applicants residing in properties in these valuation bands. See the commentary under the general note to reg 14 for further details.

Analysis

See the Analysis to reg 66 CTR(S) Regs on p1522.

Non-dependant deductions

48.–(1) Subject to the following provisions of this regulation, the non-dependant deductions in respect of a day referred to in regulation 47 (maximum council tax reduction) are–

(a) in respect of a non-dependant aged 18 or over in remunerative work, [⁹£12.55] x 1/7; and

(b) in respect of a non-dependant aged 18 or over to whom sub-paragraph (a) does not apply, [⁹£4.15] x 1/7.

(2) In the case of a non-dependant aged 18 or over to whom paragraph (1)(a) applies, where it is shown to the relevant authority that the [¹ person's] normal gross weekly income is–

(a) less than [⁹ £209.00], the deduction to be made is that specified in paragraph (1)(b);

[⁶ (b) not less than [⁹ £209.00] but less than [⁹ £363.00], the deduction to be made is [⁹ £8.30] x 1/7; and

(c) not less than [⁹ £363.00] but less than [⁹ £451.00], the deduction to be made is [⁹ £10.50] x 1/7.]

(3) Only one deduction is to be made under this regulation in respect of a couple or, as the case may be, members of a polygamous marriage and where, but for this paragraph, the amount that would fall to be deducted in respect of one member of a couple or polygamous marriage is higher than the amount (if any) that would fall to be deducted in respect of the other, or any other, member, the higher amount must be deducted.

(4) In applying the provisions of paragraph (2) in the case of a couple or, as the case may be, a polygamous marriage, regard must be had for the purpose of that paragraph to the couple's or, as the case may be, all members of the polygamous marriage's joint weekly gross income.

(5) Where in respect of a day–

(a) a person is a resident in a dwelling but is not liable for council tax in respect of that dwelling on that day;

(b) other residents in that dwelling (the liable persons) have joint and several liability for council tax in respect of that dwelling on that day otherwise than by virtue of section 77 or 77A of the Act (liability of spouses and civil partners); and

(c) the person to whom sub-paragraph (a) refers is a non-dependant of two or more of the liable persons,

the deduction in respect of that non-dependant must be apportioned equally between those liable persons.

(6) No deduction is to be made in respect of any non-dependants occupying an applicant's dwelling if the applicant or the applicant's partner is–

(a) blind or treated as blind by virtue of paragraph 7 of Schedule 1 (severe disability premium); or

(b) receiving–

(i) attendance allowance;

(ii) the care component of the disability living allowance;

[²(iia) armed forces independence payment;] or

(iii) the daily living component of personal independence payment.

(7) No deduction is to be made in respect of a non-dependant if–

(a) although the non-dependant resides with the applicant, it appears to the relevant authority that the non-dependant's normal home is elsewhere;

(b) the non-dependant is in receipt of a training allowance paid in connection with youth training established under section 2 of the 1973 Act or section 2 of the Enterprise and New Towns (Scotland) Act 1990;

(c) the non-dependant is a full-time student; [⁴]

(d) the non-dependant is not residing with the applicant because the non-dependant has been a patient for a period in excess of 52 weeks, and for these purposes where a person has been a patient for two or more distinct periods separated by one or more intervals, each not exceeding 28 days, the non-dependant is to be treated as having been a patient continuously for a period equal in duration to the total of those distinct periods [⁴; or]

[⁴ (e) the non-dependant is not residing with the applicant because the non-dependant is a member of the regular forces or the reserve forces (within the meaning of section 374 of the Armed Forces Act 2006) who is absent, while on operations, from the dwelling usually occupied as that person's home]

(8) No deduction is to be made in respect of a non-dependant–

(a) who is on income support, state pension credit, an income-based jobseeker's allowance or an income-related employment and support allowance; [⁵]

(b) to whom Schedule 1 to the Act applies (persons disregarded for purposes of discount) but this sub-paragraph does not apply to a non-dependant who is a student to whom paragraph 4 of that Schedule refers [⁵ ; or

(c) who is entitled to an award of universal credit where the award is calculated on the basis that the non-dependant does not have any earned income, within the meaning given by regulation 52 of the Universal Credit Regulations 2013].

(9) In the application of paragraph (2) there is to be disregarded from the [¹person's] weekly gross income–

(a) any attendance allowance, disability living allowance[², armed forces independence payment] or personal independence payment received by the [¹person];

(b) any payment made under or by the Trusts, the Fund, the Eileen Trust, MFET Limited, the Skipton Fund, the Caxton Foundation, [⁶ another infected blood payment scheme,] [⁵ ILF Scotland] [⁷, the London Bombings Relief Charitable Fund, the London Emergencies Trust or the We Love Manchester Emergency Fund] which, had the [¹person's] income fallen to be calculated under regulation 39 of the Council Tax Reduction Regulations (calculation of income other than earnings), would have been disregarded under paragraph 27 of Schedule 4 to those Regulations (income in kind); [⁸]

(c) any payment which, had the [¹person's] income fallen to be calculated under regulation 39 of the Council Tax Reduction Regulations, would have been disregarded under paragraph 41 of Schedule 4 to those Regulations (payments made under certain trusts and certain other payments) [⁸; and

(d) any payment made under or by the Thalidomide Trust].

Amendments

1. Amended by reg 7 of SSI 2013 No 49 as from 18.3.13.
2. Inserted by reg 12(5) of SSI 2013 No 142 as from 11.6.13.
3. Amended by reg 7 of SSI 2014 No 35 as from 1.4.14.
4. Amended by reg 18 of SSI 2015 No 46 as from 1.4.15.
5. Amended by regs 17(2)(a) and 23 of SSI 2016 No 81 as from 1.4.16.
6. Amended by reg 16 of SSI 2017 No 41 as from 1.4.17.
7. Amended by reg 11(a) of SSI 2017 No 326 as from 20.11.17.
8. Amended by regs 13 and 15 of SSI 2018 No 69 as from 1.4.18.
9. Amended by reg 11 of SSI 2019 No 29 as from 1.4.19.

General Note

The rules on non-dependant deductions for CTR purposes are broadly the same as those for HB (see reg 74 on p516). For some important differences, see the Analysis to reg 67 CTR(S) Regs on p1524.

Extended council tax reduction (qualifying contributory benefits)

49.–(1)   Except in the case of a person who is in receipt of state pension credit, a person who is entitled to council tax reduction by virtue of the general conditions of entitlement is entitled to extended council tax reduction (qualifying contributory benefits) where–

(a)   the person or the person's partner was entitled to a qualifying contributory benefit;

(b)   entitlement to a qualifying contributory benefit ceased because the person or the person's partner–

   (i)   commenced employment as an employed or self-employed earner;

   (ii)   increased their earnings from employment as an employed or self-employed earner; or

   (iii)   increased the number of hours worked in employment as an employed or self-employed earner,

and that employment, is or the increased earnings or increased number of hours are, expected to last 5 weeks or more;

(c)   the person or the person's partner had been entitled to and in receipt of a qualifying contributory benefit or a combination of qualifying contributory benefits for a continuous period of at least 26 weeks before the day on which the entitlement to a qualifying contributory benefit ceased; and

(d)   the person or the person's partner was not entitled to and not in receipt of a qualifying income-related benefit in the last reduction week in which the person or the person's partner was entitled to a qualifying contributory benefit.

(2)   For the purposes of paragraph (1), a person is entitled to council tax reduction by virtue of the general conditions of entitlement where–

(a)   the person ceased to be entitled to council tax reduction on vacating the dwelling in which the person was resident;

(b)   the first day on which the person vacated the dwelling was in the week in which entitlement to a qualifying contributory benefit ceased or in the preceding week; and

(c)   entitlement to the qualifying contributory benefit ceased in any of the circumstances listed in paragraph (1)(b).

General Note

This is similar to the HB equivalent. See p513 for the commentary.

Duration of period of entitlement to extended council tax reduction (qualifying contributory benefits)

50.–(1)   Where a person is entitled to extended council tax reduction (qualifying contributory benefits) the period of entitlement starts on the first day of the reduction week immediately following the reduction week in which the person or the person's partner ceased to be entitled to a qualifying contributory benefit.

(2)   For the purposes of paragraph (1), a person or a person's partner ceases to be entitled to a qualifying contributory benefit on the day immediately following the last day of entitlement to that benefit.

(3)   The period of entitlement to extended council tax reduction (qualifying contributory benefits) ends on the earliest of–

(a)   the end of a period of 4 weeks of that entitlement; or

(b)   the first day on which the person who is entitled to extended council tax reduction (qualifying contributory benefits) has no liability for council tax.

Amount of extended council tax reduction (qualifying contributory benefits)

51.–(1)   For any week during the period of entitlement to extended council tax reduction (qualifying contributory benefits) the amount of reduction to which the person is entitled is the higher of–

(a)   the amount of council tax reduction to which the person was entitled in the last reduction week before the person or the person's partner ceased to be entitled to a qualifying contributory benefit;

(b)   the amount of council tax reduction to which the person would be entitled for any reduction week during the period of entitlement to extended council tax reduction (qualifying contributory benefits), if regulation 49 did not apply to the person; or

(c)   the amount of council tax reduction to which the person's partner would be entitled if regulation 49 did not apply to the person.

(2)   Paragraph (1) does not apply in the case of a mover to whom regulation 52 applies.

(3)   Where a person is entitled to extended council tax reduction (qualifying contributory benefits) and the person's partner makes an application for council tax reduction, the person's partner is not entitled to council tax reduction during the existing period of entitlement to extended council tax reduction (qualifying contributory benefits).

Extended council tax reduction (qualifying contributory benefits): movers

52.–(1)   Where a mover who is entitled to extended council tax reduction (qualifying contributory benefits) for council tax to the first authority moves to reside in a dwelling in the area of the second authority that mover is entitled to extended council tax reduction in respect of any liability to pay council tax to the second authority of an amount calculated in accordance with paragraph (2).

(2)   The amount of extended council tax reduction (qualifying contributory benefit) to which the mover is entitled is the amount of council tax reduction to which the mover was entitled for the last reduction week before the mover ceased to be entitled to a qualifying contributory benefit.

(3)   The period of entitlement to extended council tax reduction (qualifying contributory benefit) in respect of liability to pay council tax to the first authority ends on the day on the earliest of–

(a)   the first Sunday after the move; or

(b)   the day on which the mover's liability to pay council tax to the first authority ends.

(4)   The period of entitlement to extended council tax reduction (qualifying contributory benefits) granted by virtue of paragraph (1)–

(a)   starts on the Monday following the day of the move; and

(b)   ends on the expiry of the period of extended council tax reduction (qualifying contributory benefits) which would have applied had the mover not moved from the area of the first authority.

Relationship between council tax reduction and extended council tax reduction (qualifying contributory benefits)

53.–(1)   Where a person's entitlement to council tax reduction would have ended when the person ceased to be entitled to a qualifying contributory benefit in the circumstances listed in regulation 49(1)(b), that entitlement does not cease until the end of the period of entitlement to extended council tax reduction.

(2)   Part 8 (effective date) does not apply to any extended council tax reduction (qualifying contributory benefits) calculated in accordance with regulation 51(1)(a) or 52(2).

Entitlement to extended council tax reduction or extended council tax reduction (qualifying contributory benefits) under the Council Tax Reduction Regulations

54.–(1)   This regulation applies where–

(a)   a person became entitled to extended council tax reduction under regulation 68 of the Council Tax Reduction Regulations or to extended council tax reduction (qualifying contributory benefits) under regulation 73 of those Regulations; and

(b)   during that period of entitlement to extended council tax reduction or extended council tax reduction (qualifying contributory benefits) these Regulations become applicable to that person or that person's partner in accordance with regulation 12 (application).

(2)   Where this regulation applies, for any week during the period of entitlement to extended council tax reduction or extended council tax reduction (qualifying contributory benefits) referred to in paragraph (1)(a) the amount of council tax reduction to which the person is entitled is the higher of–

(a)   the amount of council tax reduction to which the person is entitled under regulation 70(1)(a) of the Council Tax Reduction Regulations or the amount of council tax reduction (qualifying contributory benefits) to which the person is entitled under regulation 75(1)(a) of those Regulations, as the case may be;

(b)   the amount of council tax reduction to which the person would be entitled under the general conditions of entitlement of these Regulations, if regulation 68 (extended council tax reduction) or regulation 73 (extended council tax reduction (qualifying contributory benefits)) of the Council Tax Reduction Regulations did not apply to the person; or

(c)   the amount of council tax reduction to which the person's partner would be entitled under these Regulations if regulation 68 or regulation 73 of the Council Tax Reduction Regulations did not apply to the person.

(3)   No partner of a person to whom this regulation applies is entitled to council tax reduction.

Continuing payments where state pension credit claimed

55.–(1)   This regulation applies where–

(a)   a person is entitled to council tax reduction;

(b)   paragraph (2) is satisfied; and

(c)   either–

(i)   the person has attained the qualifying age for state pension credit or, if the person's entitlement to income-based jobseeker's allowance or income-related employment and support allowance continued beyond that age, has attained the age of 65; or

(ii)   the person's partner has claimed state pension credit.

(2)   This paragraph is satisfied if the Secretary of State has certified that the person's partner has claimed state pension credit or that–

(a)   the person's award of–

(i)   income support has terminated because the person has attained the qualifying age for state pension credit; or

(ii)   income-based jobseeker's allowance or income-related employment and support allowance has terminated because the person has attained the qualifying age for state pension credit or the age of 65; and

(b)   the person has claimed or is treated as having claimed or is required to make a claim for state pension credit.

(3)   Subject to paragraph (4), in a case to which this regulation applies, the person's entitlement to council tax reduction is to continue for the period of 4 weeks beginning on the day following the day the person's entitlement to income support, income-based jobseeker's allowance or income-related employment and support allowance ceased if and for so long as the applicant otherwise satisfies the conditions for entitlement to council tax reduction.

(4)   Where the person continues to be entitled to council tax reduction in accordance with paragraph (3) and the last day of the 4 week period of entitlement falls on a day other than the last day of a reduction week, the person's entitlement to council tax reduction continues until the end of the reduction week in which the last day of the 4 week period falls.

(5)   Throughout the period of 4 weeks specified in paragraph (3) and any further period specified in paragraph (4)–

(a)   the whole of the income and capital of the person must be disregarded; and

(b)   the appropriate maximum council tax reduction of the person is that which was applicable in the person's case immediately before that 4 week period commenced.

(6)   The appropriate maximum council tax reduction is to be calculated in accordance with regulation 47(1) if, since the date it was last calculated,–
(a)   the person's council tax liability has increased; or
(b)   a change in the deduction under regulation 48 (non-dependant deductions) falls to be made.

General Note
This is similar to the HB equivalent. See p799 for the commentary.

Alternative maximum council tax reduction
56.–(1)   Subject to paragraphs (2) and (3), the alternative maximum council tax reduction where the conditions set out in regulation 14(3) and (6) (conditions of entitlement to council tax reduction) are fulfilled is the amount determined in accordance with Schedule 5.
(2)   Subject to paragraph (3), where an applicant is jointly and severally liable for council tax in respect of a dwelling in which the applicant is resident with one or more other persons, in determining the alternative maximum council tax reduction in the applicant's case, the amount determined in accordance with Schedule 5 must be divided by the number of persons who are jointly and severally liable for that tax.
(3)   Paragraph (2) does not apply in the case of an applicant who is jointly and severally liable for council tax in respect of a dwelling with the applicant's partner only by virtue only of section 77 or 77A of the Act (liability of spouses and civil partners).

General Note
Reg 56 is broadly the same as reg 78 CTR(S) Regs on p1528.

Residents of a dwelling to whom regulation 14(6) does not apply
57.   Regulation 14(6) (conditions of entitlement to council tax reduction: alternative maximum council tax reduction) does not apply in respect of–
(a)   a person who is liable for council tax solely in consequence of the provisions of section 77 or 77A of the Act;
(b)   a person who is residing with a couple or with the members of a polygamous marriage where the applicant is a member of that couple or of that marriage and–
(i)   in the case of a couple, neither member of that couple is a person who, in accordance with Schedule 1 to the Act, falls to be disregarded for the purposes of discount; or
(ii)   in the case of a polygamous marriage, two or more members of that marriage are not persons who, in accordance with Schedule 1 to the Act, fall to be disregarded for the purposes of discount;
(c)   a person who jointly with the applicant falls within the same sub-paragraph of section 75(2)(a) to (e) of the Act (persons liable to pay council tax) as applies in the case of the applicant; or
(d)   a person who is residing with two or more persons both or all of whom fall within the same sub-paragraph of section 75(2)(a) to (e) of the Act and two or more of those persons are not persons who, in accordance with Schedule 1 to the Act, fall to be disregarded for the purposes of discount.

General Note
See the Analysis to reg 79 CTR(S) Regs on p1530.

PART 8
Effective date

Date on which entitlement begins
58.–(1)   Subject to paragraph (2), where a person–
(a)   makes, or is treated as making, an application; and
(b)   fulfils the conditions of entitlement to council tax reduction in regulation 14 [¹ or 14A],

that person is entitled to council tax reduction from the first Monday after the date on which the application is made or treated as made.

(2)   Where, a person–

(a)   becomes liable for the first time for council tax in respect of a dwelling in which the person resides;

(b)   makes, or is treated as making, an application in the reduction week in which the person first becomes liable for council tax in respect of that dwelling; and

(c)   fulfils the conditions of entitlement to council tax reduction in regulation 14 [¹ or 14A],

that person is entitled to council tax reduction from the day on which the person first becomes liable for council tax.

Amendment

1.   Amended by reg 14 of SSI 2016 No 253 as from 1.4.17.

General Note

This is similar to the HB equivalent. See p803 for the commentary.

Date on which a change of circumstances is to take effect

59.–(1)   Subject to the provisions of this regulation and regulation 60 (change of circumstances where state pension credit is in payment), a change of circumstances which affects entitlement to council tax reduction is to take effect for the purpose of calculating entitlement to council tax reduction from the first day of the reduction week starting immediately after the date on which the change actually occurs, and where that change is cessation of entitlement to any benefit under the benefit Acts, the date on which the change actually occurs is the day immediately following the last day of entitlement to that benefit.

(2)   Subject to paragraph (3), where the change of circumstances is a change in the amount of council tax payable, it takes effect for the purpose of calculating entitlement to council tax reduction from the day on which it actually occurs.

(3)   Where the change of circumstances is a change in the amount a person is liable to pay in respect of council tax in consequence of regulations under section 80 of the Act (reduced amounts of council tax) or changes in the discount to which a dwelling may be subject under section 79 of that Act, it takes effect for the purpose of calculating entitlement to council tax reduction from the day on which the change in amount has effect.

(4)   Where the change of circumstances is an amendment to these Regulations, it takes effect for the purpose of calculating entitlement to council tax reduction from the date on which the amendment to these Regulations comes into force.

(5)   Where the change of circumstances is the applicant's acquisition of a partner, it takes effect for the purpose of calculating entitlement to council tax reduction on the day on which they become partners.

(6)   Where the change of circumstances is the death of an applicant's partner or their separation, it takes effect for the purpose of calculating entitlement to council tax reduction on the day the death or separation occurred.

(7)   If two or more changes of circumstances occurring in the same reduction week would, but for this paragraph, take effect for the purpose of calculating entitlement to council tax reduction in different reduction weeks in accordance with paragraphs (1) to (6) they take effect from the day to which the appropriate paragraph from (2) to (6) refers, or, where more than one day is concerned, from the earlier day.

(8)   Where the change of circumstances is that income, or an increase in the amount of income, other than a benefit or an increase in the amount of a benefit under the 1992 Act[¹, Part 4 of the Welfare Reform Act 2012 or article 24A of the Armed Forces and Reserve Forces (Compensation Scheme) Order 2011], is paid in respect of a past period and there was no entitlement to income of that amount during that period, it takes effect for the purpose of calculating entitlement to council tax reduction from the first day on which the income, had it been paid in that period at intervals appropriate to that income, would have been taken into account for the purposes of these Regulations.

(9)   Without prejudice to paragraph (8), where the change of circumstances is the payment of income or arrears of income in respect of a past period, it takes effect for the purpose of calculating entitlement to council tax reduction from the first day on which the income, had it been timeously paid in that period at intervals appropriate to that income, would have been taken into account for the purposes of these Regulations.

(10)   Paragraph (11) applies if–

(a)   the applicant or the applicant's partner has attained the age of 65; and

(b)   either–

    (i)   a non-dependant took up residence in the applicant's dwelling; or

    (ii)   there has been a change of circumstances in respect of a non-dependant as a result of which the amount of the deduction to be made under regulation 48 (non-dependant deductions) increased.

(11)   Where this paragraph applies, the change of circumstances referred to in paragraph (10)(b) takes effect from the effective date.

(12)   Subject to paragraph (13), in paragraph (11) "the effective date" means–

(a)   where more than one change of a kind referred to in paragraph (10)(b) relating to the same non-dependant has occurred since the latest of–

    (i)   the date on which the applicant's entitlement to council tax reduction first began; or

    (ii)   the date which was the last effective date in respect of such a change, the date which falls 26 weeks after the date on which the first change occurred; and

(b)   where sub-paragraph (a) does not apply, the date which falls 26 weeks after the date on which the change referred to in paragraph (10)(b) occurred.

(13)   If in any particular case the date determined under paragraph (12) is not the first day of a reduction week, the effective date in that case is the first day of the reduction week starting immediately after the date determined under that paragraph.

Amendment

1.   Inserted by reg 12(6) of SSI 2013 No 142 as from 11.6.13.

General Note

This is similar to the HB equivalent. See p806 for the commentary.

Change of circumstances where state pension credit is in payment

60.–(1)   Paragraphs (2) to (4) apply where–

(a)   the applicant is on state pension credit;

(b)   the amount of state pension credit awarded to the applicant is changed as a result of a change in the applicant's circumstances or the correction of an official error; and

(c)   the change in the amount of state pension credit payable to the applicant results in a change in the applicant's entitlement to council tax reduction.

(2)   Where the change of circumstances is that an increase in the amount of state pension credit payable to the applicant results in–

(a)   an increase in the amount of council tax reduction to which the applicant is entitled, it takes effect from the first day of the reduction week in which state pension credit becomes payable at the increased rate; or

(b)   a decrease in the amount of council tax reduction to which the applicant is entitled, it takes effect from the first day of the reduction week starting immediately after the latest of–

    (i)   the date on which the relevant authority receives notification from the Secretary of State of the increase in the amount of state pension credit; or

    (ii)   the date on which state pension credit is increased.

(3)   Where the change of circumstances is that the applicant's state pension credit has been reduced and as a result the amount of council tax reduction to which the applicant is entitled is reduced–

(a)   in a case where the applicant's state pension credit is reduced because the applicant failed to notify the Secretary of State timeously of the change of circumstances, the change takes effect from the first day of the reduction week in which state pension credit was reduced; and

(b)   in any other case the change takes effect from the first day of the reduction week starting immediately after the latest of–

(i)   the date on which the relevant authority receives notification from the Secretary of State of the reduction in the amount of state pension credit; or

(ii)   the date on which state pension credit is reduced.

(4)   Where the change of circumstances is that state pension credit is reduced and as a result the amount of council tax reduction to which the applicant is entitled is increased, the change takes effect from the first day of the reduction week in which state pension credit becomes payable at the reduced rate.

(5)   Where the change of circumstances is that an award of state pension credit has been made to the applicant or the applicant's partner and this would result in a decrease in the amount of council tax reduction to which the applicant is entitled, the change takes effect from the first day of the reduction week starting immediately after the latest of–

(a)   the date on which the relevant authority receives notification from the Secretary of State of the award of state pension credit; or

(b)   the date on which entitlement to state pension credit begins.

(6)   Where, in the case of an applicant or any partner of an applicant who is or has been awarded state pension credit comprising only the savings credit, there is–

(a)   a change of circumstances of a kind described in any of paragraphs (2) to (5) which is the result of a relevant calculation or estimate; and

(b)   a change of circumstances which is a relevant determination,

each of which results in a change in the amount of council tax reduction to which the applicant is entitled, the change of circumstances referred to in sub-paragraph (b) takes effect from the day specified in paragraphs (2), (3), (4) or (5) as the case may be, in relation to the change referred to in sub-paragraph (a).

(7)   Where the change of circumstances is that a guarantee credit has been awarded to the applicant or any partner of the applicant and that would result in an increase in the amount of council tax reduction to which the applicant is entitled, the change takes effect from the first day of the reduction week starting immediately after the date in respect of which the guarantee credit is first payable.

(8)   Where a change of circumstances would, but for this paragraph, take effect under the preceding provisions of this regulation within the 4 week period specified in regulation 55 (continuing payments where state pension credit claimed), that change takes effect on the first day of the reduction week starting immediately after the expiry of the 4 week period.

(9)   Where the change of circumstances is an amendment of these Regulations that change takes effect from the date on which the amendment to these Regulations comes into force.

(10)   In this regulation–

(a)   "relevant calculation or estimate" means the calculation or estimate made by the Secretary of State of the applicant's or, as the case may be, the applicant's partner's income and capital for the purposes of the award of state pension credit; and

(b)   "relevant determination" means a change in the determination by the relevant authority of the applicant's income and capital using the relevant calculation or estimate, in accordance with regulation 25(1) (calculation of income in savings credit only cases).

General Note

This is similar to the HB equivalent. See p808 for the commentary.

PART 9
Applications

Who may apply

61. In the case of a couple or members of a polygamous marriage an application is to be made by whichever one of them they agree should apply or, in default of agreement, by whichever one of them the relevant authority determines is to make the application.

General Note

This is similar to the HB equivalent. See p543 for the commentary.

Time limit for making an application

62.–(1) Subject to paragraph (2), an application for council tax reduction must be made within 3 months of the date when the applicant fulfils the conditions of entitlement to council tax reduction in regulation 14 other than the condition in regulation 14(3)(c) (submission of an application).

(2) In a case where regulation 65(1)(a) (date on which an application is made) applies, paragraph (1) does not entitle an applicant to apply for council tax reduction in respect of any day earlier than 3 months before the date on which the claim for state pension credit is made (or treated as made by virtue of any provision of the Social Security (Claims and Payments) Regulations 1987).

General Note

This is similar to the HB equivalent. See p815 for the commentary.

Written applications

63.–(1) Subject to regulation 64 (telephone applications), an application must be sent to the designated office in writing and–

(a) made on a properly completed form approved for the purpose by the relevant authority; or

(b) in such written form as the relevant authority accepts as sufficient in the circumstances of any particular case or class of cases having regard to the sufficiency of the written information and evidence.

(2) Where an application is not made in the form described in paragraph (1)(a) or (b) it is defective.

(3) Where an application is defective because–

(a) it was made on the form approved for the purpose but that form is not accepted by the relevant authority as being properly completed; or

(b) it was made in writing but not on the form approved for the purpose and the relevant authority does not accept the application as being in a written form which is sufficient in the circumstances of the case, having regard to the sufficiency of the written information and evidence,

the relevant authority may–

(c) in a case to which sub-paragraph (a) applies, request the applicant to complete the defective application; or

(d) in a case to which sub-paragraph (b) applies, supply the applicant with the approved form or request further information or evidence.

(4) A defective application is to be treated as if it had been validly made in the first instance if, in any particular case, one of the conditions specified in paragraph (5) is satisfied.

(5) The conditions are that–

(a) where paragraph (3)(a) (incomplete form) applies, the relevant authority receives the properly completed application, the information requested to complete it or the evidence within one month of the authority's request, or any longer period the relevant authority considers reasonable; or

(b) where paragraph (3)(b) (application not on approved form or further information requested by relevant authority) applies–

    (i)   the approved form sent to the applicant is received by the relevant authority properly completed within one month of it having been sent to the applicant, or any longer period the relevant authority considers reasonable; or,

    (ii)   the applicant supplies whatever information or evidence was requested under paragraph (3) within one month of the request, or any longer period the relevant authority considers reasonable.

(6)   An application made on an approved form is for the purposes of these Regulations properly completed if completed in accordance with the instructions on the form, including any instructions to provide information and evidence in connection with the application.

General Note

This is similar to the HB equivalent. See p549 for the commentary.

Telephone applications

64.–(1)   Where the relevant authority has published a telephone number for the purpose of receiving applications for council tax reduction, an application may be made by telephone to that telephone number.

(2)   The relevant authority may determine that an application made by telephone is not a valid application unless the applicant approves a written statement of the person's circumstances, provided by the relevant authority.

(3)   An application made by telephone in accordance with paragraph (1) is defective unless the relevant authority is provided with all the information requested by it during the telephone call.

(4)   Where an application made by telephone in accordance with paragraph (1) is defective, the applicant must be given an opportunity to correct the defect.

(5)   If the applicant corrects the defect referred to in paragraph (4) within one month, or any longer period the relevant authority considers reasonable, of the date the authority last drew attention to the defect, the application is to be treated as if it had been validly made in the first instance.

(6)   If the person does not correct the defect within one month, or any longer period the relevant authority considers reasonable, of the date the authority last drew attention to the defect, the application may be treated as if it had not been defective if the relevant authority considers that it has sufficient information to determine the application.

General Note

This is similar to the HB equivalent. See p549 for the commentary.

Date on which an application is made

65.–(1)   Subject to paragraph (3) and regulation 5(9) (occupation of a dwelling as a home), the date on which an application is made is–

    (a)   where an award of state pension credit which comprises a guarantee credit has been made to the applicant or the applicant's partner and the application for council tax reduction is made within one month of the date on which the claim for that state pension credit which comprises a guarantee credit was received at the appropriate DWP office, the first day of entitlement to state pension credit which comprises a guarantee credit arising from that claim;

    (b)   where the applicant or the applicant's partner is in receipt of a guarantee credit and the applicant becomes liable for the first time to pay council tax in respect of the dwelling which the applicant occupies as a home and the application for council tax reduction is received within one month of the date on which the applicant first became liable to pay that council tax, the date when the applicant first became so liable;

    (c)   where the applicant is the former partner of a person who was, at the date of that partner's death or the partners' separation, entitled to council tax reduction and where the applicant makes an application for council tax reduction within one month of the date of the death or the separation, that date;

   (d)   except where sub-paragraph (a), (b) or (c) is satisfied, in a case where a properly completed application is received within one month, or any longer period the relevant authority considers reasonable, of the date on which–

        (i)   an application form was issued to the applicant following the applicant first notifying, by whatever means, the relevant authority of an intention to make an application; or

        (ii)   the applicant notifies, by whatever means, the relevant authority of an intention to make an application by telephone in accordance with regulation 64,

      the date of first notification; and

   (e)   in any other case, the date on which the application is received by the relevant authority.

   (2)   Except in the case of an application by a person living abroad, where the applicant is not liable for council tax but it is anticipated that the applicant will become liable for council tax within a period of 8 weeks, the applicant may apply for council tax reduction at any time in that 8 week period and, if liability arises within that 8 week period, the application is to be treated as having been made on the day on which the liability for council tax arises.

   (3)   Except in the case of an application by a person living abroad, where the applicant or any partner of the applicant has attained the age which is 17 weeks younger than the qualifying age for state pension credit and is not entitled to council tax reduction in the first reduction week starting after the date of the application but the relevant authority is of the opinion that the applicant will become entitled to council tax reduction for a period beginning not later than the seventeenth benefit week following the date on which the application is made, the relevant authority may treat the application as made in the reduction week immediately before the first reduction week of the period of entitlement.

   (4)   Where a relevant authority has not set or imposed its council tax by the beginning of the financial year, if an application for council tax reduction is made or treated as made and–

   (a)   the date on which the application is made or treated as made is in the period starting on 1st April of the current year and ending one month after the date on which the relevant authority imposes its council tax; and

   (b)   if the council tax had been determined by the beginning of the financial year, the applicant would have been entitled to council tax reduction from–

        (i)   the reduction week in which 1st April of the current year fell; or

        (ii)   a reduction week falling after 1st April of the current year but before the application was made,

      the relevant authority is to treat the application as made in the reduction week immediately preceding the reduction week in which the applicant would have become entitled to council tax reduction.

   (5)   In this regulation "appropriate DWP office" means an office of the Department for Work and Pensions dealing with state pension credit or a claim office which is normally open to the public for the receipt of claims for income support, a jobseeker's allowance or an employment and support allowance.

General Note

This is similar to the HB equivalent. See p549 for the commentary.

Evidence and information

   66.–(1)   Subject to paragraphs (2) and (3) an applicant must furnish any certificates, documents, information and evidence in connection with an application for council tax reduction or existing entitlement to council tax reduction as may reasonably be required by the relevant authority in order to determine that person's entitlement to, or continuing entitlement to, council tax reduction and must do so within one month of the authority requiring the applicant to do so, or any longer period the authority considers reasonable.

(2)   Nothing in this regulation requires a person to furnish any certificates, documents, information or evidence relating to a payment to which paragraph (3) applies.

(3)   This paragraph applies to–

(a)   a payment which is made under or by the Trusts, the Fund, the Eileen Trust, MFET Limited, the Skipton Fund, the Caxton Foundation [², another infected blood payment scheme] [³, the London Bombings Relief Charitable Fund, the London Emergencies Trust or the We Love Manchester Emergency Fund];

(b)   a payment which is disregarded under paragraph 16 of Schedule 4 (payments made under certain trusts and certain other payments), other than a payment [¹ by ILF Scotland]; and

(c)   a payment which is disregarded under regulation 48(9)(b) or (c) (non-dependant deductions) or paragraph 2(b) or (c) of Schedule 5 (alternative maximum council tax reduction: second adult's gross income) other than a payment [¹ by ILF Scotland].

(4)   Where a request is made under paragraph (1) the relevant authority must–

(a)   inform the applicant of the duty under regulation 69 to notify the authority of any change of circumstances; and

(b)   without prejudice to the extent of the duty owed under regulation 69, indicate to the applicant, either orally or by notice or by reference to some other document available to that applicant, on application and without charge, the kind of changes of circumstances which are to be notified.

(5)   Where an applicant or any partner of the applicant has attained the qualifying age for state pension credit and is a member of, or a person deriving entitlement to a pension under, a personal pension scheme the applicant must, where the relevant authority so requires, furnish the following information–

(a)   the name and address of the pension fund holder; and

(b)   any other information including any reference or policy number needed to enable the personal pension scheme to be identified.

(6)   In this regulation "pension fund holder" means the trustees, managers or scheme administrators, as the case may be, of the scheme concerned.

Amendments

1.   Substituted by reg 17(5) of SSI 2016 No 81 as from 1.4.16.
2.   Amended by reg 17 of SSI 2017 No 41 as from 1.4.17.
3.   Amended by reg 11(b) of SSI 2017 No 326 as from 20.11.17.

General Note

This is similar to the HB equivalent. See p556 for the commentary. Reg 66(1) is also similar to Sch 8 para 7(4) of CTRS(PR)(E) Regs, see p1181 for commentary.

Amendment of applications

67.–(1)   Subject to paragraph (2), at any time before a relevant authority has made a determination on an application the applicant may amend the application by notice in writing delivered or sent to the designated office.

(2)   Where an application is made by telephone in accordance with regulation 64 an amendment may be made by telephone to the telephone number specified by the relevant authority for the purpose of that regulation.

(3)   Any application amended in accordance with paragraph (1) or (2) is to be treated as if it had been in its amended state when it was first made.

General Note

This is similar to the HB equivalent. See p559 for the commentary.

Withdrawal of applications

68.–(1)   An applicant may withdraw the application at any time by notice in writing delivered or sent to the designated office before the relevant authority has determined the application.

(2)   Where the application was made by telephone in accordance with regulation 64, the withdrawal may be made by telephone to the telephone number specified by the relevant authority for the purpose of that regulation.

(3)   Any notice of withdrawal given in accordance with paragraph (1) or (2) has effect when it is received by the relevant authority.

General Note
This is similar to the HB equivalent. See p559 for the commentary.

PART 10
Notification of change of circumstances

Duty to notify changes of circumstances
69.–(1)   Subject to paragraphs (2) to (7) and regulation 70 (alternative means of notifying changes of circumstances), if at any time between the making of an application and it being determined or during a period of entitlement to council tax reduction, there is a change of circumstances which an applicant might reasonably be expected to know might affect entitlement to council tax reduction that applicant must notify that change of circumstances by giving notice to the relevant authority at the designated office–
(a)   in writing; or
(b)   by telephone–
    (i)   where the relevant authority has published a telephone number for that purpose or for the purposes of regulation 64 (telephone applications), unless the authority determines that in any particular case, or class of case, notification of a change of circumstances may not be given by telephone; or
    (ii)   in any case, or class of case, where the relevant authority determines that notice of a change of circumstances may be given by telephone; or
(c)   by any other means the relevant authority agrees to in any particular case.
(2)   Subject to paragraph (3), the duty imposed by paragraph (1) does not extend to notifying changes–
(a)   in the amount of council tax payable to the relevant authority;
(b)   in the age of the applicant or of any member of the applicant's family; or
(c)   to these Regulations.
(3)   Notwithstanding paragraph (2)(b) an applicant is required by paragraph (1) to notify the relevant authority of any change in thecomposition of the applicant's family arising from the fact that a person who was a member of the family is now no longer a member of the family because that person ceased to be a child or young person.
(4)   Where the amount of an entitled person's council tax reduction is the alternative maximum council tax reduction applicable to that person calculated in accordance with regulation 56, the person is required by paragraph (1) to notify the relevant authority of changes which occur in the number of adults in the dwelling or in their total gross incomes which might reasonably be expected to change the applicant's entitlement to council tax reduction and where any of those adults ceases to be in receipt of state pension credit, income support, universal credit, an income-based jobseeker's allowance or an income-related employment and support allowance the date when this occurs.
(5)   An applicant who is entitled to council tax reduction and state pension credit need only notify the changes specified in paragraphs (6) and (7).
(6)   An applicant referred to in paragraph (5) must notify–
(a)   changes affecting the residence or income of any non-dependant normally residing with the applicant or with whom the applicant normally resides; and
(b)   any absence from the dwelling which exceeds or is likely to exceed 13 weeks.
(7)   In addition to the changes required to be notified under paragraph (6), an applicant referred to in paragraph (5) whose state pension credit comprises only a savings credit must also notify–
(a)   changes affecting a child living with the person which may result in a change in the amount of council tax reduction to which the applicant is entitled, but this does not include changes in the age of the child;

(b)   any change in the amount of the applicant's capital to be taken into account
        when calculating the applicant's entitlement to council tax reduction which does
        or may take the amount of the applicant's capital to more than £16,000; and
(c)   any change in the income or capital of–
        (i)   a non-dependant whose income and capital are treated as belonging to the
                applicant in accordance with regulation 22 (circumstances in which capital
                and income of a non-dependant is to be treated as applicant's); or
        (ii)   a person to whom regulation 25(2)(e) (calculation of income in savings
                credit only cases) refers,
        and whether such a person or, as the case may be, non-dependant stops living
        with, or begins or resumes living with, the applicant.

General Note
This is similar to the HB equivalent. See p820 for the commentary.

Alternative means of notifying changes of circumstances

70.   Where a change of circumstances described in regulation 69 is a birth or death
the relevant authority may determine for a particular class of case that the duty in that
regulation to notify a change in circumstances may be discharged by personal attendance
at an office specified by that authority.

General Note
This is similar to the HB equivalent. See p562 for the commentary.

[¹PART 10A
Reviews

Amendment
1.   Inserted by reg 13 of SSI 2013 No 218 as from 1.10.13.

Review of determination on an application

70A.–(1)   A determination on an application may not be appealed to a valuation
appeal committee.
(2)   An applicant who is aggrieved by a determination on an application may serve
a written notice on the relevant authority requesting that it review its determination.
(3)   The notice under paragraph (2) must be served within two months of the
determination it relates to and must state the matter by which, and the grounds on which,
the applicant is aggrieved.
(4)   Where a notice under paragraph (2) is served on a relevant authority, that
authority must–
(a)   consider the matter to which the notice relates;
(b)   within two months of receipt of the notice, redetermine the application or decide
        that no alteration of the determination is to be made;
(c)   notify the applicant in writing of its decision and that if the applicant remains
        aggrieved then a request for further review may be made within 42 days of the
        notification, with the address to which any such a request is to be sent.]

Amendment
1.   Inserted by reg 13 of SSI 2013 No 218 as from 1.10.13. For transitional provisions, see reg 18 of SSI
        2013 No 218.

[¹Request for further review

70B.–(1)   A request for further review of a determination on an application must be
made in writing within 42 days of the notification by the relevant authority under sub-
paragraph (c) of regulation 70A(4) and be served at the address notified under that sub-
paragraph.
(2)   A request for further review of a determination on an application may also be
made where a relevant authority has not notified the applicant of a decision on a request

for review under regulation 70A(2) and more than two months have elapsed since the notice requesting review was served.

(3)　A request under paragraph (2)–

(a)　must be made in writing and be served on the relevant authority; and

(b)　prevents the relevant authority from notifying a decision on the request for review under regulation 70A(2).

(4)　A request for further review must state the matter by which, and the grounds on which, the applicant is aggrieved.

(5)　Where a relevant authority is served with a notice requesting further review it must, as soon as possible, forward it to the panel appointed by the Scottish Ministers under regulation 90C of the Council Tax Reduction Regulations.]

Amendment

1.　　　　Inserted by reg 13 of SSI 2013 No 218 as from 1.10.13.

[¹Conduct of further reviews

70C.–(1)　A further review of a determination on an application is to be undertaken by one member of the panel appointed under regulation 90C(1) of the Council Tax Reduction Regulations, except as set out in paragraph (8).

(2)　A further review is to include an oral hearing unless the parties and the member of the panel who is undertaking the review agree that the review is to be disposed of by written representations.

(3)　A party to a further review must, if requested, advise the member of the panel who is undertaking the review–

(a)　whether that party agrees that the review may be disposed of by written representations;

(b)　whether the applicant has appealed any application for housing benefit that may be relevant to the consideration of the further review, and if so whether that appeal has been determined (insofar as these matters are within the party's knowledge).

(4)　Where either party to a further review is requested by the member of the panel who is undertaking the further review to provide documents or information and fails to respond to that request within such timescale as the member considers reasonable, such inferences may be drawn from the failure as the member sees fit, including the inference that the further review should be allowed or refused.

(5)　A request for further review that has been validly made in accordance with regulation 70B may not be withdrawn other than with leave of the [² senior reviewer appointed under regulation 90C(1) of the Council Tax Reduction Regulations].

(6)　The member of the panel who is undertaking the further review–

(a)　is to decide the procedure for that review [², having regard to any guidance issued by the senior reviewer appointed under regulation 90C(1) of the Council Tax Reduction Regulations];

(b)　may hold any oral hearing in public or private, as the member sees fit;

(c)　may request, but has no power to require, the production of documents or the attendance of any person as a witness;

(d)　if satisfied that there are good and sufficient reasons for doing so, may refuse to permit a particular person to represent a party at an oral hearing; [²]

(e)　may uphold or reject the request for that review, in full or in part, but must remit any calculation of the amount of an applicant's entitlement to a council tax reduction to the relevant authority [²; and]

[² (f)　must give full reasons for the decision to uphold or reject the request for review, if asked to do so by a party to that review within 14 days of the date on which the decision was given.]

[² (6A)　A member of the panel may set aside a decision disposing of a request for further review if satisfied that it is in the interests of justice to do so.]

[² (6B)　Where a decision is set aside the further review must be undertaken again.]

[² (6C)　A request to set aside a decision must–

(a) be made within 14 days of the date on which the decision was given, and

(b) give reasons for the request.]

(7) The relevant authority must implement the decision of the member of the panel disposing of a request for further review of a determination as soon as is reasonably practicable, including any calculation of the amount of an applicant's entitlement to a council tax reduction that is required.

(8) In the circumstances of a particular case the Scottish Ministers may consider it appropriate for three members of the panel appointed under regulation 90C(1) of the Council Tax Reduction Regulations to undertake the further review, and in such a case references in this regulation to anything being done or decided by a member of the panel refer to it being done or decided by all three members, or by two of them should they not be agreed.]

Amendments

1.   Inserted by reg 13 of SSI 2013 No 218 as from 1.10.13.

2.   Amended by reg 19 of SSI 2015 No 46 as from 1.4.15.

PART 11
Electronic communication

Electronic communication

71.–(1) For the purpose of these Regulations, an applicant may send a document by electronic communication–

(a) in a form approved by the relevant authority for the purposes of this regulation;

(b) to an address notified by the relevant authority for the purposes of this regulation; and

(c) by the method set out in paragraph (4).

(2) An applicant sending a document to a relevant authority by electronic communication is taken to have agreed–

(a) to the use of electronic communication for all purposes relating to the application which are capable of being carried out electronically; and

(b) that the address for the purpose of such communication is the address incorporated into, or otherwise logically associated with, that communication.

(3) Deemed agreement referred to in paragraph (2) subsists until the applicant gives notice to revoke the agreement, and the notice takes effect from the date specified in it, being a date not less than 7 working days after the date on which the notice is given.

(4) An electronic communication must be–

(a) capable of being accessed by the recipient;

(b) legible in all other material respects; and

(c) sufficiently permanent to be used for subsequent reference.

(5) Unless the contrary is proved a document sent by the method specified in paragraph (3) is, for the purposes of any legal proceedings, to be regarded as having been–

(a) delivered when the document has been delivered to or by the relevant authority and the delivery of the document has been recorded on an official computer system; and

(b) received at the time and date of receipt recorded in an official computer system.

(6) In this regulation–

"address" includes any number or address used for the purpose of electronic communication or storage;

"document" includes an application, notice, certificate, information and evidence;

"electronic communication" has the same meaning as in section 15(1) of the Electronic Communications Act 2000;

"legible in all material respects" means that the information contained in the document is available to the recipient to no lesser extent than it would be if sent or given by means of a document in printed form; and "official computer system" means a computer system maintained by or on behalf of the relevant authority for the sending, receiving, processing or storing of an application.

[¹PART 12
Transitional provision

Transitional provision

72.–(1)   A person described in paragraph (2) is deemed to have made an application for council tax reduction on 1st April 2013.

(2)   A person referred to in paragraph (1) is a person–

(a)   who is entitled to council tax benefit on 31st March 2013;

(b)   who made an application for council tax benefit which is not determined before 1st April 2013;

(c)   whose entitlement to council tax benefit is wholly or partly suspended immediately before 1st April 2013;

(d)   other than a person described in sub-paragraphs (a) or (c), who has applied for a revision of a decision by a relevant authority under regulation 4(1) (revision of decisions) or 5(1) (late application for a revision) of the Housing Benefit and Council Tax Benefit (Decisions and Appeals) Regulations 2001 ("the 2001 Regulations") and whose application is pending immediately before 1st April 2013; and

(e)   other than a person described in sub-paragraphs (a) or (c), who has appealed against a decision of the First-tier Tribunal, the Upper Tribunal or a court in relation to a claim for council tax benefit and whose appeal is pending immediately before 1st April 2013.

(3)   For the purposes of sub-paragraph (2)(d) a revision of a decision relating to a claim for council tax benefit is pending if an application for a revision has been made but not been determined.

(4)   For the purposes of paragraph (2)(e) an appeal against a decision relating to a claim for council tax benefit is pending if–

(a)   an appeal against the decision has been brought but not determined;

(b)   an application for permission to appeal against the decision has been made but not determined; or

(c)   the time within which–

(i)   an application for permission to appeal may be made; or

(ii)   an appeal against the decision may be brought,

has not expired and one of the circumstances prescribed in regulation 11(3) of the 2001 Regulations apply.

(5)   Where an application for council tax reduction is deemed to be made in accordance with paragraph (1) and–

(a)   on 31st March 2013 the applicant by whom the application is deemed to have been made is a person to whom regulation 50(10) to (13) (date on which change of circumstances regarding non-dependants is to take effect) of the Council Tax Benefit (Persons who have attained the qualifying age for State Pension Credit) Regulations 2006 applies; and

(b)   the effective date for the purposes of the change of circumstances is a date after 31st March 2013,

that application is to be determined as though the change of circumstances has not taken place and is to be re-determined on the effective date to take account of the change of circumstances.]

Amendment

1.   Inserted by reg 8 of SSI 2013 No 49 as from 18.3.13.

SCHEDULE 1
Applicable amount

General Note

This is similar to Sch 3 HB(SPC) Regs, see p848 for the commentary. However, for CTR in Scotland, there is no 'two-child limit' for personal allowances for children and young people, as there is in some circumstances for HB and CTR in England. Instead, an applicant's applicable amount includes an allowance for each child or young person who is a member of the applicant's family. For commentary on the transitional rules determining continued eligibility for the family premium within the assessment of an applicant's applicable amount (under Part 2 of this Schedule), see below. For commentary on the need to register as blind or severely sight impaired to satisfy para 7(3) and (4) and therefore para 9(b), see the General Note to Sch 2 para 6 of The Council Tax Reduction Schemes and Prescribed Requirements (Wales) Regulations 2013 No.3029 (p1248).

From 1 April 2017, the amount included for a child or young person who is a member of the applicant's family specified in para 3 of this schedule were increased by 25 per cent.

PART 1
Personal allowances

1. In this Schedule "patient" means a person (other than a person who is serving a sentence of imprisonment or detention in a youth custody institution) who is regarded as receiving free in-patient treatment within the meaning of regulation 2(4) and (5) of the Social Security (Hospital In-Patients) Regulations 2005.

2. The amount specified in column (2) below in respect of each person or couple specified in column (1) is the amount specified for the purposes of regulation 20(a) (applicable amount)–

Column (1) Person, couple or member of a polygamous marriage	Column (2) Amount
(1) Single applicant or lone parent–	
(a) aged under 65;	[⁷ £167.25]
(b) aged 65 or over.	[⁷ £181.00]
(2) Couple–	
(a) both members aged under 65;	[⁷ £255.25]
(b) one member or both members aged 65 or over.	[⁷ £270.60]
(3) If the applicant is a member of a polygamous marriage and none of the members of the marriage have attained the age of 65–	
(a) for the applicant and one other party to the marriage;	[⁷ £255.25]
(b) for each additional party to the marriage who is a member of the same household as the applicant.	[⁷ £88.00]
(4) If the applicant is a member of a polygamous marriage and one or more members of the marriage is aged 65 or over–	
(a) for the applicant and one other party to the marriage;	[⁷ £270.60]
(b) for each additional party to the marriage who is a member of the same household as the applicant.	[⁷ £89.60].

Amendments

1. Amended by reg 9(a) of SSI 2013 No 49 as from 18.3.13.
2. Amended by reg 8(a) of SSI 2014 No 35 as from 1.4.14.
3. Amended by reg 20 of SSI 2015 No 46 as from 1.4.15.
4. Amended by reg 24(a) of SSI 2016 No 81 as from 1.4.16.
5. Amended by reg 18(a) of SSI 2017 No 41 as from 1.4.17.
6. Amended by reg 16(a) of SSI 2018 No 69 as from 1.4.18.
7. Amended by reg 12(a) of SSI 2019 No 29 as from 1.4.19.

---

3. The amount specified in column (2) below in respect of each person specified in column (1) is, for the relevant period specified in column (1), the amount specified for the purposes of regulation 20(b) (applicable amount)–

Column (1) Child or young person	Column (2) Amount
A person in respect of the period–	
(a) beginning on that person's date of birth and ending on the day preceding the first Monday in September following that person's sixteenth birthday;	[⁴£83.63]
(b) beginning on the first Monday in September following that person's sixteenth birthday and ending on the day preceding that person's twentieth birthday.	[⁴£83.63].

Amendments

1.   Amended by reg 9(b) of SSI 2013 No 49 as from 18.3.13.
2.   Amended by reg 8(b) of SSI 2014 No.35 as from 1.4.14.
3.   Amended by reg 20 of SSI 2015 No 46 as from 1.4.15.
4.   Substituted by reg 15 of SSI 2016 No 253 as from 1.4.17.

[² Part 2]

Amendments

1.   Amended by reg 8(c) of SSI 2014 No 35 as from 1.4.14.
2.   Omitted by reg 18(2) of SSI 2016 No 81 as from 1.5.16, subject to transitional provision in reg 2 of SSI 2016 No 81.

General Note

Paragraph 4 contained the rules for the family premium. This was included in an applicant's applicable amount if a child or young person was a member of her/his family. The family premium has been abolished for most applicants from 1 May 2016. From that date, only those covered by the transitional provision in reg 2 Council Tax Reduction (Scotland) Amendment Regulations 2016 No.81 can be entitled to it. Under reg 2, an applicant can still qualify for a family premium if, on 30 April 2016, s/he was entitled to CTR and was:

(1)   a member of a family which included at least one child or young person; *or*

(2)   a partner in a polygamous marriage and either s/he, or another partner of the polygamous marriage, was responsible for a child or young person who was a member of the same household.

An applicant covered by this transitional provision stop being entitled to a family premium either when the above condition 1 or 2 ceases to apply to her/him or when s/he makes a new CTR application. (A reassessment of an existing award does not count as a new CTR application.)

See p1528 of the 28th edition of this book for para 4.

'Family', 'partner', 'polygamous marriage' and 'child' are defined in reg 2. The meaning of 'young person' is defined in reg 4. Reg 10 explains when someone can be treated as responsible for a child or young person and reg 11 deals with when someone is treated as a member of the same household.

PART 3
Disability premiums

5.   For the purposes of regulation 20(d), a premium of an amount specified in Part 4 of this Schedule is applicable to an applicant who satisfies the conditions specified in this Part which relate to that premium.

6.–(1)   Subject to sub-paragraph (2), for the purposes of this Part, once a premium is applicable to an applicant under this Part, a person is to be treated as being in receipt of a benefit for–

(a)   in the case of a benefit to which the Social Security (Overlapping Benefits) Regulations 1979 applies, any period during which, but for the provisions of those Regulations, [²the person] would be in receipt of that benefit; and

(b)   any period spent by a person in undertaking a course of training or instruction provided or approved by Skills Development Scotland, Scottish Enterprise or Highlands and Islands Enterprise under section 2 of the Enterprise and New Towns (Scotland) Act 1990 or the Secretary of State under section 2 of the 1973 Act for any period during which [²the person] is in receipt of a training allowance.

(2)   For the purposes of the carer premium under paragraph 10, a person is to be treated as being in receipt of a carer's allowance by virtue of sub-paragraph (1)(a) only for so long as the person in respect of whose care the allowance has been claimed remains in receipt of attendance allowance, the care component of disability living allowance at the highest or middle rate prescribed in accordance with section 72(3) of the 1992 Act [¹, armed forces independence payment] or the daily living component of personal independence payment.

Amendments

1.   Inserted by reg 12(7)(a) of SSI 2013 No 142 as from 11.6.13.
2.   Amended by reg 14 of SSI 2013 No 218 as from 1.10.13.

Severe disability premium

7.–(1) With regard to severe disability premium the condition referred to in paragraph 5 is that the applicant is a severely disabled person.

(2)   For the purposes of sub-paragraph (1), an applicant is to be treated as being a severely disabled person if–

(a)   in the case of a single applicant, lone parent or an applicant who is treated as having no partner under sub-paragraph (3)–

(i)   the applicant is in receipt of attendance allowance, the care component of disability living allowance at the highest or middle rate prescribed in accordance with section 72(3) of the

1992 Act [¹, armed forces independence payment] or the daily living component of personal independence payment;

(ii)   subject to sub-paragraph (6), the applicant has no non-dependants aged 18 or over normally residing with the applicant or with whom the applicant normally resides; and

(iii)   no person is [³ in receipt of a carer's allowance under section 70 of the 1992 Act, or has an award of universal credit which includes the carer element under regulation 29 of the Universal Credit Regulations 2013,] in respect of caring for the applicant; and

(b)   in the case of an applicant who has a partner–

(i)   the applicant is in receipt of attendance allowance, the care component of disability living allowance at the highest or middle rate prescribed in accordance with section 72(3) of the 1992 Act [¹, armed forces independence payment] or the daily living component of personal independence payment;

(ii)   the applicant's partner is also in receipt of attendance allowance, the care component of disability living allowance at the highest or middle rate prescribed in accordance with section 72(3) of the 1992 Act [¹, armed forces independence payment] or the daily living component of personal independence payment or, if the applicant is a member of a polygamous marriage, each other member of that marriage is in receipt of such an allowance or payment; and

(iii)   subject to sub-paragraph (6), the applicant has no non-dependants aged 18 or over normally residing with the applicant or with whom the applicant normally resides,

and either a person is entitled to and in receipt of a carer's allowance [³, or has an award of universal credit which includes the carer element,] in respect of caring for only one member of the couple or, if the applicant is a member of a polygamous marriage, for one or more but not all the members of the marriage, or as the case may be, no person is entitled to and in receipt of a carer's allowance [³, or has an award of universal credit which includes the carer element,] in respect of caring for either member of the couple or any of the members of the marriage.

(3)   Where an applicant has a partner who does not satisfy the condition in sub-paragraph (2)(b)(ii), and that partner is blind or is treated as blind within the meaning of sub-paragraph (4), that partner is to be treated for the purposes of sub-paragraph (2) as if the partner was not a partner of the applicant.

(4)   For the purposes of sub-paragraph (3), a person is blind if that person has been certified as blind and in consequence is registered as blind in a register maintained by or on behalf of a local authority in Scotland or is registered as blind in a register compiled under section 29 of the National Assistance Act 1948 (welfare services) [² or is registered as severely sight impaired in a register kept by a local authority in Wales under section 18(1)(a) of the Social Services and Well-being (Wales) Act 2014].

(5)   For the purposes of sub-paragraphs (3) and (4), a person who has ceased to be registered as blind on regaining eyesight is to be treated as blind for a period of 28 weeks following the date on which the person ceased to be registered as blind.

(6)   For the purposes of sub-paragraph (2)(a)(ii) and (2)(b)(iii) no account is to be taken of–

(a)   a person receiving attendance allowance, the care component of disability living allowance at the highest or middle rate prescribed in accordance with section 72(3) of the 1992 Act [¹, armed forces independence payment] or the daily living component of personal independence payment; or

(b)   a person who is blind within the meaning of sub-paragraph (4) or is treated as blind within the meaning of sub-paragraph (5).

(7)   For the purposes of sub-paragraph (2)(b) a person is to be treated–

(a)   as being in receipt of attendance allowance, the care component of disability living allowance at the highest or middle rate prescribed in accordance with section 72(3) of the 1992 Act or the daily living component of personal independence payment, if the person would, but for being a patient for a period exceeding 28 days, be in receipt of attendance allowance, the care component of disability living allowance at the highest or middle rate prescribed in accordance with section 72(3) of the 1992 Act or the daily living component of personal independence payment, as the case may be; and

(b)   as being entitled to and in receipt of a carer's allowance [³ or as having an award of universal credit which includes the carer element] if the person would, but for the person [³ being cared for] being a patient in hospital for a period exceeding 28 days, be entitled to and in receipt of a carer's allowance [³ or would have an award of universal credit which includes the carer element].

(8)   For the purposes of sub-paragraph (2)(a)(iii) and (2)(b)–

(a)   no account is to be taken of an award of carer's allowance [³, or of universal credit which includes the carer element,] to the extent that payment of that award is back-dated for a period before the date on which the award is first paid; and

(b)   references to a person being in receipt of a carer's allowance [³ or as having an award of universal credit which includes the carer element] include references to a person who would have been in receipt of that allowance [³ or award] but for the application of a restriction under section 6B or 7 of the Social Security Fraud Act 2001 (loss of benefit).

Amendments

1.   Inserted by reg 12(7)(b) of SSI 2013 No 142 as from 11.6.13.

2.   Inserted by reg 19(3) of SSI 2016 No 81 as from 6.4.16.

3.   Amended by reg 24(b) of SSI 2016 No 81 as from 1.4.16.

Enhanced disability premium

8.–(1)   Subject to sub-paragraph (2), with regard to enhanced disability premium the condition referred to in paragraph 5 is that–

(a)   the care component of disability living allowance is, or would, but for a suspension of benefit in accordance with regulations under section 113(2) of the 1992 Act or but for an abatement as a consequence of hospitalisation, be payable at the highest rate prescribed under section 72(3) of the 1992 Act in respect of a child or young person who is a member of the applicant's family;

[²(aa)   armed forces independence payment is payable in respect of a young person within the applicant's family;] or

(b)   the daily living component of personal independence payment [¹at the enhanced rate] is, or would, but for a suspension of benefit in accordance with regulations made under section 86(1) of the Welfare Reform Act 2012 or an abatement as a consequence of hospitalisation, be payable in respect of a child or young person who is a member of the applicant's family.

(2)   Where the condition in sub-paragraph (1) ceases to be satisfied because of the death of a child or young person, the condition referred to in paragraph 5 is that the applicant or the applicant's partner is entitled to child benefit in respect of that child or young person under section 145A of the 1992 Act (entitlement after death of child or qualifying young person).

Amendments

1.   Amended by reg 9(c) of SSI 2013 No 49 as from 18.3.13.
2.   Inserted by reg 12(7)(c) of SSI 2013 No 142 as from 11.6.13.

Disabled child premium

9.   With regard to disabled child premium the condition referred to in paragraph 5 is that a child or young person for whom the applicant or applicant's partner is responsible and who is a member of the applicant's household–

(a)   is in receipt of disability living allowance or personal independence payment or is no longer in receipt of that allowance or payment because the child or young person is a patient, provided that the child or young person continues to be a member of the family;

(b)   is blind within the meaning of paragraph 7(4) or treated as blind in accordance with paragraph 7(5);

[¹(ba)   is a young person who is in receipt of armed forces independence payment;] or

(c)   is a child or young person in respect of whom section 145A of the 1992 Act (entitlement after death of child or qualifying young person) applies for the purposes of entitlement to child benefit but only for the period prescribed under that section, and in respect of whom a disabled child premium was included in the applicant's applicable amount immediately before the death of that child or young person, or ceased to be included in the applicant's applicable amount because of that child or young person's death.

Amendment

1.   Inserted by reg 12(7)(d) of SSI 2013 No 142 as from 11.6.13.

Carer premium

10.–(1)   With regard to carer premium the condition referred to in paragraph 5 is that the applicant or the applicant's partner is, or both of them are, entitled to a carer's allowance.

(2)   Where a carer premium has been awarded but–

(a)   the person in respect of whose care the carer's allowance was awarded dies; or

(b)   the person in respect of whom the premium was awarded ceases to be entitled, or ceases to be treated as entitled, to a carer's allowance,

the condition for the award of the premium must be treated as satisfied for a period of 8 weeks from the relevant date specified in sub-paragraph (3).

(3)   The relevant date for the purposes of sub-paragraph (2) is–

(a)   where sub-paragraph (2)(a) applies, the Sunday following the death of the person in respect of whose care the carer's allowance was awarded (or beginning with the date of death if the date occurred on a Sunday); and

(b)   in any other case, the date on which the person who was entitled to a carer's allowance ceases to be entitled to it.

(4)   For the purposes of this paragraph, a person is to be treated as being entitled to and in receipt of a carer's allowance for any period not covered by an award but in respect of which a payment is made in lieu of an award.

Persons in receipt of concessionary payments

11.–(1)   For the purpose of determining whether a premium is applicable to a person under paragraphs 7 to 10, any concessionary payment made to compensate that person for the non-payment of any benefit mentioned in those paragraphs is to be treated as if it was a payment of that benefit.

(2)   In this paragraph "concessionary payment" means a payment made under arrangements made by the Secretary of State with the consent of the Treasury which is charged to a Departmental Expenditure Vote to which payments of benefit or tax credits under the benefit Acts or the Tax Credits Act 2002 are charged.

Person in receipt of benefit
12.   For the purposes of this Part of this Schedule, a person is only to be regarded as being in receipt of a benefit if it is paid in respect of that person and is only to be regarded as being in receipt of that benefit for any period in respect of which the benefit is paid.

PART 4
Amount of disability premium

Premium	Amount
13.–(1) Severe disability premium–	
(a) where the applicant satisfies the condition in paragraph 7(2)(a);	[⁷ £65.85]
(b) where the applicant satisfies the condition in paragraph 7(2)(b)–	
(i) in a case where someone is in receipt of a carer's allowance [⁴ , or who has an award of universal credit which includes the carer element under regulation 29 of the Universal Credit Regulations 2013,] or if the applicant or any partner of the applicant satisfies that condition only by virtue of paragraph 7(7);	[⁷ £65.85]
(ii) in a case where no-one is in receipt of a carer's allowance [⁴ or an award of universal credit which includes the carer element].	[⁷ £131.70]
(2) Enhanced disability premium.	[⁷ £26.04] in respect of each child or young person in respect of whom the condition in paragraph 8 is satisfied.
(3) Disabled child premium.	[⁷ £64.19] in respect of each child or young person in respect of whom the condition in paragraph 9 is satisfied.
(4) Carer premium.	[⁷ £36.85] in respect of each person who satisfies the condition in paragraph 10.

Amendments
1.   Amended by reg 9(d) of SSI 2013 No 49 as from 18.3.13.
2.   Amended by reg 8(d) of SSI 2014 No 35 as from 1.4.14.
3.   Amended by reg 20 of SSI 2015 No 46 as from 1.4.15.
4.   Amended by reg 24(c) of SSI 2016 No 81 as from 1.4.16.
5.   Amended by reg 18(b) of SSI 2017 No 41 as from 1.4.17.
6.   Amended by reg 16(b) of SSI 2018 No 69 as from 1.4.18.
7.   Amended by reg 12(b) of SSI 2019 No 29 as from 1.4.19.

SCHEDULE 2
Sums to be disregarded in the calculation of earnings

General Note
This is similar to the HB equivalent. See p655 for the commentary. For commentary on the need to register as blind or severely sight impaired to satisfy para 5(b), see the General Note to Sch 2 para 6 of The Council Tax Reduction Schemes and Prescribed Requirements (Wales) Regulations 2013 No.3029 (p1248).

1.   Where two or more of paragraphs 2 to 5 apply in any particular case the overall maximum sum to be disregarded in that case is restricted to–
(a)   £25 in the case of a lone parent; and
(b)   £20 in any other case.
2.   In a case where the applicant is a lone parent, £25.
3.–(1)   In a case of earnings from any employment or employments to which sub-paragraph (2) applies, £20.
(2)   This paragraph applies to employment–
(a)   as a part time fire-fighter employed by a fire and rescue authority constituted by a scheme under section 2 of the Fire and Rescue Services Act 2004 or a scheme to which section 4 of that Act applies;
[¹ (b)   as a part-time fire-fighter employed by the Scottish Fire and Rescue Service established under section 1A of the Fire (Scotland) Act 2005;]

(c)   as an auxiliary coastguard in respect of coast rescue activities;

(d)   in the manning or launching of a lifeboat if the employment is part-time; and

(e)   as a member of any territorial or reserve force prescribed in Part 1 of Schedule 6 to the Social Security (Contributions) Regulations 2001.

(3)   If–

(a)   any of the earnings of the applicant or the applicant's partner, or both of them, are disregarded under sub-paragraph (1); and

(b)   either of them has, or both of them have, other earnings,

so much of those other earnings as would not if aggregated with the earnings disregarded under sub-paragraph (1) exceed £20.

Amendment

1.   Substituted by reg 21 of SSI 2015 No.46 as from 1.4.15.

4.–(1)   If the applicant or any partner of the applicant is a carer, or both are carers, £20 of any earnings received from that employment.

(2)   Where the carer premium is awarded in respect of the applicant and the applicant's partner, their earnings are, for the purpose of this paragraph, to be aggregated, but the amount to be disregarded in accordance with sub-paragraph (1) must not exceed £20 of the aggregated amount.

(3)   In this paragraph the applicant or the applicant's partner is a carer if paragraph 10 of Schedule 1 (carer premium) is satisfied in respect of the applicant or the applicant's partner.

5.–(1)   £20 if the applicant or any partner of the applicant–

(a)   is in receipt of–

(i)   long-term incapacity benefit under section 30A of the 1992 Act;

(ii)   severe disablement allowance under section 68 of the 1992 Act;

(iii)   attendance allowance;

(iv)   disability living allowance;

[[1](iva)   armed forces independence payment;]

(v)   personal independence payment;

(vi)   any mobility supplement under article 20 of the 2006 Order, any other supplement awarded in respect of disablement which affects a person's ability to walk and for which the person is in receipt of war disablement pension or any mobility supplement under article 25A of the Personal Injuries (Civilians) Scheme 1983;

(vii)   the disability element or the severe disability element of working tax credit under Schedule 2 to the Working Tax Credit Regulations; or

(viii) main phase employment and support allowance;

(b)   has been certified as blind and in consequence is registered as blind in a register maintained by or on behalf of a local authority in Scotland or is registered as blind in a register compiled under section 29 of the National Assistance Act 1948 (welfare services) [[3] or is registered as severely sight impaired in a register kept by a local authority in Wales under section 18(1)(a) of the Social Services and Well-being (Wales) Act 2014];

(c)   is, or is treated as, incapable of work in accordance with the provisions of, and regulations made under, Part 12A of the 1992 Act (incapacity for work) and has been incapable, or has been treated as incapable, of work for a continuous period of not less than–

(i)   in the case of an applicant who is terminally ill within the meaning of section 30B(4) of the 1992 Act, 196 days; and

(ii)   in any other case, 364 days; or

(d)   has, or is treated as having, limited [[2]capability] for work within the meaning of section 1(4) of the Welfare Reform Act 2007 or limited capability for work-related activity within the meaning of section 2(5) of that Act and either–

(i)   the assessment phase as defined in section 24(2) of the Welfare Reform Act 2007 has ended; or

(ii)   regulation 7 of the Employment and Support Allowance Regulations (circumstances where the condition that the assessment phase has ended before entitlement to the support component [[4]] arises does not apply) applies.

(2)   Subject to sub-paragraph (3), £20 if the applicant or any partner of the applicant has, within a period of 8 weeks ending on the day in respect of which the applicant or the applicant's partner attains the qualifying age for state pension credit, had an award of housing benefit or was entitled to council tax reduction and under these Regulations or the Council Tax Reduction Regulations–

(a)   £20 was disregarded in respect of earnings taken into account in that award or calculation of entitlement to council tax reduction; and

(b)   the person whose earnings qualified for the disregard continues in employment after the termination of that award of housing benefit or entitlement to council tax reduction.

(3)   The disregard of £20 specified in sub-paragraph (2) applies so long as there is no break, other than a break which does not exceed 8 weeks, in a person's entitlement to housing benefit or council tax reduction or in employment following the first day in respect of which that housing benefit is awarded or the person becomes entitled to council tax reduction.

(4)   £20 is the maximum amount which may be disregarded under this paragraph, notwithstanding that the applicant and any partner of the applicant may each satisfy the requirements of this paragraph.

Amendments

1.   Inserted by reg 12(8) of SSI 2013 No 142 as from 11.6.13.
2.   Amended by reg 15 of SSI 2013 No 218 as from 1.10.13.
3.   Inserted by reg 19(4) of SSI 2016 No 81 as from 6.4.16.
4.   Amended by reg 16 of SSI 2017 No 326 as from 20.11.17.

6.–(1)   Where–
(a)   the applicant (or if the applicant is a member of a couple, at least one member of that couple) is a person to whom sub-paragraph (5) applies;
(b)   the Secretary of State is satisfied that that person is undertaking exempt work as defined in sub-paragraph (6); and
(c)   regulation 24 (applicant in receipt of guarantee credit) does not apply,
the amount specified in sub-paragraph (7) ("the specified amount").

(2)   Where this paragraph applies, paragraphs 1 to 5 and 8 do not apply, but in any case where the applicant is a lone parent and the specified amount would be less than the amount specified in paragraph 2, paragraph 2 applies instead of this paragraph.

(3)   Notwithstanding regulation 21 (calculation of income and capital of members of applicant's family and of a polygamous marriage), if sub-paragraph (1) applies to one member of a couple ("A") it does not apply to the other member of that couple ("B") except to the extent provided for in sub-paragraph (4).

(4)   Where A's earnings are less than the specified amount, so much of B's earnings as would not when aggregated with A's earnings exceed the specified amount, but the amount of B's earnings which may be disregarded under this sub-paragraph is limited to a maximum of £20 unless the Secretary of State is satisfied that B is also undertaking exempt work.

(5)   This sub-paragraph applies to a person who is–
(a)   in receipt of a contributory employment and support allowance;
(b)   in receipt of incapacity benefit;
(c)   in receipt of severe disablement allowance; or
(d)   being credited with earnings on the grounds of incapacity for work or limited capability for work under regulation 8B of the Social Security (Credits) Regulations 1975.

(6)   In this paragraph "exempt work" means work of the kind described in–
(a)   regulation 45(2), (3) or (4) of the Employment and Support Allowance Regulations; or as the case may be;
(b)   regulation 17(2), (3) or (4) of the Social Security (Incapacity for Work) (General) Regulations 1995,
and, in determining for the purposes of this paragraph whether an applicant or a member of a couple is undertaking any type of exempt work, it is immaterial if that person or their partner is also undertaking other work.

(7)   The specified amount is the amount of money from time to time mentioned in any provision referred to in sub-paragraph (6) by virtue of which the work referred to in sub-paragraph (1) is exempt or, where more than one such provision is relevant and those provisions mention different amounts of money, the highest of those amounts.

7.   Any amount or the balance of any amount which would fall to be disregarded under paragraph 17 or 18 (parental and other contributions towards student maintenance) of Schedule 3 had the applicant's income which does not consist of earnings been sufficient to entitle the applicant to the full disregard under those paragraphs.

8.   Except where the applicant or the applicant's partner qualifies for a £20 disregard under the preceding provisions of this Schedule–
(a)   £5 if an applicant who has no partner has earnings; and
(b)   £10 if an applicant who has a partner has earnings.

9.   Any earnings, other than earnings referred to in regulation 31(8)(b) (calculation of weekly income), derived from employment which ended before the day in respect of which the applicant first satisfies the conditions for entitlement to council tax reduction in regulation 14.

10.–(1)   In a case where the applicant is a person who satisfies at least one of the conditions in sub-paragraph (2), and the applicant's net earnings equal or exceed the total of the amounts set out in sub-paragraph (3), the amount of the applicant's earnings to be disregarded must be increased by £17.10.

(2)   The conditions referred to in sub-paragraph (1) are that–
(a)   the applicant or, if the applicant is a member of a couple either the applicant or the other member of the couple, is a person to whom regulation 20(1)(c) of the Working Tax Credit Regulations applies; or
(b)   the applicant–
(i)   is, or any partner of the applicant's is, aged at least 25 and is engaged in remunerative work for on average not less than 30 hours per week;
(ii)   if the applicant is a member of a couple–
(aa)   at least one member of that couple is engaged in remunerative work for on average not less than 16 hours per week; and]

[¹ (bb) the applicant's family includes at least one child or young person]

(iii)   is a lone parent who is engaged in remunerative work for on average not less than 16 hours per week; or

(iv)   the applicant or, if the applicant is a member of a couple, at least one member of the couple is engaged in remunerative work for on average not less than 16 hours per week and paragraph 5(1) is satisfied in respect of that person.

(3)   The following are the amounts referred to in sub-paragraph (1)–

(a)   any amount disregarded under this Schedule;

(b)   the amount of child care charges calculated as deductible under regulation 29(1)(c) (treatment of child care charges); and

(c)   £17.10.

(4)   The provisions of regulation 6 (remunerative work) apply in determining whether or not a person works for on average not less than 30 hours per week, but as if the reference to 16 hours in regulation 6(1) was a reference to 30 hours.

Amendment

1.   Substituted by reg 18(3) of SSI 2016 No 81 as from 1.5.16, subject to transitional provision in reg 2 of SSI 2016 No 81.

---

11.   Where a payment of earnings is made in a currency other than sterling, any banking charge or commission payable in converting to that payment into sterling.

12.   Any payment in consequence of a reduction of council tax under section 13 or 80 of the Act.

SCHEDULE 3
Sums to be disregarded in the calculation of income other than earnings

General Note

This is similar to the HB equivalent. See p664 for the commentary.

---

1.   Each of the following payments–

(a)   a war disablement pension (except insofar as that pension is to be disregarded under paragraph 2);

(b)   a war widow's pension or war widower's pension;

(c)   a pension payable to a person as a widow, widower or surviving civil partner under any power of Her Majesty otherwise than under an enactment to make provision about pensions for or in respect of persons who have been disabled or have died in consequence of service as members of the armed forces of the Crown;

(d)   a guaranteed income payment and, if the amount of that payment has been abated to less than £10 by a pension or payment falling within article 39(3)(a) or (b) of the Armed Forces and Reserve Forces (Compensation Scheme) Order 2011, so much of that pension or payment as would not, in aggregate with the amount of any guaranteed income payment disregarded, exceed £10;

(e)   a payment made to compensate for the non-payment of a pension or payment mentioned in sub-paragraphs (a) to (d);

(f)   a pension paid by the government of a country outside Great Britain which is analogous to any of the pensions or payments mentioned in sub-paragraphs (a) to (d); and

(g)   a pension paid to victims of National Socialist persecution under any special provision made by the law of the Federal Republic of Germany, or any part of it, or of the Republic of Austria.

2.   Any mobility supplement under article 20 of the 2006 Order (including a mobility supplement under any other scheme or order) or under article 25A of the Personal Injuries (Civilians) Scheme 1983 or any payment intended to compensate for the non-payment of such a supplement.

3.   Any supplementary pension under article 23(2) of the 2006 Order (pensions to surviving spouses and surviving civil partners) and any analogous payment made by the Secretary of State for Defence to any person who is not a person entitled under that Order.

4.   In the case of a pension awarded at the supplementary rate under article 27(3) of the Personal Injuries (Civilians) Scheme 1983 (pensions to surviving spouses and surviving civil partners), the sum specified in paragraph 1(c) of Schedule 4 to that Scheme.

5.–(1)   Any payment which is–

(a)   made under any of the Dispensing Instruments to a widow, widower or surviving civil partner of a person–

(i)   whose death was attributable to service in a capacity analogous to service as a member of the armed forces of the Crown; and

(ii)   whose service in such capacity terminated before 31st March 1973; and

(b)   equal to the amount specified in article 23(2) of the 2006 Order.

(2)   In this paragraph "the Dispensing Instruments" means the Order in Council of 19th December 1881, the Royal Warrant of 27th October 1884 and the Order by His Majesty of 14th January 1922 (exceptional grants of pay, non-effective pay and allowances).

6.   £15 of any widowed parent's allowance to which the applicant is entitled under section 39A of the 1992 Act.

7.   £15 of any widowed mother's allowance to which the applicant is entitled under section 37 of the 1992 Act.

8.   Where the applicant occupies a dwelling as a home and provides in that dwelling board and lodging accommodation for a charge, an amount in respect of each person for whom the accommodation is provided for the whole or any part of a week, equal to–

(a)   where the aggregate of any payments made in respect of any one week in respect of the board and lodging accommodation provided to such persons does not exceed £20, 100 per cent of the aggregate of the payments; or

(b)   where the aggregate of any payments made in respect of any one week exceeds £20, £20 and 50 per cent of the excess of the aggregate of the payments over £20.

9.   If the applicant–

(a)   owns the freehold or leasehold interest in any property or is a tenant of any property;

(b)   occupies a part of that property; and

(c)   has an agreement with another person allowing that person to occupy another part of that property on payment of rent and–

　(i)   the amount paid by that person is less than £20 per week, the whole of that amount; or

　(ii)   the amount paid is £20 or more per week, £20.

10.   Where an applicant receives income under an annuity purchased with a loan which satisfies the following conditions–

(a)   that the loan was made as part of a scheme under which not less than 90 per cent of the proceeds of the loan were applied to the purchase by the person to whom it was made of an annuity ending with the applicant's life or with the life of the survivor of two or more persons ("the annuitants") who include the person to whom the loan was made;

(b)   that at the time the loan was made the person to whom it was made or each of the annuitants had attained the age of 65;

(c)   that the loan was secured on a dwelling in Great Britain and the person to whom the loan was made or one of the annuitants owns an interest in that dwelling;

(d)   that the person to whom the loan was made or one of the annuitants occupies the dwelling on which it was secured as a home at the time the interest is paid; and

(e)   that the interest payable on the loan is paid by the person to whom the loan was made or by one of the annuitants,

an amount, calculated on a weekly basis, equal to–

　(i)   where, or insofar as, section 369 of the Income and Corporation Taxes Act 1988 (mortgage interest payable under deduction of tax) applies to the payments of interest on the loan, the interest which is payable after deduction of a sum equal to income tax on such payments at the applicable percentage of income tax within the meaning of section 369(1A) of that Act; and

　(ii)   in any other case, the interest which is payable on the loan without deduction of such a sum.

11.–(1)   Any payment, other than a payment to which sub-paragraph (2) applies, made to the applicant by trustees in exercise of a discretion exercisable by them.

(2)   This sub-paragraph applies to payments made to the applicant by trustees in exercise of a discretion exercisable by them for the purpose of–

(a)   obtaining food, ordinary clothing or footwear or household fuel;

(b)   the payment of rent, council tax or water charges for which that applicant or the applicant's partner is liable; and

(c)   meeting housing costs of a kind specified in Schedule 2 to the State Pension Credit Regulations 2002.

(3)   In a case to which sub-paragraph (2) applies, £20 or–

(a)   if the payment is less than £20, the whole payment;

(b)   if, in the applicant's case, £10 is disregarded in accordance with paragraph 1, £10 or the whole payment if it is less than £10; or

(c)   if, in the applicant's case, £15 is disregarded under paragraph 6 or 7 and–

　(i)   the applicant has no disregard under paragraph 1, £5 or the whole payment if it is less than £5; or

　(ii)   the applicant has a disregard under paragraph 1, nil.

(4)   In this paragraph–

(a)   "ordinary clothing or footwear" means clothing or footwear for normal daily use, but does not include school uniforms or clothing and footwear used solely for sporting activities; and

(b)   "water charges" means–

　(i)   any water and sewerage charges established by Scottish Water under a charges scheme made under section 29A of the Water Industry (Scotland) Act 2002, in so far as such charges are in respect of the dwelling which the applicant occupies as a home; or

　(ii)   any water and sewerage charges under chapter 1 of Part 5 of the Water Industry Act 1991.

12.   Any increase in pension or allowance under Part 2 or 3 of the 2006 Order paid in respect of a dependent other than the pensioner's partner.

13. Any payment ordered by a court to be made to the applicant or the applicant's partner in consequence of any accident, injury or disease suffered by the person or a child of the person to or in respect of whom the payments are made.

14. Periodic payments made to the applicant or the applicant's partner under an agreement entered into in settlement of a claim made by the applicant or the applicant's partner for an injury suffered by the applicant or the applicant's partner as the case may be.

15. Any income which is payable outside the United Kingdom for a period during which there is a prohibition against the transfer to the United Kingdom of that income.

16. Any banking charges or commission payable in converting to sterling payments of income made in a currency other than sterling.

17. Where the applicant makes a parental contribution in respect of a student attending a course of study in the United Kingdom which contribution has been assessed for the purposes of calculating–

(a) under regulations made under section 49 of the Education (Scotland) Act 1980, that student's bursary, scholarship or other allowance under that section or under regulations made under section 73 of that Act, any payment to that student under that section;

(b) the student's student loan, an amount equal to the weekly amount of that parental contribution, but only in respect of the period for which that contribution is assessed as being payable; or

(c) under or pursuant to regulations made under sections 1 or 2 of the Education Act 1962 or section 22 of the Teaching and Higher Education Act 1998,

that student's award.

18.–(1) Where the applicant is the parent of a student aged under 25 who either–

(a) is not in receipt of any award, grant or student loan in respect of that education; or

(b) is in receipt of an award under section 2 of the Education Act 1962 (discretionary awards) an award bestowed by virtue of the Teaching and Higher Education Act 1998 or regulations made under that Act, a bursary, scholarship or other allowance under section 49(1) of the 1980 Act or a payment under section 73 of the 1980 Act,

and the applicant makes payments by way of a contribution towards the student's maintenance, other than a parental contribution falling within paragraph 17, an amount specified in sub-paragraph (2) in respect of each week during the student's term.

(2) For the purposes of sub-paragraph (1), the amount is the sum equal to the lesser of–

(a) the weekly amount of the payments; or

(b) the amount by way of a personal allowance for a single applicant under 25 less the weekly amount of any award, bursary, scholarship, allowance or payment referred to in sub-paragraph (1)(b).

[¹**18A.**–(1) Any payment made in respect of a person who is a member of the applicant's family–

(a) in accordance with an adoption allowance scheme made under section 71 of the Adoption and Children (Scotland) Act 2007 (adoption allowances schemes) or pursuant to regulations under section 2(6)(b), 3 or 4 of the Adoption and Children Act 2002;

(b) which is a payment made by a local authority in pursuance of section 50 of the Children Act 1975 (payments towards maintenance of children) or section 15(1) of, and paragraph 15 of Schedule 1 to, the Children Act 1989 (local authority contribution to a child's maintenance where the child is living with a person as a result of a residence order);

(c) which is a payment made by an authority, as defined in article 2 of the Children (Northern Ireland) Order 1995, in pursuance of article 15 of, and paragraph 17 of Schedule 1 to, that Order (contribution by an authority to child's maintenance); or

(d) in accordance with regulations made pursuant to section 14F of the Children Act 1989 (special guardianship support services).

(2) Any payment, other than a payment to which sub-paragraph (1)(a) applies, made to the applicant pursuant to regulations under section 2(6)(b), 3 or 4 of the Adoption and Children Act 2002.

18B. Any payment made by a local authority in accordance with section 12 of the Social Work (Scotland) Act 1968 (general social welfare services of local authorities), section 22 of the Children (Scotland) Act 1995 (promotion of welfare of children in need) or section 17 of the Children Act 1989 (provision of services for children in need, their families and others).]

Amendment

1. Inserted by reg 25 of SSI 2016 No 81 as from 1.4.16.

19.–(1) Where an applicant's [¹ family includes at least one child or young person], £15 of any payment of aliment or maintenance, whether under a court order or not, which is made or due to be made by the applicant's spouse, civil partner, former spouse or former civil partner or the applicant's partner's spouse, civil partner, former spouse or former civil partner.

(2) For the purposes of sub-paragraph (1), where more than one aliment or maintenance payment is to be taken into account in any week, all the aliment or maintenance payments must be aggregated and treated as if they were a single payment.

Amendment

1. Substituted by reg 18(4) of SSI 2016 No 81 as from 1.5.16, subject to transitional provision in reg 2 of SSI 2016 No 81.

20. In a case where the conditions of paragraph 10(2) of Schedule 2 (sums to be disregarded in the calculation of earnings) are met but the applicant's earnings are not disregarded for the purposes of that paragraph, any amount of working tax credit up to £17.10.

21. Where the total value of any capital specified in Part 2 of Schedule 4 (capital not to be treated as income under regulation 27(2)) does not exceed £10,000, any income actually derived from such capital.

22. Except in the case of income from capital specified in Part 2 of Schedule 4, any actual income from capital.

23. Where the applicant, or a person who was the partner of the applicant on 31st March 2003, was entitled on that date to income support or an income-based jobseeker's allowance but ceased to be so entitled on or before 5th April 2003 by virtue only of regulation 13 of the Housing Benefit (General) Amendment (No. 3) Regulations 1999 as in force at that date, the whole of the applicant's income.

[¹**24.** Any payment or interest on a payment made under, or in connection with, the Windrush Compensation Scheme administered by the Home Office.]

Amendment
1.   Inserted by reg 3(a) of SSI 2019 No 325 as from 26.11.19.

SCHEDULE 4

General Note
This is similar to the HB equivalent. See p683 for the commentary.

Capital disregards

PART 1
Capital to be disregarded

1. Any premises acquired for occupation by the applicant which the applicant intends to occupy as a home within 26 weeks of the date of acquisition or such longer period as is reasonable in the circumstances to enable the applicant to obtain possession and commence occupation of the premises.

2. Any premises which the applicant intends to occupy as the applicant's home, and in respect of which the applicant is taking steps to obtain possession and has sought legal advice, or has commenced legal proceedings, with a view to obtaining possession, for a period of 26 weeks from the earliest of the date on which the applicant first sought the advice or the date on which the applicant first commenced the proceedings, or such longer period as is reasonable in the circumstances to enable the applicant to obtain possession and commence occupation of those premises.

3. Any premises which the applicant intends to occupy as the applicant's home to which essential repairs or alterations are required in order to render them fit for occupation, for a period of 26 weeks from the date on which the applicant first takes steps to effect those repairs or alterations, or such longer period as is necessary to enable those repairs or alterations to be carried out.

4. Any premises occupied in whole or in part–

(a)   by a person who is a relative of the applicant or of any partner of the applicant as that person's home where the person has attained the qualifying age for state pension credit or is incapacitated; or

(b)   by a former partner of the applicant as that person's home, but this provision does not apply where the former partner is a person from whom the applicant is estranged or divorced or with whom the applicant had formed a civil partnership that has been dissolved.

5. Any future interest in property of any kind, other than land or premises in respect of which the applicant has granted a subsisting lease or tenancy, including sub-leases or sub-tenancies.

6.–(1) Where an applicant has ceased to occupy what was formerly the dwelling occupied as the applicant's home following estrangement or divorce from the applicant's former partner or the dissolution of a civil partnership with the applicant's former partner, that dwelling for a period of 26 weeks from the date on which the applicant ceased to occupy it or, where the dwelling is occupied as a home by the former partner who is a lone parent, for so long as it is so occupied.

(2) In this paragraph "dwelling" includes any garage, garden and outbuildings pertaining to the home formerly occupied by the applicant and any premises not so occupied which it is impracticable or unreasonable to sell separately, and in particular any croft land on which the dwelling is situated.

7. Any premises where the applicant is taking reasonable steps to dispose of the whole of the applicant's interest in those premises, for a period of 26 weeks from the date on which the applicant first took those steps, or any longer period as is reasonable in the circumstances to enable the applicant to dispose of the interest in the premises.

8. All personal possessions.

9. The assets of any business owned in whole or in part by the applicant and for the purposes of which the applicant is engaged as a self-employed earner or, if the applicant has ceased to be engaged as a self-employed earner, for a period that is reasonable in the circumstances to allow for disposal of those assets.

10. The assets of any business owned in whole or in part by the applicant where–

(a)　　the applicant is not engaged as a self-employed earner in that business by reason of some disease or bodily or mental disablement; but

(b)　　the applicant intends to become engaged or re-engaged as a self-employed earner in that business as soon as the applicant recovers or is able to become engaged or re-engaged in that business,

for a period of 26 weeks from the date on which the application for council tax reduction is made, or treated as made, or, if it is unreasonable to expect the applicant to become engaged or re-engaged in that business within that period, for a longer period that is reasonable in the circumstances to enable the applicant to become engaged or re-engaged as a self-employed earner in that business.

11.　　The surrender value of any policy of life insurance by which the payment of money is assured on death (except death by accident only) or the happening of any contingency dependent on human life, or any instrument evidencing a contract which is subject to payment of premiums for a term dependent on human life.

12.　　The value of any contract under which–

(a)　　the applicant makes one or more payments to another person ("the provider");

(b)　　the provider undertakes to provide, or secure the provision of, a funeral in the United Kingdom for the applicant on the applicant's death; and

(c)　　the sole purpose of the plan is to provide or secure the provision of a funeral for the applicant on the applicant's death.

13.　　Where an ex-gratia payment has been made by the Secretary of State on or after 1st February 2001 in consequence of the imprisonment or internment of–

(a)　　the applicant;

(b)　　the applicant's partner;

(c)　　the applicant's deceased spouse or deceased civil partner; or

(d)　　the applicant's partner's deceased spouse or deceased civil partner,

by the Japanese during the Second World War, an amount equal to that payment.

14.–(1)　　Subject to sub-paragraph (2), the amount of any trust payment made to an applicant or any partner of the applicant who is–

(a)　　a diagnosed person;

(b)　　a diagnosed person's partner or was a diagnosed person's partner at the time of the diagnosed person's death; or

(c)　　a parent of a diagnosed person, a person acting in place of a diagnosed person's parents or a person who was acting in place of a diagnosed person's parents at the date of the diagnosed person's death.

(2)　　Where a trust payment is made to–

(a)　　a person referred to in sub-paragraph (1)(a) or (b), sub-paragraph (1) applies for the period beginning on the date on which the trust payment is made and ending on the date on which that person dies; or

(b)　　a person referred to in sub-paragraph (1)(c), that paragraph (1) applies for the period beginning on the date on which the trust payment is made and ending 2 years after that date.

(3)　　Subject to sub-paragraph (4), the amount of any payment by a person to whom a trust payment has been made or of any payment out of the estate of a person to whom a trust payment has been made, which is made to an applicant or an applicant's partner who is–

(a)　　a diagnosed person;

(b)　　a diagnosed person's partner or was a diagnosed person's partner at the date of the diagnosed person's death; or

(c)　　a parent of a diagnosed person, a person acting in place of a diagnosed person's parents or a person who was acting in place of a diagnosed person's parents at the date of the diagnosed person's death.

(4)　　Where a payment referred to in sub-paragraph (3) is made to–

(a)　　a person referred to in sub-paragraph (3)(a) or (b), sub-paragraph (3) applies for the period beginning on the date on which the payment is made and ending on the date on which that person dies; or

(b)　　a person referred to in sub-paragraph (3)(c), sub-paragraph (3) applies for the period beginning on the date on which the payment is made and ending 2 years after that date.

(5)　　In this paragraph a reference to a person–

(a)　　being a diagnosed person's partner; or

(b)　　acting in place of a diagnosed person's parents,

at the date of the diagnosed person's death includes a person who would have been a diagnosed person's partner or a person acting in place of a diagnosed person's parents but for the diagnosed person residing in a care home or an independent hospital.

(6)　　In this paragraph–

"diagnosed person" means a person who has been diagnosed as suffering from, or who after death has been diagnosed as having suffered from, variant Creutzfeldt-Jakob disease; and

"trust payment" means a payment under a trust established out of funds provided by the Secretary of State in respect of persons who suffered, or who are suffering, from variant Creutzfeldt-Jakob disease for the benefit of persons eligible for payments in accordance with its provisions.

15.　　The amount of any payment, other than a war disablement pension, a war widow's pension or a war widower's pension to compensate for the fact that during the Second World War the applicant, the applicant's partner, the applicant's deceased spouse or civil partner or the applicant's partner's deceased spouse or civil partner–

(a)　　was a slave labourer or a forced labourer;

(b)   had suffered property loss or had suffered personal injury; or
(c)   was a parent of a child who had died.
16.–(1)   Any payment made under or by–
(a)   the Trusts, the Fund, the Eileen Trust, MFET Limited, the Skipton Fund, the Caxton Foundation [², another infected blood payment scheme] [³, the London Bombings Relief Charitable Fund,the London Emergencies Trust or the We Love Manchester Emergency Fund]; or
(b)   [¹ ILF Scotland].
(2)   Any payment by or on behalf of a person who is suffering, or who suffered, from haemophilia or who is or was a qualifying person, which derives from a payment made under or by any of the Trusts and which is made to or for the benefit of that person's partner or former partner from whom the applicant is not, or where that person has died was not, estranged or divorced or with whom the applicant has formed a civil partnership that has not been dissolved or, where that person has died, had not been dissolved at the time of that person's death.
(3)   Any payment by or on behalf of the partner or former partner of a person who is suffering, or who suffered, from haemophilia or who is or was a qualifying person provided that the partner or former partner and that person are not, or if either of them has died were not, estranged or divorced or, where the partner or former partner and that person have formed a civil partnership, the civil partnership has not been dissolved or, if either of them has died, had not been dissolved at the time of the death, which derives from a payment made under or by any of the Trusts and which is made to or for the benefit of the person who is suffering from haemophilia or who is a qualifying person.
(4)   Any payment by a person who is suffering from haemophilia or who is a qualifying person, which derives from a payment under or by any of the Trusts, where–
(a)   that person has no partner or former partner from whom the person is not estranged or divorced or with whom the applicant has formed a civil partnership that has not been dissolved, nor any child who is or had been a member of that person's household; and
(b)   the payment is made either–
        (i)   to that person's parent or step-parent; or
        (ii)   where that person at the date of the payment is a child or a student who has not completed full-time education and has no parent or step-parent, to any person standing in the place of the applicant's parent,
but only for a period from the date of the payment until the end of two years from the person's death.
(5)   Any payment out of the estate of a person who suffered from haemophilia or who was a qualifying person, which derives from a payment under or by any of the Trusts, where–
(a)   that person at the date of the person's death had no partner or former partner from whom the person was not estranged or divorced or with whom the person had formed a civil partnership that had not been dissolved, nor any child who was or had been a member of the person's household; and
(b)   the payment is made either–
        (i)   to the person's parent or step-parent; or
        (ii)   where the person at the relevant date was a child or a student who had not completed full-time education and had no parent or step-parent, to any person standing in place of the applicant's parent,
but only for a period of two years from the person's death.
(6)   In the case of a person to whom or for whose benefit a payment referred to in this paragraph is made, any capital resource which derives from any payment of income or capital made under or deriving from any of the Trusts or [¹ ILF Scotland].
(7)   In this paragraph "qualifying person" means a person in respect of whom payment has been made from the Fund, the Eileen Trust, MFET Limited, the Skipton Fund, the Caxton Foundation [², another infected blood payment scheme] [³, the London Bombings Relief Charitable Fund, the London Emergencies Trust or the We Love Manchester Emergency Fund.]
(8)   For the purposes of sub-paragraphs (2) to (6), any reference to the Trusts is to be construed as including a reference to the Fund, the Eileen Trust, MFET Limited, the Skipton Fund, the Caxton Foundation [², any other infected blood payment scheme] [³, the London Bombings Relief Charitable Fund, the London Emergencies Trust and the We Love Manchester Emergency Fund].

Amendments
    1.   Substituted by reg 17(2)(b) of SSI 2016 No 81 as from 1.4.16.
    2.   Amended by reg 19 of SSI 2017 No 41 as from 1.4.17.
    3.   Amended by regs 11(c) and 12 of SSI 2017 No 326 as from 20.11.17.

17.–(1)   Subject to sub-paragraph (2), an amount equal to the amount of any payment made in consequence of any personal injury to the applicant or to any partner of the applicant.
(2)   Where the whole or part of the payment is administered–
(a)   in accordance with an order made under Rule 36.14 of the Ordinary Cause Rules 1993 or under Rule 128 of those Rules;
(b)   by the High Court or the County Court under Rule 21.11(1) of the Civil Procedure Rules 1998, or the Court of Protection, or on behalf of a person where the payment can only be disposed of by order or direction of any such court; or

(c)   in accordance with the terms of a trust established for the benefit of the applicant or the applicant's partner,
the whole of the amount administered.

18.   Any amount specified in paragraph 19, 20, 21 or 25 for a period of one year beginning with the date of receipt.

19.   Any amount paid under a policy of insurance in connection with the loss of or damage to the property occupied by the applicant as the applicant's home or to the applicant's personal possessions.

20.   Any amount paid to the applicant or deposited in the applicant's name for the sole purpose of–
(a)   purchasing premises which the applicant intends to occupy as the applicant's home; or
(b)   effecting essential repairs or alterations to the premises occupied or intended to be occupied by the applicant as the applicant's home.

21.–(1)   Subject to paragraph 22 any amount paid–
(a)   by way of arrears of benefit;
(b)   by way of compensation for the late payment of benefit;
(c)   in lieu of the payment of benefit; or
(d)   to rectify, or compensate for [⁶ –
        (i)   an official error,
        (ii)   an error on a point of law made by an officer of the Department of Work and Pensions,
        (iii)   any error made by a member of staff of the Scottish Administration involved in the administration of social security benefits to which no person outside the Scottish Government or the Department for Work and Pensions materially contributed,]
being an amount to which that paragraph does not apply.

(2)   In sub-paragraph (1) "benefit" means–
(a)   attendance allowance under section 64 of the 1992 Act;
[⁴ (aa)   bereavement support payment under section 30 of the Pensions Act 2014;]
(b)   child tax credit;
(c)   council tax benefit;
(d)   disability living allowance;
[¹(da)   armed forces independence payment;]
(e)   personal independence payment;
(f)   housing benefit;
(g)   income-related employment and support allowance;
(h)   income support;
(i)   income-based jobseeker's allowance;
[⁹ (ia)   maternity allowance under section 35 of the 1992 Act,]
(j)   state pension credit;
(k)   working tax credit;
(l)   an increase of a disablement pension under section 104 of the 1992 Act (increase where constant attendance is needed), and any further increase of such a pension under section 105 of the 1992 Act (increase for exceptionally severe disablement);
(m)   any amount included on account of the applicant's exceptionally severe disablement or need for constant attendance in a war disablement pension, war widow's pension or war widower's pension; [²]
(n)   any discretionary housing payment paid pursuant to [⁸ regulation 2(1) of the Discretionary Financial Assistance Regulations 2001 or] [⁷ Part 5 of the Social Security (Scotland) Act 2018,] [³]
[² (o)   any social fund payment made pursuant to Part 8 of the 1992 Act] [³ ; [⁵]
(p)   universal credit]. [⁵ ; or
(q)   carer's allowance supplement made under section 81 of the Social Security (Scotland) Act 2018]

Amendments
1.   Inserted by reg 12(9) of SSI 2013 No 142 as from 11.6.13.
2.   Amended by reg 22(a) of SSI 2015 No 46 as from 1.4.15.
3.   Amended by reg 26(a) of SSI 2016 No 81 as from 1.4.16.
4.   Inserted by reg 14(a) of SSI 2017 No 326 as from 20.11.17.
5.   Amended by reg 7 of SSI 2018 No 211 as from 27.10.18.
6.   Amended by reg 7(a) of SSI 2018 No 295 as from 28.11.18.
7.   Amended by reg 14(a) of SSI 2019 No 29 as from 1.4.19.
8.   Amended by reg 3 of SSI 2019 No 133 as from 1.6.19.
9.   Inserted by reg 3(b)(i) of SSI 2019 No 325 as from 26.11.19.

22.–(1)   Subject to sub-paragraph (3), any payment of £5,000 or more which has been made to rectify, or to compensate for, [² an error described in sub-paragraph (1A)] relating to a benefit specified in paragraph 21(2) and has been received by the applicant in full on or after the day on which the applicant became entitled to council tax reduction under these Regulations or the Council Tax Reduction Regulations.

[² (1A)   Sub-paragraph (1) applies to–
(a)   an official error,

(b) an error on a point of law made by an officer of the Department of Work and Pensions,

(c) any error made by a member of staff of the Scottish Administration involved in the administration of social security benefits to which no person outside the Scottish Government or the Department for Work and Pensions materially contributed.]

(2) Subject to sub-paragraph (3), the total amount of any payments disregarded under–

(a) paragraph 7(2) of Schedule 10 to the Income Support Regulations;

(b) paragraph 12(2) of Schedule 8 to the Jobseeker's Allowance Regulations 1996;

(c) paragraph 20A of Schedule 5 to the State Pension Credit Regulations 2002; [¹]

(d) paragraph 11(2) of Schedule 9 to the Employment and Support Allowance Regulations[; or]

[² (e) paragraph 18 of Schedule 10 to the Universal Credit Regulations 2013,]

where the award in respect of which the payments last fell to be disregarded under those Regulations terminated immediately before the relevant date or is still in existence at that date.

(3) Any disregard which applies under sub-paragraph (1) or (2) has effect until expiry of the period of entitlement to council tax reduction.

(4) In this paragraph–

"period of entitlement to council tax reduction" means–

(a) the period of entitlement to council tax reduction under these Regulations during which the relevant sum or, where it is paid in more than one instalment, the first instalment of that sum is received; and

(b) where the period of entitlement to council tax reduction under these Regulations is followed by one or more further periods of entitlement to council tax reduction under these Regulations which, or each of which, begins immediately after the previous period of entitlement to council tax reduction ends, such further periods of entitlement to council tax reduction until the expiry of the last period of entitlement to council tax reduction provided that, for such further periods of entitlement to council tax reduction, the applicant–

(i) is the person who received the relevant sum;

(ii) is the partner of that person; or

(iii) was the partner of that person at the date of the applicant's death;

"the relevant date" means–

(a) in the case of an existing period of entitlement to council tax reduction under these Regulations or the Council Tax Reduction Regulations, 6th October 2003; and

(b) in any other case, the date on which the application for council tax reduction under these Regulations or the Council Tax Reduction Regulations was made; and

"the relevant sum" means the payment referred to in sub-paragraph (1) or the total amount referred to in sub-paragraph (2).

Amendments

1. Amended by reg 22(b) of SSI 2015 No 46 as from 1.4.15.

2. Amended by reg 7(b) and (c) of SSI 2018 No 295 as from 28.11.18.

---

23. Where a capital asset is held in a currency other than sterling, any banking charge or commission payable in converting that capital into sterling.

24. The value of the right to receive income from an occupational pension scheme or a personal pension scheme.

25. Any arrears of supplementary pension which are disregarded under paragraph 3 of Schedule 3 (amounts to be disregarded in the calculation of income other than earnings) or of any amount which is disregarded under paragraph 4 or 5 of that Schedule.

26. The dwelling, together with any garage, garden and outbuildings, normally occupied by the applicant as the applicant's home, including any premises not so occupied which it is impracticable or unreasonable to sell separately, and in particular any croft land on which the dwelling is situated but, notwithstanding regulation 21 (calculation of income and capital of members of applicant's family and of a polygamous marriage), only one dwelling is to be disregarded under this paragraph.

27.–(1) Subject to sub-paragraph (2), where the applicant is entitled to alternative maximum council tax reduction, the whole of the applicant's capital.

(2) Sub-paragraph (1) does not apply where in addition to satisfying the conditions in regulation 14(3) and (6) the applicant also satisfies the conditions in regulation 14(4) and (5) (conditions of entitlement to council tax reduction).

28. Any payment made under Part 8A of the 1992 Act (entitlement to health in pregnancy grant).

29. Any payment made [¹as a direct payment as defined in section 4(2) of the Social Care (Self-directed Support) (Scotland) Act 2013] or [² under] sections 12A to 12D of the National Health Service Act 2006 (direct payments for health care) or under regulations made under section 57 of the Health and Social Care Act 2001 (direct payments) [³ or under sections 50 to 53 of the Social Services and Well-being (Wales) Act 2014 (direct payments)].

Modification

The amendment made to Sch 4 para 29 by SSI 2014 No.90, which replaced "under section 12B of the Social Work (Scotland) Act 1968 (direct payments in respect of community care services)", does not have effect in respect of any payment made under s12B Social Work (Scotland) Act 1968 after 1.4.14.

Amendments

1.	Amended by art 2(3) and Sch Part 3 of SSI 2014 No 90 as from 1.4.14 subject to the saving provision in art 3 of that SSI.
2.	Amended by reg 22(c) of SSI 2015 No 46 as from 1.4.15.
3.	Inserted by reg 19(5) of SSI 2016 No81 as from 6.4.16.

30.	Any payment in consequence of a reduction of council tax under section 13 or section 80 of the Act (reduction of liability for council tax) but only for a period of 52 weeks from the date of receipt of the payment.

[¹**30A.**	Where a person elects to be entitled to a lump sum under Schedule 5 or 5A to the 1992 Act or under Schedule 1 to the Social Security (Graduated Retirement Benefit) Regulations 2005, or is treated as having made such an election, and a payment has been made pursuant to that election, an amount equal to–

	(a)	except where sub-paragraph (b) applies, the amount of any payment or payments made on account of that lump sum; or

	(b)	the amount of that lump sum,

but only for so long as that person does not change that election in favour of an increase in pension or benefit.]

Amendment

1.	Inserted by reg 26(b) of SSI 2016 No 81 as from 1.4.16.

[¹**30B.**	Any payment of bereavement suppport payment in respect of the rate set out in regulation 3(2) or (5) of the Bereavement Support Payment Regulations 2017 (rate of bereavement support payment), but only for a period of 52 weeks from the date of receipt of the payment.]

Amendment

1.	Inserted by reg 14(b) of SSI 2017 No 326 as from 20.11.17.

[¹**30C.**	Any payment made under or by the Thalidomide Trust.]

Amendment

1.	Inserted by reg 14 of SSI 2018 No 69 as from 1.4.18.

[¹**30D.**	Any early years assistance given in accordance with section 24, section 32 and schedule 6 of the Social Security (Scotland) Act 2018.]

Amendment

1.	Inserted by reg 14(b) of SSI 2019 No 29 as from 1.4.19.

[¹ **30E.**	Any funeral expense assistance given in accordance with section 24, section 34 and schedule 8 of the Social Security (Scotland) Act 2018.]

Amendment

1.	Inserted by reg 14(b) of SSI 2019 No 29 as from 1.4.19.

[¹**30F.**	Any payment or interest on a payment made under, or in connection with, the Windrush Compensation Scheme administered by the Home Office.]

Amendment

1.	Inserted by reg 3(b)(ii) of SSI 2019 No 325 as from 26.11.19.

PART 2

Capital not to be treated as income under regulation 27(2)

31.	The value of the right to receive any income under a life interest or from a life rent.

32.	The value of the right to receive any rent except where the applicant has a reversionary interest in the property in respect of which rent is due.

33.	The value of the right to receive any income under an annuity or the surrender value (if any) of such an annuity.

34.	Where property is held under a trust, other than–

	(a)	a charitable trust within the meaning of the Charities Act 2011; or

	(b)	a trust set up with any payment to which paragraph 16 of this Schedule applies,

and under the terms of the trust, payments fall to be made, or the trustees have a discretion to make payments, to or for the benefit of the applicant or any partner of the applicant, or both, that property.

SCHEDULE 5
Amount of alternative maximum council tax reduction

General Note
This is broadly the same as Sch 2 CTR(S) Regs. See p1551.

---

1. Subject to paragraphs 2 and 3, the alternative maximum council tax reduction in respect of a day for the purpose of regulation 56 is to be determined in accordance with the following table.

Table

Column (1) Second adult	Column (2) Alternative maximum council tax reduction
(a) Where the second adult is, or all second adults are, in receipt of income support, income-related employment and support allowance or state pension credit or the second adult is a person, or all second adults are persons, on an income based jobseeker's allowance [¹]or in receipt of universal credit;	25 per cent of the council tax due in respect of that day;
(b) Where the gross income of the second adult or, where there is more than one second adult, their aggregate gross income, disregarding any income of persons on income support, income-related employment and support allowance, state pension credit or an income based jobseeker's allowance–	
(i) is less than [⁸ £205.00] per week;	15 per cent of the council tax due in respect of that day;
(ii) is not less than [⁸ £205.00] per week but is less than [⁸ £268.00] per week.	7.5 per cent of the council tax due in respect of that day.
(c) Where the dwelling would be wholly occupied by one or more persons to whom regulation 20(2) of the Council Tax Reduction Regulations applies but for the presence of one or more second adults who are in receipt of income support, state pension credit, an income-related employment and support allowance or are persons on an income-based jobseeker's allowance.	100 per cent of the council tax due in respect of that day.

Amendments
1. Amended by reg 10 of SSI 2013 No 49 as from 18.3.13.
2. Amended by reg 18 of SSI 2013 No 287 as from 25.11.13.
3. Amended by reg 9 of SSI 2014 No 35 as from 1.4.14.
4. Amended by reg 23 of SSI 2015 No 46 as from 1.4.15.
5. Amended by reg 27 of SSI 2016 No 81 as from 1.4.16.
6. Amended by reg 20(a) of SSI 2017 No 41 as from 1.4.17.
7. Amended by reg 17 of SSI 2018 No 69 as from 1.4.18.
8. Amended by reg 13 of SSI 2019 No 29 as from 1.4.19.

---

2. In determining a second adult's gross income for the purposes of this Schedule, there must be disregarded from that income–
(a) any attendance allowance, disability living allowance[¹, armed forces independence payment] or personal independence payment;
(b) any payment made under or by the Trusts, the Fund, the Eileen Trust, MFET Limited, the Skipton Fund, the Caxton Foundation, [³ another infected blood payment scheme,] [² ILF Scotland] [⁴, the London Bombings Relief Charitable Fund, the London Emergencies Trust or the We Love Manchester Emergency Fund] which had the second adult's income fallen to be calculated under regulation 39 of the Council Tax Reduction Regulations (calculation of income other than earnings) would have been disregarded under paragraph 27 of Schedule 4 to those Regulations (income in kind); and
(c) any payment which had the applicant's income fallen to be calculated under regulation 39 of the Council Tax Reduction Regulations would have been disregarded under paragraph 41 of Schedule 4 to those Regulations (payments made under certain trusts and certain other payments).

Amendments
1. Inserted by reg 12(10) of SSI 2013 No 142 as from 11.6.13.
2. Substituted by reg 17(2)(c) of SSI 2016 No 81 as from 1.4.16.
3. Amended by reg 20(b) of SSI 2017 No 41 as from 1.4.17.
4. Amended by reg 11(d) of SSI 2017 No 326 as from 20.11.17.

3. Where there are two or more second adults residing with the applicant and any of those second adults falls to be disregarded for the purposes of discount in accordance with Schedule 1 to the Act, the applicant's income is to be disregarded in determining the amount of any alternative maximum council tax reduction unless that second adult is a member of a couple and the other partner does not fall to be disregarded for the purposes of discount.

4. In this Schedule–

"council tax due in respect of that day" means the council tax payable under section 78 of the Act less–

[¹(a) any reductions in liability for council tax under regulations made under section 80 of the Act or under a scheme established under section 80A of the Act, other than a reduction under these Regulations;] and

(b) in a case to which sub-paragraph (c) in column (1) of the table above applies, the amount of any discount which may be appropriate to the dwelling under the Act;

"second adult" means any person or persons residing with the applicant to whom regulation 14(6) (conditions of entitlement to council tax reduction) applies; and

"persons to whom regulation 20(2) of the Council tax Reduction Regulations applies" (persons not entitled to council tax reduction: students) includes any person to whom that regulation would apply if that person, and any partner of that person, was below the qualifying age for state pension credit.

Amendment

1. Substituted by reg 16 of SSI 2013 No 218 as from 1.10.13.

The Council Tax Reduction (Scotland) Amendment (No.2) Regulations 2013

(2013 No. 218)

Citation and commencement

1. These Regulations may be cited as the Council Tax Reduction (Scotland) Amendment (No. 2) Regulations 2013 and come into force on 1st October 2013.

Transitional provisions

17. Regulation 90A (review of determination on an application) of the Council Tax Reduction (Scotland) Regulations 2012 applies to a determination made before the date that these Regulations come into force, and for such purposes–

(a) the two month period referred to in paragraph (3) is deemed to commence on that date; and

(b) any notice of appeal relating to an application under those Regulations that has been served on the relevant authority under section 81 of the Local Government Finance Act 1992 before that date, and has not been disposed of, is to be progressed as if it were a notice served under paragraph (2) on that date.

18. Regulation 70A (review of determination on an application) of the Council Tax Reduction (State Pension Credit) (Scotland) Regulations 2012 applies to a determination made before the date that these Regulations come into force, and for such purposes–

(a) the two month period referred to in paragraph (3) is deemed to commence on that date; and

(b) any notice of appeal relating to an application under those Regulations that has been served on the relevant authority under section 81 of the Local Government Finance Act 1992 before that date, and has not been disposed of, is to be progressed as if it were a notice served under paragraph (2) on that date.

Part 6:

Valuation Tribunals and council tax reduction schemes – England and Wales

The Valuation Tribunal for England (Council Tax and Rating Appeals) (Procedure) Regulations 2009

(2009 No.2269)

PART 1
INTRODUCTION

1.   Citation, application and commencement
2.   Interpretation: general
3.   Discharge of VTE's functions: general
4.   Arbitration

PART 2
APPEALS: FUNCTIONS OF THE VTE AND GENERAL PROVISIONS

5.   Arrangements for appeals
6.   Appeal management powers
7.   Lead appeals
8.   Procedure for applying for and giving directions
9.   Failure to comply with Regulations, etc
10.   Striking out proceedings
11.   Substitution and addition of parties
12.   No power to award costs
13.   Representatives
14.   Calculating time
15.   Sending and delivery of documents
16.   Use of documents and information
17.   Evidence and submissions
18.   Summoning of witnesses, and orders to answer questions or produce documents

PART 3
PROVISIONS RELEVANT ONLY TO COUNCIL TAX APPEALS

20A.   Notices of appeal – section 16 appeals
21.   Time limits

PART 4
PROCEEDINGS BEFORE THE VTE
CHAPTER 1
Before the hearing

28.   Notices of appeal, etc

CHAPTER 2
Hearings and inspection of premises

29.   Decision with or without a hearing
30.   Notice of hearing
31.   Public and private hearings
32.   Hearing in a party's absence

CHAPTER 3
Decisions and Orders

35.   Consent orders
36.   Notice of decisions
37.   Reasons for the decision
38.   Orders other than consent orders

PART 5
CORRECTING, REVIEWING, SETTING ASIDE AND APPEALING DECISIONS
39.   Clerical mistakes and accidental slips or omissions
40.   Reviewing and setting aside decisions
41.   Records of decisions, etc
43.   Appeals to the High Court
44.   Notification of further proceedings

General Note

In England and Wales, under s16(1)(b) and (2) Local Government Finance Act 1992 and unless s16(3) applies, someone can appeal to a valuation tribunal if s/he is aggrieved by any calculation or estimate made by the authority of the amount of council tax s/he is liable to pay. Appeals on entitlement to council tax reduction (CTR) and the amount of CTR paid therefore lie to the valuation tribunal. In *SC v East Riding of Yorkshire Council* [2014] EW Misc B46 (VT), the President of the Valuation Tribunal for England (VTE) decided that appeals relating to applications for discretionary council tax reduction also come under the jurisdiction of the valuation tribunal under s16(1)(b), stating:

> "12.   In precisely the same way as council tax reduction scheme appeals come to the Tribunal under section 16(1)(b), so too do calculations of the amount payable as a result of an application for discretionary relief under section 13A(1)(c). It is difficult to see any basis for a contrary argument."

It is worth noting that a challenge relating to the lawfulness of the CTR scheme itself, or any revision of it, must be made by way of judicial review rather than to the valuation tribunal (s66 LGFA 1992).

For further commentary on appeals relating to discretionary council tax reductions, see p1075.

Before an appeal can be brought to the valuation tribunal, the authority must first have had the opportunity to reconsider its decision. This is because a person can only appeal to the valuation tribunal if s/he has served a notice on the authority stating her/his grievance (ie, the decision s/he disagrees with and the grounds for considering it wrong) and either:

1.   s/he remains aggrieved after the authority has notified her/him in writing that:
  – it believes the grievance is not well founded; *or*
  – steps have been taken to deal with the grievance; *or*
2.   the authority has not given such written notice within the two-month period starting with the date s/he notified the authority of her/his grievance.

See s16(4)–(8) LGFA 1992 and p1080 for further commentary.

These regulations set out the rules for appeals to the VTE (the rules for Wales are contained in The Valuation Tribunal for Wales Regulations 2010 No.713 – see p1684).

For the purpose of these regulations, an appeal relating to CTR and discretionary council tax reduction comes under the term "section 16 appeal". An appeal must be made in writing to the valuation tribunal (reg 20A(1)) and must contain certain information (reg 20A(2)).

Reg 21 sets out the time limit for appealing to the valuation tribunal. When a written notice has been received from the authority under s16(7)(a) or (b) LGFA 1992, the written notice of appeal must be given to the valuation tribunal within two months of the date of service of the authority's notice. When s16(7)(c) applies, the written notice of appeal must be given within four months of the date notice was served on the billing authority of the grievance (reg 21(2) and (3)). The VTE President has the power to extend these time limits if satisfied that the delay has occurred because of circumstances beyond the control of the aggrieved person (reg 21(6)). This power can be delegated to other members of the VTE under para A16, Part 1 of Sch 11 LGFA 1988.

General requirements placed on the valuation tribunal in relation to the conduct of its functions are set out in reg 3 and the powers the valuation tribunal has in the management of appeals are described in reg 6. The valuation tribunal has power to give directions (see, for example, regs 6(2), 8, 16(2) and 17). Reg 9 deals with failures of either the person appealing or the billing authority in complying with the requirements of the regulations or a direction of the valuation tribunal. Circumstances in which a failure to comply with a direction can result in the striking out of proceedings are contained in reg 10.

Standard directions for appeals to the Valuation Tribunal for England are contained in the Consolidated Practice Statement for the Valuation Tribunal for England 2017 (as amended) (VTE CPS 2017 (as amended)).

PART 1
INTRODUCTION

Citation, application and commencement

1.   These Regulations, which apply in England only, may be cited as the Valuation Tribunal for England (Council Tax and Rating Appeals) (Procedure) Regulations 2009 and shall come into force on 1st October 2009.

Interpretation: general

2.–(1)   In these Regulations–

"the 1992 Act" means the Local Government Finance Act 1992;

"the 1988 Act" means the Local Government Finance Act 1988;

"appeal", unless the context otherwise requires, means an appeal under–

(a)   section 16 of the 1992 Act (appeals: general) (in these Regulations called a "section 16 appeal");

(b)   regulation 7 or 10 of the CT Regulations (in these Regulations called a "CT appeal");

[¹ (c)   regulation 13A of the NDR Regulations;]

(d)   paragraph 4 of Schedule 4A(2) to the 1988 Act as it applies for the purposes of–
    (i)   Part 3 of the 1988 Act (non-domestic rating); and
    (ii)   Part 1 of the 1992 Act (council tax; England and Wales);

(e)   paragraph 5C(3) of Schedule 9 to the 1988 Act (in these Regulations called an "appeal against imposition of a NDR penalty"); or

(f)   paragraph 3 of Schedule 3 to the 1992 Act (in these Regulations called an "appeal against imposition of a CT penalty");

"appeal against a completion notice", except in regulations 42(1), 43(1) and 44(2)(c), means an appeal mentioned in paragraph (d) of the definition of "appeal";

"appellant", unless the context otherwise requires, means–

(a)   a person who makes a section 16 appeal;

(b)   a person who makes a CT appeal or a NDR appeal; or

(c)   where a person has been substituted under regulation 11(1), that person;

"central list" means the central non-domestic rating list;

"company", "holding company" and "subsidiary" have the meanings given by the Companies Act 2006;

"completion notice" means a notice under paragraph 1 of Schedule 4A to the 1988 Act as it applies for the purposes of Part 3 of the 1988 Act or Part 1 of the 1992 Act (council tax; England and Wales);

"competent appellant", in relation to a CT proposal, a CT appeal or the withdrawal of a CT appeal, means a person who has appealed against the LO's decision in respect of the proposal or appeal (whether or not that person's appeal proceeds);

"competent party", in relation to a CT proposal, a CT appeal or the withdrawal of a CT appeal, means an interested person ("IP") who serves a notice on the LO and the VTE in accordance with regulation 27 of these Regulations (competent party to appeal);

"CT Regulations" means the Council Tax (Alteration of Lists and Appeals) (England) Regulations 2009;

"IP" (interested person)–

(a)   in relation to a dwelling and a day, means–
    (i)   the owner;
    (ii)   where subsection (3) of section 8 of the 1992 Act has effect on the day, and regulations provide for that subsection to have effect as if, for the reference to the owner, there were substituted a reference to another person, that other person;
    (iii)   in relation to an exempt dwelling or a dwelling in respect of which the amount set under section 30 of the 1992 Act for the financial year is nil, any person (other than the owner) who would be liable to pay council tax if the dwelling were not an exempt dwelling or, as the case may be, the amount so set were other than nil; and
    (iv)   any other person who is a taxpayer in respect of the dwelling;

(b)   in relation to a hereditament which forms part of the Crown Estate and is held by the Crown Estate Commissioners under their management within the meaning of section 1 of the Crown Estate Act 1961, means the Crown Estate Commissioners;

(c)   in relation to any other hereditament, means–
    (i)   the occupier;

(ii)　any other person (other than a mortgagee not in possession) having in any part of the hereditament either a legal estate or an equitable interest such as would entitle him (after the cessation of any prior interest) to possession of the hereditament or any part of it; and

(iii)　any person having a qualifying connection with the occupier or a person described in (ii);

"list"–

(a)　in relation to a section 16 appeal or a CT appeal, means a valuation list compiled under section 22 of the 1992 Act;

(b)　in relation to a NDR appeal, means, as the circumstances require, the central list or the local list;

"LO" (listing officer), in relation to a list, means the officer charged with its maintenance under section 22 of the 1992 Act;

"local list" means a local non-domestic rating list;

[¹ "NDR appeal" means an appeal under regulation 13A of the NDR Regulations;]

"NDR Regulations" means the Non-Domestic Rating (Alteration of Lists and Appeals) (England) Regulations 2009;

"proposal" means a proposal for the alteration of a list;

"proposer" means the person making a proposal;

"qualifying connection" has the meaning given in paragraph (2);

"ratepayer", in relation to a hereditament, means the occupier or, if the hereditament is not occupied, the owner;

"relevant authority", in relation to a dwelling or a hereditament, means the billing authority in whose area the dwelling or hereditament is situated;

"taxpayer", in relation to a dwelling and a day, means the person who is liable (whether solely or jointly and severally) to pay council tax in respect of the dwelling and the day.

"VO" means valuation officer;

"VTE" means the Valuation Tribunal for England;

"VTE panel", in relation to an appeal, means the members of the VTE selected to deal with the appeal in accordance with tribunal business arrangements;

"VTE President" means the person who is for the time being the President of the VTE; and

"VTS" means the Valuation Tribunal Service.

(2)　A person shall be treated as having a qualifying connection with another–

(a)　where both persons are companies, and–

(i)　one is a subsidiary of the other, or

(ii)　both are subsidiaries of the same company; or

(b)　where only one person is a company, the other person (the "second person") has such an interest in that company as would, if the second person were a company, result in its being the holding company of the other.

(3)　Any reference in these Regulations to a party–

(a)　in relation to a section 16 appeal, means the appellant and the billing authority;

(b)　in relation to a CT appeal, includes the appellant and the LO and–

(i)　where the appeal is under regulation 10 of the CT Regulations–

(aa)　the taxpayer for the time being as regards any dwelling to which the decision notice relates;

(bb)　any competent appellant; and

(cc)　any competent party;

(ii)　where the appeal is proceeding by virtue of regulation 22 of these Regulations (CT appeals: new appellant's appeal), includes the appellant and the LO, and–

(aa)　any other person who, in response to the request in the VTE's notice under regulation 23(1) (CT appeals: other parties to new appeal), has within the period specified in the notice served a notice informing the VTE of that person's wish to be a party; and

 (bb) any other person who becomes a competent party after the date on which the VTE's notice was served under regulation 23(1)
 (c) in relation to an appeal against imposition of a CT penalty, means the appellant and the authority which imposed the penalty;
 (d) in relation to a NDR appeal or an appeal against imposition of a NDR penalty, means the appellant and the VO and includes–
  (i) where the appeal is under [¹ regulation 13A] or 19 of the NDR Regulations–
   (aa) a person whose agreement is required under regulation 12 of those Regulations (agreed alterations following proposals); and
   (bb) any other person who has been a ratepayer in relation to the hereditament since the proposal was made and who has notified the [¹ VTE] in writing before the hearing, or before determination on the basis of written representations, that the person wishes to be a party to the appeal;
  (ii) where the appeal is against a completion notice, the relevant authority;
 (e) if the proceedings on an appeal have been concluded, means a person who was a party when the VTE finally disposed of all issues in the proceedings.
 [¹ (4) A reference in these Regulations to a matter included in the notice of appeal or any document accompanying the notice of appeal does not include any particulars of the grounds of the proposal with which the VO agreed.
 (5) In paragraph (4), "particulars of the grounds of the proposal" has the meaning given in the NDR Regulations.]

Amendment
1.   Amended by reg 4 of SI 2017 No 156 as from 1.4.17, in relation to a local non-domestic rating list and a central non-domestic rating list compiled on or after 1.4.17.

Discharge of VTE's functions: general
3. In giving effect to these Regulations and in exercising any of its functions under these Regulations, the VTE must have regard to–
 (a) dealing with appeals in ways which are proportionate to the importance of the appeal, the complexity of the issues, the anticipated costs and the resources of the parties;
 (b) avoiding unnecessary formality and seeking flexibility in the proceedings;
 (c) ensuring, so far as practicable, that the parties are able to participate fully in the proceedings;
 (d) using any special expertise of the VTE effectively; and
 (e) avoiding delay, so far as compatible with proper consideration of the issues.

Arbitration
4.–(1) Where the persons mentioned in paragraph (2) agree in writing that a matter falling within the VTE's jurisdiction is to be referred to arbitration, the matter shall be so referred.
 (2) The persons are those who, if the matter were to be the subject of an appeal to the VTE, would be the parties to the appeal.
 (3) Unless the VTE considers that there is good reason not to do so, where at any time before the determination of an appeal by the VTE, the parties to the proceedings on an appeal agree in writing that any matter arising in the proceedings is to be referred to arbitration, the matter shall be so referred.
 (4) In any arbitration under this regulation the award may include any order which could have been made by the VTE in relation to the matter; and paragraph 9 of Schedule 11 to the 1988 Act shall apply to such an order as it applies to an order recorded under these Regulations.

PART 2
APPEALS: FUNCTIONS OF THE VTE AND GENERAL PROVISIONS

Arrangements for appeals

5.–(1)   It shall be the duty of the VTE President to ensure that arrangements are made for appeals to be determined in accordance with the following provisions of these Regulations.

(2)-(3)   *[Omitted]*

Appeal management powers

6.–(1)   Subject to the provisions of Part 1 of Schedule 11 to the 1988 Act and of these Regulations, the VTE may regulate its own procedure.

(2)   The VTE may give a direction in relation to the conduct or disposal of proceedings at any time, including a direction amending, suspending or setting aside an earlier direction.

(3)   In particular, and without restricting the general powers in paragraphs (1) and (2), the VTE may–

(a)   extend or shorten the time for complying with any regulation or direction;

(b)   consolidate or hear together two or more sets of proceedings or parts of proceedings raising common issues, or treat an appeal as a lead appeal (whether in accordance with regulation 7 or otherwise);

(c)   [¹ subject to paragraph (4),] permit or require a party to amend a document;

(d)   [¹ subject to regulations 17, 17A and 18A,] permit or require a party or another person to provide documents, evidence, information, or submissions to the VTE or a party;

(e)   deal with an issue in proceedings as a preliminary issue;

(f)   hold a hearing to consider any matter, including a case management issue;

(g)   decide the form of any hearing;

(h)   adjourn or postpone a hearing;

(i)   require a party to produce a bundle for a hearing;

(j)   stay proceedings; or

(k)   suspend the effect of its own decision pending the determination by the Upper Tribunal or a court of an application for permission to appeal against, and any appeal against or review of, that decision.

[¹ (4)   *[Omitted]*]]

Amendment

1.   Amended by reg 6 of SI 2017 No 156 as from 1.4.17. in relation to a local non-domestic rating list and a central non-domestic rating list compiled on or after 1.4.17.

Procedure for applying for and giving directions

8.–(1)   The VTE may give a direction on the application of one or more of the parties or on its own initiative.

(2)   An application for a direction may be made–

(a)   by sending or delivering a written application to the VTE; or

(b)   orally during the course of a hearing.

(3)   An application for a direction must state the reason for making that application.

(4)   Unless the VTE considers that there is good reason not to do so, the VTE must send written notice of any direction to every party and to any other person affected by the direction.

(5)   If a party or any other person sent notice of a direction under paragraph (4) wishes to challenge it, they may do so by applying for another direction which amends, suspends or sets aside the first direction.

Failure to comply with Regulations, etc

9.–(1)   An irregularity resulting from failure to comply with any requirement in these Regulations or a direction does not of itself render void the proceedings or any step taken in the proceedings.

(2)   If a party has failed to comply with a requirement in these Regulations or a direction, the VTE may take such action as it considers just, which may include–
(a)   waiving the requirement;
(b)   requiring the failure to be remedied; or
(c)   exercising the power under regulation 8.

Striking out proceedings

10.–(1)   The proceedings, or the appropriate part of them, will automatically be struck out if the appellant has failed to comply with a direction that stated that failure by a party to comply with the direction would lead to the striking out of the proceedings or that part of them.

(2)   The VTE must strike out the whole or part of the proceedings if the VTE does not have jurisdiction in relation to the proceedings or that part of them.

(3)   The VTE may strike out the whole or a part of the proceedings if–
(a)   the appellant has failed to comply with a direction that stated that failure by the appellant to comply with the direction could lead to the striking out of the proceedings or that part of them;
(b)   the appellant has failed to co-operate with the VTE to such an extent that the VTE cannot deal with the proceedings fairly and justly; or
(c)   the VTE considers there is no reasonable prospect of the appellant's appeal, or part of it, succeeding.

(4)   The VTE may not strike out the whole or part of the proceedings under paragraph (2) or (3)(b) or (c) without first giving the appellant an opportunity to make representations in relation to the proposed striking out.

(5)   If the proceedings, or part of them, have been struck out under paragraph (1) or (3)(a), the appellant may apply for the proceedings, or part of them, to be reinstated.

(6)   An application under paragraph (5) must be made in writing and received by the VTE within one month after the date on which the VTE sent notification of the striking out to the appellant.

(7)   This regulation applies to a party to the proceedings other than the appellant as it applies to an appellant except that–
(a)   a reference to the striking out of the proceedings is to be read as a reference to the barring of that other party from taking further part in the proceedings; and
(b)   a reference to an application for the reinstatement of proceedings which have been struck out is to be read as a reference to an application for the lifting of the bar on that other party from taking further part in the proceedings.

(8)   If a party other than the appellant has been barred from taking further part in the proceedings under this regulation and that bar has not been lifted, the VTE need not consider any response or other submission made by that party.

[[1](9)   The functions of the VTE under paragraphs (2), (3)(a) and (4) and under regulation 37, so far as they relate to the striking out of proceedings in a section 16 appeal, may be discharged on behalf of the VTE by the clerk of the VTE or by any other member of the VTE's staff.

(10)   In paragraph (9), "VTE's staff" means the staff provided to the VTE by (or under arrangements made by) the VTS.]

Amendment
1.   Inserted by reg 2(2) of SI 2013 No 465 as from 1.4.13.

Analysis
Reg 10(1) allows an appeal, or part of the appeal proceedings, to be automatically struck out if:
(1)   the appellant is given a direction which states that failure to comply with it *would* lead the appeal or part of the proceedings to being struck out; *and*
(2)   the appellant fails to comply with that direction.
Alternatively, if the appellant has failed to comply with a direction which stated a failure to comply with it *could* lead to the striking out the proceedings, or any part of the proceedings, reg 10(3)(a) gives the tribunal discretion to strike out all or part of the appeal.

In a similar vein, another party to the proceedings (in CTR cases before the VTE, this will be the billing authority) will be automatically barred from taking further part in the proceedings if it fails to comply with a direction which stated a failure to comply would lead to its being barred from taking further part. If the failure to comply relates to a direction which stated such a failure could lead to its being barred from taking further part in the proceedings, it will be up to the discretion of the VTE whether to bar the billing authority: paras 7 and 8. The tribunal also has discretion to waive the requirements in a direction or to require the failure to comply with the direction be remedied: reg 9.

In *Simpsons Malt & Ors v Jones & Ors (Valuation Officers)* [2017] UKUT 460 (LC), it was stated (para 230): "A decision to strike out an appeal is a draconian course which should only be taken if a tribunal is persuaded that it is clearly justified after exercising its discretion properly." In exercising its discretion to strike out under para (3) or to bar the billing authority (as provided by para 7), or under reg 9, the tribunal should have regard to the principles in reg 3.

It is open to an appellant or other party to the proceedings to challenge a direction under reg 8(5), which provides that a party to the proceedings who has received a direction under reg 8(4) can apply for a direction to amend, suspend or set it aside. The procedure for doing so is laid out in regs 8(2) and (3) and 15.

In *Simpsons Malt*, which concerned a number of non-domestic rating appeals by ratepayers against VTE decisions not to reinstate their appeals having struck them out for failures by the appellants to comply with procedural directions contained in the VTE's Practice Statement and standard directions, the Chamber President and Deputy Chamber President, considering the different operation of paras (1) and (3) of reg 10, stated:

"14.   Regulation 10(1) contemplates the making of orders which state explicitly that the consequence of non-compliance will be that the proceedings or some part of them will be struck out. The exercise of judicial discretion is involved in the decision whether it is appropriate to make such an order in the first place. Where such an order is made, and is broken, the striking out of proceedings, or the relevant part of them, occurs automatically, without any further judicial decision or the exercise of judicial discretion.

15.   Regulation 10(3), in contrast, allows the VTE a discretion to strike out an appeal in the situations described in sub-paragraphs (a) to (c). There is nothing automatic or inevitable in the exercise of such a discretion, which is a judicial act and requires consideration of all relevant factors. Being a judicial act, a decision to strike out an appeal under this power must be explained by sufficient reasoning, and is amenable to an appeal."

If the proceedings (or part of them) have been struck out under reg 10(1) or reg 10(3)(a), the appellant can apply for the proceedings to be reinstated under reg 10(5) by making a written application to the VTE. Such an application must be received within one month after the date the appellant is sent notification of the striking out: para (6). In the same way, a billing authority that has been barred from taking further part in the proceedings can apply for the bar to be lifted: para (7)(b).

Note, under reg 6(3)(a) the VTE has discretion to extend or shorten the time for complying with any regulation or direction, but in exercising such discretion should have regard to the principles in reg 3.

The Consolidated Practice Statement (VTE CPS 2017 (as amended)) PS14 states:

"2.   An application for reinstatement/lifting of a bar may be on the ground that either:
– there was compliance with the relevant direction and the decision to strike out was therefore in error, or
– there are good reasons to excuse the non-compliance which justify relief from the sanction of striking out/barring.

3.   Reasons to explain or excuse non-compliance may include illness, compassionate circumstances, or any other reasons or circumstances judged to be compelling and reasonable. Relevant considerations include the interests of the administration of justice, whether the application has been made promptly, whether the failure to comply was intentional, accidental or negligent, whether there is a good explanation for the failure, and the effect on the parties of granting the application.

4.   It is for the applicant to satisfy the Tribunal that the reasons are such that it is in the interests of justice to reinstate the appeal or lift the bar. There is no presumption in favour of doing so and reinstatement will not be ordered merely because the striking out will deprive the appellant of having the appeal determined on its merits."

A question arises as to whether the approach to relief from sanctions – such as here, striking out an appeal or barring a party to the proceedings – contained in the Civil Procedure Rules are relevant to CTR cases.

Part 1 of the VTE CPS 2007 (as amended) states that the tribunal's overriding objective is to deal with cases fairly and justly and, in doing so, it will, among other things, apply the principle in reg 3. In addition, it states

"2.   The Tribunal must, when administering the conduct of a case, further the overriding objective by:
(a)   exercising any power given it by statute;
(b)   applying any Practice Statement or Direction; and
(c)   interpreting any rule or practice direction to ensure that appeals proceed with due expedition.

3   In doing so, it will have regard to the decision of the Supreme Court in *BPP Holdings v HMRC* [2017] UKSC 55."

In *BPP Holdings v HMRC*, the Supreme Court considered whether the First-tier Tribunal (Tax Chamber) was entitled to make an order debarring HMRC from taking further part in an appeal against a VAT decision and assessments. Although an appeal to the Upper Tribunal against this decision was successful, the Court of Appeal restored the debarring order. The Supreme Court unanimously agreed with the Court of Appeal but did not approve all of its reasoning.

The case concerned the application of rule 8 of the Tribunal Procedure (First-tier Tribunal) (Tax Chamber) Rules 2009 No.273 which is substantially the same as reg 10 above. The First-tier Tribunal had issued a direction to HMRC to reply to questions put by *BPP*, the direction stated that that a failure to comply with the direction by a given date may result in HMRC being barred from further proceedings – ie, under the terms equivalent to para (3)(a). HMRC's late response to the direction failed to answer the questions that had been put, and no excuse or reason for the failure was given. HMRC had also been substantially late in complying with other procedural deadlines during the course of the appeal. In deciding whether to issue a debarring order, the First-tier Tribunal judge considered caselaw concerning time limits and sanctions relevant to the Civil Procedure Rules and concluded that, although they may not be directly relevant, in reaching a decision she must consider all the relevant facts including the factors in CPR 3.9 (a) and (b), according them significant weight as part of her consideration of the overriding objective to deal with cases fairly and justly. (For CPR 3.9, see p1683.)

The Supreme Court considered this was the correct approach, stating (para 23):

"...it is highly desirable, particularly in a field where the law is the same throughout the United Kingdom (as in tax), that tribunals, or at any rate tribunals in the same field, apply the same, or (at least in some cases) even similar, rules in the same way throughout the UK. In these circumstances, all tribunals and appellate courts above the level of the UT should be wary of applying or relying on the procedural jurisprudence of the English and Welsh courts without also taking into account that of the Scottish and Northern Irish courts... Further, while it would be both unrealistic and undesirable for the tribunals to develop their procedural jurisprudence on any topic without paying close regard to the approach of the courts to that topic, the tribunals have different rules from the courts and sometimes require a slightly different approach to a particular procedural issue..."

Referring to the guidance given to tribunals on tax cases given by Judge Sinfield in the Upper Tribunal in *McCarthy & Stone (Developments) Ltd v HMRC* [2014] WLR 795 para 43, the Supreme Court stated (para 26):

"It is not for this Court to interfere with the guidance given by the UT and the Court of Appeal as to the proper approach to be adopted by the Ft-T in relation to the lifting or imposing of sanctions for failure to comply with time limits (save in the very unlikely event of such guidance being wrong in law). .... In a nutshell, the cases on time-limits and sanctions in the CPR do not apply directly, but the Tribunals should generally follow a similar approach."

Further, it stated:

"the issue whether to make a debarring order on certain facts is very much one for the tribunal making that decision, and an appellate judge should only interfere where the decision is not merely different from that which the appellate judge would have made, but is a decision which the appellate judge considers cannot be justified. In the words of Lawrence Collins LJ in *Walbrook Trustee (Jersey) Ltd v Fattal* [2008] EWCA Civ 427, para 33: Page 13

"[A]n appellate court should not interfere with case management decisions by a judge who has applied the correct principles and who has taken into account matters which should be taken into account and left out of account matters which are irrelevant, unless the court is satisfied that the decision is so plainly wrong that it must be regarded as outside the generous ambit of the discretion entrusted to the judge."

In other words, before they can interfere, appellate judges must not merely disagree with the decision: they must consider that is "unjustifiable" (para 33).

The Supreme Court clarified (para 34):

"That is not to say that an appellate tribunal cannot interfere in a case where a debarring order has been imposed or confirmed. The decision to impose a debarring order (unlike case management decisions of a more routine nature) can often have the effect of determining the substantive case. Further, as already mentioned in para 27 above, an important function of the UT and the Court of Appeal is to ensure a degree of consistency of approach among Ft-T judges. In the context of court decisions, this concern was plainly in the mind of the Court of Appeal in Mitchell and Denton. There must be a limit to the permissible harshness (or indeed the permissible generosity) of a decision relating to the imposition or confirmation (or discharge) of a debarring order."

See p1682 for further commentary on the applicability of caselaw on time limits and sanctions relevant to the Civil Procedure Rules.

Substitution and addition of parties

11.–(1)   The VTE may give a direction substituting a party if–

(a)   the wrong person has been named as a party; or

(b)   the substitution has become necessary because of a change of circumstances since the start of proceedings.

(2)   The VTE may give a direction adding a person to the proceedings as a party.

(3)   If the VTE gives a direction under paragraph (1) or (2), it may give such consequential directions as it considers appropriate.

No power to award costs
12.   The VTE may not make any order in respect of costs.

Representatives
13.–(1)   A party may appoint a representative (whether a legal representative or not) to represent that party in the proceedings, but the representative must not be a member of the VTE or the VTS or an employee of the VTS.

(2)   If a party appoints a representative, that party (or the representative if the representative is a legal representative) must send or deliver to the VTE written notice of the representative's name and address unless the representative's name and address have already been given to the VO or, as the case may be, the LO.

(3)   If the VTE receives notice that a party has appointed a representative under paragraph (2), it must send a copy of that notice to each other party.

(4)   Anything permitted or required to be done by a party under these Regulations or a direction may be done by the representative of that party, except signing a witness statement.

(5)   A person who receives due notice of the appointment of a representative–

(a)   must provide to the representative any document which is required to be provided to the represented party, and need not provide that document to the represented party; and

(b)   may assume that the representative is and remains authorised as such until they receive written notification that this is not so from the representative or the represented party.

(6)   At a hearing a party may be accompanied by another person, other than a member of the VTE or the VTS or an employee of the VTS, whose name and address has not been notified under paragraph (2); and that person may act as a representative or otherwise assist in presenting the party's case at the hearing.

(7)   Paragraphs (2) to (5) do not apply in relation to a person who accompanies a party under paragraph (6).

Calculating time
14.–(1)   An act required by these Regulations or a direction to be done on or by a particular day must be done by 5pm on that day.

(2)   If the time specified by these Regulations or a direction for doing any act ends on a day other than a working day, the act is done in time if it is done on the next working day.

(3)   In this regulation "working day" means any day except a Saturday or Sunday, Christmas Day, Good Friday or a bank holiday under section 1 of the Bank and Financial Dealings Act 1971.

Sending and delivery of documents
15.–(1)   Any document to be provided to the VTE under these Regulations or a direction must be–

(a)   sent by pre-paid post or delivered by hand to the address specified for the proceedings;

(b)   sent by fax to the number specified for the proceedings; or

(c)   sent or delivered by such other method and to such address as may be agreed by the VTE and the person by whom the documents are to be sent or delivered.

(2)   Subject to paragraph (3), if a party provides a fax number, email address or other details for the electronic transmission of documents to them, that party must accept delivery of documents by that method.

(3)   If a party informs the VTE and all other parties that a particular form of communication (other than pre-paid post or delivery by hand) should not be used to provide documents to that party, that form of communication must not be used.

(4)   If the VTE or a party sends a document to a party or the VTE by email or any other electronic means of communication, the recipient may request that the sender provide a hard copy of the document to the recipient.

(5)   A request under paragraph (4) must be made as soon as reasonably practicable after the recipient receives the document electronically.

(6)   The VTE and each party may assume that the address provided by a party or its representative is and remains the address to which documents should be sent or delivered until receiving written notification to the contrary.

Use of documents and information

16.–(1)   The VTE may make an order prohibiting the disclosure or publication of–
(a)   specified documents or information relating to the proceedings; or
(b)   any matter likely to lead members of the public to identify any person whom the VTE considers should not be identified.

(2)   The VTE may give a direction prohibiting the disclosure of information to a person if–
(a)   the VTE is satisfied that such disclosure would be likely to cause that person or some other person serious harm; and
(b)   the VTE is satisfied, having regard to the interests of justice, that it is proportionate to give such a direction.

(3)   If a party ("the first party") considers that the VTE should give a direction under paragraph (2) prohibiting the disclosure of information to another party ("the second party"), the first party must–
(a)   exclude the relevant document or information from any documents that will be provided to the second party; and
(b)   provide to the VTE the excluded document or information, and the reason for its exclusion, so that the VTE may decide whether the document or information should be disclosed to the second party or should be the subject of a direction under paragraph (2).

(4)   The VTE must conduct proceedings as appropriate in order to give effect to a direction under paragraph (2).

(5)   If the VTE gives a direction under paragraph (2) which prevents disclosure to a party who has appointed a representative, the VTE may give a direction that the documents or information be disclosed to that representative if the VTE is satisfied that–
(a)   disclosure to the representative would be in the interests of the party; and
(b)   the representative will act in accordance with paragraph (6).

(6)   Documents or information disclosed to a representative in accordance with a direction under paragraph (5) must not be disclosed either directly or indirectly to any other person without the VTE's consent.

Evidence and submissions

17.–(1)   [⁴ Subject to paragraph (1A), the VTE] may give directions as to–
(a)   issues on which it requires evidence or submissions;
(b)   the nature of the evidence or submissions it requires;
(c)   whether any parties are permitted or required to provide expert evidence;
(d)   any limit on the number of witnesses whose evidence a party may put forward, whether in relation to a particular issue or generally;
(e)   the manner in which any evidence or submissions are to be provided, which may include a direction for them to be given–
    (i)   orally at a hearing; or
    (ii)   by written submissions or witness statement; and
(f)   the time at which any evidence or submissions are to be provided.
[⁴ (1A)   *[Omitted]*]

(2)   [⁴ Subject to regulation 17A, the VTE] may–
(a)   admit evidence whether or not the evidence would be admissible in a civil trial in England; or
(b)   exclude evidence that would otherwise be admissible where–
    (i)   the evidence was not provided within the time allowed by a direction;
    (ii)   the evidence was otherwise provided in a manner that did not comply with a direction; or

    (iii)   it would otherwise be unfair to admit the evidence.

(3)   Paragraph (4) applies to information–

(a)   [¹(a) supplied in pursuance of–

    (i)   paragraph 5 of Schedule 9 to the 1988 Act,

    (ii)   section 27(1) or (3) of the 1992 Act,

    (iii) regulations made under section 13 of, or Schedule 2 to, the 1992 Act, [²]

    (iv) regulation 24 of the NDR Regulations; [²]]

    [³(v) under paragraph 15A of Schedule 2 to the 1992 Act; or

    (vi) under section 131 of the Welfare Reform Act 2012 for purposes relating to council tax; and]

(b)   information contained in–

    (i)   any document which, having been produced to the Commissioners for Her Majesty's Revenue and Customs in pursuance of section 28 of the Finance Act 1931 or furnished to them in pursuance of Schedule 2 to that Act, is for the time being in their possession or under their control; or

    (ii)   any land transaction return within the meaning of Part 4 (stamp duty land tax) of the Finance Act 2003.

(4)   Information to which this paragraph applies shall not be used in any relevant proceedings by a billing authority, a LO or a VO unless–

(a)   not less than two weeks' notice, specifying in relation to any information to be so used the documents or other media in or on which that information is held and the dwelling or hereditament to which it relates, has previously been given to every other party to the proceedings; and

(b)   any person who has given not less than 24 hours' notice of his intention to do so has been permitted, at any reasonable time–

    (i)   to inspect the documents or other media in or on which such information is held; and

    (ii)   to make a copy (other than a photographic copy) of, or of any extract from, any document containing such information;

[⁴ (c) *[Omitted]*]

(5)-(10)   *[Omitted]*

(11)   In paragraphs (4) and (8) "relevant proceedings" means any proceedings on or in consequence of an appeal under section 16 of the 1992 Act, the CT Regulations, the NDR Regulations and any proceedings on or in consequence of a reference to arbitration under regulation 4.

(12)-(13)   *[Omitted]*

Amendments

1.   Substituted by reg 2(2) of SI 2011 No 434 as from 1.4.11.

2.   Omitted by reg 2(3)(i) and (ii) of SI 2013 No 465 as from 1.4.13.

3.   Inserted by reg 2(3)(iii) of SI 2013 No 465 as from 1.4.13.

4.   Amended by reg 8 of SI 2017 No 156 as from 1.4.17. in relation to a local non-domestic rating list and a central non-domestic rating list compiled on or after 1.4.17.

Summoning of witnesses, and orders to answer questions or produce documents

18.–[¹ (A1)   *[Omitted]*]

(1)   On the application of a party or on its own initiative, the VTE may–

(a)   by summons require any person to attend as a witness at a hearing at the time and place specified in the summons;

(b)   order any person to answer any questions or produce any documents in that person's possession or control which relate to any issue in the proceedings.

(2)   A summons under paragraph (1) must–

(a)   give the person required to attend 14 days' notice of the hearing or such shorter period as the VTE may direct; and

(b)   where the person is not a party, make provision for the person's necessary expenses of attendance to be paid, and state who is to pay them.

(3)   No person may be compelled to give any evidence or produce any document that the person could not be compelled to give or produce on a trial of an action in a court of law in England.

(4)   A summons or order under this regulation must–

(a)   state that the person on whom the requirement is imposed may apply to the VTE to vary or set aside the summons or order if they have not had an opportunity to object to it; and

(b)   state the consequences of failure to comply with the summons or order.

Amendment

1.   Inserted by reg 10 of SI 2017 No 156 as from 1.4.17, in relation to a local non-domestic rating list and a central non-domestic rating list compiled on or after 1.4.17.

PART 3
PROVISIONS RELEVANT ONLY TO COUNCIL TAX APPEALS

[¹Notices of appeal – section 16 appeals

20A.–(1)   A section 16 appeal shall be initiated by giving written notice of appeal to the VTE.

(2)   A notice of appeal in the case of a section 16 appeal shall include the following particulars–

(a)   full name and address of the appellant;

(b)   the address of the relevant chargeable dwelling, if different from the address referred to in sub-paragraph (a);

(c)   the date on which the written notice under section 16(4)(a) of the 1992 Act was served and the name of the authority on which it was served;

(d)   the date, if applicable, on which the appellant was notified by the authority in accordance with section 16(7)(a) or (b) of the 1992 Act;

(e)   the grounds on which the appellant is aggrieved;

(f)   brief reasons why the appellant considers that the decision or calculation made by the authority was incorrect; and

(g)   where the appellant has also made an appeal to the First-tier Tribunal in accordance with the Housing Benefit and Council Tax Benefit (Decisions and Appeals) Regulations 2001 and the appeal raises common issues of fact with the appeal made under section 16 of the 1992 Act, a statement to that effect.]

Amendment

1.   Inserted by reg 2(4) of SI 2013 No 465 as from 1.4.13.

Time limits

21.–(1)   Paragraphs (2) to (5) are subject to paragraph (6).

(2)   The VTE shall dismiss an appeal by a person in relation to whom the condition mentioned in section 16(7)(a) or (b) of the 1992 Act is fulfilled unless the appeal is initiated within two months of the date of service of the billing authority's notice under that section.

(3)   Where the condition mentioned in section 16(7)(c) of the 1992 Act is fulfilled, the VTE shall dismiss an appeal by an aggrieved person unless the appeal is initiated within four months of the date of service of the person's notice under section 16(4).

(4)   The VTE shall dismiss an appeal under paragraph 3 of Schedule 3 to the 1992 Act unless the appeal is initiated within two months of the date of service of written notice of the imposition of the penalty.

(5)   The VTE shall dismiss an appeal against a completion notice unless the appeal is initiated within 28 days of the date of service of the notice.

(6)   The VTE President may authorise an appeal to be entertained where the VTE President is satisfied that the failure of the person aggrieved to initiate the appeal as provided by this regulation has arisen by reason of circumstances beyond that person's control.

General Note
This regulation details the time limits for making an appeal to the VTE. The President of the VTE has discretion to accept a late appeal if satisfied that the failure to appeal within the time limit arose because of circumstances beyond the appellant's control. A function of the President can be delegated other members of the VTE under para A16, Part 1, LGFA 1988 and PS1 para 4 VTE CPS 2017 (as amended), indicates that a decision on an extension of the time limit will be considered either by the President or by a Senior Member of the VTE on behalf of the President. If appealing outside the time limit the Practice Statement states that the application form 'Extension of Time Limits for Appeals' must be completed and sent with the appeal form for council tax reduction to the Tribunal: PS1 para 3 VTE CPS 2017 (as amended). Both forms can be obtained from www.valuationtribunal.gov.uk/forms. In determining whether to allow a late appeal, PS1 para 7 VTE CPS 2017 (as amended) states:

"The President (or Senior Member) will have regard to the following and any other matters that appear relevant to determining the application:
– when was the notice actually received?
– was the applicant informed of the right of appeal and the time limit?
– has the applicant acted with all reasonable speed in the circumstances?
– has the applicant advanced, with sufficient proof, any reasons to justify delay, such as illness, absence from home or bereavement?
– is the delay such that it would be contrary to the interests of justice to permit the appeal to be heard or heard fairly?"

In *Sabesan v LB Waltham Forest* [2018] EWHC 2373 (Admin) (see p1683), it was argued that the test "acting with all reasonable speed" is not part of the test under reg 21(6), exceeding the requirements of the statutory test of "circumstances beyond the control of the applicant". The High Court did not need to rule on this as the appeal was dismissed under reg 43(2) for being out of time, but Deputy High Court Judge Murray stated at para 37:

"Another interpretation of that factor, which is consistent with the statutory test, is that where an appellant has acted "with all reasonable speed" and is nonetheless late in filing the appeal, that will be a factor in favour of the appellant that may tip the decision in his or her favour in a close case. It is indicative that the delay was due to circumstances beyond the control of the applicant, because, despite acting with all reasonable speed, the application was nonetheless late. Under that interpretation, whether the applicant has acted with all reasonable speed is not an independent hurdle with which the appellant must comply, but merely a factor to be considered by the President of the VTE or his delegate in determining the application."

PART 4
PROCEEDINGS BEFORE THE VTE
CHAPTER 1
Before the hearing

Notices of appeal, etc
28.–(1)   If an appellant provides notice of appeal against a completion notice or the imposition of a penalty to the VTE later than the time required by the CT Regulations or the NDR Regulations (as the case may be) or by an extension of time allowed under regulation 6(3)(a) (appeal management powers), the VTE must not admit the notice of appeal unless the VTE extends time for the notice of appeal under that provision.

(2)   The VTE must acknowledge receipt of every notice of appeal within two weeks of its receipt and must send a copy of the notice of appeal and any accompanying documents to every party (other than the appellant) as soon as reasonably practicable after receiving the notice of appeal.

(3)   *[Omitted]*

CHAPTER 2
Hearings and inspection of premises

Decision with or without a hearing
29.–(1)   Subject to the following paragraphs, the VTE must hold a hearing before making a decision which disposes of proceedings unless–
(a)   each party has consented to, or has not objected to, the matter being decided without a hearing; and
(b)   the VTE considers that it is able to decide the matter without a hearing.
(2)   The VTE may in any event dispose of proceedings without a hearing under regulation 10 (striking out proceedings).

Notice of hearing

30.–(1)   The VTE must give each party entitled to attend a hearing reasonable notice of the time and place of the hearing (including any adjourned or postponed hearing) and any changes to the time and place of the hearing.

(2)   The period of notice under paragraph (1) must be at least 14 days except that the VTE may give shorter notice–

(a)   with the parties' consent; or

(b)   in urgent or exceptional circumstances.

Public and private hearings

31.–(1)   Subject to the following paragraphs, all hearings must be held in public.

(2)   The VTE or the VTE panel may give a direction that a hearing, or part of it, is to be held in private.

(3)   Where a hearing, or part of it, is to be held in private, the VTE or the VTE panel may determine who is permitted to attend the hearing or part of it.

(4)   Where the VTE or the VTE panel considers–

(a)   that the conduct of any person is likely to disrupt the hearing;

(b)   that the presence of any person is likely to prevent another person from giving evidence or making submissions freely; or

(c)   that the presence of any person is likely to defeat the purpose of the hearing, the VTE or the VTE panel (as the case may be) may give a direction excluding the person from any hearing, or part of it.

(5)   The VTE panel may give a direction excluding from any hearing, or part of it any person whose conduct the VTE panel considers is disrupting the hearing.

(6)   The VTE or the VTE panel may give a direction excluding a witness from a hearing until that witness gives evidence.

Hearing in a party's absence

32.   If a party fails to attend a hearing the VTE panel may proceed with the hearing if–

(a)   it is satisfied that the party has been notified of the hearing or that reasonable steps have been taken to notify the party of the hearing; and

(b)   it considers that it is in the interests of justice to proceed with the hearing.

CHAPTER 3
Decisions and Orders

Consent orders

35.–(1)   The VTE may, at the request of the parties but only if the VTE considers it appropriate, make a consent order disposing of the proceedings and making such other appropriate provision as the parties have agreed.

(2)   *[Omitted]*

(3)   Notwithstanding any other provision of these Regulations, the VTE need not hold a hearing before making an order under paragraph (1), or provide reasons for the order.

Notice of decisions

36.–(1)   The VTE panel may give a decision orally at a hearing.

(2)   As soon as reasonably practicable after the VTE panel, makes a decision which finally disposes of all issues in the proceedings, the VTE must provide to each party–

(a)   a decision notice stating the VTE panel's decision;

[[1](aa) in the case of a section 16 appeal, notification of the right to request a written statement of reasons, where those written reasons have not already been provided;]

(b)   notification of any right of appeal against the decision and of any right to make an application for the review of the decision; and

(c) notification of the time within which, and the manner in which, any [²right referred to in sub-paragraph (aa) or (b)] may be exercised.

[³ (3)-(4) *[Omitted]*]

Amendments

1. Inserted by reg 2(5)(a) of SI 2013 No 465 as from 1.4.13.
2. Amended by reg 2(5)(b) of SI 2013 No 465 as from 1.4.13.
3. Inserted by reg 14 of SI 2017 No 156 as from 1.4.17. in relation to a local non-domestic rating list and a central non-domestic rating list compiled on or after 1.4.17.

Reasons for the decision

37.–(1) [¹Subject to paragraph (3) as soon] as reasonably practicable after the VTE panel makes a decision which finally disposes of all issues in the proceedings on an appeal, the VTE must send to each party a written statement of the VTE panel's reasons for the decision.

(2) *[Omitted]*

[²(3) In the case of a section 16 appeal the VTE Panel may give reasons for a decision which disposes of proceedings–

(a) orally at a hearing; or

(b) in a written statement of reasons to each party.

(4) Unless the VTE Panel has already provided a written statement of reasons under paragraph (3)(b), a party may request the VTE Panel to provide such written statement following a decision which finally disposes of all issues in the proceedings.

(5) A request under paragraph (4) must be made within two weeks beginning with the date on which the VTE Panel sent or otherwise provided to the party a decision notice relating to the decision which finally disposes of all issues in the proceedings.

(6) If a party makes a request in accordance with paragraphs (4) and (5) the VTE Panel must send a written statement of reasons to each party within two weeks beginning with the date on which the request was made or as soon as reasonably practicable after the end of that period.

(7) Where a request under paragraph (4) is made in writing, it shall be treated, for the purposes of paragraphs (5) and (6), as having been made on the date it is received by the VTE.]

Amendments

1. Amended by reg 2(6)(a) of SI 2013 No 465 as from 1.4.13.
2. Inserted by reg 2(6)(b) of SI 2013 No 465 as from 1.4.13.

Orders other than consent orders

38.–(1) After dealing with a section 16 appeal the VTE may by order require–

(a) an estimate to be quashed or altered;

(b) a penalty to be quashed;

(c) the decision of a billing authority to be reversed; or

(d) a calculation (other than an estimate) of an amount to be quashed and the amount to be re-calculated.

(2)-(7) *[Omitted]*

[¹(7A) After dealing with an appeal against imposition of a CT penalty, the VTE may by order require a penalty to be quashed.]

(8) After dealing with an appeal against the imposition of a CT penalty or a NDR penalty, the VTE may order the LO or, as the case may be, the VO whose notice is the subject of the appeal to reduce or remit the penalty.

(9) The billing authority, the LO or the VO (as the case may be) must comply with an order under this regulation within two weeks of the day of its making.

(10) An order under this regulation may require any matter ancillary to its subject matter to be attended to.

Amendment

1. Inserted by reg 2(7) of SI 2013 No 465 as from 1.4.13.

PART 5
CORRECTING, REVIEWING, SETTING ASIDE AND APPEALING DECISIONS

Clerical mistakes and accidental slips or omissions

39. The VTE may at any time correct any clerical mistake or other accidental slip or omission in a decision, direction, order or any document produced by it, by–

(a) sending notification of the amended decision, direction or order, or a copy of the amended document, to all parties; and

(b) making any necessary amendment to any information published in relation to the decision, direction, order or document.

Reviewing and setting aside decisions

40.–(1) A party may apply to the VTE in writing for the review of the whole or part of a decision which disposes of proceedings on an appeal.

(2) The VTE President may direct that a review be undertaken of the whole or part of a decision which disposes of proceedings on an appeal.

(3) An application under paragraph (1)–

(a) must be made within 28 days of the date on which notice of the decision was sent; and

(b) must be considered by the VTE President.

(4) The VTE President shall not grant an application under paragraph (1) unless at least one of the conditions in paragraph (5) is satisfied.

(5) The conditions referred to in paragraph (4) are–

(a) a document relating to the proceedings was not sent to, or was not received at an appropriate time by, a party or a party's representative;

(b) a document relating to the proceedings was not sent to the VTE at an appropriate time;

(c) a party or its representative was not present at a hearing relating to the proceedings and the party shows reasonable cause for its or its representative's absence;

(d) there has been some other procedural irregularity in the proceedings;

(e) the decision is affected by a decision of, or on appeal from, the Upper Tribunal or the High Court;

(f) where the decision relates to an appeal against a completion notice, new evidence, whose existence could not have been discovered by reasonable inquiry or could not have been foreseen, has become available since the conclusion of the proceedings.

(6) Where an application under paragraph (1) is granted or a direction is given under paragraph (2), the VTE shall review the decision or part that is the subject of the review; and if it considers–

(a) that any of the conditions specified in paragraph (5) is satisfied; and

(b) that it is in the interests of justice to do so,

the VTE shall set aside the decision or part.

(7) Tribunal business arrangements shall apply in relation to the selection of members of the VTE to review a decision or part of a decision as if the review were an appeal.

(8) If the VTE sets aside a decision it must revoke any order made in consequence of the decision and notify the parties in writing of the revocation.

(9) The VTE must notify the parties in writing–

(a) of the result of an application under paragraph (1);

(b) of the result of a review under paragraph (6); and

(c) if, under paragraph (8), it revokes an order.

(10) Where, on the day on which an application under paragraph (1) is made, an appeal to the Upper Tribunal or the High Court in relation to the same issue as is the subject of the application remains undetermined, the VTE shall notify the Upper Tribunal or the High Court as soon as reasonably practicable–

(a) after the application is made; and

(b) after notice is given under any sub-paragraph of paragraph (9).

Records of decisions, etc

41.–(1)   The VTE must make arrangements for each decision, each order under regulation 35 or 38, the effect of each correction under regulation 39, and each revocation under regulation 40(8) to be recorded.

(2)   Records may be kept in any form, whether documentary or otherwise [¹].

(3)   Each record shall be retained for the period of six years beginning on the day on which an entry was last made in it.

(4)   Any person may, at a reasonable time stated by or on behalf of the VTE and without making payment, inspect records which are required to be made by paragraph (1).

(5)   If without reasonable excuse a person having custody of records ("the custodian") intentionally obstructs a person in exercising the right conferred by paragraph (4), the custodian shall be liable on summary conviction to a fine not exceeding level 1 on the standard scale.

(6)   The production in any proceedings in any court of law of a document purporting to be certified by the VTE President or the clerk of the VTE to be a true copy of a record of the VTE shall, unless the contrary is proved, be sufficient evidence of the document and of the facts it records.

Amendment

1.   Omitted by reg 2(8) of SI 2011 No 434 as from 1.4.11.

Appeals to the High Court

43.–(1)   An appeal shall lie to the High Court on a question of law arising out of a decision or order which is given or made by the VTE on an appeal under section 16 of the 1992 Act or the CT Regulations or an appeal against a completion notice under paragraph 1 of Schedule 4A to the 1988 Act as it applies for the purposes of Part 1 of the 1992 Act (council tax; England and Wales).

(2)   Subject to paragraph (3), an appeal under paragraph (1) may be dismissed if it is not made within four weeks of the date on which notice is given of the decision or order that is the subject of the appeal. [¹or, in the case of a section 16 appeal, within two weeks of the date on which written reasons for the decision are given in accordance with regulation 37(6), if later]

(3)   Where–

(a)   the appeal is made by a person whose application under regulation 40(1) for the review of the decision relied (whether in whole or part) on satisfaction of the condition mentioned in regulation 40(5)(c); and

(b)   the VTE gave notice–

   (i)   that it would not undertake a review; or

   (ii)   having reviewed the decision or part, that it would not set aside the decision or part,

the appeal may be dismissed if it is not made within four weeks of the date of the VTE's notice.

(4)   The High Court may confirm, vary, set aside, revoke or remit the decision or order, and may make any order the VTE could have made.

(5)   Billing authorities and LOs must act in accordance with any order made by the High Court; and paragraph 10A of Schedule 11 to the 1988 Act shall have effect as if the reference to a tribunal included a reference to the High Court.

Amendment

1.   Inserted by reg 2(8) of SI 2013 No 465 as from 1.4.13.

General Note

This provides that an appeal against a decision of the VTE, which has arisen on an appeal made to the VTE under s16 of the LGFA 1992, is to the High Court only on a question of law. (A similar provision covers appeals against decisions of the VTW – see reg 44 of The Valuation Tribunal for Wales Regs 2010 on p1693.) In England, unless reg 43(3) applies, such an appeal may be dismissed if it is not made either:

(1)   within four weeks of the date of the notification of the VTE's decision; *or*

(2)   within two weeks of the date on which the written statement of reasons for the VTE's decision are given, if that is later. (If written reasons have not already been provided, a party to the appeal can request them from the tribunal but the request must be received within the two weeks starting with the date on which the VTE's decision notice is sent or given, see reg 37.)

The High Court therefore has discretion to dismiss an appeal if it is not made within these time limits. In a case in which the council tax payer had lodged his appeal two weeks and one day out of time (*Turner v South Cambridgeshire DC* [2016] EWHC 1017 (Admin)), Mr Justice Warby considered that it did not matter whether reg 43 was analysed as either:

−   imposing a time limit which may only be extended if the court, at its discretion, agrees;

−   imposing an automatic sanction from which relief must be sought; *or*

−   giving a ground on which the court may in its discretion dismiss an appeal.

In refusing the application for an extension of time, he treated the application as equivalent to an application for relief from sanctions under the Civil Procedure Rules 3.9 and applied the guidance given in *Denton v TH White* [2014] EWCA Civ 906; [2014] 1 WLR 3927(the "Denton principles"), stating:

"25.   CPR 3.9 provides as follows:

"Relief from sanctions

(1)   On an application for relief from any sanction imposed for a failure to comply with any rule, practice direction or court order, the court will consider all the circumstances of the case, so as to enable it to deal justly with the application, including the need (a) for litigation to be conducted efficiently and at proportionate cost; and (b) to enforce compliance with rules, practice directions and orders.

(2)   An application for relief must be supported by evidence."

26.   The guidance given in Denton v T H White [2014] EWCA Civ 906, [2014] 1 WLR 3927 is now very familiar. The court said this at [24]:

"…. A judge should address an application for relief from sanctions in three stages. The first stage is to identify and assess the seriousness and significance of the failure to comply with any rule, practice direction or court order which engages rule 3.9(1). If the breach is neither serious nor significant, the court is unlikely to need to spend much time on the second and third stages. The second stage is to consider why the default occurred. The third stage is to evaluate all the circumstances of the case, so as to enable [the court] to deal justly with the application including factors (a) and (b)."

27.   The reference to factors (a) and (b) is a reference to the factors specified in CPR 3.9(1)…

28.   … As the court pointed out in *Denton,* it is a mistake to think that a serious or significant default for which there is no good reason will inevitably lead to the refusal of relief. The court must always consider all the circumstances, including the two factors specifically identified."

The appropriateness of this approach was confirmed by the High Court in *Sabesan v LB Waltham Forest* [2018] EWHC 2373 (Admin).

Mr Sabesan owned the freehold of a property he let to tenants. He appealed to the VTE against Waltham Forest's decision to designate the property a house in multiple occupation (which meant he was liable for council tax on the property rather than his tenants). His appeal was made three months out of time and his request for a late appeal was rejected by Vice President Young of the VTE, who considered the requirements for allowing a late appeal (under reg 21(6)) were not met. Mr Sabesan requested a review of that decision under reg 40, but his request was rejected by the President of the VTE.

Mr Sabesan appealed against Vice President Young's decision to the High Court but his appeal was five months out of time. The Court rejected arguments made on behalf of Mr Sabesan that *Jagoo v Bristol City Council* [2017] EWHC 926 (Admin) should be followed and that it was not appropriate to take the approach outlined in *Denton* but that the wording of reg 43(2) indicated a less stringent approach should be taken. While not questioning the result in *Jagoo*, the Court confirmed that the approach taken by Warby J in *Turner* was the correct one and applied the three-stage process summarised in the *Denton* case (as detailed above). The Court concluded that it was not appropriate to allow an extension of time and Mr Sabesan's appeal was dismissed.

Notification of further proceedings

44.–(1)-(4)   *[Omitted]*

(5)   Where, in relation to a decision or order made on a section 16 appeal, a billing authority appeals to the High Court under regulation 43, or receives notice of such an appeal instituted by another party, it must, as soon as reasonably practicable afterwards, notify the VTE of the appeal.

General Note

Turner v South Cambridgeshire DC [2016] EWHC 1017 (Admin) deals with the exercise of discretion provided to the Court when deciding whether to dismiss an appeal made out of time (see the Note to reg 43).

The Valuation Tribunal for Wales Regulations 2010
(2010 No. 713 (W.69))

PART 1
GENERAL

1. Title and commencement
2. Application
3. Interpretation

PART 5
COUNCIL TAX APPEALS

27.   Interpretation
28.   Appeal Panels in special circumstances
29.   Time limits
30.   Initiating an appeal
31.   Arrangements for appeals
32.   Withdrawal
32A. Striking out proceedings
33.   Disposal by written representations
34.   Notice of hearing
35.   Disqualification from participating
36.   Representation at the hearing
37.   Conduct of the hearing – Appeal Panels
38.   Evidence: general
39.   Evidence of lists and other documents
40.   Decisions on appeals
41.   Orders
42.   Review of decisions
43.   Records of decisions, etc
44.   Appeals
45.   Arbitration
46.   Service of notices
Schedule 3 Contents of records made under Part 5

General Note

See the general note to the Valuation Tribunal for England (Council Tax and Rating Appeals) (Procedure) Regs 2009 on p1666 for information about the jurisdiction of the valuation tribunal to hear appeals relating to CTR and discretionary coincil cocil tax reduction in England and Wales under s16 Local Government Finance Act 1992 and for a discussion of the requirement to have served a grievance on the billing authority before an appeal to the Valuation Tribunal. For commentary on s16 LGFA 1992, see p1080.

These regulations set out the rules for appeals to the Valuation Tribunal for Wales (VTW). An appeal to the valuation tribunal must be made in writing to the clerk of the tribunal (reg 30(1)) and must contain certain information (reg 30(2)). Reg 46(2) deals with the acceptable methods of service of an appeal notice.

Reg 29 sets out the time limit for appealing to the valuation tribunal. When a written notice has been received from the authority under s16(7)(a) or (b) LGFA 1992, the written notice of appeal must be served on the clerk of the tribunal within two months of the date of service of the authority's notice (reg 29(1)). When s16(7)(c) LGFA 1992 applies, the written notice of appeal must be served within four months of the date the notice of the grievance was served on the billing authority, and for appeals relating to decisions to award a council tax reduction under the CTR scheme, the notice of grievance must have been served on the billing authority within one month of the authority serving the decision notice, or within one month of the authority serving a statement of written reasons for its decision, provided the written reasons were requested from the authority within one month of the date of notification of the authority's decision (reg 29(2) and (2A)). The President of the VTW has the power to extend these time limits if satisfied that the delay has occurred because of circumstances beyond the control of the aggrieved person (reg 29(5)).

General requirements placed on the valuation tribunal in relation to the conduct of the hearing are set out in reg 37.

Best Practice Protocols giving guidance on the procedures of the valuation tribunal are published on the VTW website (www.valuation-tribunals-wales.org.uk).

PART 1
General

Title and commencement
1.–(1)   The title of these Regulations is The Valuation Tribunal for Wales Regulations 2010.

(2)   Regulations 1 to 26 come into force on 1 April 2010 and the remaining regulations come into force on 1 July 2010.

Application
2.   These Regulations apply in Wales only.

Interpretation
3.–(1)   In these Regulations, unless the context otherwise requires–
"the 1988 Act" ("Deddf 1988") means the Local Government Finance Act 1988;
"the 1992 Act" ("Deddf 1992") means the Local Government Finance Act 1992;
"the 2005 Regulations" ("Rheoliadau 2005") means the Valuation Tribunals (Wales) Regulations 2005;
"appeal" ("apêl") means an appeal under–
    (a)   section 16 (appeals : general) of the 1992 Act;
    (b)   paragraph 3 of Schedule 3 (penalties) to the 1992 Act;
    (c)   regulations made under section 24 of the 1992 Act;
    (d)   regulations made under section 55 of the 1988 Act;
    (e)   paragraph 4 of Schedule 4A (completion notices) to the 1988 Act (in these Regulations called an "appeal against a completion notice");
    (f)   paragraph 5C of Schedule 9 (civil penalties) to the 1988 Act; and
    (g)   section 45 of the Land Drainage Act 1991;
"billing authority" ("awdurdod bilio") means a billing authority as defined in section 1(2) of the 1992 Act;
"Chairperson" ("Cadeirydd") means a Chairperson of the Valuation Tribunal appointed under regulation 12;
"chief executive" ("prif weithredwr") means the person appointed under regulation 15;
"Governing Council" ("Cyngor Llywodraethu") means the Governing Council of the Valuation Tribunal established under regulation 5;
"old Service" ("hen Wasanaeth") means the Valuation Tribunal Service for Wales established by the 2005 Regulations;
"old Tribunal" ("hen Dribiwnlys") means a valuation tribunal in Wales which existed immediately before 1 July 2010;
"President" ("Llywydd") means the President of the Valuation Tribunal appointed under regulation 11;
"regional representative" ("cynrychiolydd rhanbarthol") means a regional representative appointed under regulation 13; and
"Valuation Tribunal" ("Tribiwnlys Prisio") means the Valuation Tribunal for Wales established under regulation 4.

(2)   References to regulations, Parts and Schedules are, unless otherwise stated, references to regulations and Parts of, and Schedules to, these Regulations.

PART 5
Council Tax Appeals

Interpretation
27.–(1)   In this Part–
"appeal" ("apêl"), unless the context otherwise requires, means an appeal under–
    (a)   section 16 (appeals: general) of the 1992 Act;
    (b)   paragraph 3(1) of Schedule 3 (penalties) to the 1992 Act; or

(c)   paragraph 4 of Schedule 4A to the 1988 Act as it applies for the purposes of Part I of the 1992 Act (in this Part called an "appeal against a completion notice");

"Appeal Panel" ("Panel Apêl") means the members of the Valuation Tribunal convened in accordance with this Part for the purpose of disposing of an appeal;

"Clerk" ("Clerc") means–
(a)   the chief executive; and
(b)   any other employee of the Valuation Tribunal appointed under regulation 15(6) to whom some or all of the functions of the Clerk in this Part have been delegated;

[1"council tax reduction scheme" ("cynllun gostyngiadau'r dreth gyngor") means a scheme made by a billing authority in accordance with [2the Council Tax Reduction Schemes and Prescribed Requirements (Wales) Regulations 2013] or the scheme that applies in default by virtue of paragraph 6(1)(e) of Schedule 1B to the 1992 Act;]

"list" ("rhestr") means a valuation list compiled under Chapter 2 of Part 1 of the 1992 Act;

"listing officer" ("swyddog rhestru") in relation to an appeal, means the officer appointed under section 20 for the authority in whose area the dwelling to which the appeal relates is situated;

"notice of appeal" ("hysbysiad am apêl") means a notice under regulation 30(1); and

"penalty" ("cosb") means a penalty imposed under paragraph 1 of Schedule 3 to the 1992 Act.

(2)   Any reference in this Part–
(a)   to a party to an appeal, includes the appellant and any person entitled in pursuance of this Part to be served with a copy of the appellant's notice of appeal; and
(b)   to a numbered section is, unless the context otherwise requires, a reference to the section so numbered in the 1992 Act.

Modifications
The definition of "council tax reduction scheme" in reg 27(1) was amended by reg 2(2) Valuation Tribunal for Wales (Wales) (Amendment) Regulations 2014 SI No.554 (W.66) as from 31.3.14, so that the words "the Council Tax Reduction Schemes and Prescribed Requirements (Wales) Regulations 2013" were substituted for "the Council Tax Reduction Schemes and Prescribed Requirements (Wales) Regulations 2012" save that, in accordance with reg 4 of SI 2014 No.554, this amendment does not apply in respect of any appeals made to the Valuation Tribunal in relation to any applications made or reductions awarded under the provisions of a scheme made by a billing authority in accordance with the Council Tax Reduction Schemes and Prescribed Requirements (Wales) Regulations 2012 SI No.3144 or a scheme which applies in default on 1 April 2013 in accordance with Sch 1B para 6(1)(e) LFGA 1992.

Amendments
1.   Inserted by reg 2(3) of SI 2013 No 547 (W.59) as from 1.4.13.
2.   Amended by reg 2(2) of SI 2014 No 554 (W. 66) as from 31.3.14 subject to the savings provision in reg 4 of SI 2014 No 554.

Appeal Panels in special circumstances
28.–(1)   Where the appellant is–
(a)   a former member of an old Tribunal,
(b)   a former employee of an old Tribunal, of the old Service or of the Valuation Tribunal, or
(c)   an employee or member of the Valuation Tribunal;
the appeal must be dealt with by such members of the Valuation Tribunal as may be appointed for that purpose by the President.

(2)   Where it appears to the President that by reason of a conflict of interests, or the appearance of such a conflict, it would be inappropriate for an appeal to be dealt with by particular members of the Valuation Tribunal, the President must appoint other members to deal with that appeal.

Time limits

29.–(1)   An appeal by a person in relation to whom the condition mentioned in section 16(7)(a) or (b) is fulfilled will be dismissed unless it is initiated in accordance with this Part not later than the expiry of two months beginning with the date of service of the billing authority's notice under that section.

(2)   [¹Subject to paragraph (2A), when] the condition mentioned in section 16(7)(c) is fulfilled, an appeal by the aggrieved person will be dismissed unless it is initiated within four months of the date of service of that person's notice under section 16(4).

[²(2A)   When the condition mentioned in section 16(7)(c) is fulfilled and the appeal by the aggrieved person relates to a billing authority's decision to award a reduction under its council tax reduction scheme, the appeal will be dismissed unless the notice required by section 16(4) was served on the billing authority in accordance with paragraph 8(2) of Schedule 12 to the Council Tax Reduction Schemes and Prescribed Requirements (Wales) Regulations 2013 or paragraph 8(2) of Schedule 1 of the scheme prescribed in the Council Tax Reduction Schemes (Default Scheme) (Wales) Regulations 2013, as the case may be.]

(3)   An appeal under paragraph 3 of Schedule 3 to the 1992 Act will be dismissed unless it is initiated not later than the expiry of two months beginning with the date of service of written notice of the imposition of the penalty.

(4)   An appeal against a completion notice will be dismissed unless it is initiated not later than the expiry of four weeks beginning with the date of service of the notice.

(5)   Notwithstanding paragraphs (1) to (4), the President may authorise an appeal to be entertained where the President is satisfied that the failure of the person aggrieved to initiate the appeal as provided by this regulation has arisen by reason of circumstances beyond that person's control.

Modifications

In reg 29, the words "Subject to paragraph (2A)" in para (2), and sub-para (2A) were inserted by reg 2(3) Valuation Tribunal for Wales (Wales) (Amendment) Regulations 2014 SI No.554 (W. 66) as from 31.3.14, save that, in accordance with reg 4 of SI 2014 No.554, these amendments do not apply in respect of appeals made to the Valuation Tribunal in relation to any applications made or reductions awarded under the provisions of a scheme made by a billing authority in accordance with the Council Tax Reduction Schemes and Prescribed Requirements (Wales) Regulations 2012 SI No.3144 or a scheme which applies in default on 1 April 2013 in accordance with Sch 1B para 6(1)(e) LGFA 1992.

Amendments

1.   Amended by reg 2(3)(a) of SI 2014 No 554 (W.66) as from 31.3.14 subject to the savings provision in reg 4 of SI 2014 No.554.

2.   Inserted by reg 2(3)(b) of SI 2014 No 554 (W.66) as from 31.3.14 subject to the savings provision in reg 4 of SI 2014 No.554.

Initiating an appeal

30.–(1)   An appeal must be initiated by serving on the Clerk a notice in writing.

(2) Where the appeal is made under section 16, the notice of appeal must contain the following information–

(a)   the grounds on which the appeal is made;

(b)   the date on which the notice under section 16(4) was served on the billing authority;[¹]

(c)   the date, if any, on which the appellant was notified by the authority as mentioned in section 16(7)(a) or (b)[²; and]

[²(d)   where the appellant has also made an appeal to the First-tier Tribunal in accordance with the Housing Benefit and Council Tax Benefit (Decisions and Appeals) Regulations 2001 and the appeal raises common issues of fact with the appeal made under section 16 of the 1992 Act, a copy of the notice provided in accordance with regulation 20(1) of those Regulations and any other information required to be provided under regulation 20 of those Regulations.

(2A)   A notice of appeal given under paragraph (2) must be accompanied by a copy of any written notification provided by the billing authority in accordance with section 16(7)(a) or (b).]

(3)   Where the appeal is an appeal against a completion notice, the notice of appeal must be accompanied by–

(a)   a copy of the completion notice; and

(b)   a statement of the grounds on which the appeal is made.

(4)   Where the appeal is against the imposition of a penalty, the notice of appeal must contain the following information–

(a)   the grounds on which the appeal is made; and

(b)   the date of service of written notice of the imposition of a penalty.

(5)   The Clerk must, within two weeks of service of the notice of appeal, notify the appellant that the Clerk has received the notice, and must serve a copy of it on the billing authority whose decision, action or notice is the subject of the appeal, and any other billing authority appearing to the Clerk to be concerned with the matter.

Amendments

1.   Omitted by reg 2(4)(a) of SI 2013 No 547 (W.59) as from 1.4.13.
2.   Inserted by reg 2(4)(b) and (c) of SI 2013 No 547 (W.59) as from 1.4.13.

Arrangements for appeals

31.–(1)   The President must secure that arrangements are made for appeals to be determined in accordance with the following provisions of this Part.

(2)   This paragraph applies where an appeal under this Part and an appeal under one or more of the following–

(a)   regulations made under section 55 of the 1988 Act,

(b)   regulations made under section 24,

relate to the same property.

(3)   Where paragraph (2) applies–

(a)   the President will secure that the appeals are dealt with in such order as appears to the President best designed to secure the interests of justice;

(b)   the valuation officer or the listing officer (as the case may be) and the billing authority must be joined as a party to an appeal under this Part.

(4)   In paragraph (3), "valuation officer" means the officer appointed under section 61(1)(a) of the 1988 Act.

(5)   The Clerk must as soon as is reasonably practicable serve a copy of the notice of appeal on a person who has been made a party in accordance with paragraph (3).

Withdrawal

32.–(1)   An appeal may be withdrawn by notice in writing given to the Clerk before the commencement of a hearing or of consideration of written representations by an Appeal Panel.

(2)   The Clerk must notify the appellant when the notice of withdrawal has been received, and must serve a copy of the notice on all the other parties to the appeal.

[¹Striking out proceedings

32A.–(1)   The Valuation Tribunal may strike out an appeal or part of an appeal where–

(a)   the appeal, or part of the appeal, relates to a billing authority's decision to award a reduction under its council tax reduction scheme; and

(b)   the reduction awarded is the maximum reduction that the billing authority may have awarded under its scheme.

(2)   Where only part of an appeal falls within paragraph (1), the Valuation Tribunal may only strike out that part of the appeal.

(3)   The Valuation Tribunal may not strike out an appeal, or part of an appeal, without first giving the appellant an opportunity to make representations in relation to the proposed striking out.]

Amendment

1.   Inserted by reg 2(5) of SI 2013 No 547 (W.59) as from 1.4.13.

Disposal by written representations

33.–(1)   An appeal may be disposed of on the basis of written representations if all the parties have given their agreement in writing.

(2)   Where all the parties have given their agreement as mentioned in paragraph (1), the Clerk must serve notice on the parties accordingly; and, within four weeks of service of such a notice on a party, each party may serve on the Clerk a notice stating–

(a)   the reasons or further reasons for the disagreement giving rise to the appeal; or

(b)   that party does not intend to make further representations.

(3)   A copy of any notice served in pursuance of paragraph (2) must be served by the Clerk on the other party or parties to the appeal, and must be accompanied by a statement of the effect of paragraphs (4) and (5).

(4)   Any party on whom a notice is served under paragraph (3) may, within four weeks of that service, serve on the Clerk a further notice stating that party's reply to the other party's statement, or that that party does not intend to make further representations, as the case may be; and the Clerk must serve a copy of any such further notice on the other party or parties.

(5)   After the expiry of four weeks beginning with the expiry of the period of four weeks mentioned in paragraph (4) the Clerk must submit to an Appeal Panel copies of–

(a)   any information transmitted to the Clerk under these Regulations, and

(b)   any notice under paragraph (2) or (4).

(6)   The Appeal Panel to which an appeal is referred as provided in paragraph (5) may if it thinks fit–

(a)   require any party to furnish in writing further particulars of the grounds relied on and of any relevant facts or contentions; or

(b)   order that the appeal be disposed of on the basis of a hearing.

(7)   Where an Appeal Panel requires any party to furnish any particulars under paragraph (6)(a), the Clerk must serve a copy of such particulars on every other party, and each such party may within four weeks of such service serve on the Clerk any further statement they wish to make in response.

Notice of hearing

34.–(1)   Where the appeal is to be disposed of on the basis of a hearing, the Clerk must, not less than four weeks before the date in question, serve on the parties notice of the date, time and place appointed for the hearing.

(2)   The Clerk will advertise the date, time and place appointed for any hearing by causing a notice giving such information to be conspicuously displayed–

(a)   outside an office of the billing authority appointed by the authority for that purpose, or

(b)   in another place within that authority's area.

(3)   The notice required by paragraph (2) must name a place where a list of the appeals to be heard may be inspected.

(4)   Where the hearing of an appeal has been postponed, the Clerk must take such steps as are reasonably practicable in the time available–

(a)   to notify the parties of the postponement; and

(b)   to advertise the postponement.

Disqualification from participating

35.–(1)   A person will be disqualified from participating as a member in the hearing or determination of, or acting as Clerk or officer of the Valuation Tribunal in relation to, an appeal if that person is a member of the relevant billing authority.

(2)   In this regulation "relevant billing authority" means–

(a)   in the case of an appeal against a completion notice, the billing authority in whose area is situated the dwelling which is the subject matter of the appeal; and

(b)   in any other case, the billing authority whose decision is being appealed against.

(3)   A person will be disqualified from participating as a member in the hearing or determination of, or acting as Clerk or officer of the Valuation Tribunal in relation to, an

appeal if the appellant is that person's spouse, civil partner or that person supports the appellant financially or is liable to do so.

(4)   A person will not otherwise be disqualified from acting in any capacity in relation to an appeal by reason only of the fact that that person is a member of an authority which derives revenue directly or indirectly from payments in respect of council tax which may be affected by the exercise of that person's functions.

Representation at the hearing

36.   Any party to an appeal which is to be decided at a hearing may appear in person (with assistance, if wished, from any person), or be represented by counsel or solicitor, or any other representative (other than a person who is a member of the Valuation Tribunal or the Governing Council or an employee of the Valuation Tribunal).

Conduct of the hearing – Appeal Panels

37.–(1)   Subject to paragraph (2), the Valuation Tribunal's function of hearing or determining an appeal will be discharged by a panel of three members of the Valuation Tribunal ("an Appeal Panel") which must include at least one Chairperson; and a Chairperson will preside.

(2)   Where all parties to an appeal who appear so agree, the appeal may be decided by two members of an Appeal Panel, and notwithstanding the absence of a Chairperson.

[1(3)   The hearing must take place in public unless the Appeal Panel otherwise orders on being satisfied that it is in the interests of justice to hold a hearing, or part of a hearing, in private.]

[2(3A)   Where the hearing is to be held in private, the Appeal Panel may determine who is permitted to attend the hearing or part of the hearing.]

(4)   If the appellant fails to appear at the hearing, the Appeal Panel may dismiss the appeal, and if any other party does not appear the Appeal Panel may hear and determine the appeal in that party's absence.

(5)   The Appeal Panel may require any witness to give evidence under oath or affirmation, and will have power for that purpose to administer an oath or affirmation in due form.

(6)   Parties at the hearing may be heard in such order as the Appeal Panel may determine, and may examine any witness before the Appeal Panel and call witnesses.

(7)   A hearing may be adjourned for such time, to such place and on such terms (if any) as the Appeal Panel thinks fit; and reasonable notice of the time and place to which the hearing has been adjourned must be given to every party.

(8)   If it thinks fit an Appeal Panel may, after notice to the parties inviting them to be present, inspect any dwelling which is the subject of an appeal.

(9)   Subject to any provisions of this Part, the Appeal Panel–

(a)   must conduct the hearing in such manner as it considers most suitable to the clarification of the issues before it and generally to the just handling of the proceedings;

(b)   must, so far as appears to it appropriate, seek to avoid formality in its proceedings; and

(c)   will not be bound by any enactment or rule of law relating to the admissibility of evidence before courts of law.

Amendments
1.   Substituted by reg 2(6)(a) of SI 2013 No 547 (W.59) as from 1.4.13.
2.   Inserted by reg 2(6)(b) of SI 2013 No 547 (W.59) as from 1.4.13.

Evidence: general

38.–(1)   This regulation applies to information supplied in pursuance of regulations under section 13 or Schedule 2 to the 1992 Act [1 or section 131 of the Welfare Reform Act 2012].

(2)   Subject to the following provisions of this regulation, information to which this regulation applies will in any relevant proceedings be admissible as evidence of any fact

stated in it; and any document purporting to contain such information will, unless the contrary is shown, be presumed–

(a) to have been supplied by the person by whom it purports to have been supplied; and

(b) to have been supplied by that person in any capacity in which it purports to have been supplied.

(3) Information to which this regulation applies must not be used in any relevant proceedings by a billing authority unless–

(a) not less than two weeks' notice, specifying the information to be so used and the dwelling or person to which or to whom it relates, has previously been given to every other party to the proceedings; and

(b) any person who has given not less than 24 hours' notice of that person's intention to do so has been permitted by that authority at any reasonable time–

(i) to inspect the documents and other media in or on which such information is held; and

(ii) to make a copy of, or of any extract from, any document containing such information.

(4) If any information required to be made available for inspection in accordance with this regulation is not maintained in documentary form, the duty to make it so available is satisfied if a print-out, photographic image or other reproduction of the information, which has been obtained from the storage medium adopted in relation to that information, is made available for inspection.

(5) In this regulation "relevant proceedings" means any proceedings on or in consequence of an appeal, and any proceedings on or in consequence of a reference to arbitration under regulation 45.

Amendment
1.   Inserted by reg 2(7) of SI 2013 No. 547 (W.59) as from 1.4.13.

Evidence of lists and other documents

39.–(1) The contents of a list may be proved by the production of a copy of the list, or of the relevant part, purporting to be certified to be a true copy by the listing officer.

(2) The contents of a completion notice may be proved by the production of a copy of it purporting to be certified to be a true copy by the proper officer of the billing authority.

(3) In paragraph (2) "proper officer" has the same meaning as in the Local Government Act 1972.

Decisions on appeals

40.–(1) An appeal may be decided by a majority of the members participating; and where (pursuant to regulation 37(2)) it falls to be disposed of by two members and they are unable to agree, it must be remitted by the Clerk to be decided by an Appeal Panel consisting of three different members.

(2) Where an appeal is disposed of on the basis of a hearing, the decision of the Appeal Panel may be reserved or given orally at the end of the hearing.

(3) Subject to paragraph (4), as soon as is reasonably practicable after a decision has been made, it must–

(a) in the case of a decision given orally, be confirmed,

(b) in any other case, be communicated,

by notice in writing to the parties; and the notice must be accompanied by a statement of the reasons for the decision.

(4) Nothing in paragraph (3) will require notice to be given to a party if it would be repetitive of any document supplied to that person in accordance with regulation 43.

(5) In the case of an appeal against a completion notice, the Clerk must send notice of the decision to the listing officer appointed for the billing authority which is a party to the appeal.

(6) In this regulation, "member" means a member of an Appeal Panel.

Orders

41.–(1)   On or after deciding an appeal the Appeal Panel may, in consequence of the decision, by order require–

(a)   an estimate to be quashed or altered;

(b)   a penalty to be quashed;

(c)   the decision of a billing authority to be reversed;

(d)   a calculation (other than an estimate) of an amount to be quashed and the amount to be recalculated.

(2)   An order may require any matter ancillary to its subject-matter to be attended to.

Review of decisions

42.–(1)   Subject to paragraphs (2) and (3), an Appeal Panel constituted as provided in paragraph (4) will have power on written application by a party to review or set aside by certificate under the hand of the presiding member–

(a)   any decision on any of the grounds mentioned in paragraph (5), and

(b)   a decision on an appeal against a completion notice, on the additional ground mentioned in paragraph (6).

(2)   Paragraph (1) does not apply where an appeal against the decision in question has been determined by the High Court.

(3)   An application under paragraph (1) may be dismissed if it is not made within the period of four weeks beginning on the day on which notice is given (whether in accordance with regulation 40(3) or regulation 43(3)) of the decision in question.

(4)   So far as is reasonably practicable, the Appeal Panel appointed to review a decision will consist of the same members as constituted the Appeal Panel which took the decision.

(5)   The grounds referred to in paragraph (1)(a) are–

(a)   that the decision was wrongly made as a result of clerical error;

(b)   that a party did not appear and can show reasonable cause why that party did not do so;

(c)   that the decision is affected by a decision of, or a decision on appeal from, the High Court or the Upper Tribunal in relation to an appeal in respect of the dwelling which, or, as the case may be, the person who, was the subject of the Appeal Panel's decision; and

(d)   the interests of justice otherwise require such a review.

(6)   The ground mentioned in paragraph (1)(b) is that new evidence, the existence of which could not have been ascertained by reasonably diligent inquiry or could not have been foreseen, has become available since the conclusion of the proceedings to which the decision relates.

(7)   If an Appeal Panel sets aside a decision in pursuance of this regulation, it must revoke any order made in consequence of that decision and must order a re-hearing or redetermination before either the same or a different Appeal Panel.

(8)   The Clerk must as soon as reasonably practicable notify the parties to the appeal in writing of–

(a)   a determination that the Appeal Panel will not undertake a review under paragraph (1);

(b)   the determination of the Appeal Panel, having undertaken a review under paragraph (1), that it will not set aside the decision concerned;

(c)   the issue of any certificate under paragraph (1); and

(d)   the revocation of any order under paragraph (7).

(9)   Where in relation to a decision in respect of which an application under paragraph (1) is made, an appeal to the High Court remains undetermined on the relevant day, the Clerk must notify the High Court as soon as reasonably practicable after the occurrence of the relevant event.

(10)   In paragraph (9)–

"the relevant day" ("diwrnod perthnasol") means the day on which, as the case may be–

(a)   the application under paragraph (1) is made;

(b)   the event referred to in any of sub-paragraphs (a) to (d) of paragraph (8) occurs; and

"the relevant event" ("digwyddiad perthnasol"), in relation to a relevant day, means the event occurring on that day.

(11)   In this regulation, "member" means a member of an Appeal Panel.

Records of decisions, etc

43.–(1)   It will be the duty of the Clerk to make arrangements for each decision, each order made under regulation 41 and the effect of each certificate and revocation under regulation 42 to be recorded.

(2)   Records may be kept in any form, whether documentary or otherwise, and must contain the particulars specified in Schedule 3.

(3)   A copy, in documentary form, of the relevant entry in the record must, as soon as reasonably practicable after the entry has been made, be sent to each party to the appeal to which the entry relates.

(4)   Each record must be retained for the period of six years beginning on the day on which an entry was last made in it.

(5)   Any person may, at a reasonable time stated by or on behalf of the Valuation Tribunal and without making payment, inspect the records which are required to be made by paragraph (1).

(6)   If, without reasonable excuse, a person having custody of the record intentionally obstructs a person in exercising the right conferred by paragraph (5), that person will be liable on summary conviction to a fine not exceeding level 1 on the standard scale.

(7)   The member who presided at the hearing or determination of an appeal may authorise the correction of any clerical error in the record, and a copy of the corrected entry must be sent to the persons to whom a copy of the original entry was sent.

(8)   The production in any proceedings in any court of law of a document purporting to be certified by the Chief Executive or Clerk of an Appeal Panel to be a true copy of a record or decision of that Panel will, unless the contrary is proved, be sufficient evidence of the document and of the facts it records.

Appeals

44.–(1)   An appeal will lie to the High Court on a question of law arising out of a decision or order which is given or made by an Appeal Panel on an appeal and may be made by any party to the appeal.

(2)   Subject to paragraph (3), an appeal under paragraph (1) may be dismissed if it is not made within four weeks of the date on which notice is given of the decision or order that is the subject matter of the appeal.

(3)   Where in relation to an application under paragraph (1) of regulation 42 made within four weeks of the date on which notice was given of the decision which is the subject matter of the appeal–

(a)   notice is given as mentioned in paragraph (8)(a) of that regulation, or

(b)   notice is given as mentioned in paragraph (8)(b) of that regulation,

the appeal may be dismissed if it is not made within four weeks of the service of the notice under that paragraph (8)(a) or (b).

(4)   The High Court may confirm, vary, set aside, revoke or remit the decision or order of an Appeal Panel, and may make any order which the Appeal Panel could have made.

(5)   Billing authorities must act in accordance with any order made by the High Court; and paragraph 10A of Schedule 11 to the 1988 Act will have effect subject to this requirement.

Arbitration

45.–(1)   Where at any time before the beginning of a hearing or the consideration by an Appeal Panel of written representations it is so agreed in writing between the persons who, if a dispute were to be the subject of an appeal to the Valuation Tribunal, would be the parties to the appeal, the question will be referred to arbitration.

(2)   In any arbitration in pursuance of this regulation, the award may include any order which could have been made by an Appeal Panel in relation to the question; and paragraph 10A of Schedule 11 to the 1988 Act will apply to such an order as it applies to orders recorded in pursuance of this Part.

Service of notices

46.–(1)   Without prejudice to section 233 of the Local Government Act 1972, any notice to be served by the Clerk or listing officer under this Part may be served–

(a)   by delivering it–
   (i)   to the person on whom it is to be served; or
   (ii)   to any other person authorised by them to act as their agent for the purpose;
(b)   by leaving it at or forwarding it by post to–
   (i)   the usual or last-known place of business of that person, or
   (ii)   in the case of a company, its registered office, or
   (iii)   the usual or last-known place of business or registered office of any other person authorised as mentioned in sub-paragraph (a)(ii);
(c)   by delivering it to some person on the premises to which it relates or, if there is no person on the premises to whom it can so be delivered, by fixing it to some conspicuous part of the premises;
(d)   without prejudice to the foregoing provisions of this regulation, where premises to which the notice relates are a place of business of the person on whom it is to be served, by leaving it at, or forwarding it by post addressed to that person at, that place of business; or
(e)   by electronic communication in accordance with paragraph (3) but subject as mentioned in that paragraph.

(2)   Any notice to be served on the Valuation Tribunal, the Clerk, the valuation officer or the listing officer under these Regulations must be–

(a)   sent by pre-paid post or delivered by hand to the address specified for the proceedings;
(b)   sent by fax to the number specified for the proceedings; or
(c)   sent or delivered by such other method and to such address as may be agreed by the Clerk, the valuation officer or the listing officer (as the case may be) and the person by whom the notice is to be served.

(3)   Subject to paragraph (4), if a party provides a fax number, email address or other details for the electronic transmission of documents to them, that party must accept service of notices and delivery of documents by that method.

(4)   If a party informs the Clerk and all other parties that a particular form of communication (other than post or delivery) should not be used to serve notice on, or provide documents to, that party, that form of communication must not be used.

(5)   If the Clerk or a party sends a notice to a party or the Clerk by email or any other electronic means of communication, the recipient may request that the sender provide a hard copy of the notice to the recipient.

(6)   A request under paragraph (5) must be made as soon as reasonably practicable after the recipient receives the notice or document electronically.

(7)   If the name of any taxpayer on whom a notice is required or authorised to be served cannot after reasonable inquiry be ascertained, the notice may be served by addressing it to "The Council Tax Payer" of the dwelling concerned (naming the dwelling), without further name or description.

(8)   For the purpose of any legal proceedings, a notice given by electronic communication, shall, unless the contrary is proved, be treated as served on the second business day after it was sent.

(9)   A person who has notified an address for the purpose of electronic communication shall, by notice in writing to the Clerk and the other parties, advise the Clerk and the other parties of any change in that address; and the change shall take effect on the third business day after the date on which the notice is received by the Clerk and the other parties, as the case may be.

(10)   The Clerk and each party may assume that the address provided by a party or its representative is and remains the address to which documents should be sent or delivered until receiving written notification to the contrary.

(11)   In this regulation–

(a)   "electronic communication" has the meaning given in section 15(1) of the Electronic Communications Act 2000;

(b)   any reference to a notice includes a reference to any other document required or authorised to be served; and

(c)   any reference to such requirement or authorisation is to a requirement or authorisation under these Regulations.

SCHEDULE 3

Regulation 43

Contents of records made under Part 5

The appellant's name and address
The date of the appeal
The matter appealed against
The name of the billing authority whose decision was appealed against
The date of the hearing or determination
The names of the parties who appeared, if any
The decision of the Appeal Panel and its date
The reasons for the decision
Any order made in consequence of the decision
The date of any such order
Any certificate setting aside the decision
Any revocation under regulation 42(7).

Part 7

Other primary legislation

Housing Act 1996
(1996 c52)

Functions of rent officers in connection with housing benefit and rent allowance subsidy

122.–(1) The Secretary of State may by order require rent officers to carry out such functions as may be specified in the order in connection with housing benefit and council tax benefit.

(2) Without prejudice to the generality of subsection (1), an order under this section may contain provision–

(a) enabling a prospective landlord to apply for a determination for the purposes of any application for housing benefit which may be made by a tenant of a dwelling which he proposed to let;

(b) as to the payment of a fee by the landlord for that determination;

(c) requiring the landlord to give a copy of the determination to the appropriate local authority; and

(d) enabling the appropriate local authority to seek a redetermination when a claim for housing benefit or rent allowance subsidy is made.

(3) Regulations under section 130(4) of the Social Security Contributions and Benefits Act 1992 (housing benefit: manner of determining appropriate maximum benefit) may provide for benefit to be limited by reference to determinations made by rent officers in exercise of functions conferred under this section.

(4) In relation to rent allowance subsidy, the Secretary of State may by order under section 140B of the Social Security Administration Act 1992–

(a) provide for any calculation under subsection (2) of that section to be made,

(b) specify any additions and deductions as are referred to in that subsection, and

(c) exercise his discretion as to what is unreasonable for the purposes of subsection (4) of that section,

by reference to determinations made by rent officers in exercise of functions conferred on them under this section.

(5) The Secretary of State may by any such regulations or order as are mentioned in subsection (3) or (4) require a local authority in any prescribed case–

(a) to apply to a rent officer for a determination to be made in pursuance of the functions conferred on them under this section; and

(b) to do so within such time as may be specified in the order or regulations.

(6) An order under this section–

(a) shall be made by statutory instrument which shall be subject to annulment in pursuance of a resolution of either House of Parliament;

(b) may make different provision for different cases or classes of case and for different areas; and

(c) may contain such transitional, incidental and supplementary provisions as appear to the Secretary of State to be desirable.

(7) In this section "housing benefit" and "rent allowance subsidy" have the same meaning as in Part VIII of the Social Security Administration Act 1992.

Commencement
1.4.97.

General Note
This section allows the Secretary of State to expand the role of rent officers in HB matters. See the Rent Officers (Housing Benefit Functions) Order 1997 (p879) and the Scottish equivalent (p909).

Subs (1) is a general power to give rent officers additional functions in relation to HB and rent allowance subsidy. The Secretary of State's powers are not restricted to those in Subs (2).

Subs (2) allows landlords to know, prior to the entry of a tenancy agreement, precisely what level of rent will be met by a rent allowance. It is the landlord's responsibility to obtain that assessment. Note, however, that provision may be made for a local authority to seek a fresh determination on a claim for HB. See also reg 14(1)(e) of both the HB and the HB(SPC) Regs, and for cases prior to 1 April 2011, reg 13D(8) of those regulations.

Subs (3) authorises the form of regs 13 and 13D of both the HB and the HB(SPC) Regs.

Welfare Reform and Pensions Act 1999
(1999 c30)

General Note to the Act

The principal innovation made by the Act, as far as this book is concerned, was an expanded role for local authorities as providers of benefit services.

Miscellaneous

Supply of information for certain purposes

72.–(1) The Secretary of State may by regulations make such provision for or in connection with any of the following matters, namely–

(a) the use by a person within subsection (2) of social security information [⁵ , or information relating to employment or training,] held by that person,

(b) the supply (whether to a person within subsection (2) or otherwise) of social security information [⁵ , or information relating to employment or training,] held by a person within that subsection,

(c) the relevant purposes for which a person to whom such information is supplied under the regulations may use it, and

(d) the circumstances and extent (if any) in and to which a person to whom such information is supplied under the regulations may supply it to any other person (whether within subsection (2) or not), as the Secretary of State considers appropriate in connection with any provision to which subsection (3) applies or in connection with any scheme or arrangements to which subsection (4) applies.

(2) The persons within this subsection are–

(a) a Minister of the Crown;

(b) a person providing services to, or designated [⁷ (specifically or by description)] for the purposes of this section by an order of, a Minister of the Crown;

(c) a local authority (within the meaning of the Administration Act); [⁴]

[⁶ (ca) a county council in England; and]

(d) a person providing services to, or authorised to exercise any function of, [⁶ any authority mentioned in paragraph (c) or (ca)].

(3) This subsection applies to any provision made by or under–

(a) any of the sections of the Administration Act inserted by section 57, 58 or 71 of this Act,

[¹ (aa) section 2AA of the Administration Act,]

(b) section 60 of this Act, [³]

(c) the Jobseekers Act 1995. [² or

(d) Part 1 of the Welfare Reform Act 2007.] [⁸ ;or]

[⁸ (e) Part 1 of the Welfare Reform Act 2012.]

(4) This subsection applies to–

(a) any scheme designated by regulations under subsection (1), being a scheme operated by the Secretary of State (whether under arrangements with any other person or not) for any purposes connected with employment or training in the case of persons of a particular category or description;

(b) any arrangements of a description specified in such regulations, being arrangements made by the Secretary of State for any such purposes.

(5) Regulations under subsection (1) may, in particular, authorise information supplied to a person under the regulations–

(a) to be used for the purpose of amending or supplementing other information held by that person; and

(b) if it is so used, to be supplied to any other person, and used for any purpose, to whom or for which that other information could be supplied or used.

(6) In this section–

"relevant purposes" means purposes connected with–

(a) social security, child support or war pensions, or

(b)   employment or training;

"social security information" means [7 [6]] information relating to social security, child support or war pensions; and in this subsection "war pensions" means war pensions within the meaning of section 25 of the Social Security Act 1989 (establishment and functions of war pensions committees).

[7 [6 (6A)]]

(7)   Any reference in this section to [5 information relating to, or purposes connected with, employment or training includes information relating to, or purposes connected with,] the existing or future employment or training prospects or needs of persons, and (in particular) assisting or encouraging persons to enhance their employment prospects.

Commencement
11.11.99: see s89(4)(c).

Amendments
1.   Inserted by the Employment Act 2002 s53 and Sch 7 para 55 (5.7.03).
2.   Inserted by WRA s28 and Sch 3 para 18 (18.3.08 for making regulations and 27.10.08).
3.   Omitted by WRA s67 and Sch 8 (27.10.08).
4.   Amended by Education and Skills Act 2008 s169 and Sch 2 as from 26.1.09.
5.   Inserted by Welfare Reform Act 2009 s34(4) as from 12.1.09.
6.   Amended by Education and Skills Act 2008 s169 and Sch 1 para 74 as from 30.3.10.
7.   Amended by WRA 2012 s134 as from 8.5.12.
8.   Amended by reg 15 of SI 2013 No 630 as from 29.4.13.

General Note
This permits regulations governing the passing of information between the people listed in sub-section (2), including between a local authority and other public officials.

Supplementary

Regulations and orders

83.–(1)   Any power under this Act to make regulations or orders (other than orders under section 72(2)) shall be exercisable by statutory instrument.

(2)   A statutory instrument–

(a)   which contains (whether alone or with other provisions) regulations made under this Act, and

(b)   which is not subject to any requirement that a draft of the instrument be laid before and approved by a resolution of each House of Parliament, shall be subject to annulment in pursuance of a resolution of either House of Parliament.

(3)   A statutory instrument containing an order under section 27(3) shall be subject to annulment in pursuance of a resolution of either House of Parliament.

(4)   Any power under this Act to make regulations or orders may be exercised–

(a)   either in relation to all cases to which the power extends, or in relation to those cases subject to specified exceptions, or in relation to any specified cases or classes of case;

(b)   so as to make, as respects the cases in relation to which it is exercised–

(i)   the full provision to which the power extends or any less provision (whether by way of exception or otherwise);

(ii)   the same provision for all cases in relation to which the power is exercised, or different provision for different cases or different classes of case or different provision as respects the same case or class of case for different purposes of this Act;

(iii)   any such provision either unconditionally or subject to any specified condition.

(5)   Where any such power is expressed to be exercisable for alternative purposes it may be exercised in relation to the same case for any or all of those purposes.

(6)   Any such power includes power–

(a)   to make such incidental, supplementary, consequential, saving or transitional provision (including provision amending, repealing or revoking enactments) as appears to the authority making the regulations or order to be expedient; and

(b)   to provide for a person to exercise a discretion in dealing with any matter.

(7)   Any power to make regulations or an order for the purposes of any provision of this Act is without prejudice to any power to make regulations or an order for the purposes of any other provision of this or any other Act.

(8)   Any power conferred by this Act to make regulations or an order relating to–

(a)   housing benefit, or

(b)   council tax benefit, includes power to make different provision for different areas or different authorities; and regulations under section 60 or 79 may make different provision for different areas.

(9)   Without prejudice to the generality of any of the preceding provisions of this section, regulations under section 60 or 72 may provide for all or any of the provisions of the regulations to apply only in relation to any area or areas specified in the regulations.

(10)   Any power to make regulations under Part IV, except sections 28 and 48, shall, if the Treasury so direct, be exercisable only in conjunction with them.

(11)   Before exercising any power to make regulations under Part IV, the authority on whom the power is conferred, or, if the power is the subject of a direction under subsection (10), that authority and the Treasury acting jointly, shall consult such persons as the authority, or the authority and the Treasury, may consider appropriate.

Consequential amendments etc

84.–(1)   The consequential amendments specified in Schedule 12 shall have effect.

(2)   The Secretary of State may by regulations make such amendments or revocations of any instrument made under an Act as he thinks necessary or expedient in consequence of the coming into force of any of the provisions specified in subsection (4).

(3)   The Secretary of State may, for the purposes of or in connection with the coming into force of any of the provisions specified in subsection (4), make by regulations any provision which could be made by an order bringing the provision into force.

(4)   The provisions mentioned in subsections (2) and (3) are–

(a)   Part IV;

(b)   subsection (1) above so far as relating to paragraphs 14 to 63 of Schedule 12; and

(c)   section 88 so far as relating to Part III of Schedule 13.

Transitional provisions

85.–(1)   The Secretary of State may, for the purposes of or in connection with the coming into force of any provisions of Parts I and II, by regulations make such transitional adaptations or modifications–

(a)   of those provisions, or

(b)   in connection with those provisions, of any provisions of–

(i)   this Act,

(ii)   the Pension Schemes Act 1993, or

(iii)   the Pensions Act 1995, then in force, as he considers necessary or expedient

(2)-(8)   *[Omitted]*

General financial provisions

86.–(1)   There shall be paid out of money provided by Parliament–

(a)   any expenditure incurred by a Minister of the Crown or government department under this Act; and

(b)   any increase attributable to this Act in the sums which under any other Act are payable out of money so provided.

(2)   There shall be paid into the Consolidated Fund any increase attributable to this Act in the sums which under any other Act are payable into that Fund.

Repeals

88.   The enactments specified in Schedule 13 (which include certain enactments no longer of practical utility) are hereby repealed to the extent specified in the third column of that Schedule.

Commencement

89.–(1)   Subject to the provisions of this section, the provisions of this Act shall not come into force until such day as the Secretary of State may by order appoint.

(2)   The following provisions shall not come into force until such day as the Lord Chancellor may by order appoint–

(a)   sections 19, 21 and 22;

(b)   section 84(1) so far as relating to paragraphs 1 to 4 and 64 to 66 of Schedule 12;

(c)   section 85(3) and (4); and

(d)   section 88 so far as relating to the entries in Part II of Schedule 13 in respect of the Matrimonial Causes Act 1973, the Matrimonial and Family Proceedings Act 1984 and sections 9(8) and 16 of the Family Law Act 1996.

(3)   The following provisions shall not come into force until such day as the Treasury may by order appoint–

(a)   sections 73 to 78;

(b)   section 84(1) so far as relating to paragraphs 74, 76 to 78 and 84 to 86 of Schedule 12; and

(c)   section 88 so far as relating to Parts VI and VII of Schedule 13.

(4)   The following provisions come into force on the day on which this Act is passed–

(a)   sections 52, 57, 58, 60, 68 and 71;

(b)   section 70 so far as relating to Part V of Schedule 8;

(c)   section 72;

(d)   sections 79 to 83;

(e)   section 84(1) so far as relating to paragraphs 13, 79 to 83 and 87 of Schedule 12;

(f)   section 84(2) to (4);

(g)   section 85(1), (2), (6) and (7); and

(h)   sections 86 and 87, this section and sections 90 and 91.

(5)   The following provisions come into force on the day on which this Act is passed, but for the purpose only of the exercise of any power to make regulations–

(a)   Parts I to IV;

(b)   sections 59 and 61; and

(c)   section 70 so far as relating to paragraph 23 of Schedule 8.

(6)   Without prejudice to section 83, an order under this section may appoint different days for different purposes or different areas.

Extent

90.–(1)   The following provisions extend to England and Wales only–

(a)   section 15;

(b)   paragraph 2 of Schedule 2, and section 18 so far as relating thereto;

(c)   sections 19, 21 and 22 and Schedules 3 and 4;

(d)   paragraphs 1 to 4, 64 to 66 and 70 to 72 of Schedule 12, and section 84(1) so far as relating thereto; and

(e)   section 85(3) and (4).

(2)   The following provisions extend to Scotland only–

(a)   sections 13 and 16;

(b)   paragraph 1 of Schedule 2, and section 18 so far as relating thereto;

(c)   section 20;

(d)   paragraphs 5 to 12 and 67 to 69 of Schedule 12, and section 84(1) so far as relating thereto; and

(e)   section 85(5).

(3)   The following provisions extend to England and Wales and Scotland only–

    (a)   Part I;

    (b)   sections 9 to 12, 14 and 17;

    (c)   Schedule 2 (except for paragraphs 1, 2, 3(1), 7(2) and 16), and section 18 so far as relating thereto;

    (d)   sections 23, 24 and 26;

    (e)   Part IV except sections 42 to 44;

    (f)   Chapter I of Part V (except paragraph 1 of Schedule 8, and section 70 so far as relating thereto);

    (g)   sections 73, 75 and 77 and Schedule 9;

    (h)   section 79;

    (i)   paragraphs 1 to 8, 20 to 23, 32(b), 33, 35 and 37 of Schedule 11, and section 81 so far as relating thereto;

    (j)   paragraphs 14 to 63, 66(17), 76 to 80, 82, 83 and 87 of Schedule 12, and section 84(1) so far as relating thereto; and

    (k)   section 84(2) to (4).

    (4)   The following provisions extend to England and Wales, Scotland and Northern Ireland–

    (a)   paragraphs 3(1) and 16 of Schedule 2, and section 18 so far as relating thereto;

    (b)   sections 42 to 44;

    (c)   paragraph 1 of Schedule 8, and section 70 so far as relating thereto;

    (d)   section 80;

    (e)   paragraphs 29 to 31 and 32(a) of Schedule 11, and section 81 so far as relating thereto;

    (f)   sections 82 and 83;

    (g)   paragraphs 13, 73 to 75 and 81 of Schedule 12, and section 84(1) so far as relating thereto;

    (h)   sections 85(1), (2), (6) and (7) and 86; and

    (i)   section 89, this section and section 91.

    (5)   The following provisions extend to Northern Ireland only–

    (a)   paragraph 7(2) of Schedule 2, and section 18 so far as relating thereto;

    (b)   sections 74, 76 and 78 and Schedule 10;

    (c)   paragraphs 9 to 19, 24 to 28, 34, 36 and 38 of Schedule 11, and section 81 so far as relating thereto;

    (d)   paragraphs 84 to 86 of Schedule 12, and section 84(1) so far as relating thereto; and

    (e)   section 87.

    (6)   Nothing in the preceding provisions of this section applies to any repeal made by this Act; and the extent of any such repeal is the same as that of the enactment repealed.

Short title, general interpretation and Scottish devolution

    91.–(1)   This Act may be cited as the Welfare Reform and Pensions Act 1999.

    (2)   In this Act–

"the Administration Act" means the Social Security Administration Act 1992;

"the Contributions and Benefits Act" means the Social Security Contributions and Benefits Act 1992.

    (3)   In this Act, except sections 84(2) and (3), 85(1) and (6) and 89, and in any Act amended by this Act, references to the coming into force of any provision of this Act are to its coming into force otherwise than for the purpose of authorising the making of regulations.

    (4)   For the purposes of the Scotland Act 1998, the following provisions shall be taken to be pre-commencement enactments within the meaning of that Act–

    (a)   paragraphs 8(3) and (4) and 10 of Schedule 12; and

    (b)   so far as relating to those provisions, sections 83, 84(1) and 89(1) and (5).

SCHEDULE 8

Part VIII
Administration of benefits

34.–(1)   In each of the provisions of the Administration Act to which this paragraph applies–

(a)   any reference to a person authorised to exercise any function of a relevant authority relating to housing benefit or council tax benefit shall include a reference to a person providing services to a relevant authority which relate to such a benefit; and

(b)   any reference to the exercise of any function relating to such a benefit shall include a reference to the provision of any services so relating.

(2)   This paragraph applies to the following provisions of the Administration Act–

(a)   [¹ . . .];

(b)   sections 122C, 122D and 122E (supply of information in connection with administration of housing benefit or council tax benefit);

(c)   section 126A (power to require information from landlords etc. in connection with claims for housing benefit);

(d)   section 182B (information about redirection of post); and

(e)   Schedule 4 (persons covered by offence relating to unauthorised disclosures).

(3)   In this paragraph "relevant authority" means an authority administering housing benefit or council tax benefit.

Commencement

6.4.03. See SI 2003 No.936.

Amendment

1.   Repealed by CSPSSA s85(1) and Sch 9 Pt VI (1.4.01).

Immigration and Asylum Act 1999

(1999 c33)

PART VI

Support for Asylum-Seekers
Exclusions

Exclusion from benefits

115.–(1) No person is entitled to income-based jobseeker's allowance under the Jobseekers Act 1995 or to–

(a)-(l) *[Omitted]*

(j) housing benefit, or

[² (k)]

under the Social Security Contributions and Benefits Act 1992 while he is a person to whom this section applies.

(2) No person in Northern Ireland is entitled to–

(a) [...]

(b) any of the benefits mentioned in paragraphs (a) to (j) of subsection (1),

under the Social Security Contributions and Benefits (Northern Ireland) Act 1992 while he is a person to whom this section applies.

(3) This section applies to a person subject to immigration control unless he falls within such category or description, or satisfies such conditions, as may be prescribed.

(4) Regulations under subsection (3) may provide for a person to be treated for prescribed purposes only as not being a person to whom this section applies.

(5) In relation to [¹ child benefit], "prescribed" means prescribed by regulations made by the Treasury.

(6) In relation to the matters mentioned in subsection (2) (except so far as it relates to [¹ child benefit]), "prescribed" means prescribed by regulations made by the Department.

(7) Section 175(3) to (5) of the Social Security Contributions and Benefits Act 1992 (supplemental power in relation to regulations) applies to regulations made by the Secretary of State or the Treasury under subsection (3) as it applies to regulations made under that Act.

(8) Sections 133(2), 171(2) and 172(4) of the Social Security Contributions and Benefits (Northern Ireland) Act 1992 apply to regulations made by the Department under subsection (3) as they apply to regulations made by the Department under that Act.

(9) "A person subject to immigration control" means a person who is not a national of an EEA State and who–

(a) requires leave to enter or remain in the United Kingdom but does not have it;

(b) has leave to enter or remain in the United Kingdom which is subject to a condition that he does not have recourse to public funds;

(c) has leave to enter or remain in the United Kingdom given as a result of a maintenance undertaking; or

(d) has leave to enter or remain in the United Kingdom only as a result of paragraph 17 of Schedule 4.

(10) "Maintenance undertaking", in relation to any person, means a written undertaking given by another person in pursuance of the immigration rules to be responsible for that person's maintenance and accommodation.

Commencement

1.1.2000 for the purpose only of making regulations: Immigration and Asylum Act 1999 (Commencement No.1) Order 1999 SI No.3190.

3.4.2000 for all other purposes: Immigration and Asylum Act 1999 (Commencement No.3) Order 2000 SI No.464.

Amendments

1. Amended by TCA Sch 4 para 21 (1.4.03).

2. Repealed by WRA 2012 s147 and Sch 14 Part 1 (1.4.13).

General Note

Although s115 appears in Part VI of the Act headed "Support for Asylum-Seekers", it has an impact on the entitlements of a wider range of claimants than asylum seekers. The section introduced a general exclusion from HB in respect of "persons subject to immigration control" with exceptions to be set out in regulations: sub-section (1)(j).

To work out whether a claimant is excluded from entitlement, it is necessary to consider two separate questions.

(1)   Is the claimant a "person subject to immigration control" within the meaning of s115? If so, s/he is excluded from entitlement to HB, unless s/he can show that s/he falls within para (1), (4)(a) or (6) of reg 2 Social Security (Immigration and Asylum) Consequential Amendments Regulations 2000 (see p1747).

(2)   Is the claimant a "person from abroad" within the meaning of reg 10 of both the HB and the HB(SPC) Regs (see p297)? If so, s/he is excluded from benefit. It was confirmed in *Yesiloz v LB Camden and SSWP* [2009] EWCA Civ 145 (reported as *R(H) 7/09*) that those subjected to immigration control who were not excluded from benefit because they were within the Consequential Amendments Regulations still needed to have a right to reside.

Note, however, that following the landmark decision of the ECJ in *Zambrano v Office national de l'emploi* (ONEm) (Case C-34/09) [2011] ECR I-01177, s115(1) must arguably be set aside in any case where a person subject to Immigration control is in fact the primary carer of a British child: see the commentary at reg 10 HB Regs on p305 for a more detailed discussion of the scope of the decision in the context of the right to reside test and, in particular, whether the amendments to that test from 8 November 2012 are compatible with EU law. Whether *Zambrano* can also be relied upon to defeat s115(1) by a person who would otherwise be excluded from HB as a person subject to immigration control involves the same considerations.

Analysis

Subsections (1) to (6): The general exclusion

Subs (1)(j) excludes a person to whom s115 applies from entitlement to HB in England, Wales and Scotland and subs (2) makes similar provision in relation to Northern Ireland in respect of the separate HB scheme there.

Subs (3) states that s115 applies to "a person subject to immigration control" subject to the wide powers to make regulations provided for in that subsection. This critical phrase is defined in subs (9) and is discussed below. It should be noted that the regulation-making powers do *not* include powers to create further categories of people within the definition; the powers are to exclude people from the effect of s115 only: subs (4).

Subsections (9) and (10): "Person subject to immigration control"

Two general points need to be made at the outset. Firstly, it is for the decision-making body (the local authority for HB) to show that a claimant is a person subject to immigration control, the onus does not lie on the claimant to show that s/he is not a person subject to immigration control: *CIS 1697/2004*. In cases where the position is not clear (eg, what part a sponsorship undertaking in fact played in the decision to grant the claimant leave to remain in the UK), the responsibility for obtaining the information necessary to decide the point rests with the decision maker: *R(PC) 1/09*. Secondly, for the purposes of s115, a national of a member state of the European Economic Area (EEA) can never be a person subject to immigration control (whatever may be the effect of other immigration legislation in relation to her/him). The member states are: UK (until Brexit), Austria, Belgium, Bulgaria, Croatia, Cyprus, the Czech Republic, Denmark, Estonia, Finland, France, Germany, Greece, Hungary, Iceland, Ireland, Italy, Latvia, Liechtenstein, Lithuania, Luxembourg, Malta, the Netherlands, Norway, Poland, Portugal, Romania, Slovakia, Slovenia, Spain and Sweden.

Subject to that consideration, there are four categories of "person" listed in subs (9).

(1)   ***"A person who requires leave to enter or remain in the United Kingdom but does not have it"***. The Immigration Rules (HC 395) para 7 defines such a person as someone who is not a British citizen, a person with a right of residence under the Immigration (European Economic Area) Regulations 2006 (SI 2006 No.1003) (that means an EEA citizen without a right of residence under those Regulations needs leave to enter but still cannot be a person subject to immigration control given the opening words of the definition in subs (9)), or a Commonwealth citizen with a right of abode.

For those who fall into the latter category, see s2(1)(b) Immigration Act 1971 which requires that the person should have fallen within s2(1)(d) or (2) of the 1971 Act at the time that the British Nationality Act 1981 came into force on 30 October 1981. Those that fall into this category of claimant will include illegal entrants, overstayers and those with temporary admission under Sch 2 para 21 Immigration Act 1971 – ie, asylum seekers who had been entitled to HB and CTB under reg 7A HB Regs 1987 and reg 4A CTB Regs 1992 prior to April 2000.

With regard to the 2006 regulations, note that although, as mentioned above, EEA nationals cannot be persons subject to immigration control for the purposes of s115 due to the wording of subs (9), it is also possible for non-EEA nationals to have rights of residence under the 2006 Regulations as the family member of an EEA national with such a right. Furthermore, s7 Immigration Act 1988 provides that a person with an "enforceable Community right" also does not require leave to enter or remain in the UK and therefore those who have a right of residence in EU law, provision for which is not mirrored in the 2006 regulations, are not persons subject to immigration control for the purposes of s115.

(2) **"A person who has leave to enter or remain in the United Kingdom which is subject to a condition that he does not have recourse to public funds"**. It should be clear from the stamp on a claimant's passport whether or not there is such a condition. Most of the categories of limited leave granted under the Immigration Rules are subject to such a condition: see, for example, para 41(vi) (visitors), para 56K(vii) (students), para 128(v) (holders of work permits) and para 281(v) (spouses). An eventual grant of indefinite leave to remain which carries no public funds condition operates from the date of grant and is not retrospective: *SSWP v IG* [2008] UKUT 5 (AAC).

(3) **"A person who has leave to enter or remain in the UK given as a result of a maintenance undertaking"**. See the definition in subs (10). Under para 35 of the Immigration Rules a person may be given leave to enter as a result of a sponsor giving an undertaking to be responsible for her/his maintenance and accommodation. Typically such an undertaking is given for five years (unless a shorter period of leave is granted). The undertaking need not be on the standard RON 112 form but may be, for example, in a letter: see *R (Begum) v SSWP* [2003] EWHC 3380 Admin (reported as *R(IS) 11/04*). There must be a necessary causal connection between the giving of the undertaking and the granting of leave to enter or remain, which must be investigated by the First-tier Tribunal if necessary (see *SJ v SSWP (SPC)* [2015] UKUT 505 (AAC); [2016] AACR 17 where the First-tier Tribunal needed to carefully determine the basis on which leave had been granted in order to determine whether the undertaking had been a factor). However, it need not be shown that the undertaking was the sole matter taken into account by the immigration officer as long as it was taken into account: *Shah v Secretary of State for Social Security* [2002] EWCA Civ 285, CA (reported as *R(IS) 2/02*); *CIS 3508/2001* paras 10, 24; *CIS 47/2002* para 27. Note, however, to count as an undertaking it must amount to a promise, and not simply a general willingness, to maintain the person: *SSWP v Ahmed* [2005] EWCA Civ 535 (reported as *R(IS) 8/05*).

A person who falls within s115(9)(c) because of a maintenance undertaking would be excluded from HB indefinitely but for the fact that regulations have been made under s115(4) of the Act. These regulations operate to make such people eligible once they have been resident in the UK for five years from the later of their date of entry to the UK or the date on which the maintenance undertaking was given. That rule is relaxed further if the person (or all persons) who gave the undertaking ("the sponsor(s)") die before the end of that period – see the commentary to Schedule para 2 Social Security (Immigration and Asylum) Consequential Amendment Regulations 2000 on p1749.

(4) **"A person who has leave to enter or remain in the United Kingdom only as a result of paragraph 17 of Schedule 4"**. The entirety of Sch 4 was repealed by Sch 9 para 1 Nationality, Immigration and Asylum Act 2002. *EE v City of Cardiff* (HB) [2018] UKUT 418 (AAC) decides that the reference to Sch 4 para 17 is to be construed as a reference to that provision as re-enacted in section 3C(1) and (2)(b) and (c) of the Immigration Act 1971, but it is not as a reference to the former section 3D of the 1971 Act.

As indicated above, if a person falls within the definition of "person subject to immigration control" explained here, s/he is excluded from entitlement to HB unless either s/he is within the exceptions provided for in reg 2 Social Security (Immigration and Asylum) Consequential Amendments Regulations 2000 (see p1747), can rely upon the *Zambrano* ruling as the primary carer of a British child (see the discussion on p305 – amendments from 8 November 2012 attempt to exclude such persons on the basis, not that they are persons subject to immigration control, but rather that a right to reside on this basis is not a sufficient one to obtain entitlement to HB) or have some other EEA right of residence. Finally, it is worth noting that it is only the HB *claimant* who can be caught by the exclusion of persons subject to immigration control. Where a couple have different immigration statuses such that one is a person subject to immigration control and the other is either not or is within an exception to the general exclusion of such persons, then the latter may claim. In a case where the former person is subject to immigration control because s/he has leave to remain subject to a condition that s/he does not have recourse to public funds, consideration should be given to whether a claim would represent an additional recourse to funds and place her/him in breach of her/his conditions of leave. That would typically only be the case where the amount of benefit paid to the claimant is more than what would have been paid had the partner subject to immigration control not been there.

Back-dating of benefits where person recorded as refugee
[⁴**123.**]

Amendments

1. Inserted by TCA Sch 4 para 22(2) (1.4.03).
2. Amended by TCA Sch 4 para 22(3) (1.4.03).
3. Amended by SPCA Sch 2 para 42 (2.7.02 for making regulations). Commencement from October 2003.
4. Repealed by the Asylum and Immigration (Treatment of Claimants, etc.) Act 2004 s12(1) (for those recorded as refugees after 14.6.07).

Commencement

1.1.2000 for the purpose only of making regulations: Immigration and Asylum Act 1999 (Commencement No.1) Order 1999 SI No.3190.

3.4.2000 for all other purposes: Immigration and Asylum Act 1999 (Commencement No.3) Order 2000 SI No.464.

General Note

The section ceased to have effect from 14 June 2007 for those recorded as refugees after that date: s12(1) Asylum and Immigration (Treatment of Claimants, etc.) Act 2004, brought into effect by the Asylum and Immigration (Treatment of Claimants, etc.) Act 2004 (Commencement No.7 and Transitional Provisions) Order 2007 SI No.1602. For these purposes, a person is "recorded as a refugee" on the day the Secretary of State notifies her/him that s/he has been recognised as a refugee and granted asylum in the UK. For the full text of the section, see pp985-86 of the 19th edition.

The section authorised the making of regulations to permit backdated claims by asylum seekers who succeeded in establishing refugee status for benefits for the whole of that period. The relevant provisions in relation to HB and CTB were reg 10A and Sch A1 of both the HB and the HB(SPC) Regs and reg 7A and Sch A1 of both the CTB and the CTB(SPC) Regs as inserted by Sch 4 HB&CTB(CP) Regs (see p1805). There were specific powers to provide for one authority to determine all the entitlement over the period during which a person's status was being determined. The power to deduct the value of any asylum support provided was not exercised in relation to HB or CTB (compare reg 3(5) Social Security (Immigration and Asylum) Consequential Provisions Regulations 2000 which provided for the value of support to be deducted from backdated IS).

Children (Leaving Care) Act 2000

(2000 c35)

General Note to the Act

The Children (Leaving Care) Act 2000 makes provision for assistance by local authority social services departments to children formerly "looked after" by a local authority. The Act makes detailed provision for a package of assistance for children in such a position, of a financial and practical nature. Such children are generally excluded from entitlement to IS, income-based JSA and HB to prevent duplication of provision. However, children will always be entitled either to assistance or to benefits and advisers should be prepared to press authorities to act where there is a dispute between benefits and social services departments as to whether a child has a right to assistance. Note that, to date, such children have not been excluded from entitlement to ESA. Note also that such children can qualify for UC in limited cases.

The bulk of this Act only applies to England and Wales, but by s8(6), s6 also applies to Scotland.

Exclusion from benefits

6.–(1)   No person is entitled to income-based jobseeker's allowance under the Jobseekers Act 1995, or to income support or housing benefit under the Social Security Contributions and Benefits Act 1992, while he is a person to whom this section applies.

(2)   Subject to subsection (3), this section applies to–

(a)   an eligible child for the purposes of paragraph 19B of Schedule 2 to the Children Act 1989;

(b)   a relevant child for the purposes of section 23A of that Act; and

[¹ (ba) a category 1 young person within the meaning of section 104 of the Social Services and Well-being (Wales) Act 2014;

(bb)   a category 2 young person within the meaning of section 104 of the Social Services and Well-being (Wales) Act 2014;]

(c)   any person of a description prescribed in regulations under subsection (4).

(3)   The Secretary of State may by regulations provide that this section does not apply to a person who falls within subsection (2)(a) or (b) but who also falls within such category or description, or satisfies such conditions, as may be prescribed in the regulations.

(4)   The Secretary of State may make regulations prescribing descriptions of person who do not fall within subsection (2)(a) or (b) but who–

(a)   have been looked after by a local authority in Scotland (within the meaning of section 17(6) of the Children (Scotland) Act 1995); and

(b)   otherwise correspond (whether or not exactly) to eligible or relevant children.

(5)   The Secretary of State may in regulations make such transitional, consequential and saving provision as he considers necessary or expedient in connection with the coming into force of this section.

(6)   Section 175(3) to (5) of the Social Security Contributions and Benefits Act 1992 (supplemental power in relation to regulations) applies to regulations made under this section as it applies to regulations made under that Act.

(7)   Powers to make regulations under this section include power to make different provision for different areas.

(8)   Powers to make regulations under this section are exercisable by statutory instrument.

(9)   No statutory instrument containing regulations under subsection (4) is to be made unless a draft of the instrument has been laid before Parliament and approved by a resolution of each House of Parliament.

(10)   A statutory instrument containing regulations under subsection (3) or (5) shall be subject to annulment in pursuance of a resolution of either House of Parliament.

Commencement

10.9.01 for making regulations and 1.10.01 for other purposes: art 2 of SI 2001 No.3070.

Amendment

1.   Inserted by reg 178 of SI 2016 No.413 as from 6.4.16.

General Note
This section excludes young people who receive assistance under the 2000 Act from entitlement to IS, income-based JSA and HB. Subs (2) to (4) refer to regulation-making powers. The relevant regulations are the Children (Leaving Care) Social Security Benefits Regulations 2001 SI No.3074 made under subs (3) and the Children (Leaving Care) Social Security Benefits (Scotland) Regulations 2004 No.747 made under subs (4).

Analysis
Subs (1) has the effect of excluding children to whom the arrangements apply from entitlement to HB, unless such a child is brought back into entitlement by regulations made under subs (3) or (4). The Children (Leaving Care) Social Security Benefits Regulations 2001 SI No.3074, made under subs (3), do not apply to HB. The Children (Leaving Care) Social Security Benefits (Scotland) Regulations 2004 No.747 bring certain children back into entitlement to IS and income-based JSA, but not to HB. So at present any child falling within subs (2) is excluded from HB.

Subs (2) and (4) set out the categories of children to whom the exclusion applies.
(1)   An "eligible child". Sch 2 para 19B Children Act 1989, inserted by s1 of the 2000 Act, defines such a child as being aged 16/17 who has been looked after by a local authority. S/he must have been looked after for at least 13 weeks and have been looked after at some point since the age of 14: reg 40(1) Care Planning, Placement and Case Review (England) Regulations 2010 SI No.959 (the CPPCR(E) Regs). The regulations then exclude specified categories of child. Regs 40(2) and 48 CPPCR(E) Regs exclude a child who has had a series of short-term placements before returning to her/his parent or guardian. The local authority social services department is required to prepare for the child to become independent by preparing a "pathway plan".
(2)   A "relevant child", which is defined by s23A(2) of the 1989 Act, as inserted by s2(4) of the 2000 Act, is a child aged 16/17 who is not presently being looked after by a local authority in England or Wales but who was an "eligible child" when last looked after. By s23A(3)(a), there is power to prescribe additional categories of "relevant child", and by s23A(3)(b), there is a power to exclude people from the definition. Reg 3(2) Care Leavers (England) Regulations 2010 SI No.2571 (the CL(E) Regs) includes a child who was in detention or in hospital at the age of 16 and who has been accommodated by the local authority for at least 13 weeks between the ages of 14 and 16, provided that there is no care order in force in respect of the child. Reg 3(5) CL(E) Regs excludes a child who has had a family placement of at least six months' duration, except where the placement breaks down and it is more than six months since the placement began, save where the family placement "breaks down": see reg 3(6).
(3)   A "category 1 young person". s104(2) of the 2014 Act defines such a child as a child aged 16 or 17 who is being looked after by a local authority, and has been looked after by a local authority in Wales or in England for a period, or periods amounting in all to 13 weeks , which began after the child reached the age of 14 and ended after the child reached the age of 16: reg 47 Care Planning, Placement and Case Review (Wales) Regulations 2015 SI No.1818 (CPPCR(W) Regs). Reg 62 CPPCR(W) Regs excludes a child who has had a series of short-term placements. The local authority is required to prepare a care and support plan.
(4)   A "category 2 young person", also defined in s104(2) of the 2014 act, is a child aged 16 or 17 who is not being looked after by a local authority in Wales or in England, and immediately before ceasing to be looked after, was a category 1 young person. Reg 3 (2) of the Care Leavers (Wales) Regulations 2015 SI No.1820 (the CL(W) Regs) includes a child who was in detention or hospital and who immediately before being detained or admitted to hospital was looked after by a local authority for at least 13 weeks after s/he turned 14. Reg 3(4) CL(W) Regs excludes a child who has lived for a continuous period of six months or more with her/his parent, someone who had parental responsibility for her/him or a person named in a child arrangements order as the person with whom s/he was to live.
(5)   Those prescribed under subs (4). See the note to subs (1).

Social Security Fraud Act 2001
(2001 c11)

General Note to the Act

This was the second Act of Parliament in four years, following the Social Security Administration (Fraud) Act 1997, to be explicitly dedicated in its short title to the prevention of social security fraud. It amended the provisions for obtaining information in Pt VI of the SSAA 1992. In addition, controversial provisions were put into place for reducing the entitlement of recidivist benefit fraud offenders. There is an expansion of the powers to offer the payment of a penalty rather than prosecution.

Sections 6A, 6B and 7 to 13, provide "loss of benefit" provisions. See p1761 for the Social Security (Loss of Benefit) Regulations 2001, made under those sections.

Obtaining and sharing information

Code of practice about use of information powers

3.–(1)   The Secretary of State shall issue a code of practice relating to the exercise of–

(a)   the powers that are exercisable by an authorised officer under section 109B of the Administration Act in relation to the persons mentioned in subsection (2A) of that section; and

(b)   the powers conferred on an authorised officer by sections 109BA and 110AA of that Act.

(2)   The Secretary of State may from time to time–

(a)   revise the whole or any part of the code for the time being in force under this section; and

(b)   issue a revised code.

(3)   Before issuing or revising the code of practice under this section, the Secretary of State shall–

(a)   prepare and publish a draft of the code, or of the revised code; and

(b)   consider any representations made to him about the draft;

and the Secretary of State may incorporate in the code he issues any modifications made by him to his proposals after their publication.

(4)   The Secretary of State shall lay before each House of Parliament the code of practice, and every revised code, issued by him under this section.

(5)   The code of practice issued under this section and any revisions of the code shall come into force at the time at which the code or, as the case may be, the revised code is issued by the Secretary of State.

(6)   An authorised officer exercising any power in relation to which provision must be made by the code of practice under this section shall have regard, in doing so, to the provisions (so far as they are applicable) of the code for the time being in force under this section.

(7)   A failure on the part of any person to comply with any provision of the code of practice for the time being in force under this section shall not of itself render him liable to any civil or criminal proceedings.

(8)   The code of practice for the time being in force under this section shall be admissible in evidence in any civil or criminal proceedings.

(9)   In this section "authorised officer" has the same meaning as in Part 6 of the Administration Act.

Commencement

28.1.02: SI 2002 No.117.

General Note

This welcome provision, added during passage of the Act through Parliament as a result of concerns about the absence of any comprehensive guidance for investigators, requires a Code of Practice to be issued. The critical provision is subs (6), which only requires an officer to "have regard" to the provisions. It is therefore clear that a breach of the Code will not require evidence to be excluded in a criminal prosecution, although such a breach would no doubt be a ground on which to base a submission to exclude such evidence under s78 Police and

Criminal Evidence Act 1984. Under subs (7), a failure to comply with the Code cannot give rise to civil or criminal proceedings and so could not give rise, for example, to a claim for misfeasance in a public office unless the elements of that tort were present in the absence of a breach of the Code.

A copy of the Code of Practice is available at www.gov.uk/government/publications/social-security-fraud-code-of-practice-on-obtaining-information.

Arrangements for payments in respect of information

4.–(1)   It shall be the duty of the Secretary of State to ensure that such arrangements (if any) are in force as he thinks appropriate for requiring or authorising, in such cases as he thinks fit, the making of such payments as he considers appropriate in respect of compliance with relevant obligations by any of the following–

(a)   a credit reference agency (within the meaning given by section 145(8) of the Consumer Credit Act 1974 (c. 39)) or any servant or agent of such an agency;

(b)   a person providing a telecommunications service (within the meaning of the Regulation of Investigatory Powers Act 2000 (c. 23)) or any servant or agent of such a person;

(c)   a water undertaker or [¹ Scottish Water] or any servant or agent of such an undertaker or [¹ that body];

(d)   any person who (within the meaning the Gas Act 1986 (c. 44)) supplies gas conveyed through pipes, or any servant or agent of such a person;

(e)   any person who (within the meaning of the Electricity Act 1989 (c. 29)) supplies electricity conveyed by distribution systems, or any servant or agent of such a person;

(f)   any person added to the list of persons falling within subsection (2A) of section 109B of the Administration Act by an order under subsection (6) of that section, or any person's servant or agent who falls within that subsection by virtue of such an order.

(2)   In subsection (1) "relevant obligation"–

(a)   in relation to a person falling within paragraph (a), (b) or (f) of that subsection, means–

(i)   an obligation to provide information in pursuance of a requirement imposed on that person under section 109B of the Administration Act by virtue only of his falling within subsection (2A) of that section; or

(ii)   any obligation to comply, for the purpose of enabling an authorised officer to obtain information which might otherwise be obtained by the imposition of such a requirement, with any requirements imposed on that person under section 109BA or 110AA of that Act; and

(b)   in relation to a person falling within any of paragraphs (c) to (e) of that subsection, means any obligation to provide information in pursuance of a requirement imposed by such an exercise of the powers conferred by section 109B of that Act as is mentioned in subsection (2D) of that section.

(3)   For the purpose of complying with his duty under this section, the Secretary of State may make arrangements for payments to be made out of money provided by Parliament.

(4)   It shall be the duty of an authority administering housing benefit or council tax benefit to comply with such general or specific directions as to the making of payments as may be given by the Secretary of State in accordance with any arrangements for the time being in force for the purposes of subsection (1).

Commencement

1.4.02: SI 2002 No.1222.

Amendment

1.   Amended by art 2 and Sch para 19 of SI 2004 No. 1822 as from 14.7.04.

General Note

Section 4 gives powers to pay for information. Not every body will be paid; only those bodies specified in subs (1) and then only to the extent that they have complied with "relevant obligations" as defined in subs (2).

The Secretary of State may issue directions under subs (4) to local authorities to make payments.

Loss of benefit provisions

Meaning of "disqualifying benefit" and "sanctionable benefit" for purposes of sections 6B and 7

6A.–(1)   In this section and sections 6B and 7–

"disqualifying benefit" means (subject to any regulations under section 10(1))–

[³ (za) any benefit under Part 1 of the Welfare Reform Act 2012 (universal credit) or under any provision having effect in Northern Ireland corresponding to that Part;]

(a)   any benefit under the Jobseekers Act 1995 or the Jobseekers (Northern Ireland) Order 1995;

(b)   any benefit under the State Pension Credit Act 2002 or the State Pension Credit Act (Northern Ireland) 2002;

(c)   any benefit under Part 1 of the Welfare Reform Act 2007 or Part 1 of the Welfare Reform Act (Northern Ireland) 2007 (employment and support allowance);

[⁴ (ca) any benefit under Part 4 of the Welfare Reform Act 2012 (personal independence payment) or under any provision in Northern Ireland which corresponds to that Part;]

(d)   any benefit under the Social Security Contributions and Benefit Act 1992 or the Social Security Contributions and Benefits (Northern Ireland) Act 1992 other than–

(i)   maternity allowance;

(ii)   statutory sick pay and statutory maternity pay;

(e)   any war pension;

[¹ (f) child tax credit;]

[¹ (g) working tax credit;]

"sanctionable benefit" means (subject to subsection (2) and to any regulations under section 10(1)) any disqualifying benefit other than–

(a)   joint-claim jobseeker's allowance;

(b)   any retirement pension;

(c)   graduated retirement benefit;

[⁴ (ca) personal independence payment;]

(d)   disability living allowance;

(e)   attendance allowance;

(f)   child benefit;

[² (fa) child tax credit;]

[² (fb) working tax credit;]

(g)   guardian's allowance;

(h)   a payment out of the social fund in accordance with Part 8 of the Social Security Contributions and Benefits Act 1992;

(i)   a payment under Part 10 of that Act (Christmas bonuses).

(2)   In their application to Northern Ireland sections 6B and 7 shall have effect as if references to a sanctionable benefit were references only to a war pension.

Commencement
Inserted by WRA 2009 s24 as from 12.1.10 for making regulations; 1.4.10 for all other purposes.

Amendments
1.   Inserted by WRA 2012 s117(1) and (2) (1.4.13).
2.   Inserted by WRA 2012 s117(3) (6.4.13).
3.   Amended by WRA 2012 s31 and Sch 2 para 57 (1.4.13).
4.   Amended by WRA 2012 s91 and Sch 9 para 46 (8.4.13).

General Note
This section provides the definitions of "disqualifying benefit" and "sanctionable benefit" for the purposes of the schemes for loss of benefit following commission of offences under ss6B and 7, often referred to as the "one strike" and the "two strikes" schemes respectively. "Disqualifying benefit" and "sanctionable benefit" both include HB within the definition, subject to subs (2). Note:

(1) Until CTB was abolished on 1 April 2013, it was a benefit under the SSCBA 1992 (sub-section (1)(d)) and was thus both a "disqualifying benefit" and a "sanctionable benefit". Although CTB is no longer a benefit under that Act, for the savings and transitional provisions, see regs 9 and 10 of the Welfare Reform Act 2012 (Commencement No.8 and Savings and Transitional Provisions) Order 2013 SI No.358. Local help with payment of council tax (under any of the council tax reductions schemes) is neither a "disqualifying benefit" nor a "sanctionable benefit".

(2) CTC and WTC are both "disqualifying benefits" but are not "sanctionable benefits". However, under separate rules, a claimant can be disqualifed from receiving WTC: ss36A and 36B Tax Credits Act 2002.

Loss of benefit in case of conviction, penalty or caution for benefit offence

6B.–(1)   Subsection (4) applies where a person ("the offender")–

(a)   is convicted of one or more benefit offences in any proceedings,

(b)   after being given a notice under subsection (2) of the appropriate penalty provision by an appropriate authority, agrees in the manner specified by the appropriate authority to pay a penalty under the appropriate penalty provision to the appropriate authority [¹], in a case where [¹ the offence to which the notice relates] is a benefit offence,

(c)   is cautioned in respect of one or more benefit offences.

(2)   In subsection (1)(b)–

(a)   "the appropriate penalty provision" means section 115A of the Administration Act (penalty as alternative to prosecution) or section 109A of the Social Security Administration (Northern Ireland) 1992 (the corresponding provision for Northern Ireland);

(b)   "appropriate authority" means–

(i)   in relation to section 115A of the Administration Act, the Secretary of State or an authority which administers housing benefit *[or council tax benefit]*, and

(ii)   in relation to section 109A of the Social Security Administration (Northern Ireland) Act 1992, the Department (within the meaning of that Act) or the Northern Ireland Housing Executive.

(3)   Subsection (4) does not apply by virtue of subsection (1)(a) if, because the proceedings in which the offender was convicted constitute the [³ current] set of proceedings for the purposes of section 7, the restriction in subsection (2) of that section applies in the offender's case.

(4)   If this subsection applies and the offender is a person with respect to whom the conditions for an entitlement to a sanctionable benefit are or become satisfied at any time within the disqualification period, then, even though those conditions are satisfied, the following restrictions shall apply in relation to the payment of that benefit in the offender's case.

(5)   Subject to subsections [⁴ (5A)][⁵ and (8)], the sanctionable benefit shall not be payable in the offender's case for any period comprised in the disqualification period.

(5A)   *[Omitted]*

(6)-(9)   *[Omitted]*

(10)   The Secretary of State may by regulations provide that, where the sanctionable benefit is housing benefit *[or council tax benefit]*, the benefit shall be payable, during the whole or a part of any period comprised in the disqualification period, as if one or more of the following applied–

(a)   the rate of the benefit were reduced in such manner as may be prescribed;

(b)   the benefit were payable only if the circumstances are such as may be prescribed.

(11)   For the purposes of this section the disqualification period, in relation to any disqualifying event, means [² the relevant period] beginning with such date, falling after the date of the disqualifying event, as may be determined by or in accordance with regulations made by the Secretary of State.

[² (11A)   For the purposes of subsection (11) the relevant period is–

(a)   in a case falling within subsection (1)(a) where the benefit offence, or one of them, is a relevant offence, the period of three years,

(b)   in a case falling within subsection (1)(a) (but not within paragraph (a) above)), the period of 13 weeks, or

(c)   in a case falling within subsection (1)(b) or (c), the period of four weeks.]

(12)   This section has effect subject to section 6C.

(13)   In this section and section 6C–

"benefit offence" means–

(a)   any post-commencement offence in connection with a claim for a disqualifying benefit;

(b)   any post-commencement offence in connection with the receipt or payment of any amount by way of such a benefit;

(c)   any post-commencement offence committed for the purpose of facilitating the commission (whether or not by the same person) of a benefit offence;

(d)   any post-commencement offence consisting in an attempt or conspiracy to commit a benefit offence;

"disqualifying event" means the conviction falling within subsection (1)(a), the agreement falling within subsection (1)(b) or the caution falling within subsection (1)(c);

"post-commencement offence" means any criminal offence committed after the commencement of this section.

[² (14)   In this section and section 7 "relevant offence" means–

(a)   in England and Wales, the common law offence of conspiracy to defraud, or

(b)   a prescribed offence which, in the offender's case, is committed in such circumstances as may be prescribed, and which, on conviction–

(i)   is found by the court to relate to an overpayment (as defined in section 115A(8) of the Administration Act) of at least £50,000,

(ii)   is punished by a custodial sentence of at least one year (including a suspended sentence as defined in section 189(7)(b) of the Criminal Justice Act 2003), or

(iii)   is found by the court to have been committed over a period of at least two years.]

[² (15)   The Secretary of State may by order amend subsection (11A)(a), (b) or (c), or (14)(b)(i), (ii) or (iii) to substitute a different period or amount for that for the time being specified there.]

Commencement

Inserted by WRA 2009 s24 as from 12.1.10 for the power to make regulations; 1.4.10 for all other purposes.

Amendments

1.   Amended by WRA 2012 s113(8)(a) (8.5.12).

2.   Amended by WRA 2012 s118 (1.4.13).

3.   Amended by WRA 2012 s119(2) (1.4.13).

4.   Amended by WRA 2012 s31 and Sch 2 para 58(2) (1.4.13).

5.   Amended by WRA 2012 s33 and Sch 3 para 16 (1.4.13).

Modification

Section 6B(2)(b)(i) was amended and s6B(10) was repealed by WRA 2012 s147 and Sch 14 part 1 on 1.4.13 in so far as it related to CTB.

General Note

This section sets up the "one strike" scheme for loss of benefit following commission of one or more benefit offences. A conviction for the offence is not always required. Note that where a person is convicted of one or more benefit offences and there is a further "disqualifying event" within five years (for which see subs (13)), a longer sanction can be imposed under s7, instead of a sanction under s6B.

The regulations made under this section are the Social Security (Loss of Benefit) Regulations 2001 (see p1761).

In essence, the scheme operates by providing for loss of benefit for an offender (under s6B) or a member of her/his family (under s9). HB is both a "disqualifying benefit" (those which can trigger a sanction if an offence is committed) and a "sanctionable benefit" (those which may be affected by an offence). HB can be partly reduced, though only in circumstances where a claimant is not in receipt of IS, income-based JSA, income-related ESA or PC in which case the sanction applies to those benefits alone: reg 18 Social Security (Loss of Benefit) Regulations 2001 (see p1767). Section 6C deals with matters supplementary to s6B, including what is to happen if a conviction is quashed or a person withdraws agreement to pay a penalty.

As the decision to impose the sanction is one made by the Secretary of State (not the local authority), an appeal lies to the First-tier Tribunal against a decision made under s6B by virtue of Sch 3 para 3(f) SSA 1998.

Analysis

Subsections (1) to (4) and (12): The conditions for operation of the scheme

A sanction may be applied in three situations.

(1)   The claimant has been convicted of one or more "benefit offences": subs (1)(a). However, a sanction cannot be applied on this ground if the proceedings in which the claimant was convicted are a current set of proceedings for the purposes of s7 and hence the longer sanction under s7(2) applies: subs (3). s6C(5)(a) deals with the date of the conviction and s6C(b) with what references to a conviction includes.

(2)   The claimant has agreed to pay a penalty instead of being prosecuted for an offence ("the appropriate penalty provision", defined in subs (2)): subs (1)(b). The offence must be one mentioned in s115A SSAA 1992 or the equivalent Northern Ireland provision which means that there must be grounds for instituting proceedings for an offence.

(3)   The claimant has been cautioned in respect of one or more "benefit offences": subs (1)(c). Note that "cautioned" is defined in s13 (on p1726) and means cautioned after the person concerned has admitted the offence.

"Benefit offence" is widely defined in subs (13) to cover offences relating to claims and receipt of benefit, as well as aiding and abetting or attempting or conspiring to commit such an offence. Critically, it does not include any offence committed on or before the commencement date – ie, 1 April 2010: see the definition of "post-commencement offence", also in subs (13).

In all three cases, the offender must be a person who is, or is to become, entitled to a "sanctionable benefit" at any time within the "disqualification period", defined in subs (11): subs (4). "Sanctionable benefit" is defined in s6A and includes HB.

Section 6B has effect subject to s6C: subs (12). See s6C(1) where a a sanction is based on a conviction for an offence and the conviction is quashed and s6C(2) and (3) where the sanction is based on an agreement to pay a penalty and the agreement is withdrawn or it is decided on appeal that the overpayment to which the agreement related is not recoverable or due.

Subsections (5) and (10): Imposition of the sanction

The general rule under subs (5) is that the "sanctionable benefit" shall not be payable in respect of any period during the "disqualification period", defined in subs (11). However, in the case of HB, subs (10) and reg 17 Social Security (Loss of Benefit) Regulations 2001 provide for a reduction of benefit instead (see p1767). However, no reduction is to be made to HB where reg 18 of those regulations applies – ie, where a claimant is in receipt of IS, income-based JSA, income-related ESA or PC, the sanction applies to those benefits alone. Note the transitional provisions made if payments of benefit are subject to restriction under s6B and an award of UC is made to a claimant who is an offender: reg 35 UC(TP) Regs (on p1875).

Subsections (11) and (11A): The disqualification period

The disqualification period is "the relevant period" beginning from the date specified in reg 2 Social Security (Loss of Benefit) Regulations 2001: subs (11).

The "relevant period", defined in subs (11A), depends on the reason for the sanction as follows.

(1)   If the case falls within subs (1)(a) and the offence is a "relevant offence", the disqualification period is three years. "Relevant offence" is defined in a subs (14) as the common law offence of conspiracy to defraud (in England and Wales only) or a prescribed offence which on conviction is found to relate to an overpayment of £50,000 or more, is punished by a custodial sentence of at least one year (including a suspended sentence) or is found to have been committed over a period of two years or more. The prescribed offences are found in reg 2A Social Security (Loss of Benefit) Regulations 2001 (on p1766).

(2)   If the case falls within subs (1)(a) but is not a "relevant offence", the disqualification period is 13 weeks.

(3)   If the case falls within subs (1)(b) or (c), the disqualification period is four weeks.

Prior to 1 April 2013 the disqualification period was four weeks in all cases.

Subsection (15): Amendment of subsections (11A) and (14)

This gives the Secretary of State discretion to amend by order the length of the periods or amounts specified.

Section 6B: supplementary provisions

6C.–(1)   Where–

(a)   the conviction of any person of any offence is taken into account for the purposes of the application of section 6B in relation to that person, and

(b)   that conviction is subsequently quashed,

all such payments and other adjustments shall be made as would be necessary if no restriction had been imposed by or under section 6B that could not have been imposed if the conviction had not taken place.

(2)   Where, after the agreement of any person ("P") to pay a penalty under the appropriate penalty provision is taken into account for the purposes of the application of section 6B in relation to that person–

(a)   P's agreement to pay the penalty is withdrawn under subsection (5) of the appropriate penalty provision, or

(b)   it is decided on an appeal or in accordance with regulations under the Social Security Act 1998 or the Social Security (Northern Ireland) Order 1998 that [¹ any overpayment made] to which the agreement relates is not recoverable or due,

all such payments and other adjustments shall be made as would be necessary if no restriction had been imposed by or under section 6B that could not have been imposed if P had not agreed to pay the penalty.

(3)   Where, after the agreement ("the old agreement") of any person ("P") to pay a penalty under the appropriate penalty provision is taken into account for the purposes of the application of section 6B in relation to P, the amount of [¹ any overpayment made] to which the penalty relates is revised on an appeal or in accordance with regulations under the Social Security Act 1998 or the Social Security (Northern Ireland) Order 1998–

(a)   section 6B shall cease to apply by virtue of the old agreement, and

(b)   subsection (4) shall apply.

(4)   Where this subsection applies–

(a)   if there is a new disqualifying event consisting of–

(i)   P's agreement to pay a penalty under the appropriate penalty provision in relation to the revised overpayment, or

(ii)   P being cautioned in relation to the offence to which the old agreement relates,

the disqualification period relating to the new disqualifying event shall be reduced by the number of days in so much of the disqualification period relating to the old agreement as had expired when section 6B ceased to apply by virtue of the old agreement, and

(b)   in any other case, all such payments and other adjustments shall be made as would be necessary if no restriction had been imposed by or under section 6B that could not have been imposed if P had not agreed to pay the penalty.

(5)   For the purposes of section 6B–

(a)   the date of a person's conviction in any proceedings of a benefit offence shall be taken to be the date on which the person was found guilty of that offence in those proceedings (whenever the person was sentenced) or in the case mentioned in paragraph (b)(ii) the date of the order for absolute discharge; and

(b)   references to a conviction include references to–

(i)   a conviction in relation to which the court makes an order for absolute or conditional discharge or a court in Scotland makes a probation order,

(ii)   an order for absolute discharge made by a court of summary jurisdiction in Scotland under section 246(3) of the Criminal Procedure (Scotland) Act 1995 without proceeding to a conviction, and

(iii)   a conviction in Northern Ireland.

(6)   In this section "the appropriate penalty provision" has the meaning given by section 6B(2)(a).

Commencement

Inserted by WRA 2009 s24 as from 12.1.10 for the power to make regulations; 1.4.10 for all other purposes.

Modifications

In England, Wales and Northern Ireland only, in para (5)(b)(i), the words "or a court in Scotland makes a probation order" are repealed with effect from 16 September 2011 by art 3 and para 13 of the Schedule, the Criminal Justice and Licensing (Scotland) Act 2010 (Consequential Provisions and Modifications) Order 2011, SI No.2298.

Amendment

1.   Amended by WRA 2012 s113(8)(b) (8.5.12).

Analysis

Section 6B is subject to this section which contains supplementary provisions.

Subs (1) provides that where a conviction taken into account for the purposes of a sanction under s6B is quashed, and the sanction could not have been applied unless that conviction stood, payment of the sanctionable benefit should be made as normal. The words "could not have been imposed" are, however, of importance. If a claimant is convicted of two offences and only one is quashed, then if the remaining conviction falls to be taken into account under s6B(1)(a) the sanction will remain in place.

Subs (2) sets out when, after an agreement to pay a penalty has been taken into account for the purposes of a sanction under s6B, payment of the sanctionable benefit should be made as normal. There are two possible situations.

(1)   The agreement to pay a penalty is withdrawn: subs (2)(a).

(2)   It is decided on appeal or in accordance with regulations made under specified provisions (eg, on revision) that any overpayment to which the agreement relates is not recoverable or due: subs (2)(b).

In both cases, this only applies if the sanction could not have been applied had the claimant not agreed to pay the penalty. As with subs (1) above, the words "could not have been imposed" are of importance.

Subs (3) and (4) deal with the situation when the amount of any overpayment to which a penalty relates is revised on appeal or in accordance with regulations made under specified provisions and this happens after the agreement to pay a penalty is taken into account for the purposes of a sanction under s6B. In this case, the sanction under s6B ceases to apply in relation to the old agreement and payment of the sanctionable benefit should be made as normal: subs (4)(b). However, if there is a new agreement to pay a penalty in relation to the revised overpayment, or the claimant is cautioned in relation to the offence to which the old agreement applied (a now "disqualifying event", defined in s6D(13)), a new sanction may be applied. In this case, the days in the disqualification period relating to the old agreement are offset against the days in the new disqualification period: subs (4)(a).

Subs (5)(a) confirms that the date of conviction is the date the claimant was "found guilty" rather than the date of sentence. "Found guilty" will include cases where the defendant pleads guilty as well as those where s/he is convicted on a plea of not guilty. If a guilty plea is subsequently changed to a plea of not guilty, it is suggested that the relevant date will be the date on which either a subsequent plea of guilty is entered or on which the claimant is convicted.

Subs (5)(b) confirms that "conviction" includes convictions in Northern Ireland or a conditional discharge in England. South of the border, s14(1) Powers of Criminal Courts (Sentencing) Act 2000 provides that absolute and conditional discharges are not to be treated as convictions, and s14(3) prevents either type of discharge biting in relation to legislation which imposes a "disqualification or disability" on convicted persons. Quite clearly, this Act falls within that description. There is no specific exception to s14(3) for other legislation which specifically imposes a disqualification on those subjected to a conditional discharge, so there is a conflict between s14(3) of the 2000 Act and s6C(5)(b) of this Act. It is likely that the courts will apply the rule of statutory construction that the general provision is overridden by the specific provision and that s6C(5)(b) of this Act prevails over s14(3) of the 2000 Act, particularly since this Act was passed on a later date.

Loss of benefit for [⁵ [⁷ repeated benefit fraud]]

7.–(1)   If–

[⁷ (a) a person ("the offender") is convicted of one or more benefit offences in a set of proceedings ("the current set of proceedings"),]

[⁷ (b) within the period of five years ending on the date on which the benefit offence was, or any of them were, committed, one or more disqualifying events occurred in relation to the offender (the event, or the most recent of them, being referred to in this section as "the earlier disqualifying event"),]

[⁷ (c) the current set of proceedings has not been taken into account for the purposes of any previous application of this section or section 8 or 9 in relation to the offender or any person who was then a member of his family,]

[⁷ (d) the earlier disqualifying event has not been taken into account as an earlier disqualifying event for the purposes of any previous application of this section or either of those sections in relation to the offender or any person who was then a member of his family, and]

[⁷ (e) the offender is a person with respect to whom the conditions for an entitlement to a sanctionable benefit are or become satisfied at any time within the disqualification period,]

then, even though those conditions are satisfied, the following restrictions shall apply in relation to the payment of that benefit in the offender's case.

[⁶ (1A)   The following restrictions do not apply if the benefit offence referred to in subsection (1)(a), or any of them, is a relevant offence.]

(2)   Subject to subsections [⁸ (2A)][⁹ and (4A)] , the sanctionable benefit shall not be payable in the offender's case for any period comprised in the disqualification period.

(2A)   *[Omitted]*

(3)-(4)   *[Omitted]*

[² (4A)]   *[Omitted]*
[⁴ (4B)]   *[Omitted]*
(5)   The Secretary of State may by regulations provide that, where the sanctionable benefit is housing benefit *[or council tax benefit]*, the benefit shall be payable, during the whole or a part of any period comprised in the disqualification period, as if one or both of the following applied–
    (a)   the rate of the benefit were reduced in such manner as may be prescribed;
    (b)   the benefit were payable only if the circumstances are such as may be prescribed.
(6)   For the purposes of this section the disqualification period, [⁷ in an offender's case, means the relevant period beginning with a prescribed date falling after the date of the conviction in the current set of proceedings].
[⁷ (6A)   For the purposes of subsection (6) the relevant period is–
    (a)   in a case where, within the period of five years ending on the date on which the earlier disqualifying event occurred, a previous disqualifying event occurred in relation to the offender, the period of three years;
    (b)   in any other case, 26 weeks.]
(7)   Where–
    (a)   the conviction of any person of any offence is taken into account for the purposes of the application of this section in relation to that person, and
    (b)   that conviction is subsequently quashed,
all such payments and other adjustments shall be made as would be necessary if no restriction had been imposed by or under this section that could not have been imposed if the conviction had not taken place.
[⁷ (7A)   Subsection (7B) applies where, after the agreement of any person ("P") to pay a penalty under the appropriate penalty provision is taken into account for the purposes of the application of this section in relation to that person–
    (a)   P's agreement to pay the penalty is withdrawn under subsection (5) of the appropriate penalty provision,
    (b)   it is decided on an appeal or in accordance with regulations under the Social Security Act 1998 or the Social Security (Northern Ireland) Order 1998 (S.I. 998/1506 (N.I. 10)) that any overpayment to which the agreement relates is not recoverable or due, or
    (c)   the amount of any overpayment to which the penalty relates is revised on an appeal or in accordance with regulations under the Social Security Act 1998 or the Social Security (Northern Ireland) Order 1998 and there is no new agreement by P to pay a penalty under the appropriate penalty provision in relation to the revised overpayment.]
[⁷ (7B)   In those circumstances, all such payments and other adjustments shall be made as would be necessary if no restriction had been imposed by or under this section that could not have been imposed if P had not agreed to pay the penalty.]
(8)   In this section–
[⁷ "appropriate penalty provision" has the meaning given in section 6B(2)(a);]
"benefit offence" means–
    (a)   any post-commencement offence in connection with a claim for a disqualifying benefit;
    (b)   any post-commencement offence in connection with the receipt or payment of any amount by way of such a benefit;
    (c)   any post-commencement offence committed for the purpose of facilitating the commission (whether or not by the same person) of a benefit offence;
    (d)   any post-commencement offence consisting in an attempt or conspiracy to commit a benefit offence;
[⁷ "disqualifying event" has the meaning given in section 6B(13).]
[⁵ "post-commencement offence" means an offence committed on or after 1 April 2002 (the day on which this section came into force).]
[⁵]
[⁵]

[⁷ (8A)   Where a person is convicted of more than one benefit offence in the same set of proceedings, there is to be only one disqualifying event in respect of that set of proceedings for the purposes of this section and–

(a)   subsection (1)(b) is satisfied if any of the convictions take place in the five year periods mentioned there;

(b)   event is taken into account for the purposes of subsection (1)(d) if any of the convictions have been taken into account as mentioned there;

(c)   in the case of the earlier disqualifying event mentioned in subsection (6A)(a), the reference there to the date on which the earlier disqualifying event occurred is a reference to the date on which any of the convictions take place;

(d)   in the case of the previous disqualifying event mentioned in subsection (6A)(a), that provision is satisfied if any of the convictions take place in the five year period mentioned there.]

(9)   For the purposes of this section–

(a)   the date of a person's conviction in any proceedings of a benefit offence shall be taken to be the date on which he was found guilty of that offence in those proceedings (whenever he was sentenced [⁵ or in the case mentioned in paragraph (b)(ii) the date of the order for absolute discharge]); and

[⁵ (b)   references to a conviction include references to–

(i)   a conviction in relation to which the court makes an order for absolute or conditional discharge or a court in Scotland makes a probation order,

(ii)   an order for absolute discharge made by a court of summary jurisdiction in Scotland under section 246(3) of the Criminal Procedure (Scotland) Act 1995 without proceeding to a conviction, and

(iii)   a conviction in Northern Ireland.]

(10)   In this section references to any previous application of this section or section 8 or 9–

(a)   include references to any previous application of a provision having an effect in Northern Ireland corresponding to provision made by this section, or either of those sections; but

(b)   do not include references to any previous application of this section, or of either of those sections, the effect of which was to impose a restriction for a period comprised in the same disqualification period.

[⁷ (10A)   The Secretary of State may by order amend subsection (6A) to substitute different periods for those for the time being specified there.]

[⁷ (10B)   An order under subsection (10A) may provide for different periods to apply according to the type of earlier disqualifying event or events occurring in any case]

[⁵ (11)]

Commencement

17.11.01 for making regulations and 1.4.02 generally: SI 2001 No.3689.

Amendments

1.   Repealed by TCA Sch 6 (8.4.03).

2.   Amended by SPCA Sch 2 para 45 (2.7.02 (for making regulations) and 6.10.03).

3.   Amended by WRA 2007 s49(1) (1.4.08).

4.   Amended by WRA 2007 s28 and Sch 3 para 23 (18.3.08 (for making regulations) and 27.10.08).

5.   Amended by WRA 2009 s24 and Sch 4 para 2 (12.1.10 for making regulations; 1.4.10 for all other purposes).

6.   Amended by WRA 2012 s118(7) (1.4.13).

7.   Amended by WRA 2012 s119(3)-(11) (1.4.13).

8.   Amended by WRA 2012 s31 and Sch 2 para 59(2) (1.4.13).

9.   Amended by WRA 2012 s33 and Sch 3 para 17 (1.4.13).

Modifications

In England, Wales and Northern Ireland only, in para (9)(b)(i), the words "or a court in Scotland makes a probation order" are repealed with effect from 16 September 2011 by art 3 and para 13 of the Schedule, the Criminal Justice and Licensing (Scotland) Act 2010 (Consequential Provisions and Modifications) Order 2011, SI No.2298.

Section 7(3), (4), (4B) and (5) were repealed and s7(10) was amended by WRA 2012 s147 and Sch 14 part 1 on 1.4.13 in so far as they related to CTB.

General Note

This section sets up the "two strikes" scheme for loss of benefit following commission of one or more benefit offences and a further "disqualifying event" (for which see s6B(13)). Note also the "one strike" scheme under ss6B and 6C.

The regulations made under this section are the Social Security (Loss of Benefit) Regulations 2001.

In essence, the scheme operates by providing for loss of benefit for a repeat offender (under s7) or a member of her/his family (under s9). HB is both a "disqualifying benefit" (those which can trigger a sanction if an offence is committed) and a "sanctionable benefit" (those which may be affected by a repeat offence). HB can be partly reduced, though only in circumstances where a claimant is not in receipt of IS, income-based JSA, income-related ESA or PC in which case the sanction applies to those benefits alone: reg 18 Social Security (Loss of Benefit) Regulations 2001 (see p1767).

As the decision to impose the sanction is one made by the Secretary of State (not the local authority), an appeal lies to the First-tier Tribunal against a decision made under s7 by virtue of Sch 3 para 3(f) SSA 1998.

Analysis

Subsection (1): The conditions for operation of the scheme

There are three conditions under s7(1), all of which must be met for the scheme to bite upon a particular claimant who has been guilty of repeated benefit fraud offences.

(1)   The claimant has been convicted of one or more benefit offences in "the current set of proceedings": subs (1)(a). Note the definition of conviction in subs (9). There are provisions in paras (c) and (d) and in subs (10)(b) to prevent a particular set of proceedings being taken into account more than once. Para (c) provides that the current conviction can only affect benefit entitlement of the claimant, or a member of his family under s9 on one occasion. Para (d) prevents an earlier "disqualifying event" (defined in s6B(13)) triggering a loss of benefit in relation to a third conviction. This applies if any of the offences have already been taken into account: subs (8A)(b). Subs (10)(b) prevents double counting if, for example, both s7 and s9 can apply because both a claimant and a member of her/his family are convicted twice. However, it is clear that a fourth conviction would then trigger a second loss of benefit. By subs (10)(a), the previous offence may have been committed in Northern Ireland.

This condition is not met if the benefit offence is a "relevant offence" (defined in s6B(14)). These are the serious offences that result in a three-year disqualification period. Such offences are dealt with under s6B and not s7.

(2)   The offence giving rise to the current conviction was (or any of the offences were) committed within five years of at least one "disqualifying event": subs (1)(b). "Disqualifying event" is defined in s6B(13) – ie, the claimant has been convicted for a benefit offence, has agreed to pay a penalty instead of being prosecuted for a benefit offence, or has been cautioned for a benefit offence.

Note that even if the person is convicted of more than one benefit offence in a set of proceedings, it only counts as one "disqualifying event", and that this condition is satisfied if any of the convictions occurred in the five-year period: subs (8A)(a).

See subs (9)(a) for the date of a conviction. There may be some difficulties in determining when an offence was committed where it involves an omission to notify a change of circumstances. It is suggested that the wording of the charge will be critical. Thus if the claimant is charged with a failure to notify, the date on which it is said in the charge that notification should have occurred will be the relevant date for the purposes of subs (1)(b). If no date is specified in the charge, it will have to be determined at what point the offence was committed.

(3)   The claimant must be, or must become, entitled to a "sanctionable benefit" during the "disqualification period" which is defined in subs (6): subs (1)(e). "Sanctionable benefit" is defined in s6A and includes HB.

Subsections (2), (5), (7), (7A) and (7B): Imposition of the sanction

The general rule under subs (2) is that the "sanctionable benefit" is not payable for any period during the "disqualification period". However, in the case of HB, subs (5) and reg 17 Social Security (Loss of Benefit) Regulations 2001 provide for a reduction of benefit instead. However, no reduction is to be made to HB where reg 18 of those regulations applies – ie, where a claimant is in receipt of IS, income-based JSA, income-related ESA or PC, the sanction applies to those benefits alone. Note the transitional provisions made if payments of benefit are subject to restriction under s7 and an award of UC is made to a claimant who is an offender: reg 35 UC(TP) Regs (on p1875).

See s7(7) where a sanction is based on a conviction for an offence and the conviction is quashed. See s7(7A) and (7B) where the sanction is based on an agreement to pay a penalty and the agreement is withdrawn or it is decided on appeal that the overpayment to which the agreement related is not recoverable or due, or the amount of an overpayment to which a penalty relates is revised on appeal or in accordance with regulations under specified provisions (eg, on revision) and there is no new agreement to pay a penalty. In all cases, the sanctionable benefit should be paid as normal. The words "could not have been imposed" in both s7(7) and s7(B) are, however, of importance. For example, if a claimant is convicted of two offences on the current occasion and only one is quashed, if the remaining conviction falls to be taken into account under subs (1), the sanction remains in place.

Subsection (6 and (6A)): The disqualification period
The disqualification period is "the relevant period" beginning from the date specified in reg 2 Social Security (Loss of Benefit) Regulations 2001 that falls after the date of conviction in the current proceedings (for which see subs (1)). The "relevant period" is defined in sub (6A).

(1)   The disqualification period is three years where the "disqualifying event" referred to in subs (1)(b) itself occurred within five years of a previous one: subs (6A)(a). Note if the person is convicted of more than one benefit offence in a set of proceedings, it only counts as one "disqualifying event". The date on which it occurred is the date any of the convictions took place. In the case of a previous disqualifying event, if any of the convictions took place within the five-year period, the three-year disqualification period applies: subs (8A)(c) and (d).

(2)   The disqualification period is 26 weeks in any other case: subs (6A)(b).
The disqualification period was 13 weeks in all cases prior to 1 April 2013.

Example
The claimant accepts a caution in respect of a benefit offence ("disqualifying event" A) in 2010. The disqualification period under s6B(11A)(c) is four weeks. In 2013, he commits a further benefit offence ("disqualifying event" B) and agrees to pay a penalty instead of being prosecuted. The disqualification period under s7(6A)(b) is 26 weeks. In 2014, he is convicted of a third benefit offence (the "current set of proceedings"). It is not a "relevant offence". The current benefit offence was committed within five years of "disqualifying event" B. "Disqualifying event" B occurred within five years of "disqualifying event" A. Therefore, the disqualification period is three years: s7(6A)(a).

Subsections (8) and (9): Definitions
The definition of *"benefit offence"* is the same as in s6B (see the discussion on p1717) save that here, the commencement date is 1 April 2002: see the definition of "post-commencement offence" also in subs (8).

Subs (9) is identical to s6C(5), for which see the discussion on p1719.

Subsections (10A) and (10B): Amendment of subsection (6A)
Subsections (10A) and (10B) give the Secretary of State discretion to amend by order, the length of the periods in subs (6A) and to set different periods according to the type of "disqualifying event".

Effect of offence on benefits for members of offender's family
9.–(1)   This section applies to–
[⁵ (za) universal credit;]
(a)   income support;
(b)   jobseeker's allowance;
[¹ (bb) state pension credit;]
[² (bc) employment and support allowance;]
(c)   housing benefit; and
[(d)   council tax benefit.]
(2)   The Secretary of State may by regulations make provision in accordance with the following provisions of this section in relation to any case in which–
(a)   the conditions for entitlement to any benefit to which this section applies are or become satisfied in the case of any person ("the offender's family member");
(b)   that benefit falls to be paid in that person's case for the whole or any part of a period comprised in a period ("the relevant period") which is the disqualification period in relation to restrictions imposed under [³ section 6B or 7] in the case of a member of that person's family; [⁵ and]
(c)   that member of that family ("the offender") is a person by reference to whom–
(i)   the conditions for the entitlement of the offender's family member to the benefit in question are satisfied; or
(ii)   the amount of benefit payable in the case of the offender's family member would fall (apart from any provision made under this section) to be determined.
(2A)   *[Omitted]*
(3)-(4B)   *[Omitted]*
(5)   In relation to cases in which the benefit is housing benefit *[or council tax benefit]*, the provision that may be made by virtue of subsection (2) is provision that, in the case of the offender's family member, the benefit shall be payable, during the whole or a part of any period comprised in the relevant period, as if one or both of the following applied–

(a)   the rate of the benefit were reduced in such manner as may be prescribed;

(b)   the benefit were payable only if the circumstances are such as may be prescribed.

(6)   Where–

(a)   the conviction of any member of a person's family for any offence is taken into account for the purposes of any restriction imposed by virtue of any regulations under this section, and

(b)   that conviction is subsequently quashed,

all such payments and other adjustments shall be made in that person's case as would be necessary if no restriction had been imposed that could not have been imposed had the conviction not taken place.

[³ (7)   Where, after the agreement of any member of a person's family ("M") to pay a penalty under the appropriate penalty provision is taken into account for the purposes of any restriction imposed by virtue of any regulations under this section–

(a)   M's agreement to pay the penalty is withdrawn under subsection (5) of the appropriate penalty provision, or

(b)   it is decided on an appeal or in accordance with regulations under the Social Security Act 1998 or the Social Security (Northern Ireland) Order 1998 that [⁴ any overpayment made] to which the agreement relates is not recoverable or due,

all such payments and other adjustments shall be made as would be necessary if no restriction had been imposed that could not have been imposed had M not agreed to pay the penalty.

(8)   Where, after the agreement ("the old agreement") of any member of a person's family ("M") to pay a penalty under the appropriate penalty provision is taken into account for the purposes of any restriction imposed by virtue of any regulations under this section, the amount of [⁴ any overpayment made] to which the penalty relates is revised on an appeal or in accordance with regulations under the Social Security Act 1998 or the Social Security (Northern Ireland) Order 1998–

(a)   if there is a new disqualifying event for the purposes of section 6B consisting of M's agreement to pay a penalty under the appropriate penalty provision in relation to the revised overpayment or M being cautioned in relation to the offence to which the old agreement relates, the new disqualification period for the purposes of section 6B falls to be determined in accordance with section 6C(4)(a), and

(b)   in any other case, all such payments and other adjustments shall be made as would be necessary if no restriction had been imposed by or under this section that could not have been imposed had M not agreed to pay the penalty.

(9)   In this section "the appropriate penalty provision" has the meaning given by section 6B(2)(a).]

Commencement

17.11.01 for making regulations and 1.4.02 generally: SI 2001 No.3689.

Amendments

1.   Inserted by SPCA Sch 2 para 46 (2.7.02 (for making regulations) and 6.10.03).

2.   Amended by WRA 2007 s28 and Sch 3 para 23 (18.3.08 (for making regulations) and 27.10.08).

3.   Amended by WRA 2009 s24 and Sch 4 para 4 (12.1.10 (for making regulations) and 1.4.10 for all other purposes).

4.   Amended by WRA 2012 s113(8)(b) (8.5.12).

5.   Amended by WRA 2012 s31 and Sch 2 para 61(2)-(4) (25.2.13).

Modification

Section 9(1)(a), (b), (bc), (c) and (d) and (3), (4), (4B) and (5) were repealed by WRA 2012 s147 and Sch 14 part 1 on 1.4.13 in so far as they related to CTB.

General Note

This section deals with cases where the offender is not the person claiming benefit on behalf of the family. The effect is that equivalent reductions in HB are still imposed.

The effect of s9 may in some cases be to impose a sanction on a blameless claimant. There is no requirement that the offender should have been part of the claimant's family at the time that the offence was committed. There may well be arguments that the imposition of a sanction in such a case infringes Art 8 of the European Convention on Human Rights (because it shows a lack of respect for the home which cannot be justified) or Art 14 (because there is discrimination in comparison with those who do not have a benefit offender in their households).

As the decision to impose a sanction is taken by the Secretary of State (not the local authority), an appeal lies to the First-tier Tribunal against a decision made under s6B or s7 by virtue of Sch 3 para 3(f) SSA 1998.

Analysis
Subsection (2): Cases where section 9 is applicable
The conditions for imposing a sanction under s9 are the following.
(1)   A person is claiming benefit to which s9 applies: subs (2)(a). The benefits are listed in s9(1) and include HB.
(2)   The claimant will be paid that benefit for a period which forms part or the whole of the "disqualification period" under ss6B or 7 in respect of a member of the claimant's family: subs (2)(b). "Member of ... family" refers to a person falling to be treated as part of the claimant's family under s137(1) SSCBA and Pt 4 HB and HB(SPC) Regs: see the definition of "family" in s13 on p1727.
(3)   The offender is a person in relation to whom the conditions of entitlement are satisfied (such as where HB is claimed in respect of a partner's liability for rent) or who falls to be taken into account in calculating benefit: subs (2)(c). Although non-dependents fall within the latter description, it is suggested that s9 cannot bite in such cases because they are not members of the claimant's family for the purposes of subs (2)(b).

Subsections (5) to (7): Imposition of the sanction
Subs (5) imposes identical sanctions in s9 cases to those imposed by ss6B(10) and 7(5). Subs (6) is the equivalent of ss6C(1) and 7(7). Subs (7) to (9) are the equivalent of s6C(3) to (6). Note the transitional provisions made if payments of benefit are subject to restriction under s9 and an award of UC is made to a claimant who is an offender: reg 35 UC(TP) Regs (on p1875).

Power to supplement and mitigate loss of benefit provisions
10.–(1)   The Secretary of State may by regulations provide for any social security benefit to be treated for the purposes of [⁴ sections 6A to 9]–
(a)   as a disqualifying benefit but not a sanctionable benefit; or
(b)   as neither a sanctionable benefit nor a disqualifying benefit.
(2)   The Secretary of State may by regulations provide for any restriction in section [⁴ 6B,] 7, 8 or 9 not to apply in relation to payments of benefit to the extent of any deduction that (if any payment were made) would fall, in pursuance of provision made by or under any enactment, to be made from the payments and paid to a person other than the offender or, as the case may be, a member of his family.
(3)   In this section "social security benefit" means–
(a)   any benefit under the Social Security Contributions and Benefits Act 1992 or the Social Security Contributions and Benefits (Northern Ireland) Act 1992; [²]
(b)   any benefit under the Jobseekers Act 1995 or the Jobseekers (Northern Ireland) Order 1995;
[¹ (bb) any benefit under the State Pension Credit Act 2002 or under any provision having effect in Northern Ireland corresponding to that Act;
[² (bc) any benefit under Part 1 of the Welfare Reform Act 2007 (employment and support allowance) or under any provision having effect in Northern Ireland corresponding to that Part;] or]
[⁵ (bd) any benefit under Part 1 of the Welfare Reform Act 2012 (universal credit) or under any provision having effect in Northern Ireland corresponding to that Part;]
[⁶ (be) any benefit under Part 4 of the Welfare Reform Act 2012 (personal independence payment) or under any provision in Northern Ireland which corresponds to that part;]
(c)   any war pension.

Commencement
17.11.01 for making regulations and 1.4.02 generally: SI 2001 No.3689.

Amendments
1.   Inserted by SPCA Sch 2 para 47 (2.7.02 (for making regulations) and October 2003).
2.   Amended by SPCA Sch 3 (2.7.02 (for making regulations) and October 2003).
3.   Amended by WRA s28 and Sch 3 para 23 (18.3.08 (for making regulations) and 27.10.08).
4.   Amended by WRA 2009 s24 and Sch 4 para 5 (12.1.10 (for making regulations) and 1.4.10).
5.   Amended by WRA 2012 s31 and Sch 2 para 62 (1.4.13).
6.   Amended by WRA 2012 s91 and Sch 9 para 47 (8.4.13).

General Note
None of the powers conferred by subs (1) or (2) have been exercised in relation to HB.

Loss of benefit [⁵ orders and] regulations

11.–(1)   In [³ sections 6B to 10] "prescribed" means prescribed by or determined in accordance with regulations made by the Secretary of State.

(2)   Regulations under any of the provisions of [³ sections 6B to 10] shall be made by statutory instrument which (except in the case of regulations to which subsection (3) applies) shall be subject to annulment in pursuance of a resolution of either House of Parliament.

(3)   A statutory instrument containing (whether alone or with other provisions)–

(a)   a provision by virtue of which anything is to be treated for the purposes of section [³ 6B or] 7 as a disqualifying benefit but not a sanctionable benefit,

(b)   a provision prescribing the manner in which the applicable amount is to be reduced for the purposes of section [³ 6B(6),] 7(3) or 9(3),

(c)   a provision the making of which is authorised by [⁷ section 6B(5A) or (8), 7(2A) or (4A) or 9(2A) or (4A), or

(d)   a provision prescribing the manner in which the amount of joint-claim jobseeker's allowance is to be reduced for the purposes of section 8(3)(a),

[⁵ (e)   regulations under section 6B(14) or an order under section 6B(15), or]

[⁶ (f)   an order under section 7(10A),]

shall not be made unless a draft of the instrument has been laid before, and approved by a resolution of, each House of Parliament.

(4)   Subsections (4) to (6) of section 189 of the Administration Act (supplemental and incidental powers etc.) shall apply in relation to a power to make [⁵ an order or] regulations that is conferred by any of the provisions of [³ sections 6B to 10] as they apply in relation to the powers to make [⁵ and order or] regulations that are conferred by that Act.

(5)   The provision that may be made in exercise of the powers to make regulations that are conferred by [³ sections 6B to 10] shall include different provision for different areas.

Commencement
17.11.01 for making regulations and 1.4.02 generally: SI 2001 No.3689.

Amendments
1.   Amended by SPCA Sch 2 para 48 (2.7.02 (for making regulations) and 6.10.03).
2.   Amended by WRA s28 and Sch 3 para 23 (18.3.08 (for making regulations) and 27.10.08).
3.   Amended by WRA 2009 s24 and Sch 4 para 6 (12.1.10 (for making regulations) and 1.4.10).
4.   Amended by WRA 2012 s31 and Sch 2 para 63(1) and (2) (25.2.13).
5.   Amended by WRA 2012 s118(8) (1.4.13).
6.   Amended by WRA 2012 s119(12) (1.4.13).
7.   Amended by WRA 2012 s33 and Sch 3 para 18 (1.4.13).

Interpretation of [³ sections 6A to 12]

13.   In this section and [³ sections 6A to 12]–

"benefit" includes any allowance, payment, credit or loan;

[³ "cautioned", in relation to any person and any offence, means cautioned after the person concerned has admitted the offence; and "caution" is to be interpreted accordingly;]

[³]

"family" has the same meaning as in Part VII of the Social Security Contributions and
Benefits Act 1992;
"income-based jobseeker's allowance", "joint-claim jobseeker's allowance" and "joint-
claim couple" have the same meanings as in the Jobseekers Act 1995;
[² "income-related allowance" has the same meaning as in Part 1 of the Welfare Reform
Act 2007 (employment and support allowance);]
[³]
"sanctionable benefit" has the meaning given by [³ section 6A(1)];
[¹ "state pension credit" means state pension credit under the State Pension Credit Act
2002;]
"war pension" has the same meaning as in section 25 of the Social Security Act 1989
(establishment and functions of war pensions committees).

Commencement

17.11.01 for making regulations and 1.4.02 generally: SI 2001 No.3689.

Amendments

1.   Amended by SPCA Sch 2 para 49 (2.7.02 (for making regulations) and 6.10.03).
2.   Inserted by WRA s28 and Sch 3 para 24 (18.3.08 (for making regulations) and 27.10.08).
3.   Amended by WRA 2009 s24 and Sch 4 para 7 (12.1.10 (for making regulations) and 1.4.10).

Supplemental

Meaning of "the Administration Act"
   18.   In this Act "the Administration Act" means the Social Security Administration
Act 1992 (c. 5).

Commencement
   20.–(1)   The preceding provisions of this Act shall come into force on such day as
the Secretary of State may by order made by statutory instrument appoint.
   (2)   Subject to subsection (3), different days may be appointed under this section for
different purposes.
   (3)   The power under this section to appoint a day for the coming into force of the
provisions of sections 1 and 2 shall not authorise the appointment for those purposes of
any day before the issue of the code of practice that must be issued under section 3.

Short title and extent
   21.–(1)   This Act may be cited as the Social Security Fraud Act 2001.
   (2)   Sections 5(2), [¹ 6A, 6B and 6C] 7, 10, 11, 12(3), 13 and 20, and this section,
extend to Northern Ireland; and the other provisions of this Act do not so extend.

Amendment

1.   Amended by WRA 2009 s24 and Sch 4 para 8 (12.1.10 (for making regulations) and 1.4.10).

Tax Credits Act 2002
(2002 c21)

General Note to the Act
The Tax Credits Act 2002 replaced working families' tax credit, disabled person's tax credit, personal allowances and premiums for children within the IS and JSA schemes, increases to non-means-tested benefits for children and other allowances with two tax credits: working tax credit (WTC) and child tax credit (CTC). Child benefit is paid in addition to CTC. HB continues to contain personal allowances and premiums for children who are members of the claimant's "family".

WTC and CTC are administered by HM Revenue and Customs (HMRC). For full details of the rules for WTC and CTC, see CPAG's *Welfare Benefits and Tax Credits Handbook*.

For HB (and formerly for CTB), the only directly relevant parts of the Act are those concerning the sharing of information between local authorities and HMRC.

SCHEDULE 5
USE AND DISCLOSURE OF INFORMATION

Exchange of information between Board and authorities administering certain benefits

7.–(1) This paragraph applies to information which is held for the purposes of functions relating to tax credits, child benefit or guardian's allowance–
  (a)   by the Board, or
  (b)   by a person providing services to the Board, in connection with the provision of those services.
  (2)   Information to which this paragraph applies may be supplied by or under the authority of the Board–
  (a)   to an authority administering housing benefit or council tax benefit, or
  (b)   to a person authorised to exercise any function of such an authority relating to such a benefit,
for use in the administration of such a benefit.
  (3)   Information supplied under this paragraph is not to be supplied by the recipient to any other person or body unless it is supplied–
  (a)   to a person to whom the information could be supplied directly by or under the authority of the Board,
  (b)   for the purposes of any civil or criminal proceedings relating to the Social Security Contributions and Benefits Act 1992 (c. 4), the Social Security Administration Act 1992 (c. 5) or the Jobseekers Act 1995 (c. 18) or to any provision of Northern Ireland legislation corresponding to any of them, or
  (c)   under paragraph 8 below.

8.–(1) The Board may require–
  (a)   an authority administering housing benefit or council tax benefit, or
  (b)   a person authorised to exercise any function of such an authority relating to such a benefit,
to supply benefit administration information held by the authority or other person to, or to a person providing services to, the Board for use for any purpose relating to tax credits, child benefit or guardian's allowance.
  (2)   In sub-paragraph (1) "benefit administration information", in relation to an authority or other person, means any information which is relevant to the exercise of any function relating to housing benefit or council tax benefit by the authority or other person.

Civil Partnership Act 2004
(2004 c33)

General Note

The Civil Partnership Act 2004 (Relationships Arising Through Civil Partnership) Order 2005 SI No.3137 sets out the provisions to which s246 of this Act applies for HB (and formerly for CTB) purposes (see p1772).

Interpretation of statutory references to stepchildren etc.

246.–(1)   In any provision to which this section applies, references to a stepchild or step-parent of a person (here, "A"), and cognate expressions, are to be read as follows–

A's stepchild includes a person who is the child of A's civil partner (but is not A's child);

A's step-parent includes a person who is the civil partner of A's parent (but is not A's parent);

A's stepdaughter includes a person who is the daughter of A's civil partner (but is not A's daughter);

A's stepson includes a person who is the son of A's civil partner (but is not A's son);

A's stepfather includes a person who is the civil partner of A's father (but is not A's parent);

A's stepmother includes a person who is the civil partner of A's mother (but is not A's parent);

A's stepbrother includes a person who is the son of the civil partner of A's parent (but is not the son of either of A's parents);

A's stepsister includes a person who is the daughter of the civil partner of A's parent (but is not the daughter of either of A's parents).

(2)   For the purposes of any provision to which this section applies–

"brother-in-law" includes civil partner's brother,

"daughter-in-law" includes daughter's civil partner,

"father-in-law" includes civil partner's father,

"mother-in-law" includes civil partner's mother,

"parent-in-law" includes civil partner's parent,

"sister-in-law" includes civil partner's sister, and

"son-in-law" includes son's civil partner.

Provisions to which section 246 applies: Acts of Parliament etc.

247.–(1)   Section 246 applies to–

(a)   any provision listed in Schedule 21 (references to stepchildren, in-laws etc. in existing Acts),

(b)   except in so far as otherwise provided, any provision made by a future Act, and

(c)   except in so far as otherwise provided, any provision made by future subordinate legislation.

(2)   A Minister of the Crown may by order–

(a)   amend Schedule 21 by adding to it any provision of an existing Act;

(b)   provide for section 246 to apply to prescribed provisions of existing subordinate legislation.

(3)   The power conferred by subsection (2) is also exercisable–

(a)   by the Scottish Ministers, in relation to a relevant Scottish provision;

(b)   by a Northern Ireland department, in relation to a provision which deals with a transferred matter;

(c)   by the National Assembly for Wales, if the order is made by virtue of subsection (2)(b) and deals with matters with respect to which functions are exercisable by the Assembly.

(4)   Subject to subsection (5), the power to make an order under subsection (2) is exercisable by statutory instrument.

(5)   Any power of a Northern Ireland department to make an order under subsection (2) is exercisable by statutory rule for the purposes of the Statutory Rules (Northern Ireland) Order 1979 (S.I. 1979/1573 (N.I. 12)).

(6)   A statutory instrument containing an order under subsection (2) made by a Minister of the Crown is subject to annulment in pursuance of a resolution of either House of Parliament.

(7)   A statutory instrument containing an order under subsection (2) made by the Scottish Ministers is subject to annulment in pursuance of a resolution of the Scottish Parliament.

(8)   A statutory rule containing an order under subsection (2) made by a Northern Ireland department is subject to negative resolution (within the meaning of section 41(6) of the Interpretation Act (Northern Ireland) 1954 (c. 33 (N.I.))).

(9)   In this section—

"Act" includes an Act of the Scottish Parliament;

"existing Act" means an Act passed on or before the last day of the Session in which this Act is passed;

"existing subordinate legislation" means subordinate legislation made before the day on which this section comes into force;

"future Act" means an Act passed after the last day of the Session in which this Act is passed;

"future subordinate legislation" means subordinate legislation made on or after the day on which this section comes into force;

"Minister of the Crown" has the same meaning as in the Ministers of the Crown Act 1975 (c. 26);

"prescribed" means prescribed by the order;

"relevant Scottish provision" means a provision that would be within the legislative competence of the Scottish Parliament if it were included in an Act of that Parliament;

"subordinate legislation" has the same meaning as in the Interpretation Act 1978 (c. 30) except that it includes an instrument made under an Act of the Scottish Parliament;

"transferred matter" has the meaning given by section 4(1) of the Northern Ireland Act 1998 (c. 47) and "deals with" in relation to a transferred matter is to be construed in accordance with section 98(2) and (3) of the 1998 Act.

Social security, child support and tax credits

254.–(1)   Schedule 24 contains amendments relating to social security, child support and tax credits.

(2)   Subsection (3) applies in relation to any provision of any Act, Northern Ireland legislation or subordinate legislation which–

(a)   relates to social security, child support or tax credits, and

(b)   contains references (however expressed) to persons who are living or have lived together as husband and wife.

(3)   The power under section 259 to make orders amending enactments, Northern Ireland legislation and subordinate legislation is to be treated as including power to amend the provision to refer to persons who are living or have lived together as if they were civil partners.

(4)   Subject to subsection (5), section 175(3), (5) and (6) of the Social Security Contributions and Benefits Act 1992 (c. 4) applies to the exercise of the power under section 259 in relation to social security, child support or tax credits as it applies to any power under that Act to make an order (there being disregarded for the purposes of this subsection the exceptions in section 175(3) and (5) of that Act).

(5)   Section 171(3), (5) and (6) of the Social Security Contributions and Benefits (Northern Ireland) Act 1992 (c. 7) applies to the exercise by a Northern Ireland department of the power under section 259 in relation to social security and child support as it applies to any power under that Act to make an order (there being disregarded for the purposes of this subsection the exceptions in section 171(3) and (5) of that Act).

(6)   The reference in subsection (2) to an Act or Northern Ireland legislation relating to social security is to be read as including a reference to–

(a)   the Pneumoconiosis etc. (Workers' Compensation) Act 1979 (c. 41), and

(b)   the Pneumoconiosis, etc., (Workers' Compensation) (Northern Ireland) Order 1979 (S.I. 1979/925 (N.I. 9));

and the references in subsections (4) and (5) to social security are to be construed accordingly.

SCHEDULE 21

SECTION 247

REFERENCES TO STEPCHILDREN ETC. IN EXISTING ACTS

24	Section 113(2) of the Housing Act 1985 (c. 68) (members of a person's family).
25	Section 186(2) of that Act (members of a person's family).
44	Section 62(2) of the Housing Act 1996 (c. 52) (members of a person's family: Part 1).
45	Section 140(2) of that Act (members of a person's family Chapter 1).
46	Section 143P(3) of that Act (members of a person's family: Chapter 1A).
47	The definition of "relative" in section 178(3) of that Act (meaning of associated person).

Part 8:

Other secondary legislation – Common and transitional provisions

The Housing Benefit (Permitted Totals) Order 1996
(SI 1996 No.677)

General Note

This Order sets out the basis for calculating the permitted totals of rebates or allowances for the year 1996/97 and subsequent years for authorities granting rebates or allowances under Part VIII of the Social Security Administration Act 1992. The Order limits the amount by which HB payments may be increased on the exercise of the discretions formerly provided by reg 61(2) and (3) HB Regs 1987, and to war widows through modified schemes.

Note that the Council Tax Benefit (Permitted Totals) Order 1996 SI No.678 set out the basis for calculating the permitted totals of CTB and limited the amount by which CTB could be increased on the excercise of the discretions formerly provided by regs 51(5) and 54(4) of the CTB Regs 1992, and to war widows where the authority's scheme had been modified. See p1205 of the 25th edition.

Citation, commencement and interpretation

1.–(1)   This Order may be cited as the Housing Benefit (Permitted Totals) Order 1996 and shall come into force on 1st April 1996.

(2)   In this Order–

"the Act" means the Social Security Administration Act 1992;

"housing benefit" means either rent rebate or rent allowance as the circumstances may require;

"the Housing Benefit Regulations" means the Housing Benefit (General) Regulations 1987;

"increase in housing benefit" means the difference between–

(a)   the amount of housing benefit granted in a case in which an authority makes a determination under regulation 61(2) of the Housing Benefit Regulations (increase in the appropriate maximum housing benefit)(e), and

(b)   the amount of housing benefit which would have been granted in that case if the authority had not made a determination under regulation 61(2) of those Regulations; and

"increase above maximum rent" means the difference between–

(a)   the amount of housing benefit granted in a case in which an authority makes a determination under regulation 61(3) of the Housing Benefit Regulations, and

(b)   the amount of housing benefit which would have been granted in that case if the authority had not made a determination under regulation 61(3) of those Regulations.

Permitted total of benefit awarded in exercise of a discretion

2.   For the purpose of section 134(11) of the Act, the permitted total of housing benefit–

[¹ (a)   for the year commencing on 1st April 1996 in relation to an authority shall be the total of the amounts obtained by the calculations set out in articles 3 and 4 below.

(b)   for the year commencing on 1st April 1997 in relation to an authority shall be the total of the amounts obtained by the calculations set out in articles 3 and 4 below; and

(c)   for any year commencing on or after 1st April 1998 in relation to an authority shall be the total of the amount obtained by the calculation in article 3 below and the amount specified in the Schedule to this Order.]

Amendment

1.   Amended by reg 2 of SI 1998 No 566 from 31.3.98.

Increase in housing benefit

3.   The calculation referred to in article 2 above shall be the amount obtained by deducting 100% of any increases in housing benefit in cases in which that authority has during that year made a determination under regulation 61(2) of the Housing Benefit

Regulations from the total housing benefit granted by that authority during that year, after deduction of any increase above maximum rent, and multiplying the resulting figure by [¹100.025%].

Amendment

1.　　Amended by reg 2 SI 2001 No 1129 as from 1.04.01.

Increase above maximum rent

4.–(1)　　The calculation referred to in article 2 above shall be the amount obtained by deducting 100% of any increases above maximum rent in cases in which that authority has during that year made a determination under regulation 61(3) of the Housing Benefit Regulations from the total housing benefit granted by that authority during that year, less the deductions specified in paragraph (2) below, and multiplying the resulting figure by [¹ 101.08%]

(2)　　The deductions referred to in paragraph (1) above are–

(a)　　all rent rebates granted during that year;

(b)　　subject to paragraph (3) below, all rent allowances granted during that year in cases where the local authority did not refer a claim for housing benefit, in relation to the dwelling in respect of which that allowance was granted, to the rent officer pursuant to regulation 12A of the Housing Benefit Regulations; and

(c)　　any increase in housing benefit.

(3)　　No rent allowance shall be deducted pursuant to paragraph (2) above, if that case was not referred to the rent officer by reason of paragraph (2) of regulation 12A of those Regulations.

Amendment

1.　　101.08% substituted for 100.9% by art 2 of SI 1996 No 2326 as from 7.10.96.

Permitted total of benefit in modified schemes

5.　　For the purpose of section 134(9) of the Act (modifications other than war disablement pension or war widows pension within the Act), the permitted total of housing benefit for [¹ any year commencing on or after] 1st April 1996 in relation to an authority shall be the total of the amounts obtained by deducting 100% of any housing benefit awarded as a consequence of any determination to disregard made by that authority during that year pursuant to a modification adopted by them under section 134(8) of the Act (power to modify housing benefit schemes as prescribed) and regulation 7 of the Income Related Benefits Schemes Amendment (No. 2) Regulations 1995 (power to modify in respect of certain pensions to war widows) from the total housing benefit granted by that authority during that year and multiplying the resulting figure by 100.7%.

Amendment

1.　　Amended by reg 3 of SI 1998 No 566 from 31.3.98.

Revocation

6.　　The Housing Benefit (Permitted Totals) Order 1995 is hereby revoked.

SCHEDULE 1

ARTICLE 2

[² TOTALS FOR INCREASES ABOVE MAXIMUM RENT

Authority	Permitted total £	Authority	Permitted total £
Adur	11,073	Babergh	10,044
Allerdale	14,001	Barking	38,065
Alnwick	2,832	Barnet	133,375
Amber Valley	12,361	Barnsley	31,155
Arun	41,402	Barrow in Furness	23,278
Ashfield	12,423	Basildon	21,576
Ashford	12,112	Basingstoke and Deane	12,982
Aylesbury Vale	13,412	Bassetlaw	14,013

Authority	Permitted total £	Authority	Permitted total £
Bath and NE Somerset	31,322	Daventry	4,365
Bedford	25,697	Derby	48,483
Berwick upon Tweed	3,833	Derbyshire Dales	3,813
Bexley	49,763	Derwentside	10,221
Birmingham	198,165	Doncaster	39,071
Blaby	4,376	Dover	36,954
Blackburn with Darwen	33,307	Dudley	21,784
Blackpool	117,965	Durham	5,937
Blyth Valley	8,004	Ealing	158,493
Bolsover	13,007	Easington	10,063
Bolton	46,138	East Cambridgeshire	7,026
Boston	5,138	East Devon	18,050
Bournemouth	95,696	East Dorset	6,974
Bracknell Forest	13,822	East Hampshire	11,956
Bradford	123,752	East Hertfordshire	10,036
Braintree	14,434	East Lindsey	32,105
Breckland	12,774	East Northamptonshire	8,204
Brent	193,395	East Riding of Yorkshire	57,413
Brentwood	7,087	East Staffordshire	12,968
Bridgnorth	4,120	Eastbourne	42,495
Brighton and Hove	180,857	Eastleigh	12,311
Bristol	96,138	Eden	5,083
Broadland	8,928	Ellesmere Port and Neston	5,910
Bromley	50,991	Elmbridge	22,072
Bromsgrove	4,359	Enfield	109,407
Broxbourne	13,260	Epping Forest	20,508
Broxtowe	11,299	Epsom and Ewell	9,885
Burnley	25,828	Erewash	13,294
Bury	29,838	Exeter	35,462
Calderdale	28,108	Fareham	9,844
Cambridge	16,167	Fenland	17,307
Camden	132,750	Forest Heath	6,146
Cannock Chase	6,657	Forest of Dean	10,316
Canterbury	33,324	Fylde	17,760
Caradon	20,600	Gateshead	27,463
Carlisle	13,889	Gedling	12,914
Carrick	24,764	Gloucester	38,822
Castle Morpeth	3,056	Gosport	11,207
Castle Point	21,278	Gravesham	21,343
Charnwood	17,868	Great Yarmouth	40,174
Chelmsford	14,838	Greenwich	56,280
Cheltenham	24,155	Guildford	17,990
Cherwell	23,520	Hackney	159,737
Chester	16,699	Halton	17,626
Chester le Street	5,524	Hambleton	8,380
Chesterfield	14,802	Hammersmith and Fulham	92,023
Chichester	15,367	Harborough	4,066
Chiltern	4,842	Haringey	254,022
Chorley	9,480	Harlow	10,481
Christchurch	6,318	Harrogate	24,943
City of London	1,439	Harrow	74,970
Colchester	28,238	Hart	6,633
Congleton	4,887	Hartlepool	20,158
Copeland	12,193	Hastings	70,070
Corby	12,013	Havant	15,981
Cotswold	9,367	Havering	36,693
Coventry	67,163	Herefordshire	31,035
Craven	6,118	Hertsmere	10,520
Crawley	7,786	High Peak	11,583
Crewe and Nantwich	13,121	Hillingdon	48,018
Croydon	145,919	Hinckley and Bosworth	6,864
Dacorum	13,429	Horsham	11,381
Darlington	19,355	Hounslow	81,898
Dartford	15,715	Huntingdonshire	12,412

Authority	Permitted total £	Authority	Permitted total £
Hyndburn	23,110	Nuneaton and Bedworth	14,606
Ipswich	23,448	Oadby and Wigston	4,630
Isle of Wight	48,692	Oldham	34,150
Isles of Scilly	112	Oswestry	4,760
Islington	75,538	Oxford	48,078
Kennet	6,553	Pendle	19,716
Kensington and Chelsea	95,011	Penwith	23,242
Kerrier	23,573	Peterborough	41,089
Kettering	11,336	Plymouth	95,680
Kings Lynn & West Norfolk	19,448	Poole	29,167
Kingston upon Hull	61,181	Portsmouth	67,055
Kingston upon Thames	23,020	Preston	23,230
Kirklees	61,583	Purbeck	7,603
Knowsley	24,691	Reading	51,780
Lambeth	166,917	Redbridge	142,324
Lancaster	52,083	Redcar and Cleveland	22,464
Leeds	161,079	Redditch	5,822
Leicester	51,758	Reigate and Banstead	13,661
Lewes	24,395	Restormel	32,194
Lewisham	118,483	Ribble Valley	5,025
Lichfield	3,550	Richmond upon Thames	34,918
Lincoln	20,575	Richmondshire	4,019
Liverpool	201,524	Rochdale	43,229
Luton	63,742	Rochford	10,624
Macclesfield	16,110	Rossendale	11,986
Maidstone	17,903	Rother	22,310
Maldon	18,921	Rotherham	23,596
Malvern Hills	7,025	Rugby	7,523
Manchester	195,674	Runnymede	9,170
Mansfield	14,897	Rushcliffe	9,619
Medway	108,499	Rushmoor	11,126
Melton	3,109	Rutland	1,986
Mendip	21,594	Ryedale	5,138
Merton	57,194	Salford	77,097
Mid Bedfordshire	8,266	Salisbury	19,512
Mid Devon	12,064	Sandwell	31,220
Mid Suffolk	6,806	Scarborough	37,313
Mid Sussex	13,107	Sedgefield	7,215
Middlesbrough	30,388	Sedgemoor	21,337
Milton Keynes	30,589	Sefton	84,267
Mole Valley	6,461	Selby	6,559
New Forest	19,869	Sevenoaks	10,096
Newark and Sherwood	12,775	Sheffield	52,222
Newcastle under Lyme	8,317	Shepway	51,579
Newcastle upon Tyne	75,679	Shrewsbury and Atcham	12,479
Newham	236,456	Slough	36,269
North Cornwall	22,078	Solihull	11,316
North Devon	33,937	South Bedfordshire	10,573
North Dorset	5,647	South Bucks	3,586
North East Derby	5,846	South Cambridgeshire	8,860
North East Lincoln	42,198	South Derbyshire	11,106
North Hertfordshire	15,823	South Gloucestershire	20,227
North Kesteven	6,418	South Hams	19,260
North Lincolnshire	20,707	South Holland	5,045
North Norfolk	19,096	South Kesteven	13,603
North Shropshire	6,383	South Lakeland	15,835
North Somerset	58,091	South Norfolk	9,469
North Tyneside	49,049	South Northants	5,306
North Warwickshire	3,801	South Oxfordshire	19,106
North West Leicester	5,509	South Ribble	6,160
North Wiltshire	9,457	South Shropshire	6,168
Northampton	32,163	South Somerset	22,317
Norwich	26,986	South Staffordshire	4,463
Nottingham	59,030	South Tyneside	32,453

Authority	Permitted total £
Southampton	73,593
Southend on Sea	97,336
Southwark	90,007
Spelthorne	10,818
St Albans	9,953
St Edmundsbury	8,585
St Helens	23,507
Stafford	7,452
Staffordshire Moorlands	7,006
Stevenage	9,376
Stockport	51,884
Stockton on Tees	28,021
Stoke on Trent	34,205
Stratford on Avon	11,053
Stroud	14,432
Suffolk Coastal	17,852
Sunderland	53,243
Surrey Heath	7,169
Sutton	34,929
Swale	41,749
Swindon	23,721
Tameside	36,307
Tamworth	9,172
Tandridge	7,092
Taunton Deane	21,426
Teesdale	2,865
Teignbridge	29,864
Telford and Wrekin	18,049
Tendring	44,271
Test Valley	6,818
Tewkesbury	8,100
Thanet	88,716
Three Rivers	8,128
Thurrock	24,684
Tonbridge and Malling	9,546
Torbay	85,563
Torridge	18,849
Tower Hamlets	45,003
Trafford	35,417
Tunbridge Wells	14,206
Tynedale	3,800
Uttlesford	6,206
Vale of White Horse	9,747
Vale Royal	7,303
Wakefield	27,358
Walsall	18,945
Waltham Forest	158,176
Wandsworth	121,014
Wansbeck	6,844
Warrington	13,911
Warwick	15,350
Watford	16,358
Waveney	51,698
Waverley	13,121
Wealdon	21,509
Wear Valley	7,507
Wellingborough	10,445
Welwyn Hatfield	9,713
West Berkshire	10,976
West Devon	12,775
West Dorset	11,805
West Lancashire	13,010
West Lindsey	9,532
West Oxfordshire	11,866

Authority	Permitted total £
West Somerset	10,899
West Wiltshire	20,797
Westminster	189,131
Weymouth and Portland	23,141
Wigan	26,933
Winchester	8,637
Windsor and Maidenhead	17,452
Wirral	104,453
Woking	10,638
Wokingham	11,843
Wolverhampton	28,921
Worcester	24,231
Worthing	33,956
Wychavon	6,710
Wycombe	12,804
Wyre	22,173
Wyre Forest	11,956
York	29,336
Scotland	
Aberdeen	17,118
Aberdeenshire	15,810
Angus	10,333
Argyll and Bute	17,435
Comhairle Nan Eilean Sair	2,249
Clackmannanshire	3,067
Dumfries and Galloway	19,846
Dundee	23,135
East Ayrshire	8,128
East Dunbartonshire	5,812
East Lothian	12,140
East Renfrewshire	5,656
Edinburgh	116,558
Falkirk	8,674
Fife	43,080
Glasgow	122,279
Highland	18,909
Inverclyde	9,892
Midlothian	5,423
Moray	9,487
North Ayrshire	17,642
North Lanarkshire	12,042
Orkney	2,857
Perth and Kinross	21,140
Renfrewshire	14,138
Scottish Borders	7,350
Shetland	775
South Ayrshire	22,019
South Lanarkshire	17,803
Stirling	7,290
West Dunbartonshire	5,438
West Lothian	12,617
Wales	
Blaenau Gwent	10,753
Bridgend	25,789
Caerphilly	24,394
Cardiff	60,004
Carmarthenshire	32,572
Ceredigion	18,702
Conwy	37,048
Denbighshire	30,347
Flintshire	16,400
Gwynedd	31,422

Housing Benefit (Permitted Totals) Order 1996

Authority	Permitted total £
Isle of Anglesey	18,958
Merthyr Tydfil	9,430
Monmouthshire	9,465
Neath and Port Talbot	20,810
Newport	22,985
Pembrokeshire	26,943
Powys	16,586
Rhondda Cynon Taff	38,661
Swansea	52,344
Torfaen	7,729
Vale of Glamorgan	30,658
Wrexham	14,500

Amendments

1. Schedule added by reg 2 of SI 1998 No 566 from 31.3.98.
2. Amended by reg 3 of SI 2001 No 1129 as from 1.04.01.

The Housing Benefit (Information from Landlords and Agents) Regulations 1997
(SI 1997 No.2436)

General Note

These regulations implemented s126A SSAA 1992 by setting out the circumstances in which local authorities may require information from landlords and agents, the information which must be supplied, the time limit for supplying it and the manner in which the information must be provided. Failure to comply with a notice requiring information under s126A is a criminal offence and would be a factor which a local authority could take into account when considering whether a landlord is a "fit and proper person" to receive payments of HB under regs 95 and 96 HB Regs (or regs 76 and 77 HB(SPC) Regs).

These regulations were not amended or revoked when the consolidating HB regulations came into force on 6 March 2006. However, the provisions are now also in the HB and the HB(SPC) Regs as follows.

Reg 1 is now, in part, reg 113 HB Regs (see p610) and reg 94 HB(SPC) Regs (see p835).

Reg 2 is now reg 117 HB Regs (see p615) and reg 98 HB(SPC) Regs (see p840).

Reg 3 is now reg 118 HB Regs (see p615) and reg 99 HB(SPC) Regs (see p840).

Reg 4 is now reg 119 HB Regs (see p615) and reg 100 HB(SPC) Regs (see p840).

Reg 5 is now reg 120 HB Regs (see p618) and reg 101 HB(SPC) Regs (see p842).

Reg 6 was indentical to reg 121 HB Regs (see p618) and reg 102 HB(SPC) Regs (see p842), both of which have now been substituted.

See the commentary to regs 117–121 HB Regs (pp615-618).

Citation, commencement and interpretation

1.–(1)   These Regulations, which may be cited as the Housing Benefit (Information from Landlords and Agents) Regulations 1997, shall come into force on 3rd November 1997.

(2)   In these Regulations, unless the context otherwise requires–

"the Act" means the Social Security Administration Act 1992;

"the Housing Benefit Regulations" means the Housing Benefit (General) Regulations 1987;

"the notice" means the notice prescribed in regulation 3(1)(b);

"relevant information" means such information as is prescribed in regulation 4;

"the requirer" means a person within regulation 2, who requires information pursuant to that regulation;

"the section" means section 126A of the Act and references to a subsection are to a subsection of the section;

"the supplier" means an appropriate person who is required, pursuant to regulations 2 and 3, to supply relevant information and any person who is not so required is not, for the purposes of supplying information pursuant to the section and these Regulations, an appropriate person,

and other expressions used both in these Regulations and in the Housing Benefit Regulations shall have the same meanings in these Regulations as they have in the Housing Benefit Regulations.

(3)   In these Regulations a reference to a numbered regulation is to the regulation in these Regulations bearing that number and, unless the context otherwise requires, a reference in a regulation to a numbered or lettered paragraph is to the paragraph bearing that letter or number in that regulation and a reference in a paragraph to a lettered or numbered sub-paragraph is to the sub-paragraph in that paragraph bearing that letter or number.

Requiring information

2.   Pursuant to the section, where a claim is made to an authority, on which a rent allowance may be awarded, then, in the circumstances prescribed in regulation 3, that authority, or any person authorised to exercise any function of the authority relating to housing benefit, may require an appropriate person to supply to that authority or person relevant information, in the manner prescribed in regulation 5.

Circumstances for requiring information

3.–(1)   A person is required to supply information in the following circumstances–

(a)   he is an appropriate person in relation to any dwelling in respect of which–

(i)   housing benefit is being paid to an appropriate person pursuant to regulation 93 or 94 of the Housing Benefit Regulations (circumstances in which payment is to be or may be made to a landlord); or

(ii)   a request has been made by an appropriate person or by the claimant for housing benefit to be so paid; and

(b)   the requirer serves upon that appropriate person, whether by post or otherwise, a written notice stating that the requirer–

(i)   suspects that there is or may be an impropriety in relation to a claim in respect of any dwelling wherever situate in relation to which he is an appropriate person; or

(ii)   is already investigating an allegation of impropriety in relation to that person.

(2)   Information required to be supplied under paragraph (1) shall be supplied to the requirer at the address specified in the notice.

Relevant information

4.–(1)   The information the supplier is to supply to the requirer is that prescribed in paragraphs (2) and (3) (referred to in these Regulations as "the relevant information").

(2)   For a supplier who falls within paragraph (4) or sub-section (2)(b) ("the landlord"), the information is–

(a)   where the landlord is a natural person–

(i)   his appropriate details;

(ii)   the relevant particulars of any residential property in which he has an interest; and

(iii)   the appropriate details of any body corporate, in which he is a major shareholder or of which he is a director and which has an interest in residential property;

(b)   where the landlord is a trustee, except a trustee of a charity, in addition to any information that he is required to supply in accordance with sub-paragraph (a) or (c), as the case may be, the relevant particulars of any residential property held by the trust of which he is a trustee and the name and address of any beneficiary under the trust or the objects of that trust, as the case may be;

(c)   where the landlord is a body corporate or otherwise not a natural person, other than a charity–

(i)   its appropriate details;

(ii)   the relevant particulars of any residential property in which it has an interest;

(iii)   the names and addresses of any directors of it;

(iv)   the appropriate details of any person–

(aa)   who owns 20 per cent. or more of it; or

(bb)   of whom it owns 20 per cent. or more; and

(v)   the names and addresses of its major shareholders.

(d)   where the landlord is a charity or is a recognised body the appropriate details relating to the landlord and particulars of the landlord's registration as a charity.

(3)   For a supplier who falls within subsection (2)(c) or paragraph (5) ("the agent"), the information is–

(a)   the name and address of any person ("his principal")–

(i)   to whom the agent has agreed to make payments in consequence of being entitled to receive relevant payments; or

(ii)   for whom the agent is acting on behalf of or in connection with any aspect of the management of a dwelling,

as the case may be;

(b)   the relevant particulars of any residential property in respect of which the agent–
  (i)   has agreed to make payments in consequence of being entitled to receive relevant payments; or
  (ii)   is acting on behalf of his principal in connection with any aspect of its management;
(c)   where the agent is a natural person–
  (i)   the relevant particulars of any residential property in which he has an interest;
  (ii)   the appropriate details of any body corporate or any person otherwise not a natural person, in which he is a major shareholder or of which he is a director and which has any interest in residential property; or
(d)   where the agent is a body corporate or other than a natural person–
  (i)   the relevant particulars of any residential property in which it has an interest;
  (ii)   the names and addresses of any directors of or major shareholders in the agent; and
  (iii)   the appropriate details of any person–
    (aa)   who owns 20 per cent. or more of the agent; or
    (bb)   of whom the agent owns 20 per cent. or more.

(4)   A supplier falls within this paragraph (landlord receiving the rent), if he falls within subsection (2)(a), but does not fall within paragraph (5).

(5)   A supplier falls within this paragraph (agent receiving the rent), if he falls within subsection (2)(a) and has agreed to make payments, in consequence of being entitled to receive relevant payments, to a person falling within subsection (2)(b).

(6)   For the purposes of this regulation, except where the context otherwise requires–
"appropriate details" means the name of the person and (in the case of a company) its registered office and, in any case, the full postal address, including post code, of the principal place of business of that person and the telephone and facsimile numbers (if any) of that place;
"charity" means a charity which is registered under section 3 of the Charities Act 1993 and is not an exempt charity within the meaning of that Act;
"major shareholder" means, where a body corporate is a company limited by shares, any person holding one tenth or more of the issued shares in that company and, in any other case, all the owners of that body;
"recognised body" has the same meaning as in section 1(7) of the Law Reform (Miscellaneous Provisions) (Scotland) Act 1990;
"relevant particulars" means the full postal address, including post code, and number of current lettings of or within that residential property and, if that property includes two or more dwellings, that address and the number of such lettings for each such dwelling;
"residential property" includes any premises, situated within the United Kingdom–
  (i)   used or which has, within the last six months, been used; or
  (ii)   which may be used or is adapted for use,
  as residential accommodation,
and other expressions used in this regulation and also in the Companies Act 1985 shall have the same meaning in this regulation as they have in that Act.

Manner of supply of information

[¹5.–(1)   Subject to paragraph (2) the relevant information shall be supplied–
(a)   in typewritten or printed form; or
(b)   with the written agreement of the requirer, in electronic or handwritten form,
within a period of 4 weeks commencing on the date on which the notice was sent or given.
(2)   Where–
(a)   within a period of 4 weeks commencing on the date on which the notice was sent or given, the supplier requests that the time for supply of the relevant information be extended; and

(b)   the requirer provides written agreement to that request,
the time for supply of the relevant information shall be extended to a period of 8 weeks commencing on the date on which the notice was sent or given.]

Amendment
1.   Substituted by reg 2 of SI 2000 No 4 as from 1.4.00 or 3.4.00.

Criminal offence

6.   Any failure by the supplier to supply relevant information to the requirer as, when and how required under these Regulations shall be an offence under section 113 of the Act and there may be recovered from the supplier, on summary conviction for this offence, penalties not exceeding–

(a)   for any one offence, level 3 on the standard scale; or
(b)   for an offence of continuing any such failure after conviction, £40 for each day on which it is so continued.

The Social Security (Penalty Notice) Regulations 1997
(SI 1997 No.2813)

General Note

These regulations implement the provisions of s115A SSAA 1992 which allows payment of an administrative penalty as an alternative to prosecution for an offence in relation to an overpayment of benefit. The regulations specify in detail the contents of the written notice referred to in s115A(2) in which a local authority may invite a claimant or landlord to pay such a penalty. For commentary on the penalty scheme, see p59.

The purpose of prescribing the content of a notice is to provide the recipient with the information that s/he needs to consider whether or not to accept the penalty. It is therefore suggested that a failure to supply the notice in the required form will render the penalty a nullity if the claimant is prejudiced by the omission: *Warwick DC v Freeman* (1994) 27 HLR 616, CA; *Haringey LBC v Awaritefe* (1999) 32 HLR 517.

Citation and commencement

1. These Regulations may be cited as the Social Security (Penalty Notice) Regulations 1997 and shall come into force on 18th December 1997.

Notice

2.–(1)   Where the Secretary of State or authority gives to a person a written notice under section 115A(2) of the Social Security Administration Act 1992 [¹ ("the 1992 Act") in a case to which section 115A(1) of the Act applies], the notice shall contain the information that–

(a)   the penalty [¹] applies to an overpayment which is recoverable under section 71, [¹ 71ZB,] 71A, 75 or 76 of the Social Security Administration Act 1992;

(b)   the penalty [¹] applies where it appears to the Secretary of State or authority that the making of the overpayment was attributable to an act or omission by the person and that there are grounds for instituting proceedings for an offence relating to the overpayment;

(c)   the penalty is [¹ 50 per cent of the amount of the overpayment (subject to the maximum and minimum amounts prescribed in section 115A(3) of the 1992 Act)], is payable in addition to repayment of the overpayment and is recoverable by the same methods as those by which the overpayment is recoverable;

(d)   a person who agrees to pay a penalty may withdraw the agreement within [¹ 14] days (including the date of the agreement) by notifying the Secretary of State or authority in the manner specified by the Secretary of State or authority; if the person withdraws the agreement, so much of the penalty as has already been recovered shall be repaid and he will no longer be immune from proceedings for an offence;

(e)   if it is decided on review or appeal (or in accordance with regulations) that the overpayment is not recoverable or due, so much of the penalty as has already been recovered shall be repaid;

(f)   if the amount of the overpayment is revised on review or appeal, except as covered by a new agreement to pay the revised penalty, so much of the penalty as has already been recovered shall be repaid and the person will no longer be immune from proceedings for an offence;

(g)   the payment of a penalty does not give the person immunity from prosecution in relation to any other overpayment or any offence not relating to an overpayment.

[¹ (1A)   Where the Secretary of State or authority gives to a person written notice under section 115A(2) of the 1992 Act in a case to which section 115(1A) of that Act applies, the notice shall contain the information that–

(a)   the penalty applies where it appears to the Secretary of State or authority that there are grounds for instituting proceedings against the person for an offence relating to an act or omission on the part of the person in relation to any benefit;

(b)   if an overpayment attributable to the act or omission had been made, the overpayment would have been recoverable under section 71, 71ZB, 71A, 75 or 76 of the 1992 Act;

(c)   the penalty is £350;

(d)   a person who agrees to pay the penalty may withdraw the agreement within 14 days (including the date of the agreement) by notifying the Secretary of State or authority in the manner specified by the Secretary of State or authority; if the person withdraws the agreement, so much of the penalty as has already been recovered shall be repaid and he will no longer be immune from proceedings for an offence;

(e)   if it is decided on review or appeal (or in accordance with regulations) that any overpayment attributable to the act or omission would not have been recoverable or due, so much of the penalty as has already been recovered shall be repaid;

(f)   the payment of a penalty does not give the person immunity from prosecution in relation to any overpayment or any other offence not relating to an overpayment.]

(2)   The notice [¹ in either case] shall set out–

(a)   the manner specified by the Secretary of State or authority by which the person may agree to pay a penalty;

(b)   the manner specified by the Secretary of State or authority by which the person may notify the withdrawal of his agreement to pay a penalty.

Modification

The amendments made by The Social Security (Miscellaneous Amendments) Regulations 2014 SI No.591 apply only where the offence in respect of which the notice is given is committed wholly on or after 8 May 2012: reg 5(5) of those regulations.

Amendment

1.   Amended by reg 5 of SI 2014 No 591 as from 28.4.14.

The Social Security (Immigration and Asylum) Consequential Amendments Regulations 2000
(SI 2000 No.636)

General Note

Regs 2, 12 and the Schedule to these Regulations exclude certain categories of claimant from the effect of s115 Immigration and Asylum Act 1999, which precludes a "person subject to immigration control" from claiming HB. See p1707 for a summary of the way that s115, reg 10 of both the HB and the HB(SPC) Regs and these Regulations combine.

Citation, commencement and interpretation

1.–(1) These Regulations may be cited as the Social Security (Immigration and Asylum) Consequential Amendments Regulations 2000.

(2) These Regulations shall come into force on 3rd April 2000.

(3) In these Regulations–

"the Act" means the Immigration and Asylum Act 1999;

"the Contributions and Benefits Act" means the Social Security Contributions and Benefits Act 1992;

[¹]

[¹]

"the Persons from Abroad Regulations" means the Social Security (Persons from Abroad) Miscellaneous Amendments Regulations 1996;

(4) In these Regulations, unless the context otherwise requires, a reference–

(a) to a numbered regulation or Schedule is to the regulation in, or the Schedule to, these Regulations bearing that number;

(b) in a regulation or Schedule to a numbered paragraph is to the paragraph in that regulation or Schedule bearing that number.

Amendment

1. Revoked by reg 3 and Sch 1 of SI 2006 No 217 as from 6.3.06.

Persons not excluded from specified benefits under section 115 of the Immigration and Asylum Act 1999

2.–(1) For the purposes of entitlement to income-based jobseeker's allowance, income support, a social fund payment, housing benefit [³] under the Contributions and Benefits Act, [² income-related employment and support allowance] [¹or state pension credit under the State Pension Credit Act 2002] as the case may be, a person falling within a category or description of persons specified in Part I of the Schedule is a person to whom section 115 of the Act does not apply.

(1A)-(3) *[Omitted]*

(4) For the purposes of entitlement to–

(a) income support, a social fund payment, housing benefit [³] under the Contributions and Benefits Act, [² or income-related employment and support allowance,] as the case may be, a person who is entitled to or is receiving benefit by virtue of paragraph (1) or (2) of regulation 12 of the Persons from Abroad Regulations is a person to whom section 115 of the Act does not apply;

(b) [...]

[¹(c) state pension credit under the State Pension Credit Act 2002, a person to whom sub-paragraph (a) would have applied but for the fact that they have attained the qualifying age for the purposes of state pension credit, is a person to whom section 115 of the Act does not apply.]

(5) *[Omitted]*

(6) For the purposes of entitlement to housing benefit [³] or a social fund payment under the Contributions and Benefits Act, as the case may be, a person to whom regulation 12(6) applies is a person to whom section 115 of the Act does not apply.

(7) *[Omitted]*

[⁴ (8)]

Amendments

1.   Inserted by reg 6 of SI 2003 No 2274 as from 6.10.03.
2.   Amended by reg 69 of SI 2008 No 1554 as from 27.10.08.
3.   Amended by reg 3 and Sch 1 of SI 2013 No 458 as from 1.4.13.
4.   Omitted by reg 9(2) of SI 2013 No 2536 as from 29.10.13.

General Note

Reg 2 is the primary provision which creates the six categories of claimant that are exempted from the effect of s115.

Analysis

Para (1) exempts the (currently three) categories listed in Part I of the Schedule.

Para (4) exempts those who retain their transitional protection under reg 12 Social Security (Persons from Abroad) Miscellaneous Amendments Regulations 1996 SI No.30 (see p1633 of the 26th edition). Broadly, it relates to those who did not claim asylum "on arrival".

Such claimants only retain their transitional protection if they were in receipt of HB on 5 February 1996 and their entitlements have continued since then. It only applies to those who are still receiving benefit (or to those who are not receiving benefit but have an underlying entitlement) pursuant to those rules, not to those who once did so.

The effect of the saving provision in reg 12 of the 1996 Regulations is that the rules as now found in Sch 3 para 6(1)–(4) HB&CTB(CP) Regs apply (see p1795). A person remains an asylum seeker while the Secretary of State has yet to record the claim as determined or, if the asylum claim was recorded as determined prior to 5 February 1996, while an appeal is pending. A person does not retain her/his status as an asylum seeker while a second appeal is pending from an adverse decision on the first appeal: *CIS 3418/1998* para 45. Note also the effect of reg 12(11)(b).

Para (6) exempted those falling within reg 12(6).

Transitional arrangements and savings

12.– [² (1)]

[² (2)]

(3)-(5) *[Omitted]*

[¹ (6)-(8)]

(9)   In paragraphs (4) and (7) "the Common Travel Area" means the United Kingdom, the Channel Islands, the Isle of Man and the Republic of Ireland collectively and "the Convention" means the Convention relating to the Status of Refugees done at Geneva on 28th July 1951 as extended by Article 2(1) of the Protocol relating to the Status of Refugees done at New York on 31st January 1967

(10)   *[Omitted]*

(11)   In the Persons from Abroad Regulations–

(a)   *[Omitted]*

(b)   notwithstanding the amendments and revocations in regulations 3, 6 and 7, regulations 12(1) and (2) of the Persons from Abroad Regulations shall continue to have effect as they had effect before those amendments and revocations came into force.

Amendments

1.   Revoked by reg 3 and Sch 1 of SI 2006 No 217 as from 6.3.06.
2.   Ceased to have effect by s12(1) Asylum and Immigration (Treatment of Claimants, etc.) Act 2004 (for those recorded as refugees after 14.6.07).

General Note

This regulation contained transitional arrangements and savings.

Analysis

Paragraphs (1) and (2): Amendments to backdated entitlements of refugees

Paras (1) and (2) ceased to have effect from 14 June 2007 for those recorded as refugees after that date: s12(3) Asylum and Immigration (Treatment of Claimants, etc.) Act 2004, brought into effect by the Asylum and Immigration (Treatment of Claimants, etc.) Act 2004 (Commencement No.7 and Transitional Provisions) Order 2007 SI No.1602. For these purposes, a person is "recorded as a refugee" on the day the Secretary of State notifies her/him that s/he has been recognised as a refugee and granted asylum in the UK. For the full text, see p1030 of the 19th edition. Paras (1) and (2) prevented the amendments made to the entitlements of refugees to backdated HB and CTB from having effect where the claimant sought asylum prior to 2 April 2000. Reference should be made to the version of the provisions listed in para (2) that is reproduced in the 12th edition for the provisions as they stood in relation to those claimants.

Paragraphs (6) to (9)

These paragraphs prevented certain asylum seekers either from falling foul of reg 7A HB Regs 1987 by being a person from abroad and also, by virtue of reg 2(6), from exclusion from HB under s115 of the 1999 Act. These savings rules are now to be found in Sch 3 para 6(10)–(11) HB&CTB(CP) Regs (see p1795). See the detailed commentary on p1800.

Paragraph (11)(b): Preservation of the effect of the 1996 Regulations

The effect of this provision was to prevent the repeal of large parts of reg 7A HB Regs 1987 (and reg 4A CTB 1992 Regs) from affecting the scope of the transitional protection afforded by reg 12 Social Security (Persons from Abroad) Miscellaneous Amendments Regulations 1996 SI No.30 and hence the scope of reg 2(4)(a).

SCHEDULE

REGULATION 2

Persons not excluded under section 115 of the Immigration and Asylum Act 1995 from entitlement to [...] housing benefit or council tax benefit

Amendment

1.   Amended by reg 69(5)of SI 2008 No 1554 as from 27.10.08.

General Note

These categories of claimant are exempted from the operation of s115 Immigration and Asylum Act 1999 by virtue of reg 2(1).

[¹1.]

Amendment

1.   Omitted by reg 9(2) of SI 2013 No 2536 as from 29.10.13.

Analysis

Before it was revoked, with effect from 29 October 2013, this provision, read with reg 10(4) HB Regs or reg 10(5) HB(SPC) Regs, allowed a person subject to immigration control who met three conditions to obtain HB for a period of up to 42 days. See pp1213–14 of the 25th edition for the text of the provision and a discussion of the caselaw which addressed it.

---

2.   A person who has been given leave to enter or remain in, the United Kingdom by the Secretary of State upon an undertaking given by another person or persons pursuant to the immigration rules within the meaning of the Immigration Act 1971, to be responsible for his maintenance and accommodation and who has not been resident in the United Kingdom for a period of at least five years beginning on the date of entry or the date on which the undertaking was given in respect of him, whichever date is the later and the person or persons who gave the undertaking to provide for his maintenance and accommodation has, or as the case may be, have died.

Analysis

Under the Immigration Rules, a sponsor of a person seeking leave to enter may be required to give an undertaking to be responsible for that person's maintenance and accommodation. If the sponsor is dead, para 2 excludes the sponsored person from the effect of s115 of the 1999 Act. If there is more than one sponsor, all must be deceased.

---

3.   A person who–
(a)   has been given leave to enter, or remain in, the United Kingdom by the Secretary of State upon an undertaking given by another person or persons in writing in pursuance of immigration rules within the meaning of the 1971 Act, to be responsible for his maintenance and accommodation; and
(b)   he has been resident in the United Kingdom for a period of at least five years beginning from the date of entry or the date on which the undertaking was given in respect of him, whichever date is the later.

Analysis

If a sponsored immigrant is resident for five years from the *later* of the date of entry or the date of the undertaking, para 3 excludes him/her from the effect of s115.

In *R(IS) 2/02*, Commissioner Jacobs held that where a claimant has been present with leave in the UK prior to the undertaking being given, the five-year period runs from the date the undertaking is given. When the undertaking was given before leave, time runs from the time that leave was granted: paras 67–71. He also held that the five-year period need not be continuous, but may be the sum of several different periods of residence: paras 72–75. Although this issue was discussed by one of the judges on a further appeal to the Court of Appeal – *Shah v Secretary of State for Social Security* [2002] EWCA Civ 285, CA; reported as *R(IS) 2/02* – the court did not interfere with the commissioner's conclusion on this point.

---

4. A person who is a national of a state which has ratified the European Convention on Social and Medical Assistance (done in Paris on 11th December 1953) or a state which has ratified the Council of Europe Social Charter (signed in Turin on 18th October 1961) and who is lawfully present in the United Kingdom.

Analysis

The relevant states. This paragraph applies to nationals of states that have ratified the ECSMA or the European Social Charter. All ECSMA states are at present signatories of the European Social Charter. At the time of writing, the only non-EEA states which had ratified the Social Charter were Turkey and Macedonia (as this rule is an exemption to the general exclusion from benefits for persons subject to immigration control, and as an EEA national cannot be such a person, there is no relevance under this rule in the fact that most EEA states have ratified the Charter). It is not sufficient if the state of nationality has signed but not ratified the Social Charter and so nationals of the Ukraine cannot fall within para 4.

An up-to-date list of signatories and ratifications is available at http://conventions.coe.int.

"Lawfully present" is a phrase defined in Art 11 of ECSMA. Any person who has "a permit or such other permission as is required by the laws and regulations of the country concerned to reside therein" is lawfully present in the host state. It will encompass anyone who has leave to remain in the UK. It will include those with limited leave, including those who have their leave automatically extended under the immigration legislation pending the determination of an application for an extension of leave.

A person who is present in the UK by virtue of having been granted temporary admission is "lawfully present": *Szoma v SSWP* [2005] UKHL 64, [2006] 1 All ER 1; reported as *R(IS) 2/06*.

Note, however, that for most ECSMA country nationals, entitlement to HB is now governed by whether they can satisfy the "right to reside test" in reg 10 of the HB and HB(SPC) Regs.

The Discretionary Financial Assistance Regulations 2001
(SI 2001 No.1167)

General Note to the Regulations

The DFA Regs, made under s69 CSPSSA, provide the detail of the discretionary housing payments (DHPs) scheme for increases in HB (and, until abolished, in CTB) on the grounds of exceptional circumstances of hardship. The DHP scheme replaced provisions formerly found in reg 62 HB Regs 1987 and regs 51(5) and 54(4) CTB Regs 1992. The regulations are considerably more flexible than the repealed provisions as to the circumstances in which DHPs may be made. DHPs are now seen to be a part of the package for dealing with the problems for claimants of under-occupation of accommodation and its impact on the amount of HB to which they are entitled – ie, DHPs are meant to "plug the gap": see, for example, *R (MA and Others) v SSWP* [2014] EWCA Civ 13. The government has allocated extra funding for this purpose and has provided additional guidance on good practice (see below). See the Analysis of reg 2(2) on the amount of a DHP. Note that the claimants in *R (MA) and Others* were given permission to appeal to the Supreme Court. The appeal was heard from 29 February to 2 March 2016 with *R (Rutherford and Others and A) v SSWP and New Forest DC and Others* and judgment was given on 9 November 2016. See p378 for a discussion.

Note:

(1) DHPs have not been available for help with council tax since 1 April 2013.

(2) From 10 June 2013, DHPs are available if the claimant is entitled to HB *or* to a "relevant award of universal credit" (defined in reg 1).

(3) The Scottish government has had the power to make rules on DHPs in Scotland since 1 April 2017. It was expected that the legal basis for paying DHPs in Scotland would change from April 2019. The rules on eligibility are not, however, expected to change significantly. The Social Security (Scotland) Act 2018 makes provision for DHPs in ss88 to 93. At the time of writing, these sections had not yet been brought into force.

The scheme is excluded from the right of appeal to the First-tier Tribunal. The government's reason for doing this was to keep the discretion firmly in the hands of the relevant local authority, and it is said that as the making of DHPs is discretionary, there is no breach of Art 6 of the European Convention of Human Rights in failing to provide for an appeal. See the commentary to Art 6 on p124 for a discussion and the commentary to Art 8 on p127 on the question of whether a refusal to make a DHP might interfere with the right to respect for the home.

The absence of a right of appeal means that there is some scope for judicial review proceedings in relation to DHPs.

DHPs are disregarded as income for the purposes of the HB Regs: Sch 5 para 62 HB Regs They do not come within the definition of income under the HB(SPC) Regs. Arrears of (or concessionary payments of) DHPs are disregarded as capital for HB purposes: Sch 6 para 9(1)(d) HB Regs; Sch 6 para 21 HB(SPC) Regs.

Local authority guidance is provided in the DWP's *Discretionary Housing Payments Guidance Manual*, March 2018, which includes guidance on good practice, and is available at www.gov.uk/government/uploads/system/uploads/attachment_data/file/453392/discretionary-housing-payments-guide-aug-15.pdf.

Citation, commencement and interpretation

1.–(1) These Regulations may be cited as the Discretionary Financial Assistance Regulations 2001 and shall come into force on 2nd July 2001.

[¹ (2)   In these Regulations–

"the Housing Benefit Regulations" means the Housing Benefit Regulations 2006; and

"the Housing Benefit (State Pension Credit) Regulations" means the Housing Benefit (Persons who have attained the qualifying age for state pension credit) Regulations 2006.]

[² "the Universal Credit Regulations" means the Universal Credit Regulations 2013;]

[² "relevant award of universal credit" means an award of universal credit the calculation of which includes an amount under section 11 of the Welfare Reform Act 2012, calculated in accordance with Schedule 4 to the Universal Credit Regulations, or would include such an amount but for [³ paragraph 3(h) or (i)] of Schedule 1 to those Regulations;]

[² "universal credit" means universal credit under Part 1 of the Welfare Reform Act 2012.]

Amendments

1.   Inserted by reg 5 and Sch 2 para 18(2) of SI 2006 No 217 as from 6.3.06.

2.   Inserted by reg 2(2) of SI 2013 No 1139 as from 10.6.13.

3.   Amended by reg 2(a) of SI 2018 No 65 as from 11.4.18, subject to saving and transitional provision in reg 8(2) and (3).

Discretionary housing payments

2.–(1)   Subject to paragraphs (2) and (3) and the following regulations, a relevant authority may make payments by way of financial assistance ("discretionary housing payments") to persons who–

(a)   are entitled to housing benefit or [² a relevant award of universal credit] [¹]; and

(b)   appear to such an authority to require some further financial assistance (in addition to the benefit [¹] to which they are entitled) in order to meet housing costs.

(2)   Subject to paragraph (3) and regulations 4 and 5, a relevant authority has a discretion–

(a)   as to whether or not to make discretionary housing payments in a particular case; and

(b)   as to the amount of the payments and the period for, or in respect of which, they are made.

(3)   Paragraphs (1) and (2) shall not apply in respect of housing costs incurred in any period before 2nd July 2001–

[¹ (a)]

(b)   in the case of a person entitled to housing benefit [² or a relevant award of universal credit] who requires further financial assistance in order to meet housing costs (other than costs in respect of council tax) arising from his liability to make periodical payments in respect of the dwelling which he occupies as his home.

Amendments

1.   Amended by reg 3 and Sch 1 of SI 2013 No 458 as from 1.4.13.

2.   Amended by reg 2(3) of SI 2013 No 1139 as from 10.6.13.

Analysis

Para (1). To qualify for discretionary housing payments (DHPs), a claimant must be entitled to HB or a "relevant award of UC": sub-para (a). "Relevant award of UC" is defined in reg 1 as an award of UC the calculation of which includes a housing costs element under Sch 4 UC Regs (ie, where the claimant is liable for rent payments), or would include a housing element but for Sch 1 para 3(h) or (i) UC Regs (ie, but for the rent payments being made in respect of "specified accommodation" (defined in Sch 1 para 3A UC Regs as specified types of supported or temporary accommodation – broadly as in Sch 3 para 4(10) HB&CTB(CP) Regs on p1777) or "temporary accommodation" defined in Sch 1 para 3B US Regs as specified types of homeless accommodation where rent is payable to a local authority or provider of social housing). Note that between 3 November 2014 and 11 April 2018, the definition referred to Sch 1 para 3(e) UC Regs which was deleted by reg 2(2)(b) Housing Benefit and Universal Credit (Supported Accommodation) (Amendment) Regulations 2014 No.771. Thus, between those dates, if the claimant was on UC but was not, in addition, entitled to HB (ie, for specified types of supported accommodation or of temporary accommodation), the UC had to include a housing costs element for rent payments.

It must appear to the local authority that the claimant needs financial assistance in addition to HB or UC in order to meet "housing costs": sub-para (b). *"Housing costs"* is not defined and so in principle could cover any expenditure that is related to the provision of accommodation for the claimant and her/his family including rent in advance, deposits and removal expenses. Reg 3 excludes certain categories of need but does not otherwise cut down the breadth of the phrase. It would appear that it could cover, for example, payments of capital to a mortgagee – eg, where a claimant has a shared ownership tenancy and is in danger of losing her/his home. It could also cover payments in respect of a second home that are not met by HB. The DWP's guidance, *Discretionary Housing Payments Guidance Manual,* sets out suggestions as to the types of shortfall that DHPs could cover. These include reductions in HB or UC because the "benefit cap" has been applied or because of local housing allowance (LHA) rates or because the claimant's accommodation exceeds the number of bedrooms allowed under the size criteria (eg, under the social sector or LHA schemes), and reductions because of non-dependant deductions or income tapers, or rent shortfalls to prevent a household becoming homeless while the housing authority explores alternative options. These also include situations where a claimant has to pay rent for two homes, but can only qualify for HB or UC for one of the homes – eg, s/he does not satisfy the criteria for payment of HB on two homes in reg 7 HB Regs. It may be possible to argue that DHPs should also cover shortfalls due to increases in essential work-related expenditure (eg, travel costs) if a claimant had to move because s/he could not afford to live near her/his workplace following a reduction in LHA rates. Note: it is understood that the Scottish government wants local authorities use DHPs to mitigate the effects of the social sector rent restriction scheme.

The claimant must *"require some further financial assistance"*, which is not defined. While there is no need to show that the claimant's circumstances are exceptional, it is likely that authorities will impose a fairly high threshold. If, for example, a claimant has any savings or other realisable capital asset at all, it is unlikely that an application for a DHP would succeed unless it could be shown that there was a need to utilise those savings in some other way (eg, to discharge a different debt) or to retain the asset. However, it is suggested that a claimant need not show that her/his circumstances are desperate – eg, by showing that eviction is imminent. It would be sufficient to show that the household budget simply cannot be balanced and that debts will inevitably mount up unless a DHP is paid. An authority considering refusal of a DHP on the ground that the claimant could obtain a loan would have to be prepared to show how such a loan could be financed.

While a claimant is not "entitled" to benefits unless they are claimed, there seems to be no reason why an authority could not refuse a DHP on the basis that a claimant should be entitled to some other benefit if a claim is made. The same would apply where other forms of social assistance are available such as social fund budgeting loans, or UC budgeting advances, social services assistance and housing grants.

Para (2) gives a very broad discretion as to the amount of a DHP and the form that the payments take. Except as specified in reg 4, there is no restriction on the amount of a DHP and one-off payments may be made as well as weekly or monthly payments. However, as s73(14) SSCBA requires the mobility component of DLA to "be disregarded in applying any enactment or instrument under which regard is to be had to a person's means", it is suggested that any amount of that benefit must be ignored. Note that no comparable provision appears to have been made for the mobility component of PIP.

In *R (Hardy) v Sandwell MBC* [2015] EWHC 890 (Admin), the High Court considered whether a local authority could take DLA care component into account in determining the amount of a DHP. Mr Hardy's HB entitlement had been reduced under reg B13 HB Regs for underoccupying his accommodation. He and his wife were both disabled and in receipt of DLA. The local authority awarded DHPs to plug the gap. In so doing, it disregarded the couple's DLA mobility component, but took the care component fully into account. This decision was successfully challenged on a number of grounds.

(1)   The local authority's policy was contrary to the DWP's DHP Guidance Manual and Good Practice Guide and was an unlawful fetter on the council's discretion. Mr Justice Phillips decided that the local authority's blanket policy of always taking DLA care component into account and ignoring only DLA mobility component, was based on a misunderstanding of its powers, that is, that it adopted its policy to take DLA care component into account because it incorrectly understood that it was not allowed to exclude it. The local authority, therefore, had not given proper consideration to the DHP Guidance and Good Practice Guide and had not exercised its discretion on the issue properly or at all.

(2)   Taking DLA care component into account in determining the amount of a DHP constituted unlawful discrimination arising from disability contrary to Art 14 of the European Convention on Human Rights. Mr Justice Phillips considered DHPs in the context of the HB scheme as a whole, in particular because it had been established that, unless the availability of DHPs is taken into account, reg B13 HB Regs discriminates against disabled HB claimants (see p377 for commentary on the caselaw and in particular on *R (MA and Others) v SSWP* [2014] EWCA Civ 13). He decided that DHPs come within the ambit of Art 1 Protocol 1, and Art 14 is engaged in decisions whether to award a DHP to a disabled claimant. The judge also said that awards of DHPs to disabled applicants are sufficiently related to their Art 8 rights that Art 14 is also engaged in that regard. He said:

> "52. ... the Government has provided additional funding for DHPs for the very purpose of ensuring that disabled persons affected by the HB size criteria are not forced to leave their accommodation (where that would otherwise be the avowed purpose of the reduction in HB), not least because it is recognised that the accommodation may well have been adapted to meet their disability needs. It is therefore plain that DHPs are provided to protect the private and family life of disabled applicants, in particular their recognised need to keep their existing home. Further, the decision of a local authority as to whether to reduce such DHPs below the shortfall in rent directly impacts on those interests."

In his judgment, the local authority's' approach amounted to indirect discrimination against the claimant on grounds of disability. Because the discriminatory effect of the HB size criteria could only be justified by the availability of DHPs to make up any shortfall, and additional government funding had been provided to local authorities for this purpose, the discrimination could not be justified. Agreeing with *R (MA and Others)* he said that local authorities were acting wrongly by including DLA care component in household income when determining the amount of DHPs. It is arguable that this reasoning should also apply to AA and PIP. The DWP Discretionary Housing Payments Guidance Manual (at para 3.9) reminds local authorities to "consider each DHP application on a case by case basis having regard to the purpose of those disability related benefits and whether the money from those benefits has been committed to other liabilities associated with disability."

It is suggested that the amounts specified in the Discretionary Housing Payments (Grants) Order 2001 may provide some indication as to the annual expenditure that each authority should be making on DHPs. If an authority is spending considerably less, then it may be possible to challenge a decision by way of judicial review on the ground that it is adopting an approach to its discretion that is too restrictive, as its permitted expenditure is a relevant factor in the exercise of its discretion: *R v Gloucestershire CC ex p Barry* [1997] AC 584, HL. However, in *CH 1175/2002* (para 10), Commissioner Fellner expressed scepticism about a similar suggestion made in this book in relation to the old exceptional hardship payments: see p399 of the 14th edition.

There is also a broad discretion as to the period for, or in respect of which, payments can be made, subject to reg 5.

Para (3) prevents a DHP being paid in respect of the liabilities set out arising prior to 2 July 2001.

Circumstances in which discretionary housing payments may be made

3.   For the purposes of section 69(2)(a) of the Child Support, Pensions and Social Security Act 2000, the prescribed circumstance in which discretionary housing payments may be made is where a person has made a claim for a discretionary housing payment and the requirement for financial assistance does not arise as a consequence of–

(a)   a liability to meet any of the ineligible service charges specified in [³ Schedule 1 to the Housing Benefit Regulations or Schedule 1 to the Housing Benefit (State Pension Credit) Regulations] (ineligible service charges);

[¹⁰ (aa) a liability to meet any payment in respect of service charges other than a payment listed in paragraph 7 of Schedule 1 to the Universal Credit Regulations;]

(b)   a liability to meet charges for water, sewerage or allied environmental services;

(c)   a liability to meet council tax payments [⁹];

[⁹ (d)]

[⁹ (e)]

(f)   a liability to meet the increase in such payment as is referred to in [⁴ regulation 11(3) of the Housing Benefit Regulations or regulation 11(2) of the Housing Benefit (State Pension Credit) Regulations];

(g)   a reduction of an amount of benefit by virtue of [⁴ section 46(5)] of the Child Support Act 1991;

(h)   a reduction of a specified amount of benefit by virtue of section 2A of the Social Security Administration Act 1992;

(i)   a reduction in the amount of a jobseeker's allowance payable by virtue of section 17 of the Jobseekers Act 1995;

(j)   the non-payability of a jobseeker's allowance or a reduction in the amount of a jobseeker's allowance payable, pursuant to a decision made by virtue of [⁶ regulation 27A of the Jobseeker's Allowance Regulations 1996 or] section 19 or 20A [⁸ or regulations made under section 17A] of the Jobseekers Act 1995;

(k)   the suspension of payment of an amount of benefit by virtue of section 21, 22 or 24 of the Social Security Act 1998 or section 68 of, and paragraphs 13 and 14 of Schedule 7 to, the Child Support, Pensions and Social Security Act 2000.

[¹(l)   a restriction in relation to the payment of benefit imposed pursuant to [⁵] [² section [⁷ 6B,] 7, 8 or 9 of the Social Security Fraud Act 2001] (loss of benefit provisions).]

[(m)   See Modifications below]

[⁴ (n)   a reduction in the amount of benefit due to recovery of an overpayment under Part 13 of the Housing Benefit Regulations or Part 12 of the Housing Benefit (State Pension Credit) Regulations, or recovery of excess benefit under Part 11 of the Council Tax Benefit Regulations 2006 or Part 10 of the Council Tax Benefit (Persons who have attained the qualifying age for state pension credit) Regulations 2006.]

[¹⁰ (o) a reduction in the amount of universal credit due to recovery of an overpayment pursuant to section 71ZB of the Social Security Administration Act 1992;]

[¹⁰ (p) a reduction in the amount of universal credit pursuant to a decision made under section 26 or 27 of the Welfare Reform Act 2012.]

Modifications

Reg 3 was modified in respect of people to whom the Housing Benefit (Loss of Benefit) (Pilot Scheme) (Supplementary) Regulations 2007 SI No.2474 applied. See pp1188–92 of the 22nd edition. Sub-paragrah (m) was inserted. The modification applied until 31 October 2009.

Amendments

1.   Inserted by reg 2(6) of SI 2001 No 1711 as from 15.10.01.

2.   Amended by reg 10 of SI 2002 No 490 as from 1.4.02.
3.   Amended by reg 5 and sch 2 para 18(3) of SI 2006 No 217 as from 6.3.06.
4.   Amended by reg 2 of SI 2008 No 637 as from 7.4.08.
5.   Amended by reg 5 of SI 2010 No 424 as from 2.4.10.
6.   Amended by reg 4(3) of SI 2010 No 509 as from 6.4.10.
7.   Amended by reg 8 of SI 2010 No 1160 as from 1.4.10.
8.   Inserted by reg 17 of SI 2011 No 688 as from 25.4.11.
9.   Amended by reg 3 and Sch 1 of SI 2013 No 458 as from 1.4.13.
10.   Amended by reg 2(4) of SI 2013 No 1139 as from 10.6.13.

Analysis

Reg 3 requires a claim to be made for a DHP. In addition, it sets out a number of circumstances in which DHPs cannot be paid, that is, where the need for financial assistance arises as a consequence of the following.

(1)   A liability for ineligible service charges: sub-paras (a) and (aa). For HB, these are the ineligible service charges specified in Sch 1 HB Regs on p620. For UC, they are any service charges not specified in Sch 1 para 7 UC Regs.

(2)   A liability for water, sewerage or "allied environmental services": sub-para (b). The latter phrase would cover, for example, charges for the emptying of a septic tank.

(3)   Council tax liabilities: sub-para (c). Note that prior to 1 April 2013, this only applied if the person was entitled to HB but not to CTB, or was not entitled to main CTB but was entitled to "alternative maximum CTB": sub-para (e). Also excluded were liabilities for payments listed in reg 12 of both the HB Regs and the HB(SPC) Regs if the person was entitled to CTB but not to HB: sub-para (d).

(4)   Increases in rent to cover arrears of rent or other charges as referred to in reg 11(3) HB Regs or reg 11(2) HB(SPC) Regs, whether on the present or a previous claim: sub-para (f).

(5)   Reductions in benefit for failure to co-operate in the pursuit of child support maintenance or for failing to participate in a work-focused interview: sub-paras (g) and (h). The benefit being reduced may be a benefit other than HB.

(6)   JSA paid under a severe hardship direction (ie, to a 16 or 17 year old) being reduced – eg, because the claimant gave up a place on a training scheme or failed to attend without a "good reason": sub-para (i).

(7)   JSA not being paid, or JSA or UC being paid at a reduced or nil rate because the claimant has been sanctioned under specified rules: sub-paras (j) and (p). Note that from 22 October 2012, s19 JSA 1995 was substituted under s46 WRA 2012 and reg 27A JSA Regs was revoked by SI 2012 No.2568, but at the time this book was written, no consequential amendments had been made to this provision. Note also that no amendments have yet been made to reflect the different JSA sanction provisions for JSA claimants to whom ss6J and 6K JSA 1995 apply (for which see s49 WRA 2012) – ie, for those entitled to contribution-based JSA who come under the UC system. Therefore, some JSA sanction decisions might no longer preclude a successful claim for a DHP.

(8)   Suspension of benefit under the provisions listed – eg, pending an appeal or for non-provision of information: sub-para (k). The benefit being reduced may be a benefit other than HB.

(9)   Reductions in benefit under the provisions of ss6B, 7, 8 or 9 Social Security Fraud Act 2001 (loss of benefit for benefit offences): sub-para (l). The benefit being reduced may be a benefit other than HB.

(10)   Reductions in benefit due to recovery of an overpayment of HB or CTB: sub-para (n). The benefit being reduced may be a benefit other than HB.

(11)   Reductions in UC due to the recovery of an overpayment under s71ZB SSAA 1992: sub-para (o). Currently s71ZB allows for recovery of UC, JSA or ESA and will eventually allow for the recovery of the housing credit of PC.

[⁴ **Limit on the amount of the discretionary housing payment that may be made**

4.–(1)   Where a person is entitled to housing benefit the amount of the discretionary housing payment (if calculated as a weekly sum) shall not exceed–

(a)   the aggregate of the payments specified in regulation 12(1) of the Housing Benefit Regulations less the aggregate of the amounts referred to in regulation 12B(2) of those Regulations calculated on a weekly basis in accordance with regulations 80 and 81 of those Regulations; or

(b)   the aggregate of the payments specified in regulation 12(1) of the Housing Benefit (State Pension Credit) Regulations less the aggregate of the amounts referred to in regulation 12B(2) of those Regulations, calculated on a weekly basis in accordance with regulations 61 and 62 of those Regulations.

(2)   Where a person is entitled to a relevant award of universal credit the amount of the discretionary housing payment (if calculated as a monthly sum) shall not exceed–

(a)   the amount calculated in accordance with Schedule 4 to the Universal Credit Regulations; or

(b)   where [⁵ paragraph 3(h) and (i)] of Schedule 1 to the Universal Credit Regulations applies, the aggregate of the payments referred to in paragraph 3 of Schedule 4 to those Regulations, calculated on a monthly basis.]

Amendments

1.   Amended by reg 5 and Sch 2 para 18(4) of SI 2006 No 217 as from 6.3.06.
2.   Substituted by reg 5 of SI 2007 No 2870 as from 7.4.08 (or if reg 1(3) of that SI applies, on the day on or after 7.4.08 when the first of the events specified in reg 1(4) applies, or from 6.4.09 if none have before that date).
3.   Amended by reg 3 and Sch 1 of SI 2013 No 458 as from 1.4.13.
4.   Substituted by reg 2(5) of SI 2013 No 1139 as from 10.6.13.
5.   Amended by reg 2(b) of SI 2018 No 65 as from 11.4.18, subject to saving and transitional provision in reg 8(2) and (3).

Analysis

Reg 4 imposes a limit on the amount of DHPs if calculated as a weekly sum (if the claimant is entitled to HB) or a monthly sum (if the claimant is entitled to UC). There is no restriction on amounts paid as one-off payments (eg, for rent in advance or deposits). Larger sums could, therefore, be paid by way of a lump sum.

If the claimant is entitled to HB and the DHP is calculated as a weekly sum, it may not be more than the weekly amount of the payments which can be met by HB, less the amounts referred to in reg 12B(2) of both the HB and the HB(SPC) Regs: para (1). However, HB entitlement need not be deducted and so, in theory, the total payment (of HB and DHPs) could be greater than the amount of the rent liability. The amount of any liabilities that do not fall within reg 12(1) HB Regs (reg 12(1) HB(SPC) Regs), such as those listed in reg 12(2), cannot be included in the maximum weekly amount, though that does not prevent a lump sum for these being awarded.

If the claimant is entitled to a "relevant award of UC" (for the definition, see reg 1 on p1751), and the DHP is calculated as a monthly sum, it may not be more than the amount of the UC housing costs element as calculated under Sch 4 UC Regs: para (2)(a). Under para (2)(b), if the DHP is calculated as a monthly sum and the claimant's payments are excluded from being "rent payments" for UC purposes because they are made in respect of "specified accommodation" or "temporary accommodation" (defined in Sch 1 paras 3A and 3B UC Regs), the DHP cannot not be more than the monthly amount of rent payments (other than those in respect of the "specified accommodation" or "temporary accommodation" if any) and service charges. Help with payments for "specified accommodation" and "temporary accommodation" is not met by UC, but is provided by local authorities under existing HB rules.

Note that between 3 November 2014 and 11 April 2018, para (2)(b) was of no effect. See p1676 of the 29th edition of this book for details and commentary.

In *Gargett, R (on the application of) v Lambeth LB* [2008] EWCA Civ 1450, the Court of Appeal considered whether a local authority could exercise its power to make DHPs by paying arrears of rent, if the claimant was currently in receipt of full HB and CTB. The claimant had asked for a lump sum DHP to pay rent arrears. The local authority argued that by reg 2(1)(b) Discretionary Financial Assistance Regulations 2001, there had to be a continuing shortfall between the benefits which the claimant was currently receiving and the housing costs which s/he was currently incurring (up to the eligible rent then applying). The Court of Appeal disagreed. It held that the regulations do not expressly place such a limit on the council's discretion. The limit imposed by reg 4 applies to a DHP, whether it takes the form of a lump sum payment for the past, or a weekly payment for the future. Once a local authority has used reg 5 to determine the past or future period in respect of which the DHP is to be restricted, that period must then be divided into weeks for the purpose of calculating the amount of the DHP as a weekly sum (or now months for calculating it as a monthly sum). Reg 4 sets the amount that the DHP must not exceed. Note though that although the amount of HB already received for the relevant period is not expressly specified as a deduction under reg 4, by virtue of the provisions in reg 2 that DHPs are "further financial assistance" with "housing costs", the Court decided that HB already paid for past housing costs must also be deducted. The same would apply for UC already paid.

[¹ Period for, or in respect of which, discretionary housing payments may be made

5.–(1)   Subject to paragraph (2), a relevant authority may restrict the period for or in respect of which discretionary housing payments may be made to such period as it considers appropriate in the particular circumstances of a case.

(2)   A relevant authority may make discretionary housing payments to a person only in respect of a period during which that person is or was entitled to housing benefit *[or a]* [³ relevant award of universal credit] [²].]

Amendments

1.   Substituted by reg 3 of SI 2008 No 637 as from 7.4.08.
2.   Amended by reg 3 and Sch 1 of SI 2013 No 458 as from 1.4.13.
3.   Amended by reg 2(6) of SI 2013 No 1139 as from 10.6.13.

General Note

It is important to note that claims can be made for a past period as well as the future, without any need to explain a delay in seeking a DHP. However, the claimant must have been entitled to HB or a "relevant award of UC" (defined in reg 1) during the period. Note: the italicised words in square brackets were added by the author. These did not appear in the amendment made from 10 June 2013.

Form, manner and procedure for claims

6.–(1)   A relevant authority may accept a claim for discretionary housing payments–

(a)   in such form and manner as it approves;

(b)   from–

(i)   a person entitled to either housing benefit or [² relevant award of universal credit] [¹]; or

(ii)   where it appears reasonable in the circumstances of a particular case, a person acting on behalf of a person so entitled.

(2)   A relevant authority may pay discretionary housing payments to either the person entitled to housing benefit [² relevant award of universal credit][¹], or where it appears reasonable in the circumstances of a particular case, such other person as the authority thinks appropriate.

(3)   A relevant authority shall give a person who has claimed discretionary housing payments or who has requested a review of a decision made in respect of his claim, written notice of its decision in respect of that claim or review and the reasons for that decision as soon as is reasonably practicable.

Amendments

1.   Amended by reg 3 and Sch 1 of SI 2013 No 458 as from 1.4.13.
2.   Amended by reg 2(7) of SI 2013 No 1139 as from 10.6.13.

Analysis

Para (1) gives an authority a broad discretion as to the form that claims for DHPs may take. An authority could accept an oral claim and interesting arguments could arise as to the circumstances in which an individual officer can bind the authority as to the validity of a claim. Claims may be accepted from agents where it appears reasonable to do so. Authorities ought to be ready, for example, to accept claims made by solicitors and social landlords on behalf of claimants.

Para (2) gives a power to make payments to a third party where it appears reasonable to do so. Thus rent arrears can be directed to a landlord.

Para (3) is an important provision. First, it is suggested that it confers a right to a review of a DHP decision, even though reg 8(1) appears to make it discretionary as to whether a review is carried out. It is suggested that reg 8(1) is concerned with the situation where a local authority wishes to review a decision of its own motion rather than on a request. If that is right, there is no specific time limit for a request, although a substantial delay in applying for a review could possibly be relevant to the exercise of a discretion on the review. The review need not take any particular form, although good administrative practice suggests that, at minimum, a different officer should reconsider the case.

Secondly, there must be a written decision for which adequate reasons must be given. It is likely that the courts would expect, as a minimum, a clear explanation for why an application had failed or only succeeded in part. A failure to comply with reg 6(3) would render a decision liable to be quashed on judicial review, although it is likely that a court would expect a claimant to seek a review first where one was available.

Provision of information

7.   A person claiming or receiving discretionary housing payments shall provide a relevant authority with the following information–

(a)   particulars of the grounds of claim or, as the case may be, particulars of the grounds for a review;

(b)   changes in circumstances which may be relevant to the continuance of discretionary housing payments,

and such other information as may be specified by the relevant authority within such time as that authority thinks appropriate.

Analysis

The requirement to specify particulars of the grounds for a review is a further indication that there is a right to a review rather than it purely being discretionary. Changes of circumstances which may be relevant must be disclosed by the claimant, but other information must be specified by the authority. Note that there is no prohibition on requiring information about payments such as those specified in reg 86(4) HB Regs (see p555).

Reviews

8.–(1)   A relevant authority may review any decision it has made with respect to the making, cancellation or recovery of discretionary housing payments in such circumstances as it thinks fit.

(2)   Without prejudice to the generality of paragraph (1) above, a relevant authority may, on any such review, cancel the making of further such payments and recover a payment already made where that authority has determined that–

(a)   whether fraudulently or otherwise, any person has misrepresented, or failed to disclose, a material fact and, as a consequence of that misrepresentation or failure to disclose, a payment has been made; or

(b)   an error has been made when determining the application for a payment, and as a consequence of that error, a payment had been made which would not have been made but for that error.

Analysis

Para (1) states that an authority "may" review a decision on whatever grounds it sees fit. However, it is suggested that reg 6(3) has the effect of conferring a right to a review on application – eg, by the claimant. If that is not right, then the discretion to review must still be exercised reasonably and the decisions in *R (Sibley) v West Dorset DC* [2001] EWHC Admin 365, Silber J and *R (Naghshbandi) v Camden LBC* [2001] EWHC Admin 813; (2003) HLR 280, CA, Rafferty J may assist as to the circumstances in which a refusal to review may be challenged.

Para (2) deals with the effect of a review. The making of further payments may be cancelled on any basis, but the circumstances in which there can be recovery of overpayments are limited to those in sub-paras (a) or (b).

A review of the decision awarding a DHP is a necessary precondition of recovery.

Sub-para (b) requires the error to take place during the course of the determination, but need not necessarily be that of the officer making the decision. It would be sufficient if an officer carrying out some inquiries made an error. "Error" must, however, mean a mistake as to law or fact. It cannot apply to a situation where a reviewing officer takes the view that s/he disagrees with the first officer's judgement or exercise of discretion.

The Social Security (Notification of Change of Circumstances) Regulations 2001
(SI 2001 No.3252)

General Note to the Regulations

Possible offences under ss111A and 112 SSAA 1992 include where someone fails to give prompt notification of a change of circumstances. Reg 4 of these regulations prescribes to whom, and the manner in which, a change affecting HB must be reported for these purposes.

Citation and commencement

1. These Regulations may be cited as the Social Security (Notification of Change of Circumstances) Regulations 2001 and shall come into force on 18th October 2001.

Notification for purposes of sections 111A and 112 of the Social Security Administration Act 1992

2. Regulations 3 to 5 below prescribe the person to whom, and manner in which, a change of circumstances must be notified for the purposes of sections 111A(1A) to (1G) and 112(1A) to (1F) of the Social Security Administration Act 1992 (offences relating to failure to notify a change of circumstances).

Change affecting housing benefit or council tax benefit

4.-[³ (1) Subject to paragraphs (1A) to [⁴ (1D)], where the benefit affected by the change of circumstances is housing benefit or council tax benefit, notice must be given to the relevant authority at the designated office–

(a) in writing; or

(b) by telephone–

    (i) where the relevant authority has published a telephone number for that purpose or for the purposes of making a claim unless the authority determines that in any particular case or class of case notification may not be given by telephone; or

    (ii) in any case or class of case where the relevant authority determines that notice may be given by telephone; or

(c) by any other means which the relevant authority agrees to accept in any particular case.]

[² (1A) In such cases and subject to such conditions as the Secretary of State may specify, notice may be given to the Secretary of State–

(a) where the change of circumstances is a birth or death, through a relevant authority, or a county council in England, by personal attendance at an office specified by that authority or county council, provided the Secretary of State has agreed with that authority or county council for it to facilitate such notification; or

(b) where the change of circumstances is a death, by telephone to a telephone number specified for that purpose by the Secretary of State.

(1B) Paragraph (1A) only applies if the authority administering the claimant's housing benefit or council tax benefit agrees with the Secretary of State that notifications may be made in accordance with that paragraph.]

[³ (1C) Notice may be given to the appropriate DWP office by telephone where all the following conditions are met–

(a) the claimant or the claimant's partner is in receipt of income support or a jobseeker's allowance;

(b) the change of circumstances is that the claimant or the claimant's partner starts employment;

(c) as a result of the change, either entitlement to housing benefit or council tax benefit will end, or the amount of benefit will be reduced; and

(d) a telephone number has been provided for that purpose.]

[⁴ (1D)   Where–
(a)   the change of circumstances required to be notified is a death; and
(b)   the authority administering the claimant's housing benefit or council tax benefit agrees with the Secretary of State that notifications may be made in accordance with paragraph (1A),

notice in writing may be given or sent to the Secretary of State by an electronic communication in accordance with the provisions set out in Schedule 9ZC to the Social Security (Claims and Payments) Regulations 1987 (electronic communication).

(1E)   The provisions set out in that Schedule shall apply to such a notice as they apply for the purposes of regulation 32ZA of the Social Security (Claims and Payments) Regulations 1987 (information given electronically).]

(2)   In this regulation [³ "appropriate DWP office",] [² "claimant",] "designated office" and "relevant authority" have the same meaning as in the Housing Benefit (General) Regulations 1987 and the Council Tax Benefit (General) Regulations 1992.

Amendments

1.   Amended by reg 5 and Sch 2 para 19 of SI 2006 No 217 as from 6.3.06.
2.   Amended by reg 4(3) of SI 2010 No 444 as from 5.4.10.
3.   Amended by reg 7 of SI 2010 No 2449 as from 1.11.10.
4.   Amended by reg 3(2) of SI 2011 No 2943 as from 23.1.12.

General Note

Reg 4 prescribes to whom, and the manner in which, a change affecting HB must be reported for the purposes of possible offences under ss111A and 112 SSAA 1992 (failure to give prompt notification of a change of circumstances). Note that reg 4 also applies to changes affecting CTB and may still be of relevance for changes of circumstance affecting awards of CTB prior to 1 April 2013.

Paras (1)–(1E). The notice of a change of circumstances must generally be given in writing to the "relevant authority" at its "designated office" (both defined in para (2)). It is always best for a claimant to give notice in writing, keeping a copy for her/his records. However, in specified circumstances notice can be given as follows.

(1)   Notice can be given by telephone to the relevant authority at its designated office in the circumstances set out in para (1)(b)(i) and (ii).
(2)   Notice can be given by telephone to the appropriate DWP office (defined in para (2)) where the conditions in para (1C) are met.
(3)   Where the change is a birth or a death, the change can be reported in person at a local authority office (or in England a county council office), if such an office has been specified for reporting these changes: paras (1A) and (1B). If the change is a death, this can also be notified to the DWP by telephone to a number specified for this purpose or by electronic communication: paras (1A)(b) and (1D). This provision is sometimes referred to as "Tell Us Once". Further information about this service is available at www.gov.uk/after-a-death/organisations-you-need-to-contact-and-tell-us-once.

Note that for the purposes of the general duty to report a change of circumstances in reg 88 HB Regs and reg 69 HB(SPC) Regs, and formerly in reg 74 CTB Regs and reg 59 CTB(SPC) Regs, notice could, from as early as 20 December 2006, be accepted in a form other than in writing. However, for the purposes of ss111A and 112, until 1 November 2010 notice had to generally be in writing. The only exception was where reg 4(1A) applied, and then only from 5 April 2010.

Para (2) defines various terms used in reg 4. Note that Sch 2 para 19 of SI 2006 No.217 says to substitute "Housing Benefit Regulations 2006, Housing Benefit (Persons who have attained the qualifying age for state pension credit) Regulations 2006, Council Tax Benefit Regulations 2006, Council Tax Benefit (Persons who have attained the qualifying age for state pension credit) Regulations 2006" for the regulations referred to, by reference to a non-existent provision in reg 4.

The Social Security (Loss of Benefit) Regulations 2001
(SI 2001 No.4022)

General Note to the Regulations

Sections 6A to 13 of the Social Security Fraud Act 2001 (see p1712) provide "loss of benefit" provisions where a claimant or a member of her/his family is convicted of repeat benefit offences. These regulations deal with the commencement of the disqualification period and the amount by which HB can be reduced.

PART I
GENERAL

Citation, commencement and interpretation

1.–(1)   These Regulations may be cited as the Social Security (Loss of Benefit) Regulations 2001 and shall come into force on 1st April 2002.

(2)   In these Regulations, unless the context otherwise requires–

[⁴ "the 2007 Act" means the Welfare Reform Act 2007;]

[⁴ "the 2012 Act" means the Welfare Reform Act 2012;]

"the Act" means the Social Security Fraud Act 2001;

[⁴ "the Administration Act" means the Social Security Administration Act 1992;]

[⁶ "armed forces independence payment" means armed forces independence payment under the Armed Forces and Reserve Forces (Compensation Scheme) Order 2011;]

"the Benefits Act" means the Social Security Contributions and Benefits Act 1992;

[⁴ "the ESA Regulations" means the Employment and Support Allowance Regulations 2008;]

[¹ "the Council Tax Benefit Regulations" means the Council Tax Benefit Regulations 2006;]

[¹ "the Council Tax Benefit (State Pension Credit) Regulations" means the Council Tax Benefit (Persons who have attained the qualifying age for state pension credit) Regulations 2006;]

[³ "the determination day" means (subject to paragraph (2A)) the day on which the Secretary of State determines that a restriction under–

(a)   section 6B or 7 of the Act would be applicable to the offender were the offender in receipt of a sanctionable benefit;

(b)   section 8 of the Act would be applicable to the offender were the offender a member of a joint-claim couple which is in receipt of a joint-claim jobseeker's allowance; or

(c)   section 9 of the Act would be applicable to the offender's family member were that member in receipt of income support, jobseeker's allowance, state pension credit, employment and support allowance, housing benefit or council tax benefit;]

[¹ "the Housing Benefit Regulations" means the Housing Benefit (General) Regulations 1987;]

[¹ "the Housing Benefit (State Pension Credit) Regulations" means the Housing Benefit (Persons who have attained the qualifying age for state pension credit) Regulations 2006;]

"the Income Support Regulations" means the Income Support (General) Regulations 1987;

"the Jobseekers Act" means the Jobseekers Act 1995;

"the Jobseeker's Allowance Regulations" means the Jobseeker's Allowance Regulations 1996;

[⁷ "the UC Regulations" means the Universal Credit Regulations 2013;]

[⁷ "assessment period" has the same meaning as in the UC Regulations;]

"claimant" in a regulation means the person claiming the sanctionable benefit referred to in that regulation;

"disqualification period" means the period in respect of which the restrictions on payment of a relevant benefit apply in respect of an offender in accordance with section

[² 6B(11) or] 7(6) of the Act and shall be interpreted in accordance with [²
regulations 1A and 2]; and

[⁷ "income-based jobseeker's allowance" means an income-based allowance under the
Jobseekers Act as it has effect apart from the amendments made by Part 1 of
Schedule 14 to the 2012 Act (to remove references to an income-based
allowance);]

[⁷ "income-related employment and support allowance" means an income-related
allowance under the Part 1 of the 2007 Act as it has effect apart from the
amendments made by Schedule 3 and Part 1 of Schedule 14 to the 2012 Act (to
remove references to an income-related allowance);]

[⁷ "joint claimant" means each of joint claimants as defined in section 40 of the 2012
Act;]

"offender" means the person who is subject to the restriction in the payment of his benefit
in accordance with section [² 6B or] 7 of the Act.

[³ "pay day" in relation to a sanctionable benefit means the day on which that benefit is
due to be paid;]

[⁵ "personal independence payment" means the allowance under Part 4 of the 2012 Act;]

[³ "relevant authority" in relation to housing benefit or council tax benefit means the
relevant authority administering the benefit of the offender or the offender's
family member.]

[⁷ "universal credit" means the benefit payable under Part 1 of the 2012 Act.]

[³ (2A)   Where, for the purposes of section 6B of the Act, the disqualifying event is
an agreement to pay a penalty as referred to in section 6B(1)(b) of the Act, the
determination day is the 28th day after the day referred to in the definition of that term in
paragraph (2).]

(3)   Expressions used in these Regulations which are defined either for the purposes
of the Jobseekers Act or for the purposes of the Jobseeker's Allowance Regulations shall,
except where the context otherwise requires, have the same meaning as for the purposes
of that Act or, as the case may be, those Regulations.

(4)   In these Regulations, unless the context otherwise requires, a reference–

(a)   to a numbered regulation is to the regulation in these Regulations bearing that
number;

(b)   in a regulation to a numbered paragraph is to the paragraph in that regulation
bearing that number.

Amendments

1.   Amended by reg 5 and Sch 2 para 20(2) of SI 2006 No 217 as from 6.3.06.
2.   Amended by reg 2(2) of SI 2010 No 1160 as from 1.4.10.
3.   Inserted by reg 2(2) and (3) of SI 2010 No 1160 as from 1.4.10.
4.   Inserted by reg 3 of SI 2013 No 385 as from 1.4.13.
5.   Inserted by reg 3 of SI 2013 No 285 as from 8.4.13.
6.   Inserted by art 7 and Sch para 22(1) of SI 2013 No 591 as from 8.4.13.
7.   Inserted by reg 3 of SI 2013 No 385 as from 29.4.13.

[¹ Disqualification period: section 6B(11) of the Act

1A.–(1)   The first day of the disqualification period for the purposes of section 6B(11)
of the Act ("DQ-day") shall be as follows.

(2)   This paragraph applies where on the determination day–

(a)   the offender is in receipt of a sanctionable benefit [² other than a benefit to which
paragraph (5A) applies] [³ or universal credit];

(b)   the offender is a member of a joint-claim couple which is in receipt of a joint-
claim jobseeker's allowance; or

(c)   the offender's family member is in receipt of income support, jobseeker's
allowance, state pension credit, employment and support allowance, housing
benefit or council tax benefit.

(3)   Where paragraph (2) applies and paragraph (4) does not apply (but subject to
paragraph (7))–

(a)   in relation to a sanctionable benefit which is paid in arrears, DQ-day is the day following the first pay day after the end of the period of 28 days beginning with the determination day; and

(b)   in relation to a sanctionable benefit which is paid in advance, DQ-day is the first pay day after the end of the period of 28 days beginning with the determination day.

(4)   This paragraph applies where on the determination day the offender or (as the case may be) the offender's family member is in receipt of–

(a)   either housing benefit or council tax benefit or both of those benefits; and

(b)   no other sanctionable benefit.

(5)   Where paragraph (4) applies–

(a)   in relation to housing benefit or council tax benefit which is paid in arrears, DQ-day is the day following the first pay day after the end of the period of 28 days beginning with the first day after the determination day on which the Secretary of State is notified by the relevant authority that the offender or the offender's family member is in receipt of either housing benefit or council tax benefit (or both of those benefits) or has been awarded either or both of those benefits; and

(b)   in relation to housing benefit or council tax benefit which is paid in advance, DQ-day is the first pay day after the end of the period of 28 days beginning with the first day after the determination day on which the Secretary of State is so notified by the relevant authority.

[² (5A)   This paragraph applies where on the determination day the offender or, as the case may be, the offender's family member is in receipt of a sanctionable benefit which is neither payable wholly in advance nor wholly in arrears and no other sanctionable benefit.]

(6)   Where [²paragraph (5A) applies or where there is no sanctionable benefit payable on the determination day] , DQ-day is the first day after the end of the period of 28 days beginning with the determination day.

[³ (6A)   Paragraph (6B) applies where, on the determination day, the offender or, as the case may be, the offender's family member is in receipt of universal credit.]

[³ (6B)   Where this paragraph applies, DQ-day is–

(a)   if the first day after the end of the period of 28 days beginning with the determination day is the first day of an assessment period, that day;

(b)   if the first day after the end of the period of 28 days beginning with the determination day is not the first day of an assessment period, the first day of the next assessment period after that day.]

(7)   Where on the determination day–

(a)   paragraph (2) [³ or (6A)] applies in the case of an offender or (as the case may be) the offender's family member, but

(b)   that person ceases to be in receipt of a benefit referred to in [³those paragraphs] before the first day of the disqualification period that would apply by virtue of paragraph (3) [³ or (6B)],

DQ-day is the first day after the end of the period of 28 days beginning with the determination day.]

Amendments
1.   Inserted by reg 2(3) of SI 2010 No 1160 as from 1.4.10.
2.   Amended by reg 4 of SI 2013 No 385 as from 1.4.13.
3.   Amended by reg 4 of SI 2013 No 385 as from 29.4.13.

Definitions
"determination day" – reg 1(2).
"disqualification period" – reg 1(2).
"pay day" – see reg 1(2).
"sanctionable benefit" – s6A(1) SSFA 2001.

General Note
Made under s6B(11) SSFA 2001 (see p1715), reg 1A sets the commencement date ("DQ-day") of the "disqualification period" for those subject to loss of benefit under the "one strike" scheme. Note that the length of

the disqualification period is set by s6B(11) and (11A) SSFA 2001 and is three years, thirteen weeks or four weeks as the case may be (see p1717). For HB purposes, DQ-day is set as follows. If on the "determination day" (defined in reg 1):

(1)   the offender or a family member of the offender is in receipt of HB and no other sanctionable benefit, DQ-day is set under paras (4) and (5);

(2)   the offender is in receipt of UC or a sanctionable benefit other than HB (or in addition to HB) or the offender is in receipt of joint-claim JSA, or a family member of the offender is in receipt of HB, IS, JSA, ESA or PC, DQ-day is set by para (3). However, where the offender or the family member ceases to be in receipt of any of the benefits referred to in para (2) before the first day of the disqualification period, DQ-day is instead set by para (7). Note that if the offender or family member is an HB claimant and is in receipt of IS, *income-based* JSA, *income-related* ESA or PC, the reduction is applied to those benefits and not to HB: reg 18;

(3)   the offender or a family member is in receipt of HB that is paid partly in advance or partly in arrears and no other sanctionable benefit, or no sanctionable benefit is payable on the determination day, DQ day is the day set under para (6). The former has only limited application – ie, it would apply only to those with the transitional protection provided by Sch 3 para 7 HB&CTB(TP) Regs as otherwise, HB is paid wholly in arrears (see reg 92(2) HB Regs and reg 73(2) HB(SPC) Regs).

The procedure is that the Secretary of State determines whether a restriction is applicable and notifies local authorities of the people in relation to whom a restriction is imposed. The local authority then notifies the Secretary of State that an award of benefit has been made. The Secretary of State then requires a reduction in HB to be imposed. Note: if a reduction to HB is imposed and the claimant is then awarded UC, see regs 35 and 36 Universal Credit (Transitional Provisions) Regulations 2014 on p1875 and p1877 for the effect of transition to UC.

[⁵ Disqualification period: section 7(6) of the Act

2.–(1)   The first day of the disqualification period for the purposes of section 7(6) of the Act ("DQ-day") shall be as follows.

(2)   This paragraph applies where on the determination day–

(a)   the offender is in receipt of a sanctionable benefit [⁶other than a benefit to which paragraph (5A) applies] [⁷ or universal credit];

(b)   the offender is a member of a joint-claim couple which is in receipt of a joint-claim jobseeker's allowance; or

(c)   the offender's family member is in receipt of income support, jobseeker's allowance, state pension credit, employment and support allowance, housing benefit or council tax benefit.

(3)   Where paragraph (2) applies and paragraph (4) does not apply–

(a)   in relation to a sanctionable benefit which is paid in arrears, DQ-day is the day following the first pay day after the end of the period of 28 days beginning with the determination day; and

(b)   in relation to a sanctionable benefit which is paid in advance, DQ-day is the first pay day after the end of the period of 28 days beginning with the determination day.

(4)   This paragraph applies where on the determination day the offender or (as the case may be) the offender's family member is in receipt of–

(a)   either housing benefit or council tax benefit or of both of those benefits; and

(b)   no other sanctionable benefit.

(5)   Where paragraph (4) applies–

(a)   in relation to housing benefit or council tax benefit which is paid in arrears, DQ-day is the day following the first pay day after the end of the period of 28 days beginning with the first day after the determination day on which the Secretary of State is notified by the relevant authority that the offender or the offender's family member is in receipt of either housing benefit or council tax benefit (or both of those benefits) or has been awarded either or both of those benefits; and

(b)   in relation to housing benefit or council tax benefit which is paid in advance, DQ-day is the first pay day after the end of the period of 28 days beginning with the first day after the determination day on which the Secretary of State is so notified by the relevant authority.

[⁶ (5A)   This paragraph applies where on the determination day the offender or, as the case may be, the offender's family member is in receipt of a sanctionable benefit which is neither payable wholly in advance nor wholly in arrears and no other sanctionable benefit.]

(6) Where [⁶ paragraph (5A) applies or where there is no sanctionable benefit payable on the determination day], DQ-day is the first day after the end of the period of 28 days beginning with the determination day on which the Secretary of State decides to award–

(a) a sanctionable benefit to the offender;

(b) a joint-claim jobseeker's allowance to a joint-claim couple of which the offender is a member; or

(c) [⁷ universal credit,] income support, jobseeker's allowance, state pension credit or employment and support allowance to the offender's family member.

[⁷ (6A) Paragraph (6B) applies where on the determination day, the offender or, as the case may be, the offender's family member is in receipt of universal credit.]

[⁷ (6B) Where this paragraph applies, DQ-day is–

(a) if the first day after the end of the period of 28 days beginning with the determination day is the first day of an assessment period, that day;

(b) if the first day after the end of the period of 28 days beginning with the determination day is not the first day of an assessment period, the first day of the next assessment period after that day.]

(7) For the purposes of the preceding provisions of this regulation [⁶ but except where paragraph (8) applies], DQ-day is to be no later than 5 years and 28 days after the date of the conviction of the offender for the benefit offence in the later proceedings referred to in section 7(1) of the Act; and section 7(9) of the Act (date of conviction and references to conviction) shall apply for the purposes of this paragraph as it applies for the purposes of section 7 of the Act.]

[⁶ (8) Where the date of the conviction of the offender for the benefit offence in the later proceedings is on or after 1st April 2013 and on the determination day–

(a) paragraph (2) or (6A) applies in the case of an offender or, as the case may be, an offender's family member; but

(b) that person ceases to be in receipt of a benefit referred to in those paragraphs before the first day of the disqualification period that would apply by virtue of paragraph (3) or (6B),

DQ-day is the first day after the end of the period of 28 days beginning with the determination day.]

Amendments

1.   Amended by reg 2 of SI 2002 No 486 as from 1.4.02.
2.   Amended by reg 25(2) of SI 2002 No 1792 as from 6.10.03
3.   Amended by art 3 of SI 2008 No 787 as from 1.4.08.
4.   Amended by reg 56 of SI 2008 No 1554 as from 27.10.08.
5.   Substituted by reg 2(3) of SI 2010 No 1160 as from 1.4.10.
6.   Amended by reg 5 of SI 2013 No 385 as from 1.4.13.
7.   Amended by reg 5 of SI 2013 No 385 as from 29.4.13.

Definitions

"determination day" – reg 1(2).
"pay day" – see reg 1(2).
"sanctionable benefit" – s6A(1) SSFA 2001.

General Note

Made under s7(6) SSFA 2001 (see p1715), reg 2 sets the commencement date ("DQ-day") of the "disqualification period" for those subject to loss of benefit under the "two strikes" scheme. Note that the length of the disqualification period is set by s7(6) and (6A) and is three years or 26 weeks as the case may be (see p1723). For HB purposes, DQ-day is set as follows. If on the "determination day" (defined in reg 1):

(1)   the offender or a family member of the offender is in receipt of HB and no other sanctionable benefit, DQ-day is set under paras (4) and (5);

(2)   the offender is in receipt of UC or a sanctionable benefit other than HB (or in addition to HB) or the offender is in receipt of joint-claim JSA, or a family member of the offender is in receipt of HB, IS, JSA, ESA or PC, DQ-day is set by para (3). Note that if the person ceases to be entitled to one of these benefits

before the first day of the disqualification period, DQ day is set under para (8). Note also that if the offender or family member is an HB claimant and is in receipt of IS, *income-based* JSA, *income-related* ESA or PC, the reduction is applied to those benefits and not to HB: reg 18;

(3) the offender or a family member is in receipt of HB that is paid partly in advance or partly in arrears and no other sanctionable benefit, or no sanctionable benefit is payable on the determination day, DQ day is the day set under para (6). The former has only limited application – ie, it would apply only to those with the transitional protection provided by Sch 3 para 7 HB&CTB(TP) Regs as otherwise, HB is paid wholly in arrears (see reg 92(2) HB Regs and reg 73(2) HB(SPC) Regs).

Unless para (8) applies, the date cannot be more than five years and 28 days after the conviction for the later offence: reg 2(7). The period was three years and 28 days prior to 1 April 2008. See also the transitional provisions in s49(2) WRA 2007 on p166.

The procedure is the same as under reg 1A (see p1762).

Note: if a reduction to HB is imposed and the claimant is then awarded UC, see regs 35 and 36 Universal Credit (Transitional Provisions) Regulations 2014 on p1875 and p1877 for the effect of transition to UC.

[¹ Prescribed offences: section 6B(14)(b) of the Act

2A.–(1) Paragraphs (2) to (4) prescribe offences which are relevant offences for the purpose of sections 6B and 7 of the Act where section 6B(14)(b)(i), (ii) or (iii) of the Act applies.

(2) In England and Wales, offences under–

(a) section 8 of the Accessories and Abettors Act 1861;

(b) section 1 of the Criminal Law Act 1977;

(c) section 1, 3, 4 or 5 of the Forgery and Counterfeiting Act 1981;

(d) section 6 or 7 of the Fraud Act 2006; and

(e) section 44, 45 or 46 of the Serious Crime Act 2007.

(3) In England, Wales or Scotland, offences under–

(a) section 182 of the Administration Act;

(b) section 327, 328 or 329 of the Proceeds of Crime Act 2002; and

(c) section 4, 5 or 6 of the Identity Documents Act 2010.

(4) In Scotland–

(a) the common law offences of–

(i) conspiracy to defraud;

(ii) embezzlement;

(iii) fraud;

(iv) fraudulent scheme; and

(v) uttering;

(b) offences under–

(i) section 44 of the Criminal Law (Consolidation) (Scotland) Act 1995;

(ii) section 28 or 30 of the Criminal Justice and Licensing (Scotland) Act 2010 ("the 2010 Act"); and

(c) offences to which section 29 of the 2010 Act (offences aggravated by connection with serious organised crime) applies.

(5) Paragraphs (6) and (7) prescribe offences which are relevant offences for the purpose of sections 6B and 7 of the Act where section 6B(14)(b)(i) or (ii) of the Act applies.

(6) In England and Wales, offences under section 1 of the Fraud Act 2006.

(7) In England, Wales or Scotland, offences under–

(a) section 111A of the Administration Act;

(b) section 35 of the Tax Credits Act 2002.]

Amendment

1. Inserted by reg 6 of SI 2013 No 385 as from 29.4.13.

PART V
HOUSING BENEFIT AND COUNCIL TAX BENEFIT

Circumstances where a reduced amount of housing benefit and council tax benefit is payable
  17.–(1) Subject to [³[²]] regulation 18, any payment of housing benefit or, as the case may be, council tax benefit which falls to be made to an offender in respect of any week in the disqualification period or to an offender's family member in respect of any week in the relevant period shall be reduced–
  (a) where the claimant or a member of his family is pregnant or seriously ill, by a sum equivalent to 20 per cent.;
  (b) in any other case, by a sum equivalent to 40 per cent.,
of the amount which is or, where he is not the claimant or is not single, would be applicable to the offender in respect of a single claimant for those benefits on the first day of the disqualification period or, where the payment falls to be made to an offender's family member, on the first day of the relevant period and specified in [¹ paragraph 1 of Schedule 3 to the Housing Benefit Regulations or, as the case may be, in paragraph 1(1) of Schedule 3 of the Housing Benefit (State Pension Credit) Regulations, in paragraph 1(1) of Schedule 1 to the Council Tax Benefit Regulations, or in paragraph 1(1) of Schedule 1 of the Council Tax Benefit (State Pension Credit) Regulations.
  (2) A reduction under paragraph (1) shall, if it is not a multiple of 5p, be rounded to the nearest such multiple or, if it is a multiple of 2.5p but not of 5p, to the next lower multiple of 5p.
  (3) Where the rate of housing benefit or council tax benefit payable to a claimant changes, the rules set out above for a reduction in the benefit payable shall be applied to the new rates and any adjustment to the reduction shall take effect from the beginning of the first benefit week to commence for the claimant following the change and in this paragraph "benefit week" shall have the same meaning as in [¹ regulation 2(1) of the Housing Benefit Regulations or, as the case may be, regulation 2(1) of the Housing Benefit (State Pension Credit) Regulations, regulation 2(1) of the Council Tax Benefit Regulations, or regulation 2(1) of the Council Tax Benefit (State Pension Credit) Regulations.]
  [³ [² (4)]]
  [³ [² (5)]]

Amendments
  1. Amended by reg 5 and Sch 2 para 20(3) of SI 2006 No 217 as from 6.3.06.
  2. Inserted by reg 7 of SI 2007 No 2202 as from 1.11.07. The amendment ceases to have effect on 31.10.09 unless revoked with effect from an earlier date.
  3. Omitted by reg 2(9) of SI 2010 No 1160 as from 1.4.10.

General Note
  The amount of the HB reduction imposed is normally 40 per cent of the personal allowance for a single claimant of the offender's age as at the first day of the disqualification period (for which see regs 1A and 2) or the relevant period (for which see s9(2) SSFA 2001 on p1723). If, however, the claimant or any member of the family is pregnant or seriously ill, the reduction is 20 per cent. Reference is also made to CTB but note that CTB was abolished from 1 April 2013.
  A reduction must be recalculated from the next benefit week where there is a change in the rate of HB that is payable: para (3).
  Note: if a reduction to HB is imposed and the claimant is then awarded UC, see regs 35 and 36 Universal Credit (Transitional Provisions) Regulations 2014 on p1875 and p1877 for the effect of transition to UC.

Circumstances where housing benefit and council tax benefit is payable
  18. Regulation 17 shall not apply and housing benefit or, as the case may be, council tax benefit shall be payable to an offender or to an offender's family member–
  (a) where the offender is the claimant, he is entitled to either of those benefits during the disqualification period;
  (b) where the offender's family member is the claimant, he is entitled to either of those benefits during the relevant period,

and the claimant is, at the same time, also entitled to income support [¹ , an income-related employment and support allowance, state pension credit,] or to an income-based jobseeker's allowance.

Amendment

1.   Amended by reg 2(10) of SI 2010 No 1160 as from 1.4.10.

General Note

Where the HB claimant is entitled to IS, income-based JSA, income-related ESA or PC, the reductions are applied to those benefits and not to HB. Reg 18 was not amended to include entitlement to UC. Reference is also made to CTB but note that CTB was abolished from 1 April 2013.

The Contracting Out (Functions of Local Authorities: Income-Related Benefits) Order 2002

(2002 No.1888)

General Note to the Order

The Deregulation and Contracting Out Act 1994 confers power on ministers to make orders permitting public bodies to contract out work to private contractors. Prior to this, powers of delegation and contracting out were limited. This Order permits local authorities to contract out most of their benefit-related functions, with the limited exceptions set out in art 3(2). Authorities are not obliged to contract the functions out.

Local authorities are obliged to carry out random checks on decisions made by contractors: art 4. Art 5 prohibits any contractor or employee of a contractor making a decision on a claim if s/he is a person to whom rent is payable for a dwelling in respect of which the claim is made or in which s/he has a financial interest by reason of payment of HB under that claim.

The Order was made on 18 July 2002 and so came into force, by virtue of art 1, on 25 July 2002.

Citation and commencement

1. This Order may be cited as the Contracting Out (Functions of Local Authorities: Income-Related Benefits) Order 2002 and shall come into force on the seventh day after the day on which it is made.

Interpretation

2. In this Order–

"the Administration Act" means the Social Security Administration Act 1992;

"the Benefits Act" means the Social Security Contributions and Benefits Act 1992;

"council tax benefit" means the benefit to which section 123(1)(e) of the Benefits Act refers;

"decisions on claims" means any decisions in relation to those benefits or payments referred to in article 3(1) that fall to be made under or by virtue of–

(a)   the Administration Act;

(b)   the Benefits Act;

(c)   section 34 of the Social Security Act 1998; and

(d)   the Child Support, Pensions and Social Security Act 2000

and any Regulations and Orders made under those provisions for the time being in force and, for the purposes of this Order, references to decisions include references to any determinations embodied in, or necessary to, a decision;

"discretionary housing payment" means any payment made by virtue of regulations under section 69 of the Child Support, Pensions and Social Security Act 2000;

"housing benefit" means the benefit to which section 123(1)(d) of the Benefits Act refers;

"local authority" means a billing authority, housing authority or local authority as they are defined in section 191 of the Administration Act;

"subsidy" means rent rebate subsidy, rent allowance subsidy or council tax benefit subsidy as referred to in section 140A(2) of the Administration Act or any grant made under section 70 of the Child Support, Pensions and Social Security Act 2000 (grants towards costs of discretionary housing payments).

Functions which may be contracted out

3.–(1)   In so far as it is not already lawful for functions of a local authority in relation to council tax benefit, discretionary housing payments and housing benefit under the provisions of–

(a)   the Benefits Act,

(b)   the Administration Act,

(c)   section 34 of the Social Security Act 1998, and

(d)   the Child Support, Pensions and Social Security Act 2000,

and any Regulations and Orders made under those provisions for the time being in force, to be exercised by, or by employees of, such a person (if any) authorised to do so by that authority, any such function of an authority under those provisions (not being a function excluded from section 70 of the Deregulation and Contracting Out Act 1994 by section

71(1) of that Act), other than a function specified in paragraph (2), may, if and in so far as that authority may authorise, be so exercised.

(2)   The functions referred to in paragraph (1) are–

(a)   any function relating to the claiming and receipt of subsidy;

(b)   the issue of a certificate under section 116(3)(b) of the Administration Act (as to the date on which evidence sufficient to justify prosecution came to the local authority's knowledge);

(c)   the grant or withdrawal of authorisations under section 110A(3) to (7) of the Administration Act (to exercise the powers of inspection);

(d)   the function of requiring a person to enter into arrangements under section 110AA of the Administration Act (to allow access to electronic records); and

(e)   any function under sections 139D to 139H of the Administration Act (directions by the Secretary of State).

Checking requirement attaching to the exercise of functions

4.–(1)   Subject to paragraph (5) an authorisation given under this Order in relation to any function involving decisions on claims shall include the checking requirement specified in paragraph (2), and the authorisation shall be subject to the inclusion of that requirement.

(2)   The checking requirement shall require the authorised person to–

(a)   provide a random sample of decisions on claims made on a day, of not less than 10 per cent. of those decisions, to the local authority for checking within two working days of that day;

(b)   take all reasonable steps to prevent errors identified by the local authority from recurring.

(3)   When providing a random sample for the purposes of paragraph (2)(a) above, the authorised person shall use such method of random selection as may be specified by the local authority in the authorisation or, where no such method has been specified, the authorised person shall notify the local authority of the method of random selection that has been used.

(4)   When taking reasonable steps to prevent identified errors from recurring for the purposes of paragraph (2)(b) above, the authorised person shall take such steps to prevent that error from recurring as may be required by the local authority.

(5)   An authorised person shall be subject to the checking requirement only if he employs at least one other person to carry out the work in relation to the exercise of any function involving decisions on claims.

(6)   For the purposes of this article "working day" means any day other than a Saturday, a Sunday, Christmas Day, Good Friday or a day which is a bank holiday under the Banking and Financial Dealings Act 1971 in any part of the United Kingdom.

Extent of an authorisation

5.–(1)   An authorisation given under this Order in relation to any function involving decisions on claims shall not extend to any decisions on any claims where the authorised person–

(a)   is a person to whom rent is payable for a dwelling in respect of which the claim is made; or

(b)   may otherwise be affected financially by reason of a payment of housing benefit under that claim.

(2)   An authorisation given under this Order in relation to any function involving decisions on claims shall not extend to a decision made by an employee of an authorised person on any claim where that employee–

(a)   is a person to whom rent is payable for a dwelling in respect of which that claim is made; or

(b)   may otherwise be affected financially by reason of a payment of housing benefit under that claim.

The Social Security (Habitual Residence) Amendment Regulations 2004

(SI 2004 No.1232)

Citation, commencement and interpretation

1.–(1)　These Regulations shall be cited as the Social Security (Habitual Residence) Amendment Regulations 2004 and shall come into force on 1st May 2004.

(2)　In these Regulations–

[¹]

Amendment

1.　Revoked by reg 3 and Sch 1 of SI 2006 No 217 as from 6.3.06.

Transitional arrangements and savings

6.–(1)　Paragraph (2) shall apply where a person–

(a)　is entitled to a specified benefit in respect of a period which includes 30th April 2004;

(b)　claims a specified benefit on or after 1st May 2004 and it is subsequently determined that he is entitled to that benefit in respect of a period which includes 30th April 2004;

(c)　claims a specified benefit on or after 1st May 2004 and it is subsequently determined that he is entitled to such a benefit in respect of a period which is continuous with a period of entitlement to the same or another specified benefit which includes 30th April 2004;

(d)　*[Omitted]*

(2)　Where this paragraph applies–

[¹ (a)]

(b)-(d) [Omitted]

(3)　The provisions saved by paragraph (2) shall continue to have effect until the date on which entitlement to a specified benefit for the purposes of paragraph (1) ceases, and if there is more than one such specified benefit, until the last date on which such entitlement ceases.

(4)　In this regulation "specified benefit" means income support, housing benefit, council tax benefit, jobseeker's allowance and state pension credit.

Amendment

1.　Revoked by reg 3 and Sch 1 of SI 2006 No 217 as from 6.3.06.

General Note

The transitional protection provided by reg 6 is now replicated in Sch 3 para 6(5)–(7) HB&CTB(CP) Regs (see p1795). Reg 10 of both the HB and the HB(SPC) Regs are modified for those with transitional protection by those paras.

　　Note that the amendments made by SI 2006 No.1026 to the HB Regs, HB(SPC) Regs, CTB Regs and CTB(SPC) Regs do not affect the continued operation of the transitional and savings provided for in reg 12 Social Security (Persons From Abroad) Miscellaneous Amendments Regulations 1996 (see p1633 of the 26th edition), reg 6 Social Security (Habitual Residence) Amendment Regulations 2004 or para 6 Sch 3 HB&CTB(CP) Regs (on p1795). See reg 11 of SI 2006 No.1026 (on p1807).

The Civil Partnership Act 2004 (Relationships Arising Through Civil Partnership) Order 2005

(2005 No.3137)

Citation and commencement

1. This Order may be cited as the Civil Partnership Act 2004 (Relationships Arising Through Civil Partnership) Order 2005 and comes into force on 5th December 2005.

References to stepchildren etc. in existing subordinate legislation

3.–(1) Section 246 of the Civil Partnership Act 2004 (interpretation of statutory references to stepchildren etc.) applies to the provisions of existing subordinate legislation listed in the Schedule.

(2) The application of section 246 of the Civil Partnership Act 2004 to the provisions in the Regulations set out in paragraphs 24 and 44 of the Schedule applies to those Regulations as modified in their application to persons to whom regulations 2(1) and 12(1) of the Housing Benefit and Council Tax Benefit (State Pension Credit) Regulations 2003 apply and to those Regulations as not so modified.

(3) The application of section 246 of the Civil Partnership Act 2004 to the provisions in the Regulations set out in paragraphs 27 and 47 of the Schedule applies to those Regulations as modified in their application to persons to whom regulations 2(1) and 12(1) of the Housing Benefit and Council Tax Benefit (State Pension Credit) Regulations 2003 apply.

SCHEDULE

ARTICLE 3

REFERENCES TO STEPCHILDREN ETC. IN EXISTING SUBORDINATE LEGISLATION

24. The definition of "close relative" in regulation 2(1) of the Housing Benefit (General) Regulations 1987 (interpretation).

25. Paragraphs 34(4)(b)(i) and (ii) and 34(5)(b)(i) and (ii) of Schedule 4 to those Regulations (sums to be disregarded in the calculation of income other than earnings).

26. Paragraphs 23(4)(b)(i) and (ii) and 23(5)(b)(i) and (ii) of Schedule 5 to those Regulations (capital to be disregarded).

27. Paragraphs 16(4)(b)(i) and (ii) and 16(5)(b)(i) and (ii) of Schedule 5ZA to those Regulations (Part I: capital to be disregarded).

44. The definition of "close relative" in regulation 2(1) of the Council Tax Benefit (General) Regulations 1992 (interpretation).

45. Paragraphs 35(4)(b)(i) and (ii) and 35(5)(b)(i) and (ii) of Schedule 4 to those Regulations (sums to be disregarded in the calculation of income other than earnings).

46. Paragraphs 23(4)(b)(i) and (ii) and 23(5)(b)(i) and (ii) of Schedule 5 to those Regulations (capital to be disregarded).

47. Paragraphs 16(4)(b)(i) and (ii) and 16(5)(b)(i) and (ii) of Schedule 5ZA to those Regulations (Part I: capital to be disregarded).

The Housing Benefit and Council Tax Benefit (Consequential Provisions) Regulations 2006

(2006 No.217)

Citation, commencement and interpretation

1.–(1)   These Regulations may be cited as the Housing Benefit and Council Tax Benefit (Consequential Provisions) Regulations 2006 and shall come into force on 6th March 2006.

(2)   In these Regulations–

"the Act" means the Social Security Contributions and Benefits Act 1992;

"the 1987 Regulations" means the Housing Benefit (General) Regulations 1987;

"the 1992 Regulations" means the Council Tax Benefit (General) Regulations 1992;

"Council Tax Benefit Regulations" means the Council Tax Benefit Regulations 2006;

"the Council Tax Benefit (State Pension Credit) Regulations" means the Council Tax Benefit (Persons who have attained the qualifying age for state pension credit) Regulations 2006;

"the Housing Benefit Regulations" means the Housing Benefit Regulations 2006;

"the Housing Benefit (State Pension Credit) Regulations" means the Housing Benefit (Persons who have attained the qualifying age for state pension credit) Regulations 2006;

"the consolidating Regulations" means the Council Tax Benefit Regulations, the Council Tax Benefit (State Pension Credit) Regulations, the Housing Benefit Regulations and the Housing Benefit (State Pension Credit) Regulations.

Continuity of the law

2.–(1)   The coming into force of the consolidating Regulations does not affect the continuity of the law.

(2)   Anything done or having effect as if done under or for the purposes of a provision revoked by these Regulations has effect, if it could have been done under or for the purposes of the corresponding provision of the consolidating Regulations, as if done under or for the purposes of that provision.

(3)   Any reference, whether express or implied, in the consolidating Regulations or any other instrument or document to a provision of the consolidating Regulations shall, in so far as the context permits, be construed as including, in relation to the times, circumstances and purposes in relation to which the corresponding provision of any regulation revoked by these Regulations has effect, a reference to that corresponding provision.

(4)   Any reference, whether express or implied, in any instrument or document to a provision of a regulation revoked by these Regulations shall be construed, so far as is required for continuing effect, as including a reference to the corresponding provision of the consolidating Regulations.

Documents referring to revoked provisions

4.   Any document made, served or issued after the consolidating Regulations comes into force which contains a reference to any of the regulations revoked by these Regulations shall be construed, except so far as a contrary intention appears, as referring or, as the context may require, including a reference to the corresponding provision of the consolidating Regulations.

Transitional provisions and savings

6.–(1)   The provisions of Schedule 3 to these Regulations (which contains transitional provisions and savings) shall have effect.

(2)   The revocation by these Regulations of any provision previously repealed subject to savings does not affect the continued operation of those savings.

Transitory modifications
7. The transitory modifications in Schedule 4 to these Regulations shall have effect.

Amending Orders
8. An order which is made under section 150 of the Social Security Administration Act 1992 after the consolidating Regulations have been made and which amends any of the Regulations scheduled to be revoked by these Regulations shall have the effect also of making a corresponding amendment of the consolidating Regulations.

SCHEDULE 3

REGULATION 6(1)

Transitional and Savings Provisions

1.–(1)   Where a change of circumstances occurs as a result of the payment of arrears of any income (and for the avoidance of doubt income includes any benefit within the meaning of the Act) which affects a determination or decision in respect of entitlement to, or the amount of, housing benefit or council tax benefit before 6th March 1995, the provisions specified in paragraph (2) shall apply subject to the omissions specified in relation to that provision.

(2)   The provisions specified in this paragraph (which all relate to the date on which changes of circumstances are to take effect) are–
- (a)   regulations 79 of the Housing Benefit Regulations which shall apply as if paragraph (7) was omitted;
- (b)   regulation 59 of the Housing Benefit (State Pension Credit) Regulations which shall apply as if paragraph (7) was omitted;
- (c)   regulation 67 of the Council Tax Benefit Regulations which shall apply as if paragraph (9) was omitted;
- (d)   regulation 50 of the Council Tax Benefit (State Pension Credit) Regulations which shall apply as if paragraph (9) was omitted.

General Note
This is a saving provision. The Housing Benefit and Council Tax Benefit (Amendment) Regulations 1995 SI No.511 amended reg 68 HB Regs 1987 following the decision in *R v Middlesborough BC ex p Holmes* [1995] unreported, 15 February, QBD. The transitional protection provided in that SI is now in para 1. The sub-paras in the regulations cited in para 1(2) are not to have affect where arrears of income are to be taken into account for a period prior to 6 March 1995. The amendment may be of continuing relevance in overpayment cases involving a failure to disclose receipt of income.

Persons incapable of work
2.–(1)   Where, on 12th April 1995, the disability premium was applicable to a claimant by virtue of paragraph 12(1)(b) of Schedule 2 to the 1987 Regulations or paragraph 13(1)(b) of Schedule 1 to the 1992 Regulations, as in force on that date, the disability premium shall continue to be applicable to that claimant from 13th April 1995 and for so long as he is incapable of work in accordance with the provisions of, and regulations made under, Part 12A of the Act (incapacity for work).

(2)   Where, on 12th April 1995, the disability premium was applicable to a claimant and in the period from 13th April 1995 to 1st October 1995 paragraph (1) either did not apply or ceased to apply in his case, if–
- (a)   for the period for which paragraph (1) did not apply or ceased to apply, the claimant was incapable of work or was treated as incapable of work in accordance with the provisions of, and regulations made under, Part 12A of the Act (the period of incapacity); and
- (b)   any break in the period of incapacity did not exceed a period of 56 continuous days,

with effect from 2nd October 1995 for so long as he is incapable of work or is treated as incapable of work, the disability premium shall be applicable in his case.

(3)   Paragraphs (1) and (2) shall not apply to a claimant who ceases to be incapable of work or ceases to be treated as incapable of work in accordance with the provisions of, and regulations made under, Part 12A of the Act (incapacity for work) for a period of more than 56 continuous days.

(4)   Where, in any period immediately preceding 13th April 1995, the circumstances mentioned in paragraph 12(6) of Schedule 2 to the 1987 Regulations, or paragraph 13(6) of Schedule 1 to the 1992 Regulations, as in force on 12th April 1995, applied to a claimant to whom the disability premium was not applicable, that claimant shall be treated for the purposes of–
- (a)   regulations 28(8)(c) and 56(2)(e) of, and paragraph 13(1)(b) of Schedule 3 to, the Housing Benefit Regulations;
- (b)   regulations 18(11)(e) and 45(3)(e) of, and paragraph 13(1)(b) of Schedule 1 to, the Council Tax Benefit Regulations; or as the case may be,

as if he had been incapable of work in accordance with the provisions of, and regulations made under, Part 12A of the Act (incapacity for work) throughout that period.

General Note to paras 2 and 3

The Housing Benefit and Council Tax Benefit (Miscellaneous Amendments) (No.2) Regulations 1995 SI No.626 introduced amendments to the conditions for qualifying for various premiums payable as part of HB and CTB. The transitional and savings provisions for those receiving the disability or higher pensioner premium on 12 April 1995 are now in paras 2 and 3.

Analysis

Prior to 12 April 1995, the requirement for the disability premium under, for example, Sch 2 para 12(1)(b) HB Regs 1987 was that the claimant was incapable of work for the purposes of the sickness and invalidity benefit legislation. Under para 2, the disability premium continues to be applicable to a claimant to whom it was applicable on 12 April 1995 so long as s/he is incapable of work. Gaps of up to 56 days in incapacity between 13 April and 1 October 1995 were ignored if the claimant was incapable of work on 2 October 1995. A subsequent gap of 56 days in incapacity will destroy the transitional protection. For the text of para 12(1)(b), see the 1994/95 edition of this book.

Most of those claiming IS "on the grounds of disability", IB or SDA were assessed and, if they qualified (ie, if they had limited capability for work or could be treated as having it), were transferred to ESA. This process of transfer was largely completed by the end of April 2018. Note that the transfer process did not apply to those who reached state pension age before 6 April 2014 and that such claimants getting SDA can continue to qualify for that benefit. The disability premium is not applicable to a claimant if s/he has (or is treated as having) limited capability for work: see Sch 3 para 13(9) HB Regs. Note also that those transferred to *income-related* ESA will eventually be transferred to UC under a "managed migration" process. At the time of writing, this process was due to take place between 2020 and 2023, with testing of the process with up to 10,000 claimants taking place from July 2019.

3.–(1)   Where the higher pensioner premium was applicable to a claimant on, or at any time during the 56 days immediately preceding, 12th April 1995 by virtue of [¹ paragraph 12(1)(a)(ii) of Schedule 2 to the 1987 Regulations], or paragraph 13(1)(a)(ii) of Schedule 1 to the 1992 Regulations, as in force on that date, paragraph 13 of each of the Schedules specified in sub-paragraph (2) shall, in so far as it applies to those claimants, apply subject to the amendments specified in sub-paragraph (3).

(2)   Those Schedules (which all relate to the applicable amount) are–

(a)   Schedule 3 to the Housing Benefit Regulations; and

(b)   Schedule 1 to the Council Tax Benefit Regulations.

(3)   The amendments specified in this sub-paragraph are–

(a)   in sub-paragraph (1)(a)(i), for the words "long-term incapacity benefit", substitute "an invalidity pension" and for the words "in the case of long-term incapacity benefit", substitute "in the case of invalidity pension";

(b)   in sub-paragraph (1)(a)(ii) for the words "long-term incapacity benefit" substitute "invalidity pension";

(c)   for head (b) of sub-paragraph (1), substitute–

"(b)   the circumstances of the claimant fall, and have fallen, in respect of a continuous period of not less than 28 weeks, within sub-paragraph (6) or, if he was in Northern Ireland for the whole or part of that period, within one or more comparable Northern Irish provisions.";

(d)   in sub-paragraph (3), for the words "or to be incapable of work", substitute "for the purposes of the provisions specified in that provision";

(e)   for sub-paragraphs (6) and (7), substitute–

"(6)   For the purposes of sub-paragraph (1)(b) the circumstances of a claimant fall within this sub-paragraph if–

(a)   he provides evidence of incapacity in accordance with regulation 2 of the Social Security (Medical Evidence) Regulations 1976 (evidence of incapacity for work) in support of a claim for sickness benefit, invalidity pension or severe disablement allowance within the meaning of sections 31, 33 or 68 of the Act, provided that an adjudication officer has not determined he is not incapable of work, or

(b)   he is in receipt of statutory sick pay within the meaning of Part 11 of the Act.".

Amendment

1.   Amended by reg 7(2) of SI 2008 No 1042 as from 19.5.08.

Analysis

Prior to 12 April 1995, the requirement for the higher pensioner premium under, for example, Sch 2 para 12(1)(a)(ii) HB Regs 1987 was that the claimant or her/his partner was receiving invalidity pension. The transitional rules apply where the higher pensioner premium was "applicable" (as to which see *CIS 11293/1996*) to a claimant on 12 April 1995 or during the 56 days preceding that day. *R v Secretary of State for Social Security ex p Smithson* (Case C-243/90) [1992] ECR I-467, ECJ dealt with the former version of Sch 3 para 11 HB Regs (the conditions for receipt of higher pensioner premium). It was an attempt to argue that the paragraph offended against EC Directive 79/7 in that it discriminated on the grounds of sex because women lost their right to opt for invalidity benefit at 65 and not 70. It was held that HB did not fall within the directive because it was a benefit calculated on the basis of the relationship between notional and actual income, even though the notional income was calculated by reference to a risk which was within the directive – ie, sickness or invalidity.

Note that higher pensioner and other pensioner premiums were omitted from the HB Regs by SI 2008 No.1042 as from 19 May 2008 and are not relevant for the HB(SPC) Regs.

[¹ Eligible rent

Modifications

Paras 4 and 5 substituted by reg 6(2) Housing Benefit (Local Housing Allowance, Miscellaneous and Consequential) Amendment Regulations 2007 SI No.2870 as from 7 April 2008, save that for a person to whom reg 1(3) of those regulations applied (see p1816), the amendments came into force on the day on or after 7 April 2008 when the first of the events specified in reg 1(4) applied to her/him, or on 6 April 2009 if none had before that date.

4.–(1)   Subject to the following provisions of this paragraph, the eligible rent of a person–
(a)   who was entitled to housing benefit on both the first date and the second date; or
(b)   who is liable to make payments in respect of a dwelling occupied by him as his home, which is exempt accommodation,
shall be determined in accordance with–
    (i)   regulations 12 (rent) and 13 (maximum rent) of the Housing Benefit Regulations, or, as the case may be,
    (ii)   regulations 12 (rent) and 13 (maximum rent) of the Housing Benefit (State Pension Credit) Regulations,
    as set out in paragraph 5.
(2)   Sub-paragraph (1)(a) shall not apply to–
(a)   any determination of a person's eligible rent in a case where a relevant authority is required to determine a maximum rent (LHA) by virtue of regulation 13C of the Housing Benefit Regulations or, as the case may be, regulation 13C of the Housing Benefit (State Pension Credit) Regulations; [²]
[² (aa)   a determination of eligible rent in a case where a person's landlord is a registered housing association within the meaning of regulation 2 of the Housing Benefit Regulations or any case where housing benefit is payable in the form of a rent rebate unless–
    (i)   the claimant or the claimant's partner has attained the qualifying age for state pension credit, or both have attained that age;
    (ii)   a relevant authority has, on or before 31st March 2013, reduced that person's eligible rent in accordance with regulation 13(3) of the Housing Benefit Regulations as set out in paragraph 5 of this Schedule; or
    (iii)   a relevant authority has, on or before 31st March 2013, made a determination that the person's dwelling is larger than is reasonably required or that the person's rent is unreasonably high in accordance with regulation 13(3) of the Housing Benefit Regulations as set out in paragraph 5 of this Schedule, but has not, in accordance with paragraph (4), (5) or (7) of that regulation, reduced that person's eligible rent; or]
(b)   any subsequent determination of his eligible rent.
(3)   Sub-paragraph (1)(a) shall only apply in a case where–
(a)   either–
    (i)   the dwelling occupied as his home by a person to whom sub-paragraph (1)(a) refers is the same on both the first date and the second date; or
    (ii)   the dwelling so occupied was not the same by reason only that the change was caused by a fire, flood, explosion or natural catastrophe rendering the dwelling occupied as the home on the first date uninhabitable; and
(b)   the person–
    (i)   was continuously entitled to and in receipt of housing benefit between the first date and the second date in respect of the dwelling to which head (a) above applies; or
    (ii)   was not entitled to or receiving housing benefit for a period not exceeding 4 weeks, but was in continuous occupation of the dwelling to which head (a) above refers between the first date and the second date; or
    (iii)   is a person to whom sub-paragraph (4) applies.
(4)   This sub-paragraph applies in the case of a person ("the claimant") who becomes, or whose partner becomes, a welfare to work beneficiary, and–
(a)   the claimant ceases to be entitled to housing benefit in respect of his residence in the dwelling he occupies as his home;
(b)   the claimant subsequently becomes re-entitled to housing benefit–
    (i)   in respect of the same dwelling, or
    (ii)   in respect of a different dwelling in a case to which sub-paragraph (3)(a)(ii) applies; and

(c)   the first day of that entitlement is within 52 weeks of the claimant or his partner becoming a welfare to work beneficiary.

(5)   A person shall be deemed to fulfil the requirements of sub-paragraphs (1)(a) and (3), where–

(a)   he occupies the dwelling which he occupied on the relevant date;

(b)   this paragraph applied to the previous beneficiary on the relevant date; and

(c)   the requirements of sub-paragraphs (6) and (7) are satisfied in his case.

(6)   The requirements of this sub-paragraph are that the person was, on the relevant date–

(a)   the partner of the previous beneficiary; or

(b)   in a case where the previous beneficiary died on the relevant date, was a person to whom sub-paragraph (10)(b), (c) or (d) of regulation 13 (restrictions on unreasonable payments), as specified in paragraph 5, applied and for the purposes of this sub-paragraph "claimant" in that paragraph of that regulation shall be taken to be a reference to the previous beneficiary.

(7)   The requirements of this sub-paragraph are that a claim for housing benefit is made within 4 weeks of the relevant date and where such a claim is made it shall be treated as having been made on the relevant date.

(8)   The eligible rent of a person to whom–

(a)   regulation 10A of and Schedule A1 to the Housing Benefit Regulations (entitlement to housing benefit by refugees), or, as the case may be,

(b)   regulation 10A of and Schedule A1 to the Housing Benefit (State Pension Credit) Regulations (entitlement to housing benefit by refugees)

apply, shall be determined in accordance with–

(i)   regulations 12 (rent) and 13 (maximum rent) of the Housing Benefit Regulations, or, as the case may be,

(ii)   regulations 12 (rent) and 13 (maximum rent) of the Housing Benefit (State Pension Credit) Regulations,

as set out in paragraph 5.

(9)   Sub-paragraphs (1) to (8) above shall continue to have effect in the case of a claimant who has ceased to be a welfare to work beneficiary or whose partner has ceased to be such a beneficiary where the claimant is entitled to housing benefit at the end of the 52 week period to which sub-paragraph (4)(c) refers.

(10)   In this paragraph–

"the first date" means 1st January 1996, except in a case to which sub-paragraph (5) applies, when it shall be the relevant date;

"the second date" means any day after the first date for which a claimant's entitlement to housing benefit is to be determined;

"eligible rent" means as the case may require, an eligible rent determined in accordance with–

(a)   regulations 12B (eligible rent), [² 12BA (eligible rent and maximum rent (social sector)),] 12C (eligible rent and maximum rent), 12D (eligible rent and maximum rent (LHA)) or any of regulations 12E to 12K (transitional protection for pathfinder cases) ; or

(b)   regulations 12 (rent) and 13 (restrictions on unreasonable payments) as set out in paragraph 5 of Schedule 3 to the Consequential Provisions Regulations in a case to which paragraph 4 of that Schedule applies;

"exempt accommodation" means accommodation which is–

(a)   a resettlement place provided by persons to whom the Secretary of State has given assistance by way of grant pursuant to section 30 of the Jobseekers Act 1995 (grants for resettlement places); and for this purpose "resettlement place" shall have the same meaning as it has in that section; or

(b)   provided by a non-metropolitan county council in England within the meaning of section 1 of the Local Government Act 1972, a housing association, a registered charity or voluntary organisation where that body or a person acting on its behalf also provides the claimant with care, support or supervision;

"imprisoned" means detained in custody pending sentence upon conviction or under a sentence imposed by a court;

"previous beneficiary" means a person–

(a)   who died, left the dwelling or was imprisoned, as the case may be;

(b)   who was on that date in receipt of housing benefit or was on that date within 52 weeks of having become a welfare to work beneficiary; and

(c)   to whom this regulation applied on that date;

and, in this paragraph, a reference to a person occupying a dwelling as his home shall be taken to include a person who is treated as occupying a dwelling as his home by virtue of regulation 7 of the Housing Benefit Regulations or, as the case may be, regulation 7 of the Housing Benefit (State Pension Credit) Regulations;

"the qualifying age for state pension credit" means (in accordance with section 1(2)(b) and (6) of the State Pension Credit Act 2002)–

(a)   in the case of a woman, pensionable age; or

(b)   in the case of a man, the age which is pensionable age in the case of a woman born on the same day as the man;

"relevant authority" means an authority administering housing benefit;

"the relevant date" means the date–

(a)   of the death of a previous beneficiary;

(b)   on which a previous beneficiary who was the claimant's partner left the dwelling so that he and the claimant ceased to be living together as husband and wife; or

(c)   on which a previous beneficiary, other than a beneficiary to whom regulation 7(13) of the Housing Benefit Regulations or, as the case may be, regulation 7(13) of the Housing Benefit (State Pension Credit) Regulations applied, was imprisoned, but only where on that date he was the partner of the claimant,

as the case may be;

"state pension credit" means state pension credit under the State Pension Credit Act 2002;

"welfare to work beneficiary" means a person to whom regulation 13A(1) of the Social Security (Incapacity for Work) (General) Regulations 1995 applies.

Amendments

1.   Substituted by reg 6(2) of SI 2007 No 2870 as from 7.4.08 (or if reg 1(3) of that SI applies, on the day on or after 7.4.08 when the first of the events specified in reg 1(4) applies, or from 6.4.09 if none have before that date).

2.   Amended by reg 3 of SI 2014 No.212 as from 3.3.14.

General Note

Reg 10 Housing Benefit (General) Amendment Regulations 1995 SI No.1644 provided important transitional protection for the residents of certain types of supported accommodation ("exempt accommodation") and for certain then existing claimants (referred to here as "exempt claimants") and their families, from the "local reference rent" rules on rent restrictions which were originally introduced on 2 January 1996. For those residents and categories of claimant, reg 11 HB Regs 1987 applied in its old form. This scheme, referred to in this book as the "pre-January 1996" rules, is now in paras 4 and 5. Those to whom the "pre-January 1996" rules apply are also exempt from the "local housing allowance" rules on rent restriction. In limited cases, "exempt claimants" are also exempt from the "social sector" rules on rent restriction.

See p348 for a summary of the four rent restriction schemes and when these can potentially apply.

If the pre-January 1996 rules apply, "rent" and "eligible rent" for the purposes of para 4(1) are assessed under reg 12 and "maximum rent" under reg 13 of both the HB Regs and the HB(SPC) Regs as set out in para 5. In simple terms, "eligible rent" is the contractual rent, minus ineligible services unless the authority decides that it should be restricted. If it does, it reduces eligible rent to the amount it considers appropriate. Reductions can also be made if eligible rent increases during an award of HB: reg 13ZA as inserted by para 5(3). In some cases, a reduction can be delayed: reg 13(5)–(8) as inserted by para 5(2).

The rules before 3 March 2014

Para 4(1) requires the authority to determine the eligible rent in "pre-January 1996" cases under the versions of regs 12 and 13 HB Regs and HB(SPC) Regs set out in para 5. Thus, until the insertion of para 4(2)(aa) from 3 March 2014, although the rules did not specify it, a HB claimant who came under para 4(1)(a) (ie, an "exempt claimant" who had been entitled to HB continuously since 1 January 1996 and who (generally) had continued to occupy the same dwelling), was also exempt from the "social sector" rules on rent restriction. This could include someone who was a local authority tenant or the tenant of a registered housing association. Para 4(1)(a) can now only apply to such tenants in limited cases: para 4(2)(aa)(i)–(iii).

Local authorities may have applied the "social sector" rules in error to HB claimants to whom para 4(1)(a) applied. In such cases, they should have tried to identify those affected from their records, if still available. Affected claimants can apply for a revision of the local authority's decision (eg, on grounds of official error) or appeal against it (if within the absolute time limit for doing so) and should provide sufficient evidence to enable the local authority or tribunal to decide that s/he is or was an "exempt claimant" under para 4(1)(a).

Supported accommodation under the universal credit system

The government is considering how best to provide help to those in supported accommodation when UC is rolled out fully. However, in a letter to the Social Security Advisory Committee (available on its website), it was confirmed that help with housing costs for those in "exempt accommodation" (defined for HB in para 4(10) and for UC in Sch 1 para 1 UC Regs by reference to the definition in para 4(10)) will be provided separately to UC. Payments in respect of "exempt accommodation" are currently excluded from eligibility for UC: Sch 1 paras 3(h) and 3A(2) UC Regs.

Although entitlement to HB is generally precluded if a person has an award of UC, those entitled to UC can qualify for HB, or if entitled to HB when the UC claim is made, can continue to be entitled to HB, if this is for "exempt accommodation", under the provisions in Sch 3 paras 4 and 5 of the HB&CTB(CP) Regs: see the UC(TP) Regs 2014 on p1857. The UC(TP) Regs 2014 allow UC claimants to claim and be entitled to HB for specified types of supported accommodation, the definition of which includes "exempt accommodation" and some forms of "temporary accommodation" for homeless people. However, the "pre-January 1996" rules are only relevant for "exempt accommodation" as defined in para 4(10).

For HB purposes, all of the earnings, income and capital of a "person on UC" are ignored: Sch 4 para 2, Sch 5 para 4 and Sch 6 para 5 HB Regs. For this reason, it may be in the claimant's interests to increase her/his earnings or income, although this could affect the amount of her/his UC.

UC was initially introduced in pilot areas in which entitlement to UC depended on a person meeting "gateway conditions". People subject to "gateway conditions" could not meet these, and thus could not claim and be awarded UC, if they lived in accommodation "in which care, supervision, counselling, advice or other support services (other than services connected solely with the provision of adequate accommodation) were made available to the claimant by or on behalf of the person by whom the accommodation is provided, with a view to enabling the claimant to live there": Sch 5 para 5(b) Welfare Reform Act 2012 (Commencement No.9 and Transitional and Transitory Provisions and Commencement No.8 and Savings and Transitional Provisions (Amendment) Order 2012 No.983 (the No.9 Order). However, if someone entitled to UC moved to such accommodation, s/he could qualify for HB if it was "specified accommodation", including "exempt accommodation", or "temporary accommodation".

Future changes

The government intended to introduce rules from 1 April 2019 that would cap the amount of HB payable to social sector tenants at the local housing allowance (LHA) rate that would apply to them under the LHA rules (for which see reg 13D HB Regs), if this was lower than the amount as calculated under reg B13 HB Regs. It said this would apply to a claimant who took on a new, or renewed a, social sector tenancy agreement on or after 1 April 2016 (or 1 April 2017 if s/he lived in supported accommodation). However, at Prime Minister's question time on 25 October 2017, the Prime Minister said: "as part of our response to the review [*of supported housing*], we will not be applying the local housing allowance cap to supported housing; indeed, we will not be implementing it in the wider social rented sector. The full details will be made available when we publish our response to the consultation." The response, *Funding Sheltered Housing*, was published on 31 October 2017. The government's intention is, from April 2020, to continue to fund sheltered and extra care housing, as well as long-term supported accommodation, via the benefit system with a "sheltered rent" introduced from April 2020. In England, short-term supported housing will be funded via a ring-fenced grant to local authorities.

Analysis

The general rule, as set out in sub-para (1), is that there are two categories of claimants whose eligible rent is to be assessed under the "pre-January 1996" rules. The eligible rent of those in "exempt accommodation" is assessed under these rules indefinitely. The eligible rent of those who have been entitled to HB since 1 January 1996 (referred to here as "exempt claimants") is assessed under these rules while they retain transitional protection, as is the eligible rent of those who inherit the protection.

Sub-paragraphs (1)(b) and (10): Exempt accommodation

Under sub-para (1)(b), the eligible rent of claimants living in "exempt accommodation" must be determined under regs 12 and 13 as set out in para 5 (on p1783). The language of para 4(1) makes this mandatory, even though such claimants are not excluded from the requirement for an authority to apply to the rent officer for a determination under reg 14 of both the HB Regs and the HB(SPC) Regs (the "local reference rent" rules). Such claimants are excluded from assessment under the "local housing allowance" rules by reg 13C(5)(b) of both the HB Regs and the HB(SPC) Regs.

The "benefit cap". Note that where HB is awarded for "exempt accommodation", it is disregarded in the calculation of total welfare benefits for the purposes of the "benefit cap" under the HB Regs – "exempt accommodation" comes within the definition of "specified accommodation" for these purposes: regs 75C(2) and 75H(2) HB Regs.

"Exempt accommodation" is defined in sub-para (10). It is the dwelling occupied by the claimant as her/his home which must come within the definition. If a building contains two or more dwellings, the definition of "exempt accommodation" must be applied in relation to each dwelling, and not in relation to the building as a whole: *CH 1289/2007*. The accommodation must either be a "resettlement place" (as described in sub-para (a) of the definition) or accommodation provided by specified bodies where care, support or supervision is provided to the claimant by that body or a person acting on its behalf (as described in sub-para (b) of the definition).

"Provided by ..." means that the accommodation is provided by the owner or other person (eg, a tenant or intermediate landlord) who, but for the grant to the claimant of the tenancy or licence, would have the right to possession, and therefore the right to permit occupation of it, and to whom the obligation to pay rent or licence fee is owed: *CH 2726/2008*; *Chorley BC v IT (HB)* [2009] UKUT 107 (AAC); [2010] AACR 2. The definition does not encompass people who have played a part, however important, in the accommodation becoming available, but who have no proprietary interest in the accommodation and no entitlement to the rent. In *CH 3900/2005*, Commissioner Pacey said that the accommodation must actually be provided by one of the bodies listed. This does *not* include instructing, arranging or facilitating privately rented accommodation through a third party: *R(H) 2/07* considered and applied.

"a non-metropolitan county council ... a housing association, a registered charity or voluntary organisation ...". The accommodation must be provided by one of the bodies listed. For "housing association" and "voluntary organisation", see reg 2 HB Regs on p228 and p234. *Wirral MBC v Furlong, Perry and Salisbury Independent Living and SSWP (HB)* [2013] UKUT 291 (AAC); [2014] AACR 12 considered the meaning and application of the definitions of "housing association" and "voluntary organisation". For both, there is what the judge referred to as a "non-profit-making condition". In considering that condition, he pointed out that in the real world it is obviously possible (if not inevitable) that the body providing accommodation and support (the "provider")

may enter into arrangements with other individuals or bodies (eg, the owners of the accommodation) whose purpose is to make a profit, and that this means that Parliament could not have intended that this would prevent the provider from satisfying the non-profit making condition. The judge also concluded that the objects of the provider are of central importance and an obvious starting point for determining whether the non-profit making condition is satisfied because they dictate what the provider can do lawfully. He pointed out (at paragraph 59):

"It is important to remember that the ability to make, or the making of a surplus regularly, or from time to time, does not mean that a company is trading for profit and so, for example, in breach of its memorandum of association if it provides that it is not to trade for profit. This reflects the commercial inevitability and thus the reality that, for each accounting period, a company or other body providing accommodation or other service or product will not be able to balance its books. So, whether a company or entity does or does not trade for profit engages the issue what it can or does do with any surplus or profit".

The judge made suggestions for a sequential approach by decision makers as follows.

(1)   The objects, and powers of the provider should be considered, on the basis that they are complied with. Then its accounts should be considered on the basis that they give an accurate picture of the activities and affairs of the provider.

(2)   Any other activities or matters that might be relevant to either, or both, of the definition of "exempt accommodation" (ie, the status of the provider) or any anti-abuse provision (eg, in reg 9(1)(l) HB Regs) should be considered.

"where that body or a person acting on its behalf also provides the claimant with care, support or supervision". The care, support or supervision must be provided either by, or on behalf of, the landlord. The words "or acting on its behalf" in sub-para (b) of the definition means acting on its behalf in providing the care support, or supervision. It is not sufficient that a third party is acting on behalf of the landlord in some other respect. The third party must also be acting on the landlord's behalf in providing care, etc: *R(H) 6/08*, an interim decision of Commissioner Turnbull.

In *AG v South Ayrshire Council (HB)* [2017] UKUT 110 (AAC); [2018] AACR 18, the First-tier Tribunal had decided that the claimant's accommodation was not "exempt accommodation". It said that although his landlord was providing support that was more than minimal, the landlord was required to register under s59 of the Public Services Reform (Scotland) Act 2010 and, because it had not done so, the services it provided were unlawfully provided. The Upper Tribunal allowed the appeal. The judge said that:

"... a tribunal does not have an independent jurisdiction to determine whether or not a provider is complying with some other regulatory regime. The situation would be different if a court having jurisdiction had determined that *[the landlord]* could not lawfully provide care services. Then that would be a fact to be taken into account by the FtT in determining whether or not care services were being provided that fell within the definition of "care, support or supervision" under regulation 4(10). *[R v HBRB for Allerdale District Council ex p Doughty [2000] COD 462 QBD]* is an example. In that case the application for registration as a small residential home was rejected by the Registered Homes Tribunal. The fact that registration had been rejected by the regulator meant that care services could not be lawfully provided. The Housing Board then made their decision on the basis of the fact that the proper regulatory body had refused registration and so care could not be provided."

In *CH 1289/2007*, Commissioner Turnbull said that the definition of "exempt accommodation" turns on whether the landlord provides "the claimant" with care, support or supervision. A claimant's accommodation will not be exempt if no (or only minimal) care, support or supervision is provided to her/him, however much care, support or supervision may be provided to other tenants of the landlord. He pointed out that this "does not of course mean that it will always, or perhaps even usually, be necessary, in a case where a landlord has a number of tenants in a building (or even several buildings) to obtain and present evidence directed to the provision of care, support or supervision to each occupant individually. The landlord may be able to present evidence showing that the level of support provided is broadly similar in relation to all of them. Or there may be evidence of an assessment process whereby only applicants with at least a particular level of need are accepted as tenants."

In *R(H) 2/07*, Commissioner Turnbull concluded – when dealing with the same definition of exempt accommodation in reg 10(6) Housing Benefit (General) Amendment Regulations 1995 No.1644, which the definition in sub-para (10) replaces – that the definition does not extend to a situation where the accommodation provider (ie, the landlord) neither provides nor has provided on its behalf the care, support or supervision. The landlord must either actually provide the care itself or have contracted for it to be provided on its behalf. Accordingly if the care provider is not the landlord and instead has a contract with the local authority to provide support, the accommodation will not normally be exempt. The same commissioner, in *R(H) 7/07*, emphasises that if the landlord is providing the care, support or supervision s/he need not be the main provider, nor must s/he be providing it pursuant to some contractual or statutory obligation; but the care support or supervision provided by the landlord must be more than a token or minimal amount. Note that an application for judicial review was dismissed in *R (S) v a Social Security Commissioner and Another* [2009] EWHC 2221 (Admin), in which the claimant sought to argue that *R(H) 2/07* was wrongly decided.

In *MMcF v Sefton BC (HB)* [2016] UKUT 403 (AAC), a support package for the claimant had been commissioned by the local authority and was provided by an organisation other than his landlord. His landlord also provided regular support. However, the local authority decided that the claimant did not live in "exempt accommodation", it said because support or supervision provided by a landlord must not duplicate functions and tasks already covered in a main support plan, and this was accepted by the First-tier Tribunal. Judge Brunner QC pointed out that there was nothing in the regulations to support this view. Following *R(H) 7/07*, she allowed the claimant's appeal. She said that duplication may be a useful evidential consideration to enable a local authority or tribunal to address the relevant legal issues, but it is not a legal hurdle in itself.

In his interim decision in *R(H) 4/09*, Commissioner Turnbull considered to what extent it is permissible to take into account support which is available to tenants generally, but not taken advantage of by a particular tenant. "Care" and "supervision" must actually be provided by the landlord. It is not enough that they are available should the tenant wish to call for them. However, it may be that the making available of certain types of service itself amounts to the provision of "support", but the support provided must be more than minimal. He said that there were at least two factors to which regard must be had. The first is the extent of the support services which are in reality available, having regard to the resources devoted by the landlord to providing the support and the number of tenants among whom those resources are spread. The second factor is the extent to which there is in practice any real likelihood that the claimant would need the available support.

In *Salford CC v PF* [2009] UKUT 150 (AAC), Judge Turnbull decided that provided the support would benefit the claimant to a significant extent, and therefore is needed, there is no additional test of whether it is in all the circumstances reasonable to provide support. He said that what matters is simply whether support is provided to more than a minimal extent, and that it was implicit that support is not "provided" unless there is in fact some need for it.

In *Bristol CC v AW* [2009] UKUT 109 (AAC), the claimant's rent of £503.75 included a sum of £10 for "supporting people charges". The local authority argued that the amount indicated support at only a minimal level. However, Judge Turnbull said that £10 was not an amount so small that it indicated that the support to be provided by the landlord, over and above its ordinary property management functions, must be minimal. £10 a week is not an obviously nominal or token payment. The judge accepted an argument from the claimant that a satisfactory test for determining whether support of more than a minimal amount is provided is to ask whether the support provided was likely to make a real difference to the claimant's ability to live in the property.

The final decisions in *R(H) 4/09* and *R(H) 6/08* (and a third appeal, *CH 2805/2007*) were made by Commissioner Turnbull after a joint hearing. In all three cases, he found that the claimants did not have "exempt accommodation". In his decision, he made a number of points about what amounted to "provides ... support" for the purposes of the definition in sub-para (10)(b).

(1)   The word "support" connotes the giving of advice and assistance to the claimant in coping with the practicalities of everyday life. It does not extend to scrutinising the arrangements for the provision of care, support and supervision by some other body, with a view to remedying perceived defects or to recommending improvements.

(2)   The word "support" involves the landlord doing something more than, or different from, the exercise of its ordinary property management functions. A landlord does not "provide ... support" to a tenant by doing what any prudent landlord would do in the management of its property – eg, by complying with its repairing obligations.

(3)   The making available of certain types of support is capable of amounting to the provision of support within the ordinary meaning of the words "provides ... support", even if no advantage is taken of it in the period under consideration, if what is being offered by way of advice and remedial action extends beyond ordinary housing management. The commissioner cited the example of a landlord making a properly staffed telephone service available whereby tenants could seek advice which, if given, amounts to "support". This would amount to the provision of support during any particular period, whether or not the tenant in fact makes use of the service during that period, subject to the proviso that there had to be a real prospect that the tenant would find the service of use from time to time. In determining whether such a service or facility amounts to the provision of support to any particular tenant to a more than minimal extent, regard must be had to the degree of likelihood that the particular tenant will ever need to take advantage of it and in determining that regard must be had to the extent to which support is available from elsewhere.

(4)   The words "provides ... support" imply a degree of continuity in the available support. They therefore do not include any activities of the landlord which were involved in setting up the scheme nor, for example, advice and consultation in relation to the acquisition of the building and the tenant's move to it, nor the making of adaptations to the building which are carried out before or within a short time after the commencement of the tenancy.

(5)   The willingness and ability to intervene in situations where there appears to be a serious failing in the care and support regime in exceptional cases does not fall within the words "provides ... support".

In *Chorley BC v IT (HB)* [2009] UKUT 107 (AAC); [2010] AACR 2, Judge Turnbull decided that "support" is not confined to counselling, advising, encouraging etc, the claimant. Although carrying out repairs is normally no more than the fulfilment of the landlord's repairing obligations, and therefore does not go beyond ordinary housing management, if the landlord is arranging for the carrying out of repairs which clearly go beyond ordinary housing management, this can amount to support. For example, if, owing to the nature of the tenant's disabilities, performance of the landlord's repairing obligations imposes a materially greater burden on the landlord than would otherwise be the case, performance of that greater burden may be capable of amounting to the provision of support. The same judge concluded that carrying out or arranging adaptations to accommodate a tenant's disability could also amount to "support": *DW v Oxford City Council (HB)* [2012] UKUT 52 (AAC).

In *Bristol CC v AW*, Judge Turnbull said that a landlord's help in taking an appeal to the First-tier Tribunal could not be taken into account as an item of "support" going beyond ordinary property management. He said that if a landlord is not providing support within the meaning of the definition of "exempt accommodation", accommodation cannot be brought within the definition by virtue of the fact that the landlord intends to support the tenant by taking an adverse decision on an HB claim to appeal. In his judgment, it could not be right that what would otherwise be a bad case can be made into a good one by virtue simply of the landlord's willingness to support the tenant by taking the case to appeal.

Sub-paragraphs (1) to (4): Entitlement to HB since 1 January 1996 "exempt claimants"

Unless transitional protection ends under sub-para (2), under sub-para (1)(a), it continues for those who have been continuously entitled to HB since 1 January 1996, who (generally) continue to occupy the same dwelling, and who fulfil other conditions – referred to here as "exempt claimants": definitions of "the first date" and "the second date" in sub-para (10) and sub-paras (3) to (7) and (9). If sub-para (1)(a) applies, eligible rent must be determined under regs 12 and 13 as set out in para 5.

Sub-para (2): When transitional protection ends. The transitional protection provided by sub-para (1)(a) ends when the local authority determines a person's eligible rent in two situations. Para (1)(a) cannot then apply on any subsequent determinations the local authority makes: sub-para (2)(b). The two situations are as follows.

(1) The authority is required to determine a "maximum rent (LHA)" by virtue of reg 13C HB Regs – ie, the "local housing allowance" rules apply: sub-para (2)(a). Unless any of the exceptions in reg 13C(5) apply (for which see p385), an authority is required to determine a maximum rent (LHA) where a claim for HB is made on or after 7 April 2007 (eg, where there has been a break in entitlement to HB) or where there is a change of dwelling during an award of HB after that date: reg 13C(2)(a) to (c) of both the HB Regs and the HB(SPC) Regs.

(2) The landlord is a "registered housing association" (defined in reg 2(1) HB Regs) or HB is paid in the form of a rent rebate – eg, where the landlord is a local authority: sub-para (2)(aa). The "social sector" rules in regs A13 and B13 may instead apply. However, sub-para (1)(a) *can* apply and, if it does, the claimant is an "exempt claimant", in either of the following situations.

– The claimant or her/his partner is at least the qualifying age for PC (defined in s137 SSCBA 1992): sub-para (2)(aa)(i).

– Before 31 March 2014, the local authority had used the "pre-January 1996" rules to restrict the person's eligible rent or had decided that her/his accommodation was too large or her/his rent was too high but did not restrict eligible rent because the rules for those in a protected group applied (for which see reg 13(4), (5) and (7) HB Regs as set out para 5 of this Schedule): sub-para (2)(aa)(ii) and (iii).

Linking rules are provided in sub-paras (3) and (4) where there is a break in entitlement to, and receipt of, HB of no more than four weeks (52 weeks if the claimant or her/his partner is a welfare to work beneficiary). In addition, there is provision for protection to be inherited under sub-paras (5) to (7). However, because of the effect of sub-para (2), the linking rules only apply where the authority is *not* required to determine a "maximum rent (LHA)" by virtue of reg 13C HB Regs – ie, where any of reg 13C(5)(a) to (e) of either the HB Regs or the HB(SPC) Regs applies, or where any of the exceptions in sub-para (2)(aa) apply.

Sub-para (3): Further conditions. The claimant must be occupying the same dwelling throughout the whole period, save for any period in which the dwelling was uninhabitable as a result of one of the disasters mentioned in sub-para (3)(a)(ii). If the dwelling is permanently uninhabitable, the transitional protection is presumably retained at the claimant's new property, unless sub-para (2) now applies: see, for example, reg 13C(2)(c) HB Regs. If the property is repaired, it appears that the transitional protection is lost unless the claimant moves back. Clearly, a certain period of time will have to be allowed to enable her/him to move back in. By virtue of the definition of "previous beneficiary" in sub-para (10), the question of whether a person can be treated as occupying a dwelling must be resolved by reference to reg 7 of both the HB Regs and the HB(SPC) Regs.

Sub-paras (3)(b)(ii) and (4). Breaks in entitlement to (or receipt of) HB of up to four weeks are ignored, extended to 52 weeks if the claimant or her/his partner is a "welfare to work beneficiary", as defined in sub-para (10) (but see the discussion above on the application of sub-para (2)). Note: the 52-week linking period was not extended when the linking period for welfare to work beneficiaries was extended to 104 weeks.

Welfare to work beneficiaries are broadly those who stopped receiving benefits claimed on the basis of their incapacity for work (eg, IS or incapacity benefit) to try out paid work or training. The rules allowed the welfare to work beneficiary to return to the same level of benefit that s/he was receiving before starting the work or training, so long as this was within a 104-week linking period. Note that this provision will now only have limited application.

Sub-paragraphs (5) to (7): Inherited protection

Under these provisions, a claimant is deemed to fall within sub-paras (1)(a) and (3) if s/he fulfils four conditions. The common theme is that the claimant takes over the protection from a "previous beneficiary" who was claiming in respect of the same home. That person must have died, left the dwelling or been imprisoned. However, see the discussion above about the application of sub-para (2).

(1)   The claimant must occupy the same dwelling as was occupied on the relevant date: sub-para (5)(a). "Relevant date" is defined in sub-para (10).

(2)   The previous beneficiary must have had the benefit of the transitional protection: sub-para (5)(b). It appears that it is sufficient if the previous beneficiary also inherited the transitional protection under these provisions.

(3)   Under sub-para (6), the claimant must either have been the partner of the previous beneficiary or a person to whom para (10)(b), (c) or (d) of reg 13 as set out in para 5(2) applied in relation to the previous beneficiary. See the Analysis of reg 13ZA HB Regs on p383 which refers to the same categories of person.

(4)   The claimant must claim HB within four weeks of the relevant date: sub-para (7). The claim is then treated as made on the relevant date.

[¹**5.**–(1)   For the purposes of paragraph 4(1), regulation 12 of both the Housing Benefit Regulations and the Housing Benefit (State Pension Credit) Regulations is as follows–

"**Rent**

12.–(1)   Subject to the following provision of this regulation, the payments in respect of which housing benefit is payable in the form of a rent rebate or allowance are the following periodical payments which a person is liable to make in respect of the dwelling which he occupies as his home–

(a)   payments of, or by way of, rent;

(b)   payments in respect of a licence or permission to occupy the dwelling;

(c)   payments by way of mesne profits or, in Scotland, violent profits;

(d)   payments in respect of, or in consequence of, use and occupation of the dwelling;

(e)   payments of, or by way of, service charges payment of which is a condition on which the right to occupy the dwelling depends;

(f)   mooring charges payable for a houseboat;

(g)   where the home is a caravan or a mobile home, payments in respect of the site on which it stands;

(h)   any contribution payable by a person resident in an almshouse provided by a housing association which is either a charity of which particulars are entered in the register of charities established under section 3 of the Charities Act 1993 (register of charities) or an exempt charity within the meaning of that Act, which is a contribution towards the cost of maintaining that association's almshouses and essential services in them;

(i)   payments under a rental purchase agreement, that is to say an agreement for the purchase of a dwelling which is a building or part of one under which the whole or part of the purchase price is to be paid in more than one instalment and the completion of the purchase is deferred until the whole or a specified part of the purchase price has been paid; and

(j)   where, in Scotland, the dwelling is situated on or pertains to a croft within the meaning of section 3(1) of the Crofters (Scotland) Act 1993, the payment in respect of the croft land.

(2)   A rent rebate or, as the case may be, a rent allowance shall not be payable in respect of the following periodical payments–

(a)   payments under a long tenancy except a shared ownership tenancy granted by a housing association or a housing authority;

(b)   payments under a co-ownership scheme;

(c)   payments by an owner;

(d)   payments under a hire purchase, credit sale or conditional sale agreement except to the extent the conditional sale agreement is in respect of land; and

(e)   payments by a Crown tenant.

(3)   Subject to any apportionment in accordance with paragraphs (4) and (5) and to regulations 13 and 13ZA (restrictions on unreasonable payments and rent increases), the amount of a person's eligible rent shall be the aggregate of such payments specified in paragraph (1) as he is liable to pay less–

(a)   except where he is separately liable for charges for water, sewerage or allied environmental services, an amount determined in accordance with paragraph (6);

(b)   where payments include service charges which are wholly or partly ineligible, an amount in respect of the ineligible charges determined in accordance with Schedule 1; and

(c)   where he is liable to make payments in respect of any service charges to which paragraph (1)(e) does not apply, but to which paragraph 3(2) of Schedule 1 (unreasonably low service charges) applies in the particular circumstances, an amount in respect of such charges determined in accordance with paragraph 3(2) of Schedule 1.

(4)   Where the payments specified in paragraph (1) are payable in respect of accommodation which consists partly of residential accommodation and partly of other accommodation, only such proportion thereof as is referable to the residential accommodation shall count as eligible rent for the purposes of these Regulations.

(5)   Where more than one person is liable to make payments in respect of a dwelling, the payments specified in paragraph (1) shall be apportioned for the purpose of calculating the eligible rent for each such person having regard to all the circumstances, in particular, the number of such persons and the proportion of rent paid by each such person.

(6) The amount of the deduction referred to in paragraph (3) shall be–

(a) except in a case to which sub-paragraph (c) applies, if the dwelling occupied by the claimant is a self-contained unit, the amount of the charges;

(b) in any other case except one to which sub-paragraph (c) applies, the proportion of those charges in respect of the self-contained unit, which is obtained by dividing the area of the dwelling occupied by the claimant by the area of the self-contained unit of which it forms part; or

(c) where the charges vary in accordance with the amount of water actually used, the amount which the appropriate authority considers to be fairly attributable to water and sewerage services, having regard to the actual or estimated consumption of the claimant.

[¹ (6A) Where a reduction in any of the payments listed in paragraph (1) for which a person would otherwise be liable is applied by a provider of social housing under an approved tenant incentive scheme, for the purposes of paragraph (1) the amount of the payment is to be treated as if no such reduction had been applied.

(6B) For the purposes of paragraph (6A)–

"approved tenant incentive scheme" means a scheme which is–

(a) operated by a provider of social housing and designed to avoid rent arrears by allowing reductions in the payments listed in paragraph (1) or other advantages in return for meeting specified conditions; and

(b) approved by the Secretary of State;

"provider of social housing" means–

(a) a local authority;

(b) a non-profit registered provider of social housing;

(c) in relation to accommodation which is social housing, a profit-making registered provider of social housing;

(d) a registered social landlord;

"registered social landlord" means–

(a) a body which is registered in the register maintained by the Welsh Ministers under Chapter 1 of Part 1 of the Housing Act 1996;

(b) a body which is registered in the register maintained by the Scottish Housing Regulator under the Housing (Scotland) Act 2010;

"social housing" has the meaning given in section 68 of the Housing and Regeneration Act 2008.]

(7) In this regulation and Schedule 1–

"service charges" means periodical payments for services, whether or not under the same agreement as that under which the dwelling is occupied, or whether or not such a charge is specified as separate from or separately identified within other payments made by the occupier in respect of the dwelling; and

"services" means services performed or facilities (including the use of furniture) provided for, or rights made available to, the occupier of a dwelling."

Amendment

1.   Inserted by reg 22 of SI 2017 No 995 as from 7.11.17.

General Note

As noted above, reg 10 of SI 1995 No.1644 provided important protection for the residents of "exempt accommodation" (certain types of supported accommodation) and for certain existing claimants and their families ("exempt claimants") from the rules on rent restrictions which were introduced on 2 January 1996, and subsequently provided protection from later rent restriction schemes. For those categories of claimant, reg 10 HB Regs 1987 applied in its old form. The old form of reg 10 is now provided in the version of reg 12 of both the HB Regs and the HB(SPC) Regs as set out in para 5(1). The regulation is largely the same as the current version of provisions in the HB Regs and the HB(SPC) Regs, so reference to the commentary in the HB Regs can be made. For:

– paras (1), (2) and (8), see reg 12(1), (2) and (8) HB Regs;

– paras (4) to (6), see reg 12B(3) to (5) HB Regs;

– para (3)(a) to (c), see reg 12B(2)(a) to (c) HB Regs.

Note that under the version of reg 12 in para 5(1), eligible rent is, subject to any apportionment under paras (4) and (5), and to reg 13 (as set out in para 5(2)) and reg 13ZA (as set out in para 5(3)), the aggregate of the payments specified in para (1), less the charges set out in para (3)(a) to (c). Note also the effect of paras (6A) and (6B) where a reduction in rent is applied under an approved tenant incentive scheme.

(2) For the purposes of paragraph 4(1), regulation 13 of both the Housing Benefit Regulations and the Housing Benefit (State Pension Credit) Regulations is as follows–

"**Restrictions on unreasonable payments**

13.–(1) Where a rent is registered in respect of a dwelling under Part 4 or 5 of the Rent Act 1977 or Part 4 or 7 of the Rent (Scotland) Act 1984 and the rent recoverable from a claimant is limited to the rent so registered, his eligible rent determined in accordance with regulation 12 (rent) shall not exceed the rent so registered.

(2)   Where a rent has been determined by a rent assessment committee or a private rented housing committee in respect of a dwelling under Part 1 of the Housing Act 1988 or Part 2 of the Housing (Scotland) Act 1988, the claimant's eligible rent determined in accordance with regulation 12 shall not exceed the rent determined by the committee during the twelve months beginning with the first day on which that determination had effect.

(3)   The relevant authority shall consider–

(a)   whether by reference to a determination or re-determination made by a rent officer in exercise of a function conferred on him by an order under section 122 of the Housing Act 1996 or otherwise, whether a claimant occupies a dwelling larger than is reasonably required by him and others who also occupy that dwelling (including any non-dependants of his and any person paying rent to him) having regard in particular to suitable alternative accommodation occupied by a household of the same size; or

(b)   whether by reference to a determination or re-determination made by a rent officer in exercise of a function conferred on him by an order under section 122 of the Housing Act 1996 or otherwise, whether the rent payable for his dwelling is unreasonably high by comparison with the rent payable in respect of suitable alternative accommodation elsewhere,

and, where it appears to the authority that the dwelling is larger than is reasonably required or that the rent is unreasonably high, the authority shall, subject to paragraphs (4) to (7), treat the claimant's eligible rent, as reduced by such amount as it considers appropriate having regard in particular to the cost of suitable alternative accommodation elsewhere and the claimant's maximum housing benefit shall be calculated by reference to the eligible rent as so reduced.

(4)   If any person to whom paragraph (10) applies–

[⁴ (a)   has attained the qualifying age for state pension credit; or]

[¹ (b)   is incapable of work for the purposes of Part 12A of the Act; or]

(c)   is treated as capable of work in accordance with regulations made under section 171E of the Act; or

[² (ca)   has limited capability for work [³ within the meaning of section 1(4)] of the Welfare Reform Act 2007; or

(cb)   is treated as not having limited capability for work in accordance with regulations made under paragraph 1(a) of Schedule 2 to that Act (employment and support allowance: supplementary provisions); or]

(d)   is a member of the same household as a child or young person for whom he or his partner is responsible,

no deduction shall be made under paragraph (3) unless suitable cheaper alternative accommodation is available and the authority considers that, taking into account the relevant factors, it is reasonable to expect the claimant to move from his present accommodation.

(5)   No deduction shall be made under paragraph (3) for a period of 12 months from the date of death of any person to whom paragraph (10) applied or, had a claim been made, would have applied, if the dwelling which the claimant occupies is the same as that occupied by him at that date except where the deduction began before the death occurred.

(6)   For the purposes of paragraph (5), a claimant shall be treated as occupying the dwelling if paragraph (13) of regulation 7 (circumstances in which a person is to be treated as occupying a dwelling) is satisfied and for that purpose sub-paragraph (b) of that paragraph shall be treated as if it were omitted.

(7)   Without prejudice to the operation of paragraph (4), but subject to paragraph (8), where the relevant authority is satisfied that a person to whom paragraph (10) applies was able to meet the financial commitments for his dwelling when they were entered into, no deduction shall be made under paragraph (3) during the first 13 benefit weeks of the claimant's award of housing benefit.

(8)   Paragraph (7) shall not apply where a claimant was previously entitled to benefit in respect of an award of housing benefit which fell wholly or partly less than 52 weeks before the commencement of his current award of housing benefit.

(9)   For the purposes of this regulation–

(a)   in deciding what is suitable alternative accommodation, the relevant authority shall take account of the nature of the alternative accommodation and the facilities provided having regard to the age and state of health of all the persons to whom paragraph (10) applies and, in particular, where a claimant's present dwelling is occupied with security of tenure, accommodation shall not be treated as suitable alternative accommodation unless that accommodation will be occupied on terms which will afford security of tenure reasonably equivalent to that presently enjoyed by the claimant; and

(b)   the relevant factors in paragraph (4) are the effects of a move to alternative accommodation on–

(i)   the claimant's prospects of retaining his employment; and

(ii)   the education of any child or young person referred to in paragraph (4)(d) if such a move were to result in a change of school.

(10)   This paragraph applies to the following persons–

(a)   the claimant;

(b)   any member of his family;

(c)   if the claimant is a member of a polygamous marriage, any partners of his and any child or young person for whom he or a partner is responsible and who is a member of the same household;

(d)   subject to paragraph (11), any relative of the claimant or his partner who occupies the same dwelling as the claimant, whether or not they reside with him.

(11)   Paragraph (10)(d) shall only apply to a relative who has no separate right of occupation of the dwelling which would enable him to continue to occupy it even if the claimant ceased his occupation of it."

Amendments

1.   Amended by reg 7(3) of SI 2008 No 1042 as from 19.5.08.
2.   Inserted by reg 2 of SI 2008 No 1082 as from 27.10.08.
3.   Amended by reg 25 of SI 2008 No 2428 as from 27.10.08.
4.   Substituted by reg 41 of SI 2009 No 1488 as from 6.4.10.

General Note

Reg 10 of SI 1995 No.1644 provided important protection for the residents of "exempt accommodation" (and for certain existing claimants and their families – "exempt claimants") from the rules on rent restrictions which were introduced on 2 January 1996 and subsequently provided protection from later rent restriction schemes. For those residents and categories of claimant, reg 11 HB Regs 1987 applied in its old form. The old form of reg 11 is now provided in the version of reg 13 of both the HB Regs and the HB(SPC) Regs as set out in para 5(2).

Analysis of reg 13 as set out in para 5(2)

Paragraphs (1) and (2): Set rents

Para (1) only affects tenancies created before 15 January 1989 or, in Scotland, 2 January 1989. The Rent Acts do not apply to any tenancies created after those dates. Where they do apply – and a rent has been registered – the tenant is not legally liable to pay the landlord more than the registered rent so the eligible rent could never exceed the registered rent in any event. This paragraph merely makes that explicit.

A register of the accommodation in respect of which a fair rent has been registered in any particular area is maintained by the local Valuation Office Agency and is open to public inspection. Information is also available at www.gov.uk/check-register-rents.

If a "fair rent" has been registered but the authority uses its powers under para (3) to restrict the eligible rent to a lower figure, the tenant remains liable to the landlord for the balance. This is unlikely to happen in practice unless the claimant's accommodation is unreasonably large under sub-para (3)(a).

Para (2). Rent Assessment Committees (in Scotland, Private Rented Housing Committees) have the power to assess market rents for certain assured and assured shorthold tenancies under the 1988 Acts. These were created on or after 15 January 1989 or, in Scotland, 2 January 1989. The reference to the Rent Assessment Committee should, presumably, now be read as a reference to the First-tier Tribunal (Property Chamber). The restriction of eligible rent imposed by this paragraph lasts only for 12 months from the time when the Committee's determination first takes effect. Again, this requirement is in addition to the general power under para (3).

Paragraph (3): Introduction

The scope of this provision requires careful application by authorities. First, the local authority must consider whether the circumstances of the claimant's tenancy are such as are set out in sub-paras (a) or (b), that is, it must decide if the claimant's dwelling is larger than is reasonably required or the rent for the dwelling is unreasonably high. It is plain from the word "or" at the end of sub-para (a) that the authority is obliged to reduce the claimant's eligible rent if either of the sub-paras is satisfied. It is not necessary that both should be satisfied: *R v Kensington and Chelsea RBC ex p Pirie* [1997] unreported, 26 March, QBD.

Second, if either of sub-paras (a) or (b) apply, the local authority must reduce the eligible rent and decide the amount of the reduction. The amount of the reduction is discretionary, ie it is the amount which the local authority "considers appropriate having regard in particular to the cost of suitable alternative accommodation elsewhere". Para (3) is subject to para (4) (under which in some circumstances no reduction can be made unless specified conditions are met) and paras (5) to (7) (under which a reduction must be delayed in specified circumstances). Under both sub-paras (a) and (b), the authority is to consider the circumstances by reference to determinations or re-determinations made by a rent officer (ie, following referral under reg 14 HB Regs) or otherwise. For the importance of the rent officer's determinations generally, see the Analysis of para (3)(b). For a discussion as to what "suitable alternative accommodation" is and the evidence that must be produced by the authority, see the Analysis to para (9)(a) on p1791.

Paragraph (3)(a): Size of the accommodation

The authority must consider whether the accommodation is "larger than is reasonably required" by the claimant's household. In reaching a decision, the authority must have regard to any suitable alternative accommodation occupied by a "household of the same size". The use of the phrases "or otherwise" and "in particular" make it clear that other factors may also be relevant. Some assistance may be obtained from the size criteria set out in Sch 2 Rent Officers (Housing Benefit Functions) Order 1997 and its Scottish equivalent, but the regulation requires a more general approach and the particular needs of any person in the household need close consideration. For the importance of the rent officer's determination generally, see the Analysis of para (3)(b).

In *Pirie*, it was confirmed that the word "required" means "needed" and not, as the claimant suggested, "demanded" (transcript at 2F–3B).

Although the regulation refers to the comparison being with alternative accommodation "occupied by a household of the same size", it is suggested that "household" in this context cannot be restricted to its normal meaning in social security law, which requires a degree of financial and social interdependence between the members of the household: see the Analysis to s137 SSCBA 1992 on p17. This is because the regulation provides that the requirements of others occupying the dwelling are to be taken into account, including non-dependants and lodgers, who need not be living in the same "household" as the claimant. The comparison must be with alternative accommodation which is suitable for that group, not with a narrower group comprised simply of the claimant and the members of her/his household within the dwelling.

Paragraph (3)(b): Cost of the accommodation

The authority must consider whether the claimant's rent "is unreasonably high by comparison with the rent payable in respect of suitable alternative accommodation elsewhere". "Rent" for these purposes includes all payments eligible under reg 12: *R v Beverley DC HBRB ex p Hare* (1995) 27 HLR 637, QBD.

In determining the application of para (3)(b), a number of principles can be derived from the authorities and are set out below.

The rent must be "unreasonably" higher. The question is not whether the restricted rent is reasonable but whether the full rent is unreasonably higher than rents for comparable properties. In any market for rented property there will be a range of rents which are being charged for similar properties. The fact that one such rent is higher than another does not per se make the former rent unreasonably high. That conclusion can only be justified if the rent is beyond the top end of the range of rents which a landlord might reasonably charge. Authority for this approach may be found in the decision of Lord Clyde in *Malcolm v Tweeddale District HBRB* [1994] SLT 1212, CS(OH) Discussing the examples of alternative accommodation provided by the authority, Lord Clyde said at 1215E–G:

> "Even if the examples given were of comparable accommodation and even if the rents quoted were reasonable, it does not follow that the petitioner's rent, although higher, was unreasonably high. There may well be a band of rentals within which all may be reasonable. That one is higher than the others does not necessarily mean that it is unreasonably higher."

On this point *Malcolm* followed the earlier decision of Lord Weir in *McLeod v HBRB for Banff and Buchan District HBRB* [1988] SLT 753, CS(OH). Although these were Scottish cases and the former was concerned with the meaning of a pre-1987 predecessor of the old reg 11 rather than this version of reg 13, they should be treated as highly persuasive authority in England and Wales. *McLeod*, in particular, has been cited with approval by Hutchison J in *R v Sefton MBC ex p Cunningham* (1991) 23 HLR 534 at 538, QBD and by the Court of Appeal in *R v East Devon DC HBRB ex p Gibson* (1993) 25 HLR, CA – although in the latter case it was suggested that in some respects the test which *McLeod* imposes may be "higher than the statute strictly requires".

The comparison is with the range of rents charged for suitable alternative accommodation. This is another point originating in the judgment of Lord Weir in *McLeod*. The Housing Benefit Review Board in that case had decided that because the claimant's rent was higher than the lowest rents charged for suitable alternative accommodation, it was entitled to apply the regulation then being considered (under the pre-1988 HB scheme). Lord Weir made it clear, at 756C, that this approach was incorrect and that there had to be an "overall examination of the spectrum of rents".

It follows from this that, where it is demonstrated that the claimant's rent falls into the "spectrum of rents" charged elsewhere, it will be impossible for the authority to conclude rationally that para (3)(b) is applicable. In one of the cases heard together in *R v Coventry CC ex p Waite* [1995] unreported, 7 July, QBD (also known as *R v Coventry City Council, ex p Morgan*), the bracket of comparable rents was said to be £25 to £37. The claimant's rent was £37. A finding that the rent was unreasonably high was quashed. In *R v Kensington and Chelsea RBC ex p Abou-Jaoude* [1996] unreported, 10 May, QBD, the evidence before the Housing Benefit Review Board was that two-thirds of comparable properties had rents of below £240 and the rest had higher rents. The claimant's rent was £275, but Turner J held that in the absence of more detail of the rents payable under the more expensive comparators, it was impossible to conclude that his rent was unreasonably high.

The combination of the first two principles produces the result that even if the claimant's rent is in excess of the top end of the spectrum of rents, a conclusion that the rent was unreasonably high will still not be justified where the difference is small: *Waite* (transcript at 31F–G).

In *SS v Birmingham City and SSWP (HB)* [2013] UKUT 418 (AAC), the claimant was the tenant of a charity (Roshni) providing accommodation to women fleeing domestic violence. Roshni had lost its public funding (due to public sector cut-backs as opposed to any failings on its part) and thus had increased its rents. The local authority decided that the claimant's rent was unreasonably high, having used as a comparitor, other suitable alternative accommodation that was subsidised. The Upper Tribunal decided that "suitable alternative accommodation" must not necessarily exclude subsidised accommodation, but for an unsubsidised rent to be unreasonably high in comparison with a subsidised rent, it would normally have to be shown that the unsubsidised rent was higher than what the subsidised rent could be expected to be were it unsubsidised. The local authority appealed. The Court of Appeal in *Birmingham City Council v SSWP and Others* [2016] EWCA Civ 1211; [2017] AACR 8 considered whether it was appropriate to take into account the degree of public subsidy received by the owner of a claimant's accommodation and by the owner of "suitable alternative accommodation" and decided that the Upper Tribunal had erred in law. It said:

> "It seems to me therefore that the concept of a rent being "unreasonably" high in regulation 13(3) is that the rent is unreasonably high for the claimant to have to pay, rather than unreasonably high for a particular

landlord to charge. An "unreasonably high" rent under regulation 13(3) will be a rent higher than the rent one could reasonably be expected to pay in what Evans L.J. in *ex parte Gibson* described as the "relevant active market in property of the relevant description, type or class" – the "ascertainable market rent". I see no justification for reading into this concept artificial constraints on the relevant market in which that other accommodation exists, or on the market rent for such accommodation. If there is a "relevant active market" and an "ascertainable market rent" for suitable, alternative accommodation – supported by evidence of the range of rents being paid for accommodation of the appropriate type, occupied with the appropriate security of tenure, in the appropriate general location – the comparison between rents must be objective, realistic and complete."

The local authority's financial position is irrelevant. The use of concepts of "reasonableness" and "appropriateness" in para (3) mean that the decision to be made by the authority does contain elements of discretion and judgment. However, this discretion is a narrow one and the only factors which are relevant to its exercise are those which relate to the personal circumstances of the claimant and her/his household and the existence and state of the market in suitable alternative accommodation. Successive Subsidy Orders have contained strong incentives to authorities to restrict eligible rents to a "threshold" level or to the level specified in the rent officer's determination and authorities have often succumbed to the temptation to do so, some even adopting formal policies to this effect.

However tempting this may be for authorities, it is clear from the case of *R v Brent LBC HBRB ex p Connery* (1989) 22 HLR 40 at 44, QBD, that to take the amount of subsidy payable into consideration under sub-paras (a) or (b) is impermissible.

The role of the rent officer's determination. On one reading of sub-paras (a) and (b), the authority would seem to be entitled to make decisions under those sub-paragraphs solely "by reference to" a determination under s122 Housing Act 1996. However, such a conclusion cannot always be reconciled with the terms of the Rent Officers (Housing Benefit Functions) Orders made under that section.

For example, Art 3 and Sch 1 para 1 obliges rent officers to make a "rent determination" as to whether the rent "is significantly higher than the rent which the landlord might reasonably have been expected to obtain from the tenancy at that time" having regard to "the level of rent under similar tenancies of similar dwellings in the vicinity" but on the assumption that no one who would have been entitled to HB has sought or is seeking the tenancy. The following points need to be made.

(1) A "significantly high" rent is not necessarily the same as an "unreasonably high" one.

(2) "Similar" accommodation is not necessarily the same as "suitable" alternative accommodation: the former concept does not pay as much regard to the individual circumstances of the claimant and her/his household as the latter, and those circumstances are directly relevant to the decision to be made by the authority under para (3).

(3) As the rent officer's determination is predominantly for subsidy purposes, it includes an artificial assumption as to the type of tenant who is seeking the tenancy which is not reflected in the real world. The result is that the rent officer's determination is unlikely ever to be the same as an actual market rent. Under reg 13(3) no such assumption is made and, as stated above, it is impermissible to take subsidy considerations into account when reaching decisions under sub-paras (a) and (b).

Although the link between a rent officer determination and an unreasonably high rent may be stronger if the rent officer makes an exceptionally high rent determination (the assumptions underlying the determination are different and an "exceptionally" high rent is more likely to be unreasonably high than a "significantly" high one), the distinction between "suitable" and "similar" accommodation still remains. In these circumstances, it is inconceivable that an authority could, in practice, be satisfied of all matters which must be established before applying para (3) simply on the basis of a rent officer's significantly high rent determination.

It follows that, while an authority may have regard to such a determination in reaching its decision, the simple fact that the reasonable rent determined by the rent officer is lower than the contractual rent is not sufficient on its own to justify a reduction under sub-para (b).

This is supported by *R v Coventry CC ex p Waite* [1995] unreported, 7 October, QBD. However, it is clear that the rent officer's determination will often be a factor of great weight and may be conclusive in some cases: *Waite*; *R v East Devon DC HBRB ex p Gibson* (1993) 25 HLR, CA. In the absence of any evidence to the contrary, it is to be assumed that the rent officer is doing her/his job properly and the local authority may simply produce the determinations to a tribunal: *R v Manchester CC ex p Harcup* (1993) 26 HLR 402 at 408, QBD; *R v Kensington and Chelsea RBC ex p Pirie* [1997] unreported, 26 March, QBD.

In *R v Sandwell MBC ex p Wilkinson* (1998) 31 HLR 22, QBD, Laws J emphasised the separation of the functions of the rent officer and the Housing Benefit Review Board in determining whether a claimant's rent should be restricted under the old reg 11. He robustly rejected criticisms of the way in which the rent officer had made his recommendations, both on the basis that his decision was not the subject-matter of the application for judicial review and because, as he correctly pointed out, the valuation was only "a starting point for the Board to consider". He further confirmed that, in any case, authorities concerning the duties of rent officers and Rent Assessment Committees under the Rent Act 1977 and the Housing Act 1988 were of no assistance in examining whether the correct approach had been taken to a determination for HB the purposes of the old reg 11.

Suitable alternative accommodation. See the Analysis to para (9)(a) on p1791.

The approach of tribunals. Many of the cases brought against decisions of Housing Benefit Review Boards under the old reg 11 have complained (often successfully) of failures on the part of the Boards to comply with their statutory obligations to make findings of fact and give full reasons under the former reg 83(4) HB Regs 1987. As with other areas of the Regulations which are particularly replete with pitfalls, a systematic approach will assist the First-tier Tribunal considering a case under para (3)(b). One such approach was that put forward by Schiemann J in *R v Beverley DC HBRB ex p Hare* (1995) 27 HLR 637, QBD. It involves six stages.

(1)   Establish the rent, in the wide definition including all of the elements which are set out in reg 12(1), for the current dwelling: reg 12 as set out in para 5(1) on p1783.

(2)   Indicate what type of accommodation is regarded as a suitable alternative (this involves expressing a view on what services are necessary for this particular claimant).

(3)   Indicate the rent (in the wide sense) which is considered to be payable in respect of such accommodation.

(4)   Find whether the rent (in the wide sense) is unreasonably high in comparison with the rent payable in respect of suitable alternative accommodation elsewhere.

(5)   If so, indicate the reduction found appropriate.

(6)   Indicate how the First-tier Tribunal arrived at that amount.

Paragraph (3): The amount of the reduction

Once it has been established that either sub-para (a) or (b) is applicable, the local authority must reduce the claimant's eligible rent and the question of the amount of the reduction needs to be considered. As originally enacted, the paragraph did not oblige authorities to reduce the claimant's eligible rent but merely gave them a discretion to do so where one of the sub-paras applied. That discretion was removed by SI 1991 No.235 with effect from 1 April 1991. However, the local authority still has discretion as to the amount of the reduction. Previous editions have suggested that the authority could elect to impose a nil reduction. However, it does not appear that this is an option open to the authority in view of the removal of the discretion not to apply a reduction, though Collins J thought, without resolving the point, that this was a possible construction: *R v Coventry CC ex p Waite* [1995] unreported, 7 July, QBD (transcript at 28B–29B). However, substantially the same effect could be achieved in an appropriate case by imposing a nominal reduction, such as one penny.

The Court in *Birmingham City Council v SSWP and Others* [2016] EWCA Civ 1211; [2017] AACR 8 pointed out that a local authority is not obliged to reduce a claimant's eligible rent by the full amount of the difference between the rent s/he pays and the rent s/he would pay for suitable alternative accommodation. It is simply required to have regard, in particular, to the cost of suitable alternative accommodation.

In determining the appropriate reduction, the authority may have regard to its financial position: *R v Brent LBC HBRB ex p Connery* (1989) 22 HLR 40 at 44, QBD. However, *Connery* also makes it clear that the rent may not be reduced below the level paid for suitable alternative accommodation. Neither, it is suggested, will an authority normally be justified in reducing the eligible rent to a figure at the bottom of the rental brackets. A rough average ought to be the starting point.

The language of the closing words to reg 13(3) makes it clear that any relevant factors may be taken into account in determining the level to which the claimant's rent should be reduced. The "relevant factors" listed in para (9)(b) may also be relevant here, as may other factors which exist in individual cases. The fact that the authority must consider all relevant factors when deciding whether to reduce the claimant's eligible rent and, if so, by how much, was confirmed in *R v Westminster CC HBRB ex p Mehanne* [1999] 2 All ER 319, CA. Although the cost of suitable accommodation elsewhere was "singled out for special mention and is thereby given the status of a mandatory consideration which carries the most weight", other factors could be taken into account. In particular, the pregnancy of the claimant's wife, his difficulty in obtaining other accommodation and the consequences of having to move from his present home were all matters relevant to the claimant's ability to pay his rent and so should have been considered by the Housing Benefit Review Board. *The House of Lords* [2001] 1 WLR 539 unanimously dismissed the authority's appeal. Lord Bingham and Lord Hope, who gave the two substantial speeches, both emphasised the generality of the language in the then para (2) (now para (3)) and the breadth of the discretion thereby conferred, along with the purpose of the HB Regs as being to prevent homelessness: see paras 13 and 24–26 at 546B–C, 548E–549E.

The First-tier Tribunal must consider the amount of the reduction to be made and give reasons for its decision or it will err in law: *CH 4970/2002* para 14.

Paragraph (4): Vulnerable families

Para (4) modifies the application of para (3) if there is a relevant person in the dwelling so as to forbid any reduction unless suitable cheaper alternative accommodation is available and the authority considers it reasonable to expect the claimant to move. A local authority should consider three questions.

Is there a relevant person? A person is a relevant person if s/he falls within any of the categories of people set out in para (10) and any of the following apply.

(1)   The person is at least the qualifying age for PC (defined in reg 2(1) HB Regs): sub-para (a).

(2)   The person is, or is treated as, incapable of work: sub-paras (b) and (c). These sub-paras will now have limited application. See the p1172 of the 31st edition of this work for a discussion.

(3)   The person has limited capability for work: sub-para (ca). The test is that which arises under the ESA regime within the meaning of s1(4) WRA 2007 – ie, the person's capability for work is limited by her/his physical or mental condition and the limitation is such that is is not reasonable to require her/him to work.

(4)   The person is treated as not having limited capability for work: sub-para (cb). This includes where there has been a failure to provide information or to attend a medical examination without good cause. See the Employment and Support Allowance Regulations 2008 SI No.794 and the Employment and Support Allowance Regulations 2013 SI No.379.

(5)   The person is responsible for a child or young person who is a member of the same household: sub-para (d). For whether a relevant person is responsible for a child or young person, see reg 20 of both the HB and the HB(SPC) Regs.

Is suitable alternative accommodation available? This is discussed in the Analysis to para (9)(a) on p1791.

Is it reasonable to expect the claimant to move? This question must be considered separately by the authority, and if the First-tier Tribunal fails to mention it in its decision, it will be presumed not to have applied its mind to it: *R v Sefton MBC ex p Cunningham* (1991) 23 HLR 534 at 538, QBD; *R v Allerdale DC HBRB ex p Doughty* [2000] COD 462, QRD. The question must be determined "taking into account the relevant factors". These are those set out in para (9)(b) and are the following.

(1)   The effect of a move on claimant's prospects of retaining her/his employment: sub-para (b)(i).

(2)   The effect of a move on the education of any child or young person referred to under (6) above. This factor appears only to be relevant if the move would force a change of school. In *R v Kensington and Chelsea RBC ex p Sheikh* [1997] unreported, 14 January, QBD a Housing Benefit Review Board came to the conclusion that even if the applicant was forced to move to the other side of London, travel arrangements could be made to enable the applicant's child to remain at her school. Latham J described this conclusion as "not very sensible" but decided that enough consideration had been given to the effect of a move on the child.

The factors to be taken into account

In *R v Kensington and Chelsea RBC ex p Carney* [1997] COD 124 at 125, QBD, Carnwath J decided that only the two factors in the then para (6)(b) (now para (9)(b)) were relevant. The medical evidence produced by the applicant in that case to the effect that a move would have a detrimental effect on her health could not therefore be relied upon. The same conclusion was reached by Buxton J in *R v Oadby and Wigston DC ex p Dickman* (1995) 28 HLR 807 at 817. He pointed to the fact that the then para (3) (now para (4)) referred to "the relevant factors" and suggested that the intention was to determine what was relevant and what was not relevant.

In *R v Camden LBC HBRB ex p W* [1999] 21 May, unreported, QBD (Turner J), a case concerning an HIV-positive claimant, the judge, referring to the old reg 11 HB Regs 1987, decided that "reasonableness as to the expectation that the applicant should move finds no place in the authority's determination, unless reg 11(6)(b) is satisfied". In support of the decisions in these cases, a contrast can usefully be made with Sch 3 para 13(5) Income Support (General) Regulations 1987, which is cast in substantially wider terms than para (9)(b).

The decision in *ex p W* was upheld by the Court of Appeal (1999) 32 HLR 879. The Court held that only the two factors set out in the then para (6)(b) of old reg 11 (now para (9)(b)) may be considered by the authority in deciding whether it is reasonable for the claimant to move.

"As both of those counsel [for the authority and the Secretary of State] submit, credible reasons why a claimant cannot move can properly be considered under other aspects of regulation 11. That, as it seems to me, is a powerful argument. In my judgment, [counsel for the authority and the Secretary of State] are right in relation to this issue of construction. The authority can only properly conclude that it is reasonable to expect the claimant to move if it has regard to relevant factors and not to irrelevant ones. Paragraph 11(6)(b) sets out what, for the purposes of paragraph 11(3) are 'the relevant factors'. The use of the definite article in both paragraphs is important. It makes it clear that all other factors are irrelevant .... the closely confined wording of regulation 11(3) can be contrasted with the more open wording of regulation 11(2) where the authority makes its decision 'having regard in particular to ....'. Clearly the draftsman was well able to qualify an obligation when he chose to do so, but in the subsequent paragraph he deliberately chose precise words."

This decision must be treated as authoritatively resolving the question of whether other factors besides those set out in para (9)(b) can be taken into account. However, it is suggested that it is highly arguable that these cases were wrongly decided on this point. The use of the words "taking into account" would certainly suggest that other factors may be relevant. Schiemann J expressed doubts about the correctness of the position set out in the previous paragraph in *R v Canterbury CC ex p Woodhouse* [1994] unreported, 2 August, QBD. Moreover, the decisions are arguably inconsistent with the decision of the Court of Appeal in *R v Westminster CC HBRB ex p Mehanne* [1999] 2 All ER 319, CA (see the Analysis to para (3)). The court's conclusion in *Mehanne* was that the words "having regard to" did not require only the factors set out in para (3) to be considered, merely that those factors were to be regarded as being particularly persuasive. There is, it is suggested, no difference between the wording used in the two sections. The fact that certain matters are to be considered to be relevant does not mean that other matters are necessarily irrelevant. In *R v Allerdale DC HBRB ex p Doughty* [2000] COD 462, QBD, Elias J gave powerful reasons why the analysis in *Carney* and *Dickman* should not be followed (paras 58 to 64). However, it appears that the decision of the Court of Appeal in *ex p W* was not cited and therefore his reasoning should not be adopted by authorities or tribunals, unless the House of Lords ever has occasion to pronounce on the matter.

However, there is comfort for claimants in the acknowledgment by the Court of Appeal, dealing with the old reg 11 in *ex p W*, that "credible reasons why a claimant cannot move can properly be considered under other aspects of regulation 11". It is suggested that the Court is referring to the question of whether the alternative accommodation identified by the council is in truth suitable. If the claimant cannot move, alternative accommodation cannot be suitable for him. The Court is thereby effectively approving the approach taken in *R v Westminster CC HBRB ex p Pallas* [1997] unreported, 23 September, QBD discussed in the Analysis to para (9)(a). If correct, this allows the interpretation of para (6)(b) (now para (9)(b)) propounded in *Carney*, *Dickman* and *ex p W* to be avoided.

Paragraphs (5) to (8): Delaying the restriction
These provisions allow for the effect of para (3) to be delayed in two circumstances.

(1)   Where any of the people to whom para (10) applies dies and the claimant occupies the same dwelling as s/he did before the relevant death: paras (5) and (6). No deduction can be made for 12 months from the date of death unless a deduction began before the death occurred.

(2)   Where the financial committments for the dwelling could be met by a person to whom para (10) applies when they were taken on: paras (7) and (8). No deduction can be made for the first 13 weeks of the award, provided the claimant was not entitled to HB in the 52 weeks before her/his current award.

Paragraph (9)(a): Suitable alternative accommodation
The phrase "suitable alternative accommodation" occurs at several places in the regulation. The wording used is not always consistent. The basic concepts that must be applied, however, remain the same throughout.

Para (9)(a) does not purport to provide an exclusive definition of "suitable alternative accommodation".

There is nothing that limits the factors relevant to whether the alternative accommodation is suitable. Para (9)(a) must be read against the background of a general, undefined requirement that the accommodation be suitable: *CH 3528/2006*.

Thus other factors may be taken into account, though if the factors mentioned give rise to a satisfactory result, the accommodation will *prima facie* be considered to be suitable: *R v Waltham Forest LBC ex p Holder* (1996) 29 HLR 71. In *R v Slough BC ex p Green* [1996] unreported, 15 November, QBD, Collins J referred to the phrase as "a composite phrase .... the Court in construing it must indeed give appropriate weight to each of the words that are used". The factors specifically mentioned in para (9)(a) relate mainly to the question of suitability. It is worth making the point, however, that the accommodation must be "alternative", that is accommodation other than the present accommodation: *R v East Devon DC HBRB ex p Gibson* (1993) 25 HLR, CA.

The question for consideration is whether alternative accommodation is suitable for the claimant. In *R v Canterbury CC ex p Woodhouse* [1994] unreported, 2 August, QBD, the applicants were a brother and sister who occupied a two-bedroom flat together. They had separate tenancy agreements under which both paid £299 a month rent. Both claimed HB to meet their rent. The only evidence of suitable alternative accommodation before the Housing Benefit Review Board was that of one two-bedroom flat for rent at £380 a month. The Board's approach was to treat the applicants as paying a combined rent of nearly £600, and reduced their HB entitlement accordingly. Schiemann J held that this approach was erroneous (transcript at 13A–14A) and that each claimant had to be viewed as an individual, despite their close relationship. However, he pointed out that in view of this conclusion, the authority would have been entitled to compare the rent paid with comparable one-bedroom flats.

R(H) 2/05 concludes that the wording of old reg 11(6)(a) (now reg 13(9)(a)), and particularly the use of the word "shall", means that the authority must actually take each of the relevant factors below into account in every case and is not entitled to assume that they are met unless the claimant specifically raises them. That is, the onus of proof rests with the local authority. However, he went on:

"In the case of a claimant who is elderly, for example, it may be sufficient for the authority to show that there is a supply of accommodation to rent designed or adapted for elderly residents, and in such a case it will not be necessary for the authority to identify any specific properties actually available for occupation by the claimant": para 18.

Relevant factors in deciding suitability. Bearing those general observations in mind, the factors in determining whether accommodation is suitable for the claimant include the following.

(1)   **"the nature of the alternative accommodation".** This would encompass matters that do not relate so much to the facilities available, but have more to do with whether it comprises a flat, maisonette or house, the arrangement of the rooms, and the standard of repair it is in. For example, if a claimant was unable to walk, accommodation containing one toilet accessible only up a flight of stairs could not be said to be suitable.

(2)   **"facilities provided"** having regard to the age and state of health of all the persons to whom para (10) applies. Sufficient detail must be provided by the local authority to enable it to be demonstrated that the facilities are broadly comparable. In *R v Lambeth LBC HBRB ex p Harrington* [1996] unreported 22 November, QBD, the Board's decision was quashed because the comparable bed and breakfast accommodation was only specified to have heating, furnishings and a lounge available, which was insufficient (transcript at 17B–18D). See also *Malcolm v Tweeddale District HBRB* [1994] SLT 1212, CS(OH). For the people to whom para (10) applies, see below.

(3)   **"security of tenure reasonably equivalent".** This is to be regarded as a particularly important factor. An assured shorthold tenancy is not to be regarded as "reasonably equivalent" to an assured tenancy: *R v Coventry CC ex p Waite* [1995] unreported, 7 October, QBD (transcript at 29B–G); *R v Kensington and Chelsea RBC ex p Pirie* [1997] unreported, 26 March, QBD (transcript at 4D–E). Nor should an assured

tenancy be viewed as being equivalent to a protected tenancy under the Rent Acts: the rent control is much less strict and the grounds for seeking possession less onerous. There is a conflict of authorities on whether public sector tenancies can be taken into account when the claimant is a private sector tenant. In *McLeod v HBRB for Banff and Buchan District HBRB* [1988] SLT 753, CS(OH), it was suggested that this was possible but Collins J dissented from this view in *Waite* at 30E–G. However, in *R(H) 2/05*, the commissioner rejected an argument that it is necessary for a local authority to show a mix of public and private sector tenancies in order to show an "active market" in houses of the appropriate type (para 15) in a case involving a private sector tenancy. Different durations of assured shorthold tenancies may be permissible: *R v Sefton MBC HBRB ex p Brennan* (1996) 29 HLR 735 at 741, QBD ("very difficult" to see how six- to 12-month tenancy equivalent to five-year tenancy, though decision not perverse); *R v Kensington and Chelsea RBC ex p Sheikh* [1997] unreported, 14 January, QBD (six-month tenancy equivalent to three-year tenancy). Latham J in the latter case said (transcript at 14F–15B) that the words "security of tenure" were concerned not with the length of the tenancy but with the claimant's rights to resist possession. Such a narrow construction seems at odds with the general wording of the paragraph.

(4)   **Size of the accommodation.** Consideration should be given to accommodation of the appropriate size for the claimant – eg, by reference to the size criteria in Sch 2 RO(HBF)(O) 1997. Note that this can apply even if the claimant's current accommodation is smaller: *Aylesbury Vale DC v ER(HB)* [2011] UKUT 160 (AAC). In *Sheikh*, a claimant had been living with a friend in a three-bedroom flat, and then moved to a two-bedroom property to relieve financial difficulties. It was held that in the circumstances, the local authority should have considered some three-bedroom flats in their comparison (transcript at 20A-22C). Some flexibility therefore needs to be shown.

(5)   **Area covered by the comparators.** In *R v Waltham Forest LBC ex p Holder* (1996) 29 HLR 71, it was said that the alternative accommodation had to be reasonably local. That does not mean, however, that it has to be within the same borough, at any rate in London: *Sheikh* (transcript at 15C–16B). GM A4.1172 states that alternative accommodation need not necessarily be "in the same immediate area as the current accommodation. You may, if you consider it appropriate, compare the current accommodation with the cost of similar accommodation outside your authority's area if that would be suitable for the claimant's needs. This might be appropriate when it is not possible to make valid comparisons with accommodation within your area. However, do not make comparisons with other parts of the country where accommodation costs differ widely from those which apply locally."

(6)   **The effect of a move on the claimant.** In *R v Westminster CC HBRB ex p Pallas* [1997] unreported, 23 September, QBD there was evidence before the Housing Benefit Review Board from the claimant's GP that moving house would cause grave risk to his health. The claimant suffered from chronic heart disease. George Bartlett QC, sitting as a deputy judge, held that "if there is evidence that moving to other accommodation would be likely to give rise to the risk of the claimant's death, that is a material consideration for the purposes of deciding whether suitable alternative accommodation exists".

One factor which the local authority may leave out of account is the fact that claimants will usually have taken on a liability for rent which, if their eligible rent is reduced, they will not be in a position to meet and that no other accommodation is therefore "available" or "suitable" for the claimant. That would deprive this regulation of any real effect: *Woodhouse* (transcript at 15E–G)

Evidence of comparable accommodation. It is for the authority to provide sufficient evidence to justify restricting the rent: *CH 3528/2006*. One of the most controversial issues is the type of evidence that has to be produced by the local authority relating to the alternative accommodation. It was argued that it was necessary to identify specific comparable properties. That was accepted, at least implicitly, in *Malcolm*. However, the argument was categorically rejected by the Court of Appeal in *R v East Devon DC HBRB ex p Gibson* (1993) 25 HLR, CA. Referring to the old reg 11, Lord Bingham MR stated at 494:

"It is not part of the local authority's function and no part of the Review Board's function to identify specific property available for a recipient's occupation . . . Neither the local authority nor the Review Board is an accommodation agency; neither of them can be expected to assume what would be an inappropriate role. A situation should never arise, therefore, where the local authority or the Review Board is in the position of saying: 'Number 3, Laburnum Avenue is the same size as the house you are now occupying, it is available for letting at a rent substantially below what you are now paying; why do you not move there?' That would, as I say, be an entirely inappropriate approach to this matter. Moreover, it must be borne in mind that details of payment of HB are confidential matters and it can therefore never be incumbent on local authorities to disclose the names or addresses of beneficiaries to whom the benefit is paid. It is, in my judgment, quite sufficient if an active market is shown to exist in houses of the appropriate type in an appropriate place at the level of rent to which rent is restricted. There must, however, be evidence at least of that in a case falling within paragraph 11(3); otherwise the recipient, if he had to move, would have nowhere to go. It is, however, sufficient, as I wish to stress, to point to a range of properties, or a block of property, which is available without specific identification of particular dwelling-houses."

In that case, the Housing Benefit Review Board's decision on suitable alternative accommodation was based on the monitoring of HB claims over the previous month (and showed that there had been 400 new or renewed claims, some of which related to the type of accommodation required by the claimants and their families) and on the fact that local "surgeries" had not revealed any general difficulty in obtaining rented accommodation. The claimants, on the other hand, presented detailed evidence of the searches they had actually made for somewhere cheaper to live and the reasons why those attempts had been unsuccessful. The Court was not prepared to say that there was no evidence on which the Board could have based its decision that the actual rent was unreasonably high by comparison with that payable for suitable alternative accommodation but remitted the decision to the Board because it had failed to supply adequate reasons as to why it had reached its conclusion and rejected the claimants' evidence.

The possible inconsistency between *Gibson* and *Malcolm* would require a Scottish court to consider whether it considered itself bound by *Gibson*, but there is no doubt as to the position in England and Wales. In *R v Sandwell MBC ex p Wilkinson* (1998) 31 HLR 22, QBD, an extremely bold submission was made that *Gibson*, a decision of the Court of Appeal, was wrongly decided. Unsurprisingly, Laws J held that he was bound to apply the decision in *Gibson*.

The English courts have followed and applied *Gibson* reasonably consistently. The practice has developed of local authorities providing comparables showing properties on the market around the relevant time. These need not actually be available when the claimant, hypothetically, is looking on the market. In *Brennan*, evidence of 16 properties coming onto the market over a seven-month period was held to be sufficient. Further, the First-tier Tribunal may be entitled to use its local knowledge to conclude that some of the properties on a list provided by the authority would be suitable for the claimant: *R v Kensington and Chelsea RBC ex p Abou-Jaoude* [1996] unreported, 10 May, QBD.

If local authorities choose to provide evidence based on claims made by other claimants, then any breach of the Data Protection Act 1998 in the provision of such information to the First-tier Tribunal does not render the evidence inadmissible: *CH 4970/2002* para 19.

Availability of the accommodation. The question of the extent to which the local authority must prove the availability of the alternative accommodation has also been a vexed one. A contrast needs to be drawn between paras (3) and (4). In para (3), there is no express requirement to show that the accommodation "is available". Evans LJ stated in *Gibson* at 501–2 that it was implicit in the wording "suitable alternative" that there had to be "some degree of availability". However, this part of his judgment was *obiter* and later decisions have consistently declined to read a requirement of availability into the legislation: *Malcolm; R v Ipswich BC ex p Flowers* [1994] unreported, 1 March, QBD (transcript at 14E–15E); *Waite* (transcript at 26B–28A). So under para (3), it is not necessary to exclude properties which are not, in practice, available to a claimant because s/he cannot afford to pay a deposit: *Holder; Green.*

In *Wilkinson* at 31, it was confirmed that the words "or otherwise" now in para (3)(b) cannot require the local authority to take the personal or other circumstances of the applicant into account. All that they meant was that the Rent Officer's decision was not determinative of whether the claimant's eligible rent should be restricted.

By contrast, under para (4) the authority must prove that the accommodation is available, and the availability or otherwise of properties for which a deposit is required may then be considered: *Holder* at 79; *R v Oadby and Wigston DC ex p Dickman* (1995) 28 HLR 807 at 816. In the latter case, Buxton J referred at 816 to "material about the difficulty of new tenants in obtaining properties and difficulties about deposits" being relevant. It was reiterated that the test was whether the applicant was in fact able to obtain such accommodation and not whether it was, as had been found by the Housing Benefit Review Board in that case, generally available. Buxton J explained the *Gibson* decision as being about the *evidence* required to prove availability, stating at 816:

"I quite accept that the starting point in realistic terms must be the availability of a pool or market of accommodation in general terms. It is then in accordance with the approach in *Gibson* for the applicant to put forward grounds which are unlikely to prove persuasive unless they are supported by evidence of some sort as to why that pool is either not available to her at all or only available in such a limited way or to such a limited extent that the Review Board feels that it cannot realistically say that suitable alternative accommodation is indeed available."

The First-tier Tribunal in considering whether suitable alternative accommodation "is available" must consider evidence that a claimant requires accommodation of the same type and with the same facilities. Where a vulnerable young single mother was staying in sheltered accommodation and there was evidence from her GP and from social services stating that she required the support that the accommodation provided, if the Housing Benefit Review Board rejected that evidence it had to state explicitly that it was doing so and give reasons for that rejection. As it had failed to do so, its decision was quashed: *R v East Devon DC HBRB ex p Preston* (1998) 31 HLR 936, QBD.

The old form of reg 11 was applied to the context of sheltered accommodation in two joined cases, *CH 1992/2002* and *CH 1993/2002*. The claimants were two men with learning disabilities who had been placed in accommodation adapted to their physical needs and which had room for a carer to sleep. The local authority restricted their rent on the ground that the "bricks and mortar" element of the rent was unreasonably high in relation to other suitable alternative accommodation. The commissioner emphasised that it was for the tribunal to decide the questions of fact on the evidence before it and that he was unable to overturn the decision: paras 25–26. In para 24, he concluded that the word "is" in the phrase "suitable alternative cheaper accommodation is available" now in para (4) did not require that the accommodation was available for occupation immediately, since the claimant's existing tenancy would first have to be terminated by notice. Thus alternative accommodation could be suitable if it was capable of being easily adapted. On the other hand, it would not be suitable if it could only be provided after a delay of 18 months while modifications were carried out.

Paragraphs (10) and (11)
The categories of people in para (10) are relevant for paras (4), (5) and (7). The first three categories are self explanatory. "Family" is defined in s137 SSCBA and "partner" is defined in reg 2(1) of both the HB and the HB(SPC) Regs. The fourth category is any relative of the claimant or her/his partner ("relative" is defined in reg 2(1) of both the HB and the HB(SPC) Regs) who occupies the same dwelling as the claimant without a separate right to do so, whether or not the relative "resides with" the claimant.

(3)   For the purposes of regulation 12(3) of both the Housing Benefit Regulations and the Housing Benefit (State Pension Credit) Regulations, as inserted by paragraph (1) above, regulation 13ZA of both those Regulations is as follows–

"Restrictions on rent increases
13ZA.–(1)   Subject to paragraph (2), where a claimant's eligible rent is increased during an award of housing benefit, the relevant authority shall, if it considers, whether by reference to a determination or re-determination made by a rent officer in exercise of a function conferred on him by an order under section 122 of the Housing Act 1996, or otherwise, either–
   (a)   that the increase is unreasonably high having regard in particular to the level of increases for suitable alternative accommodation, or
   (b)   in the case of an increase which takes place less than 12 months after the date of the previous increase, that the increase is unreasonable having regard to the length of time since that previous increase,
treat the eligible rent as reduced either by the full amount of the increase or, if it considers that a lesser increase was reasonable in all the circumstances, by the difference between the full amount of the increase and the increase that is reasonable having regard in particular to the level of increases for suitable alternative accommodation, and the claimant's maximum housing benefit shall be calculated by reference to the eligible rent as so reduced.
   (2)   No deduction shall be made under this regulation for a period of 12 months from the date of death of any person to whom paragraph (11) of regulation 13 (restrictions on unreasonable payments) applied or, had a claim been made, would have applied, if the dwelling which the claimant occupies is the same as that occupied by him at that date except where the deduction began before the death occurred.
   (3)   For the purposes of paragraph (2), a claimant shall be treated as occupying the dwelling if paragraph (13) of regulation 7 (circumstances in which a person is to be treated as occupying a dwelling) is satisfied and for that purpose sub-paragraph (b) of that paragraph shall be treated as if it were omitted."]

General Note
Reg 12 of the HB Regs 1987 was repealed by reg 3(3) Housing Benefit and Council Tax Benefit (General) Amendment Regulations 1997 SI No.852 as from 6 October 1997.

Before the repeal, reg 12 dealt with an authority's powers to restrict rent and applied to claimants who were already receiving HB and whose rent was increased while they were claiming. The reason for the repeal was that, given the introduction of the January 1996 changes to the old form of reg 11 HB Regs 1987 and the abolition, also on 6 October 1997, of the 50 per cent taper a change in contractual rent during the period when a rent officer's determination is in force has no effect on the level of HB actually payable. It was, therefore, no longer possible for landlords to abuse the scheme by imposing unreasonable rent increases.

This, however, is not the case where the January 1996 changes do not apply because the accommodation (or the claimant) is exempt (see para 4 on p1776). Reg 4(3) of SI 1997 No.852 preserved reg 12 as it stood immediately before 6 October 1997. This is now in reg 13ZA as set out in para 5(3).

Analysis
Para (1). A restriction must be applied if para (1) is applicable, unless any of the following paragraphs apply. The terms on which eligible rent may be restricted are two-fold.
(1)   Where the authority thinks the increase is "unreasonably high having regard in particular to the level of increases for suitable alternative accommodation": sub-para (a).
(2)   Where the increase is considered unreasonable because it is less than 12 months since the last increase: sub-para (b).
In so deciding, as mentioned above, the authority may take a rent officer's determination into account but does not have to do so, and if the authority always simply follows the rent officer's determinations it has wrongfully fettered its discretion.

In deciding whether an increase is reasonable, GM A4.1310 suggests that the authority take into account first the general level of rent increases locally for similar accommodation, and second any improvements made to the accommodation that might justify an increase even if the last increase had taken place less than 12 months before. This view can be criticised, however, in that the comparison under reg 13ZA(1)(a) is with the level of increase for *suitable alternative* accommodation, not similar accommodation in general. "Suitable alternative" is not defined here but arguably it has a similar meaning to the version of reg 13 in para 5(2) as it is part of the same "code" of restrictive measures.

BM v Cheshire West and Chester Council [2009] UKUT 162 (AAC) is the first decision to deal directly with how reg 12 HB Regs 1987 (now reg 13ZA as inserted by Sch 3 para 5(3)) should be interpreted. It concerns the rule as it was before benefit periods were abolished in April 2004, but nothing turns on this. The claimant lived in "exempt accommodation". When her rent was increased (by 81 per cent), the authority did not include the full increase in the weekly eligible rent but allowed an increase of 3.5 per cent only. The tribunal accepted the evidence that the weekly increase was unreasonably high, accepted the comparator evidence produced as evidence of suitable alternative accommodation with rent increases significantly lower than that of the claimant's accommodation and confirmed the decision to only allow an increase of 3.5 per cent.

As regards whether a rent increase was unreasonably high, Judge Williams considered whether the reasonableness of the level of an increase should be measured in terms of a percentage increase from the base rent, or in terms of a cash increase as it merges into the resulting rent. He took the view that the regulation must be interpreted as involving consideration of both aspects. It is not enough to consider the increase simply as a percentage increase from the base rent (the rent before the increase is applied, taken in isolation from any other information). It must also be considered as a cash sum and compared for reasonableness to the equivalent weekly or other rents payable, after the increase, in comparator accommodation. This was because the power in reg 12 was a power to control individual rent increases given to local authorities and, on appeal, to local tribunals. It is a power to stop individual abusive claims. It is not a power to set a national guide figure for rent increases, such as that given to the former Housing Corporation. The judge felt this interpretation was supported by the consideration that this is an exception to the general rule that rent increases are eligible for HB. He said:

"The effect of a regulation 12 decision is to face a tenant or licensee with a shortfall in benefit as compared with rent. It is taking away resources from those who already have limited resources. Such a power is not to be interpreted too liberally."

In his view, it therefore followed that the identification of what is reasonable by reference to what is "suitable alternative accommodation" must have in mind not only the increases applied in those comparators but also the base rents from which those increases are applied and the resulting rents after they are applied in those comparators.

Prior to the decision in *BM v Cheshire West and Chester Council, CH 2214/2003* was the only decision that approached the topic. *CH 2214/2003* emphasised that it is the *increase* in rent, rather than the level of the total rent itself, with which this regulation is concerned, and holds that any decision on this issue will need to be based on adequate evidence as to the level of increases in rents for suitable alternative accommodation. On the facts, it was decided that an increase in rent from £10,920 to £15,600 a year was not unreasonably high in London where there had been no previous rent increase for three years. The decision further holds that the level of increases for suitable alternative accommodation is not the only factor which can be taken into account (because of the words "in particular"), and that other factors which may be relevant are:

(1)   Whether the claimant would have to move if the increase were not met.
(2)   The quality of the accommodation.
(3)   The effect on the claimant of having to move.
(4)   The length of time the claimant has lived in the accommodation.
(5)   The age, state of health and social mobility of the claimant.
(6)   The effects on job prospects of having to move.
(7)   The effect on other members of the household of having to move.

In *BM v Cheshire West and Chester Council*, Judge Williams' view was that *CH 2214/2003* was an "own facts" decision – ie, it would be an error to apply it generally. However, he did not agree that the factors listed, could be identified as irrelevant as a matter of law. He also concluded that the tribunal had erred in law when it said that the security of tenure of properties is not a relevant issue and did not consider the point.

If it is considered that either paragraph of reg 13ZA is satisfied, the authority must treat either the whole or part of the increase as "ineligible". However, Judge Williams stressed that if the authority or the First-tier Tribunal considers that a lesser increase is "reasonable in all the circumstances" it must identify the lesser increase and reduce the allowable increase to that amount. The levels of increase at identified suitable alternative accommodation have importance here. The authority or tribunal must consider, judged by the comparators it has already considered, what rent increase is reasonable, and any judicial decision must state why. This poses a difficult issue for the tribunal; what is required is for a local authority, and on appeal the First-tier Tribunal, to take its own view not only about whether a particular rent increase is unreasonable but also on the considerably more difficult and judgmental question of *what* rent increase is reasonable.

Paras (2) and (3) provide the same restrictions on an authority's powers under this regulation as found in reg 13(5) and (6) as set out in para 5(2) (see p1784).

Persons from abroad

6.–(1)   Where, immediately before the coming into force of the Consolidating Regulations, a person is entitled to council tax benefit or, as the case may be, housing benefit, by virtue of regulation 12(1) of the Social Security (Persons From Abroad) Miscellaneous Amendments Regulations 1996 ("the 1996 Regulations"), the modifications specified in relation to council tax benefit in paragraph (2) or, as the case may be, in relation to housing benefit in paragraph (3), shall continue to have effect both as regards that person and as regards persons who are members of his family on 5th February 1996.

(2)   The modifications specified in this paragraph are that for regulation 7 of both the Council Tax Benefit Regulations and the Council Tax Benefit (State Pension Credit) Regulations there shall be substituted–

"Persons from abroad

7. –(1)   A person from abroad is a person of a prescribed class for the purposes of section 131(3)(b) of the Act.

(2)   In paragraph (1) a "person from abroad" means a person other than a person to whom paragraph (3) or (6) applies, who has limited leave (as defined in section 33(1) of the 1971 Act) to enter or remain in the United Kingdom which was given in accordance with any provision in the immigration rules (as defined in that section) relating to–

(a)   there being, or to there needing to be, no recourse to public funds, or

(b)   there being no charge on public funds,

during that limited leave.

(3)   Subject to paragraph (7) this paragraph applies to a person who–

(a)   is a national of a European Economic Area State, a state which is a signatory to the European Convention on Social and Medical Assistance (done in Paris on 11th December 1953), a state which is a signatory to the Council of Europe Social Charter (signed in Turin on 18th October 1961), the Channel Islands or the Isle of Man; or

(b)   having, during any one period of limited leave (including any such period as extended), supported himself without recourse to public funds other than any such recourse by reason of the previous application of this sub-paragraph, is temporarily without funds during that period of leave because remittances to him from abroad have been disrupted, provided that there is a reasonable expectation that his supply of funds will be resumed.

(4)   In paragraph (1) "person from abroad" also means any person other than a person to whom paragraph (6) applies who–

(a)   having a limited leave (as defined in section 33(1) of the 1971 Act) to enter or remain in the United Kingdom, has remained without further leave under that Act beyond the time limited by the leave; or

(b)   is the subject of a deportation order being an order under section 5(1) of the 1971 Act (deportation) requiring him to leave and prohibiting him from entering the United Kingdom except where his removal from the United Kingdom has been deferred in writing by the Secretary of State; or

(c)   is adjudged by the immigration authorities to be an illegal entrant (as defined in section 33(1) of the 1971 Act) who has not subsequently been given leave under that Act to enter or remain in the United Kingdom except a person who has been allowed to remain in the United Kingdom with the consent in writing of the Secretary of State; or

(d)   is a national of a European Economic Area State and is required by the Secretary of State to leave the United Kingdom; or

(e)   is not habitually resident in the United Kingdom, the Republic of Ireland, the Channel Islands or the Isle of Man, but for this purpose no person shall be treated as not habitually resident in the United Kingdom who is–

(i)   a worker for the purposes of Council Regulation (EEC) No. 1612/68 or (EEC) No. 1251/70 or a person with a right to reside in the United Kingdom pursuant to Council Directive No. 68/360/EEC or No. 73/148/EEC; or

(ii)   a refugee within the definition in Article 1 of the Convention relating to the Status of Refugees done at Geneva on 28th July 1951, as extended by Article 1(2) of the Protocol relating to the Status of Refugees done at New York on 31st January 1967; or

(iii)   a person who has been granted exceptional leave to remain in the United Kingdom by the Secretary of State; or

(iv)   person to whom paragraph (5) applies; or

(v)   the subject of a deportation order, being an order under section 5(1) of the 1971 Act (deportation) requiring him to leave and prohibiting him from entering the United Kingdom, and whose removal from the United Kingdom has been deferred in writing by the Secretary of State; or

(vi)   adjudged by the immigration authorities to be an illegal entrant (as defined in section 33(1) of the 1971 Act), has not subsequently been given leave under that Act to enter or remain in the United Kingdom but has been allowed to remain in the United Kingdom with the consent in writing of the Secretary of State.

(5)   Subject to paragraph (7) this paragraph applies to a person who, having, during any one period of limited leave (including any such period as extended), supported himself without recourse to public funds other than any such recourse by reason of the previous application of this sub-paragraph, is temporarily without funds during that period of leave because remittances to him from abroad have been disrupted, provided that there is a reasonable expectation that his supply of funds will be resumed.

(6) This paragraph applies to a person who–
(a) is an asylum seeker, and for this purpose a person–
  (i) becomes an asylum seeker when he has submitted a claim for asylum to the Secretary of State that it would be contrary to the United Kingdom's obligations under the Convention relating to the Status of Refugees done at Geneva on 28th July 1951, and the protocol to that convention, for him to be removed from, or required to leave, the United Kingdom and that claim is recorded by the Secretary of State as having been made; and
  (ii) ceases to be an asylum seeker when his claim is recorded by the Secretary of State as having been finally determined or abandoned; or
(b) is awaiting the outcome of an appeal under Part 2 of the 1971 Act (including any period for which the appeal is treated as pending under section 33(4) of that Act); or
(c) has no or no further right of appeal under the 1971 Act but has been allowed to remain in the United Kingdom while an application so to remain is, or representations on his behalf are, being considered by the Secretary of State; or
(d) except where he is a person to whom paragraph (4)(b) applies, has been granted permission to remain in the United Kingdom pending the removal from the United Kingdom of a person who is the subject of a deportation order but whose deportation has been deferred in writing by the Secretary of State; or
(e) is subject to a direction for his removal from the United Kingdom but whose removal has been deferred in writing by the Secretary of State; or
(f) is in receipt of income support.
(7) Paragraphs (3)(b) and (5) shall not apply to a person who has been temporarily without funds for any period, or the aggregate of any periods, exceeding 42 days during any one period of limited leave (including any such period as extended).
(8) In this regulation–
"the 1971 Act" means the Immigration Act 1971; and
a "European Economic Area State" means a Member State, or Norway, Sweden, Iceland, Austria or Finland..".

(3) The modifications specified in this paragraph are that for regulation 10 of both the Housing Benefit Regulations and the Housing Benefit (State Pension Credit) Regulations, there shall be substituted–

"Persons from abroad
10.–(1) A person from abroad who is liable to make payments in respect of a dwelling shall be treated as if he were not so liable.
(2) In paragraph (1) a "person from abroad" means a person, other than a person to whom paragraph (3) or (6) applies, who has limited leave (as defined in section 33(1) of the 1971 Act) to enter or remain in the United Kingdom which was given in accordance with any provision in the immigration rules (as defined in that section) relating to–
(a) there being, or to there needing to be, no recourse to public funds, or
(b) there being no charge on public funds,
during that limited leave.
(3) Subject to paragraph (7) this paragraph applies to a person who–
(a) is a national of a European Economic Area State, a state which is a signatory to the European Convention on Social and Medical Assistance (done in Paris on 11th December 1953), a state which is a signatory to the Council of Europe Social Charter (signed in Turin on 18th October 1961), the Channel Islands or the Isle of Man; or
(b) having, during any one period of limited leave (including any such period as extended), supported himself without recourse to public funds other than any such recourse by reason of the previous application of this sub-paragraph, is temporarily without funds during that period of leave because remittances to him from abroad have been disrupted, provided that there is a reasonable expectation that his supply of funds will be resumed.
(4) In paragraph (1) "person from abroad" also means any person other than a person to whom paragraph (6) applies who–
(a) having a limited leave (as defined in section 33(1) of the 1971 Act) to enter or remain in the United Kingdom, has remained without further leave under that Act beyond the time limited by the leave; or
(b) is the subject of a deportation order being an order under section 5(1) of the 1971 Act (deportation) requiring him to leave and prohibiting him from entering the United Kingdom except where his removal from the United Kingdom has been deferred in writing by the Secretary of State; or
(c) is adjudged by the immigration authorities to be an illegal entrant (as defined in section 33(1) of the 1971 Act) who has not subsequently been given leave under that Act to enter or remain in the United Kingdom except a person who has been allowed to remain in the United Kingdom with the consent in writing of the Secretary of State.
(d) is a national of a European Economic Area State and is required by the Secretary of State to leave the United Kingdom; or
(e) is not habitually resident in the United Kingdom, the Republic of Ireland, the Channel Islands or the Isle of Man, but for this purpose no person shall be treated as not habitually resident in the United Kingdom who is–

      (i)   a worker for the purposes of Council Regulation (EEC) No. 1612/68 or (EEC) No. 1251/70 or a person with a right to reside in the United Kingdom pursuant to Council Directive No. 68/360/EEC or No. 73/148/EEC; or

      (ii)   a refugee within the definition in Article 1 of the Convention relating to the Status of Refugees done at Geneva on 28th July 1951, as extended by Article 1(2) of the Protocol relating to the Status of Refugees done at New York on 31st January 1967; or

      (iii) a person who has been granted exceptional leave to remain in the United Kingdom by the Secretary of State; or

      (iv) a person to whom paragraph (5) applies; or

      (v)   the subject of a deportation order, being an order under section 5(1) of the 1971 Act (deportation) requiring him to leave and prohibiting him from entering the United Kingdom, and whose removal from the United Kingdom has been deferred in writing by the Secretary of State; or

      (vi) adjudged by the immigration authorities to be an illegal entrant (as defined in section 33(1) of the 1971 Act), has not subsequently been given leave under that Act to enter or remain in the United Kingdom but has been allowed to remain in the United Kingdom with the consent in writing of the Secretary of State.

    (5)   Subject to paragraph (7) this paragraph applies to a person who, having, during any one period of limited leave (including any such period as extended), supported himself without recourse to public funds other than any such recourse by reason of the previous application of this sub-paragraph, is temporarily without funds during that period of leave because remittances to him from abroad have been disrupted, provided that there is a reasonable expectation that his supply of funds will be resumed.

    (6)   This paragraph applies to a person who–

    (a)   is an asylum seeker, and for this purpose a person–

      (i)   becomes an asylum seeker when he has submitted a claim for asylum to the Secretary of State that it would be contrary to the United Kingdom's obligations under the Convention relating to the Status of Refugees done at Geneva on 28th July 1951, and the protocol to that convention, for him to be removed from, or required to leave, the United Kingdom and that claim is recorded by the Secretary of State as having been made; and

      (ii)   ceases to be an asylum seeker when his claim is recorded by the Secretary of State as having been finally determined or abandoned; or

    (b)   is awaiting the outcome of an appeal under Part 2 of the 1971 Act (including any period for which the appeal is treated as pending under section 33(4) of that Act); or

    (c)   has no or no further right of appeal under the 1971 Act but has been allowed to remain in the United Kingdom while an application so to remain is, or representations on his behalf are, being considered by the Secretary of State; or

    (d)   except where he is a person to whom paragraph (4)(b) applies, has been granted permission to remain in the United Kingdom pending the removal from the United Kingdom of a person who is the subject of a deportation order but whose deportation has been deferred in writing by the Secretary of State; or

    (e)   is subject to a direction for his removal from the United Kingdom but whose removal has been deferred in writing by the Secretary of State; or

    (f)   is in receipt of income support.

    (7)   Paragraphs (3)(b) and (5) shall not apply to a person who has been temporarily without funds for any period, or the aggregate of any periods, exceeding 42 days during any one period of limited leave (including any such period as extended).

    (8)   In this regulation–

"the 1971 Act" means the Immigration Act 1971;

a "European Economic Area State" means a Member State or Norway, Sweden, Iceland, Austria or Finland..".

    (4)   Where, immediately before the coming into force of the Consolidating Regulations, a person is entitled to council tax benefit or, as the case may be, housing benefit, by virtue of regulation 12(2) of the Social Security (Persons From Abroad) Miscellaneous Amendments Regulations 1996–

    (a)   the Council Tax Benefit Regulations shall have effect in relation to him subject to the modifications set out in paragraph (2);

    (b)   the Housing Benefit Regulations shall have effect in relation to him subject to the modifications set out in paragraph (3).

    (5)   Sub-paragraph (6) applies where a person–

    (a)   is entitled to a specified benefit in respect of a period which includes 30th April 2004;

    (b)   claims a specified benefit on or after 1st May 2004 and it is subsequently determined that he is entitled to that benefit in respect of a period which includes 30th April 2004;

    (c)   claims a specified benefit on or after 1st May 2004 and it is subsequently determined that he is entitled to such a benefit in respect of a period which is continuous with a period of entitlement to the same or another specified benefit which includes 30th April 2004;

    (d)   claims jobseeker's allowance on or after 1st May 2004 and it is subsequently determined that he is entitled to jobseeker's allowance in respect of a period of entitlement to that benefit which is linked to a previous period of entitlement which includes 30th April 2004 by virtue of regulations made under paragraph 3 of Schedule 1 to the Jobseekers Act 1995.

(6) Where this sub-paragraph applies–

(a) the Council Tax Benefit Regulations and the Council Tax Benefit (State Pension Credit) Regulations shall both have effect as if in regulation 7 (persons from abroad)–

    (i) in paragraph (2)(a) the words "or a person who is an accession State worker requiring registration who is treated as a worker for the purpose of the definition of "qualified person" in regulation 5(1) of the Immigration (European Economic Area) Regulations 2000 pursuant to regulation 5 of the Accession (Immigration and Worker Registration) Regulations 2004" were omitted; and

    (ii) paragraph (3) were omitted.

(b) the Housing Benefit Regulations and the Housing Benefit (State Pension Credit) Regulations shall both have effect as if in regulation 10 (persons from abroad)–

    (i) in paragraph (2)(a) the words "or a person who is an accession State worker requiring registration who is treated (i) as a worker for the purpose of the definition of "qualified person" in regulation 5(1) of the Immigration (European Economic Area) Regulations 2000 pursuant to regulation 5 of the Accession (Immigration and Worker Registration) Regulations 2004" were omitted; and

    (ii) paragraph (3) were omitted.

(7) The provisions saved by sub paragraph (6) shall continue to have effect until the date on which entitlement to a specified benefit for the purposes of sub-paragraph (5) ceases, and if there is more than one such specified benefit, until the last date on which such entitlement ceases.

(8) In sub-paragraphs (5) and (7), "specified benefit" means income support, housing benefit, council tax benefit, jobseeker's allowance and state pension credit.

(9) In regulation 12 of the 1996 Regulations–

(a) in paragraph (1), for the words "those provisions" to the end of the paragraph, substitute "the provisions of the Income Support Regulations as then in force shall continue to have effect as if regulation 8(2) and (3)(c) of these Regulations had not been made"; and

(b) in paragraph (2), for the words "those Regulations as then in force" to the end of the paragraph, substitute "the Income Support Regulations as then in force shall have effect as if regulation 8 of these Regulations had not been made".

(10) For the purposes of–

(a) regulation 10(1) of the Housing Benefit Regulations;

(b) regulation 10(1) of the Housing Benefit (State Pension Credit) Regulations;

(c) regulation 7(1) of the Council Tax Benefit Regulations; and

(d) regulation 7(1) of the Council Tax Benefit (State Pension Credit) Regulations,

a person who is an asylum seeker within the meaning of sub-paragraph (11) who has not ceased to be an asylum seeker by virtue of sub-paragraph (12), is not a person from abroad within the meaning of paragraph (1) of those regulations.

(11) An asylum seeker within the meaning of this paragraph is a person who–

(a) submits on his arrival (other than on his re-entry) in the United Kingdom from a country outside the Common Travel Area a claim for asylum on or before 2nd April 2000 to the Secretary of State that it would be contrary to the United Kingdom's obligations under the Convention for him to be removed or required to leave, the United Kingdom and that claim is recorded by the Secretary of State as having been made before that date; or

(b) on or before 2nd April 2000 becomes, while present in Great Britain, an asylum seeker when–

    (i) the Secretary of State makes a declaration to the effect that the country of which he is a national is subject to such a fundamental change of circumstances that he would not normally order the return of a person to that country; and

    (ii) he submits, within a period of three months from the date that declaration was made, a claim for asylum to the Secretary of State under the Convention relating to the Status of Refugees; and

    (iii) his claim for asylum under that Convention is recorded by the Secretary of State has having been made.

(12) A person ceases to be an asylum seeker for the purposes of this paragraph when his claim for asylum is recorded by the Secretary of State as having been decided (other than on appeal) or abandoned.

(13) In paragraph (11) "the Common Travel Area" means the United Kingdom, the Channel Islands, the Isle of Man and the Republic of Ireland collectively and "the Convention" means the Convention relating to the Status of Refugees done at Geneva on 28th July 1951 as extended by Article 2(1) of the Protocol relating to the Status of Refugees done at New York on 31st January 1967.

General Note

Paras (1)–(4). The Social Security (Persons from Abroad) Miscellaneous Amendments Regulations 1996 SI No.30 provided a savings provision for entitlement to HB and CTB by some asylum seekers. The modifications to the HB and HB(SPC) Regs to effect this are now in para 6(1)–(4).

Paras (5)–(8). The Social Security (Habitual Residence) Amendment Regulations 2004 SI No.1232 provided a savings provision for those entitled to HB and CTB when the "right to reside" test was introduced from 1 May

2004. The modifications of the HB and HB(SPC) Regs to effect this are now in para 6(5)–(7). See the commentary on p1771.

The amendments made by SI 2006 No.1026 to the HB Regs, HB(SPC) Regs, CTB Regs and CTB(SPC) Regs do not affect the continued operation of the transitional and savings provisions in reg 12 Social Security (Persons From Abroad) Miscellaneous Amendments Regulations 1996 (for which see p1633 of the 26th edition), reg 6 Social Security (Habitual Residence) Amendment Regulations 2004 (on p1771) or para 6 Sch 3 HB&CTB(CP) Regs. See reg 11 of SI 2006 No.102 on p1807.

Analysis
Paragraphs (10) to (13): Introduction
These prevent certain asylum seekers either from falling foul of reg 10 of either the HB or the HB(SPC) Regs (or until 1 April 2013 reg 7 of either the CTB or CTB(SPC) Regs) by being a person from abroad and also, by virtue of reg 2(4) Social Security (Immigration and Asylum) Consequential Amendments Regulations 2000 SI No.636, from exclusion from HB under s115 of the 1999 Act. In summary, they are those who claimed asylum on or before 2 April 2000, and either claimed asylum "on...arrival" in the UK or who were present in the UK and claimed asylum within three months of an "upheaval declaration" having been made in relation to the country of her/his nationality.

The notes below discuss these two categories of asylum seeker in more detail and then go on to outline how a person loses her/his status as a relevant asylum seeker.
Paragraphs (11)(a) and (13): Those who claimed asylum "on … arrival"
"On his arrival". For the (now almost moribund) debate on whether these three words mean claiming asylum on the very moment of a person arriving in the UK (ie, before s/he passes immigration control), see pp1073–75 of the 19th edition.

A definitive answer to this debate has been given in *Kola and Another v SSWP* [2007] 28 November, UKHL 54; reported as *R(IS) 1/08*. The House of Lords decided that an asylum seeker could have submitted her/his asylum claim "on arrival" even if s/he did not submit the claim to an immigration officer on duty at the port of entry. It held that the provision is ambiguous as to what is meant by "on arrival" and that the Secretary of State's very narrow interpretation of it would produce obvious unfairness in many cases. Lord Brown of Eaton-Under-Haywood said: "If the asylum seeker could not reasonably have been expected to claim asylum any earlier than he did, having regard both to his practical opportunity for doing so and to his state of mind at the time, including the effect on him of anything said by his facilitating agent, then I see no good reason why his claim should not properly be accepted as one made 'on his arrival'."

"other than on his re-entry". This is presumably intended to prevent a person present in the UK who wants to claim asylum but who wishes to avoid being found to be a person from abroad from simply leaving the UK and re-entering to claim asylum "on his arrival". It is suggested that it does not mean that a person cannot come within the exception if s/he has visited the UK before. It only makes sense if it is read as meaning "re-entry during the same period of limited leave". That prevents the possible evasion of the "on his arrival" requirement while ensuring that a person who has visited the UK 20 years previously is not prevented from fulfilling the criterion.

"in the United Kingdom from a country outside the Common Travel Area". The common travel area (CTA) is the UK, Channel Islands, Isle of Man and the Republic of Ireland: para (13). The phrase does not prevent the claimant from having been in another part of the CTA before arrival in the UK. If that were so, an asylum seeker from Colombia who landed in Ireland before claiming asylum in the UK could not fulfil the "on his arrival" criterion. It is suggested that a period of travel through another part of the CTA must be ignored.

"a claim for asylum". There is no set procedure for making a claim for asylum under the Immigration Rules, save that para 328 provides that an application made at a port or airport will be referred to the Secretary of State by the immigration officer. In particular, it does not need to be done in writing and it is probable that most applications are made orally. In *CIS 1137/1997*, the claimant asserted that he had tried to speak to an official at the airport and a policeman but had been unable to communicate with them. The fact that the commissioner remitted the case for further consideration of these points (para 9) suggests that such attempts could amount to a claim for asylum. Note also *CIS 4341/1998*.

"and that claim is recorded by the Secretary of State as having been made before that date". In order for the claimant to fall within the scope of para (11)(a), or indeed para (6)(b), the claim for asylum must not merely have been made but must have been recorded by the Secretary of State prior to 3 April 2000. The date on the claimant's Standard Acknowledgment Letter will be the best available evidence of this.
Paragraph (11)(b): Asylum seekers claiming after declarations
In conditions of extreme turmoil in a state, the Home Secretary may make a declaration that there will normally be no return of people to that country. These vary according to the conditions of the moment and last for three months at a time.

Any national of such a state making a claim for asylum from within the UK within three months of the declaration falls within this category of asylum seekers. It only applies to nationals of that state and not to those of other states: *R v Secretary of State for Social Security ex p Grant* [1997] unreported, 31 July, QBD.

The relevant claimants are nationals of the former Zaire who claimed asylum between 16 May–16 August 1997 and those from Sierra Leone who claimed between 1 January–1 October 1997.

Paragraph (12): Loss of asylum seeker status

By para (12), a person ceases to be an asylum seeker on the date on which her/his claim is "recorded as determined" by the Secretary of State. The question then arises as to when a claim is "recorded as determined". In *R (Anufrijeva) v SSHD* [2003] 3 WLR 353, HL, the House of Lords ruled that it was contrary to fundamental constitutional principles for an uncommunicated administrative decision to affect the rights of a person to whom that decision related. Accordingly, the claimant did not lose her entitlement to IS until the refusal of her asylum claim was communicated to her. The same will apply to HB entitlement.

Frequency of payment of rent allowance

7.–(1)   The regulations specified in sub-paragraphs (3) to (5) shall apply in accordance with the amendments so specified where the claimant–

(a)   was entitled to and in receipt of housing benefit on account of his liability to make payments in respect of a dwelling, which he occupied or was treated as occupying as his home, on 06 October 1996;

(b)   regulation 11 of the Housing Benefit (General) Amendment Regulations 1996 applied in the case of payments made to the claimant immediately before the consolidating Regulations came into force; and

(c)   continues to be entitled to and in receipt of housing benefit on account of such occupation of that dwelling.

(2)   In this regulation, "claimant" includes the deceased partner of a claimant in any case where a claim is made by the surviving partner within 4 weeks of the death, provided that this regulation or regulation 11 of the Housing Benefit (General) Amendment Regulations 1996 applied to that deceased on the day of his death.

(3)   Regulation 91 of the Housing Benefit Regulations shall have effect as if, in paragraph (3), for the words "Subject to regulations 92 to 97 (frequency of payment of and payment on account of rent allowance, payment provisions)," there are substituted the words "Subject to regulations 93 to 97 (payment on account of rent allowance, payment provisions)".

(4)   Regulation 72 of the Housing Benefit (State Pension Credit) Regulations shall have effect as if, in paragraph (3), for the words "Subject to regulations 73 to 78 (frequency of payment of and payment on account of rent allowance, payment provisions)," there are substituted the words "Subject to regulations 74 to 78 (payment on account of rent allowance, payment provisions)".

(5)   Regulation 92 of the Housing Benefit Regulations and regulation 73 of the Housing Benefit (State Pension Credit) Regulations (frequency of payment of a rent allowance) shall both have effect as if–

(a)   for paragraph (2), there is substituted–

"(2)   A payment of a rent allowance in accordance with paragraph (1) shall be made insofar as it is practicable to do so, 2 weeks before the end of the period in respect of which it is made unless the liability to pay rent of the person entitled is in respect of a past period, in which case payment of the rent allowance may be made at the end of that period.";

(b)   paragraphs (3) and (4) are omitted;

(c)   in paragraphs (5) and (6), the words "Except in a case to which paragraph (3) applies," are omitted; and

(d)   in paragraph (7) the words "Subject to paragraphs (2), (3) and (5)," are omitted.

General Note

The effect of this saving provision, formerly found in reg 11 Housing Benefit (General) Amendment Regulations 1996 SI No.965, is that the rules for payment of HB in the form of a rent allowance in arrears (either payment to the claimant or direct to the landlord – see, for example, reg 92(2) HB Regs) do not apply to claimants who were entitled to and in receipt of HB in respect of dwellings which they occupied on 6 October 1996, and who continue to be entitled to and in receipt of HB for the same dwelling. New claimants are also protected if they were the partner of a former claimant who would have been entitled to the protection of the savings rule but who has died. Such new claimants must claim HB in their own name within four weeks from the date of death: sub-para (2).

If para 7 applies, HB in the form of a rent allowance is paid, if practicable, two weeks before the end of period in respect of which it is made. So payments for two weeks are made in advance and payments for four weeks or a month, mid-way through the period: reg 92(2) HB Regs and reg 73(2) HB(SPC) Regs as substituted by sub-para (5)(a).

A dispute has arisen in at least one authority as to the meaning of "in receipt of" in reg 11(1)(a) of SI 1996 No.965 (now in para 7(1)(a)). The circumstances were that a number of former council tenants had their homes transferred into the ownership of a registered social landlord, which was then paid the HB entitlements of those tenants direct. The social landlord argued that the transitional protection continued to apply to claimants who had been in continuous receipt of HB since 1996. It is suggested that the wording "in receipt of" is loose enough to include a claimant whose HB is paid direct to her/his landlord, since it cannot have been intended that the mode of payment should make a difference. The words "in receipt of" are used in a number of other contexts in the HB Regs where the mode of payment cannot have been intended to affect their applicability: see, for example, the definition of "prospective occupier" in reg 14(8) HB Regs as well as reg 50(2) HB Regs. The matter may, however, be open to argument.

[¹ **Local reference rent taper**

8.–(1)   Regulation 13 of both the Housing Benefit Regulations and the Housing Benefit (State Pension Credit) Regulations (maximum rent) shall have effect in the case of a claimant to whom any of sub-paragraphs (3) to (6) applies subject to the amendment specified in sub-paragraph (2).

(2)   In paragraph (3) of regulation 13 at the end, add "plus 50 per cent. of the amount by which the claim related rent exceeds the local reference rent."

(3)   This sub-paragraph applies to a claimant who has been continuously entitled to and in receipt of housing benefit–

(a)   in respect of the same dwelling for a period which includes 5th October 1997; and

(b)   which included an addition by virtue of paragraph (3) or (4) of regulation 11 of the 1987 Regulations as they had effect on 5th October 1997.

(4)   Sub-paragraph (3) above shall continue to have effect in the case of a person who has ceased to be a welfare to work beneficiary or whose partner has ceased to be such a beneficiary where the person is entitled to housing benefit at the end of the 52 week period to which sub-paragraph (5) refers.

(5)   This sub-paragraph applies in the case of a person–

(a)   who was entitled to housing benefit in respect of the dwelling he occupied as his home on or before 5th October 1997;

(b)   whose entitlement to housing benefit in respect of that dwelling was continuous from that date until it ceased because either the person or his partner became a welfare to work beneficiary;

(c)   who on the day before entitlement to housing benefit ceased, was in receipt of an addition to benefit by virtue of paragraph (4) or (5) of regulation 11 of the 1987 Regulations as they had effect on 5th October 1997; and

(d)   who subsequently becomes re-entitled to housing benefit in respect of that dwelling within 52 weeks of him or his partner becoming a welfare to work beneficiary.

(6)   In this paragraph, "welfare to work beneficiary" means a person to whom regulation 13A(1) of the Social Security (Incapacity for Work) (General) Regulations 1995 applies.]

Amendment

1.   Substituted by reg 6(3) of SI 2007 No 2870 as from 7.4.08 (or if reg 1(3) of that SI applies, on the day on or after 7.4.08 when the first of the events specified in reg 1(4) applies, or from 6.4.09 if none have before that date).

Modifications

Para 8 substituted by reg 6(3) Housing Benefit (Local Housing Allowance, Miscellaneous and Consequential) Amendment Regulations 2007 SI No.2870 as from 7 April 2008, save that for a person to whom reg 1(3) of those regulations applied (see p1816), the amendments came into force on the day on or after 7 April 2008 when the first of the events specified in reg 1(4) applied to her/him, or on 6 April 2009 if none had before that date.

General Note

Para 8 preserves a 50 per cent taper (see p383) for specified claimants whose maximum rent is calculated under the "local reference rent" scheme for which see regs 13 and 14 of the HB Regs and the HB(SPC) Regs.

Analysis

Sub-paras (1) and (2) provide an amended version of reg 13 of both the HB Regs and the HB(SPC) Regs where any of sub-paras (3) to (6) apply.

Sub-para (3) provides transitional protection to a claimant if s/he was actually benefiting from a 50 per cent taper on 5 October 1997 and has been continuously entitled to, and in receipt of, HB in respect of the same dwelling since then. The transitional protection continues until the claimant ceases to be entitled to HB or moves home. It would seem that even a single day's non-entitlement to HB is sufficient to bring the protection of this sub-paragraph to an end. Note also that a new claim for HB or a move to a new dwelling during an HB award on or after 7 April 2008 may also result in the HB claim being assessed under the "local housing allowance" scheme for rent restriction instead of the "local reference rent" scheme to which para 8 applies. See Part 3 of the HB Regs, and in particular, regs 12D, 13C and 13D.

Sub-paras (4) and (5). The transitional protection under sub-para (3) is also retained even if the claimant or her/his partner ceased to be a welfare to work beneficiary as long as entitlement to HB was re-established by the end of the specified 52-week period. These paragraphs will now have limited application, Note that this period was not extended when the linking period for welfare to work beneficiaries was extended to 104 weeks.

Sub-para (5) applies to a welfare to work beneficiary (or her/his partner) who would, under sub-para (3), have been entitled to transitional protection but for the fact that s/he had returned to work. S/he could regain the protection if s/he had to reclaim HB within 52 weeks.

"Welfare to work beneficiary" is defined in sub-para (6) by reference to reg 13A Social Security (Incapacity for Work) Regulations 1995 SI No.311.

A "welfare to work beneficiary" is a claimant who had been incapable of work for at least 196 days and comes off benefit to try out paid work or training. Welfare to work beneficiaries enjoyed a number of advantages in the social security system as an incentive to return to work where possible.

Para 8 was not amended when ESA was introduced in October 2008.

Care homes

9.–(1) In regulation 2(1) of both the Housing Benefit Regulations and the Housing Benefit (State Pension Credit) Regulations there shall be inserted in the appropriate place–

" "the 1987 Regulations" means the Housing Benefit (General) Regulations 1987;"

(2)   Sub-paragraph (3) shall apply to a person who, on 3rd October 2005 was a person to whom paragraph (2) of regulation 7 of the 1987 Regulations as in force on that date applied.

(3)   Where this paragraph applies–

(a)   regulation 9 of both the Housing Benefit Regulations and the Housing Benefit (State Pension Credit) Regulations shall have effect as if–

    (i)   in paragraph (1)(k), at the beginning there were inserted the words "except where paragraph (1A) applies";

    (ii)   after paragraph (1) there were inserted–

"(1A)   This paragraph applies to a person who–

(a)   was or became entitled immediately before 30th October 1990 to housing benefit in respect of residential accommodation; or

(b)   became or becomes entitled to housing benefit in respect of such accommodation on or after that date but only if the claim was made or, as the case may be, the appropriate authority is satisfied that the claim was sent or delivered to the appropriate DWP office or designated office in accordance with regulation 83(4) [¹ regulation 64(5) *[substituted for regulation 83(4) in respect of reg 9 of the HB(SPC) Regs]*] (time and manner in which claims are made), before that date.";

    (iii)   for paragraph (4) there were substituted paragraph (3) of regulation 7 of the 1987 Regulations as in force on 23rd October 2005;

(b)   regulation 52 of the Housing Benefit Regulations shall have effect as if–

    (i)   paragraph (4) there were substituted–

"(4)   For the purposes of paragraph (3), the prescribed circumstances are that the claimant–

(a)   occupies residential accommodation as his home; or

(b)   is a person to whom paragraph (1A), as inserted by paragraph 9(3)(a)(ii) of Schedule 3 to the Consequential Provisions Regulations (exceptions to circumstances in which a person is to be treated as not liable to make payments in respect of a dwelling) applies.";

    (ii)   for paragraph (9), there were substituted–

"(9)   Paragraph (8) shall not apply to residential accommodation of the type referred to in sub-paragraph (b) or (c) of paragraph (8) where such accommodation is residential accommodation for the purposes of regulation 9 and paragraph (4)(b) does not apply to the claimant in respect of that accommodation.".

(4)   Sub-paragraph (5) shall apply to a person who, on 3rd October 2005, was a person to whom paragraph (5) of regulation 7 of the 1987 Regulations as in force on that date applied.

(5)   Where this paragraph applies–

(a)   regulation 9 of both the Housing Benefit Regulations and the Housing Benefit (State Pension Credit) Regulations shall have effect as if–

    (i)   for paragraph (4) there were substituted paragraph (3) of regulation 7 of the 1987 Regulations as in force on 23rd October 2005;

    (ii)   after paragraph (4), there was inserted–

"(5)   Subject to the following provisions of this regulation, paragraph (6) applies to a person who–

(a)   occupies or is treated by regulation 6(8) of the 1987 Regulations as occupying residential accommodation on 31st March 1993;

(b)   is or was liable to pay rent in respect of that accommodation for that day;

(c)   is a person to whom sub-paragraph (a) or (b) of paragraph (2) of regulation 7 of the 1987 Regulations applies immediately before 1st April 1993; and

(d)   is or was entitled to housing benefit in respect of the liability mentioned in sub-paragraph (b).

(6)   In the case of a person to whom this paragraph applies, regulation 9 of these Regulations shall continue to apply to him as if the amendments to the 1987 Regulations specified in regulation 5(2) of the Social Security Benefits (Amendments Consequential Upon the Introduction of Community Care) Regulations 1992 had not been made.

(7)   Subject to paragraph (8), where on 1st April 1993 paragraph (6) applies to a person that paragraph shall cease to apply to him–

(a)   on the day on which he is first absent from the accommodation which he occupied or was treated under regulation 7(8) of the 1987 Regulations as occupying on 31st March 1993; and

(b)   on any day which falls after that day.

(8)   For the purposes of paragraph (7), any absence shall be disregarded during which the person is treated as occupying the accommodation as his home pursuant to regulation 7(12), (13) or (17) of these Regulations.

(9)   Where a person–

(a)   ceases to be entitled to housing benefit; and

(b)   was before he ceased to be entitled a person to whom paragraph (6) applied,

that paragraph shall not apply to him in the case of any subsequent claim for housing benefit.";

(b)   regulation 52 of the Housing Benefit Regulations shall have effect as if–
        (i)   for paragraph (4) there were substituted–

"(4)   For the purposes of paragraph (3), the prescribed circumstances are that the claimant–

(a)   occupies residential accommodation as his home; or

(b)   is a person to whom paragraph (6), as inserted by paragraph 9(5)(a)(ii) of Schedule 3 to the Consequential Provisions Regulations (exceptions to circumstances in which a person is to be treated as not liable to make payments in respect of a dwelling) applies.";

        (ii)   for paragraph (9), there were substituted–

"(9)   Paragraph (8) shall not apply to residential accommodation of the type referred to in sub-paragraph (b) or (c) of paragraph (8) where such accommodation is residential accommodation for the purposes of regulation 9 and paragraph (4)(b) does not apply to the claimant in respect of that accommodation.".

(6)   Sub-paragraph (7) shall apply to a person who, on 3rd October 2005, was a person to whom paragraph (7) of regulation 7 of the 1987 Regulations as in force on that date applied.

(7)   Where this paragraph applies–

(a)   regulation 9 of both the Housing Benefit Regulations and the Housing Benefit (State Pension Credit) Regulations shall have effect as if–
        (i)   for paragraph (4) there were substituted paragraph (3) of regulation 7 of the 1987 Regulations as in force on 23rd October 2005;
        (ii)   after paragraph (4), there was inserted–

"(5)   Subject to the following provisions of this regulation, paragraph (6) applies to a person who–

(a)   occupies or is treated under regulation 5(7C), (8) or (8C) of the 1987 Regulations as occupying accommodation in an establishment which on 1st April 1993 is registered as a small home under Part I of the Registered Homes Act 1984 or is deemed to be so registered under section 2(3) of the Registered Homes (Amendment) Act 1991 (registration of small homes where application for registration not determined);

(b)   was occupying, or was treated under regulation 7(8) of the 1987 Regulations as occupying, that accommodation on 31st March 1993;

(c)   is or was liable to pay rent in respect of that accommodation for 31st March 1993; and

(d)   is or was entitled to housing benefit in respect of that liability.

(6)   In the case of a person to whom this paragraph applies, paragraph (4), as substituted by paragraph 9(7)(a)(i) of Schedule 3 to the Consequential Provisions Regulations, shall apply as if sub-paragraph (a) of the substituted paragraph was omitted.

(7)   Subject to paragraph (8), where on 1st April 1993 paragraph (6) applies to a person that paragraph shall cease to apply to him–

(a)   on the day on which he is first absent from the accommodation which he occupied or was treated under regulation 7(8) of the 1987 Regulations as occupying on 31st March 1993; and

(b)   on any day which falls after that day.

(8)   For the purposes of paragraph (7), any absence shall be disregarded during which the person is treated as occupying the accommodation as his home pursuant to regulation 7(12), (13) or (17) of these Regulations.

(9)   Where a person–

(a)   ceases to be entitled to housing benefit; and

(b)   was before he ceased to be entitled a person to whom paragraph (6) applied,

that paragraph shall not apply to him in the case of any subsequent claim for housing benefit.

(10)   Where on 31st March 1993 a person occupies or is treated as occupying an establishment mentioned in paragraph (5)(a) and on a day subsequent to that date the establishment–

(a)   if it was registered under Part I of the Registered Homes Act 1984, ceases to be so registered; or

(b)   if it was deemed to be so registered is neither registered nor deemed to be registered,

then on that day and on any day thereafter paragraph (9) shall not apply to that person.

(11)   In this regulation, "small home" has the same meaning as it had in Part 1 of the Registered Homes Act 1984 by virtue of section 1(4A) of that Act.".

(b)   regulation 52 of the Housing Benefit Regulations shall have effect as if–

(i)   for paragraph (4) there were substituted–

"(4)   For the purposes of paragraph (3), the prescribed circumstances are that the claimant–
(a)   occupies residential accommodation as his home; or
(b)   is a person to whom paragraph (6), as inserted by paragraph 9(7)(a)(ii) of Schedule 3 to the Consequential Provisions Regulations (exceptions to circumstances in which a person is to be treated as not liable to make payments in respect of a dwelling) applies.";

(ii)   for paragraph (9), there were substituted–

"(9)   Paragraph (8) shall not apply to residential accommodation of the type referred to in sub-paragraph (b) or (c) of paragraph (8) where such accommodation is residential accommodation for the purposes of regulation 9 and paragraph (4)(b) does not apply to the claimant in respect of that accommodation.".

Amendment
1.   Amended by reg 7(4) of SI 2008 No 1042 as from 19.5.08.

SCHEDULE 4

REGULATION 7

Transitory Modifications

Provisions not yet in force
1.–(1)   If–
(a)   no date has been appointed as the date on which a provision mentioned in column 1 of the following Table is to come into force before 24th February 2006; or
(b)   a date has been appointed which is later than 24th February 2006,
then the paragraph of this Schedule mentioned in column 2 of the Table opposite that provision shall have effect until the appointed day.

TABLE

Provision	Paragraph of this Schedule
Section 12(2)(e) of the Asylum and Immigration (Treatment of Claimants, etc.) Act 2004.	Paragraph 2
Section 12(2)(g) of the Asylum and Immigration (Treatment of Claimants, etc.) Act 2004.	Paragraph 3
Section 12(3) of the Asylum and Immigration (Treatment of Claimants, etc.) Act 2004.	Paragraph 4

(2)   If a date has been appointed as the date on which a provision mentioned in column 1 of the Table above is to come into force for some purposes of that provision but not for others, then the paragraph of this Schedule mentioned in column 2 of the Table opposite that provision shall have effect for those other purposes of that provision (in so far as it is capable of doing so) until the provisions are brought into force for the remaining purposes.

General Note
Section 12 Asylum and Immigration (Treatment of Claimants, etc.) Act 2004 came into force on 14 June 2007 by the Asylum and Immigration (Treatment of Claimants, etc.) Act 2004 (Commencement No.7 and Transitional Provisions) Order 2007 SI No.1602. The commencement does not apply to those recorded as refugees on or before 14 June 2007. For these purposes, a person is "recorded as a refugee" on the day the Secretary of State notifies her/him that s/he has been recognised as a refugee and granted asylum in the UK. For those to whom the commencement applies, the following provisions lapse.
(1)   Reg 10A and Sch A1 of both the HB Regs and the HB(SPC) Regs, as inserted by Sch 4 para 2(1) and (2). These dealt with a refugee's retrospective entitlement to HB.
(2)   Paras 55A and 55B of Sch 5 and paras 48A and 48B of Sch 6 of the HB Regs, as inserted by Sch 4 para 2(5) and (6). These provided income and capital disregards for retrospective HB and IS paid to the refugee.
(3)   Reg 7A and Sch A1 of both the CTB Regs and the CTB(SPC) Regs, as inserted by Sch 4 para 3(1) and (2). These made similar provisions to those in (1) above for CTB. Note that the CTB and the CTB(SPC) Regulations were revoked with effect from 1 April 2013.
(4)   Paras 56A and 56B of Sch 4 and paras 53A and 53B of Sch 5 of the CTB Regs, as inserted by Sch 4 para 3(5) and (6). These made similar provisions to those in (2) above for CTB. Note that the CTB and the CTB(SPC) Regulations were revoked with effect from 1 April 2013.
(5)   The modifications made to the above, as made by Sch 4 para 4.
See pp1125-33 of the 20th edition for the full text of the provisions and commentary.

Note that reg 10A and paras 3 and 7 of Sch A1 of both the HB regs and the HB(SPC) Regs, as inserted by para 2, were substituted by reg 6 Housing Benefit (Local Housing Allowance, Miscellaneous and Consequential) Amendment Regulations 2007 SI No.2870 as from 7 April 2008, save that for a person to whom reg 1(3) of those regulations applied, the amendments came into force on the day on or after 7 April 2008 when the first of the events specified in reg 1(4) applied to her/him, or on 6 April 2009 if none had before that date. Sch 4 para 3(4) was amended by reg 7(5) Social Secuity (Miscellaneous Amendments) (No.2) Regulations 2008 SI No.1042 as from 19 May 2008.

Note also that paras 4(2)(b) and (c) and 4(4)(b) and (c) of Sch 4 were omitted by reg 9 of SI 2008 No.3157 as from 5 January 2009.

The Social Security (Persons from Abroad) Amendment Regulations 2006

(SI 2006 No.1026)

Citation and commencement

1. These Regulations shall be cited as the Social Security (Persons from Abroad) Amendment Regulations 2006 and shall come into force on 30th April 2006.

Nationals of Norway, Iceland, Liechtenstein and Switzerland

10. The following provisions shall apply in relation to a national of Norway, Iceland, Liechtenstein or Switzerland or a member of his family (within the meaning of Article 2 of Council Directive No. 2004/38/EC) as if such a national were a national of a member State–

(a) regulation 7(4A)(a) to (e) of the Council Tax Benefit Regulations 2006;

(b) regulation 7(4A)(a) to (e) of the Council Tax Benefit (Persons who have attained the qualifying age for state pension credit) Regulations 2006;

(c) regulation 10(3B)(a) to (e) of the Housing Benefit Regulations 2006;

(d) regulation 10(4A)(a) to (e) of the Housing Benefit (Persons who have attained the qualifying age for state pension credit) Regulations 2006;

(e)-(h) *[Omitted]*

Revocations and savings

11.–(1) *[Omitted]*

(2) Nothing in these Regulations shall affect the continued operation of the transitional arrangements and savings provided for in–

(a) regulation 12 of the Social Security (Persons From Abroad) Miscellaneous Amendments Regulations 1996;

(b) regulation 6 of the Social Security (Habitual Residence) Amendment Regulations 2004; or

(c) paragraph 6 of Schedule 3 to the Housing Benefit and Council Tax Benefit (Consequential Provisions) Regulations 2006.

General Note

The amendments made by SI 2006 No.1026 to the HB Regs and HB(SPC) Regs do not affect the continued operation of the provisions listed. For reg 12 Social Security (Persons From Abroad) Miscellaneous Amendments Regulations 1996 see p1633 of the 26th), for reg 6 Social Security (Habitual Residence) Amendment Regulations 2004 see p1771 and for Sch 3 para 6 HB&CTB(CP) Regs see p1795. Note that amendments made to the CTB Regs and the CTB(SPC) Regs did not affect the continued operation of these provisions for CTB purposes, prior to its abolition on 1 April 2013.

The Housing Benefit and Council Tax Benefit (War Pension Disregards) Regulations 2007

(SI 2007 No.1619)

General Note on the Regulations
In the assessment of income for HB, £10 of certain war pensions must be disregarded. Sections 134(8) and 139(6) SSAA 1992 allow an authority to resolve to disregard more of (or all of) prescribed war pensions as income for the purposes of its HB (and formerly its CTB) schemes. The prescribed pensions are in the Schedule to these regulations. Note that "war widow's pension" includes any corresponding pension payable to a widower or a surviving civil partner: see, for example, s134(14) SSAA on p80.

Citation and commencement
1. These Regulations may be cited as The Housing Benefit and Council Tax Benefit (War Pension Disregards) Regulations 2007 and shall come into force on 3rd July 2007.

War disablement pensions
2. The war disablement pensions that are prescribed for the purpose of sections 134(8)(a) and 139(6)(a) of the Social Security Administration Act 1992, are specified in Part 1 of the Schedule.

War widow's pensions
3. The war widow's pensions that are prescribed for the purpose of sections 134(8)(a) and 139(6)(a) of the Social Security Administration Act, are specified in Part 2 of the Schedule.

[¹ [³ THE SCHEDULE
REGULATIONS 2 AND 3
War disablement and war widow's pensions

PART 1

War disablement pensions
1. The war disablement pensions prescribed are–
(a) any retired pay or pension or allowance payable in respect of disablement under an instrument specified in section 639(2) of the Income Tax (Earnings and Pensions) Act 2003;
(b) any retired pay or pension payable, to a member of the armed forces of the Crown in respect of a disablement which is attributable to service, under–
(i) an Order in Council made under section 3 of the Naval and Marine Pay and Pensions Act 1865,
(ii) the Army Pensions Warrant 1977,
[⁴ (iia) the Army Pensions (Armed Forces Pension Scheme 1975 and Attributable Benefits Scheme) Warrant 2010;]
(iii) any order or regulations made under section 2 of the Air Force (Constitution) Act 1917,
(iv) any order or regulations made under section 4 of the Reserve Forces Act 1996,
(v) any instrument amending or replacing any of the instruments referred to in paragraphs (i) to (iv), or
(vi) any power of Her Majesty otherwise than under an enactment to make provision about pensions for or in respect of persons who have been disabled or have died in consequence of service as members of the armed forces of the Crown; and
(c) a payment made under article 14(1)(b) of the Armed Forces and Reserve Forces (Compensation Scheme) Order 2005.

PART 2

War widow's pensions
2. The war widow's pensions prescribed are–
(a) any pension or allowance payable to a widow, widower or surviving civil partner under an instrument specified in section 639(2) of the Income Tax (Earnings and Pensions) Act 2003 in respect of the death or disablement of any person;
(b) a pension payable, to a widow, widower or surviving civil partner of a member of the armed forces of the Crown in respect of death which is attributable to service, under–

(i)   an Order in Council made under section 3 of the Naval and Marine Pay and Pensions Act 1865,

(ii)   the Army Pensions Warrant 1977,

[⁴ (iia) the Army Pensions (Armed Forces Pension Scheme 1975 and Attributable Benefits Scheme) Warrant 2010;]

(iii)   any order or regulations made under section 2 of the Air Force (Constitution) Act 1917,

(iv)   any order or regulations made under section 4 of the Reserve Forces Act 1996,

(v)   any instrument amending or replacing any of the instruments referred to in paragraphs (i) to (iv), or

(vi)   any power of Her Majesty otherwise than under an enactment to make provision about pensions for or in respect of persons who have been disabled or have died in consequence of service as members of the armed forces of the Crown; and

(c)   a payment made under article 21(1)(a) of the Armed Forces and Reserve Forces (Compensation Scheme) Order 2005.]]

Amendments

1.   Substituted by reg 10 of SI 2008 No 3157 as from 5.1.09.
2.   Omitted by reg 10 of SI 2009 No 2655 as from 26.10.09.
3.   Substituted by reg 2 of SI 2009 No 3389 as from 26.1.10.
4.   Amended by reg 8 of SI 2010 No 2449 as from 1.11.10.

The Social Security (Claims and Information) Regulations 2007

(SI 2007 No.2911)

Citation, commencement and interpretation

1.–(1) These Regulations may be cited as the Social Security (Claims and Information) Regulations 2007 and shall come into force on 31st October 2007.

(2) In regulations 4 and 5 "the Administration Act" means the Social Security Administration Act 1992.

(3) In regulations 2 to 4–

"specified benefit" means one or more of the following benefits–

    (a)   attendance allowance;

    (b)   bereavement allowance;

    (c)   bereavement payment;

    (d)   carer's allowance;

    (e)   disability living allowance;

    [¹ (ee) employment and support allowance;]

    (f)   incapacity benefit;

    (g)   income support;

    (h)   jobseeker's allowance;

    (i)   retirement pension;

    (j)   state pension credit;

    (k)   widowed parent's allowance;

    (l)   winter fuel payment;

"the Secretary of State" includes persons providing services to the Secretary of State;

"local authority" includes persons providing services to a local authority and persons authorised to exercise any function of a local authority relating to housing benefit or council tax benefit.

Amendment

1.   Inserted by reg 8 of SI 2010 No 840 as from 28.6.10.

Use of social security information: local authorities

2.–(1) This regulation applies where social security information held by a local authority was supplied by the Secretary of State to the local authority and this information–

    (a)   was used by the Secretary of State in connection with a person's claim for, or award of, a specified benefit; and

    (b)   is relevant to that person's claim for, or award of, council tax benefit or housing benefit.

(2) The local authority must, for the purposes of the person's claim for, or award of, council tax benefit or housing benefit, use that information without verifying its accuracy.

(3) Paragraph (2) does not apply where–

    (a)   the information is supplied more than twelve months after it was used by the Secretary of State in connection with a claim for, or an award of, a specified benefit; or

    (b)   the information is supplied within twelve months of its use by the Secretary of State but the local authority has reasonable grounds for believing the information has changed in the period between its use by the Secretary of State and its supply to the local authority; or

    (c)   the date on which the information was used by the Secretary of State cannot be determined.

Use of social security information: Secretary of State

3.–(1) This regulation applies where social security information held by the Secretary of State was supplied by a local authority to the Secretary of State and this information–

    (a)   was used by the local authority in connection with a person's claim for, or award of, council tax benefit or housing benefit; and

(b) is relevant to that person's claim for, or award of, a specified benefit.

(2) The Secretary of State must, for the purposes of the person's claim for, or award of, a specified benefit, use that information without verifying its accuracy.

(3) Paragraph (2) does not apply where–

(a) the information is supplied more than twelve months after it was used by a local authority in connection with a claim for, or an award of, council tax benefit or housing benefit; or

(b) the information is supplied within twelve months of its use by the local authority but the Secretary of State has reasonable grounds for believing the information has changed in the period between its use by the local authority and its supply to the Secretary of State; or

(c) the date on which the information was used by the local authority cannot be determined.

Social security information verified by local authorities

4.–(1) This regulation applies where social security information is verified by a local authority by virtue of regulations made under section 7A(2)(e) of the Administration Act and forwarded by that local authority to the Secretary of State.

(2) The Secretary of State must, for the purposes of a person's claim for, or award of, a specified benefit, use this information without verifying its accuracy.

(3) Paragraph (2) does not apply where–

(a) the Secretary of State has reasonable grounds for believing the social security information received from the local authority is inaccurate; or

(b) the Secretary of State receives the information more than four weeks after it was verified by the local authority.

Specified benefits for the purpose of section 7B(3) of the Administration Act

5. The benefits specified for the purpose of section 7B(3) of the Administration Act are–

(a) a "specified benefit" within the meaning given in regulation 1(3);

(b) housing benefit; and

(c) council tax benefit.

The Housing Benefit (Local Housing Allowance and Information Sharing) Amendment Regulations 2007

(SI 2007 No.2868)

Citation and commencement

1.–(1) These Regulations may be cited as the Housing Benefit (Local Housing Allowance and Information Sharing) Amendment Regulations 2007.

(2) This regulation and regulations 2 (amendment of the Housing Benefit Regulations 2006) and 3 (amendments relating to information sharing) shall come into force on 7th April 2008.

(3) Subject to paragraph (6) (which relates to non-local housing allowance cases), regulations 4 to 19 (amendment of the Housing Benefit Regulations 2006 relating to determination of appropriate maximum housing benefit) shall come into force on 7th April 2008 immediately following the coming into force of regulation 3.

(4) *[Omitted]*

(5) This paragraph applies to a case where no reference was made to a maximum rent (standard local rate) in determining the amount of the eligible rent which applied immediately before 7th April 2008 and in this paragraph–

"eligible rent" shall be construed in accordance with–

(i) regulations 12 or 12A of the Housing Benefit Regulations 2006 as in force immediately before 7th April 2008; or

(ii) in a case to which paragraph 4 of Schedule 3 to the Housing Benefit and Council Tax Benefit (Consequential Provisions) Regulations 2006 applies, regulations 12 and 13 of those Regulations as set out in paragraph 5 of that Schedule as in force immediately before 7th April 2008; and

"maximum rent (standard local rate)" means a maximum rent (standard local rate) determined in accordance with regulation 13A of the Housing Benefit Regulations 2006 as in force immediately before 7th April 2008.

(6) In a case to which paragraph (5) applies regulations 4 to 19 shall come into force on the day when, on or after 7th April 2008, the first of the following sub-paragraphs applies–

(a) a relevant authority is required to apply to a rent officer by virtue of regulation 14 of the Housing Benefit Regulations;

(b) sub-paragraph (a) would apply but for the case falling within regulation 14(4)(a) of, or 14(4)(b) of and paragraph 2 of Schedule 2 to, the Housing Benefit Regulations (no application to rent officer required as an existing rent officer determination may be used);

(c) a relevant authority is required to determine an eligible rent in accordance with regulation 12(3)(b) of the Housing Benefit Regulations; or

(d) a relevant authority is required to determine an eligible rent in accordance with regulation 12(3) of the Housing Benefit Regulations 2006 as set out in paragraph 5 of Schedule 3 to the Consequential Provisions Regulations,

and in this paragraph "relevant authority" means an authority administering housing benefit.

(7) Where paragraph (6) does not apply before 6th April 2009, regulations 4 to 19 shall come into force on that date.

(8) In this regulation–

(a) "the Housing Benefit Regulations" means the Housing Benefit Regulations 2006 as in force immediately before the coming into force of regulations 4 to 19 in that case; and

(b) "the Consequential Provisions Regulations" means the Housing Benefit and Council Tax Benefit (Consequential Provisions) Regulations 2006 as in force immediately before the coming into force of regulations 4 to 19 in that case.

Analysis

These regulations provided for the national introduction of the "local housing allowance" scheme for HB rent restriction, found in regs 12D, 13C and 13D HB Regs, which had been piloted in Pathfinder areas from 2003. They made many amendments to the HB Regs, all of which are incorporated into the relevant provisions in this book. Note that the equivalent regulations for those of at least the qualifying age for state pension credit are on p1814.

Reg 1 is reproduced here because of the rather complex commencement provisions found in it. In most situations, the amendments came into force on 7 April 2008. So the amended HB regulations applied on any new claim for HB on or after 7 April 2008, or where a claimant with an award of HB moved to a new dwelling on or after that date. However, for those to whom para (5) applied, all claimants with a current award of HB on 7 April 2008, the amendments did not come into force until the first of various specific events occurred, or on 6 April 2009 if earlier: paras (6) and (7). In these cases, "eligible rent" continued to be determined under the old form of regs 12 and 12A HB Regs or Sch 3 para 4 HB&CTB(CP) Regs, as the case may be. This did not apply if the claimant's HB was determined by reference to a "maximum rent (standard local rate)", that is, in a former Pathfinder area under the pilot local housing allowance scheme rules (for which see pp510–18 of the 20th edition).

For any individual claimant, the specific events in para (6) are as follows.

(1)   The authority is required to apply to a rent officer for determinations under the old version of reg 14, or would have been required to do so were there not existing determinations it could use, that is, where "eligible rent was determined under the "local reference rent" rules: sub-paras (a) and (b). This would occur, for example, where the number of occupiers has changed.

(2)   The authority is required to determine an "eligible rent" under the old version of reg 12(3)(b), that is, where no rent restriction rules applied: sub-para (c). This would occur, for example, where there has been a rent increase or where a non-dependant moves in or out of the household.

(3)   The authority is required to determine an "eligible rent" under the old version of reg 12(3) set out in Sch 4 para 5 HB&CTB(CP) regs, that is where the "pre-January 1996" rules applied: sub-para (d).

It is important to note that the effect of the amendments coming into force for an individual claimant does not mean that the claim is necessarily dealt with under a particular, or a different, rent restriction scheme. It is important to consider all the provisions in Part 3 HB Regs carefully and, in particular, any modifications or transitional protection provided.

The Housing Benefit (State Pension Credit) (Local Housing Allowance and Information Sharing) Amendment Regulations 2007

(SI 2007 No.2869)

Citation and commencement

1.–(1)   These Regulations may be cited as the Housing Benefit (State Pension Credit) (Local Housing Allowance and Information Sharing) Amendment Regulations 2007.

(2)   This regulation and regulations 2 (amendment of the Housing Benefit (Persons who have attained the qualifying age for state pension credit) Regulations 2006) and 3 (amendments relating to information sharing) shall come into force on 7th April 2008.

(3)   Subject to paragraph (6) (which relates to non-local housing allowance cases), regulations 4 to 19 (amendment of the Housing Benefit (Persons who have attained the qualifying age for state pension credit) Regulations 2006 relating to determination of appropriate maximum housing benefit) shall come into force on 7th April 2008 immediately following the coming into force of regulation 3.

(4)   [*Omitted*]

(5)   This paragraph applies to a case where no reference was made to a maximum rent (standard local rate) in determining the amount of the eligible rent which applied immediately before 7th April 2008 and in this paragraph–
"eligible rent" shall be construed in accordance with–
  (i)   regulations 12 or 12A of the Housing Benefit (Persons who have attained the qualifying age for state pension credit) Regulations 2006 as in force immediately before 7th April 2008; or
  (ii)   in a case to which paragraph 4 of Schedule 3 to the Housing Benefit and Council Tax Benefit (Consequential Provisions) Regulations 2006 applies, regulations 12 and 13 of those Regulations as set out in paragraph 5 of that Schedule as in force immediately before 7th April 2008; and
"maximum rent (standard local rate)" means a maximum rent (standard local rate) determined in accordance with regulation 13A of the Housing Benefit (Persons who have attained the qualifying age for state pension credit) Regulations 2006 as in force immediately before 7th April 2008.

(6)   In a case to which paragraph (5) applies regulations 4 to 19 shall come into force on the day when, on or after 7th April 2008, the first of the following sub-paragraphs applies–
  (a)   a relevant authority is required to apply to a rent officer by virtue of regulation 14 of the Housing Benefit (State Pension Credit) Regulations;
  (b)   sub-paragraph (a) would apply but for the case falling within regulation 14(4)(a) of, or 14(4)(b) of and paragraph 2 of Schedule 2 to, the Housing Benefit (State Pension Credit) Regulations (no application to rent officer required as an existing rent officer determination may be used);
  (c)   a relevant authority is required to determine a new eligible rent in accordance with regulation 12(3)(b) of the Housing Benefit (State Pension Credit) Regulations; or
  (d)   a relevant authority is required to determine a new eligible rent in accordance with regulation 12(3) of the Housing Benefit (Persons who have attained the qualifying age for state pension credit) Regulations 2006 as set out in paragraph 5 of Schedule 3 to the Consequential Provisions Regulations,
and in this paragraph "relevant authority" means an authority administering housing benefit.

(7)   Where paragraph (6) does not apply before 6th April 2009, regulations 4 to 19 shall come into force on that date.

(8)   In this regulation–
"the Housing Benefit (State Pension Credit) Regulations" means the Housing Benefit (Persons who have attained the qualifying age for state pension credit) Regulations 2006 as in force immediately before the coming into force of regulations 4 to 19 in that case; and

"the Consequential Provisions Regulations" means the Housing Benefit and Council Tax
    Benefit (Consequential Provisions) Regulations 2006 as in force immediately
    before the coming into force of regulations 4 to 19 in that case.

General Note

See the General Note to the Housing Benefit (Local Housing Allowance and Information Sharing) Amendment
Regulations 2007 on p1813 on these rather complex commencement provisions.

The Housing Benefit (Local Housing Allowance, Miscellaneous and Consequential) Amendment Regulations 2007

(SI 2007 No.2870)

Citation, commencement and interpretation

1.–(1)   These Regulations may be cited as the Housing Benefit (Local Housing Allowance, Miscellaneous and Consequential) Amendment Regulations 2007.

(2)   This regulation and, subject to paragraph (4) (which relates to non-local housing allowance cases), regulations 2 to 6, shall come into force on 7th April 2008.

(3)   This paragraph applies to a case where no reference was made to a maximum rent (standard local rate) in determining the amount of the eligible rent which applied immediately before 7th April 2008 and in this paragraph–

"eligible rent" shall be construed in accordance with–

    (i)   regulations 12 or 12A of the Housing Benefit Regulations 2006 or the Housing Benefit (Persons who have attained the qualifying age for state pension credit) Regulations 2006 as in force immediately before 7th April 2008; or

    (ii)   in a case to which paragraph 4 of Schedule 3 to the Housing Benefit and Council Tax Benefit (Consequential Provisions) Regulations 2006 applies, regulations 12 and 13 of the Housing Benefit Regulations 2006 or the Housing Benefit (Persons who have attained the qualifying age for state pension credit) Regulations 2006 as set out in paragraph 5 of that Schedule as in force immediately before 7th April 2007.

"maximum rent (standard local rate)" means a maximum rent (standard local rate) determined in accordance with regulation 13A of the Housing Benefit Regulations 2006 or the Housing Benefit (persons who have attained the qualifying age for state pension credit) Regulations 2006 as in force immediately before 7th April 2008.

(4)   In a case to which paragraph (3) applies, these Regulations shall come into force on the day when, on or after 7th April 2008, the first of the following sub-paragraphs applies–

    (a)   a relevant authority is required to apply to a rent officer by virtue of regulation 14 of the Housing Benefit Regulations or the Housing Benefit (State Pension Credit) Regulations;

    (b)   sub-paragraph (a) would apply but for the case falling within regulation 14(4)(a) of, or regulations 14(4)(b) of and paragraph 2 of Schedule 2 to, the Housing Benefit Regulations or the Housing Benefit (State Pension Credit) Regulations (no application to rent officer required as an existing rent officer determination may be used);

    (c)   a relevant authority is required to determine an eligible rent in accordance with regulation 12(3)(b) of the Housing Benefit Regulations or the Housing Benefit (State Pension Credit) Regulations; or

    (d)   a relevant authority is required to determine an eligible rent in accordance with regulation 12(3) of the Housing Benefit Regulations 2006 or regulation 12(3) of the Housing Benefit (Persons who have attained the qualifying age for state pension credit) Regulations 2006 as set out in paragraph 5 of Schedule 3 to the Consequential Provisions Regulations,

and in this paragraph "relevant authority" means an authority administering housing benefit.

(5)   Where paragraph (4) does not apply before 6th April 2009, these Regulations shall come into force on that date.

(6)   In paragraph (4) of this regulation–

"the Housing Benefit Regulations" means the Housing Benefit Regulations 2006 as in force immediately before the coming into force of regulations 4 to 19 of the Housing Benefit (Local Housing Allowance and Information Sharing) Amendment Regulations 2007 in that case;

"the Housing Benefit (State Pension Credit) Regulations" means the Housing Benefit (persons who have attained the qualifying age for state pension credit) Regulations 2006 as in force immediately before the coming into force of regulations 4 to 19 of the Housing Benefit (State Pension Credit) (Local Housing Allowance and Information Sharing) Amendment Regulations 2007 in that case;

"the Consequential Provisions Regulations" means the Housing Benefit and Council Tax Benefit (Consequential Provisions) Regulations 2006 as in force immediately before the coming into force of regulations 2 to 6 of these regulations in that case.

General Note

See the General Note to the Housing Benefit (Local Housing Allowance and Information Sharing) Amendment Regulations 2007 on p1813 on these rather complex commencement provisions.

The Welfare Reform Act 2007 (Commencement No.4, and Savings and Transitional Provisions) Order 2007

(SI 2007 No.2872)

Citation and interpretation

1.–(1) This Order may be cited as the Welfare Reform Act 2007 (Commencement No.4, and Savings and Transitional Provisions) Order 2007.

(2) In this Order–

"the Act" means the Welfare Reform Act 2007;

"the Administration Act" means the Social Security Administration Act 1992;

"the Contributions and Benefits Act" means the Social Security Contributions and Benefits Act 1992;

"the Consequential Provisions Regulations" means the Housing Benefit and Council Tax Benefit (Consequential Provisions) Regulations 2006;

"the Housing Act" means the Housing Act 1996;

"the Housing Benefit (State Pension Credit) Regulations" means the Housing Benefit (Persons who have attained the qualifying age for state pension credit) Regulations 2006;

"the Regulations" means the Housing Benefit Regulations 2006.

Appointed days

2.–(1) 7th April 2008 is the appointed day for the coming into force of–

(a)-(b) *[Omitted]*

(c) Schedule 8 to the Act (repeals), in so far as it relates to the repeal of–

  (i) section 130(4) of the Contributions and Benefits Act (housing benefit);

  (ii) section 5(3) of the Administration Act (power to make regulations about information or evidence required by rent officer);

  (iii) section 122(3) of the Housing Act (functions of rent officers in connection with housing benefit and rent allowance subsidy);

  (iv) in section 122(5)(b) of the Housing Act, the words "or regulations"; and

  (v) paragraph 3(2) of Schedule 13 to the Housing Act (housing benefit and related matters: consequential amendments);

  and section 67 of the Act (repeals) in so far as it relates to those repeals; and

(d) paragraph 12 of Schedule 5 to the Act (minor and consequential amendments relating to Part 2) so far as it relates to the amendment of section 122(5) of the Housing Act and section 40 of the Act in so far as it relates to that consequential amendment.

(2)-(3) *[Omitted]*

(4) This article is subject to the savings and transitional provisions in articles 3 to 5.

Transitional provisions and savings in relation to section 130(4) of the Contributions and Benefits Act and section 122(3) and (5) of the Housing Act

3.–(1) Notwithstanding article 2 and subject to article 4–

(a) section 130(4) of the Contributions and Benefits Act and section 122(3) and (5) of the Housing Act shall continue to have effect as they were in force immediately before 7th April 2008 so far as is required for the purpose of conferring power to amend or revoke the regulations referred to in paragraph (2), until 7th April 2009; and

(b) any regulations made under any of the provisions referred to in sub-paragraph (a) shall continue to have effect in relation to the period ending on the date specified in paragraph (3), (4), (5) or (6) except for paragraphs 11 and 12 of Schedule 2 to the Consequential Provisions Regulations.

(2) The regulations are–

(a) the Regulations;

(b) the Housing Benefit (State Pension Credit) Regulations; and

(c) the Consequential Provisions Regulations.

(3)   In relation to a case in which reference was made to a maximum rent (standard local rate) in determining the eligible rent which applied immediately before 7th April 2008, the date is 7th April 2008.

(4)   In relation to a case where–

(a)   either–

(i)   a claim for housing benefit is made, delivered or received on or after 7th April 2008 but the date the claim is made or is treated as being made is a date before 7th April 2008 by virtue of regulations 83, 83A, 84 or 85 of the Regulations or regulations 64, 64A, 65 or 66 of the Housing Benefit (State Pension Credit) Regulations; or

(ii)   a claim was made or was treated as made before 7th April 2008 but the decision on the claim was not made by that date; and

(b)   reference to a maximum rent (standard local rate) would have been made in determining the eligible rent which applied immediately before 7th April 2008 had the decision on the claim been made before that date,

the date is 7th April 2008.

(5)   In relation to a non-local housing allowance case the date is the relevant date for that case.

(6)   In relation to a case where–

(a)   either–

(i)   a claim for housing benefit is made, delivered or received on or after the 7th April 2008 but the date the claim is made or is treated as being made is a date before that date by virtue of regulations 83, 83A, 84 or 85 of the Regulations or regulations 64, 64A, 65 or 66 of the Housing Benefit (State Pension Credit) Regulations; or

(ii)   a claim was made or was treated as made before 7th April 2008 but the decision on the claim was not made by that date; and

(b)   the case would have been a non-local housing allowance case had the decision on the claim been made before 7th April 2008,

the date is the relevant date for that case.

(7)   In this article–

"eligible rent" shall be construed, except in the definition of "the relevant date", in accordance with–

(a)   regulations 12 or 12A of the Regulations or the Housing Benefit (State Pension Credit) Regulations as in force immediately before the 7th April 2008; or

(b)   in a case to which paragraph 4 of Schedule 3 to the Consequential Provisions Regulations applies, regulations 12 and 13 of the Housing Benefit Regulations 2006 or the Housing Benefit (Persons who have attained the qualifying age for state pension credit) Regulations 2006 as set out in paragraph 5 of that Schedule as in force immediately before the 7th April 2008;

"maximum rent (standard local rate)" means a maximum rent (standard local rate) determined in accordance with regulation 13A of the Regulations or the Housing Benefit (State Pension Credit) Regulations as in force immediately before 7th April 2008;

"non-local housing allowance case" means a case where no reference was made to a maximum rent (standard local rate) in determining the amount of the eligible rent which applied immediately before 7th April 2008;

"the relevant date" means, in relation to a non-local housing allowance case–

(a)   the day on or after 7th April 2008 when any of the following sub-paragraphs first applies–

(i)   a relevant authority is required to apply to a rent officer by virtue of regulation 14 of the Regulations or the Housing Benefit (State Pension Credit) Regulations as in force immediately before that day;

(ii)   sub-paragraph (i) would apply but for the case falling within regulation 14(4)(a) of, or 14(4)(b) of and paragraph 2 of Schedule 2 to, the Regulations or the Housing Benefit (State Pension Credit) Regulations as in force immediately before that day;

(iii)   a relevant authority is required to determine an eligible rent in accordance with regulation 12(3)(b) of the Regulations or the Housing Benefit (State Pension Credit) Regulations as in force immediately before that day;

(iv)   a relevant authority is required to determine an eligible rent in accordance with regulation 12(3) of the Housing Benefit Regulations 2006 or the Housing Benefit (Persons who have attained the qualifying age for state pension credit) Regulations 2006 as set out in paragraph 5 of Schedule 3 to the Consequential Provisions Regulations as in force immediately before that day; or

(b)   6th April 2009 in any case where paragraph (a) does not apply before that date; "relevant authority" means an authority administering housing benefit.

Transitional provisions and savings in relation to section 130(4) of the Contributions and Benefits Act and extended payments

4.–(1)   Notwithstanding article 2, regulations 72 and 73 of, and Schedules 7 and 8 to, the Regulations, and regulation 53 of, and Schedule 7 to, the Housing Benefit (State Pension Credit) Regulations shall continue to have effect in relation to the period ending on 6th October 2008 or such later date as is provided by paragraphs (2) or (3).

(2)   Where an extended payment award is determined before 6th October 2008 and the extended payment period will end after that date, the date shall be the end of that extended payment period.

(3)   Where a claim for an extended payment is made or treated as made on a date before 6th October 2008 but the extended payment award was not determined by that date, the date shall be the end of that extended payment period.

(4)   In this Article–

"extended payment" means a payment of housing benefit pursuant to–

(a)   regulation 72 of the Regulations (extended payments);

(b)   regulation 73 of the Regulations (extended payments (severe disablement allowance and incapacity benefit)); or

(c)   regulation 53 of the Housing Benefit (State Pension Credit) Regulations (extended payments severe disablement allowance and incapacity benefit),

where the date on which the claimant ceased to be entitled to housing benefit in accordance with regulation 77 or 78 of the Regulations or regulation 58 of the Housing Benefit (State Pension Credit) Regulations was before 6th October 2008; and

"extended payment period" means the period during which a person is entitled to housing benefit in accordance with regulation 72(6) or 73(6) of the Regulations or regulation 53(6) of the Housing Benefit (State Pension Credit) Regulations.

Transitional provisions and savings in relation to section 5(3) of the Administration Act

5.   Notwithstanding article 2, any regulations made under both section 5(1)(h) and 5(3) of the Administration Act shall continue to have effect for all purposes relating to the furnishing of information or evidence required by a rent officer under section 122 of the Housing Act 1996 in relation to a claim for or an award of housing benefit which relates to any period before 7th April 2008.

The Social Security (Local Authority Investigations and Prosecutions) Regulations 2008

(SI 2008 No.463)

Citation, commencement and interpretation

1.–(1) These Regulations may be cited as the Social Security (Local Authority Investigations and Prosecutions) Regulations 2008.

(2) These Regulations shall come into force on 7th April 2008.

(3) In these Regulations, "the Act" means the Social Security Administration Act 1992.

Authorisations by local authorities

2.–(1) An authority must not proceed for a purpose mentioned in section 109A(2)(a)(authorisations for investigators) of the Act unless the authorisation concerns one or more of the benefits listed in paragraph (5).

(2) An authority must not proceed for a purpose mentioned in section 109A(2)(c) of the Act unless the authorisation concerns relevant social security legislation relating to one or more of the benefits listed in paragraph (5).

(3) An authority must not proceed for a purpose mentioned in section 109A(2)(d) of the Act unless the authorisation concerns a benefit offence relating to one or more of the benefits listed in paragraph (5).

(4) An authorisation made for a purpose mentioned in section 109A(2)(a), (c) or (d) of the Act has effect in relation to a particular case only if in relation to that case an authorised officer has commenced an investigation for a purpose mentioned in section 110A(2) of that Act.

(5) The benefits are–

(a) income support;

(b) a jobseeker's allowance;

(c) incapacity benefit;

(d) state pension credit;

(e) an employment and support allowance.

Exercise of powers by local authorities to prosecute benefit fraud

3. For the purposes of paragraph (2)(a) of section 116A of the Act (local authority powers to prosecute benefit fraud), the benefits prescribed are all relevant social security benefits except for–

(a) income support;

(b) a jobseeker's allowance;

(c) incapacity benefit;

(d) state pension credit;

(e) an employment and support allowance.

The Welfare Reform Act 2007 (Commencement No.7, Transitional and Savings Provisions) Order 2008

(SI 2008 No.2101)

Citation and interpretation

1.–(1)   This Order may be cited as the Welfare Reform Act 2007 (Commencement No. 7, Transitional and Savings Provisions) Order 2008.

(2)   In this Order "the Act" means the Welfare Reform Act 2007.

Transitional and savings provisions

3.–(1)   The following provisions of the Local Government Act 2000 continue to have effect after 31st August 2008 in relation to information supplied on or before that date by virtue of section 94 of that Act–

(a)   section 94(4), (5) and (6) (which permits the onward supply of information received by virtue of section 94(3) to a person providing qualifying welfare services); and

(b)   section 95 (under which a person is guilty of an offence if he makes an unauthorised disclosure of information).

(2)   Paragraph (1) applies notwithstanding article 2(2) (which brings into force on 1st September 2008 the repeal of sections 94 and 95).

(3)   *[Omitted]*

The Social Security (Use of Information for Housing Benefit and Welfare Services Purposes) Regulations 2008
(SI 2008 No.2112)

Citation and commencement

1. These Regulations may be cited as the Social Security (Use of Information for Housing Benefit and Welfare Services Purposes) Regulations 2008 and shall come into force on 1st September 2008.

Interpretation

2. In these Regulations–

"the 2007 Act" means the Welfare Reform Act 2007;

"benefit or welfare services information" means information falling within section 42(3) of the 2007 Act (information relating to certain benefits);

"claimant" means a person claiming housing benefit;

"excluded tenancy" means a type of tenancy falling within any of paragraphs 4 to 11 of Schedule 2 to the Housing Benefit Regulations (excluded tenancies) or paragraphs 4 to 11 of Schedule 2 to the Housing Benefit (State Pension Credit) Regulations (excluded tenancies), as the case may require;

"exempt accommodation" has the meaning given by sub-paragraph 4(10) of Schedule 3 to the Housing Benefit and Council Tax Benefit (Consequential Provisions) Regulations 2006 (transitional and savings provisions);

"hostel" has the same meaning as it has in the Housing Benefit Regulations or the Housing Benefit (State Pension Credit) Regulations, as the case may require;

"the Housing Benefit Regulations" means the Housing Benefit Regulations 2006;

"the Housing Benefit (State Pension Credit) Regulations" means the Housing Benefit (Persons who have attained the qualifying age for state pension credit) Regulations 2006;

"landlord" includes a person to whom rent is payable by the person entitled to a rent allowance for the purposes of regulation 95 of the Housing Benefit Regulations (circumstances in which payment is to be made to a landlord) or regulation 76 of the Housing Benefit (State Pension Credit) Regulations (circumstances in which payment is to be made to a landlord), as the case may require;

"registered social landlord" has the same meaning as in Part 1 of the Housing Act 1996;

"relevant person" means a person falling within any of paragraphs (c) to (h) of section 42(4) of the 2007 Act;

"rent" has the same meaning as it has in the Housing Benefit Regulations or the Housing Benefit (State Pension Credit) Regulations, as the case may require.

Prescribed purposes in section 42(2) of the 2007 Act

3. Regulations 4, 5 and 6 prescribe meanings of "prescribed purpose" in section 42(2) of the 2007 Act (information relating to certain benefits) for the purposes set out in those regulations.

Holding purposes relating to welfare services

4.–(1) This regulation prescribes the purposes for which a relevant person holds benefit or welfare services information ("holding purposes").

(2) The holding purposes are purposes relating to welfare services which may indicate–

(a) whether a claimant is likely to have difficulty in managing his financial affairs;

(b) the probability that a claimant will pay his rent;

(c) whether a landlord–

    (i) was or is to provide qualifying welfare services within the meaning of section 42(6) of the 2007 Act, but

    (ii) has not provided those services or is unlikely to provide those services;

(d) whether–
    (i) a claimant's landlord is a registered social landlord [¹ or a private registered provider of social housing],
    (ii) a claimant occupies as his home a dwelling which is exempt accommodation,
    (iii) a claimant's tenancy is an excluded tenancy,
    (iv) a claimant occupies a houseboat, caravan or mobile home as his home, or
    (v) a claimant resides in a hostel.

Amendment

1.   Amended by art 4 and Sch 1 para 71 of SI 2010 No 671 as from 1.4.10.

Using purposes relating to housing benefit

5.–(1)   This regulation prescribes meanings of "prescribed purpose" for which benefit or welfare services information may be used ("using purposes") by–
    (a) the relevant person in relation to whom regulation 4 applies; or
    (b) another relevant person to whom the benefit or welfare services information has been provided.

(2)   The using purposes are purposes relating to housing benefit connected with applying any of the following regulations–
    (a) regulation 13C(5) of the Housing Benefit Regulations (when a maximum rent (LHA) is to be determined);
    (b) regulation 96(3) and (3A)(b)(i) or (ii) of the Housing Benefit Regulations (circumstances in which payment may be made to a landlord), if a relevant authority is considering making direct payments in accordance with regulation 96(3A)(b)(i) or (ii);
    (c) regulation 13C(5) of the Housing Benefit (State Pension Credit) Regulations (when a maximum rent (LHA) is to be determined);
    (d) regulation 77(3) and (3A)(b)(i) or (ii) of the Housing Benefit (State Pension Credit) Regulations (circumstances in which payment may be made to a landlord), if a relevant authority is considering making direct payments in accordance with regulation 77(3A)(b)(i) or (ii).

Identifying purposes

6.–(1)   This regulation prescribes meanings of "prescribed purpose" for the purposes of determining whether a relevant person holds benefit or welfare services information related to any holding purpose prescribed by regulation 4 ("identifying purposes").

(2)   The identifying purposes are any purposes relating to housing benefit connected with identifying a claimant.

The Welfare Reform Act (Relevant Enactment) Order 2009
(SI 2009 No.2162)

Citation and commencement

1.–(1)   This Order may be cited as the Welfare Reform Act (Relevant Enactment) Order 2009.

(2)   It comes into force on 1st September 2009.

Relevant enactment

2.   A relevant enactment for the purposes of section 42(1) of the Welfare Reform Act 2007 (information relating to certain benefits) is section 31 of the Local Government Act 2003 (power to pay grant).

The Social Security (Information-sharing in relation to Welfare Services etc.) Regulations 2012
(SI 2012 No.1483)

PART 1
GENERAL

Citation and commencement

1. These Regulations may be cited as the Social Security (Information-sharing in relation to Welfare Services etc.) Regulations 2012 and come into force on 2nd July 2012.

Interpretation

2. In these Regulations–

"the 2012 Act" means the Welfare Reform Act 2012;

"the benefit cap" means the benefit cap (if any) which is provided for in regulations under section 96 of the 2012 Act;

[⁴ "Careers Wales" means the company with the name Career Choices Dewis Gyrfa Ltd. which is trading as Careers Wales and which is established by the Welsh Government to provide careers services in Wales under sections 2, 8 and 10 of the Employment and Training Act 1973;]

"the Contributions and Benefits Act" means the Social Security Contributions and Benefits Act 1992;

[² "council tax reduction scheme"–

    (a)   in England and Wales, has the meaning given in section 13A(9) of the Local Government Finance Act 1992(c) and (in England) includes a default scheme within the meaning of paragraph 4 of Schedule 1A to that Act; and

    (b)   in Scotland, means a means-tested reduction to an individual's council tax liability in accordance with the Council Tax Reduction (Scotland) Regulations 2012(d) or the Council Tax Reduction (State Pension Credit) (Scotland) Regulations 2012;

"disabled person's badge" means a badge issued under section 21 of the Chronically Sick and Disabled Persons Act 1970 (badges for display on motor vehicles used by disabled persons);

[² "the healthy start scheme" means the scheme established by the Healthy Start Scheme and Welfare Food (Amendment) Regulations 2005;]

"housing benefit" means housing benefit under section 130 of the Contributions and Benefits Act;

"housing benefit claimant" means a person who has made a claim for or is in receipt of housing benefit;

"the Housing Benefit Regulations" means the Housing Benefit Regulations 2006;

"the Housing Benefit (State Pension Credit) Regulations" means the Housing Benefit (Persons who have attained the qualifying age for state pension credit) Regulations 2006;

"housing support services" means–

    in England, non-statutory assistance;

    in Wales, services provided under the supporting people programme in Wales;

    in Scotland, services of a type falling within the Schedule to the Housing (Scotland) Act 2001 (Housing Support Services) Regulations 2002;

"landlord" includes a person to whom rent allowance is payable under the Housing Benefit Regulations or regulation 76 of the Housing Benefit (State Pension Credit) Regulations (circumstances in which payment is to be made to a landlord), as the case may require;

[² "local welfare provision" means occasional financial or other assistance given by a local authority, the Scottish Ministers or the Welsh Ministers, or a person

authorised to exercise any function of theirs or providing a service to them, to
or in respect of individuals for the purpose of–
  (a) meeting, or helping to meet, an immediate short term need–
      (i)   arising out of an exceptional event or exceptional circumstances; and
      (ii)   that requires to be met in order to avoid a risk to the well-being of an
individual; or
  (b) enabling individuals to establish or maintain a settled home, where those
individuals have been or, without the assistance, might otherwise be–
      (i)   in prison, hospital, a residential care establishment or other institution; or
      (ii)   homeless or otherwise living an unsettled way of life;]
"non-statutory assistance" means assistance provided by a local authority in England, in
the form of the funding, planning, monitoring or delivery of housing-related
support services for the purpose of enabling people aged 16 or over to overcome
barriers to participation in society by assisting such people to live more
independently within their home or community, but does not include the grant
of a tenancy or the provision of accommodation;
[² "offence relating to a council tax reduction" means–
  (a) any criminal offence in connection with the making of an application for a
reduction under a council tax reduction scheme;
  (b) any criminal offence in connection with the award of a reduction under a council
tax reduction scheme;
  (c) any criminal offence committed for the purpose of facilitating the commission
(whether or not by the same person) of an offence of a kind referred to in
paragraph (a) or (b); or
  (d) any attempt or conspiracy to commit an offence of a kind referred to in paragraph
(a) or (b);]
"regulations relating to under-occupation" means regulations (if any) that have been
made under section 130A of the Contributions and Benefits Act which restrict,
by reference to the number of bedrooms in relation to the number of people
occupying the dwelling as their home, the amount of housing benefit available
to housing benefit claimants whose landlord is a social landlord or local
authority;
"rent" is to be construed in accordance with regulation 2(1) of the Housing Benefit
Regulations or regulation 2(1) of the Housing Benefit (State Pension Credit)
Regulations, as the case may require;
"residential care" means–
  (a) in England [⁵], the provision of accommodation together with nursing and
personal care in a care home as defined in section 3 of the Care Standards Act
2000;
  [⁵ (aa) in Wales, the provision of a care home service within the meaning of Part 1 of
the Regulation and Inspection of Social Care (Wales) Act 2016 which is
provided wholly or mainly to persons aged 18 or over;]
  (b) in Scotland, the provision of accommodation together with nursing, personal
care or personal support by a care home service as defined in paragraph 2 of
Schedule 12 to the Public Services Reform (Scotland) Act 2010;
[³ "social landlord" means–
  (a) in a case to which the Housing Benefit Regulations apply, a landlord falling
within regulation 13C(5)(a)(i), (ii) or (iii) of those Regulations;
  (b) in a case to which the Housing Benefit (State Pension Credit) Regulations apply,
a landlord falling within regulation 13C(5)(a)(i), (ii) or (iii) of those Regulations;
  (c) in a case to which the Universal Credit Regulations 2013 apply, a provider of
social housing within the definition given in paragraph 2 of Schedule 4 (housing
costs element for renters) to those Regulations;]
"the supporting people programme in Wales" means the programme of assistance
provided by local authorities in Wales, in the form of the funding, planning,
monitoring or delivery of housing-related support services for the purpose of
enabling people aged 16 or over to overcome barriers to participation in society

by assisting such people to live more independently within their home or community, other than through the grant of a tenancy or the provision of accommodation;

[² "troubled families programme" means any programme of assistance provided by a local authority] in England, for the purpose of engaging with households who face multiple disadvantages (such as crime, worklessness, truancy and anti-social behaviour), in the form of the funding, planning, monitoring or delivery of support services which assist members of such households to obtain employment, education or training, improve school attendance, or address crime and anti-social behaviour.

[² "universal credit" means universal credit under Part 1 of the 2012 Act.]

[³ "universal credit claimant" means a person who has made a claim for or has an award of universal credit;]

[³ "universal support initiative" means any initiative under which advice, assistance or support is provided by the Secretary of State or any qualifying persons listed in regulation 10(1)(e) to a universal credit claimant for the purposes of assisting them with–

(a)   managing their claim for or award of universal credit, including accessing and using online services, or

(b)   managing their financial affairs.]

Amendments

1.   Inserted by reg 2(2) of SI 2013 No 14 as from 1.2.13.
2.   Inserted by reg 3(2) of SI 2013 No 454 as from 1.4.13.
3.   Amended by reg 2(2) of SI 2015 No 46 as from 13.2.15.
4.   Inserted by reg 2(2)(a) of SI 2017 No 1016 as from 15.11.17.
5.   Amended by reg 12 of SI 2018 No 228 as from 2.4.18.

Prescription of Welsh body

[¹**2A.**   Careers Wales is prescribed as a Welsh body for the purpose of section 131 of the 2012 Act.]

Amendment

1.   Inserted by reg 2(2)(b) of SI 2017 No 1016 as from 15.11.17.

PART 2
INFORMATION-SHARING IN RELATION TO PROVISION OF OVERNIGHT CARE ETC. UNDER SECTION 130 OF THE 2012 ACT

Prescribed information

3.–(1)   The information prescribed under section 130(2)(c) of the 2012 Act (information held by a local authority) is–

(a)   whether a resident is meeting in full the cost of the provision to them of residential care and if so the date this commenced and the period over which the cost is intended to be met;

(b)   whether the local authority is funding or has funded in full or in part the cost of the provision to a resident of residential care and if so–

(i)   the date from which the funding commenced and the period covered or intended to be covered by it;

(ii)   the date when the funding stopped or is intended to stop;

(iii)   the enactment under which the funding is being or was provided;

(iv)   whether there exists any agreement enabling the local authority to recover the cost of the funding on the sale of the resident's home and if so, whether that recovery has commenced or when it is intended to commence; and

(v)   whether the local authority has entered into a deferred payment agreement with the resident and if so the date this commenced and the period the agreement is intended to cover.

(2) In this regulation–
(a) "deferred payment agreement" has the meaning given in section 55(3) of the Health and Social Care Act 2001 or (in Scotland) section 6(2) of the Community Care and Health (Scotland) Act 2002;
(b) "resident" means a recipient of residential care.

Prescribed benefits
4. The benefits prescribed under section 130(7)(d) of the 2012 Act are–
(a) attendance allowance under section 64 of the Contributions and Benefits Act;
(b) disability living allowance under section 71 of the Contributions and Benefits Act;
(c) income-based jobseeker's allowance within the meaning given in section 1(4) of the Jobseekers Act 1995;
(d) income-related employment and support allowance payable in accordance with section 1(2)(b) of the Welfare Reform Act 2007;
(e) income support under section 124 of the Contributions and Benefits Act; and
(f) state pension credit under section 1 of the State Pension Credit Act 2002 [¹ and]
[¹(g) personal independence payment under Part 4 of the 2012 Act]

Amendment
1.   Amended by reg 8 and Sch para 48 of SI 2013 No 388 as from 8.4.13.

PART 3
INFORMATION-SHARING IN RELATION TO WELFARE SERVICES [¹] UNDER SECTIONS 131 TO 133 OF THE 2012 ACT

Amendment
1.   Amended by reg 2(3) of SI 2013 No 14 as from 1.2.13.

Supply of relevant information by the Secretary of State
5.–(1) The purposes prescribed under section 131(1) of the 2012 Act [² in relation to welfare services] (purposes for which the Secretary of State or a person providing services to the Secretary of State may supply relevant information to a qualifying person) are–
[² (a) determining a person's eligibility or continued eligibility for–
   (i)   a disabled person's badge;
   (ii)   assistance under the healthy start scheme; or
   (iii) local welfare provision;]
   determining a person's eligibility or continued eligibility for a disabled person's badge;
(b) determining whether to make to any person any grant or payment listed in paragraph (2) and if so the amount of any such grant or payment;
(c) determining whether a person applying for or receiving a welfare service listed in paragraph (3) is liable to contribute towards the cost of that service and if so the amount of that contribution; [¹]
[² (d) where the qualifying person is a local authority in England–
   (i)   identifying households eligible for support under a troubled families programme;
   (ii)   providing appropriate types of advice, support and assistance to members of such households under such programmes; and
   (iii) monitoring and evaluating such programmes;]
[² (e) discharging any functions under Part 7 of the Housing Act 1996 or (in Scotland) Part 2 of the Housing (Scotland) Act 1987; [⁴]]
[² (f) identifying, and providing appropriate types of advice, support and assistance to, persons in receipt of a relevant social security benefit who are or may be affected by–
   (i)   the benefit cap;
   (ii)   regulations relating to under-occupation.]

[³ (g) where the qualifying person is a social landlord and the relevant information is limited to information referred to in paragraph (3A), determining whether a universal credit claimant, whose award includes or is likely to include a housing costs element in respect of accommodation provided by that social landlord, needs advice, assistance or support in relation to managing their financial affairs;

(h) where the qualifying person is listed in regulation 10(1)(e) and the Secretary of State or any qualifying person listed in regulation 10(1)(e) determines that a universal credit claimant needs advice, assistance or support under a universal support initiative–
    (i) providing such advice, assistance or support to that person; and
    (ii) monitoring and evaluating the provision of such advice, assistance or support.] [⁴ and;

(i) where the qualifying person is Careers Wales–
    (i) identifying persons in Wales aged 18 or over but under 25 who are not in employment and not receiving either education or training;
    (ii) providing advice, assistance and support to such persons;
    (iii) monitoring and evaluating the provision of such advice, assistance and support.]

(2) The grants and payments referred to in paragraph (1)(b) are–
(a) a disability adaptation grant;
(b) a disabled facilities grant;
(c) a discretionary housing payment.

(3) The welfare services referred to in paragraph (1)(c) are–
(a) housing support services;
(b) the provision of domiciliary care;
(c) the provision of residential care.

[³ (3A) The information referred to in paragraph (1)(g) is information confirming–
(a) the identity of the universal credit claimant;
(b) that the universal credit claimant has a tenancy with the social landlord;
(c) the date on which the universal credit claimant made a claim for or was awarded universal credit; or
(d) in a case where universal credit has been awarded to the universal credit claimant–
    (i) the date on which the next payment of universal credit is due to be paid;
    (ii) whether the next payment is the first payment under the award; or
    (iii) the amount of housing costs element in the next payment under the award.]

(4) In this regulation–
(a) "disability adaptation grant" means a grant paid under Part 2 of the Housing (Scotland) Act 2006 to assist with the adaptation of a house for a disabled person to make it suitable for the accommodation, welfare or employment of that person;
(b) "disabled facilities grant" means a grant paid under Chapter 1 of Part 1 of the Housing Grants, Construction and Regeneration Act 1996;
(c) "discretionary housing payment" means a payment made pursuant to regulation 2(1) of the Discretionary Financial Assistance Regulations 2001;
(d) "domiciliary care" means care or assistance of any description provided to an adult person by reason of their age, health or any disability, whether provided continuously or not and whether or not provided at a place where they live, but excludes care or assistance provided to a person in residential care.
[³ (e) "housing costs element" means an amount in respect of housing costs which is included in an award of universal credit under section 11 of the 2012 Act.]

Amendments
1.   Amended by reg 2(4) of SI 2013 No 41 as from 1.2.13.
2.   Amended by reg 3(3) of SI 2013 No 454 as from 1.4.13.
3.   Amended by reg 2(3) of SI 2015 No 46 as from 13.2.15.
4.   Amended by reg 2(3) of SI 2017 No 1016 as from 15.11.17.

Holding purposes

6.–(1)   The purposes prescribed under section 131(3) of the 2012 Act [¹ in relation to welfare services] as purposes for which relevant information must be held by a qualifying person in order for them to use or supply it as set out in that subsection, are any of the following–

[³ (a) determining a person's eligibility or continued eligibility for–
    (i)   a disabled person's badge;
    (ii)   assistance under the healthy start scheme;
    (iii) housing support services; or
    (iv)   local welfare provision;]

(b) determining whether to make to any person any grant or payment listed in regulation 5(2) and if so the amount of any such grant or payment;

(c) determining whether a person applying for or receiving a welfare service listed in regulation 5(3) is liable to contribute towards the cost of that service and if so the amount of that contribution;

[³ (d) where the qualifying person is a local authority in England, a person providing services to a local authority in England relating to a troubled families programme, or a person who falls within regulation 10(1)(b)–
    (i)   identifying households eligible for support under a troubled families programme;
    (ii)   providing appropriate types of advice, support and assistance to members of such households under such programmes; and
    (iii) monitoring and evaluating such programmes;]

(e) discharging any functions under Part 7 of the Housing Act 1996 or (in Scotland) Part 2 of the Housing (Scotland) Act 1987;

(f) determining whether a person is in receipt of housing benefit;

(g) determining the size of a dwelling occupied by a [³ person in receipt of a relevant social security benefit] and the number of persons occupying that dwelling as their home;

(h) identifying [³ persons in receipt of a relevant social security benefit] who are or may be affected by regulations relating to under-occupation, and providing appropriate types of advice, support and assistance to such persons;

(i) identifying [³ persons in receipt of a relevant social security benefit] who are or may be affected by the benefit cap, and providing appropriate types of advice, support and assistance to such persons;

(j) determining the amount of housing benefit payable to a housing benefit claimant by reference to the local housing allowance;

[² (k)]

(l) determining whether a [³ person in receipt of a relevant social security benefit] is likely to have difficulty in managing their financial affairs;

(m) determining the probability that a housing benefit claimant will pay their rent;

(n) determining whether the landlord of a housing benefit claimant–
    (i)   was to provide qualifying welfare services to that housing benefit claimant but has not done so, or
    (ii)   is to provide qualifying welfare services to that housing benefit claimant but is unlikely to do so;

(o) determining whether–
    (i)   the landlord of a housing benefit claimant is a social landlord,
    (ii)   a housing benefit claimant occupies as their home a dwelling which is exempt accommodation,
    (iii) the tenancy of a housing benefit claimant is an excluded tenancy,
    (iv)   a housing benefit claimant occupies as their home a houseboat, caravan or mobile home, or
    (v)   a housing benefit claimant resides in a hostel.

[³ (p) identifying the amount of housing costs included in an award of universal credit by reference to the local housing allowance.]

[⁴ (q) where the qualifying person is listed in regulation 10(1)(e)–

(i)   providing advice, assistance or support to a universal credit claimant under a universal support initiative; and

(ii)   monitoring and evaluating the provision of such advice, assistance or support.]

[⁵ (r)   where the qualifying person is Careers Wales–

(i)   identifying persons in Wales aged 18 or over but under 25 who are not in employment and not receiving either education or training;

(ii)   providing advice, assistance and support to such persons;

(iii)   monitoring and evaluating the provision of such advice, assistance and support.]

(2)   In this regulation–

(a)   "excluded tenancy" means a tenancy of a type falling within any of paragraphs 4 to 11 of Schedule 2 to the Housing Benefit Regulations or paragraphs 4 to 11 of Schedule 2 to the Housing Benefit (State Pension Credit) Regulations, as the case may require;

(b)   "exempt accommodation" has the meaning given in paragraph 4(10) of Schedule 3 to the Housing Benefit and Council Tax Benefit (Consequential Provisions) Regulations 2006 (transitional and savings provision);

(c)   "hostel" has the meaning given in regulation 2(1) of the Housing Benefit Regulations or regulation 2(1) of the Housing Benefit (State Pension Credit) Regulations, as the case may require;

(d)   "local housing allowance" means an allowance determined in accordance with paragraph 2 of Schedule 3B to the Rent Officers Order;

(e)   "Rent Officers Order" means the Rent Officers (Housing Benefit Functions) Order 1997 or (in Scotland) the Rent Officers (Housing Benefit Functions) (Scotland) Order 1997.

Amendments

1.   Amended by reg 2(4) of SI 2013 No 41 as from 1.2.13.
2.   Deleted by reg 3 and Sch 1 of SI 2013 No 458 as from 1.4.13.
3.   Amended by reg 3(4) of SI 2013 No 454 as from 1.4.13.
4.   Amended by reg 2(4) of SI 2015 No 46 as from 13.2.15.
5.   Inserted by reg 2(4) of SI 2017 No 1016 as from 15.11.17.

Using purposes connected with welfare services and housing benefit

7.–(1)   This regulation applies to relevant information held by a qualifying person for any [¹ purposes listed in regulation 6(1)(a)(ii), (iv) or (d)] except the purpose listed in regulation 6(d).

(2)   The purposes set out in paragraph (3) are prescribed–

(a)   under section 131(3)(a) of the 2012 Act as purposes for which the information may be used by that qualifying person; and

(b)   subject to regulation 11, under section 131(3)(b) of the 2012 Act as purposes for use in relation to which the information may be supplied by that qualifying person to another qualifying person.

(3)   The purposes are any purposes connected with–

[(a)   the purposes referred to in regulation 6(1)(a)(i) or (iii), (b), (c), (e), (h) or (i);]

(b)   applying any of the following regulations–

(i)   regulation 13C(5) of the Housing Benefit Regulations (cases where a maximum rent (LHA) is not to be determined);

(ii)   regulation 96(3) or (3A) of the Housing Benefit Regulations (circumstances in which payment may be made to a landlord);

(iii)   regulation 13C(5) of the Housing Benefit (State Pension Credit) Regulations (cases where a maximum rent (LHA) is not to be determined);

(iv)   regulation 77(3) or (3A) of the Housing Benefit (State Pension Credit) Regulations (circumstances in which payment may be made to a landlord);

(c)   determining whether the qualifying person who uses the information or to whom it is supplied holds other relevant information about a [¹ person in receipt of a relevant social security benefit] for any purpose prescribed in regulation 6.

Amendment
1.   Amended by reg 3(5) of SI 2013 No 454 as from 1.4.13.

Using purposes connected with [¹ a troubled families programme]

8.–(1)   This regulation applies to relevant information held by a qualifying person which is a local authority in England [¹ or a person who falls within regulation 10(1)(b)] for the purpose listed in regulation [¹ 6(1)(d) or the purpose listed in regulation [¹ 6(1)(i).

(2)   The purposes set out in paragraph (3) are prescribed–

(a)   under section 131(3)(a) of the 2012 Act as purposes for which the information may be used by that qualifying person; and

(b)   under section 131(3)(b) of the 2012 Act as purposes for use in relation to which the information may be supplied by that qualifying person to another qualifying person.

(3)   The purposes are any purposes connected with [¹ a troubled families programme].

(4)   This regulation permits relevant information to be supplied to another qualifying person only where that other qualifying person is also a local authority in England [or a person who falls within regulation 10(1)(b).].

[¹ (5)   The references in regulations 8(1) and (4) to a local authority in England include references to a person providing services to a local authority in England relating to a troubled families programme.]

Amendment
1.   Amended by reg 3(6) of SI 2013 No 454 as from 1.4.13.

Using purposes connected with under-occupation and benefit cap

9.–(1)   This regulation applies to relevant information held by a qualifying person for any purpose listed in regulation [¹ 6(1)(f)] to (i).

(2)   The purposes set out in paragraph (3) are prescribed–

(a)   under section 131(3)(a) of the 2012 Act as purposes for which the information may be used by that qualifying person; and

(b)   under section 131(3)(b) of the 2012 Act as purposes for use in relation to which the information may be supplied by that qualifying person to another qualifying person.

(3)   The purposes are any purposes connected with–

(a)   identifying [¹ persons in receipt of a relevant social security benefit] who are or may be affected by regulations relating to under-occupation, and providing appropriate types of advice, support and assistance to such persons;

(b)   identifying [¹ persons in receipt of a relevant social security benefit] who are or may be affected by the benefit cap, and providing appropriate types of advice, support and assistance to such persons.

Amendment
1.   Amended by reg 3(7) and (8) of SI 2013 No 454 as from 1.4.13.

[¹Using purposes connected with the healthy start scheme

9A.–(1)   This regulation applies to relevant information held by the Secretary of State for Health [² and Social Care] or by a person providing services to the Secretary of State for Health, as a qualifying person for the purpose listed in regulation 6(1)(a)(ii).

(2)   The purposes set out in paragraph (3) are prescribed–

(a)   under section 131(3)(a) of the 2012 Act as purposes for which the information may be used by that qualifying person; and

(b)   under section 131(3)(b) of the 2012 Act as purposes for use in relation to which the information may be supplied by that qualifying person to another qualifying person.

(3)   The purposes are any purposes connected with the healthy start scheme.

(4)   This regulation permits relevant information to be supplied to another qualifying person only where that other qualifying person is the Secretary of State for Health [² and

Social Care] or a person providing services to the Secretary of State for Health relating to the healthy start scheme.]

Amendments
1.　Inserted by reg 3(9) of SI 2013 No 454 as from 1.4.13.
2.　Amended by the Sch para 21(p) of SI 2018 No 378 as from 11.4.18.

[¹ Using purposes connected with local welfare provision
9B.–(1)　This regulation applies to relevant information held by a qualifying person listed in regulation 10(1)(d) or section 131(11)(a) to (c) of the 2012 Act for the purpose listed in regulation 6(1)(a)(iv).
(2)　The purposes set out in paragraph (3) are prescribed–
(a)　under section 131(3)(a) of the 2012 Act as purposes for which the information may be used by a qualifying person; and
(b)　subject to regulation 11, under section 131(3)(b) of the 2012 Act as purposes for use in relation to which the information may be supplied by that qualifying person to another qualifying person.
(3)　The purposes are any purposes connected with local welfare provision.
(4)　This regulation permits relevant information to be supplied to another qualifying person only where that other qualifying person is listed in regulation 10(1)(d) or section 131(11)(a) to (c) of the 2012 Act.]

Amendment
1.　Inserted by reg 3(9) of SI 2013 No 454 as from 1.4.13.

[¹ Using purposes connected with a universal support initiative
9C.–(1)　This regulation applies to relevant information held by a qualifying person listed in regulation 10(1)(e) for the purposes listed in regulation 6(1)(q).
(2)　The purposes set out in paragraph (3) are prescribed–
(a)　under section 131(3)(a) of the 2012 Act as purposes for which the information may be used by that qualifying person; and
(b)　under section 131(3)(b) of the 2012 Act as purposes for use in relation to which the information may be supplied by that qualifying person to another qualifying person.
(3)　The purposes are any purposes connected with–
(a)　providing advice, assistance or support to a universal credit claimant under a universal support initiative; and
(b)　monitoring and evaluating the provision of such advice, assistance or support.
(4)　This regulation permits relevant information to be supplied to another qualifying person only where that other qualifying person is listed in regulation 10(1)(e).]

Amendment
1.　Inserted by reg 2(5) of SI 2015 No 46 as from 13.2.15.

Qualifying persons
[¹**10.**–(1)　The following persons are prescribed as qualifying persons under section 131(11)(g) of the 2012 Act–
(a)　for the purposes of regulations [² 5(1)(g),] 6(1)(f) to (i) and 9, a social landlord;
(b)　for the purposes of regulations 6(1)(d) and 8, a person who carries out activities in connection with a troubled families programme;
(c)　for the purposes of regulations 5(1)(a)(ii), 6(1)(a)(ii) and 9A–
(i)　the Secretary of State for Health [⁴ and Social Care];
(ii)　a person providing services to the Secretary of State for Health relating to the healthy start scheme;
(d)　for the purposes of regulations 5(1)(a)(iii), 6(1)(a)(iv) and 9B–
(i)　the Scottish Ministers;
(ii)　a person authorised to exercise any function of the Scottish Ministers relating to local welfare provision;

(iii)   a person providing to the Scottish Ministers services relating to local welfare provision;

(iv)   the Welsh Ministers;

(v)   a person authorised to exercise any function of the Welsh Ministers relating to local welfare provision;

(vi)   a person providing to the Welsh Ministers services relating to local welfare provision.

[² (e)   for the purposes of regulations 5(1)(h), 6(1)(q), 9C, 16(d) and 17(3)(c)–

(i)   a person listed in section 131(11)(a), (b) or (c) of the 2012 Act,

(ii)   a member of the National Association of Citizens Advice Bureaux or the Scottish Association of Citizens Advice Bureaux,

(iii)   a credit union within section 1 of the Credit Unions Act 1979,

(iv)   a social landlord,

(v)   a charity entered in the register of charities maintained under Part 4 of the Charities Act 2011 or a body entered on the register of charities maintained under the Charities and Trustee Investment (Scotland) Act 2005.]

[³ (f)   for the purposes of regulations 5(1)(i) and 6(1)(r), Careers Wales.]

(2)   The provisions of section 132 of the 2012 Act (offence of unlawful disclosure) apply to–

(a)   the qualifying persons listed in paragraph (1) other than the Secretary of State for Health [⁴ and Social Care], the Scottish Ministers and the Welsh Ministers; and

(b)   any person ("A") associated with a qualifying person listed in paragraph (1)(a), (c)(i), (d)(i) or (iv) by reason of A's office or employment or otherwise.]

Amendments

1.   Substituted by reg 3(10) of SI 2013 No 454 as from 1.4.13.

2.   Amended by reg 2(6) of SI 2015 No 46 as from 13.2.15.

3.   Inserted by reg 2(5) of SI 2017 No 1016 as from 15.11.17.

4.   Amended by the Sch para 21(p) of SI 2018 No 378 as from 11.4.18.

Excepted matters

11.–(1)   Regulation 7(2)(b) does not permit relevant information held by a Welsh body or a Scottish body for a purpose listed in regulation [¹ 6(1)(a)(i) or (iii)], (b), (c) or (e) to be supplied by that body to another qualifying person for use in relation to the same or any other such purpose.

[¹ (1A)   Regulation 9B(2)(b) does not permit relevant information held by a Welsh body or a Scottish body to be supplied by that body to another qualifying person for use in relation to any purpose connected with local welfare provision.]

(2)   This regulation does not apply if the information was supplied by, or is derived from information supplied to another person by, the Secretary of State or a person providing services to the Secretary of State or a person engaged in the administration of housing benefit.

Amendment

1.   Amended by reg 3(11) of SI 2013 No 454 as from 1.4.13.

PART 4

INFORMATION-SHARING IN RELATION TO COUNCIL TAX UNDER SECTIONS 131 TO 133 OF THE 2012 ACT

[¹ **Supply of relevant information by the Secretary of State**

12.   The purposes prescribed under section 131(1) of the 2012 Act in relation to council tax (purposes for which the Secretary of State or a person providing services to the Secretary of State may supply relevant information to a qualifying person) are–

(a)   making a council tax reduction scheme;

(b)   determining a person's entitlement or continued entitlement to a reduction under a council tax reduction scheme.]

Amendment
1.   Inserted by reg 2(5) of SI 2013 No 14 as from 1.2.13.

[¹ **Holding purposes**
13.   The purposes prescribed under section 131(3) of the 2012 Act in relation to council tax as purposes for which relevant information must be held by a qualifying person in order for them to use or supply it as set out in that subsection, are–
(a)   making a council tax reduction scheme;
(b)   determining a person's entitlement or continued entitlement to a reduction under a council tax reduction scheme.]

Amendment
1.   Inserted by reg 2(5) of SI 2013 No 14 as from 1.2.13.

[¹ **Using purposes**
14.–(1)   This regulation applies to relevant information held by a qualifying person for any purpose listed in regulation 12.
(2)   The purposes set out in paragraph (3) are prescribed–
(a)   under section 131(3)(a) of the 2012 Act as a purpose for which the information may by used by that qualifying person; and
(b)   subject to regulation 16, under section 131(3)(b) of the 2012 Act as a purpose for use in relation to which the information may be supplied by that qualifying person to another qualifying person.
(3)   The purposes are any purposes connected with–
(a)   making a council tax reduction scheme;
(b)   determining a person's entitlement or continued entitlement to a reduction under a council tax reduction scheme.]

Amendment
1.   Inserted by reg 2(5) of SI 2013 No 14 as from 1.2.13.

[¹ **Excepted matters**
15.–(1)   Subject to paragraph (2), regulation 14 does not permit relevant information held by a Welsh body or a Scottish body to be supplied by that body to another qualifying person for use in relation to that purpose.
(2)   Paragraph (1) does not apply if the information was supplied by, or is derived from, information supplied to another person by the Secretary of State (or a person providing services to the Secretary of State) or a person engaged in the administration of housing benefit.]

Amendment
1.   Inserted by reg 2(5) of SI 2013 No 14 as from 1.2.13.

PART 5
INFORMATION-SHARING IN RELATION TO SOCIAL SECURITY BENEFITS
UNDER SECTION 131(2) OF THE 2012 ACT

[¹ **Holding purposes**
16.   The purposes prescribed under section 131(2) of the 2012 Act (supply of information to the Secretary of State or service provider for purposes relating to relevant social security benefit) as purposes for which relevant information must be held by a qualifying person in order for them to supply it as set out in that subsection, are any of the following–
(a)   determining whether a person occupies as their home a dwelling which falls within paragraph 4(1)(b) of Schedule 3 to the Housing Benefit and Council Tax Benefit (Consequential Provisions) Regulations 2006;
(b)   determining whether a person has, or is likely to have, difficulty in managing their financial affairs;

(c) where the qualifying person is a local authority in England–
 (i) identifying households eligible for support under a troubled families programme;
 (ii) providing appropriate types of advice, support and assistance to members of such households under such programmes; and
 (iii) monitoring and evaluating such programmes.]

[² (d) where the qualifying person is listed in regulation 10(1)(e)–
 (i) providing advice, assistance or support to a universal credit claimant under a universal support initiative; and
 (ii) monitoring and evaluating the provision of such advice, assistance or support.]

Amendments

1. Inserted by reg 3(16) of SI 2013 No 454 as from 1.4.13.
2. Amended by reg 2(7) of SI 2015 No 46 as from 13.2.15.

[¹ **Prescribed purposes relating to a relevant social security benefit**

17.–(1) This regulation applies to relevant information held by a qualifying person for any purpose listed in regulation 16.

(2) The purposes set out in paragraph (3) are prescribed under section 131(2) of the 2012 Act as purposes for which the information may be supplied to the Secretary of State or a person providing services to the Secretary of State.

(3) Those purposes are–

(a) in relation to the purposes prescribed in regulation 16(a) and (b), any purpose connected with the administration of universal credit;

(b) in relation to any purpose prescribed in regulation 16(c)–
 (i) any purpose connected with providing appropriate types of advice, support and assistance to a person in connection with their receipt of a relevant social security benefit; and
 (ii) any purpose connected with monitoring and evaluating the effect of participation in a troubled families programme on receipt of a relevant social security benefit.]

[² (c) in relation to either of the purposes prescribed in regulation 16(d)–
 (i) providing advice, assistance or support to a universal credit claimant under a universal support initiative; and
 (ii) monitoring and evaluating the provision of such advice, assistance or support.]

Amendments

1. Inserted by reg 3(16) of SI 2013 No 454 as from 1.4.13.
2. Amended by reg 2(8) of SI 2015 No 46 as from 13.2.15.

The Welfare Reform Act 2012 (Commencement No.3, Savings Provision) Order 2012

(2012 No.1651)

Citation and interpretation

1. This order may be cited as the Welfare Reform Act 2012 (Commencement No.3, Savings Provision) Order 2012.

Appointed Day

2. Subject to article 3, 2nd July 2012 is the day appointed for the coming into force of section 133(6) of the Welfare Reform Act 2012.

Savings provision

3. Notwithstanding their repeal by section 133(6) of the Welfare Reform Act 2012, the following provisions of the Welfare Reform Act 2007 continue to have effect on and after 2nd July 2012–

(a) section 42 (which concerns the use, supply and provision of information) insofar as it permits the use, supply or provision by any person of information which came to that person before that date by virtue of subsection (1), (2) or (5) of that section;

(b) section 43 (which creates an offence of unlawful disclosure) insofar as it relates to the disclosure by any person of such information; and

(c) *[Omitted]*

The Social Security (Civil Penalties) Regulations 2012
(2012 No.1990)

Citation, commencement and interpretation

1.–(1) These Regulations may be cited as the Social Security (Civil Penalties) Regulations 2012 and come into force on 1st October 2012.

(2) In these Regulations, "the Act" means the Social Security Administration Act 1992.

Prescribed amount of penalty: section 115C of the Act

2. The prescribed amount of the penalty for the purpose of section 115C(2) of the Act (incorrect statements etc.) is £50.

Prescribed amount of penalty: section 115D(1) of the Act

3. The prescribed amount of the penalty for the purpose of section 115D(1) of the Act (failure to provide information) is £50.

Prescribed amount of penalty: section 115D(2) of the Act

4. The prescribed amount of the penalty for the purpose of section 115D(2) of the Act (failure to notify appropriate authority of a relevant change of circumstances) is £50.

The Social Security (Overpayments and Recovery) Regulations 2013
(SI 2013 No.384)

Citation and commencement

1.–(1) These Regulations may be cited as the Social Security (Overpayments and Recovery) Regulations 2013.

(2) The following provisions of these Regulations come into force on 8th April 2013–

(a) this Part;

(b) Part 6 and Schedules 1 and 2;

(c) *[Omitted]*

(d) regulation 33(1), (2)(a) and (c) and (3); and

(e) regulation 34(1), (2)(a) and (c) and (3).

(3) All other provisions of these Regulations come into force on 29th April 2013.

Interpretation

2. In these Regulations–

"the Act" means the Social Security Administration Act 1992;

"liable person" means the person from whom a recoverable amount is recoverable;

"recoverable amount" is to be construed in accordance with regulation 3;

PART 2

Recoverability

Recoverable amounts

3.–(1) In these Regulations, "recoverable amount" means–

(a) subject to regulations 7 to 9, the amount of any overpayment; and

(b) any other amount recoverable under any provision of the Act specified in paragraph (2).

(2) Those provisions are–

(a)-(c) *[Omitted]*

(d) section 115B(4) (recovery of penalties imposed as an alternative to prosecution);

(e) section 115C(4) (recovery of civil penalties for incorrect statements); and

(f) section 115D(4) (recovery of civil penalties for failure to disclose information).

PART 6

Recovery by deduction from earnings

Interpretation of Part 6

17.–(1) In this Part–

"appropriate authority", in relation to any recoverable amount, means–

(a) the Secretary of State; or

(b) an authority administering housing benefit if the recoverable amount is recoverable by that authority under section 115B(4)(a), 115C or 115D of the Act,

and where a notice has been issued, "the appropriate authority" means the appropriate authority which issued the notice;

"notice" means a notice issued by an appropriate authority requiring an employer to make deductions from earnings to be paid by the employer to a liable person employed by them and to pay corresponding amounts to that appropriate authority in respect of the recovery of a recoverable amount from the liable person;

"pay-day" in relation to a liable person means an occasion on which earnings are paid to them or the day on which such earnings would normally fall to be paid;

"protected earnings proportion", in relation to a deduction by an employer from a liable person's net earnings, is 60 per cent. of the liable person's net earnings during the period to which the deduction relates, as calculated by the liable person's employer on the relevant payday.

(2)   In this Part, subject to paragraph (3), "earnings" means any sums payable to a person–

(a)   by way of wages or salary (including any fees, bonus, commission, overtime pay or other emoluments payable in addition to wages or salary payable under a contract of service);

(b)   by way of pension which is paid with wages or salary (including an annuity in respect of past service, whether or not rendered to the person paying the annuity, and including periodical payments by way of compensation for the loss, abolition or relinquishment, or diminution in the emoluments, of any office or employment); or

(c)   by way of statutory sick pay.

(3)   "Earnings" does not include–

(a)   sums payable by any public department of the Government of Northern Ireland or of a territory outside the United Kingdom;

(b)   pay or allowances payable to the liable person as a member of Her Majesty's forces other than pay or allowances payable by their employer to them as a special member of a reserve force (within the meaning of the Reserve Forces Act 1996);

(c)   other pensions, allowances or benefit payable under any enactment relating to social security;

(d)   pension or allowances payable in respect of disablement or disability;

(e)   guaranteed minimum pension within the meaning of the Pension Schemes Act 1993;

(f)   working tax credit payable under section 10 of the Tax Credits Act 2002;

(g)   sums paid to reimburse expenses wholly and necessarily incurred in the course of the employment.

(4)   "Net earnings" means the residue of earnings after deduction of–

(a)   income tax;

(b)   primary Class I contributions under Part 1 of the Social Security Contributions and Benefits Act 1992;

(c)   amounts deductible by way of contributions to a superannuation scheme which provides for the payment of annuities or lump sums–

(i)   to the employee on retirement at a specified age or on becoming incapacitated at some earlier age; or

(ii)   on the employee's death or otherwise, to their personal representative, widow, surviving civil partner, relatives or dependants.

(5)   Where these Regulations refer to a notice or notification being given or sent, if sent by post to the last known address of the recipient, it is to be treated as having been given or sent on the day on which it is posted.

Exemption from this Part

18.   This Part does not impose any obligation on an employer who is carrying on a business which is–

(a)   a new business; or

(b)   an existing micro-business during the exemption period,

and Schedule 1 has effect for the purpose of this regulation.

Notices

19.–(1)   A notice must be given or sent to–

(a)   the liable person; and

(b)   any employer of the liable person who is to make deductions from the liable person's earnings in accordance with the notice.

(2)   A notice must specify–

(a) the full name and address of the liable person;

(b) the name of the employer at whom the notice is directed;

(c) where known, the liable person's place of work, the nature of their work and any staff number, pay roll number or similar identifying number;

(d) the liable person's national insurance number;

(e) the rate at which deductions are be made in accordance with regulation 20(3)(a) or as the case may be, (b) or, if applicable, the deduction to be made in accordance with regulation 20(3)(c);

(f) the protected earnings proportion;

(g) the address to which amounts deducted from earnings are to be sent if paid by cheque; and

(h) details of the account into which such amounts are to be transferred if paid by direct credit transfer.

(3) The notice has effect from the next pay-day which falls a minimum of 22 days after the day on which it is given or sent.

(4) References in paragraphs (1) to (3) to a notice include references to a notice as varied in accordance with regulation 25(1).

Amount to be deducted by employer

20.–(1) This regulation applies where an employer has received from an appropriate authority a notice in respect of a liable person in their employment.

(2) Subject to the following provisions of this regulation, the employer must, each pay-day, make a deduction in accordance with paragraph (3) from the net earnings which it would otherwise pay to the liable person on that pay-day.

(3) The amount to be deducted is–

(a) where the liable person's earnings are payable weekly, the percentage of their earnings specified in column 2 of Table A in Schedule 2 opposite the band in column 1 of that Table within which their net earnings payable on their pay-day fall;

(b) where the liable person's earnings are payable monthly, the percentage of their earnings specified in column 2 of Table B in that Schedule opposite the band in column 1 of that Table within which their net earnings payable on their pay-day fall; or

(c) a lower amount calculated in the manner specified by the appropriate authority in the notice.

(4) Where any amount calculated under paragraph (3) includes a fraction of a penny, it is to be rounded to the nearest whole penny with a result of exactly half a penny being rounded down to the nearest whole penny below.

(5) The employer must continue to make deductions in accordance with paragraph (3) unless and until they are notified by the appropriate authority that the notice–

(a) has been varied in accordance with regulation 25;

(b) has been discharged under regulation 26; or

(c) has lapsed under regulation 27.

(6) Where, on any pay-day ("the relevant pay-day"), the employer fails to deduct an amount under paragraph (3) or deducts an amount less than the amount specified in that paragraph, the employer must, on the next available pay-day or pay-days, first deduct the amount required to be deducted under paragraph (3) for that pay-day and then the difference between the amount, if any, which was deducted on the relevant pay-day and the amount which should have been deducted on that pay-day.

(7) Where a deduction made in accordance with paragraph (3) or (6) would reduce the amount paid to the liable person below the protected earnings proportion, the employer must deduct only such amount as will result in the employer paying the liable person an amount equal to the protected earnings proportion.

(8) Where, on any pay-day ("the relevant pay-day"), the employer deducts more than the amount required to be deducted under paragraph (3), the employer must, on the next available pay-day or pay-days, deduct only the amount required to be deducted

under paragraph (3) less the difference between the amount which was deducted on the relevant pay-day and the amount which should have been deducted on that pay-day.

(9)   Where, on any pay-day, an employer makes a deduction from the earnings of a liable person in accordance with the notice, they may also deduct an additional amount not exceeding £1 in respect of their administrative costs and such deduction for administrative costs may reduce the amount which the employer pays to the liable person on that pay-day below the protected earnings proportion.

Employer to notify liable person of deduction

21.–(1)   An employer making a deduction from earnings for the purposes of these Regulations must notify the liable person in writing of–

(a)   the amount of the deduction including any amount deducted for administrative costs under regulation 20(9); and

(b)   how that amount was calculated.

(2)   Such notification must be given or sent not later than the pay-day on which the deduction is made or, where that is impracticable, not later than the following pay-day.

Payment by employer to the appropriate authority

22.–(1)   Amounts deducted by an employer pursuant to regulation 20 (other than any administrative costs deducted under paragraph (9) of that regulation) must be paid by the employer to the appropriate authority by the 19th day of the month following the month in which the deduction is made.

(2)   Such payment may be made–

(a)   by cheque;

(b)   by direct credit transfer; or

(c)   by such other method as the appropriate authority may permit.

(3)   The employer must keep a record of every amount paid to an appropriate authority pursuant to paragraph (1) and of the employee in respect of whom each such amount was paid.

Information to be provided by the liable person

23.–(1)   A liable person who has been given or sent a notice in accordance with regulation 19(1)(a) must notify the appropriate authority in writing within 7 days of each occasion on which–

(a)   they leave the employment of an employer named in a notice issued by the appropriate authority in respect of them; or

(b)   they become employed or re-employed.

(2)   A notification under paragraph (1)(b) must include the following details–

(a)   the name and address of their employer or employers if more than one;

(b)   the amount of their earnings or expected earnings; and

(c)   their place of work, nature of their work and any staff number, pay roll number or similar identifying number.

Duty of employers and others to notify appropriate authority

24.–(1)   In this regulation, "P" means the liable person.

(2)   Where a notice is given or sent to a person who is believed to be an employer of P but P is not in that person's employment, that person must notify the appropriate authority of that fact in writing, at the address specified in the notice, within 10 days after the day on which the notice is given or sent.

(3)   In paragraphs (4) and (5), "E" means an employer of P.

(4)   Where a notice is given or sent to E but E believes that there is no obligation on them under this Part by virtue of regulation 18 and Schedule 1, E must notify the appropriate authority of that fact in writing, at the address specified in the notice, within 10 days after the day on which the notice is given or sent.

(5)   Where E is required to make deductions under a notice and P ceases to be in their employment, E must notify the appropriate authority of that fact in writing, at the

address specified in the notice, within 10 days after the day on which P ceased to be in their employment.

Power to vary notices
25.–(1)   The appropriate authority may vary a notice so as to–
(a)   decrease any amount to be deducted under regulation 20; or
(b)   with the agreement of the liable person, increase any such amount but only to the extent that such deductions will result in the employer paying the liable person an amount more than, or equal to, the protected earnings proportion.
(2)   Where a notice has been varied and a copy of the notice as varied has been given or sent in accordance with regulation 19(1) and (4), any employer who is liable to make deductions under the notice must comply with the notice as varied from the day it takes effect by virtue of regulation 19(3).

Discharge of notices
26.–(1)   The appropriate authority must discharge a notice where the recoverable amount is no longer outstanding.
(2)   The appropriate authority may discharge a notice where–
(a)   it appears to them to be defective;
(b)   it appears to them that it is ineffective or that some other method of recovering the recoverable amount would be more effective; or
(c)   the liable person agrees with the appropriate authority to pay the recoverable amount by another method.
(3)   A notice may be considered to be defective for the purpose of paragraph (2)(a) where it does not comply with the requirements of regulation 19(2) and such failure to comply has made it impracticable for an employer to comply with their obligations under these Regulations.
(4)   Notification of the discharge of the notice under paragraph (1) or (2) must be given or sent to the liable person and the employer from whom deductions from the liable person's earnings were being made.
(5)   Where a notice is discharged by virtue of paragraph (2)(b) or (c), regulation 22 nevertheless applies in respect of any deductions made in respect of the employment but not yet paid to the appropriate authority.

Lapse of notices
27.–(1)   Where a liable person in respect of whom deductions are being made in accordance with a notice ceases to be in the employment of an employer, subject to paragraph (2), the notice is to lapse immediately after the pay-day coinciding with, or, if none, the pay-day following, the termination of the employment.
(2)   Where a notice lapses by virtue of paragraph (1), regulation 22 nevertheless applies in respect of any deductions made or to be made in respect of the employment but not yet paid to the appropriate authority.

Crown employment
28.   There a liable person is in the employment of the Crown and a notice is to be sent in respect of that person, then for the purposes of these Regulations–
(a)   the chief officer for the time being of the Department, office or other body in which the liable person is employed is to be treated as having the liable person in their employment (any transfer of the liable person from one Department, office or body to another being treated as a change of employment); and
(b)   any earnings paid by the Crown or a minister of the Crown, or out of the public revenue of the United Kingdom, is to be treated as paid by that chief officer.

Priority as between notices and orders requiring deduction from earnings
29.–(1)   In this regulation–
"child support order" means a deduction from earnings order under Part 3 of the Child Support (Collection and Enforcement) Regulations 1992;

"other deduction order" means an order, other than a child support order, under any other enactment relating to England and Wales which requires deduction from a person's earnings.

(2)   Paragraphs (3) to (10) have effect subject to paragraph (11).

(3)   Paragraph (4) applies where an employer would otherwise be obliged, on any pay-day, to make deductions from the earnings which it would otherwise pay to the liable person on that payday under two or more notices.

(4)   Where this paragraph applies, the employer must make deductions under the notices according to the respective dates on which they were made, disregarding any later notice until deductions have been made under the earlier one.

(5)   Paragraph (6) applies where an employer would otherwise be obliged, on any pay-day, to make deductions from the earnings which it would otherwise pay to the liable person on that payday, under one or more notices and one or more child support orders.

(6)   Where this paragraph applies, the employer must first make deductions under the child support order or orders and then make deductions under the notice or notices.

(7)   In England and Wales, paragraph (8) applies where an employer would otherwise be obliged, on any pay-day, to make deductions from the earnings which it would otherwise pay to the liable person on that pay-day, under one or more notices and one or more other deduction orders.

(8)   Where this paragraph applies, the employer must–

(a)   in a case where there is at least one other deduction order in effect on the first pay-day in respect of which deductions would otherwise be made under the notice, first make deductions under the other deduction order or orders and then under any notice or notices;

(b)   in any other case, make deductions under the other deduction order and the notices according to the respective dates on which they were made, disregarding any later notice or order until deductions have been made under the earlier one.

(9)   In Scotland, paragraph (10) applies where an employer would otherwise be obliged, on any pay-day, to make deductions from the earnings which it would otherwise pay to the liable person on that pay-day, under one or more notices and one or more diligences against earnings.

(10)   Where this paragraph applies, the employer must–

(a)   in a case where there is a diligence against earnings in effect on the first pay-day in respect of which deductions would otherwise be made under the notice, first make deductions under any diligence against earnings and then under any notice;

(b)   in any other case, make deductions under any notice and then under any diligence against earnings.

(11)   An employer may only make deductions under paragraph (4), (6), (8) or (10) up to the extent that such deductions will result in the employer paying the liable person an amount equal to or greater than the protected earnings proportion.

Offences

30.   A person who fails to comply with any of the following provisions of this Part is guilty of an offence punishable on summary conviction by a fine not exceeding level 3 on the standard scale–

(a)   regulation 20(2);

(b)   regulation 22(1);

(c)   regulation 22(3);

(d)   regulation 23.

SCHEDULE 1

REGULATION 18

EXEMPTION FOR EXISTING MICRO-BUSINESSES AND NEW BUSINESSES

Micro-businesses

1.   A micro-business is a business that has fewer than 10 employees (see paragraphs 6 to 8).

Existing micro-businesses
    2.   An existing micro-business is a business that was a micro-business immediately before 8th April 2013.

New businesses
    3.–(1)   A new business is a business which a person, or a number of persons, ("P") begins to carry on during the period beginning on 8th April 2013 and ending on 31st March 2014.
    (2)   But a business is not a new business if–
    (a)   P has, at any time during the period of 6 months ending immediately before the date on which P begins to carry on the business, carried on another business consisting of the activities of which the business consists (or most of them); or
    (b)   P carries on the business as a result of a transfer (within the meaning of sub-paragraph (3)).
    (3)   P carries on a business as a result of a transfer if P begins to carry on the business on another person ceasing to carry on the activities of which it consists (or most of them) in consequence of arrangements involving P and the other person.
    (4)   For this purpose, P is to be taken to begin to carry on a business on another person ceasing to carry on such activities if–
    (a)   P begins to carry on the business otherwise than in partnership on such activities ceasing to be carried on by persons in partnership; or
    (b)   P is a number of persons in partnership who begin to carry on the business on such activities ceasing to be carried on–
        (i)   by a person, or a number of persons, otherwise than in partnership;
        (ii)   by persons in partnership who do not consist only of all the persons who constitute P; or
        (iii)   partly as mentioned in paragraph (i) and partly as mentioned in paragraph (ii).
    (5)   P is not to be regarded as beginning to carry on a business for the purposes of sub-paragraph (1) if–
    (a)   before P begins to carry on the business, P is a party to arrangements under which P may (at any time during the period beginning on 8th April 2013 and ending on 31st March 2014) carry on, as part of the business, activities carried on by any other person; and
    (b)   the business would have been prevented by sub-paragraph (2)(b) from being a new business if–
        (i)   P had begun to carry on the activities when beginning to carry on the business; and
        (ii)   the other person had at that time ceased to carry them on.
    (6)   "Arrangements" includes an agreement, understanding, scheme, transaction or series of transactions (whether or not legally enforceable).

The exemption period: existing micro-businesses
    4.–(1)   This paragraph defines the exemption period in relation to an existing micro-business.
    (2)   The exemption period starts on 8th April 2013 and ends on the day after a grace period in relation to the business ends, if the grace period is one in which the business grows (see paragraphs 5 and 6).
    (3)   The following are grace periods in relation to a business for the purposes of this paragraph–
    (a)   the 6-month period that starts with the first day after 8th April 2013 on which the business has 10 or more employees;
    (b)   the 6-month period that starts after the end of a grace period (the "earlier grace period") that is not one in which the business grows, in accordance with sub-paragraph (4) or (5).
    (4)   If the business has 10 or more employees on the day after the end of the earlier grace period, the next grace period starts on that day.
    (5)   If the business has fewer than 10 employees on that day, the next grace period starts on the next day on which the business has 10 or more employees.

Grace periods in which business grows
    5.–(1)   For the purposes of this Schedule, a grace period is one in which a business grows if A is greater than B, where–
    (a)   A is the number of days in the grace period when the business has 10 or more employees; and
    (b)   B is the number of days in the grace period when the business has fewer than 10 employees.

Number of employees of a business
    6.   For the purposes of this Schedule, the number of employees of a business is calculated as follows–

$$\frac{TH}{37.5}$$

where TH is the total number of hours per week for which all the employees of the business are contracted to work.

Employees of a business
    7.   For the purposes of this Schedule, the employees of a business are the persons who are employed for the purposes of the business in connection with any of the activities of which the business consists.

Employees

8.–(1)   In this Schedule, "employee" means an individual who has entered into, or works under, a contract of employment.

(2)   In sub-paragraph (1) "contract of employment" means a contract of service, whether express or implied, and (if it is express) whether oral or in writing.

Franchises

9.   For the purposes of this Schedule, a business that is carried on pursuant to a franchise agreement is treated as part of the business of the franchisor (and not as a separate business carried on by the franchisee).

SCHEDULE 2

REGULATION 20(2)

AMOUNTS TO BE DEDUCTED BY EMPLOYERS
TABLE A:
WHERE EARNINGS ARE PAID WEEKLY

AMOUNT OF NET EARNINGS	DEDUCTION (PER CENT. OF NET EARNINGS)
Less than £100	Nil
Exceeding £100 but not exceeding £160	3
Exceeding £160 but not exceeding £220	5
Exceeding £220 but not exceeding £270	7
Exceeding £270 but not exceeding £375	11
Exceeding £375 but not exceeding £520	15
Exceeding £520	20

TABLE B:
WHERE EARNINGS ARE PAID MONTHLY

AMOUNT OF NET EARNINGS	DEDUCTION (PER CENT. OF NET EARNINGS)
Less than £430	Nil
Exceeding £430 but not exceeding £690	3
Exceeding £690 but not exceeding £950	5
Exceeding £950 but not exceeding £1,160	7
Exceeding £1,160 but not exceeding £1,615	11
Exceeding £1,615 but not exceeding £2,240	15
Exceeding £2,240	20

The Social Security (Information-sharing in relation to Welfare Services etc) Amendment and Prescribed Bodies Regulations 2013
(SI 2013 No.454)

Citation, commencement and interpretation

1.–(1)   These Regulations may be cited as the Social Security (Information-sharing in relation to Welfare Services etc.) Amendment and Prescribed Bodies Regulations 2013.

(2)   They come into force on 1st April 2013.

(3)   In these Regulations "the 2012 Act" means the Welfare Reform Act 2012.

Prescription of Scottish bodies and Welsh bodies

2.–(1)   The following are prescribed as Scottish bodies for the purpose of paragraph (d) of the definition of that term in section 131(12) of the 2012 Act–

(a)   the Scottish Ministers;

(b)   a person authorised to exercise any function of the Scottish Ministers relating to welfare services;

(c)   a person providing to the Scottish Ministers services relating to welfare services.

(2)   The following are prescribed as Welsh bodies for the purpose of paragraph (d) of the definition of that term in section 131(12) of the 2012 Act–

(a)   the Welsh Ministers;

(b)   a person authorised to exercise any function of the Welsh Ministers relating to welfare services;

(c)   a person providing to the Welsh Ministers services relating to welfare services.

The Welfare Reform Act 2012 (Commencement No.9 and Transitional and Transitory Provisions and Commencement No.8 and Savings and Transitional Provisions (Amendment)) Order 2013

(2013 No.983)

Citation

1. This Order may be cited as the Welfare Reform Act 2012 (Commencement No. 9 and Transitional and Transitory Provisions and Commencement No. 8 and Savings and Transitional Provisions (Amendment)) Order 2013.

General Note to the No.9 Order

It is understood that this order is not currently relevant for HB but it may have historic significance. Among other things, this order provided the "gateway conditions" for claims for, and awards of, universal credit in the "relevant districts" where there were gateway conditions for claims for UC. Those who did not meet the gateway conditions were prevented from claiming UC and thus could claim HB and any of the other existing benefits (ie, IS, income-based JSA and income-related ESA) and tax credits.

From December 2018, gateway conditions were removed in all postcode areas and in areas where there were gateway conditions, new claims for UC were usually not permitted. By 12 December 2018, all gateway areas had been converted to what are known as "full service" areas. UC has now been introduced across Great Britain. Note, however, that an "SDP Gateway" was introduced from 24 July 2019 for which see reg 4A UC(TP) Regs 2014 on p1862. See also the General Note on the introduction of UC on p1857.

The only provisions included here are those that had an impact on claims and awards of HB. The version of the Articles and Schedule provided here is that which applies from 6 April 2017. See also the modifications noted below and the Universal Credit (Transitional Provisions) Regulations 2014 SI No.1230 (on p1857).

It is important to note that different versions of this order could apply, and in some cases, that this order did not apply. This depends broadly on the post code area in which the UC claim was made.

Interpretation

2.–(1) In this Order–

"the Act" means the Welfare Reform Act 2012 (apart from in Schedule 4);

[¹ [²]]

[³ "disability living allowance" means an allowance under section 71 of the Social Security Contributions and Benefits Act 1992;]

[¹ "First-tier Tribunal" has the same meaning as in the Social Security Act 1998;]

[¹ "gateway conditions" means the conditions specified in Schedule 5;]

[¹ "housing benefit" means housing benefit under section 130 of the Social Security Contributions and Benefits Act 1992;]

"relevant districts" means the postcode districts specified in Schedule 1;

[¹ "old style ESA" means an employment and support allowance under Part 1 of the 2007 Act as it has effect apart from the amendments made by Schedule 3 and Part 1 of Schedule 14, to the Act that remove references to an income-related allowance and "old style ESA award" shall be construed accordingly;]

[¹ "old style JSA" means a jobseeker's allowance under the 1995 Act as it has effect apart from the amendments made by Part 1 of Schedule 14 to the Act that remove references to an income-based jobseeker's allowance and "old style JSA award" shall be construed accordingly;]

[³ "personal independence payment" means an allowance under Part 4 of the Act;]

[¹ "the 2014 Transitional Regulations" means the Universal Credit (Transitional Provisions) Regulations 2014;]

[¹ "Upper Tribunal" has the same meaning as in the Social Security Act 1998.]

[¹ (2)   *[Omitted]*]

Modifications

The definition of "gateway conditions" is omitted for claims for UC, in relevant districts as defined in this order, made on or after 7 March 2018, by art 3(2) of the Welfare Reform Act 2012 (Commencement No.9, 21 and 23 (Amendment), Commencement No.11, 13, 17, 19, 22, 23 and 24 (Modification), Transitional and Transitory Provisions) Order 2018 SI No.138.

Amendments

1. Amended by art 4 of SI 2014 No.1452 for those to whom art 3 of that order applies where a claim for UC is made or treated as made (or an award of UC is made without a claim) on or after 16.6.14.

2. Omitted by art 4(2) of SI 2014 No.1923 for those to whom art 3 of that order applies where a claim for JSA, ESA or UC is made or treated as made (or an award of UC is made without a claim) on or after 28.7.14.

3. Inserted by art 2 of SI 2015 No.32 for those to whom art 3 of that order applies where a claim for JSA, ESA or UC is made or treated as made (or an award of UC is made without a claim) on or after 26.1.15.

[¹ [³ **Incorrect information regarding residence in a relevant district or meeting the gateway conditions**

3A.–(1)   This article applies where a claim for universal credit is made and it is subsequently discovered that the single claimant or either or both of two joint claimants gave incorrect information regarding his or her (or their) residing in one of the relevant districts or meeting the gateway conditions and the conditions referred to in paragraph (2) are met.

(2)   The conditions referred to are that, on the date on which the claim was made, the claimant–

(a)   did not reside in one of the relevant districts (unless paragraph (3) applies); or

(b)   did reside in one of the relevant districts but did not meet the gateway conditions.

(3)   This paragraph applies where the claimant resided in an area apart from the relevant districts with respect to which the provisions of the Act referred to in Schedule 2 were in force in relation to a claim for universal credit and the conditions (if any) that applied to such a claim, for those provisions to come into force, were met [⁴ (and a determination had not been made under regulation 4 of the Universal Credit (Transitional Provisions) Regulations 2014, preventing a claim for universal credit being made with respect to the area in question or the category of case in question)].

(4)   Where the discovery is made before the claim for universal credit has been decided–

(a)   the claimant is to be informed that the claimant is not entitled to claim universal credit;

(b)   *[Omitted]*

(c)   if the claimant (or, in the case of joint claimants, either of them) makes a claim for housing benefit and the date of that claim (as determined in accordance with the Housing Benefit Regulations 2006 or, as the case may be, the Housing Benefit (Persons who have attained the qualifying age for state pension credit) Regulations 2006 (together referred to as "the Housing Benefit Regulations")) is after the date on which the claim for universal credit was made, but no later than one month after the date on which the information required by sub-paragraph (a) was given–

(i)   the claim for housing benefit is to be treated as made on the date on which the claim for universal credit was made or the first date on which the claimant would have been entitled to housing benefit if a claim had been made for it on that date, if later; and

(ii)   any provision of the Housing Benefit Regulations under which the claim for housing benefit is treated as made on a later date does not apply;

(d)   *[Omitted]*

(5)   Where the discovery is made after a decision has been made that the claimant is entitled to universal credit, but before any payment has been made–

(a)   that decision is to cease to have effect immediately, by virtue of this article;

(b)   the claimant is to be informed that they are not entitled to claim universal credit; and

(c)   sub-paragraphs (b) to (d) of paragraph (4) apply.

(6)   Where the discovery is made after a decision has been made that the claimant is entitled to universal credit and one or more payments have been made in respect of the claimant, the decision is to be treated as a decision under section 8 of the Social Security Act 1998.

(7)   *[Omitted]*]

Modifications

The title of art 3A as well as paras (1) and (2) are amended for claims for UC, in relevant districts as defined in this order, made on or after 7 March 2018, by art 3(2) of the Welfare Reform Act 2012 (Commencement No.9, 21 and 23 (Amendment), Commencement No.11, 13, 17, 19, 22, 23 and 24 (Modification), Transitional and Transitory Provisions) Order 2018 SI No.138.

Amendments

1. Inserted by art 5(2) of SI 2014 No.1452 for those to whom art 3 of that order applies where a claim for UC is made or treated as made (or an award of UC is made without a claim) on or after 16 June 2014.
2. Amended by art 4(3) of SI 2014 No1661, where a claim for UC is made or treated as made on or after 30.6.14.
3. Substituted by art 4(4) of SI 2014 No.1923 for those to whom Art 3 of that order applies where a claim for JSA, ESA or UC is made or treated as made (or an award of UC is made without a claim) on or after 28.7.14.
4. Amended by art 8(2) of SI 2015 No 634, where a claim for UC is made or treated as made on or after 18.3.15.

General Note

Among other things, art 3A provided the date of a claim for HB, made after a UC claim was made, when it was subsequently discovered that a single claimant, or either or both of two joint claimants did not reside in a relevant district (post code area) or meet the "gateway conditions" in Sch 5 on the date of the UC claim. This only applied if the DWP discovered that the claimant gave incorrect information and the conditions in para (2) were met: para (1). Note that for UC claims on or after 7 March 2018, where gateway conditons were removed, this only applied if the claimant did not reside in a relevant district.

The conditions in para (2) are that, on the date of the UC claim, either the claimant did not reside in a relevant district (unless para (3) applies), or lived in a relevant district but did not meet the gateway conditions. Note that for UC claims on or after 7 March 2018, where gateway conditons were removed, this only applied if the claimant did not reside in a relevant district. Under reg 4 of the UC(TP) Regs 2014 (referred to in para (3)), the Secretary of State has the discretion to determine that claims for UC may not be made in an area or in a category of case.

It is understood that DWP intention is that the conditions in para (2) were not met if the claimant gave incorrect information about the area in which s/he lived, but lived in another relevant district and met the gateway conditions there: para (3). It is not clear that para (3) provides this result, given it describes a claimant who "resided in an area apart from the relevant districts with respect to which the provisions of the Act referred to in Schedule 2 were in force in relation to a claim for universal credit".

If the conditions were met, there were three possibilities.

(1) The discovery was made before the UC claim was decided: para (4).
(2) The discovery was made after a decision that the claimant is entitled to UC but before any payment was made: para (5).
(3) The discovery was made after a decision that the claimant is entitled to UC and after one or more payments of UC were made: para (6).

In the first two cases, the claimant had to be informed that s/he was not entitled to claim UC. Then, if a claim for HB was made, and the date of claim for HB as determined under reg 83 HB Regs (or reg 64 HB(SPC) Regs) was after the date on which the UC claim was made and within one month of the date the claimant was informed s/he was not entitled to UC, the HB claim is treated as made on the date on which the UC claim was made (or on the first date on which the claimant would have been entitled to HB had a claim for HB been made on that date).

Note that in the third case, the UC claim is effectively treated as one the claimant was entitled to make. Thus the claimant cannot generally claim or be entitled to HB (other than if this is, for example, for "specified accommodation" or "temporary accommodation", or is a transitional HB payment). See regs 5, 6 and 8(2A) UC(TP) Regs 2014 on p1862 for the situations in which new claims for HB by a "universal credit claimant" are permitted and entitlement to HB is possible. See also art 6 of the Welfare Reform Act 2012 (Commencement No.21 and Transitional and Transitory Provisions) Order 2015 (on p1882) and art 7 of the Welfare Reform Act 2012 (Commencement No.23 and Transitional and Transitory Provisions) Order 2015 (on p1885) that allow new claims for HB to be made in specified circumstances.

[¹SCHEDULE 5

Modifications

Sch 5 is omitted for claims for UC, in relevant districts as defined in this order, made on or after 7 March 2018, by art 3(2) of the Welfare Reform Act 2012 (Commencement No.9, 21 and 23 (Amendment), Commencement No.11, 13, 17, 19, 22, 23 and 24 (Modification), Transitional and Transitory Provisions) Order 2018 SI No.138.

Amendment

1. Inserted by art 16 of SI 2014 No 1452 for those to whom art 3 of that order applies where a claim for UC is made or treated as made (or an award of UC is made without a claim) on or after 16 June 2014.

The Gateway conditions

General Note

Schedule 5 of this Order sets out the "gateway conditions" that those living in some "relevant districts" had to meet to, among other things, claim and be awarded UC. See the note on the introduction of UC (on p1857) for information about relevant districts and who did and did not have to meet gateway conditions. Note that for new claims for UC on or after 7 March 2018, gateway conditions were removed for those in relevant districts as defined in this order. Note also that from 1 January 2018, new claims for UC could not usually be made by those living in a relevant district where there were gateway conditions. By 12 December 2018, all gateway areas had been converted to what are known as "full service" areas – ie, there were no longer gateway conditions in any area. Note, however, the "SDP Gateway" in reg 4A (UC)TP) Regs 2014 (on p1862), introduced from 16 January 2019.

Only para 3 of Sch 5 is included in this book as it was potentially relevant to whether a person could continue to claim and receive HB. All of the conditions are summarised below. Different versions of the gateway conditions could apply in different relevant districts, as determined by the appropriate commencement order. Note: prior to 16 June 2014, instead of "gateway conditions", there were requirements that a person had to meet to fall within a "Pathfinder Group". These were in reg 4 of the Universal Credit (Transitional Provisions) Regulations 2013 SI No.386. See p1750 of the 26th edition for details.

Para 1: personal characteristics. The person had to be at least 18 but under 60 years and six months and had to be a British citizen who met specified residence conditions. Note that in some "relevant districts", the person had to be a single person when s/he first claimed.

Para 2: fitness to work. The person had to be fit for work and could not be pregnant or within 15 weeks of the birth of her baby.

Para 3: existing benefits. The person could not be entitled to a specified benefit (ie, old style ESA, old style JSA, IS, incapacity benefit, severe disablement allowance, DLA or PIP), or awaiting a decision on a claim for old style ESA, old style JSA or IS, tax credits or HB or the outcome of a request for a revision or a decision on an appeal. See the General Note to para 3 on p1853.

Para 4: income and capital. A single person had to have capital of £6,000 or less and could not expect to earn more than £338 a month. If the person was a member of a couple, but was a single claimant, s/he had to have capital of less than £6,000. If the couple were joint UC claimants, the total of their capital had to be £6,000 or less. In either case, both members of the couple could not expect to earn more than £338 a month each and the couple's joint earnings could not be more than £541 a month.

Para 5: housing. The person could not be homeless or living in specified supported accommodation. S/he could not own or partly own her/his home. S/he could not be residing in the same household as a person who was a member of the regular forces or the reserve forces who was absent from the household in connection with that role.

Para 6: caring responsibilities. In some "relevant districts", the person could not have a child or young person living with her/him some or all of the time who was certified severely sight impaired or blind, who was entitled to DLA or PIP, or who was being looked after by a local authority under specified provisions. In other "relevant districts", the person could not have *any* child or young person living with her/him some or all of the time. In all cases, the person could not be a foster parent or be liable for child support maintenance and could not be an adopter meeting certain conditions. In addition, the person could not be responsible for caring for a person with a physical or mental impairment, other than in paid or voluntary employment.

Para 7: other requirements. The person had to have a national insurance number and an account with a bank, building society, the Post Office or a credit union and could not be self employed, a company director or a member of a limited liability partnership, or be in education or training (or in specified circumstances intend to engage in education or training) or have a deputy or receiver appointed under specified mental health legislation, or any other person acting on her/his behalf in the UC claim.

Existing benefits

3.–(1) The claimant must not be entitled to–

[¹ (a) old style ESA;]

[¹ (b) old style JSA;]

[¹ (c) income support;]

(d) incapacity benefit or severe disablement allowance, as defined in Schedule 4 to the 2007 Act;

(e) disability living allowance [²]; or

(f) personal independence payment [²].

[¹ (2)]

(3) The claimant must not be awaiting–

[¹ (a) a decision on a claim for–

(i) any benefit mentioned in sub-paragraph (1)(a) to (c);

(ii) a tax credit; or

(iii) housing benefit;]

(b) the outcome of an application–

(i)   to the Secretary of State to consider whether to revise, under section 9 of the Social Security Act 1998(a), a decision that the claimant is not entitled to old style JSA, old style ESA or income support; or

(ii)   to the relevant authority (within the meaning of the Child Support, Pensions and Social Security Act 2000(b)) to consider whether to revise, under Schedule 7 to that Act, a decision that the claimant is not entitled to housing benefit.

(4)   If the claimant has appealed against a decision that he or she is not entitled to a benefit mentioned in sub-paragraph (1)(a) to (c), the Secretary of State must be satisfied–

(a)   that the appeal to the First-tier Tribunal, and any subsequent appeal to the Upper Tribunal or to a court, is not ongoing; and

(b)   where an appeal has been finally determined, that there is no possibility of a further appeal by any party.

[¹ (5)]

[¹ (6)]]

Amendments

1.   Amended by art 4(4) of SI 2014 No 1661, where a claim for UC is made or treated as made on or after 30.6.14.

2.   Amended by art 4 of SI 2015 No 32 for those to whom art 3 of that order applies where a claim for JSA, ESA or UC is made or treated as made (or an award of UC is made without a claim) on or after 26.1.15.

General Note

A person did not meet the "gateway conditions" if s/he was entitled to any of the benefits listed in sub-para (1). Note that prior to 30 June 2014, these included HB and tax credits. From that date, so long as the person was not entitled to any of the benefits listed in para (1), entitlement to HB was not a bar on a claim for UC if the person met the other gateway conditions and lived in a "relevant district".

However, a person could not meet the gateway conditions, if s/he was awaiting a decision on a claim for a benefit specified in sub-para (3)(a) (these *do* include HB and tax credits), or the outcome of an application for a revision of a decision that s/he was not entitled to "old style ESA", "old style JSA", IS or HB (for which see sub-para (3)(b)). Sub-para (4) prevented claims for UC where an appeal was pending, but only applied to appeals against decisions on entitlement to the benefits listed in sub-para (1)(a) to (c).

Note that if someone entitled to HB is awarded UC, the HB award terminates in accordance with regs 7 or 8 UC(TP) Regs 2014, or reg 13 UC(TP) Regs 2014 in cases where there has been a revision or supersession of, or an appeal against, a decision on entitlement to HB.

Note: see regs 5 and 6 UC(TP) Regs 2014 on p1862 and p1864 for the exclusion of claims for and entitlement to HB (other than in exceptional circumstances) where there is a claim for or entitlement to UC in a relevant district. See the note on the introduction of UC on p1857 for transitional provisions for claims for HB in relevant districts where there were no "gateway conditions".

The Social Security (Persons Required to Provide Information) Regulations 2013

(2013 No.1510)

Citation and commencement

1.–(1)   These Regulations may be cited as the Social Security (Persons Required to Provide Information) Regulations 2013.

(2)   They come into force on 1st October 2013.

Persons required to provide information

2.–(1)   The following are prescribed as descriptions of persons for the purpose of section 109B(2)(ia) of the Social Security Administration Act 1992 (power of authorised officers to require information)–

(a)   a person who provides relevant childcare;

(b)   a person to whom a person in receipt of universal credit ("C") is liable to make rent payments in respect of accommodation which C occupies, or purports to occupy, as their home where C's award of universal credit includes an amount in respect of such payments;

(c)   a rent officer to the extent that the information required relates to the rent officer's functions under section 122 of the Housing Act 1996;

(d)   a local authority which administers a council tax reduction scheme to the extent that the information required relates to such a scheme.

(2)   In this regulation–

(a)   "UC Regulations" means the Universal Credit Regulations 2013;

(b)   "council tax reduction scheme"–

  (i)   in England and Wales, has the meaning given in section 13A(9) of the Local Government Finance Act 1992(c) and includes a default scheme within the meaning of paragraph 4 of Schedule 1A (or in Wales paragraph 6(1)(e) of Schedule 1B) to that Act; and

  (ii)   in Scotland, means a means-tested reduction to an individual's council tax liability in accordance with the Council Tax Reduction (Scotland) Regulations 2012 or the Council Tax Reduction (State Pension Credit) (Scotland) Regulations 2012;

(c)   "relevant childcare" has the meaning given in regulation 35 of the UC Regulations;

(d)   "rent payments" has the meaning given in paragraph 2 of Schedule 1 to the UC Regulations;

(e)   "universal credit" means universal credit under Part 1 of the Welfare Reform Act 2012.

The Age-Related Payments Regulations 2013
(SI 2013 No.2980)

Citation, commencement and interpretation

1.–(1)   These Regulations may be cited as the Age-Related Payments Regulations 2013 and come into force on the day after the day on which they are made.

(2)   *[Omitted]*

Entitlement: payments to qualifying Equitable Life annuitants

2.–(1)   A qualifying Equitable Life annuitant ("A") is entitled to a payment of £5000 under this regulation.

(2)–(8)   *[Omitted]*

Entitlement: payments to qualifying Equitable Life annuitants in receipt of pension credit or similar benefit

3.–(1)   A qualifying Equitable Life annuitant ("A") is entitled to a payment of £5000 under this regulation in addition to a payment under regulation 2(1) if A was in receipt of state pension credit on 1st November 2013.

(2)–(8)   *[Omitted]*

Payment to be disregarded for tax and social security

5.   Section 6 of the Age-Related Payments Act 2004 applies to a payment made under these Regulations as it applies to a payment made under that Act.

The Social Security (Persons Required to Provide Information) Regulations 2013
(2013 No.1510)

Citation and commencement
1.–(1)   These Regulations may be cited as the Social Security (Persons Required to Provide Information) Regulations 2013.

(2)   They come into force on 1st October 2013.

Persons required to provide information
2.–(1)   The following are prescribed as descriptions of persons for the purpose of section 109B(2)(ia) of the Social Security Administration Act 1992 (power of authorised officers to require information)–

(a)   a person who provides relevant childcare;

(b)   a person to whom a person in receipt of universal credit ("C") is liable to make rent payments in respect of accommodation which C occupies, or purports to occupy, as their home where C's award of universal credit includes an amount in respect of such payments;

(c)   a rent officer to the extent that the information required relates to the rent officer's functions under section 122 of the Housing Act 1996;

(d)   a local authority which administers a council tax reduction scheme to the extent that the information required relates to such a scheme.

(2)   In this regulation–

(a)   "UC Regulations" means the Universal Credit Regulations 2013;

(b)   "council tax reduction scheme"–

(i)   in England and Wales, has the meaning given in section 13A(9) of the Local Government Finance Act 1992(c) and includes a default scheme within the meaning of paragraph 4 of Schedule 1A (or in Wales paragraph 6(1)(e) of Schedule 1B) to that Act; and

(ii)   in Scotland, means a means-tested reduction to an individual's council tax liability in accordance with the Council Tax Reduction (Scotland) Regulations 2012 or the Council Tax Reduction (State Pension Credit) (Scotland) Regulations 2012;

(c)   "relevant childcare" has the meaning given in regulation 35 of the UC Regulations;

(d)   "rent payments" has the meaning given in paragraph 2 of Schedule 1 to the UC Regulations;

(e)   "universal credit" means universal credit under Part 1 of the Welfare Reform Act 2012.

The Universal Credit (Transitional Provisions) Regulations 2014
(SI 2014 No.1230)

Introduction of universal credit

UC was introduced in all postcode areas by mid-December 2018. This means that in most cases, claims for HB are no longer possible. However, see the note on the Welfare Reform Act 2012 on p4 and note the following.

(1)   A "universal credit claimant" (defined in reg 6) can still claim and be entitled to an award of HB if this is in respect of "specified accommodation" or "temporary accommodation", or is a transitional housing payment: regs 5, 6, 8 and 8A.

(2)   Even if a person is not a "universal credit claimant", s/he can only claim HB in limited circumstances. See the Welfare Reform Act 2012 (Commencement No.21 and Transitional and Transitory Provisions) Order 2015 (the No.21 Order on p1882) and the Welfare Reform Act 2012 (Commencement No.23 and Transitional and Transitory Provisions) Order 2015 (the No.23 Order on p1885).

(3)   Claimants who have been (or whose partner has been) entitled to a severe disability premium in their award of HB (or IS, income-based JSA or income-related ESA) in the past month are prevented from claiming UC for the time being – ie, they will not be transferred to UC: see reg 4A. Instead, they can claim HB: see the No.21 Order (on p1882) and the No.23 Order (on p1885).

(4)   A claimant who is a member of a mixed-age couple (ie, if one member was at least the qualifiying age for PC but not the other) can claim HB in limited cases. See the Welfare Reform Act 2012 (Commencement No.31 and Savings and Transitional Provisions and Commencement No.21 and 23 and Transitional and Transitory Provisions (Amendment)) Order 2019 SI No.37 (the No.31 Order on p1898), the No.21 Order (on p1882) and the No.23 Order (on p1885).

Note: prior to the amendments made from 15 May 2019, the No.21 Order and the No.23 Order allowed a claim for HB by a single claimant of at least the qualifying age for PC and by a member of a couple whose partner had reached that age (ie, a member of a couple where either or both members were at least the qualifying age for PC). It is understood that the DWP intention is that single claimants of at least the qualifying age for PC, and claimants who are members of a couple both at least that age can still make a claim for HB, but the legislative basis making good such an intention is at best unclear.

PC will eventually include a housing credit but the government says that this will not happen until completion of the UC timetable, to give greater certainty to local authorities. It appears that this will begin in October 2023.

(5)   Between 6 April 2017 and 31 January 2019, claimants responsible for three or more children could not usually claim UC and instead could claim IS, income-based JSA, income-related ESA and tax credits, and therefore HB.

Transfer from HB to UC

The government's intention is that, between January 2020 and June 2024, those with an existing entitlement to HB under the HB Regs will be notified to claim, and will be transferred to, UC – referred to as "managed migration to universal credit". See the UC (TP) Regs as amended by the Universal Credit (Transitional Provisions) (Managed Migration) Amendment Regulations 2019 SI No.1152 for the rules. Up to 10,000 claimants will be transferred earlier (from July 2019) as the managed migration process is tested. Transitional protection for those moving onto UC under managed migration is provided – ie, a transitional capital disregard (for those entitled to tax credits) and a transitional element (if the total amount of any awards of existing benefits exceeds the amount of UC).

"Relevant districts"

Until mid-December 2018, in order to claim and be awarded UC, a person had to live in a "relevant district". WRA 2012 commencement orders commenced the UC provisions in the WRA 2012 in respect of claims made by, and awards to, a person who resided in a "relevant district" (specified postcode areas set out in the Schedule to the orders). In some areas, the person had to satisfy "gateway conditions". From 1 January 2018, new claims for UC could usually only be made in relevant districts known as "full service areas" (see below) where there were no gateway conditions.

The commencement orders have been amended and modified subsequent to their commencement dates. See SI 2014 No.1452, SI 2014 No.1661, SI 2014 No.1923, SI 2014 No.3067, SI 2014 No.3094, SI 2015 No.32, SI 2015 No.101, SI 2015 No.634, SI 2015 No.740, SI 2015 No.1537, SI 2015 No.1930, SI 2016 No.33, SI 2016 No.407, SI 2016 No.596, SI 2016 No.963, SI 2017 No.57, SI 2017 No.483, SI 2017 No.584, SI 2017 No.664, SI 2017 No.952, SI 2018 No.138, SI 2018 No.532, SI 2018 No.881, SI 2019 No.37 and SI 2019 No.167.

Areas where there have been "gateway conditions"

The commencement orders, containing the "relevant districts" and the commencement dates, for areas in which there have been gateway conditions are as follows. See below for the list of orders that have been amended and modified to remove gateway conditions in these areas. From 12 December 2018, gateway conditions for new claims have been removed from all areas.

From 29 April 2013. The Welfare Reform Act 2012 (Commencement No.9 and Transitional and Transitory Provisions and Commencement No.8 and Savings and Transitional Provisions (Amendment) Order 2013 No.983 (the No.9 Order).

From 1 and 29 July 2013. The Welfare Reform Act 2012 (Commencement No.11 and Transitional and Transitory Provisions and Commencement No.9 and Transitional and Transitory Provisions (Amendment) Order 2013 No.1511 (the No.11 Order).

From 28 October 2013. The Welfare Reform Act 2012 (Commencement No.13 and Transitional and Transitory Provisions) Order 2013 No.2657 (the No.13 Order).

From 25 November 2013. The Welfare Reform Act 2012 (Commencement No.14 and Transitional and Transitory Provisions) Order 2013 No.2846 (the No.14 Order).

From 24 February 2014. The Welfare Reform Act 2012 (Commencement No.16 and Transitional and Transitory Provisions) Order 2014 No.209 (the No.16 Order).

From 23 June 2014. The Welfare Reform Act 2012 (Commencement No.17 and Transitional and Transitory Provisions) Order 2014 No.1583 (the No.17 Order).

From 15, 22 and 29 September, 6, 13, 20 and 27 October, 3, 10, 17 and 24 November and 1, 8 and 15 December 2014. The Welfare Reform Act 2012 (Commencement No.19 and Transitional and Transitory Provisions and Commencement No.9 and Transitional and Transitory Provisions (Amendment)) Order 2014 No.2321 (the No.19 Order).

From 16 and 23 February, 2, 9, 16 and 23 March, 6, 13, 20 and 27 April, 4, 11, 18 and 25 May, 1, 8, 18, 22 and 29 June and 6, 13 and 20 July 2015. The Welfare Reform Act 2012 (Commencement No.22 and Transitional and Transitory Provisions) Order 2015 SI No.101 (the No.22 Order).

From 21 and 28 September, 5, 12, 19 and 26 October, 9, 16, 23 and 30 November and 7 and 14 December 2014 and 11, 18 and 25 January 1, 8, 15, 22 and 29 February, 7 14, 21 and 28 March and 11, 18 and 25 April 2016. The Welfare Reform Act 2012 (Commencement No.24 and Transitional and Transitory Provisions and Commencement No.9 and Transitional and Transitory Provisions (Amendment)) Order 2015 SI No.1537 (the No.24 Order).

"Full service areas"

The government has rolled out the UC provisions for new claims for UC throughout Great Britain in what are known as "full service" areas. This has been done via new commencement orders, and also by amending and modifying existing commencement orders. In "full service" areas, there are no gateway conditions.

The commencement orders, containing the "relevant districts" and the commencement dates, for "full service areas" are as follows.

For claims made on or after 26 November but before 20 December 2014. The Welfare Reform Act 2012 (Commencement No.20 and Transitional and Transitory Provisions and Commencement No.9 and Transitional and Transitory Provisions (Amendment)) Order 2014 SI No.3094. Transitional provision is made for claims for HB by art 6 of the order (see p1880).

From 28 January 2015. The Welfare Reform Act 2012 (Commencement No.21 and Transitional and Transitory Provisions) Order 2015 SI No.33. Transitional provision is made for claims for HB by art 6 of the order (see p1882).

From 18 March, 10 June and 4 November 2015. The Welfare Reform Act 2012 (Commencement No.23 and Transitional and Transitory Provisions) Order 2015 SI No.634 (the No.23 Order).Transitional provision is made for claims for HB by art 7 of the order (see p1885).

From 2 December 2015. The Welfare Reform Act 2012 (Commencement No.25 and Transitional and Transitory Provisions) Order 2015 No.1930. Transitional provision is made for claims for HB by art 7 of the order (see p1888).

From 27 January and 24 February 2016. The Welfare Reform Act 2012 (Commencement No.26 and Transitional and Transitory Provisions and Commencement No. 22, 23 and 24 and Transitional and Transitory Provisions (Modification)) Order 2016 No.33. Transitional provision is made for claims for HB by art 7 of the order (see p1889).

From 23 March and 27 April 2016. The Welfare Reform Act 2012 (Commencement No.27 and Transitional and Transitory Provisions and Commencement No. 22, 23 and 24 and Transitional and Transitory Provisions (Modification)) Order 2016 No.407. Transitional provision is made for claims for HB by art 7 of the order (see p1890).

Areas where "gateway conditions" are removed

Gateway conditions began to be removed in some "relevant districts" from 23 March 2016. This was done by amending and modifying earlier commencement orders. The following orders were affected. Where gateway conditions have been removed, transitional provision is made for claims for HB by art 7 of the No.23 Order (see p1885).

For claims made on or after 23 March, 25 May, 29 June and 27 July 2016. The No.13, 14, 16, 19, 22 and 24 Orders. See SI 2016 No.596 (on p1891).

For claims made on or after 5, 12, 19 and 26 October, 2, 9, 23 and 30 November and 7 and 14 December 2016. The No.19, 22 and 24 Orders. See SI 2016 No.963.

For claims made on or after 1, 8 and 22 February, 8, 15, 22 and 29 March and 5, 12, 19 and 26 April 2017. The No.11, 13, 16, 22 and 24 Orders. See SI 2017 No.57.

For claims made on or after 3, 10 and 24 May, 7, 14 and 28 June 2017. The No.19, 22 and 24 Orders. See SI 2017 No.584.

For claims made on or after 5, 12 and 19 July and 6, 13, 20 and 27 September 2017. The No.17, 19, 22 and 24 Orders. See SI 2017 No.664.

For claims made on or after 4, 11, 18 and 25 October, 1, 8, 15, 22 and 29 November, and 6, 13 and 20 December 2017 and 10, 17 and 24 January 2018. The No. 17, 19, 22 and 24 Orders. See SI 2017 No.952.

For claims made on or after 7, 14, 21 and 28 February, 7, 21 and 28 March and 4, 11, 18, and 25 April 2018. The No.11, 13, 17, 19, 22 and 24 Orders. See SI 2018 No.138.

For claims made on or after 7 March 2018. The No.9 Order. See SI 2018 No.138.

For claims made on or after 2, 9, 16, 23 and 30 May, 6, 13, 20 and 27 June and 4, 11, 18 and 25 July 2018. The No.17, 19, 22 and 24 Orders. See SI 2018 No.532.

For claims made on or after 5, 12, 19 and 26 September, 3, 10, 17, 24 and 31 October, 7, 14, 21 and 28 November and 5 and 12 December 2018. The No.17, 19, 22 and 24 Orders. See SI 2018 No.881.

General Note

These regulations replaced the Universal Credit (Transitional Provisions) 2013 No.386 (the UC(TP) Regs 2013) subject to the savings in reg 3. They make provision for the second phase of the government's UC roll-out and the abolition of the benefits it replaces. In this phase, instead of including any requirements a person must meet to claim UC in the transitional provisions, these were included in the Welfare Reform Act 2012 (Commencement No.9 and Transitional and Transitory Provisions and Commencement No.8 and Savings and Transitional Provisions (Amendment)) Order 2013 (the No.9 Order) as "gateway conditons" – see p1849. Prior to 16 June 2014, the transitional provisions were found in the UC(TP) Regs 2013. For those relevant to HB, see p1748 of the 26th edition.

Note the following.

–   Under the UC(TP) Regs 2014, if a person is entitled to UC, s/he cannot be entitled to HB unless any of the exceptions in reg 5 apply. If a person is a "universal credit claimant" (defined in reg 6(2)), s/he cannot claim HB unless any of the exceptions in reg 6 apply. However, because the WRA 2012 commencement orders only bring into force UC provisions in the WRA 2012 (and provisions for the abolition of income-based JSA and income-related ESA) in relation to claims for UC, ESA and JSA and not in relation to the claimant), if the person's circumstances change and entitlement to UC ends, s/he may, in limited cases, be able to claim HB. See above on the introduction of UC and the note on the WRA 2012 on p4.

–   Regs 7, 8 and 13 (on p1868, p1870 and p1873) provide the end date for entitlement to HB in situations where an HB claimant becomes entitled to UC, a UC claimant becomes a member of a couple with someone who is entitled to HB, or there has been a decision on an appeal or a revision or a supersession of a decision on entitlement to UC. Note the provision in reg 8(2A) of a two-week "run-on" of HB (a transitional housing payment) where a claim for UC is made.

PART 1
INTRODUCTORY

Citation and commencement

1.–(1) These Regulations may be cited as the Universal Credit (Transitional Provisions) Regulations 2014.

(2)   These Regulations come into force on 16th June 2014.

Interpretation

2.–(1) In these Regulations–

"the Act" means the Welfare Reform Act 2012;

"assessment period" has the same meaning as in the Universal Credit Regulations;

"the Claims and Payments Regulations" means the Universal Credit, Personal Independence Payment, Jobseeker's Allowance and Employment and Support Allowance (Claims and Payments) Regulations 2013;

[⁴ "childcare costs element" *[Omitted]*

"deadline day" has the meaning in regulation 44;

"earned income" *[Omitted]*]

[¹]

"existing benefit" means income-based jobseeker's allowance, income-related employment and support allowance, income support, housing benefit and child tax credit and working tax credit under the 2002 Act, but see also [⁴ paragraph (3) and] regulation 25(2);

[⁴ "final deadline" has the meaning in regulation 46;]

"First-tier Tribunal" has the same meaning as in the Social Security Act 1998;

[4 "HMRC" *[Omitted]*]

"housing benefit" means housing benefit under section 130 of the Social Security Contributions and Benefits Act 1992;

[4 "indicative UC amount" *[Omitted]*

"migration day" *[Omitted]*

"migration notice" has the meaning in regulation 44;]

"new claimant partner" has the meaning given in regulation 7;

[4 "notified person" has the meaning in regulation 44;]

"partner" in relation to a person ("A") means a person who forms part of a couple with A;

[4 "qualifying claim" *[Omitted]*]

[3 "severe disability premium" means the premium in relation to an employment and support allowance under paragraph 6 of Schedule 4 to the Employment and Support Allowance Regulations 2008 or, as the case may be, the corresponding premium in relation to income support, old style JSA or housing benefit;]

[1 "specified accommodation" means accommodation to which one or more of subparagraphs (2) to (5) of paragraph 3A of Schedule 1 to the Universal Credit Regulations applies;]

[2 "temporary accommodation" means accommodation which falls within Case 1 or Case 2 under paragraph 3B of Schedule 1 to the Universal Credit Regulations,]

[4 "total legacy amount" *[Omitted]*

"transitional capital disregard" *[Omitted]*

"transitional element" *[Omitted]*]

"the Universal Credit Regulations" means the Universal Credit Regulations 2013;

"Upper Tribunal" has the same meaning as in the Social Security Act 1998.

(2) For the purposes of these Regulations–

(a) the date on which a claim for universal credit is made is to be determined in accordance with the Claims and Payments Regulations;

(b) where a couple is treated, in accordance with regulation 9(8) of the Claims and Payments Regulations, as having made a claim for universal credit, references to the date on which the claim is treated as made are to the date of formation of the couple;

(c) where a regulation refers to entitlement to an existing benefit on the date on which a claim for universal credit is made or treated as made, such entitlement is to be taken into account notwithstanding the effect of regulations 5, 7 and 8 or termination of an award of the benefit before that date by virtue of an order made under section 150(3) of the Act.

[4 (3)-(4) *[Omitted]*]

Amendments

1. Amended by reg 3 of SI 2014 No 1626 as from 3.11.14.
2. Inserted by reg 6(3) of SI 2018 No 65 as from 11.4.18, subject to saving and transitional provision in reg 8(2) and (3).
3. Inserted by reg 2(2) of SI 2019 No 10 as from 16.1.19.
4. Inserted by reg 3(2) of SI 2019 No 1152 as from 24.7.19.

Definition

"severe disability premium" – see Sch 3 para 14 HB Regs and Sch3 para 6 HB(SPC) Regs.

General Note

"Specified accommodation" is defined by reference to the definition in Sch 1 para 3A UC Regs 2013. That definition is broadly of the same effect as that in reg 75H HB Regs (on p531).

"Temporary accommodation" is defined by reference to the definition in Sch 1 para 3B UC Regs 2013. Broadly, this is specified types of homeless accommodation that is not "exempt accommodation" (defined effectively as in Sch 3 para 4(10) HB&CTB(CP) Regs) where rent is payable to a local authoriity or provider of social housing.

Revocation and saving of the Universal Credit (Transitional Provisions) Regulations 2013

3.–(1)   The Universal Credit (Transitional Provisions) Regulations 2013 ("the 2013 Regulations") are revoked, subject to the savings in paragraphs (2) to (4).

(2)   Chapters 2 and 3 of Part 2 (Pathfinder Group and treatment of invalid claims) of the 2013 Regulations continue to have effect in relation to a claim for universal credit–

(a)   which was made before the date on which these Regulations come into force ("the commencement date"); and

(b)   in respect of which no payment has been made to the claimant before the commencement date.

(3)   *[Omitted]*

(4)   Any other provision of the 2013 Regulations continues to have effect in so far as is necessary to give full effect to paragraphs (2) and (3).

General Note

Reg 3 provides savings on the revocation of the UC(TP) Regs 2013. Under para (2), the chapters referred to continue to have effect for UC claims made before 16 June 2014, where no payment of UC had been made to the claimant before that date.

Chapter 2 contained the requirements a person had to meet to fall within the Pathfinder Group, and hence to claim UC. See the General Note to the UC(TP) Regs 2013 on p1750 of the 26th edition for a summary of the requirements.

Reg 13 in Chapter 3 was relevant for HB as it provided the date of a claim for HB, made after a UC claim was made, when it was subsequently discovered that the claimant did not fall within the Pathfinder Group on the date of the UC claim. For reg 13 and a General Note, see pp1751–52 of the 26th edition.

PART 2
TRANSITION TO UNIVERSAL CREDIT
CHAPTER 1
ENTITLEMENT TO CLAIM UNIVERSAL CREDIT

Secretary of State discretion to determine that claims for universal credit may not be made

4.–(1)   Where the Secretary of State considers it necessary, in order to–

(a)   safeguard the efficient administration of universal credit; or

(b)   ensure the effective testing of systems for the administration of universal credit, to cease to accept claims in any area, or in any category of case (either in all areas or in a specified area), the Secretary of State may determine that claims for universal credit may not be made in that area, or in that category of case.

(2)   A determination under paragraph (1) has effect until it ceases to have effect in accordance with a further determination made by the Secretary of State.

(3)   More than one determination under paragraph (1) may have effect at the same time.

General Note

Reg 4 gives the Secretary of State the discretion to stop accepting claims for UC (ie, to prevent claims for UC) in any area or in any category of case in the circumstances set out in para (1). If this happens, the person affected can claim or continue to be entitled to any existing benefit – ie, HB, IS, income-based JSA, income-related ESA and tax credits.

Since 15 May 2019, where a claimant is a member of a "mixed-age couple" (ie, only one member of the couple is at least the qualifying age for PC), a new claim for, and entitlement to, HB is not generally allowed unless the claimant has been continuously entitled to PC or HB under the HB(SPC) Regs from before that date as part of the same mixed-age couple. See the Welfare Reform Act 2012 (Commencement No.31) Order 2019 SI No.37 (the No.31 Order) on p1898 for the detailed rules and exceptions. Note, however, that where a member of a mixed-age couple who is at least the qualifying age for PC is excluded from entitlement to PC or HB in these circumstances and is also prevented from claiming UC by virtue of reg 4, s/he is treated as not having attained that age for the purposes of reg 5 of both the HB Regs and the HB(SPC) Regs and can therefore claim and be entitled to HB under the HB Regs – ie, under the rules for working age claimants. See Art 8 of the No.31 Order on p1902.

[¹ **Restriction on claims for universal credit by persons entitled to a severe disability premium**

4A.–(1)   No claim may be made for universal credit on or after 16th January 2019 by a single claimant who, or joint claimants either of whom–

(a)   is, or has been within the past month, entitled to an award of an existing benefit that includes a severe disability premium; and

(b)   in a case where the award ended during that month, has continued to satisfy the conditions for eligibility for a severe disability premium.

[² (2)   This regulation does not apply in relation to a claim for universal credit by a single claimant who is a notified person or by joint claimants both of whom are notified persons.]

Amendments

1.   Inserted by reg 2(3) of SI 2019 No 10 as from 16.1.19.
2.   Inserted by reg 3(3) of SI 2019 No 1152 as from 24.7.19.

Definitions

"existing benefit" – see reg 2(1).
"notified person" – see regs 2(1) and 44.
"severe disability premium" – see reg 2(1).

General Note

In most cases, a new claim for HB can no longer be made: see reg 6 UC(TP) Regs 2014. Claimants who are (or were) entitled to a severe disability premium (SDP) as part of their award of an existing benefit (including HB) can be substantially worse off on UC. As a result, the government, as a temporary measure, introduced an "SDP Gateway" from 16 January 2019. From that date, no claim can be made for UC in either of the following circumstances.

(1)   The claimant (or her/his partner) is entitled to an award IS, income-based JSA, income-related ESA or HB that includes a severe disability premium.

(2)   The claimant (or her/his partner) was entitled to an award of IS, income-based JSA, income-related ESA or HB within the last month that included a severe disability premium and continued to satisfy the conditions for the premium.

A claimant prevented by the SDP gateway from claiming UC retains entitlement to, and continues to be able to make claims for, existing benefits, including CTC and WTC, until s/he is a "notified person" under what is known as "managed migration": para (2). Transitional protection will then be available. Claimants who had been entitled to an award of an existing benefit that included a severe disability premium who had before 16 January 2019 migrated to UC (known as "natural migration") are, from 24 July 2019, entitled to transitional protection. See the UC(TP) Regs 2014 as amended by SI 2019 No.1152.

By para (2) this regulation does not apply to someone who is a "notified person" (defined in regs 2(1) and 44 as a person to whom a migration notice has been issued) or to joint claimants where each is a notified person. For the time being this will only be one of the limited number of people upon whom the migration process is being tested.

Since 15 May 2019, where a claimant is a member of a "mixed-age couple" (ie, only one member of the couple is at least the qualifying age for PC), a new claim for, and entitlement to, HB is not generally allowed unless the claimant has been continuously entitled to PC or HB under the HB(SPC) Regs from before that date as part of the same mixed-age couple. See the Welfare Reform Act 2012 (Commencment No.31) Order 2019 SI No.37 (the No.31 Order) on p1898 for the detailed rules and exceptions. Note, however, that where a member of a mixed-age couple who is at least the qualifying age for PC is excluded from entitlement to PC or HB and is also prevented from claiming UC because of the "SDP Gateway" in reg 4A, s/he is treated as not having attained that age for the purposes of reg 5 of both the HB Regs and the HB(SPC) Regs and can therefore claim and be entitled to HB under the HB Regs – ie, under the rules for working age claimants. See Art 8 of the No.31 Order on p1902.

Note that reg 4A will be revoked on 27 January 2021 (reg 7 of SI 2019 No.1152).

CHAPTER 2
ENTITLEMENT TO OTHER BENEFITS

Exclusion of entitlement to certain benefits

5.–(1)   Except as provided in paragraph (2), a claimant is not entitled to–

(a)   income support;

(b)   housing benefit;

(c)   a tax credit; or

(d)   state pension credit under the State Pension Credit Act 2002,
in respect of any period when the claimant is entitled to universal credit.

(2)   Entitlement to universal credit does not preclude the claimant from entitlement–

(a)   to housing benefit in respect of [¹ specified accommodation] [², temporary accommodation or where regulation 8(2A) [³, 46(1) or 47(2)] applies]; or

(b)   during the first assessment period for universal credit, where the claimant is a new claimant partner, to–

(i)   income support, where an award to which the new claimant partner is entitled terminates, in accordance with regulation 7(4), after the first date of entitlement to universal credit;

(ii)   housing benefit, where regulation 7(5)(b) applies and an award of housing benefit to which the new claimant partner is entitled terminates after the first date of entitlement to universal credit; or

(iii)   a tax credit, where an award to which the new claimant partner is entitled terminates, in accordance with the 2002 Act, after the first date of entitlement to universal credit.

Amendments

1.   Amended by reg 3 of SI 2014 No 1626 as from 3.11.14.
2.   Amended by reg 6(4) of SI 2018 No 65 as from 11.4.18, subject (insofar as the amendment relates to temporary accommodation) to saving and transitional provision in reg 8(2) and (3).
3.   Amended by reg 3(4) of SI 2019 No 1151 as from 24.7.19.

Definitions

"assessment period" – see reg 2(1).
"new claimant partner" – see regs 2(1) and 7.
"specified accommodation" – see reg 2(1).
"temporary accommodation" – see reg 2(1).

General Note

Under reg 5, a person cannot be entitled to HB in respect of any period during which s/he is entitled to UC, unless any of four exceptions applies. Note that under reg 6, a person who is a "universal credit claimant" (for which see reg 6(2)) in most cases cannot make a claim for HB which prevents entitlement to HB. Note that the definition of "universal credit claimant" is wider than the words suggest.

Analysis

Para (1). Under para (1), unless any of the exceptions in para (2) apply, a person cannot be entitled to HB (or to IS, WTC, CTC or PC) in respect of any period when s/he is entitled to UC.

Para (2) allows entitlement to UC and HB in respect of the same period in four cases.

(1)   A person entitled to UC can be entitled to HB indefinitely if this is for "specified accommodation" (specified types of supported accommodation and of temporary accommodation provided for those who have left home as a result of domestic violence as defined in reg 2(1)): sub-para (a). Note that prior to 3 November 2014, this exception applied only if the HB was for "exempt accommodation", defined as in Sch 3 para 4(10) HB&CTB(CP) Regs.

(2)   A person entitled to UC can be entitled to HB indefinitely if this is for "temporary accommodation" (specified types of homeless accommodation that is not "exempt accommodation", where rent is payable to a local authority or provider of social housing): sub-para (a). Note that exempt accommodation *does* come within the definition of "specified accommodation".

(3)   A person entitled to UC can be entitled to HB while reg 8(2A), 46(1) or 47(2) applies – ie, during a two-week run-on of entitlement to HB: sub-para (a).

(4)   During the first assessment period for UC (the calendar month beginning with the first date of entitlement to UC – see reg 21 UC Regs), a person can continue to be entitled to HB until the termination of her/his HB award, if this is after the first date of entitlement to UC: sub-para (b)(ii). This only applies if the person is a "new claimant partner", defined in reg 7 as a person who was not entitled to UC until s/he became a member of a couple with someone who was previously entitled to UC as a single person. In addition, s/he must have left the accommodation in respect of which s/he was entitled to HB to live with her/his new partner: reg 7(5)(b). Note that entitlement to HB terminates as provided for in the HB or HB(SPC) Regs and not under reg 7. See, for example, reg 79 HB Regs and reg 59 HB(SPC) Regs.

Note: reg 5(2) will be amended from 22 July 2020 when a two-week "run-on" of income support is introduced: reg 4(2) of SI 2019 No.1152.

[¹ Entitlement to universal credit and housing benefit: universal credit work allowance

5A. Where a claimant has an award of universal credit and, in any assessment period, is also entitled to housing benefit for temporary accommodation and the award of universal credit does not include an amount for housing costs, regulation 22(2) of the Universal Credit Regulations (amount of the work allowance) is to apply in relation to that assessment period as if the award did include an amount for housing costs.]

Amendment

1.　　Inserted by reg 6(5) of SI 2018 No 65 as from 11.4.18, subject to saving and transitional provision in reg 8(2) and (3).

Definitions

"assessment period" – see reg 2(1).
"temporary accommodation" – see reg 2(1).

General Note

The UC work allowance is an earnings disregard that applies if the UC claimant or her/his partner is responsible for at least one child or has limited capability for work. If earnings exceed the work allowance, 63 per cent of the excess is taken into account as income in the UC calculation: reg 22 UC Regs. The work allowance is lower if the claimant's UC includes a housing costs element, and thus a higher amount of earnings are potentially taken into account. Under reg 5A, if a UC claimant's award does not include a housing costs element, it is treated as if it does include one if s/he is entitled to HB for "temporary accommodation".

Exclusion of claims for certain existing benefits

6.–(1)　　Except as provided in paragraphs (5) to (9) a universal credit claimant may not make a claim for income support, housing benefit or a tax credit.

(2)　　For the purposes of this regulation, a person is a universal credit claimant if–

(a)　　the person is entitled to universal credit;

(b)　　the person has made a claim for universal credit, a decision has not yet been made on that claim and the person has not been informed (in accordance with an order made under section 150(3) of the Act) that he or she is not entitled to claim universal credit;

[² (ba)(i) the conditions in regulation 6(1)(a), (b) and (c) or 6(2)(a), (b) and (c) of the Claims and Payments Regulations (claims not required for entitlement to universal credit in certain cases) are met in relation to the person;

(ii)　　he or she may be entitled to an award of universal credit without making a claim if the conditions in regulation 6(1)(d) and (e) or, as the case may be, 6(2)(d) and (e) of those Regulations are also met; and

(iii)　　either the Secretary of State has no information in relation to the person which may indicate a change of circumstances as referred to in regulation 6(1)(e) or, as the case may be, 6(2)(e) of those Regulations, or the Secretary of State has such information but no decision has been made that the person is entitled to universal credit;]

(c)　　the person was previously entitled to a joint award of universal credit which terminated because the person ceased to be a member of a couple, he or she is not exempt (by virtue of regulation 9(6) of the Claims and Payments Regulations) from the condition of entitlement to universal credit that he or she makes a claim for it and the period of one month, starting with the date on which the person notified the Secretary of State that he or she had ceased to be a member of a couple, has not expired;

[²(ca) the person may be entitled to an award of universal credit in circumstances where, by virtue of regulation 9(6), (7) or (10) of the Claims and Payments Regulations (claims for universal credit by members of a couple), it is not a condition of entitlement that he or she makes a claim for it, but no decision has yet been made as to the person's entitlement;]

(d)　　the person is treated, under the Claims and Payments Regulations, as having made a claim for universal credit, [²] but no decision has yet been made as to the person's entitlement;

(e) a decision has been made that the person is not entitled to universal credit and–
    (i) the Secretary of State is considering whether to revise that decision under section 9 of the Social Security Act 1998, whether on an application made for that purpose, or on the Secretary of State's own initiative; or
    (ii) the person has appealed against that decision to the First-tier Tribunal and that appeal or any subsequent appeal to the Upper Tribunal or to a court has not been finally determined.

(3) For the purposes of paragraph (1)–
(a) a universal credit claimant makes a claim for benefit mentioned in that paragraph if the claimant takes any action which results in a decision on a claim being required under the relevant Regulations; and
(b) except as provided in [² paragraphs (5) to (7B)], it is irrelevant that the effect of any provision of the relevant Regulations is that, for the purposes of those Regulations, the claim is made or treated as made at a time when the claimant was not a universal credit claimant.

(4) The relevant Regulations are–
(a) *[Omitted]*
(b) in relation to a claim for housing benefit, the Housing Benefit Regulations 2006 ("the 2006 Regulations") or, as the case may be, the Housing Benefit (Persons who have attained the qualifying age for state pension credit) Regulations 2006 ("the 2006 (SPC) Regulations");
(c) *[Omitted]*

(5) *[Omitted]*

(6) A universal credit claimant is not precluded from making a claim for housing benefit if–
(a) first notification of the claimant's intention to make that claim was given (within the meaning of regulation 83(5)(d) of the 2006 Regulations or, as the case may be, regulation 64(6)(d) of the 2006 (SPC) Regulations) before the date on which the claim for universal credit was made or treated as made; and
(b) in accordance with the 2006 Regulations or, as the case may be, the 2006 (SPC) Regulations, the claimant's entitlement to housing benefit in connection with the claim will (if the claimant is entitled to housing benefit) pre-date–
    (i) the date, or anticipated date, of the claimant's entitlement to universal credit in connection with the current award or claim; or
    (ii) where the claimant is a new claimant partner and regulation 7(5)(b) would apply to the award, the date on which it would terminate in accordance with the 2006 Regulations or, as the case may be, the 2006 (SPC) Regulations.

(7) A universal credit claimant is not precluded from correcting or completing a claim for housing benefit which was defective within the meaning of the 2006 Regulations or the 2006 (SPC) Regulations if–
(a) the defective claim was made before the date on which the claim for universal credit was made or treated as made; and
(b) in accordance with the 2006 Regulations or, as the case may be, the 2006 (SPC) Regulations, the claimant's entitlement to housing benefit in connection with the claim will (if the claimant is entitled to housing benefit) pre-date–
    (i) the date, or anticipated date, of the claimant's entitlement to universal credit in connection with the current award or claim; or
    (ii) where the claimant is a new claimant partner and regulation 7(5)(b) would apply to the award, the date on which it would terminate in accordance with the 2006 Regulations or, as the case may be, the 2006 (SPC) Regulations.

[²(7A) A claimant who is a universal credit claimant by virtue of sub-paragraph (ba) of paragraph (2) (and no other sub-paragraph) is not precluded from–
(a) making a claim for income support for a period starting on or after the relevant date if first notification of the claimant's intention to make that claim was made, or deemed to be made, for the purposes of regulation 6(1A)(c) or 6A of the 1987

Regulations, during the period starting with the relevant date and ending with 15th November 2015;

(b) making a claim for housing benefit for a period starting on or after the relevant date if first notification of the claimant's intention to make that claim was given (within the meaning of regulation 83(5)(d) of the 2006 Regulations or, as the case may be, regulation 64(6)(d) of the 2006 (SPC) Regulations, during the period starting with the relevant date and ending with 15th November 2015;

(c) correcting or completing a claim for housing benefit for a period starting on or after the relevant date, where that claim was defective within the meaning of the 2006 Regulations or the 2006 (SPC) Regulations and was made during the period starting with the relevant date and ending with 15th November 2015.

(7B) For the purposes of paragraph (7A), the "relevant date" is–

(a) where the conditions in regulation 6(1)(a), (b) and (c) of the Claims and Payments Regulations are met in relation to the claimant, the day after the claimant's last day of entitlement to universal credit;

(b) where the conditions in regulation 6(2)(a), (b) and (c) of the Claims and Payments Regulations are met in relation to the claimant, the first date on which the claimant would have been entitled to universal credit if the claimant had been so entitled.]

(8) A universal credit claimant is not precluded from making a claim for housing benefit in respect of [¹ specified accommodation] [³or temporary accommodation].

(9) *[Omitted]*

Amendments

1. Amended by reg 3 of SI 2014 No 1626 as from 3.11.14.
2. Amended by reg 2 of SI 2015 No 1780 as from 16.11.15.
3. Amended by reg 6(6)(a) of SI 2018 No 65 as from 11.4.18, subject to saving and transitional provision in reg 8(2) and (3).

Definitions

"new claimant partner" – see regs 2(1) and 7.
"specified accommodation" – see reg 2(1).
"temporary accommodation" – see reg 2(1).

Analysis

Paras (1) to (3). A "universal credit claimant" cannot make a claim for HB (or for IS or tax credits) unless any of the exceptions in paras (5) to (9) apply. In most cases, this applies even if the claim is made or treated as made on a date when s/he was not a "universal credit claimant" – eg, where a backdated claim for HB is made after a claim is made for UC, for a period before entitlement to UC started. Note also the siutautions in which a person is prevented from claiming UC. See the note on p4 for details.

The definition of a "universal credit claimant" is wider than the words suggest. It covers those entitled to UC as well as in other situations: para (2). Sub-paras (a), (b) and (d) of para (2) are self-explanatory.

Sub-para (ba) now only applies to those subject to the savings provisions in reg 5 of the Universal Credit (Digital Service) Amendment Regulations 2014 SI No.2887. Those regs revoked the provision cited in this sub-para from 26 November 2014. Sub-para (ba) covers a person who, under the provisions cited, is exempt from the requirement to make a claim for UC – ie, s/he is in a six-month period after a claim is refused or entitlement to UC ends because her/his earnings were too high, but s/he is now potentially entitled to UC – eg, because her/his earnings have reduced.

Sub-para (c), covers a person who was entitled to UC jointly with her/his former partner if s/he is someone who is *not* exempt from the requirement to make a claim for UC under the provision stated and it is not more than one month since s/he notified the DWP that s/he had ceased to be a member of a couple. Note that reg 9(6) Claims and Payments Regulations cited is substituted for UC claimants to whom the Universal Credit (Digital Service) Amendment Regulations 2014 SI No.2887 apply.

Sub-para (ca) covers a person who is exempt from the requirement to make a claim for UC under the provisions cited because s/he was entitled to UC jointly with her/his former partner or her/his late partner, or because s/he was a single UC claimant who is now a member of a couple with another former single UC claimant.

Sub-para (e) applies if a decision has been made that a person is not entitled to UC, but the DWP is considering whether to revise the decision or an appeal is pending against the decision.

The exceptions

The exceptions relevant for HB are in paras (6) to (8).

HB claims made before claim for UC. These are allowed in two situations, but will generally only enable HB entitlement for a short period. See reg 5 for when entitlement to HB is excluded in respect of periods when the claimant is entitled to UC and regs 7 and 8 for when an HB award terminates on entitlement to UC.

(1) So long as first notification of the intention to claim HB is made before the date the claim for UC is (or is treated as) made, the HB claim can be made (eg, via a claim form or by telephone): para (6). The claimant's entitlement to HB must pre-date the date in sub-paras (b)(i) or (ii) as the case may be. Reg 83(5)(d) HB Regs (reg 64(6)(d) HB(SPC) Regs) allows the date of the HB claim to run from the date of first notification if the claim is submitted within one month of that notification or such longer period as the local authority thinks is reasonable. Note that in the same circumstance, an HB claim could be made if the person was a "universal credit claimant" only under para (2)(ba), during the period starting with the "relevant date" (defined in para (7B) and ending on 15 November 2015); para (7A)(b).

(2) A defective claim for HB can be corrected or completed so long as it was made before the date the UC claim is (or is treated as) made: para (7). If the HB claimant is a "new claimant partner" (broadly defined in reg 7 as someone who is entitled to HB who becomes a member of a couple with a UC claimant), who has left her/his home to live with her/his new partner, entitlement to HB must pre-date the date s/he left the accommodation in respect of which HB is payable. In all other cases, HB entitlement must pre-date the date (or anticipated date) of entitlement to UC. Note that if the person was a "universal credit claimant" only under para (2)(ba), a claim for HB could be corrected or completed so long as it was made during the period starting with the "relevant date" (defined in para (7B) and ending on 15 November 2015: para (7A)(c).

In both cases, see regs 7 and 8 for when an award of HB entitlement terminates.

Specified accommodation and temporary accommodation. A "universal credit claimant" can claim HB if this is in respect of "specified accommodation" (specified types of supported accommodation and of temporary accommodation for those who have left home as a result of domestic violence) or "temporary accommodation" (specified types of homeless accommodation, that is not "exempt accommodation", where rent is payable to a local authority or provider of social housing): para (8)). Entitlement to both UC and HB at the same time is then allowed indefinitely under reg 5 (see p1862). Note that prior to 3 November 2014, this exception applied only if the HB was for "exempt accommodation", defined as in Sch 3 para 4(10) HB&CTB(CP) Regs. From 3 November 2014 to 11 April 2018, this exception only applied to "specified accommodation" (which includes "exempt accommodation").

Transitional provisions

In addition to the exclusion of claims by reg 6, transitional provision, preventing claims for HB, is made in 10 of the WRA 2012 Commencement Orders. Broadly, if one of these orders applies to a claimant, a claim for HB is prevented where, if the person made a claim for UC, the UC provisions would come into force in relation to that UC claim, even if no UC claim is actually made. However, this does not apply if the HB is for "specified accommodation" or "temporary accommodation" (for which see above). In limited cases, it does not apply if the claimant is a member of a mixed-age couple – ie, where only one member is at least the qualifying age for PC. The government intention is that it also does to apply to single claimants at least the qualifying age for PC and couples where both members are at least that age, but the legislative basis making good such an intention is at best unclear.

Transitional provision for claims is found in the following.

(1) Art 6 of the Welfare Reform Act 2012 (Commencement No.20 and Transitional and Transitory Provisions and Commencement No.9 and Transitional and Transitory Provisions (Amendment)) Order 2014 No.3094 (on p1880).

(2) Art 6 of the Welfare Reform Act 2012 (Commencement No.21 and Transitional and Transitory Provisions) Order 2015 SI No.33 (on p1882).

(3) Art 7 of the Welfare Reform Act 2012 (Commencement No.23 and Transitional and Transitory Provisions) Order 2015 No.634 (the No.23 Order on p1885).

The following modify and apply art 7 of the No.23 Order.

(1) Art 7 of the Welfare Reform Act 2012 (Commencement No.25 and Transitional and Transitory Provisions) Order 2015 No.1930 (on p1888).

(2) Art 7 of the Welfare Reform Act 2012 (Commencement No.26 and Transitional and Transitory Provisions and Commencement No.22, 23 and 24 and Transitional and Transitory Provisions (Modification)) Order 2016 No.33 (on p1889).

(3) Art 7 of the Welfare Reform Act 2012 (Commencement No.27 and Transitional and Transitory Provisions and Commencement No.22, 23 and 24 and Transitional and Transitory Provisions (Modification)) Order 2016 No.407 (on p1890).

(4) Art 12 of the Welfare Reform Act 2012 (Commencement No.13, 14, 16, 19, 22, 23 and 24 and Transitional and Transitory Provisions (Modification)) Order 2016 SI No.596 (on p1891).

(5) Art 7 of the Welfare Reform Act 2012 (Commencement No.19, 22, 23 and 24 and Transitional and Transitory Provisions (Modification)) Order 2016 No.963.

(6)   Art 19 of the Welfare Reform Act 2012 (Commencement No.11, 13, 16, 22, 23 and 24 and Transitional and Transitory Provisions (Modification)) Order 2017 SI No.57.

(7)   Art 13 of the Welfare Reform Act 2012 (Commencement No.19, 22, 23 and 24 and Transitional and Transitory Provisions (Modification)) Order 2017 SI No.584.

(8)   Art 14 of the Welfare Reform Act 2012 (Commencement No.29 and Commencement No.17, 19, 22, 23 and 24 and Transitional and Transitory Provisions (Modification)) Order 2017 SI No.664.

(9)   Art 5 of the Welfare Reform Act 2012 (Commencement No.17, 19, 22, 23 and 24 and Transitional and Transitory Provisions (Modification)) Order 2017 No.952.

(10)   Art 7 of the Welfare Reform Act 2012 (Commencement No.9, 21 and 23 (Amendment), Commencement No.11, 13, 17, 19, 22, 23 and 24 and (Modification)), Transitional and Transitory Provisions Order 2018 No.138.

(11)   Art 5 of the Welfare Reform Act 2012 (Commencement No.17, 19, 22, 23 and 24 and Transitional and Transitory Provisions (Modification)) Order 2018 SI No.532.

(12)   Art 5 of the Welfare Reform Act 2012 (Commencement No.29 and Commencement No.17, 19, 22, 23 and 24 and Transitional and Transitory Provisions (Modification)(No.2)) Order 2018 SI No.881.

Termination of awards of certain existing benefits: new claimant partners

7.–(1)   This regulation applies where–

(a)   a person ("A") who was previously entitled to universal credit as a single person ceases to be so entitled on becoming a member of a couple;

(b)   the other member of the couple ("the new claimant partner") was not entitled to universal credit as a single person immediately before formation of the couple;

(c)   the couple is treated, in accordance with regulation 9(8) of the Claims and Payments Regulations, as having made a claim for universal credit; and

(d)   the Secretary of State is satisfied that the claimants meet the basic conditions specified in section 4(1)(a) to (d) of the Act (other than any of those conditions which they are not required to meet by virtue of regulations under section 4(2) of the Act).

(2)   Subject to paragraphs (4) and (5), where this regulation applies, all awards of income support or housing benefit to which the new claimant partner would (were it not for the effect of these Regulations) have been entitled during the relevant period are to terminate, by virtue of this regulation–

(a)   on the day before the first date on which the joint claimants are entitled to universal credit in connection with the claim; or

(b)   if the joint claimants are not entitled to universal credit, on the day before the first date on which they would have been so entitled, if all of the basic and financial conditions applicable to them had been met; or

(c)   if the new claimant partner became entitled to an award after the date on which it would otherwise terminate under sub-paragraph (a) or (b), at the beginning of the first day of entitlement to that award.

(3)   For the purposes of this regulation, "the relevant period" is the period starting with the first day of the assessment period (in relation to A's award of universal credit) during which A and the new claimant partner formed a couple and ending with the date of formation of the couple.

(4)   Where the new claimant partner was entitled during the relevant period to income support, he or she was at that time a member of a couple and the award included an amount in respect of the new claimant partner and their partner at that time ("P"), the award of income support terminates, by virtue of this regulation, on the date on which the new claimant partner and P ceased to be a couple for the purposes of the Income Support (General) Regulations 1987, unless it terminates on that date in accordance with other legislative provision, or terminated on an earlier date.

(5)   An award of housing benefit to which the new claimant partner is entitled does not terminate by virtue of this regulation where–

(a)   the award is in respect of [¹ specified accommodation] [² or temporary accommodation]; or

(b)   the new claimant partner leaves the accommodation in respect of which housing benefit was paid, in order to live with A.

(6)   Where an award terminates by virtue of this regulation, any legislative provision under which the award terminates on a later date does not apply.

(7)   *[Omitted]*

Modifications

Reg 7(1)(a) and (b) are amended by reg 3(3) Universal Credit (Digital Services) Amendments Regulations 2014 SI No.2887 for UC claimants who are "digital service claimants" in the postcode area SM5 2, as from 26 November 2014. The words "as a single person" are omitted from those sub-paras.

Amendments

1.   Amended by reg 3 of SI 2014 No 1626 as from 3.11.14.
2.   Amended by reg 6(6)(b) of SI 2018 No 65 as from 11.4.18, subject to saving and transitional provision in reg 8(2) and (3).

Definitions

"assessment period" – see reg 2(1) and reg 21 Universal Credit Regulations 2013 SI No.376.
"specified accommodation" – see reg 2(1).
"temporary accommodation" – see reg 2(1).

General Note

Reg 7 provides the termination date for an award of HB in situations in which a single UC claimant becomes a member of a couple with a partner who is not entitled to UC. It does not apply if the new partner is entitled to HB for "specified accommodation" or "temporary accommodation" or if s/he has left the accommodation in respect of which HB was paid. See also reg 13 if the new partner was awaiting the outcome of an appeal on entitlement to HB, or a decision on revision or supersession. See reg 8 for the rules for other UC claimants, reg 46 (on p1878) if an HB claimant subject to "managed migration" to UC fails to claim UC before a specified deadline date and reg 47 (on p1879) if a claimant subject to "managed migration" claims UC as a different benefit unit.

Analysis

Paras (1)–(3). Reg 7 applies if a person's entitlement to UC as a single person ceases because s/he has become a member of a couple with someone who was not entitled to UC (a "new claimant partner"). In addition, the couple must be treated as having made a claim for UC, and the DWP must be satisfied that the couple meet the basic conditions for UC set out in sub-para (d). Unless either of the exceptions in para (5) applies, any award of IS or HB to which the new claimant partner would have been entitled during the "relevant period" terminates. "Relevant period" is defined in para (3) as the period starting with the first day of the assessment period during which the UC claimant and her/his "new claimant partner" became a couple and ending on the actual date they became a couple. The first day of an assessment period is generally the monthly anniversary of the UC claimant's first day of entitlement to UC: reg 21 UC Regs 2013.

The dates on which a new claimant partner's HB award terminates are provided in para (2) as follows.

(1)   If the new couple is awarded UC jointly, any award of HB to which the "new claimant partner" would be entitled terminates on the day before the first date of entitlement to the joint award of UC: sub-para (a).

(2)   If the new couple meet the basic conditions for UC, but are not awarded UC because they do not meet the financial conditions, any award of HB to which the "new claimant partner" is entitled terminates on the first date they would have been entitled to UC had they met all the conditions: sub-para (b).

(3)   If the new claimant partner's award of HB was made after the date on which it would otherwise terminate under sub-para (a) or (b), the HB award terminates at the start of the first day of entitlement to HB: sub-para (c). It is understood that the DWP intention is that this only applies in exceptional cases where entitlement to HB starts after the first date of entitlement to UC. It is difficult to see when this would ever apply given that a claim for, and entitlement to, HB is not generally possible if the claimant is entitled to UC: regs 5 and 6.

Although it is not clear that the legislation provides this result, it is assumed that the intention is that in cases where entitlement to HB and UC is allowed under reg 5(2)(b) and where a claim for HB by a "UC claimant" is allowed under reg 6(6), (7) or (7A) (eg, a backdated claim is decided or an appeal is determined in a new claimant partner's favour, after an award of UC is made), the HB award terminates under para (2)(a) or (b) as the case may be, and not under para (2)(c). Note that reg 9(8) Claims and Payments Regulations cited is amended for UC claimants to whom the Universal Credit (Digital Service) Amendment Regulations 2014 SI No.2887 apply.

Example: A single UC claimant moves in with a new claimant partner (who is entitled to HB) on 1 July. The first day of the assessment period in which they became a couple is 20 June. He and his partner are awarded UC jointly with effect from 20 June. His partner's HB entitlement terminates 19 June.

Exceptions

Para (5) provides two exceptions.

(1)   An HB award in respect of "specified accommodation" (specified types of supported accommodation and of temporary accommodation for those who have left home as a result of domestic violence) or "temporary

accommodation" (specified types of homeless accommodation that is not "exempt accommodation", where rent is payable to a local authority or provider of social housing) does not terminate: sub-para (a). Note that prior to 3 November 2014, this exception applied only if the HB was for "exempt accommodation", defined as in Sch 3 para 4(10) HB&CTB(CP) Regs. Between 3 November 2014 and 11 April 2018, this exception only applied if HB was for "specified accommodation" which includes "exempt accommodation".

(2)   An HB award does not terminate under reg 7 if the new claimant partner leaves the home in respect of which the HB was awarded and moves in with the UC claimant: sub-para (b). However, it would then terminate as provided for in the HB rules. This exception is needed because the first date on which the couple are jointly entitled to UC (governed by reg 21(3) UC Regs) is the first day of the original single claimant's "assessment period" in relation to her/his old UC award – ie, the monthly anniversary of her/his original date of claim. Sub-para (b) allows the HB award to continue if the HB claimant moves in with the UC claimant part-way through an assessment period – ie, if s/he continues to have a rent liability and entitlement to HB on her/his former home until the move. Note that reg 21 UC Regs is amended for UC claimants to whom the Universal Credit (Digital Service) Amendment Regulations 2014 SI No.2887 apply.

Termination of awards of certain existing benefits: other claimants

8.–(1)   This regulation applies where–

(a)   a claim for universal credit (other than a claim which is treated, in accordance with regulation 9(8) of the Claims and Payments Regulations, as having been made) is made; and

(b)   the Secretary of State is satisfied that the claimant meets the basic conditions specified in section 4(1)(a) to (d) of the Act (other than any of those conditions which the claimant is not required to meet by virtue of regulations under section 4(2) of the Act).

(2)   [² Where] this regulation applies, all awards of income support [²] or a tax credit to which the claimant (or, in the case of joint claimants, either of them) is entitled on the date on which the claim is made are to terminate, by virtue of this regulation–

(a)   on the day before the first date on which the claimant is entitled to universal credit in connection with the claim; or

(b)   if the claimant is not entitled to universal credit, on the day before the first date on which he or she would have been so entitled, if all of the basic and financial conditions applicable to the claimant had been met.

[² (2A)   Subject to paragraph (3), where this regulation applies, an award of housing benefit to which the claimant is entitled on the day mentioned in paragraph (2)(a) or (b) terminates on the last day of the period of two weeks beginning with the day after that day (whether or not the person is also entitled to an award of income support or a tax credit).]

(3)   An award of housing benefit to which a claimant is entitled in respect of [¹ specified accommodation] [² or temporary accommodation] does not terminate by virtue of this regulation.

(4)   *[Omitted]*

(5)   Where an award terminates by virtue of this regulation, any legislative provision under which the award terminates on a later date does not apply.

Amendments

1.   Amended by reg 3 of SI 2014 No 1626 as from 3.11.14.

2.   Amended by reg 6(7) of SI 2018 No 65 as from 11.4.18, with the amendment to paragraph (3) subject to saving and transitional provisions in reg 8(2) and (3).

Definitions

"Claim and Payments Regulations" – see reg 2(1).

"specified accommodation" – see reg 2(1).

"temporary accommodation" – see reg 2(1).

General Note

Reg 8 provides the termination date of an award of HB where a claim for UC is made. See reg 7 for the termination date for some new couples jointly claiming UC. See also reg 13 if the person was awaiting the outcome of an appeal on entitlement to HB, or a decision on revision or supersession. See reg 46 (on p1878) if an HB claimant subject to "managed migration" to UC fails to claim UC before a specified deadline date and reg 47 (on p1879) if a claimant subject to "managed migration" claims UC as a different benefit unit.

Note: reg 8 will be amended and reg 8B added from 22 July 2020 when a two-week "run-on" of IS is introduced.

Analysis

Reg 8 applies if a person makes a claim for UC, other than a claim treated as made under reg 9(8) Claims and Payments Regulations referred to in para (1)(a) and s/he meets the basic conditions for UC. Reg 9(8) of those regulations treats a couple who are joint UC claimants as having made a claim for UC where one partner was a single claimant whose UC award was terminated and who became a member of a couple with the other partner who did not have an award of UC as a single person. The termination of the other partner's award of HB is instead dealt with under reg 7, or under the normal HB rules as the case may be. Note that reg 9(8) Claims and Payments Regulations cited is amended for UC claimants to whom the Universal Credit (Digital Service) Amendment Regulations 2014 SI No.2887 apply.

The termination date

If reg 8 applies, the termination date for an HB award is fixed by para (2A) which provides a two-week run-on in entitlement to HB following a claim for UC (sometimes called a transitional HB payment). An HB award terminates on the last day of the two-week period starting with the day after the day mentioned in para (2)(a) or (b) as the case may be. Under para (2)(a), this is the first date of entitlement to UC. Under para (2)(b), if the claimant meets the basic conditions for UC, but is not entitled to UC (eg, because s/he does not meet the financial conditions in s5 WRA 2012), this is the first date s/he would have been entitled had s/he met both the basic and the financial conditions. For when entitlement to UC begins, see s7 WRA 2012 and reg 21 UC Regs. Note that it appears the claimant is entitled to the transitional payment of HB even if s/he qualifies for a housing costs element of UC for the same period.

See reg 8A where a UC claim has not yet been decided, and for when HB is to be paid to the claimant – ie, not to the landlord.

When HB award does not terminate

An award of HB in respect of "specified accommodation" or "temporary accommodation" does not terminate: para (3). Note that prior to 3 November 2014, this exception applied only if the HB was for "exempt accommodation", defined as in Sch 3 para 4(10) HB&CTB(CP) Regs. Between 3 November 2014 and 11 April 2018, this exception applied only if HB was for "specified accommodation" (which includes "exempt accommodation").

[¹ Transitional housing payment

8A. Where an award of housing benefit terminates under regulation 8 [², 46 or 47]–

(a) the claimant is to be treated for the purposes of the Housing Benefit Regulations 2006 as entitled to universal credit during the period of two weeks mentioned in regulation 8(2A) [², 46(1) or 47(2)], even if no decision has been made on the claim; [²]

(b) if a claim for universal credit is made because the claimant moves to new accommodation occupied as the claimant's home, then, notwithstanding anything in the Housing Benefit Regulations 2006, housing benefit is to be paid directly to the claimant during the period of two weeks mentioned in regulation 8(2A) [², 46(1) or 47(2); and

(c) if a claim for universal credit is made by a notified person then, notwithstanding anything in the Housing Benefit Regulations 2006, the weekly amount of housing benefit to which the person is entitled for that period of two weeks is the same as the weekly amount they were entitled to on the first day of that period.]]

Amendments

1. Inserted by reg 6(8) of SI 2018 No 65 as from 11.4.18.
2. Amended by reg 3(5) of SI 2019 No 1152 as from 24.7.19.

Definitions

"notified person" – see regs 2(1) and 44(6).

General Note

Reg 8A allows the two-week run-on of entitlement to HB (the transitional HB payment) under reg 8(2A), 46(1) or 47(2) even if no decision has been made on the UC claim: para (a). Under para (b), if a UC claimant has moved to new accommodation, the HB must be paid direct to her/him. There is no apparent requirement to pay the HB direct to the claimant in any other case. If reg 8A(b) does not apply, HB is being paid direct to the claimant's landlord at the time s/he claims UC, s/he qualifies for a UC housing costs element for the same period as the transitional HB payment and rent payments are up-to-date, the claimant will need to ask the local authority to cease direct payments or alternatively ask her/his landlord to refund any amount overpaid to the landlord.

Under para (c), if a claim for UC is made by a "notified person" (defined in regs 2(1) and 44 as a person to whom a migration notice has been issued), the weekly amount of HB for the two-week period is the weekly amount to which s/he was entitled on the first day of that period.

Treatment of overpayments

10.–(1)   This regulation applies where–

(a)   an award of universal credit is made to a claimant who was previously entitled to an existing benefit other than a tax credit or a joint-claim jobseeker's allowance; and

(b)   a payment of the existing benefit is made which includes payment ("the overpayment") in respect of a period–

    (i)   during which the claimant is not entitled to that benefit (including non-entitlement which arises from termination of an award by virtue of an order made under section 150(3) of the Act or regulation 7, 8, or 14); and

    (ii)   which falls within an assessment period for universal credit.

(2)   Where this regulation applies, for the purposes of calculating the amount of an award of universal credit in respect of an assessment period–

(a)   regulation 66 of the Universal Credit Regulations (what is included in unearned income?) applies as if the overpayment which was made in respect of that assessment period were added to the descriptions of unearned income in paragraph (1)(b) of that regulation; and

(b)   regulation 73 of the Universal Credit Regulations (unearned income calculated monthly) does not apply to the overpayment.

(3)   In so far as any overpayment is taken into account in calculating the amount of an award of universal credit in accordance with this regulation, that payment may not be recovered as an overpayment under–

(a)   the Social Security (Payments on account, Overpayments and Recovery) Regulations 1988;

(b)   the Housing Benefit Regulations 2006; or

(c)   the Housing Benefit (Persons who have attained the qualifying age for state pension credit) Regulations 2006.

Definitions

"existing benefit" – see reg 2(1).

General Note

Reg 10 allows for an overpayment of an existing benefit (including HB) paid when the person was not entitled to that benefit, but was entitled to UC, to be recovered by deducting it as unearned income in calculating the amount of UC to which the person is entitled. If an overpayment of HB is offset in this way, it cannot be recovered under Part 13 of the HB Regs or Part 12 of the HB(SPC) Regs.

[¹ Arrears of benefit disregarded as capital

10A.–(1)   This regulation applies in relation to the calculation of an award of universal credit (the "current award") where the claimant has received a payment of arrears of benefit [² or armed forces independence payment], or a payment made to compensate for arrears due to the non-payment of benefit, [² or armed forces independence payment] of £5,000 or more, and the following conditions are met–

(a)   the payment–

    (i)   is received during the current award; or

    (ii)   was received during an award of an existing benefit or state pension credit (the "earlier award") and the claimant became entitled to the current award within one month of the date of termination of the earlier award;

(b)   in the case of a payment falling within sub-paragraph (a)(i), it would be disregarded from the calculation of the claimant's capital if the claimant were entitled to an existing benefit or state pension credit;

(c)   in the case of a payment falling within sub-paragraph (a)(ii), it was disregarded from the calculation of the claimant's capital for the purposes of the earlier award;

(d)   the period of entitlement to benefit [² or armed forces independence payment] to which the payment relates commences before the first date on which, by virtue of section 33 of the Act (abolition of benefits), no claimant is entitled to an existing benefit.

(2)   Where this regulation applies, notwithstanding anything in the Universal Credit Regulations, the payment is to be disregarded from the calculation of the claimant's capital for 12 months from the date of receipt of the payment, or until the termination of the current award (if later).

[² (3)   "Armed forces independence payment" means armed forces independence payment under the Armed Forces and Reserve Forces (Compensation Scheme) Order 2011.]]

Amendments

1.   Inserted by reg 8 of SI 2018 No 932 as from 11.9.18.

2.   Inserted by reg 9(2) of SI 2019 No 1314 as from 31.10.19.

[¹ **Arrears of maternity allowance disregarded as capital**

10B.–(1)   This regulation applies in relation to the calculation of an award of universal credit where–

(a)   the conditions set out in regulation 10A(1)(a)-(d) are met; and

(b)   the claimant has received a payment of arrears of maternity allowance, or a payment made to compensate for arrears due to the non-payment of maternity allowance, of under £5,000.

(2)   Where this regulation applies, notwithstanding anything in the Universal Credit Regulations, the payment is to be disregarded from the calculation of the claimant's capital for 12 months from the date of receipt of the payment.

(3)   "Maternity allowance" means a maternity allowance under section 35 of the Social Security Contributions and Benefits Act 1992 (state maternity allowance for employed or self-empoyed earner).]

Amendment

1.   Inserted by reg 9(3) of SI 2019 No 1314 as from 31.10.19.

Appeals etc relating to certain existing benefits

13.–(1)   This regulation applies where, after an award of universal credit has been made to a claimant–

(a)   an appeal against a decision relating to the entitlement of the claimant to income support, housing benefit or a tax credit (a "relevant benefit") is finally determined;

(b)   *[Omitted]*

(c)   a decision relating to the claimant's entitlement to housing benefit is revised or superseded under Schedule 7 to the Child Support, Pensions and Social Security Act 2000; or

(d)   *[Omitted]*

(2)   Where the claimant is a new claimant partner and, as a result of determination of the appeal or, as the case may be, revision or supersession of the decision the claimant would (were it not for the effect of these Regulations) be entitled to income support or housing benefit during the relevant period mentioned in regulation 7(3), awards of those benefits are to terminate in accordance with regulation 7.

(3)   Where the claimant is not a new claimant partner and, as a result of determination of the appeal or, as the case may be, revision, supersession, variation or cancellation of the decision, the claimant would (were it not for the effect of these Regulations) be entitled to a relevant benefit on the date on which the claim for universal credit was made, awards of relevant benefits are to terminate in accordance with regulation 8.

(4)   The Secretary of State is to consider whether it is appropriate to revise under section 9 of the 1998 Act the decision in relation to entitlement to universal credit or, if that decision has been superseded under section 10 of that Act, the decision as so superseded (in either case, "the UC decision").

(5)   Where it appears to the Secretary of State to be appropriate to revise the UC decision, it is to be revised in such manner as appears to the Secretary of State to be necessary to take account of–

(a)   the decision of the First-tier Tribunal, Upper Tribunal or court, or, as the case may be, the decision relating to entitlement to a relevant benefit, as revised, superseded, varied or cancelled; and

(b)   any finding of fact by the First-tier Tribunal, Upper Tribunal or court.

Definition

"new claimant partner" – see regs 2(1) and 7.

General Note

Reg 13 applies where an appeal against an HB decision has been finally determined, or an HB decision is revised or superseded, after a claimant is awarded UC. Para (2) applies if the HB claimant is a "new claimant partner", broadly someone who was not entitled to UC when s/he became a member of a couple with a single UC claimant. "Relevant period" is defined in reg 7(3) as the period starting with the first day of the assessment period during which the UC claimant and her/his "new claimant partner" became a couple and ending on the actual date they became a couple. The first day of an assessment period is generally the monthly anniversary of the UC claimant's first day of entitlement to UC: reg 21 UC Regs 2013. Para (3) applies in other cases.

   See the commentary to regs 7, 8, 46 and 47 for the relevant termination dates and the situations in which the award of HB cannot be terminated. Paras (4) and (5) allow the DWP to revise a UC entitlement decision "as appears to be necessary" to take account of the appeal, revision or supersession, or any finding off fact made in the appeal.

   Note: reg 13 will be amended from 22 July 2020 whena two-week "run-on" of IS, income-based JSA and income-related ESA is introduced.

Appeals etc relating to universal credit

14.–(1)   This regulation applies where–

(a)   a decision is made that a claimant is not entitled to universal credit ("the UC decision");

(b)   the claimant becomes entitled to income support, housing benefit or a tax credit (a "relevant benefit");

(c)   an appeal against the UC decision is finally determined, or the decision is revised under section 9 of the Social Security Act 1998;

(d)   an award of universal credit is made to the claimant in consequence of entitlement arising from the appeal, or from the decision as revised; and

(e)   the claimant would (were it not for the effect of regulation 5 and this regulation) be entitled to both universal credit and a relevant benefit in respect of the same period.

(2)   Subject to paragraph (3), where this regulation applies–

(a)   all awards of a relevant benefit to which the claimant would (were it not for the effect of these Regulations) be entitled are to terminate, by virtue of this regulation, at the beginning of the first day of entitlement to that award; and

(b)   any legislative provision [² except regulation 8(2A)] under which an award would otherwise terminate on a later date does not apply.

(3)   An award of housing benefit to which a claimant is entitled in respect of [¹ specified accommodation] [² or temporary accommodation] does not terminate by virtue of this regulation.

Amendments

1.   Amended by reg 3 of SI 2014 No 1626 as from 3.11.14.

2.   Amended by reg 6(10) of SI 2018 No 65 as from 11.4.18, with the amendment to paragraph (3) subject to saving and transitional provisions in reg 8(2) and (3).

Definitions

"specified accommodation" – see reg 2(1).
"temporary accommodation" – see reg 2(1).

General Note

Reg 14 provides the termination date for an award of HB where a person becomes entitled to a "relevant benefit" (including HB) after a decision that s/he is not entitled to UC, but an award of UC is later made as a consequence of a decision on an appeal against, or a revision of, the UC decision. Unless reg 8(2A) applies (ie, the claimant is allowed a two-week "run-on" of HB under that provision – see para (2)) or the HB award is in respect of "specified accommodation"or "temporary accommodation" (see para (3), the HB award terminates at the start of the first day of entitlement to HB. This means that all HB paid to the claimant will be an overpayment. See reg 10 for how such an overpayment is recovered. Note that prior to 3 November 2014, the exception in para (3) applied only if the HB was for "exempt accommodation", defined as in Sch 3 para 4(10) HB&CTB(CP) Regs. From 3 November 2014 to 11 April 2018, the exception only applied if the HB was for "specified accommodation" (including "exempt accommodation"). Note that this regulation was not amended to take account of the two-week run-on of HB under regs 46(1) or 47(2).

CHAPTER 3
EFFECT OF TRANSITION TO UNIVERSAL CREDIT

Meaning of "qualifying young person"

28. Where a person who would (apart from the provision made by this regulation) be a "qualifying young person" within the meaning of regulation 5 of the Universal Credit Regulations is entitled to an existing benefit–

(a) that person is not a qualifying young person for the purposes of the Universal Credit Regulations; and

(b) regulation 5(5) of those Regulations applies as if, after "a person who is receiving" there were inserted "an existing benefit (within the meaning of the Universal Credit (Transitional Provisions) Regulations 2014),".

Loss of benefit penalties: transition from existing benefits other than tax credits

35.–(1) Subject to paragraph (6), this regulation applies in the cases set out in paragraphs (2) to (4).

(2) The first case is where–

(a) an award of universal credit is made to a claimant who is an offender;

(b) the claimant was entitled to old style JSA, old style ESA, income support or housing benefit ("the earlier award") at any time during the period of one month ending with the date on which the claim for universal credit was made or treated as made (or would have been so entitled were it not for termination of that award by virtue of an order made under section 150(3) of the Act or, as the case may be, the effect of these Regulations); and

(c) payments in respect of the earlier award were, on the relevant date, subject to a restriction under section 6B (loss of benefit in case of conviction, penalty or caution for benefit offence), 7 (repeated benefit fraud) or 8 (effect of offence on joint-claim jobseeker's allowance) of the 2001 Act.

(3) The second case is where–

(a) an award of universal credit is made to a claimant who is an offender;

(b) another person who was the offender's family member (but is no longer their family member) was entitled to old style JSA, old style ESA, income support or housing benefit ("the earlier award") at any time during the period of one month ending with the date on which the claim for universal credit was made or treated as made; and

(c) payments in respect of the earlier award were, on the relevant date, subject to a restriction under section 9 (effect of offence on benefits for members of offender's family) of the 2001 Act.

(4) The third case is where–

(a) an award of universal credit is made to a claimant who is an offender's family member;

(b) the offender, or the claimant, was entitled to old style JSA, old style ESA, income support or housing benefit ("the earlier award") at any time during the period of one month ending with the date on which the claim for universal credit was made or treated as made; and

(c) payments in respect of the earlier award were, on the relevant date, subject to a restriction under section 6B, 7, 8 or, as the case may be, 9 of the 2001 Act.

(5) Where this regulation applies–

    (a)   any subsequent payment of universal credit to the claimant in respect of an assessment period which falls wholly or partly within the remainder of the disqualification period applicable to the offender is to be reduced in accordance with regulation 36; and

    (b)   regulation 3ZB of the 2001 Regulations does not apply.

    (6)   This regulation does not apply if the earlier award was a joint-claim jobseeker's allowance and–

    (a)   payments in respect of the award were, on the relevant date, subject to a restriction under section 8(2) of the 2001 Act; or

    (b)   the award of universal credit is not made to joint claimants who were, on the relevant date, both entitled to the joint-claim jobseeker's allowance.

    (7)   In this regulation and in regulation 36–

"the 2001 Act" means the Social Security Fraud Act 2001;

"the 2001 Regulations" means the Social Security (Loss of Benefit) Regulations 2001;

"disqualification period" has the meaning given in the 2001 Act, interpreted in accordance with the 2001 Regulations;

"earlier award" is to be interpreted in accordance with paragraph (2)(b), (3)(b) or, as the case may be, (4)(b) and, for the purposes of regulation 36, where there is more than one earlier award, the term refers to the award to which the claimant became entitled most recently;

"offender" means an offender within the meaning of the 2001 Act;

"offender's family member" has the same meaning as in the 2001 Act;

"the relevant date" means–

    (a)   in relation to the first case–

        (i)   where the claimant was not entitled to the earlier award on the date on which the claim for universal credit was made or treated as made, the date on which the earlier award terminated;

        (ii)   where the claimant is not a new claimant partner and was entitled to the earlier award on the date on which the claim for universal credit was made, that date;

        (iii)   where the claimant is a new claimant partner and was entitled to the earlier award on the date on which the claim for universal credit was treated as made, that date;

    (b)   in relation to the second case, the date on which the person entitled to the earlier award ceased to be the offender's family member or, if the award terminated before that date, the date on which the earlier award terminated;

    (c)   in relation to the third case–

        (i)   where the claimant was entitled to the earlier award but that entitlement terminated before the date on which the claim for universal credit was made or treated as made, the date on which the earlier award terminated;

        (ii)   where the claimant is not a new claimant partner and was entitled to the earlier award on the date on which the claim for universal credit was made, that date;

        (iii)   where the claimant is a new claimant partner and was entitled to the earlier award on the date on which the claim for universal credit was treated as made, that date;

        (iv)   where the offender's family member was entitled to the earlier award, the date on which that person ceased to be the offender's family member or, if earlier, the date on which the earlier award terminated.

    (8)   For the purposes of this regulation, the fact that payments in respect of an earlier award were subject to a restriction is to be taken into account, even if the earlier award subsequently terminated before the date on which payments became subject to a restriction by virtue of an order made under section 150(3) of the Act (in so far as it was an award of income-based jobseeker's allowance or income-related employment and support allowance), regulation 7 or, as the case may be, regulation 8.

Loss of benefit penalties: reduction of universal credit

36.–(1)   Subject to paragraph (6) [¹ and to regulation 38], where regulation 35 applies, the amount of a reduction of universal credit in respect of an assessment period is to be calculated by multiplying the daily reduction rate by the number of days in the assessment period, unless paragraph (2) applies.

(2)   Where the disqualification period ends during an assessment period, the amount of the reduction for that assessment period is (subject to paragraph (6)) to be calculated by multiplying the daily reduction rate by the number of days in the assessment period which are within the disqualification period.

(3)   Subject to paragraphs (4) and (5), the daily reduction rate where regulation 35 applies is an amount which is equal to–

(a)   the monetary amount by which payments in respect of the earlier award were reduced in accordance with section 6B or 7 of the 2001 Act or, as the case may be, regulation 3, 3ZA(a) or 17 of the 2001 Regulations in respect of the last complete week before the relevant date (within the meaning of regulation 35);

(b)   multiplied by 52;

(c)   divided by 365; and

(d)   rounded down to the nearest 10 pence.

(4)   Where the monetary amount by which payments in respect of the earlier award would have been reduced would, if the claimant had remained entitled to the earlier award, have changed during the disqualification period because of an order made under section 150 of the Social Security Administration Act 1992 (annual up-rating of benefits)–

(a)   the daily reduction rate is to be calculated in accordance with paragraph (3), but on the basis of the new amount by which payments would have been reduced; and

(b)   any adjustment to the reduction of universal credit is to take effect from the first day of the first assessment period to start after the date of the change.

(5)   Where the earlier award was a joint-claim jobseeker's allowance, the daily reduction rate is an amount which is equal to–

(a)   the amount of the standard allowance applicable to the joint claimants under regulation 36 of the Universal Credit Regulations (table showing amounts of elements);

(b)   multiplied by 12;

(c)   divided by 365;

(d)   reduced by 60%; and

(e)   rounded down to the nearest 10 pence.

(6)   The amount of the reduction under this regulation in respect of any assessment period is not to exceed the amount of the standard allowance which is applicable to the claimant in respect of that period.

Amendment

1.   Amended by reg 6 of SI 2014 No 1626 as from 13.10.14.

[¹ PART 4
MANAGED MIGRATION TO UNIVERSAL CREDIT
The Migration Process

Amendment

1.   Part 4 inserted by reg 3(7) of SI 2019 No.1152 from 24.07.19.

Migration notice

44.–(1)   The Secretary of State may, at any time, issue a notice ("a migration notice") to a person who is entitled to an award of an existing benefit–

(a)   informing the person that all awards of any existing benefits to which they are entitled are to terminate and that they will need to make a claim for universal credit; and

(b)   specifying a day ("the deadline day") by which a claim for universal credit must be made.

(2)   The migration notice may contain such other information as the Secretary of State considers appropriate.

(3)   The deadline day must not be within the period of three months beginning with the day on which the migration notice is issued.

(4)   If the person who is entitled to an award of an existing benefit is, for the purposes of that award, a member of a couple or a member of a polygamous marriage, the Secretary of State must also issue the migration notice to the other member (or members).

(5)   The Secretary of State may cancel a migration notice issued to any person–

(a)   if it has been issued in error;

(b)   if the Secretary of State has made a determination in accordance with regulation 4 (discretion to determine that claims for universal credit may not be made) that would affect a claim by that person; or

(c)   in any other circumstances where the Secretary State considers it necessary to do so in the interests of the person, or any class of person, or to safeguard the efficient administration of universal credit.

(6)   A "notified person" is a person to whom a migration notice has been issued.

Definition
  "existing benefit" – see reg 2(1).

Extension of the deadline day

45.–(1)   The Secretary of State may determine that the deadline day should be changed to a later day either–

(a)   on the Secretary of State's own initiative; or

(b)   if a notified person requests such a change before the deadline day,

where there is a good reason to do so.

(2)   The Secretary of State must inform the notified person or persons of the new deadline day.

Definitions
  "deadline day" – see regs 2(1) and 44.
  "notified person" – see regs 2(1) and 44.

Termination of existing benefits if no claim before the deadline

46.–(1)   Where a notified person has not made a claim for universal credit on or before the deadline day, all awards of any existing benefits to which the person is entitled terminate–

(a)   in the case of housing benefit, on the last day of the period of two weeks beginning with the deadline day; and

(b)   in the case of any other existing benefit, on the day before the deadline day.

(2)   An award of housing benefit to which a claimant is entitled in respect of specified accommodation or temporary accommodation does not terminate by virtue of this regulation.

(3)   Where paragraph (1) applies and the notified person makes a claim for universal credit–

(a)   after the deadline day; and

(b)   on or before the final deadline specified in paragraph (4),

then, notwithstanding anything in regulation 26 of the Claims and Payments Regulations (time within which a claim for universal credit is to be made)(5) as modified by regulation 15 of these Regulations, the award is to commence on the deadline day.

(4)   The final deadline is the day that would be the last day of the first assessment period in relation to an award commencing on the deadline day.

(5)   This regulation is subject to regulation 47.

Definitions
  "deadline day" – see regs 2(1) and 44.
  "existing benefit" – see reg 2(1).
  "notified person" – see regs 2(1) and 44.
  "specified accommodation" – see reg 2(1).
  "temporary accommodation" – see reg 2(1).

General Note

Reg 46 sets the termination date of all awards of existing benefits (including HB) if a person has been notified under the process for "managed migration" to UC (for which see reg 44) but s/he fails to claim UC by a specified date (the deadline day). Para (1)(a) allows an HB award to "run-on" for a period of two weeks. Under para (2), an award of HB does *not* terminate if it is for "specified accommodation" or "temporary accommodation".

See reg 7 for the termination date for some new couples jointly claiming UC and reg 8 for other claimants. See reg 13 if the person was awaiting the outcome of an appeal on entitlement to HB, or a decision on revision or supersession. See reg 47 if a claimant claims UC as a different benefit unit.

Notified persons who claim as a different benefit unit

47.–(1)   This regulation applies where–

(a)   notified persons who were a couple for the purposes of an award of an existing benefit when the migration notice was issued are single persons or members of a different couple for the purposes of a claim for universal credit; or

(b)   notified persons who were members of a polygamous marriage for the purposes of an award of an existing benefit when the migration notice was issued are a couple or single persons for the purposes of a claim for universal credit.

(2)   If any of those notified persons makes a claim for universal credit on or before the deadline day then, notwithstanding anything in regulation 8 (termination of awards of certain existing benefits: other claimants), all awards of any existing benefits to which any of those persons is entitled terminate–

(a)   in the case of housing benefit, on the last day of the period of two weeks beginning with the earliest day on which any of those persons is entitled to universal credit in connection with a claim (or, in a case where the person is not entitled to universal credit, on the day they would have been entitled if all the basic and financial conditions had been met); or

(b)   in the case of any other existing benefit, on the day before the "earliest day" referred to in sub-paragraph (a).

(3)   If, where paragraph (2) applies–

(a)   a notified person makes a claim for universal credit–

(i)   on or before the deadline day, or

(ii)   after the deadline day, but on or before the "final deadline" referred to in regulation 46(4); and

(b)   there would otherwise be a gap between the termination of existing benefits and the commencement of the award,

the award is to commence on the "earliest day" referred to in paragraph (2)(a).

(4)   If none of those notified persons makes a claim for universal credit on or before the deadline day, all awards of any existing benefits to which any of them is entitled terminate in accordance with regulation 46(1), and regulation 46(3) applies in relation to any subsequent claim by any of those persons.

(5)   An award of housing benefit to which a claimant is entitled in respect of specified accommodation or temporary accommodation does not terminate by virtue of this regulation.

Definitions

"the deadline day" – see regs 2(1) and 44.
"existing benefit" – see reg 2(1).
"migration notice" – see regs 2(1) and 44.
"notified person" – see regs 2(1) and 44.

General Note

Reg 47 sets the termination date of all awards of existing benefits (including HB) if a person who has been notified under the process for "managed migration" to UC (for which see reg 44) was a member of a couple when the migration notice was issued but is now a single person or member of a different couple (or in the case of a polygamous marriage is now a member of a couple or a single person): para (1).

Para (2)(a) allows an HB award to "run-on" for a period of two weeks. Under para (5), an award of HB does *not* terminate if it is for "specified accommodation" or "temporary accommodation".

See reg 7 for the termination date for some new couples jointly claiming UC and reg 8 for other UC claimants. See reg 13 if the person was awaiting the outcome of an appeal on entitlement to HB, or a decision on revision or supersession. See reg 46 if a claimant fails to claim UC by a specified date (the deadline day).

The Welfare Reform Act 2012 (Commencement No.20 and Transitional and Transitory Provisions and Commencement No.9 and Transitional and Transitory Provisions (Amendment)) Order 2014

(SI 2014 No.3094)

Citation

1. This Order may be cited as the Welfare Reform Act 2012 (Commencement No. 20 and Transitional and Transitory Provisions and Commencement No. 9 and Transitional and Transitory Provisions (Amendment)) Order 2014.

Interpretation

2.–(1)   In this Order–

"housing benefit" means housing benefit under section 130 of the Social Security Contributions and Benefits Act 1992;

"the No. 9 Order" means the Welfare Reform Act 2012 (Commencement No. 9 and Transitional and Transitory Provisions and Commencement No. 8 and Savings and Transitional Provisions (Amendment)) Order 2013;

(2)   For the purposes of this Order–

(a)   the Claims and Payments Regulations 2013 apply for the purpose of deciding–

(i)   whether a claim for universal credit is made or treated as made; and

(ii)   the date on which such a claim is made; and

(b)   where a couple is treated, in accordance with regulation 9(8) of the Claims and Payments Regulations 2013, as making a claim for universal credit, references to the date on which the claim is treated as made are to the date of formation of the couple.

Transitional provision: claims for housing benefit, income support or a tax credit

6.–(1)   Except as provided by paragraphs (2) to (5) and (8), a person may not make a claim for housing benefit, income support or a tax credit (in the latter case, whether or not as part of a Tax Credits Act couple) on any date where, if that person made a claim for universal credit on that date (whether or not as part of a couple), the provisions of the Act listed in Schedule 2 to the No. 9 Order would come into force under article 3(1) and (2)(a) of this Order in relation to that claim for universal credit.

(2)   Paragraph (1) does not apply to a claim for housing benefit in respect of specified accommodation.

(3)   Paragraph (1) does not apply to a claim for housing benefit or a tax credit where–

(a)   in the case of a claim for housing benefit, the claim is made by a person who has reached the qualifying age for state pension credit, or by a person who is a member of a State Pension Credit Act couple the other member of which has reached that age;

(b)   *[Omitted]*

(4)-(6)   *[Omitted]*

(7)   For the purposes of this article–

(a)   a person makes a claim for income support, housing benefit or a tax credit if the person takes any action which results in a decision on a claim being required under the relevant Regulations; and

(b)   except as provided in paragraph (8), it is irrelevant that the effect of any provision of the relevant Regulations is that, for the purpose of those Regulations, the claim is made or treated as made on a date that is earlier than the date on which that action was taken.

(8)   Paragraph (1) does not apply to a claim for housing benefit or income support where–

(a)   in the case of a claim for housing benefit–

  (i)   first notification of the person's intention to make the claim is given
        (within the meaning of regulation 83(5)(d) of the Housing Benefit
        Regulations 2006 ("the 2006 Regulations") or, as the case may be,
        regulation 64(6)(d) of the Housing Benefit (Persons who have attained the
        qualifying age for state pension credit) Regulations 2006 ("the 2006 (SPC)
        Regulations")) before 26th November 2014; or
  (ii) a defective claim for housing benefit (within the meaning of the 2006
        Regulations or the 2006 (SPC) Regulations) is made before 26th November
        2014 and it is corrected or completed on or after that date;

(b)   *[Omitted]*

(9)-(10)   *[Omitted]*

(11)   For the purposes of this article–

(a)   "couple" (apart from in the expressions "State Pension Credit Act couple" and
      "Tax Credit Act couple"), has the meaning given in section 39 of the Act;

(b)   "qualifying age for state pension credit" means the qualifying age referred to in
      section 1(6) of the State Pension Credit Act 2002;

(c)   the "relevant Regulations" means–

  (i)   *[Omitted]*
  (ii) in the case of a claim for housing benefit, the 2006 Regulations or, as the
        case may be, the 2006 (SPC) Regulations;
  (iii) *[Omitted]*

(d)   "specified accommodation" means accommodation to which one or more of
      subparagraphs (2) to (5) of paragraph 3A of Schedule 1 to the Universal Credit
      Regulations 2013 applies;

(e)   "State Pension Credit Act couple" means a couple as defined in section 17 of
      the State Pension Credit Act 2002;

(f)   *[Omitted]*

The Welfare Reform Act 2012 (Commencement No.21 and Transitional and Transitory Provisions) Order 2015

(2015 No.33)

Citation
1. This Order may be cited as the Welfare Reform Act 2012 (Commencement No. 21 and Transitional and Transitory Provisions) Order 2015.

Interpretation
2.–(1) In this Order–
"the No. 9 Order" means the Welfare Reform Act 2012 (Commencement No. 9 and Transitional and Transitory Provisions and Commencement No. 8 and Savings and Transitional Provisions (Amendment)) Order 2013;

(2) For the purposes of this Order, the Claims and Payments Regulations 2013 apply for the purpose of deciding–
(a) whether a claim for universal credit is made; and
(b) the date on which such a claim is made.

Transitional provision: claims for housing benefit, income support or a tax credit

6.–(1) Except as provided by paragraphs [¹ (2) to (5), and (11)] a person may not make a claim for housing benefit, income support or a tax credit (in the latter case, whether or not as part of a Tax Credits Act couple) on any date where, if that person made a claim for universal credit on that date (in the capacity, whether as a single person or as part of a couple, in which he or she is permitted to claim universal credit under the Universal Credit Regulations 2013), the provisions of the Act listed in Schedule 2 to the No. 9 Order would come into force under article 3(1) and (2)(a) of this Order in relation to that claim for universal credit.

(2) Paragraph (1) does not apply to a claim for housing benefit in respect of specified accommodation [³ or temporary accommodation].

(3) Paragraph (1) does not apply to a claim for housing benefit [⁶] where–
[⁷ (a) in the case of a claim for housing benefit, the claim is made by a member of a State Pension Credit Act couple who has reached the qualifying age for state pension credit, where the other member has not reached that age, and entitlement begins, or in the case of claims made in advance of entitlement is to begin–
    (i) before 15th May 2019; or
    (ii) on or after 15th May 2019 where one of the savings in the sub-paragraphs of article 4(1) of the Welfare Reform Act 2012 (Commencement No. 31 and Savings and Transitional Provisions and Commencement No. 21 and 23 and Transitional and Transitory Provisions (Amendment) Order 2019 applies to that person and the saving has not ceased to have effect under article 4(2) of that Order, and
entitlement to housing benefit is to be construed in accordance with article 2 of that Order;]

[⁶ (b)]

(4)-(6) *[Omitted]*

(7) Subject to paragraph (8), for the purposes of this article–
(a) a claim for housing benefit, income support or a tax credit is made by a person on the date on which he or she takes any action which results in a decision on a claim being required under the relevant Regulations; and
(b) it is irrelevant that the effect of any provision of the relevant Regulations is that, for the purpose of those Regulations, the claim is made or treated as made on a date that is earlier than the date on which that action is taken.

(8) Where under the provisions referred to in paragraph (9), a claim for housing benefit or income support is treated as made at a date that is earlier than the date on which the action referred to in paragraph (7)(a) is taken, the claim is treated as made on that earlier date.

(9)   The provisions referred to are–

(a)   in the case of a claim for housing benefit, regulation 83(4E), (4F), (5)(d) or (8) of the Housing Benefit Regulations 2006 ("the 2006 Regulations") or, as the case may be, regulation 64(5F), (5G), (6)(d) or (9) of the Housing Benefit (Persons who have attained the qualifying age for state pension credit) Regulations 2006 ("the 2006 (SPC) Regulations")); or

(b)   *[Omitted]*

(10)   For the purposes of this article–

(a)   "couple" (apart from in the expressions "State Pension Credit Act couple" and "Tax Credit Act couple"), has the meaning given in section 39 of the Act;

(b)   "housing benefit" means housing benefit under section 130 of the Social Security Contributions and Benefits Act 1992;

(c)   *[Omitted]*

(d)   "qualifying age for state pension credit" means the qualifying age referred to in section 1(6) of the State Pension Credit Act 2002;

(e)   the "relevant Regulations" means–

    (i)   in the case of a claim for housing benefit, the 2006 Regulations or, as the case may be, the 2006 (SPC) Regulations;

    (ii)-(iii) *[Omitted]*

(f)   "specified accommodation" means accommodation to which one or more of subparagraphs (2) to (5) of paragraph 3A of Schedule 1 to the Universal Credit Regulations 2013 applies;

(g)   "state pension credit" means state pension credit under the State Pension Credit Act 2002;

(h)   "State Pension Credit Act couple" means a couple as defined in section 17 of the State Pension Credit Act 2002;

(i)-(j) *[Omitted]* [³ ;

(k)   "temporary accommodation" means accommodation which falls within Case 1 or Case 2 under paragraph 3B of Schedule 1 to the Universal Credit Regulations].

[¹ (11)   Paragraph (1) does not apply to a claim for housing benefit, income support or a tax credit where, by virtue of a determination made under regulation 4 [² , or by virtue of regulation [⁴ 4A] [⁵],] of the Universal Credit (Transitional Provisions) Regulations 2014, [⁶ or by virtue of article 4(11) of the Welfare Reform Act 2012 (Commencement No. 32 and Savings and Transitional Provisions) Order 2019] the person in question would be prevented from making a claim for universal credit as referred to in that paragraph.]

Amendments

1.   Amended by art 9(5) of SI 2015 No 634 with effect from 18.3.15.
2.   Amended by art 3(2) of SI 2017 No 483 as from 6.4.17.
3.   Amended by art 6(2) of SI 2018 No 138 as from 11.4.18.
4.   Amended by reg 3(2) of SI 2019 No 10 as from 16.1.19.
5.   Amended by reg 4(2) of SI 2019 No 27 as from 1.2.19.
6.   Amended by art 5(3) of SI 2019 No 167 with effect from 1.2.19.
7.   Substituted by art 5 of SI 2019 No 37 with effect from 15.5.19, subject to transitional provision in arts 6 and 7.

General Note

By virtue of art 6, a person cannot make a claim for HB, other than in exceptional cases, on a date when, if s/he were to claim UC on that date, and if s/he is permitted to claim, the UC provisons cited would come into force: para (1). For this purpose, a claim is treated as made on the date on which the person takes action which results in a decision on a claim being required, and it is irrelevant if the claim is made, or treated as made, earlier than the date on which action is taken: para (7). Paras (8) and (9) deal with some situations when a claim for HB is treated as made on an earlier date than the date on which action was taken. The HB Regs and HB(SPC) Regs cited cover situations when a defective claim is made and then corrected, as well as when there has been notification of an intention to claim HB prior to the actual claim being submitted.

Note also that if someone is a "universal credit claimant", s/he cannot make a claim for HB, or be entitled to HB, other than in exceptional cases. See the UC(TP) Regs (on p1857) and the note on the Welfare Reform Act 2012 (on p4).

Exceptions

(1)   An HB claim can be made if it is in respect of "specified accommodation" (specified types of supported accommodation and of temporary accommodation provided for those who have left home as a result of domestic violence) or "temporary accommodation" (specified types of homeless accommodation that is not "exempt accommodation", where rent is payable to a local authority or provider of social housing), both defined in para (10) by reference to the UC Regs; para (2).

(2)   From 15 May 2019, a claim for HB can be made by a person who a member of a "State Pension Credit Act couple" – ie, a couple as defined for PC purposes, who is at least the qualifying age for PC but whose partner is not yet that age (a member of a mixed-age couple): para (3)(a). This only applies if entitlement starts (or on and advance claim will start):

– before 15 May 2019; *or*

– on or after 15th May 2019, if the savings provision in art 4 of the No.31 Order cited applies – ie, the person has been entitled to PC or HB or both continuously since 14 May 2019 as part of the same mixed-age couple (see p1899). For these purposes, entitlement to HB means entitlement under the HB(SPC) Regs: see the closing words of para (3)(a) and art 2 of the No.31 Order (on p1898). As a claim for HB under those regulations can be backdated by up to three months, the savings can apply even if the HB claim is made on or after 15 May 2019, so long as it is made no later than 13 August 2019. See art 7 of the No.31 Order (on p1901) if the member of the couple who is at least the qualifying age for PC would be prevented from claiming HB under art 6 of this order, but could claim UC as a single person or is a member of a polygamous marriage (where two of the members are treated as a couple for UC purposes and the other or others as single).

Note that even if a member of a mixed-age couple is unable to claim HB under para (3)(a), s/he may be able to make a claim under para (2) above or (11) below.

Note: prior to the amendments made from 15 May 2019, art 6 allowed a claim for HB by a single claimant of at least the qualifying age for PC and by a member of a couple whose partner had reached that age – ie, a member of a couple where either or both members were at least the qualifying age for PC. Para (3)(a) now only allows claims by mixed-age couples. It is understood that the DWP intention is that single claimants of at least the qualifying age for PC, and claimants who are members of a couple both at least that age *can* make a claim for HB. but the legislative basis making good such an intention is at best unclear.

(3)   An HB claim can be made if the person would be prevented from claiming UC by virtue of the provisions cited in para (11). These are if:

– the Secretary of State has decided to cease to accept claims for UC in any area or category of case. See reg 4 UC(TP) Regs 2014 (on p1861); *or*

– within the last month, the claimant (or her/his partner) has been entitled to an award of HB (or IS, income-based JSA or income-related ESA) that included a severe disability premium (known as the "SDP Gateway"). See reg 4A UC(TP) Regs 2014 (see p1862); *or*

– the claimant (or her/his partner) is a "frontier worker": art 4(11) of the Welfare Reform Act 2012 (Commencement No.32 and Savings and Transitional Provisions) Order 2019.

If the claimant is also a member of a mixed-age couple, the member of the couple who is at least the qualifying age for PC is treated as not having attained that age for the purposes of an award of HB. See art 8 of the No.31 Order (on p1902).

The Welfare Reform Act 2012 (Commencement No.23 and Transitional and Transitory Provisions) Order 2015
(SI 2015 No.634)

Citation
1.   This Order may be cited as the Welfare Reform Act 2012 (Commencement No. 23 and Transitional and Transitory Provisions) Order 2015.

Interpretation
2.–(1)   In this Order–
"the No. 9 Order" means the Welfare Reform Act 2012 (Commencement No. 9 and Transitional and Transitory Provisions and Commencement No. 8 and Savings and Transitional Provisions (Amendment)) Order 2013;
(2)-(5)   *[Omitted]*

Transitional provision: claims for housing benefit, income support or a tax credit
7.–(1)   Except as provided by paragraphs (2) to (6), a person may not make a claim for housing benefit, income support or a tax credit (in the latter case, whether or not as part of a Tax Credits Act couple) on any date where, if that person made a claim for universal credit on that date (in the capacity, whether as a single person or as part of a couple, in which he or she is permitted to claim universal credit under the Universal Credit Regulations 2013), the provisions of the Act listed in Schedule 2 to the No. 9 Order would come into force under article 3(1) and [¹ (2)(a) to (c) of this Order in relation to that claim] for universal credit.

(2)   Paragraph (1) does not apply to a claim for housing benefit, income support or a tax credit where, by virtue of a determination made under regulation 4 [², or by virtue of regulation [⁴ 4A] [⁵],] of the Universal Credit (Transitional Provisions) Regulations 2014, [⁶ or by virtue of article 4(11) of the Welfare Reform Act 2012 (Commencement No. 32 and Savings and Transitional Provisions) Order 2019] the person in question would be prevented from making a claim for universal credit as referred to in that paragraph.

(3)   Paragraph (1) does not apply to a claim for housing benefit in respect of specified accommodation [³ or temporary accommodation].

(4)   Paragraph (1) does not apply to a claim for housing benefit [⁶] where–
[⁷ (a) in the case of a claim for housing benefit, the claim is made by a member of a State Pension Credit Act couple who has reached the qualifying age for state pension credit, where the other member has not reached that age, and entitlement begins, or in the case of claims made in advance of entitlement is to begin–
(i)   before 15th May 2019; or
(ii)   on or after 15th May 2019 where one of the savings in the sub-paragraphs of article 4(1) of the Welfare Reform Act 2012 (Commencement No. 31 and Savings and Transitional Provisions and Commencement No. 21 and 23 and Transitional and Transitory Provisions (Amendment) Order 2019 applies to that person and the saving has not ceased to have effect under article 4(2) of that Order, and
entitlement to housing benefit is to be construed in accordance with article 2 of that Order;]
[⁶ (b)]
(5)-(7)   *[Omitted]*
(8)   Subject to paragraph (9), for the purposes of this article–
(a)   a claim for housing benefit, income support or a tax credit is made by a person on the date on which he or she takes any action which results in a decision on a claim being required under the relevant Regulations; and
(b)   it is irrelevant that the effect of any provision of the relevant Regulations is that, for the purpose of those Regulations, the claim is made or treated as made on a date that is earlier than the date on which that action is taken.

(9)   Where under the provisions referred to in paragraph (10), a claim for housing benefit or income support is treated as made at a date that is earlier than the date on which the action referred to in paragraph (8)(a) is taken, the claim is treated as made on that earlier date.

(10)   The provisions referred to are–

(a)   in the case of a claim for housing benefit, regulation 83(4E), (4F), (5)(d) or (8) of the 2006 Regulations or, as the case may be, regulation 64(5F), (5G), (6)(d) or (9) of the the 2006 (SPC) Regulations; or

[¹ (b) *[Omitted]*]

(11)   For the purposes of this article–

(a)   "couple" (apart from in the expressions "State Pension Credit Act couple" and "Tax Credit Act couple"), has the meaning given in section 39 of the Act;

(b)   "housing benefit" means housing benefit under section 130 of the Social Security Contributions and Benefits Act 1992;

(c)   "income support" means income support under section 124 of the Social Security Contributions and Benefits Act 1992;

(d)   "qualifying age for state pension credit" means the qualifying age referred to in section 1(6) of the State Pension Credit Act 2002;

(e)   "the 2006 Regulations" means the Housing Benefit Regulations 2006;

(f)   "the 2006 (SPC) Regulations" means the Housing Benefit (Persons who have attained the qualifying age for state pension credit) Regulations 2006;

(g)   "the relevant Regulations" means–

(i)   in the case of a claim for housing benefit, the 2006 Regulations or, as the case may be, the 2006 (SPC) Regulations;

(ii)-(iii) *[Omitted]*

(h)   "specified accommodation" means accommodation to which one or more of subparagraphs (2) to (5) of paragraph 3A of Schedule 1 to the Universal Credit Regulations 2013 applies;

(i)   "State Pension Credit Act couple" means a couple as defined in section 17 of the State Pension Credit Act 2002;

(j)   "tax credit" (including "child tax credit" and "working tax credit") and "tax year" have the same meanings as in the Tax Credits Act 2002;

(k)   "Tax Credits Act couple" means a couple as defined in section 3(5A) of the Tax Credits Act 2002 [³ ;

(l)   "temporary accommodation" means accommodation which falls within Case 1 or Case 2 under paragraph 3B of Schedule 1 to the Universal Credit Regulations].

Modifications

Para (1) is modified by: art 7 of the Welfare Reform Act 2012 (Commencement No.25 and Transitional and Transitory Provisions) Order 2015 SI No.1930; art 7 of the Welfare Reform Act 2012 (Commencement No.26 and Transitional and Transitory Provisions and Commencement No.22, 23 and 24 and Transitional and Transitory Provisions (Modification)) Order 2016 SI No.33; art 7 of the Welfare Reform Act 2012 (Commencement No.27 and Transitional and Transitory Provisions and Commencement No.22, 23 and 24 and Transitional and Transitory Provisions (Modification)) Order 2016 SI No.407; art 12 of the Welfare Reform Act 2012 (Commencement No.13, 14, 16, 19, 22, 23 and 24 and Transitional and Transitory Provisions (Modification)) Order 2016 SI No.596; art 5 of the Welfare Reform Act 2012 (Commencement No.17, 19, 22, 23 and 24 and Transitional and Transitory Provisions (Modification)) Order 2017 SI No.952; art 7 of the Welfare Reform Act 2012 (Commencement No. 9, 21 and 23 (Amendment), Commencement No.11, 13, 17, 19, 22, 23 and 24 (Modification), Transitional and Transitory Provisions) Order 2018 SI No.138; art 5 of the Welfare Reform Act 2012 (Commencement No.17, 19, 22, 23 and 24 and Transitional and Transitory Provisions (Modification)) Order 2018 SI No.532; art 5 of the Welfare Reform Act 2012 (Commencement No.17, 19, 22, 23 and 24 and Transitional and Transitory Provisions (Modification) (No.2)) Order 2018 SI No.881.

Amendments

1.   Amended by art 2 of SI 2015 No 740 as from 18.3.15.
2.   Amended by reg 4 of SI 2017 No 376 as from 6.4.17.
3.   Amended by art 6(3) of SI 2018 No 138 as from 11.4.18.
4.   Amended by reg 3(3) of SI 2019 No 10 as from 16.1.19.
5.   Amended by reg 4(3) of SI 2019 No 27 as from 1.2.19.

6. Amended by art 5(4) of SI 2019 No 167 with effect from 1.2.19.
7. Substituted by art 5 of SI 2019 No 37 with effect from 15.5.19, subject to transitional provision in arts 6 and 7.

General Note

By virtue of art 7, a person cannot make a claim for HB, other than in exceptional cases, on a date when, if s/he were to claim UC on that date, and if s/he is premitted to claim, the UC provisons cited would come into force: para (1). For this purpose, a claim is treated as made on the date on which the person takes action which results in a decision on a claim being required, and it is irrelevant if the claim is made, or treated as made, earlier than the date on which action is taken: para (8). Paras (9) and (10) deal with some situations when a claim for HB is treated as made on an earlier date than the date on which action was taken. The HB Regs and HB(SPC) Regs cited cover situations when a defective claim is made and then corrected, as well as when there has been notification of an intention to claim HB prior to the actual claim being submitted.

Note also that if someone is a "universal credit claimant", s/he cannot make a claim for HB, or be entitled to HB, other than in exceptional cases. See the UC(TP) Regs (on p1857) and the note on the Welfare Reform Act 2012 (on p4).

Exceptions

(1) An HB claim can be made if the person would be prevented from claiming UC by virtue of the provisions cited in para (2). These are if:
– the Secretary of State has decided to cease to accept claims for UC in any area or category of case. See reg 4 UC(TP) Regs 2014; *or*
– within the last month, the claimant (or her/his partner) has been entitled to an award of HB (or IS, income-based JSA or income-related ESA) that included a severe disability premium (known as the "SDP Gateway"). See reg 4A UC(TP) Regs 2014; *or*
– the claimant (or her/his partner) is a "frontier worker": art 4(11) of the Welfare Reform Act 2012 (Commencement No.32 and Savings and Transitional Provisions) Order 2019.
If the claimant is also a member of a mixed-age couple, the member of the couple who is at least the qualifying age for PC is treated as not having attained that age for the purposes of an award of HB. See art 8 of the No.31 Order (on p1902).

(2) An HB claim can be made if it is in respect of "specified accommodation" (specified types of supported accommodation and of temporary accommodation provided for those who have left home as a result of domestic violence) or "temporary accommodation" (specified types of homeless accommodation that is not "exempt accommodation", where rent is payable to a local authority or provider of social housing), both defined in para (11) by reference to the UC Regs: para (3).

(3) From 15 May 2019, a claim for HB can be made by a person who a member of a "State Pension Credit Act couple" as defined for PC purposes, who is at least the qualifying age for PC but whose partner is not yet that age (a member of a mixed-age couple): para (4)(a). This applies if entitlement starts (or on and advance claim will start):
– before 15 May 2019; *or*
– on or after 15th May 2019, if the savings provision in art 4 of the No.31 Order cited applies – ie, the person has been entitled to PC or HB or both continuously since 14 May 2019 as part of the same mixed-age couple (see p1899). For these purposes, entitlement to HB means entitlement under the HB(SPC) Regs: see the closing words of para (4)(a) and art 2 of the No.31 Order (on p1898). As a claim for HB under those regulations can be backdated by up to three months, the savings can apply even if the HB claim is made on or after 15 May 2019, so long as it is made no later than 13 August 2019. See art 7 of the No.31 Order (on p1901) if the member of the couple who is at least the qualifying age for PC would be prevented from claiming HB under art 6 of this order, but could claim UC as a single person or is a member of a polygamous marriage (where two of the members are treated as a couple for UC purposes and the other or others as single).

Note that even if a member of a mixed-age couple is unable to claim HB under para (4)(a), s/he may be able to make a claim under paras (2) or (3) above.

Note: prior to the amendments made from 15 May 2019, art 7 allowed a claim for HB by a single claimant of at least the qualifying age for PC and by a member of a couple whose partner had reached that age – ie, a member of a couple where either or both members were at least the qualifying age for PC. Para (4) now only applies to mixed-age couples. It is understood that the DWP intention is that is that single claimants of at least the qualifying age for PC, and claimants who are members of a couple both at least that age *can* make a claim for HB , but the legislative basis making good such an intention is at best unclear.

The Welfare Reform Act 2012 (Commencement No.25 and Transitional and Transitory Provisions) Order 2015

(2015 No.1930)

Citation

1. This Order may be cited as the Welfare Reform Act 2012 (Commencement No. 25 and Transitional and Transitory Provisions) Order 2015.

Interpretation

2.–(1) In this Order–

"the No. 23 Order" means the Welfare Reform Act 2012 (Commencement No. 23 and Transitional and Transitory Provisions) Order 2015;

(2)-(5) *[Omitted]*

Transitional provision: claims for housing benefit, income support or a tax credit

7. Article 7 of the No. 23 Order (prevention of claims for housing benefit, income support or a tax credit) applies as though the reference in paragraph (1) of that article to article 3(1) and (2)(a) to (c) of that Order included a reference to article 3(1) and (2)(a) of this Order.

The Welfare Reform Act 2012 (Commencement No.26 and Transitional and Transitory Provisions and Commencement No.22, 23 and 24 and Transitional and Transitory Provisions (Modification)) Order 2016

(2016 No.33)

Citation

1. This Order may be cited as the Welfare Reform Act 2012 (Commencement No. 26 and Transitional and Transitory Provisions and Commencement No. 22, 23 and 24 and Transitional and Transitory Provisions (Modification)) Order 2016.

Interpretation

2.–(1) In this Order–

"the No. 22 Order" means the Welfare Reform Act 2012 (Commencement No. 22 and Transitional and Transitory Provisions) Order 2015;

"the No. 23 Order" means the Welfare Reform Act 2012 (Commencement No. 23 and Transitional and Transitory Provisions) Order 2015;

(2)-(5)*[Omitted]*

Transitional provision: claims for housing benefit, income support or a tax credit

7. Article 7 of the No. 23 Order (prevention of claims for housing benefit, income support or a tax credit) applies as though the reference in paragraph (1) of that article to article 3(1) and (2)(a) to (c) of that Order included–

(a)   a reference to article 3(1) and (2)(a) and (b) of this Order; and

(b)   a reference to paragraph (1) and sub-paragraphs (i) and (t) of paragraph (2) of article 3 of the No. 22 Order, in respect only of claims in relation to which sub-paragraphs (i) and (t) are modified by article 6(2) of this Order.

The Welfare Reform Act 2012 (Commencement No.27 and Transitional and Transitory Provisions and Commencement No.22, 23 and 24 and Transitional and Transitory Provisions (Modification)) Order 2016

(2016 No.407)

Citation

1. This Order may be cited as the Welfare Reform Act 2012 (Commencement No. 27 and Transitional and Transitory Provisions and Commencement No. 22, 23 and 24 and Transitional and Transitory Provisions (Modification)) Order 2016.

Interpretation

2.–(1) In this Order–

"the No. 22 Order" means the Welfare Reform Act 2012 (Commencement No. 22 and Transitional and Transitory Provisions) Order 2015;

"the No. 23 Order" means the Welfare Reform Act 2012 (Commencement No. 23 and Transitional and Transitory Provisions) Order 2015;

(2)-(5) *[Omitted]*

Modification of the No. 23 Order: claims for housing benefit, income support or a tax credit

7. Article 7 of the No. 23 Order (prevention of claims for housing benefit, income support or a tax credit)(1) applies as though the reference in paragraph (1) of that article to article 3(1) and (2)(a) to (c) of that Order included–

(a)   a reference to article 3(1) and (2)(a) and (b) of this Order; and

(b)   a reference to paragraph (1) and sub-paragraph (i) of paragraph (2) of article 3 of the No. 22 Order, in respect of claims in relation to which sub-paragraph (i) is modified by article 6(2) of this Order.

The Welfare Reform Act 2012 (Commencement No.13, 14, 16, 19, 22, 23 and 24 and Transitional and Transitory Provisions (Modification)) Order 2016

(2016 No.596)

Citation

1. This Order may be cited as the Welfare Reform Act 2012 (Commencement No. 13, 14, 16, 19, 22, 23 and 24 and Transitional and Transitory Provisions (Modification)) Order 2016.

Interpretation

2.–(1) In this Order–

"the No. 13 Order" means the Welfare Reform Act 2012 (Commencement No. 13 and Transitional and Transitory Provisions) Order 2013;

"the No. 14 Order" means the Welfare Reform Act 2012 (Commencement No. 14 and Transitional and Transitory Provisions) Order 2013;

"the No. 16 Order" means the Welfare Reform Act 2012 (Commencement No. 16 and Transitional and Transitory Provisions) Order 2014;

"the No. 19 Order" means the Welfare Reform Act 2012 (Commencement No. 19 and Transitional and Transitory Provisions and Commencement No. 9 and Transitional and Transitory Provisions (Amendment)) Order 2014;

"the No. 22 Order" means the Welfare Reform Act 2012 (Commencement No. 22 and Transitional and Transitory Provisions) Order 2015;

"the No. 24 Order" means the Welfare Reform Act 2012 (Commencement No. 24 and Transitional and Transitory Provisions and Commencement No. 9 and Transitional and Transitory Provisions (Amendment)) Order 2015.

(3)-(6) *[Omitted]*

Modification of the No. 23 Order: claims for housing benefit, income support or a tax credit

12. Article 7 of the No. 23 Order (prevention of claims for housing benefit, income support or a tax credit) applies as though the reference in paragraph (1) of that article to article 3(1) and (2)(a) to (c) of that Order included–

(a) a reference to paragraph (1) and sub-paragraph (a) of paragraph (2) of article 3 of the No. 13 Order, in respect of claims in relation to which sub-paragraph (a) is modified by articles 4(2)(a) and 5(2)(a) of this Order;

(b) a reference to paragraph (1) and sub-paragraph (a) of paragraph (2) of article 3 of the No. 14 Order, in respect of claims in relation to which sub-paragraph (a) is modified by articles 3(2)(a) and 4(2)(b) of this Order;

(c) a reference to paragraph (1) and sub-paragraph (a) of paragraph (2) of article 3 of the No. 16 Order, in respect of claims in relation to which sub-paragraph (a) is modified by articles 3(2)(b) and 4(2)(c) of this Order;

(d) a reference to paragraph (1) and sub-paragraphs (j) and (m) of paragraph (2) of article 3 of the No. 19 Order, in respect of claims in relation to which sub-paragraphs (j) and (m) are modified respectively by article 5(2)(b) and (c) of this Order;

(e) a reference to paragraph (1) and sub-paragraphs (a), (f), (h), (i) and (k) of paragraph (2) of article 3 of the No. 22 Order, in respect of claims in relation to which those sub-paragraphs are modified respectively by articles 4(2)(d), 3(2)(d), (e) and (f) and 4(2)(e) of this Order;

(f) a reference to paragraph (1) and sub-paragraph (e) of paragraph (2) of article 3 of the No. 22 Order, in respect of claims in relation to which sub-paragraph (e) is modified by articles 3(2)(c) and 5(2)(d) of this Order; and

(g) a reference to paragraph (1) and sub-paragraphs (a), (c), (n) and (bb) of paragraph (2) of article 3 of the No. 24 Order, in respect of claims in relation to which those sub-paragraphs are modified respectively by articles 4(2)(f) and 3(2)(g), (h) and (i) of this Order.

The Employment and Support Allowance and Universal Credit (Miscellaneous Amendments and Transitional and Savings Provisions) Regulations 2017

(2017 No.204)

Citation and commencement

1. These Regulations may be cited as the Employment and Support Allowance and Universal Credit (Miscellaneous Amendments and Transitional and Savings Provisions) Regulations 2017 and come into force on 3rd April 2017.

Consequential, transitional and savings provisions

7.–(1) Schedule 1 contains amendments to secondary legislation as a consequence of the amendments made by these Regulations.

(2) Schedule 2 contains transitional and savings provisions.

SCHEDULE 2

REGULATION 7(2)

Transitional and savings provisions
PART 1
Employment and Support Allowance: transitional and savings provisions

---

Transitional and savings provisions: General

1.–(1) The amendments made by regulations 2 and 3, paragraphs 1 to 9 of Schedule 1 and by section 15(1) to (3) of the Welfare Reform and Work Act 2016 (which amend sections 2 and 4 of the Welfare Reform Act 2007) do not apply where any of the circumstances in paragraphs 2 to 7 apply.

(2) In this Part–

"assessment phase" has the same meaning as in the Welfare Reform Act 2007;

"[¹claim]" means [¹] a claim for an employment and support allowance [¹ made] in accordance with regulations 4ZC, 4G, 4H and 4I of the Social Security (Claims and Payments) Regulations 1987 or regulations 13 to 17 of the Universal Credit, Personal Independence Payment, Jobseeker's Allowance and Employment and Support Allowance (Claims and Payments) Regulations 2013;

"employment and support allowance" means an allowance under Part 1 of the Welfare Reform Act 2007;

"ESA Regulations 2008" means the Employment and Support Allowance Regulations 2008;

"ESA Regulations 2013" means the Employment and Support Allowance Regulations 2013.

Amendment

1. Amended by reg 1(9)(a) of SI 2017 No.581 from 23.6.2017.

Claimants who have made a claim for employment and support allowance before 3rd April 2017

2. The first circumstance is where the claimant has made or is treated as having made a claim for an employment and support allowance before 3rd April 2017 and that claim results in an award of employment and support allowance.

Claimants who had been found to have limited capability for work before 3rd April 2017

3. The second circumstance is where the claimant's period of limited capability for work began on or after 3rd April 2017 and is treated as a continuation of an earlier period of limited capability for work which began before 3rd April 2017 by virtue of–

(a) regulation 145 of the ESA Regulations 2008; or

(b) regulation 86 of the ESA Regulations 2013.

Claimants on Incapacity Benefits who have or will become notified persons

4. The third circumstance is where the claimant [¹ has been,] is or becomes a notified person within the meaning of regulation 4 of the Employment and Support Allowance (Transitional Provisions, Housing Benefit and Council Tax Benefit) (Existing Awards) (No. 2) Regulations 2010 and a determination is effective as to whether that person–

(a) has or is to be treated as having limited capability for work under Part 5 of the ESA Regulations 2008;

(b) has or is to be treated as having limited capability for work under Part 5 of the ESA Regulations 2013;

(c) has or is to be treated as having limited capability for work-related activity under Part 6 of the ESA Regulations 2013.

Amendment

1.   Inserted by reg 1(9)(b) of SI 2017 No.581 from 23.6.2017.

Claimants where their award becomes payable before 3rd April 2017

5.   The fourth circumstance is where the claimant becomes entitled to an employment and support allowance before 3rd April 2017 by virtue of–

(a)   regulation 19(1) and paragraph 16 of Schedule 4 to the Social Security (Claims and Payments) Regulations 1987; or

(b)   regulation 28 of the Universal Credit, Personal Independence Payment, Jobseeker's Allowance and Employment and Support Allowance (Claims and Payments) Regulations 2013.

Claimants where their assessment phase begins before 3rd April 2017

6.   The fifth circumstance is where the first day of the claimant's assessment phase began before 3rd April 2017 by virtue of–

(a)   regulation 5 of the ESA Regulations 2008; or

(b)   regulation 6 of the ESA Regulations 2013.

Claimants where they have been entitled to maternity allowance

7.   The sixth circumstance is where–

(a)   a claimant was entitled to a maternity allowance under section 35 of the Social Security Contributions and Benefits Act 1992 and the end of that award is within 12 weeks beginning with the date that the claim for an employment and support allowance is made; and

(b)   immediately prior to their entitlement to a maternity allowance beginning the claimant was previously entitled to an employment and support allowance before 3rd April 2017.

The Social Security (Restrictions on Amounts for Children and Qualifying Young Persons) Amendment Regulations 2017
(2017 No.376)

Citation and commencement

1. These Regulations may be cited as the Social Security (Restrictions on Amounts for Children and Qualifying Young Persons) Amendment Regulations 2017 and come into force on 6th April 2017.

Housing Benefit – transitional provisions for restrictions on amounts for children and young persons

9.–(1) This regulation applies where, on 5th April 2017, a person is entitled to housing benefit and the person is, or the person and the person's partner are between them, responsible for more than two individuals who are either children or young persons and who are members of the same household (each such individual is referred to as a "protected individual").

(2) Where this regulation applies, the amendments made by regulations 7 and 8 do not apply to the person entitled to housing benefit referred to in paragraph (1) until–

(a) the person makes a new claim for housing benefit; or

(b) the person or the person's partner (if any) becomes responsible for a new individual,

whichever is the first to occur.

(3) Paragraphs (4) to (8) apply where–

(a) the amendments made by regulations 7 and 8 apply by virtue of paragraph (2)(b);

(b) the child tax credit provisions do not apply; and

(c) the person has not made a new claim for housing benefit.

(4) Notwithstanding the default provisions, a child amount shall be included in the applicable amount in relation to any protected individual, in relation to any time when the person or the person's partner (if any) is responsible for the individual and the individual is a member of the same household.

(5) Paragraph (6) applies where–

(a) the person or the person's partner (if any) is responsible for one or more protected individuals who are members of the same household; and

(b) either of them is responsible for one or more new individuals who are members of the same household.

(6) Where this paragraph applies, any protected individual for whom the person or the person's partner is responsible is to be counted for the purpose of deciding whether, under the default provisions, an additional child amount is to be included in the applicable amount with respect to the new individual or individuals referred to in paragraph (5)(b).

(7) Paragraph (8) applies where–

(a) the number of protected individuals for whom either the person or the person's partner (if any) is responsible, and who are members of the same household, is one;

(b) the number of new individuals for whom either the person or the person's partner is responsible, and who are members of the same household, is two or more; and

(c) a different child amount would apply to different individuals.

(8) Where this paragraph applies, the child amounts to be included in the applicable amount shall be–

(a) the child amount in relation to the protected individual; and

(b) a child amount in relation to such one of the new individuals as will result in the greatest possible total amount.

(9) Under paragraph (3), for the purposes of determining whether the child tax credit provisions apply, by virtue of regulation 22(3) or 23(3) of the 2006 Regulations or regulation 22(5B) of the 2006 (SPC) Regulations, where the person or the person's

partner is responsible for one or more protected individuals, the total amount that would be included in the applicable amount under the default provisions shall be taken to be the total that would be included under paragraphs (4), (6) and (8).

(10)　For the purposes of this regulation–

(a)　"the 2006 Regulations" means the Housing Benefit Regulations 2006 and "the 2006 (SPC) Regulations" means the Housing Benefit (Persons who have attained the qualifying age for state pension credit) Regulations 2006;

(b)　"applicable amount" has the same meaning as in section 135 of the Social Security Contributions and Benefits Act 1992;

(c)　"child", "partner" and "young person" have the same meanings as in the 2006 Regulations;

(d)　"child amount" means the amount determined under whichever is relevant of paragraph 2 of Schedule 3 to the 2006 Regulations or paragraph 2 of Schedule 3 to the 2006 (SPC) Regulations;

(e)　"child tax credit provisions" means whichever is relevant of regulation 22(1)(b) or 23(1)(c) of the 2006 Regulations or regulation 22(1)(b) of the 2006 (SPC) Regulations, as substituted by regulation 22(4) or 23(4) of the 2006 Regulations or regulation 22(5C) of the 2006 (SPC) Regulations respectively;

(f)　"default provisions" means whichever is relevant of regulation 22(1)(b) or 23(1)(c) of the 2006 Regulations or regulation 22(1)(b) of the 2006 (SPC) Regulations, as they apply apart from regulation 22(4) or 23(4) of the 2006 Regulations or regulation 22(5C) of the 2006 (SPC) Regulations respectively;

(g)　"new individual" means a child or young person who is not a protected individual;

(h)　any reference to an individual being part of the same household means being part of the same household with the person who is entitled to housing benefit and the person's partner (if any);

(i)　a person is to be treated as responsible for a child or young person in the circumstances set out in regulation 20 of the 2006 Regulations.

The Welfare Reform Act 2012 (Commencement No.17, 19, 22, 23 and 24 and Transitional and Transitory Provisions (Modification) (No.2)) Order 2018

(2018 No.881)

Citation

1. This Order may be cited as the Welfare Reform Act 2012 (Commencement No. 17, 19, 22, 23 and 24 and Transitional and Transitory Provisions (Modification) (No. 2)) Order 2018.

Interpretation

2.–(1) In this Order–

"claimant"–

    (a)   in relation to an employment and support allowance, has the same meaning as in Part 1 of the Welfare Reform Act 2007;

    (b)   in relation to a jobseeker's allowance, has the same meaning as in the Jobseekers Act 1995 (as it applies apart from the amendments made by Part 1 of Schedule 14 to the Welfare Reform Act 2012 that remove references to an income-based jobseeker's allowance);

    (c)   in relation to universal credit, has the same meaning as in Part 1 of the Welfare Reform Act 2012;

"the Claims and Payments Regulations 1987" means the Social Security (Claims and Payments) Regulations 1987;

"employment and support allowance" means an employment and support allowance under Part 1 of the Welfare Reform Act 2007;

"jobseeker's allowance" means a jobseeker's allowance under the Jobseekers Act 1995;

"the No. 17 Order" means the Welfare Reform Act 2012 (Commencement No. 17 and Transitional and Transitory Provisions) Order 2014;

"the No. 19 Order" means the Welfare Reform Act 2012 (Commencement No. 19 and Transitional and Transitory Provisions and Commencement No. 9 and Transitional and Transitory Provisions (Amendment)) Order 2014;

"the No. 22 Order" means the Welfare Reform Act 2012 (Commencement No. 22 and Transitional and Transitory Provisions) Order 2015;

"the No. 23 Order" means the Welfare Reform Act 2012 (Commencement No. 23 and Transitional and Transitory Provisions) Order 2015;

"the No. 24 Order" means the Welfare Reform Act 2012 (Commencement No. 24 and Transitional and Transitory Provisions and Commencement No. 9 and Transitional and Transitory Provisions (Amendment)) Order 2015.

(2) For the purposes of this Order, the Universal Credit, Personal Independence Payment, Jobseeker's Allowance and Employment and Support Allowance (Claims and Payments) Regulations 2013 apply for the purpose of deciding–

    (a)   whether a claim for universal credit is made; and

    (b)   the date on which the claim is made.

(3) For the purposes of this Order, the Claims and Payments Regulations 1987 apply, subject to paragraphs (4) and (5), for the purposes of deciding–

    (a)   whether a claim for an employment and support allowance or a jobseeker's allowance is made; and

    (b)   the date on which the claim is made or treated as made.

(4) Subject to paragraph (5), for the purposes of this Order–

    (a)   a person makes a claim for an employment and support allowance or a jobseeker's allowance if that person takes any action which results in a decision on a claim being required under the Claims and Payments Regulations 1987; and

    (b)   it is irrelevant that the effect of any provision of those Regulations is that, for the purposes of those Regulations, the claim is made or treated as made at a date that is earlier than the date on which that action is taken.

(5)   Where, by virtue of–

(a)   regulation 6(1F)(b) or (c) of the Claims and Payments Regulations 1987, in the case of a claim for an employment and support allowance; or

(b)   regulation 6(4ZA) to (4ZD) and (4A)(a)(i) and (b) of those Regulations, in the case of a claim for a jobseeker's allowance,

a claim for an employment and support allowance or a jobseeker's allowance is treated as made at a date that is earlier than the date on which the action referred to in paragraph (4)(a) is taken, the claim is treated as made on that earlier date.

Modification of the No. 23 Order: claims for housing benefit, income support or a tax credit

5.–(1)   This article applies to claims in relation to which the provisions referred to in paragraph (2)(a) to (d) are modified by article 3.

(2)   Where this article applies, article 7 of the No. 23 Order (prevention of claims for housing benefit, income support or a tax credit) applies as though the reference in paragraph (1) of that article to article 3(1) and (2)(a) to (c) of that Order included a reference to–

(a)   paragraph (1) and sub-paragraphs (c) and (i) of paragraph (2) of article 3 of the No. 17 Order;

(b)   paragraph (1) and sub-paragraphs (b) to (h) and (j) to (n) of paragraph (2) of article 3 of the No. 19 Order;

(c)   paragraph (1) and sub-paragraphs (a), (c) to (e), (g) to (k), (m) to (q), and (t) of paragraph (2) of article 3 of the No. 22 Order; and

(d)   paragraph (1) and sub-paragraphs (a) to (d), (f) to (y), (aa) and (cc) of paragraph (2) of article 3 of the No. 24 Order.

The Welfare Reform Act 2012 (Commencement No.31 and Savings and Transitional Provisions and Commencement No.21 and 23 and Transitional and Transitory Provisions (Amendment)) Order 2019

(2019 No.37 (C.1))

Citation

1. This Order may be cited as the Welfare Reform Act 2012 (Commencement No. 31 and Savings and Transitional Provisions and Commencement No. 21 and 23 and Transitional and Transitory Provisions (Amendment)) Order 2019.

Interpretation

2.–(1) In this Order–

[¹ "the 1992 Act" means the Social Security Contributions and Benefits Act 1992;]

"the 2002 Act" means the State Pension Credit Act 2002;

"the 2012 Act" means the Welfare Reform Act 2012;

"the appointed day" means the day referred to in article 3;

[¹]

"the Housing Benefit SPC Regulations" means the Housing Benefit (Persons who have attained the qualifying age for state pension credit) Regulations 2006;

"the No. 21 Order" means the Welfare Reform Act 2012 (Commencement No. 21 and Transitional and Transitory Provisions) Order 2015; "the No. 23 Order" means the Welfare Reform Act 2012 (Commencement No. 23 and Transitional and Transitory Provisions) Order 2015;

"polygamous marriage" has the same meaning as in regulation 3(5) of the Universal Credit Regulations 2013;

"the qualifying age for state pension credit" has the same meaning as in the 2002 Act;

"secondary legislation" has the same meaning as in Part 1 of the 2012 Act;

"state pension credit" has the same meaning as in the 2002 Act.

[¹ (1A)   In this Order, "couple" has the same meaning as in the 2002 Act, save–

(a) in reference to entitlement to housing benefit, where it has the same meaning as in Part VII of the 1992 Act; and

(b) in article 7(3)(a), where it has the meaning given by article 7(2)(b)(ii).]

(2)   In this Order–

(a) "mixed-age couple" means a couple, one member of which has attained the qualifying age for state pension credit and the other of which has not; and

(b) the definition in sub-paragraph (a) includes a polygamous marriage where at least one party to the marriage has attained the qualifying age for state pension credit and at least one has not.

(3)   Save as stated to the contrary in article 6(2), [¹ and article 8(2)(b)] all references in this Order to claims or entitlement to housing benefit are to claims or entitlement under the Housing Benefit SPC Regulations only.

(4)   In this Order–

(a) a person is entitled to state pension credit or housing benefit on any day where the person has made a claim for that benefit and the conditions of entitlement are met in relation to that person, regardless of whether, respectively, entitlement begins on a later day under—

(i)   regulation 16A (date of entitlement under an award of state pension credit for the purpose of payability and effective date of change of rate) of the Social Security (Claims and Payments) Regulations 1987; or

(ii)   regulation 57 (date on which entitlement is to commence) of the Housing Benefit SPC Regulations; and

(b) [¹ save in article 7(3)(a),] a reference to claiming or entitlement to state pension credit or housing benefit as part of a [¹ "mixed-age"] couple is a reference to [¹ a person claiming or] being so entitled, on the basis that [¹ the person] is a member of a couple or [¹] a polygamous marriage.

Amendment

1.   Amended by art 2(2) of SI 2019 No.935 as from 14.5.19.

General Note

The definition of "qualifying age for state pension credit" is found in s1(6) SPCA 2002. That definition is spelled out in reg 2(1) of both the HB Regs and the HB(SPC) Regs (on p232 and p725).

Under para (1A)(a), the definition of couple for HB purposes is that found in s137(1) SSCBA 1992 (see p12). Para (2) provides the definition of "mixed-age couple" for the purposes of this order. See also para (4)(b) for when references to claiming or entitlement to PC or to HB as part of a mixed-age couple includes polygamous marriage.

By para (3), all references to claims or entitlement to HB in this Order, other than to those cited, are to claims or entitlement under the HB(SPC) Regs – ie, *not* under the HB Regs.

Reg 57 HB(SPC) Regs cited in para (4)(a)(ii) provides the general rule that entitlement to HB starts from the first day of the benefit week following the first day in respect of which the claim is made, and the exceptional situations in which entitlement to HB commences from the benefit week in which the first day in respect of which the claim is made (see p803). Note that the earliest date entitlement can commence is determined by reg 64 HB(SPC) Regs – ie, three months before the date of claim determined under reg 64(6) of those regulations (see p811).

Appointed day

3.   15th May 2019 is the appointed day for the coming into force of paragraph 64 (universal credit amendments: insertion of section 4(1A) into the 2002 Act) of Schedule 2 to the 2012 Act, and section 31 of the 2012 Act in so far as it relates to that paragraph.

General Note

Section 4(1A) SPCA 2002 was brought into force on 15 May 2019 by art 3. Section 4(1A) says that a "claimant is not entitled to state pension credit if he is a member of a couple the other member of which has not attained the qualifying age" – ie, s/he is a member of a mixed-age couple. This prevents entitlement to PC on or after 15 May 2019 unless the savings provisions in art 4 apply.

The significance for HB

Although HB itself has not yet been abolished, because of s4(1A), a member of a mixed-age couple requiring financial support in addition to their other income on or after 15 May 2019 will have to claim UC, and thus as a "UC claimant" as defined in the UC(TP) Regs 2014 will not be able to claim or be entitled to HB unless this is in respect of "specified accommodation" or "temporary accommodation": see regs 5 and 6 of the UC(TP) Regs 2014 (on p1862 and p1864). Even if the person is not a UC claimant, the Welfare Reform Act 2012 (Commencement No.21 and Transitional and Transitory Provisions) Order 2015 (the No.21 Order on p1882) and the Welfare Reform Act 2012 (Commencement No.23 and Transitional and Transitory Provisions) Order 2015 (the No.23 Order on p1885) prevent new claims for HB other than in exceptional cases. Note also that under art 6 of this order, awards of HB made to a members of a mixed-age couple are terminated where entitlement to HB under the HB(SPC) Regs begins on or after 15 May 2019, unless the award is in respect of "specified" or "temporary accommodation". However, note the following.

(1)   Art 5 amends the No.21 Order and the No.23 Order to allow claims for HB by some members of a mixed-age couple who have reached the qualifying age for PC. See those orders for the amended versions.

(2)   Art 7 allows HB claims by those of at least the qualifying age for PC who are members of a mixed-age couple and whose award of HB has been terminated under art 6. It applies to those who would be treated as single UC claimants or who are in in polygamous marriages where at least two members are at least the qualifying age for PC.

(3)   Art 8 effectively modifies the rules of entitlement to HB (as well as to IS, income-based JSA and income-related ESA) to among other things allow claims where someone is both excluded from entitlement to PC and to HB, as well as prevented from claiming UC.

Savings

4.–(1)   Subject to paragraph (2), the 2002 Act shall have effect as though section 4(1A) (exclusion of mixed-age couples from state pension credit) had not come into force in relation to a member of a mixed-age couple who, on the day before the appointed day and as part of that couple, is entitled to–

(a)   state pension credit;

(b)   housing benefit; or

(c)   state pension credit and housing benefit.

(2)   The savings in the sub-paragraphs of paragraph (1) shall cease to have effect in relation to the member of the mixed-age couple referred to on any day after the appointed

day when that person is not entitled to either state pension credit or housing benefit as part of the same mixed-age couple.

Definitions
"entitlement to housing benefit" – see art 2(3).
"mixed-age couple" – see art 2(2).

General Note
Entitlement to PC as part of a mixed-age couple is not prevented if the person was entitled to PC or to HB under the HB(SPC) Regs, or to both, on 14 May 2019. Under para (2) the savings provision ceases to apply if the person's entitlement to both PC and HB as part of the same mixed-age couple ends on or after 15 May 2019.
Note that where these savings provisions apply, the Welfare Reform Act 2012 (Commencement No.21 and Transitional and Transitory Provisions) Order 2015 (the No.21 Order on p1882) and the Welfare Reform Act 2012 (Commencement No.23 and Transitional and Transitory Provisions) Order 2015 (the No.23 Order on p1885) allow new claims for HB to be made. Thus, a claim for HB can be made on or after 15 May 2019 so long as the claimant is entitled to PC, and has been entitled to some PC or HB under the HB(SPC) Regs or to both, continuously since 14 May 2019. As a claim for HB can be backdated by up to three months, a claim for HB can be made on or after 15 May 2019 but for the savings provisions to apply, the claim must made no later than 13 August 2019.

Transitional provision: termination of awards of housing benefit
6.–(1)   The awards of housing benefit referred to in paragraph (2) are to terminate on the day referred to in paragraph (3), subject to paragraph (4).

(2)   The awards are those where entitlement under the Housing Benefit SPC Regulations as part of a mixed-age couple begins on or after the appointed day and where the awards are made–
(a)   at any time, under the Housing Benefit Regulations 2006 or the Housing Benefit SPC Regulations, to a person who, after the award, becomes a member of a mixed-age couple;
(b)   at any time, under the Housing Benefit Regulations 2006, to a person who is a member of a mixed-age couple, where the award subsequently ceases to be subject to those Regulations and becomes subject to the Housing Benefit SPC Regulations; or
(c)   on or before the day of making of this Order, to a person who claimed in advance of attaining the qualifying age for state pension credit.

(3)   The termination takes effect–
(a)   in the case of an award referred to in paragraph (2)(a) or (b), on the later of the appointed day and the day entitlement under the Housing Benefit SPC Regulations as part of a mixed-age couple takes effect on the award, as a change of circumstances, in accordance with the Housing Benefit and Council Tax Benefit (Decisions and Appeals) Regulations 2001; or
(b)   in the case of an award referred to in paragraph (2)(c), on the day after the day of making of this Order.

(4)   Paragraph (1) does not apply to awards in respect of specified accommodation or temporary accommodation, as defined respectively in sub-paragraphs (h) and (l) of article 7(11) of the No. 23 Order.

Definitions
"claims or entitlement to housing benefit" – see art 2(3).
"couple" – see art 2(1A).
"mixed-age couple" – see art 2(2).

General Note
Art 6 sets out when an award of HB must terminate if entitlement under the HB(SPC) Regs as part of a mixed-age couple begins on or after 15 May 2019 – ie, when a new claim for HB is made by a member of a mixed-age couple on or after that date (unless there is transitional protection), or where there is a change of circumstances that affects an award of HB made under the HB Regs – eg, where a claimant who is a member of a working-age couple reaches the qualifying age for PC or a claimant of that age forms a new relationship with someone of working age. Note that an award does *not* terminate under these provisions if it is made in respect of "specified accommodation" or "temporary accommodation": para (4).

If entitlement to HB under the HB(SPC) Regs as part of a mixed-age couple begins on or after 15 May 2019, the rules apply as follows.

(1)   An award made at any time (ie, before *or* on or after 15 May 2019) under either the HB Regs or the HB(SPC) Regs to someone who after that award becomes a member of a mixed-age couple: para (2)(a). The termination takes effect on 15 May 2019, or if later the day entitlement under the HB(SPC) Regs as a member of a mixed-age couple takes effect as a change of circumstances (for which see regs 8 and 9 of the HB&CTB(DA) Regs on p957 and p962): para (3)(a). This could apply, for example, if a single claimant who is at least the qualifying age for PC forms a new relationship with someone who is not yet that age.

(2)   An award made at any time under the HB Regs to a person who is a member of a mixed-age couple, when that award then becomes subject to the HB(SPC) Regs: para (2)(b). The termination takes effect as under (1) above: para (3)(a). This could apply, for example, if a claimant who is a member of a couple reaches the qualifying age for PC but her/his partner has not yet reached that age, or if a claimant is a member of a mixed-age couple who is on (or whose partner is on) IS, income-based JSA or income-related ESA and entitlement to that benefit ends.

(3)   An award made on or before 14 January 2019 (the day this order was made) on a claim for HB made in advance of the claimant reaching the qualifying age for PC: para (2)(c). The termination takes effect on 15 January 2019; para (3)(b).

Note that there is no provision for a transitional housing payment (a two week run-on of HB for which see reg 8(2A) UC(TP) Regs 2014) under these rules.

Transitional provision: [¹ application of the rules in universal credit for treatment of couples and] polygamous marriages

7.–(1)   Paragraph (3) applies where a [¹ member of a mixed-age couple]–

(a)   is excluded from entitlement to state pension credit under section 4(1A) of the 2002 Act;

(b)   is prevented from claiming housing benefit under article 6 of the No. 21 Order or article 7 of the No. 23 Order; or

(c)   has an award of housing benefit terminated under article 6.

[¹ (2)   For the purposes of paragraph (3)–

(a)   all secondary legislation relevant to assessment of entitlement to state pension credit or housing benefit applies so that claims and awards may be made in respect of the party specified in paragraph (3)(a) or (b) as a part of a couple or as a single person respectively; and

(b)   the following rules in regulation 3 of the Universal Credit Regulations 2013 apply–

    (i)   the rule in paragraph (3) (treatment of certain couples), which establishes that a member of a couple may make a claim as a single person;

    (ii)   the rule in paragraph (4) (treatment of polygamous marriages), which establishes that two of the parties to a polygamous marriage are to be treated as a couple and the remaining party (or parties) as a single person (or single persons);

    (iii)   the rule in paragraph (6) (absence from the household), which establishes that members of a couple may cease to be treated as a couple.]

(3)   Where this paragraph applies and the qualifying age for state pension credit has been attained by–

(a)   both the parties to be treated as a couple by virtue of paragraph [¹ (2)(b)(ii)], one of them may claim or remain entitled to state pension credit as part of that couple and one of them may claim or remain entitled to housing benefit as part of that couple;

(b)   a party to be treated as a single person by virtue of paragraph [¹ (2)(b)(i) to (iii)], that party may claim or remain entitled to state pension credit or housing benefit as a single person.

Amendment

1.   Amended by art 2(3) of SI 2019 No.935 as from 14.5.19.

Definitions

"claims or entitlement to housing benefit" – see art 2(3)

"couple" – see art 2(1A).

"mixed-age couple" – see art 2(2).

General Note

Art 7 allows claims for and entitlement to HB for certain members of a mixed-age couple if the person is prevented from claiming HB under art 6 of the Welfare Reform Act 2012 (Commencement No.21 and Transitional and Transitory Provisions) Order 2015 (on p1882) or art 7 of the Welfare Reform Act 2012 (Commencement No.23 and Transitional and Transitory Provisions) Order 2015 (on p1885), or is excluded from entitlement to PC by s4(1A) SPCA 2002 (see the General Note to arts 3 and 4 of this order), or has her/his award of HB terminated under art 6 of this order. Art 7 allows for claims for HB (and for PC) as follows.

(1)   A member of a mixed-age couple who could claim UC as a single person – eg, because her/his partner does not meet certain conditions for UC or is a prisoner. If s/he is at least the qualifying age for PC, s/he can claim or remain entitled to HB (or PC) as a single person: art 7(2(a)(i) and (3)(b) and reg 3(3) UC Regs.

(2)   A member of a polygamous marriage where two of the members are treated as a couple for UC purposes and the other (or others) as single. If the members treated as a couple are both at least the qualifying age for PC, one of them can claim or retain entitlement to HB and one can claim or retain entitlement to PC. If the member treated as single is at least that age, s/he can claim or remain entitled to HB (and PC): art 7(2)(b)(ii) and (3)(a) and (b) and reg 3(4) UC Regs.

(3)   A member of a mixed-age couple who is no longer treated as a couple for UC purposes because her/his partner's absence from the household has exceeded or is expected to exceed six months. If s/he is at least the qualifying age for PC, s/he can claim or remain entitled to HB (or PC) as a single person: art 7(2(a)(iii) and (3)(b) and reg 3(6) UC Regs. Note that for HB purposes, someone continues to be treated as a couple for up to 52 weeks (see reg 21 of both the HB Regs and the HB(SPC) Regs).

[¹Transitional provision: where restrictions on claims for universal credit are in place

8.–(1)   This article applies to a member of a mixed-age couple who, further to articles 3 to 7, is excluded from entitlement to state pension credit or housing benefit, and is also prevented from claiming universal credit by virtue of–

(a)   regulation 4 of the Universal Credit (Transitional Provisions) Regulations 2014 (claims for universal credit may not be made in an area or category of case);

(b)   regulation 4A of those Regulations (restriction on claims for universal credit by persons entitled to a severe disability premium); or

(c)   article 4(11) of the Welfare Reform Act 2012 (Commencement No. 32 and Savings and Transitional Provisions) Order 2019 (no claims for universal credit by frontier workers).

(2)   Where this article applies, the member of the mixed-age couple who has attained the qualifying age for state pension credit is, for the purposes of an award of benefit referred to in the following sub-paragraphs to that member, to be treated as–

(a)   meeting the basic condition of entitlement (upper age limit) for–

(i)   income support, in section 124(1)(aa) of the 1992 Act;

(ii)   a jobseeker's allowance, in section 1(2)(h) of the 1995 Act; or

(iii)   an employment and support allowance, in section 1(3)(c) of the 2007 Act; and

(b)   not having attained that age for housing benefit, for the purposes of regulation 5 of the Housing Benefit Regulations 2006 and regulation 5 of the Housing Benefit SPC Regulations, so that the Housing Benefit Regulations 2006 apply to the assessment of the award.

(3)   This article continues to apply until the award of benefit referred to in paragraph (2)(a) or (b) terminates, regardless of whether paragraph (1)(a), (b) or (c) continues to apply throughout the award.

(4)   Where a member of a mixed-age couple who has attained the qualifying age for state pension credit is entitled to income support by virtue of paragraph (2)(a)(i), references to a claimant's partner in paragraphs 9 and 9A (conditions for pensioner premium) and in paragraph 10 (condition for higher pensioner premium) of Schedule 2 to the Income Support (General) Regulations 1987 have effect as though they were references to the claimant.

(5) In this article–

"the 1995 Act" means the Jobseekers Act 1995;

"the 2007 Act" means the Welfare Reform Act 2007;

"employment and support allowance" means an employment and support allowance under Part 1 of the 2007 Act as it has effect apart from the amendments made by Schedule 3, and Part 1 of Schedule 14, to the 2012 Act that remove references to an income-related employment and support allowance;

"income support" has the same meaning as in Part VII of the 1992 Act;

"jobseeker's allowance" means a jobseeker's allowance under the 1995 Act as it has effect apart from the amendments made by Part 1 of Schedule 14 to the 2012 Act that remove references to an income-based jobseeker's allowance.]

Amendment

1.   Inserted by art 2(4) of SI 2019 No.935 as from 14.5.19.

Definitions

"claims or entitlement to housing benefit" – see art 2(3).

"couple" – see art 2(1A).

"mixed-age couple" – see art 2(2).

General Note

Art 8 allows an award of HB made to a member of a mixed-age couple who has reached the qualifying age for PC to continue if s/he is both excluded from entitlement to HB or to PC under this order and is also prevented from claiming UC by virtue any of the following.

(1)   Reg 4 UC(TP) Regs. Under this regulation, the Secretary of State has the discretion to determine that claims for UC may not be made in certain areas or categories of case (see p1861).

(2)   Reg 4A UC(TP) Regs. Under this regulation, a person is prevented from claiming UC if within the last month, s/he or her/his partner has been entitled to an award of HB (or IS, income-based JSA or income-related ESA) that included a severe disability premium (see p1862). This is known as the "SDP Gateway".

(3)   Art 4(11) of the order cited. This article prevents a claim for UC by a "frontier worker".

If any of the situations above apply, for the purposes of an award of HB made to the member of the couple who has reached the qualifying age for PC, that member is treated as not having reached that age for the purposes of reg 5 of both the HB Regs and the HB(SPC) Regs (on p252 and p733): para (2)(b). This means that s/he can remain entitled to HB under the HB Regs (but not the HB(SPC) Regs) until the award terminates, even if the provisions in paras (1)(a), (b) or (c) cease to apply during that award. Note that the member of the couple is also treated as satisfying the age condition for IS, income-based JSA and income-related ESA and so can retain entitlement to one of those benefits and yet, can qualify for a pensioner premium: paras (2)(a) and (4). If the "SDP Gateway" is what prevents a claim for UC, the IS/JSA/ESA claimant can make a new claim for HB by virtue of the No.21 Order or the No.23 Order.

Index

Entries against the bold headings direct you to the general information on the subject, or where the subject is covered most fully. Sub-entries are listed alphabetically and direct you to specific aspects of the subject.

The following abbreviations are used in this index.

CTR	council tax reduction		CTR(W)	council tax reduction in Wales
CTR(E)	council tax reduction in England		HB	housing benefit
CTR(S)	coundil tax reduction in Scotland		PC	pension credit
			UC	universal credit

A
A2 nationals 320
A8 nationals 320, 323
abroad
    capital abroad
        CTR(S) 1509
        CTR(S) over PC age 1620
        HB 465
        HB over PC age 791
    dwelling outside GB
        CTR(E) 1118
        CTR(S) 1481
        CTR(W) 1211
        HB 257
        HB over PC age 734
    employment abroad
        CTR(S) 1555
        HB 662
    payment in currencies other than sterling
        CTR(S) 1555, 1560, 1567
        HB 662, 675
        HB over PC age 857
    temporary absence from GB
        HB 259
        HB over PC age 737
absence from home
    CTR(E) over PC age 1123
    CTR(S) 1467, 1472
    CTR(S) over PC age 1592
    CTR(W) 1209
    detention in custody
        CTR(S) 1470, 1480
        HB 260
        HB over PC age 738
    domestic violence
        HB 261
        HB over PC age 738
    HB 259, 409
    HB over PC age 737, 763
    repairs
        HB 257
        HB over PC age 735
    students
        CTR(S) 1470
        HB 260, 487
        HB over PC age 738
    temporary absence outside GB
        HB over PC age 737
    temporary absence within GB
        CTR(S) 1479
        HB 259, 269
        HB over PC age 738

    trial stay in care home
        CTR(S) 1469, 1479
        HB 259
        HB over PC age 736
absence from work
    CTR(S) 1471
    CTR(S) over PC age 1591
    HB 253, 520
    HB over PC age 734
academic year
    HB 480
access funds
    definition
        CTR(S) 1514
        HB 480
    treatment as capital
        CTR(S) 1521
        HB 504
    treatment as income
        CTR(S) 1520
        HB 503
adaptations to home
    claiming before moving home 736
    HB 258
administration of benefits
    benefits administration information 71
        HB 618
        HB aged 60 or over 842
    contracting out benefit functions by local
        authorities 1769
    reports on local authorities 81
    specified people 103
Administrative Appeals Chamber 173
    functions 1066
adoption
    disregard of allowances
        CTR(S) 1559
        CTR(S) over PC age 1652
        HB 672
    treatment as member of household
        CTR(S) 1473
        CTR(S) over PC age 1592
        HB 409
        HB over PC age 763
adoption leave
    definition
        CTR(S) 1455
        HB 224
    in remunerative work
        CTR(S) 1495
        CTR(S) over PC age 1609
        HB 427

HB over PC age 776
not in remunerative work
 CTR(S) 1471
 CTR(S) over PC age 1591
 HB 253
 HB over PC age 734
advance claims
 HB 258, 548, 552
 HB over PC age 815
advance payment of rent
 HB 273
 HB over PC age 741
advantage
 taking advantage of benefit scheme
  CTR(S) 1466
  CTR(S) over PC age 1586
  HB 294, 421
  HB over PC age 765
age rules 18
 mixed-age couples 718, 1898, 1899
  HB 224
 under age of 18
  HB 279
Age-Related Payments Regulations 2013 1855
agents 77
almshouses
 HB 351
 HB over PC age 745
alternative dispute resolution 987, 1033
alternative maximum council tax reduction 1537
 amount
  CTR(E) 1162
  CTR(E) over PC age 1131
  CTR(S) 1551
  CTR(S) over PC age 1630, 1659
 duty to notify change of circumstances 1537
 entitlement
  CTR(E) over PC age 1130
  CTR(S) 1528
  CTR(S) over PC age 1630
 students 1483
amending a claim
 CTR(E) 1182
 CTR(W) 1328
 HB 558
 HB over PC age 818
amount of benefit
 CTR(S) over PC age 1659
 HB 5, 504
 maximum amount
  CTR(S) 1521
  CTR(S) over PC age 1624
  HB 505
  HB over PC age 795
 minimum
  HB 521
  HB over PC age 802
 tapers
  HB 478
  HB over PC age 795
 weekly amount
  HB 538
  HB over PC age 809
annuities
 disregarded
  CTR(E) 1167
  CTR(S) 1566
  CTR(S) over PC age 1651
  HB 688
  HB over PC age 859
 self-employed earners

CTR(S) 1501
CTR(S) over PC age 1616
HB 447
HB over PC age 784
treatment as income
 HB 453
anti-social behaviour
 eviction
  HB 162
 pilot scheme 8
anti-test case rule 156
appeal tribunals
 abolition 169, 1057
 functions transferred to First-tier and Upper
  tribunals 198, 1057
 superseding decisions made by appeal
  tribunals 210
 transitional provisions 1058
appeals 135, 139, 937
 appeals structure 106
 council tax
  England 1079, 1670
  Wales 1684
 council tax benefit 937
 decisions which can be appealed 144, 963
 decisions with no right of appeal 971, 980,
  1751
 effect of other appeal 155
 late appeals 973
 legal aid 1042
 lookalike appeals 1003
 notice of appeal 975, 1004, 1045
 recovery of overpayments 147
 revised decision 971
 right to appeal to Court of Appeal 184
 right to appeal to First-tier Tribunal 145
 right to appeal to Upper Tribunal 175
 service of notices and documents 940
 setting aside tribunal decisions 205
 test case pending 970
 time limits 973
 UC 1873, 1874
 Valuation Tribunal for England 1670
 Valuation Tribunal for Wales 1684
 who has right of appeal 941
**Appeals from the Upper Tribunal to the Court of
 Appeal Order 2008** 1060
applicable amounts 9
 CTR(E) 1157
 CTR(E) over PC age 1126, 1157
 CTR(S) 1487, 1541
 CTR(S) over PC age 1600, 1643
 CTR(W) 1261, 1286
 CTR(W) over PC age 1216, 1245
 HB 411, 630
 HB over PC age 764, 848
 hospital patients
  HB 415
 personal allowance
  CTR(S) 1542
  CTR(S) over PC age 1643
  HB 630, 631
  HB over PC age 849
 polygamous marriages
  CTR(S) 1488
  HB 413
applications
 amending an application
  CTR(S) 1536
  CTR(S) over PC age 1637
 CTR(E) 1175, 1178

CTR(W) 1322, 1324
date of application
  CTR(S) 1533
  CTR(S) over PC age 1635
evidence required
  CTR(S) 1535
  CTR(S) over PC age 1636
judicial review proceedings 1048
permission to appeal 1021, 1044, 1055
telephone applications
  CTR(S) 1533
  CTR(S) over PC age 1635
who can apply
  CTR(S) 1532
  CTR(S) over PC age 1634
withdrawing an application
  CTR(S) 1536
  CTR(S) over PC age 1637
written applications
  CTR(S) 1532
  CTR(S) over PC age 1634
appointees
acting on behalf of the claimant
  HB 543
person to receive benefit for claimant
  HB 542, 572
  HB over PC age 811, 824
recovery of overpayments
  HB 596
apportionment
alternative maximum CTR(S) 1630
council tax 1522
non-dependants
  CTR(S) 1523
  CTR(S) over PC age 1625
  HB 517
  HB over PC age 800
rent 356
student grant income
  CTR(S) 1517
  HB 496
student loans
  CTR(S) 1519
  HB 500
appropriate maximum housing benefit 7
approved blood scheme
  CTR(E) 1105
  CTR(S) 1459
disregarded as capital
  HB 691
disregarded as income
  HB 675
HB 224
HB over PC age 719
approved tenant incentive scheme
definition
  HB 352
  HB over PC age 746
approved training
  HB 407
armed services
bedroom for child in armed services
  local housing allowance rules 390
  social sector maximum rent 370
mobility supplement disregarded
  CTR(S) 1556
  HB 667
temporary absence from GB
  HB 260
  HB over PC age 737

arrears
causing change of circumstances 1774
disregard of benefit arrears
  CTR(S) 1565
  CTR(S) over PC age 1656
  HB 687
  HB over PC age 866
offsetting against overpayments
  HB 581
  HB over PC age 827
rent arrears
  HB 350
  HB over PC age 744
treatment of arrears of income
  CTR(S) 1531
  CTR(S) over PC age 1631, 1632
  HB 536
  HB over PC age 805
treatment of benefit arrears
  HB 536, 538
  HB over PC age 805
assessment period
definition
  CTR(S) 1456
  CTR(S) over PC age 1577
  HB 225
  HB over PC age 719
employed earners
  CTR(S) 1496
  HB 431
income other than earnings
  CTR(S) 1497
  HB 434
self-employed earners
  CTR(S) 1497
  HB 434
assured tenancy
definition
  HB 879, 881, 909
asylum seekers 1706, 1798
calculation of income
  CTR(S) 1505
  HB 451
exclusion from benefits 1706
loss of status 1801
on arrival claims 1800
retrospective claim for benefit
  CTB 1748
  HB 1748
upheaval declarations 1800
attendance allowance
disregarded
  CTR(S) 1556
  CTR(S) over PC age 1603
  HB 667
  HB over PC age 768

B
backdating
  CTR(E) over PC age 1180
  CTR(W) 1326
  CTR(W) over PC age 1326
  HB 532, 548, 552
  HB over PC age 812, 815
  refugees 1708, 1748
  HB 619
bankruptcy
recovery of overpayments 98, 597
treatment of payments from pension
  schemes

CTR(S) 1506, 1510
HB 455, 467
bedroom
additional bedroom 389
couples who cannot share
HB 230
HB over PC age 723
definition 373
one bedroom self-contained accommodation 388
one bedroom shared accommodation 388
bedroom tax 370
beneficial interest
CTR(S) 1514, 1558
HB 476, 670
HB over PC age 794
benefit cap 207, 522
amount of reduction of HB 527
calculating benefits total 524
carer's allowance 523
challenging a decision 522
circumstances when benefit cap applies 523
exceptions 527
HB over PC age 718
information sharing 1833
lone parents 522
relevant amount 530
specified accommodation 531
who it applies to 522
benefit changes
treatment as income
HB 455, 459
HB over PC age 788
benefit offences
definition 1720
disqualification from benefit 1762
effect on family's benefit 1723
loss of benefit 166, 1715, 1719
one strike scheme 1716
prescribed offences 1766
reduction of benefit 1767
two strikes scheme 1722
benefit week
HB 225, 532
HB over PC age 719
bereavement benefits
disregarded income
CTR(S) 1557
HB 670
HB over PC age 869
bereavement premium
HB 636
Best Start Grants in Scotland 701
billing authority
definition 12
blind
definition
CTR(E) 1159
CTR(W) 1248
non-dependant deductions
CTR(S) 1523
CTR(S) over PC age 1625
HB 517
HB over PC age 800
blind homeworkers' scheme
CTR(S) 1569
HB 696
board
definition
HB over PC age 719

boarders
board and attendance determinations 611, 886, 914
board and attendance redeterminations 886, 914
date entitlement begins
HB 533
HB over PC age 803
exceptions to determinations 888
insufficient information for rent officer 888, 915
non-dependants
HB 248, 520
HB over PC age 732
payments disregarded
CTR(S) 1558
CTR(S) over PC age 1651
HB 677
HB over PC age 859
substitute determinations 887
bonus of wages
treatment as earnings
CTR(S) 1498
CTR(S) over PC age 1612
HB 438
HB over PC age 780
Brexit 300
broad rental market area
definition 392, 893, 902, 927
rent officer determinations 884, 912
business
assets disregarded as capital
CTR(S) 1564
CTR(S) over PC age 1653
HB 686
HB over PC age 863
costs of accommodation
HB 356
HB over PC age 747
exemption from deductions from earnings 1845
expenses/debts
CTR(S) 1501
CTR(S) over PC age 1615
HB 446
HB over PC age 784
business partners
calculation of net profit
HB 445
HB over PC age 784

C
campsite fees
HB 888, 908, 916, 928
HB over PC age 745
cap rent
HB 389
HB over PC age 755
transitional protection
HB 366
HB over PC age 750
capital 10
abroad
CTR(S) 1509
CTR(S) over PC age 1620
HB 465
HB over PC age 791
arrears of benefit
CTR(S) 1565
CTR(S) over PC age 1620
HB 687

HB over PC age 790
calculation
  CTR(E) over PC 1131, 1148
  CTR(S) 1508
  CTR(S) over PC age 1601, 1620
  CTR(W) 1279
  CTR(W) over PC 1237
  HB 462
  HB over PC age 766, 790
calculation of capital in UK
  CTR(E) over PC age 1149
  CTR(S) 1509
  CTR(S) over PC age 1620
  CTR(W) 1279
  CTR(W) over PC age 1237
  HB 464
  HB over PC age 790
calculation of capital outside UK
  CTR(E) over PC age 1149
  CTR(S) 1509
  CTR(S) over PC age 1620
  CTR(W) 1279
  CTR(W) over PC age 1237
  HB 465
  HB over PC age 791
capital limit 9
  CTR(E) over PC age 1118
  CTR(S) 1508
  CTR(S) over PC age 1620
  CTR(W) 1214
  HB 462
  HB over PC age 790
charitable payments
  CTR(S) 1509
  HB 463
child/young person's
  CTR(S) 1489, 1508
  CTR(S) over PC age 1601
  HB 421, 463
  HB over PC age 765
CTR(S) 1508
deprivation of capital
  CTR(S) 1509
  CTR(S) over PC age 1620
  HB 466
  HB over PC age 791
difference between income and capital
  HB 415
diminishing notional capital rule
  CTR(E) over PC age 1149
  CTR(S) 1511
  CTR(S) over PC age 1621
  CTR(W) over PC age 1238
  HB 472
  HB over PC age 791
diminution of capital
  HB 601
  HB over PC age 830
disregards
  CTR(E) 1168
  CTR(S) 1508, 1564
  CTR(S) over PC age 1620, 1653
  CTR(W) 1306
  CTR(W) over PC age 1256
  HB 462, 683, 684
  HB over PC age 790, 862
family's capital 10
  CTR(S) 1489
  CTR(S) over PC age 1601
  HB 421
  HB over PC age 765

HB 415, 460
income from capital 10
  CTR(S) 1491, 1508, 1514, 1558
  CTR(S) over PC age 1604, 1605
  HB 463, 478, 670
  HB over PC age 770, 862
income treated as capital 10
  CTR(S) 1508, 1560, 1567
  CTR(W) 1279
  HB 463, 675, 691
instalments of capital
  CTR(S) 1505
  HB 453
jointly held capital
  CTR(E) over PC age 1151
  CTR(S) 1514
  CTR(S) over PC age 1624
  CTR(W) 1282
  CTR(W) over PC age 1240
  HB 476
  HB over PC age 794
non-dependant's
  CTR(S) 1490
  CTR(S) over PC age 1601
  HB 421
  HB over PC age 765
notional capital
  CTR(E) over PC age 1149
  CTR(S) 1509
  CTR(S) over PC age 1620
  CTR(W) 1280
  CTR(W) over PC age 1237
  HB 466
  HB over PC age 791
partner's capital
  CTR(S) 1489
  CTR(S) over PC age 1601
  HB 421
  HB over PC age 765
qualifying age for PC 11
tariff income 10
  CTR(E) over PC age 1151
  CTR(S) 1491, 1514
  CTR(S) over PC age 1605
  CTR(W) 1283
  CTR(W) over PC age 1240
  HB 478
  HB over PC age 1514
third party payments
  CTR(S) 1510
  HB 466
treatment as income 10
  CTR(S) 1492, 1505
  HB 423, 450, 453
treatment of guarantee credit
  CTR(S) over PC age 1601
  HB over PC age 766
treatment of savings credit
  CTR(S) over PC age 1602
  HB over PC age 766
valuation of capital
  CTR(S) over PC age 1620
  HB 464
  HB over PC age 790
care
child/young person
  HB 409
  HB over PC age 763
care homes
absence from home
  CTR(S) 1479

HB 260
HB over PC age 738
counselling and care charges 107
definition
CTR(S) over PC age 1577
HB 262
HB over PC age 719, 740
HB 1803
local authority information sharing 1828
not liable to make payments on a dwelling
HB 281
HB over PC age 741
public bodies 116
rent officer determinations 888
residents disregarded for council tax
discount
England and Wales 1087
Scotland 1087
tariff income
HB 478
trial period
CTR(S) 1469, 1479
HB 259
HB over PC age 736
care leavers
exclusion from benefits 1710
carer premium
amount
CTR(E) 1161
CTR(S) 1548
CTR(S) over PC age 1647
CTR(W) over PC age 1250
HB 646
HB over PC age 853
CTR(E) 1160
CTR(S) 1547
CTR(S) over PC age 1646
CTR(W) 1291
CTR(W) over PC age 1249
earnings disregards
CTR(S) 1553
HB 658
HB 645
HB over PC age 852
carer's allowance
benefit cap 523
carer's allowance supplement
disregarded
HB(S) 682
carers
cost of care paid by employer
CTR(S) 1498
CTR(S) over PC age 1612
HB 438
HB over PC age 780
disregard of care payments
CTR(S) 1559
HB 674
disregarded for council tax discount 1088
earnings disregard
CTR(E) 1163
CTR(S) 1554
CTR(S) over PC age 1648
HB 658
HB over PC age 854
non-dependants
CTR(S) 1466
CTR(S) over PC age 1586
HB 248
HB over PC age 732
students entitled to benefit

CTR(S) 1485
HB 489
treatment of care payments
CTR(S) 1500
CTR(S) over PC age 1614
HB 444
HB over PC age 783
Caxton Foundation
definition
CTR(S) 1456
CTR(S) over PC age 1577
HB 225
HB over PC age 719
disregarded as capital
CTR(E) 1171
CTR(S) 1567
CTR(S) over PC age 1655
HB 691
HB over PC age 865
disregarded as income
CTR(S) 1560
HB 675
disregarded from second adult's income
CTR(S) 1552
third party payments
CTR(S) 1506
HB 454
Chamber President 172
change of circumstances
arrears of income 1774
date change takes effect
CTR(S) 1531
CTR(S) over PC age 1631
CTR(W) 1285
CTR(W) over PC age 1243
HB 535
HB over PC age 804
duty to notify
CTR(E) 1182
CTR(S) 1536
CTR(S) over PC age 1638
CTR(W) 1328
HB 559
HB over PC age 819
duty to report 1759
HB 535, 555
HB over PC age 804, 817
pension credit
CTR(S) over PC age 1632, 1638
CTR(W) over PC age 1244
HB over PC age 806, 819
supersessions 957
supersessions – late application 962
charitable payments
disregarded
CTR(S) 1557, 1568
HB 668, 694
students
CTR(S) 1518
HB 499
treatment as income and capital
CTR(S) 1509
HB 463
Charter of Fundamental Rights 340
child benefit
CTR(S) 1472
CTR(S) over PC age 1592
disregarded
CTR(S) 1563
CTR(S) over PC age 1603
HB 682

HB over PC age 769
HB 406
HB over PC age 762
child support
  payments disregarded
    CTR(S) 1562
    HB 679
Child Support, Pensions and Social Security Act 2000 135
  commencement 138
  general note 135
child tax credit 1728
  arrears treated as capital
    CTR(S) 1509
    HB 463
  calculation of average weekly income 435
    CTR(W) 1276
    CTR(W) over PC age 1234
    HB 435
    HB over PC age 777
  notional income/capital
    CTR(S) 1510
    HB 454
  transitional provision for UC claims 1880, 1882, 1885
  treatment as income
    CTR(E) over PC age 1146
    CTR(S) 1504
    CTR(S) over PC age 1604
    HB 450
    HB over PC age 770
childcare
  estimating relevant charges
    CTR(S) 1494
    CTR(S) over PC age 1608
    HB 426
    HB over PC age 774
  relevant charges
    CTR(S) 1493
    CTR(S) over PC age 1606
    HB 425
    HB over PC age 773
  student grant income – disregards
    CTR(S) 1517
    HB 495
  treatment of charges
    CTR(E) over PC age 1141
    CTR(S) 1491, 1492
    CTR(S) over PC age 1606
    CTR(W) 1273
    CTR(W) over PC age 1230
    HB 423, 424
    HB over PC age 772, 773
childminders
  calculation of net profit
    CTR(S) 1502, 1503
    CTR(S) over PC age 1616
    HB 446, 449
    HB over PC age 785, 786
  costs paid by employer
    CTR(S) 1498
    CTR(S) over PC age 1612
    HB 438
    HB over PC age 780
children
  applicable amount
    CTR(S) 1487
    CTR(S) over PC age 1600
    HB 411
    HB over PC age 764
  child who cannot share a bedroom

HB 225, 369
HB over PC age 720
claiming for a child
  HB 409
  HB over PC age 762
death of a child
  HB 407
definition 12
  CTR(S) 1456
  HB 225
  HB over PC age 719
disregarded capital
  CTR(S) 1508
  HB 463
disregarded for council tax discount 1086
duty to notify changes in family
  CTR(S) 1537
  CTR(S) over PC age 1638
  HB 559
  HB over PC age 810
earnings
  CTR(S) 1555
  HB 662
income and capital
  CTR(S) 1489, 1508
  CTR(S) over PC age 1601
  HB 421
  HB over PC age 765
landlord's child – responsibility for
  HB 280
  HB over PC age 741
leaving care 1710
member of household
  CTR(S) 1472
  CTR(S) over PC age 1592
  HB 409
  HB over PC age 762
non-dependants
  CTR(S) 1466
  CTR(S) over PC age 1586
  HB 248
  HB over PC age 732
payments from child disregarded
  CTR(S) 1558
  HB 671
responsibility for child
  CTR(E) 1114
  CTR(S) 1472, 1484
  CTR(S) over PC age 1591
  CTR(W) 1202
  HB 407, 488
  HB over PC age 762
two-child limit
  CTR(E) over PC age 1126
  CTR(S) 1541
  CTR(W) 1261
  HB 411
  HB over PC age 764
Children (Leaving Care) Act 2000 1710
children in care
  disregard of care payments
    CTR(S) 1500
    CTR(S) over PC age 1614
    HB 444, 674
    HB over PC age 783
  leaving care 1710
  treatment as member of household
    CTR(S) 1473
    CTR(S) over PC age 1592
    HB 409
    HB over PC age 763

children in need
  payments disregarded
    CTR(S) 1566
    HB 690
civil partners 14, 1729
  close relatives 1729
  stepchildren 1729, 1772
Civil Partnership Act 2004 1729
Civil Partnership Act 2004 (Relationships Arising Through Civil Partnership) Order 2005 1772
civil penalties 64
  amounts 1839
  failure to disclose 64
  incorrect statements 64
claim forms
  HB 544
  HB over PC age 811
claim-related rent 932, 934
  HB 380, 382, 894, 921
  HB over PC age 751
claims 23
  advance claims
    HB 548, 552
    HB over PC age 815
  amending a claim
    HB 558
    HB over PC age 818
  backdating
    HB 532, 548, 552
    HB over PC age 812
  claim forms
    HB 544
  claiming procedure
    HB 544
    HB over PC age 811
  date entitlement begins
    HB 532
    HB over PC age 803
  date of claim
    HB 226
    HB over PC age 720
  defective claims
    HB 547
    HB over PC age 814
  discretionary housing payments 1757
  electronic claims
    HB 554
    HB over PC age 816
  end of claim
    HB 534, 535
    HB over PC age 803
  evidence to support claim
    HB 555
    HB over PC age 817
  information required by local authority
    HB 608
    HB over PC age 833
  late claims
    HB 548, 552
    HB over PC age 812
  national insurance number requirement 23
  repeat claims
    HB 549
  retrospective effect of requirement for claim 25
  telephone claims
    HB 545
    HB over PC age 812
  where to claim
    HB 544, 549
    HB over PC age 812

  who can claim
    HB 542
    HB over PC age 811
  withdrawing a claim
    HB 558
    HB over PC age 818
  written claims
    HB 544
    HB over PC age 811
close relatives
  civil partners 1729
  definition
    CTR(S) 1456
    CTR(S) over PC age 1577
    HB 225
    HB over PC age 720
  landlord
    HB 280, 286
    HB over PC age 741
co-ownership scheme
  definition
    HB 226
    HB over PC age 720
  HB 352
  HB over PC age 745
coastguard
  earnings disregard
    CTR(E) 1163
    CTR(S) 1554
    CTR(S) over PC age 1648
    HB 659
    HB over PC age 854
  HB 659
cohabitation 14
commercial basis
  CTR(S) 1466
  CTR(S) over PC age 1586
  HB 248, 280, 281
  HB over PC age 732, 741, 742
  non-commercial agreements
    HB 282
commission
  treatment as earnings
    CTR(S) 1498
    CTR(S) over PC age 1612
    HB 438
    HB over PC age 780
common travel area 299
  right to reside 327
communal areas
  definition
    HB 624
    HB over PC age 846
  fuel charges
    HB 623
    HB over PC age 845
community care
  direct payments
    CTR(S) 1562
    HB 681
compensation
  approved blood scheme
    HB 224
    HB over PC age 719
  for unfair dismissal
    HB 438
  income/capital disregards
    CTR(S) 1566, 1569
    CTR(S) over PC age 1656
    HB 687, 689, 697

HB over PC age 867
treatment as income or capital 418
components
amounts 650
entitlement to ESA components
CTR(S) 1548
CTR(W) 1293
HB 648
comprehensive sickness insurance 331
concessionary payment
definition
CTR(S) 1456
HB 225
HB over PC age 720
treatment as benefit payment
CTR(S) 1547
HB 645
treatment as capital
CTR(S) 1565
HB 687
treatment as income
CTR(S) 1556
HB 666
conditional sale agreement
HB 352
HB over PC age 745
Constitutional Reform Act 2005 160
Contracting Out (Administrative Work of Tribunals) Order 2009 1064
Contracting Out (Functions of Local Authorities: Income-Related Benefits Order 2002 1769
contrived tenancy
CTR(S) 1466
CTR(S) over PC age 1586, 1601
HB 280, 293
HB over PC age 741
taking advantage of benefit scheme
CTR(S) 1490
HB 281, 421
HB over PC age 742, 765
convictions
conviction quashed 1717
loss of benefit 1715
council tax 1071
appeals 1079
discounts
England and Wales 1072
Scotland 1083
disregarded for discount 1086
joint liability 1522
liability
England and Wales 1071
Scotland 1082
reduced amounts
England and Wales 1072
Scotland 1083
setting amounts
England and Wales 1081
Scotland 1085
shortfall in receipts
England 1094
council tax benefit
abolition 8, 207
appeals 937
overpayments 40
Council Tax Reduction (Scotland) Amendment (No.2) Regulations 2013 1661
citation 1661
commencement 1661
transitional provisions 1661

Council Tax Reduction (Scotland) Regulations 2012 1452
citation 1455
commencement 1455
definitions 1455
general provisions
amount of reduction 1521
applicable amount 1487
application of the Regulations 1473
applications 1532
change of circumstances 1536
effective date 1530
electronic communication 1540
entitlement 1474
families 1472
general 1455
income and capital 1489
reviews 1537
students 1514
transitional provision 1540
schedules
alternative maximum CTR 1551
applicable amount 1541
consequential amendments 1573
disregarded capital 1564
disregarded earnings 1552
disregarded income 1556
savings provisions 1572
Council Tax Reduction (State Pension Credit) (Scotland) Regulations 2012 1574
citation 1576
commencement 1576
definitions 1576
general provisions
amount of reduction 1624
applicable amount 1600
application of the Regulations 1593
applications 1634
change of circumstances 1638
effective date 1630
electronic communication 1641
entitlement to CTR 1593
families 1591
general 1576
income and capital 1601
reviews 1639
transitional provision 1642
schedules
alternative maximum CTR 1659
applicable amount 1643
disregarded capital 1653
disregarded earnings 1647
disregarded income 1650
council tax reduction schemes 1073
amount of reductions
CTR(E) 1089
CTR(S) 1521
CTR(S) over PC age 1624
CTR(W) 1095, 1264
CTR(W) over PC age 1219
appeals
England 1176, 1670
Wales 1684
applications
CTR(E) 1175, 1178
CTR(S) 1532
CTR(W) 1215, 1322, 1324
claiming other benefits 33
default scheme
CTR(E) 1093
CTR(W) 1333

discretionary council tax reductions 1073
disregard of payments
    HB 677
duty of authority to set up scheme
    Wales 1205
judicial review
    England and Wales 1082
local schemes
    England 1073, 1088, 1103
    Scotland 1085, 1452, 1574
    Wales 1074, 1095, 1190
matters to be included in schemes
    CTR(E) 1088, 1120, 1175
    CTR(W) 1206
primary legislation 1071
provision for all applicants
    CTR(E) 1120
    CTR(W) 1214
requirements of scheme
    CTR(E) 1120
    CTR(W) 1206
review of schemes 1097
revisions to scheme
    CTR(E) 1093
transitional provision 1098
    CTR(E) 1094
    CTR(W) 1096, 1294
who must be included in the scheme
    CTR(E) 1117
    CTR(W) 1095, 1207
**Council Tax Reduction Schemes (Amendment)
(England) Regulations 2017** 1188
**Council Tax Reduction Schemes (Default
Scheme) (Wales) Regulations 2013** 1333
commencement 1333
schedules
    applicable amounts 1409
    applications 1402
    disregarded capital 1440
    disregarded earnings 1423
    disregarded income 1427
    notification 1447
    pensioners' applicable amounts 1404
    pensioners' disregarded capital 1434
    pensioners' disregarded earnings 1418
    pensioners' disregarded income 1421
**Council Tax Reduction Schemes (Prescribed
Requirements) (England) (Amendment)
Regulations 2015** 1187
**Council Tax Reduction Schemes (Prescribed
Requirements) (England) Regulations 2012**
1103
citation 1105
commencement 1105
definitions 1105
general provisions
    general 1105
schedules
    amount of alternative maximum CTR 1162
    applicable amounts 1157
    disregarded capital 1168
    disregarded earnings 1163
    disregarded income 1166
    pensioners 1120
    procedural matters 1175
    requirements of scheme 1177
**Council Tax Reduction Schemes (Transitional
Provision) (England) Regulations 2013**
citation 1185
commencement 1185

**Council Tax Reduction Schemes (Transitional
Provisions (Wales) Regulations 2013** 1450
commencement 1450
definitions 1450
transitional provisions 1450
**Council Tax Reduction Schemes and Prescribed
Requirements (Wales) Regulations 2013** 1190
commencement 1190
definitions 1191
schedules
    applicable amounts 1286
    disregarded capital 1306
    disregarded earnings 1296
    disregarded income 1299
    eligibility 1261
    notifications 1329
    other matters 1324
    pensioners' applicable amounts 1245
    pensioners' disregarded capital 1256
    pensioners' disregarded earnings 1250
    pensioners' disregarded income 1253
    pensioners' eligibility 1216
    procedural matters 1322
    students 1314
councillors' allowances
HB 441
counselling services
grants to organisations to provide services
    165
rent officer referrals 889, 917
service charges 107, 620
supported accommodation 1781
couples
applicable amount
    CTR(S) 1487
    HB 411
cannot share a bedroom
    HB 230
    HB over PC age 723
capital of partner
    HB 421
    HB over PC age 765
change of circumstances
    CTR(S) 1531
    CTR(S) over PC age 1631
claiming
    HB 273, 542
    HB over PC age 740, 811
definition 12
    CTR(E) 1113
    CTR(S) 1457
    CTR(S) over PC age 1578
    CTR(W) 1201
    HB 226
    HB over PC age 720, 724
estrangement
    CTR(S) 1465
eviction
    HB 8
former partner is landlord
    HB 280
    HB over PC age 741
income of partner 10
    CTR(S) 1489
    CTR(S) over PC age 1601
    HB 421
    HB over PC age 765
member of household
    CTR(S) 1472
    CTR(S) over PC age 1592
    HB 409

HB over PC age 762
mixed-age couples 718, 1898, 1899, 1901
  HB 224
non-dependant deductions
  CTR(S) 1523
  CTR(S) over PC age 1625
  HB 516
  HB over PC age 800
partner
  CTR(S) 1460
  CTR(S) over PC age 1580
  HB 231
  HB over PC age 724
recovery of overpayments
  HB 597
  HB over PC age 829
student partners
  CTR(S) 1484, 1521
  HB 273, 488, 495, 503
UC claimant becomes a couple 1868

course of study
definition
  CTR(S) 1457
  HB 481

court action
delays in payment
  HB 568
recovery of overpayments
  CTB 40
  HB 37, 600
  HB over PC age 37
recovery of penalties 36

Court of Appeal
proceedings on appeal 186
right to appeal to 184, 1060

Court of Protection
HB 542
HB over PC age 811

Court of Session
proceedings on appeal 186

covenants
CTR(S) 1515, 1517, 1518
HB 481, 498, 504

credit sale
HB 352
HB over PC age 745

Creutzfeldt-Jakob disease
payments from trusts
  CTR(E) 1170
  CTR(S) 1570
  CTR(S) over PC age 1654
  HB 698
  HB over PC age 864

criminal offences 41
disclosure of information 74, 165, 213
dishonesty 51
failure to provide information
  HB 618
  HB over PC age 842
false representations 54
obstructing inspector 50
penalty alternatives to prosecution 57, 1745
time limits 65

croft land
disregarded as capital
  CTR(S) 1564
  HB 685
HB 352
HB over PC age 729, 745

Crown tenants
definition
  HB 226
  HB over PC age 720
HB 352
HB over PC age 745

D

date of claim
CTR(E) 1178
CTR(S) 1530
CTR(S) over PC age 1630
CTR(W) 1325
HB 532
HB over PC age 803

deafness
students
  HB 488

death
appeals 978
date change of circumstances takes effect
  1531, 1631
disregard of compensation
  CTR(S) 1569
  HB 697
duty to report 1759
effect on carer premium
  HB 645
inherited protection from rent restrictions
  HB 362, 383
  HB over PC age 751
payments on death
  HB 580
  HB over PC age 826
protection from social sector rent scheme
  359
recovery of overpayments
  HB 597
retaining rigth of residence after death of
  family member 335

decisions
appeal tribunals 1016, 1053
delayed – appeal pending 154
no right of appeal 971, 980
notice of decisions which can be appealed
  963
person affected 941
quashing orders 192
relevant 139
revision of decisions 942
setting aside tribunal decisions 205
time limits for appeals 973

decisions by local authority 106
notification to claimant 106
  HB 564, 701
  HB over PC age 821, 870
statement of reasons
  HB 564
  HB over PC age 821
validation of decisions 107

deductions from benefits
non-dependant
  CTR(S) 1522
  CTR(S) over PC age 1625
  HB 516
  HB over PC age 800
prescribed benefits 36
  HB 605
  HB over PC age 831
recovery of overpayments
  HB 596, 598, 599, 605

HB over PC age 829, 831
recovery of overpayments from other
    benefits
    CTR(S) 40, 1503
    HB 37, 450
deductions from eligible rent
    HB 356, 620
    HB over PC age 843
defective claims
    HB 547
    HB over PC age 814
delays
    in making payments
        HB 567
        HB over PC age 822
    moving home
        HB 258
        HB over PC age 735
deprivation of resources
    CTR(S) 1505, 1509
    CTR(S) over PC age 1620
    diminishing notional capital rule
        CTR(S) 1511
        CTR(S) over PC age 1621
        HB 472
        HB over PC age 791
    HB 457, 466
    HB over PC age 791
designated authority
    definition
        HB 226
        HB over PC age 720
designated office
    definition
        CTR(S) 1457
        HB 226
        HB over PC age 721
detention
    absence from home
        CTR(S) 1470, 1480
        HB 260
        HB over PC age 738
    disregarded for council tax discount 1086
diminishing notional capital rule
    calculating the reduction
        HB 475
        CTR(S) 1511
        CTR(S) over PC age 1621
        CTR(W) 1281
        CTR(W) over PC age 1238
        HB 472
        HB over PC age 791
    tariff income
        HB 478
direct payments to landlord
    death of claimant
        HB 580
        HB over PC age 826
    frequency of payment
        HB 569, 573
        HB over PC age 823
    HB 577
    HB over PC age 824, 825
    information requirements
        HB 1741
    notification
        HB 565, 704
        HB over PC age 872
    obligation to make direct payments
        HB 574
    payments on account

HB 572
person affected
    HB 565
recovery of overpayments
    HB 37
disability
    childcare costs
        CTR(E) over PC age 1145
        CTR(S) 1492, 1494
        CTR(S) over PC age 1608
        CTR(W) 1233
        HB 424
        HB over PC age 773
    council tax reductions
        England and Wales 1073
        Scotland 1084
    severe disability premium and UC 1862
disability living allowance
    disregarded
        CTR(S) 1556
        CTR(S) over PC age 1603
        HB 666
        HB over PC age 768
disability premium
    amount
        CTR(S) 1547
        HB 646
    CTR(S) 1543, 1544
    CTR(W) 1288
    earnings disregard
        HB 657
    HB 636
    incapable of work 1774
disability reduction
    council tax
        England and Wales 1073
        Scotland 1084
disabled child premium
    amount
        CTR(E) 1161
        CTR(S) 1547
        CTR(S) over PC age 1647
        CTR(W) over PC age 1250
        HB 646
        HB over PC age 853
    CTR(E) 1160
    CTR(S) 1546
    CTR(S) over PC age 1646
    CTR(W) 1291
    CTR(W) over PC age 1248
    HB 644
    HB over PC age 852
disabled students
    CTR(S) 1484
disabled students' allowance
    CTR(S) 1484
    HB 488
discount
    council tax
        England and Wales 1072
        Scotland 1083
discretionary council tax reductions
    CTR(E) 1176
    CTR(W) 1323
**Discretionary Financial Assistance Regulations
2001** 1751
discretionary housing payments 135, 1751
    bedroom tax 1751
    circumstances in which payments may be
        made 1754
    claims 1755, 1757

disregard of payments
  CTR(S) 1563
  HB 682
grants to local authority 137
HB 1752
information 1757
maximum weekly payments 1755
no right of appeal 1751
reviews 1758
UC 1752
discretionary powers
  HB 79
recovery of overpayments
  HB 37
dishonesty 51
disqualification from benefit
benefit offences 1719
effect on offender's family 1723
period of disqualification 1762
disqualifying benefits
definition 1714
disregards
benefits
  HB 664
  HB over PC age 768
capital
  CTR(S) 1508, 1564
  CTR(S) over PC age 1620, 1653
  CTR(W) 1306
  CTR(W) over PC age 1256
  HB 462, 684
  HB over PC age 790, 862
changes in tax and contributions
  CTR(W) 1276
  HB 437
  HB over PC age 780
child's capital
  CTR(S) 1508
  HB 463
child's earnings
  CTR(S) 1555
  HB 662
employee's earnings
  CTR(E) 1163
  CTR(S) 1499, 1552, 1555
  CTR(S) over PC age 1647
  CTR(W) over PC age 1250
  HB 442, 655
  HB over PC age 854
income other than earnings
  CTR(E) 1166
  CTR(S) 1497, 1503, 1556
  CTR(S) over PC age 1650
  CTR(W) 1299
  CTR(W) over PC age 1253
  HB 450, 664
  HB over PC age 857
non-dependant's income
  CTR(S) 1524
  CTR(S) over PC age 1626
  HB 517
  HB over PC age 801
second adult's income
  CTR(S) 1552
self-employed earnings
  CTR(S) 1500, 1501, 1503, 1555
  CTR(S) over PC age 1614, 1615, 1616
  HB 444, 445, 449
  HB over PC age 783, 786
student loans
  CTR(S) 1519

  HB 500
student's income
  CTR(S) 1516, 1518, 1521
  HB 495, 499, 503, 504
divorce
former partner pays the mortgage
  HB 280
  HB over PC age 741
retaining right of residence after divorce 335
domestic violence
definition 531
domiciliary care 1830
dwelling
change of dwelling 225
definition 12, 101
  CTR(S) 1477
  HB 237, 880, 909
  HB over PC age 721, 729
disregarded as capital
  CTR(S) 1564, 1568
  HB 685, 692
liability to make payments
  HB 273
  over PC age 740
not liable to make payments
  HB 280
  over PC age 741
occupation of home
  CTR(S) 1467
  HB 256, 487
  HB over PC age 734
rent officer categories 900, 925
size criteria
  HB 891, 918, 1786

E
early learning grant in Scotland 701
early years assistance in Scotland 701
earnings
child/young person's earnings
  CTR(S) 1555
  HB 662
deduction of childcare costs
  CTR(S) 1492
  CTR(S) over PC age 1606
  HB 424
  HB over PC age 773
deductions to recover benefit overpayments 1840
  HB 37
deductions to recover penalties 36
definition
  CTR(S) 1498
  CTR(S) over PC age 1612
  HB 438
  HB over PC age 780
disregards from employed earnings
  CTR(E) 1163
  CTR(S) 1499, 1552, 1555
  CTR(S) over PC age 1647
  CTR(W) 1296
  CTR(W) over PC age 1225, 1250
  HB 442, 449, 655
  HB over PC age 854
disregards from self-employed earnings
  CTR(S) 1500, 1501, 1503, 1555
  CTR(S) over PC age 1614, 1615, 1616
  HB 444
  HB over PC age 783, 786
employed earner
  CTR(E) over PC age 1136

CTR(S) 1498
CTR(S) over PC age 1612
CTR(W) 1267
CTR(W) over PC age 1225
HB 438
HB over PC age 780
employed earner average weekly earnings
CTR(S) 1496
CTR(W) 1267
HB 431
employed earner calculation of net earnings
CTR(S) 1499
CTR(S) over PC age 1613
CTR(W) 1268
HB 442
HB over PC age 781
fluctuating earnings of employed earner
CTR(S) 1496
HB 431
low earnings-notional income
CTR(S) 1507
HB 455
minimum earnings threshold for EEA
nationals 307
self-employed assessment period
CTR(S) 1497
HB 434
self-employed average weekly earnings
CTR(S) 1497
HB 434
self-employed calculation of net profit
CTR(S) 1501
CTR(S) over PC age 1615
HB 445
HB over PC age 784
self-employed earner
CTR(E) over PC age 1138
CTR(S) 1500
CTR(S) over PC age 1614
CTR(W) 1269
CTR(W) over PC age 1226
HB 444
HB over PC age 782, 783
education authority
CTR(S) 1515
HB 481
education maintenance allowance
CTR(S) 1556
HB 667
EEA nationals 303
comprehensive sickness insurance 331
continuity of residence 334
EU Settled Status Scheme 300
family members 298, 317
former worker 319
minimum earnings threshold 307
pregnancy 315
qualified person 313
retaining right of residence 335
retaining worker status 314
right to reside 327
self-employed 308
CTR(S) 1481
HB 298
sickness 310
unemployment 311
workers 305
HB 298
Eileen Trust
definition
CTR(S) 1457

HB 226
disregarded as capital
CTR(E) 1171
CTR(S) 1509, 1567
CTR(S) over PC age 1655
HB 463, 691
HB over PC age 865
disregarded as income
CTR(S) 1560
HB 675
disregarded from second adult's income
CTR(S) 1552
third party payments
CTR(S) 1506, 1510
HB 454, 467
electronic communications
claims
HB 554, 712
HB over PC age 816, 877, 878
CTR(E) 1176
CTR(S) 1540
HB 226
HB over PC age 721
notification of changes
HB 562
use by local authorities
CTR(S) 1540
HB 712
HB over PC age 877
eligible housing costs
calculation
HB 538
HB over PC age 744, 809
HB 349
HB over PC age 744
rent-free periods
HB 541
HB over PC age 810
students
HB 493
eligible rent 351, 356, 746
calculation
HB 356, 538
HB over PC age 746
exempt accommodation 1776
local housing allowance
HB 362
HB over PC age 748
local reference rent
HB 361
HB over PC age 747
maximum rent
HB 361, 362
HB over PC age 747, 748
maximum rent (social sector)
HB 358
employed earners
average weekly earnings
CTR(S) 1496
HB 431
calculation of net earnings
CTR(E) over PC age 1137
CTR(S) 1499
CTR(S) over PC age 1613
HB 442
HB over PC age 781
child/young person's earnings
CTR(S) 1555
HB 662
definition
CTR 1457

CTR(S) over PC age 1578
HB 227
HB over PC age 721
disregards
CTR(S) 1499, 1552
CTR(S) over PC age 1647
CTR(W) 1296
CTR(W) over PC age 1250
HB 442
HB over PC age 854
earnings
CTR(S) 1496, 1498
CTR(S) over PC age 1612
HB 438
HB over PC age 780
fluctuating earnings
CTR(S) 1496
HB 431
loans and advances from employer
CTR(S) 1509
HB 463
employers
colluding in fraud 61
employment and support allowance
assessment phase
CTR(S) 1548
change of circumstances
CTR(S) 1537
HB 559
components
CTR(S) 1548
HB 648
converted ESA
CTR(S) 1456, 1549
HB 226, 240, 651
CTR(S) 1465
CTR(S) over PC age 1585
disregarded income
CTR(S) 1555, 1556
HB 666
HB 236
HB over PC age 729
non-dependant deductions
CTR(S) 1524
CTR(S) over PC age 1626
HB 517
HB over PC age 801
person from abroad 326
personal allowance 632
students on ESA
CTR(S) 1484
HB 487
transitional provisions 1892
**Employment and Support Allowance and
Universal Credit (Miscellaneous
Amendments and Transitional and Savings
Provisions) Regulations 2017** 1892
employment zone programme
definition
CTR(S) 1457
HB 227
disregard of payments
CTR(S) 1563, 1570
HB 682, 698
Employment, Skills and Enterprise Scheme
definition
CTR(S) 1457
disregarded as capital
CTR(S) 1564
disregarded as income
CTR(S) 1556

end of claim
date entitlement ends
HB 534, 535
HB over PC age 803
enduring power of attorney
HB 543
HB over PC age 811
enforcement notices 85
enhanced disability premium
amount
CTR(E) 1161
CTR(S) 1548
CTR(S) over PC age 1647
CTR(W) over PC age 1250
HB 646
HB over PC age 853
CTR(E) 1160
CTR(S) 1546
CTR(S) over PC age 1646
CTR(W) 1291
CTR(W) over PC age 1248
HB 643
entitlement
conditions of entitlement
CTR(S) 1474
HB 5
date entitlement begins
CTR(E) over PC age 1154
CTR(S) 1530
CTR(S) over PC age 1630
CTR(W) 1285
CTR(W) over PC age 1243
HB 532
HB over PC age 803
end of entitlement
HB 534, 535
HB over PC age 803
exclusions 9
persons from abroad
CTR(S) 1481
HB 297
HB over PC age 742
restriction in cases of error 156
work-focused interview 26
entry
inspectors' powers of entry 47
Equitable Life 1855
equity release schemes
treatment as income
CTR(S) over PC age 1604
HB over PC age 770
equity sharing schemes
HB 240
errors
civil penalties for incorrect statements 64
correction of accidental errors 158, 205, 964,
1018, 1054
First-tier Tribunal errors 1018
grounds for revision 943
mistakes 585
official error – definition 938, 939
overpayment caused by official error
HB 583, 584, 601
HB over PC age 827, 830
rent officer
HB 889, 916
rent officer application
HB 404
HB over PC age 760
restriction on benefit entitlement 156
Upper Tribunal errors 1054

estrangement
 CTR(S) 1465
 CTR(S) over PC age 1585
EU Settled Status Scheme 300
European Commission on Human Rights 112
European Convention on Human Rights 111
 Articles 124
 Convention rights 111
 declaration of incompatibility 114
 impact on UK law 113
 judicial remedies 118
 legal proceedings 116
European Court of Human Rights 112
eviction
 loss of HB 8, 162
 pilot scheme 8
evidence
 in support of claims
  HB 555
  HB over PC age 817
 judicial reviews 1051
 of liability for rent
  HB 277
 required by rent officer
  HB 613
  HB over PC age 838
 tribunals 204, 1001, 1040
exceptionally high rent
 HB 891, 918
excluded tenancies
 definition 626
 HB 625
 HB over PC age 846
 local housing allowance 386
 referrals to rent officers
  HB 398
  HB over PC age 758
 social sector rent restrictions 367, 625
exempt accommodation
 benefit cap 531
 definition 1777, 1779
 eligible rent 1776
 protection from rent restrictions 367, 1778
exempt work
 HB 660
expenses
 disregarded income
  CTR(S) 1556
  HB 666
 paid work
  CTR(S) 1556
  HB 666
 self-employed
  CTR(S) 1501
  CTR(S) over PC age 1615
 service user group
  CTR(S) 1556
 treatment as earnings
  CTR(S) 1498
  CTR(S) over PC age 1612
  HB 438
  HB over PC age 780
 tribunals 197, 205, 1004, 1037, 1043
 voluntary/charity work
  CTR(S) 1556
  HB 665
extended payments
 amount of payments
  CTR(E) over PC age 1152
  CTR(S) 1526, 1528
  CTR(S) over PC age 1627

 CTR(W) 1283
 CTR(W) over PC age 1241
 HB 509, 514
 HB over PC age 797
 CTR(E) over PC age 1152
 CTR(S) over PC age 1629
 CTR(W) over PC age 1240
 decision notice
  HB 703
  HB over PC age 871
 HB over PC age 721, 795, 799
 information to be supplied
  HB 614
  HB over PC age 839
 moving home
  CTR(E) 1177
  CTR(E) over PC age 1153
  CTR(S) 1526, 1528
  CTR(S) over PC age 1628
  CTR(W) 1284
  CTR(W) over PC age 1241
  HB 510, 515, 613
  HB over PC age 798
 payment period
  CTR(E) over PC age 1152
  CTR(S) 1525, 1527
  CTR(S) over PC age 1627
  CTR(W) 1283
  CTR(W) over PC age 1241
  HB 227, 508, 513
  HB over PC age 721, 796
 qualifying contributory benefits
  CTR(E) over PC age 1152
  CTR(S) 1527
  CTR(S) over PC age 1627
  CTR(W) 1284
  CTR(W) over PC age 1242
  HB 512
  HB over PC age 796
 starting work or increasing hours
  CTR(S) 1525
  CTR(W) 1283
  HB 162, 506

F
failure to
 disclose overpayments
  HB 592, 595, 601
  HB over PC age 828, 830
 supply information 64
  HB 618
  HB over PC age 842
fair rent
 HB 1786
families
 aggregation of applicable amounts
  CTR(S) 1487
  CTR(S) over PC age 1600
  HB 411
  HB over PC age 764
 death of a child
  HB 407
 definition 12
  CTR(E) 1113
  CTR(S) 1458
  CTR(W) 1202
  HB 405
  HB over PC age 762
 duty to notify changes in family
  CTR(S) 1537
  CTR(S) over PC age 1638

HB 559
    HB over PC age 819
EEA nationals 298, 317
membership of family
    HB 405
    HB over PC age 762
non-dependants
    CTR(S) 1466
    CTR(S) over PC age 1585
    HB 248
    HB over PC age 732
responsibility for a child
    HB 407
    HB over PC age 762
treatment of income and capital 10
    CTR(S) 1489, 1508, 1554
    CTR(S) over PC age 1601
    HB 421, 463, 659
    HB over PC age 765
family premium
    abolition 413, 634
    amount
        CTR(E) 1158
        CTR(W) 1287
        CTR(W) over PC age 1246
    CTR(E) 1158
    CTR(W) 1287
    CTR(W) over PC age 1246
firefighters
    earnings disregard
        CTR(E) 1163
        CTR(S) 1554
        CTR(S) over PC age 1647
        HB 659
        HB over PC age 854
    HB 659
First-tier Tribunal 168
    administration 201
    appealing First-tier Tribunal decisions in
        Upper Tribunal 150, 175
    application for permission to appeal 1021
    application treated as different type of
        application 1026
    case management powers 988
    composition of tribunals 169, 1061
    consent orders 1016
    costs and expenses 197, 205, 1004
    decision-making approach 145
    decisions which can be appealed 144
    decisions which cannot be appealed 144
    delegation to staff 988
    enforcement of decisions 196
    evidence and submissions 1001
    expert assistance 197
    failure to attend a hearing 1015
    failure to comply with rules 992
    fees 202
    hearings 1011
    judges 169, 171
    lookalike appeals 1003
    mediation 195, 987
    membership of tribunal 1027
    notice of appeal 1004
    notice of decisions 1016
    notice of hearings 1014
    obligation to cooperate 985
    organisation 1065
    overriding objective 985
    practice directions 194
    procedures for giving directions 991
    public and private hearings 1014

reasons for decisions 1017
representatives 998
response to the tribunal 1008
review of decisions 173, 1023
right to appeal to First-tier tribunal 144
sending documents 1000
setting aside a decision 1019
sitting places 196
striking out a case 993
time limits 1026
transfer of functions 198
transitional provisions 1058
Tribunal Procedure Rules 194, 204, 984
withdrawal of a case 1002
witnesses 1002
**First-tier Tribunal and Upper Tribunal
    (Chambers) Order 2010** 1065
**First-tier Tribunal and Upper Tribunal
    (Composition of Tribunal) Order 2008** 1061
fluctuating earnings
    CTR(S) 1496
    CTR(S) over PC age 1611
    HB 431
    HB over PC age 777, 779
fluctuating hours of work
    CTR(S) 1471
    CTR(S) over PC age 1590, 1591, 1611
    HB 253
    HB over PC age 733, 734
former pathfinder authority
    definition
        HB 619
        HB over PC age 842
    list of authorities 707, 873, 930, 934
    maximum rent 619
    transitional protection
        HB 365, 708
        HB over PC age 749, 874
fostering
    treatment as member of household
        CTR(S) 1473
        CTR(S) over PC age 1592
        HB 409
        HB over PC age 763
    treatment of allowances
        CTR(S) 1500
        CTR(S) over PC age 1614
        HB 444
        HB over PC age 783
fraud 41
    authorisation of inspectors 42
    employers colluding 61
    landlords
        HB 575
    local authorities power to prosecute 68, 1821
    local authorities requirement to prevent fraud
        82
    loss of benefit 1712
    penalties 51, 54
    penalty as alternative to prosecution 57
    powers of entry 47
    powers of investigators 43
    prevention affecting subsidy 89
    prosecution of offences 65
    recovery of overpayments
        HB 592, 601
        HB over PC age 828, 830
    redirected mail 96
    reports on local authorities administration 82

fuel
definition
HB 624
HB over PC age 846
fuel costs
communal areas
HB 623
HB over PC age 845
deductions from eligible rent
HB 623
HB over PC age 845
service charges
HB 623
HB over PC age 845
full-time course of study
definition
CTR(S) 1458
HB 481
sandwich course
HB 483
full-time education
definition
HB 481
non-advanced education
HB 406
Fund, The
definition
CTR(S) 1458
HB 227
disregarded as capital
CTR(S) 1509, 1567
HB 463, 691
disregarded as income
CTR(S) 1560
HB 675
disregarded from second adult's income
CTR(S) 1552
third party payments
CTR(S) 1506, 1510
HB 454, 467
funeral expense assistance in Scotland 701

G
George Cross payments
CTR(S) 1556, 1569
HB 667, 697
good cause
absence from work
CTR(S) 1471
CTR(S) over PC age 1591
HB 253
HB over PC age 734
for late claim
HB 548
granny annexe 250
grants
student
CTR(S) 1515, 1516
HB 482, 495
guarantee payments
treatment as earnings
CTR(S) 1498
HB 438
guaranteed income payment
disregarded
CTR(S) 1557
HB 669
guardian's allowance
CTR(S) 1562
CTR(S) over PC age 1603

HB 679
HB over PC age 769

H
habitual residence 344, 1797
CTR(E) 1118
CTR(S) 1481
CTR(W) 1211
HB 297
HB over PC age 742, 744
transitional arrangements 1771
haemophilia
CTR(S) 1560
CTR(S) over PC age 1655
HB 676, 691
HB over PC age 865
health benefits
CTR(S) 1561, 1569
HB 678
health in pregnancy grant
disregarded
CTR(S) 1569
HB over PC age 869
healthy start scheme 1833
heritable securities 5
HB 348
higher education
CTR(S) 1458
HB 482, 491
higher pensioner premium
HB 636
hire purchase agreement
HB 352
HB over PC age 745
holiday pay
CTR(S) 1498, 1508
CTR(S) over PC age 1612
HB 438, 463
HB over PC age 780
treatment as earnings
CTR(S) 1498
CTR(S) over PC age 1612
holidays
treatment of hours of work
CTR(S) 1471
CTR(S) over PC age 1591
HB 253
HB over PC age 734
home
disregarded as capital
CTR(S) 1564, 1568
CTR(S) over PC age 1653
HB 685, 692
HB over PC age 863
occupation of home
CTR(S) 1467
HB 487
HB over PC age 734
two homes
HB 257
HB over PC age 735
homeless
disregarded for council tax discount 1088
homeowner
definition
HB 230
HB over PC age 724
hospital
absence from home
CTR(S) 1470, 1480
HB 260

HB over PC age 738
applicable amount
  HB over PC age 764
child care charges
  HB 424
definition of patient
  HB 262, 430
  HB over PC age 740
disregarded for council tax discount 1087
HB 415
member of household
  HB 409
non-dependant deductions
  CTR(S) 1523
  CTR(S) over PC age 1626
  HB 517
  HB over PC age 801
students
  HB 487
hostels
benefit cap 531
date entitlement begins
  HB 533
  HB over PC age 803
definition
  HB 227, 240
NINO requirement
  HB 251
  HB over PC age 732
rent officer determinations
  HB 398, 888, 916
  HB over PC age 758
residents disregarded for council tax
  discount 1088
  England and Wales 1087
treatment as home 257
hours of work
CTR(S) 1471
CTR(S) over PC age 1590
HB 253
HB over PC age 733
house sale
CTR(S) 1564, 1568
HB 685, 693
two homes
  HB 257, 258
  HB over PC age 735
houseboats
HB 237, 351, 888, 908, 916, 928
HB over PC age 729, 745
household
definition 17
duty to notify changes in family
  CTR(S) 1537
  CTR(S) over PC age 1638
  HB 559
  HB over PC age 819
treated as member of
  CTR(E) 1114
  CTR(S) 1472
  CTR(S) over PC age 1592
  CTR(W) 1203
  HB 409
  HB over PC age 762
Housing Act 1996 1699
housing association
co-ownership scheme
  HB 226
  HB over PC age 720
definition
  HB 228

HB over PC age 722
disregard of deposits
  CTR(S) 1566
  HB 688
excluded tenancies 628
local housing allowance 386
registered housing association 232, 245
rent officer determinations 895, 922
housing authority
definition 80
housing benefit 219
absence from home 260, 738
administration 79
entitlement 5
future changes 4
over PC age 714
power to modify scheme 79
primary legislation 4
transitional provision for UC claims 1880,
  1882, 1885
**Housing Benefit (Information from Landlords
and Agents) Regulations 1997** 1741
**Housing Benefit (Local Housing Allowance and
Information Sharing) Amendment
Regulations 2007** 1812
**Housing Benefit (Local Housing Allowance,
Miscellaneous and Consequential)
Amendment Regulations 2007** 1816
Housing Benefit (Permitted Totals) Order 1996
1735
schedules
  totals for increases above maximum rent
  1736
**Housing Benefit (Persons who have attained the
qualifying age for state pension credit)
Regulations 2006** 714
arrangement 714
citation 718
commencement 718
definitions 718
general note 718
general provisions
  amount of benefit 795
  applicable amounts 764
  assessment of income and capital 765
  calculation of weekly amount 803
  claims 811
  decisions 821
  entitlement 734
  former pathfinder authorities 842
  general 718
  information 833
  membership of a family 762
  overpayments 827
  payments 822
  payments for a dwelling 744
schedules
  applicable amounts 848
  decision notice 870
  disregarded capital 862
  disregarded earnings 854
  disregarded income 857
  electronic communication 877
  excluded tenancies 846
  former pathfinder authorities 873
  ineligible service charges 843
  refugees 843

Housing Benefit (State Pension Credit) (Local Housing Allowance and Information Sharing) Amendment Regulations 2007 1814
Housing Benefit and Council Tax Benefit (Consequential Provisions) Regulations 2006 1773
Housing Benefit and Council Tax Benefit (Decisions and Appeals) Regulations 2001 937
  general provisions
    appeal tribunals 979
    general 937
    revisions and supersessions 942
    rights of appeal and procedure 971
    suspension and termination 964
  schedule 980
Housing Benefit and Council Tax Benefit (War Pension Disregards) Regulations 2007 1808
Housing Benefit Regulations 2006 219
  commencement 224
  definitions 224
  general provisions
    amount of benefit 504
    applicable amounts 411
    calculation of weekly amount 532
    claims 542
    decisions 563
    entitlement 256
    former pathfinder authorities 619
    general 224
    income and capital 415
    information 608
    membership of a family 405
    overpayments 581
    payments 567
    payments for a dwelling 348
    students 479
  schedules
    applicable amounts 630
    capital disregarded 683
    decision notices 701
    electronic communication 712
    excluded tenancies 625
    former pathfinder authorities 707
    ineligible service charges 620
    refugees 619
    sums disregarded in calculating earnings 655
    sums disregarded in calculating income 664
housing costs
  calculation
    HB 538
    HB over PC age 809
  eligible rent
    HB 356
    HB over PC age 746
  HB 349
  HB over PC age 744
  ineligible housing costs 5
  rent-free periods
    HB 541
    HB over PC age 810
  students
    HB 493
human rights
  benefits treated as possessions 132
  freedom of thought, conscience and religion 128
  limitation on use of restrictions on rights 131
  prohibition of abuse of rights 131
  prohibition of discrimination 128
  prohibition of torture 124
  protection of property 131
  public bodies – definition 115
  remedies through the courts 118
  right to a fair trial 124
  right to education 133
  right to respect for private and family life 126
  taking legal action 116
Human Rights Act 1998 111
  commencement 123
  introduction 111
  legislation 113
  public authorities 115
  remedial action 120
  Schedule 1 124

I
Iceland 1807
ILF Scotland
  definition
    CTR(S) 1459
    CTR(S) over PC age 1579
  disregarded as capital
    CTR(S) 1509
    CTR(S) over PC age 1655
  disregarded as income
    CTR(S) 1560
  disregarded from second adult's income
    CTR(S) 1552
  third party payments
    CTR(S) 1506, 1510
Immigration and Asylum Act 1999 1706
Immigration and Asylum Chamber 1065
incapacity for work 1774
  students able to claim benefit
    CTR(S) 1484
    HB 488
income 10
  arrears of income
    CTR(S) 1531
    CTR(S) over PC age 1632
    HB 536
    HB over PC age 805
  assessment period
    CTR(S) 1496
    CTR(S) over PC age 1577
    HB 225, 434
    HB over PC age 719
  average weekly income other than earnings
    CTR(S) 1497
    CTR(W) 1267
    HB 434
  calculation of income
    CTR(E) over PC age 1131
    CTR(S) 1490, 1491, 1498
    CTR(S) over PC age 1601, 1605, 1610
    CTR(W) 1265
    CTR(W) over PC age 1220
    HB 421, 423, 436, 450
    HB over PC age 765, 766, 772, 777
  calculation of income other than earnings
    CTR(S) 1503
    HB 434
  capital treated as income 10
    CTR(S) 1492, 1505, 1567
    CTR(W) 1270
    HB 423, 450, 453, 691
  change in income
    CTR(S) 1531
    CTR(S) over PC age 1631

HB 536
HB over PC age 805
chargeable income
HB 449
child/young person's income
CTR(S) 1489
CTR(S) over PC age 1601
HB 421
HB over PC age 765
CTR(S) 1490, 1491, 1503
CTR(S) over PC age 1605
definition
CTR(E) over PC age 1133
CTR(S) over PC age 1603
CTR(W) over PC age 1222
HB over PC age 768, 771
deprivation of income
CTR(S) 1505
CTR(S) over PC age 1617
HB 453
HB over PC age 787
difference between capital and income
HB 415
disregards
CTR(S) 1503, 1556
CTR(S) over PC age 1603, 1650
HB 434, 450, 664
HB over PC age 857
effect of PC on calculation
CTR(S) over PC age 1601
HB over PC age 766
family's income 10
CTR(S) 1489
CTR(S) over PC age 1601
HB 421
HB over PC age 765
HB 415
HB over PC age 766
income from capital 10
CTR(S) 1491, 1508, 1514, 1558
CTR(S) over PC age 1604, 1605
HB 423, 463, 478, 670
HB over PC age 770, 862
income other than earnings
CTR(E) 1166
CTR(S) 1556
CTR(S) over PC age 1650
CTR(W) 1269, 1299
CTR(W) over PC age 1253
HB 664
HB over PC age 857
income treated as capital 10
CTR(S) 1508, 1560
HB 463, 675
minimum earnings threshold for EEA
workers 307
non-dependant's income
CTR(S) 1490, 1523
CTR(S) over PC age 1601, 1625
CTR(W) 1265
CTR(W) over PC age 1220
HB 421, 516
HB over PC age 765, 800
notional income
CTR(S) 1492, 1505
CTR(S) over PC age 1617
CTR(W) 1271
CTR(W) over PC age 1227
HB 423, 453
HB over PC age 787
partner's income

CTR(S) 1489
CTR(S)over PC age 1601
HB 421
HB over PC age 765
qualifying age for PC 11
second adult's income
CTR(S) 1551
CTR(S) over PC age 1659
student grants
CTR(S) 1516
HB 495
student loans
CTR(S) 1519
HB 500
tariff income 10
CTR(E) over PC age 1151
CTR(S) 1491, 1514
CTR(S) over PC age 1604, 1605
HB 423, 463, 478
HB over PC age 771
third party payments
CTR(E) over PC age 1140
CTR(S) 1506
CTR(W) over PC age 1229
HB 454
treatment of guarantee credit
CTR(S) over PC age 1601
CTR(W) over PC age 1220
HB over PC age 766
treatment of savings credit
CTR(S) over PC age 1602
CTR(W) over PC age 1221
HB over PC age 766
weekly income
CTR(E) over PC age 1135
CTR(S) 1491, 1498
CTR(S) over PC age 1605, 1610
CTR(W) 1266, 1272
CTR(W) over PC age 1223, 1229
HB 423, 436
HB over PC age 772, 777
income related benefits 3
definition 101
income support
change of circumstances
CTR(S) 1537
HB 559
disregarded income
CTR(S) 1555, 1556
HB 666
information passed between authorities 78
non-dependant deductions
CTR(S) 1524
CTR(S) over PC age 1626
HB 517
HB over PC age 801
persons from abroad 326
students on IS
CTR(S) 1484
HB 487
transitional provision for UC claims 1880,
1882, 1885
income tax
calculating net profit
CTR(S) 1502
deducted from earnings
CTR(S) 1499
CTR(S) over PC age 1613, 1616
HB 442
HB over PC age 781
deducted from notional earnings

CTR(S) 1507
HB 456
deducted from self-employed net profit
CTR(S) 1502
CTR(W) 1278
HB 446, 449
HB over PC age 784, 785, 786
disregard of changes
CTR(E) over PC age 1146
CTR(W) 1276
HB 437
HB over PC age 780
disregarded income
CTR(S) 1556
HB 665
refund of tax
CTR(S) 1508, 1521, 1567
HB 463, 504, 691
Independent Living Funds
definition
HB 228
HB over PC age 722
disregarded as capital
HB 463, 691
HB over PC age 865
disregarded as income
HB 675
third party payments
HB 454, 467
indicative rent levels
HB 896, 923
information 70
benefits administration information 71
collection of information
HB 608
HB over PC age 834
disclosure by authorities
CTC/WTC 1728
disclosure by First-tier Tribunal 1000
disclosure by Upper Tribunal 1039
discretionary housing payments 1757
electronic information 49
failure to supply 842
forwarding information
HB 609
HB over PC age 834
fraud investigations 43
holding information
HB 609
HB over PC age 834
in support of claim
CTR(E) 1180
HB 555
HB over PC age 817
included in notification of decision
CTR(W) 1329
HB 702
HB over PC age 870
local authority powers
HB 608
HB over PC age 833
local housing allowances 931, 933
HB 397
HB over PC age 757
passed between benefit authorities 1700
passed between local authorities
HB 613
HB over PC age 838
payments on account
HB 571
HB over PC age 824

penalty notices 1745
possessions 8
relevant information
HB 615
HB over PC age 840
requesting information
HB 609
HB over PC age 835
required by rent officers
HB 610
HB over PC age 835, 838
required by Upper Tribunal 195
required from appropriate person
HB 615
HB over PC age 840
required from landlords and agents 77
HB 615, 1741
HB over PC age 840
social security information 35, 1810
suspension of benefit 153, 966
to Welsh Ministers 1207
to/from Secretary of State 74, 1810
CTR(E) 1094
verifying information
HB 609
HB over PC age 834
wrongful disclosure 70, 74
inspection
administration of benefits 81
authorisation of inspectors 42
directions for improvement 83
enforcement determinations 86
enforcement notices 85
obstruction of inspectors 50
power to require information 43
powers 47
powers of entry 47
instalments
capital
CTR(S) 1505, 1566
HB 453, 690
interim payments
HB 39, 571
HB over PC age 823
invalid vehicles
definition
CTR(S) 1459
CTR(S) over PC age 1579
HB 228
HB over PC age 722
investigators
administration of benefits 81
authorisation 42
code of practice 1712
powers of investigators 43, 47
investments
valuation of capital
CTR(S) 1509
CTR(S) over PC age 1620
HB 464
HB over PC age 790

J
jobseeker's allowance
change of circumstances
CTR(S) 1537
HB 559
CTR(S) 1464
CTR(S) over PC age 1584
disregarded income
CTR(S) 1555, 1556

HB 666
HB 236, 559
HB over PC age 728
information passed between authorities 78
non-dependant deductions
    CTR(S) 1524
    CTR(S) over PC age 1626
    HB 517
    HB over PC age 801
persons from abroad 326
students on JSA
    CTR(S) 1484
    HB 487
joint beneficial interest
    CTR(S) 1514
    CTR(S) over PC age 1624
    HB 242, 476
    HB over PC age 794
joint capital
    CTR(S) 1514
    CTR(S) over PC age 1624
    HB 476
    HB over PC age 794
joint liability for council tax
    CTR(E) 1184
    CTR(S) 1522
    non-dependants 1466, 1523, 1586, 1625
joint occupiers
    liability for rent
        HB 280
        HB over PC age 741
    non-dependants
        CTR(S) 1523
        CTR(S) over PC age 1625
        HB 248, 516
        HB over PC age 732, 800
joint owner
    CTR(S) 1514
    CTR(S) over PC age 1624
    HB 476
    HB over PC age 794
joint tenants
    HB 250, 476
judicial review 190, 1048
    applications for proceedings 1048
    council tax reduction scheme
        England and Wales 1082
    transfers to High Court 1051
    transfers to Upper Tribunal 1048
jury service
    allowances
        HB 677

K
kinship carers
    payments disregarded
        CTR(S) 1559
        HB 444, 672, 674

L
landlords
    assessment of rent level 1699
    close relative
        HB 280
        HB over PC age 741
    connected trust or company
        HB 280, 289
        HB over PC age 741
    direct payments
        HB 573, 577
        HB over PC age 824, 825

duty to notify change of circumstances
    HB 559
    HB over PC age 819
fit and proper person
    HB 575
former partner
    HB 287
    HB over PC age 741
information required by local authority
    HB 615, 616, 1741
    HB over PC age 840
notification of decision
    HB 704
    HB over PC age 872
overpayments which are not recoverable
    HB 591
    HB over PC age 828
payments on account
    HB 572
recovery of overpayments
    HB 607
    HB over PC age 833
resident landlord
    HB 280
    HB over PC age 741
responsibility for landlord's child
    HB 280, 288
    HB over PC age 741
late claims
    HB 552
    HB over PC age 812
learner support funds
    CTR(S) 1514
    HB 480
leave to enter or remain 1706
    EEA citizens 300
leave to remain outside the rules 326
legal aid
    funding for appeals 1042
liability to make payments for a home
    evidence of liability
        HB 277
    HB 273
    liability defined
        HB 276
    persons from abroad
        HB 297
    persons treated as not liable
        HB 280
    students 487
    who can be treated as liable
        HB 275
licence
    HB 351, 745
Liechtenstein 1807
life insurance policy
    definition
        CTR(S) over PC age 1581
        HB 231
        HB over PC age 725
    payments disregarded
        CTR(S) 1560
        HB 675
    surrender value disregarded
        CTR(S) 1566
        CTR(S) over PC age 1654
        HB 690
        HB over PC age 864
lifeboat crew
    earnings disregard
        CTR(E) 1163

CTR(S) 1554
CTR(S) over PC age 1648
HB 659
HB over PC age 854
HB 659
limited capability for work
CTR(S) 1548
HB 649
students 488
limited capability for work-related activity
CTR(S) 1548
HB 649
linked person
definition
HB 228
loans
business loans disregarded
CTR(S) 1502
CTR(S) over PC age 1616
HB 446
HB over PC age 785
from employer
CTR(S) 1509
HB 463
mortgage interest loans 348
student
CTR(S) 1519
HB 500
local authorities
acting on behalf of another authority 79
benefit administration information 71
children leaving care 1710
collection of information
HB 608
HB over PC age 834
contracting out benefit functions 1769
directions for improvement 83
disclosure of information
HB 613
duty of authority to set up scheme
CTR(E) 1073
CTR(W) 1205
duty to publicise benefit schemes 4
enforcement notices 85
forwarding information
HB 609
HB over PC age 834
holding information
HB 609
HB over PC age 834
information between authorities
HB 613
HB over PC age 838
information from landlords
HB 615, 1741
information required by rent officers
HB 610
HB over PC age 835
information to/from Secretary of State 1810
inspection of benefits administration 81
joint arrangements 91
permitted spending totals
HB 1735
power to appoint inspectors 47
powers to prosecute fraud 68, 1821
relevant decisions 139
requesting information
HB 609
HB over PC age 835
second authority
CTR(S) 1461

CTR(S) over PC age 1582
HB 233
HB over PC age 727
standards of service 85
Local Government Finance Act 1992 1071
Local Government Finance Act 2012 1097
local housing allowance
calculation of maximum rent
HB 388
HB over PC age 754
categories of dwellings 899, 900, 925
definition 391
eligible rent
HB 362
HB over PC age 748
excluded tenancies
HB 625
introduction
HB 1812
HB over PC age 1814
local authority pilot areas 929
maximum rent
HB 385
HB over PC age 753, 754
paid direct to landlord 573
publication of LHAs
HB 397
HB over PC age 757
rent officer determinations 879, 884, 900, 912, 931, 933
size criteria
HB 389
transitional protection
HB 365
HB over PC age 750
local reference rent
definition
HB 381
HB over PC age 751
eligible rent
HB 361
HB 382, 892, 919
maximum rent
HB 380
HB over PC age 750
rent officer determinations 398, 890
size criteria 897, 923
taper 1802
transitional protection 1778
local welfare provision 1834
definition
HB 228
HB over PC age 723
local authority information sharing 1829
London Bombings Relief Charitable Fund
definition
CTR(S) 1459
CTR(S) over PC age 1579
HB 229
HB over PC age 723
disregarded as capital
CTR(E) 1171
CTR(S) 1567
CTR(S) over PC age 1655
HB 691
HB over PC age 865
third party payments
CTR(S) 1510
HB 467

London Emergencies Trust
definition
CTR(E) 1108
CTR(S) 1459
HB 229
HB over PC age 723
disregarded as capital
HB 691
disregarded as income
HB 675
lone parents
benefit cap 522
childcare costs
CTR(S) 1492
CTR(S) over PC age 1606
HB 424
HB over PC age 773
definition
CTR(S) 1459
CTR(S) over PC age 1579
HB 229
HB over PC age 723
earnings disregards
CTR(E) 1163
CTR(S) 1553
CTR(S) over PC age 1647
HB 658
HB over PC age 854
students – occupation of home
HB 257
HB over PC age 734
students able to claim benefit
CTR(S) 1484
HB 488
long tenancy
definition
HB 229
HB over PC age 723
HB 352
HB over PC age 745
looked after children
leaving care 1710
treatment as member of family
CTR(S) 1473
HB 409
treatment of payments
CTR(S) 1559
HB 673
HB over PC age 783
low paid work
earnings and notional income
CTR(S) 1507
HB 455

M
Macfarlane Trusts
definition
CTR(S) 1463
CTR(S) over PC age 1579
HB 229
HB over PC age 723
disregarded as capital
CTR(E) 1171
CTR(S) over PC age 1655
HB 463, 691
HB over PC age 865
disregarded as income
HB 675
third party payments
HB 454, 467

mail
Post Office requirement to report redirected
mail 97
return of redirected mail 96
maintenance
disregard of payments
CTR(S) 1562
CTR(S) over PC age 1652
HB 678
HB over PC age 861
maintenance undertaking
definition 1706
Mandatory Work Activity Scheme
definition
CTR(S) 1460
HB 229
disregarded as capital
CTR(S) 1564
HB 684
disregarded as income
CTR(S) 1556
HB 665
married couples 14
maternity leave
definition
CTR(S) 1460
CTR(S) over PC age 1580
HB 229
HB over PC age 723
in remunerative work
CTR(S) 1495
CTR(S) over PC age 1609
HB 427
HB over PC age 776
not in remunerative work
CTR(S) 1471
CTR(S) over PC age 1591
HB 253
HB over PC age 734
maximum benefit
CTR(E) over PC age 1127
CTR(S) 1521
CTR(S) over PC age 1624
CTR(W) 1262
CTR(W) over PC age 1217
HB 5, 7, 505
HB over PC age 795
maximum rent 361, 747
calculation
HB 369, 382, 388
HB over PC age 754
definition
HB 229
HB over PC age 723
former pathfinder authorities 707
increases above
HB 1736
local housing allowance
HB 229, 362, 388
HB over PC age 723, 748
local reference rent
HB 361, 380
HB over PC age 747, 750
protection from restrictions
HB 384
HB over PC age 751
social sector
HB 358
transitional protection
HB 365, 707
HB over PC age 750

under occupation of social rented housing 370
when a social sector rent rules are used
HB 367
when LHA rules are used
HB 385
HB over PC age 753, 754
meals
excluded from HB 621, 844
service charges
HB 620, 621, 920
HB over PC age 843, 844
mediation 195, 987, 1033
medical treatment 107
absence from home
CTR(S) 1470, 1480
HB 260
HB over PC age 738
mental illness
charges for counselling/support 107
liability to pay rent
HB 279
mesne profits
HB 351
HB over PC age 745
minimum benefit 9
HB 521
HB over PC age 802
misrepresentation
criminal offences 54
overpayment
HB 592, 595, 601
HB over PC age 828, 830
mobile homes
campsite fees
HB 351
HB over PC age 745
excluded tenancies 628
HB 237, 888, 908, 916, 928
HB over PC age 729
mobility supplement
disregarded
CTR(S) 1556
CTR(S) over PC age 1650
HB 667
HB over PC age 858
mooring charges
HB 351, 888, 908, 916, 928
HB over PC age 745
mortgage interest loans 348
mortgage payments 5
disregard of mortgage protection payments
CTR(S) 1560
HB 675
HB 348, 352
HB over PC age 745
moving home
date entitlement begins
HB 532
HB over PC age 803
definition of mover
CTR(S) 1460
CTR(S) over PC age 1580
HB 230
HB over PC age 724
extended payments
CTR(E) 1177
CTR(S) 1526, 1528
CTR(S) over PC age 1628
CTR(W) 1284
CTR(W) over PC age 1241

HB 510, 515
HB over PC age 798
liaison between local authorities
HB 613
two homes
HB 257, 258
HB over PC age 735

N
national insurance contributions
deducted from earnings
CTR(S) 1499
CTR(S) over PC age 1613
HB 442
HB over PC age 781
deducted from notional income
CTR(S) 1508
HB 456
deducted from self-employed net profit
CTR(S) 1501, 1502
CTR(S) over PC age 1617
CTR(W) 1278
CTR(W) over PC age 1236
HB 446, 449
HB over PC age 784, 785, 786
disregard of changes
CTR(W) 1276
CTR(W) over PC age 1235
HB 437
HB over PC age 780
national insurance number requirement 23
HB 251
HB over PC age 732
neighbourhood
rent officer determinations
HB 892
net earnings
definition
CTR(S) 1460
CTR(S) over PC age 1580
HB 230
HB over PC age 724
net profit
CTR(S) 1501
deductions of tax and national insurance
CTR(S) 1502
definition
CTR(S) over PC age 1580
HB 230
HB over PC age 724
HB 445
HB over PC age 784
self-employed earners
CTR(S) 1501
CTR(S) over PC age 1615
CTR(W) 1277
CTR(W) over PC age 1235
New Deal
definition
HB 230
disregard of payments
CTR(S) 1510
HB 467
notional income
CTR(S) 1507
HB 455
payments treated as capital
CTR(S) 1509
self-employed earnings
HB 463

next of kin
  definition
    HB 580
    HB over PC age 826
nil award 141
no fixed abode
  disregarded for council tax discount 1088
non-advanced education
  HB 407
non-dependants
  calculation of non-dependant's income
    CTR(S) 1523
    CTR(S) over PC age 1625
    HB 516
    HB over PC age 800
  deductions
    CTR(E) over PC age 1127
    CTR(S) 1522
    CTR(S) over PC age 1625
    CTR(W) 1263
    CTR(W) over PC age 1217
    HB 516
    HB over PC age 800
  definition
    CTR(E) 1116
    CTR(S) 1466
    CTR(S) over PC age 1585
    CTR(W) 1204
    HB 248
    HB over PC age 732
  disregard of payments
    CTR(S) 1558
    HB 671
  exceptions
    CTR(S) 1466
    CTR(S) over PC age 1585
    HB 248
    HB over PC age 732
  exclusions from non-dependant deductions
    HB 517
    HB over PC age 800
  income/capital
    CTR(S) 1490
    CTR(S) over PC age 1601
    CTR(W) 1265
    HB 421
    HB over PC age 765
  notification of decisions
    HB 705
    HB over PC age 872
  taking advantage of benefit scheme
    CTR(S) 1466, 1490
    CTR(S) over PC age 1601
    HB 421
    HB over PC age 765
Norway 1807
notice
  payments in lieu
    CTR(S) 1498
    CTR(S) over PC age 1612
    HB 438, 656
    HB over PC age 780
notification
  board and attendance
    HB 886, 914
  decisions 106
    CTR(E) 1183
    CTR(W) 1329
    HB 564, 701
    HB over PC age 821, 870

  rent officer determinations
    HB 896, 922
notional capital
  CTR(S) 1509, 1511
  CTR(S) over PC age 1620
  CTR(W) over PC age 1237
  diminishing notional capital rule
    CTR(S) over PC age 1621
    CTR(W) 1281
    HB 472
    HB over PC age 791
  HB 466
  HB over PC age 791
notional income
  CTR(E) over PC age 1139
  CTR(S) 1492, 1505
  CTR(S) over PC age 1617
  CTR(W) 1271, 1280
  CTR(W) over PC age 1227
  HB 423, 453, 459
  HB over PC age 787
nursing care 107, 620

O
obstruction of inspector 50
occupation
  normally occupied
    HB 264
  of home
    CTR(S) 1467
    HB 487
    HB over PC age 734
occupational pensions
  contributions deducted from earnings
    CTR(S) 1499
    CTR(S) over PC age 1613
    HB 442
    HB over PC age 781
  contributions deducted from notional
    earnings
    CTR(S) 1508
    HB 456
  definition
    CTR(S) 1460
    CTR(S) over PC age 1580
    HB 230
    HB over PC age 724
  disregarded
    CTR(S) 1568
    HB 694
  notional capital/ income
    CTR(S) 1506
    CTR(S) over PC age 1618
    HB 454, 466
    HB over PC age 787
  third party payments
    CTR(S) 1506, 1510
    HB 454, 466
  treatment as earnings
    CTR over PC age 1612
    CTR(S) 1499
    HB 439
    HB over PC age 781
occupier
  definition
    HB 880, 881, 909
ombudsman
  HB 564

ONE 29
one bedroom self-contained accommodation
388
one bedroom shared accommodation 388
one strike scheme 1716
    disqualification period 1763
overlapping benefits
    CTR(S) 1543
    CTR(S) over PC age 1644
    HB 635
    HB over PC age 850
overnight care
    additional bedroom required
        local housing allowance rules 389
        social sector maximum rent 369, 376
    information sharing 211, 1828
    person who requires
        HB 231, 243
        HB over PC age 725
overpayments
    appeals 147
    arising from arrears
        HB 538
    bankruptcy 597
    calculation
        HB 601
        HB over PC age 830
    challenging a decision 147
    challenging a decision on recovery 147
    challenging method of recovery 147
    court action
        HB 37, 600
        HB over PC age 37
    CTB 40
    deductions from recoverable overpayments
        HB 602
        HB over PC age 830
    definition
        HB 582
        HB over PC age 827
    diminution of capital
        HB 601
        HB over PC age 830
    discretion to recover
        CTB 40
        HB 37
    HB 37
    involvement of relevant person
        HB 588
    knowledge of overpayment 589
    landlord, payments direct 37
    local housing allowance
        HB 592
        HB over PC age 828
    method of recovery
        HB 596
        HB over PC age 829
    mistakes
        HB 584
    notification of recoverable overpayments
    1841
        HB 706
        HB over PC age 872
    official error
        HB 583
        HB over PC age 827
    offsetting against arrears
        HB 581
        HB over PC age 827
    payments on account
        HB 571, 582

    HB over PC age 824
    person from whom recovery may be sought
        CTB 40
        HB 37
    prescribed benefits
        HB 605
        HB over PC age 831
    recoverable overpayments 1840
        HB 583, 591
        HB over PC age 827
    recovery from benefits
        CTB 40
        HB 37, 596, 605
        HB over PC age 828, 829, 831
    recovery from earnings 1840
        HB 37
    recovery from landlord
        HB 607
        HB over PC age 833
    time limit for recovery
        HB 600
    treatment as rent arrears
        HB 575
    two homes
        HB 266
    UC 1872
overseas assets
    CTR(S) 1509
    CTR(S) over PC age 1620
    HB 465
    HB over PC age 791
owner
    beneficial interest
        CTR(S) 1514
        CTR(S) over PC age 1624
        HB 476
        HB over PC age 794
    definition
        HB 230
        HB over PC age 724

P
parental contribution
    covenant income
        CTR(S) 1517
        HB 498
    definition
        CTR(S) 1515
        HB 480
    disregarded
        CTR(S) 1558
        CTR(S) over PC age 1652
        HB 671
        HB over PC age 861
part-time work
    definition
        CTR(S) 1555
        HB 662
    earnings disregards
        CTR(S) 1553
        HB 657
partner
    definition
        CTR(S) 1460
        CTR(S) over PC age 1580
        HB 231
        HB over PC age 724
paternity leave
    definition
        CTR(S) 1460
        CTR(S) over PC age 1580

HB 231
HB over PC age 724
in remunerative work
    CTR(S) 1495
    CTR(S) over PC age 1609
    HB 427
    HB over PC age 776
not in remunerative work
    CTR(S) 1471
    CTR(S) over PC age 1591
    HB 253
    HB over PC age 734
pay in lieu of notice
treatment as earnings
    CTR(S) 1498
    CTR(S) over PC age 1612
    HB 438
    HB over PC age 780
payment in kind
treatment as earnings
    CTR(S) 1499
    CTR(S) over PC age 1612
    HB 439
    HB over PC age 781
payment of benefit
death of person entitled
    HB 580
    HB over PC age 826
frequency of payment
    HB 567, 1801
    HB over PC age 822
HB 567
HB over PC age 822
landlord direct
    HB 573
    HB over PC age 824
late payment
    HB 567
    HB over PC age 822
method
    HB 79
power to make regulations about
    administration of payments
    HB 30
rent allowance
    HB 569
    HB over PC age 823
who is paid
    HB 572
    HB over PC age 824
payments on account 39
HB 571, 582
HB over PC age 823
penalties
alternative to prosecution 57, 61
civil penalties 64
court action to recover 36
penalty notices 1745
recovered from benefits 36
recovered from earnings 36
UC 1875
withdrawn 1717
pension age
definition 12, 731
equalisation 731
HB 245
pension credit
change of circumstances
    CTR(S) over PC age 1632
    CTR(W) over PC age 1244
    HB over PC age 806

extended payments
    CTR(S) 1629
    HB 799
future changes 1857
guarantee credit
    CTR(S) over PC age 1601
    CTR(W) over PC age 1220
    HB over PC age 766
HB over PC age 714
mixed-age couples 1898
non-dependant deductions
    CTR(S) over PC age 1626
    HB over PC age 801
notifying change of circumstances
    CTR(S) over PC age 1638
    HB over PC age 819
qualifying age 11, 13, 17
    HB 232, 252
    HB over PC age 725, 733
savings credit
    CTR(S) over PC age 1602
    CTR(W) over PC age 1221
    HB over PC age 766
pension fund holder
definition
    CTR(S) over PC age 1581
    HB 231
    HB over PC age 724
pensioner
applicable amounts
    CTR(W) 1216
    CTR(E) 1118, 1120, 1121
    CTR(W) 1208, 1214
definition
    CTR(E) 1113
    CTR(W) 1201
non-dependant deductions
    CTR(W) 1217
pensioner premium
HB 636
period of experience
definition
    CTR(S) 1516
    HB 482
period of study
definition
    CTR(S) 1515
    HB 482
permitted totals
HB 79, 1735
person affected
definition
    HB 231
    HB over PC age 725
HB 565
HB/CTB 941
person subject to immigration control
CTR(E) 1120
CTR(S) 1474, 1483
CTR(S) over PC age 1599
CTR(W) 1213
definition 1706
entitlement to claim benefits 1747, 1749
excluded from benefit entitlement 1707
personal allowances
CTR(E) 1157
CTR(S) 1542
CTR(S) over PC age 1643
CTR(W) 1286
CTR(W) over PC age 1245
HB 630

HB over PC age 849
rates
  CTR(E) 1157
  CTR(S) 1542
  CTR(S) over PC age 1643
  CTR(W) 1286
  CTR(W) over PC age 1245
  HB 631
  HB over PC age 849
personal care 620
personal injuries
disregard of compensation
  CTR(S) 1505, 1566
  CTR(S) over PC age 1652, 1655
  HB 454, 466, 689
  HB over PC age 860, 866
periodical payments
  CTR(S) 1505
  HB 453
  HB over PC age 860
personal pensions
contributions deducted from earnings
  CTR(S) 1500, 1502
  CTR(S) over PC age 1613, 1616
  HB 442, 447
  HB over PC age 782, 785
contributions deducted from notional
  earnings
  CTR(S) 1508
  HB 456
definition
  CTR(S) 1460
  CTR(S) over PC age 1581
  HB 231
  HB over PC age 725
disregarded
  CTR(S) 1568
  HB 694
information to be provided
  HB 555
  HB over PC age 817
lump sums
  HB over PC age 788
notional income/capital
  CTR(S) 1510
  CTR(S) over PC age 1618
  HB 454, 466
  HB over PC age 787
qualifying contribution
  CTR(S) 1500
  CTR(S) over PC age 1613
  HB 442
  HB over PC age 782
third party payments
  CTR(S) 1506, 1510
  HB 454, 466
persons from abroad 1795
definition
  CTR(S) 1481
  HB 297, 299
  HB over PC age 742
entitlement to claim benefits 1747, 1749
  HB 297
  HB over PC age 742
exceptions 302
  CTR(S) 1481
  HB 298
excluded from benefits 1707
students
  CTR(S) 1484

polygamous marriages
alternative maximum CTR(S) 1529, 1630
applicable amounts
  CTR(S) 1488
  CTR(W) 1262
  HB 413
claims
  HB 542
  HB over PC age 811
definition
  CTR(E) 1113
  CTR(S) 1461
  CTR(S) over PC age 1581
  CTR(W) 1202
  HB 232
  HB over PC age 725
earnings disregards
  CTR(S) 1553
  HB 657
mixed-age couples 1901
non-dependants
  CTR(S) 1466, 1523
  CTR(S) over PC age 1586, 1625
  HB 248, 516
  HB over PC age 800
occupation of home
  HB 257
  HB over PC age 734
treatment of income and capital
  CTR(S) 1489
  CTR(S) over PC age 1601
  HB 421
  HB over PC age 765
possession orders
loss of HB 8
post
return of redirected post 96
Post Office
reporting redirected mail 97
power of attorney
HB 543
HB over PC age 811
pregnancy
EEA nationals 315
premiums
amounts
  CTR(S) 1547
  CTR(W) 1292
  CTR(W) over PC age 1250
  HB 646
  HB over PC age 853
CTR(E) 1158
CTR(S) 1543
CTR(W) 1288
CTR(W) over PC age 1246
HB 634
HB over PC age 850
prescribed benefits
HB 606
HB over PC age 832
prisoners
absence from home
  CTR(S) 1470, 1480
  HB 260
  HB over PC age 738
child care charges
  CTR(S) 1492
  HB 424
disregard of payments for visits
  CTR(S) 1561, 1569
  HB 678

disregarded for council tax discount 1086
non-dependant deductions
  HB 517
  HB over PC age 801
temporary release
  CTR(S) 1470, 1480
  HB 260
  HB over PC age 738
property
benefits treated as possessions 132
valuation of capital
  HB 464
  HB over PC age 790
public authority 115
definition 115, 116
  CTR(S) over PC age 1581
  HB 232
  HB over PC age 725
public bodies
definition 115, 116
human rights 115
Public Lending Right payments
CTR(S) 1501
HB 444

Q
Qualifications for Appointment of Members to the First-tier Tribunal and Upper Tribunal Order 2008 1027
qualifying benefits
contributory benefits
  CTR(S) 1461
  CTR(S) over PC age 1581
  HB 232
  HB over PC age 726
extended payments
  CTR(S) 1525, 1527
  CTR(S) over PC age 1627
  HB 227, 512
  HB over PC age 796
income-related benefits
  CTR(S) 1461
  CTR(S) over PC age 1581
  HB 232
  HB over PC age 726
qualifying course
definition
  CTR(S) 1461
  HB 482
qualifying person
definition
  CTR(S) 1461
  HB 232
  HB over PC age 726
qualifying premium
CTR(S) 1501
CTR(S) over PC age 1615
HB 445
HB over PC age 784
quashing order 192

R
rapid reclaim
HB 549
reckonable rent
change in reckonable rent
  HB 385
  HB over PC age 752
definition
  HB 232, 385
  HB over PC age 726

recovery of benefits
appeals relating to overpayments 147
court action
  CTB 40
  HB 37, 600
  HB over PC age 37
deduction from benefits 36
  CTB 40, 1503
  HB 37, 450, 605
  HB over PC age 829, 831
discretion to recover
  CTB 40
  HB 37
from landlord
  HB 607
  HB over PC age 833
methods of recovery
  HB 596
  HB over PC age 829
notification to claimant
  HB 706
  HB over PC age 872
payments on account
  HB 571
  HB over PC age 824
person from whom recovery made
  CTB 40
  HB 37, 591
  HB over PC age 828
recoverable overpayments
  HB 583
  HB over PC age 827
redeterminations
appeals by tribunal 149
board and attendance
  HB 886, 914
challenging decision of rent officer
  HB 402
  HB over PC age 760
definition
  HB 880, 909
errors
  HB 889, 916
exceptions 888, 916
  HB 402
  HB over PC age 759
rent officer
  HB 883, 899, 911, 924
substitute redeterminations
  HB 404, 912
  HB over PC age 760
reduction of benefit 152
benefit offences 1767
  CTB 964
failure to provide information 966
  HB 964
reduction lifted 966
  UC 1877
redundancy
treatment as earnings
  CTR(S) 1498
  CTR(S) over PC age 1612
  HB 438
  HB over PC age 780
refugees
definition 325
  HB 299
evidence to support a claim
  HB 555
  HB over PC age 817
HB 347, 619

HB over PC age 744, 843
not persons from abroad
    CTR(S) 1481
    HB 298
retrospective claim for benefit 1708
    CTR(S) 1748
    HB 1748
transitional protection 1748
refuges
    HB 531
registered provider of social housing 388
rehabilitation allowance
    CTR(S) 1506
    HB 454
relative
    definition
        CTR(S) 1461
        CTR(S) over PC age 1581
        HB 232
        HB over PC age 726
relevant authority
    decisions 139
        HB 563
        HB over PC age 821
    definition
        CTR(S) 1461
        CTR(S) over PC age 1581
        HB 232
        HB over PC age 726
religious orders
    HB 281, 292
    HB over PC age 741
remunerative work
    definition
        CTR(E) 1116
        CTR(S) 1471
        CTR(S) over PC age 1590
        CTR(W) 1204
        HB 253, 254
        HB over PC age 733
rent
    advance payments
        HB 273
    claim-related rent
        HB 380, 382, 894, 921
        HB over PC age 751
    definition
        CTR(S) 1461
        CTR(S) over PC age 1581
        HB 233, 351, 353
        HB over PC age 726, 745
    disregards
        CTR(S) 1558
        HB 671
    eligible rent
        HB 356
        HB over PC age 746
    exceptionally high rent
        HB 891, 918
    increases in rent 1794
        HB 626
        HB over PC age 846
    increases to cover arrears
        HB 350
        HB over PC age 744
    indicative rent levels
        HB 896, 923
    liability to pay
        HB 273
    local reference rent
        HB 382, 892, 919

HB over PC age 751
maximum rent
    HB 229
reckonable rent
    HB 232
    HB over PC age 726
rent-free periods
    HB 273, 505, 541, 624
    HB over PC age 740, 810, 846
significantly high rent
    HB 382, 890, 918
single room rent
    HB 380, 382, 893, 920
size criteria
    HB 382, 891, 897, 918, 923
unreasonably high
    HB 1787
weekly rent
    HB 538
    HB over PC age 809
rent allowance
    definition 79, 348
    frequency of payment
        HB 569
        HB over PC age 823
    payments on account
        HB 571
        HB over PC age 823
    rent restrictions 349
    when rent allowances are paid
        HB 568
        HB over PC age 822
rent arrears
    overpayments of benefit to landlord
        HB 575
    payment direct to landlord
        HB 573, 577
        HB over PC age 824, 825
    payment on account to landlord
        HB 572
    rent increases to cover arrears
        HB 350
        HB over PC age 744
rent assessment committee determinations
    HB 1786
rent officer
    challenging decision of rent officer
        HB 402, 879
        HB over PC age 760
    claim-related rent
        HB 894, 921
    determinations 879
        HB 882, 890, 910, 918
    errors
        HB 889, 916
    excluded tenancies
        HB 625
        HB over PC age 846
    functions 1699
    indicative rent calculation
        HB 896, 923
    information from local authority
        HB 610
        HB over PC age 835
    local reference rent
        HB 380
        HB over PC age 750
    notifications
        HB 896, 922
    pre-tenancy determination
        HB 398

HB over PC age 757
redeterminations
    HB 402, 883, 899, 911, 924
    HB over PC age 759
requirement to refer to rent officers 7, 398, 757
requirement to supply information 74
substitute determinations
    HB 404
    HB over PC age 760
time limit for referrals
    HB 399
    HB over PC age 758
rent officer determinations
amended determinations
    HB 405
    HB over PC age 761
board and attendance
    HB 886, 914
broad rental market area
    HB 884, 912
categories of dwelling 900
    HB 925
definition
    HB 880, 909
definition of relevant period
    HB 880, 882, 909
definition of relevant time
    HB 880
errors
    HB 889, 916
exceptions 888, 916
indicative rent calculation
    HB 896, 923
local housing allowance 912
    HB 884
local reference rent 890
notifications
    HB 896, 922
redeterminations
    HB 402
    HB over PC age 759
significantly high rent
    HB 890
substitute determinations
    HB 404, 912
    HB over PC age 760
Rent Officers (Housing Benefit Functions) (Local Housing Allowance) Amendment Order 2003 929
Rent Officers (Housing Benefit Functions) (Local Housing Allowance) Amendment Order 2005 930
Rent Officers (Housing Benefit Functions) (Scotland) Order 1997 909
citation 909
commencement 909
definitions 909
general note 909
revocations 918
schedules
    Schedule 1 918
    Schedule 2 923
    Schedule 3 924
    Schedule 4 928
Rent Officers (Housing Benefit Functions) Amendment Order 2007 931
Rent Officers (Housing Benefit Functions) Order 1997 879
citation 879
commencement 879
definitions 879
general note 879
revocations 909
schedules
    Schedule 1 890
    Schedule 2 897
    Schedule 3 899
    Schedule 4 908
rent rebate 349
recovery of overpayment
    HB 600
subsidy 90
rent restrictions 7, 348
cap rent
    HB 389
    HB over PC age 755
increases of rent 1794
local housing allowance 348, 899
local reference rent 348
pre-Jan 96 scheme 348
protection from restrictions
    HB 359, 362, 1786
social sector scheme 348
transitional protection
    HB 365
    HB over PC age 750
rent-free period
    HB 273, 505, 541, 624
    HB over PC age 740, 795, 810, 846
rental purchase agreements
    HB 351, 888, 908, 916, 928
    HB over PC age 745
repairs
disregard of dwelling awaiting repairs
    CTR(S) 1568
    HB 694
set-off against rent
    HB 273, 541
    HB over PC age 740
temporary accommodation
    HB 257
    HB over PC age 735
resident
definition
    council tax 1476
residential accommodation
    HB 281, 293
    HB over PC age 740
retainer fee
treatment as earnings
    CTR(S) 1498
    CTR(S) over PC age 1612
    HB 438
    HB over PC age 780
retirement
annuity contracts
    CTR(S) 1506
earnings disregards
    CTR(S) 1553
    HB 655
retirement pensions
notional income
    CTR(S) over PC age 1617
    HB over PC age 787
treatment as income
    HB over PC age 768, 771
reviews
discretionary housing payments 1758
First-tier Tribunal decisions 173, 1023
replacement of reviews 139
Upper Tribunal decisions 175

revision 135, 139, 942
  any grounds revision 942
  any time revisions 947
  appeal pending 943
  appealing a revised decision 971
  date revision takes effect 951
  difference between revision and
      supersession 142
  late application 949
  official error 943
  refusal to revise 140
  revision of decisions 142, 942
  revision or supersession 953
right to reside
  Article 21 rights 337
  CTR(E) 1118
  CTR(S) 1481
  EEA nationals 298, 327
  extended right to reside 328
  HB 298
  initial right to reside 328
  permanent right to reside 332
  retaining right to reside 335
  self-sufficient people 329
rounding up of benefit
  CTR(S) 1465
  HB 539
  HB over PC age 809
royalties
  CTR(S) 1501
  HB 444

S
sanctionable benefits
  definition 1714
sanctions
  benefit offences 1719
  conviction quashed 1717
  criminal sanctions 41
  disqualification from benefit 1762
  effect on offender's family 1723
  failure to attend a work-focused interview 27
  one strike scheme 1716
  two strikes scheme 1722
Sanctuary Schemes 378
sandwich courses
  CTR(S) 1461, 1517
  HB 482, 483, 496
school age grant in Scotland 701
school holidays
  treatment of hours of work
    CTR(S) 1471
    CTR(S) over PC age 1591
    HB 253
    HB over PC age 734
Scottish basic rate
  HB 233
Scottish Infected Blood Support Scheme
  definition
    HB 233
    HB over PC age 727
  disregarded as capital
    HB 691
  disregarded as income
    HB 675
second adult
  CTR(E) 1162
  CTR(S) over PC age 1630
  duty to notify change of circumstances
    CTR(S) 1537
    CTR(S) over PC age 1638

income
  CTR(S) 1551
  CTR(S) over PC age 1659
second adult rebate 1475
Second World War
  ex-gratia payments
    CTR(S) 1570
    CTR(S) over PC age 1654
    HB 698
    HB over PC age 864
self-employed earner
  average weekly earnings
    CTR(S) 1497
    CTR(W) 1267
    HB 434
  calculation of net profit
    CTR(E) over PC age 1146
    CTR(S) 1501
    CTR(S) over PC age 1615
    CTR(W) 1277
    CTR(W) over PC age 1235
    HB 445
    HB over PC age 784
  chargeable income
    HB 449
  CTR(S) 1500
  definition
    CTR(S) 1461
    CTR(S) over PC age 1582
    HB 233
    HB over PC age 727
  disregards from earnings
    CTR(E) over PC age 1148
    CTR(S) 1500, 1503
    CTR(S) over PC age 1614, 1616
    HB 444, 445, 449, 657
    HB over PC age 783, 786
  earnings
    CTR(E) over PC age 1138
    CTR(S) 1500
    CTR(S) over PC age 1614
    HB 444
    HB over PC age 782
  earnings defined
    CTR(E) over PC age 1138
    CTR(S) 1501
    CTR(S) over PC age 1615
    HB 444
    HB over PC age 783
  EEA nationals 308
    CTR(S) 1481
    HB 298
  expectation of payment
    HB 254
  notional capital
    CTR(S) 1511
    HB 467
self-employment route
  definition
    CTR(S) 1462
    HB 233
Senior President of Tribunals 168, 173
  reports 202
separation
  date change of circumstances takes effect
    CTR(S) 1531
    CTR(S) over PC age 1631
  disregard of home
    CTR(S) 1568
    HB 692
  estrangement

CTR(S) 1465
CTR(S) over PC age 1585
former partner
  HB 273
  HB over PC age 740
former partner is landlord
  HB 280, 287
  HB over PC age 741
service charges
  counselling and support 107
  definition
    HB 352
    HB over PC age 746
  excessive
    HB 623
    HB over PC age 845
  fuel
    HB 623
    HB over PC age 845
  HB 351
  HB over PC age 745
  ineligible charges 932, 933
    HB 356, 620, 893, 895, 920, 921
    HB over PC age 843
  meals
    HB 620
    HB over PC age 843
  rent officer determinations
    HB 893, 917, 920
  validated charges 107
service of notices for appeals 940
service user
  definition
    CTR(S) 1462
    CTR(S) over PC age 1582
    HB 237
    HB over PC age 729
  disregard of expenses
    HB 666
  notional income
    CTR(S) 1508
    CTR(S) over PC age 1618
    HB 456
  treatment of expenses
    HB 439
services
  definition
    HB 352
    HB over PC age 746
setting aside decision 158, 205, 1019, 1054
severe disability premium
  amount
    CTR(E) 1161
    CTR(S) 1547
    CTR(S) over PC age 1647
    CTR(W) over PC age 1250
    HB 646
    HB over PC age 853
  CTR(E) 1158
  CTR(S) 1545
  CTR(S) over PC age 1644
  CTR(W) 1290
  CTR(W) over PC age 1247
  earnings disregards
    CTR(S) 1553
    HB 657
  HB 641
  HB over PC age 850
  SDP Gateway 1862
  UC claims 1862

severe mental impairment
  disregarded for council tax discount 1086
share fishermen
  CTR(S) 1501
  HB 445
shared accommodation
  HB 248
shared ownership tenancy
  definition
    HB 233
    HB over PC age 727
  HB 352
shared parental leave
  definition
    CTR(E) 1110
    CTR(S) 1462
    CTR(W) 1199
    HB 233
    HB over PC age 727
  in remunerative work
    CTR(S) 1495
    CTR(S) over PC age 1609
    HB 427
    HB over PC age 776
  not in remunerative work
    CTR(S) 1471
    CTR(S) over PC age 1591
    HB 253
    HB over PC age 734
shares
  valuation of capital
    CTR(S) 1509
    CTR(S) over PC age 1620
    HB 464
    HB over PC age 790
sickness
  EEA nationals 310
  not in remunerative work
    CTR(S) 1471
    CTR(S) over PC age 1591
    HB 253
    HB over PC age 734
  students entitled to benefit
    CTR(S) 1485
    HB 489
significantly high rent
  HB 382, 890, 918
single room rent
  definition
    HB 233
  HB 380, 382, 893, 920
  transitional arrangements
    HB 882, 911
site fees
  HB 351, 908, 928
size criteria
  definition
    HB 880, 910
  HB 891, 897, 918, 923
  local housing allowance
    HB 389, 394
    HB over PC age 754
  social sector maximum rent 369
  transitional protection
    HB 365
    HB over PC age 749, 750
  under-occupation 370
Skipton Fund
  definition
    CTR(S) 1462
    CTR(S) over PC age 1582

HB 233
HB over PC age 727
disregarded as capital
CTR(E) 1171
CTR(S) 1567
CTR(S) over PC age 1655
HB 691
HB over PC age 865
third party payments
HB 467
Social Entitlement Chamber 173
functions 984, 1065
social housing 388
social sector maximum rent scheme 370
determination of maximum rent 369
excluded tenancies 367, 625
future changes 371, 1779
HB over PC age 718
maximum rent 358
size criteria 369
when a maximum rent is to be determined 367
Social Security (Civil Penalties) Regulations 2012 1839
Social Security (Claims and Information) Regulations 2007 1810
Social Security (Consequential Provisions) Act 1992 105
Social Security (Habitual Residence) Amendment Regulations 2004 1771
Social Security (Immigration and Asylum) Consequential Amendments Regulations 2000 1747
Social Security (Information-sharing in relation to Welfare Services etc.) Amendment and Prescribed Bodies Regulations 2013 1848
Social Security (Information-sharing in relation to Welfare Services etc.) Regulations 2012 1826
Social Security (Local Authority Investigations and Prosecutions) Regulations 2008 1821
Social Security (Loss of Benefit) Regulations 2001 1761
Social Security (Notification of Change of Circumstances) Regulations 2001 1759
Social Security (Overpayments and Recovery) Regulations 2013 1840
Social Security (Penalty Notice) Regulations 1997 1745
Social Security (Persons from Abroad) Amendment Regulations 2006 1807
Social Security (Persons Required to Provide Information) Regulations 2013 1854, 1856
Social Security (Restrictions on Amounts for Children and Qualifying Young Persons) Amendment Regulations 2017 (2017 No.376) 1894
Social Security (Use of Information for Housing Benefit and Welfare Services Purposes) Regulations 2008 1823
Social Security Act 1998 106
commencement 109
definitions 109
parliamentary control 109
regulations and orders 108
Social Security Administration Act 1992 21
commencement 103
definitions 100
parliamentary control 100
regulations and orders 98

Social Security Advisory Committee 92
Social Security Commissioners
abolition 169, 1057
functions transferred to First-tier and Upper Tribunals 170, 198, 1057
transitional provisions 1058
Social Security Contributions and Benefits Act 1992 3
commencement 20
parliamentary control 20
regulations, orders and schemes 19
Social Security Fraud Act 2001 1712
spare room subsidy 370
special account 233
specified accommodation
HB 531
UC 1866
sports award
definition
CTR(S) 1462
CTR(S) over PC age 1582
HB 233
HB over PC age 727
disregard of payments
CTR(S) 1563, 1569
CTR(S) over PC age 1615
HB 444, 681
HB over PC age 784
not in remunerative work
CTR(S) 1471
CTR(S) over PC age 1591
HB 253
HB over PC age 734
standard maintenance allowance
CTR(S) 1516
HB 482
statement of reasons
decisions which can be appealed 963
HB 564
HB over PC age 821
statutory adoption pay
treatment as earnings
CTR(S) 1499
CTR(S) over PC age 1612
HB 438
HB over PC age 781
statutory maternity pay
treatment as earnings
CTR(S) 1499
CTR(S) over PC age 1612
HB 438
HB over PC age 780
statutory paternity pay
treatment as earnings
CTR(S) 1499
HB 438
HB over PC age 781
statutory shared parental pay
treatment as earnings
CTR(S) 1499
CTR(S) over PC age 1612
HB 438
HB over PC age 781
statutory sick pay
treatment as earnings
CTR(S) 1499
CTR(S) over PC age 1612
HB 438
HB over PC age 780

student loans
  definition
    CTR(S) 1463
    HB 483
  fee loans
    CTR(S) 1520
    HB 502
  giving up course
    CTR(S) 1504
    HB 450
  treatment as income
    CTR(S) 1504
students
  absence from home
    CTR(S) 1470, 1480
    HB 260
    HB over PC age 738
  academic year
    CTR(S) 1455
    HB 480
  accommodation during vacations
    HB 487
  accommodation owned by institution
    HB 493
  alternative maximum CTR(S) 1483
  breaks from study
    HB 492
  course of study
    CTR(S) 1457
    HB 481
  covenants
    CTR(S) 1517, 1518
    CTR(W) 1319
    HB 498
  CTR(S) 1514
  CTR(W) 1314
  deaf students
    CTR(S) 1485
    HB 488
  definition
    CTR(S) 1463
    HB 483, 484
  disabled students
    CTR(S) 1484
    HB 488
  disregarded for council tax discount 1086
  disregards
    CTR(S) 1516
    HB 495, 499
  eligible housing costs
    HB 493
  entitlement to benefit
    CTR(S) 1484
    CTR(W) 1317
    HB 487
  excluded from benefit
    CTR(S) 1484
    CTR(W) 1317
    HB 487
  exemptions from exclusion from benefits
    CTR(S) 1484
    HB 487, 490
  failing exams
    HB 493
  frequency of payment
    HB 570
    HB over PC age 823
  full-time course
    CTR(S) 1458
    HB 481
  giving up course

    CTR(S) 1504
    HB 450
  grant income
    CTR(S) 1515, 1516
    CTR(W) 1318
    HB 482, 495
  HB 479
  income
    CTR(S) 1516
    HB 495
  income treated as capital
    CTR(S) 1521
    HB 504
  last day of course
    CTR(S) 1515
    HB 482
  loans
    CTR(S) 1519
    CTR(W) 1320
    HB 500
  lone parents
    CTR(S) 1484
    HB 488
  modular courses
    HB 485
  non-dependant deductions
    CTR(S) 1523
    CTR(S) over PC age 1626
    HB 517
  occupation of home
    HB 257, 487
    HB over PC age 734
  overseas students
    CTR(S) 1484
  period of study
    CTR(S) 1515
    HB 482
  receiving IS/JSA/ESA
    CTR(S) 1484
    HB 487
  student partners
    CTR(S) 1484
    HB 273, 488, 503
    HB over PC age 741
  summer vacations
    CTR(S) 1521
    HB 504
  two homes
    HB 257
    HB over PC age 735
subsidiary limit
  HB 79
subsidy 88
  calculation 88
  discretionary housing payments 137
  fraud prevention 89
  payment 89
  rent rebate 90
suitable alternative accommodation
  HB 1786, 1791
supersession 139, 143, 942, 951
  change of circumstances after decision 141
  closed period supersessions 142
  date of taking effect 957
  decisions of former appeal tribunals 210
  difference between supersession and
    revision 142
  grounds for 951, 954
  refusal to supersede 140
  revision or supersession 953

support charges
ineligible charges
HB 620, 895, 921
rent officer referrals 889
support component
amount
CTR(S) 1549
CTR(W) 1293
HB 650
CTR(S) 1548
CTR(W) 1293
HB 649
supported accommodation
benefit cap 531
definition 1778
future changes 1778
protection from rent restrictions 1778
UC claimants 1867
supporting people programme in Wales 1827
Supreme Court
appeals to Supreme Court 187
surrender value
valuation of investments
CTR(S) 1509
CTR(S) over PC age 1620
HB 464
HB over PC age 790
suspension of benefit 152
CTB 964
failure to provide information 966
HB 964
lifting of suspension 966
suspension leading to termination 968
Switzerland 1807

T
tapers
HB 383, 478, 506, 1794
HB over PC age 795
transitional protection
HB 1802
tariff income 10
CTR(E) over PC age 1151
CTR(S) 1514
CTR(S) over PC age 1604
HB 423, 478
HB over PC age 771
Tax Credits Act 2002 1728
tax year
definition
HB 234
HB over PC age 727
teachers
student loans disregarded
CTR(S) 1557
temporary accommodation
accommodation for homeless people 1778
exempt from social sector rent restrictions
367
fear of violence 266
HB on two homes 257, 735
UC 1860, 1863, 1866
tenancy
definition
HB 578, 880, 910
tenancy in common
HB 476
tenant incentive scheme
HB 352
HB over PC age 746

termination of benefit 968
termination of employment
earnings disregards
CTR(S) 1553
HB 655
Territorial Army
earnings disregard
CTR(E) 1163
CTR(S) 1554
CTR(S) over PC age 1648
HB 659
HB over PC age 854
test case pending 955, 970
third party payments
capital
CTR(S) 1510
HB 466
income
CTR(S) 1506
notional capital
CTR(S) 1510
HB 466
notional income
CTR(S) 1506
HB 454, 458
HB over PC age 789
tied accommodation
HB 281, 292
HB over PC age 741
time limits 821
appeals 973
applying for revision of decision 942
challenging decision of rent officer
HB 403
HB over PC age 760
criminal proceedings 65
first payment of benefit
HB 567
HB over PC age 822
First-tier Tribunals 204, 1026
landlord to supply information
HB 618
HB over PC age 842
notice of appeal 1026
notice of decisions which can be appealed
963
notification of decision
HB 564
HB over PC age 821
notification of rent officer determinations
HB 896
recovery of overpayment
HB 600
referrals to rent officers
HB 399
HB over PC age 758
statement of reasons
HB 564
HB over PC age 822
supplying information to support a claim
HB 555
HB over PC age 817
Upper Tribunals 204
training
definition of training course
HB 262
HB over PC age 740
disregard of payments
CTR(S) 1557
HB 668, 695

training allowance
definition
CTR(S) 1463
CTR(S) over PC age 1583
HB 234
HB over PC age 727
disregarded
CTR(S) 1557
HB 668
non-dependant deductions
CTR(S) 1523
CTR(S) over PC age 1626
HB 517
HB over PC age 801
Transfer of Tribunal Functions Order 2008 1057
transitional arrangements
council tax reduction schemes
CTR(E) 1185, 1187, 1188
CTR(S) 1540
CTR(S) over PC age 1642, 1661
CTR(W) 1450
employment and support allowance
CTR(S) 1549
HB 651
former pathfinder cases
HB 365, 708
HB over PC age 749
habitual residence 1771
housing payments 1871
rent restrictions 365, 749
single room rent 882
UC 1875, 1880, 1882, 1885
travel expenses
treated as earnings
CTR(S) 1498, 1556
CTR(S) over PC age 1612
HB 438
HB over PC age 780
voluntary/charity work
HB 665
Tribunal Procedure (First-tier Tribunal) (Social Entitlement Chamber) Rules 2008 983
Tribunal Procedure (Upper Tribunal) Rules 2008 1029
definitions 1030
Tribunals, Courts and Enforcement Act 2007 167
administrative matters 201
First-tier and Upper Tribunals 168
orders and regulations 203
oversight 202
transfer of tribunal functions 197
troubled families programme 1833
definition 1828
trusts
CTR(S) 1505, 1509
HB 454, 466
landlord is a connected trust
HB 280, 289
HB over PC age 741
two homes
HB 257
HB over PC age 735
students
HB 257
HB over PC age 734
two strikes scheme 1722
two-child limit
CTR(E) over PC age 1126
CTR(S) 1541
CTR(W) 1261
HB 411

HB over PC age 764
transitional provisions 1894

U
udal tenure
definition
HB 243
under-occupation 1827
discretionary housing payments 1751
information sharing 1833
rent restrictions 370
underpayments
CTB 41
offsetting against overpayments
HB 581
HB over PC age 827
payments on account
HB 571
HB over PC age 824
unemployment
EEA nationals 311
unfair dismissal
CTR(S) 1498
HB 438, 656
universal credit 1857
appeals 1873, 1874
change of circumstances
CTR(S) 1537
claiming HB 1850, 1859, 1865
entitlement to claim 1861
exclusion from existing benefits 1852, 1862, 1864
full service areas 1858
gateway conditions 1849, 1852, 1857
managed migration 1877
migration notice 1877
mixed-age couples 1898
overpayments 1872
penalties 1875
relevant districts 1857
required to provide information 1854, 1856
roll out of UC 1858
single claimant becomes a couple 1868
specified accommodation 1866
termination of HB award 1870
transfer from HB to UC 1857
transition 1861, 1875
transitional provision 1880, 1882, 1885
Universal Credit (Transitional Provisions) Regulations 2014 1857
universal support 1834
unmarried couple 14
unreasonable rent restriction
HB 628
HB over PC age 847
transitional protection 1784
unreasonably large accommodation
HB 891, 897, 918, 1786
HB over PC age 847
size criteria
HB 923
Upper Tribunal 168
administration 201
appealing against an Upper Tribunal decision 150, 184, 1060
appeals against First-tier Tribunal decisions 150, 175
appeals to Supreme Court 187
application for permission to appeal 1044, 1055
case management powers 1034

composition 170, 1061
consent orders 1053
costs and expenses 197, 205, 1037, 1043
delegation to staff 1033
enforcement of decisions 196
evidence and submissions 1040
expert assistance 197
failure to comply with rules 1035
fees 202
hearings 1051
judges 170, 171
judicial review powers 190
judicial review proceedings 1048
mediation 195, 1033
membership of tribunal 1027
notice of appeal 1045
notice of decisions 1053
notice of hearings 1052
obligation to cooperate 1032
organisation 1066
overriding objective 1032
practice directions 194
procedures 1029
procedures for giving directions 1034
proceedings on appeal 183
public and private hearings 1052
quashing order 192
representatives 1038
review of decisions 175, 1056
right to appeal to 175
sending documents 1039
setting aside a decision 1054
sitting places 196
striking out a case 1035
transfer of functions 198
transitional provisions 1058
Tribunal Procedure Rules 194, 204
withdrawal of a case 1041
witnesses 1041

V
vacations
summer vacations for students
CTR(S) 1521
HB 504
treatment of hours of work
CTR(S) 1471
CTR(S) over PC age 1591
HB 253
HB over PC age 734
vaccine damage payment
HB 458
validated charges 107
valuation of capital
CTR(S) 1509
CTR(S) over PC age 1620
HB 464, 465
HB over PC age 790, 791
Valuation Tribunal for England 1665
appeal management powers 1670
appeals to the High Court 1681
calculating time 1674
correcting decisions 1681
decisions and orders 1679
directions 1670
evidence and submissions 1675
failure to comply with Regulations 1670
functions 1670
hearings 1678
notices of appeal 1677, 1678
powers to award costs 1674

representatives 1674
reviewing decisions 1681
sending a delivery of documents 1674
setting aside decisions 1681
striking out proceedings 1671
substitution and addition of parties 1673
summoning witnesses 1676
time limits 1677
use of documents and information 1675
Valuation Tribunal for England (Council Tax and Rating Appeals) (Procedure) Regulations 2009 1665
commencement 1666
definitions 1667
general provisions
appeals 1670
correcting, reviewing, setting aside and appealing decisions 1681
council tax appeals 1677
proceedings 1678
Valuation Tribunal for Wales 1684
Appeal Panels 1690
appeals 1693
arbitration 1693
arrangements for appeals 1688
decisions on appeals 1691
disqualification 1689
evidence 1690
evidence of lists 1691
initiating an appeal 1687
notice of hearing 1689
orders 1692
records of decisions 1693
representation 1690
review of decisions 1692
service of notices 1693
special circumstances 1686
striking out 1688
time limits 1687
withdrawal 1688
written representations 1689
Valuation Tribunal for Wales Regulations 2010 1684
commencement 1685
definitions 1685
general provisions
council tax appeals 1685
schedules 1695
vicinity
rent officer determinations
HB 891
Victoria Cross payments
CTR(S) 1556, 1569
HB 667, 697
violence
absence from home
HB 261
HB over PC age 738
housing costs for two homes
HB 257, 258
HB over PC age 735, 736
refuges
HB 531
treated as occupying former home
HB 258
HB over PC age 736
violent profits
HB 351
HB over PC age 745

voluntary payments
  disregarded
    CTR(S) 1557
    HB 668
  students
    CTR(S) 1518
    HB 499
  treatment as income/capital
    CTR(S) 1509
    HB 463
voluntary work
  expectation of payment
    CTR(S) 1471
    HB 254
  expenses
    HB 665
  unpaid work and notional income
    CTR(S) 1507
    HB 455
  voluntary organisation defined
    CTR(S) 1463
    CTR(S) over PC age 1583
    HB 234
    HB over PC age 728
vouchers
  non-cash vouchers
    HB 439
    HB over PC age 780

W
waiting days
  HB 236
  HB over PC age 728
war disablement pension
  definition 1808
  disregarded
    CTR(E) 1166
    CTR(S) 1557, 1808
    CTR(S) over PC age 1650, 1808
    HB 79, 669, 1808
    HB over PC age 1808
war pension scheme
  definition 13
war pensions
  definition
    CTR(S) 1463
    HB 234
    HB over PC age 728
  disregarded
    CTR(E) 1166
    CTR(S) 1557, 1568, 1808
    CTR(S) over PC age 1650, 1808
    HB 79, 669, 695, 1808
    HB over PC age 1808
water and sewerage charges
  deductions from rent 356
  definition
    CTR(S) 1463
    HB 234
    HB over PC age 728
We Love Manchester Emergency Fund
  definition
    CTR(S) 1464
    HB 234
    HB over PC age 728
  disregarded as capital
    HB 691
  disregarded as income
    HB 675

week
  definition
    HB 225
    HB over PC age 719
welfare fund
    CTR(S) 1464
    CTR(S) over PC age 1584
Welfare Reform Act (Relevant Enactment) Order 2009 1825
Welfare Reform Act 2007 162
Welfare Reform Act 2007 (Commencement No.4, and Savings and Transitional Provisions) Order 2007 1818
Welfare Reform Act 2007 (Commencement No.7, Transitional and Savings Provisions) Order 2008 1822
Welfare Reform Act 2012 4, 207
Welfare Reform Act 2012 (Commencement No.3, Savings Provision) Order 2012 1838
Welfare Reform Act 2012 (Commencement No.9 and Transitional and Transitory Provisions and Commencement No.8 and Savings and transitional provisions (Amendment)) Order 2013 1849
Welfare Reform Act 2012 (Commencement No.13, 14, 16, 19, 22, 23 and 24 and Transitional and Transitory Provisions (Modification)) Order 2016 1891
Welfare Reform Act 2012 (Commencement No.17, 19, 22, 23 and 24 and Transitional and Transitory Provisions (Modification) (No.2)) Order 2018 1896
Welfare Reform Act 2012 (Commencement No.21 and Transitional and Transitory Provisions) Order 2015 1882
Welfare Reform Act 2012 (Commencement No.23 and Transitional and Transitory Provisions) Order 2015 1885
Welfare Reform Act 2012 (Commencement No.25 and Transitional and Transitory Provisions) Order 2015 1888
Welfare Reform Act 2012 (Commencement No.26 and Transitional and Transitory Provisions and Commencement No.22, 23 and 24 and Transitional and Transitory Provisions (Modification)) Order 2016 1889
Welfare Reform Act 2012 (Commencement No.27 and Transitional and Transitory Provisions and Commencement No.22, 23 and 24 and Transitional and Transitory Provisions (Modification)) Order 2016 1890
Welfare Reform Act 2012 (Commencement No.31 and Savings and Transitional Provisions and Commencement No.21 and 23 and Transitional and Transitory Provisions (Amendment)) Order 2019 1898
Welfare Reform Act 2012(Commencement No. 20 and Transitional and Transitory Provisions and Commencement No.9 and Transitional and Transitory Provisions (Amendment)) Order 2014 1880
Welfare Reform and Pensions Act 1999 1700
  commencement 1703
welfare services 213
  information sharing 165, 212
welfare to work beneficiary 639
withdrawal of claim 139
    CTR(E) 1182
    CTR(W) 1328
    HB 558
    HB over PC age 818

witnesses
allowances
HB 677
summoned to tribunals 204, 1002, 1041
Upper Tribunal's power to call 195
work
exempt work
HB 660
starting or increasing work
extended CTR(S) 1525
extended HB 162, 506
working away from home
HB 409
HB over PC age 763
work experience 456, 1507
work-focused interview
condition of benefit entitlement 26
definition 28
optional 29
work-related activity component 649
abolition 647
amount
CTR(S) 1549
CTR(W) 1293
CTR(S) 1548
CTR(W) 1293
work-related activity group
definition
HB 230
HB over PC age 724
ESA 632
workers
A2 nationals 322
definition 305
minimum earnings threshold for EEA
workers 307
not persons from abroad
CTR(S) 1481
HB 298
retaining worker status 314
working tax credit 1728
arrears treated as capital
CTR(S) 1509
HB 463
calculation of average weekly income 435
CTR(S) 1497
CTR(S) over PC age 1610
CTR(W) 1276
CTR(W) over PC age 1234
HB 435
HB over PC age 777
income/notional capital
CTR(S) 1510
HB 454
transitional provision for UC claims 1880,
1882, 1885
treatment as income
CTR(E) over PC age 1146
CTR(S) 1504
CTR(S) over PC age 1604
HB 450
HB over PC age 770

Y
young individual
age limit 382
definition
HB 234, 246
one bedroom shared accommodation 388
rent officer determinations
HB 888, 916

single room rent
HB 382, 893, 920
young people
applicable amount
CTR(S) 1487
CTR(S) over PC age 1600
HB 411
HB over PC age 764
definition
CTR(S) 1467
HB 406
HB over PC age 762
disregarded for council tax discount 1086
duty to notify changes in family
CTR(S) 1537
CTR(S) over PC age 1638
HB 559
HB over PC age 819
earnings
CTR(S) 1555
income and capital
CTR(S) 1489
HB 421, 463, 662
leaving care 1710
liability to pay rent
HB 279
member of household
CTR(S) 1472
CTR(S) over PC age 1592
HB 407
HB over PC age 762
non-dependants
CTR(S) 1466
CTR(S) over PC age 1586
HB 248
HB over PC age 732
payments from young person disregarded
CTR(S) 1558
HB 671
responsibility for
CTR(S) 1472, 1484
CTR(S) over PC age 1591
HB 407, 488
HB over PC age 762

Z
Zambrano right 328